Reverse
Acronyms, Initialisms &
Abbreviations Dictionary

Reverse Acronyms, Initialisms & Abbreviations Dictionary

A Companion Volume to *Acronyms, Initialisms & Abbreviations Dictionary*,
with Terms Arranged Alphabetically by Meaning of Acronym, Initialism, or Abrreviation

Covering: Aerospace, Associations, Banking, Biochemistry, Business, Data Processing,
Domestic and International Affairs, Economics, Education, Electronics, Genetics,
Government, Information Technology, Internet, Investment, Labor, Language, Law, Medicine, Military
Affairs, Pharmacy, Physiology, Politics, Religion, Science, Societies, Sports, Technical
Drawings and Specifications, Telecommunications, Trade, Transportation, and Other Fields

29th Edition

Volume 3

Part 1

A-C

Mary Rose Bonk,
Editor

GALE GROUP

Detroit
New York
San Francisco
London
Boston
Woodbridge, CT

Editor: Mary Rose Bonk

Associate Editor: Pamela Dear
Assistant Editor: Phyllis Spinelli

Data Capture Manager: Ronald D. Montgomery
Project Administrator: Gwendolyn S. Tucker
Data Capture Specialist: Constance Wells
Data Capture Associate: Nikkita Bankston
Data Capture Assistants: Katrina Coach, Cynthia Jones, Elizabeth Pilette
Administrative Assistant, Editorial Services: Mary Pamula

Manufacturing Manager: Dorothy Maki
Buyer: NeKita McKee

Graphic Services Manager: Barbara J. Yarrow
Graphic Artist: Mike Logusz

Director, Technical Support Services: Theresa A. Rocklin
Oracle Applications Specialist: Carolin V. Jones

TRADEMARKS AND PROPRIETARY RIGHTS

Library of Congress Catalog Card Number 84-643188
ISBN 0-7876-4112-X (Volume 3 Complete)
ISBN 0-7876-4113-8 (Part 1: A-C only)
ISBN 0-7876-4114-6 (Part 2: D-I only)
ISBN 0-7876-4115-4 (Part 3: J-P only)
ISBN 0-7876-5805-7 (Part 4: Q-Z only)
ISSN 0270-4404

Printed in the United States of America

Contents

Gale's publications in the acronyms and abbreviations field include:

Acronyms, Initialisms & Abbreviations Dictionary series:

Acronyms, Initialisms & Abbreviations Dictionary (Volume 1). A guide to acronyms, initialisms, abbreviations, and similar contractions, arranged alphabetically by abbreviation.

Acronyms, Initialisms & Abbreviations Dictionary Supplement (Volume 2). An interedition supplement in which terms are arranged alphabetically both by abbreviation and by meaning.

Reverse Acronyms, Initialisms & Abbreviations Dictionary (Volume 3). A companion to Volume 1 in which terms are arranged alphabetically by meaning of the acronym, initialism, or abbreviation.

Acronyms, Initialisms & Abbreviations Dictionary Subject Guide series:

Computer & Telecommunications Acronyms (Volume 1). A guide to acronyms, initialisms, abbreviations, and similar contractions used in the field of computers and telecommunications in which terms are arranged alphabetically both by abbreviation and by meaning.

Business Acronyms (Volume 2). A guide to business-oriented acronyms, initialisms, abbreviations, and similar contractions in which terms are arranged alphabetically both by abbreviation and by meaning.

International Acronyms, Initialisms & Abbreviations Dictionary series:

International Acronyms, Initialisms & Abbreviations Dictionary (Volume 1). A guide to foreign and international acronyms, initialisms, abbreviations, and similar contractions, arranged alphabetically by abbreviation.

Reverse International Acronyms, Initialisms & Abbreviations Dictionary (Volume 2). A companion to Volume 1, in which terms are arranged alphabetically by meaning of the acronym, initialism, or abbreviation.

Periodical Title Abbreviations series:

Periodical Title Abbreviations: By Abbreviation (Volume 1). A guide to abbreviations commonly used for periodical titles, arranged alphabetically by abbreviation.

Periodical Title Abbreviations: By Title (Volume 2). A guide to abbreviations commonly used for periodical titles, arranged alphabetically by title.

Highlights

Over 200,000 New Terms
Arrangement by Meaning
Comprehensive Coverage
Subject Categories
Source Citations

Reverse Acronyms, Initialisms, and Abbreviations Dictionary (RAIAD) enables you to determine the generally accepted short forms of organization names and technical terms in hundreds of fields. It contains essentially the same entries as its companion volume *(Acronyms, Initialisms, and Abbreviations Dictionary)* but arranges these entries alphabetically by meaning, rather than by acronym or initialism. The twenty-ninth edition offers increased coverage in all fields of human endeavor. Many of the 200,000 new terms are from the subject areas of:

- Arts
- Associations
- Business
- Education
- Internet
- Medicine
- Military affairs
- Science
- Technology

Of major value to librarians and researchers is the inclusion of:

- airlines/airports
- information systems
- library symbols
- organizations
- radio/television station call letters
- research centers
- stock exchange symbols

Subject Categories Provided

Where possible, and if not already implied in the entry itself, a category or identifier follows many terms. It provides a subject context for those entries that require clarification.

Major Sources Cited

Codes are provided to indicate the source from which the information was obtained. This feature allows you to verify the entries and may, in some instances, lead to additional information. Complete bibliographic data about the publications cited can be found in the List of Selected Sources following the acknowledgments. Terms that are obtained from miscellaneous newspapers and newsmagazines, are provided by outside contributors, or are discovered through independent research by the editorial staff remain uncoded.

OUTSTANDING
ALA
RUSA
REFERENCE SOURCE

Acronyms, Initialisms
& Abbreviations
Dictionary
was named an
***"Outstanding
Reference Source,"***
*the highest honor
given by the
American Library
Association Reference
and User Services
Association.*

Preface

Acronyms, initialisms, and other abbreviated letter symbols make up what is perhaps the fastest growing "language" in contemporary society. Whether one views the phenomenon with disdain or delight, it is apparent that the abbreviated form has established a lasting and ever-widening influence on both written and spoken communication.

For over thirty years, Gale's *Acronyms, Initialisms, and Abbreviations Dictionary (AIAD)* has served as a reliable and up-to-date reference, guiding librarians, businesspeople, technical writers, and other researchers through this alphabetical maze. Its scope has been broadened by publication of this companion volume, *Reverse Acronyms, Initialisms, and Abbreviations Dictionary (RAIAD)*, which is Volume 3 of the *AIAD* series.

Useful in Sorting Out Inconsistencies

If all abbreviated terms were as logically formed as Royal Artillery-RA, there would be little need for a tool such as *RAIAD*. The countless exceptions to this generalized formation, however, make a guide essential. Receipt Acknowledged, for instance, is not necessarily shortened to RA, but often to REACK; Sisters of the Most Holy Sacrament is abbreviated as MHS, not SMHS; and the military designation for First Available Air Transportation is not FAAT, but FAIRTRANS.

Sometimes, *all* words in a term are represented in the initialism, including articles, prepositions, etc.:

    Radiation, Detection, and Computation .... RADIAC

Or, the first syllables or a part of each word, rather than initial letters, are used to form the acronym:

    Quick FORTRAN .... QWIKTRAN

Often, terms that are particularly long are shortened by representing only the first several words:

    Easter Seal Research Foundation of the National Easter Seal Society .... ESRF

Yet another method uses only *selected* words to create a telescoped form:

    International Information Centre for Terminology .... INFOTERM

Another popular practice is to tack on a stray letter that has no connection with the acronym's translation, but that renders it pronounceable or gives it an appropriate meaning:

    Greater Underwater Propulsive Power [*Type of submarine*] .... GUPPY

It is obvious from these cited examples that *RAIAD* can take the guesswork out of acronym and initialism formation and usage.

Mistaken Identity Avoided

An incorrect initialism can not only cause confusion, but may even change the meaning of a term. A Bachelor of Interior Architecture is designated BI Arch. Abbreviating it as BIA confers on the subject a Bachelor of Industrial Arts degree.

Some commercial firms and associations use their entire corporate name in their initials: Cancer Care, Inc.-CCI; while others use only the principal part of their name: American Airlines, Inc.-AA. If Cancer Care, Inc., is abbreviated to CC, it may indicate Chrysler Corporation; lengthening the initialism for American Airlines, Inc., to AAI may result in translation as Alliance of American Insurers. Even terms in the same subject field are not always shortened the same way. The abbreviation for Luggage and Leather Goods Manufacturers of America is formed as one might expect-LLGMA; however, the Luggage and Leather Goods Salesman's Association of America is shortened simply to LLG.

A Valuable Key to Abbreviations and Symbols

Because simple abbreviations are also included in the *AIAD* series, a user will be able to find in *RAIAD* that the common abbreviated forms for Commission include CMSN, COM, COMM, COMMN, and COMSN. This type of information is often sought by users of data processing systems, where limited space makes the use of abbreviated terms necessary.

Both *AIAD* and *RAIAD* contain a number of letter symbols as well. These do not meet the criteria for being acronyms, initialisms, or abbreviations, but are included as an important part of an alphabetical reference. *Reverse Acronyms, Initialisms, and Abbreviations Dictionary* is especially valuable in assigning correct symbols to given terms, since the symbol often bears little or no resemblance to what it represents. For example, the meteorological symbol for Hail is A; the Navy symbol for a Cruiser Submarine is SSC; the New York Stock Exchange symbol for Borden, Inc. is BN; the research code symbol for Travenol Laboratories is BAX.

Airport code names may also seem baffling. A few are apparent, such as the symbol for Denver-DEN. But in many cases the connection between subject and symbol seems remote at best; Michigan's Willow Run Airport is represented by YIP, illogical unless one realizes the airport's proximity to the city of Ypsilanti; the giant Chicago O'Hare Airport is represented by ORD-few remember that this is because its original name was Orchard Field.

Available in Electronic Format

RAIAD is available for licensing on magnetic tape or diskette in a fielded format. Either the complete database or a custom selection of entries may be ordered. The database is available for internal data processing and nonpublishing purposes only. For more information, call 800-877-GALE.

Suggestions Are Welcome

Many suggestions concerning individual terms to be included or subjects to be covered have been received from individual users and have been most helpful. The editors invite all such comments and will make every effort to incorporate them in future editions.

Acknowledgments

For suggestions, contributions of terms, permission to take material from personal or published sources, and for other courtesies extended during the preparation of previous editions and the present one, the editors are indebted to the following:

James Aguirre, former staff writer and editor, Quality Evaluation Laboratory, United States Naval Weapons Station, Concord, California

O.T. Albertini, Plans and Policy Directorate, Joint Chiefs of Staff, Department of Defense (retired)

Irving Allen, Professor of Sociology, University of Connecticut

American Library Association (publisher of *Pugh's Dictionary of Acronyms & Abbreviations*)

Associated Press

Associated Spring Corp., B-G-R Division (publisher of *Civilian's Dictionary,* a dictionary of wartime abbreviations)

Association of American Railroads

Paul Axel-Lute

Janice Badash

Burroughs Corp. (publisher of *Computer Acronyms and Abbreviations Handbook*)

Butterworth & Co. (Publishers) Ltd. (publisher of *Index to Legal Citations and Abbreviations*)

Ethel M. Fair

John Fobian

David Glagovsky

Jack Gordon

Hoyt Hammer, Jr.

Hanley & Belfus Inc. (publisher of *Dictionary of Medical Acronyms & Abbreviations*)

William S. Hein Co. (publisher of *Bieber's Dictionary of Legal Abbreviations*)

Charles C. Hinckley, executive vice president, Union Central Life Insurance Co.

Roy Hubbard

Mildred Hunt, editorial consultant

International Business Machines Corp., Data Processing Division (publisher of *IBM Glossary for Information Processing*)

David J. Jones, compiler of *Australian Dictionary of Acronyms and Abbreviations* and *Australian Periodical Title Abbreviations*

Kogan Page Ltd. (publisher of *Dictionary of British Qualifications*)

Steven C. Krems, computer specialist, Internal Revenue Service

Ktav Publishing House, Inc. (publisher of *Biblical and Judaic Acronyms*)

Robert E. Lacey, journalist

Lund Humphries Publishers Ltd. (publisher of *Dictionary of Graphic Arts Abbreviations*)

David MacLaren

Lawrence Marwick, late editor of *Biblical and Judaic Acronyms*

David Mattison

Mamie Meredith, late Professor of English, University of Nebraska

National Association of Securities Dealers (publisher of the *NASDAQ Company Directory*)

National Library of Canada

National Library of Medicine

Morgan Oates, late librarian, *Detroit Free Press*

Charles Parsons, formerly of Translation Research Institute

Eric Partridge, late author of *A Dictionary of Slang and Unconventional English; A Dictionary of Abbreviations, with Especial Attention to War-Time Abbreviations;* and other books

James U. Rose

Janet I. Rose

Stuart E. Rose

Rynd Communications (publisher of *Dictionary of Health Services Management*)

Harry Schechter, late chairman, Government Printing Office Style Board

Edward A. Schmerler

Brian Scott, editor of *Dictionary of Military Abbreviations*

Peter Sikli

Standard & Poor's Corporation (publisher of *Security Owner's Stock Guide*)

Edwin B. Steen, professor emeritus of biology, Western Michigan University, author of *Abbreviations in Medicine and Dictionary of Biology*

Miriam M. Steinert, editorial consultant

A. Marjorie Taylor, editor, *Language of World War II*

Edith Thompson

Toronto Stock Exchange

David J. Trotz, editor of *Defense Weapon Systems Glossary*

Tracey Head Turbett

The University Press of Virginia (publisher of *Dictionary of Sigla and Abbreviations to and in Law Books before 1607*)

U.S. Air Force, Translation Section HQ

VCH Publishers (publisher of *Index of Acronyms and Abbreviations in Electrical and Electronic Engineering*)

Donald Weeks

Witherby & Co. Ltd. (publisher of *Aviation Insurance Abbreviations, Organisations, and Institutions; Dictionary of Commercial Terms and Abbreviations; Dictionary of Shipping International Trade Terms and Abbreviations*)

Harvey J. Wolf

User's Guide

The following examples illustrate possible elements of entries in *RAIAD*:

①   ②   ③   ④
Force Aerienne Tactique [*Tactical Air Force*] [*French*] (NATG) ....FATAC

⑤   ⑥
Multiple-Mirror Telescope [*Mount Hopkins, AZ*] [*Jointly operated by
Smithsonian Institution and the University of Arizona*] [*Astronomy*].......................MMT
                                                            ⑦   ⑧

①   Meaning or Phrase

②   English Translation

③   Language (for non-English entries)

④   Source code (Allows you to verify entries or find additional information. Decoded in the List of Selected Sources)

⑤   Location or Country of origin (Provides geographic identifiers for airports, colleges and universities, libraries, military bases, political parties, radio and television stations, and others)

⑥   Sponsoring organization

⑦   Subject category (Clarifies entries by providing appropriate context)

⑧   Acronym, Initialism, or Abbreviation

The completeness of a listing is dependent upon both the nature of the term and the amount of information provided by the source. If additional information becomes available during future research, an entry is revised.

Arrangement of Entries

Terms are arranged in alphabetical order, according to the meaning of the acronym, initialism, or abbreviation. If a particular translation has more than one initialism representing it, the various choices are then arranged alphabetically. Thus:

        Liquid Nitrogen..LIN
        Liquid Nitrogen..LN

Articles, conjunctions, prepositions, etc., generally are not considered in the alphabetizing:

        Master Switch...MS
        Master *of* Textile Chemistry...MTC
        Not Less Than ....NLT
        Not *in* Line *of* Duty...NLD

List of Selected Sources

Each of the sources included in the following list contributed at least 50 terms. It would be impossible to cite a source for every entry because the majority of terms are sent by outside contributors, are uncovered through independent research by the editorial staff, or surface as miscellaneous broadcast or print media references.

For sources used on an ongoing basis, only the latest edition is listed. For most of the remaining sources, the edition that was used is cited. The editors will provide further information about these sources upon request.

Unless further described in an annotation, the publications listed here contain no additional information about the acronym, initialism, or abbreviation cited.

(AABC)   *Catalog of Abbreviations and Brevity Codes*. Washington, DC: U.S. Department of the Army, 1981. [Use of source began in 1969]

(ABAC)   "Abbreviations, Acronyms, and Initialisms." <http://www.pnl.gov/ag/usage/acroel.html> (27 January 2000)

(AAEL)   *Common Abbreviations and Acronyms in Electronics.* By Gunham Kaytaz. <http://www.seas.smu.edu/~kaytaz/menu.html> (27 April 1999)

(AAG)   *Aerospace Abbreviations Glossary*. Report Number AG60-0014. Prepared by General Dynamics/Astronautics. San Diego, CA: 1962.

(AAGC)   *Acronyms and Abbreviations in Government Contracting*. 2d ed. By Patricia A. Tobin and Joan Nelson Phillips. Washington, DC: George Washington University, 1997.

(AAMN)   *Abbreviations and Acronyms in Medicine and Nursing*. By Solomon Garb, Eleanor Krakauer, and Carson Justice. New York, NY: Springer Publishing Co., 1976.

(ABBR)   *Abbreviations: The Comprehensive Dictionary of Abbreviations and Letter Symbols*. Vol. 1 C. By Edward Wall. Ann Arbor, MI: The Pierian Press, 1984.

(AC)   *Associations Canada 1995/96.* Edited by Ward McBurney. Toronto, Canada: Canadian Almanac & Directory Publishing Co. Ltd., 1995.

(ACAE)   *Aerospace and Defense Acronyms.* 2d ed. Compiled by Fernando B. Morinigo. Washington, DC: American Institute of Aeronautics and Astronautics, 1992

(ACII)   *"Acronym and Initials Index."* 7 February 1996. <http://www.ioi.ie/~readout/cl.html> (7 November 1996)

(AD)   *Abbreviations Dictionary*. 8th ed. By Ralph De Sola. Boca Raton, FL: CRC Press, 1992.

(ADA)   *The Australian Dictionary of Acronyms and Abbreviations*. 2nd ed. Compiled by David J. Jones. Leura, NSW, Australia: Second Back Row Press Pty. Ltd., 1981.

(ADDR)   *Army Dictionary and Desk Reference*. By Tim Zurick. Harrisburg, PA: Stackpole Books, 1992.

(ADWA)   *Abbreviations Dictionary; A Practical Compilation of Today's Acronyms and Abbreviations.* By Robert S. Wachal. Boston: Houghton Mifflin Co., 1999.

(AEBE)   *Acronyms in Electronics Business and Engineering.* By Ken Westover. Boulder, CO: Cliff Canyon Publishing Co., 1998.

(AEBS)   *Acronyms in Education and the Behavioral Sciences.* By Toyo S. Kawakami. Chicago, IL: American Library Association, 1971.

(AEE)   *American Educators' Encyclopedia.* By Edward L. Dejnozka and David E. Kapel. Westport, CT: Greenwood Press, 1991.

(AEPA)   U.S. Environmental Protection Agency. *ACCESS EPA.* 1995/96 ed. Washington, DC: Office of Information Resources Management, 1996.

(AF)   *Reference Aid: Abbreviations in the African Press.* Arlington, VA: Joint Publications Research Service, 1979.

(AFIT)   *Compendium of Authenticated Systems and Logistics.* Washington, DC: Air Force Institute of Technology, 1984.

(AFM)   *Air Force Manual of Abbreviations.* Washington, DC: U.S. Department of the Air Force, 1975. [Use of source began in 1969]

(AIA)   *Aviation Insurance Abbreviations, Organisations and Institutions.* By M.J. Spurway. London, England: Witherby & Co. Ltd., 1983.

(AIE)   *Acronyms and Initialisms in Education.* 6th ed. Compiled by John Hutchins. Norwich, England: Librarians of Institutes and Schools of Education, 1995.

(AL)   *"Acronyms & Abbreviations."* American Library Association. <http://www.ala.org/> (2 December 1997)

(ALHF)   *"Alaska Housing Finance Corporation Glossary"* <http://www.ahfc.state.ak.us.index.htm> (18 October Glossary)

(ANA)   *"Abbreviations" - U.S. Navy Dictionary.* 3rd revision. Washington, DC: DCP, 1989.

(APTA)   *Australian Periodical Title Abbreviations.* Compiled by David J. Jones. Leura, NSW, Australia: Second Back Row Press Pty. Ltd., 1985.

(ARC)   *Agricultural Research Centres: A World Directory of Organizations and Programmes.* 2 vols. Edited by Nigel Harvey. Harlow, Essex, England: Longman Group, 1983.
       A world guide to official, educational, industrial, and independent research centers which support research in the fields of agriculture, veterinary medicine, horticulture, aquaculture, food science, forestry, zoology, and botany.

(ARCH)   *Dictionary of Architecture and Construction.* Edited by Cyril M. Harris. New York, NY: McGraw-Hill, Inc., 1975.

(ARMP)   "Global Change Acronyms and Abbreviations." <http://www.arm.gov/docs/index/html> (8 February 2000)

(ASC)   *Associations Canada 1995/96.* Edited by Ward McBurney. Toronto, Ontario: Canadian Almanac & Directory Publishing Co Ltd., 1995.

(ASF)   *Guide to Names and Acronyms of Organizations, Activities, and Projects.* By Food and Agriculture Organization of the United Nations. Fishery Information, Data, and Statistics Service and U.S. National Oceanic and Atmospheric Administration. Aquatic Sciences and Fisheries Information System Reference Series, Number 10, 1982. n.p.

(AUEG)   "Acronyms Used by Environmental Groups and Agencies." <http://www.etd.ameslab.gov/etd/library/acronyms/acronym.html> (2000)

(AVGL)   *"Aircraft Owners and Pilots Association Aviation Glossary."* <http://www.aopa.ch/xgloss.htm> (20 October 1999)

(BABM)   *Bailliere's Abbreviations in Medicine.* 5th ed. By Edwin B. Steen. London, England: Bailliere Tindall, 1984.

(BARN)   *The Barnhart Abbreviations Dictionary.* Edited by Robert K. Barnhart. New York, NY: John Wiley & Sons, Inc., 1995.

(BCP)   *BCP Guidebook.* <http://www.dtic.dla.mil/environdod/> (Fall 1995)

(BEE)   "The Beeline." http://www.bton.com/tb17/abbr/a.html (17 November 1999)

(BI)   *British Initials and Abbreviations.* 3rd ed. By Ian H. Wilkes. London, England: Leonard Hill Books, 1971.

(BIB)   *Bibliotech.* Ottawa, Canada: National Library of Canada, 1988-89.

(BJA)   *Biblical and Judaic Acronyms.* By Lawrence Marwick. New York, NY: Ktav Publishing House, Inc., 1979.

(BRI)   *Book Review Index.* 1997 Cumulation. Edited by Beverly Baer. Detroit, MI: Gale Research, 1998.

(BROA)   *Broadcasting and Cable Yearbook 2000.* Donald V. West, Group Editor in Chief. New Providence, NJ: R.R. Bowker, 2000.

(BTTJ)   *Breaking Through Technical Jargon: A Dictionary of Computer and Automation Acronyms.* By Mark S. Merkow. New York, NY: Van Nostrand Reinhold, 1990.

(BUAC)   *Buttress's World Guide to Abbreviations of Organizations.* 11th ed. Revised by L.M. Pitman. London, England: Blackie Academic and Professional, 1997.

(BUR)   *Computer Acronyms and Abbreviations Handbook.* Tokyo, Japan: Burroughs Co. Ltd., 1978.

(BYTE)   *Byte: The Small Systems Journal.* Peterborough, NH: McGraw-Hill Information Systems, Inc., 1987-89.

(CAAL)   *CAAL COMOPTEVFOR Acronym and Abbreviation List.* Norfolk, VA: (CAAL-U) Operational Test and Evaluation Force, 1981.

(CARB)   "Carbon Dioxide Information Analysis Center--Acronyms and Abbreviations." <http://www.cdiac.esd.oorni.gov/cdiac/pns/acronyms.html> (18 July 1996)

(CB) *Centres & Bureaux: A Directory of Concentrations of Effort, Information and Expertise*. Edited by Lindsay Sellar. Beckenham, Kent, England: CBD Research Ltd., 1987.
  A guide to British organizations which include the words "centre" or "bureau" in their names. Entries include name and address; telephone and telex numbers; chief official; and a description of the purposes, activities, and services of the organization.

(CCCA) *ABC Pocket Guide for the Field on C3 Acronyms; An Anthology of Command, Control, and Communications Acronyms and Abbreviations*. 2d. ed. Edited by Charles R. Wolfson. Geneva, IL: ABC TeleTraining, Inc., 1986.

(CDAI) *Concise Dictionary of Acronyms and Initialisms*. By Stuart W. Miller. New York, NY: Facts on File Publications, 1988.

(CDE) *The Computer Desktop Encyclopedia*. By Alan Freedman. New York, NY: AMACOM, 1996.

(CDI) *The Cancer Dictionary*. By Roberta Altman and Michael Sarg, M.D. New York, NY: Facts on File, 1992.

(CED) *Current European Directories*. 2nd ed. Edited by G.P. Henderson. Beckenham, Kent, England: CBD Research, 1981.

(CET) *Communications-Electronics Terminology*. AFM 11-1. Vol. 3. U.S. Department of the Air Force, 1973.

(CGWS) *The Comprehensive Guide to Wireless Resources; Definitions and Acronyms, and National Trade Shows, Association and Publication Listings*. By Lawrence Harte and Steven Kellogg. Fuquay-Varina, NC: APDG Publishing, 1998.

(CINC) *A CINCPAC Glossary of Commonly Used Abbreviations and Short Titles*. By Ltc. J.R. Johnson. Washington, DC: 1968.

(CIST) *Computer & Information Science & Technology Abbreviations & Acronyms Dictionary*. Edited by David W. South. Boca Raton, FL: CRC Press, Inc., 1994.

(CMD) *Complete Multilingual Dictionary of Computer Terminology*. Compiled by Georges Nania. Chicago, IL: National Textbook Co., 1984.
  Computer-related terms in Spanish, French, Italian, Portuguese, and English. Indexes in French, Italian, Spanish, and Portuguese are also provided.

(CNC) *American National Standard Codes for the Representation of Names of Countries, Dependencies, and Areas of Special Sovereignty for Information Interchange*. U.S. National Bureau of Standards. Washington, DC: Government Printing Office, 1986. [Use of source began in 1977]
  These standard codes, approved by the International Organization for Standardization and the American National Standards Institute, are used in the international interchange of data in many fields.

(COBU) "Common Business and Professional Abbreviations and Acronyms." <http://www.instantaccess.co.uk/infozone/abbraviations.html> (27 January 2000)

(COE) *Cooper's Comprehensive Environmental Desk Reference*. Edited by Andre R. Cooper. New York, NY: John Wiley & Sons, 1990.

(CPGU) *Canadian Parliamentary Guide, Parlementaire Canadien, 1998-1999.* Edited by Kathryn O'Handley. Farmington Hills, MI: Gale Group, Inc., 1999.

(CPH) *The Charles Press Handbook of Current Medical Abbreviations.* 3rd ed. Philadelphia, PA: The Charles Press Publishers, Inc., 1991.

(CRD) *Computer-Readable Databases: A Directory and Data Sourcebook.* 6th ed. Edited by Kathleen Young Marcaccio. Detroit, MI: Gale Research, 1990.
> A guide to online databases, offline files available in various magnetic formats, and CD-ROM files. Entries include producer name, address, telephone number, description of coverage, vendors, and contact person.

(CROSS) *Cross-Border Links: A Directory of Organizations in Canada, Mexico, and the United States.* Edited by Ricardo Hernandez and Edith Sanchez. Albuquerque, NM: Inter-Hemispheric Education Resource Center, 1992.

(CSR) *Computer Science Resources: A Guide to Professional Literature.* Edited by Darlene Myers. White Plains, NY: Knowledge Industry Publications, Inc., 1981.
> Covers several types of computer-related literature including journals, technical reports, directories, dictionaries, handbooks, and university computer center newsletters. Five appendices cover career and salary trends in the computer industry, user group acronyms, university computer libraries, and trade fairs and shows.

(CTAS) "CTAS Acronym Dictionary." <http://www.ctas.arc.nase.gov/acronyms> (10 October 2000)

(CTT) *Corporate TrendTrac.* Edited by A. Dale Timpe. Detroit, MI: Gale Research, 1988-89.
> Covers mergers and acquisitions, stock exchange listings and suspensions, company name changes, bankruptcies, liquidations, and reorganizations.

(CWA) *"Civil War Acronyms.*<http://www.antiqueresources.com/articles/cwacronyms.html>(1998)

(DA) *Dictionary of Aviation.* By R. J. Hall and R. D. Campbell. Chicago, IL: St. James Press, 1991.

(DAS) *Dictionary of Abbreviations and Symbols.* By Edward Frank Allen. London, England: Cassell and Co. Ltd., 1949.

(DAVI) *Medical Abbreviations; 14,000 Conveniences at the Expense of Communications and Safety.* 9th ed. By Neil M. Davis. Huntingdon Valley, PA: Neil M. Davis Associates, 1999.

(DB) *Dictionary of Biomedical Acronyms and Abbreviations.* 2nd ed. By Jacques Dupayrat. New York, NY: John Wiley & Sons, 1990.

(DBA) *Directory of British Associations.* Edited by G. P. Henderson and S. P. A. Henderson. Beckenham, Kent, England: CBD Research, Ltd., 1990.

(DBQ) *A Dictionary of British Qualifications.* London, England: Kogan Page Ltd., 1985.

(DCTA) *Dictionary of Commercial Terms and Abbreviations.* By Alan E. Branch. London, England: Witherby & Co. Ltd., 1984.

(DD) *The Financial Post Directory of Directors 1997.* Toronto, Canada: The Financial Post, 1996.

(DDC) *The International Dictionary of Data Communications.* By Robert A. Saigh. Chicago, IL: The Glenlake Publishing Company, Ltd., 1998.

(DDSO)   *D & D Standard Oil Abbreviator.* 4th ed. Compiled by the Association of Desk and Derrick Clubs. Tulsa, OK: PennWell Books, 1994.

(DEMM)   "Department of Emergency Management Master List of Acronyms." <http://bcem.co.bay.fl.us/dem/htm> (27 January 2000)

(DEN)   *Dictionary of Electronics and Nucleonics.* By L.E.C. Hughes, R.W.B. Stephens and L. D. Brown. New York, NY: Barnes & Noble, 1969.

(DET)   *Dictionary of Educational Terms.* Edited by David Blake and Vincent Hanley. Brookfield, VT: Ashgate Publishing Co., 1995.

(DFIT)   *Dictionary of Finance and Investment Terms.* 4th ed. Edited by John Downes and Jordan Elliot Goodman. Hauppauge, NY: Barron's Educational Series, 1995.

(DGA)   *Dictionary of Graphic Arts Abbreviations.* By L. W. Wallis. Rockport, MA: Rockport Publishers, Inc., 1986.

(DHP)   *Dictionary of Abbreviations and Acronyms in Helping Professions.* By John W. Hollis. Muncie, IN:
Accelerated Development, Inc., 1987.

(DHSM)   *Dictionary of Health Services Management.* 2nd ed. By Thomas C. Timmreck. Owings Mills, MD: Rynd Communications, 1987.

(DI)   *The Dictionary of Initials--What They Mean.* Compiled and edited by Harriette Lewis. Kingswood, Surrey, England: Paper Fronts Elliot Right Way Books, 1983.

(DICI)   *The Dictionary of Initials.* By Betsy M. Parks. Secaucus, NJ: Citadel Press, 1981.

(DIPS)   *The Dictionary of Psychology.* By Raymond J. Corsini. Philadelphia: Taylor and Francis, 1999.

(DIT)   *Dictionary of Informatics Terms in Russian and English.* By G.S. Zhdanov, E.S. Kolobrodov, V.A. Polushkin, and A.I. Cherny. Moscow: Nauka, 1971.

(DLA)   *Bieber's Dictionary of Legal Abbreviations.* 3rd ed. By Mary Miles Prince. Buffalo, NY: William S. Hein & Co., 1988.

(DMA)   *Dictionary of Military Abbreviations: British, Empire, Commonwealth.* By B.K.C. Scott. Hastings, East Sussex, England: Tamarisk Books, 1982.

(DMAA)   *Dictionary of Medical Acronyms and Abbreviations.* 3rd ed. Edited by Stanley Jablonski. Philadelphia, PA: Hanley & Belfus, Inc., 1998.

(DMC)   *Webster's New World Dictionary of Media and Communications.* Revised ed. By Richard Weiner. New York, NY: Macmillan, 1996.

(DNAB)   *Dictionary of Naval Abbreviations.* 3rd ed. Compiled and edited by Bill Wedertz. Annapolis, MD: Naval Institute Press, 1984.

(DOAD)   *The Dictionary of Advertising.* Edited by Laurence Urdang. Lincolnwood, IL: NTC Business Books, 1986.

(DOG)   *A Dictionary of Genetics.* 5th ed. By Robert C. King and William D. Stansfield. New York, NY:

Oxford University Press, 1997.

(DOGT)   *"List of Acronyms."* <http://www.em.doe.gov/rtc1994/loa.html> (5 March 1997)

(DOM)   *The Dictionary of Multimedia: Terms & Acronyms.* By Brad Hansen. Wilsonvillee, OR: Franklin, Beedle & Associates, 1997.

(DOMA)   *Dictionary of Military Abbreviations.* By Norman Polmar, Mark Warren, and Eric Wertheim. Annapolis, MD: Naval Institute Press, 1994.

(DS)   *Dictionary of Shipping International Trade Terms and Abbreviations.* 3rd ed. By Alan E. Branch. London, England: Witherby & Co. Ltd., 1986.

(DSA)   *Dictionary of Sigla and Abbreviations to and in Law Books before 1607.* By William Hamilton Bryson. Charlottesville, VA: University Press of Virginia, 1975.

(DSUE)   *A Dictionary of Slang and Unconventional English.* 8th ed. By Eric Partridge. New York, NY: Macmillan Publishing Co., 1984.

(DUND)   *Directory of United Nations Databases and Information Services.* 4th ed. Compiled by the Advisory Committee for the Coordination of Information Systems. New York, NY: United Nations, 1990.
          A guide to computerized databases and information systems/services. Entries
          include sponsoring organization, year established, type, scope, coverage, timespan,
          and contact information.

(DWSG)   *Defense Weapon Systems Glossary.* By David Trotz. Piscataway, NJ: Target Marketing, 1992.

(EA)   *Encyclopedia of Associations.* 34th ed. Vol. 1, National Oranizations of the U.S. Edited by Christine Maurer and Tara E. Sheets. Farmington Hills, MI: Gale Group, 1999.
          [Use of source began in 1960]
          A guide to trade, professional, and other nonprofit associations that are national and
          international in scope and membership and that are headquartered in the United
          States. Entries include name and address; telephone and telex number; chief official;
          and a description of the purpose, activities, and structure of the organization.

(EAAP)   *Encyclopedia of Associations: Association Periodicals.* 3 vols. Edited by Denise M. Allard and Robert C. Thomas. Detroit, MI: Gale Research, 1987.
          A directory of publications issued by all types of national nonprofit organizations in
          the United States. Entries include title and organization name, address, telephone
          number; description of periodical, frequency of publication, and price.

(EAIO)   *Encyclopedia of Associations: International Organizations.* 29th ed. Edited by Linda Irvin. Detroit, MI: Gale Research, 1995. [Use of source began in 1985]
          A guide to trade, professional, and other nonprofit associations that are national or
          international in scope and membership and that are headquartered outside the
          United States. Entries include name and address; principal foreign language name;
          telephone and telex number; chief official; and a description of the purpose,
          activities, and structure of the organization.

(EBF)   *Encyclopedia of Banking and Finance.* 10th ed. Edited by Charles J. Woelfel. Chicago, IL: Probus Publishing Co., 1994.

(ECED)   *The European Communities Encyclopedia and Directory 1992*. London, England: Europa Publications Ltd., 1991; distributed in U.S. by Gale Research, Detroit, MI.
A comprehensive guide to the European Communities. Entries explain widely-used acronyms and include address, telephone, telex, fax numbers and chief officers for EC-level organizations.

(ECII)   *Electronics, Computers and Industrial Instrumentation Abbreviations and Acronyms.* Edited by Sergio Sobredo. Miami, FL: Sergio Sobredo Technical Services, 1986.

(ECON)   *The Economist*. London, England: The Economist Newspaper Ltd., 2001. [Use of source began in 1988]

(EDAC)   *Dictionary of Educational Acronyms, Abbreviations, and Initialisms.* 2nd ed. Edited by James C. Palmer and Anita Y. Colby. Phoenix, AZ: Oryx Press, 1985.

(EDCT)   *Encyclopedic Dictionary of Chemical Technology.* By Dorit Noether and Herman Noether. New York, NY: VCH Publishers, Inc., 1993.

(EE)   *Eastern Europe and the Commonwealth of Independent States 1992.* London, England: Europa Publications Ltd., 1992; distributed in U.S. by Gale Research, Detroit, MI.

(EECA)   *Dictionary of Electrical, Electronics, and Computer Abbreviations.* By Phil Brown. London, England: Buttersworth, 1985.

(EES)   *A Dictionary of Ecology, Evolution and Systematics.* 2nd edition. Edited by Roger Lincoln, Geoff Boxshall and Paul Clark. New York, NY: Cambridge University Press, 1998.

(EEVL)   *Environmental Engineering Dictionary.* 3rd ed. Edited by C.C. Lee. Rockville, MD: Government Institutes, 1998.

(EFIS)   *Corporate Acronym Resource Guide, 1800s-1995.* Seattle, WA: Environmental Financial Information Services, Inc. (EFIS), 1996.

(EG)   *Environmental Glossary.* 4th ed. Edited by G. William Frick and Thomas F.P. Sullivan. Rockville, MD: Government Institutes, Inc., 1986.

(EGAO)   *Encyclopedia of Governmental Advisory Organizations.* 9th ed. Edited by Donna Batten. Detroit, MI: Gale Research, 1994-95 (and supplement, 1995). [Use of source began in 1975]
A reference guide to permanent, continuing, and ad hoc U.S. presidential advisory committees, interagency committees, and other government-related boards, panels, task forces, commissions, conferences, and other similar bodies serving in a consultative, coordinating, advisory, research, or investigative capacity. Entries include name and address, telephone number, designated federal employee, history, recommendation and findings of the committee, staff size, publications, and subsidiaries. Also includes indexes to personnel, reports, federal agencies, presidential administration, and an alphabetical and keyword index.

(EMRF)   *The St. James Encyclopedia of Mortgage & Real Estate Finance.* By James Newell, Albert Santi, and Chip Mitchell. Chicago, IL: St. James Press, 1991.

(EOSA)   "Earth Observing System (EOS) Acronyms and Abbreviations." http://eospso.gsfc.nasa/eos_homepage/misc (5 October 1999)

(EPA)   *Glossary of EPA Acronyms.* Washington, DC: Environmental Protection Agency, 1987.

(EPAT)   "Terms of Environment." http://www.epa.gov/OCEPAterms/aaad.html (3 November 1999)

(ERG)   *Environmental Regulatory Glossary.* 5th ed. Edited by G. William Frick and Thomas F.P. Sullivan. Rockville, MD: Government Institutes, Inc., 1990.

(EY)   *The Europa World Year Book 1992.* London: Europa Publications Ltd., 1992. distributed in U.S. by Gale Research, Detroit, MI.
           An annual survey containing detailed information about the political, economic, statistical, and commercial situation of the regions and countries covered.

(FAAC)   *Contractions Handbook.* Changes. U.S. Department of Transportation. Federal Aviation Administration, 1993. [Use of source began in 1969]

(FAAL)   *Location Identifiers.* U.S. Department of Transportation. Federal Aviation Administration. Air Traffic Service, 1982.

(FEA)   *The Far East and Australasia 1987.* 18th ed. London, England: Europa Publications Ltd., 1986; distributed in U.S. by Gale Research, Detroit, MI.
           An annual survey containing detailed information about the political, economic, statistical, and commercial situation of the regions and countries covered.

(FFDE)   *The Facts on File Dictionary of Environmental Science.* By L. Harold Stevenson and Bruce Wyman. New York, NY: Facts on File, 1991.
           Defines terms from disciplines as diverse as biology, chemistry, geology, physics, engineering, meteorology, social science, medicine, and economics.

(FUCW)   *"Frequently Used Contractions in National Weather Service Products."* <http://www.awc-kc.noaa.gov/info/domestic_contractions.html>

(GAAI)   *"Glossary of Abbreviations, Acronyms, and Initialisms."* <http://www.em.doe.gov/idb97/acropdf.html> (17 February 1998)

(GAVI)   *"Glossary of Aviation Acronyms and Abbreviations."* <http://olias.arc.nasa.gov/AFO_Acronyms_.html> (5 March 1997)

(GEA)   *Government Economic Agencies of the World: An International Directory of Governmental Organisations Concerned with Economic Development and Planning.* A Keesing's Reference Publication. Edited by Alan J. Day. Harlow, Essex, England: Longman Group Ltd., 1985.
           Covers over 170 countries and territories. Two introductory sections for each area cover economic data and prevailing economic and political conditions. Individual entries provide title, address, and names of chief officials of each agency. Current activities and financial structure of each agency are also detailed. An index of agency officials is provided.

(GEAB)   "Genealogy Abbreviations." http://www.genweb.net/~samcasey/abbre.html (17 November 1999)

(GEOI)   "Dictionary of Abbreviations and Acronyms in Geographic Information Systems, Cartography, and Remote Sensing." By Philip Hoehn and Mary Lynette Larsgaard. http://www.lib.berkeley.edu/EART/abbrev.html (June 1999)

(GFGA)   *Guide to Federal Government Acronyms.* Edited by William R. Evinger. Phoenix, AZ: The Oryx Press, 1989.

(GNE)   *The Green Encyclopedia.* By Irene Franck and David Brownstone. New York, NY: Prentice Hall General Reference, 1992.

(GPO)   *Style Manual.* Washington, DC: Government Printing Office, 1984. [Terms are included in Chapter 24, Foreign Languages]

(GRD)   *Government Research Directory.* 8th ed. Edited by Joseph M. Palmisano. Detroit, MI: Gale Research, 1994. (and supplement, 1994).
        A descriptive guide to U.S. government research and development centers, institutes, laboratories, bureaus, test facilities, experiment stations, data collection and analysis centers, and grants management and research coordinating offices in agriculture, business, education, energy, engineering, environment, the humanities, medicine, military science, and basic applied sciences.

(GRST)   *"Glossary of Remote Sensing Terms."* <http://ceo1409.ceo.sai.jrc.it:8080...2/tutorials/glossary> (5 October 1999)

(GVA)   "Glossary of Veterinary Acronyms." http://www/spvs.org.uk/glossary.htm (October 1999)

(HCT)   *Health Care Terms.* 2nd ed. By Vergil N. Slee and Debora A. Slee. St. Paul, MN: Tringa Press, 1991.

(HEAS)   "Acronyms and Abbreviations Used in Health and Safety Executive Information Services." <http://www.healthandsafety.co.uk/acronyms.html> (26 September 2000)

(HGAA)   *The Handy Guide to Abbreviations and Acronyms for the Automated Office.* By Mark W. Greenia. Seattle, WA: Self-Counsel Press, Inc., 1986.

(HGEN)   *Human Genome Acronym List.* <http://www.ornl.gov/hgmis/acronym.html> (2 December 1998)

(HLLA)   "Honeywell Abbreviation and Acronym Dictionary." <http://www.cas.honeywell.com/ats/acronym.html> (27 January 2000)

(HRG)   *The Human Resources Glossary: The Complete Desk Reference for HR Executives, Managers, and Practitioners.* 2nd ed. By William R. Tracey. Boca Raton, FL: St. Lucie Press, 1998.

(IAA)   *Index of Acronyms and Abbreviations in Electrical and Electronic Engineering.* Compiled by Buro Scientia. New York, NY: VCH Publishers, 1989.

(IAS)   *"International Arctic Science Committee."* <http://www.iasc.no/acronyms.htm> (20 October 1999)

(IUSS)   "IUSS Acronyms." http://206.239.241.41/Acronym/1.html (12 October 1999)

(IBMDP)   *IBM Data Processing Glossary.* 6th ed. White Plains, NY: IBM Corp., 1977.

(ICAO)   *Aircraft Type Designators.* 13th ed. International Civil Aviation Organization, August, 1981.

(ICDA)   *Designators for Aircraft Operating Agencies, Aeronautical Authorities and Services.* 49th ed. International Civil Aviation Organization, June, 1982.
        Document also includes telephony designators and postal and telegraphic addresses of government civil aviation authorities.

(ICLI)   *Location Indicators.* 51st ed. International Civil Aviation Organization, February, 1987.

Document also contains addresses of flight information centers.

(IDAI)   *The International Dictionary of Artificial Intelligence*. By William Raynor. Chicago: Glenlake Publishing Co., Ltd., 1999.

(IDOE)   *The Illustrated Dictionary of Electronics*. 6th ed. By Stan Gibilisco. New York, NY: TAB Books, 1994.

(IEEE)   *IEEE Standard Dictionary of Electrical and Electronics Terms*. Edited by Frank Jay. New York, NY: The Institute of Electrical and Electronics Engineers, Inc., 1977, 1984.
Includes definitions for thousands of electrical and electronics terms. Each entry includes a numeric source code.

(IGQR)   *The Internet Glossary & Quick Reference Guide.* By Alan Freedman, Alfred Glossbrenner and Emily Glossbrenner. New York, NY: AMACOM, 1998.

(IIA)   *Index of Initials and Acronyms*. Compiled by Richard Kleiner. New York, NY: Auerbach Publishers, 1971.

(IID)   *Information Industry Directory*. 15th ed. Edited by Annette Novallo. Detroit, MI: Gale Research, 1995. (and supplement, 1995).
An international guide to computer-readable databases, database producers, and publishers, online vendors and time-sharing companies, telecommunications networks, and many other information systems and services. Entries include name and address, telephone number, chief official, and a detailed description of the purpose and function of the system or service.

(ILCA)   *Index to Legal Citations and Abbreviations*. By Donald Raistrick. Abingdon, Oxfordshire, England: Professional Books Ltd., 1981.

(IMH)   *International Marketing Handbook*. 2nd ed. Edited by Frank Bair. Detroit, MI: Gale Research, 1985.
An in-depth guide to commercial and trade data on 142 countries of the world. Features include a list of European trade fairs and a report on growth markets in Western Europe.

(INF)   *Infantry*. Fort Benning, GA: U.S. Army Infantry Training School, 1996. [Use of source began in 1983]

(IOWA)   *"Iowa Department of Natural Resources Quick Facts."*
<http://www.state.ia.us/government/dnr/part1.htm> (19 October 1999)

(IRC)   *International Research Centers Directory 1992-93*. 6th ed. Edited by Annette Piccirelli. Detroit, MI: Gale Research, 1991.
A world guide to government, university, independent, nonprofit, and commercial research and development centers, institutes, laboratories, bureaus, test facilities, experiment stations, and data collection and analysis centers, as well as foundations, councils, and other organizations which support research.

(IRUK)   *Industrial Research in the United Kingdom*. 12th ed. Harlow, Essex, England: Longman Group UK Ltd., 1987.
A guide to all groups conducting or funding research relevant to British industrial development. Entries include name, address, telephone and telex numbers; chief officials; and scope of activities.

(IT)   *Information Today: The Newspaper for Users and Producers of Electronic Information Services*. Medford, NJ: Learned Information, Inc., 1988-89.

(ITCA)   *Internet Terms and Computer Acronyms, A Useful Guide*. By Mary Brookhart. Charlotte, NC: Southeast Consulting, Inc., 1998.

(ITD)   *International Tradeshow Directory*. 5th ed. Frankfurt, Germany: M + A Publishers for Fairs, Exhibitions and Conventions Ltd., 1989.
            A guide to trade fairs and exhibitions throughout the world. Entries include event name, dates, frequency, location, description of purpose, profile of exhibitors and attendees.

(IYR)   *The 1989-92 International Yacht Racing Rules*. London, England: International Yacht Racing Union, 1989.

(KSC)   *A Selective List of Acronyms and Abbreviations*. Compiled by the Documents Department, Kennedy Space Center Library, 1971, 1973.

(LAIN)   *Latest Intelligence: An International Directory of Codes Used by Government, Law Enforcement, Military, and Surveillance Agencies*. By James E. Tunnell. Blue Ridge Summit, PA: TAB BOOKS, 1990.

(LCCP)   *MARC Formats for Bibliographic Data*. Appendix II. Washington, DC: Library of Congress, 1982.

(LCLS)   *Symbols of American Libraries*. 14th ed. Edited by the Enhanced Cataloging Division. Washington, DC: Library of Congress, 1992. [Use of source began in 1980]

(LWAP)   *Legal Words and Phrases: Speed Abbreviations*. By Joel Larus. Boston, MA: Aurico Publishing, 1965.

(MAE)   *Medical Abbreviations and Eponyms*. By Sheila B. Sloane. Philadelphia, PA: W.B. Saunders Co., 1985.

(MARI)   "Glossary of Marine Abbreviations." <http://www.royalsunalliance.ca/rsa.arine/glossabbrevdisp.html> (26 September 2000)

(MAH)   *Medical Abbreviations Handbook*. 2nd ed. Oradell, NJ: Medical Economics Co., Inc., 1983.

(MCD)   *Acronyms, Abbreviations, and Initialisms*. Compiled by Carl Lauer. St. Louis, MO: McDonnell Douglas Corp., 1989. [Use of source began in 1969]

(MDG)   *Microcomputer Dictionary and Guide*. By Charles J. Sippl. Champaign, IL: Matrix Publishers, Inc., 1975.
            A listing of definitions for over 5,000 microelectronics terms. Seven appendices.

(ME)   *The Marine Encyclopaedic Dictionary*. 5th ed. By Eric Sullivan. London, England: LLP Ltd., 1996.

(MEC)   *Macmillan Encyclopedia of Chemistry*. Vol. 1. Edited by Joseph J. Lagowski. New York, NY: Macmillan Reference USA, 1997.

(MED)   *McGraw-Hill Electronic Dictionary*. 5th ed. Edited by John Markus and Neil Sclater. New York, NY: McGraw-Hill, Inc., 1994.

(MEDA)   *Medical Acronyms*. 2nd ed. By Marilyn Fuller Delong. Oradell, NJ: Medical Economic Books, 1989.

(MELL) *Melloni's Illustrated Dictionary of Medical Abbreviations.* By John Melloni and Ida G. Dox. Pearl River, NY: Parthenon Publishing Group, Inc., 1998.

(MENA) *The Middle East and North Africa 1987.* 33rd ed. London, England: Europa Publications Ltd., 1986; distributed in U.S. by Gale Research, Detroit, MI.
An annual survey containing detailed information about the political, economic, statistical, and commercial situation of the regions and countries covered.

(MGMA) *"Medical Group Management Associations Book of Acronyms for Medical Practice Executives."* <http://www.mgma.com/library/acronyms.html> (19 October 1999)

(MHDB) *McGraw-Hill Dictionary of Business Acronyms, Initials, and Abbreviations.* By Jerry M. Rosenberg. New York, NY: McGraw-Hill, Inc., 1992.

(MHDI) *McGraw-Hill Dictionary of Information Technology and Computer Acronyms, Initials, and Abbreviations.* By Jerry M. Rosenberg. New York, NY: McGraw-Hill, Inc., 1992.

(MHDW) *McGraw-Hill Dictionary of Wall Street Acronyms, Initials, and Abbreviations.* By Jerry M. Rosenberg. New York, NY: McGraw-Hill, Inc., 1992.

(MILB) *The Military Balance 1998/99.* London: Oxford University Press for the International Institute for Strategic Studies, 1998.

(MLOA) "Marconi--List of Acronyms." <http://www.fore.com/atm-edu/acronyms.html> (1999)

(MSA) *Military Standard Abbreviations for Use on Drawings, and in Specifications, Standards, and Technical Documents.* MIL-STD-12D. U.S. Department of Defense, 1981. [Use of source began in 1975]

(MSC) *Annotated Acronyms and Abbreviations of Marine Science Related Activities.* 3rd ed. Revised by Charlotte M. Ashby and Alan R. Flesh. Washington, DC: U.S. Department of Commerce. National Oceanographic and Atmospheric Administration. Environmental Data Service. National Oceanographic Data Center, 1976, 1981.

(MUGU) *The Mugu Book of Acronyms and Abbreviations.* Missile Range, CA: Management Engineering Office, 1963, 1964.

(MUSM) *Dictionary of Modern United States Military.* By S.F. Tomajczyk. Jefferson, NC: McFarland and Co., Inc., 1996.

(NADA) *The New American Dictionary of Abbreviations.* By Mary A. De Vries. New York, NY: Signet, 1991.

(NAKS) *"NASA/KSC Aronym List."* <http://www.ksc.nasa.gov/facts/acronyms.html> (27 May 1999)

(NASA) *Space Transportation System and Associated Payloads: Glossary, Acronyms, and Abbreviations.* Washington, DC: U.S. National Aeronautics and Space Administration, 1985.

(NATG) *Glossary of Abbreviations Used in NATO Documents.* AAP 15(B), n.p., 1979. [Use of source began in 1976]

(NAU) *"The Nautical Institute: Acronyms & Abbreviations."* <http://www.nautinst.org/Acronyms.htm> (20 October 1999)

(NAV) *"Navoceano Acronym List."* <http://www.navo.hpc.mil> (12 November 1993)

(NCC) *NCC The National Centre for Information Technology. Guide to Computer Aided Engineering, Manufacturing and Construction Software.* Manchester, England: NCC Publications, The National Computing Centre Ltd., 1985.
  Includes software classifications and descriptions, names and addresses of suppliers, processor manufacturers, and operating systems.

(NDBD) *The New Dickson Baseball Dictionary.* By Paul Dickson. San Diego, CA: Harcourt, Brace, and Co., 1999.

(NFD) *The NSFRE Fund-Raising Dictionary.* Edited by Barbara R. Levy. New York, NY: John Wiley & Sons, Inc., 1996.

(NFLA) "National Football League Abbreviations and Team Histories." http://maxwell.uhh.hawaii.edu/football/archive/nflAbbreviations.html (1998)

(NFPA) *Standard for Fire Safety Symbols/NFPA170.* Quincy, MA: National Fire Protection Association, 1994.

(NG) *NAVAIR Glossary of Unclassified Common-Use Abbreviated Titles and Phrases.* NAVAIRNOTE 5216 AIR-6031, n.p., July, 1969.

(NGC) *Catalogue of the National Gallery of Canada.* Compiled by National Gallery of Canada. Ottawa, Canada: National Gallery of Canada, 1998.

(NHD) *The New Hacker's Dictionary.* Edited by Eric Raymond. Cambridge, MA: MIT Press, 1991.

(NITA) *Dictionary of New Information Technology Acronyms.* 2nd ed. By Michael Gordon, Alan Singleton, and Clarence Rickards. London, England: Kogan Page, Ltd., 1986.

(NLC) *Symbols of Canadian Libraries.* 12th ed. National Library of Canada. Minister of Supply and Services Canada, 1987.

(NOAA) *NOAA Directives Manual.* 66-13 Acronyms. 1977.

(NQ) *NASDAQ Company Directory.* New York, NY: National Association of Securities Dealers, Inc., 1990. [Use of source began in 1983]

(NRCH) *A Handbook of Acronyms and Initialisms.* Washington, DC: U.S. Nuclear Regulatory Commission. Division of Technical Information and Document Control, 1985.

(NTCM) *NTC's Mass Media Dictionary.* R. Terry Ellmore. Lincolnwood, IL: National Textbook Co., 1991.

(NTIO) *NTC's Dictionary of Acronyms and Abbreviations.* Compiled by Steven R. Kleinedler. Edited by Richard A. Spears. Lincolnwood, IL: NTC Publishing Group, 1996.

(NTPA) *NTPA '97: National Trade and Professional Associations of the United States.* 32nd ed. Edited by John J. Russell. Washington, DC: Columbia Books, Inc., 1997.

(NUCP) *A Dictionary of Nuclear Power and Waste Management with Abbreviations and Acronyms.* Foo-Sun Lau. Letchworth, England: Research Studies Press Ltd., 1987.

(NUJO) "Initials, Credentials, Abbreviations Found on Medical Resumes." <http://www.nursesearch.net/initials.html> (1 February 2000)

(NUMA)   *The Numa Dictionary of Derivatives Acronyms.* <http://www.numa.com/ref/acronym.html> (24 February 1999)

(NVT)   *Naval Terminology.* NWP3. Rev. B. U.S. Department of the Navy. Office of the Chief of Naval Operations, 1980. [Use of source began in 1974]

(OA)   *Ocran's Acronyms: A Dictionary of Abbreviations and Acronyms Used in Scientific and Technical Writing.* By Emanuel Benjamin Ocran. London, England: Routledge & Kegan Paul Ltd., 1978.

(OAG)   *Official Airline Guide Worldwide Edition.* Oak Brook, IL: Official Airlines Guide, Inc., 1984. [Use of source began in 1975]

(OCD)   *Oxford Classical Dictionary.* 2nd ed. Edited by N.G. Hammond and H.H. Scullard. London, England: Oxford University Press, 1970.

(OCLC)   *OCLC Participating Institutions Arranged by OCLC Symbol.* Dublin, OH: OCLC, 1981.

(ODBW)   *The Oxford Dictionary for the Business World.* New York, NY: Oxford University Press, Inc., 1993.

(ODCC)   *The Oxford Dictionary of the Christian Church.* Edited by F.L. Cross and E.A. Livingstone. New York, NY: Oxford University Press, 1997.

(OICC)   *Abbreviations and Acronyms.* Des Moines, IA: Iowa State Occupational Information Coordinating Committee, 1986.

(OLDSS)   *Online Database Search Services Directory.* 2nd ed. Edited by Doris Morris Maxfield. Detroit, MI: Gale Research, 1988.
> Provides detailed descriptions of the online information retrieval services offered by libraries, private information firms, and other organizations in the United States and Canada. Entries include name and address, telephone number, and key contact, as well as online systems accessed, frequently searched databases, and access hardware.

(OPSA)   *"Official Postal Service Abbreviations."* <http://www.usps.gov/ncsc/lookups/abbr_suffix.txt> (17 December 1996)

(OSI)   *OSI Standards and Acronyms.* 3rd ed. Compiled by Adrian V. Stokes. United Kingdom: Stokes, 1991.

(OTD)   *Official Telecommunications Dictionary.* Edited by Thomas F.P. Sullivan. Rockille, MD: Government Institutes, Inc., 1997.

(PA)   *Planning Acronyms.* <http://www.planning.org/info/acronyms/html> (24 February 1999)

(PAZ)   *Parenting A to Z.* By Irene M. Franck and David M. Brownstone. New York, NY: HarperCollins Publishers, Inc., 1996.

(PCM)   *PC Magazine.* New York, NY: Ziff-Davis Publishing Co., 1997. [Use of source began in 1987]

(PD)   *Political Dissent: An International Guide to Dissident, Extra-Parliamentary, Guerrilla and Illegal Political Movements.* A Keesing's Reference Publication. Compiled by Henry W. Degenhardt. Edited by Alan J. Day. Harlow, Essex, England: Longman Group, 1983.
> Includes the history and aims of approximately 1,000 organizations, with details of their leaderships.

(PDAA)   *Pugh's Dictionary of Acronyms and Abbreviations: Abbreviations in Management, Technology and Information Science.* 5th ed. By Eric Pugh. Chicago, IL: American Library Association, 1987.

(PGP)   *Peterson's Graduate Programs in the Humanities, Arts & Social Sciences.* 31st ed. Princeton, NJ: Peterson's 1997.

(PHSD)   *1998/1999 Public Human Services Directory.* Vol 59. Washinton, DC: American Public Human Services Association, 1998.

(PIAV)   "Pilot's Magazine's A to Z Aviation Jargon." Compiled by James Allan and Mike Jerran. <http://web1.hiway.co.uk/avaition/pterms.html> (10 October 2000)

(PIPO)   *Pilot's Pocket Handbook.* 4th ed. N.p.: Flight Time Publishing, 1999.

(PPE)   *Political Parties of Europe.* 2 vols. Edited by Vincent E. McHale. The Greenwood Historical Encyclopedia of the World's Political Parties. Westport, CT: Greenwood Press, 1983.
           One of a series of reference guides to the world's significant political parties. Each guide provides concise histories of the political parties of a region and attempts to detail the evolution of ideology, changes in organization, membership, leadership, and each party's impact upon society.

(PPW)   *Political Parties of the World.* 2nd ed. A Keesing's Reference Publication. Compiled and edited by Alan J. Day and Henry W. Degenhardt. Harlow, Essex, England: Longman Group, 1980, 1984.
           Covers historical development, structure, leadership, membership, policy, publications, and international affiliations. For each country, an overview of the current political situation and constitutional structure is provided.

(PROS)   *Prospector's Choice.* User's Guide. Detroit: The Taft Group, 1997.

(PS)   *Popular Science.* New York, NY: Times-Mirror Magazines, Inc., 2001. [Use of source began in 1992]

(PSS)   *Peterson's Sports Scholarships & College Athletic Programs.* 3rd ed. Edited by Ron Walker. Princeton, NJ: Peterson's, 1998.

(QUAC)   "Dictionary of Quaternary Acronyms." http://www.ualberta.ca/abeaudoi/cap/diction/atoc.html (12 October 1999)

(RALS)   *Encyclopedia of Computer Science.* 4th ed. Edited by Anthony Ralston, Edwin E. Reilly, and David Hemmendinger. London: Nature Publishing Group, 2000.

(RCD)   *Research Centers Directory.* 19th ed. Edited by Thomas J. Cichonski. Detroit, MI: Gale Research, 1994. [Use of source began in 1986]
           A guide to university-related and other nonprofit research organizations carrying on research in agriculture, astronomy and space sciences, behavioral and social sciences, computers and mathematics, engineering and technology, physical and earth sciences and regional and area studies.

(RDA)   *Army RD and A Magazine.* Alexandria, VA: Development, Engineering, and Acquisition Directorate, Army Materiel Command, 1997. [Use of source began in 1979]

(REAL)   *Abbreviations.* <http://www.reboc.on.ca/abbreviations.html> (24 February 1999)

(RIMS)   "Rimship AS Forkortelser." <http://www.rimship.no/sider/liste.html> (26 September 2000)

(ROAS)   "Acronym and Abbreviation Server Results." <http://www.ucc.ie/cgi-bin/acronym>
         (20 September 1999)

(ROG)   *Dictionary of Abbreviations.* By Walter T. Rogers. London, England: George Allen & Co. Ltd.,
         1913; reprinted by Gale Research, 1969.

(SAA)   *Space-Age Acronyms, Abbreviations and Designations.* 2nd ed. By Reta C. Moser. New York,
         NY: IFI/Plenum, 1969.

(SAG)   *Stock Abbreviation Guide.* New York, NY: Associated Press. [Database]

(SARE)   "Safety and Related Acronyms." <http://www.labsafety.org/acro.htm> (1999)

(SAUO)   *International Encyclopedia of Abbreviations and Acronyms of Organizations.* 3rd ed. Compiled
         by Paul Spillner and Peter Wennrich. 6 vol. set. Munchen: K. G. Saur, 1990.

(SAUS)   *International Encyclopedia of Abbreviations and Acronyms in Science and Technology.*
         Compiled by Michael Peschke. 8 vol. set. Munchen: K.G. Saur, 1996.

(SDI)   *Report to the Congress on the Strategic Defense Initiative.* U.S. Department of Defense. Strategic
         Defense Initiative Organization, April, 1987.

(SEIS)   *Seismograph Station Codes and Characteristics.* Geological Survey. Circular 791. By Barbara
         B. Poppe, Debbi A. Naab, and John S. Derr. Washington, DC: U.S. Department of the Interior,
         1978.

(SG)   *Standard & Poor's Stock Guide.* New York, NY: Standard & Poor's, 2000.

(SLS)   *World Guide to Scientific Associations and Learned Societies/Internationales Verzeichnis
         Wissenschaftlicher Verbande und Gesellschaften.* 4th ed. Edited by Barbara Verrel. New York,
         NY: K.G. Saur, 1984.
            A directory of more than 22,000 societies and associations in all fields of science,
            culture, and technology. International, national, and regional organizations from 150
            countries are also included.

(SPSG)   *Security Owner's Stock Guide.* New York, NY: Standard & Poor's Corp., 1994. [Use of source
         began in 1988]

(SPST)   "Space Station Acronyms." <http://www.spacefllight.nasa.gov/cgi-bi> (1999)

(SRA)   *State and Regional Associations of the United States.* 9th ed. Edited by Tracey E. Chirico, Buck
         J. Downs and John J. Russell. Washington, DC: Columbia Books, Inc., 1997.

(SSD)   *Space Station Directory and Program Guide.* Edited and compiled by Melinda Gipson, Jane
         Glass, and Mary Linden. Arlington, VA: Pasha Publications, Inc., 1988.

(STED)   *Stedman's Abbreviations, Acronyms and Symbols.* Edited by William R. Hensyl. Baltimore,
         MD: Williams & Wilkins, 1992.

(TAD)   *The AIDS Dictionary.* By Sarah Barbara Watstein and Karen Chandler. New York, NY: Facts
         on File, Inc., 1998.

(TAG)   *Transportation Acronym Guide 1996.* U.S. Department of Transportation. Washington, DC:
         Bureau of Transportation Statistics, 1996.

(TBD)	*Thomson Bank Directory.* Skokie, IL: Thomson Financial Publishing, 1991.
(TDOB)	*The Dictionary of Banking.* By Charles J. Woelfel. Chicago, IL: Probus Publishing Company, 1994.
(TEL)	*Telephony's Dictionary.* 2nd ed. By Graham Langley. Chicago, IL: Telephony Publishing Corp., 1986. Includes definitions for U.S. and international telecommunications terms. Ten appendices.
(TELE)	*List of Libraries Abbreviations Encountered in the Context of EU R&D.* <http://www2.echo.lu/libraries/en/acronym.html> (24 February 1999)
(TES)	*Tests: A Comprehensive Reference for Assessments in Psychology, Education, and Business.* 3rd ed. Austin, TX: PRO-ED, Inc., 1991.
(TMMY)	*The Thirteenth Mental Measurements Yearbook.* Edited by James C. Impara and Barbara S. Plake. Lincoln: NE: The Buros Institute of Mental Measurements of the University of Nebraska-Lincoln, 1998.
(TNIG)	*Telecommunications, Networking and Internet Glossary.* By George S. Machovec. Chicago, IL: American Library Association, 1993.
(TOCD)	*The Official Catholic Directory 1997.* New Providence, NJ: P.J. Kennedy & Sons, 1997.
(TRID)	"Travel Industry Dictionary." <http://www.hometravelagency.com/dictionary/itra/html> (15 August 2000)
(TSPED)	*Trade Shows and Professional Exhibits Directory.* 2nd ed. Edited by Robert J. Elster. Detroit, MI: Gale Research, 1987. [Use of source began in 1986] A guide to scheduled events providing commercial display facilities including conferences, conventions, meetings, fairs and festivals, etc. Entries include name of trade show; sponsor name, address, and telephone number; attendance figures; principal exhibits; special features; publications; and date and location of shows.
(TSSD)	*Telecommunications Systems and Services Directory.* 4th ed. (and supplement). Edited by John Krol. Detroit, MI: Gale Research, 1989. [Use of source began in 1985] An international descriptive guide to telecommunications organizations, systems, and services. Entries include name and address, telephone number, chief official, and a description of the purposes, technical structure, and background of the service or system.
(USCA)	*"U.S. Census Bureau Abbreviations and Acronyms."* <http://www.census.gov/cgi-bin/main/allacro.pl> (20 October 1999)
(USDC)	*"Glossary of Acronyms."* U.S. Department of Commerce. <http://www.pmel.noaa.gov/pubs/acronym.html> (5 March 1997)
(USGC)	*"U.S. Government Commonly Used Abbreviations and Acronyms."* <http://www.fed.gov/hptext/infohwy/gov_acro.html> (5 March 1997)
(USMO)	*The Military Online: A Directory for Internet Access to the Development of Defense.* Edited by William M. Arkin. Washington, DC: Brassey's, 1997.
(VERA)	*VERA-Virtual Entity of Relevant Acronyms.* <http://www/thphy.uni~duesseldorf.de/~gnu/info/VERA/vera_2.html#SEC3> (1 December 1998)

(VNW)   *Words of the Vietnam War.* By Gregory R. Clark. Jefferson, NC: McFarland and Co., Inc., 1990.

(VRA)   *VRA Special Bulletin. No. 2, 1987: Standard Abbreviations for Image Descriptions for Use in Fine Arts Visual Resources Collections.* Compiled by Nancy S. Schuller. Austin, TX: Visual Resources Association, 1987.

(WA)   *Whitakers Almanack 1998.* London: The Stationery Office, Ltd., 1997.

(WDAA) *Webster's New World Dictionary of Acronyms and Abbreviations.* By Auriel Douglas and Michael Strumpf. New York, NY: Webster's New World, 1989.

(WDMC) *Webster's New World Dictionary of Media and Communications.* Revised and updated ed. By Richard Weiner. New York, NY: Webster's New World, 1996.

(WEAT) "Weather Abbreviations." <http://www.ukweather.freeserve.co.uk/abbrev.html> (16 November 1999)

(WGA)   *Webster's Guide to Abbreviations.* Springfield, MA: Merriam-Webster, Inc., 1985.

(WORL) *World Guide to Libraries.* Edited by Willemina van der Meer. 14th ed. Munich, Germany: Saur, 1999.

(WPI)   *Selected Acronyms and Abbreviations for Wood Products, Forest Industry and Governmental Affairs.* <http://www.ari.net/awpi/acronyms.html> (3 March 1999)

(WYGK) *HR Words You Gotta Know!* By William R. Tracey. New York, NY: AMACOM,

Numerics
By Meaning

1 dimensional U/S exam of length of eye (SAUS) .... A scan
1-Brommercuri-2-hydro-Propan (SAUS) .... BMHP
1-Methyl-4-Phenyl-1,2,3,6-Tetrahydropyridin (SAUS) .... MPTP
1-Naphthaleneacetic Acid (LDT) .... NAA
1st Bancorp Ind [NASDAQ symbol] (TTSB) .... FBCV
1st Bergen Bancorp [NASDAQ symbol] (TTSB) .... FBER
1st Canadian Destroyer Flotilla (SAUO) .... CANDESFLOT 1
1st County of London Yeomanry (SAUO) .... DCH
1st Fighter Association (EA) .... FFGA
1st Marine Division Association (EA) .... FMDA
1st United Bancorp(FL) [NASDAQ symbol] (TTSB) .... FUBC
1st Washington Bancorp [NASDAQ symbol] (TTSB) .... WFSB
2 dimensional U/S exam of eye (SAUS) .... B scan
2-Amino-2-(Hydroxymethyl)-1,3-Propanediol (DAVI) .... THAM
2-Aminoethylisothiouronium Bromide (DB) .... AET
2-(Aminomethyl)phenylacetic Acid (DB) .... AMPA
2-Hydroxy-4-Methylpentanoic Acid Dehydrogenase (DB) .... HMPDH
2-Mercaptobenzimidazol (SAUS) .... MBI
2nd Bomb Wing Association (EA) .... SBWA
2-Spirited of the First Nations (AC) .... TPFN
3CI Complete Compliance [NASDAQ symbol] (TTSB) .... TCCC
3Com Corp. [NASDAQ symbol] (TTSB) .... COMS
3-D Geophysical [NASDAQ symbol] (TTSB) .... TDGO
3-D Systems Corp. [NASDAQ symbol] (TTSB) .... TDSC
3D0 Company [NASDAQ symbol] (TTSB) .... THDO
3-Dimensional Finite-Element Model of Flow And Transport [Computer science] 3DFEMFAT
3-Dimensional Ozone Mapping with Ultraviolet Imaging Spectrometer (EOSA) .... TOMUIS
3-Dimensional Subsurface Flow and FAte and Transport of MIcrobes and Chemicals Model [Computer science] 3DFATMIC
3-Hydroxytyramine [Dopamine] [Medicine] (STED) 3-HT
3i Co-Information Interscience (SAUO) 3i
3rd Generation Language [Computer science] (EERA) 3GL
4 Front Software Intl [NASDAQ symbol] (TTSB) .... FFST
4 Kids Entertainment [NYSE symbol] .... KDE
4 Kids Entertainment [NASDAQ symbol] (TTSB) .... KIDE
4G Data Systems, Inc. (SAUO) .... GGGG
4-Hydroxy-3-Methoxymandelic Acid (STED) .... HMMA
4th Field Artillery (Pack) Association (EA) .... FFAA
4th Generation Language [Computer science] (EERA) 4GL
4th Infantry Division [Army] 4ID
4th Marine Division Association WWII (EA) .... FMDA
4th/7th Royal Dragoon Guards (SAUO) 4/7DG
5-amino-3-nitro-1H-1,2,4-triazole (SAUS) .... ANTA
5-Bromodeoxyuridine (DOG) .... Brdu
5-Bromodeoxyuridine (DOG) .... BUDR
5-Fluorouracil [Medicine] 5-FU
5-Hydroxy-L-Tryptophan 5HTP
5-Hydroxymethylfurfural .... HMF
5-Hydroxytryptamine [Serotonin] [Medicine] (STED) 5-HT
5-Methyltetrahydrofolate [Biochemistry] (DAVI) .... MF
5th Royal Inniskilling Dragoon Guards (SAUO) 5DG
5th Royal Inniskilling Dragoon Guards (SAUO) .... 5 INNIS DG
6-Aminopenicillanic Acid (EDCT) 6-APA
6-Benzylaminopurine (DOG) .... BAP
6-Mercaptopurin, Vincristine, Methotrexate, Citrovorum Factor [Chemotherapy] (DAVI) .... PIP
6-Mercaptopurine [Medicine] 6-MP

6-Thioguanine [Medicine] 6-TG
7-Amino-Cephalosporanic Acid 7-ACA
7-Eleven,Inc. [NASDAQ symbol] (SG) .... SVEV
7th Army Training Command (RDA) 7ATC
7th Infantry Division Association (EA) .... SIDA
7th Level Inc. [NASDAQ symbol] (TTSB) .... SEVL
0.8 cm wavelength radar (SAUS) .... ka-band
9 to 5 Working Women Education Fund [An association] (EA) ...... WWEF
10³ (K) of Instructions Per Second [Unit of computer processing speed] (NITA) .... KIPS
11th Armored Cavalry's Veterans of Vietnam and Cambodia (EA) .... 11th ACVVC
12th Royal Lancers (SAUO) .... 12 L
17 Division/Malaya District (SAUO) .... 17 Div
17-Ketogenic Steroid (STED) 17-KGS
17-Ketosteroid (STED) 17K
17th Bomb Group Reunion Association (EA) .... 17th BGRA
17th/21st Lancers (SAUO) .... 17/21 L
18 Square Meter Sailing Association (EA) .... ESMSA
20th Century Indus [NYSE symbol] (TTSB) .... TW
2,4 Dichlorophenoxyacetic Acid (DOG) 2,4D
2,5-Dimethoxy-4-Methylamphetamine [Also, Methyldimethoxy-Amphetamine and DOM] [An illicit hallucinogenic drug] (DAVI) ..... STP
25-Hydroxycholecalciferol (STED) 25-HCC
30th Infantry Division Association (EA) .... TIDA
36Onetworks, Inc. [NASDAQ symbol] (SG) .... TSIX
37th Division Veterans Association (EA) .... TDVA
50% Dextrose injection (SAUS) D50
50-Off Stores [NASDAQ symbol] (TTSB) .... FOFF
51st Medical Battalion Association (EA) .... FMBA
85 Percent/15 Percent Unleaded Gasoline [BTS] (TAG) M85
91st General Hospital Association (EA) .... NGHA
99th Infantry Division Association (EA) .... NIDA
100 (WDMC) C
1,1,2-Trichlortrifluorethan (SAUS) R113
127th Infantry Veterans Association (EA) .... OIVA
129 digit cryptographic security number (SAUS) RSA129
135 Airways [FAA designator] (FAAC) .... KHC
135th Medical Regiment Association (EA) .... OMRA
187th Airborne Regimental Combat Team Association (EA) ...... RAKKASANS
304th Fighter Squadron Association (EA) .... TFSA
360 (Degrees) Communic [NYSE symbol] (TTSB) .... XO
369th Veterans' Association (EA) .... TVA
381st Bomb Group Memorial Association (EA) .... 381 BGMA
390 to 1,550 MHz (SAUS) .... L-BAND
483rd Bombardment Group (H) Association (EA) .... FBGHA
504th Parachute Infantry Regiment Association (EA) .... FPIA
505th Ordnance Company (EA) .... FOC
550th Airborne Infantry Association (EA) .... FAIA
605th Ordnance Battalion Association (EA) .... SOBA
611 897 Alberta Ltd. [Canada] [FAA designator] (FAAC) .... THD
724 Solutions [NASDAQ symbol] (SG) .... SVNX
1015 British Thermal Units/Year .... QUADS
1838 Bond-Deb Trad'g [NYSE symbol] (TTSB) .... BDF
2002 Target Term Trust [NYSE symbol] (TTSB) .... TTR
[The] 49-99 Cooperative Library System, Stockton, CA [Library symbol] [Library of Congress] (LCLS) .... CStoF
5,000 [Film] (WDMC) .... FK
15.250 to 17.250 GHz (SAUS) .... KU-BAND
36,000 to 46,000 Megacycles per Second .... Q-BAND
225-390 Megacycles per Second .... P-BAND

A
By Meaning

A. A. Weinman [*Designer's mark, when appearing on US coins*] .... AW

A Address Register (SAUS) .... AAR

A & A Foods Ltd. [*Vancouver Stock Exchange symbol*] .... AA

A & A Foods Ltd. [*Associated Press*] (SAG) .... A & A Fd

A & A Foods Ltd. [*NASDAQ symbol*] (SAG) .... ANAF

A & A Foods Ltd [*NASDAQ symbol*] (TTSB) .... ANAFF

A. Barton Hepburn Hospital, Ogdensburg, NY [*Library symbol*] [*Library of Congress*] (LCLS) .... NOgH

A Basic Coursewriter (SAUS) .... ABAC

A Battuta [*Music*] .... A Batt

A Be, Inc. Operating System (SAUO) .... BeOS

A Better Administrative Computer Utility System (SAUS) .... ABACUS

A Better Language Experiment (SAUS) .... ABLE

A Biographical Register of the University of Cambridge to 1500 [*A publication*] [*British*] (ODCC) .... BRUC

A Biographical Register of the University of Oxford to A.D. 1500 [*A publication*] [*British*] (ODCC) .... BRUO

A Broad Band Imaging X-Ray All-Sky Survey (SAUS) .... ABRIXAS

A Broadband Imaging X-ray All-Sky Survey (SAUS) .... ABRIXAS

A Brotherhood Against Totalitarian Enactments (SAUO) .... ABATAE

A. C. Dougherty Memorial Township Library, Dupo, IL [*Library symbol*] [*Library of Congress*] (LCLS) .... IDup

A. C. Owners Club - American Centre (EA) .... ACOC

A Caenorhabditis Elegans Database (SAUS) .... ACEDB

A Cappella [*Unaccompanied*] [*Music*] .... A Capp

A Capriccio [*At One's Fancy*] [*Music*] (ROG) .... A CAPO

A. Carotis Externa .... ACE

A. Carotis Interna (SAUS) .... ACI

A Cembalo [*Music*] .... A Cemb

A. Christiaens [*Belgium*] [*Research code symbol*] .... AC

A Classification of Residential Neighborhoods [*Database*] [*CACI*] [*Information service or system*] (CRD) .... ACORN

A Classification Of Residential Neighbourhoods (SAUS) .... ACORN

A Coeur Joie International [*An association*] (EAIO) .... ACJI

A Common Operational Software (SAUS) .... ACOS

A Company that Makes Everything (SAUO) .... ACME

A Complete Computerized Examination System (SAUS) .... ACCESS

A computer company (SAUO) .... Be

A Computer Series [*Nippon Electric Co.*] [*Japan*] .... ACOS

A Computerised London Information Service [*Greater London Council Research Library*] [*British*] .... ACOMPLIS

A Computerised London Information System Online [*Greater London Council Research Library*] [*Bibliographic database*] [*British*] .... ACOMPLINE

A Computerized London Information Service (SAUO) .... ACOMPLIS

A Computerized London Online Information Network (SAUS) .... ACOMPLINE

A Confusing Racket Of Naming Your Meaning (SAUS) .... ACRONYM

A Consortium for the Application of Climate Impact Assessments (SAUS) .... ACACIA

A Consortium on Restorative Dentistry Education (SAUO) .... ACORDE

A Contrived Reduction Of Nouns, Yielding Mnemonics (SAUS) .... ACRONYM

A Convenient Reduction of Nomenclature Yielding Mnemonic Syllables (SAUS) .... ACRONYMS

A Cooperative Community Educational School System (SAUS) .... ACCESS

A Cost Estimating/Order Control System (SAUS) ACE/OCS-1/LSG

A Data Base Management System (SAUS) .... ADBMS

A data communications company (SAUO) .... Adaptec

A Data Interchange System (SAUS) .... ADIS

A Data Management System (NITA) .... ADAM

A. de Lara Limited Edition Recordings [*Now Orfeo with same numbers*] [*Record label*] [*Great Britain*] .... AdL

A Debugger (SAUS) .... ADB

A Departmental Reporting System (SAUS) .... ADRS

A Design Language for Indicating Behavior (SAUS) .... ADLIB

A Destra [*To the Right*] [*Italian*] (ADA) .... A DES

A Direction Finder .... ADF

A Drink .... AD

A. E. Lepage Capital Prop. [*Limited Partnership Units*] [*Toronto Stock Exchange symbol*] .... AEP

A Favor [*In Favor*] [*Spanish*] .... AF

A Flip-Flop (SAUS) .... AFF

A Focus for Analytical Chemistry in Europe (SAUS) .... EURACHEM

A Fortiori [*With More Reason*] [*Latin*] (ROG) .... A FORT

A. G. Ruthven Museums Building (SAUS) .... MUS

A. H. Brown Public Library, Mobridge, SD [*Library symbol*] [*Library of Congress*] (LCLS) .... SdMo

A. H. Robins Co. [*Research code symbol*] .... AHR

A. H. Robins Co., Richmond, VA [*OCLC symbol*] (OCLC) .... VIR

A. H. Robins Co., Richmond, VA [*Library symbol*] [*Library of Congress*] (LCLS) .... ViRRob

A. J. Hurley Ltd., London, United Kingdom [*Library symbol*] [*Library of Congress*] (LCLS) .... UkLHu

A. K. Smiley Public Library, Redlands, CA [*Library symbol*] [*Library of Congress*] (LCLS) .... CRedl

A Kind of (SAUS) .... AKO

A Kinder and Gentler America .... AKAGA

A la Carte [*According to the Menu, each item ordered individually*] [*French*] (ADA) .... ALC

A la Gloire du Grand Architecte de l'Univers [*Freemasonry*] [*French*] (ROG) .... ALGDGADLU

A Language for Automation (SAUS) .... ALFA

A Language for Decision Information (SAUS) .... ALADIN

A Language for Financial Analysis (SAUS) .... ALFA

A Later Date (SAUS) .... ALD

A Library Management System (SAUS) .... ALMS

A Long-term Oligotrophic Habitat Assessment (SAUS) .... ALOHA

A l'Orient [*At the East*] [*Freemasonry*] [*French*] (ROG) .... AI'O

A l'Orient [*At the East*] [*Freemasonry*] [*French*] .... A l'OR

A Lover's Complaint [*Poem usually attributed to Shakespeare*] (BARN) .... Compl

A Low Budget Easy Retrieval Technique (SAUS) .... ALBERT

A. M. Best Electronic Retrieval Services [*A. M. Best Co.*] [*Database*] .... AMBERS

A Manufacturing Language (SAUS) .... AML

A Manuscript Preparation Language (SAUS) .... AMPL

A Mediterranean Undercurrent Seeding Experiment (SAUS) .... AMUSE

A Microprogramming Language (SAUS) .... AMIL

A Mind Forever Voyaging [*Infocom*] [*Computer gaming*] .... AMFV

A Minus (SAUS) .... A-

A Mon Ordre [*To My Order*] [*French*] [*Business term*] (ROG) .... AM/O

A Multi-access Online System (SAUS) .... AMOS

A Multi-Programming Language-Extended (SAUS) .... AMPLE

A. N. Tupolev [*Initialism used as designation for Russian aircraft designed by Tupolev*] .... ANT

A. Nattermann & Cie [*Germany*] [*Research code symbol*] .... CH

A Navigator of Natural Language Organized Data (SAUS) .... ANNOD

A Negative (SAUS) .... A-

A+ Network [*NASDAQ symbol*] (TTSB) .... ACOM

A New Genesis (TOCD) .... ANG

A New Life for You Inc. (SAUO) .... ALFY

A package from GEAC (SAUS) .... ADVANCE

A Parse Request Language (SAUS) .... APAREL

A Perspicious Language (SAUS) .... APL

A. Philip Randolph Educational Fund (EA) .... APREF

A. Philip Randolph Institute (EA) .... APRI

A Plus Communications, Inc. [*NASDAQ symbol*] (SAG) .... ACOM

A Plus Network, Inc. [*Associated Press*] (SAG) .... A Plus

A Portable EMACS Library (SAUS) .... APEL

A Positive (SAUS) .... A+

A Posteriori Probabilities (or Probability) (SAUS) .... APP

A Posteriori Probability (MCD) .... APP

A Posteriori Probability Distribution [*Mathematics*] .... PPD

A Priori Stochastic-Optimal (SAUS) .... APSO

A programming language (SAUS) C

A Programming Language with Shared Files (SAUS) .... APLSF

A Programming Language-Structured (SAUS) .... APL-S

A project for cooperation between higher education institutes around the Mediterranean (SAUO) .... MED-CAMPUS

A Protester [*To Be Protested*] [*French*] [*Business term*] .... AP

A Public Library/Community Access Tool [*Acronym used by Community Information Database*] [*Dallas Public Library*] [*Texas*] [*Information service or system*] (IID) .... APL/CAT

A Pulse (SAUS) .... AP

A Query and Retrieval Interactive Utility System (SAUS) .... AQUARIUS

A Query Language (SAUS) .... AQL

A Rat in the House May Eat the Ice Cream [*Mnemonic guide for spelling "arithmetic"*] .... ARITHMETIC

A Real-Time Interface Coprocessor (SAUS) .... ARTIC

A Recording Stray Energy Monitor (SAUS) .... ARESTEM

A Relational Information System (SAUS) .... ARIS

A Retrieval Process Language (SAUS) .... ARPL

A Scientific Application Programmer (SAUS) .... ASAP

A Search Tree Underlying the Experiment [*University of Michigan's experimental online catalog*] .... ASTUTE

A Selective Strategy for Utilization Review Effectiveness [*Health insurance*] (GHCT) ... ASSURE

A Severity Characterization of Trauma [*Medicine*] (DMAA) ... ASCOT

A Simple Systematic Integration of Statistical Techniques (SAUS) ... ASSIST

A Society to Help the Morale of Asthmatics (SAUO) ... ASTHMA

A Spolecnost [*and Company*] [*Czech*] (BARN) ... A spol

A Stack Based Abstraction Language (SAUS) ... ASBAL

A subsidiary of Control Data Corporation that manufactures supercomputers (SAUO) ... ETA

A System for Programmers (SAUS) ... ASP

A System for Storage and Subsequent Selection of Information (SAUS) ... ASSASSIN

A Tempo [*In Strict Time*] [*Music*] ... AT

A Tempo [*In Strict Time*] [*Music*] ... A Tem

A Tempo [*In Strict Time*] [*Music*] ... A TEMP

A Test Application Facility (SAUS) ... ATAF

A Test Specification Language (SAUS) ... ATSL

A Third World development agency (SAUO) ... GOAL

A Total Library Automation System (SAUS) ... ATLAS

A Tutorial System (SAUS) ... ATS

A. V. Roe & Co. Ltd. [*Acronym used as designation for a British aircraft and is formed from the name of the aircraft's manufacturer*] ... AVRO

A. W. Wright Nuclear Structure Laboratory [*Yale University*] [*Research center*] (RCD) ... WNSL

A While Ago (SAUS) ... AWA

A While Back (SAUS) ... AWB

A Windows News Client. (SAUS) ... WinVN

A. Y. Jackson High School, Kanata, Ontario [*Library symbol*] [*National Library of Canada*] (BIB) ... OKAYJ

AA for Tracking and Data Acquisition (SAUS) ... AA/TDA

AAA Stamp & Coin [*Vancouver Stock Exchange symbol*] ... ASJ

Aab Bank for Investment and Foreign Trade (SAUO) ... ABIFT

AABBAX International Financial [*Vancouver Stock Exchange symbol*] ... AXF

AABCO Ventures, Inc. [*Vancouver Stock Exchange symbol*] ... AAB

Aabiter (SAUS) ... APB

Aachen [*Federal Republic of Germany*] [*Seismograph station code, US Geological Survey*] [*Closed*] (SEIS) ... AAC

Aachen Aphasia Test [*Medicine*] (DMAA) ... AAT

Aachen/Merzbruck [*Germany*] [*ICAO location identifier*] (ICLI) ... EDCM

AAHL Board of Management (SAUO) ... ABOM

AAHL Industry Liaison Committee (SAUO) ... AILC

AAHL Policy Advisory Committee (SAUO) ... APAC

AAL Common Part (SAUS) ... AALCP

AAL Management (SAUS) ... AALM

AAL Protocol Data Unit (SAUS) ... AALPDU

AAL Type 1. Protocol standard used for the transport of Constant Bit Rate traffic (SAUS) ... AAL1

AAL Type 2. Protocol standard for supporting time-dependent Variable Bit Rate (SAUS) ... AAL2

AAL Type 3 and 4. Protocol standard for supporting both connectionless and connection-oriented Variable Bit Rate (SAUS) ... AAL3/4

AAL Type 5. Protocol standard for supporting the transport of Lightweight Variable Bit Rate (SAUS) ... AAL5

Aaland Islands ... AI

Aalborg [*Denmark*] [*Airport symbol*] (OAG) ... AAL

Aalborg Airtaxi [*Denmark*] [*ICAO designator*] (FAAC) ... DAX

Aalen-Heidenheim/Elchingen [*Germany*] [*ICAO location identifier*] (ICLI) ... EDTA

Aalenian [*Geology*] ... Aal

Aalesund [*Norway*] [*Airport symbol*] (OAG) ... AES

Aalog Multiplexer (SAUS) ... ANAMUX

Aalst [*Belgium*] [*ICAO location identifier*] (ICLI) ... EBAL

Aames Financial Corp. [*NYSE symbol*] (SAG) ... AAM

Aames Financial Corp. [*Associated Press*] (SAG) ... Aames

a-Aminoguanidinopropionic Acid (SAUS) ... AGPA

a-Aminoisobutyric acid (SAUS) ... AIB acid

AAMR Adaptive Behavior Scale-Residential and Community, Second Edition [*Test*] (TMMY) ... ABS-RC

AAMR Adaptive Behavior Scale-School, Second Edition [*Test*] (TMMY) ... ABS-S

Aanderaa current meter (SAUS) ... ACM

Aantekening [*Note*] [*Netherlands*] (ILCA) ... aant

AAO Aquaculture [*Vancouver Stock Exchange symbol*] ... AAO

AAON, Inc. [*NASDAQ symbol*] (SAG) ... AAON

AAR Corp. [*Associated Press*] (SAG) ... AAR

AAR Corp. [*NYSE symbol*] (SPSG) ... AIR

Aargang [*Annual Volume*] [*Sweden*] (BARN) ... aarg

Aarhus [*Denmark*] [*Airport symbol*] (OAG) ... AAR

Aarhus University (SAUO) ... AU

Aaron Burr Association (EA) ... ABA

Aaron Burr Association (SAUO) ... ARA

Aaron Diamond AIDS Research Center ... ADARC

Aaron Mining Ltd. [*Vancouver Stock Exchange symbol*] ... AOM

Aaron Rents [*NASDAQ symbol*] (TTSB) ... ARON

Aaron Rents [*NYSE symbol*] (SG) ... RNT

Aaron Rents Cl'A' [*NASDAQ symbol*] (TTSB) ... ARONA

Aaron Rents, Inc. [*Associated Press*] (SAG) ... AarnRt

Aaron Rents, Inc. [*Associated Press*] (APAG) ... AaronRt

Aaron Rents, Inc. [*NASDAQ symbol*] (NQ) ... ARON

Aaronson, Huchra, and Moruld [*Method of determining age of the universe*] ... AHM

AARP GNMA & U.S.Treasury [*Mutual fund ticker symbol*] (SG) ... AGNMX

AARP Growth & Income Fund [*Mutual fund ticker symbol*] (SG) ... AGIFX

Aarskog Syndrome [*Medicine*] (MELL) ... AS

Aasche Transport Svcs Wrrt [*NASDAQ symbol*] (TTSB) ... ASHEW

Aasche Transportation [*NASDAQ symbol*] (TTSB) ... ASHE

Aasche Transportation Services [*Associated Press*] (SAG) ... Aasche

Aasche Transportation Services [*Associated Press*] (SAG) ... AascheT

Aasche Transportation Services [*NASDAQ symbol*] (SAG) ... ASHE

AASL [*American Association of School Librarians*] **Non-Public Schools Section** ... AASL NPSS

AASL [*American Association of School Librarians*] **School Library Media Educators Section** ... AASL SLMES

AASL [*American Association of School Librarians*] **Supervisors Section** ... AASL SS

A-Associate Response [*Computer science*] (TNIG) ... AARE

AASTRA Aerospace, Inc., Downsview, Ontario [*Library symbol*] [*National Library of Canada*] (BIB) ... OTAA

AAU [*Amateur Athletic Union of the United States*]**/USA Junior Olympics** (EA) ... AAU/USA JO

Aavahelukka [*Finland*] [*ICAO location identifier*] (ICLI) ... EFAA

Aavid Thermal Technologies [*NASDAQ symbol*] (TTSB) ... AATT

Aavid Thermal Technologies, Inc. [*NASDAQ symbol*] (SAG) ... AATT

Aavid Thermal Technologies, Inc. [*Associated Press*] (SAG) ... AavidTh

Aaxico Air Lines ... AXO

Ab Abraham [*The chronological reckoning from the first year of Abraham; St. Jerome's translation and enlargement of Eusebius' Chronicle*] [*Classical studies*] (OCD) ... ab Abr

A/B Astra [*Sweden*] [*Research code symbol*] ... A

AB Bofors [*Sweden*] [*Research code symbol*] ... LAC

AB Bookman's Weekly [*A publication*] (BRI) ... AB

A.B. Dick & Co. (SAUO) ... ABD

Ab Extra [*From Without*] [*Latin*] ... ABEX

Ab Initio [*From the Beginning*] [*Latin*] ... AB INIT

A.B. Middle School, International Falls, MN [*Library symbol*] [*Library of Congress*] (LCLS) ... MnIfM

AB Nyge Aero [*Sweden*] [*FAA designator*] (FAAC) ... TGT

A/B Rederi Transatlantic [*Pacific Australia Direct Line*] (MHDB) ... ABRT

AB Svensk Exp Cap Sec [*NYSE symbol*] (TTSB) ... SEPPr

Ab Urbe Condite [*From the Year of the Founding*] [*Latin*] ... AUC

Aba [*Zaire*] [*ICAO location identifier*] (ICLI) ... FZJF

ABA [*American Bar Association*] **Center on Children and the Law** (EA) ... ABACCL

ABA Journal [*A publication*] (BRI) ... ABA Jour

Ababa [*Ethiopia*] [*Airport symbol*] (AD) ... ABA

ABAC Resources [*Vancouver Stock Exchange symbol*] ... ABS

Abacan Resource [*NASDAQ symbol*] (TTSB) ... ABACE

Abacan Resource Corp. [*NASDAQ symbol*] (SAG) ... ABAC

Abacan Resource Corp. [*Associated Press*] (SAG) ... Abacan

abacterial (SAUS) ... abact

Abacus ... ABCS

Abacus Air (SAUS) ... VM

Abacus Direct [*NASDAQ symbol*] (SG) ... ABDR

Abacus Direct Corp. [*Associated Press*] (SAG) ... AbacDir

Abacus Direct Corp. [*NASDAQ symbol*] (SAG) ... ABDR

Abacus Fund (SAUO) ... ABJ

Abacus Programming Corp. ... APC

Abadan [*Iran*] [*Airport symbol*] (OAG) ... ABD

Abadan [*Iran*] [*ICAO location identifier*] (ICLI) ... OIAT

Abadan/International [*Iran*] [*ICAO location identifier*] (ICLI) ... OIAA

Abadeh [*Iran*] [*ICAO location identifier*] (ICLI) ... OISA

Abaiang [*Kiribati*] [*Airport symbol*] (OAG) ... ABF

Abaiang [*Kiribati*] [*ICAO location identifier*] (ICLI) ... NGAB

Abakan [*Former USSR*] [*ICAO location identifier*] (ICLI) ... UNKA

Abakan-Avia [*Former USSR*] [*FAA designator*] (FAAC) ... ABG

Abalone (VRA) ... abal

Abalone Management Advisory Committee [*Australia*] ... ABMAC

Abamectin (LDT) ... ABM

Abampere (SAUS) ... AA

Abampere [*Also, Bi*] [*Unit of electric current*] ... aA

Abampere (SAUS) ... ab-a

Abampere (SAUS) ... abamp

A-Band (MELL) ... A

Abandon [*Legal shorthand*] (LWAP) ... ABAN

Abandon (SAUS) ... ABND

Abandon Call and Retry [*Telecommunications*] ... ACR

Abandon Ship (MSA) ... ABDNSHP

Abandoned ... ABAND

Abandoned (ABBR) ... ABDND

Abandoned Lighthouse ... ABAND LT HO

Abandoned Military Reservations Act [*1884*] ... AMRA

Abandoned Mine Land [*Department of the Interior*] ... AML

Abandoned Mine Land Reclamation [*Department of the Interior*] ... AMLR

Abandoned Police Post [*Board on Geographic Names*] ... PPQ

Abandoned Private Property ... APP

Abandoned Property Collection Act [*1863*] ... APCA

Abandoned Site Program Information System (SARE) ... ASPIS

Abandoner (ABBR) ... ABDNR

Abandonment (ABBR) ... ABANDMT

Abandonment ... ABANDT

Abandonment [*Legal shorthand*] (LWAP) ... ABANM

Abandonment (ABBR) ... ABDMT

Abandonment (ABBR) ... ABDNNT

Abandonment [*Insurance*] ... Abdnt

Abandonment (ABBR) ... ABNDMNT

Abarghou [*Iran*] [*ICAO location identifier*] (ICLI) ... OISU

Abarth Register, USA (EA) ... ARUSA

Abasement (ABBR) ... ABASNT

Abasement (ABBR) ... ABAST

Abashian-Booth-Crowe anomaly (SAUS) ... ABC-anomaly

Abashiri [*Japan*] [*Seismograph station code, US Geological Survey*] ... ABJ

Abasing (ABBR) ... ABASG

Abastumani [*Former USSR*] [*Seismograph station code, US Geological Survey*] [*Closed*] ... ABS

Abastumani Astrophysical Laboratory (SAUO) ... AAO
Abatable (ABBR) ... ABATB
Abatement [*Legal term*] (DLA) ... ABAT
Abatement (ABBR) ... ABATMT
Abatement (ABBR) ... ABATNT
Abatement and Control [*Environmental Protection Agency*] (GFGA) ... A & C
Abatement and Control (SAUS) ... A&C
Abatement and Residual Forecasting Model (SAUS) ... ABTRES
Abatement Council of the Midwest (SRA) ... ACM
Abatement of Nuisances Caused by Air Transport ... ANCAT
Abaterra Energy Ltd. [*Toronto Stock Exchange symbol*] [*Vancouver Stock Exchange symbol*] ... ABR
Abating (ABBR) ... ABATG
Abatix Environmental [*NASDAQ symbol*] (TTSB) ... ABIX
Abatix Environmental Corp. [*Associated Press*] (SAG) ... Abatix
Abatix Environmental Corp. [*NASDAQ symbol*] (NQ) ... ABIX
Abaton Resources Ltd. [*Vancouver Stock Exchange symbol*] ... AAT
abattoir (SAUS) ... abat
Abau [*Papua*] [*Airport symbol*] (AD) ... ABW
Abaxial (MSA) ... ABXL
Abaxial Leaflet Pubescence - Curly [*Botany*] ... ABPC
Abaxis, Inc. [*NASDAQ symbol*] (SAG) ... ABAX
Abaxis, Inc. [*Associated Press*] (SAG) ... Abaxis
ABB AB [*NASDAQ symbol*] (SAG) ... ABB AB
ABB AB [*NASDAQ symbol*] (SAG) ... ABBB
ABB AB ADR [*NASDAQ symbol*] [*Formerly, ASEA AB ADR*] (SG) ... ABBBY
Abbas Air Ltd. [*British*] [*ICAO designator*] (FAAC) ... ABA
Abbas Antiquus [*Deceased, 1296*] [*Authority cited in pre-1607 legal work*] (DSA) ... Ab
Abbas Siculus [*Deceased, 1445*] [*Authority cited in pre-1607 legal work*] (DSA) ... Sicu Ab
Abbassamento [*Music*] ... Abb
Abbaye de Saint-Benoit-Du-Lac, Comte De Brome, PQ, Canada [*Library symbol*] [*Library of Congress*] (LCLS) ... CaQStBL
Abbaye de Saint-Benoit-Du-Lac, Comte De Brome, Quebec [*Library symbol*] [*National Library of Canada*] (NLC) ... QSTBL
Abbe Sine Condition ... ASC
Abberrant (ABBR) ... ABER
Abbe's Sine Law ... ASL
Abbess (ADWA) ... Abb
Abbess ... ABS
Abbeville [*France*] [*ICAO location identifier*] (ICLI) ... LFOI
Abbeville, AL [*AM radio station call letters*] (RBYB) ... WARI
Abbeville, AL [*FM radio station call letters*] (RBYB) ... WIZB
Abbeville, LA [*AM radio station call letters*] ... KROF
Abbeville, LA [*FM radio station call letters*] ... KROF-FM
Abbeville, SC (SAUS) ... WABV
Abbeville, SC [*AM radio station call letters*] (BROA) ... WABV-AM
Abbeville, SC [*FM radio station call letters*] ... WZLA
Abbeville-Greenwood Regional Library, Greenwood, SC [*Library symbol*] [*Library of Congress*] (LCLS) ... ScGrw
Abbey ... A
Abbey [*or Abbot*] ... AB
Abbey (GEAB) ... ab
Abbey ... ABB
Abbey [*Record label*] ... Abb
Abbey Exploration, Inc. [*Toronto Stock Exchange symbol*] ... ABB
Abbey Lane Elementary School, Levittown, NY [*Library symbol*] [*Library of Congress*] (LCLS) ... NLevAE
Abbey Natl. [*Associated Press*] (SAG) ... AbbyNtl
Abbey Natl. [*NYSE symbol*] (SAG) ... ANB
Abbey of Gethsemani, Trappist, KY [*Library symbol*] [*Library of Congress*] (LCLS) ... KyTrA
Abbey Woods Development [*Vancouver Stock Exchange symbol*] ... AWD
Abbie J. Lane Memorial Hospital, Halifax, NS, Canada [*Library symbol*] [*Library of Congress*] (LCLS) ... CaNSHALMH
Abbildungen [*Illustration, Figure*] [*German*] (BJA) ... Abb
Abbot Biological and Chemical Data (SAUS) ... ABCD
Abbot Energy Corp. [*Vancouver Stock Exchange symbol*] ... ABT
Abbot Public Library Marblehead, Ma [*Library symbol*] [*Library of Congress*] (LCLS) ... MMh
Abbotsbury [*England*] ... ABBOTSB
Abbotsford [*Canada*] [*Airport symbol*] ... YXX
Abbotsford Air Services [*Canada*] [*ICAO designator*] (FAAC) ... ABE
Abbotsford, BC [*ICAO location identifier*] (ICLI) ... CYXX
Abbotsford-Matsqui, AB [*FM radio station call letters*] ... CFSR
Abbotsford-Matsqui, BC [*AM radio station call letters*] ... CKMA
Abbott and Costello Fan Club (EA) ... ACFC
Abbott Consortium for Technology ... ACT
Abbott Laboratories [*Research code symbol*] ... A
Abbott Laboratories ... Abb
Abbott Laboratories [*NYSE symbol*] (SPSG) ... ABT
Abbott Laboratories [*Research code symbol*] ... AG
Abbott Laboratories [*Research code symbol*] ... MO
Abbott Laboratories [*Research code symbol*] ... PR
Abbott Laboratories [*Research code symbol*] ... PS
Abbott Laboratories Ltd. [*Associated Press*] (SAG) ... AbtLab
Abbott Laboratories Ltd. [*Great Britain*] [*Research code symbol*] ... ES
Abbott Laboratories Ltd., Montreal, PQ, Canada [*Library symbol*] [*Library of Congress*] (LCLS) ... CaQMALL
Abbott Laboratories Ltd., Montreal, Quebec [*Library symbol*] [*National Library of Canada*] (NLC) ... QMALL
Abbott Laboratories, North Chicago, IL [*Library symbol*] [*Library of Congress*] (LCLS) ... INcA
Abbott Laboratories, North Chicago, IL [*OCLC symbol*] (OCLC) ... ITB
Abbott Mead Vickers [*Commercial firm*] [*British*] ... AMV
Abbott Memorial Library, Pomfret, VT [*Library symbol*] [*Library of Congress*] (LCLS) ... VtPom
Abbott on Civil Jury Trials [*A publication*] (ILCA) ... Abbott Civ Jur Tr
Abbott on Civil Jury Trials [*A publication*] (DLA) ... Abbott Civ Jury Trials
Abbott on Criminal Trial Practice [*A publication*] (DLA) ... Abbott Crim Tr Pr
Abbott on Merchant Ships and Seaman [*1802-1901*] [*A publication*] (DLA) ... Abbott
Abbott on Shipping [*A publication*] (DLA) ... Abb Sh
Abbott on Shipping [*A publication*] (DLA) ... Abb Ship
Abbott. United States Circuit and District Court Reports [*A publication*] (DLA) ... Abb
Abbottabad [*Pakistan*] [*Airport symbol*] (AD) ... AOT
Abbottabad [*Pakistan*] [*ICAO location identifier*] (ICLI) ... OPAB
Abbott-Northwestern Hospitals, Inc., Minneapolis, MN [*Library symbol*] [*Library of Congress*] (LCLS) ... MnMAb
Abbott's Admiralty Reports [*United States*] [*A publication*] (DLA) ... Abb Ad
Abbott's Admiralty Reports [*United States*] [*A publication*] (DLA) ... Abb Adm
Abbott's Admiralty Reports [*United States*] [*A publication*] (DLA) ... Abb Ad R
Abbott's Admiralty Reports [*United States*] [*A publication*] (DLA) ... Abbott's Adm
Abbott's Admiralty Reports [*United States*] [*A publication*] (DLA) ... Abbott's Ad Rep
Abbott's Circuit Court Reports [*United States*] [*A publication*] (DLA) ... Abb CC
Abbott's Circuit Court Reports [*United States*] [*A publication*] (DLA) ... Abb US
Abbott's Clerks and Conveyancers' Assistant [*A publication*] (DLA) ... Abb Cl Ass
Abbott's Court of Appeals Decisions [*New York*] [*A publication*] (DLA) ... Abb Ap Dec
Abbott's Court of Appeals Decisions [*New York*] [*A publication*] (DLA) ... Abb App Dec
Abbott's Court of Appeals Decisions [*New York*] [*A publication*] (DLA) ... Abb Ct App
Abbott's Court of Appeals Decisions [*New York*] [*A publication*] (DLA) ... Abb Ct of App Dec
Abbott's Court of Appeals Decisions [*New York*] [*A publication*] (DLA) ... Abb NY App
Abbott's Decisions [*A publication*] (DLA) ... Abb Dec
Abbott's Dictionary [*A publication*] (DLA) ... Abb Dict
Abbott's Dictionary [*A publication*] (DLA) ... Abbott
Abbott's Digest of the Law of Corporations [*A publication*] (DLA) ... Abb Dig Corp
Abbott's Forms of Pleading [*A publication*] (DLA) ... Abb F
Abbott's Forms of Pleading, Supplement [*A publication*] (DLA) ... Abb F Sup
Abbott's Indiana Digest [*A publication*] (DLA) ... Abb Ind Dig
Abbott's Introduction to Practice under the Codes [*A publication*] (DLA) ... Abb Int
Abbott's Law Dictionary [*1879*] [*A publication*] (DLA) ... Abb Law Dict
Abbott's Law Dictionary [*1879*] [*A publication*] (DLA) ... Abb L Dic
Abbott's Legal Remembrancer [*A publication*] (DLA) ... Abb Leg Rem
Abbott's Merchant Ships and Seamen, by Story [*A publication*] (DLA) ... Story Merchants
Abbott's Monthly Index [*A publication*] (DLA) ... Abb Mo Ind
Abbott's National Digest [*A publication*] (DLA) ... Abb Nat Dig
Abbott's New Cases [*New York*] [*A publication*] (DLA) ... Abb NC
Abbott's New Cases [*New York*] [*A publication*] (DLA) ... Abb N Cas
Abbott's New Cases [*New York*] [*A publication*] (DLA) ... Abb New Cas
Abbott's New Cases [*New York*] [*A publication*] (DLA) ... Abbott's NC
Abbott's New Cases [*New York*] [*A publication*] (DLA) ... AN
Abbott's New Cases [*New York*] [*A publication*] (DLA) ... ANC
Abbott's New York Digest [*A publication*] (DLA) ... Abb Dig
Abbott's New York Digest [*A publication*] (DLA) ... Abb NY Dig
Abbott's New York Digest, Second [*A publication*] (DLA) ... Abb NY Dig 2d
Abbott's Pleadings under the Code [*A publication*] (DLA) ... Abb Pl
Abbott's Practice in the United States Courts [*A publication*] (DLA) ... Abb US Pr
Abbott's Practice Reports [*New York*] [*A publication*] (DLA) ... Abbott PR
Abbott's Practice Reports [*New York*] [*A publication*] (DLA) ... Abbott Pract Cas
Abbott's Practice Reports [*New York*] [*A publication*] (DLA) ... Abbott Pr Rep
Abbott's Practice Reports [*New York*] [*A publication*] (DLA) ... Abbott's Prac Rep
Abbott's Practice Reports [*New York*] [*A publication*] (DLA) ... Abbott's Pr Rep
Abbott's Practice Reports [*New York*] [*A publication*] (DLA) ... Abb PR
Abbott's Practice Reports [*New York*] [*A publication*] (DLA) ... Abb Prac
Abbott's Practice Reports [*New York*] [*A publication*] (DLA) ... Abb Pr Rep
Abbott's Practice Reports, New Series [*New York*] [*A publication*] (DLA) ... Abb NS
Abbott's Practice Reports, New Series [*New York*] [*A publication*] (DLA) ... Abb Prac NS
Abbott's Practice Reports, New Series [*New York*] [*A publication*] (DLA) ... Abb Pr NS
Abbott's Real Property Statutes [*A publication*] (DLA) ... Abb RPS
Abbott's Reports of the Beecher Trial [*A publication*] (DLA) ... Abb Beech Tr
Abbott's Trial Evidence [*A publication*] (DLA) ... Abb Tr Ev
Abbott's United States Circuit and District Courts Reports [*A publication*] (DLA) ... Abbott USR
Abbott's United States Circuit and District Courts Reports [*A publication*] (DLA) ... Abbott US Rep
Abbott's United States Circuit and District Courts Reports [*A publication*] (DLA) ... Abb USCC
Abbott's Year Book of Jurisprudence [*A publication*] (DLA) ... Abb Y Bk
Abbreviate (ADWA) ... abbr
Abbreviate (SAUS) ... ABBR
Abbreviate (ADWA) ... abbrev
Abbreviated (ABBR) ... ABBRD
Abbreviated (DAVI) ... abbrev
Abbreviated Address Calling (SAUS) ... AAC
Abbreviated Address Dialling (SAUS) ... AAD
Abbreviated Analysis [*Military*] ... AA
Abbreviated Antibiotic Drug Application [*Food and Drug Administration*] ... AADA

Abbreviated Blood Count [Medicine] (MELL) ...... ABC
Abbreviated COBOL Preprocessor [Computer science] (IEEE) ...... ACOPP
Abbreviated COBOL Pre-Processor (SAUS) ...... ACOPP
Abbreviated Coded Rendition of Name Yielding Meaning (SAUS) ...... ACRONYM
Abbreviated Conners Parent/Teacher Rating Scale (EDAC) ...... ACRS
Abbreviated Cost Form (MCD) ...... ACF
Abbreviated Dial (DNAB) ...... ABD
Abbreviated Dialing Number (SAUS) ...... ADN
Abbreviated Dialling (SAUS) ...... AD
Abbreviated Effectiveness Report [Air Force] ...... AER
Abbreviated Injury Scale [Medicine] (PDAA) ...... AIS
Abbreviated Item Description (NASA) ...... AID
Abbreviated New Animal Drug Application [Food and Drug Administration] ...... ANADA
Abbreviated New Drug Application [FDA] ...... ANDA
Abbreviated Operational Evaluation (MCD) ...... AOE
Abbreviated Outline Test Plan [DoD] ...... AOTP
Abbreviated Parent Symptom Questionnaire [Medicine] (DMAA) ...... APSQ
Abbreviated Performance Campaign (SAUS) ...... APC
Abbreviated Performance Characteristics [Army] ...... APC
Abbreviated Precision Approach Path Indicator [Aviation] (DA) ...... APAPI
Abbreviated Purchase Order ...... ABBR PO
Abbreviated Registered Address ...... ARA
Abbreviated Symptom Questionnaire [Medicine] (AAMN) ...... ASQ
Abbreviated Test Language for All Systems [Electronics] (AAEL) ...... ATLAS
Abbreviated Test Language for Avionics Systems ...... ATLAS
Abbreviated Tracking and Reporting Form (IUSS) ...... ATARF
Abbreviated Transportation Accounting Classification [Army] ...... ATAC
Abbreviated Trouble History (SAUS) ...... ATH
Abbreviated Visual Approach Slope Indicator [Aviation] ...... AVASI
Abbreviated Visual Approach Slope Indicator System [Aviation] (DA) ...... AV
Abbreviated Visual Approach Slope Indicator System [Aviation] ...... AVASIS
Abbreviating (ABBR) ...... ABBRG
Abbreviation (IAA) ...... A
Abbreviation (ROG) ...... AB
Abbreviation (ADWA) ...... ab
Abbreviation (WDAA) ...... abb
Abbreviation (ROG) ...... ABB
Abbreviation (AFM) ...... ABBR
Abbreviation (DMAA) ...... abbr
Abbreviation (EY) ...... ABBREV
Abbreviation (ABBR) ...... ABBRN
Abbreviation (ROG) ...... ABBRON
Abbreviation (IAA) ...... ABR
abbreviations (SAUS) ...... abbrevia
Abbreviations and Acronyms (SAUS) ...... AAA
Abbreviations and Acronyms (SAUS) ...... A&A
Abbreviations and Acronyms Associated with Astronomy and a Bunch of Related Activities (SAUS) ...... ABRAC
Abbreviations and Related Acronyms Associated with Defense, Astronautics, Business (SAUS) ...... ABRACADABRA
Abbreviations and Related Acronyms Associated with Defense, Astronautics, Business, and Radio-Electronics [Raytheon Co. publication] ...... ABRACADABRA
Abbreviator (ABBR) ...... ABBRR
Abbreviomania (ABBR) ...... ABBREVIO
Abbs [Yemen] [ICAO location identifier] (ICLI) ...... OYAS
Abbs Surname Organization (EA) ...... ASO
Abbse [Yemen Arab Republic] [Airport symbol] (OAG) ...... EAB
Abby Investment [Vancouver Stock Exchange symbol] ...... ABY
ABC [Air Business Contact] [France] [ICAO designator] (FAAC) ...... ACB
ABC + Drugs/EKG/ Flimmern/Gauging/Hypothermie/Intensive (SAUS) ...... ABCDEFGHI
ABC Airlines, Inc. (SAUS) ...... SUP
ABC Bancorp [NASDAQ symbol] (SAG) ...... ABCB
ABC Bancorp [Associated Press] (SAG) ...... ABC Bc
ABC Consolidated Corporation (SAUO) ...... ABC
ABC Dispensing Technologies, Inc. [NASDAQ symbol] (SAG) ...... ABCC
ABC Dispensing Technologies, Inc. [NASDAQ symbol] (SAG) ...... ABC Dsp
ABC Rail Products [NASDAQ symbol] (TTSB) ...... ABCR
ABC Rail Products [Associated Press] (SAG) ...... ABC Rail
ABC Technology, Inc. [Vancouver Stock Exchange symbol] ...... ABW
ABC World Airways Guide [ICAO designator] (FAAC) ...... ABC
ABC-Naco Inc. [NASDAQ symbol] (SG) ...... ABCR
Abcoulomb (IDOE) ...... abC
Abcoulomb (SAUS) ...... AC
Abcoulomb [Unit of electric charge] ...... aC
Abcoulomb Centimeter (SAUS) ...... aCcm
Abcoulomb per Cubic Centimeter (SAUS) aCcm3
Abcoulomb per Square Centimeter (SAUS) ...... aCcmy
Abdanan [Iran] [ICAO location identifier] (ICLI) ...... OICD
Abdicate (ABBR) ...... ABDI
Abdicated (ROG) ...... ABD
Abdicated (GEAB) ...... abd
Abdicated (ABBR) ...... ABDID
Abdication (ABBR) ...... ABDIN
Abdomen [Medicine] ...... AB
Abdomen [or Abdominal] ...... ABD
abdomen (SAUS) ...... abd
Abdomen (DB) ...... Abd
Abdomen (ABBR) ...... ABDM
Abdomen ...... ABDOM
Abdomen (DMAA) ...... abdom
Abdominal (MELL) ...... AB
abdominal (SAUS) ...... abd

Abdominal (ABBR) ...... ABDML
Abdominal (SAUS) ...... abdom
Abdominal (ADWA) ...... adbom
Abdominal Aorta [Medicine] (DB) ...... AO
Abdominal Aortic Aneurysm [or Aneurismectomy] [Medicine] ...... AAA
Abdominal Auscultation [Medicine] (MELL) ...... AA
Abdominal Bloating [Medicine] (MELL) ...... AB
Abdominal Circumference [Neonatology and pediatrics] (DAVI) ...... AC
Abdominal Diameter [Roentgenology] ...... AD
Abdominal Diaphragmatic Breathing (SAUS) ...... AD
Abdominal Distention [Medicine] (MELL) ...... AD
Abdominal Fluid [Medicine] (DAVI) ...... ABD
Abdominal Girth (MELL) ...... AG
Abdominal Herniorrhaphy [Medicine] (MELL) ...... AH
Abdominal Hysterectomy [Gynecology] (CPH) ...... Abd Hyst
Abdominal Hysterectomy [Medicine] ...... AH
Abdominal Incontinence Operation [Medicine] (MELL) ...... AIO
Abdominal Irradiation [Medicine] (MELL) ...... AI
Abdominal Muscles (ADWA) ...... abs
Abdominal Pad [Orthopedics] (DAVI) ...... ABD
Abdominal Paracentesis [Medicine] (MELL) ...... APC
Abdominal Perineal [Medicine] (CPH) ...... A-P
Abdominal Surgery [Medical specialty] (DHSM) ...... ABS
Abdominal Surgery (journ.) (SAUS) ...... Abdom Surg
Abdominal Trauma Index [Medicine] (DMAA) ...... ATI
Abdominal Tympany [Medicine] (AAMN) ...... AT
Abdominal Vena Cava (SAUS) ...... AVBR
Abdominal Vena Cava [Medicine] ...... AVC
Abdominal Wall [Medicine] (MELL) ...... AW
Abdominal X-Ray [Medicine] ...... AXR
Abdominally (ABBR) ...... ABDMLY
Abdominally (ABBR) ...... ABDMY
Abdomino-Jugular Reflex [Medicine] (MELL) ...... AJR
Abdominojugular Reflux Maneuver [Medicine] (DMAA) ...... AJR
Abdomino-Perineal Resection (SAUS) ...... APR
Abdominoperineal Resection [Medicine] ...... APR
Abducens Motoneuron [Neuroanatomy] ...... ABM
Abducent Nerve [Medicine] (MELL) ...... AN
Abduct [or Abductor] [Neurology and orthopedics] (DAVI) ...... abd
Abduct [or Abduction] [Neurology and orthopedics] (DAVI) ...... abdc
Abducted (ABBR) ...... ABDCD
Abducting (ABBR) ...... ABDCG
Abduction [FBI standardized term] ...... ABD
Abduction (ABBR) ...... ABDCN
Abduction ...... ABDUC
Abduction, External Rotation [Physiology] ...... ABDER
Abduction, Internal Rotation [Physiology] ...... ABDIR
Abduction Stress Test (MELL) ...... AST
Abductive Logic Programming (RALS) ...... ALP
Abductor (MELL) ...... AB
Abductor (SAUS) ...... ABD
Abductor (ABBR) ...... ABDCR
Abductor Digiti Minimi [Muscles of Hands or Feet] [Anatomy] (DAVI) ...... ADM
Abductor Digiti Quinti [Muscles of Hands or Feet] [Anatomy] (DAVI) ...... ADQ
Abductor Pollicis [Muscle] [Anatomy] (DAVI) ...... abd poll
Abductor Pollicis Brevis [Muscle] [Anatomy] (DAVI) ...... APB
Abductor Pollicis Longus [Medicine] (DMAA) ...... APL
Abdy and Walker's Gaius and Ulpian [A publication] (DLA) ...... A & W Gai
Abdy and Walker's Gaius and Ulpian [A publication] (DLA) ...... Abdy & W Gai
Abdy and Walker's Justinian [A publication] (DLA) ...... A & W Just
Abdy and Walker's Justinian [A publication] (DLA) ...... Abdy & W Just
Abdy's Roman Civil Procedure [A publication] (DLA) ...... Abdy R Pr
Abdy's Roman Civil Procedure [A publication] (DLA) ...... Ab Rom Proc
Abe-Ali [Iran] [ICAO location identifier] (ICLI) ...... OIIA
Abeam ...... ABM
abecedarium (SAUS) ...... abc
Abeche [Chad] [Seismograph station code, US Geological Survey] [Closed] .... ABC
Abeche [Chad] [ICAO location identifier] (ICLI) ...... FTTC
Abecher [Chad] [Airport symbol] (AD) ...... AEH
A'Beckett's Comic Blackstone [A publication] (DLA) ...... Com Black
A'Beckett's Reserved Judgements [Victoria] [A publication] (ILCA) ...... A'Beckett Res Judg
A'Beckett's Reserved Judgements [A publication] (ILCA) ...... A'Beck Res Judg
A'Beckett's Reserved Judgements [Port Phillip] [A publication] (ILCA) ...... RJ
Abel Bibliographic Control System (SAUS) ...... ABCS
Abelag Airways [Belgium] [ICAO designator] (ICDA) ...... VY
Abelag Aviation [Belgium] [ICAO designator] (FAAC) ...... AAB
Abelard (SAUS) ...... Abel
Abell Cluster Inertial Frame [Cosmology] ...... ACIF
Abell-Corwin-Olowin Clusters [Galaxy cluster] ...... ACO
Abelson Leukemia Virus ...... ALV
Abelson Lymphosarcoma [Oncology] ...... ABLS
Abelson Murine Leukemia Virus [Medicine] (DB) ...... AmuLV
Abelson Plasmacytoid Lymphosarcoma [Oncology] ...... ABPL
Abelson Plasmacytoma [Oncology] ...... ABPC
Abelson Virus Transformed [Medicine] (DMAA) ...... ATV
Abelson Virus Transformed [Cells] [Medicine] (DB) ...... AVT
Abelson-Murine Leukemia [Virus] ...... AbL
Abelson-Murine Leukemia Virus ...... A-MuLV
Abelson-Murine Leukemia Virus (SAUS) ...... A-MULV
Abemama [Kiribati] [Airport symbol] (OAG) ...... AEA
Abemama [Kiribati] [ICAO location identifier] (ICLI) ...... NGTB
Abengourou [Ivory Coast] [ICAO location identifier] (ICLI) ...... DIAU
Abengourou [Ivory Coast] [Airport symbol] (OAG) ...... OGO
Abequose Residue [Medicine] (BABM) ...... abe

Aber Resource Ltd. [*NASDAQ symbol*] (TTSB) .... ABERE
Aber Resources Ltd. [*NASDAQ symbol*] (NQ) .... ABER
Aber Resources Ltd. [*Associated Press*] (SAG) .... AberRs
Aber Resources Ltd. [*Toronto Stock Exchange symbol*] .... ABZ
Aberation (SAUS) .... ab
Aberbeeg [*Welsh depot code*] .... ABEEG
Aberbrombie & Fitch (SAUO) .... A&F
Abercrombie & Fitch [*Retail stores*] .... A & F
Abercrombie & Fitch Co. [*Associated Press*] (SAG) .... AberFit
Abercrombie & Fitch Co. [*NYSE symbol*] (SAG) .... ANF
Abercynon [*Cardiff*] [*Welsh depot code*] .... AYN
Aberdare [*Welsh depot code*] .... ABDR
Aberdare National Park (SAUS) .... ANP
Aberdeen [*City and county in Scotland*] (ROG) .... ABD
Aberdeen [*Scotland*] [*Seismograph station code, US Geological Survey*]
  (SEIS) .... ABE
Aberdeen [*City and county in Scotland*] (ROG) .... ABER
Aberdeen (SAUS) .... Aber
Aberdeen [*City and county in Scotland*] .... ABERD
Aberdeen (SAUS) .... Abn
Aberdeen [*South Dakota*] [*Airport symbol*] (OAG) .... ABR
Aberdeen [*Scotland*] [*Airport symbol*] (OAG) .... ABZ
Aberdeen Airways [*British*] [*ICAO designator*] (FAAC) .... AAW
Aberdeen Airways [*Airline flight code*] (ODBW) .... SM
Aberdeen Airways Ltd. .... AAW
Aberdeen and North of Scotland Library and Information Cooperative
  Service (SAUS) .... ANSLICS
Aberdeen and North Scotland Library and Information Cooperative
  Services (NITA) .... ANSLICS
Aberdeen & Rockfish Railroad Co. [*AAR code*] .... AR
Aberdeen & Rockfish Railroad Company (SAUO) .... A&R
Aberdeen Art Society (SAUO) .... AAS
Aberdeen Association of Civil Engineers (SAUO) .... AACE
Aberdeen Cable Services [*Cable TV*] (NITA) .... ACS
Aberdeen Fishing Vessel Owners Association (SAUO) .... AFVOA
Aberdeen Ground/Materiel Testing Directorate [*Maryland*] [*Army*] .... APG/MT
Aberdeen Hospital, New Glasgow, Nova Scotia [*Library symbol*] [*National
  Library of Canada*] (NLC) .... NSNGA
Aberdeen Marine Laboratory .... AML
Aberdeen, MD [*Location identifier*] [*FAA*] (FAAL) .... APG
Aberdeen, MD [*Location identifier*] [*FAA*] (FAAL) .... PPM
Aberdeen, MD [*AM radio station call letters*] .... WAMD
Aberdeen Medico-Chirurgical Society (SAUO) .... AMCS
Aberdeen, MS [*AM radio station call letters*] .... WWZQ
Aberdeen, MS [*FM radio station call letters*] .... WWZQ-FM
Aberdeen, NC [*AM radio station call letters*] .... WQNX
Aberdeen Philosophical Society (SAUO) .... APS
Aberdeen Press and Journal (journ.) (SAUS) .... APJ
Aberdeen Proving Ground [*Maryland*] [*Army*] .... APG
Aberdeen Proving Ground/Ballistics Research Laboratory [*Army*] .... APGBRL
Aberdeen Proving Ground/Human Engineering Laboratory [*Army*] .... APG/HEL
Aberdeen Proving Ground-Materiel Testing Directorate (SAUO) .... APG/MT
Aberdeen Proving Ground/Ordnance Bomb Disposal Center [*Army*]
  (KSC) .... APG/OBDC
Aberdeen Proving Ground/Ordnance Training Command (SAUS) .... APC/OTC
Aberdeen Proving Ground/Ordnance Training Command [*Army*]
  (KSC) .... APG/OTC
Aberdeen Public Library, Aberdeen, ID [*Library symbol*] [*Library of
  Congress*] (LCLS) .... IdAb
Aberdeen Public Library, Aberdeen, WA [*Library symbol*] [*Library of
  Congress*] (LCLS) .... WaA
Aberdeen Pulsed Reactor Facility (SAUS) .... APR
Aberdeen Pulsed Reactor Facility .... APRF
Aberdeen Research and Development Center (MCD) .... ARDC
Aberdeen, SD [*Television station call letters*] .... KABY
Aberdeen, SD [*FM radio station call letters*] (BROA) .... KBFO-FM
Aberdeen, SD [*Television station call letters*] .... KDSD
Aberdeen, SD [*AM radio station call letters*] .... KGIM
Aberdeen, SD [*AM radio station call letters*] .... KKAA
Aberdeen, SD [*FM radio station call letters*] .... KQAA
Aberdeen, SD [*AM radio station call letters*] .... KSDN
Aberdeen, SD [*FM radio station call letters*] .... KSDN-FM
Aberdeen Test Center .... ATC
Aberdeen University Library (SAUO) .... AUL
Aberdeen University Press (SAUO) .... AUP
Aberdeen University Research and Industrial Services (AIE) .... AURIS
Aberdeen University Research & Industrial Services Ltd. [*British*] [*Research
  center*] (IRUK) .... AURIS
Aberdeen University Review (journ.) (SAUS) .... AUR
Aberdeen, WA [*FM radio station call letters*] .... KAYO-FM
Aberdeen, WA [*AM radio station call letters*] (RBYB) .... KBKW
Aberdeen, WA [*AM radio station call letters*] .... KDUX
Aberdeen, WA [*AM radio station call letters*] .... KXRO
Aberdeen/Amory, MS [*Location identifier*] [*FAA*] (FAAL) .... HWF
Aberdeen-Angus Journal, Webster City, IA [*Library symbol*] [*Library of
  Congress*] (LCLS) .... IaWecAJ
Aberdeen/Dyce [*British*] [*ICAO location identifier*] (ICLI) .... EGPD
Aberford Resources Ltd. [*Toronto Stock Exchange symbol*] .... ABC
Aberfoyle [*Scotland*] [*Seismograph station code, US Geological Survey*]
  (SEIS) .... EAB
Abermarle County Historical Society, Charlottesville, VA [*Library symbol*]
  [*Library of Congress*] (LCLS) .... ViCAHi
Abermin Corp. [*Toronto Stock Exchange symbol*] .... ABM
Aberporth [*British*] [*ICAO location identifier*] (ICLI) .... EGUC
Aberrance (ABBR) .... ABRN

Aberrancy (ABBR) .... ABRNC
Aberrant (DMAA) .... aber
Aberrant (ABBR) .... ABRNT
Aberrant Banding Region [*Genetics*] .... ABR
Aberrant Behavior Center (SAUO) .... ABC
Aberrant Behavior Checklist [*Treatment effectiveness test*] [*Psychology*] .... ABC
Aberrant Congenital Venous Loop [*Medicine*] (MELL) .... ACVL
Aberrant Ventricular Conduction [*Medicine*] (MELL) .... AVC
Aberrantly (ABBR) .... ABRNTY
Aberratio (LDT) .... ab
Aberration (IAA) .... ABER
Aberration (ABBR) .... ABERN
Aberration (ABBR) .... ABRAN
Aberrational (ABBR) .... ABERNL
Aberrational (ABBR) .... ABRANL
Aberration-Compensated Input Lens [*Optics*] .... ACIL
Aberystwyth [*Borough in Wales*] .... ABERY
Aberystwyth [*Welsh depot code*] .... ABH
Aberystwyth University College (SAUO) .... AUC
A-Beta-Lipoproteinemia [*Medicine*] (MAH) .... ABL
Abetment (ABBR) .... ABETMT
Abetment (ABBR) .... ABETNT
Abetted (ABBR) .... ABETD
Abetting (ABBR) .... ABETG
Abettor (ABBR) .... ABETR
Abeve Proof (SAUS) .... AP
Abex, Inc. [*NYSE symbol*] (SPSG) .... ABE
Abeyance (ABBR) .... ABYNC
Abeyant (ABBR) .... ABYNT
Abfarad (IDOE) .... abF
Abfarad [*Unit of capacitance*] .... aF
Abgekuerzt [*Abbreviated*] [*German*] .... ABGK
Abgeordneter [*Member of Parliament*] [*German*] (BARN) .... Abg
Abha [*Saudi Arabia*] [*Airport symbol*] (OAG) .... AHB
Abha [*Saudi Arabia*] [*ICAO location identifier*] (ICLI) .... OEAB
Abhandlungen [*Transactions*] [*German*] [*Business term*] .... ABH
Abhandlungen der Preussische Akademie der Wissenschaften zu Berlin
  [*A publication*] (OCD) .... Berl Abh
Abhandlungen. Saechsische Gesellschaft der Wissenschaften
  [*A publication*] (OCD) .... Abh Sachs Ges Wiss
Abhandlungen zur Geschichte der Mathematischen Wissenschaften
  [*A publication*] (OCD) .... Abh zu Gesch d Math
Abhandlungen zur Geschichte der Naturwissenschaften und der Medizin
  [*A publication*] (OCD) .... Abh zu Gesch d Med
Abhazian Autonomous Soviet Socialist Republic (SAUO) .... AASR
Abhenry (IDOE) .... abH
Abhenry [*Unit of inductance*] .... aH
Abhorred (ABBR) .... ABHRD
Abhorrence (ABBR) .... ABHRNC
Abhorrent (ABBR) .... ABHRNT
Abhorrent (ABBR) .... ABHRT
Abhorrently (ABBR) .... ABHRNTY
Abhorrently (ABBR) .... ABHRTY
Abhorrer (ABBR) .... ABHRR
Abhorring (ABBR) .... ABHRG
[*The*] Abibi Jazz Artists [*British*] .... TAJA
Abidance (ABBR) .... ABIDNC
Abiding (ABBR) .... ABIDG
Abidingly (ABBR) .... ABIDGY
Abidjan [*Ivory Coast*] [*Airport symbol*] (OAG) .... ABJ
Abidjan [*Ivory Coast*] [*ICAO location identifier*] (ICLI) .... DIAV
Abidjan [*Ivory Coast*] [*ICAO location identifier*] (ICLI) .... DIII
Abidjan/Port Bouet [*Ivory Coast*] [*ICAO location identifier*] (ICLI) .... DIAP
Abigail Adams Historical Society (EA) .... AAHS
Abigail Adams Historical Society, Weymouth, MA [*Library symbol*] [*Library of
  Congress*] (LCLS) .... MWeyAA
Abigail Adams National Bancorp, Inc. [*NASDAQ symbol*] (SAG) .... AANB
Abigail Adams National Bancorp, Inc. [*Associated Press*] (SAG) .... AbigAd
Abigail Adams Smith Museum, New York City (SAUS) .... AASM
Abilene [*Texas*] [*Airport symbol*] (OAG) .... ABI
Abilene & Southern (SAUS) .... AS
Abilene & Southern Railway Co. [*AAR code*] .... AS
Abilene and Southern Railway Company (SAUO) .... A&S
Abilene Christian College (SAUO) .... ACC
Abilene Christian University (SAUO) .... ACU
Abilene Christian University, Abilene, TX [*Library symbol*] [*Library of
  Congress*] (LCLS) .... TxAbC
Abilene Christian University, Abilene, TX [*OCLC symbol*] (OCLC) .... TXC
Abilene Free Public Library, Abilene, KS [*Library symbol*] [*Library of
  Congress*] (LCLS) .... KAb
Abilene, KS [*AM radio station call letters*] .... KABI
Abilene, KS [*FM radio station call letters*] .... KSAJ
Abilene Municipal Airport (SAUO) .... ABI
Abilene Public Library, Abilene, TX [*Library symbol*] [*Library of Congress*]
  (LCLS) .... TxAb
Abilene Public Library, Abilene, TX [*OCLC symbol*] (OCLC) .... TXB
Abilene, TX [*Location identifier*] [*FAA*] (FAAL) .... DYS
Abilene, TX [*FM radio station call letters*] .... KACU
Abilene, TX [*FM radio station call letters*] (RBYB) .... KAQD-FM
Abilene, TX [*AM radio station call letters*] .... KBBA
Abilene, TX [*AM radio station call letters*] .... KEAN
Abilene, TX [*FM radio station call letters*] .... KEAN-FM
Abilene, TX [*FM radio station call letters*] .... KEYJ
Abilene, TX [*FM radio station call letters*] .... KFXJ
Abilene, TX [*AM radio station call letters*] (BROA) .... KGMM

Abilene, TX [*FM radio station call letters*]	KGNZ
Abilene, TX [*FM radio station call letters*]	KHXS
Abilene, TX [*AM radio station call letters*] (BROA)	KMPC
Abilene, TX [*AM radio station call letters*]	KNTS
Abilene, TX [*FM radio station call letters*]	KORQ-FM
Abilene, TX [*Television station call letters*]	KRBC
Abilene, TX [*Television station call letters*]	KTAB
Abilene, TX [*FM radio station call letters*] (BROA)	KULL-FM
Abilene, TX [*AM radio station call letters*]	KYYD
Abilene, TX [*Location identifier*] [*FAA*] (FAAL)	TQA
Abilene, TX (SAUS)	TYV
Abilene, TX [*Location identifier*] [*FAA*] (FAAL)	TYY
Abilene/Dyess Air Force Base [*Texas*] [*ICAO location identifier*] (ICLI)	KDYS
Abilene/Municipal [*Texas*] [*ICAO location identifier*] (ICLI)	KABI
Ability (ABBR)	ABIL
Ability (ABBR)	ABLT
Ability Based on Long Experience	ABLE
Ability Grouped Active Teaching (EDAC)	AGAT
Ability of Solder Paste to Retain Components [*Electronics*] (AAEL)	ASPaRC
Abingdon [*Australia*] [*Airport symbol*] (OAG)	ABG
Abingdon [*England*]	ABING
Abingdon [*British*] [*ICAO location identifier*] (ICLI)	EGUD
Abingdon Mile [*Newmarket Racecourse*] [*Horseracing*] [*British*]	ABM
Abingdon Pottery Club (EA)	APC
Abingdon Press [*Publisher*]	AP
Abingdon, VA [*Location identifier*] [*FAA*] (FAAL)	ATX
Abingdon, VA [*AM radio station call letters*]	WABN
Abingdon, VA [*FM radio station call letters*]	WABN-FM
Abinger [*United Kingdom*] [*Later, HAD*] [*Geomagnetic observatory code*]	ABN
Abington Free Library, Abington, PA [*Library symbol*] [*Library of Congress*] (LCLS)	PAb
Abington Library Society, Jenkintown, PA [*Library symbol*] [*Library of Congress*] [*Obsolete*] (LCLS)	PJA
Abington Savings Bank [*NASDAQ symbol*] (NQ)	ABBK
Abington Savings Bank [*Associated Press*] (SAG)	AbingSB
Abington Township Public Library, Abington, PA [*OCLC symbol*] (OCLC)	ABG
Abiomed, Inc. [*Associated Press*] (SAG)	Abiomd
Abiomed, Inc. [*NASDAQ symbol*] (SAG)	ABMD
Abisko [*Sweden*] [*Seismograph station code, US Geological Survey*] [*Closed*]	ABK
Abisko [*Sweden*] [*ICAO location identifier*] (ICLI)	ESHA
Abitibi Asbestos Mining Co. Ltd. [*Vancouver Stock Exchange symbol*]	ABS
Abitibi Resources Ltd. [*Vancouver Stock Exchange symbol*]	AIR
Abitibi-Consolidated [*NYSE symbol*] (SG)	ABY
Abitibi-Price [*NYSE symbol*] (TTSB)	ABY
Abitibi-Price, Inc. [*Associated Press*] (SAG)	Abitibi
Abitibi-Price, Inc. [*NYSE symbol*] (SPSG)	ABY
Abitibi-Price, Inc., Mississauga, ON, Canada [*Library symbol*] [*Library of Congress*] (LCLS)	CaOMABP
Abitibi-Price, Inc., Mississauga, Ontario [*Library symbol*] [*National Library of Canada*] (NLC)	OMABP
Abitur [*School Exit Examination*] [*German*]	Abit
Abject (ABBR)	ABJT
Abjection (ABBR)	ABJTN
Abjectly (ABBR)	ABJTY
Abjectness (ABBR)	ABJTNS
Abjuration (ABBR)	ABJRN
Abjure (ABBR)	ABJR
Abjured (ABBR)	ABJRD
Abjurer (ABBR)	ABJRR
Abjuring (ABBR)	ABJRG
Abkuerzungsfimmel [*Abbreviation Craze*]	ABKUFI
Abkurzung [*Abbreviation*] [*German*] (BARN)	Abk
Ablating Blunt Body	ABB
Ablating Inner Surface	AIS
Ablative	ABL
Ablative (WDAA)	abl
Ablative (KSC)	ABLAT
Ablative (ABBR)	ABLTV
Ablative Absolute (ADWA)	abl absol
Ablative Heat Rate (MCD)	AHR
Ablative Heat Shield	AHS
Ablative Insulative Plastic	AIP
Ablative Photo Decomposition [*Physics*]	APD
Ablative Thrust Chamber [*NASA*]	ATC
Ablative Thrust Chamber Engine [*NASA*]	ATCE
Ablative Thrust Control (MCD)	ATC
Ablative Toroidal Compressor	ATC
Ablator Insulated Ramjet Study [*NASA*] (KSC)	AIRS
Ablaze (ABBR)	ABLZ
Able (ABBR)	ABL
Able and Available [*Unemployment insurance*] (OICC)	AA
Able Chief (MCD)	AC
Able Seaman [*Navy*]	AB
Able Seaman Clearance Diver	ABCD
Able Telcom Holding Corp. [*Associated Press*] (SAG)	AbleTel
Able Telcom Holding Corp. [*NASDAQ symbol*] (SAG)	ABTE
Able Telecom Holding [*NASDAQ symbol*] (TTSB)	ABTE
Able to Work (MELL)	AW
Ableauctions.comInc. [*AMEX symbol*] (SG)	AAC
Able-Bodied Seaman	AB
Able-Bodied Seaman	ABS
Able-Bodied Seaman, Air Technical Aircraft [*Navy*]	ABATA
Able-Bodied Seaman, Air Technical Communications [*Navy*]	ABATC
Able-Bodied Seaman, Air Technical Weapons Electrical [*Navy*]	ABATWL

Able-Bodied Seaman Cook [*Navy*]	ABCK
Able-bodied Seaman Coxswain [*Navy*]	ABCOX
Able-Bodied Seaman Dental, NV	ABDEN
Able-Bodied Seaman Electrical Technical Power [*Navy*]	ABETP
Able-Bodied Seaman Electrical Technical Weapons [*Navy*]	ABETW
Able-Bodied Seaman Electronic Technical Communications [*Navy*]	ABETC
Able-Bodied Seaman Electronic Warfare [*Navy*]	ABEW
Able-Bodied Seaman Fire Control [*Navy*]	ABFC
Able-Bodied Seaman Firefighter [*Navy*]	ABFF
Able-Bodied Seaman Marine Technical Hull [*Navy*]	ABMTH
Able-Bodied Seaman Marine Technical Propulsion [*Navy*]	ABMTP
Able-Bodied Seaman Medical [*Navy*]	ABMED
Able-Bodied Seaman Meteorology [*Navy*]	ABMET
Able-Bodied Seaman Mine Warfare [*Navy*]	ABMW
Able-Bodied Seaman Motor Transport Driver [*Navy*]	ABMTD
Able-Bodied Seaman Musician [*Navy*]	ABMUSN
Able-Bodied Seaman Photography [*Navy*]	ABPH
Able-Bodied Seaman Physical Training [*Navy*]	ABPT
Able-Bodied Seaman Quartermaster Gunner [*Navy*]	ABQMG
Able-Bodied Seaman RADAR Plotter [*Navy*]	ABRP
Able-Bodied Seaman Radio Operator [*Navy*]	ABRO
Able-Bodied Seaman Signalman [*Navy*]	ABSIG
Able-Bodied Seaman Steward [*Navy*]	ABSTD
Able-Bodied Seaman Stores Naval [*Navy*]	ABSN
Able-Bodied Seaman Stores Victualling [*Navy*]	ABSV
Able-Bodied Seaman Survival Equipment [*Navy*]	ABSE
Able-Bodied Seaman Underwater Control [*Navy*]	ABUC
Able-bodied Seaman Work Study [*Navy*]	ABWS
Able-Bodied Seaman Writer [*Navy*]	ABWTR
Able-Bodied Sick Bay Attendant [*Navy*]	ABBA
Abler (ABBR)	ABLR
Ablest (ABBR)	ABLT
Abloom (ABBR)	ABLM
Ablow [*Vanuatu*] [*ICAO location identifier*] (ICLI)	NVSA
Ablution (ABBR)	ABLUN
Ablutionary (ABBR)	ABLUNRY
Ablutionary (ABBR)	ABLUNY
ABM Industries, Inc. [*Associated Press*] (SAG)	ABM
ABM Industries, Inc. [*NYSE symbol*] (SG)	ABM
ABN AMRO Holding ADS [*NYSE symbol*] (SG)	AAN
ABN AMRO Holdings N.V. [*AM Symbol*] (TTSB)	ALGEE
Abnegate (ABBR)	ABNG
Abnegate (ABBR)	ABNGA
Abnegated (ABBR)	ABNGAD
Abnegated (ABBR)	ABNGD
Abnegates (ABBR)	ABNGS
Abnegating (ABBR)	ABNGAG
Abnegating (ABBR)	ABNGG
Abnegation (ABBR)	ABNGN
Abnegator (ABBR)	ABNGR
Abner (SAUS)	Ab
Abnormal (MAE)	AB
Abnormal [*or Abnormality*] [*Medicine*] (AAMN)	ABN
Abnormal (MSA)	ABNL
Abnormal [*or Abnormality*]	ABNOR
Abnormal [*Medicine*] (AAMN)	ABNORM
Abnormal Banding Region [*Genetics*]	ABR
Abnormal Blood Gas	ABG
Abnormal Condition Control [*Environmental science*] (COE)	ACC
Abnormal Control Plasma [*Clinical chemistry*]	ACP
Abnormal Curve [*Biochemistry*] (DAVI)	ABNC
Abnormal Development & Involution [*Medicine*] (WDAA)	ANDI
Abnormal End [*Computer science*]	ABEND
Abnormal End [*Computer science*] (IAA)	ABNED
Abnormal End of Task (ADWA)	ABEND
Abnormal Fluctuation in the Economy (MCD)	AFIE
Abnormal Forms Percent [*Sperm count*] [*Urology*] (DAVI)	ABN F%
Abnormal Frequency	AF
Abnormal Glucose Tolerance [*Medicine*] (MELL)	AGT
Abnormal Glucose Tolerance Test [*Medicine*]	AGTT
Abnormal Involuntary Movement Disorder [*Medicine*] (DMAA)	AIMD
Abnormal Involuntary Movement Scale [*Medicine*]	AIMS
Abnormal Left Axis Deviation (MAE)	ALAD
Abnormal Liver Function Test [*Medicine*] (DMAA)	ALFT
Abnormal Localization of Immature P recursors [*Clinical hematology*]	ALIP
Abnormal Localization of Immature Precursors (SAUS)	ALIP
Abnormal Lungs [*Medicine*]	AL
Abnormal Mission Routine	AMR
Abnormal Mucopolysacchariduria [*Medicine*] (MAE)	AMPS
Abnormal Occurrence (NRCH)	AO
Abnormal Occurrence Report	AOR
Abnormal Occurrence Reporting System (MHDB)	AORS
Abnormal Operating Condition (GFGA)	AOC
Abnormal Operating Conditions (SAUS)	AOC
Abnormal Operating Procedure (NRCH)	AOP
Abnormal Oxygen Affinity [*Hematology*] (DAVI)	AOA
Abnormal Posterior Vector [*Medicine*] (DMAA)	APV
Abnormal Psychology (SAUS)	ABPSY
Abnormal Record Compatible with Myocardial Disease [*Lower-case c in acronym means "with"*] [*Cardiology*]	ARCcMD
Abnormal Record Compatible with Myocardial Drug Effect [*Lowercase c in acronym means "with"*] [*Cardiology*]	ARCcMDE
Abnormal [*or Anomalous*] Retinal Correspondence [*Ophthalmology*]	ARC
Abnormal Retinal Correspondence (SAUS)	ARC
Abnormal Return Address (SAUS)	ARA

Abnormal Return Address (SAUS) ARD
Abnormal Skin Reflex [*Medicine*] (DMAA) AbSR
Abnormal Spinal Posture [*Medicine*] (MELL) ASP
Abnormal Spindle asp
Abnormal Statement (SAUS) AS
Abnormal Steady State Limits (MCD) ASSL
Abnormal Test Procedure Operator Guidelines (SAUS) ATOG
Abnormal Transient (SAUS) AT
Abnormal Transient Operational Guidelines [*Nuclear energy*] (NRCH) ATOG
Abnormal Uterine Bleeding [*Gynecology*] (DMAA) AUB
Abnormal Voltage AV
Abnormal Wall Motion [*Medicine*] (DMAA) AWM
Abnormal Xylem Elements [*Botany*] AX
Abnormality (ABBR) ABNMT
Abnormally (ABBR) ABNMY
Abnormally Polarized Waves (SAUS) APW
Abo Akademi [*Swedish University of Abo*], **Turku, Finland** [*Library symbol*] [*Library of Congress*] (LCLS) FiTA
ABO Resource Corp. [*Vancouver Stock Exchange symbol*] ABU
Aboard (SAUS) ABD
Aboard (BARN) abd
Aboard (ABBR) ABRD
Aboce Clouds (SAUS) AC
Aboda Zara (BJA) AbZ
Aboda Zara (BJA) AbZar
Aboda Zara (BJA) AZ
Abode (ABBR) ABOD
Abogada Internacional [*A publication*] (DLA) Abogada Int'l
Abohoy [*Indonesia*] [*ICAO location identifier*] (ICLI) WAKH
Aboisso [*Ivory Coast*] [*ICAO location identifier*] (ICLI) DIAO
Aboitiz Air Transport Corp. [*Philippines*] [*ICAO designator*] (FAAC) BOI
Abolish (ABBR) ABLH
Abolish All Abortion Laws (SAUO) AAAL
Abolishable (ABBR) ABLHB
Abolished ABOL
Abolished (ABBR) ABOLD
Abolisher (ABBR) ABLHR
abolisher (SAUS) abol
Abolishing (ABBR) ABOLG
Abolishment (ABBR) ABLHNT
abolishment (SAUS) abol
Abolishment (ABBR) ABOLT
Abolition (ABBR) ABOLN
abolitionism (SAUS) abol
Abolitionism (ABBR) ABOLNM
Abolitionist abol
abolitionist (SAUS) abol
Abolitionist (ABBR) ABOLNST
Abolitionist (ABBR) ABOLNT
Abominable (ABBR) ABMNB
Abominable (ABBR) ABOML
Abominably (ABBR) ABMNBY
Abominate (ABBR) ABMNA
Abominate (ABBR) ABOM
Abominated (ABBR) ABOMD
Abominating (ABBR) ABMNAG
Abominating (ABBR) ABOMG
Abomination (ABBR) ABMNAN
Abomination (ABBR) ABOMN
Abong-M'Bang [*Cameroon*] [*ICAO location identifier*] (ICLI) FKAG
Abonminated (ABBR) ABMNAD
Abopo [*Bolivia*] [*ICAO location identifier*] (ICLI) SLAB
Abori Guidance Section (SAUS) AGS
Aboriginal (ABBR) ABO
Aboriginal (ADWA) Aborg
Aboriginal (ABBR) ABORL
Aboriginal (ABBR) ABRGNL
Aboriginal Advancement Trust Account [*Australia*] AATA
Aboriginal Affairs Foundation [*Australia*] AAF
Aboriginal Affairs Victoria (SAUO) AAV
Aboriginal and Islander Child Care Agencies [*Australia*] AICCA
Aboriginal and Islander Forum [*A publication*] Abo Island Forum
Aboriginal and Islander Teacher Education Program [*Australia*] AITEP
Aboriginal and Torres Strait Islander Commission [*Australia*] ATSIC
Aboriginal and Torres Strait Islander Commission Regional Information Syste ARIS
Aboriginal and Torres Strait Islander Legal Service [*Australia*] ATSILS
Aboriginal and Torres Strait Islander Library and Resource Network [*Australia*] ATSILRN
Aboriginal Areas Protection Authority [*Northern Territory, Australia*] AAPA
Aboriginal Cadetship Program (SAUS) ACP
Aboriginal Child at School [*A publication*] Abo Child School
Aboriginal Children's Services [*Australia*] ACS
Aboriginal Community Affairs Panel [*Australia*] ACAP
Aboriginal Community Liaison Officer [*Australia*] ACLO
Aboriginal Community Recreation Health Services Centre [*Australia*] ACRHSC
Aboriginal Community Recreation Health Services Centre of South Australia ACRHSCSA
Aboriginal Coordinating Council [*Australia*] ACC
Aboriginal Cultural Centre and Keeping Place [*University of New England*] [*Australia*] ACCKP
Aboriginal Cultural Foundation [*Australia*] ACF
Aboriginal Development Assistance Association [*Australia*] ADAA
Aboriginal Economic and Employment Development Officer [*Australia*] AEEDO
Aboriginal Education Council (New South Wales) [*Australia*] AEC(NSW)
Aboriginal Education Direct Assistance Program [*Australia*] AEDAP
Aboriginal Education Foundation of South Australia AEFSA
Aboriginal Education Worker [*Australia*] AEW
Aboriginal Electoral Assistant [*Australia*] AEA
Aboriginal Electoral Information Service [*Australia*] AEIS
Aboriginal English (SAUS) Abo Eng
Aboriginal Environmental Health Worker [*Australia*] AEHW
Aboriginal Evangelical Fellowship of Australia AEFA
Aboriginal freehold/National Park (SAUO) FINP
Aboriginal Government, Resources, Economy and Environment (SAUO) AGREE
Aboriginal Health Development Group [*Australia*] AHDG
Aboriginal Health Policy Review Team [*Australia*] AHPRT
Aboriginal Health Service [*Australia*] AHS
Aboriginal Health Worker Education Program [*Australia*] AHWEP
Aboriginal Heritage Branch [*South Australia*] AHB
Aboriginal Home Care Service [*Australia*] AHCS
Aboriginal Housing Development Committee [*Australia*] AHDC
Aboriginal Independent Community Schools [*Australia*] AICS
Aboriginal Issues Unit [*Australia*] AIU
Aboriginal Land Fund Commission [*Australia*] ALFC
Aboriginal Lands Council [*Australia*] ALC
Aboriginal Lands of Hawaiian Ancestry [*Hawaiian group seeking compensation for land*] ALOHA
Aboriginal Language Maintenance Project [*Australia*] ALMP
Aboriginal Languages Education Strategy [*Australia*] ALES
Aboriginal Legal Service of Western Australia ALSWA
Aboriginal Loans Commission [*Australia*] ALC
Aboriginal Mental Health Network [*Western Australia*] AMHN
Aboriginal Middle Management Program [*Australia*] AMMP
Aboriginal Multi-Media Society of Alberta (AC) AMMSA
Aboriginal National Theatre Trust [*Australia*] ANTT
Aboriginal Nurses Association of Canada [*Association des Infirmieres et Infirmiers Autochtones du Canada*] [*Indian & Inuit Nurses of Canada*] (AC) ANAC
Aboriginal People's Business Association (AC) APBA
Aboriginal Programs Management Information System [*Australia*] APMIS
Aboriginal Protection Board [*Australia*] APB
Aboriginal Protection Society (SAUS) APS
Aboriginal Reconciliation Unit [*Australia*] ARU
Aboriginal Recruitment Training and Career Development (SAUO) ARTCD
Aboriginal Research Club (EA) ARC
Aboriginal Resource and Development Services [*Australia*] ARDS
Aboriginal Resource Unit [*University of New England*] [*Australia*] ARU
Aboriginal Rights Coalition [*Coalition pour les Droits des Autochtones*] [*Project North*] (AC) ARC
Aboriginal Sacred Sites Protection Authority [*Northern Territory, Australia*] ASSPA
Aboriginal Staff Cadetship Program [*Australia*] ASCP
Aboriginal Studies Electronic Data Archive (SAUO) ASEDA
Aboriginal Teaching Assistant [*Australia*] ATA
Aboriginal Trappers Federation of Canada (AC) ATFC
Aboriginal Visitors' Scheme [*Australia*] AVS
Aboriginal Welfare Board [*New South Wales, Australia*] AWB
Aboriginal Work Experience Program [*Australia*] AWEP
Aboriginally (ABBR) ABORLY
Aborigine (ABBR) ABO
Aborigine (SAUO) Abo
Aborigine ABOR
Aborigine (ABBR) ABRGN
Aborigines (SAUS) ABOS
Aborigines Inland Mission of Australia AIMA
Aborigines Protection Society [*Later, Anti-Slavery Society for the Protection of Human Rights*] APS
Aborigines Protection Society (SAUO) APS
Abort (MCD) ABRT
Abort ABT
Abort Accept [*Telecommunications*] (OSI) AA
Abort Advisory Channel [*NASA*] (KSC) AAC
Abort Advisory Equipment [*NASA*] (KSC) AAE
Abort Advisory System [*NASA*] AAS
Abort Electronics [*Apollo*] [*NASA*] AE
Abort Electronics Assembly [*Apollo*] [*NASA*] AEA
Abort Guidance Section [*NASA*] (KSC) AGS
Abort Guidance System [*or Subsystem*] [*Apollo*] [*NASA*] AGS
Abort Inertial Digital System [*NASA*] (KSC) AIDS
Abort Interface Unit [*NASA*] AIU
Abort Motor Facility [*NASA*] (NASA) AMF
Abort Once Around [*NASA*] AOA
Abort Once around Cutoff (MCD) ACO
Abort Output (SAUS) AO
Abort Programmer Assembly (SAUS) APA
Abort Programmer Assembly [*NASA*] (KSC) APA
Abort Programmer Assembly (SAUS) APA
Abort Request (MCD) ABRTREQ
Abort Sensing and Implementation System ASIS
Abort Sensing Control Unit ASCO
Abort Sensor Assembly [*Apollo*] [*NASA*] ASA
Abort Solid Rocket Motor [*NASA*] (NASA) ASRM
Abort Time Assembly [*NASA*] (NASA) ATA
Abort Timer (HGAA) ABT
Abort Timing Assembly (SAUS) ATA
Abort To Orbit (SAUS) ATO
Aborted (ABBR) ABRTD
aborted fetus (SAUS) abortus

Abort/Hold/Orbit [*NASA*] ... A/H/O
Aborting (ABBR) ... ABRTG
Abortion (SAUS) ... AB
Abortion [*Medicine*] (DMAA) ... ab
Abortion [*Obstetrics*] (DAVI) ... ABO
Abortion [*Medicine*] ... ABOR
Abortion (DMAA) ... Abor
Abortion (ABBR) ... ABRTN
Abortion and Contraception Counselling and Research Association (SAUO) ... ACCRA
Abortion Fund (EA) ... AF
Abortion Information Data Bank [*of Zero Population Growth, Inc.*] [*Defunct*] ... AID
Abortion Information Databank (SAUS) ... AID
Abortion Law Reform Association (EAIO) ... ALRA
Abortion Law Reform Association. News Letter [*A publication*] (DLA) ... ALRANL
Abortion Law Reporter [*A publication*] (DLA) ... Abortion L Rep
Abortion Patient [*Medicine*] ... AB
Abortion Pill (SAUS) ... A Pill
Abortion Rights League (SAUS) ... ARL
Abortion Rights Mobilization (EA) ... ARM
Abortion Sydney [*An association*] [*Australia*] ... AS
Abortionist (ABBR) ... ABRTNST
Abortionist (ABBR) ... ABRTNT
Abortive (ABBR) ... ABRTV
Abortively (ABBR) ... ABRTVY
Abortiveness (ABBR) ... ABRTVNS
Abort-Sensing Implementation System (SAUS) ... ASIS
Abort-to-Orbit [*NASA*] (NASA) ... ATO
Abortus Bang Ringprobe [*Test*] [*Medicine*] ... ABR
Abortus, Militensis, Suis [*Microbiology*] ... AMS
Aboth (BJA) ... Ab
Aboth [*or Avot*] **d'Rabbi Nathan** (BJA) ... ARN
Abou Deia [*Chad*] [*Airport symbol*] (AD) ... AOD
Abound (ABBR) ... ABND
About ... A
About (WDMC) ... a
About (BEE) ... ab
About ... AB
About (MUGU) ... ABT
About [*Internet language*] [*Computer science*] ... abt
About Books, Inc. [*An association*] (EA) ... ABI
About Buttonhooks, Spoons, and Patents [*An association*] [*Defunct*] (EA) ... ABSP
About Buttonhooks, Spoons and Patents (SAUO) ... ABSP
About Clinical Trials (SAUO) ... ACT
About Face [*An association*] (EAIO) ... AF
About Face/Let's Face It (EA) ... AFLFI
About Good [*Numismatic term*] ... AG
About or On (MCD) ... A/O
About Proof (WDAA) ... AP
About Uncirculated [*Numismatic term*] ... AU
About.com, Inc. [*NASDAQ symbol*] (SG) ... BOUT
About-Face (ABBR) ... ABT-FC
Above (MSA) ... ABV
Above (ADWA) ... abv
Above Aerodrome Elevation [*Aviation*] (PIAV) ... aae
Above Aerodrome Level (SAUS) ... AAL
Above Airport Elevation (SAUS) ... AAE
above and beyond the call of duty (SAUS) ... abcd
Above Average Terrain (OTD) ... AAT
Above Baseline ... ABL
Above Bridges (SAUS) ... ab
Above Burst Height (DNAB) ... ABH
Above Client Expectations [*Program*] ... ACE
Above Clouds [*Aviation*] (FAAC) ... ACLD
Above Core Load Pad [*Nuclear energy*] (NRCH) ... ACLP
Above Core Load Plane [*Nuclear energy*] (NRCH) ... ACLP
Above Deck [*of a ship*] (DS) ... AD
Above Detection Limit (SAUS) ... ADL
Above Elbow [*Amputation*] [*Medicine*] (DMAA) ... A/E
Above Elbow Amputation (SAUS) ... AE-Amp
Above Field Height (PIPO) ... AFH
Above Field Level [*Aerospace*] (AAG) ... AFL
Above Finished Floor [*Technical drawings*] ... AFF
Above Grade (DAC) ... AG
Above Ground Biomass Density (SAUS) ... AGBD
Above Ground Level (PIAV) ... agl
Above Ground Level ... AGL
Above Ground Net Primary Production [*Ecology*] ... ANPP
Above Ground Net Primary Productivity (SAUS) ... ANPP
Above Ground Storage Tank ... AST
Above Ground Test [*Defense Nuclear Agency*] ... AGT
Above Knee [*Amputation*] [*Medicine*] (DMAA) ... A/K
Above Knee Amputation [*Medicine*] ... AKA
Above Local Terrain (MCD) ... ALT
Above Lower Limit (SAUS) ... ALL
Above Mean Sea Level (PIAV) ... amsl
Above Mean Sea Level [*Navigation*] ... AMSL
Above Mentioned ... AM
Above Modern River Level [*Geology*] ... AMRL
Above Mountains [*ICAO*] (FAAC) ... MON
Above Named (ADWA) ... an
Above Normal Loss [*Insurance*] ... ANL
Above or Equal (SAUS) ... AE
Above Ordnance Datum [*Military*] (DA) ... AOD
Above Platen Device (SAUS) ... APD
Above Proof ... AP
Above Scale [*Laboratory*] (DAVI) ... AS
Above Sea Level ... ASL
Above Sea Level (QUAC) ... asl
Above Suspended Ceiling [*Technical drawings*] ... ASC
Above Target Elevation (MCD) ... ATE
Above the Elbow (SAUS) ... AE
Above the Horizon ... ATH
Above Transmitted as Received (FAAC) ... ATAR
Above Transmitted As Received (SAUS) ... ATAR
Above Upper Limit (MHDB) ... AUL
Above Waist [*Medicine*] ... AW
Above Water ... AW
Above Water Thrown Torpedo [*Navy*] (CAAL) ... AWTT
Above Water Torpedo Tube [*Navy*] (NVT) ... AWTT
Above Water Warfare [*Navy*] (NVT) ... AWW
Above-Board (ABBR) ... ABV-BRD
Above-Elbow Amputation [*Orthopedics*] (DAVI) ... AEA
Aboveground Biomass [*Of vegetation*] ... AGB
Aboveground Net Primary Production [*Of biomass*] ... AGNPP
Above-Ground Pool (SAUS) ... AGP
Above-Knee Amputation [*Orthopedics*] (DAVI) ... AK Amp
Above-Mentioned (SAUS) ... AM
Above-Named ... AN
Above-Named Officer [*Army orders*] ... ANO
Above-Threshold Dissociation ... ATD
Above-Threshold Ionization (MCD) ... ATI
ABR Information Services [*NASDAQ symbol*] (TTSB) ... ABRX
ABR Information Services, Inc. [*Associated Press*] (SAG) ... ABR Inf
ABR Information Services, Inc. [*NASDAQ symbol*] (SAG) ... ABRX
Abra De Llog [*Philippines*] [*Seismograph station code, US Geological Survey*] [*Closed*] ... ABP
Abracadabra (DSUE) ... ABRAC
Abracos (SAUS) ... ARCS
Abrade (ABBR) ... ABRAD
Abrade (ABBR) ... ABRD
Abraded (ABBR) ... ABRADD
Abraded (ABBR) ... ABRDD
Abrading (ABBR) ... ABRADG
Abrading (ABBR) ... ABRDG
Abraham (ABBR) ... ABR
Abraham (ABBR) ... ABRA
Abraham (ABBR) ... ABRAM
Abraham & Straus [*Retail store*] ... A & S
Abraham and Straus (SAUO) ... A&S
Abraham Baldwin Agricultural College [*Tifton, GA*] ... ABAC
Abraham Baldwin Agricultural College, Tifton, GA [*Library symbol*] [*Library of Congress*] (LCLS) ... GTiA
Abraham Baldwin Agricultural College, Tifton, GA [*OCLC symbol*] (OCLC) ... GTM
Abraham Lincoln [*US president, 1809-1865*] ... AL
Abraham Lincoln Association (EA) ... ALA
Abraham Lincoln Birthplace National Monument ... ABLI
Abraham Lincoln High School (SAUO) ... ALHS
Abraham Lincoln National Park (SAUS) ... ALNP
Abraham Lincoln Quarterly (journ.) (SAUS) ... ALQ
ABRAMEX Group (SAUO) ... ABRAMEX
Abrams Industries [*NASDAQ symbol*] (TTSB) ... ABRI
Abrams Industries, Inc. [*Associated Press*] (SAG) ... Abrams
Abrams Industries, Inc. [*NASDAQ symbol*] (NQ) ... ABRI
Abrams Power Train Evolution ... APTE
Abrasion (DAVI) ... ABR
Abrasion (ABBR) ... ABRAN
Abrasion (ABBR) ... ABRAS
Abrasion (ABBR) ... ABRSN
Abrasion-Resistant Print Coating [*for plastic laminates*] [*Nevamar*] ... ARP
Abrasions (SAUS) ... ABRAS
Abrasive (ABBR) ... ABR
Abrasive (ABBR) ... ABRAV
Abrasive (MSA) ... ABRSV
Abrasive Ceramic Mosiac (DICI) ... ACM
Abrasive Engineering Society (EA) ... AES
Abrasive Engineering Society Magazine (SAUO) ... Abrasive Eng Soc Mag
Abrasive Flow Machining [*Mechanical engineering*] ... AFM
Abrasive Grain Association (EA) ... AGA
Abrasive Industries Association (MHDB) ... AIA
Abrasive Jet Machining (PDAA) ... AJM
Abrasive Machining (IAA) ... AM
Abrasive Paver (DICI) ... AP
Abrasive Water Jet Machining [*Factory automation*] (BTTJ) ... AWJM
Abrasive-Resistant (SAUS) ... ABRSV RES
Abraxas Petroleum [*NASDAQ symbol*] (TTSB) ... AXAS
Abraxas Petroleum Corp. [*Associated Press*] (SAG) ... Abraxas
Abraxas Petroleum Corp. [*NASDAQ symbol*] (SAG) ... AXAS
Abreast (SAUS) ... ABR
Abreast (ABBR) ... ABRST
Abreviated Test Language for All Systems (SAUS) ... ATLAS
Abreviation by Croping Names that Yield Meaning (SAUS) ... ACRONYM
Abri Technique Mobile. ISO Shelter (SAUS) ... ATM
Abridge (ABBR) ... ABRG
Abridgeable (ABBR) ... ABRGB
Abridged ... ABR
Abridged (WDMC) ... abr
Abridged (ABBR) ... ABRGD

Abridged (ABBR)	ABRID
Abridged and American Nautical Almanac (SAUS)	AANA
Abridged Arrival Report [Navy] (NVT)	HAVREP
Abridged Building Classification (SAUS)	ABC
Abridged Building Classification for Architects, Builders, and Civil Engineers	ABC
Abridged Call Sign (SAUS)	ACS
Abridged Index Medicus [A publication] (MELL)	AIM
Abridged Index Medicus Accessed by Teletypewriter Exchange Service [National Library of Medicine]	AIM-TWX
Abridged Index Medicus-Teletype-writer Exchange (SAUS)	AIM-TWX
Abridged Ocular Chart [Ophthalmology] (DAVI)	AOC
Abridged Readers Guide	AbRG
Abridgement	ab
Abridger (ABBR)	ABRGR
Abridging (ABBR)	ABRGG
Abridgment (DLA)	Ab
Abridgment (WDMC)	abr
Abridgment (ABBR)	ABRGNT
Abridgment (ABBR)	ABRGT
Abridgment of Cases in Equity [1667-1744] [A publication] (DLA)	Abr Ca Eq
Abridgment of Cases in Equity [1667-1744] [A publication] (DLA)	Eq Ab
Abridgment of Cases in Equity [1667-1744] [A publication] (DLA)	Eq Ca Abr
Abril [April] [Spanish] (BARN)	Abl
Abr-Nahrain (BJA)	AbN
Abr-Nahrain (BJA)	AN
Abroad (ABBR)	ABRD
Abroad (ABBR)	ABROD
Abrogate (ABBR)	ABRGA
Abrogate (ABBR)	ABROG
Abrogated (ABBR)	ABRGAD
Abrogated (ABBR)	ABROGD
Abrogating (ABBR)	ABROGAG
Abrogating (ABBR)	ABROGGG
Abrogation (ABBR)	ABRGAN
Abrogation (ABBR)	ABROGN
Abrupt (ABBR)	ABRP
Abrupt Change in Resistivity (SAUS)	ACR
Abrupt Climate Change (SAUS)	ACC
Abrupt Junction Varactor Doubler	AJVD
Abrupt Pacemaker Inhibition [Medicine] (MELL)	APMI
Abrupt Space Charge Edge [Algorithm]	ASCE
Abrupt Symmetrical Pull Up (MCD)	ASPU
Abrupt Withdrawal (MELL)	AW
Abruptio Placentae [Medicine] (MELL)	AP
Abruptness (ABBR)	ABRPNS
ABS Industries [Associated Press] (SAG)	ABS
ABS Industries, Inc. [NASDAQ symbol] (NQ)	ABSI
ABS Resources Ltd. [Vancouver Stock Exchange symbol]	ABL
ABS [Australian Bureau of Statistics] Time-Series Database [Information service or system] (CRD)	ABSTD
Absatz [Paragraph] [German] (ILCA)	Abs
Absatzwirtschaft Data Bank [Dusseldorf, Federal Republic of Germany] [Database producer] [Information service or system] (IID)	ASW
Abscess (ABBR)	AB
Abscess (SAUS)	Ab
Abscess (ABBR)	ABCS
Abscessed (ABBR)	ABCSD
Abscesses (ABBR)	ABS
Abscessing (ABBR)	ABCSG
Abschnitt [Section, Part, Chapter, or Division] [German] (BARN)	Abs
Abschnitt [Paragraph, Chapter] [German] (ILCA)	Abschn
Abschnittsbevollmaechtiger [Section Deputy] [German]	ABV
Abscisic Acid [Biochemistry]	ABA
Abscissa [Mathematics] (AAMN)	ABSC
Abscissa (IDOE)	x
Abscissa of a Coordinate (BARN)	X
Abscission Zone [Botany]	AZ
Abscond (ABBR)	ABSC
Abscond (ABBR)	ABSCD
Absence (ABBR)	ABSC
Absence (ABBR)	ABSNC
Absence and Turnover Rates [Database]	ABSTURN
Absence Card (SAUS)	AC
Absence of Immunoglobulin [Immunology] (DAVI)	AIGA
Absence of Immunoglobulin G [Biochemistry] (DAVI)	ABIG
Absence of Immunoglobulin M [Immunology] (DAVI)	AIGM
Absence of Sex Chromosome (DAVI)	O
Absence Over Leave (SAUS)	AOL
Absence Seizure [Medicine] (MELL)	AS
Absend Subscriber (SAUS)	ABS
Absent (ADWA)	a
Absent	A
Absent (ROG)	AB
Absent (AFM)	ABS
Absent (ADWA)	abs
Absent (ABBR)	ABSNT
Absent and/on Temporary Additional Duty (SAUS)	ATAD
Absent Bed Occupancy [Medicine]	ABO
Absent Bed Occupancy (or Occupant) (SAUS)	ABO
Absent Bed Occupant (MELL)	ABO
Absent by Reason of Being Held by Civil Authorities [Military]	HCA
Absent On Duty [Military]	AOD
Absent on Temporary Additional Duty [Navy]	ATAD
Absent on Temporary Duty [Navy]	ATD
Absent over Leave [Navy]	AOL
Absent Sick in Hospital (DAVI)	ASIH
Absent Subscriber, Office Closed (WDMC)	ABS
Absent Testes Syndrome [Medicine] (MELL)	ATS
Absent With Leave [Military]	AWL
Absent Without Leave [Military] [British]	AWL
Absent without Official Leave [Military]	AWOL
Absent Without Official Leave (SAUS)	AWOL
Absent without Pay (MCD)	AWOP
Absente Febre [In the Absence of Fever] [Pharmacy]	ABS FEB
Absente Febre [In the Absence of Fever] [Pharmacy] (ROG)	ABS FEBR
Absente Reo [The Defendant Being Absent] [Legal term] [Latin] (ADA)	ABSE RE
Absente Reo [The Defendant Being Absent] [Legal term] [Latin] (ADA)	ABS RE
Absented (ABBR)	ABSD
Absentee (ABBR)	ABSNTE
Absentee (ABBR)	ABST
Absentee	ABSTEE
absentee voting (SAUS)	abs vot
Absenteeism (ABBR)	ABSNTEM
Absenteeism (ABBR)	ABSTM
Absenting (ABBR)	ABSG
Absently (ABBR)	ABSY
Absent-Minded Club [Defunct] (EA)	AMC
Absiemens (IDOE)	abS
Absiemens [Unit of conductance]	aS
Absolute [Temperature in Fahrenheit degrees]	A
Absolute [Flowchart]	ABS
Absolute (ABAC)	abs
Absolute (ABBR)	ABSLT
Absolute	ABSOL
Absolute (ADWA)	absol
Absolute Address (AAG)	AA
Absolute Alcohol (SAUS)	AA
Absolute Altitude [Navigation]	AA
Absolute Ampere	ABAMP
Absolute Assembly Language [Programming language] (BUR)	AAL
Absolute Average Percent Deviation [Mathematics]	AAPD
Absolute Band Count [Biochemistry] (DAVI)	ABC
Absolute Basophil Count [Hematology] (MAE)	ABC
Absolute Bed Rest [Medicine]	ABR
Absolute Binody Final (SAUS)	ABF
Absolute Boiling Point	ABP
Absolute Cardiac Dullness [Medicine]	ACD
Absolute Catabolic Rate [Medicine] (DMAA)	ACR
Absolute Category Rating (SAUS)	ACR
Absolute Cavity Radiomter (SAUS)	ACR
Absolute Ceiling	ABCLG
Absolute Ceiling [Aviation]	ABS CLG
Absolute Ceiling [Aviation]	AC
Absolute Cephalopelvic Disproportion [Medicine] (MELL)	ACPD
Absolute Claudication (DB)	ACD
Absolute Claudication Distance (DB)	ACD
Absolute Code (SAUS)	AC
Absolute Coding (SAUS)	AC
Absolute Coefficient of Yawing Moments	CN
Absolute Convergence (SAUS)	AC
Absolute Coulomb (SAUS)	ABCOULOMB
Absolute Counter (SAUS)	AC
Absolute Cryogenic Radiometer	ACR
Absolute Cumulative Frequency (SAUS)	ACF
Absolute Delay (SAUS)	AD
Absolute Determination (SAUS)	AD
Absolute Deviation (SAUS)	AD
Absolute Dullness [on Auscultation] [Medicine] (DAVI)	M_3
Absolute Electrical Unit (SAUS)	AEU
Absolute Electrical Unit Scale	AEUS
Absolute Electromagnetic Unit (SAUS)	AEMU
Absolute Electrometer (SAUS)	AE
Absolute Electrostatic Unit (SAUS)	ABSTAT Unit
Absolute Electrostatic Unit (IAA)	AESU
Absolute Error (IAA)	ABSE
Absolute Error	AE
Absolute Essential Equipment	AEE
Absolute Expression (SAUS)	AE
Absolute Filtration Rating	AFR
Absolute Function (SAUS)	AF
Absolute Global Warming Potential (SAUS)	AGWP
Absolute Global Warming Potential (CARB)	AGWP
Absolute Granulocyte Count [Medicine] (DMAA)	AGC
Absolute Ground Level (MCD)	AGL
Absolute Henry (SAUS)	ABHENRY
Absolute Humidity (MELL)	AH
Absolute Interferometric LASER (SAA)	AIL
Absolute Iodine Uptake [Medicine]	AIU
Absolute Judgement (SAUS)	AJ
Absolute Jump (SAUS)	AJ
Absolute Level (SAUS)	AL
Absolute Limen [Psychophysics]	AL
Absolute Loader [Computer science]	ABSLDR
Absolute Location Error (SAUS)	ALE
Absolute Lymphocyte Count [Medicine]	ALC
Absolute Magnitude [Astronomy]	M
Absolute Magnitude Difference Function (PDAA)	AMDF
Absolute Maximum Loss	AML
Absolute Memory Image (MCD)	AMI

Absolute MKS (SAUS)	MKSA
Absolute Name (SAUS)	AN
Absolute Neutrophe Count (SAUS)	ANC
Absolute Neutrophil Count [Medicine] (MELL)	ANA
Absolute Neutrophil Count [Hematology]	ANC
Absolute Ohm (SAUS)	ABOHM
Absolute Output [Computer science]	AO
Absolute Pardon (ADA)	AP
Absolute Peak (SAUS)	AP
Absolute Permeability (SAUS)	AP
Absolute Permissive Block Scheme (SAUS)	APB Scheme
Absolute Permissive Block Signalling (SAUS)	APB Signalling
Absolute Permissive Block System (SAUS)	APB System
Absolute Permitivity (SAUS)	AP
Absolute Phagocyte Count [Medicine] (MELL)	APC
Absolute Pitch [Physiology]	AP
Absolute Plate Motion [Geophysics]	APM
Absolute Pollen Frequency (SAUS)	APF
Absolute Position Indication [Nuclear energy] (NRCH)	API
Absolute Position Register (SAUS)	APR
Absolute Power Level (SAUS)	APL
Absolute Pressure (SAUS)	AP
Absolute Pressure Control	APC
Absolute Pressure in Vessel	APV
Absolute Pressure Sensor [Automotive engineering]	APS
Absolute Programming (SAUS)	AP
Absolute Proximal Reabsorption [Medicine] (DMAA)	APR
Absolute Radiation Scale (PDAA)	ARS
Absolute Radio Frequency Channel Number (CGWS)	ARFCN
Absolute Rate Theory [Statistics]	ART
Absolute Reaction of Degeneration	ARD
Absolute Reaction Rate Theory [Physical chemistry]	ARRT
Absolute Refractory Period	ARP
Absolute Retention Time (MAE)	ART
Absolute Rod Position Indication [Nuclear energy] (NRCH)	ARPI
Absolute Sensation Threshold	AST
Absolute Sensitivity (SAUS)	AS
Absolute Skip (SAUS)	AS
Absolute Solar Transmission Interferometer (SAUS)	ASTI
Absolute Solar Transmittance Interferometer (ARMP)	ASTI
Absolute Space Time (SAUS)	AST
Absolute Specular Reflectance [Spectroscopy]	ASR
Absolute spektrale Empfindlichkeit der Eichdiode (SAUS)	sd
Absolute spektrale Strahlungsempfindlichkeit (SAUS)	sabs
Absolute spektrale Strahlungsempfindlichkeit nach DIN 5032 (SAUS)	xs/i
Absolute Symbol (SAUS)	AS
Absolute System (SAUS)	AS
Absolute Temperature [Symbol] [IUPAC]	T
Absolute Temperature or Transformer symbol (SAUS)	T-1-1
Absolute Temperature Scale	ATS
Absolute Term (IAA)	AT
Absolute Terminal Innervation Ratio [Psychiatry]	ATIR
Absolute Text and Storage Project (SAUS)	ATSP
Absolute Thermoelectric Power (SAUS)	ATP
Absolute Threshold	AT
Absolute Time (SAUS)	A T
Absolute Time Base Accuracy (SAUS)	ATBA
Absolute Time Base Error [Computer science] (IAA)	ATBE
Absolute Time Command (NAKS)	ATC
Absolute Time in Pregroove (VERA)	ATIP
Absolute Title [Business term]	AT
Absolute Total and Complete Camouflage [Hunting]	ATACC
[The] Absolute Truth [In Julian Barnes' novel "Staring at the Sun"]	TAT
Absolute Unsicherheit bei der Erfas-sung der Grauwerte durch den Analog-Digital-Wandler der Kamera (SAUS)	d ADC
Absolute Value (IAA)	ABSV
Absolute Value (BUR)	ABV
Absolute Value Amplifier (SAUS)	AVA
Absolute Value BIT [Binary Digit] Synchronizer	AVBS
Absolute Value Computer (SAUS)	AVC
Absolute Value Device (SAUS)	AVD
Absolute Value Representation (SAUS)	AVR
Absolute Value Sign (SAUS)	AVS
Absolute Vapour Pressure	AVP
Absolute Vapour Pressure, in Liquid State	AVP (L)
Absolute Virtual Address [Computer science]	AVA
Absolute Volt (SAUS)	ABSVOLT
Absolute Voltmeter (IAA)	ABSVM
Absolute Wet Center Manifold Pressure (SAUS)	AWCWP
Absolute Worst Case	AWC
Absolute Zero (SAUS)	Abs Z
Absolute Zero [Temperature] (MAE)	K
Absolutely (ABBR)	ABSLTY
Absolutely (ROG)	ABSLY
Absolutely (ABBR)	ABSOLY
Absolutely Bloody Final [Especially with reference to a drink]	ABF
Absolutely Convergent (SAUS)	AbsConv
absolutely fabulous (SAUS)	abfab
Absolutely Fabulous (DSUE)	ABFAB
Absolutely Incredible Counting Page (SAUS)	AICP
Absolutely Integral Algebraic Function (SAUS)	AIAF
Absolutely to Die [Slang]	ATD
Absoluteness (ABBR)	ABSOLNS
Absolution (ABBR)	ABSLTN
Absolution (ABBR)	ABSOLN
Absolution (BARN)	Absoluo
Absolutism (ABBR)	ABSLTM
Absolutist (ABBR)	ABSLTST
Absolutus Iuris [Absolute Jurisdiction] [Latin]	Abs Iur
Absolvable (ABBR)	ABSLVB
Absolve (ABBR)	ABSLV
Absolved (ABBR)	ABSLVD
Absolvent (SAUS)	Abs
Absolver (ABBR)	ABSLVR
Absolving (ABBR)	ABSLVG
Absolvo [I Acquit] [Used by Romans in criminal trials] [Latin]	A
Absonant (ABBR)	ABS
Absorb [or Absorption]	ABS
Absorb (ABBR)	ABSB
Absorbability (ABBR)	ABSBBT
Absorbable (ABBR)	ABSBB
Absorbable Gelatin Sponge (MELL)	AGS
Absorbance [Internal transmission density] [Symbol] [IUPAC]	A
Absorbance (ABBR)	ABSBNC
Absorbance Expanded [Spectroscopy]	ABEXed
Absorbance Unit [Physical chemistry]	AU
Absorbance Units Full Scale [Physical chemistry]	AUFS
Absorbance-Detected Magnetic Resonance [Physics]	ADMR
Absorbancy (SAUS)	A
Absorbed (ABBR)	ABSBD
Absorbed Burden (SAUS)	AB
Absorbed Dose [Environmental science] (COE)	D
Absorbed Energy	AE
Absorbed Photosynthetically Active Radiation [Botany]	APAR
Absorbed Power (SAUS)	AP
Absorbed Voltage (SAUS)	AV
Absorbency (ABBR)	ABSBCY
Absorbency (ABBR)	ABSBNC
Absorbent (SAUS)	Abs
Absorbent (ABBR)	ABSBT
Absorbent Paper Manufacturers Association [Defunct]	APMA
Absorber (ABBR)	ABSBR
Absorber (EEVL)	AS
Absorber Circuit (SAUS)	AC
Absorber Open Test Assembly [Nuclear energy] (NRCH)	AOTA
Absorbing (ABBR)	ABSBG
Absorbing Field (SAUS)	AF
Absorbing Filter (SAUS)	AF
Absorbing Power (SAUS)	AP
Absorbing Trunk (SAUS)	ABT
Absorbtion Heat Transformer	AHT
Absorp (SAUS)	ABS
Absorption (DMAA)	Abs
Absorption (ABBR)	ABSBN
Absorption	ABSORB
Absorption (DMAA)	absorp
Absorption (ABBR)	ABSPN
Absorption Capacity (SAUS)	AC
Absorption Circuit (SAUS)	AC
Absorption Coefficient, Linear [Symbol] [IUPAC]	a
Absorption Coil (SAUS)	AC
Absorption Cross Section (SAUS)	ACS
Absorption, Distribution, and Elimination (MELL)	ADE
Absorption, Distribution, Metabolism, Excretion [Medicine]	ADME
Absorption Edge Modulator (SAUS)	AEM
Absorption Equivalent Thickness	AET
Absorption Fading (SAUS)	AF
Absorption Filter (SAUS)	AF
Absorption Frequency Meter (SAUS)	AFM
Absorption Heat Pumping [Engineering]	AHP
Absorption Index (SAUS)	K
Absorption index for the daylight end of a day-night electromagnetic transmission path	KI
Absorption Limiting Frequencies (SAUS)	ALFs
Absorption Limiting Frequency (DEN)	ALF
Absorption Limiting Frequency (SAUS)	ALM Frequency
Absorption Modulation (SAUS)	AM
Absorption of Conversion Electrons (IAA)	ACE
Absorption Peak Wavelength (SAUS)	APW
Absorption Power Meter (SAUS)	APM
Absorption Rate (MELL)	AR
Absorption Signal (SAUS)	AS
Absorption Switch (SAUS)	AS
Absorption Trap (SAUS)	AT
Absorption Wavemeter (SAUS)	AW
Absorptive (ABBR)	ABSPV
Absorptive Hypercalciuria [Medicine] (DMAA)	AH
Absorptive Power	AP
Absorptive Stripping Voltametry (ABAC)	ASV
Absorptive Technology, Inc. [Vancouver Stock Exchange symbol]	ABV
Absorptivity	A
Absorptivity (ABBR)	ABSPT
Absorptivity Emissivity Ratio (SAUS)	AERATIO
Absorptivity-Emissivity [Ratio]	A/E
Absque Ulla Nota [Without Any Marking or Note] [Latin] (ROG)	ABS U N
Absque Ulla Nota [Without Any Marking or Note] [Latin]	AUN
Abstain (ILCA)	Abs
Abstain (ABBR)	ABSTA
Abstained (ABBR)	ABSTAD
Abstaining (ABBR)	ABSTAG

Abstaining Motorists' Association (EA) ... AMA
Abstemious (ABBR) ... ABSTMS
Abstemiously (ABBR) ... ABSTMSY
Abstemiousness (ABBR) ... ABSTMSNS
Abstention (ABBR) ... ABSTN
Abstinence (ABBR) ... ABSTNC
Abstinent (ABBR) ... ABSTNT
Abstract [*Online database field identifier*] ... AB
Abstract (GEAB) ... abs
Abstract ... ABST
Abstract ... ABSTR
Abstract (ADWA) ... abstr
Abstract ... ABSTRCT
Abstract [*Legal*] [*British*] (ROG) ... ABSTT
Abstract and Book Title Index Card Service [*United Kingdom*] ... ABTICS
abstract art (SAUS) ... abs art
Abstract Bulletin of the Institute of Paper Chemistry (SAUS) ... ABIPC
Abstract Code (SAUS) ... AC
Abstract Computer (SAUS) ... AC
Abstract Data Type [*Computer science*] ... ADT
Abstract Enterprise [*Vancouver Stock Exchange symbol*] ... AEP
Abstract Evolution Equation (PDAA) ... AEE
Abstract Expressionism (BARN) ... Ab Ex
abstract expressionism (SAUS) ... abs exp
Abstract Family of Acceptors (SAUS) ... AFA
Abstract Family of Deterministic Acceptors (SAUS) ... AFDA
Abstract Family of Deterministic Languages (PDAA) ... AFDL
Abstract Family of Languages [*Computer science*] ... AFL
Abstract Family of Processors [*Computer science*] (PDAA) ... AFP
Abstract Family of Relations (PDAA) ... AFR
Abstract Information Digest Service [*Forest Products Research Society*] [*Information service or system*] (IID) ... AIDS
Abstract Information Unit (SAUS) ... AIU
Abstract Machine Description Language [*1977*] [*Computer science*] (CSR) ... AMDL
Abstract Mathematics (SAUS) ... AM
Abstract Number [*Database terminology*] (NITA) ... AN
Abstract of New Technology (ACAE) ... ANT
Abstract Planning Tool ... ABT
Abstract Service Primitive [*Telecommunications*] (OSI) ... ASP
Abstract Syntax [*Data structure*] [*Computer science*] (TNIG) ... AS
Abstract Syntax Notation [*Computer science*] ... ASN
Abstract Syntax Notation One (SAUS) ... ASN1
Abstract Syntax Notation One (VERA) ... ASNI
Abstract Syntax Tree (SAUS) ... AST
Abstract Test Method [*Telecommunications*] (OSI) ... ATM
Abstract Test Suite [*Telecommunications*] (OSI) ... ATS
Abstract Window Toolkit (SAUS) ... AET
Abstract Window Toolkit [*Computer science*] ... AWT
Abstract Windowing Toolkit [*Sun Microsystems*] (IGQR) ... AWT
Abstract Windows Toolkit-Application Programmer Interface [*Computer science*] (VERA) ... AWTAPI
Abstracted (ABBR) ... ABSTRD
Abstracted Business Information (SAUS) ... ABI
Abstracted Business Information, Inc. ... ABI
Abstracted Business/Information (SAUS) ... ABB/INFORM
Abstracted Reappraisement Decisions [*A publication*] (DLA) ... R
Abstracted Valuation Decisions [*A publication*] (DLA) ... V
Abstracted Valuation Decisions (SAUS) ... V
Abstracter (ABBR) ... ABSTRR
Abstracting and Indexing ... A & I
Abstracting and Indexing Services Directory [*A publication*] ... AISD
Abstracting Automatic (SAUS) ... AA
Abstracting Board [*International Council of Scientific Unions*] [*Information service or system*] (IID) ... AB
Abstraction (ABBR) ... ABSTRN
Abstractly (ABBR) ... ABSTRY
Abstractness (ABBR) ... ABSTRNS
Abstracts ... A
Abstracts in Bio-Commerce (SAUS) ... ABC
Abstracts Information Dissemination System (SAUS) ... AIDS
Abstracts Information Dissemination Systems (SAUS) ... AIDS
Abstracts of Bioanalytic Technology [*Council of American Bioanalysts*] [*A publication*] (AEBS) ... ABT
Abstracts of Classified Reports [*A publication*] ... ACR
Abstracts of Computer Literature (journ.) (SAUS) ... Abstr Comput Lit
Abstracts of Declassified Documents [*A publication*] ... ADD
Abstracts of Hospital Management Studies (journ.) (SAUS) ... AIIMS
Abstracts of Instructional Materials in Vocational and Technical Education (OICC) ... AIMVTE
Abstracts of Instructional Materials in Vocational and Technical Education (journ.) (SAUS) ... AIM
Abstracts of Instructional Materials/Abstracts of Research Materials ... AIM/ARM
Abstracts of New World Archaeology [*A publication*] ... ANWA
Abstracts of North American Geology [*A publication*] ... ANAG
Abstracts of papers delivered at the annual meeting of the American Philological Association (SAUO) ... AAPh
Abstracts of Papers of the American Chemical Society (SAUO) ... Abs Pap ACS
Abstracts of Photographic Science and Engineering Literature [*A publication*] ... APSE
Abstracts of Photographic Sciences and Engineering Literature (SAUS) ... APSE
Abstracts of Star Chamber Proceedings [*1550-58*] [*A publication*] (DLA) ... Mundy
Abstracts of Title [*A publication*] (DLA) ... Abstr T
Abstracts of Treasury Decisions [*United States*] [*A publication*] (DLA) ... Ab
Abstracts of Treasury Decisions [*A publication*] (DLA) ... Abs
Abstracts of Treasury Decisions, New Series [*A publication*] (DLA) ... Ab N
Abstracts of Treasury Decisions, New Series [*A publication*] (DLA) ... Ab NS
Abstracts of Treasury Decisions, New Series [*A publication*] (DLA) ... Abs (NS)
Abstracts of Working Papers in Economics [*Cambridge University Press*] [*Information service or system*] (IID) ... AWPE
Abstrene (ABBR) ... ABS
Abstruse (ABBR) ... ABSTRS
Abstruse (ABBR) ... ABSTRU
Abstrusely (ABBR) ... ABSTRUY
Abstruseness (ABBR) ... ABSTRUNS
Absurd (ABBR) ... ABSRD
Absurd Special Interest Group (EA) ... ASIG
Absurdity (ABBR) ... ABSDT
Absurdity (ABBR) ... ABSRDT
Absurdly (ABBR) ... ABSRDY
Absurdness (ABBR) ... ABSRDNS
ABT Building Products [*NASDAQ symbol*] (TTSB) ... ABTC
ABT Building Products Corp. [*Associated Press*] (SAG) ... ABT Bld
ABT Building Products Corp. [*NASDAQ symbol*] (SAG) ... ABTC
Abteilung [*Department, Division, Section*] [*German*] ... ABT
Abtesla [*Unit of magnetic induction*] ... abT
Abu Dhabi [*United Arab Emirates*] [*Airport symbol*] (OAG) ... AUH
Abu Dhabi Air Force (SAUS) ... ADAF
Abu Dhabi Defence Force (SAUO) ... ADDF
Abu Dhabi Defense Force (SAUS) ... ADDF
Abu Dhabi Fund (SAUO) ... ADF
Abu Dhabi Gas Industries Ltd. (BUAC) ... GASCO
Abu Dhabi International Bank, Inc. ... ADIB
Abu Dhabi Investment Company ... ADIC
Abu Dhabi Marine Areas Ltd. (SAUO) ... ADMA
Abu Dhabi National Oil Co. (ODBW) ... ADNOC
Abu Dhabi Oil Co. [*United Arab Emirates*] (EY) ... ADOC
Abu Dhabi Oil Company (SAUO) ... ADCO
Abu Dhabi/Al Dhafra [*United Arab Emirates*] [*ICAO location identifier*] (ICLI) ... OMAM
Abu Dhabi/Bateen [*United Arab Emirates*] [*ICAO location identifier*] (ICLI) ... OMAD
Abu Dhabi/International [*United Arab Emirates*] [*ICAO location identifier*] (ICLI) ... OMAA
Abu Nidal Organization (SAUS) ... ANO
Abu Simbel [*Egypt*] [*Airport symbol*] (OAG) ... ABS
Abu Simbel [*Egypt*] [*ICAO location identifier*] (ICLI) ... HEBL
Abuja [*Nigeria*] [*Airport symbol*] (OAG) ... ABV
Abuja [*Nigeria*] [*ICAO location identifier*] (ICLI) ... DNBJ
Abuja/International [*Nigeria*] [*ICAO location identifier*] (ICLI) ... DNAA
Abulia (ABBR) ... ABUL
abulia (SAUS) ... abul
abulic (SAUS) ... abul
Abuliomania (ABBR) ... ABUL
Abumumbazi [*Zaire*] [*ICAO location identifier*] (ICLI) ... FZFE
Abumusa Island [*Iran*] [*ICAO location identifier*] (ICLI) ... OIBA
Abundance (ABBR) ... ABNDNC
Abundance (ABBR) ... ABUNDNC
Abundant [*With respect to occurrence of species*] ... A
Abundant (ABBR) ... ABNDNT
Abundant (ABBR) ... ABT
Abundant (BARN) ... abund
Abundant (ABBR) ... ABUNDT
Abundant Life Seed Foundation (EA) ... ALSF
Abundant Wildlife Society of North America (EA) ... AWS
Abundantly (ABBR) ... ABNDNTY
Abundantly (ABBR) ... ABUNDTY
Abundantly Yours (EA) ... AY
Aburra (VRA) ... abu
Abuse (ABBR) ... ABS
Abuse (ABBR) ... ABUS
Abuse Resistant Key Distribution (SAUS) ... ARKD
Abused (ABBR) ... ABSD
Abused (ABBR) ... ABUSD
Abused Child Unit (SAUO) ... ACU
Abused Deaf Women's Advocacy Services (ADWA) ... ADWAS
Abused Women and Girls Project (SAUO) ... AWAG
Abused Women's Aid in Crisis (EA) ... AWAIC
Abuser (ABBR) ... ABSR
Abuser (ABBR) ... ABUSR
Abusing (ABBR) ... ABSG
Abusing (ABBR) ... ABUSG
Abusing Men Exploring New Directions (SAUO) ... AMEND
Abusive (ABBR) ... ABSV
Abusive (ABBR) ... ABUSV
Abusive Men Exploring New Directions [*In association name AMEND Network*] ... AMEND
Abusively (ABBR) ... ABSVY
Abusively (ABBR) ... ABUSVY
Abusiveness (ABBR) ... ABSVNS
Abusiveness (ABBR) ... ABUSVNS
Abutment (ABBR) ... ABTNT
Abutment (ABBR) ... ABUT
Abutment (ABBR) ... ABUTMT
Abutted (ABBR) ... ABTD
Abutted (ABBR) ... ABUTD
Abutting (ABBR) ... ABTG
Abutting (ABBR) ... ABUTG
Abuyama [*Japan*] [*Seismograph station code, US Geological Survey*] ... ABU
Abvolt (IDOE) ... abV
Abvolt (SAUS) ... AV

Abvolt [*Unit of electromotive force*] ... aV
ABW Ministries [*Formerly, American Baptist Women's Ministries*] (EA) ... ABW
Abwatt (IDOE) ... abW
Abweber [*Also, Mx*] [*Unit of magnetic flux*] ... abWb
Abwehrdienst [*Counterintelligence Service*] [*German military - World War II*] ... AD
Abwehroffizier [*Counterintelligence Officer*] [*German military - World War II*] ... AO
Abyek [*Iran*] [*ICAO location identifier*] (ICLI) ... OIIE
Abysmal (ABBR) ... ABSML
Abysmal (ABBR) ... ABYSM
Abyss (ABBR) ... ABYS
Abyssal Plain (SAUS) ... AP
Abyssinia ... AB
Abyssinia ... Aby
Abyssinia ... ABYSS
Abyssinian [*Cat species*] ... ABY
Abyssinian cat (SAUS) ... Abs cat
Abzahlungsgesetz [*Law on hire purchase agreements*] [*German*] (ILCA) ... AbzG
AC [*Alternating Current*] **Amperometric** [*Electromagnetics*] ... ACAmp
A.C. Cars Ltd. (SAUO) ... AC
AC [*Alternating Current*] **Control Unit** ... ACU
AC Network (MCD) ... ACNET
AC Resistance (IDOE) ... R_{ac}
AC Spark Plug Co., Electronics Division, Milwaukee, WI [*Library symbol*] [*Library of Congress*] (LCLS) ... WMACS
AC Spark Plug Co., General Motors Corp., Flint, MI [*Library symbol*] [*Library of Congress*] (LCLS) ... MiFliACS
AC Thin Film Electro-Luminescence (SAUS) ... ACTFEL
AC [*Alternating Current*] **Voltage** (ACII) ... VAC
Acacia [*Gum Arabic*] [*Chemistry*] (ROG) ... ACAC
Acacia Confusa Trypsin Inhibitor [*Biochemistry*] ... ACTI
Acacia Mineral [*Vancouver Stock Exchange symbol*] ... AMD
Acacia Research Corp. [*Associated Press*] (SAG) ... AcaciaR
Acacia Research Corp. [*NASDAQ symbol*] (SAG) ... ACRI
academ (SAUS) ... acad
Academe (ABBR) ... ACDM
Academia Brasileira de Ciencias [*Brazil*] (MCD) ... ABC
Academia Cosmologica Nova [*International Free Academy of New Cosmology - IFANC*] (EAIO) ... ACN
Academia de Ciencias de Cuba (GEOI) ... ACC
Academia Europaea ... AE
Academia Maria Reina, Rio Piedras, PR [*Library symbol*] [*Library of Congress*] (LCLS) ... PrRA
Academia Mexicana de Derechos Humanos [*The Mexican Academy for Human Rights*] (CROSS) ... AMDH
Academia Ophthalmologica Internationalis (EAIO) ... AOI
Academia R.S. Romania [*Academy of Romania*], **Bucharest, Romania** [*Library symbol*] [*Library of Congress*] (LCLS) ... RoBA
Academiae Americanae Socius [*Fellow of the American Academy (Academy of Arts and Sciences)*] [*Latin*] (GPO) ... AAS
Academiae Antiquarinae Societales Socius ... AASS
Academic (ABBR) ... ACAD
academic (SAUS) ... acad
Academic (AL) ... Acad
Academic (ADWA) ... acad
Academic (ABBR) ... ACADC
Academic ... ACDMC
Academic (ABBR) ... ACDMK
Academic Abstracts ... AcAB
Academic Administration Internship Program (SAUO) ... AAIP
Academic Administration Internship Program [*Later, AFP*] (EA) ... AAIP
Academic Alertness Test [*Education*] (AEBS) ... AA
Academic Alliances (EA) ... AA
Academic American Encyclopedia Database [*Computer science*] (CIST) ... AAED
Academic and Creative Thinking Skills ... ACTS
Academic and Research Network of Slovenia (SAUO) ... ARNES
Academic and Social Anxiety Program [*Cornell University*] ... ASAP
Academic Aptitude Test [*Vocational guidance test*] ... AAT
Academic Audit Unit [*British*] (DET) ... AAU
Academic Book Center, Portland, OR [*Library symbol*] [*Library of Congress*] (LCLS) ... OrPAB
Academic Class Year (DNAB) ... ACAD CL YR
Academic Clinical Laboratory Physicians and Scientists ... ACLPS
Academic Clinical Laboratory Physi-cians and Scientists (SAUS) ... ACLPS
Academic Collective Bargaining Information Service (EA) ... ACBIS
Academic Committee on Soviet Jewry (EA) ... ACSJ
Academic Computation Center [*Georgetown University*] [*Research center*] (RCD) ... ACC
Academic Computation (or Computer) Center (SAUS) ... ACC
Academic Computer Center [*University of Washington*] [*Research center*] (RCD) ... ACC
Academic Computer Facility [*Roosevelt University*] [*Research center*] (RCD) ... ACF
Academic Computer Group (SAUO) ... ACCOMP Group
Academic Computer Service [*Generic*] [*Research center*] (RCD) ... ACS
Academic Computer Services Division [*Milwaukee School of Engineering*] [*Research center*] (RCD) ... ACSD
Academic Computing and Network Services [*Northwestern University*] [*Information service or system*] (IID) ... ACNS
Academic Computing Center [*University of California, Riverside*] [*Research center*] (RCD) ... ACC
Academic Computing Center [*University of Vermont*] [*Research center*] (RCD) ... ACC
Academic Computing Group ... ACCOMP
Academic Computing Services Network (VERA) ... ACSNET
Academic Consortium for Economic and Social Surveys [*Australia*] ... ACCESS
Academic Council on the United Nations System ... ACUNS
Academic Courseware Exchange [*Combined Apple University Consortium and Kinko's project*] [*Software distributor*] ... ACE
academic dismissal (SAUS) ... ac dis
Academic Emergency Medicine (SAUS) ... AEM
Academic English ... AE
Academic Evaluation Report [*Military*] (INF) ... AER
Academic Guidance Service (SAUO) ... AGS
Academic Health Center ... AHC
Academic Health Services Complexes (SAUS) ... AHSC
Academic Index ... AcI
Academic Individual Advanced Development [*Military*] (RDA) ... AIAD
Academic Information Management Center (NITA) ... AIMC
Academic Instructional Measurement System [*Academic achievement and aptitude test*] ... AIMS
Academic Instructor and Allied Officer School [*Military*] (AFM) ... AIAOS
Academic Instructor and Foreign Officer School [*Military*] ... AIFOS
Academic Instructors School [*Air Force*] ... AIS
Academic Language Therapy Association (NTPA) ... ALTA
Academic Learning Time (SAUS) ... ALT
Academic Librarians Assisting the Disabled [*ASCLA*] (AL) ... ALAD
Academic Librarians Assisting the Disabled Discussion Group [*Association of Specialized and Cooperative Library Agencies*] ... ALAD
Academic Libraries of Brooklyn [*Library network*] ... ALB
Academic Library Book Review [*A publication*] (BRI) ... ALBR
Academic Library Development Program (SAUS) ... ALDP
Academic Map Analysis Package (SAUS) ... AMAP
Academic Medical Center ... AMC
Academic Member of Trinity College (SAUS) ... AMTC
Academic Networking Workshop (SAUO) ... ANW
Academic Nursing Home (DMAA) ... ANH
Academic Operating System ... AOS
Academic Orthopaedic Society (NTPA) ... AOS
Academic Physical Plant Association (SAUO) ... APPA
Academic Potential Coding [*Military*] (DNAB) ... APC
Academic Practice Assembly (SAUO) ... APA
Academic Press (DGA) ... ACAD PR
Academic Press, Inc. [*Publishers*] ... AP
Academic Press, Inc. [*Publishers*] (MCD) ... API
Academic Press of Arkansas (SAUS) ... Acad Pr Ark
Academic Press Print and Electronic Access License ... APPEAL
Academic Profile Code [*Military*] (DNAB) ... APC
Academic Program Evaluation Project (EDAC) ... APEP
Academic Programs Committee (SAUS) ... APC
Academic Promise Test [*Psychology*] (AEBS) ... APT
Academic Psychiatry (SAUS) ... AP
Academic Radio League (SAUO) ... ARL
Academic Ranking (EDAC) ... AR
Academic Remedial Training [*Navy*] ... ART
Academic Research Enhancement Award [*NIH*] ... AREA
Academic Research Information System, Inc. (SAUS) ... ARIS
Academic Salaries Tribunal (SAUO) ... AST
Academic Self-Concept Scale (EDAC) ... ASCS
Academic Senate for California Community Colleges (EDAC) ... ASCCC
Academic Staff Association of Curtin University of Technology [*Australia*] ... ASACUT
Academic Staff Association of University College, University of New South Wales [*Australia*] ... ASAUCUNSW
Academic Staff Training and Development Programme [*British*] (AIE) ... ASTDP
Academic Strategic Alliances Program ... ASAP
Academic Therapy Publications (SAUS) ... Acad Therapy
Academic Training Division [*Military*] (DNAB) ... ATD
Academic Travel Abroad (EA) ... ATA
Academic Travel Abroad (SAUO) ... ATA
Academic Women Allied for Rights and Equality (SAUO) ... AWARE
Academic Women for Equality (SAUO) ... ACE
Academic Year (MCD) ... AY
Academic Year Institute [*National Science Foundation*] ... AYI
Academica Posteriora [*of Cicero*] [*Classical studies*] (OCD) ... Acad Post
Academica Priora [*of Cicero*] [*Classical studies*] (OCD) ... Acad Pr
Academicae Quaestiones [*of Cicero*] [*Classical studies*] (OCD) ... Acad
Academical (ABBR) ... ACADL
Academical (ABBR) ... ACDMKL
Academical Rank of Civil Engineers ... ARCE
Academically (ABBR) ... ACADCLY
Academically (ABBR) ... ACDMKY
Academically Separated Budgeted Research (SAUS) ... ASBR
Academically Talented (DAVI) ... AT
Academically Talented Student ... ATS
Academically-Related Research ... ARR
Academician [*or Academy*] ... A
Academician [*or Academy*] (EY) ... ACAD
Academician (ABBR) ... ACADCN
Academician (ABBR) ... ACDMN
Academician of the National Academy of Design, New York [*1825*] (NGC) ... NA
Academics for the Second Amendment ... A2A
Academic-Technical Aptitude Tests for Coloured Pupils in Standards 6, 7, and 8 (TES) ... ATA
Academie Canadienne de Medecine Sportive (AC) ... ACMS
Academie Canadienne d'Endodontie [*Canadian Academy of Endodontics*] (EAIO) ... ACE
Academie Canadienne des Arts et des Sciences de l'Enregistrement (AC) ... ACASE
Academie Canadienne du Genie [*Canadian Academy of Engineering*] (EAIO) ... ACG

Academie Canadienne Francaise [*French-Canadian Academy*] [*French*] (BARN) ... ACF
Academie de Medecine Veterinaire du Quebec (GVA) ... AMVQ
Academie de Musique du Quebec (AC) ... AMQ
Academie des Sciences [*Academy of Science*] [*French*] ... ADS
Academie des Sciences: Comptes Rendus, Serie 2 (MEC) ... Comp Rend Acad Sci
Academie Europeenne des Sciences, des Arts, et des Lettres [*European Academy of Arts, Sciences, and Humanities*] (EAIO) ... AESAL
Academie Europeenne d'Histoire [*European Academy of History - EAH*] (EAIO) ... AEH
Academie Internationale d'Astronautique [*France*] (EAIO) ... AIA
Academie Internationale de Droit et de Sante Mentale (AC) ... AIDSM
Academie Internationale de la Ceramique [*International Academy of Ceramics - IAC*] (EAIO) ... AIC
Academie Internationale de Medecine Aeronautique et Spatiale [*International Academy of Aviation and Space Medicine IAASM*] [*Canada*] (EA) ... AIMAS
Academie Internationale d'Heraldique [*Bridel, Luxembourg*] (EAIO) ... AIH
Academie Internationale d'Histoire de la Pharmacie [*International Academy of the History of Pharmacy*] (EAIO) ... AIHP
Academie Internationale du Tourisme [*International Academy of Tourism*] (EAIO) ... AcIT
Academie Internationale Olympique [*International Olympic Academy*] [*Athens, Greece*] (EAIO) ... AIO
Academie Royale des Arts du Canada [*Royal Canadian Academy of Arts - RCA*] ... ARAC
Academy (SAUO) ... Ac
Academy (SAUO) ... Acad
Academy [*Record label*] ... Acad
Academy (ABBR) ... ACDMY
Academy Award [*Academy of Motion Picture Arts and Sciences film award*] ... AA
Academy Board (VRA) ... acad bd
Academy for Catholic Health Care Leadership [*Defunct*] (EA) ... ACHCL
Academy for Contemporary Problems (SAUO) ... ACP
Academy for Educational Development (EA) ... AED
Academy for Educational Development (SAUS) ... AFED
Academy for Electronic Information Technology (SAUO) ... AEIT
Academy for Friends of Secretarial Arts and Sciences [*Defunct*] (EA) ... AFSAS
Academy for Guided Imagery (SAUO) ... AGI
Academy for Health Services Marketing [*Chicago, IL*] (EA) ... AHSM
Academy for Healthcare Management (SAUO) ... AHM
Academy for Implants and Transplants (EA) ... AIT
Academy for International Health Studies (SAUO) ... AIHS
Academy for Interscience Methodology (EA) ... AIM
Academy for Peace Research (EA) ... APR
Academy for Regional research and regional planning (SAUO) ... ARL
Academy for Sports Dentistry (EA) ... ASD
Academy for State and Local Government (EA) ... ASLG
Academy for the Development of a Democratic Environment (SAUO) ... AZAD
Academy for the Psychology of Sports International [*Later, ASPI*] (EA) ... APSI
Academy Introduction Mission [*Military*] ... AIM
Academy of Accounting Historians (EA) ... AAH
Academy of Agricultural and Forest Sciences (SAUO) ... ASAS
Academy of Air Traffic Control Medicine ... AATCM
Academy of Ambulatory Foot Surgery (EA) ... AAFS
Academy of American Franciscan History (EA) ... AAFH
Academy of American Poets (EA) ... AAP
Academy of American Poets Fellowship (SAUO) ... AAPF
Academy of American Poets Fellow-ship (SAUS) ... AAPF
Academy of Ancient Music (SAUO) ... AAM
Academy of Aphasia (EA) ... AA
Academy of Applied Osteopathy (SAUO) ... AAO
Academy of Applied Science (EA) ... AAS
Academy of Art and Literature [*British*] ... AAL
Academy of Art and Literature (SAUO) ... AAL
Academy of Arts and Sciences of the Americas (EA) ... AASA
Academy of Behavioral Medicine Research (EA) ... ABMR
Academy of Canadian Cinema [*Academie du Cinema Canadien*] ... ACC
Academy of Canadian Cinema & Television [*Academie Canadienne du Cinema et de la Television*] (AC) ... ACCT
Academy of Canadian Cinema and Television [*Canada*] (WWLA) ... ACCTV
Academy of Certified Social Workers ... ACSW
Academy of Chief Executive Nurses of Teaching Hospitals (AC) ... ACEN
Academy of Christian Art (SAUO) ... ACA
Academy of Clinical and Applied Thrombosis/Hemostasis (SAUO) ... ACAT/H
Academy of Clinical Laboratory Physicians and Scientists (SAUO) ... ACLPS
Academy of Clinical Psychiatrists (SAUO) ... AACP
Academy of Comic Book Artists ... ACBA
Academy of Comic-Book Fans and Collectors [*Defunct*] ... ACBFC
Academy of Country Music (EA) ... ACM
Academy of Country Music Entertainment [*Canada*] ... ACME
Academy of Criminal Justice Science (SAUO) ... ACJS
Academy of Criminal Justice Sciences (EA) ... ACJS
Academy of Dental Materials (EA) ... ADM
Academy of Dentistry for Persons with Disabilities (NTPA) ... ADPD
Academy of Dentistry for the Handicapped (EA) ... ADH
Academy of Dentistry International (EA) ... ADI
Academy of Denture [*or Dental*] **Prosthetics** (EA) ... ADP
Academy of Dispensing Audiologists (EA) ... ADA
Academy of Economics (SAUO) ... AEIIE
Academy of Electrical Contracting (EA) ... AEC
Academy of Family Films and Family Television (EA) ... AFFFT
Academy of Family Mediators (EA) ... AFM
Academy of Family Psychology (SAUO) ... AFP
Academy of Fine Arts (SAUO) ... AFA
Academy of Florida Trial Lawyers (SRA) ... AFTL
Academy of Forensic and Industrial Chiropractic Consultants (SAUO) ... AFICC
Academy of General Dentistry (EA) ... AGD
Academy of General Practice (SAUO) ... AGP
Academy of Geology (SAUO) ... CAGS
Academy of Gp Orthodontics (SAUO) ... AGpO
Academy of Hazard Control Management (EA) ... AHCM
Academy of Health Care Consultants [*Defunct*] (EA) ... AHCC
Academy of Health Information Professionals (NUJO) ... AHIP
Academy of Health Sciences [*Health Services Command*] [*Fort Sam Houston, TX*] [*Army*] ... AHS
Academy of Homiletics (EA) ... AH
Academy of Hospice Physicians (NTPA) ... AHP
Academy of Hospital Counselors [*Later, AHCC*] (EA) ... AHC
Academy of Hospital Public Relations [*Later, Hospital Academy - HA*] ... AHPR
Academy of Human Rights ... AHR
Academy of Independent Scholars [*Defunct*] (EA) ... AIS
Academy of International Business [*Cleveland, OH*] (EA) ... AIB
Academy of International Dental Studies (EAIO) ... AIDS
Academy of International Law (SAUO) ... AIL
Academy of International Military History (SAUO) ... AIMH
Academy of International Military History [*Later, IMA*] (EA) ... AIMH
Academy of Interscience Methodology (SAUO) ... AIM
Academy of Irish Art ... AIA
Academy of Laser Dentistry (NTPA) ... ALD
Academy of Legal Studies in Business (NTPA) ... ALSB
Academy of Lighting Arts ... ALA
Academy of Live and Recorded Arts [*British*] ... ALRA
Academy of Managed Care Pharmacy (NTPA) ... AMCP
Academy of Management (SAUO) ... Acad Mgmt
Academy of Management [*Mississippi State, MS*] (EA) ... AM
Academy of Management (NTPA) ... AOM
Academy of Marketing Science [*Coral Gables, FL*] (EA) ... AMS
Academy of Master Wine Growers (EA) ... AMWG
Academy of Medical Sciences (SAUO) ... ASM
Academy of Medical-Surgical Nurses (NTPA) ... AMSN
Academy of Medical-Surgical Nursing (SAUO) ... AMSN
Academy of Medicine (SAUO) ... Acad Med
Academy of Medicine (SAUO) ... AOM
Academy of Medicine of New Jersey (SRA) ... AMNJ
Academy of Medicine of New Jersey, Bloomfield, NJ [*Library symbol*] [*Library of Congress*] (LCLS) ... NjBlM
Academy of Medicine, Toronto (SAUO) ... AMT
Academy of Medicine Toronto, Canada (SAUS) ... AMT
Academy of Medicine, Toronto, ON, Canada [*Library symbol*] [*Library of Congress*] (LCLS) ... CaOTA
Academy of Medicine, Toronto, Ontario [*Library symbol*] [*National Library of Canada*] (NLC) ... OTA
Academy of Military Science (ACAE) ... AMS
Academy of Model Aeronautics (EA) ... AMA
Academy of Motion Picture Arts and Sciences (EA) ... AMPAS
Academy of Motion Picture Arts and Sciences aperture (SAUS) ... Acad aper
Academy of Motion Picture Arts and Sciences, Los Angeles, CA [*Library symbol*] [*Library of Congress*] (LCLS) ... CLAc
Academy of Motion Picture Arts and Sciences mask (SAUS) ... Acad mask
Academy of Music (SAUO) ... Acad Mus
Academy of Music and Dramatic Art (SAUO) ... AMDA
Academy of Natural Science (BARN) ... Acad Nat Sci
Academy of Natural Sciences (SAUO) ... ANS
Academy of Natural Sciences [*Academy of Natural Sciences of Philadelphia*] [*Acronym is based on former name,*] (EA) ... ANSP
Academy of Natural Sciences, Journal (SAUS) ... Acad of Nat Sci Jour
Academy of Natural Sciences of Philadelphia (SAUS) ... ANSP
Academy of Natural Sciences of Philadelphia, Philadelphia, PA [*OCLC symbol*] (OCLC) ... ANS
Academy of Natural Sciences of Philadelphia, Philadelphia, PA [*Library symbol*] [*Library of Congress*] (LCLS) ... PPAN
Academy of Natural Sciences of Philadelphia Proceedings (journ.) (SAUS) ... Acad Natur Sci Phila Proc
Academy of Operative Dentistry (EA) ... AOD
Academy of Oral Diagnosis, Radiology, and Medicine (EA) ... AODRM
Academy of Oral Dynamics (EA) ... AOD
Academy of Organizational and Occupational Psychiatry (SAUO) ... AOOP
Academy of Orthomolecular Medicine (EA) ... AOM
Academy of Orthomolecular Psychiatry (SAUO) ... AAOM
Academy of Orthomolecular Psychiatry [*Later, AOM*] (EA) ... AOP
Academy of Osseointegration (NTPA) ... AO
Academy of Osteopathic Directors of Medical Education (EA) ... AODME
Academy of Parapsychology and Medicine [*Defunct*] (EA) ... APM
Academy of Parish Clergy (EA) ... APC
Academy of Periodontology (SAUO) ... AP
Academy of Pharmaceutical Research and Science (NTPA) ... APRS
Academy of Pharmaceutical Sciences (EA) ... APS
Academy of Pharmacy Practice (EA) ... APP
Academy of Pharmacy Practice and Management (SAUO) ... APPM
Academy of Physical Medicine (MELL) ... APM
Academy of Political and Social Science (SAUS) ... APSS
Academy of Political and Social Sciences (SAUO) ... APSS
Academy of Political Science (EA) ... APS
Academy of Product Safety Management [*Defunct*] (EA) ... APSM
Academy of Psychic Arts and Sciences (EA) ... APAS
Academy of Psychologists in Marital Counseling [*Later, APMSFT*] ... APMC
Academy of Psychologists in Marital Sex and Family Therapy (EA) ... APMSFT
Academy of Psychosomatic Medicine (EA) ... APM
Academy of Radiology Research (NTPA) ... ARR

Academy of Rehabilitative Audiology (EA) ARA
Academy of Rehabilitative Audiometry (MELL) ARA
Academy of Religion and Mental Health [*Later, Institutes of Religion and Health*] ARMH
Academy of Religion and Psychical Research (EA) ARPR
Academy of Richmond County, Augusta, GA [*Library symbol*] [*Library of Congress*] (LCLS) GAuAR
Academy of Roofing Contractors [*Defunct*] (EA) ARC
Academy of Science (SAUO) Acad Sci
Academy of Science (SAUO) A of S
Academy of Science (SAUS) A of S
Academy of Science Fiction, Fantasy and Horror Films (SAUO) ASFFHF
Academy of Science (Union of Soviet Socialist Republics) ASUSSR
Academy of Sciences AS
Academy of Sciences of the Czech Republic ASCR
Academy of Sciences of the USSR (SAUO) ASUSSR
Academy of Scientific Hypno Therapy (EA) ASH
Academy of Screen Printing Technology (EA) ASPT
Academy of Security Educators and Trainees (EA) ASET
Academy of Social and Political Sciences (SAUO) ASSP
Academy of Sports Psychology International (EA) ASPI
Academy of Stress and Chronic Disease (EA) ASCD
Academy of Students of Pharmacy (EA) APhA-ASP
Academy of Students of Pharmacy (SAUO) ASP
Academy of Teachers of Occupations [*Defunct*] (EA) ATO
Academy of Television Arts and Sciences (EA) ATAS
Academy of the Arts and Sciences of the Americas (SAUO) AASA
Academy of the New Church ANC
Academy of the New Church, Bryn Athyn, PA [*Library symbol*] [*Library of Congress*] (LCLS) PBa
Academy of the Street of Puerto Rican Congress (EA) ASPRC
Academy of Underwater Arts and Sciences [*Defunct*] (EA) AUAS
Academy of Veterinary Allergy (EA) AVA
Academy of Veterinary Allergy and Clinical Immunology (NTPA) AVACI
Academy of Veterinary Cardiology (EA) AVC
Academy of Veterinary Emergency & Critical Care Technicians (GVA) AVECCT
Academy of Veterinary Homeopathy (GVA) AVH
Academy of Visual Arts (SAUO) AVA
Academy of Wind and Percussion Arts (EA) AWAPA
Academy of Wind and Percussion Arts (SAUO) AWPA
Academy of Zoology [*Uttar Pradesh, India*] (EA) AZ
Academy on Architecture for Health (SAUO) AAH
Academy on Computers (SAUO) AoC
Academy on Computers (SAUS) A o C
Academy on Human Rights and Peace (EA) AHRP
Academy Resources Ltd. [*Vancouver Stock Exchange symbol*] AMY
Academy Sergeant-Major [*British military*] (DMA) AcSM
Acadernic Press (SAUO) ISBN 0-12
Acadia (ABBR) ACAD
Acadia (SAUS) Acad
Acadia Health Education Coalition (SRA) AHEC
Acadia Mineral Ventures Ltd. [*Toronto Stock Exchange symbol*] ALV
Acadia National Park ACAD
Acadia National Park (SAUS) ANP
Acadia Parish Library, Crowley, LA [*Library symbol*] [*Library of Congress*] (LCLS) LCrA
Acadia Realty Trust [*Formerly, Mark Centers Trust*] [*NYSE symbol*] AKR
Acadia University (SAUO) Acad
Acadia University (SAUO) Acad U
Acadia University (SAUO) Ac Univ
Acadia University (SAUO) AU
Acadia University, Department of Geography, Wolfville, NS, Canada [*Library symbol*] [*Library of Congress*] (LCLS) CaNSWAG
Acadia University, Wolfville, Nova Scotia [*Library symbol*] [*National Library of Canada*] (NLC) NSWA
Acadia University, Wolfville, NS, Canada [*Library symbol*] [*Library of Congress*] (LCLS) CaNSWA
Acadian Friendship Committee [*See also CAA*] (EAIO) AFC
Acadian Genealogical and Historical Association [*Defunct*] (EA) AGHA
Acadian Home Builders Association (SRA) AHBA
Acadiana Bancshares, Inc. [*Associated Press*] (SAG) Acadiana
Acadiana Bancshares, Inc. [*AMEX symbol*] (SAG) ANA
Acalculous Cholecystitis [*Medicine*] (MELL) ACC
Acandi [*Colombia*] [*Airport symbol*] (OAG) ACD
Acanthiomeatal Line [*Medicine*] (MEDA) AML
Acanthocephala (SAUS) Acanth
Acanthosis Factor (MELL) AF
Acanthosis Nigricans [*Medicine*] AN
Acanthrocytes [*Hematology*] (DAVI) ACAN
Acanthrocytes [*Hematology*] (DAVI) ACANTH
Acanthus (VRA) acant
Acao Libertadora National [*Brazilian Action for National Liberation*] [*Political party*] (LAIN) ALN
Acapulco [*Mexico*] [*Airport symbol*] ACA
Acapulco [*Mexico*] (ABBR) ACAP
Acapulco gold (SAUS) Acap gold
Acapulco/General Juan N. Alvarez Internacional [*Mexico*] [*ICAO location identifier*] (ICLI) MMAA
Acarigua [*Venezuela*] [*Airport symbol*] (OAG) AGV
Acarigua, Portuguesa [*Venezuela*] [*ICAO location identifier*] (ICLI) SVAC
ACARS [*ARINC Communications and Address Reporting System*] **Management Unit** (GAVI) ACARS MU
ACB [*American Council of the Blind*] **Radio Amateurs** [*An association*] (EA) ACBRA
ACC Consumer Finance [*NASDAQ symbol*] (TTSB) ACCI
ACC Consumer Finance Corp. [*Associated Press*] (SAG) ACC Cns
ACC Consumer Finance Corp. [*NASDAQ symbol*] (SAG) ACC Cns
ACC Consumer Finance Corp. [*NASDAQ symbol*] (SAG) ACCI
ACC Corp. [*Associated Press*] (SAG) ACC
ACC Corp. [*NASDAQ symbol*] (NQ) ACCC
ACC Corp. [*Associated Press*] (SAG) ACC Cp
ACC Levels by Altimetrics and Island Measurements (SAUS) ACCLAIM
Accademia [*Academy*] [*Italian*] (BJA) Acc
Accademia ACCAD
Accao Nacional Popular [*National Popular Action*] [*Angola*] [*Political party*] (AF) ANP
Accao Social Democratica [*Social Democratic Action*] [*Portugal*] [*Political party*] (PPE) ASD
Accao Socialista Portugues [*Portuguese Socialist Action*] (PPE) ASP
ACCE Institute for Communication Development and Research (SAUO) ACCE/CDR
ACCE Institute for Communication Development and Research (SAUO) ACCE/ICDR
ACCE Institute for Communication Development and Research (SAUO) ACCE/ICOR
Accede (ABBR) ACD
Accede (ABBR) ACED
Acceded (ABBR) ACDD
Acceded to Throne (ROG) AC
Accedence (ABBR) ACDNC
Acceder (ABBR) ACDR
Acceding (ABBR) ACDG
Accel International Corp. [*Associated Press*] (SAG) Accel
Accel International Corp. [*Formerly, Acceleration Corp.*] [*NASDAQ symbol*] (NQ) ACLE
Accel International Corp. Productivity Interface [*Computer science*] (BYTE) API
Accel Intl. [*NASDAQ symbol*] (TTSB) ACLE
Accelerando [*Quickening the Pace*] [*Music*] ACC
Accelerando [*Quickening the Pace*] [*Music*] ACCEL
Accelerando [*Quickening the Pace*] [*Music*] (ROG) ACCELO
Accelerate (AABC) ACCEL
Accelerate (ABBR) ACEL
Accelerate (ABBR) ACLRA
Accelerate (BARN) ACLT
Accelerated (ABBR) ACELD
Accelerated (ABBR) ACLRAD
Accelerated Accounting and Reporting System AARS
Accelerated Acquisition Approach [*Pronounced "a-cubed"*] [*Air Force*] A^3
Accelerated Active Search System (CAAL) A^{2S2}
Accelerated Apprenticeship Training (ADA) AAT
Accelerated Assemblies (NASA) AA
Accelerated Business Collection and Delivery [*Postal Service*] ABCD
Accelerated Capabilities Initiative [*Office of naval research*] ACI
Accelerated Capital Cost Allowance [*Accounting*] ACCA
Accelerated Capital Recovery System [*Accounting*] ACRS
Accelerated Carrier Return (SAUS) ACR
Accelerated Cathode Excitation [*Electricity*] (IAA) ACE
Accelerated Christian Education [*An association*] ACE
Accelerated Claimant Match ACM
Accelerated Climatic Simulator (PDAA) ACS
Accelerated College Examination Board (PAZ) ACE
Accelerated Computing Environment (SAUS) ACE
Accelerated Constrained Simplex Technique (PDAA) ACSIM
Accelerated Constrained Simplex Technique (SAUS) ACSIM Technique
Accelerated Construction Completion Date (NATG) ACCD
Accelerated Cooled/Direct Quenched programme (SAUS) AC/DQ
Accelerated Co-Pilot Enrichment [*Program*] ACE
Accelerated Corrosion Test Facility [*Army*] ACTF
Accelerated Cost Recovery [*Accounting*] (ADA) ACR
Accelerated Cost Recovery Schedule [*Accounting*] ACRS
Accelerated Cost Recovery System [*Accounting*] ACRS
Accelerated Deactivation Test [*Chemistry*] ADT
Accelerated Declassification System (NVT) ADS
Accelerated Depreciation (SAUS) AD
Accelerated Depreciation Range (SAUS) ADR
Accelerated Development, Inc. (DHP) AD
Accelerated Development Test (MUGU) ADT
Accelerated Development Test Program (AAG) ADTP
Accelerated Evaluation Method AEM
Accelerated File Access (SAUS) AFA
Accelerated Free Fall (SAUS) AFF
Accelerated Freeze-Drying [*Food processing*] AFD
Accelerated Graphics Port [*Computer science*] AGP
Accelerated Growth Area [*Embryology*] AGA
Accelerated Hypertension [*Medicine*] AH
Accelerated Idioventricular Rhythm [*Cardiology*] (DAVI) AIR
Accelerated Idioventricular Rhythm [*Cardiology*] AIVR
Accelerated Individual and Company Development (PDAA) AICD
Accelerated Inspection System (DNAB) AIS
Accelerated Intelligence Report (NATG) CELINTREP
Accelerated Inverse Voltage AIV
Accelerated Investment Mortgage AIM
Accelerated Item Reduction [*Military*] AIR
Accelerated Learning of Logic ALL
Accelerated Life Testing ALT
Accelerated Loading Facility (ADA) ALF
Accelerated Mental Process (MEDA) AMP
Accelerated Mission Endurance Test (MCD) AMET

Accelerated Mission Testing (IEEE) ... AMT
Accelerated Networks [*NASDAQ symbol*] ... ACCL
Accelerated Pacification Campaign [*South Vietnam*] ... APC
Accelerated Pacification Program [*Vietnam, 1968*] (VNW) ... APP
Accelerated Painless Labor (MAE) ... APL
Accelerated Pavement Testing [*FHWA*] (TAG) ... APT
Accelerated Photosynthetic System [*Sewage purification*] ... APS
Accelerated Project to Automate Critical Hardware Hardcore Systems ... APACHE
Accelerated Project to Automate Critical Hardware Systems (SAUS) ... APACHE
Accelerated Promotion Scheme (WDAA) ... APS
Accelerated Propagation System [*Gardening*] ... APS
Accelerated Provisioning Concept (ACAE) ... APC
Accelerated Public Works [*Program*] [*Department of the Interior*] ... APW
Accelerated Public Works Program [*Department of the Interior*] ... APWP
Accelerated Random Search (MCD) ... ARS
Accelerated Ray-Tracing System (VERA) ... ARTS
Accelerated Reaction (MELL) ... AR
Accelerated Readiness Analysis (NG) ... ARA
Accelerated Reeducation of Emotions, Behavior, and Attitudes [*Rehabilitation program*] ... AREBA
Accelerated Refuge Maintenance Management [*Department of the Interior*] ... ARMM
Accelerated Relaxation Algorithm (SAUS) ... ARA
Accelerated Relaxation Method (PDAA) ... ARM
Accelerated Remittance Cycle [*Business term*] (EMRF) ... ARC
Accelerated Research Initiative (SAUO) ... ARI
Accelerated Research Initiative [*Marine science*] (OSRA) ... ART
Accelerated Retirement of Vehicles Program [*Air quality implementation plans*] ... ARVP
Accelerated Rural Development ... ARD
Accelerated Service Test (MCD) ... AST
Accelerated Service Test Program (SAA) ... ASTP
Accelerated Simulated Mission Endurance Test (MCD) ... ASMET
Accelerated Solicitation to Award Process [*National Institutes of Health*] ... ASAP
Accelerated Specialized Inspection Sites [*Customs inspection at airports*] ... ASIST
Accelerated Storage Adapter (IAA) ... ASA
Accelerated Strategic Computing Initiative [*Department of Energy*] ... ASCI
Accelerated Strike Aircraft Program (ACAE) ... ASAP
Accelerated Strike Aircraft Program Requirement [*DoD*] (MCD) ... ASAPR
Accelerated Surface Post [*British*] (DCTA) ... ASP
Accelerated Take-Off [*British military*] (DMA) ... ATO
Accelerated Test Technology ... ATT
Accelerated Training Program (NAKS) ... ATP
Accelerated Turnover to the Vietnamese (SAUO) ... ACTOV
Accelerated Turn-Over to Vietnamese [*Military*] ... ACTOV
Accelerated Ventricular Rhythm [*Cardiology*] (DMAA) ... AVR
Accelerated Vesication Test (AAEL) ... AVT
Accelerated View of Input Data ... AVOID
Accelerates (ABBR) ... ACELS
Accelerate-Stop Distance Available [*Aviation*] (FAAC) ... ASDA
accelerating (SAUS) ... accel
Accelerating (ABBR) ... ACELG
Accelerating (ABBR) ... ACLRAG
Accelerating Contactor or Relay (IEEE) ... A
Accelerating Rate Calorimeter [*Instrumentation*] ... ARC
Accelerating Rate Calorimetry (SAUS) ... ARC
Accelerating Relay (SAUS) ... AccR
Acceleration (NTIO) ... a
Acceleration [*or Accelerator*] ... A
Acceleration ... ACC
Acceleration (IDOE) ... acc
Acceleration (ABBR) ... ACELN
Acceleration (ABBR) ... ACLRAN
Acceleration [*Symbol*] (DEN) ... f
Acceleration Command ... AC
Acceleration Compensation [*or Control*] **Unit** [*Aviation*] ... ACU
Acceleration Compensation Unit (SAUS) ... ACU
Acceleration Control Unit (SAUS) ... ACU
Acceleration Correction ... C
Acceleration, Cruising, Idling, Deceleration (MHDI) ... ACID
Acceleration Curve Restraint Seat [*Automotive safety systems*] ... ACRS
acceleration due to gravity (SAUS) ... g
Acceleration Enrichment [*Automotive fuel systems*] ... AE
Acceleration Force (DMAA) ... G
Acceleration forces (SAUS) ... G forces
Acceleration, High Voltage (SAUS) ... AHV
acceleration in feet per second (SAUS) ... a
Acceleration Monitoring Experiment (SAUS) ... AME
Acceleration Monitoring Guidance System (MCD) ... AMGS
Acceleration of Free Fall [*Symbol*] ... g
Acceleration of Gravity Force (PIPO) ... G
Acceleration Position Sensor [*Diesel engines*] ... APS
Acceleration Restraint Curve [*Automotive engineering*] ... ARC
Acceleration Slip Regulation [*Automotive engineering*] ... ASR
Acceleration Spectral Density (PDAA) ... ASD
Acceleration Spectral Density (SAUS) ... ASD
Acceleration Switching Valve ... ASV
Acceleration Time ... ACT
Acceleration Vector Control ... AVC
Acceleration-Deceleration Unit ... ADU
Acceleration-Type Control Law ... ATCL
Accelerative (ABBR) ... ACELV
Accelerative (ABBR) ... ACLRAV
Accelerator (AAG) ... AC
Accelerator [*Automotive engineering*] ... ACCEL
Accelerator (ABBR) ... ACELR
Accelerator (ABBR) ... ACLRTR
Accelerator (MSA) ... ACLTR
Accelerator and Reactor Improvement and Modification ... ARIM
Accelerator for Physics and Chemistry of Heavy Elements (SAUS) ... APACHE
Accelerator for Physics and Chemistry of Heavy Metals ... APACHE
Accelerator Free Fall [*Parachuting*] ... AFF
Accelerator Globulin [*Medicine*] ... AcG
Accelerator Globulin [*Medicine*] (DB) ... ACG
Accelerator Globulin (ADWA) ... ac-g
Accelerator Heel Point [*Automotive engineering*] ... AHP
Accelerator, High Voltage (SAA) ... AHV
Accelerator Information Center [*ORNL*] ... AIC
Accelerator Mass Spectrometer (or Spectrometry) (SAUS) ... AMS
Accelerator Mass Spectrometry ... AMS
Accelerator Pedal Position Sensor [*Automotive engineering*] ... APS
Accelerator Pedal with Idler [*Automotive engineering*] ... API
Accelerator Performance Demonstration Facility (SAUS) ... APDF
Accelerator Production of Tritium [*Physics*] ... APT
Accelerator Pulsed Fast Assembly ... APFA
Accelerator Research (SAUS) ... AR
Accelerator Technology (SAUS) ... AT
Accelerator Test Stand (SAUS) ... ATS
Accelerator Test Stand Upgrade (SAUS) ... ATSU
Accelerator Transmutation of Waste [*Nuclear waste*] ... ATW
Accelerator-Based Conversion (SAUS) ... ABC
Accelerator-Pulsed Fast Assembly (SAUS) ... APFA
Accelerator-Pulsed Reactor (SAUS) ... APR
Accelerator-Tritium Producer [*Nuclear physics*] ... ATP
Accelerin-Convertin [*Medicine*] (MELL) ... ACC
Accelerometer ... ACCEL
Accelerometer ... ACCLRM
Accelerometer Assembly [*NASA*] ... AA
Accelerometer Calibration Vibration Exciter ... ACVE
Accelerometer Monitoring Program [*NASA*] (KSC) ... AMP
Accelerometer Package (KSC) ... AP
Accelerometer Package (KSC) ... APK
Accelerometer Parameter Shift ... APS
Accelerometer Pulse Converter ... APC
Accelerometer Scale Factor Error ... ASFE
Accelerometer Scale Factor Input Panel ... ASFIP
Accelerometer Signal Conditioner (KSC) ... ASC
Accelerometer Signal Processing (ACAE) ... ASP
Accelerometer Timer Switch (SAUS) ... ATS
Accelerometer-Timer (SAA) ... AT
Accelerometer-Timer Switch (IAA) ... ATS
Accellerated Cathode Excitation (SAUS) ... ACE
Accelr8 Technology Corp. [*Associated Press*] (SAG) ... Accelr8
Accelr8 Technology Corp. [*NASDAQ symbol*] (SAG) ... ACLY
Accenet Flexible Digital Access Service (SAUS) ... AFDAS
Accent (NTCM) ... A
Accent ... ACCT
Accent (ABBR) ... ACNT
Accent before Cooking [*Advertising slogan*] ... ABC
Accent Color Sciences, Inc. [*Associated Press*] (SAG) ... AccCSci
Accent Color Sciences, Inc. [*NASDAQ symbol*] (SAG) ... ACLR
Accent on Developing Abstract Processes of Thought ... ADAPT
Accent on Information (EA) ... AI
Accent on Information [*Databank for the handicapped and rehabilitation professionals*] [*Accent on Living*] (IID) ... AOI
Accent Software International Inc. [*Associated Press*] (SAG) ... AccentS
Accent Software International Ltd. [*Associated Press*] (SAG) ... Accent
Accent Software International Ltd. [*NASDAQ symbol*] (SAG) ... ACNT
Accent Software International Ltd. [*NASDAQ symbol*] (SAG) ... ACNW
Accent Software Intl. [*NASDAQ symbol*] (TTSB) ... ACNTF
Accent Software Intl. Ltd. [*Associated Press*] (SAG) ... AccSftl
Accent Software Intl. Ltd. [*NASDAQ symbol*] (SAG) ... ACNU
Accented (WDAA) ... ACCTD
Accented (ABBR) ... ACNTD
Accenting (ABBR) ... ACNTG
Accentual (ABBR) ... ACNTL
Accentuate (ABBR) ... ACNTU
Accentuated (ABBR) ... ACNTUD
Accentuating (ABBR) ... ACNTUG
Accentuation (ABBR) ... ACNTUN
Accept (EBF) ... Acc
Accept [*or Acceptance*] [*Banking*] (KSC) ... ACCPT
Accept (AABC) ... ACPT
Accept Data State [*Computer science*] (IAA) ... ACDS
Accept No Verbal Orders ... ANVO
Accept or Reject (ACAE) ... A/R
Accept Request (IAA) ... ARQ
Accept Response (IAA) ... ARP
Acceptability (ABBR) ... ACPTBT
Acceptability (ABBR) ... ACPTBY
Acceptable (ABBR) ... ACPTB
Acceptable Biological Catch [*Fishery management*] (MSC) ... ABC
Acceptable Biological Removal [*Fishery management*] ... ABR
Acceptable Container Condition [*Shipping*] (DS) ... ACC
Acceptable Contractions of Randomly Organized Names Yielding Meritorious Spontan (SAUS) ... ACRONYMS
Acceptable Contrast Ratio (SAUS) ... ACR
Acceptable Daily Dose (LDT) ... ADD

Acceptable Daily Intake [*Toxicology*] ... ADI
Acceptable Data Base (EEVL) ... ADABA
Acceptable Defect Level ... ADL
Acceptable Environmental Range Test ... AERT
Acceptable Failure Rate ... AFR
Acceptable Hazard Rate (IEEE) ... AHR
Acceptable Hazard Rate (ODBW) ... ahr
Acceptable Intake Daily [*of foods and additives*] ... AID
Acceptable Intake for Chronic Exposure [*Environmental science*] (COE) ... AIC
Acceptable Intake for Chronic Exposures (SAUS) ... AIC
Acceptable Intake for Subchronic Exposure [*Environmental science*] (COE) ... AIS
Acceptable Level (GNE) ... AL
Acceptable Level of Competence (SAUS) ... ALOC
Acceptable Limit for Dispersion ... ALD
Acceptable Means of Compliance (DA) ... AMC
Acceptable Periodic Inspection ... API
Acceptable Process Level ... APL
Acceptable Productivity Level [*Quality control*] ... APL
Acceptable Qualifying (or Quality) Level (SAUS) ... AQL
Acceptable Quality Level [*Quality control*] ... AQL
Acceptable Quality Rate [*Quality control*] ... AQR
Acceptable Quality Test [*Quality control*] (MSA) ... AQT
Acceptable Reliability Level [*Quality control*] ... ARL
Acceptable Residue Level in Drinking Water ... ARLDW
Acceptable Risk [*Toxicology*] (LDT) ... AR
Acceptable Supplier List ... ASL
Acceptable Tissue Concentration (EEVL) ... ATC
Acceptable Use Policy ... AUP
Acceptable Variation (SAUS) ... AV
Acceptable Workload Factor [*Management*] ... AWF
Acceptableness (ABBR) ... ACPTNS
Acceptably (ABBR) ... ACPTY
Acceptance [*Banking*] ... ACC
Acceptance [*Banking*] ... ACCE
Acceptance [*Business term*] (EBF) ... Acce
Acceptance [*Banking*] (ROG) ... ACCEPTCE
Acceptance ... ACCEPTN
Acceptance [*Banking*] (TBD) ... Accpt
Acceptance [*Business term*] (EBF) ... Acpt
Acceptance (WDMC) ... acpt
Acceptance (ABBR) ... ACPTNC
Acceptance Advice Form ... AAF
Acceptance and Certification Branch [*Social Security Administration*] ... ACB
Acceptance and Checkout / Maintenance Ground Equipment (SAA) ... ACO/MGE
Acceptance and Checkout/Maintenance Ground Equipment (SAUS) ... ACO/MGE
Acceptance and Commitment Therapy [*Developed by Steven Hayes*] (DIPS) ... ACT
Acceptance and Ferry Flight [*NASA*] (NASA) ... AFF
Acceptance and Operational Checkout Requirements Document [*NASA*] (NASA) ... AOCRD
Acceptance and Takeover Date [*Telecommunications*] (TEL) ... ATD
Acceptance and Transfer ... A & T
Acceptance and Transfer (SAUS) ... A/T
Acceptance Checkout [*NASA*] (NASA) ... ACO
Acceptance Checkout and Evaluation System [*NASA*] (NASA) ... ACES
Acceptance Checkout Equipment [*NASA*] ... ACE
Acceptance Checkout Equipment - Spacecraft [*NASA*] (KSC) ... ACE-S/C
Acceptance Checkout Procedure (KSC) ... ACP
Acceptance, Checkout, Retest, and Backout Criteria (NAKS) ... ACRBC
Acceptance, Conforming, and Qualification Test ... AC & QT
Acceptance, Conforming and Qualification Test (SAUS) ... AC&QT
Acceptance Control Equipment Section [*or System*] [*NASA*] (NASA) ... ACES
Acceptance Control Equipment System (SAUS) ... ACES
Acceptance Data Package (KSC) ... ADP
Acceptance Data Package System (NAKS) ... ADPS
Acceptance Failure Rate (SAUS) ... AFR
Acceptance for Honor [*Business term*] ... AFH
Acceptance Functional Test (SAUS) ... AFT
Acceptance Functional Test Procedure [*NASA*] (KSC) ... A/FTP
Acceptance Inspection Equipment [*Army*] (AABC) ... AIE
Acceptance Inspection Instruction ... AII
Acceptance Inspection Package (KSC) ... AIP
Acceptance Insurance Companies [*NYSE symbol*] (SPSG) ... AIF
Acceptance Insurance Companies, Inc. [*Associated Press*] (SAG) ... Acpt Ins
Acceptance Into Naval Service (SAUS) ... AINS
Acceptance Message [*Aviation code*] ... ACP
Acceptance Number [*Business term*] ... Ac
Acceptance of Others Scale [*Psychology*] (EDAC) ... AOS
Acceptance Quality Level (AAEL) ... AQL
Acceptance Quality Test (ACAE) ... AQT
Acceptance Readiness (NASA) ... AR
Acceptance Requirement ... AR
Acceptance Requirements (ACAE) ... AR
Acceptance Requirements Document (ACAE) ... ARD
Acceptance Review (NASA) ... AR
Acceptance Review/Integration Readiness Review (SAUS) ... AR/IRR
Acceptance Sampling (SAUS) ... AS
Acceptance Standard (SAUS) ... QAAS
Acceptance Summary Report ... ASR
Acceptance Tag (NRCH) ... AT
Acceptance Test (NRCH) ... AT
Acceptance Test and Launch Operations [*NASA*] (MCD) ... ATLO
Acceptance Test Equipment (MCD) ... ATE
Acceptance Test Facility [*Nuclear energy*] ... ATF
Acceptance Test of Launch Language [*NASA*] ... ATOLL
Acceptance Test or Launch Language (SAUS) ... ATOLL
Acceptance Test Plan [*or Procedure*] ... ATP
Acceptance Test Procedure (IUSS) ... ATP
Acceptance Test Report (MCD) ... ATR
Acceptance Test Review (CTAS) ... ATR
Acceptance Test Specification [*DoD*] ... ATS
Acceptance Tester (SAUS) ... AT
Acceptance Thermal Test [*or Testing*] [*NASA*] (NASA) ... ATT
Acceptance, Transfer and Training Unit (SAUO) ... ACTRU
Acceptance Trials [*Shipbuilding*] ... AT
Acceptance Vibration Testing [*NASA*] (NASA) ... AVT
Acceptation [*Acceptance*] [*French*] [*Banking*] (ROG) ... ACCEPN
Accepte sous Protet pour Compte [*Accepted under Protest for Account*] [*French*] ... ASPC
Accepted ... A
Accepted (ROG) ... AC
Accepted (ABBR) ... ACPTD
Accepted Alternative Designation Of ... AADO
Accepted Applicants (SAUS) ... Accp App
Accepted Batch Listing [*Accounting*] ... ABL
Accepted Dental Remedies [*A publication*] ... ADR
Accepted Dental Remedy (DAVI) ... ADR
Accepted Dental Therapeutics ... ADT
Accepted on Hire ... AOH
Accepted Point Mutation 250 (SAUS) ... PAM 250
Accepted Position (SAUS) ... Ac Psn
Accepted Record (SAUS) ... Acc Rec
Accepted Test Procedures (SAUS) ... ATP
Accepted Weight/Estimate [*Ships*] ... AWE
Accepting (ABBR) ... ACPTG
Accepting Challenges of Today in Our New-world (SAUS) ... ACTION
Accepting Challenges of Today in our Newworld (SAUO) ... ACTION
Accepting Houses Committee [*Banking*] [*British*] ... AHC
Accepting Individual Differences Curriculum (EDAC) ... AID
Acceptor [*Physiology*] ... A
Acceptor (MSA) ... ACPTR
Acceptor Bound Exciton [*Electronics*] (AAEL) ... ABE
Acceptor Circuit (SAUS) ... AC
Acceptor Energy Level ... AEL
Acceptor Handshake (MHDI) ... AH
Acceptor Idle State (SAUS) ... AIDS
Acceptor Level (SAUS) ... AL
Acceptor not Ready State (SAUS) ... ANRS
Acceptor of Action Results (DIPS) ... AAR
Acceptor Ready State (SAUS) ... ACRS
Acceptor Wait for New cycle State (SAUS) ... AWNS
Accept/Refuse message (SAUS) ... A/R
Accept-Reject Rule [*Statistics*] ... AR
Accepts Transfer as Offered (NOAA) ... ATRSO
Access [*Credit card*] [*British*] ... A
Access [*Telecommunications*] (TEL) ... AC
Access ... ACC
Access ... ACCSS
Access [*Telecommunications*] (MSA) ... ACS
Access ... AXS
Access Access Control Set (SAUS) ... ACS
Access Address (SAUS) ... AA
Access America [*Commercial firm*] (EA) ... AA
Access and Amendment Refusal Authority [*Army*] (AABC) ... AARA
Access and Control Point [*Telecommunications*] (TEL) ... A & CP
Access and Control Point (SAUS) ... A&CP
Access Anytime Bancorp, Inc. [*NASDAQ symbol*] (SAG) ... AABC
Access Anytime Bancorp, Inc. [*Associated Press*] (SAG) ... AccessAny
Access Area Digital Switching System (MCD) ... AADS
Access Area Digital Switching System (ACAE) ... AADSS
Access Area Digital Switching System (SAUS) ... AADS System
Access ATM Network, Inc. [*Toronto Stock Exchange symbol*] ... ATM
Access Authorization [*Nuclear energy*] ... AA
Access Barred Signal (SAUS) ... ACB Signal
Access Beyond, Inc. [*NASDAQ symbol*] (SAG) ... ACCB
Access Beyond, Inc. [*Associated Press*] (SAG) ... AccByndl
Access Block Diagram ... ABD
Access Bus Industry Group (SAUO) ... ABIC
Access Characteristics Estimation System [*Computer science*] (MHDI) ... ACCESS
Access Coding (SAUS) ... AC
Access Colorado Library and Information Network (AEPA) ... ACLIN
Access Committee Centre on Environment for the Handicapped [*British*] ... ACCEH
Access Compatibility Layer (SAUS) ... ACL
Access Control (SAA) ... AC
Access Control Block [*Computer science*] (CIST) ... ACB
Access Control Center (SAUO) ... ACC
Access Control Committee ... ACC
Access control Decision Function (SAUS) ... ADF
Access Control Document [*NASA*] (NASA) ... ACD
Access Control Encryption (SAUS) ... ACE
Access control Enforcement Function (SAUS) ... AEF
Access Control Entry (SAUS) ... ACE
Access Control Facilities (or Facility) (SAUS) ... ACF
Access Control Facility ... ACF
Access Control Field [*Computer science*] (ACRL) ... ACF
Access Control List [*Computer science*] (HGAA) ... ACL
Access Control List Facility (VERA) ... ACLF
Access Control Logging and Reporting (SAUS) ... ACLR

Access Control Machine ... ACM
Access Control Register [*Computer science*] ... ACR
Access Control Server (SAUS) ... ACS
Access Control Set (SAUS) ... ACS
Access Control System [*Computer science*] (VERA) ... ACS
Access Control Unit (SAUS) ... ACU
Access Control Verification [*Computer science*] (HGAA) ... ACV
Access Control Word [*Computer science*] (MHDI) ... ACW
Access Control-Logging and Reporting [*Computer science*] (MHDI) ... ACLR
Access Cost Factor [*Telecommunications*] (TEL) ... ACF
Access Course Recognition Group [*British*] (DET) ... ACRG
Access Cycle (IAA) ... AC
Access Decision Binding Time (MHDI) ... ADBT
Access Deficit Contributions (SAUS) ... ADC
Access Developer's Toolkit [*Microsoft Corp.*] (PCM) ... ADT
Access Device Messaging Specification (SAUS) ... ADMS
Access Division Binding Time (SAUS) ... ADBT
Access Door ... AD
Access Electronic Payment Terminals [*for credit cards*] [*British*] ... ACCEPT
Access Enable (SAUS) ... ACEN
Access File Attribute (SAUS) ... AFA
Access Floor [*Technical drawings*] ... ACFL
Access Floor Manufacturing Association (EA) ... AFMA
Access Flooring Association [*British*] (DBA) ... AFA
Access for Disabled People to Arts Today (WDAA) ... ADAPT
Access for the Handicapped [*Defunct*] (EA) ... AH
Access Function Register ... AFR
Access Grant Channel (SAUS) ... AGCH
Access Health [*NASDAQ symbol*] (TTSB) ... ACCS
Access Health, Inc. [*Associated Press*] (SAG) ... AccesHlt
Access Health Marketing, Inc. [*NASDAQ symbol*] (SAG) ... ACCS
Access Health Marketing, Inc. [*Associated Press*] (SAG) ... AcesHlt
Access HealthNet, Inc. [*Associated Press*] (SAG) ... AccesH
Access HealthNet, Inc. [*NASDAQ symbol*] (SAG) ... AHNT
Access Hole (SAUS) ... AH
Access Instruction (SAUS) ... AI
Access Interface (SAUS) ... AI
Access Isolation Mechanism [*Computer science*] (NITA) ... AIM
Access Link (SAUS) ... A Link
Access Manager [*Computer science*] ... AM
Access Manway (SAUS) ... AM
Access Matrix (SAUS) ... AM
Access Mechanism (SAUS) ... AM
Access Method [*Computer science*] ... AM
[*The*] **Access Method** (IAA) ... TAM
Access Method Control Block [*Computer science*] (BUR) ... ACB
Access Method Control Block (SAUS) ... AMCB
Access Method Executor (SAUS) ... AME
Access Method for Indexed Data Generalized for Operating System [*Computer science*] ... AMIGOS
Access Method Service [*Computer science*] (BUR) ... AMS
Access Method Services Cryptographic Option (MHDI) ... AMSCO
Access Methods, Inc. (NITA) ... AMI
Access Methods Service Macros [*Computer science*] (HGAA) ... AMSM
Access Methods Services Utilities [*Computer science*] (HGAA) ... AMSU
Access Michigan Periodical List-Full Text ... AMPL-FT
Access Module (SAUS) ... AM
Access Module Processor (RALS) ... AMP
Access Network, Media Resource Center [*UTLAS symbol*] ... ACN
Access Node (VERA) ... AN
Access Node Hub Router (VERA) ... ANHR
Access Node Router (VERA) ... ANR
Access Now for Gay and Lesbian Equality [*An association*] ... ANGLE
Access Opening (AAG) ... ACS-O
Access Opening [*Technical drawings*] ... AO
Access Opening (SAUS) ... ASC-O
Access Overload Class (CGWS) ... ACCOLC
Access Panel [*Technical drawings*] (IAA) ... ACSPNL
Access Panel [*Technical drawings*] ... AP
Access Path Specification Language [*Computer science*] (CIST) ... APSL
Access Permit [*or Permittee*] [*Nuclear energy*] ... AP
Access Permit Holder ... APH
Access Pharmaceuticals [*AMEX symbol*] (SG) ... AKC
Access Point (SAUS) ... ap
Access Point [*Telecommunications*] (TEL) ... AP
Access Point Pace (KSC) ... APP
Access Prefix (SAUS) ... AP
[*The*] **Access Program for the CompuServe Information Service** (PCM) ... TAPCIS
Access Protection and Priority Control Mechanism (VERA) ... APPCM
ACCESS Query Interface (SAUS) ... AQI
Access Refusal and Barrier Interface Terminal [*Hardware-based security device from Computer Security Systems*] ... ARBITER
Access Regulation Mechanism (SAUS) ... ARM
Access Relay Set (SAUS) ... ARS
Access Rights List (VERA) ... ARL
Access Service for Profitable Informa-tion Resource Exchanges (SAUS) ... ASPIRE
Access Service Request [*Telecommunications*] (ITD) ... ASR
Access Solutions International, Inc. [*Associated Press*] (SAG) ... AccSol
Access Solutions International, Inc. [*NASDAQ symbol*] (SAG) ... ASIC
Access Speed (SAUS) ... AS
Access Stack Node (SAUS) ... ASN
Access Station (SAUS) ... AS
Access Store Address (SAUS) ... ASA
Access Stored Knowledge via Symbolic Access Method (SAUS) ... ASKSAM
Access Switch (SAUS) ... AS
Access Tandem ... AT
Access Technique (SAUS) ... AT
Access Technologies Forum (SAUO) ... ACTEF
Access Technology Association (NTPA) ... ATA
Access Time ... ACST
Access Time ... AT
Access Time of/to Reading (SAUS) ... ATR
Access to Careers in Technology (SAUO) ... ACT
Access to Information and Reading Service (AIE) ... AIRS
Access to Information for Medicine (SAUS) ... AIM
Access to Information for Medicine [*Allegheny General Hospital, Health Sciences Library*] [*Information service or system*] (IID) ... AIM
Access to Information on Multicultural Educational Resources (AIE) ... AIMER
Access to Learning for Adults (AIE) ... ALFA
Access to Remote Catalogues by Implementing SR Target Functions (SAUS) ... ARCA
Access to Source of Knowledge (SAUS) ... ASK
Access to Voluntary and Safe Contraception (ADWA) ... AVSC
Access Type Bit (SAUS) ... ATB
Access Type BIT [*Binary Digit*] [*Computer science*] ... ATB
Access Unit [*Computer science*] (TNIG) ... AU
Access Upsizing Tools [*Microsoft Corp.*] (PCM) ... AUT
ACCESS.bus Industry Group [*Computer science*] (PCM) ... ABIG
Accessed (SAUS) ... A
Accessed BIT [*Binary Digit*] [*Computer science*] ... A
Access/Egress Roadway System (SAUS) ... AERS
Accessibility (ABBR) ... ACSBT
Accessibility and Dissemination of Data (SAUS) ... ADD
Accessibility to Gate Arrays through Technology and Engineering (PDAA) ... AGATE
Accessible (ABBR) ... ACSB
Accessible Emission Limit [*Environmental science*] (COE) ... AEL
Accessible Operand Affiliation (SAUS) ... AOA
Accessibleness (ABBR) ... ACSBNS
Accessibly (ABBR) ... ACSBY
Access/Information [*Information service or system*] (IID) ... AI
Accessing the Internet Via Email (SAUS) ... ACCMAIL
Accession (ABBR) ... ACSN
Accession Compensatory Account (DCTA) ... ACA
Accession Designation Number [*Military*] ... ADN
Accession Document (SAUS) ... AD
Accession List ... AL
Accession Number [*Online database field identifier*] ... ACN
Accession Number [*Online database field identifier*] ... AN
Accession Number Year [*Computer science*] (CIST) ... AY
Accession Treaty and Decision Concerning the European Coal and Steel Community [*A publication*] (DLA) ... ATD
Accessional (ABBR) ... ACSNL
Accessioned (ABBR) ... ACSND
Accessioning (ABBR) ... ACSNG
Accessions (AL) ... Acc
Accessions Document [*Air Force*] ... AD
Accessorial (AABC) ... ACCSL
Accessorial Service (SAUS) ... AS
Accessories ... Acc
Accessories Bulletin (MCD) ... AB
Accessories for Electronics Inc. (SAUO) ... AFE
Accessory [*Protein synthesis*] ... A
Accessory ... ACC
Accessory ... ACCES
Accessory (KSC) ... ACCESS
Accessory ... Access
Accessory (KSC) ... ACCRY
Accessory (AFM) ... ACCY
Accessory (IAA) ... ACESS
Accessory (ABBR) ... ACSRY
Accessory and Equipment Technical Committee (KSC) ... AETC
Accessory Boring Organ [*of a gastropod*] ... ABO
Accessory Bulletin (MCD) ... AYB
Accessory Bundle (SAUS) ... AcB
Accessory Cells [*Histology*] ... AC
Accessory Change (MCD) ... AYC
Accessory Clinical Findings [*Medicine*] ... ACF
Accessory Conduction Pathway [*Medicine*] (DMAA) ... ACP
Accessory Control Document (SAUS) ... ACD
Accessory Defenses (SAUS) ... Acc Def
Accessory Drive Gear Box (MCD) ... ADG
Accessory Drive Gear Box (MCD) ... ADGB
Accessory Drive System (NG) ... ADS
Accessory Dwelling Unit (PA) ... ADU
Accessory Gear Box ... AGB
Accessory Gland ... AG
Accessory Kit (SAUS) ... AK
Accessory Manufacturers Racing Association [*British*] (BI) ... AMRA
Accessory Meningeal Artery [*Anatomy*] ... AMA
Accessory Nerve [*Medicine*] (MELL) ... AN
Accessory Olfactory Bulb [*Anatomy*] ... AOB
Accessory Optic Nucleus [*Neuroanatomy*] ... AON
Accessory Optic System [*Neuroanatomy*] ... AOS
Accessory Pancreatic Duct [*Medicine*] (MELL) ... APD
Accessory Pathway [*Medicine*] (DMAA) ... AP
Accessory Pedal Ganglia ... APG
Accessory Power Supply (AABC) ... APS

Accessory Power System (SAUS) .... APS
Accessory Power Unit (MUGU) .... APU
Accessory Record Card (DNAB) .... ARC
Accessory Sex Organ [Anatomy] .... ASO
Accessory Supply System .... ASS
Accident .... Ac
Accident .... ACC
Accident .... ACCD
Accident (AAMN) .... ACCID
Accident (MELL) .... accid
Accident (SAUS) .... ACCT
Accident .... ACDNT
Accident (AABC) .... ACDT
Accident Analysis Branch (SAUO) .... AAB
Accident Anatomy Method [Engineering] .... AAM
Accident and Emergency [Ward, Department, or Services] [Medicine] .... A & E
Accident and Emergency .... A&E
Accident and Health (ADWA) .... a&h
Accident and Health (SAUS) .... A&H
Accident and Health (SAUS) .... A and H
Accident and Health Insurance .... A & H
Accident and Illness Reporting System (SAUS) .... AIRS
Accident and Indemnity [Insurance] .... A & I
Accident and Sickness Insurance .... A & S
Accident Benefits [Insurance] .... AB
Accident Compensation Commission (BARN) .... ACC
Accident Compensation Corporation (SAUO) .... ACC
Accident Compensation Journal [Madhya Pradesh, India] [A publication] (DLA) .... ACJ (Mad Pr)
Accident Cost Indicator Model [US Bureau of Mines] .... ACIM
Accident Data Recorder [Aviation] (AIA) .... ADR
Accident Data Recorder (or Recording) (SAUS) .... ADR
Accident Dispensary [Medicine] .... AD
Accident Documentation System [Safety research] [Automotive engineering] .... ADS
Accident Evolution and Barrier [Engineering] .... AEB
Accident Frequency Rate [Employment] (ODBW) .... AFR
Accident, Incident, Deficiencies (AFM) .... AID
Accident Information Retrieval System (RDA) .... AIRS
Accident Initiation and Progression Analysis (SAUO) .... AIPA
Accident Injury .... ACCI
Accident Insurance Policy (MHDB) .... AIP
Accident Intelligence [British police term] .... AI
Accident Investigation [Aviation] .... AIG
Accident Investigation Branch (SAUO) .... AIB
Accident Investigation Methodology [Engineering] .... AIM
Accident Investigation Unit (SAUO) .... AIU
Accident Investigative Bureau (SAUO) .... AIB
Accident Investigator (SARE) .... AI
Accident Legal Advise Service [British] .... ALAS
Accident Management (SAUS) .... AM
Accident Mitigation System [Industrial engineering] .... AMS
Accident Model Document [NASA] (KSC) .... AMD
Accident Notice (SAUS) .... ACNOT
Accident Offices Association [British] (BI) .... AOA
Accident Prevention Advisory Unit (HEAS) .... APAU
Accident Prevention Council (ABAC) .... APC
Accident Prevention Measures for Regulated Substances [Environmental science] (COE) .... APMRS
Accident Prevention Plan .... APP
Accident Prevention Regulations for Hazardous Substances [Environmental science] (COE) .... APRHS
Accident Prevention Risk Management Plan [Environmental science] (COE) .... APRMP
Accident Progression Event Tree (SAUS) .... APET
Accident Reconstruction Criminology (LAIN) .... ACC
Accident Records Bureau (SAUO) .... ARB
Accident Response Capabilities Coordinating Committee [Environmental science] (COE) .... ARCCC
Accident Response Group [Department of Energy] .... ARG
Accident Risk Assessment Report (ACAE) .... ARAR
Accident Sequence Evaluation Program [Nuclear energy] (NRCH) .... ASEP
Accident Sequence Precursor Study [Nuclear Regulatory Commission] .... ASP
Accident Site Liaison Officer (SAUS) .... ASLO
Accident Source Term Program Office [Nuclear energy] (NRCH) .... ASTPO
Accidental [Injury Insurance] (BARN) .... Acc
Accidental (ABBR) .... ACDNTL
Accidental (ABBR) .... ACDTL
Accidental Breakdown (SAUS) .... AB
Accidental Damage (WDAA) .... AD
Accidental Death and Disability [Insurance] .... ADD
Accidental Death and Dismemberment [Insurance] .... AD and D
Accidental Death and Dismemberment (SAUS) .... AD&D
Accidental Death Benefit (ADWA) .... adb
Accidental Death Benefit [Insurance] .... ADB
Accidental Discharge [Firearms] .... AD
Accidental Earth (SAUS) .... AE
Accidental Error (SAUS) .... AE
Accidental Hypothermia [Medicine] .... AH
Accidental Incident Sabotage Assistance Request (MCD) .... AISAR
Accidental Injuries (or Injury) (SAUS) .... AI
Accidental Injury .... AI
Accidental Launch Prevention System (DOMA) .... ALPS
Accidental Launch Protection System [Military] .... ALPS
Accidental Loss [Nuclear energy] .... AL

Accidental Nuclear War Prevention Project [Nuclear Age Peace Foundation] (EA) .... ANWPP
Accidental Printing (SAUS) .... AP
Accidental Release Information Program [Environmental science] (COE) .... ARIP
Accidentally (ABBR) .... ACDNTLY
Accidentally Incurred .... AI
Accidentally Killed (SAUS) .... ACK
Accidentally Wounded (SAUS) .... AW
Accident-Experience Learning Curve (PDAA) .... AELC
Accident/Incident [FRA] (TAG) .... ACC/INC
Accident/Incident .... A/I
Accident/Incident Analysis (PDAA) .... AIA
Accident-incident Data Reporting (SAUS) .... ADREP
Accident/Incident Data System [Database] [FAA] .... AIDS
Accident/Incident Reporting System [National Transportation Safety Board] [Information service or system] (IID) .... AIRS
Accident/Injury/Damages (DLA) .... AID
Accidents and Road Safety [British] .... ARS
Accidents Investigation Branch [Air Force] [British] .... AIB
Accidents, Poisonings and Violence (SAUS) .... APV
Accion Chilena Anticomunista [Chilean Anticommunist Action] [Political party] (EY) .... ACHA
Accion Ciudadana Liberal [Liberal Citizens' Action] [Spain] [Political party] (PPE) .... ACL
Accion del Pueblo [Costa Rica] [Political party] (EY) .... AP
Accion Democratica [Democratic Action] [Venezuela] [Political party] (PPW) .... AD
Accion Democratica 86 [Democratic Action 1986] [Aruba] [Political party] (EY) .... AD 86
Accion Democratica Ecuadoriana [Ecuadorean Democratic Action] [Political party] (PPW) .... ADE
Accion Democratica Nacionalista [Nationalist Democratic Action] [Bolivia] [Political party] (PPW) .... ADN
Accion Democratica Popular [Popular Democratic Action] [Costa Rica] [Political party] .... ACP
Accion Democratico Nacional [National Democratic Action] [Aruba] [Political party] (EY) .... ADN
Accion Espanola [Spanish Action] [Political party] (PPE) .... AE
Accion International [An association] (EA) .... ACCION
ACCION International (EA) .... AI
Accion Nacional [National Action] [Spain] [Political party] (PPE) .... AN
Accion Nacional Vasca [Basque National Action] [Spain] [Political party] (PPE) .... ANV
Accion Politica Progresista [Progressive Political Action] [Ecuador] [Political party] (PPW) .... APP
Accion Politica Socialista [Socialist Political Action] [Peru] [Political party] (PPW) .... APS
Accion Popular [Popular Action] [Peru] [Political party] (PPW) .... AP
Accion Popular [Popular Action] [Spain] [Political party] (PPE) .... AP
Accion Revolucionaria Nacional Ecuatoriana [National Revolutionary Action] [Ecuador] [Political party] .... ARNE
Accion Revolucionaria Socialista [Socialist Revolutionary Action] [Peru] [Political party] (PPW) .... ARS
Accion Socialista Revolucionaria [Peru] [Political party] (EY) .... ASR
accismus (SAUS) .... accis
Acclaim (ABBR) .... ACLM
Acclaim Entertainment [NASDAQ symbol] (TTSB) .... AKLM
Acclaim Entertainment, Inc. [Associated Press] (SAG) .... Acclaim
Acclaim Entertainment, Inc. [NASDAQ symbol] (NQ) .... AKLM
Acclamation (ABBR) .... ACLMAN
Acclamation (ABBR) .... ACLMN
Acclamatory (ABBR) .... ACLMY
Acclimate (ABBR) .... ACLIM
Acclimate (ABBR) .... ACLMA
Acclimated (ABBR) .... ACLIMD
Acclimated (ABBR) .... ACLMAD
Acclimating (ABBR) .... ACLIMG
Acclimating (ABBR) .... ACLMAG
Acclimation (ABBR) .... ACLIMN
Acclimatization (ABBR) .... ACLIMZN
Acclimatization (ABBR) .... ACLMATZN
Acclimatization Experiences Institute [Later, IEE] (EA) .... AEI
Acclimatization Experiences Institute (SAUS) .... AEI
Acclimatize (ABBR) .... ACLIMZ
Acclimatize (ABBR) .... ACLMATZ
Acclimatized (ABBR) .... ACLIMZD
Acclimatized (ABBR) .... ACLMATZD
Acclimatizing (ABBR) .... ACLIMZG
Acclimatizing (ABBR) .... ACLMATZG
Accokeek Foundation (EA) .... AF
Accolade (ABBR) .... ACLD
Accom, Inc. [Associated Press] (SAG) .... Accom
Accom, Inc. [NASDAQ symbol] (SAG) .... ACMM
Accomac, VA [FM radio station call letters] .... WVES
Accommodate [or Accommodation] (AFM) .... ACCOM
Accommodate (ABBR) .... ACMD
Accommodated (ABBR) .... ACMDD
Accommodating (ABBR) .... ACMDG
Accommodation .... A
Accommodation .... ACC
Accommodation .... ACCN
Accommodation (ROG) .... ACCOMMODON
Accommodation (ABBR) .... ACMDN
Accommodation Address (LAIN) .... AA
Accommodation and Messenger Service, Admiralty [Obsolete] [British] .... AMS
Accommodation Convergence [Ophthalmology] .... AC

Accommodation Endorsement [Banking]	AE
Accommodation Ladder (SAUS)	AL
Accommodation Sales Authorization (MCD)	ASA
Accommodation Sales Order	ASO
Accommodation Sales Requisition	ASR
Accommodation Service Unit (SAUO)	ASU
Accommodation Weight Investigation (KSC)	AWI
Accommodative (ABBR)	ACMDV
Accommodative Convergence (SAUS)	AC
Accommodative Convergence/ Accommodation (SAUS)	AC/A
Accommodative Convergence to Accommodation ratio (SAUS)	AC/A
Accommodative Convergence/Accommodation (ADWA)	AC/A
Accommodative Insufficiency (SAUS)	AI
Accomodative Convergence/Accomodation (Ratio) [Ophthalmology]	AC/A
Accompagnamento [Accompaniment] [Music]	ACC
Accompanied	ACC
Accompanied (ABBR)	ACMPD
Accompanied (ABBR)	ACMPYD
Accompanied by Adult [British Board of Film Censors]	AA
Accompaniment (WDAA)	acc
Accompaniment [Music]	ACCOM
Accompaniment [Music]	ACCOMP
Accompaniment (ADWA)	accomp
Accompaniment (WGA)	ACCPT
Accompaniment [Music]	ACCT
Accompaniment (ABBR)	ACMPNT
Accompaniment (ABBR)	ACMPT
Accompaniment (ABBR)	ACOMP
Accompaniment ad Libitum [Music]	Accom ad Lib
accompaniment ad libitum (SAUS)	accom ad lib
accompaniment obligato (SAUS)	accom oblto
Accompaniment Obligato [Music]	Accom Oblto
accompanist (SAUS)	acc
Accompanist (ABBR)	ACMPST
Accompany (AFM)	ACCOM
Accompany (ROG)	ACCOY
Accompany (SAUO)	accpy
Accompany (AABC)	ACMP
Accompany (ABBR)	ACMPY
Accompany (ABBR)	ACOMP
Accompany (FAAC)	ACPY
Accompanying (ABBR)	ACMPG
Accompanying Artillery (SAUO)	Ac Arty
Accompanying Battery (SAUO)	Acc Bty
Accompanying Spare Parts Kit [Navy]	ASPK
Accompanying Tanks (SAUO)	Acc Tks
Accomplice [FBI standardized term]	ACCPL
Accomplice (ABBR)	ACMPL
Accomplice (ABBR)	ACMPLS
Accomplish (AFM)	ACCOMP
Accomplish (MUGU)	ACCOMPL
Accomplish (ABBR)	ACMPLH
Accomplish (ABBR)	ACOMP
Accomplishable (ABBR)	ACMPLHB
Accomplishable (ABBR)	ACOMPB
Accomplished (ABBR)	ACMPLHD
Accomplished (ABBR)	ACOMPD
Accomplisher (ABBR)	ACOMPR
Accomplishing (ABBR)	ACOMPG
Accomplishment	ACCMPLSMNT
Accomplishment (ABBR)	ACMPLHNT
Accomplishment (ABBR)	ACOMPT
Accomplishment of Assigned Mission Impeded by Deadline [Army] (AABC)	AAMID
Accomplishment Quotient	AQ
Accomplishment Ratio (ADA)	AR
Accomplishment Utilization Report	AUR
Accomplishment/Cost Procedure	ACP
accord (SAUS)	ac
Accord (DLA)	Acc
Accord (AABC)	ACD
Accord (ABBR)	ACRD
Accord Dangereuse Routier [European agreement on the carriage of dangerous goods by road]	ADR
Accord European Relative au Transport International par Route des Marchandises Dangereuses par Route [European Agreement on the International Transport of Dangerous Goods by Road] (PDAA)	ADR
Accord General sur les Tarifs Douaniers et le Commerce [General Agreement on Tariffs and Trade] [Switzerland] (EAIO)	AGTDC
Accord Transports Permissables [European agreement on the transport of perishable foodstuffs]	ATP
Accordance (ROG)	ACCDCE
Accordance (ROG)	ACCORDCE
Accordance (ABBR)	ACRDNC
Accordance With (MSA)	A/W
Accordant (ABBR)	ACRDT
Accorded (ABBR)	ACRDD
According (ADWA)	acc
According	ACCORD
According (ROG)	ACCORDG
According (ABBR)	ACRDG
According (To)	ACC
according to (SAUS)	acc to
According to the Custom of the Port (SAUS)	ACC/COP
According to Value (EBF)	Ad Val

According to Value (EBF)	A/V
Accordingly (ABBR)	ACRDGY
Accordion [Music]	Accord
Accordion (SAUS)	ACD
Accordion	acn
Accordion Federation of North America (EA)	AFNA
Accordion for All International [An association] (EAIO)	AAI
Accordion Symphony Society (SAUO)	ASS
Accost (ABBR)	ACOS
Accost (ABBR)	ACST
Accosted (ABBR)	ACOSD
Accosting (ABBR)	ACOSG
Account	A
Account	AC
Account (WA)	a/c
Account (EBF)	Acc
Account [Internet language] [Computer science]	acc
Account (EY)	ACC
Account (GEAB)	acco
Account [Banking] (TBD)	Acct
Account (WDMC)	acct
Account [or Accountant] (AFM)	ACCT
Account (ABBR)	ACONT
Account Access Layer [Computer science]	AAL
Account and Risk [Investment term]	A & R
Account and Risk (SAUS)	A&R
Account Balance Pension (WYGK)	ABP
Account Book (DGA)	A/C BK
Account branch (SAUO)	A
Account Card (SAUS)	AC
Account Code (SAUS)	AC
Account Control (AFM)	AC
Account Current [Business term]	A/C
Account Current (ADWA)	a/c
Account Current Company Information System (SAUO)	ACCIS
Account Data List Management (SAUS)	ADLM
Account Directory [Computer science] (OA)	AD
Account Distribution (SAUS)	AD
Account Executive [Advertising, securities]	AE
Account Identification and Description Services [Dun & Bradstreet] (IID)	AIDS
Account Identification and Description Smices (SAUS)	AIDS
Account Identifier [Computer science]	ACCTID
Account Manager Code (TEL)	AMC
Account Mechanical (FAAC)	AMECH
Account Number	AN
Account Number Change File [IRS]	ANCF
Account Number File [Integrated Data Retrieval System] [IRS]	ANF
Account Number Request (ACAE)	ANR
Account Number Update File [IRS]	ANUF
Account Of (ACAE)	AO
account of (SAUS)	a o
Account Of (EBF)	a/o
Account Paid	AP
Account Reconciliation Plan	ARP
Account Resource Management (SAUS)	ARM
Account Resources Manager	ARM
Account Sales (SAUS)	AS
Account Sales (EBF)	as
Account Sales (EBF)	A/S
Account Sales	ASLE
Account Sequence (SAUS)	AS
Account Sheet (SAUS)	AS
Account Stated (SAUS)	AS
Account Traffic [Aviation] (FAAC)	ATFC
Accountability (ABBR)	ACCTBT
Accountability (ABBR)	ACONTBT
Accountability Data Package (MCD)	ADP
Accountability in Data Entry (SAUS)	AIDE
Accountable (ABBR)	ACCTB
Accountable (ABBR)	ACONTB
Accountable Activity	AA
Accountable Area [Environmental science] (EPAT)	AA
Accountable Entertainment Allowance [British]	AEA
Accountable Health Partnership [Medicine]	AHP
Accountable Health Plan [Medicine]	AHP
Accountable Indirect Representational Supplement [British]	AIR
Accountable Inventory Adjustment Document (ACAE)	AIAD
Accountable Property Officer [Military] (AABC)	ACTPO
Accountable Property Officer [Military]	APO
Accountable Strength (AABC)	ACCTSTR
Accountable Strength (SAUS)	ACCT STR
Accountable Supply Distribution Activity (MCD)	ASDA
Accountableness (ABBR)	ACCTBNS
Accountably (ABBR)	ACCTBY
Accountably (ABBR)	ACONTBLY
Accountancy	ACCT
Accountancy	ACCTCY
Accountancy	ACCTNCY
Accountancy (ABBR)	ACCTY
Accountancy (AFM)	ACCY
Accountancy (ABBR)	ACONTNC
Accountancy & Legal Professions Selection Ltd. [British] (ECON)	ALPS
Accountancy Law Reporter [A publication] (DLA)	Accountancy L Rep
Accountant	ACCNT
Accountant (TBD)	Accnt

Accountant (ADWA) ... acct
Accountant (ABBR) ... ACCT
Accountant (DLA) ... ACCTANT
Accountant (ABBR) ... ACCTNT
Accountant (MUGU) ... ACTNT
Accountant (ABBR) ... ACTT
Accountant and Auditor (SAUS) ... Acc&Aud
Accountant Computer Users Technical Exchange (SAUS) ... ACUTE
Accountant General ... AG
Accountant Law Reports [*England*] [*A publication*] (DLA) ... Acct L Rep
Accountant of Courts Clerical Association (SAUO) ... ACCA
Accountant [*or Accounting*] **Officer** ... AO
Accountants and Controllers ... AC
Accountants Association of Iowa (SRA) ... AAI
Accountants Computer Users Technical Exchange (EA) ... ACUTE
Accountants' Fellowship of New South Wales [*Australia*] ... ACFNSW
Accountants for the Public Interest [*Washington, DC*] ... API
Accountants International Study Group [*Later, International Federation of Accountants*] ... AISG
Accountants Joint Parliamentary Committee (SAUO) ... AJPC
Accountant's Resource Network [*Information service or system*] (IID) ... ARNE
Accountants Trial Balance (SAUO) ... ATB
Accounted (ABBR) ... ACCTD
Accounting ... ACCTG
Accounting (DD) ... acctg
Accounting ... ACCTNG
Accounting (ABBR) ... ACONTG
Accounting ... ACTNG
Accounting and Auditing Enforcement Release [*Securities and Exchange Commission*] (EBF) ... AAER
Accounting and Auditing Enforcement Releases (TDOB) ... AAER
Accounting and Auditing Releases (SAUS) ... AAER
Accounting and Budget Distribution System [*Air Force*] ... ABDS
Accounting and Budgetary Control (DNAB) ... ABC
Accounting and Data Processing Abstracts (journ.) (SAUS) ... ADPA
Accounting and Disbursing (MCD) ... A & D
Accounting and Disbursing (MCD) ... AD
Accounting and Disbursing Station Number [*Air Force*] (AFM) ... ADSN
Accounting and Finance (AFIT) ... AAF
Accounting and Finance (AFM) ... A & F
Accounting and Finance (SAUS) ... A&F
Accounting and Finance Office [*or Officer*] ... AFO
Accounting & Finance Office of the Future (SAUS) ... AFOOF
Accounting and Finance Office of the Future (SAUO) ... AFOOF
Accounting and Finance Officer [*Air Force*] ... ACCTG & FINO
Accounting and Financial Management Division [*GAO*] (AAGC) ... AFMD
Accounting and Reporting Management Improvement Program [*Army*] (AABC) ... ARMIP
Accounting Association of Australia and New Zealand (SAUO) ... AAANZ
Accounting Authority Identification Code (SAUS) ... AAIC
Accounting Authority Identification Codes [*Telecommunications*] (OTD) ... AAIC
Accounting Automaton (SAUS) ... AA
Accounting, Budget and Cost System (SAUS) ... ABC
Accounting Calculation (SAUS) ... AC
Accounting Card (SAUS) ... AC
Accounting Careers Council (SAUO) ... ACC
Accounting Careers Council [*Later, AICPA*] ... ACC
Accounting Carriage (SAUS) ... AC
Accounting Classification Code (AFM) ... ACC
Accounting Classification Reference Number (MCD) ... ACRN
Accounting Code Reference Number ... ACRN
Accounting Computer (IAA) ... AC
Accounting Computer System [*Burroughs Corp.*] ... ACSYS
Accounting Control Office (SAUS) ... ACO
Accounting Control System ... ACS
Accounting Control Table (CMD) ... ACT
Accounting Controllers Committee ... ACC
Accounting, Cost, Estimating ... ACE
Accounting Data System ... ADS
Accounting Department Instructions ... ADI
Accounting Detail Card (SAUS) ... ADC
Accounting Firms Associated (NTPA) ... AFAi
Accounting Firms Associated, Inc. (SAUO) ... AFA
Accounting Form (SAUS) ... AF
Accounting Group International (SAUO) ... AGI
Accounting Incomplete Records System [*Software package*] (NCC) ... AIRS
Accounting Information System (BUR) ... AIS
Accounting Line Number (CINC) ... ALN
Accounting Management Information System (SAUS) ... AMIS
Accounting Management System (SAUS) ... AMS
Accounting Master of Business Administration (GAGS) ... AMBA
Accounting Method (SAUS) ... AM
Accounting Operations Office (COE) ... AOO
Accounting Package (SAUS) ... ACCPAC
Accounting Period (SAUS) ... AP
Accounting Point (GFGA) ... AP
Accounting Policy Division (AAGC) ... PACO
Accounting Policy Division (AAGC) ... PAD
Accounting Principles Board [*Later, Financial Accounting Standards Board*] [*American Institute of Certified Public Accountants*] ... APB
Accounting Principles Board Interpretations (SAUO) ... APBI
Accounting Principles Board Opinions (SAUO) ... APBO
Accounting Principles Board Opinions [*A publication*] (DLA) ... APB Op
Accounting Principles Board Statements (SAUO) ... APBS
Accounting Principles Committee (SAUO) ... APC
Accounting Processing Code (AABC) ... APC
Accounting Program [*Association of Independent Colleges and Schools specialization code*] ... AC
Accounting Property Officer ... APO
Accounting Rate of Return (ADA) ... ARR
Accounting Requirements Code [*Military*] (AABC) ... ARC
Accounting Research and Education Centre [*McMaster University*] [*Canada*] [*Research center*] (RCD) ... ARC
Accounting Research Association (SAUO) ... ARA
Accounting Research Board Opinion [*A publication*] (DLA) ... ARB
Accounting Research Bulletin [*A publication*] ... ARB
Accounting Research Centre [*University of Sydney*] [*Australia*] ... ARC
Accounting Research Committee (SAUO) ... ARC
Accounting Research Study ... ARS
Accounting Researchers International Association [*Defunct*] (EA) ... ARIA
Accounting Review [*A publication*] (BRI) ... AR
Accounting Routine (SAUS) ... AR
Accounting Sequence (SAUS) ... AS
Accounting Series Release [*Securities and Exchange Commission*] ... ASR
Accounting Series Releases (TDOB) ... ASR
Accounting Specialist (SAUS) ... acctg sp
Accounting Standards Board [*British*] (ECON) ... ASB
Accounting Standards Committee [*British*] ... ASC
Accounting Standards Executive Committee ... AccSEC
Accounting Standards Executive Committee (TDOB) ... AcSEC
Accounting Standards Executive Committee Statements of Position (SAUO) ... ACC-SOP
Accounting Standards Steering Committee (ODBW) ... ASSC
Accounting Symbol (SAUS) ... AS
Accounting System (SAUS) ... AS
Accounting Systems International World Group [*Consortium of resellers*] (PCM) ... ASI
Accounting Tabulating [*Card*] (AAG) ... AT
Accounting Tabulating Form (AAG) ... ATF
Accounting Technique (SAUS) ... AT
Accounting Terminology Bulletins (SAUS) ... ATB
Accounting Transfer Function (SAUS) ... ATF
Accounting Unit (NATG) ... AU
Accounting Work Order ... AWO
Account-Purchase (ADA) ... A/P
Accounts [*Secondary school course*] [*British*] ... ACCTS
Accounts and Collection Unit Circulars [*A publication*] (DLA) ... A & C Cir
Accounts, Collection, and Taxpayer Service [*Internal Revenue Service*] ... ACTS
Accounts Control Area (AFM) ... ACA
Accounts Department (SAUS) ... AD
Accounts Enquiry Sales and Order Processing (ADA) ... AESOP
Accounts Maintenance [*IRS*] ... AM
Accounts of Chemical Research [*A publication*] (MEC) ... Acc Chem Res
Accounts Office [*Army*] (AABC) ... AO
Accounts Payable (HGAA) ... A/csPay
Accounts Payable ... AP
Accounts Receivable [*Business term*] (MHDB) ... A/C Rec
Accounts Receivable [*Accounting*] ... A/CS REC
Accounts Receivable (ADWA) ... A/cs rec
Accounts Receivable [*Accounting*] ... AR
Accounts Receivable Management System (SAUS) ... ARMS
Accounts Receivable Statement (SAUS) ... ARS
Accounts Register [*Computer science*] ... AR
Accoustic Information Processing System [*Navy*] (DOMA) ... ACIPS
Accoustics (SAUS) ... ACOUS
Accra [*Ghana*] [*Airport symbol*] (OAG) ... ACC
Accra [*Ghana*] [*ICAO location identifier*] (ICLI) ... DGAC
Accra [*Ghana*] [*ICAO location identifier*] (ICLI) ... DGFC
Accra/Kotoka International [*Ghana*] [*ICAO location identifier*] (ICLI) ... DGAA
Accredit (ABBR) ... ACRD
Accredit (ABBR) ... ACRT
Accreditation ... ACCRDTN
Accreditation ... acred
Accreditation and Institutional Eligibility Staff [*Office of Education*] ... AIES
Accreditation Association for Ambulatory Health Care (EA) ... AAAHC
Accreditation Board for Engineering and Technology (EA) ... ABET
Accreditation Council for Accountancy [*Later, ACAT*] (EA) ... ACA
Accreditation Council for Accountancy (SAUO) ... ACA
Accreditation Council for Accountancy and Taxation (EA) ... ACAT
Accreditation Council for Continuing Medical Education (MELL) ... AACME
Accreditation Council for Continuing Medical Education (EA) ... ACCME
Accreditation Council for Facilities for the Mentally Retarded ... ACF-MR
Accreditation Council for Graduate Medical Education [*American Medical Association*] ... ACGME
Accreditation Council for Gynecologic Endoscopy (SAUO) ... ACGE
Accreditation Council for Services for Mentally Retarded and Other Developmentally Disabled Persons [*Later, ACDD*] (EA) ... AC/MRDD
Accreditation Council on Services for People with Developmental Disabilities (EA) ... ACDD
Accreditation Maintenance Report [*Environmental science*] (COE) ... AMR
Accreditation Manual for Ambulatory Health Care (SAUO) ... AMAHC
Accreditation Manual for Hospitals (SAUO) ... AMH
Accreditation Manual for Long Term Care (SAUO) ... AMLTC
Accreditation Manual for Managed Behavioral Health Care (SAUO) ... AMMBHC
Accreditation of Prior Achievement [*Education*] (AIE) ... APA
Accreditation of Prior Learning (AIE) ... APL
Accreditation Program / Ambulatory Health Care (MEDA) ... AP/AHC
Accreditation Program / Home Health Care (MEDA) ... AP/HHC
Accreditation Program / Hospice (MEDA) ... AP/HC
Accreditation Program / Long Term Care [*Medicine*] (MEDA) ... AP/LTC

Accreditation Program / Psychiatric Facilities (MEDA) .... AP/PF
Accreditation Review Committee on Education for Physicians Assistants (EA) .... ARC-PA
Accreditation Review Committee on Education in Surgical Technology [*Formerly, Accreditation Review Committee for Educational Programs in Surgical Technology*] (EA) .... ARC-ST
Accreditation Review Council for Educational Programs in Surgical Technology (HCT) .... ARC-ST
Accreditation Review Team [*Environmental science*] (COE) .... ART
Accredited .... ACCRDTRD
Accredited (EY) .... ACCRED
Accredited (ABBR) .... ACRTD
Accredited Adviser in Insurance .... AAI
Accredited Agents Scheme .... AAS
Accredited Airport Executive [*American Association of Airport Executives*] [*Designation awarded by*] .... AAE
Accredited Appraiser, Canadian Institute .... AACI
Accredited Center [*Youth Training Scheme*] [*British*] (AIE) .... AC
Accredited Clinical Polysomnographer (CMD) .... ACP
Accredited Dosimetry Calibration Laboratories .... ADCL
Accredited Farm Manager [*Designation given by American Society of Farm Managers and Rural Appraisers*] .... AFM
Accredited Financial Examiner [*Society of Financial Examiners*] [*Designation awarded by*] .... AFE
Accredited Financial Examiner (SAUS) .... AFE
Accredited Gemologists Association (EA) .... AGA
Accredited Genealogist (SAUS) .... AG
Accredited Home Newspapers of America [*Later, SNA*] .... AHNA
Accredited in Public Relations [*Canadian Public Relations Society, Inc.*] (DD) .... APR
Accredited Leasing Officer [*Canada*] (DD) .... ALO
Accredited Management Organization [*Institute of Real Estate Management*] [*Designation awarded by*] .... AMO
Accredited Member of the Canadian Public Relations Society (ASC) .... APR
Accredited Off-Campus Instruction .... AOCI
Accredited Pet Cemetary Society .... APCS
Accredited Poultry Breeders Federation (SAUO) .... APBF
Accredited Poultry Breeding Station (SAUS) .... APBS
Accredited Quality Assurance .... AQA
Accredited Record Technician [*American Medical Record Association*] .... ART
Accredited Resident Manager [*Institute of Real Estate Management of the N ational Association of Realtors*] [*Designation awarded by*] .... ARM
Accredited Review Appraisers Council (EA) .... ARAC
Accredited Rural Appraiser [*American Society of Farm Man agers and Rural Appraisers*] [*Designation awarded by*] .... ARA
Accredited Safety Auditor [*International Loss Control Institute*] (SARE) .... ASA
Accredited Standards Committee (AAGC) .... ASC
Accredited Training Centre [*Education*] [*British*] (AIE) .... ATC
Accrediting (ABBR) .... ACRTG
Accrediting and Recording Centralized System (MCD) .... ARCS
Accrediting Association of Bible Colleges [*Later, American Association of BibleColleges*] (EA) .... AABC
Accrediting Bureau of Health Education Schools (EA) .... ABHES
Accrediting Bureau of Medical Laboratory Schools [*Later, ABHES*] .... ABMLS
Accrediting Bureau of Medical Laboratory Schools (SAUS) .... ABMLS
Accrediting Commission for Business Schools (EA) .... ACBS
Accrediting Commission for Continuing Education Training [*National Court Reporters Association*] .... ACCET
Accrediting Commission for Specialized Colleges [*Defunct*] (EA) .... ACSC
Accrediting Commission on Education for Health Services Administration (EA) .... ACEHSA
Accrediting Commission on Education for Health Services Administration (SAUO) .... ACEHSA
Accrediting Council for Continuing Education and Training (NTPA) .... ACCET
Accrediting Council for Independent Colleges and Schools (PGP) .... ACICS
Accrediting Council for Theological Education in Africa [*of the Association of Evangelicals of Africa and Madagascar*] [*See also COHETA*] (EAIO) .... ACTEA
Accrediting Council on Education in Journalism and Mass Communications (EA) .... ACEJMC
Accrediting Council on Education in Journalism and Mass Communications (SAUO) .... ACEJMC
Accrescinto [*Increased*] [*Music*] (ROG) .... ACCRES
Accrete (ABBR) .... ACCR
Accreted (ABBR) .... ACCRD
Accreted Crystaline Anthropoid Homologue .... ACAH
Accreting (ABBR) .... ACCRG
Accretion (ABBR) .... ACCRN
Accretion (ABBR) .... ACRN
Accretion Disk Corona [*Astrophysics*] .... ADC
Accretion-Induced Collapse [*Astrophysics*] .... AIC
Accretion-Induced Rotational Fragmentation [*Astrophysics*] .... ARF
Accretive (ABBR) .... ACCRV
Accretive (ABBR) .... ACRV
Accretive Industrial Development Syndrome [*Real estate phenomenon*] .... AIDS
Accrington Public Library, Accrington, United Kingdom [*Library symbol*] [*Library of Congress*] (LCLS) .... UkAc
Accrual Accounting and Reporting System .... AARS
Accrue [*Banking*] (TBD) .... Accr
Accrue (ABBR) .... ACRU
Accrued (AFM) .... ACCR
Accrued (ADWA) .... accrd
accrued (SAUS) .... acrd
Accrued (ABBR) .... ACRD
Accrued (ABBR) .... ACRUD
Accrued Comprehensive Income (DICI) .... ACI
Accrued Dividend .... AD
Accrued Expenditure [*Accounting*] (AFM) .... AE
Accrued Expenditure Paid [*Accounting*] (AFM) .... AEP
Accrued Expenditure Unpaid [*Accounting*] (AFM) .... AEU
Accrued Interest [*Finance*] (BARN) .... accrd int
Accrued Interest [*Investment term*] .... AI
Accrued Leave [*Military*] .... ACLV
Accrued Liability [*Accounting*] .... AL
Accrued Rights Premium (MARI) .... ARP
Accruement (ABBR) .... ACRUT
Accruing (ABBR) .... ACRUG
Accruing Return Investments [*Business term*] .... ARI
ACCS OSI Library (SAUS) .... AOLib
ACCS Surveillance Exploratory Prototype (SAUS) .... ASEP
Acctex Information Systems (NITA) .... AIS
Accugraph Corp. [*NASDAQ symbol*] (SAG) .... ACCU
Accugraph Corp. [*NASDAQ symbol*] (TTSB) .... ACCUF
Accugraph Corp. [*Associated Press*] (SAG) .... Accugph
Accugraph Corp. [*Associated Press*] (SAG) .... Accugrph
Accugraph Corp. [*Toronto Stock Exchange symbol*] .... ACU
Accumaster Consolidated Workstation [*Computer science*] (TNIG) .... ACW
AccuMed International, Inc. [*Associated Press*] (SAG) .... AccuM
AccuMed International, Inc. [*Associated Press*] (SAG) .... AccuMed
AccuMed International, Inc. [*NASDAQ symbol*] (SAG) .... ACMI
AccuMed Intl. Wrrt [*NASDAQ symbol*] (TTSB) .... ACMIW
Accumulable (ABBR) .... ACUMB
Accumulate (KSC) .... ACCUM
Accumulate (ADWA) .... accum
Accumulate (ABBR) .... ACMLA
Accumulate (ABBR) .... ACUM
Accumulated (ABBR) .... ACMLAD
Accumulated (ABBR) .... ACUMD
Accumulated Adjustments Account (SAUS) .... AAA
Accumulated Alveolar Ventilatory Volume [*Respiratory testing*] (DAVI) .... AAVV
Accumulated Benefit Obligation (TDOB) .... ABO
Accumulated Data Set (SAUS) .... ADS
Accumulated Data Tape (SAUS) .... ACDT
Accumulated Deductible Employee Contributions .... ADEC
Accumulated Dose Special Process (SAUS) .... PKAD
Accumulated Error (SAUS) .... AE
Accumulated Heat Unit (OA) .... AHU
Accumulated Interest [*Banking*] .... AI
Accumulated Leading (DGA) .... ACL
Accumulated Operating Results .... AOR
Accumulated Standardized Data Tape (SAUS) .... ASDT
Accumulated Standardized Data Tape (SAUS) .... ASD Tape
Accumulated Surplus [*Profit margin*] .... AS
Accumulated Total Punching (SAUS) .... ATP
Accumulated Value (SAUS) .... AV
Accumulated Visits (WDAA) .... AV
Accumulating (SAUS) .... ACCG
Accumulating (ABBR) .... ACMLAG
Accumulating (ABBR) .... ACUMG
Accumulating Counter (SAUS) .... AC
Accumulating Reproducer (SAUS) .... AR
Accumulating Shift (SAUS) .... AS
Accumulating Speed (SAUS) .... AS
Accumulation (ROG) .... ACCUMULON
Accumulation (ABBR) .... ACMLAN
Accumulation (ABBR) .... ACUMN
Accumulation and Distributing Unit (SAUS) .... ADU
Accumulation Area Ratio .... AAR
Accumulation Distribution Unit [*Computer science*] .... ADU
Accumulation Factor (DEN) .... AF
Accumulation Mode Charge Injection Device (MCD) .... AMCID
Accumulation Time .... ACT
Accumulations [*Finance*] .... ACCUM
Accumulations (EBF) .... Accum
Accumulative (ABBR) .... ACMLAV
Accumulative (ABBR) .... ACUMV
Accumulative Hours (SAUS) .... Acc Hrs
Accumulative Multiplication (SAUS) .... AM
Accumulative Register (SAUS) .... AR
Accumulator [*Computer science*] (MDG) .... A
Accumulator [*Computer science*] .... AC
Accumulator [*Flowchart*] (MSA) .... ACC
Accumulator [*Computer science*] .... ACCUM
Accumulator (DNAB) .... ACM
Accumulator (ABBR) .... ACMLATR
Accumulator (ABBR) .... ACUMR
Accumulator and Buffer [*Computer science*] (IAA) .... AB
Accumulator Area Communication Controller (SAUS) .... ACC
Accumulator Bit (SAUS) .... AB
Accumulator Buffer Register [*Computer science*] (MHDI) .... ACBR
Accumulator Contents (SAUS) .... AC
Accumulator Gating [*Naval Space Surveillance System*] (DNAB) .... ACCGAT
Accumulator High [*Computer science*] .... AH
Accumulator High-Pressure Air .... AHPA
Accumulator Injection System [*Nuclear energy*] (NRCH) .... AIS
Accumulator Left Shift (SAA) .... ALS
Accumulator Low [*Computer science*] .... AL
Accumulator Makers' Association [*British*] (BI) .... AMA
Accumulator Overflow (SAUS) .... AO
Accumulator Quotient register (SAUS) .... AQ
Accumulator Read Track (SAUS) .... ART

Accumulator Read Truck (SAUS) ... ART
Accumulator Read-In Module (OA) ... ARM
Accumulator Register [*Computer science*] (IAA) ... ACR
Accumulator Register [*Computer science*] ... AR
Accumulator Register [*Computer science*] (IAA) ... AREG
Accumulator Reservoir Manifold Assembly ... ARMA
Accumulator Right Shift (SAA) ... ARS
Accumulator Shift Right (SAUS) ... ASR
Accumulator Sign (SAUS) ... AS
Accumulator Specification (SAUS) ... AS
Accumulator Storage Battery (SAUS) ... ASB
Accumulator Switch [*Computer science*] ... ACS
Accumulator, Temporary ... ACT
Accumulator Track Read (SAUS) ... ATR
Accumulator Track Write (SAUS) ... ATW
Accumulator Volume (SAUS) ... AV
Accumulator/Multiplicand Divisor (SAUS) ... ACC-MD
Accumulator/Reservoir (MCD) ... A/R
Accumulators Shift Right [*Computer science*] (BUR) ... ASR
Accunet Bandwidth Manager (SAUS) ... ABM
Accunet Reserved Digital Service [*AT&T*] (CIST) ... ARDS
Accunet Spectrum of Digital Services [*AT&T*] (CIST) ... ASDS
ACCUPLACER: Computerized Placement Tests (TMMY) ... CPT
Accura Resources [*Vancouver Stock Exchange symbol*] ... ACR
Accuracy (SAUS) ... Acc
Accuracy ... ACCRCY
Accuracy (AFM) ... ACCRY
Accuracy (ABBR) ... ACRCY
Accuracy (ABBR) ... ACURC
Accuracy Check (SAUS) ... AC
Accuracy Control Analysis (ACAE) ... ACA
Accuracy Control Document (NASA) ... ACD
Accuracy Factor (SAUS) ... AF
Accuracy Figure [*British and Canadian*] [*World War II*] ... AF
Accuracy Improvement Program (IUSS) ... AIP
Accuracy in Academia (EA) ... AA
Accuracy in Academia ... AIA
Accuracy in Media (EA) ... AIM
Accuracy Landing (SAUS) ... AL
Accuracy Level Test [*R. Carver*] (TES) ... ALT
Accuracy Limit Factor (SAUS) ... ALF
Accuracy of Fire (SAUS) ... Acc of F
Accuracy of Position (MCD) ... AOP
Accuracy, Reliability, Supportability Improvement Program (SAUS) ... ARSIP
Accurate ... ACCRT
Accurate (GEAB) ... accu
Accurate [*or Accurately*] (MSA) ... ACCUR
Accurate (ABBR) ... ACRA
Accurate (ABBR) ... ACUR
Accurate and Reliable Prototype Earth Sensor Head [*NASA*] ... ARPESH
Accurate, Brief, Clear (WDAA) ... ABC
Accurate Calibration Technology (SAUS) ... ACT
Accurate Graphics (SAUS) ... ACCUGRAF
Accurate Piston Motion (SAUS) ... APM
Accurate Position Finder ... APF
Accurate Position Indicator ... API
Accurate Programming (SAUS) ... AP
Accurate Surgical and Scientific Instruments Corp. (DAVI) ... ASSI
Accurate Tracking (MUGU) ... ACTRAC
Accurate Traffic Volume [*BTS*] (TAG) ... ATV
Accurately (ABBR) ... ACRAY
Accurately (ABBR) ... ACURY
Accurately Defined System [*Computer science*] ... ADS
Accurateness (ABBR) ... ACRANS
Accurateness (ABBR) ... ACURNS
Accuratissime [*Most Carefully*] [*Pharmacy*] (DAVI) ... accur
Accured (SAUS) ... ACCR
Accured (SAUS) ... ACRD
Accured Interest (SAUS) ... AI
Accured Leave (SAUS) ... aclv
Accured Military Pay System (SAUS) ... AMPS
Accursed (ABBR) ... ACRSD
Accursedly (ABBR) ... ACRSDY
Accursedness (ABBR) ... ACRSDNS
Accursius [*Deceased, 1263*] [*Authority cited in pre-1607 legal work*] (DSA) ... A
Accursius [*Deceased, 1263*] [*Authority cited in pre-1607 legal work*] (DSA) ... Ac
Accursius [*Deceased, 1263*] [*Authority cited in pre-1607 legal work*] (DSA) ... Acc
Accursius [*Deceased, 1263*] [*Authority cited in pre-1607 legal work*] (DSA) ... Accur
Accursius [*Deceased, 1263*] [*Authority cited in pre-1607 legal work*] (DSA) ... Acsius
Accursius [*Deceased, 1263*] [*Authority cited in pre-1607 legal work*] (DSA) ... Acu
Accurst (ABBR) ... ACRST
Accusation (ABBR) ... ACUSN
Accusative [*Grammar*] (ROG) ... A
Accusative ... ACC
Accusative (WDAA) ... acc
Accusative (NTIO) ... accus
Accusative ... ACCUS
Accusative (ABBR) ... ACSTV
Accusative (ABBR) ... ACUSV
Accusatorial (ABBR) ... ACUSTL
Accusatory (ABBR) ... ACUSTRY
Accusatory (ABBR) ... ACUSTY
Accuse (ABBR) ... ACUS
Accused (ABBR) ... ACUSD
Accuser (ABBR) ... ACUSR
Accusing (ABBR) ... ACUSG
Accusingly (ABBR) ... ACUSGY
AccuStaff, Inc. [*Associated Press*] (SAG) ... AccuStff
AccuStaff, Inc. [*NYSE symbol*] (SAG) ... ASI
AccuStaff, Inc. [*NASDAQ symbol*] (SAG) ... ASTF
Accustom (ABBR) ... ACSTM
Accustomed (ABBR) ... ACSTMD
Accustoming (ABBR) ... ACSTMG
Ace ... A
Ace Air Cargo Express, Inc. [*ICAO designator*] (FAAC) ... AER
Ace Bandage (HGAA) ... ab
Ace Cash Express [*NASDAQ symbol*] (SAG) ... AACE
Ace Cash Express [*Associated Press*] (SAG) ... AceCsh
ACE [*Allied Command Europe*] **Communication Management Organization** [*NATO*] (NATG) ... ACMO
ACE Communications Security (SAUS) ... ACE COMSEC
ACE Developments [*Vancouver Stock Exchange symbol*] ... AE
ACE [*American Council on Education*] **Fellows Program** (EA) ... AFP
ACE Limited [*NYSE symbol*] (TTSB) ... ACL
ACE Long-term Infrastructure Plan (SAUS) ... ACELIP
ACE Ltd. [*Associated Press*] (SAG) ... ACE Ltd.
ACE Ltd. [*NYSE symbol*] (SPSG) ... ACL
ACE [*Allied Command Europe*] **Mobile Force** [*NATO*] ... AMF
ACE Mobile Force (SAUS) ... AMF
ACE Mobile Force-Air (SAUS) ... AMF-A
ACE Mobile Force-Land (SAUS) ... AMF-L
ACE Operational Telegraph Network (MCD) ... AOTN
ACE Rapid Reaction Corps (SAUO) ... ARRC
ACE Rapid Reaction Force (SAUO) ... ARRF
ACE Reaction Forces Planning Staff (SAUS) ... ARFPS
ACE Target Data Base (MCD) ... ATDB
ACE troposcatter communications system (SAUS) ... ACE High
ACEC Research and Management Foundation (SAUO) ... ACEC/RMF
ACEC [*American Consulting Engineers Council*] **Research and Management Foundation** (EA) ... ACEC/RMF
Aceco Tool Corp. (SAUO) ... Aceco
ACECO/Creusot-Loire/Framatome/ Westinghouse Electric Energy Systems Europe (SAUO) ... ACLE
Acedemic Computing Services Network (SAUS) ... ACSNET
Aceglutamide Aluminum [*Biochemistry*] ... AGA
Aceite [*Acceptance*] [*Portuguese*] [*Business term*] ... A
Acellular Vaccine [*Medicine*] ... ACV
Acentric Chromosome [*Medicine*] (MELL) ... ACC
Aceosteolysis (SAUS) ... AOL
Acepromazine ... ACP
Acer Laboratories, Inc. (SAUO) ... ALI
Acerbity (ABBR) ... ACRBT
Aces [*ICAO designator*] (AD) ... VX
Acess Stored Knowledge via Symbolic Access Method [*Computer science*] (VERA) ... ASKSAM
Acet Cellulose Acetate (SAUS) ... CEL
Acetabulum (MELL) ... A
Acetal (ACAE) ... ACL
Acetaldehyde Dehydrogenase (SAUS) ... AHD
Acetaldehyde Monoperacetate (PDAA) ... AMP
Acetaldehyde Oxime [*Organic chemistry*] ... AAO
(Acetamidol)Aminoethanesulfonic Acid [*A buffer*] ... ACES
(Acetamidol)Iminodiacetic Acid [*A buffer*] ... ADA
Acetamidomethyl (SAUS) ... Acm
Acetaminophen [*Medicine*] (DMAA) ... APAP
acetaminophen (SAUS) ... apap
Acetaminophen (SAUS) ... Tylenol
Acetate (MELL) ... A
Acetate [*Also, ACTT*] [*Organic chemistry*] ... AC
Acetate (SAUS) ... ACE
Acetate (VRA) ... acet
Acetate (ABBR) ... ACTA
Acetate [*Also, AC*] [*Organic chemistry*] (MSA) ... ACTT
Acetate Base Tape (SAUS) ... ABT
Acetate Cloth Tape ... ACT
Acetate Film Tape ... AFT
Acetate Halftone Litho [*Du Pont*] ... AHL
Acetazolamide-Responsive Familial Paroxysmal Ataxia [*Medicine*] (DMAA) ... AREPA
Acetic (ABBR) ... ACE
Acetic Acid [*Organic chemistry*] (MAE) ... AA
Acetic Acid [*Organic chemistry*] (OA) ... AC
Acetic Acid (SAUS) ... HAc
Acetic Acid, Alcohol, Formalin [*Biology*] ... AAF
Acetic Acid Esters of Mono/Diglycerides ... AMG
Acetic Derivation of DDT (SAUS) ... DDA
Acetic-Alcohol-Formalin (SAUS) ... AAF
Acetl (LDT) ... Ac
Aceto Corp. [*NASDAQ symbol*] (NQ) ... ACET
Aceto Corp. [*Associated Press*] (SAG) ... Aceto
Acetoacetanilide [*Organic chemistry*] ... AAA
Acetoacetate Decarboxylase [*An enzyme*] ... AAD
Acetoacetat-Meta-Xylidide (SAUS) ... AAMX
Aceto-Acetic Acid [*Medicine*] (MELL) ... AAA
Acetoacetic Acid [*Biochemistry*] (DAVI) ... AcAcOH
Aceto-Acet-Meta-Xylidid (SAUS) ... AAMX
Acetoacet-m-xylidide [*Organic chemistry*] ... AAMX
Acetoacet-o-anisidide [*Organic chemistry*] ... AAOA
Acetoacet-o-chloroanilide [*Organic chemistry*] ... AAOC

Acetoacet-o-toluidide [*Organic chemistry*] ... AAOT
Acetoacetoxyethyl Methacrylate [*Organic chemistry*] ... AAEM
Acetocoenzyme A Acetyltransferase (DMAA) ... ACAT
Acetohexamide [*Pharmacology*] (DAVI) ... AH
Acetohydroxamic Acid [*Medicine*] (DMAA) ... AHA
Acetohydroxy Acid Synthase (SAUS) ... AHAS
Acetohydroxyacidsynthase [*An enzyme*] ... AHAS
Acetolactate Decarboxylase [*An enzyme*] ... ALDC
Acetolactate Synthase [*An enzyme*] ... ALS
Acetone (MELL) ... ace
Acetone [*Medicine*] ... Acet
Acetone (SAUS) ... ACET
Acetone (ADWA) ... acet
Acetone (ABBR) ... ACTNE
Acetone, Butanol, and Ethanol [*Fermentation products*] ... ABE
Acetone, Butanol and Ethanol (SAUS) ... ABE
Acetone Cyanohydrin [*Organic chemistry*] (PDAA) ... ACH
Acetone Cyanohydrin [*Organic chemistry*] ... ACN
Acetone Cyanohydrin Process (EDCT) ... ACN
Acetone Powder Extract (MAE) ... APE
Acetone Producers Association [*Belgium*] (EAIO) ... APA
Acetone-Dicarboxylic Acid (WDAA) ... ADA
Acetonedicarboxylic Acid (SAUS) ... ADA
Acetone-Extracted Serum (DB) ... AES
Acetone/Water [*Medicine*] (AAMN) ... AC/W
acetonide (SAUS) ... acet
Acetonitrile [*Organic chemistry*] (BABM) ... ACE
Acetonitrile [*Organic chemistry*] ... ACN
Acetonitrile [*Organic chemistry*] ... AN
Acetophenone [*Organic chemistry*] ... ACP
Acetosyringone [*Organic chemistry*] ... AS
Acetoxy [*Biochemistry*] ... AcO
(Acetoxyacetylamino)fluorene [*Organic chemistry*] ... AAAF
Acetoxycycloheximide [*Biochemistry*] ... AXM
Acetoxycyclopentenone [*Organic chemistry*] ... ACP
Acetoxymethyl Ester ... AM
Acetoxy-N-trimethylanilinium Iodide [*Organic chemistry*] ... ANTI
Acetoxypregnenolone [*Pharmacology*] ... AOP
Acetum [*Medicine*] (DMAA) ... A
Acetyl [*As substituent on nucleoside*] [*Biochemistry*] ... ac
Acetyl (SAUS) ... AC
Acetyl Benzoyl Peroxide [*Organic chemistry*] ... ABP
Acetyl Carrier Protein [*Biochemistry*] (DB) ... ACP
Acetyl Coenzyme A [*Biochemistry*] ... AcCoA
Acetyl Coenzyme A (SAUS) ... ACETYL-CO
Acetyl Coenzyme A (MELL) ... ACoA
Acetyl Epsilon Aminocaproic Acid (SAUS) ... AEACA
Acetyl Esterase (DB) ... Acest
Acetyl Ethyl Tetramethyl Tetralin [*Musk fragrance, neuro-toxic compound*] ... AETT
Acetyl Levo-Carnitine Chloride [*Biochemistry*] ... ALCC
Acetyl Salicylic Acid (SAUS) ... ASA
Acetyl Tributylcitrate [*Organic chemistry*] ... ATBC
Acetyl Xylan Esterase [*An enzyme*] ... AXE
Acetylacetonate [*Organic chemistry*] ... Acac
Acetyl-Acetonate (SAUS) ... ACAC
Acetylacetone [*Organic chemistry*] ... ACAC
Acetylacrolein [*Organic chemistry*] ... AA
(Acetylalanyl)histidine Aluminum [*Biochemistry*] ... AAHA
Acetyl(alanyl)phenylalanylchloromethyl Ketone [*Biochemistry*] ... AAPCK
Acetylaminobiphenyl [*Biochemistry*] (OA) ... AABP
Acetylaminofluorene [*Also, AcAF, AcNHFln, FAA*] [*Organic chemistry*] ... AAF
Acetylaminofluorene [*Also, AAF, AcNHFln, FAA*] [*Organic chemistry*] ... AcAF
Acetylaminofluorene [*Also, AAF, AcAF, FAA*] [*Organic chemistry*] ... AcNHFln
acetylaminofluorine (SAUS) ... aaf
Acetylamino(formylamino)methyluracil [*Biochemistry*] ... AFMU
Acetylarginine Methyl Ester [*Biochemistry*] (AAMN) ... AAME
Acetylated Low-Density Lipoprotein [*Biochemistry*] ... AcLDL
Acetylbutyrolactone [*Organic chemistry*] ... ABL
Acetylchlorine (DIPS) ... Ach
Acetylcholine [*Biochemistry*] (IIA) ... AC
Acetylcholine [*Biochemistry*] (AAMN) ... AcCh
Acetylcholine [*Biochemistry*] ... ACh
Acetylcholine ... ACH
Acetylcholine (WDAA) ... ACL
Acetylcholine Mustard (SAUS) ... AChM
Acetylcholine Receptor [*Also, AChR*] [*Biochemistry*] ... AcChR
Acetylcholine Receptor [*Also, AcChR*] [*Biochemistry*] ... AChR
Acetyl-Choline Receptor (SAUS) ... AChR
Acetylcholine Receptor [*Medicine*] (MELL) ... ACR
Acetylcholine Receptor Antibody [*Immunology*] ... AChRAb
Acetylcholine Receptor-Inducing Activity [*Biochemistry*] ... ARIA
Acetylcholinesterase [*An enzyme*] (MAE) ... AcCHS
Acetylcholinesterase [*An enzyme*] (PDAA) ... ACH
Acetylcholinesterase [*An enzyme*] (OA) ... AChE
Acetylcholinesterase (SAUS) ... AchE
Acetyl-CoA Carboxylase [*An enzyme*] ... ACC
Acetyl-CoA Carboxylase [*An enzyme*] ... ACCase
Acetylcoenzyme A [*Biochemistry*] (DAVI) ... acetyl-CoA
Acetylcysteine [*Biochemistry*] (AAMN) ... AC
Acetylcysteine [*Biochemistry*] ... ACC
Acetyle Tetrabromide (SAUS) ... ATB
Acetylene (MSA) ... ACET
Acetylene (ABBR) ... ACETL
Acetylene (ABBR) ... ACTYLN
Acetylene Reduction Activity (DB) ... ARA
Acetylene Reduction Assay [*Botany*] ... ARA
Acetylene-Terminated Bisphel [*Organic chemistry*] ... ATB
Acetylene-Terminated Imide [*Polymer technology*] ... ATI
Acetylene-Terminated Phenylquinoxaline [*Polymer technology*] ... ATPQ
Acetylene-Terminated Sulfone [*Organic chemistry*] ... ATS
Acetyl-Glyceryl-Ether Phosphoryl-choline (SAUS) ... AGEPC
(Acetylglycyl)lysine Methyl Ester Acetate [*Biochemistry*] ... AGLME
Acetylhomocysteinethiolactone [*Citiolone*] [*Organic chemistry*] ... AHCTL
Acetyl-L-Tyrosine Ethyl Ester [*Biochemistry*] (MAE) ... ALTEE
Acetyllysine Methyl Ester [*Biochemistry*] ... ALME
acetyl-lysine methyl ester (SAUS) ... alme
Acetylneuraminic Acid [*Also, NAN, NANA*] [*Biochemistry*] ... AcNeu
Acetylneuraminic Acid [*Biochemistry*] (MAE) ... ANA
Acetyl-para-aminophenol [*Pharmacology*] ... APAP
Acetyl-Phenyl-Alanyl-Tyrosine (SAUS) ... APAT
Acetylphenylhydrazine (SAUS) ... APH
Acetyl(p-nitrophenyl)sulfanilamide [*Pharmacology*] ... APNPS
Acetylpyridineadenine Dinucleotide [*Biochemistry*] ... APAD
Acetylsalicylic Acid [*Aspirin*] ... ASA
Acetylsalicylic Acid [*Aspirin*], **Phenacetin, and Caffeine Compound** [*Slang translation is, "All Purpose Capsules"*] [*Pharmacy*] ... APC
Acetylselenocholine (SAUS) ... ASECH
Acetylstrophanthidin [*Organic chemistry*] ... ACS
Acetylstrophanthidin [*Organic chemistry*] (MAE) ... AS
Acetylsulfanilyl Chloride [*Organic chemistry*] ... ASC
Acetyl-Thiocholine Iodide (SAUS) ... AThChI
Acetyltyrosine Ethyl Ester [*Biochemistry*] ... ATEE
Acetyltyrosine Hydrazide (MAE) ... ATH
ACF Industries, Inc., Albuquerque, NM [*Library symbol*] [*Library of Congress*] (LCLS) ... NmAACF
ACFOT Coordinating Team (SAUO) ... ACT
Achaete-Scute Homologue [*Genetics*] ... ASH
Achaguas, Apure [*Venezuela*] [*ICAO location identifier*] (ICLI) ... SVCH
Achard-Thiers [*Syndrome*] [*Medicine*] (DB) ... AT
Achard-Thiers Syndrome [*Medicine*] (DMAA) ... ATS
Acharnenses [*Acharnians*] [*of Aristophanes*] [*Classical studies*] (OCD) ... Ach
Achates Resources Ltd. [*Vancouver Stock Exchange symbol*] ... ATR
Ached (ABBR) ... ACHD
Achenbach Child Behavior Checklist (EDAC) ... ACBC
Acheron Resources Ltd. [*Vancouver Stock Exchange symbol*] ... ACZ
Aches (ABBR) ... ACHS
Achiasaph (BJA) ... Ach
Achievable (ABBR) ... ACHVB
Achievable Benefit Achieved ... ABA
Achievable Benefit Not Achieved ... ABNA
Achievable Data Rate (MCD) ... ADR
Achieve (ABBR) ... ACHV
Achieve (ABBR) ... ACHVE
Achieve Successful Performance. Intensify Reliability Effort (SAUS) ... ASPIRE
Achieved (ABBR) ... ACHVD
Achieved Availability (MCD) ... AA
Achievement (ABBR) ... ACHIEV
Achievement (ADWA) ... achiev
Achievement (SAUS) ... Achiev
Achievement (SAUS) ... Achvit
Achievement ... ACHVIT
Achievement ... ACHVMNT
Achievement (ABBR) ... ACHVNT
Achievement (ABBR) ... ACHVT
Achievement Age [*Psychology*] ... AA
Achievement Anxiety Scale [*Psychology*] ... AAS
Achievement Anxiety Test (SAUS) ... AAT
Achievement Anxiety Text [*Psychology*] (EDAC) ... AAT
Achievement Drive [*Psychology*] (AAMN) ... AD
Achievement Identification Measure [*Educational test*] ... AIM
Achievement Identification Measure-Teacher Observation [*Test*] [*Sylvia B. Rimm*] (TES) ... AIM-TO
Achievement Motivation (MELL) ... AM
Achievement of Test Readiness (SAUS) ... ATR
Achievement Orientation [*Psychology*] (AAMN) ... AO
Achievement Quotient ... AQ
Achievement Ratio ... AR
Achievement Regards for College Scientists (SAUS) ... ARCS
Achievement Rewards for College Scientists [*Foundation*] ... ARCS
Achievement Test ... AT
Achievement Test for Accounting Graduates (TMMY) ... ATAG
Achievement through Counselling and Treatment ... ACT
Achievement via Independence (SAUS) ... AI
Achiever (ABBR) ... ACHVR
Achieving (ABBR) ... ACHVG
Achieving Behavioral Competencies [*Test*] (TMMY) ... ABC
Achieving the Competitive Edge (ABAC) ... ACE
Achilleis [*of Statius*] [*Classical studies*] (OCD) ... Achil
Achilles Heel Cleavage (DOG) ... AHC
Achilles Resources [*Vancouver Stock Exchange symbol*] ... ACL
Achilles Tectonic Exhibit ... ATE
Achilles Tendon [*Anatomy*] ... AT
Achilles Tendon Inflammation [*Medicine*] (MELL) ... ATI
Achilles Tendon Lengthening [*Medicine*] ... ATL
Achilles Tendon Reflex [*Neurology*] ... ATR
Achilles Tendon Reflex; atrophy (SAUS) ... ATR
Achilles Tendon Reflex Test [*Neurology and orthopedics*] (DAVI) ... ART
Achilles Track Club (EA) ... ATC
Achillobursitis [*Medicine*] (MELL) ... AB
Aching (ABBR) ... ACHG

Acholi [*MARC language code*] [*Library of Congress*] (LCCP) .... ach
Achondroplasia [*Medicine*] .... ACH
Achondroplasia [*Medicine*] (MELL) .... ACP
Achromatic (ABBR) .... ACHR
Achromatic (ABBR) .... ACHRMTK
Achromatic Color Removal (DGA) .... ACR
Achromatically (ABBR) .... ACHRY
Achromaticity (ABBR) .... ACHRT
Achromatism (ABBR) .... ACHRM
Achromatism (ABBR) .... ACHROM
Achromatism (SAUS) .... Achrom
Achutupo [*Panama*] [*Airport symbol*] (OAG) .... ACU
ACI Telecentrics, Inc. [*NASDAQ symbol*] (SAG) .... ACIT
ACI Telecentrics, Inc. [*Associated Press*] (SAG) .... ACI TIcn
acicular (SAUS) .... acic
Acicular (ABBR) .... ACIC
Acid [*or Acidity*] .... A
Acid (AAMN) .... AC
Acid [*Pharmacy*] (ROG) .... ACI
Acid Addition System (SAUS) .... AAS
Acid and Alkaline (MELL) .... A&A
Acid and Base Washed and Silanized (SAA) .... ABS
Acid and Neutral (SAUS) .... A/N
Acid Base Characteristics Phototropism (ACAE) .... ABCP
Acid Bismuth Yeast [*Agar*] (MAE) .... ABY
Acid Calcium Phosphate (WDAA) .... ACP
Acid Cholesteryl Ester Hydrolase [*An enzyme*] .... ACEH
Acid Citrate Dextrose (SAUS) .... ACD
Acid Concentrator (SAUS) .... AC
Acid Concentrator Feed [*Nuclear energy*] (NRCH) .... ACF
Acid Copper Chromate [*Wood preservative*] .... ACC
Acid Degree Value [*Food technology*] .... ADV
Acid Deposition and Atmospheric Research Division [*Environmental Protection Agency*] (GFGAG) .... ADARD
Acid Deposition and Oxidant Model [*for acid rain*] [*Canada and Federal Republic of Germany*] .... ADOM
Acid Deposition Assessment Staff [*Environmental Protection Agency*] (GFGA) .... ADAS
Acid Deposition Control Program [*Environmental science*] (COE) .... ADCP
Acid Deposition Data Network [*Environmental Protection Agency*] (CARB) .... ADDNET
Acid Deposition Modeling Project (SAUS) .... ADMP
Acid Deposition Planning Staff [*Environmental Protection Agency*] (GFGA) .... ADPS
Acid Deposition Report [*Environmental science*] (COE) .... ADR
Acid Deposition System [*EPA*] (AUEG) .... ADS
Acid Deposition System Database (SAUS) .... ADS
Acid Detergent Fiber Nitrogen [*Organic chemistry*] (DICI) .... ADF-N
Acid Detergent Fiber (or Fibre) (SAUS) .... ADF
Acid Dew Point .... ADP
Acid Dip (SAUS) .... A/DP
Acid Equivalent (GNE) .... AE
Acid Fractionator Distillate (GFGA) .... AFD
Acid Fractionator Off-Gas [*Nuclear energy*] (NRCH) .... AOG
Acid Fractionator Recycle [*Nuclear energy*] (NRCH) .... AFR
Acid Gas Removal System [*Chemical engineering*] .... AGRS
Acid Generator [*Chemistry*] .... AG
Acid Glycoprotein [*Biochemistry*] .... AGP
Acid Hematine (SAUS) .... AH
Acid Ionization Constant [*Physics*] (DAVI) .... K_a
Acid Laboratory (SAUS) .... A-Lab
Acid Maltase Deficiency (DB) .... AMD
Acid Mine Drainage [*Mining technology*] .... AMD
Acid Mucopolysaccharide [*Biochemistry*] .... AMP
Acid Mucopolysaccharide [*Biochemistry*] .... AMPS
Acid Number [*Chemistry*] .... AN
Acid Open Hearth (PDAA) .... AOH
Acid Output [*Physiology*] .... AO
Acid Perfusion Test [*Medicine*] (MELL) .... APT
Acid Phosphatase (MELL) .... acid p'tase
Acid Phosphatase [*Also, ACPH, AP*] [*An enzyme*] .... ACP
Acid Phosphatase [*Also, ACP, AP*] [*An enzyme*] .... ACPH
Acid Phosphatase (MELL) .... AcPh
Acid Phosphatase [*An enzyme*] (CPH) .... ac phos
Acid Phosphatase [*Also, ACP, ACPH*] [*An enzyme*] .... AP
Acid Phosphatase Prostatic Fluid [*Biochemistry*] (DAVI) .... ACPP PF
Acid Phosphatase Test [*Medicine*] (MELL) .... APT
Acid Phosphatase Test for Semen [*Medicine*] (MELL) .... APTS
Acid Phosphatase with Tartrate [*Clinical chemistry*] .... ACPT
Acid Precipitable Material (SAUS) .... APM
Acid Precipitation Act of 1980 (COE) .... APA
Acid Precipitation Experiment .... APEX
Acid Precipitation Mitigation Program (SAUS) .... APMP
Acid Precipitation Research Program [*Environmental science*] (COE) .... APRP
Acid Precipitation Task Force [*Environmental science*] (COE) .... APTF
Acid Rain Advisory Committee [*Environmental Protection Agency*] (EPAT) .... ARAC
[*The*] Acid Rain Foundation (EA) .... TARF
Acid Rain Information Centre (SAUO) .... ARIC
Acid Rain Information Clearinghouse (GNE) .... ARIC
Acid Rain Information System (SAUS) .... ARIS
Acid Rain Mitigation Strategies .... ARMS
Acid Rain National Early Warning Systems (EPAT) .... ARNEWS
Acid Rain Policy Office [*Environmental Protection Agency*] (GFGA) .... ARPO
Acid Rain Research Program [*Environmental Protection Agency*] (GFGA) ..... ARRP

Acid Reflux Test [*Medicine*] (MELL) .... ART
Acid Resistant Cement .... ARC
Acid Resisting [*Technical drawings*] .... AR
Acid Rock Draining [*Mining technology*] .... ARD
Acid Rutile (SAUS) .... AR
Acid Scrubber (EEVL) .... ACS
Acid Test Solution (DB) .... ATS
Acid Value [*Chemistry*] .... AV
Acid Waste .... AW
Acid-Ash Diet [*Medicine*] (MELL) .... AAD
Acid-Balance Control [*Biochemistry*] (DB) .... ABC
Acid/Base [*Ratio*] (AAMN) .... A/B
Acid-Base Balance [*Medicine*] (MELL) .... ABB
Acid/Base Electrolyte [*Disorder diagnosed by an experimental medical system of the same name*] .... ABEL
Acid/Base Electrolyte Disorders (MHDB) .... ABED
Acid-Citrate-Dextrose [*Hematology*] .... ACD
Acid-Detergent Fiber [*Food analysis*] .... ADF
Acid-Detergent Lignin [*Food analysis*] .... ADL
Acid-Detergent Residue [*Food analysis*] .... ADR
Acide Nucleique [*French*] [*Medicine*] .... AN
Acid-Fast [*Microbiology*] .... AF
Acid-Fast Bacillus [*Microbiology*] .... AFB
Acid-Fast Culture [*Biochemistry*] (DAVI) .... ACF
Acid-Fast Smear [*Biochemistry*] (DAVI) .... AFS
Acidic and Neutral [*Chemical analysis*] .... A/N
Acidic Fibroblast Growth Factor [*Biochemistry*] .... AFGF
Acidic Glycoaminoglycan [*Biochemistry*] .... AGAG
Acidic Gneisses and Schists [*Agronomy*] .... AC GN SCH
Acidic Proline-Rich Protein [*Medicine*] (DMAA) .... APRP
Acidification Chemistry Information Data Base (SAUS) .... ACID
Acidified Boiling Water (SAUS) .... ABW
Acidified Glycerol Lysis Test [*Clinical chemistry*] .... AGLT
Acidified Potato-Dextrose Agar [*Microbiology*] .... APDA
Acid-Insoluble Residue .... AIR
Acidity Index, Bohreiskerne (SAUS) .... AI
Acidity Oxidation Potential [*Chemistry*] .... AOP
Acidium tranexamicum (SAUS) .... AMCHA
Acid-Loading Test [*Medicine*] (MELL) .... ALT
Acid-Modified Flour (OA) .... AMF
Acid-Neutralizing Capacity [*Chemistry*] .... ANC
Acidophil [*Medicine*] (DMAA) .... A
acidosis (SAUS) .... acid
Acid-Precipitable Globulin [*Clinical chemistry*] .... APG
Acid-Precipitable Material [*Antiviral agent*] .... APM
Acid-Precipitated Protein [*Food analysis*] .... APP
Acid-Prepared Mesostructure [*Inorganic chemistry*] .... APM
Acidproof .... AP
Acidproof Cement Manufacturers Association [*Defunct*] (EA) .... ACMA
Acidproof Floor [*Technical drawings*] .... APF
Acid-Rinsing Solution [*Clinical chemistry*] .... ARS
Acid-Saline Giemsa (SAUS) .... ASG
Acid-Soluble Collagen [*Biochemistry*] .... ASC
Acid-Soluble Oil [*Petroleum refining*] .... ASO
acidulated drop (SAUS) .... acid
Acidulated Phosphofluoride .... APF
Acidus [*Acid*] [*Latin*] (ROG) .... AC
Acidus [*Acid*] [*Latin*] (ROG) .... ACID
Acid-Volatile Sulfide [*Chemistry*] .... AVS
Acier Haut Resistance [*Bicycling*] (DICI) .... AHR
Acinetobacter Calcoaceticus Varanitratus [*Microbiology*] .... ACV
Acinic Cell Carcinoma [*Medicine*] .... ACC
Aciodistoincisal [*Medicine*] (MEDA) .... ADI
Acis of Andrew (SAUS) .... ActAndr
Aciual Measurement Weight (SAUS) .... AMW
Ack [*Phonetic alphabet*] [*Pre-World War II*] (DSUE) .... A
Ackerley Communications [*AMEX symbol*] (TTSB) .... AK
Ackerley Communications, Inc. [*Associated Press*] (SAG) .... AckCom
Ackerley Communications, Inc. [*AMEX symbol*] (SPSG) .... AK
Ackerley Group [*Associated Press*] (SAG) .... AckGrp
Ackerley Group [*NYSE symbol*] (SG) .... AK
Ackerman Computer Sciences (SAUS) .... ACS
Ackerman Institute for Family Therapy (EA) .... AIFT
Ackerman, MS [*FM radio station call letters*] .... WFCA
Acklands Ltd. [*Toronto Stock Exchange symbol*] .... ACK
Ackley Public Library, Ackley, IA [*Library symbol*] [*Library of Congress*] (LCLS) .... IaAc
Acknoledgment Signal Unit (SAUS) .... ASU
Acknowledge (ADWA) .... ack
Acknowledge (AFM) .... ACK
Acknowledge .... ACKNE
Acknowledge (ABBR) .... ACNWLG
Acknowledge character (SAUS) .... ACK
Acknowledge Control (IAA) .... ACC
Acknowledge Enable [*Computer science*] (IAA) .... ACE
Acknowledge Hold [*Computer science*] (IAA) .... ACH
Acknowledge Input [*Computer science*] (IAA) .... ACKI
Acknowledge Output [*Computer science*] (IAA) .... ACKO
Acknowledge Receipt Of [*Telecommunications*] (TEL) .... AKRO
Acknowledgeable (ABBR) .... ACKB
Acknowledgeable (ABBR) .... ACNWLGB
Acknowledged [*Business term*] (EBF) .... ack
Acknowledged (SAUS) .... ACK
Acknowledged (GEAB) .... ackd
Acknowledged [*Business term*] .... ACK'D

Acknowledged [Business term] (EBF) .... ackn
Acknowledged (ABBR) .... ACNWLGD
Acknowledged (ROG) .... AKGD
Acknowledged Information Transfer Service [Telecommunications]
(ACRL) .... AITS
Acknowledged Sequence Number (SAUS) .... ASN
Acknowledgement (WDMC) .... ack
Acknowledgement [Telecommunications] (OSI) .... ACK
Acknowledgement (WDMC) .... ackl
Acknowledgement (DLA) .... ACKNOWL
Acknowledgement (SAUS) .... ACKO
Acknowledgement Code [Computer science] (IGQR) .... ACK
Acknowledgement Due (SAUS) .... AD
Acknowledgement flag (SAUS) .... ACK
Acknowledgement of Debt (SAUS) .... AOD
Acknowledgement Signal Unit [Telecommunications] (TEL) .... ASU
Acknowledgement Unit [Telecommunications] (TEL) .... ACU
Acknowledger (ABBR) .... ACNWLGR
Acknowledging (ABBR) .... ACKG
Acknowledging (ABBR) .... ACNWLGG
Acknowledging Switch (SAUS) .... AS
Acknowledgment [Business term] (EBF) .... Ackgt
Acknowledgment .... ACKGT
Acknowledgment (ROG) .... ACKNT
Acknowledgment (ABBR) .... ACKT
Acknowledgment (ABBR) .... ACNWLGNT
Acknowledgment Character [Keyboard] [Computer science] .... ACK
Acknowledgment Due .... AD
Acknowledgment of Receipt [Message handling] [Telecommunications] .... AR
Acknowledgment of Receipt [Message handling] [Telecommunications] .... R
ACLANT [Allied Command, Atlantic] Planning Guidance [NATO] .... APG
Aclara BioSciences [NASDAQ symbol] (SG) .... ACLA
Aclinomycin-C (SAUS) .... Act-C
ACM Government Income Fund [NYSE symbol] (SPSG) .... ACG
ACM Government Income Fund, Inc. [Associated Press] (SAG) .... ACMIn
ACM Government Opportunity Fund [NYSE symbol] (SAG) .... ACF
ACM Government Opportunity Fund, Inc. [Associated Press] (SAG) .... ACM Op
ACM Government Opportunity Fund, Inc. [NYSE symbol] (CTT) .... AOF
ACM Government Securities [NYSE symbol] (SPSG) .... GSF
ACM Government Securities Fund, Inc. [Associated Press] (SAG) .... ACM Sc
ACM Government Spectrum Fund [NYSE symbol] (SPSG) .... SI
ACM Government Spectrum Fund, Inc. [Associated Press] (SAG) .... ACMSp
ACM Gvt Income Fund [NYSE symbol] (TTSB) .... ACG
ACM Gvt Opportunity Fd [NYSE symbol] (TTSB) .... AOE
ACM Gvt Securities [NYSE symbol] (TTSB) .... GSF
ACM Gvt Spectrum Fund [NYSE symbol] (TTSB) .... SI
ACM Managed Dollar Income [NYSE symbol] (TTSB) .... ADF
ACM Managed Dollar Income Fund [NYSE symbol] (SPSG) .... ADF
ACM Managed Dollar Income Fund, Inc. [Associated Press] (SAG) .... ACMMD
ACM Managed Income Fund [NYSE symbol] (TTSB) .... AMF
ACM Managed Income Fund, Inc. [Associated Press] (SAG) .... ACM MI
ACM Managed Income Fund, Inc. [NYSE symbol] (CTT) .... AMF
ACM Muni Securities Income [NYSE symbol] (TTSB) .... AMU
ACM Municipal Securities Income [Associated Press] (SAG) .... ACMMu
ACM [Association for Computing Machinery] Municipal Securities Income
[NYSE symbol] (SPSG) .... AMU
ACM [Association for Computing Machinery] Standards Committee .... ACMSC
ACMAT Corp. [NASDAQ symbol] (NQ) .... ACMT
ACMAT Corp'A' [NASDAQ symbol] (TTSB) .... ACMTA
ACMD [Advanced Concepts and Missions Division] Combined Control and
EnergyStorage System (SSD) .... ACCESS
Acme [Spain] [ICAO designator] (FAAC) .... AKM
Acme Aviation Ltd. [British] [ICAO designator] (FAAC) .... ADP
Acme Electric [NYSE symbol] (TTSB) .... ACE
Acme Electric Corp. [NYSE symbol] (SPSG) .... ACE
Acme Electric Corp. [Associated Press] (SAG) .... AcmeE
Acme Metals [NASDAQ symbol] (SAG) .... ACME
Acme Metals [Associated Press] (SAG) .... AcmeMet
Acme Metals [Associated Press] (SAG) .... AcmeMt
Acme Metals [NYSE symbol] (SAG) .... AMI
Acme Municipal Library, Acme, AB, Canada [Library symbol] [Library of
Congress] (LCLS) .... CaAAM
Acme Municipal Library, Alberta [Library symbol] [National Library of
Canada] (NLC) .... AAM
Acme Screw Thread (SAUS) .... ACME
Acme Steel Co., Chicago, IL [Library symbol] [Library of Congress] (LCLS) .... ICAS
Acme Steel Co., Chicago, IL [Library symbol] [Library of Congress]
(LCLS) .... ICASC
Acme Steel Company (SAUO) .... ACO
Acme United [AMEX symbol] (TTSB) .... ACU
Acme United Corp. [Associated Press] (SAG) .... AcmeU
Acme United Corp. [AMEX symbol] (SPSG) .... ACU
Acme Zone (SAUS) .... AZ
Acme-Cleveland [NYSE symbol] (TTSB) .... AMT
Acme-Cleveland Corp. [Associated Press] (SAG) .... AcmeC
Acme-Cleveland Corp. [NYSE symbol] (SPSG) .... AMT
Acmite [CIPW classification] [Geology] .... ac
Acne (MELL) .... A
Acne Neonatorum [Medicine] (DMAA) .... AN
Acne Research Institute (EA) .... ARI
Acne Rosacea [Medicine] (MELL) .... AR
Acne Vulgaris [Medicine] (MELL) .... AV
ACNielsen Corp. [NYSE symbol] (SAG) .... ART
ACOA [Administrative and Clerical Officers Association] Journal
[A publication] .... ACOA Jl

Acolyte (ABBR) .... ACLYT
Acomb Reunion (EA) .... AR
Acompanying Sound Trap (SAUO) .... AST
Aconcagua (SAUS) .... Acon
Aconite, Belladonna and Chloroform (SAUS) .... ABC
Aconite, Belladonna, and Chloroform [Liniment compound] .... ABC
Acordia, Inc. [NYSE symbol] (SPSG) .... ACO
Acordia, Inc. [Associated Press] (SAG) .... Acordia
Acorn Fund [Mutual fund ticker symbol] .... ACRNX
Acorn Interactive System [Videodisc control system] (NITA) .... AIS
Acorn International Fund [Mutual fund ticker symbol] (SG) .... ACINX
Acorn Library District, Oak Forest, IL [Library symbol] [Library of Congress]
(LCLS) .... IOf
Acorn Resources Ltd. [Vancouver Stock Exchange symbol] .... ARN
Acorn RISC Machine [Acorn Computers] [Reduced instruction set computer]
(NITA) .... ARM
Acorn Venture Cap [NASDAQ symbol] (TTSB) .... AVCC
Acorn Venture Capital Corp. [Associated Press] (SAG) .... AcrnVn
Acorn Venture Capital Corp. [NASDAQ symbol] (NQ) .... AVCC
Acoustic (IAA) .... A
Acoustic (IUSS) .... ACC
Acoustic [or Acoustical] (KSC) .... ACOUS
Acoustic (ABBR) .... ACOUST
Acoustic (MSA) .... ACST
Acoustic (ADWA) .... acst
Acoustic .... ACSTC
Acoustic Add-on Unit (SAUS) .... AAU
Acoustic Add-On Unit (MCD) .... AAU
Acoustic Analysis Memo (SAUS) .... AAM
Acoustic Artillery Location System (DNAB) .... AALS
Acoustic Artillery Observer Subsystem (SAUS) .... AAOS
Acoustic Backscatter Probes (SAUS) .... ABP
Acoustic Beacon Ranging and Location (PDAA) .... ABRALOC
Acoustic Bullet Detector [Military] (VNW) .... ABD
Acoustic Charge Transport [Computer science] .... ACT
Acoustic Charge Transport Device (ACAE) .... ACTD
Acoustic Charged Transport Electronic Warfare (SAUS) .... ACTEW
Acoustic Comfort Index .... ACI
Acoustic Communication Program .... ACP
Acoustic Computer Signal (SAUS) .... ACS
Acoustic Containerless Experiment System [Materials processing] .... ACES
Acoustic Containerless Processing Facility .... ACPF
Acoustic Containerless Processing Module (MCD) .... ACPM
Acoustic Control (NVT) .... ACCON
Acoustic Control and Telemetry System .... ACTS
Acoustic Control Induction System [Automotive engineering] .... ACIS
Acoustic Corporation of America (SAUO) .... ACA
Acoustic Correlation and Detection System .... ACCORDS
Acoustic Counter-Countermeasures [Navy] (NG) .... ACCM
Acoustic Countermeasures [Navy] (NG) .... ACM
Acoustic Coupler [Computer MODEM] .... AC
Acoustic Data Analysis Center .... ADAC
Acoustic Data Base Management System (IUSS) .... ADBMS
Acoustic Data Base System (IUSS) .... ADBSS
Acoustic Data Capsule [Oceanography] (MSC) .... ACODAC
Acoustic Data Processor (MCD) .... ADP
Acoustic Data Reduction Program (CAAL) .... ADRP
Acoustic Data Relay (IUSS) .... ADR
Acoustic Data Vessel Identification, Classification & Explanation
(SAUS) .... ADVICE
Acoustic Database (IUSS) .... ADB
Acoustic Deception Device (CAAL) .... ADD
Acoustic Decoupler (DNAB) .... AD
Acoustic Delay Line .... ADL
Acoustic Depth Finder .... ADF
Acoustic Detection and Ranging [Geophysics] .... ACDAR
Acoustic Detection Device (MCD) .... ADD
Acoustic Detection Range Prediction Model (MCD) .... ADRPM
Acoustic Detection System (SAUS) .... ADS
Acoustic Device, Countermeasure (CAAL) .... ADC
Acoustic Digital Memory .... ADM
Acoustic Dimension Compiler (SAUS) .... ADC
Acoustic Directed Energy Pulse Train (BARN) .... ADEPT
Acoustic Discrimination of Decoys .... ADD
Acoustic Display Console (IUSS) .... ADC
Acoustic Distribution Box (CAAL) .... ADB
Acoustic Doppler Current Profiler [Oceanography] .... ADCP
Acoustic Doppler Profilers (SAUS) .... ACP
Acoustic Doppler Sounder (MCD) .... ADS
Acoustic Doppler Velocimeter [Instrumentation] .... ADV
Acoustic Echo Canceler (SAUS) .... AEC
Acoustic Electron Paramagnetic Resonance (SAUS) .... AEPR
Acoustic Emission .... AE
Acoustic Emission Technology Corp. (SAUO) .... AET
Acoustic Emission Testing (MHDB) .... AET
Acoustic Emission Weld Monitor (PDAA) .... AEWM
Acoustic Environment Support Detachment (SAUO) .... AESD
Acoustic Environmental Support Detachment [Office of Naval Research]
[Arlington, VA] .... AESD
Acoustic Evoked Potential [Physiology] .... AEP
Acoustic Evoked Response [Neurophysiology] (DMAA) .... AER
Acoustic Fast Motion (SAUS) .... AFM
Acoustic Fatigue Test Article (NASA) .... AFTA
Acoustic Firing Device (CAAL) .... AFD
Acoustic Flaw Detector (SAUS) .... AFD

Acoustic Generator (SAUS) ... AG
Acoustic Guidance SONAR (HGAA) ... AGS
Acoustic Helicopter Overflight Detector (MCD) ... ACHOD
Acoustic Homing Torpedo ... AHT
Acoustic Imaging System (SAUS) ... AIS
Acoustic Impact Technique [*Test*] (PDAA) ... AIT
Acoustic Impact Test (SAUS) ... AIT
Acoustic Impedance (SAUS) ... AI
Acoustic Intelligence [*Military*] (NG) ... ACINT
Acoustic Intelligence Data System [*Navy*] ... AIDS
Acoustic Intelligence Gathering System [*Military*] (CAAL) ... AIGS
Acoustic Intensity (SAUS) ... AI
Acoustic Intercept Receiver [*Navy*] ... AIR
Acoustic Intercept Receiver/Multimode Hydrophone System [*Navy*] ... AIR/MMH
Acoustic Intercept System (IUSS) ... AIS
Acoustic Isolation Chamber ... AIC
Acoustic Lens SONAR System (MCD) ... ALSS
Acoustic Levitation (or Levitator) Furnace (SAUS) ... ALF
Acoustic Levitator (SAUS) ... AL
Acoustic Locating Device (SAA) ... ALD
Acoustic Low-Flying-Aircraft Detector (MCD) ... ALFAD
Acoustic Match Filter ... AMF
Acoustic Material Signature (MCD) ... AMS
Acoustic Materials Association (SAUO) ... AMA
Acoustic Measurement System (KSC) ... AMS
Acoustic Memory (SAUS) ... AM
Acoustic, Meteorological, and Oceanographic Survey ... AMOS
Acoustic Midflight Deck Module (SAUS) ... AMDM
Acoustic Mine Sweeping (SAUS) ... AMNSWP
Acoustic Minesweeping ... AMNSWP
Acoustic Mismatch Model (AAEL) ... AMM
Acoustic Miss Distance Indicator (PDAA) ... AMDI
Acoustic Model Evaluation Committee [*Woods Hole Oceanographic Institution*] (MSC) ... AMEC
Acoustic Model Test Facility [*NASA*] (NASA) ... AMTF
Acoustic Modulator-Demodulator (SAUS) ... Acoustic Modem
Acoustic Monitor System (SAUS) ... AMS
Acoustic Myography [*Otorhinolaryngology*] (DAVI) ... AMG
Acoustic Neuroma [*Medicine*] (DMAA) ... AN
Acoustic Neuroma Association (EA) ... ANA
Acoustic Neuroma Association of Australasia ... ANAA
Acoustic Neuroma Association of Canada [*Association pour les Neurinomes Acoustiques du Canada*] (AC) ... ANAC
Acoustic Noise Canceling [*Headsets*] [*Bose Corp.*] ... ANC
Acoustic Noise Environment ... ANE
Acoustic Noise Generator ... ANG
Acoustic Noise Making (CAAL) ... ANM
Acoustic Noise Test ... ANT
Acoustic Nuclear Magnetic Resonance (SAUS) ... ANMR
Acoustic Optical RADAR Classification System (CAAL) ... ARCS
Acoustic Paramagnetic Resonance [*Physics*] ... APR
Acoustic Performance Monitor ... APM
Acoustic Performance Prediction [*Navy*] (MSC) ... APP
Acoustic Performance Prediction Program (IUSS) ... APPP
Acoustic Performance Prediction System (IUSS) ... APPS
Acoustic Plate Mode (AAEL) ... APM
Acoustic Playback System [*Army*] ... APS
Acoustic Projector Pressure Relief and Equalization System (SAUS) ... APPRES
Acoustic Radar (SAUS) ... ACDAR
Acoustic Radiation Element ... ARE
Acoustic Range Prediction System (SAUS) ... ARPS
Acoustic Range Project (ACAE) ... AUTEC
Acoustic Range-Finder (MCD) ... ARF
Acoustic Rate Sensor (PDAA) ... ARS
Acoustic Ray Trace Indicator (PDAA) ... ARTI
Acoustic Reflex ... AR
Acoustic Reflex Ear Defender ... ARED
Acoustic Reflex Ear Defender System (RDA) ... AREDS
Acoustic Reflex Test [*Audiology*] ... ART
Acoustic Research Center (MCD) ... ARC
Acoustic Research International (SAUO) ... AR
Acoustic Resistance Unit ... ARU
Acoustic Resonance Densitometry (SAUS) ... ARD
Acoustic Response of Reusable Shuttle Tiles (MCD) ... ARREST
Acoustic Seismic Intrusion Detector (SAUS) ... ACOUSID
Acoustic Self-Ranging system (SAUS) ... ASR
Acoustic Sensor Operator ... ASO
Acoustic Sensor Pattern Assessment System (MCD) ... ASPAS
Acoustic Sensor Range and Prediction (SAUS) ... ASRAP
Acoustic Sensor [*or SONAR*] **Range Prediction** (NVT) ... ASRAP
Acoustic Sensor [*or SONAR*] **Range Prediction System** (NVT) ... ASRAPS
Acoustic Sensor Signal Generator (SAUS) ... ASSG
Acoustic Sensor Training Aids Program [*Navy*] (CAAL) ... ASTAP
Acoustic Sensor Unit [*Navy*] (CAAL) ... ASU
Acoustic Shield Thermal/Variable Cycle Engine (MCD) ... AST/VCE
Acoustic Ship Positioning - Advanced (MCD) ... ASPA
Acoustic Ship Positioning System ... ASPS
Acoustic Short-Pulse Echo Classification Technique (NVT) ... ASPECT
Acoustic Short-Pulse Echo Classifi-cation Technique (SAUS) ... ASPECT
Acoustic Signal Data Analysis and Conversion System [*Navy*] ... ASDACS
Acoustic Signal Generator System ... ASGE
Acoustic Signal Processing System (SAUS) ... ASPS
Acoustic Signal Processor (MHDB) ... ASP
Acoustic Simulation Unit (SAUS) ... ASU
Acoustic Sonar Range Prediction System (SAUS) ... ASRAPS
Acoustic Sound Intrusion Device [*Military*] (VNW) ... ACOU-SID
Acoustic Source (SAUS) ... A
Acoustic Stapedius Reflex [*Medicine*] ... ASR
Acoustic Storage (or Store) (SAUS) ... AS
Acoustic Support Function (SAUS) ... ASF
Acoustic Surface Analysis Technology ... ASAT
Acoustic Surface Wave ... ASW
Acoustic Target Generator ... ATG
Acoustic Target Sensor ... ATS
Acoustic Telemetry Bathythermometer ... ATBT
Acoustic Telemetry Subsystem (MCD) ... ATS
Acoustic Telephone Interface [*Telecommunications*] ... ATI
Acoustic Test Laboratory ... ATL
Acoustic Test Signal Generator (CAAL) ... ATSG
Acoustic Thermography of Ocean Climate (SAUS) ... ATOC
Acoustic Thermometry of Ocean Climate [*International oceanographic project*] ... ATOC
Acoustic Thermometry of Ocean Climates (SAUS) ... ATOC
Acoustic Tile Ceiling (SAUS) ... ATC
Acoustic Torpedo Countermeasures (SAUS) ... ATC
Acoustic Tracking System (SAUS) ... ATS
Acoustic Transmission System ... ATS
Acoustic Transponder Navigation (PDAA) ... ATNAV
Acoustic Travel Time Ocean Current Monitor (SAUS) ... ATTOM
Acoustic Traveling Wave Lens ... ATWL
Acoustic Trials (NVT) ... ACTRL
Acoustic Underwater Range Determination (SAUS) ... ACURAD
Acoustic Underwater Range Determination Systems ... ACURAD
Acoustic Underwater Sound Experiment (MCD) ... AUSEX
Acoustic Value Operating System (CIST) ... AVOS
Acoustic Valve Leak Detector (DNAB) ... AVLD
Acoustic Valve Operating System (PDAA) ... AVOS
Acoustic Variable Density (CARB) ... AVD
Acoustic Velocity (SAUS) ... AV
Acoustic Velocity Meter (NOAA) ... AVM
Acoustic Video Processor (DWSG) ... AVP
Acoustic Video Processor Integrated Display Station ... AVPIDS
Acoustic Warfare (NVT) ... AW
Acoustic Warfare Support Measures (NVT) ... ACSM
Acoustic Warfare Support Measures (NVT) ... AWSM
Acoustic Warfare System [*Navy*] (MCD) ... AWS
Acoustic Wave ... AW
Acoustic Wave Analysis ... AWA
Acoustic Wave Analysis System ... AWAS
Acoustic Zone Plate (SAUS) ... AZP
Acoustical [*Technical drawings*] ... AC
Acoustical (ABBR) ... ACSTL
Acoustical Absorption Coefficient ... AAC
Acoustical Absorption Loss ... AAL
Acoustical Analysis Memo [*Navy*] (MCD) ... AAM
Acoustical and Board Products Association ... ABPA
Acoustical and Insulating Materials Association [*Later, ABPA*] (EA) ... AIMA
Acoustical Assurance Period (EEVL) ... AAP
Acoustical Attenuation Constant ... AAC
Acoustical Conductance (SAUS) ... g
Acoustical Displacement (BARN) ... W
Acoustical Door Institute [*Defunct*] (EA) ... ADI
Acoustical Emission Monitoring (NASA) ... AEM
Acoustical Institute, Academy of Sciences (SAUS) ... AKIN
Acoustical Intelligence [*Military*] (AABC) ... ACOUSTINT
Acoustical Materials Association [*Later, ABPA*] (EA) ... AMA
Acoustical Paper (SAUS) ... ACP
Acoustical Phase Constant ... APC
Acoustical Physics (SAUS) ... Acoust Phys
Acoustical Plaster [*Technical drawings*] ... ACPL
Acoustical Plaster Ceiling [*Technical drawings*] ... APC
Acoustical Propagation Constant ... APC
Acoustical Signal Classification and Analysis Center [*Navy*] (CAAL) ... ASCAC
Acoustical Society of America ... ACSA
Acoustical Society of America ... ACSOC
Acoustical Society of America (SAUO) ... Ac Soc A
Acoustical Society of America (EA) ... ASA
Acoustical Society of Scandinavia [*Formerly, Nordic Acoustics Society*] (EA) ... ASS
Acoustical Standards Board (MUGU) ... ASB
Acoustical Standards Management Board ... ASMB
Acoustical Test Chamber ... ATC
Acoustical Tile [*Technical drawings*] ... ACT
Acoustical Tile Ceiling [*Technical drawings*] ... ATC
Acoustically (ABBR) ... ACSTLY
Acoustically Navigated Geological Underwater Survey [*Unmanned vehicle*] ... ANGUS
Acoustic-Daylight, Ambient-Noise Imaging System ... ADONIS
Acoustic-Gravity Wave ... AGW
Acoustic-Impedance Profile (SAUS) ... AIP
Acoustic-Magnetic (NVT) ... AM
Acoustic-Magneto-Electric (PDAA) ... AME
Acoustic-Optic [*Ophthalmology and otorhinolaryngology*] (DAVI) ... A-O
Acoustic-Optic Modulator (SAUS) ... AOM
Acoustic/Optical (SAUS) ... AO
Acoustic-Pressure (NVT) ... AP
Acoustics (ROG) ... ACOUST
Acoustics and Signal Analysis (SAUS) ... A/SA
Acoustics and Vibration Data Center (MCD) ... AVDC
Acoustics Associates (AAG) ... AA

Acoustics Laboratory .... AL
Acoustics of the Target .... ACTAR
Acoustics Propellant Utilization .... APU
Acoustics, Speech, and Signal Processing (MCD) .... ASSP
Acoustics, Speech and Signal Processing (SAUS) .... ASSP
Acoustic-Seismic Intrusion Detector (MCD) .... ACOUSID
Acousto-Electric (PDAA) .... AE
Acoustoelectric Oscillator (IEEE) .... AEO
Acousto-Electric Oscillator (SAUS) .... AEO
Acoustographic Imaging System (PDAA) .... AGIS
Acoustomagnetoelectric (SAUS) .... AME
Acousto-Optic (MCD) .... A-O
Acousto-Optic Beam Deflector [Instrumentation] .... AOBD
Acousto-Optic Mode Locker and Frequency Doubler (MCD) .... AMOL-FD
Acousto-Optic Mode-Locker / Frequency Doubles (PDAA) .... AOML/FD
Acousto-Optic Modulator .... AOM
Acousto-Optic Q-Switch (SAUS) .... AOQS
Acousto-Optic Tunable Filter [Instrumentation] .... AOTF
Acousto-Optic Tunable Scanning [Instrumentation] .... AOTS
Acousto-Optical Imaging .... AOI
Acousto-Optical Spectrograph (ADA) .... AOS
Acousto-Optics Device .... AOD
Acousto-Ultrasonic (SAUS) .... AU
Acoyapa [Nicaragua] [Seismograph station code, US Geological Survey] (SEIS) .... ACY
ACPA [Affiliated Conference of Practicing Accountants] International (EA) ..... ACPA
ACP/EEC Consultative Assembly (SAUO) .... ACP/EEC
ACPI Control Method Source Language (SAUS) .... ASL
ACPI Machine Language (SAUS) .... AML
Acqua (SAUS) .... AQARD
Acquaint (ABBR) .... ACQNT
Acquaintance (ABBR) .... ACQNTNC
Acquaintanceship (ABBR) .... ACQNTNCSP
Acquainted (ABBR) .... ACQNTD
Acquainting (ABBR) .... ACQNTG
Acqualin Resources Ltd. [Vancouver Stock Exchange symbol] .... AQU
Acquest Enterprises Ltd. [Vancouver Stock Exchange symbol] .... ACQ
Acquiesce (ABBR) .... ACQS
Acquiesced (ABBR) .... ACQSD
Acquiescence (DLA) .... A
Acquiescence (ABBR) .... ACQSNC
Acquiescent (ABBR) .... ACQSNT
Acquiescently (ABBR) .... ACQSNTY
Acquiescing (ABBR) .... ACQSG
Acquirable (ABBR) .... ACQRB
Acquire (ROG) .... ACQ
Acquire (ADWA) .... acq
Acquire (ABBR) .... ACQR
Acquire on Jam .... AOJ
Acquired (ABBR) .... ACQRD
Acquired Aplastic Anemia [Medicine] (DMAA) .... AAA
Acquired Artery Immune Augmentation [Cardiology] (DAVI) .... AAIA
Acquired Artery Immune Augmentation [Medicine] (DAVI) .... AIA
Acquired Brain Injury (ADWA) .... ABI
Acquired Chromosomal Abnormalities [Medicine] (MELL) .... ACA
Acquired Community Immune Deficiency Syndrome [Medicine] (TAD) ...... ACIDS
Acquired Cystic Disease of the Kidney [Medicine] (MELL) .... ACDK
Acquired Cystic Kidney Disease [Medicine] (DMAA) .... ACKD
Acquired Drug Resistance (MELL) .... ADR
Acquired Epidermolysis Bullosa [Medicine] .... AEB
Acquired Fanconi's Syndrome [Medicine] (DB) .... AFS
Acquired Heart Disease (MELL) .... AHD
Acquired Hemolytic Anemia [Medicine] (MAE) .... AHA
Acquired Hepatocellular Degeneration [Medicine] (DMAA) .... AHCD
Acquired Idiopathic Sideroblastic Anemia [Medicine] (DMAA) .... AISA
Acquired Immune Deficiency Syndrome [Also, AID, GRID] [Medicine] .... AIDS
Acquired Immune Deficiency Syndrome with Kaposi's Sarcoma [Medicine] (DMAA) .... AIDS-KS
Acquired Immune Hemolytic Disease [Medicine] (DMAA) .... AIHD
Acquired Immunodeficiency [Also, AIDS, GRID] [Medicine] .... AID
Acquired Immunodeficiency Syndrome [Medicine] (DAVI) .... AIDS
Acquired Immunodeficiency Syndrome [Medicine] [French, Spanish and other Romance languages] (TAD) .... SIDA
Acquired Immunodeficiency Syndrome Associated Virus [Medicine] (TAD) .... AAV
Acquired Immunodeficiency Syndrome Clinical Trials Group [Medicine] (TAD) .... ACTU
Acquired Immunodeficiency Syndrome Control and Prevention Project (SAUO) .... AIDSCAP
Acquired Immunodeficiency Syndrome Drug Assistance Program [Medicine] (TAD) .... ADAP
Acquired Immunodeficiency Syndrome Education and Training Centers [Medicine] (TAD) .... AETC
Acquired Immunodeficiency Syndrome, Information Online (MELL) ...... AIDSLINE
Acquired Immunodeficiency Syndrome Self-Help and Care [Medicine] (DMAA) .... ASHAC
Acquired Immunodeficiency Syndrome Service Organization [Medicine] (TAD) .... ASO
Acquired Immunodeficiency Syndrome Treatment Evaluation Unit [Medicine] (TAD) .... ATEU
Acquired Intelligence, Inc. [Information service or system] (IID) .... AII
Acquired Intelligence Incorporated (SAUO) .... AII
Acquired Monosaccharide Intolerance [Medicine] (DMAA) .... AMI
Acquired Pattern Addiction [Telecommunications] (PCM) .... APA
Acquired Red Cell Anemia [Medicine] (MELL) .... ARCA

Acquired Red Cell Aplasia [Hematology] .... ARCA
Acquired Severe Aplastic Anemia [Hematology] (DAVI) .... ASAA
Acquired Valvular Heart Disease [Medicine] (MELL) .... AVHD
Acquirement (ABBR) .... ACQRNT
Acquirement (ABBR) .... ACQRT
Acquirer (ABBR) .... ACQRR
Acquiring (ABBR) .... ACQRG
Acquisicorp Capital [Vancouver Stock Exchange symbol] .... AQ
Acquisition (AFM) .... ACQ
Acquisition (TBD) .... Acq
Acquisition (ABBR) .... ACQIS
Acquisition (IAA) .... ACQN
Acquisition (ABBR) .... ACQSN
Acquisition .... ACQSTN
Acquisition .... ACQUIS
Acquisition (KSC) .... AQUIS
Acquisition Adjustment (IAA) .... ACQADJ
Acquisition Adjustment (SAUS) .... ACQ ADJ
Acquisition Advice Code [NASA] (KSC) .... AAC
Acquisition Advisory Board (MCD) .... AAB
Acquisition Advisory Group [Business term] .... AAG
Acquisition Aid .... AQUAID
Acquisition Aid Vehicle [Army] (AABC) .... AADV
Acquisition Aiding (SAUS) .... AA
Acquisition and Command Support (MCD) .... ACS
Acquisition & Command Vehicle (SAUS) .... ACV
Acquisition and Control Module (MCD) .... ACM
Acquisition and Control Query Executive [Programming language] .... ACQE
Acquisition and Distribution of Commercial Products [Also, ADCP] [Department of Defense program] .... ADCOP
Acquisition and Distribution of Commercial Products [Also, ADCOP] [Department of Defense program] (MCD) .... ADCP
Acquisition and Improvement District (SAUS) .... A&ID
Acquisition and Inoculation Access Period [Immunology] .... AAP
Acquisition and Logistics (MCD) .... AL
Acquisition and Serials Control (SAUS) .... ASC
Acquisition and Synchronization Unit (LAIN) .... ASU
Acquisition and Technology .... A & T
Acquisition and Track Simulation (ACAE) .... ATSIM
Acquisition and Tracking Electronics (MCD) .... A & TE
Acquisition and Tracking Electronics (MCD) .... ATE
Acquisition and Tracking Seeker (ACAE) .... ATS
Acquisition and Tracking Station (SAUS) .... ATS
Acquisition and Tracking Subsystem (MUGU) .... ATSS
Acquisition and Tracking System .... ATS
Acquisition Based on Consideration of Logistic Effects [Air Force] .... ABLE
Acquisition Basic Course [DSMC] (AAGC) .... ABC
Acquisition Beacon .... AB
Acquisition Bus Monitor [Computer science] (MCD) .... ABM
Acquisition Career Enhancement .... ACE
Acquisition Career Field [Army] (RDA) .... ACF
Acquisition Career Management Advocate [Army] (RDA) .... ACMA
Acquisition Career Management Office [Army] .... ACMO
Acquisition Career Record Brief [Army] .... ACRB
Acquisition Career Record Briefs [Army] .... ACRD
Acquisition, Cataloguing, and Circulation Working Party of the Aslib Computer Applications Group [Banking] (NITA) .... ACCWP
Acquisition, Cataloguing, Technical System (SAUS) .... ACTS
Acquisition Category (AAGC) .... ACAT
Acquisition Circular (AAGC) .... AC
Acquisition Civilian Record Brief [Army] .... ACRB
Acquisition Command [Army] .... AC
Acquisition Command Headquarters (AFIT) .... ACH
Acquisition, Construction, and Improvement (DNAB) .... AC & I
Acquisition, Construction and Improvement (SAUS) .... AC&I
Acquisition, Control of Test [Units] (NASA) .... ACT
Acquisition Control Unit (SAUS) .... ACU
Acquisition Coordinating Group (IUSS) .... ACG
Acquisition Corps [Army] .... AC
Acquisition Cost Evaluation (ACAE) .... ACE
Acquisition Costs .... AC
Acquisition Data Facility (MCD) .... ADF
Acquisition Data Input Equipment (AABC) .... ADIE
Acquisition Decision Memorandum (MCD) .... ADM
Acquisition, Development, and Construction [Real estate loan] .... ADC
Acquisition Director .... AD
Acquisition Education and Training Program [Army] .... AETP
Acquisition Education Learning Center [Army] .... AELC
Acquisition Education, Training, and Experience [Army] .... AETE
Acquisition Engineer [Military] (IUSS) .... AE
Acquisition Enhancement [Program] (DOMA) .... ACE
Acquisition Executive [Military] (DOMA) .... AE
Acquisition Gate Enable (ACAE) .... AGE
Acquisition Improvement Program (ACAE) .... AIP
Acquisition Information Management Program [Army] .... AIM
Acquisition Institute [Defunct] (EA) .... AI
Acquisition Instruction (ACAE) .... AI
Acquisition Integrated Data Base [Army] (RDA) .... AID
Acquisition Law Specialist (AAGC) .... ALS
Acquisition Lead Time .... ALT
Acquisition Letter [Replaced PIL] (AAGC) .... AL
Acquisition Life Cycle .... ALC
Acquisition Logistician (NG) .... AL
Acquisition Logistics Division (SAUO) .... ALD
Acquisition Logistics Management Information System (SAUS) .... ALMIS

Acquisition Management Branch [*Army*] .... AMB
Acquisition Management Guide [*Military*] (AFIT) .... AMG
Acquisition Management Information System [*Air Force*] .... AMIS
Acquisition Management Institute (SAUS) .... AMI
Acquisition Management Milestone System [*DoD*] .... AMMS
Acquisition Management Mission Cluster Group [*Army*] (RDA) .... AMMCG
Acquisition Management Plan [*Navy*] .... AMP
Acquisition Management System Control (AAGC) .... AMSC
Acquisition Management System Control Officer (MCD) .... AMSCO
Acquisition Management System Data List [*Military*] (DOMA) .... AMSDL
Acquisition Management System List (MCD) .... AMSL
Acquisition Management Systems and Data Control List .... AMSDCL
Acquisition Management Systems and Data Control List .... AMSDL
Acquisition Management Systems and Data Requirements Control List [*A publication*] (AAGC) .... AMSDL
Acquisition Management Systems and Data Requirements Control Program [*Navy*] .... AMSDRP
Acquisition Management Systems Control Aviation Structural Mechanic, Structures,Chief [*Navy rating*] (DNAB) .... AMSC
Acquisition Management Systems Review Committee (SAUO) .... AMSRC
Acquisition Manager .... AM
Acquisition Material List (MCD) .... AML
Acquisition Message .... AQ
Acquisition Method Coding (MCD) .... AMC
Acquisition Method Suffix Code (AAGC) .... AMSC
Acquisition of Land Act [*Town planning*] [*British*] .... AL
Acquisition of Monographs and Bibliographical Enquiry Remotely [*Computer software*] (NITA) .... AMBER
Acquisition of Satellite [*Telecommunications*] .... AOS
Acquisition of Sight (SAUS) .... AOS
Acquisition of Signal [*Telecommunications*] .... AOS
Acquisition Officer Selection Board [*Army*] (INF) .... AOSB
Acquisition on Target (ACAE) .... ACQUOT
Acquisition on Target .... AOT
Acquisition on Target Held (ACAE) .... AOTH
Acquisition Orbit Determination Program (SAUS) .... AODP
Acquisition Orbit Determination Program Assembly [*Space Flight Operations Facility, NASA*] .... AODP
Acquisition Plan .... AP
Acquisition Plan (Procurement) .... APP
Acquisition Plan Review Board [*Army*] .... APRB
Acquisition Planning and Tracking System .... APATS
Acquisition Planning Conference .... APC
Acquisition Planning Executive Council (AAGC) .... APEC
Acquisition Planning System (IUSS) .... APS
Acquisition Point (MUGU) .... AP
Acquisition Pointing and Tracking (ACAE) .... APT
Acquisition Policy .... AP
Acquisition Policy Working Group (IUSS) .... APWG
Acquisition Processor Display (SAUS) .... APD
Acquisition Processor Subsystem (NAKS) .... APS
Acquisition Professional Development Program [*DoD*] .... APDP
Acquisition Program Baseline (DOMA) .... APB
Acquisition Program Office [*DoD*] .... APO
Acquisition Program Review Board (IUSS) .... APRB
Acquisition Program Sponsor (IUSS) .... APS
Acquisition Project Manager .... APM
Acquisition Project Officer (IUSS) .... APO
Acquisition RADAR .... AR
Acquisition RADAR and Control System .... ARCS
Acquisition Radar & Control System (SAUS) .... ARCS
Acquisition RADAR Jamming .... ARJ
Acquisition Radar Repair Helper (SAUS) .... ACQ RDR REP HLPR
Acquisition Radar Repairman (SAUS) .... ACQ RDR REPM
Acquisition Reform Communications Center .... ARCC
Acquisition Reform Implementation Assessment Team [*Army*] .... ARIAT
Acquisition Reform Working Group [*Coalition of nine industry groups*] (AAGC) .... ARWG
Acquisition Request (IUSS) .... AR
Acquisition Requirements Tracking System (MCD) .... ARTS
Acquisition Review Board [*Military*] (CAAL) .... ARB
Acquisition Review Committee [*Navy*] (CAAL) .... ARC
Acquisition Review Council (IUSS) .... ARC
Acquisition Review Quarterly [*A publication*] (AAGC) .... ARQ
Acquisition Section (SAUS) .... AS
Acquisition Select Switch (MCD) .... ACQSEL
Acquisition Select Switch (SAUS) .... ACQSEL Switch
Acquisition Sponsor Project Officer [*USMC*] (AAGC) .... ASPO
Acquisition Strategy (AAGC) .... Acq/Strat
Acquisition Strategy [*Army*] (RDA) .... AS
Acquisition Strategy Comparison Model (MCD) .... ASCM
Acquisition Strategy Meeting (AAGC) .... ASM
Acquisition Strategy Report [*Military*] (DOMA) .... ASR
Acquisition Strategy/Plan [*Military*] (CAAL) .... AS/P
Acquisition Streamlining and Standardization Electronic Transfer System (AAGC) .... ASSETS
Acquisition Streamlining and Standardization Information System (AAGC) .... ASSIST
Acquisition Streamlining Initiative (IUSS) .... ASI
Acquisition Sun Sensor (ACAE) .... ACSS
Acquisition Sun Sensor (MCD) .... ASS
Acquisition System Integration Program (DWSG) .... ASIP
Acquisition Systems Protection Office [*DoD*] (RDA) .... ASPO
Acquisition Target and Search .... ATS
Acquisition Task Force on Modeling and Simulation [*Army*] .... ATFM & S

Acquisition Team (IUSS) .... AT
Acquisition Team [*Army*] (RDA) .... A-TEAM
Acquisition Track Techniques (ACAE) .... ATT
Acquisition, Tracking, and Pointing [*Military*] (SDI) .... ATP
Acquisition, Tracking & Pointing & Fire Control (SAUS) .... ATPFC
Acquisition Tracking and Recognition [*Aviation*] .... ATAR
Acquisition, Tracking, Pointing, and Fire Control [*Military*] (SDI) .... ATP-FC
Acquisition Trigger at Zero Beat .... ATZ
Acquisition Workforce Support Specialist [*Army*] .... AWSS
Acquisition Workforce Support Specialists [*Army*] .... AWSS
Acquisitions (AL) .... Acq
Acquisitions and Development Directory (SAUO) .... ADD
Acquisitions Bibliographic Support Project .... ABSP
Acquisitions, Cataloguing, Technical Systems [*Library service*] .... ACTS
Acquisitions Section [*Resources and Technical Services Division of ALA*] .... AS
Acquisiton Civilian Record Brief [*Army*] .... ACRB
Acquisitor Mines Ltd. [*Vancouver Stock Exchange symbol*] .... AQT
Acquistion Data Input Equipment (SAUS) .... ADIE
Acquistion Reform Network .... ARNet
Acquit (ABBR) .... ACQT
Acquittal (AFM) .... ACQ
Acquittal (ABBR) .... ACQTL
Acquittance (ABBR) .... ACQTNC
Acquittance (SAUS) .... Aq
Acquitted (ABBR) .... ACQTD
Acquitting (ABBR) .... ACQTG
ACR Group [*Associated Press*] (SAG) .... ACR
ACR Group [*NASDAQ symbol*] (SAG) .... ACRG
ACR Irradiance Monitor (SAUS) .... ACRIM
Acral Lentiginous Melanoma [*Medicine*] .... ALM
Acral Lick Dermatitis [*Medicine*] .... ALD
Acre .... A
Acre (SAUS) .... A
Acre (IDOE) .... a
Acre .... AC
Acre Foot (ABBR) .... AC FT
Acreage (ABBR) .... ACRG
Acreage Conservation Reserve .... ACR
Acreage Diversion [*Agriculture*] .... ADV
Acreage Marketing Guide .... AMG
Acreage Reduction Program [*Department of Agriculture*] (GFGA) .... ARP
Acre-Feet (ADWA) .... AF
Acre-Feet par Day (SAUS) .... ACRE-FT/D
Acre-Feet per Day .... ACRE-FT/D
Acre-Feet per Year (ADWA) .... AFY
Acre-Foot .... AF
acres (SAUS) .... a
Acres American, Inc., Buffalo, NY [*Library symbol*] [*Library of Congress*] (LCLS) .... NBuAA
Acres Consulting Services Ltd., Niagara Falls, ON, Canada [*Library symbol*] [*Library of Congress*] (LCLS) .... CaONfA
Acres Consulting Services Ltd., Niagara Falls, Ontario [*Library symbol*] [*National Library of Canada*] (NLC) .... ONFA
Acres Consulting Services Ltd., Toronto, ON, Canada [*Library symbol*] [*Library of Congress*] (LCLS) .... CaOTAC
Acres Consulting Services Ltd., Toronto, Ontario [*Library symbol*] [*National Library of Canada*] (NLC) .... OTAC
Acres Gaming [*NASDAQ symbol*] (TTSB) .... AGAM
Acres Gaming, Inc. [*Associated Press*] (SAG) .... AcreG
Acres Gaming, Inc. [*Associated Press*] (SAG) .... AcresGm
Acres Gaming, Inc. [*NASDAQ symbol*] (SAG) .... AGAM
Acres Gaming Wrrt [*NASDAQ symbol*] (TTSB) .... AGAMW
Acres, Roods, Perches [*Land measurement*] [*British*] (ROG) .... ARP
Acrid (ABBR) .... ACRI
Acridine Orange [*Dye*] .... AO
Acridine Orange Direct Count (CARB) .... AODC
Acridine Orange Stain [*Medicine*] (MELL) .... AOS
Acridine-Orange Diagnosis (SAUS) .... AO DIAG
Acridine-Orange Technique (SAUS) .... AO TECHNIQUE
Acridinyl Ansidide [*Antineoplastic drug*] (DAVI) .... m-AMSA
(Acridinylamino)methanesulfon-m-anisidide [*Antineoplastic drug regimen*] .... AMSA
Acridity (ABBR) .... ACRDT
Acridity (ABBR) .... ACRIT
Acriflavine [*Anti-infective mixture*] .... Acr
ACRIM Satellite (SAUS) .... ACRIMSAT
Acrimonious (ABBR) .... ACRMNIS
Acrimonious (ABBR) .... ACRMS
Acrimony (ABBR) .... ACRM
Acrimony (ABBR) .... ACRMNY
ACRL [*Association of College and Research Libraries*] **Anthropology and Sociology Section** .... ACRL ANSS
ACRL [*Association of College and Research Libraries*] **Anthropology and Sociology Section** .... ACRL ASS
ACRL [*Association of College and Research Libraries*] **Art Section** .... ACRL ARTS
ACRL [*Association of College and Research Libraries*] **Art Section** .... ACRL AS
ACRL [*Association of College and Research Libraries*] **Asian and African Section** .... ACRL AAS
ACRL [*Association of College and Research Libraries*] **Bibliographic Instruction Section** .... ACRL BIS
ACRL [*Association of College and Research Libraries*] **College Libraries Section** .... ACRL CLS
ACRL [*Association of College and Research Libraries*] **Community and Junior College and Research Libraries** .... ACRL CJCLS

ACRL [*Association of College and Research Libraries*] **Education and Behavioral Sciences Section** .... ACRL EBSS
ACRL [*Association of College and Research Libraries*] **Law and Political Science Section** .... ACRL LPSS
ACRL [*Association of College and Research Libraries*] **Rare Books and Manuscripts Section** .... ACRL RBMS
ACRL [*Association of College and Research Libraries*] **Science and Technology Section** .... ACRL STS
ACRL [*Association of College and Research Libraries*] **Slavic and East European Section** .... ACRL SEES
ACRL [*Association of College and Research Libraries*] **University Libraries Section** .... ACRL ULS
ACRL [*Association of College and Research Libraries*] **Western European Specialists Section** .... ACRL WESS
ACRL [*Association of College and Research Libraries*] **Women's Studies Section** .... ACRL WSS
Acrobat (DSUE) .... ACRO
Acrobatic (FAAC) .... ACRBT
Acrobatic (ABBR) .... ACRBTC
Acrobatically (ABBR) .... ACRBTCY
Acrocentric Chromosome [*Medicine*] (MELL) .... ACC
Acrocephalopolysyndactyly (DMAA) .... ACPS
Acrocephalosyndactyly [*Medicine*] (DMAA) .... ACS
Acrodermatitis Chronica Atrophicans [*Dermatology*] .... ACA
Acrodermatitis Enteropathica [*Medicine*] .... AE
Acrodyne Communications [*NASDAQ symbol*] (TTSB) .... ACRO
Acrodyne Communications, Inc. [*NASDAQ symbol*] (SAG) .... ACRO
Acrodyne Communications, Inc. [*Associated Press*] (SAG) .... Acrodyne
Acrodyne Communicns Wrrt [*NASDAQ symbol*] (TTSB) .... ACROW
Acrodyne Holdings, Inc. [*NASDAQ symbol*] (SAG) .... ACRO
Acrodyne Holdings, Inc. [*Associated Press*] (SAG) .... Acrody
Acrokeratoelastoidosis (DMAA) .... AKE
Acrolect (ABBR) .... ACROL
acromegaly (SAUS) .... acromeg
Acromial Spur Index [*Medicine*] (MELL) .... ASI
Acromio-Clavicular (SAUS) .... AC
acromioclavicular (SAUS) .... ac
Acromioclavicular [*Joint*] [*Medicine*] (DHSM) .... AC
Acromioclavicular Joint [*Anatomy*] (DAVI) .... ACJ
Acromioclavicular Joint [*Medicine*] (MELL) .... AC joint
Acromioclavicular Joint (SAUS) .... ACJT
Acromioclavicular Joint Dislocation (MELL) .... ACJD
Acromioclavicular Line [*Anatomy*] (DAVI) .... ACL
Acromion (MELL) .... A
Acronym (ABBR) .... ACRNM
Acronym (WDAA) .... ACRON
Acronym Control Officer (SAUS) .... ACO
Acronym Data Base [*Defunct*] .... ACRODABA
Acronym Free Zone (SAUS) .... AFZ
[*The*] **Acronym Generator** [*An RCA computer program*] .... TAG
[*The*] **Acronym Generator Converter Program** [*RCA computer program*] (IAA) .... TCP
[*The*] **Acronym Generator Reference** [*RCA computer program*] (IAA) .... TAREF
Acronym Master List (SAUS) .... AML
Acronym May Be Ignored Totally (SAUS) .... AMBIT
Acronym May Be Ignored Totally [*Computer science*] (CSR) .... AMBIT/L
Acronym Production Particularly at Lavish Level Is No Good [*Term coined by Theodore M. Bernstein*] .... APPALLING
acronymization (SAUS) .... acronymiz
acronymizing (SAUS) .... acronymiz
Acronym-Oriented Nut .... ACORN
Acronyms, Abbreviations and Initialisms (SAUS) .... AA&I
Acronyms and Initialisms Dictionary [*Later, AIAD*] [*A publication*] .... AID
Acronyms in Moderation [*Term coined by Ralph Slovenko*] .... AIM
Acronyms, Initialisms, and Abbreviations Dictionary [*Formerly, AID*] [*A publication*] .... AIAD
Acronyms, Initials, and Abbreviations (DAVI) .... AIA
Acro-Osteolysis [*Medicine*] .... AOL
Acropectorovertebral Dysplasia [*Medicine*] (MELL) .... APVD
Acrophobe [*or Acrophobia*] (ABBR) .... ACRO
acrophobe (SAUS) .... acro
Acrophobia (ABBR) .... ACPHOB
Acrophobia (SAUS) .... ACRO
Acropolis (VRA) .... acrpl
Acrorenal Field Defect, Ectodermal Dysplasia, Lipotrophic Diabetes [*Medicine*] (DMAA) .... AREDYLD
Acrosome Reaction [*Fertilization*] .... AR
Across (ADWA) .... A
Across .... ACR
Across (BARN) .... acrs
Across Data Systems [*NASDAQ symbol*] (TTSB) .... ACRS
Across Data Systems, Inc. [*Associated Press*] (SAG) .... Across
Across Data Systems, Inc. [*NASDAQ symbol*] (SAG) .... ACRS
Across Flats .... ACRFLT
Across Flats .... AF
Across North America Tracer Experiment (SAUS) .... ANATEX
Across Shoulder (WDMC) .... XS
Across Tape [*Curve*] .... AT
Across the Board .... ATB
Across the Fence [*Real estate*] (DICI) .... ATF
Acrostic (ABBR) .... ACROS
acrostic (SAUS) .... across
Acrosyndactyly (MELL) .... ASD
Acroteria (VRA) .... acrt
Acryl Cyclic Sulfonium Zwitterion (SAUS) .... ACSZ

Acryl Group [*Organic chemistry*] (DAVI) .... Ac
Acryl Hydrocarbon Hydroxylase (SAUS) .... AHH
Acrylamide (EDCT) .... AM
Acrylamide Bis-Acrylamide .... ACRYL-BIS
Acrylamide Gel Electrophoresis (MAE) .... AGE
Acrylamide Producers Association (EA) .... APA
Acrylamidomethylbutyl Trimethylammonium Chloride [*Organic chemistry*] .... AMBTAC
(Acrylamido)methylpropanesulfonic Acid [*Trademark of Lubrizol*] [*Organic chemistry*] .... AMPS
Acrylate-Butadiene Rubber .... ABR
Acrylate-Styrene-Acrylonitrile Terpolymer (EDCT) .... ASA
Acrylic [*Organic chemistry*] .... Acr
Acrylic .... ACRY
Acrylic (MSA) .... ACRYL
Acrylic Acid [*Organic chemistry*] .... AA
Acrylic acid ester rubber (SAUS) .... ACM
Acrylic Council (NTPA) .... AC
Acrylic Eye Illustrator [*Medicine*] .... AEI
Acrylic Jacket Crown (MELL) .... AJC
Acrylic on Canvas (VRA) .... ac/c
Acrylic Optics Corp. (SAUO) .... AOP
Acrylic Rubber (EDCT) .... AR
Acrylic Styrene [*Plastics technology*] .... AS
Acrylic Styrene Acrylonitrile (SAUS) .... ASA
Acrylic Veneer Crown (MELL) .... AVC
Acrylic-Styrene-Acrylonitrile [*Organic chemistry*] .... ASA
Acrylonitrile [*Organic chemistry*] .... ACN
Acrylonitrile [*Organic chemistry*] .... AN
Acrylonitrile Butadiene Acrylate (SAUS) .... ABA
Acrylonitrile Butadiene Alternating Copolymer Rubber (PDAA) .... ABACR
Acrylonitrile Chlorinated polyethylene Styrene (SAUS) .... ACS-poly
Acrylonitrile Ethylene Styrene [*Organic chemistry*] .... AES
[*The*] **Acrylonitrile Group** (EA) .... TAG
Acrylonitrile Methyl Methacrylate [*Organic chemistry*] .... AMMA
Acrylonitrile Styrene Acrylate [*Plastics*] [*Organic chemistry*] .... ASA
Acrylonitrile-Butadiene [*Organic chemistry*] .... AB
Acrylonitrile/Butadiene [*Organic chemistry*] .... AC/BD
Acrylonitrile-Butadiene-Acrylate [*Organic chemistry*] .... ABA
Acrylonitrile-Butadiene-Styrene [*Organic chemistry*] .... ABS
Acrylonitrile-Butadiene-Styrene and Styrene-Acrylonitrile [*Organic chemistry*] (ERG) .... ABS/SAN
Acrylonitrile-Butadiene-Styrene Resin (EDCT) .... ABS
Acrylonitrile-Chlorinated PE-Styrene (SAUS) .... ACS
Acrylonitrile-Ethylene-Propylene-Styrene (EDCT) .... AES
Acrylonitrile-Isoprene Rubber (SAUS) .... NIR
Acrylonitrile-Methyl Methacrylate Copolymer (EDCT) .... AMMA
Acrylonitrile/Styrene/Acrylate (SAUS) .... ASA
Acryloyloxyethyl N-Methylcarbamate [*Organic chemistry*] .... AEMC
ACS Biblio-information, Inc., Brossard, Quebec [*Library symbol*] [*National Library of Canada*] (BIB) .... QBRA
ACS Symposium Series (SAUS) .... ACS Symp Ser
ACSE [*Association Control Service Element*]**-Associate-Request** [*Telecommunications*] (OSI) .... AARE
ACSE [*Association Control Service Element*]**-Associate-Request** [*Telecommunications*] (OSI) .... AARQ
ACSEC Practice Bulletins (SAUS) .... ASECPB
Act (SAUS) .... A
Act Australian Heritage Commission Act (SAUO) .... AHC
Act Day [*Financial Services*] [*British*] .... A-(Day)
Act Environment Protection [*Alligator Rivers Region*] [*Act 1978*] [*Commonwealth*] (EERA) .... EP (ARR)
Act for Better Child Care Services .... ABC
Act for International Development (ACAE) .... AID
Act in Crisis Today [*Fund sponsored by the Lutheran Church in America*] .... ACT
Act Inside the Army [*European antiwar group*] .... AITA
ACT Land Information Forum (SAUO) .... ACTLIF
ACT Manufacturing [*NASDAQ symbol*] (TTSB) .... ACTM
ACT Manufacturing, Inc. [*NASDAQ symbol*] (SAG) .... ACTM
ACT Manufacturing, Inc. [*Associated Press*] (SAG) .... ACT Mf
ACT Networks [*NASDAQ symbol*] (TTSB) .... ANET
ACT Networks, Inc. [*Associated Press*] (SAG) .... ACT Net
ACT Networks, Inc. [*NASDAQ symbol*] (SAG) .... ANET
Act of Sederunt (DLA) .... Act of Sed
Act of Sederunt (DLA) .... AS
Act Teleconferencing [*NASDAQ symbol*] (TTSB) .... ACTT
Act Teleconferencing, Inc. [*NASDAQ symbol*] (SAG) .... ACTT
Act Teleconferencing, Inc. [*Associated Press*] (SAG) .... ActTele
Act Teleconferencing Unit [*NASDAQ symbol*] (TTSB) .... ACTTU
Act Teleconferencing Wrrt [*NASDAQ symbol*] (TTSB) .... ACTTW
Act Together [*Defunct*] (EA) .... AT
Acta Apostolicae Sedis [*A publication*] (ODCC) .... AAS
Acta Archaeologica (journ.) (SAUS) .... AARch
Acta Cancellariae [*England*] [*A publication*] (DLA) .... Monro
Acta Cancellariae, by Monroe [*England*] [*A publication*] (DLA) .... Act Can
Acta Cancellariae by Monroe (journ.) (SAUS) .... ActCan
Acta Chimica Scandinavica [*A publication*] (MEC) .... Acta Chim Scand
Acta Conciliorum Oecumenicorum [*A publication*] (ODCC) .... ACO
Acta Dominorum Concili [*3 vols.*] [*1839-1943*] [*Scotland*] [*A publication*] (DLA) .... ADC
Acta Geographica Lodziensia (journ.) (SAUS) .... SAGLBQ
Acta Geologica Taiwanica (journ.) (SAUS) .... SRTUAW
Acta Juridica [*South Africa*] [*A publication*] (ILCA) .... AJ
Acta Pathologica, Microbiologica et Immunologica Scandinavica (SAUS) .... APMIS

Acta Physica Austriaca Supplementum (journ.) (SAUS) ... Acta Phgys Austr Suppl
Acta Psychologica (journ.) (SAUS) ... APsych
Acta Sanctae Sedis [*A publication*] (ODCC) ... ASS
Acta Sanctorum [*A publication*] (ODCC) ... AASS
Acta Sanctorum [*Acts of the Saints*] [*Latin*] ... ASS
Actas Ciba (journ.) (SAUS) ... Act Ci
Actas Clinica Yodice (journ.) (SAUS) ... Actas Clin Yodice
Acted (ABBR) ... ACTD
Actel Corp. [*Associated Press*] (SAG) ... Actel
Actel Corp. [*NASDAQ symbol*] (SAG) ... ACTL
Actifed [*Burroughs-Wellness, Inc.*] [*Pharmacology*] (DAVI) ... ACTIFD
Actin [*Muscle physiology*] ... A
Actin-Binding Protein [*Cytology*] ... ABP
Acting ... A
Acting (ROG) ... AC
Acting ... ACT
Acting (PHSD) ... Act
Acting (ADWA) ... actg
Acting (AFM) ... ACTG
Acting (ADA) ... AG
Acting Air Vice-Marshal [*British*] (DAS) ... AAVM
Acting Air-Marshal [*British*] ... AAM
Acting Appointment ... AA
Acting Army (SAUS) ... AA
Acting Assistant (SAUS) ... A/A
Acting Assistant Adjutant-General [*Military*] [*British*] (ROG) ... AAAG
Acting Assistant Quartermaster [*Marine Corps*] ... AAQM
Acting Bureau Chief (DEMM) ... ABC
Acting Chief (SAUS) ... ACTG CHF
Acting Chief Petty Officer (SAUS) ... ACPO
Acting Commander, Royal Engineers (SAUS) ... ACRE
Acting Commissary General of Subsistence [*Army*] ... ACGS
Acting Commissary of Subsistence ... ACS
Acting Director (SAUS) ... Act Dir
Acting Fort Major [*Military*] [*British*] (ROG) ... AFM
Acting Grand Master [*Freemasonry*] ... AGM
Acting Group Captain (SAUO) ... A/GC
Acting Inspector of Constabulary (SAUS) ... AIC
Acting Judge (ADA) ... AJ
Acting Justice (ADA) ... AJ
Acting Lieutenant [*Navy*] [*British*] ... A/L
Acting Pay Clerk [*Navy*] ... ACTPC
Acting Paymaster Sub-Lieutenant [*Navy*] [*British*] ... APSL
Acting Paymaster Sub-Lieutnant (SAUS) ... APSL
Acting Petty Officer Air Mechanic [*British military*] (DMA) ... APOAM
Acting Pilot Officer [*British*] ... APO
Acting Secretary (SAUS) ... ACTG SEC
Acting Secretary (BARN) ... Actg Sec
Acting Secretary General (SAUS) ... ASG
Acting Secretary of Defense (SAA) ... ACTSECDEF
Acting Secretary of the Navy (SAUS) ... ACTSECNAN
Acting Secretary of the Navy ... ACTSECNAV
Acting Sergeant-Major [*Military*] (WDAA) ... ASM
Acting Sub-Lieutenant (SAUS) ... Actg Sub-Lt
Acting Sub-Lieutenant [*Navy*] [*British*] ... ASL
Acting Sub-Lieutenant [*Canadian*] ... ASLT
Acting Transportation Officer ... ATRO
Acting Transporting Officer (SAUS) ... ATRO
Acting Wing Commander (SAUS) ... AWC
Acting Wing-Commander [*British*] ... AWC
Acting-Lieutenant (SAUS) ... Actg-Lt
Actinic Keratosis [*Ophthalmology*] (DAVI) ... AK
Actinic Reticuloid Syndrome [*Medicine*] (DMAA) ... AR
Actinide Nitride-Fueled Reactor (NRCH) ... ANF
Actinidin ... ACT
Actinium [*Chemical element*] ... Ac
Actinium A (SAUS) ... Ac A
Actinium B (SAUS) ... Ac B
Actinium C (SAUS) ... Ac C
Actinium D (SAUS) ... AcD
Actinium Emanation [*Chemistry*] (MAE) ... ACE
Actinium Emanation [*Chemistry*] (IAA) ... ACEM
Actinium K (SAUS) ... AcK
Actinium Uranium (SAUS) ... AcU
Actinium X (SAUS) ... Ac X
Actinolite (SAUS) ... AK
Actinomicin D (SAUS) ... AMD
Actinomyces (MAE) ... A
Actinomycin [*Also, act*] [*Antibiotic compound*] ... A
Actinomycin [*Also, A*] [*Generic form*] [*Antibiotic compounds*] ... act
Actinomycin C (LDT) ... ACC
Actinomycin D [*Medicine*] (DMAA) ... ACD
Actinomycin D (SAUS) ... AD
Actinomycin D, Bleomycin, Vincristine [*Antineoplastic drug regimen*] ... ABV
Actinomycin D, Fluorouracil, Cyclophosphamide [*Antineoplastic drug regimen*] ... ACFUCY
Actinomycin D, Vincristine, Cisplatin [*Antineoplastic drug regimen*] (DAVI) ... AVP-II
Actinomycin D, Vincristine, Platinol [*Cisplatin*] [*Antineoplastic drug regimen*] ... AVP
Actinomycin Dactinomycin [*Antineoplastic drug regimen*] (DAVI) ... ACTIN-D
Actinomycin-C [*Antineoplastic drug*] ... act-C
Actinomycin-D [*Also, AMD, DACT*] [*Antineoplastic drug*] ... act-D
Actinomycin-D [*Also, act-D, DACT*] [*Antineoplastic drug*] ... AMD
Actinomycin-D, Dacarbazine, Vincristine [*Antineoplastic drug regimen*] ... ADV
Actinomycosis (MELL) ... AM
Actinon (MAE) ... An
Actinouranium (MED) ... AcU
Action ... A
Action [*NATO*] ... ACT
Action ... ACTN
Action Against Allergy [*British*] (EAIO) ... AAA
Action Against Armageddon Project [*Defunct*] (EA) ... AAAP
Action Against Burns [*Formerly, APBIC*] (EA) ... AAB
Action Aid (SAUO) ... AA
Action Aid of the Asia Foundation (SAUO) ... ACN
Action and Reply Notice (SAA) ... ARN
Action and/or Reply [*Control system*] ... A/R
Action at a Distance Electrodynamics (SAUS) ... ADE
Action Bell Canada ... ABC
Action by Christians Against Torture (EAIO) ... ACT
Action by Churches Together (SAUO) ... ACT
Action by the Community Relating to the Environment [*EC*] (ECED) ... ACE
Action Canada Network [*Coalition formed in 1987 opposed to free trade*] (CROSS) ... ACN
Action Cards for Engineers and Scientists (ACAE) ... ACES
Action Center for Educational Service and Scholarships ... ACCESS
Action Change Card ... ACC
Action Chretienne pour l'Eglise du Silence [*Belgium*] ... ACES
Action Civile [*Civil Action*] [*French*] (ILCA) ... AC
Action Coalition to Create Opportunities for Retirement with Dignity (SAUO) ... ACCORD
Action Code (SAUS) ... AC
Action Committee against Narcotics (SAUO) ... ACAN
Action Committee Against Narcotics ... ACAN
Action Committee for a United States of Europe [*EC*] (ECED) ... ACUSE
Action Committee for European Aerospace (SAUO) ... ACEA
Action Committee for Higher Education [*Defunct*] (EA) ... ACHE
Action Committee for Narcotics Education (SAUS) ... ACNE
Action Committee for Narcotics Education and Enforcement ... ACNEE
Action Committee for Rural Electrification (EA) ... ACRE
Action Committee of Public Transport of the European Communities GG2 [*See also CATPCE*] (EAIO) ... ACPTEC
Action Committee on American-Arab Relations [*Later, AARC*] ... ACAAR
Action Committee on American-Arab Relations (SAUO) ... ACAAR
Action Congress Party [*Ghana*] [*Political party*] (PPW) ... ACP
Action Contre la Faim (SAUO) ... ACF
Action Control Number [*Army*] (MCD) ... ACN
Action Control Point [*Telecommunications*] ... ACP
ACTION Cooperative Volunteer Program ... ACV
Action Coordinating Committee to End Segregation in the Suburbs ... ACCESS
Action Coordinating Council for Comprehensive Child Care ... ACC-CCC
Action Council of Regional Dissemination Directors ... ACORDD
Action Current Potential (IAA) ... ACP
Action Current, Potential (SAUS) ... ACP
Action Cutout (SAUS) ... ACO
Action Cut-Out ... ACO
Action Data Automation [*British*] (NATG) ... ADA
Action Data Automation - Small (SAA) ... ADA-S
Action Data Automation Language [*Computer science*] (MHDB) ... ADAL
Action Data Automation System (SAUS) ... ADAS
Action Data Automation Weapon System (SAUS) ... ADAWS
Action Data Automation Weapons System (MCD) ... ADAWS
Action Data Automation-Large (SAUS) ... ADA-L
Action Data Network (MCD) ... ADNET
Action Decision [*or Determination*] **Taken** ... ADTAKE
Action Decision Taken Advice Decision Taken (SAUS) ... ADTAD
Action Delay Character (SAUS) ... ADC
Action Democratique Guyanaise [*French Guiana*] [*Political party*] (EY) ... ADG
Action des Chretiens pour l'Abolition de la Torture [*Action by Christians for the Abolition of Torture*] (EAIO) ... ACAT
Action Description Memoranda [*Environmental science*] (COE) ... ADM
Action Description Memorandum (SAUS) ... ADM
Action Determination Taken Advice Determination Taken (SAUS) ... ADTAD
Action Directe [*Direct Action*] [*Terrorist group*] [*French*] (PD) ... AD
Action Driver [*Computer science*] ... AD
ACTION Drug Prevention Program ... ADPP
Action d'Urgence Internationale [*International Emergency Action - IEA*] [*Paris, France*] (EAIO) ... AUI
Action Error Analysis [*Engineering*] ... AEA
Action Figure ... AF
Action for Better Living [*Defunct*] (EA) ... ABL
Action for Blind People (SAUO) ... ABP
Action for Boston Community Development (SAUO) ... ABCD
Action for Brain-Handicapped Children [*Defunct*] (EA) ... ABC
Action for Brain-injured Children (SAUS) ... ABC
Action for Child Protection (EA) ... ACP
Action for Child Transportation Safety [*Defunct*] (EA) ... ACTS
Action for Children in Trouble (EA) ... ACT
Action for Children's Television [*Defunct*] (EA) ... ACT
Action for Children's Television ... AFCTV
Action for Corporate Accountability [*An association*] (EA) ... ACTION
Action for Development [*FAO*] [*United Nations*] ... AD
Action for Development (SAUO) ... AFORD
Action for Disabled Customers [*British Telecom*] ... ADC
Action for Dysphasic Adults [*British*] ... ADA
Action for Food Production (SAUO) ... AFPRO
Action for Former Military Wives [*Later, NAFMW*] [*An association*] (EA) ... AFMW
Action for Gay & Lesbian Ordinands (WDAA) ... AGLO
Action for Independent Maturity (SAUO) ... AIM

Action for Independent Maturity [*Later, AARP*] .... AIM
Action for Industrial Recycling [*An association*] .... AIR
Action for Interracial Understanding [*Defunct*] (EA) .... AIU
Action for Life (EA) .... AL
Action for Non-Violence in Learning [*British*] (DI) .... ANVIL
Action for Nuclear Disarmament Education Fund (EA) .... ANDEF
Action for Post-Soviet Jewry [*An association*] (EA) .... APSJ
Action for Prevention of Bum Injuries to Children (SAUO) .... APBIC
Action for Prevention of Burn Injuries to Children [*Later, AAB*] (EA) .... APBIC
Action for Rational Transit (SAUS) .... ART
Action for Resisting Invasion, Colonialism and Apartheid Fund (SAUO) .... AFRICA Fund
Action for Soviet Jewry (EA) .... ASJ
Action for Victims of Medical Accidents [*British*] [*An association*] (DBA) .... AVMA
Action for World Development (SAUO) .... AWD
Action from Ireland [*An association*] (EAIO) .... AFRI
Action Group [*United National Independence Party Alliance of Nigeria*] [*Political party*] .... AG
Action Group Against Harassment & Discrimination in the Workplace [*Groupe d'Action Contre le Harcelement et Discrimination au Travail*] [*Action Against Harassment*] (AC) .... AGAHD
Action Group for the Construction Industry Institute (SAUO) .... CIAG
Action Group on Immigration and Nationality [*British*] (DI) .... AGIN
Action Health 2000-International Voluntary Health Association (SAUO) .... AH 2000
Action Identifier (SAUS) .... AI
Action in Distress [*British*] (DI) .... AID
Action in Error Condition (SAUS) .... AEC
Action Indus [*AMEX symbol*] (TTSB) .... ACZ
Action Industries [*AMEX symbol*] (SAG) .... ACZ
Action Industries, Inc. [*Associated Press*] (SAG) .... Action
Action Industries, Inc. [*AMEX symbol*] (SPSG) .... ACX
Action Information Control Officer [*Navy*] .... AICO
Action Information Display System .... AIDS
Action Information Operations Tactical Trainer (ADA) .... AIOTT
Action Information Organization .... AIO
Action Information System (SAUS) .... AIS
Action Information Training Center .... AITC
Action International Ministries (EAIO) .... ACTION
Action Internationale Contre la Faim [*International Action Against Hunger*] [*Paris, France*] (EAIO) .... AICF
Action Internationale pour les Droits de l'Enfant [*International Action for the Rights of the Child - IARC*] [*Paris, France*] (EAIO) .... AIDE
Action Item (NASA) .... AI
Action Item Assignment (DNAB) .... AIA
Action Item Closeout Sheet (MCD) .... AICS
Action Item Control Card (SAUS) .... AICC
Action Item Directive (AAG) .... AID
Action Item List (MCD) .... AIL
Action Item Report (NASA) .... AIR
Action Item Sheet (MCD) .... AIS
Action Item System .... AIS
Action Item Tracking System [*Radiation measurement*] (NRCH) .... AITS
Action League for Physically Handicapped Advancement (SAUO) .... ALPHA
Action League of Physically Handicapped Adults [*Canada*] .... ALPHA
Action Leakage Rate [*Environmental science*] (EPAT) .... ALR
Action Learning (PDAA) .... AL
Action [*Indicator*] **Level** [*Radiation measurement*] (NRCH) .... AL
Action Library, Washington, DC [*OCLC symbol*] (OCLC) .... ACT
Action Limit (SAUS) .... AL
Action Linkage [*An association*] (EA) .... AL
Action Linkage Network (EA) .... AL
Action Memorandum (BCP) .... AM
Action Monegasque [*Monegasque Action*] [*Political party*] (PPE) .... AM
Action Nationale [*National Action for People and Homeland*] [*Switzerland*] [*Political party*] (PPE) .... AN
Action of Instant Recording [*Video technology*] .... AIR
Action Officer [*Army*] (AABC) .... ACTO
Action Officer [*Air Force*] (AFM) .... AO
Action on Alcohol Abuse [*British*] .... AAA
Action on Disability and Development [*Tamale, Ghana*] .... ADD
Action on Smoking and Health (EA) .... ASH
Action on Smoking and Health - Northern Ireland (EAIO) .... ASH-NI
Action on Smoking and Health - Scotland (EAIO) .... ASH-S
Action on Smoking and Health in Wales (EAIO) .... ASHW
Action on Violence and Family Intervention (SAUO) .... AVFI
Action Organization for the Liberation of Palestine (SAUO) .... AOLP
Action Peace International (SAUO) .... AP
Action Performance Companies [*NASDAQ symbol*] (SAG) .... ACTN
Action Performance Companies [*Associated Press*] (SAG) .... ActPerf
Action Performance Cos. [*NASDAQ symbol*] (TTSB) .... ACTN
Action Pharmaceutique (journ.) (SAUS) .... Act Pharm
Action Plan (SAUS) .... AP
Action Plan Element (SAUS) .... APE
Action Plan for Coordinated Aid to Poland and Hungary (SAUS) .... PHARE
Action Plan for Marine Biodiversity Conservation in China (SAUS) .... APMBCC
Action Planning Conference (SAUO) .... APC
Action Point (SAUS) .... ACP
Action Post (SAUS) .... AP
Action Potential [*of auditory nerve*] .... AP
Action Potential Amplitude [*Physiology*] .... APA
Action Potential Duration [*Electrophysiology*] .... APD
Action pour la Renaissance de Corse [*Action for the Rebirth of Corsica*] [*French*] .... ARC
Action Print Only [*Cinematography*] (WDMC) .... APO
Action Products International, Inc. [*Associated Press*] (SAG) .... ActnPr
Action Products International, Inc. [*NASDAQ symbol*] (NQ) .... APII
Action Products Intl. [*NASDAQ symbol*] (TTSB) .... APII
Action Program for Women .... APW
Action Public Library, Action, ON, Canada [*Library symbol*] [*Library of Congress*] (LCLS) .... CaOAc
Action Register .... AR
Action Republicaine et Sociale [*Republican and Social Action*] [*France*] [*Political party*] (PPE) .... ARS
Action Requests (SAUS) .... ARs
Action Research for the Crippled Child (SAUO) .... ARCC
Action Research into Multiple Sclerosis [*See also Arms of America - AA*] [*British*] .... ARMS
Action Research Model [*Program of Keep America Beautiful, Inc.*] .... ARM
Action Resource Centre [*British*] (CB) .... ARC
Action Resource Development Center (SAUO) .... ARDC
Action Revolutionnaire Corse [*Corsican Revolutionary Action*] (PD) .... ARC
Action Sociale Tchadienne [*Chadian Social Action*] .... AST
Action Socialiste [*Socialist Action*] [*Congo*] .... AS
Action Socialiste Congolaise [*Congolese Socialist Action*] .... ASC
Action Speed Tactical .... AST
Action Sports Entertainment Cable [*Cable TV programming service*] .... ASEC
Action Surveys, Inc. [*Information service or system*] (IID) .... ASI
Action Table Print (SAA) .... ATP
Action Taken .... AT
Action Taken (SAUS) .... A/T
Action Taken Code (MCD) .... ATC
Action Tape In (SAUS) .... ATI
Action Technical Order .... ATO
Action through Creative Organization, Research, and Discussion [*An association*] (EA) .... ACORD
Action through Creative Organization, Research and Discussion (SAUS) .... ACORD
Action Time (SAUS) .... AT
Action Time [*Air Force*] .... A/T
Action Tracking System [*Environmental Protection Agency*] (GFGA) .... ATS
Action Training Coalition [*Defunct*] (EA) .... ATC
Action Variable [*Physics*] (BARN) .... J
Action Volunteers for Animals (AC) .... AVA
Action Will Be Cancelled (NOAA) .... ACWCN
Actionable (ABBR) .... ACTNB
ActionAid [*British*] (EAIO) .... AA
Action-Centered Leadership [*Management term*] .... ACL
Action-Centred Leadership (SAUS) .... ACL
Action-Chart Diagramer [*Computer science*] .... ACD
Actions Having Significant Personnel Implications (MCD) .... AHSPI
Actions per Time Interval .... APTI
Action-Speed Tactical Trainer (SAUS) .... ASTT
Action-Study Center for a Governed World [*Defunct*] (EA) .... ASCGW
Activ Card SA ADS [*NASDAQ symbol*] (SG) .... ACTI
Activate (AFM) .... ACTV
Activate (ABBR) .... ACTVA
Activate (MSA) .... ACTVT
Activate Logical Unit [*IBM Co.*] (ACRL) .... ACTLU
Activate Physical Unit [*IBM Co.*] (ACRL) .... ACTPU
Activate Test Article [*Military*] (NASA) .... ACTA
Activated (ABBR) .... ACTVAD
Activated (ABBR) .... ACTVTD
Activated Carbon .... AC
Activated Carbon Fiber .... ACF
Activated Carbon Treatment System (MCD) .... ACTS
Activated Carbons Producers' Association [*European Council of Chemical Manufacturers Federations*] [*Brussels, Belgium*] (EAIO) .... ACPA
Activated Carbons Producers Association (SAUS) .... ACPA
Activated Cell (DB) .... ATC
Activated Charcoal [*Medicine*] (DB) .... AC
Activated Charcoal Artificial Cell [*Medicine*] (DB) .... ACAC
Activated Charcoal Granule (PDAA) .... ACG
Activated Charcoal Granules (SAUS) .... ACG
Activated Clotting (or Coagulation) Time (SAUS) .... ACT
Activated Clotting [*or Coagulation*] **Time** [*Medicine*] .... ACT
Activated Clotting Time for Dactinomycin [*Clinical medicine*] .... ACT-D
Activated Cloud Condensation Nuclei (SAUS) .... ACCN
Activated Coagulation Time (SAUS) .... ACT
Activated Data Sheet (SAUS) .... ADS
Activated Dough Development (OA) .... ADD
Activated Factor X (SAUS) .... Xa
Activated Human Protein [*Biochemistry*] (DB) .... APC
Activated Low Structure (SAUS) .... ALS
Activated Partial Thromboplastin Time [*Hematology*] .... APTT
Activated Partial Thromboplastin Time [*Medicine*] (MELL) .... aPTT
Activated Partial Thromboplastin Time, Control [*Hematology*] (DAVI) .... PTT-CT
Activated Protein C .... APC
Activated Reactive Evaporation [*Coating technology*] .... ARE
Activated Sludge Process .... ASP
Activated Sludge Process Control Series (journ.) (SAUS) .... Act Sludge Process Control Ser
Activated Thymus Cell [*s*] [*Immunochemistry*] .... ATC
Activated Towed Array Sonar (SAUS) .... ACTAS
Activated/Non-Activated [*Cytology*] .... A/NA
Activating (ABBR) .... ACTVAG
Activating (ABBR) .... ACTVTG
Activating Event [*or Experience*], **Belief System, Consequence** [*Irrational behavior theory*] [*Psychotherapy*] .... ABC
Activating Factor [*Biochemistry*] .... AF

Activating Reticular System [*Medicine*] (MELL) .... ARS
Activating Transcription Factors [*Genetics*] .... ATF
Activation (NVT) .... ACT
Activation (NASA) .... ACTIV
Activation (ABBR) .... ACTVAN
Activation (ABBR) .... ACTVTN
Activation Acceptance Team [*NASA*] (NASA) .... AAT
Activation Analysis [*Chemistry*] .... AA
Activation Analysis (MSA) .... ACTVNANAL
Activation Analysis Unit [*British*] .... AAU
Activation and Checkout [*NASA*] (SPST) .... A&C
Activation Ballistic Missile Site (SAA) .... ABMS
Activation Coefficient .... AC
Activation Domain [*Biochemistry*] .... AD
Activation Energy (MAE) .... AE
Activation Energy (SAUS) .... E
Activation Engineering Information Bulletin (AAG) .... AEIB
Activation Management Group [*NASA*] (NASA) .... AMG
Activation Project Control Plan .... APCP
Activation Sequence Factor [*Genetics*] .... ASF
Activation Test Program (MCD) .... ATP
Activation Work Notice .... AWN
Activation Working Group [*Military*] (MCD) .... AWG
Activation/Conversion (DNAB) .... ACT/CONV
Activation-Induced Cell Death [*Immunology*] .... AICD
Activator [*Genetics*] .... AC
Activator (ABBR) .... ACTVOR
Activator (MSA) .... ACTVTR
Activator Protein .... AP
Activator-Dissociation System (DOG) .... Ac Ds System
Active (VRA) .... act
Active (AFM) .... ACT
Active (FAAC) .... ACTV
Active Accounts (SAUS) .... AA
Active Acoustic Correlation Detection System (ACAE) .... ACCORDS
Active Acoustic Device .... AAD
Active Acquisition Aid .... AAA
Active Adjunct (SAUS) .... AA
Active Adjunct Undersea Surveillance (SAUS) .... AAUS
Active Aero Charter [*FAA designator*] (FAAC) .... JUS
Active Air Defence [*British*] [*World War II*] .... AA
Active Air Target Fuse (MCD) .... AATF
Active Airborne Expendable Decoy .... AAED
Active Aircraft Plume Suppression (MCD) .... AAPS
Active Alcohol (MELL) .... AA
Active Alkali [*Chemistry*] .... AA
Active and Equal (SAUS) .... AE
Active Antenna Array (MCD) .... AAA
Active Apparel Group [*NASDAQ symbol*] (TTSB) .... AAGP
Active Apparel Group, Inc. [*NASDAQ symbol*] (SAG) .... AAGP
Active Apparel Group, Inc. [*Associated Press*] (SAG) .... ActApp
Active Area .... AA
Active Arm External Load Stabilization System [*Army*] .... AAELSS
Active Army .... AA
Active Army Locator System (SAUS) .... AALC
Active Army Locator System (AABC) .... AALS
Active Army Military Manpower Program .... AAMMP
Active Army Personnel Reporting System [*Europe*] (MCD) .... AAPERS
Active Array Radar (ACAE) .... AAR
Active Assertive Range of Motion [*Medicine*] (DMAA) .... AAROM
Active Assets .... AA
Active Assisted (HGAA) .... AA
Active Assistive Exercise [*Medicine*] .... AAE
Active Assistive Range of Motion [*Medicine*] .... AAROM
Active Asynchronous Quenching (SAUS) .... AAQ
Active Attached Reserve [*Military*] .... AA
Active Attached Reserve [*Royal Australian Naval Reserve*] .... AAR
Active Avoidance [*Medicine*] (DMAA) .... AA
Active Avoidance Reaction [*Medicine*] (DMAA) .... AAR
Active Band-Pass [*Electronics*] (IAA) .... ABP
Active Beacon Collision Avoidance System [*Aviation*] (DA) .... A-BCAS
Active Bilaterally (HGAA) .... ab
Active Bioprosthetic Composition [*Artificial ligament*] .... ABC
Active Body Control [*Automotive engineering*] .... ABC
Active Boom Suspension [*Engineering*] .... ABS
Active Buffer Address (SAUS) .... ABA
Active Business Records [*Bell & Howell Co.*] .... ABR
Active Capital [*Investment term*] .... AC
Active Cavity Radiometer .... ACR
Active Cavity Radiometer Irradiance Monitor .... ACRIM
Active Cavity Radiometer Irradiance Monitor (SAUS) .... ACRIM II
Active Certificate Information Program [*for stock certificates*] [*Computer science*] .... ACIP
Active Change Initiating Document (IUSS) .... ACID
Active Chronic Gastritis [*Medicine*] (MELL) .... ACG
Active Chronic Hepatitis [*Medicine*] (DMAA) .... ACH
Active Cirrhosis [*Medicine*] .... AC
Active Citizen Force [*British military*] (DMA) .... ACF
Active Citizen Force (SAUO) .... ACF
Active Citizenship Campaign .... ACC
Active Cleaning Technique [*Optical surface*] .... ACT
Active Clearance Control (PDAA) .... ACC
Active Color Enhancement [*Proxima Corp.*] [*Computer science*] (PCM) .... ACE
Active Commission Base Date [*Military*] .... ACBD
Active Communications Satellite .... ACS

Active Component .... AC
Active Components and Reserve Components .... AC & RC
Active Components and Reserve Components (SAUS) .... AC&RC
Active Compression-Decompression Cardiopulmonary Resuscitation [*Medicine*] (MELL) .... ACDCPR
Active Computer (SAUS) .... AC
Active Concentration (SAUS) .... AC
Active Configuration Profile [*Computer science*] (VERA) .... ACP
Active Contamination Control Subsystem (SSD) .... ACCS
Active Contract Data Review Board [*Air Force*] (AFIT) .... ACDRB
Active Contract File [*DoD*] .... ACF
Active Contrast Reduction System (MCD) .... ACRS
Active Control Device (SSD) .... ACD
Active Control Equivalence Studies .... ACES
Active Control Evaluation for Spacecraft (SAUS) .... ACES
Active Control for Total In-Flight Simulator (MCD) .... ACTIFS
Active Control of Space Structures .... ACOSS
Active Control Station (IUSS) .... ACS
Active Control System (ACAE) .... ACS
Active Control Technique [*or Technology*] .... ACT
Active Control Technique (or Technology) (SAUS) .... ACT
Active Control Torque System [*Automotive engineering*] (PS) .... ACTS
Active Corps of Executives [*Maintained by the Service Corps of Retired Executives Association*] .... ACE
Active Correlation Track-on-Jam .... ACTOJ
Active Countermeasures .... ACM
Active Damping and Precision Pointing (ACAE) .... ADAPP
Active Data Objects (SAUS) .... ADO
Active Defense (SAUS) .... Act Def
Active Deferral Service (MCD) .... ADS
Active Delay Phase Shift (SAUS) .... ADPS
Active Delayed Phase Shift (IAA) .... ADPS
Active Device Mount (SAUS) .... ADM
Active Diffusion Control (MCD) .... ADC
Active Dipping Sonar (MCD) .... ADS
Active Directory (SAUS) .... AD
Active Directory Service Interface [*Computer science*] .... ADSI
Active Directory Services [*Computer science*] .... ADS
Active Disease (MELL) .... AD
Active Disk Table [*Computer science*] (IBMDP) .... ADT
Active Dosimeter .... AD
Active Duty .... ACDU
Active Duty (DNAB) .... ACTDU
Active Duty (ACAE) .... AD
Active Duty Agreement .... ADA
Active Duty Assistance Program (DNAB) .... ADAP
Active Duty Assistance Program Team .... ADAPT
Active Duty Base Date [*Later, PSD*] [*Navy*] .... ADBD
Active Duty Commitment (SAUS) .... ACD
Active Duty Commitment .... ADC
Active Duty Dates of Rank [*Army*] (INF) .... ADOR
Active Duty for Training [*Army*] (MCD) .... ACDUTRA
Active Duty for Training [*Army*] (AABC) .... ADT
Active Duty in a Flying Status, Involving Operational or Training Flights [*Navy*] (DNAB) .... ACDIFOPS
Active Duty in a Flying Status, Involving Proficiency in Flying [*Navy*] (DNAB) .... ACDIFPRO
Active Duty in a Flying Status, Not Involving Flying [*Navy*] (DNAB) .... ACDIFDEN
Active Duty in a Flying Status, Operational and Training Flights [*Navy*] .... ACDIFOT
Active Duty in a Flying Status, Operational and Training Flights as Crewmember [*Navy*] .... ACDIFOTCREW
Active Duty in a Flying Status, Operational and Training Flights as Noncrewmember [*Navy*] .... ACDIFOTNONCREW
Active Duty List [*Army*] (INF) .... ADL
Active Duty Nondisability Retirement Branch (SAUS) .... ANDPB
Active Duty Nondisability Retirement Branch [*BUPERS*] [*Navy*] .... ANDRB
Active Duty Obligation [*DoD*] .... ACDUOBLI
Active Duty Service Commitment [*Military*] (AFM) .... ADSC
Active Duty Service Date [*Military*] (DNAB) .... ADSD
Active Duty Under Instruction [*Navy*] .... ACDUINS
Active Duty Under Instruction (SAUS) .... ACDUINS
Active Duty under Instruction in a Flying Status, Involving Operational or Training Flights [*Navy*] (DNAB) .... ACDIFINOPS
Active Duty under Instruction in a Flying Status, Involving Proficiency Flying [*Navy*] (DNAB) .... ACDIFINSPRO
Active Duty under Instruction in a Flying Status, Not Involving Flying [*Navy*] (DNAB) .... ACDIFDENIS
Active Duty under Instruction in a Flying Status, Operational and Training Flights [*Navy*] .... ACDIFOTINS
Active Duty under Instruction in a Flying Status, Operational and Training Flights as Crewmember [*Navy*] .... ACDIFOTINSCREW
Active Duty under Instruction in a Flying Status, Operational and Training Flights as Noncrewmember [*Navy*] .... ACDIFOTINSNONCREW
Active Electromagnetic System [*Electronics*] (IAA) .... AES
Active Electronic Buoy (DWSG) .... AEB
Active Electronic Counter-Measure (PDAA) .... AECM
Active Electronic Countermeasures (IUSS) .... AECCM
Active Electronic Countermeasures (SAUS) .... AECM
Active Electronic Decoy (CAAL) .... AED
Active Electronic Gimballess Inertial System .... AEGIS
Active Electronically Scanned Array (SAUS) .... AESA
Active Element Array .... AEA
Active Element Group [*QCR*] .... AEG
Active Emitter File (IUSS) .... AEF

Active Employment Strategy ..... AES
Active Employment Training Organization ..... AETO
Active Engine Mount [*Automotive engineering*] ..... AEM
Active Enhancement (MCD) ..... AE
Active Enlisted Plans Branch [*BUPERS*] ..... AEPB
Active Euthanasia (MELL) ..... AE
Active Exercise [*Rehabilitation*] (DAVI) ..... Act Ex
Active Exercise (MELL) ..... AE
Active Expendable Decoy (SAUS) ..... AED
Active Expendable Decoy System (SAUS) ..... AEDS
Active Experiment Working Group (SAUO) ..... AEWG
Active Federal Commissioned Service ..... AFCS
Active Federal Service (DOMA) ..... AFS
Active Feedback Block (SAUS) ..... AFB
Active File Table [*Computer science*] (IBMDP) ..... AFT
Active Filter (SAUS) ..... ACTER
Active Filter Design ..... AFD
Active Filter Network ..... AFN
Active Filter Unit (SAUS) ..... AFU
Active Fleet Ships (IUSS) ..... AFS
Active Flight Load System (MCD) ..... AFLS
Active Framework for Data Warehousing (RALS) ..... AFDW
Active Fuel Length [*Nuclear energy*] (NRCH) ..... AFL
Active Fuzing System ..... AFS
Active Galactic Nuclei ..... AGN
Active Galactic Nucleus [*Astronomy*] ..... AGN
Active Guard and Reserve [*Military*] (DOMA) ..... AGR
Active Guard Reserve [*DoD*] ..... AGR
Active High Resolution (MCD) ..... AHR
Active History File [*Army*] ..... AHF
Active Homing (SAUS) ..... AH
Active Hostile Battery (SAUS) ..... AH Bty
Active Hostility Index [*Psychology*] ..... AHI
Active Imaging Pointer-Tracker System (SAUS) ..... AIPTS
Active In Commission (SAUS) ..... ACT/IC
Active in Commission [*Vessel status*] [*Navy*] ..... ACT/IC
Active in Service [*Vessel status*] [*Navy*] ..... ACT/IS
Active Index Register (SAUS) ..... AIR
Active Inert Missile ..... AIM
Active Ingredient ..... AI
Active Input Interface [*Computer science*] (VERA) ..... AII
Active Instability Control (HEAS) ..... AIC
Active Integral Defense (AFM) ..... AID
Active Integrated Module ..... AIM
Active Interface (SAUS) ..... AI
Active Interference Suppression (SAUS) ..... AIS
Active Isolated Stretching ..... AIS
Active Isolation/Balance System [*for aircraft*] (RDA) ..... AIBS
Active Item Balance Tape in (SAUS) ..... AIBT in
Active Item Balance Tape out (SAUS) ..... AIBT out
Active Lane Control [*Image control and lane positioning*] [*Automotive engineering*] ..... ALC
Active Laser Homing (SAUS) ..... ALH
Active Laser Resonator Techniques (ACAE) ..... ALERT
Active LASER Seeker (MCD) ..... ALS
Active Launch Normal (ACAE) ..... ALN
Active Life Expectancy (MELL) ..... ALE
Active Lift Distribution Control Center (SAUO) ..... ALDCC
Active Lift Distribution Control System [*Aerospace*] ..... ALDCS
Active Line Rotation [*Telecommunications*] (TEL) ..... ALR
Active Line State (SAUS) ..... ALS
Active Link (SAUS) ..... ALINK
Active List (NDBD) ..... AL
Active Long Term Archive (SAUS) ..... ALTA
Active Long-Term Archive (EOSA) ..... ALTA
Active Look-Aside Table (SAUS) ..... ALAT
Active Low-Light-Level Television [*Night vision device*] [*Air Force*] (MCD) ..... ALLTV
Active Magnetic Bearing [*Mechanical engineering*] ..... AMB
Active Magnetosphere Particle Explorers (SAUS) ..... AMPTEs
Active Magnetospheric Particle Tracer Experiment (SAUS) ..... AMPTE
Active Magnetospheric Particle Tracer Explorer [*Project*] [*NASA/West Germany*] ..... AMPTE
Active Magnetospheric Particle Tracer Explorers (SAUS) ..... AMPTE
Active Magnetospheric Plasma Tracer Explorers (SAUS) ..... AMPTE
Active Maintenance Downtime ..... AMDT
Active Maintenance Time ..... AMT
Active Maintenance Training Simulator [*Military*] ..... AMTS
Active Mariner Program [*Military*] (DNAB) ..... A-M
Active Market [*Investment term*] ..... AM
Active Matrix (VERA) ..... AM
Active Matrix Color Display (VERA) ..... AMCD
Active Matrix Display (VERA) ..... AMD
Active Matrix Display Advanced Micro Devices, Inc. (SAUO) ..... AMD
Active Matrix Electro Luminescent (SAUS) ..... AMEL
Active Matrix Electroluminescent (RDA) ..... AMEL
Active Matrix Liquid Crystal Display ..... AMLCD
Active Matrix Technology (VERA) ..... AMT
Active Matrix Thin-Film Transistor [*Electronics*] (MED) ..... AMTFT
Active Medium Propagation [*Amplifier*] ..... AMP
Active Memory Technology (ECON) ..... AMT
Active Messages (SAUS) ..... AM
Active Microwave Imager Synthetic Aperture Radar (GEOI) ..... AMISAR
Active Microwave Instrument ..... AMI
Active Microwave Instrument 2 (SAUS) AMI-2
Active Microwave Instrumentation (ACAE) ..... AMI
Active Microwave Pressure Sounder (SAUS) ..... AMPS
Active Microwave Workshop ..... AMW
Active Militia (SAUO) ..... AM
Active Monitor [*Telecommunications*] ..... AM
Active Monitor Present (ACRL) ..... AMP
Active Movie Streaming Format (SAUS) ..... ASF
Active Name Table (HGAA) ..... ANT
Active Neighbourhood Pattern (SAUS) ..... ANP
Active Neighbourhood Pattern Sensitive Fault (SAUS) ..... ANPSF
Active Network Sensitivity Study (ACAE) ..... ANSS
Active Network Synthesis ..... ANS
Active Night Covert Viewing [*or Vision*] **System** ..... ANCOVS
Active Night Covert Viewing System (SAUS) ..... ANCOVS
Active Noise Control [*Noise pollution technique*] ..... ANC
Active Noise Reduction (MCD) ..... ANR
Active Noise System (SAUS) ..... ANS
Active Nutation Control ..... ANC
Active Nutation Damper ..... AND
Active Nutation Damper Electronics ..... ANDE
Active Officer Promotion Branch [*BUPERS*] ..... AOPB
Active On Target (SAUS) ..... AOT
Active Operations (SAUS) ..... Act Opns
Active Optical Fuze ..... AOF
Active Optical Fuzing System ..... AOFS
Active Optical Proximity Fuze (ACAE) ..... AOPF
Active Optical Sensor (MCD) ..... AOS
Active Optical Target Detecting Device (ACAE) ..... AOTDD
Active Optical Target Detector (NVT) ..... AOTD
Active Optical Target Housing (MCD) ..... AOTH
Active Optics Simulation Program [*NASA*] (KSC) ..... AOSP
Active Optics Simulation System [*NASA*] ..... AOSS
Active out of Commission [*Vessel status*] [*Navy*] ..... ACT/OC
Active out of Service [*Vessel status*] [*Navy*] ..... ACT/OS
Active Output Interface [*Computer science*] (VERA) ..... AOI
Active Oxygen (EDCT) ..... AO
Active Oxygen Loss (ACAE) ..... AOL
Active Oxygen Method [*Food fat stability test*] ..... AOM
Active Oxygen Species [*Biochemistry*] ..... AOS
Active Page Register [*Computer science*] (MHDI) ..... APR
Active Parenting [*Publishers*] (DHP) ..... AP
Active Participation Rental Real Estate [*IRS*] ..... APRRE
Active Pass, BC [*ICAO location identifier*] (ICLI) ..... CUAP
Active Personnel Dosimeter ..... APD
Active Phased-Array Antenna (SAUS) ..... APAA
Active Pixel Sensor (SAUS) ..... APS
Active Plasma Experiments (SAUS) ..... APEX
Active Position Backward (SAUS) ..... APB
Active Position Down (SAUS) ..... APD
Active Position Forward (SAUS) ..... APF
Active Position Home (SAUS) ..... APH
Active Position Return (SAUS) ..... APR
Active Position Up (SAUS) ..... APU
Active Prominence Region (SAUS) ..... APR
Active Protection System [*Military*] (INF) ..... APS
Active Pulse Compression Network ..... APCN
Active Purchase Request File [*DoD*] ..... APRF
Active RADAR Augmentor Beacon System (MCD) ..... ARABS
Active Radar Demonstrator (SAUS) ..... ARD
Active Radar Homing (SAUS) ..... ARH
Active RADAR Seeker ..... ARS
Active RADAR Test System (MCD) ..... ARTS
Active Range (MCD) ..... AR
Active Range of Motion [*Medicine*] ..... AROM
Active Range of the Day (MCD) ..... ARD
Active Rate (SAUS) ..... AR
Active Reconnaissance Zone ..... ARZ
Active Recording Program (SAA) ..... ARP
Active Records/Fiche-Oriented Retrieval (DNAB) ..... AR/FOR
Active Reduction of Contrast (MCD) ..... ARC
Active Reference Table (HGAA) ..... ART
Active Relaxed Static Stability (MCD) ..... ARSS
Active Relief Sensor (SAUS) ..... ARES
Active Repeater Satellite [*Air Force*] ..... ARS
Active Requisition Control and Status File [*DoD*] ..... ARCSF
Active Resistance [*Occupational therapy*] ..... AR
Active Resistance Training [*Medicine*] (MELL) ..... ART
Active Resistive Exercise ..... ARE
Active Responsive Factor [*Biochemistry*] ..... ARF
Active Rest Point (IAA) ..... ARP
Active Retirees in Israel [*An association*] ..... ARI
Active Retrodirective Array (MCD) ..... ARA
Active Roll Stabilization [*Automotive suspension*] ..... ARS
Active Rosette-Forming T-Cell (DB) ..... ARFC
Active Routine (SAUS) ..... AR
Active Satellite Attitude Control ..... ASAC
Active Scattering Aerosol Spectrometer [*Aerosol measurement device*] ..... ASAS
Active Scattering Aerosol Spectrometer Probe (MCD) ..... ASASP
Active Security [*Investment term*] ..... AS
Active Segment Field [*Computer science*] (MHDI) ..... ASF
Active Segment Table (HGAA) ..... AST
Active Seismic Experiment [*NASA*] (MCD) ..... ASE
Active Server Application (SAUS) ..... ASA
Active Server Page [*Microsoft Corp.*] ..... ASP
Active Service (SAUS) ..... ASV

Active Service Base Date (DNAB) ... ASBD
Active Service Career for Reserve Officers ... ASCRO
Active Service Unit [*Irish Republican Army*] [*Northern Ireland*] ... ASU
Active Siedband Optimum (SAUS) ... ASO
Active Signal Correction [*Video technology*] ... ASC
Active Singles Quest [*Technique*] [*In book title*] ... ASQ
Active Site Peptide [*Immunochemistry*] ... ASP
Active Sleep [*Physiology*] ... AS
Active Sodium Transport Inhibitor [*Biochemistry*] ... ASTI
Active Sonar for Entrance Surveillance (SAUS) ... ASES
Active SONAR Frequency Analysis and Recording ... ASFAR
Active SONAR Processor ... ASP
Active Sonar Unit (SAUS) ... ASU
Active Spacecraft Potential Control [*Instrumentation*] ... ASPOC
Active Status Register ... ASR
Active Stock Record Card (SAUS) ... ASRC
Active Storage Element [*Computer science*] (VERA) ... ASE
Active Store (SAUS) ... AS
Active Streaming Format [*Microsoft Corp.*] (IGQR) ... ASF
Active Surface Area (MCD) ... ASA
Active Swept Frequency Interferometer Radar (SAUS) ... ASFIR
Active Swept-Frequency Interferometer RADAR [*RADC*] ... ASFIR
Active Switching Element (SAUS) ... ASE
Active Systems (journ.) (SAUS) ... Act Syst
Active Target List (ACAE) ... ATL
Active Task List [*Computer science*] (MHDI) ... ATL
Active Television System (MCD) ... ATS
Active Template Library (SAUS) ... ATL
Active Test Article (MCD) ... ACTA
Active Thermal Control ... ATC
Active Thermal Control Subsystem [*NASA*] (MCD) ... ATCS
Active Thermal Control System [*NASA*] (MCD) ... ACTCS
Active Thermal Feedback (PCM) ... ATF
Active Thermal Protection for Avionics Crew and Heat-Sensitive Equipment [*Air Force*] (MCD) ... APACHE
Active Thermal System (SPST) ... ATS
Active Thermo-Atmosphere Combustion (PDAA) ... ATAC
Active Time List [*Computer science*] ... ATL
Active to Inert Conversion [*Environmental science*] (EPAT) ... AIC
Active Token Collectors Organization (EA) ... ATCO
Active Torque Transfer System ... ATTS
Active Towed Array Sonar (SAUS) ... ATAS
Active Towed Array System (SAUS) ... ATAS
Active Training [*Army*] ... AT
Active Transfer and Conversion, Army ... ATCAR
Active Transfer Bias (ACAE) ... ATB
Active Transfer Command ... ATC
Active Transfer Initiate (ACAE) ... ATI
Active Tuition Assistance Plan [*UAW-General Motors Corp.*] ... ATAP
Active Unattached Reserve [*Royal Australian Navy*] ... AUR
Active Universal Joints ... AUJ
Active Valve Train [*Automotive engineering*] ... AVT
Active Van Atta Array (SAUS) ... AVA Array
Active Vibration Isolation System ... AVIS
Active Vibration Isolator (MCD) ... AVI
Active Voice [*NASDAQ symbol*] (TTSB) ... ACVC
Active Voice Corp. [*Associated Press*] (SAG) ... ActVoic
Active Voice Corp. [*NASDAQ symbol*] (SAG) ... ACVC
Active Voltage Controlled Oscillator (ACAE) ... AVCO
Active Wavelength Demodulation System (SAUS) ... AWDS
Active Well Coincidence Counter [*Nuclear energy*] (NRCH) ... AWCC
Active Work Space [*Computer science*] (NITA) ... AWS
Active X Data Objects (SAUS) ... ADO
Active Zone ... AZ
Active-Assistive [*Range of motion*] [*Orthopedics*] (DAVI) ... AA
Active-Gated Television (PDAA) ... AGTV
Active-In Service (SAUS) ... ACT/IS
Actively (ABBR) ... ACTVY
Actively Shared Knowledge [*Data processing system*] ... ASK
Activeness (ABBR) ... ACTVNS
Active-Out of Commission (SAUS) ... ACT-OC
Active-Out of Service (SAUS) ... ACT/OS
Active/Passive (ACAE) ... AP
Active/Passive Reliable Acoustic Path SONAR (MCD) ... APRAPS
Active-Resistance Exercise (SAUS) ... ARE
Active-Retired Lighthouse Service Employees' Association (EA) ... ARLSEA
ActiveX Data Objects [*Computer science*] ... ADO
Activin [*Biochemistry*] ... ATV
Activin Receptor Gene [*Medicine*] (MELL) ... ARG
Activin Responsive Element [*Biochemistry*] ... ARE
Activision, Inc. [*Associated Press*] (SAG) ... Activisn
Activision, Inc. [*NASDAQ symbol*] (SAG) ... ATVI
Activists for Protecive Animal Legislation (SAUS) ... A-PAL
Activities (SAUS) ... ACT
Activities Committee on New Directions for ALA [*American Library Association*] ... ACONDA
Activities Control Number (SAUS) ... ACN
Activities File [*CSIRO database*] (ADA) ... ACTF
Activities for Daily Living ... ADL
Activities Implemented Jointly [*Between nations*] ... AIJ
Activities Integrating Math and Science ... AIMS
Activities of Daily Living [*Medicine*] ... ADL
Activities Report [*Shipping*] ... ACTREP
Activities Report. Research and Development Associates for Military Food and Packaging Systems, Inc. (journ.) (SAUS) ... Act Rep Res Dev Assoc Mil Food Packag Syst Inc
Activities Report. Research and Development Associates for Military Food and Packaging Systems. Incorporated (SAUO) ... Act Rep Res Dev Assoc Mil Food Packag Syst Inc
Activity ... A
Activity (WDAA) ... AC
Activity (MSA) ... ACT
Activity (ABBR) ... ACTIV
Activity (AABC) ... ACTV
Activity ... ACTVTY
Activity (AFM) ... ACTY
Activity Account ... AA
Activity Accreditation Schedule (MCD) ... AAS
Activity Address Code [*DoD*] ... AAC
Activity Area (SAUS) ... AA
Activity as Tolerated [*Medicine*] (MELL) ... AAT
Activity Assembly Area (SAUS) ... AAA
Activity Automatic Data Process Security Plan (MCD) ... AADPSP
Activity Balance Line Evaluation [*PERT*] ... ABLE
Activity Based Costing [*Financial management*] ... ABC
Activity Based Risk Evaluation Model of Auditing ... ABREMA
Activity Bit (SAUS) ... ACT
Activity Captain (MCD) ... AC
Activity Career Program Manager [*Military*] ... ACPM
Activity Characteristics Sheet [*Agency for International Development*] ... ACS
Activity Civil Engineer (DNAB) ... ACE
Activity Classification Number [*NASA*] (GFGA) ... ACN
Activity Code [*DoD*] ... AC
activity coefficient (SAUS) ... f
Activity Completion Technique [*Personality development test*] [*Psychology*] ... ACT
Activity Control Number ... ACM
Activity Control Number [*Navy*] ... ACN
Activity Credit Unit (DNAB) ... ACU
Activity Data Control System (ACAE) ... ADCS
Activity Data Method (IEEE) ... ADM
Activity Data Sheet (IEEE) ... ADS
Activity Elements (MCD) ... A/E
Activity File (SAUS) ... AF
Activity Identification Code [*Navy*] ... AIC
Activity Index ... AI
Activity Indication Monitor (ACAE) ... AIM
Activity Information Data System (SAUS) ... AIDS
Activity, Interest, and Opinion [*Factor scores*] [*Marketing*] ... AIO
Activity Level Dependent (KSC) ... ALD
Activity Level Dependent Operations (NASA) ... ALDO
Activity Level Independent (KSC) ... ALI
Activity Level Independent Operations (NASA) ... ALIO
Activity Median Aerodynamic Diameter ... AMAD
Activity Metabolic Rate ... AMR
Activity Metabolic Request (SAUS) ... AMR
Activity Mission Code (DNAB) ... AMC
Activity Monitoring Completion Detection (SAUS) ... AMCD
Activity Operating Schedule ... AOS
Activity Order and Shipping Quantity (AFIT) ... AOSQ
Activity Performing Inspection (SAA) ... API
Activity Processing Code ... APC
Activity Providing Telephone Service (DNAB) ... APTS
Activity Readiness Code (DNAB) ... ARC
Activity Reorder Point [*Military*] (AFIT) ... AROP
Activity Report (MCD) ... AR
Activity Reporting Information System (PDAA) ... ARIS
Activity Request Packet (SAUS) ... ARP
Activity Resume (SAUS) ... AR
Activity Routing Indicator (MCD) ... ARI
Activity Safety Level (AFIT) ... ASL
Activity Scheduling Processor [*NASA*] ... ASP
Activity Scheduling Program [*NASA*] ... ASP
Activity Sections Council [*Association of College and Research Libraries*] ... ASC
Activity Start (SAUS) ... AS
Activity Support Date (ACAE) ... ASD
Activity Support File (DNAB) ... ASF
Activity Test ... AT
Activity Therapy center ... ATC
Activity Time Status Report (MCD) ... ATSR
Activity Value Analysis (ACAE) ... AVA
Activity Vector Analysis [*Psychology*] ... AVA
Activity-Based Cost [*Management accounting system*] ... ABC
Activity-Based Management (AAEL) ... ABM
Actoma Resources Ltd. [*Vancouver Stock Exchange symbol*] ... ATA
Actomyosin [*Biochemistry*] ... AM
Acton High School, Acton, ON, Canada [*Library symbol*] [*Library of Congress*] (LCLS) ... CaOAcH
Acton High School, Ontario [*Library symbol*] [*National Library of Canada*] (NLC) ... OACH
Acton Laboratory, Inc. (SAUS) ... ALI
Acton, MA [*FM radio station call letters*] (RBYB) ... WHAB
Acton Public Library, Ontario [*Library symbol*] [*National Library of Canada*] (NLC) ... OAC
Acton Society [*British*] (EAIO) ... AS
Acton, TX [*Location identifier*] [*FAA*] (FAAL) ... AQN
Acton's Prize Cases, Privy Council [*A publication*] (DLA) ... Act
Acton's Prize Cases, Privy Council [*A publication*] (DLA) ... Acton

Acton's Reports, Prize Cases [England] [A publication] (DLA)	Act Pr C
Actons Reports, Prize Cases (journ.) (SAUS)	Act Pr C
actor (SAUS)	act
Actor	ACTR
Actors and Others for Animals (EA)	A & O
Actors and Others for Animals (SAUO)	AOA
Actors' Benevolent Fund [Australia]	ABF
Actors' Church Union [Episcopalian]	ACU
Actor's Conservatory Theater	ACT
Actors' Equity Association (EA)	AEA
Actors Equity Association (SAUS)	AEA
Actors' Equity of Australia	AEA
Actors' Feature Film Award [Australia]	AFFA
Actors' Fund of America (EA)	AFA
Actors Studio (EA)	AS
Actors Working for an Actors Guild (EA)	AWAG
Actrade International Ltd. [NASDAQ symbol] (SAG)	ACRT
Actrade International Ltd. [Associated Press] (SAG)	Actrade
Actrade Intl Ltd. [NASDAQ symbol] (TTSB)	ACRT
Actress (SAUS)	Act
Actress (ABBR)	ACTRE
Actress (ABBR)	ACTRS
Actresses' Franchise League [British]	AFL
Actron Microprocessor Software Support System (SAUS)	AMSSS
Acts and Joint Resolutions of South Carolina (SAUS)	SC Acts
Acts and Joint Resolutions of the State of Iowa [A publication] (DLA)	Iowa Acts
Acts and Joint Resolutions of the State of South Carolina [A publication] (DLA)	SC Acts
Acts and Joint Resolutions of the State of South Carolina (journ.) (SAUS)	SC Acts
Acts & Ordinances of South Australia 1837-1866 (SAUS)	S Austl Acts&Ord
Acts and Ordinances of the Interregnum [1642-60] [British] [A publication] (ILCA)	Acts & Ords Interreg
Acts and Ordinances of the Interregnum [1642-60] [United Kingdom] [A publication] (DLA)	Acts & Ords Interregnum
Acts and Resolves of Massachusetts [A publication] (DLA)	Mass Acts
ACTS Mobile Terminal (SAUS)	AMT
Acts of Alabama [A publication] (DLA)	Ala Acts
Acts of Andrew (BJA)	ActAndr
Acts of Indiana [A publication] (DLA)	Ind Acts
Acts of John (BJA)	ActJn
Acts of Lawting Court [Scotland] [A publication] (DLA)	Act Lawt Ct
Acts of Lords Auditors of Causes [Scotland] [A publication] (DLA)	Act Ld Aud C
Acts of Lords of Council in Civil Causes [1478-1501] [Scotland] [A publication] (DLA)	Act Ld Co CC
Acts of Lords of Council in Public Affairs [Scotland] [A publication] (DLA)	Act Ld Co Pub Aff
Acts of Paul (BJA)	ActPaul
Acts of Peter (BJA)	ActPet
Acts of South Australia (journ.) (SAUS)	Acts S Aust
Acts of Tasmania (journ.) (SAUS)	Acts Tasm
Acts of the Apostles [New Testament book] (BJA)	AA
Acts of the Apostles [New Testament book] (BJA)	Ac
Acts of the Apostolic See	AAS
Acts of the Australian Parliament [A publication] (ILCA)	Acts Austl Parl
Acts of the Australian Parliament [A publication] (DLA)	Austl Acts
Acts of the Australian Parliament (journ.) (SAUS)	Acts Austi P
Acts of the Australian Parliament (journ.) (SAUS)	Acts AustJ Parl
Acts of the General Assembly, Church of Scotland [1638-1842] [A publication] (DLA)	Act Ass
Acts of the General Assembly, Church of Scotland (journ.) (SAUS)	Act Ass
Acts of the General Assembly, Commonwealth of Virginia [A publication] (DLA)	VA Acts
Acts of the General Assembly of the Commonwealth of Virginia (SAUS)	Va Acts
Acts of the Gods (BJA)	AG
Acts of the Legislature of West Virginia [A publication] (DLA)	W Va Acts
Acts of the Legislature of West Virginia (SAUS)	WVa Acts
Acts of the Parliament of Victoria (journ.) (SAUS)	Acts Vict
Acts of the Parliaments of Scotland	APS
Acts of the Parliaments of Scotland (DLA)	Scot Parl Acts
Acts of the Privy Council [England] [A publication] (DLA)	PCA
Acts of the Privy Council, Colonial Series [England] [A publication] (DLA)	Act Pr C Col S
Acts of the Privy Council, Colonial Series [A publication] (DLA)	PCC
Acts of the Privy Council, Colonial Series (journ.) (SAUS)	ActPrCColS
Acts of the Privy Council (Dasent) [England] [A publication] (DLA)	Act PC
Acts of the Privy Council (Dasent) [England] [A publication] (DLA)	Dasent
Acts of the Privy Council (journ.) (SAUS)	Act PC
Acts of the Privy Council, New Series (Dasent) [England] [A publication] (DLA)	Act PC NS
Acts of the Privy Council, New Series (journ.) (SAUS)	Act PC NS
Acts, Resolves, and Constitutional Resolutions of the State of Maine [A publication] (DLA)	ME Acts
Actual (ADA)	A
Actual (KSC)	ACT
Actual (MSA)	ACTL
Actual Acquisition Cost	AAC
Actual Address (SAUS)	AA
Actual Argument (SAUS)	AA
Actual Availability (MCD)	AA
Actual Block Processor [IBM Corp.] [Computer science] (BUR)	ABP
Actual Bodily Harm [Legal term] (WDAA)	ABH
Actual Body Weight (DAVI)	ABW
Actual Bottom Time	ABT
Actual Calculated Landing Time [FAA] (TAG)	ACLT
Actual Cash Value (ADWA)	acv
Actual Cash Value [Accounting]	ACV
Actual Commitment (EPAT)	AC
Actual Completion Date of Activity [Business term]	AA
Actual Cost [Accounting]	AC
Actual Cost for Work Performed [Accounting]	ACWP
Actual Cost Incurred [Accounting] (MCD)	ACI
Actual Cost of Work Association (SAUO)	ACWP
Actual Cost of Work Flow [Accounting]	ACWF
Actual Cost of Work Performed (SAUS)	ACWP
Actual Cost of Work Scheduled (ACAE)	ACWS
Actual Cost Report (NASA)	ACR
Actual Count (MHDI)	AC
Actual Count (SAUS)	Act ct
Actual Cubic Feet per Minute (NRCH)	ACFM
Actual Current on Board (DNAB)	ACOB
Actual Cycle Time (AAEL)	ACT
Actual Departure Time (CINC)	ADT
Actual Development Cost Certification [HUD]	ADCC
Actual Device Code (SAUS)	ADC
Actual Device Number (SAUS)	ADN
Actual Direct Costs (ACAE)	ADC
Actual Dive Time	ADT
Actual Elapsed Time	AET
Actual Equipment Trainer (MCD)	AET
Actual Evapotranspiration [Biology]	AET
Actual Expenses Allowable [Military] (AFM)	AEA
Actual Exposure Time (MUGU)	AET
Actual Flying Time [Travel industry] (TRID)	AFT
Actual Gross Weight	agw
Actual Gross Weight [Railroads]	AGW
Actual Ground Zero [Nuclear explosions]	AGZ
Actual Ground Zone (MUGU)	AGZ
Actual Hours (SAUS)	AH
Actual Instruction (SAUS)	AI
Actual Leaf Area [Botany]	ALA
Actual Loss Ratio [Insurance]	ALR
Actual Loss Sustained - No Specified Daily Indemnity [Insurance]	ALS-NSDI
Actual Measured Loss [Telecommunications] (TEL)	AML
Actual Measurement Weight [Railroads]	AMW
Actual Mechanical Advantage [Physics]	AMA
Actual Military Service (SAUS)	AMS
Actual Minus Sign (SAUS)	AMS
Actual Miss [Distance]	AM
Actual Navigation Performance (HLLA)	ANP
Actual Net Weight (SAUS)	ANWT
Actual Noise Silencer (SAUS)	ANS
Actual Obtained Achievement (SAUS)	ach
Actual Operating Time (MCD)	AOT
Actual Operation (SAUS)	AO
Actual Parade State (SAUS)	APS
Actual Parameter Area (SAUS)	APT
Actual Parameter List (SAUS)	APL
Actual Parameter Part (SAUS)	APP
Actual Plus Sign (SAUS)	APS
Actual Price Index (OTD)	API
Actual Production History Program	APH
Actual Projected on Board [Allowance] (DNAB)	APOB
Actual Range (IAA)	AR
Actual Range Angle (IAA)	ARA
Actual Reality (WDAA)	AR
Actual Retention Time (SAUS)	ART
Actual Ship Position	ASP
Actual Sign (SAUS)	AS
Actual Target Labor Auditing System (SAUS)	ATLAS
Actual Test Number [NASA]	ATN
Actual Time Enroute	ATE
Actual Time of Arrival	ATA
Actual Time of Departure	ATD
Actual Time of Fall	ATF
Actual Time of Interception	ATI
Actual Time of Penetration [Aviation] (FAAC)	ATP
Actual Time of Refueling (SAA)	ATR
Actual Time of Release [Aviation]	ATRLS
Actual Time of Return to Operation (AFM)	ATRO
Actual Time Over (MCD)	ATO
Actual Time Over Target (SAUS)	ATOT
Actual Total Loss (SAUS)	atl
Actual Total Loss	ATL
Actual Track Pointer (SAUS)	ATP
Actual Unit Price [Billing] (MCD)	AUP
Actual Value [Business term] (MHDB)	Act Val
Actual Value	AV
Actual Velocity	AV
Actual Volume of the Lung [Medicine] (DAVI)	V_L
Actual Weight [Business term]	AW
Actual Weight [Business term] (ODBW)	aw
Actual Weight of an Aircraft (SAUS)	A
Actual Weight Report	AWR
Actual Wind Factor [NWS] (FAAC)	ALWF
Actual Work Time [Bell System]	AWT
Actual Working Pressure	AWP
Actual Working Pressure (SAUS)	awp

Actualite Automobile (journ.) (SAUS)	Actual Auto
Actualite Juridique [*A publication*] (ILCA)	AJ
Actuality (ABBR)	ACTLT
Actualization (ABBR)	ACTLZAN
Actualization (ABBR)	ACTLZN
Actualize (ABBR)	ACTLZ
Actualized (ABBR)	ACTLZD
Actualizing (ABBR)	ACTLZG
Actualizing Assessment Battery [*Personality development test*] [*Psychology*]	AAB
Actually (ABBR)	ACTLY
Actually Time Used to Count (RIMS)	ATUTC
actuarial (SAUS)	act
Actuarial	ACTRL
Actuarial Approach for Financial Risks (SAUO)	AFIR
Actuarial Common Claims File [*Health insurance*] (GHCT)	ACCF
Actuarial Data Assembly (SAUS)	ADA
Actuarial Data Base [*I. P. Sharp Associates*] [*Database*]	ACT
Actuarial Engine Life (AFIT)	AEL
Actuarial Life Expectancy (AFIT)	ALE
Actuarial Life Table (SAUS)	ALT
Actuarial Mail File [*IRS*]	AMF
Actuarial Programming Language (SAUS)	APL
Actuarial Removal Interval (AFIT)	ARI
Actuarial Science (DD)	ActSc
Actuarial Science (SAUS)	AS
Actuarial Society of America [*Later, SA*]	ASA
Actuarial Statistics (SAUS)	AS
Actuarial Studies in Non-Life Insurance [*of the International Actuarial Association*] [*Brussels, Belgium*] (EA)	ASTIN
Actuary [*Insurance*]	ACT
Actuary (ABBR)	ACTRY
Actuary (ABBR)	ACTUR
Actuary (ROG)	ACTY
Actuate (KSC)	ACT
Actuate	ACTE
Actuate (ABBR)	ACTU
Actuated (ABBR)	ACTAD
Actuated (ABBR)	ACTUD
Actuating (ABBR)	ACTAG
Actuating (KSC)	ACTG
Actuating (ABBR)	ACTUG
Actuating Transfer Function (SAA)	ATF
Actuation (SAUS)	ACT
Actuation (ABBR)	ACTAN
Actuation (ABBR)	ACTUN
Actuation Data Communication [*Naval Ordnance Laboratory*]	ADC
Actuation Mechanism Subsystem (MCD)	AMS
Actuation Mine Simulator (MCD)	AMS
Actuation Test Mode [*Automotive service*]	ATM
Actuator (SAUS)	ACT
Actuator (ABBR)	ACTAR
Actuator (KSC)	ACTR
Actuator Control Electronics (SAUS)	ACE
Actuator Drive (SAA)	AD
Actuator Drive and Monitor Computer (SAUS)	ADMC
Actuator Mechanism (NASA)	AM
Actuator Selection Logic (SAA)	ASL
Actuator Sensor Interface (ACII)	ASI
Actuator/Indicator (SAUS)	AI
Actum Fide [*Done in Faith*] [*Latin*] (WGA)	AF
Actum ut Supra [*Done as Above*] [*Latin*]	AUS
ACTV, Inc. [*Associated Press*] (SAG)	ACTV
ACTV, Inc. [*NASDAQ symbol*] (SAG)	IATV
Acuerdo Nacional [*Paraguay*] [*Political party*] (EY)	AN
acuity (SAUS)	acu
Acuity of Color Vision [*Ophthalmology*] (DAVI)	VC
Acule Mesenteric Venous Thrombosis (SAUS)	AMVT
aculeat (SAUS)	acu
Acumen (ABBR)	ACMN
acumen (SAUS)	acu
acuminate (SAUS)	acu
acupressure (SAUS)	acu
Acupuncture	ACPNCTR
Acupuncture (ABBR)	ACUP
Acupuncture Analgesia [*Medicine*] (DMAA)	AA
Acupuncture and Electro-Therapeutics Research (SAUS)	Acupunct Electrother Res
Acupuncture and Transcutaneous Electrical Nerve Stimulation [*Orthopedics and neurology*] (DAVI)	ACUTENS
Acupuncture Association and Register Ltd. [*British*]	AAR
Acupuncture Association of Minnesota (SRA)	AAM
Acupuncture Association of South Australia (SAUS)	AASA
Acupuncture Association of Southern California (SAUO)	AASC
Acupuncture Clinic [*British*]	AC
Acupuncture Foundation of Canada	AFC
Acupuncture Foundation of Canada Institute (SAUO)	AFCI
Acupuncture International Association (EA)	AIA
Acupuncture Research Institute (EA)	ARI
Acupuncture Society of Virginia (SRA)	ASVA
acupuncturist (SAUS)	acupunc
Acuson Corp. [*NYSE symbol*] (CTT)	ACN
Acuson Corp. [*Associated Press*] (SAG)	Acuson
Acusto Optical Modulator (SAUS)	AOM
Acute	A

Acute [*Medicine*]	AC
Acute Abdomen [*Medicine*] (MELL)	AA
Acute Abdominal Series [*Medicine*] (MEDA)	AAS
Acute Abdominal Tympany [*Medicine*] (AAMN)	AAT
Acute Agitated Delirium [*Medicine*] (MELL)	AAD
Acute Allergic Encephalitis [*Medicine*] (MAE)	AAE
Acute Allergic Encephalitis [*Medicine*] (MELL)	AEE
Acute Alveolar Respiratory Failure [*Medicine*] (CPH)	AARF
Acute Amebic Dysentery [*Medicine*] (MELL)	AAD
Acute Angle (SAUS)	AA
Acute Angle Closure Glaucoma [*Ophthalmology*]	AACG
Acute Anterior Uveitis [*Medicine*] (MEDA)	AAU
Acute Anxiety Attack [*Medicine*]	AAA
Acute Aortic Regurgitation [*Medicine*] (MELL)	AAR
Acute Appendicitis [*Medicine*]	AA
Acute Articular Rheumatism [*Medicine*] (DMAA)	AAR
Acute Aseptic Meningitis [*Medicine*] (MELL)	AAM
Acute Aseptic Meningitis Syndrome [*Medicine*] (DMAA)	AAMS
Acute Asthma [*Medicine*] (MELL)	AA
Acute Atrophic Spinal Paralysis [*Medicine*] (DMAA)	AASP
Acute Axial Load [*Medicine*] (MELL)	AAL
Acute Bacterial Endocarditis [*Medicine*]	ABE
Acute Bacterial Exacerbation of Chronic Bronchitis [*Medicine*]	ABECB
Acute Bacterial Meningitis [*Medicine*]	ABM
Acute Bacterial Prostatitis [*Medicine*] (MELL)	ABP
Acute Bilateral Upper Tract Obstruction [*Medicine*] (MELL)	ABUTO
Acute Biliary Pancreatitis [*Medicine*] (MELL)	ABP
Acute Bisectrix [*Crystallography*]	AB
Acute Bovine Pulmonary Emphysema [*Cattle disease*]	ABPE
Acute Bovine Pulmonyra Emphysema (SAUS)	ABPE
Acute Brain Syndrome [*Medicine*]	ABS
Acute Bronchitis [*Medicine*] (MELL)	AB
Acute Bronchopulmonary Asthma [*Medicine*] (MEDA)	ABPA
Acute Canine Idiopathic Polyneuropathy [*Veterinary science*] (DMAA)	ACIP
Acute Cardiac Ischemia [*Medicine*] (MELL)	ACI
Acute Cardiovascular Disease [*Medicine*] (AAMN)	ACVD
Acute Care Admission [*Medicine*]	ACA
Acute Care Bed Need Methodology [*Hospital management*]	ACBNM
Acute Care Center [*Medicine*] (DAVI)	ACC
Acute Care Facility [*Medicine*]	ACF
Acute Care Hospital (MELL)	ACH
Acute Care Journal. International Society on Biotelemetry (journ.) (SAUS)	Acute Care
Acute Care Nurse Practitioner	ACNP
Acute Care Unit [*Medicine*]	ACU
Acute Cerebellar Ataxia [*Medicine*] (MELL)	ACA
Acute Cerebrospinal Meningitis [*Medicine*] (DMAA)	ACM
Acute Cervical Strain (SAUS)	ACS
Acute Cervical Trauma Syndrome (SAUS)	ACTS
Acute Cervical Traumatic Sprain [*Medicine*] (MELL)	ACTS
Acute Chest Syndrome [*Medicine*] (MELL)	ACS
Acute Cholecystitis [*Medicine*] (MELL)	AC
Acute Cholestatic Jaundice [*Medicine*] (MELL)	ACJ
Acute Circulatory Failure [*Medicine*] (MELL)	ACF
Acute Colonic Pseudo-Obstruction [*Medicine*] (MELL)	ACPO
Acute Conditioned Necrosis (SAUS)	ACN
Acute Conditioned Neurosis	ACN
Acute Confusional State [*Medicine*] (MEDA)	ACS
Acute Cor Pulmonale [*Medicine*] (MELL)	ACP
Acute Coronary Care Unit [*Medicine*]	ACCU
Acute Coronary Disease [*Medicine*] (PDAA)	ACD
Acute Coronary Event [*Medicine*] (DB)	ACE
Acute Coronary Infarction [*Medicine*] (DB)	ACI
Acute Coronary Insufficiency (HGAA)	ACI
Acute Coronary Occlusion [*Medicine*] (DMAA)	ACO
Acute Coronary Syndromes (SAUS)	ACS
Acute Death Syndrome (MELL)	ADS
Acute Demyelinating Polyneuropathy [*Medicine*] (MELL)	ADP
Acute Diarrhea [*Medicine*] (MELL)	AD
Acute Diarrheal Syndrome [*Medicine*] (DMAA)	ADS
Acute Diarrhoea in Childhood Symposium (journ.) (SAUS)	Acute Diarrhoea Child Symp
Acute Disseminated Encephalitis [*Neurology*] (DAVI)	ADE
Acute Disseminated Encephalomyelitis [*Medicine*]	ADE
Acute Disseminated [*or Disseminating*] Encephalomyelitis [*Medicine*]	ADEM
Acute Dystonic Reaction [*Neurology*] (DAVI)	ADR
Acute Emergency Guideline Levels [*EPA*]	AEGL
Acute Encephalography and Fatty Degeneration of the Viscera [*Reye's syndrome*]	AEFDV
Acute Erosion Gastritis [*Medicine*]	AEG
Acute Erythroblastopenia (DB)	AEB
Acute Erythroleukemia [*Oncology*]	AEL
Acute Exacerbation (MELL)	AE
Acute Exertional Rhabdomyolysis (DB)	AER
Acute Extrapyramidal Syndrome [*Medicine*]	EPS
Acute Fatty Liver of Pregnancy [*Medicine*]	AFLP
Acute Fear Regarding AIDS	AFRAIDS
Acute Febrile Illness [*Medicine*] (MELL)	AFI
Acute Febrile Neutrophilic Dermatosis [*Medicine*] (DMAA)	AFND
Acute Febrile Polyneuritis [*Medicine*] (MELL)	AFP
Acute Febrile Respiratory Disease [*Medicine*]	AFRD
Acute Febrile Respiratory Illness [*Medicine*]	AFRI
Acute Fibrinopurulent Pneumonia [*Medicine*]	AFPP
Acute Fibrinoserous Pneumonia [*Medicine*]	AFSP
Acute Flaccid Paralysis [*Medicine*]	AFP

Acute Fluid Replacement in the Therapy of Shock. Proccedings. Conference (journ.) (SAUS) .... Acute Fluid Replacement Ther Shock Pro Conf
Acute Focal Appendicitis [*Medicine*] .... AFA
Acute Focal Cerebral Ischemia [*Medicine*] (DMAA) .... AFCI
Acute Gastritis [*Medicine*] (MELL) .... AG
Acute Gastroenteritis [*Medicine*] (DAVI) .... AGE
Acute Generalized Tuberculosis [*Medicine*] (DB) .... AGT
Acute Glomerulonephritis [*Medicine*] .... AGN
Acute Gonococcal Arthritis [*Medicine*] (CPH) .... AGA
Acute Gouty Arthritis [*Medicine*] (MELL) .... AGA
Acute Granulocytic Leukemia [*Medicine*] .... AGL
Acute Haemorragic Encephalomyelitis (SAUS) .... AHE
Acute Haemorrhagic Conjunctivitis (SAUS) .... AHC
Acute Hallucinatory Paranoia [*Medicine*] (MELL) .... AHP
Acute Hantavirus-Associated Respiratory Disease [*Medicine*] (MELL) ...... AHARD
Acute Heart Disease (MELL) .... AHD
Acute Heart Failure [*Medicine*] .... AHF
Acute Hemolytic Anemia [*Medicine*] (DB) .... AHA
Acute Hemolytic Transfusion Reaction [*Medicine*] .... AHTR
Acute Hemolytic Uremic [*Syndrome*] [*Medicine*] (DB) .... AHU
Acute Hemorrhagic Conjunctivitis [*Ophthalmology*] (AAMN) .... AHC
Acute Hemorrhagic Cystitis [*Urology*] (AAMN) .... AHC
Acute Hemorrhagic Encephalomyelitis [*Medicine*] (MAE) .... AHE
Acute Hemorrhagic Leukoencephalitis [*Medicine*] (MAE) .... AHLE
Acute Hemorrhagic Leukoencphalitis [*Medicine*] (MELL) .... AHL
Acute Hemorrhagic Pancreatitis [*Medicine*] (MAE) .... AHP
Acute Hepatitis [*Medicine*] (DB) .... AH
Acute Herpetic Gingival Stomatitis [*Dentistry*] .... AHGS
Acute Hospital Syndrome [*Used facetiously to explain the popularity of a West German soap opera*] .... AHS
Acute Idiopathic Blind Spot Enlargement (SAUS) .... AIBSE
Acute Idiopathic Demyelinating Polyneuropathy [*Medicine*] (DMAA) .... AIDP
Acute Idiopathic Pericarditis [*Medicine*] (DMAA) .... AIP
Acute Idiopathic Thrombocytopenic Purpura [*Medicine*] (MELL) .... AITP
Acute Inclusion Body Encephalitis [*Medicine*] (DMAA) .... AIE
Acute Infantile Diarrhea [*Medicine*] (MELL) .... AID
Acute Infarction Ramipril Efficacy [*Cardiology study*] .... AIRE
Acute Infectious Disease [*Medicine*] .... AID
Acute Infectious Disease Series [*Medicine*] (DAVI) .... AIDS
Acute Infectious Encephalitis [*Medicine*] (MELL) .... AIE
Acute Infectious Endocarditis [*Medicine*] (DMAA) .... AIE
Acute Infectious Lymphocytosis [*Medicine*] (DMAA) .... AIL
Acute Infectious Polyneuritis [*Medicine*] (DMAA) .... AIP
Acute Infero-Posterior Myocardial Infarction [*Medicine*] .... AIPMI
Acute Insulin Response [*Endocrinology*] .... AIR
Acute Intensive Treatment [*Medicine*] (DMAA) .... AIT
Acute Intermittent Porphyria [*Medicine*] .... AIP
Acute Interstitial Nephritide [*or Nephritis*] [*Medicine*] (MAE) .... AIN
Acute Interstitial Nephritis (SAUS) .... AIN
Acute Intestinal Infection [*Medicine*] (DMAA) .... AII
Acute Intestinal Pseudoobstruction [*Ogilivie's Syndrome*] [*Medicine*] (MELL) .... AIPO
Acute Intrapartum Fetal Distress [*Medicine*] (MELL) .... AIFD
Acute Ionization Detector [*Medicine*] (DMAA) .... AID
Acute Irritant Contact Dermatitis [*Medicine*] (MELL) .... AICD
Acute Joint Syndrome [*Medicine*] (DMAA) .... AJS
Acute Laryngotracheobronchitis [*Virus*] .... ALTB
Acute Laryngotracheobronchitis [*Commonly known as croup*] (PAZ) .... LTB
Acute Lateral Sclerosis [*Medicine*] .... ALS
Acute Launch Emergency Reliability Tip [*NASA*] (KSC) .... ALERT
Acute Left Ventricular Failure [*Cardiology*] (DMAA) .... ALVF
Acute Lethal Catatonia [*Neurology and psychiatry*] (DAVI) .... ALC
Acute Leukemia [*Medicine*] .... AL
Acute Lower Repiratory Infection [*Medicine*] (CPH) .... ALRI
Acute Lumbar Strain (SAUS) .... ALS
Acute Lumbar Trauma Syndrome (SAUS) .... ALTS
Acute Lumbar Traumatic Sprain (HGAA) .... ALTS
Acute Lung Injury [*Medicine*] (DMAA) .... ALI
Acute Lupus Pericarditis [*Medicine*] (AAMN) .... ALP
Acute Lymphatic [*or Lymphoblastic or Lymphocytic*] **Leukemia** [*Medicine*] ...... ALL
Acute Lymphatic Leukemia (SAUS) .... ALL
Acute Lymphoblastic Leukemia (SAUS) .... ALL
Acute Lymphocytic Leukemia (SAUS) .... ALL
Acute Lymphocytic Leukemia Antigen [*Medicine*] (DMAA) .... ALLA
Acute Mallet Finger [*Medicine*] (MELL) .... AMF
Acute Megakaryoblastic Leukemia [*Medicine*] (MELL) .... AMBL
Acute Megakaryoblastic Leukemia [*Medicine*] (DMAA) .... AMEGL
Acute Megakaryoblastic Leukemia [*Medicine*] (MELL) .... AMKL
Acute Mesenteric Ischemia [*Medicine*] .... AMI
Acute Mesenteric Vascular Insufficiency [*Medicine*] (AAMN) .... AMVI
Acute Mesenteric Venous Thrombosis [*Medicine*] .... AMVT
Acute Metabolic Acidosis [*Medicine*] (MELL) .... AMA
Acute Migraine Headache (MELL) .... AMH
Acute Military Tuberculosis [*Medicine*] (DMAA) .... AMT
Acute Monoblastic Leukaemia [*Medicine*] (BABM) .... AMOL
Acute Monoblastic Leukemia [*Also, AMoL*] [*Medicine*] .... AMonoL
Acute Monocytic Leukemia [*Medicine*] (DAVI) .... AML
Acute Monocytic Leukemia [*Also, AMonoL*] [*Medicine*] .... AMoL
Acute Monomyelocytic Leukemia [*Medicine*] (DB) .... AMML
Acute Mountain Sickness .... AMS
Acute Mucocutaneous Ocular [*Syndrome*] [*Medicine*] (DB) .... AMO
Acute Multifocal Placoid Pigment Epitheliopathy [*Ophthalmology*] .... AMPPE
Acute Multifocal Posterior Placoid Pigment Epitheliopathy [*Dermatology*] (DAVI) .... AMPPPE
Acute Myeloblastic Leukaemia (SAUS) .... AML
Acute Myeloblastic Leukemia [*Hematology and oncology*] (DAVI) .... AMBL
Acute Myeloblastic Leukemia Surface Glycoprotein Antigen [*Medicine*] (DB) .... AMLSGA
Acute Myelocytic Leukaemia (SAUS) .... AML
Acute Myelogenous Leukemia [*Medicine*] .... AML
Acute Myeloid [*or Myeloblastic or Myelocytic*] **Leukemia** [*Medicine*] .... AML
Acute Myelomonoblastic Leukemia [*Medicine*] (MELL) .... AMMBL
Acute Myelomonoblastic Leukemia [*Medicine*] .... AMMOL
Acute Myelomonocytic Leukemia [*Medicine*] .... AMML
Acute Myoblastic Leukemia (SAUS) .... AML
Acute Myocardial Infarction [*Medicine*] .... AMI
Acute Myocardial Insufficiency (SAUS) .... AMI
Acute Narrow Angle Glaucoma [*Opthamology*] (DMAA) .... ANAG
Acute Necrosis of Intestinal Mucosa [*Gastroenterology*] .... ANIM
Acute Necrotic Myelopathy [*Medicine*] .... ANM
Acute Necrotizing Gingivitis [*Medicine*] (MELL) .... ANG
Acute Necrotizing Hemorrhagic Encephalopathy [*Medicine*] (MELL) .... ANHE
Acute Necrotizing Ulacerative Muscositi [*Medicine*] (MELL) .... ANUM
Acute Necrotizing Ulcerative Gingivitis [*Dentistry*] .... ANUG
Acute Necrotzing Pancreatitis [*Medicine*] (MELL) .... ANP
Acute Nephritic Syndrome [*Medicine*] (MELL) .... ANS
Acute Nephritis [*Medicine*] (MELL) .... AN
Acute Nerve Irritation (HGAA) .... ANI
Acute Nerve Root Irritation (HGAA) .... ANRI
Acute Nongranulomatous Anterior Uveitis (SAUS) .... ANGAU
Acute Nonlymphoblastic Leukemia [*Medicine*] .... ANL
Acute Nonlymphoblastic Leukemia [*Medicine*] (DAVI) .... ANLL
Acute Nonlymphocytic Leukemia [*Medicine*] .... ANLL
Acute Nonlymphoid Leukemia [*Medicine*] (MELL) .... ANLI
Acute Obstructive Suppurative Cholangitis [*Medicine*] (MELL) .... AOSC
Acute Optic Neuritis [*Medicine*] (MELL) .... AON
Acute Oral Toxicity for Birds, Mice, Rats (SAUS) .... ORALTOX
Acute Organic Brain Syndrome [*Medicine*] (DMAA) .... AOBS
Acute Osteomyelitis [*Medicine*] (MELL) .... AOM
Acute Otitis Media [*Medicine*] .... AOM
Acute Outflow Obstruction [*Medicine*] (MELL) .... AOO
Acute Pain (MELL) .... AP
Acute Painful Neuropathy [*Medicine*] (MELL) .... APN
Acute Pancreatitis [*Medicine*] (MELL) .... AP
Acute Panniculitis [*Medicine*] (MELL) .... AP
Acute Parenteral [*Medicine*] (MELL) .... APA
Acute Parotitis [*Medicine*] (MELL) .... AP
Acute Pericarditis [*Medicine*] (MELL) .... APC
Acute Peritonitis [*Medicine*] (MELL) .... AP
Acute Pernicious Beriberi [*Medicine*] (PDAA) .... APB
Acute Pharyngoconjunctival Fever [*Medicine*] (MEDA) .... APC
Acute Pharyngo-Conjunctival Fever [*Medicine*] .... APCF
Acute Phase [*Laboratory*] (DAVI) .... ACUT
Acute Phase Reactant [*Medicine*] .... APR
Acute Phase Reactant Protein [*Medicine*] (DMAA) .... APRP
Acute Phase Response [*Medicine*] .... APR
Acute Physiology and Chronic Health Evaluation .... APACHE
Acute Physiology Score [*In evaluating impact of intensive care*] .... APS
Acute Pneumonia [*Medicine*] (MELL) .... AP
Acute Polioencephalitis [*Medicine*] (DB) .... APE
Acute Posterior Multifocal Placoid Pigment Epitheliopathy [*Ophthalmology*] .... APMPPE
Acute Postinfectious Polyneuropathy [*Medicine*] (MELL) .... APIP
Acute Postoperative Renal Failure [*Medicine*] (AAMN) .... APORF
Acute Poststreptococcal Glomerulonephritis [*Immunology*] .... APSGN
Acute Progranulocytic [*or Promyelocytic*] **Leukemia** [*Hematology*] .... APL
Acute Progranulocytic Leukemia (SAUS) .... APL
Acute Progranulocytic Leukemia [*Hematology*] (DAVI) .... AProL
Acute Proliferative [*or Proliferation*] (MAE) .... AP
Acute Proliferative Glomerulonephritis [*Medicine*] (MELL) .... APG
Acute Promyelocytic Leukemia [*Medicine*] .... APL
Acute Promyelocytic Leukemia [*Hematology*] (MAE) .... AProL
Acute Psychotic Episode .... APE
Acute Pulmonary Edema (DAVI) .... APE
Acute Pyelonephritis [*Medicine*] (MAE) .... APN
Acute Radiation Disease [*Medicine*] (MELL) .... ARD
Acute Radiation Nephritis [*Medicine*] (MELL) .... ARN
Acute Radiation Syndrome [*Medicine*] .... ARS
Acute Reactive Psychotic Episode [*Medicine*] (MELL) .... ARPF
Acute Renal Dysfunction [*Medicine*] (MELL) .... ARD
Acute Renal Failure [*Medicine*] .... ARF
Acute Renal Failure and Chronic Renal Failure [*Nephrology*] (DAVI) .... ARF/CRF
Acute Repetitive Seizure [*Medicine*] (MELL) .... ARS
Acute Repetitive Seizure Disorder [*Medicine*] (MELL) .... ARSD
Acute Respiratory Acidosis [*Medicine*] (MELL) .... ARA
Acute Respiratory Akalosis [*Medicine*] (MELL) .... ARA
Acute Respiratory Disease [*Medicine*] .... ARD
Acute Respiratory Distress [*Medicine*] (MELL) .... ARD
Acute Respiratory Distress Syndrome [*Medicine*] .... ARDS
Acute Respiratory Failure [*Medicine*] .... ARF
Acute Respiratory Illness [*Medicine*] (DMAA) .... ARI
Acute Respiratory Infection [*Medicine*] .... ARI
Acute Respiratory System Malfunction [*Medicine*] .... ARSM
Acute Respiratory Tract Illness .... ARTI
Acute Retinal Necrosis [*Medicine*] (MELL) .... ARN
Acute Retinal Necrosis Syndrome [*Medicine*] (MELL) .... ARNS
Acute Retroviral Syndrome [*Medicine*] (MELL) .... ARVS
Acute Rheumatic Carditis [*Medicine*] (MELL) .... ARC
Acute Rheumatic Fever [*Medicine*] .... ARF
Acute Salpingitis [*Medicine*] (MEDA) .... AS

Acute Schistosomiasis [*Medicine*] (MELL) ... ASS
Acute Sclerosing Hyaline Necrosis [*Medicine*] (MAE) ... ASHN
Acute Serum Sickness [*Medicine*] (DMAA) ... ASS
Acute Soft Tissue Injury [*Medicine*] (MELL) ... ASTI
Acute Spinal Cord Injury (DMAA) ... ASCI
Acute Spinal Stenosis [*Medicine*] (MELL) ... ASS
Acute Splenic Sequestration Crisis [*Medicine*] (DMAA) ... ASSC
Acute Stress Erosion [*Gastroenterology*] (DAVI) ... ASE
Acute Stroke Unit [*Medicine*] (DAVI) ... ASU
Acute Subdural Hematoma [*Medicine*] ... ASDH
Acute Suppurative Parotitis [*Otorhinolaryngology*] (DAVI) ... ASP
Acute Symmetric Polyarthritis [*Medicine*] (MELL) ... ASP
Acute Thromboembolism [*Medicine*] (MELL) ... ATE
Acute Toxic Encephalopathy [*Medicine*] (MELL) ... ATE
Acute Toxicity Endpoint (EEVL) ... ATE
Acute Transient Radiation Myelopathy [*Oncology*] ... ATRM
Acute Transmural Myocardial Infarction [*Medicine*] (MELL) ... ATMI
Acute Transverse Myelopathy [*Medicine*] (DMAA) ... ATM
Acute Traumatic Brain Injury [*Medicine*] (MELL) ... ATBI
Acute Tubular Necrosis [*Nephrology*] ... ATN
Acute Tubulointerstitial Nephritis [*Medicine*] (MELL) ... ATIN
Acute Tumor Lysis Syndrome [*Medicine*] (MELL) ... ATLS
Acute Ulcerative Gingivitis [*Medicine*] (MELL) ... AUG
Acute Uncomplicated Back Pain [*Medicine*] (MELL) ... AUBP
Acute Undifferentiated Leukemia [*Hematology*] ... AUL
Acute Upper Gastrointestinal Bleeding [*Medicine*] (MELL) ... AUGIB
Acute Upper Gastrointestinal Hemorrhage [*Medicine*] (MELL) ... AUGH
Acute Uremic Encephalopathy [*Medicine*] (MELL) ... AUE
Acute Urethral Syndrome [*Medicine*] (MELL) ... AUS
Acute Uric Acid Nephropathy [*Medicine*] (MELL) ... AUAN
Acute Urinary Retention [*Medicine*] (MELL) ... AUR
Acute Urinary Tract Infection [*Medicine*] (MELL) ... AUTI
Acute Variceal Haemorrhage [*Medicine*] (PDAA) ... AVH
Acute Vasomotor Nephropathy [*Medicine*] (DAVI) ... AVN
Acute Vertebral Collapse [*Medicine*] ... AVC
Acute Viral Hepatitis [*Medicine*] ... AVH
Acute Viral Meningitis [*Medicine*] ... AVM
Acute Viral Respiratory Infection [*Medicine*] (DMAA) ... AVRI
Acute Yellow Atrophy [*Medicine*] (DMAA) ... AYA
Acute-Fatty Liver [*Medicine*] (MELL) ... AFL
Acutely (ABBR) ... ACTY
Acutely Hazardous Material ... AHM
Acuteness (ABBR) ... ACTNS
Acuteness (ABBR) ... ACUTNS
Acute-Phase Protein (MELL) ... APP
Acute-Phase Response Element [*Biochemistry*] ... APRE
Acute-Phase Response Factor [*Biochemistry*] ... APRF
Acute-to-Chronic Ratio [*Toxicology*] (LDT) ... ACR
Acuvision Systems, Inc. [*Vancouver Stock Exchange symbol*] ... AVI
Acvila Air-Romanian Carrier [*FAA designator*] (FAAC) ... RRM
ACX Technologies [*NYSE symbol*] (SAG) ... ACX
ACX Technologies [*NASDAQ symbol*] (SAG) ... ACXT
ACX Technologies [*Associated Press*] (SAG) ... ACX Tc
Acxiom Corp. [*Associated Press*] (SAG) ... Acxiom
Acxiom Corp. [*NASDAQ symbol*] (NQ) ... ACXM
Acxiom Corp. (SAUO) ... Acxm
Acyclic Process (SAUS) ... AP
Acycloguanosine [*Also, ACV, Acyclovir*] [*Antiviral compound*] ... ACG
Acycloguanosine (SAUS) ... acyclovir
Acyclovir [*Pharmacology*] (DAVI) ... ACA
Acyclovir [*Also, ACG, Acycloguanosine*] [*Antiviral compound*] ... ACV
Acyclovir Diphosphate [*Antiviral compound*] ... ACV-DP
Acyclovir Monophosphate [*Antiviral compound*] ... ACV-MP
Acyclovir Monophosphate (SAUS) ... ACV-MP
Acyclovir Triphosphate (SAUS) ... ACVTP
Acyclovir Triphosphate [*Antiviral compound*] ... ACVTP
Acyl [*Organic chemistry*] ... Ac
Acyl Carrier Protein [*Biochemistry*] ... ACP
Acyl Cholesterol Acyl [*Medicine*] (MELL) ... ACAT
Acyl Cholesterol Acyl Transferase Inhibitor [*Medicine*] (MELL) ... ACATI
Acyl Coenzyme A Oxidase (DMAA) ... ACAO
Acyl Coenzyme A: Retinal Acyltransferase [*An enzyme*] ... ARAT
Acyl Lyso-glycerophosphocholine (SAUS) ... LPC
Acylaied Plasminogen-Streplokinase Activator Complex (SAUS) ... APS
Acylaminocephalosporanic Acid [*Medicine*] (DMAA) ... AACA
Acylated Octapeptide [*Biochemistry*] ... A-OP
Acylated Plasminogen-Streptokinase Activator Complex [*Anticlotting agent*] ... APSAC
Acylcholine Acyl-Hydrolase [*Same as PCE*] [*An enzyme*] ... ACAH
Acyltransferase [*An enzyme*] ... AT
acyrologia (SAUS) ... acyro
acyrology (SAUS) ... acyro
Ad [*To or At*] [*Latin*] (ROG) ... A
AD 2000: a Journal of Religious Opinion [*A publication*] (APTA) ... AD
Ad Annum [*Up to the Year*] [*Latin*] ... AD AN
Ad Aperturam Libri [*As the Book Opens*] [*Latin*] (BARN) ... AA
Ad Captandum [*For the Purpose of Captivating*] [*Latin*] ... Ad Capt
Ad Com Marketing, Inc. [*Vancouver Stock Exchange symbol*] ... ADO
Ad Defectionem Animi [*To the Point of Fainting*] [*Pharmacy*] ... AD DEF AN
Ad Deliquium [*To Fainting*] [*Pharmacy*] (DAVI) ... ad Deliq
Ad Duas Vices [*For Two Doses*] [*Pharmacy*] ... AD 2 VIC
Ad Effectum [*Until Effectual*] [*Pharmacy*] ... AD EFFECT
Ad Eundem Gradum [*To the Same Degree*] [*Of the admission of a graduate of one university to the same degree at another without examination*] [*Latin*] ... AD EUND
Ad Eundem Gradum [*To the Same Degree*] [*Of the admission of a graduate of one university to the same degree at another without examination*] [*Latin*] ... AEG
Ad Extremum [*To the Extreme, To the End*] [*Latin*] ... AD EX
Ad Finem [*At or To the End*] [*Latin*] ... AD FIN
Ad Finem [*At or To the End*] [*Latin*] ... AF
Ad Finem [*At or To the End*] [*Latin*] (ADA) ... FIN
Ad Gentes [*Decree on the Church's Missionary Activity*] [*Vatican II document*] ... AG
Ad Gratum Aciditatem [*To an Agreeable Sourness*] [*Pharmacy*] ... AD GR ACID
Ad Gratum Aciditatem [*To an Agreeable Sourness*] [*Pharmacy*] ... Ad Grat Acid
Ad Gratum Gustum [*To an Agreeable Taste*] [*Pharmacy*] ... AD GR GUST
Ad Hanc Vocem [*At This Word*] [*Latin*] ... AHV
Ad Helviam [*of Seneca the Younger*] [*Classical studies*] (OCD) ... Helv
Ad Hoc Advisory Group on Science Programs [*Terminated, 1976*] [*National Science Foundation*] (EGAO) ... AGOSP
Ad Hoc Collective Protection (SAUS) ... AHCP
Ad hoc Committee (SAUO) ... AC
Ad Hoc Committee for American Silver (EA) ... AHCAS
Ad Hoc Committee for Competitive Communication (CIST) ... ACCC
Ad hoc Committee for Competitive Communications (SAUO) ... ACCC
Ad Hoc Committee for Competitive Communications (SAUS) ... ACCC
Ad Hoc Committee for Lebanese Freedom [*Defunct*] (EA) ... AHCLF
Ad Hoc Committee on Copyright Law (EA) ... AHCCL
Ad Hoc Committee on Equipment Interoperability [*NATO*] (NATG) ... AHCEI
Ad Hoc Committee on Freedom of Scholarly Inquiry [*Defunct*] (EA) ... AHCFSI
Ad Hoc Committee on New Directions of the Research and Technical Services Division of the ALA [*American Library Association*] (NITA) ... AHONDA
Ad Hoc Committee on the Baltic States and the Ukraine (EA) ... AHCBSU
Ad Hoc Committee on the Cumulative Regulatory Effects on the Cost of Automotive Transportation [*Terminated, 1972*] (EGAO) ... RECAT
Ad Hoc Conference (SAUS) ... HOCO
Ad Hoc Congressional Committee for Irish Affairs (EA) ... AHCCIA
Ad Hoc Congressional Committee on the Baltic States and the Ukraine (EA) ... AHCCBSU
Ad Hoc Congressional Committee on the Baltic States and the Ukraine (SAUO) ... AHCCBSU
Ad Hoc Crypto-Coordination Agency (MUGU) ... ACCA
Ad Hoc Group for Medical Research Funding (EA) ... AHGMRF
Ad Hoc Group on Missile Reliability (SAA) ... AHGMR
Ad hoc Group on the Berlin Mandate (SAUO) ... AGBM
Ad Hoc Group on US Policy toward the UN [*Defunct*] (EA) ... AHGUSPTUN
Ad Hoc Intelligence Working Group (SAUO) ... AHIWG
Ad Hoc Mixed Exploratory Working Group (SAUO) ... AHMEWG
Ad Hoc Mixed Working Group (SAA) ... AHMWG
Ad Hoc Monitoring Group on Southern Africa [*Defunct*] (EA) ... AHMGSA
Ad Hoc Requirements Committee [*Later, COMOR*] ... ARC
Ad Hoc Schedule Message (DA) ... ASM
Ad hoc Study Group on Implications and Implementation of IOC Functional Autonomy (SAUO) ... III-FA
Ad hoc Study Group on IOC Development, Operations, Structure and Statutes (SAUO) ... DOSS
Ad hoc Task Team to Study the Implications, for the Commission, of the United Nations Convention on the Law of the Sea and the New Ocean Regime (SAUS) ... LOSI
Ad Hoc Technical Air Intelligence Working Group (SAUO) ... AHTAIWG
Ad Hoc Working Group [*Army*] ... AHWG
Ad Hoc Working Group on Biosafety (SAUS) ... BSWG
Ad Hominem [*To the man*] [*A debating technique that attacks the person not his ideas*] [*Latin*] (BARN) ... ad hom
Ad Hunc Locum [*To (or At) This Place*] [*Latin*] ... AD HL
Ad Hunc Locum [*To (or At) This Place*] [*Latin*] ... AHL
Ad Infinitum [*To Infinity*] [*Latin*] ... AD INF
Ad Initium [*At the Beginning*] [*Latin*] ... AD INIT
Ad Interim [*In the Meantime*] [*Latin*] ... AD INT
Ad Interim [*For the Present*] [*Latin*] (EES) ... ad int
Ad Interim [*In the Meantime*] [*Latin*] (EY) ... AI
Ad Interim Specification [*Navy*] ... INT
Ad Jesum per Mariam [*To Jesus through Mary*] [*Latin*] ... AJPM
A.D. Johnson Family Association (EA) ... ADJFA
Ad Libitum [*At Pleasure, As Desired*] [*Music*] (ROG) ... AD L
Ad Libitum [*At Pleasure, As Desired*] [*Music*] ... AD LIB
Ad Libitum [*At Pleasure*] [*Music*] (WA) ... ad lib
Ad Libitum [*At Pleasure, As Desired*] [*Music*] ... AD LIBIT
Ad Locum [*To (or At) the Place*] [*Latin*] ... AD LOC
Ad Majorem Dei Gloriam [*To the Greater Glory of God*] [*Latin*] (WGA) ... AMDG
Ad Manus Medici [*To Be Delivered into the Hands of the Physician*] [*Pharmacy*] ... AD MAN MED
Ad Nationes [*of Tertullian*] [*Classical studies*] (OCD) ... Ad Nat
Ad Nauseum [*To the Extent of Producing Nausea*] [*Latin*] ... AD NAUS
Ad Neutralizandum [*To Neutralization*] [*Pharmacy*] ... AD NEUT
Ad Partes Dolentes [*To the Painful Parts*] [*Pharmacy*] ... Ad Part Dol
Ad Partes Dolentes [*To the Painful Parts*] [*Pharmacy*] ... ad part dolent
Ad Pondus Omnium [*To the Weight of the Whole*] [*Pharmacy*] ... AD POND OM
Ad Saeculum [*To the Century*] [*Latin*] (ADA) ... AD SAEC
Ad Saturandum [*To Saturation*] [*Pharmacy*] ... AD SAT
Ad Saturandum [*To Saturation*] [*Pharmacy*] ... AD SATUR
Ad Sectam [*At the Suit Of*] [*Legal term*] [*Latin*] ... Ads
ad sectam (SAUS) ... ad sec
Ad Tertiam Vicem [*Three Times*] [*Pharmacy*] ... AD TERT VIC
Ad Universiterrarum Orbis Summi Architecti Gloriam [*To the Glory of the GrandArchitect of the Universe*] [*Freemasonry*] [*Latin*] ... AUTOSAG
Ad Usum [*According to Custom*] [*Pharmacy*] ... Ad Us
Ad Usum [*According to Custom*] [*Pharmacy*] ... AU

Ad Usum Externum [For External Use] [Pharmacy] ..... AD US EXTER
Ad Valorem [According to the Value] [Latin] [Business term] ..... ADV
Ad Valorem [According to the Value] [Latin] [Business term] ..... AD VAL
Ad Valorem (EBF) ..... Ad Val
Ad Valorem [According to Value] [Latin] (NTIO) ..... A/V
Ad Valorem [According to the Value] [Latin] [Business term] ..... AV
Ad Valorem [According to the Value] Equivalent ..... AVE
Ad Valorem Tax [Added Value Tax] ..... AVT
Ada [Byron] [The name of a computer language] (BARN) ..... Ada
Ada (SAUS) ..... Addy
Ada [Oklahoma] [Airport symbol] (AD) ..... ADH
Ada [Ghana] [ICAO location identifier] (ICLI) ..... DGAD
ADA Air [Albania] [FAA designator] (FAAC) ..... ADE
ADA and Software Engineering Technology [British] (NITA) ..... ASET
Ada Based Integrated Control System (ACAE) ..... ABICS
ADA Based Integrated Control System (SAUS) ..... ABICS
Ada Compiler Evaluation Capability (ACAE) ..... ACEC
ADA Compiler Evaluation Criteria (SAUS) ..... ACEC
ADA Compiler Validation Capability (or Capacity) (SAUS) ..... ACVC
ADA Compiler Validation Capacity [Computer science] ..... ACVC
ADA Compiler Validation Criteria (SAUS) ..... ACVC
Ada County District Library, Boise, ID [Library symbol] [Library of Congress] (LCLS) ..... IdBC
ADA Design and Coping Standards [DoD] ..... ADCS
Ada Design Language [Computer science] (ODBW) ..... ADL
Ada Development Environment (SSD) ..... ADVENT
ADA Development Environment Portable Tools [A programming language] (NITA) ..... ADEPT
Ada Elementary School, Ada, MN [Library symbol] [Library of Congress] (LCLS) ..... MNAdaE
Ada High School, Ada, MN [Library symbol] [Library of Congress] (LCLS) ..... MnAdaH
Ada Improvement Programme (SAUS) ..... ADIMP
Ada Information Clearinghouse (SAUO) ..... AdaIC
ADA Information Clearinghouse (SAUS) ..... AdaIC
Ada Information Management System (ACAE) ..... AIMS
ADA Integrated Methodology (MCD) ..... AIM
Ada Joint Program Office [Later, Ada Board] [DoD] (RDA) ..... AJPO
Ada Joint Users Group (SAUO) ..... Ada JUG
ADA Language System (MCD) ..... ALS
Ada Language System/Navy (SSD) ..... ALS/N
Ada, MI [AM radio station call letters] (BROA) ..... WJNZ
Ada, MN [FM radio station call letters] ..... KRJB
Ada, OH [FM radio station call letters] ..... WONB
Ada, OK [Location identifier] [FAA] (FAAL) ..... ADH
Ada, OK [Location identifier] [FAA] (FAAL) ..... AMR
Ada, OK [AM radio station call letters] ..... KADA
Ada, OK [FM radio station call letters] ..... KADA-FM
Ada, OK [Television station call letters] ..... KTEN
Ada, OK [FM radio station call letters] (BROA) ..... KTGS-FM
Ada, OK [FM radio station call letters] ..... KTLS
Ada Programming Support Environments [Computer science] (RDA) ..... APSE
[The] Ada Project [World Wide Web] ..... TAP
ADA Project Support Environment (SAUS) ..... APSE
Ada Public Library, Ada, MN [Library symbol] [Library of Congress] (LCLS) ..... MnAda
Ada Public Library, Ada, OK [Library symbol] [Library of Congress] (LCLS) ..... OkAd
ADA Real-Time System (SAUS) ..... ARTS
Ada Runtime Environment Working Group (SAUO) ..... ARTEWG
Ada Software Repository ..... ASR
ADA Software Repository (SAUS) ..... ASR
Ada Test and Verification System (ACAE) ..... ATVS
Ada Validation Office (SAUO) ..... AVO
Adaba [Ethiopia] [ICAO location identifier] (ICLI) ..... HAAD
ADABAS [Adaptable Database System] network software [Computer] (NITA) ..... ADANET
Ada-Based Design Approach for Real Time Systems (CIST) ..... ADARTS
ADAC Laboratories [NASDAQ symbol] (NQ) ..... ADAC
ADAC Laboratories [Associated Press] (SAG) ..... AdacLb
Adagdak [Alaska] [Seismograph station code, US Geological Survey] (SEIS) AD8
Adage (ABBR) ..... ADG
Adage Graphics Terminal ..... AGT
Adage, Inc. [Associated Press] (SAG) ..... Adage
Adage, Inc. [NASDAQ symbol] (NQ) ..... ADGE
Adagio [Slow] [Music] ..... ADAG
Adagio [Slow] [Music] (ROG) ..... ADAGO
Adagio [Slow] [Music] ..... ADGO
Adagio [Slow] [Music] ..... ADO
Adair County Free Press, Greenfield, IA [Library symbol] [Library of Congress] (LCLS) ..... IaGrefFP
Adair News, Adair, IA [Library symbol] [Library of Congress] (LCLS) ..... IaAdN
Adair on Law Libels [A publication] (DLA) ..... Adair Lib
Adair on Libels [A publication] (DLA) ..... Ad Lib
Adair-Dighton [Syndrome] [Medicine] (DB) ..... AD
Adair-Koshland-Nemethy-Filmer [Enzyme model] ..... AKNF
Adak, AK [Location identifier] [FAA] (FAAL) ..... NUD
Adak Island [Alaska] [Seismograph station code, US Geological Survey] [Closed] (SEIS) ..... ADA
Adak Island [Alaska] [Seismograph station code, US Geological Survey] (SEIS) ..... ADK
Adak Island [Alaska] [Airport symbol] (OAG) ..... ADK
Adak [Alaska] Search and Rescue Coordinator [Coast Guard] (DNAB) ..... ADAKSARCOORD
Adak/Davis [Alaska] [ICAO location identifier] (ICLI) ..... PADK

Ada/Lattice ICE [Integrated Conceptual Environment] [Computer science] ..... ALICE
Adam and Eve (EA) ..... AE
Adam and Eve (SAUS) ..... A-E
Adam, Harding & Lueck [Commercial firm] [British] ..... AHL
Adam Hilger (SAUO) ..... ISBN 0-7503
Adam Language Processor (SAUS) ..... ALP
Adam on the Law of Slavery in British India [A publication] (DLA) ..... Adam Sl
Adam on Trial by Jury [A publication] (DLA) ..... Adam Jur Tr
Adam Smith Institute (EA) ..... ASI
A.D.A.M. Software [NASDAQ symbol] (TTSB) ..... ADAM
ADAM Software, Inc. [NASDAQ symbol] (SAG) ..... ADAM
ADAM Software, Inc. [Associated Press] (SAG) ..... AdamSft
Adam Walsh Child Resource Center (EA) ..... AWCRC
Adamant (ABBR) ..... ADAMT
Adamant (ABBR) ..... ADMNT
Adamantane [Organic chemistry] ..... AD
Adamantine (ABBR) ..... ADAM
Adamantly (ABBR) ..... ADAMTY
Adamantly (ABBR) ..... ADMNTY
Adamantylsulphonyl (DB) ..... ADS
Adams [New York] [Seismograph station code, US Geological Survey] [Closed] (SEIS) ..... ADN
Adams and Durham on Real Property [A publication] (DLA) ..... AD & Dur RP
Adams & Rountree Technology, Inc. [Information service or system] (IID) ..... A & RT
Adams County Free Press, Corning, IA [Library symbol] [Library of Congress] (LCLS) ..... IaCornFP
Adams County Juvenile Detention Center, Brighton, CO [Library symbol] [Library of Congress] (LCLS) ..... CoBriJ
Adams County Legal Journal [Pennsylvania] [A publication] (DLA) ..... Adams
Adams County Legal Journal [Pennsylvania] [A publication] (DLA) ..... Adams LJ
Adams County Public Library, Bennett, CO [Library symbol] [Library of Congress] (LCLS) ..... CoBen
Adams County Public Library, Brighton, CO [Library symbol] [Library of Congress] (LCLS) ..... CoBri
Adams County Public Library, Northglenn, CO [Library symbol] [Library of Congress] (LCLS) ..... CoNgA
Adams County School District No. 12, Northglenn, CO [Library symbol] [Library of Congress] (LCLS) ..... CoNgSD
Adams County School District No. 12, Northglenn, CO [OCLC symbol] (OCLC) ..... DVA
Adams Drug Company (SAUO) ..... ADG
Adams Elementary School, Fergus Falls, MN [Library symbol] [Library of Congress] (LCLS) ..... MnEfAE
Adams' Equity [A publication] (DLA) ..... Adams Eq
Adams' Equity [A publication] (DLA) ..... Ad Eq
Adams' Essay on Anglo-Saxon Law [A publication] (DLA) ..... Ad Ang Sax L
Adams Exploration Ltd. [Vancouver Stock Exchange symbol] ..... ADM
Adams Express [NYSE symbol] (TTSB) ..... ADX
[The] Adams Express Co. [Associated Press] (SAG) ..... AdaEx
[The] Adams Express Co. [NYSE symbol] (SPSG) ..... ADX
Adams Express Company (SAUO) ..... ADX
Adams Family Association (EA) ..... AFA
Adams Field [FAA] (TAG) ..... LIT
Adams Golf [NASDAQ symbol] (SG) ..... ADGO
Adams International Ltd. ..... AIL
Adam's Justiciary Reports [1893-1906] [Scotland] [A publication] (ILCA) ..... A
Adams' Justiciary Reports [Scotland] [A publication] (DLA) ..... Ad Jus
Adams' Legal Journal [Pennsylvania] [A publication] (DLA) ..... Adams Leg J (PA)
Adams Library (Chelmsford Public Library), Chelmsford, MA [Library symbol] [Library of Congress] (LCLS) ..... MChelm
Adams, MA [Television station call letters] ..... WCDC
Adams Mansion, Quincy, MA [Library symbol] [Library of Congress] (LCLS) ..... MQA
Adams National Historic Site ..... ADAM
Adams National Historic Site (SAUS) ..... ANHS
Adams on Ejectment [A publication] (DLA) ..... Ad Ej
Adams on the Education Act [A publication] (DLA) ..... Ad Ed Act
Adams on Trade Marks [A publication] (DLA) ..... Ad Tr M
Adams Public Library, Adams, OR [Library symbol] [Library of Congress] (LCLS) ..... OrAd
Adams' Reports [1 New Hampshire] [A publication] (DLA) ..... Adams
Adams' Reports [41, 42 Maine] [A publication] (DLA) ..... Adams
Adams Res & Energy [AMEX symbol] (TTSB) ..... AE
Adams Resources & Energy, Inc. [Associated Press] (SAG) ..... AdmRsc
Adams Resources & Energy, Inc. [AMEX symbol] (SPSG) ..... AE
Adams' Roman Antiquities [A publication] (DLA) ..... Adams Rom Ant
Adams' Roman Antiquities [A publication] (DLA) ..... Ad Rom Ant
Adams State College (GAGS) ..... Adams St C
Adams State College [Alamosa, CO] ..... ASC
Adams State College, Alamosa, CO [Library symbol] [Library of Congress] (LCLS) ..... CoAlC
Adams State College of Colorado (SAUO) ..... ASCC
Adams, WI [FM radio station call letters] ..... WDKM
Adams-Brown County Bookmobile, Winchester, OH [Library symbol] [Library of Congress] (LCLS) ..... OWin
Adamsite [Army] ..... ADM
Adams-Stokes [Cardiology] ..... A-S
Adams-Stokes Attack [Cardiology] (MAE) ..... ASA
Adams-Stokes Syndrome [Medicine] (MELL) ..... ASS
Adamsville, TN [AM radio station call letters] ..... WEAB
Adana [Turkey] [Airport symbol] (OAG) ..... ADA
Adanac Mining & Exploration Ltd. [Toronto Stock Exchange symbol] [Vancouver Stock Exchange symbol] ..... ADN
Adana/Incirlik [Turkey] [ICAO location identifier] (ICLI) ..... LTAG

Adana/Sakirpasa [Turkey] [ICAO location identifier] (ICLI) .... LTAF
Adapt .... AD
Adapt II Structural Activities (SAUS) .... ADAPT
Adaptability (ABBR) .... ADPBT
Adaptability, Partnership, Growth, Affection, and Resolve [Family Therapy Questionnaire] .... APGAR
Adaptable .... A
Adaptable (ABBR) .... ADAPB
Adaptable (ABBR) .... ADPB
Adaptable Board Computer [Signetics] .... ABC
Adaptable Computerized Type Setting (SAUS) .... ACTYS
Adaptable Data Base Management System (COE) .... ADABAS
Adaptable Data Manager [Hitachi Ltd.] [Japan] .... ADM
Adaptable Database System (SAUS) .... ADA
Adaptable Database System [Database management system] [Registered trademark of Software AG, Darmstadt, Germany] .... ADABAS
Adaptable Hydrologic Data Acquisition System (GEOI) .... AHDAS
Adaptable Low-Cost Shop-Floor Control Systems (SAUO) .... LOW-COST CONTROL
Adaptable Microcomputer Realtime User System (SAUS) .... AMCRUS
Adaptable Space Propulsion System [Military] .... ASPS
Adaptable Surface Interface Terminal (MCD) .... ASIT
Adaptable Terminal Interface Configuration [Military] (MCD) .... ATIC
Adaptable-Programmable Assembly System [Computer science] (PDAA) .... APAS
Adaptably (ABBR) .... ADAPY
Adaptation (ABBR) .... ADAPN
Adaptation (ABBR) .... ADAPT
Adaptation (ADWA) .... adapt
Adaptation (ABBR) .... ADAPTTN
Adaptation Controlled Environment System (ADWA) .... ACES
Adaptation der AppleTalk-Architektur (SAUS) .... EtherTalk
Adaptation Kit (ACAE) .... AK
Adaptation Level .... AL
Adaptation Mathematical Processor .... AMP
Adaptation Of [Etymology] .... AD
Adaptation of Meso-beta-scale Models for Operational and Research Applications (SAUS) .... AMMORA
Adaptation to Premises and Equipment Scheme [Education] (AIE) .... APE
Adaptec, Inc. [Associated Press] (SAG) .... Adaptec
Adaptec, Inc. [NASDAQ symbol] (NQ) .... ADPT
Adaptec RAIDport Option [Computer science] .... ARO
Adapted (ABBR) .... ADAPD
Adapted (SAUS) .... adpt
Adapted Child [Psychology] (DHP) .... AC
Adapted Delivered Source Instruction .... ADSI
Adapted Identification Decision Equipment .... AIDE
Adapted Payload Carrier (SAUS) .... APC
Adapted Physical Educator (SAUS) .... APE
Adapted Swimming-pool Tank Reactor, Austria (SAUS) .... ASTRA
Adapted Uzgiris-Hunt Scales (EDAC) .... AUHS
Adapter (ADWA) .... ad
Adapter (ABBR) .... ADAPR
Adapter .... ADAPT
Adapter [MARC relator code] [Library of Congress] (LCCP) .... adp
Adapter (KSC) .... ADPT
Adapter (MSA) .... ADPTR
Adapter, Binding Post .... ABP
Adapter Booster .... AB
Adapter Building Units (ACAE) .... ABU
Adapter, Bulkhead .... AB
Adapter Cable .... AC
Adapter Cluster (SAUS) .... AC
Adapter Common Card (SAUS) .... ACC
Adapter Control Block [Computer science] (IBMDP) .... ACB
Adapter Control Detector [Computer science] .... ACD
Adapter Definition File (BYTE) .... ADF
Adapter Description File [Computer science] (PCM) .... ADF
Adapter Device Driver (VERA) .... ADD
Adapter Fault Tolerance [Intel] [Computer science] .... AFT
Adapter Interface (ADWA) .... AI
Adapter Kit (MCD) .... AK
Adapter Panel .... AP
Adapter, Right Angle .... ARA
Adapter Section [NASA] (KSC) .... AS
Adapter Service Area (MCD) .... ASA
Adapter, Straight .... AS
Adapter Sub-Unit Tester (SAUS) .... ASUT
Adapter Support Interface [Computer science] (VERA) .... ASI
Adapter, Tee .... AT
Adapter Unit (NG) .... ADU
Adapter-Binding Post (SAUS) .... ABP
Adapting (ABBR) .... ADAPG
Adaption (ABBR) .... ADAPN
Adaption (SAUS) .... ADAPT
Adaption Binary Load [Program] (CET) .... ABL
Adaption Box Assembly (SAUS) .... ABA
Adaption Error Note .... AEN
Adaption Kit .... AK
Adaption Layer Controller [Computer science] (VERA) .... ALC
Adaption Level (SAUS) .... AL
Adaption Mathematical Processor (SAUS) .... AMP
Adaption of Automatically Programmed Tools (SAUS) .... ADAPT
Adaptive (ABBR) .... ADAPTV
Adaptive (ABBR) .... ADAPV
Adaptive Agile RADAR ECCM [Electronic Counter-Countermeasures] (MCD) .... AAREC

Adaptive and Integrated Decision Expeditor (MCD) .... AIDE
Adaptive Angle Bias .... AAB
Adaptive Antenna Control (MCD) .... AAC
Adaptive Antenna Receiver System .... ADARS
Adaptive Arithmetical Method .... ADAM
Adaptive Array (ACAE) .... AA
Adaptive Array Processor (SAUS) .... AAP
Adaptive Assembly Robotic Machine (SAUS) .... AARM
Adaptive Battery Life Extender (SAUS) .... ABLE
Adaptive Beam Forming (NVT) .... ABF
Adaptive Behavior [Psychology] .... AB
Adaptive Behavior Inventory [Test] (TES) .... ABI
Adaptive Behavior Inventory for Children [Psychology] .... ABIC
Adaptive Behavior Scale [American Association on Mental Deficiency] [Psychology] .... ABS
Adaptive Behavior Scale for Infants and Early Childhood [Child development test] .... ABSI
Adaptive Behavior Scale, School Edition [Child development test] .... ABS-SE
Adaptive Bounding Algorithm (SAUS) .... ABA
Adaptive Braking System (SAUS) .... ABS
Adaptive Break-in Control Function (SAUS) .... ABCF
Adaptive Broadband [NASDAQ symbol] .... ADAP
Adaptive Bus Controller (SAUS) .... ABC
Adaptive Character Reader (SAUS) .... ACR
Adaptive Code System (SAUS) .... ACS
Adaptive Communication (MHDB) .... ADAPTICOM
Adaptive Communication Live Controller (MCD) .... ACLC
Adaptive Communications and Control Subsystem (ACAE) .... ACCS
Adaptive Communications Processor (SAUS) .... ACP
Adaptive Computer Experiment (SAUS) .... ACE
Adaptive Computer Technologies [San Jose, CA] .... ACT
Adaptive Computerized Training System (ACAE) .... ACTS
Adaptive Control [Manufacturing term] .... AC
Adaptive Control Constrained [Manufacturing term] .... ACC
Adaptive Control Constraint (SAUS) .... ACC
Adaptive Control Drilling System (SAUS) .... ACDS
Adaptive Control Geometrical (SAUS) .... ACG
Adaptive Control of Thought [Psychology] .... ACT
Adaptive Control Optimization (or Optimized) (SAUS) .... ACO
Adaptive Control Optimized [Manufacturing term] .... ACO
Adaptive Control Process .... ACP
Adaptive Control System .... ACS
Adaptive Control Unit (SAUS) .... ACU
Adaptive Control Voltage Module (SAUS) .... ACVM
Adaptive Controlled Phased Array (CAAL) .... ACPA
Adaptive Controlling System (SAUS) .... ACS
Adaptive Counseling and Therapy (DHP) .... ACT
Adaptive Data Compression [Computer science] .... ADC
Adaptive Data Reporting System (SAUS) .... ADRS
Adaptive Decision Maker in an Information Retrieval Environment [Stanford University] (NITA) .... ADMIRE
Adaptive Delta Modulation [Electronics] .... ADM
Adaptive Delta Pulse Code Modulation (TELE) .... ADPCM
Adaptive Delta Voice Modulation [Air Force] .... ADVM
Adaptive Detection, Estimation, and Correlation (IUSS) .... ADEC
Adaptive Diagnostic Approach to Performance Testing (SAUS) .... ADAPT
Adaptive Differential Pulse Code Modulated Transcoder [Telecommunications] .... ADPCMT
Adaptive Differential Pulse Code Modulation [Computer science] .... ADCPM
Adaptive Differential Pulse Code Modulation [Computer science] (IGQR) .... ADPCM
Adaptive Differential Pulse-Code Modulators (SAUS) .... ADPCMs
Adaptive Digital Acquisition Sampling (SAUS) .... ADAS
Adaptive Digital Avionics Module .... ADAM
Adaptive Digital Signal Processor (MCD) .... ADSP
Adaptive Dynamic Analysis and Maintenance (MHDI) .... ADAM
Adaptive Dynamic Decision-Aiding Method .... ADDAM
Adaptive Dynamic Range Coding (SAUS) .... ADRC
Adaptive Echo Cancellation [Navy] (MCD) .... AEC
Adaptive Environmental Assessment and Management .... AEAM
Adaptive Escalator Predictor (MCD) .... AEP
Adaptive Ferroelectric Transformer (OA) .... AFT
Adaptive Fire Control System [Military] (IUSS) .... AFCS
Adaptive Flight Control System .... AFCS
Adaptive Flight Training System (MCD) .... AFTS
Adaptive Fuel Control (SAUS) .... AFC
Adaptive Functioning Index [Nancy F. Marlett] (TES) .... AFI
Adaptive Fuzzy Associative Memory (IDAI) .... AFAM
Adaptive Gain Computer (SAUS) .... AGC
Adaptive Ground-Implemented Phased Array [NASA] .... AGIPA
Adaptive Head Lamp .... AHL
Adaptive Hopping Permit (SAUS) .... AHP
Adaptive Hough Transform [Computer science] .... AHT
Adaptive Inferential Control [Control technology] .... AIC
Adaptive Information Selector .... AIS
Adaptive Injection Molding [Engineering] .... AIM
Adaptive Injection Moulding (SAUS) .... AIM
Adaptive Intelligent Control of Radio Networks (SAUS) .... AICORN
Adaptive Intelligent Dialog (PDAA) .... AID
Adaptive Intercommunication Requirement (MCD) .... ADAP
Adaptive Intercommunication Requirement .... AICR
Adaptive Intercommunication Requirement (NASA) .... AIR
Adaptive Interface Suppression (ACAE) .... AIS
Adaptive Interference Cancellation System (CAAL) .... AICS
Adaptive Interferometer Processor (SAUS) .... AIP

Adaptive Internetwork Management System [*Ungermann-Bass, Inc.*] .... AIM
Adaptive Intrusion Data System (MCD) .... AIDS
Adaptive Iterated Extended Kalman Filtering (MCD) .... AIEKF
Adaptive Jam-Resistant Tranceiver (PDAA) .... AJRT
Adaptive LASER Optics Techniques (MCD) .... ALOT
Adaptive Laser Oscillator Technique (ACAE) .... ALOT
Adaptive LASER Resonator Technique (MCD) .... ALERT
Adaptive Lattice Filter (SAUS) .... ADLAT
Adaptive Lattice Linear Prediction (PDAA) .... ALLP
Adaptive Learn Processor [*Fuel systems*] [*Automotive engineering*] .... ADP
Adaptive Learning Environments Model (EDAC) .... ALEM
Adaptive Learning Environments Program .... ALEP
Adaptive Learning Network [*Computer science*] .... ALN
Adaptive Lempel-Ziv Data Compression [*Computer science*] .... ALDC
Adaptive Lens Array (MCD) .... ADLAR
Adaptive Library Management System [*Lipman Management Resources Ltd.*] [*Information service or system*] (IID) .... ADLIB
Adaptive Library Management System (SAUS) .... ADLIB Management System
Adaptive Light Pattern .... ALP
Adaptive Line Canceller and Enhancer (CAAL) .... ALICE
Adaptive Line Enhancement (SAUS) .... ALE
Adaptive Line Enhancer [*Telecommunications*] (CAAL) .... ALE
Adaptive Linear (KSC) .... ADALINE
Adaptive Linear Combiner [*Computer science*] .... ALC
Adaptive Linear Element (SAUS) .... ADALINE Element
Adaptive Linear Predictive Coding (TEL) .... ALPC
Adaptive Location of Internetworked Bases of Information (SAUS) .... ALIBI
Adaptive Logic Circuit .... ALC
Adaptive Long-Range Infrared Tracker .... ALIRT
Adaptive Lossless Data Compression (SAUS) .... ADLC
Adaptive Lossless Data Compression [*IBM Corp*] (VERA) .... ALDC
Adaptive Maneuvering Logic (MCD) .... AML
Adaptive Maneuvering Logic Score (MCD) .... AMLS
Adaptive Man-Machine Nonarithmetic Information Processing [*Documentation*] .... AMNIP
Adaptive Man-machine Non-arithmetic Information Processing (SAUS) .... AMNIP
Adaptive Man/Machine Non-Numeric Information Processing System [*IBM Corp.*] (NITA) .... AMNIPS
Adaptive Mathematical Model .... AMM
Adaptive Mesh Refinement (SAUS) .... AMR
Adaptive Microprogrammed Control System (SAUS) .... AMCS
Adaptive Microwave Proximity [*Military*] (MCD) .... AMP
Adaptive Mission-Oriented Software System (MCD) .... AMOSS
Adaptive Mobile Access Protocol (MCD) .... AMAP
Adaptive Mobile Torpedo Decoy [*Navy*] (MCD) .... AMTD
Adaptive Mode Planning System [*Computer program*] .... AMPS
Adaptive Mode Planning System Input [*Computer program*] .... AMPSIN
Adaptive Mode Planning System Input (SAUS) .... AMPSLIN
Adaptive Moving Target Detection (SAUS) .... AMTD
Adaptive Moving Target Indicator [*Military*] .... AMTI
Adaptive Multibeam Experiment for Aeronautical and Maritime Services (SAUS) .... AMEAMS
Adaptive Multibeam Phased Array [*RADAR*] (MCD) .... AMPA
Adaptive Multifunction Antenna (MCD) .... AMA
Adaptive Multi-function Antenna (SAUS) .... AMA
Adaptive Multiplexer (CAAL) .... AM
Adaptive Narrowband FM [*Frequency Modulation*] **MODEM** [*Telecommunications*] (TEL) .... ANBFM
Adaptive Network Analysis Connected with Defence Applications (SAUS) .... ANACONDA
Adaptive Network Cognitive Processor (ACAE) .... ANCP
Adaptive Network Sensor Processor (ACAE) .... ANSP
Adaptive Noise Cancelling (MCD) .... ANC
Adaptive Noise Control [*Automotive engineering*] .... ADC
Adaptive Noise Processor (SAUS) .... ANP
Adaptive Null Aerial (or Antenna) (SAUS) .... ANA
Adaptive Null Antenna .... ANA
Adaptive Optical Camouflage (SAUS) .... AOC
Adaptive Optics (ACAE) .... AO
Adaptive Packet Assembly (VERA) .... APA
Adaptive Pattern Recognition Processing [*Computer science*] .... APRP
Adaptive Pattern-Perceiving Electronic Computer System .... APPECS
Adaptive Payload Carrier (NAKS) .... APC
Adaptive Phase Array RADAR .... APAR
Adaptive Phase Velocimeter .... APV
Adaptive Phased Array [*Military*] (IUSS) .... APA
Adaptive Physical Education .... APE
Adaptive Planning and Control Sequence [*Marketing*] .... APACS
Adaptive Planning System .... APS
Adaptive Plate Cabinet (SAUS) .... APC
Adaptive Polarization Electronic Countermeasure (MCD) .... APECM
Adaptive Power Applique (SAUS) .... APA
Adaptive Predictive Coding [*Telecommunications*] (TEL) .... APC
Adaptive Predictive Coding with Maximum-Likelihood Quantization (SAUS) .... APC-MLQ
Adaptive Predictive Correction (CGWS) .... APC
Adaptive Problem-Oriented Software (SAUS) .... APOS
Adaptive Process Symposium (SAUS) .... ADPSYM
Adaptive Processing Control (SAUS) .... APC
Adaptive Processor (SAUS) .... APROC
Adaptive Processor, SONAR (CAAL) .... APS
Adaptive Processor System (SAUS) .... APS
Adaptive Programmable Interface Unit (SAUS) .... APIU
Adaptive Programming Technology .... APT
Adaptive Pulse Code Modulation [*Telecommunications*] (TEL) .... APCM
Adaptive Pulse Width Modulation (ACAE) .... APWM
Adaptive Quantization (SAUS) .... AQ
Adaptive Random Search Technique [*Computer science*] (MHDI) .... ARSTEC
Adaptive Rapid Turnaround Communication (ACAE) .... ARTC
Adaptive Rate Based (SAUS) .... ARB
Adaptive Rate System (SAUS) .... ARS
Adaptive Recognition Technology [*Calera Recognition Systems, Inc.*] [*Computer science*] (PCM) .... ART
Adaptive Reliability Control System [*Electronics*] (IAA) .... ARCS
Adaptive Residual Coding (MCD) .... ARC
Adaptive Resonance Theory [*Computer science*] .... ART
Adaptive Search and Track Array (SAUS) .... ASTA
Adaptive Seating Device [*Occupational therapy*] .... ASD
Adaptive Security Algorithm (SAUS) .... ASA
Adaptive Sensing Vehicle [*Robot*] .... ASV
Adaptive Sensitivity Time Control (ACAE) .... ASTC
Adaptive Side-Lobe Cancellation (ACAE) .... ASLC
Adaptive Side-Lobe Canceller [*RADAR*] (MCD) .... ASLC
Adaptive Signal Control Optimization Techniques .... ASCOT
Adaptive Signal Correcting (or Correction) (SAUS) .... ASC
Adaptive Signal Correction (IAA) .... ASC
Adaptive Signal Masking (ACAE) .... ASM
Adaptive Solution Domain .... ASD
Adaptive Solutions [*NASDAQ symbol*] (TTSB) .... ADSO
Adaptive Solutions, Inc. [*Associated Press*] (SAG) .... AdapSl
Adaptive Solutions, Inc. [*Associated Press*] (SAG) .... AdapSol
Adaptive Solutions, Inc. [*NASDAQ symbol*] (SAG) .... ADSO
Adaptive Solutions Wrrt [*NASDAQ symbol*] (TTSB) .... ADSOW
Adaptive Source Routing Transparent [*Computer science*] (PCM) .... ASRT
Adaptive Spectral Perceptual Entropy Encoding (SAUS) .... ASPEC
Adaptive Speed Control (PDAA) .... ASC
Adaptive Speed Levelling [*US Robotics*] (VERA) .... ASL
Adaptive Static Margin Controller (MCD) .... ASMC
Adaptive Statistical Processor [*Computer science*] (MHDI) .... APROC
Adaptive Step-Size Random Search [*Computer science*] (IAA) .... ASSRS
Adaptive Style Inventory (TMMY) .... ASI
Adaptive Subband Coding (SAUS) .... ASC
Adaptive Subbands Excited Transform [*Telecommunications*] (OSI) .... ACIT
Adaptive Subbands Excited Transform [*Computer science*] .... ASET
Adaptive Surface Interface Terminal (SAUS) .... ASIT
Adaptive Surface-Signal Recognition and Direction Indicator [*Navy*] ...... ASRADI
Adaptive System (IAA) .... ASM
Adaptive Tactical Navigation (MCD) .... ATN
Adaptive Target Data Link (SAUS) .... ATDL
Adaptive Technologies (SAUS) .... ADT
Adaptive Technologies (Canada) [*Vancouver Stock Exchange symbol*] .... ADT
Adaptive Technology Resource Center (SAUO) .... ATRC
Adaptive Threshold Detection with Estimated Sequence (LAIN) .... ATDES
Adaptive Threshold Gate (PDAA) .... ATG
Adaptive Threshold Learning [*Computer science*] (VERA) .... ATL
Adaptive Tolerant Protocol (SAUS) .... ATP
Adaptive Tracker Unit (ACAE) .... ATU
Adaptive Traffic Control [*Automotive engineering*] .... ATC
Adaptive Transform Acoustic Coding [*Sony*] (VERA) .... ATRAC
Adaptive Transform Coding (PDAA) .... ATC
Adaptive Triangular Mesh (GEOI) .... ATM
Adaptive User Interface (SAUS) .... AUI
Adaptive Vehicular Antenna (SAUS) .... AVA
Adaptive Video Guidance System (MCD) .... AVGS
Adaptive Video Processor .... AVP
Adaptive Wafer Scale Integration (MCD) .... AWSI
Adaptive Waveform Recognition .... AWR
Adaptively Data Equalized MODEM .... ADEM
Adaptively Data Equalized Modem (SAUS) .... ADEM
Adaptor (KSC) .... ADAP
Adaptronics, Inc. .... ADI
Adas [*or Adath*] **Israel** (BJA) .... AI
Adas Israel Congregation, Washington, DC [*Library symbol*] [*Library of Congress*] (LCLS) .... DAdI
Adas [*or Adath*] **Jeshurun** (BJA) .... AJ
Adastra Aviation Ltd. [*Canada*] [*ICAO designator*] (FAAC) .... ADD
Adastral Resources Ltd. [*Vancouver Stock Exchange symbol*] .... ASA
Adavanced Spaceborne Thermal Emission and Radiometer (SAUS) .... ASTER
ADAWS Improvement Programme (SAUS) .... ADIMP
Adaxial Leaflet Pubescence - Curly [*Botany*] .... ADPC
Adbominal Compression [*Medicine*] (MELL) .... AC
Adbuct (ABBR) .... ABBC
ADC Telecommunications [*NASDAQ symbol*] (TTSB) .... ADCT
ADC Telecommunications, Inc. [*NASDAQ symbol*] (NQ) .... ADCT
ADC Telecommunications, Inc. [*Associated Press*] (SAG) .... ADCTel
Adco Technologies [*NASDAQ symbol*] (TTSB) .... ADCO
Adco Technologies, Inc. [*NASDAQ symbol*] (SAG) .... ADCO
ADCOM Current Intelligence Center (SAUO) .... ACIC
ADCOM Intelligence Center (SAUO) .... ADIC
ADCOM [*Air Defense Command*] **Intelligence Memorandum** (MCD) .... AIM
Adcom Technologies, Inc. [*Associated Press*] (SAG) .... AdcoTc
ADCOM Weekly Intelligence Review Support (MCD) .... AWIR
Add [*Computer science*] [*Telecommunications*] .... a
Add Address (SAUS) .... AA
Add and Carry Logical Word (SAA) .... ACL
Add BCD [*Binary Coded Decimal*] **Number with Extend** [*Computer science*] .... ABCD
Add Carry (SAUS) .... AC
Add Command Execution (SAUS) .... ACE
Add Delete Rework Instruction (SAUS) .... ADRI

Add Fixed Point (SAUS) .... AFP
Add Halfword (SAUS) .... AH
Add Impulse (SAUS) .... AI
Add In Utility (SAUS) .... ADN
Add Index (SAUS) .... ADX
Add Index Register [*Computer science*] (IAA) .... ADX
Add, Initial, Multiprecision .... AIM
Add Logical (SAUS) .... AL
Add Lot (AAEL) .... ADL
Add Magnitude [*Computer science*] (IAA) .... ADM
Add Memory (SAUS) .... ADM
Add, Multi-Precision (SAUS) .... AMP
Add Normalized Short (SAUS) .... ANS
Add Numeric (SAUS) .... ADDN
Add On (SAUS) .... ADDON
Add One Right (SAUS) .... AOR
Add One to Memory [*Computer science*] .... AOM
Add One to the Right (SAA) .... AOR
Add or Subtract .... AOS
Add Or Subtract (SAUS) .... AOS
Add Order Execution (SAUS) .... AOE
Add Packed [*Computer science*] .... AP
Add Punch Machine (SAUS) .... APM
Add Row and Constant (SAUS) .... ARC
Add Row and Row (SAUS) .... ARR
Add Statement (SAUS) .... AS
Add Time (SAUS) .... AT
Add Unnormalized Long (SAUS) .... AUL
Add Unnormalized Short (SAUS) .... AUS
Add with Carry .... ADC
Add Word (SAUS) .... AW
Addams' Ecclesiastical Reports [*A publication*] (DLA) .... Ad
Addams' Ecclesiastical Reports [*A publication*] (DLA) .... Add
Addams' Ecclesiastical Reports [*A publication*] (DLA) .... Addams
Addams' Ecclesiastical Reports [*A publication*] (DLA) .... Addams Ecc (Eng)
Addams' Ecclesiastical Reports [*A publication*] (DLA) .... Add Ecc
Addams' Ecclesiastical Reports [*A publication*] (DLA) .... Add Eccl
Addams' Ecclesiastical Reports [*A publication*] (DLA) .... Add Eccl Rep
Addams' Ecclesiastical Reports [*A publication*] (DLA) .... Add ER
Addantur [*Let Them Be Added*] [*Latin*] .... add
Add/Drop Multiplexer [*Telecommunications*] (ACRL) .... ADM
Add-Drop-Multiplexer (SAUS) .... ADM
Adde [*Add or Up To*] [*Pharmacy*] .... AD
Adde [*Add or Up To*] [*Pharmacy*] .... ADD
Adde Cum Tritu [*Add Trituriton*] [*Pharmacology*] (DAVI) .... add C Trit
Adde cum Tritu [*Add Trituration*] [*Pharmacy*] .... ADD c TRIT
Added Belly Band [*Military*] (CAAL) .... ABB
Added Entry [*Online database field identifier*] .... AE
Added Name [*Travel industry*] (TRID) .... AN
Added Reference Transmission (SAUS) .... ART
Added Segment (TRID) .... AS
Added Thermal Barrier (CAAL) .... ATB
Added Value Tax (SAUS) .... AVT
Added-Value-Agriculture (EDCT) .... AVA
Addend (ABBR) .... ADND
Addend Register (SAUS) .... AR
Addenda (SAUS) .... ADD
Addenda (ABBR) .... ADNDA
Addenda and Corrigenda (ADA) .... A & C
Addenda and Corrigenda (SAUS) .... A&C
Addendum .... AD
Addendum (KSC) .... ADD
Addendum (WDMC) .... add
Addendum (ABBR) .... ADDNDM
Addendum (ABBR) .... ADNDM
Addendum to Monthly Collection [*IRS*] .... ADDM
Addendus [*To Be Added*] [*Pharmacy*] .... ADDEND
Adder [*Computer device*] .... A
Adder [*Computer device*] .... ADDR
Adder [*Computer device*] (MDG) .... ADR
Adder, Algebraic (SAUS) .... Addr Alg
Adder Carry (SAUS) .... AC
Adder Center Input Register (SAUS) .... ACIR
Adder Circuit (SAUS) .... AC
Adder for Multiple Operands (SAUS) .... AMO
Adder Gate (SAUS) .... AG
Adder Left Input Register (SAUS) .... ALIR
Adder Left Output Register (SAUS) .... ALOR
Adder, Logical, and Transfer Unit [*Computer*] .... ALTU
Adder of Multiple Operands (SAUS) .... AMO
Adder Output (SAUS) .... AO
Adder Output Buffer (SAUS) .... AOB
Adder Stage (SAUS) .... AS
Adder Tree (SAUS) .... AT
Adder Unit (SAUS) .... AU
Adder/Substracter (SAUS) .... A/S
ADD-H [*Attention Deficit Disorder with Hyperactivity*] **Comprehensive Teachers Rating Scale** .... ACTERS
Addict [*Drug*] [*Slang*] .... AD
Addict (ABBR) .... ADDC
Addict Rehabilitation Counselor .... ARC
Addicted (ABBR) .... ADDCD
Addicting (ABBR) .... ADDCG
Addiction (SAUS) .... ADD
Addiction (ABBR) .... ADDCN
Addiction [*Chemical dependency*] (DAVI) .... Addict
Addiction (SAUS) .... Addict
Addiction Research and Treatment Center (SAUO) .... ARTC
Addiction Research and Treatment Corp. (EA) .... ARTC
Addiction Research and Treatment Corporation [*An association*] (EA) .... ARTC
Addiction Research Center [*Baltimore, MD*] [*Department of Health and Human Services*] .... ARC
Addiction Research Center (SAUS) .... ARC
Addiction Research Center Inventory [*Psychology*] .... ARCI
Addiction Research Foundation [*Fondation de la Recherche sur la Toxicomanie*] [*Formerly, Alcoholism & Drug Addiction Research Foundation*] (AC) .... ARF
Addiction Research Foundation Library [*Canada*] (DI) .... ARFL
Addiction Research Foundation of Ontario Library [*UTLAS symbol*] .... ARF
Addiction Research Foundation, Toronto, ON, Canada [*Library symbol*] [*Library of Congress*] (LCLS) .... CaOTAD
Addiction Research Foundation, Toronto, Ontario [*Library symbol*] [*National Library of Canada*] (NLC) .... OTAD
Addiction Services Agency (SAUO) .... ASA
Addiction Severity Index [*Medicine*] (MELL) .... ASI
Addiction Workers Alerted to Rehabilitation and Education (SAUO) .... AWARE
Addictions Community Centres for Education, Prevention, Treatment, and Research [*British*] (AIE) .... ACCEPT
Addictive Behavior Group [*Psychology*] (DAVI) .... abg
Addictive Diseases Trust (WDAA) .... ADT
Addicts Anonymous (SAUO) .... AA
Addicts Anonymous (EA) .... AA
Addicts Rehabilitation Center (SAUO) .... ARC
Add-In (SAUS) .... XLA
Adding (ABBR) .... ADDG
Adding (SAUS) .... Addg
Adding Circuit (SAUS) .... AC
Adding Counter (SAUS) .... AC
Adding Jump (SAUS) .... AJ
Adding Listing Machine (SAUS) .... ALM
Adding Machine (SAUS) .... AM
Adding Mechanism (SAUS) .... AM
Adding Operator (SAUS) .... AO
Adding Punch (SAUS) .... AP
Adding Wheel (SAUS) .... AW
Addington Association (EA) .... AA
Addington Resources [*NASDAQ symbol*] (TTSB) .... ADDR
Addington Resources, Inc. [*NASDAQ symbol*] (NQ) .... ADDR
Addington Resources, Inc. [*Associated Press*] (SAG) .... Adingtn
Addington's Abridgment of Penal Statutes [*A publication*] (DLA) .... Add Abr
Addis Ababa [*Ethiopia*] [*Seismograph station code, US Geological Survey*] .... AAE
Addis Ababa [*Ethiopia*] [*Airport symbol*] (OAG) .... ADD
Addis Ababa [*Ethiopia*] [*ICAO location identifier*] (ICLI) .... HAAA
Addis Ababa, Ethiopia (SAUS) .... Addis
Addis Ababa/Bole International [*Ethiopia*] [*ICAO location identifier*] (ICLI) .... HAAB
Addis Ababa/Liddetta [*Ethiopia*] [*ICAO location identifier*] (ICLI) .... HAAL
Addis Abeba Water and Sewerage Authority (SAUO) .... AAWSA
Addison, AL [*FM radio station call letters*] (BROA) .... WYAM-FM
Addison Charges [*Addison's Pennsylvania Reports*] [*A publication*] (DLA) .... Add Ch
Addison Foster [*Record label*] .... AF
Addison Gallery of American Art (SAUO) .... AGAA
Addison Gilbert Hospital, Gloucester, Mass. (SAUS) .... AGH
Addison on Contract [*A publication*] (ILCA) .... Ad Cont
Addison on Contracts [*A publication*] (DLA) .... Ad Con
Addison on Contracts [*A publication*] (DLA) .... Add C
Addison on Contracts [*A publication*] (DLA) .... Add Con
Addison on Contracts [*A publication*] (DLA) .... Add Cont
Addison on the Agricultural Holdings Act [*A publication*] (DLA) .... Add Agr Act
Addison on Torts [*A publication*] (DLA) .... Add T
Addison on Torts [*A publication*] (DLA) .... Add Tor
Addison on Torts [*A publication*] (DLA) .... Add Torts
Addison on Torts [*A publication*] (DLA) .... Ad Torts
Addison on Torts, Abridged [*A publication*] (DLA) .... Add Torts Abr
Addison on Torts, Dudley and Baylies' Edition [*A publication*] (DLA) .... Add Torts D & B
Addison on Torts, Woods Edition [*A publication*] (DLA) .... Add Torts Woods
Addison Public Library, Addison, NY [*Library symbol*] [*Library of Congress*] (LCLS) .... NAd
Addison, TX [*Location identifier*] [*FAA*] (FAAL) .... TBQ
Addison's County Court Reports [*Pennsylvania*] [*A publication*] (DLA) .... Addis
Addison's County Court Reports [*Pennsylvania*] [*A publication*] (DLA) .... Addison (PA)
Addison's County Court Reports [*Pennsylvania*] [*A publication*] (DLA) .... Add PA
Addison's County Court Reports [*Pennsylvania*] [*A publication*] (DLA) .... Add Rep
Addison's Disease [*Medicine*] (MELL) .... AD
Addison's Pennsylvania Supreme Court Reports [*A publication*] (DLA) .... Add
Addison-Wesley [*Publisher*] .... A-W
Addison-Wesley (SAUO) .... ISBN 0-201
Addison-Wesley Publishing Company (SAUO) .... A-WPC
Addition (AABC) .... ADD
Addition (ADWA) .... add
Addition (ADWA) .... addn
Addition .... ADDN
Addition .... ADDTN
Addition (ABBR) .... ADTN
Addition Formula (SAUS) .... AF
Addition Key (SAUS) .... AK
Addition Matrix (SAUS) .... AM
Addition Nucleophile Ring Opening Ring Closure [*Organic chemistry*] .... ANRORC

Addition Position (SAUS)	AP
Addition Register (SAUS)	AR
Addition Slip (SAUS)	AS
Addition, Subtraction, Timing, and Ratio	ASTR
Addition Theorem (SAUS)	AT
Additional (DLA)	addit
Additional (KSC)	ADDL
Additional	ADDNL
Additional (ADWA)	addnl
Additional	ADDTL
Additional (SAUS)	Addtl
Additional (DA)	ADNI
Additional (ABBR)	ADTNL
Additional Air Force Speciality Code (SAUS)	AAFSC
Additional Authorization Item [Military] (INF)	AAI
Additional Authorization List [Army] (AABC)	AAL
Additional Benefits [Unemployment insurance]	AB
Additional Billet Requirements [Military]	ABR
Additional Bit (SAUS)	AB
Additional Budget Submissions [DoD]	ABS
Additional Claim [Unemployment insurance] (OICC)	AC
Additional Clergy Society (SAUO)	ACIS
Additional Clock Resolution (SAUS)	ACR
Additional Code (SAUS)	AC
Additional Collection [Travel industry] (TRID)	add/col
Additional Conditional Purchase [Business term] (ADA)	ACP
Additional Core Enhancements (SAUS)	ACE
Additional Core Storage (SAUS)	ACS
Additional Crew Member [Military] (AFM)	ACM
Additional Curates' Society [British]	ACS
Additional Curates Society, Harpenden, Herts (SAUO)	ACS
Additional Data (SAUS)	AD
Additional Day Off	ADO
Additional Days Added [Legal term] (WDAA)	ADA
Additional Days Remitted (WDAA)	ADR
Additional Dealer Markup [Automobile retailing]	ADM
Additional Dealer Profit [Automobile retailing]	ADP
Additional Delay in Reporting [Military] (DNAB)	ADDELREP
Additional Dialogue Replacement	ADR
Additional Duty	ADDU
Additional Duty (AABC)	ADY
Additional Education	ADDED
Additional Equipment Interface (SAUS)	AEI
Additional Expediting Expense [Insurance]	AEE
Additional Expenses	AE
Additional Extended Coverage [Insurance]	AEC
Additional Fiscal Year Money Is Authorized by the Secretary of the Army (AABC)	AFYMOSAP
Additional Flight Training Period (AABC)	AFTP
Additional Government Requirement (AAGC)	AGR
Additional Gunner Training (MCD)	AGT
Additional High Layer Functions (SAUS)	AHLF
Additional Information Form	AIF
Additional Information Request (MCD)	AIR
Additional Instruction (SAUS)	AI
Additional Listing [Telecommunications] (TEL)	AL
Additional Living Expense [Insurance]	ALE
Additional Low Layer Functions (SAUS)	ALLF
Additional Material Required to Complete Fabrication Order	AMRCFO
Additional Member System [Electoral reform] [British]	AMS
Additional Memory Module	AMM
Additional Military Production	AMP
Additional Mobile SAM [Surface-to-Air Missile] Site (NATG)	AMOSS
Additional Network Feature (SAUS)	ANF
Additional Nonresidential Conditional Purchase (ADA)	ANRCP
Additional Pension/Benefit	AP/B
Additional Peripheral Unit (SAUS)	APU
Additional Personal Allowance (DLA)	APA
Additional Personal Injury Protection [Insurance]	APIP
Additional Places	ADDPLA
Additional Planning Capability (SAA)	APC
Additional Platen Roller (SAUS)	APR
Additional Premium [Insurance]	AP
Additional Premium (WDAA)	ap
Additional Print Position Feature (SAUS)	APPF
Additional Product Documentation (VERA)	APD
Additional Programming Language (IAA)	APL
Additional Qualification Designation/ Utilization (SAUS)	AQDIU
Additional Qualification Designation/Utilization (DNAB)	AQD/U
Additional Qualification Designator (NVT)	AQD
Additional Qualifying Symptom [Medicine] (MAE)	AQS
Additional Reference Carrier Transmission [Telecommunications] (TEL)	ART
Additional Reference Number [NASA] (NASA)	ARN
Additional Reference Transmission (SAUS)	ART
Additional Reference-carrier Transmission (SAUS)	ART
Additional Requirements (DLA)	AR
Additional Secondary Phase [Navigation]	ASP
Additional Selection Factor	ASF
Additional Sense Byte (SAUS)	ASB
Additional Skill Identifier [Army] (INF)	ASI
Additional Sources	AS
Additional Specialty [Military] (INF)	ADSPEC
Additional Specialty Indicator [Army]	ASI
Additional Specialty Training [Military]	AST
Additional Tape Attachment (SAUS)	ATA

Additional Traffic [Air Traffic Control] (FAAC)	ADNL TFC
Additional Training Assemblies	ATA
Additional Training Assembly [Army]	ATA
Additional Trunk Capacity (SAUS)	ATC
Additional Uniform Allowance [Military]	ADDUNIFALW
Additional Voluntary Contribution [Employee's wage contribution toward a company pension plan]	AVC
Additional Word (SAUS)	AW
Additionally (ABBR)	ADDNLY
Additionally (ABBR)	ADTNLY
Additionally Awarded Military Occupational Specialty	AMOS
Additionat Information Request (SAUS)	AIR
Additions (SAUS)	ADDNS
Additions (WDMC)	adds
Additions and Amendments (ADA)	A & A
Additions and Amendments (SAUS)	A&A
Additions in Progress (SAUS)	AIP
Additions to Esther [Apocrypha] (BJA)	AddEsther
Additive (MSA)	ADDT
Additive (ABBR)	ADDV
Additive (ABBR)	ADTV
Additive Bernoulli Noise Linear Sequential Circuit (SAUS)	ABNLSC
Additive Card Code (SAUS)	ACC
Additive Cell Rate (SAUS)	AIR
Additive Color Process	ACP
Additive Color Viewer Printer	ACVP
Additive Controlling Ignition (SAUS)	ACI
Additive Delivery System	ADS
Additive Full-Time Manning (MCD)	AFTM
Additive Gaussian Noise	AGN
Additive Histologic Assessment [Medicine]	AHA
Additive Increase Rate (SAUS)	AIR
Additive Links Online Hawaii Area System (SAUS)	ALOHA System
Additive Noise Linear Sequential Circuit	ANLSC
Additive Noise Machine (SAUS)	ANM
Additive Operational Project [Army]	ADOP
Additive Operational Project [Army] (MCD)	AOP
Additive Process (SAUS)	AP
Additive Source Current (SAUS)	ASC
Additive System of Photographic Exposure (DICI)	APEX
Additive Unit Codes (SAUS)	AUC
Additive Voice Gaussian Noise [Telecommunications] (NITA)	AWGN
Additive White Gaussian Noise [Telecommunications] (TEL)	AWGN
Additive-Free Hard Gold [Metallurgy]	AFHG
Additives and Containments Committee [British]	ACC
Additivity and Variance Stabilization (IDAI)	AVAS
Addtitive Links On-Line Hawaii Area System [Computer science]	ALOHA
Addo Elephant Park (SAUS)	AEP
Addo Elephant Park near Port Elizabeth, South Africa (SAUS)	Addo
Ad-Dome International Ltd. [Vancouver Stock Exchange symbol]	ADI
Add-On (SAUS)	AO
Add-on Audio Unit (SAUS)	AAU
Add-On Audio Unit (MCD)	AAU
Add-On Conference Call [Telecommunications] (DOM)	CONF
Add-On Header [Computer science] (CIST)	AOH
Add-On Main Memory (SAUS)	AOMM
Add-On Memory (SAUS)	AOM
Add-On Module (SAUS)	ADM
Add-On Non-Stop Reliability (PDAA)	ANSR
Add-On Pollution Control Devices (AAEL)	APCD
Add-On Stabilisation (SAUS)	AOS
Add-On Stabilization (MCD)	AOS
Add-Ons and Upgrades (ACAE)	AUG
Address [Computer character] [Computer science]	A
Address (IAA)	AD
Address	ADD
Address (AL)	Add
Address [Computer character] [Computer science]	ADDR
Address (ECII)	ADDSS
Address [Computer character] [Computer science]	ADR
Address [Computer character] [Computer science] (AFM)	ADRS
Address (FAAC)	ADS
Address Accumulator (SAUS)	AA
Address Addend Register (SAUS)	AAR
Address Adder [Computer science] (IAA)	AAD
Address Adder (IAA)	ADA
Address Adding (SAUS)	ADA
Address Algorithm (SAUS)	AA
Address Allocation (SAUS)	AA
Address and Control Field Compression (VERA)	ACFC
Address and Data Interface Unit (SAUS)	ADIU
Address and Instruction Bus (SAUS)	AIB
Address Appendix (SAUS)	AA
Address Arithmetic Unit [Computer science]	AAU
Address Array (SAUS)	AA
Address Assignment (SAUS)	AA
Address Base (SAUS)	AB
Address Blank (SAUS)	AB
Address Book Synchronization (SAUS)	ABS
Address Buffer (MCD)	AB
Address Bus [Computer science]	AB
Address Byte (SAUS)	AB
Address Calculation Machine [Compagnie Honeywell Bull] (NITA)	ACM
Address Card (SAUS)	AC
Address Carry [Computer science] (IAA)	AC

Address Census [*or Control*] File [*Bureau of the Census*] (GFGA)	ACF
Address Census File (SAUS)	ACF
Address Chain (SAUS)	AC
Address Change Service [*Postal Service*] [*United States*] (WDMC)	ACS
Address Character (SAUS)	AC
Address Check (SAUS)	Adr Chk
Address Code Multiplex (SAUS)	ACM
Address Coding [*Business term*]	AC
Address Coding Guide	ACG
Address Commission (RIMS)	ADCOM
Address Comparing (SAUS)	AC
Address Compilation Instruction (SAUS)	ACI
Address Complete, Charge [*Telecommunications*] (TEL)	ADC
Address Complete, Coin-Box [*Telecommunications*] (TEL)	ADX
Address Complete Message [*Telecommunications*] (ACRL)	ACM
Address Complete, No-Charge [*Telecommunications*] (TEL)	ADN
Address Complete, Subscriber Free, Coin-Box [*Telecommunications*] (TEL)	AFX
Address Complete, Subscriber Free, No-Charge [*Telecommunications*] (TEL)	AFN
Address Constant [*Computer science*]	ADCON
Address Control File [*US Census Bureau*]	ACF
Address Control List (SAUS)	ACL
Address Control Register [*Computer science*] (MHDI)	ACR
Address Control Unit [*Computer science*] (MDG)	ACU
Address Control Vector (SAUS)	ACV
Address Conversion Table (SAUS)	ACT
Address Correction Requested	ACR
Address Counter [*Computer science*] (MHDI)	AC
Address Data	AD
Address Data Latch (SAUS)	ADL
Address Data Strobe [*Electronics*]	ADS
Address Decoding [*Computer science*] (IAA)	ADEC
Address Decoding Unit (SAUS)	ADU
Address Definition (SAUS)	ADD
Address Disable [*Computer science*] (CIST)	ADDSB
Address Display System [*or Subsystem*]	ADS
Address Distribution Facility (SAUS)	ADF
Address Effective [*Computer science*] (IAA)	AE
Address Enable [*Computer science*] (IAA)	ADE
Address Enable [*Computer science*]	AEN
Address Error (NITA)	ADE
Address Extension Register [*Computer science*] (IAA)	AER
Address Family (SAUS)	AF
Address Field (SAUS)	ADDF
Address Field Extension (SAUS)	EA
Address File (SAUS)	AF
Address Format (SAUS)	AF
Address Frame (SAUS)	AF
Address Generation/Execute Cycle [*Computer science*]	AGEX
Address Generator	ADGEN
Address Generator (SAUS)	AG
Address Generator Module	ADGM
Address Group (SAUO)	AG
Address Incomplete [*Telecommunications*] (TEL)	ADI
Address Incomplete [*Telecommunications*] (TEL)	AI
Address Incomplete Signal (SAUS)	ADI Signal
Address Index (SAUS)	AI
Address Indicating Group [*Computer science*]	AIG
Address Indicator Group (SAUO)	AIG
Address Information Center [*Memphis, TN*] [*US Postal Service*]	AIC
Address Information System (AUEG)	AIS
Address Instruction (SAUS)	AI
Address Key Register	AKR
Address Kind (SAUS)	AK
Address Language (SAUS)	AL
Address Latch Enable [*Computer science*]	ALE
Address Level (SAUS)	AL
Address Lifetime Expectancy (SAUS)	ALE
Address Lifetime Expectation (VERA)	ALE
Address Line (SAUS)	AL
Address List (SAUS)	AL
Address List Compilation Test (SAUS)	ALCT
Address Locator Logic [*Computer science*]	ALL
Address Management System (SAUS)	AMS
Address Mapping Table (RALS)	AMT
Address Mark [*Microprocessors*]	AM
Address Mark Bit (SAUS)	AMB
Address Mark Detection (SAUS)	AMD
Address Mark Gate (SAUS)	AMG
Address Mark Write Data (SAUS)	AMWD
Address Match (SAUS)	AM
Address Matching Software (SAUS)	ADMATCH
Address Matching Software Package [*Bureau of the Census*] (GFGA)	ADMATCH
Address Memory (SAUS)	AM
Address Mode [*Computer science*]	AM
Address Modification Register (SAUS)	AMR
Address Modifier	AM
Address Operation (SAUS)	AO
Address Order	AO
Address Out (SAUS)	ADDROUT
Address Out [*Computer science*] (IAA)	ADO
Address Out Buffer (SAUS)	AO Buffer
Address Parity Enable (SAUS)	APAREN
Address Part (SAUS)	AP

Address Pass Through (SAUS)	APT
Address Plate Cabinet	APC
Address Portion (SAUS)	AP
Address Printing (SAUS)	AP
Address Punched Card (SAUS)	APC
Address Queue (SAUS)	AQ
Address Range (SAUS)	AR
Address Read Wire (SAUS)	AR-Wire
Address Recall Register (CIST)	ARR
Address Recognition Unit	ARU
Address Record Buffer (SAUS)	ARB
Address Reference File (SAUS)	ARF
Address Reference Number (SAUS)	ARN
Address Reference Register (SAUS)	ARR
Address Register	ADDR
Address Register (BUR)	ADR
Address Register (CMD)	AR
Address Register Area [*Bureau of the Census*] (GFGA)	ARA
Address Register Decoding (SAUS)	ARD
Address Register Modification (SAUS)	ARM
Address Register Position	ARP
Address Registers (SAUS)	ARs
Address Resolution Protocol [*Telecommunications*] (BYTE)	ARP
Address Retrieval System (SAUS)	ARS
Address Search (SAUS)	AS
Address Section (SAUS)	AS
Address Selective (SAUS)	ADSEL
Address Selector (SAUS)	AS
Address Shift Register [*Computer science*] (NITA)	ASR
Address Space Control Block [*Computer science*] (MHDI)	ASCB
Address Space Control Task [*Fujitsu*] (NITA)	ASCT
Address Space Identification	ASID
Address Space Identifier (BUR)	ASID
Address Space Identifier (SAUS)	ASSI
Address Space Manager [*Computer software*] (NITA)	ASM
Address Space Register (SAUS)	ASR
Address Start Register [*Computer science*] (IAA)	ASR
Address Statement (SAUS)	AS
Address Status Changed (SAUS)	ADSC
Address Store (SAUS)	AS
Address Strobe [*Signal*] [*Computer science*]	AS
Address Supporting Organization (SAUO)	ASO
Address Syllable (IAA)	AS
Address Synchronizing Track (SAUS)	AST
Address System (SAUS)	AS
Address Table (SAUS)	AT
Address Tape (SAUS)	AT
Address to Index, True	AXT
Address Trace Block (SAUS)	ATB
Address Track (SAUS)	AT
Address Transfer Sequence (SAUS)	ATS
Address Transition Detection Circuit (SAUS)	ATDC
Address Translation Buffer [*Telecommunications*] (TEL)	ATB
Address Translation Cache [*Motorola, Inc.*] [*Computer science*]	ATC
Address Translation Chip	ATC
Address Translation Controller [*Computer science*] (VERA)	ATC
Address Translation Gateway	ATG
Address Translation Memory [*Computer science*] (IAA)	ATM
Address Translation Table [*Computer science*] (CIST)	ATT
Address Translation Unit (NITA)	ATU
Address Translator [*Computer science*]	AT
Address Unit [*Computer science*]	AU
Address Validity (SAUS)	AV
Address Validity (MCD)	AVL
Address Verification Pulse (KSC)	AVP
Address Verification System (SAUS)	AVS
Address Verification System Plus [*Information Design, Inc.*] [*Information service or system*] (IID)	AVS+
Address Word (SAUS)	AW
Addressable Asynchronous Receiver Transmitter	AART
Addressable Clock (SAUS)	AC
Addressable Core Memory (SAUS)	ACM
Addressable Core Store (SAUS)	ACS
Addressable Data (SAUS)	AD
Addressable Location (SAUS)	AL
Addressable Remote Multiplexer Unit (MCD)	ARMU
Addressable Secondary Surveillance Radar (SAUS)	ADSS Radar
Addressable Store (SAUS)	AS
Addressable Unit (SAUS)	AU
Addressable Word (SAUS)	AW
Addresse (SAUS)	Addr
Addresse (SAUS)	ADEE
Addresse (SAUS)	ADSE
Addressed (ABBR)	ADDRD
Addressed (ABBR)	ADDSD
Addressed [*Computer science*] (IAA)	ADSD
Addressed Cable Delivery (IAA)	ACD
Addressed Core (SAUS)	AC
Addressed Device (SAUS)	AM
Addressed Memory (SAUS)	AM
Addressed Packet System (SAUS)	APS
Addressee (NVT)	ADDEE
Addressee (SAUS)	ADDRE
Addressee (ECII)	ADDSSEE
Addressee (CINC)	ADEE

Addressee (ABBR) .... ADRSE
Addressee .... ADSE
Address-Generation Unit [Computer science] .... AGU
Addressing (SAUS) .... ADDR
Addressing (ABBR) .... ADDRG
Addressing Error (SAUS) .... AE
Addressing Format (SAUS) .... AF
Addressing Machine (SAUS) .... AM
Addressing Matrix (SAUS) .... AM
Addressing Method (SAUS) .... AM
Addressing Mode (SAUS) .... AM
Addressing Operation (SAUS) .... AO
Addressing Scheme (SAUS) .... AS
Addressing Signal (SAUS) .... AS
Addressing System (SAUS) .... AS
Addressing Systems International (NITA) .... ASI
Addressing Technique (SAUS) .... AT
Addressing Toroidal Core Matrix (SAUS) .... ATCM
Addressless (SAUS) .... AL
Addressograph Multigraph [Later, AM International] (DGA) .... AM
Addressograph Multigraph Copier Duplicator (SAUS) .... AMCD
Addressograph-Multigraph-International (SAUS) .... AM International
Address-Selective [British] (MCD) .... ADSEL
Add-Substract Counter (SAUS) .... ASC
Add-Substract Time (SAUS) .... AST
Add-Subtract .... AS
Add-Subtract Unit (SAUS) .... ASU
Adducable (ABBR) .... ADUCB
Adduce (ABBR) .... ADC
Adduce (ABBR) .... ADUC
Adduced (ABBR) .... ADUCD
Adducing (ABBR) .... ADUCG
Adduct (ABBR) .... ADCT
Adducted (ABBR) .... ADUCTD
Adducting (ABBR) .... ADUCTG
Adduction (ABBR) .... ADCTN
Adduction [or Adductor] [Medicine] .... ADD
Adduction [Neurophysiology] (DAVI) .... A-D-Duct
Adduction (ABBR) .... ADUCTN
Adduction Stress Test (MELL) .... AST
Adductive (ABBR) .... ADCTV
Adductive (ABBR) .... ADUCTV
Adductor (MELL) .... AD
Adductor (SAUS) .... ADD
Adductor Longus [Anatomy] .... AL
Adductor Longus Muscle [Medicine] (MELL) .... ALM
Adductor Magnus Muscle [Medicine] (MELL) .... AMM
Adductor Pollicis [Muscle] [Antomy] (DAVI) .... Add Poll
Adductor Pollicis Muscle [Medicine] (MELL) .... APM
Addult Support Network (EA) .... ASN
AddValue Communications [Telecommunications service] (TSSD) .... AVC
ADE Corp. [Associated Press] (SAG) .... ADECp
ADE Corp. [NASDAQ symbol] (SAG) .... ADEX
Adecco SA [Associated Press] (SAG) .... AdccoSA
Adecco SA [NASDAQ symbol] (SAG) .... ADEC
Adecco SA ADS [NYSE symbol] (SG) .... ADO
Adel, GA [AM radio station call letters] (BROA) .... WAXD
Adel, GA [AM radio station call letters] .... WBIT
Adel, GA [FM radio station call letters] .... WDDQ
Adelaide [Mount Bonython] [Australia] [Seismograph station code, US Geological Survey] (SEIS) .... ADE
Adelaide [South Australia] (BARN) .... Adel
Adelaide [Australia] [Airport symbol] (OAG) .... ADL
Adelaide [Australia] [ICAO location identifier] (ICLI) .... APAA
Adelaide [Australia] [ICAO location identifier] (ICLI) .... APAD
Adelaide [Australia] [ICAO location identifier] (ICLI) .... APAR
Adelaide [Australia] [ICAO location identifier] (ICLI) .... APAX
Adelaide [Australia] [ICAO location identifier] (ICLI) .... APRM
Adelaide [South Africa] [ICAO location identifier] (ICLI) .... FAAD
Adelaide Airways Limited (SAUS) .... AAL
Adelaide Airways Ltd. [Australia] .... AAL
Adelaide, Australia (SAUS) .... Adee
Adelaide College of Divinity .... ACD
Adelaide Convention and Tourism Authority [Australia] .... ACTA
Adelaide Entertainment Centre [Australia] .... AEC
Adelaide Festival of Arts [Australia] .... AFA
Adelaide Gem and Mineral Club [Australia] .... AGMC
Adelaide Harriers Athletic Club [Australia] .... AHAC
Adelaide Historical Bottle Club [Australia] .... AHBC
Adelaide Junior Chamber of Commerce [Australia] .... AJCC
Adelaide Medical Centre for Women and Children [Australia] .... AMCWC
Adelaide Pistol Shooting Club [Australia] .... APSC
Adelaide Potters' Club [Australia] .... APC
Adelaide Produce Market [Australia] .... APM
Adelaide Review [A publication] .... Adel R
Adelaide Steamship Co. (MHDB) .... ASC
Adelaide University (SAUO) .... ADU
Adelaide University Hockey Club [Australia] .... AUHC
Adelaide Wool Brokers' Association [Australia] .... AWB
Adelaide/Parafield [Australia] [ICAO location identifier] (ICLI) .... APPF
Adelanto, CA [Location identifier] [FAA] (FAAL) .... HAK
Adelbert College (SAUO) .... AC
Adelphi College (SAUO) .... AC
Adelphi Parent Administered Readiness Test [Educational development test] .... APART

Adelphi University (GAGS) .... Adelphi U
Adelphi University, Garden City, NY [Library symbol] [Library of Congress] (LCLS) .... NGcA
Adelphi University, Garden City, NY [OCLC symbol] (OCLC) .... VJA
Adelphia Communic'A' [NASDAQ symbol] (TTSB) .... ADLAC
Adelphia Communications Corp. [Associated Press] (SAG) .... Adelph
Adelphia Communications Corp. [NASDAQ symbol] (SAG) .... ADLAC
Adelphoe [of Terence] [Classical studies] (OCD) .... Ad
Adelson-Velskii and Landis Trees [Computer science] .... AVL
Aden [People's Democratic Republic of Yemen] [Airport symbol] (OAG) .... ADE
Aden [People's Democratic Republic of Yemen] .... ADN
Aden [People's Democratic Republic of Yemen] [ICAO location identifier] (ICLI) .... ODAF
Aden Airways .... AD
Aden Airways Ltd. (SAUO) .... AD
Aden and Protectorate of South Arabia (SAUO) .... A&PSA
Aden Colony (SAUS) .... AC
Aden Law Reports [A publication] (ILCA) .... Aden LR
Aden Law Reports (SAUS) .... ALR
Aden News Agency [People's Democratic Republic of Yemen] (MENA) .... ANA
Aden Protectorate Levies [British military] (DMA) .... APL
Aden Trade Union Congress .... ATUC
Adenal Cortical Hormone (SAUS) .... ACH
Adenin, Thymine, Guanine [Medicine] (BABM) .... ATG
Adenine [Also, Ade] [Biochemistry] .... A
Adenine [Also, A] [Biochemistry] .... Ade
Adenine (SAUS) .... ADN
Adenine Adenine Adenine [A triplet of bases coding for the amino acid, lysine] (EES) .... AAA
Adenine Adenine Cytosine [A triplet of bases coding for the amino acid, asparagine] (EES) .... AAC
Adenine Adenine Guanine [A triplet of bases coding for the amino acid, lysine] (EES) .... AAG
Adenine Adenine Uracil [A triplet of bases coding for the amino acid, asparagine] (EES) .... AAU
Adenine and Thymine [Genetics] (DAVI) .... AT
Adenine and Thymine type (SAUS) .... AT type
Adenine Arabinoside [Medicine] (DMAA) .... AA
Adenine Arabinoside [Also called vidarabine] [Antineoplastic drug] (DAVI) .... ARA-A
Adenine Arabinoside Monophosphate [Biochemistry] .... ara-AMP
Adenine Arabinoside Triphosphate [Biochemistry] .... ara-ATP
Adenine Cytosine Adenine [A triplet of bases coding for the amino acid, threonine] (EES) .... ACA
Adenine Cytosine Cytosine [A triplet of bases coding for the amino acid, threonine] (EES) .... ACC
Adenine Cytosine Guanine [A triplet of bases coding for the amino acid, threonine] (EES) .... ACG
Adenine Cytosine Uracil [A triplet of bases coding for the amino acid, threonine] (EES) .... ACU
Adenine Diphosphate (EDCT) .... ADP
Adenine Guanine Adenine [A triplet of bases coding for the amino acid, arginine] (EES) .... AGA
Adenine Guanine Cytosine [A triplet of bases coding for the amino acid, serine] (EES) .... AGC
Adenine Guanine Guanine [A triplet of bases coding for the amino acid, arginine] (EES) .... AGG
Adenine Guanine Uracil [A triplet of bases coding for the amino acid, serine] (EES) .... AGU
Adenine Nucleotide Translocator [Genetics] .... ANT
Adenine Phosphoribosyltransferase [An enzyme] .... APRT
Adenine Phosphoribosyltransferase Deficiency [Medicine] (MELL) .... APRTD
Adenine Ribose Naphthaline Imide [Genetics] .... ARNI
Adenine Ribose Thymine [Genetics] .... ART
Adenine, Thymine, Guanine [Genetics] (DAVI) .... ATG
Adenine Uracil Adenine [A triplet of bases coding for the amino acid, isoleucine] (EES) .... AUA
Adenine Uracil Cytosine [A triplet of bases coding for the amino acid, isoleucine] (EES) .... AUC
Adenine, Uracil, Guanine [Biochemistry] .... AUG
Adenine Uracil Uracil [A triplet of bases coding for the amino acid, isoleucine] (EES) .... AUU
Adenine-D-ribose-phosphate-phosphate-D-ribose-nicotinamide [Also, NAD, DPN] [Biochemistry] .... ARPPRN
Adenine-Guanine-Cytosine-Thymine (PDAA) .... AGCT
Adenine-Thymine (MELL) .... A-T
Adenine-Thymine/Guanine-Cytosine [Ratio] [Medicine] (MELL) .... AT/GC
Adenine-Uridine-Guanine [Medicine] (MELL) .... AUG
Aden/International [People's Democratic Republic of Yemen] [ICAO location identifier] (ICLI) .... ODAA
(Adeninyl)hydroxypropanoic Acid [Antiviral] .... AHPA
Adeninylhydroxypropanoic Acid (SAUS) .... AHPA
Adeno-Associated Virus .... AAV
Adenocarcinoma [Medicine] (DB) .... AC
Adenocarcinoma [Medicine] (MAE) .... ACA
Adenocarcinoma [Medicine] .... adenoca
adenocarcinoma (SAUS) .... adeno-Ca
Adenocarcinoma-Squamous Cell Carcinoma [Oncology] .... Adeno-SCC
Adeno-Conjunctival-Pharyngeal Virus (SAUS) .... ACP-Virus
Adenohypophyseal Hormone [Medicine] (MELL) .... AHH
Adenoid [Otorhinolaryngology] (DAVI) .... adn
Adenoid Cystic Carcinoma [Medicine] .... ACC
Adenoid Cystic Carcinoma of Bartholin Gland [Medicine] (MELL) .... ACCBG
Adenoid Cystic Carcinoma of Salivary Glands [Medicine] (MELL) .... ACCSG
Adenoid Degeneration Virus (SAUS) .... AD-Virus
Adenoid Degenerative [Viruses] .... AD

Adenoidal-Pharyngeal-Conjunctival [*Virus*] [*Obsolete usage*] .... APC
Adenoidectomy [*Otorhinolaryngology*] (DAVI) .... adn
Adeno-Like Virus [*Medicine*] (DMAA) .... ALV
Adenoma (MELL) .... A
Adenoma Malignum of the Cervix [*Oncology*] .... AMC
Adenomatosis of the Colon and Rectum [*Medicine*] .... ACR
Adenomatous Hyperplasia [*Medicine*] .... AH
Adenomatous Polyp [*Medicine*] (MELL) .... AP
Adenomatous Polyposis [*Medicine*] (MELL) .... AP
Adenomatous Polyposis Coli [*Genetics*] .... APC
Adenomatous Polyposis Coli [*Medicine*] .... APE
Adenosine [*One-letter symbol; see Ado*] [*A nucleoside*] .... A
Adenosine [*Also, A*] [*A nucleoside*] .... Ado
Adenosine Deaminase [*An enzyme*] .... ADA
Adenosine Deaminase [*An enzyme*] (DMAA) .... ADD
Adenosine Deaminase Complexing Protein (DMAA) .... ADCP
Adenosine Deaminase Deficiency [*Medicine*] (MELL) .... ADD
Adenosine Deaminase Inhibitor (PDAA) .... ADAI
Adenosine Deceminase Binding Protein [*Biochemistry*] .... ADABP
Adenosine Deminase [*An enzyme*] (DMAA) .... ADase
Adenosine Diphosphatase [*An enzyme*] .... ADPase
Adenosine Diphosphate [*Biochemistry*] .... ADP
Adenosine Diphosphate Ribosyltransferase [*An enzyme*] .... ADPRT
Adenosine Diphosphoribose (DB) .... ADPR
Adenosine Disphosphoglucose (SAUS) .... ADPG
Adenosine Kinase (DMAA) .... ADK
Adenosine Kinase [*An enzyme*] .... AK
Adenosine Monophosphate [*Biochemistry*] .... AMP
Adenosine Monophosphate Deaminase [*An enzyme*] .... AMPDA
Adenosine Monophosphate Succinate [*Biochemistry*] .... AMPS
Adenosine Phosphate [*Pharmacology*] (DAVI) .... B$_8$
Adenosine Phosphate Phosphosulfate [*Also, PAPS*] [*Biochemistry*] .... APPS
Adenosine Phosphate Phosphosulfate (SAUS) .... APPS
Adenosine Phosphoribosyltransferase [*An enzyme*] .... ADPT
Adenosine Phosphosulfate [*Biochemistry*] .... APS
Adenosine Tetraphosphate [*Biochemistry*] .... Atetra P
Adenosine Triphosphatase [*An enzyme*] .... ATPase
Adenosine Triphosphatase .... ATP-ase
Adenosine Triphosphatase (Na, K-Activated) [*An enzyme*] .... Na K-ATPase
Adenosine Triphosphate [*Biochemistry*] (AAMN) .... ADT
Adenosine Triphosphate [*Biochemistry*] .... ATP
Adenosine-5-Monophosphate [*Muscle adenylic acid*] (EDCT) A5MP
Adenosine-5-Monophosphoric Acid (SAUS) .... A 5 MP
Adenosine-5-Phosphat (SAUS) A5P
Adenosinediphosphatase (SAUS) .... ADPase
Adenosis Pattern [*Medicine*] .... AP
Adenosne Regulating Agent [*Medicine*] (MELL) .... ARA
Adenosyl Homocysteine (DB) .... AHCy
Adenosylcobalamin [*A vitamin*] (BABM) .... Abe Cbl
Adenosylcobalamin [*Biochemistry*] (DAVI) .... Ade Cbl
Adenosylcobalamin [*Also, DBC*] [*A vitamin*] .... ADOCBL
Adenosyldiaminobutyric Acid [*Biochemistry*] (DB) .... AdoDABA
Adenosylhomocysteine [*Biochemistry*] .... AdoHcy
Adenosylmethionine [*Also, SAM, SAMe*] [*Biochemistry*] .... AdoMet
Adenotonsillectomy [*Medicine*] (MELL) .... ATE
Adenovirus [*Also, ADV*] .... AD
Adenovirus [*Also, AD*] .... ADV
Adenovirus [*Medicine*] (MELL) .... AV
Adenovirus Infection [*Medicine*] (MELL) .... AVI
Adenovirus Major Late .... ADML
Adenovirus Major Late Promoter [*Genetics*] .... ADMLP
Adenovirus Respiratory Disease [*Medicine*] (PDAA) .... ARD
Adenovirus-Associated Virus (SAUS) .... AAV
Adenylatcyclase (SAUS) .... ADC
Adenylate Clyclase Inhibitor (SAUS) .... ACI
Adenylate Cyclase [*An enzyme*] .... AC
Adenylate Cyclase (DMAA) .... AdC
Adenylate Cyclase Inhibitor [*Biochemistry*] .... ACI
Adenylate Cyclase-Stimulating Activity [*Medicine*] (DMAA) .... ACSA
Adenylate Energy Charge (BARN) .... AEC
Adenylate Kinase [*An enzyme*] .... ADK
Adenylate Kinase [*An enzyme*] .... AK
Adenylatkinase (SAUS) .... Ak
Adenylic Acid [*Biochemistry*] .... AA
Adeodato (SAUS) .... Ad
Adept (ABBR) .... ADPT
ADEPT Subsystem for Scanning of Electronic Received Traffic
    (SAUS) .... ASSERT
Adept Technology [*NASDAQ symbol*] (TTSB) .... ADTK
Adept Technology, Inc. [*Associated Press*] (SAG) .... AdeptT
Adept Technology, Inc. [*NASDAQ symbol*] (SAG) .... ADTK
Adeptly (ABBR) .... ADPY
Adeptness (ABBR) .... ADEPNS
Adeptness (ABBR) .... ADPNS
Adequacy (ABBR) .... ADQC
Adequacy (ABBR) .... ADQCY
Adequate .... A
Adequate (DAVI) .... ADEQ
Adequate (DMAA) .... adeq
Adequate (ABBR) .... ADQA
Adequate (FAAC) .... ADQT
Adequate Public Facilities Ordinance (PA) .... APFO
Adequately (ABBR) .... ADQAY
Adequately (ABBR) .... ADQTY
Adequateness (ABBR) .... ADQTNS

Adera Financial Corp. Ltd. [*Vancouver Stock Exchange symbol*] .... ADF
ADF Data System (SAUS) .... ADS
ADF Distributed Intelligence System (SAUS) .... ADFDIS
ADFlex Solutions [*Associated Press*] (SAG) .... ADFlex
ADFlex Solutions [*NASDAQ symbol*] (SAG) .... AFLX
AdForce, Inc. [*NASDAQ symbol*] .... ADFC
Adhere (MSA) .... ADH
Adhere (ABBR) .... ADHR
Adhered (ABBR) .... ADHRD
Adherence (ABBR) .... ADHRNC
Adherence Group (SAUS) .... TAG
Adherence Ratio [*Medicine*] (DMAA) .... AR
Adherens Junction [*Cytology*] .... AJ
Adherent (ABBR) .... ADHRNT
Adherent (ABBR) .... ADHRT
Adherent Cell (AAMN) .... AC
Adherently (ABBR) .... ADHRTY
Adhering (ABBR) .... ADHRG
Adhesion [*Medicine*] (DMAA) .... adh
Adhesion (ABBR) .... ADHN
Adhesion Index [*Medicine*] (MELL) .... AI
Adhesion Molecule on Glia (DMAA) .... AMOG
Adhesion Promoter [*Electronics*] (AAEL) .... AP
Adhesion Proteoglycan [*Biochemistry*] .... AP
Adhesion Society (EA) .... AS
Adhesions (SAUS) .... ADH
Adhesive (KSC) .... ADH
Adhesive (SAUS) .... Adh
Adhesive (ROG) .... ADHEVE
Adhesive (ABBR) .... ADHSV
Adhesive (ABBR) .... ADNV
Adhesive Active [*Tire manufacturing*] .... AA
Adhesive and Sealant Council (EA) .... ASC
Adhesive and Sealant Council, Inc. (SAUO) .... ASC
Adhesive Bonding [*Welding*] .... ABD
Adhesive Bonding Repair .... ABR
Adhesive Capsulitis of Shoulder [*Medicine*] (MELL) .... ACS
Adhesive Component System (PDAA) .... ACS
Adhesive Film Mechanism .... AFM
Adhesive Insulation Material .... AIM
Adhesive Interconnect System [*Electronics*] (AAEL) .... AIS
Adhesive Tape Manufacturers Association (EAIO) .... ATMA
Adhesively (ABBR) .... ADHSVY
Adhesively Bonded Joint [*or Junction*] .... ABJ
Adhesively Bonded Junction (SAUS) .... ABJ
Adhesiveness (ABBR) .... ADHSVNS
Adhesiveness (ABBR) .... ADHVNS
Adhesives Manufacturers Association (EA) .... AMA
Adhesives Manufacturers Association of America [*Later, AMA*] (EA) .... AMAA
Adhibendus [*To Be Used*] [*Pharmacy*] (ROG) .... A
Adhibendus [*To Be Used*] [*Pharmacy*] (ROG) .... ADH
Adhibendus [*To Be Administered*] [*Pharmacy*] (DAVI) .... ADHIB
Adhibendus [*To Be Used*] [*Pharmacy*] .... ADHIBEND
Ad-Hoc Committee .... AHC
Ad-Hoc Committee for Competitive Telecommunications (SAUS) .... ACCT
Ad-hoc Committee for Guided Missile Reliability (SAUO) .... ACGMR
Adi Dassler [*Founder of German sporting goods company; acronym used as
    brand name of shoes manufactured by the firm*] .... ADIDAS
ADI Minesweeping and Surveillance System (SAUS) .... AMASS
Adia SA [*Associated Press*] (SAG) .... AdiaSA
Adia S.A. ADS [*NASDAQ symbol*] (TTSB) .... ADIAY
Adia Services, Inc. [*NASDAQ symbol*] (NQ) .... ADIA
Adiabatic Demagnetization Refrigeration (SAUS) .... ADR
Adiabatic Fast Equilibration (SAUS) .... AFEQ
Adiabatic Fast Passage (OA) .... AFP
Adiabatic Film Cooling .... ADFC
Adiabatic Flame Temperature (SAUS) .... AFT
Adiabatic Isochoric Complete Combustion (SAUS) .... AICC
Adiabatic Low-Energy Injection and Capture Experiment .... ALICE
Adiabatic Rapid Passage [*Physics*] .... ARP
Adiabatic Storage Test [*For hazardous chemicals*] .... AST
Adiabatic Toroidal Compression (or Compressor) (SAUS) .... ATC
Adiabatic Toroidal Compressor [*Nuclear energy*] .... ATC
Adiake [*Ivory Coast*] [*ICAO location identifier*] (ICLI) .... DIAD
Adie-Holmes [*Syndrome*] [*Medicine*] (DB) .... AH
A-Digit Hunter (SAUS) .... ADH
Adiamycin, Cyclophosphamide/X-Ray Therapy (SAUS) .... AC/XRT
Adios My Friend (SAUS) .... AMF
Adipic, Glutaric, and Succinic [*Acids for flue-gas cleaning*] .... AGS
Adipic, Glutaric, Succinic Acids (EDCT) .... AGS
Adipocyte Lipid-Binding Protein .... ALBP
Adipokinetic Hormone [*Endocrinology*] .... AKH
Adiponitrile [*Organic chemistry*] .... ADN
Adipose Differentiation-Related Protein [*Medicine*] (DMAA) .... ADRP
Adipose Fin [*Fish anatomy*] .... AD
Adipose Fin and Left Pectoral Fin Clips [*Pisciculture*] .... ADLP
Adipose Fin and Left Ventral Fin Clips [*Pisciculture*] .... ADLV
Adipose Fin and Right Pectoral Fin Clips [*Pisciculture*] .... ADRP
Adipose Fin and Right Ventral Fin Clips [*Pisciculture*] .... ADRV
Adipose Fin Clip with Coded Wire Tag [*Pisciculture*] .... ADCWT
Adipose Tissue Extract [*Biochemistry*] (MAE) .... ATE
Adipose Tissue Lipoprotein Lipase [*Medicine*] (MELL) .... ATLPL
Adiposis Dolorosa [*Medicine*] (MELL) .... AD
Adiposity Index (DB) .... AI
Adiposity-Oligomenorrheaparotid Swelling [*Syndrome*] [*Medicine*] (MELL) .... AOP

Adirondac Conference (SAUS) .... AC
Adirondack (FAAC) .... ADRNDCK
Adirondack Community College (SAUO) .... ACC
Adirondack Community College, Glens Falls, NY [Library symbol] [Library of Congress] (LCLS) .... NGlfAC
Adirondack Council (EA) .... AC
Adirondack Forty-Sixers (EA) .... AFS
Adirondack Historical Association (EA) .... AHA
Adirondack Historical Association Museum Library, Blue Mountain Lake, NY [Library symbol] [Library of Congress] (LCLS) .... NBmlA
Adirondack Lake Survey Corporation (SAUO) .... ALSC
Adirondack Mountain Club (EA) .... ADK
Adirondack Mountains, New York (SAUS) .... Adirondacks
Adirondack Park Agency (SAUS) .... APA
Adirondack Park Agency (SAUO) .... APa
Adirondack Trail Improvement Society (EA) .... ATIS
Adirondack Watershed Data Base (SAUS) .... AWDB
Adirondack World Affairs Resources for Education .... AWARE
ADIS [Australasian Drug Information Services] Drug Information Retrieval System [ADIS Press Ltd.] [Auckland, New Zealand] .... ADIRS
Adiuretin (SAUS) .... Adi
Adizes Network International [Santa Monica, CA] (EA) .... ANI
Adjacency (ABBR) .... ADJC
Adjacency (ABBR) .... ADJCNC
Adjacens [Adjacent] [Pharmacy] (ROG) .... ADJAC
Adjacent .... ADJ
Adjacent (WDAA) .... Adj
Adjacent (ABBR) .... ADJA
Adjacent (ABBR) .... ADJCNT
Adjacent (AFM) .... AJA
Adjacent and across-the-river cities of Rock Island, East Moline and Moline, Illinois, plus Davenport, Iowa (SAUS) .... Quad Cities
Adjacent Arctic Ocean (ARMP) .... AAO
Adjacent Carrier Interference Protection Ratio (CGWS) .... ACIPR
Adjacent Channel (IAA) .... AC
Adjacent Channel Attenuation .... ACA
Adjacent Channel Coupled Power Ratio (SAUS) .... ACCPR
Adjacent Channel Interface Power Ratio (SAUS) .... ACIPR
Adjacent Channel Interference .... ACI
Adjacent Channel Rejection .... ACR
Adjacent Charging Group [Telecommunications] (TEL) .... ACG
Adjacent DRG (SAUS) .... ADRG
Adjacent Fire Platoon [Army] .... ADJFP
Adjacent Link Station [IBM Corp] (VERA) .... ALS
Adjacent Phase Pulse Generator [Electronics] (OA) .... APPG
Adjacent Tone (IAA) .... AT
Adjacent Tone-Reference Phase-Shift Keying [Computer science] (IAA) .... ATPSK
Adjacent-Channel Power (SAUS) .... ACP
Adjacently (ABBR) .... ADJAY
Adjacently (ABBR) .... ADJCNTY
Adjal [Former USSR] [FAA designator] (FAAC) .... ADJ
Adjarian Autonomous Soviet Socialist Republic (SAUO) .... AASR
Adjectival (ADWA) .... adj
adjectival (SAUS) .... adj
Adjectival (ABBR) .... ADJVL
Adjective .... A
Adjective (ROG) .... AD
Adjective .... ADJ
Adjective (WA) .... adj
Adjective (ABBR) .... ADJV
Adjective Check List [Psychology] .... ACL
Adjective Noun [Used in correcting manuscripts, etc.] .... AjN
Adjective (or Adjectival) Phrase (SAUS) .... AP
Adjective Phrase [Linguistics] .... AP
adjectives (SAUS) .... aa
Adjoin (ABBR) .... ADJN
Adjoining .... ADJ
Adjoining (ABBR) .... ADJNG
Adjoining (ROG) .... ADJOING
Adjoining Landowner (DLA) .... ADJ L
Adjoint (ABBR) .... ADJ
Adjoint Gamma-Ray Moments [Computer code] .... ADJMOM
Adjoint Matrix (SAUS) .... AM
Adjoint Neutron Transport Equation (PDAA) .... ANTE
Adjoint Wave Function .... AWF
Adjornator [British] .... ADJ
Adjourn (ROG) .... ADJN
Adjourn (ABBR) .... ADJRN
Adjourned .... ADJ
Adjourned (WDAA) .... adj
Adjourned (ROG) .... ADJD
Adjourned (ABBR) .... ADJRND
Adjourned Session (DLA) .... Adj Sess
Adjourned Summons (BARN) .... adjd sumns
Adjourning (ABBR) .... ADJRNG
Adjournment (ABBR) .... ADJRNNT
Adjournment (ABBR) .... ADJRNT
Adjournment in Contemplation of Dismissal [Law] .... ACD
Adjournment in Contemplation of Dismissal [Law] .... ACOD
Adjudge (ABBR) .... ADJDG
Adjudged (ROG) .... ADJ
Adjudged (ABBR) .... ADJDGD
Adjudging (ABBR) .... ADJDGG
Adjudicate (ABBR) .... ADJDCA
Adjudicate (ABBR) .... ADJUD

Adjudicated (ADA) .... ADJD
Adjudicated (ABBR) .... ADJDCAD
Adjudicated (ABBR) .... ADJUDD
Adjudicating (ABBR) .... ADJDCAG
Adjudicating (ABBR) .... ADJUDG
Adjudication (ABBR) .... ADJDCAN
Adjudication (ABBR) .... ADJUDN
Adjudication (ROG) .... ADJUN
Adjudicator (ABBR) .... ADJDCR
Adjudicator (ABBR) .... ADJUDR
Adjudicatory (ABBR) .... ADJUDRY
Adjunct [Linguistics] .... A
Adjunct .... ADJ
Adjunct (WDAA) .... adj
Adjunct (ABBR) .... ADJNC
Adjunct in Arts .... Adj A
Adjunct Processor (SAUS) .... AP
Adjunct Unit (SAUS) .... AU
Adjunctive (ABBR) .... ADJNCV
Adjunctive Therapy [Medicine] .... AT
Adjunct/Switch Applications Interface [Tekelec] .... ASAI
Adjuntas, PR [AM radio station call letters] .... WPJC
Adjunto [Enclosure] [Spanish] [Business term] .... adj
Adjuration (ABBR) .... ADJRAN
Adjuratory (ABBR) .... ADJRAY
Adjure (ABBR) .... ADJR
Adjured (ABBR) .... ADJRD
Adjurer (ABBR) .... ADJRR
Adjuring (ABBR) .... ADJRG
Adjust .... ADJ
Adjust (ABBR) .... ADJS
Adjust Mode [Computer science] .... ADMD
Adjust Requested Privilege Level (SAUS) .... ARPL
Adjustable .... ADJ
Adjustable .... ADJBLE
Adjustable (ABBR) .... ADJSB
Adjustable [Technical drawings] .... ADJT
Adjustable Bed (SAUS) .... AJB
Adjustable Bed Press (SAUS) .... AJB Press
Adjustable Buoyancy Jacket .... ABJ
Adjustable Buoyancy Life Jacket .... ABLJ
Adjustable Center (or Centre) Distance (SAUS) .... ACD
Adjustable Chain Clutch (PDAA) .... ACC
Adjustable Focus Control (MCD) .... AFC
Adjustable Frequency Power Supply (SAUS) .... AFPS
Adjustable Leg and Ankle Repositioning Mechanism (DMAA) .... ALARM
Adjustable Mortgage Loan [Business term] (EMRF) .... AML
Adjustable Multi-Class Organizing System (MHDI) .... AMOS
Adjustable Muzzle Stabilizer [Rifles] [Army] (INF) .... AMS
Adjustable Objective .... AO
Adjustable Pawl Fastener .... APF
Adjustable Pitch Device .... APD
Adjustable Point (SAUS) .... AP
Adjustable Premium Policy (MARI) .... APP
Adjustable Pressure Conveyor .... APC
Adjustable Ranging Telescope [Army] (MCD) .... ART
Adjustable Rate Mortgage .... ARM
Adjustable Rate Preferred Stock .... ARPS
Adjustable Rear Plate [Air conditioning systems] [Automotive engineering] .... ARP
Adjustable Shock Absorber .... ASA
Adjustable Speed (IAA) .... ADJSPD
Adjustable Speed Drive .... ASD
Adjustable Stroke Kit .... ASK
Adjustable Thermal Wire Stripper .... ATWS
Adjustable Thigh Antiembolism Stockings [Cardiology] (DAVI) .... ATS
Adjustable Voltage Inverter (PDAA) .... AVI
Adjustable Voltage Rectifier (IAA) .... AVR
Adjustable Voltage Screwdown .... AVS
Adjustable Voltage Screw-down (SAUS) .... AVS
Adjustable Wire Stripper .... AWS
Adjustable Zero, Adjustable Range .... AZAR
Adjustable Zero Adjustable Span (SAUS) .... AZAS
Adjustable-Rate Preferred Stock (MHDB) .... ARP
Adjustably (ABBR) .... ADJSBY
Adjusted (MILB) .... adj
Adjusted (ABBR) .... ADJSD
Adjusted Acceptable Daily Intake .... AADI
Adjusted Agreement Index (EDAC) .... AAI
Adjusted Air Speed [Navigation] .... AAS
Adjusted Average per Capita Cost .... AAPC
Adjusted Average per Capita Cost .... AAPCC
Adjusted Balance Method .... ABM
Adjusted Calving Interval [Dairy science] (OA) .... ACI
Adjusted Charge (SAUS) .... AC
Adjusted Clinical Groups (SAUO) .... ACG
Adjusted Community Rate .... ACR
Adjusted Community Rate Proposal .... ACRP
Adjusted Community Rating .... ACR
Adjusted Compensation Payment Act [1936] .... ACPA
Adjusted Current Earnings .... ACE
Adjusted Daily Average (ADA) .... ADA
Adjusted Daily Average (SAUS) .... ADA
Adjusted Debit Balance [Accounting] .... ADB
Adjusted Decibel (AAEL) .... dBa
Adjusted Family Income (GFGA) .... AFI

Adjusted Gross Income [*Income taxes*] ... AGI
Adjusted Gross Weight (MCD) ... AGW
Adjusted Insured Unemployment Rate ... AIUR
Adjusted Interest-Bearing Liabilities ... ADJ IBL
Adjusted Internal Rate of Return (SAUS) ... AIRR
Adjusted Liquid Capital ... ALC
Adjusted Loaded Vehicle Weight (EEVL) ... ALVW
Adjusted Main Ring Length (SAUS) ... AMRL
Adjusted Mapping Support Data (GEOI) ... AMSD
Adjusted Market Value [*Automobile retailing*] ... AMV
Adjusted Maximum Dive Time ... AMDT
Adjusted Megaton Equivalent (MCD) ... AMTE
Adjusted Monetary Base [*Economics*] ... AMB
Adjusted Negotiated Unit Target Cost (ACAE) ... ANUTC
Adjusted Net Present Value (MCD) ... ANPV
Adjusted on Basis of Photostat or Reviewed Copy of Temporary Pay Record from Finance Center, United States Army (AABC) ... ADJFCUSA
Adjusted Output [*Computer science*] ... AO
Adjusted Performance Percentile (DNAB) ... APP
Adjusted Permanent Pay Record [*Military*] (DNAB) ... ADJ/PPR
Adjusted Range Correction (SAUS) ... ARC
Adjusted Reviewed Copy of Temporary Pay Record [*Military*] (DNAB) ... ADJ/RCT
Adjusted Ring Length (SAUS) ... ARL
Adjusted Running Book Inventory (SAUS) ... ARBI
Adjusted Sequential Probability Ratio Test [*Statistics*] ... ASPRT
Adjusted Service Rating Score [*Military*] ... ASRS
Adjusted Total Financial Assistance Requirement ... ATFAR
Adjusted Transcript Deserter's Account [*Military*] (DNAB) ... ADJ/TDA
Adjusted Volume (COE) ... AV
Adjuster [*Business term*] (EBF) ... Adj
Adjuster [*Finance*] ... ADJ
Adjuster (ABBR) ... ADJSR
Adjuster ... ADJSTER
Adjuster (ABBR) ... ADJSTR
adjustieren (SAUS) ... adj
Adjusting (SAUS) ... ADJ
Adjusting (ABBR) ... ADJSG
Adjusting Journal Entry [*Accounting*] ... AJE
Adjusting Schedule of Reinforcement (DIPS) ... ADJ
Adjustment (IAA) ... A
Adjustment (AFM) ... ADJ
Adjustment [*Business term*] (EBF) ... Adj
Adjustment (WDAA) ... adj
Adjustment ... ADJMT
Adjustment (ABBR) ... ADJSNT
Adjustment (ABBR) ... ADJST
Adjustment [*Accounting*] ... AJ
Adjustment and Preventative (MCD) ... AP
Adjustment Assistance ... AA
Adjustment Bond [*Investment term*] ... AB
Adjustment Disorder with Anxious Mood (MELL) ... ADAM
Adjustment Disorder with Depressed Mood (MELL) ... ADDM
Adjustment File [*IRS*] ... ADJF
Adjustment Inventory [*Psychology*] ... AI
Adjustment of Scheduled Maintenance Requirements through Analysis (MCD) ... ASMRA
Adjustment Payment Level [*Social Security Administration*] ... APL
Adjustment Reaction to Adult Life [*Medicine*] (DMAA) ... ARAL
Adjustment Sleep Disorder (MELL) ... ASD
Adjustment With a Human Face [*UNICEF phrase to describe African adjustment programs*] ... AWAHF
Adjustment-Calibration ... AC
Adjustor ... ADJTOR
Adjutancy (ABBR) ... ADJTNC
Adjutant ... A
Adjutant (AFM) ... ADJ
Adjutant (GEAB) ... adj
Adjutant (WDAA) ... Adj
Adjutant (WDAA) ... Adjt
Adjutant ... ADJT
Adjutant and Inspector General (SAUO) ... AIG
Adjutant, Battalion Level and Below [*Army*] ... S1
Adjutant General (DNAB) ... ADJG
Adjutant General (SAUO) ... Adj Gen
Adjutant General ... AG
[*The*] **Adjutant General** [*Army*] ... TAG
Adjutant General, Air Force (SAUS) ... A-G AF
[*The*] **Adjutant General Center** [*Army*] (AABC) ... TAGCEN
Adjutant General Inspection (DNAB) ... AGI
Adjutant General Management Information System ... AGMIS
Adjutant General Management Infor-mation System (SAUS) ... AGMIS
Adjutant General of the Army (SAUS) ... AGA
Adjutant General Pool [*for Army officers*] ... AGP
Adjutant General Pool for Army Officers (SAUO) ... AGP
Adjutant General Publications Center [*Army*] ... AGPC
Adjutant General, Royal Marines (SAUO) ... AGRM
Adjutant General, Royal Marines (SAUS) ... AGRM
Adjutant General to the Forces (SAUS) ... AGF
Adjutant General, War Department [*Obsolete*] ... AGWAR
[*The*] **Adjutant General's Board, United States Army** ... TAGBDUSA
Adjutant Generals Board, United States Army (SAUS) ... TAGBDUSA
Adjutant General's Corps ... AGC
Adjutant General's Corps (AAGC) ... AG Corps
Adjutant General's Department [*Army*] ... AGD
Adjutant Generals Department (SAUS) ... AGD
Adjutant General's Office [*Washington, DC*] [*Army*] ... AGO
Adjutant Generals Office (SAUS) ... TAGO
[*The*] **Adjutant General's Office** [*Army*] ... TAGO
Adjutant Generals Pool (SAUS) ... AGP
Adjutant Generals Publications Depot (SAUS) ... AGPUBLDEP
[*The*] **Adjutant General's Research and Development Command, United States Army** ... TAGRDCUSA
[*The*] **Adjutant General's School** [*United States*], **Army** ... TAGSUSA
Adjutant Inspector General [*Military*] ... AIG
Adjutant to the Corps of Royal Engineers (SAUS) ... ACRE
Adjutant-General (DAS) ... Adj-Gen
Adjutant-General [*British military*] (DMA) ... Adjt-Gen
Adjutant-General and Quartermaster-General [*British*] ... AG & QMG
Adjutant-General and Quartermaster-General (SAUO) ... AG&QMG
Adjutant-General to the Forces [*British*] ... AGF
Adjutants (ABBR) ... ADJTS
Adjutants General Association of the United States [*Later, AGAUS*] (EA) ... AGA
Adjutants General Association of the Unites States (SAUO) ... AGAUS
Adjutants Section (SAUS) ... Adj Sec
Adjuvant Arthritis ... AA
Adjuvant Chemotherapy [*Oncology*] ... ACT
Adjuvant Disease (SAUS) ... AD
Adjuvant Radiation Therapy [*Medicine*] (MELL) ... ART
Adjuvant Therapy [*Antineoplastic drug regimen*] (DAVI) ... AT
Adkins Life Skills Program (EDAC) ... ALSP
Adkinson on Township and Town Law in Indiana [*A publication*] (DLA) ... Adk Town
ADL [*Avionics Development Laboratory*] **Master Control Program** [*NASA*] (NASA) ... AMCP
ADL Master Control Program (SAUS) ... AMCP
Adlai (SAUS) ... Ad
Adlai E. Stevenson (ADWA) ... AES
Adlai Stevenson Institute of International Affairs (SAUO) ... ASIIA
Adler Computer Series (SAUS) ... TA
Adler. Handbuch der Musikgeschichte [*A publication*] ... AdHM
Adler Planetarium (SAUS) ... Adler
Adler Planetarium and Astronomical Museum (SAUO) ... AP&AM
ADLER Port (SAUS) ... ADLER Pt
Adlerian Psychological Association of British Columbia (AC) ... APABC
Adlerian Society of Great Britain (BI) ... ASGB
Adler/Sochi [*Former USSR*] [*Airport symbol*] (OAG) ... AER
ADM Tronics Unlimited [*NASDAQ symbol*] (TTSB) ... ADMT
ADM Tronics Unlimited [*Associated Press*] (SAG) ... ADM Tr
ADM Tronics Unltd. [*NASDAQ symbol*] (SAG) ... ADMT
Admar Group, Inc. [*Associated Press*] (SAG) ... Admar
[*The*] **Admar Group, Inc.** [*NASDAQ symbol*] (NQ) ... ADMR
Administaff, Inc. [*NYSE symbol*] (SG) ... ASF
Administer (CPH) ... admin
Administer (ABBR) ... ADMN
Administer (ABBR) ... ADMSTR
Administered (ABBR) ... ADMND
Administering (ABBR) ... ADMNG
Administering Agency (SARE) ... AA
Administracion de Aeropuertos [*Bolivia*] [*ICAO designator*] (FAAC) ... XXV
Administradora de Fondos ADS [*NYSE symbol*] (TTSB) ... PVD
Administradora de Fondos de Pensiones (SAUS) ... AFP
Administradora de Fondos de Pensiones Provida SA [*Associated Press*] (SAG) ... AFProv
Administradora de Fondos de Pensiones Provida SA [*NYSE symbol*] (SAG) ... PVD
Administradoras de Fondos de Pensione [*Chile*] (ECON) ... AFP
Administrate (SAUS) ... ADMIN
Administrate (ABBR) ... ADMNT
Administrate (ABBR) ... ADMSTRA
Administrated (ABBR) ... ADMNTD
Administrates (ABBR) ... ADMNTS
Administrateur Agree [*Canada*] (DD) ... AdmA
Administrating (ABBR) ... ADMNTG
Administration ... A
Administration (DLA) ... Ad
Administration [*or Administrator*] (EY) ... ADM
Administration (EBF) ... Adm
Administration (NTIO) ... adm
Administration (DD) ... admin
Administration (DMAA) ... Admin
Administration [*or Administrator*] (EY) ... ADMIN
Administration (DLA) ... Administrn
Administration ... ADMN
Administration (ABBR) ... ADMNTN
Administration (ROG) ... ADMON
Administration (ABBR) ... ADMSTRAN
Administration ... ADOM
Administration above the Company (MCD) ... AAC
Administration and Data Server (SAUS) ... ADS
Administration and Logistics (SAUS) ... A&L
Administration and Logistics [*Military*] (INF) ... A & L
Administration and Maintenance Order (SAUS) ... AMO
Administration and Management operations (SAUS) ... AM
Administration and Management Services (SAUO) ... AMS
Administration and Planning (SAUS) ... Admin&Plng
Administration and Program Support (SAUS) ... A&PS
Administration and Program Support [*George C. Marshall Space Flight Center Directorate*] [*NASA*] (NASA) ... A & PS
Administration and Services Bureau (SAUO) ... ADB
Administration and Storage Building ... ASB

Administration Area Unit (SAUO) ... AAU
Administration Branch, Manitoba Department of Municipal Affairs, Winnipeg, Manitoba [*Library symbol*] [*National Library of Canada*] (NLC) ... MWAMA
Administration Building Library, Canada Institute for Scientific and Technical Information [*Bibliotheque de l'Edifice de l'Administration, Institut Canadien de l'Information Scientifique et Technique*] **Ottawa, Ontario** [*Library symbol*] [*National Library of Canada*] (NLC) ... OONAB
Administration by Competency [*Business term*] ... ABC
Administration by Objectives ... ABO
Administration Center ... ADMCEN
Administration Communication Language (SAUS) ... ACL
Administration de la Voie Maritime du Saint-Laurent [*St. Lawrence Seaway Authority - SLSA*] [*Canada*] ... AVMS
Administration de l'Assistance Technique des Nations Unies [*United Nations Technical Assistance Administration*] ... AATNU
Administration des Mesures d'Encouragement du Secteur Petrolier [*Petroleum Incentives Administration*] [*Canada*] ... AMESP
Administration du Petrole et du Gaz des Terres du Canada [*Canada Oil and Gas Lands Administration*] ... APGTC
Administration du Pipeline du Nord Canada [*Northern Pipeline Agency Canada - NPAC*] ... APNC
Administration du Retablissement Agricole des Prairies [*Prairie Farm Rehabilitation Administration - PFRA*] ... ARAP
Administration Duty Officer (NATG) ... ADO
Administration Engineering Information Management System (SAUS) ... AEIMS
Administration for Children and Families [*Department of Health and Human Services*] ... ACF
Administration for Children, Youth, and Families [*Office of Human Development Services*] ... ACYF
Administration for Children, Youth and Families (SAUO) ... ACYF
Administration for Civil Affairs in Liberated Areas [*World War II*] ... ACALA
Administration for Native Americans [*Office of Human Development Services*] ... ANA
Administration for Native Americans Research Analysis Project (EDAC) ... ANARAP
Administration for Native Americans-HEW (SAUO) ... ANA/HEW
Administration for Public Services [*Office of Human Development Services*] ... APS
Administration for Public Services-HEW (SAUO) ... APS/HEW
Administration Group Office ... AGO
Administration Information Display Equipment (SAUS) ... AIDE
Administration Information System (SAUS) ... AIS
Administration Laboratory Project File [*University of Alberta*] [*Canada*] [*Information service or system*] (CRD) ... ALP
Administration Management Domain [*Telecommunications*] (TEL) ... ADMD
Administration Management Society (SAUO) ... AMS
Administration Manager (HEAS) ... AM
Administration Module (MCD) ... ADMIN MOD
Administration of Correction (SAUO) ... AC
Administration of Designed Services (TEL) ... ADS
Administration of Designed Services Review (SAUO) ... ADSR
Administration of Justice ... AJ
Administration of Justice (SAUO) ... AOJ
Administration of Justice Branch [*US Military Government, Germany*] ... AJB
Administration of Territories Committee (Balkans) [*World War II*] ... AT(B)
Administration of Territories Committee (Europe) [*World War II*] ... AT(E)
Administration of Territories Committee (Europe), Shipping and Supply Subcommittee [*World War II*] ... AT(E)SSS
Administration of the Customs Union [*EEC*] (DS) ... ACU
Administration of Veterans Affairs [*Army*] ... AVA
Administration Office ... AO
Administration on Aging [*HEW*] [*Defunct*] ... AA
Administration on Aging (SAUO) ... AA
Administration on Aging [*Defunct*] [*Department of Health and Human Services*] ... AOA
Administration on Children, Youth and Families (SAUS) ... ACYF
Administration on Developmental Disabilities [*Human Development Services*] ... ADD
Administration, Operation, and Maintenance (COE) ... AO&M
Administration (or Administrative) Center (SAUS) ... AdmCen
Administration Planning Group (HEAS) ... APG
Administration Publique [*A publication*] (ILCA) ... Admin pub
Administration, Ryukyu Islands, Army (AABC) ... ARIA
Administration Sciences Research Centre [*University of Moncton*] [*Canada*] [*Research center*] (RCD) ... CRSA
Administration Services Division (SAUO) ... ASD
Administration Support Equipment (MCD) ... ASE
Administration Use Vehicle (ACAE) ... AUV
Administration/Logistics (INF) ... A/L
Administration-Logistics [*Military*] (INF) ... ALOG
Administrative (DLA) ... Ad
Administrative (WDAA) ... adm
Administrative (DLA) ... Adminstrv
Administrative ... ADMINV
Administrative (FAAC) ... ADMIV
Administrative ... ADMNSTRV
Administrative (ABBR) ... ADMNTV
Administrative (ABBR) ... ADMSTRAV
Administrative (PHSD) ... Admv
Administrative Adjustment Report [*Supply*] [*Military*] ... AAR
Administrative Agreement ... AA
Administrative Aircraft [*When a suffix to Navy plane designation*] ... Z
Administrative Aircraft Standardization Office [*NASA*] ... AASO
Administrative Analysis, Information, and Statistics [*Red Cross*] ... AAIS
Administrative and Accounting Purposes ... ADANDAC
Administrative and Clerical (ADA) ... A & C
Administrative and Clerical Officers Association (SAUO) ... ACOA
Administrative and Customer Services Division (SAUS) ... ACSD
Administrative and Direct Support Logistics [*Company*] [*Army*] ... A & DSL
Administrative and Direct Support Logistics (SAUS) ... A&DSL
Administrative and Financial Services (SAUO) ... AFS
Administrative and Information Services (SAUO) ... AIS
Administrative and Logistical Downtime (SAUS) ... ALDT
Administrative and Logistics Delay [*or Down*] **Time** (MCD) ... ALDT
Administrative and Logistics Operations Center [*Military*] (INF) ... ALOC
Administrative and Management Services (OICC) ... AMS
Administrative and Management Services [*DoD*] (GFGA) ... AMSD
Administrative and Management Services Division (SAUO) ... AMSD
Administrative and Miscellaneous Duties [*RAF*] [*British*] ... AMD
Administrative and Network Support Office (SAUS) ... ANSO
Administrative and Operational Procedure (MCD) ... AOP
Administrative and Overhead [*Costs*] (KSC) ... AO
Administrative and Publications Management Information System (SAUS) ... APMIS
Administrative and Publications Services Division (SAUS) ... APSD
Administrative Appeals Reports [*Australia*] [*A publication*] ... AAR
Administrative Appeals Tribunal (ADA) ... AAT
Administrative Appeals Tribunal Decisions [*Australia*] [*A publication*] ... ADMN
Administrative Applications Division (SAUO) ... AAD
Administrative Area Control Centre [*Military*] [*British*] ... AACC
Administrative Area Unit [*Army*] ... AAU
Administrative Arrangements Order (ADA) ... AAO
Administrative Assistant ... AA
Administrative Assistant to the Secretary of the Army ... AASA
Administrative Audit (SAUS) ... AU
Administrative Authority (SAUS) ... AA
Administrative Authority Identifier [*Computer science*] ... AAI
Administrative Base Unit [*British military*] (DMA) ... ABU
Administrative Battalion [*British military*] (DMA) ... AB
Administrative Board - Dress Industry (EA) ... ABDI
Administrative Board-Dress Industry (SAUO) ... ABDI
Administrative Bulletin (MCD) ... AB
Administrative, Business, and Commercial (AIE) ... ABC
Administrative, Business, and Commercial Training Group (AIE) ... ABCTG
Administrative Center (SAUO) ... Adm
Administrative Center of Social Security of Rhine Boatmen (SAUO) ... ACSSRB
Administrative Central (SAUS) ... AC
Administrative Centre of Social Security for Rhine Boatmen (SAUS) ... ACSSRB
Administrative Circular ... ADCIR
Administrative Clerical and Technical Programs [*Department of Labor*] ... ACT
Administrative Code [*A publication*] (DLA) ... Admin Cd
Administrative Command ... ADCOM
Administrative Command [*Navy*] [*British*] ... ADCOMD
Administrative Command, Amphibious Forces, Atlantic Fleet (SAUO) ... ADCOMPHIBSLANT
Administrative Command, Amphibious Forces, Pacific Fleet ... ADCOMPHIBSPAC
Administrative Command, Amphibious Forces, Pacific Fleet, Subordinate Command (SAUO) ... ADCOMSUBORDCOMPHIBSP
Administrative Command, Amphibious Forces, Pacific Fleet, Subordinate Command ... ADCOMSUBORDCOMPHIBSPAC
Administrative Command, Minecraft, Pacific Fleet ... ADCOMINPAC
Administrative Commission (SAUO) ... AD
Administrative Commitment Document ... ACD
Administrative Committee (SAUS) ... ADCOM
Administrative Committee on Administration [*United Nations*] ... ACA
Administrative Committee on Coordination [*of the United Nations*] [*Aviation*] ... ACC
Administrative Committee on Coordination - Subcommittee on Nutrition [*United Nations*] (EAIO) ... ACC/SCN
Administrative Committee on Coordination/Sub Committee on Nutrition (SAUO) ... ACC/SCN
Administrative Committee on Research (SAUO) ... ACR
Administrative Communications Distribution Center [*Air Force*] (AFM) ... ACDC
Administrative Communications Requirement (IAA) ... ACR
Administrative Communications Requirements (SAUS) ... ACR
Administrative Computing and Systems (SAUS) ... ACS
Administrative Computing Service ... ACS
Administrative Conference of the United States [*Independent government agency*] [*Washington, DC*] ... ACUS
Administrative Consent Order [*Environmental Protection Agency*] ... ACO
Administrative Contract Document (MCD) ... ACD
Administrative Contracting Office [*or Officer*] ... ACO
Administrative Contracting Officer (ACAE) ... ACO
Administrative Control ... ADCON
Administrative Control System [*Telecommunications*] (TEL) ... ACS
Administrative Coordination Committee (SAUO) ... ACC
Administrative County (WDAA) ... Ad Co
Administrative Court Digest [*A publication*] (DLA) ... Ad Ct Dig
Administrative Data Entry for Processing Transmission (SAUS) ... ADEPT
Administrative Data Processing (KSC) ... ADP
Administrative Data Systems ... ADS
Administrative Data Systems - Teleprocessing (IEEE) ... ADS-TP
Administrative Decisions [*A publication*] (DLA) ... Admin Dec
Administrative Decisions under Immigration and Nationality Laws of the United States [*A publication*] (DLA) ... BIA
Administrative Department (ADA) ... AD
Administrative Design Service Information (SAUS) ... ADSI
Administrative Detail Program (SAUS) ... ADP
Administrative Determination of Fault ... ADF

Administrative Directive (MCD) ... AD
Administrative Directives System [*Social Security Administration*] (DHP) ... ADS
Administrative Directory User Agent (SAUS) ... ADUA
Administrative Discharge [*Military*] (VNW) ... AD
Administrative Dispute Resolution Act (AAGC) ... ADRA
Administrative Dispute Resolution Act of 1996 (AAGC) ... ADRA
Administrative Distributed Network (GFGA) ... ADNET
Administrative District (ADA) ... AD
Administrative Districts (SAUS) ... Distads
Administrative Division (SAUO) ... AD
Administrative Division [*Municipality*] [*Board on Geographic Names*] ... ADMD
Administrative Domain (SAUS) ... AD
Administrative Engineer (SAUS) ... Admin Engr
Administrative Engineering Information Management System ... AEIMS
Administrative Entity [*Job Training and Partnership Act*] (OICC) ... AE
Administrative Exception Note (SAUS) ... AEN
Administrative, Executive, and Clerical (HEAS) ... AEC
Administrative Fact Sheet [*Vocational education*] (OICC) ... AFS
Administrative Flagship [*Navy symbol*] [*Obsolete*] ... APF
Administrative Function (SAUS) ... AF
Administrative Identification (MHDI) ... ADMINID
Administrative Information and Management System (SAUS) ... AIMS
Administrative Information Data System (AFM) ... AIDS
Administrative Inspection [*Military*] (NVT) ... ADINSP
Administrative Inspection [*Military*] (NVT) ... ADMININSP
Administrative Instructions ... ADMINI
Administrative Instructions ... ADMININST
Administrative Instructions ... AI
Administrative Interpretations [*A publication*] (DLA) ... Adm Interp
Administrative Law (DLA) ... Ad L
Administrative Law (DLA) ... ADMIN L
Administrative Law Bulletin [*A publication*] (DLA) ... Ad LB
Administrative Law Bulletin [*A publication*] (ILCA) ... Ad L Bull
[*The*] **Administrative Law Journal of The American University** [*A publication*] (AAGC) ... Admin LJ
Administrative Law Judge [*Also, HE*] [*Federal trial examiner*] ... ALJ
Administrative Law Judge in Charge [*Social Security Administration*] (DHP) ... ALJIC
Administrative Law Judge of the Department [*Department of Labor*] (OICC) ... ALJD
Administrative Law News [*A publication*] (DLA) ... Ad L News
Administrative Law Newsletter [*A publication*] (DLA) ... Ad L Newsl
Administrative Law Notes [*Australia*] [*A publication*] ... ALN
Administrative Law Reporter, Second (Pike and Fischer) [*A publication*] (DLA) ... Ad L Rep 2d (P & F)
Administrative Law Review [*A publication*] [*ABA*] (AAGC) ... Admin L Rev
Administrative Law Reviews (SAUS) ... Adm Law Rev
Administrative Lead Time ... ALT
Administrative Leave (GFGA) ... AL
Administrative Liaison Officer ... ALO
Administrative License Revocation [*Laws*] ... ALR
Administrative Machine Branch [*Army*] (AABC) ... AMB
Administrative Machine Division [*Army*] (AABC) ... AMD
Administrative Management by Objectives Appraisal System (EDAC) ... AMOAS
Administrative Management Division [*Coast Guard*] ... CAM
Administrative Management Domain (SAUS) ... ADMD
Administrative Management Society [*Willow Grove, PA*] (EA) ... AMS
Administrative Management Staff [*Environmental Protection Agency*] (GFGA) ... AMS
Administrative Management Staff (SAUS) ... AMS
Administrative Management System (SAUS) ... AMS
Administrative Manual ... AM
Administrative Medical Officer [*British*] ... AMO
Administrative Medicine (AAMN) ... ADM
Administrative Memo (NATG) ... ADMM
Administrative Message [*Telecommunications*] (OTD) ... ADR
Administrative Message (SAUS) ... AM
Administrative Module [*AT&T*] (ACRL) ... AM
Administrative Module Processor (ACRL) ... AMP
Administrative Motor Vehicle Management ... AMVM
Administrative Names Diagram (WDAA) ... AND
Administrative Network (SAUS) ... ADINET
Administrative Note ... AN
Administrative Office [*or Officer*] (CINC) ... ADMINO
Administrative Office (SAUO) ... Admin Off
Administrative Office (SAUO) ... Adm Off
Administrative Office - Navy ... AO-N
Administrative Office Instruction ... AOINST
Administrative Office, Navy Department ... AOND
Administrative Office, Navy Department (SAUO) ... AO-ND
Administrative Office of the Courts. Newsletter [*A publication*] (DLA) ... AOC Newsl
Administrative Office of the US Courts (SAUO) ... AC
Administrative Office of United States Courts ... AOUSC
Administrative Officer [*Army*] ... Admo
Administrative Officer (GFGA) ... AO
Administrative Officer for Commander in Chief, Pacific (SAUO) ... ADMINOCINCPAC
Administrative Officer of the Day (DAVI) ... AOD
Administrative Officer on Duty ... AOD
Administrative Operation and Support Services [*Kennedy Space Center*] [*NASA*] (NASA) ... AD
Administrative Operations ... AO
Administrative operations and support service (SAUS) ... AD
Administrative Operations Branch [*NTIS*] ... AOB
Administrative Operations Office (SAUS) ... AOO
Administrative Order ... ADMINO
Administrative Order (NVT) ... ADMINORD
Administrative Order [*Army*] ... Admo
Administrative Order (DLA) ... AO
Administrative Order on Consent [*Environmental Protection Agency*] (ERG) ... AOC
Administrative Organs Department (LAIN) ... AOD
Administrative Plan (NVT) ... ADMINPLAN
Administrative Planning Department (SAUO) ... APD
Administrative Planning Division (SAUO) ... APD
Administrative Policy Office (SAUS) ... APO
Administrative Procedure (NRCH) ... AP
Administrative Procedure Act (SAUS) ... APA
Administrative Procedures Act [*1946*] ... APA
Administrative Processor (TEL) ... AP
Administrative Professional and Technical Evaluation System (DNAB) ... APTES
Administrative, Professional, Technical, and Clerical Grades [*Education*] (AIE) ... APT&C
Administrative Protective Order [*Department of Commerce*] (GFGA) ... APO
Administrative Publication [*Navy*] ... AP
Administrative Radio Conference [*International Telecommunications Union*] ... ARC
Administrative Real Time Express Mortgage and Investment System (MHDB) ... ARTEMIS
Administrative Record (BCP) ... AR
Administrative Records Information System (SAUS) ... ARIS
Administrative Reform Unit ... ARU
Administrative Report (NVT) ... ADMINREP
Administrative Report (SAUS) ... Adm Rep
Administrative Request (SAUS) ... AR
Administrative Request Acknowledge (SAUS) ... ARA
Administrative Requirement (SAUS) ... AR
Administrative Research Bulletin ... ARB
Administrative Review [*A publication*] ... Admin Rev
Administrative Rule (SAUS) ... AR
Administrative Rules and Regulations of the Government of Guam [*A publication*] (DLA) ... Guam Admin R
Administrative Rules for Courts of Limited Jurisdiction (SAUO) ... ARLJ
Administrative Rules of Montana [*A publication*] (AAGC) ... ARM
Administrative Rules of Montana [*A publication*] (DLA) ... Mont Admin R
Administrative Rules of South Dakota [*A publication*] (AAGC) ... ARSD
Administrative Rules of South Dakota [*A publication*] (DLA) ... SD Admin R
Administrative Rules of South Dakota (SAUS) ... SD Admin R
Administrative Rules of Utah [*A publication*] (DLA) ... Utah Admin R
Administrative Rules of Utah (journ.) (SAUS) ... Utah Admin R
Administrative Ruling [*US*] ... AR
Administrative Science (DD) ... AdminSc
Administrative Sciences Association of Canada [*Association des Sciences Administratives du Canada*] ... ASAC
Administrative Sciences Corp. ... ASC
Administrative Section for Technical Cooperation [*United Nations*] ... ASTC
Administrative Service (SAUO) ... ASC
Administrative Service Center (SAUS) ... ASC
Administrative Service Centers (AABC) ... ASC
Administrative Service Company (SAUO) ... Admin Svc Co
Administrative Service Office ... ASO
Administrative Service Officer Class ... ASOC
Administrative Service Officer Structure ... ASOS
Administrative Service Only ... ASO
Administrative Service Oversight Center (SAUS) ... ASOC
Administrative Service Test ... AST
Administrative Service Unit ... ASU
Administrative Services (SAUS) ... Adm Serv
Administrative Services Contract [*Health insurance*] (GHCT) ... ASC
Administrative Services Department [*Queensland, Australia*] ... ASD
Administrative Services Division [*Census*] (OICC) ... ASD
Administrative Services Only (SAUS) ... ASO
Administrative Services Section (SAUS) ... ADM
Administrative Site Procedures [*Nuclear energy*] (NRCH) ... ASP
Administrative Specialist (SAUS) ... ADM SP
Administrative, Staff, and Technical [*Budget term*] ... AS & T
Administrative Staff College [*British*] (DI) ... ASC
Administrative Staff College (SAUO) ... ASC
Administrative Staff Officer ... Admin SO
Administrative Support (NVT) ... ADMINSUP
Administrative Support (MCD) ... ADMSPT
Administrative Support ... AS
Administrative Support Airlift (MCD) ... ASA
Administrative Support and Logistic Company [*Military*] ... AS & L
Administrative Support Center [*Marine science*] (OSRA) ... ASC
Administrative Support Center (SAUS) ... ASC
Administrative Support Group [*Army*] ... ASG
Administrative Support Manual (DNAB) ... ASM
Administrative Support Operations Center [*Army*] ... ADSOC
[*The*] **Administrative Support Theaters Army** ... TASTA
Administrative Support Unit (DNAB) ... ADMINSUPP
Administrative Support Unit ... ASU
Administrative Support/Utilization (SAUS) ... ASUS
Administrative Survey Detachment [*Army*] (LAIN) ... ASD
Administrative Systems Testing Section [*Social Security Administration*] ... ASTS
Administrative Telecommunications Agency [*Canada*] ... ATA
Administrative Telephone System (ACAE) ... ATS
Administrative Terminal Management System [*Computer science*] (HGAA) ... ATMS

Administrative Terminal System [IBM Corp.] .... ATS
Administrative Trainee [Civil Service] [British] .... AT
Administrative Transport Management Survey (MCD) .... ATMS
Administrative Tribunal of the International Labour Organization (SAUS) .... ILOAT
Administrative Unit (SAUO) .... AU
Administrative Unit/Medical Inspection Room (SAUS) .... AU/MIR
Administrative Use Vehicle [Military] (AABC) .... AUV
Administrative Use Vehicle Management Information System [Military] (MCD) .... AUVMIS
Administrative Veterinary Office (SAUO) .... AVO
Administrative Veterinary Officer [British military] (DMA) .... AVO
Administrative Vice President (HGAA) .... AVP
Administrative Watch Officer (DNAB) .... AWO
Administrative Weight Limitation [Military] (AABC) .... AWL
Administrative/Intelligence/Logistics [Military] .... AIL
Administrative/Logistics Center [Military] (INF) .... ALC
Administratively (ABBR) .... ADMNTVY
Administratively Uncontrollable Overtime .... AUO
Administrative-Material Inspection [Military] (NVT) .... ADMAT
Administrative/Network Management (COE) .... A/NM
Administrative-Supply Technician [Army] (AABC) .... AST
Administrator (DLA) .... Ad
Administrator (PHSD) .... Adm
Administrator (GEAB) .... admin
Administrator .... ADMINR
Administrator (DLA) .... Adminstr
Administrator .... ADMNSTR
Administrator (ABBR) .... ADMNTR
Administrator (ROG) .... ADMOR
Administrator .... ADMR
Administrator (WGA) .... ADMS
Administrator .... ADMSTR
Administrator (EBF) .... Admstr
Administrator (ABBR) .... ADMSTRATR
Administrator .... ADMTR
Administrator, Deputy (SAA) .... AD
Administrator of General Services (ACAE) .... AGS
Administrator Professional Leadership Scale .... APLS
Administrators' Bulletin [A publication] .... Admin Bull
Administrator's Discretionary Fund [Marine science] (OSRA) .... ADF
Administrators Discretionary Fund (SAUS) .... ADF
Administrators in Medicine (SAUO) .... AIM
Administrators in Oncology/Hematology Assembly (ADWA) .... AOHA
Administrators of Medium-sized Public Libraries in Ontario (SAUO) .... AMPLO
Administrator's Office (EEVL) .... AO
Administrators Office (SAUS) .... AX
Administrators Pesticide Advisory Committee (SAUS) .... APAC
Administrator's Pesticide Advisory Committee [Terminated, 1985] [Environmental Protection Agency] .... APAC
Administrator's Tracking System [Environmental Protection Agency] (GFGA) .... ATS
Administrators Tracking System (SAUS) .... ATS
Administrators's Discretionary Fund (USDC) .... ADF
Administratrices [Legal shorthand] (LWAP) .... ADMRCS
Administratrix [Business term] (ADA) .... ADMIN
Administratrix [Business term] (ROG) .... ADMIX
Administratrix (ABBR) .... ADMNTX
Administratrix (SAUS) .... Admr
Administratrix [Business term] (ROG) .... ADMRX
Administratrix [Business term] (ROG) .... ADMTRX
Administratrix [Business term] (ROG) .... ADMX
Adminstrative Data Transmission Network [FAA] (TAG) .... ADTN
Admirable (ABBR) .... ADMRB
Admirably (ABBR) .... ADMRY
Admiral .... A
Admiral .... ADM
Admiral (WA) .... Adm
Admiral (BARN) .... Adml
Admiral [Navy] O10
Admiral, Benelux & Netherlands (SAUS) .... ABNL
Admiral Commanding .... AC
Admiral Commanding Aircraft-Carriers [Navy] [British] .... ACAC
Admiral Commanding Battlecruisers [Obsolete] [Navy] [British] .... ACQ
Admiral Commanding Cruiser Squadron (SAUO) .... ACSqn
Admiral Commanding North Atlantic Station [Navy] [British] (DMA) .... ACNAS
Admiral Commanding Reserves [Navy] [British] .... ACR
Admiral Commanding Reserves (SAUO) .... ACR
Admiral Commanding Submarines (SAUO) .... ACS
Admiral Commanding, Submarines (SAUS) .... ACS
Admiral Corporation (SAUO) .... ADL
Admiral of Mine Sweepers (SAUS) .... AMS
Admiral of the Fleet (SAUO) .... AF
Admiral of the Fleet [British] .... AF
Admiral of the Fleet [British] .... A of F
Admiral of the Ocean Sea (SAUS) .... A of OS
Admiral of the Ocean Sea [Annual award of US Merchant Marine; title originally bestowed on Christopher Columbus by the Spanish government] .... AOTOS
Admiral Superintendent [Obsolete] [British] .... AS
Admiral Togo Heihachiro (SAUS) .... Togo
Admirally Islands (SAUS) .... AI
Admiral's Club [American Airlines' club for frequent flyers] [Dallas/Ft. Worth Airport] [Texas] (EA) .... AC
Admiralstabsoffizier (SAUS) .... Asto

Admiralty (GEOI) .... Adm
Admiralty [British] .... ADM
Admiralty (SAUO) .... Adm
Admiralty (ABBR) .... ADMLT
Admiralty (ABBR) .... ADMRLT
Admiralty (SAUO) .... Admt
Admiralty (NATG) .... ADMTY
Admiralty [British] .... ADMY
Admiralty (SAUO) .... Admy
Admiralty (SAUO) .... Ady
Admiralty and Ecclesiastical (DLA) .... A & E
Admiralty Berthing Officer (SAUS) .... ABO
Admiralty Berthing Officer [British] .... ABQ
Admiralty Board [British] .... AB
Admiralty Center (SAUO) .... Adm
Admiralty Center (SAUO) .... AdmCen
Admiralty Centre for Scientific Information and Liaison [British] .... ACSIL
Admiralty Chart Datum (PDAA) .... ACD
Admiralty Civilian Shore Wireless Service [British] (IAA) .... ACSWS
Admiralty Civilian Shore Wireless Service (SAUO) .... ACSWS
Admiralty Coast Organization (SAUO) .... ACO
Admiralty Compass Observatory [British] (DEN) .... ACO
Admiralty Computing Service [British] (SAA) .... ACS
Admiralty Computing Service (SAUO) .... ACS
Admiralty Constabulary (SAUO) .... AC
Admiralty Corrosion Committee [British] (KSC) .... ACC
Admiralty Court (SAUO) .... AdmCo
Admiralty Court (BARN) .... Adm Ct
Admiralty Decisions of Hopkinson in Gilpin's Reports [A publication] (DLA) .... Hopk Adm Dec
Admiralty Decisions Tempore Hay and Marriott [England] [A publication] (DLA) .... Dec T H & M
Admiralty Design (SAUS) .... AD
Admiralty Distilling Experimental Station (SAUO) .... ADES
Admiralty Division (DLA) .... Admir
Admiralty Dockmaster (SAUO) .... AD
Admiralty Dockyard (SAUO) .... AD
Admiralty Emergency Service (SAUO) .... AES
Admiralty Engineering Laboratory (SAUO) .... AEL
Admiralty Engineering Laboratory [British] (MCD) .... AEL
Admiralty Experiment Works [British] .... AEW
Admiralty Experimental Diving Unit [British] .... AEDU
Admiralty Fleet Confidential Order [British] (DMA) .... AFCO
Admiralty Fleet Order [Obsolete] [British] .... AFO
Admiralty Floating Dock [British] .... AFD
Admiralty Forecast Section (SAUO) .... AFS
Admiralty Fuel Experimental Station [British] .... AFES
Admiralty Fuel Research (SAUS) .... AFR
Admiralty Fuels and Lubricants Advisory Committee (SAUO) .... AFLAC
Admiralty General Message [Obsolete] [British] .... AGM
Admiralty Gunnery Establishment [British] .... AGE
Admiralty House (SAUO) .... AH
Admiralty Inspection Officer (SAUS) .... AIO
Admiralty Instruction [A publication] (DLA) .... AI
Admiralty Instructions (SAUS) .... AI
Admiralty Interview Board [British] .... AIB
Admiralty Islands .... AI
Admiralty Letter [British military] (DMA) .... AL
Admiralty Liaison Officer [British] .... ALO
Admiralty Lines Limited (SAUO) .... ALL
Admiralty List of Lights [British] .... ALL
Admiralty List of Radio Signals [British] .... ALRS
Admiralty List of Wireless-signals (SAUS) .... ALW
Admiralty Machinery Depot (SAUO) .... AMD
Admiralty Marine Engineering Establishment [British] .... AMEE
Admiralty Marine Technology Establishment [Research center] [British] (IRC) .... AMTE
Admiralty Marine Training Establishment (Physiological Laboratory) [Research center] [British] .... AMTE(PL)
Admiralty Materials Laboratory [British] .... AML
Admiralty Medical Board [British military] (DMA) .... AMB
Admiralty Merchant Ship Defense Instructions [British] .... AMDI
Admiralty Merchant Shipping Instructions [British] .... AMSI
Admiralty Mining Establishment [British] (MCD) .... AME
Admiralty Monthly Order [British military] (DMA) .... AMO
Admiralty Naval Staff [British] .... ANS
Admiralty Naval Staff (SAUO) .... ANS
Admiralty Net Defence [Antitorpedo nets] [British] [World War II] .... AND
Admiralty Notice to Mariners [British] (DI) .... ANM
Admiralty Office [Navy] [British] (ROG) .... AO
Admiralty Office, London (ROG) .... AOL
Admiralty Oil Laboratory [British] .... AOL
Admiralty Overseeing Staff Association (SAUO) .... AOSA
Admiralty Pattern [The right procedure, the correct thing to do] [British] .... AP
Admiralty Press Division [British military] (DMA) .... APD
Admiralty Press Division (SAUO) .... APD
Admiralty Prize Court (SAUO) .... APC
Admiralty Raster Chart Service (WDAA) .... ARCS
Admiralty Reactor Test Establishment (MCD) .... ARTE
Admiralty Recruiting Service [British] .... ARS
Admiralty Recruiting Service (SAUO) .... ARS
Admiralty Regional Electrical Engineer (SAUO) .... AREE
Admiralty Regional Electrical Engineer [British] (IAA) .... AREE
Admiralty Regional Office (SAUO) .... ARO
Admiralty Representative (SAUS) .... AR

Admiralty Research Establishment [*British*] (IRUK) ... ARE
Admiralty Research Laboratory [*British*] ... ARL
Admiralty Research Laboratory Extension [*British*] ... ARLE
Admiralty Sailing Directions for the World (BARN) ... ASDW
Admiralty Salvage Department (SAUO) ... ASD
Admiralty Salvage Department [*British military*] (DMA) ... ASD
Admiralty Signal and RADAR Establishment [*British*] ... ASRE
Admiralty Signal Establishment [*British*] ... ASE
Admiralty Small Vessels Pool (SAUO) ... ASVP
Admiralty Standard Range (SAUS) ... ASR
Admiralty Standard Stockless [*Anchor*] (PDAA) ... ASS
Admiralty Stores Depot (SAUO) ... ASD
Admiralty Supply Item ... ASI
Admiralty Surface Weapons Establishment [*British Ministry of Defense*] [*Research center*] ... ASWE
Admiralty Test Rating (SAUS) ... ATR
Admiralty Trawler (SAUS) ... AT
Admiralty Vickers Gearing Research Association (SAUO) ... AVGRA
Admiralty Weekly Order (SAUS) ... AWO
Admiralty Weekly Order [*British military*] (DMA) ... AWO
Admiralty Wireless-Signals List (SAUS) ... AWL
Admiralty Works Department Employees Association [*A union*] [*British*] ... AWDEA
Admiration (ABBR) ... ADMRAN
Admiration (ABBR) ... ADMRN
Admire (ABBR) ... ADMR
Admired (ABBR) ... ADMRD
Admirer (ABBR) ... ADMRR
Admiring (ABBR) ... ADMRG
Admiringly (ABBR) ... ADMRGY
Admissibility (ABBR) ... ADMSBLT
Admissibility (ABBR) ... ADMSBT
Admissible (ABBR) ... ADMSB
Admissible Linear Unbiased Estimator [*Statistics*] ... ALUE
Admissible Rank Test [*Statistics*] ... ART
Admission ... ADM
Admission (GEAB) ... adm
Admission (WA) ... Adm
Admission [*Medicine*] (DAVI) ... admit
Admission (ROG) ... ADMON
Admission (AFM) ... ADMSN
Admission and Discharge ... A & D
Admission and Discharge (SAUS) ... AD
Admission and Disposition [*Military*] (AABC) ... AAD
Admission and Disposition [*Medicine*] (DAVI) ... A & D
Admission and Dispositions Section [*Field or evacuation hospital*] (VNW) ... A & D
Admission Multiphasic Screening [*Medicine*] (CPH) ... AMS
Admission Pattern Monitoring [*Medicine*] (HCT) ... APM
Admission Referral and Information Center [*Commission on Independent Colleges and Universities*] ... ARIC
Admission Scheduling and Control System [*Hospital management*] ... ASCS
Admission Temporaire-temporary Admission (SAUO) ... ATA
Admission Test for Graduate Study in Business ... ATGSB
Admission to Practice Rules (SAUO) ... APR
Admission/Discharge/Transfer [*Hospital records*] (DHSM) ... ADT
Admissions ... ADMIS
Admissions Committee (SAUO) ... AC
Admissions Liaison Officer (SAUS) ... ALO
Admissions per Thousand [*Hospitalization*] ... APT
Admissions Testing Program ... ATP
Admissive (ABBR) ... ADMSV
Admit (WGA) ... ADM
Admit (ABBR) ... ADMT
Admittance (MAE) ... A
Admittance (ABBR) ... ADMTNC
Admittance [*Symbol*] [*IUPAC*] ... Y
Admitted [*Medicine*] (DAVI) ... Adm
Admitted (SAUS) ... ADM
Admitted (ABBR) ... ADMTD
Admitted from Other Ward (MELL) ... AOW
Admittedly (ABBR) ... ADMTDY
Admitting (MSA) ... ADMG
Admitting (ABBR) ... ADMTG
Admitting Blood Sugar [*Medicine*] ... ABS
Admitting Diagnosis [*Medicine*] (MAE) ... AD
Admitting Diagnosis (SAUS) ... Ad Diag
Admitting Room (MELL) ... AR
Admixture (ABBR) ... ADMXR
Admixture-Lathe-Cut + Eutectic [*Dental alloy*] ... ALE
Admixture-Lathe-Cut + Single Composition Spherical [*Dental alloy*] ... ALSCS
Admonish (ABBR) ... ADMNH
Admonish (ABBR) ... ADMON
Admonished (ABBR) ... ADMOND
Admonisher (ABBR) ... ADMNHR
Admonisher (ABBR) ... ADMONR
Admonishing (ABBR) ... ADMONG
Admonishingly (ABBR) ... ADMONGY
Admonishment (ABBR) ... ADMONT
Admonition (ABBR) ... ADMNN
Admonition (ABBR) ... ADMONTN
Admonitions (ABBR) ... ADMNTNS
Admove [*Apply*] [*Pharmacy*] ... ADM
Admove [*Apply*] [*Pharmacy*] ... ADMOV
Adnexa [*Medicine*] (CPH) ... ad
Adnexal Carcinoma of Skin [*Medicine*] (MELL) ... ACS
Adobe (VRA) ... adb
Adobe Binary Screen Font (SAUS) ... ABF
Adobe Certified Expert (SAUS) ... ACE
Adobe Developers Association (SAUO) ... ADA
Adobe Document Structuring Conventions (SAUS) ... ADSC
Adobe Font Binary (SAUS) ... AFB
Adobe Font Manager (SAUS) ... AFM
Adobe Font Metrics (SAUS) ... AFM
Adobe Font Metrics File (CDE) ... AFM File
Adobe Glyph Bitmap Distribution Format (SAUS) ... BDF
Adobe Illustrator [*Computer science*] (PCM) ... AI
Adobe Point (SAUS) ... APT
Adobe Postscript Point (SAUS) ... APT
Adobe Press (SAUO) ... ISBN 0-672
Adobe Systems [*NASDAQ symbol*] (TTSB) ... ADBE
Adobe Systems [*Associated Press*] (SAG) ... AdobeSy
Adobe Systems, Inc. [*NASDAQ symbol*] (NQ) ... ADBE
Adobe Systems Inc. (SAUS) ... ADBE
Adobe Type Manager [*Computer software*] [*Adobe Systems, Inc.*] (PCM) ... ATM
Adobe Virtual Network (SAUS) ... AVN
Adola Mining Corp. [*Vancouver Stock Exchange symbol*] ... ADA
Adolescence (ABBR) ... ADLSNC
Adolescence (DMAA) ... adol
Adolescence [*A publication*] (BRI) ... Adoles
Adolescence Directory On-Line (SAUO) ... ADOL
Adolescent (ABBR) ... ADLSNT
Adolescent (ABBR) ... ADLST
Adolescent ... ADOL
Adolescent Abuse Inventory (EDAC) ... AAI
Adolescent Alienation Index [*Personality development test*] [*Psychology*] ... AAI
Adolescent and Adult Psychoeducational Profile [*Educational testing*] ... AAPEP
Adolescent and Adult Psychoeduca-tional Profile (SAUS) ... AAPEP
Adolescent Argumentativeness Scale [*Roberto and Finucane, 1997*] ... ADARG
Adolescent Behavior Rating Scale [*Devereaux*] [*Also, DAB*] [*Psychology*] ... ABRS
Adolescent Behaviour Rating Scale (SAUS) ... ABRS
Adolescent Chemical Dependency Inventory (TES) ... ACDI
Adolescent Coercive Sex (MELL) ... ACS
Adolescent Coping Scale [*Test*] (TMMY) ... ACS
Adolescent Drug Abuse Unit [*Medicine*] (DMAA) ... ADAU
Adolescent Family Life Act [*of 1981*] ... AFLA
Adolescent Family Life Program [*Department of Health and Human Services*] ... AFL
Adolescent Language Quotient (PAZ) ... ALQ
Adolescent Language Screening Test [*Speech development test*] ... ALST
Adolescent Medicine [*Medical specialty*] (DHSM) ... ADL
Adolescent Medicine [*Medicine*] (DMAA) ... ADO
Adolescent Medicine (MELL) ... AM
Adolescent Multiphasic Personality Inventory [*Personality development test*] [*Psychology*] ... AMPI
Adolescent Pregnancy [*Medicine*] (MELL) ... AP
Adolescent Psychiatry (journ.) (SAUS) ... ADPSDJ
Adolescent Verbal Aggressiveness Scale [*Roberto and Finucane, 1997*] ... ADVA
Adolescent-Coping Orientation for Problem Experiences [*Psychology*] ... A-COPE
Adolescent-Family Inventory of Life Events and Changes [*Psychology*] ... A-FILE
Adolf Schild ... AS
Adolf Stieler (GEOI) ... AdSt
Adolfo [*Couturier*] ... A
Adolph Meyer Mental Health Center, Decatur, IL [*Library symbol*] [*Library of Congress*] (LCLS) ... IDecM
Adolph Schild, S.A. ... ASSA
Adolphus and Ellis' English King's Bench Reports [*A publication*] (DLA) ... Ad & E
Adolphus and Ellis' English King's Bench Reports [*A publication*] (DLA) ... Ad & El
Adolphus and Ellis' English King's Bench Reports [*A publication*] (DLA) ... Ad & El (Eng)
Adolphus and Ellis' English King's Bench Reports [*A publication*] (DLA) ... Adol & El
Adolphus and Ellis' English King's Bench Reports [*A publication*] (DLA) ... Adolph & E
Adolphus and Ellis' English Queen's Bench Reports [*A publication*] (DLA) ... A & E
Adolphus and Ellis' English Queen's Bench Reports, New Series [*A publication*] (DLA) ... A & E (NS)
Adolphus and Ellis' English Queen's Bench Reports, New Series [*A publication*] (DLA) ... Ad & Ell NS
Adolphus and Ellis' English Queen's Bench Reports, New Series [*A publication*] (DLA) ... Adol & El NS
Adolphus and Ellis' Reports, New Series [*A publication*] (ILCA) ... Ad & El NS
Adominal Pregnancy (MELL) ... AP
Adopt a Special Kid (PAZ) ... AASK
Adopt A Special Kid (SAUO) ... AASK
Adoptable (ABBR) ... ADOPB
Adopt-a-Native-Elder ... ANE
Adopted (ABBR) ... ADOPD
Adopted By ... AD
Adopted Child ... AC
Adopted Child [*Legal shorthand*] (LWAP) ... ADC
Adopted From [*or Adoption Of*] [*Etymology*] ... A
Adoptee-Birthparent Center [*An association*] (EA) ... ABC
Adoptee-Birthparent Searches [*An association*] (EA) ... ABC
Adoptee-Birthparent Support Network (EA) ... ABSN
Adoptee/Natural Parent Locators [*Later, ANPLI*] (EA) ... ANPL

Adoptee/Natural Parent Locators - International [*Formerly, ANPL*] [*Later, MPI*] (EA) ... ANPLI
Adoptees and Natural Parents Organization (EA) ... ANPO
Adoptees in Search [*An association*] (EA) ... AIS
Adoptees Liberty Movement Association (EA) ... ALMA
Adoptees' Liberty Movement Association (PAZ) ... ALMA Society
Adopter (ABBR) ... ADOPR
Adopting (ABBR) ... ADOPG
Adoption (ABBR) ... ADOP
Adoption (ABBR) ... ADOPN
Adoption (DLA) ... ADOPT
Adoption ... ADPTN
Adoption Act [*British*] ... AA
Adoption Agency (SAUS) ... AA
Adoption and Family Reunion Center (EA) ... AFRC
Adoption Directory [*A publication*] ... AD
Adoption Identity Movement (EA) ... AIM
Adoption Information Services (EA) ... AIS
Adoption of Automatically Programmed Tools [*Computer science*] (IEEE) ... ADAPT
Adoption Resource Exchange [*British*] (DI) ... ARE
Adoption Resource Exchange of North America [*Later, NAIES*] (EA) ... ARENA
Adoption Search Institute [*Inactive*] (EA) ... ASI
Adoption Taxpayer Identification Number ... ATIN
Adoption Triangle Ministries [*Later, AFRC*] (EA) ... ATM
Adoptive (ABBR) ... ADOPV
Adoptive Bit Rate Encoding [*Computer science*] ... ABRE
Adoptive Families of America [*Formerly, OURS (Organization for United Response)*] (PAZ) ... AFA
Adoptive Families Of America (SAUO) ... AFA
Adoptive Family Network [*Formerly, Families Adopting Children Everywhere (FACE)*] (PAZ) ... AFN
Adoptive Triangle New South Wales [*Australia*] [*An association*] ... ATNSW
Adorability (ABBR) ... ADORBT
Adorable (ABBR) ... ADORB
Adorableness (ABBR) ... ADORBNS
Adorably (ABBR) ... ADORBL
Adorably (ABBR) ... ADORBY
Adoration (ABBR) ... ADORAN
Adoration (ABBR) ... ADORTN
Adoratrici Perpetuae del Santissimo Sacramento [*Nuns of the Perpetual Adoration of the Blessed Sacrament*] [*Roman Catholic religious order*] ... AP
Adored (ABBR) ... ADORD
Adorers of the Blood of Christ (SAUO) ... ABC Sisters
Adorers of the Blood of Christ [*Roman Catholic women's religious order*] ... ASC
Adorers of the Precious Blood (TOCD) ... APB
Adoring (ABBR) ... ADORG
Adoringly (ABBR) ... ADORGY
Adornment (ABBR) ... ADORNT
Adornment (ABBR) ... ADRNT
Adorno Fathers (TOCD) ... crm
Adorno Fathers (TOCD) ... CRM
adoxographer (SAUS) ... adoxograph
adoxography (SAUS) ... adoxograph
ADP [*Automatic Data Processing, Inc.*] **Brokerage Information Services Group** [*Also, an information service or system*] (IID) ... ADP/BISG
ADP [*Automatic Data Processing, Inc.*] **Electronic Financial Services** [*Telecommunications service*] (TSSD) ... ADP-EFS
ADP [*American Defense Preparedness*] **Equipment** (DOMA) ... ADPE
ADP [*Automatic Data Processing, Inc.*] **Financial Information Services, Inc.** [*Later, ADP/BISG*] [*Information service or system*] (IID) ... ADP/FIS
ADP [*Adenosine Diphosphate*] **Ribosylated Enzyme** ... ADPR
ADP System Security Officer (SAUS) ... ADPSSO
ADP [*Automatic Data Processing*] **Systems Resources Analysis** ... ASRA
ADP [*Automatic Data Processing, Inc.*] **Telephone Computing Services, Inc.** [*Telecommunications service*] (TSSD) ... ADP/TCS
Ad-Page Exposure (NTCM) ... APX
ADPE [*Automatic Data Processing Equipment*] **Resources Management System** (AFM) ... ARMS
ADPE System Sizing Tool (SAUS) ... ASSIST
ADP [*Adenosine Diphosphate*]**-Ribosylation Factor** [*Biochemistry*] ... ARF
Ad-Print, Belleville, NJ [*Library symbol*] [*Library of Congress*] (LCLS) ... NjBeA
Adrar [*Algeria*] [*Airport symbol*] (OAG) ... AZR
Adrar/Touat [*Algeria*] [*ICAO location identifier*] (ICLI) ... DAUA
Adrema Pitney Bowes (SAUS) ... APB
Adrenal [*Medicine*] ... Ad
Adrenal [*Gland*] (ABBR) ... ADREN
Adrenal Androgen [*Medicine*] (DMAA) ... AA
Adrenal Androgen Corticotropic Stimulating Hormone [*Medicine*] (DMAA) ... AACSH
Adrenal Androgen Stimulating Hormone [*Medicine*] ... AASH
Adrenal Androgenic Hyperfunction (DB) ... AAH
Adrenal [*or Adrenocortical*] **Autoantibody** ... AA
Adrenal Autoantibody (SAUS) ... AA
Adrenal Cortex [*Medicine*] ... AC
Adrenal Cortex [*Medicine*] ... AdC
Adrenal Cortex Inner Zone (SAUS) ... X zone
Adrenal Cortical Extract [*Endocrinology*] ... ACE
Adrenal Cortical Hormone [*Endocrinology*] ... ACH
Adrenal Cortical Insufficiency [*Endocrinology*] (MAE) ... ACI
Adrenal Dysfunction [*Medicine*] (MELL) ... AD
Adrenal Gland [*Anatomy*] ... ADGL
Adrenal Gland [*Medicine*] (MELL) ... AG
Adrenal Gland Sympathogonioma [*Medicine*] (DB) ... AGS
Adrenal Glands (SAUS) ... adrenals
Adrenal Growth Factor [*Medicine*] (MELL) ... AGF
Adrenal Hypoplasia Congenita [*Metabolic disease*] ... AHC
Adrenal Insufficiency [*Medicine*] (MELL) ... AI
Adrenal Medulla [*Anatomy*] ... AdM
Adrenal Medulla [*Anatomy*] ... AM
Adrenal Metabolic Research Society of the Hypoglycemia Foundation (EA) ... AMRSHF
Adrenal Regeneration Hypertension [*Medicine*] (DB) ... ARH
Adrenal Weight Factor [*Endocrinology*] ... AWF
Adrenalectomized [*Medicine*] (MELL) ... ADE
Adrenalectomized [*Medicine*] ... ADX
Adrenalectomized Alloxan Diabetic (SAUS) ... AAD
Adrenalectomized rats (SAUS) ... ADX rats
Adrenalectomy [*Medicine*] (DAVI) ... Adrenex
Adrenalin, Atropine, and Cocaine (MELL) ... AAC
Adrenaline [*Endocrinology*] (MAE) ... A
Adrenaline [*Endocrinology*] ... Adr
Adrenaline (ABBR) ... ADRN
Adrenaline Acid Tartrate [*Medicine*] (MELL) ... AAT
Adrenergic ¤-Inhibitors (SAUS) ... AI
Adrenergic ¤-Stimulators (SAUS) ... AS
Adrenergic Blocking Agent (DIPS) ... aba
Adrenergic Blocking Agent (DIPS) ... ABA
Adrenergic Blocking Drug [*Medicine*] (MELL) ... ABD
Adrenergic Receptor [*Physiology*] ... AR
Adrenergic Receptor Binder [*Physiology*] (DMAA) ... ARB
Adrenergic Receptor Kinase (DB) ... ARK
Adrenergic Receptor Material [*Physiology*] (DMAA) ... ARM
Adrenocortical Carcinoma [*Medicine*] ... ACC
Adreno-Cortical Hormone (SAUS) ... ACH
Adrenocortical Renin Inhibitory Peptide [*Biochemistry*] ... ACRIP
Adrenocorticoid [*Medicine*] ... AC
Adrenocorticopolypeptide [*Endocrinology*] ... ACPP
Adrenocorticosteroid [*Medicine*] (OA) ... ACS
Adrenocorticotrophic Hormone [*Endocrinology*] ... ACTH
Adrenocorticotrophic Polypeptide [*Endocrinology*] ... ACTP
Adrenocorticotrophin (PDAA) ... ACT
Adrenocorticotrophin (LDT) ... ACTH
Adrenocortico-Trophin (SAUS) ... ACTN
Adrenocorticotrophin-Like Immunoreactivity [*Immunochemistry*] ... ACTH-LI
Adrenocorticotropic hormone (SAUS) ... ACTA
Adrenocorticotropic Hormone (LDT) ... ACTH
Adreno-Corticotropic Hormone (SAUS) ... ACTH
Adrenocorticotropic Hormone Deficiency [*Medicine*] (MELL) ... AHD
Adrenocorticotropic Hormone Receptor [*Medicine*] (DMAA) ... ACTHR
Adrenocorticotropic Hormone-Releasing Factor [*Endocrinology*] (MAE) ... ACTH-RF
Adrenocorticotropic Polypeptide (SAUS) ... ACTP
Adrenocorticotropin [*Endocrinology*] (MAE) ... ACTN
Adrenocortiotrophin (SAUS) ... ACT
Adrenogenital Syndrome [*Medicine*] ... AGS
Adreno-Genitales-Syndrom (SAUS) ... AGS
Adrenoglomerulotrophin [*Medicine*] (MEDA) ... AGT
Adrenoglomerulotrophin [*Also, ASH*] [*Endocrinology*] ... AGTr
Adrenoglomerulotropin Hormone [*Endocrinology*] (MAE) ... AGTH
Adrenoleukodystrophy [*Medicine*] (DB) ... ADL
Adrenoleukodystrophy [*Medicine*] ... ALD
Adrenoleukodystrophy Protein [*Biochemistry*] ... ALDP
Adrenomedullin [*Endocrinology*] ... ADM
Adrenomyeloneuropathy [*Neurology*] ... AMN
Adrenotropic Hormone (LDT) ... ACTH
Adress Resolution Protocol (SAUS) ... ARP
Adressable (SAUS) ... Addrb
Adressograph Multigraph Corp. (SAUO) ... AM
Adria Aero Lloyd (SAUO) ... AAL
Adria Airways [*Yugoslavia*] [*ICAO designator*] (FAAC) ... ADR
Adria Airways [*Airline flight code*] (ODBW) ... JP
Adria Laboratories, Inc., Columbus, OH [*OCLC symbol*] (OCLC) ... OAD
Adriamcin, Cyclophosphamide, Cisplatin [*Antineoplastic drug regimen*] (DAVI) ... CAD-I
Adriamycin [*Also, ADM, ADR, D, H*] [*Antineoplastic drug*] ... A
Adriamycin (DB) ... AD
Adriamycin [*Also, A, ADR, D, H*] [*Antineoplastic drug*] ... ADM
Adriamycin (SAUS) ... ADM
Adriamycin (SAUS) ... ADR
Adriamycin [*Also, A, ADM, D, H*] [*Antineoplastic drug*] ... ADR
Adriamycin (DMAA) ... Adr
Adriamycin [*Also called doxorubicin*] [*Antineoplastic drug*] (DAVI) ... ADRIA
Adriamycin, ARA-C [*Cytosine Arabinoside*] [*Antineoplastic drug*] (CDI) ... AA
Adriamycin, ARA-C [*Cytarabine*] [*Antineoplastic drug*] (CDI) ... AA
Adriamycin, BCNU [*Carmustine*]**, Cyclophosphamide** [*Antineoplastic drug regimen*] ... ABC
Adriamycin, Bleomycin, CCNU [*Lomustine*]**, Dacarbazine** [*Antineoplastic drug regimen*] ... ABCD
Adriamycin, Bleomycin, Cisplatin, Radiation Therapy [*Antineoplastic drug regimen*] (DAVI) ... ABCX
Adriamycin, Bleomycin, Cyclophosphamide, Mitomycin C [*Antineoplastic drug regimen*] ... ABCM
Adriamycin, Bleomycin, Dacarbazine [*Antineoplastic drug regimen*] ... ABD
Adriamycin, Bleomycin, Dacarbazine, CCNU [*Lomustine*] [*Antineoplastic drug regimen*] ... ABDIC
Adriamycin, Bleomycin, Dacarbazine, Vinblastine [*Antineoplastic drug regimen*] ... ABDV
Adriamycin, Bleomycin, Prednisone [*Antineoplastic drug regimen*] ... ABP
Adriamycin, Bleomycin, Vinblastine [*Antineoplastic drug regimen*] ... ABV

Adriamycin, Bleomycin, Vinblastine [Oncovin], Dacarbazine [Antineoplastic drug regimen] .... ABVD
Adriamycin, Carmustine [Antineoplastic drug] (CDI) .... AC
Adriamycin, CCNU [Lomustine] [Antineoplastic drug regimen] .... AC
Adriamycin Cisplatin [Antineoplastic drug] (CDI) .... AP
Adriamycin, Cisplatin, Arabinosylcytosine, Adrenocorticoid [Antineoplastic drug] (CDI) .... ASHAP
Adriamycin, Cyclophosphamide [Antineoplastic drug regimen] .... AC
Adriamycin, Cyclophosphamide [Antineoplastic drug regimen] .... ACe
Adriamycin, Cyclophosphamide, 5-Fluorouracil, Actinomycin D [Antineoplastic drug regimen] (DAVI) .... ADCONFU
Adriamycin, Cyclophosphamide, Dacarbazine [Antineoplastic drug regimen] .... A-CY-DIC
Adriamycin, Cyclophosphamide, Dacrabazine [DTIC], Actinomycin D [Antineoplastic drug regimen] (DAVI) .... ACID
Adriamycin [Doxorubicin], Cyclophosphamide, Etoposide [VP-16] [Antineoplastic drug regimen] (DAVI) .... ACE
Adriamycin, Cyclophosphamide, Methotrexate [Antineoplastic drug regimen] .... ACM
Adriamycin, Cyclophosphamide, Oncovin [Vincristine], Prednisone [Antineoplastic drug regimen] .... ACOP
Adriamycin, Cyclophosphamide, Oncovin [Vincristine], Procarbazine, Prednisone [Antineoplastic drug regimen] .... ACOPP
Adriamycin, Cyclophosphamide, Oncovin, Procarbazine, Prednisone (SAUS) .... ACOPP
Adriamycin, Cyclophosphamide, Vincristine, 5-Fluorouracil, [Antineoplastic drug regimen] (DAVI) .... ADCONFU
Adriamycin, Cyclophosphamide, Vincristine, Cytosine Arabinoside, Prednisone [Antineoplastic drug regimen] (DAVI) .... ACOAP
Adriamycin, Cyclophosphamide/X-Ray Therapy [Antineoplastic drug regimen] .... AC/XRT
Adriamycin [Doxorubicin], Cyclophosphanide, and Etoposide in High Dose Infusion [Vepeside] [Antineoplastic drug regimen] (DAVI) ACE-11
Adriamycin [Doxorubicin], Cytosine Arabinoside , Vincristine, Prednisone [Cytarabine] [Antineoplastic drug regimen] (DAVI) .... ADOAP
Adriamycin, Dacarbazine [Antineoplastic drug regimen] .... A-DIC
Adriamycin, Dacarbazine, Bleomycin, CCNU [Lomustine] [Antineoplastic drug regimen] .... ADBC
Adriamycin, Dacarbazine, Dactinomycin [Antineoplastic drug regimen] .... A-DIC-DACT
Adriamycin, Dactinomycin [Antineoplastic drug regimen] .... A-DACT
Adriamycin, Ifosfamide, Dacarbazine [Antineoplastic drug regimen] .... AID
Adriamycin, Leukeran [Chlorambucil], Oncovin , Methotrexate, Actinomycin D, Dacarbazine [Vincristine] [Antineoplastic drug regimen] .... ALOMAD
Adriamycin, L-Phenylalanine Mustard [Antineoplastic drug regimen] .... Adria-L-PAM
Adriamycin, Oncovin, ara-C, Prednisone [Antineoplastic drug regimen] ..... ADOAP
Adriamycin, Oncovin [Vincristine], Prednisone [Antineoplastic drug regimen] .... ADOP
Adriamycin, Oncovin, Prednisone (SAUS) .... ADOP
Adriamycin, Prednisone, Oncovin [Vincristine] [Antineoplastic drug regimen] .... APO
Adriamycin, Vinblastine, Methotrexate [Antineoplastic drug regimen] (DAVI) .... AVM
Adriamycin, Vincristine [Antineoplastic drug regimen] .... AV
Adriamycin, Vincristine, Cyclophosphamide [Antineoplastic drug regimen]..... AVC
Adriamycin, Vincristine, Procarbazine [Antineoplastic drug regimen] (DAVI) .... AVP
Adriamycin-Symposium (journ.) (SAUS) .... Adriamycin-Symp
Adrian C. and Leon Israel [in company name "ACLI International"] .... ACLI
Adrian College (SAUO) .... AC
Adrian College, Adrian, MI [OCLC symbol] (OCLC) .... EEA
Adrian College, Adrian, MI [Library symbol] [Library of Congress] (LCLS) .... MiAdC
Adrian, MI [Location identifier] [FAA] (FAAL) .... ADG
Adrian, MI [AM radio station call letters] .... WABJ
Adrian, MI [FM radio station call letters] .... WLEN
Adrian, MI [FM radio station call letters] .... WQTE
Adrian, MI [FM radio station call letters] .... WVAC
Adrian Public Library, Adrian, MI [Library symbol] [Library of Congress] (LCLS) .... MiAd
Adrian Resources [Vancouver Stock Exchange symbol] .... ADL
Adrian Resources [NASDAQ symbol] (TTSB) .... ADLRF
Adrian Resources Ltd. [NASDAQ symbol] (SAG) .... ADLR
Adrian Resources Ltd. [Associated Press] (SAG) .... AdrianR
Adrian Van Reypen Egerton [Near-acronym used as shortened first name of detective-story character Average Jones, in stories by Samuel Hopkins Adams] .... AVERAGE
Adriance Memorial Library, Poughkeepsie, NY [Library symbol] [Library of Congress] (LCLS) .... NP
Adriatic (SAUS) .... Adr
Adriatic (ABBR) .... ADR
Adriatic Base Command [Military] .... ABC
Adriatic Force [Military] .... ADFOR
Adriatic Mercantile & Trading Co. Ltd. (SAUO) .... AMAT
Adriatic Resources Corp. [Vancouver Stock Exchange symbol] .... AIC
Adriatic Sea (SAUS) .... Adr S
Adria-Wien-Pipeline (SAUS) .... AWP
Adrien Arpel [AMEX symbol] [Formerly, Alfin, Inc.] .... RPL
Adroit (ABBR) .... ADRT
Adroitly (ABBR) .... ADRTY
Adroitness (ABBR) .... ADRTNS
Adsorb (ABBR) .... ADSB
Adsorbed (SAUS) .... ADS
Adsorbed Normal Pool Plasma [Clinical chemistry] .... A-NPP
Adsorbent (ABBR) .... ADSBNT

Adsorbent (ABBR) .... ADSBT
Adsorbent .... ADSORB
Adsorbierbare Organische Halogenverbindungen (SAUS) .... AOX
Adsorption .... Ads
Adsorption (ABBR) .... ADSPN
Adsorption Isotherm Test [Environmental chemistry] (FFDE) .... AI
Adsorption Layer Open Tubular Column [Chromatography] .... ALOT
Adsorption Thin-Layer Chromatography (DB) .... ATLC
Adsorption Wall Open Tubular Column [Chromatography] .... AWOT
Adsorption/Temperature/Vacuum Process (SAUS) .... ADTEVAC PROCESS
Adsorptive Heat Recovery [Chemical engineering] .... AHR
Adstante Febre [When Fever Is Present] [Pharmacy] .... AD FEB
Adstante Febre [When Fever Is Present] [Pharmacy] .... ADST FEB
Adstar Distributed Storage Manager (SAUS) .... ADSM
ADT Aviation Ltd. [British] [ICAO designator] (FAAC) .... AUC
ADT Limited [NYSE symbol] (TTSB) .... ADT
ADT Ltd. [NYSE symbol] (SPSG) .... ADT
Adtec, Inc. (SAUO) .... JAIL
Adtran, Inc. [NASDAQ symbol] (SAG) .... ADTN
Adtran, Inc. [Associated Press] (SAG) .... Adtran
Adulate (ABBR) .... ADLA
Adulate (ABBR) .... ADUL
Adulated (ABBR) .... ADLAD
Adulated (ABBR) .... ADULD
Adulating (ABBR) .... ADLAG
Adulating (ABBR) .... ADULG
Adulation (ABBR) .... ADLAN
Adulation (ABBR) .... ADULN
Adulator (ABBR) .... ADLAR
Adulator (ABBR) .... ADULR
Adulatory (ABBR) .... ADLARY
Adulatory (ABBR) .... ADULY
Adult [Film certificate] [British] .... A
Adult (WGA) .... AD
Adult (AL) .... Ad
Adult (ABBR) .... ADLT
Adult Accompaniment [Restricted to age 14 and up unless accompanied by an adult] [Movie rating] [Canadian] .... AA
Adult Acquired Immunodeficiency Syndrome [Medicine] (DAVI) .... AAIDS
Adult Adrenogenital Syndrome [Medicine] (DAVI) .... AAGS
Adult Album Alternative [Radio broadcasting] .... AAA
Adult Alternative Album [Radio stations] .... Triple-A
Adult and Community Education .... ACE
Adult and Community Learning Services .... ACLS
Adult and Vocational Educational Electronic Mail Network [National Center for Research in Vocational Education] [Columbus, OH] [Telecommunications] (TSSD) .... ADVOCNET
Adult Assessment and Coordination Team .... AACT
Adult Attention Deficit Disorder Behavior Rating Scale [Test] (TMMY) .... AADDBRS
Adult Authority (OICC) .... AA
Adult Basic and Continuing Education (EDAC) .... ABCE
Adult Basic Education .... ABE
Adult Basic Education Resource and Information Service [Australia] .... ARIS
Adult Basic Learning Examination (NVT) .... ABLE
Adult Basic Skill Training (NVT) .... ABST
Adult Bovine Serum [Medicine] (DMAA) .... ABS
Adult, Career, and Vocational Education [Educational Resources Information Center (ERIC) Clearinghouse] [Ohio State University] (PAZ) .... CE
Adult Career Concerns Inventory [Test] .... ACCI
Adult Celiac Disease [Medicine] (CPH) .... ACD
Adult Certificate [Board of Film Censors] [British] (WDMC) .... A certificate
Adult Child of a Dysfunctional Family [Psychology] (DAVI) .... ACDF
Adult Child of Alcoholic [Psychology] (DAVI) .... ACOA
Adult Children Anonymous (EA) .... ACA
Adult Children Anonymous, Region 8 [An association] (EA) .... ACA/Region 8
Adult Children Educational Foundation (EA) .... ACEF
Adult Children of Alcoholics [Support group] .... ACA
Adult Children of Alcoholics [Bestseller by Janet Geringer Woititz] .... ACoA
Adult Children of Alcoholics (DIPS) .... ACOA
Adult Children of Alcoholics [Chemical dependency] [Psychology] (DAVI) ..... ADA
Adult Christian Education Foundation (EA) .... ACEF
Adult Community Movement for Equality [Civil rights] .... ACME
Adult Congregate Living Facilities [Military] .... ACLF
Adult Continuing Education (OICC) .... ACE
Adult Correctional Institution (SAUS) .... ACI
Adult Cost per Entered Employment [Job Training and Partnership Act] (OICC) .... ACEE
Adult Cystic Fibrosis Committee of Quebec (SAUO) .... ACFCQ
Adult Daily Minimum Requirement (HGAA) .... ADMR
Adult Day Health Care (GFGA) .... ADHC
Adult Day-Care Center (MELL) .... ADCC
Adult Diabetes Education Program and Training .... ADEPT
Adult Diphtheria and Tetanus Virus .... ADT
Adult Diploma Program .... ADP
Adult Disease (SAUS) .... AD
Adult Education .... AE
Adult Education Act .... AEA
Adult Education and Lifelong Learning .... ADELL
Adult Education Association (SAUO) .... AEA
Adult Education Association of the United States of America (SAUO) .... AEAUSA
Adult Education Association of the USA (EA) .... AEA
Adult Education Association of Victoria [Australia] .... AEAV
Adult Education Board (SAUO) .... AEB
Adult Education Centre [British] .... AEC

Adult Education Council (SAUO) .... AEC
Adult Education Institute (AIE) .... AEI
Adult Education Journal Review [*A publication*] (ADA) .... AEJR
Adult Education Movement (SAUO) .... AEM
Adult Education Program .... AEP
Adult Education Quarterly [*A publication*] (BRI) ...... AE
Adult Education Tutors' Association [*Australia*] ...... AETA
Adult Emergency Service [*In TV series "A.E.S. Hudson Street"*] ...... AES
Adult Employment Training Programme [*British*] (AIE) ...... ATP
Adult Entered Employment Rate [*Job Training and Partnership Act*]
  (OICC) .... AEER
Adult Erythrocyte [*Medicine*] (DMAA) .... AE
Adult Fanconi's Syndrome [*Medicine*] (DB) ...... AFS
Adult Female (HGAA) .... AF
Adult Females, Density Of [*Ecology*] .... AFDEN
Adult Fiction [*Library science*] (TELE) .... AF
Adult Film Association of America (EA) .... AFAA
Adult Foster Care .... AFC
Adult Growth Examination [*Test*] .... AGE
Adult Haemoglobin (SAUS) .... HbA
Adult Heart .... AH
Adult Independent Living Center (ADWA) .... AILC
Adult Information on Drugs [*Referral service*] ...... AID
Adult Institutions (SAUO) .... AI
Adult Inventory of Reading Interests and Attitudes (EDAC) ...... AIRIA
Adult Jewish Education .... AJE
Adult Language Use Survey (AIE) .... ALUS
Adult Learning [*A publication*] (BRI) .... Adult L
Adult Learning Association (EA) .... ALA
Adult Learning Satellite Service [*Public Broadcasting Service*]
  [*Telecommunications service*] (TSSD) .... ALSS
Adult Learning Service (SAUS) .... ALS
Adult Life Long Learning Section [*Public Library Association*] ...... ALLS
Adult Literacy and Basic Education .... ALBE
Adult Literacy and Basic Skills Action Coalition [*Australia*] ...... ALBSAC
Adult Literacy and Basic Skills Unit [*British*] ...... ALBSU
Adult Literacy and Numeracy Scale .... ALAN
Adult Literacy Initiative .... ALI
Adult Literacy Resource Institute .... ALRI
Adult Literacy Support Services Fund (AIE) ...... ALSSF
Adult Literacy Unit [*British*] .... ALU
Adult Literary Resource Agency (SAUO) .... ALRA
Adult Literary Unit (SAUO) .... ALU
Adult Male (MELL) .... AM
Adult Male Unit (SAUS) .... AMU
Adult Males, Density Of [*Ecology*] .... AMDEN
Adult Migrant Education [*Department of Labor*] ...... AME
Adult Migrant Education Home Tutor Scheme ...... AMEHTS
Adult Migrant English Services [*New South Wales, Australia*] ...... AMES
Adult Migrant Information System [*Australia*] ...... AMIS
Adult Movies and Magazines Association (SAUO) ...... AMMA
Adult Neuropsychological Questionnaire [*Psychology*] (DHP) ...... ANQ
Adult Non-Fiction [*Library science*] (TELE) ...... ANF
Adult Normal [*Medicine*] (DMAA) .... AN
Adult Numeracy Practitioners Network .... ANPN
Adult Nurse Practitioner (DAVI) .... ANP
Adult Onset Diabetes [*Medicine*] (DMAA) .... AOD
Adult onset Diabetes Mellitus (SAUS) .... ADM
Adult Operculum .... AO
Adult Opportunity Center [*State employment service*] ...... AOC
Adult Oriented Rock [*Music*] .... AOR
Adult Outpatient Psychotherapy Clinic (DMAA) ...... AOPC
Adult Parole Authority (SAUO) .... APA
Adult Performance Level .... APL
Adult Performance Level Project [*Defunct*] (EA) ...... APL
Adult Personal Data Inventory [*Medicine*] (DMAA) ...... APDI
Adult Polycystic Disease [*Nephrology*] (DAVI) ...... APCD
Adult Polycystic Disease [*Medicine*] .... APD
Adult Polycystic Kidney Disease [*Medicine*] (MELL) ...... APKD
Adult Polycystic Renal Disease [*Medicine*] (MELL) ...... APRD
Adult Porcine Tyorid Gland (SAUS) .... APTG
Adult Protective Services .... APS
Adult Rat Growth Hormone [*Endocrinology*] ...... ARGH
Adult Reading Improvement Association .... ARIA
Adult Recovery Services [*Chemical dependency and rehabilitation*] (DAVI) ...... ARS
Adult Referral and Information Service in Education (SAUS) ...... ARISE
Adult Rehabilitation Centre [*Canada*] .... ARC
Adult Residential Colleges Association [*British*] (DBA) ...... ARCA
Adult Respiratory Distress [*Medicine*] .... ARD
Adult Respiratory Distress Syndrome [*Medicine*] ...... ARDS
Adult Retraining Program .... ARP
Adult Secondary Education .... ASE
Adult Services Division [*American Library Association*] [*Later, RASD*] (EA) ...... ASD
Adult Services Division-American Library Association (SAUO) ...... ASD-ALA
Adult Situation Stress Reaction [*Psychology*] (DAVI) ...... ASSR
Adult T cell Lymphoma (SAUS) .... ATL
Adult T-Cell Leukemia [*Medicine*] (DMAA) ...... ATCl
Adult T-Cell Leukemia [*Medicine*] .... ATL
Adult T-Cell Leukemia Antigen [*Medicine*] ...... ATLA
Adult T-Cell Leukemia Virus .... ATLV
Adult T-Cell Leukemia-Lymphoma [*Medicine*] ...... ATLL
Adult Training Strategy (AIE) .... ATS
Adult Unemployed Project [*Department of Education and Science*] [*British*]
  (AIE) .... AUP
Adult Use of Tobacco Survey [*1986*] .... AUTS

Adult Verification System [*Computer science*] (VERA) ...... AVS
Adult Video Association (EA) .... AVA
Adult, Vocational and Technical Education (SAUS) ...... AVTE
Adult Vocational Training [*HEW*] .... AVT
Adult Vocational Training Program [*HEW*] .... AVTP
Adult Xanthogranuloma [*Medicine*] (DMAA) ...... AXG
Adult-Child Interaction [*Test*] .... ACI
Adult-Contemporary [*Music*] .... AC
Adulterant (ABBR) .... ADLTNT
Adulterant (ABBR) .... ADLTRNT
Adulterant (ABBR) .... ADULT
adulterant (SAUS) .... adult
Adulterate (ABBR) .... ADLTA
Adulterate (ABBR) .... ADLTRA
Adulterate (ABBR) .... ADULT
adulterate (SAUS) .... adult
Adulterated (ABBR) .... ADLTAD
Adulterated (ABBR) .... ADLTRAD
Adulterating (ABBR) .... ADLTAG
Adulterating (ABBR) .... ADLTRAG
Adulteration (ABBR) .... ADLTRAN
Adulteration (ABBR) .... ADULT
adulteration (SAUS) .... adult
adulterer (SAUS) .... a
Adulterer (ABBR) .... ADLTR
Adulterer (ABBR) .... ADLTRR
Adulteress [*Letter embroidered on Hester Prynne's dress in Nathaniel
  Hawthorne's "The Scarlet Letter"*] .... A
adulteress (SAUS) .... a
Adulteress (ABBR) .... ADLTRES
Adulteress (ABBR) .... ADLTRS
Adulterous (ABBR) .... ADLTRU
Adulterous (ABBR) .... ADLTUS
Adulterously (ABBR) .... ADLTUSY
Adultery (ABBR) .... ADLTRY
Adultery [*FBI standardized term*] .... ADLTY
Adultery (DLA) .... ADULT
Adulthood (ABBR) .... ADLTHD
Adult-Onset Diabetes (SAUS) .... AOD
Adult-Onset Diabetes Mellitus [*Medicine*] (DAVI) ...... ADODM
Adult-Onset Diabetes Mellitus [*Endocrinology*] ...... AODM
Adult-Onset Polycystic Kidney Disease [*Medicine*] ...... APCKD
Adult-Onset Polycystic Kidney Disease [*Medicine*] ...... APKD
Adult-Onset Still's Disease [*Medicine*] (DAVI) ...... AOSD
Adults Molested as Children United (EA) .... AMACU
Adults Molested as Children United (EA) .... AMCU
Adults Only (ADA) .... AO
Adult-Versus-Child [*Medicine*] (DMAA) .... A-C
Adumbrate (ABBR) .... ADMB
Adumbrate (ABBR) .... ADMBRA
Adumbrated (ABBR) .... ADMBD
Adumbrated (ABBR) .... ADMBRAD
Adumbrating (ABBR) .... ADMBG
Adumbrating (ABBR) .... ADMBRAG
Advaced Clearing Station (SAUS) .... Adv Clr Sta
Advance [*Wire service code*] (NTCM) .... A
Advance [*Flowchart*] (AFM) .... ADV
Advance (ADWA) .... adv
Advance (EBF) .... Adv
Advance (FAAC) .... ADVN
Advance (ABBR) .... ADVNC
Advance Acquisition Notification (SAUS) .... AAN
Advance Acquisition Planning (AAGC) .... AAP
Advance Air Charters [*Canada*] [*ICAO designator*] (FAAC) ...... ADV
Advance Airborne Launch Center (SAUS) .... AALC
Advance Airlines [*Australia*] .... AA
Advance Airlines [*ICAO designator*] (AD) ...... DR
Advance Alteration Notice (MSA) .... AAN
Advance Antitank Weapon System - Medium (DWSG) ...... AAWS-M
Advance Australia [*A publication*] .... Advance Aust
Advance Australia Party [*Political party*] .... AAP
Advance Aviation Services, Inc. [*ICAO designator*] (FAAC) ...... XTJ
Advance Base Air Task Unit (SAUO) .... ABATU
Advance Base Aviation Training Unit (SAUS) .... ABATU
Advance Base Components [*Military*] (AFIT) .... ABC
Advance Base Ordnance Depot (SAUS) .... Adv BOD
Advance Base Sea Dock (SAUS) .... ABSD
Advance Base Section Dock [*Floating drydock, first used in World War II*] ...... ABSD
Advance Baseline Configuration (MCD) .... ABC
Advance Bill of Material (SAUS) .... ABM
Advance Book Information [*Publishing*] .... ABI
Advance Booking Charter [*Airline fare*] .... ABC
Advance Booking Fare [*Airlines*] .... ABF
Advance Boundary Information (DA) .... ABI
Advance Calling (SAUS) .... AC
Advance Capability (MCD) .... ADVCAP
Advance Carrier Training Group [*Navy*] .... ACTG
Advance Cash Allowance Authorized .... ADCASHAL
Advance Census Report (SAUS) .... ACR
Advance Change (DNAB) .... ADVCHG
Advance Change Authorization (SAA) .... ACA
Advance Change Notice (AAG) .... ACN
Advance Change Order (SAUS) .... ACO
Advance Charges (SAUS) .... adv chgs

Advance Circuit Order and Layout Information [*Telecommunications*] (TEL) ... ACOLI
Advance Circuits, Inc. (EFIS) ... ACI
Advance Circuits, Inc. (SAUO) ... ADVC
Advance Command ... ADCOM
Advance Command Post (NATG) ... ACP
Advance Components through Increased Volumetric Efficiency (SAA) ... ACTIVE
Advance Computerized Execution System [*Business term*] (EBF) ... ACES
Advance Concepts (ACAE) ... ADCON
Advance Concepts for Terrain Avoidance ... ADCON
Advance Contracting Officer (AAG) ... ACO
Advance Corporate Contract Directive (MCD) ... ACCD
Advance Corporation Tax [*British*] ... ACT
Advance Count Switch ... ACS
Advance Data (journ.) (SAUS) ... Adv Data
Advance Data System (SAUS) ... ADS
Advance Decoy Missile (MCD) ... ADM
Advance Delivery of Correspondence [*Military*] ... ADC
Advance Deposit Agreement (SAUS) ... ADA
Advance Design Aids (SAUS) ... ADA
Advance Development Engineering Order ... ADEO
Advance Development Group [*Army*] (AABC) ... ADG
Advance Deviations Report (AAG) ... ADR
Advance Devices and Material Committee [*British*] ... ADMG
Advance Discontinuance of Allotment ... ADVDISC
Advance Discontinuance of Allotment (SAUS) ... ADVDISC
Advance Document Storage and Retrieval ... ADSTAR
Advance Drawing Release Notice (KSC) ... ADRN
Advance Electronic Diagnostics [*Automotive industry supplier*] ... AED
Advance Element of the Emergency Response Team (SAUO) ... ERT-A
Advance Engineering Change Proposal (MSA) ... AECP
Advance Engineering Material Order ... AEMO
Advance Engineering Memorandum (AAGC) ... AE
Advance Engineering Memorandum ... AEM
Advance Engineering Order ... AEO
Advance Evaluation Note ... AEN
Advance Exit Common (SAUS) ... AEC
Advance Feature Extractor Processor (ACAE) ... AFXP
Advance Feed Tape (SAUS) ... AFT
Advance Financial Bancorp [*Associated Press*] (SAG) ... AdvFnlB
Advance Financial Bancorp [*NASDAQ symbol*] (SAG) ... AFBC
Advance Freight [*Shipping*] (MHDW) ... Adv Frt
Advance Freight [*Shipping*] ... AF
Advance in Antimicrobial and Antineoplastic Chemotherapy (journ.) (SAUS) ... Adv Antimicrob Antineoplast Chemother
Advance In Schedule (SAUS) ... AIS
Advance in Schedule (KSC) ... AIS
Advance in Schedule (KSC) ... AVS
Advance Information Document (MCD) ... AID
Advance Information Letter [*Military*] (AABC) ... AIL
Advance Information Memo (MCD) ... AIM
Advance Information Memory (SAUS) ... AIM
Advance Informed Agreement ... AIA
Advance Investors Corp. (SAUO) ... AIV
Advance Leave [*Military*] ... ADV/L
Advance Light Imaging with Computer Enhancement [*First projection television that houses a computer system*] ... ALICE
Advance Linebacker Radar (ACAE) ... ALR
Advance List of Oversea-Resumees for Reassignment (SAUS) ... AOR
Advance List of Oversea-Returnees for Reassignment [*Army*] ... AOR
Advance Logistical Command [*Army*] ... ADLOG
Advance Low-Altitude Infrared-Reconnaissance Sensor (SAUS) ... ALAIRS
Advance Maneuvering Propulsion System (SAUS) ... AMPS
Advance Manned Mission (SAA) ... AMM
Advance Manufacturing Directive ... AMD
Advance Market Protection (MCD) ... AMP
Advance Master Schedule Change Notice (SAA) ... AMSCN
Advance Material List (DNAB) ... AML
Advance Material Order [*Manufacturing*] ... AMO
Advance Material Request ... AMR
Advance Materials Process Program [*Department of Energy*] ... AMPP
Advance Matter (SAUS) ... A Matter
Advance Medium-Range Air-to-Air (MED) ... Amraam
Advance Message Center (SAUS) ... AMC
Advance Missile Deviation Report ... AMDR
Advance Monthly Retail Trade Survey (SAUO) ... MARTS
Advance Murgor [*Vancouver Stock Exchange symbol*] ... AVR
Advance Notice of Proposed Rulemaking [*Also, ANPRM*] [*US Government agencies*] ... ANPR
Advance Notice of Proposed Rulemaking [*Also, ANPR*] [*US Government agencies*] ... ANPRM
Advance of Pay and Allowances (AABC) ... APA
Advance Opinions [*A publication*] (DLA) ... Adv Ops
Advance Opinions in Lawyers' Edition of United States Reports [*A publication*] (DLA) ... Adv O
Advance Ordering Information ... AOI
Advance Paradigm, Inc. [*NASDAQ symbol*] (SAG) ... ADVP
Advance Paradigm, Inc. [*Associated Press*] (SAG) ... AdvPara
Advance Pay (MCD) ... AP
Advance Payment [*Finance*] ... ADVPMT
Advance Payment of Dislocation Allowance to Dependents [*Air Force*] (AFM) ... ADVDLA-DEP
Advance Payment of Mileage Authorized [*Army*] ... APMA
Advance Payment of Monetary Allowance in Lieu of Transportation Authorized (SAUS) ... APMA
Advance Payment of Monetary Allowance in Lieu of Transportation Is Authorized [*Army*] ... APMALTA
Advance Payment of Subsistence and Quarters ... APSQ
Advance Payment of Travel per Diem Authorized [*Army*] ... APTPDA
Advance Payment Plan (SAUS) ... APP
Advance Payment Plan [*Airlines*] ... APX
Advance Performance Algorithm (AAEL) ... APA
Advance Performance Interceptor (SAUS) ... API
Advance Personnel Requirements Research Note (SAUS) ... APPRN
Advance Personnel Requirements Research Note ... APRRN
Advance Planning Group (SAUO) ... APG
Advance Planning Procedure Change (SAA) ... APPC
Advance Planning Procurement Information [*Army*] (MCD) ... APPI
Advance Port Purchase [*Investment term*] (ECON) ... APP
Advance Post Office Check [*Bureau of the Census*] (GFGA) ... APOC
Advance Prediction Computer Program ... APCP
Advance Preparation (SAUS) ... AP
Advance Process Engineering Order [*Manufacturing*] (MCD) ... APEO
Advance Procurement Data Worksheets [*Air Force*] (AFIT) ... APDW
Advance Procurement List (MCD) ... APL
Advance Procurement Plan [*Navy*] ... APP
Advance Procurement Plan (AAGC) ... AP Plan
Advance Procurement Planning Council [*DoD*] (PDAA) ... APPC
Advance Production Release (NRCH) ... APR
Advance Program Feature (SAUS) ... APF
Advance Programming and Proposal Operations (SAUS) ... AP&PO
Advance Programming and Proposal Operations (MCD) ... AP & PO
Advance Purchase Excursion Fare [*Aviation*] (DA) ... APEX
Advance Purchase Required [*Also, AP*] [*Airline fare code*] ... AB
Advance Purchase Required [*Also, AB*] [*Airline fare code*] ... AP
Advance RADAR Maintenance Target Set (DWSG) ... ARMTS
Advance Ratio Design Co. Inc. (SAUO) ... ARDCO
Advance Reading (SAUS) ... AR
Advance Reading Copy [*Publishing*] (WDMC) ... ARC
Advance Release [*Military*] ... ADVR
Advance Release (SAUS) ... AR
Advance Release Record (AAG) ... ARR
Advance Remote Display System [*Computer science*] (PDAA) ... ARDS
Advance Research Projects Agency Network [*Australia*] ... ARPNET
Advance Ross Corp. [*Associated Press*] (SAG) ... AdvRoss
Advance Ross Corp. [*NASDAQ symbol*] (NQ) ... AROS
Advance Sciences, Inc. (GAAI) ... ASI
Advance Section (SAUO) ... ADSEC
Advance Section [*Military*] ... AD SEC
Advance Selector (SAUS) ... AS
Advance Sensor Development Program [*Military*] (MCD) ... ASDP
Advance Services of Supply [*Army*] ... ADSOS
Advance Sheet (DLA) ... Ad Sh
Advance Sheet (DLA) ... Adv Sh
Advance Simulation Facility Interconnection and Setup System [*or Subsystem*] [*Air Force*] ... ASFISS
Advance Space System Hardening (MCD) ... ASSH
Advance Space Vehicle Engineering Operation (SAUS) ... ASVEO
Advance Spaceborne Thermal Emission and Reflectance Radiometer ... ASTER
Advance Stack Network Management [*Computer science*] (VERA) ... ASNM
Advance STOL [*Short Takeoff and Landing*] **Transport (Medium)** [*Aviation*] (MCD) ... ASTM
Advance Stoppage (MUGU) ... ADVST
Advance Strike Gully [*Mining engineering*] ... ASG
Advance Study Response [*Psychology*] (DHP) ... ASR
Advance Supplement Testing Systems ... ASTS
Advance Surface-to-Air Weapons System ... ASAWS
Advance Synthetic Aperture RADAR System (MCD) ... ASARS
Advance Tax Rulings [*Also, Tax Advance Rulings*] [*Database*] (IID) ... ATR
Advance Technical Requirements (MCD) ... ATR
Advance Technology Alert System [*United Nations*] (DUND) ... ATAS
Advance Technology Corp. (SAUO) ... ATC
Advance telegraphic notification relating to the operation of the Marine Meteorological Services (SAUS) ... WIFMA
Advance telegraphic notification relating to the operation of WWW (SAUS) ... METNO
Advance Test Plant (AAG) ... ATP
Advance to Minister for Finance (SAUO) ... AMF
Advance Tracker Prototype (IUSS) ... ATP
Advance Transportation Control and Movement Document ... ATCMD
Advance Warfighting Experiment (SAUS) ... AWE
Advance Warning Equipment (SAUS) ... AWARE
Advance Weapon Ammunition Support Point ... AWASP
Advance Winding (SAUS) ... AW
Advanced ... ADV
Advanced ... ADVNCD
Advanced Academic Degree (AFM) ... AAD
Advanced Academic Degree Management System (AFM) ... AADMS
Advanced Accounting System ... AAS
Advanced Acoustic Decoy [*Military*] (IUSS) ... AAD
Advanced Acoustic Search Sensor (SAUS) ... AASS
Advanced Acoustic Search Sensors (MCD) ... AASS
Advanced Acquisition Plan (MCD) ... AAP
Advanced Acquisition Planning System (ACAE) ... AAPS
Advanced Action Manipulator System ... ADAMS
Advanced Action Taken (SAUS) ... ADTAK
Advanced Active Microwave Instruments (SAUS) ... AAMI
Advanced Active Sonobuoy (MCD) ... AAS
Advanced Adaptive Control (SSD) ... AAC
Advanced Adaptive Protocol (SAUS) ... AAP

Advanced Address Space Facility [*IBM*] [*Computer science*] (CIST) .... AASF
Advanced Administration System (SAUS) .... AAS
Advanced Administrative System [*IBM Corp.*] .... AAS
Advanced AERA Concepts [*FAA*] (TAG) .... AAC
Advanced Aerial Armed Recon-naissance Vehicle (SAUS) A3RV
Advanced Aerial Fire Support System [*Military*] (IUSS) .... AAFS
Advanced Aerial Fire Support System [*Army*] .... AAFSS
Advanced Aerial Fire Support System Office [*Army*] (MCD) .... AAFSSO
Advanced Aerial Gunnery TOW Target System .... AAGTTS
Advanced Aerial Refuelling Boom (SAUS) .... AARB
Advanced Aerial System (SAUS) .... AAS
Advanced Aerodynamics & Structures, Inc. [*Associated Press*] (SAG) .... AA&S
Advanced Aerodynamics and Structures, Inc. (ECON) .... AASI
Advanced Aerodynamics & Structures, Inc. [*Associated Press*] (SAG) .... AdA&S
Advanced Aerodynamics & Structures, Inc. [*Associated Press*] (SAG) .... AdvA&S
Advanced Aerospace Vehicle (MCD) .... AAV
Advanced Aero-Wing Systems Corp. [*Vancouver Stock Exchange symbol*] .... AAS
Advanced Air Cycle Machine (MCD) .... AACM
Advanced Air Defense Electro-Optic Sensor [*Army*] .... AADEOS
Advanced Air Defense Electro-Optical System (SAUS) .... AADEOS
Advanced Air Defense System .... AADS
Advanced Air Defense Weapon .... AADW
Advanced Air Depot Area [*Air Force*] .... AADA
Advanced Air Park (SAUS) .... AAP
Advanced Air Refueling Boom [*Air Force*] (MCD) .... AARB
Advanced Air Station (DAS) .... AAS
Advanced Air Striking Force [*British*] .... AASF
Advanced Air Striking Force (SAUO) .... AASF
Advanced Air to Air Missile Launch Envelope (ACAE) .... AAAMLE
Advanced Air Traffic Management System [*Department of Transportation*] .... AATMS
Advanced Air Traffic Management Systems (SAUS) .... AATMS
Advanced Air Training Base (SAUO) .... AATB
Advanced Air Training Command [*Military*] .... AATC
Advanced Airborne Anti-Armour Weapon (SAUS) .... AAAW
Advanced Airborne Command Post .... AABCP
Advanced Airborne Command Post .... AACP
Advanced Airborne Computer (SAUS) .... AAC
Advanced Airborne Demonstrator .... AAD
Advanced Airborne Digital Computer (SAUS) .... AADC
Advanced Airborne Expendable Decoy (SAUS) .... AAED
Advanced Airborne Expendable Decoy and Launcher Control (DWSG) .... AED & LC
Advanced Airborne Flight Experiment (SAUS) .... AAFE
Advanced Airborne Launch Center (MCD) .... AALC
Advanced Airborne Long Range Interceptor (ACAE) .... ALRI
Advanced Airborne Multispectral Scanner (SAUS) .... AMSS
Advanced Airborne National Command Post (DOMA) .... AABNCP
Advanced Airborne National Command Post [*Air Force*] (PDAA) .... AANCP
Advanced Airborne RADAR System (MCD) .... AARS
Advanced Airborne Radar System (SAUS) .... AARS
Advanced Airborne Radio Position Location System [*Army*] (MCD) .... AARPLS
Advanced Airborne Remote Instrumentation (SAUS) .... AARI
Advanced Airborne Signal Reconnaissance (ACAE) .... AASRS
Advanced Airborne Surveillance Antenna (ACAE) .... AASA
Advanced Airborne Surveillance Radar (ACAE) .... AASR
Advanced Airborne Surveillance Sensor (MCD) .... AASS
Advanced Airburst Fuze (ACAE) .... AAF
Advanced Airburst Fuze System (ACAE) .... AAFS
Advanced Aircraft Anti Submarine Avionics (ACAE) .... AASWA
Advanced Aircraft Concept Formulation (ACAE) .... AACF
Advanced Aircraft Early Warning RADAR (MCD) .... AAEWR
Advanced Aircraft Early Warning Radar (SAUS) .... AAEWR
Advanced Aircraft Electrical System [*Navy*] .... AAES
Advanced Aircraft Programs Office .... AAPO
Advanced Aircrew Escape/rescue Capability (SAUS) .... AERCAB
Advanced Aircrew Mask (ACAE) .... ADAM
Advanced Airframe Assembly Program [*Aviation*] .... AAAP
Advanced Air-Launched Anti-Armor Weapon [*Military*] (MUSM) .... AALAW
Advanced Air-Launched Anti-Armour Weapon (SAUS) .... AALAAW
Advanced Air-Launched Missile (MCD) .... AALM
Advanced Air-Launched Motor (MCD) .... AALM
Advanced Airport Ground Traffic Control System (ACAE) .... AGTC
Advanced Air-to-Air Missile [*Military*] .... AAAM
Advanced Air-to-Surface Missile (MCD) .... AASM
Advanced Air-to-Surface Missile Seeker [*Navy*] (MCD) .... AASMS
Advanced Algebra (SAUS) .... AA
Advanced Allied Headquarters [*World War II*] .... AAHQ
Advanced Allied Headquarters (SAUO) .... AAHQ
Advanced Along Track Scanning Radiometer .... AATSR
Advanced Alternative Minuteman Defense Study [*Military*] .... AAMDS
Advanced Ammunition Depot .... AAD
Advanced Amphibious Assault [*Marine Corps*] (DOMA) .... AAA
Advanced Amphibious Assault Vehicle [*Marine Corps*] .... AAAV
Advanced Amphibious Training Base [*Navy*] .... AATB
Advanced Analytical (SAUS) .... AA
Advanced and Applied Concepts Office [*MERDC*] [*Army*] .... AACO
Advanced Animal Breeder (journ.) (SAUS) .... Adv Anim Breed
Advanced Antenna System [*Air Force*] .... AAS
Advanced Anthracite Technology and Research. Proceedings of the Conference (journ.) (SAUS) .... Adv Anthracite Technol Res Proc Conf
Advanced Anti Armor Weapon System (ACAE) .... AAAWS
Advanced Anti-Aircraft and Anti-Tank Guided-Missile System (ECON) .... ADATS
Advanced Anti-Armor Missile Systems (SAUS) .... AAAMS
Advanced Antiarmor Vehicle Evaluation Test (RDA) .... ARMVAL
Advanced Antiarmor Weapon System, Medium [*Army*] (INF) .... AAWS-M
Advanced Antiradiation Missile (MCD) .... AARM
Advanced Anti-Radiation Missile (SAUS) .... AARM
Advanced Anti-Satellite (SAUS) .... AA-SAT
Advanced Antisubmarine Rocket (SAA) .... AASROC
Advanced Antisubmarine Warfare Exercise (NVT) .... ADEX
Advanced Antitank Missile System (MCD) .... AAMS
Advanced Antitank Weapon [*Army*] (MCD) .... AATW
Advanced Anti-Tank Weapon (SAUS) .... AATW
Advanced Anti-tank Weapon System (SAUS) .... AAWS
Advanced Antitank Weapon System - Heavy .... AAWS-H
Advanced Antitank Weapon System - Medium [*Pronounced "awesome"*] (RDA) .... AAWS-M
Advanced Antitank Weapon System-Heavy (SAUS) .... AAWS-H
Advanced Antitank Weapon System-Medium (SAUS) .... AAWS-M
Advanced APC (SAUS) .... AAPC
Advanced Application Rotary Launcher (DWSG) .... AARL
Advanced Applications and Research Laboratory (SAUS) .... AARL
Advanced Applications Consultants Inc. (SAUO) .... AACI
Advanced Applications Flight Equipment (MCD) .... AAFE
Advanced Applications Flight Experiment Radiometer-Scatterometer Sensor [*Aviation*] (PDAA) .... AAFE RADSCAT
Advanced Applications Flight Experiments [*NASA*] (MCD) .... AAFE
Advanced Applications Research Laboratory (SAUO) .... AARL
Advanced Applications Rotary Launcher (SAUS) .... AARL
Advanced Architecture Microprocessor (MCD) .... AAMP
Advanced Army Airborne Indicating System (SAUS) .... AAAIS
Advanced Army Aircraft Instrument System (MCD) .... AAAIS
Advanced Army Aircraft Instrumentation Program (SAUO) .... AAAIP
Advanced Army Aircraft Instrumentation Program (SAUS) .... AAAIP
Advanced Army Aircraft Instrumentation System (SAUS) .... AAAIS
Advanced (Army) Base Supply Depot (SAUO) .... ABSD
Advanced Army Defense System (SAUS) .... AADS
Advanced Army System Requirements .... AASR
Advanced Array Sensor [*Military*] (IUSS) .... AAS
Advanced Assembly Outline (MCD) .... AAO
Advanced Assembly Sequence Record Sheet (MCD) .... ASRS
Advanced Atmosphere Sounder and Imaging Radiometer (SAUS) .... AASIR
Advanced Atmospheric Burst Location (MCD) .... AABL
Advanced Atmospheric Sounder and Imaging Radiometer [*NASA*] (NASA) .... AAIR
Advanced Atmospheric Sounder and Imaging Radiometer [*NASA*] (MCD) .... AASIR
Advanced Atmospheric Sounder Imaging (ACAE) .... AASI
Advanced Atmospheric Sounding and Imaging Radiometer (SAUS) .... AASIR
Advanced Attack Aircraft (CAAL) .... AAA
Advanced Attack Aircraft [*Military*] (MUSM) .... AX
Advanced Attack Airframe [*Army*] .... AAAF
Advanced Attack Helicopter [*Army*] .... AAH
Advanced Attack Helicopter TOW Missile Equipment (ACAE) .... AAHTME
Advanced Authoring Format [*Computer science*] .... AAF
Advanced Authoring Tools (SAUS) .... AAT
Advanced Automated Directional Solidification Furnace [*Materials processing*] .... AADSF
Advanced Automated Sample Processor .... AASP
Advanced Automated System .... AAS
Advanced Automatic Compilation System [*Computer science*] (MHDI) .... AACS
Advanced Automatic Film Titles System (MCD) .... AAFTS
Advanced Automatic Flight Control System (MCD) .... AAFCS
Advanced Automatic Monitoring System (ACAE) .... AAMS
Advanced Automation [*FAA*] (TAG) .... AAP
Advanced Automation Research Laboratory [*Purdue University*] .... AARL
Advanced Automation System .... AAS
Advanced Automative Power Systems Program (SAUS) .... AAPSP
Advanced Automotive Power System (SAUS) .... AAPS
Advanced Automotive Power Systems .... AAPS
Advanced Automotive Power Systems Program (SAUO) .... AAPSP
Advanced Aviation Base Ship [*Navy symbol*] [*Obsolete*] .... AVB
Advanced Aviation Forward Area Refueling System (SAUS) .... AAFARS
Advanced Aviation Transportation Technology (GAVI) .... AATT
Advanced Avionic Display Processor (MCD) .... AADP
Advanced Avionic Fault Isolation System [*Navy*] (MCD) .... AAFIS
Advanced Avionic System (MCD) .... AAS
Advanced Avionic System for Multi-Mission Application (MCD) .... AASMMA
Advanced Avionic Systems for Multi-Mission Application (PDAA) .... AASMA
Advanced Avionics Architecture (SAUS) A3
Advanced Avionics Data Handling System [*Air Force*] (MCD) .... AADHS
Advanced Avionics Digital Computer [*Naval Air Systems Command*] .... AADC
Advanced Avionics Interface Program (SAUO) .... AAIP
Advanced Avionics Test Bed [*The Boeing Co.*] .... AAT
Advanced Avionics Testbed (SAUS) .... AAT
Advanced Backplane Technology (SAUS) .... ABT
Advanced Ballistic Computer (SAUS) .... ABC
Advanced Ballistic Missile Defense [*Army*] .... ABMD
Advanced Ballistic Missile Defense Agency [*Alexandria, VA*] [*Army*] .... ABMDA
Advanced Ballistic Missile Systems (KSC) .... ABMS
Advanced Ballistic Reentry System .... ABRES
Advanced Ballistic Reentry System (SAUS) .... Abres
Advanced Ballistic Reentry Vehicle (MCD) .... ABRV
Advanced Ballistics Concepts [*Air Force*] (MCD) .... ABC
Advanced Ballistic-Type Logistic Spacecraft System (MCD) .... ABLSS
Advanced Ballistic-type Logistic Spacecraft System (SAUS) .... ABLSS
Advanced Baltistic Re-Entry System (SAUS) .... ABRES
Advanced Banking On-line System (SAUS) .... ABOS
Advanced Banking On-Line System (BUR) .... ABOS

Advanced Base (SAUS) .... Adv Bse
Advanced Base Air Task Unit (SAUS) .... ABATU
Advanced Base Aviation Training Unit [*Navy*] .... ABATU
Advanced Base Camp (SAUS) .... ABC
Advanced Base Combat Communication Training Center (SAUS) .... ABCCTC
Advanced Base Combat Communication Training Center [*Pearl Harbor*] .... ABCCTC
Advanced Base Combat Communications Training Center (SAUO) .... ABCCTC
Advanced Base Components [*Military*] .... ABCO
Advanced Base Construction Depot .... ABCD
Advanced Base Depot [*or Dock*] [*Obsolete*] [*Navy*] .... ABD
Advanced Base Depot Area Command (SAUO) .... ABADACOM
Advanced Base Depot Area Command .... ABDACOM
Advanced Base Functional Component [*Military*] .... ABFC
Advanced Base Functional Component System [*Military*] .... ABFCS
Advanced Base Hospital [*British*] .... ABH
Advanced Base Hospital (SAUO) .... ABH
Advanced Base Initial Outfitting List [*Military*] .... ABIOL
Advanced Base Initial Outfitting List (SAUS) .... ABSIOL
Advanced Base Initial Support Lists [*Navy*] (AFIT) .... ABISL
Advanced Base Ordnance Depot (SAUO) .... ABOD
Advanced Base Ordnance Depot (SAUO) .... AdvBOD
Advanced Base Personnel Administration .... ABPA
Advanced Base Personnel Officer .... ABPO
Advanced Base Personnel Unit .... ABPU
Advanced Base Proving Ground .... ABPG
Advanced Base Receiving Barracks .... ABRB
Advanced Base Receiving Depot .... ABRD
Advanced Base Repair Depot .... ABRD
Advanced Base Reshipment Depot .... ABRD
Advanced Base Supply Depot .... ABSD
Advanced Base Support Aircraft (SAUS) .... ABSA
Advanced Base Torpedo Unit [*Navy*] .... ABTU
Advanced Base Training Unit [*Navy*] .... ABTU
Advanced Base Workshop (SAUO) .... ABW
Advanced Basic Input Output System (SAUS) .... ABIOS
Advanced Basic Input/Output System [*Computer science*] (DOM) .... ABIOS
advanced battalion headquarters (SAUO) .... Adv Bn Hq
Advanced [*or Alternate*] **Battery Acquisition RADAR** .... ABAR
Advanced Battlefield Computer Simulation (SAUS) .... ABACUS
Advanced Battlefield Simulation (RDA) .... ABS
Advanced Beach Signal Station (IAA) .... ABSS
Advanced Beam Control System (SAUS) .... ABCS
Advanced Beamformer (MCD) .... ABF
Advanced Beam-Former (SAUS) .... ABF
Advanced Beam-Weapon Concept Definition (ACAE) .... ABCD
Advanced Beam-Weapon Concept Evaluation Study (ACAE) .... ACES
Advanced Beef Breeds Federation (EA) .... ABBF
Advanced BiCMOS Technology (SAUS) .... ABT
Advanced BiCMOS Technology/ Enhanced Transceiver Logic (SAUS) .... ABTE/ETL
Advanced Bill of Material [*Accounting*] (AAG) .... ABM
Advanced Bio-Mechanical Linkage Enablement [*Rehabilitation technology*] .... ABLE
Advanced Bio-mechanical Linkage Enablement (SAUS) .... ABLE
Advanced Biomedical Capsule .... ABC
Advanced Biophysical Research Accelerator (BARN) .... ABRA
Advanced BIOS (SAUS) .... ABIOS
Advanced Biotechnologies Inc. (SAUO) .... ABI
Advanced Biotechnologies, Inc. .... ABI
Advanced Bipolar and CMOS (SAUS) .... ABCMOS
Advanced Blade Concept Advancing (SAUS) .... ABC
Advanced Blown Lift Enhancement (MCD) .... ABLE
Advanced Boiling Water Reactor .... ABWR
Advanced Bomb Family [*Navy*] (DOMA) .... ABF
Advanced Bombardment Sub-System (SAUS) .... ABOSS
Advanced Bombardment System .... ABOSS
Advanced Book Exchange (SAUS) .... ABE
Advanced Booking Charter (SAUS) .... ABC
Advanced Booking Charters [*Travel industry*] (TRID) .... ABC
Advanced Boolean Expression Language (VERA) .... ABEL
Advanced Boost Phase Track Satellite .... ABPTS
Advanced Booster Technology (MCD) .... ABT
Advanced Boresight Equipment [*Army*] .... ABE
Advanced Brake Control System (MCD) .... ABCS
Advanced Branch [*Training*] [*Military*] (DNAB) .... ADV-BR
Advanced Breast Biopsy Instrumentation [*Medicine*] .... ABBI
Advanced Breast Cancer [*Medicine*] .... ABC
Advanced Bridge Erection Boat (SAUS) .... ABEB
Advanced Building Block for Large Area Exploitation (ACAE) .... ABLE
Advanced Built-In Test (SAUS) .... ABIT
Advanced Bus Interface (SAUS) .... ABI
Advanced Business Application Programming (SAUS) .... ABAP
Advanced Business Application Programming/4 (VERA) ABAP4
Advanced Business Communications, Inc. [*McLean, VA*] [*Telecommunications*] (TSSD) .... ABCI
Advanced Business Communications Inc. (SAUS) .... ABCI
Advanced Business Communications Incorporated (SAUO) .... ABCI
Advanced Business Communications via Satellite (SAUS) .... ABCS
Advanced Business Processor [*Datapoint Corp.*] .... ABP
Advanced Business Unit (SAUS) .... ABU
Advanced Byte-Oriented [*Computer science*] (HGAA) .... ABO
Advanced C3 Systems Laboratory (ACAE) AC3SL
Advanced Cab and Visual System [*Army*] (RDA) .... ACAVS
Advanced Cabin Entertainment and Services System [*Aircraft*] .... ACESS
Advanced Cabin Interphone System (ACAE) .... ACIS
Advanced Cableship Navigation Aid System (TEL) .... ACNAS
Advanced Calculator Attachment (SAUS) .... ACA
Advanced Capabilities Anti-Radar Missile (SAUS) .... ADCAPARM
Advanced Capabilities RADAR .... ACR
Advanced Capabilities Radar (SAUS) .... ACR
Advanced Capability .... ADCAP
Advanced Capability Tanker (MCD) .... ACT
Advanced Capabiltiy Torpedo [*Military*] (MUSM) .... ADCAP
Advanced Carbon-Carbon (MCD) .... ACC
Advanced Card Technology Association of Canada (AC) .... ACT Canada
Advanced Cardiac Life Support (CMD) .... ACLS
Advanced Cardiac Life Support System .... ACLS
Advanced Cardiovascular Systems .... ACS
Advanced Career Training .... ACT
Advanced Cargo Aircraft .... ACA
Advanced Cargo Rotorcraft [*Later, Advanced Cargo Aircraft - ACA*] .... ACR
Advanced Cargo Rotorcraft (SAUS) .... ACR
Advanced Cargo Vehicle (SAUS) .... ACV
Advanced Cargo/Tanker Aircraft .... ACTA
Advanced Carry-on ELINT/ESM Suite (SAUS) .... ACES
Advanced Cartographic Data Digitizing System (MCD) .... ACDDS
Advanced Cartographic Environment (GEOI) .... ACE
Advanced Cartographic Equipment (GEOI) .... ACE
Advanced Cartographic Systems (GEOI) .... ACS
Advanced Cathode Ray Tube Controller (SAUS) .... ACRTC
Advanced CCD Imaging Spectrometer (SAUS) .... ACIS
Advanced Cell Technology .... ACT
Advanced Cell Technology, Inc. .... ACT
Advanced Central Interface Unit (SAUS) .... ACIU
Advanced Ceramic System .... ACS
Advanced Certificate (PGP) .... AC
Advanced Certificate (PGP) .... Adv C
Advanced Certificate .... AdvCert
Advanced Certificate in Applied Management Communication .... AdvCertApplMgtComm
Advanced Certificate in Banking and Finance .... AdvCertBankFin
Advanced Certificate in Building Construction .... AdvCertBuildCons
Advanced Certificate in Building Inspection .... AdvCertBuildInsp
Advanced Certificate in Customs Agent Procedures .... AdvCertCustomsAgProc
Advanced Certificate in Education (GAGS) .... ACE
Advanced Certificate in Education .... Adv Cert in Ed
Advanced Certificate in Estate Agency .... AdvCertEstateAg
Advanced Certificate in Furniture Production .... AdvCertFurnProd
Advanced Certificate in Management .... AdvCertMgt
Advanced Certificate in Music Education .... Adv Cert in Mus Ed
Advanced Certificate in Office Management .... AdvCertOffMgt
Advanced Certificate in Personnel .... AdvCertPers
Advanced Certificate in Sales Management .... AdvCertSalesMgt
Advanced Certificate of Education (AIE) .... ACE
Advanced Certificate of the Welsh College of Music and Drama [*British*] (DBQ) .... WCMD
Advanced Certification [*Canadian Association of Medical Radiation Technologists*] (ASC) .... AC
Advanced Certified Fund Raising Executive [*National Society of Fund Raising Executives*] .... ACFRE
Advanced Chain Home [*RADAR*] .... ACH
Advanced Change In Design (SAUS) .... ACID
Advanced Change Study Notice [*Aerospace*] .... ACSN
Advanced Channel Service Unit (CIST) .... ACSU
Advanced Channel Testing System (SAUS) .... ACTS
Advanced Charged Coupled Mosaics (ACAE) .... ACCM
Advanced Chassis Technology [*Automotive engineering*] .... ACT
Advanced Chemical Agent Detector Alarm (MCD) .... ACADA
Advanced Chemical Defense Aircrew Respirator (ACAE) .... ACDAR
Advanced Chemical Diagnostics Facility (SAUS) .... ACDF
Advanced Chemical Rocket Engine [*Air Force*] .... ACRE
Advanced Chemistry Development .... ACD
Advanced Chip Interconnect [*Computer science*] .... ACI
Advanced Circuit Design (SAUS) .... ACD
Advanced Circuit Module .... ACM
Advanced Circuit Packaging Extended (SAUS) .... ACPX
Advanced Circuits International (SAUS) .... ACI
Advanced Circular Scan Thermal Imaging System (MCD) .... ACSTIS
Advanced Circular Scan Thermal Imaging System (MCD) .... ACTIS
Advanced Civil Schooling [*Army*] (INF) .... ACS
Advanced Civilian Earth Remote Sensing System (SAUS) .... ACERSS
Advanced Civilian Technology Agency (AAGC) .... ACTA
Advanced Civil/Military Aircraft (MCD) .... ACMA
Advanced Clean Emission [*Automotive engineering*] .... ACE
Advanced Climate Model (SAUS) .... ACM
Advanced Clothing Subsystem [*SIPE*] [*Military*] (RDA) .... ACS
Advanced CMOS Logic [*Texas Instruments, Inc.*] .... ACL
Advanced CMOS logic using TTL voltage levels (SAUS) .... ACT
Advanced CMOS logic using TTL voltage levels (SAUS) ACT11
Advanced CMOS logic with center ground and power pins (SAUS) AC11
Advanced Coastal Zone Color Scanner (MCD) .... ACZCS
Advanced Coherent Deception Countermeasure (MCD) .... ACDC
Advanced Collaborative Filtering [*Firefly Network*] [*Computer science*] .... ACF
Advanced Collective Protection Shelter (ACAE) .... ACPS
Advanced Color Technology Inc. (SAUO) .... ACT
Advanced Color Technology, Inc. [*Chelmsford, MA*] [*Printer manufacturer*] .... ACT
Advanced Color Work Station (SAUS) .... ACWS
Advanced Combat Air Patrol (MCD) .... ACAP
Advanced Combat Aircraft (MCD) .... ACA

Advanced Combat Arms Team Trainer (ACAE) ACATT
Advanced Combat Direction System (MCD) ACDS
Advanced Combat Experimental (SAUS) ACX
Advanced Combat Optical Gunsight [*Military*] (INF) ACOG
Advanced Combat Rifle [*Military*] (INF) ACR
Advanced Combat Surveillance RADAR ACSR
Advanced Combat Surveillance Radar (SAUS) ACSR
Advanced Combat Training Academy [*Army*] (AABC) ACTA
Advanced Combustion Engineering ACE
Advanced Command (SAUS) ADCOM
Advanced Command and Control Architectural Testbed (MCD) ACCAT
Advanced Command Data System (NG) ACDS
Advanced Common Intercept Missile (MCD) ACIM
Advanced Common Intercept Missile Demonstration (MCD) ACIMD
Advanced Communication and Timekeeping Technology [*Seiko Telecommunications Systems*] [*FM data receiver chip set*] (PCM) ACTT
Advanced Communication Enhancement [*Multimedia modem*] [*Telecommunications*] (PCM) ACE
Advanced Communication Facility ACF
Advanced Communication for Training (SAUS) ACT
Advanced Communication Function (SAUS) ACF
Advanced Communication Function/ Virtual Terminal Access Method (SAUS) ACF/VTAM
Advanced Communication Function/Telecommunications Access Method (SAUS) ACFTCAM
Advanced Communication System [*Computer science*] (TNIG) ACS
Advanced Communication Technology Satellite Program [*Office of Space Scie nce and Applications*] [*Washington, DC*] [*NASA*] (GRD) ACTS
Advanced Communication Technology Satellite Program (SAUS) ACTS
Advanced Communications (DNAB) ADCOM
Advanced Communications Control System (CAAL) ACCS
Advanced Communications Corporation (ACAE) ACC
Advanced Communications Course (SAUS) ACC
Advanced Communications Electronics Requirements Plan (SAUS) ACERP
Advanced Communications Equipment Depot (NATG) ACED
Advanced Communications Function [*IBM Corp.*] [*Computer science*] ACF
Advanced Communications Function for the Telecommunications Access Method (ITCA) ACF/TCAM
Advanced Communications Function for the Virtual Telecommunications Access Method Entry (ITCA) ACF/VTAME
Advanced Communications Function/Network Control Program (ITCA) ACF/NCP
Advanced Communications Group [*NYSE symbol*] ADG
Advanced Communications Grp. [*NYSE symbol*] (SG) ADG
Advanced Communications Interface [*Computer science*] (DGA) ACI
Advanced Communications Network Service (MHDI) ACNS
Advanced Communications Processor (ACAE) ACP
Advanced Communications Satellite (ACAE) ACS
Advanced Communications Service [*Later, AIS*] [*AT & T*] ACS
Advanced Communications Support System [*Sytek, Inc.*] [*Computer science*] (TNIG) ACSS
Advanced Communications System (SAUS) ACS
Advanced Communications Technol-ogies and Services (SAUS) ACTS
Advanced Communications Technologies and Services (VERA) ACTS
Advanced Communications Technology [*Tymshare, Inc.*] ACT
Advanced Communications Tracking Satellite (SAUS) ACTS
Advanced Communications-Electronics Requirements Plan [*Air Force*] ACERP
Advanced Compact Thermal Imaging System (SAUS) ACTIS
Advanced Compatible Television [*Wide-screen, high-resolution system utilizing standard broadcast channels*] [*RCA Corp.*] ACTV
Advanced Compilation Equipment (MCD) ACE
Advanced Complementory Metal Oxide Semiconductor (SAUS) ACMOS
Advanced Composite Aircraft Primary Structure (ACAE) ACAPS
Advanced Composite Aircraft Program (SAUS) ACAP
Advanced Composite Airframe Program [*Air Force*] ACAP
Advanced Composite Cost Estimating Model (MCD) ACCEM
Advanced Composite Materials Corporation (SAUO) ACMC
Advanced Composite Products, Inc. ACP
Advanced Composite Technology [*Materials science*] ACT
Advanced Composite Thermoplastic (SAUS) ACTP
Advanced Composite Vertical Fin (MCD) ACVF
Advanced Composite Vertical Fine (SAUS) ACVF
Advanced Composite Wing Cover-to-Substructure Attachment (MCD) CTSA
Advanced Composites Programs Office (SAUS) ACPO
Advanced Composites Technology Transfer Consortium ACTTC
Advanced Composition Explorer [*Satellite*] [*NASA*] (USDC) ACE
Advanced Compound Engine ACE
Advanced Computational Element (MCD) ACE
Advanced Computational Facility (ACAE) ACF
Advanced Computational Processor ACP
Advanced Computer Applications (CARB) ACA
Advanced Computer Audit Techniques [*Arthur Andersen & Co.*] ACAT
Advanced Computer Communications [*Santa Barbara, CA*] ACC
Advanced Computer Environmental Systems Support Inc. (SAUO) ACESS
Advanced Computer Environmental Systems Support, Inc. (SAUS) ACESS
Advanced Computer Flight Plan [*Air Force*] (GFGA) ACFP
Advanced Computer for Array Processing ACAP
Advanced Computer for Medical Research [*Stanford University*] ACME
Advanced Computer for Medical Research (SAUS) ACMR
Advanced Computer Image Generator (MCD) ACIG
Advanced Computer Oriented System (BUR) ACOS
Advanced Computer Program Multiple Array Processor System ACMAPS
Advanced Computer Services [*Honeywell Information Systems*] (IEEE) ACS
Advanced Computer System [*IBM Corp.*] (IEEE) ACS
Advanced Computer System Interface (SAUS) ACSI
Advanced Computer Tape Standards Association (SAUO) ACTSA
Advanced Computer Technique (SAUO) ACT
Advanced Computer Technique Corporation (SAUO) ACTC
Advanced Computer Techniques (MCD) ACT
Advanced Computer Techniques Corporation (SAUO) ACT Corporation
Advanced Computer Techniques Project (KSC) ACTP
Advanced Computer Technology Project [*British*] (EECA) ACTP
Advanced Computer Training In a Versatile Environment (SAUS) ACTIVE
Advanced Computer Training Institute [*Springfield, VA*] ACTI
Advanced Computer-Aided Design ACAD
Advanced Computer-Oriented System (SAUS) ACOS
Advanced Computing Attachment (SAUS) ACA
Advanced Computing Center for the Arts and Design [*Ohio State University*] [*Research center*] (RCD) ACCAD
Advanced Computing Environment [*Personal computer standard*] (ECON) ACE
Advanced Computing Group [*Marine science*] (OSRA) ACG
Advanced Computing Initiative (SAUS) ACI
Advanced Computing Laboratory (SAUS) ACL
Advanced Computing Systems Professional and Technical Association (SAUS) USENIX
Advanced Concept and Technology Demonstration [*Military*] (RDA) ACTD
Advanced Concept Cost Model (MCD) ACCM
Advanced Concept Ejection Seat [*Aviation*] (MCD) ACES
Advanced Concept Escape System (MCD) ACES
Advanced Concept Excursion [*Army*] ACE
Advanced Concept Team (SAUO) ACT
Advanced Concept Technology Demonstration ACTD
Advanced Concept Technology Demonstration [*DoD*] ATCD
Advanced Concept Tire [*Firestone Tire & Rubber Co.*] ACT
Advanced Concept Train [*Aerospace*] ACT
Advanced Concepts and Engineering [*Military*] (IUSS) AC&E
Advanced Concepts and Missions Division [*NASA*] ACMD
Advanced Concepts and Technology Demonstration [*Military*] (INF) ACTD
Advanced Concepts and Technology II (SAUS) ACT II
Advanced Concepts and Technology Program [*Army*] (RDA) ACT
Advanced Concepts Center [*General Motors Corp.*] [*Automotive engineering*] ACC
Advanced Concepts Flight Simulator (GAVI) ACFS
Advanced Concepts for Ordnance ACORD
Advanced Concepts Group ACG
Advanced Concepts Missile (MCD) ACM
Advanced Concepts Team [*Army*] (RDA) ACT
Advanced Concepts Test (MCD) ACT
Advanced Conceptual Design (ABAC) ACD
Advanced Confidential Report (MCD) ACR
Advanced Configuration and Power Interface (PCM) ACPI
Advanced Configuration Management System ACMS
Advanced Conformal Antenna Technique ACAT
Advanced Conformal Submarine Acoustic Sensor ACSAS
Advanced Connector Unit [*Telecommunications*] (TSSD) ACU
Advanced Conservative Studies (SAUS) ACS
Advanced Construction Technology Show (SAUS) ACTS
[*The*] **Advanced Construction Technology Show** [*British*] (ITD) ACTS
Advanced Consumer Marketing ACM
Advanced Contingency Theater Sensor [*Military*] (DOMA) ACTS
Advanced Continuous Simulation Language [*Pronounced "axle"*] [*Computer science*] (CSR) ACSL
Advanced Continuous System Language (MCD) ACSL
Advanced Continuous Wave Acquisition Radar (ACAE) ACWAR
Advanced Contract Administrator ACA
Advanced Control Evaluation for Structures Facility (ACAE) ACES-I
Advanced Control Experiment (SAUS) ACE
Advanced Control Experiments (MCD) ACE
Advanced Control Function/Virtual Telecommunication Access Method (SAUS) ACF/VTAM
Advanced Control Function/Virtual Telecommunications Access Method [*IBM Corp.*] (NITA) ACF/Vtam
Advanced Control Programmer (SAUS) ADCP
Advanced [*Flight*] **Control Programmer** ADCP
Advanced Control Signal Processor [*For spacecraft*] ACSP
Advanced Control System [*IBM Corp.*] (NITA) ACS
Advanced Control Technology for Integrated Vehicles (SAUS) ACTIVE
Advanced Control Technology Program [*Oak Ridge National Laboratory*] ACTP
Advanced Control Test Operation [*Oak Ridge National Laboratory*] ACTO
Advanced Controls Technology for Integrated Vehicles (ADWA) ACTIVE
Advanced Conventional Munitions ACM
Advanced Conventional Standoff Missile (MCD) ACSM
Advanced Conventional Stand-off Missile (SAUS) ACSM
Advanced Conventional Standoff Weapon ACSW
Advanced Conversion Technology (MCD) ACT
Advanced Converter Reactor [*Atomic energy*] ACR
Advanced Cooperative Countermeasure (MCD) ADCCM
Advanced Cooperative Countermeasure (MCD) ADCOM
Advanced Cooperative Project [*NASA*] ACP
Advanced Copies Delivered ACD
Advanced Core Performance Reactor (NRCH) ACPR
Advanced Core Pulsed Reactor (NRCH) ACPR
Advanced Core Test [*Nuclear energy*] ACT
Advanced Coronal Observing System (SAUS) ACOS
Advanced Coronary Treatment [*Cardiology*] (DAVI) ACT
Advanced Coronary Treatment Foundation ACT
Advanced Corporation Tax Act [*British*] (ECON) ACT
Advanced Cosmic-ray Composition Experiment for the Space Station (SAUS) ACCESS
Advanced Cost Management System (AAGC) ACMS

Advanced Count Switch (SAUS) ..... ACS
Advanced Counter Air Fighter (ACAE) ..... ACAF
Advanced CounterMeasure Systems [*Commercial firm*] (RDA) ..... ACMS
Advanced Countermeasures Dispenser System (SAUS) ..... ACDS
Advanced Course in Astrophysics (journ.) (SAUS) ..... Adv Course Astrophys
Advanced Course Studentships [*British*] ..... ACS
Advanced Course. Swiss Society of Astronomy and Astrophysics (journ.) (SAUS) ..... Adv Course Swiss Soc Astron Astrophys
Advanced Cracking Reactor [*Fuel technology*] ..... ACR
Advanced Credit Information System ..... ACIS
Advanced Credit Information System (SAUS) ..... ACIS
Advanced Crew Escape System (ACAE) ..... ACES
Advanced Crew-Served Weapon [*Army*] (INF) ..... ACSW
Advanced Critical Pulse Reactor [*Nuclear energy*] ..... ACPR
Advanced CRT Controller [*Computer chip*] ..... ACRTC
Advanced Cruise Missile ..... ACM
Advanced Cruise Missile Combustor (MCD) ..... ACMC
Advanced Cruise Missile Program [*Navy*] ..... ACMP
Advanced Cruise Missile Technology (MCD) ..... ACMT
Advanced Cruiser (SAUS) ..... AK
Advanced Cryogenic Rocket Engineering (PDAA) ..... ACRE
Advanced Cryogenics (journ.) (SAUS) ..... Adv Cryog
Advanced Cryptographic System [*Air Force*] (MCD) ..... ACS
Advanced Data Access Method [*Computer science*] (IAA) ..... ADAM
Advanced Data Acquisition Routine [*Computer science*] (OA) ..... ADAR
Advanced Data Adapter/Processor Tester (SAUS) ..... ADAPT
Advanced Data and Picture Transformation System (SAUS) ..... ADAPTS
Advanced Data Broadcasting System (SAUS) ..... ADBS
Advanced Data Collection - Position Location (MCD) ..... ADC/PL
Advanced Data Collection and Location System ..... ADCLS
Advanced Data Collection-Position Location (SAUS) ..... ADC/PL
Advanced Data Communication for Stores (SAUS) ..... ADCS
Advanced Data Communication Protocol [*Computer science*] ..... ADCP
Advanced Data Communications [*Computer science*] (ECII) ..... ADC
Advanced Data Communications Control Procedure [*American National Standards Institute*] ..... ADCCP
Advanced Data Communications Utility [*IBM*] (CIST) ..... ADCU
Advanced Data Connector [*Computer science*] ..... ADC
Advanced Data Control (SAUS) ..... ADC
Advanced Data Controller (SAUS) ..... ADC
Advanced Data Delivery System (ACAE) ..... ADDS
Advanced Data Dictionary System (ITCA) ..... ADDS
Advanced Data Display System (DNAB) ..... ADDS
Advanced Data Entry ..... ADE
Advanced Data Entry Executive [*Computer science*] (CIST) ..... ADEX
Advanced Data Handling Inter-Service Working Party (SAUO) ..... ADHWP
Advanced Data Link Control [*Computer science*] ..... ADLC
Advanced Data Management ..... ADAM
Advanced Data Management [*Information service or system*] (IID) ..... ADM
Advanced Data Processing (NITA) ..... ADP
Advanced Data Processing (SAUS) ..... AQL
Advanced Data Processing Control Subsystem (ACAE) ..... ADPCS
Advanced Data Processing System Investigation (ACAE) ..... ADPSI
Advanced Data Scalar ..... ADS
Advanced Data System [*DoD*] ..... ADS
Advanced Data Technologies, Inc. (GEOI) ..... ADT
Advanced Database Linkages in Biotechnology (SAUO) ..... ADLIB
Advanced Database System ..... ADBS
Advanced Data-Base System (SAUS) ..... ADBS
Advanced Dated Remittances [*IRS*] ..... ADR
Advanced Debugging System ..... ADS
Advanced Deck-Launched Interceptor (MCD) ..... ADLI
Advanced Declassification Schedule (MCD) ..... ADS
Advanced Decoy Dispenser System (SAUS) ..... ADDS
Advanced Decoy Technology (SAA) ..... ADTEC
Advanced Decoy Technology (MCD) ..... ADTECH
Advanced Deep Diving Submersible ..... ADDS
Advanced Deep-Dive System (NVT) ..... ADS
Advanced Deep-dive System (SAUS) ..... ADS
Advanced Deep-Running Acoustic Torpedo (MCD) ..... ADRAT
Advanced Defence Radar Controller (SAUS) ..... ADRC
Advanced Defence Radar Unit (SAUS) ..... ADRU
Advanced Defense Communications Satellite [*Air Force*] (AFM) ..... ADCS
Advanced Defense Communications Satellite Program [*Air Force*] ..... ADCSP
Advanced Defense Communications Satellite System (ACAE) ..... ADCSS
Advanced Defense Intelligence Support System (MCD) ..... ADISS
Advanced Defense Satellite Communications Project (SAUO) ..... ADSCP
Advanced Defense Satellite Communications System (ACAE) ..... ADSCS
Advanced Defense Suppression Antiradiation Missile ..... ADSARM
Advanced Defense Suppression Weapon ..... ADSW
Advanced Defensive Avionics Response Strategy (SAUS) ..... ADARS
Advanced Definition Television (AAEL) ..... ADTV
Advanced Degree in Education (GAGS) ..... EdA
Advanced Degree in Education ..... Ed A2
Advanced Degree Program for ROTC Instructor Duty (MCD) ..... ADPRID
Advanced Degree Requirements Information System (SAUS) ..... ADRIS
Advanced Delivery of Correspondence (SAUS) ..... ADC
Advanced Demonstration Model (SAUS) ..... ADM
Advanced Deployability Posture [*Military*] (DOMA) ..... AD
Advanced Deployable Digital Imagery Support System [*Military*] (DOMA) ..... ADDISS
Advanced Deployable Digital Imagery Support System (ACAE) ..... ADISS
Advanced Deployable Systems program (SAUS) ..... ADS
Advanced Deployment Demonstration & Engineering Risk reduction (SAUS) ..... ADDER
Advanced Deployment Model (MCD) ..... ADM
Advanced Deposition Tech [*NASDAQ symbol*] (TTSB) ..... ADTC
Advanced Deposition Tech Wrrt [*NASDAQ symbol*] (TTSB) ..... ADTCW
Advanced Deposition Technologies [*NASDAQ symbol*] (SAG) ..... ADTC
Advanced Deposition Technologies [*Associated Press*] (SAG) ..... AdvD
Advanced Deposition Technologies [*Associated Press*] (SAG) ..... AdvDep
Advanced Deposition Technologies [*Associated Press*] (SAG) ..... AdvDp
Advanced Depot (SAUO) ..... Adv Dep
Advanced Depot of Medical Stores (SAUO) ..... ADMS
Advanced Design (IEEE) ..... AD
Advanced Design (SAUS) ..... A/D
Advanced Design Aluminum Metal Shelter [*A prefabricated building known as an ADAMS hut*] ..... ADAMS
Advanced Design Array RADAR ..... ADAR
Advanced Design Array Radar (SAUS) ..... ADAR
Advanced Design [*or Drawing*] **Change** ..... ADC
Advanced Design [*or Drawing*] **Change Notice** ..... ADCN
Advanced Design Composite Aircraft (MCD) ..... ADCA
Advanced Design Electronic Key System [*Telecommunications*] ..... ADEKS
Advanced Design Methods Laboratory [*Ohio State University*] [*Research center*] (RCD) ..... ADML
Advanced Design Special Processor (LAIN) ..... ADSP
Advanced Design Team ..... ADT
Advanced Destroyer/Aircraft Lightweight Torpedo (MCD) ..... AD/ALT
Advanced Destroyer/Aircraft Light-weight Torpedo (SAUS) ..... AD/ALT
Advanced Detection Technology Sensor (SAUS) ..... ADTS
Advanced Developing Country (ADWA) ..... ADC
Advanced Developing Institutions Program ..... ADIP
Advanced Development ..... AD
Advanced Development [*Army*] (AABC) ..... ADDEV
Advanced Development [*Army*] ..... ADV DEV
Advanced Development Activity (SAUO) ..... ADA
Advanced Development Aims Processor Transponder [*Military*] (MCD) ..... ADAPT
Advanced Development Analysis ..... ADA
Advanced Development Array Radar (SAUS) ..... ADAR
Advanced Development Concept (CAAL) ..... ADC
Advanced Development Design (CAAL) ..... ADD
Advanced Development Environment (AAEL) ..... ADE
Advanced Development Experimental [*Army*] (AABC) ..... ADX
Advanced Development Facility [*Branch*] [*Marine science*] (OSRA) ..... ADF
Advanced Development Facility Branch [*Forecast Systems Laboratory*] (USDC) ..... ADF
Advanced Development Hardware (SSD) ..... ADH
Advanced Development Hardware Phase (ACAE) ..... ADHP
Advanced Development Implementation (ACAE) ..... ADI
Advanced Development Laboratory (CCCA) ..... ADL
Advanced Development Memory (MCD) ..... ADM
Advanced Development Model ..... ADM
Advanced Development Objective [*Military*] ..... ADO
Advanced Development Phase (IUSS) ..... ADP
Advanced Development Plan [*Air Force*] (MCD) ..... ADP
Advanced Development Plan (System) ..... ADP(S)
Advanced Development Program (IUSS) ..... ADP
Advanced Development Program Office ..... ADPO
Advanced Development Project (SAUS) ..... ADP
Advanced Development Prototype (MHDI) ..... ADEPT
Advanced Development Report [*NASA*] (KSC) ..... ADR
Advanced Development Technology (KSC) ..... ADT
Advanced Development Unit Test [*Army*] ..... ADUT
Advanced Development Vehicle (ACAE) ..... ADV
Advanced Development Verification Test (RDA) ..... ADVT
Advanced Development Verification Test - Coordinator (MCD) ..... ADVT-C
Advanced Development Verification Test - Government (MCD) ..... ADVT-G
Advanced Development Verification Test-Government (SAUS) ..... ADVT-G
Advanced Developmental Model Subsystem (ACAE) ..... ADMS
Advanced Diagnostic Engine Monitoring System [*Air Force*] ..... ADEMS
Advanced Diagnostic Executive System ..... ADES
Advanced Diagnostic Research [*Medicine*] (DB) ..... ADR
Advanced Digital Avionics Map (ACAE) ..... ADAM
Advanced Digital Avionics System (MCD) ..... ADAS
Advanced Digital Dispensing System (SAUS) ..... ADDS
Advanced Digital Electronic Displays ..... ADEDS
Advanced Digital Engine Control System (SAUS) ..... ADECS
Advanced Digital Inertial Optical Sensor ..... ADIOS
Advanced Digital Information Corp. (PCM) ..... ADIC
Advanced Digital Information Corp. [*Associated Press*] (SAG) ..... AdvDIn
Advanced Digital Network [*Computer science*] (IGQR) ..... ADN
Advanced Digital Processing System ..... ADPS
Advanced Digital Processor (ACAE) ..... ADP
Advanced Digital RADAR Imagery Exploitation System ..... ADRIES
Advanced Digital Radar Imagery Exploitation System (SAUS) ..... ADRIES
Advanced Digital Radar Imagery Exploitation System (SAUS) ..... ADRTIES
Advanced Digital Ranging System [*NASA*] (KSC) ..... ADRAN
Advanced Digital Recording ..... ADR
Advanced Digital SAR Processor (MCD) ..... ADSP
Advanced Digital Signal Processor ..... ADSP
Advanced Digital Simulation System (MCD) ..... ADSS
Advanced Digital Stereophoto-grammetric System (SAUS) ..... ADSS
Advanced Digital Switch (SAUS) ..... ADS
Advanced Digital System (SAUS) ..... ADS
Advanced Digital Systems [*Commercial firm*] (NITA) ..... ADS
Advanced Digital Systems, Inc. [*NASDAQ symbol*] ..... ADVA
Advanced Digital Television Service ..... ACATS
Advanced Digital/Optical Control System ..... ADOCS
Advanced Diploma ..... AdvDip

Advanced Diploma, Australian Risk Management ... A Dip ARM
Advanced Diploma in Art Education [British] ... ADAE
Advanced Diploma in Education (ADA) ... AdvDipEd
Advanced Diploma in Midwifery [British] ... ADM
Advanced Diploma in Teaching ... AdvDipT
Advanced Direct Memory Access [Siemens Corp.] (NITA) ... ADMA
Advanced Direct Support Unit (SAUO) ... ADDSU
Advanced Direct Support Unit (NATG) ... ADSU
Advanced Directional Solidification Furnace (NAKS) ... ADSE
Advanced Directional Warhead (MCD) ... ADWAR
Advanced Directive [Medicine] (MELL) ... AD
Advanced Direct-Landing Apollo Mission [NASA] (IEEE) ... ADAM
Advanced Directory Services Interface (SAUS) ... ADSI
Advanced Disk Array [Computer science] ... ADA
Advanced Disk File (SAUS) ... ADF
Advanced Diskette Operating System ... ADOS
Advanced Dispenser Technology (MCD) ... ADT
Advanced Display and Debriefing Subsystem (DWSG) ... ADDS
Advanced Display & Intelligent Interface (SAUS) ... ADII
Advanced Display Computer (SAUS) ... ADC
Advanced Display System ... ADS
Advanced Display Systems Branch (SAUS) ... ADSB
Advanced Display Terminal (SAUS) ... ADT
Advanced Disposal Fee ... ADF
Advanced Distributed Aperture Infra-Red System (SAUS) ... ADAIRS
Advanced Distributed Onboard Processor (SDI) ... ADOP
Advanced Distributed Simulation [Army] ... ADS
Advanced Distributed Simulation Program (SAUS) ... ADSP
Advanced Distributed Simulation Technology [Army] (RDA) ... ADST
Advanced Diving System ... ADS
Advanced Divisional Headquarters (SAUO) ... ADHq
Advanced Divisional Headquarters (SAUS) ... AD Hq
Advanced Document Engineering (SAUS) ... ADE
Advanced Document Revision Notice [NASA] (KSC) ... ADRN
Advanced Dosimetry System (PDAA) ... ADS
Advanced Double Pass Reverse Osmosis Water Purification Unit (SAUS) ... ADROWPU
Advanced Dressing Station [British] ... ADS
Advanced Driver and Vehicle Advisory Navigation Concept ... ADVANC
Advanced Driver And Vehicle Advisory Navigation Concept [FHWA] (TAG) ... ADVANCE
Advanced Driver and Vehicle Navigation Concept ... ADVANCE
Advanced Driver Information System [Automotive engineering] ... ADIS
Advanced Driver Training [British military] (DMA) ... ADT
Advanced Dual Band Forward Looking Infrared (ACAE) ... ADBFLIR
Advanced Ducted Propulsor (SAUS) ... ADP
Advanced Dungeons & Dragons (SAUS) ... AD&D
Advanced Dungeons and Dragons ... AD & D
Advanced Dynamic Anthropomorphic Manikin [Air Force] ... ADAM
Advanced Early Warning System [Military] (IUSS) ... AEWS
Advanced Earned Income Credit [IRS] ... AEIC
Advanced Earth Location Data System (ADWA) ... AELDS
Advanced Earth Observation (or Observing) Satellite (SAUS) ... ADEOS
Advanced Earth Observation Satellite ... AEOS
Advanced Earth Observation System (SAUS) ... ADEOS
Advanced Earth Observing Mission (NAKS) ... ADEOS
Advanced Earth Observing Satellite (GEOI) ... ADEO
Advanced Earth Observing satellite (SAUS) ... ADEO
Advanced Earth Observing Satellite [Japan] ... ADEOS
Advanced Earth Observing Satellite 2 (SAUS) ... ADEOS 2
Advanced Earth Observing System (SAUS) ... ADEOS
Advanced Earth Orbiting Satellite (SAUS) ... ADEOS
Advanced Earth Resources Observation Satellite (SAUS) ... AEROS
Advanced Earth Resources Observation System ... AEROS
Advanced Earth Resources Observational Satellite (SAUS) ... AEROS
Advanced Earth Resources Satellite (GEOI) ... AERS
Advanced Earth Satellite Weapon System [Air Force] ... AEWS
Advanced Echelon [Marine Corps] ... ADVON
Advanced Echolon (SAUS) ... ADVON
Advanced Economic Order Quantity (ACAE) ... AEOQ
Advanced Education Institution ... AEI
Advanced Educational Technology (SAUS) ... AET
Advanced Elect Support Pds [NASDAQ symbol] (SG) ... AESP
Advanced Electric Distribution System ... AEDS
Advanced Electric Reactor (SAUS) ... AER
Advanced Electrical Development Package (MCD) ... AEDP
Advanced Electrical Reactor (EEVL) ... AER
Advanced Electro Optical System (ACAE) ... AEOS
Advanced Electrochemical Depolarized Concentrator Module [NASA] ... AEDCM
Advanced Electronic and Digital Sensor Technology ... AEADST
Advanced Electronic Control Unit (SAUS) ... AECU
Advanced Electronic Design ... AED
Advanced Electronic Display System [FAA] ... ADEDS
Advanced Electronic Guidance and Instrumentation System (VERA) ... AEGIS
Advanced Electronic Publishing System (NITA) ... AEPS
Advanced Electronic Warfare Evaluation Display System (ACAE) ... AEWEDS
Advanced Electronic Warfare System (MCD) ... AEWS
Advanced Electronic Warfare Test Set (MCD) ... AEWTS
Advanced Electronic Warfare Trainer System (ACAE) ... AEWTS
Advanced Electronically Tuned Radio [Automotive accessory] ... AETR
Advanced Electronics Design [Commercial firm] [British] (NITA) ... AED
Advanced Electronics Field ... AEF
Advanced Electronics Network [British] (NITA) ... AEON
Advanced Electronics Systems International (ACAE) ... AESI
Advanced Electro-Optical Sensor Simulation ... AEOSS
Advanced Electro-Optical Tracker/ Ranger (SAUS) ... AEOTR
Advanced Electro-Optical Tracker/Ranger (MCD) ... AEOTR
Advanced Embedded Codes Gateway (SAUS) ... AECG
Advanced Emergency Medical Technician (HCT) ... A-EMT
Advanced Encapsulated Hypertext (SAUS) ... AEH
Advanced Encryption Standard (SAUS) ... AES
Advanced Energetic Materials Corp. (SAUO) ... AEMC
Advanced Energy Industries [NASDAQ symbol] (TTSB) ... AEIS
Advanced Energy Industries, Inc. [Associated Press] (SAG) ... AdvEnId
Advanced Energy Industries, Inc. [NASDAQ symbol] (SAG) ... AEIS
Advanced Energy Projects [Department of Energy] ... AEP
Advanced Energy System Division (SAUS) ... AESD
Advanced Energy Systems Division (SAUO) ... AESD
Advanced Energy Technology ... AET
Advanced Engine Aerospace ... AEA
Advanced Engine, Aerospike (SAUS) ... AEA
Advanced Engine Bell ... AEB
Advanced Engine Control System (SAUS) ... AECS
Advanced Engine Development [Automotive industry supplier] ... AED
Advanced Engine Overhaul Base ... AEOB
Advanced Engine Quality Control (SAUS) ... AEQC
Advanced Engineering Data Set (SAUS) ... AEDS
Advanced Engineering Services [General Motors Corp.] [Automotive engineering] ... AES
Advanced Engineering Test Reactor ... AETR
Advanced Engine/Gearbox Integrated System (SAUS) ... AEGIS
Advanced Enhanced Interface for Open Universal Systems (SAUS) ... AEIOUS
Advanced Entry Control System [Air Force] ... AECS
Advanced Envirn Recycl Tech [NASDAQ symbol] (TTSB) ... AERTA
Advanced Environ Recycling Technologies, Inc. [Associated Press] (SAG) ... AdvEnv
Advanced Environ Recycling Technologies, Inc. [NASDAQ symbol] (SAG) ... AERT
Advanced Environmental Control System (MCD) ... AECS
Advanced Environmental Control Technology Research Center [University of Illinois] [Environmental Protection Agency] [Research center] (RCD) ... AECTRC
Advanced Environmental Recycling Technology, Inc. [NASDAQ symbol] (NQ) ... AERT
Advanced Environmental Research and Technology (MCD) ... AERT
Advanced Environmental Research Group [Commercial firm] ... AERG
Advanced Environmental Technology Corp. (EFIS) ... AETC
Advanced Environm'l Recyclg Wrrt [NASDAQ symbol] (TTSB) ... AERTZ
Advanced Epithermal Thorium Reactor ... AETR
Advanced Equipment Controller (AAEL) ... AEC
Advanced Equipment Repair Program [Military] (DNAB) ... AERP
Advanced Error Correction [Computer science] (VERA) ... AEC
Advanced ESA Resource Satellite (SAUS) ... AERS
Advanced Escape/Rescue Capability (SAUS) ... AERCAB
Advanced [or Aircrew] Escape/Rescue Capability [Navy - Air Force] ... AERCAB
Advanced EW Evaluation Display System (SAUS) ... AEWEDS
Advanced Executive Master of Business (PGP) ... AEMBA
Advanced Experimental Vehicle - 5th Generation [Toyota] ... AXV-V
Advanced Extendable Integration Support Facility (ACAE) ... AEISF
Advanced Extension Course (SAUS) ... AEC
Advanced Extravehicular Protective System [NASA] ... AEPS
Advanced Extravehicular Suit [NASA] ... AES
Advanced Facility Intrusion Detection System (DWSG) ... AFIDS
Advanced Fast Time Acoustic Analysis System (MCD) ... AFTAAS
Advanced Fault Recognition [Computer science] (NITA) ... AFR
Advanced Fault Resolution (SAUS) ... AFR
Advanced Fault Tree Analysis Program [SIA Computer Services] [Software package] (NCC) ... AFTP
Advanced Feature Connector. (SAUS) ... VAFC
Advanced Fermentation System ... AFS
Advanced Fiber Optic Digital Autopilot [Military] ... AFDAP
Advanced Fiber Optic Echelle [Spectrograph] ... AFOE
Advanced Fibre Communications [Associated Press] (SAG) ... AdvFCm
Advanced Fibre Communications [NASDAQ symbol] (SAG) ... AFCI
Advanced Field Array RADAR ... AFAR
Advanced Field Artillery System ... AFAS
Advanced Field Artillery System - Armaments [Army] (RDA) ... AFAS-ARM
Advanced Field Artillery System - Cannon ... AFAS-C
Advanced Field Artillery System - Future Armored Resupply Vehicle [Army] (RDA) ... AFAS-FARV
Advanced Field Artillery System - Mobility [Army] (RDA) ... AFAS-MOB
Advanced Field Artillery Tactical Data System [Army] ... AFADS
Advanced Field Artillery Tactical Data System (SAUS) ... AFATDS
Advanced Field Operating System [National Weather Service] ... AFOS
Advanced Field Site Facility ... AFSF
Advanced Fighter Capability (MCD) ... AFC
Advanced Fighter Capability Demonstrator (MCD) ... AFCD
Advanced Fighter Control Flight Simulator [Military] (PDAA) ... AFCFS
Advanced Fighter Crew Protection System (SAUS) ... APS
Advanced Fighter Diagnostic System (MCD) ... AFDS
Advanced Fighter RADAR System ... AFRS
Advanced Fighter Technology Integration [Air Force] ... AFTI
Advanced Figure Sensor (KSC) ... AFS
Advanced Filament Wound Structure ... AFWS
Advanced File Organization ... AFO
Advanced File System (SAUS) ... AFS
Advanced Fileable Processor ... AFP
Advanced Financial [AMEX symbol] (TTSB) ... AVF
Advanced Financial, Inc. [Associated Press] (SAG) ... AdvFin
Advanced Financial, Inc. [Associated Press] (SAG) ... AdvFn

Advanced Financial, Inc. [*AMEX symbol*] (SPSG) .... AVF
Advanced Financial, Inc. [*NASDAQ symbol*] (SAG) .... AVFI
Advanced Financial Reporting System (SAUS) .... AFRS
Advanced Finl 10.50% Cv'B' Pfd [*NASDAQ symbol*] (TTSB) .... AVFIP
Advanced Fire Control (MCD) .... AFC
Advanced Fire Control RADAR System (MCD) .... AFCORS
Advanced Fire Support Avionics System .... AFSAS
Advanced Fire Support System [*Army*] .... AFSS
Advanced Firefighter [*Military*] .... AFF
Advanced Firefinder System (SAUS) .... AFFS
Advanced Fire/Flight Control System (MCD) .... AFFC
Advanced Fire/Flight Control System (SAUS) .... AFFC System
Advanced Firing System (SAUS) .... AFS
Advanced Firing Systems (MSA) .... AFS
Advanced First-Term Avionics (DNAB) .... AFTA
Advanced Flash X-Ray Facility .... AFXF
Advanced Flash X-ray Facility (SAUS) .... AFXF
Advanced Fleet Reactor [*Navy*] (DOMA) .... AFR
Advanced Fleet Training (SAUS) .... Adv Flt Trng
Advanced Flexible Processor (MCD) .... AFP
Advanced Flexible Reusable Surface Insulation [*For space shuttles*] .... AFRSI
Advanced Flexiple Processor (SAUS) .... AFP
Advanced Flight Control Actuation System [*Navy*] (MCD) .... AFCAS
Advanced Flight Control Actuation System-All Electric (SAUS) .... AFCAS-AE
Advanced Flight Control Programmer .... AFCP
Advanced Flight Control System (MCD) .... AFCS
Advanced Flight Deck Simulator [*Aviation*] (PDAA) .... AFDS
Advanced Flight Management System (DA) .... AFMS
Advanced Flight Research Model (SAA) .... AFRM
Advanced Flow LASER (MCD) .... AFL
Advanced Flow Laser (SAUS) .... AFL
Advanced Flying School [*British military*] (DMA) .... AFS
Advanced Flying Training School (SAUS) .... AFTS
Advanced Flying Unit (SAUS) .... AFU
Advanced Flying Unit [*Air Force*] .... AFU
Advanced Force Commander (IUSS) .... AFC
Advanced Foreign System Requirements .... AFSR
Advanced Forward Air Defense System [*Missiles*] (IEEE) .... AFADS
Advanced Forward Area Air Defense System .... AFAADS
Advanced Forward Area Air Defense Weapon .... AFAADW
Advanced Forward Looking Infrared (SAUS) .... AFLIR
Advanced Free-Electron Laser (SAUS) .... AFEL
Advanced Freephone Service (SAUS) .... AFS
Advanced Fuel Accessories Test System (DWSG) .... AFATS
Advanced Fuel Assembly [*Nuclear energy*] (NUCP) .... AFA
Advanced Fuel Electronics [*Automotive engineering*] .... AFE
Advanced Fullscreen Debug (SAUS) .... AFD
Advanced Function of Communications (SAUS) .... AFC
Advanced Function Presentation [*IBM Corp*] (VERA) .... AFP
Advanced Function Printing (IAA) .... AFP
Advanced Function Printing Architecture [*IBM Corp*] (VERA) .... AFPA
Advanced Function Printing Data Stream [*IBM Corp*] (VERA) .... AFPDS
Advanced Furnace Technology (SAUS) .... AFT
Advanced Fuze Function Control System (MCD) .... AFFCS
Advanced Gas Centrifuge .... AGC
Advanced Gas Turbine .... AGT
Advanced Gas-cooled Graphite Moderated Reactor (SAUS) .... AGGMR
Advanced Gas-cooled Maritime Reactor (SAUS) .... AGMR
Advanced Gas-Cooled Reactor [*British*] .... AGR
Advanced Gear Box Technology (ACAE) .... AGBT
Advanced GEM Task Force (SAUS) .... A-GEMTF
Advanced General Aviation Transport Experiments (GAVI) .... AGATE
Advanced General Purpose Bomb (MCD) .... AGPB
Advanced General Purpose Processor Element (SAUS) .... AGPPE
Advanced Generator Technology (SAUS) .... AGT
Advanced Generic Equipment Model Task Force (AAEL) .... A-GEMTF
Advanced Genetic Sciences, Inc. .... AGS
Advanced Genetic Sciences, Incorporated (SAUO) .... AGSI
Advanced Geometry Blade [*Military*] (RDA) .... AGB
Advanced Geosynchronous Observation Environment Satellite [*NASA*] (NASA) .... AGOES
Advanced Geosynchronous Platform (SAUS) .... AGP
Advanced Gigahertz Input Snap Shot (ACAE) .... AGISS
Advanced Gimbal System (SAUS) .... AGS
Advanced Glass Melter .... AGM
Advanced Global Atmospheric Gases Experiment (SAUS) .... AGAGE
Advanced Glycosylated End-Product [*Biochemistry*] .... AGE
Advanced GPS/Inertial Integration (MCD) .... ADGINT
Advanced Graduate Certificate .... AGC
Advanced Graduate Specialist (GAGS) .... AGS
Advanced Graduate Specialist Certificate (PGP) .... AGSC
Advanced Graphic Chip Set .... AGCS
Advanced Graphical User Interface (SAUS) .... AGUI
Advanced Graphics Adapter [*Computer science*] (VERA) .... AGA
Advanced Graphics and Alphanumerics Controller (SAUS) .... AGAC
Advanced Graphics Architecture .... AGA
Advanced Graphics Avionics Display System (MCD) .... AGADS
Advanced Graphics Engine (SAUS) .... AGE
Advanced Graphics Package (SAUS) .... AGP
Advanced Graphics Port [*Intel*] [*Computer science*] .... AGP
Advanced Graphics Software, Inc. (PCM) .... AGS
Advanced Graphics Workstation [*Auto-trol Technology Corp.*] (NITA) .... AGW
Advanced Graphite Experiments Testing [*Military*] .... AGENT
Advanced Graphite Reactor (SAUS) .... AGR
Advanced Gravis [*Vancouver Stock Exchange symbol*] .... AED

Advanced Gravis ComputerTechnology Ltd. (SAUO) .... GRVS
Advanced Ground Receiving Equipment Experiment [*NASA*] (PDAA) .... AGREE
Advanced Ground Segment Design (SSD) .... AGSD
Advanced Ground Surveillance RADAR (MCD) .... AGSR
Advanced Ground Systems Engineering Corp. (SAUO) .... AGSE
Advanced Ground Transport .... AGT
Advanced Ground Transportation Vehicle (PDAA) .... AGTV
Advanced Ground Vehicle Technology (SAUS) .... AGVT
Advanced Ground Vehicle Technology Project [*Army*] .... AGVT
Advanced Ground Vehicle Technology Project (SAUS) .... AGVT Project
Advanced Growth Systems, Inc. [*Vancouver Stock Exchange symbol*] .... AVG
Advanced Guard [*British military*] (DMA) .... Adv Gd
Advanced Guard .... AG
Advanced Guidance and Control System (MCD) .... AGCS
Advanced Guidance Evaluation Program (SAUS) .... AGEP
Advanced Guidance System .... AGS
Advanced Guidance Technology [*SAMSO*] [*Air Force*] (MCD) .... AGT
Advanced Guided Projectile (MCD) .... AGP
Advanced Guided Vehicle Technology (ACAE) .... AGVT
Advanced Gun System (ACAE) .... AGS
Advanced Gun Technology (DOMA) .... AGT
Advanced Gun Weapon System (MCD) .... AGWS
Advanced Gun Weapon System Technology (SAUS) .... AGWST
Advanced Gunnery Target Systems (MCD) .... AGTS
Advanced Gust Front Algorithm (SAUS) .... AGFA
Advanced Hadron Facility (SAUS) .... AHF
Advanced Hardened Guidance Computer (MCD) .... AHGC
Advanced Hardware Architectures (SAUS) .... AHA
Advanced Hardware Exploitation Program (ACAE) .... AHEP
Advanced Harpoon Guidance System (MCD) .... AHGS
Advanced Headquarters (MUGU) .... ADVHED
Advanced Headquarters (SAUO) .... AHQ
Advanced Health [*NASDAQ symbol*] .... AHTC
Advanced Health Corp. [*Associated Press*] (SAG) .... AdHlthC
Advanced Health Corp. [*NASDAQ symbol*] (SAG) .... ADVH
Advanced Heat Rejection System (ACAE) .... AHRS
Advanced Heavy Anti Armor Missile System (ACAE) .... AHAAMS
Advanced Heavy Antitank Missile System [*Army*] (MCD) .... AHAMS
Advanced Heavy Antitank Weapon System (MCD) .... AHAWS
Advanced Heavy Weight Torpedo (ACAE) .... AHWT
Advanced Helicopter Development (DNAB) .... AHD
Advanced Helicopter Improvement Program [*Army*] (RDA) .... AHIP
Advanced Helicopter Pilotage (SAUS) .... AHP
Advanced Helmet Sight Reticle Assembly [*Air Force*] (MCD) .... AHRA
Advanced High Energy Laser (ACAE) .... ADHEL
Advanced High Performance Nuclear Attack Submarine (SAUS) .... AHPNAS
Advanced High Resolution Imaging Spectrometer (SAUS) .... AHRIS
Advanced High Resolution Radiometer (SAUS) .... AHRR
Advanced High Resolution Visible Imager (SAUS) .... AHRV
Advanced High Speed CMOS (SAUS) .... AHC
Advanced Highway Advisory Radio [*FHWA*] (TAG) .... AHAR
Advanced Hit Efficiency and Destruction (SAUS) .... AHEAD
Advanced Homing Sensor .... AHS
Advanced Hover Intercept Technology (SAUS) .... AHIT
Advanced Human Systems Institute [*San Jose State University*] [*Research center*] (RCD) .... AHSI
Advanced Humionics Platform [*Military*] .... AHP
Advanced Hybrid Computer System .... AHCS
Advanced Hybrid Computing System (SAUS) .... AHCS
Advanced hydraulic Piston Corer (SAUS) .... APC
Advanced Hypersonic Manned Aircraft .... AHMA
Advanced Icing Severity Indication System [*Military*] (RDA) .... AISIS
Advanced Identification Friend or Foe (SAUS) .... AIFF
Advanced Identification Techniques (MCD) .... AIT
Advanced Image Compression (MCD) .... AIC
Advanced Image Digitizing System (SAUS) .... AIDS
Advanced Image Management Software [*Computer science*] .... AIMS
Advanced Image Processing Terminal (SAUS) .... AIPT
Advanced Imagery Exploitation System (CCCA) .... AIES
Advanced Imagery Manipulation System .... AIMS
Advanced Imagery Requirements and Exploitation System (MCD) .... AIRES
Advanced Imaging Communications System (MCD) .... AICS
Advanced Imaging Software (DGA) .... AIS
Advanced Imaging Tracker .... AIT
Advanced Impact Drilling System (HGAA) .... AIDS
Advanced Impact Location System (SAA) .... AILS
Advanced Impact Management System [*Padding for sportswear*] .... AIMS
Advanced Indentification System .... AIDS
Advanced Indication Technology Experiment (MCD) .... AITE
Advanced Indications Structure (MCD) .... AIS
Advanced Indications System (MCD) .... AIS
Advanced Indirect Fire System (ACAE) .... AIFS
Advanced Individual Combat Weapon [*Army*] (INF) .... AICW
Advanced Individual Training [*Army*] .... AIT
Advanced Individual Training Attrition Analysis (MCD) .... AITAA
Advanced Individual Training Available [*Military*] .... AITA
Advanced Industrial Instrumentation Project (SAUO) .... AIIP
Advanced Industrial Management .... AIM
Advanced Industrial Materials (SAUS) .... AIM
Advanced Inert Missile Simulator (DWSG) .... AIMS
Advanced Inertial Measurement System .... AIMS
Advanced Inertial Measurement Unit (ACAE) .... AIMU
Advanced Inertial Navigation System (MCD) .... AINS
Advanced Inertial Reference Sphere [*ICBM technology*] .... AIRS
Advanced Infantry Training .... AIT

Advanced Infared Studies (SAUS) .... AIRS
Advanced Information and Management Systems (NITA) .... AIMS
Advanced Information in Medicine .... AIM
Advanced Information Leaflets (SAUS) .... AIL
Advanced Information Management [*Information service or system*] (IID) .... AIM
Advanced Information Manager [*Fujitsu Ltd.*] [*Japan*] .... AIM
Advanced Information Memos (SAUS) .... AIMs
Advanced Information Processing (SAUS) .... AIP
Advanced Information System/Net 1 Service [*Formerly, ACS*] [*American Bell, Inc.*] .... AIS
Advanced Information Systems Company (SAUO) .... AIS
Advanced Information Systems Company (ACAE) .... AISC
Advanced Information Technology (NITA) .... AIT
Advanced Information Technology (SAUS) .... AITEC
Advanced Information Technology in Design and Manufacturing (SAUS) .... AIT
Advanced Information Transmission System (SAUS) .... AITS
Advanced Infrared Entertainment System (ACAE) .... AIRES
Advanced Infra-red Imaging Seeker (SAUS) AI2S
Advanced Infrared Imaging Seeker (MCD) .... AIRIS
Advanced Infra-Red imaging Seeker (SAUS) .... AIRS
Advanced Infrared Search and Track (ADWA) .... AIRST
Advanced Infrared Seeker (ACAE) .... AIRS
Advanced Infrared Sounder (GAVI) .... AIRS
Advanced Institutional Development Program [*Under Title III of the Higher Education Act*] .... AIDP
Advanced Institutional Management Software Inc. (SAUO) .... AIMS
Advanced Institutional Management Software, Inc. (SAUS) .... AIMS
Advanced Instruction Flying School (SAUO) .... AIFS
Advanced Instruction Technique (DA) .... AIT
Advanced Instructional System (MCD) .... AIS
Advanced Instrument Course (SAUS) .... AIC
Advanced Instrumentation and Data Analysis System .... AIDAS
Advanced Instrumentation for Industry Project (SAUS) .... AIIP
Advanced Instrumentation for Reflood Studies [*Nuclear energy*] (NRCH) .... AIRS
Advanced/ Instrumentation Subsystem (SAUS) .... AIS
Advanced Instrumentation Unit [*National Physical Laboratory*] (PDAA) .... AIU
Advanced Integrated Circuit Design Aids [*ESPRIT*] (NITA) .... AIDA
Advanced Integrated Data System (AFM) .... AIDS
Advanced Integrated Diagnostics (BUR) .... AID
Advanced Integrated Digital Avionics System (SAUS) .... AIDAS
Advanced Integrated Display System [*Military*] .... AIDS
Advanced Integrated Electronic Warfare System (SAUS) .... AIEWS
Advanced Integrated Flight System (MCD) .... AIFS
Advanced Integrated Landing System .... AILS
Advanced Integrated Life-Support System .... AILSS
Advanced Integrated MAD System (SAUS) .... AIMS
Advanced Integrated Magnetic Anomaly Detection System (MCD) .... AIMS
Advanced Integrated Maintenance Support System .... AIMSS
Advanced Integrated Modular Instrumentation System (MCD) .... AIMIS
Advanced Integrated Power Supply .... AIPS
Advanced Integrated Propulsion System [*Aerospace*] .... AIPS
Advanced Integrated Reconnaissance System (SAUS) .... Airs
Advanced Integrated Safety and Optimizing Computer .... ADVISOR
Advanced Integrated-circuit Design Aids (SAUS) .... AIDA
Advanced Integration Research [*PC motherboard*] [*Computer science*] (PCM) .... AIR
Advanced Intelligence Center [*Navy*] .... ADINTELCEN
Advanced Intelligence Center [*Navy*] .... ADV INTEL CEN
Advanced Intelligence Center (SAUO) .... ADVINTELCEN
Advanced Intelligence Center [*Navy*] .... AIC
Advanced Intelligence Center, Pacific Ocean Area (SAUO) .... AICPOA
Advanced Intelligence Center Pacific Ocean Area (SAUS) .... AICPOA
Advanced Intelligence Center, Pacific Ocean Areas [*Navy*] .... AICPOA
Advanced Intelligence Processing System (ACAE) .... AIPS
Advanced Intelligent Network [*Computer science*] (ACRL) .... AIN
Advanced Intelligent Tape [*Sony Corp.*] (PCM) .... AIT
Advanced Interactive Data Entry / Transaction Processing System [*Computer science*] (PDAA) .... AIDE/TPS
Advanced Interactive Debugging System .... AIDS
Advanced Interactive Display System (SAUS) .... AIDS
Advanced Interactive Draughting [*McGrane Computer Systems Ltd.*] [*Software package*] (NCC) .... AID
Advanced Interactive Enterprise Systems Architecture (SAUS) .... AIXESA
Advanced Interactive Executive [*IBM RT Personal Computer*] (BYTE) .... AIX
Advanced Interactive Executive for RS-6000 (SAUS) AIX/6000
Advanced Interactive Executive Systems Architecture (SAUS) .... AIXESA
Advanced Interactive Executive/Enterprise Systems Architecture [*Computer science*] (VERA) .... AIXESA
Advanced Interactive Presentation System .... AIPS
Advanced Interactive Software (DGA) .... AIS
Advanced Interactive Symbolic Evaluator of Reliability (SAUS) .... ADVISER
Advanced Interactive Video .... AIV
Advanced Intercept Missile .... AIM
Advanced Interceptor Air-to-Air Missile (MCD) .... AIAAM
Advanced Interceptor Missile Subsystem [*Military*] .... AIMS
Advanced Interceptor Propulsion (MCD) .... AIP
Advanced Interceptor Technology (MCD) .... AIT
Advanced Interconnection Development System (SAUS) .... AIDS
Advanced Intercontinental Missile System .... AIMS
Advanced Interdiction Weapon System [*Military*] .... AIWS
Advanced Interface Module (SAUS) .... AIM
Advanced Interference Blanker Unit (SAUS) .... AIBU
Advanced Interferometer Radiometer Sounder (SAUS) .... AIRS
Advanced Interior Communication System .... AICS
Advanced Internally Blown Jet Flag (MCD) .... AIBF
Advanced International Studies Institute (EA) .... AISI
Advanced Interrogation, Recording and Location System (SAUS) .... AIRLS
Advanced Interventional Systems (SAUS) .... LAIS
Advanced Invar Mask [*Computer science*] (VERA) .... AIM
Advanced Inventory Management System .... AIMS
Advanced Ion Exchange Cellulose [*Analytical biochemistry*] .... AIEC
Advanced Ionization Detector .... AID
Advanced Ionization Development (MCD) .... AID
Advanced Ionospheric Sounder [*A ground-based instrument*] .... AIS
Advanced IR Imaging Seeker (MCD) .... AIIS
Advanced IRST (SAUS) .... AIRST
Advanced Isotope Separation [*Process*] [*Nuclear energy*] .... AIS
Advanced IT [*Information Technology*] **Transfer** [*British*] .... AIT[3]
Advanced Jaguar [*Jaguar PLC*] [*Automotive engineering*] .... AJ
Advanced Jet Trainer .... AJT
Advanced Keyboarding System (SAUS) .... AKS
Advanced Kick Stage [*Missile launching*] (MCD) .... AKS
Advanced Kinematic Bombing System .... AKBS
Advanced Kinetic Energy Missile (SAUS) .... ADKEM
Advanced Laminate Analysis Code (SPST) .... ADVLAM
Advanced LAMP Design Demonstration Integration (SAUS) .... ALADDIN
Advanced Land Combat (SAUS) .... ALC
Advanced Land Combat Systems [*Army*] (RDA) .... ALCOS
Advanced Land Navigation (MCD) .... ALN
Advanced Land Observation (or Observing) Satellite (SAUS) .... ALOS
Advanced Land Observation Satellite (ARMP) .... ALOS
Advanced Land Observing Satellite [*Sponsored by Japan Space Agency*] .... ALOS
Advanced Land SAR (SAUS) .... ALSAR
Advanced Landing Field (SAUS) .... ALFd
Advanced Landing Ground [*Air Force*] .... ALG
Advanced Landing System .... ALS
Advanced Landsat Sensor (SAUS) .... ALS
Advanced Language Processor (SAUS) .... ALP
Advanced Language Program [*Institute for Defense Analysis*] .... ALP
Advanced Large Object Recovery System (SAUS) .... ALORS
Advanced Large-Area Infra-Red Transducer (SAUS) .... ALIRT
Advanced Laser Communication Experiment (SAUS) .... ALCE
Advanced LASER Designator .... ALD
Advanced Laser Designator Pod (ACAE) .... ALDP
Advanced LASER Flow Analysis (MCD) .... ALFA
Advanced LASER Intercept Receiver (MCD) .... ALIR
Advanced Laser Reconnaissance Set (ACAE) .... ALRS
Advanced LASER Requirements Assessment (MCD) .... ALRA
Advanced Laser Search and Track Set (ACAE) .... ALSTS
Advanced LASER Spot Tracker (MCD) .... ALAST
Advanced Laser System (ACAE) .... ALS
Advanced LASER System Study .... ALSS
Advanced Laser Warning (ACAE) .... ALW
Advanced LASER-Aided Defect Inspection in Nondestructive Testing (IAA) .... ALADIN
Advanced Laser-Aided Defect Inspection in Nondestructive Testing (SAUS) .... ALADIN Testing
Advanced Laser-Guided Missile System (SAUS) .... ALGMS
Advanced Launch Development (SAUS) .... ALD
Advanced Launch Development Program (SAUS) .... ALDP
Advanced Launch System [*Rocketry*] .... ALS
Advanced Legal Education, Hamline University School of Law (DLA) .... ALEHU
Advanced Legal Software [*Computer science*] (HGAA) .... ALS
Advanced Level [*School graduating grade*] [*British*] .... A
Advanced Level (ODBW) .... A level
Advanced Level Telecommunications Centre (SAUS) .... ALTCENTRE
Advanced Levitation Unit [*Materials processing*] .... ALU
Advanced Liaison Forward Area (MCD) .... ALFA
Advanced Libraries & Information, Inc. [*Information service or system*] (IID) .... ALII
Advanced Libraries & Information Incorporated (SAUO) .... ALII
Advanced Library Concepts, Inc. [*Later, ALI'I*] [*Information service or system*] (IID) .... ALC
Advanced Library Concepts, Inc. (SAUS) .... ALC
Advanced Library Systems, Inc. [*Information service or system*] (IID) .... ALS
Advanced Library Systems Inc. (SAUO) .... ALS
Advanced Life Information System [*Computer science*] .... ALIS
Advanced Life Support [*System*] .... ALS
Advanced Life Support System (MCD) .... ALSS
Advanced Light Antitank Weapon (RDA) .... ALAW
Advanced Light Armored Amphibious Vehicle System (SAUS) .... ALAAVS
Advanced Light Helicopter [*Air Force*] (PDAA) .... ALH
Advanced Light Rapid Transit .... ALRT
Advanced Light Source [*For Synchrotron radiation*] [*High-energy physics*] .... ALS
Advanced Lighting Technol [*NASDAQ symbol*] (TTSB) .... ADLT
Advanced Lighting Technologies, Inc. [*NASDAQ symbol*] (SAG) .... ADLT
Advanced Lighting Technologies, Inc. [*Associated Press*] (SAG) .... AdvLight
Advanced Lightning Mapper (SAUS) .... ALM
Advanced Lightweight SONAR [*Military*] .... ALWS
Advanced Lightweight Tactical Antenna (SAUS) .... ALTA
Advanced Lightweight Torpedo [*Navy*] .... ALWT
Advanced Limb Scanner (MCD) .... ALS
Advanced Linear Programming System [*Operational research technique*] .... ALPS
Advanced Linux Sound Architecture (SAUS) .... ALSA
Advanced Liquid Feed Experiment (SAUS) .... ALFE
Advanced Liquid Hydrogen (ADWA) .... ALH
Advanced Liquid Metal Reactors [*Nuclear energy*] .... ALMR
Advanced Liquid Propulsion System [*NASA*] .... ALPS
Advanced List of Materials .... ALM
Advanced Lithography Research Initiative [*British*] .... ALRI

Advanced Location Strike System [*Formerly, Airborne Location and Strike System*] [*Air Force*] .... ALSS
Advanced Logic Design (MHDB) .... ALD
Advanced Logic Processing System (SAUS) .... ALPS
Advanced Logic Research [*NASDAQ symbol*] (SAG) .... AALR
Advanced Logic Research (SAUS) .... ALR
Advanced Logic Research Access 386 [*Microcomputer*] .... ALR
Advanced Logic Research, Inc. [*Associated Press*] (SAG) .... AdvLog
Advanced Logic Research, Inc. (PCM) .... ALR
Advanced Logical Programming Environments Support [*ESPRIT project*] (NITA) .... ALPES
Advanced Logical Utility (PDAA) .... ALU
Advanced Logistic Support Site [*Environmental science*] (COE) .... ALSS
Advanced Logistic System (AFM) .... ALS
Advanced Logistics Development .... ALD
Advanced Logistics Information and Control System [*Air Force*] .... ALICS
Advanced Logistics Spacecraft .... ALS
Advanced Logistics Support Base [*Navy*] .... ALSB
Advanced Logistics System Center (SAUO) .... ALSC
Advanced Logistics System Project Advisory Committee [*Terminated, 1977*] [*DoD*] (EGAO) .... ALSPAC
Advanced Logistics Systems Center [*Air Force*] .... ADVLOGSYSCEN
Advanced Logistics Systems Center (SAUS) .... ALSC
Advanced Long-Range Air-to-Air Missile (SAUS) .... ALRAAM
Advanced Long-Range All-Weather Interceptor (MCD) .... ALRAWI
Advanced Long-Range Interceptor .... ALRI
Advanced Long-Wave IR Circuit and Array Technology (MCD) .... ALICAT
Advanced Low Altitude Reconnaissance Sensor (SAUS) .... ALAIRS
Advanced Low Altitude Technique (SAUS) .... ADLAT
Advanced Low Altitude Terrain [*Missile*] (DOMA) .... ADLAT
Advanced Low Voltage Technology [*Electronics*] (AAEL) .... ALVT
Advanced Low-Altitude RADAR Model (MCD) .... ALARM
Advanced Low-Altitude SAM (MCD) .... ALASAM
Advanced Low-Altitude Technique .... ADLAT
Advanced Low-Altitude Terrain System (MCD) .... ADLAT
Advanced Low-Cost G-Cueing System .... ALCOGS
Advanced Low-Level Wind Shear Alert System (SAUS) .... ALWAS
Advanced Low-Power Schottky (MCD) .... ALS
Advanced Low-power Schottky Transistor-Transistor Logic (SAUS) .... ALS-TTL
Advanced Low-Voltage CMOS (SAUS) .... ALVC
Advanced Low-Volume Ramjet .... ALVRJ
Advanced Lunar Operation .... ALO
Advanced Lunar Orbital Rendezvous (IEEE) .... ALOR
Advanced Lunar Projects .... ALP
Advanced Lunar Projects Laboratory .... ALPL
Advanced Lunar Studies .... ALS
Advanced Lunar Transportation System (SAUS) .... ALTS
Advanced Lunar Transportation Systems .... ALTS
Advanced Mach Vision Ci'A' [*NASDAQ symbol*] (SG) .... AMVC
Advanced Mach Vision Ci'A' [*NASDAQ symbol*] .... AMVC
Advanced Machining Program (SAUS) .... AMP
Advanced Machining System (SAUS) .... AMS
Advanced Magnetic Helmet-Mounted Sight (SAUS) .... AMHMS
Advanced Magnetic Minesweeping (MCD) .... AMMS
Advanced Magnetic Silencing Project [*Military*] (DNAB) .... AMSP
Advanced Magnetics [*Associated Press*] (SAG) .... AdvMag
Advanced Magnetics [*AMEX symbol*] (SAG) .... AVM
Advanced Magnetics, Inc. (SAUO) .... MIT
Advanced Mail Coding System (MCD) .... AMCS
Advanced Maintenance Recorder System (SAUS) .... AMRS
Advanced Mammography Sys [*NASDAQ symbol*] (TTSB) .... MAMO
Advanced Mammography Systems [*Associated Press*] (SAG) .... AdvMam
Advanced Mammography Systems [*NASDAQ symbol*] (SAG) .... MAMO
Advanced Management Information and Retrieval System (SAUS) .... ADMIRES
Advanced Management Information Service [*or System*] [*Air Force*] .... AMIS
Advanced Management Information System (SAUS) .... AMIS
Advanced Management Journal (journ.) (SAUS) .... Advan Manage J
Advanced Management Program .... AMP
Advanced Management Program for Clinician (PGP) .... AMPC
Advanced Management Research [*A publication*] (DLA) .... AMR
Advanced Maneuvering Demonstration Aircraft .... AMDA
Advanced Maneuvering FLAP [*Flight Application Software*] (MCD) .... AMF
Advanced Maneuvering Orbit-to-Orbit Shuttle [*NASA*] (NASA) .... AMOOS
Advanced Maneuvering Propulsion System .... AMPS
Advanced Maneuvering Propulsion Technology [*NASA*] (KSC) .... AMPT
Advanced Maneuvering Reentry Vehicle (MCD) .... AMARV
Advanced Maneuvering Re-entry Vehicle (SAUS) .... AMRV
Advanced Manned Aerial Scout (ACAE) .... AMAS
Advanced Manned Interceptor [*US Air Force Artillery Spotting Division interceptor*] .... AMI
Advanced Manned Launch System [*NASA*] .... AMLS
Advanced Manned Missions Program [*NASA*] (MCD) .... AMMP
Advanced Manned Penetrator Strike System (SAUS) .... AMPSS
Advanced Manned Penetrator .... AMP
Advanced Manned Penetrator System .... AMPS
Advanced Manned Precision Strike System [*Proposed Air Force plane*] .... AMPSS
Advanced Manned Space Simulator .... AMSS
Advanced Manned Spacecraft .... AMS
Advanced Manned Strategic Aircraft [*Facetious translation: "America's Most Studied Aircraft"*] [*Air Force*] .... AMSA
Advanced Manoeuvring Re-entry Vehicle (SAUS) .... AMARV
Advanced Manportable Weapons System (Provisional) [*Army*] (RDA) .... AMWS
Advanced Manpower Control System (SAUS) .... AMCS
Advanced Manual Line (SAUS) .... AML
Advanced Manufacturing, Accounting and Production System (SAUS) .... AMAPS

Advanced Manufacturing, Accounting, and Production System (MCD) .... AMAPS
Advanced Manufacturing, Accounting, and Production System for Government Contractors (MCD) .... AMAPS/G
Advanced Manufacturing Engineering (SAUS) .... AME
Advanced Manufacturing Engineering Council .... AMEC
Advanced Manufacturing Feasibility Studies (SAUS) .... AMFS
Advanced Manufacturing Initiative [*Department of Energy*] .... AMI
Advanced Manufacturing Methods (MHDB) .... AMM
Advanced Manufacturing Online .... AMO
Advanced Manufacturing System (MCD) .... AMS
Advanced Manufacturing Systems Exposition and Conference (ITD) .... AMS
Advanced Manufacturing Techniques (NITA) .... AMT
Advanced Manufacturing Technology [*Technical Insights, Inc.*] [*Information service or system*] (CRD) .... AMT
Advanced Manufacturing Technology Centre [*University of Manchester*] [*British*] (NITA) .... AMTC
Advanced Manufacturing Technology Centre [*Research center*] [*British*] (CB) .... AMTeC
Advanced Manufacturing Technology Research Institute [*Research center*] [*British*] (IRC) .... AMTRI
Advanced Mapping and Surveying Equipment (IIA) .... AMASE
Advanced Mapping System [*Geography*] .... AMS
Advanced Marine Airborne Signal Intelligence System (IUSS) .... AMASS
Advanced Marine Helicopter Squadron (SAUS) .... HMX
Advanced Maritime Patrol Aircraft (PDAA) .... AMPA
Advanced Marketing Services [*Book supplier*] .... AMS
Advanced Marketing Services, Inc. [*NASDAQ symbol*] (NQ) .... ADMS
Advanced Marketing Svcs [*NASDAQ symbol*] (TTSB) .... ADMS
Advanced Marketing Systems [*Associated Press*] (SAG) .... AdMkSv
Advanced Marksman Series (SAUS) .... AMS
Advanced Marksmanship Unit (SAUO) .... AMU
Advanced Masking Systems [*Automotive engineering*] [*3M Co.*] .... AMS
Advanced Master (PGP) .... Adv M
Advanced Master of Education (GAGS) .... AdMEd
Advanced Master of Education .... AME
Advanced Master of Library Science (GAGS) .... AdMLS
Advanced Material Concepts Laboratory (SAUO) .... AMCL
Advanced Material Order Form (SAUS) .... AMOF
Advanced Materials and Fluid Processes (SAUS) .... AMFP
Advanced Materials at Tuskegee University (RDA) .... CEAM-TU
Advanced Materials Cargo Sling System (MCD) .... AMCSS
Advanced Materials Engineering Ltd. (SAUO) .... AME
Advanced Materials Fabrication Facility [*Manufacturing*] (MCD) .... AMFF
Advanced Materials Group, Inc. [*NASDAQ symbol*] (SAG) .... ADMG
Advanced Materials Group, Inc. [*Associated Press*] (SAG) .... AdvMat
Advanced Materials Technology [*Information service or system*] (IID) .... AMT
Advanced Materials Testing & Evaluation Laboratory (SAUS) .... AMTEL
Advanced Materiel Concepts Agency [*Alexandria, VA*] [*Army*] .... AMCA
Advanced Materiel Segmented Combustor (SAUS) .... AMSC
Advanced Math Library [*Computer science*] (MHDI) .... AML
Advanced Matts Group [*NASDAQ symbol*] (TTSB) .... ADMG
Advanced Measurement Instruments, Inc. (SAUO) .... AMI
Advanced Meat Recovery [*Food Technology*] .... AMR
Advanced Mechanical Transport Depot (SAUS) .... AMTD
Advanced Mechanically Scanned Radiometer (SAUS) .... AMSR
Advanced Medical Communications [*Commercial firm*] [*British*] (NITA) .... AMC
Advanced Medical, Inc. [*Associated Press*] (SAG) .... AdMd
Advanced Medical, Inc. [*Associated Press*] (SAG) .... AdvMed
Advanced Medical, Inc. [*AMEX symbol*] (SPSG) .... AMA
Advanced Medium Anti Missile System (ACAE) .... AMAMS
Advanced Medium Antitank Missile (MCD) .... AMAMS
Advanced Medium Antitank Weapon (MCD) .... AMAW
Advanced Medium Assault Weapons System (ACAE) .... AMAWS
Advanced Medium Caliber Aircraft Weapon System (SAUS) .... AMCAWS
Advanced Medium or Long Range Air to Air Missile (ACAE) .... AM/LRAAM
Advanced Medium Resolution Infrared Radiometer .... AMRIR
Advanced Medium Resolution Visible Imager .... AMRVI
Advanced Medium Rocket (MCD) .... AMR
Advanced Medium STOL [*Short Takeoff and Landing*] Transport .... AMST
Advanced Medium-Caliber Aircraft Weapon System (MCD) .... AMCAWS
Advanced Medium-Range Air-to-Air Missile (MCD) .... AMRAAM
Advanced Medium-Resolution Imaging Radiometer .... AMRIR
Advanced Med'l 10% cm Pfd [*AMEX symbol*] (TTSB) .... AMAPr
Advanced Memory Concepts (MCD) .... AMC
Advanced Memory Development (SAUS) .... AMD
Advanced Memory Management Architecture [*Computer science*] (BYTE) .... AMMA
Advanced Memory Specification [*Computer science*] .... AMS
Advanced Memory Systems, Inc. (IEEE) .... AMS
Advanced Memory Systems Inc. (SAUO) .... AMS
Advanced Message Center (SAUS) .... AdvMsgCen
Advanced Message Centre (SAUO) .... Adv Msg Cen
Advanced Metal Evaporated .... AME
Advanced Metal Oxide Semiconductor (SAUS) .... AMOS
Advanced Metal Powder (SAUS) .... AMP
Advanced Metallic Air Vehicle Structure (MCD) .... AMAVS
Advanced Metallic Structures [*Program*] [*Air Force*] .... AMS
Advanced Metals Research Corporation (SAUO) .... AMRC
Advanced Meteoroid Program (ACAE) .... AMP
Advanced Meteorological & Temperature Sounder (SAUS) .... AMTS
Advanced Meteorological Ground Station (SAUS) .... AMGS
Advanced Meteorological Image and Graphics Analysis System (SAUS) .... AMIGAS
Advanced Meteorological Processing System (SAUS) .... AMPS
Advanced Meteorological Satellite (SAUS) .... AMS

Advanced Meteorological Sounding System .... AMSS
Advanced Meteorological System (MCD) .... AMS
Advanced Meteorological Temperature Sounder (MCD) .... AMTS
Advanced Meteorological Temperature Sounding Study (SAUS) .... AMTS
Advanced Meterological Sounding System (SAUS) .... AMSS
Advanced Micro Dev [*NYSE symbol*] (TTSB) .... AMD
Advanced Micro Devices, Inc. .... ADV
Advanced Micro Devices, Inc. [*NYSE symbol*] (SPSG) .... AMD
Advanced Micro Devices-Metal Oxide Semiconductor (SAUS) .... AMD-MOS
Advanced Microcomputer Development System (CIST) .... AMDS
Advanced Microcomputer System-Multibus-architecture (SAUS) .... AMS-M
Advanced Microcontroller Bus Architecture (SAUS) .... AMBA
Advanced Microdevices, Inc. (NITA) .... ADM
Advanced Micro-Electronics Converter (SAUS) .... AMC
Advanced Micrographic Access and Retrieval System (SAUS) .... AMARS
Advanced Microprocessor Laboratory (SAUS) .... AMPL
Advanced Microprocessor Programming Language [*Texas Instruments, Inc.*] .... AMPL
Advanced Microprocessor Prototyping Laboratory [*Texas Instruments, Inc.*] .... AMPL
Advanced Microprocessor Prototyping Language (SAUS) .... AMPL
Advanced Microprogrammable Processor (SAUS) .... AMPP
Advanced Microprogrammable Processors (MCD) .... AMPP
Advanced Microscopy and Imaging Laboratory (SAUS) .... AMIL
Advanced Microstructure Profiler [*Instrumentation, oceanography*] .... AMP
Advanced Microwave (SAUS) .... AMW
Advanced Microwave Circuit Analysis Programme (HGAA) .... AMCAP
Advanced Microwave Imaging Radiometer (SAUS) .... AMIR
Advanced Microwave Imaging Sensor (SAUS) .... AMIS
Advanced Microwave Moisture Sensor (MCD) .... AMMS
Advanced Microwave Moisture Sounder (SAUS) .... AMMS
Advanced Microwave Precipitation Radiometer (ACAE) .... AMPR
Advanced Microwave Radiometer (SSD) .... AMR
Advanced Microwave Scanner Radiation (SAUS) .... AMSR
Advanced Microwave Scanning Radiometer (ARMP) .... AMRS
Advanced Microwave Scanning Radiometer (MCD) .... AMSR
Advanced Microwave Sounding Radiometer (SAUS) .... AMSR
Advanced Microwave Sounding Unit [*Satellite instrument for meteorology*] .... AMSU
Advanced Microwave Sounding Unit-A (EOSA) .... AMSU-A
Advanced Midcourse Active System (MCD) .... AMAS
Advanced Military Occupational Specialty [*Army*] (AABC) .... ADVMOS
Advanced Military Spaceflight Capability .... AMSC
Advanced Military Spaceflight Technology (MCD) .... AMST
Advanced Military Spacelift Capability (SAUS) .... AMSC
Advanced Military Studies Program [*DoD*] .... AMSP
Advanced Millimeter Wave Atmospheric Sounder (SAUS) .... AMAS
Advanced Millimeter Wave Device .... AMWD
Advanced Mine Countermeasures (MCD) .... AMCM
Advanced Mine Detection System [*Navy*] (DOMA) .... AMDS
Advanced Mine Hunting Sonar (ACAE) .... AMHS
Advanced Mine-Hunting SONAR System (MCD) .... AMSS
Advanced Miniature High Frequency System (ACAE) .... AMHFS
Advanced Minuteman Accelerometer .... AMA
Advanced Minuteman Computer .... AMC
Advanced Minuteman Platform .... AMP
Advanced Minuteman Platform/Electronic (ACAE) .... AMP/E
Advanced Minuteman System .... AMS
Advanced Missile Control System (SAA) .... AMCS
Advanced Missile Ejector Launch Technology (ACAE) .... AMELT
Advanced Missile Materials Research Technical Advisory Group [*Terminated, 1975*] [*DoD*] (EGAO) .... AMMRES
Advanced Missile Model (ACAE) .... AMM
Advanced Missile Propulsion Definition Study [*NASA*] (KSC) .... AMPDS
Advanced Missile Receiver (MCD) .... AMR
Advanced Missile System .... AMS
Advanced Missile System - Heavy (MCD) .... AMS-H
Advanced Missile Technology Installation (ACAE) .... AMTI
Advanced Missile Technology Integration (SAUS) .... AMTI
Advanced Mission Materials Preparation Program (ACAE) .... AMMPS
Advanced Mission Planning Aid (SAUS) .... AMPA
Advanced Mission Sensor System (ACAE) .... AMSS
Advanced Mission Studies [*NASA*] (KSC) .... AMS
Advanced Missions Docking Subsystem (SAUS) .... AMDS
Advanced Missions Docking System [*or Subsystem*] [*NASA*] (NASA) .... AMDS
Advanced Mobile Integration in General Operating Systems (SAUS) .... AMIGOS
Advanced Mobile Phone Service [*Bell System*] .... AMPS
Advanced Mobile Phone System (ACRL) .... AMPS
Advanced Mobile Telephone System (MCD) .... AMTS
Advanced Mobile Traffic Information and Communications System [*Automotive engineering*] .... AMTICS
Advanced Mode Control and High Power Optics Techniques (ACAE) .... AMCHIPOT
Advanced Model Builder Shell [*Programming language*] [*1970*] (CSR) .... AMBUSH
Advanced Model of the FV-432 (SAUS) FV-1609
Advanced Modeling Extension [*Computer science*] (PCM) .... AME
Advanced Modular Artillery Command System (SAUS) .... AMACS
Advanced Modular Audio Visual Unit (MHDI) .... AMAVU
Advanced Modular Processor (SAUS) .... AMP
Advanced Modular RADAR (MCD) .... AMR
Advanced Moisture and Temperature Sounder (CARB) .... AMTS
Advanced Monopulse Countermeasures (ACAE) .... AMC
Advanced Monopulse Seeker .... AMS
Advanced Mortgage Online System [*Computer science*] (HGAA) .... AMOS
Advanced Motor Case (MCD) .... AMC
Advanced Moving Target Indicator, RADAR .... AMTIR
Advanced Multi Role Combat Aircraft (ACAE) .... AMRCA
Advanced Multi Spectral Scanner (ACAE) .... AMSS
Advanced Multichannel Microwave Radiometer (SAUS) .... AMMR
Advanced Multichannel Microwave Sensor (SAUS) .... AMMS
Advanced Multifunctions Radar (ACAE) .... AMR
Advanced Multimission RADAR .... AMMR
Advanced Multimission Reconnaissance System [*Military*] (MCD) .... AMMRS
Advanced Multimission Remotely Piloted Vehicle (MCD) .... AMRPV
Advanced Multimission Sensor System .... AMSS
Advanced Multimission Torpedo (MCD) .... AMMT
Advanced Multi-Mode Radar Altimeter (SAUS) .... AMRA
Advanced Multiplatform Navy Computer System (MCD) .... AMNCS
Advanced Multiple Environment Simulator (SAUS) .... AMES
Advanced Multiple-Beam Equalization Radiography [*Medicine*] (DMAA) .... AMBER
Advanced Multiprogramming Analysis Procedure (SAUS) .... AMAP
Advanced Multi-Programming Processor (SAUS) .... AMPP
Advanced Multipurpose Armor System (ACAE) .... AMAS
Advanced Multipurpose Gas Turbine Program .... AMPGATP
Advanced Multipurpose Large Launch Vehicle (MCD) .... AMLLV
Advanced Multipurpose Missile (MCD) .... AMM
Advanced Multi-Purpose Radar (SAUS) .... AMPR
Advanced Multipurpose Surfacing System (MCD) .... AMSS
Advanced Multi-Sensor System (SAUS) .... AMSS
Advanced Multispectral Image Descriptor System [*Photography*] .... AMIDS
Advanced Multispectral Tracking Adjunct (ACAE) .... AMTA
Advanced Multi-Stage Axial-Flow Compresor Program [*NASA*] (PDAA) .... AMSAC
Advanced Multivision Radar (SAUS) .... AMMR
Advanced Munitions Office (SAUS) .... AMO
Advanced Mutual Security Act .... AMSA
Advanced Narrow-band Digital Voice Terminal (SAUS) .... ANDVT
Advanced National Certificate [*Education*] (WDAA) .... ANC
Advanced National Radio Data Service [*Joint venture of IBM and Motorola*] (CDE) .... Ardis
Advanced Natural Gas Vehicle .... ANGV
Advanced Naval Gun Weapon System (MCD) .... ANGWS
Advanced Naval System Requirements .... ANSR
Advanced Naval Training School .... ANTS
Advanced Naval Vehicle (CAAL) .... ANV
Advanced Naval Vehicle Concepts Evaluation (MCD) .... ANVCE
Advanced Naval Vehicle Concepts Evaluation programme (SAUS) .... ANVCE
Advanced Navigation School [*British military*] (DMA) .... ANS
Advanced Navigation System Inertial Reference (HLLA) .... ANSIR
Advanced Navigator [*Air Force*] .... AN
Advanced Navy Display System .... ANDS
Advanced Navy Tactical Command and Control System (NG) .... ANTACCS
Advanced Negative Resist [*Materials science*] .... ANR
Advanced Netware (SAUS) .... ANW
Advanced Network & Services, Inc. [*Nonprofit company formed to manage the National Science Foundation Network*] (IID) .... ANS
Advanced Network Design and Management System [*Computer science*] (MHDB) .... ANDMS
Advanced Network Integration (TEL) .... ANI
Advanced Network Management Protocol (SAUS) .... ANMP
Advanced Network Routing (SAUS) .... ANR
Advanced Network Support System [*Computer science*] (PCM) .... ANSS
Advanced Network System [*Computer science*] (ECON) .... ANS
Advanced Network System Architecture (BUR) .... ANSA
Advanced Network System Performance and Application Group [*Computer science*] (VERA) .... ANSPAG
Advanced Networking Test Center (VERA) .... ANTC
Advanced Networks and Services (SAUS) .... ANS
Advanced Neutron Detection Analysis System (SAUS) .... ANDAS
Advanced Neutron Source [*Proposed nuclear reactor*] .... ANS
Advanced Night Reconnaissance Sensor (ACAE) .... ANRS
Advanced Night Viewer Subsystem (MCD) .... ANVS
Advanced Night Vision [*Goggles*] .... ANVIS
Advanced NMR Sys Wrrt [*NASDAQ symbol*] (TTSB) .... ANMRW
Advanced NMR Systems [*Associated Press*] (SAG) .... AdNMR
Advanced NMR Systems [*Associated Press*] (SAG) .... ANMR
Advanced NMR Systems, Inc. [*NASDAQ symbol*] (NQ) .... ANMR
Advanced Noncommissioned Officer Course [*Army*] (INF) .... ANCOC
Advanced Noncommissioned Officer Course [*Army*] .... ANOC
Advanced Noncommissioned Officer Education System (MCD) .... ANCOES
Advanced Non-Rigid Airship [*British*] .... ANR
Advanced Nosetip Test [*AEC*] (MCD) .... ANT
Advanced Nozzle Concepts (MCD) .... ANC
Advanced Nuclear Attack Submarine Program (MCD) .... ANASP
Advanced Nuclear Fuels Corp. (ABAC) .... ANF
Advanced Nuclear Gamma-ray Analysis System (SAUS) .... ANDAS
Advanced Nuclear Gamma-ray Spectrometer (SAUS) .... ANGAS
Advanced Nuclear Systems Engineering (SAUO) .... ANSE
Advanced Nuclear Thermal Rocket Engine Simulator (SAUS) .... ANTARES
Advanced Nucleic Acid Analyzer .... ANAA
Advanced Nurse Practitioner (MEDA) .... ANP
Advanced Nursing Practice in Acute & Critical Care (SAUO) .... ANPACC
Advanced Ocean Drilling Program [*National Science Foundation*] .... AODP
Advanced Ocean Engineering Laboratory [*Scripps Institution of Oceanography*] .... AOEL
Advanced Office Computer [*Northern Telecom, Inc.*] (NITA) .... AOC
Advanced Office Concepts Corp. [*Defunct*] [*Information service or system*] (IID) .... AOC
Advanced Office Concepts Corp. [*Defunct*] (TSSD) .... AOCC
Advanced Office System (SAUS) .... AOS
Advanced Officer's Course [*Army*] .... AOC

Advanced On-Board Processor [*Computer*] ... AOP
Advanced Onboard Processor (SAUS) ... AOP
Advanced Onboard Signal Processor (ACAE) ... AOSP
Advanced On-Screen Information System (SAUS) ... ADONIS
Advanced On-the-job Training System (SAUS) ... AOTS
Advanced Operating Facility [*Computer Technology, Inc.*] ... AOF
Advanced Operating System [*Data General Corp.*] ... AOS
Advanced Operating System/Virtual Storage [*Data General Corp.*] ... AOS/VS
Advanced Operational Base [*Navy*] ... AOB
Advanced Operational Studies Fellowship (SAUS) ... AOSF
Advanced Operations Support System (SAUS) ... AOSS
Advanced Operations Unit [*Navy*] ... ADVON
Advanced Optical Adjunct (LAIN) ... AOA
Advanced Optical Character Reader ... AOCR
Advanced Optical Character Recognition (SAUS) ... AOCR
Advanced Optical Counter Measures (SAUS) ... AOCM
Advanced Optical Position Transducer (SAUS) ... AOPT
Advanced Optical Power Spectrum Analyzer (MCD) ... AOPSA
Advanced Optical Rate Sensor ... AORS
Advanced Optics Technology (MCD) ... ADOPT
Advanced (or Advancing) Blade Concept (SAUS) ... ABC
Advanced Orbit Laboratory Operations (SAUS) ... AOLO
Advanced Orbital Launch Operations ... AOLO
Advanced Orbital Test Satellite [*European Space Agency*] ... AOTS
Advanced Orbit/Ephemeris Subsystem ... AOES
Advanced Orbiting Astronautical Observatory ... AOAO
Advanced Orbiting Geophysical Observatory ... AOGO
Advanced Orbiting Solar Observatory [*NASA*] ... AOSO
Advanced Orbiting Solar Panel (ACAE) ... AOSP
Advanced Orbiting System (SAUS) ... AOS
Advanced Order Entry [*Investment system*] (ECON) ... AOE
Advanced Ordnance Department [*British*] ... AOD
Advanced Ordnance Depot ... AOD
Advanced Ordnance Test Station (SAUS) ... Adv Ord Test Sta
Advanced Organisation (SAUS) ... AO
Advanced Organisation Saint Hill (SAUS) ... AOSH
Advanced Orthopedic Tech [*NASDAQ symbol*] (TTSB) ... AOTI
Advanced Orthopedic Technologies, Inc. [*Associated Press*] (SAG) ... AdvOrtho
Advanced Orthopedic Techs [*NASDAQ symbol*] (SAG) ... AOTI
Advanced Other Network (SAUS) ... EON
Advanced Oxidation Process [*Chemistry*] ... AOP
Advanced Packet Exchange (VERA) ... APEX
Advanced Panoramic Helmet Interface Demonstrator System (SAUS) ... APHIDS
Advanced Panoramic Sonar-Hull-mounted (SAUS) ... APSOH
Advanced Papyrological Information System ... APIS
Advanced Parallel Technology (SAUS) ... APT
Advanced Paris Release (SAUS) ... APR
Advanced Park (SAUO) ... Adv Pk
Advanced Park (SAUS) ... AP
Advanced Particles and Fields Observer (EOSA) ... APAFO
Advanced Parts List (SAA) ... APL
Advanced Parts Procurement (MCD) ... APP
Advanced Parts Release (NASA) ... APR
Advanced Passenger Information System (SAUS) ... APIS
Advanced Passenger Train [*British*] ... ADP
Advanced Passenger Train [*British*] ... APT
Advanced Passenger Trains (SAUS) ... APTS
Advanced Passenger Transport (OA) ... APT
Advanced Passive Array Sonobuoy [*Navy*] (CAAL) ... APAS
Advanced Passive Light Water Reactor [*Nuclear energy*] ... APLWR
Advanced Passive Sensors [*Military*] (IUSS) ... APAS
Advanced Patent Technique ... APT
Advanced Patrol Sensor System (MCD) ... ADPASS
Advanced Pay ... ADV/P
Advanced Pay Grade (DNAB) ... APG
Advanced Pediatric Life Support (NUJO) ... APLS
Advanced Peer-to-Peer Communications [*IBM Corp.*] (VERA) ... APPC
Advanced Peer-to-Peer Internetworking (SAUS) ... APPI
Advanced Peer-to-Peer Network [*Computer science*] (DDC) ... APPN
Advanced Peer-to-Peer Networking [*Computer science*] ... APPN
Advanced Penetration Model (MCD) ... APM
Advanced Performance Algorithm (SAUS) ... APA
Advanced Performance Computer ... APC
Advanced Performance Interceptor ... API
Advanced Personal Computer (NITA) ... APC
Advanced Personal Defense Weapon [*Army*] (INF) ... APDW
Advanced Personal (or Personnel) Data System (SAUS) ... ADPS
Advanced Personnel Data System (MCD) ... APDS
Advanced Personnel System ... APS
Advanced Personnel Testing (ADWA) ... APT
Advanced Phased Array Chemical High Energy laser equipment (SAUS) ... APACHE
Advanced Phased-array Active Radar (SAUS) ... APAR
Advanced Photo System [*Camera and film system introduced in 1996*] [*Eastman Kodak Co.*] ... APS
Advanced Photon Research Facility [*Proposed, 1986, for high-energy physics*] ... APRF
Advanced Photon Source [*Particle accelerator*] [*Argonne National Laboratory*] ... APS
Advanced Photonix, Inc. [*Associated Press*] (SAG) ... AdvPhot
Advanced Photonix, Inc. [*AMEX symbol*] (SPSG) ... API
Advanced Photonix'A' [*AMEX symbol*] (TTSB) ... API
Advanced Photoscale Technology (PCM) ... APT
Advanced Photosynthetic System ... APS
Advanced Photovoltaic & Electronics Experiment (SAUS) ... APEX
Advanced Physical Fitness Test (INF) ... APFT
Advanced Pilot Training (PDAA) ... APT
Advanced Pilotage System Program (SAUS) ... APSP
Advanced Pioneering Performance by Leading Engineering ... APPLE
Advanced Piston Corer (SAUS) ... APC
Advanced Piston Coring [*Drilling technology*] ... APC
Advanced Placement [*Education*] ... AP
Advanced Placement Program ... APP
Advanced Planetary Mission Technology [*NASA*] ... APMT
Advanced Planetary Probe ... APP
Advanced Planetary Spacecraft System ... APSS
Advanced Planner and Optimizer (SAUS) ... APO
Advanced Planning (ODBW) ... ADPLAN
Advanced Planning Acquisition Information (AAGC) ... APAI
Advanced Planning and Design [*NASA*] (KSC) ... AP & D
Advanced Planning and Design (SAUS) ... AP&D
Advanced Planning and Technology Office [*Kennedy Space Center Directorate*] (NASA) ... PT
Advanced Planning Briefing [*Program*] [*DoD*] (RDA) ... APB
Advanced Planning Briefs [*or Briefings*] **for Industry** (MCD) ... APBI
Advanced Planning Data Sheet ... APDS
Advanced Planning Division (SAUS) ... APD
Advanced Planning Document [*DoD*] (AABC) ... APD
Advanced Planning Procurement Information (SAUS) ... APPI
Advanced Planning Program Scheduling ... APPS
Advanced Planning System (ACAE) ... APS
Advanced Platform Technologies (SAUS) ... APT
Advanced Point Defense Missile System [*Navy*] ... APDMS
Advanced Point Defense Surface Missile System [*Navy*] ... APDSMS
Advanced Pointing Tracking (MCD) ... APT
Advanced Polar Orbiting Satellite ... APOS
Advanced Polaris Guidance Information ... APOGI
Advanced Polarization Diversity Autotrack Receiver (SAUS) ... APDAR
Advanced Polymer Composite [*Materials science*] ... APC
Advanced Polymer Sys [*NASDAQ symbol*] (TTSB) ... APOS
Advanced Polymer Systems, Inc. [*Associated Press*] (SAG) ... AdvPoly
Advanced Polymer Systems, Inc. [*NASDAQ symbol*] (NQ) ... APOS
Advanced Polysilicon Self-Aligned (SAUS) ... APSA
Advanced Pork Technology Association (AC) ... APTA
Advanced Portable Coronary Observation Radio (SAUS) ... APCOR
Advanced Post [*Military*] ... AP
Advanced Post Boost System [*Military*] ... APBS
Advanced Post Boost Vehicle (MCD) ... APBV
Advanced Post Office [*Military*] ... APO
Advanced Power Conversion Experimental Facility ... APCEF
Advanced Power Conversion Skid Experiment (SAUS) ... APCSE
Advanced Power Management [*Computer science*] (PCM) ... APM
Advanced Power Management System [*Jammer*] (MCD) ... APMS
Advanced Power Source (SAUS) ... APS
Advanced Power System ... APS
Advanced Power Technology [*Army*] ... APT
Advanced Power Train Electronic Controller [*Automotive engineering*] ... APTEC
Advanced Practice Nurse (NUJO) ... APN
Advanced Practice Registered Nurse (SAUO) ... APRN
Advanced Pressure Tube Reactor [*Nuclear energy*] ... APTR
Advanced Pressurized [*In name of nuclear reactor, AP 600, developed by Westinghouse Electric Corp.*] ... AP
Advanced Pressurized-Water Reactor [*Nuclear energy*] ... APWR
Advanced Printer Function [*Computer science*] (VERA) ... APE
Advanced Printer Function (SAUS) ... APF
Advanced Printing Service (SAUS) ... APS
Advanced Probe Technology (AAEL) ... APT
Advanced Process Control (AAEL) ... APC
Advanced Process Control Framework Initiative (AAEL) ... APCFI
Advanced Process Equipment Control (AAEL) ... APEC
Advanced Processing Science Center [*Oak Ridge National Laboratory*] ... APSC
Advanced Processing Technology (ABAC) ... APT
Advanced Processing Technology Institute (ABAC) ... APTI
Advanced Processor [*Honeywell, Inc.*] (NITA) ... AP
Advanced Processor Technology Air to Air Missile (ACAE) ... APTAAM
Advanced Processor Temperature Control (SAUS) ... APTC
Advanced Procurement (NG) ... AP
Advanced Procurement & Logistics Systems conference (SAUS) ... APLS
Advanced Procurement Change [*or Check*] (MCD) ... APC
Advanced Procurement Engineering (MCD) ... APE
Advanced Procurement Funding (MCD) ... APF
Advanced Procurement Information (MCD) ... API
Advanced Procurement Package (MCD) ... APP
Advanced Procurement Plan [*Navy*] [*British*] ... APP
Advanced Procurement Planning Program ... APPP
Advanced Procurement Planning System for Security Assistance ... APPSSA
Advanced Product Change Notice ... APCN
Advanced Product Evaluation Laboratory ... APEL
Advanced Product Line (IAA) ... APL
Advanced Product Planning Operation (MUGU) ... APPO
Advanced Product Planning Organization (SAUS) ... APPO
Advanced Production Engineering ... APE
Advanced Production Release (SAUS) ... APR
Advanced Production System (SAUS) ... APS
Advanced Productivity Research and Technology (MCD) ... APRT
Advanced Products & Technologies, Incorporated (SAUO) ... APTI
Advanced Products NV (SAUS) ... APNV
Advanced Profession Computer (SAUS) ... APC
Advanced Professional Certificate (PGP) ... APC
Advanced Professional Computer (HGAA) ... APC

Advanced Professional Programs, University of Southern California Law Center (SAUS) .... USCAPP
Advanced Professional Sales, Incorporated (SAUO) .... APSI
Advanced Program Authorization (SAUS) .... APA
Advanced Program Development .... APD
Advanced Program Management Course [Army] .... APMC
Advanced Program to Program Communications Protocol [Computer science] (VERA) .... APPCP
Advanced Program Weight Control System .... APWCS
Advanced Programmable Interrupt Controller .... AIPC
Advanced Programmable Interrupt Controller [Computer science] .... APIC
Advanced Programming Course [Computer science] .... APC
Advanced Programming Language [Computer science] .... APL
Advanced Programming Language Statistical Package (MCD) .... APLSTATPACK
Advanced Programming Option (SAUS) .... APO
Advanced Programs Authorization .... APA
Advanced Program-to-Program Communication [Computer science] .... APPC
Advanced Program-to-Program Communication/Personal Computer [IBM Corp.] (BYTE) .... APPC/PC
Advanced Progressive Matrices [Intelligence test] .... APM
Advanced Project Planning .... APP
Advanced Promotion Technologies, Inc. [Associated Press] (SAG) .... AdvPro
Advanced Promotion Technology (SAUS) .... APT
Advanced Promotion Technology [NASDAQ symbol] (SPSG) .... APTV
Advanced Propellant System .... APS
Advanced Propulsion Comparison Study [NASA] (NASA) .... APC
Advanced Propulsion Cooling .... APC
Advanced Propulsion Packaged Liquid Engine (SAUS) .... APPLE
Advanced Propulsion Payload Effects [NASA] (NASA) .... APPLE
Advanced Propulsion Subsystem Integration [Air Force] .... APSI
Advanced Propulsion System (SAUS) .... APS
Advanced Propulsion Test (SSD) .... APT
Advanced Protein Crystal Growth (SAUS) .... APCG
Advanced Protein Crystal Growth Facility (SSD) .... APCGF
Advanced Protein Purification System .... APPS
Advanced Protocol Controller [Adax, Inc.] .... APC
Advanced Proton Source [Physics] .... APS
Advanced Public Transportation System (SAUO) .... APTS
Advanced Public Transportation Systems .... APTS
Advanced Publishing Technology (SAUS) .... APT
Advanced Purification [Chromatography] .... AP
Advanced PVO [Protivo-Vozdushnaia Oborona] Intercepter [Military] (MCD) .... APVOI
Advanced Qualification Program [FAA] (TAG) .... AQP
Advanced Qualitative and Quantitative Personnel Requirements Information [Army] .... AQQPRI
Advanced Qualitative and Quantitative Personnel Requirements Information (SAUS) .... AQQPRI
Advanced Query Language (SAUS) .... AQL
Advanced Quick Look [Army] .... AQL
Advanced Quickfix [Military] .... AQF
Advanced Quickfix sensor (SAUS) .... AQF
Advanced Quick-Look sensor (SAUS) .... AQL
Advanced Radar Altimeter (EOSA) .... ADALT
Advanced Radar Altimeter (SAUS) .... ARA
Advanced Radar Altimeter (SAUS) RA-2
Advanced RADAR Experimental Systems Technology [Army] .... AREST
Advanced RADAR Information Evaluation System .... ARIES
Advanced Radar Maintenance Training Set (SAUS) .... ARMTS
Advanced Radar Missile Scoring System (SAUS) .... ARMS
Advanced Radar Modelling System (SAUS) .... ARMS
Advanced RADAR Pattern Recognition .... ARPR
Advanced RADAR Processing System .... ARPS
Advanced Radar Target Identification System (ACAE) .... ARTIS
Advanced Radar Techniques for Improved Surveillance & Tracking (SAUS) .... ARTIST
Advanced RADAR Terminal System (IEEE) .... ARTS
Advanced Radar Test-Bed [Military] (DOMA) .... ARTB
Advanced Radar Tracking System (SAUS) .... ARTS
Advanced RADAR Traffic Control System [Air Force] (AFM) ..... ARTCS
Advanced RADAR Traffic Control System [Air Force] .... ARTS
Advanced Radar Traffic System (SAUS) .... ARTS
Advanced Radar Warning Receiver (SAUS) .... ARWAR
Advanced RADAR Warning Receiver (MCD) .... ARWR
Advanced RADAR Warning System (MCD) .... ARWS
Advanced Radiation Effects Simulation .... ARES
Advanced Radiation Space Defense Application (MCD) .... ARSDA
Advanced Radiation Technology (ACAE) .... ART
Advanced Radiation Technology Facility (SAUO) .... ARTF
Advanced Radiation Technology Office [Military] .... ARTO
Advanced Radio Astronomy Explorer (PDAA) .... ARAE
Advanced Radio Data Information Service [IBM Corp., Motorola, Inc.] .... ARDIS
Advanced Radio Interferometry Between Space and Earth ...... ARISE
Advanced Radio Local Area Network (CIST) .... ARLAN
Advanced Radio Technology Subcommittee (CGWS) .... ARTS
Advanced Radio Telecom [NASDAQ symbol] (SG) .... ARTT
Advanced Radio Telecom Corp. [Associated Press] (SAG) ...... AdvRdio
Advanced Radio Telecom Corp. [NASDAQ symbol] (SAG) ...... ARTT
Advanced Railroad Electronics System [A space guidance system made by Collins Air Transport] .... ARES
Advanced Railway Depot (SAUO) .... ARD
Advanced Range Data System [Air Force] .... ARDS
Advanced Range Instrumentation Aircraft .... ARIA
Advanced Range Instrumentation Ship [Navy symbol] .... ARIS
Advanced Range Instrumentation Systems (MCD) .... ARIS

Advanced Range (or Ranging) Testing, Reporting and Control (SAUS) .... ARTRAC
Advanced Range Testing, Reporting, and Control .... ARTRAC
Advanced Raster-Graphics System (MHDB) .... ARGS
Advanced Reactivity Measurement Facility [Idaho Falls, ID] [Department of Energy] .... ARMF
Advanced Reactivity Measurement Facility (SAUS) .... ARMF
Advanced Reactor (KSC) .... AR
Advanced Reactor Development Associates .... ARDA
Advanced Reactor Technology (IEEE) .... ART
Advanced Reactors Division [of the Nuclear Regulatory Commission] (NRCH) .... ARD
Advanced Readiness (MCD) .... AR
Advanced Real Time Total Information System (SAUS) .... ARTTIS
Advanced Real-time Executive (SAUS) .... ARE
Advanced Real-Time Processing System (PDAA) .... ARPS
Advanced Real-Time Range Control (IEEE) .... ARTRAC
Advanced Real-Time Simulation (MCD) .... ARTS
Advanced Real-Time System (MCD) .... ARTS
Advanced Reasoning Tool (IDAI) .... ART
Advanced Receiver Model System .... ARMS
Advanced Recoilless Weapon (MCD) .... ARW
Advanced Reconfigurable Computer System .... ARCS
Advanced Reconnaissance and Target Acquisition Capabilities .... ARTAC
Advanced Reconnaissance Electrically Propelled Spacecraft (SAUS) ..... AREPS
Advanced Reconnaissance Electrically-Propelled Spacecraft [Military] (PDAA) .... AREPS
Advanced Reconnaissance Helicopter .... ARH
Advanced Reconnaissance Satellite .... ARS
Advanced Reconnaissance Sensor [Military] (IUSS) .... ADRES
Advanced Reconnaissance System (ACAE) .... ADRES
Advanced Reconnaissance System (MUGU) .... ARS
Advanced Record System [Air Force] .... ARS
Advanced Recovery Mode [Computer science] .... ARM
Advanced Recovery Sequencer (DWSG) .... ARS
Advanced Recovery System (MCD) .... ADRECS
Advanced Recovery System (SAUS) .... ARS
Advanced Reentry Concepts [Aerospace] .... ARC
Advanced Reentry Program [Aerospace] .... ARP
Advanced Reentry System (SAUS) .... ARES
Advanced Reentry System [Aerospace] .... ARS
Advanced Regional Prediction System [Marine science] (OSRA) ..... ARPS
Advanced Registered Nurse Practitioner .... ARNP
Advanced Regulating Station [British military] (DMA) .... ARS
Advanced Relay and Technology Mission Satellite (SAUS) ..... ARTEMIS
Advanced Relay Technology Mission .... ARTEMIS
Advanced Remote Display Station (IAA) .... ARDS
Advanced Remote Minehunting System (SAUS) .... ARMS
Advanced Remote Node [Bay Networks] [Computer science] .... ARN
Advanced Remote Tracking Station (MCD) .... ARTS
Advanced Remotely Operated Underwater Vehicle (SAUS) ..... ARDROV
Advanced Remotely Piloted Modular Aircraft (MCD) .... ARPMA
Advanced Remotely Piloted Vehicle [Aviation] (AIA) .... ARPV
Advanced Repeater for Aeronautic and Maritime Integrated Services (ACAE) .... ARAMIS
Advanced Reproductive Technology [Medicine] .... ART
Advanced Requirements Tasking Information and Support System (MCD) .... ARTISS
Advanced Rescue and Recovery System [Proposed VTOL aircraft] [Also, ARS] (MCD) .... ARRS
Advanced Rescue System [Proposed VTOL aircraft] [Also, ARRS] ...... ARS
Advanced Reseach and Development Agency .... ARDA
Advanced Research Agency Project Tempo (MCD) .... ARAPT
Advanced Research & Applications (SAUS) .... Aracor
Advanced Research and Development .... AR & D
Advanced Research and Development Activity (SAUS) .... AR&DA
Advanced Research and Global Observation Satellite (ADWA) ..... ARGOS
Advanced Research and Global Observation Satellite/Extreme Ultraviolet Imaging Photometer (SAUS) .... ARGOS/EUVIP
Advanced Research and Global Observation Satellite/Unconventional Stellar Aspect (SAUS) .... ARGOS/USA
Advanced Research and Technology (MUGU) .... AR & T
Advanced Research and Technology .... ART
Advanced Research and Technology Development Program [Department of Energy] .... AR & TD
Advanced Research Center [Aerospace] .... ARC
Advanced Research Consultants (MCD) .... ARCON
Advanced Research Craft Hydrokeel (MCD) .... ARCK
Advanced Research Division .... ARD
Advanced Research Electromagnetic Simulation (or Simulator) (SAUS) .... ARES
Advanced Research Engine (MCD) .... ARE
Advanced Research Environmental Test Satellite (SAUS) ...... ARENTS
Advanced Research Geophysical Observatory (IAA) .... ARGO
Advanced Research Instrument System (SAUS) .... ARIS
Advanced Research Instrument System, Inc. .... ARIS
Advanced Research Objective (MCD) .... ARO
Advanced Research on Groups Under Stress (SAUO) .... ARGUS
Advanced Research Perspectives Program (SAUS) .... ARPPS
Advanced Research Planning Document .... ARPD
Advanced Research Program Directive (MCD) .... ARPD
Advanced Research Project Agency Measurement Radar (IUSS) ..... AMRAD
Advanced Research Projects .... ARP
Advanced Research Projects Agency [Later, DARPA] [DoD] ...... ARPA
Advanced Research Projects Agency Network [DoD] .... ARPANET

Advanced Research Projects Agency Research Center [*DoD*] (DNAB) .... ARPARSCHCEN
Advanced Research Projects Agency Terminal [*DoD*] .... ARPAT
Advanced Research Projects Agency-Network Information Center (SAUS) .... ARPA-NIC
Advanced Research Testbed for Medical Informatics (ADWA) .... ARTEMIS
Advanced Research Workshop .... ARW
Advanced Resident Training Plan [*Military*] (AABC) .... ARTP
Advanced Resolution Gunnery Simulator (SAUS) .... ARGS
Advanced Resolution Technology [*Minolta*] (VERA) .... ART
Advanced Resource Tracking Spreadsheet [*Scitor Corp.*] [*Computer science*] (PCM) .... ARTS
Advanced Restricted Report .... ARR
Advanced Rifle Grenade Munition [*Army*] (INF) .... ARGM
Advanced Rifle Marksmanship [*Military*] (INF) .... ARM
Advanced RISC [*Reduced Instruction Set Computer*] **Computing** (CDE) .... ARC
Advanced RISC [*Reduced Instruction-Set Computerizing*] **Machine** (ECON) .... ARM
Advanced Road Profile Measurement Vehicle [*Suspension design and testing*] [*Automotive engineering*] .... ARPMV
Advanced Robotics Research .... ARR
Advanced Rocket Engine Storable (MCD) .... ARES
Advanced Rocket Ramjet (MCD) .... ARR
Advanced Rocket Ramjet .... ARRJ
Advanced Rocket System [*Military*] (DOMA) .... ARS
Advanced Rotocraft Technology Integration (SAUS) .... ARTI
Advanced Rotorcraft Transmission (SAUS) .... ART
Advanced Routing Protocol (CIST) .... ARP
Advanced Ruling Expiration Date [*IRS*] .... AD
Advanced Run Length Limited [*Computer science*] .... ARLL
Advanced Rural Transportation Systems [*FHWA*] (TAG) .... ARTS
Advanced Russian Proficiency Test (TES) .... ARPT
Advanced Safe Device (ACAE) .... ASD
Advanced Safety Vehicle [*Automotive engineering*] .... ASV
Advanced SAGE [*Semiautomatic Ground Environment*] **Tracking Study** [*Military*] (IAA) .... ASTS
Advanced Sales Index [*LIMRA*] .... ASI
Advanced Salvo Rifle (MCD) .... ASR
Advanced Satellite .... ASAT
Advanced Satellite for Cosmology and Astrophysics [*Japanese spacecraft*] .... ASCA
Advanced Satellite Products Project [*Madison, WI*] [*NOAA/NESDIS*] (GRD) .... ASPP
Advanced Satellite Tracking Center .... ASTC
Advanced Saturn Data Adapter (SAUS) .... ASDA
Advanced Saturn Guidance Computer (SAUS) .... ASGC
Advanced Scanning Array Module (ACAE) .... ASAM
Advanced Scatterable Mine [*Air Force*] (MCD) .... ASM
Advanced Scatterometer (CARB) .... A-SCAT
Advanced Scatterometer (CARB) .... ASCATT
Advanced School (SAUO) .... ADVSCOL
Advanced School of Automobile Engineering (SAUO) .... ASAE
Advanced Schools (MUGU) .... ADVSCOL
Advanced Schottky (AEBE) .... AS
Advanced Schottky Transitor-Transistor Logic (AAEL) .... ASTTL
Advanced Science Education Program [*National Science Foundation*] .... ASEP
Advanced Sciences Research Group (SAA) .... ASRG
Advanced Scientific Array Processor (SAUS) .... ASAP
Advanced Scientific Array Processors (GEOI) .... ASAP
Advanced Scientific Computer [*Texas Instruments, Inc.*] .... ASC
Advanced Scientific Instrument (IAA) .... ASIS
Advanced Scientific Instruments [*AMR, Inc.*] .... ASI
Advanced Scientific Instruments Symbolic Translator [*Assembly program*] (DEN) .... ASIST
Advanced Scout Helicopter [*Military*] .... ASH
Advanced Scout Helicopter Task Force [*Army*] (RDA) .... ASH-TF
Advanced SCSI Architecture (SAUS) .... ASA
Advanced SCSI Programmer (or Programming) Interface (SAUS) .... ASPI
Advanced SCSI [*Small Computer System Interface*] **Programming Interface** (PCM) .... ASPI
Advanced Sea Ice Zone (SAUS) .... ASIZ
Advanced Sea Mine (SAUS) .... ASM
Advanced Sea-Based Deterrent [*Navy*] .... ASBD
Advanced Seal Delivery System [*Formerly, Advanced Swimmer Delivery System*] [*Navy*] (DOMA) .... ASDS
Advanced SEAL Delivery System (SAUS) .... ASDS
Advanced Sea-Launched Cruise Missile (MCD) .... ASLCM
Advanced Secondary Treatment [*Environmental science*] (EPAT) .... AST
Advanced Secondary Wastewater Treatment (EEVL) .... AST
Advanced Secretarial Language Certificate [*British*] (DI) .... ASLC
Advanced Section Communication Zone [*World War II*] .... ADSC
Advanced Security Agency (SAUS) .... ASA
Advanced Security and Identification Technology (SAUS) .... ASIT
Advanced Seeker Development Program (SAUS) .... ASDP
Advanced Seeker Homing (SAUS) .... ASH
Advanced Seeker Technology for Air-to-Air Missiles (SAUS) .... ASTAAM
Advanced Seismic Computer (SAUS) .... ASC
Advanced Self-Contained Chemical Energy Propulsion (SAUS) .... ADSCEPTS
Advanced Self-Protection [*Jammer*] (MCD) .... ASP
Advanced Self-Protection Integrated Suite [*Military*] (DOMA) .... ASPIS
Advanced Self-Protective Jammer (SAUS) .... ASPJ
Advanced Self-Timed Random Access Memory [*Computer science*] (CIST) .... ASTRAM
Advanced Semi. Eng. ADS [*NYSE symbol*] .... ASX
Advanced Semi Mat's [*NASDAQ symbol*] (TTSB) .... ASMIF
Advanced Semiconductor Equipment Exposition (TSPED) .... ASEE
Advanced Semiconductor Materials .... ASM
Advanced Semiconductor Materials International (MHDW) .... ASMIF
Advanced Semiconductor Materials International NV [*Associated Press*] (SAG) .... AdvSem
Advanced Semiconductor Materials International NV [*NASDAQ symbol*] (NQ) .... ASMI
Advanced Sensor Analog Relay System [*Army*] (MCD) .... ASARS
Advanced Sensor Demonstration (ACAE) .... ASD
Advanced Sensor Development Program (SAUS) .... ASDP
Advanced Sensor Evaluation and Test [*NASA*] .... ASET
Advanced Sensor Exploitation (ACAE) .... ASE
Advanced Sensor Exploration [*Military*] (IUSS) .... ASE
Advanced Sensors Demonstration Program (ACAE) .... ASDP
Advanced Series 400 (SAUS) AS/400
Advanced Series of Tactical Air Defence Radars (SAUS) .... ASTAR
Advanced Server [*Computer science*] (VERA) .... AS
Advanced Server Environment (SAUS) .... ASE
Advanced Server Management [*Acer*] [*Computer science*] (VERA) .... ASM
Advanced Servomanipulator .... ASM
Advanced Shared Aperture Program (SAUS) .... ASAP
Advanced Ship Communications (SAUS) .... ADSCOM
Advanced Ship Concept Development .... ASCD
Advanced Ship Concepts .... ASC
Advanced Ship Development .... ASD
Advanced Ship Types and Combatant Craft (MCD) .... ASTACC
Advanced Shipboard Command Communications System (SAA) .... ASCCS
Advanced Shipboard Communications (MCD) .... ADSCOM
Advanced Shipboard Satellite Communications (DNAB) .... ASSC
Advanced Shipment Notification [*Inventory control*] [*Automotive manufacturing*] .... ASN
Advanced Ship-to-Shore Automatic Telegraph System (SAUS) .... ASSATS
Advanced Short Takeoff and Vertical Landing [*Military*] .... ASTOVL
Advanced Short-Range Air Defense System (MCD) .... ASHORAD
Advanced Short-Range Air-to-Air Missile (MCD) .... ASRAA
Advanced Short-Range Air-to-Air Missile (RDA) .... ASRAAM
Advanced Short-to-Median-Range (SAUS) .... ASMR
Advanced Short-to-Medium Range .... ASMR
Advanced Signal Processing (VERA) .... ASP
Advanced Signal Processing System (VERA) .... ASPS
Advanced Signal Processor [*Computer science*] .... ASP
Advanced Signal Processor (SAUS) .... ASPRO
Advanced Signals (SAUS) .... AD Sigs
Advanced Signals Assistant Director of Signals (SAUS) .... ADSIGS
Advanced Simulation [*Missions project*] .... ADSIM
Advanced Simulation Center [*Army*] (MCD) .... ASC
Advanced Simulation Facility [*Army*] (MCD) .... ASF
Advanced Simulation Initiative (SAUS) .... ASI
Advanced Simulation Language (SAUS) .... ASL
Advanced Simulation Technology [*DoD*] (IEEE) .... AST
Advanced Simulator for Pilot Training (MCD) .... ASPT
Advanced Simulator for Undergraduate Pilot Training [*Air Force*] .... ASUPT
Advanced Size Reduction Facility (MCD) .... ASRF
Advanced Skewed Sensory Electronic Triad [*Navy*] .... ASSET
Advanced Skills Education Program [*Army*] .... ASEP
Advanced Sleep Phase Syndrome [*Medicine*] (DMAA) .... ASPS
Advanced Small Axial Turbine Technology (RDA) .... ASATT
Advanced Small Computer Systems Interface (VERA) .... ASCSI
Advanced Small Computer Systems Interface (ADWA) .... ASPI
Advanced Small Launch Vehicle .... ASLV
Advanced Small-Axial-Turbine Technology (SAUS) .... ASATT
Advanced Smokeless Technology Demonstration Motor (MCD) .... ASTDM
Advanced Sodium Cooled Reactor (SAUS) .... ASCR
Advanced Software Products, Inc. (SAUS) .... ASP
Advanced Software System (SAUS) .... ADSS
Advanced Software Technology and Algorithms (SAUS) .... ASTA
Advanced Solar Coronal Explorer (SAUS) .... ASCE
Advanced Solar Observatory (DEN) .... ASO
Advanced Solar Turbo-Electric Concept (SAUS) .... ASTEC
Advanced Solar Turbo-Electric Conversion .... ASTEC
Advanced Solid Axial Stage programme (SAUS) .... ASAS
Advanced Solid Logic Technology [*Computer science*] .... ASLT
Advanced Solid Rocket Motor [*Proposed*] [*NASA*] .... ASRM
Advanced Solid State Array Sensor (CARB) .... ASAS
Advanced Solid State Array Spectrometer (ACAE) .... ASAS
Advanced Solidification Experiment Activity (SAUS) .... ASEA
Advanced Solid-State Array Sensor (SAUS) .... ASASP
Advanced Sonobuoy Communications Link [*Navy*] (MCD) .... ASC
Advanced Sonobuoy Communications Link [*Navy*] (MCD) .... ASCL
Advanced Soviet [*Combined with GENS to form A Group*] [*Division of National Security Agency*] .... ADVA
Advanced Space Applications Program [*Military*] .... ASAP
Advanced Space Computer (SAUS) .... ASC
Advanced Space Engine (NASA) .... ASE
Advanced Space Ground Link Subsystem (MCD) .... ASGLS
Advanced Space Guidance System (IIA) .... ASGS
Advanced Space Propellant Demonstration (MCD) .... ASPD
Advanced Space Station .... ASS
Advanced Space Structure Technology Research Experiments (MCD) .... ASTREX
Advanced Space Technology Division [*NASA*] (NASA) .... ASTD
Advanced Space Technology Program [*Military*] (DOMA) .... ASTP
Advanced Space Vehicle Engineering Operation (SAUS) .... ASVEO
Advanced Spaceborne Computer Module (IUSS) .... ASCM
Advanced Spaceborne Thermal Emission and Reflection Radiometer (NAKS) .... ASTER

Advanced Spaceborne Thermal Emission Reflectance (SAUS) ASTER
Advanced Spacecraft Subsystem Cost Analysis Structure (MCD) ASSCAS
Advanced Spacecraft Thermal Analysis Routine (ACAE) ASTAR
Advanced Spacecraft Trainer [*or Transport or Truck*] **Reusable Orbiter** [*NASA*] (MCD) ASTRO
Advanced Spacecraft Truck/Trainer/ Transport Reusable Orbiter (SAUS) ASTRO
Advanced Spatial Disorientation Demonstrator (SAUS) ASDD
Advanced Special Electronics Mission Aircraft (SAUS) ASEMA
Advanced Special Projects in Radiation Effects ASPIRE
Advanced Special Receiver (SAUS) ASR
Advanced Specialist in Education Certificate (GAGS) ASEdCert
Advanced Spectre Entropy Coding (VERA) ASPEC
Advanced Speech Processing Station (ACAE) ASPS
Advanced Speech Processor (ACRL) ASP
Advanced Squadron (SAUO) ASq
Advanced Stack Network Management (SAUS) ASNM
Advanced Standard Buried Collector (IAA) ASBC
Advanced Stand-off Area Weapon (SAUS) ASAW
Advanced STANO [*Surveillance, Target Acquisition, and Night Observation*] **Data Link** [*Military*] (MCD) ASDL
Advanced Star/Target Reference Optical Sensor (SSD) ASTROS
Advanced Static Test Recording Apparatus ASTRA
Advanced Station (MHDI) ADVAST
Advanced Statistical Analysis Program [*Computer science*] (MCD) ASTAP
Advanced Status Threat Generator (DWSG) ASTG
Advanced Stepper Application Program (AAEL) ASAP
Advanced Stirling Conversion System [*Mechanical engineering*] ASCS
Advanced Stokes polarimeter (SAUS) ASP
Advanced Storage Control Test (SAUS) ASCOT
Advanced Storage Magneto Optical (SAUS) ASMO
Advanced Stored Chemical Energy Propulsion System (ACAE) ADSCEPS
Advanced STOVL aircraft (SAUS) ASTOVL
Advanced Strategic Aerodynamic Configuration Technology (MCD) ASACT
Advanced Strategic Aerospace Crew Systems (ACAE) ADSACS
Advanced Strategic Air Defense ASAD
Advanced Strategic Air Launced Missile (ACAE) ALSAM
Advanced Strategic Air Launched multimission Missile (SAUS) ASALM
Advanced Strategic Airborne RADAR System ASARS
Advanced Strategic Aircraft (SAUS) AMSAS
Advanced Strategic Air-Launched Missile (MCD) ASALM
Advanced Strategic Computing Initiative [*Department of Energy*] ASCI
Advanced Strategic Missile System [*DoD*] ASM
Advanced Strategic Missile System [*DoD*] (MCD) ASMS
Advanced Strategic Missile Systems [*Air Force*] (DOMA) ASMS
Advanced Strategic Penetrator (ACAE) ASP
Advanced Strategic Penetrator Aircraft (MCD) ASPA
Advanced Strategic Processing (ACAE) ASP
Advanced Strategic Reconnaissance System [*Air Force*] ASRS
Advanced Strategic Standoff Aircraft (MCD) ASSA
Advanced Strategic Standoff Attack Missile (MCD) ASSAM
Advanced Strategic Transport Aircraft ASTA
Advanced Streaming Format [*Computer science*] ASF
Advanced Strike Radar Technology System (ACAE) ASRATS
Advanced Strike Weapon System (MCD) ASWS
Advanced Striking Force (SAUO) ASF
Advanced Strip and Passivation (AAEL) ASP
Advanced Strip Processor ASP
Advanced Structural Concept and Evaluation Program [*Military*] (DNAB) ADCEP
Advanced Structural (or Structure) Analyzer (SAUS) ASTRA
Advanced Structures Technology Demonstration ASTD
Advanced Student in Law [*British*] (ROG) ASL
Advanced Studies Group [*Air Force*] ASG
Advanced Studies Institute (SAUO) ASI
Advanced Study Institute (SAUS) ASI
Advanced Study Institute on Underwater Acoustics and Signal Processing (SAUO) ASI
Advanced Study Institute/NATO (SAUO) ASI/NATO
Advanced Study Institutes (NATG) ASI
Advanced Study of Human Sexuality (SAUS) ASHS
Advanced Study Program ASP
Advanced Submarine Combat System [*Military*] (IUSS) ASCS
Advanced Submarine Control Program (MCD) ASCOP
Advanced Submarine Detection (MCD) ASD
Advanced Submarine Tactical ESM Combat System (SAUS) ASTECS
Advanced Submarine Weapon Handling System (MCD) ASWHS
Advanced Subsonic Aerial Target (SAUS) ASAT
Advanced Super Thin layer and High-Output Metal Media [*Fuji*] (VERA) ATOMM
Advanced Supersonic All-Purpose Dispenser (MCD) ASAP
Advanced Supersonic Technology AST
Advanced Supersonic Transport ASST
Advanced Supersonic Transport AST
Advanced Supplementary [*Education level*] [*British*] AS
Advanced Supplementary Level Examination [*Education*] (WDAA) A/S level
Advanced Supply Depot (SAUO) ASD
Advanced Supply Point (SAUO) ASP
Advanced Support Helicopter (SAUS) ASH
Advanced Support Processor [*Computer science*] (IAA) ASP
Advanced Surface Engineering Technologies ASET
Advanced Surface Machinery System (SAUS) ASMS
Advanced Surface Missile ASM
Advanced Surface Missile System ASMS
Advanced Surface Ship Towed Array Surveillance System (SAUS) ASSTASS
Advanced Surface/Air Missile (IUSS) ASAM
Advanced Surface-to Air Weapon System (SAUS) ASAWS
Advanced Surface-to-Air Missile (SAUS) ASAM
Advanced Surface-to-Air Missile System (SAUS) AdSAMS
Advanced Surface-to-Air Ramjet [*Navy*] ASAR
Advanced Surface-to-Air Ramjet, Extended Range (MCD) ASAR-ER
Advanced Surface-to-Air Ramjet, Medium Range (MCD) ASAR-MR
Advanced Surface-to-Air Rocket Ramjet (MCD) ASARR
Advanced Surgical Centre [*British and Canadian*] [*World War II*] ASC
Advanced Surgical, Inc. [*Associated Press*] (SAG) AdvSu
Advanced Surgical, Inc. [*Associated Press*] (SAG) AdvSurg
Advanced Surgical, Inc. [*NASDAQ symbol*] (SAG) ASUR
Advanced Surgical Suite for Trauma Casualties ASSTC
Advanced Surveillance Aircraft (MCD) ASA
Advanced Surveillance and Reconnaissance Systems ASURS
Advanced Surveillance and Target Acquisition RADAR ASTAR
Advanced Surveillance and Tracking System (ACAE) ASTS
Advanced Surveillance & Tracking Technology (SAUS) ASTT
Advanced Surveillance Drone (MCD) ASD
Advanced Surveillance RADAR ASR
Advanced Surveillance Workstation [*Military*] (IUSS) ASWS
Advanced Survivability Test Bed [*Military*] (INF) ASTB
Advanced Survival Avionics Program (MCD) ASAP
Advanced Survival Techniques and Analysis (ACAE) ASTAP
Advanced Switching Commun. [*NASDAQ symbol*] ASCX
Advanced Symbolic Artwork Preparation (MCD) ASAP
Advanced Synchronous Meteorological Satellite ASMS
Advanced Synthetic Aperture Radar (EOSA) A-SAR
Advanced Synthetic Aperture RADAR System-2 [*RADAR*] ASARS-2
Advanced Synthetic Aperture RADER [*Marine science*] (OSRA) ASAR
Advanced System [*NAS*] AS
Advanced System and Evaluation Technique (SAUS) ASSET
Advanced System Architecture (ACAE) ASA
Advanced System Architecture for Postscript [*Printer technology*] [*QMS, Inc.*] [*Computer science*] (PCM) ASAP
Advanced System Architectures Ltd. (SAUO) ASA
Advanced System Avionics [*Air Force*] ASA
Advanced System Buffering (SAUS) ASB
Advanced System Computer Center (SAUS) ASCC
Advanced System Concept (MCD) ASC
Advanced System Concepts Laboratory [*Army*] ASCL
Advanced System Control/ Processor and Memory (SAUS) ASC/PAM
Advanced System Data Processing Simulation (AABC) ASDPSIM
Advanced System Environment and Threat Simulation ASETS
Advanced System for Communications and Education in National Development (SAUS) ASCEND
Advanced System for Process Engineering ASPEN
Advanced System for Radiological Assessment (SAUS) ASTRA
Advanced System Integration Demonstration [*Military*] ASID
Advanced System Management (SAUS) ASM
Advanced System Planning [*Air Force*] (MCD) ASP
Advanced System Synthesis and Evaluation Technique [*Lockheed Aircraft*] ASSET
Advanced System Technology AST
Advanced System Time Domain ASYSTD
Advanced Systematic Analysis Production (ACAE) ASAP
Advanced Systematic Techniques for Reliable Operational Software [*Computer science*] (MHDI) ASTROS
Advanced Systems and Design ASD
Advanced Systems and Technologies Study Centre (SAUS) CESTA
Advanced Systems and Technology (MCD) AS & T
Advanced Systems and Technology Programme [*European Space Agency*] ASTP
Advanced Systems Buying ASB
Advanced Systems Computer Center (SAUS) ASCC
Advanced Systems Concept Office (SAUO) ASCO
Advanced Systems Concepts Office [*Army*] (RDA) ASCO
Advanced Systems Development Division (SAUO) ASDD
Advanced Systems Development Inc. (SAUO) ASDI
Advanced Systems Division [*IBM Corp.*] ASD
Advanced Systems Engineer (SAUS) Adv Syst Engr
Advanced Systems Engineering ASE
Advanced Systems Group (SAUS) ASG
Advanced Systems Incorporated (SAUO) ASI
Advanced Systems Laboratory ASL
Advanced Systems Planning, Research, Development, and Engineering Course [*Army*] ASPRDEC
Advanced Systems Project Office (SAA) ASPO
Advanced Systems Requirements ASR
Advanced Systems Research and Analysis Office [*Army and NASA joint operation*] (RDA) ASRAO
Advanced Systems Research & Analysis Office (SAUS) ASRAO
Advanced Systems Research Department ASRD
Advanced Systems Synthesis and Evaluation Technique (SAUS) ASSET
Advanced Systems Technology (IEEE) ASTEC
Advanced Systems Technology and Integration Office [*Army*] ASTIO
Advanced Table Look-up (SAUS) ATL
Advanced Tactical ATAC
Advanced Tactical Aerial Reconnaissance System [*Cancelled 1993*] [*Air Force*] (DOMA) ATARS
Advanced Tactical Air Combat Simulation ATACS
Advanced Tactical Air Command and Control System (MCD) ATACCS
Advanced Tactical Air Command Center [*Marine Corps*] (DOMA) ATACC
Advanced Tactical Air Command Central (AAGC) ATACC
Advanced Tactical Air Command Missile Systems (AAGC) ATACMS

Advanced Tactical Air Control Central .... ATACC
Advanced Tactical Air Control System (ACAE) .... ATACS
Advanced Tactical Air Warfare System (SAUS) .... ATAWS
Advanced Tactical Airborne Battle Control System (ACAE) .... ATABCS
Advanced Tactical Airborne Radar Emitter System (SAUS) .... ATARES
Advanced Tactical Airborne Reconnaissance System [*Air Force*] (MCD) .... ATARS
Advanced Tactical Aircraft [*Army*] .... ATA
Advanced Tactical Aircraft (SAUS) .... ATTA
Advanced Tactical Aircraft Command and Control System (SAUS) .... ATACCS
Advanced Tactical Aircraft Launch and Recovery System (MCD) .... ATALARS
Advanced Tactical Aircraft Program System .... ATAPS
Advanced Tactical Aircraft Protection System (ACAE) .... ATAPS
Advanced Tactical Air-to-Air Missile (MCD) .... ATAAM
Advanced Tactical All Weather Strike (ACAE) .... ATAWS
Advanced Tactical Assault Weapon .... ATAW
Advanced Tactical Attack System (MCD) .... ATAS
Advanced Tactical Attack System Mission Analysis (MCD) .... ATASMA
Advanced Tactical Attacks/Manned System (IEEE) .... ATAMS
Advanced Tactical Avionics RADAR .... ATAR
Advanced Tactical Ballistic Missile [*AMC - Missile*] .... ATBM
Advanced Tactical Command and Control Capabilities .... ATCCC
Advanced Tactical Control System (MCD) .... ATCS
Advanced Tactical Cruise System (ACAE) .... ATACS
Advanced Tactical Electronic Warfare System (AFM) .... ATEWS
Advanced Tactical Fighter [*Air Force*] (MCD) .... ATF
Advanced Tactical Fighter Engine (ACAE) .... ATFE
Advanced Tactical Fighter Mission Analysis (MCD) .... ATFMA
Advanced Tactical Inertial Guidance System [*Navy*] .... ATIGS
Advanced Tactical Jamming System [*Aircraft*] .... ATJS
Advanced Tactical Lightweight Air Superiority [*RADAR*] [*Air Force*] (MCD) .... ATLAS
Advanced Tactical Lightweight Avionics System .... ATLAS
Advanced Tactical Mini-drone (SAUS) .... ATM
Advanced Tactical Missile (ACAE) .... ATM
Advanced Tactical Missile System (SAUS) .... ATACMS
Advanced Tactical Parachute System [*Army*] .... ATPS
Advanced Tactical Processor .... ATP
Advanced Tactical Prototype (DOMA) .... ATP
Advanced Tactical RADAR [*Army*] (MCD) .... ATR
Advanced Tactical Radar System (IUSS) .... ATRS
Advanced Tactical Reconnaissance System (MCD) .... ATRS
Advanced Tactical Stand-off Missile (SAUS) .... ATSM
Advanced Tactical Strike (MCD) .... ATS
Advanced Tactical Support [*Aircraft*] [*Navy*] (DOMA) .... ATS
Advanced Tactical Support Aircraft [*Navy*] (DOMA) .... ATSA
Advanced Tactical Support Base [*Navy*] (NVT) .... ATSB
Advanced Tactical Support System (DOMA) .... ATSS
Advanced Tactical Surveillance (SAUS) .... ATS
Advanced Tactical Surveillance Radar (ACAE) .... ATSR
Advanced Tactical Surveillance System (ACAE) .... ATSS
Advanced Tactics & Engagement Simulation System (SAUS) .... ATESS
Advanced Takeoff and Landing System (MCD) .... ATOLS
Advanced Tank Cannon (DOMA) .... ATAC
Advanced Tank Cannon system (SAUS) .... ATAC
Advanced Tank Cannon System [*Army*] .... ATACS
Advanced Tank Cannon System (SAUS) .... ATCS
Advanced Tank Fire Control System (SAUS) .... ATFCS
Advanced Tank Target Auto Kill (ACAE) .... ATTAK
Advanced Tanker Cargo [*Aircraft*] (MCD) .... ATAC
Advanced Tanker/Cargo Aircraft (SAUS) .... ATCA
Advanced Target Acquisition Counterfire System (SAUS) .... ATACS
Advanced Target Acquisition Sensor [*Air Force*] (MCD) .... ATAS
Advanced Target Acquisition System [*Air Force*] .... ATAS
Advanced Target Attack programme (SAUS) .... ATACK
Advanced Target Location and Strike .... ATLAS
Advanced Target Study (ACAE) .... ATS
Advanced TDRSS (SAUS) .... ATDRSS
Advanced Technical Demonstration (SAUS) .... ATD
Advanced Technical Education Program .... ATEP
Advanced Technical Engagement Model (MCD) .... ATEM
Advanced Technical Experimental Translation (SAUS) .... ATET
Advanced Technical Experimental Transportation (MCD) .... ATET
Advanced Technical Fighter (SAUS) .... ATF
Advanced Technical, Limited (ACAE) .... ATL
Advanced Technical Objective Working Group .... ATOWG
Advanced Technical Payload (SAA) .... ATP
Advanced Technical Products [*NASDAQ symbol*] (SG) .... ATPX
Advanced Technical Requirements [*DoD*] .... ATR
Advanced Technical Service School (SAUO) .... ATSS
Advanced Technical Solutions (SAUS) .... ATS
Advanced Technical Training Center [*Military*] (MUGU) .... ATTC
Advanced Technical Training Facility [*Military*] .... ATTF
Advanced Technical Workstation (IUSS) .... ATW
Advanced Technician's Test (MCD) .... ATT
Advanced Techniques for Electrical Power Management, Control, and Distribution Systems [*Army*] (RDA) .... ATEPS
Advanced Techniques for Imagery Interpretation (AABC) .... ATII
Advanced Techniques Integration into Efficient Scientific Application Software [*ESPRIT project*] (NITA) .... ATES
Advanced Techniques integration into Efficient scientific Software (SAUS) .... ATES
Advanced Technological Education (SAUS) .... ATE
Advanced Technologies ASW Display (SAUS) .... ATAD
Advanced Technologies for Tactical Aircraft (MCD) .... ATTAC
Advanced Technologies (or Technology) Incorporated (SAUO) .... ATI
Advanced Technologies Testing Aircraft System [*NASA*] .... ATTAS
Advanced Technology [*In PC AT, model name of a computer*] [*IBM Corp.*] .... AT
Advanced Technology Advisory Committee (SAUO) .... ATAC
Advanced Technology Airfoil Tests (MCD) .... ATAT
Advanced Technology Anti-G Suit (ADWA) .... ATAGS
Advanced Technology Applications Facility [*UNCHS*] [*United Nations*] (DUND) .... ATAF
Advanced Technology Assessment Center (SAUS) .... ATAC
Advanced Technology Attachment [*Hard disk interface*] [*Computer science*] .... ATA
Advanced Technology Attachment Interface with Extensions [*Computer science*] (ITCA) ATA-2
Advanced Technology Attachment Software Programming Interface (VERA) .... ATASPI
Advanced Technology Attention (SAUS) .... AT
Advanced Technology Axial-Centrifugal Compression (SAUS) .... ATACC
Advanced Technology Ballistic Missile (SAUS) .... ATBM
Advanced Technology Bomber [*Air Force*] .... ATB
Advanced Technology Center [*Aerospace*] .... ATC
Advanced Technology Centre, Honeywell Ltd., Willowdale, Ontario [*Library symbol*] [*National Library of Canada*] (NLC) .... OTHL
Advanced Technology Classroom (IUSS) .... ATC
Advanced Technology Components [*Program*] [*Army, Navy*] (RDA) .... ATC
Advanced Technology Crew Protection (MCD) .... ATCP
Advanced Technology Cruise Missile (MCD) .... ATCM
Advanced Technology Cruise Missile Study (SAUS) .... ATCMS
Advanced Technology Demonstration .... ATD
Advanced Technology Demonstration Aircraft .... ATDA
Advanced Technology Demonstration LASER Gyro (MCD) .... ATDLG
Advanced Technology Demonstration Network [*Telecommunications*] .... ATDNet
Advanced Technology Demonstrator Engine .... ATDE
Advanced Technology Development (SAUO) .... ATD
Advanced Technology Developments (MCD) .... ATD
Advanced Technology Directorate [*Army Strategic Defense Command*] [*Huntsville, AL*] .... ATD
Advanced Technology Energy Efficient Demonstrator (MCD) .... ATEED
Advanced Technology Engine (MCD) .... ATE
Advanced Technology Experimental Transport (SAUS) .... ATET
Advanced Technology Extended [*Computer science*] (VERA) .... ATX
Advanced Technology Fighter .... ATF
Advanced Technology Fighter (SAUS) ATF-2
Advanced Technology for Large Area Space Structures (SAUS) .... ATLASS
Advanced Technology for Large Structural Systems [*National Science Foundation*] .... ATLASS
Advanced Technology Ground Attack Fighter [*Air Force*] .... ATGAF
Advanced Technology Group [*Navy*] .... ATG
Advanced Technology Innovation [*Computer science*] .... ATI
Advanced Technology Insertion Module (SAUS) .... ATIM
Advanced Technology Laboratories, Inc. [*Associated Press*] (SAG) .... AdvTLb
Advanced Technology Laboratories, Inc. [*Formerly, Westmark International, Inc.*] [*NASDAQ symbol*] (SPSG) .... ATLI
Advanced Technology Laboratories (or Laboratory) (SAUS) .... ATL
Advanced Technology Laboratory [*Navy*] (MCD) .... ATL
Advanced Technology Labortories, Inc. (DAVI) .... ATL
Advanced Technology Labs [*NASDAQ symbol*] (TTSB) .... ATLI
Advanced Technology LADAR System (SAUS) .... ATLAS
Advanced Technology Large Aircraft System [*Air Force*] (MCD) .... ATLAS
Advanced Technology Launcher (SAUS) .... ATL
Advanced Technology Light Twin Engine Aircraft (MCD) .... ATLIT
Advanced Technology Light Twin Engine Research Aircraft [*Air Force*] (MCD) .... ATLIT
Advanced Technology Maintenance [*British*] (NITA) .... ATM
Advanced Technology Materials [*Commercial firm*] [*Associated Press*] (SAG) .... AdvTch
Advanced Technology Materials [*NASDAQ symbol*] (SAG) .... ATMI
Advanced Technology Matr'l [*NASDAQ symbol*] (TTSB) .... ATMI
Advanced Technology Microelectronic Array Computer (MCD) .... ATMAC
Advanced Technology Multimedia Communications (MCD) .... ATMC
Advanced Technology of Management (SAA) .... ATOM
Advanced Technology Park .... ATP
Advanced Technology Partner (SAUS) .... ATP
Advanced Technology Program [*Department of Commerce*] .... ATP
Advanced Technology Pultrusion .... ATP
Advanced Technology Reader Sorter (SAUS) .... ATRS
Advanced Technology Reconnaissance Aircraft (ACAE) .... ATRA
Advanced Technology Rotor System (MCD) .... ATRS
Advanced Technology Satellite .... ATS
Advanced Technology Spacecraft [*NASA*] (MCD) .... ATS
Advanced Technology Systems, Inc. [*Arlington, VA*] [*Telecommunications*] (TSSD) .... ATS
Advanced Technology Systems Inc. (SAUO) .... ATS
Advanced Technology Tactical Transport (SAUS) AT3
Advanced Technology Tactical Transport [*Proposed low-altitude long-range airlifter*] [*Military*] .... AT^3
Advanced Technology Tactical Transport [*Proposed low-altitude long-range airlifter*] [*Military*] (MCD) .... ATTT
Advanced Technology Test Demonstrator (SAUS) .... ATTD
Advanced Technology Testing Aircraft System (SAUS) .... ATTAS
Advanced Technology Training [*Army*] (VNW) .... ATT
Advanced Technology Transition Demonstration [*Army*] (INF) .... ATTD
Advanced Technology Transport .... ATT
Advanced Technology Upper Stage (MCD) .... ATUS
Advanced Technology Validation and Integration (ACAE) .... ATVI
Advanced Technology Vehicle .... ATV

Advanced Technology Vessel (SAUS)	ATV
Advanced Technology Workstation [Computer system]	ATW
Advanced Technology/Libraries [Information service]	AT/L
Advanced Telecommunication Research	ATR
Advanced Telecommunications Corp. [Atlanta, GA] (TSSD)	ATC
Advanced Telecommunications Research (SAUS)	ATR
Advanced Telecommunications Sciences Office [STRATCOM] [Army] (RDA)	ATSO
Advanced Telecommunications Services (TELE)	ATS
Advanced Telecomunications Institute (VERA)	ATI
Advanced Teleoperating Retrieval System (ACAE)	ATRS
Advanced Teleprocessing System (IAA)	ATS
Advanced Telescope Mission [Skylab] [NASA]	ATM
Advanced Telescope Project (SAUS)	ATP
Advanced Telescopes Project [University of Colorado] [Research center] (RCD)	ATP
Advanced Television [See also HDTV]	ATV
Advanced Television Infrared Observation Satellite (SAUS)	TIROS-N
Advanced Television Research Consortium (PS)	ATRC
Advanced Television Seeker (MCD)	ATVS
Advanced Television Services [FCC] (NTCM)	ATS
Advanced Television Systems Committee [FCC] (NTCM)	ATSC
Advanced Television Test Center [Telecommunications] (TSSD)	ATTC
Advanced Terminal Aerial Weapon Delivery Simulation (MCD)	ATAWDS
Advanced Terminal Controller (SAUS)	ATC
Advanced Terminal Defense Interceptor (MCD)	ATDI
Advanced Terminal for Operation and Maintenance (SAUS)	ATOM
Advanced Terminal Guidance System	ATGS
Advanced Terminal Interceptor	ATI
Advanced Terminal Interceptor Technology	ATIT
Advanced Terminal Interceptor Technology Program	ATITP
Advanced Terminal Management System (SAUS)	ATMS
Advanced Terminal System (SAUS)	ATS
Advanced Test Accelerator [Lawrence Livermore National Laboratory]	ATA
Advanced Test Battery [Aptitude and skills test]	ATB
Advanced Test in Psychology	ATP
Advanced Test Module (ACAE)	ATM
Advanced Test Prototype Reactor (SAUS)	ATPR
Advanced Test Reactor [Nuclear energy]	ATR
Advanced Test Reactor Critical Experiment [Nuclear energy]	ATRCE
Advanced Test Reactor Critical Facility [Nuclear energy]	ATRC
Advanced Test Reactor Critical Facility [Nuclear energy] (GFGA)	ATRCF
Advanced Test Vehicle (MCD)	ATV
Advanced Testing Line for Actinide Separations (SAUS)	ATLAS
Advanced Testing Technology (IUSS)	ATT
Advanced Tethered Vehicle [Navy]	ATV
Advanced Text Management System [IBM Corp.]	ATMS
Advanced Theater Transport (ACAE)	ATT
Advanced Therapeutic Sys [AMEX symbol] (TTSB)	ATH
Advanced Therapeutic Systems Ltd. [Associated Press] (SAG)	AdvThr
Advanced Therapeutic Systems Ltd. [AMEX symbol] (SAG)	ATH
Advanced Thermal Analysis (MCD)	ATHAS
Advanced Thermal Flight Experiment (MCD)	ATFE
Advanced Thermal Imaging Focal Plane Array (ACAE)	ATIFPA
Advanced Thermal Imaging Scanner [or System]	ATIS
Advanced Thermal Reactor	ATR
Advanced Thermal-Hydraulic Energy Network Analyzer (SAUS)	ATHENA
Advanced Thermodynamic Cycle (SAUS)	ATC
Advanced Threat Emitter Simulator (SAUS)	ATEMS
Advanced Threat Infra-Red Countermeasures (SAUS)	ATIRCM
Advanced Threat Infrared Countermeasures Program (DWSG)	ATIRCM
Advanced Threat Radar Jammer [DoD]	ATRJ
Advanced Threat Training Emitter System (SAUS)	ATTES
Advanced Threat-Reactive Receiver (SAUS)	ATRR
Advanced Throttling Slurry Engine (KSC)	ATSE
Advanced Time Division Multiple Access (SAUS)	ATDMA
Advanced Time Sharing (SAUS)	ATS
Advanced TIROS [Television Infrared Observation Satellite] Operational Vertical Sounder	ATOVS
Advanced Tissue Sci [NASDAQ symbol] (TTSB)	ATIS
Advanced Tissue Sciences [NASDAQ symbol] (SG)	ATIS
Advanced Tissue Sciences, Inc. [Associated Press] (SAG)	AdvTiss
Advanced Tissue Sciences, Inc. [NASDAQ symbol] (SAG)	ATIS
Advanced Tomahawk Weapon Control System (SAUS)	ATWCS
Advanced Tool Development Facility (AAEL)	ATDF
Advanced Toroidal Facility [Oak Ridge National Laboratory]	ATF
Advanced Torpedo Decoy (CAAL)	ATD
Advanced Torsion Bar (MCD)	ATB
Advanced Total Traction Engineering System for All-Terrain [Automotive engineering]	ATTESA
Advanced TOVS (SAUS)	ATOVS
Advanced Tracker Radar (SAUS)	ATR
Advanced Tracking and Data Relay Satellite (ADWA)	ATDRS
Advanced Tracking Program (MCD)	ATP
Advanced Tracking System (SAUS)	ATS
Advanced Traffic Information Supply System [Highway traffic management]	ATISS
Advanced Traffic Management [FAA] (GFGA)	ATF
Advanced Traffic Management (PA)	ATM
Advanced Traffic Management System (SAUO)	ATM
Advanced Traffic Management System	ATMS
Advanced Traffic Observation and Management Information Collection System (SAUS)	ATOMICS
Advanced Traffic Signal System	ATSS
Advanced Train Control System [Union Pacific Railroad Co.]	ATCS

Advanced Trainer [Air Force]	AT
Advanced Trainer Aircraft (SAUS)	ATTA
Advanced Training [Military] (NVT)	ADVTNG
Advanced Training Airplane (SAUS)	AT Ap
Advanced Training Command (MCD)	ATC
Advanced Training Solution	ATS
Advanced Training Squadron (SAUO)	ATS
Advanced Training System [Air Force]	ATS
Advanced Training Systems Inc. (SAUO)	ATS
Advanced Training Technology Associates [Commercial firm] [British]	ATTA
Advanced Training Unit	ATU
Advanced Transit Association (EA)	ATRA
Advanced Transonic Technology (MCD)	ATT
Advanced Transport Aircraft (MCD)	ATA
Advanced Transport Operating System (MCD)	ATOPS
Advanced Transport Operations System (SAUS)	ATOPS
Advanced Transport Technology Mission Analysis (MCD)	ATTMA
Advanced Transport Technology Program [NASA] (OA)	ATTP
Advanced Transport Technology Program Office [NASA]	ATTPO
Advanced Transport Telematics [Traffic management] (ECON)	ATT
Advanced Trauma Life Support (CMD)	ATLS
Advanced Trauma Life Support System	ATLS
Advanced Trauma Life Support training course (SAUS)	ATLS
Advanced Trauma Management [Army]	ATM
Advanced Travel Information Systems [Formerly, ADI] [Highway safety research]	ATIS
Advanced Treatment (GNE)	AT
Advanced Triga Prototype Reactor	ATPR
Advanced Triple Ejector Rack (SAUS)	ATER
Advanced Turbine Engine Gas Generator [Air Force]	ATEGG
Advanced Turbine Engine Studies (SAUS)	ATES
Advanced Turbine Systems (SAUS)	ATS
Advanced Turbine Technology Program (ACAE)	ATTAP
Advanced Turbo Systems [Automotive industry supplier]	ATS
Advanced Turbocharged Intercooled [Truck engineering]	ATi
Advanced Turbofan Engine	ATE
Advanced Turboprop [Aeronautics]	ATP
Advanced Turboshaft Development Engine (ACAE)	ATDE
Advanced TV Enhancement Forum (SAUS)	ATVEF
Advanced TV Systems Committee (EA)	ATSC
Advanced TV Systems Committee (EA)	ATVSC
Advanced UHF Communication System (MCD)	AUCS
Advanced Undersea (SAUS)	A/U
Advanced Underseas Weapons [Army]	AUW
Advanced Underseas Weapons Circuitry	AUWC
Advanced Underwater Missile	AUM
Advanced Underwater Search System (MCD)	AUSS
Advanced Underwater Warfare [Navy]	AUW
Advanced Underwater Weapons System [Military] (IUSS)	AUWS
Advanced Underwatr Weapon [Military] (MUSM)	AUW
Advanced Underwriting Service [Database] [R & R Newkirk] [Information service or system] (CRD)	AUS
Advanced Unit Record System (SAUS)	AURS
Advanced Unit Training [Army]	AUT
Advanced Universal Jamming System	AUJS
Advanced Unmanned Cargo Vehicle (ACAE)	ACUV
Advanced Upper Stage Motor (MCD)	AUSM
Advanced User Terminal [Navy] (MCD)	AUT
Advanced Utility Simulation Model [Environmental Protection Agency] (GFGA)	AUSM
Advanced Vector Computer (SAUS)	AVC
Advanced Vehicle Control System [Automotive engineering]	AVCS
Advanced Vehicle Design Department	AVDD
Advanced Vehicle Highway System [Automotive engineering]	AVHS
Advanced Vehicle Identification	AVI
Advanced Vehicle Reception Park (SAUO)	AVRP
Advanced Vehicle Simulation Technique	AVST
Advanced Vehicle System [Automotive engineering]	AVS
Advanced Vehicle Technologies [Military] (RDA)	AVT
Advanced Vertical Processor (AAEL)	AVP
Advanced Vertical Speed Indicator	AVSI
Advanced Vertical Strike (SAUS)	AVS
Advanced Vertical Strike Fighter (MCD)	AVS
Advanced Vertical Strike Fighter	AVSF
Advanced Very High Resolution Radar (SAUS)	AVHRR
Advanced Very-High-Resolution Radiometer [NASA]	AVHRR
Advanced Very-Large-Scale Integration [Electronics]	AVLSI
Advanced Vibration Reducer (SAUS)	AVR
Advanced Videcon Camera Systems (SAUS)	AVCS
Advanced Video Attribute Terminal Assembler and Recreator (VERA)	AVATAR
Advanced Video Display Controller (SAUS)	AVD Controller
Advanced Video Imaging [Zenith Electronics Corp.]	AVI
Advanced Video Interface.	VAVI
Advanced Video Processor (SAUS)	AVP
Advanced Video Signal Processor (SAUS)	AVSP
Advanced Video Tape Recorder	AVTR
Advanced Video Terminal	AVT
Advanced Vidicon Camera (ACAE)	AVC
Advanced Vidicon Camera Service (SAUS)	AVCS
Advanced Vidicon Camera Subsystem (ACAE)	AVCS
Advanced Virtual Machine (IAA)	AVM
Advanced Virtual Machine/Extended Facility (SAUS)	AVM/EF
Advanced Visible and Near Infrared Radiometer (SAUS)	AVNIR
Advanced Visible and Near-Infrared Radiometer [Instrumentation]	AVNIR
Advanced Visual [Near Visual] Electro-Optic Sensor [Simulator] (MCD)	AVEOS

Advanced Visual Extension (PCM) ... AVE
Advanced Visual Information Display ... AVID
Advanced Visual Interface (SAUS) ... AVI
Advanced Visual System ... AVS
Advanced Visual Target Acquisition System (MCD) ... AVTAS
Advanced Visual Technology System [*NASA*] ... AVTS
Advanced Visualization System (AAEL) ... AVS
Advanced VLF/LF [*Very Low Frequency/Low Frequency*] **Receiver** (DWSG) ... AVR
Advanced Voice Technol Wrrt [*NASDAQ symbol*] (TTSB) ... HMWKW
Advanced Voice Technologies [*NASDAQ symbol*] (TTSB) ... HMWK
Advanced Voice Technologies, Inc. [*Associated Press*] (SAG) ... AdVoic
Advanced Voice Technologies, Inc. [*Associated Press*] (SAG) ... AdvVoic
Advanced Voice Technologies, Inc. [*NASDAQ symbol*] (SAG) ... HMWK
Advanced Voice Tehcnol's 'Unit' [*NASDAQ symbol*] (TTSB) ... HMWKU
Advanced Vortex System (MCD) ... AVS
Advanced Voyager ... AV
Advanced V/STOL [*Vertical/Short Takeoff and Landing*] **Weapon System** (MCD) ... AVS
Advanced Vulcan Air Defense System (MCD) ... AVADS
Advanced Wafer Imaging System (ACAE) ... AWIS
Advanced Warfighter [*or Warfighting*] **Experiment** [*Military*] (RDA) ... AWE
Advanced Warfighting Experiment [*Military*] (INF) ... AWE
Advanced Warfighting Experiments (SAUS) ... AWE
Advanced Warning Airborne Command System ... AWACS
Advanced Warning and Control System (IEEE) ... AWACS
Advanced Warning and Control System/Combat Air Patrol [*Air Force*] ... AWACS/CAP
Advanced Warning of Active Radar Emissions (SAUS) ... AWARE
Advanced Warning System ... AWS
Advanced Waste Treatment [*of water*] ... AWT
Advanced Waste Treatment Laboratory [*National Environmental Research Center*] ... AWTL
Advanced Waste Treatment Processes (PDAA) ... AWTR
Advanced Wastewater Treatment (ADWA) ... AWT
Advanced Wave Effects [*Sound synthesis*] (DOM) ... AWE
Advanced Wave Memory (SAUS) ... AWM
Advanced Weapon Carriage Integration Technology (MCD) ... AWCIT
Advanced Weapon Delivery RADAR ... AWDR
Advanced Weapon Delivery Radar (ACAE) ... AWPR
Advanced Weapon System (SAUS) ... AWS
Advanced Weapon/Aircraft Requirements Evaluation (MCD) ... AWARE
Advanced Weapons Carriage Configured Vehicle (MCD) ... AWCCV
Advanced Weapons Radiochemical Diagnostics Facility (SAUS) ... AWRDF
Advanced Weapons Support Command [*Army*] (AABC) ... AWSCOM
Advanced Weapons System (MCD) ... AWS
Advanced Weather Analysis and Prediction System (ACAE) ... AWAPS
Advanced Weather Interactive Processing System [*National Oceanic and Atmospheric Administration*] ... AWIPS
Advanced Weather Interactive Processing System for the 90s (SAUS) ... AWIPS-90
Advanced Weather Interactive Processing System of the 1990's [*National Oceanic and Atmospheric Administration*] ... AWIPS-90
Advanced Weather RADAR (MCD) ... AWR
Advanced Web Creations ... AWC
Advanced WESTAR (MCD) ... AW
Advanced Wet Station (AAEL) ... AWS
Advanced Wide Area Defense Missile (MCD) ... AWADM
Advanced Wide-Angle Reflective Display System (SAUS) ... AWARDS
Advanced Wide-Area Antipersonnel Mine (MCD) ... AWAAPM
Advanced Wide-Area Missile (MCD) ... AWAM
Advanced Wild Weasel [*RADAR warning system*] ... AWW
Advanced Wind Energy Conversion System (MCD) ... AWECS
Advanced Wind Scatterometer (SAUS) ... ASCAT
Advanced Windowing Toolkit (PCM) ... AWT
Advanced Workflow Engine (SAUS) ... AWE
Advanced Workshop Detachment [*British and Canadian*] [*World War II*] ... AWD
Advanced Workstation Environment (SAUS) ... AWE
Advanced Workstation Products [*El Segundo, CA*] (ECON) ... AWP
Advanced Workstations and Systems (SAUS) ... AWS
Advanced X.25 Connection Services (SAUS) ... AXCS
Advanced X-ray Astronomical Facility (SAUS) ... AXAF
Advanced X-Ray Astrophysics Facility [*Great Observatory Program*] [*NASA*] ... AXAF
Advanced X-Ray Astrophysics Facility-Imaging [*NASA*] ... AXAF-I
Advanced X-ray Facility (SAUS) ... AXF
Advanced X-Ray Facility ... AXF
Advanced X-Ray System (DWSG) ... AXS
Advanced-Booking Charter (PDAA) ... ABC
Advanced-Composite Thermoplastic [*Materials engineering*] ... ACTP
Advanced-Core Military Engine (SAUS) ... ACME
Advance/Decline (MCD) ... A/D
Advance-Decline Line [*Investment term*] ... A-D
Advanced-Far Infrared Search/Track (SAUS) ... A-FIRST
Advanced/Innovative Wind Energy Concept (MCD) ... AIWEC
Advanced-Level Examination [*Education*] (AIE) ... A
Advanced-Technology Medium-Range Transport ... ATMR
Advanced-Technology Vehicle (SAUS) ... ATV
Advanced-Visual Information System (SAUS) ... AVIS
Advance-Enable-Sequence (SAUS) ... ADV-EN-SEQ
Advancement (DLA) ... ADVANCEM
Advancement ... ADVMNT
Advancement (ABBR) ... ADVNCNT
Advancement (ABBR) ... ADVNCT
Advancement of Computing in Education ... AACE
Advancement of Management (SAA) ... AM
Advancement of Medical Instrumentation (MELL) ... AMI
Advancement of Science (journ.) (SAUS) ... ADSCAH
Advancement Planning (SAUS) ... ADPLAN
Advancement, Strength, and Training Plan System ... ADSTAP
Advance-Purchase Excursion [*Airline fare code*] ... APEX
Advance-Purchase Excursion Fare [*Airline fare code*] (ADA) ... APEF
Advances for Mutual Defense Assistance ... AMDA
Advances Gas Reactor (SAUS) ... AGR
Advances in Activation Analysis(journ.) (SAUS) ... Adv Activ Anal
Advances in Agronomy (SAUS) ... Adv Agron
Advances in Analytical Toxicology [*A publication*] (MEC) ... Adv Anal Toxicol
Advances in Anatomy, Embryology and Cell Biology (SAUS) ... Adv Anat Embryol Cell Biol
Advances in Andrology (journ.) (SAUS) ... Adv Androl
Advances in Animal Physiology and Animal Nutrition (journ.) (SAUS) ... Adv Anim Physiol Anim Nutr
Advances in Astronomy and Astro-physics (journ.) (SAUS) ... Adv Astron Astrophys
Advances in Atmospheric Sciences (SAUS) ... Adv Atmos Sci
Advances in Atomic and Molecular Physics (journ.) (SAUS) ... Adv At Mol Phys
Advances in Audiology (journ.) (SAUS) ... Adv Audiol
Advances in Automated Analysis. Technicon International Congress (journ.) (SAUS) ... Adv Autom Anal Technicon Int Congr
Advances in Automatic Testing Technology (SAUS) ... AATT
Advances in Behavioral Biology (journ.) (SAUS) ... Adv Behav Biol
Advances in Behavioral Pharmacology (journ.) (SAUS) ... Adv Behav Pharmacol
Advances in Behaviour Research and Therapy (SAUO) ... ABRAT
Advances in Behaviour Research and Therapy (journ.) (SAUS) ... Adv Behav Res Ther
Advances in Biochechemical Engineer-ing (journ.) (SAUS) ... Adv Biochem Eng
Advances in Biochemical Engineering/Biotechnology (SAUS) ... Adv Biochem Eng Biotechnol
Advances in Biochemical Psychopharmacology (journ.) (SAUS) ... Adv Biochem Psychopharmacol
Advances in Biochemistry and Biophysics (journ.) (SAUS) ... Adv Biochem Biophys
Advances in Bioengineering and Instrumentation (journ.) (SAUS) ... Adv Bioeng Instrum
Advances in Bioengineering (journ.) (SAUS) ... Adv Bioeng
Advances in Biological and Medical Physics (journ.) (SAUS) ... Adv Biol Med Phys
Advances in Biological Psychiatry (journ.) (SAUS) ... Adv Biol Psychiatry
Advances in Biology of the Skin (journ.) (SAUS) ... Adv Biol Skin
Advances in Biomedical Engineering and Medical Physics (journ.) (SAUS) ... Adv Biomed Eng Med Phys
Advances in Biomedical Engineering (journ.) (SAUS) ... Adv Biomed Eng
Advances in Biophysics (journ.) (SAUS) ... Adv Biophys
Advances in Biotechnology Processes (journ.) (SAUS) ... Adv Biotechnol Processes
Advances in Blood Grouping (journ.) (SAUS) ... Adv Blood Grouping
Advances in Botanical Research (journ.) (SAUS) ... Adv Bot Res
Advances in Bryology (journ.) (SAUS) ... Adv Bryol
Advances in Cancer Chemotherapy (journ.) (SAUS) ... Adv Cancer Chemother
Advances in Cancer Research (journ.) (SAUS) ... Adv Cancer Res
Advances in Carbohydrate Chemistry (journ.) (SAUS) ... Adv Carbohydr Chem
Advances in Cardiology (journ.) (SAUS) ... Adv Cardiol
Advances in Cardiopulmonary Diseases (journ.) (SAUS) ... Adv Cardiopulm Dis
Advances in Cardiovascular Physics (journ.) (SAUS) ... Adv Cardiovasc Phys
Advances in Catalysis and Related Subjects (journ.) (SAUS) ... Adv Catal
Advances in Cell and Molecular Biology (journ.) (SAUS) ... Adv Cell Moi Biol
Advances in Cell Biology (journ.) (SAUS) ... Adv Cell Biol
Advances in Cell Culture (journ.) (SAUS) ... Adv Cell Cult
Advances in Cellular Neurobiology (journ.) (SAUS) ... Adv Cell Neurobiol
Advances in Cereal Science and Technology (journ.) (SAUS) ... Adv Cereal Sei Technol
Advances in Chemical Physics (journ.) (SAUS) ... Adv Chem Phys
Advances in Chemoreception (journ.) (SAUS) ... Adv Chemoreception
Advances in Chemotherapy (journ.) (SAUS) ... Adv Chemother
Advances in Child Development and Behavior (journ.) (SAUS) ... Adv Child Dev Behav
Advances in Chromatography (journ.) (SAUS) ... Adv Chromatogr
Advances in Cladistics (journ.) (SAUS) ... Adv Cladistics
Advances in Clinical Enzymology (journ.) (SAUS) ... Adv Clin Enzymol
Advances in Clinical Nutrition. Proceedings. International Symposium (journ.) (SAUS) ... Adv Clin Nutr Proc Int Symp
Advances in Clinical Pharmacology (journ.) (SAUS) ... Adv Clin Pharmacol
Advances in Colloid Science (journ.) (SAUS) ... Adv Colloid Sci
Advances in Comparative Leukemia Research. Proccedings. International Syrnposium on Comparative Re-search on Leukemia and Related Diseases (journ.) (SAUS) ... Adv Comp Leuk Res Proc Int Symp
Advances in Comparative Physiology and Biochemistry (journ.) (SAUS) ... Adv Comp Physiol Biochem
Advances in Computers (journ.) (SAUS) ... AdvComp
Advances in Contraception (journ.) (SAUS) ... Adv Contracept
Advances in Contraceptive Delivery Systems (journ.) (SAUS) ... Adv Contracept Delivery Syst
Advances in Control Systems (journ.) (SAUS) ... Adv Control Syst
Advances in Cornposite Materials. Proceedings. International Conference on Coinposite Materials (journ.) (SAUS) ... Adv Compos Mater Proc Int Conf
Advances in Corrosion Science and Technology (journ.) (SAUS) ... Adv Corros Sci Technol
Advances in Cyclic Nucleotide and Protein Phosphorylation Research (journ.) (SAUS) ... Adv Cyclic Nucleotide Protein Phosphorylation Res
Advances in Cyclic Nucleotide Research (journ.) (SAUS) ... Adv Cyclic Nucleotide Res
Advances in Cycloaddition (journ.) (SAUS) ... Adv Cycloaddit
Advances in Cytopharmacology (journ.) (SAUS) ... AdvCytopharmacol

Advances in Desalination. Proceedings. National Symposium on Desalination (journ.) (SAUS) ... Adv Desalin Proc Nat Symp Desalin
Advances in Desert and Arid Land Technology and Development (journ.) (SAUS) ... Adv Desert Arid Land Technol Dev
Advances in Digital Libraries (SAUS) ... ADL
Advances in Digital Libraries [*Conference*] (VERA) ... ADL
Advances in Ecological Research (SAUS) ... Adv Ecol Res
Advances in Environmental Science and Technology (SAUS) ... Adv Environ Sci Technol
Advances in Enzymology [*A publication*] (MEC) ... Advances in Enzymol
Advances in Enzymology and Related Subjects (SAUS) ... Adv Enzymol Relat Subj
Advances in Enzymology and Related Subjects of Biochemistry (SAUS) ... Adv Enzymol Relat Subj Biochem
Advances in Food Research (journ.) (SAUS) ... Adv Food Res
Advances in Geophysics (SAUS) ... Adv Geophys
Advances in Gerontology Research (journ.) (SAUS) ... AGNRAO
Advances in Heat Transfer (journ.) (SAUS) ... Adv Heat Transfer
Advances in Heat Transfer (journ.) (SAUS) ... AHTRA
Advances in ihe Biology of Disease (journ.) (SAUS) ... Adv Biol Dis
Advances in Immunology (journ.) (SAUS) ... Advances Immun
Advances in Inorganic Biochemistry (journ.) (SAUS) ... AIB
Advances in Inorganic Chemistry and Radiochemistry (journ.) (SAUS) ... Adv Inorg Chem Radiochem
Advances in Internal Medicine [*A publication*] (MEC) ... Adv Inter Med
Advances in Internal Medicine (journ.) (SAUS) ... Advances Int Med
Advances in Knee Joint Technology (journ.) (SAUS) ... Adv Artif Hip Knee Jt Technol
Advances in Marine Biology (SAUS) ... Adv Mar Biol
Advances in Mathematics. Supplementary Studies (journ.) (SAUS) ... Ad- vances in Math Suppl Studies
Advances in Molecular Relaxation Processes (journ.) (SAUS) ... Advan Mol Relaxation Processes
Advances in Nephrology from the Necker Hospital (SAUS) ... Adv Nephrol Necker Hosp
Advances in Nephrology (journ.) (SAUS) ... ANGYBQ
Advances in Neurological Sciences (journ.) (SAUS) ... SKNSAF
Advances in Nuclear Physics (journ.) (SAUS) ... Adv Nucl Phys
Advances in Nuclear Physics (journ.) (SAUS) ... ANUPB
Advances in Nuclear Science and Technology (journ.) (SAUS) ... Adv Nucl Sci Technol
Advances in Nuclear Science and Technology (journ.) (SAUS) ... ANUTA
Advances in Obstetrics and Gynecology (journ.) (SAUS) ... Adv Obstet Gynecol
Advances in Obstetrics and Gynecology (journ.) (SAUS) ... AOGYA
Advances in Ophthalmic, Plastic and Reconstructive Surgery (SAUS) ... Adv Ophthalmic Plast Reconstr Surg
Advances in Optical and Electron Microscopy (journ.) (SAUS) ... AOEM
Advances in Organic Chemistry (journ.) (SAUS) ... Adv Org Chem
Advances in Organic Geochemistry (SAUS) ... Adv Org Geochem
Advances in Organometallic Chemistry [*A publication*] (MEC) ... Adv Organomet Chem
Advances in Organometallic Chemistry (journ.) (SAUS) ... AOMCA
Advances in Osteoporosis (ADWA) ... AIO
Advances in Oto-Rhino-Laryngology (SAUS) ... Adv Otorhinolaryngol
Advances in Parasitology (journ.) (SAUS) ... ADPRA
Advances in Pediatrics (journ.) (SAUS) ... Advances Pediat
Advances in Pharmaceutical Sciences (journ.) (SAUS) ... APHMAS
Advances in Pharmacology (SAUS) ... Adv Pharmacol
Advances in Pharmacology (journ.) (SAUS) ... Advances Pharmacol
Advances in Physical and Organic Chemistry [*A publication*] (MEC) ... Adv Phys Org Chem
Advances in Physical Organic Chemistry (journ.) (SAUS) ... APORA
Advances in Physical Sciences (journ.) (SAUS) ... Advances Phys Sci
Advances in Physics [*A publication*] (MEC) ... Adv in Phys
Advances in Plasma Physics (journ.) (SAUS) ... Adv Plasma Phys
Advances in Plasma Physics (journ.) (SAUS) ... APLPB
Advances in Plastic and Reconstructive Surgery (journ.) (SAUS) ... APRSEC
Advances in Pollen-Spore Research (journ.) (SAUS) ... APSRDD
Advances in Polyamine Research (journ.) (SAUS) ... APLRDC
Advances in Polymer Science [*A publication*] (MEC) ... Adv Polym Sci
Advances in Polymer Science (journ.) (SAUS) ... APSID
Advances in Prostaglandin and Thromboxane Research (journ.) (SAUS) ... APTRDI
Advances in Prostaglandin, Thromboxane and Leukotriene Research (SAUS) ... Adv Prostaglandin Thromboxane Leukot Res
Advances in Protein Chemistry (journ.) (SAUS) ... APC
Advances in Psychoanalysis Theory, Research, and Practice (journ.) (SAUS) ... APTPED
Advances in Psychosomatic Medicin (SAUS) ... Adv Psychosom Med
Advances in Quantum Chemistry [*A publication*] (MEC) ... Adv Quantum Chem
Advances in Quantum Electronics (journ.) (SAUS) ... ADQEA
Advances in Radiation Biology (journ.) (SAUS) ... Adv Radiat Biol
Advances in Renal Replacement Therapy (SAUS) ... ARRT
Advances in Space Research (SAUS) ... Adv Space Res
Advances in Space Science and Technology (journ.) (SAUS) ... Adv Space Sci Technol
Advances in Structure Research by Diffraction Methods (journ.) (SAUS) ... Adv Struct Res Diffr Metho
Advances in Surgery (journ.) (SAUS) ... ADSU
Advances in Surgery (journ.) (SAUS) ... Advances Surg
Advances in Teratology (journ.) (SAUS) ... ADTL
Advances in Thanatology (journ.) (SAUS) ... Advan Thanatol
Advances in the Astronautical Sciences (journ.) (SAUS) ... Adv Astronaut Sci
Advances in the Biosciences (journ.) (SAUS) ... Adv Biosci
Advances in Theoretical Physics (journ.) (SAUS) ... Adv Theor Phys
Advances in Tracer Methodology (journ.) (SAUS) ... Adv Tracer Methodol
Advances in Virus Research (journ.) (SAUS) ... Advan Virus Res
Advances in Water Resources (SAUS) ... Adv Water Resour
Advances in X-Ray Analysis (journ.) (SAUS) ... Adv X-Ray Anal
Advances Network Systems Architecture (SAUS) ... ANSA
Advances Systems Institute (SAUO) ... ASI
Advancing (IAA) ... ADVG
Advancing (ABBR) ... ADVNCG
Advancing Blade Concept [*Helicopter*] ... ABC
Advancing Careers in Engineering ... ACE
Advancing Developing Countries [*Economics*] ... ADC
Advancing Frontiers of Plant Sciences (journ.) (SAUS) ... Advan Front Plant Sd
Advancing Key (SAUS) ... AK
Advancing the Consumer Interest [*A publication*] ... ACI
Advanta Corp. [*Associated Press*] (SAG) ... Advant
ADVANTA Corp. [*Associated Press*] (SAG) ... Advanta
Advanta Corp. [*Associated Press*] (SAG) ... AdvantB
Advanta Corp. [*NASDAQ symbol*] (SAG) ... ADVN
ADVANTA Corp. Cl'A' [*NASDAQ symbol*] (TTSB) ... ADVNA
ADVANTA Corp. Cl'B' [*NASDAQ symbol*] (TTSB) ... ADVNB
ADVANTA Corp. Dep Shrs [*NASDAQ symbol*] (TTSB) ... ADVNZ
Advantage (WGA) ... AD
Advantage ... ADV
Advantage (ABBR) ... ADVATG
Advantage (MSA) ... ADVG
Advantage (ABBR) ... ADVNTG
Advantage ... ADVTG
Advantage (ROG) ... ADVTGE
Advantage [*Tennis*] (BARN) ... van
Advantage Bancorp [*NASDAQ symbol*] (TTSB) ... AADV
Advantage Bancorp, Inc. [*NASDAQ symbol*] (SAG) ... AADV
Advantage Bancorp, Inc. [*Associated Press*] (SAG) ... AdvBcp
Advantage Companies, Inc. [*NASDAQ symbol*] (SAG) ... ADVG
Advantage Companies, Inc. [*Associated Press*] (SAG) ... AdvntCos
Advantage Enterprises, Inc. [*Vancouver Stock Exchange symbol*] ... ADG
Advantage Health Corp. [*NASDAQ symbol*] (SAG) ... ADHC
Advantage Health Corp. [*Associated Press*] (SAG) ... AdvHlt
Advantage Life Products [*Associated Press*] (SAG) ... AdvLfe
Advantage Life Products [*NASDAQ symbol*] (NQ) ... ADVT
Advantage Marketing System [*AMEX symbol*] (SG) ... AMM
Advantage Mktg. Sys. Wrrt. [*AMEX symbol*] ... AMMWS
Advantage Mktg. Sys. Wrrt'A [*AMEX symbol*] ... AMMWSA
Advantaged (ABBR) ... ADVNTGD
Advantageous (ABBR) ... ADVATGUS
Advantageous (ABBR) ... ADVNTGU
Advantageously (ABBR) ... ADVATGUSY
Advantageously (ABBR) ... ADVNTGUY
Advantaging (ABBR) ... ADVNTGG
Advection [*NWS*] (FAAC) ... ADVCTN
Advection (ABBR) ... ADVEC
Advection (ABBR) ... ADVECT
Advection-Dominated Accretion Flow [*Planetary science*] ... ADAF
advective (SAUS) ... advect
Advent (ADWA) ... Adv
Advent ... ADV
Advent (ABBR) ... ADVNT
Advent Christian General Conference of America (EA) ... ACGC
Advent Christian General Conference of America (EA) ... ACGCA
Advent Orbital Test and Operation Plan (SAA) ... AOTOP
Advent Software [*NASDAQ symbol*] (TTSB) ... ADVS
Advent Software, Inc. [*Associated Press*] (SAG) ... Advent
Advent Software, Inc. [*NASDAQ symbol*] (SAG) ... ADVS
Adventist Board of Missions (SAUO) ... ABM
Adventist Community Services (EA) ... ACS
Adventist Community Services (EA) ... CS
Adventist Development and Relief Agency (SAUO) ... ADRA
Adventist Development and Relief Agency, International (EA) ... ADRA
Adventist Health Network of North America [*Defunct*] (EA) ... AHN
Adventist Language Teachers Association [*Defunct*] (EA) ... ALTA
Adventist Network of Georgia, Cumberland Elementary Library, Collegedale, TN [*OCLC symbol*] (OCLC) ... TCA
Adventist Network of Georgia, Cumberland Elementary Library, Collegedale, TN (SAUS) ... TCA
Adventist Radio Television Services [*Canada*] ... ARTS
Adventist World Radio (NTCM) ... AWR
Adventist-Laymen's Services and Industries (EA) ... ASI
Adventitious Root Formation [*Botany*] ... ARF
Adventura Energy [*Vancouver Stock Exchange symbol*] ... AVU
Adventure ... Adv
Adventure (SAUS) ... ADVEN
Adventure ... ADVNTR
Adventure Activities Industry Advisory Committee (HEAS) ... AAIAG
Adventure Definition Language (SAUS) ... ADL
Adventure Description Language [*Computer science*] (VERA) ... ADL
Adventure Unlimited Retail Association [*Commercial firm*] (EA) ... AURA
Adventure Vehicle [*Vancouver Stock Exchange symbol*] ... AVH
Adventured (ABBR) ... ADVNTRD
Adventurer (SAUS) ... ADVECT
Adventurer (SAUS) ... ADVEN
Adventurer ... adven
Adventurer (ABBR) ... ADVNTRR
Adventurers Club of New York [*Defunct*] (EA) ... ACNY
Adventurers' Guild [*British*] (DBA) ... AG
Adventures Club of New York (SAUO) ... ACNY
Adventures in Fantasy (SAUS) ... AF
Adventures in Movement for the Handicapped (EA) ... AIM

Adventures in Travel [Oakland, CA] [Information service or system] (IID) .... AIT
Adventures of Batman and Robin .... AB&R
[The] Adventures of Buckaroo Banzai across the Eighth Dimension [1984 movie title] .... TAOBBATED
Adventuresome (ABBR) .... ADVNTRSM
Adventuress (ABBR) .... ADVNTRES
Adventuring (ABBR) .... ADVNTRG
Adventurous (ABBR) .... ADVNTRU
Adventurous (ABBR) .... ADVNTRUS
Adventurously (ABBR) .... ADVNTRUSY
Adverb (ROG) .... AD
Adverb [or Adverbial] .... ADV
Adverb (WA) .... adv
Adverbial (WDAA) .... adv
Adverbial (ADWA) .... advb
Adverbial .... ADVB
Adverbial (ABBR) .... ADVBL
Adverbial (ABBR) .... ADVL
Adverbial (SAUS) .... Advl
Adverbs (ADWA) .... advs
Adverbs (ADA) .... ADVV
Adversary (ABBR) .... ADVRSRY
Adversary (ABBR) .... ADVSY
Adversary Information System [Military] (RDA) .... AIS
Adversary Threat Training Group [Military] .... ATTG
Adversative (ABBR) .... ADVERSAT
adversative (SAUS) .... adversat
Adverse (ABBR) .... ADVRS
Adverse Action (EEVL) .... AA
Adverse Channel Enhancement .... ACE
Adverse Drug Event [Food and Drug Administration] .... ADE
Adverse Drug Event .... ADEs
Adverse Drug Reaction [Medicine] .... ADR
Adverse Effect Wage Rate (GFGA) .... AEWR
Adverse Effects [Medicine] .... AE
Adverse Environment Effect .... AEE
Adverse Event .... AE
Adverse Patient Occurence [Medicine] (HCT) .... APO
Adverse Patient Occurrences [Medicine] (MEDA) .... APO
Adverse Political Event (SAUO) .... APE
Adverse Possession [Legal term] (DLA) .... ADV POSS
Adverse Possession (SAUS) .... Adv Poss
Adverse Reaction [Medicine] (DB) .... AR
Adverse Reaction Monitoring System [Food and Drug Administration] (PAZ) .... ARMS
Adverse Reaction Report [Medicine] (MELL) .... ARR
Adverse Reactions Reporting System [FDA] .... ARRS
Adverse Reactions Terminology (SAUS) .... ART
Adverse State Detector .... ASD
Adverse Weather Aerial Delivery System (SAUS) .... AWADS
Adverse Weather [or All-Weather] Aerial Delivery System [Ordnance delivery method] .... AWADS
Adverse Weather Close Air Support [Military] (MCD) .... AWCAS
Adverse Weather Close Air Support Study (ACAE) .... AWCAS
Adverse Weather Maverick (ACAE) .... AWM
Adverse Weather Precision Guided Munition [Air Force] (DOMA) .... AWPGM
Adversely (ABBR) .... ADVRSY
Adverseness (ABBR) .... ADVRSNS
Adversity (ABBR) .... ADVRST
Adversity Quotient [Psychology] .... AQ
Adversus [Against] [Latin] (ROG) .... ADS
Adversus [or Adversum] [Against] [Latin] .... ADV
Adversus Indoctum [of Lucian] [Classical studies] (OCD) .... Ind
Adversus Iovinianum [of St. Jerome] [Classical studies] (OCD) .... Adv Iovinian
Adversus Mathematicos [of Sextus Empiricus] [Classical studies] (OCD) .... Math
Adversus Valentinianos [of Tertullian] [Classical studies] (OCD) .... Adv Valent
Advertence (ABBR) .... ADVERTNC
Advertent (ABBR) .... ADVRTNT
Advertise .... ADVT
advertise (SAUS) .... advt
Advertise and Award (SAUS) .... A&A
Advertise and Award (KSC) .... A & A
Advertised (ABBR) .... ADVTD
Advertised Computer Technologies [Data Courier, Inc.] [Information service or system] [Defunct] (IID) .... ACT
Advertised Recruitment and Consultancy .... ARC
Advertisement .... AD
Advertisement (WDMC) .... ad
Advertisement (WDAA) .... adv
Advertisement .... ADV
Advertisement (BARN) .... advers
Advertisement .... ADVERT
Advertisement (SAUS) .... ADVMT
Advertisement (ABBR) .... ADVRTZNT
Advertisement (AABC) .... ADVT
Advertisement (WDMC) .... advt
Advertisement (ABBR) .... ADVTMT
Advertisement Contractors' Association [British] (BI) .... ACA
Advertisement Contractors Association (SAUO) .... ACA
Advertisement Curtain (SAUS) .... Ad Curtain
Advertisement Digest [A publication] .... AD
Advertisement Format Selection [Marketing] .... ADFORS
Advertisement Investigation Department, Advertising Association (SAUO) .... AID
Advertisement Manager (SAUS) .... Ad Man

Advertisement Transmission System (SAUS) .... ATS
Advertisements (SAUS) .... Ads
Advertisements (SAUS) .... Adverts
Advertiser (ABBR) .... ADVRTZR
Advertiser .... ADVT
advertiser (SAUS) .... advt
Advertiser (ABBR) .... ADVTR
Advertiser (Adelaide) [A publication] .... Adv (Adel)
Advertiser, Franklinville, NJ [Library symbol] [Library of Congress] (LCLS) .... NjFrvA
Advertiser Syndicated Television Association (NTCM) .... ASTA
Advertisers Casting Service .... ACS
Advertising (WDMC) .... ad
Advertising (WDMC) .... adv
Advertising (DLA) .... ADVERTIS
Advertising .... advg
Advertising (ABBR) .... ADVRTZG
Advertising (WDMC) .... advt
Advertising (DD) .... advtg
Advertising (ABBR) .... ADVTG
Advertising .... ADVTSNG
Advertising Advisory Board of the Canadian Advertising Foundation .... AAB
Advertising Age (journ.) (SAUS) .... ADA
Advertising Agencies Association of India (SAUO) .... AAA of I
Advertising Agency (NTCM) .... AA
Advertising Agency Association of British Columbia (AC) .... AAABC
Advertising Agency Print Production Association (AC) .... AAPPA
Advertising Agency Production Association (DGA) .... AAPA
Advertising Agency Production Club (SAUO) .... AAPC
Advertising Agency Production Club of New York [Later, APC] (EA) .... AAPC
Advertising Agency Service Interchange [Defunct] (EA) .... AASI
Advertising and Graphic Arts Techniques (journ.) (SAUS) .... Ad Techniq
Advertising and Marketing Association .... A & MA
Advertising and Marketing Association (SAUO) .... A&MA
Advertising and Marketing Intelligence [The New York Times Co.] [Information service or system] (CRD) .... AMI
Advertising and Marketing Intelligence Service (SAUS) .... AMI Service
Advertising and Marketing International Network [Stamford, CT] (EA) .... AMIN
Advertising and Marketing Law Bulletin [Australia] [A publication] .... AMLB
Advertising & Mass Media Effect (SAUS) .... ADMASS
Advertising and Promotion Exchange (SAUS) .... APEX
Advertising and Publicity (WDMC) .... ADPUB
Advertising and Publicity [Theater] (WDMC) .... ad-pub
Advertising Antique (SAUS) .... Advertique
Advertising Association (EAIO) .... AA
Advertising Association of the West [Later, AAF] (EA) .... AAW
Advertising Association of the West (SAUO) .... AAW
Advertising Checking Bureau .... ACB
Advertising Club of New York [New York, NY] (EA) .... ACNY
Advertising Club of Victoria [Australia] .... ACV
Advertising Communications International (SAUS) .... ACI
Advertising Control for Television [Advertising testing service] (WDMC) .... ACT
Advertising Council (EA) .... AC
Advertising Council (NTPA) .... AD Concil
[The] Advertising Council, Inc. (NTCM) .... ACI
Advertising Council of America, Inc. (NTCM) .... ACA
Advertising Creative Circle (DGA) .... ACC
Advertising Cup and Mug Collectors of America (EA) .... ACMCA
Advertising Dimensions Standards [American Newspaper Publishers Association] .... ADS
Advertising Educational Foundation (EA) .... AEF
Advertising Federation of America [Later, AAF] .... AFA
Advertising Federation of Minnesota (SRA) .... Ad-Fed
Advertising Film and Videotape Producers' Association [British] .... AFVPA
Advertising Film Producers Association [British] (BI) .... AFPA
Advertising Information Services .... AIS
Advertising Inquiry Council (DGA) .... AIC
Advertising Institute of New Zealand (SAUO) .... AINZ
Advertising Investigation Department [British] .... AID
Advertising Law Anthology [A publication] (ILCA) .... Advert L Anth
Advertising Link Exchange (SAUS) .... ALEX
Advertising Mail Marketing Association (NTPA) .... AMMA
Advertising Management System (SAUS) .... AMS
Advertising Manager (DGA) .... AD MAN
Advertising Matter [Freight] .... ADV MTR
Advertising Media Credit Executives Association [Toledo, OH] (EA) .... AMCEA
Advertising Media Representation Agency (DGA) .... AMRA
Advertising News of New York (journ.) (SAUS) .... Army
Advertising Photographers of America (EA) .... APA
Advertising Photographers of America, National (NTPA) .... APAN
Advertising Planning (SAUS) .... ADPLAN
Advertising Production Club of New York (EA) .... APC
Advertising Provider (WDMC) .... AP
Advertising Research Foundation (EA) .... ARF
Advertising Specialty Guild of America .... ASGA
Advertising Specialty Institute (WDMC) .... ASI
Advertising Specialty National Association (SAUO) .... ASNA
Advertising Standards Authority [British] .... ASA
Advertising Standards Authority of Singapore (SAUO) .... ASAS
Advertising Standards Council [Canada] [Australia] .... ASC
Advertising Training Center [New York, NY] .... ATC
Advertising, Typesetting and Foundry Employers Federation (DGA) .... ATFEF
Advertising Typographers Association (EA) .... ATA
Advertising Typographers Association (SAUO) .... ATA
Advertising Typographers Association of America (SAUO) .... ATA

Advertising Typographers Association of America (DGA) .... ATAA
Advertising Video (WDMC) .... advid
Advertising Videotape .... ADVID
Advertising Women of New York [*New York, NY*] (EA) .... AWNY
Advertising-Press Club [*Republic of Ireland*] (BI) .... APC
Advertising-Press Club, Dublin (SAUO) .... APC
Advertising/Sales Ratio (WDMC) .... A/S
Advest Group [*NYSE symbol*] (TTSB) .... ADV
[*The*] **Advest Group, Inc.** [*NYSE symbol*] (SPSG) .... ADV
[*The*] **Advest Group, Inc.** [*Associated Press*] (SAG) .... Advest
Advice (AABC) .... AD
Advice (ROG) .... ADV
Advice (WDAA) .... Adv
Advice Allotment (SAUS) .... A/A
Advice and Consent of the Senate (SAUS) .... ADCONSEN
Advice by Message (SAUS) .... ADSMG
Advice by Teletype (SAUS) .... ADTELP
Advice Called Subscriber (SAUS) .... ACS
Advice Decision [*or Determination*] **Taken** .... ADTAKE
Advice Duration and Charge (SAUS) .... AD and C
Advice Note (ADA) .... AN
Advice of Allotment (AFM) .... A/A
Advice of Allotment (SAUS) .... ADVALT
Advice of Charge [*Telecommunications*] (TEL) .... AC
Advice of Charge [*Telecommunications*] (DOM) .... AOC
Advice of Charge, at the End of the call (SAUS) .... AOCE
Advice of Charge, During the call (SAUS) .... AOCD
Advice of Duration and Charge (ODBW) .... ADC
Advice of Payment .... AP
Advice of Payment (SAUS) .... A-P
Advice of Receipt .... AR
Advice of Rights [*Legal term*] (BARN) .... AOR
Advice Services Alliance [*British*] (DBA) .... ASA
Advices of Allowance (EEVL) .... AA
Advieskomitee vir Internasionale Samewerking op Wetenskaplike Gebied [*International Council of Scientific Unions*] .... AISWG
Advisability (ABBR) .... ADVSBT
Advisable (ABBR) .... ADVSB
Advisably (ABBR) .... ADVSBY
Advise [*Legal term*] .... ADV
Advise (EBF) .... Adv
Advise (AFM) .... ADVS
Advise .... ADZ
Advise Acceptance (NOAA) .... ADVAC
Advise Action Taken (NOAA) .... ADACT
Advise Action to Be Taken by This Office (NOAA) .... ADATT
Advise All Concerned .... ADALCON
Advise [*or Issue Instructions to*] **All Concerned** .... ADCON
Advise Appropriate Command Having Cognizance of Transportation when Available for Transportation [*Military*] (DNAB) .... ADVAILTRANS
Advise Appropriate Command Having Cognizance of Transportation when Available for Transportation to Continental United States [*Military*] .... ADVAILTRANSCONUS
Advise Approximate Date (NOAA) .... ADADA
Advise Arrival [*Aviation*] (FAAC) .... ADZAR
Advise as Soon as Possible (NOAA) .... ADSAP
Advise as to Names [*Travel industry*] (TRID) .... ADVN
Advise as to Rate [*Travel industry*] (TRID) .... ADVR
Advise at What Time Able [*Aviation*] (FAAC) .... AAWTA
Advise Availability [*Army*] .... ADAVAL
Advise Availability [*Army*] .... ADVAL
Advise by Admiral (SAUS) .... ADAML
Advise by Air Mail as Soon as Possible (FAAC) .... ADMAP
Advise by Airmail [*Army*] .... ADAML
Advise by [*Electronically Transmitted*] **Message** [*Army*] (AABC) .... ADMSG
Advise by Message (SAUS) .... ADMSG
Advise by Message of Action the Following Individual Is Taking [*Military*] .... ADPERSACT
Advise by Message Reduction Current Period of Active Duty [*Military*] .... ADREDPRED
Advise by Message Why Individual Is Being Reduced [*Military*] .... ADPRORED
Advise by Wire (MHDB) .... ABW
Advise Customs [*Aviation*] (FAAC) .... ADCUS
Advise Data of Reporting in Compliance with Orders (SAUS) .... ADARCO
Advise [*Command Designated*] **Date Available for Transportation from Port ofEmbarkation** [*Military*] .... ADVAILTRANSPOE
Advise Date of Receipt (NOAA) .... ADARE
Advise Date of Shipment (NOAA) .... ADASH
Advise Disposition [*Aviation*] (FAAC) .... ADSPN
Advise Duration and Charge [*British telephone term*] .... AD and C
Advise Duration and Charge (SAUS) .... ADC
Advise Earliest Date (NOAA) .... ADSDA
Advise Effective Date (NOAA) .... ADEDA
Advise if Able [*Aviation*] (FAAC) .... AIA
Advise if Able to Proceed [*Aviation*] (FAAC) .... AAP
Advise if Duplicate Booking [*Travel industry*] (TRID) .... ADB
advise if not correct (SAUS) .... adnoc
Advise if Not Correct [*Aviation*] (FAAC) .... ADNOK
Advise if Not Okay [*Travel industry*] (TRID) .... ADNO
Advise if Ticketed [*Travel industry*] (TRID) .... ADTK
Advise Immediately by Dispatch (NOAA) .... ADIMD
advise immediately by dispatch (SAUS) .... adimd
Advise Individual Concerned of Change of Assignment [*Military*] .... CHASG
Advise Intentions [*Aviation*] (FAAC) .... ADZI
Advise Latest Address [*Military*] (AABC) .... ADLATAD
Advise Method and Date of Shipment (NOAA) .... ADMAD
Advise Method, Bill of Lading and Data Shipped (SAUS) .... AMBLADS
Advise on Arrival [*Travel industry*] (TRID) .... ADOA
Advise Present Grade, Status, Physical Condition, and Mailing Address of Following Named [*Military*] .... STATREP
Advise Present Grade, Status, Physical Condition and Mailing Address of Following Named (SAUS) .... STATREP
Advise Present Position and Altitude [*Aviation*] (FAAC) .... APPA
Advise Reason for Delay [*Aviation*] (FAAC) .... ADRDE
Advise [*names of*] **Representatives, Accommodations, and Transportation** [*desired*] [*Army*] (AABC) .... ARAT
Advise Shipping Data (AABC) .... ADSHIPDA
Advise Shipping Date .... ADSHIPDA
Advise Shipping Date .... ADSHPDAT
Advise Soldier Write Home .... ASWH
Advise Status and/or Disposition [*Army*] .... ADSTADIS
Advise Status and/or Disposition [*Army*] (DNAB) .... ASTADIS
Advise Stock on Hand [*Army*] .... ADSTKOH
Advise This Headquarters of Complete Action [*Army*] .... ADHCA
Advise This Office (NOAA) .... ADVOF
Advise This Office (FAAC) .... ADZOF
Advise What Action Has Been Taken [*Military*] (NVT) .... ADTAKE
Advise When Able [*Aviation*] (FAAC) .... AWA
Advise When Established [*Aviation*] (FAAC) .... AWE
Advise Whether Individual May Be Properly Utilized in Your Installation [*Army*] (AABC) .... ADIPU
Advised (SAUS) .... ADV
Advised (ABBR) .... ADVSD
Advised and Released [*Medicine*] .... A & R
Advised and Released (SAUS) .... A&R
Advised Not to Move Dependents until Suitable Quarters Located [*Military*] .... ADNOMOVPEN
Advisedly (ABBR) .... ADVSDY
Advisement (ABBR) .... ADVSNT
Advisement (ABBR) .... ADVST
Adviser (AL) .... Adv
Adviser (SAUS) .... Adv
Adviser Business Oriented Language [*Programming language*] .... ABOL
Adviser Business-Oriented Language (SAUS) .... ABOL
Adviser on Combined Operations [*British*] .... ACO
Adviser on Militia (SAUS) .... AOM
Adviser on War Administration to the Viceroy of India (SAUO) .... AWAVI
Advising (ABBR) .... ADVSG
Advising Schedule Change [*Travel industry*] (TRID) .... ASC
Advisor (AABC) .... ADVR
Advisor .... ADVSR
Advisor (TBD) .... Advsr
Advisor Business-Oriented Language (SAUS) .... ABOL
Advisor, Middletown, NJ [*Library symbol*] [*Library of Congress*] (LCLS) .... NjMiA
Advisor Virtual Memory Operating System [*Computer science*] (MHDI) .... AVOS
Advisory .... ADV
Advisory (AL) .... Adv
Advisory (DD) .... adv
Advisory .... ADVRY
Advisory (ABBR) .... ADVSRY
Advisory (AFM) .... ADVSY
Advisory [*NWS*] (FAAC) .... ADVY
Advisory (FAAC) .... ADZY
Advisory Agricultural Meteorologist (NOAA) .... AAM
Advisory and Coordinating Committee on Child Abuse [*Western Australia*] .... ACCCA
Advisory Area (SAUS) .... ADA
Advisory Board .... AB
Advisory Board for Cooperative Systems [*of ICIREPAT*] .... ABCS
Advisory Board for Medical Specialties (DAVI) .... ABMS
Advisory Board for Research Development (SAUO) .... ABRD
Advisory Board for the Research Councils (SAUO) .... ABRC
[*The*] **Advisory Board for the Research Councils** [*British*] .... ABRC
Advisory Board of Accountancy Education (SAUO) .... ABAE
Advisory Board on Chaplaincy Services (SAUO) .... ABCS
Advisory Board on Counceling Services (SAUO) .... ABCS
Advisory Board on Economic Growth and Stability (SAUO) .... ABEGS
Advisory Board on Energy (SAUO) .... ABE
Advisory Board on Justice Compensation (SAUO) .... ABJC
Advisory Board on Scientific and Technical Information (SAUO) .... ABSTI
Advisory Board on the Built Environment [*Formerly, BRAB*] (EA) .... ABBE
Advisory Board on the Built Environment (SAUS) .... ABBE
Advisory Board on the Law of the Sea (SAUS) .... ABLOS
Advisory Board on Veterinary Specialties (EA) .... ABVS
Advisory Body of Experts on the Law of the Sea (SAUS) .... ABE-LOS
Advisory, Caution And Warning System (SAUS) .... ACAWS
Advisory Caution Panel (MCD) .... ACP
Advisory Centre for Education [*British*] .... ACE
Advisory Centre for Education Ltd. (SAUO) .... ACE
Advisory Centre on Technology for Industry in Victoria [*Australia*] .... ACTIV
Advisory Circular .... AC
Advisory Circular (journ.) (SAUS) .... AC
Advisory Commission on Conferences in Ocean Shipping (WPI) .... ACCOS
Advisory Commission on Electronic Commerce .... ACEC
Advisory Commission on Information (SAUO) .... ACI
Advisory Commission on Intergovernmental Relations [*Washington, DC*] .... ACIR
Advisory Commission on Parliamentary Accommodation [*Canada*] .... ACPA
Advisory Commission on Textbook Specifications .... ACTS
Advisory Commission on the Realm (SAUO) .... ACR
Advisory Committee (NRCH) .... AC

Advisory Committee for Atmospheric Sciences (SAUS) ..... ACAS
Advisory Committee for Biology and Medicine [*AEC*] ..... ACBM
Advisory Committee for Chemical, Biochemical, and Thermal Engineering [*Washington, DC*] [*National Science Foundation*] (EGAO) ..... CBTE
Advisory Committee for Civil and Environmental Engineering [*Terminated, 1 985*] [*National Science Foundation*] (EGAO) ..... CEE
Advisory Committee for Earthquake Hazard Mitigation [*Washington, DC*] [*National Science Foundation*] (EGAO) ..... EHM
Advisory Committee for Electrical, Computer, and Systems Engineering [*Terminated, 1985*] (EGAO) ..... ECSE
Advisory Committee for Immunization Practices (SAUO) ..... ACIP
Advisory Committee for Information Technology Standardisation (SAUO) ..... ACITS
Advisory Committee for Innovation and Technology Transfer [*EC*] (ECED) ..... CIT
Advisory Committee for Land Mobile Radio Services (SAUO) ..... ACLMRS
Advisory Committee for Land-Mobile Radio Services (NTCM) ..... ACLMRS
Advisory Committee for Mechanical Engineering and Applied Mechanics [*Washington, DC*] [*Terminated, 1985*] [*National Science Foundation*] (EGAO) ..... MEAM
Advisory Committee for Neuclear Facility Safety (SAUO) ..... ACNFS
Advisory Committee for Operational Hydrology [*WMO*] (MSC) ..... ACOH
Advisory Committee for Research on Information Transfer [*Netherlands*] (NITA) ..... ACRIT
Advisory Committee for Scientific and Technical Information [*British*] ..... ACSTI
Advisory Committee for Scientific, Technological, and International Affairs [*National Science Foundation*] (EGAO) ..... ACSTIA
Advisory Committee for Teacher Education in the Mid-South (AIE) ..... ACTEMS
Advisory Committee for the Application of Science (SAUS) ..... ACAST
Advisory Committee for the Coordination of Information Systems (SAUO) ..... ACCIS
Advisory Committee for the Co-Ordination of Information Systems [*Database producer*] [*Geneva, Switzerland*] [*United Nations*] ..... ACCIS
Advisory Committee for the Definition of the Metre (SAUO) ..... ACDM
Advisory Committee for the Education of Romany and Other Travellers ..... ACERT
Advisory Committee for the Research and Development Department [*British Library*] (AIE) ..... ACORDD
Advisory Committee for the Supply and Education of Teachers, Further Education Sub-Committee (AIE) ..... ACSET(FE)
Advisory Committee for the US Meat Animal Research Center [*Terminated, 1977*] (EGAO) ..... USMARC
Advisory Committee for the World Climate Applications and Data Programmes (SAUO) ..... ACCAD
Advisory Committee for Trade Policy and Negotiations [*US Trade Representative*] (EGAO) ..... ACTPN
Advisory Committee for Vocational Training (AIE) ..... ACVT
Advisory Committee of Experts on Marine Resources Research [*Marine science*] (OSRA) ..... ACMRR
Advisory Committee of Fundamental Research on the Composition and Properties of Petroleum (SAUO) ..... ACFPCPP
Advisory Committee of Permanent Representatives and other Representatives Designated by Members of the Commission (SAUO) ..... ACPR
Advisory Committee of Reactor Safety [*Environmental science*] (COE) ..... ACRS
Advisory Committee of the Federal Register (SAUO) ..... ACFR
Advisory Committee of the Supply and Training of Teachers [*British*] ..... ACSTT
Advisory Committee on Administrative and Budgetary Questions [*United Nations*] ..... ACABQ
Advisory Committee on Advanced Automotive Power Systems (SAUO) ..... ACAAPS
Advisory Committee on Advanced Research and Development (SAUO) ..... ACARD
Advisory Committee on Advanced Television Service [*FCC high-definition television*] (NTCM) ..... ACATS
Advisory Committee on Advanced Television Systems (SAUO) ..... ACATS
Advisory Committee on Agricultural and Veterinary Chemicals (AUEG) ..... ACAVC
Advisory Committee on Agricultural Product Health and Safety [*European Union*] (GVA) ..... ACAPHS
Advisory Committee on Air Quality [*Australia*] ..... ACAQ
Advisory Committee on Allotments [*New Deal*] ..... ACA
Advisory Committee on Animal Feedingstuffs (GVA) ..... ACAF
Advisory Committee on Antarctic Feature Names [*Board on Geographic Names*] (NOAA) ..... ACAN
Advisory Committee on Applications of Science and Technology (SAUS) ..... ACAST
Advisory Committee on Asbestos (SAUO) ..... ACA
Advisory Committee on Business and the Environment (SAUO) ..... ACBE
Advisory Committee on Chemicals in the Environment [*Australia*] ..... ACCE
Advisory Committee on Civilian Policy [*World War II*] ..... ACCP
Advisory Committee on Climate Applications and Data [*Marine science*] (OSRA) ..... ACCAD
Advisory Committee on Climate Applications and Data (SAUO) ..... ACCI
Advisory Committee on Colonial Colleges of Arts, Science and Technology (SAUO) ..... ACCAST
Advisory Committee on Conservation of Biological Diversity (AUEG) ..... ACCBD
Advisory Committee on Construction Safety and Health (SARE) ..... ACCSH
Advisory Committee on Coordination in the Field of Industrial Development (SAUS) ..... UNIDAC
Advisory Committee on Dangerous Pathogens [*British*] ..... ACDP
Advisory Committee on Dangerous Substances [*British*] ..... ACDS
Advisory Committee on Electrical Appliances and Accessories ..... ACEAA
Advisory Committee on Electronics and Telecommunications [*International Electrotechnical Commission*] [*ISO*] (DS) ..... ACET
Advisory Committee on Energy Research and Development [*British government*] ..... ACORD
Advisory Committee on Energy Re-search and Development (SAUS) ..... ACORD
Advisory Committee on Environmental Employment Opportunities (SAUO) ..... ACCEEO
Advisory Committee on Environmental Resources (AUEG) ..... ACER
Advisory Committee on Export Policy [*Department of Commerce*] ..... ACEP
Advisory Committee on Fisheries Applications of Remote Sensing [*Australia*] ..... ACFARS
Advisory Committee on Fisheries Research (SAUS) ..... ACFR
Advisory Committee on Flight Information [*FAA*] ..... ACFI
Advisory Committee on Genetic Manipulation [*Health and Safety Executive*] [*British*] ..... ACGM
Advisory Committee on Health Research (SAUO) ..... ACHR
Advisory Committee On Highway Policy [*MTMC*] (TAG) ..... ACHP
Advisory Committee on Human Radiation Experiments ..... ACHRE
Advisory Committee on Immunization Practices [*Public Health Service*] ..... ACIP
Advisory Committee on Industrial Development (SAUO) ..... ACID
Advisory Committee on Industrial Development (SAUO) ..... CADI
Advisory Committee on Industrial Research and Development (SAUO) ..... CORDI
Advisory Committee on Information Dissemination in Science and Technology ..... CIDST
Advisory Committee on Information Technology Standardization [*Commission of the European*] (NITA) ..... ACITS
Advisory Committee on International Oceanographic Affairs [*British*] ..... ACIOA
Advisory Committee on Irradiated and Novel Foods [*Government body*] [*British*] ..... ACINF
Advisory Committee on Isotopes and Radiation Development (SAUO) ..... ACIRD
Advisory Committee on Legal Units of Measurement (SAUO) ..... ACLUM
Advisory Committee on Live Fish [*Australia*] ..... ACLF
Advisory Committee on Major Hazards [*British*] ..... ACMH
Advisory Committee on Marine Pollution (SAUO) ..... ACMP
Advisory Committee on Marine Resources Research (USDC) ..... ACMR
Advisory Committee on Marine Resources Research ..... ACMRR
Advisory Committee on Medical Uses of Isotopes [*Nuclear energy*] (NRCH) ..... ACMI
Advisory Committee on Networking [*British*] (TELE) ..... ACN
Advisory Committee on Northern Development [*Canada*] ..... ACND
Advisory Committee on Novel Foods and Processes [*British*] ..... ACNFP
Advisory Committee on Nuclear Facility Safety (SAUS) ..... ACNFS
Advisory Committee on Nuclear Materials Safeguards ..... ACNMS
Advisory Committee on Nuclear Safety [*Canada*] ..... ACNS
Advisory Committee on Nuclear Waste [*United States Nuclear Regulatory Commission*] ..... ACNW
Advisory Committee on Oceanic Meteorological Research [*Marine science*] (OSRA) ..... ACOMR
Advisory Committee on Oceanic Meterological Research (SAUO) ..... ACOMR
Advisory Committee on Personal Dosimetry Services [*National Science Foundation*] (NRCH) ..... ACPDS
Advisory Committee on Pesticides [*British*] ..... ACP
Advisory Committee on Polar Programs [*National Science Foundation*] (MSC) ..... ACPP
Advisory Committee on Pollution of the Sea (EAIO) ..... ACOPS
Advisory Committee on Program Management (MHDB) ..... ACPM
Advisory Committee on Programme Management (SAUO) ..... ACPM
Advisory Committee on Protection of the Sea [*Marine science*] (OSRA) ..... ACOPS
Advisory Committee on Radiological Protection [*Canada*] ..... ACRP
Advisory Committee on Reactor Safeguards [*Nuclear Regulatory Commission*] ..... ACRS
Advisory Committee on Releases into the Environment (SAUO) ..... ACRE
Advisory Committee on Releases to the Environment [*British*] ..... ACRE
Advisory Committee on Resource Use (SAUS) ..... ACRU
Advisory Committee on Safety [*International Electrotechnical Commission*] [*ISO*] (DS) ..... ACOS
Advisory Committee on Science and Technology [*British*] ..... ACOST
Advisory Committee on Science and Technology (SAUO) ..... ACST
Advisory Committee on Science and Technology and Foreign Affairs [*Terminated, 1975*] [*Department of State*] (EGAO) ..... ACSTFA
Advisory Committee on Technology Innovation [*Board on Science and Technology for International Development*] [*Office of International Affairs*] [*National Research Council*] (EGAO) ..... ACTI
Advisory Committee on Techology Innovation (SAUO) ..... ACTI
Advisory Committee on Telecommunications for Disabled and Elderly People (SAUO) ..... DIEL
Advisory Committee on Telecommunications for Small Businesses (SAUO) ..... BACT
Advisory Committee on the Application of Science and Technology to Development [*Also, ACASTD, ACST*] [*United Nations*] ..... ACAST
Advisory Committee on the Application of Science and Technology to Development [*Also, ACAST, ACST*] [*United Nations*] ..... ACASTD
Advisory Committee on the Application of Science and Technology to Development [*Also, ACAST, ACASTD*] [*United Nations*] ..... ACST
Advisory Committee on the Arts [*Terminated, 1973*] (EGAO) ..... ACA
Advisory Committee on the Biological Effects of Ionizing Radiations (SAUO) ..... BEIR
Advisory Committee on the Carriage of Dangerous Goods in Ships (SAUS) ..... SAC
Advisory Committee on the Environment (SAUO) ..... ACE
Advisory Committee on the Law of the Sea [*Department of State*] [*Terminated, 1983*] (NOAA) ..... ACLOS
Advisory Committee on the Marine Environment [*Marine science*] (OSRA) ..... ACME
Advisory Committee on the Microbiological Safety of Food (GVA) ..... ACMSV
Advisory Committee on the NAIC [*National Astronomy and Ionosphere Center*] **Nation-Wide Marine Definition** (EA) ..... COI

Advisory Committee on the Safety of Nuclear Installations [*British*] (NUCP) ... ACSNI
Advisory Committee on the Supply and Education of Teachers [*British*] ... ACSET
Advisory Committee on the Supply and Education of Teachers (SAUS) ... ACSTT
Advisory Committee on the Supply and Training of Teachers (SAUO) ... ACSTT
Advisory Committee on the Transport of Radioactive Materials [*British*] ... ACTRAM
Advisory Committee on Toxic Substances [*British*] ... ACTS
Advisory Committee on Undersea Feature Names [*Board on Geographic Names*] (NOAA) ... ACUF
Advisory Committee on Undersea Features (SAUS) ... ACUF
Advisory Committee on Vehicle Emissions and Noise (SAUO) ... ACVEN
Advisory Committee on Vehicle Performance (SAUO) ... ACVP
Advisory Committee on Veterinary Training [*European Union*] (GVA) ... ACVT
Advisory Committee on Voluntary Foreign Aid [*Department of State*] ... ACVA
Advisory Committee on Voluntary Foreign Aid [*Department of State*] ... ACVFA
Advisory Committee on Voter Education [*Defunct*] (EA) ... ACVE
Advisory Committee on Weather Control [*Terminated, 1957*] ... ACWC
Advisory Committee, Statistics [*British*] ... AC(S)
Advisory Committee to the Board and to the Committee on Commodities [*UNCTAD*] ... ACBCC
Advisory Committee to the Canada Centre for Inland Waters (PDAA) ... ACCC
Advisory Committee to the Department of Housing and Urban Development ... ACHUD
Advisory Committee to the Depart-ment of Housing and Urban Development (SAUO) ... ACHUD
Advisory, Conciliation and Arbitration Service (SAUO) ... ACAS
Advisory, Conciliation, and Arbitration Service [*London, England*] ... ACAS
Advisory Council (SAUO) ... AC
Advisory Council, Allied Control Commission [*Italy*] [*World War II*] ... ACACC
Advisory Council for Adult and Continuing Education [*British*] ... ACACE
Advisory Council for Applied Research and Development [*British government*] ... ACARD
Advisory Council for Energy Conservation (SAUS) ... ACEC
Advisory Council for Historic Preservation (SAUO) ... ACHP
Advisory Council for Minority Enterprise [*Department of Commerce*] ... ACME
Advisory Council for Orthopaedic Resident Education (EA) ... ACORE
Advisory Council for Scientific and Industrial Research (SAUO) ... ACSIR
Advisory Council for the Church's Ministry [*Church of England*] ... ACCM
Advisory Council for the Elimination of Tuberculosis ... ACET
Advisory Council for the International Geophysical Year (SAUO) ... ACIGY
Advisory Council for/on Applied Research and Development (SAUO) ... ACARD
Advisory Council for/on Energy Conservation (SAUO) ... ACEC
Advisory Council of National Organizations [*Corporation for Public Broadcasting*] (NTCM) ... ACNO
Advisory Council of the International Geophysical Year ... ACIGY
Advisory Council of the National Arboretum (SAUO) ... ACNA
Advisory Council on Applied Research and Development (SAUS) ... ACARD
Advisory Council on Australia's Languages Policy ... ACALP
Advisory Council on Calibration and Measurement (ACII) ... ACCM
Advisory Council on Camps (EA) ... ACC
Advisory Council on Clean Air Compliance Analysis [*Environmental Protection Agency*] ... ACCACA
Advisory Council on College Chemistry ... ACCC
Advisory Council on Community Relations in Defence (SAUO) ... ACCORD
Advisory Council on Education and Training (AIE) ... ACET
Advisory Council on Education Statistics [*Department of Education*] (GFGA) ... ACES
Advisory Council on Energy Conservation [*British*] ... ACEC
Advisory Council on Exhibition Birds [*Australia*] ... ACEB
Advisory Council on Federal Reports ... ACFR
Advisory Council on Historic Preservation (NRCH) ... ACHP
Advisory Council on Industrial Research (SAUO) ... ACIR
Advisory Council on Intergovernmental Relations (SAUO) ... ACIR
Advisory Council on Medical Education ... ACME
Advisory Council on Naval Affairs ... ACNA
Advisory Council on Naval Affairs (SAUO) ... ACONA
Advisory Council on Naval Affairs of the Navy League ... ACONA
Advisory Council on Personnel Policy [*Canada*] ... ACPP
Advisory Council on Research and Development for Fuel and Power (SAUO) ... ACORD
Advisory Council on Research and Redevelopment for Fuel and Power (NUCP) ... ACORD
Advisory Council On Science and Technology (SAUO) ... ACOST
Advisory Council on Scientific Policy ... ACSP
Advisory Council on Scientific Research and Technical Development [*British*] ... AC
Advisory Council on Technology [*British*] ... ACT
Advisory Council on the Misuse of Drugs (HEAS) ... ACMD
Advisory Council on the Penal System (SAUO) ... ACPS
Advisory Council on the Status of Women [*Canada*] ... ACSW
Advisory Council on the Treatment of Offenders (SAUO) ... ACTO
Advisory Council to the University Librarian (SAUO) ... ACUL
Advisory County Cricket Committee (SAUO) ... ACCC
Advisory Defense Committee ... ADC
Advisory Direction (NATG) ... AD
Advisory Engineer (SAUS) ... Adv Engr
Advisory Group [*Military*] ... ADGRU
Advisory Group ... ADVGP
Advisory Group (SAUO) ... AdvGp
Advisory Group [*Military*] ... AG
Advisory Group for Aeronautical Research and Development (SAUO) ... AGARD
Advisory Group for Aerospace Research and Development [*NATO*] ... AGARD
Advisory Group for Central American Economic Integration (SAUS) ... GAFICA
Advisory Group for Increasing Productivity by Standardisation (SAUO) ... AGIPS
Advisory Group for International Training of Cooperators (SAUO) ... AGITCOOP
Advisory Group for Ocean Engineering [*Society of Naval Architects and Marine Engineers*] (DNAB) ... AGOE
Advisory Group for/on Aerospace Research and Development (SAUO) ... AGARD
Advisory Group On Computer Graphics (SAUO) ... AGOCG
Advisory Group on Data Transmission (SAUO) ... AGDT
Advisory Group on Electron Devices [*Army*] [*Washington, DC*] ... AGED
Advisory Group on Electronic Devices (SAUO) ... AGED
Advisory Group on Electronic Parts [*Military*] ... AGEP
Advisory Group on Energy [*Army*] (RDA) ... AGE
Advisory Group on Greenhouse Gases [*Australia*] ... AGGG
Advisory Group on Harmonization of Classification and Labeling (SAUO) ... AGHCL
Advisory Group on Management of Electronic Parts Specifications ... AGMEPS
Advisory Group on National Bibliographic Control ... AGNBC
Advisory Group on Ocean Research (SAUO) ... AGOR
Advisory Group on Reliability of Electronic Equipment [*Military*] ... AGREE
Advisory Group on Science Programs (SAUO) ... AGOSP
Advisory Group on Systems Definitions (SAUO) ... AGSD
Advisory Leaflet ... AL
Advisory Light Panel (MCD) ... ALP
Advisory Map Display (HLLA) ... AMD
Advisory Panel (SAUO) ... ADPAN
Advisory Panel (SAUO) ... AP
Advisory Panel for Oceanography [*National Science Foundation*] (MSC) ... APO
Advisory Panel for Operations Research ... APOR
Advisory Panel of Alternative Means of Financing and Managing Radioactive Waste Facilities [*Terminated, 1984*] [*Department of Energy*] (EGAO) ... AMFM
Advisory Panel on Environmental Change (SAUS) ... APEC
Advisory Panel on Management Education (SAUO) ... APME
Advisory Panel on Microscopic Analysis (SAUO) ... APMA
Advisory Panel on Safeguarding Special Nuclear Material ... APSSNM
Advisory Panel on Safety Matters (SAUO) ... APSM
Advisory Report (SAUS) ... AR
Advisory Review Panel ... ARP
Advisory Route [*Aviation*] (FAAC) ... ADR
Advisory Rule (DA) ... ADR
Advisory Service for the Building Industry (SAUO) ... ASBI
Advisory Service Leaflet. Research and Development Association (journ.) (SAUS) ... Ad Serv Leafl Timb Res Developm Ass
Advisory Services. Sea Grant Program. Southern California University (SAUO) ... Advis Serv Sea Grant Program South Calif Univ
Advisory Support Force [*Military*] ... ASF
Advisory Tax Board Recommendation [*Internal Revenue Bureau*] [*United States*] [*A publication*] (DLA) ... TBR
Advisory Team ... ADVTM
Advisory, Training, and Operaions Mission (VNW) ... ATOM
Advisory Unit for Computer Based Education [*Hatfield, England*] [*Information service or system*] [*Telecommunications*] (TSSD) ... AUCBE
Advo, Inc. [*NYSE symbol*] (SAG) ... AD
Advo, Inc. [*Associated Press*] (SAG) ... Advo Inc
Advocaat [*Barrister*] [*Netherlands*] (ILCA) ... adv
Advocacy (ABBR) ... ADVCY
Advocacy Centre for the Elderly (AC) ... ACE
Advocacy Group for the Environmentally Sensitive [*Association Groupant les Malades de l'Environnement*] (AC) ... AGES
Advocacy Institute (EA) ... AI
Advocacy Resource Centre for the Handicapped [*Canada*] ... ARCH
Advocat, Inc. [*Associated Press*] (SAG) ... Advocat
Advocat, Inc. [*NYSE symbol*] (SAG) ... AVC
Advocate [*Cleveland*] [*1929*] [*A publication*] (ILCA) ... Adv
Advocate [*Canada*] [*1943*] [*A publication*] (ILCA) ... Adv
Advocate [*Ife, Nigeria*] [*1968*] [*A publication*] (ILCA) ... Adv
Advocate (SAUS) ... ADV
Advocate (ABBR) ... ADVCA
Advocate (ABBR) ... ADVO
Advocate (DLA) ... ADVOC
Advocate, East Orange, NJ [*Library symbol*] [*Library of Congress*] (LCLS) ... NjEoA
Advocate Health Care [*An association*] (EA) ... AHC
Advocate, Pictou, Nova Scotia [*Library symbol*] [*National Library of Canada*] (NLC) ... NSPA
Advocated (ABBR) ... ADVCAD
Advocated (ABBR) ... ADVOD
Advocates (ABBR) ... ADVOS
Advocates Against Psychic Abuse [*Defunct*] (EA) ... AAPA
Advocates' Chronicle [*India*] [*A publication*] (DLA) ... Adv Chron
Advocates for a Safe Vaccine (EA) ... ASV
Advocates for Better Communication [*An association*] ... ABC
Advocates for Border Law Enforcement (SAUO) ... ABLE
Advocates for Communication Technology for Deaf/Blind People ... ACT
Advocates for Community Based Training & Education for Women (AC) ... ACTEW
Advocates for Library Outreach [*Office for Literacy and Outreach*] [*American Library Association*] ... AFLO
Advocates for Self-Government (EA) ... ASG
Advocates for Women [*Defunct*] (EA) ... AFW
Advocates for Women (SAUO) ... AW
Advocates of International Trade and Comity [*Defunct*] (EA) ... AITC
Advocates to Save Legal Services [*Inactive*] [*Defunct*] (EA) ... ASLS
Advocating (ABBR) ... ADVCAG

Advocating (ABBR) ... ADVOG
Advocating Legislation for Adoption Reform Movement (EA) ... ALARM
Advocation (ABBR) ... ADVCAN
Advocation (ABBR) ... ADVON
Advocator (ABBR) ... ADVOR
Advokatbladet [*Denmark*] [*1921-*] [*A publication*] (ILCA) ... Adv Bl
Adye on Courts-Martial [*A publication*] (DLA) ... Adye CM
Adygey (SAUS) ... Adyg
Adzhar (SAUS) ... Adzh
A/E Contract Administrative Support System (SAUO) ... ACASS
AE Developments Ltd. [*Research center*] [*British*] ... AED
A.E. Staley Manufacturing Co., Decatur, IL [*Library symbol*] [*Library of Congress*] (LCLS) ... IDecS
AEC XML Working Group (SAUO) ... AECXML
AEC XML Working Group (SAUS) ... aecXML
AECL International, Mississauga, ON, Canada [*Library symbol*] [*Library of Congress*] (LCLS) ... CaOMAECL
AECL International, Mississauga, Ontario [*Library symbol*] [*National Library of Canada*] (NLC) ... OMAECL
AECMA Certification Service (SAUS) ... AECMA-CERT
Aedh (SAUS) ... Ad
Aedicula (VRA) ... aed
AEELS [*Airborne ELINT Emitter Location System*] **Fixed Downlink Terminal** (MCD) ... AFDT
AEERL Dual Alkali FGD Process Demonstration (SAUS) ... DAPD
AEG Telefunken (NAKS) ... AEG
Aegean (SAUS) ... Aeg
Aegean Aviation [*Greece*] [*ICAO designator*] (FAAC) ... AEE
Aegean Islands (SAUS) ... Aegeans
Aegean Sea (SAUS) ... Aegean
Aegean Sea (SAUS) ... Aeg S
Aegean Sea ... AEG S
Aegirine (SAUS) ... AE
Aegirine (SAUS) ... ae
Aegis Combat System [*Navy*] (LAIN) ... ACS
Aegis Combat Training System (SAUS) ... ACTS
Aegis Consumer Funding [*NASDAQ symbol*] (TTSB) ... ACAR
Aegis Consumer Funding Group [*NASDAQ symbol*] (SAG) ... ACAR
Aegis Consumer Funding Group [*Associated Press*] (SAG) ... Aegis
AEGIS Display System (DNAB) ... ADS
Aegis Realty [*AMEX symbol*] ... AER
Aegis Surface Action Group [*Military*] (DOMA) ... ASAG
AEGIS [*Airborne Early Warning Ground Environment Integrated Segment*] **Tactical Executive Program** ... ATEP
Aegis Training Support Group (SAUO) ... ATSG
Aegis Training Unit (SAUS) ... ATU
AEGIS Weapon System (SAUS) ... AWS
AEGON N.V. [*NYSE symbol*] (SPSG) ... AEG
AEGON NV [*Associated Press*] (SAG) ... Aegon
AEGON N.V. Ord [*NYSE symbol*] (SG) ... AEG
Aegrus [*or Aegra*] [*The Patient*] [*Medicine*] ... AEG
AEI Corp. of Bethlehem (SAUO) ... AEI
AEL Industries, Inc. [*Associated Press*] (SAG) ... AEL
AEL Industries, Inc. [*NASDAQ symbol*] (NQ) ... AELN
Aelianus [*c. 170-235AD*] [*Classical studies*] (OCD) ... Ael
Aelius Donatus [*Fourth century AD*] [*Classical studies*] (OCD) ... Donat
Aemilius Ferretus [*Deceased, 1552*] [*Authority cited in pre-1607 legal work*] (DSA) ... Aemil Ferret
Aemilius Papinianus [*Deceased, 212*] [*Authority cited in pre-1607 legal work*] (DSA) ... Aemil Pap
Aemilius Paulus [*of Plutarch*] [*Classical studies*] (OCD) ... Aem
Aeneid [*of Vergil*] [*Classical studies*] (OCD) ... Aen
Aeolian (or Aeolic) (SAUS) ... Aeol
Aeolian-Skinner Organ Co. [*Record label*] ... ASK
Aeon [*10^9 years*] [*Geology*] ... AE
AEP Industries [*NASDAQ symbol*] (TTSB) ... AEPI
AEP Industries [*Associated Press*] (SAG) ... AEP Ind
AEP Industries, Inc. [*Moonachie, NJ*] [*NASDAQ symbol*] (NQ) ... AEPI
Aequales [*Equal*] [*Latin*] ... AEQ
Aequitron Medical [*NASDAQ symbol*] (TTSB) ... AQTN
Aequitron Medical, Inc. [*Associated Press*] (SAG) ... Aequtrn
Aequitron Medical, Inc. [*Minneapolis, MN*] [*NASDAQ symbol*] (NQ) ... AQTN
Aer Arann Teo [*ICAO designator*] (AD) ... RE
Aer Arann Teoranta [*Ireland*] [*ICAO designator*] (ICDA) ... II
Aer Arann Teoranta [*Ireland*] [*ICAO designator*] (FAAC) ... REA
AER Energy Resources [*Associated Press*] (SAG) ... AER En
AER Energy Resources [*NASDAQ symbol*] (SAG) ... AERN
AER Lingus (SAUO) ... AER
Aer Lingus Teoranta [*Ireland*] ... ALT
Aer Lingus Teoranta [*Ireland*] [*ICAO designator*] (FAAC) ... EIN
AER Local Forecast and Assimilation (SAUS) ... ALFA
Aer Turas Teoranta [*Republic of Ireland*] [*ICAO designator*] (FAAC) ... ATT
Aer Turas Teoranta (SAUS) ... QT
Aera Electricity Board (SAUS) ... AEB
Aerated Autoclaved Concrete ... AAC
Aerated Bread Co. [*Chain of restaurants in London*] ... ABC
Aerated Bread Company (SAUO) ... ABC
Aerated Concrete (SAUS) ... AC
Aerated Drain Tank [*Nuclear energy*] (NRCH) ... ADT
Aerated Stabilization Basin [*For water purification*] ... ASB
Aerated Waters Trade Board (SAUS) ... AWTB
Aerated Waters Trade Board (SAUO) ... AWTB
Aeration (ABBR) ... AERA
Aeration (SAUS) ... Aerea
Aeration Test Burner [*Heating*] ... ATB
Aeredrome (or Airport) Of Entry (SAUS) ... AOE
Aereo Postal de Mexico SA de CV [*ICAO designator*] (FAAC) ... PTX
Aereo Taxi de Leon SA de CV [*Mexico*] [*ICAO designator*] (FAAC) ... TXL
Aereotaxis SA de CV [*Mexico*] [*ICAO designator*] (FAAC) ... TXI
AERI Front End Processor (SAUS) ... AERI-FEP
Aerial (IAA) ... A
Aerial (IAA) ... ADX
Aerial (IAA) ... AER
Aerial (AFM) ... AERL
Aerial ... ARL
Aerial (SAUS) ... Arl
Aerial Ambulance Co. [*Army*] (AABC) ... AAC
Aerial Ambulance Company (SAUO) ... AAC
Aerial Armored Reconnaissance Vehicle ... AARV
Aerial Array (SAUS) ... AA
Aerial Aspect Processor (SAUS) ... AAP
Aerial Assembly (SAUS) ... AS
Aerial Attack (SAUS) ... Ae Atk
Aerial Base Spring (SAUS) ... ABS
Aerial Beam-shape Factor (SAUS) ... ABF
Aerial Biosensing Association (EA) ... ABA
Aerial Board of Control (SAUO) ... ABC
Aerial Bomb (SAUS) ... AB
Aerial Bulk Fuel Delivery System [*Military*] (AFIT) ... ABFDS
Aerial Burst Bombs ... AB
Aerial Caltographic and Geodetic Squadron (SAUS) ... ACGS
Aerial Cartographic and Geodetic Squadron (SAUO) ... ACGS
Aerial Cartographic and Geodetic Squadron [*Air Force*] (AFM) ... ACGSq
Aerial Cartographics of America (GEOI) ... ACA
Aerial Color Infrared Management System (MCD) ... ACIMS
Aerial Colour Infrared Management System (SAUS) ... ACIMS
Aerial Combat and Surveillance System (SAA) ... AC & SS
Aerial Combat Engagement Display (ACAE) ... ACED
Aerial Combat Engagement Simulator (ACAE) ... ACES
Aerial Combat Evaluator (MCD) ... ACE
Aerial Combat Maneuvering Training (MCD) ... ACMT
Aerial Combat Maneuvres (SAUS) ... ACM
Aerial Combat Reconnaissance ... ACR
Aerial Combat Tactics (SAA) ... ACT
Aerial Common Sensor [*Military*] (RDA) ... ACS
Aerial Common Sensor-Corps (SAUS) ... ACS-C
Aerial Communications [*NASDAQ symbol*] (SG) ... AERL
Aerial Communications, Inc. [*Associated Press*] (SAG) ... AerialC
Aerial Communications, Inc. [*NASDAQ symbol*] (SAG) ... AERL
Aerial Communications Point [*Military*] (DOMA) ... ACP
Aerial Control Bay (SAUS) ... ACB
Aerial Control Console (SAUS) ... ACC
Aerial Control Display (IAA) ... ACD
Aerial Control Point [*Military*] (DOMA) ... ACP
Aerial Control Unit (SAUS) ... ACU
Aerial Coupler Receiver (SAUS) ... ACR
Aerial Coupling Regulator (SAUS) ... ACR
Aerial Cross Talk (SAUS) ... ACT
Aerial Current (IAA) ... AC
Aerial Data Reduction Associates Inc. (SAUO) ... ADR
Aerial Delivered Land Mine (AFM) ... ADLM
Aerial Delivery (MCD) ... AD
Aerial Delivery Equipment (MCD) ... ADE
Aerial Delivery System ... ADS
Aerial Demonstration Squadron (MCD) ... ADS
Aerial Demonstration Team (MCD) ... ADT
Aerial Direction Finding ... ADF
Aerial Directive Gain (SAUS) ... ADG
Aerial Dish Control (SAUS) ... ADC
Aerial Distribution Wire [*Telecommunications*] (TEL) ... ADW
Aerial Dummy Load (SAUS) ... ADL
Aerial Effective Height (SAUS) ... AEH
Aerial Effective Resistance (SAUS) ... AER
Aerial Elevation Angle (SAUS) ... AEA
Aerial Embarkation Center (SAUS) ... AEC
Aerial Enterprises Ltd. [*British*] [*ICAO designator*] (FAAC) ... AEG
Aerial Experimental Component [*Military*] (IUSS) ... AEC
Aerial Exploitation Battalion (MCD) ... AEB
Aerial Exposure Index ... AEI
Aerial Feed Horn (SAUS) ... AFH
Aerial Feed System (SAUS) ... AFS
Aerial Field Artillery (MCD) ... AFA
Aerial Field Artillery Multi-Mode (MCD) ... AFAMM
Aerial Field Charge Kit (SAUS) ... AFCK
Aerial Field Gain (SAUS) ... AFG
Aerial Film Speed ... AFS
Aerial Fire Support ... AFS
Aerial Fire Support Officer [*Army*] (INF) ... AFSO
Aerial Firefighting Industry Association (NTPA) ... AFIA
Aerial Free Gunnery Instruction School (SAUO) ... AFGIS
Aerial Free Gunnery Instructions School [*Obsolete*] ... AFGIS
Aerial Free Gunnery Unit ... AFGU
Aerial Geological and Geophysical Survey of Northern Australia. Report [*A publication*] ... AGGSNA Rept
Aerial Gunner-Scanner Simulator (SAUS) ... AGSS
Aerial Gunnery Advanced Technology Evaluation (ACAE) ... AGATE
Aerial Gunnery Part Task Trainer (MCD) ... AGPTT
Aerial Gunnery Target System (MCD) ... AGTS
Aerial Gunnery TOW Target (MCD) ... AGTT
Aerial Homing System (SAUS) ... AHS

Aerial Image Interpretation System (SAUS)	AIIS
Aerial Impedance (SAUS)	AI
Aerial Independent Model (OA)	AIM
Aerial Inspection Instrument	AII
Aerial Intercept Missile	AIM
Aerial Intercept Mobile (ACAE)	AIM
Aerial Laboratory (SAUS)	AL
Aerial Ladder Platform (WDAA)	ALP
Aerial Lentiginous Melanoma [Medicine] (DMAA)	ALM
Aerial Lightning Arrester (SAUS)	ALA
Aerial Loading Coil (SAUS)	ALC
Aerial Locations of Hazardous Atmospheres (GEOI)	ALOHA
Aerial Mail Terminal (AFM)	AMT
Aerial Manufacturers Association [British] (DBA)	AMA
Aerial Matching Unit (SAUS)	AMU
Aerial Measurement Station (SAUS)	AMS
Aerial Measurement System (SAUS)	AMS
Aerial Measuring System [Environmental science] (COE)	AMS
Aerial Mission Photographic Indoctrination (MCD)	AMPHI
Aerial Monitoring System [Nuclear energy] (NRCH)	AMS
Aerial Multi-Mission Integrated Test-bed (SAUS)	AMMIT
Aerial Noise Temperature (SAUS)	ANT
Aerial Nurse Corps of America (SAUO)	ANCO
Aerial Nurse Corps of America	ANCOA
Aerial Observation Post (SAUO)	AOP
Aerial Observer [Military] (NVT)	AO
Aerial Ohmic Resistance (SAUS)	AOR
Aerial Pattern Error Analysis (SAUS)	APEA
Aerial Pattern Recorder (SAUS)	APR
Aerial Pattern Test System (SAUS)	APATS
Aerial Phenomena Research Group (SAUO)	APRG
Aerial Phenomena Research Organization [Defunct] (EA)	APRO
Aerial Phenomena Research Organization, Inc., Information Services Division, Tucson, AZ [Library symbol] [Library of Congress] (LCLS)	AzTAP
Aerial Photo Interpretation (AUEG)	API
Aerial Photo Summary Records System (SAUS)	APSRS
Aerial Photographic Analysis Center	APAC
Aerial Photographic Analysis Centre (SAUO)	APAC
Aerial Photographic Reconnaissance	APR
Aerial Photography Contract Management System (GEOI)	APCM
Aerial Photography Field Office [Department of Agriculture] (GFGA)	APFO
Aerial Photography Information System (GEOI)	APIS
Aerial Photography Micrographic Index (GEOI)	APMI
Aerial Photography Micrographic Index System (SAUS)	APMI
Aerial Photography of the Eclipse of the Quiet Sun (SAUS)	APEQS
Aerial Photography Progress Summary Report (GEOI)	APPSR
Aerial Photography Quad File (GEOI)	APQF
Aerial Photography Summary Record (GEOI)	APSR
Aerial Photography Summary Record System (GEOI)	APSRS
Aerial Pointing Angle Change (SAUS)	APAC
Aerial Pointing Subsystem (SAUS)	APS
Aerial Port	AP
Aerial Port (SAUO)	APORT
Aerial Port Control Center (SAUO)	APCC
Aerial Port Detachment	APD
Aerial Port Documentation and Management System	ADAM II
Aerial Port Documentation and Management System-111 (SAUS)	ADAM 111
Aerial Port Exploitation Squadron (SAUO)	APES
Aerial Port Flight [Air Force]	APF
Aerial Port Group [Air Force] (AFM)	APG
Aerial Port Group [Air Force]	APGp
Aerial Port Group [Air Force] (AFM)	APOG
Aerial Port Liaison Office [or Officer] [Air Force] (AFM)	APLO
Aerial Port Logistics Office [Air Force]	APLO
Aerial Port of Debarkation [Military]	APOD
Aerial Port of Embarkation [Military]	APE
Aerial Port of Embarkation [Military]	APOE
Aerial Port Operations Center	APOC
Aerial Port Squadron [Air Force]	APS
Aerial Port Squadron [Air Force] (AFM)	APSq
Aerial Ports [And Air Operating Base File] [Military] (DOMA)	APORTS
Aerial Position Indicator (SAUS)	API
Aerial Position Programmer (SAUS)	APP
Aerial Position Recorder (SAUS)	APR
Aerial Positioning Device (SAUS)	ANPOD
Aerial Positioning Mechanism (SAUS)	APM
Aerial Power Gain (SAUS)	APG
Aerial Profiling of Terrain [System] [Department of the Interior]	APT
Aerial Profiling of Terrain System (GEOI)	APTS
Aerial RADIAC Instrument	ARI
Aerial RADIAC Instrument System	ARIS
Aerial Radiac System (SAUS)	ARS
Aerial Radiation Pattern (SAUS)	ARP
Aerial Radiation Resistance (SAUS)	ARR
Aerial Radio Instrument System	ARIS
Aerial Radiological Measurement and Survey [Program]	ARMS
Aerial Radiological Measurements and Survey (SAUS)	ARMS
Aerial Radiological Measurements Study (ACAE)	ARMS
Aerial Radiological Measurements System [Nuclear energy] (NRCH)	ARMS
Aerial Radiological Measuring Survey (SAUS)	ARMS
Aerial Radiological Measuring System (SAUS)	ARMS
Aerial Radiological Monitoring System (SAUS)	ARMS
Aerial Radome Heater (SAUS)	ARH
Aerial Range Equipment (SAUS)	ARE
Aerial Reconnaissance and Security	ARS
Aerial Reconnaissance and Security Troop	ARST
Aerial Reconnaissance and Surveillance Penetration Analysis [Army]	ARSPA
Aerial Reconnaissance and Surveillance Survivability Analysis [Army]	ARSSA
Aerial Reconnaissance Camera [Military] (PDAA)	ARC
Aerial Reconnaissance Helicopter [Army]	ARH
Aerial Reconnaissance Laboratory	ARL
Aerial Reconnaissance Surveillance (MCD)	ARS
Aerial Reconnaissance Weather System (ACAE)	ARWS
Aerial Reconnoiterer (SAUS)	AR
Aerial Refueling Area	ARA
Aerial Refueling Group (ACAE)	ARG
Aerial Refueling Master Plan (ACAE)	ARMP
Aerial Refueling Operator (MCD)	ARO
Aerial Refueling Receptacle (MCD)	ARR
Aerial Refueling Squadron (DNAB)	AERREFRON
Aerial Refueling Squadron (SAA)	ARS
Aerial Refueling Squadron [Navy symbol] (DNAB)	VAK
Aerial Refueling Systems Advisory Group [Military] (CAAL)	ARSAG
Aerial Refueling Systems Development Plan (ACAE)	ARSDP
Aerial Refueling Wing [Aeronautics]	ARW
Aerial Refuelling Operator (SAUS)	ARO
Aerial Refuelling Systems Advisory Group (SAUS)	ARSAG
Aerial Relay Transportation System (MCD)	ARTS
Aerial Resistance (SAUS)	AR
Aerial Resupply and Communications [Air Force] (LAIN)	ARC
Aerial Rocket Antitank Program (MCD)	ARAT
Aerial Rocket Artillery	ARA
Aerial Rocket Control System [or Subsystem] (MCD)	ARCS
Aerial Ropeways Association [British] (BI)	ARA
Aerial Ropeways Association (SAUO)	ARA
Aerial Rotation Period (SAUS)	ARP
Aerial Rotation Rate (SAUS)	ARR
Aerial Scout Helicopter (MCD)	ASH
Aerial Scout Program (ACAE)	ASP
Aerial Sensing System of US Coast Guard (SAUS)	AIREYE
Aerial Sensor	AS
Aerial Signal Processing (SAUS)	ASP
Aerial Slave Data Equipment (SAUS)	ASDE
Aerial Stores Lift Truck (MCD)	ASLT
Aerial Superiority Program (ACAE)	ASP
Aerial Surveillance (MCD)	AS
Aerial Surveillance and Target Acquisition (SAUS)	ASTA
Aerial Surveillance and Target Acquisition Platoon (SAUO)	ASTAP
Aerial Survey and Target Acquisition [Military]	ASTA
Aerial Survey Team (AFM)	AST
Aerial Surveys (1980) Ltd. [New Zealand] [ICAO designator] (FAAC)	SUY
Aerial Survival Equipment	ASE
Aerial Switching Matrix (SAUS)	ASM
Aerial Tape (SAUS)	AT
Aerial Tape Armor [Telecommunications] (TEL)	AT
Aerial Target	AT
Aerial Target Control Center (SAUS)	ATCC
Aerial Target Control Central (NG)	ATCC
Aerial Test Facility (SAUS)	ATF
Aerial Test Model (SAUS)	ATM
Aerial Torpedo	AT
Aerial Training Squadron (SAUO)	ATRS
Aerial Transit Co. [ICAO designator] (FAAC)	AEZ
Aerial Transmit-Receive (SAUS)	ATR
Aerial Tuning Capacitor (SAUS)	ATC
Aerial Tuning Condenser	ATC
Aerial Tuning Inductance	ATI
Aerial Tuning Unit [Telecommunications] (OA)	ATU
Aerial Turning Motor (SAUS)	ATM
Aerial Unmanned Vehicle [Military]	AUV
Aerial Vehicle (SAUS)	AV
Aerial View (VRA)	arl vw
Aerial Weapons Company [Military] (VNW)	AWC
Aerialift Industries Association [Defunct] (EA)	AIA
Aerialist (ABBR)	AERLT
Aerially Deployed Ice Thickness Transponder (SAUS)	ADITT
Aerially Deployed Soil Penetrometer (SAUS)	ADSP
Aerial-Receiver-Transmitter (SAUS)	ART
Aerials and Propagation (SAUS)	A/P
Aeriantur-M Airlines [Moldova] [FAA designator] (FAAC)	TUM
Aerie Airlines (SAUO)	LTL
Aeritalia (NAKS)	AIT
Aeritalia SpA [Italy] [ICAO aircraft manufacturer identifier] (ICAO)	AY
Aerliest Arriving Time (SAUS)	EAT
Aerline Eireann (SAUS)	IIA
Aerlinte Eireann Teoranta [Irish Air Lines]	AET
Aermacchi SpA [Italy] [ICAO aircraft manufacturer identifier] (ICAO)	MC
Aermediterranea Linee Aeree Mediterranee SpA (SAUS)	VQ
Aero [Denmark] [ICAO location identifier] (ICLI)	EKAE
Aero 1 Prop-Jet, Inc. [Canada] [ICAO designator] (FAAC)	SSM
Aero Albatros [Mexico] [ICAO designator] (FAAC)	ALB
Aero Algarve Lda. [Portugal] [FAA designator] (FAAC)	DSK
Aero America, Inc. [ICAO designator] (ICDA)	EO
Aero Asia [Pakistan] [ICAO designator] (FAAC)	RSO
Aero Astra [Mexico] [ICAO designator] (FAAC)	OSA
Aero Aviation Centre Ltd. [Canada] [ICAO designator] (FAAC)	AAD
Aero Barloz SA de CV [Mexico] [ICAO designator] (FAAC)	BLZ
Aero Belize Ltd. [FAA designator] (FAAC)	ABZ
Aero Calif Airlines (SAUS)	ACA
Aero Campeche SA de CV [Mexico] [ICAO designator] (FAAC)	CPC

Aero Car (SAA) .... ACAR
Aero Chasqui SA [Peru] [ICAO designator] (FAAC) .... XYC
Aero Chombo SA [Mexico] [ICAO designator] (FAAC) .... CHM
Aero Club of America [Later, National Aeronautic Association of the USA] ... ACA
Aero Club of America (SAUS) ACA-4
Aero Club of India (SAUO) .... ACI
Aero Club of the United Kingdom (SAUO) .... ACUK
Aero Coach Aviation International, Inc. [ICAO designator] (FAAC) ... DFA
Aero Continente [Peru] [ICAO designator] (FAAC) .... ACQ
Aero Contractors Company of Nigeria Ltd. [ICAO designator] (FAAC) ... NIG
Aero Control Air Ltd. [Canada] [ICAO designator] (FAAC) ... LFC
Aero Costa Rica [ICAO designator] (FAAC) .... AEK
Aero Ejecutiva SA [Mexico] [ICAO designator] (FAAC) ...... EJT
Aero Ejecutivo de Baja California SA de CV [Mexico] [ICAO designator]
   (FAAC) .... EBC
Aero Ejecutivo SA de CV [Mexico] [ICAO designator] (FAAC) ... AJO
Aero Ejecutivos CA [Venezuela] [ICAO designator] (FAAC) ... VEJ
Aero Empresa Mexicana SA [Mexico] [ICAO designator] (FAAC) ... AFO
Aero Energy Ltd. [Toronto Stock Exchange symbol] .... AEY
Aero Engine Services Ltd. (SAUO) .... AESL
Aero Fe SA [Mexico] [ICAO designator] (FAAC) .... RFE
Aero Fiesta Mexicana SA de CV [Mexico] [FAA designator] (FAAC) ... FIT
Aero Filipanas Ltd. [Philippines] [ICAO designator] (FAAC) ... AFI
Aero Flight Service, Inc. [FAA designator] (FAAC) .... AGY
Aero Flotilla [Airline] [Former USSR] .... AEROFLOT
Aero Flugzeugbau [Germany] [ICAO aircraft manufacturer identifier] (ICAO) ... AE
Aero Geo Astro Corp. (SAUO) .... AGA
Aero Geo Astro Corp. .... AGAC
Aero Gun Sights .... AGS
Aero Industries, Inc. [ICAO designator] (FAAC) .... WAB
Aero Industry Development Center (SAUO) .... AIDC
Aero Insurance Underwriters .... AIU
Aero Jalisco SA de CV [Mexico] [ICAO designator] (FAAC) ... AJL
Aero Jets Corporativos, SA de C.V. [Mexico] [FAA designator] (FAAC) ... AJP
Aero Leasing Italiana SpA [Italy] [ICAO designator] (FAAC) ... ALJ
Aero Lider SA de CV [Mexico] [ICAO designator] (FAAC) ... LDR
Aero Lloyd Flugreisen GmbH [Germany] [ICAO designator] (FAAC) ... AEF
Aero Lloyd Flugreisen GmbH & Co. KG (SAUO) LL
Aero Madrid [Spain] [ICAO designator] (FAAC) .... AEM
Aero Medical Association of the United States (SAUS) .... AMAUS
Aero Medical Equipment Laboratory (SAUS) .... AMEL
Aero North Aviation Services [Canada] [ICAO designator] (FAAC) ... SKP
Aero North Icelandic, Inc. [ICAO designator] (FAAC) .... ANF
Aero O/Y [Finnish airline] .... FINNAIR
Aero Personal SA de CV [Mexico] [ICAO designator] (FAAC) ... PNL
Aero Peru [ICAO designator] (AD) .... PL
Aero Premier de Mexico, SA de CV [Mexico] [FAA designator] (FAAC) ... MIE
Aero Products (SAUS) .... APD
Aero Products International SAS (SAUS) .... API
Aero Quick [Mexico] [ICAO designator] (FAAC) .... QIC
Aero Quimmco SA de CV [Mexico] [ICAO designator] (FAAC) ... QUI
Aero Renta de Coahuila SA de CV [Mexico] [ICAO designator] (FAAC) ... RCO
Aero Repair (MCD) .... AR
Aero Rifle Platoon [Military] (VNW) .... ARP
Aero Sami SA de CV [Mexico] [ICAO designator] (FAAC) ... SMI
Aero Santos SA de CV [Mexico] [ICAO designator] (FAAC) ... STO
Aero Scout Platoon [Military] (VNW) .... ASP
Aero Service Bolivia [ICAO designator] (FAAC) .... GHM
Aero Services [Barbados] [ICAO designator] (FAAC) .... BAS
Aero Services Executive [France] [ICAO designator] (FAAC) ... BES
Aero Servicio de Carga Mexicana SA de CV [Mexico] [ICAO designator]
   (FAAC) .... SCM
Aero Servicio del Norte SA de CV [Mexico] [ICAO designator] (FAAC) ... SNV
Aero Servicios Ejecutivas del Pacifico, SA de CV [Mexico] [FAA
   designator] (FAAC) .... SEF
Aero Servicios Especializados SA de CV [Mexico] [ICAO designator]
   (FAAC) .... SVE
Aero Servicios Pro-Bajio, SA de CV [Mexico] [FAA designator] (FAAC) ... PRJ
Aero Sierra Eco SA de CV [Mexico] [ICAO designator] (FAAC) ... ACO
Aero Sierra Eco, SA de CV [Mexico] [FAA designator] (FAAC) ... ECO
Aero Slovakia [FAA designator] (FAAC) .... ASO
Aero Sonora SA de CV [Mexico] [ICAO designator] (FAAC) ... SNR
Aero Space Technologies of Australia (ACAE) .... ASTA
Aero Spacelines [Air carrier designation symbol] .... AERX
Aero Spacelines [ICAO aircraft manufacturer identifier] (ICAO) ... AP
Aero Sudpacifico SA [Mexico] [ICAO designator] (FAAC) ... SDP
Aero Sun International, Inc. (SAUS) .... UR
Aero Sys Engr [NASDAQ symbol] (TTSB) .... AERS
Aero Systems Engineering, Inc. [NASDAQ symbol] (NQ) .... AERS
Aero Systems Engineering, Inc. [Associated Press] (SAG) ... AerSyE
Aero Systems Engineering Inc. (SAUO) .... ASE
Aero Talleres Boero SRL [Argentina] [ICAO aircraft manufacturer identifier]
   (ICAO) .... AB
Aero Taxi [Canada] [ICAO designator] (FAAC) .... QAT
Aero Taxi Aviation, Inc. [ICAO designator] (FAAC) .... QKC
Aero Tec Laboratories Inc. (SAUO) .... ATL
Aero Toluca Internacional, SA de CV [Mexico] [FAA designator] (FAAC) ... TUL
Aero Tonala [Mexico] [ICAO designator] (FAAC) .... TON
Aero Top SRL Societa [Italy] [ICAO designator] (FAAC) .... TOP
Aero Trade International [Romania] [ICAO designator] (FAAC) ... AON
Aero Trades (Western) Ltd. [Canada] [ICAO designator] (FAAC) ... ATW
Aero Transporte SA [Peru] [ICAO designator] (FAAC) ...... AMP
Aero Transportes (SAUS) .... ATSA
Aero Transportes Sociedad Anonima [Mexican airline] ...... ATSA
Aero Transporti Italiani [ICAO designator] (AD) .... BM

Aero Transporti Italiani SpA [Italy] [ICAO designator] (FAAC) ... ATI
Aero Veracruz SA de CV [Mexico] [ICAO designator] (FAAC) ... VRZ
Aero Vics SA de CV [Mexico] [ICAO designator] (FAAC) ... ARI
Aero Virgin Islands [ICAO designator] (AD) .... QY
Aero Weapons Platoon (VNW) .... AWP
Aero West Airlines, Inc. [ICAO designator] (FAAC) .... RWE
Aero Zambia Ltd. [FAA designator] (FAAC) .... RZI
Aero/Acoustic Detection System [Army] (MCD) .... AADS
Aero/Acoustic Rotor (RDA) .... A/AR
Aero-Alentejo, Servicos Aereos Lda. [Portugal] [ICAO designator] (FAAC) ... ANJ
Aeroamerica [ICAO designator] (AD) .... EO
Aeroamerica, Inc. [Air carrier designation symbol] .... AAIX
Aeroamistad SA de CV [Mexico] [ICAO designator] (FAAC) ... MST
Aeroassist Flight Experiment (NAKS) .... AAFE
Aeroassist Flight Experiment [NASA] (ACAE) .... AFE
Aeroassisted Orbital Transfer Vehicle .... AOTV
Aerobacter [Microbiology] .... Aero
Aeroballistic Range Association (SAUO) .... ARA
Aeroballistic Reentry Vehicle .... ARV
Aeroballistic Rocket (ADWA) .... ABR
Aeroballistics (SAA) .... AERO
Aeroballistics - Aerodynamics Analysis (SAA) .... AERO-A
Aeroballistics - Director (SAA) .... AERO-DIR
Aeroballistics - Dynamics Analysis (SAA) .... AERO-D
Aeroballistics - Experimental Aerodynamics (SAA) ... AERO-E
Aeroballistics - Flight Evaluation (SAA) .... AERO-F
Aeroballistics - Future Projects (SAA) .... AERO-P
Aeroballistics - Program Coordination and Administration (SAA) ... AERO-PCA
Aeroballistics - Project Staff (SAA) .... AERO-PS
Aeroballistics - Technical and Scientific Staff (SAA) ... AERO-TS
Aerobeira, Sociedade de Transporties Aeros [Portugal] [ICAO designator]
   (FAAC) .... ARA
Aerobic Chair Exercise (MEDA) .... ACE
Aerobic Dive Limit [Psysiology] .... ADL
Aerobic Plate Count [Microbiology] .... APC
Aerobic Way Association [Defunct] (EA) .... AWA
Aerobically Thioglycolate Broth Disk (PDAA) .... AeTBD
Aerobic-Media Trickling Filter (PDAA) .... AMTF
Aerobics and Fitness Association of America (EA) .... AFAA
Aerobics and Fitness Foundation of America (EA) .... AFFA
Aerobics International Research Society (EA) .... AIRS
Aerobiochemical (SAUS) .... ABC
Aerobiology and Evaluation Laboratory [Army] (KSC) ..... AEL
Aerobiospheric Genetic Adaptation System (DB) .... AGAS
Aerocalifornia SA [Mexico] [ICAO designator] (FAAC) ...... SER
Aerocancun [Mexico] [ICAO designator] (FAAC) .... ACU
Aerocardal [Chile] [FAA designator] (FAAC) .... CDA
Aerocentury Corp. [AMEX symbol] (SG) .... ACY
Aerocer SA [Mexico] [ICAO designator] (FAAC) .... RCE
Aerocesar, Aerovias del Cesar [Colombia] [ICAO designator] (FAAC) ... AEC
Aero-Chaco [ICAO designator] (AD) .... CQ
Aerochago [Dominican Republic] [ICAO designator] (FAAC) ... AHG
Aerocharter [Czechoslovakia] [ICAO designator] (FAAC) ... STX
Aerocharter GmbH [Austria] [ICAO designator] (FAAC) ... MOZ
Aerocharter, Inc. [Canada] [ICAO designator] (FAAC) ...... MRM
Aerocharter Midlands Ltd. [British] [ICAO designator] (FAAC) ... ACC
Aero-Chem Research Laboratories, Inc. (KSC) .... ACRL
Aerochemical Metal-Oxide Kinetics [Program] (MCD) ..... AMOK
Aerochiapas SA de CV [Mexico] [ICAO designator] (FAAC) ... AHP
Aeroclub of America (SAUO) .... ACA
Aeroclub of America (SAUS) .... ACA
Aerocombi SA [Spain] [ICAO designator] (FAAC) .... HSW
Aerocomponentes Internacionales, SA de CV [Mexico] [FAA designator]
   (FAAC) .... CPE
Aerocontrol Electronics Unit [NASA] (NASA) .... ACEU
Aerocozumel SA [Mexico] [ICAO designator] (FAAC) ...... AZM
Aerodan, SA de CV [Mexico] [FAA designator] (FAAC) ...... ROD
Aerodespachos de El Salvador [ICAO designator] (FAAC) ... DNA
Aerodienst GmbH [Germany] [ICAO designator] (FAAC) ... ADN
Aerodin SA de CV [Mexico] [ICAO designator] (FAAC) ...... DIN
Aerodrome .... AD
Aerodrome .... ADRM
Aerodrome (IAA) .... AER
Aerodrome (SAUS) .... Aer
Aerodrome Advisory Area (PIPO) .... ADA
Aerodrome Beacon (IAA) .... ABCN
Aerodrome Beacon (DA) .... ABE
Aerodrome Beacon [ICAO] (FAAC) .... ABN
Aerodrome Control [British] .... ADC
Aerodrome Control RADAR (IAA) .... ACR
Aerodrome Control Radar (SAUS) .... ACR
Aerodrome Control Service .... ACS
Aerodrome Control Tower (SAUS) .... TWR
Aerodrome Control Tower [ICAO designator] (ICDA) .... ZT
Aerodrome Control Tower [FAA designator] (FAAC) .... ZTZ
Aerodrome Control Zone [Aviation] (PIAV) .... ACZ
Aerodrome Damage Repair [NATO] .... ADR
Aerodrome Defence Corps [British] .... ADC
Aerodrome Defence Corps (SAUO) .... ADC
Aerodrome Emergency Service (DA) .... AES
Aerodrome Fire Service [British] (AIA) .... AFS
Aerodrome Flight Information Service .... AFIS
Aerodrome Flight Information Service (Officer) (DA) ... AFIS(O)
Aerodrome Flight Information Service Officer's Licence [British]
   (DBQ) .... AFISOL

Aerodrome Forecast (SAUS)	TAF
Aerodrome Information Zone [Aviation] (PIAV)	AIZ
Aerodrome Obstruction Chart	AOC
Aerodrome [or Airport] of Entry	AOE
Aerodrome of Entry (SAUO)	AoE
Aerodrome Of Entry (SAUS)	AOE
Aerodrome Officer-of-the-Day (DNAB)	AOD
Aerodrome Operation (DA)	AOP
Aerodrome Owners Association [British] (BI)	AOA
Aerodrome RADAR/Radio Approach Aid	ARAA
Aerodrome Reference Code Panel [ICAO] (DA)	ARCP
Aerodrome Reference Point [Aviation] (PIAV)	ARP
Aerodrome Report [Aviation] (DA)	Ae
Aerodrome Security Services (SAUS)	ZY
Aerodrome Security Services [FAA designator] (FAAC)	ZYZ
Aerodrome Surface Movement Control	AMC
Aerodrome Surface Movement Indicator (SAA)	ASMI
Aerodrome to Aerodrome	A/A
Aerodrome Traffic Frequency (PIPO)	ATF
Aerodrome Traffic Zone	ATZ
Aerodrome Warning (DA)	AW
Aerodromes, Air Routes, and Ground Aids [Aviation]	AGA
Aerodromes and Ground Aids (SAUS)	AGA
Aerodromes Environmental Federation (PIAV)	aef
Aerodromes Protection Agency [British] (PIAV)	APA
Aerodynamic (IAA)	AER
Aerodynamic (ABBR)	AERDYN
Aerodynamic (NASA)	AERO
Aerodynamic (KSC)	AERODYN
Aerodynamic Accounting Technique (MCD)	AAT
Aerodynamic and Propulsion Test Unit	APTU
Aerodynamic Center (IDOE)	ac
Aerodynamic Center (SAUO)	AC
Aerodynamic Coefficient Identification Package (NASA)	ACIP
Aerodynamic Coefficient Instrumentation Package (NASA)	ACIP
Aerodynamic Coefficient Instrumenta-tion Package (SAUS)	ACIP
Aerodynamic Configuration Drivers (MCD)	ACD
Aerodynamic Configured Missile (MCD)	ACM
Aerodynamic Damping Moment in Pitch [Helicopter rotor]	ADMP
Aerodynamic Data Analysis and Integration System [Computer science]	ADAIS
Aerodynamic Data Analysis Program [Computer science] (SSD)	ADAP
Aerodynamic Data Book (NASA)	ADB
Aerodynamic Data Correlation (MCD)	ADC
Aerodynamic Decelerator (AAG)	AD
Aerodynamic Deployable Decelerator Performance Evaluation Program	ADDPEP
Aerodynamic Design and Analysis System for Supersonic Aircraft (MCD)	ADASSA
Aerodynamic Equivalent Diameter (PDAA)	AED
Aerodynamic Flight Control (MCD)	AFC
Aerodynamic Flight Test (NASA)	AFT
Aerodynamic Heat Test Plans	AHTP
Aerodynamic Heating (NG)	AEROHEAT
Aerodynamic Heating Indicator (MCD)	AHI
Aerodynamic Influence Coefficients with Interference (PDAA)	AIC/INT
Aerodynamic Load Balanced Elliptical Nozzle (MCD)	ALBEN
Aerodynamic Maneuver Capability (SAA)	AMC
Aerodynamic Mean Chord (DA)	AMC
Aerodynamic Missile Guidance Analysis Program (ACAE)	AMGAP
Aerodynamic Model Test Plan (SAA)	AMTP
Aerodynamic Model Test Report (SAA)	AMTR
Aerodynamic Modeling [Module]	AEROMOD
Aerodynamic Modelling (SAUS)	AEROMOD
Aerodynamic Particle Size (SAUS)	APS
Aerodynamic Postprocessing (SAUS)	AEROPOST
Aerodynamic Post-Processing [Module]	AEROPOST
Aerodynamic Propulsive Interactive Force [Air Force]	APIF
Aerodynamic Report	AR
Aerodynamic (Research Inc.) Communication and Recording System (SAUO)	ACARS
Aerodynamic Research Incorporated Communication (SAUO)	ARINC
Aerodynamic Source of Power (SAUS)	ASP
Aerodynamic Spacecraft Two-Stage Reusable Orbiter [NASA]	ASTRO
Aerodynamic Stability Augmentation Subsystem (NASA)	ASAS
Aerodynamic Stability Augmentation System [or Subsystem] [NASA] (NASA)	ASAS
Aerodynamic Surface Assembly and Checkout [NASA] (NASA)	ASAC
Aerodynamic Test Vehicle (MCD)	ATV
Aerodynamic Test Vehicles (ACAE)	ATV
Aerodynamic Threat Analysis System (ACAE)	ATAS
Aerodynamic Yaw Coupling	AYC
Aerodynamic Yaw Coupling Parameters	AYCP
Aerodynamically Neutral Spin Stabilized Rocket (SAUS)	ANSSR
Aerodynamically Neutral Spin-Stabilized Rocket Artillery System [Army] (MCD)	ANSSRAS
Aerodynamically Regenerated Trap	ART
Aerodynamic-Influence Coefficient	AIC
Aerodynamics (ADWA)	aerodyn
Aerodynamics	ARODYN
Aerodynamics Advisory Panel [AEC] (MCD)	AAP
Aerodynamics and Flight Mechanics (SAUS)	A&FM
Aerodynamics Center [NASA]	AC
Aerodynamics Department (SAUO)	AD
Aerodynamics Laboratory [Naval Ship Research and Development Center]	AL

Aerodynamics Measurements Projects (ACAE)	AEROP
Aerodynamics Note	AN
Aerodynamics Surface Control (MCD)	ASC
Aerodynamics-Thermodynamics-Acoustic Wind Tunnel [Automotive research]	ATAWT
Aerodyne Charter [ICAO designator] (FAAC)	AQZ
Aerodyne Executive Aviation Services [ICAO designator] (FAAC)	ADY
Aerodyne Research, Inc.	ARI
Aeroejecutivos, Aeroservicios Ejecutivos [Colombia] [ICAO designator] (FAAC)	AJS
Aeroel Airways Ltd. [Israel] [FAA designator] (FAAC)	ROL
Aeroelastic and Structures Research Laboratory [Massachusetts Institute of Technology]	ASRL
Aero-elastic and Structures Research Laboratory (SAUS)	ASRL
Aero-Elastic Research Laboratory [MIT] (MCD)	AERL
Aeroelastic Research Wing (MCD)	ARW
Aeroelastic Rotor Experimental System (MCD)	ARES
Aeroelastic Wind Tunnel	AWT
Aero-elastic Wind Tunnel (SAUS)	AWT
Aeroelastically Conformable Rotor (RDA)	ACR
Aeroelectronic (IEEE)	AE
Aero-Electronic Technology Department [Navy] (MCD)	AETD
Aeroequipment Corporation (SAUO)	AEQ
Aeroexpreso Bogota [Colombia] [ICAO designator] (FAAC)	ABO
Aeroexpreso Interamerican [Colombia] [ICAO designator] (FAAC)	AEI
Aerofer, SL [Spain] [ICAO designator] (FAAC)	ARF
Aeroflex, Inc. [Associated Press] (SAG)	Aeroflex
Aeroflex, Inc. [NYSE symbol] (SAG)	ARX
Aeroflightdynamics Directorate [Army and NASA joint operation] (RDA)	AFDD
Aeroflot - Russian International Airlines [Russian Federation] [ICAO designator] (FAAC)	AFL
Aerofrance [France] [ICAO designator] (FAAC)	ROF
Aerofrisco [Mexico] [ICAO designator] (FAAC)	FCO
Aerographer	AERO
Aerographer's Mate [Navy rating]	AERM
Aerographer's Mate [Navy rating]	AG
Aerographers Mate (SAUS)	AG
Aerographer's Mate, Chief [Navy rating]	AGC
Aerographers Mate First Class (SAUS)	AERM 1c
Aerographer's Mate, First Class [Navy rating]	AG1
Aerographer's Mate, Master Chief [Navy rating]	AGCM
Aerographers Mate Second Class (SAUS)	AERM 2c
Aerographer's Mate, Second Class [Navy rating]	AG2
Aerographer's Mate, Senior Chief [Navy rating]	AGCS
Aerographers Mate Third Class (SAUS)	AERM 3c
Aerographer's Mate, Third Class [Navy rating]	AG3
Aeroguayacan [Chile] [ICAO designator] (FAAC)	AGY
Aero-Industries Technical Institute (SAUO)	AITI
Aerojelk, SA de CV [Mexico] [FAA designator] (FAAC)	JEL
Aerojet de Costa Rica SA [ICAO designator] (FAAC)	ARJ
Aerojet Differential Analyzer	ADA
Aerojet Electrosystems Co. (MCD)	AESC
Aerojet Electrosystems Co., Azusa, CA [Library symbol] [Library of Congress] (LCLS)	CAzA
Aerojet Electrosystems Company (SAUO)	AESC
Aerojet Energy Conversion Company (SAUO)	AECC
Aerojet General Corporation (SAUO)	AEROJET
Aerojet General Corporation (SAUO)	AG
Aerojet General Corporation (SAUO)	AGC
Aerojet Liquid Rocket Company (SAUO)	ALRC
Aerojet Liquid Rocket Corporation (SAUO)	ALRC
Aerojet Manufacturing Co.	AMCO
Aerojet Manufacturing Company (SAUS)	AMCO
Aerojet Mass Analyzer Program (MCD)	AMAP
Aerojet Network Analyzer	ANA
Aerojet Nuclear Co., Idaho Falls, ID [Library symbol] [Library of Congress] (LCLS)	IdIfA
Aerojet Nuclear Company (ABAC)	ANC
Aerojet Nuclear Corporation (SAUO)	ANC
Aerojet Ordnance & Manufacturing Company (SAUO)	AOMC
Aero-Jet SA [Switzerland] [ICAO designator] (FAAC)	AOJ
Aerojet Services Co.	ASC
Aerojet Solid Propulsion Co.	ASPC
Aerojet Solid Propulsion Company (SAUO)	ASPC
Aerojet Techsystems Company (ACAE)	ATC
Aerojet/Bumblebee [Navy missile]	AEROBEE
Aerojet/Bumblebee (SAUS)	Aerobee
Aerojet-General Corporation (ACAE)	AEROJ
Aerojet-General Nucleonics [of Aerojet-General Corp.]	AGN
Aerojobeni SA de CV [Mexico] [ICAO designator] (FAAC)	JOB
Aerokuznetsk, Joint Stock Company [Former USSR] [FAA designator] (FAAC)	AKZ
Aerolab Development Company (ACAE)	AERLAB
Aerolastic Wind-Tunnel (SAUS)	AWT
Aeroleasing SA [Switzerland] [ICAO designator] (FAAC)	FPG
Aerolift, Inc. [Vancouver Stock Exchange symbol]	AER
Aerolift Philippines Corp. [ICAO designator] (FAAC)	LFT
Aerolik [Former USSR] [FAA designator] (FAAC)	AKR
Aerolinas Nacionales del Ecuador SA [ICAO designator] (FAAC)	EDA
Aerolinas Uruguayas SA [Uruguay] [ICAO designator] (FAAC)	AUY
Aerolinea Federal Argentina [Argentine Federal Airline] (EY)	ALFA
Aerolinea Federal Argentina [ICAO designator] (AD)	CQ
Aerolinea Muri [Mexico] [ICAO designator] (FAAC)	MUR
Aerolineas Argentinas [Argentina] [ICAO designator] (FAAC)	ARG
Aerolineas Argentinas (SAUS)	ENT

Aerolineas Centrales de Colombia [*Airline*] [*Colombia*] .... ACES
Aerolineas Centrales de Colombia [*ICAO designator*] (FAAC) .... AES
Aerolineas Centroamericanas SA [*Central American Airlines*] [*Nicaragua*] [*ICAO designator*] (FAAC) .... ACN
Aerolineas Coco Club Hoteles de Mexico SA de CV [*ICAO designator*] (FAAC) .... CCO
Aerolineas Colonia SA [*Airline*] [*Uruguay*] .... ARCO
Aerolineas Cordillera Ltda. [*Chile*] [*ICAO designator*] (FAAC) .... AEROCOR
Aerolineas Cordillera Ltda. [*Chile*] [*ICAO designator*] (FAAC) .... CRD
Aerolineas de El Salvador [*Airline*] [*El Salvador*] .... AESA
Aerolineas de El Salvador SA [*ICAO designator*] (FAAC) .... SZA
Aerolineas de Honduras, SA [*Honduras*] [*FAA designator*] (FAAC) .... AHB
Aerolineas de Michoacan [*Mexico*] [*ICAO designator*] (FAAC) .... MIC
Aerolineas Del Mayab, SA de CV [*Mexico*] [*FAA designator*] (FAAC) .... MYB
Aerolineas del Oeste SA de CV [*Mexico*] [*ICAO designator*] (FAAC) .... AST
Aerolineas del Sol, SA de CV [*Mexico*] [*FAA designator*] (FAAC) .... LSO
Aerolineas del Sureste SA [*Mexico*] [*ICAO designator*] (FAAC) .... SUE
Aerolineas Dominicanas [*ICAO designator*] (AD) .... YU
Aerolineas Dominicanas SA [*Dominican Republic*] [*ICAO designator*] (FAAC) .... ADM
Aerolineas Dominicanas SA (SAUS) .... SS
Aerolineas Ejecutivas de San Luis Potosi SA de CV [*Mexico*] [*ICAO designator*] (FAAC) .... ELP
Aerolineas Ejecutivas SA [*Mexico*] [*ICAO designator*] (FAAC) .... LET
Aerolineas Especiales de Colombia [*ICAO designator*] (FAAC) .... ALE
Aerolineas Internacionales, SA de CV [*Mexico*] [*FAA designator*] (FAAC) .... LNT
Aerolineas Latinas CA [*Venezuela*] [*ICAO designator*] (FAAC) .... LTN
Aerolineas Marcos SA de CV [*Mexico*] [*ICAO designator*] (FAAC) .... MCO
Aerolineas Medellin [*Colombia*] [*ICAO designator*] (FAAC) .... AMD
Aerolineas Mexicanas JS SA de CV [*Mexico*] [*ICAO designator*] (FAAC) .... LMX
Aerolineas Nacionales del Ecuador [*Airline*] .... ANDES
Aerolineas Nicaraguenses [*Nicaragua Airlines*] (EY) .... AERONICA
Aerolineas Nicaraguenses [*ICAO designator*] (AD) .... RL
Aerolineas Pacifico Atlantico SA [*Spain*] [*ICAO designator*] (FAAC) .... APP
Aerolineas Peruanas Sociedad Anonima [*Peruvian Air Lines*] .... APSA
Aerolineas Yasi, SA de CV [*Mexico*] [*FAA designator*] (FAAC) .... RLY
Aerolinee Italiane Internazionali [*Italian International Airline*] [*Facetious translation: Always Late in Takeoffs, Always Late in Arrivals*] .... ALITALIA
Aerological (SAUS) .... AERLGL
Aerological .... AEROL
Aerological Duty Officer (SAUS) .... AEDO
Aerological Officer (SAUS) .... Aer Of
Aerological Officer .... AER OF
Aerologist .... AEROG
Aerologist (SAUS) .... AEROL
Aerology [*NAO code*] (DNAB) .... A
Aeromagnetic Data System (SAUS) .... AERODAS
Aeromak [*Yugoslavia*] [*ICAO designator*] (FAAC) .... AMK
Aeromaritime (CAAA) [*France*] [*ICAO designator*] (FAAC) .... QKL
Aeromarket Express [*Spain*] [*ICAO designator*] (FAAC) .... ARM
Aeromech Commuter Airlines (SAUS) .... KCI
Aero-Mechanical Engineering Laboratory [*Army*] (RDA) .... AMEL
Aero-Mechanics Department [*Navy*] (MCD) .... AMD
Aeromechanics Department (SAUO) .... AMD
Aeromechanics Laboratory [*Army*] (GRD) .... AL
Aeromedial Airlift Wing (SAUS) .... AAWg
Aeromedical .... AEROMED
Aero-Medical Acceleration Laboratory (DMAA) .... AMAI
Aero-Medical Acceleration Laboratory (SAUO) .... AMAL
Aeromedical Airlift Group [*Air Force*] .... AAG
Aeromedical Airlift Group [*Air Force*] (AFM) .... AAGp
Aeromedical Airlift Squadron [*Air Force*] .... AAS
Aeromedical Airlift Squadron [*Air Force*] (AFM) .... AASq
Aeromedical Airlift Wing [*Air Force*] (MCD) .... AAW
Aeromedical Airlift Wing [*Air Force*] (AFM) .... AAWg
Aero-Medical Association (SAUO) .... AeMA
Aero-Medical Association (SAUO) .... AMA
Aeromedical Association of France (SAUO) .... AAMF
Aero-Medical Association of the United States of America (SAUO) .... AMAUS
Aeromedical Data .... AMD
Aeromedical Education Division [*FAA*] .... AED
Aeromedical Environmental Health Laboratory (SAUS) .... AEHL
Aeromedical Equipment Laboratory .... AMEL
Aero-Medical Equipment Laboratory (SAUO) .... AMEL
Aeromedical Evacuation [*Later, AME*] (AFM) .... AE
Aeromedical Evacuation [*Later, AME*] .... AMDLEVAC
Aeromedical Evacuation [*Formerly, AE, AMDLEVAC*] (AABC) .... AME
Aero-Medical Evacuation (SAUS) .... AME
Aeromedical Evacuation Control Center [*Military*] (MCD) .... AECC
Aeromedical Evacuation Control Element (SAUO) .... AECE
Aeromedical Evacuation Control Officer [*Military*] (AABC) .... AECO
Aeromedical Evacuation Flight [*Air Force*] .... AEF
Aeromedical Evacuation Group [*Air Force*] .... AEG
Aeromedical Evacuation Group [*Air Force*] (AFM) .... AEGp
Aeromedical Evacuation Liaison Officer [*Air Force*] (AFM) .... AELO
Aeromedical Evacuation Liaison Team [*Environmental science*] (COE) .... AELT
Aeromedical Evacuation Operations Office [*or Officer*] [*Military*] (MCD) .... AEOO
Aeromedical Evacuation Squadron [*Air Force*] .... AES
Aeromedical Evacuation Squadron [*Air Force*] (DAVI) .... AESQ
Aeromedical Evacuation Squadron (SAUO) .... AESq
Aeromedical Evacuation Support Team .... AEST
Aeromedical Evacuation System [*Environmental science*] (COE) .... AES
Aeromedical Evacuation System [*Air Force*] (AFM) .... AMES
Aeromedical Evacuation Technician .... AET
Aeromedical Evacuation Unit (SAUO) .... AEU
Aeromedical Field Laboratory (SAUS) .... AFB
Aeromedical Field Laboratory (SAUO) .... AFL
Aeromedical Laboratory .... AML
Aeromedical Liaison Office [*or Officer*] [*Air Force*] (AFM) .... AMLO
Aeromedical Liaison Officer (SAUS) .... AMLO
Aeromedical Library, 6571st Aeromedical Research Laboratory, Holloman AFB, NM [*Library symbol*] [*Library of Congress*] (LCLS) .... NmHARL
Aeromedical Monitor (SAA) .... AM
Aeromedical Monitor Console .... AMC
Aeromedical Research Laboratory [*Army*] (KSC) .... ARL
Aeromedical Research Unit [*Army*] (MCD) .... ARU
Aeromedical Staging Facility .... ASF
Aeromedical Staging Flight [*Air Force*] .... ASF
Aeromedical Staging Unit (AFM) .... ASU
Aeromedicare Ltd. [*British*] [*ICAO designator*] (FAAC) .... AMQ
Aeromega Ltd. [*British*] [*ICAO designator*] (FAAC) .... OMG
Aeromere SpA [*Italy*] [*ICAO aircraft manufacturer identifier*] (ICAO) .... AO
Aerometric and Emissions Reporting System [*Environmental Protection Agency*] .... AEROS
Aero-Metric Engineering, Inc. (GEOI) .... AME
Aerometric Information Retrieval System [*Environmental Protection Agency*] [*Information service or system*] (CRD) .... AIRS
Aeromexico [*Airline*] (DS) .... AM
Aeromexpress, SA de CV [*Mexico*] [*FAA designator*] (FAAC) .... MPX
Aeromonterrey SA [*Mexico*] [*ICAO designator*] (FAAC) .... MOT
Aeromorelos SA de CV [*Mexico*] [*ICAO designator*] (FAAC) .... MRL
Aeromundo Ejecutivo, SA de CV [*Mexico*] [*FAA designator*] (FAAC) .... MUN
Aeromyl SA de CV [*Mexico*] [*ICAO designator*] (FAAC) .... MYL
Aeron International Airlines, Inc. [*ICAO designator*] (FAAC) .... AXI
Aeronardi SpA [*Italy*] [*ICAO designator*] (FAAC) .... NRD
Aeronaut (ABBR) .... AERN
Aeronaut (SAUS) .... Aeron
Aeronaut Society (EA) .... AS
Aeronautic Department (SAUO) .... AD
Aeronautica and Air Label Collectors Club (EA) .... AAL
Aeronautica and Air Label Collectors Club (EA) .... AALCC
Aeronautica Industrial SA [*Spain*] [*ICAO aircraft manufacturer identifier*] (ICAO) .... AI
Aeronautica Interespacial SA de CV [*Mexico*] [*ICAO designator*] (FAAC) .... ITS
Aeronautica Venezolana CA [*Venezuela*] [*ICAO designator*] (FAAC) .... AEROVENCA
Aeronautica Venezolana, CA [*Venezuela*] [*ICAO designator*] (FAAC) .... AVC
Aeronautical (ABBR) .... AE
Aeronautical (ABBR) .... AERNL
Aeronautical (ADWA) .... aero
Aeronautical .... AERON
Aeronautical .... AERONL
Aeronautical .... ARNTCL
Aeronautical Administration Communication [*A class of communication which supports administrative communication*] (GAVI) .... AAC
Aeronautical Advisory Council .... AAC
Aeronautical Advisory Station Operating on 122.8 mc (SAUS) .... UNICOM
Aeronautical and Aircraft Experimental Establishment (SAUO) .... AAEE
Aeronautical and Astronautical Engineering (MCD) .... AAE
Aeronautical and Astronautical Research Laboratory (SAUO) .... ARL
Aeronautical & General Instruments Ltd. (SAUO) .... AGI
Aeronautical and Maritime Satellite Communications (ACAE) .... AMSC
Aeronautical and Mechanical Engineering Branch, Canada Institute for Scientific and Technical Information [*Division du Genie Aeronautique et Mecanique, Institut Canadien de l'Information Scientifique et Technique*] **Ottawa, Ontario** [*Library symbol*] [*National Library of Canada*] (NLC) .... OONAM
Aeronautical and Navigational Electronics (MCD) .... ANE
Aeronautical Approach Chart [*Air Force*] .... AAC
Aeronautical Approach Chart [*Air Force*] .... AC
Aeronautical Army and Navy (AAG) .... AAN
Aeronautical Assignment Group (SAUO) .... AAG
Aeronautical Board [*Air Force*] .... AB
Aeronautical Broadcast Station [*ITU designation*] (CET) .... FAB
Aeronautical Center [*FAA*] .... AC
Aeronautical Chamber of Commerce of America [*Later, AIA*] .... ACCA
Aeronautical Chamber of Commerce of America (SAUO) .... ACCA
Aeronautical Chart and Information Center [*St. Louis, MO*] [*Later, DMAAC*] [*Air Force*] .... ACIC
Aeronautical Chart and Information Center Technical Translation Section [*Air Force*] .... ACIC-TC
Aeronautical Chart and Information Office [*Air Force*] (SAA) .... ACIO
Aeronautical Chart and Information Squadron [*Air Force*] (DNAB) .... ACIS
Aeronautical Chart and Information Squadron [*Air Force*] .... ACISQ
Aeronautical Chart and Information Squadron (SAUO) .... ACISq
Aeronautical Chart Automation Project [*Military*] (DA) .... ACAP
Aeronautical Chart Service (SAUO) .... ACS
Aeronautical Charting and Cartography (SAUS) .... AC&C
Aeronautical Charting and Information Center [*Marine science*] (OSRA) .... ACIC
Aeronautical Charting Division (SAUO) .... ACD
Aeronautical Charting Division (GEOI) .... ADC
Aeronautical Command Systems [*Air Force*] .... ACS
Aeronautical Communications Equipment Corp. .... AEROCOM
Aeronautical Communications Equipment Corporation (SAUO) .... AERCOM
Aeronautical Communications Equipment Corporation (SAUO) .... AEROCOM
Aeronautical Communications Satellite System .... AEROSAT
Aeronautical Computer Laboratory (SAUS) .... ACL
Aeronautical Computers Laboratory [*Johnsville, PA*] [*Navy*] .... ACL
Aeronautical Data .... AD
Aeronautical Data Communication Network (DA) .... ADCN
Aeronautical Data Interchange System Panel (OA) .... ADISP

Aeronautical Data Link Program (SAUS) .... ADLP
Aeronautical Data Report [Navy] .... ADR
Aeronautical Data Reproducer (SAUS) .... ADR
Aeronautical Data-Link [FAA] (TAG) .... ADL
Aeronautical Depot Maintenance Industrial Technology [Navy] (AFIT) ...... ADMIT
Aeronautical Design Standard [Army] .... ADS
Aeronautical Development Establishment (SAUS) .... ADE
Aeronautical Development Group [Military] (AFIT) ...... ADG
Aeronautical Digital Information Display System (DA) .... ADIDS
Aeronautical Earth Station (DA) .... AES
Aeronautical Electronic and Electrical Laboratory (SAUO) .... AEEL
Aeronautical Engine Laboratory [Later, NAPC] [Navy] .... AEL
Aeronautical Engineer .... AE
Aeronautical Engineer .... AeE
Aeronautical Engineer (IEEE) .... AeEng
Aeronautical Engineer (ADA) .... AerE
Aeronautical Engineering (SAUS) .... EE
Aeronautical Engineering and Electronic Laboratory [Johnsville, PA] [Navy] .... AEEL
Aeronautical Engineering Department [NASA] (KSC) .... AED
Aeronautical Engineering Division [Air Force] (DOMA) .... AED
Aeronautical Engineering Duty [Navy] .... AED
Aeronautical Engineering Duty Officer [Navy] (DOMA) .... AEDO
Aeronautical Engineering Laboratory [NASA] (KSC) .... AEL
Aeronautical Engineering Report .... AER
Aeronautical Enroute Information Service (DA) .... AEIS
Aeronautical Equipment Reference (SAA) .... AER
Aeronautical Equipment Reference Number [Military] .... AERNO
Aeronautical Equipment Service Record (MCD) .... AESR
Aeronautical Fixed Service .... AFS
Aeronautical Fixed Station [ITU designation] (CET) .... FAX
Aeronautical Fixed Station [ICAO designator] (ICDA) .... YF
Aeronautical Fixed Systems Planning for Data Interchange Panel [ICAO] (DA) .... ASPP
Aeronautical Fixed Telecommunication Network [United Kingdom] .... AFTN
Aeronautical Fixed Telecommunications Service .... AFTS
Aeronautical Frequency Management Committee [British] (DA) .... AFMLC
Aeronautical Ground Station (SAUS) .... AGS
Aeronautical Icing Research Laboratory .... AIRL
Aeronautical Information Circular (FAAC) .... AIC
Aeronautical Information Data (SAUS) .... AID
Aeronautical Information Documents Unit (SAUS) ..... AIDU
Aeronautical Information Manual [FAA] (TAG) .... AIM
Aeronautical Information Publication [FAA] (TAG) ..... AIP
Aeronautical Information Regulation and Control ...... AIRAC
Aeronautical [or Aerospace] Information Report (MCD) .... AIR
Aeronautical Information Report (SAUS) .... AIR
Aeronautical Information Section .... AIS
Aeronautical Information Service .... AIS
Aeronautical Information Service Automation Group [ICAO] (DA) .... AAG
Aeronautical Information Service Automation Group [ICAO] (DA) .... AISAG
Aeronautical Information Service Automation Specialist Panel [ICAO] (DA) .... AISAP
Aeronautical Information Service Unit [ICAO designator] (ICDA) .... YO
Aeronautical Information Specialist (FAAC) .... AIS
Aeronautical Inspection Directorate [British] (MCD) .... AID
Aeronautical Instruments Laboratory [Military] .... AIL
Aeronautical Laboratory .... AL
Aeronautical Maintenance Duty Officer .... AMDO
Aeronautical Maintenance Facility (SAUS) .... T-ARVH
Aeronautical Maintenance Support Equipment List [Military] (AFIT) .... AMSEL
Aeronautical Manufacturers' Planning Report [NASA] .... AMPR
Aeronautical Manufacturers Planning Report (SAUS) .... AMPR
Aeronautical Manufacturers Progress Report [NASA] .... AMPR
Aeronautical Manufactures Planning Report (SAUS) .... AMPR
Aeronautical Maps and charts (SAUS) .... MAP
Aeronautical Marker Beacon [ITU designation] (CET) .... RLA
Aeronautical Material Screening Unit (AFIT) .... AMSU
Aeronautical [or Aerospace] Material Specification ... AMS
Aeronautical Material Support Equipment (DNAB) ..... AMSE
Aeronautical Materials Laboratory .... AML
Aeronautical Medical Acceleration Laboratory [Air Force] .... AMAL
Aeronautical Meteorology Programme (SAUS) .... AeMP
Aeronautical Military Standards .... AMS
Aeronautical Mobile .... AEM
Aeronautical Mobile Satellite for Service and Safety (ACAE) .... AMSS
Aeronautical Mobile Satellite Service [ICAO designator] (FAAC) .... AMSS
Aeronautical Mobile Satellite Service Panel [ICAO] (DA) .... AMSSP
Aeronautical Museum (SAUS) .... AEROMUS
Aeronautical National Taper Pipe Threads .... ANPT
Aeronautical Navigator Association (NTPA) .... ANNA
Aeronautical Operating Systems Division [NASA] ..... AOSD
Aeronautical Operation Control [Communications which support safety and regularity of flight that normally take place between aircraft and the operator] (GAVI) .... AOC
Aeronautical Operational Control .... AOC
Aeronautical Order (AFM) .... AO
Aeronautical Passenger Communication [A class of communication which supports passenger communication] (GAVI) .... APC
Aeronautical Photographic Experimental Laboratory [Johnsville, PA] [Navy] .... APEL
Aeronautical Planning Chart [Military] .... APC
Aeronautical Production Control System .... APCS
Aeronautical Propulsion Division [NASA] .... APD
Aeronautical Public Correspondence (DA) .... APC

Aeronautical Quality Assurance Directorate [British] (PDAA) .... AQAD
Aeronautical Quality Assurance Directorate [British] .... AQD
Aeronautical Quality Assurance Field Office (SAUS) .... AQAFO
Aeronautical Quality Directorate (SAUO) .... AQD
Aeronautical RADAR Research Complex .... ARRC
Aeronautical Radio (IAA) .... AR
Aeronautical Radio and RADAR Laboratory [Navy] ... ARRL
Aeronautical Radio, Inc. (KSC) .... ARI
Aeronautical Radio, Inc. .... ARINCO
Aeronautical Radio, Inc. [ICAO designator] (FAAC) .... XAA
Aeronautical Radio Inc. Communications, Addressing the Reporting System (SAUS) .... ACARS
Aeronautical Radio Incorporated (SAUO) .... ARI
Aeronautical Radio Incorporated (SAUO) .... ARINC
Aeronautical Radio Incorporated (SAUO) .... ARINCO
Aeronautical Radio Incorporated Communications, Addressing the Reporting System (SAUO) .... ACARS
Aeronautical Radio Incorporation (SAUO) .... ARINC
Aeronautical Radio Navigation Services (SAUS) .... ARNS
Aeronautical Radio of Canada .... ARCAN
Aeronautical Radio Range [Nautical charts] .... AERO R Rge
Aeronautical Radiobeacon [Nautical charts] .... AERO R Bn
Aeronautical Radio-navigation (SAUS) .... AR
Aeronautical Radionavigation Glide Path (IAA) .... ARGP
Aeronautical Radionavigation Land Station [ITU designation] .... AL
Aeronautical Radionavigation Mobile Station [ITU designation] .... AM
Aeronautical Radionavigation RADAR .... ARR
Aeronautical [or Aerospace] Recommended Practice .... ARP
Aeronautical Recommened Practice (SAUS) .... ARP
Aeronautical Repair Station Association (EA) .... ARSA
Aeronautical [or Aircraft] Requirement [Military] (MCD) .... AR
Aeronautical Requirement (SAUS) .... AR
Aeronautical Research (IAA) .... AR
Aeronautical Research and Development (SAUS) ...... AR&D
Aeronautical Research & Test Institute (SAUS) .... ARTI
Aeronautical Research Association of Princeton (SAUO) .... ARAP
Aeronautical Research Board (SAUO) .... ARB
Aeronautical Research Council (SAUO) .... AEC
Aeronautical Research Council [British] .... ARC
Aeronautical Research Division [NASA] .... ARD
Aeronautical Research Establishment (SAUS) .... ARE
Aeronautical Research Foundation .... ARF
Aeronautical Research, Inc. (MCD) .... ARINC
Aeronautical Research Incorporated (SAUO) .... ARINC
Aeronautical Research Institute of Sweden (MCD) .... ARIS
Aeronautical Research Laboratory (SAUS) .... ARL
Aeronautical Research Scientist .... ARS
Aeronautical Satellite (SAUS) .... AEROSAT
Aeronautical Satellite .... AEROSAT
Aeronautical Satellite Communications Center (NITA) .... ASCC
Aeronautical Satellite Communications Processor (DA) .... ASCAP
Aeronautical Satellite Data Link (SAUS) .... ASDL
Aeronautical Satellite Datalink System [Mitre Corp.] (NITA) .... ASDL
Aeronautical Satellite Earth Terminal (SAUS) .... ASET
Aeronautical Services Communication Center [Great Britain] .... ASCC
Aeronautical Services Communication Centre (SAUO) .... ASCC
Aeronautical Services Earth Terminal (OA) .... ASET
Aeronautical Shipboard Installation Representative (NVT) .... ASIR
Aeronautical Society of Great Britain (BI) .... ASGB
Aeronautical Society of India (SAUO) .... ASI
Aeronautical Specifications .... AS
Aeronautical Staging Flight (DNAB) .... ASF
Aeronautical Standards .... AS
Aeronautical Standards Group [Military] .... AG
Aeronautical Standards Group [Military] .... ASG
Aeronautical Standards Group [Military] (AFIT) .... ASGP
Aeronautical Standards Group (SAUO) .... ASGp
Aeronautical Standards Group Air Force and Navy (SAUS) .... ASG
Aeronautical Station [ITU designation] (CET) .... FA
Aeronautical Station [ICAO designator] (ICDA) .... YS
Aeronautical Station [FAA designator] (FAAC) .... YSY
Aeronautical Structures Laboratory [Navy] .... ASL
Aeronautical Supply Office (SAUO) .... ASO
Aeronautical Support Equipment Type Designation System .... ASETDS
Aeronautical System Development (NG) .... ASD
Aeronautical System Training Equipment (SAA) .... ASTE
Aeronautical Systems (ACAE) .... AS
Aeronautical Systems Center [Air Force] .... ASC
Aeronautical Systems Division [Wright-Patterson Air Force Base, OH] [Air Force] .... ASD
Aeronautical Systems Division A-10 System Program Office [Wright-Patterson Air Force Base, OH] ASD/A-10-SPO
Aeronautical Systems Division Form .... ASDF
Aeronautical Systems Division Manual .... ASDM
Aeronautical Systems Division Regulation .... ASDR
Aeronautical Technical Directive Requirement [Obsolete] .... ATDR
Aeronautical Telecommunications Network .... ATN
Aeronautical Telecommunications Officers (ADA) .... ATO
Aeronautical Telecommunications Operator .... ATO
Aeronautical Training Society .... ATS
Aeronautical Turbine Laboratories (SAUS) .... ATL
Aeronautical Turbine Laboratory [Navy] .... ATL
Aeronautical Vehicles Division .... AVD
Aeronautical Video Charts (MCD) .... AVC
Aeronautical Video Plates (MCD) .... AVP

Aeronautical weather report (SAUS) .... AERO
Aeronautically (ABBR) .... AERNLY
Aeronautically Fixed .... AF
Aeronautics (IAA) .... A
Aeronautics (MCD) .... AER
Aeronautics (ABBR) .... AERNC
Aeronautics (AFM) .... AERO
Aeronautics (DD) .... Aero
Aeronautics .... Aeron
Aeronautics (ADWA) .... aeron
Aeronautics (ADWA) .... aeronaut
Aeronautics Advisory Committee (SAUO) .... AAC
Aeronautics and Astronautics Coordinating Board [*NASA*] .... AACB
Aeronautics and Astronautics Coordination Board (SAUS) .... AACB
Aeronautics and Astronautics, University of Southampton [*British*] (SAA) .... AASU
Aeronautics and Space .... AEROSPACE
Aeronautics and Space Historical Center (EA) .... ASHC
Aeronautics Division, Ford Motor Company (SAUO) .... ADF
Aeronautics Division, Philco Corporation (ACAE) .... AERONT
Aeronautics Maintenance .... AERO
Aeronautics Supply Officer (MUGU) .... ASO
Aeronautics Upper Atmosphere Impact Program [*NASA*] .... AUAIP
Aeronave Militar Espanola, Ministerio de Defensa [*Spain*] [*FAA designator*] (FAAC) .... AME
Aeronaves de Mexico SA [*Mexican airline*] (MCD) .... ADM
Aeronaves de Mexico SA [*Mexico*] [*ICAO designator*] (ICDA) .... AM
Aeronaves del Centro [*Venezuela*] [*ICAO designator*] (FAAC) .... AGA
Aeronaves del Peru SA [*ICAO designator*] (FAAC) .... WPL
Aeronavs La Dprada SA [*Spain*] [*ICAO designator*] (FAAC) .... ALD
Aeronca Aviators Club (EA) .... AAC
Aeronca Club (EA) .... AC
Aeronca Lovers Club (EA) .... ALC
Aeronca Manufacturing [*ICAO aircraft manufacturer identifier*] (ICAO) .... AR
Aeronca Sedan Club (EA) .... ASC
Aeronias Nacionales de Honduras Sociedad Anonima [*Airline*] [*Honduras*] .... ANHSA
Aeronoleggi e Lavoro Aereo (AERAL) [*Italy*] [*ICAO designator*] (ICDA) .... HS
Aeronomic South Hemisphere and Antarctic Year (PDAA) .... ASHAY
Aeronomy and Space Data Center [*Later, NGSDC*] [*National Oceanic and Atmospheric Administration*] .... ASDC
Aeronomy Laboratory [*National Institute of Standards and Technology*] .... AL
Aeronomy Satellite (SAUS) .... AEROS
Aeronomy Satellite - Neutral Atmosphere Temperature Experiment .... AEROS-NATE
Aeronomy Satellite-Neutral Atmosphere Temperature Experiment (SAUS) .... AEROS-NATE
Aeronorte - Transportes Aereos Lda. [*Portugal*] [*ICAO designator*] (FAAC) .... RTE
Aeronorte SA [*Colombia*] [*ICAO designator*] (FAAC) .... ANR
Aeronutronic Ford Corp., Newport Beach, CA [*Library symbol*] [*Library of Congress*] (LCLS) .... CNbAF
Aeronutronic General Perturbations Differential Correction Program .... AGPDC
Aeronutronics Division, Ford Motor Co. (AAG) .... ADF
Aero-Palma SA [*Spain*] [*ICAO designator*] (FAAC) .... AET
Aeropelican .... AP
Aeropelican Air Services Pty Ltd. [*Australia*] [*ICAO designator*] (FAAC) .... PEL
Aeropelican Intercity Commuter Air Services [*ICAO designator*] (AD) .... PO
Aeropeninsular, SA de CV [*Mexico*] [*FAA designator*] (FAAC) .... PSU
Aeropesca [*ICAO designator*] (AD) .... RS
Aeropetrel [*Chile*] [*ICAO designator*] (FAAC) .... PET
Aerophilatelic Federation of the Americas (EA) .... AFA
Aerophysics - Curtiss-Wright (SAA) .... A-CW
Aerophysics and Aerospace Engineering Research Report (SAUS) .... AAERR
Aerophysics Development Corp. .... ADC
Aerophysics Development Corporation (SAUO) .... ADC
Aerophysics Laboratories Memorandum (SAUS) .... ALM
Aerophysics Laboratory (MCD) .... AL
Aerophysics Laboratory Memorandum [*NASA*] (KSC) .... ALM
Aerophysics Research Corp. .... ARC
Aeropiloto-Sociedade Exploradora de Servicos Aereos Lda. [*Portugal*] [*ICAO designator*] (FAAC) .... AOP
Aeroplane (ADA) .... AER
Aeroplane and Armament Experimental Establishment [*British*] .... AAEE
Aeroplane and Armament Experimental Establishment (SAUO) .... A&AAE
[*The*] **Aeroplane Collection** [*British*] .... TAC
Aeroplane Flag [*Navy*] [*British*] .... AP
Aeroplane (or Aerospace) & Armament Experimental Establishment (SAUO) .... A&AEE
Aeroplane Repair Section (SAUO) .... ARS
Aeroplane Repair Section (SAUS) .... ARS
Aeroposta SA [*Argentina*] [*ICAO designator*] (FAAC) .... POS
Aeroposta, SA [*Argentina*] [*FAA designator*] (FAAC) .... RPO
Aeropro [*Canada*] [*ICAO designator*] (FAAC) .... APO
Aero-Propulsion Fuels Laboratory [*Air Force*] .... APFL
Aero-Propulsion Laboratory [*Air Force*] .... APL
Aeropropulsion Systems Test Facility [*Arnold Air Force Station, TN*] [*Air Force*] (MCD) .... ASTF
Aeropuerto del Norte [*Mexico*] [*ICAO location identifier*] (ICLI) .... MMAN
Aeropuma SA [*El Salvador*] [*ICAO designator*] (FAAC) .... APU
Aeroput [*Yugoslavia*] [*ICAO designator*] (FAAC) .... PUT
Aeropycsa SA de CV [*Mexico*] [*ICAO designator*] (FAAC) .... PYC
Aeroquetzal [*ICAO designator*] (AD) .... AW
Aeroquip Corporation (SAUO) .... AQP
Aerora SA [*Mexico*] [*ICAO designator*] (FAAC) .... ARR
Aero-Rent SA de CV [*Mexico*] [*ICAO designator*] (FAAC) .... REN
Aerorepresentaciones Tupac Amaru [*Peru*] [*ICAO designator*] (ICDA) .... XU
Aerorepresentaciones Tupac Amaru [*Peru*] [*ICAO designator*] (FAAC) .... XUT
Aerorepublica [*Columbia*] [*FAA designator*] (FAAC) .... RPB
Aero-Rey SA de CV [*Mexico*] [*ICAO designator*] (FAAC) .... REY
Aerosaba SA de CV [*Mexico*] [*FAA designator*] (FAAC) .... ESB
Aeroservice [*Kazakhstan*] [*FAA designator*] (FAAC) .... AVZ
Aeroservicio Sipse SA de CV [*Mexico*] [*ICAO designator*] (FAAC) .... PSE
Aeroservicios Carabobo CA [*Venezuela*] [*ICAO designator*] (FAAC) .... ASERCA
Aeroservicios Carabobo CA (ASERCA) [*Venzuela*] [*ICAO designator*] (FAAC) .... OCA
Aeroservicios del Bajio, SA de CV [*Mexico*] [*FAA designator*] (FAAC) .... RBJ
Aeroservicios Ejecutivos del Occidente SA de CV [*Mexico*] [*ICAO designator*] (FAAC) .... AEO
Aeroservicios Ejecutivos del Pacifico SA [*Mexico*] [*ICAO designator*] (FAAC) .... SPO
Aeroservicios Ejecutivos Sinaloenses SA [*Mexico*] [*ICAO designator*] (FAAC) .... SLS
Aeroservicios Monterrey SA de CV [*Mexico*] [*ICAO designator*] (FAAC) .... SVM
Aerosevicios Ecuatorianos CA [*Ecuador*] [*ICAO designator*] (FAAC) .... EAE
Aerosi SA de CV [*Mexico*] [*ICAO designator*] (FAAC) .... OSI
Aerosierra de Durango [*Mexico*] [*ICAO designator*] (FAAC) .... SDG
Aerosiyusa, SA [*Mexico*] [*FAA designator*] (FAAC) .... SIY
Aerosol (ABBR) .... AERSL
Aerosol Analyzer (KSC) .... AA
Aerosol Assisted Chemical Vapor Deposition (SAUS) .... AACVD
Aerosol Characterization and Process Studies (SAUS) .... ACAPS
Aerosol Characterization Experiment [*Marine science*] (OSRA) .... ACE
Aerosol Characterization Experiment (PDAA) .... ACHEX
Aerosol Chemistry Experiment (SAUS) .... ACE
Aerosol Climatic Effects [*NASA*] .... ACE
Aerosol Collector and Pyrolyzer (ACAE) .... ACP
Aerosol Extinction-to-Backscatter Ratios (ARMP) .... AEBR
Aerosol Inhalation Measurement [*Medicine*] .... AIM
Aerosol Lidar (SAUS) .... AELID
Aerosol Lidar Experiment in Space (SAUS) .... ALEX S
Aerosol liquid (SAUS) .... AER
Aerosol liquid with Adapter (SAUS) .... ARA
Aerosol Mask [*Medicine*] (DAVI) .... Aer M
Aerosol Monitoring & Analysis (EFIS) .... AMA
Aerosol Obscurant (MCD) .... AO
Aerosol Observing System (ARMP) .... AOS
Aerosol Optical Depth (USDC) .... AOD
Aerosol Optical Thickness [*Climatology factor*] .... AOT
Aerosol Photoemission (HEAS) .... APE
Aerosol Physical Properties of the Stratosphere [*NASA*] (MCD) .... APPS
Aerosol Protective (DICI) .... AP
Aerosol Radiative Forcing (ARMP) .... ARF
Aerosol Release and Transport [*Nuclear energy*] (NRCH) .... ART
Aerosol Sampling System .... ASS
Aerosol Scattering Coefficient [*Climatology factor*] .... ASC
Aerosol Scattering Ratio (ARMP) .... ASR
Aerosol Scattering Spectrometer Probe [*Marine science*] (OSRA) .... ASSP
Aerosol Solar Radiation (SAUS) .... ASR
Aerosol solid (SAUS) .... ARO
Aerosol solid with adapter (SAUS) .... ARD
Aerosol Techniques, Incorporated (SAUO) .... ATI
Aerosol Tent [*Medicine*] (DAVI) .... Aer T
Aerosol Time-of-Flight Mass Spectrometer .... ATOFMS
Aerosol-Cloud Interactions (QUAC) .... ACI
Aerosolized Aluminium Chlorhydrate (DB) .... ACH
Aerosonic Corp. [*Associated Press*] (SAG) .... Aeroson
Aerosonic Corp. [*AMEX symbol*] (SPSG) .... AIM
Aerososel [*Chile*] [*FAA designator*] (FAAC) .... AOE
Aerospace (MCD) .... A
Aerospace .... AERO
Aerospace (MSA) .... AEROSP
Aerospace (ABBR) .... AERSPC
Aerospace .... ARSPC
Aerospace (IEEE) .... AS
Aerospace Amplifier (MCD) .... ASA
Aerospace Ancillary Equipment (SAUS) .... AAE
Aerospace & Defense Sales Inc. (SAUS) .... ADSI
Aerospace & Defense Sales, Inc. (SAUO) .... ADSI
Aerospace and Electronic (SAUS) .... A&E
Aerospace and Electronic Systems Society (NITA) .... AESC
Aerospace and Electronics Systems (IEEE) .... AESS
Aerospace and Electronics Systems Society (SAUO) .... AESS
Aerospace and Environmental Medicine Information System (IID) .... AEMIS
Aerospace and Equipment (SAUS) .... A&E
Aerospace and Flight Test Radio Coordinating Council (MCD) .... AFTRCC
Aerospace and Flight Test Range Coordinating Company (ACAE) .... AFTRCC
Aerospace and Nagigational Electronics (SAUS) .... ANE
Aerospace and Strategic Technology Office (ACAE) .... ASTO
Aerospace Application Studies Comitee (SAUO) .... AASC
Aerospace Applications Studies Committee [*NATO*] (PDAA) .... AASC
Aerospace Audiovisual Service [*Air Force*] (MCD) .... AAVS
Aerospace Audio-Visual Service (SAUO) .... AAVS
Aerospace Auxiliary Equipment (SAUS) .... AABA
Aerospace Auxiliary Equipment [*NASA*] .... AAE
Aerospace Bearing Support Inc. (SAUO) .... ABS
Aerospace Business Environment Simulator [*Computer-programmed management game*] .... ABES
Aerospace Business Environment Simulator (SAUS) .... abes
Aerospace Cartographic and Geodetic Service .... ACGS
Aerospace Catalog Automated Microfilm, Inc. (MCD) .... ASCAM

Aerospace Center [*Defense Mapping Agency*] ... AC
Aerospace Command and Control System (SAA) ... ACCS
Aerospace Communication and Controls Division [*NASA*] (KSC) ... ACCD
Aerospace Communications ... AEROSPACECOM
Aerospace Communications (SAUS) ... AIRCOM
Aerospace Communications Complex [*Air Force*] ... AIRCOM
Aerospace Communications Squadron (SAUO) ... ACOMMW
Aerospace Communications Wing [*Air Force*] ... ACOMMW
Aerospace Computer Program [*Air Force*] ... ACP
Aerospace Computer Program Model [*Air Force*] (IAA) ... ACPM
Aerospace Contract Engineers (MCD) ... ACE
Aerospace Control [*Air Force*] (MCD) ... ASC
Aerospace Control Environment [*Air Force*] ... ACE
Aerospace Control Squadron [*Air Force*] ... ACONS
Aerospace Corp. (AAG) ... AC
Aerospace Corp., El Segundo, CA [*Library symbol*] [*Library of Congress*] (LCLS) ... CEsA
Aerospace Corporation (SAUO) ... AC
Aerospace Crew Equipment Development ... ACED
Aerospace Crew Equipment Laboratory [*Philadelphia, PA*] (MCD) ... ACEL
Aerospace Data Acquisition System (SAUS) ... ADAS
Aerospace Data Adapter Programmable Tester (SAUS) ... ADAPT
Aerospace Data Facility (ACAE) ... ADF
Aerospace Data Systems (MCD) ... ADS
Aerospace Data Systems Standard (SSD) ... ADSS
Aerospace Defence Command (SAUO) ... ADC
Aerospace Defense Command [*Formerly, Air Defense Command*] [*Air Force*] ... ADC
Aerospace Defense Command (CCCA) ... ADCOM
Aerospace Defense Command Intelligence Center (SAUO) ... ADIC
Aerospace Defense Command Region [*Military*] ... ADCOMR
Aerospace Defense Division [*Air Force*] ... ADD
Aerospace Defense Flight [*Air Force*] ... AERODF
Aerospace Defense Software Engineering Environment (SAUS) ... ASD/SEE
Aerospace Defense Squadron [*Military*] (MUSM) ... ADS
Aerospace Defense Squadron [*Air Force*] ... AERODS
Aerospace Defense Systems Officer [*Air Force*] (AFM) ... ADSO
Aerospace Defense Wing [*Air Force*] ... AERODW
Aerospace Department Chairmen's Association (EA) ... ADCA
Aerospace Department Chairmens Association (SAUO) ... ADCA
Aerospace Deployment Device (ACAE) ... ADD
Aerospace Design and Development, Inc. (AAGC) ... ADD
Aerospace Design Hugo Marom Ltd. (SAUO) ... ADHM
Aerospace Digital Development ... ADD
Aerospace Division Commitment Record (SAA) ... ADCR
Aerospace Draftsman's Education and Proficiency Training (MCD) ... ADEPT
Aerospace Draftsmans Education and Proficiency Training (SAUS) ... ADEPT
Aerospace Driver (GFGA) ... ASDE
Aerospace Education ... AE
Aerospace Education Association (EA) ... AEA
Aerospace Education Foundation (EA) ... AEF
Aerospace Education Instructor (AFM) ... AEI
Aerospace Education Workshop Project ... AEWP
Aerospace Electrical Division (SAA) ... AED
Aerospace Electrical Society (EA) ... AES
Aerospace Electronics Laboratories (MCD) ... AEL
Aerospace Electronics Laboratory (SAUS) ... AEL
Aerospace Electronics System (IAA) ... AES
Aerospace Electronics Systems (SAUS) ... AES
Aerospace Energy Conversion Committee (SAUO) ... AECC
Aerospace Engine Life Committee [*Air Force*] (AFIT) ... AELC
Aerospace Engineer (PGP) ... AE
Aerospace Engineering and Engineering Mechanics (SAUS) ... AEEM
Aerospace Engineering Conference and Exhibits (ACAE) ... AECS
Aerospace Engineering Process Institute ... AEPI
Aerospace Engineering Test Establishment [*Canada*] ... AETE
Aerospace Engineering Test Establishment, Canadian Forces Base Coal Lake, Medley, Alberta [*Library symbol*] [*National Library of Canada*] (NLC) ... AMECFA
Aerospace Environment (MCD) ... AE
Aerospace Environment Simulation System ... ASESS
Aerospace Environmental Support Unit [*Air Weather Service*] (IID) ... AESU
Aerospace Facilities Engineer ... AFE
Aerospace Facts and Figures (SAUS) ... Aero F&F
Aerospace Flight Test Radio Coordinating Council (SAUS) ... AFTRCC
Aerospace Flight Vehicle ... AFV
Aerospace Ground Equipment [*NASA*] ... AGE
Aerospace Ground Equipment Department ... AGED
Aerospace Ground Equipment Illustration [*Air Force*] (SAA) ... AGEI
Aerospace Ground Equipment Installation ... AGEI
Aerospace Ground Equipment Not Operationally Ready Supply (ACAE) ... AGENORS
Aerospace Ground Equipment Out of Commission for Parts [*Air Force*] ... AGEOCP
Aerospace Ground Equipment Out of Commission for Parts [*Air Force*] (SAA) ... AGEOP
Aerospace Ground Equipment Plan (ACAE) ... AGEP
Aerospace Ground Equipment Recommendation Data (SAUS) ... AGERD
Aerospace Ground Equipment Requirements Data ... AGERD
Aerospace Ground Equipment/Support Equipment (MCD) ... AGE/SE
Aerospace Ground Support Equipment ... AGSE
Aerospace Ground Unit ... AGU
Aerospace Group ... AG
Aerospace Group Configuration Management (ACAE) ... AGCM
Aerospace Group Configuration Management Manual (ACAE) ... AGCMM
Aerospace Group Directive Document System (ACAE) ... AGDDS
Aerospace Group Management Directive (ACAE) ... AGMD
Aerospace Group Property Administrator (ACAE) ... AGPA
Aerospace Group Property Engineering (ACAE) ... AGPE
Aerospace Group Property Management (ACAE) ... AGPM
Aerospace Guidance and Metrology Center [*Air Force*] (AFIT) ... AG
Aerospace Guidance and Metrology Center [*Newark Air Force Station, OH*] ... AG & MC
Aerospace Guidance and Metrology Center [*Air Force*] ... AGE
Aerospace Guidance and Metrology Center [*Newark Air Force Station, OH*] (AFM) ... AGMC
Aerospace High School (SAUO) ... AHS
Aerospace Human Factors Association (SAUO) ... ASHA
Aerospace Industrial Association (SAUO) ... AIA
Aerospace Industrial Life Sciences Association [*of Aerospace Medical Association*] (MCD) ... AILSA
Aerospace Industrial Modernization ... AIM
Aerospace Industries Association of America (EA) ... AIA
Aerospace [*formerly, Aircraft*] **Industries Association of America** (MCD) ... AIAA
Aerospace Industries Association of America (SAUO) ... AIAA
Aerospace Industries Association of Canada [*Association des Industries Aerospatiales du Canada*] [*Formerly, Air Industries Association of Canada*] (AC) ... AIAC
Aerospace Industries Association of Canada (SAUS) ... ORAE
Aerospace Industry Standards Committee (SAUO) ... AISC
Aerospace Information Division [*Library of Congress*] ... AID
Aerospace Information Report [*SAE*] (AAGC) ... AIR
Aerospace [*or Aircraft*] **Installation Diagnostic Equipment** (KSC) ... AIDE
Aero-Space Institute (SAUO) ... ASI
Aerospace Instrumentation Committee (SAUO) ... ASIC
Aerospace Instrumentation Laboratory [*Air Force*] (MCD) ... AIL
Aerospace Instrumentation Range Station ... AESIR
Aerospace Intelligence Data System [*IBM Corp.*] (DIT) ... AIDS
Aerospace Intelligence File (CINC) ... AIF
Aerospace Intelligence (journ.) (SAUS) ... AI
Aerospace Intelligence Squadron [*Air Force*] ... AEROIS
Aerospace Intelligence Squadron [*Air Force*] ... AISq
Aerospace Internal Data Report [*Air Force*] (MCD) ... AIDR
Aerospace Maintenance and Development Unit (MCD) ... AMDU
Aerospace Maintenance and Operational Status (AFM) ... AMOS
Aerospace Maintenance and Regeneration Center [*Air Force*] ... AMARC
Aerospace Management Liaison Section (SAUO) ... AMLS
Aerospace Manufacturers Council [*Defunct*] (EA) ... AMC
Aerospace, Maritime and Military Systems (SAUS) ... AMMS
Aerospace Material Document (SAUS) ... AMD
Aerospace Material Specification (MCD) ... AMS
Aerospace Materials Document (MCD) ... AMD
Aerospace Materials Information ... AMI
Aerospace Materials Information Center [*Air Force*] (MCD) ... AMIC
Aerospace Materials Specifications (AAGC) ... AMS
Aerospace Mechanical Fastening Requirements (MCD) ... AMFR
Aerospace Medical Association (MCD) ... AMA
Aerospace Medical Association (EA) ... AsMA
Aerospace Medical Association (SAUO) ... ASMA
Aerospace Medical Association of the Philippines (SAUO) ... AMAP
Aerospace Medical Command [*Air Force*] ... AMC
Aerospace Medical Division [*Brooks Air Force Base, TX*] [*Air Force*] ... AMD
Aerospace Medical Laboratory (Clinical) [*Lackland Air Force Base, TX*] (MCD) ... AMLC
Aerospace Medical Operations Office [*NASA*] (KSC) ... AMOO
Aerospace Medical Panel (SAUS) ... AMP
Aerospace Medical Panel (SAUO) ... ASMP
Aerospace Medical Research ... AMR
Aerospace Medical Research Laboratory [*Later, MRL*] [*Wright-Patterson Air Force Base, OH*] ... AMRL
Aerospace Medicine (MCD) ... AM
Aerospace Medicine and Biology ... AMB
Aerospace Medicine (journ.) (SAUS) ... Aerosp Med
Aerospace Multiple Station Analysis (MCD) ... AMSA
Aerospace Nuclear Safety Information Center (MCD) ... ANSIC
Aerospace Observation Platform ... AOP
Aerospace (or Air) Defense Command Post (SAUO) ... ADCP
Aerospace (or Air) Defense Communications Office (SAUO) ... ADCO
Aerospace Photographic Reconnaissance Equipment ... APRE
Aerospace Physiologists Society (SAUO) ... ASPS
Aerospace Physiology Officer (SAUS) ... APO
Aerospace Plane ... ASP
Aerospace Planning Charts ... ASC
Aerospace Planning, Execution, and Control System (ACAE) ... APECS
Aerospace Power Division [*Air Force*] ... APD
Aerospace Primus Club ... APC
Aerospace Products Division, SED Systems Ltd., Saskatoon, Saskatchewan [*Library symbol*] [*National Library of Canada*] (NLC) ... SSSEDA
Aerospace Products Division, SED Systems Ltd., Saskatoon, Saskatchewan (SAUS) ... SSSEDA
Aerospace Program-Oriented Language [*Computer science*] (PDAA) ... APOL
Aerospace Radioisotope Power Information Center (KSC) ... ARPIC
Aerospace Recommened Practice (SAUS) ... ARP
Aerospace Reconnaissance Technical Squadron [*Air Force*] ... ARTSq
Aerospace Reconnaissance Technical Wing (MCD) ... ARTW
Aerospace Recovery Facility (MCD) ... ARF
Aerospace Reference Project [*Formerly, ATP*] [*Library of Congress*] ... ARP
Aerospace Remote Calculator (MCD) ... ARC
Aerospace Rescue and Recovery ... ARR
Aerospace Rescue and Recovery Center [*Air Force*] (AFM) ... ARRC

Aerospace Rescue and Recovery Group [*Air Force*] ... ARRG
Aerospace Rescue and Recovery Group [*Air Force*] (AFM) ... ARRGp
Aerospace Rescue and Recovery Service [*Air Force*] (PDAA) ... AARS
Aerospace Rescue and Recovery Service [*Scott Air Force Base, IL*] (MCD) ... ARRS
Aerospace Rescue and Recovery Squadron [*Air Force*] ... AR & RSq
Aerospace Rescue and Recovery Squadron (ACAE) ... ARRS
Aerospace Rescue and Recovery Squadron [*Air Force*] (AFM) ... ARRSq
Aerospace Rescue and Recovery Training Center [*Air Force*] (AFM) ... ARRTC
Aerospace Rescue and Recovery Wing [*Air Force*] (MCD) ... ARRW
Aerospace Rescue and Recovery Wing [*Air Force*] (AFM) ... ARRWg
Aerospace Research and Testing Committee (SAA) ... ARTC
Aerospace Research Applications Center [*Indiana University*] [*NASA*] ... ARAC
Aerospace Research Associates (SAUS) ... ARA
Aerospace Research Associates Inc. (SAUO) ... ARA
Aerospace Research Association (MCD) ... ARA
Aerospace Research Chamber ... ARC
Aerospace Research Laboratory [*Wright-Patterson Air Force Base, OH*] (AFM) ... ARL
Aerospace Research Pilot School [*Air Force*] ... ARPS
Aerospace Research Pilot School - Edwards Air Force Base [*Air Force*] ... ARPSE
Aerospace Research Pilot School-Edwards Air Force Base (SAUS) ... ARPS-E
Aerospace Research Satellite ... ARS
Aerospace Research Support Program [*Air Force*] ... ARSP
Aerospace Research USAF Test Pilot School [*Later, USAFTESTPLTSCH*] ... AEROSPRSCHPLTSCH
Aerospace Research Vehicle ... ARV
Aerospace Resource Information Network (SAUS) ... ARIN
Aerospace Safety Advisory Panel (SAUS) ... ASAP
[*The*] **Aerospace Safety Advisory Panel** [*NASA/Air Force*] (NASA) ... ASAP
Aerospace Safety Research and Data Institute [*Lewis Research Center*] [*NASA*] ... ASRDI
Aerospace Security Force (AFM) ... ASF
Aerospace Services Division [*NASA*] (KSC) ... ASD
Aerospace Spin-Off Laboratory ... AEROSOL
Aerospace Standards ... AS
Aerospace Static Converter ... ASC
Aerospace Static Inverter ... ASI
Aerospace Structural Material ... ASM
Aerospace Structures Information and Analysis Center [*Wright-Patterson Ai r Force Base, OH*] [*Air Force*] (MCD) ... ASIAC
Aerospace Structures Test Facility [*Air Force*] ... ASTF
Aerospace Studies [*AFROTC*] (AFM) ... AS
Aerospace Studies Institute [*Air Force*] (MCD) ... ASI
Aerospace Support Equipment ... ASE
Aerospace Support Group [*Air Force*] ... AEROSG
Aerospace Support Squadron [*Air Force*] ... AEROSS
Aerospace Support Squadron [*Air Force*] ... AEROSSq
Aerospace Support Systems (MCD) ... ASS
Aerospace Surveillance and Control [*Air Force*] (AFM) ... AS & C
Aerospace Surveillance and Control (SAUS) ... AS&C
Aerospace Surveillance and Control Squadron [*Air Force*] ... ASCS
Aerospace Surveillance and Warning ... ASSAW
Aerospace Surveillance and Warning System (SAUS) ... ASWS
Aerospace Surveillance System ... ASS
Aerospace Surveillance Warning System (MCD) ... ASWS
Aerospace System Test and Evaluation Complex (KSC) ... ASTEC
Aerospace Systems Center [*Dayton, OH*] [*Air Force*] (MCD) ... ASC
Aerospace Systems Division (SAUO) ... ASD
Aerospace Systems, Inc. ... ASI
Aerospace Systems Safety Society (MCD) ... ASSS
Aerospace Systems Security Program (AFM) ... ASSP
Aerospace Systems Test Environment ... ASTE
Aerospace Systems Test Reactor [*Formerly, Aircraft Shield Test Reactor*] ... ASTR
Aerospace Technical Council (SAUO) ... ATC
Aerospace Technical Intelligence Center ... ATIC
Aerospace Technologies of Australia (SAUS) ... ATA
Aerospace Technologies of Australia Pty Ltd. (SAUS) ... ASTA
Aerospace Technologist [*or Technology*] [*NASA*] ... AST
Aerospace Technology (SAUS) ... AST
Aerospace Technology Division [*Formerly, Aerospace Information Division; later, ARP*] [*Library of Congress*] ... ATD
Aerospace Technology Division [*Formerly, Aerospace Information Division; later, ARP*]**/Library of Congress** (AFM) ... ATD/LC
Aerospace Test Equipment ... ATE
Aerospace Test Group (NASA) ... ASTG
Aerospace Test System (MCD) ... ATS
Aerospace Test Wing [*Air Force*] ... ASTW
Aerospace Test Wing [*Air Force*] (AFM) ... ASTWg
Aerospace Test Wing [*Air Force*] ... ATW
Aerospace Traffic Control Center ... ATCC
Aerospace Vehicle (KSC) ... ASV
Aerospace Vehicle (AFM) ... AV
Aerospace Vehicle Detection ... AVD
Aerospace Vehicle Distribution Office [*or Officer*] [*Air Force*] (AFM) ... AVDO
Aerospace Vehicle Distribution Officer (SAUS) ... AVDO
Aerospace Vehicle Electronics (MCD) ... AVE
Aerospace [*or Airborne*] **Vehicle Equipment** ... AVE
Aerospace Vehicle Equipment (SAUS) ... AVE
Aerospace Vehicle Interactive Design (MCD) ... AVID
Aerospace Vehicle Inventory, Status, and Utilization Reporting System ... AVISURS
Aerospace Vehicle Simulation (PDAA) ... AVS
Aerospace Vehicle System (MCD) ... AVS
Aerospace Warning and Control (MCD) ... ASWAC
Aerospatial Helicopter Corporation (SAUO) ... AHC
Aerospatiale [*Societe Nationale Industrielle Aerospatiale*] [*France*] [*ICAO aircraft manufacturer identifier*] (ICAO) ... ND
Aerospatiale Helicopter Corporation (ACAE) ... AHC
Aerospatiale (SOCATA) Stark KG [*Germany*] [*ICAO aircraft manufacturer identifier*] (ICAO) ... TB
Aerospatiale [*Societe Nationale Industrielle Aerospatiale*] **(Sud Aviation)** [*France*] [*ICAO aircraft manufacturer identifier*] (ICAO) ... S
Aerospray [*Ionization*] [*Physics*] ... AS
Aerospun Cluster Munitions (MCD) ... ACM
Aerostar Airlines, Inc. [*ICAO designator*] (FAAC) ... FNT
Aerostar Owners Association (EA) ... AOA
Aerostat ... ARSTT
Aerosucre SA [*Colombia*] [*ICAO designator*] (FAAC) ... HRE
Aerosucre, SA [*Colombia*] [*FAA designator*] (FAAC) ... KRE
AeroSun International, Inc. [*ICAO designator*] (FAAC) ... ASI
Aerosuper AS de CV [*Mexico*] [*ICAO designator*] (FAAC) ... SUP
Aerosurface Amplifier (NASA) ... ASA
Aerosurface Control [*NASA*] (NASA) ... ASC
Aerosurface Driver Electronics (SAUS) ... ASDE
Aerosurface Driver/Monitor [*NASA*] (MCD) ... ASDM
Aerosurface End-to-End Test (MCD) ... AET
Aerosurface Position (NASA) ... ASP
Aerosurface Position Indicator (MCD) ... ASPI
Aerosurface Servo Amplifier [*NASA*] (NASA) ... ASA
Aerosurfaces (NASA) ... AERO
Aerotal Aerolineas Territoriales de Colombia Ltd. [*ICAO designator*] (FAAC) ... ART
Aerotamatan SA de CV [*Mexico*] [*ICAO designator*] (FAAC) ... TAA
Aerotaxi (SAUS) ... DX
Aerotaxi Casanare Ltda. [*Colombia*] [*ICAO designator*] (FAAC) ... ATK
Aerotaxi del Valle [*Colombia*] [*ICAO designator*] (FAAC) ... AOX
Aerotaxi Villa Rica, SA de CV [*Mexico*] [*FAA designator*] (FAAC) ... VRI
Aerotaxis Calzada SA de CV [*Mexico*] [*ICAO designator*] (FAAC) ... CLZ
Aerotaxis Corporativo SA de CV [*Mexico*] [*ICAO designator*] (FAAC) ... CRP
Aerotaxis de Aguascalientes SA de CV [*Mexico*] [*ICAO designator*] (FAAC) ... GUA
Aerotaxis del Centro SA [*Mexico*] [*ICAO designator*] (FAAC) ... CTO
Aerotaxis del Golfo, SA de CV [*Mexico*] [*FAA designator*] (FAAC) ... TGF
Aerotaxis Latinoamericanos SA de CV [*Mexico*] [*ICAO designator*] (FAAC) ... LTI
Aerotaxis Pegaso SA de CV [*Mexico*] [*ICAO designator*] (FAAC) ... APG
Aerotec [*Sociedade Aerotec Ltda.*] [*Brazil*] [*ICAO aircraft manufacturer identifier*] (ICAO) ... T
Aerotherm Axisymmetric Transient Heating and Material Ablation [*Program*] ... ASTHMA
Aerotherm Axi-Symmetric Transient Heating and Material Ablation (SAUS) ... ASTHMA
Aerotherm Prediction Procedure for LASER Effects (MCD) ... APPLE
Aerothermal Re-Entry Experiment (MCD) ... ARE
Aerothermal Structure (ACAE) ... ATS
Aerothermal Structures (ACAE) ... AST
Aerothermodynamic Data Book [*NASA*] (NASA) ... ATDB
Aerothermodynamic Duct ... ATHODYD
Aerothermodynamic Elastic Structural System Environmental Tests (SAUS) ... ASSET
Aerothermodynamic Elastic Vehicle ... AEV
Aerothermodynamic Environmental Vehicle (ACAE) ... AEV
Aerothermodynamic Integration Model ... AIM
Aerothermodynamic Structural Systems Environmental Test [*Military*] ... ASSET
Aerothermodynamic Structural Vehicle [*Air Force*] ... ASV
Aerothermodynamic-Aerothermoelastic Structural Systems Environmental Test (SAUS) ... ASSET
Aero-Thermo-Dynamic-Duct (SAUS) ... ATHODYD
Aerotours Dominican, C por A [*Dominican Republic*] [*ICAO designator*] (FAAC) ... ATD
Aerotranscolombiana de Carga Ltda. [*Columbia*] [*FAA designator*] (FAAC) ... TCO
Aerotransporte Peruanos Internacionales SA [*Peru*] [*ICAO designator*] (FAAC) ... APS
Aerotransportes Barlovento SA de CV [*Mexico*] [*ICAO designator*] (FAAC) ... BLO
Aerotransportes Entre Rios SRL [*Argentina*] [*ICAO designator*] (FAAC) ... SFA
Aerotransportes Especiales Ltda. [*Colombia*] [*ICAO designator*] (FAAC) ... ATP
Aerotransportes Mas de Carga SA de CV [*Mexico*] [*ICAO designator*] (FAAC) ... MAA
Aerotransportes Privados SA de CV [*Mexico*] [*ICAO designator*] (FAAC) ... PVA
Aero-Triangulation (GEOI) ... AT
Aerotronic Associate (IAA) ... AA
Aerotronic Associates, Inc. (SAUO) ... AA
Aerotur SA [*Mexico*] [*ICAO designator*] (FAAC) ... TUR
Aerovaradero SA [*Cuba*] [*FAA designator*] (FAAC) ... AVY
Aerovekel SA [*Mexico*] [*ICAO designator*] (FAAC) ... VKL
Aeroventas SA [*Mexico*] [*ICAO designator*] (FAAC) ... AEV
Aerovia del Altiplano SA de CV [*Mexico*] [*ICAO designator*] (FAAC) ... APN
Aerovia Sud Americana ... ASUD
Aeroviajes Ejecuitvos SA de CV [*Mexico*] [*ICAO designator*] (FAAC) ... AVJ
Aerovial [*Chile*] [*ICAO designator*] (FAAC) ... AVL
Aerovias Bueno Ltd. [*Colombia*] [*ICAO designator*] (FAAC) ... ABU
Aerovias Caribe SA [*Mexico*] [*ICAO designator*] (FAAC) ... CBE
Aerovias Castillo SA [*Mexico*] [*ICAO designator*] (FAAC) ... CLL
Aerovias Condor de Colombia Ltda. [*Condor Airlines of Colombia Ltd.*] ... AEROCONDOR
Aerovias Condor de Colombia Ltda. (AEROCONDOR) [*Colombia*] [*ICAO designator*] (ICDA) ... OD
Aerovias Dap [*Chile*] [*ICAO designator*] (FAAC) ... DAP
Aerovias de Lagos SA de CV [*Mexico*] [*ICAO designator*] (FAAC) ... LAG

Aerovias de Mexico SA de CV [*ICAO designator*] (FAAC) .... AMX
Aerovias de Poniente SA de CV [*Mexico*] [*ICAO designator*] (FAAC) .... PNI
Aerovias del Atlantico Ltd. [*Colombia*] [*ICAO designator*] (FAAC) .... AOK
Aerovias Ecuatoriana SA .... AREA
Aerovias Especiales de Carga Ltda. [*Colombia*] [*ICAO designator*] (FAAC) .... AVESCA
Aerovias Especiales de Carga Ltda. [*Colombia*] [*ICAO designator*] (FAAC) .... VSC
Aerovias Interamericanas de Panama SA .... AVISPA
Aerovias Las Amricas, SA [*Panama*] [*FAA designator*] (FAAC) .... AVL
Aerovias Montes Azules, SA de CV [*Mexico*] [*FAA designator*] (FAAC) .... MZL
Aerovias Nacionales de Colombia [*Colombian National Airways*] .... AVIANCA
Aerovias Oaxaquenas SA [*Mexico*] [*ICAO designator*] (FAAC) .... AVO
Aerovias Panama Airways .... APA
Aerovias Quisqueyana [*Airlines*] [*Dominican Republic*] [*ICAO designator*] (OAG) .... QQ
Aerovias Venezolanas Sociedad Anonima [*Airline*] [*Venezuela*] .... AVENSA
Aerovias Xalitic SA de CV [*Mexico*] [*ICAO designator*] (FAAC) .... XAL
Aerovilla Ltda. [*Columbia*] [*FAA designator*] (FAAC) .... VVG
Aerovironment, Inc. .... AV
Aerovitro SA de CV [*Mexico*] [*ICAO designator*] (FAAC) .... VRO
Aerovox, Inc. [*Associated Press*] (SAG) .... Aerovx
Aerovox, Inc. [*NASDAQ symbol*] (SAG) .... ARVX
Aes [*Obverse*] [*Numismatics*] .... AE
AES China Generating Co. [*Associated Press*] (SAG) .... AES Chn
AES China Generating Co. [*NASDAQ symbol*] (SAG) .... CHGN
AES China Generating'A' [*NASDAQ symbol*] (TTSB) .... CHGNF
AES Corp. [*NYSE symbol*] (SAG) .... AES
AES Corp. [*NASDAQ symbol*] (SAG) .... AESC
AES Corp. [*Associated Press*] (SAG) .... AES Cp
AES Regina Weather Office, Environment Canada [*Bureau Meteorologique du SEA de Regina, Environnement Canada*] **Saskatchewan** [*Library symbol*] [*National Library of Canada*] (NLC) .... SREAE
AES Regina Weather Office, Environment Canada Saskatchewan (SAUS) .... SREAE
Aeschines [*c. 397-322BC*] [*Classical studies*] (OCD) .... Aeschin
Aeschylus [*Greek poet, 525-456BC*] [*Classical studies*] (ROG) .... AESCH
Aesculapian Club (EA) .... AC
Aesculapius International Medicine (EA) .... AIM
Aesop (BARN) .... Aes
Aesop Basic Machine Language (ACAE) .... ABML
Aesthete (ABBR) .... AESTH
aesthete (SAUS) .... aesth
aesthetic (SAUS) .... aesth
Aesthetic .... ASTHTC
Aesthetic Realism Foundation (EA) .... ARF
Aesthetically (ABBR) .... AESTHY
aesthetician (SAUS) .... aesth
Aestheticians International Association (EA) .... AIA
Aesthetics .... AESTH
aesthetics (SAUS) .... aesth
Aesthetics and Visual Literacy Council [*Australia*] .... AVLC
Aetas [*or Aetatis*] [*Age or Aged*] [*Latin*] .... aet
Aetatis [*Age*] [*Latin*] .... AE
Aetatis [*Age*] [*Latin*] .... AETAT
Aethelred [*King of England*] (ILCA) .... Athlr
Aether [*Ether*] (ROG) .... AETH
Aetherius Society (EA) .... AS
Aethestan [*King of England, 895-940*] (ILCA) .... As
Aetia [*of Callimachus*] [*Classical studies*] (OCD) .... Aet
Aetiology [*or Etiology*] [*Medicine*] (DAVI) .... aet
Aetiology [*or Etiology*] [*Medicine*] (DAVI) .... aetiol
Aetna Capital 9.50%'MIPS' [*NYSE symbol*] (TTSB) .... AETPrA
Aetna Capital LLC [*NYSE symbol*] (SAG) .... AET
Aetna Capital LLC, Inc. [*Associated Press*] (SAG) .... AetnaC
Aetna, Inc. [*NYSE symbol*] [*Formerly, Aetna Life & Casualty*] (SG) .... AET
Aetna, Inc. [*Associated Press*] (SAG) .... Aetna Inc
Aetna Life & Casualty [*NYSE symbol*] (TTSB) .... AET
Aetna Life & Casualty Co. [*NYSE symbol*] (SAG) .... AET
Aetna Life & Casualty Co. [*Associated Press*] (SAG) .... AetnLf
Aetna Life Insurance Co. of America (EFIS) .... ALICA
Aetna Life Insurance Co. of Canada [*Toronto Stock Exchange symbol*] .... ALI
Aetna Telecommunications Consultants [*Centerville, MA*] [*Telecommunications*] (TSSD) .... ATC
Aetrium, Inc. [*Associated Press*] (SAG) .... Aetrium
Aetrium, Inc. [*NASDAQ symbol*] (SAG) .... ATRM
AF JINTACCS Program Office (SAUO) .... AFJPO
AF Maui Optical Station (SAUO) .... AMOS
AF Small Computer (SAUS) .... TSCT
Afan Cooperative Development Agency [*British*] .... ACDA
Afar Democratic Union [*Ethiopia*] .... ADU
Afar Liberation Front [*Ethiopia*] (PD) .... ALF
Afar Locality [*Paleoanthropology*] .... AL
Afar People's Democratic Organisation [*Ethiopia*] .... APDO
Afar Revolutionary Democratic Union [*Eritrea*] .... ARDU
Afar Revolutionary Democratic Unity Front [*Eritrea*] .... ARDUF
Afareaitu [*Society Islands*] [*Seismograph station code, US Geological Survey*] (SEIS) .... AFR
Afars and Issas, Republic of Djibouti (SAUS) .... A&I
AFC Cable Systems [*Associated Press*] (SAG) .... AFC Cbl
AFC Cable Systems [*NASDAQ symbol*] (SAG) .... AFCX
AFCAP Review Group (SAUO) .... ARG
AFCAP Technical Coordinating Group (SAUO) .... ATCG
AFCAP Users Group (SAUO) .... AUG
AFCEA Computing Conference & Exhibition (SAUS) .... ACCE
AFCENT Logistic Land Panel (SAUO) .... ALLP
Afebrile [*Medicine*] (MELL) .... AF
Afebrile [*Free from fever*] [*Medicine*] (DAVI) .... afeb
Afebrile, Vital Signs Stable [*Medicine*] (DAVI) .... AFVSS
Afebrile, Vital Signs Stable [*Medicine*] (DAVI) .... AVSS
Affability (ABBR) .... AFBT
Affable (ABBR) .... AFB
Affably (ABBR) .... AFBY
Affair .... AFFR
Affaires des Anciens Combattants du Canada [*Department of Canadian Veterans Affairs - DVA*] .... AACC
Affaires Exterieures Canada [*External Affairs Canada*] .... AEC
Affairs (AFM) .... AFF
Affairs (ADWA) .... aff
Affairs (PROS) .... Aff
affdavit (SAUS) .... afft
Affect .... A
Affect .... AFCT
Affect Adjective Check List [*Psychology*] .... AACL
Affect Elaboration [*Scale*] [*Psychology*] .... AE
Affectation (ABBR) .... AFCTAN
affectation (SAUS) .... affiec
Affected (ABBR) .... AFCTD
Affected Areas .... AA
Affected Pair Method [*Statistics*] .... APM
Affectedly (ABBR) .... AFCTDY
Affected-Pedigree-Member [*Technique for genetic study*] .... APM
Affecting (ABBR) .... AFCTG
Affecting (ROG) .... AFF
Affectingly (ABBR) .... AFCTGY
Affection (ABBR) .... AFCTN
affection (SAUS) .... affec
Affectionate (ABBR) .... AFCTNA
Affectionate (ABBR) .... AFCTNT
Affectionate (ADA) .... AFFEC
Affectionate [*Correspondence*] (ROG) .... AFFTE
Affectionately (ABBR) .... AFCTNAY
Affectionately (ABBR) .... AFCTNTY
Affectionately [*Correspondence*] .... AFF
Affectionately [*Correspondence*] (ROG) .... AFFECTLY
Affectionately [*Correspondence*] (ROG) .... AFFLY
Affectionately [*Correspondence*] (ROG) .... AFFY
affective (SAUS) .... affec
Affective Disorder (MELL) .... AD
Affective Disorder Rating Scale [*Medicine*] (DB) .... ADRS
Affective Disorders Clinic (MELL) .... ADC
Affective Perception Inventory [*Student personality test*] .... API
Affective Sensitivity Scale .... ASS
Affective Spectrum Disorder [*Psychiatry*] (ECON) .... ASD
Affective System .... AS
Affective Work Competencies Inventory (EDAC) .... AWCI
Affects Balance Scale [*Personality development test*] [*Psychology*] .... ABS
Affenpinscher Club of America [*Later, AAA*] .... ACA
Affenpinscher Club of America (SAUO) .... ACA
Afferent [*Medicine*] .... AFF
Afferent Glomerular Arteriole [*Medicine*] (MELL) .... AGA
Afferent Nerve [*Medicine*] (MELL) .... AN
Afferent Pupillary Defect [*Ophthalmology*] (DAVI) .... APD
Afferent Renal Vein (SAUS) .... ARV
Afferent Vein to Nephridial Gland (SAUS) .... AVNG
Afferent Vessel (SAUS) .... AV
Affettuoso [*With Expression*] [*Music*] .... AFFET
Affettuoso [*With Expression*] [*Music*] .... AFFETT
Affettuoso [*With Expression*] [*Music*] .... AFFETTO
Affezionatissimo [*Very Tenderly, Pathetically*] [*Music*] (ROG) .... AFFMO
Aficultural Information Bulletin (SAUS) .... AIB
Affidavit (GEAB) .... af
Affidavit .... AFDVT
Affidavit [*Legal term*] (DLA) .... AFFI
Affidavit .... AFFT
Affidavit (ADWA) .... afft
Affiliate (SAUS) .... AF
Affiliate .... AFFIL
Affiliate (MUGU) .... AFFL
Affiliate (TBD) .... Affl
Affiliate .... AFFLT
Affiliate and Immigration Services (SAUS) .... AIS
Affiliate Artists (EA) .... AA
Affiliate Assembly [*American Association of School Librarians*] .... AA
Affiliate, Association of Medical Secretaries, Practice Administrators, and Receptionists [*British*] (DBQ) .... AMS(Aff)
Affiliate Information System (SAUS) .... AIS
Affiliate of the Company Directors' Association of Australia .... ACDA
Affiliate of the Institute of Plumbing [*British*] (DBQ) .... AffIP
Affiliate of the Institute of Sales Management [*British*] (DI) .... AffInstSM
Affiliate of the Institution of Works and Highways Technician Engineers (SAUS) .... AffIWHTE
Affiliate of the Royal Society of Health [*British*] .... Affil RSH
Affiliate of the Society of Licensed Aircraft Engineers and Technologists [*British*] (DBQ) .... AffilSLAET
Affiliate, Royal Society of Medicine [*British*] (CMD) .... ARSM
Affiliated (ADA) .... AFF
Affiliated (AL) .... Affil
Affiliated .... AFFLTD
Affiliated Advertising Agencies International (EA) 3AI
Affiliated Advertising Agencies International [*Aurora, CO*] (EA) .... AAAI

Affiliated Advertising Agencies Network (SAUS) .... AAAN
Affiliated Boards of Officials (EA) .... ABO
Affiliated Chiropodists-Podiatrists of America (EA) .... ACPA
Affiliated Community Bancorp [*NASDAQ symbol*] (TTSB) .... AFCB
Affiliated Community Bancorp, Inc. [*NASDAQ symbol*] (SAG) .... AFCB
Affiliated Community Bancorp, Inc. [*Associated Press*] (SAG) .... AffCom
Affiliated Computer Services 'A' [*NYSE symbol*] (SG) .... ACS
Affiliated Computer Services, Inc. [*NASDAQ symbol*] (SAG) .... ACSA
Affiliated Computer Services, Inc. [*Associated Press*] (SAG) .... AffCmpS
Affiliated Computer Services'A' [*NASDAQ symbol*] (TTSB) .... ACSA
Affiliated Computer System Inc. (SAUS) .... ACSI
Affiliated Computer System Incorporated (SAUO) .... ACSI
Affiliated Computer Systems [*Later, MPEC Co.*] [*Telecommunications*] (TSSD) .... ACS
Affiliated Computer Systems (SAUS) .... ACS
Affiliated Conference of Practicing Accountants International [*Later, ACPA*] (EA) .... ACPAI
Affiliated Conference of Practicing Accountants International (NTPA) .... ACPA Int'l
Affiliated Data Center (CARB) .... ADC
Affiliated Distributed Active Archive Center (EOSA) .... ADAAC
Affiliated Distributed Active Archive Centers (SAUS) .... ADAACS
Affiliated Dress Manufacturers (EA) .... ADM
Affiliated Dress Manufacturers, Inc. (SAUO) .... ADM
Affiliated Drug Stores (EA) .... ADS
Affiliated Employers of California (SRA) .... AEC
Affiliated Gas Equipment (SAUS) .... AGE
Affiliated Government Employees' Distributing Co. [*California*] .... AGE
Affiliated Inventors Foundation (EA) .... AIF
Affiliated Leadership League of and for the Blind of America (EA) .... ALL
Affiliated League of Emergency Radio Teams (SAUS) .... ALERT
Affiliated Managers Group [*NYSE symbol*] .... AMG
Affiliated Medical Research, Inc. [*Research code symbol*] .... AMR
Affiliated National Coaches Council (EA) .... ANCC
Affiliated National Riding Commission (EA) .... ANRC
Affiliated Nutritional Retailers Association [*Commercial firm*] (EA) .... ANRA
Affiliated Resources Corp. (EFIS) .... ARC
Affiliated Schools and Seminars for International Study and Training (SAUO) .... ASSIST
Affiliated Warehouse Companies (EA) .... AWC
Affiliated Woodcarvers Ltd. (EA) .... AFWC
Affiliation (PROS) .... affil
Affiliation .... AFFILTN
Affiliation Code [*IRS*] .... AFC
Affiliation of Author [*Online database field identifier*] .... AF
Affiliation of First Author [*Used to define searchable field*] (NITA) .... AF
Affiliation of Multicultural Societies & Service Agencies of BC (AC) .... AMSSA
Affiliation Officer [*British*] .... AO
Affiliation Testing Program [*for Catholic secondary schools*] (AEBS) .... ATP
Affinely Connected Space .... ACS
Affinis [*Having an Affinity with but Not Identical To*] [*Latin*] (MAE) .... aff
Affinitty Teleproductions, Inc. [*Associated Press*] (SAG) .... AffinTel
Affinity [*Laboratory analysis*] .... Affin
Affinity Capillary Electrophoresis [*An enzyme*] .... ACE
Affinity Chromatography [*Biopharmaceutical Purification*] .... AC
Affinity Column [*Chromatography*] .... Aff
Affinity Cross-Flow Filtration .... ACFF
Affinity Entertainment, Inc. [*Associated Press*] (SAG) .... AffinEnt
Affinity Entertainment, Inc. [*NASDAQ symbol*] (SAG) .... AFTY
Affinity Group of Evolutionary Anarchists (EA) .... AGEA
Affinity Technology Gp [*NASDAQ symbol*] (TTSB) .... AFFI
Affinity Technology Group, Inc. [*NASDAQ symbol*] (SAG) .... AFFI
Affinity Technology Group, Inc. [*Associated Press*] (SAG) .... AffTech
Affinity Teleproductions, Inc. [*NASDAQ symbol*] (SAG) .... AFTY
Affinity-Based-Collection [*Immunoassay*] .... ABC
Affirmation [*Linguistics*] .... A
Affirmation (ROG) .... AFFRMN
Affirmation Book [*Self-help advice*] .... AFFIE
Affirmation: United Methodists for Lesbian, Gay and Bisexual Concerns (EA) .... AUMLGBC
Affirmation: United Methodists for Lesbian/Gay Concerns (EA) .... AUMLGC
Affirmative .... AFF
Affirmative (AABC) .... AFIRM
Affirmative [*ICAO designator*] (FAAC) .... AFM
Affirmative Acknowledge [*Computer Science*] (NITA) .... ACK
Affirmative Action [*Employment policies for minorities*] .... AA
Affirmative Action Clause .... AAC
Affirmative Action committee (SAUS) .... AA
Affirmative Action Compliance Manual [*BNA*] [*A publication*] (AAGC) .... AACM
Affirmative Action Coordinating Center [*Defunct*] (EA) .... AACC
Affirmative Action Employer (MEDA) .... AAE
Affirmative Action Officer .... AAO
Affirmative Action Plan [*or Program*] [*Equal opportunity employment*] .... AAP
Affirmative Action Planning Guide [*Executive Telecom System, Inc.*] [*Information service or system*] (CRD) .... AAPG
Affirmative Action Program Plans [*DoD*] .... AAPP
Affirmative Action Program/Plan (SAUO) .... AAP
Affirmative Action Representative (SAUS) .... AAR
Affirmative Action/Equal Employment Opportunity (SAUS) .... AA/EEO
Affirmative Action/Equal Opportunity Employer (SAUS) .... AA/EOE
Affirmative Employment Plan (SAUS) .... AEP
Affirmative Fair Housing Marketing Regulations [*Department of Housing and Urban Development*] (GFGA) .... AFHM
Affirmative Flag [*Navy*] [*British*] .... AF
Affirmative Marketing Agreement [*Business term*] (EMRF) .... AMA
Affirmative Poll Response State (IAA) .... APRS
Affirmative Replies Neither Required nor Desired (MUGU) .... NOAFIRM
Affirmed (DLA) .... A
Affirmed .... AFFD
Affirmed (ADWA) .... affd
Affirmed [*or Affirming*] **on Rehearing** [*Legal term*] (DLA) .... Aff Reh
Affirming (ROG) .... AFF
Affirming .... AFFG
Affirming (ADWA) .... affg
Affirming Apostolic Order (WDAA) .... AAO
Affirmist Society [*Defunct*] (EA) .... AS
Affix [*Linguistics*] .... A
Affix [*Linguistics*] .... AF
Affix (ADWA) .... af
affixed (SAUS) .... affd
afflatus (SAUS) .... afflat
Afflizione [*Afflictedly*] [*Music*] (ROG) .... AFFLIZ
Affluent .... AFFL
Afford Service Member Opportunity to Apply for Ordinary Leave [*Army*] (AABC) .... ASMOLV
affordability (SAUS) .... affd
Affordable Basic Floppy Disk [*Computer science*] (MHDI) .... ABFD
Affordable Housing Action Group (AC) .... AHAG
Affordable Housing Management Association - Pacific Southwest (SRA) .... AHMA-PSW
Affordable Housing Program [*Federal Home Loan Bank*] .... AHP
Affordable Housing Tax Credit Coalition (NTPA) .... AHTCC
Afforestation (SAUS) .... Affores
Affray [*FBI standardized term*] .... AFFR
Affretair [*Zimbabwe*] [*ICAO designator*] (FAAC) .... AFM
Affrettando [*Hurrying the Pace*] [*Music*] .... AFFRET
Affrettando [*Tenderly*][*Music*] [*Italian*] [*Music*] (BARN) .... affrett
Affrettando [*Hurrying the Pace*] [*Music*] .... AFFRETTO
Affymetrix, Inc. [*NASDAQ symbol*] (SAG) .... AFFX
Affymetrix, Inc. [*Associated Press*] (SAG) .... Affymet
Afghan (ADWA) .... Af
Afghan (SAUS) .... Afg
Afghan Border Cruisade (SAUO) .... ABC
Afghan Border Crusade [*Later, NWFF*] (EA) .... ABC
Afghan Community in America (EA) .... ACA
Afghan Construction Unit Kabul (SAUO) .... ACUK
Afghan Express (SAUS) .... Ghan
Afghan Geodesy and Cartography Office (SAUS) .... ACGO
Afghan Hound Club of America (EA) .... AHCA
Afghan Institute of Technology (SAUO) .... AIT
Afghan National Movement Party [*Political party*] (EY) .... ANMP
Afghan Refugee Aid Committee (AC) .... ARAC
Afghan Refugee Fund (EA) .... ARF
Afghan Refugee Information Network [*British*] [*Defunct*] .... ARIN
Afghan Republican Air Force (SAUS) .... ARAF
Afghan Tourist Organization (MENA) .... ATO
Afghan Youth Council in America (EA) .... AYCA
Afghani [*Monetary unit*] [*Afghanistan*] .... AF
Afghani .... AFG
Afghanistan [*MARC geographic area code*] [*Library of Congress*] (LCCP) .... a-af-
Afghanistan [*MARC country of publication code*] [*Library of Congress*] (LCCP) .... af
Afghanistan [*ANSI three-letter standard code*] (CNC) .... AFG
Afghanistan (ADWA) .... Afg
Afghanistan (VRA) .... Afgh
Afghanistan .... AFGH
Afghanistan Information Center [*Later, ASAP*] (EA) .... AIC
Afghanistan National Liberation Front .... ANLF
Afghanistan Relief Committee (EA) .... ARC
Afghanistan Rural Rehabilitation Programme .... ARRP
Afghanistan Studies Association (EA) .... ASA
Afghanistan-Iran-Pakistan (SAUS) .... A-I-P
Afghanite [*A zeolite*] .... AFG
Afghans (SAUS) .... Afg
AFGL Interactive Meteorological System (SAUS) .... AIMS
AFGL International, Inc. [*NASDAQ symbol*] (SAG) .... AFGL
AFGL Intl. [*NASDAQ symbol*] (TTSB) .... AFGL
Afiamalu [*Samoa Islands*] [*Seismograph station code, US Geological Survey*] (SEIS) .... AFI
AFIWC Data Warehouse (SAUS) .... ADW
AFLAC, Inc. [*NYSE symbol*] (SPSG) .... AFL
AFLAC, Inc. [*Associated Press*] (SAG) .... AFLAC
Aflatoxicol [*Metabolite of AFB*] [*Biochemistry*] .... AFL
Aflatoxin [*A toxic factor*] [*Biochemistry*] (DAVI) .... AF
Aflatoxin [*Mycotoxin*] [*Generic form*] .... AFT
Aflatoxin (SAUS) .... Atlatox
Aflatoxin B [*Mycotoxin*] .... AFB
Aflatoxin G [*Mycotoxin*] .... AFG
Aflatoxin M [*Mycotoxin*] .... AFM
Aflatoxin P [*Mycotoxin*] .... AFP
Aflatoxin Q [*Mycotoxin*] .... AFQ
AFLC Management System Acquisition (SAUS) .... PACER ACQUIRE
AFLC Teletypewriter Communications System (SAUO) .... LOGCOMNET
AFLC/Logistics Management Support Center (SAUO) .... AFMC/LMSC
Afloat (SAUS) .... Aflt
Afloat Command and Control System (CAAL) .... ACCS
Afloat Communications Management Office [*Naval Ship Engineering Center*] (IEEE) .... ACMO
Afloat Consumption Cost and Effectiveness Surveillance System [*Navy*] .... ACCESS

Afloat Consumption, Cost and Effectiveness Surveillance System (SAUO) .... ACCESS
Afloat Contingency Command Center [*Military*] (IUSS) .... ACCC
Afloat Correlation System [*Navy*] .... ACS
Afloat Cryptologic Support System [*Military*] (IUSS) .... ACCS
Afloat Intelligence System Manager Overview (DOMA) .... AISMO
Afloat Planning System [*Navy*] (DOMA) .... APS
Afloat Prepositioned Force (SAUS) .... APF
Afloat Prepositioned Ship [*Navy*] (DOMA) .... APS
Afloat Pre-Positioning Force (ACAE) .... AFP
Afloat Prepositioning Force (DOMA) .... APF
AFloat Prepositioning Ship (DOMA) .... AFS
Afloat Supply Systems Improvement and Support Team (MCD) .... ASSIST
Afloat Training Group (SAUO) .... ATG
Afluidal Variant [*Bacteriology*] .... AFV
Afobaka [*Surinam*] [*ICAO location identifier*] (ICLI) .... SMAF
Afore [*Papua New Guinea*] [*Airport symbol*] (OAG) .... AFR
Aforesaid (SAUS) .... AFS
Aforesaid .... AFSD
AFOS [*Automation of Field Operations and Services*] **Regional Representative** [*National Weather Service*] (NOAA) .... ARR
AFP Imaging [*NASDAQ symbol*] (TTSB) .... AFPC
AFP Imaging Corp. [*Associated Press*] (SAG) .... AFP
AFP Imaging Corp. [*NASDAQ symbol*] (NQ) .... AFPC
AFPS Forecast Working Group (USDC) .... AFWG
afraid (SAUS) .... fraid
Afram Films (NTPA) .... AF
A-Frame .... AF
Africa .... AA
Africa .... AF
Africa .... AFR
Africa (VRA) .... Afr
Africa [*MARC geographic area code*] [*Library of Congress*] (LCCP) .... f----
Africa - Middle East Theater [*World War II*] .... AMET
Africa Air Links [*Sierra Leone*] [*ICAO designator*] (FAAC) .... AFK
Africa and Asia .... AFRASIA
Africa Auxiliary Pioneer Corps (SAUO) .... AAPC
Africa Bibliographic Centre (SAUO) .... ABC
Africa, Central [*MARC geographic area code*] [*Library of Congress*] (LCCP) .... fc---
Africa Church Information Service (EAIO) .... ACIS
Africa Circle and Correspondence Association for Thematicists (EAIO) .... AC & CAT
Africa Committee [*British*] [*World War II*] .... A
Africa Community Technical Service [*Formerly, Red Sea Desert Development*] (AC) .... ACTS
Africa Container Lines (SAUS) .... AFCL
Africa Co-operative Savings and Credit Association (SAUO) .... ACECA
Africa Development Fund (SAUO) .... AFDF
Africa Diary [*A publication*] .... AD
Africa, East [*MARC geographic area code*] [*Library of Congress*] (LCCP) .... fe---
Africa, Eastern Mediterranean and Europe Regional Office (SAUO) .... AEMERO
Africa Economic Digest [*A publication*] .... AED
Africa Educational Trust [*British*] .... AET
Africa Emergency Locust/ Grasshopper Assistance (SAUO) .... AELGA
Africa, Equatorial [*MARC geographic area code*] [*Library of Congress*] (LCCP) .... fq---
Africa (Ethiopia) Committee [*British*] [*World War II*] .... A(E)
Africa, Europe, Middle East of Wetlands International (SAUO) .... AEME
Africa Evangelical Fellowship (EA) .... AEF
Africa Faith and Justice Network (EA) .... AFJN
Africa Food Security Initiative (SAUO) .... AFSI
Africa Fund (SAUO) .... AF
[*The*] **Africa Fund** (EA) .... AF
Africa Guild [*Defunct*] (EA) .... AG
Africa Information Center (SAUO) .... AIC
Africa Inland Church-Hurri Hills Project (SAUO) .... AIC
Africa Inland Mission International (EAIO) .... AIM
Africa Inland Transport [*British*] [*World War II*] .... A(IT)
Africa Institute (SAUO) .... AI
Africa Italiana (journ.) (SAUS) .... AI
Africa Music International [*Lorient, France*] (EAIO) .... AMI
Africa Network [*An association*] (EA) .... AN
Africa Network and Churches Participation in Development (SAUO) .... ANCPD
Africa Network on Churches Participation in Development (SAUO) .... ANCDP
Africa Network on Churches Participation in Development (SAUO) .... ANCPFD
Africa New Zealand Service (SAUO) .... ANZS
Africa News [*A publication*] .... AN
Africa News Service (EA) .... AFRICA NEWS
Africa, North [*MARC geographic area code*] [*Library of Congress*] (LCCP) .... ff---
Africa north of the Tropic of Cancer (SAUS) .... North Africa
Africa Policy Information Center (SAUS) .... APIC
Africa Press Service [*A publication*] .... APS
Africa Project Development Facility [*United Nations*] (EY) .... APDF
Africa Publications Trust [*British*] .... APT
Africa Quarterly (journ.) (SAUS) .... AQ
Africa Report [*A publication*] (BRI) .... Afr Rep
Africa Report [*A publication*] .... Afr Rpt
Africa Report [*A publication*] .... AR
Africa Research and Publications Project (EA) .... ARPP
Africa Research Bulletin [*A publication*] .... ARB
Africa Resource Center (SAUO) .... ARC
Africa Resources Trust .... ART
Africa Service Institute (SAUO) .... ASI
Africa Service Institute of New York [*Defunct*] .... ASI
Africa South of the Sahara [*A publication*] .... AFSS
Africa South of the Sahara [*Military*] (EA) .... ASOTS
Africa, Southern [*MARC geographic area code*] [*Library of Congress*] (LCCP) .... fs---
Africa Special Project (SAUO) .... ASP
Africa, Sub-Saharan [*MARC geographic area code*] [*Library of Congress*] (LCCP) .... fb---
Africa, the Caribbean and the Pacific (SAUS) .... ACP
Africa Today [*A publication*] (BRI) .... Africa T
Africa Trade and Investment Pprogram (SAUO) .... ATRIP
Africa Travel Association (EA) .... ATA
Africa Watch [*An association*] (EA) .... AW
Africa, West [*MARC geographic area code*] [*Library of Congress*] (LCCP) .... fw---
Africa-Asia (or Afro-Asian) Islamic Organization (SAUO) .... AAIO
Africair Service [*Senegal*] [*ICAO designator*] (FAAC) .... FFB
African [*Derogatory nickname for blacks in Zimbabwe and South Africa*] .... Af
African (NTIO) .... Afr
African .... AFRCN
African , Caribbean and Pacific countries (SAUS) .... ACP
African Adult Education Association (SAUO) .... AAEA
African Adult Education Association [*Later, AALAE*] (EAIO) .... AAEA
African Affairs [*A publication*] .... AA
African Affairs Bureau, Accra (SAUO) .... AAB
African African Regional Organization of the International Federation of Commercial, Clerical, Professional and Technical Employees (SAUO) .... AFRO-FIET
African Air Traffic Conference (SAUO) .... AFRATC
African Airlines Association [*Kenya*] (AF) .... AFRAA
African Airlines International Ltd. [*Kenya*] [*ICAO designator*] (FAAC) .... AIK
African American (MELL) .... AA
African American Family History Association (EA) .... AAFHA
African American Labor Center (SAUS) .... AALC
African American Museums Association (EA) .... AAMA
African American Review [*A publication*] (BRI) .... Afr Am R
African American Study of Kidney Diseases and Hypertension Pilot Study (DMAA) .... AASK
African American Travel and Tourism Association (NTPA) .... AATTA
African American Vernacular English [*Language*] .... AAVE
African and Madegascan Organization for Economic Cooperation (SAUO) .... AMOEC
African and Malagasa Esperanto Centre (SAUO) .... AMEC
African and Malagasy Postal and Telecommunications Union (SAUO) .... AMPTU
African and Mauritian Union of Development Banks (EAIO) .... AMUDB
African ans American (SAUS) .... Aframerican
African Anti-Colonial Movement of Kenya .... AACM
African Association for Biological Nitrogen Fixation (SAUO) .... AABNF
African Association for Biological Nitrogen-Fixation [*Egypt*] (EAIO) .... AABNF
African Association for Corres-pondence (or Correspondense) Education (SAUO) .... AACE
African Association for Literacy and Adult Education (EA) .... AALAE
African Association for the Advancement of Science (SAUS) .... AAAST
African Association for the Study of Liver Diseases (EAIO) .... AASLD
African Association of Cartography (EA) .... AAC
African Association of Education for Development (EAIO) .... AFASED
African Association of Liturgy, Music and art (SAUO) .... AALMA
African Association of Tax Administrators (EAIO) .... AATA
African Bank [*South Africa*] .... AFBANK
African Bar Association (EAIO) .... ABA
African Bibliographic Center (EA) .... ABC
African Bibliographic Center, Washington, DC [*Library symbol*] [*Library of Congress*] (LCLS) .... DABC
African Biosciences Network [*International Council of Scientific Unions*] .... ABN
African Business [*A publication*] .... AB
African Business (journ.) (SAUS) .... AGC
African Capacity Building Foundation (ECON) .... ACBF
African, Caribbean, and Pacific Countries [*Associated with the EEC*] (AF) .... ACP
African, Caribbean and Pacific Group of States (SAUO) .... ACP Group
African, Caribbean and Pacific States (SAUO) .... ACP States
African Cassanova Mosaic Disease [*Botany*] .... ACMD
African Cavalry Guard [*British military*] (DMA) .... ACG
African Center for Meteorological Applications to Development (SAUS) .... ACMAD
African Center (or Centre) for Technology Studies (SAUO) .... ACTS
African Centre for Applied Research and Training in Social Developement (SAUO) .... ACARTSOD
African Centre for Applied Research and Training in Social Development (EAIO) .... ACARTSD
African Centre for Technology Studies (SAUO) .... AACTS
African Centre for Technology Studies [*Kenya*] (EAIO) .... ACTS
African Centre for/of Meteorological Applications for Development (SAUO) .... ACMAD
African Civil Aviation Commission [*See also CAFAC*] (EAIO) .... AFCAC
African Coastal Security (DOMA) .... ACS
African Coasters [*Steamship*] (MHDB) .... AC
African Colonial Forces [*British military*] (DMA) .... ACF
African Commission on Agricultural Statistics (EA) .... ACAS
African Commission on Agricultural Statistics [*Ghana*] (EAIO) .... AFCAS
African Commune of Bad Relevant Artists [*Chicago*] .... AFRICOBRA
African Communications Liaison Service (EA) .... ACLS
African Communist (SAUO) .... AC
African Comprehensive Party [*Jamaica*] [*Political party*] (EY) .... ACP
African Computer Institute (SAUO) .... ACI
African Confederation of Cooperative Savings and Credit Associations [*See also ACECA*] [*Nairobi, Kenya*] (EAIO) .... ACCOSCA
African Conservation Trust (SAUO) .... ACT
African Continental Bank Ltd. .... ACB

African Cooperative Alliance (SAUO) ... ACA
African Cooperative Savings and Credit Association [*See also ACECA*] [*Later, ACCOSCA*] (EAIO) ... ACOSCA
African Council of Food and Nutrition Sciences (SAUO) ... AFRONUS
African Council on Remote Sensing (SAUO) ... ACRS
African Cultural Centre (SAUO) ... ACE
African Cultural Foundation (EA) ... ACF
African Curriculum Organisation (AIE) ... ACO
African Defence Federation (SAUO) ... ADF
African Democratic Party [*Political party*] ... ADP
African Development [*A publication*] ... AFD
African Development Bank [*Also, AfDB*] ... ADB
African Development Bank (SAUO) ... ADB
African Development Bank [*Also, ADB*] (EY) ... AfDB
African Development Bank (SAUO) ... AIDB
African Development Foundation (EGAO) ... ADF
African Development Fund ... AFDF
African Development Fund (SAUO) ... AIDF
African Development Information Association (SAUO) ... ADIA
African Division (SAUO) ... ADiv
African Drought Monitoring Integrative Technique (SAUS) ... ADMIT
African Economic Affairs Committee [*London*] [*World War II*] ... AEA
African Economic Development News [*Kenya*] [*A publication*] (EY) ... AEDN
African Economic Research Consortium ... AERC
African EDIFACT Board (SAUS) ... AFEB
African Elected Members Organization ... AEMO
African Elephant and Rhino Specialist Group [*of the International Union for Conservation of Nature and Natural Resources*] (EA) ... AERSG
African Elephant and Rhino Specialist Group (SAUO) ... AFRSG
African Elephant Conservation Coordinating Group ... AECCG
African Elephant Conservation Coordinating (or Coordination) Group (SAUO) ... AECCG
African Elephant Conservation Group (SAUO) ... AECG
African English (SAUS) ... Afr Eng
African Entomology (SAUS) ... Afr Entomol
African Environmental Research and Consulting Group (SAUO) ... AERGC
African Export Import Bank ... AFREXIMBANK
African Farmers Committee [*See also CPA*] (EAIO) ... AFC
African Financial Community (SAUO) ... AFC
African Financial Community (SAUO) ... CFA
African Football Association (SAUO) ... AFA
African Football Confederation (EAIO) ... AFC
African Force Headquarters [*World War II*] ... AFHQ
African Forestry Commission [*UN Food and Agriculture Organization*] ... AFC
African Friends Service Committee (SAUO) ... AFSC
African Graduate Fellowship Program [*African-American Institute*] (AEBS) ... AFGRAD
African Green Monkey Immunodeficiency Virus ... AGMIV
African Green Monkey Kidney [*Type of cell line*] ... AGMK
African Green Monkey Kidney [*Type of cell line*] [*Medicine*] (DMAA) ... AGMkK
African Green Monkeys [*Virology*] ... AGM
African Groundnut Council [*See also CAA*] [*Nigeria*] ... AGC
African Heritage Center for African Dance and Music (EA) ... AHCADM
African Heritage Federation of the Americas [*Defunct*] (EA) ... AHFA
African Heritage Studies Association (EA) ... AHSA
African Horse Sickness [*Medicine*] (DMAA) ... AHS
African Horsesickness Virus [*Veterinary medicine*] ... AHSV
African Household Survey Capability Programme [*United Nations*] (EY) ... AHSCP
African Human Rights Research Association [*Formerly, African Human Rights Study Group*] (EA) ... AHRA
African Human Rights Research Association (SAUO) ... AHRA
African Imprint Library Services, Bedford, NY [*Library symbol*] [*Library of Congress*] (LCLS) ... AfrI
African Index Medicus (SAUO) ... AIM
African India Ocean Region [*USTTA*] (TAG) ... AFI
African Institute for Economic Development and Planning (SAUS) ... AICB
African Institute for Economic Development and Planning (SAUO) ... IDEP
African Institute for Economic Planning of the United Nations (SAUO) ... IDEP
African Institute of Human Rights (EAIO) ... AIHR
African Integrated Malaria Initiative (SAUO) ... AIMI
African Intellectual Property Organization (SAUO) ... AIPO
African Inter-Ministerial Committee for Food (SAUO) ... AIMCF
African International Airlines [*Lesotho*] [*ICAO designator*] (FAAC) ... AFN
African International Airways [*Swaziland*] [*ICAO designator*] (FAAC) ... AIN
African International Airways (West Africa) Ltd. [*Nigeria*] [*FAA designator*] (FAAC) ... ROB
African International Movement of Catholic Students (EA) ... AIMCS
African International Reservation System (PDAA) ... AIRS
African Internet Development Action Team [*South Africa*] (DDC) ... AIDAT
African Irrigated Rice Advanced Trial (SAUO) ... AIRAT
African Irrigated Rice Observational Nursery (SAUO) ... AIRON
African Irrigated Rice Preliminary Screening Set (SAUO) ... AIRPSS
African Jazz Art Society Studios ... AJASS
African Journal of Ecology (SAUS) ... Afr J Ecol
African Journal of Medical Practice [*A publication*] ... AJMP
African Journal of Reproductive Health (SAUS) ... AJRH
African Journal of the Health Sciences [*A publication*] ... AJHS
African Language Review [*A publication*] ... ALR
African Language Studies (journ.) (SAUS) ... AfrLS
African Languages Association of Southern Africa (SAUO) ... ALASA
African Law Association in America (SAUO) ... ALAA
African Law Association in America [*Later, INTWORLSA*] (EA) ... ALAA
African Law Digest [*A publication*] (ILCA) ... African LD
African Law Reports [*A publication*] (DLA) ... Afr LR
African Law Reports, Appellate Division [*A publication*] (DLA) ... AD
African Law Reports, Commercial Series [*A publication*] (DLA) ... African LR Comm
African Law Reports, Malawi Series [*A publication*] (DLA) ... African LR Mal
African Law Reports, Malawi Series [*A publication*] (DLA) ... Afr LR Mal Ser
African Law Reports, Malawi Series [*A publication*] (DLA) ... ALR Mal
African Law Reports, Malawi Series [*A publication*] (DLA) ... ALR (Malawi Ser)
African Law Reports, Sierra Leone Series [*A publication*] (DLA) ... African LRSL
African Law Reports, Sierra Leone Series [*A publication*] (DLA) ... Afr LR Sierre L Ser
African Law Reports, Sierra Leone Series [*A publication*] (DLA) ... ALR (Sierra L Ser)
African Law Reports, Sierra Leone Series [*A publication*] (DLA) ... ALRSL
African Law Studies [*A publication*] (DLA) ... Af L Studies
African Liberation Front (SAUO) ... ALF
African Library [*Belgium Ministry of Foreign Affairs*] [*Information service or system*] (CRD) ... AFLI
African Literature Association (EA) ... ALA
African Love Bird Society (EA) ... ALBS
African Lowland Rice Evaluation and Screening Set (SAUO) ... ALRESS
African Magnetic Mapping Project (SAUS) ... AMMP
African Mathematical Union (EA) ... AMU
African Medical and Research Foundation (SAUS) ... AM&RF
African Medical and Research Foundation (EA) ... AMRF
African Medical and Research Foundation, USA (EA) ... AMREF
African Metals Corporation Limited (SAUO) ... AMCL
African Methodist Episcopal [*Church*] ... AME
African Methodist Episcopal Church (SAUO) ... AFMEC
African Methodist Episcopal Church (SAUO) ... AMECH
African Methodist Episcopal Mission (SAUO) ... AMEM
African Methodist Episcopal Mission ... AMEM
African Methodist Episcopal Zion [*Church*] ... AMEZ
African Methodist Episcopal Zion Church (SAUO) ... AMEZC
African Mineworkers Union (SAUO) ... AMU
African Mineworkers Union (SAUO) ... AMWU
African Ministerial (or Ministers) Conference on the Environment (SAUO) ... AMCEN
African Mountains Association (SAUS) ... AMA
African National Action (SAUO) ... ANA
African National Congress [*South Africa*] (PD) ... ANC
African National Congress of South Africa ... ANCSA
African National Congress Youth League [*South Africa*] (PD) ... ANCYL
African National Council (SAUO) ... Afr Nat Cnl
African National Council [*Later, UANC*] [*Zimbabwe*] [*Political party*] (PPW) ... ANC
African National People's Empire Re-Established (EA) ... AFANPERA
African Nationalist Pioneer Movement [*Defunct*] ... ANPM
African Nations' Cup [*Soccer*] ... ANC
African Network (SAUO) ... AN
African Network for Public Administration and Management (SAUS) ... ANPAM
African Network for Scientific and Technological Institutions (SAUS) ... ANSTI
African Network for the Development and Ecological Agriculture (SAUO) ... ANDEA
African Network for/of Administrative Information (SAUO) ... ANAI
African Network of Administrative Information (SAUO) ... ANA
African Network of Administrative Information [*Information service or system*] (IID) ... ANAI
African Network of Scientific and Technological Institutes [*Kenya*] [*Research center*] ... ANSTI
African Network on Churches Participation in Development (SAUO) ... ANCPD
African Networks for Health Research & Development (SAUO) ... AFRO-NETS
African News Bulletin [*A publication*] ... ANB
African News Service (SAUO) ... ANS
African NGOs [*Nongovernmental Organizations*] **Environment Network** (EAIO) ... ANEN
African NGOs Environment Network (SAUS) ... ANEN
African Notes [*Ibadan*] [*A publication*] ... AN
African Organization for Cartography and Remote Sensing (SAUO) ... AOCARS
African Organization of Supreme Audit Institutions [*Lome, Togo*] (EAIO) ... AFROSAI
African Peanut (Groundnut) Council ... APC
African People's Democratic Union of South Africa (PD) ... Apdusa
African Peoples Movement (SAUS) ... APM
African People's Organization (WDAA) ... APO
African People's Party [*Kenya*] (AF) ... APP
African Postal (or Posts) and Telecommunications Union (SAUO) ... APTU
African Postal Union (SAUO) ... AFPU
African Preferential Trade Area (SAUS) ... PTA
African pygmy (SAUS) ... baka
African Refugee Housing Action Group [*British*] ... ARHAG
African Region Traffic Analysis Forecasting Group [*ICAO*] (DA) ... ATAFG
African Regional Agricultural Credit Association (EAIO) ... AFRACA
African Regional Agricultural (or Agriculture) Credit Association (SAUO) ... AFRACA
African Regional Centre for Engineering Design and Manufacturing (SAUO) ... AECEDEM
African Regional Centre for Engineering Design and Manufacturing (EA) ... ARCEDEM
African Regional Centre for Technology [*See also CRAT*] (EA) ... ARCT
African Regional Coordinating Committee for the Integration of Women in Development (SAUO) ... ARCC
African Regional Documentation Centre on Communication Research and Policies (SAUO) ... ACCE/CDR Documentation Centre
African Regional Documentation Centre on Communication Research and Policies (SAUO) ... ACCE/ICDR Documentation Centre
African Regional Office (SAUO) ... AFRO
African Regional Organization for Standardization [*Kenya*] ... ARSO

African Regional Organization of the Public Services and Teachers (SAUO) ... AFROFEDOP
African Regional Trade Information System [*ECA*] [*United Nations*] (DUND) ... ARTIS
African Reinsurance Corporation (SAUO) ... AFRICA RE
African Research Foundation (EA) ... ARF
African Research Institute [*La Trobe University*] [*Australia*] ... ARI
African Research Network for Agricultural Byproducts (SAUO) ... ARNAB
African Resistance Movement [*South Africa*] (PD) ... ARM
African Rhino Group (EA) ... ARG
African Rice Blast Nursery (SAUO) ... ARBN
African Safari Airways (SAUS) ... QS
African Safari Airways Ltd. [*Kenya*] [*ICAO designator*] (FAAC) ... QSC
African Safari Club of Philadelphia (EA) ... ASCP
African Satellite ... AFROSAT
African Scholarship Program of American Universities [*Joint undertaking, headquartered in Cambridge, MA, to provide aid to African applicants for admission to American universities*] ... ASPAU
African Scientific Institute (EA) ... ASI
African Sleeping Sickness [*Medicine*] (MELL) ... ASS
African Social and Environmental Studies Programme [*Formerly, African Social Studies Programme*] [*Kenya*] (EAIO) ... ASSP
African Social Studies Programme (SAUO) ... AASP
African Social Studies Programme (EA) ... ASSP
African Society for Cultural Relationship to Independent Africa (SAUO) ... ASCRIA
African Society for Human Rights [*Defunct*] (EA) ... ASHR
African Special Project (SAUS) ... ASP
African Star [*Decoration*] [*British*] ... AS
African Starvation and Hunger Relief Fund (EA) ... ASHRF
African Steamship Company (SAUO) ... ASC
African Studies [*Johannesburg*] [*A publication*] ... AFS
African Studies and Research Program [*Howard University*] [*Research center*] (RCD) ... ASRP
African Studies Association (EA) ... ASA
African Studies Association, Brandeis University, Waltham, MA [*Library symbol*] [*Library of Congress*] (LCLS) ... MWalAF
African Studies Association of Australasia & the Pacific (SAUO) ... AFSAAP
African Studies Association United Kingdom ... ASAUK
African Studies Bulletin (journ.) (SAUS) ... ASB
African Studies Center [*Michigan State University*] [*Research center*] (RCD) ... ASC
African Studies Centre (SAUO) ... ASC
African Studies (journ.) (SAUS) ... AfrS
African Succulent Plant Society [*Defunct*] (EA) ... ASPS
African Swine Fever [*Veterinary medicine*] ... ASF
African Swine Fever Virus ... ASFV
African Swine Pox [*Medicine*] (DMAA) ... ASP
African Technical Association (SAUO) ... ATA
African Technical Regional Environment Group (SAUS) ... ATREG
African Telecommunication Union (SAUO) ... ATU
African Timber Organization (EAIO) ... ATO
African Trade Union Confederation [*Later, OATUU*] ... ATUC
African Trades Union Congress of Southern Rhodesia ... ATUC(SR)
African Training and Research Centre For Women (SAUS) ... ATRCW
African Transair [*Nigeria*] [*FAA designator*] (FAAC) ... FTS
African Union for Scientific Development (SAUO) ... AUSD
African Union of Physics [*See also UAP*] (EAIO) ... AUP
African Unity Organisation (SAUO) ... AUO
African Upland Rice Advanced Trial (SAUO) ... AURAT
African Upland Rice Observational Nursery (SAUO) ... AURON
African Upland Rice Preliminary Screening Set (SAUO) ... AURPSS
African Violet Association of Australia ... AVAA
African Violet Society of America (EA) ... AVSA
African West Air [*Senegal*] [*ICAO designator*] (FAAC) ... AFC
African West Air [*Senegal*] [*ICAO designator*] (FAAC) ... AWA
African Wild Dog Conservation Fund (SAUO) ... AWDCF
African Wildlife Foundation (EA) ... AWF
African Wildlife Leadership Foundation ... AWLF
African Wildlife Resource (SAUO) ... AWR
African Workers Federation [*Kenya*] (AF) ... AWF
African Writers Series [*A publication*] ... AWS
Africana Bulletin [*Warsaw*] [*A publication*] ... AB
Africana Bulletin [*Warsaw*] [*A publication*] ... Africana
Africana Research Bulletin (journ.) (SAUS) ... ARB
African-American (BEE) ... Afro-Amer
African-American (SAUS) ... Afro-American
African-American Almanac [*A publication*] ... AAA
African-American English [*A dialect*] ... AAE
African-American Historical and Cultural Society (EA) ... AAHCS
African-American Institute (EA) ... AAI
African-American, Latino, Asian and Native American (SAUS) ... ALANA
African-American Library and Information Science Association ... AALISA
African-American Natural Foods Association (EA) ... AANFA
African-American Reference Library [*A publication*] ... AARL
African-American Scholars Conference [*Defunct*] (EA) ... AASC
African-American Women's Clergy Association (NTPA) ... AAWCA
African-American Women's Clergy Association (EA) ... AWCA
African-Atlantic Coast Association of Round Tables ... AACART
African-Belgian-American Diamond Industry S.A. (SAUO) ... ABADISA
African-Canadian Council (AC) ... ACC
African-Eurasian Migratory Waterbird Agreement (SAUS) ... AEWA
African/Indian Ocean [*Aviation*] ... AFI
Africanized Honey Bee ... AHB
Afrihili [*MARC language code*] [*Library of Congress*] (LCCP) ... afh
Afrika Malagasa Esperanto-Centro (SAUO) ... AMEC
Afrikaans (ADWA) ... Afk
Afrikaans [*MARC language code*] [*Library of Congress*] (LCCP) ... afr
Afrikaans ... AFRIK
Afrikaans (ADWA) ... Afrik
Afrikaans English (SAUS) ... Afrik Eng
Afrikan Airlines Ltd. (SAUO) ... KW
Afrikaner Volkfront [*An association*] ... AVF
Afrikaner Weerstandsbeweging [*Afrikaner Resistance Movement*] [*South Africa*] [*Political party*] (ECON) ... AWB
Afrique Equatoriale Francaise [*French Equatorial Africa*] [*French*] (AF) ... AEF
Afrique Occidentale Francaise [*French West Africa*] [*French*] ... AOF
Afriwest Airlines Ltd. [*Nigeria*] [*FAA designator*] (FAAC) ... AFW
Afro International Ent. Ltd. [*Nigeria*] [*FAA designator*] (FAAC) ... AOR
Afro Unity Airways [*Benin*] [*ICAO designator*] (FAAC) ... AFU
Afro-Academic Cultural Technological and Scientific Olympics (SAUS) ... ACT SO
Afro-American Art Institute (EA) ... AAAI
Afro-American Association of Performing Artists (EA) ... AAAPA
Afro-American Cultural and Historical Society [*Later, AACHSM*] ... AACHS
Afro-American Cultural and Historical Society Museum (EA) ... AACHSM
Afro-American Cultural Foundation (EA) ... AACF
Afro-American Cultural Technological Scientific Olympics ... ACT-SO
Afro-American Historical and Genealogical Society (EA) ... AAHGS
Afro-American Liberation Army (SAUO) ... AALA
Afro-American Men Against Narcotics (SAUS) ... A-A MAN
Afro-American Museum (SAUS) ... A-AM
Afro-American Museum of Detroit (EA) ... AAM
Afro-American Music Foundation (EA) ... AAMF
Afro-American Music Opportunities Association (EA) ... AAMOA
Afro-American Police League (EA) ... AAPL
Afro-American Policemens League (SAUS) ... AAPL
Afro-American Purchasing Center (PDAA) ... AAPC
Afro-American Resources and Library Manpower Project [*Columbia University*] (NITA) ... AARLMP
Afro-American Society for International Relations (EA) ... AASIR
Afro-American Student Association (EA) ... AASA
Afro-American Student Union (SAUO) ... AASU
Afro-American Students Society (SAUO) ... AASS
Afro-American Studies Librarians Section [*Association of College and Research Libraries*] ... AASLS
Afro-American Studies Librarians Section [*Association of College and Research Libraries*] ... AFAS
Afro-Asian Center (EA) ... AAC
Afro-Asian Documentation Centre (SAUO) ... AADC
Afro-Asian Documentation Service (SAUO) ... AADS
Afro-Asian Housing Organization [*Cairo, Egypt*] (EAIO) ... AAHO
Afro-Asian Journalists' Association (NATG) ... AAJA
Afro-Asian Latin-American Students Organization (SAUS) ... AALASO
Afro-Asian Lawyers' Conference (NATG) ... AALC
Afro-Asian Organization for Economic Cooperation ... AFRASEC
Afro-Asian People's Solidarity Organization [*Cairo, Egypt*] (EAIO) ... AAPSO
Afro-Asian Reconstruction Organization (SAUO) ... AARO
Afro-Asian Rural Construction Organisation (SAUO) ... AARCO
Afro-Asian Rural Reconstruction Organization [*New Delhi, India*] ... AARRO
Afro-Asian Rural Reconstruction Organization (EAIO) ... ARRO
Afro-Asian Solidarity Organization (NATG) ... AASO
Afro-Asian Solidarity Secretariat (NATG) ... AASS
Afro-Asian Workers' Organization (NATG) ... AAWO
Afro-Asian Workers Organization (SAUS) ... AAWO
Afro-Asian Workers Organization, Djarkarta (SAUO) ... AAWO
Afro-Asian Writers' Permanent Bureau (NATG) ... AAWPB
Afro-Asian Youth Solidarity Organization (NATG) ... AAYSO
Afro-Asiatic [*MARC language code*] [*Library of Congress*] (LCCP) ... afa
Afro-Brasiliero (SAUS) ... Afro-Bras
Afro-Caribbean (SAUS) ... Afro-Carib
Afro-Caribbean Action Group [*British*] ... ACAG
Afro-Caribbean Alliance [*British*] ... ACA
Afro-Caribbean Educational Resource Centre [*British*] ... ACER
Afro-Caribbean Educational Resource Project (AIE) ... ACER
Afro-Hispanic Institute (EA) ... AHI
Afrolit Society [*Defunct*] (EAIO) ... AS
Afro-Malagasy Common Organization (SAUS) ... OCAM
Afro-Mauritian Common Organization ... AMCO
Afro-Mediterranean Orbital System [*Israel*] ... AMOS
Afro-Saxon (SAUS) ... Af Sax
Afro-Shirazi Party [*Zanzibar*] ... ASP
Afro-Shirazi Party [*Tanzania*] (AF) ... ASP
Afro-Shirazi Youth League [*Tanzania*] (AF) ... ASYL
AFS [*American Field Service*] **International-Intercultural Programs** (CDAI) ... AFSIIP
AFS International/Intercultural Programs Inc. (SAUO) ... AFS
AFSA Consumer Credit Education Foundation [*Formerly, Consumer Credit Education Foundation*] (EA) ... CCEF
Afsala Bancorp, Inc. [*NASDAQ symbol*] (SAG) ... AFED
Afsala Bancorp, Inc. [*Associated Press*] (SAG) ... AfsalaBc
AFSC Data Tie Line Network (SAUS) ... SYSDATA
AFSC Technical Information Center, Washington, DC [*OCLC symbol*] (OCLC) ... SCH
AFSC Voice Tie Line Network (SAUS) ... SYSVOICE
Aft ... A
Aft Across the Hatch [*Stowage*] (DNAB) ... A/AC
Aft Cargo Carrier (IEEE) ... ACC
Aft Cargo Compartment (MCD) ... ACC
Aft Crew Station [*NASA*] (MCD) ... ACS

Aft End Assembly	AEA
Aft End Cone [*NASA*] (NASA)	AEC
Aft Engineering Operating Station (DNAB)	AEOS
Aft Equipment Bay [*NASA*] (KSC)	AEB
Aft Events Controller [*NASA*] (MCD)	AEC
Aft Flight Deck (NASA)	AFD
Aft Flight Deck Control Panel (MCD)	AFDCP
Aft Flight Deck Operator (MCD)	AFDO
Aft Flight Deck Power Distribution Box (MCD)	AFDPDB
Aft Frame Tilt Actuator [*Aviation*] (NASA)	AFTA
Aft Fuselage (NASA)	AF
Aft Left (MCD)	AL
Aft Load Control Assembly (MCD)	ALCA
Aft Load Controller (MCD)	ALC
Aft Master Events Controller [*NASA*] (NASA)	AMEC
Aft Motor Control Assembly (NASA)	AMCA
Aft or Forward (SAUS)	a or f
Aft Peak Tank [*Shipping*]	APT
Aft Perpendicular [*Naval engineering*]	AP
Aft Power Controller (MCD)	APC
Aft Power Controller Assembly [*NASA*] (MCD)	APCA
Aft Propulsion Subsystem (SAUS)	APS
Aft Propulsion System [*or Subsystem*] [*NASA*] (NASA)	APS
Aft Provision Stage (ACAE)	APF
Aft Reaction Control Subsystem (SAUS)	ARCS
Aft Reaction Control System [*or Subsystem*] [*NASA*] (NASA)	ARCS
Aft Right (MCD)	AR
Aft Shroud (SAUS)	AS
Aft Station Command and Data Systems (SAUS)	ASCADS
Aft Utility Bridge (NASA)	AUB
After	A
After (KSC)	AFT
After (VRA)	aft
After Acid Treatment (SAUS)	AAT
After Action Report [*Military*]	AAR
After Action Review [*Military*] (MCD)	AAR
After All [*Message handling*]	AA
After Arrival	AA
After Arrival (MARI)	aa
After Beginning of Time (SAUS)	ABT
After Body	AB
After Born Antibiotic [*Medicine*] (MELL)	ABA
After Bottom Center [*Valve position*]	ABC
After Bottom Center (or Centre) (SAUS)	ABC
After Bottom Dead Center [*Valve position*]	ABDC
After Bulkhead in Hatch [*Stowage*] (DNAB)	AF/B
after cant frames (SAUS)	a cant
After Care Association of New South Wales [*Australia*]	ACANSW
After Christ	AC
After Clean Inspection (AAEL)	ACI
After Conning Position [*British military*] (DMA)	ACP
After Cooler	AFTCLR
After Dark [*NWS*] (FAAC)	AFDK
After Date [*Business term*]	AD
After Date (EBF)	ad
After Date of Award (MCD)	ADAD
After Date of Award of Contract [*Telecommunications*] (TEL)	ADA
After Deducting Freight [*Billing*]	ADF
After Delivery Economies	ADE
After Develop Inspection (AAEL)	ADI
After Diastase Digestion [*Biochemistry*] (DAVI)	PASD
After Digital [*Post-computer revolution*]	AD
After Dinner Opera Co.	ADOCo
After Diversity Demand (IAA)	ADD
After Drain (SAUS)	AD
After Effective Date of Contract (ACAE)	AEDOC
After Egg Laying (DB)	AEL
After End [*Naval engineering*] (DAS)	AE
After End of the Hatch [*Stowage*] (DNAB)	AF/E
After Engine Room	AER
After Engineering Operating Station (CAAL)	AEOS
After England Failed [*Soldier slang for American Expeditionary Force in World War I*]	AEF
After Etch Inspection (AAEL)	AEI
After Extra Time (WDAA)	AET
After Flame Ratio (SAUS)	AFR
After Ford [*Calendar used in Aldous Huxley's novel, "Brave New World;" refers to Henry Ford*]	AF
After Full Moon [*Freemasonry*] (ROG)	AFM
After Glucose Infusion Started [*Biochemistry*] (DAVI)	POSG
After Goetz [*A reference to "vigilante" Bernhard Goetz, who shot four youths on a New York subway in 1984 after allegedly being threatened by them*] [*See also BG*]	AG
After Hangup (SAUS)	AHU
After Hatch [*Shipping*]	AH
After Hours (ADA)	AH
After Image [*Psychology*]	AI
After Image-Datei (SAUS)	AFIM-Datei
After Initial Release (MCD)	AIR
After Inspection (SAUS)	ai
After Japan [*Industry*]	AJ
After Market [*Investment term*]	AM
After New Moon [*Freemasonry*] (ROG)	ANM
After Orders (MCD)	AO
After Overhaul Inspection	AOHI

After Parturition (SAUS)	AP
After Passage (SAUS)	APSG
After Passing [*ICAO*] (FAAC)	APSG
After Peak (MSA)	AP
After Peak Bulkhead [*Shipping*] (DS)	APBH
After Peak Tank (SAUS)	APT
After Perpendicular (SAUS)	AP
After Power Unit (SAUS)	APU
After Puparium Formation [*Entomology*]	APF
After Quarter Day [*Freemasonry*] (ROG)	A Qr D
After Receipt of Funds (SAUS)	ARF
After Receipt of Order	ARO
After Receipt of Proposal	ARP
After Right (SAUS)	AR
After Sale Assurance Program	ASAP
After Sale Price	ASP
After Sales Manager (DCTA)	ASM
After Sight (EBF)	as
After Sight (EBF)	A/S
After Sight (SAUS)	AS
After Tax Cash Flow	ATCF
After the Christian Era (BJA)	ACE
After the Dish [*Description of TV viewing via satellite transmission vs traditional or cable TV*] (PS)	AD
After the Fact (MCD)	ATF
After Top Center [*Valve position*]	ATC
After Top Dead Center [*Valve position*]	ATDC
After Torpedo Room	ATRM
After Total (SAUS)	Aft Tot
After Women or Liquor [*Slang*]	AWOL
Afterbirth (MELL)	AB
Afterburner (AFIT)	A3
Afterburner [*on jet engines*]	AB
Afterburner [*on jet engines*]	AFTB
Afterburner Control (SAUS)	AB/C
Afterburner Pump (SAUS)	AB/P
Afterburning Turbojet (SAUS)	ABTJ
After-Care Instructions [*Medicine*] (DAVI)	ACI
Aftercoming Head [*Obstetrics*]	ACH
Aftercooled [*Automotive engineering*]	A
After-Death Communication	ADC
After-Depolarization [*Neurophysiology*]	ADP
Afterdischarge [*Electrophysiology*]	AD
After-Effect [*Medicine*] (DB)	AE
After-Hyperpolarization [*Also, AHP*] [*Neurophysiology*]	AH
Afterhyperpolarization [*Also, AH*] [*Neurophysiology*]	AHP
Afterloaded Quick Release [*Physiology*]	AQR
Aftermarket Body Parts Association (EA)	ABPA
Aftermarket Body Parts Distributors Association [*Later, ABPA*] (EA)	ABPDA
Aftermarket Technology [*NASDAQ symbol*] (SG)	ATAC
Aftermarket Technology Corp. [*Associated Press*] (SAG)	Aftmarkt
Aftermarket Technology Corp. [*NASDAQ symbol*] (SAG)	ATAC
Aftermath (SAUS)	A
Afternoon	A
Afternoon	AFT
Afternoon (WDMC)	aft
Afternoon (FAAC)	AFTN
Afternoon (ROG)	ARNOON
Afterpiece Kisser [*Slang*] [*Bowdlerized version*]	AK
Aftersight [*Billing*]	AS
Aftertouch (SAUS)	AT
Afterwards (ROG)	AFTWDS
Afterwards (ROG)	ARWDS
Afton, OK [*Location identifier*] [*FAA*] (FAAL)	AGB
Afton Star-Enterprise, Afton, IA [*Library symbol*] [*Library of Congress*] (LCLS)	IaAfSE
Afton, WY [*Location identifier*] [*FAA*] (FAAL)	AFO
Afton, WY [*AM radio station call letters*]	KRSV
Afton, WY [*FM radio station call letters*]	KRSV-FM
Afton, WY [*FM radio station call letters*] (BROA)	KUWA-FM
Afunctional Neutrophil (DMAA)	AFN
Afwaj al-Muqawimah al-Lubnaniyah [*Lebanese Resistance Battalions*]	AMAL
AFWAL [*Air Force Wright Aeronautical Laboratories*] Technical Information Center, Wright-Patterson AFB, OH [*OCLC symbol*] (OCLC)	SCW
AFWL [*Air Force Weapons Laboratory*] LASER Engineering and Applications to Prototype Systems (MCD)	AFWL/LEAPS
Afyon [*Turkey*] [*Airport symbol*] (AD)	AFY
Afyon [*Turkey*] [*ICAO location identifier*] (ICLI)	LTAH
AG Associates [*NASDAQ symbol*] (TTSB)	AGAI
AG Associates, Inc. [*NASDAQ symbol*] (SAG)	AGAI
AG Associates, Inc. [*Associated Press*] (SAG)	AG Asc
Ag Electronics Association (NTPA)	AEA
Ag Services of America, Inc. [*NASDAQ symbol*] (SAG)	AGSV
Ag Services of America, Inc. [*Associated Press*] (SAG)	AgSvcs
Ag Services of America, Inc. [*NYSE symbol*] (SAG)	ASV
Aga Khan Foundation [*Switzerland*] (EAIO)	AKF
Aga Khan Fund for Economic Development	AKFED
Aga Khan University [*Karachi, Pakistan*]	AKU
Agada (BJA)	Ag
Agades [*Niger*] [*Airport symbol*] (OAG)	AJY
Agades-Sud [*Niger*] [*ICAO location identifier*] (ICLI)	DRZA
Agadir [*Morocco*] [*Airport symbol*] (OAG)	AGA
Agadir/Inezgane [*Morocco*] [*ICAO location identifier*] (ICLI)	GMAA
Again [*Telecommunications*] (TEL)	AG
Again	AGN

Against (ROG)	AG
Against (EBF)	ag
Against (ROG)	AGNST
Against	AGST
Against (ADWA)	agst
Against	AGT
Against (EBF)	Contra
Against Actuals (NUMA)	AA
Against All Risks [Business term] (EBF)	aar
Against All Risks [Insurance]	AAR
Against All Risks [Marine] (EBF)	ar
Against All Risks [Marine] (EBF)	A/R
Against Apion [Josephus] (BJA)	AgAp
Against Apion [Josephus] (BJA)	JAp
Against Apion [Josephus] (BJA)	JosApion
Against Drunk Driving [Also, The Neil Gray Memorial Fund] (AC)	ADD
Against Grain	AG
Against Gravity (HGAA)	AG
Against Investment Discrimination (SAUO)	AID
Against Leocrates [of Lycurgus] [Classical studies] (OCD)	Leoc
Against Leptines [of Demosthenes] [Classical studies] (OCD)	Lept
Against Manufacturing Defects [Automotive engineering]	AMD
Against Medical Advice	AMA
Against Meidias [of Demosthenes] [Classical studies] (OCD)	Meid
Against Testing on Mururoa [An association] [Australia]	ATOM
Against Tests on Moruroa (SAUO)	ATOM
Against Wind (SAUS)	A/W
Agamemnon [of Aeschylus] [Classical studies] (OCD)	Ag
Agammaglobulinemia [Medicine]	AGG
Agammaglobulinemia Leukemia [Medicine] (DAVI)	AGG
Agana [Diocesan abbreviation] [Guam] (TOCD)	AGN
Agana (SAUS)	ZUA
Agana, GU [Television station call letters]	KGTF
Agana, GU [AM radio station call letters]	KGUM
Agana, GU [FM radio station call letters]	KOKU
Agana, GU [FM radio station call letters] (RBYB)	KPRG
Agana, GU [FM radio station call letters]	KSTO
Agana, GU [AM radio station call letters]	KTWG
Agana, GU [AM radio station call letters]	KUAM
Agana, GU [FM radio station call letters]	KUAM-FM
Agana, GU [Television station call letters]	KUAM-TV
Agana, GU [FM radio station call letters]	KZGZ
Agana, GU [Location identifier] [FAA] (FAAL)	ZUA
Agana, Guam [Television station call letters] (BROA)	KAXM
Agana Naval Air Station [FAA] (TAG)	NGM
Agana Naval Air Station, Guam Island [Mariana Islands] [ICAO location identifier] (ICLI)	PGUM
Agape Force (EA)	AF
Agar [Biochemistry] (DAVI)	a
Agar Gel Diffusion (SAUS)	AGD
Agar Gel Double Diffusion [Medicine] (DMAA)	AGDD
Agar Gel Immunodiffusion Test (SAUS)	AGDT
Agar Gel Precipitation [Biochemistry] (DMAA)	AGP
Agar Gel Precipitin Inhibition (DMAA)	AGPI
Agar GelI Immunodiffusion [Veterinary medicine]	AGID
Agar Immersion, Plating, and Contact (PDAA)	AIPC
Agar-Gel Diffusion [Clinical chemistry]	AGD
Agar-Gel Diffusion Test [Clinical chemistry] (MAE)	ADT
Agar-gel Diffusion Test (SAUS)	ADT
Agar-Gel Precipitation Test [Clinical chemistry]	AGPT
Agarose (DB)	AG
Agarose Diffusion [Method] [Cardiology] (DAVI)	AGD
Agarose Diffusion Method [Medical device safety test]	ADM
Agarose Electrophoresis (DB)	AE
Agarose Gel Zone Electrophoresis	AGE
Agartala [India] [Airport symbol] (OAG)	IXA
Agartala [India] [ICAO location identifier] (ICLI)	VEAT
Agarwal Resources Ltd. [Vancouver Stock Exchange symbol]	AWL
Agassiz National Wildlife Refuge (SAUS)	ANWR
Agassiz Resources Ltd. [Toronto Stock Exchange symbol]	AGZ
Agassiz-Harrison Historical Society, Agassiz, British Columbia [Library symbol] [National Library of Canada] (BIB)	BHLH
Agat, GU [FM radio station call letters]	KSDA
Agate [Typography] (DGA)	AG
Agate (VRA)	ag
Agate Fossil Beds National Monument (SAUS)	AFBNM
Agateware (VRA)	agwr
Agatha Christie Appreciation Society: Postern of Murder (EA)	ACAS
Agathon Publication Services, Inc. [Later, APS Publications]	APS
Agats [Indonesia] [ICAO location identifier] (ICLI)	WAKG
AG-Bag International Ltd. [Associated Press] (SAG)	AGBag
AG-Bag International Ltd. [NASDAQ symbol] (SAG)	AGBG
Ag-Bag Intl. Ltd. [NASDAQ symbol] (TTSB)	AGBG
Agboville [Ivory Coast] [ICAO location identifier] (ICLI)	DIAE
AG-Chem Equipment [NASDAQ symbol] (TTSB)	AGCH
Ag-Chem Equipment Co., Inc. [NASDAQ symbol] (SAG)	AGCH
Ag-Chem Equipment Co. Inc. [Associated Press] (SAG)	Ag-Chm
AGCO Corp. [NYSE symbol] (SAG)	AG
AGCO Corp. [Associated Press] (SAG)	AGCO
Agderfly AS [Norway] [ICAO designator] (FAAC)	AGD
Age	A
Age Action Year [1976] (DI)	AAY
Age Anaesthesia Association (SAUO)	AAA
Age and Ageing (SAUS)	Age Ageing
Age at Time of Bomb [Of survivors at Hiroshima]	ATB

Age Concern England [An association] [British]	ACE
Age Concern Scotland [An association] (EAIO)	ACS
Age Controlled Item (NASA)	ACI
Age Discrimination and Employment Act (SAUS)	ADEA
Age Discrimination Claims Assistance Act [1988]	ADCAA
Age Discrimination in Employment Act [1967] [Department of Labor]	ADEA
Age Equivalent [Development level] [Education]	AE
Age Equivalent (MAE)	AEq
Age Exemption (WDAA)	AE
AGE [Air-Ground Equipment] Module Test Set (MCD)	AMTS
Age Monthly Review [A publication]	Age MR
Age of Date, Clock (SSD)	AODC
Age of Date, Ephermis (SSD)	AODE
Age of Onset (MELL)	AOO
Age of Primary Taxpayer [IRS]	AG
Age; Prior Service; Physical, Legal, Educational, and Marital Status; and Dependents [Army recruiting questionnaire]	APPLE-MD
Age, Prior Service, Physical, Legal, Educational and Marital Status and Dependents (SAUS)	APPLE-MD
Age Progression Technique [Criminology] (LAIN)	APT
Age Regression (MELL)	AR
Age Replacement	AR
Age Replacement Policy (PDAA)	ARP
Age Run Length	ARL
Age Standardized Mortality Ratio	ASMR
Age Weighted Pupil Unit [Education] (AIE)	AWPU
Age-Appropriately Immunized [Children]	AAI
Age-Associated Memory Disorder [Medicine] (CPH)	AAMD
Age-Associated Memory Impairment [Medicine]	AAMI
aged (SAUS)	ae
Aged, Adrenalectomized Animals [Endocrinology]	AX
Aged and Community Care Division (SAUS)	ACC
Aged and Community Care Division. Australian Department of Health & Aged Care (SAUO)	ACC
Aged and Invalid Pensioners' Association of South Australia	AIPASA
Aged and Invalid Pensioners' Home	AIPH
Aged, Blind, or Disabled [HEW]	ABD
Aged Care Australia [An association]	ACA
Aged Care Support Program [Australia]	ACSP
Aged Individual [Title XVI] [Social Security Administration] (OICC)	AI
Aged Intact Animal [Endocrinology]	AI
Aged Persons Homes Act [Australia]	APHA
Aged Persons' Residential Program [Australia]	APRP
Aged Services Australia [Australia]	ASA
Aged Spouse [Social Security Administration] (OICC)	AS
Age-Dependent Epileptic Encephalopathy [Medicine] (DMAA)	ADEE
Aged-Related Eye Disease Study [National Eye Institute]	AREDS
Ageing & Disability Department (SAUO)	ADD
Ageing and Surveillance Test Program (SAUS)	ASTP
Agen [France] [Airport symbol] (OAG)	AGF
Agena Class Lunar Orbiter [NASA]	ACLO
Agena Control System [NASA]	ACS
Agena Detailed Maneuver Table [NASA] (SAA)	ADMT
Agena Ephemeris Data [NASA] (SAA)	AED
Agena Systems/Power-On Test [NASA] (KSC)	AS/POT
Agena Target Vehicle [NASA] (KSC)	ATV
Agenahambo [Papua New Guinea] [Seismograph station code, US Geological Survey] [Closed] (SEIS)	AGE
Agence Africaine d'Information [African Information Agency] [Zaire]	AAI
Agence Africaine d'Information et de Documentation [African Information and Documentation Agency]	AAID
Agence Angolaise de Presse et d'Information [Angolan Press and Information Agency]	API
Agence Camerounaise de Presse [Cameroon Press Agency]	ACAP
Agence Canadienne de Developpement International [Canadian International Development Agency - CIDA]	ACDI
Agence Centrafricaine des Communications Fluviales [Central African Agency for River Communications] (AF)	ACCF
Agence Centrale des Approvisionnements [Central Supplies Agency] (NATG)	ACA
Agence Centrale Parisienne de Presse [Parisian Central Press Agency] [French] (AF)	ACP
Agence Civile OTAN [Organisation du Traite de l'Atlantique Nord] du Temps de Guerre [NATO Civil Wartime Agency] (NATG)	ACOG
Agence Congolaise de Presse [Congolese Press Agency]	ACP
Agence Congolaise d'Information [Congolese Information Agency] (AF)	ACI
Agence Dahomeene de Presse [Dahomean Press Agency]	ADP
Agence Dahomeenne de Presse [Dahomean Press Agency]	ADP
Agence de Cooperation Culturelle et Technique [Agency for Cultural and Technical Cooperation] (EAIO)	ACCT
Agence de Cooperation Internationale Pour l'Integration Economique et Sociale des Personnes Handicapees (AC)	ACIPH
Agence de l'OCDE pour l'Energie Nucleaire [OECD Nuclear Energy Agency - NEA] (EAIO)	AEN
Agence de Presse de l'OPEC [OPEC News Agency - OPECNA] [Vienna, Austria] (EAIO)	APOPEC
Agence de Presse Ivoirienne [Ivorian Press Agency]	API
Agence de Presse Libre du Quebec [Free Press Agency of Quebec] [Canada]	APLQ
Agence de Presse Senegalaise [Senegalese Press Agency]	APS
Agence de Surveillance du Secteur Petrolier [Petroleum Monitoring Agency, Energy, Mines & Resources, Canada]	ASSP
Agence des Telecommunications Administratives [Administrative Telecommunications Agency] [Canada]	ATA

Agence des Telecommunications Gouvernementales [*Government Telecommunications Agency*] [*Canada*] ... ATG
[*French Rating Agency*] **Agence d'Evaluation Financiere** (ODBW) ... ADEF
Agence d'Examen de l'Investissement Etranger [*Foreign Investment Review Agency - FIRA*] [*Canada*] ... AEIE
Agence d'Illustrations pour la Presse [*Press Illustrations Agency*] [*French*] (AF) ... AGIP
Agence Djiboutienne de Presse (EY) ... ADP
Agence Europeenne d'Approvisionnement ... AEA
Agence Europeenne pour l'Energie Nucleaire [*France*] (NUCP) ... AEEN
Agence France-Presse [*French Press Agency*] (IID) ... AFP
Agence Gabonaise de Presse [*Gabonese Press Agency*] (AF) ... AGP
Agence Gabonaise d'Information [*Gabonese Information Agency*] (AF) ... AGI
Agence Generale de Transit en Afrique [*General Transit Agency in Afica*] [*Congo*] ... AGTA
Agence Generale d'Editions Professionnelles [*Agency General of Professional Publishing*] [*Canada*] ... AGEP
Agence Guineenne de Presse [*Guinean Press Agency*] (AF) ... AGP
Agence Internationale de l'Energie Atomique ... AIEA
Agence Internationale d'Information du Mali [*Press agency*] [*Mali*] ... ANIM
Agence Internationale pour le Developpement [*Paris, France*] (EAIO) ... AIDE
Agence Ivoirienne de Presse [*Ivory Coast*] (AF) ... AIP
Agence Khmere de Presse [*Cambodian Press Agency*] ... AKP
Agence Lao Presse [*Laos Press Agency*] ... ALP
Agence Madagascar - Presse [*Press agency*] [*Malagasy Republic*] ... AMP
Agence Malgache de Presse [*Malagasy Press Agency*] (AF) ... AMP
Agence Maritime Internationale [*International Maritime Agency*] ... AMI
Agence Mauritanienne de l'Information [*News Agency*] (EY) ... AMI
Agence Nationale de Valorisation de la Recherche [*National Agency for the Promotion of Research*] [*Information service or system*] (IID) ... ANVAR
Agence Nationale d'Edition et de Publicite [*National Publication and Advertising Agency*] [*Algeria*] (AF) ... ANEP
Agence Nationale des Aerodromes et de la Meteorologie [*Ivory Coast*] [*ICAO designator*] (FAAC) ... ZZM
Agence Nationale d'Information Malienne [*Malian National Information Agency*] (AF) ... ANIM
Agence Nigerienne de Presse [*News Agency*] [*Niger*] (EY) ... ANP
Agence Parisienne de Presse [*Parisian Press Agency*] [*French*] (AF) ... APP
Agence pour la Securite de la Navigation Aerienne en Afrique et a Madagascar (ASECNA) [*ICAO designator*] (ICDA) ... XK
Agence pour la Securite de la Navigation Aerienne en Afrique et Madagascar [*Agency for Air Navigation Safety in Africa and Madagascar*] (AF) ... ASECNA
Agence pour la Securite de la Navigation Afrique-Madagascar [*France*] [*FAA designator*] (FAAC) ... XKX
Agence Presse Voltaique [*Upper Voltan Press Agency*] (AF) ... APV
Agence Spatiale Europeenne [*European Space Agency*] (EAIO) ... ASE
Agence Tchadienne de Presse [*Chadian Press Agency*] (AF) ... ATP
Agence Telegraphique Suisse [*Swiss News Agency*] [*Berne, Switzerland*] ... ATS
Agence Transcongolaise des Communications [*Trans-Congolese Communications Agency*] (AF) ... ATC
Agence Transcontinentale de Presse [*Transcontinental Press Agency*] [*France*] (AF) ... ATP
Agence Transequatoriale des Communications [*Trans-Equatorial Communications Agency*] [*Africa*] (AF) ... ATEC
Agence Tunis Afrique Press (SAUS) ... TAP
Agence Zaire-Presse [*Zaire Press Agency*] ... AZAP
Agencement en Rames Automatisees de Modules Independants dans les Stations [*Arrangement in automated trains of independent modules in stations*] [*A satirical novel by Bruno Latour*] [*Based on an actual Personal Rapid Transit program pursued by the French government*] ... ARAMIS
Agencia Centroamericana de Noticias SA [*Press agency*] [*Panama*] ... ACAN
Agencia Latinoamericana de Informacion [*Latin American Information Agency*] [*Canada*] ... ALAI
Agencia Mexicana de Noticias SA [*Press agency*] [*Mexico*] ... AMEX
Agencia Nacional [*National Agency*] [*Press agency*] [*Brazil*] ... AN
Agencia Nacionale de Informacoes [*National Information Agency*] [*Portugal*] ... ANI
Agencia Nicaraguense de Noticias [*News agency*] (EY) ... ANN
Agencia Noticiosa Corporacion de Periodistas [*Press agency*] [*Chile*] ... COPER
Agencia Noticiosa Saporiti [*Press agency*] [*Argentina*] ... ANS
Agencies (EY) ... AGS
Agencja Robotricza [*Press agency*] [*Poland*] ... AR
Agency ... A
Agency (EY) ... AG
Agency (AFM) ... AGCY
Agency (WDMC) ... agcy
Agency ... AGNCY
Agency (ADA) ... AGY
Agency (EBF) ... Agy
Agency ... AY
Agency Accounting Control System (SAUS) ... AACON
Agency Action Notice (SAUS) ... AAN
Agency Activity Analysis [*LIMRA*] ... AAA
Agency Broadcast Producers Workshop [*Defunct*] (EA) ... ABPW
Agency Confirmation Agreement (SAUO) ... ACR
Agency Coordinating Body for Afghan Relief [*Afghanistan/Pakistan*] (ECON) ... ACBAR
Agency for Agricultural Research and Development (SAUO) ... AARD
Agency for Air Safety in Africa and Madagascar (SAUS) ... ASECNA
Agency for Assessment and Application of Technology (SAUS) ... BPPT
Agency for Business and Career Development (EA) ... ABCD
Agency for Consumer Advocacy (SAUO) ... ACA
Agency for Cooperation and Research in Development [*International consortium on Africa*] (ECON) ... ACORD
Agency for Coordination of Transportation in the Mediterranean (SAUO) ... ACTIME
Agency for Cultural Affairs (SAUO) ... ACA
Agency for Cultural and Technical Cooperation (SAUO) ... ACCT
Agency for Cultural and Technical Cooperation (SAUO) ... AGECOOP
Agency for Defence Development (SAUS) ... ADD
Agency for Health Care Administration (DEMM) ... AHCA
Agency for Health Care Policy and Research [*Department of Health and Human Services*] ... AHCPR
Agency for Healthcare Research and Quality ... AHRQ
Agency for Industrial Mission [*Canada*] ... AIM
Agency for Information and Cultural Exchange (SAUO) ... AICE
Agency for Instructional Technology (SAUS) ... AIT
Agency for Instructional Television (NTCM) ... AIT
Agency for Instructional TV (SAUO) ... AIT
Agency for International Development [*State Department*] [*Also, USAID*] [*US International Development Cooperation Agency*] ... AID
Agency for International Development Acquisition Regulation [*A publication*] (AAGC) ... AIDAR
Agency for International Development, Bureau for Technical Assistance [*Department of State*] ... AID/TA
Agency for International Development, Bureau for Technical Assistance (SAUS) ... AIDBTA
Agency for International Development, Procurement Regulations ... AIDPR
Agency for International Development, Washington, DC [*OCLC symbol*] (OCLC) ... AID
Agency for International Development/Private Enterprise Promotion ... AID/PEP
Agency for Middle East Research (SAUO) ... AMER
Agency for Navigation on the Rhine and the Moselle (NATG) ... RHIMO
Agency for Technical Cooperation (SAUS) ... GTZ
Agency for Technical Cooperation and Development (SAUO) ... ACTED
Agency for Tele-Education in Canada ... ATEC
Agency for the Assessment and Application of Technology (SAUS) ... BPTT
Agency for the Coordination of Transport in the Mediterranean [*NATO*] (MCD) ... ACTIME
Agency for the Coordination of Transport in the Mediterranean [*NATO*] (NATG) ... ACTIMED
Agency for the Prohibition of Nuclear Weapons in Latin America and the Caribbean (SAUS) ... OPANAL
Agency for the Safety of Aerial Navigation in Africa (SAUS) ... ASECNA
Agency for the Safety of Aerial Navigation in Africa and Madagascar (SAUO) ... ASECNA
Agency for the Security of Air Navigation (AFM) ... ASECNA
Agency for Toxic Substances and Disease Registry (BCP) ... ASTDR
Agency for Toxic Substances and Disease Registry [*Atlanta, GA*] [*Department of Health and Human Services*] ... ATSDR
Agency for Toxic Substances and Emergency Response ... ATSER
Agency Investigation Board ... AIB
Agency Logistics Center (SAUO) ... ALC
Agency Management Conference [*LIMRA*] ... AMC
Agency Management Information Systems [*DCAA*] (AAGC) ... AMIS
Agency Manager Survey [*LIMRA*] ... AMS
Agency Name [*Database terminology*] (NITA) ... AN
Agency of Applied Science (SAUO) ... AAS
Agency of Broadcast Producers Workshop (SAUO) ... ABPW
Agency of National Resources and Energy (SAUO) ... ANRE
Agency of Natural Resources and Energy (SAUO) ... ANRE
Agency of Record [*An advertising agency*] (WDMC) ... AOR
Agency Officers School [*Formerly, FOS*] [*LIMRA*] ... AOS
Agency Owners Roundtable [*Formerly, Canadian Association of Professional Advertising Agencies*] (AC) ... AOR
Agency Planning Team (SAUO) ... APT
Agency Procedure ... AP
Agency Procurement Officer (SAUO) ... APO
Agency Procurement Request ... APR
Agency Progress Report ... APR
Agency Ranking Committee [*Environmental Protection Agency*] (GFGA) ... ARC
Agency Sales Magazine [*Manufacturers' Agents National Association*] [*A publication*] ... ASM
Agency State [*Database Terminology*] (NITA) ... AS
Agency Subcommittee (SAUO) ... ASC
Agency Technical Representative (SAUO) ... ATR
Agency Technology Transfer Staff (SAUO) ... ATTS
Agency to Prevent Evil [*Organization in TV series "Lancelot Link"*] ... APE
Agency-Company Organization for Research and Development ... Acord
Agency-Wide Coding Structure [*Military*] ... AWCS
Agency-Wide Information Management System [*Department of Agriculture*] (GFGA) ... AIMS
Agenda Item (MCD) ... AI
Agenda of Science for Environment and Development into the 21st Century (SAUO) ... ASCEND
Agen/La Garenne [*France*] [*ICAO location identifier*] (ICLI) ... LFBA
Agent (ODBW) ... ag
Agent ... AGNT
Agent (WDMC) ... agt
Agent (EBF) ... Agt
Agent (AABC) ... AGT
Agent Building Environment (SAUS) ... ABE
Agent Collaboration Language [*Computer science*] (RDA) ... ACL
Agent Communication Language (SAUS) ... ACL
Agent Control Language (SAUS) ... ACL
Agent Development Program [*LIMRA*] ... ADP
Agent Distributor Service [*Departments of State and Commerce*] ... ADS
Agent Distributor Service (SAUO) ... A/DS
Agent General ... AG

Agent in Charge [Criminology] (LAIN) ... AIC
Agent in London for Government of Northern Ireland (SAUO) ... ALGNI
Agent Job Review [LIMRA] ... AJR
Agent Kernel Language (SAUS) ... AKL
Agent Orange [Herbicide] (MELL) ... AO
Agent Orange Victims International [Later, VVAOVI] (EA) ... AOVI
Agent Orange Working Group [Cabinet Council on Human Resources] ... AOWG
Agent Reference Material [Used by airline agents] ... ARM
Agent Report (MCD) ... AR
Agent Report [Army] (AABC) ... AREPT
Agent Selection Kit [LIMRA] ... ASK
Agent to the Governor-General [British] ... AGG
Agents and Brokers Automated Computer Users System (MHDI) ... ABACUS
Agents and Brokers Legislative Council ... ABL
Agents' Association, Totalizator Agency Board, New South Wales ... AATAB
Agent's Discount (TRID) ... AD
Agents Master File [IRS] ... AGMF
Agents of Biological Origin [Military] ... ABO
Agent's Vehicle Record (DS) ... AVR
Agentstvo Pechati Novosti [News agency] [Former USSR] ... APN
Agenzia Europea per L'Energia Nucleare (NUCP) ... AEEN
Agenzia Giornalistica Italia [Press agency] [Italy] ... AGI
Agenzia Internazionale Fides [News agency] [Vatican City] (EY) ... AIF
Agenzia Nazionale Stampa Associata [Associated National Press Agency] [Italy] ... ANSA
Agenzia Spaziale Italiana [Italy] (EOSA) ... ASI
Age-Related Macular Degeneration [Ophthalmology] ... AMD
Age-Related Macular Degeneration [Ophthalmology] (CPH) ... ARMD
Age-Related Pain Perception [Medicine] (MELL) ... ARPP
Agerpres Information Bulletin (journ.) (SAUS) ... AP Inf B
Age/Sex (SAUS) ... A/S
Age/Sex Rate ... ASR
Age/Sex/Location (SAUS) ... A/S/L
Agesilaus [of Xenophon] [Classical studies] (OCD) ... Ages
Agesilaus [of Plutarch] [Classical studies] (OCD) ... Ages
Age-Specific Fertility Rate ... ASFR
Age-Specific Mortality Rate ... ASMR
AGF Management Ltd. [Toronto Stock Exchange symbol] ... AGF
Agfa Publishing Systems Environment (SAUS) ... APSE
Aggadah (BJA) ... Agg
Aggadic (BJA) ... Agg
Aggeneys [South Africa] [Airport symbol] (OAG) ... AGZ
Aggeneys [South Africa] [ICAO location identifier] (ICLI) ... FAAG
Agglomerate [Geology] ... A
Agglutination [Immunology] ... AGG
Agglutination [Immunology] ... AGGL
Agglutination (DMAA) ... aggl
Agglutination (DMAA) ... agglut
Agglutination [Immunology] (AAMN) ... AGGLUT
Agglutination Activating Factor [Medicine] ... AAF
Agglutination Negative, Absorption Positive [Medicine] (MAE) ... ANAP
Agglutination Test for Brucellosis [Immunology] (DMAA) ... ABr
Agglutination-Flocculation Test [Immunology] (DMAA) ... AFT
Agglutination-Inhibition Test [Clinical chemistry] ... AIT
Aggragate Supply (SAUS) ... AS
aggravate (SAUS) ... agg
Aggravated (MAE) ... agg
Aggravated Burglary [Legal term] (WDAA) ... AB
Aggravated in Military Service (MAE) ... AMS
Aggravation (DSUE) ... AGGRO
aggravation (SAUS) ... agro
Aggrediente Febre [When the Fever Increases] [Pharmacy] ... AG FEB
Aggrediente Febre [When the Fever Increases] [Pharmacy] ... Aggred Feb
Aggregate ... AGG
Aggregate (EES) ... agg
Aggregate (AABC) ... AGGR
Aggregate ... AGGRGT
Aggregate (VRA) ... agr
Aggregate Abrasion Value (SAUS) ... AAV
Aggregate and Concrete Executives (NTPA) ... ACE
Aggregate Base Course (DAC) ... ABC
Aggregate Concrete Block Association [British] (DBA) ... ACBA
Aggregate Data Manager (SAUS) ... ADM
Aggregate Data Rate (SAUS) ... ADR
Aggregate Defensive Simulation Protocol (SAUS) ... ALSP
Aggregate Demand ... AD
Aggregate Demand Potential (PDAA) ... ADP
Aggregate Estimated Net Pool Return [Business term] ... AENPR
Aggregate Exercise Price [Investment term] ... AEP
Aggregate Expenditure [Economics] ... AE
Aggregate Expense Analysis [Insurance] ... AEA
Aggregate Field Expense Study [LIMRA] ... AFES
Aggregate Level Simulation Protocol (SAUS) ... ALPS
Aggregate Level Simulation Protocol ... ALSP
Aggregate Measure of Support [International trade] (ECON) ... AMS
Aggregate Producers Association of Ontario (AC) ... APAO
Aggregate Production Planning (PDAA) ... APP
Aggregate Ready-Mix of Minnesota (SRA) ... ARM
Aggregate Signal ... AS
Aggregate Supply ... AS
Aggregate Value (SAUS) ... AV
aggregated (SAUS) ... agg
Aggregated Albumin (MAE) ... AA
Aggregated Human Gamma-Globulin (DB) ... AHGG
Aggregated Human Globulin [Biochemistry] (DAVI) ... AHG

Aggregated School Budget (AIE) ... ASB
Aggregated Switch Procurement (SAUS) ... ASP
Aggregated Switch Procurement Program [General Services Administration] (GFGA) ... ASP
Aggregates of P-Protein [Botany] ... AgPp
Aggregation [Medicine] (AAMN) ... AGGREG
Aggregation Factor [Biochemistry] ... AF
Aggregation Half Time [Medicine] (DMAA) ... AHT
Aggregation Index (DB) ... AI
Aggregation of Red Blood Cells [Hematology] ... ARC
Aggregation-Attachment Pheromone [Entomology] ... AAP
Aggregator (ACAE) ... AGG
Aggressive Behavioral Disturbance [Medicine] (DMAA) ... ABD
Aggressive Growth [Investment term] ... AG
Aggressive Packet Adaptive Assembly (SAUS) ... APAA
Aggressor Squadron [Air Force] ... AS
Aggrevation (SAUS) ... AGG
Aghajari [Iran] [ICAO location identifier] (ICLI) ... OIAG
Agiate (SAUS) ... AG
Agicultural Climate Service System (SAUS) ... AGRICLIMSS
Agiicultural Electricity Institute Report (journ.) (SAUS) ... Agric Electr Inst Rep
Agile Beam Director (SAUS) ... ABD
Agile Beam Laser Radar (ACAE) ... ABLR
Agile Beam System (ACAE) ... ABS
Agile Beam Tracker/Illuminator (ACAE) ... ABTI
Agile Combat Aircraft [Proposed] ... ACA
Agile Continuous Wave Acquisition Radar (SAUS) ... ACWAR
Agile Control Experiment (ACAE) ... ACE
Agile Intelligent Manufacturing [Computer-assisted manufacturing] ... AIM
AGILE [Autonetics General Information Learning Equipment] Interceptor Defense ... AID
Agile Manufacturing Information Infrastructure (SAUS) ... AMII
Agile Response Effective Support (SAUS) ... ARES
AGILE [Autonetics General Information Learning Equipment] Responsive Effective Support [Army/Air Force] ... ARES
Agile Seeker Program (ACAE) ... ASP
Agile Target System (SAUS) ... ATS
Agile-Beam Illuminator (MCD) ... ABI
Agility Excellent ... AX
Agincourt [Canada] [Later, OTT] [Geomagnetic observatory code] ... AGN
Agincourt Exploration, Inc. [Vancouver Stock Exchange symbol] ... AGX
Aging ... AGNG
Aging Activities, Adaptation and Aging (journ.) (SAUS) ... Act Adapt
Aging Aircraft Nondestructive Inspection Development and Demonstration Center [Federal Aviation Administration] ... AANC
Aging Aircraft Program [FAA] (DA) ... AAP
Aging and Health Programme [World Health Organization] ... AHE
Aging Brain Syndrome [Medicine] (MELL) ... ABS
Aging, Federal Council (OICC) ... AC
Aging Health Policy Center [Research center] (RCD) ... AHPC
Aging in America (EA) ... AIA
Aging Research Centre (SAUO) ... ARC
Aging Research Institute [Defunct] (EA) ... ARI
Aging Waste Facility (SAUS) ... AWF
Agio Resources Corp. [Vancouver Stock Exchange symbol] ... AGI
Agita [Shake] [Pharmacy] ... AGIT
Agita Ante Sumendum [Shake Before Taking] [Latin] [Pharmacy] (WDAA) ... AGIT ANTE SU
Agita ante Usum [Shake before Using] [Pharmacy] ... AGIT A US
Agita Bene [Shake Well] [Pharmacy] ... AGIT BENE
Agitate (MSA) ... AG
Agitation and Propaganda [Military] ... AGIT-PROP
Agitato [Agitatedly] [Music] ... Agit
Agitato [Agitatedly] [Music] ... AGITO
Agitato [Agitatedly] [Music] (ROG) ... AGO
Agitato Vase [The Vessel Being Shaken] [Pharmacy] ... Agit Vas
Agitator [FBI standardized term] ... AGTR
Agkistrodon Contortrix Thrombin-Like Enzyme ... ACTE
AGL Resources [NYSE symbol] [Formerly, Atlanta Gas Light] (SG) ... ATG
AGL Resources, Inc. [NYSE symbol] (SAG) ... ATG
AGLA [Australian Government Lawyers' Association] Bulletin [A publication] ... AGLA
Aglets Workbench (SAUS) ... AWB
Aglow International (EA) ... AI
a-Glycerol Phosphate ... GP
Agmatine Iminohydrolase [An enzyme] ... AIH
Agmnomia Sulriograndense (journ.) (SAUS) ... Agron Sulriograndense
Agnes Etherington Art Centre, Queen's University, Kingston, Ontario [Library symbol] [National Library of Canada] (NLC) ... OKQA
Agnes Scott College [Decatur, GA] ... ASC
Agnes Scott College, Decatur, GA [OCLC symbol] (OCLC) ... EGA
Agnes Scott College, Decatur, GA [Library symbol] [Library of Congress] (LCLS) ... GDS
Agness Community Library, Agness, OR [Library symbol] [Library of Congress] (LCLS) ... OrAg
Agnetha Faltskog, Bjorn Ulvaeus, Benny Andersson, Anni-Frid Lyngstad [Swedish singing group; acronym formed from first letters of their first names] ... ABBA
Agnew Association of America (EA) ... AA
Agnew on Patents [A publication] (DLA) ... Agn Pat
Agnew on Patents (journ.) (SAUS) ... Agn Pat
Agnew on the Statute of Frauds [A publication] (DLA) ... Agn Fr
Agni Yoga Society (EA) ... AYS
Agnico Eagle Mines [NASDAQ symbol] (TTSB) ... AEM
Agnico-Eagle Mines, Inc. [NYSE symbol] (SAG) ... AEM

Agnico-Eagle Mines, Inc. [*Associated Press*] (SAG) ... Agnico
Agnico-Eagle Mines Ltd. [*Toronto Stock Exchange symbol*] ... AGE
Agnogenic Myeloid (MELL) ... AMMMF
Agnogenic Myeloid Metaplasia [*Medicine*] ... AMM
agnomen (SAUS) ... agn
Agnosia [*Medicine*] ... AGN
Agnostic ... AGNOS
Agnostic Christians for Equality for Dignity (EA) ... ACED
Agnostics' Adoption Society [*British*] (BI) ... AAS
Agnostics/Atheists (SAUS) ... A/A
Agnus Dei [*Lamb of God*] [*Latin*] ... AD
Agnus Dei [*Lamb of God*] [*Latin*] ... Ag
Agora/Documentaire [*Agence France-Presse*] [*French*] [*Information service or system*] (CRD) ... ADOC
Agora-Economie [*Agence France-Presse*] [*French*] [*Information service or system*] (CRD) ... AECO
AGORA-GENERAL [*Agence France-Presse*] [*Information service or system*] (CRD) ... AGRA
Agoraphobic Foundation of Canada Inc. [*Fondation Canadienne pour les Agoraphobes Inc.*] (AC) ... AFC
Agoraphobics Anonymous (EA) ... AA
Agoraphobics in Motion [*An association*] (EA) ... AIM
AGORA-SPORTS [*Agence France-Presse*] [*Information service or system*] (CRD) ... ASPO
Agordat [*Ethiopia*] [*ICAO location identifier*] (ICLI) ... HAAG
Agorot [*Monetary unit*] [*Israel*] ... AG
Agostiniani Secolari Agustinos Seculares [*Order Secular of St. Augustine - OSSA*] [*Rome, Italy*] (EAIO) ... ASAS
Agouron Pharmaceuticals, Inc. [*Associated Press*] (SAG) ... Agourn
Agouron Pharmaceuticals, Inc. [*NASDAQ symbol*] (NQ) ... AGPH
AGP & Co., Inc. [*NASDAQ symbol*] (SAG) ... AGPC
AGP & Company, Inc. [*Associated Press*] (SAG) ... AGP & Co
AGR. University of Kentucky. Cooperative Extension Service (journ.) (SAUS) ... AGR Univ KY Coop Ext Serv
Agra [*India*] [*Airport symbol*] (OAG) ... AGR
Agra [*India*] [*Seismograph station code, US Geological Survey*] [*Closed*] (SEIS) ... AGR
Agra [*India*] [*ICAO location identifier*] (ICLI) ... VIAG
Agra Full Bench Rulings [*India*] [*A publication*] (ILCA) ... Agra FB
Agra High Court Reports [*India*] [*A publication*] (ILCA) ... Agra
Agra High Court Reports [*India*] [*A publication*] (DLA) ... Agra HC
Agra Industries Ltd. [*Toronto Stock Exchange symbol*] ... AGR
Agra University (SAUO) ... Agra U
Agra University Journal of Research: Science (SAUS) ... Agra Univ J Res: Sci
Agranular Endoplasmic Reticulum (SAUS) ... AER
Agranulocytic Angina [*Medicine*] (DMAA) ... AA
Agrar-Aviacion SA [*Spain*] [*ICAO designator*] (FAAC) ... AGI
agrarian (SAUS) ... agrar
Agrarian Party [*Albania*] [*Political party*] (EY) ... AP
Agrarian Party [*Czech Republic*] (BUAC) ... ZS
Agrarian Research and Intelligence Service (SAUO) ... ARIS
Agrarian Research & Traininn Institute (SAUO) ... ARTI
agrarianism (SAUS) ... agrar
agrarians (SAUS) ... agrar
Agrarmeteorologische Datenbank Rheinland-Pfalz (SAUS) ... AGMEDA
Agrartudomanyi Egyetem, Keszthely, Hungary [*Library symbol*] [*Library of Congress*] (LCLS) ... HuKeAgE
Agrartudomanyi Egyetem Koezlemenyei [*A publication*] ... Agrartud Egy Kozl
Agrarwirtschaft (journ.) (SAUS) ... AGR
Agrecol Development Information (SAUO) ... AGRECOL
Agree (ILCA) ... Ag
Agree (FAAC) ... AGR
Agree en Relations Publiques [*Canada*] (DD) ... ARP
Agree Reality Corp. [*NYSE symbol*] (SAG) ... ADC
Agree Realty Corp. [*Associated Press*] (SAG) ... AgreeRit
Agreed ... AGD
Agreed Case [*Legal term*] (DLA) ... AGR C
Agreed, Cease Fire Line [*Military*] (INF) ... AFCL
Agreed Characteristics (SAUS) ... ACs
Agreed Industry Standard (SAUS) ... AIS
Agreed Medical examiner (DAVI) ... AME
Agreed Operational Characteristics (DNAB) ... AOC
Agreed Set of Security Rules (SAUS) ... ASSR
Agreed Syllabus Conference [*Education*] (AIE) ... ASC
Agreement (ODBW) ... ag
Agreement (ADA) ... AG
Agreement (ROG) ... AGMT
Agreement (ROG) ... AGREET
Agreement (AABC) ... AGRM
Agreement (FAAC) ... AGRMT
Agreement ... AGRT
Agreement ... AGT
Agreement (WDMC) ... agt
Agreement and Account of Crew (ADA) ... AAC
Agreement for Fighter Interceptor Operations ... AFIO
Agreement for the International Transport of Perishable Products ... ATP
Agreement in Principle (COE) ... AIP
Agreement Item (MCD) ... AGI
Agreement on a global system of trade preferences among developing countries (SAUO) ... GSTP
Agreement on Defence Co-operation (SAUS) ... ADC
Agreement on Government Procurement (AAGC) ... AGP
Agreement on minimum requirements for the issue and validity of driving permits (SAUO) ... APC
Agreement on Peaceful Uses of Atomic Energy (SAUS) ... PUAE
Agreement on the Conservation of African-Eurasian Migratory Waterbirds (SAUO) ... AEWA
Agreement on the Conservation of Bats in Europe (SAUO) ... EUROBATS
Agreement on the Conservation of Cetaceans of the Black Sea, Mediterranean Sea and Contiguous Atlantic Area (SAUO) ... ACCOBAMS
Agreement on the Conservation of Small Cetaceans of the Baltic and North Seas (SAUO) ... ASCOBANS
Agreement on the international carriage of passengers by road by means of occasional coach and bus service (SAUO) ... ASOR
Agreement on Trade-Related Aspects of Intellectual Property Rights ... TRIP
Agreement on Trade-Related Investment Measures ... TRIM
Agreement to Extend Enlistment [*Military*] ... AEX
Agreement to Remain on Active Duty Until Date (SAUS) ... GREEMAIN
Agreement to Remain on Active Duty Until Date Specified (DNAB) ... GREEMAIN
Agreements for Recreation and Conservation [*Canada*] ... ARC
Agree-Undecided-Disagree [*Multiple choice test*] (BARN) ... AUD
Agrement Dangereuse Routier [*Agreement on the International Carriage of Dangerous Goods by Road*] [*1968*] ... ADR
Agri [*Turkey*] [*Airport symbol*] (AD) ... AGZ
Agri [*Turkey*] [*ICAO location identifier*] (ICLI) ... LTCB
AGRI Industries (SAUO) ... AGRI
AgriBioTech, Inc. [*NASDAQ symbol*] (SAG) ... ABTX
AgriBioTech, Inc. [*Associated Press*] (SAG) ... AgriBio
Agribrands International [*NYSE symbol*] ... AGX
Agribrands Intl. [*NYSE symbol*] (SG) ... AGX
Agribusiness Accountability Project [*Public interest research group*] [*Defunct*] ... AAP
Agribusiness Association of Australia and New Zealand ... AAANZ
Agribusiness Association of Iowa (SRA) ... AAI
Agribusiness Council (EA) ... AC
Agri-Business Council of Arizona (SRA) ... ABC
Agri-Business Council of Oregon (SRA) ... ABC
Agribusiness Foundation of Australia ... AFA
Agribusiness Information [*G. V. Olsen Associates*] [*Information service or system*] (CRD) ... AGBIZ
Agribusiness Management Information System (SAUS) ... AMIS
Agrichemical Age (journ.) (SAUS) ... Agrichem Age
Agrichemical West (journ.) (SAUS) ... Agrichem W
Agrico Chemical Co., Memphis, TN [*Library symbol*] [*Library of Congress*] (LCLS) ... TMAC
Agricola [*of Tacitus*] [*Classical studies*] (OCD) ... Agr
Agricultual Machinery Advisory Group (HEAS) ... AMAG
Agricultural ... ACRCLTL
Agricultural (ADWA) ... ag
Agricultural (TBD) ... Ag
Agricultural (ROG) ... AGL
Agricultural [*or Agriculture*] ... AGR
Agricultural (ADWA) ... agr
Agricultural (DD) ... Agr
Agricultural (ADWA) ... agri
Agricultural (ADWA) ... agric
Agricultural ... AGRL
Agricultural Adjustment Act [*1933, 1938, 1980*] [*Department of Agriculture*] ... AAA
Agricultural Adjustment Administration [*or Agency*] [*Production and Marketing Administration*] [*Department of Agriculture*] ... AAA
Agricultural Adjustment Agency (SAUO) ... AAA
Agricultural Adjustment Unit (SAUO) ... AAU
Agricultural Advisory Council (SAUO) ... AAC
Agricultural Advisory Council for England and Wales (BI) ... AAC
Agricultural Advisory Meteorologist (NOAA) ... AAM
Agricultural Aids Foundation ... AAF
Agricultural Aircraft Association [*Later, CAAA*] (EA) ... AAA
Agricultural Aircraft Association (SAUO) ... AAA
Agricultural Ammonia Institute (SAUO) ... AAI
Agricultural Ammonia Institute [*Later, The Fertilizer Institute*] (EA) ... AAI
Agricultural and Allied Workers' National Trade Group [*British*] ... AAWTG
Agricultural and Biosystems Engineering (SAUS) ... ABE
Agricultural and Dairy Educational Political Trust ... ADEPT
Agricultural and Engineering (SAUS) ... A&E
Agricultural and Food Chemistry (journ.) (SAUS) ... Agric Fd Chemy
Agricultural and Food Policy Center [*Texas A & M University*] [*Research center*] (RCD) ... AFPC
Agricultural and Food Products Market Development Assistance Program [*Canada*] ... AGMAP
Agricultural and Food Research Council (SAUO) ... AFCR
Agricultural and Food Research Council [*Research center*] [*British*] (IRC) ... AFRC
Agricultural and Food Research Service [*Ministry of Agriculture, Fisheries, and Food*] [*British*] (IRUK) ... AFRS
Agricultural and Forest Meteorology (journ.) (SAUS) ... Agric For Meteorol
Agricultural and Forestry Committee (SAUO) ... A&F
Agricultural and Horticultural ... A & H
Agricultural and Horticultural (SAUS) ... A&H
Agricultural and Horticultural Engineering Abstracts [*A publication*] ... AHA
Agricultural and Horticultural Engineering Abstracts (journ.) (SAUS) ... Agric Hort Engng Abstr
Agricultural and Industrial [*In a college name*] ... A & I
Agricultural and Industrial Chemistry (SAUS) ... AIC
Agricultural and Industrial Manufacturers' Representatives Association (EA) ... AIMRA
Agricultural and Industrial Manufacturers Representatives Association (SAUO) ... AIMRA
Agricultural and Industrial Process Heat (MCD) ... AIPH

Agricultural and Livestock Research Center for the Semi-Arid Tropic (SAUO) ... EMBRAPA
Agricultural and Mechanical (SAUS) ... A&M
Agricultural and Mechanical [*In a college name*] ... A & M
Agricultural and Mechanical College (SAUO) ... A & M Coll
Agricultural and Mechanical College of Texas (SAUO) ... A&M
Agricultural and Natural Resources ... ANR
Agricultural and Pastoral (ADA) ... A & P
Agricultural and Pastoral (SAUS) ... A&P
Agricultural and Pastoral Society of New Zealand (SAUO) ... A&P
Agricultural and Rural Development Act [*Canada*] ... ARDA
Agricultural and Rural Development Corporation (SAUO) ... ARDC
Agricultural and Technical [*In a college name*] ... A & T
Agricultural and Technical Institute (SAUO) ... A&TI
Agricultural and Veterinary Chemical ... AVC
Agricultural and Veterinary Chemicals Act (SAUO) ... AVCA
Agricultural and Veterinary Chemicals (journ.) (SAUS) ... Agr Vet Chem
Agricultural and Veterinary Chemicals Policy Committee (SAUO) ... AVCPC
Agricultural and Veterinary Products Index [*A publication*] ... AVPI
Agricultural Automation ... AGRIMATION
Agricultural Aviation Research Unit [*British*] (ARC) ... AARU
Agricultural Bank of China ... ABoC
Agricultural Biological Literature Evaluation (SAUS) ... ABLE
Agricultural Biological Literature Exploitation (SAUS) ... ABLE
Agricultural Biotechnology Center [*University of Maryland*] [*Research center*] ... ABC
Agricultural Biotechnology International Conference (HGEN) ... ABIC
Agricultural Biotechnology News (journ.) (SAUS) ... Agric Biotechnol News
Agricultural Bulletin. Federated Malay States (journ.) (SAUS) ... Agric Bull Fed Malay States
Agricultural Bulletin. Saga University (journ.) (SAUS) ... Agric Bull Saga Univ
Agricultural Bureau of New South Wales [*Australia*] ... ABNSW
Agricultural Bureau of New South Wales. State Congress (journ.) (SAUS) ... Agric Bur NSW State Congr
Agricultural Bureau of South Australia ... ABSA
Agricultural Business (SAUS) ... AGRIBUSINESS
Agricultural Business and Commerce ... ABC
Agricultural Central Cooperation Association (SAUO) ... ACCA
Agricultural Central Cooperative Association Ltd. [*British*] (BI) ... ACCA
Agricultural Central Trading [*British*] ... ACT
Agricultural Central Trading, Ltd. (SAUO) ... ACT
Agricultural Chemical Computerized Information System (SAUS) ... ACCIS
Agricultural Chemicals Consultative Group [*Australia*] ... ACCG
Agricultural Chemicals (journ.) (SAUS) ... AGCHAZ
Agricultural Climatological Office [*Department of Commerce*] ... ACO
Agricultural Code [*A publication*] (DLA) ... Agric C
Agricultural Code (journ.) (SAUS) ... Agric C
Agricultural College (SAUS) ... AGCOL
Agricultural Colony (GEOI) ... COL
Agricultural Commodities Data Base [*Alberta Department of Agriculture*] [*Information service or system*] (IID) ... AGDATA
Agricultural Communications Network [*Purdue University*] [*Telecommunications service*] (TSSD) ... ACN
Agricultural Communications Networks (SAUS) ... ACN
Agricultural Communicators in Education (EA) ... ACE
Agricultural Computer Association [*Defunct*] (EA) ... ACA
Agricultural Conservation and Adjustment Administration [*New Deal*] ... ACAA
Agricultural Conservation Program [*Department of Agriculture*] ... ACP
Agricultural, Construction, and Earthmoving Equipment [*Acronym is the name of ametal coating painting product*] [*Imperial Chemical Industries Ltd.*] [*British*] ... ACE
Agricultural Construction Industry Association [*British*] (EAIO) ... ACIA
Agricultural Co-operation & Marketing Services, Ltd. (SAUO) ... ACMS
Agricultural Cooperative Association (SAUO) ... ACA
Agricultural Cooperative Council of Oregon (SRA) ... ACCO
Agricultural Cooperative Development Institute (SAUO) ... ACDI
Agricultural Cooperative Development International (EA) ... ACDI
Agricultural Cooperative Development International/Volunteers in Overseas Cooperative Assistance (SAUO) ... ACDI/VOCA
Agricultural Cooperative Federation (SAUO) ... ACF
Agricultural Cooperative Managers Association (SAUO) ... ACMA
Agricultural Cooperative Service [*Washington, DC*] [*Department of Agriculture*] (GRD) ... ACS
Agricultural Co-operatives Bank of Iran (SAUO) ... ACBI
Agricultural Council of America (SAUO) ... ACA
Agricultural Council of Arkansas (SRA) ... ACA
Agricultural Council of California (SRA) ... ACC
Agricultural Credit and Cooperative Financing Administration (SAUO) ... ACCFA
Agricultural Credit Corp. Act [*1932*] ... ACCA
Agricultural Credit Corp. Ltd. [*British*] (BI) ... ACC
Agricultural Decisions [*A publication*] ... AD
Agricultural Decisions [*A publication*] (DLA) ... Agric Dec
Agricultural Department (SAUO) ... AC
Agricultural Department (SAUS) ... AD
Agricultural Department (SAUO) ... AgrIDept
Agricultural Development Advisory Service (SAUS) ... ADAS
Agricultural Development Agencies in Bangladesh (SAUO) ... ADAB
Agricultural Development and Advisory Service [*British*] (ARC) ... ADAS
Agricultural Development and Credit Bank (SAUO) ... ADCB
Agricultural Development and Marketing Authority [*Northern Territory, Australia*] ... ADMA
Agricultural Development and Marketing Board [*Northern Territory Australia*] ... ADMB
Agricultural Development Branch, Agriculture Canada [*Direction Generale du Developpement Agricole, Agriculture Canada*], **New Westminster, British Columbia** [*Library symbol*] [*National Library of Canada*] [*Obsolete*] (BIB) ... BNWAG
Agricultural Development Center (SAUS) ... ADC
Agricultural Development Corporation (SAUO) ... ADC
Agricultural Development Council [*Later, WIIAD*] (EA) ... ADC
Agricultural Development Planning Center [*ASEAN*] [*Thailand*] [*Research center*] (IRC) ... ADPC
Agricultural Development Planning Center (or Centre) (SAUS) ... ADPC
Agricultural Development Planning Centre (SAUO) ... ADPC
Agricultural Development Project [*London, England*] ... ADP
Agricultural Development Service (SAUO) ... ADS
Agricultural Documentation (SAUS) ... AGDOC
Agricultural Drainage Well (GEOI) ... ADW
Agricultural Drought Monitoring Integrative Technique (SAUS) ... ADMIT
Agricultural, Ecological, and Geographical Information System ... AEGIS
Agricultural Economic Report (SAUS) ... AER
Agricultural Economic Reports ... AER
Agricultural Economics [*Database*] [*Department of Agriculture*] [*Washington, DC*] ... AGECON
Agricultural Economics and Farm Management Occasional Paper. Department of Agriculture. Univer-sity of Queensland (journ.) (SAUS) ... Agric Econ Fm Mgmt Occ Pap Dep Agric Qd Univ
Agricultural Economics Association of Southeast Asia (SAUO) ... AESSEA
Agricultural Economics Bulletin for Africa [*A publication*] ... AEBA
Agricultural Economics Division [*of AMS, Department of Agriculture*] ... AEC
Agricultural Economics Extension Series. University of Kentucky. Cooperative Extension Service (journ.) (SAUS) ... Agric Econ Ext Ser Univ KY Coop Ext Serv
Agricultural Economics Reference Organization (SAUO) ... AERO
Agricultural Economics Report. Department of Agricultural Economics. Michigan State University (journ.) (SAUS) ... Agric Econ Rep Dep Agric Econ Mich State Univ
Agricultural Economics Research Council of Canada (SAUO) ... AERCC
Agricultural Economics Research Institute (or Institution) (SAUS) ... AERI
Agricultural Economics Research Institute, Oxford (SAUO) ... AERI
Agricultural Economics Research Institution [*British*] ... AERI
Agricultural Economics Research Report. Mississippi Agricultural and Forestry Experiment Station (journ.) (SAUS) ... Agric Econ Res Rep Miss Agric For Exp Sta
Agricultural Economics Research Unit (SAUO) ... AERU
Agricultural Economics Research. United States Department of Agri-culture. Economic Research Service (journ.) (SAUS) ... Agric Econ Res US Dep Agric Econ Res Serv
Agricultural Economics Society (EAIO) ... AES
Agricultural Economist (journ.) (SAUS) ... Agric Econ
Agricultural Education Association [*British*] ... AEA
Agricultural Education (journ.) (SAUS) ... Agric Educ
Agricultural Education Magazine (journ.) (SAUS) ... Agric Educ Mag
Agricultural Electronic Fund Transfer (SAUO) ... AGEFT
Agricultural Engineer ... AE
Agricultural Engineer ... AgE
Agricultural Engineering (DD) ... AgrEng
Agricultural Engineering Journal (journ.) (SAUS) ... AgricEngJ
Agricultural Engineering Research and Development [*Canada*] ... AERD
Agricultural Engineering Research Division [*of ARS, Department of Agriculture*] ... AE
Agricultural Engineering Research Division (SAUO) ... AERD
Agricultural Engineering Society, Australia (SAUO) ... AESA
Agricultural Engineers Association [*British*] (DS) ... AEA
Agricultural Enterprise Institute (SAUO) ... AEI
Agricultural Environmental Quality Institute [*Department of Agriculture*] [*Beltsville, MD*] ... AEQI
Agricultural Equipment Advisory Committee [*Australia*] ... AEAC
Agricultural Equipment Liaison Committee [*Victoria, Australia*] ... AELC
Agricultural Estimates (SAUS) ... AES
Agricultural Estimates Division [*of AMS, Department of Agriculture*] ... AES
Agricultural Executive Committee (SAUO) ... AEC
Agricultural Executive Council [*British*] ... AEC
Agricultural Experiment Station (SAUO) ... AES
Agricultural Experiment Station. University of Vermont. Bulletin (journ.) (SAUS) ... Agric Exp Stn Univ VT Bull
Agricultural Experiment Station. University of Vermont. Bulletin (journ.) (SAUS) ... VAEBAI
Agricultural Export Company Ltd. (SAUO) ... Agrexco
Agricultural Extension and Research Liaison Service [*Nigeria*] (IRC) ... AERLS
Agricultural Extension and Rural Development Centre [*University of Reading*] [*British*] (CB) ... AERDC
Agricultural Extension Service (OICC) ... AES
Agricultural Fair Practices Act (SAUS) ... AFPA
Agricultural Fair Practices Act of 1967 ... AFPA
Agricultural Finance Federation, Ltd. (SAUO) ... AFFL
Agricultural Finance Review. United States Department of Agriculture. Economics, Statistics and Coopera-tive Service (journ.) (SAUS) ... Agric Financ Rev US Dep Agric Econ Stat Coop Serv
Agricultural Forecaster (NOAA) ... AF
Agricultural Foreign Investment Disclosure Act [*1978*] ... AFIDA
Agricultural Futures Exchange [*London, England*] ... AFE
Agricultural Gazette of Canada (journ.) (SAUS) ... Agric Gaz Can
Agricultural Gazette of New South Wales (journ.) (SAUS) ... AGNSAR
Agricultural Gazette of New South Wales (journ.) (SAUS) ... Agric Gaz NSW
Agricultural Gazette of Tasmania (journ.) (SAUS) ... Agric Gaz Tasm
Agricultural Genetics Co. Ltd. [*British*] (IRUK) ... AGC
Agricultural Genetics Company (SAUO) ... AGC

Agricultural History (journ.) (SAUS) ... AgricHist
Agricultural History Society (EA) ... AHS
Agricultural Homestead (SAUS) ... ah
Agricultural, Horticultural and Forestry Industry Training Board (SAUO) ... AH&FITB
Agricultural Implements Hand [*Freight*] ... AG IMPS HND
Agricultural Implements Hand (SAUS) ... Ag Imps Hnd
Agricultural Implements other than Hand (SAUS) ... Ag Imps ot Hand
Agricultural Implements Other Than Hand [*Freight*] ... AG IMPS O T HND
Agricultural Improvement Council [*British*] ... AIC
Agricultural Index [*Edinburgh School of Agriculture*] [*Information service or system*] [*British*] (NITA) ... AGDEX
Agricultural Index ... AI
Agricultural Index (journ.) (SAUS) ... Agric Index
Agricultural, Industrial, and Development [*Bank*] [*Dominica*] (EY) ... AID
Agricultural Industrial Development (SAUS) ... AID
Agricultural Industries and Food Committee (SAUO) ... AIFC
Agricultural Industry Development Advisory Service (ODBW) ... AIDAS
Agricultural Information (SAUS) ... AGROINFORM
Agricultural Information and Documentation Section [*Royal Tropical Institute*] [*Netherlands*] [*Information service or system*] (IID) ... AIDS
Agricultural Information and Marketing Services [*Department of Agriculture*] [*Information service or system*] (IID) ... AIMS
Agricultural Information Association for Australasia ... AIAA
Agricultural Information Bank for Asia [*Southeast Asian Regional Center for Graduate Study and Research in Agriculture*] [*Information service or system*] (IID) ... AIBA
Agricultural Information Bulletin ... AIB
Agricultural Information Bulletin USDA Forest Service (SAUS) ... Agric Inf Bull USDA For Serv
Agricultural Information Development Scheme (EAIO) ... AIDS
Agricultural Information Services [*HUD*] [*Information service or system*] (IID) ... AGROINFORM
Agricultural Information System (NITA) ... ARIS
Agricultural Insecticide and Fungicide Association (SAUO) ... AIFA
Agricultural Institute of Canada ... AIC
Agricultural Institute Review (journ.) (SAUS) ... Agric Inst Rev
Agricultural Institution (SAUS) ... AI
Agricultural Institution (SAUO) ... AI
Agricultural Investment Corporation S.A. (SAUO) ... Aicsa
Agricultural Investment Grant Scheme (SAUS) ... AIGS
Agricultural Journal and Mining Record. Maritzburg (journ.) (SAUS) ... Agric J&Mining Rec Maritzburg
Agricultural Journal. Department of Agriculture. Fiji Islands (journ.) (SAUS) ... Agric J Dep Agric Fiji Isl
Agricultural Journal of British Guiana (journ.) (SAUS) ... Agric J Br Guiana
Agricultural Journal of Egypt (journ.) (SAUS) ... Agric J Egypt
Agricultural Journal of India (journ.) (SAUS) ... Agric J India
Agricultural Journal of South Africa (journ.) (SAUS) ... Agric J S Afr
Agricultural Journal of the Cape of Good Hope (journ.) (SAUS) ... AgricJ Cape GH
Agricultural Journal of the Union of South Africa (journ.) (SAUS) ... Agric J Union S Afr
Agricultural Labor Relations Act (SAUO) ... ALRA
Agricultural Labor Relations Board (SAUO) ... ALRB
Agricultural Laboratory Technology ... ALT
Agricultural Labourer ... AL
Agricultural Land Commission [*British*] (BI) ... ALC
Agricultural Land Service [*Later, ADAS*] [*British*] ... ALS
Agricultural Land Tribunal (SAUO) ... ALT
Agricultural Librarians in Colleges and Universities (AIE) ... ALCU
Agricultural Libraries and Documentation Centres Network (SAUO) ... AGLINET
Agricultural Libraries and Information Services in the South-East (SAUS) ... ALISSE
Agricultural Libraries Information Network [*Department of Agriculture*] [*Library network*] ... AGLINET
Agricultural Libraries Information Network [*Department of Agriculture*] [*Library network*] ... ALIN
Agricultural Library Networks [*IAALD*] [*United Kingdom*] ... AGLINET
Agricultural Lime Department (SAUO) ... ALD
Agricultural Limestone Institute ... ALI
Agricultural Literature of Czecho-slovakia (journ.) (SAUS) ... Agric Lit Czech
Agricultural Machinery Development Board (SAUS) ... AMDB
Agricultural Machinery Development Board (SAUO) ... AMDB
Agricultural Machinery Journal (journ.) (SAUS) ... Agric Mach J
Agricultural Machinery Operation and Management Office (SAUO) ... AMONO
Agricultural Machinery Parts Association (SAUO) ... AMPA
Agricultural Machinery Research Association (SAUO) ... AMRA
Agricultural Machinery Testing and Evaluation Center (SAUO) ... AMTEC
Agricultural Machinery Training Development Society (SAUO) ... AMTDS
Agricultural Management Information System [*European Economic Community*] (ADA) ... AMIS
Agricultural Manpower Society [*British*] (EAIO) ... AMS
Agricultural Manufacturers' Association [*Australia*] ... AMA
Agricultural Marketing ... AM
Agricultural Marketing Administration [*World War II*] ... AMA
Agricultural Marketing Development Executive Committee (SAUO) ... AMDEC
Agricultural Marketing (journ.) (SAUS) ... Agric Mark
Agricultural Marketing Project [*Defunct*] (EA) ... AMP
Agricultural Marketing Service [*Formerly, CMS*] [*Washington, DC*] [*Department of Agriculture*] ... AMS
Agricultural Marketing Service, P and S Docket [*United States*] [*A publication*] (DLA) ... AMS P & S
Agricultural Marketing Transition Act (SAUO) ... AMTA
Agricultural Materials Analysis Information Service [*Laboratory of the Government Chemist*] [*British*] (NITA) ... AMAIS
Agricultural Materials in Libraries [*Later, Agriculture Library*] [*Online Computer Library Center, Inc.*] [*Information service or system*] (CRD) ... AgMIL
Agricultural Meteorological Data Logging System (NOAA) ... AMDLS
Agricultural Meteorology Programme (SAUS) ... AgMP
Agricultural Missions (EA) ... AM
Agricultural Mortgage Corp. [*Finance*] [*British*] ... AMC
Agricultural Mortgage Corporation Ltd. (SAUO) ... AMC
Agricultural Network Serving Extension and Research [*University of Kentucky*] [*Lexington*] [*Information service or system*] [*Research center*] (IID) ... ANSER
Agricultural News Letter. E.1. Du Pont De Nemours and Company (journ.) (SAUS) ... Agric News Lett E1 Du Pont De Nemours Co
Agricultural Newsletter (journ.) (SAUS) ... Ag NL
Agricultural Non-Point Source [*Environmental science*] ... AGNPS
Agricultural Nonpoint Source Pollution Model (SAUS) ... AGNPS
Agricultural Online (SAUS) ... AGLINE
Agricultural On-Line Access [*Formerly, CAIN*] [*National Agricultural Library, Information Systems Division*] [*Bibliographic database*] [*Information service or system*] (IID) ... AGRICOLA
Agricultural (or Agriculture) and Food Research Council (SAUO) ... AFRC
Agricultural (or Agriculture) and Resource Management Council of Australia and New Zealand (SAUO) ... ARMCANZ
Agricultural (or Agriculture) Conservation Program (SAUO) ... ACP
Agricultural (or Agriculture) Cooperative Development International (SAUO) ... ACDI
Agricultural (or Agriculture) Network Information Center (SAUO) ... AgNIC
Agricultural Organization Society (SAUO) ... AOS
Agricultural Pest Destruction Council (SAUO) ... APDC
Agricultural Pilots Association [*Defunct*] (EA) ... APA
Agricultural Pipe Drain ... APD
Agricultural Planning and Coordinating Committee (SAUO) ... APCC
Agricultural Policy Review (journ.) (SAUS) ... Agr Policy Rev
Agricultural Power (SAUS) ... AGRIPOWER
Agricultural Procurement Regulations ... AGPR
Agricultural Producers Labor Committee (SAUO) ... APLC
Agricultural Production and Management ... APM
Agricultural Production Systems Research Unit (SAUS) ... APSRU
Agricultural Productivity Commission (SAUO) ... APC
Agricultural Program (NTCM) ... A
Agricultural Progress (journ.) (SAUS) ... AGPGAZ
Agricultural Projects Services Centre (SAUO) ... APROSC
Agricultural Property and Client System (SAUO) ... AGPACS
Agricultural Property Management Regulations ... AGPMR
Agricultural Protection Board (SAUO) ... APB
Agricultural Publishers Association (EA) ... APA
Agricultural Real Time Imaging Satellite System (PDAA) ... ARTISS
Agricultural Record (journ.) (SAUS) ... Agric Rec
Agricultural Record. South Australia Department of Agriculture (journ.) (SAUS) ... Agric Rec South Aust Dep Agric
Agricultural Refinance and Development Corporation (SAUO) ... ARDC
Agricultural Refinance Corporation (SAUO) ... ARC
Agricultural Rehabilitation and Development Agency (SAUO) ... ARDA
Agricultural Rehabilitation and Development Association (SAUO) ... ARDA
Agricultural Relations Council (EA) ... ARC
Agricultural Representative [*Canada*] ... Ag Rep
Agricultural Requirements Board [*Queensland, Australia*] ... ARB
Agricultural Requisites and Mechanization (SAUS) ... ARM
Agricultural Research ... AR
Agricultural Research Administration [*Superseded by ARS, 1953*] [*Department of Agriculture*] ... ARA
Agricultural Research and Advisory Station [*New South Wales, Australia*] ... ARAS
Agricultural Research and Education Center, Belle Glade [*University of Florida*] [*Research center*] (RCD) ... AREC
Agricultural Research and Education Center, Fort Lauderdale [*University of Florida*] [*Research center*] (RCD) ... AREC
Agricultural Research and Educational Center [*American University of Beirut*] ... AREC
Agricultural Research and Veterinary Centre [*New South Wales, Australia*] ... ARVC
Agricultural Research Center [*of ARS, Department of Agriculture*] ... ARC
Agricultural Research Center Operations [*of ARS, Department of Agriculture*] ... ARCO
Agricultural Research Council [*Research center*] [*British*] (IRC) ... ARC
Agricultural Research Council Computerized Information System (SAUO) ... ARCIS
Agricultural Research Council Radiobiological Laboratory (SAUO) ... ARCRL
Agricultural Research Council Radiological Laboratory [*British*] ... ARCRL
Agricultural Research Council Unit of Statistics [*British*] (ARC) ... ARCUS
Agricultural Research Council Weed Research Organization [*British*] ... ARCWRO
Agricultural Research Current Information System (SAUS) ... ARCIS
Agricultural Research Department, Ministry of Agriculture, Nature Conservation and Fisheries (SAUO) ... DLO
Agricultural Research, Education, Extension Organization (SAUO) ... AREEO
Agricultural Research Foundation [*Oregon State University*] [*Research center*] (RCD) ... ARF
Agricultural Research Information Centre [*Indian Council of Agricultural Research*] (IID) ... ARIC
Agricultural Research Information Index [*United Nations*] ... AGRINDEX
Agricultural Research Institute (SAUS) ... RALA
Agricultural Research Institute and Agricultural College (SAUO) ... ARIAC
Agricultural Research Institute Ukiriguru. Progress Report (journ.) (SAUS) ... PRAUD9
Agricultural Research (journ.) (SAUS) ... NOGKAV
Agricultural Research Journal of Kerala (journ.) (SAUS) ... Agr Res J Kerala

Agricultural Research Management Information System (SAUS) .... ARMIS
Agricultural Research Organization. Preliminary Report (journ.) (SAUS) .... PRAODP
Agricultural Research Organizations on the Web (SAUO) .... AROW
Agricultural Research Policy Advisory Committee [*Terminated, 1977*] [*Department of Agriculture*] .... ARPAC
Agricultural Research Program and Facilities Subcommittee (SAUO) .... ARPF
Agricultural Research Review (journ.) (SAUS) .... AGRRA
Agricultural Research. Seoul National University (journ.) (SAUS) .... NYSTDL
Agricultural Research Service [*Washington, DC*] [*Department of Agriculture*] [*Also, an information service or system*] .... ARS
Agricultural Research Service (SAUS) MV-678
Agricultural Research Service National Research Program (SAUO) .... ARS-NRP
Agricultural Research Service Special Research Program (SAUO) .... ARS-SRP
Agricultural Research Service/ United States Department of Agriculture (SAUO) .... ARS/USDA
Agricultural Research Service Water Conservation Laboratory [*Tempe, AZ*] .... WCL-ARS
Agricultural Research Services, Animal Health Division [*Department of Agriculture*] [*ICAO designator*] (FAAC) .... AGR
Agricultural Research Station (ADA) .... ARS
Agricultural Resources Center (SAUO) .... ARC
Agricultural Resources Conservation Program [*Department of Agriculture*] .... ARCP
Agricultural Retailers Association (NTPA) .... ARA
Agricultural Runoff Model [*Environmental Protection Agency*] (AEPA) .... ARM
Agricultural Safety (HEAS) .... AS
Agricultural School (SAUO) .... AgSch
Agricultural Science and Technology Information Management System (SAUS) .... ASTIMS
Agricultural Science Information Center (SAUS) .... ASIC
Agricultural Science Journal. (journ.) (SAUS) .... Ag Sci J
Agricultural Science Review [*A publication*] .... ASR
Agricultural Science Review (journ.) (SAUS) .... ASR
Agricultural Sciences Advisory Panel (GEOI) .... ASAP
Agricultural Sciences Information Network [*National Agricultural Library*] [*Beltsville, MD*] .... ASIN
Agricultural Security Coordinating Committee (SAUO) .... ASCC
Agricultural Service Information Network [*Database producer*] (NITA) .... ASIN
Agricultural Show Council of Tasmania [*Australia*] .... ASCT
Agricultural Show Exhibitors' Association [*British*] (BI) .... ASEA
Agricultural Situation (journ.) (SAUS) .... Agr Situation
Agricultural Societies Council of New South Wales [*Australia*] .... ASCNSW
Agricultural Society (SAUO) .... AS
Agricultural Society of Nigeria. Proceedings [*A publication*] .... ASNP
Agricultural Soil Moisture Estimation (MCD) .... ASME
Agricultural Space Informatics Network Experiment (SAUS) .... AGRISPINE
Agricultural Special Fund [*Asian Development Bank*] [*United Nations*] (EY) .... ASF
Agricultural Stabilization and Conservation .... ASC
Agricultural Stabilization and Conservation Service [*Department of Agriculture*] .... ASCS
Agricultural Statistical Information System (SAUS) .... AGIS
Agricultural Statistics Board [*Department of Agriculture*] [*Information service or system*] (IID) .... ASB
Agricultural Statistics. North Dakota Crop and Livestock Reporting Service (journ.) (SAUS) .... Agr Statist N Dak Crop Livestock Rep Serv
Agricultural Subterminal Facilities Act of 1980 .... ASFA
Agricultural System for Storage and Subsequent Selection of Information (SAUS) .... ASSASSIN
Agricultural System for Storage and Subsequent Selection of Information [*British*] [*Information service or system*] (NITA) .... ASSASSIN
Agricultural Systems Research Institute [*Beltsville, MD*] [*Department of Agriculture*] (GRD) .... ASRI
Agricultural Teachers' Association of the Australian Capital Territory .... ATAACT
Agricultural Technical Assistance Foundation [*Defunct*] (EA) .... ATAF
Agricultural Technologist [*A publication*] .... Agric Tech
Agricultural Trade Council (EA) .... ATC
Agricultural Trade Office [*Foreign Agricultural Service*] .... ATO
Agricultural Training Board (COBU) .... ATB
Agricultural Training Institute (SAUO) .... ATI
Agricultural Wages Board [*British*] .... AWB
Agricultural Wages Board (SAUO) .... AWB
Agricultural Wages Committee (SAUO) .... AWC
Agricultural Wages Committee [*British*] (DAS) .... AWC
Agricultural Wastes (journ.) (SAUS) .... Agr Wastes
Agricultural Water Management (SAUS) .... Agric Water Manage
Agricultural Water Quality Protection Program [*Department of Agriculture*] .... AWQPP
Agricultural Weather Service Center [*National Oceanic and Atmospheric Administration*] .... AWSC
Agricultural Wholesale Society (SAUO) .... AWS
Agricultural Workers Organization (SAUS) .... AWO
Agricultural Workers Organizing Committee [*Later, UFWA*] [*AFL-CIO*] .... AWOC
Agricultural Workers' Union (DAS) .... AWU
Agricultural Workers Union (SAUO) .... AWU
Agricultural-Biological Literature Exploitation [*Systems study of National Agricultural Library*] .... ABLE
Agricultural-Energy Transportation Digest (journ.) (SAUS) .... Agric-Energy Transp Dig
Agriculture .... AG
Agriculture (NTIO) .... agr
Agriculture (DD) .... Agr
Agriculture .... AGRCLT
Agriculture (DLA) .... AGRI
Agriculture .... AGRIC
Agriculture .... Agric
Agriculture (SAUS) .... DG VI
Agriculture Act of 1970 (COE) .... AA
Agriculture and Agri-Food Canada .... AAFC
Agriculture and Agro-Industries Journal (journ.) (SAUS) .... Agric Agroind J
Agriculture and Animal Husbandry (journ.) (SAUS) .... Agric Anim Hub
Agriculture and Consumer Protection Act of 1973 .... ACPA
Agriculture and Engineering (SAUS) .... A&E
Agriculture and Environment (journ.) (SAUS) .... Agric Env
Agriculture and Financial Statistics Division (SAUS) .... AGFS
Agriculture and Fishery Development Corp. [*South Korea*] .... AFDC
Agriculture and Fishery Development Fund (SAUO) .... AFDC
Agriculture and Forestry (SAUS) .... A&F
Agriculture and Forestry Bulletin (journ.) (SAUS) .... Agric For Bull
Agriculture and Forestry Committee [*US Senate*] .... A & F
Agriculture and Forestry Secretariat .... AFS
Agriculture and Industrial (SAUS) .... A&I
Agriculture and Livestock in India (journ.) (SAUS) .... Agric Livestock India
Agriculture and Livestock Professional Photographers Association (EA) .... ALPPA
Agriculture and Markets [*A publication*] (DLA) .... Agric & Mkts
Agriculture and Markets (journ.) (SAUS) .... Agric&Mkts
Agriculture & Resources Inventory Surveys Thru Aerospace Remote Sensing (SAUO) .... AgRISTARS
Agriculture and Rural Development Subsidiary Agreement [*Canada*] .... ARDSA
Agriculture and Technical (SAUS) .... A&T
Agriculture and Veterinary Chemicals Association (SAUO) .... AVCA
Agriculture and Veterinary Chemicals Association of Australia (SAUO) .... AVCAA
Agriculture and Veterinary Chemicals Unit (SAUS) .... AVCU
Agriculture and Water Project (SAUS) .... AGWAT
Agriculture Asia (journ.) (SAUS) .... Agric Asia
Agriculture Biotechnology Research Advisory Committee [*Department of Agriculture*] (EGAO) .... ABRAC
Agriculture Board of Contract Appeals (AAGC) .... AGBCA
Agriculture Bulletin (journ.) (SAUS) .... Agric Bull
Agriculture Canada .... AGC
Agriculture Canada .... AGRIC
Agriculture Canada. Annual Report (journ.) (SAUS) .... Agric Can Annu Rep
Agriculture Canada, Lethbridge, Alberta [*Library symbol*] [*National Library of Canada*] (NLC) .... ALAG
Agriculture Canada Library [*UTLAS symbol*] .... DAG
Agriculture Canada. Monograph (journ.) (SAUS) .... Agric Can Monogr
Agriculture Canada, Montreal, Quebec [*Library symbol*] [*National Library of Canada*] (NLC) .... QMPCA
Agriculture Canada. Rapport Annual (journ.) (SAUS) .... Agric Can Rapp Annu
Agriculture Canada. Research Branch Report (journ.) (SAUS) .... Agric Can Res Brauch Rep
Agriculture Canada, Saint Hyacinthe Food Research Centre, Saint Hyacinthe, PQ, Canada [*Library symbol*] [*Library of Congress*] (LCLS) .... CaQStHAG
Agriculture Canada, Vancouver, British Columbia [*Library symbol*] [*National Library of Canada*] (NLC) .... BVAAG
Agriculture Canada. Weed Survey Series (journ.) (SAUS) .... Agric Can Weed Sury Ser
Agriculture Circular. United States Department of Agriculture (journ.) (SAUS) .... Agric Circ US Dep Agric
Agriculture Conservation Program (EBF) .... ACP
Agriculture Control Program [*Environmental Protection Agency*] (EPAT) .... ACP
Agriculture Control Program [*Water quality management*] (EEVL) .... ACP
Agriculture Cooperative Service (SAUS) .... ACS
Agriculture Council of America (EA) .... ACA
Agriculture Council of America (NTPA) .... Ag Council
Agriculture Department [*US government*] .... A
Agriculture Department Automated Manpower (SAUS) .... ADAM
Agriculture Department (US) (AAGC) .... Ag
Agriculture Department's Automated Manpower .... ADAM
Agriculture Development Bank of Nepal (SAUS) .... ADBN
Agriculture Division [*Census*] (OICC) .... AGR
Agriculture, Ecosystems and Environment (journ.) (SAUS) .... Agric Ecosyst&Environ
Agriculture Engineers Association (SAUO) .... AEA
Agriculture Fact Sheet US Department of Agriculture (journ.) (SAUS) .... Agric Fact Sh US Dep Agric
Agriculture Forestry and Other Human Activities Subgroup (SAUO) .... AFOS
Agriculture, Forestry, Fishing [*Department of Employment*] [*British*] .... AFF
Agriculture Handbook (SAUS) .... Agric Handb
Agriculture Handbook .... AH
Agriculture Handbook. United States Department of Agriculture. Agricultural Research Service (journ.) (SAUS) .... Agric Flandb US Dep Agric Agric Res Serv
Agriculture Handbook. United States Department of Agriculture (journ.) (SAUS) .... Agric Ilandb US Dep Agric
Agriculture, Hydrology and Meteorology (SAUS) .... AGRHYMET
Agriculture in the Americas (journ.) (SAUS) .... Ag Am
Agriculture Industry Advisory Committee (HEAS) .... AIAC
Agriculture International (journ.) (SAUS) .... Agric Int
Agriculture Labor (SAUS) .... ALA
Agriculture Labor Administration (SAUO) .... ALA
Agriculture Labor Relations Board (SAUO) .... ALRB
Agriculture Labor Relations Bureau (SAUO) .... ALRB
Agriculture Lime Industry Ltd. (SAUO) .... ALIL
Agriculture, Marine, Scientific, and Industrial Research Ministry (SAUO) .... AMSIR
Agriculture Mechanized (SAUS) .... AGRIMECH
Agriculture Network Information Center [*Internet resource*] .... AgDB

Agriculture, Nutrition, and Forestry (DLA) .... ANF
Agriculture Online [*Doane Western, Inc.*] (NITA) .... AGLINE
Agriculture Pakistan (journ.) (SAUS) .... AGRPAK
Agriculture Stabilization and Conservation Service (SAUO) .... ASCS
Agriculture Western Australia commercial unit (SAUO) .... AG WEST
Agriculture Working Group .... AWG
Agricultured Engineering (journ.) (SAUS) .... Agric Eng
Agriculturist (SAUS) .... Agri
AgriData Network [*AgriData Resources, Inc.*] [*Milwaukee, WI*] [*Telecommunications service*] (TSSD) .... ADN
AgriDyne Technologies, Inc. [*NASDAQ symbol*] (SAG) .... AGRI
AgriDyne Technologies, Inc. [*Associated Press*] (SAG) .... AgriDyn
Agri-Energy Roundtable (EA) .... AER
Agri-Food Development Branch [*Canada*] .... AFDB
Agri-Markets Data Service [*Capitol Publications, Inc.*] [*Database*] [*Defunct*] .... AMDS
Agrinion [*Greece*] [*Airport symbol*] (AD) .... AGQ
Agrinion [*Greece*] [*ICAO location identifier*] (ICLI) .... LGAG
Agri-Nutrition Group [*Associated Press*] (SAG) .... AgriNutr
Agri-Nutrition Group Ltd. [*NASDAQ symbol*] (SAG) .... AGNU
Agri-Products Exporters Association (EA) .... APEA
Agri-residue Dry Matter Content (SAUS) .... ADMC
Agri-residue used for animal Feed (SAUS) .... AF
Agri-residue Utilized for Energy supply (SAUS) .... EU
Agriservices Foundation (EA) .... AF
Agri-Silviculture Institute (EA) .... ASI
Agristar, Inc. (SAUO) .... AGRS
Agritope, Inc. [*NASDAQ symbol*] .... AGTO
Agrium, Inc. [*Associated Press*] (SAG) .... Agrium
Agrium, Inc. [*NYSE symbol*] (SAG) .... AGU
Agro Sur (journ.) (SAUS) .... UCASBJ
agrobiological (SAUS) .... agro
Agroborealis (journ.) (SAUS) .... AGBO
Agrochemophysica (journ.) (SAUS) .... AGPYAL
Agrociencia (journ.) (SAUS) .... AGCCBR
Agrociencia. Serie A (journ.) (SAUS) .... AGCNCR
Agroecological Zone (SAUO) .... AEZ
Agro-Ecosystems (SAUS) .... Agro-Ecosyst
Agro-Environmental Monitoring System [*Computerized Data Collection*] .... AEMS
Agroforestry Systems (SAUS) .... Agrofor Syst
Agrogeology (SAUS) .... Agrogeol
Agroindustrialization (SAUS) .... Agroind
Agroindustry (SAUS) .... Agroind
Agrolet-Mci Ltd. [*Slovakia*] [*FAA designator*] (FAAC) .... AGZ
Agrology (SAUS) .... Ag
Agronmeteorology and Operational Hydrology and Their Applications (SAUS) .... AGRHYMET
Agronomic Research for Food. Papers Presented at the Annual Meeting of the American Society of Agronomy (journ.) (SAUS) .... Agron Res Food Pap Annu Meet Am Soc Agron
Agronomics (SAUS) .... Agro
Agronomist (SAUS) .... Agro
Agronomy .... AGRON
Agronomy (ADWA) .... agron
Agronomy and Soils Research Series. Clemson Agricultural Experiment Station (journ.) (SAUS) .... Agron Soils Res Ser Clemson Agr Exp Sta
Agronomy Journal (journ.) (SAUS) .... Agron J
Agronomy (journ.)j (SAUS) .... AGRYAV
Agronomy. Mimeograph Circular. North Dakota Agricultural Experi-ment Station (journ.) (SAUS) .... Agron Mimeogr Circ N Dak Agr Exp Sta
Agronomy Pamphlet. South Dakota Agricultural Experiment Station (journ.) (SAUS) .... Agron Pam S Dak Agr Exp Sta
Agronomy, Plant Physiology and Agroecology Division (SAUO) .... APPA
Agronomy Research Center [*Southern Illinois University at Carbondale*] [*Research center*] (RCD) .... ARC
Agronomy Research Report. Louisiana State University and Agricultural and Mechanical College. Department of Agronomy (journ.) (SAUS) .... Agron Res Rep LA State Univ Agric Mech Coll Dep Agron
Agronomy Society of America (SAUO) .... ASA
Agronomy Society of New Zealand. Special Publication (journ.) (SAUS) .... Agron Soc NZ Spec Publ
Agronomy Society of New Zealand. Special Publication (journ.) (SAUS) SPAZD9
Agronomy Views. University of Nebraska. College of Agriculture and Home Economics. Extension Service (journ.) (SAUS) .... Agron Views Univ Nebr Coll Agr Home Econ Ext Sery
Agrophysics Breeding Control Device [*Birth-control device for dogs*] .... ABCD
Agroplantae (journ.) (SAUS) .... AGPLAG
Agropyron Mosaic Virus [*Plant pathology*] .... AGMV
Agrotikon Komma [*Agrarian Party*] [*Greek*] [*Political party*] (PPE) .... AGROT
Agrotikon Komma Ellados [*Agrarian Party of Greece*] [*Political party*] .... AKE
Agrupacián Nacional de Fabricantes de Maquinaria Agr²cola (SAUO) .... ANFAMA
Agrupacion de Exportadores del Centro de Espana [*Trade association*] [*Spain*] (EY) .... AGRECE
Agrupacion Herrena Independiente [*Spain*] [*Political party*] (EY) .... AHI
Agrupaciones Independientes de Canarias [*Spain*] [*Political party*] (EY) .... AIC
Agrupament Democratic Andorra (SAUO) .... ADA
Agrupament Democratic d'Andorra [*Andorran Democratic Association*] [*Political party*] (PPW) .... ADA
Agryrophil, Fluorescent, Granulated Cells (SAUS) .... AFG Cells
AGS Computers, Inc. (SAUO) .... AGS
Aguacate Mountains, Costa Rica (SAUS) .... Aguacates
Aguada, PR [*FM radio station call letters*] .... WNNV
Aguadilla [*Puerto Rico*] [*Airport symbol*] (OAG) .... BQN
Aguadilla, PR [*Location identifier*] [*FAA*] (FAAL) .... JFF
Aguadilla, PR [*AM radio station call letters*] .... WABA
Aguadilla, PR [*Television station call letters*] .... WELU
Aguadilla, PR [*FM radio station call letters*] .... WIVA
Aguadilla, PR [*AM radio station call letters*] .... WNOZ
Aguadilla, PR [*Television station call letters*] .... WOLE
Aguadilla, PR [*FM radio station call letters*] .... WTPM
Aguadilla, PR [*Television station call letters*] .... WVEO
Aguadilla/Borinquen [*Puerto Rico*] [*ICAO location identifier*] (ICLI) .... TJBQ
Aguan [*Papua New Guinea*] [*Airport symbol*] (OAG) .... AUP
Aguarico [*Ecuador*] [*ICAO location identifier*] (ICLI) .... SERI
Aguas Blancas [*Peru*] [*ICAO location identifier*] (ICLI) .... SPCB
Aguas Calientes [*Peru*] [*ICAO location identifier*] (ICLI) .... SPAT
Aguascalientes [*Mexico*] [*Airport symbol*] (OAG) .... AGU
Aguascalientes [*Mexico*] [*ICAO location identifier*] (ICLI) .... MMAS
Agudas Harabonim [*Union of Orthodox Rabbis of the United States and Canada*] .... AH
Agudas Israel World Organization [*Jerusalem, Israel*] .... AIWO
Agudath Israel [*Union of Israel*] [*World organization of Orthodox Jews*] .... AI
Agudath Israel of America (EA) .... AIA
Agudath Israel Organization (SAUO) .... AIWO
Agudath Shofte ha-Hakhra'ah ha-Yehudit (BJA) .... ASHY
Aguelhoc [*Mali*] [*ICAO location identifier*] (ICLI) .... GAGL
Aguilar Public Library, Aguilar, CO [*Library symbol*] [*Library of Congress*] (LCLS) .... CoAg
Agulhas Current (SAUS) .... Agu Cur-106
Aguni [*Japan*] [*Airport symbol*] (OAG) .... AGJ
Aguni [*Ryukyu Islands*] [*ICAO location identifier*] (ICLI) .... RORA
Agusta [*Construzioni Aeronautiche Giovanni Agusta SpA*] [*Italy*] [*ICAO aircraft manufacturer identifier*] (ICAO) .... A
Agusta Aerospace Services (SAUS) .... AAS
Agway, Inc., Library, Syracuse, NY [*OCLC symbol*] (OCLC) .... ZUL
Agway, Inc., Syracuse, NY [*Library symbol*] [*Library of Congress*] (LCLS) .... NSyAg
AHA Automotive Technologies Corp. [*Toronto Stock Exchange symbol*] .... AHA
Ah-Ah [*Lava-Flow*] [*Hawaiian*] .... AA
Ahar [*Iran*] [*ICAO location identifier*] (ICLI) .... OITQ
Aharonov-Bohm [*Physics*] .... AB
Ahavah, Zedakah, Ahdut (BJA) .... AZA
Ahead (FAAC) .... AHD
Ahead Flag [*Navy*] [*British*] .... AD
Ahead-Throwing Weapon [*Antisubmarine*] .... ATW
AHERA Designated Person (SAUS) .... ADP
AHI Healthcare Systems, Inc. [*Associated Press*] (SAG) .... AHIHlth
AHI Healthcare Systems, Inc. [*NASDAQ symbol*] (SAG) .... AHIS
Ahikar (BJA) .... Ah
Ahilot (BJA) .... Ah
AHL Group [*Formerly, Automotive Hardware Ltd.*] [*Toronto Stock Exchange symbol*] .... AHL
Ahlhorn [*Germany*] [*ICAO location identifier*] (ICLI) .... EDNA
Ahmadabad [*India*] [*ICAO location identifier*] (ICLI) .... VAAH
Ahmadiyya Muslim Association (EAIO) .... AMA
Ahmanson [*H. F.*] **& Co.** [*NYSE symbol*] (SPSG) .... AHM
Ahmanson [*H.F.*] **& Co.** [*Associated Press*] (SAG) .... Ahmans
Ahmanson [*H.F.*] **& Co.** [*Associated Press*] (SAG) .... Ahmn
Ahmedabad [*India*] [*Airport symbol*] (OAG) .... AMD
Ahnapee and Western Railroad Co (SAUO) .... AW
[*The*] **Ahnapee & Western Railway Co.** [*Formerly, AW*] [*AAR code*] .... AHW
[*The*] **Ahnapee & Western Railway Co.** [*Later, AHW*] [*AAR code*] .... AW
Aho, Weinberger and Kernighan (SAUS) .... AWK
Aho Weinberger Kernigan (SAUS) .... AWK
Aho Weinberger Kernighan (CDE) .... awk
Ahold Ltd. [*NYSE symbol*] (SAG) .... AHO
Ahold Ltd. [*Associated Press*] (SAG) .... Ahold
A-horizon (SAUS) .... A-horiz
Ahoskie, NC [*Location identifier*] [*FAA*] (FAAL) .... ASJ
Ahoskie, NC [*FM radio station call letters*] .... WQDK
Ahoskie, NC [*AM radio station call letters*] .... WRCS
Ahoskie Public Library, Ahoskie, NC [*Library symbol*] [*Library of Congress*] (LCLS) .... NcAh
Ahoy [*Slang*] (DNAB) .... AY
Ahrens-Fox Fire Buffs Club [*Defunct*] (EA) .... AFFBC
AHT Corp. [*NASDAQ symbol*] (SG) .... AHTC
Ahtari [*Finland*] [*ICAO location identifier*] (ICLI) .... EFHT
Ahua [*Hawaii*] [*Seismograph station code, US Geological Survey*] (SEIS) .... AHA
Ahuachapan [*El Salvador*] [*Seismograph station code, US Geological Survey*] (SEIS) .... AHU
Ahvenanmaan Kokoomus; Alaendsk Samling [*Aland Coalition*] [*Finland*] (PPE) .... ALSAML
Ahwaz [*Iran*] [*Airport symbol*] [*Obsolete*] (OAG) .... AWZ
Ahwaz [*Iran*] [*ICAO location identifier*] (ICLI) .... OIAW
AIA Industries, Inc. (SAUO) .... AIAI
Aiborne Mechanical Special Mission System (SAUS) .... AMSMS
Albright College (SAUS) .... AC
AICPA Personal Liability Umbrella Security Plan (SAUO) .... AICPA PLUS
Aid and Attendance (MAE) .... A & A
Aid and Attendance (SAUS) .... A&A
Aid and Trade Provision [*Shipping*] (DS) .... ATP
Aid Association for Lutherans (EA) .... AAL
Aid Auto Stores, Inc. [*NASDAQ symbol*] (SAG) .... AIDA
Aid Auto Stores, Inc. [*Associated Press*] (SAG) .... AidAut
Aid Auto Stores, Inc. [*Associated Press*] (SAG) .... AidAuto
AID [*Agency for International Development*] **Consultant Registry InformationSystem** (IID) .... ACRIS
Aid Detachment (SAUO) .... AD
Aid for Afghan Refugees [*An association*] (EA) .... AAR
Aid for Afghan Refugees [*An association*] (EA) .... AFAR

Aid for Commonwealth English Scheme [*British*] ... ACE
Aid for Commonwealth Teaching of Science Scheme [*British*] ... ACTS
Aid for Dependent Children (SAUO) ... AFDC
Aid for India [*An association*] [*British*] (EAIO) ... AFI
Aid for International Medicine (EA) ... AIM
Aid for the Elderly in Government Institutions [*British*] ... AEGIS
Aid in Decision Making (SAUS) ... ADM
Aid of International Medicine (SAUS) ... AIM
Aid of the United States of America (SAUS) ... AUSA
Aid Refugee Chinese Intellectuals [*Defunct*] (EA) ... ARCI
Aid to Adoption of Special Kids [*An association*] (EA) ... AASK
Aid to Artisans (EA) ... ATA
Aid to Believers in the Soviet Union [*See also ACU*] [*Paris, France*] (EAIO) ... ABSU
Aid to Children with Tracheostomies [*British*] [*An association*] (DBA) ... ACT
Aid to Dependent Children ... ADC
Aid to Dependent Children of Unemployed (DHP) ... ADC-U
Aid to Displaced Persons and Its European Villages (EAIO) ... ADPEV
Aid to Families and/with Dependent Children (SAUO) ... AFDC
Aid to Families with Dependent Children ... AFDC
Aid to Families with Dependent Children of Unemployed Fathers ... AFDCUF
Aid to Families with Dependent Children-Unemployed Parents (SAUO) ... AFDC-UP
Aid to Improved Marksmanship [*Army training aid*] (INF) ... AIM
Aid to Incarcerated Mothers (EA) ... AIM
Aid to Refugee Chinese Intellectuals (SAUO) ... ARCI
Aid to Russia Fund (SAUO) ... ARF
Aid to the Aged, Blind, or Disabled [*Department of Health and Human Services*] ... AABD
Aid to the Blind ... AB
Aid to the Church in Need (EA) ... ACN
Aid to the Disabled ... AD
Aid to the Permanently and Totally Disabled [*HEW*] ... APTD
Aid to the Potentially Self-supporting Blind (SAUO) ... APSB
Aid to the Totally and Permanently Disabled [*Social Security Administration*] (OICC) ... ATPD
Aid to the Totally Disabled (IIA) ... ATD
AID Worldwide Accounting and Control System (SAUO) ... AWACS
AIDAB Centre for Pacific Development and Training (SAUO) ... ACPAC
Aide aux Personnes Deplacees et Ses Villages Europeens [*Aid to Displaced Persons and Its European Villages*] (EAIO) ... APDVE
Aide Informatisee pour le Developpement des Entreprises [*Automated Information for Management - AIM*] ... AIDE
Aided ... AID
Aided Card (LAIN) ... AC
Aided Display Submarine Control System [*Navy*] (MCD) ... ADSCS
Aided LASER Tracking System (RDA) ... ALTS
Aided School [*British*] ... A
Aided Target Detection / Classification [*Military*] ... ATD/C
Aided Target Recognition [*Army*] ... ATR
Aided Tracking ... ADT
Aided Tracking System (IAA) ... ATS
Aided Visual Development Program ... AVDP
Aided Visual Homing Missile (MCD) ... AVHOM
Aided Visual Sensor System ... AVSS
Aided Visual System ... AVS
Aide-de-Camp [*Military*] [*French*] ... ADC
Aide-de-Camp [*Military*] (MUSM) ... Aide
Aide-de-Camp General [*Appointment to the Queen*] [*British*] ... ADCGEN
Aide-de-Camp Personal [*Appointment to the Queen*] [*British*] ... ADC(P)
Aiding Leukemia Stricken American Children [*Later, ALSAC - St. Jude Children's Research Hospital*] [*Fund-raising organization*] ... ALSAC
Aiding Mothers Experienceing Neonatal Death [*Medicine*] (MEDA) ... AMEND
AIDS Action Council (EA) ... AAC
Aids Clinical Review (SAUS) ... AIDS Clin Rev
AIDS Clinical TRIALS (SAUO) ... AIDSTRIALS
AIDS [*Acquired Immune Deficiency Syndrome*] **Clinical Trials Group** (EA) ... ACTG
AIDS [*Acquired Immune Deficiency Syndrome*] **Clinical Trials Information Service** (IID) ... ACTIS
AIDS Clinical Trials Information Service (SAUO) ... ACTIS
AIDS Coalition to Unleash Power [*An association*] (NTIO) ... ACT-UP
AIDS [*Acquired Immune Deficiency Syndrome*] **Coalition to Unleash Power** ... ACT UP
AIDS Committee of Cambridge, Kitchener/Waterloo & Area (AC) ... ACCKWA
AIDS Committee of Guelph & Wellington County (AC) ... ACGWC
AIDS Committee of London (AC) ... ACOL
AIDS Committee of North Bay & Area [*Comite du Sida de North Bay et de la Region*] (AC) ... ACNBA
AIDS Committee of Simcoe County (AC) ... ACSC
AIDS Committee of Thunder Bay (AC) ... ACT-B
AIDS Committee of Toronto (AC) ... ACT
AIDS Committee of Windsor (AC) ... ACW
AIDS Community Care Montreal [*Sida Benevoles Montreal*] (AC) ... ACCM
AIDS Control and Prevention Project (SAUO) ... AIDSCAP
AIDS Cost and Services Utilization Survey (SAUO) ... ACSUS
AIDS [*Acquired Immune Deficiency Syndrome*] **Council of Central Australia** ... ACOA
AIDS Council of Central Australia (SAUO) ... ACOCA
AIDS [*Acquired Immune Deficiency Syndrome*] **Council of South Australia** ... ACOSA
AIDS Council of South Australia (SAUO) ... ACSA
AIDS [*Acquired Immune Deficiency Syndrome*] **Dementia Complex** [*Medicine*] ... ADC
Aids Distribution List [*Military*] (SAA) ... ADL
AIDS [*Acquired Immuno-Deficiency Syndrome*] **Drug Assistance Program** ... ADAP
AIDS drug Hivid (SAUS) ... ddC
AIDS drug Videx (SAUS) ... ddI
AIDS drug Zerit (SAUS) ... d4T
Aids Education and Prevention (SAUS) ... AIDS Educ Prev
AIDS Education Global Information Service (SAUO) ... AEGIS
AIDS Education Global Information System (ADWA) ... AEGIS
AIDS Education/Services for the Deaf [*An association*] ... AESD
AIDS Follow-Up Assessment Questionnaire [*Department of Health and Human Services*] (GFGA) ... AFA
AIDS Follow-up Assessment Questionnaire (SAUS) ... AFA
AIDS Housing Group of Ottawa (AC) ... AHGO
AIDS Information On-Line (SAUO) ... AIDSLINE
AIDS Initial Assessment Questionnaire [*Department of Health and Human Services*] (GFGA) ... AIA
AIDS Knowledge, Attitudes and Practices (SAUS) ... AIDS KAP
AIDS Malignancy Bank [*National Cancer Institute*] ... AMB
AIDS Medical Foundation (SAUO) ... AMF
Aids Navigation Radio Control (SAUS) ... ANRAC
Aids Production and Distribution List (SAA) ... APDL
AIDS Project Los Angeles (SAUO) ... APLA
AIDS [*Acquired Immune Deficiency Syndrome*] **Related Virus** [*Immunology*] (DAVI) ... ARV
AIDS Research Advisory Committee [*National Institutes of Health*] (EGAO) ... ARAC
Aids Research and Human Retroviruses (SAUS) ... AIDS Res Hum Retroviruses
AIDS Resource Foundation for Children (EA) ... ARFC
AIDS Saint John (AC) ... ASJ
AIDS Services and Prevention Coalition (EA) ... ASAP
AIDS Society for Asia and the Pacific ... ASFAP
AIDS Support Network of San Luis Obispo County (SAUO) ... ASN
AIDS [*Acquired Immune Deficiency Syndrome*] **Targeted Information Newsletter** [*Williams & Wilkins*] [*A publication*] ... ATIN
Aids to Communication in Education (AIE) ... ACE
Aids to Identification in Difficult Groups of Animals and Plants (SAUO) ... AIDGAP
Aids to Navigation ... AN
Aids to Navigation ... ATON
Aids to Navigation Boat ... ANB
Aids to Navigation Radio Control [*Military*] ... ANRAC
Aids to Navigation Subcommittee (SAUO) ... ANSC
AIDS Training and Information Centres (SAUO) ... ATICS
AIDS Treatment Update (SAUO) ... ATU
Aids Vaccine Advocacy Coalition ... AVAC
AIDS Vancouver Island [*Also Vancouver Island AIDS Society*] (AC) ... AVI
AIDS Virus Education and Research Trust [*British*] ... AVERT
AIDS Volunteer Clearinghouse (SAUO) ... AVC
AIDS-Associated Nephropathy [*Medicine*] (MELL) ... AAN
AIDS-Associated Neutropenia [*Medicine*] (MELL) ... AAN
AIDS [*Acquired Immune Deficiency Syndrome*]**-Associated Retrovirus** ... ARV
AIDS-Induced Panic Syndrome (SAUS) ... AIPS
Aids-Related Complex (SAUS) ... ARC
AIDS [*Acquired Immune Deficiency Syndrome*]**-Related Complex** [*Medicine*] ... ARC
AIDS-related virus (SAUS) ... Aw
Aidu [*Inawashino*] [*Seismograph station code, US Geological Survey*] [*Closed*] (SEIS) ... AID
Aiea, HI [*FM radio station call letters*] ... KGMZ
Ai-Electronics Computer (SAUS) ... AICOM
Aigen/Ennstal [*Austria*] [*ICAO location identifier*] (ICLI) ... LOXA
Aigle Azur [*France*] [*ICAO designator*] (FAAC) ... AAF
Aigner Holdings [*Vancouver Stock Exchange symbol*] ... AHS
All India Reporter, Hyderabad (journ.) (SAUS) ... Hyd
All India Reporter, Sind (journ.) (SAUS) ... Sind
Aikawa [*Japan*] [*Seismograph station code, US Geological Survey*] (SEIS) ... AIK
Aiken Dahlgren Electronic Calculator (MCD) ... ADEC
Aiken Dynamic Algebra (MCD) ... ADA
Aiken Dynamic Algebra Air Data Assembly (SAUS) ... ADA
Aiken Relay Calculator ... ARC
Aiken, SC [*Location identifier*] [*FAA*] (FAAL) ... AIK
Aiken, SC [*FM radio station call letters*] ... WKXC
Aiken, SC [*FM radio station call letters*] ... WLJK
Aiken, SC [*FM radio station call letters*] ... WRXR
Aiken Technical College, Aiken, SC [*Library symbol*] [*Library of Congress*] (LCLS) ... ScAiTC
Aiken-Bamberg-Barnwell-Edgefield Regional Library, Aiken, SC [*Library symbol*] [*Library of Congress*] (LCLS) ... ScAi
Aiken's Digest of Alabama Statutes [*A publication*] (DLA) ... Aik Dig
Aiken's Digest of Alabama Statutes [*A publication*] (DLA) ... Aik Stat
Aikens, Macaulay & Thoralldson Law Firm, Winnipeg, MB, Canada [*Library symbol*] [*Library of Congress*] (LCLS) ... CaMWAMT
Aikens' Vermont Reports [*A publication*] (DLA) ... Aikens' Rep
Aikens' Vermont Reports [*A publication*] (DLA) ... Aikens (VT)
Aikens' Vermont Reports [*A publication*] (DLA) ... Aik Rep
Aikens' Vermont Reports [*A publication*] (DLA) ... Aik (VT) Rep
Aikens' Vermont Supreme Court Reports [*1825-28*] [*A publication*] (DLA) ... Aik
Aikins, MacAulay, and Thorvaldson Law Firm, Winnipeg, Manitoba [*Library symbol*] [*National Library of Canada*] (NLC) ... MWAMT
AIL Absorbent Industry [*Vancouver Stock Exchange symbol*] ... AIJ
Aileen, Inc. [*NYSE symbol*] (SPSG) ... AEE
Aileen, Inc. (IIA) ... AIL
Aileen, Inc. [*Associated Press*] (SAG) ... Aileen
Aileron [*Martinique*] [*Seismograph station code, US Geological Survey*] (SEIS) ... AIL
Aileron [*Aviation*] ... AIL
Aileron Rudder Interconnect (MCD) ... ARI
Aileron Station (MCD) ... AS

Ailing-In Difficulty ... AID
Ailuk [*Marshall Islands*] [*Airport symbol*] (OAG) ... AIM
AIM Aggressive Growth Fund [*Mutual fund ticker symbol*] (SG) ... AAGFX
AIM Balanced Fund Cl.A [*Mutual fund ticker symbol*] (SG) ... AMBLX
AIM Charter Cl.A [*Mutual fund ticker symbol*] (SG) ... CHTRX
AIM Constellation Cl.A [*Mutual fund ticker symbol*] (SG) ... CSTGX
AIM Global Utilities Cl.A [*Mutual fund ticker symbol*] (SG) ... AUTLX
AIM High Yield Fund Cl.A [*Mutual fund ticker symbol*] (SG) ... AMHYX
AIM Income Cl.A [*Mutual fund ticker symbol*] (SG) ... AMIFX
AIM Intermed. Govt. Fund Cl.A [*Mutual fund ticker symbol*] (SG) ... AGOVX
AIM Intl. Equity Cl.A [*Mutual fund ticker symbol*] (SG) ... AIIEX
AIM Limited Maturity Treas. Shs. [*Mutual fund ticker symbol*] (SG) ... SHTIX
AIM Municipal Bond Cl.A [*Mutual fund ticker symbol*] (SG) ... AMBDX
Aim Point Bias [*Military*] ... APB
Aim Point Initiative (SAUS) ... API
Aim Safety Co. [*Vancouver Stock Exchange symbol*] ... ASF
AIM Select Growth Cl.A [*Mutual fund ticker symbol*] (SG) ... AGWFX
AIM Strategic Income Fd [*AMEX symbol*] (TTSB) ... AST
AIM Strategic Income Fund [*Associated Press*] (SAG) ... AIM Str
AIM Strategic Income Fund [*AMEX symbol*] (SPSG) ... AST
AIM Value Cl.A [*Mutual fund ticker symbol*] (SG) ... AVLFX
AIM Weingarten Cl.A [*Mutual fund ticker symbol*] (SG) ... WEINX
Aimed Controlled-Effect Anti-Tank Mine (SAUS) ... ACEATM
AimGlobal Technologies [*AMEX symbol*] (SG) ... AGT
Aiming & Firing Limitations Computer (SAUS) ... AFLC
Aiming and Guidance [*Military*] (IUSS) ... A&G
Aiming & Pointing System (SAUS) ... APS
Aiming Circle (SAUS) ... AC
Aiming Date Chart (SAUS) ... ADC
Aiming Point ... AP
Aiming Point Determination ... APD
Aiming Symbol (DNAB) ... AS
Aimpoint Correlator [*Weaponry*] (MCD) ... APC
Aimpoint Display Unit (SAUS) ... ADU
Aim-Point-Miss ... APM
Aims College, Greeley, CO [*Library symbol*] [*Library of Congress*] (LCLS) ... CoGrA
Aims of Industry (SAUS) ... A o I
Ain Oussera [*Algeria*] [*ICAO location identifier*] (ICLI) ... DAAQ
Ain Shams University. Faculty of Agriculture. Research Bulletin (journ.) (SAUS) ... RBAADT
Ain Shems (BJA) ... AS
AIN Switch Capabilities (SAUS) ... ASC
Ain Zalah [*Iraq*] [*ICAO location identifier*] (ICLI) ... ORBZ
Ainahou [*Hawaii*] [*Seismograph station code, US Geological Survey*] (SEIS) ... AIN
Ainsworth, NE [*Location identifier*] [*FAA*] (FAAL) ... ANW
Ainsworth, NE [*AM radio station call letters*] ... KBRB
Ainsworth, NE [*FM radio station call letters*] ... KBRB-FM
Ainsworth's Latin-English Dictionary [*1837*] [*A publication*] (DLA) ... Ainsworth Lex
Ainsworth's Lexicon [*A publication*] (DLA) ... Ainsw
Aintree Resources [*Vancouver Stock Exchange symbol*] ... ANJ
A-inverse Hyperbolic Sine (SAUS) ... ARSINH
Aiome [*Papua New Guinea*] [*Airport symbol*] (OAG) ... AIE
Aioun El Atrouss [*Mauritania*] [*Airport symbol*] (OAG) ... AEO
Aioun El Atrouss [*Mauritania*] [*ICAO location identifier*] (ICLI) ... GQNA
Aiquile [*Bolivia*] [*ICAO location identifier*] (ICLI) ... SLAQ
Air ... A
Air 2000 Airlines Ltd. [*Canada*] [*ICAO designator*] (FAAC) ... CMM
Air 2000, Ltd, [*British*] [*ICAO designator*] (FAAC) ... AMM
Air 21, Inc. [*FAA designator*] (FAAC) ... RKT
Air 500 Ltd. [*Canada*] [*ICAO designator*] (FAAC) ... BRM
Air Abort (SAA) ... A/A
Air Abrasive Trimming (PDAA) ... AAT
Air Accident ... AIRACCDT
Air Accident Investigation Branch [*British*] (ACAE) ... AAIB
Air Accidents Investigation Branch (SAUO) ... AAIB
Air Accounting and Finance Center [*Air Force*] ... AAFC
Air Acetylene Welding ... AAW
Air ACG [*France*] [*FAA designator*] (FAAC) ... QSP
Air Acoustic Echo Ranging System [*Automotive safety systems*] ... AAERS
Air Activities Logistic Information System (MCD) ... AIRACLIS
Air Adjutant General (SAUO) ... AAG
Air Adjutant-General [*Military*] ... AAG
Air Administrative Net [*Army*] (AABC) ... AIRAD
Air Adviser (SAUS) ... AA
Air Affaires EJA France [*ICAO designator*] (FAAC) ... AEJ
Air Afrique (MCD) ... AFQ
Air Afrique [*Ivory Coast*] [*ICAO designator*] (ICDA) ... RK
Air Afrique [*Ivory Coast*] [*ICAO designator*] (FAAC) ... RKA
Air Afrique Vacances [*Ivory Coast*] [*FAA designator*] (FAAC) ... AFV
Air Aide-de-Camp [*RAF*] [*British*] ... AADC
Air Alba Ltd. [*British*] [*ICAO designator*] (FAAC) ... RLB
Air Alfa Hava Yollari Ve Tec, AS [*Turkey*] [*FAA designator*] (FAAC) ... LFA
Air Algerie [*ICAO designator*] (AD) ... AH
Air Algerie [*Algeria*] [*ICAO designator*] (FAAC) ... DAH
Air Alliance, Inc. [*Canada*] [*ICAO designator*] (FAAC) ... AAQ
Air Alma, Inc. [*Canada*] [*ICAO designator*] (FAAC) ... AAJ
Air Almanac (SAUS) ... AA
Air Alpes [*ICAO designator*] (AD) ... LP
Air Alpha, AS [*Denmark*] [*ICAO designator*] (FAAC) ... AHA
Air Alpha, Inc. [*ICAO designator*] (FAAC) ... DBA
Air Alsace [*ICAO designator*] (AD) ... SY
Air Alsie, AS [*Denmark*] [*ICAO designator*] (FAAC) ... ALS
Air Ambulance Network [*MTMC*] (TAG) ... AAN
Air America (SAUO) ... AA
Air America [*ICAO designator*] (AD) ... GM
Air America Inc. (SAUO) ... AA
Air America, Inc. [*Air carrier designation symbol*] ... AAMX
Air Ammunition Depot (SAUO) ... AAD
Air & Air Defence Force (SAUS) ... AADF
Air and Earth Shock (MCD) ... AES
Air and Energy Engineering Research Laboratory [*Research Triangle Park, NC*] [*Environmental Protection Agency*] (GRD) ... AEERL
Air and Energy Staff [*Environmental Protection Agency*] (GFGA) ... AES
Air and Expedited Motor Carriers Conference (EA) ... AEMCC
Air and Ground Forces Resources and Technical Staff [*Army*] ... AGFRTS
Air and Naval Gunfire Liaison Company (SAUO) ... AIRNAVGUNFIRELCO
Air and Naval Gunfire Liaison Company [*Military*] ... ANGLICO
Air and Radiation (COE) ... A&R
Air and Radiation Division [*Environmental Protection Agency*] (GFGA) ... AR
Air and Radiation Division [*Environmental Protection Agency*] (GFGA) ... ARD
Air and Radiation Docket and Information Center [*Environmental Protection Agency*] (AEPA) ... ARDIC
Air and Rail [*Shipping*] ... A & R
Air and Rail (SAUS) ... A&R
Air and Space Lawyer [*A publication*] (DLA) ... Air & Space Law
Air & Space/Smithsonian [*A publication*] (BRI) ... A & S Sm
Air and Special Operations Division (SAUO) ... AIROPS
Air and Surface Transport (SAUS) ... AST
Air and Toxics Division [*Environmental Protection Agency*] (GFGA) ... ATD
Air and Waste Management (OICC) ... AWM
Air and Waste Management Association (NTPA) ... A&WMA
Air and Waste Management Association (SAUO) ... APCA
Air and Waste Management Association (FFDE) ... AWMA
Air and Waste Management Division [*Environmental Protection Agency*] (GFGA) ... AWMD
Air & Water Tech'A' [*AMEX symbol*] (TTSB) ... AWT
Air & Water Technologies Corp. [*Associated Press*] (SAG) ... AirWat
Air & Water Technologies Corp. [*AMEX symbol*] (SPSG) ... AWT
Air Anglia [*ICAO designator*] (AD) ... AQ
Air Angouleme [*France*] [*ICAO designator*] (FAAC) ... AGL
Air Antares Ltd. [*Romania*] [*ICAO designator*] (FAAC) ... AAY
Air Antilles [*Airline*] (MHDB) ... GD
Air Antisubmarine Squadron [*Navy*] ... AIRANTISUBRON
Air Antisubmarine Squadron [*Navy*] ... VS
Air [*Defense*] **Anti-Tank System** (DOMA) ... ATATS
Air Approach Control (MCD) ... AAC
Air Aquitaine [*France*] [*ICAO designator*] (FAAC) ... AQE
Air Arc Heater ... AAH
Air Arc Heater Housing ... AAHH
Air [*Traffic*] **Area Control** (DOMA) ... AAC
Air Armament (NATG) ... AA
Air Armament Evaluation Detachment (SAUO) ... AAED
Air Armament School [*British military*] (DMA) ... AAS
Air Armorique [*France*] [*FAA designator*] (FAAC) ... RMQ
Air Aruba [*ICAO designator*] (FAAC) ... ARU
Air Aruba [*ICAO designator*] (AD) ... FQ
Air Assault [*Military*] (DOMA) ... AA
Air Assault [*Army*] (AABC) ... AASLT
Air Assault Badge [*Military decoration*] (GFGA) ... AIRASLT
Air Assault Brigade (MCD) ... AAB
Air Assault Division [*Army*] ... AAD
Air Assault Task Force [*Army*] (ADDR) ... AATF
Air Assault Task Force [*Army*] (INF) ... AATFC
Air at Atmosphere Pressure (SAUS) ... AAP
Air at Atmospheric Pressure (MAE) ... AAP
Air at High Pressure (SAUS) ... AHP
Air Atlantic [*Canada*] [*ICAO designator*] (FAAC) ... ATL
Air Atlantic Airlines [*ICAO designator*] (AD) ... OX
Air Atlantic Uruguay [*ICAO designator*] (FAAC) ... AUM
Air Atlantique [*British*] [*ICAO designator*] (FAAC) ... AAG
Air Atlantique [*ICAO designator*] (AD) ... ES
Air Atlantique [*ICAO designator*] (AD) ... KL
Air Atlantique Air Publicite [*France*] [*ICAO designator*] (FAAC) ... APB
Air Atlas/Air Maroc ... ATM
Air, Atmospheric Chemistry and Air Pollution. Seminar (journ.) (SAUS) ... Air Atmos Chem Air Pollut Semin
Air Atonabee Ltd. [*Canada*] [*ICAO designator*] (FAAC) ... OUL
Air Attache [*British*] ... AA
Air Attache [*Air Force*] ... AIRA
Air Attack RADAR ... AAR
Air Attack Radar (SAUS) ... AAR
Air Augmented Propulsion (ACAE) ... AAP
Air Aurora, Inc. [*ICAO designator*] (FAAC) ... AAI
Air Austral [*France*] [*FAA designator*] (FAAC) ... REU
Air Bag Impact Attentuation System (MCD) ... ABIAS
Air Bag Skid System (MCD) ... ABSS
Air Bag System Diagnostic Module [*Automotive engineering*] ... ASDM
Air Bags ... AB
Air Balance Consultants (EA) ... ABC
Air Balear [*ICAO designator*] (ICDA) ... JI
Air Ballistics Missile Division [*Air Force*] ... ABMD
Air Ban Ltd. [*Bulgaria*] [*FAA designator*] (FAAC) ... BAN
Air Barrier Exercise [*Military*] (NVT) ... AIRBAREX
Air Base ... AB
Air Base Advisory Team (CINC) ... ABAT
Air Base Air Defense [*Air Force*] (MCD) ... ABAD
Air Base Argentia (SAUO) ... ABA
Air Base Augmentation Support Set [*Air Force*] (AFM) ... ABASS
Air Base Borinquenfield (SAUO) ... ABB
Air Base Commander ... AIRBASECOM

Air Base Damage Assessment (ACAE) .... AIDA
Air Base Damage Assessment Model (MCD) .... ADAM
Air Base Damage Assessment Model (MCD) .... AIDA
Air Base Defense Simulator (SAUS) .... ABDS
Air Base Defense Weapon (ACAE) .... ABDW
Air Base Defense/Sensor Communications and Display System [Air Force] (MCD) .... ABD/SCADS
Air Base Flight [Air Force] .... ABF
Air Base Ground Defence (SAUS) .... ABGD
Air Base Ground Defense (ACAE) .... ABGD
Air Base Group (SAUO) .... ABG
Air Base Group [Obsolete] [Navy] .... ABG
Air Base Group [Air Force] .... ABGP
Air Base Group (SAUO) .... AB Gp
Air Base Harmonfield (SAUO) .... ABH
Air Base Operability (ACAE) .... ABO
Air Base Service (SAUO) .... ABSv
Air Base Simulator [Air Force] .... ABS
Air Base Squadron (SAUO) .... ABRON
Air Base Squadron [Air Force] .... ABS
Air Base Squadron [Air Force] .... ABSq
Air Base Stephenville (SAUO) .... ABS
Air Base Survivability .... ABS
Air Base Wallerfield (SAUO) .... AB Wa
Air Base Wing [Air Force] (MCD) .... ABW
Air Base Wing [Air Force] .... ABWG
Air Base Wing (SAUO) .... ABWg
Air Bases Command, 1st Naval District .... AB ONE
Air Bases Command, First Naval District (SAUO) .... AB ONE
Air Bath Chamber .... ABC
Air Battalion Royal Engineers [Later, Royal Aircraft Establishment] [British] .... ABRE
Air Battalion Royal Engineers (SAUS) .... ABRE
Air Battle Analysis Center Utility System [Air Force] .... ABACUS
Air Battle Analysis Division [Air Force] .... ABAD
Air Battle Captain (DOMA) .... ABC
Air Battle Management [Military] .... ABM
Air Battle Management Demonstration (ACAE) .... ABMD
Air Battle Management Operation Center (SAUS) .... ABMOC
Air Battle Management Operations Center (ACAE) .... ABMOC
Air Battle Net [Military] (INF) .... ABN
Air BC Ltd. [Canada] [ICAO designator] (FAAC) .... ABL
Air Bearing (KSC) .... AB
Air Bearing Lift Pad (KSC) .... ABLP
Air Bearing Platform .... ABP
Air Beechcraft Seminole transport aircraft (SAUS) .... Beech Queen
Air Belgium [ICAO designator] (FAAC) .... ABB
Air Benin (SAUS) .... TS
Air Berlin (SAUS) .... AB
Air Berlin USA [ICAO designator] (ICDA) .... AB
Air Berlin, USA [Germany] [ICAO designator] (FAAC) .... BER
Air Blast (MSA) .... AB
Air Blast Circuit Breaker .... ABCB
Air Blast Cooled (IAA) .... ABC
Air Blast Heat Exchanger [Nuclear energy] (NRCH) .... ABHX
Air Blast Landing (SAUS) .... ABL
Air Blast Loading .... ABL
Air Blast Time-of-Arrival Detector (PDAA) .... ABTOAD
Air Blast Transformer (MSA) .... ABT
Air Blast Value (SAUS) .... ABV
Air Blast Valve .... ABV
Air Bleed Actuator Valve [Automotive engineering] .... ABAV
Air Board [RAF] [British] .... AB
Air Board (SAUO) .... AB
Air Board Order .... ABO
Air Bomber .... AB
Air Bombers Training Unit [Navy] .... ABTU
Air Booking Centre (SAUO) .... ABC
Air Botnia OY, AB, Finland [FAA designator] (FAAC) .... KFB
Air Botswana [ICAO designator] (AD) .... BP
Air Botswana (Pty) Ltd. [ICAO designator] (FAAC) .... BOT
Air Brake [Automotive engineering] .... AB
Air Brake Association (EA) .... ABA
Air Branch (SAUO) .... AB
Air Bras d'Or [Canada] [ICAO designator] (FAAC) .... BRL
Air Bravo [Uganda] [ICAO designator] (FAAC) .... BRF
Air Break [Mechanical engineering] (IAA) .... AB
Air Breather [Aerospace] .... A/B
Air Breathing Engine (SAUS) .... ABE
Air Breathing Engine System (SAUS) .... ABES
Air Breathing Missile [Military] (LAIN) .... ABM
Air Breathing System (SAUS) .... ABS
Air Breathing Threat (SAUS) .... ABT
Air Bremen [ICAO designator] (AD) .... HR
Air Brick .... AB
Air Bridge Carriers [ICAO designator] (AD) .... AG
Air Bridge to Canada (SAUS) .... ABC
Air Bristol, Ltd. [British] [FAA designator] (FAAC) .... AZX
Air Brousse, Inc. [Canada] [ICAO designator] (FAAC) .... ABT
Air Bubble Craft .... ABC
Air Bubble Vehicle .... ABV
Air Bubble Vehivle (SAUS) .... ABV
Air Budapest Club Ltd. [Hungary] [ICAO designator] (FAAC) .... BUD
Air Bug (SAUS) .... AB
Air Burkina [Burkina Faso] [ICAO designator] (FAAC) .... VBW

Air Burkina [ICAO designator] (AD) .... VH
Air Burst Contact Maker .... ABCM
Air Burst Effect .... ABE
Air Burst Fuze .... ABF
Air Burst/Surface Burst (MCD) .... ABSB
Air Burundi [ICAO designator] (AD) .... PB
Air Business Contact [France] [ICAO designator] (FAAC) .... ABC
Air Busol [Ukraine] [FAA designator] (FAAC) .... BUA
Air BVI [ICAO designator] (AD) .... BL
Air Bypass Valve [Automotive engineering] .... ABV
Air Cadet Central Gliding School [British] .... ACCGS
Air Cadet League of Canada [World War II] .... ACLC
Air Cadet Liaison Officer (SAUS) .... ACLO
Air Cadets School [RAF] [British] [ICAO designator] (FAAC) .... ACW
Air Caledonia, Inc. [Canada] [ICAO designator] (FAAC) .... ACM
Air Caledonia International (SAUS) .... SB
Air Caledonie [France] [ICAO designator] (FAAC) .... TPC
Air Caledonie [ICAO designator] (AD) .... TY
Air Caledonie International [France] [ICAO designator] (FAAC) .... ACI
Air Caledonie International [ICAO designator] (AD) .... SB
Air California [Air carrier designation symbol] .... ACAX
Air California (MCD) .... ACF
Air California (SAUO) .... AIRCAL
Air California [Air carrier designation symbol] (AD) .... OC
Air Call Medical Services [British] .... ACMS
Air Cameroun (SAUS) .... VY
Air Campaign Planning Tool [Military] (IUSS) .... ACPT
Air Canada [ICAO designator] (OAG) .... AC
Air Canada [ICAO designator] (FAAC) .... ACA
Air Canada (MHDW) .... AIR CAN
Air Canada (SAUO) .... Air Can
Air Canada (SAUS) .... TC
Air Canada Cargo Enquiry and Service System (SAUS) .... ACCESS
Air Canada Corp. [Vancouver Stock Exchange symbol] [Toronto Stock Exchange symbol] .... AC
Air Canada Corp. [NASDAQ symbol] (SAG) .... ACNA
Air Canada Corp. [Associated Press] (SAG) .... AirCan
Air Canada Library [UTLAS symbol] .... ACA
Air Canada, Montreal, PQ, Canada [Library symbol] [Library of Congress] (LCLS) .... CaQMTC
Air Canada, Montreal, Quebec [Library symbol] [National Library of Canada] (NLC) .... QMTC
Air Canada'A' [NASDAQ symbol] (TTSB) .... ACNAF
Air Canarias S. Coop Ltd. [Spain] [ICAO designator] (FAAC) .... CAN
Air Cannon Impact Tester (SAUS) .... ACIT
Air Capable Ship (MCD) .... ACS
Air Cape [ICAO designator] (FAAC) .... ACK
Air Cape [South Africa] [ICAO designator] (FAAC) .... ACP
Air Capitol [Italy] [ICAO designator] (FAAC) .... ACL
Air Caravane [ICAO designator] (AD) .... EN
Air Carbon Arc Cutting [Welding] .... AAC
Air Carcinogen Policy [Environmental Protection Agency] (GFGA) .... ACP
Air Care Alliance [An association] (EA) .... ACA
Air Cargo (SAUS) .... ACO
Air Cargo America, Inc. [ICAO designator] (FAAC) .... MVM
Air Cargo Belize Ltd. [FAA designator] (FAAC) .... CGB
Air Cargo Carriers, Inc. [ICAO designator] (FAAC) .... PRT
Air Cargo Carriers, Inc. [ICAO designator] (FAAC) .... SNC
Air Cargo Exhibition [British] (ITD) .... ACE
Air Cargo Express, Inc. .... ACG
Air Cargo Fast Flow (DA) .... ACFF
Air Cargo Glider .... ACG
Air Cargo Inc. (SAUS) .... ACI
Air Cargo Incorporated (SAUO) .... ACI
Air Cargo Integrated System (MCD) .... ACIS
Air Cargo Masters, Inc. [FAA designator] (FAAC) .... RNR
Air Cargo Processing in the 80's [British Telecom] .... ACP 80
Air Cargo Transport (SAUS) .... ACT
Air Caribe [ICAO designator] (AD) .... QA
Air Caribe International [ICAO designator] (AD) .... ZE
Air Carolina [ICAO designator] (AD) .... FN
Air Carrier (SAUS) .... ACR
Air Carrier Activity Information System [BTS] [FAA] (TAG) .... ACAIS
Air Carrier Contract Personnel .... AACP
Air Carrier District Office .... ACDO
Air Carrier Economic Regulation Act .... ACERA
Air Carrier Engineering Service .... ACES
Air Carrier Engineering Service, Inc. (SAUO) .... ACES
Air Carrier Flight Engin (SAUS) .... ACFEA
Air Carrier Flight Engineers Association .... ACFEA
Air Carrier Mechanic Association .... ACMA
Air Carrier Mechanics Association (SAUO) .... ACM
Air Carrier Safety District Office .... ACSDO
Air Carrier Service Corp. .... ACSC
Air Carrier Service Corporation (SAUO) .... ACSC
Air Carrier Standard Security Programs [FAA] (TAG) .... ACSSP
Air Cavalry (BARN) .... Aircav
Air Cavalry Attack Brigade (MCD) .... ACAB
Air Cavalry Combat Brigade [Army] .... ACCB
Air Cavalry Combat Brigade/Triple Capability Division [Army] (MCD) .... ACCB/TRICAP
Air Cavalry Division [Army] .... ACD
Air Cavalry Regiment .... ACR
Air Cavalry Troop (DOMA) .... ACT
Air Center Commander .... ACC

Air Central [*ICAO designator*] (AD) ... HV
Air Ceylon (SAUO) ... AE
Air Ceylon Ltd. ... AIRCEY
Air Change per Hour [*Ventilation and infiltration rates*] ... ACH
Air Change per Hour [*Ventilation and infiltration rates*] ... ACPH
Air Characteristic Improvement Board [*Navy*] (DOMA) ... ACIB
Air Charter [*France*] [*ICAO designator*] (FAAC) ... ACF
Air Charter Association (SAUO) ... ACA
Air Charter Carriers Association (MHDB) ... ACCA
Air Charter Express [*France*] [*ICAO designator*] (FAAC) ... CHX
Air Charter Express AS [*Norway*] [*ICAO designator*] (FAAC) ... ECR
Air Charter Ltd. (Leiguflug Isleifs Ottesen) [*Iceland*] [*FAA designator*] (FAAC) ... LIO
Air Charter Services [*Zaire*] [*ICAO designator*] (FAAC) ... CHR
Air Charter Services (Pty) Ltd. South Africa [*ICAO designator*] (FAAC) ... IPL
Air Charter World [*ICAO designator*] (FAAC) ... XAC
Air Charters [*Senegal*] [*ICAO designator*] (ICDA) ... JV
Air Charters, Inc. [*Canada*] [*ICAO designator*] (FAAC) ... ACX
Air Chathams [*Airline code*] [*Australia*] ... CV
Air Chico [*ICAO designator*] (AD) ... FZ
Air Chief Commandant [*British*] ... ACC
Air Chief Marshal [*RAF*] [*British*] ... ACM
Air Chief Marshal (SAUS) ... Air Chf Mshl
Air China [*ICAO designator*] (FAAC) ... CCA
Air Circuit Breaker ... ACB
Air Circulating ... ACIRC
Air City SA [*Switzerland*] [*ICAO designator*] (FAAC) ... ACY
Air Class Teachers Certificate (SAUS) ... ACTC
Air Classification of Solid Wastes (journ.) (SAUS) ... Air Classif Solid Wastes
Air Cleaner [*Automotive engineering*] ... A/CLNR
Air Cleaner ... AIRCLNR
Air Cleaner Bi-Metal Sensor [*Automotive engineering*] ... ACLBIMET
Air Cleaner Cold Weather Modulator [*Automotive engineering*] ... ACCWM
Air Cleaner Duct and Valve [*Automotive engineering*] ... ACLDV
Air Cleaner Gasket [*Automotive engineering*] ... ACL
Air Cleaner Housing [*Automotive engineering*] ... ACH
Air Cleanup Unit [*Nuclear energy*] (NRCH) ... ACU
Air Clearance Authorities (SAUO) ... ACAs
Air Clearance Authority ... ACA
Air Club International [*Canada*] [*FAA designator*] (FAAC) ... CLI
Air Clutch Antislack Device (CAAL) ... ACASD
Air Co. Ltd. [*Romania*] [*FAA designator*] (FAAC) ... RMR
Air Coach Transport Association ... ACTA
Air Coalition (SAUO) ... Air Coal
Air Coating System (PDAA) ... ACS
Air Collection and Enrichment ... ACE
Air Collection and Enrichment System ... ACES
Air Collection Engine System ... ACES
Air Colombia [*ICAO designator*] (FAAC) ... ACO
Air Columbus SA [*Portugal*] [*ICAO designator*] (FAAC) ... CNB
Air Combat Analysis ... ACA
Air Combat and Surveillance System (MCD) ... ACSS
Air Combat Command [*Air Force*] ... ACC
Air Combat Command Intelligence Network (ADWA) ... ACCINTNET
Air Combat Direction System (SAUS) ... ACDS
Air Combat Element (MCD) ... ACE
Air Combat Emulator [*Computer game*] ... ACE
Air Combat Engagement (MCD) ... ACE
Air Combat Engagement Experiment ... ACEE
Air Combat Environment Test & Evaluation Facility (SAUS) ... ACETEF
Air Combat Environment Test and Evaluation Facility (SAUO) ... ACETEF
Air Combat Evaluation (MCD) ... ACEVAL
Air Combat Evaluation / Air Intercept Missile Evaluation (PDAA) ... ACEVAL/AIMVAL
Air Combat Evaluation Model (ACAE) ... ACEM
Air Combat Expert Simulation [*Military*] (RDA) ... ACES
Air Combat Fighter (MCD) ... ACF
Air Combat Information ... ACI
Air Combat Intelligence [*Obsolete*] [*Navy*] ... ACI
Air Combat Intelligence Office [*or Officer*] [*Navy*] ... ACIO
Air Combat Interference Techniques (ACAE) ... ACIT
Air Combat Maneuvering (AFM) ... ACM
Air Combat Maneuvering Instrumentation (ACAE) ... ACMI
Air Combat Maneuvering Instrumentation System [*Air Force*] (DWSG) ... ACMIS
Air Combat Maneuvering Performance Measurement (MCD) ... ACMPM
Air Combat Maneuvering Range (DOMA) ... ACMR
Air Combat Maneuvering Range/Instrumentation (ACAE) ... ACMR/I
Air Combat Maneuvering Simulator (MCD) ... ACMS
Air Combat Maneuvering Visual System (MCD) ... ACMVS
Air Combat Manoeuvring Expert Systems Trainer (SAUS) ... ACMEST
Air Combat Mode (ACAE) ... ACM
Air Combat Part Task Trainer ... ACPTT
Air Combat Simulator (SAUS) ... ACS
Air Combat Tactics (AFM) ... ACT
Air Combat Tactics Instructor (DOMA) ... ACTI
Air Combat Training (SAUS) ... ACT
Air Combat Training System [*Army*] ... ACTS
Air Command (ADA) ... AC
Air Command (MCD) ... AIRCOM
Air Command Acoustic Processing (IUSS) ... ACAP
Air Command and Control Improvement System [*NATO*] ... ACCIS
Air Command and Control Improvement System (SAUS) ... ACCIS
Air Command and Control System [*NATO*] ... ACCS
Air Command and Staff College [*Maxwell AFB, AL*] [*Air Force*] ... AC & SC
Air Command and Staff College [*Maxwell AFB, AL*] [*Air Force*] (MCD) ... ACSC
Air Command and Staff College [*Air Force*] ... AIRCSC
Air Command and Staff School [*Air Force*] ... AC & SS
Air Command and Staff School [*Air Force*] ... ACSS
Air Command Headquarters, Canadian Forces Base, Westwin, Manitoba [*Library symbol*] [*National Library of Canada*] (NLC) ... MWAC
Air Command Net [*Army*] (AABC) ... AIRCOMD
Air Command Net (SAUS) ... AIRCOMD Net
Air Command Operations Center [*NATO*] (NATG) ... ACOC
Air Command Operations Center (or Centre) (SAUO) ... ACOC
Air Command Post [*Military*] ... ACPT
Air Command, Southeast Asia ... ACSEA
Air Command Squadron (SAUO) ... ACS
Air Commandant [*British*] ... A CDT
Air Commandant [*British*] (DMA) ... A Ct
Air Commandant (SAUS) ... Air Comdt
Air Commander (SAUO) ... Air Cdr
Air Commander, Canadian Atlantic Subarea ... COMAIRCANLANT
Air Commander, Central Atlantic (SAUS) ... COMAIRCENTLANT
Air Commander, Central Atlantic Subarea ... COMAIRCENTLANT
Air Commander Eastern Atlantic Area (SAUO) ... COMAIREASTLANT
Air Commander Home Defence Forces (SAUS) ... ACHDF
Air Commander in Chief, Eastern Atlantic Area (SAUO) ... CINCAirEastLant
Air Commander North Norway (SAUO) ... ACNN
Air Commander, North Norway [*NATO*] (NATG) ... ACNN
Air Commander, Northeast Subarea Channel ... COMAIRNORECHAN
Air Commander, Northern Atlantic Subarea ... COMAIRNORLANT
Air Commander Norway (SAUO) ... ACN
Air Commander, Norway [*NATO*] (NATG) ... ACN
Air Commander, Plymouth Subarea Channel ... COMAIRPLYMCHAN
Air Commander-in-Chief, Eastern Atlantic Area ... CINCAIREASTLANT
Air Commando Association (EA) ... ACA
Air Commando Squadron [*Air Force*] ... ACMDOSq
Air Commando Squadron (CINC) ... ACS
Air Commerce [*Yugoslavia*] [*ICAO designator*] (FAAC) ... ACS
Air Commerce Bulletin (journ.) (SAUS) ... Air Commerce Bul
Air Commerce Manual ... ACM
Air Commerce Type Certificate (SAUS) ... ACTC
Air Commodore [*RAF, RCAF*] ... A/C
Air Commodore [*RAF, RCAF*] ... A CDE
Air Commodore [*RAF, RCAF*] (DMA) ... A Cdre
Air Commodore [*RAF, RCAF*] (DAS) ... A Comm
Air Commodore (SAUS) ... Air Cdre
Air Commodore (SAUO) ... Air Cmdre
Air Communication Officer [*Military*] (IAA) ... ACO
Air Communications (SAUS) ... AIRCOM
Air Communications and Weather [*Group*] [*Navy*] ... AC & W
Air Communications and Weather (SAUO) ... AC&W
Air Communications and Weather (SAUS) ... ACAW
Air Communications and Weather Group [*Navy*] (IAA) ... ACAW
Air Communications Network ... AIRCOMNET
Air Communications System (SAUS) ... AIRCOM System
Air Commuter, Inc. (SAUS) ... ACI
Air Commuter Incorporated (SAUO) ... ACI
Air Comores [*ICAO designator*] (AD) ... OR
Air Component (SAUS) ... AC
Air Component Command [*Military*] (MCD) ... ACC
Air Component Commander [*Air Force*] (DOMA) ... ACC
Air Component Commander, Southeast Asia Treaty Organization (CINC) ... ACCSEATO
Air Compressor (AAG) ... AC
Air Compressor Research Council [*Defunct*] ... ACRC
Air Concept [*Germany*] [*ICAO aircraft manufacturer identifier*] (ICAO) ... VW
Air Condal SA [*Spain*] [*ICAO designator*] (FAAC) ... JID
Air Condensate Drain [*Aerospace*] (AAG) ... ACD
Air Condition [*Technical drawings*] (DAC) ... AIR COND
Air Conditioned (TRID) ... ACON
Air Conditioned Microclimate System [*Army*] (RDA) ... ACMS
Air Conditioner ... Air
Air Conditioner Air Transportable (MCD) ... ACAT
Air Conditioner, cooling only (SAUS) ... ACR
Air Conditioner Technical Data Package (DWSG) ... ACTDP
Air Conditioning (KSC) ... AC
Air Conditioning (IDOE) ... a/c
Air Conditioning [*Automotive engineering*] ... A/COND
Air Conditioning Advisory Bureau (SAUO) ... ACAB
Air Conditioning Analytical Simulation Package (PDAA) ... A/CASP
Air Conditioning Analytical Simulation Package (SAUS) ... ACASP
Air Conditioning and Mechanical Contractors' Association of Queensland [*Australia*] ... ACMCAQ
Air Conditioning and Mechanical Contractors' Association of South Australia ... ACMCASA
Air Conditioning and Mechanical Contractors' Association of Victoria [*Australia*] ... ACMCAV
Air Conditioning and Oil Heat (journ.) (SAUS) ... Air Cond Oil Heat
Air Conditioning and Refrigerating Machinery Association (SAUO) ... ACRMA
Air Conditioning and Refrigeration Contractors Association of New Jersey (SRA) ... ARCA
Air Conditioning & Refrigeration Industry Association of British Columbia (AC) ... ARIA
Air Conditioning and Refrigeration Institute (SAUO) ... ACRI
Air Conditioning and Refrigeration News (journ.) (SAUS) ... Air Cond&Refrig N
Air Conditioning and Refrigeration Program [*Association of Independent Colleges and Schools specialization code*] ... AR
Air Conditioning and Temperature Control System [*Aerospace*] ... ACTCS
Air Conditioning Association (SAUO) ... ACA

Air Conditioning Clutch Compressor [*Automotive engineering*] ACC
Air Conditioning Contractors of America (EA) ACCA
Air Conditioning Engineer (SAUS) Air Cond Engr
Air Conditioning Equipment (SAUS) ACE
Air Conditioning Equipment Room [*NFPA pre-fire planning symbol*] (NFPA) AC
Air Conditioning, Heating and Ventilating (SAUS) ACHVA
Air Conditioning, Heating and Ventilating (journ.) (SAUS) Air CHV
Air Conditioning Institute (SAUS) ACI
Air Conditioning Institute (SAUO) ACI
Air Conditioning Manufacturers Association (SAUO) ACMA
Air Conditioning Sensor [*Automotive engineering*] ACS
Air Conditioning System ACS
Air Conditioning Trade Association of California (SRA) ACCACA
Air Conduction AC
Air Conduction and Bone Conduction [*Otorhinolaryngology*] (DAVI) AC & BC
Air Conformity Applicability Model [*Environmental science*] (BCP) ACAM
Air Congo [*Zaire*] AC
Air Consignment Note (ADA) ACN
Air Contact Area Commander (SAUS) ACAC
Air Contact Officer (SAUS) ACO
Air Contact System (SAUS) ACS
Air Containment Atmosphere Dilution [*Nuclear energy*] (NRCH) ACAD
Air Continental, Inc. [*ICAO designator*] (FAAC) NAR
Air Contrast Barium Enema [*Medicine*] ACBE
Air Contrast Myelography (MELL) ACM
Air Control (SAUS) AC
Air Control and Reporting (NATG) ACR
Air [*or Aircraft*] **Control and Warning** [*Military*] AC & W
Air [*or Aircraft*] **Control and Warning** [*Military*] ACW
Air Control and Warning Station (SAUS) ACWS
Air Control Area Commander (NVT) ACAC
Air Control Center [*Military*] ACC
Air Control Center (or Centre) (SAUS) ACC
Air Control Commission (AAG) ACC
Air Control Component ACPC
Air Control Intercept ACI
Air [*or Airborne*] **Control Officer** [*or Contract*] [*Military*] [*British*] ACO
Air Control Officer (SAUS) ACO
Air Control Point ACP
Air Control Post (SAUO) ACP
Air Control Products, Inc. (SAUO) AIR
Air Control RADAR ACR
Air Control Radar (SAUS) ACR
Air Control Room (MUGU) ACR
Air Control Supervisor [*Military*] (IUSS) ACS
Air Control Team [*Air Force*] ACT
Air Control Valve (MCD) ACV
Air Controller (NVT) AC
Air Controlman [*Navy rating*] AC
Air Controlman, Chief [*Navy rating*] ACC
Air Controlman, First Class [*Navy rating*] AC1
Air Controlman, Master Chief [*Navy rating*] ACCM
Air Controlman, Second Class [*Navy rating*] AC2
Air Controlman, Senior Chief [*Navy rating*] ACCS
Air Controlman, Third Class [*Navy rating*] AC3
Air Cooled (IAA) AC
Air Cooled Heat Exchanger Manufacturers Association [*Defunct*] (EA) ACHEMA
Air Cooled Triode [*Chemistry*] (IAA) ACT
Air Cooperation Command [*RAF*] [*British*] AC/OC
Air Co-operation Command (SAUO) AC/OC
Air Coordinating Committee [*Governmental policy body for civil aviation in US; terminated, 1960*] ACC
Air Coordinating Committee [*Terminated*] **Airspace Subcommittee** ACCASP
Air Coordinating Committee [*Terminated*] **Communications Subcommittee** ACC/COM
Air Coordinating Committee [*Terminated*] **Meteorological Subcommittee** ACC/MET
Air Coordinating Committee Meteorological Subcommittee (SAUS) ACC/MET
Air Coordinator [*Air Force*] AIRCO
Air Corporations Engineering Apprentice School (SAUO) ACEAS
Air Corporations Joint Medical Services (SAUO) ACJMS
Air Corps [*Obsolete*] AC
Air Corps Board [*Obsolete*] (MCD) ACB
Air Corps Information Circular [*Obsolete*] ACIC
Air Corps Medical Forces [*Obsolete*] ACMF
Air Corps Reserve [*Obsolete*] ACR
Air Corps Reserve (SAUO) Air Res
Air Corps Tactical School [*Obsolete*] ACTS
Air Corps Technical Report [*Obsolete*] ACTR
Air Corps Training Center (SAUO) ACTC
Air Correction Jet [*Automotive engineering*] ACJ
Air Correction Jet-Primary [*Automotive engineering*] ACJP
Air Correction Jet-Secondary [*Automotive engineering*] ACJS
Air Correlation Tracker (ACAE) ACT
Air Corse [*France*] [*ICAO designator*] (FAAC) ARK
Air Cote d'Opale [*France*] [*ICAO designator*] (FAAC) OPL
Air Council (ADA) AC
Air Council (SAUO) AC
Air Council for Training [*British*] (DAS) ACT
Air Council Instruction [*World War II*] ACI
Air Courier Conference of America (EA) ACCA
Air Couriers International, Inc. [*Defunct*] (TSSD) ACI
Air Courses of Action Assessment Model [*Navy*] ACAAM
Air Court-Martial ACM
Air Craft Energy Efficiency ACEE
Air Crash Equipment (SAUS) ACE
Air Creebec [*Canada*] [*ICAO designator*] (FAAC) CRQ
Air Crew (ACAE) AC
Air Crew Association Canada ACAC
Air Crew Bulletin (SAUS) ACB
Air Crew Bulletin (ACAE) ACR
Air Crew Change ACC
Air Crew Combat Mission Enhancement (ACAE) ACME
Air Crew Equipment Laboratory (MCD) ACEL
Air Crew Error (MCD) ACE
Air Crew Rescue (CINC) ACR
Air Crew System Bulletin (MCD) ACB
Air Crew Training System ACTS
Air Curtain Incinerator (MCD) ACI
Air Cushion Aircraft (SAUS) ACA
Air Cushion Equipment (MHDB) ACE
Air Cushion Ferry (SAUS) ACF
Air Cushion Landing System (SAUS) ACLS
Air Cushion Launch Platform (MCD) ACLP
Air Cushion Recovery System (MCD) ACRS
Air Cushion Relief Equipment (PDAA) ACRE
Air Cushion Restraint System (SAUS) ACRS
Air Cushion Restraint System Module ACRSM
Air Cushion Rig Mover (PDAA) ACRM
Air Cushion Take-Off and Landing [*Aviation*] (PDAA) ACTOL
Air Cushion Trailer (SAUS) ACT
Air Cushion Transporter (SAUS) ACT
Air Cushion Valve (SAUS) ACV
Air Cushion Vessel (SAUS) ACV
Air Cycle Air-Conditioning System (MCD) ACACS
Air Cycle Air-Conditioning System (MCD) ACAS
Air Cycle Engine / Liquid Air Cycle Engine (SAA) ACE/LACE
Air Cycle Machine [*Aerospace*] ACM
Air Dan [*Nigeria*] [*FAA designator*] (FAAC) DMT
Air Data (MCD) AD
Air Data and Inertial Reference System (SAUS) ADAIRS
Air Data & Inertial Reference System (SAUS) ADIRS
Air Data Assembly (NASA) ADA
Air Data Computer [*or Computing*] (MCD) ADC
Air Data Computer Set ADCS
Air Data Computer Static Pressure Compensator (MCD) ADCSPC
Air Data Computing (SAUS) ADC
Air Data Computing System ADCS
Air Data Converter ADC
Air Data Inertial Reference System (DA) ADIRS
Air Data Inertial Reference Unit ADIRU
Air Data Ltd. [*British*] [*FAA designator*] (FAAC) AFS
Air Data Measuring Unit (NATG) ADMU
Air Data Module (HLLA) ADM
Air Data Package ADP
Air Data Probe [*Aerospace*] (MCD) ADP
Air Data Probe Assemblies [*Aerospace*] (NASA) ADPA
Air Data Reference (HLLA) ADR
Air Data Relay (SAUS) ADR
Air Data Screening System [*Environmental Protection Agency*] (GFGA) ADSS
Air Data Sensor [*Aerospace*] (MCD) ADS
Air Data Sensor Unit (MCD) ADSU
Air Data System [*or Subsystem*] (RDA) ADS
Air Data Terminal (SAUS) ADT
Air Data Test System ADTS
Air Data Tester (HLLA) ADT
Air Data Transducer [*Aerospace*] (MCD) ADT
Air Data Transducer Assembly [*Aerospace*] (NASA) ADTA
Air Data Unit (SAUS) ADU
Air Decoy Missile (SAUS) ADI
Air Decoy Missile (AFM) ADM
Air Defence Anti-Missile System (SAUS) ADAMS
Air Defence Artillery Commander [*Military*] [*British*] ADAC
Air Defence Battle Management Technology (SAUS) ADBMT
Air Defence Brigade (SAUO) ADBrig
Air Defence Cadet Corps (SAUO) ADCC
Air Defence Cadet Corps [*Military*] [*British*] ADCC
Air Defence Centre (SAUO) ADC
Air Defence Command Information System (SAUS) ADCIS
Air Defence Commander (SAUS) ADC
Air Defence Control Center (SAUO) ADCC
Air Defence Control Centre (SAUS) ADCC
Air Defence Control Ship (SAUS) ADCS
Air Defence Control Unit (SAUO) ADCU
Air Defence Data Centre (SAUS) ADDC
Air Defence Element (SAUO) ADE
Air Defence Exercise (SAUO) ADEX
Air Defence Exercise (SAUO) AIRDEX
Air Defence Experimental Establishment [*Later, ADRDE, RRE*] [*British*] ADEE
Air Defence Fighter (SAUS) ADF
Air Defence Gun Sight (SAUS) ADGS
Air Defence Institute (SAUO) ADI
Air Defence Interoperability Validation System (SAUS) ADIVS
Air Defence Master Plan (SAUS) ADMP
Air Defence National Centre (SAUO) ADNC
Air Defence Notification Centre (SAUO) ADNC
Air Defence of Great Britain (SAUO) ADGB
Air Defence of Great Britain Command (SAUO) ADGBC
Air Defence Officer [*Navy*] [*British*] ADO

Air Defence Operations Centre (SAUS)	ADOC
Air Defence (or Defense) (SAUO)	AD
Air Defence (or Defense) Canada-United States (SAUO)	ADCANUS
Air Defence (or Defense) Command (SAUO)	ADC
Air Defence (or Defense) Group (SAUO)	ADG
Air Defence (or Defense) Operations Center (or Centre) (SAUO)	ADOC
Air Defence (or Defense) Operations Liaison Team (SAUO)	ADOLT
Air Defence (or Defense) Software Committee (SAUO)	ADSC
Air Defence (or Defense) Software Committee-Support Office (SAUO)	ADSC-SO
Air Defence (or Defense) Technical Center (or Centre) (SAUO)	ADTC
Air Defence Region (SAUO)	ADR
Air Defence Research and Development Establishment (SAUO)	ADRDE
Air Defence Research and Development Establishment [*Later, RRE*] [*British*]	ADRDE
Air Defence Research and Development Establishment (SAUS)	ADRDE
Air Defence Research Committee (SAUO)	ADRC
Air Defence Tactical Training Theatre (SAUS)	ADT3
Air Defence Tactical Training Theatre (SAUS)	ADTTT
Air Defence Technology programme (SAUS)	ADT
Air Defence Unit (SAUS)	ADU
Air Defence Weapon (SAUS)	ADW
Air Defence Zone (SAUS)	ADAZ
Air Defences, Eastern Mediterranean [*British military*] (DMA)	ADEM
Air Defense [*Air Force*]	AD
Air Defense - Surface-to-Air Missile	AD/SAM
Air Defense Action Area [*Military*]	ADAA
Air Defense Advanced Mobile System (SAUS)	ADAMS
Air Defense Agency (SAUO)	ADA
Air Defense Aircraft (MCD)	AD/AC
Air Defense Air-to-Ground Engagement [*Simulation*]	ADAGE
Air Defense Alert Facility (SAUO)	ADAF
Air Defense Alert Unit (SAUO)	ADAU
Air Defense Alerting Device [*Military*]	ADAD
Air Defense Analysis Model (ACAE)	ADAM
Air Defense and Targets Office (SAUO)	ADCAT
Air Defense Annual Service Practice (AABC)	ADASP
Air Defense Antimissile	ADAM
Air Defense Antitank System	ADATS
Air Defense Anti-Tank System (SAUS)	ADATS
Air Defense Area [*Army*]	ADA
Air Defense Area [*Army*]	ADAR
Air Defense Area Monthly Report [*Army*]	ADAM
Air Defense Artillery [*Army*]	ADA
Air Defense Artillery Board [*Army*]	ADABD
Air Defense Artillery Command and Control (SAUS)	ADAC2
Air Defense Artillery Command Post (SAUO)	ADACP
Air Defense Artillery Complex (MCD)	ADAC
Air Defense Artillery Control Station [*Army*]	ADACS
Air Defense Artillery, Director [*Air Force*]	ADAD
Air Defense Artillery Director (SAUS)	ADAD
Air Defense Artillery Fire Control Direction Center (SAUO)	ADA FDC
Air Defense Artillery Magazine (journ.) (SAUS)	Air D Arty
Air Defense Artillery Officer (SAA)	ADAO
Air Defense Artillery Operations Detachment	ADAOD
Air Defense Artillery Office [*or Officer*]	ADAOO
Air Defense Artillery Threat Simulator (MCD)	ADATS
Air Defense Board [*Army*] (AAG)	ADB
Air Defense, Canada-United States (SAUS)	ADCANUS
Air Defense Center (AAG)	ADC
Air Defense Combat Operations Staff (SAUO)	ADCOS
Air Defense Combined Arms Tactical Trainer [*Army*]	ADCATT
Air Defense Command [*Peterson Air Force Base, CO*]	ADC
Air Defense Command [*Army*]	ADCOM
Air Defense Command (SAUO)	AD Comd
Air Defense Command and Control [*MICOM*] (RDA)	ADCC
Air Defense Command and Control System (MCD)	ADCCS
Air Defense Command & First Air Region (SAUO)	MACEN
Air Defense Command Center	ADCC
Air Defense Command Commendation Certificate	ADCCC
Air Defense Command Communications Network [*Military*] (IAA)	ADCCOMNET
Air Defense Command Communica-tions Network (SAUS)	ADC COMNET
Air Defense Command Computer [*Military*] (IAA)	ADCC
Air Defense Command, Control, and Coordination System (AABC)	ADCCCS
Air Defense Command, Control and Coordination System (SAUS)	ADCCCS
Air Defense Command Headquarters, St. Hubert, Province of Quebec, Canada	CANAIRDEF
Air Defense Command Interoperability System [*Army*]	ADCOINS
Air Defense Command Manual (SAA)	ADCM
Air Defense Command Operation Control (SAUS)	ADCOC
Air Defense Command Post	ADCOP
Air Defense Command Post (AABC)	ADCP
Air Defense Command Regulation (SAA)	ADCR
Air Defense Command Unit Proficiency Directive (SAUS)	ADCUPD
Air Defense Commander	AIRDEFCOM
Air Defense Command/North American Air Defense (SAUO)	ADC/NORAD
Air Defense Command-Office of Operations Analysis [*Peterson Air Force Base, CO*]	ADC-OA
Air Defense Communication Equipment [*Military*]	ADCE
Air Defense Communications Jammer [*Military*] (PDAA)	ADCJ
Air Defense Communications Office (AABC)	ADCO
Air Defense Communications Officer (SAUS)	ADCO
Air Defense Computer (AAG)	ADC
Air Defense Control and Coordination System (SAUS)	ADCCS
Air Defense Control and Targets Office [*Army*]	ADCAT

Air Defense Control Center [*Air Force*]	ADCC
Air Defense Control Facility (FAAC)	ADCF
Air Defense Control System [*Military*]	ADCS
Air Defense Controller (SAUS)	ADC
Air Defense Coordination Center (SAUO)	ADCC
Air Defense Defended Area [*Army*]	ADDA
Air Defense Defended Point [*Army*]	ADDP
Air Defense Demonstration System (MCD)	ADDS
Air Defense Development	ADD
Air Defense Direction Center [*Air Force*]	ADDC
Air Defense District (NATG)	ADD
Air Defense Division [*NATO*] (SAA)	ADD
Air Defense Division [*NATO*] (NATG)	AIRDEF
Air Defense Early Warning (NATG)	ADEW
Air Defense Effectiveness Demonstration [*Army*] (MCD)	ADED
Air Defense Electro Optical Laboratory (ACAE)	ADEOL
Air Defense Electro Optical Support (ACAE)	ADEOS
Air Defense Electronic Environment (SAA)	ADEE
Air Defense Electronic Warfare System (MCD)	ADEWS
Air Defense Element (AABC)	ADE
Air Defense Emergency [*Military*] (AABC)	ADE
Air Defense Engagement System (MCD)	ADES
Air Defense Engineering Service (MCD)	ADES
Air Defense Evaluation	ADE
Air Defense Evaluation Tests (MCD)	ADVAL
Air Defense Exercise (NVT)	ADEX
Air Defense Exercise [*Army/Air Force*] (AABC)	ADX
Air Defense Filter Center [*Military*]	ADFC
Air Defense Firing Unit (MCD)	ADFU
Air Defense Force	ADF
Air Defense Force Headquarters (SAA)	ADFHQ
Air Defense Ground Environment [*NATO*] (MCD)	ADGE
Air Defense Group [*Air Force*] (MCD)	ADG
Air Defense Group [*Air Force*] (AFM)	ADGp
Air Defense Guard [*Military*]	ADG
Air Defense Gun Missile Experiment [*Army*]	ADGILE
Air Defense Hardware Committee [*NATO*] (NATG)	ADHC
Air Defense Hardware Committee (SAUS)	ADHC
Air Defense High Energy Laser (SAUS)	ADHEL
Air Defense High Energy LASER (MCD)	ADHEL
Air Defense Identification Line [*Air Force*]	ADIL
Air Defense Identification Zone [*Air Force, FAA*]	ADIZ
Air Defense Initiative [*DoD*]	ADI
Air Defense Initiative Simulation for Command and Control (ACAE)	ADISCC
Air Defense Inspector Provost Marshall (SAA)	ADIPM
Air Defense Institute	ADI
Air Defense Integrated System [*Military*]	ADIS
Air Defense Intercept [*Air Force*]	ADI
Air Defense, Interdiction, and Photographic	ADIP
Air Defense, Interdiction and Photographic (SAUS)	ADIP
Air Defense Liaison Officer	ADLO
Air Defense Machine Gun (MCD)	ADMG
Air Defense Management Office (MCD)	ADMO
Air Defense Missile	ADM
Air Defense Missile Base (SAA)	ADMB
Air Defense Missile Battalion [*Army*] (AABC)	ADMSLBN
Air Defense Missile Command (AABC)	ADMC
Air Defense Missile Squadron [*Air Force*]	ADMS
Air Defense Missile Wing (SAUO)	ADMWg
Air Defense Mission [*Army*]	ADM
Air Defense Monitor and Control (ACAE)	ADMAC
Air Defense National Center (NATG)	ADNC
Air Defense Notification Center (NATG)	ADNC
Air Defense of Great Britain	ADGB
Air Defense of North American Continent [*Army*] (AABC)	ADNAC
Air Defense of the Division (MCD)	ADDIV
Air Defense of the North American Continent (SAUS)	ADNAC
Air Defense Operations (NATG)	ADO
Air Defense Operations Area [*Army*] (ADDR)	ADDA
Air Defense Operations Area [*Army*]	ADOA
Air Defense Operations Center [*Air Force*]	ADOC
Air Defense Planning Board (MCD)	ADPB
Air Defense Planning Group (MCD)	ADPG
Air Defense Position [*Military*]	ADP
Air Defense Radar Control (SAUS)	ADRC
Air Defense Region (NATG)	ADR
Air Defense Requirement (SAA)	ADR
Air Defense Reticle (SAUS)	ADR
Air Defense School (SAUO)	AirDefSch
Air Defense School (SAUO)	AirDefScol
Air Defense Sector [*Air Force*]	ADS
Air Defense Sector (SAUS)	Air Def Sec
Air Defense Service Medal [*Military decoration*] (GFGA)	ADSM
Air Defense Ship (NATG)	ADS
Air Defense Simulator Evaluation (SAUS)	ADSE
Air Defense Simulator Evaluation (MCD)	ADSVAL
Air Defense Software Committee (NATG)	ADSC
Air Defense Software Evaluation Team (MCD)	ADSET
Air Defense Special Weapons Support Organization	ADSWSO
Air Defense Special Weapons Support Organization (SAUS)	ADSWSO
Air Defense Squadron [*Air Force*]	ADEFSq
Air Defense Squadron [*Air Force*]	ADS
Air Defense Squadron [*Vietnam*] [*Air Force*] (AFM)	ADSq
Air Defense Suppression Missile (ACAE)	ADSM
Air Defense Suppression System (MCD)	ADSS

Air Defense System	ADS
Air Defense System Engineering Committee	ADSEC
Air Defense System Management Office [*Air Force*]	ADSMO
Air Defense Systems Command	ADSC
Air Defense Systems Directorate (NATG)	ADSD
Air Defense Systems Engineering Committee (SAUO)	ADSEC
Air Defense Systems Integration Division [*Air Force*]	ADSID
Air Defense Systems Operation Division (SAA)	ADSOD
Air Defense Tactical Air Command (SAUO)	ADTAC
Air Defense Tactical Air Commander [*Air Force*]	ADTAC
Air Defense Tactical Data Systems (SAUS)	ADTC
Air Defense Tactical Data Systems [*Missile minder*] (RDA)	ADTDS
Air Defense Tactical Operations Centre (SAUS)	ADTOC
Air Defense Tactical Replacement Aircraft (ACAE)	ADTRAC
Air Defense Technical Center (NATG)	ADTC
Air Defense Test Center (SAUO)	ADTC
Air Defense Variant	ADV
Air Defense Version (SAUS)	ADV
Air Defense Vulnerability Simulation [*Simulation game*]	ADVUL
Air Defense Warning [*Air Force*]	ADW
Air Defense Warning Key Point [*Air Force*]	ADWKP
Air Defense Warning System (SAUS)	ADWS
Air Defense Weapon	ADW
Air Defense Weapon Simulation System (MCD)	ADWSS
Air Defense Weapon System (MCD)	ADWS
Air Defense Weapons Center [*Tyndall Air Force Base, FL*] (MCD)	ADWC
Air Defense Weapons Center Regulation (MCD)	ADWCR
Air Defense Weapons Cost Effectiveness Study (AABC)	ADWEPS
Air Defense Wing [*Air Force*]	ADW
Air Defense Zone [*Army/Airforce*] (NATG)	ADZ
Air Defense/Surface-to-Air Missile (SAUS)	AD/SAM
Air Defense/Theater Missile Defense	AD/TMD
Air Deflection and Modification [*NASA*] (KSC)	ADAM
Air Deflection and Modulation [*Air Force*] (MCD)	ADAM
Air Delivery Equipment Division [*Natick Laboratories*] [*Army*]	ADED
Air Delivery Operations [*Aerial resupply*] [*Military*] (NVT)	AIRDELOPS
Air Delivery Platoon (DNAB)	ADP
Air Delivery Platoon	AIRDELPLT
Air Denial Weapon (SAUS)	ADW
Air Density [*Explorer satellite*] [*NASA*]	AD
Air Density [*Explorer satellite*] [*NASA*]	ADE
Air Density A [*Explorer satellite*] [*NASA*]	AD-A
Air Density Explorer (SAUS)	ADE
Air Density Gauge [*Aviation*]	ADG
Air Density/Injun [*Explorer satellite*]	AD/I
Air Department of the Admiralty [*British*]	AD
Air Deployable Active Reservoir [*Military*] (DOMA)	ADAR
Air Deployable Airborne Deception Device System	ADS
Air Deployable Anti-Pollution Transfer System (SAUS)	ADAPTS
Air Deployable Drifting Linear Array SONAR System (MCD)	ADDLASS
Air Deployable Ice Beacon (SAUS)	ADIB
Air Deployed Oceanographic Mooring (PDAA)	ADOM
Air Deployment & Control Squadron (SAUO)	ADCS
Air Deployment Delivery System [*Military*] (NVT)	ADDS
Air Depot	AD
Air Depot (SAUO)	A/D
Air Depot [*Army*]	ADEP
Air Depot Group (SAUO)	ADG
Air Depot Wing (SAUO)	ADW
Air Depot Wing (SAUO)	A/D Wg
Air Deputy [*NATO*] (NATG)	AIRDEP
Air Deputy [*NATO*] (NATG)	DEPAIR
Air Design Review (MCD)	ADR
Air Despatch [*British military*] (DMA)	AD
Air Despatch Company (SAUO)	ADC
Air Despatch Group (SAUO)	ADG
Air Detector/Tracker (CAAL)	AD/T
Air Development Center [*Air Force*]	ADC
Air Development Center (SAUO)	AirDevCen
Air Development Delivery System (DNAB)	ADDS
Air Development Force	ADF
Air Development Service (MCD)	ADS
Air Development Squadron [*Navy*]	AIRDEVRON
Air Development Squadron [*Navy*]	VX
Air Development Station [*Navy*]	ADS
Air Development System (SAUS)	ADS
Air Device Systems [*Honda Motor Co.*] [*Automotive air conditioning*]	ADSYS
Air Diffusion and Components Council of South Australia	ADCCSA
Air Diffusion Council (EA)	ADC
Air Diffusion Institute (EA)	ADI
Air Diffusion Perfomance Index [*Of room ventilation*]	ADPI
Air Direct Ltd. [*British*] [*ICAO designator*] (FAAC)	DFT
Air Direction Center	ADC
Air Direction Control Centre (SAUS)	ADCC
Air Direction Finder	ADF
Air Director (DAS)	AD
Air Director (SAUO)	AD
Air Discount Bulletin [*Travel industry*] (TRID)	ADB
Air Dispatch Letter Service [*Navy*]	ADLS
Air Distance (SAA)	AD
Air Distance Measuring Unit	ADMU
Air Distribution Institute (EA)	ADI
Air Distribution Unit [*Portable cooling system*] [*Air Force*]	ADU
Air Diverter Valve [*Automotive engineering*]	ADV
Air Division [*Air Force*]	AD
Air Division (SAUO)	AD

Air Division (SAUO)	ADiv
Air Division [*Air Force*]	A DIV
Air Division [*Air Force*]	AIRDIV
Air Division Advisor [*Air Force*] (SAA)	ADA
Air Division Defense [*Air Force*] (MUGU)	AIRDIVDEF
Air Division Warning Center (SAUO)	ADWC
Air Djibouti [*ICAO designator*] (AD)	DJ
Air Djibouti [*ICAO designator*] (FAAC)	DJB
Air Dolomiti [*Italy*] [*ICAO designator*] (FAAC)	DLA
Air Dorval Ltd. [*Canada*] [*ICAO designator*] (FAAC)	ADT
Air Dose [*Also called air exposure, referring to radiation exposure*] (DAVI)	E
Air Driven Pump	ADP
Air Drop Operator	ADO
Air Drop System [*Army*]	ADS
Air Droppable, Expendable Ocean Sensor [*Oceanography*] (MSC)	ADEOS
Air Droppable Measurement System [*Oceanography*] (MSC)	ADRAMS
Air Duct (MSA)	AD
Air East Africa Ltd. [*Kenya*] [*FAA designator*] (FAAC)	JND
Air Economy [*Ukraine*] [*FAA designator*] (FAAC)	AYY
Air Ecosse [*ICAO designator*] (AD)	EC
Air Ecosse Ltd. [*British*]	AE
Air Education and Recreation Organization (SAUO)	AERO
Air Education and Training Command [*Air Force*] (DOMA)	AETC
Air Education Recreation Organization [*British*] (DA)	AERO
Air Education Section of the Irish Aviation Council (EAIO)	AESIAC
Air Education Training Center [*Environmental science*] (BCP)	AETC
Air Efficiency Award [*RAF*] [*British*] (DMA)	AE
Air Efficiency Award [*RAF*] [*British*]	AEA
Air Efficiency Medal [*RAF*] [*British*]	AEM
Air Efficiency Medal (SAUS)	AEM
Air Efficieny Award (SAUS)	AEA
Air Ejection Off Gas (IEEE)	AEOG
Air Ejector	AE
Air Electrical [*NATO*] (NATG)	AE
Air Electrical [*Special duties officer*] [*Military*] [*British*]	AL
Air Electrical Officer	AIRELO
Air Electrical Officer's Writer [*British military*] (DMA)	ALOW
Air Electronic Warfare (SAUS)	AEW
Air Electronics Officer [*British*]	AEO
Air Element Coordinator [*Military*] (CAAL)	AREC
Air Eligibility Code	AEC
Air Embolism (MUSM)	AE
Air, Emergency Breathing System (DNAB)	AEB
Air Emplaced Classifier (MCD)	AEC
Air Encephalogram [*Medicine*]	AEG
Air Encephalography [*Medicine*] (MELL)	AEG
Air Enforcement Division [*Office of Enforcement and Compliance Monitoring*] [*Environmental Protection Agency*] (EPA)	AED
Air Engiadina [*Switzerland*] [*ICAO designator*] (FAAC)	RQX
Air Engineer (SAUS)	AE
Air Engineer Officer	AEO
Air Engineer Officer	AIREO
Air Engineer Officer's Writer [*British military*] (DMA)	AEOW
Air Engineering [*British*]	AE
Air Engineering Development Center (SAUS)	AEDC
Air Engineering Development Division [*Air Force*]	AEDD
Air Engineering (journ.) (SAUS)	Air Eng
Air Enterprise [*France*] [*ICAO designator*] (FAAC)	AEN
Air Entraining Agent [*Freight*]	AEA
Air Entry [*Respiration*] (DAVI)	AE
Air Equipment and Naval Photography Department (SAUO)	AED
Air Equipment and Support [*Army*] (AABC)	AE & S
Air Equipment and Support (SAUS)	AE&S
Air Equipment and Support [*Army*] (AFIT)	AEAS
Air Equipment Authority (SAUO)	AEA
Air Equipment Department (SAUO)	AED
Air Equipment Department [*British military*] (DMA)	AED
Air Equivalence Ratio [*For hydrocarbon combustion*]	AER
Air Escape [*Technical drawings*]	AE
Air et Cosmos. Special 1000 (journ.) (SAUS)	Air Cos S
Air Europa [*Spain*] [*ICAO designator*] (FAAC)	AEA
Air Europe [*ICAO designator*] (AD)	AE
Air Europe SpA [*Italy*] [*ICAO designator*] (FAAC)	AEL
Air Evacuation	AEVAC
Air Evacuation	AIREVAC
Air Evacuation of Wounded (SAUS)	AEW
Air Evacuation Patients (AFIT)	AEP
Air Evacuation Unit [*Military*]	AEU
Air Evacuation Wing	AIREVACWING
Air Evacuation Wounded Aircraft (SAUS)	AEW acft
Air Evasion [*France*] [*ICAO designator*] (FAAC)	IVS
Air Event Conference (SAUO)	AEC
Air Evex GmbH [*Germany*] [*ICAO designator*] (FAAC)	EVE
Air EW Working Group (SAUO)	AEWWG
Air Exchange, Inc. [*ICAO designator*] (FAAC)	EXG
Air Exel [*France*] [*ICAO designator*] (FAAC)	RXL
Air Exel Belgique [*Belgium*] [*ICAO designator*] (FAAC)	BXL
Air Exel Executive [*France*] [*ICAO designator*] (FAAC)	AOL
Air Exel Netherlands BV [*ICAO designator*] (FAAC)	AXL
Air Experienc Flight [*British*] [*ICAO designator*] (FAAC)	AED
Air Experience Flight [*British military*] (DMA)	AEF
Air Explorer Squadron	AESQ
Air Express	AXPS
Air Express AS [*Norway*] [*ICAO designator*] (FAAC)	AXP
Air Express Division of the Railway Express Agency	AIRYX

Air Express in Norrkoping AB [*Sweden*] [*ICAO designator*] (FAAC) ... GOT
Air Express, Inc. [*ICAO designator*] (FAAC) ... ARX
Air Express International Corp. ... AEI
Air Express International Corp. [*NASDAQ symbol*] (SAG) ... AEIC
Air Express International Corp. (EFIS) ... AEX
Air Express International Corp. [*Associated Press*] (SAG) ... AirExp
Air Express Intl. [*NASDAQ symbol*] (TTSB) ... AEIC
Air Facility (DNAB) ... AFY
Air Facility (SAUO) ... AIRFAC
Air Fall (SAUS) ... AF
Air Fecteau Ltd. [*Canada*] [*ICAO designator*] (FAAC) ... AFH
Air Ferry Squadron [*Navy*] ... AIRFERRON
Air Field (SAUS) ... A/F
Air Field Attack Munition (MCD) ... AFAM
Air Fighting Development Squadron (SAUO) ... AFDS
Air Fighting Development Squadron (SAUS) ... AFDS
Air Fighting Development Unit [*British*] ... AFDU
Air Filter ... AF
Air F.ilter (SAUS) ... AF
Air Filter [*Freight*] ... AIR FIL
Air Filter Institute [*Later, ARI*] (EA) ... AFI
Air Filtration Unit (SAUS) ... AFU
Air Fire Support (SAUS) ... AFS
Air Fitter (SAUS) ... AF
Air Fleet, Marine Force (SAUO) ... AFMF
Air Fleet Marine Force (AFIT) ... AIRFMF
Air Fleet, Marine Force, Atlantic (SAUO) ... AirFMFLant
Air Fleet, Marine Force, Pacific (SAUO) ... AirFMFPac
Air Fleet, Marine Forces (SAUO) ... AirFMF
Air Flight (SAUS) ... AF
Air Florida [*Air carrier designation symbol*] ... AFLX
Air Florida [*ICAO designator*] (FAAC) ... FLA
Air Florida, Inc. (SAUS) ... QH
Air Flow Actuated Switch ... AFAS
Air Flow and Pressure Test Station (ACAE) ... AFPTS
Air Flow Control [*Automotive engineering*] ... AFC
Air Flow Indicator ... AFI
Air Flow Meter [*Automotive engineering*] ... AFM
Air Flow Relay (SAUS) ... AFR
Air Flow Sensor [*Automotive engineering*] ... AFS
Air Flow Thermal Balance Calorimeter ... AFTBC
Air Foil Design System [*Automotive engineering*] ... AFDS
Air Forager [*Ornithology*] ... AF
Air Force ... AF
Air Force - Military Interdepartmental Purchase Requests ... AF-MIPR
Air Force - Navy ... AFNA
Air Force - Navy Aeronautical ... ANA
Air Force - Navy Aeronautical Bulletin ... AFNAB
Air Force - Navy Aeronautical Bulletin (NASA) ... ANA
Air Force - Navy Aeronautical Standard ... AFNAS
Air Force - Navy Standard (SAA) ... AFNS
Air Force Academy ... AFA
Air Force Academy and Aircrew Examining Center ... AFAAEC
Air Force Academy Board ... AFAB
Air Force Acceptance Team (MCD) ... AFAT
Air Force Accountable Property Officer (AAG) ... AFAPO
Air Force Accounting and Finance Center ... AFAFC
Air Force Achievement Medal [*Military decoration*] ... AFAM
Air Force Acquisition Circular (MCD) ... AFAC
Air Force Acquisition Document (MCD) ... AFAD
Air Force Acquisition Executive (MCD) ... AFAE
Air Force Acquisition Executive System (AAGC) ... AFAES
Air Force Acquisition Logistics Center (MCD) ... AFALC
Air Force Acquisition Logistics Division [*Wright Patterson Air Force Base*] (MCD) ... AFALD
Air Force Acquisition Logistics Division (AAGC) ... AFLD
Air Force Acquisition Model (AAGC) ... AFAM
Air Force Act [*British military*] (DMA) ... AFA
Air Force Administration and Organization (SAUS) ... AFAO
Air Force Administrative Order [*Canada, 1946-1964*] ... AFAO
Air Force Advanced Flying School (SAUO) ... AFAFS
Air Force Advanced Management Class ... AFADVMC
Air Force Advisory ... AFA
Air Force Advisory Group (CINC) ... AFADGRU
Air Force Advisory Group ... AFAG
Air Force Advisory Group ... AFGP
Air Force Advisory Team ... AFAT
Air Force Aero Propulsion Directorate (SAUS) ... AFAPD
Air Force Aeronautical Chart and Information Center (SAUO) ... AFAC&IC
Air Force Aeronautical Chart and Information Center (MUGU) ... AFAC & IC
Air Force Aeronautical Research Laboratory (SAUO) ... AFARL
Air Force Aeronautical Systems Command ... AFASC
Air Force Aeronautical Systems Division ... AFASD
Air Force Aero-Propulsion Laboratory [*Wright-Patterson Air Force Base, OH*] (AFM) ... AFAPL
Air Force Aerospace Fuel Petroleum Supply Office ... AFAFPSO
Air Force Aerospace Fuels Field Office (AFM) ... AFAFFO
Air Force Aerospace Materials Information Center (SAUO) ... AFAMIC
Air Force Aerospace Medical Research Laboratory [*Wright-Patterson Air Force Base, OH*] ... AFAMRL
Air Force Aerospace Rescue and Recovery Service (SAA) ... AARRS
Air Force Aerospace Rescue and Recovery Service (MCD) ... AARS
Air Force Agent Installation (AFM) ... AFAI
Air Force Aid Society (EA) ... AFAS
Air Force Air Base ... AAB
Air Force Air Materiel Area ... AFAMA
Air Force Alaskan Long Line System [*Communications*] (MCD) ... AFALLS
Air Force Alternate Command Post (SAUO) ... AFALT
Air Force Alternate Headquarters ... AFALT
Air Force Ammunition Depot (SAUO) ... AFAD
Air Force Ammunition Ordnance Depot (SAUO) ... AFAMMOD
Air Force & Anti-Aircraft Command (SAUS) ... AFAAC
Air Force & Anti-Aircraft Logistics Command (SAUS) ... AFAALC
Air Force & Anti-Aircraft Training Command (SAUS) ... AFAATC
Air Force Arctic Broadcasting Squadron [*New York, NY*] (EY) ... AFABS
Air Force Armament Center [*Eglin Air Force Base, FL*] ... AFAC
Air Force Armament Development and Test Center (MCD) ... AFADTC
Air Force Armament Museum ... AFAM
Air Force Armament Technology Laboratory [*Eglin Air Force Base, FL*] (AFM) ... AFATL
Air Force Armament Technology Laboratory (SAUO) ... AFATLE
Air Force Armament Testing Laboratory (DOMA) ... AFATL
Air Force Armaments Laboratory (ACAE) ... AFAI
Air Force Assistance Fund ... AFAF
Air Force Assistant Chief of Staff, Director of Policy, Plans, & Programs (SAUS) ... AF/INX
Air Force Association (EA) ... AFA
Air Force Association - Space Education Foundation ... AFA-SEF
Air Force Association-Space Education Foundation (SAUO) ... AFA-SEF
Air Force Astronautics Laboratory [*Edwards Air Force Base, CA*] (GRD) ... AFAL
Air Force, Atlantic Command (SAUO) ... AFLANT
Air Force Atlantic Test Range (SAA) ... AFATR
Air Force Audit Agency ... AFAA
Air Force Audit Branch (AFM) ... AFAB
Air Force Audit, Inspection & Investigations Council (SAUO) ... AFAIIC
Air Force Auditor General ... AFAUD
Air Force Authorization Document (MCD) ... AFAD
Air Force Automated Information Systems Review Council (SAUO) ... AFAISRC
Air Force Automated Message Processing Exchange (SAUS) ... AFAMPE
Air Force Automated Systems Project Office ... AFASPO
Air Force Auxiliary [*British*] ... AFA
Air Force Auxiliary Field ... AFAF
Air Force Auxiliary Field ... AFAUX
Air Force Avionics Laboratory [*Wright-Patterson Air Force Base, OH*] ... AFAL
Air Force Bailment Property ... AFBP
Air Force Ballistic Missile (KSC) ... AFBM
Air Force Ballistic Missile Arsenal ... AFBMA
Air Force Ballistic Missile Center ... AFBMC
Air Force Ballistic Missile Committee ... AFBMC
Air Force Ballistic Missile Division [*Inglewood, CA*] ... AFBMD
Air Force Ballistic Missile Division - Field Operations (SAA) ... AFBMD-FO
Air Force Ballistic Missile Installation Regulation ... AFBMIR
Air Force Ballistic Missile Office (SAUS) ... AFBMO
Air Force Ballistic Missile Training Center ... AFBMTC
Air Force Ballistic Systems Division [*Later, Space and Missile Systems Operations*] ... AFBSD
Air Force Base ... AFB
Air Force Base Conversion Agency ... AFBCA
Air Force Base Development Center (SAUO) ... AFBDC
Air Force Base Disposal Agency (DOMA) ... AFBDA
Air Force Base Group (SAUO) ... AFB Gp
Air Force Base Information Transfer System (MCD) ... AFBITS
Air Force Base Squadron (SAUO) ... AFB Sq
Air Force Base Unit ... AFBU
Air Force Base/Station (MILB) ... AFB/S
Air Force Basic Flying School (SAUO) ... AFBFS
Air Force Bent Fin Artillery Rocket (MCD) ... AFBFAR
Air Force Board (SAUS) ... AFB
Air Force Board for Correction of Military Records (GFGA) ... AFBCMR
Air Force Board of Review ... AFBR
Air Force Board Structure (MCD) ... AFBS
Air Force Broadcasting Service (DOMA) ... AFBS
Air Force Bulletin ... AFB
Air Force Business Research Management Center [*Wright-Patterson Air Force Base, OH*] ... AFBRMC
Air Force Business Research Manage-ment Center (SAUS) ... AFBRMC
Air Force C3CM Support Data Base (SAUO) ... AFC3CMSDB
Air Force Cambridge Research Center [*Obsolete*] ... AFCRC
Air Force Cambridge Research Computer (SAUS) ... AFCRC
Air Force Cambridge Research Laboratories [*Later, AFGL*] [*Hanscom Air Force Base, MA*] ... AFCRL
Air Force Cambridge Research Laboratories-Physical Sciences Research Paper (SAUS) ... AFCRL-PSRP
Air Force Cambridge Research Library (MCD) ... AFCRL
Air Force Capability Assessment Program (GFGA) ... AFCAP
Air Force Center (IUSS) ... AFC
Air Force Center for Environmental Excellence (DOMA) ... AFCEE
Air Force Center for International Programs ... AFCIP
Air Force Center for Studies and Analyses [*Washington, DC*] ... AFCSA
Air Force Center, Guided Missiles (SAUS) ... AFCGM
Air Force Central Museum (SAUS) ... AFCM
Air Force Central NOTAM Facility (SAUO) ... AFCNF
Air Force Central Notice to Airmen Facility ... AFCNF
Air Force Central Review Board (AAG) ... AFCRB
Air Force Ceramics and Graphite Information Center (SAUO) ... AFCGIC
Air Force Change (AAGC) ... AFC
Air Force Chaplain School [*Maxwell Air Force Base, AL*] ... AF Ch Sch
Air Force, Chief of Flight Safety (SAUS) ... AFCFS
Air Force Chief of Operations Analysis (MUGU) ... AFCOA
Air Force Chief of Staff (SAA) ... AFCS

Air Force Chief of Staff, Studies and Analysis (SAA) .... AFCSA
Air Force Chief Scientist (SAUS) .... AFCCN
Air Force Circulars .... AFC
Air Force Civil Engineer (journ.) (SAUS) .... AFCE
Air Force Civil Engineering Center [Tyndall Air Force Base, FL] .... AFCEC
Air Force Civil Engineering Support Agency (DOMA) .... AFCESA
Air Force Civil Engineering Unit (MCD) .... AFCE
Air Force Civilian Appellate Review Agency .... AFCARA
Air Force Civilian Automated Pay System (GFGA) .... AFCAPS
Air Force Civilian Personnel Management Center .... AFCPMC
Air Force Civilian Personnel Manual (SAUS) .... AFCPM
Air Force Civilian Welfare Fund (AFM) .... AFCWF
Air Force Cleaner "C" [Chemical warfare decontaminant] (ACAE) .... AFC
Air Force Clothing and Textile Office (AFIT) .... AFC & TO
Air Force Clothing and Textile Office (SAUS) .... AFC&TO
Air Force Coated Aluminum Metal (MCD) .... AFCAM
Air Force Coding System (SAA) .... AFCS
Air Force Combat Ammunition Center (SAUO) .... AFCOMAC
Air Force Combat Ammunitions Center .... AFCOMAC
Air Force Combat Climatology Center (SAUO) .... AFCCC
Air Force Combat Command .... AFCC
Air Force Combat Operations Staff .... AFCOS
Air Force Combat Theater Communications (SAUS) .... AFTC
Air Force Combat Theater Communications Program (AFIT) .... AFCTCP
Air Force Combined Tomography System (MCD) .... AFCTS
Air Force Command and Control Development Center .... AFCCDC
Air Force Command and Control Development Division [Bedford, MA]
   (AAG) .... AFCCDD
Air Force Command and Control Network AFC2N
Air Force Command and Control Post .... AFCCP
Air Force Command and Control System .... AFCCS
Air Force Command and Control System Graphic Operator Macros
   (MCD) .... AFGOM
Air Force Command and Control Systems Systems Program Office
   (SAUO) AFC2SSPO
Air Force Command and Staff College .... AFCSC
Air Force Command Post .... AFCP
Air Force Commander (SAUO) .... Com AF
Air Force Commendation Medal [Military decoration] (AFM) .... AFCM
Air Force Commendation Medal [Military decoration] .... AFCOM
Air Force Commissary Commission (ACAE) .... AFCOMS
Air Force Commissary Service .... AFCOMS
Air Force Communication Center .... AFCC
Air Force Communication Complex (SAUS) .... AIRCOM
Air Force Communications [Satellite] .... AFCOM
Air Force Communications Agency .... AFCA
Air Force Communications Center (SAUO) .... AFCC
Air Force Communications Command .... AFCC
Air Force Communications Complex (SAUO) .... AIRCOM
Air Force Communications Computer Programming Center .... AFCCPC
Air Force Communications Network (SAUS) .... AIRCOMNET
Air Force Communications Program .... AIRCOM
Air Force Communications Project (SAUS) .... AIIRCOM
Air Force Communications Security .... AFCOMSEC
Air Force Communications Security Center (AFM) .... AFCOMSECCEN
Air Force Communications Security Letter .... AFCSL
Air Force Communications Security Manual .... AFCOMSECM
Air Force Communications Security Manual .... AFCSM
Air Force Communications Security Pamphlet (MCD) .... AFCSP
Air Force Communications Service [or System] [Scott Air Force Base, IL] .... AFCS
Air Force Communications Service, Engineering and Installation
   (CET) .... AFCS E & I
Air Force Communications Service Manual .... AFCSM
Air Force Communications Service, Scott AFB, IL [OCLC symbol]
   (OCLC) .... ACS
Air Force Communications Service-Engineering and Installations
   (SAUO) .... AFCS E&I
Air Force Communications Service-Ground Electronics Engineering
   Installation A (SAUS) .... AFCS-GEEIA
Air Force Communications Service-Ground Electronics Engineering
   Installation Agency (SAUO) .... AFCS-GEEIA
Air Force Communications Squadron (MCD) .... AFCS
Air Force Communications Station .... AFCOMMSTA
Air Force Communications Support System .... AFCSS
Air Force Communications System (SAUS) .... AFCS
Air Force Communications Systems Integration Office (SAUS) .... AFCSIO
Air Force Communications-computer Systems Doctrine Office
   (SAUS) .... AFCSDO
Air (force) Component (SAUO) .... AC
Air Force Component .... AFC
Air Force Component Command Post (AFM) .... AFCCP
Air Force Component Commander (AFM) .... AFCC
Air Force Component Headquarters .... AFCH
Air Force Composite (SAUS) .... AF Comp
Air Force Comptroller .... AFAAC
Air Force Comptroller (AAG) .... AFC
Air Force Comptroller .... AFOC
Air Force Comptroller (journ.) (SAA) .... AFOC
Air Force Comptroller Management Engineering Team .... AFCOMPMET
Air Force Computer Acquisition Center .... AFCAC
Air Force Computer Acquisition Office .... AFCAO
Air Force Computer Program Library .... AFCPL
Air Force Computer Security Program Office (SAUO) .... AFCSPO
Air Force Computer Systems Integration Office (SAUS) .... AFCSIO
Air Force Configuration Control Board (AAG) .... AFCCB

Air Force Consolidation and Containerization Point (DOMA) .... AF-CCP
Air Force Container System Development Group .... AFCSDG
Air Force Contingency Operations Staff (SAUO) .... AFCOS
Air Force Contract Adjustment Board (AAGC) .... AFCAB
Air Force Contract Law Center .... AFCLC
Air Force Contract Maintenance Center (AFM) .... AFCMC
Air Force Contract Management Division [Los Angeles, CA] .... AFCMD
Air Force Contract Management Division Directorate of Quality Assurance
   [Los Angeles, CA] .... AFCMD/QA
Air Force Contract Management Office .... AFCMO
Air Force Contracting Office Approval .... AFCOA
Air Force Contracting Officer .... AFCO
Air Force Contractor (SAA) .... AFCON
Air Force Contractor Experience List (AFM) .... AFCEL
Air Force Control Office (AAG) .... AFCO
Air Force Controlled [Units] .... AFCON
Air Force Coordinating Office for Logistics Research (MCD) .... AFCOLR
Air Force Coronary Atherosclerosis Prevention Study .... AFCAPS
Air Force Cost Analysis Agency (DOMA) .... AFCAA
Air Force Cost Center .... AFCCE
Air Force Cost Center (ACAE) .... AFCSTC
Air Force Cost Reduction Program (AFM) .... AFCRP
Air Force Council [Advisory board to Air Force] .... AFC
Air Force Court of Military Review (ACAE) .... AFCMR
Air Force Cross [US and British] [Military decoration] .... AFC
Air Force Cryptographic Aid, General .... AFKAG
Air Force Cryptographic Aid, Recognition and Identification Systems
   (CET) .... AFKAI
Air Force Cryptographic Code System (CET) .... AFKAC
Air Force Cryptographic Maintenance Manual (CET) .... AFKAM
Air Force Cryptographic One Time Pads (CET) .... AFKAP
Air Force Cryptologic Depot (AFM) .... AFCD
Air Force Cryptologic Support Center .... AFCSC
Air Force Data Automation Agency (AFM) .... AFDAA
Air Force Data Automation Management Engineering Team .... AFDAMET
Air Force Data Automation Planning (SAUS) .... AFDAP
Air Force Data Automation Planning Concepts [Manual] .... AFDAP
Air Force Data Communications (SAUS) .... AFDATACOM
Air Force Data Communications System .... AFDATACOM
Air Force Data Services Center .... AFDSC
Air Force Data Station .... AFDASTA
Air Force Data Station (CET) .... AFDATASTA
Air Force Data System Design Center (SAUS) .... AFDSDC
Air Force Data Systems Design Center [Gunter Air Force Station, AL]
   (AFM) .... AFDSDC
Air Force Data Systems Evaluation Center .... AFDSEC
Air Force Decision Coordinating Paper (MCD) .... AFDCP
Air Force Decorations Board .... AFDB
Air Force Defence Control Centre (SAUS) .... ADFCC
Air Force Defense Acquisition Regulation Supplement [Superseded by
   AFFARS in 1984] (AAGC) .... AFDARS
Air Force Defense Acquisition Regulations (MCD) .... AFDAR
Air Force Defense Metals Information Center (SAUO) .... AFDMIC
Air Force Department (SAUS) .... AFT
Air Force Department Constabulary [British military] (DMA) .... AFDC
Air Force Department Fire Service [British military] (DMA) .... AFDFS
Air Force Departmental Catalog Coordinating Office .... AFDCCO
Air Force Departmental Industrial Equipment Reserve (SAA) .... AFDIER
Air Force Departmental Industrial Equipment Reserve Storage Site .... AFDIERSS
Air Force Departure Point (SAUS) .... AFDP
Air Force Depot .... AFD
Air Force Depot Equipment Performance Tester (AAG) .... ADEPT
Air Force, Deputy for Foreign Development (SAUS) .... AFDFD
Air Force Designated Acquisition Program .... AFDAP
Air Force Detachment .... AFD
Air Force Development Field Office (SAUO) .... AFDFO
Air Force Development Field Representative (AAG) .... AFDFR
Air Force Development Test Center (DOMA) .... AFDTC
Air Force Development Unit (SAUS) .... AFDU
Air Force Digital Graphics System (COE) .... AFDIGS
Air Force Directive (AAG) .... AFD
Air Force Directive .... AFDIR
Air Force Director for Strategic Force Analysis (SAUS) .... AFSAS
Air Force Director of Accounting and Financing (AAG) .... AFAF
Air Force Director of Administration (ACAE) .... AFDA
Air Force Director of Command Control and Communications .... AFOCC
Air Force Director of Data Automation (IEEE) .... AFDDA
Air Force Director of Development and Planning (SAA) .... AFDAP
Air Force Director of Inspection Services (MUGU) .... AFDIS
Air Force Director of Management Analysis (SAUS) .... AFDMA
Air Force Director of Personnel Planning (SAA) .... AFDPP
Air Force Director of Reconnaissance and Electronic Warfare (IEEE) .... AFDRDR
Air Force Director of Requirements .... AFDRQ
Air Force Director [or Directorate] of Research and Development .... AFDRD
Air Force Director of Research and Development (SAUO) .... AFDRD
Air Force Director of Research and Technology (SAA) .... AFDRT
Air Force Director of Special Investigations (SAA) .... AFDSI
Air Force Directorate of Advanced Technology .... AFDAT
Air Force Directorate of Materials and Processes (KSC) .... AFDMP
Air Force Directorate of Requirement (AAG) .... AFDR
Air Force Directorate of Research and Development (SAUS) .... AFDRD
Air Force Directory of Resident Inspection Facilities (AAG) .... AFDRIF
Air Force Disability Review Board .... AFDRB
Air Force Disaster Preparedness Resource Center .... AFDPRC
Air Force Discharge Review Board .... AFDRB

Air Force Disciplinary Board (SAUO) ... AFDCB
Air Force Discrepancy Report (SAUS) ... AFDR
Air Force Dispersion Assessment Model (ACAE) ... ADAM
Air Force Distribution Agency ... AFDA
Air Force Distribution Control Office ... AFDCO
Air Force District of Washington ... AFDW
Air Force District of Washington Accounting and Finance Office ... AFDWAFO
Air Force Doctrine Center (COE) ... AFDC
Air Force Doctrine Command (SAUS) ... AFDC
Air Force Doctrine Document ... AFDD
Air Force Drug Testing Laboratory [*Brooks Air Force Base, TX*] (GRD) ... AFDTL
Air Force Duty Officer ... AFDO
Air Force Eastern Test Range [*Later, ESMC*] [*Patrick Air Force Base, FL*] ... AFETR
Air Force Eastern Test Range Manual [*A publication*] (MCD) ... AFETRM
Air Force Educational Requirements Board (AFM) ... AFERB
Air Force Edwards Research Center ... AFERC
Air Force Electronic Combat Office (ACAE) ... AFECO
Air Force Electronic Data Processing Center (AAG) ... AFEDPC
Air Force Electronic Failure Report (SAA) ... AFEFR
Air Force Electronic Properties Information Center (PDAA) ... AFEPIC
Air Force Electronic Security Command ... AFESC
Air Force Electronic Systems Division ... AFESD
Air Force Electronic Warfare Center (CAAL) ... AFEWC
Air Force Electronic Warfare Effectiveness Simulator (ADWA) ... AFEWES
Air Force Electronic Warfare Evaluation Simulator ... AFEWES
Air Force Electro-Optical Site (CET) ... AFEOS
Air Force Emergency Force ... AFEF
Air Force Emergency Operations Center (CET) ... AFEOC
Air Force Engineering and Logistic Information System (ACAE) ... AFELIS
Air Force Engineering and Logistics Information System (IEEE) ... AFELIS
Air Force Engineering & Sciences Center (SAUS) ... AFESC
Air Force Engineering and Services Agency (SAUO) ... AFESA
Air Force Engineering and Services Center [*Tyndall Air Force Base, FL*] ... AFESC
Air Force Engineering and Services Center/Engineering and Services Laboratory [*Tyndall Air Force Base, FL*] ... AFESC/ESL
Air Force Engineering & Services Laboratory (SAUO) ... AFESL
Air Force Engineering and Services Management Engineering Team ... AFESMET
Air Force Engineering and Services Quarterly (journ.) (SAUS) ... Air Force Eng Serv Q
Air Force Engineering and Technical Service (AFM) ... AFETS
Air Force Engineering Data Service Center (SAUO) ... AFEDSC
Air Force Engineering Responsibility (CET) ... AFER
Air Force Engineering Technology Office [*Tyndall Air Force Base, FL*] ... AFETO
Air Force English Syntax Project (SAUS) ... AFESP
Air Force Environmental Rocket-Sounding System [*Meteorology*] ... AFERSS
Air Force Environmental Technical Applications Center (MCD) ... AFETAC
Air Force Equipment Maintenance Management Information System (MCD) ... AFEMMIS
Air Force Equipment Management Survey Team ... AFEMST
Air Force Equipment Management System (AFM) ... AFEMS
Air Force Equipment Management Team (AFIT) ... AFEMT
Air Force Equipment Procurement Instruction ... AFEPI
Air Force Escape and Evasion Society (SAUO) ... AFEES
Air Force Escape & Evasion Society (SAUS) ... AFEES
Air Force European Broadcasting Squadron ... AFEBS
Air Force European Office of Aerospace Research (KSC) ... AFEOAR
Air Force Examination Board (SAUO) ... AFEB
Air Force Exchange (SAUO) ... AFEX
Air Force Exchange Service (AFM) ... AFES
Air Force Experiment ... AFE
Air Force Far East ... AFFE
Air Force Federal Acquisition Regulation Supplement [*Replaced AFDARS in 1984*] (AAGC) ... AFFARS
Air Force Field Office Manager (AAG) ... AFFOM
Air Force Field Technical Center [*Edwards Air Force Base, CA*] (MCD) ... AFFTC
Air Force Film Library Center ... AFFLC
Air Force Finance Center ... AFFC
Air Force Finance Center ... AFN
Air Force Financial Postal Clerk (AFM) ... AFFPC
Air Force Flight Dynamics Laboratory [*Wright-Patterson Air Force Base, OH*] (AFM) ... AFFDL
Air Force Flight Standards Agency (DOMA) ... AFFSA
Air Force Flight Test Center (SAUO) ... AAFTC
Air Force Flight Test Center [*Edwards Air Force Base, CA*] ... AFFTC
Air Force Flight Test Center [*Edwards Air Force Base, CA*] (MCD) ... AFFTEC
Air Force Flight Test Instrumentation System ... AFFTIS
Air Force Flight Training Command ... AFTC
Air Force Flying Safety (SAUS) ... AFFS
Air Force Flying Training Command (SAUO) ... AFFTC
Air Force Forces [*Element of a joint task force*] ... AFFOR
Air Force Forces Deputy [*or Director*] **Communications-Electronics** (AFIT) ... AFFOR/DC
Air Force Foreign Technology Division (KSC) ... AFFTD
Air Force Foreign Technology Intel Center (SAUO) ... AFFTIC
Air Force, Forward Area, Central Pacific (SAUO) ... AIRFORWARD
Air Force Frequency Management Agency (DOMA) ... AFFMA
Air Force Frequency Management Center (SAUO) ... AFFMC
Air Force General Orders (SAUS) ... AFGO
Air Force Geographic Information Handling System (ADWA) ... AFGIHS
Air Force Geophysics Laboratory [*Formerly, AFCRL*] [*Hanscom Air Force Base, MA*] ... AFGL
Air Force Geophysics Laboratory Research Library, Hanscom AFB, MA [*OCLC symbol*] (OCLC) ... SCG
Air Force Global Weather Center (SAUS) ... AWGWC
Air Force Global Weather Central [*or Control*] [*Offutt Air Force Base, NE*] ... AFGWC
Air Force Global Weather Reconnaissance Program ... AFGWRP
Air Force Good Conduct Medal [*Military decoration*] (AFM) ... AFGCM
Air Force Group (SAUO) ... AFGp
Air Force Guide for Writing ... GW
Air Force Guide Specification (MCD) ... AFGS
Air Force Headquarters ... AFHQ
Air Force Headquarters Command ... AFHC
Air Force Headquarters, Ottawa, Ontario, Canada ... CANAIRHED
Air Force Health Professions Scholarship Program ... AFHPSP
Air Force Historical Foundation (EA) ... AFHF
Air Force Historical Research Agency (DOMA) ... AFHRA
Air Force Historical Society (SAUO) ... AFHS
Air Force Hospital ... AFH
Air Force Human Relations Laboratory (SAUS) ... AFHRL
Air Force Human Resources Laboratory [*Brooks Air Force Base, TX*] (AFM) ... AFHRL
Air Force Human Resources Laboratory/Flying Training Division [*Williams Air Force Base, AZ*] ... AFHRL/FT
Air Force Human Resources Laboratory/Manpower Development Division [*Alexandria, VA*] ... AFHRL/MD
Air Force Hurricane Liaison Office (SAUO) ... AFHLO
Air Force in Europe ... AFE
Air Force Industrial Assistance Management Survey (ACAE) ... AFIAMS
Air Force Industrial Fund (AFM) ... AFIF
Air Force Industrial Security Regulations ... AFISR
Air Force Information for Industry Office (DOMA) ... AFIFIO
Air Force Information For Industry Offices (SAUS) ... AFIFIO
Air Force Information Management Study ... AFIMS
Air Force Information Network (SAUS) ... AFIN
Air Force Information Program (SAA) ... AFIP
Air Force Information Systems Architecture (SAUS) ... AFISA
Air Force Information Warfare Center (SAUO) ... AFIWC
Air Force Inspection Agency (DOMA) ... AFIA
Air Force Inspection and Safety Center ... AFISC
Air Force Inspector General (SAUS) ... AFCIG
Air Force Inspector General (SAA) ... AFIG
Air Force Inspector General Activities Center ... AFIGAC
Air Force Inspector General Activities Center (SAUS) ... AFIGAC
Air Force Installation Representative ... AFIR
Air Force Installation Representative Officer ... AFIRO
Air Force Installations Representative Officer (SAUO) ... AFIRO
Air Force Institute of Pathology (DAVI) ... AFIP
Air Force Institute of Technology (GAGS) ... AF Inst
Air Force Institute of Technology [*Wright-Patterson Air Force Base, OH*] ... AFIT
Air Force Institute of Technology, Residence School ... AFIT(RS)
Air Force Institute of Technology School of Systems and Logistics (SAUO) ... AFIT/LS
Air Force Institute of Technology School of Systems and Logistics [*Wright-Patterson Air Force Base, OH*] ... AFIT/SL
Air Force Institute of Technology, Wright-Patterson AFB, OH [*OCLC symbol*] (OCLC) ... SCT
Air Force Instruction ... AFI
Air Force Instruction and Military Training School (SAUO) ... AFIMTS
Air Force Integrated Command and Control System (AFM) ... AFICCS
Air Force Intelligence (SAUO) ... AFI
Air Force Intelligence (CCCA) ... AFIN
Air Force Intelligence Agency (ACAE) ... AFIA
Air Force Intelligence Center ... AFIC
Air Force Intelligence Command [*Established 1991*] (DOMA) ... AFIC
Air Force Intelligence Data Handling System [*ESD*] ... AIDS
Air Force Intelligence Data System (ACAE) ... AIDS
Air Force Intelligence Information Systems Plan (ACAE) ... AFIISP
Air Force Intelligence Management Engineering Team ... AFINTELMET
Air Force Intelligence Officer (CCCA) ... AFIO
Air Force Intelligence Publication (SAA) ... AFIP
Air Force Intelligence Reserve programme (SAUS) ... AFIR
Air Force Intelligence Service ... AFIS
Air Force Intelligence Study ... AFIS
Air Force Intelligence Support Agency (DOMA) ... AFISA
Air Force Intelligent System (IUSS) ... AFIS
Air Force Interim Command and Control System (SAUS) ... AFICCS
Air Force International Standard ... AIR-STD
Air Force Inventory Manager ... AFIM
Air Force JAG Bulletin [*A publication*] (AAGC) ... AF JAG Bull
Air Force Jet ... AFJ
Air Force Job Knowledge Test ... AFJKT
Air Force Joint Project Office (SAA) ... AFJPO
Air Force Journal of Logistics (journ.) (SAUS) ... Air F J Log
Air Force Judge Advocate General ... AFJAG
Air Force Judge Advocate General School ... AFJAGS
Air Force Junior Reserve Officers Training Corps (AFM) ... AFJROTC
Air Force Justification for Major System New Start (MCD) ... AFJMSNS
Air Force Knowledge Test (SAA) ... AFKT
Air Force Language Aptitude Test ... AFLAT
Air Force Law Enforcement Terminal System ... AFLETS
Air Force Legal Services Agency (DOMA) ... AFLSA
Air Force Legal Services Center ... AFLSC
Air Force Legislative Item ... AFLI
Air Force Letter ... AFL
Air Force Liaison ... AFL
Air Force Library Service (SAUO) ... AFLS
Air Force List [*British military*] (DMA) ... AFL

Air Force Local Area Network Systems Program Office (SAUO) .... AFLANSPO
Air Force Logistic Command Manual (SAUS) .... AFLCM
Air Force, Logistics and Engineering (DOMA) .... AF/LE
Air Force Logistics Center (MCD) .... AFLC
Air Force Logistics Command [*Formerly, Air Materiel Command*] [*Wright-Patterson Air Force Base, OH*] .... AFLC
Air Force Logistics Command - Operations Analysis Office (SAUO) .... AFLC-OAO
Air Force Logistics Command Form .... AFLCF
Air Force Logistics Command Letter (MCD) .... AFLCL
Air Force Logistics Command Operations Analysis Office [*Wright-Patterson Air Force Base, OH*] .... AFLC-OA
Air Force Logistics Command Operations Network (MCD) .... AFLCON
Air Force Logistics Command Pamphlets .... AFLCP
Air Force Logistics Command Regulations .... AFLCR
Air Force Logistics Command Support Office (SAUO) .... AFLCSO
Air Force Logistics Communications Network (AFM) .... AFLCON
Air Force Logistics Control Group .... AFLCG
Air Force Logistics Management (MUSM) .... AFLMA
Air Force Logistics Management Agency .... AFLMA
Air Force Logistics Management Center [*Gunter Air Force Station, AL*] (AFM) .... AFLMC
Air Force Logistics Management Engineering Team .... AFLOGMET
Air Force Longevity Service Award [*Military decoration*] (AFM) .... AFLSA
Air Force Lumber Stock Control Office (SAUO) .... AFLSCO
Air Force Machinability Data Center (MCD) .... AFMDC
Air Force Maintenance and Supply Management Engineering Team [*Wright-Patterson Air Force Base, OH*] .... AFMSMET
Air Force Maintenance Management Engineering Team .... AFMAINMET
Air Force Management Analysis Group (MCD) .... AFMAG
Air Force Management Engineering Agency .... AFMEA
Air Force Management Improvement Group (ACAE) .... AFMIG
Air Force Manpower and Personnel Center (MCD) .... AFMPC
Air Force Manpower & Personnel Management Engineering Team (SAUS) .... AFMPMET
Air Force Manpower Standards .... AFMS
Air Force Manual [*A publication*] .... AFM
Air Force Manual of Procurement and Productions [*A publication*] (AAGC) .... AFMPP
Air Force Manuals of National Technical Criteria of Compromising Emanations (ACAE) .... AFNAG
Air Force Manufacturing Technology .... AFMT
Air Force Material Command .... AFMC
Air Force Material Review Board (MCD) .... AFMRB
Air Force Material Supply and Services (SAA) .... AFMSS
Air Force Materials Information Center (DIT) .... AFMIC
Air Force Materials Laboratory [*Wright-Patterson Air Force Base, OH*] .... AFML
Air Force Materiel Command Support Center, Europe (SAUO) .... AFMCSCE
Air Force Maui Optical Site (SAUS) .... AMOS
Air Force Maui Optical Station .... AMOS
Air Force Maui Optical System (SAUS) .... AMOS
Air Force Measurement Standards Laboratories (AFIT) .... AFMSL
Air Force Mechanical Properties Data Center (SAUO) .... AFMPDC
Air Force Medal [*British*] .... AFM
Air Force Medical Center (SAUS) .... AFMC
Air Force Medical Logistics Office .... AFMLO
Air Force Medical Management Engineering Team .... AFMEDMET
Air Force Medical Material Field Office (SAUO) .... AFMMFO
Air Force Medical Materiel Field Office (AFM) .... AFMMFO
Air Force Medical Materiel Letter .... AFMML
Air Force Medical Operations Agency (DOMA) .... AFMOA
Air Force Medical Publications Agency .... AFMPA
Air Force Medical Service .... AFMS
Air Force Medical Service Center (MCD) .... AFMSC
Air Force Medical Specialist Corps .... AFMSC
Air Force Medical Support Agency (DOMA) .... AFMSA
Air Force Meteorological Center (SAUO) .... AFMeTC
Air Force Meteorological Center (SAUS) .... AFMETC
Air Force Meteorological Satellite Program (NOAA) .... AFMSP
Air Force Military Personnel Center [*Randolph Air Force Base, TX*] .... AFMPC
Air Force Military Training Center (AFM) .... AFMTC
Air Force Military Training Center (SAUS) AFMTC-83B
Air Force MIPR [*Military Interdepartmental Purchase Request*] **Management Office** (AFIT) .... AFMMO
Air Force Missile Development Center [*AFSC*] .... AFMDC
Air Force Missile Division (SAA) .... AFMD
Air Force Missile Test Center [*Later, AFETR*] [*Patrick Air Force Base, FL*] .... AFMTC
Air Force Mission Element Need Statement .... AFMENS
Air Force Mission Support System (DOMA) .... AFMSS
Air Force Morale, Welfare & Recreation Agency (SAUS) .... AFMWRA
Air Force Mortuary Services Office .... AFMSO
Air Force Motor Vehicle Operator Test (SAUS) .... AFMVOP
Air Force Museum .... AFM
Air Force National Guard (SAUO) .... AFNG
Air Force National Range Division .... AFNRD
Air Force NATO Agreement (MCD) .... AFNAG
Air Force Navigators Observers Association (EA) .... AFNOA
Air Force Negotiation Team (AAGC) .... AFNT
Air Force Network (SAUS) .... AFNET
Air Force Networks Station .... AFNETSTA
Air Force News Agency (DOMA) .... AFNEWS
Air Force News Service .... AFNS
Air Force Noncommissioned Officer Academy [*Graduate*] **Ribbon** [*Military decoration*] (AFM) .... AFNCOAR
Air Force Noncommissioned Officer Academy Ribbon (SAUS) .... AFNCOAR
Air Force NOTAM [*Notice to Airmen*] **Exchange Area** .... AFNEA
Air Force NOTAM [*Notice to Airmen*] **Exchange Office** .... AFNEO
Air Force Nuclear Engineering Test Facility [*Reactor*] .... AF NETF
Air Force Nuclear Engineering Test Reactor (SAA) .... AFNETR
Air Force Nurse Corps .... AFNC
Air Force Objective Series [*Papers*] .... AFOS
Air Force Occupational and Environmental Health Laboratory (SAUS) .... AFOEHL
Air Force Occupational and Health Standard (ACAE) .... AFOSH
Air Force Occupational Safety and Health [*Standards*] .... AFOSH
Air Force of the People Chinese Liberation Army .... AFPCA
Air Force of the Republic of Viet Nam (SAUO) .... AFRVN
Air Force of the Unites States (SAUO) .... AFUS
Air Force Office for Aerospace Research (SAUS) .... AFOAR
Air Force Office for Atomic Energy (SAUO) .... AFOAT
Air Force Office for Logistic Technology Applications (ACAE) .... AFOLTA
Air Force Office of Aerospace Research [*AFSC*] .... AFOAR
Air Force Office of Aerospace Sciences [*AFOAR*] .... AFOAS
Air Force Office of Atomic Energy (SAUO) .... AFOAE
Air Force Office of Atomic Energy .... AFOAT
Air Force Office of Civil Engineering (SAA) .... AFOCE
Air Force Office of Manpower and Organization .... AFOMO
Air Force Office of Medical Support .... AFOMS
Air Force Office of Public Affairs .... AFOPA
Air Force Office of Research Analysis (AFM) .... AFORA
Air Force Office of Scientific Research [*Bolling Air Force Base*] [*Washington, DC*] .... AFOSR
Air Force Office of Security Police .... AFOSP
Air Force Office of Special Investigation .... AFOSI
Air Force Office of Special Investigations (ACAE) .... AFOIS
Air Force Office of Technology (ACAE) .... AFOT
Air Force Officer Education and Commissioning Program (SAUO) .... AFOECP
Air Force Officer Education Program (AFM) .... AFOEP
Air Force Officer in Charge .... AFOIC
Air Force Officer Qualifying Test .... AFOQT
Air Force One (SAUS) .... AFO
Air Force On-Line Bulletin Board Systems (SAUS) .... DIAL-A-LOG
Air Force On-Line Data System .... AFOLDS
Air Force Operational Report (AFM) .... AFOREP
Air Force Operational Service (SAA) .... AFOS
Air Force Operational Test and Evaluation Center [*Kirtland Air Force Base, NM*] .... AFOTEC
Air Force Operational Test Center (MCD) .... AFOTC
Air Force Operations Analysis Office (KSC) .... AFOAO
Air Force Operations Base .... AFOB
Air Force Operations Center .... AFOC
Air Force Operations Resource Management System (SAUS) .... AFORMS
Air Force Operations Room [*British military*] (DMA) .... AFOR
Air Force Order (SAUS) .... AFO
Air Force Organization Status Change Report .... AFOSCR
Air Force Orientation Group (ACAE) .... AFOG
Air Force Outstanding Unit Award [*Military decoration*] (AFM) .... AFOUA
Air Force Outstanding Unit Award Ribbon [*Military decoration*] .... AFOUAR
Air Force Outstanding Unit Emblem [*Military decoration*] .... AFOUE
Air Force Overseas Replacement (SAUS) .... AFOR
Air Force Overseas Replacement Depot [*World War II*] .... AFORD
Air Force Overseas Replacement Group [*World War II*] .... AFORG
Air Force Pacific Broadcasting Squadron .... AFPBS
Air Force Packaging Evaluation Agency (MCD) .... AFPEA
Air Force Packaging Laboratory .... AFPL
Air Force Pamphlet .... AFP
Air Force Pamphlet .... AFPAM
Air Force Personnel and Training Research Center [*Later, Air Force Personnel Research Laboratory*] [*Lackland Air Force Base, TX*] .... AFPTRC
Air Force Personnel Board .... AFPB
Air Force Personnel Center .... AFPC
Air Force Personnel Council .... AFPC
Air Force Personnel on Duty with Army .... AFWAR
Air Force Personnel on Duty with Navy .... AFWN
Air Force Personnel Processing Group .... AFPG
Air Force Personnel Research Laboratory (SAUS) .... AFPRL
Air Force Personnel Test (AFM) .... AFPT
Air Force Personnel Training and Research Center (SAUO) .... AFPTRC
Air Force Petroleum Retail Distribution Station (AFM) .... AFPRDS
Air Force Phillips Laboratory .... AFPL
Air Force Physical Disability Appeal Board .... AFPDAB
Air Force Pictorial Service (SAUO) .... AFAPS
Air Force Plan (MCD) .... AFP
Air Force Planning Element .... AFPE
Air Force Planning Guide .... AFPG
Air Force Planning Guide (ACAE) .... APG
Air Force Plant .... AFP
Air Force Plant Office (SAUO) .... AFPO
Air Force Plant Representative .... AFPR
Air Force Plant Representative Office .... AFPRO
Air Force Polaris Material Office .... AFPMO
Air Force Police (NATG) .... AFP
Air Force Policy Council (AAG) .... AFPC
Air Force Policy Letter for Commanders .... AFPLC
Air Force Policy on Disclosure of Classified Military Information (SAA) .... AFDCMI
Air Force Postal Clerk (AFM) .... AFPC
Air Force Postal Unit .... AFPU
Air Force Potential Contractor Program (MCD) .... AFPCP
Air Force Preliminary Evaluation (MCD) .... AFPE
Air Force Procurement Circular (SAUS) .... AFPC

Air Force Procurement Circulars ... AFPC
Air Force Procurement District (SAUO) ... AFPD
Air Force Procurement Instructions ... AFPI
Air Force Procurement Officer (SAUS) ... AFPO
Air Force Procurement Officer (AAGC) ... APO
Air Force Procurement Procedures ... AFPP
Air Force Procurement Regulation ... AFPR
Air Force Procurement Representative ... AFPR
Air Force Production Reserve Policy ... AFPRP
Air Force Professional Entertainment Branch ... AFPEB
Air Force Professional Manpower and Personnel Management School ... AFPMPMS
Air Force Professionel Entertainment Branch (SAUO) ... AFPEB
Air Force Program (SAUS) ... AFP
Air Force Program Executive Office (DOMA) ... AFPEO
Air Force Program Executive Offices (BARN) ... AFPEO
Air Force Program for Joint Interoperability of Tactical Command and Control Systems (SAUO) ... AFJINTACCS
Air Force Program Objectives Memorandum (MCD) ... AFPOM
Air Force Program Representative Office (MCD) ... AFPRO
Air Force programme for the Joint Interoperability of TACCS (SAUS) ... AFJINTACCS
Air Force, Programs and Evaluation (DOMA) ... AF/PR
Air Force Programs Executive Officer, Director of Strategic Programs (SAUS) ... AFPEO/ST
Air Force Project Representative ... AFPR
Air Force Property Officer (MCD) ... AFPO
Air Force Publications and Distribution Center (SAUS) ... AF-PDC
Air Force Purchase Item Description ... AFPID
Air Force Purchasing Office (MUGU) ... AFPO
Air Force Qualification Test (SAUS) ... AFQT
Air Force Qualified Products List (SAUS) ... AFQPL
Air Force Quality Assurance (KSC) ... AFQA
Air Force Quality Assurance Representative ... AFQAR
Air Force Quality Control ... AFQC
Air Force Quality Control Representative ... AFQCR
Air Force Radiation Effects Information Center (SAUO) ... AFREIC
Air Force Range Support Facility ... AFRSF
Air Force Real Estate Agency (MUSM) ... AFREA
Air Force Records Center ... AFRC
Air Force Recoverable Assembly Management (PDAA) ... AFRAM
Air Force Recoverable Assembly Management System (AFM) ... AFRAMS
Air Force Recruiter Assistance Program (MCD) ... AFRAP
Air Force Recruiting Office (SAUO) ... AFRO
Air Force Recurring Publication (AFM) ... AFRP
Air Force Regional Civil Engineer (SAUO) ... AFRC
Air Force Regional Civil Engineers ... AFRCE
Air Force Regional Civil Engineers (SAUO) ... AFRLC
Air Force Regulation ... AFR
Air Force Replacement Squadron (SAUO) ... AF Repl Sq
Air Force Representative (SAUS) ... AFREP
Air Force Rescue Coordination Center ... AFRCC
Air Force Rescue Service ... AFRS
Air Force Research and Development Branch ... AFRDB
Air Force Research and Technology Division ... AFRTD
Air Force Research Center (SAUO) ... AFRC
Air Force Research Directorate (KSC) ... AFRD
Air Force Research Division ... AFRD
Air Force Research in Aircraft Propulsion Technology Program [*West Lafayette, IN*] (GRD) ... AFRAPT
Air Force Research Laboratory ... AFRL
Air Force Research Objectives ... AFRO
Air Force Research Training Center ... AFRTC
Air Force Reserve (DOMA) ... AFR
Air Force Reserve (SAUO) ... AFRes
Air Force Reserve ... AFRES
Air Force Reserve - Base Level Military Personnel System (SAUO) ... ARF-BLMPS
Air Force Reserve Base Support Group (SAUO) ... AFRBSG
Air Force Reserve Base Support Group (SAUO) ... AFRBSGp
Air Force Reserve Base Support Group ... AFRBSGP
Air Force Reserve Combat Support Training Center ... AFRCSTC
Air Force Reserve Combat Training Center ... AFRCTC
Air Force Reserve Command ... AFRC
Air Force Reserve Coordination Center (AFM) ... AFRCC
Air Force Reserve Division ... AFRD
Air Force Reserve Facility (SAUO) ... AFRESF
Air Force Reserve Flying Training Center ... AFRFTC
Air Force Reserve Navigation Squadron ... AFRESNAVSQ
Air Force Reserve Officers Training Corps [*Washington, DC*] ... AFROTC
Air Force Reserve Orders ... AFRO
Air Force Reserve Policy Committee ... AFRPC
Air Force Reserve Recovery Group (SAUO) ... AFRRG
Air Force Reserve Recovery Group (AFM) ... AFRRGp
Air Force Reserve Region (SAUO) ... AFRESR
Air Force Reserve Regions (AFM) ... AFRR
Air Force Reserve Regions Base Support Group ... AFRESBSGP
Air Force Reserve Regions Group ... AFRESRGP
Air Force Reserve Sector (SAUO) ... AFRESS
Air Force Reserve Sector (SAUO) ... AFRS
Air Force Reserve Sectors (AFM) ... AFRS
Air Force Reserve Specialist Training Center ... AFRSTC
Air Force Reserve Training Center ... AFRTC
Air Force Resident Officer in Charge ... AFROIC
Air Force Resident Representative (AAG) ... AFRR
Air Force Retired Officer's Community ... AFROC
Air Force Retiring Board ... AFRB
Air Force Review Boards Agency (DOMA) ... AFRBA
Air Force Review Boards Office ... AFRBO
Air Force Rocket Propulsion Laboratory [*Later, AFAL*] [*Edwards Air Force Base, CA*] ... AFRPL
Air Force Rome Air Development Center ... AF/RADC
Air Force Rome Air Development Center (SAUO) ... AFRADC
Air Force Route (DA) ... AFR
Air Force Routine Order [*Canada, 1920-1945*] ... AFRO
Air Force Royal Aeronautical Society (SAUO) ... AFRAeS
Air Force Safety Agency (DOMA) ... AFSA
Air Force Salary Impact Report ... AFSIR
Air Force Satellite (CCCA) ... AFSAT
Air Force Satellite Communications System (AFM) ... AFSATCOM
Air Force Satellite Communications System (CCCA) ... AFSCF
Air Force Satellite Communications System (MCD) ... AFSCS
Air Force Satellite Control Center (CET) ... AFSCC
Air Force Satellite Control Facility ... AFSATLCF
Air Force Satellite [*or Spacecraft*] **Control Facility** [*Sunnyvale Air Force Station, CA*] (AFM) ... AFSCF
Air Force Satellite Control Network (MCD) ... AFSCN
Air Force Satellite Facility ... AFSF
Air Force Satellite Test Center (MCD) ... AFSTC
Air Force School (SAUO) ... AFS
Air Force School of Applied Tactics (SAUO) ... AFSAT
Air Force School of Aviation Medicine ... AFSAM
Air Force Science Advisory Board (SAUS) ... AFSAB
Air Force Scientific Advisory Board (SAUS) ... AFNB
Air Force Scientific Advisory Board (MCD) ... AFSAB
Air Force Section (SAUO) ... AFS
Air Force Section (AFM) ... AFSec
Air Force Section, Military Assistance Advisory Group ... AFSMAAG
Air Force Security Clearance Office ... AFSCO
Air Force Security Communications Center (MCD) ... AFSCC
Air Force Security Police (VNW) ... AFSP
Air Force Security Police Agency (DOMA) ... AFSPA
Air Force Security Police Management Engineering Team (SAUS) ... AFSPMET
Air Force Security Policy Management Engineering Team ... AFSPMET
Air Force Security Service [*Later, AFESC*] (AFM) ... AFSS
Air Force Security Service Office of Production ... AFSSOP
Air Force Senior Advisory ... AFSA
Air Force Senior Advisory - Jefferson Barracks ... AFSA-JB
Air Force Senior Non-Commissioned Officer Academy (SAUS) ... AFSNCOA
Air Force Sergeants Association (EA) ... AFSA
Air Force Serial Number ... AFSN
Air Force Service Center [*or Command*] ... AFSC
Air Force Service Command (SAUO) ... AFSC
Air Force Service Command (SAUO) ... AF Sv Comd
Air Force Service Contract Advisory Group (MCD) ... AFSCAG
Air Force Service Information and News Center ... AFSINC
Air Force Service Number ... AFSN
Air Force Service Office (AFM) ... AFSO
Air Force Service Statement ... AFSS
Air Force Skill Code ... AFSC
Air Force Small Computer/ Office Automation Service Organization (SAUO) ... AFSCOASO
Air Force Solar Observing Optical Network (MCD) ... AFSOON
Air Force Space and Missile Organization (SAUO) ... AFSMO
Air Force Space and Missile Systems Organization (KSC) ... AFSAMSO
Air Force Space Command (DOMA) ... AFSC
Air Force Space Command (DOMA) ... AFSPACECOM
Air Force Space Command ... AFSPC
Air Force Space Command (SAUS) ... SPACECMD
Air Force Space Division (MCD) ... AFSD
Air Force Space Forecast Center (SAUS) ... AFSFC
Air Force Space Forecasting Center (ADWA) ... AFSFC
Air Force Space Intelligence Plan (ACAE) ... AFSIP
Air Force Space Intelligence Program (ACAE) ... AFSIP
Air Force Space Operations Center (COE) ... AFSPOC
Air Force Space Plan (SAUS) ... AFSP
Air Force Space Plane (AAG) ... AFSP
Air Force Space Program ... AFSP
Air Force Space Systems Division ... AFSSD
Air Force Space Technology Center [*Kirtland Air Force Base, NM*] (MCD) ... AFSTC
Air Force Space Technology Satellite (SAUS) ... AFSTS
Air Force Space Test Center [*Later, Western Test Range*] ... AFSTC
Air Force Spacecraft Control Facility (SAUS) ... AFSCF
Air Force Spare (SAA) ... AFSP
Air Force Special Activities Center ... AFSAC
Air Force Special Activities Wing ... AFSAW
Air Force Special Air Warfare Center (MCD) ... AFSAWC
Air Force Special Communications Center (CET) ... AFSCC
Air Force Special Communications Center (AFM) ... AFSPCOMMCEN
Air Force Special Elements Activity [*American Embassy security*] (VNW) ... AFSEA
Air Force Special Operations Base (SAUO) ... AFSOB
Air Force Special Operations Command ... AFSOC
Air Force Special Operations Forces (SAUO) ... AFSOF
Air Force Special Security Office [*or Officer*] (AFM) ... AFSSO
Air Force Special Security Officer (SAUS) ... AFSSO
Air Force Special Staff Management Engineering Team ... AFSSMET
Air Force Special Weapons Center [*AFSC*] [*Kirtland Air Force Base, NM*] ... AFSWC
Air Force Special Weapons Project (SAUS) ... AFSWP

Air Force Specialty ... AFS
Air Force Specialty Code ... AFSC
Air Force Specification Bulletin ... AFSB
Air Force Squadron (SAUO) ... AFSq
Air Force Staff College (SAUO) ... AFSC
Air Force Staff Requirement ... AFSR
Air Force Standard (NASA) ... AFS
Air Force Standard Information Systems Center (SAUO) ... AFSISC
Air Force Standard Intelligence Publication (AFM) ... AFSIP
Air Force Standard Items and Equipment (SAA) ... AFSIE
Air Force Standard Practice ... AFSP
Air Force Station ... AFS
Air Force Stock (AAG) ... AFS
Air Force Stock Data (SAA) ... AFSD
Air Force Stock Fund ... AFSF
Air Force Stock Number ... AFSN
Air Force Stock Record Account Number (AAG) ... AFSRAN
Air Force Strike Command (MCD) ... AFSTRIKE
Air Force Studies and Analyses Agency (DOMA) ... AFSAA
Air Force Studies and Analysis (IUSS) ... AF/SA
Air Force Supply ... AFS
Air Force Supply Catalog ... AFSC
Air Force Supply Code ... AFSC
Air Force Supply Date ... AFSD
Air Force Supply Depot ... AFSD
Air Force Supply Directive (MCD) ... AFSD
Air Force Supply Force ... AFSF
Air Force Supply Services System ... AFSS
Air Force Supply Services System (SAUS) ... AFSS System
Air Force Support Base (SAA) ... AFSB
Air Force Surveys in Geophysics (SAUS) ... AFSIC
Air Force System (SAUS) ... AFS
Air Force System Acquisition Review Council ... AFSARC
Air Force Systems Acquisition Review Council (SAUO) ... AFSARC
Air Force Systems Command [*Andrews Air Force Base, MD*] ... AFSC
Air Force Systems Command Design Handbook (SAUS) ... AFSC-DH
Air Force Systems Command Design Handbooks ... AFSC-DH
Air Force Systems Command Director of Laboratories ... AFSC/DL
Air Force Systems Command Form ... AFSCF
Air Force Systems Command Inspection Center ... AFSCIC
Air Force Systems Command Letter ... AFSCL
Air Force Systems Command Manual ... AFSCM
Air Force Systems Command Pamphlet ... AFSCP
Air Force Systems Command Procurement Production (MCD) ... AFSCPP
Air Force Systems Command Regulation ... AFSCR
Air Force Systems Command Scientific Technical Liaison Office (SAUO) ... AFSC/STLO
Air Force Systems Command/Space Systems Division (SAUS) ... AFSC/SSD
Air Force Systems Concept Paper (MCD) ... AFSCP
Air Force Systems Maintenance Engineering (ACAE) ... AFSME
Air Force Systems Project Division (MCD) ... AFSPD
Air Force Tactical Air Command (MCD) ... AFTAC
Air Force Tactical Center (SAUS) ... AFTAC
Air Force Tactical Exploitation of National Capability [*Air Force*] ... AFTENCAP
Air Force Tactical Fighter Weapons Center (MCD) ... AFTFWC
Air Force Tactical Imagery Exploitation (ACAE) ... AFTACIE
Air Force Tactical Imagery Exploitation System (ACAE) ... AFTACIES
Air Force Tactical Shelter (MCD) ... AFTS
Air Force Tactical Shelter Systems Development Office (SAUS) ... AFTSSDO
Air Force Task Force (AFM) ... AFTF
Air Force Technical Applications Center [*Patrick Air Force Base, FL*] ... AFTAC
Air Force Technical Approval Team (AAG) ... AFTAT
Air Force Technical Headquarters (SAUO) ... AFTH
Air Force Technical Intelligence Center ... AFTIC
Air Force Technical Objectives Documents ... AFTOD
Air Force Technical Order ... AFTO
Air Force Technical Order Management Center (MCD) ... AFTOC
Air Force Technical Order Standardization Board ... AFTOSB
Air Force Technical Report ... AFTR
Air Force Technical Service Command ... AFTSC
Air Force Technical Training Center (SAUO) ... AFTTC
Air Force Technical Training Command (SAUS) ... AFTRC
Air Force Technical Training Command (SAUO) ... AFTTRC
Air Force Technical Training Headquarters ... AFTTH
Air Force Telecom Association (AC) ... AFTA
Air Force Telecommunications Certification Office (SAUO) ... AFTCO
Air Force Teleprocessing Center (SAUO) ... AFTPC
Air Force Test and Evaluation Center [*Kirtland Air Force Base, NM*] (AFM) ... AFTEC
Air Force Test Base ... AFTB
Air Force Test Director (MCD) ... AFTD
Air Force Test Pilot School (MCD) ... AFTPS
Air Force Test Team (ACAE) ... AFTT
Air Force Test Unit (MCD) ... AFTU
Air Force Test Unit, Vietnam ... AFTU-V
Air Force Theater Command (SAUO) ... AFFOR
Air Force Thermionic Engineering and Research [*Stanford University*] (PDAA) ... AFTER
Air Force Thermophysical Properties Research Center (SAUO) ... AFTPRC
Air Force Training & Support Command (SAUS) ... AF T&S C
Air Force Training Auxiliary [*British*] ... ATA
Air Force Training Camp (SAUO) ... AFTC
Air Force Training Category [*48 inactive duty training periods and 15 days active duty training per year*] ... A
Air Force Training Category [*24 inactive duty training periods and 15 days active duty training per year*] ... B
Air Force Training Category [*Inactive duty training periods and 15 days active duty training per year*] ... D
Air Force Training Category [*Inactive duty training periods and 30 days active duty training per year*] ... E
Air Force Training Category [*No inactive duty periods and 4 months minimum initial active duty training per year*] ... F
Air Force Training Category [*12 training periods and zero days active duty training per year*] ... G
Air Force Training Category ... H
Air Force Training Category [*No training*] ... I
Air Force Training Category [*Officer training program*] ... J
Air Force Training Center (SAUS) ... AFTRC
Air Force Training Command ... AFTRC
Air Force Transportation Management Engineering Team ... AFTRANSMET
Air Force Troop Carrier Command [*British military*] (DMA) ... AFTCC
Air Force Undergraduate Navigator Training System (SAUS) ... AFUNTS
Air Force Uniform Board (SAUO) ... AFUB
Air Force Unit Post Office ... AFUPO
Air Force Units ... AFU
Air Force Visual Aid ... AFVA
Air Force Wargaming Center (SAUO) ... AFWC
Air Force Wartime Manpower and Personnel Readiness Team (ACAE) ... AFWMPRT
Air Force Wartime Manpower Personnel Readiness Team (SAUO) ... AFWMPRT
Air Force Weapon ... AFW
Air Force Weapon Supply [*or System*] (SAA) ... AFWS
Air Force Weapon System Improvement Group (SAUO) ... AFWSIG
Air Force Weapons Effectiveness Testing (AFM) ... AFWET
Air Force Weapons Effectiveness Testing System ... AFWETS
Air Force Weapons Laboratory [*Kirtland Air Force Base, NM*] ... AFWL
Air Force Weapons Laboratory, Kirtland AFB, NM [*OCLC symbol*] (OCLC) ... SCK
Air Force Weapons Support Improvement Group (SAUO) ... AFSIG
Air Force Weapons Training Facility (ACAE) ... AFWTF
Air Force Weather Agency (SAUS) ... AFWA
Air Force Weather Observing and Forecasting System ... AFWOFS
Air Force Weather Wing (SAA) ... AFWW
Air Force Welfare Board (AFM) ... AFWB
Air Force Western Development Division (SAUO) ... AFWDD
Air Force Western Test Range [*Later, Space and Missile Test Center*] [*Vandenberg Air Force Base, CA*] ... AFWTR
Air Force Western Test Range Manual (MCD) ... AFWTRM
Air Force Wide Mission Area Analysis (MCD) ... AFWMAA
Air Force Wing (SAUO) ... AFW
Air Force with Army ... AFWA
Air Force With Navy (SAUS) ... AFNA
Air Force With Navy (SAUS) ... AFWN
Air Force with Navy (SAUO) ... AFWN
Air Force World Wide Military Command and Control System (MCD) ... AFWWMCCS
Air Force Wright Aeronautical Laboratories [*Wright-Patterson Air Force Base, OH*] ... AFWAL
Air Force Wright Aeronautical Laboratories Materials Laboratory [*Wright-Patterson Air Force Base, OH*] ... AFWAL/ML
Air Force WWMCCS [*Worldwide Military Command and Control System*] **Information System** (GFGA) ... AFWIS
Air Force Zone of Interior (SAUS) ... AFZIN
Air Force/Armed Service Procurement Regulation ... AF/ASPR
Air Force-Military Interdepartmental Purchase Requests (SAUS) ... AF-MIPR
Air Force/Navy (AAG) ... AF/N
Air Force-Navy (SAUO) ... AN
Air Force/Navy Aeronautical ... AF/NA
Air Force-Navy Aeronautical Design Standard (SAUS) ... AND
Air Force-Navy Design ... AND
Air Force-Navy Ground RADAR (SAA) ... AN/GRA
Air Force-Navy-Civil (SAUS) ... ANC
Air Force-Navy-Civil Committee on Aircraft Design Criteria (SAUO) ... ANC
Air Force-Navy-Civil Committee on Aircraft Requirements ... ANC
Air Force-Navy-NASA-Army (SAUS) ... ANNA
Air Forces Anti-Submarine Command (SAUS) ... AFSUB
Air Forces, Arabian Peninsula [*British military*] (DMA) ... AFAP
Air Forces, Atlantic ... AFLANT
Air Forces, Atlantic Fleet [*Navy*] ... AIRLANT
Air Forces, [*US*] Central Command (DOMA) ... AIRCENT
Air Forces Europe Exchange ... AFEX
Air Forces Ferry Command ... AFFC
Air Forces Flight Safety Committee Europe (SAUO) ... AFFSCE
Air Forces Gulf (SAUO) ... AFG
Air Forces, Iceland (MCD) ... AFI
Air Forces, Iceland ... AFICE
Air Forces Korea (SAUO) ... AFK
Air Forces, Pacific Advanced (SAUO) ... AIRPAC/ADV
Air Forces Pacific Advanced ... AIRPAC(ADV)
Air Forces, Pacific Fleet ... AIRPAC
Air Forces Pacific, Pearl Harbor ... AIRPAC(PEARL)
Air Forces Pacific, Pearl Harbor (SAUO) ... AIRPAC/PEARL
Air Forces Pacific, Subordinate Command, Forward Area (SAUO) ... AIRPACSUBCOMFORD
Air Forces Southern Europe Command [*NATO*] ... AFSOUTHCOM
Air Forces, Southern Region (SAUO) ... AIRSOUTH
Air Forces Subordinate Command, Forward Area ... AIRPACSUBCOMFORD
Air Forces Tactical Center ... AFTAC
Air Forces, Western Europe [*NATO*] (NATG) ... AFWE
Air Forward Observer (ACAE) ... AFO

Air Foundation ... AF
Air Foyle Airways Ltd. [*British*] [*FAA designator*] (FAAC) ... UPC
Air Foyle Charter Airways Ltd. [*British*] [*FAA designator*] (FAAC) ... UPD
Air Foyle (Executive) Ltd. [*British*] [*ICAO designator*] (FAAC) ... AFY
Air Foyle Ltd. (SAUS) ... UP
Air Foyle Ltd. [*British*] [*ICAO designator*] (FAAC) ... UPA
Air Frame (MCD) ... AF
Air Frame Assembly (MCD) ... AFA
Air France [*ICAO designator*] ... AF
Air France [*ICAO designator*] (FAAC) ... AFR
Air Freight [*Air carrier designation symbol*] ... AFFX
Air Freight (FAAC) ... AFRT
Air Freight Association of America (EA) ... AFA
Air Freight Association of America (NTPA) ... AFAA
Air Freight Bill (SAUS) ... A/B
Air Freight Bill [*Shipping*] ... AFB
Air Freight Control Centre (SAUO) ... AFCC
Air Freight Decision Tool (MCD) ... AFDT
Air Freight Express, Inc. [*ICAO designator*] (FAAC) ... AFX
Air Freight Forwarders Association of America [*Later, AFA*] (EA) ... AFFA
Air Freight Forwarders Association of America (SAUO) ... AFFA
Air Freight List (SAUS) ... AFL
Air Freight Motor Carriers Conference [*Later, AEMCC*] (EA) ... AFMCC
Air Freight Motor Carriers Conference Inc. (SAUO) ... AFM
Air Freight Motor Carriers Conference, Inc., Arlington VA [*STAC*] ... AFM
Air Freight Terminal ... AFT
Air Freighters [*Air carrier designation symbol*] ... AFIX
Air Fret Senegal [*FAA designator*] (FAAC) ... ABN
Air Gabon [*ICAO designator*] (AD) ... GN
Air Gambia [*ICAO designator*] (FAAC) ... AGS
Air Gambia [*Airline flight code*] (ODBW) ... iv
Air Gap ... AG
Air Gap Width ... AGW
Air Gauge ... AG
Air GEFCO [*France*] [*ICAO designator*] (FAAC) ... GEF
Air General Staff (SAUO) ... G/A
Air General-Head-Quarters (SAUO) ... Air GHQ
Air Georgia [*Former USSR*] [*FAA designator*] (FAAC) ... GEO
Air Georgian [*Canada*] [*FAA designator*] (FAAC) ... GGN
Air Glaciers SA [*Switzerland*] [*ICAO designator*] (FAAC) ... AGV
Air Goyle Charter Ltd. [*British*] [*FAA designator*] (FAAC) ... UPB
Air Grap (SAUS) ... AG
Air Grease System (PDAA) ... AGS
Air Great Lakes [*ICAO designator*] (AD) ... BB
Air Great Wall [*CHINA*] [*FAA designator*] (FAAC) ... CGW
Air Greece SA [*FAA designator*] (FAAC) ... AGJ
Air Ground Chart (SAUS) ... AGC
Air Ground Engagement [*Military*] (DOMA) ... AGE
Air Ground Liaison Officer (SAUS) ... AGLO
Air Group ... AG
Air Group ... AIRGRP
Air Group Headquarters (SAUO) ... GARIM
Air Guadeloupe [*ICAO designator*] (AD) ... OG
Air Guam [*ICAO designator*] (FAAC) ... AGM
Air Guinea [*Guinea*] [*ICAO designator*] (FAAC) ... GIB
Air Guinee [*ICAO designator*] (AD) ... GI
Air Gunner [*British*] ... AG
Air Gunnery Instructor [*British military*] (DMA) ... AGI
Air Gunnery Officer ... AGO
Air Gunnery Officers School (SAUO) ... AGOS
Air Gunnery School [*British*] (OA) ... AGS
Air Gunnery Target System (SAUS) ... AGTS
Air Guyane [*France*] [*ICAO designator*] (FAAC) ... GUY
Air Guyane [*ICAO designator*] (AD) ... KJ
Air Hainaut [*France*] [*ICAO designator*] (FAAC) ... AHN
Air Haiti [*ICAO designator*] (FAAC) ... HJA
Air Handling [*Nuclear energy*] (NRCH) ... A/H
Air Hanson Ltd. [*British*] [*ICAO designator*] (FAAC) ... AHL
Air Hawaii [*ICAO designator*] (AD) ... HP
Air Header ... AHDR
Air Headquarters (SAUO) ... AH
Air Headquarters ... AHQ
Air Headquarters, Malta (SAUS) ... AHqM
Air Heater (CARB) ... AH
Air Heater Blower ... AHB
Air Height Surveillance RADAR ... AHSR
Air, High Pressure (DNAB) ... AHP
Air Historical Branch [*Air Ministry*] [*British*] ... AHB
Air History (SAUS) ... AH
Air Holland Regional (AHR) [*ICAO designator*] (FAAC) ... AHR
Air Hong Kong Ltd. [*ICAO designator*] (FAAC) ... AHK
Air Horsepower [*Air Force*] ... AHP
Air Ile de France [*ICAO designator*] (FAAC) ... AIF
Air Iliria [*Yugoslovia*] [*ICAO designator*] (FAAC) ... ILR
Air Illinois [*ICAO designator*] (AD) ... UX
Air Illinois, Inc. [*ICAO designator*] (FAAC) ... AIL
Air Illinois, Inc. [*Air carrier designation symbol*] ... AILX
Air Images [*British*] [*FAA designator*] (FAAC) ... IMS
Air Incident Message ... AIM
Air Incident Report ... AIR
Air Independent Propulsion [*Submarine*] (DOMA) ... AIP
Air Independent Propulsion (SAUS) ... AIP
Air India [*ICAO designator*] (AD) ... AI
Air India [*ICAO designator*] (FAAC) ... AIC
Air India Corp. (SAUO) ... AI
Air India International ... AII
Air Indicator Not Operating (SAUS) ... ARNO
Air Induction ... AINDTN
Air Induction Control System [*Air Force*] ... AICS
Air Industriel (journ.) (SAUS) ... Air Ind
Air Industries and Transports Association (MCD) ... AITA
Air Infiltration Measurement Service [*National Association of Home Builders National Research Center*] ... AIMS
Air Inflatable Retarder [*for bombs*] (MCD) ... AIR
Air Information Center (NATG) ... AIC
Air Information Codification (NATG) ... AIC
Air Information Dataset (SAUS) ... AID
Air Information Device (SAUS) ... AID
Air Information Division [*Library of Congress*] (MCD) ... AID
Air Injection [*Automotive engineering*] ... AI
Air Injection Reactor ... AIR
Air Injection Relief Valve [*Automotive engineering*] ... AIRV
Air Injection Tube [*Automotive engineering*] ... AIT
Air Inlet [*Automotive engineering*] ... A/INL
Air Inlet Control System ... AICS
Air Inlet Control System Test Set ... AICSTS
Air Inlet Controller (MCD) ... AIC
Air Inlet Damper (NRCH) ... AID
Air Inspection Directorate [*British*] ... AID
Air Inspector ... AI
Air Inspector General (MCD) ... AIG
Air Installation Compatible Use Zones (SAUO) ... AICUZ
Air Installation Compatible Use Zoning [*Air Force*] ... AICUZ
Air Installation Office ... AIO
Air Installations ... AI
Air Insurance (SAUS) ... airsurance
Air Intake Duct (DNAB) ... AID
Air Intake Panel ... AIP
Air Intake Temperature (SAUS) ... AIT
Air Integra, Inc. [*Canada*] [*ICAO designator*] (FAAC) ... AII
Air Integrated Data System (SAUS) ... AIDS
Air Intelligence (NVT) ... AI
Air Intelligence Agency [*Air Force*] ... AIA
Air Intelligence Command (SAA) ... AIC
Air Intelligence Duty Officer (DNAB) ... AIDO
Air Intelligence Force ... AIF
Air Intelligence Group [*Military*] (MCD) ... AIG
Air Intelligence Group [*Military*] (MCD) ... AINTELG
Air Intelligence Information Report (SAUS) ... AIIR
Air Intelligence Liaison [*British*] ... AIL
Air Intelligence Liaison Officer [*British*] ... AILO
Air Intelligence Officer (SAUS) ... A-2
Air Intelligence Officer [*Air Force*] ... AINTELO
Air Intelligence Officer [*Navy*] (NVT) ... AIO
Air Intelligence Organization (NATG) ... AIO
Air Intelligence Section [*Army*] ... AINTSEC
Air Intelligence Section (SAUO) ... AIntSec;
Air Intelligence Service ... AIS
Air Intelligence Services Squadron [*Defunct*] [*Air Force*] ... AISS
Air Intelligence Squadron [*Air Force*] ... AINTELS
Air Intelligence Support Team (ACAE) ... AIST
Air Intelligence Training Center (MCD) ... AITC
Air Inter (SAUS) ... INT
Air Inter [*ICAO designator*] (AD) ... IT
Air Inter Gabon [*ICAO designator*] (FAAC) ... AIG
Air Inter Gabon [*ICAO designator*] (AD) ... GB
Air Inter, Societe [*France*] [*ICAO designator*] (ICDA) ... IT
Air Inter, Societe [*France*] [*ICAO designator*] (FAAC) ... ITF
Air Intercept Battle Analysis ... AIBA
Air Intercept [*or Interception*] **Control** [*or Controller*] ... AIC
Air Intercept Control Command (SAA) ... AICC
Air Intercept Control School ... AICS
Air Intercept Controller Supervisor (NVT) ... AICS
Air Intercept Missile Package ... AIMP
Air Intercept Officer (MCD) ... AIO
Air Intercept Radar (SAUS) ... AIR
Air Intercept Rocket (IEEE) ... AIR
Air Interception (ACAE) ... AI
Air Interception Committee [*Air Ministry*] [*British*] ... AIC
Air Interception Control (SAUS) ... AIC
Air Interception Missile (SAUS) ... AIM
Air Interception Radar (SAUS) ... AI Radar
Air Interceptor, Centimeter (SAUS) ... AIC
Air Interceptor Fuze ... AIF
Air Interdiction (MCD) ... AI
Air Interdiction (COE) ... AIR
Air Interface Standards Working Group (SAUO) ... AISWG
Air Interface Sub-Working Group [*NATO*] (NATG) ... AISWG
Air International [*British*] [*ICAO designator*] (FAAC) ... AIX
Air International Formation SA (SAUS) ... AIF
Air International (Holdings) PLC [*British*] [*ICAO designator*] (FAAC) ... JPR
Air International (journ.) (SAUS) ... Air Int
Air Inuit Ltd. [*Canada*] [*ICAO designator*] (FAAC) ... AIE
Air Isolated Monolithic [*Circuit*] ... AIM
Air Ivoire [*ICAO designator*] (AD) ... VU
Air Ivoire Societe [*Ivory Coast*] [*ICAO designator*] (FAAC) ... VUN
Air Jamaica (SAUO) ... Air Jam
Air Jamaica [*ICAO designator*] (FAAC) ... AJM
Air Jamaica Ltd. [*ICAO designator*] (OAG) ... JM
Air Jet [*ICAO designator*] (FAAC) ... AIJ

Air Jet Control Unit	AJCU
Air Jet Distortion Generator (MCD)	AJDG
Air Jordan [Airline]	AJ
Air Jordan Company, Ltd. (SAUO)	AJ
Air Kangaroo Island [Airline code] [Australia]	UV
Air Kentucky [ICAO designator] (AD)	KN
Air Kiev [Ukraine] [FAA designator] (FAAC)	KIV
Air Kilroe Ltd. [British] [ICAO designator] (FAAC)	AKL
Air Korea Co. Ltd. [South Korea] [ICAO designator] (FAAC)	AKA
Air Koryo [North Korea] [ICAO designator] (FAAC)	KOR
Air La [ICAO designator] (AD)	UE
Air LA, Inc. [ICAO designator] (FAAC)	UED
Air Land (ACAE)	AL
Air Land Force Application Agency (SAUO)	ALFA
Air, Land, Sea Application centre (SAUS)	ALSA
Air Landing Exercise [Military] (NVT)	AIRLEX
Air Lanka [Sri Lanka] [ICAO designator] (FAAC)	ALK
Air Lanka (SAUS)	UJ
Air Lanka [ICAO designator] (AD)	UL
Air Launch [or Lift] (SAA)	A/L
Air Launch Control Center (SAUO)	ALCC
Air Launch Sounding Rocket	ALSOR
Air Launchable Concept	ALC
Air Launched Air-to-Air Rocket (SAUS)	ALAAR
Air Launched Anti Satellite (ACAE)	ALASAT
Air Launched Anti-Ballistic Missile (SAUS)	ALABM
Air Launched Boost Intercept (ACAE)	ALABINT
Air Launched Cruise Missiles (SAUS)	ALCMs
Air Launched Interceptor (SAUS)	ALI
Air Launched Propulsion System (ACAE)	ALPS
Air Launched Surface Attack Missile (SAUS)	ALSAM
Air Launched Vehicle	ALV
Air Launched Weapon (SAUS)	ALW
Air Launched Weapon School (ACAE)	ALWS
Air Launcher Low Volume Ramjet (SAUS)	ALVRT
Air League (SAUO)	AL
Air League [An association] (EAIO)	AL
Air League of India (SAUO)	ALI
Air League of New Zealand (SAUO)	ALNZ
Air League of the British Empire (SAUO)	ALBE
Air Letter	AL
Air Liaison	AL
Air Liaison Net (SAUS)	ALN
Air Liaison Officer [Air Force]	AIRLO
Air Liaison Officer	ALO
Air Liaison Officer Net (NATG)	ALON
Air Liaison Party	ALP
Air Liaison Post (SAUS)	ALP
Air Liaison Section [British and Canadian] [World War II]	AL Sec
Air Liberia [ICAO designator] (FAAC)	ALI
Air Liberia [ICAO designator] (AD)	NL
Air Liberte [France] [ICAO designator] (FAAC)	LIB
Air Liberte Tunisie [Tunisia] [ICAO designator] (FAAC)	LBT
Air Licensing Authority (SAUO)	ALA
Air Lietuva [Lithuania] [ICAO designator] (FAAC)	KLA
Air Lift (SAUS)	AL
Air Lift Forces (SAUO)	ALF
Air Lift International (SAUS)	RD
Air Lift Management System (SAUS)	ALMS
Air Lifting Unit (WDAA)	ALU
Air Light Beacon (WDAA)	ALB
Air Limousin TA [France] [ICAO designator] (FAAC)	LMT
Air Lincoln, Inc. [ICAO designator] (FAAC)	ALN
Air Line Communication Employees Association	ACEA
Air Line Communication Employees Association	ALCEA
Air Line Communications Employees Association (SAUO)	ALCEA
Air Line Dispatchers Association [Defunct]	ALDA
Air Line Employees Association, International (EA)	ALEA
Air Line of Communication [Air Force]	ALOC
Air Line Pilots Association	ALPA
Air Line Pilots Association, International (EA)	ALPA
Air Line Pilots Association, International (EA)	ALPAI
Air Line Stewards and Stewardesses Association (EA)	ALSSA
Air Lines Circuit (SAA)	ALC
Air Lines of Communication	AIRLOC
Air Lingus [ICAO designator] (AD)	EI
Air Link [ICAO designator] (AD)	FF
Air Link Charters [Canada] (FAAC)	FSR
Air Link Corp. (SAUO)	LNK
Air Liquide Canada Ltee., Montreal, Quebec [Library symbol] [National Library of Canada] (NLC)	QMAL
Air Liquide, Montreal, PQ, Canada [Library symbol] [Library of Congress] (LCLS)	CaQMAL
Air Littoral [ICAO designator] (AD)	FU
Air Littoral [France] [ICAO designator] (FAAC)	LIT
Air Loadmaster (SAUS)	ALM
Air Lock [Technical drawings]	AL
Air Lock (NAKS)	A/L
Air Lock System (MCD)	ALS
Air Logistic Coordination Center	ALCORCEN
Air Logistics (SAUS)	ALG
Air Logistics Center [McClellan Air Force Base, CA] (MCD)	ALC
Air Logistics Center Augmentation Squadron [Air Force]	ALCAS
Air Logistics Chain (MCD)	ALOC
Air Logistics Command [Air Force]	ALC

Air Logistics Command Local Area Network	ALCLAN
Air Logistics Coordination Center (SAUO)	ALCorCen
Air Logistics Coordination Center (SAUS)	ALCORCEN
Air Logistics Message (SAUS)	LOGHOLDAIR
Air Logistics Officer (AAGC)	ALO
Air Logistics Pipeline Study (MCD)	ALP
Air Logistics Service [or System] [Military]	ALS
Air London [British] [ICAO designator] (FAAC)	ACG
Air, Low Pressure (DNAB)	ALP
Air Lubricated Free Attitude [NASA] (KSC)	ALFA
Air Lubricated Free Axis Trainer (SAUS)	AFLA
Air Madagascar (SAUO)	Air Mad
Air Madagascar [ICAO designator] (AD)	MD
Air Madagascar, Societe Nationale Malgache de Transports Aeriens [ICAO designator] (FAAC)	MDG
Air Mahe [ICAO designator] (AD)	HM
Air Mail Center	AMC
Air Mail Facility [Post Office]	AMF
Air Mail Field	AMF
Air Mail Letter (SAUS)	AML
Air Mail Only (SAUS)	AMO
Air Mail Pioneers (EA)	AMP
Air Mail Processing Center (SAUS)	AMPC
Air Mail Route Number 2	AM2
Air Mail Service	AMS
Air Mail Terminal (ACAE)	AMT
Air Mail Transfer (ODBW)	amt
Air Mail Transfer (ADA)	AMT
Air Mail Transmission	AMT
Air Maintenance and Repair Station (SAUS)	AMRS
Air Maintenance Control Office (SAUO)	AMCO
Air Maintenance Group (SAUO)	AMG
Air Maintenance Squadron (SAUS)	AMS
Air Malawi [ICAO designator] (FAAC)	AML
Air Malawi [ICAO designator] (AD)	QM
Air Maldives [ICAO designator] (FAAC)	AMI
Air Mali [ICAO designator] (AD)	MY
Air Malta [ICAO designator] (AD)	KM
Air Malta Co. Ltd. [ICAO designator] (FAAC)	AMC
Air Management Division [Environmental Protection Agency] (GFGA)	AMD
Air Management Information System (SAUS)	AMIS
Air Management Oversight System [Environmental science] (EPAT)	AMOS
Air Management Research Group (SAUO)	AMRG
Air Management Sector Group (SAUO)	AMSG
Air Management Station	AMS
Air Management System	AMS
Air Manila, Inc. (SAUS)	UM
AIR [All India Law Reporter] Manual: Unrepealed Central Acts [2nd ed.] [India] [A publication] (DLA)	India AIR Manual
Air Margarita [Venezuela] [ICAO designator] (FAAC)	MAG
Air Marshal (SAUS)	Air Mshl
Air Marshal [British]	AM
Air Marshall Islands [Airline code] [Australia]	CW
Air Martinique (Satair) [ICAO designator] (AD)	BT
Air Mass [Solar energy research]	AM
Air Mass (FAAC)	AMS
Air Mass and Front Analysis (SAUS)	AMAFA
Air Mass and Frontal Analysis [Meteorology]	AMAFA
Air Mass Flow (SAUS)	AMF
Air Mass Transformation Experiment (SAUO)	AMTEX
Air Mass Transportation Experiment [Global Atmospheric Research Program] (USDC)	AMTEX
Air Mass Zero (SAUS)	AMO
Air Mass Zero (SAUS)	AMO
Air Mass Zero (SAUS)	AMZ
Air Material (SAUS)	AM
Air Material AG [Switzerland] [ICAO designator] (FAAC)	AMG
Air Material and Supply Officer (SAUS)	A-4
Air Material Area Stock Control Point (NG)	AMASCP
Air Material Armament Test Center	AMATC
Air Material Armament Test Center [Air Force] (MCD)	AMTC
Air Material Base (SAUO)	AMB
Air Material Command [Later, Air Force Logistics Command] [Air Force]	AIMACO
Air Material Command Communications Network (SAUS)	AMCCOMNET
Air Material Command [later, Air Force Logistics Command] Compiling [System]	AIMACC
Air Material Command Compiling System (SAUS)	AIMACC System
Air Material Command Headquarters, Ottawa, Ontario, Canada	CANAIRMAT
Air Material Computer (MCD)	AIMACO
Air Material Force (SAUO)	AMF
Air Material Force, European Area (SAUO)	AMFEA
Air Material Office [Military] (DNAB)	AMO
Air Material Proving Ground	AMPG
Air Materiel Area [Later, Air Logistics Centers] [Air Force]	AMA
Air Materiel Area System Management [Air Force]	AMASM
Air Materiel Armament Test Center	AMATC
Air Materiel Command [Later, Air Force Logistics Command]	AMC
Air Materiel Command (SAUO)	AMC
Air Materiel Command [later, Air Force Logistics Command] - Air Force	AMC-AF
Air Materiel Command [later, Air Force Logistics Command] Ballistic Missile Center (IEEE)	AMCBMC
Air Materiel Command [later, Air Force Logistics Command] Forms	AMCF
Air Materiel Command Forms (SAUS)	AMCF
Air Materiel Command [later, Air Force Logistics Command] Headquarters	AMCHQ

Air Materiel Command Headquarters (SAUO) .... AMCHQ
Air Materiel Command [later, Air Force Logistics Command] Letter .... AMCL
Air Materiel Command Letter .... AMCL
Air Materiel Command Logistics Officer (SAUS) .... AMCLO
Air Materiel Command Manual (SAUS) .... AMCM
Air Materiel Command [later, Air Force Logistics Command] Manual .... AMCM
Air Materiel Command [later, Air Force Logistics Command] Missile Field Office .... AMCMFO
Air Materiel Command [later, Air Force Logistics Command] Regulations..... AMCR
Air Materiel Command Research and Development (SAUS) .... AMCRD
Air Materiel Command System (ACAE) .... AMCS
Air Materiel Command Test Site Office (SAUO) .... AMCTSO
Air Materiel Command [later, Air Force Logistics Command] Test Site Office .... AMCTSO
Air Materiel Command-Aeronautical Systems Center (SAUO) .... AMC-ASC
Air Materiel Department (SAUO) .... AMD
Air Materiel Force, Pacific Area .... AMFPA
Air Mattress [Medicine] .... AM
Air Mauritanie [Mauritania] [ICAO designator] (ICDA) .... MR
Air Mauritanie [Mauritania] [ICAO designator] (FAAC) .... MRT
Air Mauritius [ICAO designator] (AD) .... MK
Air Mauritius Ltd. [ICAO designator] (FAAC) .... MAU
Air Mechanic (SAUS) .... Air Mech
Air Mechanic (SAUS) .... AM
Air Mechanic (Engines) [British military] (DMA) .... AE
Air Mechanician .... AM
Air Med Jetoperations [Austria] [ICAO designator] (FAAC) .... JDE
Air Medal (SAUS) .... Am
Air Medal [Military decoration] .... AM
Air Medical Ltd. [British] [ICAO designator] (FAAC) .... MCD
Air Medical Research Laboratory [Later, MRL] (MCD) .... AMRL
Air Melanesiae [ICAO designator] (AD) .... HB
Air Member, Canadian Joint Staff (SAUO) .... CanAirLon
Air Member, Canadian Joint Staff, London, England .... CANAIRLON
Air Member, Canadian Joint Staff, Washington, DC .... CANAIRWASH
Air Member for Accounts and Finance [British and Canadian] [World War II] .... AMAF
Air Member for Aeronautical Engineering [British and Canadian] [World War II] .... AMAE
Air Member for Air Staff [British and Canadian] [World War II] .... AMAS
Air Member for Development and Production [Air Ministry] [British] .... AMDP
Air Member for Engineering and Supply [British and Canadian] [World War II] .... AMES
Air Member for Organization [British and Canadian] [World War II] .... AMO
Air Member for Organization and Training [British and Canadian] [World War II] .... AMOT
Air Member for Personnel [Air Ministry] [British] .... AMP
Air Member for Research and Development [Later, TRE] [Air Ministry] [British] .... AMRD
Air Member for Supply [British and Canadian] [World War II] .... AMS
Air Member for Supply and Organisation [Air Ministry] [British] .... AMSO
Air Member for Supply and Research [Air Ministry] [British] .... AMSR
Air Member for Technical Services (SAUS) .... AMTS
Air Member for Training [British and Canadian] [World War II] .... AMT
Air Mercury International [Belgium] [ICAO designator] (FAAC) .... AMI
Air Methods [NASDAQ symbol] (TTSB) .... AIRM
Air Methods Corp. [NASDAQ symbol] (SAG) .... AIRM
Air Methods Corp. [Associated Press] (SAG) .... AirMeth
Air Meuse - Dat Wallonie [Belgium] [ICAO designator] (FAAC) .... AMZ
Air Midwest [ICAO designator] (AD) .... ZV
Air Midwest, Inc. [ICAO designator] (FAAC) .... AMW
Air Midwest, Incorporated (SAUO) .... AMWI
Air Mileage Indicator [Navigation] .... AMI
Air Mileage Unit [Navigation] .... AMU
Air Ministry [British] .... AM
Air Ministry (SAUO) .... AM
Air Ministry Bulletin [British military] (DMA) .... AMB
Air Ministry Command Order (SAUS) .... AMCO
Air Ministry Confidential Order (SAUS) .... AMCO
Air Ministry Constabulary [British military] (DMA) .... AMC
Air Ministry Experimental Station [British] .... AMES
Air Ministry Local Staff Union [Singapore] .... AMLSU
Air Ministry, London (SAUO) .... Airmin Ldn
Air Ministry Message (SAUS) .... AM/M
Air Ministry Navigational Warning (SAUO) .... AMNW
Air Ministry News Service (SAUO) .... AMNS
Air Ministry Order [British] .... AMO
Air Ministry Plans Department (SAUO) .... AMPD
Air Ministry Radio (SAUS) .... AM RD
Air Ministry Radio Station (SAUO) .... AMRS
Air Ministry Reconnaissance Department [British] (DAS) .... AMRE
Air Ministry Research Establishment [British military] (DMA) .... AMRE
Air Ministry Secret Intelligence Summary [British military] (DMA) .... AMSIS
Air Ministry Technical and Stores Department (SAUO) .... AMTSD
Air Ministry War Room [British] [World War II] .... AMWR
Air Ministry Warden [British military] (DMA) .... AMW
Air Ministry Works Directorate (SAUO) .... AMWD
Air Ministry's Accident Branch [British] .... AMAB
Air Ministrys Meteorological Office (SAUS) .... AMMO
Air Missile Space Threat (ACAE) .... AMST
Air Missile System (NG) .... AMS
Air Mission [Air Force] .... AIRMSN
Air Mission Brief [Air Force] (INF) .... AMB
Air Mission Commander [Military] (INF) .... AMC
Air Mission Unit [Air Force] .... AMU

Air Mobile .... AM
Air Mobile Aircraft Refueling System .... AMARS
Air Mobile Assault Brigade (MCD) .... AMAB
Air Mobile Ground Security and Surveillance System [Army] .... AMGSSS
Air Mobile, Light Helicopter [Army] (VNW) .... AML
Air Mobile Refueling Equipment .... ARE
Air Mobile Task Force .... AMTF
Air Mobile Van [Trailer unit for use on ground or in air] [Military] .... AIRVAN
Air Mobility Branch [Environmental science] (COE) .... AMB
Air Mobility Command [Air Force] .... AMC
Air Mobility Element [Army] .... AME
Air Mobility Research and Development Laboratory [Also, USAMR & DL] [Army] .... AMR & DL
Air Mobility Research & Development Laboratory (SAUS) .... AMR&DL
Air Mobility Research and Development Laboratory [Also, AMR & DL, USAMR & DL] [Army] (MCD) .... AMRD
Air Moldova [ICAO designator] (FAAC) .... MLD
Air Moldova International, SA [FAA designator] (FAAC) .... MLV
Air Molokai-Tropic Airlines [ICAO designator] (FAAC) .... TRO
Air Mongol [ICAO designator] (AD) .... OM
Air Monitor System (ACAE) .... AMS
Air Monitoring Analysis and Prediction [System] .... AIRMAP
Air Monitoring Center [Rockwell International Corp.] .... AMC
Air Montenegro [Yugoslavia] [ICAO designator] (FAAC) .... AMN
Air Montreal, Inc. [Canada] [ICAO designator] (FAAC) .... AMO
Air Moorea [France] [ICAO designator] (FAAC) .... TAH
Air Moravia [Czechoslovakia] [ICAO designator] (FAAC) .... MAI
Air Motor Servo Unit (MCD) .... AMSU
Air Mounting Centre [British military] (DMA) .... AMC
Air Movement [Message] (NVT) .... AIRMOVE
Air Movement and Control Association (EA) .... AM & CA
Air Movement and Control Association (EA) .... AMCA
Air Movement and Control Association, Inc. .... AMCA
Air Movement Data [Air Force] .... AMD
Air Movement Designator [Army] .... AMD
Air Movement Exercise [Military] (NVT) .... AIRMOVEX
Air Movement Information Center [NATO] (NATG) .... AMIC
Air Movement Institute (EA) .... AMI
Air Movement Officer [Military] .... AMO
Air Movement Recorder .... AMR
Air Movements (SAA) .... AM
Air Movements (SAUO) .... AMs
Air Movements British Empire Routes (SAUO) .... AMBER
Air Movements Group (SAUO) .... AMG
Air Movements Identification System (SAUO) .... AMIS
Air Movements Information Section .... AMIS
Air Movements Information Service (SAUO) .... AMIS
Air Movements Section (SAUO) .... AMS
Air Movements Talker (SAA) .... AMT
Air Movements Training Flight .... AMTF
Air Movements Unit (SAUO) .... AMU
Air Moving and Conditioning Association (SAA) .... AMCA
Air Moving and Control Association, Inc. (SAUO) .... AMCA
Air Munitions .... AMUN
Air Munitions Development Laboratory (MUGU) .... AMDL
Air Munitions Requirements and Development (SAUO) .... AMRAD
Air Munitions Requirements and Development Committee [DoD] (MCD) .... AMRAD
Air Musketry Range (SAUS) .... AMR
Air Muskoka [Canada] [ICAO designator] (FAAC) .... AMS
Air National (SAUS) .... ANE
Air National Guard (SAUO) .... Air NG
Air National Guard .... ANG
Air National Guard Base .... ANGB
Air National Guard Fighter Weapons Office [Tucson, AZ] .... ANG-FWO
Air National Guard Installation (SAUO) .... ANGI
Air National Guard of the United States .... ANGUS
Air National Guard Operational Support Aircraft [Air Force] (DOMA) ...... ANGOSA
Air National Guard Operational Support Aircraft (SAUO) .... ANGOSTA
Air National Guard Operational Support Transport Aircraft (ACAE) ...... ANGOSTA
Air National Guard Optometric Society (EA) .... ANGOS
Air National Guard Policy Council .... ANGPC
Air National Guard Support Aircraft (SAUS) .... ANGSA
Air National Guard Support Center .... ANGSC
Air Nauru [ICAO designator] (AD) .... ON
Air Nauru [ICAO designator] (FAAC) .... RON
Air Naval School (SAUO) .... ANS
Air Navigation .... AN
Air Navigation Act [British] .... ANA
Air Navigation and Bombing School .... ANBS
Air Navigation & Management System (SAUS) .... ANMS
Air Navigation and Tactical Control .... ANTAC
Air Navigation & Trading Co. Ltd. [British] [ICAO designator] (FAAC) .... ANB
Air Navigation and Traffic Control .... ANATC
Air Navigation Board [Military] (SAA) .... ANB
Air Navigation Bureau [British] (AIA) .... ANB
Air Navigation Charge (ADA) .... ANC
Air Navigation Commission (SAUS) .... ANC
Air Navigation Commission (or Conference (SAUO) .... ANC
Air Navigation Committee [NATO] (NATG) .... ANC
Air Navigation Computer Unit (MCD) .... ANCU
Air Navigation Conference [ICAO] .... ANC
Air Navigation Data Center (SAA) .... ANDAC
Air Navigation Development Board [Functions absorbed by the FAA] .... ANDB
Air Navigation Device .... AND

Air Navigation Directions	AND
Air Navigation Facilities (or Facility) (SAUS)	ANF
Air Navigation Facilities (or Facility) (SAUS)	NAVAID
Air Navigation Facility	ANF
Air Navigation (General) Regulation [British] (DA)	ANGR
Air Navigation Multiple Indicator (PDAA)	ANMI
Air Navigation Office [Navy]	AIRNAVO
Air Navigation Office [Navy]	ANO
Air Navigation Order	ANO
Air Navigation Plan (DA)	ANP
Air Navigation Radio Aids	ANRA
Air Navigation Regulations (ADA)	ANR
Air Navigation Routes (SAUS)	ANR
Air Navigation School [British]	ANS
Air Navigation Services (SAUS)	ANS
Air Navigation Technical Committee (SAA)	ANTC
Air Navigation Traffic Control	ANTC
Air Navigation Trainer (SAUS)	ANT
Air Navigation Training Unit	ANTU
Air Navigational Aid [Navy] (NG)	AIRNAVAID
Air Navigational Terminal (ACAE)	ANT
Air Nebraska (SAUS)	ANB
Air Nebraska [ICAO designator] (AD)	DF
Air Nelson Ltd. [New Zealand] [ICAO designator] (FAAC)	RLK
Air Nevada [ICAO designator] (AD)	LW
Air Nevada Airlines, Inc. [ICAO designator] (FAAC)	ANV
Air New England [ICAO designator] (AD)	NE
Air New Zealand (SAUO)	Air NZ
Air New Zealand Ltd. [Airline]	Air NZ
Air New Zealand Ltd. [ICAO designator] (FAAC)	ANZ
Air New Zealand Ltd. (SAUS)	TE
Air New Zealand Ltd. (Domestic Division) [ICAO designator] (ICDA)	NZ
Air Newark, Inc. [ICAO designator] (FAAC)	NER
Air Niagara Express, Inc. [Canada] [ICAO designator] (FAAC)	DBD
Air Nicaragua (SAUO)	AN
Air Niger [ICAO designator] (FAAC)	AWN
Air Nippon Co. Ltd. [Japan] [ICAO designator] (FAAC)	ANK
Air Niugini (SAUS)	Air Niu
Air Niugini [Papua New Guinea] [ICAO designator] (FAAC)	ANG
Air Niugini [Air New Guinea] [ICAO designator] (AD)	PX
Air Niugini New Guinea (SAUO)	Air Niu
Air, Noise, and Radiation Health Research Division [Environmental Protection Agency] (GFGA)	ANRHRD
Air, Non-Ventilated (SAUS)	ANV
Air Nordic in Vasteras AB [Sweden] [ICAO designator] (FAAC)	NOX
Air Nordic SWE Aviation, AB [Sweden] [FAA designator] (FAAC)	NDC
Air Nordic Sweden [ICAO designator] (AD)	EO
Air Normandie [France] [ICAO designator] (FAAC)	RNO
Air North [ICAO designator] (AD)	GD
Air North [ICAO designator] (AD)	NO
Air North [ICAO designator] (AD)	XG
Air North Charter [Canada] [ICAO designator] (FAAC)	ANT
Air North Ltd. [Australia] [ICAO designator] (FAAC)	ANO
Air Nova [British] [ICAO designator] (FAAC)	HMT
Air Nova, Inc. [Canada] [ICAO designator] (FAAC)	ARN
Air Objective Folder (SAA)	AOF
Air Observation Plane (SAUS)	AOP
Air Observation Post	AOP
Air Observation Post Flight [British military] (DMA)	AOPF
Air Observer (SAUS)	Air Obs
Air Observer [Military] [British]	AO
Air Observer [Military] (AFM)	AOBSR
Air Observer School [British]	AOS
Air Observer School (SAUO)	AOS
Air Observers Navigation School [Military] (OA)	AONS
Air Ocean Exchange Experiment (SAUS)	AEROCE
Air Officer [RAF] [British]	AO
Air Officer Commander-in-Chief (SAUO)	AO C-in-C
Air Officer Commander-in-Chief, Strike Command (SAUS)	AOCSTC
Air Officer Commanding [RAF] [British]	AOC
Air Officer Commanding Base Air Forces [RAF] [British]	AOCBAF
Air Officer Commanding, Coastal Area (SAUS)	AOCCA
Air Officer Commanding, Scotland & Northern Ireland (SAUS)	AOSNI
Air Officer Commanding-in-Chief [RAF] [British]	AOCIC
Air Officer Commanding-in-Chief [RAF] [British] (NATG)	AOCINC
Air Officer Commanding-in-Chief British Air Force Occupation [RAF]	AOC in CBAFO
Air Officer Commanding-in-Chief, Coastal Command (SAUS)	AOCCC
Air Officer in Charge of Administration [RAF] [British]	AOA
Air Officer in charge of Engineering (SAUS)	AOEng
Air Officer of the Day [Air Force] (AFM)	AOD
Air Oil Cooler	AOC
Air Oil Separator	AOS
Air One (SAUS)	AONE
Air Ontario Ltd. [Canada] [ICAO designator] (FAAC)	ONT
Air Operated Unit (SAUS)	AOU
Air Operating Base (CCCA)	AOB
Air Operation Central (SAUS)	AOC
Air Operational Network [Air Force]	AIROPNET
Air Operational Training	APTRA
Air Operations [Military]	AIROPS
Air Operations [Military] (NVT)	AOPS
Air Operations and Training Officer (SAUS)	A-3
Air Operations Center [Air Force]	AOC
Air Operations Centre (SAUS)	AirOpsCen
Air Operations Control Center (IUSS)	AOCC
Air Operations Control Centre (SAUS)	AOCC
Air Operations Coordination Center (SAUO)	AOCC
Air Operations Officer [Air Force]	AIROPNSO
Air Operations Officer [Military] (IUSS)	AOO
Air Operations Room	AOR
Air Operations Specialist	AOS
Air Operator (NRCH)	AO
Air Operators Certificate [British] (AIA)	AOC
Air (or Aerospace) Crew Equipment Laboratory, Philadelphia (SAUO)	ACEL
Air Order of Battle (AFM)	AOB
Air Order of Battle Textual Summary (MCD)	AOBTS
Air Ordnance [Special duties officer] [British]	AO
Air Oregon (SAUS)	JT
Air Organisation and Training Division [British military] (DMA)	AOTD
Air Orkney [British] [ICAO designator] (FAAC)	ORK
Air Ostrava Ltd. [Czechoslovakia] [FAA designator] (FAAC)	VTR
Air Outlet [Automotive engineering]	A/OUT
Air Over (MSA)	AO
Air Over Hydraulic (AAG)	A/H
Air Over Hydraulic [Automotive engineering]	AOH
Air Over Motor (SAUS)	AOM
Air Overseas (SAUS)	AO
Air Pacific [ICAO designator] (AD)	AIRPAC
Air Pacific [ICAO designator] (AD)	FJ
Air Pacific Airlines [ICAO designator] (FAAC)	APM
Air Pacific Crake [Philippines] [ICAO designator] (FAAC)	CRK
Air Pacific Limited (SAUO)	APL
Air Pacific Ltd. [Fiji] [ICAO designator] (FAAC)	FJI
Air Panama Internacional [ICAO designator] (FAAC)	API
Air Panama Internacional [ICAO designator] (AD)	OP
Air Parcel Express [ICAO designator] (FAAC)	APE
Air Parcel Post [Shipping] (AABC)	APP
Air Paris [ICAO designator] (AD)	IO
Air Park	APRK
Air Park Aviation Ltd. [Canada] [ICAO designator] (FAAC)	APA
Air Particulate Detector (IEEE)	APD
Air Particulate Matter [Environmental science]	APM
Air Particulate Monitor [Nuclear energy] (NRCH)	APM
Air Passage (MSA)	AP
Air Pathway Analyses [Environmental chemistry]	APA
Air Patrol (DNAB)	AP
Air Patrol Area (NVT)	APA
Air Patrol Zone (NVT)	APZ
Air Pennsylvania [ICAO designator] (AD)	ZY
Air Permeability Meter	APM
Air Personnel Department (SAUO)	APD
Air Personnel Officer (SAUS)	A-1
Air, Pesticides, and Toxics Management Division [Environmental Protection Agency] (GFGA)	APTMD
Air Philippines Corporation, Inc. [ICAO designator] (FAAC)	APQ
Air Photo Interpreter (SAUS)	API
Air Photo Production Unit [Canada]	APPU
Air Photo Reader (SAUS)	APR
Air Photographic and Charting Service	APCS
Air Photographic Charting Service (SAUS)	APCS
Air Photographic Interpretation Unit (SAUS)	APIU
Air Pictorial Service (SAUO)	APR
Air Pictorial Service	APS
Air Pilot	AP
Air Pilots, Engineers and Navigators Association of Canada (SAUO)	APENA
Air Plan International [Zaire] [FAA designator] (FAAC)	APV
Air Plot (DNAB)	AP
Air Point (WDAA)	AP
Air Police [By extension, a person who is a member of the Air Police]	AP
Air Police Squadron (SAUO)	APRON
Air Policy Commission (SAUO)	APC
Air Pollutant Emissions Report [Environmental Protection Agency]	APER
Air Pollution (KSC)	AP
Air Pollution Action Network (SAUO)	AIRPLAN
Air Pollution Control	APC
Air Pollution Control Act (MELL)	APCA
Air Pollution Control Agency (COE)	APCA
Air Pollution Control Association (EA)	APCA
Air Pollution Control Association. Journal (journ.) (SAUS)	Air Pollut Assoc J
Air Pollution Control Association. Journal (journ.) (SAUS)	J Air Pollut Contr A
Air Pollution Control Board (SAUO)	APCB
Air Pollution Control Code (SAA)	APCC
Air Pollution Control Department (SAUO)	APCD
Air Pollution Control Device (EEVL)	APCD
Air Pollution Control District	APCD
Air Pollution Control Equipment Manufacturers' Association	APCEMA
Air Pollution Control Office [Obsolete] [Environmental Protection Agency]	APCO
Air Pollution Control Regulation (MCD)	APCR
Air Pollution Control Regulations (SAUS)	APC Regulations
Air Pollution Control System (EEVL)	APCS
Air Pollution Division (SAUO)	APD
Air Pollution Emissions Notice (COE)	APEN
Air Pollution Emissions Report (SAUS)	APER
Air Pollution Engineer (SAUS)	APE
Air Pollution Engineer (SAUO)	APE
Air Pollution Episode Game (SAUS)	ARPEGE
Air Pollution Exercise	APEX
Air Pollution Index (SAUS)	API
Air Pollution Information and Computation System	APICS

Air Pollution Information and Computer System (SAUS) .... APICS
Air Pollution Meteorologist (NOAA) .... APM
Air Pollution Potential .... APP
Air Pollution Research Advisory Committee .... APRAC
Air Pollution Research Group (SAUO) .... APRG
Air Pollution Syndrome .... APS
Air Pollution Technical Data [Series] [A publication] .... APTD
Air Pollution Technical Information Center [Also, NAPTIC] [Bibliographic database] [Environmental Protection Agency] .... APTIC
Air Pollution Technical Information Center (SAUS) .... APTIC
Air Pollution Training Institute [Environmental Protection Agency] (GFGA) .... APTI
Air Polynesie [ICAO designator] (AD) .... VT
Air Port Signal Unit (SAUS) .... APSU
Air Portable Bridge (PDAA) .... APB
Air Portugal (SAUS) .... Air Port
Air Position .... AP
Air Position Indicating Station [Air Force] (IAA) .... APIS
Air Position Indicator [Air Force] .... API
Air Position Indicator (SAUS) .... api
Air Post Office (MCD) .... APO
Air Postal Group (SAUO) .... APSTLGRU
Air Postal Squadron [Air Force] .... AIRPS
Air Postal Squadron (SAUS) .... APSTRON
Air Power History [A publication] .... APH
Air Power League (SAUO) .... APL
Air Power Management (SAUS) .... APM
Air Power Museum (SAUO) .... APM
Air Pressure (MCD) .... AP
Air Pressure Analysis Program [Bell System] .... AIRPAP
Air Pressure Switch .... APS
Air Primary Training .... PRIMTRA
Air Priority (ACAE) .... APR
Air Priority .... APRI
Air Priority Board (SAUO) .... APB
Air Priority Rating .... APR
Air Prisoner of War Interrogation .... APWI
Air Processing Subsystem (MCD) .... AP
Air Procurement Directive (MCD) .... APD
Air Procurement District [Air Force] .... APD
Air Procurement District Commander [Air Force] .... APDC
Air Procurement Office .... APO
Air Procurement Region, Europe (AFM) .... APRE
Air Procurement Region, Far East (AFM) .... APRFE
Air Procuring Subsystein (SAUS) .... AP
Air Products & Chem [NYSE symbol] (TTSB) .... APD
Air Products & Chemicals, Inc. [Associated Press] (SAG) .... AirProd
Air Products and Chemicals, Inc. (SAUO) .... APCI
Air Products & Chemicals, Inc. [NYSE symbol] (SPSG) .... APD
Air Products & Chemicals, Inc., Allentown, PA [OCLC symbol] (OCLC) .... APA
Air Products & Chemicals, Inc., Allentown, PA [Library symbol] [Library of Congress] (LCLS) .... PAtA
Air Programs Office [Environmental Protection Agency] .... APO
Air Progress (SAUS) .... Air Prog
Air Project Coordinator [Military] (DNAB) .... APC
Air Proving Ground .... APG
Air Proving Ground Center [or Command] [Eglin Air Force Base, FL] .... APGC
Air Proving Ground Center-Eglin Air Force Base (SAUS) .... APGCE
Air Proving Ground Command (SAUO) .... APGC
Air Proving Ground-Eglin, Florida (SAUO) .... APGOEF
Air Provost Marshal (SAUS) .... APL
Air Provost Marshal .... APM
Air Public Relations Association [British] (BI) .... APRA
Air Public Relations Association (SAUO) .... APRA
Air Publication [Navy] .... AP
Air Publications and Forms Centre (SAUO) .... APFC
Air Publications and Forms Centre (SAUS) .... APFC
Air Publications and Forms Store (SAUO) .... APFS
Air Pullmans Croydon, Limited (SAUO) .... APCL
Air Pump Diverter Valve [Automotive engineering] .... APDV
Air Quality Act .... AQA
Air Quality Advisory Board (SAUS) .... AQAB
Air Quality and Chemical Tracking Division/Air Programs [Environmental science] (COE) .... AQCTD/AP
Air Quality and Emission Limitations [Environmental science] (COE) .... AQEL
Air Quality Assessment Model [Air Force] .... AQAM
Air Quality Committee (EEVL) .... AQC
Air Quality Control Act (SAUS) .... AQCA
Air Quality Control Program [Environmental Protection Agency] (EPAT) ...... AQCP
Air Quality Control Region [Environmental Protection Agency] .... AQCR
Air Quality Control Regulation (SAUS) .... AQCR
Air Quality Criteria and Control Techniques [Environmental Protection Agency] (GFGA) .... AQCCT
Air Quality Criteria Document [Environmental Protection Agency] (AEPA) .... AQCD
Air Quality Data Handling System [or Subsystem] [Environmental Protection Agency] .... AQDHS
Air Quality Digest [Environmental science] (COE) .... AQD
Air Quality Dispersion Model (SAUS) .... AQDM
Air Quality Display Model .... AQDM
Air Quality Forecast .... AQF
Air Quality Guideline Values [World Health Organization] .... AQGV
Air Quality Improvement Research Program [Automotive industry, research consortium] .... AQIRP
Air Quality Index .... AQI
Air Quality Maintenance Area [Environmental Protection Agency] (GFGA)..... AQMA
Air Quality Maintenance Plan [Environmental Protection Agency] (GFGA) .... AQMP

Air Quality Management .... AQM
Air Quality Management District .... AQMD
Air Quality Management District (SAUS) .... AQNM
Air Quality Management Division [Environmental science] (COE) .... AQMD
Air Quality Management Plan (SAUS) .... AQMP
Air Quality Region .... AQR
Air Quality Related Values/Visibility Test [Environmental Protection Agency] .... AQRV
Air Quality Simulation Model [Environmental Protection Agency] .... AQSM
Air Quality Standard .... AQS
Air Quality Subsystem (SAUS) .... AIRS
Air Quality Subsystem [Environmental Protection Agency] (AEPA) .... AQS
Air Quality Technical Assistance Demonstration [Environmental Protection Agency] (GFGA) .... AQTAD
Air quality, urban environment, noise, transport and energy (SAUS) .... DG XI-D3
Air Quartermaster (SAUO) .... AQM
Air Queensland [Australia] .... AQ
Air Queensland [Australia] [ICAO designator] (FAAC) .... AQN
Air Quenched (IAA) .... AQ
Air Radar Support Team (SAUO) .... ARST
Air Radio [Special duties officer] [British] .... AR
Air Radio Officer .... ARO
Air Raid Casualties Services (SAUO) .... ARCS
Air Raid Precautions [British] [World War II] .... ARP
Air Raid Precautions Controller [British] [World War II] .... ARPC
Air Raid Precautions Department (SAUO) .... ARPD
Air Raid Precautions Department (SAUO) .... ARPD
Air Raid Precautions Officer [British] [World War II] .... ARPO
Air Raid Precautions Service (SAUO) .... ARPS
Air Raid Precautions Service (SAUS) .... ARPS
Air Raid Protection (NATG) .... ARP
Air Raid Reporting & Control Station (SAUS) .... ARRCS
Air Raid Reporting Control Ship [Navy] (NVT) .... ARRCS
Air Raid Reporting Net (SAUS) .... ARRN
Air Raid Reporting Officer (SAUS) .... ARRO
Air Raid Warden .... ARW
Air Raid Warning [Air Force] .... ARW
Air Rarotonga [ICAO designator] (AD) .... GZ
Air Reactor Experiment .... ARE
Air Receive .... AR
Air Reconnaissance (IAA) .... AR
Air Reconnaissance Detection Force (CINC) .... ARDF
Air Reconnaissance Liaison Officer .... ARLO
Air Reconnaissance Low [Army] (RDA) .... ARL
Air Reconnaissance Support (AABC) .... ARSPT
Air Reconnaissance Support Battalion .... ARSB
Air Recovery and Rescue Service (NASA) .... ARRS
Air Recreational Vehicle .... ARV
Air Reduction (SAUS) .... AN
Air Reduction Center [NASA] (KSC) .... ARC
Air Reduction Chemical Company (SAUS) .... AIRCO
Air Reduction Co., Inc., Central Research Department Library, Murray Hill, NJ [Library symbol] [Library of Congress] (LCLS) .... NjMuA
Air Reduction Company (SAUS) .... AIRCO
Air Refueling [Aviation] (FAAC) .... AIRFL
Air Refueling .... AR
Air Refueling Boom (MCD) .... ARB
Air Refueling Control Point (AFM) .... ARCP
Air Refueling Control Time (AFM) .... ARCT
Air Refueling Egress Point [Aviation] (FAAC) .... AREP
Air Refueling Exit [Aviation] (FAAC) .... AREX
Air Refueling Facility [Military] (DOMA) .... ARF
Air Refueling Group (ACAE) .... AREFG
Air Refueling Group [Air Force] (DOMA) .... ARG
Air Refueling Ingress Point (SAUS) .... ARIP
Air Refueling Initial Point [Air Force] (AFM) .... ARIP
Air Refueling Part Task Trainer .... ARPTT
Air Refueling Probe .... ARP
Air Refueling Squadron .... AREFS
Air Refueling Squadron .... AREFSQ
Air Refueling Squadron [Air Force] (MUSM) .... ARS
Air Refueling Squadron (SAUO) .... ARSq
Air Refueling Wing .... AREFW
Air Refueling Wing [Air Force] (MUSM) .... ARW
Air Refuelling Group (SAUO) .... AREFG
Air Refuelling Squadron (SAUS) .... AREFS
Air Refuelling Squadron (SAUS) .... ARS
Air Refuelling Wing (SAUS) .... AREFW
Air Refuelling Wing (SAUS) .... ARW
Air Regenerative Exhaust .... ARX
Air Regional Library (PGSL), Transport Canada [Bibliotheque Regionale de l'Air (PGSL), Transports Canada] Vancouver, British Columbia [Library symbol] [National Library of Canada] (NLC) .... BVATCA
Air Regional Representative .... ARR
Air Register [Combustion emission control] .... AR
Air Registration Board [British] .... ARB
Air Regulating Squadron .... ARS
Air Regulator .... AR
Air Reinforcement Squadron (SAUS) .... ARS
Air Release Capacity [Aviation] .... ARC
Air Report [Aviation] [ICAO designator] (FAAC) .... AIREP
Air Report [Aviation] .... ARP
Air Reporting Control (NVT) .... ARC
Air Reporting Net (NATG) .... ARN
Air Request Net (SAUS) .... ARN

Air Requirement (SAUS) ... AR
Air Rescue (CINC) ... AIRRES
Air Rescue ... AR
Air Rescue and Recovery Squadron ... ARRS
Air Rescue Center (SAUO) ... ARC
Air Rescue Group (SAUO) ... ARG
Air Rescue Kit (SAUS) ... ARK
Air Rescue Operations Center [*Air Force*] ... AROC
Air Rescue Science (NASA) ... ARS
Air Rescue Service [*Air Force*] ... ARS
Air Rescue Service Manual (SAUS) ... ARSM
Air Rescue Service Regulation (SAUS) ... ARSR
Air Rescue Ship ... ARS
Air Rescue Squadron (SAUO) ... ARS
Air Rescue Squadron (SAUO) ... ARSq
Air Rescue Unit (SAUS) ... ARU
Air Research and Development (SAUS) ... AR&D
Air Research and Development (SAUS) ... AR and D
Air Research and Development ... AR & D
Air Research and Development Center [*Later, Air Force Systems Command*] ... ARDC
Air Research and Development Center (SAUS) ... ARDC
Air Research and Development Command [*Washington, DC*] [*Air Force*] ... ARDC
Air Research and Development Command - Andrews Air Force Base ... ARDCA
Air Research and Development Command, Ballistic Missile Department (SAUS) ... ARDC-BMD
Air Research and Development Command Forms ... ARDCF
Air Research and Development Command Manual [*Air Force*] ... ARDCM
Air Research and Development Command Regulations ... ARDCR
Air Research and Development Command-Andrews Air Force Base (SAUO) ... ARDCA
Air Research and Development Council [*NATO*] (NATG) ... ARDC
Air Research and Testing Committee (MUGU) ... ARTC
Air Research Bureau ... ARB
Air Research, Los Angeles (SAUO) ... AiResearch
Air Research Organization (SAA) ... ARO
Air Research Vehicle (MCD) ... ARV
Air Reservations Interline Message Procedure ... AIRIMP
Air Reserve ... AR
Air Reserve Association [*Later, Air Force Association*] ... ARA
Air Reserve Base ... ARB
Air Reserve Center (SAUO) ... Air Res Cen
Air Reserve Center ... ARC
Air Reserve Center (SAUO) ... ARCen
Air Reserve Component (SAUS) ... ARC
Air Reserve Components [*Military*] ... ARC
Air Reserve Component-Survivability Augmentation for Transport (SAUS) ... ARC-SATIN
Air Reserve District ... ARD
Air Reserve Facility (ACAE) ... ARF
Air Reserve Flying Center [*Air Force*] ... ARFC
Air Reserve Forces ... ARF
Air Reserve Forces Facility [*Military*] ... ARFF
Air Reserve Forces Meritorious Service Award [*Military decoration*] ... ARFMSA
Air Reserve Forces Meritorious Service Medal [*Military decoration*] (GFGA) ... ARFMS
Air Reserve Forces Meritorious Service Ribbon [*Military decoration*] (AFM) ... ARFMSR
Air Reserve Forces Personnel Data System (AFM) ... ARFPDS
Air Reserve Group (SAUO) ... ARG
Air Reserve Officers' Training Corps [*Air Force*] ... AROTC
Air Reserve Pay and Allowance System ... ARPAS
Air Reserve Pay System (AFM) ... ARPS
Air Reserve Personnel Center [*Air Force*] ... ARPC
Air Reserve Records Center ... ARRC
Air Reserve Specialist Training Squadron ... ARSTS
Air Reserve Squadron (SAUO) ... Air Res Squad
Air Reserve Squadron [*Air Force*] ... ARS
Air Reserve Technician [*Air Force*] ... ART
Air Reserve Technician Program [*Air Force*] ... ARTP
Air Reserve Unit ... ARU
Air Reserve Unit (General Training) ... ARUG
Air Reserve Unit (General Training, Nonpay) ... ARUSNP
Air Reserve Unit (General Training, Pay) ... ARUSP
Air Reserve Volunteer Support Group ... ARVSG
Air Reserve Wing [*Canada*] (DD) ... ARW
Air Reserve Wing Headquarters (SAUO) ... ARWH
Air Resistance ... AR
Air Resorts [*ICAO designator*] (FAAC) ... ARZ
Air Resorts Airlines [*ICAO designator*] (AD) ... UZ
Air Resources Atmospheric Turbulence and Diffusion Laboratory [*National Oceanic and Atmospheric Administration*] (NOAA) ... ARATDL
Air Resources Board [*California*] ... ARB
Air Resources Control Board (SAUO) ... ARCB
Air Resources Element Coordinator (IUSS) ... AREC
Air Resources Environmental Research Laboratory [*National Oceanic and Atmospheric Administration*] (NOAA) ... AREL
Air Resources Information Clearinghouse [*Also, an information service or system*] (EA) ... ARIC
Air Resources Laboratory [*Silver Spring, MD*] [*National Oceanic and Atmospheric Administration*] ... ARL
Air Resources Laboratory - Field Research Office [*National Oceanic and Atmospheric Administration*] (NOAA) ... ARL-FRO
Air Resources Management [*Environmental Protection Agency*] (GFGA) ... ARM
Air Resources Regional Pollution Assessment Model [*Environmental Protection Agency*] (GFGA) ... ARRPA
Air Resources Solar Radiation Laboratory [*National Oceanic and Atmospheric Administration*] (NOAA) ... ARRL
Air Resupply and Communication Service ... ARCS
Air Resupply and Communications Service (SAUO) ... ARCS
Air Resupply and Communications Wing (SAUO) ... ARCW
Air Reunion [*France*] [*ICAO designator*] (FAAC) ... REU
Air Revitalization System (MCD) ... ARS
Air Rhodesia (SAUS) ... RH
Air Risk Information Support Center [*Environmental Protection Agency*] (AEPA) ... AIR RISC
Air Roberval [*Canada*] [*ICAO designator*] (FAAC) ... RBV
Air Route Surveillance RADAR ... ARSR
Air Route Traffic Control [*Aviation*] ... ARTC
Air Route Traffic Control Center [*Aviation*] ... ARTCC
Air Route Traffic Control Center (SAUO) ... ATC
Air Routes and Ground Aids (SAA) ... AGA
Air Routing International Corp. [*ICAO designator*] (FAAC) ... ARC
Air Royal [*France*] [*ICAO designator*] (FAAC) ... RFO
Air Run Landing (SAUS) ... ARL
Air Run Take-Off (SAUS) ... ARTO
Air Russia Airlines [*Russian Federation*] [*ICAO designator*] (FAAC) ... RUS
Air Rwanda [*ICAO designator*] (FAAC) ... RWD
Air Rwanda [*ICAO designator*] (AD) ... RY
Air Rwanda [*Rwanda*] [*ICAO designator*] (ICDA) ... UW
Air Sacculitis [*Avian pathology*] ... AS
Air Safaris & Services (NZ) Ltd. [*New Zealand*] [*ICAO designator*] (FAAC) ... SRI
Air Safety Board ... ASB
Air Safety Foundation (SAUO) ... ASF
Air Safety Group [*British*] ... ASG
Air Safety Incident Reporting ... ASIR
Air Safety Reporting System [*NASA*] ... ASRS
Air Safety Review Board (SAUO) ... ASRB
Air Saigon [*Vietnam*] [*ICAO designator*] (FAAC) ... SGA
Air Saint-Pierre SA [*France*] [*ICAO designator*] (FAAC) ... SPM
Air Salomons Command (SAUO) ... AIRSOLS
Air Sampling System ... ASS
Air Sandy, Inc. [*Canada*] [*ICAO designator*] (FAAC) ... SNY
Air Sardinia International [*ICAO designator*] (FAAC) ... ARS
Air Sardinia SpA [*Italy*] [*ICAO designator*] (FAAC) ... ASZ
Air Sarthe Organisation - Societe [*France*] [*ICAO designator*] (FAAC) ... ASO
Air Satellite [*ICAO designator*] (AD) ... QR
Air Satellite, Inc. [*Canada*] [*ICAO designator*] (FAAC) ... ASJ
Air Savoie [*France*] [*ICAO designator*] (FAAC) ... ASV
Air Scatterable Antipersonnel Mine (MCD) ... ASPM
Air Schefferville, Inc. [*Canada*] [*ICAO designator*] (FAAC) ... ASF
Air Screw ... AS
Air, Sea and Land Defense (SAUS) ... TRIAD
Air, Sea, and Space Club (EA) ... ASSC
Air Sea Experiment (SAUS) ... ASE
Air Sea Fluxes (SAUS) ... ASF
Air Sea International [*British*] ... ASI
Air Sea Rescue Kit [*Military*] ... ASRK
Air Search Acquisition RADAR (CAAL) ... ASAR
Air Search Attack Team [*Military*] ... ASAT
Air Search Attack Unit [*Military*] ... ASAU
Air Search RADAR ... ASR
Air Search RADAR Receiver [*Shipborne*] ... SR
Air Search Radar Receiver (SAUS) ... SR
Air Seasoned (IAA) ... AS
Air Section (SAUO) ... AIR SEC
Air Section ... AS
Air Sector (SAUO) ... AIR SEC
Air Sector Operations Center (SAUO) ... ASOC
Air Security Agency (MCD) ... ASA
Air Sedona [*ICAO designator*] (AD) ... UJ
Air Self Defence (or Defense) Force (SAUO) ... ASDF
Air Self-Defense Force [*Japan*] (CINC) ... ASDF
Air Senegal [*ICAO designator*] (AD) ... DS
Air Senegal, Societe Nationational de Transport Aerien [*ICAO designator*] (FAAC) ... DSB
Air Sensors, Inc. [*Associated Press*] (SAG) ... AirSen
Air Sensors, Inc. [*NASDAQ symbol*] (SAG) ... ARSN
Air Separation Unit [*For oxygen production*] ... ASU
Air Service ... AS
Air Service (SAUO) ... AS
Air Service [*Poland*] [*ICAO designator*] (FAAC) ... ASQ
Air Service ... A/Svc
Air Service [*Mali*] [*ICAO designator*] (FAAC) ... ODB
Air Service Affaires [*France*] [*ICAO designator*] (FAAC) ... RSA
Air Service Area Command ... ASAC
Air Service Command ... ASC
Air Service Command Advisory Team ... ASCAT
Air Service Coordination Office [*Military*] (DNAB) ... ASCO
Air Service Coordination Office, Mediterranean [*Military*] (DNAB) ... ASCOMED
Air Service Force (IIA) ... ASF
Air Service Group [*Air Force*] ... ASG
Air Service Information Circular ... ASIC
Air Service Information Circular (journ.) (SAUS) ... ASIC
Air Service Mechanic (SAUS) ... ASM
Air Service Signal Corps ... ASSC
Air Service Signal Corps (SAUO) ... ASSC
Air Service State Co. [*Hungary*] [*ICAO designator*] (FAAC) ... RSZ
Air Service Support Squadron [*Army*] ... ASSRON

Air Service Training (SAUO)	AST
Air Service Training Ltd.	AST
Air Service Training Ltd. [British] [ICAO designator] (FAAC)	ATZ
Air Service Vosges [France] [ICAO designator] (FAAC)	VGE
Air Services [Military] (NVT)	AIRSVC
Air Services Agreement (DA)	ASA
Air Services Ltd. [Czechoslovakia] [ICAO designator] (FAAC)	RIS
Air Services Nantes [France] [ICAO designator] (FAAC)	ASN
Air Services of India Ltd. (SAUO)	ASI
Air Seychelles [ICAO designator] (FAAC)	SEY
Air Shutoff	ASHOF
Air Shutoff Valve	ASV
Air Shutter	AIRSHTR
Air Shuttle (CDAI)	A-S
Air Sicilia, SRL [Italy] [FAA designator] (FAAC)	SIC
Air Sierra [ICAO designator] (AD)	SI
Air Signal Officer	ASO
Air Sinai [Egypt] [ICAO designator] (FAAC)	ASD
Air Sinclair Ltd. [British] [ICAO designator] (FAAC)	SCK
Air Situation Coordinator (SAA)	ASC
Air Situation Display (SAA)	ASD
Air Slovakia BWJ Ltd. [FAA designator] (FAAC)	SVK
Air Society, International (EA)	ASI
Air Sofia [Bulgaria] [ICAO designator] (FAAC)	SFB
Air Solenoid Valve	ASV
Air Solomons Command [US]	AIRSOLS
Air Solomons Command (SAUS)	AIRSOLS Command
Air Sorel Ltd. [Canada] [ICAO designator] (FAAC)	WHY
Air South Australia	AirSA
Air South, Inc. [Airline code]	KQ
Air South, Inc. [ICAO designator] (FAAC)	SHW
Air South West [British] [FAA designator] (FAAC)	PIE
Air Southwest [Canada] [ICAO designator] (FAAC)	ASW
Air Space	ASPA
Air Space Management (SAUS)	ASM
Air Space Paper Core	ASPC
Air Space Paper Core Cable (SAUS)	ASPC cable
Air Space Transportation	ASTRA
Air Space Travel Research Organization	ASTRO
Air Special [Czechoslovakia] [ICAO designator] (FAAC)	ASX
Air Specialties Corp. [ICAO designator] (FAAC)	AMR
Air Specification (NG)	AS
Air Spirit, Inc. [ICAO designator] (FAAC)	SIP
Air St. Pierre [ICAO designator] (AD)	PJ
Air St. Thomas [ICAO designator] (FAAC)	STT
Air staff (SAUO)	A
Air Staff (SAUO)	AS
Air Staff [Air Force]	AS
Air Staff Board [Air Force] (AFM)	ASB
Air Staff Defense Force (CINC)	ASDF
Air Staff Information Systems Plan (ACAE)	ASISP
Air Staff Management Aid (SAUS)	ASMA
Air Staff Office (ACAE)	ASO
Air Staff Office Automation System [Air Force] (GFGA)	ASOAS
Air Staff Officer	ASO
Air Staff Orientation (AFM)	ASO
Air Staff Requirement	ASR
Air Staff Target [Royal Air Force] [British]	AST
Air Staff Trainee [or Training] [Air Force]	ASTRA
Air Staff Training (SAUS)	ASTRA
Air Staff Training Program (SAUO)	ASTRA
Air Stagnation Advisories [National Weather Service]	ASA
Air Stagnation Model	ASM
Air Standard Efficiency	ASE
Air Standardization Coordinating Committee	ASCC
Air Standardization Coordination Program [NATO]	ASCP
Air Standards Coordinating Committee (SAUO)	ASCC
Air Star Corp. [Canada] [ICAO designator] (FAAC)	ASC
Air Star Zanzibar [Tanzania] [ICAO designator] (FAAC)	AZU
Air Starline AG [Switzerland] [ICAO designator] (FAAC)	ASA
Air Starting	ASTRG
Air Station	AS
Air Station [Air Force]	ASTN
Air Stations Weekly Orders [Navy]	ASWO
Air Steward [British military] (DMA)	AS
Air Storage System Energy Transfer (SAUS)	ASSET
Air Stord AS [Norway] [ICAO designator] (FAAC)	SOR
Air Store Establishment (SAUO)	ASE
Air Store Establishment (SAUS)	ASE
Air Store Issuing Ship	AIRIS
Air Stores Depot [Navy]	AIRSTORDEP
Air Stores Park [British military] (DMA)	ASP
Air Stores Park (SAUO)	ASP
Air Straubing Luftfahrtgesellschaft MbH, Atting [Germany] [FAA designator] (FAAC)	ASN
Air Strike	A/S
Air Suction Valve [Automotive engineering]	ASV
Air Sunshine, Inc. [ICAO designator] (FAAC)	RSI
Air Superiority (MCD)	AS
Air Superiority Fighter	ASF
Air Superiority Mission (SAUS)	ASM
Air Superiority Program	ASP
Air Supplemented Solid Rocket Motor (MCD)	ASSRM
Air Supply (NRCH)	AS
Air Supply	ASUP

Air Supply (SAUS)	ASUPP
Air Supply Board [Ministry of Aircraft Production] [British]	ASB
Air Supply Fan Club (EA)	ASFC
Air Supply Officer (SAUS)	ASO
Air Support	AS
Air Support Command	ASC
Air Support Command Operations Centre (SAUO)	ASCOC
Air Support Control	ASC
Air Support Control Unit (SAUO)	ASCU
Air Support Control Units	ASCU
Air Support Coordination and Control (MCD)	ASCC
Air Support Coordinator (MCD)	ASC
Air Support Director [Military] (NVT)	ASD
Air Support Officer [Military]	ASO
Air Support Operations (CAAL)	ASO
Air Support Operations Center [Air Force]	ASOC
Air Support Operations Center Squadron [Air Force]	ASOCS
Air Support Operations Group [Air Force]	ASOG
Air Support Program (SAUS)	ASP
Air Support RADAR Team [Marine Corps]	ASRT
Air Support Signal Unit (NATG)	ASSU
Air Support Tactics	AST
Air Support Test Unit	ASTU
Air Support Training Unit (SAUO)	ASTU
Air Support Training Units	ASTU
Air Supported Threat	AST
Air Sur [Spain] [ICAO designator] (FAAC)	NCR
Air, Surface, and Electronic Warfare Division [Navy] (MCD)	AS & EWD
Air Surface Coordinating Office Mediterranean (SAUO)	ASCOMED
Air Surface Missile Digital Differential Analyzer (SAUS)	ASMDDA
Air Surface Zone (SAUS)	ASZ
[The] Air Surgeon [Army]	TAS
Air Surveillance [Air Force]	AS
Air Surveillance and Airspace Control (MCD)	ASAC
Air Surveillance & Gun Control console (SAUS)	AS/GC
Air Surveillance & Targeting Radar, L-band (SAUS)	ASTRAL
Air Surveillance Broadcast (MCD)	ASB
Air Surveillance Evaluation (SAA)	ASE
Air Surveillance Group (SAA)	ASG
Air Surveillance Officer [Air Force]	ASO
Air Surveillance RADAR (AFM)	ASR
Air Surveillance RADAR/Operations Center System	ASR/OPS
Air Surveillance Subsystem Evaluation and Training [Air Force] (IAA)	ASSET
Air Surveillance System	ASS
Air Surveillance Technician [Air Force]	AST
Air Survey Co. of India Ltd. (SAUO)	IS
Air Suspension [Automotive engineering]	A/SUSP
Air Swazi Cargo (Pty) Ltd. [Swaziland] [ICAO designator] (FAAC)	CWS
Air Swift [British] [ICAO designator] (FAAC)	SWF
Air System Interrogator (SAUS)	AIS
Air Systems Command [Navy]	AIRSYSCOM
Air Systems Command [Navy]	ASC
Air Tactical Actions Control Officer (COE)	ATACO
Air Tactical Communications [FAA] (TAG)	ATC
Air Tactical Control Officer (NVT)	ATACO
Air Tactical Control Operator	ATACO
Air Tactical Data System (MCD)	ATDS
Air Tactical Missile (ACAE)	ATM
Air Tactical Operations Center [Military]	ATOC
Air Tactical Publication	ATP
Air Tactical School [Air Force]	ATS
Air Tactics Officer [Air Force]	ATO
Air Tahiti (SAUS)	QE
Air Tahiti [France] [ICAO designator] (FAAC)	VTA
Air Tanzania [ICAO designator] (FAAC)	ATC
Air Tanzania [ICAO designator] (AD)	TC
Air Tara Ltd. [Republic of Ireland] [ICAO designator] (FAAC)	AGP
Air Target Chart (CINC)	ATC
Air Target Indicator	ATI
Air Target Intelligence Liaison Program [Air Force]	ATIL
Air Target Intelligence Liaison Program (SAUS)	ATIL Program
Air Target Materials [Military]	ATM
Air Target Materials Program [Military] (AFM)	ATMP
Air Target Mosaic (MCD)	ATM
Air Targets Officer	ATO
Air Task Force	ATF
Air Task Force Commander (MUGU)	ATFC
Air Tasking Officer (SAUO)	ATO
Air Tasking Order	ATO
Air Tasking Order Center (SAUO)	ATOC
Air Tasmania [ICAO designator] (AD)	XZ
Air Taxi (SAUS)	ATX
Air Taxi and Commercial Pilots Association [Defunct] (EA)	ATCPA
Air Taxi Operators Association (SAUO)	AROA
Air Taxi Operators Association (SAUO)	ATOA
Air Taxi-Commercial Operator	ATCO
Air Tchad [ICAO designator] (AD)	HT
Air Tchad, Societe de Transport Aeriens [Chad] [ICAO designator] (FAAC)	HTT
Air Team, AS [Norway] [FAA designator] (FAAC)	TTX
Air Technical Analysis Division (SAA)	ATAD
Air Technical Battalion (MCD)	ATB
Air Technical Index [Air Force]	ATI
Air Technical Information [Used by Armed Services Technical Information Agency - later, Defense Documentation Center - to accession and identify documents]	ATI

Air Technical Intelligence [*Air Force*] ... ATI
Air Technical Intelligence Center ... ATIC
Air Technical Intelligence Liaison Office (SAUS) ... ATILO
Air Technical Intelligence Service (SAUO) ... ATIS
Air Technical Intelligence Services Command [*Air Force*] ... ATISC
Air Technical Intelligence Study [*Air Force*] ... ATIS
Air Technical Library, Department of National Defence [*Bibliotheque Techniquede l'Aviation, Ministere de la Defense Nationale*] **Ottawa, Ontario** [*Library symbol*] [*National Library of Canada*] (NLC) ... OONDAT
Air Technical Service (IAA) ... ATS
Air Technical Service Command [*Air Force*] ... ATSC
Air Technical Training [*Navy*] ... TECHTRA
Air Technician [*Air National Guard*] (AFM) ... AT
Air Temperature ... AT
Air Temperature (SAUS) ... TAIR
Air Temperature Control (IEEE) ... ATC
Air Temperature Correction ... T
Air Temperature Sensor [*Automotive engineering*] ... ATS
Air Tenglong [*China*] [*ICAO designator*] (FAAC) ... CTE
Air Terminal ... ATERM
Air Terminal (SAUO) ... ATerm
Air Terminal Identifier Code ... ATIC
Air Terminal Management Control Team (SAUO) ... ATMCT
Air Terminal Officer [*Air Force*] ... ATO
Air Terminal Operations Center (ACAE) ... ATOC
Air Terminal Team ... ATT
Air Terrex [*Czechoslovakia*] [*ICAO designator*] (FAAC) ... TRX
Air Test and Evaluation Squadron (SAUS) ... VX
Air Test Vehicle ... ATV
Air Texana [*ICAO designator*] (AD) ... OJ
Air Texana (SAUS) ... TEX
Air Thanet [*British*] [*ICAO designator*] (FAAC) ... THL
Air Threat Conference (SAUO) ... ATC
Air Threat to Central Europe ... ATCE
Air to Air Attack Management (ACAE) ... AAAM
Air to Air Covert Sensor Technology (ACAE) ... AACSENT
Air to Air Electro Optical Fire Control System (ACAE) ... AAEOFCS
Air to Air Missile Seeker (ACAE) ... AAMS
Air to Air Recognition System (ACAE) ... ATARS
Air to Air Search (ACAE) ... AAS
Air to Air Search and Track (ACAE) ... A/ASTR
Air to Air Target Indentification System (ACAE) ... AATIDS
Air to Air Track (ACAE) ... AAT
Air to Ground Automatic Tracking Equipment (ACAE) ... AGATE
Air to Ground Missile Excalibur (ACAE) ... AGMX
Air to Heat Exchanger [*Aerospace*] (AAG) ... AHE
Air to Pneumatic Distribution [*Aerospace*] ... APD
Air to Service (ACAE) ... A/S
Air to Underwater (SAA) ... AU
Air Today, Inc. [*ICAO designator*] (FAAC) ... TDY
Air Tonga [*ICAO designator*] (FAAC) ... ATO
Air Toronto [*ICAO designator*] (AD) ... CS
Air Toronto, Inc. [*Canada*] [*ICAO designator*] (FAAC) ... CNE
Air Torpedo-Firing (DNAB) ... ATF
Air Toulon [*France*] [*ICAO designator*] (FAAC) ... ATU
Air Toulouse [*France*] [*ICAO designator*] (FAAC) ... TLE
Air Tour Management Plan ... ATMP
Air Toxics and Radiation Monitoring Research Division [*Environmental Protection Agency*] (EPA) ... ATRMRD
Air, Toxics, and Radiation Staff [*Environmental Protection Agency*] (GFGA) ... ATRS
Air Toxics Control Measure (SARE) ... ATCM
Air Toxics Exposure and Risk Information System (SAUS) ... ATERIS
Air Toxics Task Force [*Environmental Protection Agency*] (GFGA) ... ATTF
Air Tracker (DNAB) ... A/T
Air Tracker/Long-Range (DNAB) ... AT/LR
Air Tracker/Short-Range (DNAB) ... AT/SR
Air Traffic [*FAA*] (TAG) ... AT
Air Traffic Communication System [*NASA*] (KSC) ... ATCS
Air Traffic Communications (MCD) ... ATCOM
Air Traffic Communications Operators Guild (SAUO) ... ATCOG
Air Traffic Communications Service (MCD) ... ATCS
Air Traffic Communications Station ... ATCS
Air Traffic Compiler (SAUS) ... ATCOM
Air Traffic Conference (SAUO) ... ATC
Air Traffic Conference of America [*Defunct*] (EA) ... ATC
Air Traffic Conference of America [*Defunct*] (EA) ... ATCA
Air Traffic Control [*or Controller*] ... ATC
Air Traffic Control [*ICAO designator*] (ICDA) ... ZG
Air Traffic Control [*FAA designator*] (FAAC) ... ZGZ
Air Traffic Control Advises (FAAC) ... ATCA
Air Traffic Control Advisory Committee [*Department of Transportation*] ... ATCAC
Air Traffic Control and Landing System [*DoD*] ... ATCALS
Air Traffic Control and Navigation (SAUS) ... ATC/NAV
Air Traffic Control and Navigation Board ... ATCNB
Air Traffic Control and Warning (IAA) ... ATCW
Air Traffic Control Area Maintenance Facilities (SAUO) ... ATCAMF
Air Traffic Control Assigned Airspace [*FAA*] (TAG) ... ATCAA
Air Traffic Control Assistant (DA) ... ATCA
Air Traffic Control Association (EA) ... ATCA
Air Traffic Control Automated (or Automation) System (SAUS) ... ATCAS
Air Traffic Control Automatic System [*Sweden*] ... ATCAS
Air Traffic Control Automation Panel [*International Civil Aviation Organization*] ... ATCAP
Air Traffic Control Beacon Ground Station ... ATCBGS
Air traffic control beacon IFF Mk XII system (SAUS) ... AIM
Air Traffic Control Beacon Interrogator ... ATCBI
Air Traffic Control Board (SAUO) ... ATCB
Air Traffic Control Center [*Air Force*] ... ATCC
Air Traffic Control Chief Engineer (SAUS) ... ATCCE
Air Traffic Control Clears (FAAC) ... ATCC
Air Traffic Control Command Center [*FAA*] (TAG) ... ATCCC
Air Traffic Control Communication ... ATCC
Air Traffic Control Communications Switching System (ACAE) ... ATCCSS
Air Traffic Control Coordination Center (IAA) ... ATCCC
Air Traffic Control Evaluation Unit [*British*] ... ATCEU
Air Traffic Control Experimental Unit (SAUO) ... ATCEU
Air Traffic Control Facility ... ATCF
Air Traffic Control Flight ... ATCF
Air Traffic Control Flight Advisory Service (MCD) ... ATCFAS
Air Traffic Control in European NATO Countries (SAUS) ... EURO-CONTROL
Air Traffic Control Line (AFM) ... ATCL
Air Traffic Control Office [*or Operations*] [*Air Force*] ... ATCO
Air Traffic Control Operations Representative (SAUS) ... ATCOR
Air Traffic Control Procedures ... ATCP
Air Traffic Control Product [*Army*] ... ATCP
Air Traffic Control Proficiency Training System [*Navy*] ... APTS
Air Traffic Control Project for Satellite (DA) ... ATCPROSAT
Air Traffic Control RADAR Beacon ... ATCRB
Air Traffic Control Radar Beacon/ Identification Friend or Foe/Mark XII/System (SAUS) ... AIMS
Air Traffic Control RADAR Beacon System ... ATCRBS
Air Traffic Control RADAR Beacon/Identification Friend or Foe/Mark XII/ System ... AIMS
Air Traffic Control RADAR System ... ATCRS
Air Traffic Control RADAR Unit (AFM) ... ATCRU
Air Traffic Control Request (FAAC) ... ATCR
Air Traffic Control Satellite (IIA) ... ATCS
Air Traffic Control Service (OA) ... ATCS
Air Traffic Control Signalling System (SAUS) ... ATCSS
Air Traffic Control Simulation Facility ... ATCSF
Air Traffic Control Specialist (SAUS) ... ATCS
Air Traffic Control Station (SAUS) ... ATCS
Air Traffic Control Subsystem (SAUS) ... ATCS
Air Traffic Control System (IUSS) ... ATCS
Air Traffic Control System Command Center (GAVI) ... ATCSCC
Air Traffic Control Systems Command Center (SAUS) ... ATCSC
Air Traffic Control Tower (SAUS) ... ATCT
Air [*or Airport*] **Traffic Control Tower** ... ATCT
Air Traffic Control Tower, Approach Control and Departure Control Facility (SAUS) ... TAD
Air Traffic Control Transponder ... ATCT
Air Traffic Coordinating Office (SAUS) ... ATCO
Air Traffic Coordinator ... ATCOR
Air Traffic Coordinator Europe ... ATCOREU
Air Traffic Data Processor ... ATDP
Air Traffic Delay ... ATD
Air Traffic Division [*Air Traffic Control*] (FAAC) ... ATD
Air Traffic Engineer [*British*] (DA) ... ATE
Air Traffic Flow [*Later, ATIF*] (MCD) ... ATF
Air Traffic Flow Control Unit [*ICAO designator*] (ICDA) ... ZD
Air Traffic Flow Control Unit [*FAA designator*] (FAAC) ... ZDZ
Air Traffic Flow Management [*ICAO designator*] (FAAC) ... ATEM
Air Traffic Flow Management (DA) ... ATFM
Air Traffic Flow Management Unit (DA) ... ATFMU
Air Traffic GmbH [*Germany*] [*ICAO designator*] (FAAC) ... ATJ
Air Traffic GmbH (SAUS) ... TJ
Air Traffic Incident Report (SAUS) ... ATIR
Air Traffic Information Service (DA) ... ATIS
Air Traffic Management ... ATM
Air Traffic Management System [*Army*] (AABC) ... ATMS
Air Traffic Managements Automated Center (SAUO) ... ATMAC
Air Traffic Navigation, Integration and Coordination System [*Army*] ... ATNAVICS
Air Traffic Navigation, Integration & Co-ordination System (SAUS) ... ATNAVICS
Air Traffic Operations (CTAS) ... ATO
Air Traffic Operations Management System [*FAA*] (TAG) ... ATOMS
Air Traffic Operations Service [*FAA*] (TAG) ... ATO
Air Traffic Plans and Requirements Service (CTAS) ... ATR
Air Traffic Procedures ... ATP
Air Traffic Procedures Advisory Committee [*FAA*] (TAG) ... ATPAC
Air Traffic Regulation Center (AFM) ... ATRC
Air Traffic Regulation Identification System [*Army*] ... ATRIS
Air Traffic Regulations ... ATR
Air Traffic Representative (FAAC) ... ATREP
Air Traffic Requirements (CTAS) ... ATR
Air Traffic Rules (SAUS) ... ATR
Air Traffic Section (AFM) ... ATS
Air Traffic Service (SAUS) ... AAT
Air Traffic Service (SAUO) ... AT
Air Traffic Service [*of FAA*] [*Also known as AAT, AT*] ... ATS
Air Traffic Service Communications [*Communications related to air traffic services.*] (GAVI) ... ATSC
Air Traffic Service Contingency Command Post (FAAC) ... ATSCCP
Air Traffic Service Flight Services Division [*of FAA*] ... ATSFSD
Air Traffic Service System Error Analysis (SAA) ... ATESSEA
Air Traffic Service Unit (OA) ... ATSU
Air Traffic Services (SAUO) ... ATS
Air Traffic Services Organization [*Military*] (DOMA) ... ATSO
Air Traffic Services Outside Regulated Airspace [*British*] (DA) ... ATSORA
Air Traffic Services Planning Manual (DA) ... ATSPM

Air Traffic Services Reporting Office [*Aviation*] ... ARO
Air Traffic Services Reporting Office [*ICAO designator*] (ICDA) ... ZP
Air Traffic Services Reporting Office [*FAA designator*] (FAAC) ... ZPZ
Air Traffic System (SAUS) ... ATS
Air Traffic Transponder ... ATT
Air Trails [*ICAO designator*] (AD) ... NN
Air Training (SAUS) ... AT
Air Training Advisor (NATG) ... ATA
Air Training Advisory Group ... ATAG
Air Training Association [*British*] (DA) ... ATA
Air Training Camp (SAUO) ... ATC
Air Training Command [*Randolph Air Force Base, TX*] ... ATC
Air Training Command (SAUO) ... ATCOM
Air Training Command [*Air Force*] ... ATRC
Air Training Command Headquarters (SAUO) ... CANAIRTRAIN
Air Training Command Manual [*Air Force*] ... ATCM
Air Training Command Pamphlet [*Air Force*] ... ATCP
Air Training Command Regulation [*Air Force*] ... ATCR
Air Training Communications Division [*Air Force*] ... ATCD
Air Training Control [*Military*] (MUSM) ... ATC
Air Training Corps (SAUS) ... AIRTC
Air Training Corps [*RAF*] [*British*] ... ATC
Air Training Corps Cadet [*British*] ... ATCC
Air Training Corps of America ... ATCA
Air Training Group (SAUO) ... ATG
Air Training Information Systems Division (SAUO) ... ATISD
Air Training Manual (SAUS) ... ATM
Air Training Memorandum (SAUS) ... ATM
Air Training Missile (ACAE) ... ATM
Air Training Officer [*Air Force*] ... ATO
Air Training Scheme (SAUS) ... ATS
Air Training School (SAUO) ... ATS
Air Training Squadron (MUGU) ... AIRTRAINRON
Air Training Squadron ... AIRTRARON
Air Training Squadron (SAUO) ... AIRTRATON
Air Training Team (NATG) ... ATT
Air Tran Holdings [*NASDAQ symbol*] [*Formerly, ValuJet, Inc.*] (SG) ... AAIRD
Air Tranport School [*Former USSR*] [*ICAO designator*] (FAAC) ... AIS
Air Trans NG Group Moldova [*FAA designator*] (FAAC) ... NGG
Air Transafrik Ltd. [*Ghana*] [*ICAO designator*] (FAAC) ... TRF
Air Transat [*Canada*] [*ICAO designator*] (FAAC) ... TSC
Air Transfer Order ... ATO
Air Transmit ... AT
Air Transn Hldgs [*NASDAQ symbol*] (TTSB) ... AIRT
Air Transport [*Military*] ... AT
Air Transport Advisory Council [*British*] ... ATAC
Air Transport and Allied Undertakings (SAUO) ... ATAU
Air Transport and Delivery (SAUO) ... ATAD
Air Transport & Movements Officer (SAUO) ... ATMO
Air Transport and Travel Industry Training Board (SAUO) ... ATTITB
Air Transport Association ... ATA
Air Transport Association International (SAUO) ... ATAI
Air Transport Association Meteorological Committee (SAUO) ... ATAMC
Air Transport Association of America (EA) ... ATA
Air Transport Association of America ... ATAA
Air Transport Association of Canada ... ATAC
Air Transport Auxiliary [*British*] [*World War II*] ... ATA
Air Transport Auxiliary (SAUO) ... ATA
Air Transport, Auxiliary (SAUS) ... ATA
Air Transport Auxiliary Association (DA) ... ATAA
Air Transport Auxiliary Service [*British*] [*World War II*] ... ATAS
Air Transport Auxiliary Service (SAUO) ... ATAS
Air Transport Board (SAUS) ... ATB
Air Transport Bureau [*ICAO*] ... ATB
Air Transport Bureau (SAUO) ... ATP
Air Transport Certificate (SAUS) ... ATC
Air Transport (Chatham Island) Ltd. [*New Zealand*] [*ICAO designator*] (FAAC) ... CVA
Air Transport Command [*Air Force*] ... ATC
Air Transport Command Headquarters (SAUO) ... CanAirLift
Air Transport Command Headquarters, Rockcliffe, Ontario, Canada ... CANAIRLIFT
Air Transport Committee [*ICAO*] ... ATC
Air Transport Coordinator, United States (SAUS) ... ATCORUS
Air Transport Corp. (SAUS) ... TPT
Air Transport Council [*New South Wales, Australia*] ... ATC
Air Transport Development Unit [*British*] ... ATDU
Air Transport Electronics Council (SAUO) ... ATEC
Air Transport Force ... ATF
Air Transport, Inc. [*FAA designator*] (FAAC) ... CYO
Air Transport Indicator (HLLA) ... ATI
Air Transport Industry Training Association (DA) ... ATITA
Air Transport International [*ICAO designator*] (FAAC) ... ATN
Air Transport Liaison [*Military*] [*British*] ... ATL
Air Transport Liaison Officer [*British*] ... ATLO
Air Transport Licensing Authority [*British*] ... ATLA
Air Transport Licensing Authority (SAUO) ... ATLA
Air Transport Licensing Board ... ATLB
Air Transport Ltd. [*Slovakia*] [*ICAO designator*] (FAAC) ... EAT
Air Transport Movement Control Center ... ATMC
Air Transport Movement Control Center [*Military*] ... ATMCC
Air Transport of Radiation ... ATR
Air Transport Operation Centre [*Military*] [*British*] ... ATOC
Air Transport Operators Association (EAIO) ... ATOA
Air Transport Pressurizing Unit (SAUS) ... APTU
Air Transport Pressurizing Unit ... ATPU
Air Transport Pyrenees [*France*] [*ICAO designator*] (FAAC) ... TPR
Air Transport Rack (ACAE) ... ATR
Air Transport Radio [*NASA*] (NASA) ... ATR
Air Transport Rating (SAUS) ... ATR
Air Transport Regulation Panel [*ICAO*] (DA) ... ATRP
Air Transport Schiphol [*Netherlands*] [*ICAO designator*] (FAAC) ... ATQ
Air Transport Service [*Navy*] ... ATS
Air Transport Service [*Zaire*] [*ICAO designator*] (FAAC) ... ATS
Air Transport Squadron ... AIRTRANSRON
Air Transport Squadron (SAUO) ... AIRTRASRON
Air Transport Squadron [*Air Force*] (MCD) ... ATS
Air Transport Squadron [*Air Force*] ... ATSq
Air Transport Squadron, Atlantic ... AIRTRANSRONLANT
Air Transport Squadron, Pacific ... AIRTRANSRONPAC
Air Transport Squadron, West Coast ... AIRTRANSRONWESTCOAST
Air Transport Statistical Programme [*International Civil Aviation Authority*] [*Canada*] (NITA) ... ATSP
Air Transport Statistics ... ATS
Air Transport Support (SAUS) ... ATS
Air Transport Systems (HLLA) ... ATS
Air Transport Users' Association [*British*] (DA) ... ATUA
Air Transport Wing [*Air Force*] ... ATW
Air Transport Wing [*Air Force*] (AFM) ... ATWg
Air Transportability Test Loading Agency ... ATTLA
Air Transportability Training Center (SAUS) ... ATTC
Air Transportability Training Centre (SAUO) ... ATTC
Air Transportable Acoustic Communications (CAAL) ... ATAC
Air Transportable Armament Control (ACAE) ... AIRTRAC
Air Transportable Buffet Lab (DWSG) ... ATBL
Air Transportable Clinic (MCD) ... ATC
Air Transportable Communications Complex ... ATRAX
Air Transportable Communications Unit (NVT) ... ATCU
Air Transportable Dispensary (AFM) ... ATD
Air Transportable Earth Station (IAA) ... ATES
Air Transportable Hospital (AFM) ... ATH
Air Transportable Pantograph Fueling System (MCD) ... ATPFS
Air Transportable Racking (SAUS) ... ATR
Air Transportable Radio Installations ... ATRI
Air Transportable SONAR Surveillance System ... ATSSS
Air Transportable Telecommunications Unit ... ATTU
Air Transportation Association (AAGC) ... ATA
Air Transportation Board ... ATB
Air Transportation Coordination Office (CINC) ... ATCO
Air Transportation Corps (SAUO) ... ATC
Air Transportation Exercise [*Military*] (NVT) ... AIRTRANSEX
Air Transportation Holding Co., Inc. [*NASDAQ symbol*] (NQ) ... AIRT
Air Transportation Holding Co., Inc. [*Associated Press*] (SAG) ... AirTrans
Air Transportation Hydrant Refueling System (AFIT) ... ATHRS
Air Transportation Management (GAVI) ... ATM
Air Transportation Rack [*NASA*] (NASA) ... ATR
Air Transportation Research Information Service [*National Academy of Sciences*] [*Information service or system*] ... ATRIS
Air Transportation Research International Forum (MCD) ... ATRIF
Air Transportation Squadron (Medium) ... ATS(M)
Air Transportation Training Flight [*Military*] ... ATTF
Air Trapping (SAUS) ... AT
Air Travel Card [*Airline notation*] ... ATC
Air Travel Card of High Credit [*Airline notation*] ... ATCQ
Air Travel Corp. [*ICAO designator*] (FAAC) ... ATH
Air Travel Organisers Licence [*British*] ... ATOL
Air Travel Plan (IIA) ... ATP
Air Travel Reserve Fund Agency (SAUO) ... ATRFA
Air Travel Security Unit ... ATSU
Air Trial Unit (SAUS) ... ATU
Air Troika [*Russian Federation*] [*ICAO designator*] (FAAC) ... TKA
Air Truck [*Spain*] [*ICAO designator*] (FAAC) ... TRK
Air Tungaru [*British*] [*ICAO designator*] (FAAC) ... TUN
Air Tungaru [*ICAO designator*] (AD) ... VK
Air Tungaru (Gilbert Islands) [*British*] [*ICAO designator*] (ICDA) ... RT
Air Turbine Alternator ... ATA
Air Turbine Drive (NG) ... ATD
Air Turbine Generator ... ATG
Air Turbine Motor ... ATM
Air Turbine Pump (SAUS) ... ATP
Air Turbine Starter (NG) ... ATS
Air Turbine Starter, Cartridge (MCD) ... ATSC
Air Turbine Starter Control Value (MCD) ... ATSCV
Air Turbine Starter/Accessory Drive (MCD) ... ATS/AD
Air Turbo Rocket ... ATR
Air Turbo-Ram (WDAA) ... ATR
Air Turks and Caicos [*ICAO designator*] (AD) ... QW
Air UK (Leisure) Ltd. [*British*] [*ICAO designator*] (FAAC) ... LEI
Air UK Ltd. (SAUS) ... UK
Air UK Ltd. [*British*] [*ICAO designator*] (FAAC) ... UKA
Air Ukraine [*ICAO designator*] (FAAC) ... UKR
Air Ukraine Cargo [*FAA designator*] (FAAC) ... UKC
Air Ukraine International [*ICAO designator*] (FAAC) ... AUI
Air Unit Risk [*Environmental Science*] ... AUR
Air University (SAUO) ... Air U
Air University (MCD) ... AIRU
Air University [*Maxwell Air Force Base, AL*] ... AU
Air University (SAUO) ... AU
Air University (SAUO) ... AUV
Air University Board of Visitors ... AUBV

Air University Center for Professional Development [*Military*] ..... AUCPD
Air University Institute for Professional Development (SAUO) ..... AUIPD
Air University Library ..... AUL
Air University Press ..... AUP
Air University. Review [*A publication*] (DLA) ..... Air U Rev
Air University-Airpower Research Institute [*Maxwell Air Force Base, AL*] ..... AU-ARI
Air Urga [*Ukraine*] [*FAA designator*] (FAAC) ..... URG
Air Users' Committee [*British*] ..... AUC
Air Valve Silencer ..... AVS
Air Vane Erection System (MCD) ..... AVES
Air Vanuatu [*ICAO designator*] (FAAC) ..... AVN
Air Vanuatu [*Airline code*] [*Australia*] ..... NF
Air Varna Co. [*Bulgaria*] [*ICAO designator*] (FAAC) ..... BAV
Air Vectors [*ICAO designator*] (AD) ..... ZB
Air Vegas Airlines, Inc. [*FAA designator*] (FAAC) ..... VGA
Air Vehicle (COE) ..... AV
Air Vehicle / Swivel Nozzle [*Military*] ..... AV/SN
Air Vehicle Detection (MCD) ..... AVD
Air Vehicle Digital Computer Unit ..... ADCU
Air Vehicle Field Maintenance Evaluation Requirement (MCD) ..... AVFMER
Air Vehicle Functional Group [*Military*] ..... AVFG
Air Vehicle Handler (SAUS) ..... AVH
Air Vehicle Nuclear Radiation ..... AVNR
Air Vehicle Specification (MCD) ..... AVS
Air Vehicle Synthesis [*Program*] ..... AVSYN
Air Vehicle System (ACAE) ..... AVS
Air Vehicle/Jet Vane ..... AV/JV
Air Vehicle/Launch Module ..... AV/LM
Air Vehicles Ltd. (SAUS) ..... AVL
Air Velocity Detector ..... AVD
Air Velocity Index ..... AVI
Air Velocity Meter ..... AVM
Air Velocity Transducer ..... AVT
Air Vendee [*France*] [*ICAO designator*] (FAAC) ..... AVD
Air Vent ..... AV
Air Ventilation Garment [*NASA*] ..... AVG
Air Vibrating Table ..... AVT
Air Vibration Table (SAUS) ..... AVT
Air Vice-Marshal [*British*] ..... AVM
Air Vietnam (SAUO) ..... AVN
Air Viet-Nam ..... VNA
Air Virginia [*ICAO designator*] (AD) ..... CE
Air Volcano Team [*Army*] ..... AVT
Air Volta [*ICAO designator*] (AD) ..... VH
Air Volume Totalizer [*Navy*] ..... AVT
Air War College [*Air Force*] ..... AIRWC
Air War College [*Maxwell Air Force Base, AL*] ..... AWC
Air War College Associate Program (AFM) ..... AWCAP
Air War Plans Division (SAUS) ..... AWPD
Air Warfare Analysis Section [*British*] ..... AWA
Air Warfare Analysis Section [*British*] ..... AWAS
Air Warfare Center [*Air Force*] (DOMA) ..... AWC
Air Warfare Control (MCD) ..... AWC
Air Warfare Control Officer ..... AWCO
Air Warfare Co-Ordination [*British military*] (DMA) ..... AWC
Air Warfare Course (SAUO) ..... AWS
Air Warfare Division [*Navy*] ..... AWD
Air Warfare Instructor [*Navy*] [*British*] ..... AWI
Air Warfare Research Department [*Navy*] (MCD) ..... AWRD
Air Warfare Simulation [*Military*] ..... ACOSIM
Air Warfare Simulation (SAUS) ..... AWSIM
Air Warfare Simulation Complex (MCD) ..... AWSC
Air Warfare Simulation Model [*Military*] (IUSS) ..... AWSIM
Air Warfare Simulation System (SAUS) ..... AWSIMS
Air Warfare Systems Analysis ..... AWSA
Air Warfare Systems Development (DNAB) ..... AWSD
Air Warfare Training Division [*Navy*] [*British*] ..... AWTD
Air Warfare Training Division (SAUO) ..... AWTD
Air Warning ..... AW
Air Warning Service (SAUO) ..... AWngSvc
Air Warning Service (IAA) ..... AWSVC
Air Warning Squadron [*Marine Corps*] ..... AWS
Air Warning System ..... AWS
Air Washer (SAUS) ..... AW
Air Waybill [*Shipping*] ..... AWB
Air Waybill (EBF) ..... awb
Air Waybill/Consignment Note (SAUS) ..... AWB/CN
Air Weapon [*British military*] (DMA) ..... AW
Air Weapon Systems [*Air Force*] ..... AWS
Air Weapons Control System [*Air Force*] ..... AWCS
Air Weapons Controller ..... AWC
Air Weapons Group (SAUO) ..... AWG
Air Weapons Systems Management ..... AWSM
Air Weapons Systems Plan ..... AWSP
Air Weapons Training Installation (NATG) ..... AWTI
Air Weather Association (EA) ..... AWA
Air Weather Flight [*Military*] ..... AWF
Air Weather Group (SAUO) ..... AWG
Air Weather Network (SAUS) ..... AIRWEANET
Air Weather Network ..... AWN
Air Weather Officer (SAUS) ..... AWO
Air Weather Service [*Scott Air Force Base, IL*] (IAA) ..... AWEASVC
Air Weather Service [*Scott Air Force Base, IL*] ..... AWS
Air Weather Service Manual ..... AWSM
Air Weather Service Master Station Catalog (SAUS) ..... AWSMSC
Air Weather Service Office ..... AWSWO
Air Weather Service Regulation (COE) ..... AWSR
Air Weather Service Technical Library [*Air Force*] [*Information service or system*] (IID) ..... AWSTL
Air Weather Service, Technical Library, Scott AFB, IL [*OCLC symbol*] (OCLC) ..... SCA
Air Weather Service Training Guide ..... AWSTG
Air Weather Service Washington Office (ACAE) ..... AWSWO
Air Weather Wing (SAUO) ..... Air Wea Wg
Air West [*Canada*] [*ICAO designator*] (FAAC) ..... AWT
Air West Airlines [*ICAO designator*] (AD) ..... ZX
Air West Airlines, Inc. [*ICAO designator*] (FAAC) ..... LEP
Air Whitsunday [*Australia*] [*ICAO designator*] (FAAC) ..... RWS
Air Wing Commander ..... AWC
Air Wing Duty Officer (DNAB) ..... AWDO
Air Wing Staff [*Air Force*] ..... AWS
Air Wisconsin [*ICAO designator*] (FAAC) ..... AWI
Air Wisconsin [*Airline code*] ..... ZW
Air Works Incorporated (SAUO) ..... AWI
Air Workshop (SAUO) ..... AWks
Air World Company (SAUO) ..... AW Co
Air World Ltd. [*British*] [*FAA designator*] (FAAC) ..... AWD
Air Yendis Ltd. [*Zambia*] [*FAA designator*] (FAAC) ..... SYD
Air Youth of America (SAUO) ..... AYA
Air Yugoslavia (SAUS) ..... JR
Air Yugoslavia [*ICAO designator*] (FAAC) ..... YRG
Air Zaire SA [*Zaire*] [*ICAO designator*] (ICDA) ..... QC
Air Zaire, Societe [*ICAO designator*] (FAAC) ..... AZR
Air Zanzibar [*Tanzania*] [*ICAO designator*] (FAAC) ..... AZL
Air Zero ..... AZ
Air Zero Gas ..... AZG
Air Zimbabwe [*ICAO designator*] (FAAC) ..... AZW
Air Zimbabwe [*Zimbabwe*] [*ICAO designator*] (ICDA) ..... RH
Air Zimbabwe [*ICAO designator*] (AD) ..... UM
Air Zory [*Bulgaria*] [*FAA designator*] (FAAC) ..... MZA
Air-Aid-to-Intercept (SAUS) ..... AAI
Air-Air Forced Cooling (SAUS) ..... AAFA
Air-Air-Cooling (SAUS) ..... AAC
Air-Arming Impact Rocket (SAUS) ..... AIR
Air-Assisted Fuel Injection [*Automotive engineering*] ..... AAFI
Air-Augmented Propulsion for Short-Range Air Defense (MCD) ..... AAP/SHORAD
Air-Augmented Rocket ..... AAR
Air-Augmented Rocket Propulsion System ..... AARPS
Airavia [*France*] [*ICAO designator*] (FAAC) ..... IAV
Airbag Central Sensor [*Automotive safety*] ..... ACS
Air-Base Damage Assessment Model (SAUS) ..... ADAM
Airbase Survivability Program (SAUS) ..... ASP
Air-Based Electronics (MCD) ..... ABE
Air-based Free-Electron Laser (SAUS) ..... ABFEL
Airblast Fuel Injection Tube [*Gas turbine engine*] ..... AFIT
Airborne (IAA) ..... A
Airborne [*ICAO designator*] (FAAC) ..... AB
Airborne (AFM) ..... ABN
Airborne (ADWA) ..... abn
Airborne (ACAE) ..... A/BR
Airborne Acoustic Information System (Intelligence) ..... ACINF
Airborne Active Expendable Decoy (ACAE) ..... AAED
Airborne Activity Confinement Systems [*Environmental science*] (COE) ..... AACS
Airborne Activity Monitor [*Nuclear energy*] (NRCH) ..... AAM
Airborne Adaptive Controlled Phased Array Antenna System (ACAE) ..... ACPA
Airborne Advanced Communications System (SAUS) ..... AACS
Airborne Advanced Reconfigurable Computer System (PDAA) ..... ARCS
Airborne Advanced Standoff Jammer (ACAE) ..... ASOJ
Airborne Adverse Weather Weapons System (MCD) ..... AAWWS
Airborne Aerial System (SAUS) ..... AAS
Airborne Airfield Lighting System (SAUS) ..... AALS
Airborne Alert (AFM) ..... AA
Airborne Alert (SAUS) ..... A/A
Airborne Alert (IIA) ..... ABA
Airborne Alert Indoctrination (AFM) ..... AAI
Airborne Alert Weapon System ..... AAWS
Airborne Alternate Command Center (ACAE) ..... AACC
Airborne Alternate Command Echelon [*NATO*] (NATG) ..... AACE
Airborne and Communications Electronics Board (SAUO) ..... ACEBD
Airborne and Communications-Electronics Board [*Army*] (RDA) ..... ACEBD
Airborne and Electronics Board [*Army*] (MCD) ..... AEB
Airborne and Ground Communications Central (MCD) ..... AGCC
Airborne and Helicopter Division [*Aeroplane and Armament Experimental Establishment*] [*British*] ..... AHD
Airborne and Surface Early Warning ..... ASEW
Airborne Angular Position Sensor ..... AAPS
Airborne Antarctic Ozone Experiment [*Marine science*] (OSRA) ..... AAOE
Airborne Antenna System ..... AAS
Airborne Anti Sea Launched Ballistic Missile (ACAE) ..... AA/SLBM
Airborne Antiaircraft (SAUS) ..... ABAA
Airborne Antiaircraft Artillery (SAUO) ..... Abn AAA
Airborne Antiarmor Defense Concept (MCD) ..... AADC
Airborne Anti-Armour Defence (SAUS) ..... AAAD
Airborne Antiship Missile Defense (MCD) ..... AASMD
Airborne Anti-Ship Missile Defense (SAUS) ..... AASMD
Airborne Antisubmarine Warfare ..... AASW
Airborne Anti-Submarine Warfare Coordination Aircraft (IUSS) ..... AACA
Airborne Anti-Submarine Warfare Tactical Coordinator (IUSS) ..... AATC
Airborne Anti-Submarine-Launched Ballistic Missile [*Military*] (IUSS) ..... AASLBM

Airborne Antitank Armor Air Defense (SAUS) .... AAAAD
Airborne Antitank Armor Air Defense (MCD) .... AAAD
Airborne Arctic Stratospheric Expedition .... AASE
Airborne Arctic Stratospheric Experiment [*Marine science*] (OSRA) .... AASE
Airborne Area of Operation (SAUS) .... AAO
Airborne Argon Ion LASER .... AAIL
Airborne Armament Control [*Air Force*] (MCD) .... AAC
Airborne Armament Maintenance (ACAE) .... AAM
Airborne Assault (CINC) .... ABA
Airborne Assault Division (MCD) .... AAD
Airborne [*or Amphibious or Armored*] **Assault Vehicle** .... AAV
Airborne Associate Array Processor (SAUS) .... AAAP
Airborne Associative Array Processor .... AAAP
Airborne Astrographic Camera System [*Air Force*] (MCD) .... AACS
Airborne Attack Recorder (MCD) .... AAR
Airborne Audio Frequency Coder .... AAFC
Airborne Audio Visual Instrumentation System (ACAE) .... AVIS
Airborne Automatic Voice Communications System (MCD) .... AAVCRS
Airborne Automatic Voice Communications System (SAUS) .... AAVCS
Airborne Autonomous Orbit Determination System (ACAE) .... AAODS
Airborne Auxiliary Memory System .... AAMS
Airborne Auxiliary Power Plant (SAUS) .... AAPP
Airborne Auxiliary Power Unit .... AAPU
Airborne Backing Store .... ABS
Airborne Ballistic Missile Intercept System .... ABMIS
Airborne Ballistics Division [*NASA*] (KSC) .... ABD
Airborne Battalion Combat Team [*Army*] .... ABCT
Airborne Battlefield Command and Control (SAUS) .... ABCC
Airborne Battlefield Command and Control Center (SAA) ABC3
Airborne Battlefield Command and Control Center (MCD) .... ABCC
Airborne Battlefield Command and Control Center [*Air Force*] (AFM) .... ABCCC
Airborne Battlefield Light Equipment System [*Army*] .... ABLES
Airborne Beacon Electronic Test Set .... ABETS
Airborne Beacon Interference Locator (MCD) .... ABIL
Airborne Beacon Processing System .... ABPS
Airborne Beacon Processor .... ABP
Airborne Beam Control System (ACAE) .... ABCS
Airborne Bombing Evaluation .... ABE
Airborne Central Data Tape Recorder (MCD) .... ACDTR
Airborne Chromatograph for Atmospheric Trace Species [*Instrumentation*] .... ACATS
Airborne Cloud-Radiation Observing System (ARMP) .... ACROS
Airborne Collection Electronic Signals (SAUS) .... ACES
Airborne Collision Avoidance System (SAUS) .... ACAS
Airborne Collision Warning .... ACW
Airborne Collision-Avoidance System [*Later, TCAS*] .... ACAS
Airborne Combat Group (SAUO) .... Abn Cbt Gr
Airborne Combat Operations Center (SAUO) .... ACOC
Airborne COMINT DF System (SAUO) .... GUARDRAIL
Airborne Command (SAUO) .... ABC
Airborne Command (SAUO) .... A/B Comd
Airborne Command and Control Center (ROAS) .... ABCCC
Airborne Command & Control Squadron (SAUO) .... ACCS
Airborne Command and Control System .... ACCS
Airborne Command and Launch Subsystem (ACAE) .... ACALS
Airborne Command Center .... ABCC
Airborne Command Control Squadron [*Air Force*] (CINC) .... ACCS
Airborne Command Control Squadron (CCCA) .... ACCSQ
Airborne Command Control Squadron (SAUO) .... ACCSq
Airborne Command Element [*Air Force*] (DOMA) .... ACE
Airborne Command Post (MCD) .... ABCP
Airborne Command Post [*Air Force*] .... ABNCP
Airborne Command Post [*Air Force*] .... ACP
Airborne Command-Launch Control Subsystem (CAAL) .... ACLCS
Airborne Communication Relay Station [*Air Force*] .... ACRES
Airborne Communications and Electronics (MCD) .... ACE
Airborne Communications Center [*Military*] .... ABCC
AirBorne Communications, Command, and Control System (SAUS) .... ABCCS
Airborne Communications Location Identification and Collection System (SAUS) .... ACLICS
Airborne Communications Location Identification and Collection System .... ACLICS
Airborne Communications Mode Selector Control (ACAE) .... ACMSC
Airborne Communications Reconnaissance Platform .... ACRP
Airborne Communications Reconnaissance Program (AFM) .... ACRP
Airborne Communications Restoral Relay (SAUS) .... ACRR
Airborne Communications Squadron [*Air Force*] .... ACSQ
Airborne Computer (SAUS) .... ABC
Airborne Computer Unit (SAUS) .... ACU
Airborne Computing & Communications System (SAUS) .... ACCS
Airborne Contingency Operations Director (SAUS) .... AIRCOD
Airborne Control [*System*] .... ABC
Airborne Control Computer .... ACC
Airborne Control System (SAUS) .... ACS
Airborne Control Unit [*Telecommunications*] (TSSD) .... ACU
Airborne Controlled Intercept [*Air Force*] .... ACI
Airborne Cooperational Equipment .... ACE
Airborne Coordinating Group .... ACG
Airborne Coordination Group (SAUO) .... ACG
Airborne Corps (IUSS) .... ABC
Airborne Corps Operation Plan [*Military*] (AABC) .... ACOP
Airborne Countermeasures Environment and RADAR Target Simulation .... ACEARTS
Airborne Countermeasures Environment and Radar Target Simulation (or Simulator) (SAUS) .... ACEARTS
Airborne Crew Trainer (SAUS) .... ACT
Airborne Damage Assessment System (ACAE) .... ADAS
Airborne Data Acquisition and Recording System .... ADARS
Airborne Data Acquisition and Registration [*Trademark and service mark of Positive Systems, Inc.*] .... ADAR
Airborne Data Acquisition Multifunction System (MCD) .... ADAMS
Airborne Data Acquisition System .... ADAS
Airborne Data Analysis and Monitoring System (MCD) .... ADAMS
Airborne Data Automation (AFM) .... ADA
Airborne Data Insertion Unit (DNAB) .... ADIU
Airborne Data Link .... ADL
Airborne Data Link Equipment (SAUS) .... DOLLY
Airborne Data Link System .... ADLS
Airborne Data Link Terminal (SAUS) .... ADLT
Airborne Data Loader [*Aviation*] .... ADL
Airborne Data Marketing Ltd. [*Vancouver Stock Exchange symbol*] .... ABD
Airborne Data Processing Unit (SAUS) .... ADPU
Airborne Data Processor [*Air Force*] .... ADP
Airborne Data Recorder (MCD) .... ADR
Airborne Data Requisition Center (SAA) .... ADAC
Airborne Data System (ACAE) .... ADS
Airborne Data Terminal (MCD) .... ADT
Airborne Data Transfer System (MCD) .... ADTS
Airborne Deception Device .... ADD
Airborne Decommutation System (ACAE) .... ADS
Airborne Defense Control Center (ACAE) .... ADCC
Airborne Defensive Electronic Countermeasures (ACAE) .... ADEC
Airborne Designation and Discrimination Study (SAUS) .... ADDS
Airborne Designator (MCD) .... AD
Airborne Detection Discrimination Sensor .... ADDS
Airborne Development Aid Program (ACAE) .... ADAP
Airborne Digital Automatic Collection System (SAUS) .... ADACS
Airborne Digital Avionics Test System (ACAE) .... ADATS
Airborne Digital Computer [*Air Force*] .... ADC
Airborne Digital Data Acquisition System (SAUS) .... ADDAS
Airborne Digital Decoder (SAUS) .... ADD
Airborne Digital Instrumentation System .... ADIS
Airborne Digital Processing Unit .... ADPU
Airborne Digital Recorder .... ADR
Airborne Digital Recording System .... ADRS
Airborne Digital Symbology Generator (ACAE) .... ADSG
Airborne Digital Timer .... ADT
Airborne Digital Voltmeter .... ADV
Airborne Digitizing Unit (ACAE) .... ADU
Airborne Direct Air Support Center (SAUO) .... Abn DASC
Airborne Direct Air Support Center .... ABNDASC
Airborne Directed Energy Weapons (ACAE) .... ADEW
Airborne Direction Finder (MCD) .... ADF
Airborne Display Electrical Management System (MCD) .... ADEMS
airborne division (SAUO) .... AB Div; A/B Div
Airborne Division (SAUO) .... AbnDiv
Airborne Division, Territorial Army (SAUO) .... ADTA
Airborne Doppler Lidar System (SAUS) .... ADLS
Airborne Doppler Velocity Altitude Navigation Compass Equipment (MCD) .... ADVANCE
Airborne Drone Missile Target [*DOD missile designation*] (MCD) .... BQM
Airborne Dual Detector Indicator (MCD) .... ADDI
Airborne Dual-channel Variable Input Severe Environmental Recorder (SAUS) .... ADVISER
Airborne Dual-Channel Variable Input Severe Environmental Recorder/ Reproducer [*Air Force*] (MCD) .... ADVISER
Airborne Dual-frequency Microwave Radiometer/Scatterometer (SAUS) .... ADMSR
Airborne Dynamic Alignment System (MCD) .... ADAS
Airborne Early Control and Warning Squadron (SAUO) .... AECWRon
Airborne Early Control and Warning Wing (SAUO) .... AECWWg
Airborne Early Warning Aircraft .... AEWA
Airborne Early Warning and Control [*Army*] (AFM) .... AEW & C
Airborne Early Warning and Control [*Army*] (AABC) .... AEWC
Airborne Early Warning and Control [*Air Force*] (IAA) .... AEWCON
Airborne Early Warning and Control Squadron [*Air Force*] .... AEW & CSq
Airborne Early Warning and Control Squadron (SAUS) .... AEW&CSq
Airborne Early Warning and Control Wing (SAUS) .... AEW&Con Wg
Airborne Early Warning and Control Wing (SAUO) .... AEW & Con Wg
Airborne Early Warning and Interceptor Control System .... AEWICS
Airborne Early Warning Combat Air Patrol (NVT) .... AEWCAP
Airborne Early Warning Control Center [*Military*] (IUSS) .... AEWCC
Airborne Early Warning Fighter .... AEWF
Airborne Early Warning Ground Integration Segment (SAUS) .... AEGIS
Airborne Early Warning RADAR [*Air Force*] (IAA) .... AEWRADAR
Airborne Early Warning Squadron .... AEWRON
Airborne Early Warning Squadron (SAUO) .... AEWRon
Airborne Early Warning Squadron (SAUO) .... AEW Sq
Airborne [*or Aircraft*] **Early Warning Station** .... AEW
Airborne Early Warning Training Unit .... AEWTU
Airborne Early Warning Wing (MUGU) .... AEWW
Airborne Early Warning Wing, Pacific Fleet (ACAE) .... AEWINGPAC
Airborne Early Warning/Ground Integration Segment .... AEGIS
Airborne Electrical Support Equipment (NAKS) .... AESE
Airborne Electrical Test Set (SAUS) .... ABETS
Airborne Electromagnetic (SAUS) .... AEM
Airborne Electromechanical Bombing .... AEMB
Airborne Electron Beam Recorder .... AEBR
Airborne Electronic Equipment Modification .... AEEM
Airborne Electronic LASER System .... AELS

Airborne Electronic Ranging Instrumentation System	AERIS
Airborne Electronic Sensor Operator [Canadian Navy]	AESO
Airborne Electronic Terrain Map System (MCD)	AETMS
Airborne Electronic Warfare (NG)	AEW
Airborne Electronic Warfare School (SAUO)	AELW
Airborne Electronic Warfare School (SAUS)	AELW School
Airborne Electronics (MCD)	AE
Airborne Electronics Operator (IAA)	AEO
Airborne Electronics Research Activity [Lakehurst, NJ] [United States Army Communications-Electronics Command] (GRD)	AERA
Airborne Electronics Unit (SAUS)	AEU
Airborne Electronics Warfare (SAUS)	AELW
Airborne Electronics Warfare Course (DNAB)	AELW
Airborne Electro-optical Special Operations Payload (SAUS)	AESOP
Airborne ELINT Emitter Location System (MCD)	AEELS
Airborne Emergency Actions Officer [SAC]	AEAO
Airborne Emergency Alternate Command Post (CINC)	AEACP
Airborne Emergency Reaction Unit	ABERU
Airborne Emission Spectrometer (ARMP)	AES
Airborne Engineer Aviation Battalion (SAUO)	A/B Engr Avn Bn
Airborne Engineer Battalion (SAUO)	Abn Engr Bn
Airborne Engineer Contraction Equipment (MCD)	AECE
Airborne Environmental Reporting System	AERS
Airborne Equipment (AAG)	A/BE
Airborne Equipment Division [Bureau of Aeronautics; later, NASC] [Navy]	AE
Airborne Equipment Failure [Air Force]	AEF
Airborne Equipment for Remote Imaging of the Environment (SAUS)	AERIE
Airborne Equipment Repair Squadron (MCD)	AERS
Airborne Evaluation Equipment (IEEE)	AEE
Airborne Expendable Bathythermograph	AXBT
Airborne Expendable Current Profiler [Marine science] (OSRA)	AXCP
Airborne Expendable Rocket System (MCD)	AERS
Airborne Experiment to Study Ozone Production [Marine science] (OSRA)	AESOP
Airborne Express, Inc. [ICAO designator] (FAAC)	ABX
Airborne Extended Range	AER
Airborne Field Mill Program (SAUS)	ABFM
Airborne Fill-and-Drain (AAG)	A/BF&D
Airborne Fill-and-Drain (AAG)	A/B F & D
Airborne Fire Control RADAR Set (MCD)	AFCRS
Airborne Fire Fighting Equipment [Air Force] (MCD)	AFFE
Airborne Fixed Array RADAR (MSA)	AFAR
Airborne Flat Plate Array	AFPA
Airborne Flight Detection Measurement System (MCD)	AFDMS
Airborne Flight Information Service (HLLA)	AFIS
Airborne Flight Test System (MCD)	AFTS
Airborne Flight Training Command (SAUO)	AFTC
Airborne Force, Army Air Base (SAUO)	ABFAAB
Airborne Forces Experimental Establishment (SAUO)	AFEE
Airborne Forces Liaison Officer (SAUS)	AFLO
Airborne Forces Security Fund (SAUO)	AFSF
Airborne Formation Flight Simulator (MCD)	AFFSIM
Airborne Forward Air Controller	AFAC
Airborne Forward Delivery Airfield Group	AFDAG
Airborne Frauenhofer Line Discriminator (SAUS)	AFLD
Airborne Fraunhofer Line Discriminator	AFLD
Airborne Freight [NYSE symbol] (TTSB)	ABF
Airborne Freight Corp. [NYSE symbol] (SPSG)	ABF
Airborne Freight Corp. (EFIS)	ABX
Airborne Freight Corp. [Associated Press] (SAG)	AirFrt
Airborne Frequency Doubler	AFD
Airborne Frequency Multiplexing System	AFMS
Airborne Fuze Test Jammer (CAAL)	AFTJ
Airborne Gamma-Ray Spectrometer (SAUS)	AGRS
Airborne Gas Accumulator (ACAE)	AGA
Airborne General Illumination Light	AGIL
Airborne Ground Fire Locating System	AGFLS
Airborne Ground Fire Locator	AGFL
Airborne Gun-Laying	AGL
Airborne Gun-Laying for Turrets	AGLT
Airborne Gun-Laying RADAR (AFM)	AGLR
Airborne Gunsight	AGS
Airborne Hardware Simulator (MCD)	AHS
Airborne Heading-Attitude Reference System (ACAE)	AHARS
Airborne Height-Surveillance RADAR (IAA)	AHSR
Airborne Helmet Mounted Display	AHMD
Airborne HF/VHF/UHF Intercept And Location System (SAUO)	GUARDRAIL V
Airborne Identification Kit (DEN)	ABK
Airborne Identification, Mark XII System	AIMS
Airborne Identification, Mobile System [Military] (NVT)	AIMS
Airborne Image Transmission (ACAE)	ABIT
Airborne Imagery Transmission [Military] (IUSS)	ABIT
Airborne Imaging Microwave Radiometer (SAUS)	AIMR
Airborne Imaging Radar (SAUS)	AIR
Airborne Imaging Spectrometer	AIS
Airborne Imaging Spectrometer for Different Applications (SAUS)	AISA
Airborne Inertial Data System (SAUS)	AIDS
Airborne Inertial Navigation System (SAUS)	AINS
Airborne Infantry [Military] (SAA)	ABINF
Airborne Infantry [Military]	ABNINF
Airborne Infantry (SAUO)	AbnInf
Airborne Infantry Combat Group (SAUO)	AICG
Airborne Infantry Regiment (SAUO)	AIR
Airborne Information Correlation (MCD)	AIC
Airborne Information Correlation Program (ACAE)	AIC

Airborne Information Display System (SAUS)	AIDS
Airborne Information Systems Squadron (SAUO)	AISS
Airborne Infrared Decoy Evaluation System (MCD)	AIDES
Airborne Infrared Early Warning	AIREW
Airborne Infrared Equipment for Target Analysis	AIETA
Airborne Infrared Gunfire Locator	AIRGLO
Airborne Infrared Linescan System (SAUS)	AIRSS
Airborne Infrared Live Scanner	AILS
Airborne Infrared Mapper	AIM
Airborne Infrared Mapper	AIRM
Airborne Infrared Measurement Instrument	AIMI
Airborne Infrared Observatory [NASA]	AIO
Airborne Infrared Radiometer System	AIRS
Airborne Infrared Spectrometer	AIS
Airborne Infrared Surveillance Set	AISS
Airborne Initial Data System (SAUS)	Aids
Airborne Initiation System	AIS
Airborne Inlet Control System (ACAE)	AICS
Airborne Insertion Display Equipment	AIDE
Airborne Installation Unit (SAUS)	AIU
Airborne Institute Laboratories, Melville, NY [Library symbol] [Library of Congress] (LCLS)	NMelA
Airborne Instrument Landing Approach system (SAUS)	AILA
Airborne Instrumentation Platform	AIP
Airborne Instrumentation Research Project (SAUS)	AIRP
Airborne Instrumentation Subsystem (MCD)	AIS
Airborne Instrumentation Subsystem Internal (MCD)	AISI
Airborne Instrumentation System (ACAE)	AIS
Airborne Instruments Laboratories (or Laboratory) (SAUO)	AIL
Airborne Instruments Laboratory [Mineola, NY]	AIL
Airborne Instruments Laboratory Approach	AILA
Airborne Integrated Antenna System (SAUS)	AIAS
Airborne Integrated Data System	AIDS
Airborne Integrated Display System (SAUS)	AIDS
Airborne Integrated Flight Test Data System [NASA]	AIFTDS
Airborne Integrated Light Avionics System	AILAS
Airborne Integrated Maintenance System	AIMS
Airborne Integrated Mapping System (GEOI)	AIMS
Airborne Integrated Reconnaissance System (MCD)	AIRS
Airborne Integration Area (MCD)	AIA
Airborne Intelligent Display (MCD)	AID
Airborne Intercept [RADAR] [Air Force] (AFM)	AI
Airborne Intercept (SAUS)	I
Airborne Intercept Missile (ACAE)	AIM
Airborne Intercept Missile Evaluation (MCD)	AIMEVAL
Airborne Intercept Radar (SAUS)	AIR
Airborne Intercept RADAR (MED)	AI radar
Airborne Interception and Gun Direction (SAUS)	AIGD
Airborne Interception Fire Control System [Air Force]	AIFCS
Airborne Interception of Aircraft (SAUS)	AIA
Airborne Interception RADAR and Pilot's Attack Sight System	AIRPASS
Airborne Interceptor All Weather (ACAE)	AIWX
Airborne Interceptor Day (ACAE)	AIDAY
Airborne Interceptor Equipment	AIE
Airborne Interceptor Missile (SAA)	AIM
Airborne Interceptor Officer (MCD)	AIO
Airborne Interceptor RADAR	AIR
Airborne Interceptor Radar Counter Low Observables (ACAE)	AIRCLOP
Airborne Interceptor Rocket (AFM)	AIR
Airborne Intercommunication System (ACAE)	AICS
Airborne Intruder Engagement System (ACAE)	AIES
Airborne Investigations of Mesoscale Convective Systems (SAUS)	AIMCS
Airborne Ion Laser (SAUS)	AAIL
Airborne Ionospheric Observatory (MCD)	AIO
Airborne LASER (MCD)	ABL
Airborne LASER Bathymeter (PDAA)	ALB
Airborne Laser Densitometer (ACAE)	ALD
Airborne Laser Designator Pod (SAUS)	ALDP
Airborne Laser Electronic warfare Receiver Training System (SAUS)	ALERTS
Airborne LASER Equipment Real-Time Surveillance	ALERTS
Airborne LASER Experiment [Strategic Defense Initiative]	ALE
Airborne LASER Illuminator	ALI
Airborne LASER Illuminator Ranging and Tracking System	ALIRATS
Airborne LASER Laboratory [Air Force]	ALL
Airborne LASER Locator Designator (MCD)	ALLD
Airborne Laser Locator Designator System (ACAE)	ALLDS
Airborne Laser Polarization Sensor (SAUS)	ALPS
Airborne LASER Propagation Experiment (MCD)	ALPE
Airborne Laser Radar Mine Sensor (SAUS)	ALARMS
Airborne LASER Range-Finder	ALR
Airborne Laser Rangefinder and Designator (SAUS)	ALRAD
Airborne Laser Ranging System for Measuring Crustal Dynamics (SAUS)	ALRS
Airborne LASER Receiver Module (MCD)	ALARM
Airborne LASER System (SAUS)	ALS
Airborne Laser Terrain Scanner (SAUS)	ALTS
Airborne LASER Tracker [System]	ALT
Airborne Launch (ACAE)	A/L
Airborne Launch Control and Recovery System (MCD)	ALCARS
Airborne Launch Control Center	ALCC
Airborne Launch Control System [Air Force] (MCD)	ALCS
Airborne Launching [Aviation] (FAAC)	ABLCHG
Airborne Law Enforcement Association (NTPA)	ALEA
Airborne Lidar Bathymetry Technical Center of Expertise [US Army Corps of Engineers]	ALBTCX

Airborne Lidar Observations and Hawaiian Airglow (SAUS) ... ALOHA
Airborne LIDAR [*Light Detection and Ranging*] **Oceanographic Probing Experiment** [*NASA*] ... ALOPE
Airborne LIDAR Oceanographic Probing Experiment (SAUS) ... ALOPE
Airborne LIDAR Plume and Haze Analyzer (SAUS) ... ALPHA-1
Airborne Light Observation System (SAUS) ... ALOS
Airborne Light Optical Fiber Technology ... ALOFT
Airborne Light Regiment (SAUO) ... AB Lt Reg
Airborne Lighting System [*Air Force*] (MCD) ... AIRLIGHT
Airborne Lightweight Optical Tracker (SAUS) ... ALOT
Airborne Lightweight Optical Tracking [*Air Force*] ... ALOT
Airborne Lightweight Optical Tracking System [*Air Force*] ... ALOTS
Airborne Line Discriminator ... ALD
Airborne Line Printer ... ALP
Airborne Linescan Image Processor (SAUS) ... ALICE
Airborne Link Segment [*Military*] (IUSS) ... ALS
Airborne Live Scanner ... ALS
Airborne Location and Strike System (MCD) ... ALSS
Airborne Locator Laser Designator (SAUS) ... ALLD
Airborne Longe-Range Intercept (SAUS) ... ALRI
Airborne Long-Range Input (KSC) ... ALRI
Airborne Long-Range Input Electronic (SAUS) ... ALRIE
Airborne Long-Range Input System (SAA) ... ALRIS
Airborne Long-Range Intercept ... ALRI
Airborne Long-Range RADAR Input (MUGU) ... ALRRI
Airborne Low-Frequency SONAR [*Sound Navigation and Ranging*] [*Navy*] ... ALFS
Airborne Low-Frequency Sonar (SAUS) ... ALFS
Airborne Magnetic Recorder ... AMR
Airborne Maintenance Battalion (SAUO) ... Abn Maint Bn
Airborne Maintenance System ... AMS
Airborne Maritime Situation Control System (SAUS) ... AMASCOS
Airborne Maritime Situation Control System (SAUS) ... AMSCOS
Airborne Maritime Surveillance (SAUS) ... AMS
Airborne Measurement System (SAUS) ... AMS
Airborne Microwave Moisture Sounder (SAUS) ... AMMS
Airborne Microwave Radiometer System (SAUS) ... AMRS
Airborne Microwave Rain-Scatterometer/Radiometer (SAUS) ... AMRS
Airborne Microwave Refractometer (CAAL) ... AMR
Airborne Microwave Scattermeter [*For measuring wind speed and direction*] ... AMSCAT
Airborne Microwave Scatterometer (SAUS) ... AMSCAT
Airborne Mine Countermeasure Equipment ... AMCM
Airborne Mine Countermeasure System (NG) ... AMCMS
Airborne Mine Countermeasures (SAUS) ... AMCM
Airborne Mine Detection and Surveillance System [*Navy*] (DOMA) ... AMDAS
Airborne Mine Detection and Surveillance System (SAUS) ... AMDASS
Airborne Mine Detection System (MCD) ... AMDS
Airborne Mine Detection System (ACAE) ... AMIDS
Airborne Mine Neutralization Equipment (DWSG) ... AMNE
Airborne Mine Neutralization System (DOMA) ... AMNSYS
Airborne Minefield Detection and Reconnaissance System (SAUS) ... AMIDARS
Airborne Minefield Detection System (SAUS) ... AMIDS
Airborne Minefield Detector System (MCD) ... AMIDS
Airborne Missile Control Subsystem ... AMCSS
Airborne Missile Control System ... AMCS
Airborne Missile Maintenance Squadron [*Air Force*] ... AMMSq
Airborne Missions and Applications Division [*Ames Research Center*] (GEOI) ... AMAD
Airborne Mode Control ... AMC
Airborne Modular Integrated System (MCD) ... AMIS
Airborne Molecular Contamination (AAEL) ... AMC
Airborne Moving Attack Target (SAA) ... AMAT
Airborne Moving Target Attack ... AMTA
Airborne Moving Target Indicator (CAAL) ... AMTI
Airborne Moving Target Indicator System (SAUS) ... AMTIS
Airborne Multi Purpose Avionics Computer (ACAE) ... AMPAC
Airborne Multi-role Solid-state Active-array Radar (SAUS) ... AMSAR
Airborne Multispectral Scanner (SAUS) ... AMSS
Airborne National Command Force (SAUS) ... ABNCF
Airborne National Command Force [*DoD*] ... ABNCP
Airborne National Command Post (SAUO) ... Abn CP
Airborne Navigation Computer ... ANC
Airborne Navigation Sensor ... ANS
Airborne Navigation System (SAUS) ... ANS
Airborne Navigational Multiple Indicators (MCD) ... ANMI
Airborne Night Classification System (MCD) ... ANCS
Airborne Night Observation Device (MCD) ... ANOD
Airborne Night Television System [*Obsolete*] [*Army*] (MCD) ... ANTS
Airborne Nuclear Operations Center (ACAE) ... ABNOC
Airborne Observation Adjunct (ACAE) ... AOA
Airborne Observation Post (SAUO) ... AOP
Airborne Observer [*Military*] (VNW) ... AO
Airborne Ocean Colour Imager (SAUS) ... AOCI
Airborne Oceanographic Lidar (SAUS) ... AOL
Airborne Oceanographic LIDAR [*Light Detection and Ranging*] (PDAA) ... AOL
Airborne of Sweden AB [*ICAO designator*] (FAAC) ... MIW
Airborne Oil Surveillance System ... AOSS
Airborne Operation (SAUS) ... AIROP
Airborne Operational Computer Program (MCD) ... AOCP
Airborne Operational Equipment ... AOE
Airborne Operations Center (SAUO) ... Abn CP
Airborne Operations Center [*NATO*] (NATG) ... ABNOC
Airborne Optical Adjunct [*Army*] (RDA) ... AOA
Airborne Optical Beacon ... AOB
Airborne Optical Platform ... AOP
Airborne Optical Sensor [*Military*] (SDI) ... AOS
Airborne Optical Sensor Adjunct (SAUS) ... AOSA
Airborne Optical Surveillance (MCD) ... AOS
Airborne Optical System (LAIN) ... AOS
Airborne Optics (ACAE) ... AO
Airborne over the Horizon Radar (ACAE) ... AOHR
Airborne Overland RADAR ... AOR
Airborne Parabolic Arc Computer ... APAC
Airborne Particle Monitoring System (MCD) ... APMS
Airborne Particulate and Precipitation Data (SAUS) ... ERFD
Airborne Passive Indentification System (ACAE) ... APIS
Airborne Passive Infrared Imaging System (ACAE) ... APIIS
Airborne Photography of the Eclipse of the Quiet Sun ... APEQS
Airborne Platform (DWSG) ... AP
Airborne Platform Versus Airbreathing Strategic Threats (MCD) ... APVAST
Airborne Pointer and Tracker ... APT
Airborne Pointing and Tracking System (ACAE) ... APTS
Airborne Position and Altitude Camera System (OA) ... APACS
Airborne Positive Hostile Indentification System (ACAE) ... APHIDS
Airborne Power Adapter ... APA
Airborne Power Supply (KSC) ... APS
Airborne Power System (IAA) ... APS
Airborne Power Unit (IAA) ... APU
Airborne Precision Emitter Location System (MCD) ... APELS
Airborne Processing Unit ... APU
Airborne Profile Recorder (SAUS) ... APR
Airborne Propellant System (AAG) ... A/BPS
Airborne Provisioning Parts Breakdown ... APPB
Airborne Proximity Warning Indicator (DA) ... APWI
Airborne Public Correspondence (SAUS) ... APC
Airborne Pulse Search RADAR after Passing [*Aviation*] (FAAC) ... APS
Airborne RADAR and Doppler ... ARAD
Airborne Radar and Radio Installation Team (SAUS) ... ABNRADARARADIOINSTLTM
Airborne RADAR Approach (AFM) ... ARA
Airborne RADAR Approach Control (DNAB) ... ARAC
Airborne Radar Attachement (SAUS) ... ARA
Airborne Radar Control (SAUO) ... ARC
Airborne Radar Demonstrator System (SAUS) ... ARDS
Airborne Radar Extension (SAUS) ... ARE
Airborne Radar for Detecting Surface Vessels (SAUS) ... ASV
Airborne RADAR Inflight Monitoring System ... ARIMS
Airborne Radar Jamming System (ACAE) ... AJARS
Airborne RADAR Jamming System (MCD) ... ARJS
Airborne RADAR Navigational Aid (MCD) ... ARN
Airborne Radar Optical System (ACAE) ... AROS
Airborne RADAR Orbital Determination System ... ARODS
Airborne RADAR Platform [*Air Force*] ... ARP
Airborne RADAR Target Simulator ... ARTS
Airborne Radar Technician (SAUS) ... ART
Airborne RADAR Unit [*Aviation*] (FAAC) ... ARU
Airborne RADARscope Used in NAVAR (SAUS) ... NAVASCOPE
Airborne Radiation Detection and Fixing [*Military*] ... ARDF
Airborne Radiation Thermometer ... ART
Airborne Radio & Intercom Control system (SAUS) ... ARIC
Airborne Radio Communicating ... ARC
Airborne Radio Communicating (or Communication) (SAUS) ... ARC
Airborne Radio Control ... ARC
Airborne Radio Direction Finding (AFM) ... ARDF
Airborne Radio Direction Finding (SAUS) ... ARDF
Airborne Radio Installation [*RADAR*] ... ARI
Airborne Radio Instrument ... ARI
Airborne Radio Maintenance Team (SAUS) ... ABNRADIOMAINTTM
Airborne Radio Navigation ... ARN
Airborne Radio Receiver ... ARR
Airborne Radioactivity Removal System (NRCH) ... ARRS
Airborne Rain Mapping Radar (SAUS) ... ARMAR
Airborne Range Instrumentation Aircraft (SAUS) ... ARIA
Airborne Range Instrumentation Station ... ARIS
Airborne Range Only [*RADAR ranging set for use with various gun computers*] ... ARO
Airborne Ranging and Orbit Determination (SAUS) ... AROD
Airborne Ranging and Orbit Determination System ... AROD
Airborne Ranging and Orbit Determination System (SAUS) ... AROD System
Airborne Ranging System ... ARS
Airborne Rapid-Blooming Off-Board Chaff (DOMA) ... AIRBOC
Airborne Rapid-Scan Spectrometer ... ARS
Airborne Real-Time Instrumentation System (MCD) ... ARTIS
Airborne Recce Low (DOMA) ... ARL
Airborne Receiver ... AR
Airborne Receiving Antenna ... ARA
Airborne Reconnaissance Integrated Electronic System (MCD) ... ARIES
Airborne Reconnaissance Low programme (SAUS) ... ARL
Airborne Reconnaissance-Low (SAUS) ... AR-L
Airborne Recording & Training System (SAUS) ... ARTS
Airborne Reference Noise Source (MCD) ... ARNS
Airborne Reference RADAR (PDAA) ... ARR
Airborne Refrigeration System ... ARS
Airborne Regimental Combat Team (SAUO) ... ARCT
Airborne Relay [*Military*] (IUSS) ... ABR
Airborne Relay Facility (MCD) ... ARF
Airborne Relay Stations (MCD) ... ARS
Airborne Relay System (ACAE) ... ARS
Airborne Relay Vehicle ... ARV
Airborne Remote Control Officer (SAUS) ... ARCO
Airborne Remote Control Operator (DNAB) ... ARCO

Airborne Remote Mapping (GEOI) .... ARM
Airborne Remote Sensing Oceanography Project .... ARSOP
Airborne Remote Sensing System [*Coast Guard*] (MCD) .... ARSS
Airborne Remotely Operated Device [*Marine Corps*] .... AROD
Airborne Research Australia .... ARA
Airborne Research Capsule .... ARC
Airborne Research Instrumentation System (SAUS) .... ARIS
Airborne Research Integration Engineering Support (MCD) .... ARIES
Airborne Resupply (CINC) .... ABR
Airborne Rocket Artillery (SAUS) .... ARA
Airborne Ruggedized Memory System (SAUS) .... ARMS
Airborne Sample Data Reduction (SAUS) .... ASDR
Airborne Satellite Receiving Station .... ASRS
Airborne Satellite Receiving System (SAUS) .... ASRS
Airborne Scanning Radiometer .... ASR
Airborne Science Office (SAUO) .... ASO
Airborne Science Program [*NASA*] (NASA) .... ASP
Airborne Science Shuttle [*or Spacelab*] **Experiment System Simulation** [*NASA*] (MCD) .... ASSESS
Airborne Science Shuttle Experiment System Simulation (SAUS) .... ASSESS
Airborne Science Shuttle Experiments System Simulation [*NASA*] (NASA) .... ASSESS
Airborne Science Spacelab Experiments-Simulation System (SAUS) .... ASSESS
Airborne Sea Swell Recorder (SAUS) .... ASSR
Airborne Search and Attack Plotter .... ABSAP
Airborne Search & Rescue System (SAUS) .... ASARS
Airborne Search Equipment (SAUS) .... ase
Airborne Search Equipment .... ASE
Airborne Search for Surface Vessels (SAUS) .... ASV
Airborne Search Target Attack RADAR (MCD) .... ASTAR
Airborne Sea/Swell Recorder [*Oceanography*] (MSC) .... ASSR
Airborne Seeker Evaluation Test Set (SAUS) .... ASETS
Airborne Seeker Evaluation Test System [*Air Force*] .... ASETS
Airborne Self-Defence Laser (SAUS) .... ASDL
Airborne Self-Propelled Gun .... ASU
Airborne Self-Protection Jammer (MCD) .... ASPJ
Airborne Self-Protection Jammer Rack Assembly (DWSG) .... ASPJRA
Airborne Sensor Platform (MCD) .... ASP
Airborne Shared Aperture Program (SAUS) .... ASAP
Airborne SHORAD Target Acquisition Radar (SAUS) .... S-STAR
Airborne SIGINT Reconnaissance Program (MCD) .... ASRP
Airborne Signal Battalion (IAA) .... ABNSIGBN
Airborne Signal Battalion (SAUO) .... Abn Sig Bn
Airborne Software Change (MCD) .... ASC
Airborne Sonobuoy Communications Center .... ASCC
Airborne Sonobuoy Communications Link .... ASCL
Airborne Southern Hemisphere Ozone Expedition [*Marine science*] (OSRA) .... ASHOE
Airborne Southern Hemisphere Ozone Experiment (SAUS) .... ASHOE
Airborne Special Bombing .... ASB
Airborne Special-Type Auxiliary Assembly (MCD) .... ASTAA
Airborne Special-Type Navigational Aid (MCD) .... ASN
Airborne Spiral Gun (ACAE) .... ASG
Airborne Stabilized Viewing System .... ASVS
Airborne Standoff Minefield Detection System [*Military*] (RDA) .... ASTAMIDS
Airborne Stand-Off Radar (SAUS) .... ASTOR
Airborne Strategic Communication System (IUSS) .... ASCS
Airborne Subsystem (ACAE) .... ABSS
Airborne Supply and Transport Company (SAUO) .... Abn Sup & Trans Co
Airborne Support Equipment (MCD) .... ASE
Airborne Support Platform [*Army*] .... ASP
Airborne Surface Vessel Detection [*RADAR device*] .... ASV
Airborne Surface Vessel Detection (SAUS) .... ASV Detection
Airborne Surveillance, Airborne Control (SAUS) .... ASAC
Airborne Surveillance and Control System [*ASD*] .... ASACS
Airborne Surveillance and Intercept Defense System .... ASIDS
Airborne Surveillance and Reconnaissance System (ACAE) .... ASARS
Airborne Surveillance and Target Acquisition (SAA) .... AS & TA
Airborne Surveillance and Warning Control System (SAUS) .... ASWACS
Airborne Surveillance, Ground Control (SAUS) .... ASGC
Airborne Surveillance RADAR (IEEE) .... ASR
Airborne Surveillance Set .... ASS
Airborne Surveillance Testbed [*Military*] (MUSM) .... AST
Airborne Surveillance Warning and Control RADAR [*ASD/ADC*] .... ASWCR
Airborne Survivable Tracking System (ACAE) .... ASTS
Airborne Synthetic Aperture RADAR [*Instrumentation*] .... AIRSAR
Airborne Synthetic Aperture Radar System (CCCA) .... ASARS
Airborne System for Evaluation and Testing (ACAE) .... ASSET
Airborne System, Gun (SAUS) .... ASG
Airborne Systems Functional Test Stand (IAA) .... ASFTS
Airborne Systems Group (ACAE) .... ASG
Airborne Systems Laboratory (ACAE) .... ASL
Airborne Systems Support Center .... ASSC
Airborne Tactical Air Battle Control System .... ATABCS
Airborne Tactical Air Command and Control System (SAUS) .... ATACCS
Airborne Tactical Air Control Capability [*Air Force*] (AFM) .... ATACC
Airborne Tactical Air Coordinator [*Navy*] (NVT) .... ATAC
Airborne Tactical Air Support Team (ACAE) .... ATAST
Airborne Tactical Command System [*Formerly, ATDS*] (MCD) .... ATCS
Airborne Tactical Control and Surveillance (ACAE) .... ATCAS
Airborne Tactical Data Processing System .... ATDPS
Airborne Tactical Data System [*Later, ATCS*] .... ATDS
Airborne Tactical Jamming System [*Air Force*] .... ATJS
Airborne Tanker, Boom (NVT) .... TAB
Airborne Tanker, Drogue (NVT) .... TAD
Airborne Tanker, General (NVT) .... TAG
Airborne Target Acquisition and Fire Control System (MCD) .... ATAFCS
Airborne Target Acquisition Control System (MCD) .... ATACS
Airborne Target Area (ACAE) .... ATA
Airborne Target Assessment System (ACAE) .... ATAS
Airborne Target Augmenter .... ATA
Airborne Target Augmeter (SAUS) .... ATA
Airborne Target Hand-off System (SAUS) .... ATHS
Airborne Target Handover System [*Military*] (DOMA) .... ATHS
Airborne Targeting Low Altitude Navigation Thermal Imaging & Cueing (SAUS) .... ATLANTIC
Airborne Task Force .... ABTF
Airborne Technical Data System (SAUS) .... ATDS
Airborne Teletypewriter Equipment .... ATE
Airborne Terminal (SAUS) .... AIRTERM
Airborne Test Bed .... ATB
Airborne Test Bed Mode Control .... ATBMC
Airborne Test Bed Turret .... ATBT
Airborne Test Conductor (MUGU) .... ATC
Airborne Test Equipment (MCD) .... ATE
Airborne Test Instrumentation System [*Air Force*] (MCD) .... ATIS
Airborne Test Reactor (SAA) .... ATR
Airborne Test Safety Board (MCD) .... ATSB
Airborne Thematic Mapper (SAUS) .... ATM
Airborne Time-Frequency Range-Altitude Monitor (SAUS) .... ATFRAM
Airborne Time/Frequency Range/Altitude Monitor (MCD) .... ATFRAM
Airborne TOW [*Tube-Launched, Optically Tracked, Wire-Guided Weapon*] **USAREUR Repair Facility** [*United States Army, Europe*] (MCD) .... ATURF
Airborne Towed Array Experimental Modules (ACAE) .... AIRTASS
Airborne Towed Array SONAR System (MCD) .... AIRTASS
Airborne Toxic Control Measure .... ATCM
Airborne Toxic Elements and Organic Species .... ATEOS
Airborne Track Illuminator [*Military*] (DOMA) .... ATI
Airborne Tracking (MCD) .... ABT
Airborne Tracking, Acquisition, and Recognition .... ATAR
Airborne Tracking, Acquisition & Recognition (SAUS) .... ATAR
Airborne Tracking LASER Identification System .... ATLIS
Airborne Traffic and Situation Display (SAUS) .... ATSD
Airborne Traffic Situation Display [*FAA*] .... ATSD
Airborne Transmitter Control Center (SAUO) .... ATCC
Airborne Transponder Subsystem .... ABTSS
Airborne Troops [*British and Canadian*] [*World War II*] .... airtps
Airborne Turnable Laser Absorption Spectrometer (CARB) .... ATLAS
Airborne Two-Way Acoustic and Control System (MCD) .... ATAC
Airborne Ultraviolet LASER .... AUVL
Airborne Uninhabited Fighter (SAUS) .... AUF
Airborne Unit .... AU
Airborne Vapour Monitor (SAUS) .... AVM
Airborne Vehicle Equipment (MCD) .... AVE
Airborne Vehicle Identification .... AVI
Airborne Vehicle Identification (AABC) .... AVID
Airborne Vehicle Identification System (ACAE) .... AVID
Airborne Very Low Frequency (SAUS) .... AVLF
Airborne Very-Low-Frequency (NG) .... AVLF
Airborne Vibration Monitor (NG) .... AVM
Airborne Video Recorder [*Automotive engineering*] .... AVR
Airborne Video Recording System (SAUS) .... AVRS
Airborne Video Tape Recorder (MCD) .... AVTR
Airborne Videocassette Tape Recorder (SAUS) .... AVTR
Airborne Viewing System .... AVS
Airborne Visible and Infrared Data Processing System (SAUS) .... AIR
Airborne Visible and Infrared Imaging Spectrometer (SAUS) .... AVIRIS
Airborne Visible-Infrared Imaging Spectrometer .... AVIRIS
Airborne Visible-LASER Optical-Communications .... AVLOC
Airborne V/STOL [*Vertical/Short Takeoff and Landing*] **Simulator** (MCD) .... AVS
Airborne Warning and Command System (SAUS) .... AWACS
Airborne Warning and Command System (SAUS) .... AWAC System
Airborne Warning and Control (SAUS) .... AWAC
Airborne Warning and Control Division (SAUO) .... AWACD
Airborne Warning and Control Group [*Air Force*] .... AWACG
Airborne Warning and Control Squadron [*Air Force*] .... AWACS
Airborne Warning and Control Squadron [*Military*] (MUSM) .... AW&CS
Airborne Warning and Control Squadron [*Air Force*] .... AWCSq
Airborne Warning and Control Support Squadron (SAUS) .... AWACSS
Airborne [*or Aircraft*] **Warning and Control System** [*Air Force*] .... AWACS
Airborne Warning and Control Training Squadron [*Air Force*] .... AWACTS
Airborne Warning and Control Wing [*Air Force*] .... AWACW
Airborne Warning and Control Wing [*Military*] (MUSM) .... AW&CW
Airborne Warning and Recording Equipment .... AWARE
Airborne Waveguide Slot Array Aerial (or Antenna) (SAUS) .... AWSAA
Airborne Waveguide Slotted Array .... AWSA
Airborne Waveguide Slotted Array Antenna .... AWSAA
Airborne Weapon and Control .... AWAC
Airborne Weapon Control System (MCD) .... AWCS
Airborne Weapon Guided (ACAE) .... AWG
Airborne Weapon Maintenance (ACAE) .... AWM
Airborne Weapons Control .... AWC
Airborne Weapons Corrective Action Program (MCD) .... AWCAP
Airborne Weather and Reconnaissance System (MCD) .... AWARS
Airborne Weather and Reconnaissance System (MCD) .... AWRS
Airborne Weather Radar (SAUS) .... WX
Airborne Weather RADAR System .... AWRS
Airborne Wind-Shear Alert Sensor (PDAA) .... AWAS
Airborne Workshop (SAUO) .... AB Works
Airborne Workshop (SAUS) .... AB WORKS

Airborne XBT [*Expendable Bathythermograph*] (USDC) ... AXBT
Airborne-Delivered Multipurpose Submunition (MCD) ... ARDEMS
Airborne/Shipboard Universal Recovery Device (IUSS) ... ABSURD
Airboss of America [*Toronto Stock Exchange symbol*] (SG) ... BOS
Airbourne School of Flying [*British*] [*FAA designator*] (FAAC) ... RGT
Air-Brake Switch ... ABS
Air-Brake Switch ... ABSW
Airbreak (SAUS) ... AB
Airbreak Switch (SAUS) ... Abr SW
Air-Breathing Electric Laser (SAUS) ... ABEL
Air-Breathing Electric LASER (MCD) ... ABEL
Air-Breathing Engine (KSC) ... ABE
Air-Breathing Engine System ... ABES
Air-Breathing Launch Vehicle [*Military*] (PDAA) ... ABLV
Air-Breathing Propulsion System [*or Subsystem*] [*NASA*] ... ABPS
Air-Breathing Propulsion System [*or Subsystem*] [*NASA*] (NASA) ... APS
Air-Breathing System ... ABS
Air-Breathing Target [*Military*] ... ABT
Air-Breathing Threat [*Military*] ... ABT
Air-Britain Historians [*An association*] (EAIO) ... ABH
Airbrush (VRA) ... airbr
Air-Burundi [*ICAO designator*] (FAAC) ... PBU
Airbus Industrie [*France*] [*ICAO designator*] (FAAC) ... AIB
Airbus Industrie [*France*] [*ICAO aircraft manufacturer identifier*] (ICAO) ... EA
Airbus Industries Group [*FAA*] (TAG) ... AIG
Aircab-System (SAUS) ... AC-System
Aircam Aviation Ltd. [*British*] [*ICAO designator*] (FAAC) ... RCM
Aircarrier (DA) ... AC
Air-Charged Temperature [*Automotive engineering*] ... ACT
Aircleaning (SAUS) ... ARC
Airco Speer Research & Development Laboratories, Niagara Falls, NY [*Library symbol*] [*Library of Congress*] (LCLS) ... NNiaA
AIRCOA Hotel Ltd. [*AMEX symbol*] (SPSG) ... AHT
Aircoa Hotel Partners Ltd. [*Associated Press*] (SAG) ... Aircoa
Aircoach Transport Association (SAUS) ... ACTA
Air-Commodore-in-Chief [*RAF, RCAF*] (DAS) ... A-Com-in-C
Aircompany Karat [*Former USSR*] [*FAA designator*] (FAAC) ... AKT
Aircompany Liana JSA [*Ukraine*] [*FAA designator*] (FAAC) ... NSG
Air-Conditioning Advisory Bureau (SAUS) ... ACAB
Air-Conditioning and Pneumatic System (MCD) ... ACPS
Air-Conditioning and Refrigerating Machinery Association [*Later, ARI*] (KSC) ... ACRMA
Air-Conditioning and Refrigerating Machinery Association (SAUS) ... ACRMA
Airconditioning and Refrigeration Business (journ.) (SAUS) ... Aircond Refrig Bus
Air-Conditioning and Refrigeration Industry Safety Committee (SAUO) ... ARISC
Air-Conditioning and Refrigeration Institute (MSA) ... ACRI
Air-Conditioning and Refrigeration Institute (EA) ... ARI
Air-conditioning and Refrigeration Wholesalers (SAUO) ... ARW
Air-Conditioning Apparatus [*JETDS nomenclature*] [*Military*] (CET) ... HD
Air-Conditioning Equipment (AAG) ... ACE
Air-Conditioning Pack ... ACP
Air-Conditioning Power Panel (DAC) ... PP-AC
Air-conditioning Protection and Diagnostic System [*Automotive electronics*] ... APADS
Air-Conditioning Room (AAG) ... AC/RM
Air-Conditioning Unit ... ACU
Air-Controlled Interception (SAUS) ... ACI
Air-Cool (ADWA) ... ac
Aircooled (MSA) ... ACLD
aircooled (SAUS) ... acld
Aircooled Beryllium Oxide with Integrated Gas Turbine ... ABORIGINE
Air-Cooled Compact Reactor (SAA) ... ACR
Aircooled Fluidized Bed [*Chemical engineering*] ... AFB
Air-Cooled Motor (SAUS) ... AM
Air-Cooled Triode (SAUS) ... ACT
Air-Cooled Vault Storage Facility (SAUS) ... ACVSF
Air-Coooled Vault Storage Facility (SAUO) ... ACVSF
Air-Core Gauge (RDA) ... ACG
Aircorp Airlines, Inc. [*Canada*] [*ICAO designator*] (FAAC) ... BBJ
Aircraft [*or Airplane*] ... A
Aircraft [*Public-performance tariff class*] [*British*] ... AC
Aircraft [*FAA*] (TAG) ... A/C
Aircraft (IDOE) ... a/c
Aircraft (ADWA) ... acft
Aircraft (AFM) ... ACFT
Aircraft ... ACRFT
Aircraft ... Aircft
Aircraft ... ARCRFT
Aircraft [*Wind triangle problems*] ... P
Aircraft Accessories & Components Co. (SAUO) ... AACC
Aircraft Accessories Corporation (SAUO) ... AAC
Aircraft Accident Authority [*ICAO designator*] (ICDA) ... YL
Aircraft Accident Authority [*FAA designator*] (FAAC) ... YLY
Aircraft Accident Board ... AAB
Aircraft Accident Investigation (DNAB) ... AAI
Aircraft Accident Investigation Board ... AAIB
Aircraft Accident Investigation School (SAUO) ... AAIS
Aircraft Accident Investigation System ... AAIS
Aircraft Accident Notification Procedures (SAUS) ... AANP
Aircraft Accident Record [*Obsolete*] [*Military*] ... AAR
Aircraft Accident Report [*Military*] ... AAR
Aircraft Accident/Incident Reporting System [*International Civil Aviation Organization*] [*Information service or system*] (IID) ... ADREP
Aircraft Acquisition and Support (NG) ... AIRACS
Aircraft Actually Possessed [*Air Force*] (AFIT) ... AAP
Aircraft Adapter Group (DWSG) ... AAG
Aircraft Adapter Groups (SAUO) ... AAGS
Aircraft Airworthiness Certification Authority (DA) ... AACA
Aircraft Airworthiness Section ... AAS
Aircraft Alerting Cockpit Equipment (DWSG) ... AACE
Aircraft Alerting Communications Electromagnetic Pulse (MCD) ... AACE
Aircraft Alerting Communications Electromagnetic Pulse ... AACEP
Aircraft Alerting Communications EMP (SAUS) ... AACE
Aircraft and Adventure Factory [*Mallard*] ... AAF
Aircraft and Armament Development ... AAD
Aircraft and Armament Experimental Establishment [*British*] ... A & AEE
Aircraft and Armament Experimental Establishment (SAUS) ... A&AEE
Aircraft and Engine Mechanic ... AEM
Aircraft and Engineering (MCD) ... A & E
Aircraft and Engineering (SAUS) ... A&E
Aircraft and Engines (SAUS) ... A&E
Aircraft and Engines (AAG) ... A & E
Aircraft and Equipment Configuration List (MCD) ... AECL
Aircraft and Facilities [*Navy appropriation*] ... A & F
Aircraft and Facilities (SAUS) ... A&F
Aircraft & Instrument Demisting Ltd. [*British*] ... AID
Aircraft and Missiles (journ.) (SAUS) ... Aircr Missiles
Aircraft and Related Procurement, Navy ... ARPN
Aircraft and Rocket Design Engineers ... ARDE
Aircraft and Warning (SAUS) ... AC&W
Aircraft and Weapons Control Interceptor ... AWCI
Aircraft and Weapons Control Interceptor System ... AWCIS
Aircraft Anticollision Beacon System High-Intensity Light [*Army*] (PDAA) ... AABSHIL
Aircraft Anticollision Beacon System High-Intensity Light [*Army*] (MCD) ... AABSHILL
Aircraft Antisubmarine Development Detachment, Atlantic Fleet ... AIRASDEVLANT
Aircraft Antisubmarine Squadron (DNAB) ... AIRASRON
Aircraft Appliances & Equipment Ltd. (SAUO) ... AAE
Aircraft Approach Light (MSA) ... AAL
Aircraft Approach Limitation ... AAL
Aircraft Approach Overlay (SAUS) ... AAO
Aircraft Armament Bulletin [*Navy*] [*A publication*] (MCD) ... AAB
Aircraft Armament Change ... AAC
Aircraft Armament, Incorporated (ACAE) ... AIRARM
Aircraft Armament Laboratory [*Naval Air Development Center*] ... AAL
Aircraft Armament Unit ... AIRARMUNIT
Aircraft Armaments, Inc. (DNAB) ... AAI
Aircraft Arresting Gear (NG) ... A/G
Aircraft Arresting System ... AAS
Aircraft Artificer [*British*] ... AA
Aircraft, Asiatic Fleet ... AIRAF
Aircraft Assembly Plant ... AAP
Aircraft Assignment Directive ... AAD
Aircraft Assignment Letter ... AAL
Aircraft Assignment Order (SAUS) ... Acft Asgmt O
Aircraft Attack, Experimental-Light [*Navy*] ... VAX-L
Aircraft Availability Model (MCD) ... AAM
Aircraft Avionics Tradeoff Study (ACAE) ... AATS
Aircraft Battle Damage Repair (ACAE) ... ABDR
Aircraft Battle Force [*Obsolete*] [*Navy*] ... ABF
Aircraft Battle Force, Pacific Fleet [*Navy*] ... AIRBATFORPAC
Aircraft Battle-Damage Repair (SAUS) ... ABDR
Aircraft Blast Interaction Tests (MCD) ... ABIT
Aircraft Builders Council [*British*] (AIA) ... ABC
Aircraft Bulletin ... A/B
Aircraft Cabin Water Spray System (SAUS) ... ACWAS
Aircraft Camera Parameter Control ... ACPC
Aircraft Cannon (SAUS) ... AC
Aircraft Capable of Satellite Operations ... ACSO
Aircraft Cargo Loader (DWSG) ... ACL
Aircraft Carrier ... A/CC
Aircraft Carrier (ABBR) ... ACFTC
Aircraft Carrier (SAUS) ... Acft C
Aircraft Carrier [*Navy symbol*] ... CV
Aircraft Carrier (SAUO) ... CVS
Aircraft Carrier Firefighting Assistance Team (DNAB) ... ACFAT
Aircraft Carrier Flag [*Navy*] [*British*] ... AC
Aircraft Carrier General Memorandum ... ACGM
Aircraft Carrier, Helicopter [*NATO*] ... CVH
Aircraft Carrier Intelligence Center (NVT) ... CVIC
Aircraft Carrier Landing System (PDAA) ... ACLS
Aircraft Carrier Landing Trainer (SAUS) ... ACLT
Aircraft Carrier, Medium Sized [*Navy symbol*] (MCD) ... CVV
Aircraft Carrier, Nuclear Propulsion [*Navy symbol*] (NVT) ... CVN
Aircraft Carrier Squadron [*British military*] (DMA) ... ACS
Aircraft Castings Association (SAUO) ... ACA
Aircraft Catering Equipment [*British airlines*] ... ACE
Aircraft Central Computer Interface Subsystem (SAUS) ... ACCIS
Aircraft Certification Systems Evaluation Program [*FAA*] (TAG) ... ACSEP
Aircraft Change Analysis (AAG) ... ACA
Aircraft Change Application List (MCD) ... ACAL
Aircraft Change Control Board [*DoD*] ... ACCB
Aircraft Change Directive (ACAE) ... ACD
Aircraft Chart Viewing Device (ACAE) ... ACVD
Aircraft Checker's Report (AAG) ... ACR
Aircraft Checkers Report (SAUS) ... ACR
Aircraft Circular Letter (MCD) ... ACL
Aircraft Classification Number [*Aviation*] (FAAC) ... ACN

Aircraft Classification Number/Pavement Classification Number (DA)	ACN/PCN
Aircraft Collision Avoidance System (PDAA)	ACAS
Aircraft Coloring and Marking (NATG)	ACM
Aircraft Combat Maneuvering Instrument (DWSG)	ACMI
Aircraft Commander	AC
Aircraft Commander [MTMC] (TAG)	ACC
Aircraft Commander Time	ACT
Aircraft Communication and Recording System (CARB)	ACARS
Aircraft Communication Control and Electronic Signaling System [Air Force]	ACCESS
Aircraft Communication Procedures [Navy] (MCD)	ACP
Aircraft Communications Addressing and Reporting System (IEEE)	ACARS
Aircraft Communications System	ACCS
Aircraft Communications System	ACS
Aircraft Communicator [Signaling device] [Aviation] (IAA)	ACCOM
Aircraft Compatibility Control Drawing (MCD)	ACCD
Aircraft Component Intensive Management System [Military] (AABC)	ACIMS
Aircraft Component Management System (SAUS)	ACIMS
Aircraft Component Mating Evaluation (MCD)	ACME
Aircraft Condition Evaluation [Navy] (MCD)	ACE
Aircraft Condition Inspection (MCD)	ACI
Aircraft Condition Monitoring System (GAVI)	ACMS
Aircraft Configuration Allowance List (DNAB)	ACAL
Aircraft Configuration Change Board	ACCB
Aircraft Configuration Control Board [DoD]	ACCB
Aircraft Control (MUGU)	AC
Aircraft Control and Surveillance [Air Force]	ACS
Aircraft Control and Warning (MCD)	ACAW
Aircraft Control and Warning (SAA)	ACW
Aircraft Control and Warning Group [Air Force]	ACWG
Aircraft Control and Warning Officer [Military]	ACWO
Aircraft Control and Warning Service (SAUO)	ACWS
Aircraft Control and Warning Squadron [Air Force]	AC & WSq
Aircraft Control and Warning Squadron [Military]	ACWRON
Aircraft Control and Warning Squadron [Air Force]	ACWS
Aircraft Control and Warning Stations [Military]	AC & WS
Aircraft Control and Warning System [Military]	ACWS
Aircraft Control and Warning System Station [Military] (IAA)	ACWSS
Aircraft Control Equipment (ACAE)	ACCE
Aircraft Control Link	ACL
Aircraft Control Operator (MUGU)	ACO
Aircraft Control Room	ACR
Aircraft Control Room Officer [British military] (DMA)	ACRO
Aircraft Control System (MUGU)	ACS
Aircraft Control Unit (NVT)	ACU
Aircraft Controlling Custodian (MCD)	ACC
Aircraft Corp. of Great Britain (OA)	ACGB
Aircraft Corporation of Great Britain (SAUO)	ACGB
Aircraft Crash Rescue Field Assistance and Evaluation Team [Air Force] (AFM)	ACRFAET
Aircraft Crashworthiness Program Plan (MCD)	ACPP
Aircraft Crew Interphone System (MCD)	ACIS
Aircraft Crewman Badge [Military decoration] (GFGA)	ACCMB
Aircraft Crewman Badge [Military decoration] (AABC)	AcftCrmnBad
Aircraft Crewman Badge (SAUS)	Acft CrmnBad
Aircraft Cross-Servicing Program [Military]	ACSP
Aircraft Damage (ADA)	ACD
Aircraft Damage Sensing System	ADSS
Aircraft Data Entry (DNAB)	ADE
Aircraft Data Line (MCD)	ADL
Aircraft Data Link (ACAE)	ADL
Aircraft Data Link Kit (ACAE)	ADLK
Aircraft Data Link Processor [Mode S subnetwork function onboard the aircraft that implements OSI network layer protocols] (GAVI)	ADLP
Aircraft Data Recording Evaluation System (PDAA)	ADRES
Aircraft Data Systems (SAUS)	ADS
Aircraft Decontaminating, Deicing, Cleaning System (MCD)	ADDCS
Aircraft Defense Analysis (MCD)	ADA
Aircraft De-Ice and Inhibitor [MTMC] (TAG)	ADI
Aircraft Delivery Group [Air Force]	ADG
Aircraft Delivery Unit [Air Force]	ADU
Aircraft Depot [British military] (DMA)	AD
Aircraft Depot (SAUS)	A Dep
Aircraft Depot (SAUS)	Adpo
Aircraft Depth [Bomb] (DNAB)	AD
Aircraft Design Research Division [Navy]	ADR
Aircraft Design-Induced Pilot Error [National Transportation Safety Board]	ADIPE
Aircraft Destination Record (MCD)	ADR
Aircraft Development Service [Air Force]	ADS
Aircraft Development Test Activity [Army] (MCD)	ADTA
Aircraft Development Test Activity [Army] (MCD)	ATA
Aircraft Diagnostics and Integrated Test System (MCD)	ADITS
Aircraft Direction Room [Navy]	ADR
Aircraft Directives Configuration [Navy] (NG)	ADC
Aircraft Discrepancy Report	ADR
Aircraft Distributors and Manufacturers Association (SAUO)	ADMA
Aircraft Division (MCD)	AD
Aircraft Division/Department List [Air Force]	AD/DL
Aircraft Dummy Deck Landing [Navy]	ADDL
Aircraft Early Warning System (SAUS)	AEWS
Aircraft Earth Station [ICAO designator] (FAAC)	AES
Aircraft Ejection Kit	AEK
Aircraft Ejection Seat	AES
Aircraft Ejection Seat System	AESS
Aircraft Electrical Power System	AEPS
Aircraft Electrical Society (SAA)	AES
Aircraft Electrical System Component Tester (DWSG)	AESCOT
Aircraft Electronics Association (EA)	AEA
Aircraft Electronics Warfare Self-Protection System [Army]	AEWSP
Aircraft Electronics Warfare Self-Protection System [Army]	AEWSPS
Aircraft Emergency Procedures over Water	AEPW
Aircraft Emission Estimator (MCD)	ACEE
Aircraft Energy Efficiency (SAUS)	ACEE
Aircraft Engine Business Group (SAUO)	AEBG
Aircraft Engine Component Improvement Program (ACAE)	AECIP
Aircraft Engine Laboratory	AEL
Aircraft Engine Management System (MCD)	AEMS
Aircraft engine overhaul and structural repair ship (SAUS)	ARV
Aircraft Engine Record Card (DNAB)	AERC
Aircraft Engineering & Jigs Ltd. (SAUO)	AEJ
Aircraft Engineering District Office	AEDO
Aircraft Engineering Foundation	AEF
Aircraft Engineering (journ.) (SAUS)	Aircraft
Aircraft Engineering Maintenance Co.	AEMCO
Aircraft Engineering Maintenance Company (SAUO)	AEMCO
Aircraft Engineering Squadron (SAA)	AES
Aircraft Engineering Support Wing (SAUS)	AESW
Aircraft Engineering Wing (SAUS)	AEW
Aircraft Engineers (SAUS)	LAEs
Aircraft Engineers Association	AEA
Aircraft Engines Emission Study Group (SAUO)	AEESG
Aircraft Environmental Support Office [Naval Air Rework Facility] [North Island, CA]	AESO
Aircraft Equipment	AE
Aircraft Equipment Failure	AEF
Aircraft Equipment List (MCD)	AEL
Aircraft Equipment Overhauls & Sales Pty Ltd. (SAUO)	AEOS
Aircraft Equipment Procedures (MCD)	AEP
Aircraft Equipment Reliability and Maintainability Program (ACAE)	AERMIP
Aircraft Equipment Requirement Schedule	AERS
Aircraft Equipment Trainer (MCD)	AET
Aircraft Escape System Maintenance Data (MCD)	AESMD
Aircraft Escort Vessel [Navy symbol] [Obsolete]	AVG
Aircraft Establishment (SAUS)	AE
Aircraft Evaluation Group [FAA] (TAG)	AEG
Aircraft Expendable Bathythermograph Program in the Pacific [National Science Foundation] (MSC)	AIRPAX
Aircraft Explosive Device (MCD)	AED
Aircraft Familiarization	AIRFAM
Aircraft Fatigue Data Analysis System (ADA)	AFDAS
Aircraft Fault Indentification System [Aviation] (PDAA)	AFIS
Aircraft Ferry Squadron (SAUO)	AIRFERON
Aircraft Ferry Squadron (SAUO)	AIRFERRON
Aircraft Ferry Squadron [Navy]	VRF
Aircraft Field Material Evaluation Report (ACAE)	AFMER
Aircraft Finance Association [Later, NAFA] (EA)	AFA
Aircraft, Fleet Marine Force, Atlantic [Obsolete]	AIRFMFLANT
Aircraft, Fleet Marine Force, Pacific [Obsolete]	AFMFP
Aircraft, Fleet Marine Force, Pacific [Obsolete]	AIRFMFPAC
Aircraft Flight Correlator (SAUS)	AFC
Aircraft Flight Report (AAG)	AFR
Aircraft Flighting Zone (SAUS)	AFZ
Aircraft Flying Training	ACFT
Aircraft Force Projection Model [Computer] [Navy]	AFPM
Aircraft Gas and Turbine	AGT
Aircraft General Standards [British]	AGS
Aircraft General Stores (SAUS)	AGS
Aircraft Generation Squadron (MCD)	AGS
Aircraft Generation Squadron [Air Force]	AGSq
Aircraft Ground Equipment Ltd. (SAUO)	AGE
Aircraft Ground Fire Suppression and Rescue [Air Force] (MCD)	AGFSR
Aircraft Ground Fire Suppression and Rescue Systems [Wright-Patterson Air Force Base, OH] [Air Force]	AGFSRS
Aircraft Ground Mishap (DOMA)	AGM
Aircraft Ground Mobility System (MCD)	AGMS
Aircraft Ground Support Equipment (MCD)	AGSE
Aircraft Grounded for Lack of Parts	AGP
Aircraft Gun Pod (NG)	AGP
Aircraft Gunfire Detector	AGD
Aircraft Gurt Pod (SAUS)	AGP
Aircraft Handler [British]	AH
Aircraft Handling Vehicle (MCD)	AHV
Aircraft Hangar (MCD)	ACH
Aircraft Holding Station (SAUO)	AHS
Aircraft Holding Unit (SAUO)	AHU
Aircraft Homing System (SAUS)	YE
Aircraft Identification (KSC)	ACID
Aircraft Identification (AAG)	AI
Aircraft Identification Control	AIC
Aircraft Identification Determination (SAA)	AID
Aircraft Identification Military System (ACAE)	AIMS
Aircraft Identification Monitoring System (ACAE)	AIMS
Aircraft Identification Number (SAUS)	AIN
Aircraft Identifier (CTAS)	AID
Aircraft IFF [Identification, Friend or Foe] Mark XII System (AABC)	AIMXS
Aircraft In Commission	AIC
Aircraft in Flight [ICAO designator] (ICDA)	ZZ
Aircraft in Flight [FAA designator] (FAAC)	ZZZ

Aircraft Incident Report [*Navy*] (NG) ... AIR
Aircraft Indentification (CTAS) ... AID
Aircraft Industries Association (BARN) ... AIA
Aircraft Industries Center (AAG) ... AIC
Aircraft Industries Research Organization (SAUO) ... AIRO
Aircraft Industries Research Organization on Housing (SAUO) ... AIROH
Aircraft Industry (AAG) ... AI
Aircraft Industry Conference [*Navy*] ... AIC
Aircraft Inflight Monitoring System (MCD) ... AIMS
Aircraft Information Correlator (CAAL) ... AIC
Aircraft Information Subsystem (SAUS) ... AIS
Aircraft Inspection and Survey Party (SAUO) ... AISP
Aircraft Inspection Department (SAUO) ... AID
Aircraft Inspection System ... AIS
Aircraft Inspections and Repair ... AIR
Aircraft Inspector (SAUS) ... acft insp
Aircraft Installation Delay (DA) ... AID
Aircraft Installation Diagnostic Equipment (MCD) ... AIDE
Aircraft Installation Report (ACAE) ... AIR
Aircraft Instrument Bulletin [*Navy*] (NG) ... AIB
Aircraft Instrument Laboratory [*Navy*] (AAG) ... AIL
Aircraft Instrument Mechanic (SAUS) ... Acft Instr Mech
Aircraft Instrument Repair Facility ... AIRF
Aircraft Instrument Subsystem [*Navy*] (MCD) ... AIS
Aircraft Instrumentation System (ACAE) ... AIS
Aircraft Instruments and Aircrew Stations [*NATO*] (NATG) ... AI
Aircraft Integrated Crew Station Concepts (MCD) ... AICSC
Aircraft Integrated Data System (MCD) ... AIDS
Aircraft Integrated Design System (MCD) ... AIDS
Aircraft Integrated Munition System (MCD) ... AIMS
Aircraft Integrated Test Equipment ... AITE
Aircraft Integration Social Test Equipment (ACAE) ... AISTE
Aircraft Intelligence Department (SAUO) ... AID
Aircraft Intensively Managed Items ... AIMI
Aircraft Interception Special Weapon (SAUS) ... AISW
Aircraft Interceptor (SAUS) ... AI
Aircraft Interceptor (MCD) ... AI
Aircraft Intercommunication (SAUS) ... AIC
Aircraft Interface Data Summaries (MCD) ... AIDS
Aircraft Interface Device (DWSG) ... AID
Aircraft Interface Unit (SAUS) ... AIU
Aircraft Intermediate Maintenance [*Detachment*] [*Navy*] [*Marine Corps*] (DOMA) ... AIM
Aircraft Intermediate Maintenance Department [*Navy*] (NVT) ... AIMD
Aircraft Intermediate Maintenance Department (SAUO) ... AIMO
Aircraft Intermediate Maintenance Support Office (DNAB) ... AIMSO
Aircraft International Register (SAUS) ... AIR
Aircraft Interphone & Mixer (SAUS) ... AIM
Aircraft Intrusion Detection System [*RADAR*] ... AIDS
Aircraft Inventory Management Group [*Military*] (AFIT) ... AIM
Aircraft Inventory Record (NVT) ... AIR
Aircraft Inventory Reporting System (AABC) ... AIRS
Aircraft Kill Indicator ... AKI
Aircraft Laboratory (SAUO) ... AL
Aircraft Landing Gear ... ALG
Aircraft Landing Lamp ... ALL
Aircraft Landing Measurement System (MCD) ... ALMS
Aircraft Landing System ... ALS
Aircraft Laser Infrared Absorption Spectrometer (CARB) ... ALIAS
Aircraft Latitude (MCD) ... ALAT
Aircraft Launch and Recovery Equipment [*Navy*] (MCD) ... ALRE
Aircraft Launch and Recovery Equipment Maintenance Program [*Navy*] (NG) ... ALREMP
Aircraft Launch Interface Computer (SAUS) ... ALIC
Aircraft Launched Boost Intercept Study (ACAE) ... ALBIS
Aircraft Launching Accessory Service Change (MCD) ... ALASC
Aircraft Launching Bulletin ... ACLB
Aircraft Launching Bulletin (MCD) ... ALB
Aircraft Life Support Equipment [*Military*] (DOMA) ... ALSE
Aircraft Limited Model ... ALM
Aircraft Load ... ACL
Aircraft Load Generator (SAUO) ... LOGEN
Aircraft Loaders Control Assembly ... ALCA
Aircraft Locknut Manufacturers Association (EA) ... ALMA
Aircraft Logistics (SAUS) ... AL
Aircraft Logistics Division [*Bureau of Aeronautics*] [*Later, NASC*] [*Navy*] ... AL
Aircraft Logistics Planning Board (MCD) ... ALPB
Aircraft Longitude (MCD) ... ALON
Aircraft Loss, Utilization, Combat, and Repair Damage (MCD) ... ALUCARD
Aircraft Machine Gunner ... AIRMG
Aircraft Machine Gunner ... AMG
Aircraft Maintenance and Repair Department [*British military*] (DMA) ... AMRD
Aircraft Maintenance and Repair Department (SAUO) ... AMRD
Aircraft Maintenance and Support Equipment Exhibition & Conference (SAUS) ... AMASE
Aircraft Maintenance Base ... AMB
Aircraft Maintenance Branch (SAUO) ... AMB
Aircraft Maintenance Co. [*Egypt*] [*ICAO designator*] (FAAC) ... AMV
Aircraft Maintenance Control System (SAUS) ... AMCS
Aircraft Maintenance Delayed for Parts [*Military*] ... AMDP
Aircraft Maintenance Department [*Military*] (AFIT) ... AMD
Aircraft Maintenance Effectiveness Simulation (MCD) ... AMES
Aircraft Maintenance Group (SAUO) ... AMG
Aircraft Maintenance Irregularity Control System (PDAA) ... AMICS
Aircraft Maintenance Management Information System ... AMMIS
Aircraft Maintenance Manpower Information System [*Air Force*] ... AMMIS
Aircraft Maintenance Manpower Requirement [*Air Force*] (AFM) ... AMMR
Aircraft Maintenance Manual ... AMM
Aircraft Maintenance Material Readiness List [*Navy*] (NG) ... AMMRL
Aircraft Maintenance Officer ... AMO
Aircraft Maintenance Qualification Program (SAUS) ... AMQP
Aircraft Maintenance Support Equipment (MCD) ... AMSE
Aircraft Maintenance Unit (SAUS) ... AMU
Aircraft Management Computer (SAUS) ... AMC
Aircraft Management System (SAUS) ... AMS
Aircraft Manufacturers Association [*Superseded by MAA*] (EA) ... AMA
Aircraft Manufacturer's Council ... AMC
Aircraft Manufacturers Progress Report (SAUS) ... AMPR
Aircraft Manufacturing Company (SAUO) ... AMC
Aircraft Manufacturing Factory (SAUS) ... AMF
Aircraft Material Management Center [*Air Force*] ... AMMC
Aircraft Material Officer ... AMO
Aircraft Material Specifications [*Society of Automotive Engineers*] ... AMS
Aircraft Mechanician [*British military*] (DMA) ... AMN
Aircraft Mechanics Fraternal Association (EA) ... AMFA
Aircraft Meteorological (NATG) ... AC/M
Aircraft Meteorological Data Relay (SAUS) ... AMDAR
Aircraft Microwave Refractometer (ACAE) ... AMR
Aircraft Military Mission ... AIRMILMIS
Aircraft Mishap Board (DNAB) ... AMB
Aircraft Mishap Prevention programme (SAUS) ... AMP
Aircraft Missile Parts Mfg. Co. (SAUO) ... AMPM
Aircraft Mission Equipment (MCD) ... AME
Aircraft Model Change ... AMC
Aircraft Modernization Program (ACAE) ... AMP
Aircraft Modification Center (SAUS) ... AMC
Aircraft Monitor and Control (NG) ... AMAC
Aircraft Motion Compensation ... AMC
Aircraft Mounted Control System ... AMCS
Aircraft Movement Element (MCD) ... AME
Aircraft Movement Information Section (SAUO) ... AMIS
Aircraft Movement Information Service [*Air Force*] ... AMIS
Aircraft Multiband Scanner (SAUS) ... AMS
Aircraft Multichannel Scanner System (SAUS) ... AMSS
Aircraft Multiengine Land [*Pilot rating*] (IEEE) ... AMEL
Aircraft Multiengine Sea [*Pilot rating*] (AIA) ... AMES
Aircraft Multiplex Intercommunications ... AMI
Aircraft Multiplex Intercommunications System ... AMIS
Aircraft Multipurpose Test Inspection and Diagnostic Equipment ... AMTIDE
Aircraft Multispectral Photographic System [*NASA*] ... AMPS
Aircraft Nationality and Registration Marks ... REG
Aircraft Navigation (SAUS) ... Avigation
Aircraft Noise Prediction Office [*NASA*] ... ANOPO
Aircraft Noise Prediction Program [*NASA*] ... ANOPP
Aircraft Nonflying-Electronics (CINC) ... ANFE
Aircraft, Northern Salomons (SAUO) ... AIRNORSOLS
Aircraft, Northern Solomons [*Military*] ... AIRNORSOLS
Aircraft Not Combat Ready (MCD) ... ANCR
Aircraft Not Fully Equipped ... ANFE
Aircraft Not Operationally Ready Due to Lack of Equipment (SAA) ... ANORE
Aircraft Not Operationally Ready Due to Lack of Parts (SAA) ... ANORP
Aircraft Not Operationally Ready Supply (AFIT) ... ANOPS
Aircraft Not Operationally Ready-Maintenance (SAUS) ... ANORM
Aircraft Not Operationally Ready-Supplies (SAUS) ... ANORS
Aircraft Nuclear Power [*or Propulsion*] ... ANP
Aircraft Nuclear Power Plant Facility ... ANPPF
Aircraft Nuclear Propulsion Department (SAUO) ... ANP
Aircraft Nuclear Propulsion Department [*Navy*] ... ANPD
Aircraft Nuclear Propulsion Department, General Electric (SAUS) ... ANPDGE
Aircraft Nuclear Propulsion Office [*of AEC*] [*Defunct*] ... ANPO
Aircraft Nuclear Propulsion Program ... ANPP
Aircraft Nuclear Propulsion Project (SAUO) ... ANPP
Aircraft Number (SAUS) ... AN
Aircraft Observer (SAUS) ... AOB
Aircraft Observer, Bombardment (SAUS) ... AOB
Aircraft Observer Training Wing (SAUS) ... Acft Obsr Tng Wg
Aircraft of Bomber Command [*British*] ... ABC
Aircraft on Ground [*Navy*] ... ACOG
Aircraft on Ground [*Navy*] ... AOG
Aircraft Operating Company, Ltd. (SAUO) ... AOC
Aircraft Operating Cost Report (NG) ... AOCR
Aircraft Operating Fee (ADA) ... AOF
Aircraft Operating Manual (GAVI) ... AOM
Aircraft Operating Report (MCD) ... AOR
Aircraft Operational Capability (DNAB) ... AOC
Aircraft Operations Center (OSRA) ... AOC
Aircraft Operations Division [*Johnson Space Center*] [*NASA*] (NASA) ... AOD
Aircraft Operations Group Association ... AOGA
Aircraft Operator (DA) ... AO
Aircraft or advanced Multichannel Microwave Radiometer (SAUS) ... AMMR
Aircraft Out for Parts (MCD) ... AOP
Aircraft Out of Commission for Maintenance [*Military*] ... AOCM
Aircraft out of Commission for Parts [*MTMC*] (TAG) ... AOCM
Aircraft Out of Commission for [*Lack of*] **Parts** [*Obsolete*] [*Military*] ... AOCP
Aircraft Overations Group Association (SAUO) ... AOGA
Aircraft Overhaul Work Stoppage (NG) ... AOWS
Aircraft Owners and Pilots Association (EA) ... AOPA
Aircraft Parachute Flare (SAA) ... APF
Aircraft Parameters Handled in Real time Over Data link to Improve Trajectory Estimation (SAUS) ... APHRODITE

Aircraft Parts Corp. (SAUO)	APC
Aircraft Penetration Model (MCD)	ACPEN
Aircraft per Hour (CTAS)	AC/HR
Aircraft Performance (SAA)	ACP
Aircraft Performance Indicator (ACAE)	API
Aircraft Personnel Group [Military] (MUSM)	APG
Aircraft Plume Analysis	APA
Aircraft Porous Media, Incorporated (ACAE)	APM
Aircraft Position Information Converter [Air Force]	APICON
Aircraft Position Sensor (PDAA)	APS
Aircraft Precision Position Location Equipment (DA)	APPL
Aircraft Prepared for Service	APS
Aircraft Procurement (Appropriations), Army/Navy/Air Force (AAGC)	AP/A/N/AF
Aircraft Procurement, Army (AABC)	APA
Aircraft Procurement, Navy (NVT)	APN
Aircraft Procurement-Army (SAUS)	APA
Aircraft Produced Ice Particles (SAUS)	APIP
Aircraft Production Advisory Council (SAUO)	APAC
Aircraft Production Board (SAUO)	APB
Aircraft Production (journ.) (SAUS)	Aircr Prod
Aircraft Production Resources Agency	APRA
Aircraft Production Resources Ageny (SAUO)	APRA
Aircraft Program Data File	APDF
Aircraft Propulsion Subsystem Integration	APSI
Aircraft Propulsion Unit	APU
Aircraft Proximity Hazard (DA)	APHAZ
Aircraft Proximity Warning Device	APWD
Aircraft Proximity Warning System	APWS
Aircraft Pulse Navigation	APN
Aircraft Quality (AAG)	AQ
Aircraft Radio Control of Aerodrome Lighting (PIAV)	ARCAL
Aircraft Radio Corporation (SAUO)	AEC
Aircraft Radio Corporation (SAUO)	ARC
Aircraft Radio Incorporated (SAUO)	ARINC
Aircraft Radio Instrument (SAUS)	ARI
Aircraft Radio Laboratory	ARL
Aircraft Radio Mechanic (SAUS)	ARM
Aircraft Radio Regulations	ARR
Aircraft Radio Sight (IAA)	ARS
Aircraft Radiosight (SAUS)	ARS
Aircraft Reactor Equipment	ARE
Aircraft Reactor Experiment (NUCP)	ARE
Aircraft Reactor Test (IAA)	ART
Aircraft Reactors Branch	ARB
Aircraft Readiness Maintainability Simulator (MCD)	ARMS
Aircraft Ready (AFIT)	AR
Aircraft Reception Unit (SAUO)	ARU
Aircraft Recommended Practice (DNAB)	ARP
Aircraft Recording Instrumentation System [British]	ARIS
Aircraft Recovery (CINC)	AIR
Aircraft Recovery Association (EA)	ARA
Aircraft Recovery Bulletin (MCD)	ARB
Aircraft Recovery Equipment	ARE
Aircraft Reference Point	ARP
Aircraft Refueling and Rearming System (SAUS)	ARRS
Aircraft Refuel/Rearm Study (MCD)	ARRS
Aircraft Regression Model (MCD)	ARM
Aircraft Reliability and Maintainability Simulation	ARMS
Aircraft Reliability, Maintainability, Availability Design Analysis (SAUS)	ARMADA
Aircraft Repair and Supply Base (AFIT)	ARSB
Aircraft Repair and Supply Center	ARSC
Aircraft Repair Division (SAA)	AIREDIV
Aircraft Repair Division [Military]	AIREPDIV
Aircraft Repair Division [Military]	AIREPDN
Aircraft Repair Section (SAUO)	ARS
Aircraft Repair Ship [Navy]	ARS
Aircraft Repair Ship [Navy symbol]	ARV
Aircraft Repair Ship (Aircraft) [Navy symbol]	ARVA
Aircraft Repair Ship (Engine) [Navy symbol]	ARVE
Aircraft Repair Ship for Engines (SAUS)	ARVE
Aircraft Repair Ship for Helicopter (SAUS)	ARVH
Aircraft Repair Ship (Helicopter) [Navy symbol]	ARVH
Aircraft Replaceable Assemblies	ARA
Aircraft Reply and Interference Environment Simulator (MCD)	ARIES
Aircraft Report (SAUS)	ACRT
Aircraft Report	AIREP
Aircraft Report, Special (ADA)	ARS
Aircraft Reports (WEAT)	Aireps
Aircraft Requirements Computer System	ARCS
Aircraft Requiring Overhaul (AFIT)	AOH
Aircraft Rescue and Fire Fighting Vehicle	ARFFV
Aircraft Rescue Association (SAUO)	ARA
Aircraft Rescue Boat [Navy symbol]	AVH
Aircraft Rescue Vessel [Navy] (MCD)	ARV
Aircraft [or Aviation] Rescue Vessel [Navy symbol] [Obsolete]	AVR
Aircraft Research and Development Unit [Australia]	ARDU
Aircraft Research and Testing Committee (MCD)	ARTC
Aircraft Research Association (EAIO)	ARA
Aircraft Research Instrumentation System	ARIS
Aircraft Resources Control Office	ARCO
Aircraft Resources Management System [Military]	ARMS
Aircraft Resources Management System, Pacific [Military] (NVT)	ARMSPAC
Aircraft Response to Wind Spectrum (MCD)	ARWS
Aircraft Rocket (NVT)	AR
Aircraft Rocket Subsystem [Army/Air Force]	ARS
Aircraft Routeing Right-of-Way (SAUS)	ARROW
Aircraft Safety Beacon	ASB
Aircraft Salvage-Handling Equipment (DNAB)	ASHE
Aircraft Sampling Inspection (MCD)	ASI
Aircraft Schedule for Delivery to Fleet	AIRSKEDELFLT
Aircraft Scheduling Unit	ASU
Aircraft Scouting Flotilla (SAUO)	Airscoflot
Aircraft Scouting Force (SAUO)	Airscofor
Aircraft Scouting Force, Pacific Fleet	AIRSCOFORPAC
Aircraft Search Equipment (SAUS)	ASE
Aircraft Security (SAUS)	A/C S
Aircraft Security System (MCD)	ASS
Aircraft Security Vessel	A/CS
Aircraft Sensor Correlation Device (MCD)	ASCD
Aircraft Service Association (SAUO)	ASA
[The] Aircraft Service Association	TASA
Aircraft Service Change [Navy]	ASC
Aircraft Service Period Adjustments [Air Force] (DOMA)	ASPA
Aircraft Services Base	ASB
Aircraft Services Facility	ASF
Aircraft Servicing Platform (DA)	ASP
Aircraft Shield Test Reactor (SAA)	ASTR
Aircraft Shipment Readiness Date [Army] (AABC)	ASRD
Aircraft Single Engine Sea [Pilot rating] (AIA)	ASES
Aircraft Situation Display [FAA] (TAG)	ASD
Aircraft Situational Display (CTAS)	ASD
Aircraft Sound Description System [FAA]	ASDS
Aircraft, South Pacific Force [Navy]	AIRSOPAC
Aircraft, Southwest Pacific Force [Navy]	AIRSOWESPAC
Aircraft Space Position Measurement System (MCD)	ASPMS
Aircraft Specialties Lines	ASL
Aircraft Specification Form Committee (SAUO)	ASFC
Aircraft Specification Forum Committee	ASFC
Aircraft Squadron (SAUO)	ACSqn
Aircraft Stabilization Equipment [Aviation] (PDAA)	ASE
Aircraft Standard Communication Bus (SAUS)	ASCB
Aircraft Standard Parts (NATG)	ASP
Aircraft Starting Unit	ASU
Aircraft Station Keeper (MCD)	ASK
Aircraft Stations [ITU designation] (CET)	MA
Aircraft Statistical Data	ASD
Aircraft Storage and Disposition Group [Air Force]	ASDG
Aircraft Storage Facility (SAA)	ACSF
Aircraft Storage Unit [Military] [British]	ASU
Aircraft Stores Establishment [Navy]	ASE
Aircraft Stores Interface Data Systems	ASIDS
Aircraft Stores Interface Manual (MCD)	ASIM
Aircraft Strength (SAUS)	acft str
Aircraft Structural Integrity Management Information System [Air Force] (AFIT)	ASIMIS
Aircraft Structural Integrity Program	ASIP
Aircraft Structural Integrity Program Recorder	ASPR
Aircraft Summary List	ASL
Aircraft Supply Council [Ministry of Aircraft Production] [British]	ASC
Aircraft Supply Council (SAUO)	ASC
Aircraft Supply Depot (SAUO)	ASD
Aircraft Supply Group	ASG
Aircraft Supply Officer (SAUS)	ASO
Aircraft Support and Service Equipment Tug (PDAA)	ASSET
Aircraft Surface Detection Equipment (SAUS)	ASDE
Aircraft Surge Launch and Recovery [FAA] (TAG)	ASLAR
Aircraft Survivability Equipment	ASE
Aircraft Survivability Equipment - Product Manager	ASE-PM
Aircraft Survivability Equipment Trainer (SAUS)	ASET
Aircraft Survival Measures Program (SAUS)	ASM Program
Aircraft Survival Measures Programme [NATO]	ASM
Aircraft Synthesis [Computer science]	ACSYNT
Aircraft Synthesis Analysis Program	ASAP
Aircraft Synthetic Aperture Radar (SAUS)	AIRSAR
Aircraft Systems Activation Program [Military]	ASAP
Aircraft Systems Co. (EFIS)	ASC
Aircraft Systems Trainer (MCD)	AST
Aircraft Tactical Air Battle Control System (SAUS)	ATABCS
Aircraft Tactical Control System	ATCS
Aircraft Tail Warning	ATW
Aircraft Tail-Warning (SAUS)	ATW
Aircraft Target Unit	ATU
Aircraft Technical Bulletin	ATB
Aircraft Technical Committee [Aerospace Industries Association] (MCD)	ATC
Aircraft Technical Order	ATO
Aircraft Technical Publishers [Information service or system] (IID)	ATP
Aircraft Tender (SAUS)	AT
Aircraft Test Equipment Modification	ATEM
Aircraft Thermal Management (MCD)	ATM
Aircraft to Be Identified [Aviation] (AIA)	ACFTTBI
Aircraft Torpedo Development Unit [British]	ATDU
Aircraft Torpedo Maintenance Unit [Navy]	ATMU
Aircraft Traffic Advisory Resolution System	ATARS
Aircraft Trailing Vortices	ATV
Aircraft (Training) [Navy symbol]	VTD
Aircraft Transfer Order	ATO
Aircraft Transmitter Receiver (SAUS)	ATR
Aircraft Transportation Lighter [Navy symbol]	YCK

Aircraft Transportation Lighter [*Non-self-propelled*] [*Navy symbol*] .... YCV
Aircraft Transportation Officer [*Navy*] (DOMA) .... ATO
Aircraft Trouble Report .... ATR
Aircraft Trouble-Shooting System (MCD) .... ATS
Aircraft Tube-Launched Recoilless System (MCD) .... ATLRS
Aircraft Turbine Service (SAUO) .... ATS
Aircraft Undersea Sound Experiment (SAUO) .... AUSEX
Aircraft Unitized Diagnostic Inspection and Test [*Boeing*] .... AUDIT
Aircraft Utilization Rate (SAUS) .... UTE
Aircraft Utilization Report .... AUR
Aircraft Vehicle Manufacturer (SAUS) .... AVM
Aircraft Velocity (MCD) .... AVEL
Aircraft Vertical Accelerometer Reports .... AVARs
Aircraft Warning (IAA) .... AW
Aircraft Warning Company [*Army*] .... AWCo
Aircraft Warning Company [*Marine Corps*] .... AWRNCO
Aircraft Warning Interface System (ACAE) .... AWIS
Aircraft Warning Service [*Military*] .... AWS
Aircraft Warning Set (SAUS) .... AWS
Aircraft Warning System (SAUS) .... AWS
Aircraft Warning Unit Training Center (SAUS) .... AWUTC
Aircraft Weapons Electronics (SAUS) .... AWE
Aircraft Weapons Handling Vehicle .... AWHV
Aircraft Weapons Release Set [*or System*] (NG) .... AWRS
Aircraft Weapons Release Unit [*DoD*] (MCD) .... AWRU
Aircraft Weapons Tactics Trainer (ACAE) .... AWTT
Aircraft Weather Report (SAUS) .... AIRE
Aircraft weather Report (SAUS) .... AIREP
Aircraft Wide-Angle Reflective Display System [*Singer Co., Link Division*] .... AWARDS
Aircraft Wireless Intercom (DWSG) .... AWIC
Aircraft Work Order (ACAE) .... AWO
Aircraft Working Party (SAUO) .... AWP
Aircraft/Aeronautical Directive Requirements (ACAE) .... ADR
Aircraft-Based Infrared Detector .... ABIRD
Aircraft-derivative Gas Turbine (SAUS) .... AGT
Aircraft-Expendable Bathythermograph (SAUS) .... AXBT
Aircrafthand [*British*] .... ACH
Aircraftman [*British*] .... AC
Aircraftman, First Class [*Canadian*] AC1
Aircraftman, Second Class [*Canadian*] AC2
Aircraft-Marine Products, Inc. (SAUO) .... A-MP
Aircraft/Missile Maintenance - Production Compression Report .... AMREP
Aircraft/Missile Project (AFM) .... AMP
Aircraft-Missile Project (SAUO) .... AMP
Aircraft-Mounted Accessory Drive (SAUS) .... AMAD
Aircrafts Departing at Minimum Intervals (SAUS) .... ADMIS
Aircraft-Ship Integrated Secure & Traverse (SAUS) .... ASIST
Aircraftsman Second Class (SAUS) .... AC 2
Aircraftsman Third Class (SAUS) .... AC 3
Aircraftswoman (SAUS) .... ACW
Aircraft-to-Satellite Data Relay [*Meteorology*] .... ASDAR
Aircraft-to-Satellite Data Relay System (ADWA) .... ASDAR
Aircraft-to-Surface Vessel [*Navy*] .... ASV
Aircraftwoman [*Military*] .... AC
Aircraftwoman [*British*] .... ACW
Aircraftwoman, First Class [*Canadian*] AW1
Aircraftwoman, Second Class [*Canadian*] AW2
Aircrew .... ACREW
Aircrew (AFM) .... ACRW
Aircrew Association (EAIO) .... ACA
Aircrew Body Armor [*System*] [*Army*] .... ACBA
Aircrew Body Armor System (SAUS) .... ACBA System
Aircrew Classification Battery Test (SAUS) .... ACCBT
Aircrew Classification Test (AFM) .... ACT
Aircrew Classification Test Battery .... ACTB
Aircrew Combat Mission Enhancement (SAUS) .... ACME
Aircrew Egress Trainer (MCD) .... AET
Aircrew Electronic Warfare Tactics Facility (NATG) .... AEWTF
Aircrew Escape Propulsion System [*Navy*] .... AEPS
Aircrew Evaluation Board (ACAE) .... AEB
Aircrew Eye/Respiratory Protection (SAUS) .... AERP
Aircrew Eyes Respiratory Protection (DWSG) .... AERP
Aircrew Flight Training Period (AABC) .... AFTP
Aircrew Gliding Escape System (MCD) .... AGES
Aircrew Holding Unit [*British military*] (DMA) .... ACHU
Aircrew Instruction System (ACAE) .... AIS
Aircrew Integrated Helmet System (SAUS) .... AIHS
Aircrew Integrated Protection System (ACAE) .... AIPS
Aircrew Life Support System (CAAL) .... ALSS
Aircrew Microclimate Conditioning System (SAUS) .... AMCS
Aircrew Microclimate Cooling System [*Military*] (DOMA) .... AMCS
Aircrew Modular Survival System (SAUS) .... AMSS
Aircrew Omification Test Battery (SAUS) .... ACRB
Aircrew Part Task Trainer (MCD) .... APTT
Aircrew Reception Centre [*British military*] (DMA) .... ARC
Aircrew Resource Management System (ACAE) .... ARMS
Aircrew Respiratory Protection .... ARP
Aircrew Standardization & Evaluation Team (SAUS) .... ASET
Aircrew Station Standardization Panel .... ASSP
Aircrew Survival Equipmentman [*Navy rating*] .... PR
Aircrew Systems Advisory Panel [*NASA, Air Force*] (MCD) .... ASAP
Aircrew Systems Change (MCD) .... ASC

Aircrew Training and Test Squadron [*Air Force*] .... ATTSq
Aircrew Training Device (MCD) .... ATD
Aircrew Training Manual [*A publication*] (MCD) .... ATM
Aircrew Training System (MCD) .... ATS
Aircrew Training Test Wing [*Air Force*] .... ATTW
Aircrew Uniform, Integrated Battlefield [*Army*] .... AUIB
Aircrewman .... AC
Aircrewman [*British military*] (DMA) .... ACMN
Air-Cure Environmental [*NASDAQ symbol*] (SPSG) .... AIRE
Air-Cure Technologies [*NASDAQ symbol*] (TTSB) .... ATSS
Air-Cure Technologies, Inc. [*Associated Press*] (SAG) .... AirCure
Air-Cure Technologies, Inc. [*AMEX symbol*] (SAG) .... ATS
Air-Cure Technologies, Inc. [*NASDAQ symbol*] (SAG) .... ATSS
Air-Cushion Barge (MCD) .... ACB
Air-Cushion Equipment Transportation System .... ACETS
Air-Cushion Equipment Transporter (SAUS) .... ACET
Air-Cushion Landing Gear .... ACLG
Air-Cushion Landing System .... ACLS
Air-Cushion Logistic Vehicle [*Helicopter*] .... ACLV
Air-Cushion Restraint System [*General Motors*] .... ACRS
Air-Cushion Takeoff System (MCD) .... ACTS
Air-Cushion Take-off System (SAUS) .... ACTS
Air-Cushion Trailer [*or Transporter*] .... ACT
Air-Cushion Vehicle .... ACV
Air-Cushion Vehicle built by Air Bearings [*England*] [*Usually used in combination with numerals*] .... AB
Air-Cushion Vehicle built by Air Vehicles [*England*] [*Usually used in combination with numerals*] .... AV
Air-Cushion Vehicle built by Ajax Hovercraft [*England*] [*Usually used in combination with numerals*] .... AH
Air-Cushion Vehicle built by Canadian Cushion Craft [*Usually used in combination with numerals*] [*Canada*] .... CANAIR
Air-Cushion Vehicle built by Commercial Hovercraft Industries [*New Zealand*] [*Usually used in combination with numerals*] .... CH
Air-Cushion Vehicle built by Cushioncraft [*England*] [*Usually used in combination with numerals*] CC
Air-Cushion Vehicle built by DeHavilland Aircraft Co. of Canada [*Usually used in combination with numerals*] [*Canada*] .... DHC
Air-Cushion Vehicle built by Denny Brothers [*England*] [*Usually used in combination with numerals*] .... D
Air-Cushion Vehicle built by Flygtekniska Forsoksanstalen [*Sweden*] [*Usually used in combination with numerals*] .... FFA
Air-Cushion Vehicle built by Hover Vehicles [*New Zealand*] [*Usually used in combination with numerals*] .... HV
Air-Cushion Vehicle built by Hovercraft Development [*England*] [*Usually used in combination with numerals*] .... HD
Air-Cushion Vehicle built by Hoverjet [*Usually used in combination with numerals*] [*Canada*] .... HJ
Air-Cushion Vehicle Built by Hovermarine [*Usually used in combination with numerals*] .... HM
Air-Cushion Vehicle built by Hoversport [*US*] [*Usually used in combination with numerals*] .... HS
Air-Cushion Vehicle built by Mitsubishi [*Japan*] [*Usually used in combination with numerals*] .... MH
Air-Cushion Vehicle built by Nakamura Seisakusho [*Usually used in combination with numerals*] [*Japan*] .... NAMCO
Air-Cushion Vehicle built by Research Vehicle Department [*Brazil*] [*Usually used in combination with numerals*] .... DEPV
Air-Cushion Vehicle built by Rhein Flugzeugbau [*Usually used in combination with numerals*] [*Germany*] .... RFB
Air-Cushion Vehicle built by Saunders Roe [*England*] [*Usually used in combination with numerals*] .... SR
Air-Cushion Vehicle built by Sealand Air Cushion Vehicles [*US*] [*Usually used in combination with numerals*] .... SAVC
Air-Cushion Vehicle built by Sealand Hovercraft [*England*] [*Usually used in combination with numerals*] .... SH
Air-Cushion Vehicle built by Societe National Industrielle Aerospatiale [*France*] [*Usually used in combination with numerals*] .... SA
Air-Cushion Vehicle built by Universal Hovercraft [*US*] [*Usually used in combination with numerals*] .... UH
Air-Cushion Vehicle built by Vosper Thorneycroft [*England*] [*Usually used in combination with numerals*] .... VT
Aird. Blackstone Economised [*1873*] [*A publication*] (ILCA) .... Aird Black
Aird Blackstone Economised (journ.) (SAUS) .... Aird Black
Air-Dale Ltd. [*Canada*] [*ICAO designator*] (FAAC) .... ADL
Airdance, Inc. [*Formerly, Bellanca-Champion Club*] (EA) .... BCC
Air-Deliverable Anti-Pollution Transfer System (SAUS) .... ADAPTS
Air-Deliverable Antipollution Transfer System .... ADAPTS
Air-Delivered Attack Marker [*Air Force*] (MCD) .... ADAM
Air-Delivered Land Mine System [*Military*] .... ADLMS
Air-Delivered Seismic Instruction Detector (SAUS) .... ADSID
Air-Delivered Seismic Intrusion Detectors .... ADSID
Air-Delivered Target-Activated Munitions (AFM) .... ADTAM
Air-Deployable Array Sonobuoy [*Military*] (IUSS) .... ADAS
Air-Deployed Expendable Bathythermographs (SAUS) .... AXBT
Air-Deployed Towed-Array Surveillance System (MCD) .... AIRTAS
Air-Derived Separation Assurance [*Aviation*] .... ADSA
Air-Derived Separation Assurance System [*Aviation*] .... ADSAS
Airdrie Municipal Library, Airdrie, AB, Canada [*Library symbol*] [*Library of Congress*] (LCLS) .... CaAAiM
Airdrie Municipal Library, Alberta [*Library symbol*] [*National Library of Canada*] (NLC) .... AAIM
Air-Dried [*Lumber*] .... AD
Air-Dried Ton .... ADT
Air-Driven Air Amplifier .... ADAA

Air-Driven Generator (MCD)	ADG
Airdrome	AD
Airdrome Battalion	ADROBN
Airdrome Beacon (SAUS)	A/Ben
Airdrome Control [British] (SAA)	AC
Airdrome Control Point (SAUS)	ACP
Airdrome Defense Corps [Air Force]	ADC
Airdrome Officer	AO
Airdrome Squadron (SAUO)	A Sq
Airdrome to Airdrome (SAUS)	A/A
Airdrop [Military] (AABC)	ADRP
Air-Dropped Sensors	ADSIDS
Air-Dry (SAUS)	AD
Aird's Civil Laws of France [A publication] (DLA)	Aird Civ Law
Airedale Terrier Association of New South Wales [Australia]	ATANSW
Airedale Terrier Club of America (EA)	ATCA
Aires, Aerovias de Integracion Regional SA [Colombia] [ICAO designator] (FAAC)	ARE
AiResearch Manufacturing Co.	AMC
Air-Espace Techniques (journ.) (SAUS)	Air-Espace Tech
Aire-Sur-L'Addour [France] [ICAO location identifier] (ICLI)	LFDA
Aireworth Volunteer Corps [British military] (DMA)	AVC
Airfast Service Indonesia PT [ICAO designator] (FAAC)	AFE
Airfield (NATG)	A/F
Airfield (AFM)	AFLD
Airfield (SAUS)	Airfd
Airfield Ammunition Park (SAUO)	AFAP
Airfield and Carrier Requirements Department (SAUO)	ACRD
Airfield and Carrier Requirements Department (SAA)	ACRD
Airfield and Seaplane Stations of the World (MUGU)	ASSOTW
Airfield Attack Ammunition (SAUS)	AFAM
Airfield Attack Munition (ACAE)	AAM
Airfield Attack Weapon (ACAE)	AAW
Airfield Capabilities Application (SAUS)	PACCA
Airfield Chemical Alarm System (SAUS)	ACAS
Airfield Clearance Plough (SAUS)	ACP
Airfield Construction Branch (SAUO)	ACB
Airfield Construction Branch [British military] (DMA)	ACB
Airfield Construction Group (SAUO)	ACG
Airfield Construction Service [Military] (WDAA)	ACS
Airfield Control RADAR [Air Force]	ACR
Airfield Damage Assessment System (SAUS)	ADAS
Airfield Damage Information & Reporting System (SAUS)	ADIRS
Airfield Damage Repair [Military]	ADR
Airfield Damage Repair Squadron (SAUS)	ADRS
Airfield Delay Simulation Model [FAA] (TAG)	ADSIM
Airfield Heliport	AH
Airfield Index	AI
Airfield Landing Mat (SAUS)	ALM
Airfield Lighting System	ALS
Airfield Marking and Lighting (NATG)	AML
Airfield Operations Designator [Air Force/Army]	AOD
Airfield Pavement [Air Force]	AFPAV
Airfield Rescue & Fire Fighting (SAUS)	ARFF
Airfield Spare Parts Depot (SAUO)	AFSPD
Airfield Surface Detection Radar (SAUS)	ASDER
Airfield Surface Movement Indication (SAUO)	ASMI
Airfield Surface Movement Indication (or Indicator) (SAUS)	ASMI
Airfield Surface Movement Indicator [RADAR] [Aviation] (IAA)	ASM
Airfield Surface Movement Indicator [RADAR] [Aviation] (SAUS)	ASMI
Airfield Surface Movement Indicator (SAUO)	ASMI
Airfield Surveillance Radar (SAUS)	ASR
Airfield Vehicle Obstacle Device (SAUS)	AVOID
Airfield Vehicle Obstacle Indicating (or Indication) Device (SAUS)	AVOID
Airfields Environment Federation (EAIO)	AEF
Airfields Environment Trust [British]	AET
Airfields, Pavements, and Mobility Information Analysis Center [Military]	APMIAC
Airfile (SAUS)	AF
Air-Filled Cushion [Medicine] (DAVI)	AFC
Air/Firing Mechanism (SAUS)	A/FM
Airflex Clutch (DS)	AFC
Airflow Club of America (EA)	ACA
Airflow per Unit of Time [Medicine] (DAVI)	V_E
Airfoil Design and Analysis Center [Ohio State University] (MCD)	ADAC
Airfoil Leading Edge Separation (MCD)	ALESEP
Airfoil Temperature Thickness (SAUS)	t
Airforce Magazine (journ.) (SAUS)	AirFMgz
Air-Force Navy-Army Guided-Missiles (SAUS)	ANG
Airforce Post Office (SAUS)	APO
Air-Force Training Auxiliary (SAUS)	ATA
Airforce-Navy Aeronautical Bulletin (SAUS)	ANA
Airframe	AFME
Airframe	AFR
Airframe (AABC)	AFRM
Airframe and Engine	A and E
Airframe and Powerplant [Aviation]	A & P
Airframe and Powerplant (SAUS)	A&P
Airframe and System Assembly/Test (MCD)	ASA/T
Airframe Bulletin (MCD)	AFB
Airframe Change	AC
Airframe Change (MCD)	AFC
Airframe Change Control Board (MCD)	ACCB
Airframe Design (SAUS)	AD
Airframe Design Division [Bureau of Aeronautics; later, NASC] [Navy]	AD

Airframe Fatigue Data Analysis System (MCD)	AFDAS
Airframe Flight Qualification	AFQ
Airframe Integrated Nozzle (MCD)	AIN
Airframe Manufacturers Planning Report (SAUS)	AMPR
Airframe Manufacturing Equipment Committee	AMEC
Airframe Manufacturing Tooling Committee (SAUO)	AMTC
Airframe Mechanical and Fluid Subsystems (MCD)	AMFS
Airframe Mounted Accessory Drive (SAUS)	AMAD
Airframe Nose Up (SAUS)	ANU
Airframe Repair Technician-Repairman (AAG)	ART/R
Airframe Unit Weight	AUW
Airframe-Mounted Accessory Drive System	AMADS
Airfreight Container [Shipping] (DCTA)	AC
Air/Fuel [Mixture ratio]	A/F
Air-Fuel Ratio (ADA)	AFR
Air-Fuel Ratio Control Device [Automotive engineering]	AFRCD
Air-Gap Separation [Environmental science] (COE)	AG
Airgas, Inc. [Associated Press] (SAG)	Airgas
Airgas, Inc. [NYSE symbol] (SPSG)	ARG
Airglow Measurements of Infrared Measurements Emissions (SAUS)	AMIE
Airglow Measurements of Infrared Measurements Emissions (GEOI)	AMIF
Airglow Solar Spectrometer Instrument	ASSI
Airgraph (ADA)	A/G
Air/Ground (SAUS)	A/G
Air/Ground Anti-jam Transmission from Helicopter or Aircraft (SAUS)	AGATHA
Air-Ground Chart (AFM)	AGC
Air-Ground Communications (CET)	AGC
Air-Ground Communications Channel	AGCC
Air-Ground Communications System (SAA)	AGCS
Air-Ground Cooling Unit (MCD)	AGCU
Air-Ground Cooperation Officer	AGCO
Air-Ground Correlation Factor (AABC)	AGCF
Air-Ground Data Telemetry System (SAUS)	AGDATS
Air-Ground Engagement Simulation (RDA)	AGES
Air-Ground Information Center (or Centre) (SAUS)	AGIC
Air-Ground Integration System	AGIS
Air-Ground Liaison Officer [Marine Corps]	AGLO
Air-Ground Operations School (SAUO)	AGOS
Air-Ground Operations Section [or School or System]	AGOS
Air-Ground Radiotelephone Automated Service (CGWS)	AGRAS
Air-Ground Radiotelephone Automated Service Credit Card Number (CGWS)	AGRASCCN
Air-Ground System	AGS
Air-Ground-Air Communications System	AGACS
Air-Ground-Air Communications System (SAUS)	AGA-CS
Air-Handling Unit [Mechanical engineering] (OA)	AHU
Air-Hardened (SAUS)	AH
Airhead [Army] (AABC)	AH
Airhead Air Traffic Coordination Center [Army] (AFIT)	AATCC
Airhead Air Traffic Coordination Center (SAUO)	AATOC
Airhead Maintenance Area [Military] [British]	AMA
Air-Independent (SAUS)	AI
Air-Independent Propulsion System [Navy]	AIP
Air-India International (SAUO)	A-II
Air-Land Assault (CINC)	ALA
Air-Land Battle (MCD)	ALB
Airland battle Force (SAUO)	ALF
Air-Land Battle Management	ALBM
Air/Land Battlefield Environment [Army] (RDA)	ALBE
Air-Land Battle-Future [Army] (INF)	ALB-F
Air-Land Forces Agency [Air Force] [Army] (MCD)	ALFA
Air-Land Forces Application Agency (SAUS)	ALFA
Air-Land Forces Applications	ALFA
Air-Land Forces Applications Agency [TAC-TRADOC] (MCD)	ALFAA
Air-Land Forces Integration (MCD)	ALFI
Air-Land Forces Interface	ALFI
Air-Land Operations Manual (MCD)	ALOM
Air-Land Programs Office	ALPO
Air-Land Resupply (CINC)	ALR
Air/Land Warfare (SAUS)	ALW
Air-Landing [British military] (DMA)	A/L
Airlanding Antitank Battery (SAUS)	ALATB
Airlantic Transport [Air carrier designation symbol]	ATIX
Air-Launch Sounding Rock	ALSOR
Air-Launched [Missile launch environment symbol]	A
Air-Launched Advanced Ramjet Missile (KSC)	ALARM
Air-Launched Air-Recoverable Rocket (SAUS)	ALARR
Air-Launched Antiradiation Missile	ALARM
Air-Launched Ballistic Intercept	ALBI
Air-Launched Ballistic Intercept System (MCD)	ALBIS
Air-Launched Ballistic Missile	ALBM
Air-Launched Balloon System (MCD)	ALBS
Air-Launched Boost Intercept (MSA)	ALBI
Air-Launched Booster (MCD)	ALB
Air-Launched Conventional Attack Missile (SAUS)	ALCAM
Air-Launched Cruise Missile	ALCM
Air-Launched Cruise Missile Guidance Set (MCD)	ALCMGS
Air-launched Decoy Missile	ADM
Air-launched Expendable Bathythermograph (SAUS)	AXBT
Air-launched Expendable Sound Velocimeter (SAUS)	ASXV
Air-Launched Guided Missile [Military]	AGM
Air-Launched Guided Weapons Modification Committee (SAUO)	ALGWMC
Air-Launched High-Altitude Reconnaissance Drone (MCD)	ALHARD
Air-Launched Instrumented Vehicle Evaluation (MCD)	ALIVE

Air-Launched Intercept Missile ... ALIM
Air-Launched Intercept Missile Record System ... AIMS
Air-Launched Interceptor Missile (MCD) ... AIM
Air-Launched Low-Altitude Cruise Missile (MCD) ... ALLACM
Air-Launched Low-Volume Ramjet (MCD) ... ALLVRJ
Air-Launched Low-Volume Ramjet ... ALVRJ
Air-Launched Medium-Intermediate Range Ballistic Missile (MCD) ... ALMIRBM
Air-Launched Miniature Vehicle ... ALMV
Air-Launched Missile ... ALM
Air-Launched Missile Ballistics (MCD) ... ALMB
Air-launched Missile Bulletin (SAUS) ... AMB
Air-Launched Missile Change (DNAB) ... ALMC
Air-Launched Missile Change (MCD) ... AMC
Air-Launched Missile Intermediate Maintenance System Program [*Navy*] (MCD) ... ALMIMSIP
Air-Launched Missile Inventory Objectives Study (MCD) ... ALMIOS
Air-Launched Missile Propulsion Technology (MCD) ... ALMPT
Air-Launched Missile System ... ALMS
Air-Launched Nonnuclear Ordnance (DNAB) ... ALNN
Air-Launched Non-Nuclear Ordnance (SAUS) ... ALNNO
Air-Launched Nuclear Weapon (DNAB) ... ALNW
Air-Launched Platform (NVT) ... ALP
Air-Launched Probe System (MCD) ... ALPS
Air-Launched Projected Sonobuoy (MCD) ... ALPS
Air-Launched Report [*Navy*] (NG) ... ALREP
Air-Launched Rocket Recovery (SAUS) ... ALARR
Air-Launched Saturation System missile (SAUS) ... ALSS
Air-Launched Segment (ACAE) ... ALS
Air-Launched Ship-Attack Missile ... ALSAM
Air-Launched Sortie Vehicle [*Aviation*] (AIA) ... ALSV
Air-Launched Sounding Rocket (SAUS) ... ALSOR
Air-Launched Strategic Missile ... ALSM
Air-Launched Surface Attack Missile ... ALSAM
Air-Launched Trainer Rocket (AFM) ... ATR
Air-Launched Unit ... ALU
Airlease Ltd. [*Associated Press*] (SAG) ... Airlease
Airlease Ltd. [*NYSE symbol*] (SPSG) ... FLY
Airlease Ltd L.P. [*NYSE symbol*] (TTSB) ... FLY
Airlec [*France*] [*ICAO designator*] (FAAC) ... ARL
Airlen [*Russian Federation*] [*ICAO designator*] (FAAC) ... LNA
Airless Spray Gun (SAUS) ... ASG
Airless Spraying (SAUS) ... AS
Airletter Mail Express [*American Express Co.*] ... AMEX
Airlie Beach [*Australia*] [*Airport symbol*] ... WSY
AirLifeLine (EA) ... ALL
Airlift (AABC) ... AL
Airlift [*International*] ... ALF
Airlift ... ALFT
Airlift ... ARLFT
Airlift and Training Division [*Air Force*] (MCD) ... ATD
Air-Lift Associates, Inc. [*ICAO designator*] (FAAC) ... WPK
Airlift Association (EA) ... AA
Airlift Center [*Air Force*] (MCD) ... ALCENT
Airlift Circulator (SAUS) ... ALC
Airlift Clearance Authority (AFM) ... ACA
Airlift Command Post (AFM) ... ACP
Airlift Communications Division [*Military*] ... ACD
Airlift Concepts and Requirements Agency ... ACRA
Airlift Concepts & Requirements Agency (SAUS) ... ACRA
Airlift Contingency Battalion Landing Team (NVT) ... ACBLT
Airlift Contingency Forces [*Marine Corps*] (DOMA) ... ACF
Airlift Control Center (AFM) ... ALCC
Airlift Control Element (AFM) ... ALCE
Airlift Control Squadron (SAUO) ... ALCS
Airlift Coordinating Office [*or Officer*] (AFIT) ... ALCO
Airlift Coordination Center [*Air Force*] (DOMA) ... ACC
Airlift Coordination Center (SAUO) ... ALCC
Airlift Coordination Center/Military Airlift Support Squadron (SAUO) ... ACC/MASS
Airlift Division [*Air Force*] ... ALD
Airlift Execution Planning System (ACAE) ... AEPS
Airlift Field Maintenance Section ... AFMS
Airlift Group (SAUO) ... AG
Airlift Group [*Military*] ... ALG
Airlift Industrial Services Flight [*Military*] ... AISF
Airlift Information Systems Division (ACAE) ... AISD
Airlift International, Inc. [*ICAO designator*] (FAAC) ... AIR
Airlift International, Inc. (IIA) ... ALI
Airlift International, Inc. [*ICAO designator*] ... RD
Airlift International, Inc. [*Air carrier designation symbol*] ... RDLX
Airlift Launch Control Officer [*Air Force*] (AFM) ... ALCO
Airlift Liaison Coordination Officer [*Air Force*] ... ALCO
Airlift Loading Model ... ALM
Airlift Logistics Readiness Center (SAUO) ... ALRC
Air-Lift Management System [*Air Force*] (PDAA) ... ALMS
Airlift Management System (SAUS) ... Alms
Airlift Master Plan (SAUS) ... AMP
Airlift Mission Planning and Scheduling System [*Air Force*] (MCD) ... AMPSS
Airlift Operational Report ... ALOREP
Airlift Operations Center (SAUO) ... AOC
Airlift Operations Directive (AFM) ... AOD
Airlift Operations School (SAUS) ... AOS
Airlift Operations School Library, Scott AFB, IL [*OCLC symbol*] (OCLC) ... AOS
Airlift Readiness Center (SAUO) ... ARC
Airlift Requirements Center (SAUO) ... ARC
Airlift Requirements Forecast System (SAUO) ... FORECAST
Airlift Service Industrial Fund [*Military*] ... ASIF
Airlift Simulation Model ... ASM
Airlift Squadron (SAUO) ... ALS
Airlift Squadron (SAUS) ... AS
Airlift Summary (SAUS) ... LIFSUM
Airlift Summary Report [*Air Force*] ... LIFSUM
Airlift Summary Report (SAUS) ... LIFUM
Airlift Task Force [*Air Force*] (AFM) ... ALTF
Airlift Total Force Plan (SAUS) ... ATFP
Airlift Wing (SAUS) ... AW
Airlift/Tanker Association (EA) ... AA
Airline ... ARLN
Airline Administrative Message (DA) ... AAM
Airline Aviation Academy, Inc. [*ICAO designator*] (FAAC) ... ACD
Airline Cargo Services, Inc. [*British*] [*FAA designator*] (FAAC) ... ACV
Airline Carrier code (SAUS) ... EI
Airline Carriers of Goods ... ACG
Airline Carriers of Passengers ... ACP
Airline Carriers Passengers (SAUS) ... ACP
Airline Charter Service ... ACS
Airline Computer Tracing System (SAUS) ... ACTS
Airline Control Program / Transaction Processing Facility [*Computer science*] (BTTJ) ... ACP/TPF
Airline Control Program Transaction Processing Facility [*IBM Corp.*] (NITA) ... ACP/TF
Airline Credit Union Association (EA) ... ACUA
Airline Economic Modeling System (HGAA) ... AEMS
Airline Electrical Engineering Council (ACAE) ... AEEC
Airline Feed System ... AFS
Airline Flight Attendants Association [*Defunct*] (EA) ... AFAA
Airline Ground Transportation Association [*Defunct*] (EA) ... AGTA
Airline Group of International Federation of Operational Research Societies [*Denmark*] (MCD) ... AGIFORS
Airline Hostess (SAUS) ... AH
Airline Industrial Relations Conference (EA) ... AIR
Airline Industrial Relations Conference (NTPA) ... AIRCON
Air-Line Industrial Relations Conference Air Reduction Sales Company (SAUO) ... AIRCO
Airline Industry Affairs Committee (SAUO) ... AIAC
Airline Interline Development ... AID
Airline Interline Reservations System (SAUS) ... AIRS
Airline Inventory Redistribution System ... AIRS
Airline Link Control (HGAA) ... ALC
Airline Maintenance and Operation Support System (HLLA) ... AMOSS
Airline Mechanics Association (SAUO) ... AMA
Airline Medical Directors Association (EA) ... AMDA
Airline Modifiable Information (HLLA) ... AMI
Airline Mutual Insurance [*International Air Transport Association*] ... AMI
Airline of Adriatic [*Croatia*] [*ICAO designator*] (FAAC) ... ADC
Airline of the Marshall Islands [*ICAO designator*] (FAAC) ... MRS
Airline Operational Control Society [*Defunct*] (EA) ... AOCS
Airline Operations Center (CTAS) ... AOC
Airline Operations Planning Model (SAUS) ... AOP
Airline Operations Planning Model (NASA) ... AOPM
Airline Operations Services, Inc. [*ICAO designator*] (FAAC) ... XAO
Airline Operations Simulation Model (MCD) ... AOSM
Airline Operators Committee (SAUO) ... AOC
Airline Passenger Association (SAUO) ... APA
Airline Passenger Tariff [*Travel industry*] (TRID) ... APT
Airline Passengers Association (SAUO) ... APA
Airline Passengers Association of North America (EA) ... APANA
Airline Passengers of America (SAUS) ... APA
Airline Passengers of America [*Defunct*] (EA) ... AP/USA
Airline Public Relations Organization [*British*] (DBA) ... APRO
Airline Request Communication System (DA) ... ARCS
Airline Reservation System [*Aviation*] (ECII) ... ARS
Airline Reservations System (SAUS) ... ARS
Airline Revenue (DA) ... ARE
Airline Schedules and Interline Availability Study [*IATA*] (DS) ... ASIAS
Airline Service Quality Performance [*FAA*] (TAG) ... ASQP
Airline Services Association [*ARSA*] [*Absorbed by*] (EA) ... ASA
Airline Sports and Cultural Association (SAUO) ... ACA
Airline Stewards and Hostess Union (SAUO) ... ASHU
Airline System Simulator ... ALSS
Airline Tariff Analysis (DA) ... ATA
Airline Tariff Publishing Co. ... ATP
Airline Tariff Publishing Company (SAUO) ... ATPCO
Airline Traffic Association ... ALTA
Airline Transport Pilot [*Certificate*] [*British*] (IEEE) ... ATP
Airline Transport Pilot's Licence [*British*] (AIA) ... ALTP
Airline Transport Pilot's Licence [*British*] (DBQ) ... ATPL
Airline Transport Rating (IIA) ... ATR
Airline Travel Clubs (EA) ... ATC
Airline Users Committee (SAUO) ... AUC
Airline-Like Maintenance (DNAB) ... AIRLMAINT
Airlines Carriers of Goods (SAUS) ... ACG
Airlines Communications Administrative Council ... ALCAC
Airlines Computer Tracing System [*Luggage retrieving system*] ... ACTS
Airlines Control Program [*IBM Corp.*] ... ACP
Airlines Deregulation Act [*1978*] ... ADA
Airlines Electronic Engineering Committee ... AEEC
Airlines Engineering Electronics Committee (SAUO) ... AEEC
Airlines Load Optimization Recording and Display (SAUS) ... AIRLORD

Airlines Load Optimization Recording and Display Passenger Name Check-in (SAUS) .... AIRLORD PNC
Airlines Load Optimization Recording and Display System [*Airport passenger-moving sidewalk*] .... AIRLORDS
Airlines Medical Directors Association (SAUS) .... AMDA
Airlines of Hainan Province [*China*] [*ICAO designator*] (FAAC) .... CHH
Airlines of South Australia Pty (SAUO) .... ASAP
Airlines of Tasmania [*Australia*] [*ICAO designator*] (FAAC) .... ATM
Airlines of Tasmania [*ICAO designator*] (AD) .... IP
Airlines of Western Australia [*Australia*] [*ICAO designator*] (ICDA) .... MV
Airlines Reporting Corporation (TRID) .... ARC
Airlines Sports and Cultural Association (EA) .... ASCA
Airlines Staff International Association (EAIO) .... ASIA
Airline-Selected Equipment (HLLA) .... ASE
Airlink Airlines (Pty) Ltd. [*South Africa*] [*ICAO designator*] (FAAC) .... LNK
Airlink Luftverkehrsgesellschaft GmbH [*Austria*] [*ICAO designator*] (FAAC) .... JAR
Airlis SA [*Spain*] [*ICAO designator*] (FAAC) .... LIS
Airlock Adapter Plate (MCD) .... AAP
Airlock Audio Terminal (SAUS) .... ATU
Airlock Illumination Subassembly (MCD) .... AIS
Airlock Module [*NASA*] .... AM
Airlock Module and Multiple Docking Adapter (PDAA) .... AM/MDA
Airlock Module Station [*NASA*] (MCD) .... AMS
Airlock Multiple Docking Adapter [*NASA*] (MCD) .... ALMDA
Airlock Outfitting (SSD) .... AO
Airlock Signal Conditioning Electronics (MCD) .... ASCE
Airlock Stowage Bag [*NASA*] (MCD) .... ASB
Airlock Support Subsystem [*NASA*] (NASA) .... ASS
Airlock Support System [*or Subsystem*] [*NASA*] (MCD) .... ALSS
Airlock System (SAUS) .... ALS
Airlock Systems Test [*NASA*] (MCD) .... AST
Airlock Wall (MCD) .... AW
Air-locked Module (SAUS) .... AM
Airlock/Extravehicle Mobility Unit [*NASA*] (MCD) .... AL/EMU
Airlock/Extravehicular Mobility Unit (SAUS) .... AL/EMU
Airluxor Ltda. [*Portugal*] [*ICAO designator*] (FAAC) .... LXR
Airmail .... AM
Airmail (FAAC) .... ARML
Airmail Facility (SAUO) .... AMF
Airmail Notice (SAUS) .... AN
Air-Mail Pioneer (SAUS) .... AMP
Airmail Service (SAUO) .... ARS
Airmailgram .... AMGM
Airman .... A
Airman (AFM) .... AMN
Airman (ADWA) .... Amn
Airman [*Nonrated enlisted man*] [*Navy*] .... AN
Airman [*British military*] (DMA) .... ARMN
Airman [*Air Force*] E2
Airman, Aerographer's Mate, Striker [*Navy rating*] .... AGAN
Airman, Air Controlman, Striker [*Navy rating*] .... ACAN
Airman Apprentice [*Navy rating*] .... AA
Airman Apprentice, Aerographer's Mate, Striker [*Navy rating*] .... AGAA
Airman Apprentice, Air Controlman, Striker [*Navy rating*] .... ACAA
Airman Apprentice, Aviation ASW [*Antisubmarine Warfare*] Operator, Striker [*Navy rating*] .... AWAA
Airman Apprentice, Aviation ASW [*Antisubmarine Warfare*] Technician, Striker [*Navy rating*] .... AXAA
Airman Apprentice, Aviation Boatswain's Mate, Striker [*Navy rating*] .... ABAA
Airman Apprentice, Aviation Electrician, Striker [*Navy rating*] .... AEAA
Airman Apprentice, Aviation Fire Control Technician, Striker [*Navy rating*] .... AQAA
Airman Apprentice, Aviation Machinist's Mate, Reciprocating Engine Mechanic, Striker [*Navy rating*] .... ADRAA
Airman Apprentice, Aviation Machinists Mate, Reciprocating Engine Mechanic, Striker (SAUS) .... ADRAA
Airman Apprentice, Aviation Maintenance Administrationman, Striker [*Navy rating*] .... AZAA
Airman Apprentice, Aviation Storekeeper [*Navy rating*] .... AKAA
Airman Apprentice, Aviation Structural Mechanic, Striker [*Navy rating*] .... AMAA
Airman Apprentice, Aviation Support Equipment Technician, Striker [*Navy rating*] .... ASAA
Airman Apprentice (High School) .... AA(HS)
Airman Apprentice High School (SAUS) .... AAHS
Airman Apprentice, Jet Striker [*Navy rating*] .... ADJAA
Airman Apprentice, Parachute Rigger, Striker [*Navy rating*] .... PRAA
Airman Apprentice, Photographer's Mate, Striker [*Navy rating*] .... PHAA
Airman Apprentice, Photographic Intelligenceman, Striker [*Navy rating*] .... PTAA
Airman Apprentice, Tradevman (SAUS) .... TDAA
Airman Apprentice, TRADEVMAN [*Training Devices Man*], Striker [*Navy rating*] .... TDAA
Airman, Aviation ASW [*Antisubmarine Warfare*] Operator, Striker [*Navy rating*] .... AWAN
Airman, Aviation ASW [*Antisubmarine Warfare*] Technician, Striker [*Navy rating*] .... AXAN
Airman, Aviation Boatswain's Mate, Striker [*Navy rating*] .... ABAN
Airman, Aviation Electrician, Striker [*Navy rating*] .... AEAN
Airman, Aviation Electronics Technician [*Navy rating*] .... ATAN
Airman, Aviation Fire Control Technician, Striker [*Navy rating*] .... AQAN
Airman, Aviation Machinist's Mate, Reciprocating Engine Mechanic, Striker [*Navy rating*] .... ADRAN
Airman, Aviation Machinists Mate, Reciprocating Engine Mechanic, Striker (SAUS) .... ADRAN
Airman, Aviation Maintenance Administrationman, Striker [*Navy rating*] .... AZAN
Airman, Aviation Storekeeper [*Navy rating*] .... AKAN

Airman, Aviation Structural Mechanic, Striker [*Navy rating*] .... AMAN
Airman, Aviation Support Equipment Technician, Striker [*Navy rating*] .... ASAN
Airman Basic .... AB
Airman, Basic (SAUS) AB/3C
Airman Classification Battery (SAUS) .... ACB
Airman Classification Squadron [*Air Force*] .... ACS
Airman Classification Test (SAUS) .... ACT
Airman Commissioning Program [*Air Force*] (AFM) .... ACP
Airman Education and Commissioning Program .... AECP
Airman Education & Commissioning Program (SAUS) .... AECP
Airman Effectiveness Report [*Air Force*] .... AER
Airman First Class (SAUS) A/1C
Airman, First Class (IIA) .... AFC
Airman, First Class E3
Airman High School (SAUS) .... ANHS
Airman (High School) (DNAB) .... AN(HS)
Airman, Jet Striker [*Navy rating*] .... ADJAN
Airman Memorial Foundation (EA) .... AMF
Airman Military Record [*Air Force*] .... AMR
Airman, Parachute Rigger, Striker [*Navy*] .... PRAN
Airman Performance Report Review Board (AFM) .... APRRB
Airman, Photographer's Mate, Striker [*Navy rating*] .... PHAN
Airman, Photographic Intelligenceman, Striker [*Navy rating*] .... PTAN
Airman Proficiency Test (SAUS) .... APT
Airman Qualifying Examination .... AQE
Airman Qualifying Test (SAUS) .... AQT
Airman Records [*Air Force*] (AFM) .... AR
Airman Recruit .... AR
Airman Recruit (High School) (DNAB) .... AR(HS)
Airman Scholarship & Commissioning Program (SAUS) .... ASCP
Airman Second Class (SAUS) A/2C
Airman Third Class (SAUS) A/3C
Airman, Tradevman (SAUS) .... TDAN
Airman, TRADEVMAN [*Training Devices Man*], Striker [*Navy rating*] .... TDAN
Airman's Guide [*A publication*] .... AIRGI
Airman's Information Manual [*FAA*] .... AIM
Airmans Information Manual (SAUS) .... AIM
Airman's Medal [*Military decoration*] (AFM) .... AmnM
Airman's Meteorological Information [*FAA*] (TAG) .... AIRMET
Airmans Qualification Card (SAUS) .... AQC
Airmanship Training Squadron [*Air Force*] .... ATS
Airmark Aviation, Inc. [*ICAO designator*] (FAAC) .... TRH
Air-Mass Transformation Experiment [*National Science Foundation/ Japan*] .... AMTEX
Airmen Classification Battery [*Military tests*] .... ACB
Airmen Qualifying Examination (SAUS) .... AQE
Airmens Advisory (SAUS) .... AIRAD
Airmens Meteorological Information (SAUS) .... AIRMET
Air-Mining Mission [*Military*] .... AMM
Airmobile (AABC) .... AMBL
Airmobile Aircraft Maintenance Shop (SAUO) .... AAMS
Airmobile Cavalry (SAUO) .... Air Cav
Air-Mobile Van (SAUS) .... AIRVAN
Air-Moving Device [*Technical drawings*] (DAC) .... AMD
Air-Natural, Air-Natural Cooling (SAUS) .... ANAN Cooling
AirNet Systems [*NYSE symbol*] (SG) .... ANS
AirNet Systems [*NASDAQ symbol*] (TTSB) .... ANSY
AirNet Systems, Inc. [*Associated Press*] (SAG) .... AirNetS
AirNet Systems,Inc. [*NASDAQ symbol*] (SAG) .... ANSY
Air-Nitrogen Pressurization Control .... ANPC
Airnman Basic (SAUS) .... A/B
Air-Ocean Environmental Specialist (DNAB) .... AOES
Air/Oil Ratio (SAUS) .... AOR
Air-operated Circuit Breaker (SAUS) .... ACB
Air-Operated Plastic Valve .... AOPV
Air-Operated Unit .... AOU
Air-Operated Valve (NRCH) .... AOV
Airpac Airlines, Inc. [*ICAO designator*] (FAAC) .... APC
Airpac, Inc. (SAUO) .... APM
Air-Piloted Control Valve .... APCV
Air-Piloted Valve .... APV
Airplane (ABBR) .... A
Airplane [*Freight*] .... AIRPL
Airplane .... AP
Airplane (KSC) .... APL
Airplane & Armament Experimental Establishment (SAUS) .... AAEE
Airplane and Engine License (SAUS) .... AEL
Airplane Armada (SAUS) .... AIRMADA
Airplane Avionics (NASA) .... AA
Airplane Avionics/AUTOLAND (NASA) .... AA/AL
Airplane Avionics/Autoland (SAUS) .... AA/AL
Airplane Change Analysis (SAUS) .... ACA
Airplane Condition Monitoring System [*Aviation*] .... ACMS
Airplane Configuration System .... ACS
Airplane Economic Design Evaluator [*Boeing Co.*] .... AEDE
Airplane Engine, Propeller, and Accessory Overhaul [*Navy*] .... AIRENGPROPACCOVERHAUL
Airplane Flight Manual [*Federal Aviation Administration*] .... AFM
Airplane, General (MCD) .... APG
Airplane Glue (SAUS) .... A-Glue
Airplane Group (MCD) .... AG
Airplane Hotel (SAUS) .... AEROTEL
Airplane Information Management System [*Honeywell, Inc.*] .... AIMS
Airplane Mechanic .... AM
Airplane Messenger (SAUS) .... Ap Msgr

Airplane Model List of America ... AMLA
Airplane Multi-Engine Land (PIPO) ... AMEL
Airplane Multi-Engine Sea (PIPO) ... AMES
Airplane Nose Down ... AND
Airplane Nose Up (NG) ... ANU
Airplane Observation (SAUS) ... APOB
Airplane Operating Empty Weight (OA) ... AOEW
Airplane Pilot ... AP
Airplane Responsive Engine Selection (MCD) ... ARES
Airplane Single-Engine Land [*Aviation rating*] ... ASEL
Airplane Single-Engine Sea (PIPO) ... ASES
Airplane Sizing and Mission Performance [*Computer program*] ... ASAMP
Airplane Splint (MELL) ... APS
Airplane Test Equipment (SAUS) ... ATE
Airplanes, Inc. [*ICAO designator*] (FAAC) ... REZ
Air-Pollutants Index ... API
Air-Pollution Control Equipment (SAUS) ... APCE
Airport (VRA) ... airpt
Airport ... AP
Airport (AFM) ... APRT
Airport (AFIT) ... APT
Airport ... ARPRT
Airport ... ARPT
Airport Acceptance Rate [*FAA*] (TAG) ... AAR
Airport Acceptance Rate [*Aviation*] (FAAC) ... AARTE
Airport Advisory Service [*FAA*] (TAG) ... AAS
Airport and Airspace Delay Model (PDAA) ... AADM
Airport and Airspace Simulation Model [*FAA*] (TAG) ... SIMMOD
Airport and Airway Development Act (SAUS) ... AADA
Airport and Airway Improvement Act [*OST*] (TAG) ... AAIA
Airport and Airways (OICC) ... A/A
Airport and Airways Surveillance RADAR [*Air Force*] ... AASR
Airport and Airways Surveillance Radar (SAUS) ... AASR
Airport and Surveillance Radar (SAUS) ... AASR
Airport Area (PIPO) ... A
Airport Art (SAUS) ... Airpt Art
Airport Associations Coordinating Council [*Geneva Airport, Switzerland*] (EAIO) ... AACC
Airport Bird Detection Equipment ... ABDE
Airport Business Center, Inc. [*Minneapolis, MN*] [*Telecommunications*] (TSSD) ... ABCI
Airport Business Center Incorporated (SAUO) ... ABCI
Airport Capacity Enhancement [*FAA*] (TAG) ... ACE
Airport Capital Improvement Program [*OST*] (TAG) ... ACIP
Airport Catering Service Ltd. (SAUO) ... ACS
Airport Characteristics Data Bank [*International Civil Aviation Organization*] [*Information service or system*] (IID) ... ACDB
Airport Coalition (SAUS) ... Air Coal
Airport Consultants Council (EA) ... ACC
Airport Control Station [*ITU designation*] (DEN) ... FAC
Airport Control Tower ... ACT
Airport Control Tower (SAUS) ... APT
Airport Council International (SAUO) ... ACI
Airport Data Information System (DA) ... ADIS
Airport Data System [*FAA*] ... ADS
Airport Development Aid Program [*FAA*] ... ADAP
Airport Development Program ... ADP
Airport Directory [*FAA*] ... APD
Airport District Office (SAUS) ... ADO
Airport Electronic Project (SAUS) ... AEP
Airport Engineering Data Sheet [*FAA*] (MCD) ... AEDS
Airport Engineering Hugo Marom Ltd. (SAUO) ... AEHM
Airport Environmental Protection Areas (ACAE) ... AEPA
Airport Facilities Directory (PIPO) ... A/FD
Airport Facility Directory [*FAA*] (TAG) ... AFD
Airport Field Office (SAUO) ... AFO
Airport Fire Officer (DA) ... AFO
Airport Ground Traffic Control [*Department of Transportation*] ... AGTC
Airport Ground Transportation Association (EA) ... AGTA
Airport Group International, Inc ... AGI
Airport Handling Agreements Sub-Committee [*IATA*] (DS) ... AHASC
Airport Handling Committee [*IATA*] (DS) ... AHC
Airport Handling Equipment Sub-Committee [*IATA*] (DS) ... AHESC
Airport Handling Manual [*IATA*] (DS) ... AHM
Airport Handling Procedures Sub-Committee [*IATA*] (DS) ... AHPSC
Airport Hangar [*New York*] [*Seismograph station code, US Geological Survey*] (SEIS) ... APH
Airport Hotel (SAUO) ... airtel
Airport Hotel Directory [*National Association of Business Travel Agents*] [*A publication*] ... AHD
Airport Improvement Program [*FAA*] (TAG) ... AIP
Airport in Sight (FAAC) ... AIS
Airport Income Management System (SAUS) ... AIMS
Airport Information Desk ... AID
Airport Information Retrieval System [*FAA*] ... AIRS
Airport Instrument Laboratories (SAUO) ... AIL
Airport Landing Equipment (MCD) ... ALE
Airport Layout Plan [*FAA*] (TAG) ... ALP
Airport Lighting Equipment (NASA) ... ALE
Airport Lights [*FAA*] (TAG) ... APL
Airport Location Point (SAUS) ... ALP
Airport Mail Facility (AFM) ... AMF
Airport Management and Information Display System (DA) ... AMIDS
Airport Management Information System ... AMIS
Airport Manager (FAAC) ... AMGR
Airport Managers Association of South Dakota (SRA) ... AMASD
Airport Movement Area Safety System [*FAA*] (TAG) ... AMASS
Airport Movement RADAR (DA) ... AMR
Airport Network Flow Simulator (MCD) ... ANFS
Airport Network Simulation Model [*FAA*] (TAG) ... AIRNET
Airport Noise Abatement Plan (PDAA) ... ANAP
Airport Noise Evaluation Process (PDAA) ... ANEP
Airport of Entry (DA) ... AOE
Airport of Entry (PIAV) ... AoE
Airport Operation Area (DA) ... AOA
Airport Operators' Association (PIAV) ... AOA
Airport Operators Council [*Later, AOCI*] (EA) ... AOC
Airport Operators Council International (EA) ... AOCI
Airport Overlay District (SAUO) ... AOP
Airport Parking Company of America (SAUO) ... APCOA
Airport RADAR Service Area [*Aeronautics*] ... ARSA
Airport Reference Point ... ARP
Airport Reporting Office (SAUO) ... ARO
Airport Rescue and Fire Fighting Alarm Checked (FAAC) ... ARFFOK
Airport Reservation Function [*FAA*] (TAG) ... ARF
Airport Reservation Office [*FAA*] (TAG) ... ARO
Airport Reservations Office (FAAC) ... ARO
Airport Security Council (EA) ... ASC
Airport Site (ACAE) ... APS
Airport Special Information and Regulations (SAUS) ... ASIR
Airport Surface Detection Equipment [*RADAR*] ... ASDE
Airport Surface Detection Equipment [*RADAR*] (IAA) ... ASE
Airport Surface Detection RADAR ... ASDR
Airport Surface Movement Equipment ... ASME
Airport Surface Movement Indicator (SAUO) ... ASMI
Airport Surface Surveillance RADAR (DA) ... ASSR
Airport Surface Traffic Automation [*FAA*] (TAG) ... ASTA
Airport Surface Traffic Control (OA) ... ASTC
Airport Surface Traffic RADAR Equipment (MCD) ... ASTRE
Airport Surface Traffic Simulator ... ASTS
Airport Surveillance RADAR (MSA) ... APSR
Airport Surveillance RADAR ... ASR
Airport Systems [*NASDAQ symbol*] (SAG) ... ASII
Airport Systems International, Inc. [*Associated Press*] (SAG) ... AirSys
Airport Systems International Inc. (SAUO) ... ASI
Airport Systems Intl [*NASDAQ symbol*] (TTSB) ... ASII
Airport Systems Intl. [*AMEX symbol*] ... ASY
Airport Terminal Information System (SAUS) ... ATIS
Airport Ticket Office (TRID) ... ATO
Airport Tower (SAUS) ... APT
Airport Traffic [*ICAO*] [*Information service or system*] [*United Nations*] (DUND) ... AT
Airport Traffic Area (MCD) ... ATA
Airport [*or Airway*] **Traffic Control** ... ATC
Airport Traffic Controller (IAA) ... APTC
Airport Trailing Vortex Warning System ... ATVWS
Airport Transportation ... AIRTRANS
Airport Transportation System (SAUS) ... AIRTRANS
Airport Vicinity Air Pollution ... AVAP
Airportable [*British military*] (DMA) ... APT
Airportable Cargo Trailer (SAUS) ... ACT
Air-Portable Fuel Container (SAUS) ... APFC
Airportable Lifting Equipment [*British military*] (PDAA) ... APLE
Airport-radar Terminal System (SAUS) ... ATS
Airports [*Public-performance tariff class*] [*British*] ... ARP
Airports and Construction Services, Transport Canada [*Service des Aeroports et de la Construction, Transports Canada*] **Ottawa, Ontario** [*Library symbol*] [*National Library of Canada*] (NLC) ... OOTAC
Airports Association Council International [*Switzerland*] (EAIO) ... AACI
Airports Authority Group [*Transport Canada*] (DA) ... AAG
Airports Council International/North America (NTPA) ... ACI/NA
Airports Development Agency (SAUO) ... ADA
Airports Economic Panel [*ICAO*] (DA) ... AEP
Airports Field Office ... AFO
Airports National Network [*British Airports Authority*] (NITA) ... ANN
Airports Program Report (FAAC) ... APR
Airports Service [*of FAA*] ... AS
Airpower Research Institute [*Air University*] [*Research center*] (RCD) ... ARI
Air-Purifying Respirator (FFDE) ... APR
Air-quality Data Monitoring (SAUS) ... ADAM
Air-Quality Management Plan [*Environmental Protection Agency*] (EPAT) ... AQMP
Air-Raid Defence [*British*] [*World War II*] ... ARD
Air-Refuelling Part-Task Trainer (SAUS) ... ARPTT
Air-Refuelling Transport (SAUS) ... ART
Air-Rep [*FAA designator*] (FAAC) ... XPR
Air-Resistance Horsepower [*Automotive engineering*] ... HPAR
AIRS [*Aerometric Information Retrieval System*] **Facility Subsystem** [*Environmental Protection Agency*] (GFGA) ... AFS
AIRS Facility Subsystem (SAUO) ... AFS
AIRS Facility Users Group (SAUO) ... AFUG
Airscoop ... AS
Air-Scooping Orbital Rocket (PDAA) ... A-SCOOR
Air-Sea Convective Intraseasonal Interaction (SAUS) ... ASCII
Air-Sea Interaction (SAUS) ... ASI
Air-Sea Interaction, Cloud and Precipitation Experiment over the Baltic Sea (SAUS) ... ASCAP
Air-Sea Rescue ... ASR
Air-Sea Rescue Craft ... ASRC
Air-Sea Rescue Flight [*British military*] (DMA) ... ASRF
Air-Sea Rescue Service [*British military*] (DMA) ... ASRS

Air-Sea Rescue Service (SAUS)	A-S RS
Air/Sea Warfare Development Unit (SAUS)	ASWDU
Air/Sea Warfare Development Unit (SAUO)	ASWDU
Air-Sea-Ice Interaction (SAUS)	ASII
Airsearch Manufacturing Co., Los Angeles, CA [Library symbol] [Library of Congress] (LCLS)	CLAi
AirSensors Wrrt [NASDAQ symbol] (TTSB)	ARSNW
Air-Service-Gabon [ICAO designator] (FAAC)	AGB
Airshed Model Data-Handling System [Environmental Protection Agency] (GFGA)	ASMDHS
Airship	ASHP
Airship, Air-Sea Rescue [Navy symbol]	ZNH
Airship Association [British] (EAIO)	AA
Airship Association - US (EA)	AA
Airship Detachment (SAUO)	AD
Airship Experimental Center [Navy]	AEC
Airship Group	AIRSHIPGR
Airship Group [Navy symbol]	ZPG
Airship Industries Ltd. [British]	AI
Airship (Nonrigid) [Navy symbol]	ZN
Airship Rigger	AR
Airship Squadron	AIRSHIPRON
Airship Tender [Navy symbol] [Obsolete]	AZ
Airship Training Unit (SAUO)	ATU
Airship, Utility [Navy symbol]	ZNJ
Airship Utility Squadron [Navy symbol]	ZUTRON
Air-Shuttle (SAUS)	AS
Airsignal International (SAUS)	ASI
Air-Sol Longue Portee (SAUS)	ASLP
Air-Sol Moyenne Portee. Air-to-surface medium-range missile (SAUS)	ASMP
Airspace (IAA)	AS
Airspace and Traffic Management [ICAO] (DA)	ATM
Airspace and Traffic Management Center (DA)	ATMC
Air-Space Cable (SAUS)	AS CABLE
Airspace Control & Operations Training simulator (SAUS)	ASCOT
Airspace Control Authority [Air Force] (DOMA)	ACA
Airspace Control Center (MCD)	ACC
Airspace Control Command [South Africa] [ICAO location identifier] (ICLI)	FAAC
Airspace Control [or Coordination] Element [Army]	ACE
Airspace Control Element (SAUS)	ACE
Airspace Control Order (SAUS)	ACO
Airspace Coordination Area (MCD)	ACA
Airspace Coordination Center [NATO] (DOMA)	ACC
Airspace Coordination Element (SAUO)	ACE
Airspace Flight Inspection Pilot (FAAC)	ASIP
Airspace Management (DA)	ASM
Airspace Management (DA)	ASMT
Airspace Management and Control (MCD)	AMC
Airspace Management Cell (SAUS)	AMC
Airspace Management Center (MCD)	AMC
Airspace Management Element (MCD)	AME
Airspace Management Element Liaison Officer	AME LNO
Airspace Management Liaison Section (MCD)	AMLS
Airspace Management Systems (SAUS)	AMS
Air-Space Multiple-Twin (IAA)	ASMT
Airspace Reservation Coordination Office (SAUO)	ARCO
Airspace Reservation Unit [Canada] (FAAC)	ARU
Airspace Subcommittee [ACC]	ASP
Airspace Surveillance Display & Control System (SAUS)	ASDCS
Airspace Surveillance Station	ASS
Airspace Warning (DNAB)	AW
Airspeed	AS
Air-Speed (PIPO)	A/S
Airspeed	ASP
Airspeed and Altitude Computer Set (CAAL)	AACS
Airspeed and Direction Sensor (PDAA)	AADS
Airspeed Aviation, Inc. [Canada] [ICAO designator] (FAAC)	SPD
Airspeed, forward Velocity (SAUS)	V
Airspeed Indicator (MSA)	AI
Airspeed Indicator	ASI
Airspeed Indicator	ASI
Airspeed Indicator Reading	ASIR
Airspeed Mach Indicator (MCD)	AMI
Air-Spray 1967 Ltd. [Canada] [ICAO designator] (FAAC)	ASB
Airspur Helicopters, Inc. (SAUS)	SPL
Air-Start Diesel Engine (DNAB)	AD
Airstream Direction Detector (PDAA)	ADD
Airstream Direction Sensing Unit (MCD)	ADSU
Air-Supported Threat [Army]	AST
Air-Supported Threat Defense [Army] (AABC)	ASTD
Air-Supported Threat Defense System [Army]	ASTDS
Air/Surface Laser Ranger (SAUS)	ASLR
Air-Surveillance Vehicle (SAUS)	ASVEH
Airtaxi Bedarfsluftverkehrsges GmbH [Austria] [ICAO designator] (FAAC)	JOK
Airtaxi Wings AG [Switzerland] [ICAO designator] (FAAC)	AWG
Airtech Firearms Training System (SAUS)	AFTS
Airtight [Technical drawings]	AT
Airtight Containers [Freight]	AT C
Airtight Drywall Approach	ADA
Air-to-Air [NASA]	AA
Air-to-Air	ATA
Air-to-Air Aftercooling	AAA
Air-to-Air Aftercooling System [Pronounced "attack"]	ATAAC
Air-to-Air Armament Mission Analyses [Air Force] (MCD)	AAAMA
Air-to-Air Banner (SAUS)	AAB

Air-to-Air Battle Management (SAUS)	AABM
Air-to-Air Combat Environment (DOMA)	AACE
Air-to-Air Doppler Clutter (SAUS)	AADC
Air-to-Air Guided Weapons (NATG)	AAGW
Air-to-Air Gunnery (SAUS)	AAG
Air-to-Air Gunnery Assessment (MCD)	ATAGAS
Air-to-Air Gunnery Range [Army]	AAGR
Air-to-Air Identification [Air Force]	AAI
Air-to-Air Identification Control Panel [Air Force] (MCD)	AAICP
Air-to-Air Identification Friend or Foe [Air Force] (MCD)	AAIFF
Air-to-Air Intercept (MCD)	AAI
Air-to-air Interceptor Radar Training (SAUS)	AIRT
Air-to-Air Interrogation (MCD)	AAI
Air-to-Air MEP/Weapons Demonstrator (SAUS)	AAMWD
Air-to-Air Missile [Army]	AAM
Air-to-Air Missile [RDA]	ATAM
Air-to-Air Missile Guidance Element	AAMGE
Air-to-Air Missile Weapons System Flight Report (NG)	AAMREP
Air-to-Air Missile/Refuelling (MILB)	AAM/R
Air-To-Air Mistral missile (SAUS)	ATAM
Air-to-Air Operations (SAUS)	AAO
Air-To-Air Recognition device (SAUS)	ATAR
Air-to-Air Recovery [Air Force] (AFM)	ATAR
Air-to-Air Refueling [Military] (MUSM)	AAR
Air-to-Air Refueling Squadron	AARS
Air-to-Air Refuelling Area (DA)	AARA
Air-to-Air Stinger (MCD)	ATAS
Air-To-Air Stinger missile (SAUS)	ATAS
Air-to-Air Visual Recognition [Aviation]	ATAR
Air-to-Boil Temperature [Mechanical engineering]	ATB
Air-to-Cloth [Air pollution control] (FFDE)	A/C
Air-to-Fuel Ratio (MCD)	AF
Air-to-Ground [Photos, missiles, etc.]	AG
Air-to-Ground (SAUS)	A/G
Air-to-Ground [Photos, missiles, etc.]	ATG
Air-to-Ground Acquisition and Tracking Equipment	AGATE
Air-to-Ground Code (SAUS)	AGC
Air-to-Ground Data Link System (SAUS)	AGDLS
Air-to-Ground Engagement System (MCD)	AGES
Air-to-Ground Engagement/Air Defence (SAUS)	AGES/AD
Air-to-Ground Gunnery (MCD)	ATOG
Air-to-Ground Gunnery Range	AGGR
Air-to-Ground Liaison Code [Air Force]	AGLC
Air-to-Ground Missile	AGM
Air-to-Ground Missile System (RDA)	AGMS
Air-to-Ground Moving Target Indicator	AGMTI
Air-to-Ground Ranging	AGR
Air-to-Ground Rocket (MCD)	AGR
Air-to-Ground Stand-off Weapon (SAUS)	AGSW
Air-to-Ground Voice System [or Subsystem] (MCD)	AGVS
Air-to-Ground-to Air (SAUS)	A-G-A
Air-to-Ground-to Air (SAUS)	AGA
Air-to-Heat Exchanger (SAUS)	AHE
Air-to-Land Ballistic Missile (SAUS)	ALBM
Air-to-Ship (SAUS)	ats
Air-to-Ship (DNAB)	ATS
Air-to-Ship Launched Ballistic Missile [Navy] (IAA)	ASLBM
Air-to-Surface [Missiles] (NATG)	AS
Air-to-Surface [Missiles] (MCD)	ATS
Air-to-Surface Ballistic Missile	ASBM
Air-to-Surface Missile	ASM
Air-to-Surface Missile (SAUS)	GAM
Air-to-Surface Missile Development (MCD)	ASMD
Air-to-Surface Transport System (SAUS)	ASTS
Air-to-Surface Vessel (SAUS)	ASV
Air-to-Surface Weapon	ASW
AirTouch Communications [Associated Press] (SAG)	AirTch
AirTouch Communications [NYSE symbol] (TTSB)	ATI
AirTouch Communications Co. [Formerly, PacTel Corp.] [Associated Press] (SAG)	AirTouch
Airtouch Communications Co. [Formerly, PacTel Corp.] [NYSE symbol] (SAG)	ATI
Air-to-Umbilical Junction Box	AUJ
Air-to-Umbilical Junction Box (SAUS)	AUJ Box
Air-to-Underwater Missile [Air Force]	AUM
Air-to-Underwater Missile - Nuclear [Air Force] (IAA)	AUMN
Airtours International Airways Ltd. [British] [ICAO designator] (FAAC)	AIH
Air-to-Vessel (IAA)	ATV
Air-to-Water	AW
AirTran Airways, Inc. [FAA designator] (FAAC)	MTE
AirTran Corp. [NASDAQ symbol] (SPSG)	ATCC
AirTran Hldgs [NASDAQ symbol] (SG)	AAIR
Air-Transportable Communications Complex (SAUS)	ATRAX
Air-Transportable Loading Dock (SAUS)	ATLD
Air-Transportable Towed System (SAUS)	ATTS
Airtrooper (SAUS)	Airtpr
Air-Turbo Exchanger (SAUS)	ATE
Airung AEP [Ukraine] [FAA designator] (FAAC)	UNG
Airvallee SpA-Services Aeriens de Val d'Aoste [Italy] [ICAO designator] (FAAC)	RVL
AirVantage, Inc. [ICAO designator] (FAAC)	AVV
Airventure, BVBD [Belgium] [FAA designator] (FAAC)	RVE
Air-Via [Bulgaria] [ICAO designator] (FAAC)	VIM
Airvias SA Linhas Aereas [Brazil] [FAA designator] (FAAC)	AIV
Airvolga [Former USSR] [FAA designator] (FAAC)	VOG

Air/Water Pollution Report [*Business Publishers, Inc.*] [*Information service or system*] (CRD) .... A/WPR
Air/Water Ratio (SAUS) .... AWR
Airwave Transport, Inc. [*Canada*] [*ICAO designator*] (FAAC) .... AWV
Airway .... ARWY
Airway (PIAV) .... Awy
Airway .... AWY
Airway (IAA) .... AY
Airway Bill (SAUS) .... AWB
Airway, Breathing, and Circulation [*Medicine*] (DAVI) .... ABC
Airway, Breathing, Circulation, Cervical Spine, Consciousness Level [*Medicine*] (MEDA) .... ABC & C & C
Airway, Breathing, Circulation, Intravenous Crystalloid [*Medicine*] (DMAA) .... ABCIC
Airway Centre, AES Data Ltd., Mississauga, Ontario [*Library symbol*] [*National Library of Canada*] (NLC) .... OMADA
Airway Conductance [*Medicine*] (DAVI) .... Ga
Airway Conductance [*The reciprocal of airway resistance*] [*Medicine*] (DAVI) .... GAW
Airway Facilities [*FAA*] (TAG) .... AF
Airway Facilities Service (SAUO) .... AFS
Airway Obstruction [*Medicine*] (MELL) .... AO
Airway Obstruction [*Medicine*] (MELL) .... AWO
Airway Opened, Breathing Restored, and Circulation Restored [*Cardiopulmonary resuscitation*] [*Medicine*] .... ABC
Airway Opened, Breathing Restored, Circulation Restored, and Definitive Therapy [*Cardiopulmonary resuscitation*] [*Medicine*] .... ABCD
Airway Operations Specialist [*Airport*] .... AOSAP
Airway Operations Specialist, Airport (SAUS) .... AOSAP
Airway Planning Standard [*FAA*] (TAG) .... APS
Airway Pressure [*Pulmonary ventilation*] .... AP
Airway Pressure [*Pulmonary ventilation*] .... AWP
Airway Radio Station (IAA) .... ARSTN
Airway Reactivity Index [*Physiology*] .... ARI
Airway Resistance [*Medicine*] (MELL) .... AR
Airway Resistance [*Medicine*] (MAE) .... Ra
Airway Resistance [*Medicine*] .... RAW
Airway Traffic Control (SAUS) .... ATC
Airway Traffic Controller (IAA) .... AWTC
Airway/Breathing/Circulation (SAUS) .... ABC
Airways .... AW
Airways [*Medicine*] (DAVI) .... aw
Airways and Air Communications Service [*Air Force*] .... AACS
Airways and Air Communications Service Manual .... AACSM
Airways and Air Communications Service Regulation [*Air Force*] (IAA) ..... AACSR
Airways and Air Communications Service Squadron [*Air Force*] (IAA) .... AACSRON
Airways and Air Communications Service Wing [*Air Force*] (IAA) .... AACSWG
Airways and Air Communications Service Wing (SAUO) .... AACSWg
Airways Communication Station (NATG) .... ACS
Airways Communications (SAUS) .... AIRCOM
Airways Communications System .... AIRCOM
Airways Control (SAUS) .... AC
Airways Corp. [*NASDAQ symbol*] (SAG) .... AAIR
Airways Corp. [*Associated Press*] (SAG) .... Airways
Airways Corp. of New Zealand Ltd. [*ICAO designator*] (FAAC) .... XFX
Airways Corporations Joint Pensions (SAUO) .... ACJP
Airways Data Collection and Distribution [*Computer science*] .... ADCAD
Airways Engineer .... AENG
Airways Engineering Corp. (SAUO) .... AEC
Airways Engineering Society [*Defunct*] (EA) .... AES
Airways Environmental RADAR Information System (IEEE) .... AERIS
Airways Environmental Radar Information System (SAUS) .... AERIS
Airways Facilities Sector Field Office (FAAC) .... AFSFO
Airways Facilities Sector Field Office Plus Unit (FAAC) .... AFSFOU
Airways Facilities Sector Office (FAAC) .... AFSO
Airways Facilities Shop (SAUO) .... AFS
Airways Failities Sector (FAAC) .... AFS
Airways Flight Inspector .... AFINS
Airways India Ltd., Calcutta (SAUO) .... AIL
Airways Inspector .... AI
Airways Integrating and Monitoring System (MCD) .... AIMS
Airways International [*ICAO designator*] (AD) .... HO
Airways International, Inc. [*ICAO designator*] (FAAC) .... AWB
Airways Modernization Board [*Functions transferred to FAA*] .... AMB
Airways of New Mexico (SAUS) .... ANM
Airways Operations Evaluation Center .... AOEC
Airways Operations Specialist (SAA) .... AOS
Airways Operations Specialist .... AOSS
Airways Operations Specialist, General (SAUS) .... AOSG
Airways Operations Supervisor .... AOSPV
Airways Technical District Office (SAUO) .... ATDO
Airways Technical District Office [*FAA*] .... ATDO
Airways Technical District Supervisor [*FAA*] .... ATDS
Airways Technical Field Office (SAUO) .... ATFC
Airways Technical Field Office [*FAA*] .... ATFO
Airways Weather Office (SAUO) .... AWO
Airwolf Recovery Team [*An association*] [*Defunct*] (EA) .... ART
Airwoman .... Awmn
Airwork Atlantic Limited (SAUS) .... AIRWORK
Airwork Ltd. [*British*] .... AW
Airwork Ltd. [*British*] [*ICAO designator*] (FAAC) .... HRN
Airwork (New Zealand) Ltd. [*ICAO designator*] (FAAC) .... PST
Airwork Service Training [*British*] [*ICAO designator*] (FAAC) .... AWK
Air-World Co. .... AW

Airworthiness and Flight Characteristics (MCD) .... AFC
Airworthiness Assurance Center of Excellence [*Federal Aviation Administration*] .... AACE
Airworthiness Certificate (MCD) .... AC
Airworthiness Circular (DA) .... AC
Airworthiness Committee .... AC
Airworthiness Directive .... AD
Airworthiness Examination Committee (SAUO) .... AEC
Airworthiness Library, Atlantic Region, Transport Canada [*Bibliotheque de la Navigabilite Aerienne, Region de l'Atlantique, Transports Canada*], Moncton, New Brunswick [*Library symbol*] [*National Library of Canada*] (NLC) .... NBMOTA
Airworthiness Library, Central Region, Transport Canada [*Bibliotheque de la Navigabilite Aerienne, Region Centrale, Transports Canada*], Winnipeg, Manitoba [*Library symbol*] [*National Library of Canada*] (NLC) .... MWTA
Airworthiness Library, Ontario Region, Transport Canada [*Bibliotheque de la Navigabilite Aerienne, Region de l'Ontario, Transports Canada*], Willowdale, Ontario [*Library symbol*] [*National Library of Canada*] (NLC) .... OWTAI
Airworthiness Library, Transport Canada [*Bibliotheque de la Navigabilite Aerienne, Transports Canada*], Ottawa, Ontario [*Library symbol*] [*National Library of Canada*] (NLC) .... OOTA
Airworthiness Qualification Plan .... AQP
Airworthiness Qualification Program .... AQL
Airworthiness Qualification Program (MCD) .... AQP
Airworthiness Qualification Specification .... AQS
Airworthiness Qualification Test Directorate [*Military*] (RDA) .... AQTD
Airworthiness Requirements Board [*British*] (AIA) .... ARB
Airworthiness Requirements Committee .... ARC
Airworthiness Review Board (PIAV) .... ARB
Airworthiness Standards Evaluation Committee [*FAA*] .... ASEC
Airworthiness Substantiation Document [*Army*] (RDA) .... ASD
Airworthy (ADA) .... A/W
Airy Township Public Library, Whitney, Ontario [*Library symbol*] [*National Library of Canada*] (NLC) .... OWAIT
AIS Met Information Equipment (SAUS) .... AMIE
AIS Resources Ltd. [*Vancouver Stock Exchange symbol*] .... AIS
Aisan Buddhist Conference for Peace (SAUO) .... ABCP
Aisan Pacific Dental Students Association (SAUO) .... APDSA
Aishalton [*Guyana*] [*ICAO location identifier*] (ICLI) .... SYAH
Aisin Warner [*Automotive industry supplier*] [*Japan*] .... AW
Aitape [*Papua New Guinea*] [*Airport symbol*] (OAG) .... ATP
Aitken Double Star catalog (SAUS) .... ADS
Aitken Jr.-Sr. High School Media Center, Aitken, MN [*Library symbol*] [*Library of Congress*] (LCLS) .... MnAJ
Aitken Public Library, Aitken, MN [*Library symbol*] [*Library of Congress*] (LCLS) .... MnA
Aitkin, MN [*Location identifier*] [*FAA*] (FAAL) .... AIT
Aitkin, MN [*FM radio station call letters*] .... KEZZ
Aitkin, MN [*AM radio station call letters*] .... KKIN
Aitkin, MN [*FM radio station call letters*] (RBYB) .... KKIN-FM
Aitutaki [*Cook Islands*] [*Airport symbol*] (OAG) .... AIT
Aitutaki [*Cook Islands*] [*ICAO location identifier*] (ICLI) .... NCAI
Aix-En-Provence [*France*] [*ICAO location identifier*] (ICLI) .... LFMB
Aix-En-Provence [*France*] [*ICAO location identifier*] (ICLI) .... LFMM
Aix-Les-Milles [*France*] [*ICAO location identifier*] (ICLI) .... LFMA
AIXwindows Interface Composer (SAUS) .... AIC
Aiyar's Company Cases [*India*] [*A publication*] (DLA) .... Aiyar
Aiyar's Company Cases [*India*] [*A publication*] (DLA) .... Aiyar CC
Aiyar's Leading Privy Council Cases [*India*] [*A publication*] (DLA) .... Aiyar LPC
Aiyar's Unreported Decisions [*India*] [*A publication*] (DLA) .... Aiyar Unrep D
Aiyura [*Papua New Guinea*] [*Airport symbol*] [*Obsolete*] (OAG) .... AYU
Aizwal [*India*] [*ICAO location identifier*] (ICLI) .... VEAZ
AJ Services Ltd. [*British*] [*ICAO designator*] (FAAC) .... AJA
Ajaccio [*Corsica*] [*Airport symbol*] (OAG) .... AJA
Ajaccio/Campo Dell'Oro, Corse [*France*] [*ICAO location identifier*] (ICLI) .... LFKJ
Ajax [*of Sophocles*] [*Classical studies*] (OCD) .... Aj
Ajax Magnethermic (IIA) .... AJX
Ajax, ON [*FM radio station call letters*] (RBYB) .... CJKX
Ajax Public Library, Ajax, ON, Canada [*Library symbol*] [*Library of Congress*] (LCLS) .... CaOAj
Ajax Public Library, Ontario [*Library symbol*] [*National Library of Canada*] (NLC) .... OAJ
Ajax Resources Ltd. [*Vancouver Stock Exchange symbol*] .... AJR
Ajax Resources, Inc. [*Vancouver Stock Exchange symbol*] .... AJY
Ajay Sports [*NASDAQ symbol*] (TTSB) .... AJAY
Ajay Sports 10% Cv Pfd [*NASDAQ symbol*] (TTSB) .... AJAYP
Ajay Sports, Inc. [*NASDAQ symbol*] (NQ) .... AJAY
Ajay Sports Wrrt [*NASDAQ symbol*] (TTSB) .... AJAYW
Ajiro [*Japan*] [*Seismograph station code, US Geological Survey*] (SEIS) .... AJI
AJL Peps Trust [*Associated Press*] (SAG) .... AJL
AJL Peps Trust [*NYSE symbol*] (SAG) .... AJP
Ajmer-Merwara Law Journal [*India*] [*A publication*] (DLA) .... Ajmer-Merwara LJ
Ajmer-Merwara Law Journal [*India*] [*A publication*] (DLA) .... AMLJ
Ajo, AZ [*FM radio station call letters*] .... KTTZ
Ajoutez [*Add*] [*Music*] .... AJ
AJR: American Journalism Review [*A publication*] (BRI) .... AJR
AJS [*Albert John Stevens*] and Matchless Owners Club [*Mount Sorrel, Leicestershire, England*] .... AJSMOC
Ajstra Resources Corp. [*Vancouver Stock Exchange symbol*] .... ARC
AJT Air International [*Russian Federation*] [*ICAO designator*] (FAAC) .... TRJ
Ajustable (ABBR) .... ADJSTB
Ajustable Rate Convertible Note (EBF) .... ARCN
Ajusted Permanent Pay Record (SAUS) .... ADJ/PPR
AK Steel Hldg 7%'SAILS' [*NYSE symbol*] (TTSB) .... AKSPr

AK Steel Holding Corp. [*NYSE symbol*] (SAG) ..... AKS
AK Steel Holding Corp. [*Associated Press*] (SAG) ..... AK Steel
AK Steel Holding Corp. [*Associated Press*] (SAG) ..... AK Stl
Akademie [*Academy*] [*German*] (BJA) ..... Ak
Akademie der Wissenschaften, Berlin (SAUS) ..... AdW
Akademiet for de Tekniska Videnskaber [*Academy of Technical Sciences*] [*Denmark*] ..... ATV
Akademiia Nauk Belorusskaia SSR, Fundamemtalnaia Biblioteka Imeni Ia. Kolasa [*Academy of Sciences of the Belorussian SSR, J. Kolasa Fundamental Library*], Minsk, Belorussian SSR, Soviet Union [*Library symbol*] [*Library of Congress*] (LCLS) ..... RuBeMiA
Akademiia Nauk Kirgizskoi SSR, Tsentralnaia Nauchaia Biblioteka [*Academy of Sciences of the Kirghiz SSR, Central Scientific Library*], Frunze, Kirghiz SSR,Soviet Union [*Library symbol*] [*Library of Congress*] (LCLS) ..... RuKiFrA
Akademiia Nauk Moldavskoi SSR, Tsentralnaia Nauchnaia Biblioteka [*Academy of Sciences of the Moldavian SSR, Central Scientific Library*], Kishivev, Moldavian SSR, Soviet Union [*Library symbol*] [*Library of Congress*] (LCLS) ..... RuMoKisA
Akademiia Nauk SSSR [*Academy of Sciences of the USSR*], Leningrad, Soviet Union [*Library symbol*] [*Library of Congress*] (LCLS) ..... RuLA
Akademiia Nauk Turkmenskoi SSR, Tsentralnaia Nauchnaia Biblioteka [*Academy ofSciences of Turkmen SSR, Central Scientific Library*], Ashkhabad, Turkmen, SS R, Soviet Union [*Library symbol*] [*Library of Congress*] (LCLS) ..... RuTuAsA
Akademio Internacia de la Sciencoj [*International Academy of Sciences - IAS*] (EAIO) ..... AIS
Akademio Internacia de la Sciencoj San Marino (SAUO) ..... AIS
Akademischer Senat (SAUS) ..... AS
Akademisches Computer Netz [*Academic Computer Network*] [*Computer science*] [*Austria*] (TNIG) ..... ACONet
Akaflieg Muenchen Mitsubishi Heavy Industries [*Germany*] [*Japan*] [*ICAO aircraft manufacturer identifier*] (ICAO) ..... MU
Akaitcho Yellowknife Gold Mines Ltd. [*Toronto Stock Exchange symbol*] ..... AKY
Akan National Park (SAUS) ..... ANP
Akan National Park on Hokkaido Island, Japan (SAUS) ..... Akan
Akatsi [*Ghana*] [*ICAO location identifier*] (ICLI) ..... DGAP
Akciova Spolecnost [*Joint-Stock Company*] ..... as
Akdeniz Hava Tasimacilik TIC, Ve San A.S. [*Turkey*] [*FAA designator*] (FAAC) ..... AKD
Akeley Elementary School, Akeley, MN [*Library symbol*] [*Library of Congress*] (LCLS) ..... MnAkE
Akeley High School, Akeley, MN [*Library symbol*] [*Library of Congress*] (LCLS) ..... MnAkH
Akeno [*Japan*] [*ICAO location identifier*] (ICLI) ..... RJOE
Akeno Giant Air Shower Array (SAUS) ..... AGASA
Akerman, Senterfitt, Eidson, Law Library, Orlando, FL [*Library symbol*] [*Library of Congress*] (LCLS) ..... FOAS
Akers Medical Technology Ltd. [*Vancouver Stock Exchange symbol*] ..... AKE
Akersberga [*Sweden*] [*ICAO location identifier*] (ICLI) ..... ESHR
Aketi [*Zaire*] [*ICAO location identifier*] (ICLI) ..... FZKN
Akhal [*Turkmenistan*] [*ICAO designator*] (FAAC) ..... AKH
Akhalkalaki [*Former USSR*] [*Seismograph station code, US Geological Survey*] [*Closed*] (SEIS) ..... AKH
Akhal-Teke Registry of America (EA) ..... A-TRA
Akhiok [*Alaska*] [*Airport symbol*] (OAG) ..... AKK
Akhisar [*Turkey*] [*Airport symbol*] (AD) ..... AKH
Akhisar [*Turkey*] [*ICAO location identifier*] (ICLI) ..... LTBT
Akhmos-I [*Belarus*] [*FAA designator*] (FAAC) ..... AKS
Akiachak [*Alaska*] [*Airport symbol*] (OAG) ..... KKI
Akiak [*Alaska*] [*Airport symbol*] (OAG) ..... AKI
Akieni [*Gabon*] [*Airport symbol*] (OAG) ..... AKE
Akieni [*Gabon*] [*ICAO location identifier*] (ICLI) ..... FOGA
Akiko-Lori Gold [*Vancouver Stock Exchange symbol*] ..... AKI
Akim Oda [*Ghana*] [*ICAO location identifier*] (ICLI) ..... DGKA
Akimuga [*Indonesia*] [*ICAO location identifier*] (ICLI) ..... WAKA
Akinetic ..... A
Akinetic-Rigid Syndrome [*Medicine*] (MELL) ..... ARS
Akita [*Japan*] [*Seismograph station code, US Geological Survey*] (SEIS) ..... AKI
Akita [*Japan*] [*Airport symbol*] (OAG) ..... AXT
Akita [*Japan*] [*ICAO location identifier*] (ICLI) ..... RJSK
Akita Club of America (EA) ..... ACA
Akita Television (SAUO) ..... AKT
Akjoujt [*Mauritania*] [*Airport symbol*] (AD) ..... AJJ
Akjoujt [*Mauritania*] [*ICAO location identifier*] (ICLI) ..... GQNJ
Akkadian (SAUS) ..... Akk
Akkadian [*MARC language code*] [*Library of Congress*] (LCCP) ..... akk
Akkadian [*A publication*] (BJA) ..... Akkad
Akkadische Fremdworter als Beweis fuer Babylonischen Kultureinfluss [*A publication*] (BJA) ..... AFw
Akkadische Goetterepitheta [*A publication*] (BJA) ..... AGe
Akkadische Keilschrifttexte [*A publication*] (BJA) ..... ASKT
Akkadisches Handwoerterbuch [*A publication*] (BJA) ..... AHw
Aklak Air Ltd. [*Canada*] [*ICAO designator*] (FAAC) ..... AKK
Aklavik [*Canada*] [*Airport symbol*] (OAG) ..... LAK
Akobo [*Sudan*] [*ICAO location identifier*] (ICLI) ..... HSAK
Akola [*India*] [*ICAO location identifier*] (ICLI) ..... VAAK
Akorn, Inc. [*Associated Press*] (SAG) ..... Akorn
Akorn, Inc. [*NASDAQ symbol*] (NQ) ..... AKRN
Akridinorange (SAUS) ..... AO
Akro Agate Art Association [*Defunct*] (EA) ..... AAAA
Akron [*Ohio*] [*ICAO location identifier*] (ICLI) ..... KAKR
[The] Akron & Barberton Belt Railroad Co. [*AAR code*] ..... ABB
Akron & Barberton Belt Railroad Company (SAUO) ..... ABB
Akron Art Institute (SAUS) ..... AAI

Akron Barberton Belt (SAUS) ..... ABB
Akron, Canion & Youngstown Railroad Co. (SAUO) ..... ACY
[The] Akron, Canton & Youngstown Railroad Co. (IIA) ..... AC & Y
[The] Akron, Canton & Youngstown Railroad Co. [*AAR code*] ..... ACY
Akron, Canton and Youngstown Railroad Company (SAUO) ..... AC&Y
Akron Carnegie Public Library, Akron, IN [*Library symbol*] [*Library of Congress*] (LCLS) ..... InAk
Akron Child Guidance Center, Akron, OH [*Library symbol*] [*Library of Congress*] (LCLS) ..... OAkCh
Akron, CO [*Location identifier*] [*FAA*] (FAAL) ..... AKO
Akron Council of Engineering and Scientific Societes (SAUO) ..... ACESS
Akron, OH [*Location identifier*] [*FAA*] (FAAL) ..... ACO
Akron, OH [*Location identifier*] [*FAA*] (FAAL) ..... AKR
Akron, OH [*Location identifier*] [*FAA*] (FAAL) ..... GGZ
Akron, OH [*Location identifier*] [*FAA*] (FAAL) ..... RGO
Akron, OH [*Television station call letters*] ..... WAKC
Akron, OH [*AM radio station call letters*] ..... WAKR
Akron, OH [*FM radio station call letters*] ..... WAPS
Akron, OH [*Television station call letters*] ..... WBNX
Akron, OH [*Television station call letters*] ..... WEAO
Akron, OH [*AM radio station call letters*] ..... WHLO
Akron, OH [*FM radio station call letters*] ..... WKDD
Akron, OH [*FM radio station call letters*] ..... WONE
Akron, OH [*AM radio station call letters*] ..... WTOU
Akron, OH [*Television station call letters*] (BROA) ..... WVPX
Akron, OH [*FM radio station call letters*] ..... WZIP
Akron Polymer Lecture Group (SAUO) ..... APLG
Akron Public Library (SAUO) ..... APL
Akron Public Library, Akron, CO [*Library symbol*] [*Library of Congress*] (LCLS) ..... CoAk
Akron Public Library, Akron, OH [*Library symbol*] [*Library of Congress*] (LCLS) ..... OAk
Akron Register-Tribune, Akron, IA [*Library symbol*] [*Library of Congress*] (LCLS) ..... IaAkRT
Akron Rubber Group (SAUO) ..... ARG
Akron Symphony Orchestra (SAUO) ..... ASO
Akron University College of Engineering [*Ohio*] ..... AUE
Akron/Canton [*Ohio*] [*Airport symbol*] ..... CAK
Akron-Canton, OH [*Location identifier*] [*FAA*] (FAAL) ..... HJM
Akron-Summit County Public Library, Akron, OH [*OCLC symbol*] (OCLC) ..... APL
Akrotiri [*Cyprus*] [*ICAO location identifier*] (ICLI) ..... LCRA
Aksjeselskap [*Joint-Stock Company*] [*Norway*] (GPO) ..... A/S
Aksu [*China*] [*Airport symbol*] (OAG) ..... AKU
Aksu [*China*] [*ICAO location identifier*] (ICLI) ..... ZWAK
Aksys Ltd. [*NASDAQ symbol*] (SAG) ..... AKSY
AKsys Ltd [*NASDAQ symbol*] (TTSB) ..... AKSYS
Aksys Ltd. [*Associated Press*] (SAG) ..... AksysL
Aktiebolag [*or Aktiebolaget*] [*Joint-Stock Company*] [*Sweden*] ..... AB
Aktiebolaget Aero Transport [*Swedish airline*] ..... ABA
Aktiebolaget Atomenergi [*Swedish nuclear development company*] ..... ABA
Aktiebolaget Atomenergi Computer-Based User-Oriented Service ..... ABACUS
Aktiekomitee Zuidelyk Afrika [*Belgium*] ..... AKZA
Aktiengesellschaft [*Corporation*] [*German*] ..... AG
Aktiengesellschaft fuer Anilinfabrikaten [*German photographic manufacturer*] ..... AGFA
Aktiengesetz [*Law governing public companies*] [*German*] (ILCA) ..... AktG
Aktieselskab [*Joint-Stock Company*] [*Sweden*] ..... A/S
Aktinon (SAUS) ..... An
Aktion Demokratischer Fortschritt [*Action for Democratic Progress*] [*Germany*] (PPE) ..... ADF
Aktion Soziale Gemeinschaft, die Partei der Sozialversicherten Arbeitnehmer und Rentner [*Social Community Action (Party of Socially Insured Employees and Pensioners)*] [*Germany*] [*Political party*] (PPW) ..... ASG
Aktionsgemeinschaft Unabhaengiger Deutscher [*Action Group of Independent Germans*] [*Germany*] [*Political party*] (PPE) ..... AUD
Aktionsgemeinschaft Vierte Partei [*Fourth Party Action Group*] [*Germany*] [*Political party*] (PPW) ..... AVP
Aktiv [*Active*] [*German*] ..... akt
Aktiv Hinten Kinematik [*Active Rear-Axle Movement*] [*German*] ..... AHK
Aktyubinsk [*Former USSR*] [*ICAO location identifier*] (ICLI) ..... UATT
Akulik, AK [*Location identifier*] [*FAA*] (FAAL) ..... AKU
Akulivik [*Canada*] [*Airport symbol*] (OAG) ..... AKV
Akureyri [*Iceland*] [*Airport symbol*] (OAG) ..... AEY
Akureyri [*Iceland*] [*Seismograph station code, US Geological Survey*] (SEIS) ..... AKU
Akureyri [*Iceland*] [*ICAO location identifier*] (ICLI) ..... BIAR
Akuse [*Ghana*] [*ICAO location identifier*] (ICLI) ..... DGAK
Akutan [*Alaska*] [*Airport symbol*] (OAG) ..... KQA
Akutan, AK [*Location identifier*] [*FAA*] (FAAL) ..... KQA
Akwesasne, ON [*FM radio station call letters*] ..... CKON
Akyab [*Burma*] [*Airport symbol*] (AD) ..... AKY
Akyab [*Myanmar*] [*Airport symbol*] (OAG) ..... AKY
Akzo Nobel N.V. ADS [*NASDAQ symbol*] (TTSB) ..... AKZOY
Akzo NV [*Associated Press*] (SAG) ..... Akzo
Akzo NV [*NASDAQ symbol*] (NQ) ..... AKZO
Al Ain [*United Arab Emirates*] [*ICAO location identifier*] (ICLI) ..... OMAL
Al Akhawayn University, Ifrane [*Morocco*] ..... AUI
Al Arish [*Egypt*] [*Airport symbol*] (OAG) ..... AAC
Al Bahrain Arab African Bank ..... AL-BAAB
Al Bawardi Enterprises ..... ABE
Al Bayda [*Libya*] [*Airport symbol*] (AD) ..... LAQ
AL Environmental Protection Agency (SAUS) ..... AL/EPD
AL Facilities Planning & Maintenance Division (SAUS) ..... AL/FPMD
Al Fine [*To the End*] [*Music*] ..... AF
Al Ghaydah [*Aden*] [*Airport symbol*] (AD) ..... AAY

Al Hamra [*United Arab Emirates*] [*ICAO location identifier*] (ICLI) .... OMAH
AL Health Protection Division (SAUS) .... AL/HPD
Al Hoceima [*Morocco*] [*Airport symbol*] (OAG) .... AHU
Al Hoceima/Cote Du Rif [*Morocco*] [*ICAO location identifier*] (ICLI) .... GMTA
AL Kirtland Area Office (SAUS) .... AL/KAO
AL Laboratories, Inc. [*NYSE symbol*] (SPSG) .... BMD
AL Management Review Division (SAUS) .... AL/MRD
AL Office of Environment, Safety and Health (SAUS) .... AL/OESH
AL Office of Intergovernmental and External Affairs (SAUS) .... AL/OIEA
AL Operation Safety Division (SAUS) .... AL/OQD
AL Personnel, Industrial Relations Division (SAUS) .... AL/PIRD
AL Pharmaceuticals, Inc. [*Later, AL Labs*] [*NYSE symbol*] (SAG) .... ALO
AL Pharmaceuticals, Inc. [*Associated Press*] (SAG) .... Alpharma
Al Pharmaceuticals, Inc. [*Associated Press*] (SAG) .... Alphm
Al Segno [*At the Sign*] [*Music*] .... AL SEG
Al Segno [*At the Sign*] [*Music*] (ROG) .... AS
Al Sigl Center Library, Rochester, NY [*OCLC symbol*] (OCLC) .... VQA
AL Special Programs Division (SAUS) .... AL/SPD
AL Waste Management & Operational Surety Division (SAUS) .... AL/WMOSD
Ala Abaete Linhas Aereas, SA [*Brazil*] [*FAA designator*] (FAAC) .... ABJ
Ala Pwr Cap 17.375% Tr Pfd Sec [*NYSE symbol*] (TTSB) .... ALPPrQ
Alabama [*Postal code*] .... AL
Alabama .... ALA
Alabama (BEE) .... Ala
Alabama (SAUO) .... Ala
Alabama [*MARC country of publication code*] [*Library of Congress*] (LCCP) .... alu
Alabama [*MARC geographic area code*] [*Library of Congress*] (LCCP) .... n-us-al
Alabama Acupuncture Council (SRA) .... AAC
Alabama Administrative Monthly [*A publication*] (AAGC) .... Ala Admin Month
Alabama Aggregates Association (SRA) .... AAA
Alabama Agricultural and Mechanical University (GAGS) .... Ala A&M U
Alabama Agricultural and Mechanical University (SAUO) .... ANA
Alabama Agricultural and Mechanical University, Normal, AL [*Library symbol*] [*Library of Congress*] (LCLS) .... ANA
Alabama Agricultural Experiment Station (SAUS) .... Ala Agric Exp Stn
Alabama. Agricultural Experiment Station. Leaflet (SAUS) .... LAEADA
Alabama. Agricultural Experiment Station. Progress Report Series (journ.) (SAUS) PRASD3
Alabama Air National Guard (ACAE) .... ALANG
Alabama Alliance of Business and Industry (SRA) .... AABI
Alabama Appellate Court (DLA) .... Ala A
Alabama Appellate Court Reports [*A publication*] (DLA) .... Ala App
Alabama, Arkansas, Florida, Georgia, Louisiana, Mississippi, North Carolina, South Carolina, Tennessee and Virginia (SAUS) .... Southeast Sun Belt
Alabama Army Ammunition Plant (AABC) .... ALAAP
Alabama Asphalt Pavement Association (SRA) .... AAPA
Alabama Association of Credit Executives (SRA) .... AACE
Alabama Association of Elementary School Administrators (SAUO) .... AAESA
Alabama Association of Health Maintenance Organizations (SRA) .... AAHMO
Alabama Association of Independent Colleges and Universities (SRA) .... AAICU
Alabama Association of Realtors (SRA) .... AAR
Alabama Association of School Boards (SRA) .... AASB
Alabama Automated Clearing House Association (TBD) .... ALACHA
Alabama Bankers Association (SRA) .... ABA
Alabama Basic Competency Test (EDAC) .... ABCT
Alabama Cable Telecommunications Association (SRA) .... ACTA
Alabama Cattlemen's Association (SRA) .... ACA
Alabama Central R. R. [*AAR code*] .... ALC
Alabama Central Railroad Company (SAUO) .... ACR
Alabama Central Railroad Company (SAUO) .... ALC
Alabama Chiropractic Association (SRA) .... ASCA
Alabama Christian School of Religion, Montgomery, AL [*Library symbol*] [*Library of Congress*] (LCLS) .... AMAC
Alabama Civil Appeals [*A publication*] (DLA) .... Ala Civ App
Alabama Coal Association (SRA) .... ACA
Alabama Code [*A publication*] (AAGC) .... Ala Code
Alabama College (SAUO) .... AC
Alabama Commission of Higher Education (SAUO) .... ACHE
Alabama Commission on Higher Education (SAUS) .... ACHE
Alabama Concrete Industries Association (SRA) .... ACIA
Alabama Constitution [*A publication*] (DLA) .... Ala Const
Alabama Council for School Administration and Supervision (SRA) .... ACSAS
Alabama Council of Association Executives (SRA) .... ACAE
Alabama Counseling Association (SRA) .... ALCA
Alabama Court of Appeals (DLA) .... Ala App
Alabama Credit Union League (SRA) .... ACUL
Alabama Criminal Appeals [*A publication*] (DLA) .... Ala Cr App
Alabama Crop Improvement Association (SRA) .... ACIA
Alabama Dental Association (SRA) .... ALDA
Alabama Department of Archives and History, Montgomery, AL [*OCLC symbol*] (OCLC) .... AAR
Alabama Department of Archives and History, State Documents, Montgomery, AL [*OCLC symbol*] (OCLC) .... AAS
Alabama Department of Public Health (SAUO) .... ADPH
Alabama District Attorneys Association (SRA) .... ADAA
Alabama Education Association (SRA) .... AEA
Alabama Energy Management Board (SAUS) .... AEMB
Alabama Environmental Quality Association (SAUO) .... AEQA
Alabama Fan Club (EA) .... AFC
Alabama Farm and Power Equipment Dealers Association (SRA) .... AFPEDA
Alabama Farmers Federation (SRA) .... AFF
Alabama Financial Services Association (SRA) .... AFSA
Alabama Food and Agriculture Council (SRA) .... AFAC
Alabama Forest Owners' Association (SRA) .... AFOA
Alabama Forestry Association (SRA) .... AFA
Alabama Funeral Directors Association (SRA) .... AFDA
Alabama Gas (SAUS) .... AGA
Alabama Gas Corp. (EFIS) .... ALAGASCO
Alabama Gas Corporation (SAUO) .... AGA
Alabama Geological Survey (SAUS) .... Ala Geol Surv
Alabama Great Southern Railroad Co. (SAUO) .... AGS
[*The*] **Alabama Great Southern Railroad Co.** [*AAR code*] .... AGS
Alabama Great Southern Railroad Corp. (SAUO) .... AGT
Alabama High School Graduation Examination (EDAC) .... AHSGE
Alabama Historical Quarterly (journ.) (SAUS) .... AlaHQ
Alabama Home Builders Association (SRA) .... AHBA
Alabama Hospital Association (SRA) .... AlaHA
Alabama Hospitality Association (SRA) .... AHA
Alabama Independent Automobile Dealers Association (SRA) .... AIADA
Alabama Independent Insurance Agents (SRA) .... AIIA
Alabama Independent School Association (SRA) .... AISA
Alabama Industrial Development Training .... AIDT
Alabama Information Development System (SAUS) .... AIDS
Alabama Initial Teacher Certification Test (EDAC) .... AITCT
Alabama Inspection and Rating Buerau (SAUO) .... AIRB
Alabama International Trade Center [*University of Alabama*] [*Research center*] (RCD) .... AITC
Alabama Journal of Medical Sciences (SAUS) .... AlaJMed Sci
Alabama Junior and Community College Conference (PSS) .... AJCC
Alabama League of Municipalities (SRA) .... ALM
Alabama Lenders Association (SRA) .... ALA
Alabama Library Association (SRA) .... AlaLA
Alabama Lutheran College, Selma, AL [*Library symbol*] [*Library of Congress*] (LCLS) .... ASeLC
Alabama Manufactured Housing Institute (SRA) .... AMHI
Alabama Marine and Recreation Association (SRA) .... AMRA
Alabama Marine Resources (SAUS) .... Ala Mar Resour
Alabama National Bancorporation [*NASDAQ symbol*] (SAG) .... ALAB
Alabama National Bancorporation [*Associated Press*] (SAG) .... AlaNBcp
Alabama Natl Bancorp [*NASDAQ symbol*] (TTSB) .... ALAB
Alabama Nurserymen's Association (SRA) .... ANA
Alabama Nursing Home Association (SRA) .... ANHA
Alabama Oilmen's Association and Alabama Association of Convenience Stores (SRA) .... AOA/AACS
Alabama Optometric Association (SRA) .... ALOA
Alabama Ordnance Works (SAUO) .... AOW
Alabama Pawnbrokers Association (SRA) .... APA
Alabama Peace Officers Association (SRA) .... APOA
Alabama Peanut Producers Association (SRA) .... APPA
Alabama Personnel and Guidance Association (SAUO) .... APGA
Alabama Petroleum Council (SRA) .... APC
Alabama Pharmacy Association (SRA) .... APA
Alabama Polytechnic Institute (MCD) .... API
Alabama Poultry and Egg Association (SRA) .... AP&EA
Alabama Power Capital Trust I [*Associated Press*] (SAG) .... AlaPC
Alabama Power Capital Trust I [*NYSE symbol*] (SAG) .... ALP
Alabama Power Co. [*Associated Press*] (SAG) .... AlaP
Alabama Power Co., Birmingham, AL [*Library symbol*] [*Library of Congress*] (LCLS) .... ABAP
Alabama Power Company (SAUO) .... ALP
Alabama Power Company (SAUO) .... APCO
Alabama Power Company Reactor (SAUO) .... APCR
Alabama Press Association (SRA) .... APA
Alabama Primary Health Care Association (SRA) .... APHCA
Alabama Propane Gas Association (SRA) .... APGA
Alabama Public Library Service, Montgomery, AL [*Library symbol*] [*Library of Congress*] (LCLS) .... A
Alabama Public Library Service, Montgomery, AL [*OCLC symbol*] (OCLC) .... ASL
Alabama Public Service Commission Decisions [*A publication*] (DLA) .... APSC
Alabama Pwr 6.40% 'A'Pfd [*NYSE symbol*] (TTSB) .... ALPPrC
Alabama Pwr 6.80% 'A'Pfd [*NYSE symbol*] (TTSB) .... ALPPrB
Alabama Pwr 7.60% 2nd'A'Pfd [*NYSE symbol*] (TTSB) .... ALPPrH
Alabama Pwr 7.60%'A'Pfd [*NYSE symbol*] (TTSB) .... ALPPrA
Alabama Recreation and Parks Association (SRA) .... ARPA
Alabama Reports [*A publication*] (DLA) .... Ala
Alabama Reports [*A publication*] (DLA) .... Alabama Rep
Alabama Reports [*A publication*] (DLA) .... Alab Rep
Alabama Reports [*A publication*] (DLA) .... Ala R
Alabama Reports [*A publication*] (DLA) .... Ala Rep
Alabama Reports [*A publication*] (DLA) .... Ala Reps
Alabama Reports [*A publication*] (DLA) .... AL Rep
Alabama Reports, New Series [*A publication*] (DLA) .... Alab (NS)
Alabama Reports, New Series [*A publication*] (DLA) .... Ala NS
Alabama Reports, New Series [*A publication*] (DLA) .... Ala Rep NS
Alabama Reports, New Series [*A publication*] (DLA) .... Ala RNS
Alabama Resources Information System [*Auburn University*] [*Information service or system*] (IID) .... ARIS
Alabama Restaurant Association (SRA) .... ARA
Alabama Retail Association (SRA) .... ARA
Alabama Road Builders Association (SRA) .... ARBA
Alabama Roofing, Sheet Metal, Heating and Air Conditioning Contractors Association (SRA) .... ARSM-HACCA
Alabama Rural Electric Association of Cooperatives (SRA) .... AREAC
Alabama Rural Water Association (SRA) .... ARWA
Alabama Select Cases (Supreme Court), by Shepherd [*37, 38, 39*] [*A publication*] (DLA) .... Ala Sel Cas
Alabama Sheriff's Association (SRA) .... ASA
Alabama Society of Physician Assistants (SAUO) .... ASPA
Alabama Society of Professional Engineers (SRA) .... ASPE

Alabama Society of Professional Land Surveyors (SRA) .... ASPLS
Alabama Soft Drink Association (SRA) .... ASDA
Alabama Space and Rocket Center (ACAE) .... ASRC
Alabama State Bar (SRA) .... ASB
Alabama State Bar Foundation. Bulletin [*A publication*] (DLA) .... Ala St B Found Bull
Alabama State College (SAUO) .... ASC
Alabama State Employees Association (SRA) .... ASEA
Alabama State Foundation (SAUO) .... Ala St Found
Alabama State Foundation Bulletin [*A publication*] (ILCA) .... Ala St Found Bull
Alabama State Normal School, Daphne, AL [*Library symbol*] [*Library of Congress*] [*Obsolete*] (LCLS) .... ADaN
Alabama State Nurses Association (SRA) .... ASNA
Alabama State Society of Anesthesiologists (SAUO) .... ASSA
Alabama State Supreme Court Library, Montgomery, AL [*Library symbol*] [*Library of Congress*] (LCLS) .... A-SC
Alabama State Training School (SAUO) .... ASTS
Alabama State University, Montgomery, AL [*Library symbol*] [*Library of Congress*] (LCLS) .... AMS
Alabama State University, Montgomery, AL [*OCLC symbol*] (OCLC) .... AMU
Alabama Supercomputer Center (SAUS) .... ASC
Alabama Supreme Court and State Law Library, Montgomery, AL [*OCLC symbol*] (OCLC) .... ALS
Alabama Supreme Court Reports [*A publication*] (DLA) .... Ala
Alabama, Tennessee & Northern R. R. [*AAR code*] .... ATN
Alabama, Tennessee and Northern Railroad Company (SAUO) .... AT&N
Alabama Textile Manufacturers Association (SRA) .... ATMA
Alabama Tobacco and Candy Distributors Association (SRA) .... AT&CDA
Alabama Travel Council (SRA) .... ATC
Alabama Trial Lawyers Association (SRA) .... ATLA
Alabama Trucking Association (SRA) .... ATA
Alabama Trucking Association, Montgomery AL [*STAC*] .... ALT
Alabama University (SAUO) .... AU
Alabama Vending Association (SRA) .... AVA
Alabama Veterinary Medical Association (SRA) .... AVMA
Alabama Virtual Library .... AVL
Alabama Vocational Association (SRA) .... AVA
Alabama Water Resources Research Institute [*Auburn, AL*] [*Department of the Interior*] (GRD) .... WRRI
Alabama Wholesale Beer and Wine Association (SRA) .... AWBWA
Alabama World Trade Association (SRA) .... AWTA
Alabama-Mississippi Telephone Association (SRA) .... AMTA
Alabamian (SAUS) .... Ala
Alabamine [*Superseded by astatine*] [*Chemical element*] .... Ab
Alabamine [*Chemical element*] (BARN) .... Am
Alabamium (SAUS) .... Ab
Alabamla Polytechnic Institute (SAUS) .... API
Alabaster, AL [*Location identifier*] [*FAA*] (FAAL) .... AOA
Alabaster, AL [*AM radio station call letters*] .... WGTT
Alabaster Cavern State Park [*Oklahoma*] [*Seismograph station code, US Geological Survey*] (SEIS) .... ACO
Alabat, Quezon [*Philippines*] [*ICAO location identifier*] (ICLI) .... RPXT
Alachua, FL [*FM radio station call letters*] (RBYB) .... WNDT-FM
Aladdin Ghostscript Free Punlic License (SAUS) .... AGFPL
Aladdin Knights of the Mystic Light (EA) .... AKML
Aladdin Knowledge Systems [*Commercial firm*] [*Associated Press*] (SAG) .... AladnKn
Aladdin Knowledge Systems [*NASDAQ symbol*] (SAG) .... ALDN
Aladdin Knowledge Systems [*NASDAQ symbol*] (TTSB) .... ALDNF
Aladdin Smartcard Environment (SAUS) .... ASE
Aladdin Systems (SAUS) .... Aladdin
Alagappa Chettiar College of Technology (SAUO) .... ALTECH
Alah [*Philippines*] [*Airport symbol*] (OAG) .... AAV
Al-Ahli Bank of Qatar (MENA) .... QSC
Al-Ahsa [*Saudi Arabia*] [*ICAO location identifier*] (ICLI) .... OEAH
Alain Boublil Music Limited [*Publisher*] .... BOU
Alajuela [*Costa Rica*] [*ICAO location identifier*] (ICLI) .... MRAL
Alak [*Former USSR*] [*ICAO designator*] (FAAC) .... LSV
Alakanuk [*Alaska*] [*Airport symbol*] (OAG) .... AUK
[*The*] **Alalakh Tablets** (BJA) .... AT
Alamar Biosciences, Inc. [*Associated Press*] (SAG) .... Alamar
Alamar Biosciences, Inc. [*Associated Press*] (SAG) .... Alamr
Alamar Biosciences, Inc. [*NASDAQ symbol*] (SAG) .... ALMR
Alamco, Inc. [*Associated Press*] (SAG) .... Alamco
Alamco, Inc. [*AMEX symbol*] (SPSG) .... AXO
Alamdeh [*Iran*] [*ICAO location identifier*] (ICLI) .... OINL
Alameda Administration Center (SAUS) .... AAC
Alameda Belt Line [*AAR code*] .... ABL
Alameda, CA [*FM radio station call letters*] (RBYB) .... KZSF
Alameda, CA [*Location identifier*] [*FAA*] (FAAL) .... NGZ
Alameda County Health Department, Oakland, CA [*Library symbol*] [*Library of Congress*] (LCLS) .... COH
Alameda County Law Library, Oakland, CA [*Library symbol*] [*Library of Congress*] (LCLS) .... COAL
Alameda County Library, Fremont, CA [*Library symbol*] [*Library of Congress*] (LCLS) .... CFrA
Alameda County Public Library, Hayward, CA [*Library symbol*] [*Library of Congress*] (LCLS) .... CHA
Alameda Free Library, Alameda, CA [*Library symbol*] [*Library of Congress*] (LCLS) .... CAla
Alameda Naval Air Base [*California*] (SAA) .... ANAB
Alameda/Alameda Naval Air Station [*California*] [*ICAO location identifier*] (ICLI) .... KNGZ
Alameda-Oakland Tunnel (SAUS) .... AOT
Alamethicin [*An antibiotic*] .... ALA
Alamo [*Nevada*] [*Seismograph station code, US Geological Survey*] (SEIS) .... ALA
Alamo Community, NM [*AM radio station call letters*] .... KABR
Alamo Commuter Airlines [*ICAO designator*] (AD) .... JZ
Alamo Developments [*Vancouver Stock Exchange symbol*] .... ALO
Alamo Group [*NYSE symbol*] (TTSB) .... ALG
Alamo Group, Inc. [*Associated Press*] (SAG) .... AlamoGp
Alamo Group, Inc. [*NYSE symbol*] (SAG) .... ALG
Alamo Heights, TX [*AM radio station call letters*] .... KDRY
Alamo Personal Computer Organization (PCM) .... APCO
Alamo, TN [*AM radio station call letters*] .... WCTA
Alamo, TN [*FM radio station call letters*] .... WWGM
Alamo, TX [*FM radio station call letters*] .... KJAV
Alamogordo [*New Mexico*] [*Airport symbol*] (OAG) .... ALM
Alamogordo, NM [*Location identifier*] [*FAA*] (FAAL) .... HMN
Alamogordo, NM [*AM radio station call letters*] .... KINN
Alamogordo, NM [*FM radio station call letters*] (RBYB) .... KNMZ-FM
Alamogordo, NM [*AM radio station call letters*] .... KPSA
Alamogordo, NM [*FM radio station call letters*] .... KYEE
Alamogordo, NM [*FM radio station call letters*] .... KZZX
Alamogordo, NM [*Location identifier*] [*FAA*] (FAAL) .... MUK
Alamogordo Public Library, Alamogordo, NM [*OCLC symbol*] (OCLC) .... AMO
Alamogordo Public Library, Alamogordo, NM [*Library symbol*] [*Library of Congress*] (LCLS) .... NmAl
Alamogordo/Holloman Air Force Base [*New Mexico*] [*ICAO location identifier*] (ICLI) .... KHMN
Alamogordo/Holloman Air Force Base (SAUS) .... KliMN
Alamosa [*Colorado*] [*Airport symbol*] (OAG) .... ALS
Alamosa, CO [*FM radio station call letters*] .... KALQ
Alamosa, CO [*FM radio station call letters*] .... KASF
Alamosa, CO [*AM radio station call letters*] .... KGIW
Alamosa, CO [*FM radio station call letters*] .... KRZA
Alan Cobham Engineering Ltd. (SAUO) .... ACE
Alan Feinstein Fan Club (EA) .... AFFC
Alan Guttmacher Institute (EA) .... AGI
Alan Hutchison Publishing Ltd. [*British*] .... AH
Alan Mann Helicopters Ltd. [*British*] [*FAA designator*] (FAAC) .... AMH
Alan Pascoe Associates [*British*] .... APA
Alan R. Barton Nuclear Plant (NRCH) .... ABNP
Alan Stratford and Associates [*Aviation consultants*] [*British*] (ECON) .... ASA
Alan Thicke Fan Club (EA) .... ATFC
Alanaine-amino Transferase (SAUS) .... ALT
Alanco Environmental Res [*NASDAQ symbol*] (TTSB) .... ALAN
Alanco Resources Corp. [*NASDAQ symbol*] (SAG) .... ALAN
Alanco Resources Corp. [*Associated Press*] (SAG) .... Alanco
Aland islanders (SAUS) .... Alanders
Aland Islands (SAUS) .... Alands
Alanine [*One-letter symbol; see Ala*] .... A
Alanine [*Also, A*] [*An amino acid*] .... Ala
Alanine Aminotransferase [*Also, ALAT, ALT, GPT*] [*An enzyme*] .... AAT
Alanine Aminotransferase [*Formerly, SGPT*] [*Pharmacology*] (DAVI) .... ALAT
Alanine Aminotransferase [*Also, AAT, ALAT, GPT*] [*An enzyme*] .... ALT
Alanine Beta-Naphthylamide [*Medicine*] (MELL) .... ANA
Alanine Nitroanilide [*Biochemistry*] .... ANA
Alanine Nitrogen Mustard [*L-PAM*] [*Antineoplastic drug*] .... A
Alanine Transaminase [*Also, AAT, ALT, GPT*] [*An enzyme*] .... ALAT
Alanine Transaminase [*Biochemistry*] (DAVI) .... ALT
Alanine-Aspartate Aminotransferase (DB) .... ASAT
Al-Anon Family Group Headquarters (EA) .... AAFGH
ALANON Family Group Headquarters (EA) .... AFG
Alanson Public Library, Alanson, MI [*Library symbol*] [*Library of Congress*] (LCLS) .... MiAln
Alantec Corp. [*Associated Press*] (SAG) .... Alantec
Alantec Corp. [*NASDAQ symbol*] (SAG) .... ALTC
Alantic Canada Centre for Environmental Science (AC) .... ACCES
Alanus Anglicus [*Flourished, 1208-10*] [*Authority cited in pre-1607 legal work*] (DSA) .... A
Alanus Anglicus [*Flourished, 1208-10*] [*Authority cited in pre-1607 legal work*] (DSA) .... Al
Alanus Anglicus [*Flourished, 1208-10*] [*Authority cited in pre-1607 legal work*] (DSA) .... Ala
Alaris Medical [*NASDAQ symbol*] (SG) .... ALRS
Alarm [*Telecommunications*] (TEL) .... AL
Alarm (MSA) .... ALM
Alarm (ADWA) .... alm
Alarm .... ALRM
Alarm and Control System [*Telecommunications*] (TEL) .... ACS
Alarm & Distributed Access Control System (SAUS) .... ADACS
Alarm and Jettison Panel .... AJP
Alarm & Power Remote-Control Unit (SAUS) .... APCU
Alarm and Status Module .... ASM
Alarm Apparatus (SAUS) .... AA
Alarm Association of Florida (SRA) .... AAF
Alarm Bell (SAUS) .... ABE
Alarm Buzzer (SAUS) .... ABU
Alarm Check Value (SAUS) .... ACV
Alarm Check Valve (MSA) .... ACV
Alarm Communications and Display Segment (MCD) .... ACADS
Alarm Communications and Display System (MCD) .... ACAD
Alarm Control and Display (TEL) .... ACD
Alarm Control & Display (SAUS) .... ACD
Alarm Control Center (NVT) .... ACC
Alarm Control Module [*Telecommunications*] (TEL) .... ACM
Alarm Control Panel .... ACP
Alarm Control Unit [*Bell System*] [*Telecommunications*] .... ACU
Alarm Data Interface (SAUS) .... ADI

Alarm Device (SAUS) ... AD
Alarm Display and Control Unit [*Telecommunications*] (TEL) ... ADCU
Alarm Equipment Rack (SAUS) ... AER
Alarm Group Register (SAUO) ... AGR
Alarm Identification on Demand (SAUS) ... AID
Alarm Identification Reporting System (ACRL) ... AIRS
Alarm Indicating (or Indication) Monitor (SAUS) ... AIM
Alarm Indication Signal [*Telecommunications*] (TEL) ... AIS
Alarm Indication Signal-External (VERA) ... AISE
Alarm Industry Committee for Combating Crime [*Defunct*] (EA) ... AICCC
Alarm Inhibit Signal [*Telecommunications*] (TEL) ... AIS
Alarm Integrated Signal (SAUS) ... AIS
Alarm Interface Unit [*Telecommunications*] (TEL) ... AIU
Alarm Master (SAUS) ... ALM
Alarm Message (SAUS) ... AM
Alarm Monitor Computer ... AMC
Alarm Monitor Group [*Army*] ... AMG
Alarm Monitor Unit [*Telecommunications*] (TEL) ... AMU
Alarm Monitoring System ... AMS
Alarm Network Group ... ANG
Alarm Panel Monitor (AFM) ... APM
Alarm Reaction [*Psychology*] ... AR
Alarm Receiving and Reporting Equipment [*Telecommunications*] (TEL) ... ARRE
Alarm Relay (SAUS) ... AL
Alarm Reporting Telephone [*Telecommunications*] (TEL) ... ART
Alarm Reset (SAUS) ... ALR
Alarm Response and Assessment Performance Test [*Environmental science*] (COE) ... ARAPT
Alarm Response Team [*Military*] ... ART
Alarm Signal Input Device (SAUS) ... ASID
Alarm Signal Processing Routine (SAUS) ... ASPR
Alarm System [*Automotive advertising*] ... ALRM
Alarm System Control Unit ... ASCU
Alarm System Improvement Guide (MCD) ... ASIG
Alarm System Operation ... ASO
Alarm Termination Subsystem [*Telecommunications*] (TEL) ... ATS
Alarm Valve (SAUS) ... AIV
Alarmformation (SAUS) ... Al Fo
Alarms and Shutdown Process (SAUS) ... ASP
Alarms By Carner (SAUS) ... ABC
Alarms by Carrier (PDAA) ... ABC
Alas Nacionales SA [*Dominican Republic*] [*ICAO designator*] (FAAC) ... ALW
Alas Panamenas SA [*Panama*] [*ICAO designator*] (FAAC) ... ALPANSA
Alas Panamenas SA [*Panama*] [*ICAO designator*] (FAAC) ... PWI
ALAS, SA [*Uruguay*] [*ICAO designator*] (ICDA) ... HP
Alasehir [*Turkey*] [*ICAO location identifier*] (ICLI) ... LTBC
Alaska (SAUS) ... Aaa
Alaska ... AAA
Alaska [*Postal code*] ... AK
Alaska (ROG) ... AKA
Alaska [*MARC country of publication code*] [*Library of Congress*] (LCCP) ... aku
Alaska (AFM) ... ALAS
Alaska (NTIO) ... Alas
Alaska (SAUS) ... Alas
Alaska (BEE) ... Alsk
Alaska [*MARC geographic area code*] [*Library of Congress*] (LCCP) ... n-us-ak
Alaska Administrative Code [*A publication*] (AAGC) ... AAC
Alaska Administrative Code [*A publication*] (DLA) ... Alaska Admin Code
Alaska Administrative Journal [*A publication*] (AAGC) ... AAJ
Alaska Aeronautical Industries [*ICAO designator*] (AD) ... YC
Alaska Agricultural Experiment Station, Palmer, AK [*Library symbol*] [*Library of Congress*] (LCLS) ... AkPalA
Alaska Air Carriers Association (SRA) ... AACA
Alaska Air Command [*Air Force*] ... ALAC
Alaska Air Group [*NYSE symbol*] (TTSB) ... ALK
Alaska Air Group, Inc. [*NYSE symbol*] (SPSG) ... ALK
Alaska Air Group, Inc. [*Associated Press*] (SAG) ... AlskAir
Alaska Air Lines (SAUO) ... AAL
Alaska Airlines [*ICAO designator*] (AD) ... Alaska
Alaska Airlines (SAUO) ... AS
Alaska Airlines, Inc. (IIA) ... ALK
Alaska Airlines, Inc. [*ICAO designator*] (OAG) ... AS
Alaska Airlines, Inc. [*ICAO designator*] (FAAC) ... ASA
Alaska Airways and Air Communications Service (SAUO) ... ALAACS
Alaska Anthropological Association (QUAC) ... AAA
Alaska Apollo Gold Mines [*Associated Press*] (SAG) ... AlskAplo
Alaska Apollo Gold Mines [*NASDAQ symbol*] (SAG) ... APLO
Alaska Apollo Gold Mines Ltd. (SAUO) ... APLO
Alaska Apollo Gold Mines Ltd. [*Vancouver Stock Exchange symbol*] ... ASK
Alaska Apollo Res Ltd [*NASDAQ symbol*] (TTSB) ... APLOF
Alaska Association of Legal Assistants (SAUO) ... AALA
Alaska Association of Realtors (SRA) ... AAR
Alaska Bar Association (SRA) ... ABA
Alaska Bar Brief [*A publication*] (DLA) ... Alaska B Brief
Alaska Bar Journal [*A publication*] (DLA) ... Alaska BJ
Alaska British Columbia Transportation Co. [*AAR code*] ... ABCK
Alaska Broadcasters Association (SRA) ... ABA
Alaska Building Science Network (SAUO) ... ABSN
Alaska, Canada, Unites States (SAUO) ... ALCANUS
Alaska Carriers Association Inc. (SAUO) ... ACA
Alaska Carriers Association, Inc., Anchorage AK [*STAC*] ... ACA
Alaska Census Data Network [*Alaska State Department of Labor*] [*Juneau*] [*Information service or system*] (IID) ... ACDN
Alaska Civil Liberties Union (SAUO) ... ACLU
Alaska Coal Association (SRA) ... ACA
Alaska Coalition (EA) ... AC
Alaska Coastal Airlines ... ACA
Alaska Coastal Current [*Marine science*] (OSRA) ... ACC
Alaska Coastal Management Office ... ACMO
Alaska Coastal-Ellis Airlines (SAUS) ... AK
Alaska Codes (Carter) [*A publication*] (DLA) ... Alaska Co
Alaska Communication System Industrial Fund (AFM) ... ACSIF
Alaska Communications (SAUS) ... ALASCOM
Alaska Community Development Corporation (SAUO) ... ACDC
Alaska Conference on Library and Information Service (SAUS) ... ACLIS
Alaska Conservation Society (EA) ... ACS
Alaska Constitution [*A publication*] (DLA) ... Alaska Const
Alaska Cooperative Wildlife Research Unit (journ.) (SAUS) ... ACWR
Alaska Council of School Administrators (SRA) ... ACSA
Alaska Craftsman Home Program (SAUO) ... ACHP
Alaska Credit Union League (SRA) ... ACUL
Alaska Current (SAUS) ... Alas Cur
Alaska Defense Command [*Known to many of the soldiers who served in it as "All Damn Confusion"*] [*World War II*] ... ADC
Alaska Defense Frontier [*Military*] ... ADF
Alaska Dental Society (SRA) ... ADS
Alaska Department of Emergency Services (SAUO) ... ADES
Alaska Department of Environmental Conservation, Juneau, AK [*Library symbol*] [*Library of Congress*] (LCLS) ... AkJEC
Alaska Department of Fish and Game (GEOI) ... ADFG
Alaska Department of Fish and Game Habitat, Anchorage, AK [*Library symbol*] [*Library of Congress*] (LCLS) ... AkAEG
Alaska Department of Fish and Game, Juneau, AK [*Library symbol*] [*Library of Congress*] (LCLS) ... AkJFG
Alaska Department of Fisheries Research Report (SAUS) ... Alsk Dep Fish Res Rep
Alaska Department of Health & Social Services (SAUO) ... DHSS
Alaska Department of Highways (SAUO) ... ADH
Alaska Department of Natural Resources (GEOI) ... ADNR
Alaska Department of Transportation and Public Facilities (GEOI) ... ADOTPF
Alaska Detroit Diesel Allison [*Commercial firm*] ... ADDA
Alaska Division of Policy Development and Planning (GEOI) ... ADPDP
Alaska Early Childhood Certification Process (EDAC) ... AECCP
Alaska Engineering Commission [*Later, the Alaska Railroad*] ... AEC
Alaska Eskimo Whaling System (USDC) ... AEWC
Alaska Federal Reports [*A publication*] (DLA) ... AF Rep
Alaska Federal Reports [*A publication*] (DLA) ... Alaska Fed
Alaska Federal Reports [*A publication*] (DLA) ... Alaska Fed Rep
Alaska Federation of Natives (EA) ... AFN
Alaska Ferry Service (SAUO) ... AFS
Alaska Field Operations Center [*Anchorage, AK*] [*Department of the Interior*] (GRD) ... AFOC
Alaska Fish and Game Library, Douglas, AK [*Library symbol*] [*Library of Congress*] (LCLS) ... AkDFG
Alaska Fishery Research Bulletin (SAUS) ... Alsk Fish Res Bull
Alaska Forest Association (SRA) ... AFA
Alaska Forest Fire Council ... AFFCO
Alaska Game Commission [*Terminated, 1959*] ... AGC
Alaska Health Sciences Library, Anchorage, AK [*Library symbol*] [*Library of Congress*] (LCLS) ... AkAAH
Alaska High-altitude Aerial Photography (SAUS) ... AHAP
Alaska High-Altitude Aerial Photography (GEOI) ... AHAP
Alaska Historical Library (SAUO) ... AHL
Alaska Historical Library and Museum, Juneau, AK [*Library symbol*] [*Library of Congress*] (LCLS) ... AkHi
Alaska Home Properties (SAUO) ... AHP
Alaska Hotel and Motel Association (SRA) ... AKHMA
Alaska Housing Finance Corporation (SAUO) ... AHFC
Alaska Housing Market Indicators (SAUO) ... AHMI
Alaska Human Resources Investment Council (SAUO) ... AHRIC
Alaska Hydraulic Train (SAUS) ... AHT
Alaska Hydrography Digitizing System (SAUS) ... AHDS
Alaska Hydro-Train [*AAR code*] ... AHT
Alaska Independent Insurance Agents and Brokers (SRA) ... AIIAB
Alaska Independent Radio, Reading & Education Services (SAUO) ... AIRRES
Alaska Industrial Development and Export Authority (SAUO) ... AIDEA
Alaska Initial Attack Management System (SAUS) ... AIAMS
Alaska Institute for Fisheries Development ... AIFD
Alaska Integrated Communications System (SAUS) ... ALICS
Alaska Integrated Resource Inventory System (SAUS) ... AIRIS
Alaska International Air, Inc. [*Air carrier designation symbol*] ... AIAX
Alaska International Rail and Highway Commission [*Terminated, 1961*] ... AIRHC
Alaska Interstate Co. (SAUO) ... AKI
Alaska Island Air, Inc. [*ICAO designator*] (FAAC) ... AAK
Alaska Juneau Aeronautics, Inc. [*ICAO designator*] (FAAC) ... WAK
Alaska Land and Resources System (GEOI) ... ALARS
Alaska Landscape Flux Study (OSRA) ... ALFS
Alaska Legal Services (SAUO) ... ALS
Alaska Legislative Affairs Agency, Legislative Reference Library, Juneau, AK [*Library symbol*] [*Library of Congress*] (LCLS) ... AkJL
Alaska Legislative Teleconference Network [*Alaska State Legislative Affairs Agency*] [*Juneau, AK*] [*Telecommunications service*] (TSSD) ... LTN
Alaska Library Association ... AkLA
Alaska Manufactured Housing Association (SRA) ... AMHA
Alaska Marine Highway Authority (SAUO) ... AMHS
Alaska Mental Health Trust Authority (SAUO) ... AMHTA
Alaska Methodist University ... AMU
Alaska Methodist University, Anchorage, AK [*Library symbol*] [*Library of Congress*] (LCLS) ... AkAM
Alaska Military Highway ... AMH

Alaska Mineral Resource Assessment Program [*Department of the Interior*] .... AMRAP
Alaska Miners Association (SRA) .... AMA
Alaska Mortgage Bankers Association (SAUO) .... AMBA
Alaska Municipal League (SRA) .... AML
Alaska National Bank of the North (SAUS) .... AreN
Alaska National Interest Land Conservation Act [*1980*] .... ANILCA
Alaska National Interest Lands Conservation (COE) .... ANILCA
Alaska National Interest Lands Conservation Act (SAUO) .... ANILCA
Alaska Native Arts and Crafts Cooperative Association .... ANAC
Alaska Native Claims Appeals Board (in United States Interior Decisions) [*A publication*] (DLA) .... ANCAB
Alaska Native Claims Settlement Act [*1971*] .... ANCSA
Alaska Native Health Service (SAUO) .... ANHS
Alaska Native Industries Cooperative Association (SAUO) .... ANICA
Alaska Native Land Claims Act (SAUS) .... ANLCA
Alaska Native Language Center [*Research center*] (RCD) .... ANLC
Alaska Native Management Report (journ.) (SAUS) .... ANMR
Alaska Native Medical Center (SAUS) .... ANMC
Alaska Native Regional Corp. (GEOI) .... ANRC
Alaska Native Science Commission (SAUO) .... ANSC
Alaska Native Service (SAUO) .... ANS
Alaska Native Village (GEOI) .... ANV
Alaska Native Village Statistical Area (GEOI) .... ANVSA
Alaska Natural Gas Transportation Act (SAUS) .... ANGTA
Alaska Natural Gas Transportation Act of 1976 .... ANGTA
Alaska Natural Gas Transportation System .... ANGTS
Alaska Network (SAUS) .... AN
Alaska Nurses Association (SRA) .... AaNA
Alaska Oil and Gas Association (SRA) .... AOGA
Alaska Oil and Gas News (journ.) (SAUS) .... AOGN
Alaska Pacific University (SAUO) .... APU
Alaska Pacific University, Anchorage, AK [*Library symbol*] [*Library of Congress*] (LCLS) .... AkAAPU
Alaska Power Administration (SAUO) .... ALPOWAD
Alaska Power Administration (SAUO) .... AP
Alaska Power Administration [*Department of Energy*] .... APA
Alaska Psychiatric Institute (SAUO) .... API
Alaska Public Employees Association (SAUO) .... APEA
Alaska Public Interest Research Group [*Research center*] (RCD) .... AKPIRG
Alaska Public Lands Information Center .... APLIC
Alaska Public Offices Commission (SAUO) .... APOC
Alaska Public Radio Network (SAUS) .... AFIRN
Alaska Public Radio Network .... APRN
Alaska Public Utilities Commission (SAUO) .... APUC
Alaska Quaternary Center [*University of Alaska, Fairbanks*] [*Research center*] (RCD) .... AQC
Alaska Railroad (SAUO) .... ALSK
Alaska Railroad (SAUO) .... ARR
[*The*] Alaska Railroad [*AAR code*] .... ARR
Alaska Reporter [*A publication*] (DLA) .... Alaska
Alaska Reports [*A publication*] (AAGC) .... Alaska
Alaska Reports [*A publication*] (DLA) .... Alk
Alaska Resources for the Moderately/Severely Impaired (EDAC) .... ARMSI
Alaska Rural Electric Cooperative Association (SRA) .... ARECA
Alaska Rural Teacher Training Corps (EDAC) .... ARTTC
Alaska Salmon Industry (SAUO) .... ASI
Alaska SAR Facility (SAUS) .... ASF
Alaska Seafood Marketing Institute (SAUO) .... ASMI
Alaska Seismic Network .... ASN
Alaska Session Laws [*A publication*] (DLA) .... Alaska Sess Laws
Alaska Society of Professional Land Surveyors (GEOI) .... ASPLS
Alaska Specialized Education & Training Services (SAUO) .... ASETS
Alaska Standard Time .... ALST
Alaska State Chamber of Commerce (SRA) .... ASCC
Alaska State Court System, Law Library, Anchorage, AK [*Library symbol*] [*Library of Congress*] (LCLS) .... Ak-L
Alaska State Data Center [*Alaska State Department of Labor*] [*Information service or system*] (IID) .... ASDC
Alaska State District Council of Laborers (SRA) .... ASDCL
Alaska State Employees Association (SAUO) .... ASEA
Alaska State Homebuilders Association (SRA) .... ASHBA
Alaska State Hospital and Nursing Home Association (SRA) .... ASHNHA
Alaska State Housing Authority (SAUO) .... ASHA
Alaska State Library, Juneau, AK [*Library symbol*] [*Library of Congress*] (LCLS) .... Ak
Alaska State Medical Association (SRA) .... ASMA
Alaska State Pension Investment Board (SAUO) .... ASPIB
Alaska State Troopers .... AST
Alaska Statutes [*A publication*] (DLA) .... Alaska Stat
Alaska Steamship Company (SAUO) .... A
Alaska Steamship Company (SAUO) .... ASC
Alaska Synthetic Aperture RADAR Facility [*NASA*] (GRD) .... ASF
Alaska Telephone Association (SRA) .... ATA
Alaska Territorial Medical Association (SAUO) .... ATMA
Alaska Tourism Marketing Council (SAUO) .... ATMC
Alaska Transportation Commission (SAUO) .... ATC
Alaska Trucking Association (SRA) .... ATA
Alaska Tsunami Warning Center [*Army*] (OSRA) .... ATWC
Alaska Tsunami Warning System [*National Oceanic and Atmospheric Administration*] (GFGA) .... ATWS
Alaska University of California Los Angeles-Alaska (SAUS) .... UCLA
Alaska Village Demonstration Project [*Environmental Protection Agency*] .... AVDP
Alaska Visitors Association (SRA) .... AVA
Alaska Wine and Spirits Wholesalers Association (SRA) .... AWSWA

Alaska-Canada (ADWA) .... Alcan
Alaska-Canada [*Highway*] .... ALCAN
Alaska-Canada (SAUS) .... AlCan
Alaskagold Mines Ltd. [*Vancouver Stock Exchange symbol*] .... AKG
Alaska-Hawaii Daylight (SAUS) .... AHD
Alaska-Hawaii Standard (SAUS) .... AHS
Alaska-Hawaii Standard Time (WGA) .... AHST
Alaska-Hawaii Time (SAUS) .... A-H
Alaskan ADCOM Region [*Military*] .... AKADCOMRGN
Alaskan AIDS Assistance Association .... AAAA
Alaskan Air Command [*Elmendorf Air Force Base*] .... AAC
Alaskan Air Command (SAUO) .... ALAC
Alaskan Air Command [*Elmendorf Air Force Base*] [*Air Force*] .... ALAIRC
Alaskan Air Defense Region (SAUO) .... AADR
Alaskan Air Depot (SAUO) .... AAD
Alaskan Arctic National Wildlife Refuge (EEVL) .... AANWR
Alaskan Arctic Training Center (SAUS) .... AATC
Alaskan Building Equity (SAUO) .... ABE
Alaskan Collectors Club (EA) .... ACC
Alaskan Command [*Discontinued, 1975*] [*Military*] .... AC
Alaskan Command [*Discontinued, 1975*] [*Military*] .... ALCOM
Alaskan Communication System (SAUO) .... ACS
Alaskan Communications Region [*Air Force*] .... ACR
Alaskan Communications System [*Air Force*] .... ACS
Alaskan Daylight Saving Time (SAUS) .... Alas DST
Alaskan Daylight Time .... ADT
Alaskan Department of Fish and Game (SAUO) .... ADFG
Alaskan District Corps of Engineers (SAUO) .... ALDISTCE
Alaskan DX Certificate (SAUS) .... ADXC
Alaskan Forces Radio Network (SAUO) .... AFRN
Alaskan General Depot (SAUO) .... AGD
Alaskan General Depot (SAUO) .... ALGENDEP
Alaskan Health Sciences Information Center (SAUS) .... AHSIC
Alaskan Integrated Air Defense System .... ALIADS
Alaskan Integrated Communications Exchange .... ALICE
Alaskan Long-Period Array .... ALPA
Alaskan Long-Period Array (SAUS) .... ALPO
Alaskan Malamute Club of America (EA) .... AMCA
Alaskan Malamute Protection League (EA) .... AMPL
Alaskan Meteorological Data System (ACAE) .... ALMEDS
Alaskan Native Village Statistical Area (SAUS) .... ANVSA
Alaskan NICS [*FAA*] (TAG) .... ANICS
Alaskan NORAD Region .... ANR
Alaskan NORAD Region Control Center (SAUO) .... ANRCC
Alaskan NORAD Region Operations Control Center (SAUO) .... ANROCC
Alaskan Projects Office, Fort Wainwright, AK [*Library symbol*] [*Library of Congress*] (LCLS) .... AkFwP
Alaskan Railroad (SAUS) .... ARR
Alaskan Region Operations Control Center (SAUO) .... AKROCC
Alaskan SAR Facility (SAUO) .... ASF
Alaskan Sea Frontier [*Navy*] .... AL SEA FRON
Alaskan Sea Frontier [*Navy*] .... ASF
Alaskan Sector .... AL SEC
Alaskan Standard Time [*Aviation*] (SAA) .... AST
Alaskan Territorial Guard .... ATG
Alaskans Concerned for Neglected Environments (SAUS) .... ACNE
Alaska-Yukon Pacific (SAUS) .... AYP
Alaskon Resources [*Vancouver Stock Exchange symbol*] .... AKN
Alatenn Resources, Inc. [*Associated Press*] (SAG) .... Alaten
AlaTenn Resources, Inc. [*NASDAQ symbol*] (NQ) .... ATNG
Alavus [*Finland*] [*ICAO location identifier*] (ICLI) .... EFAL
Alawas Gold Corp. [*Vancouver Stock Exchange symbol*] .... ALW
Al-Azhar University (SAUO) .... AAU
Albacete [*Spain*] [*ICAO location identifier*] (ICLI) .... LEAB
Al-Baha [*Saudi Arabia*] [*Airport symbol*] (OAG) .... BBH
Alban Exploration Ltd. [*Vancouver Stock Exchange symbol*] .... ABN
Alban Institute (EA) .... AI
Albania [*MARC country of publication code*] [*Library of Congress*] (LCCP) .... aa
Albania [*ANSI two-letter standard code*] (CNC) .... AL
Albania [*ANSI three-letter standard code*] (CNC) .... ALB
Albania (VRA) .... Alb
Albania .... Alban
Albania [*MARC geographic area code*] [*Library of Congress*] (LCCP) .... e-aa-
Albania [*License plate code assigned to foreign diplomats in the US*] .... GP
Albania, Bulgaria, Czechoslovakia, East Germany, Hungary, Poland, Romania, Yugoslavia .... East Bloc
Albania Education Development Project .... AEDP
Albania, France, Italy, Yugoslavia (SAUS) .... Southern Alplands
Albania Society of Britain [*British*] (EAIO) .... ASB
Albania Workers' Party [*Political party*] .... AWP
Albanian [*MARC language code*] [*Library of Congress*] (LCCP) .... alb
Albanian (ADWA) .... Alb
Albanian Airline Co. [*ICAO designator*] (FAAC) .... LBC
Albanian Airways [*ICAO designator*] (FAAC) .... ABW
Albanian Catholic Information Center (EA) .... ACIC
Albanian Catholic Institute (EA) .... ACI
Albanian Communist Party [*Political party*] .... ACP
Albanian Kosovar Youth in the Free World (EA) .... AKYFW
Albanian People's Army .... APA
Albanian Republican Party [*Partia Republikane Shqiptare*] [*Political party*] (EY) .... ARP
Albanian Society (EAIO) .... AS
Albanian Society Jusuf Gervalla (EA) .... ASJG
Albanian Telegraph Agency (SAUS) .... ATA
Albanian Telegraphic Agency [*News agency*] (EY) .... ATA

Albanian-American Enterprise Fund (SAUO) ... AAEF
Albanian-American National Organization ... AANO
Albank Financial Corp. [*Associated Press*] (SAG) ... Albank
Albank Financial Corp. [*NASDAQ symbol*] (SAG) ... ALBK
ALBANK Finl [*NASDAQ symbol*] (TTSB) ... ALBK
Albany [*Georgia*] [*Airport symbol*] (OAG) ... ABY
Albany [*New York*] [*Airport symbol*] (OAG) ... ALB
Albany (SAUS) ... Alb
Albany [*Australia*] [*Airport symbol*] (OAG) ... ALH
Albany [*Australia*] [*ICAO location identifier*] (ICLI) ... APAL
Albany & Northern Railway Co. (IIA) ... A & N
Albany & Northern Railway Co. [*AAR code*] ... ALN
Albany & Northern Railway Company (SAUO) ... ALN
Albany Area Board of Cooperative Education Services, Colonie, NY [*Library symbol*] [*Library of Congress*] (LCLS) ... NColnA
Albany Avenue Elementary School, North Massapequa, NY [*Library symbol*] [*Library of Congress*] (LCLS) ... NNomAE
Albany Business College, Albany, NY [*Library symbol*] [*Library of Congress*] (LCLS) ... NAIBC
Albany College of Pharmacy, Albany, NY [*Library symbol*] [*Library of Congress*] (LCLS) ... NAIP
Albany Corp. [*Toronto Stock Exchange symbol*] ... AYO
Albany County Public Library, Laramie, WY [*Library symbol*] [*Library of Congress*] (LCLS) ... WyLar
Albany Free Public Library, Albany, CA [*Library symbol*] [*Library of Congress*] (LCLS) ... CAlb
Albany, GA [*Location identifier*] [*FAA*] (FAAL) ... NHX
Albany, GA [*Television station call letters*] ... WALB
Albany, GA [*AM radio station call letters*] ... WALG
Albany, GA [*AM radio station call letters*] ... WANL
Albany, GA [*Television station call letters*] ... WFXL
Albany, GA [*FM radio station call letters*] ... WGNP
Albany, GA [*AM radio station call letters*] ... WGPC
Albany, GA [*FM radio station call letters*] ... WGPC-FM
Albany, GA [*FM radio station call letters*] ... WJIZ
Albany, GA [*AM radio station call letters*] ... WJYZ
Albany, GA [*FM radio station call letters*] ... WKAK
Albany, GA [*FM radio station call letters*] ... WUNV
Albany General Hospital, Albany, OR [*Library symbol*] [*Library of Congress*] (LCLS) ... OrAlH
Albany Institute of History of Art, Albany, NY [*Library symbol*] [*Library of Congress*] (LCLS) ... NAII
Albany International Corp. [*NYSE symbol*] (CTT) ... AIN
Albany International Corp. [*Associated Press*] (SAG) ... AlbnyIn
Albany Intl. 'A' [*NYSE symbol*] (TTSB) ... AIN
Albany Jr. H.S./Elementary Library, Albany, MN [*Library symbol*] [*Library of Congress*] (LCLS) ... MnAlJ
Albany Junior College, Albany, GA [*Library symbol*] [*Library of Congress*] (LCLS) ... GAIJC
Albany, KY [*AM radio station call letters*] ... WANY
Albany, KY [*FM radio station call letters*] ... WANY-FM
Albany Law Journal [*A publication*] (DLA) ... Alb LJ
Albany Law Journal [*A publication*] (DLA) ... ALJ
Albany Law School (SAUS) ... Alb LS
Albany Law School (SAUS) ... NAILS
Albany Law School, Albany, NY [*Library symbol*] [*Library of Congress*] (LCLS) ... NAILS
Albany Law School, Albany, NY [*OCLC symbol*] (OCLC) ... YZA
Albany Law School Journal [*A publication*] (DLA) ... Alb LS Jour
Albany Medical Center (SAUO) ... AMC
Albany Medical College (GAGS) ... Albany Med C
Albany Medical College (SAUO) ... AMC
Albany Medical College, Albany, NY [*Library symbol*] [*Library of Congress*] (LCLS) ... NAIA
Albany Medical College, Schaffer Library of Health Sciences, Albany, NY [*OCLC symbol*] (OCLC) ... VXL
Albany, MN [*AM radio station call letters*] ... KASM
Albany, MN [*FM radio station call letters*] ... KASM-FM
Albany, MN [*FM radio station call letters*] (BROA) ... KDDG-FM
Albany, NY [*Location identifier*] [*FAA*] (FAAL) ... DEJ
Albany, NY [*AM radio station call letters*] ... WABY
Albany, NY [*FM radio station call letters*] ... WAMC
Albany, NY [*FM radio station call letters*] ... WCDB
Albany, NY [*AM radio station call letters*] (RBYB) ... WDCD
Albany, NY [*AM radio station call letters*] ... WGNA
Albany, NY [*FM radio station call letters*] ... WGNA-FM
Albany, NY [*FM radio station call letters*] ... WHRL
Albany, NY [*FM radio station call letters*] ... WKLI
Albany, NY [*Television station call letters*] ... WNYT
Albany, NY [*FM radio station call letters*] ... WPYX
Albany, NY [*AM radio station call letters*] ... WROW
Albany, NY [*Television station call letters*] ... WTEN
Albany, NY [*Television station call letters*] ... WXXA
Albany, NY [*FM radio station call letters*] ... WYJB
Albany, OR [*FM radio station call letters*] ... KHPE
Albany, OR [*AM radio station call letters*] ... KRKT
Albany, OR [*FM radio station call letters*] ... KRKT-FM
Albany, OR [*AM radio station call letters*] ... KWIL
Albany Port District [*AAR code*] ... APD
Albany Port District Commission (SAUO) ... APDC
Albany Public Library (SAUO) ... APL
Albany Public Library, Alabany, MN [*Library symbol*] [*Library of Congress*] (LCLS) ... MnAl
Albany Public Library, Albany, GA [*Library symbol*] [*Library of Congress*] (LCLS) ... GAI
Albany Public Library, Albany, NY [*Library symbol*] [*Library of Congress*] (LCLS) ... NAI
Albany Public Library, Albany, OR [*Library symbol*] [*Library of Congress*] (LCLS) ... OrAl
Albany Resources [*Vancouver Stock Exchange symbol*] ... ALX
Albany Senior High School, Albany, MN [*Library symbol*] [*Library of Congress*] (LCLS) ... MnAIS
Albany State College [*Georgia*] ... ASC
Albany State College, Albany, GA [*Library symbol*] [*Library of Congress*] (LCLS) ... GAISC
Albany Symphony Orchestra (SAUO) ... ASO
Albany Yacht Club (SAUO) ... AYC
Albany/Albany [*New York*] [*ICAO location identifier*] (ICLI) ... KALB
Albany/Albany Naval Air Station [*Georgia*] [*ICAO location identifier*] (ICLI) ... KNAB
Albany-Corvallis [*Oregon*] [*Airport symbol*] (AD) ... CVO
Albaraka Algeria Islamic Bank (EY) ... AAIB
Albatros Airline, Inc. [*Turkey*] [*ICAO designator*] (FAAC) ... ABK
Albatrosz Ltd. [*Hungary*] [*ICAO designator*] (FAAC) ... ALT
Alba-Waldensian [*AMEX symbol*] (TTSB) ... AWS
Alba-Waldensian, Inc. [*Associated Press*] (SAG) ... AlbaW
Alba-Waldensian, Inc. [*AMEX symbol*] (SPSG) ... AWS
Albedo [*Psychology*] ... A
Al-Beida [*Yemen*] [*ICAO location identifier*] (ICLI) ... OYBI
Albemarle Corp. [*Associated Press*] (SAG) ... Albemr
Albemarle, NC [*Location identifier*] [*FAA*] (FAAL) ... SWY
Albemarle, NC [*FM radio station call letters*] ... WABZ
Albemarle, NC [*AM radio station call letters*] ... WSPC
Albemarle, NC [*AM radio station call letters*] ... WZKY
Albemarle-Stanly County Public Library, Albemarle, NC [*Library symbol*] [*Library of Congress*] (LCLS) ... NcAlb
Albendazole [*Anthelmintic*] ... ABZ
Albenga [*Italy*] [*Airport symbol*] (AD) ... ALL
Albenga [*Italy*] [*ICAO location identifier*] (ICLI) ... LIMG
Albericus de Maletis [*Flourished, 1431-33*] [*Authority cited in pre-1607 legal work*] (DSA) ... Alber de Malet
Albericus de Porta Ravennate [*Flourished, 1165-94*] [*Authority cited in pre-1607 legal work*] (DSA) ... A
Albericus de Porta Ravennate [*Flourished, 1165-94*] [*Authority cited in pre-1607 legal work*] (DSA) ... Al
Albericus de Porta Ravennate [*Flourished, 1165-94*] [*Authority cited in pre-1607 legal work*] (DSA) ... Alb
Albericus de Porta Ravennate [*Flourished, 1165-94*] [*Authority cited in pre-1607 legal work*] (DSA) ... Albri
Albericus de Rosate [*Deceased, 1360*] [*Authority cited in pre-1607 legal work*] (DSA) ... Alb
Albericus de Rosate [*Deceased, 1360*] [*Authority cited in pre-1607 legal work*] (DSA) ... Alb de Ros
Albericus de Rosate [*Deceased, 1360*] [*Authority cited in pre-1607 legal work*] (DSA) ... Albe
Albericus de Rosate [*Deceased, 1360*] [*Authority cited in pre-1607 legal work*] (DSA) ... Alber
Albericus de Rosate [*Deceased, 1360*] [*Authority cited in pre-1607 legal work*] (DSA) ... Alberic de Rosat
Albericus de Rosate [*Deceased, 1360*] [*Authority cited in pre-1607 legal work*] (DSA) ... Albri de Rosa
Albermarle Corp. [*NYSE symbol*] (SAG) ... ALB
Albermarle Corp. [*Associated Press*] (SAG) ... Albemar
Albermarle Regional Library, Winton, NC [*Library symbol*] [*Library of Congress*] (LCLS) ... NcWintA
Alberni [*British Columbia*] [*Seismograph station code, US Geological Survey*] (SEIS) ... ALB
Alberni Airway [*Canada*] [*ICAO designator*] (FAAC) ... BNI
Alberni District Archives, Port Alberni, British Columbia [*Library symbol*] [*National Library of Canada*] (BIB) ... BPADA
Alberni Valley Museum, Port Alberni, BC, Canada [*Library symbol*] [*Library of Congress*] (LCLS) ... CaBPaM
Alberni Valley Museum, Port Alberni, British Columbia [*Library symbol*] [*National Library of Canada*] (NLC) ... BPAM
Albers-Schonberg's Disease [*Medicine*] (MELL) ... ASD
Albert Achillodynia (MELL) ... AA
Albert Arbitration [*Lord Cairns' Decisions*] [*A publication*] (DLA) ... Alb Arb
Albert Campbell Branch, Scarborough Public Library, Ontario [*Library symbol*] [*National Library of Canada*] (NLC) ... OTSPA
Albert Canal connecting Antwerp and Liege (SAUS) ... Albert
Albert Champion [*Automotive industrialist whose company is now part of General Motors*] ... AC
Albert County Historical Society, Inc., Hopewell Cape, New Brunswick [*Library symbol*] [*National Library of Canada*] (NLC) ... NBHCA
Albert Einstein College of Medicine (SAUO) ... AECM
Albert Einstein Foundation (SAUO) ... AEF
Albert Einstein Institution (EA) ... AEI
Albert Einstein International Academy Foundation (EA) ... AEIAF
Albert Einstein Medical Center ... AEMC
Albert Einstein Medical Center, Northern Division, Philadelphia, PA [*Library symbol*] [*Library of Congress*] (LCLS) ... PPAEM
Albert Einstein Medical College (DAVI) ... AEMD
Albert Einstein Peace Prize Foundation (EA) ... AEPPF
Albert Einstein School of Medicine (SAUS) ... AESM
Albert Einstein-Archiv, Hebrew University Jerusalem (SAUS) ... AEA
Albert F. Simpson Historical Research Center (AFM) ... AFSHRC
Albert Hofmann Foundation (SAUO) ... AHF
Albert Kahn Associates [*Founded in 1895, one of the oldest architectural firms in the US*] ... AKA
Albert Lea, MN [*Location identifier*] [*FAA*] (FAAL) ... AEL

Albert Lea, MN [*Location identifier*] [*FAA*] (FAAL) .... FYB
Albert Lea, MN [*AM radio station call letters*] .... KATE
Albert Lea, MN [*FM radio station call letters*] .... KCPI
Albert Lea, MN [*FM radio station call letters*] .... KQPR
Albert Lea Public Library, Albert Lea, MN [*Library symbol*] [*Library of Congress*] (LCLS) .... MnAlb
Albert Medal [*British*] .... AM
Albert National Park (SAUS) .... ANP
Albert National Park in Zaire (SAUS) .... Albert
Albert Rolland [*France*] [*Research code symbol*] .... ANP
Albert Rolland [*France*] [*Research code symbol*] .... Rd
Albert Schweitzer Fellowship (EA) .... ASF
Albert Schweitzer Friendship House (SAUO) .... ASFH
Albert South Library, Regina, Saskatchewan [*Library symbol*] [*National Library of Canada*] (NLC) .... SRAS
Albert South Library, Regina, SK, Canada [*Library symbol*] [*Library of Congress*] (LCLS) .... CaSRAS
Albert W. Thompson Memorial Library, Clayton, NM [*Library symbol*] [*Library of Congress*] (LCLS) .... NmCla
Albert W. Thompson Memorial Library, Clayton, NM [*Library symbol*] [*Library of Congress*] (LCLS) .... NmClaP
Alberta [*Canadian province*] [*Postal code*] .... AB
Alberta [*MARC country of publication code*] [*Library of Congress*] (LCCP) .... abc
Alberta [*Canadian province*] .... ALB
Alberta [*Canadian province*] .... ALBA
Alberta (ADWA) .... Alba
Alberta [*Canada*] (DD) .... Alta
Alberta [*Canadian province*] .... ALTA
Alberta [*MARC geographic area code*] [*Library of Congress*] (LCCP) .... n-cn-ab
Alberta 5 Pin Bowlers' Association (AC) A5-PBA
Alberta Advanced Education, Edmonton, Alberta [*Library symbol*] [*National Library of Canada*] (NLC) .... AEAE
Alberta Agriculture, Edmonton, Alberta [*Library symbol*] [*National Library of Canada*] (NLC) .... AEAG
Alberta Agriculture Library [*UTLAS symbol*] .... AAG
Alberta Alcoholism and Drug Abuse Commission Library, Edmonton, AB, Canada [*OCLC symbol*] (OCLC) .... AAD
Alberta Amateur Softball Association [*Also Softball Alberta*] (AC) .... AASA
Alberta & Southern Gas Co. Ltd., Calgary, Alberta [*Library symbol*] [*National Library of Canada*] (BIB) .... ACASG
Alberta Arbitration & Mediation Society (AC) .... AAMS
Alberta Association for Community Living [*Alberta Association for the Mentally Handicapped*] (AC) .... AACL
Alberta Association for Marriage & Family Therapy (AC) .... AAMFT
Alberta Association for Multicultural Education [*Association de l'Education Multiculturelle de l'Alberta*] (AC) .... AAME
Alberta Association of Agricultural Fieldmen (AC) .... AAAF
Alberta Association of Agricultural Societies (AC) .... AAAS
[*The*] **Alberta Association of Animal Health Technologists** (AC) .... AAAHT
Alberta Association of Architects [*1906*] [*Canada*] (NGC) .... AAA
Alberta Association of College Librarians (AC) .... AACL
Alberta Association of Designers & Architectural Technologists (AC) .... AADAT
Alberta Association of Landscape Architects (AC) .... AALA
Alberta Association of Legal Assistants (AC) .... AALA
Alberta Association of Library Technicians (AC) .... AALT
Alberta Association of Medical Radiation Technologists (AC) .... AAMRT
Alberta Association of Midwives (AC) .... AAM
Alberta Association of Registered Nurses (AC) .... AARN
Alberta Association of Registered Nurses, Edmonton, AB, Canada [*Library symbol*] [*Library of Congress*] (LCLS) .... CaAEARN
Alberta Association of Registered Nurses, Edmonton, Alberta [*Library symbol*] [*National Library of Canada*] (NLC) .... AEARN
Alberta Association of Registered Occupational Therapists (AC) .... AAROT
Alberta Association of Rehabilitation Centres (AC) .... AARC
Alberta Association of Services for Children & Families [*Formerly, Alberta Association of Child Care Centres*] (AC) .... AASCF
Alberta Association of the Appraisal Institute of Canada (AC) .... AA-AIC
Alberta Association of the Canadian Institute of Planners (AC) .... AACIP
Alberta Association of Translators & Interpreters [*Association des Traducteurs et Interpretes de l'Alberta*] (AC) .... AATI
Alberta Attorney General, Edmonton, Alberta [*Library symbol*] [*National Library of Canada*] (NLC) .... AEATG
Alberta Attorney General, Provincial Court Libraries [*UTLAS symbol*] .... PCL
Alberta Attorney General, Queen's Bench Libraries [*UTLAS symbol*] .... AQB
Alberta Attorney Generat Queens Bench Libraries (SAUS) .... AQB
Alberta Ballet Co. [*Canada*] .... ABC
Alberta Beach Municipal Library, Alberta [*Library symbol*] [*National Library of Canada*] (NLC) .... AABM
Alberta Beef Cattle Performance Association (SAUO) .... ABCPA
Alberta Bureau of Surveying and Mapping [*Canada*] (GEOI) .... ABSM
Alberta Camping Association (AC) .... ACA
Alberta Cancer Clinic, Edmonton, AB, Canada [*Library symbol*] [*Library of Congress*] (LCLS) .... CaAECC
Alberta Cancer Clinic, Edmonton, Alberta [*Library symbol*] [*National Library of Canada*] (NLC) .... AECC
Alberta Case Locator [*University of Alberta*] [*Canada*] [*Information service or system*] (CRD) .... ACL
Alberta Chess Association (AC) .... ACA
Alberta Children's Hospital, Calgary, AB, Canada [*Library symbol*] [*Library of Congress*] (LCLS) .... CaACACH
Alberta Children's Hospital, Calgary, Alberta [*Library symbol*] [*National Library of Canada*] (NLC) .... ACACH
Alberta Children's Hospital Research Centre [*Canada*] (IRC) .... ACHRC
Alberta Choral Federation (AC) .... ACF
Alberta Citylink [*Canada*] [*FAA designator*] (FAAC) .... ABK
Alberta College of Art (SAUO) .... ACA
Alberta College of Art, Calgary, AB, Canada [*Library symbol*] [*Library of Congress*] (LCLS) .... CaACSAA
Alberta College of Art, Calgary, Alberta [*Library symbol*] [*National Library of Canada*] (NLC) .... ACSAA
Alberta Committee of Citizens with Disabilities (AC) .... ACCD
Alberta Conservation Tillage Society (AC) .... ACTS
Alberta Construction Association (AC) .... ACA
Alberta Consumer and Corporate Affairs, Edmonton, Alberta [*Library symbol*] [*National Library of Canada*] (NLC) .... AECA
Alberta Council on Aging (AC) .... ACA
Alberta Craft Council (AC) .... ACC
Alberta Crown Attorneys' Association (AC) .... ACAA
Alberta Culture, Edmonton, AB, Canada [*Library symbol*] [*Library of Congress*] (LCLS) .... CaAECL
Alberta Culture, Edmonton, AB, Canada [*Library symbol*] [*Library of Congress*] (LCLS) .... CaAECYR
Alberta Culture, Edmonton, Alberta [*Library symbol*] [*National Library of Canada*] (NLC) .... AECL
Alberta Culture, Heritage Resources Development, Edmonton, AB, Canada [*Library symbol*] [*Library of Congress*] (LCLS) .... CaAECYRH
Alberta Culture Library Services, Edmonton, AB, Canada [*Library symbol*] [*Library of Congress*] (LCLS) .... CaAECLS
Alberta Culture Library Services, Edmonton, Alberta [*Library symbol*] [*National Library of Canada*] (NLC) .... AECLS
Alberta Curling Federation (AC) .... ACF
Alberta Deaf Sports Association (AC) .... ADSA
Alberta Debate & Speech Association (AC) .... ADSA
Alberta Dental Assistants Association [*Formerly, Alberta Dental Nurses & Assistants Association*] (AC) .... ADAA
Alberta Dental Association (SAUO) .... ADA
Alberta Department of Advanced Education and Manpower, Edmonton, AB, Canada [*Library symbol*] [*Library of Congress*] (LCLS) .... CaAEAE
Alberta Department of Agriculture, Dairy Division, Wetaskiwin, AB, Canada [*Library symbol*] [*Library of Congress*] (LCLS) .... CaAWAD
Alberta Department of Agriculture, Edmonton, AB, Canada [*Library symbol*] [*Library of Congress*] (LCLS) .... CaAEAg
Alberta Department of Agriculture, Farm Business Management Branch, Olds, AB, Canada [*Library symbol*] [*Library of Congress*] (LCLS) .... CaAOAF
Alberta Department of Agriculture, Field Crops Branch, Lacombe, AB, Canada [*Library symbol*] [*Library of Congress*] (LCLS) .... CaALaAF
Alberta Department of Agriculture, Horse Industry Branch, Calgary, AB, Canada [*Library symbol*] [*Library of Congress*] (LCLS) .... CaACAH
Alberta Department of Agriculture, Irrigation Division, Lethbridge, AB, Canada [*Library symbol*] [*Library of Congress*] (LCLS) .... CaALAI
Alberta Department of Agriculture, Laboratory, Edmonton, AB, Canada [*Library symbol*] [*Library of Congress*] (LCLS) .... CaAEAgL
Alberta Department of Agriculture, O. S. Longman Building, Edmonton, AB, Canada [*Library symbol*] [*Library of Congress*] (LCLS) .... CaAEAO
Alberta Department of Agriculture, Regional Office, Airdrie, AB, Canada [*Library symbol*] [*Library of Congress*] (LCLS) .... CaAAAR
Alberta Department of Agriculture, Regional Office, Barrhead, AB, Canada [*Library symbol*] [*Library of Congress*] (LCLS) .... CaABaAR
Alberta Department of Agriculture, Regional Office, Fairview, AB, Canada [*Library symbol*] [*Library of Congress*] (LCLS) .... CaAFAAR
Alberta Department of Agriculture, Regional Office, Lethbridge, AB, Canada [*Library symbol*] [*Library of Congress*] (LCLS) .... CaALAR
Alberta Department of Agriculture, Regional Office, Red Deer, AB, Canada [*Library symbol*] [*Library of Congress*] (LCLS) .... CaARDAR
Alberta Department of Agriculture, Regional Office, Vermilion, AB, Canada [*Library symbol*] [*Library of Congress*] (LCLS) .... CaAVAR
Alberta Department of Agriculture, Veterinary Laboratory, Fairview, AB, Canada [*Library symbol*] [*Library of Congress*] (LCLS) .... CaAFAAV
Alberta Department of Business Development and Tourism, Edmonton, AB, Canada [*Library symbol*] [*Library of Congress*] (LCLS) .... CaAEIC
Alberta Department of Consumer and Corporate Affairs, Edmonton, AB, Canada [*Library symbol*] [*Library of Congress*] (LCLS) .... CaAECA
Alberta Department of Culture Library [*UTLAS symbol*] .... AEC
Alberta Department of Economic Development, Edmonton, AB, Canada [*Library symbol*] [*Library of Congress*] (LCLS) .... CaAEEC
Alberta Department of Education, Audio Visual Services Branch, Edmonton, AB, Canada [*Library symbol*] [*Library of Congress*] (LCLS) .... CaAEEAV
Alberta Department of Education, Edmonton, AB, Canada [*Library symbol*] [*Library of Congress*] (LCLS) .... CaAEE
Alberta Department of Education, Special Education, Materials Resource Centre, Edmonton, AB, Canada [*Library symbol*] [*Library of Congress*] (LCLS) .... CaAEESE
Alberta Department of Energy and Natural Resources, Edmonton, AB, Canada [*Library symbol*] [*Library of Congress*] [*Obsolete*] (LCLS) .... CaAEMM
Alberta Department of Energy and Natural Resources, Edmonton, AB, Canada [*Library symbol*] [*Library of Congress*] (LCLS) .... CaAENR
Alberta Department of Energy and Natural Resources, Renewable Resources Division, Edmonton, AB, Canada [*Library symbol*] [*Library of Congress*] [*Obsolete*] (LCLS) .... CaAELF
Alberta Department of Federal and Intergovernmental Affairs, Edmonton, AB, Canada [*Library symbol*] [*Library of Congress*] (LCLS) .... CaAEFIA
Alberta Department of Government Services, Computing and Systems Division, Edmonton, AB, Canada [*Library symbol*] [*Library of Congress*] (LCLS) .... CaAEDC
Alberta Department of Government Services, Edmonton, AB, Canada [*Library symbol*] [*Library of Congress*] (LCLS) .... CaAEGS
Alberta Department of Housing and Public Works, Edmonton, AB, Canada [*Library symbol*] [*Library of Congress*] (LCLS) .... CaAEPW

Alberta Department of Labour, Edmonton, AB, Canada [Library symbol] [Library of Congress] (LCLS) .... CaAEML

Alberta Department of Labour, Occupational Health and Safety Division, Edmonton, AB, Canada [Library symbol] [Library of Congress] (LCLS) .... CaAEMLOH

Alberta Department of Municipal Affairs, Edmonton, AB, Canada [Library symbol] [Library of Congress] (LCLS) .... CaAEMA

Alberta Department of Recreation, Parks, and Wildlife, Edmonton, AB, Canada [Library symbol] [Library of Congress] (LCLS) .... CaAERPW

Alberta Department of Social Services and Community Health, Edmonton, AB, Canada [Library symbol] [Library of Congress] (LCLS) .... CaAEHSD

Alberta Department of the Attorney General, Edmonton, AB, Canada [Library symbol] [Library of Congress] (LCLS) .... CaAEAtG

Alberta Department of the Attorney General, Planning, Research, and Development Division, Edmonton, AB, Canada [Library symbol] [Library of Congress] (LCLS) .... CaAEPRD

Alberta Department of the Environment, Calgary, AB, Canada [Library symbol] [Library of Congress] (LCLS) .... CaACEN

Alberta Department of the Environment, Edmonton, AB, Canada [Library symbol] [Library of Congress] (LCLS) .... CaAEEN

Alberta Department of the Environment, Lethbridge, AB, Canada [Library symbol] [Library of Congress] (LCLS) .... CaALEn

Alberta Department of the Environment, Peace River, AB, Canada [Library symbol] [Library of Congress] (LCLS) .... CaAPrEN

Alberta Department of Transportation, Edmonton, AB, Canada [Library symbol] [Library of Congress] (LCLS) .... CaAEHT

Alberta Department of Transportation, Highways Testing Laboratory, Edmonton, AB, Canada [Library symbol] [Library of Congress] (LCLS) .... CaAEHTT

Alberta Department of Utilities and Telephones, Edmonton, AB, Canada [Library symbol] [Library of Congress] (LCLS) .... CaAEUT

Alberta Dragoons (SAUO) .... Alta Dns

Alberta Economic Development and Trade, Edmonton, Alberta [Library symbol] [National Library of Canada] (NLC) .... AEED

Alberta Education, Edmonton, Alberta [Library symbol] [National Library of Canada] (NLC) .... AEE

Alberta Education Libraries [Professional collection] [UTLAS symbol] .... ACL

Alberta Education Materials Resource Centre [UTLAS symbol] .... AMR

Alberta Education Materials Resource Centre, Edmonton, AB, Canada [Library symbol] [Library of Congress] (LCLS) .... CaAEEM

Alberta Education Materials Resources Centre, Calgary, AB, Canada [Library symbol] [Library of Congress] (LCLS) .... CaACEM

Alberta Energy [NYSE symbol] (TTSB) .... AOG

Alberta Energy and Natural Resources, Edmonton, Alberta [Library symbol] [National Library of Canada] (NLC) .... AENR

Alberta Energy and Natural Resources Library [UTLAS symbol] .... ANR

Alberta Energy and Natural Resources Library, Edmonton, AB, Canada [Library symbol] [Library of Congress] (LCLS) .... CaAEENR

Alberta Energy and Utilities Board (SAUO) .... EUB

Alberta Energy Co., Calgary, AB, Canada [Library symbol] [Library of Congress] (LCLS) .... CaACAE

Alberta Energy Co., Calgary, Alberta [Library symbol] [National Library of Canada] (NLC) .... ACAE

Alberta Energy Co. Ltd. [Toronto Stock Exchange symbol] [Vancouver Stock Exchange symbol] .... AEC

Alberta Energy Co. Ltd. [Associated Press] (SAG) .... AlbrtE

Alberta Energy Co. Ltd. [NYSE symbol] (SAG) .... AOG

Alberta Energy Resources Conservation Board, Calgary, AB, Canada [Library symbol] [Library of Congress] (LCLS) .... CaACER

Alberta Energy Resources Conservation Board, Calgary, Alberta [Library symbol] [National Library of Canada] (NLC) .... ACER

Alberta Environment, Calgary, Alberta [Library symbol] [National Library of Canada] (NLC) .... ACEN

Alberta Environment Centre, Vegreville, Alberta [Library symbol] [National Library of Canada] (NLC) .... AVEE

Alberta Environment, Edmonton, Alberta [Library symbol] [National Library of Canada] (NLC) .... AEEN

Alberta Environment, Lethbridge, Alberta [Library symbol] [National Library of Canada] (NLC) .... ALEN

Alberta Environment Library [UTLAS symbol] .... AEL

Alberta Environment, Peace River, Alberta [Library symbol] [National Library of Canada] (NLC) .... APREN

Alberta Environmental Centre Library [UTLAS symbol] .... AEN

Alberta Environmental Centre, Vegreville (SAUO) .... AECV

Alberta Environmental Centre, Vegreville, AB, Canada [Library symbol] [Library of Congress] (LCLS) .... CaAVeE

Alberta Environmental Network (AC) .... AEN

Alberta Environmental Protection and Enhancement Act [Canada] .... AEPA

Alberta Equestrian Federation (AC) .... AEF

Alberta Exploration [Vancouver Stock Exchange symbol] .... AXO

Alberta Family Histories Society (AC) .... AFHS

Alberta Federal and Intergovernmental Affairs, Edmonton, Alberta [Library symbol] [National Library of Canada] (NLC) .... AEFIA

Alberta Federation of Labour [Federation du Travail de l'Alberta] (AC) .... AFL

Alberta Fire Training School, Alberta Labour, Vermilion, Alberta [Library symbol] [National Library of Canada] (NLC) .... AVLF

Alberta Forest Development Research Trust Fund [Also Forest Research Program - Environmental Protection & Enhancement Fund] (AC) .... AFDRTF

Alberta Forest Products Association (AC) .... AFPA

Alberta Gas Ethylene Co., Calgary, AB, Canada [Library symbol] [Library of Congress] (LCLS) .... CaACAG

Alberta Gas Ethylene Co., Calgary, Alberta [Library symbol] [National Library of Canada] (NLC) .... ACAG

Alberta Gas Trunk Line Co. Ltd., Calgary, AB, Canada [Library symbol] [Library of Congress] (LCLS) .... CaACGTL

Alberta Gas Trunk Line Co. Ltd., Calgary, Alberta [Library symbol] [National Library of Canada] (NLC) .... ACGTL

Alberta Gas Trunkline Co. Ltd. (SAUO) .... AGTL

Alberta Gas Trunkline Co. Ltd., Calgary (SAUS) .... AGTL

Alberta Gazette [A publication] (DLA) .... Alta Gaz

Alberta Genealogical Society (AC) .... AGS

Alberta Geological Survey [Canada] (GEOI) .... AGS

Alberta Government [Canada] [ICAO designator] (FAAC) .... GOA

Alberta Government Civil Lawyers Association (AC) .... AGCLA

Alberta Government Libraries' Council (AC) .... AGLC

Alberta Government Libraries Union Catalogue, Edmonton, Alberta [Library symbol] [National Library of Canada] (NLC) .... AEAUC

Alberta Government Services, Operating and Maintenance Division, Edmonton, AB, Canada [Library symbol] [Library of Congress] (LCLS) .... CaAEAGS

Alberta Government Telephones [Part of Telecom Canada] [Calgary, AB] [Telecommunications service] (TSSD) .... AGT

Alberta Government Telephones Commission, Edmonton, AB, Canada [Library symbol] [Library of Congress] (LCLS) .... CaAEGT

Alberta Government Telephones, Edmonton, Alberta [Library symbol] [National Library of Canada] (NLC) .... AEGT

Alberta Government Union Catalogue, Edmonton Concordia College, Edmonton, AB, Canada [Library symbol] [Library of Congress] (LCLS) .... CaAEAUC

Alberta Health Record Association (AC) .... AHRA

Alberta Healthcare Association [Formerly, Alberta Hospital Association] (AC) .... AHA

Alberta Heritage Foundation for Medical Research [Canada] .... AHFMR

Alberta Historical Resources, Alberta Culture and Multiculturalism, Edmonton, Alberta [Library symbol] [National Library of Canada] (NLC) .... AEA

Alberta Historical Resources, Edmonton, AB, Canada [Library symbol] [Library of Congress] (LCLS) .... CaAEA

Alberta Historical Resources Foundation (AC) .... AHRF

Alberta Hog Producers Marketing Board (SAUO) .... AHPMB

Alberta Horticultural Research Centre, Brooks, AB, Canada [Library symbol] [Library of Congress] (LCLS) .... CaABAH

Alberta Horticultural Research Centre, Brooks, Alberta [Library symbol] [National Library of Canada] (NLC) .... ABAH

Alberta Hospital Association [Edmonton] .... AHA

Alberta Hospital Association, Resource Library, Edmonton, AB, Canada [Library symbol] [Library of Congress] (LCLS) .... CaAEAHA

Alberta Hospital, Edmonton, AB, Canada [Library symbol] [Library of Congress] (LCLS) .... CaAEAH

Alberta Hospital, Edmonton, Alberta [Library symbol] [National Library of Canada] (BIB) .... AEAH

Alberta Hospital Library, Oliver, Alberta [Library symbol] [National Library of Canada] (NLC) .... AEHO

Alberta Hospital, Oliver, AB, Canada [Library symbol] [Library of Congress] (LCLS) .... CaAEHO

Alberta Hospital, Ponoka (SAUS) .... APH

Alberta Hospital, Ponoka, Alberta [Library symbol] [National Library of Canada] (NLC) .... APH

Alberta Hospital, Staff Library, Ponoka, AB, Canada [Library symbol] [Library of Congress] (LCLS) .... CaAPH

Alberta Hospitals & Medical Care, Edmonton, Alberta [Library symbol] [National Library of Canada] (NLC) .... AEHSC

Alberta Housing Corp., Edmonton, AB, Canada [Library symbol] [Library of Congress] (LCLS) .... CaAEHC

Alberta Human Rights Commission, Edmonton, AB, Canada [Library symbol] [Library of Congress] (LCLS) .... CaAEHR

Alberta Information Retrieval Association (SAUO) .... AIRA

Alberta Information Retrieval for Health, Physical Education and Recreation (SAUS) .... AIRHPER

Alberta Institute of Law Research and Reform [Canada] (ILCA) .... Alberta LRR

Alberta Irrigation Projects Association (AC) .... AIPA

Alberta Journal of Educational Research (journ.) (SAUS) .... AJER

Alberta Labour, Alberta Fire Training School, Vermilion, AB, Canada [Library symbol] [Library of Congress] (LCLS) .... CaAVLF

Alberta Labour, Edmonton, Alberta [Library symbol] [National Library of Canada] (NLC) .... AEML

Alberta Labour-Building Standards Library, Edmonton, AB, Canada [Library symbol] [Library of Congress] (LCLS) .... CaAELBS

Alberta Land Surveyors' Association (AC) .... ALSA

Alberta Land Use Planning Data Bank [Alberta Municipal Affairs] [Information service or system] [Defunct] (IID) .... LANDUP

Alberta Law [A publication] (DLA) .... Alta L

Alberta Law Foundation (AC) .... ALF

Alberta Law Quarterly [A publication] (DLA) .... Alb LQ

Alberta Law Quarterly [A publication] (DLA) .... Alta LQ

Alberta League for Environmentally Responsible Tourism (AC) .... ALERT

Alberta Legislation Information [Alberta Public Affairs Bureau] [Canada] [Information service or system] (CRD) .... ALI

Alberta Legislature Library, Edmonton, AB, Canada [Library symbol] [Library of Congress] (LCLS) .... CaAEP

Alberta Legislature Library, Edmonton, Alberta [Library symbol] [National Library of Canada] (NLC) .... AEP

Alberta Library Trustees' Association (AC) .... ALTA

Alberta Light Horse (SAUO) .... Alta LH

Alberta Limousin Association (AC) .... ALA

Alberta Livestock Cooperative (SAUS) .... ALC

Alberta Manpower, Edmonton, AB, Canada [Library symbol] [Library of Congress] (LCLS) .... CaAEMAN

Alberta Manpower, Edmonton, Alberta [Library symbol] [National Library of Canada] (NLC) .... AEMAN

Alberta Marine Trades Association (AC) .... AMTA

Alberta Materials Exchange [Formerly, Alberta Waste Materials Exchange] (AC) .... AME
Alberta Medal [Canada] (DD) .... AM
Alberta Microelectronic Centre [University of Alberta] [Research center] (RCD) .... AMC
Alberta Motion Picture Industries Association [Canada] (WWLA) .... AMPIA
Alberta Municipal Affairs, Edmonton, Alberta [Library symbol] [National Library of Canada] (NLC) .... AEMA
Alberta Native Plants Council (AC) .... ANPC
Alberta Natural Gas Co. Ltd. [Toronto Stock Exchange symbol] [Vancouver Stock Exchange symbol] .... ANG
Alberta Occupation Health and Safety, Edmonton, Alberta [Library symbol] [National Library of Canada] (NLC) .... AEOH
Alberta Office of the Ombudsman, Edmonton, Alberta [Library symbol] [National Library of Canada] (NLC) .... AEOM
Alberta Oil Sands Index [Alberta Oil Sands Technology and Research Authority] [Information service or system] .... AOSI
Alberta Oil Sands Information Centre, Edmonton, AB, Canada [Library symbol] [Library of Congress] (LCLS) .... CaAEAOS
Alberta Oil Sands Information Centre, Edmonton, Alberta [Library symbol] [National Library of Canada] (NLC) .... AEAOS
Alberta Oil Sands Technology and Research Authority (IID) .... AOSTRA
Alberta Ombudsman, Edmonton, AB, Canada [Library symbol] [Library of Congress] (LCLS) .... CaAEOM
Alberta Orienteering Association (AC) .... AOA
Alberta Personnel Administration, Edmonton, AB, Canada [Library symbol] [Library of Congress] (LCLS) .... CaAEAPA
Alberta Personnel Administration, Edmonton, Alberta [Library symbol] [National Library of Canada] (NLC) .... AEAPA
Alberta Pesticide Action Network (AC) .... APAN
Alberta Petroleum Marketing Commission, Calgary, AB, Canada [Library symbol] [Library of Congress] (LCLS) .... CaACPMC
Alberta Petroleum Marketing Commission, Calgary, Alberta [Library symbol] [National Library of Canada] (NLC) .... ACPMC
Alberta Pharmaceutical Association (AC) .... APha
Alberta Pilot Projects for Television (SAUS) .... APPT
Alberta Plastics Recycling Association (AC) .... APRA
Alberta Printed Circuits, Ltd. (SAUO) .... APC
Alberta Provincial Courts, Edmonton, AB, Canada [Library symbol] [Library of Congress] (LCLS) .... CaAEPC
Alberta Provincial Courts, Edmonton, Alberta [Library symbol] [National Library of Canada] (NLC) .... AEPC
Alberta Psychiatric Association (AC) .... APA
Alberta Public Affairs Bureau, Bibliography Section, Edmonton, AB, Canada [Library symbol] [Library of Congress] (LCLS) .... CaAEPA
Alberta Public Health Association (AC) .... APHA
Alberta Public Utilities Board, Edmonton, AB, Canada [Library symbol] [Library of Congress] (LCLS) .... CaAEPU
Alberta Public Utilities Board, Edmonton, Alberta [Library symbol] [National Library of Canada] (NLC) .... AEPU
Alberta Public Works, Supply and Services, Edmonton, Alberta [Library symbol] [National Library of Canada] (NLC) .... AEGS
Alberta RCMP Century Library, Beaverlodge, AB, Canada [Library symbol] [Library of Congress] (LCLS) .... CaABeaAr
Alberta RCMP Century Library, Beaverlodge, Alberta [Library symbol] [National Library of Canada] (NLC) .... ABAR
Alberta Real Estate Association (AC) .... AREA
Alberta Recording Industry Association (AC) .... ARIA
Alberta Recreation and Parks, Edmonton, Alberta [Library symbol] [National Library of Canada] (NLC) .... AERPW
Alberta Recreation, Parks & Wildlife Foundation (AC) .... RPW Foundation
Alberta Registered Dietitians Association (AC) .... ARDA
Alberta Registered Music Teachers' Association (AC) .... ARMTA
Alberta Registered Professional Foresters Association (AC) .... ARPFA
Alberta Reports (journ.) (SAUS) .... AR
Alberta Research Council [Canada] (QUAC) .... ARC
Alberta Research Council, Clover Bar Branch, Edmonton, AB, Canada [Library symbol] [Library of Congress] (LCLS) .... CaAERC
Alberta Research Council, Edmonton, Alberta [Library symbol] [National Library of Canada] (NLC) .... AER
Alberta Research Council, Solar and Wind Energy Research Program Information Centre, Edmonton, AB, Canada [Library symbol] [Library of Congress] (LCLS) .... CaAERSWE
Alberta Research Council, Southern Branch Library, Calgary, AB, Canada [Library symbol] [Library of Congress] (LCLS) .... CaACRS
Alberta Research Council, Terrace Plaza Branch Library, Edmonton, AB, Canada [Library symbol] [Library of Congress] (LCLS) .... CaAERTP
Alberta Research Council, University Branch, Edmonton, AB, Canada [Library symbol] [Library of Congress] (LCLS) .... CaAERU
Alberta Research, Edmonton, AB, Canada [Library symbol] [Library of Congress] (LCLS) .... CaAER
Alberta Research Network [Computer science] [Canada] (TNIG) .... ARnet
Alberta Restaurant & Foodservices Association (AC) .... ARFA
Alberta Revised Statutes [Canada] [A publication] (DLA) .... Alta Rev Stat
Alberta Roofing Contractors Association Ltd. (AC) .... ARCA
Alberta School Boards Association [Formerly, Alberta School Trustees' Association] (AC) .... ASBA
Alberta School for the Deaf, Edmonton, AB, Canada [Library symbol] [Library of Congress] (LCLS) .... CaAESD
Alberta School for the Deaf, Edmonton, Alberta [Library symbol] [National Library of Canada] (NLC) .... AESD
Alberta Schools Athletic Association (AC) .... ASAA
Alberta Scuba Divers Council (AC) .... ASDC
Alberta Section of Rural Medicine (SAUO) .... ASRM

Alberta Securities Commission, Edmonton, AB, Canada [Library symbol] [Library of Congress] (LCLS) .... CaAEASC
Alberta Securities Commission, Edmonton, Alberta [Library symbol] [National Library of Canada] (NLC) .... AEASC
Alberta Senior Citizens Sport & Recreation Association (AC) .... ASCSRA
Alberta Sheep Breeders Association (AC) .... ASBA
Alberta Simmental Association (AC) .... ASA
Alberta Snowmobile Association (AC) .... ASA
Alberta Social Services and Community Health, Edmonton, Alberta [Library symbol] [National Library of Canada] (NLC) .... AEHSD
Alberta Society of Artists [1931] [Canada] (NGC) .... ASA
Alberta Society of Artists (SAUO) .... ASA
Alberta Society of Engineering Technologists (AC) .... ASET
Alberta Society of Professional Biologists (AC) .... ASPB
Alberta Solicitor General, Edmonton, Alberta [Library symbol] [National Library of Canada] (NLC) .... AESG
Alberta Solicitor General's Department, Edmonton, AB, Canada [Library symbol] [Library of Congress] (LCLS) .... CaAESG
Alberta Speleological Society (AC) .... ASS
Alberta Sports & Recreation Association for the Blind (AC) .... ASRAB
Alberta Statistical Information System [Alberta Treasury, Bureau of Statistics] [Database] .... ASIST
Alberta Statutes [Canada] [A publication] (DLA) .... Alta Stat
Alberta Stock Exchange [Canada] .... A
Alberta Stock Exchange (HGAA) .... ASE
Alberta Sulphur Research Ltd. (AC) .... ASRL
Alberta Swine Breeders' Association (AC) .... ASBA
Alberta Table Tennis Association (AC) .... ATTA
Alberta Teachers' Association [Association des Enseignants de l'Alberta] (AC) .... ATA
Alberta Therapeutic Riding Association (AC) .... ATRA
Alberta Tourism and Small Business, Edmonton, Alberta [Library symbol] [National Library of Canada] (NLC) .... AEIC
Alberta Transportation, Edmonton, Alberta [Library symbol] [National Library of Canada] (NLC) .... AEHT
Alberta Treasury Department, Bureau of Statistics, Edmonton, AB, Canada [Library symbol] [Library of Congress] (LCLS) .... CaAETBS
Alberta Treasury Department, Corporate Tax Administration, Edmonton, AB, Canada [Library symbol] [Library of Congress] (LCLS) .... CaAETCT
Alberta Treasury Department, Edmonton, AB, Canada [Library symbol] [Library of Congress] (LCLS) .... CaAET
Alberta Treasury, Edmonton, Alberta [Library symbol] [National Library of Canada] (NLC) .... AET
Alberta Tree Nursery and Horticultural Centre, Edmonton, Alberta [Library symbol] [National Library of Canada] (BIB) .... AETN
Alberta Union of Civil Service Employees, Edmonton, AB, Canada [Library symbol] [Library of Congress] (LCLS) .... CaAECS
Alberta Union of Provincial Employees [Canada] (BARN) .... AUPE
Alberta Union of Provincial Employees, Edmonton, Alberta [Library symbol] [National Library of Canada] (NLC) .... AECS
Alberta Urban Municipalities Association (AC) .... AUMA
Alberta Utilities and Telephones, Edmonton, Alberta [Library symbol] [National Library of Canada] (NLC) .... AEUT
Alberta, VA [FM radio station call letters] (BROA) .... NEW FM
Alberta, VA [FM radio station call letters] (BROA) .... WAQD-FM
Alberta Veterinary Medical Association (AC) .... AVMA
Alberta Vocational Centre, Calgary (SAUS) .... ACVC
Alberta Vocational Centre, Calgary, AB, Canada [Library symbol] [Library of Congress] (LCLS) .... CaACVC
Alberta Vocational Centre, Calgary, Albert [Library symbol] [National Library of Canada] (NLC) .... ACVC
Alberta Vocational Centre, Edmonton, AB, Canada [Library symbol] [Library of Congress] (LCLS) .... CaAEVC
Alberta Vocational Centre, Edmonton, Alberta [Library symbol] [National Library of Canada] (NLC) .... AEVC
Alberta Vocational Centre, Grouard, AB, Canada [Library symbol] [Library of Congress] (LCLS) .... CaAGVC
Alberta Vocational Centre, Grouard, Alberta [Library symbol] [National Library of Canada] (NLC) .... AGVC
Alberta Vocational Centre, Lac La Biche, AB, Canada [Library symbol] [Library of Congress] (LCLS) .... CaALLbVC
Alberta Vocational Centre, Lac La Biche, Alberta [Library symbol] [National Library of Canada] (NLC) .... ALLBVC
Alberta Volleyball Association (AC) .... AVA
Alberta Water Polo Association (AC) .... AWPA
Alberta Water Well Drilling Association (AC) .... AWWDA
Alberta Weekly Newspapers Association (AC) .... AWNA
Alberta Wilderness Association (AC) .... AWA
Alberta Women's Institutes (AC) .... AWI
Alberta Worker's Health, Safety, and Compensation, Edmonton, AB, Canada [Library symbol] [Library of Congress] (LCLS) .... CaAEOH
Albert/Bray [France] [ICAO location identifier] (ICLI) .... LFAQ
Albertine Sisters (Krakow, Poland) (TOCD) .... CSA
Alberto Culver (DB) .... A-C
Alberto Culver [NYSE symbol] (SAG) .... ACV
Alberto Culver Co. [Associated Press] (SAG) .... Alberto
Alberto Culver Co. [Associated Press] (SAG) .... AlCulA
Alberto-Culver Cl'A' [NYSE symbol] (TTSB) .... ACVA
Alberto-Culver Cl'B' [NYSE symbol] (TTSB) .... ACV
Alberto-Culver Co., Melrose Park, IL [Library symbol] [Library of Congress] (LCLS) .... IMelpA
Alberto-Culver Company (SAUO) .... ACV
Alberton High School, Alberton, MT [Library symbol] [Library of Congress] (LCLS) .... MtAHS
Albertson College of Idaho (GAGS) .... Albertson C (ID)

Albertson's, Inc. [*NYSE symbol*] (SPSG) … ABS
Albertsons, Inc. (SAUO) … ABS
Albertson's, Inc. [*Associated Press*] (SAG) … Albertsn
Albertus Beneventanus [*Deceased, 1187*] [*Authority cited in pre-1607 legal work*] (DSA) … A
Albertus Beneventanus [*Deceased, 1187*] [*Authority cited in pre-1607 legal work*] (DSA) … Al
Albertus Brunus [*Deceased, 1541*] [*Authority cited in pre-1607 legal work*] (DSA) … Alb Brun
Albertus Brunus [*Deceased, 1541*] [*Authority cited in pre-1607 legal work*] (DSA) … Alber Bru
Albertus de Saliceto [*Authority cited in pre-1607 legal work*] (DSA) … Alb
Albertus Denarii de Odofredo [*Deceased, 1300*] [*Authority cited in pre-1607 legal work*] (DSA) … Alb de Odofre
Albertus Electus Imperator Optimus Vivat [*Inscription used by Albert II, 15th-century German king*] … AEIOU
Albertus Longobardista [*Flourished, 12th century*] [*Authority cited in pre-1607 legal work*] (DSA) … a
Albertus Longobardista [*Flourished, 12th century*] [*Authority cited in pre-1607 legal work*] (DSA) … Al
Albertus Longobardista [*Flourished, 12th century*] [*Authority cited in pre-1607 legal work*] (DSA) … Alb
Albertus Magnus [*Teutonicus*] [*Deceased, 1280*] [*Authority cited in pre-1607 legal work*] (DSA) … Al
Albertus Magnus College [*New Haven, CT*] … AMC
Albertus Magnus College, New Haven, CT [*Library symbol*] [*Library of Congress*] (LCLS) … CtNhA
Albertus Magnus Guild (EA) … AMG
Albertus Papiensis [*Flourished, 1211-40*] [*Authority cited in pre-1607 legal work*] (DSA) … Alb Pp
Albertus Papiensis [*Flourished, 1211-40*] [*Authority cited in pre-1607 legal work*] (DSA) … Al Pa
Albertus Papiensis [*Flourished, 1211-40*] [*Authority cited in pre-1607 legal work*] (DSA) … Al Pp
Albertus Ranconis [*Flourished, 1369-72*] [*Authority cited in pre-1607 legal work*] (DSA) … Al
Albertville [*France*] [*ICAO location identifier*] (ICLI) … LFKA
Albertville, AL [*Location identifier*] [*FAA*] (FAAL) … ARF
Albertville, AL [*AM radio station call letters*] … WAVU
Albertville, AL [*FM radio station call letters*] … WQSB
Albertville, AL [*AM radio station call letters*] (BROA) … WXBK-AM
Albertville Elementary School, Albertville, MN [*Library symbol*] [*Library of Congress*] (LCLS) … MnAlvE
Albertville Olympic Organizing Committee [*Albertville, France*] (EAIO) … AOOC
Albert-Westmorland-Kent Regional Library, Moncton, NB, Canada [*Library symbol*] [*Library of Congress*] (LCLS) … CaNBMoW
Albert-Westmorland-Kent Regional Library, Moncton, New Brunswick [*Library symbol*] [*National Library of Canada*] (NLC) … NBMOW
Albi [*France*] [*Airport symbol*] (OAG) … LBI
Albia, IA [*AM radio station call letters*] … KLBA
Albia, IA [*FM radio station call letters*] … KLBA-FM
Albia Public Library, Albia, IA [*Library symbol*] [*Library of Congress*] (LCLS) … IaAlb
Albia Union-Republican, Albia, IA [*Library symbol*] [*Library of Congress*] (LCLS) … IaAlbUR
Albian (SAUS) … Alb
Albi/Le Sequestre [*France*] [*ICAO location identifier*] (ICLI) … LFCI
Albin, WY [*FM radio station call letters*] (BROA) … KKAW-FM
Albina [*Surinam*] [*ICAO location identifier*] (ICLI) … SMBN
Albinism World Alliance … AWA
Albinism-Deafness [*Syndrome*] [*Medicine*] (DMAA) … ADFN
Albino Guinea Pig [*Medicine*] (DMAA) … A
Albion (SAUS) … Alb
Albion Banc Corp. [*NASDAQ symbol*] (SAG) … ALBC
Albion Banc Corp. [*Associated Press*] (SAG) … AlbionBc
Albion College (SAUO) … AC
Albion College, Albion, MI [*OCLC symbol*] (OCLC) … EXA
Albion College, Albion, MI [*Library symbol*] [*Library of Congress*] (LCLS) … MiAlbC
Albion Community Library, Albion, ID [*Library symbol*] [*Library of Congress*] (LCLS) … IdAl
Albion, IL [*FM radio station call letters*] (RBYB) … WBJW-FM
Albion, MI [*AM radio station call letters*] … WALM
Albion, MI [*FM radio station call letters*] … WUFN
Albion, NE [*Television station call letters*] … KCAN
Albion, NE [*Television station call letters*] (RBYB) … KLKE
Albion Public Library, Albion, IL [*Library symbol*] [*Library of Congress*] (LCLS) … IAlb
Albion Public Library, Albion, MI [*Library symbol*] [*Library of Congress*] (LCLS) … MiAlb
Albion State Normal School, Albion, ID [*Library symbol*] [*Library of Congress*] (LCLS) … IdAlN
Albion-Bolton Branch, Town of Caledon Public Libraries, Bolton, Ontario [*Library symbol*] [*National Library of Canada*] (NLC) … OBCAB
Albis Wire Telephone (SAUS) … AWITEL
Albite [*CIPW classification*] [*Geology*] … ab
Alborg [*Denmark*] [*ICAO location identifier*] (ICLI) … EKYT
Alborn Elementary School, Alborn, MN [*Library symbol*] [*Library of Congress*] (LCLS) … MnAbnE
Al-Bough [*Yemen*] [*ICAO location identifier*] (ICLI) … OYBO
Albrecht Durer [*German artist, 1471-1528*] … AD
Albrecht Durer Study Unit [*American Topical Association*] (EA) … ADSU
Albright & Wilson Ltd. (SAUO) … AW
[*Secretary of State Madeleine*] **Albright,** [*National-Security Adviser Sandy*] **Berger,** [*and Defense Secretary William*] **Cohen** [*A troika known in Washington*] … ABC
Albright College (SAUO) … AC
Albright College, Reading, PA [*Library symbol*] [*Library of Congress*] (LCLS) … PRA
Albright-Butler-Bloomberg Syndrome [*Medicine*] (DMAA) … ABB
Albright-Butler-Lightwood [*Syndrome*] [*Medicine*] (DB) … ABL
Albright-Knox Art Gallery [*Buffalo, NY*] … AK
Albright-Knox Art Gallery (SAUO) … AKAG
Albright-Knox Art Gallery Library, Buffalo Fine Arts Academy, Buffalo, NY [*Library symbol*] [*Library of Congress*] (LCLS) … NBuAK
Albright-Lightwood [*Syndrome*] [*Medicine*] (DB) … AL
Albright's Hereditary Osteodystrophy [*Medicine*] … AHO
Albrook High School, Saginaw, MN [*Library symbol*] [*Library of Congress*] (LCLS) … MnSagHS
Album (VRA) … alb
Album Adult Alternative [*Music classification*] … AAA
Album Oriented Rock [*Facetious translation: Another Old Record*] [*Broadcasting*] … AOR
Albumen (ADWA) … alb
Albumen (VRA) … ALPT
Albumin [*Also, ALB*] [*Biochemistry*] … AL
Albumin [*Also, AL*] [*Biochemistry*] … ALB
Albumin Clearance (DMAA) … ALBC
Albumin Clearance [*Biochemistry*] (DAVI) … C_{alb}
Albumin, Dextrose, Catalase [*Media*] … ADC
Albumin Excretion Rate [*Physiology*] … AER
Albumin-Buffered Saline [*Clinical chemistry*] … ABS
Albumin-Calcium-Magnesium [*Biochemistry*] (MAE) … ACM
Albumin-Calcium-Magnesium (SAUS) … A-C-M
Albumin-Coagulin Ratio [*Biochemistry*] (MAE) … A/C
Albumin/Coagulin Ratio (SAUS) … A/C Ratio
Albumin-Free [*Medicine*] … AF
Albumin/Globulin [*Medicine*] … A/G
Albumin-Globulin Ratio (ADWA) … A/G ratio
Albumin/Globulin Ratio [*Gastroenterology*] (DAVI) … ALB/GLOB
Album-Oriented Radio [*Radio station format*] (WDMC) … AOR
Albuq [*Yemen*] [*Airport symbol*] (OAG) … BUK
Albuquerque [*New Mexico*] [*Airport symbol*] (OAG) … ABQ
Albuquerque [*New Mexico*] [*Seismograph station code, US Geological Survey*] (SEIS) … ABQ
Albuquerque [*New Mexico*] [*Seismograph station code, US Geological Survey*] (SEIS) … ALQ
Albuquerque [*New Mexico*] [*Seismograph station code, US Geological Survey*] (SEIS) … ANMO
Albuquerque [*New Mexico*] [*ICAO location identifier*] (ICLI) … KZAB
Albuquerque Academy, Albuquerque, NM [*Library symbol*] [*Library of Congress*] (LCLS) … NmAAc
Albuquerque Bar Journal [*A publication*] (DLA) … Albuquerque BJ
Albuquerque Budget Reform Task (SAUS) … ALBURT
Albuquerque Field Office (SAUS) … AL
Albuquerque, NM [*Location identifier*] [*FAA*] (FAAL) … ILT
Albuquerque, NM [*AM radio station call letters*] … KABQ
Albuquerque, NM [*FM radio station call letters*] … KANW
Albuquerque, NM [*FM radio station call letters*] … KASY
Albuquerque, NM [*Television station call letters*] … KASY-TV
Albuquerque, NM [*Television station call letters*] … KAZQ
Albuquerque, NM [*AM radio station call letters*] … KDAZ
Albuquerque, NM [*AM radio station call letters*] … KDEF
Albuquerque, NM [*AM radio station call letters*] … KDZZ
Albuquerque, NM [*FM radio station call letters*] (BROA) … KEZF-FM
Albuquerque, NM [*FM radio station call letters*] … KFLQ
Albuquerque, NM [*FM radio station call letters*] … KHFM
Albuquerque, NM [*AM radio station call letters*] (RBYB) … KHTL
Albuquerque, NM [*AM radio station call letters*] (BROA) … KHTZ
Albuquerque, NM [*AM radio station call letters*] … KKIM
Albuquerque, NM [*AM radio station call letters*] … KKOB
Albuquerque, NM [*FM radio station call letters*] … KKOB-FM
Albuquerque, NM [*Television station call letters*] … KLUZ
Albuquerque, NM [*FM radio station call letters*] … KLYT
Albuquerque, NM [*FM radio station call letters*] … KMGA
Albuquerque, NM [*Television station call letters*] … KNAT
Albuquerque, NM [*Television station call letters*] … KNME
Albuquerque, NM [*AM radio station call letters*] (RBYB) … KNOS
Albuquerque, NM [*Television station call letters*] … KOAT
Albuquerque, NM [*Television station call letters*] … KOB
Albuquerque, NM [*FM radio station call letters*] (RBYB) … KPEK-FM
Albuquerque, NM [*Television station call letters*] … KRQE
Albuquerque, NM [*FM radio station call letters*] … KRST
Albuquerque, NM [*FM radio station call letters*] … KRZN
Albuquerque, NM [*AM radio station call letters*] … KRZY
Albuquerque, NM [*FM radio station call letters*] (RBYB) … KTBL-FM
Albuquerque, NM [*FM radio station call letters*] (RBYB) … KTEG
Albuquerque, NM [*FM radio station call letters*] … KUNM
Albuquerque, NM [*AM radio station call letters*] … KXKS
Albuquerque, NM [*FM radio station call letters*] … KZRR
Albuquerque, NM [*AM radio station call letters*] … KZSS
Albuquerque, NM [*Location identifier*] [*FAA*] (FAAL) … SPT
Albuquerque, NM [*Location identifier*] [*FAA*] (FAAL) … ZAB
Albuquerque Operations Office (DOGT) … AL
Albuquerque Operations Office [*Department of Energy*] … ALO
Albuquerque Operations Office [*Department of Energy*] (GRD) … ALOO
Albuquerque Operations Office (SAUO) … AOO
Albuquerque Operations, Weapons Development Division (SAUS) … AL-WDD
Albuquerque Public Library (SAUO) … APL
Albuquerque Public Library, Albuquerque, NM [*Library symbol*] [*Library of Congress*] (LCLS) … NmA

Albuquerque Public Library, Albuquerque, NM [*OCLC symbol*] (OCLC) .... QUE
Albuquerque Public Library, Ernie Pyle Memorial Branch, Albuquerque, NM [*Library symbol*] [*Library of Congress*] (LCLS) .... NmA-EP
Albuquerque Public Library, Los Griegos Branch, Albuquerque, NM [*Library symbol*] [*Library of Congress*] (LCLS) .... NmA-LG
Albuquerque Public Library, Prospect Park Branch, Albuquerque, NM [*Library symbol*] [*Library of Congress*] (LCLS) .... NmA-PP
Albuquerque Symphony Orchestra (SAUO) .... ASO
Albuquerque Testing Laboratory (AAGC) .... ATL
Albuquerque Urban Regional Information System (SAUS) .... AURIS
Albuquerque/International [*New Mexico*] [*ICAO location identifier*] (ICLI) ...... KABQ
Albury [*New South Wales*] [*Airport symbol*] (AD) .... ABX
Albury [*Australia*] [*Airport symbol*] (OAG) .... ABX
Albury [*Australia*] [*ICAO location identifier*] (ICLI) .... AMAY
Albury-Wodonga Environment Center [*Australia*] .... AWEC
Albury-Wodonga Environment Centre (SAUO) .... AWEC
Albus [*White*] [*Pharmacy*] .... ALB
Alcadd Test [*Psychology*] .... AT
Alcaeus [*Seventh century BC*] [*Classical studies*] (OCD) .... Alc
Alcan Aluminium Ltd. [*NYSE symbol*] [*Toronto Stock Exchange symbol*] [*Vancouver Stock Exchange symbol*] (SPSG) .... AL
Alcan Aluminum Co., Cleveland, OH [*Library symbol*] [*Library of Congress*] (LCLS) .... OClA
ALCAN Aluminum Ltd. [*Associated Press*] (SAG) .... Alcan
ALCAN International Ltee. [*ALCAN International Ltd.*] **Jonquiere, Quebec** [*Library symbol*] [*National Library of Canada*] (NLC) .... QAA
ALCAN Research & Development Ltd., Kingston, ON, Canada [*Library symbol*] [*Library of Congress*] (LCLS) .... CaOKA
ALCAN Smelters Chemical Ltd., Technical Library, Kitimat, BC, Canada [*Library symbol*] [*Library of Congress*] (LCLS) .... CaBKAS
ALCAN [*Aluminum Co. of Canada Ltd.*] **World Price** [*Obsolete*] (FEA) .... AWP
Alcatel ADS [*Formerly, Alcatel Alsthom ADS*] [*NYSE symbol*] .... ALA
Alcatel Alsthom ADS [*NYSE symbol*] (TTSB) .... ALA
Alcatel Alsthom Compagnie General d'Electricite [*NYSE symbol*] (SPSG) .... ALA
Alcatel Alsthom Compagnie General d'Electricite [*Associated Press*] (SAG) .... Alcatel
Alcatel Espace Systems (SAUS) .... ATES
Alcatel Plasma Vapor Deposition [*Alcatel-France*] (AAEL) .... APVD
Alcatel Thomson Gigadisc [*Optical disk*] .... ATG
Alcester Public Library, Alcester, SD [*Library symbol*] [*Library of Congress*] (LCLS) .... SdAl
Alcestis [*of Euripides*] [*Classical studies*] (OCD) .... Alc
Alchemical Medicine Research and Teaching Association (SAUO) .... AMRTA
Alchemy (VRA) .... alch
Alchemy .... ALCH
Alcian Blue [*A biological stain*] .... AB
Alcian Blue-Aldehyde Fuchsin [*Dyes*] (OA) .... AB-AF
Alcian Blue-Periodic Acid Schiff-Lead Hematoxylin Procedure [*Biotechnology*] .... AB-PAS-Pbh
Alcibiades [*of Plato*] [*Classical studies*] (OCD) .... Alc
Alcibiades [*of Plutarch*] [*Classical studies*] (OCD) .... Alc
Alcide Corp. [*NASDAQ symbol*] (NQ) .... ALCD
Alcide Corp. [*Associated Press*] (SAG) .... Alcide
Alcina Development Corp. [*Vancouver Stock Exchange symbol*] .... AIV
Alclad [*Metallurgy*] .... ALCD
Alclare Resources [*Vancouver Stock Exchange symbol*] .... ALS
Alclometasone Dipropionate [*Glucocorticoid*] .... ADP
Alcman [*Seventh century BC*] [*Classical studies*] (OCD) .... Alcm
Alco Products, Inc. (SAUO) .... AP
Alco Standard [*NYSE symbol*] (TTSB) .... ASN
Alco Standard Corp. [*Associated Press*] (SAG) .... AlcoSt
Alco Standard Corp. [*NYSE symbol*] (SPSG) .... ASN
Alco Std $5.04 Cv Dep Pfd [*NYSE symbol*] (TTSB) .... ASNPrB
Alcoa, Inc. [*NASDAQ symbol*] (SG) .... AA
Alcoa Picturephone Remote Information System [*AT&T Co.*] (NITA) .... APRIS
ALCOA Smelting Process .... ASP
Alcoa Steamship Company (SAUO) .... A
ALCOA Steamship Company (SAUS) .... A
Alcoa, TN [*AM radio station call letters*] .... WBCR
Alcoa, TN [*FM radio station call letters*] .... WYLV
Alcobaca [*Brazil*] [*Airport symbol*] (OAG) .... ABC
Alcock and Napier's Irish King's Bench Reports [*A publication*] (DLA) .... A & N
Alcock and Napier's Irish King's Bench Reports [*A publication*] (DLA) ...... Al & N
Alcock and Napier's Irish King's Bench Reports [*A publication*] (DLA) .... Al & Nap
Alcock and Napier's Irish King's Bench Reports [*A publication*] (ILCA)..... Alc & N
Alcock and Napier's Irish King's Bench Reports [*A publication*] (DLA) .... Alc & Nap
Alcock and Napier's Irish King's Bench Reports [*A publication*] (DLA) .... Alcock & N
Alcock on Personal Property [*A publication*] (DLA) .... Alc Per Prop
Alcock's Registry Cases [*1832-41*] [*Ireland*] [*A publication*] (DLA) .... Alc
Alcock's Registry Cases [*Ireland*] [*1832-41*] [*A publication*] (ILCA) .... Alc Reg
Alcock's Registry Cases [*1832-41*] [*Ireland*] [*A publication*] (DLA) .... Alc Reg C
Alcock's Registry Cases [*1832-41*] [*Ireland*] [*A publication*] (DLA) .... Alc Reg Cas
Alcohol (ADA) .... A
Alcohol (ADWA) .... al
Alcohol (ADWA) .... alc
Alcohol (KSC) .... ALC
Alcohol .... ALCH
Alcohol .... ALCOH
Alcohol .... ALCOL
Alcohol (SAUS) .... Alcol
Alcohol 5%, Dextrose 5%, in Water (SAUS) A5D5W
Alcohol 5%, Dextrose 5% in Water A5D5W
Alcohol and Acid (SAUS) .... ALCID
Alcohol and Dependency Intervention Council [*Military*] (AABC) .... ADDIC
Alcohol and Drug [*Type of addiction*] .... A & D
Alcohol and Drug (SAUS) .... A&D
Alcohol and Drug Abuse Action Panel (SAUO) .... ADAAP
Alcohol and Drug Abuse Education Act (GFGA) .... ADAEA
Alcohol and Drug Abuse Prevention and Control Program [*Military*] (AABC) .... ADAPCP
Alcohol and Drug Abuse Prevention Team (SAUS) .... ADAPT
Alcohol and Drug Abuse Prevention Treatment .... ADAPT
Alcohol and Drug Control Office [*Military*] (AABC) .... ADCO
Alcohol and Drug Control Officer (SAUO) .... ADCO
Alcohol and Drug Counseling Office [*Army*] .... ADCO
Alcohol and Drug Dependence Service (SAUO) .... ADDS
Alcohol and Drug Dependence Unit (SAUS) .... ADDU
Alcohol and Drug Dependency Clinic (DAVI) .... ADD
Alcohol and Drug Dependency Unit [*Medicine*] (DAVI) .... ADDU
Alcohol and Drug Education Service, Winnipeg, Manitoba [*Library symbol*] [*National Library of Canada*] (NLC) .... MWAD
Alcohol and Drug Foundation of Victoria [*Australia*] .... ADFV
Alcohol & Drug Foundation Queensland (SAUO) .... ADFQ
Alcohol & Drug Information Service (SAUO) .... ADIS
Alcohol and Drug Institute, Seattle, WA [*Library symbol*] [*Library of Congress*] (LCLS) .... WaSAD
Alcohol and Drug Problems Association of North America (EA) .... ADPA
Alcohol and Drug Programs, Vancouver, BC, Canada [*Library symbol*] [*Library of Congress*] (LCLS) .... CaBVaADP
Alcohol and Drug Programs, Vancouver, British Columbia [*Library symbol*] [*National Library of Canada*] (NLC) .... BVAADP
Alcohol and Drug Programs, Victoria, British Columbia [*Library symbol*] [*National Library of Canada*] (BIB) .... BVIADP
Alcohol and Drug Services Study (ADWA) .... ADSS
Alcohol and Drug Treatment and Rehabilitation Block Grant [*Department of Health and Human Services*] (GFGA) .... ADTR
Alcohol and Nutrition (SAUS) .... ALCOTRICIAN
Alcohol and Other Drug (MELL) .... AOD
Alcohol and Other Drug Abuse (MELL) .... AODA
Alcohol and Other Drug Thesaurus (SAUO) .... AOD
Alcohol and other Drugs Council of Australia (SAUO) .... ADCA
Alcohol and Public Health Research Unit (SAUO) .... APHRU
Alcohol and Tobacco Tax (SAUS) .... A&TT
Alcohol and Tobacco Tax Division [*Internal Revenue Service*] [*United States*] (DLA) .... AT
Alcohol and Tobacco Tax Division [*Internal Revenue Service*] .... ATTD
Alcohol Beverage Legislative Council (EA) .... ABLC
Alcohol, Chloroform, Ether [*An early anesthetic mixture*] .... ACE
Alcohol Community Centre for Education, Prevention, and Treatment [*British*] (DI) .... ACCEPT
Alcohol Concentration (TAG) .... AC
Alcohol Counselling Service [*British*] (DI) .... ACS
Alcohol Dehydrogenase [*Also, ADH*] [*An enzyme*] .... AD
Alcohol Dehydrogenase [*Also, AD*] [*An enzyme*] .... ADH
Alcohol Dependence (MELL) .... AD
Alcohol Dependence Scale (MELL) .... ADS
Alcohol Dependency Treatment Program (DAVI) .... ADTP
Alcohol, Drug Abuse, and Mental Health [*Block grant*] .... ADA/MH
Alcohol, Drug Abuse, and Mental Health Administration [*Formerly, HSMHA*] [*Department of Health and Human Services*] [*Rockville, MD*] .... ADAMHA
Alcohol, Drug Abuse, and Mental Health Administration [*Formerly, HSMHA*] [*Department of Health and Human Services*] (OICC) .... ADMHA
Alcohol, Drug Abuse, and Mental Health Block Grant [*Public human service program*] (PHSD) .... ADAMHBG
Alcohol Drug Motorsensory Impairment Test [*Pharmometrics Corp.*] .... ADMIT
Alcohol, Drug or Mental disorder (SAUS) .... ADM
Alcohol, Drug or Mental Disorder .... ADM
Alcohol, Drugs, Driving, and You [*An association*] .... ADDY
Alcohol Education Centre [*British*] (DI) .... AEC
Alcohol Education for Youth (EA) .... AEY
Alcohol Education for Youth [*An association*] .... AYE
Alcohol Education for Youth and Community [*Defunct*] (EA) .... AEYC
Alcohol, Ether, Acetone [*Solvent mixture*] .... AEA
Alcohol Ether Sulfate (EDCT) .... AES
Alcohol Ethoxylate (EDCT) .... AE
Alcohol Glyceryl Ether Sulfonate (EDCT) .... AGES
Alcohol Insoluble Solid (SAUS) .... AIS
Alcohol Insoluble Solids [*Food analysis*] .... AIS
Alcohol Intake Sheet [*Medicine*] (DB) .... AIS
Alcohol Level Evaluation Road Tester .... ALERT
Alcohol on Breath [*Police term*] .... AOB
Alcohol Oxidase (SAUS) .... AOD
Alcohol Policy Council (EA) .... APC
Alcohol Quotient .... AQ
Alcohol Recovery [*or Rehabilitation*] **Drydock** (DNAB) .... ARD
Alcohol Recovery Service (DNAB) .... ARS
Alcohol Rehabilitation Center (NVT) .... ARC
Alcohol Rehabilitation Services Unit (SAUO) .... ARSU
Alcohol Rehabilitation Unit (DNAB) .... ARU
Alcohol Related (MELL) .... AR
Alcohol Related Brain Injury Association (SAUO) .... ARBIAS
Alcohol Research Group [*Research center*] (RCD) .... ARG
Alcohol Research Information Service (EA) .... ARIS
Alcohol Rub [*Medicine*] .... AlcR
Alcohol Rub (SAUS) .... ALc R
Alcohol Safety Action Program (SAUO) .... ASAP
Alcohol Safety Action Project [*Department of Transportation*] .... ASAP

Alcohol Safety Interlock System .... ASIS
Alcohol Sensors International Ltd. [*NASDAQ symbol*] (SAG) .... ASIL
Alcohol Sensors Intl. Ltd. [*Associated Press*] (SAG) .... AlSens
Alcohol Sensors Intl. Ltd. [*Associated Press*] (SAG) .... AlSns
Alcohol Sensors Intl Unit [*NASDAQ symbol*] (TTSB) .... ASILU
Alcohol Soluble Propionate [*Press coating*] (DGA) .... ASP
Alcohol Sreening Test (MELL) .... AST
Alcohol Studies Centre [*British*] (CB) .... ASC
Alcohol Sulfate (EDCT) .... AS
Alcohol Tax Unit [*Department of the Treasury*] .... ATU
Alcohol, Tobacco, and Firearms Cumulative Bulletin [*A publication*] (DLA) .... ATFCB
Alcohol, Tobacco and Firearms Summary Statistics. US Internal Revenue Service (journ.) (SAUS) .... IRS Alcohl
Alcohol, Tobacco, and Other Drugs (MELL) .... ATOD
Alcohol, Tobacco, Firearms Bureau [*Department of the Treasury*] (PDAA) .... ATFB
Alcohol, Tobacco Tax and Firearms (SAUO) .... ATT&F
Alcohol Treatment Center (SAUO) .... ATC
Alcohol Treatment Program .... ATP
Alcohol Use Disorders Identification Test .... AUDIT
Alcohol Use Inventory [*Medicine*] (DMAA) .... AUI
Alcohol Withdrawal (MELL) .... AW
Alcohol Withdrawal (MELL) .... AWD
Alcohol Withdrawal Syndrome (MELL) .... AWS
Alcohol Withdrawal Unit (MELL) .... AWU
Alcohol-Chloroform-Ether (SAUS) .... ACE
Alcohol-Dependent Sleep Disorder (MELL) .... ADSD
Alcohol-Drug Education Association in Alberta (AC) .... ADEAA
Alcohol-Formaldehyde-Acetic [*Fixative*] [*Medicine*] (DMAA) .... AFA
Alcohol-free variety of ethyl iodoacetate (SAUS) .... KSK
Alcoholic .... ALCHLC
Alcoholic (SAUS) .... Alcoh
Alcoholic (SAUS) .... Alcolic
Alcoholic [*Freight*] .... ALCOLIC
Alcoholic Abstinence Syndrome (MELL) .... AAS
Alcoholic and Narcotic Addict Rehabilitation Amendments .... ANARA
Alcoholic Beverage (DLA) .... Alco Bev
Alcoholic Beverage Control [*Board*] .... ABC
Alcoholic Beverage Control (DLA) .... Alco Bev Cont
Alcoholic Beverage Control Department-California (SAUO) .... ABCDCAL
Alcoholic Hepatitis [*Medicine*] .... AH
Alcoholic Intoxication [*Medicine*] (MELL) .... AI
Alcoholic Ketoacidosis [*Endocrinology and gastroenterology*] (DAVI) .... AKA
Alcoholic Liver Cirrhosis [*Medicine*] (MELL) .... ALC
Alcoholic Liver Disease [*Medicine*] .... ALD
Alcoholic Myopathy (MELL) .... AM
Alcoholic Onion Extract .... AOE
Alcoholic Rehabilitation Center (SAUO) .... ARC
Alcoholic Rehabilitation Inc. (SAUO) .... ARI
Alcoholics Anonymous (AC) .... AA
Alcoholics Anonymous Family Groups (ADA) .... ALANON
Alcoholics Anonymous members (SAUS) .... AAs
Alcoholics Anonymous Teens (BARN) .... Alateen
Alcoholics Anonymous World Services [*Canada*] .... AAWS
Alcohol-Induced Hyperlipidemia [*Medicine*] (PDAA) .... AHL
Alcohol-Induced Hypoglycemia [*Medicine*] (MELL) .... AIH
Alcohol-Insoluble Glutamine (SAUS) .... AIG
Alcohol-Insoluble Glutelin (SAUS) .... AIG
Alcoholism [*Chemical dependency and psychiatry*] (DAVI) .... AL
Alcoholism [*Chemical dependency*] (DAVI) .... alc
Alcoholism .... ALCHLSM
Alcoholism (SAUS) .... Alcism
Alcoholism and Drug Abuse Commission, Calgary, AB, Canada [*Library symbol*] [*Library of Congress*] (LCLS) .... CaACAD
Alcoholism and Drug Abuse Commission, Calgary, Alberta [*Library symbol*] [*National Library of Canada*] (NLC) .... ACAD
Alcoholism and Drug Abuse Commission, Edmonton, AB, Canada [*Library symbol*] [*Library of Congress*] (LCLS) .... CaAEAD
Alcoholism and Drug Abuse Commission, Edmonton, Alberta [*Library symbol*] [*National Library of Canada*] (NLC) .... AEAD
Alcoholism and Drug Abuse Commission, Vancouver, British Columbia [*Library symbol*] [*National Library of Canada*] (NLC) .... BVAAD
Alcoholism and Drug Addiction Research Foundation (SAUO) .... ADARF
Alcoholism and Drug Addiction Treatment Center (MELL) .... ADATC
Alcoholism Center for Women (EA) .... ACW
Alcoholism, Clinical and Experimental Research (SAUS) .... Alcohol Clin Exp Res
Alcoholism Commission of Saskatchewan, Regina (SAUS) .... SRAC
Alcoholism Commission of Saskatchewan, Regina, Saskatchewan [*Library symbol*] [*National Library of Canada*] (NLC) .... SRAC
Alcoholism Commission of Saskatchewan, Regina, SK, Canada [*Library symbol*] [*Library of Congress*] (LCLS) .... CaSRAC
Alcoholism Council of Greater Los Angeles (SAUO) .... ACGLA
Alcoholism Counseling and Education Center (SAUO) .... ACEC
Alcoholism Foundation of Manitoba, Winnipeg, Manitoba [*Library symbol*] [*National Library of Canada*] (NLC) .... MWAF
Alcoholism Treatment Facility (SAUO) .... ATF
Alcoholism Treatment Unit (MELL) .... ATU
Alcohol-Related Birth Defect [*Medicine*] (LDT) .... ARBD
Alcohol-Related Brain Damage Association [*Australia*] .... ABDA
Alcohol-Related End-Stage Liver Disease [*Medicine*] .... ARESLD
Alcohol-Related Liver Disease [*Medicine*] .... ARLD
Alcohol-Related Traffic Fatalities (MELL) .... ARTF
Alcohol-Related Treatment [*Medicine*] (MELL) .... ART
Alcohol-Soluble Glutelin (SAUS) .... ASG
Alcohol-Tobacco Amblyopia (MELL) .... ATA
Alcoma Community Library, Rainier, AB, Canada [*Library symbol*] [*Library of Congress*] (LCLS) .... CaARaC
Alcoma Community Library, Rainier, Alberta [*Library symbol*] [*National Library of Canada*] (NLC) .... ARAC
Alcon Laboratories (SAUO) .... ALB
Alcon Laboratories, Inc., Fort Worth, TX [*Library symbol*] [*Library of Congress*] (LCLS) .... TxFAl
Alcona County Library, Harrisville, MI [*Library symbol*] [*Library of Congress*] (LCLS) .... MiHarv
Alconbury [*British*] [*ICAO location identifier*] (ICLI) .... EGWZ
Alcor Life Extension Foundation (EA) .... ALEF
Alcorn Agricultural and Mechanical College, Lorman, MS [*Library symbol*] [*Library of Congress*] (LCLS) .... MsAM
Alcove (ABBR) .... A
Alcove [*Classified advertising*] (ADA) .... ALC
ALCTS [*Association for Library Collections and Technical Services*] **Cataloging and Classification Section** .... ALCTS CCS
ALCTS [*Association for Library Collections and Technical Services*] **Reproduction of Library Materials Section** .... ALCTS RLMS
ALCTS [*Association for Library Collections and Technical Services*] **Resources Section** .... ALCTS RS
Alcuin Club (EAIO) .... AC
Alcuin Club (SAUO) .... AC
Alcuin Society (EA) .... AS
Aldehyde Dehydrogenase [*An enzyme*] .... ALDH
Aldehyde Ferredoxin Oxidoreductase [*An enzyme*] .... AOR
Aldehyde Fuchsin [*A dye*] .... AF
Aldehyde Oxidase [*An enzyme*] .... AO
Aldehyde Reductase (DMAA) .... ALR
Aldehyde Reductase [*Medicine*] (DB) .... AR
Aldehyde-Fuchsin (SAUS) .... AF
Aldehydes [*Organic chemistry*] .... HCHO
Alden and Van Hoesen's Digest of Mississippi Laws [*A publication*] (DLA) .... Ald & VH
Alden Electronic and Recording Equipment (SAUS) .... AERE
Alden Electronics, Inc. [*NASDAQ symbol*] (NQ) .... ADNE
Alden Electronics, Inc. [*Associated Press*] (SAG) .... Alden
Alden Electronics'A' [*NASDAQ symbol*] (TTSB) .... ADNEA
Alden [*John*] **Financial Corp.** [*Associated Press*] (SAG) .... JAlden
Alden Kindred of America (EA) .... AKA
Alden Ocean Shell Association (EA) .... AOSA
Alden Public Library, Alden, IA [*Library symbol*] [*Library of Congress*] (LCLS) .... IaAld
Alden Terrace Elementary School, Elmont, NY [*Library symbol*] [*Library of Congress*] (LCLS) .... NElmoAE
Alden Terrace Elementary School, Valley Stream, NY [*Library symbol*] [*Library of Congress*] (LCLS) .... NVsAE
Alden's Abridgment of Law [*A publication*] (DLA) .... Ald Abr
Alden's Condensed Reports [*Pennsylvania*] [*A publication*] (DLA) .... Ald
Alden's Index of United States Reports [*A publication*] (DLA) .... Ald Ind
Alden's Law Reports [*A publication*] (DLA) .... ALR
Alder Flats Public Library, Alberta [*Library symbol*] [*National Library of Canada*] (NLC) .... AAF
Alderbourne Valley Environmental Protection Society (SAUO) .... AVEPS
Alderman (WDAA) .... Ald
Alderman (GEAB) .... ald
Alderman .... ALD
Alderman .... ALDM
Alderman (ROG) .... ALDMN
Aldermaston Mechanised Cataloging and Ordering System [*British*] (DIT) .... AMCOS
Aldermaston Mechanized Cataloguing and Ordering Systems [*British*]..... AMCOS
Aldermaston Multi-Access Configura-tion (SAUS) .... AMAC
Aldermaston Project for the Application of Computers to Engineering (SAUS) .... APACE
Aldermaston Project for the Application of Computers to Engineering [*United Kingdom Atomic Energy Authority*] (NITA) .... APACE
Alderney [*Channel Islands*] [*Airport symbol*] (OAG) .... ACI
Alderney [*International vehicle registration*] (ODBW) .... GBA
Alderney, Channel Islands [*British*] [*ICAO location identifier*] (ICLI) .... EGJA
Aldershot Command (SAUO) .... AC
Aldershot Command (SAUS) .... AC
Aldershot Detention Barracks (SAUO) .... ADB
Aldershot District (SAUS) .... AD
Aldershot Military Corrective Establishment (SAUS) .... AMCE
Aldershot Military Corrective Establishment (SAUO) .... AMCE
Alderson-Broaddus College, Philippi, WV [*OCLC symbol*] (OCLC) .... WVA
Alderson-Broaddus College, Philippi, WV [*Library symbol*] [*Library of Congress*] (LCLS) .... WvPhA
Alderwoman (ADWA) .... Ald
Aldila, Inc. [*NASDAQ symbol*] (SAG) .... ALDA
Aldila, Inc. [*Associated Press*] (SAG) .... Aldila
Aldindicarboxylic Acid (SAUS) .... ADA
Aldine [*of Aldus Manutius*] (DGA) .... ALD
Aldo Ray Fan Club (EA) .... ARFC
Aldolase [*An enzyme*] .... ALD
Aldolase [*An enzyme*] (DAVI) .... ALDOL
Aldolase [*An enzyme*] .... ALS
Aldose Reductase Inhibitor [*Organic chemistry*] (DAVI) .... ARI
Aldosterone [*Endocrinology*] .... ALDO
Aldosterone (SAUS) .... Aldo
Aldosterone [*Endocrinology*] (DAVI) .... ALDOST
Aldosterone Excretion Rate [*Endocrinology*] .... AER
Aldosterone Secret in Rate (SAUS) .... ASR
Aldosterone Secretion Defect [*Endocrinology*] (MAE) .... ASD

Aldosterone Secretion Inhibitory Factor [*Endocrinology*] .... ASIF
Aldosterone Secretion Rate [*Endocrinology*] .... ASR
Aldosterone-Binding Protein [*Endocrinology*] .... ABP
Aldosterone-Induced Polypeptide (SAUS) .... AIP
Aldosterone-Induced Protein [*Biochemistry*] .... AIP
Aldosterone-Producing (MELL) .... APAA
Aldosterone-Producing Adenoma [*Clinical chemistry*] .... APA
Aldosterone-Stimulating Hormone [*Also, AGTr*] [*Endocrinology*] .... ASH
Aldracus [*Flourished, 13th century*] [*Authority cited in pre-1607 legal work*] (DSA) .... Aldra
Aldred's Questions on the Law of Property [*A publication*] (DLA) .... Ald Ques
Aldrich's Edition of Ansen on Contracts [*A publication*] (DLA) .... Ald Ans Cont
Aldricus [*Flourished, 1154-72*] [*Authority cited in pre-1607 legal work*] (DSA) .... Ald
Aldricus [*Flourished, 1154-72*] [*Authority cited in pre-1607 legal work*] (DSA) .... Aldri
Aldridge. History and Jurisdiction of the Courts of Law [*1835*] [*A publication*] (ILCA) .... Ald
Aldridge. History and Jurisdiction of the Courts of Law [*A publication*] (DLA) .... Ald Hist
Aldrindicarboxylic Acid (SAUS) .... ADA
Aldus Books London (SAUO) .... AB
Aldus Color file (SAUS) .... ACS
Ale, Bread, and Cheese .... ABC
Ale, Bread and Cheese (SAUS) .... ABC
ale firkin (SAUS) .... af
Ale Firkin [*Unit of measurement*] (ROG) .... AF
Aledo, IL [*FM radio station call letters*] .... WRMJ
Aleg [*Mauritania*] [*Airport symbol*] (AD) .... LEG
ALE/Global Atmospheric Gases Experiment (SAUS) .... ALE/GAGE
Alegrete [*Brazil*] [*Airport symbol*] [*Obsolete*] (OAG) .... ALQ
Aleknagik [*Alaska*] [*Airport symbol*] (OAG) .... WKK
Aleknagik, AK [*Location identifier*] [*FAA*] (FAAL) .... WKK
Aleksandr Solzhenitsyn Society for Freedom and Justice (EA) .... ASSFJ
Alena Enterprises of Canada (SAUO) .... ALENCA
Alencon/Valframbert [*France*] [*ICAO location identifier*] (ICLI) .... LFOF
Alenia Elsag Sistemi Navali (SAUS) .... AESN
Alenquer [*Brazil*] [*Airport symbol*] (AD) .... AQR
Aleph Zadik Aleph [*Society*] .... AZA
Aleppo [*Syria*] [*Airport symbol*] (OAG) .... ALP
Aleppo/Neirab [*Syria*] [*ICAO location identifier*] (ICLI) .... OSAP
Alergic Encephalomyelitis [*Medicine*] (BARN) .... AE
Alert [*Northwest Territories*] [*Seismograph station code, US Geological Survey*] (SEIS) .... ALE
Alert (SAUS) .... ALR
Alert and Oriented (CPH) .... A & O
Alert and Oriented Times Four [*Neurology and psychiatry*] (DAVI) .... A & OX4
Alert and Oriented Times Three [*Neurology and psychiatry*] (DAVI) .... A & OX3
Alert and Oriented to Person, Place, and Time [*Neurology and psychiatry*] (DAVI) .... A & OX3
Alert and Oriented to Person, Place, Time, and Date [*Neurology and psychiatry*] (DAVI) .... A & OX4
Alert Area [*Military*] .... A
Alert Area Supervisor [*Military*] (AFM) .... AAS
Alert Availability (MCD) .... AA
Alert Bay, BC [*ICAO location identifier*] (ICLI) .... CYAL
Alert Bay Public Library and Museum, British Columbia [*Library symbol*] [*National Library of Canada*] (NLC) .... BABM
Alert Building (NATG) .... AB
Alert Centre, Inc. [*Associated Press*] (SAG) .... AlertC
Alert Centre, Inc. [*Associated Press*] (SAG) .... AlertCt
Alert Centre, Inc. [*AMEX symbol*] (SAG) .... ALT
Alert Citizens for Environmental Safety [*Formed to protect West Texas and the US/Mexico border region's natural resources*] (CROSS) .... ACES
Alert Condition (SAUS) .... AC
Alert Condition [*Military*] (AABC) .... LERTCON
Alert Condition System (SAUO) .... LERTCON
Alert Conditions (MCD) .... ALERTCONS
Alert, Cooperative, and Oriented (HGAA) .... ACO
Alert, Cooperative, Oriented (SAUS) .... ACO
Alert Crew Billet Security (AFM) .... ACBS
Alert Exercise (NATG) .... ALEX
Alert Force Capability Test (MCD) .... AFCAT
Alert Force Capability Test (MCD) .... AFCT
Alert Holding Area [*Military*] (DOMA) .... AHA
Alert Implementation Report (MCD) .... ALIMREP
Alert Implementation Reports (NATG) .... ALIMPREPS
Alert Locate and Report Missiles [*Military*] (MUSM) .... ALARM
Alert Manager (SAUS) .... Alt Mgr
Alert Message (CINC) .... AM
Alert Monitoring System Computer (SAUS) .... AMCS
Alert, Northwest Territories, Canada (SAUS) .... ALT
Alert Notice .... ALNOT
Alert, NT [*FM radio station call letters*] .... CHAR
Alert, NT [*ICAO location identifier*] (ICLI) .... CYLT
Alert Pending [*Military*] (IUSS) .... A/P
Alert Phase [*Aviation code*] .... ALERFA
Alert Reaction Time .... ART
Alert Severe Weather Watch (PIPO) .... AWW
Alert Stage Declaration (SAUS) .... ALERTDECL
Alert State Declaration (SAUS) .... ALERTDECL
Alert Team (ACAE) .... AT
Alert Transmit Console (SAA) .... ATC
Alert Transmit Panel (SAA) .... ATP
Alert Transport Service Facility [*IBM*] (CIST) .... ATSF
Alert Velocity Track (ACAE) .... AT
Alert, Verbal, Pain, Unresponsive (SAUS) .... AVPU
Alert, Verbal, Painful, Unresponsive [*Neurologic test*] [*Medicine*] (DMAA) .... AVPU
Alert Weather Watch [*Meteorology*] (DA) .... AWW
Alert, Well and Keeping Energetic Network (SAUO) .... AWAKE
Alert With Info (SAUS) .... AWI
Alerta [*Peru*] [*ICAO location identifier*] (ICLI) .... SPAR
Alerting (SAUS) .... ALERT
Alerting and Status (SAA) .... ALS
Alerting Automatic Telling Status (SAA) .... AAS
Alerting Long-Range Airborne RADAR for MTI [*Moving Target Indicator*] .... ALARM
Alerting Message (SAUS) .... ALM
Alerting Message [*Aviation code*] .... ALR
Alerting Search Service from Kinokuniya [*Kinokuniya Co. Ltd.*] [*Japan*] [*Information service or system*] (IID) .... ASK
Alertness, Airway, Breathing, Circulation, Cervical Spine [*Medicine*] (DMAA) .... AABCC
AlertVIEW [*Virtual Interface Environment Workstation*] **Manager** [*Shany, Inc.*] (PCM) .... AVM
AlertVIEW [*Virtual Interface Environment Workstation*] **Station** [*Shany, Inc.*] [*Computer science*] (PCM) .... AVS
Ales/Deaux [*France*] [*ICAO location identifier*] (ICLI) .... LFMS
Alesis Digital Audio Tape (SAUS) .... ADAT
Alesund/Vigra [*Norway*] [*ICAO location identifier*] (ICLI) .... ENAL
Aleta Resource Industries [*Vancouver Stock Exchange symbol*] .... ALH
Aleut [*MARC language code*] [*Library of Congress*] (LCCP) .... ale
Aleutian (SAUS) .... Aleut
Aleutian (FAAC) .... ALUTN
Aleutian Current (SAUS) .... Aleut Cur
Aleutian Disease [*of mink*] [*Veterinary medicine*] .... AD
Aleutian Disease Virus [*of mink*] .... ADV
Aleutian Housing Authority (SAUO) .... AFA
Aleutian Islands .... ALUTS
Aleutian Islands National Wildlife Refuge (SAUS) .... AINWR
Aleutian Mountains (SAUS) .... Aleutians
Aleutian Sector (SAUS) .... AL SEC
Alex [*Aarons*] **and Vinton** [*Freedley*] [*Theatrical producers of the 1920's and 1930's, after whom the Alvin Theatre in New York City was named*] .... ALVIN
Alex Brown Inc. [*NYSE symbol*] (TTSB) .... AB
Alex Brown, Inc. [*Associated Press*] (SAG) .... AlexBr
Alex Brown, Inc. [*Associated Press*] (SAG) .... AlexBrn
Alex de Tocqueville Society (SAUO) .... A de T S
Alex File System (SAUS) .... AFS
Alex Lindsay String Orchestra (SAUO) .... ALSO
Alex von Falkenhausen Motorenwerke [*Automobile manufacturer*] .... AFM
Alexa Ventures, Inc. [*Vancouver Stock Exchange symbol*] .... AXA
Alexandair, Inc. [*Canada*] [*ICAO designator*] (FAAC) .... JMR
Alexander [*of Lucian*] [*Classical studies*] (OCD) .... Alex
Alexander [*of Plutarch*] [*Classical studies*] (OCD) .... Alex
Alexander & Alex Sv [*NYSE symbol*] (TTSB) .... AAL
Alexander & Alexander Services, Inc. [*NYSE symbol*] (SPSG) .... AAL
Alexander & Alexander Services, Inc. [*Associated Press*] (SAG) .... AlexAlx
Alexander & Baldwin [*NASDAQ symbol*] (TTSB) .... ALEX
Alexander & Baldwin, Inc. [*NASDAQ symbol*] (NQ) .... ALEX
Alexander & Baldwin, Inc. [*Associated Press*] (SAG) .... AlexBld
Alexander Archipelago (SAUS) .... Alexanders
Alexander Bay [*South Africa*] [*Airport symbol*] (OAG) .... ALJ
Alexander Bay [*New York*] [*Seismograph station code, US Geological Survey*] (SEIS) .... ALX
Alexander Bay [*South Africa*] [*ICAO location identifier*] (ICLI) .... FAAB
Alexander Bonaparte Cust [*Antagonist of Agatha Christie's novel "The ABC Murders"*] .... ABC
Alexander Brown, Inc. [*NYSE symbol*] (SPSG) .... AB
Alexander City, AL [*Location identifier*] [*FAA*] (FAAL) .... ALX
Alexander City, AL [*AM radio station call letters*] .... WRFS
Alexander City, AL [*FM radio station call letters*] .... WSTH
Alexander City State Junior College, Alexander City, AL [*Library symbol*] [*Library of Congress*] (LCLS) .... AAcC
Alexander County Public Library, Taylorsville, NC [*Library symbol*] [*Library of Congress*] (LCLS) .... NcTayA
Alexander Energy [*NASDAQ symbol*] (TTSB) .... AEOK
Alexander Energy Corp. [*NASDAQ symbol*] (NQ) .... AEOK
Alexander Energy Corp. [*Associated Press*] (SAG) .... AlexEng
Alexander Graham Bell Association for the Deaf (EA) .... AGBA
Alexander Graham Bell Association for the Deaf (EA) .... AGBAD
Alexander Haagen Properties [*AMEX symbol*] (TTSB) .... ACH
Alexander Haagen Property, Inc. [*AMEX symbol*] (SPSG) .... ACH
Alexander Haagen Property, Inc. [*Associated Press*] (SAG) .... AHaagen
Alexander Hamilton High School (SAUO) .... AHHS
Alexander Islands (SAUS) .... Alexanders
Alexander M. Poniatoff, Excellence [*Acronym is name of electronics company and brand name of its products; formed from name of firm's founder, plus "excellence"*] .... AMPEX
Alexander Marx Jubilee Volume [*A publication*] (BJA) .... AMJV
Alexander Mitchell Library, Aberdeen, SD [*Library symbol*] [*Library of Congress*] (LCLS) .... SdAbA
Alexander on Life Insurance in New York [*A publication*] (DLA) .... Alex Ins
Alexander Railroad Co. [*AAR code*] .... ARC
Alexander Raxlen Memorial Library, Doctors Hospital, Toronto, Ontario [*Library symbol*] [*National Library of Canada*] (NLC) .... OTDAR
Alexander Severus [*of Scriptores Historiae Augustae*] [*Classical studies*] (OCD) .... Alex Sev
Alexander Tartagna de Imola [*Deceased, 1477*] [*Authority cited in pre-1607 legal work*] (DSA) .... Alex

Alexander Tartagna de Imola [*Deceased, 1477*] [*Authority cited in pre-1607 legal work*] (DSA) .... Alexan
Alexander Tartagna de Imola [*Deceased, 1477*] [*Authority cited in pre-1607 legal work*] (DSA) .... Alexand
Alexander Turnbull Library (SAUO) .... ATL
Alexander von Humbolt Foundation (SAUO) .... AvH
Alexander Zakreski (GEOI) .... AZ
Alexander Zonjic Fan Club (EA) .... AZFC
Alexander's British Statutes in Force in Maryland [*A publication*] (DLA) .... Alex Br Stat
Alexander's Chancery Practice in Maryland [*A publication*] (DLA) .... Alex Ch Pr
Alexander's, Inc. [*Associated Press*] (SAG) .... Alexdr
Alexander's, Inc. [*NYSE symbol*] (SPSG) .... ALX
Alexanders, Laing & Cruickshank [*Broker*] [*British*] .... ALC
Alexander's Practice of the Commissary Courts, Scotland [*A publication*] (DLA) .... Alex Com Pr
Alexander's Reports [*66-72 Mississippi*] [*A publication*] (DLA) .... Alexander
Alexander's Texas Digest [*A publication*] (DLA) .... Alex Dig
Alexandra [*of Lycophron*] [*Classical studies*] (OCD) .... Alex
Alexandra [*New Zealand*] [*Airport symbol*] (OAG) .... ALR
Alexandra Day Fund (SAUO) .... ADF
Alexandra Docks & Railway (SAUO) .... AD
Alexandra [*Newport and South Wales*] **Docks & Railway** [*Wales*] .... AD
Alexandra Rose Day Fund (SAUO) .... ARDF
Alexandra Yacht Club (SAUO) .... AYC
Alexandria [*Diocesan abbreviation*] [*Louisiana*] (TOCD) .... ALX
Alexandria (SAUS) .... Alx
Alexandria [*Egypt*] [*Airport symbol*] (OAG) .... ALY
Alexandria [*Minnesota*] [*Airport symbol*] [*Obsolete*] (OAG) .... AXN
Alexandria [*Louisiana*] [*Airport symbol*] (OAG) .... ESF
Alexandria [*Egypt*] [*ICAO location identifier*] (ICLI) .... HEAX
Alexandria [*Greece*] [*ICAO location identifier*] (ICLI) .... LGAX
Alexandria [*Virginia*] [*Airport symbol*] (AD) .... WVA
Alexandria Branch, Stormount, Dundas, and Glengarry County Public Library, Ontario [*Library symbol*] [*National Library of Canada*] (NLC) .... OASDG
Alexandria Digital Library (GEOI) .... ADL
Alexandria Drafting Company (GEOI) .... ADC
Alexandria Flying Club (SAUO) .... AFC
Alexandria, IN [*FM radio station call letters*] .... WAXT
Alexandria, LA [*Location identifier*] [*FAA*] (FAAL) .... AEX
Alexandria, LA [*Location identifier*] [*FAA*] (FAAL) .... ERJ
Alexandria, LA [*Location identifier*] [*FAA*] (FAAL) .... ESF
Alexandria, LA [*Television station call letters*] .... KALB-TV
Alexandria, LA [*FM radio station call letters*] (RBYB) .... KAPM-FM
Alexandria, LA [*AM radio station call letters*] (RBYB) .... KDBS-AM
Alexandria, LA [*FM radio station call letters*] (BROA) .... KEDG-FM
Alexandria, LA [*FM radio station call letters*] .... KFAD
Alexandria, LA [*Television station call letters*] .... KLAX-TV
Alexandria, LA [*AM radio station call letters*] (RBYB) .... KLBG
Alexandria, LA [*Television station call letters*] .... KLPA
Alexandria, LA [*FM radio station call letters*] .... KLSA
Alexandria, LA [*FM radio station call letters*] (RBYB) .... KOUZ
Alexandria, LA [*FM radio station call letters*] .... KQID
Alexandria, LA [*AM radio station call letters*] .... KRRV
Alexandria, LA [*FM radio station call letters*] .... KRRV-FM
Alexandria, LA [*AM radio station call letters*] .... KSYL
Alexandria, LA [*AM radio station call letters*] .... KZMZ
Alexandria Library, Alexandria, VA [*Library symbol*] [*Library of Congress*] (LCLS) .... ViAl
Alexandria, MN [*Location identifier*] [*FAA*] (FAAL) .... AJW
Alexandria, MN [*Television station call letters*] .... KCCO
Alexandria, MN [*FM radio station call letters*] .... KIKV
Alexandria, MN [*Television station call letters*] .... KSAX
Alexandria, MN [*FM radio station call letters*] .... KSTQ
Alexandria, MN [*AM radio station call letters*] .... KXRA
Alexandria, MN [*FM radio station call letters*] .... KXRA-FM
Alexandria News, Alexandria, IN [*Library symbol*] [*Library of Congress*] (LCLS) .... InAleN
Alexandria Public Library, Alexandria, IN [*Library symbol*] [*Library of Congress*] (LCLS) .... InAle
Alexandria Public Library, Alexandria, MN [*Library symbol*] [*Library of Congress*] (LCLS) .... MnAle
Alexandria Public Library, Alexandria, SD [*Library symbol*] [*Library of Congress*] (LCLS) .... SdAle
Alexandria Public Library, Alexandria, VA [*OCLC symbol*] (OCLC) .... VAX
Alexandria R.E. Equities [*NYSE symbol*] (SG) .... ARE
Alexandria Runestone Museum, Alexandria, MN [*Library symbol*] [*Library of Congress*] (LCLS) .... MnAleR
Alexandria Shipping & Navigation Co. [*Egypt*] (IMH) .... ALEXSHIP
Alexandria Technical Institute, Alexandria, MN [*Library symbol*] [*Library of Congress*] (LCLS) .... MnAleTI
Alexandria Times-Tribune, Alexandria, IN [*Library symbol*] [*Library of Congress*] (LCLS) .... InAleTT
Alexandria, VA [*AM radio station call letters*] (RBYB) .... WBZS
Alexandria/England Air Force Base [*Louisiana*] [*ICAO location identifier*] (ICLI) .... KAEX
Alexandria/Esler Field [*Louisiana*] [*ICAO location identifier*] (ICLI) .... KESF
Alexandrian Free Public Library, Mount Vernon, IN [*Library symbol*] [*Library of Congress*] (LCLS) .... InMtv
Alexandroupolis [*Greece*] [*Airport symbol*] (OAG) .... AXD
Alexandroupolis [*Greece*] [*ICAO location identifier*] (ICLI) .... LGAL
Alexian Brothers (TOCD) .... cfa
Alexian Brothers (TOCD) .... CFA
Alexion Pharmaceuticals [*NASDAQ symbol*] (TTSB) .... ALXN
Alexion Pharmaceuticals, Inc. [*Associated Press*] (SAG) .... Alexion

Alexion Pharmaceuticals, Inc. [*NASDAQ symbol*] (SAG) .... ALXN
Alexipharmaca [*of Nicander*] [*Classical studies*] (OCD) .... Alex
Alexis De Tocqueville Society (EA) .... ATS
Alexis de Tocqueville Society (SAUO) .... ATS
Alexis Nihon Finance, Inc. [*Toronto Stock Exchange symbol*] .... AXN
Alexis Nihon Finance, Inc. [*Vancouver Stock Exchange symbol*] .... AXV
Aleyn's English King's Bench Reports [*A publication*] (DLA) .... Al
Aleyn's English King's Bench Reports [*A publication*] (DLA) .... Allen
Aleyn's Select Cases, English King's Bench [*82 English Reprint*] [*A publication*] (DLA) .... Aleyn
Aleyn's Select Cases, English King's Bench [*82 English Reprint*] [*A publication*] (DLA) .... Aleyn (Eng)
Alfa [*Phonetic alphabet*] [*International*] (DSUE) .... A
Alfa Air [*Czechoslovakia*] [*ICAO designator*] (FAAC) .... AFA
Alfa Corp. [*NASDAQ symbol*] (NQ) .... ALFA
Alfa Corp. [*Associated Press*] (SAG) .... AlfaCp
Alfa Jet [*Spain*] [*ICAO designator*] (FAAC) .... AJE
Alfa Romeo Club of Canada (AC) .... ARCC
Alfa Romeo Nissan Autoveicoli [*Italian-Japanese alliance for the joint manufacture of automobiles with Alfa engines and Nissan bodies*] .... ARNA
Alfa Romeo Owners Club (EA) .... AROC
Alfa Romeo Owners' Club of Australi .... AROCA
Alfacell Corp. [*NASDAQ symbol*] (SAG) .... ACEL
Alfacell Corp. [*Associated Press*] (SAG) .... Alfacell
Alfalfa Club (EA) .... AC
Alfalfa Cryptic Virus [*Plant pathology*] .... ACV
Alfalfa Mosaic Virus .... AMV
Alfalfa Pest Management .... APM
Alfalfa Temperate Virus [*Plant pathology*] .... ATEV
Alfarbandishe Gezelshaft far Ainordenen Yidn af Erd in FSSR [*A publication*] (BJA) .... GEZERD
Alfa-Romeo Distributors of North America .... ARDONA
Alfin Fragrances, Inc. [*AMEX symbol*] (SPSG) .... AFN
Alfin Inc. [*AMEX symbol*] (TTSB) .... AFN
Alfin, Inc. [*Associated Press*] (SAG) .... Alfin
Alfred [*New York*] [*Seismograph station code, US Geological Survey*] (SEIS) .... ALF
Alfred A. Knopf, Publisher (SAUO) .... AAK
Alfred Adler Institute (EA) .... AAI
Alfred Adler Institute for Individual Psychology (SAUO) .... AAIIP
Alfred C. Kinsey Institute for Sex Research, Bloomington, IN [*Library symbol*] [*Library of Congress*] (LCLS) .... InBloKi
Alfred Dickey Free Library, Jamestown, ND [*Library symbol*] [*Library of Congress*] (LCLS) .... NdJ
Alfred E. Packer Society (EA) .... AEPS
Alfred E. Smith High School (SAUO) .... AESHS
Alfred Holbrook College, Manchester, OH [*Library symbol*] [*Library of Congress*] [*Obsolete*] (LCLS) .... OMancAH
Alfred Holt [*Blue Funnel Line*] [*Steamship*] (MHDB) .... AH
Alfred Kinsey Institute (SAUO) .... AKI
Alfred Metzner Verlag, Frankfurt (SAUO) .... AMV
Alfred, NY [*FM radio station call letters*] .... WALF
Alfred, NY [*FM radio station call letters*] .... WETD
Alfred, NY [*FM radio station call letters*] (RBYB) .... WZKZ-FM
Alfred Township Public Library, Bibliotheque Publique du Canton d'Alfred, Lefaivre, ON, Canada [*Library symbol*] [*Library of Congress*] (LCLS) .... CaOLAL
Alfred University (GAGS) .... Alfred U
Alfred University (SAUO) .... AU
Alfred University, Alfred, NY [*Library symbol*] [*Library of Congress*] (LCLS) .... NAlf
Alfred University, Alfred, NY [*OCLC symbol*] (OCLC) .... YAH
Alfred University, School of Theology, Alfred, NY [*Library symbol*] [*Library of Congress*] [*Obsolete*] (LCLS) .... NAlf-ST
Alfred Wegener Institute for Polar and Marine Research (SAUO) .... AWI
Alfred-Wegener Institute for Polar and Marine Research (SAUS) .... AWI
Alfven Ion Cyclotron (SAUS) .... AIC
Alfven Number [*IUPAC*] .... Al
Alfven Propulsion Engine [*Aerospace*] .... APE
Alga Bloom Task Force (SAUO) .... ABTF
algae (SAUS) .... alg
Algal (SAUS) .... Alg
Algarvilara Transportes Aereos Algarvios SA [*Portugal*] [*ICAO designator*] (FAAC) .... ALR
Algas Resources Ltd., Halifax, Nova Scotia [*Library symbol*] [*National Library of Canada*] (NLC) .... NSHAR
Algas Resources Ltd., Halifax, NS, Canada [*Library symbol*] [*Library of Congress*] (LCLS) .... CaNSHAR
Algebra (BEE) .... Alg
Algebra (ADWA) .... alg
Algebra .... ALG
Algebra .... ALGEB
Algebra of Logic (SAUS) .... A of L
Algebra Package [*Computer science*] .... ALPAK
Algebraic (SAUS) .... Alg
Algebraic Adder (SAUS) .... ALGADDR
Algebraic Addition (SAUS) .... AA
Algebraic and Differential Equations Processor and Translator (SAUS) .... ADEPT
Algebraic Automated Digital Iterative Network [*Computer science*] (MHDI) .... ALADIN
Algebraic Calculation (SAUS) .... AC
Algebraic Calculator Language (SAUS) .... ALCAL
Algebraic Code Excited Linear Prediction (SAUS) .... ACELP
Algebraic Code-Excited Linear Prediction (ACRL) .... ACELP
Algebraic Compiler [*or Computer*] [*Computer science*] .... ALCOM
Algebraic Compiler and Translator [*Computer science*] .... ACT
Algebraic Components and Coefficients (SAUS) .... ALEC
Algebraic Computer (SAUS) .... ALCOM

Algebraic Curve (SAUS) .... AC
Algebraic Dependency (SAUS) .... AD
Algebraic Equation (SAUS) .... AE
Algebraic Exponents and Coefficients (SAUS) .... ALEC
Algebraic Function (SAUS) .... AF
Algebraic Interpretive Dialogue [Computer science] (BUR) .... AID
Algebraic Language (SAUS) .... ALCAL
Algebraic Language Translator (SAUS) .... ALT
Algebraic Logic Investigation of Apollo Systems (MCD) .... ALIAS
Algebraic Logic Network Analysis (SAUS) .... ALNA
Algebraic Manipulation by Identify Translation (SAUS) .... AMBIT
Algebraic Manipulation Language (SAUS) .... AML
Algebraic Methodology And Software Technology (SAUS) .... AMAST
Algebraic Multigrid [Computation method] .... AMG
Algebraic Operating System [Texas Instruments, Inc.] [Computer science] ..... AOS
Algebraic Oriented Language (SAUS) .... ALGOL
Algebraic Reconstruction Technique .... ART
Algebraic Sign (SAUS) .... AS
Algebraic Solution for Queues .... ASQ
Algebraic Specifications and Implementations Kit (SAUS) .... ASPIK
Algebraic Stress Model (MCD) .... ASM
Algebraic Technological Function [Computer science] .... ATF
Algebraic Transistorized Automatic Computer (SAUS) .... ALTAC
Algebraic Translator [Programming language] [1969] .... ALTRAN
Algebraic Translator and Compiler [Computer science] (MCD) .... ALTAC
Algebraic Translator Assembler Compiler (SAUS) .... ALTAC
Algebraical (SAUS) .... Alg
Algebraical Sum .... AS
Algebraically Oriented Language (SAUS) .... ALGOL
Algemeen Nederlandisch Persbureau [Press agency] [Netherlands] .... ANP
Algemeen Rijksarchief te s'Gravenhage (Central State Archives), The Hague, Netherlands [Library symbol] [Library of Congress] (LCLS) .... Ne
Algemeen Vrijzinning Vakverbond in Nederland [General Liberal Labor Federation] [Netherlands] .... AVV
Algemene Bond van Rooms Katholieke Kiesverenigingen [General League of Roman Catholic Election Societies] [Netherlands] (PPE) .... BRKKV
Algemene Kunstzijde Unie [Later, AKZO] [Netherlands] [Commercial firm] .... AKU
Algemene Maatregel van Bestuur [Order in Council] [Netherlands] (ILCA) .... AMvB
Algemene Spaar- en Lijfrentekas/Caisse Generale d'Espargne et de Retraite [Commercial bank] [Belgium] (EY) .... ASLK-CGER
Alger [Algeria] [ICAO location identifier] (ICLI) .... DAAA
Alger [Algeria] [ICAO location identifier] (ICLI) .... DAAL
Alger [Algeria] [ICAO location identifier] (ICLI) .... DAMM
Alger Small Cap. Portfolio Cl.B [Mutual fund ticker symbol] (SG) .... ALSCX
Alger-Bouzareah [Algeria] [Seismograph station code, US Geological Survey] .... ABA
Alger/Houari Boumediene [Algeria] [ICAO location identifier] (ICLI) .... DAAG
Algeria [Aircraft nationality and registration mark] (FAAC) 7T
Algeria [MARC country of publication code] [Library of Congress] (LCCP) .... ae
Algeria (MILB) .... Ag
Algeria [IYRU nationality code] (IYR) .... AL
Algeria .... ALG
Algeria (VRA) .... Alg
Algeria [ANSI two-letter standard code] (CNC) .... DZ
Algeria [ANSI three-letter standard code] (CNC) .... DZA
Algeria [MARC geographic area code] [Library of Congress] (LCCP) .... f-ae-
Algeria - Palma, Spain [Submarine cable] [Telecommunications] .... ALPAL
Algeria, Egypt, Libya, Morocco, Tunisia (SAUS) .... North Africa
Algerian (ADWA) .... Alg
Algerian-Franc (ABBR) .... A-FR
Algerie Presse Service [Algerian Press Service] (AF) .... APS
Algernon (SAUS) .... Alger
Alger's Law in Relation to Promoters and Promotion of Corporations [A publication] (DLA) .... Alger's Law Promoters & Prom Corp
Algers, Winslow & Western Railway Co. [AAR code] .... AWW
Al-Gheida [People's Democratic Republic of Yemen] [ICAO location identifier] (ICLI) .... ODAG
Alghero [Italy] [Airport symbol] (OAG) .... AHO
Alghero [Italy] [ICAO location identifier] (ICLI) .... LIEA
Algiers [Algeria] [Airport symbol] (OAG) .... ALG
Algiers [Algeria] [Seismograph station code, US Geological Survey] (SEIS) ...... ALG
Algo Group, Inc. [Toronto Stock Exchange symbol] .... AO
Algo Resources Ltd. [Vancouver Stock Exchange symbol] .... AGO
ALGOL Compiler [Computer science] (DIT) .... ALCOM
ALGOL Conversion (SAUS) .... ALCOR
ALGOL Extended for Design [1967] [Computer science] .... AED
Algol Management Strategy (SAUS) .... AMS
ALGOL Realtime Language (SAUS) .... ARL
ALGOL-to-FORTRAN Translator [Computer science] (MCD) .... ALFTRAN
Algoma Airways, Inc. [Canada] [ICAO designator] (FAAC) .... AGG
Algoma Central and Hudson Bay (Ontario) (SAUO) .... AC&HB(Ont)
Algoma Central & Hudson Bay Railroad (IIA) .... AC & HB
Algoma Central and Hudson Bay Railway (SAUO) .... AC&HBR
Algoma Central and Hudson Bay Railway Company (SAUO) .... AC
Algoma Central Railway [AAR code] .... AC
Algoma Central Railway (SAUS) .... ACR
Algoma Central Railway [Toronto Stock Exchange symbol] .... ALC
Algoma College, Sault Ste. Marie, ON, Canada [Library symbol] [Library of Congress] (LCLS) .... CaOStMA
Algoma College, Sault Ste. Marie, Ontario [Library symbol] [National Library of Canada] (NLC) .... OSTMA
Algoma Eastern Railway (SAUS) .... AE
Algoma Steel (SAUO) .... Algoma
Algoma Steel [NASDAQ symbol] (TTSB) .... ALGSE

Algoma Steel Corp. Ltd. [Toronto Stock Exchange symbol] [Vancouver Stock Exchange symbol] .... ALG
Algoma Steel Corp., Quality Control and Research Department, Sault Ste. Marie, ON, Canada [Library symbol] [Library of Congress] (LCLS) ..... CaOStMAS
Algoma Steel, Inc. [Associated Press] (SAG) .... Algma
Algoma Steel, Inc. [NASDAQ symbol] (SAG) .... ALGS
Algoma, WI [FM radio station call letters] .... WBDK
Algoma, WI [FM radio station call letters] (BROA) .... WRLU-FM
Algona, IA [Location identifier] [FAA] (FAAL) .... AXA
Algona, IA [AM radio station call letters] .... KLGA
Algona, IA [FM radio station call letters] .... KLGA-FM
Algona Public Library, Algona, IA [Library symbol] [Library of Congress] (LCLS) .... IaAlg
Algoneurodystrophy [Medicine] (DMAA) .... AND
Algonquian [MARC language code] [Library of Congress] (LCCP) .... alg
Algonquian (BEE) .... Algon
Algonquian Syllabic Texts in Canadian Repositories [Bibliographic project] .... ASTIC
Algonquin Arts Council (AC) .... AAC
Algonquin College, Colonel By Campus, Ottawa, ON, Canada [Library symbol] [Library of Congress] (LCLS) .... CaOOACC
Algonquin College of Applied Arts and Technology, Heron Park Campus, Ottawa, ON,Canada [Library symbol] [Library of Congress] (LCLS) ..... CaOOACH
Algonquin College of Applied Arts and Technology, Library Technician Program, Ottawa, ON, Canada [Library symbol] [Library of Congress] (LCLS) .... CaOOACL
Algonquin College of Applied Arts and Technology, Ottawa, Ontario [Library symbol] [National Library of Canada] (NLC) .... OOAC
Algonquin College of Applied Arts and Technology, School of Lanark County, Resource Centre, Perth, ON, Canada [Library symbol] [Library of Congress] (LCLS) .... CaOPAC
Algonquin College, Ottawa, ON, Canada [Library symbol] [Library of Congress] (LCLS) .... CaOOAC
Algonquin College, Rideau Campus, Ottawa, ON, Canada [Library symbol] [Library of Congress] (LCLS) .... CaOOACR
Algonquin College, Upper Ottawa Valley Campus Resource Centre, Pembroke, ON, Canada [Library symbol] [Library of Congress] (LCLS) .... CaOPemAC
Algonquin Mercantile Corp. [Toronto Stock Exchange symbol] .... AM
Algonquin Minerals [Vancouver Stock Exchange symbol] .... AMF
Algonquin Peak (SAUS) .... Algonquin
Algonquin Provincial Park (SAUS) .... APP
Algonquin Radio Observatory [Research center] (RCD) .... ARO
Algonquin Regional Library, Parry Sound, ON, Canada [Library symbol] [Library of Congress] (LCLS) .... CaOPsA
Algonquin Regional Library, Parry Sound, Ontario [Library symbol] [Obsolete] [National Library of Canada] (NLC) .... OPSA
Algonquin Regional Library System, Sturgeon Falls Branch, Sturgeon Falls, ON, Canada [Library symbol] [Library of Congress] (LCLS) .... CaOSfAR
Algood, TN [AM radio station call letters] .... WATX
Algorithm (SAUS) .... ALGO
Algorithm Control (SAUS) .... AC
Algorithm Description Section (SAUS) .... ADS
Algorithm Development Facility [for spacecraft data] [Jet Propulsion Laboratory] .... ADF
Algorithm for Non-Synchronized Waveform Error Reduction (MHDB)..... ANSWER
Algorithm Intercomparison Programme (SAUS) .... AIP
Algorithm Intercomparison Project-1 (SAUS) AIP-1
Algorithm Intercomparison Project-2 (SAUS) AIP-2
Algorithm Intercomparison Project-3 (SAUS) AIP-3
Algorithm Mass-Factoring Method (MCD) .... AM-FM
Algorithm Programming Language [Computer science] (HGAA) .... APL
Algorithm Simulation Test and Evaluation Program [NASA] .... ASTEP
Algorithm Support Team (SAUS) .... AST
Algorithm Theoretical Basis Document (SAUS) .... ATBD
Algorithm Theory (SAUS) .... AT
Algorithm Translation (SAUS) .... AT
Algorithmic and Business Oriented Language (SAUS) .... ABABOL
Algorithmic and Business Oriented Language [Computer science] .... ALABOL
Algorithmic Block (SAUS) .... AB
Algorithmic Element (SAUS) .... AE
Algorithmic Key Selection, Entry and Summarization System (SAUS) .... AKSESS
Algorithmic Language [1958] [Formerly, IAL] [Computer science] .... ALGOL
Algorithmic Language Compiler (SAUS) .... ALGOL Compiler
Algorithmic Language for Economic Calculations [Computer science] .... ALGEC
Algorithmic Language Symbol (SAUS) .... ALGOL Symbol
Algorithmic Language System (SAUS) .... ALGOL System
Algorithmic Problem-Oriented Language (SAUS) .... ALGOPOL
Algorithmic Procedural Language [Computer science] (IAA) .... APL
Algorithmic Procedure (SAUS) .... AP
Algorithmic Processor Description Language (SAUS) .... ADPL
Algorithmic Processor Description Language [Computer science] (MHDI) .... APDL
Algorithmic Programming Language (SAUS) .... APL
Algorithmic Remote Manipulation [Programming language] .... ARM
Algorithmic State Machine [Computer science] (ODBW) .... ASM
Algorithmic System (SAUS) .... AS
Algorithmic Variable (SAUS) .... AV
Algorithmic Wiswesser Notation (CIST) .... ALWIN
Algorithmic-Oriented Language (ADWA) .... ALGOL
Algorothm Intercomparison Projects (SAUS) .... AIP
Algos Pharmaceutical [NASDAQ symbol] (SG) .... ALGO
Algos Pharmaceutical Corp. [NASDAQ symbol] (SAG) .... ALGO
Algos Pharmaceutical Corp. [Associated Press] (SAG) .... AlgosPh
Algram Engineering Co. Ltd. (SAUO) .... AGE

Alhambra (BARN) .... Alh
Alhambra *[Record label] [Spain]* .... Ambra
Alhambra Public Library, Alhambra, CA *[Library symbol] [Library of Congress]* (LCLS) .... CAlh
Al-Hazm *[Yemen] [ICAO location identifier]* (ICLI) .... OYZM
Alia *[Others] [Latin]* .... AL
Alia Editione *[Another Edition] [Latin]* (ROG) .... AL E
Alia Editione *[Another Edition] [Latin]* (ADA) .... AL ED
Alia Lectio *[Another Reading] [Latin]* .... Al L
ALIA, Royal Jordanian Airlines (SAUO) .... ALIA
ALI-ABA *[American Law Instutute - American Bar Association]* **Committee on Continuing Professional Education** (EA) .... ALI-ABA
Alianca Anticomunista Brasileira *[Brazilian Anti-Communist Alliance]* (PD) .... AAB
Alianca Democratica *[Democratic Alliance] [Portugal] [Political party]* (PPE) .... AD
Alianca Democratica *[Democratic Alliance] [Brazil] [Political party]* (EY) .... AD
Alianca Libertadora Nacional *[National Liberation Alliance] [Brazil] [Political party]* (PD) .... ALN
Alianca Operaria Camponesa *[Peasants and Workers Alliance] [Portugal] [Political party]* (PPE) .... AOC
Alianca Popular Unida/Alianca Povo Unido *[United People's Alliance] [Portugal] [Political party]* (PPW) .... APU
Alianca Renovadora Nacional *[Alliance for National Renewal] [Brazil] [Political party]* (PPW) .... ARENA
Alianca Socialista de Juventude *[Socialist Youth Alliance] [Portugal] [Political party]* (PPE) .... ASJ
Aliant Communications, Inc. *[Associated Press]* (SAG) .... AliantCm
Aliant Communications, Inc. *[NASDAQ symbol]* (SAG) .... ALNT
Alianza Anticomunista Argentina *[Argentine Anti-Communist Alliance]* (PD) .... AAA
Alianza Apostolica Anticomunista *[Anti-Communist Apostolic Alliance] [Spain]* (PD) .... AAA
Alianza Apostolica Antigua *[Apostolic Ancient Alliance] [Spain] [Political party]* (EY) .... AAA
Alianza Campesina de Organizaciones Nacionales de Honduras *[Peasant Alliance of National Organizations of Honduras] [Political party]* (PD) .... ALCONH
Alianza del Movimiento Nacionalista Revolucionario *[Bolivia]* (PPW) .... A-MNR
Alianza Democratica *[Democratic Alliance] [Chile] [Political party]* (PPW) .... AD
Alianza Democratica de Oposicion Civilista *[Panama] [Political party]* (EY) .... ADOC
Alianza Democratica Revolucionaria *[Democratic Revolutionary Alliance] [Bolivia]* .... ADR
Alianza Federal des Pueblos Libres *[An association]* (NTCM) .... AFPL
Alianza Interamericana *[Defunct]* (EA) .... AI
Alianza Nacional *[National Alliance] [Spain] [Political party]* (PPE) .... AN
Alianza Nacional Cristiana *[Costa Rica] [Political party]* (EY) .... ANC
Alianza Nacional Popular *[National Popular Alliance] [Colombia]* (PD) .... ANAPO
Alianza para el Progreso *[Alliance for Progress] [Washington, DC]* .... ALPRO
Alianza para el Progreso *[Alliance for Progress] [Washington, DC]* .... AP
Alianza Patriotica *[Bolivia] [Political party]* (EY) .... AP
Alianza Popular *[Popular Alliance] [Madrid, Spain]* (PPW) .... AP
Alianza Popular Conservadora *[Nicaragua] [Political party]* (EY) .... APC
Alianza Popular de Integracion Nacional *[Bolivia] [Political party]* (PPW) .... APIN
Alianza Popular Revolucionaria Americana *[American Popular Revolutionary Alliance] [Peru] [Political party]* (PPW) .... APRA
Alianza Popular Revolucionaria Ecuatoriana *[Ecuadorean Popular Revolutionary Alliance] [Political party]* (PPW) .... APRE
Alianza pour Accion Anticommunista *[Honduras] [Political party]* (EY) .... AAA
Alianza Republicana Nacionalista *[Nationalist Republican Alliance] [El Salvador] [Political party]* (PPW) .... ARENA
Alianza Revolucionaria Barrientista *[Bolivia] [Political party]* (PPW) .... ARB
Alianza Revolucionaria Democratica *[Democratic Revolutionary Alliance] [Nicaragua] [Political party]* (PD) .... ARDE
Alias *[Computer science] [Telecommunications]* .... a
Alias *[Otherwise] [Latin]* .... AL
alias (SAUS) .... al
Alias *[Otherwise] [Latin]* .... ALS
Alias (GEAB) .... als
Alibag *[India] [Geomagnetic observatory code]* .... ABG
Alibert-Bazin *[Disease] [Medicine]* (DB) .... AB
Alibi *[Elsewhere] [Latin]* (ROG) .... AL
Alibi *[Elsewhere] [Latin]* .... Ali
ALIBI Fan Club (EA) .... AFC
Aliblu Airways SpA *[Italy] [ICAO designator]* (FAAC) .... KRO
Alicahue *[Chile] [Seismograph station code, US Geological Survey]* (SEIS) .... ALH
Alicante *[Spain] [Airport symbol]* (OAG) .... ALC
Alicante *[Spain] [Seismograph station code, US Geological Survey]* (SEIS) .... ALI
Alicante *[Spain] [ICAO location identifier]* (ICLI) .... LEAL
Alice Arm/Kitsault *[Canada] [Airport symbol]* (OAG) .... ZAA
Alice Heim *[Psychology]* (WDAA) .... AH
Alice Lake Mines *[Vancouver Stock Exchange symbol]* .... ALM
Alice Lloyd College, Pippa Passes, KY *[Library symbol] [Library of Congress]* (LCLS) .... KyPpA
Alice Lloyd Junior College (SAUO) .... ALJC
Alice Meynell *[British poet, 1847-1922]* .... AM
Alice Springs *[Australia] [ICAO location identifier]* (ICLI) .... ABAS
Alice Springs *[Australia] [Seismograph station code, US Geological Survey]* (SEIS) .... ASP
Alice Town/South Bimini, Bimini Island *[Bahamas] [ICAO location identifier]* (ICLI) .... MYBS
Alice, TX *[Location identifier] [FAA]* (FAAL) .... ALI
Alice, TX *[AM radio station call letters]* .... KDSI
Alice, TX *[FM radio station call letters]* (RBYB) .... KNDA
Alice, TX *[AM radio station call letters]* (RBYB) .... KOPY-AM
Alice, TX *[FM radio station call letters]* (RBYB) .... KOPY-FM
Alice, TX *[FM radio station call letters]* .... KQNN
Alice/International *[Texas] [ICAO location identifier]* (ICLI) .... KALI
Aliceville, AL *[Location identifier] [FAA]* (FAAL) .... AIV
Alico, Inc. *[NASDAQ symbol]* (TTSB) .... ALCO
Alico, Inc. *[Associated Press]* (SAG) .... Alico
Alicudi *[Lipari Islands] [Seismograph station code, US Geological Survey]* (SEIS) .... ACL
Alicyclic *[Chemistry]* .... ac
Alidade *[Engineering]* .... ALDD
Alidaunia SRL *[Italy] [ICAO designator]* (FAAC) .... LID
Alien Cell .... AC
Alien Critic (journ.) (SAUS) .... TAC
Alien Declared Intention .... ADI
Alien Documentation, Identification, and Telecommunications *[Immigration and Naturalization Service]* .... ADIT
Alien Firearms Act .... AFA
Alien Grange .... AGR
Alien Hand Syndrome *[Medicine]* (WDAA) .... AHS
Alien Life Force *[Acronym is name of title character in television series]* .... ALF
Alien Life-Form .... ALF
Alien, Penumbral, Umbral, Penumbral, Alien .... APUPA
Alien Priory .... APR
Alien Property Custodian *[World War II]* .... APC
Alien Property Division *[Department of Justice]* (DLA) .... APD
Alien Status Verification Index *[Immigration and Naturalization Service]* (GFGA) .... ASVI
Alienation Index Survey (TES) .... Al SURVEY
alienist (SAUS) .... alien
Aligarh *[India] [ICAO location identifier]* (ICLI) .... VIAH
Aligarh Muslim University (SAUO) .... Alig
Aligator Rivers Region Research Institute (SAUS) .... ARRRI
Alighting (SAUS) .... ALGTG
Alighting Area (SAUS) .... ala
Alighting Area *[Aviation]* .... ALA
Aligiulia SpA *[Italy] [ICAO designator]* (FAAC) .... RWA
Align .... ALN
Align Control Box (SAUS) .... ACB
Align Control Panel (SAUS) .... ACP
Align Control Unit (SAUS) .... ACU
Aligned Short Fiber Sheet Molding Compound (MCD) .... ASSM
Aligner .... ALGNR
Aligning .... ALGNNG
Alignment (KSC) .... ALGN
Alignment .... ALIGN
Alignment (SAUS) .... ALN
Alignment (AAG) .... ALNMT
Alignment and Diagnostic Display Console .... ADDC
Alignment and Test Facility for Optical Systems *[Navy]* .... ATFOS
Alignment Control Panel .... ACP
Alignment Countdown Set *[Aerospace]* (AAG) .... A-CS
Alignment Countdown Set Inertial Guidance *[Aerospace]* (AAG) .... ACSIG
Alignment Display Unit (SAUS) .... ADU
Alignment Error Rate Monitor (SAUS) .... AERM
Alignment Group .... AG
Alignment Group Sensing Platform (AAG) .... AGSP
Alignment Lab .... AL
Alignment Level Signal (SAUS) .... ALS
Alignment Mark *[On cardiography] [Cardiology]* (DAVI) .... AL
Alignment Mark (SAUS) .... AM
Alignment Optical Telescope .... AOT
Alignment Periscope .... AP
Alignment Procedures .... AP
Alignment Progress Indicator (KSC) .... API
Alignment Requirements Outline (MCD) .... ARO
Alignment Signal (SAUS) .... AS
Alignment Technique (SAUS) .... AT
Alignment Unit .... AU
Alignment Window .... AW
Alignment-Off-Time *[Instrumentation]* .... AOT
Align-Rite International, Inc. *[Associated Press]* (SAG) .... AligrR
Align-Rite International, Inc. *[NASDAQ symbol]* (SAG) .... MASK
Align-Rite Intl. *[NASDAQ symbol]* (TTSB) .... MASK
Aligoodarz *[Iran] [ICAO location identifier]* (ICLI) .... OICZ
Alijo *[Portugal] [ICAO location identifier]* (ICLI) .... LPJO
Alimentary Sleep *[Medicine]* (BABM) .... AS
Alimentary System *[Medicine]* .... AS
Alimentary Toxic Aleukia *[Medicine]* (MELL) .... ATA
Alimentos para Animales, SA *[Feed plant] [Guatemala]* .... ALIANSA
Alimony *[Legal shorthand]* (LWAP) .... ALI
Alina International Industries *[Vancouver Stock Exchange symbol]* .... ALA
Alindao *[Central African Republic] [ICAO location identifier]* (ICLI) .... FEFA
Alinea *[Paragraph] [Italian]* (ILCA) .... Al
Alinea *[Paragraph] [Dutch]* (ILCA) .... Al
Alingsas *[Sweden] [ICAO location identifier]* (ICLI) .... ESGI
Alinine, Sulphur, and Formaldehyde *[Medicine]* (BABM) .... ASF
Alinord *[Italy] [ICAO designator]* (FAAC) .... DNO
Aliorum *[Of Others] [Latin]* (EES) .... al
Aliphatic Acyl Radical *[Biochemistry]* (DAVI) .... RCO
Aliphatic Ammonium Nitrate (MCD) .... AAN
Aliquippa and Southern Railroad Co. (SAUO) .... ALQS
Alis *[Former USSR] [FAA designator]* (FAAC) .... LSI
Alisarda *[ICAO designator]* (AD) .... IG
ALISARDA SpA *[Italy] [ICAO designator]* (ICDA) .... IG
Aliserio *[Italy] [ICAO designator]* (FAAC) .... ALL
Alishan *[Republic of China] [Seismograph station code, US Geological Survey]* (SEIS) .... ALS

Alison Mortgage Investment Trust (SAUO) ... AMV
Alison's Practice [*Scotland*] [*A publication*] (DLA) ... Alison Pr
Alison's Principles of the Criminal Law of Scotland [*A publication*] (DLA) ... Alis Princ Scotch Law
Alison's Principles of the Criminal Law of Scotland [*A publication*] (ILCA) ... Alis Princ Scot Law
Alison's Principles of the Criminal Law of Scotland [*A publication*] (DLA) ... Al Pr
Alison's Principles of the Criminal Law of Scotland [*A publication*] (DLA) ... Al Sc CrL
Alister Hardy Research Centre [*Manchester College*] [*British*] (CB) ... AHRC
Alitak [*Alaska*] [*Airport symbol*] (OAG) ... ALZ
ALITALIA [*Aerolinee Italiane Internazionali*] [*Italian airline*] (MCD) ... ALI
ALITALIA [*Aerolinee Italiane Internazionali*] [*Italian airline*] [*ICAO designator*] ... AZ
ALITALIA, Lufthansa, Air France, Sabena [*Consortium of airlines*] (MCD) ... ATLAS
Alitalia-Linee Aeree Italiane SpA [*Italy*] [*ICAO designator*] (FAAC) ... AZA
Alitaxi SRL [*Italy*] [*ICAO designator*] (FAAC) ... ALX
Aliter [*Otherwise*] [*Latin*] (ADA) ... ALR
Alitude Reference Unit (ACAE) ... ARU
Alive ... A
Alive and Healthy (SAUS) ... A&H
Alive and Well (SAUS) ... A&W
Alive and Well ... A & W
Alive No Evidence of Disease [*Medicine*] ... ANED
Alive with Disease [*Medicine*] ... AWD
Aliwal North [*South Africa*] [*ICAO location identifier*] (ICLI) ... FAAN
Alix Public Library, Alberta [*Library symbol*] [*National Library of Canada*] (NLC) ... AALI
Alizarin (DMAA) ... AZR
Alizarin Red S [*An indicator*] [*Chemistry*] ... ARS
Aljamia [*MARC language code*] [*Library of Congress*] (LCCP) ... ajm
Al-Jouf [*Saudi Arabia*] [*ICAO location identifier*] (ICLI) ... OESK
Al-Jubail Fertiliser Company (SAUS) ... SAMA
Alkair [*Denmark*] [*ICAO designator*] (ICDA) ... KA
Alkair Flight Operations APS [*Denmark*] [*ICAO designator*] (FAAC) ... LKA
Alkali (SAUS) ... Alk
Alkali (ADWA) ... alk
Alkali and Clean Air Inspectorate [*British*] (DCTA) ... ACAI
Alkali and Radiochemical Inspectorate [*British*] (NUCP) ... ARCI
Alkali Cellulose [*Chemistry*] ... AC
Alkali Flame Ionization Detector [*Instrumentation*] ... AFID
Alkali Light Chain (SAUS) ... ALC
Alkali Metal Cleaning Facility [*Nuclear energy*] (NRCH) ... AMCF
Alkali Metal Thermoelectric Converter [*Power source*] ... AMTEC
Alkali Plasma Hall Accelerator (MCD) ... ALPHA
Alkali Resistant Factor (SAUS) ... ARF
Alkali-Extractable Light Chain [*Biochemistry*] ... ALC
Alkali-Gravity-Viscosity [*Glass technology*] ... AGV
Alkali-Metal Turbine ... AMT
Alkaline (KSC) ... ALK
Alkaline (SAUS) ... Ta
Alkaline Calcium Petroleum Sulfonate ... ACPS
Alkaline Contaminant Material [*In used frying oils*] ... ACM
Alkaline Copper Quat [*Wood preservative*] (WPI) ... ACQ
Alkaline Earth Precipitate (SAUS) ... AEP
Alkaline Electrolyte Fuel Cell ... AEFC
Alkaline Fuel Cell ... AFC
Alkaline Peptone Water (DMAA) ... APW
Alkaline Permanganate [*Nuclear energy*] (NUCP) ... AP
Alkaline Permanganate Ammonium Citrate (OA) ... APAC
Alkaline Phosphalase/Antialkaline Phosphatase (SAUS) ... APAAP
Alkaline Phosphatase (DMAA) ... AKP
Alkaline Phosphatase [*An enzyme*] (DAVI) ... ALK-P
Alkaline Phosphatase [*An enzyme*] (CPH) ... alk phos
Alkaline Phosphatase (SAUS) ... Alk Phos
Alkaline Phosphatase [*An enzyme*] (CPH) ... alk ptase
Alkaline Phosphatase [*Also, AP*] [*An enzyme*] ... ALP
Alkaline Phosphatase [*Also, ALP*] [*An enzyme*] ... AP
Alkaline Phosphatase (MELL) ... APh
Alkaline Phosphatase [*An enzyme*] (DAVI) ... KA
Alkaline Phosphatase [*Biochemistry*] (DAVI) ... p'ase
Alkaline Phosphatase Activity [*Marine science*] (OSRA) ... APA
Alkaline Phosphatase Activity (SAUS) ... APA
Alkaline Phosphatase Activity, Granular Leukocytes [*Immunochemistry*] (MAE) ... APGL
Alkaline Phosphatase Isoenzymes [*Biochemistry*] (DAVI) ... ALKISO
Alkaline Phosphatase:Antialkaline Phosphatase [*Immunochemistry*] ... APAAP
Alkaline Polyethylene Glycol (EEVL) ... APEG
Alkaline Protease Inhibitor (DB) ... API
Alkaline Reflux Gastritis [*Medicine*] (MELL) ... ARG
Alkaline Rust Remover (SAUS) ... ARR
Alkalinity (ADWA) ... alky
Alkalinity (MSA) ... ALKY
Alkalinity Factor (SAUS) ... pOH
Alkali-Refined Linseed Oil [*Organic chemistry*] ... ARLO
Alkalisilica Reaction [*Chemistry*] ... ASR
Alkali-Soluble Nitrogen (MAE) ... ASN
Alkali-Stable Pepsin (DB) ... ASP
Alkali-Tin-Silicate [*Glass for possible nuclear waste storage*] ... ATS
Alkali-Treated Straw (PDAA) ... ATS
Alkalyzing Agent ... AA
Alkan Air Ltd. [*Canada*] [*ICAO designator*] (FAAC) ... AKN
Alkan Air Ltd. [*ICAO designator*] (AD) ... TO
Alkan Society [*Surrey, England*] (EAIO) ... AS
Alkane [*Organic chemistry*] ... AL
Alkaril Chemicals Ltd., Mississauga, ON, Canada [*Library symbol*] [*Library of Congress*] (LCLS) ... CaOMAC
Alkaril Chemicals Ltd., Mississauga, Ontario [*Library symbol*] [*National Library of Canada*] (NLC) ... OMAC
Alkenyl Succinic Anhydride [*Organic chemistry*] ... ASA
Alkermes, Inc. [*Associated Press*] (SAG) ... Alkerm
Alkermes, Inc. [*NASDAQ symbol*] (SPSG) ... ALKS
Al-Kharj [*Saudi Arabia*] [*ICAO location identifier*] (ICLI) ... OEKJ
Alkoxyglycerol [*Organic chemistry*] ... AKG
Alkyd Moulding Compound (PDAA) ... AMC
Alkyl [*Chemistry*] ... Alk
Alkyl Amines Council (EA) ... AAC
Alkyl Ammonium Compound [*Wood preservative*] (WPI) ... AAC
Alkyl Benzene Sulfonate (SAUS) ... ABS
Alkyl Benzenesulfonate [*Organic chemistry*] ... ABS
Alkyl Glyceryl Sulfonate (EDCT) ... AGS
Alkyl Ketene Dimer [*Organic chemistry*] ... AKA
Alkyl Lysophospholipid [*Biochemistry*] ... ALP
Alkyl Polyglycoside [*Organic chemistry*] ... APG
Alkyl Sulfate [*Surfactant*] [*Organic chemistry*] ... AS
Alkylated Chlorsulfonated Polyethylene [*Plastics technology*] ... ACSM
Alkylation Unit Acid [*Petroleum refining*] ... AUA
Alkylbenzyl Sulfonates (SAUS) ... ABS
Alkyldimethylamine [*Acronym is a trademark of Ethyl Corp. for its brand of alkyldimethylamine products*] ... ADMA
Alkylethoxylated Sulfate [*Surfactant*] [*Organic chemistry*] ... AES
Alkylketene Dimer [*Organic chemistry*] ... AKD
Alkylosing Spinal Hyperostosis [*Medicine*] (MELL) ... ASH
Alkylphenol Ethoxylate [*Organic chemistry*] ... APE
Alkylphenol Polyethoxylate [*Organic chemistry*] ... APEO
Alkylsuccinic Anhydride [*Organic chemistry*] ... ASA
All Ability School [*British*] ... AA
All Abnormal [*Clinical hematology*] ... AA
All About Issues American [*An association*] (EA) ... AAIA
All About Marilyn [*An association*] (EA) ... AAM
All Accident Notice Offices (FAAC) ... ALANO
All Africa Church Music Association (SAUO) ... AACMA
All Africa Conference of Churches (SAUO) ... AACC
All Africa Leprosy and Rehabilitation Training Center (or Centre) (SAUO) ... ALERT
All Africa Students Union [*See also UPE*] (EAIO) ... AASU
All Africa Teachers' Organization (EAIO) ... AATO
All Africa Teachers Organization (SAUS) ... AATO
All African Award (SAUS) ... AAA
All African Peoples Conference (SAUS) ... AAPC
All After [*Aviation*] (DA) ... AA
All [*Text*] **After** [*Specified Point*] [*Message handling*] ... AA
All Air Carrier Field Offices (FAAC) ... ALACFO
All Air Defense Liasion Officers in Region (FAAC) ... ALADLO
All Air Route Traffic Control Centers in Region (FAAC) ... ALARTC
All Air Traffic (Area) Supervisors in Region (FAAC) ... ALATAS
All Air Traffic Field Facilities (FAAC) ... ALATF
All Air Traffic Field Offices (FAAC) ... ALATFO
All Air Traffic Service Personnel in Region (FAAC) ... ALAT
All Airway Facilities Sector and Field Offices (FAAC) ... ALAFFO
All Along (ADA) ... AA
All Aluminum Alloy Conductor (MCD) ... AAAC
All Aluminum Conductor ... AAC
All Amer Communications'B' [*NASDAQ symbol*] (TTSB) ... AACIB
All Amer Semiconductor [*NASDAQ symbol*] (TTSB) ... SEMI
All America Cables and Radio (SAUS) ... AACR
All America Girls Professional Baseball League [*In 1992 movie, "A League of Their Own"*] [*Also, GPBL*] ... AAGPBL
All America Rose Selections (SAUO) ... AARS
All American Association of Contest Judges (EA) ... AAACJ
All American Aviation (SAUS) ... AAA
All American Aviation, Wilmington (SAUO) ... AAA
All American Cables & Radio, Inc. ... AAC & R
All American Canal (SAUS) ... AAC
All American Commun [*NASDAQ symbol*] (TTSB) ... AACI
All American Communications, Inc. [*NASDAQ symbol*] (SAG) ... AACI
All American Communications, Inc. [*Associated Press*] (SAG) ... AllACm
All American Engineering Company (SAUO) ... AAE
All American Food Group, Inc. [*NASDAQ symbol*] (SAG) ... AAFG
All American Food Group, Inc. [*Associated Press*] (SAG) ... AllAFG
All American Life & Financial Corp. (SAUO) ... AAL
All American Semiconductor, Inc. [*Associated Press*] (SAG) ... AllASem
All American Semiconductor, Inc. [*NASDAQ symbol*] (NQ) ... SEMI
All American Target Term Trust [*NYSE symbol*] (SAG) ... AAT
All American Target Term Trust [*Associated Press*] (SAG) ... AllAmTar
All Amhamra People's Organisation [*Ethiopia*] ... AAPO
All Applications Digital Computer [*Navy*] ... AADC
All Arms Air Defence (SAUS) ... AAAD
All Arms Anti Armor Weapon System (ACAE) ... AAAAWS
All Arms Classroom Trainer (SAUS) ... AACT
All Arms Training Centre (SAUO) ... AATC
All Arms Trencher (SAUS) ... AAT
All Army Activities (AABC) ... ALARACT
All Asia Anti-Communist Youth League (SAUO) ... AAACYL
All Aspect Gunsight Evaluation (MCD) ... AAGE
All Attitude Bombing System (SAUS) ... AABS
All Attitude Indicator (SAUS) ... AAI
All Australian Register of Massage Therapists Organizations (SAUS) ... AARMTO
All Average Recoverable (SAUS) ... AAR
All Before (SAUS) ... AB

All [*Text*] **Before** [*Specified Point*] [*Message handling*] ... AB
All Biota Taxonomic Inventory (SAUS) ... ABTI
All Body Type [*Army*] (AABC) ... ABT
All Brit Karate Organisation (DBA) ... TABKO
All Bureaus [*Navy*] ... ALBUS
All Busy Low [*AT & T*] ... ABL
All But Dissertation (SAUS) ... ABD
All But Not Only (SAUS) ... ABNO
All but Not Only ... ABNO
All But the Dissertation [*PhD candidates*] ... ABD
All But their Dissertations (SAUS) ... ABDs
All Canada Insurance Federation ... ACIF
All Canada Poetry Contests ... ACPC
All Canadian Congress of Labour ... ACCL
All Cards Printed (SAUS) ... ACP
All Cargo Airlines Ltd. (SAUS) ... UF
All Ceylon Federation of Free Trade Unions ... ACFFTU
All Ceylon Harbour and Dock Workers Union (SAUO) ... ACHDWU
All Charter Ltd. [*British*] [*ICAO designator*] (FAAC) ... BLA
All Chiefs, No Indians [*Slang*] (AAG) ... ACNI
All Clad (SAUS) ... alcd
All Colors (SAUS) ... ac
All Commands [*A dispatch to all commands in an area*] [*Navy*] ... ALCOM
All Commands, [*US*] **Atlantic Fleet** [*Navy*] (NVT) ... ALCOMLANT
All Commands, [*US*] **Pacific Fleet** [*Navy*] (NVT) ... ALCOMPAC
All Commands Process as Attached [*Army*] (AABC) ... ACPATT
All Comment Listing (SAUS) ... ACL
All Composite Aircraft (MCD) ... ACA
All Composite Evaluator (SAUS) ... ACE
All Concerned [*Army*] (AABC) ... ALCON
All Concerned Notified ... ACN
all correct (SAUS) ... ok
All Courses and Quadrants (SAUS) ... ACQ
All Culture [*Broth*] [*Biochemistry*] (DAVI) ... AC
All Cycles (SAUS) ... ACy
All Dielectric Filter ... ADF
All Digital Control Run (SAUS) ... ADCR
All Digital Data Tape (SAUS) ... ADDT
All Digital Phase Locked Loop (SAUS) ... ADPLL
All Digital Video Imaging System for Atmospheric Research (SAUS) ... ADVISAR
All Edges Gilt [*Bookbinding*] (ADA) ... AEG
All Electrical Kitchen (ADWA) ... AEK
All Electronic Equipment (SAUS) ... AEE
All Engines Operating [*Aviation*] ... AEO
All England ... AE
All England Club (SAUO) ... AEC
All England Law Reports [*A publication*] ... AER
All England Law Reports [*A publication*] ... All ER
All England Law Reports (Reprint) [*1558-1935*] [*A publication*] (DLA) ... AER Rep
All England Law Reports (Reprint) [*1558-1935*] [*A publication*] (DLA) ... All ER Rep
All England Law Reports (Reprint) [*1558-1935*] [*A publication*] (DLA) ... All ER Repr
All England Law Reports (Reprint) Australian Extension Volumes [*A publication*] (DLA) ... AER Rep Ext
All England Law Reports (Reprint), Australian Extension Volumes [*A publication*] (DLA) ... All ER Rep Ext
All England Lawn Tennis Club ... AELTC
All England Netball Association (EAIO) ... AENA
All England Women's Hockey Association (EAIO) ... AEWHA
All England Women's Lacrosse Association (EAIO) ... AEWLA
All Equipment OK [*Expression meaning "in perfect working order." Popularized during early development of NASA's space program*] ... A-OK
All Equipment Production Reliability Test (SAUS) ... AEPRT
All Equipment Production Reliability Tests (MCD) ... AEPRT
All Ethiopia Socialist Union ... MEISONE
All European Academies (SAUO) ... ALLEA
All European Academies Network (SAUS) ... ALLEA
All Events Trace (SAUS) ... AET
All Faiths for One Race (AIE) ... AFFOR
All Figure Number [*Telecommunications*] (TEL) ... AFN
All Flight Service Station (SAUS) ... ALFSS
All Flight Service Stations in Region (FAAC) ... ALFSS
All Flight Standards Field Offices (FAAC) ... ALFSFO
All Food Activities [*DoD*] ... ALFOODACT
All for the Children Foundation [*Defunct*] (EA) ... ACF
All Former Buyers ... AFB
All Fouled-Up [*Bowdlerized version*] (AAG) ... AFU
All Going Well (RIMS) ... AGW
All Got Up (ADA) ... AGU
All Hope Abandoned [*Union*] [*British*] (DGA) ... AHA
All in Hand (ADA) ... AIH
All In Hand (SAUS) ... AIH
All in One (SAUS) ... AIO
All in the Family [*TV program*] ... AITF
All In the Family TV Program (SAUS) ... AITF TV Program
All India Automobile Association (SAUO) ... AIAA
All India Congress Committee (SAUO) ... AICC
All India Coordinated Agronomic Research Project (SAUO) ... AICARP
All India Coordinated Oilseeds Research Project (SAUO) ... AICORP
All India Coordinated Rice Improvement Programme (SAUO) ... AICRIP
All India Coordinated Rice Improvement Project (SAUO) ... AICRIP
All India Coordinated Scheme of Micronutrients in Soils and Plants (SAUO) ... AICSMSP
All India Council for Technical Education (SAUO) ... AICTE
All India Criminal Decisions [*A publication*] (DLA) ... Al Cr D
All India Criminal Decisions [*A publication*] (ILCA) ... All Ind Crim Dec
All India Criminal Decisions [*A publication*] (DLA) ... All India Crim Dec
All India Criminal Times [*A publication*] (DLA) ... All Ind Cr T
All India Federation of Educational Associations (SAUO) ... AIFEA
All India Federation of Electricity Employees (SAUO) ... AIFEE
All India Institute of Hygiene and Public Health (SAUS) ... AIIHPH
All India Institute of Medical Sciences (SAUO) ... AIIMS
All India Institute of Mental Health (SAUO) ... AIIMH
All India Institute of Physical Medicine and Rehabilitation (SAUO) ... AIIPMR
All India Law Reporter [*Usually followed by a province abbreviation*] [*as AIR All., for Allahabad, Bom. for Bombay, Dacca for Dacca, HP for Himachal Pradesh, Hyd. for Hyderabad, etc.*] [*A publication*] (DLA) ... AIR
All India League (SAUO) ... AIL
All India Library Association (SAUO) ... ILA
All India Management Association (SAUO) ... AIMA
All India Moslem League (SAUO) ... AIML
All India National Congress (SAUO) ... AINC
All India National Trade Union Congress (SAUO) ... AINTUC
All India Plastics Manufacturers Association (SAUO) ... AIPMA
All India Reporter, Ajmer Series [*A publication*] (ILCA) ... AIR Aj
All India Reporter, Ajmer Series [*A publication*] (ILCA) ... Aj
All India Reporter, Allahabad Series [*A publication*] (ILCA) ... AIRA
All India Reporter, Allahabad Series [*A publication*] (ILCA) ... AIR All
All India Reporter, Andhra Pradesh Series [*A publication*] (ILCA) ... AIR Andh Pra
All India Reporter, Andhra Pradesh Series [*A publication*] (DLA) ... Andh Pra
All India Reporter, Andhra Series [*A publication*] (ILCA) ... AIR And
All India Reporter, Andhra Series [*A publication*] (ILCA) ... AIR Andh
All India Reporter, Andhra Series [*A publication*] (DLA) ... And
All India Reporter, Andhra Series [*A publication*] (DLA) ... Andh
All India Reporter, Assam Series [*A publication*] (ILCA) ... AIR Asm
All India Reporter, Assam Series [*A publication*] (ILCA) ... AIR Assam
All India Reporter, Assam Series [*A publication*] (DLA) ... Asm
All India Reporter, Bhopal Series [*A publication*] (ILCA) ... AIR Bhop
All India Reporter, Bhopal Series [*A publication*] (DLA) ... Bhop
All India Reporter, Bhopal Series (journ.) (SAUS) ... AIR Bhop
All India Reporter, Bilaspur Series [*A publication*] (ILCA) ... AIR Bilas
All India Reporter, Bilaspur Series [*A publication*] (DLA) ... Bilas
All India Reporter, Bilaspur Series (journ.) (SAUS) ... AIR Bilas
All India Reporter, Bombay Series [*A publication*] (ILCA) ... AIRB
All India Reporter, Bombay Series [*A publication*] (ILCA) ... AIR Bom
All India Reporter, Bombay Series [*A publication*] (DLA) ... B
All India Reporter, Bombay Series (journ.) (SAUS) ... AIPB
All India Reporter, Calcutta Series [*A publication*] (ILCA) ... AIRC
All India Reporter, Calcutta Series [*A publication*] (ILCA) ... AIR Cal
All India Reporter, Calcutta Series [*A publication*] (DLA) ... C
All India Reporter, Calcutta Series [*A publication*] (DLA) ... Cal
All India Reporter, Dacca Series [*A publication*] (ILCA) ... AIR Dacca
All India Reporter, Dacca Series [*1949-50*] [*A publication*] (DLA) ... Dacca
All India Reporter, Dacca Series (journ.) (SAUS) ... AIR Dacca
All India Reporter, East Punjab [*1948-50*] [*A publication*] (DLA) ... East Punjab
All India Reporter, East Punjab Series [*A publication*] (ILCA) ... AIR East Punjab
All India Reporter, Federal Court [*1947-50*] [*A publication*] (DLA) ... FC
All India Reporter, Federal Court Series [*A publication*] (ILCA) ... AIRFC
All India Reporter, Himachal Pradesh [*A publication*] (DLA) ... Him Pra
All India Reporter, Himachal Pradesh [*A publication*] (DLA) ... HP
All India Reporter, Himachal Pradesh Series [*A publication*] (ILCA) ... AIR Him Pra
All India Reporter, Himachal Pradesh Series [*A publication*] (ILCA) ... AIRHP
All India Reporter, Hyderabad [*A publication*] (DLA) ... Hy
All India Reporter, Hyderabad Series [*A publication*] (ILCA) ... AIR Hy
All India Reporter, Hyderabad Series [*A publication*] (ILCA) ... AIR Hyd
All India Reporter, Indian Digest [*A publication*] (ILCA) ... AIR Ind Dig
All India Reporter, Indian Digest [*1946-52*] [*A publication*] (DLA) ... Ind Dig
All India Reporter, Jammu and Kashmir [*A publication*] (DLA) ... J & K
All India Reporter, Jammu and Kashmir Series [*A publication*] (ILCA) ... AIRJ & K
All India Reporter, Jammu and Kashmir Series (journ.) (SAUS) ... AIRJ&K
All India Reporter, Kerala Series [*A publication*] (ILCA) ... AIR Kerala
All India Reporter, Kerala Series (journ.) (SAUS) ... AIR Kerala
All India Reporter, Kutch [*1949-56*] [*A publication*] (DLA) ... Kutch
All India Reporter, Kutch Series [*A publication*] (ILCA) ... AIR Kutch
All India Reporter, Lahore Series [*A publication*] (ILCA) ... AIR Lahore
All India Reporter, Lahore Series [*A publication*] (ILCA) ... Lahore
All India Reporter, Madhya Bharat [*1950-57*] [*A publication*] (DLA) ... MB
All India Reporter, Madhya Bharat Series [*A publication*] (ILCA) ... AIRMB
All India Reporter, Madhya Pradesh [*A publication*] (DLA) ... Madh Pra
All India Reporter, Madhya Pradesh [*A publication*] (DLA) ... MP
All India Reporter, Madhya Pradesh Series [*A publication*] (ILCA) ... AIR Madh Pra
All India Reporter, Madhya Pradesh Series [*A publication*] (ILCA) ... AIRMP
All India Reporter, Madras [*A publication*] (DLA) ... Mad
All India Reporter, Madras Series [*A publication*] (ILCA) ... AIRM
All India Reporter, Madras Series [*A publication*] (ILCA) ... AIR Mad
All India Reporter, Madras Series [*A publication*] (ILCA) ... M
All India Reporter, Manipur [*A publication*] (DLA) ... Manip
All India Reporter, Manipur Series [*A publication*] (ILCA) ... AIR Manip
All India Reporter, Mysore [*A publication*] (DLA) ... Mys
All India Reporter, Mysore Series [*A publication*] (ILCA) ... AIR My
All India Reporter, Mysore Series [*A publication*] (ILCA) ... My
All India Reporter, Nagpur [*A publication*] (DLA) ... All India Rep
All India Reporter, Nagpur [*A publication*] (DLA) ... Nag
All India Reporter, Nagpur Series [*A publication*] (ILCA) ... AIRN
All India Reporter, Nagpur Series [*A publication*] (ILCA) ... AIR Nag
All India Reporter, Nagpur Series [*A publication*] (ILCA) ... N
All India Reporter, New Series [*A publication*] (DLA) ... All Ind Rep NS
All India Reporter, Orissa [*A publication*] (DLA) ... Oris
All India Reporter, Orissa [*A publication*] (DLA) ... Orissa
All India Reporter, Orissa Series [*A publication*] (ILCA) ... AIR Oris

All India Reporter, Oudh Series [*A publication*] (ILCA) ... AIR Oudh
All India Reporter, Patiala and East Punjab States Union [*1950-57*] [*A publication*] (DLA) ... PEPSU
All India Reporter, Patiala and East Punjab States Union Series [*A publication*] (ILCA) ... AIR PEP
All India Reporter, Patiala and East Punjab States Union Series [*A publication*] (ILCA) ... AIR PEPSU
All India Reporter, Patiala and East Punjab States Union Series [*A publication*] (ILCA) ... PEP
All India Reporter, Patna [*A publication*] (DLA) ... P
All India Reporter, Patna Series [*A publication*] (ILCA) ... AIRP
All India Reporter, Patna Series [*A publication*] (ILCA) ... AIR Pat
All India Reporter, Patna Series [*A publication*] (ILCA) ... Pat
All India Reporter, Peshawar [*1933-50*] [*A publication*] (DLA) ... Peshawar
All India Reporter, Peshawar Series [*A publication*] (ILCA) ... AIR Pesh
All India Reporter, Privy Council [*A publication*] (ILCA) ... AIRPC
All India Reporter, Privy Council [*1914-50*] [*A publication*] (DLA) ... PC
All India Reporter, Punjab [*A publication*] (DLA) ... Pun
All India Reporter, Punjab (journ.) (SAUS) ... Pun
All India Reporter, Punjab Series [*A publication*] (ILCA) ... AIR Pun
All India Reporter, Rajasthan [*A publication*] (DLA) ... R
All India Reporter, Rajasthan [*A publication*] (DLA) ... Raj
All India Reporter, Rajasthan Series [*A publication*] (ILCA) ... AIRR
All India Reporter, Rajasthan Series [*A publication*] (ILCA) ... AIR Raj
All India Reporter, Saurashtra [*1950-57*] [*A publication*] (DLA) ... Sau
All India Reporter, Saurashtra (journ.) (SAUS) ... Sau
All India Reporter, Saurashtra Series [*A publication*] (ILCA) ... AIR Sau
All India Reporter, Simla [*1951*] [*A publication*] (DLA) ... Simla
All India Reporter, Simla (journ.) (SAUS) ... Simla
All India Reporter, Simla Series [*A publication*] (ILCA) ... AIR Simla
All India Reporter, Sind [*1914-50*] [*A publication*] (DLA) ... Sind
All India Reporter, Sind. (journ.) (SAUS) ... Sind
All India Reporter, Sind Series [*A publication*] (ILCA) ... AIR Sind
All India Reporter, Supreme Court [*A publication*] (ILCA) ... AIRSC
All India Reporter, Supreme Court Reports [*A publication*] (DLA) ... SC
All India Reporter, Supreme Court Reports (journ.) (SAUS) ... SC
All India Reporter, Travancore-Cochin [*1950-57*] [*A publication*] (DLA) ... TC
All India Reporter, Travancore-Cochin Series [*A publication*] (ILCA) ... AIRTC
All India Reporter, Tripura [*A publication*] (DLA) ... Trip
All India Reporter, Tripura Series [*A publication*] (ILCA) ... AIR Trip
All India Reporter, Vindhya Pradesh [*1951-57*] [*A publication*] (DLA) ... VP
All India Reporter, Vindhya Pradesh Series [*A publication*] (ILCA) ... AIRVP
All India Reports [*A publication*] (DLA) ... All IR
All India Rubber Industries Association (SAUO) ... AIRIA
All India Television (SAUS) ... AIT
All India Trade Union Congress (SAUO) ... AITUC
All India Youth Federation (SAUO) ... AIYF
All Indian Criminal Reports [*A publication*] (DLA) ... All ICR
All Indian Criminal Reports [*A publication*] (DLA) ... All Ind Cr R
All Indian Law Reports, Kerala Series [*A publication*] (DLA) ... Kerala
All Indian Pueblo Council (EA) ... AIPC
All Indian Student Federation (SAUO) ... AISF
All Indian Temperance Association (SAUO) ... AITA
All Individuals Deserve Support [*Alternative translation of AIDS, Acquired Immune Deficiency Syndrome, used as a slogan by AWARE*] ... AIDS
All Indonesian Labor Federation (IMH) ... FBSI
All Inertial (SAA) ... AI
All Inertial Guidance [*Aerospace*] (AAG) ... AIG
All Inertial Guidance System [*Aerospace*] ... AIGS
All International Air Traffic Communications Stations [*FAA*] ... ALIATCS
All International Air Traffic Switching Centers (FAAC) ... AIATSC
All International Field Offices (FAAC) ... ALIFO
All International Flight Service Stations (SAUS) ... ALIFSS
All International Flight Service Stations in Region (FAAC) ... ALIFSS
All Iron ... AI
All Is Well [*Search and rescue symbol that can be stamped in sand or snow*] ... LL
All Island Air [*ICAO designator*] (AD) ... AJ
All Known Allergies [*Medicine*] (DAVI) ... AKA
All Leisure Aviation Ltd. [*British*] [*FAA designator*] (FAAC) ... ALT
All Lengths [*Lumber*] ... AL
All Letters Answered (WDAA) ... ALA
All Light Level Television (SAUS) ... ALLTV
All Line Repeat Printing (SAUS) ... ALRP
All London Parents' Action Group [*British*] (AIE) ... ALPAG
All London Teachers Against Racism and Fascism [*British*] (AIE) ... ALTARF
All Major Commands ... ALMAJCOM
All Major Commands (MCD) ... AMC
All Malaya Council of Joint Action (SAUO) ... AMCJA
All Malignant Neoplasm [*Medicine*] ... AMN
All Marine Corps Activities (NVT) ... ALMAR
All Marines ... ALMAR
All Media Floppy (SAUS) ... AMF
All Military Activities (AFM) ... ALMILACT
All Mobile Tactical Air Force (ACAE) ... AMTAF
All Muslim National Union of Tanganyika (SAUO) ... AMNUT
All My Best Wishes (SAUS) ... AMBW
All My Children [*Television program title*] ... AMC
All Nationals Congress [*Fiji*] [*Political party*] (EY) ... ANC
All Nations Christian College [*British*] ... ANCC
All Nations Sports and Cultural Association (SAUO) ... ANSCA
All Nations Women's League (EA) ... ANWL
All Naval Activities Employing Civilians (MCD) ... ANAEC
All Naval Station (SAUS) ... ALNASTA
All Naval Stations [*A dispatch to all Naval stations in an area*] ... ALLNAVSTAS
All Naval Stations [*A dispatch to all Naval stations in an area*] ... ALNAVSTA
All Navy Activities [*A dispatch to all activities in an area*] ... ALNAV
All Navy Activities [*A dispatch to all activities in an area*] ... NAVACT
All Nigeria Law Reports [*A publication*] (DLA) ... All Nig LR
All Nigeria Law Reports [*A publication*] (DLA) ... All NLR
All Nigeria Trade Union Federation (SAUO) ... ANTUF
All Nippon [*ICAO designator*] (AD) ... NH
All Nippon Airways ... ANA
All Nippon Airways Co. Ltd. [*Japan*] [*ICAO designator*] (FAAC) ... ANA
All Nippon Airways Co. Ltd. (SAUS) ... NH
All Nippon News (SAUO) ... ANN
All Normal [*Hematology*] ... AN
All Numbers Calling [*Telephone*] ... ANC
All Officers Meeting [*Military*] (DNAB) ... AOM
All Offices Having Send-Receive Teletypewriter Service on Circuit (FAAC) ... ALCKT
All OK (SAUS) ... AOK
All Ones Counter (SAUS) ... AOC
All Operator Letter (MCD) ... AOL
All or None [*Investment, securities*] ... AON
All Other Contents (MARI) ... AOC
All Other Perils [*Insurance*] ... AOP
All Other Things Being Equal (SAUS) ... AOTBE
All Others [*Later, G Group*] [*Division of National Security Agency*] ... ALLO
All Out-of-Kilter [*Slang*] ... AOK
All Over Pattern [*Quilting*] ... AOP
All Over Set [*Quilting*] ... AOS
All Over the Hatch [*or Hold*] [*Stowage*] (DNAB) ... A/O
All Pakistan Confederation of Labour (SAUO) ... APCL
All Pakistan Confederation of Labour (SAUO) ... APCOL
All Pakistan Federation of Labour (SAUO) ... APFL
All Pakistan Legal Decisions [*A publication*] (ILCA) ... PLD
All Pakistan Post and Telegraph Union (SAUO) ... APPTU
All Parties Administration (SAUO) ... APA
All Party Alliance [*British*] ... APA
All Party Penal Affairs Group (SAUO) ... APPAG
All Pass Network ... APN
All Patient Diagnosis Related Groups (SAUO) ... AP-DRG
All Patient Refined Diagnosis Related Groups (SAUO) ... APR-DRG
All Peoples' Republican Party [*Ghana*] (AF) ... APRP
All Personnel Communication [*Military*] (AFM) ... ALPERSCOM
All Picture Transfer (SAUS) ... APT
All Pilots Meeting [*Military*] (DNAB) ... APM
All Points Addressable [*Computer science*] ... APA
All Points Bulletin [*Police call*] ... APB
All Power Controller Assembly (SAUS) ... APCA
All Praise and Credit (SAUS) ... APAC
All Present or Accounted For ... APOAF
All Present Or Accounted Force (SAUS) ... APOAF
All Propulsive Orbited Transfer Vehicle [*NASA*] ... APOTV
All Purpose Carrier (SSD) ... APC
All Purpose Electronic x Computer [*Early computer*] [*Birkbeck College*] [*British*] ... APExC
All Purpose Fast Memory (SAUS) ... APFM
All Purpose Linotype (SAUS) ... APL
All Purpose Paper [*Euphemism for toilet paper*] ... APP
All Purpose Room (SAUS) ... APR
All Purpose Structure Eurocontrol RADAR Information Exchange (DA) ... ASTERIX
All Purpose Tracker [*Military*] (IUSS) ... APT
All Quadrants (FAAC) ... ALQDS
All Quotes, Inc. [*Associated Press*] (SAG) ... AllQt
All Quotes, Inc. [*Associated Press*] (SAG) ... AllQuote
All Quotes, Inc. [*NASDAQ symbol*] (SAG) ... ALQT
All RADAR Air Traffic Control Facilities in Region [*FAA*] ... ALRAFAC
All Radio Marketing Study [*Business term*] (DOAD) ... ARMS
All Rail [*Railroad*] ... AR
All Rail [*Marine*] (EBF) ... ar
All Rail [*Marine*] (EBF) ... A/R
All Red Series [*A publication*] ... ARS
All Regional Offices (FAAC) ... ALRGN
All Returned (DGA) ... A/R
All Right [*From Oll Korrect; or from Old Kinderhook, a political club that supported the 1840 presidential campaign of Martin Van Buren*] ... OK
All Risk Management [*Insurance*] ... ARM
All Risks [*Insurance*] ... AR
All Risks [*Marine*] (EBF) ... ar
All Risks [*Marine*] (EBF) ... A/R
All Roads Ministry [*An association*] (EA) ... ARM
All Rock-and-Roll Oldies [*Radio station format*] (WDMC) ... ARRO
All Rods Out [*Nuclear energy*] (NRCH) ... ARO
All Round [*Price*] (ROG) ... A/R
All Round Defence (SAUS) ... ARD
All Routes Busy [*Telecommunications*] (TEL) ... ARB
All Routes Explorer [*Computer science*] (VERA) ... ARE
All Russian Central Executive Committee (SAUO) ... ARCEC
All Russian Research Institute (SAUS) ... VNII
All Safety Commands [*Air Force*] (AFM) ... ALSAFECOM
All Saints' Day ... ASD
All Saints Sisters of the Poor (SAUO) ... ASSP
All Savers Certificate [*Banking*] ... ASC
All Seasons Aviation Ltd. (SAUO) ... JC
All Seasons Global Fund [*Associated Press*] (SAG) ... AllSeasG
All Seasons Global Fund [*NASDAQ symbol*] (TTSB) ... FUND
All Sectors (FAAC) ... ALSEC
All Service Postal Chess Club (EA) ... ASPCC

All Ships and Stations Letters ... AS & SL
All Ships and Stations Letters (SAUS) ... AS&SL
All sky monitor on Spectrum-X-Gamma (SAUS) ... MOXE
All Solid Source MBE (SAUS) ... ASSMBE
All Solid Source Molecular Beam Epitaxy (AAEL) ... ASSMBE
All Souls College (SAUO) ... All S
All Souls College (SAUO) ... ASC
All Source Analysis Center (MCD) ... ASAC
All Source Analysis System [*Military*] (DOMA) ... ASAR
All Source Analysis System [*DoD*] ... ASAS
All Source Analysis System/Software [*Military*] (RDA) ... ASAS/SFT
All Source Document Index [*Army*] ... ASDI
All Source Imagery Program (ACAE) ... ASIP
All Source Intelligence Center (MCD) ... ASIC
All Sources Analysis System-Warlord (SAUS) ... ASAS-WL
All South Africa Law Reports [*A publication*] (DLA) ... ASAR
All South Pole (IAA) ... ASP
All Sports Federation of China (SAUO) ... ASFC
All Star Airlines, Inc. [*ICAO designator*] (FAAC) ... ASR
All Star Dairy Association (EA) ... ASDA
All Star Resources [*Vancouver Stock Exchange symbol*] ... ASR
All States Hobby Club [*Later, NASHC*] ... ASHC
All Stations (SAUS) ... ALLSTNS
All Stations (KSC) ... ALSTA
All Stations, Continental United States (MUGU) ... ALSTACON
All Steps Control (SAUS) ... ASC
All Systems Test [*NASA*] (KSC) ... AST
All Systems Test Equipment Group ... ASTEG
All Systems Vehicle ... ASV
All Tariffs Computerized [*Project*] ... ATAC
All Taxa Biodiversity Inventory [*Proposed*] [*National Science Foundation*] ... ATBI
All Terrain Lifter Articulated System [*MTMC*] (TAG) ... ATLAS
All Terrain Tow Vehicle (SAUS) ... ATTV
All Terrain Vehicle (SAUS) ... ATV
All Test Go (MCD) ... ATG
All Tests Pass (SAUS) ... ATP
All The Acronyms In The Known Universe (SAUS) ... ATAITKU
All The Best (SAUS) ... ATB
All the Best Dog Poems [*A publication*] ... AIBD
All the Conveniences ... A/C
All the Worlds Aircraft (SAUS) ... AWA
All Things Considered [*Radio program*] ... ATC
All Thrust Terminate Relay (MUGU) ... ATTR
All Thrust Termination (MUGU) ... ATT
All Time Saved, Both Ends (SAUS) ... ATSBE
All Together (EA) ... AT
All Told (SAUS) ... AT
All Transistor (IAA) ... ATR
All Trunks Busy [*Telecommunications*] ... ATB
All Union Central Council of Trade Unions [*Former USSR*] ... AUCCTU
All Union Central Scientific Research Laboratory for the Restoration of Valuable (SAUS) ... AUCSRLFRVWAM
All Union Scientific Research Institute of Radio Equipment (SAUO) ... AUSRIRE
All Up (ADA) ... AU
All Up Weight (DOMA) ... AUW
All Vehicle Test ... AVT
All Volatile Treatment [*Nuclear energy*] (NRCH) ... AVT
All Wales Ladies Lacrosse Association (BI) ... AWLLA
All Water ... AW
All Water (EBF) ... aw
All Water (SAUS) ... A/W
All Wave Aerial (or Antenna) (SAUS) ... AWA
All Wave Antenna ... AWA
All Weather Attack Control System (ACAE) ... ALLWACS
All Weather Carrier Landing (ACAE) ... AWCI
All Weather Electronic System (ACAE) ... AWES
All Weather Flare (SAUS) ... AWF
All Weather Flying Division [*Air Force*] ... AWAF
All Weather Interceptor (SAUS) ... AWI
All Weather Low Altitude Route (ACAE) ... AWLAR
All Weather Operations (DA) ... AWO
All Weather Reconnaissance System (ACAE) ... AWAR
All Weather Yaw Damper Computer (SAUS) ... AWYDC
All Widths [*Lumber*] ... AW
All Women's Archaeological Research Expedition ... AWARE
All Wood Screw (DAC) ... AWS
All Wool (SAUS) ... AW
All Working Time Saved (SAUS) ... AWTS
All Year Round Chrysanthemum Growers' Association (EAIO) ... AYRCGA
Alla Cacia [*In the Hunting Style*] [*Music*] (ROG) ... AL CAC
Alla Capella [*In Church Style*] [*Music*] (ROG) ... AL CAP
Alla Militaire [*In Military Style*] [*Music*] (ROG) ... AL MIL
Alla Moderna [*In Modern Style*] [*Music*] (ROG) ... AL MOD
All-Activity Vehicle ... AAV
All-Africa Conference of Churches [*Nairobi, Kenya*] (AF) ... AACC
All-African Farmers Union (SAUS) ... AAFU
All-African Peoples Organization (SAUS) ... AAPO
All-African People's Revolutionary Party (EA) ... A-APRP
All-African Trade Union Federation (SAUS) ... AATUF
All-African Women's Conference [*or Congress*] ... AAWC
Allagash [*Maine*] [*Seismograph station code, US Geological Survey*] (SEIS) ... AGM
Allagash River and Allagash Wilderness Waterway, Maine (SAUS) ... Allagash
Allahabad (SAUS) ... Alld
Allahabad [*India*] [*Airport symbol*] (OAG) ... IXD
Allahabad [*India*] [*ICAO location identifier*] (ICLI) ... VIAL
Allahabad Criminal Cases [*India*] [*A publication*] (DLA) ... ACC
Allahabad Criminal Cases [*India*] [*A publication*] (DLA) ... A Cr C
Allahabad Criminal Cases [*India*] [*A publication*] (DLA) ... All Cr Cas
Allahabad Criminal Reports [*India*] [*A publication*] (DLA) ... A Cr R
Allahabad Law Journal [*India*] [*A publication*] (DLA) ... All LJ
Allahabad Law Review [*India*] [*A publication*] (DLA) ... All LR
Allahabad Law Times [*India*] [*A publication*] (DLA) ... All LT
Allahabad Series, Indian Law Reports [*A publication*] (DLA) ... All Ser
Allahabad University (SAUO) ... Alld
Allahabad University (SAUO) ... AU
Allahabad Weekly Notes [*India*] [*A publication*] (DLA) ... AWN
Allahabad Weekly Notes (and Supplement) [*India*] [*A publication*] (DLA) ... All WN
Allahabad Weekly Reporter [*India*] [*A publication*] (DLA) ... All WR
Allahabad Weekly Reporter [*India*] [*A publication*] (DLA) ... AWR
Allaire [*Stock market symbol*] ... ALLR
Allaire Corp. [*NASDAQ symbol*] (SG) ... ALLR
Allakaket [*Alaska*] [*Airport symbol*] (OAG) ... AET
All-Altitude Air-Bearing Research and Training Simulator ... ARTS
All-Altitude Control Capability (SAUS) ... AACC
All-Altitude Spin Projected [*Munition*] ... ASP
All-Aluminium Conductor (SAUS) ... AAC
Allama Iqbal Open University (SAUO) ... AIOU
Allamakee County Courthouse, Waukon, IA [*Library symbol*] [*Library of Congress*] (LCLS) ... IaWaukAC
Allamakee County Courthouse, Waukon, IA [*Library symbol*] [*Library of Congress*] (LCLS) ... IaWaukCoC
Allamakee Journal, Lansing, IA [*Library symbol*] [*Library of Congress*] (LCLS) ... IaLanJ
All-America Football Conference [*Major league 1946-49, merged with NFL 1950*] ... AAFC
All-America Rose Selections [*An association*] (EA) ... AARS
All-America Selections (EA) ... AAS
All-American Amateur Baseball Association (EA) ... AAABA
All-American Boy [*Lifestyle classification*] (ECON) ... AAB
All-American Bronze Club (EA) ... AABC
All-American Cable Company (SAUO) ... ALAMCABDO
All-American Challenge [*Auto racing*] ... AAC
All-American Collegiate Golf Foundation (EA) ... AACGF
All-American Conference to Combat Communism (EA) ... AACCC
All-American Girl [*Lifestyle classification*] (ECON) ... AAG
All-American Gladiolus Selections (SAUO) ... AAGS
All-American Indian Motorcycle Club (EA) ... AAIMC
All-American Racers [*Automobile racing team*] ... AAR
All-American Selections (SAUO) ... AAS
All-American Term Trust [*NYSE symbol*] (TTSB) ... AAT
All-American Youth Orchestra ... AAYO
Allamin Gorkij Konyvtar, Budapest, Hungary [*Library symbol*] [*Library of Congress*] (LCLS) ... HuBG
Allamvedelmi Hivatal [*Hungarian secret police*] ... AVH
Allan Blair Memorial Clinic, Regina, Saskatchewan [*Library symbol*] [*National Library of Canada*] (NLC) ... SRAB
Allan Blair Memorial Clinic, Regina, SK, Canada [*Library symbol*] [*Library of Congress*] (LCLS) ... CaSRAB
Allan Hancock College [*Santa Maria, CA*] ... AHC
Allan Hancock College, Santa Maria, CA [*Library symbol*] [*Library of Congress*] (LCLS) ... CStmaAH
Allan Hancock Foundation. Occasional Papers (journ.) (SAUS) ... OPAFD7
Allan Hancock Foundation. Technical Reports (journ.) (SAUS) ... TAHFDQ
Allan Hancock Monographs in Marine Biology (SAUS) ... Allan Hancock Monogr Mar Biol
Allan Hancock Occasional Papers (SAUS) ... Allan Hancock Occas Pap
Allan Hancock Pacific Expeditions (SAUS) ... Allan Hancock Pac Exped
Allan Hills [*Antarctic meteorology*] ... ALH
Allan Memorial Institute, Montreal, Quebec [*Library symbol*] [*National Library of Canada*] (NLC) ... QMAM
Allanco Iolite Monitor Corp. [*Vancouver Stock Exchange symbol*] ... AIT
Allantic Geoscience Association (SAUO) ... AGS
Allantic Provinces Trucking Association (SAUO) ... APTA
Allanto-Amnio-Chorion (SAUS) ... AAC
Allantoin Vaginal Cream [*Gynecology*] (MAE) ... AVC
All-Application Digital Computer (SAUS) ... AADC
Allarcom Pay Television Ltd. [*Canada*] ... APT
Allard Owners Club [*British*] (EAIO) ... AOC
Allard Owners Club USA (EA) ... AOC-USA
Allard Register (EA) ... AR
All-Arms Training Center (SAUS) ... AATC
All-Around [*Rodeo term*] ... AA
All-Articles Configuration Inspection Log [*Aerospace*] (AAG) ... AACIL
All-Aspect Capability (SAUS) ... AAC
All-Aspect Maneuvering Index (MCD) ... AAMI
Allative (BJA) ... All
All-Attitude Control Capability [*Aerospace*] (AAG) ... AACC
All-Attitude Indicator Bombing System (MCD) ... AABS
All-Attitude Vertical Reference System [*Aerospace*] ... AAVRS
All-Band Intercept Receiver ... ABIR
All-Breeds Rescue Conservancy (EA) ... ARC
All-Burma Peasants Organisation (SAUO) ... ABPO
All-Bus Instrumentation System (SAUS) ... ABIS
Allcanada Express Ltd. [*Canada*] [*ICAO designator*] (FAAC) ... CNX
All-Canada Weekly Summaries [*Canada Law Book Ltd.*] [*Database*] ... ACWS
All-Ceylon Harbor and Dock Workers' Union ... ACHDWU
All-Channel Television Society [*UHF interest group*] (NTCM) ... ACTS
All-China Democratic Youth Federation (SAUO) ... ACDYF
All-China Federation of Democratic Women (SAUO) ... ACFDW
All-China Federation of Democratic Youth (SAUO) ... ACFDY

All-China Federation of Labour (SAUO) ... ACFL
All-China Federation of Trade Unions [*Communist China*] ... ACFTU
Allcity Insurance [*NASDAQ symbol*] (TTSB) ... ALCI
Allcity Insurance Co. [*NASDAQ symbol*] (NQ) ... ALCI
Allcity Insurance Co. [*Associated Press*] (SAG) ... AllCity
All-Comm Media [*NASDAQ symbol*] (TTSB) ... ALCM
All-Comm Media Corp. [*NASDAQ symbol*] (SAG) ... ALCM
All-Comm Media Corp. [*Associated Press*] (SAG) ... AllCom
All-Commodity Volume [*Marketing*] (WDMC) ... ACV
All-Craft Foundation (EA) ... ACF
All-Delivered acoustic-implant Seismic-intrusion Detector (SAUS) ... ADSID
All-Digital Answering Machine [*PhoneMate, Inc.*] ... ADAM
All-Digital Attack Center (MCD) ... ADAC
All-Digital Data Tape (KSC) ... ADDT
All-Digital Phase-Locked Loop (KSC) ... ADPLL
All-Digital Simulator ... ADS
Alle Macht aan de Arbeiders [*All Power to the Workers*] [*Belgium*] [*Political party*] (PPW) ... AMADA
Alleberg [*Sweden*] [*ICAO location identifier*] (ICLI) ... ESGC
Allegan, MI [*FM radio station call letters*] (RBYB) ... WNTX
Allegan, MI [*FM radio station call letters*] (BROA) ... WZUU-FM
Allegan Public Library, Allegan, MI [*Library symbol*] [*Library of Congress*] (LCLS) ... MiAlle
Allegany Community College, Cumberland, MD [*Library symbol*] [*Library of Congress*] (LCLS) ... MdCuAC
Allegany County Library, Cumberland, MD [*Library symbol*] [*Library of Congress*] (LCLS) ... MdCu
Allegata [*Schedules, Enclosures*] [*Italian*] (ILCA) ... all
Allegato (SAUS) ... All
Alleged Discrimination Official (MCD) ... ADO
Alleged Onset Date [*of disability*] [*Social Security Administration*] (OICC) ... AOD
Alleged Quarter [*of the year*] **Disability Began** [*Social Security Administration*] (OICC) ... AQD
Alleged Vegetarian (SAUS) ... AV
Alleged Year Disability Began [*Social Security Administration*] (OICC) ... AYD
Allegemeine Elektrizitats Gesellschaft [*Federal Republic of Germany*] (NUCP) ... AEG
Alleghany Corp. [*NYSE symbol*] (SPSG) ... Y
Alleghany County Public Library, Sparta, NC [*Library symbol*] [*Library of Congress*] (LCLS) ... NcSpa
Allegheny (GAVI) ... AL
Allegheny (FAAC) ... ALGHNY
Allegheny (SAUS) ... Alleg
Allegheny Airlines [*Air carrier designation symbol*] ... AAA
Allegheny Airlines [*ICAO designator*] (AD) ... AL
Allegheny Airlines (IIA) ... ALA
Allegheny Airlines (MCD) ... ALL
Allegheny & South Side [*AAR code*] ... AYSS
Allegheny & Western Energy Corp. [*NASDAQ symbol*] (NQ) ... ALGH
Allegheny & Western Railroad Co. (SAUO) ... AY
Allegheny Ballistic Laboratory (SAUS) ... ABL
Allegheny Ballistics Laboratory [*Cumberland, MD*] (MCD) ... ABL
Allegheny College (SAUO) ... AC
Allegheny College (GAGS) ... Allegheny C
Allegheny College, Meadville, PA [*OCLC symbol*] (OCLC) ... AVL
Allegheny College, Meadville, PA [*Library symbol*] [*Library of Congress*] (LCLS) ... PMA
Allegheny Corp. [*Associated Press*] (SAG) ... AllegCp
Allegheny County Law Library, Pittsburgh, PA [*OCLC symbol*] (OCLC) ... PAL
Allegheny County Law Library, Pittsburgh, PA [*Library symbol*] [*Library of Congress*] (LCLS) ... PPiAL
Allegheny Energy [*NYSE symbol*] [*Formerly, Allegheny Power System*] (SG) ... AYE
Allegheny Housing Rehabilitation Corporation (SAUO) ... AHRCO
Allegheny International ... AI
Allegheny International, Inc., Brackenridge, PA [*Library symbol*] [*Library of Congress*] (LCLS) ... PBracAL
Allegheny Ludlum [*NYSE symbol*] (TTSB) ... ALS
Allegheny Ludlum Corp. [*Associated Press*] (SAG) ... AlgLud
Allegheny Ludlum Corp. [*NYSE symbol*] (SPSG) ... ALS
Allegheny Ludlum Industries, Inc. (SAUO) ... AG
Allegheny Ludlum Steel (SAUS) ... AG
Allegheny Ludlum Steel Company ... ALS
Allegheny Ludlum Steel Corp. (SAUO) ... AL
Allegheny Mountain Collegiate Conference (PSS) ... AMCC
Allegheny Portage Railroad National Historic Site ... ALPO
Allegheny Power Sys [*NYSE symbol*] (TTSB) ... AYP
Allegheny Power System, Inc. [*Associated Press*] (SAG) ... AllgPow
Allegheny Power System, Inc. ... APS
Allegheny Power System, Inc. [*NYSE symbol*] (SPSG) ... AYP
Allegheny Region ... AR
Allegheny Teledyne [*NYSE symbol*] (SG) ... ALT
Allegheny-Ludlum (SAUS) ... A-L
Alleghery Power System, Inc. (SAUO) ... APS
Allegiance (GEAB) ... alleg
Allegiance ... ALLEG
Allegiance Banc [*NASDAQ symbol*] (TTSB) ... ALLG
Allegiance Banc Corp. [*Associated Press*] (SAG) ... Allegian
Allegiance Banc Corp. [*NASDAQ symbol*] (SAG) ... ALLG
Allegiance Corp. [*NYSE symbol*] (SAG) ... AEH
Allegiance Corp. [*Associated Press*] (SAG) ... Allegnc
Allegiance Telecom [*NASDAQ symbol*] (SG) ... ALGX
Allegiant Bancorp [*NASDAQ symbol*] (TTSB) ... ALLE
Allegiant Bancorp, Inc. [*NASDAQ symbol*] (SAG) ... ALLE
Allegiant Bancorp, Inc. [*Associated Press*] (SAG) ... Allegiant
Allegiant Physician Services, Inc. [*Associated Press*] (SAG) ... AllegPhy
Allegiant Physician Services, Inc. [*NASDAQ symbol*] (SAG) ... ALPS
Allegory (ADA) ... ALLEG
Allegory (VRA) ... alleg
Allegretto [*Moderately Quick*] [*Music*] (ROG) ... ALLEGTO
Allegretto [*Moderately Quick*] [*Music*] ... Allgett
Allegretto [*Moderately Quick*] [*Music*] (ROG) ... ALLGTTO
Allegretto [*Moderately Quick*] [*Music*] (ROG) ... ALLTO
Allegro [*Quick*] [*Music*] (ROG) ... ALL
Allegro [*Quick*] [*Music*] ... ALLO
Allegro [*Lively*] [*Italian*] [*Music*] (WDAA) ... Allo
Allegro New Media [*NASDAQ symbol*] (TTSB) ... ANMI
Allegro New Media, Inc. [*Associated Press*] (SAG) ... Allegro
Allegro New Media, Inc. [*NASDAQ symbol*] (SAG) ... ANMI
Allegro New Media, Inc. [*NASDAQ symbol*] (SAG) ... SPCO
Allegro-Elite [*Formerly, Allegro*] [*Record label*] ... Allo
Allein bei Christo die Ewige Freude [*With Christ Alone Is Eternal Joy*] [*Motto of Albrecht Gunther, Count Schwarzburg (1582-1634)*] [*German*] ... ABCDEF
Allein Gott Traue Ich [*I Trust in God Alone*] [*Motto of Dorothee, Duchess of Braunschweig-Lunebert (1546-1617)*] [*German*] ... AGTI
Allele [*Genetics*] ... A
allele (SAUS) ... a
All-Electric Aircraft [*Aviation*] (PDAA) ... AEA
All-Electric Kitchen (SAUS) ... AEK
All-Electronics Show (SAUS) ... AES
Allele-Specific Oligonucleotide [*Genetics*] ... ASO
Allelix, Inc., Mississauga, ON, Canada [*Library symbol*] [*Library of Congress*] (LCLS) ... CaOMAI
Allelix, Inc., Mississauga, Ontario [*Library symbol*] [*National Library of Canada*] (NLC) ... OMAI
Alleluia [*An old abbreviation, formed from the vowels of the word*] ... AEUIA
Alleluia ... ALL
Allemating Continuous Wave (SAUS) ... ACW
Allen Academy, Bryan, TX [*Library symbol*] [*Library of Congress*] (LCLS) ... TxBryA
Allen & Hanburys [*Great Britain*] [*Research code symbol*] ... AH
Allen & Hanburys [*Great Britain*] [*Research code symbol*] ... CB
Allen and Morris' Trial [*A publication*] (DLA) ... All & Mor Tr
Allen and Wright [*Root beer*] [*Initialism also used as name of franchised drive-in restaurants*] ... A & W
Allen Avicraft Radio, Inc. (SAUO) ... AAR
Allen Blue Test [*Medicine*] (MELL) ... ABT
Allen, Brady & Marsh [*British advertising agency*] ... ABM
Allen Cognitive Levels Test ... ACL
Allen County Law Library, Lima, OH [*Library symbol*] [*Library of Congress*] (LCLS) ... OLimaAL
Allen County Public Library, Fort Wayne, IN [*OCLC symbol*] (OCLC) ... IMF
Allen County Times, New Haven, IN [*Library symbol*] [*Library of Congress*] (LCLS) ... InNhvAT
Allen County-Fort Wayne Historical Society Library, Fort Wayne, IN [*Library symbol*] [*Library of Congress*] (LCLS) ... InFwAHi
Allen Group [*NYSE symbol*] (TTSB) ... ALN
[*The*] **Allen Group, Inc.** [*Associated Press*] (SAG) ... AllenGp
[*The*] **Allen Group, Inc.** [*NYSE symbol*] (SPSG) ... ALN
Allen Head (SAUS) ... AH
Allen Industries, Inc. (SAUO) ... ANL
Allen, KY [*FM radio station call letters*] ... WMDJ
Allen on Sheriffs [*A publication*] (DLA) ... All Sher
Allen Organ Cl'B' [*NASDAQ symbol*] (TTSB) ... AORGB
Allen Organ Co. [*Associated Press*] (SAG) ... AlnOrg
Allen Organ Co. (SAUO) ... AOR
Allen Organ Co. [*NASDAQ symbol*] (NQ) ... AORG
Allen Osborne Associates, Inc. (GEOI) ... ADA
Allen Parish Library, Oberlin, LA [*Library symbol*] [*Library of Congress*] (LCLS) ... LObA
Allen Park Public Library, Allen Park, MI [*Library symbol*] [*Library of Congress*] (LCLS) ... MiAp
Allen Products (SAUO) ... ALPO
Allen Telecom [*NYSE symbol*] (SG) ... ALN
Allen Township Consolidated Community School District 65, Ransom, IL [*Library symbol*] [*Library of Congress*] (LCLS) ... IRanASD
Allen University (SAUO) ... AU
Allen University, Columbia, SC [*Library symbol*] [*Library of Congress*] (LCLS) ... ScCoA
Allen Video-Enhanced Contrast [*Microscopy*] ... AVEC
Allen Video-Enhanced Differential Interference Contrast [*Microscopy*] ... AVEC DIC
Allen Vision Test [*Ophthalmology*] (DAVI) ... AVT
Allen-Bradley Company (SAUO) ... A-B
Allendale, MI [*FM radio station call letters*] ... WGVU
Allendale, SC [*Location identifier*] [*FAA*] (FAAL) ... ALD
Allendale, SC [*AM radio station call letters*] ... WDOG
Allendale, SC [*FM radio station call letters*] ... WDOG-FM
Allendale, SC [*Television station call letters*] ... WEBA
Allendale Township Library, Allendale, MI [*Library symbol*] [*Library of Congress*] (LCLS) ... MiAll
Allendale-Hampton-Jasper Regional Library, Allendale, SC [*Library symbol*] [*Library of Congress*] (LCLS) ... ScAl
Allendorf/Eder [*Germany*] [*ICAO location identifier*] (ICLI) ... EDFQ
Allenford Branch, Bruce County Public Library, Ontario [*Library symbol*] [*National Library of Canada*] (NLC) ... OALL
All-England Lawn Tennis Club (SAUO) ... AELTC
All-England Netball Association (SAUO) ... AENA
All-England Series ... AES
Allenmore Community Hospital, Tacoma, WA [*Library symbol*] [*Library of Congress*] (LCLS) ... WaTAC

Allens Creek [*Nuclear power plant*] (NRCH) ... AC
Allens Creek Nuclear Generating Station (NRCH) ... ACNGS
Allen's Massachusetts Reports [*A publication*] (DLA) ... All
Allen's Massachusetts Supreme Judicial Court Reports [*1861-67*] [*A publication*] (DLA) ... Allen
Allen's New Brunswick Reports [*Canada*] [*A publication*] (DLA) ... All
Allen's New Brunswick Reports [*Canada*] [*A publication*] (DLA) ... Allen
Allen's New Brunswick Reports [*Canada*] [*A publication*] (DLA) ... Allen NB
Allen's New Brunswick Reports [*Canada*] [*A publication*] (DLA) ... All NB
Allen's New Brunswick Reports [*Canada*] [*A publication*] (DLA) ... NBR All
Allen's Telegraph Cases [*A publication*] (DLA) ... Allen Tel Cas
Allen's Telegraph Cases [*A publication*] (DLA) ... All Tel Cas
Allen's Telegraph Cases [*A publication*] (DLA) ... Al Tel Ca
Allens Telegraph Cases (SAUS) ... Al Tel Ca
Allen's Washington Territory Reports [*1854-85*] [*A publication*] (DLA) ... Allen
Allen's Washington Territory Reports, New Series [*A publication*] (DLA) ... Wash Ter NS
Allens Washington Territory Reports, New Series (SAUS) ... Wash Ter NS
Allention Control Training (SAUS) ... ACT
Allentown [*Diocesan abbreviation*] [*Pennsylvania*] (TOCD) ... ALN
Allentown Borough Hall, Allentown, NJ [*Library symbol*] [*Library of Congress*] (LCLS) ... NjAlB
Allentown College of Saint Francis De Sales, Center Valley, PA [*OCLC symbol*] (OCLC) ... ALL
Allentown College of Saint Francis De Sales, Center Valley, PA [*Library symbol*] [*Library of Congress*] (LCLS) ... PCvA
Allentown Historical Society, Allentown, NJ [*Library symbol*] [*Library of Congress*] (LCLS) ... NjAlHi
Allentown, PA [*FAA*] [*Location identifier*] (FAAL) ... BXY
Allentown, PA [*AM radio station call letters*] ... WAEB
Allentown, PA [*FM radio station call letters*] ... WAEB-FM
Allentown, PA [*FM radio station call letters*] ... WDIY
Allentown, PA [*FM radio station call letters*] ... WFMZ
Allentown, PA [*Television station call letters*] (BROA) ... WFMZ-DT
Allentown, PA [*Television station call letters*] ... WFMZ-TV
Allentown, PA [*AM radio station call letters*] ... WHOL
Allentown, PA [*FM radio station call letters*] (RBYB) ... WJCS-FM
Allentown, PA [*AM radio station call letters*] (RBYB) ... WKAP
Allentown, PA [*Television station call letters*] ... WLVT
Allentown, PA [*FM radio station call letters*] ... WMUH
Allentown, PA [*AM radio station call letters*] ... WTKZ
Allentown Printing Service, Allentown, NJ [*Library symbol*] [*Library of Congress*] (LCLS) ... NjAlA
Allentown Public Library, Allentown, NJ [*Library symbol*] [*Library of Congress*] (LCLS) ... NjAl
Allentown Public Library, Allentown, PA [*OCLC symbol*] (OCLC) ... AYP
Allentown Public Library, Allentown, PA [*Library symbol*] [*Library of Congress*] (LCLS) ... PAt
Allentown State Hospital, Allentown, PA [*OCLC symbol*] (OCLC) ... PHL
Allentown/Bethlehem/Easton [*Pennsylvania*] [*Airport symbol*] ... ABE
Aller Ehren Ist Oesterreich Voll [*Austria Is Crowned with All Honor*] [*Variation of 15th-century inscription*] ... AEIOU
Aller Erst Ist Oesterreich Verdorben [*Variation of 15th-century inscription*] ... AEIOU
Allergan, Inc. [*NYSE symbol*] (SPSG) ... AGN
Allergan, Inc. [*Associated Press*] (SAG) ... Alergn
Allergan Ligand Retinoid Therapeutics [*Associated Press*] (SAG) ... AllLig
Allergan Ligand Retinoid Therapeutics [*NASDAQ symbol*] (SAG) ... ALRI
Allergan Ligand Retinoid (Unit) [*NASDAQ symbol*] (TTSB) ... ALRIZ
Allergen Challenge Test [*Medicine*] (DAVI) ... ACT
Allergen Tachyphylaxis [*Immunology*] ... AT
Allergenic Unit [*Medicine*] (DAVI) ... AU
Allergen-Induced Asthma [*Medicine*] (MELL) ... AIA
allergic (SAUS) ... alg
Allergic Angutis [*Medicine*] (MELL) ... AA
Allergic Asthma [*Medicine*] (MELL) ... A
Allergic Asthma [*Medicine*] (MELL) ... AA
Allergic Bronchopulmonary Aspergillosis [*Medicine*] ... ABA
Allergic Bronchopulmonary Aspergillosis [*Medicine*] ... ABPA
Allergic Conjunctivitis [*Ophthalmology*] ... AC
Allergic Contact Dermatitis [*Dermatology*] ... ACD
Allergic Disease ... AD
Allergic Drug Reaction (MELL) ... ADR
Allergic Eczematous Contact Dermatitis [*Dermatology*] (DMAA) ... AECD
Allergic Reaction [*Immunology*] ... AR
Allergic Respiratory Disease [*Medicine*] (MELL) ... ARD
Allergic Rhinitis [*Medicine*] ... AR
Allergic to Combat [*A play on the initialism for the Air Transport Command*] ... ATC
Allergic Vasculitis [*Medicine*] (MELL) ... AV
allergical (SAUS) ... alg
allergisch (SAUS) ... allerg
Allergist [*Medicine*] (DAVI) ... A
Allergist ... ALLRGST
Allergologist [*Medicine*] (DMAA) ... A
Allergro New Media, Inc. [*Associated Press*] (SAG) ... Allegro
Allergy ... A
Allergy (AAMN) ... ALL
Allergy (SAUS) ... All
Allergy ... ALLRGY
Allergy and Asthma Network/ Mothers of Asthmatics (SAUO) ... AANïMA
Allergy and Asthma Network/Mothers of Asthmatics (PAZ) ... AAN/MA
Allergy and Asthma Network/Mothers of Asthmatics (SAUS) ... AANïMA
Allergy & Clinical Immunology International (SAUS) ... ACI International
Allergy and Immunology (DMAA) ... A&I
Allergy and Immunology [*Medical specialty*] (DHSM) ... AI
Allergy Eczematous Contact Dermatitis (SAUS) ... AECD
Allergy Foundation of America [*Later, A & AFA*] ... AFA
Allergy Foundation of America (SAUO) ... AFA
Allergy, Immunology, and Transplantation Program [*NIH*] ... AITP
Allergy Immunotherapy [*Medicine*] (MELL) ... AIT
Allergy Index [*Medicine*] (DAVI) ... AI
Allergy Information Association [*Canada*] ... AIA
Allergy Infornation Association (SAUO) ... AIA
Allergy Relief Medicine [*Pharmacology*] (DAVI) ... ARM
Allergy Relief Medicine (SAUS) ... ARM
Allergy Society of South Africa (SAUO) ... ALLSA
Allergy to Latex Education and Resource Team (SAUO) ... ALERT
Allergy/Asthma Information Association ... AAIA
Allergy/Asthma Information Association of Canada (EA) ... AAIAC
Allergy-Suppressing Factor [*Medicine*] (DB) ... ASF
Allerton Public Library, Allerton, IA [*Library symbol*] [*Library of Congress*] (LCLS) ... IaAll
Allerton Public Library, Monticello, IL [*Library symbol*] [*Library of Congress*] (LCLS) ... IMont
Alles Erdreich Ist Oesterreich Unterthan [*Variation of 15th-century inscription*] ... AEIOU
Alles mit Gott [*Everything with God*] [*Motto of Georg Albrecht, Margrave of Brandenburg-Baireuth (1619-66)*] [*German*] ... AMG
Alles nach Gottes Willen [*Everything According to the Will of God*] [*Motto for a number of members of German and Bavarian royalty during the 16th and 17th centuries*] ... ANGW
All-Ethiopia Socialist League (SAUS) ... Meison
All-Ethiopia Trade Union (SAUO) ... AETU
Alley (WDAA) ... A
Alley (WGA) ... AL
Alley ... ALL
Alley [*Commonly used*] (OPSA) ... ALLEE
Alley [*Commonly used*] (OPSA) ... ALLY
Alley ... ALY
Alley Cat Allies [*An association*] (EA) ... ACA
Alleyne. Legal Decrees of Marriage [*1810*] [*A publication*] (DLA) ... All LD of Mar
Allgemaine Elektizitaetsgesellschaft [*Automotive industry supplier*] ... AEG
Allgemein [*General*] [*Music*] ... Allgem
Allgemeine Geschaftsbedingungen [*General Conditions of Contracts, Transactions, Etc.*] [*German*] (DLA) ... AGB
Allgemeine Geschaftsbedingungen [*General conditions of contracts, transactions, etc.*] [*German*] (ILCA) ... Allg Gesch Bed
Allgemeine Nahrungs und Genussmittel Ausstellung [*General Food and Delicacies Fair*] [*West Germany*] ... ANUGA
Allgemeine Unabhaengige Juedische Wochenzeitung (BJA) ... AUJW
Allgemeine Versicherungsbedingungen [*General conditions of insurance*] [*German*] (ILCA) ... Allg VersBed
Allgemeine Versicherungsbedingungen [*General conditions of insurance*] [*German*] (ILCA) ... AVB
Allgemeine Verwaltungsvorschrift [*or Vorschrift*] [*General Administrative Regulation*] [*German*] (ILCA) ... AV
Allgemeiner Deutscher Automobil Club [*German Automobile Association*] ... ADAC
Allgemeiner Deutscher Nachrichtendienst [*German General News Service*] [*Germany*] (EG) ... ADN
Allgemeiner Energie Verein (SAUS) ... AEV
Allgemeiner Variablenvektor (SAUS) ... x
Allgemeines Bucher-Lexikon [*A publication*] ... ABI
Allgemeines Buergerliches Gesetzbuch [*Austrian Civil Code*] (DLA) ... ABGB
Allgemeines Deutsches Handelsgesetzbuch von 1861 [*German commercial code*] (ILCA) ... ADHGB
Allgemeines Krankenhaus [*Austria*] [*Largest hospital in Europe*] ... AKH
Alliance [*Uganda*] [*FAA designator*] (FAAC) ... AFJ
Alliance [*Nebraska*] [*Airport symbol*] (OAG) ... AIA
Alliance ... ALLNCE
Alliance Against Fraud in Telemarketing (EA) ... AAFT
Alliance Against Intoxicated Motorists [*An association*] ... AAIM
Alliance Against Sexual Coercion (EA) ... AASC
Alliance All Market Advantage Fund, Inc. [*Associated Press*] (SAG) ... AlliAM
Alliance All Market Advantage Fund, Inc. [*Associated Press*] (SAG) ... AlliAMkt
Alliance All Market Advantage Fund, Inc. [*NYSE symbol*] (SAG) ... AMO
Alliance All-Mkt Adv Fd [*NYSE symbol*] (TTSB) ... AMO
Alliance and Dublin Consumers Gas Company (SAUO) ... A&DGC
Alliance Atlantis Communications [*Formerly, Alliance Communic. "B"*] [*NASDAQ symbol*] ... ALLIF
Alliance Atlantis Communic'B' [*NASDAQ symbol*] (SG) ... AACB
Alliance Balanced Shs: Cl.A [*Mutual fund ticker symbol*] (SG) ... CABNX
Alliance Balkanique [*Balkan Alliance*] ... AB
Alliance Bancorp New England [*AMEX symbol*] [*Formerly, Tolland Bank*] (SG) ... ANE
Alliance Biblique Universelle ... ABU
Alliance Cabinet Makers Association [*A union*] [*British*] ... ACMA
Alliance Canadienne des Responsables et Enseignants en Francais [*Canadian Association for the Teachers of French as a First Language*] (AC) ... ACREF
Alliance Cap Mgmt L.P. [*NYSE symbol*] (TTSB) ... AC
Alliance Capital Management LP [*NYSE symbol*] (SPSG) ... AC
Alliance Capital Management Ltd. [*Associated Press*] (SAG) ... AlnCap
Alliance Carpenters and Joiners Society [*A union*] [*British*] ... ACJS
Alliance Centriste et Democrate [*Algeria*] [*Political party*] (EY) ... ACD
Alliance College (SAUO) ... AC
Alliance College, Cambridge Springs, PA [*Library symbol*] [*Library of Congress*] (LCLS) ... PCamA
Alliance Communic 'B' [*NASDAQ symbol*] (TTSB) ... ALLIF
Alliance Communications Corp. [*Associated Press*] (SAG) ... AllCom

Alliance Communications Corp. [*NASDAQ symbol*] (SAG) .... ALLI
Alliance Co-Operative Internationale [*International Co-Operative Alliance*] (EAIO) .... ACI
Alliance Corporate Bond Ptfl. Cl.B [*Mutual fund ticker symbol*] (SG) .... CBFBX
Alliance de Baboma-Bateke du Kwamouth [*Alliance of Baboma-Bateke People of Kwamouth*] .... ABAKWA
Alliance de Jeunesse Angolaise pour la Liberte [*Alliance of Angolan Youth for Freedom*] .... AJEUNAL
Alliance de la Fonction Publique du Canada [*Public Service Alliance of Canada - PSAC*] .... AFPC
Alliance Defense Industry and Technology (NATG) .... ADIT
Alliance Democratique pour le Progres du Cameroun [*Political party*] (EY) .... ADPC
Alliance Democratique pour le Progres et l'Emancipation [*Cameroon*] [*Political party*] (EY) .... ADPE
Alliance Democratique Senegalaise [*Allied Democratic Party of Senegal*] [*Political party*] .... ADS
Alliance des Bahemba au Katanga [*Alliance of the Bahemba in Katanga*] [*Zaire*] .... ALLIBAKAT
Alliance des Bakongo [*Alliance of the Bakongo People*] .... ABAKO
Alliance des Bateke [*Alliance of Bateke*] .... ABATE
Alliance des Bayanzi [*Alliance of Bayanzis*] .... ABAZI
Alliance des Communautes Culturelles pour l'Egalite dans la Sante et les Services Sociaux (AC) .... ACCESS
Alliance des Independants [*Independent Party*] [*Switzerland*] [*Political party*] (PPE) .... AdI
Alliance des Jeunes pour le Socialisme [*Alliance of Youth for Socialism*] [*France*] [*Political party*] (PPE) .... AJS
Alliance des Moniteurs de Ski du Canada [*Canadian Ski Instructors' Alliance*] .... AMSC
Alliance des Patriotes Independents du Congo [*Alliance of Independent Patriots of the Congo*] .... APIC
Alliance des Pays Producteurs de Cacao [*Cocoa Producers' Alliance*] [*Use COPAL*] (AF) .... APC
Alliance des Professeures et Professeurs de Montreal (AC) .... APPM
Alliance des Proletaires Independents du Congo [*Alliance of Independent Proletarians of the Congo*] .... APIC
Alliance Entertainment Corp. [*Associated Press*] (SAG) .... AlnEnt
Alliance Entertainment Corp. [*NYSE symbol*] (SAG) .... CDS
Alliance Europeenne des Agences de Presse .... AEAP
Alliance for a Clean Rural Environment (EA) .... ACRE
Alliance for a Drug-Free Canada [*Alliance pour un Canada sans Drogues*] (AC) .... ADFC
Alliance for a Paving Moratorium (EA) .... APM
Alliance for Acid Rain Control (EA) .... AARC
Alliance for Aging Research (EA) .... AAR
Alliance for Alternative Health Care (SAUO) .... AAHC
Alliance for Alternatives in Healthcare (EA) .... AAH
Alliance For America (SAUO) .... AFA
Alliance for America [*An association*] (WPI) .... AFA
Alliance for Arts Education (EA) .... AAE
Alliance for Balanced Environmental Solutions [*Defunct*] (EA) .... ABES
Alliance for Best Clinical Practices in Dentistry (SAUO) .... ABCPD
Alliance for Canadian New Music Projects [*Alliance pour des Projets de Musique Canadienne Nouvell*] [*Also Contemporary Showcase*] (AC) .... ACNMP
Alliance for Cannabis Therapeutics (EA) .... ACT
Alliance for Cannabis Therapeutics (SAUS) .... AC-T
Alliance for Capital Access [*Defunct*] (EA) .... ACA
Alliance for Chemical Sciences & Technologies in Europe .... AllChemE
[*The*] **Alliance for Children & Television** [*The Children's Broadcast Institute*] (AC) .... ACT
Alliance for Clean Energy [*Defunct*] (EA) .... ACE
Alliance for Coal and Competitive Transportation .... ACCT
Alliance for Communities in Action (EA) .... ACA
Alliance for Community Media (NTPA) .... ACM
Alliance for Consumer Rights (EA) .... ACR
Alliance for Continuing Medical Education (NTPA) .... ACME
Alliance for Cultural Democracy (EA) .... ACD
Alliance for Democracy [*Malawi*] [*Political party*] (ECON) .... AFORD
Alliance for Democracy in Korea [*Defunct*] (EA) .... ADK
Alliance for Electronic Communications (SAUS) .... AAEC
Alliance for Engineering in Medicine and Biology [*Defunct*] (EA) .... AEMB
Alliance for Environmental Education (EA) .... AEE
Alliance for Environmental Education (GEOI) .... AEF
Alliance for Environmental Technology .... AET
Alliance for Fair Competition [*Falls Church, VA*] (EA) .... AFC
Alliance for Fire and Emergency Management (NTPA) .... AFEM
Alliance for Gay and Lesbian Artists in the Entertainment Industry [*Defunct*] (EA) .... AGLA
Alliance for Guidance of Rural Youth (SAUO) .... AGRY
Alliance for Healthcare Strategy and Marketing (NTPA) .... AHSM
Alliance for International Reforestation (SAUS) .... AIR
Alliance for Justice (EA) .... AJ
Alliance for Labor Action [*1968-1971*] .... ALA
Alliance for Leadership Development [*Defunct*] (EA) .... ALD
Alliance for Monetary Education (EA) .... AME
Alliance for Neighborhood Government [*Later, NAN*] (EA) .... ANG
Alliance for Opportunity [*Defunct*] (EA) .... AO
Alliance for Our Common Future (EA) .... AOCF
Alliance for Parental Involvement in Education (PAZ) .... ALLPIE
Alliance for Patriotic Re-Orientation and Construction [*Gambia*] [*Political party*] .... APRC
Alliance for Perinatal Research and Services (EA) .... APRS
Alliance for Philippine Concerns (EA) .... APC
Alliance for Photonic Technology (SAUS) .... APT
Alliance for Progress [*OAS*] .... AP
Alliance for Psychosocial Nursing (SAUO) .... APN
Alliance for Rail Commuter Progress [*Later, ARCP*] (EA) .... ARC
Alliance for Rehabilitative Medical Services (NTPA) .... ARMS
Alliance for Responsible CFC [*Chlorofluorocarbon*] **Policy** (EA) .... ARCFCP
Alliance for Simple, Equitable, and Rational Truck Taxation (EA) .... ASERTT
Alliance for Social Security and Disability Recipients (EA) .... ASSDR
Alliance for South Asian AIDS Prevention (AC) .... ASAP
Alliance for Strategic Token Ring Advancement a Leadership (SAUS) .... ASTRAL
Alliance for Strategic Token Ring Advancement and Leadership (SAUO) .... ASTRAL
Alliance for Technology Access .... ATA
Alliance for Telecommunications Industry Solutions [*Washington, DC*] (DDC) .... ATIS
Alliance for the Preservation of English in Canada .... APEC
Alliance for the Preservation of Religious Liberties (DICI) .... APRL
Alliance for the Prudent Use of Antibiotics (EA) .... APUA
Alliance for Traffic Safety (EA) .... ATS
Alliance for Transportation Research (SAUS) .... ATR
Alliance for Transportation Research (SAUS) .... ATRAP
Alliance for Undesirable but Necessary Tasks [*From book title, "The Woman from AUNT"*] .... AUNT
Alliance for Volunteerism [*Defunct*] (EA) .... AFV
Alliance Forest Prod [*NYSE symbol*] (SG) .... PFA
Alliance Francaise de New York [*Later, FIAF*] .... AFNY
Alliance Fund: Cl.A [*Mutual fund ticker symbol*] (SG) .... CHCLX
Alliance Gaming [*NASDAQ symbol*] (TTSB) .... ALLY
Alliance Gaming Corp. [*Associated Press*] (SAG) .... AlliGam
Alliance Gaming Corp. [*NASDAQ symbol*] (SAG) .... ALLY
Alliance Global Enviro Fd [*NYSE symbol*] (TTSB) .... AEF
Alliance Global Environmental Fund, Inc. [*NYSE symbol*] (SPSG) .... AEF
Alliance Global Environmental Fund, Inc. [*Associated Press*] (SAG) .... AllGIE
Alliance Global: Small Cap.Cl.A [*Mutual fund ticker symbol*] (SG) .... GSCAX
Alliance Global Strategic Income Trust Cl.A [*Mutual fund ticker symbol*] (SG) .... AGSAX
Alliance Graphique Internationale [*International League of Graphic Artists*] [*Zurich, Switzerland*] (EAIO) .... AGI
Alliance Growth & Income: Cl.A [*Mutual fund ticker symbol*] (SG) .... CABDX
Alliance Growth Fund Cl.B [*Mutual fund ticker symbol*] (SG) .... AGBBX
Alliance High Yield Cl.B [*Mutual fund ticker symbol*] (SG) .... AHHBX
Alliance Imaging [*NASDAQ symbol*] (TTSB) .... SCAN
Alliance Imaging, Inc. [*Associated Press*] (SAG) .... AllnImg
Alliance Imaging, Inc. [*NASDAQ symbol*] (SPSG) .... SCAN
Alliance International Cl.A [*Mutual fund ticker symbol*] (SG) .... ALIFX
Alliance Internationale de la Distribution par Cable [*International Alliance for Distribution by Cable*] (EAIO) .... AID
Alliance Internationale de la Distribution par Cable [*International Alliance for Distribution by Cable - IADC*] (EAIO) .... AIDC
Alliance Internationale de Tourisme [*International Touring Alliance*] (EAIO) .... AIT
Alliance Internationale des Femmes [*International Alliance of Women - IAW*] [*Valetta, Malta*] (EAIO) .... AIF
Alliance Internationale Jeanne d'Arc [*Saint Joan's International Alliance - SJIA*] (EAIO) .... AIJA
Alliance Internationale pour le Merite (EA) .... AIM
Alliance Israelite Universelle [*Universal Israelite Alliance*] .... AIU
Alliance Libre Europeenne [*European Free Alliance - EFA*] [*Political party*] [*Brussels, Belgium*] (EAIO) .... ALE
Alliance Missionnaire Evangelique [*Missionary Evangelical Alliance - MEA*] [*Renens, Switzerland*] (EAIO) .... AME
Alliance Muni Bond: Insur.Natl.Cl.A [*Mutual fund ticker symbol*] (SG) .... CABTX
Alliance Muni Bond: Natl. Cl.A [*Mutual fund ticker symbol*] (SG) .... ALTHX
Alliance Muni Income: Cal.Cl.A [*Mutual fund ticker symbol*] (SG) .... ALCAX
Alliance Muni Income: Insur.Cal.Cl.A [*Mutual fund ticker symbol*] (SG) .... BUICX
Alliance Muni Income: N.Y.Cl.A [*Mutual fund ticker symbol*] (SG) .... ALNYX
Alliance Nationale pour la Democratie et le Progres [*Haiti*] [*Political party*] (EY) .... ANDP
Alliance, NE [*Location identifier*] [*FAA*] (FAAL) .... AOQ
Alliance, NE [*FM radio station call letters*] .... KAAQ
Alliance, NE [*AM radio station call letters*] .... KCOW
Alliance, NE [*FM radio station call letters*] .... KPNY
Alliance, NE [*FM radio station call letters*] .... KTNE
Alliance, NE [*Television station call letters*] .... KTNE-TV
Alliance New Europe Fund (SAUS) .... ANE
Alliance New Europe Fund, Inc. [*Mutual fund ticker symbol*] (SG) .... ANEAX
Alliance North Amer. Govt. Inc. Cl.B [*Mutual fund ticker symbol*] (SG) .... ANABX
Alliance of American Insurers [*Schaumburg, IL*] (EA) .... AAI
Alliance of Associations for the Advancement of Education [*Defunct*] (EA) .... AAAE
Alliance of Atomic Veterans [*International Alliance of Atomic Vetrans*] [*Acronym is based on former name,*] (EA) .... IAAV
Alliance of Black Entertainment Technicians (NTPA) .... ABET
Alliance of British Clubs (EAIO) .... ABC
Alliance of Business Brokers and Intermediaries (NTPA) .... ABBI
Alliance of Business Consultants (COBU) .... ABC
Alliance of Canadian Cinema, Television & Radio Artists [*Alliance des Artistes Canadiens du Cinema, de la Television et de la Radio*] [*Formerly, Association of Canadian Television & Radio Artists*] (AC) .... ACTRA
Alliance of Canadian Regional Motion Picture Industry Associations .... ACRMPIA
Alliance of Canadian Travel Associations .... ACTA
Alliance of Canadian Travel Associations - Saskatchewan (AC) .... SATA
Alliance of Clinical Educators (SAUS) .... ACE
Alliance of Cooperatives for Rural Development (SAUO) .... ACORDSDR
Alliance of Female Owned Businesses Involved in Construction (EA) .... AFOBIC
Alliance of Free Democrats [*Hungary*] [*Political party*] (EY) .... AFD

Alliance of Free Democrats [*Hungary*] [*Political party*] ... SZDSZ
Alliance of Free Democrats (SAUS) ... SzDSz
Alliance of Gay Artists (EA) ... AGA
Alliance of Genetic Support Groups (EA) ... AGSG
Alliance of Independent Colleges of Art (EA) ... AICA
Alliance of Independent Retailers (EAIO) ... AIR
Alliance of Independent Telephone Unions [*Later, TIU*] (EA) ... AITU
Alliance of Independent Telephone Unions [*Later, TIU*] ... ATU
Alliance of Individual Grocers [*British*] (BI) ... AIG
Alliance of Information and Referral Systems (EA) ... AIRS
Alliance of Latin Artistes Society [*Defunct*] (EA) ... ALAS
Alliance of Manufacturing and Management Organizations (MHDB) ... AMMO
Alliance of Medical Internet Professionals (SAUO) ... AMIP
Alliance of Metalworking Industries (EA) ... AMI
Alliance of Minority Women for Business and Political Development (EA) ... AMWBPD
Alliance of Natives of Zombo [*Angola*] ... ALIAZO
Alliance of NGOs [*Nongovernmental Organizations*] **on Crime Prevention and Criminal Justice** (EA) ... ANCPCJ
Alliance of Nonprofit Mailers (EA) ... ANM
Alliance of Pan-American Round Tables (SAUO) ... APART
Alliance of Poles of America (EA) ... APA
Alliance of Progressive and Left-Wing Forces [*Greek*] (PPE) ... APLF
Alliance of Rail Citizens for Progress (EA) ... ARCP
Alliance of Reform Forces [*Macedonia*] [*Political party*] ... ARF
Alliance of Resident Theatres/New York (EA) ... ART/NY
Alliance of Retail Travel Agency Consortia (SAUO) ... ARTAC
Alliance of Small Firms and Self Employed People [*British*] (DBA) ... ASP
Alliance of Small Island States ... AOSIS
Alliance of State Aftermarket Associations ... ASAAA
Alliance of State Car and Truck Renting and Leasing Associations [*Defunct*] (EA) ... ASCTRLA
Alliance of States Supporting Indians in Science and Technology [*Montana State University*] ... ASSIST
Alliance of Telephone Unions (SAUS) ... ATU
Alliance of Television Film Producers [*Later, Association of Motion Picture andTelevision Producers*] (EA) ... ATFP
Alliance of the American Dental Association (EA) ... AADA
Alliance of Theatrical Stage Employees (SAUO) ... ATSE
Alliance of Transylvanian Saxons [*Cleveland, OH*] (EA) ... ATS
Alliance of Unitarian Women (SAUO) ... AUW
Alliance of Warehouses and Federations [*Defunct*] (EA) ... AWF
Alliance of Women Bikers (EA) ... AWB
Alliance of Women for Equality ... AWE
Alliance of Women in Architecture (EA) ... AWA
Alliance of Women Road Riders and Associates (EA) ... AWRRA
Alliance, OH [*AM radio station call letters*] ... WDPN
Alliance, OH [*Television station call letters*] ... WNEO
Alliance, OH [*FM radio station call letters*] ... WRMU
Alliance, OH [*FM radio station call letters*] ... WZKL
Alliance Oil Development (SAUO) ... AOD
Alliance Party [*Fiji*] [*Political party*] (EY) ... AP
Alliance Party of Northern Ireland [*Political party*] (EAIO) ... APNI
Alliance Pharmaceutical Corp. [*Associated Press*] (SAG) ... AlianPh
Alliance Pharmaceutical Corp. [*NASDAQ symbol*] (NQ) ... ALLP
Alliance Pharmaceuticals [*Associated Press*] (SAG) ... AlianPh
Alliance pour la Democratie au Mali - Parti Pan-Africain pour la Liberte, la Solidarite, et la Justice [*Political party*] (EY) ... ADEMA-PPLSJ
Alliance pour la Democratie et la Federation [*Burkina Faso*] [*Political party*] (EY) ... ADF
Alliance pour la Democratie et le Progres [*Benin*] [*Political party*] (EY) ... ADP
Alliance pour la Democratie et l'Emancipation Sociale [*Burkina Faso*] [*Political party*] (EY) ... ADES
Alliance pour la Social-Democratie [*Benin*] [*Political party*] (EY) ... ASD
Alliance pour l'Enfant et la Television [*The Children's Broadcast Institute*] (AC) ... AET
Alliance pour Une Mauritanie Democratique [*Alliance for One Democratic Mauritania*] (PD) ... AMD
Alliance Premier Growth Cl.B [*Mutual fund ticker symbol*] (SG) ... APGBX
Alliance Property and Construction [*Commercial firm*] [*British*] ... APC
Alliance Public Library, Alberta [*Library symbol*] [*National Library of Canada*] (NLC) ... AAL
Alliance Quasar Fund Cl.B [*Mutual fund ticker symbol*] (SG) ... QUABX
Alliance Reformee Mondiale [*World Alliance of Reformed Churches - WARC*] [*Geneva, Switzerland*] (EAIO) ... ARM
Alliance Republicaine pour les Libertes et le Progres [*Republican Alliance for Liberties and Progress*] [*France*] [*Political party*] (PPE) ... ARLP
Alliance Research Center [*Nuclear energy*] (NRCH) ... ARC
Alliance Resources Ltd. [*Vancouver Stock Exchange symbol*] ... ALE
Alliance Revolutionnaire Caraibe [*Guadeloupe*] [*Political party*] (EY) ... ARC
Alliance Semiconductor [*NASDAQ symbol*] (TTSB) ... ALSC
Alliance Semiconductor Corp. [*Associated Press*] (SAG) ... AlnSem
Alliance Semiconductor Corp. [*NASDAQ symbol*] (SAG) ... ALSC
Alliance Telecommunications Frequency Management Group [*Telecommunications service*] (TSSD) ... ATFMG
Alliance to End Childhood Lead Poisoning (PAZ) ... AECLP
Alliance to End Repression (EA) ... AER
Alliance to Fight Eating Disorders (SAUO) ... AFED
Alliance to Save Energy (EA) ... ASE
Alliance Universelle des Ouvriers Diamantaires [*Universal Alliance of Diamond Workers - UADW*] [*Antwerp, Belgium*] (EAIO) ... AUOD
Alliance Universelle des Unions Chretiennes de Jeunes Gens [*World Alliance of Young Men's Christian Associations*] ... UCJG
Alliance World Dollar Government Fund [*Associated Press*] (SAG) ... AllWrld
Alliance World Dollar Government Fund [*NYSE symbol*] (SPSG) ... AWF
Alliance World Dollar Government Fund [*NYSE symbol*] (SPSG) ... AWG
Alliance World Dollar Government Fund 2 [*Associated Press*] (SAG) ... AllWrld2
Alliance World Dollar Gvt Fd [*NYSE symbol*] (TTSB) ... AWG
Alliance World Dollar Gvt Fd II [*NYSE symbol*] (TTSB) ... AWF
Alliance World Fellowship (EA) ... AWF
Alliances for Minority Participation [*National Science Foundation*] ... AMP
Alliant Energy [*NYSE symbol*] (SG) ... LNT
Alliant Techsystems [*Associated Press*] (SAG) ... AllTch
Alliant Techsystems [*NYSE symbol*] (TTSB) ... ATK
Allied (SAUS) ... Al
Allied ... ALLD
Allied Administrative Publication [*NATO*] ... AAP
Allied Aerial Photographic Interpretation Unit [*Obsolete*] ... AAPIU
Allied African Economic Affairs Committee [*World War II*] ... AAEA
Allied Agencies Center, Peoria, IL [*Library symbol*] [*Library of Congress*] (LCLS) ... IPA
Allied Air Cooperation (SAUS) ... AAC
Allied Air Defense Ground Environment (MCD) ... AADGE
Allied Air Force Europe, Chaplaincy Consultative Committee (SAUO) ... AAFECCC
Allied Air Forces (SAUO) ... AAF
Allied Air Forces ... AAF
Allied Air Forces, Baltic Approaches [*NATO*] (NATG) ... AIRBALTAP
Allied Air Forces, Central Europe [*Later, AIRCENT*] [*NATO*] (MCD) ... AAFCE
Allied Air Forces, Central Europe [*Formerly, AAFCE*] [*NATO*] ... AIRCENT
Allied Air Forces in Italy [*World War II*] ... AAFI
Allied Air Forces, North Norway [*NATO*] (NATG) ... AIRNON
Allied Air Forces, Northern Europe [*Later, AIRNORTH*] [*NATO*] ... AAFNE
Allied Air Forces, Northern Europe [*Formerly, AAFNE*] [*NATO*] ... AIRNORTH
Allied Air Forces, Northern Norway (SAUS) ... AIRNON
Allied Air Forces, South Norway [*NATO*] (NATG) ... AIRSONOR
Allied Air Forces, South West Pacific Area [*NATO*] (ADA) ... AAFSWPA
Allied Air Forces, Southern Europe [*Later, AIRSOUTH*] [*NATO*] ... AAFSE
Allied Air Forces, Southern Europe [*Formerly, AAFSE*] [*NATO*] ... AIRSOUTH
Allied Air Forces Southern Europe (SAUO) ... AIRSOUTH
Allied Air Forces, Southern Norway (SAUS) ... AIRSONOR
Allied Air Forces Western Europe (SAUO) ... AAFWE
Allied Air Headquarters [*Obsolete*] ... AAHQ
Allied Air Intelligence Center ... AAIC
Allied Air Photograph Interpretation Unit (SAUS) ... AAPIU
Allied Air Support Command [*Mediterranean*] ... AASC
Allied Airborne Association (EA) ... AAA
Allied Airborne Association (EA) ... AABA
Allied and Alternative Medicine (ADWA) ... AMED
Allied Armies in Italy [*Obsolete*] ... AAI
Allied Army Procedures (NATG) ... AAP
Allied Army Publications (NATG) ... AAP
Allied Artists (SAUO) ... AA
Allied Artists of America (EA) ... AAA
Allied Artists of America, New York (SAUO) ... AAA
Allied Artists Pictures (SAUO) ... AAP
Allied Association of Bleachers, Dyers and Finishers (SAUO) ... AABDF
Allied Authorized Publication ... AAP
Allied Bank Capital, Inc. [*NASDAQ symbol*] (SAG) ... ABCI
Allied Bank Capital, Inc. [*Associated Press*] (SAG) ... AlBCap
Allied Bank Commission (SAUO) ... ABC
Allied Bank of Nigeria Ltd. ... ABN
Allied Banking Commission (SAUS) ... ABC
Allied Bankshares [*Associated Press*] (SAG) ... AlldBksh
Allied Bankshares (GA) [*NASDAQ symbol*] (TTSB) ... ABGA
Allied Bankshares, Inc. [*NASDAQ symbol*] (NQ) ... ABGA
Allied Bankshares, Inc. [*Associated Press*] (SAG) ... AlldBk
Allied Beauty Association (AC) ... ABA
Allied Board of Trade ... ABT
Allied Boating Association of Canada (AC) ... ABC
Allied Brewery Traders' Association [*British*] (DI) ... ABTA
Allied British-Canadian Army (SAUO) ... ABCA
Allied Business System Ltd. (SAUS) ... ABS
Allied Camouflage and Concealment Publication [*NATO*] (NATG) ... ACAMP
Allied Capital [*NASDAQ symbol*] (SG) ... ALLC
Allied Capital Advisers [*NASDAQ symbol*] (TTSB) ... ALLA
Allied Capital Advisers, Inc. [*Associated Press*] (SAG) ... AldCAdv
Allied Capital Advisers, Inc. [*NASDAQ symbol*] (SAG) ... ALLA
Allied Capital Commercial [*NASDAQ symbol*] (TTSB) ... ALCC
Allied Capital Commercial Corp. [*NASDAQ symbol*] (SAG) ... ALCC
Allied Capital Commercial Corp. [*Associated Press*] (SAG) ... AldCapC
Allied Capital Corp. [*NASDAQ symbol*] (SAG) ... ALLC
Allied Capital Corp. [*Associated Press*] (SAG) ... AlldCap
Allied Capital Corp II [*Associated Press*] (SAG) ... AldCaII
Allied Capital Corp II [*NASDAQ symbol*] (TTSB) ... ALII
Allied Capital Corp. II [*NASDAQ symbol*] (SAG) ... ALLI
Allied Capital Lending [*NASDAQ symbol*] (TTSB) ... ALCL
Allied Capital Lending Corp. [*NASDAQ symbol*] (SAG) ... ALCL
Allied Capital Lending Corp. [*Associated Press*] (SAG) ... AldCap
Allied Captured Intelligence Center [*US and Britain*] ... ACIC
Allied Cellular [*Vancouver Stock Exchange symbol*] ... ALY
Allied Central Air Bureau [*World War II*] ... ACAB
Allied Central Interpretation Unit [*World War II*] ... ACIU
Allied Central Mediterranean Force [*Later, AAI*] [*World War II*] ... ACMF
Allied Chemical & Dye Corporation (SAUO) ... A-C
Allied Chemical Corp. [*Later, Allied Corp.*] (MCD) ... ACC
Allied Chemical Corp., Fibers Division, Technical Center Library, Petersburg (SAUS) ... ViPetA
Allied Chemical Corp., Fibers Division, Technical Center Library, Petersburg, VA [*Library symbol*] [*Library of Congress*] (LCLS) ... ViPetA

Allied Chemical Corp., Library, Solvay, NY [*OCLC symbol*] (OCLC) ... ZUB
Allied Chemical Corporation (SAUO) ... ACC
Allied Chemical Corporation (SAUO) ... ACD
Allied Chemical Nuclear Services (SAUO) ... ACNS
Allied Chemical Technology [*Trademark*] ... ACT
Allied Chemicals (SAUS) ... AC
Allied Chief Commissioner [*World War II*] ... ACC
Allied Chiefs of Staff [*World War II*] ... ACS
Allied Citizens Representing Other New York Minorities ... ACRONYM
Allied Civil Affairs Office (SAUO) ... ACAO
Allied Civil Affairs Office [*World War II*] ... ACAO
Allied Civil Defense [*World War II*] ... ACD
Allied Civil Engineers (SAUO) ... ACE
Allied Collection Point [*World War II*] ... ACP
Allied Combat Operations Center (SAUO) ... ACOC
Allied Command (ACAE) ... AC
Allied Command and Control System (ACAE) ... ACCS
Allied Command, Atlantic (SAUO) ... ACA
Allied Command Atlantic (EAIO) ... ACA
Allied Command Atlantic [*NATO*] ... ACLANT
Allied Command Atlantic Frequency Allocation Panel [*Obsolete*] [*NATO*] (NATG) ... LANTFAP
Allied Command Atlantic Reporting System [*NATO*] (MCD) ... ACLANTREP
Allied Command Baltic Approaches (SAUO) ... ACBA
Allied Command Baltic Approaches [*NATO*] ... COMBALTAP
Allied Command Baltic Approaches Command Control and Information System (SAUO) ... ACBACCIS
Allied Command Channel [*NATO*] ... ACCHAN
Allied Command Channel Intelligence Plan [*NATO*] (NATG) ... CHIP
Allied Command Europe [*NATO*] ... ACE
Allied Command Europe [*NATO*] ... ACEUR
Allied Command Europe (SAUO) ... AE
Allied Command Europe [*ICAO designator*] (FAAC) ... ALF
Allied command europe ACCIS Implementation Strategy (SAUS) ... AAIS
Allied Command Europe Air Defence Ground Environment (SAUO) ... AADGE
Allied Command Europe Automated Command Control and Information System [*Proposed*] [*NATO*] ... ACE-ACCIS
Allied Command Europe Command Control Information System (CCCA) ... ACECCIS
Allied Command Europe Communication Management Organization (SAUO) ... ACMO
Allied Command Europe Communications Network [*NATO*] (NATG) ... ACENET
Allied Command Europe Report (AFM) ... ACEREP
Allied Command Europe Reporting System ... ACERS
Allied Command Europe Strike Command (SAUO) ... ACESTRIKE
Allied Command, North Norway (SAUS) ... ACNN
Allied Command Operations Center ... ACOC
Allied Command South East Asia (SAUS) ... ACSEA
Allied Command Southeast Asia [*World War II*] ... ACSEA
Allied Command South-East Asia (SAUO) ... ACSEA
Allied Commander-in-Chief [*World War II*] ... ACC
Allied Commander-in-Chief, Channel (MCD) ... CINCCHAN
Allied Commission [*World War II*] ... AC
Allied Commission, Agriculture Subcommission [*World War II*] ... ACAGR
Allied Commission, Austria [*World War II*] ... ACA
Allied Commission, Austria, British Element [*World War II*] ... ACABRIT
Allied Commission, Commerce Subcommission, Exports [*World War II*] ... ACCCE
Allied Commission, Economic Section [*World War II*] ... ACECO
Allied Commission for Austria (SAUO) ... ACA
Allied Commission, Industry Subcommission [*World War II*] ... ACIDY
Allied Commission, Military Government Subcommission [*World War II*] ... ACMG
Allied Commission, Mining Subcommission [*World War II*] ... ACMNG
Allied Commission on Reparations ... ACR
Allied Commission, Requisitions Subcommittee [*World War II*] ... ACREQ
Allied Communications and Computer Security Agency (SAUO) ... ACCSA
Allied Communications Procedures (SAUS) ... ACP
Allied Communications Publications [*Military*] ... ACP
Allied Communications Security Agency [*Brussels, Belgium*] [*NATO*] ... ACSA
Allied Communications Support Area ... ACSA
Allied Container Advisory Committee [*Obsolete*] ... ACAC
Allied Control Authority [*Allied German Occupation Forces*] ... ACA
Allied Control Authority for Germany (SAUO) ... ACAG
Allied Control Center [*NATO*] (NATG) ... ACC
Allied Control Commission [*World War II*] ... ACC
Allied Control Commission (British Element) (SAUO) ... ACC(BE)
Allied Control Commission for Austria [*World War II*] ... AACA
Allied Control Commission for Austria (SAUO) ... ACCA
Allied Control Commission for Bulgaria [*World War II*] ... AACB
Allied Control Commission for Hungary [*World War II*] ... AACH
Allied Control Commission for Italy [*World War II*] ... AACI
Allied Control Commission for Rumania [*World War II*] ... AACR
Allied Control Council [*World War II*] ... ACC
Allied Control Council for Germany [*World War II*] ... AACG
Allied Control Council for Germany (SAUO) ... ACCG
Allied Control Council for Japan [*World War II*] ... AACJ
Allied Corp. [*Initialism is trademark*] ... A-C
Allied Corp., Hopewell, VA [*Library symbol*] [*Library of Congress*] (LCLS) ... ViHopA
Allied Corp., Solvay Process Division, Syracuse, NY [*Library symbol*] [*Library of Congress*] (LCLS) ... NSyA
Allied Corp., Specialty Chemicals Division, Buffalo, NY [*Library symbol*] [*Library of Congress*] (LCLS) ... NBuA
Allied Council for Japan, Tokyo (SAUO) ... ACJ
Allied Data processing Publication (SAUS) ... ADATP
Allied Data Processing Publications (NATG) ... ADatP
Allied Data Publication (IUSS) ... ADATP
Allied Data Publications (SAUS) ... ADatP
Allied Data Sciences (SAUS) ... ADS
Allied Data System Interoperability Agency [*Brussels, Belgium*] [*NATO*] ... ADSIA
Allied Defense Initiative (ACAE) ... ADI
Allied Defense Publications (NATG) ... ADP
Allied Demands, Supplies [*World War II*] ... AD(S)
Allied Devices Corp. [*Associated Press*] (SAG) ... AldDevic
Allied Devices Corp. [*NASDAQ symbol*] (SAG) ... ALDV
Allied Digital Tech [*AMEX symbol*] (TTSB) ... ADK
Allied Digital Technologies [*Formerly, AMG Digital Technologies*] [*AMEX symbol*] (SAG) ... ADK
Allied Digital Technologies [*Formerly, AMG Digital Technologies*] [*Associated Press*] (SAG) ... AldD
Allied Digital Technologies [*Formerly, AMG Digital Tchnologies*] [*Associated Press*] (SAG) ... AlldDgtl
Allied Distribution [*An association*] (EA) ... AD
Allied Distribution (EA) ... ADI
Allied Electrical Industry Publications (SAUS) ... AEIP
Allied Electrical Publication [*Military*] ... AELP
Allied Electrical Publications (NATG) ... AEIP
Allied Electrical Publications (SAUS) ... AELP
Allied Electronics Publications (NATG) ... AEtP
Allied Engineering Publications (NATG) ... AEP
Allied Equipment Publications ... AEP
Allied Equipment Publications (NATG) ... AEqP
Allied Exercise Publications [*NATO*] ... AXP
Allied Expeditionary Air Force ... AEAF
Allied Expeditionary Force ... AEF
Allied Expeditionary Force Long Lines Control [*British military*] (DMA) ... AEFLLC
Allied Explosive Ordnance Disposal Publication (MCD) ... AEODP
Allied Explosive Ordnance Disposal Publications (NATG) ... AEoP
Allied Finance Adjusters Conference [*Greensboro, NC*] (EA) ... AFAC
Allied Financial Agency [*World War II*] ... AFA
Allied Fiscal Administration [*World War II*] ... AFA
Allied Forces (SAUO) ... AF
Allied Forces ... ALFOR
Allied Forces Baltic Approaches [*NATO*] (MCD) ... AFBALTAP
Allied Forces Baltic Approaches [*NATO*] ... BALTAP
Allied Forces Center (SAUS) ... AFCENT
Allied Forces Central Europe [*NATO*] (MCD) ... ACE
Allied Forces Central Europe [*NATO*] (MCD) ... AFCE
Allied Forces Central Europe [*NATO*] ... AFCENT
Allied Forces, Central Mediterranean (SAUO) ... MEDCENT
Allied Forces Europe (SAUO) ... AFE
Allied Forces Headquarters [*Might refer to any theater of war*] [*World War II*] ... AFHQ
Allied Forces Headquarters (Counter Intelligence Corps) [*World War II*] ... AFHQ (CIC)
Allied Forces Headquarters Petroleum Section [*World War II*] ... AFHQPS
Allied Forces Italy (SAUO) ... AFI
Allied Forces Local Resources Section [*World War II*] ... AFLRS
Allied Forces Mediterranean [*NATO*] ... AFMED
Allied Forces North Norway [*NATO*] (MCD) ... AFNON
Allied Forces Northern Europe [*NATO*] ... AFNE
Allied Forces Northern Europe [*NATO*] ... AFNORTH
Allied Forces, Northwest Europe (SAUS) ... AFNORTHWEST
Allied Forces Soroptimist Clubs (SAUO) ... AFSC
Allied Forces South Norway [*NATO*] (MCD) ... AFSONOR
Allied Forces Southern Europe [*NATO*] (NATG) ... AFSE
Allied Forces Southern Europe [*NATO*] ... AFSOUTH
Allied Forces, Southern Europe, Mediterranean East (SAUO) ... MEDEAST
Allied Forces, Southern Europe, Mediterranean North East (SAUO) ... MEDNOREAST
Allied Forces, Southern Europe, Mediterranean South East (SAUO) ... MEDSOUTHEAST
Allied Forces, Southern Europe, Mediterranean West (SAUO) ... MEDOC
Allied Forces Southern Norway (SAUS) ... SONOR
Allied Freighter Guard (NATG) ... AFG
Allied Friendship Travel Association (SAUO) ... Afta
Allied Fund for Capital Appreciation (SAUO) ... Afca
Allied General Nuclear Services (SAUO) ... AGNS
Allied Geographic Section [*Southwest Pacific*] [*Obsolete*] ... AGS
Allied Group [*NASDAQ symbol*] (SAG) ... ALGR
Allied Group [*Associated Press*] (SAG) ... AlliedGp
Allied Gulf Nuclear Services (SAUS) ... AGNS
Allied Hat Manufacturers Association (EA) ... AHMA
Allied Headquarters ... AHQ
Allied Health Professionals ... AHP
Allied Health Professions Admissions Test [*Admissions and selection test*] ... AHPAT
Allied Health Program [*Association of Independent Colleges and Schools specialization code*] ... AH
Allied Healthcare Prod [*NASDAQ symbol*] (SG) ... AHPI
Allied Healthcare Products, Inc. [*NASDAQ symbol*] (SAG) ... AHPI
Allied Healthcare Products, Inc. [*Associated Press*] (SAG) ... AldHlPd
Allied High Commission [*Germany*] (NATG) ... AHC
Allied High Commission for Germany (SAUO) ... AHCG
Allied High Control Commission for Germany (SAUO) ... HICOCOM
Allied Holdings [*NYSE symbol*] (SG) ... AHI
Allied Holdings [*NASDAQ symbol*] (TTSB) ... HAUL
Allied Holdings, Inc. [*Associated Press*] (SAG) ... AlldHldg
Allied Holdings, Inc. [*NASDAQ symbol*] (SAG) ... HAUL

Allied Home Health Association (SAUO) .... AHHA
Allied Hydrographic Publication [*NATO*] .... AHP
Allied Impex Corp. (EFIS) .... AIC
Allied Independent Unions [*Lebanon*] .... AIU
Allied Indian Metis Society [*Canada*] .... AIMS
Allied Information Service (SAUO) .... AIS
Allied Intelligence Bureau (ADA) .... AIB
Allied Intelligence Center (SAUO) .... AIC
Allied Intelligence Committee [*London*] .... AIC
Allied Intelligence Publication (SAUS) .... AIP
Allied Intelligence Publications [*NATO*] (NATG) .... AIP
Allied Interrogating Organization .... AIO
Allied Interrogation and Captured Documents Unit (SAUO) .... AICDU
Allied Interrogation Organization (SAUO) .... AIO
Allied Invasion Forces (SAUO) .... AIF
Allied Invasion Forces [*World War II*] .... AIF
Allied Irish Banks ADS [*NYSE symbol*] (SPSG) .... AIB
Allied Irish Banks Ltd. [*Associated Press*] (SAG) .... AldIrish
Allied Irish Banks PLC [*Associated Press*] (SAG) .... AldIrish
Allied Irish Banks PLC [*Associated Press*] (SAG) .... ALIrish
Allied Irish Investment Bank .... AIIB
Allied Kid Company (SAUO) .... AKD
Allied Kinetic Energy Recovery Rope [*Army*] (INF) .... AKERR
Allied Kommandantura (SAUS) .... AK
Allied Kommandantura Berlin (SAUO) .... AKB
Allied Kommandatura, (SAUO) .... AK
Allied Land Forces .... ALF
Allied Land Forces Central Europe [*NATO*] (NATG) .... ALFCE
Allied Land Forces Central Europe (SAUS) .... ALFCENT
Allied Land Forces Central Europe [*NATO*] .... LANDCENT
Allied Land Forces Denmark [*NATO*] .... LANDENMARK
Allied Land Forces North Norway [*NATO*] (NATG) .... LANDNON
Allied Land Forces, North Norway (SAUO) .... LANDNOR
Allied Land Forces Northern Europe [*NATO*] (NATG) .... LANDNORTH
Allied Land Forces Norway [*NATO*] .... LANDNORWAY
Allied Land Forces Schleswig-Holstein [*NATO*] (NATG) .... ALFSH
Allied Land Forces Schleswig-Holstein and Jutland [*NATO*] (NATG) .... LANDJUT
Allied Land Forces South East Europe (SAUO) .... ALFSEE
Allied Land Forces South Norway [*NATO*] (NATG) .... LANDSONOR
Allied Land Forces Southeast (SAUO) .... ALFSE
Allied Land Forces Southeast Asia [*NATO*] .... ALFSEA
Allied Land Forces Southeastern Europe [*NATO*] .... ALFSEE
Allied Land Forces Southeastern Europe [*NATO*] .... LANDSOUTHEAST
Allied Land Forces Southern Europe [*NATO*] .... ALFSE
Allied Land Forces Southern Europe [*NATO*] .... LANDSOUTH
Allied Land Forces Zealand [*NATO*] (NATG) .... LANDZEALAND
Allied Land Headquarters [*World War II*] .... LHQ
Allied Liaison and Protocol [*Military*] .... ALP
Allied Liaison Office [*Military*] .... ALO
Allied Life Financial [*Commercial firm*] [*Associated Press*] (SAG) .... AldLife
Allied Life Financial [*NASDAQ symbol*] (SAG) .... ALFC
Allied Linens and Domestics Association [*Defunct*] (EA) .... ALDA
Allied Logistic Publication (SAUS) .... ALP
Allied Logistics Publication [*Military*] .... ALP
Allied Longline Agency [*NATO*] .... ALLA
Allied Longline Agency Annual Conference [*NATO*] (NATG) .... AAC
Allied Maintenance Corporation (SAUO) .... ALM
Allied Maritime Air Commander-in-Chief, Channel .... CINCMAIRCHAN
Allied Masonic Degrees [*Freemasonry*] .... AMD
Allied Medical Group [*British*] .... AMG
Allied Medical Publications (NATG) .... AMed P
Allied Mediterranean Commission [*World War II*] .... AMC
Allied Meteorological Office (NATG) .... AMO
Allied Middle East Command (SAUO) .... AMEC
Allied Military Administration Civil Affairs Branch [*World War II*] .... AMACAB
Allied Military Communications Electronics Committee (SAUO) .... AMCEC
Allied Military Communications Panel .... AMCP
Allied Military Communications-Electronics Committee (AABC) .... AMCEC
Allied Military Financial Agency [*World War II*] .... AMFA
Allied Military Government [*of occupied territory*] [*Formerly, AMGOT*] [*Post-World War II*] .... AMG
Allied Military Government in Occupied Territories (SAUO) .... AMGOT
Allied Military Government of Occupied Territory [*Later, AMG*] [*Post-World War II*] .... AMGOT
Allied Military Government Venezia Giulia (SAUO) .... AMGVG
Allied Military Liaison [*Balkans*] [*World War II*] .... AML
Allied Military Liaison, Greece [*World War II*] .... AMLG
Allied Military Mission [*World War II*] .... AMM
Allied Military Security General (SAUS) .... AMSG
Allied Military Security Publication .... AMSP
Allied Military Staff Conference [*Quebec, Yalta, etc.*] [*World War II*] .... AMSC
Allied Mills, Inc. (SAUO) .... ADS
Allied Minimum Imports Program [*World War II*] .... AMIP
Allied Mining and Mine Countermeasures Publications [*NATO*] (NATG) .... AMP
Allied Mobile Force [*NATO*] .... AMF
Allied Mobile Force (Air) [*NATO*] .... AMF(A)
Allied Mobile Force (Land) [*NATO*] .... AMF(L)
Allied Naval Commander, Expeditionary Force (SAUS) .... ANCXF
Allied Naval Commander Expeditionary Forces .... ANCXF
Allied Naval Commander-in-Chief [*World War II*] .... ANC-in-C
Allied Naval Commander-in-Chief, Expeditionary Forces (SAUO) .... ANCXF
Allied Naval Communications Agency [*London, England*] [*NATO*] .... ANCA
Allied Naval Expeditionary Force [*British military*] (DMA) .... ANXF
Allied Naval Forces [*NATO*] .... ANF
Allied Naval Forces, Baltic Approaches [*NATO*] (NATG) .... NAVBALTAP
Allied Naval Forces Central Europe [*NATO*] .... ANFCE
Allied Naval Forces, Central Europe [*NATO*] .... NAVCENT
Allied Naval Forces, North Norway [*NATO*] (NATG) .... NAVNON
Allied Naval Forces, Northern Europe [*NATO*] .... NAVNORTH
Allied Naval Forces, Scandinavian Approaches [*NATO*] (NATG) .... NAVSCAP
Allied Naval Forces, South Norway (SAUS) .... NAVSONOR
Allied Naval Forces, Southern Europe [*NATO*] (NATG) .... NAVSOUTH
Allied Naval Maneuvering Instructions [*NATO*] (NATG) .... ANMI
Allied Navigation Publication (SAUS) .... ANP
Allied Navigation Publications [*NATO*] (NATG) .... ANP
Allied Non-Theatrical Film Association (AEBS) .... ANFA
Allied Nuclear Force (SAUO) .... ANF
Allied Nuclear Power Program [*Military*] (GFGA) .... ANPP
Allied Operational Center [*Military*] (IUSS) .... AOC
Allied Ordnance Publications (NATG) .... AOP
Allied Papers .... A/P
Allied Petroleum Service Organization .... APSO
Allied Pilots Association (EA) .... APA
Allied Political and Military Commission [*World War II*] .... APMC
Allied Political and Military Commission (SAUO) .... APMC
Allied Press Information Center [*NATO*] (NATG) .... APIC
Allied Printing Trades Council (DGA) .... APTC
Allied Procedural Publication (SAUS) .... APP
Allied Procedures Publications (NATG) .... APP
Allied Products [*NYSE symbol*] (TTSB) .... ADP
Allied Products Corp. [*NYSE symbol*] (SPSG) .... ADP
Allied Products Corp. [*Associated Press*] (SAG) .... AlldPd
Allied Provincial Securities [*British*] (ECON) .... APS
Allied Publication (RDA) .... AP
Allied Publications Board [*World War II*] .... APB
Allied Purchasing Co. (EA) .... APC
Allied Quality Assurance Provision [*NATO*] (MCD) .... AQAP
Allied Quality Assurance Publication [*NATO*] (NATG) .... AQAP
Allied Radio Frequency Agency (SAUO) .... AREA
Allied Radio Frequency Agency [*Formerly, ERFA*] [*Brussels, Belgium*] [*NATO*] .... ARFA
Allied Railway Supply Association [*Later, RSA*] .... ARSA
Allied Record Sales [*Record label*] .... Ald
Allied Record Sales [*Record label*] .... Alld
Allied Reliability and Maintainability Publication (MCD) .... ARMP
Allied Research Associates, Inc. [*Associated Press*] (SAG) .... AlldRsh
Allied Research Associates, Inc. (MCD) .... ARA
Allied Research Association, Inc. (SAUO) .... ARA
Allied Research Corp. [*AMEX symbol*] (SPSG) .... ALR
Allied Research Corp. (SAUO) .... ARAI
Allied Research Corp. International (SAUO) .... ARCI
Allied Research Corporation (SAUO) .... ARC
Allied Research Institute [*Later, Aluminum Recycling Association*] (EA) .... ARI
Allied Secretariat [*Allied German Occupation Forces*] .... ASEC
Allied Sector Operations Center [*NATO*] (MUSM) .... ASOC
Allied Signal - Kansas City Division (SAUO) .... AS-KCD
Allied Signal Aerospace Company (ACAE) .... ASAC
Allied Signal, Inc. [*Associated Press*] (SAG) .... Aldsignl
Allied Signal, Inc., Baltimore, MD [*Library symbol*] [*Library of Congress*] (LCLS) .... MdBASI
Allied Signal, Inc., Communications Diviaion, Baltimore, MD [*Library symbol*] [*Library of Congress*] (LCLS) .... MdBASI-C
Allied Signal Training Center [*NATO*] (IAA) .... ASTC
Allied Signals Training Centre (SAUO) .... ASTC
Allied Social Science Associations (EA) .... ASSA
Allied Staff, Berlin [*Post-World War II*] .... ASB
Allied Staff Chiefs [*World War II*] .... ASC
Allied Standard Avionics Architecture Council (SAUO) .... ASAAC
Allied Standing Procedure [*NATO*] (NATG) .... ASP
Allied States Association of Motion Picture Exhibitors [*Later, NATO*] .... ASAMPE
Allied Steel and Wire, Ltd. [*British*] .... ASW
Allied Stone Industries (EA) .... ASI
Allied Stores Corp. (SAUO) .... ALS
Allied Stores Corporation (SAUO) .... ASC
Allied Submarine Detection & Investigation Committee (SAUS) .... ASDIC
Allied Submarine Detection Investigation Committee (SAUO) .... ASDIC
Allied Supermarkets, Inc. (SAUO) .... ASU
Allied Supply Executive [*World War II*] .... ASE
Allied Supply Executive, China [*World War II*] .... ASE(C)
Allied Supply Executive, Chinese Oil Supplies [*World War II*] .... ASE(OC)
Allied Supply Executive, Middle East [*World War II*] .... ASE(ME)
Allied Supply Executive, Other Allies [*World War II*] .... ASE(OA)
Allied Supply Executive, Persian Gulf [*World War II*] .... ASE(PG)
Allied Supply Executive, Russia and Persian Gulf [*World War II*] .... ASE(R)
Allied Supply Executive, Transportation [*World War II*] .... ASE(T)
Allied Supreme Commander in Europe (SAUO) .... ASCE
Allied Supreme Commander in Europe (SAUS) .... ASCE
Allied Supreme Council (SAUO) .... ASC
Allied Supreme Council [*World War II*] .... ASC
Allied Tactical Air Force [*NATO*] .... ATAF
Allied Tactical Air Force, Northern Norway [*NATO*] .... TAFNORNOR
Allied Tactical Air Force, South Norway [*NATO*] (NATG) .... TAFSONOR
Allied Tactical Communications Agency [*Brussels, Belgium*] [*NATO*] (NATG) .... ATCA
Allied Tactical Data Systems Interoperability Agency [*NATO*] (NATG) .... ATADSIA
Allied Tactical Data Systems Interoperability Agency (SAUS) .... ATDSIA
Allied Tactical Operations Center [*Military*] .... ATOC
Allied Tactical Publication [*Army*] [*NATO*] .... ATP
Allied Tanker Coordinating Committee in London .... ATCC (L)
Allied Tanker Coordinating Committee in Washington .... ATCC (W)

Allied Task Force Commander, North Norway [*NATO*] (NATG) ATFCNN
Allied Task Force Commander Northern Norway (SAUO) ATFCNN
Allied Task Force, North Norway [*NATO*] (NATG) TASKFORNON
Allied Technical Publication [*Navy*] [*NATO*] ATP
Allied Telecommunications Committee [*Allied Control Commission for Italy*] ATC
Allied Telesyn International (SAUS) ATI
Allied Telesyn International Corp. ATI
Allied Textiles Companies [*British*] ATC
Allied Trades of the Banking Industry (SAUO) ATBI
Allied Training Publication (SAUS) ATrP
Allied Training Publications [*NATO*] (NATG) ATrP
Allied Translator and Interpreter Service ATIS
Allied Travel Office (NATG) ATO
Allied Underwear Association (EA) AUA
Allied Vehicle Testing Publication [*Army*] (RDA) AVTP
Allied Wartime Navigational Information System (SAUS) AWNIS
Allied Waste, Inc. [*NYSE symbol*] AW
Allied Waste Ind [*NYSE symbol*] (SG) AW
Allied Waste Ind [*NASDAQ symbol*] (TTSB) AWIN
Allied Waste Industries [*NASDAQ symbol*] (SPSG) AWIN
Allied Waste Industries, Inc. [*Associated Press*] (SAG) AldWste
Allied Weather Publications [*NATO*] (NATG) AWP
Allied Workers Association (SAUO) AWA
Allied Workers International Union (SAUO) AWIU
Allied Workers International Union (Independent) AWIU(I)
Allied Works Council [*World War II*] AWC
Allied Youth [*Later, AYFCC*] AY
Allied Youth and Family Counseling Center (EA) AYFCC
Allied-Lyons [*Toronto Stock Exchange symbol*] ALD
Allied/Neutral [*Military*] A/N
Allied-Signal Aerospace Service Corp. (SAUO) ASASCO
Allied-Signal, Inc. [*Toronto Stock Exchange symbol*] ACD
Allied-Signal, Inc. [*NYSE symbol*] (SPSG) ALD
Alligator Rivers Research Institute [*Australia*] ARRI
Alligatorweed Stunting Virus [*Plant pathology*] AWSV
All-Important Box Score [*Baseball term*] (NDBD) AIBS
All-Important Loss Column [*Baseball term*] (NDBD) AILC
Allin Communications Corp. [*Associated Press*] (SAG) AllinCm
Allin Communications Corp. [*NASDAQ symbol*] (SAG) ALLN
All-Inclusive Trust Deed [*Insurance*] AITD
All-India Anna Dravida Munnetra Kazhagam [*Political party*] (PPW) ADMK
All-India Anna Dravida Munnetra Kazhagam [*Tamil Nadu*] [*Political party*] AIADMK
All-India Bank Employeee Federation (SAUS) AIBEF
All-India Bank Employees Association (SAUS) AIBEA
All-India Confederation of Bank Officers Organisations (SAUO) AICOBO
All-India Congress Committee AICC
All-India Coordinated Millet Improvement Programme AICMIP
All-India Federation of Electricity Employees AIFEE
All-India Federation of University and College Teachers Organization (SAUO) AIFUCTO
All-India Institute of Medial Sciences AIMS
All-India Insurance Employees' Association AIIEA
All-India International Corporation (SAUO) AIIC
All-India Jute Textile Workers' Federation AIJWF
All-India Port and Dock Workers' Federation AIPDWF
All-India Radio AIR
All-India Railwaymen's Federation AIRF
All-India Sikh Students Federation (SAUO) AISSF
All-India Trade Union Congress AITUC
All-India Trade Union Congress (SAUO) ALTUC
All-Industrial (or Industry) Research Advisory Council (SAUO) AIRAC
All-Industrial Research Advisory Council (SAUS) AIRAC
All-Industry Electronics Conference AIEC
All-Industry Radio Music Licensing Committee (NTCM) AIRMLC
All-Industry Research Advisory Council [*Later, IRC*] (EA) AIRAC
All'Ingrosso [*wholesale*] [*Italian*] (ODBW) all'ingr
All-in-One Business Contactbook [*A publication*] ABC
Allinson's Pennsylvania Superior and District Court Reports [*A publication*] (DLA) Allin
Allinson's Pennsylvania Superior and District Court Reports [*A publication*] (DLA) Allinson
All-Ireland Distress (DI) AID
Allis-Chalmers Corp. AC
Allis-Chalmers Corp. (SAUO) AH
Allis-Chalmers Critical Experimental Facility AC-CEF
Allis-Chalmers Mfg. Co. (SAUO) A-C
Allis-Chalmers Power System Inc. (SAUO) A-CPSI
Allison Gas Turbine [*Engine*] AGT
Allison Smith Fan Club (EA) ASFC
Allison Transmission Electronic Control [*Detroit Diesel Allison*] ATEC
Allison's American Dictionary [*A publication*] (DLA) Allison's Am Dict
Alliston Memorial Public Library, Ontario [*Library symbol*] [*National Library of Canada*] (BIB) OAL
Alliston Procedure [*Medicine*] (MELL) AP
Alliston Public Library, Alliston, ON, Canada [*Library symbol*] [*Library of Congress*] (LCLS) CaOAL
alliterative (SAUS) allit
All-Japan Cotton Spinners Association (SAUO) AJCSA
All-Japanese Districts (SAUS) AJD
All-Language Services, Inc. ALS
All-Logic Level (SAUS) ALL
Allmaenna Svenska Electriska Aktiebolaget (SAUS) ASEA
Allmerica Financial [*NYSE symbol*] (TTSB) AFC
Allmerica Financial Corp. [*NYSE symbol*] (SAG) AFC
Allmerica Financial Corp. [*Associated Press*] (SAG) AllmrFn
Allmerica Prop & Cas Cos. [*NYSE symbol*] (TTSB) APY
Allmerica Property & Casualty [*Associated Press*] (SAG) AllmerPr
Allmerica Property & Casualty [*NYSE symbol*] (SAG) APY
Allmerica Sec Tr [*NYSE symbol*] (TTSB) ALM
Allmerica Securities Trust [*Formerly, State Mutual Securities Trust*] [*Associated Press*] (SAG) AllmrST
Allmerica Securities Trust [*Formerly, State Mutual Securities Trust*] [*NYSE symbol*] (SAG) ALM
Allmerican Financial Corp. [*Associated Press*] (SAG) AllmrFn
All-Movie Guide (SAUS) AMG
All-Music Guide (SAUS) AMG
Allnat. Law of Partition [*1820*] [*A publication*] (DLA) Alln Part
Allnat on Wills [*A publication*] (DLA) Alln Wills
All-Navy Message ALNAV
Allnet Communication Services, Inc. (EFIS) ALC
All-North Resources Ltd. [*Vancouver Stock Exchange symbol*] ANH
Allo-Activated Killer [*Medicine*] (DMAA) AAK
Allocable Installment Indebtedness (MHDB) AII
Allocate ALLCT
Allocate [*or Allocation*] (AFM) ALLOC
Allocate [*or Allocation*] (AABC) ALOC
Allocate Control Block (SAUS) ACB
Allocate on Demand [*Computer science*] (BYTE) AOD
Allocate to Order (SAUS) ATO
Allocated ALLOT
Allocated Baseline (MCD) ABL
Allocated Configuration Audit (MCD) ACA
Allocated Configuration Documentation (AAGC) ACD
Allocated Configuration Identification [*NASA*] (KSC) ACI
Allocated Configuration Item [*Navy*] ACI
Allocated Configuration Management [*NASA*] (NASA) ACM
Allocated Prime Costs (SAUS) APC
Allocated Queue Element (SAUS) AQE
Allocated Reserve AR
Allocated Transfer Risk Reserve [*Banking*] ATRR
Allocation ALLCTN
Allocation and Control Through Identification of Ongoing Situations (SAUS) ACTIONS
Allocation Assessment and Analysis [*Report*] AAA
Allocation Carry (SAUS) AC
Allocation Counter [*Computer science*] (IAA) AC
Allocation Engineering Division (SAUO) AED
Allocation Engineering Division (ACAE) AET
Allocation Register (SAUS) AR
Allocation Strategy Module (IAA) ASM
Allocation Voucher (SAUS) AV
Allocations (SAUS) ALC
Allocations for Budgetary Control ABC
Allocator A
Allogeneic Effect Factor [*Immunochemistry*] AEF
Allograft-Bound Lymphocytes [*Biochemistry*] (DAVI) ABL
Alloisoleucine (ADWA) alle
allonym (SAUS) allo
Allophone (SAUS) ALLOP
Allophycocyanin [*Also, APC*] [*Biochemistry*] AP
Allophycocyanin [*Also, AP*] [*Biochemistry*] APC
All-Optic Towed Array (SAUS) AOTA
All-Optical Towed-Array SONAR [*Navy*] (DOMA) AOTA
Allopurinol Phosphate [*Biochemistry*] APP
Allopurinol Phosphate Ribonucleotide [*Biochemistry*] APPR
All-Ordnance Destruct System AODS
All-Ordnance Thrust Termination (KSC) AOTT
Allorhythmia [*Medicine*] (MELL) ALL
Allos Therapeutics [*NASDAQ symbol*] (SG) ALTH
Allosteric [*Biochemistry*] AI
Alloted (SAUS) ALLOT
Alloted (SAUS) Altd
Allotetrahydrocortisol [*Organic chemistry*] (DAVI) ATHC
Allotetrahydrocortisol (SAUS) ATHE
Allotment (SAUS) ALMT
Allotment (AABC) ALOT
Allotment (AFM) ALOTM
Allotment (DNAB) ALOTMT
Allotment Advice (FAAC) ADVALT
Allotment Division [*Navy*] NAVALOT
Allotment Gardens (WDAA) Allot Gdns
Allotment Key (SAUS) AK
Allotment Serial Number (AFM) ASN
Allotment-of-Probability Shares (PDAA) APS
All'Ottava [*At the Octave*] [*Music*] ALL'OTT
All'Ottava [*At the Octave*] [*Music*] All'Ova
Allotted (SAUS) ALOT
Allotter Switch (SAUS) AS
Allou Health & Beauty Care ALU
Allou Health & Beauty Care, Inc. [*Associated Press*] (SAG) AllouH
Allou Health & Beauty Care, Inc. [*AMEX symbol*] (SPSG) ALU
Allou Health&Beauty'A' [*AMEX symbol*] (TTSB) ALU
Allouez, WI [*FM radio station call letters*] (RBYB) WJLW-FM
All-Over Good (IIA) AOG
Allow Enable Intercept [*Military*] (CAAL) AEI
Allowable (SAUS) ALLOW
Allowable Biological Catch ABC
Allowable Cabin Load [*in an aircraft*] ACL

Allowable Cargo Load [*Air Force*] (AFIT) .... ACL
Allowable Cleanliness Level [*Industrial maintenance and engineering*] .... ACL
Allowable Container Load [*in an aircraft*] (NASA) .... ACL
Allowable Cost (OICC) .... AC
Allowable Daily Intake [*Toxicology*] .... ADI
Allowable Deficiency (MCD) .... AD
Allowable Expense Level [*Department of Housing and Urban Development*] (GFGA) .... AEL
Allowable [*Takeoff*] Gross Weight [*for an aircraft*] .... AGW
Allowable Gross Weight (SAUS) .... AGW
Allowable Lead Angle (ACAE) .... ALA
Allowable Limit of Intake (ABAC) .... ALI
Allowable Limits of Error (MELL) .... ALE
Allowable Outage Time [*Environmental science*] (COE) .... AOT
Allowable Sale Quantity (WPI) .... ASQ
Allowable Ship Turn .... AST
Allowable Steering Error .... ASE
Allowable Supply List [*Military*] (DOMA) .... ASL
Allowable Takeoff Gross [*Weight*] [*for an aircraft*] .... ATOG
Allowable Take-Off Gross Weight (SAUS) .... ATOG Weight
Allowable Utilities Consumption Level [*Department of Housing and Urban Development*] (GFGA) .... AUCL
Allowance (ROG) .... ALLCE
Allowance .... ALLOW
Allowance (AFM) .... ALW
Allowance (ADWA) .... alw
Allowance Appendix Package .... AAPG
Allowance Appendix Page .... AAP
Allowance Change Request .... ACR
Allowance Change Request-Fixed (IUSS) .... ACR-F
Allowance Components List (IUSS) .... ACL
Allowance Equipage List .... AEL
Allowance for Funds Used during Construction .... AFUDC
Allowance for Loan and Lease Losses (TDOB) .... ALLI
Allowance for Program Adjustment (SAUS) .... APA
Allowance for Project Adjustment .... APA
Allowance Holder [*Environmental Protection Agency*] (GFGA) .... AH
Allowance Holder Monthly [*Environmental Protection Agency*] (GFGA) .... AHM
Allowance in Lieu of Overtime .... AILOT
Allowance Item Code .... AIC
Allowance List .... AL
Allowance Load List (AFIT) .... ALL
Allowance Officer Desk Code (DNAB) .... AODC
Allowance Override Requirement (CAAL) .... AOR
Allowance Parts List .... APL
Allowance Parts List Master Index (MCD) .... APLMI
Allowance Parts List/Component Identification Number .... APL/CID
Allowance Prescribed in Joint Travel Regulation (SAUS) .... AJTR
Allowance Prescribed in Joint Travel Regulations [*Military*] (AABC) .... AJTR
Allowance Quality (DNAB) .... AQTY
Allowance Quantity (IUSS) .... AQ
Allowance Race [*Horse racing*] .... ALW
Allowance Regulations (SAUS) .... AR
Allowance Requirement Register (MCD) .... ARR
Allowance Source Code [*Military*] (AFM) .... ASC
Allowance Summary Code .... ASC
Allowance Support Code (IUSS) .... ASC
Allowance Tracking System [*Environmental science*] (EPAT) .... ATS
Allowance Type [*Military*] (AFIT) .... A/T
Allowances (SAUS) .... ALWS
Allowed .... ALLD
Allowed Cell Rate (SAUS) .... ACR
Allowed Failure Effect .... AFE
Allowed Off Aircraft Time (SAUS) .... AOAT
Allowed Off-Engine Time (AFIT) .... AOET
Allowed-Off Aircraft Time .... AOAT
Alloxazine Adenine Dinucleotide [*Biochemistry*] .... AAD
Alloxazine Mononucleotide [*Pharmacology*] .... AMN
Alloy .... ALLY
Alloy (VRA) .... aly
Alloy .... ALY
Alloy Bulk Diffusion (IAA) .... ABD
Alloy Bulk Diffusion Transistor (SAUS) .... ABD Transistor
Alloy Casting Institute [*Later, SFSA*] (EA) .... ACI
Alloy Casting Institute (SAUO) .... ACI
Alloy Container [*Shipping*] (DCTA) .... A
Alloy Data Center [*National Institute of Standards and Technology*] .... ADC
Alloy Development for Irradiation Performance (MCD) .... ADIP
Alloy Diffused (IAA) .... AD
Alloy Junction .... AJ
Alloy Phase Diagram .... APD
Alloy Products Corporation (SAUO) .... APC
Alloy Restoration [*Medicine*] (DMAA) .... AR
Alloy Semiconductor (SAUS) .... AlGaAs
Alloy Semiconductor (SAUS) .... InGaAs
Alloy Semiconductor (SAUS) .... InGaP
Alloy Steel (IAA) .... AS
Alloy Test (SAUS) .... MOTA-IC
Alloy Undercooling Experiment (SAUS) .... AUE
Alloy-Coated Aluminum (KSC) .... ALCAL
Alloy-Diffused (SAUS) .... AD
Alloyed Diffused Transistor (SAUS) .... ADTRANSISTOR
Alloyed Nickel Cobalt Steel (SAUS) .... ALNICO
Alloyed Zinc Sheet .... AZS
Alloys Index [*METADEX*] (NITA) .... AI

Alloy-Steel Protective Plating .... ASPP
Alloy-Tin Couple (SAUS) .... ATC
All-Party Hill Leaders' Conference [*India*] [*Political party*] (PPW) .... APHLC
All-Party Parliamentary Committee for the Release of Soviet Jewry (EAIO) .... PCSJ
All-Pass Error Spectrum Shaping Quantizer (SAUS) .... AP-ESSQ
All-Pass Loop (SAUS) .... APL
All-People's Congress [*Sierra Leone*] [*Political party*] (PPW) .... APC
Allport-Vernon [*Psychology*] (BARN) .... AV
Allport-Vernon-Lindzey [*Study of values*] .... AVL
All-Purpose .... AP
All-purpose Ballastable Crawler (SAUS) .... ABC
All-purpose Battle Computer (SAUS) .... ABC
All-Purpose Communications System .... ALPURCOMS
All-Purpose Decontaminant (MCD) .... APD
All-Purpose Electronic Computer (IEEE) .... APEC
All-Purpose Interface [*Computer science*] (HGAA) .... API
All-purpose Lightweight Carrying Equipment (SAUS) .... ALICE
All-Purpose Lightweight Individual Carrying Equipment [*Army*] (RDA) .... ALICE
All-Purpose Lightweight Individual Carrying Equipment (SAUS) .... ALICE
All-Purpose Lightweight Individual Carrying Equipment [*Army*] .... ALICW
All-Purpose Linotype (DGA) .... APL
All-Purpose Rocket for Collecting Atmospheric Samples (SAUS) .... ARCAS
All-Purpose Rocket for Collecting Atmospheric Soundings [*Navy*] (IAA) .... APRCAS
All-Purpose Rocket for Collecting Atmospheric Soundings [*Navy*] .... ARCAS
All-Purpose Terminal [*Computer technology*] .... APT
All-Purpose Ticket Issuing System (PDAA) .... APTIS
All-Purpose Tween [*Microorganism growth medium*] .... APT
All-Purpose Vehicle [*Automotive engineering*] .... APV
All-Radio Methodology Study [*Audience ratings*] (NTCM) .... ARMS
Allred Interaction Analysis (SAUS) .... AIA
All-Reflecting Schmidt Telescope (PDAA) .... ARST
All-Round Defense (SAUS) .... AR Def
All-Round Fire (SAUS) .... ARF
All-Round Thermal Surveillance (SAUS) .... ARTS
All-Russia Research Institute of Marine Fisheries and Oceanography (SAUS) .... VNIRO
All-Russian Cooperative Society [*English equivalent of AMTORG*] .... ARCOS
All-Russian Institute of Hydrometeorological Information-World Data Center (SAUS) .... VNIIGMI-MCD
All-Russian Monarchist Front [*Defunct*] (EA) .... ARMF
All-Russian Radiotechnical Institute (SAUS) .... VNIIFTRI
All-Russian Research Institute of Ocean Geology (SAUS) .... VNIIO
All-Russian Scientific Research Institute of Drilling Technology (SAUS) .... VNIIBT
All-Russian Scientific Research Institute of Marine Fisheries and Oceanography (SAUS) .... VNIRO
All's Well That Ends Well [*Shakespearean work*] .... AWW
Allscripts, Inc. [*NASDAQ symbol*] (SG) .... MDRX
All-Season .... AS
All-Season Performance .... ASP
All-Season Touring .... AST
All-Seems-Well Signal (SAUS) .... ASWSignal
All-Service Close Air Support [*Military*] .... ASCAS
All-Services Evaluation Group [*Military*] .... ASEG
All-Sky Camera .... ASC
All-Sky Imaging Photometer .... ASIP
All-Sky Monitor [*Optics*] .... ASM
Allsopp, Morgan Engineering Ltd., Edmonton, AB, Canada [*Library symbol*] [*Library of Congress*] (LCLS) .... CaAEAME
Allsopp, Morgan Engineering Ltd., Edmonton, Alberta [*Library symbol*] [*National Library of Canada*] (NLC) .... AEAME
All-Source Imagery Processing System [*Marine Corps*] (IUSS) .... ASIP
All-Source Production [*Army*] (ADDR) .... ASP
All-Source Production Section [*Army*] (ADDR) .... ASPS
Allstar Inns Ltd. (SAUS) .... SAI
Allstar Systems [*NASDAQ symbol*] (SG) .... ALLS
Allstate Corp. [*NYSE symbol*] (SPSG) .... ALL
Allstate Corp. [*Associated Press*] (SAG) Allst98
Allstate Corp. [*Associated Press*] (SAG) .... Allstate
Allstate Corp. [*NYSE symbol*] (SAG) .... PME
Allstate Cp 6.76% Exch Nts '98 [*NYSE symbol*] (TTSB) .... PME
Allstate Financial [*NASDAQ symbol*] (TTSB) .... ASFN
Allstate Financial Corp. [*Associated Press*] (SAG) .... AllstFn
Allstate Financial Corp. [*NASDAQ symbol*] (NQ) .... ASFN
Allstate Insurance Co., Barrington, IL [*Library symbol*] [*Library of Congress*] (LCLS) .... IBarAS
Allstate Insurance, Inc., Corporate Library, Northbrook, IL [*Library symbol*] [*Library of Congress*] (LCLS) .... INbAS
Allstates-Programming and Systems Incorporated (SAUO) .... APSI
All-Steel Equipment, Inc. .... ASE
Allstrom (SAUS) .... DC/AC
Allted Air Forces (SAUS) .... AAF
ALLTEL Corp. [*Formerly, Allied Telephone Co.*] [*Associated Press*] (SAG) .... Alltel
ALLTEL Corp. [*Formerly, Allied Telephone Co.*] [*NYSE symbol*] (SPSG) .... AT
ALLTEL Corp. $2.06 Cv Pfd [*NYSE symbol*] (TTSB) .... ATPr
Allternating Light (SAUS) .... AltLt
All-Terrain All Climate (SAUS) .... ATAC
All-Terrain All-Purpose Cart [*Military*] (INF) .... ATAC
All-Terrain Amphibious Carrier (SAUS) .... ATAC
All-Terrain Bike .... ATB
All-Terrain Carrier [*Roscoe Brown Corp.*] .... ATC
All-Terrain Cycle .... ATC
All-Terrain Lightweight Articulating Suspension .... ATLAS

All-Terrain Mobile Platform .... ATMP
All-Terrain Racing Association (EA) .... ATRA
All-Terrain Remote Control Vehicle (MCD) .... ATRCV
All-Through Training School (SAUO) .... ATTS
All-Through Training School (SAUS) .... ATTS
All-to-All Broadcast (SAUS) .... AAB
All-to-All Scatter (SAUS) .... AAS
Alltransport International Group .... AIG
All-Trans-Retinoc Acid [*Medicine*] .... ATRA
All-Trans-Retinylester .... atRY
Alltrista Corp. [*NYSE symbol*] (SG) .... ALC
Alltrista Corp. [*Associated Press*] (SAG) .... Alltrista
Alltrista Corp. [*NASDAQ symbol*] (SAG) .... JARS
All-Ukrainian Evangelical Baptist Fellowship (EA) .... AUEBF
All-Union Central Council of Trade Unions (SAUO) .... ACCTU
All-Union Central Scientific Research Laboratory for the Restoration of Valuable Works of Art in Museums (SAUO) .... AUCSRLFRVWAM
All-Union Council of Trade Unions (SAUO) .... AUCTU
All-Union State Library of Foreign Literature (SAUO) .... AUSLFL
All-Up-Round (SAUS) .... AUR
Allure Industries Corp. [*Vancouver Stock Exchange symbol*] .... ARU
Allusion .... ALLUS
Allusion (ADWA) .... allus
alluvial (SAUS) .... alluv
alluvium (SAUS) .... alluv
All-Valence-Electron (DB) .... AVE
All-Volunteer Force [*Army*] .... AVF
All-Volunteer Force Program Action Request [*Military*] (DNAB) .... AVF/PAR
All-Volunteer Army (SAUO) .... A-V A
Allwaste, Inc. [*Associated Press*] (SAG) .... Allwaste
Allwaste, Inc. [*NYSE symbol*] (SAG) .... ALW
Allwe [*Former USSR*] [*FAA designator*] (FAAC) .... LWE
All-Weather [*As applied to fighter aircraft, etc.*] .... AW
Allweather (SAUS) .... A/W
All-Weather Aerial Delivery System (SAUS) .... AWADS
All-Weather Air Delivery System (SAA) .... AWADS
All-Weather Airborne Reconnaissance System (SAUS) .... AWARS
All-Weather Aircraft [*Air Force*] (NATG) .... AWX
All-Weather Aircraft Guided Missile (MCD) .... AWAG
All-Weather Air-to-Air Missile (MCD) .... AWAAM
All-Weather Attack .... AWA
All-Weather Attack Avionics System (MCD) .... AWAAS
All-Weather Attack Squadron (SAUO) .... AWATKRON
All-Weather Carrier Landing System [*Navy*] .... ACLS
All-Weather Carrier Landing System [*Navy*] .... AWCLS
All-Weather Chassis Dynamometer (PDAA) .... AWCD
All-Weather Electronics .... AWE
All-Weather Fighter (SAUS) .... AWF
All-Weather Fighter .... AWX(F)
All-Weather Fighter Squadron (SAUO) .... AWFS
All-Weather Flare .... AWF
All-Weather Ground Surveillance RADAR .... AGSR
All-Weather Guidance (MCD) .... AWG
All-Weather Identification Sensor .... AWIS
All-Weather Interceptor (SAUS) .... AWX
All-Weather Intruder .... AWX(I)
All-Weather Landing .... AWL
Allweather Landing (SAUS) .... AWL
All-Weather Landing System [*Also, AWLS*] .... ALS
All-Weather Landing System [*Also, ALS*] .... AWLS
All-Weather Long-Range Fighter .... AWLRF
All-Weather Operations (SAUO) .... AWO
All-Weather Operations Committee [*ATA*] .... AWOC
All-Weather Operations Division [*ICAO*] (MCD) .... AWOD
All-Weather Operations Panel [*International Civil Aviation Organization*] .... AWOP
All-Weather Radial Tire [*Automotive accessory*] .... AWR
All-Weather Reconnaissance System .... AWRS
All-Weather Sea Target Acquisition System [*Navy*] (MCD) .... AWSTAS
All-Weather Short-Range Air Defense Missile System (MCD) .... AW-SHORADS
All-Weather Sleepout (ADA) .... AWSO
All-Weather Stand-off Aircraft Control System (SAUS) .... AWSACS
All-Weather Stand-off Attack Control System (SAUS) .... AWSACS
All-Weather Stand-off Attack System (SAUS) .... AWSAS
All-Weather Station .... AWSTA
All-Weather Surface Observations [*NASA*] (PDAA) .... AWSO
All-Weather System (MCD) .... AWS
All-Weather Tactical Bombing System .... AWTBS
All-Weather Tactical Strike System [*Air Force*] (MCD) .... AWTSS
All-Weather Test Bed (MCD) .... AWTB
All-Weather Topographic Mapping System [*Army*] .... AWTMS
All-Weather Training Unit (SAUS) .... ALL Wea Tra U
All-Weather Training Unit, Atlantic Fleet (SAUO) .... AllWeaTraULant
All-Weather Training Unit, Pacific Fleet (SAUO) .... AllWeaTraUPac
All-Wheel Control [*Mitsubishi*] [*Transmisssion systems*] .... AWC
All-Wheel Drive [*Automotive engineering*] .... AWD
Allwood's Appeal Cases under the Weights and Measures Act [*England*] [*A publication*] (DLA) .... Allwood
Allyl Alcohol (SAUS) .... AA
Allyl Chloride [*Organic chemistry*] .... AC
Allyl Diglycol Carbonate [*Organic chemistry*] .... ADC
Allyl Elthenesulphonate (PDAA) .... AES
Allyl Glycidyl Ether [*Organic chemistry*] .... AGE
Allyl Isothiocyanate [*Organic chemistry*] .... AITC
Allyl Methacrylate [*Organic chemistry*] .... ALMA
Allyl(dimethyl)chlorosilane [*Organic chemistry*] .... ADMCS
Allylisopropylacetamide [*Biochemistry*] .... AIA
Allyl-Isopropyl-Acetamide (SAUS) .... AIA
Allyltrimethyl-Ammoniumbromide (SAUS) .... AMAB
[*The*] **Alma & Jonquieres Railway Co.** [*AAR code*] .... AJ
Alma & Jonquieres Railway Co. (SAUO) .... AJ
Alma College (SAUO) .... AC
Alma College, Alma, MI [*OCLC symbol*] (OCLC) .... EZA
Alma College, Alma, MI [*Library symbol*] [*Library of Congress*] (LCLS) .... MiAC
Alma, GA [*Location identifier*] [*FAA*] (FAAL) .... AMG
Alma, GA [*AM radio station call letters*] .... WAJQ
Alma, GA [*FM radio station call letters*] .... WAJQ-FM
Alma Mater Society [*Canada*] .... AMS
Alma, MI [*Location identifier*] [*FAA*] (FAAL) .... AMN
Alma, MI [*Location identifier*] [*FAA*] (FAAL) .... GTX
Alma, MI [*AM radio station call letters*] .... WFYC
Alma, MI [*FM radio station call letters*] .... WQAC
Alma, MI [*FM radio station call letters*] (RBYB) .... WQBX
Alma, PQ [*AM radio station call letters*] .... CFGT
Alma, PQ [*FM radio station call letters*] (RBYB) .... CKYK-FM
Alma Public Library, Alma, MI [*Library symbol*] [*Library of Congress*] (LCLS) .... MiA
Alma Urbis [*Beloved City*] [*Rome*] .... AU
Alma White College [*New Jersey*] .... AWC
Alma White College, Zarephath, NJ [*Library symbol*] [*Library of Congress*] (LCLS) .... NjZaA
Alma-Ata [*Former USSR*] [*Seismograph station code, US Geological Survey*] (SEIS) .... AAA
Alma-Ata [*Former USSR*] [*Airport symbol*] (OAG) .... ALA
Alma-Ata (SAUS) .... Al-At
Alma-Ata [*Former USSR*] [*ICAO location identifier*] (ICLI) .... UAAA
Almacenes Maritimos (SAUS) .... AM
Almaden [*California*] [*Seismograph station code, US Geological Survey*] (SEIS) .... AMC
Almaden Resources Corp. [*Vancouver Stock Exchange symbol*] .... AMH
Almagest [*of Ptolemy*] [*Classical studies*] (OCD) .... Alm
Almagro [*Spain*] [*ICAO location identifier*] (ICLI) .... LEAO
Almaguin Highlands Community Living (AC) .... AHCL
Almanac (ROG) .... ALK
Almanac (ROG) .... ALMC
[*The*] **Almanac of American Politics** [*National Journal Inc.*] [*Database*] [*A publication*] .... AMPOL
Almanach der Psychoanalyse (journ.) (SAUS) .... Adp
Almandine (SAUS) .... AL
Almanor Railroad Co. [*AAR code*] .... AL
Almas Gemelas (SAUS) .... ALGEM
Almazy Rossii-Sakha .... ARS
Almenara [*Brazil*] [*Airport symbol*] [*Obsolete*] (OAG) .... AMJ
Almeria [*Spain*] [*Seismograph station code, US Geological Survey*] (SEIS) .... ALM
Almeria [*Spain*] [*ICAO location identifier*] (ICLI) .... LEAM
Almeria [*Spain*] [*Airport symbol*] (OAG) .... LEI
Almeta Air [*Austria*] [*FAA designator*] (FAAC) .... AAW
Almine Resources [*Vancouver Stock Exchange symbol*] .... ART
Almirall [*Spain*] [*Research code symbol*] .... LAS
Almond Board of California (EA) .... ABC
Almond Hullers and Processors Association (SRA) .... AHPA
Almond Leaf Scorch [*Plant pathology*] .... ALS
Almond Leaf Scorch Bacterium [*Plant pathology*] .... ALSB
Almondsbury [*England*] .... ALMOND
Almonte Public Library, Ontario [*Library symbol*] [*National Library of Canada*] (NLC) .... OA
Almost [*Philately*] .... alm
almost A-1 in quality (SAUS) A-2
Almost Difference Quasiternary Code (PDAA) .... ADQC
Almost Differential Quasiternary Code [*Telecommunications*] (TEL) .... ADQ
Almost Everywhere .... AE
Almost Exactly Prism (SAUS) .... AXP
Almost Ideal Demand System [*Agriculture*] .... AIDS
Almost Letter Quality [*Refers to the quality of print or of a printer*] (NITA) .... ALQ
Almost Periodic Amplitude Variation Coding (SAUS) .... APAVC
Almost Periodical (SAUS) .... AP
Almost Ready to Fly [*Remote-control plane*] .... ARF
Almost Uncirculated [*Condition of coins*] [*Numismatics*] .... AU
Almost Verbatim (AAGC) .... AV
Almost-Developed Country .... ADC
Almquist Shell (SAUS) .... ASH
ALO Advance Planning Division (SAUS) .... AL/APD
Aloe Technology Association (EA) .... ATA
Aloette Cosmetics [*NASDAQ symbol*] (TTSB) .... ALET
Aloette Cosmetics, Inc. [*NASDAQ symbol*] (NQ) .... ALET
Aloette Cosmetics, Inc. [*Associated Press*] (SAG) .... Aloette
Alofi/Niue International [*Niue Island*] [*ICAO location identifier*] (ICLI) .... NIUE
Aloft (FAAC) .... ALF
Aloha Airlines [*ICAO designator*] (FAAC) .... AAH
Aloha Airlines (SAUO) .... ALO
Aloha Airlines [*ICAO designator*] (AD) .... AQ
Aloha Airlines, Inc. (SAUS) .... ALOHA
Aloha Airlines, Inc. (SAUO) .... AQ
Aloha Airlines, Inc. [*Air carrier designation symbol*] .... TSA
Aloha International [*An association*] (EA) .... AI
Aloha Islandair [*ICAO designator*] (AD) .... WP
Aloha Society of Association Executives - Hawaii (SRA) .... ASAE-HI
Aloin, Extract of Belladonna, and Strychnine Pill [*A laxative*] [*Pharmacology*] (DAVI) .... ABS
Aloin, Strychnine, and Belladonna [*Pharmacy*] .... AS & B
Aloin, Strychnine, Belladonna, and Ipecac [*Pharmacy*] .... ASB & I

Aloin/Strychnine/Belladonna (DB) ... ASB
Aloin/Strychnine/Belladonna/Ipecac (DB) ... ASBI
Alon, Inc. [*ICAO aircraft manufacturer identifier*] (ICAO) ... FO
Alone Unit Record System (SAUS) ... AURS
Along (FAAC) ... ALG
Along [*India*] [*Airport symbol*] (AD) ... IXV
Along [*India*] [*ICAO location identifier*] (ICLI) ... VEAN
Along The Same Line (SAUS) ... ATSL
Along Track Scanning Radiometer with Microwave Sounder (SAUS) ... ATSR-M
Alongside ... AS
Along-Slope (SAUS) ... AS
Along-Track Scanning Radiometer ... ATSR
Alopecia Areata [*Medicine*] ... AA
Alopecia Universalis [*Dermatology*] ... AU
Alor [*Indonesia*] [*Airport symbol*] (OAG) ... ARD
Alor Setar [*Malaysia*] [*Airport symbol*] (OAG) ... AOR
Alor Setar/Sultan Abdul Halim [*Malaysia*] [*ICAO location identifier*] (ICLI) ... WMKA
Alotau [*Papua New Guinea*] [*Airport symbol*] (OAG) ... GUR
Alotta Resources Ltd. [*Vancouver Stock Exchange symbol*] ... AOS
Alouette Topside Sounder Synoptic [*NASA*] ... ALOSYN
Alpavia [*France*] [*ICAO aircraft manufacturer identifier*] (ICAO) ... AL
Alpena [*Michigan*] [*Airport symbol*] (OAG) ... APN
Alpena Community College [*Michigan*] ... ACC
Alpena Community College, Alpena, MI [*Library symbol*] [*Library of Congress*] (LCLS) ... MiAlpC
Alpena County Library, Alpena, MI [*Library symbol*] [*Library of Congress*] (LCLS) ... MiAlp
Alpena, MI [*Location identifier*] [*FAA*] (FAAL) ... CLO
Alpena, MI [*AM radio station call letters*] ... WATZ
Alpena, MI [*FM radio station call letters*] ... WATZ-FM
Alpena, MI [*Television station call letters*] ... WBKB
Alpena, MI [*FM radio station call letters*] ... WCML
Alpena, MI [*Television station call letters*] ... WCML-TV
Alpena, MI [*FM radio station call letters*] ... WHSB
Alpenair GmbH & Co. KG [*Austria*] [*ICAO designator*] (FAAC) ... LPN
Alperin Jet-Diffuser Ejector (MCD) ... AJDE
Alpes Maritimes [*French*] ... AM
Alpha ... A
Alpha [*Australia*] [*Airport symbol*] (OAG) ... ABH
Alpha ... ALPH
Alpha 1 National Association (SAUO) ... A1NA
Alpha 1-Antitrypsin Deficiency [*Genetic disorder*] (PAZ) ... a1AT
Alpha Activity Median Diameter [*Nuclear energy*] (NRCH) ... AMD
Alpha Antiprotease [*Biochemistry*] ... AAP
Alpha Aviation, Inc. [*ICAO designator*] (FAAC) ... ALH
Alpha Aviation, Inc. [*ICAO designator*] (FAAC) ... APH
Alpha Benzene Hexachloride [*Organic chemistry*] (ADA) ... ABH
Alpha Beta Gamma International (EA) ... ABG
Alpha Block Control Number [*Computer science*] ... ABC
Alpha Block Control Number (SAUS) ... ABC Number
Alpha Chi (EA) ... AX
Alpha Communication Network (SAUO) ... ACN
Alpha Control Guidance ... ACG
Alpha Counter Tube ... ACT
Alpha Cutoff ... ACO
Alpha Cut-Off (SAUS) ... ACO
Alpha Delta [*Society*] ... AD
Alpha Delta Phi [*Fraternity*] ... ADP
Alpha Delta Pi [*Sorority*] ... ADP
Alpha Delta Sigma [*Fraternity*] (NTCM) ... ADS
Alpha Disintegration Energy ... ADE
Alpha Energy Analysis (ABAC) ... AEA
Alpha Energy Range Discrimination [*Analysis of radioactivity*] ... AERD
Alpha Epsilon (EA) ... AE
Alpha Epsilon Rho [*Also, AERho*] [*Fraternity*] (NTCM) ... AER
Alpha Extended Processor (SAUS) ... AXP
Alpha Fetal Globulin [*Biochemistry*] (DAVI) ... AFG
Alpha Gamma Rho [*An association*] (NTPA) ... AGR
Alpha Hand and Shoe Monitor [*Radiation detection*] ... AHSM
Alpha Hospitality [*NASDAQ symbol*] (TTSB) ... ALHY
Alpha Hospitality Corp. [*NASDAQ symbol*] (SAG) ... ALHY
Alpha Hospitality Corp. [*Associated Press*] (SAG) ... AlphH
Alpha Hospitality Corp. [*Associated Press*] (SAG) ... AlphHsp
Alpha Hospitality Wrrt [*NASDAQ symbol*] (TTSB) ... ALHYW
Alpha Hydroxy Acid (SAUS) ... AHA
Alpha Hydroxybutyrat-Dehydrogenase (SAUS) ... AHBDH
Alpha Indus [*NASDAQ symbol*] (SG) ... AHAA
Alpha Industries, Inc. [*AMEX symbol*] (SPSG) ... AHA
Alpha Industries Inc. (SAUO) ... AI
Alpha Industries, Inc. [*Associated Press*] (SAG) ... AlphaIn
Alpha Kappa Alpha (SAUO) ... AKA
Alpha Kappa Kappa [*Fraternity*] ... AKK
Alpha Kappa Psi [*An association*] (NTPA) ... AKPsi
Alpha Magnetic Spectrometer ... AMS
Alpha Meter (MCD) ... AM
Alpha Micro Devices (AAEL) ... AMD
Alpha Micro Users Society (EA) ... AMUS
Alpha Microsystems [*NASDAQ symbol*] (NQ) ... ALMI
Alpha Microsystems [*Associated Press*] (SAG) ... AlpMic
Alpha Microsystems Operating System ... AMOS
Alpha Microsystems Wrrt [*NASDAQ symbol*] (TTSB) ... ALMIW
Alpha Motoneuron (SAUS) ... AMN
Alpha Omega Computer System (IEEE) ... AOCS
Alpha Omega International Dental Fraternity [*An association*] (NTPA) ... AO
Alpha Park Public Library, Bartonville, IL [*Library symbol*] [*Library of Congress*] (LCLS) ... IBart
Alpha Park Public Library District, Pekin, IL [*OCLC symbol*] (OCLC) ... ISF
Alpha Particle (ADWA) ... A-part
Alpha Particle (ADA) ... A-PART
Alpha Particle Spectrometer (KSC) ... AP
Alpha Phi Delta (EA) ... APD
Alpha Pi Omega (SAUS) ... APO
Alpha Portland Cement Co. (SAUO) ... AHP
Alpha Portland Industries (SAUO) ... APC
Alpha Proton X-Ray Spectrometer ... APXS
ALPHA [*AMC Logistics Program - Hardcore Automated*] **Remote Terminal Interactive System** ... ARTIS
Alpha Repertory Television Service [*Cable-television system*] ... ARTS
Alpha Research and Development (SAUS) ... A&RD
Alpha Research and Development (KSC) ... ARAD
Alpha Roster Locator List (United States Army Reserve) Colonels ... ARLLUC
Alpha Scattering Instrument (ACAE) ... ASI
Alpha Scattering Instrument Sensor (ACAE) ... ASIS
Alpha Scattering Instrument Sensor Head (ACAE) ... ASISH
Alpha Solar Array Drive (SSD) ... ASAD
Alpha Solarco [*NASDAQ symbol*] (TTSB) ... ASCO
Alpha Solarco, Inc. [*Associated Press*] (SAG) ... AlphaSo
Alpha Solarco, Inc. [*NASDAQ symbol*] (NQ) ... ASCO
Alpha Tau Alpha (EA) ... ATA
Alpha Tau Delta [*An association*] (NTPA) ... ATD
Alpha Tau Omega [*Fraternity*] ... ATO
Alpha Technologies Grp [*NASDAQ symbol*] (TTSB) ... ATGI
Alpha Technology Group, Inc. [*Associated Press*] (SAG) ... AlphaTch
Alpha Technology Group, Inc. [*NASDAQ symbol*] (SAG) ... ATGI
Alpha Temperature Probe Assembly [*NASA*] (MCD) ... ATPA
Alpha Test of Phonology [*Robert J. Lowe*] (TES) ... ALPHA
Alpha Track (GNE) ... AT
Alpha Track Detection (EEVL) ... AT
Alpha Track Detector (ABAC) ... ATD
Alpha Trans-Inducing Factor [*Genetics*] ... ATIF
Alpha Waste Storage Facility [*Nuclear energy*] ... AWSF
Alpha Xi Delta [*Sorority*] ... AXD
Alpha Zeta (EA) ... AZ
Alpha Zeta Omega [*Fraternity*] ... AZO
Alpha-1 Antitrypsin Deficiency (DB) ... AAD
Alpha-1-Antitrypsin [*Protease inhibitor*] [*Serology*] ... A_1AT
Alpha-2HS-Glycoprotein (DMAA) ... AHSG
Alpha-66 [*An association*] (EA) ... A-66
Alpha-activity Median Diameter (SAUS) ... AMD
Alpha-Adrenergic Agonist (MELL) ... AAA
Alpha-Adrenergic Blocker [*Medicine*] (MELL) ... AAB
Alpha-Adrenergic Blocking Drug [*Medicine*] (MELL) ... AABD
Alpha-Adrenergic Receptor [*Medicine*] (MELL) ... AAR
Alpha-Adrenergic Receptor Blocker [*Medicine*] (MELL) ... AARB
Alpha-Amino Nitrogen (MAE) ... AAN
Alpha-Amino-Butyric Acid (MELL) ... AANB
Alpha-Aminoisobulyric Acid (SAUS) ... AIBA
Alpha-Aminoisobutyric (DB) ... AAIB
Alpha-Aminoisobutyric Acid [*Organic chemistry*] ... AIBA
Alpha-Amino-N-Butyric acid (SAUS) ... AANB
Alpha-Antitrypsin [*Biochemistry*] ... AAT
Alpha-Atrial Natriuretic Polypeptide [*Biochemistry*] (DAVI) ... ANP
Alpha-Benzene-Hexachloride (SAUS) ... ABH
alphabet (SAUS) ... abc
[*The*] **Alphabet** (BARN) ... ABC
Alphabet Arithmetic (SAUS) ... Alphametic
Alphabet Soup Index for Health and Environmental Science and Engineering (EEVL) ... ASIFHESE
Alpha-Beta Pseudo-Coincidence Difference Method (SAUS) ... ABPD-Method
Alphabeta Pseudocoincidence Discrimination [*Analysis of radioactivity*] ... ABDP
Alpha-Beta Technology [*NASDAQ symbol*] (TTSB) ... ABTI
Alpha-Beta Technology, Inc. [*NASDAQ symbol*] (SAG) ... ABTI
Alpha-Beta Technology, Inc. [*Associated Press*] (SAG) ... AlphaBta
Alphabetic ... A
Alphabetic (SAUS) ... Alpha
Alphabetic 1 Bit (SAUS) ... AL 1 B
Alphabetic Character (SAUS) ... AC
Alphabetic Code (SAUS) ... AC
Alphabetic Collating Device (SAUS) ... ACD
Alphabetic Collator (SAUS) ... AC
Alphabetic Duplicating Punch (SAUS) ... ADP
Alphabetic Field (SAUS) ... AF
Alphabetic File (SAUS) ... AF
Alphabetic Information (SAUS) ... AI
Alphabetic Interpreter (SAUS) ... AI
Alphabetic Item (SAUS) ... AI
Alphabetic Letters (SAUS) ... AL
Alphabetic Listing (SAUS) ... AL
Alphabetic numeric (SAUS) ... Alphameric
Alphabetic Order (SAUS) ... AO
Alphabetic Phonogram [*Egyptology*] (ROG) ... ALPH
Alphabetic Print Control (SAUS) ... APC
Alphabetic Register (SAUS) ... AR
Alphabetic Sequence (SAUS) ... AS
Alphabetic Sort (SAUS) ... AS
Alphabetic Storage (SAUS) ... AS
Alphabetic Store Device (SAUS) ... ASD
Alphabetic String (SAUS) ... AS
Alphabetic Subject Index [*A publication*] ... ASI

Alphabetic Typewriter Keyboard (SAUS)	ATK
Alphabetic Verifier (SAUS)	AV
Alphabetic Word (SAUS)	AW
Alphabetical (WDAA)	ALPH
Alphabetical [Flowchart]	ALPHA
Alphabetical (WDMC)	alpha
Alphabetical Accounting Machine (SAUS)	AAM
Alphabetical and Numerical (ADWA)	alphanumeric
Alphabetical Block (SAUS)	AB
Alphabetical British [Railway Guide of Timetables] (BARN)	ABC
Alphabetical Code Punching (SAUS)	ACP
Alphabetical Index of Names	AION
Alphabetical Indication Store (SAUS)	AIS
Alphabetical Information Recording (SAUS)	AIR
Alphabetical Information Storage (SAUS)	AIS
Alphabetical Numerical (SAUS)	Alphanumeric
Alphabetical Order (SAUS)	Alpha Order
Alphabetical Tabulator (SAUS)	AT
Alphabetisches Sachregister (SAUS)	ASR
Alpha-Cedrene	ACDR
Alpha-Comp Simulation Package [Alpha-Comp Ltd.] [Software package] (NCC)	ASIM
Alpha-Delta Sleep (MELL)	ADS
Alphafetoprotein	AFP
Alpha-Fetoprotein [Clinical chemistry]	AFP
Alphafetoprotein Test	AFP
Alphaglucosylrutin [Antioxidant]	AGR
Alpha-Hydrazine analog of Histidine (SAUS)	AHH
Alpha-Hydrazine Analogue of Histidine (MAE)	AHH
Alpha-Hydroxy Acid [Organic chemistry]	AHA
Alpha-Hydroxybutyric Acid (DMAA)	AHB
Alpha-Hydroxybutyric Dehydrogenase [An enzyme] (MAH)	AHB
Alpha-Hydroxybutyric Dehydrogenase [An enzyme]	AHBD
Alpha-I Antitrypsin (SAUS)	AAT
Alpha-Interferon [Medicine] (TAD)	IFN-A
Alpha/LAMP Integration (SAUS)	ALI
Alphalytic Protease [An enzyme]	ALP
Alpha/Mach Indicator (NASA)	AMI
Alpha-Macroglobulin [Biochemistry]	AMG
Alphameric (SAUS)	ALPH
Alphameric (SAUS)	AN
Alpha-Methyldopa [Also, MD] [Antihypertensive compound]	AMD
Alpha-Methylmannoside [Biochemistry]	AMM
Alpha-Methyl-m-tyrosine [Pharmacology]	MMT
Alphamethyl-Penethylamine (SAUS)	Amphetamine
Alpha-Methylphenethylamine [CNS stimulant]	AMPHETAMINE
Alpha-Methyl-p-tyrosine [Also, MPT] [Pharmacology]	AMPT
Alpha-Methyl-p-tyrosine [Also, AMPT] [Pharmacology]	MPT
Alpha-Methylstyrene [Organic chemistry]	AMS
Alpha-Methyltyrosine [Pharmacology] (MAE)	AMT
Alpha-Naphthalenic Acid (SAUS)	ANA
Alpha-Naphthoflavone [Biochemistry]	ANF
Alpha-Naphthyl Acetate [Organic chemistry]	ANA
Alpha-Naphthyl Butyrate [Organic chemistry]	ANB
Alpha-Naphthyl Butyrate Esterase [An enzyme]	ANBE
Alpha-Naphthyl Isothiocyanate (SAUS)	ANIT
Alpha-Naphthylisothiocyanate [Organic chemistry]	ANIT
Alpha-Naphthylthiourea [Organic chemistry]	ANTU
Alphanaphthylthiourea (SAUS)	ANTU
Alpha-Naphtyl Acetate (SAUS)	ANA
AlphaNet Solutions [NASDAQ symbol] (TTSB)	ALPH
AlphaNet Solutions, Inc. [NASDAQ symbol] (SAG)	ALPH
AlphaNet Solutions, Inc. [Associated Press] (SAG)	AlphNet
Alpha-Nitrose-Beta-Naphthol (SAUS)	ANBN
Alphanumeric (SAUS)	ALF
Alphanumeric	ALPHANUM
Alphanumeric (SAUS)	ALPM
Alphanumeric	AN
Alphanumeric Accounting Computer (SAUS)	AAC
Alphanumeric Address (SAUS)	AA
Alphanumeric Block Printer (SAUS)	ABP
Alphanumeric Channel Set (SAUS)	ANCS
Alphanumeric Character (SAUS)	AC
Alphanumeric Character Generator (SAUS)	Anchor
Alpha-Numeric Character Generator [Computer science] (MHDB)	ANCHOR
Alphanumeric Character Graphic [Computer science] (ECII)	ACG
Alphanumeric Code for Music Analysis [Input code for music notation] (NITA)	ALMA
Alphanumeric Code (or Coding) (SAUS)	AC
Alphanumeric Command (SAUS)	AC
Alphanumeric Data Printer (SAUS)	ADP
Alphanumeric Data Recorder (or Recording) (SAUS)	ADR
Alphanumeric Device (SAUS)	AD
Alphanumeric Digital Display (CAAL)	ADD
Alphanumeric Display	AND
Alphanumeric Display Equipment	ADE
Alphanumeric Display Equipment	ANDE
Alphanumeric Display for Sumery (SAUS)	TOTE
Alphanumeric Display Terminal	ADT
Alphanumeric Display Tube (SAUS)	ADT
Alphanumeric Displays (SAUS)	ANDS
Alphanumeric Electronic Bit Analyzer (SAUS)	ANEBA
Alphanumeric Entry Device	AED
Alphanumeric Expression (SAUS)	AE
Alphanumeric Impact Printer	AIP
Alphanumeric Information (SAUS)	AI
Alphanumeric Instruction (SAUS)	AI
Alphanumeric Item (SAUS)	AI
Alphanumeric Keyboard	ANK
Alphanumeric Keyboard	ANKB
Alphanumeric Language for Music Analysis	ALMA
Alphanumeric Logging System (SAUS)	ALS
Alpha-Numeric Logic Package [Computer science] (MHDI)	ANLP
Alphanumeric Optical Reader (SAUS)	AOR
Alphanumeric Order	AO
Alpha-Numeric Output (SAUS)	ANO
Alphanumeric Output	ANO
Alphanumeric Page Reader (SAUS)	APR
Alphanumeric Photocomposer System (IEEE)	APS
Alphanumeric Publishing System, Inc. (SAUS)	APS-INC
Alphanumeric Publishing System Incorporated (SAUO)	APS-INC
Alphanumeric Punching (SAUS)	AP
Alphanumeric Replacement (SAUS)	ANR
Alphanumeric Representation (SAUS)	AR
Alphanumeric Standard Keyboard (SAUS)	ASK
Alphanumeric Store (SAUS)	AS
Alphanumeric System for Classification of Recordings	ANSCR
Alphanumeric Terminal Display Unit (SAUS)	ATDU
Alphanumeric Terminal Executive (SAUS)	ANTEX
Alphanumeric Universal Keyboard (SAUS)	AUK
Alpha/Numeric Wall Display (CCCA)	ANWD
Alphanumeric Warning Display (SAUS)	ANVM
Alphanumeric Warning Display (MCD)	ANWD
Alphanumerical Reader (SAUS)	AR
Alphanumerics (SAUS)	A/N
Alpha-Olefin Sulfonate [Surfactant] [Organic chemistry]	AOS
Alpha-Omega Industries, Inc. [Vancouver Stock Exchange symbol]	ALF
Alphaprodine [Anesthesiology]	AP
Alpha-Ray Spectrometer (SAUS)	ARS
Alpha-Ray Spectrometric Equipment (SAUS)	ARSE
Alpharel, Inc. [Associated Press] (SAG)	Alpharl
Alpharel, Inc. [Associated Press] (SAG)	Alphr
Alpharel, Inc. [NASDAQ symbol] (SAG)	AREL
Alpharetta, GA [AM radio station call letters] (BROA)	WLTA
Alpharetta, GA [AM radio station call letters]	WVNF
Alpharm, Inc. [NYSE symbol] (SAG)	ALO
Alpharm, Inc. [Associated Press] (SAG)	Alpharma
Alpharm, Inc. [Associated Press] (SAG)	Alphm
ALPHARMA, Inc. [NYSE symbol] [Formerly, A. L. Pharma] (SG)	ALO
ALPHARMA INC.'A' [NYSE symbol] (TTSB)	ALO
ALPHARMA Inc.Wrrt [NYSE symbol] (TTSB)	ALO WS
Alpha-Tocopherol (MELL)	ATB
Alphen (SAUS)	Alp
Alphonsus College, Woodcliff Lake, NJ [Library symbol] [Library of Congress] (LCLS)	NjWolA
Alpi Eagles SpA [Italy] [ICAO designator] (FAAC)	ELG
Alpine (ADWA)	alp
Alpine (SAUS)	Alp
Alpine and Mediterranean Hydrology component of FRIENDS (SAUS)	AMHY
Alpine Aviation [ICAO designator] (AD)	ZA
Alpine Aviation Inc. [ICAO designator] (FAAC)	AIP
Alpine Biodiversity (SAUO)	ALPNET
Alpine Club [British]	AC
Alpine Club, Banff, AB, Canada [Library symbol] [Library of Congress] (LCLS)	CaABAC
Alpine Club, Banff, Alberta [Library symbol] [National Library of Canada] (NLC)	ABAC
Alpine Club of Canada (EA)	ACC
Alpine Experiment [International Council of Scientific Unions]	ALPEX
Alpine Experiment (SAUO)	Alpex
Alpine Exploration [Vancouver Stock Exchange symbol]	AXC
Alpine Flight Approach by GPS/NAVSTAR (SAUO)	ALFASTAR
Alpine Garden Society (EA)	AGS
Alpine Group [NYSE symbol] (SG)	AGI
Alpine Group [Associated Press] (SAG)	AlpineGr
Alpine Group, Inc. [AMEX symbol] (SPSG)	AGI
Alpine Group, Inc. [Associated Press] (SAG)	AlpinGr
Alpine International Corp. (SAUO)	APIN
Alpine Journal (journ.) (SAUS)	APJL
Alpine Lace Brands [NASDAQ symbol] (SPSG)	LACE
Alpine Lace Brands, Inc. [Associated Press] (SAG)	AlpLce
Alpine Luft-Transport AB [Switzerland] [ICAO designator] (FAAC)	ALU
Alpine Mountains of south central Europe (SAUS)	Alps
Alpine Science Information Service (SAUS)	ASIS
Alpine Science Information Service [Information service or system] (IID)	ASISS
Alpine Silver Ltd. [Vancouver Stock Exchange symbol]	ASV
Alpine Technology Training Association Center (SAUO)	ATTAC
Alpine Tourist Commission [See also TGA] [Switzerland] (EAIO)	ATC
Alpine, TX [Location identifier] [FAA] (FAAL)	BWR
Alpine, TX [FM radio station call letters]	KALP
Alpine, TX [AM radio station call letters]	KVLF
Alpines International (EA)	AI
Alpinopolis/Furnas [Brazil] [ICAO location identifier] (ICLI)	SBFU
Alpliner AG [Switzerland] [ICAO designator] (FAAC)	ALP
Alpnet, Inc. [NASDAQ symbol] (NQ)	AILP
Alpnet, Inc. [Associated Press] (SAG)	Alpnet
Alport Syndrome [Medicine]	AS
Alport Syndrome Home Page (SAUO)	ASHP
Alprazolam [Tranquilizer]	ALP
Alps Region [MARC geographic area code] [Library of Congress] (LCCP)	ea---

Al-Rajhi Co. for Currency Exchange and Commerce [*Saudi Arabia*] .... ARCCEC
Already Been Chewed [*Gum*] .... ABC
Already Been Converted (PDAA) .... ABC
Alrenco, Inc. [*Associated Press*] (SAG) .... Alrenco
Alrenco, Inc. [*NASDAQ symbol*] (SAG) .... RNCO
Alright Auto Parks, Inc. (SAUO) .... ALR
ALS [*Amyotrophic Lateral Sclerosis*] **and Neuromuscular Research**
  Foundation (EA) .... ALSNRF
Als Forbes Norris Research Center (EA) .... ALSNRF
Alsager's Dictionary of Business Terms (DLA) .... Alsager
Alsair Societe [*France*] [*ICAO designator*] (FAAC) .... LSR
Alsands Energy Ltd., Library and Records Centre, Calgary, AB, Canada
  [*Library symbol*] [*Library of Congress*] (LCLS) .... CaACAEL
Alsatian Yiddish (BJA) .... AY
Alsavia, Societe [*France*] [*ICAO designator*] (FAAC) .... ALV
Alsip-Merrionette Park Library District, Alsip, IL [*Library symbol*] [*Library of
  Congress*] (LCLS) .... IAlsA
Also Completed (SAUS) .... AC
Also Known As .... AKA
Also Known As [*Pseudonym*] (WDMC) .... aka
Also Printed As (ADWA) .... APA
ALSTOM ADS [*NYSE symbol*] (SG) .... ALS
Alston & Bird, Law Library, Atlanta, GA [*Library symbol*] [*Library of
  Congress*] (LCLS) .... GAAB
Alston Wilkes Society (EA) .... AWS
Alt Tuberculin [*Old Tuberculin*] [*German*] .... AT
Alta [*Utah*] [*Seismograph station code, US Geological Survey*] [*Closed*]
  (SEIS) .... AAU
Alta [*Norway*] [*Airport symbol*] (OAG) .... ALF
Alta [*Norway*] [*ICAO location identifier*] (ICLI) .... ENAT
Alta Advertiser, Alta, IA [*Library symbol*] [*Library of Congress*] (LCLS) .... IaAltaA
Alta Flights Ltd. [*Canada*] [*ICAO designator*] (FAAC) .... ALZ
Alta Gold Co. [*NASDAQ symbol*] (NQ) .... ALTA
Alta Gold Co. [*Associated Press*] (SAG) .... AltaGld
Alta, IA [*FM radio station call letters*] (BROA) .... KBVU-FM
Alta Public Library, Alta, IA [*Library symbol*] [*Library of Congress*] (LCLS) ..... IaAlta
ALTA [*American Library Trustee Association*] **Specialized Outreach Services**
  Committee [*American Library Association*] .... ALTA SOSC
Alta Velocidad Espanola [*Spain*] [*High speed train*] .... AVE
Alta Vista Branch, Ontario Cancer Foundation, Ottawa, Ontario [*Library
  symbol*] [*National Library of Canada*] (NLC) .... OOACF
Altach Points Only (SAUS) .... APO
Altadena Library District, Altadena, CA [*OCLC symbol*] (OCLC) .... ALD
Altadena Library District, Altadena, CA [*Library symbol*] [*Library of
  Congress*] (LCLS) .... CAlt
Altai Mountains (SAUS) .... Altais
Altair [*Airline*] (MHDB) .... AK
Altair Aviation Ltd. [*Canada*] [*ICAO designator*] (FAAC) .... ALQ
Altamira [*Brazil*] [*Airport symbol*] (OAG) .... ATM
Altamira [*Brazil*] [*ICAO location identifier*] (ICLI) .... SBHT
Altamira De San Carlos [*Costa Rica*] [*ICAO location identifier*] (ICLI) .... MRAT
Altamont, OR [*FM radio station call letters*] .... KCHQ
Altamont, OR [*FM radio station call letters*] (BROA) .... KRAT-FM
Altamont Public Library, Altamont, IL [*Library symbol*] [*Library of Congress*]
  (LCLS) .... IAlta
Altar [*Constellation*] (WDAA) .... Ara
Altar Gold & Resources [*Vancouver Stock Exchange symbol*] .... ALT
Altaramaeische Urkunden aus Assur [*A publication*] (BJA) .... AaUA
Altarpiece (VRA) .... altpc
Altavista Business Card Directory (SAUS) .... ABCD
Altavista, VA [*AM radio station call letters*] .... WKDE
Altavista, VA [*FM radio station call letters*] .... WKDE-FM
Altay [*China*] [*Airport symbol*] (OAG) .... AAT
Altbabylonische Briefe im Umschrift und Uebersetzung [*A publication*]
  (BJA) .... AbB
Alte Exploration (SAUS) .... ANE
Alte Kaempfer [*Old Fighters*] [*German*] .... AK
Altemaria citri Rough Lemon-specific Toxins .... ACRL
Altemate National Military Intelligence Center (SAUS) .... ANMIC
Altemeier's Procedure [*Medicine*] (MELL) .... AP
Altena/Hegenscheid [*Germany*] [*ICAO location identifier*] (ICLI) .... EDKD
Altenrhein [*Switzerland*] [*ICAO location identifier*] (ICLI) .... LSZR
Altenstadt [*Germany*] [*ICAO location identifier*] (ICLI) .... EDPL
Altenstadt [*Germany*] [*ICAO location identifier*] (ICLI) .... EDZT
Alteon, Inc. [*Associated Press*] (SAG) .... Alteon
Alteon, Inc. [*NASDAQ symbol*] (SPSG) .... ALTN
Alter .... ALTR
Alter Course [*Navigation*] .... A/C
Alter Ego [*My Other Self*] [*Latin*] .... Alt Eg
Alter Heading [*Navigation*] .... AH
Alter Idem [*Another Self*] [*Latin*] .... Alt Id
Alter Orient und Altes Testament [*Kevelaer/Neukirchen*] [*A publication*]
  (BJA) .... AltOrAT
Alter Orient und Altes Testament. Veroeffentlichungen zur Kultur und
  Geschichte des Alten Orients und des Alten Testaments [*Kevelaer/
  Neukirchen/Vluyn*] [*A publication*] (BJA) .... AOAT
Alter Ridge [*Washington*] [*Seismograph station code, US Geological Survey*]
  (SEIS) .... ALD
Alter Statement (SAUS) .... AS
Altera Corp. [*Associated Press*] (SAG) .... Altera
Altera Corp. [*NASDAQ symbol*] (NQ) .... ALTR
Altera Hardware Description Language (SAUS) .... AHDL
Alterable Control Memory .... ACM
Alterable Gate Array (SAUS) .... AGA
Alterable Read-Only Memory [*Computer science*] .... AROM

Alterable Read-Only Operating System [*Computer science*] .... AROS
Alteration .... ALT
Alteration (ADWA) .... alt
Alteration (BEE) .... alter
Alteration (ROG) .... ALTER
Alteration .... ALTERON
Alteration [*Technical drawings*] (DAC) .... ALTN
Alteration (AABC) .... ALTR
Alteration (MSA) .... ALTRN
Alteration (ROG) .... ALTRON
Alteration and Improvement (SAUS) .... A&I
Alteration and Improvement Program [*Navy*] .... A & I
Alteration and Inspection .... A & I
Alteration and Inspection (SAUS) .... A&I
Alteration and Project Report (DNAB) .... APR
Alteration Equivalent to a Repair .... AER
Alteration Identification .... ALTID
Alteration Management System (NVT) .... AMS
Alteration of Instruments [*Legal term*] (DLA) .... ALT INST
Alteration of Instruments (SAUS) .... alt of inst
Alteration Request Number .... ARN
Alteration Work Requirements (ACAE) .... AWR
Alterations (ROG) .... ALTS
Alterations in Respiratory Function [*Medicine*] (DMAA) .... AIRF
Alterations Notice (ACAE) .... AN
Altercate Minimum Tax (TDOB) .... AMT
Altered (DCTA) .... ALT
Altered (MSA) .... ALTRD
Altered Commercial Item (MCD) .... ACI
Altered Course (SAUS) .... AC
Altered from a Detail (SAA) .... A/FD
Altered Item Drawing (SSD) .... AID
Altered Keyword in Context (SAUS) .... AKWIC
Altered Mental Status (MEDA) .... AMS
Altered Oceanic Crust [*Geology*] .... AOC
Altered State of Consciousness [*Parapsychology*] .... ASC
Altered State of Consciousness Induction Device [*Parapsychology*] .... ASCID
Altering [*FBI standardized term*] .... ALT
altering (SAUS) .... alt
Alterio Resources Ltd. [*Toronto Stock Exchange symbol*] .... AWO
Alteriovenous Concentration Difference (SAUS) .... A-V Difference
Alterius Diebus [*Every Other Day*] [*Pharmacy*] .... Al Dieb
Alternamoi (SAUS) .... AOH
Alternant Molecular Orbit (SAUS) .... AMO
Alternant Molecular Orbital [*Physical chemistry*] .... AMO
Alternaria [*A fungus*] .... Alt
Alternaria alternata f lycopersici [*A toxin-producing fungus*] .... AL
Alternaria Citri (Lemon race) [*A toxin-producing fungus*] .... ACL
Alternaria citri (Tangerine race) [*A toxin-producing fungus*] .... ACT
Alternaria kikuchiana [*A toxin-producing fungus*] .... AK
Alternaria mali [*A toxin-producing fungus*] .... AM
Alternariol [*Biochemistry*] .... AOH
Alternariol Methyl Ether [*Biochemistry*] .... AME
Alternate [*Approach and landing charts*] [*Aviation*] .... A
Alternate .... ALT
Alternate (TBD) .... Alt
Alternate (VRA) .... alt
Alternate .... ALTER
Alternate (AFM) .... ALTN
Alternate (KSC) .... ALTR
Alternate Acquisition RADAR (MCD) .... AAR
Alternate Acquisition Radar (SAUS) .... AAR
Alternate Address (SAUS) .... AADR
Alternate aerodrome (SAUS) .... ALTN
Alternate Air Defense Weapon System (ACAE) .... AADWS
Alternate Air Force Command Post (SAUO) .... AAFCOP
Alternate Aircraft Takeoff System (MCD) .... AATS
Alternate Airport (FAAC) .... ALTPT
Alternate Alerting Network [*Air Force*] .... ALTAN
Alternate Antiair Warfare Commander (NVT) .... AAAWC
Alternate Area (SAUS) .... AA
Alternate Attachment Unit Interface [*Computer science*] .... AAUI
Alternate Attitude Determination System (ACAE) .... ADDS
Alternate Battery Acquisition Radar (SAUS) .... ABAR
Alternate Binaural Loudness Balance [*Otorhinolaryngology*] (DAVI) .... ABLB
Alternate Binaural Loudness Balancing [*Audiometry*] .... ABLB
Alternate Binaural Loundness Balance (or Balancing) (SAUS) .... ABLB
Alternate Birthing Center [*Obstetrics*] (DAVI) .... ABC
Alternate Call (SAUS) .... AC
Alternate Call Listing [*Telecommunications*] (TEL) .... AC
Alternate Cancellation (SAUS) .... AC
Alternate Captain [*Sports*] .... A
Alternate Care Plan [*Health Care Financing Administration*] .... ACP
Alternate Central Computer Complex (MCD) .... ACCC
Alternate Code (SAUS) .... AC
Alternate Coding Key (SAUS) .... ACK
Alternate Command [*or Commander*] [*Navy*] (NVT) .... ALTCOM
Alternate Command and Control Center [*Air Force*] (MCD) .... ACCC
Alternate Command, Atlantic Fleet (MCD) .... ALTCOM
Alternate Command, Atlantic Fleet .... ALTCOMLANTFLT
Alternate Command Center [*Navy*] (CINC) .... ACC
Alternate Command Center [*Navy*] (NVT) .... ALTCOMCEN
Alternate Command Elements [*Navy*] (CINC) .... ACE
Alternate Command Facility [*Navy*] (NVT) .... ACF
Alternate Command Operations Center (SAUO) .... ACOC

Alternate Command Operations Centre (SAUS)	ACOC
Alternate Command Post [Military] (CET)	ACP
Alternate Command Post [Military] (AFM)	ALCOP
Alternate Command Post	ALCP
Alternate Commander, Atlantic [Navy] (NVT)	ALTCOMLANT
Alternate Commander, Indian (SAUO)	ALTCOMIND
Alternate Commander, Pacific [Navy] (NVT)	ALTCOMPAC
Alternate Communications Facility [Military]	ACF
Alternate Competition Advocate (AAGC)	ACA
Alternate Concentration Level [Environmental science] (COE)	ACL
Alternate Concentration Limit [Environmental science] (COE)	ACL
Alternate Concentration Limits (ADWA)	ACLs
Alternate Core Spray [Nuclear energy] (NRCH)	ACS
Alternate CPU [Central Processing Unit] Recovery [IBM Corp.] [Computer science] (BUR)	ACR
Alternate Current (SAUS)	AC
Alternate Current Charging Unit (SAUS)	ACCU
Alternate Data Retry (SAUS)	ADR
Alternate Days (SAUS)	AD
Alternate Days (EBF)	A/D
alternate days	alt dieb
Alternate Definition of Accident [Insurance]	A/D
Alternate Delivery System [Medicine] (DHSM)	ADS
Alternate Deoxyribonucleic Acid (SAUS)	a-DNA
Alternate Departure Route [Air Traffic Control] (FAAC)	ADRT
Alternate Detection and Control Unit (MCD)	ADCU
Alternate Device Support [NASA]	ADS
Alternate Diesel or Gas-Turbine (SAUS)	A-Dog
Alternate Digit Inversion [Computer science] (IAA)	ADI
Alternate Dispute Resolution (EEVL)	ADR
Alternate Document Control Officer (SAUO)	ADCO
Alternate Drop [Electroanalysis]	AD
Alternate Emergency Action Center (CINC)	AEAC
Alternate Emergency Information and Coordination Center (SAUO)	AEICC
Alternate Energy Institute [Defunct] (EA)	AEI
Alternate Feature Identification Code (SAUS)	FEAT
Alternate Field (SAUS)	ALTF
Alternate Fighter Engine (MCD)	AFE
Alternate Financial Mechanisms [Health insurance] (GHCT)	AFM
Alternate Flight Plan	AFP
Alternate Geologies (SAUS)	AG
Alternate Geology Test Facility (SAUS)	AGTF
Alternate Gothic	Alt Got
Alternate Gradient (SAUS)	AG
Alternate Gross Weight (MCD)	AGW
Alternate Guidance Section (ACAE)	AGS
Alternate Hardened Headquarters (ACAE)	AHHQ
Alternate Headquarters [Military] (NVT)	AH
Alternate Headquarters [Military] (AABC)	ALTHQ
Alternate Headquarters Battle Staff (SAUO)	ALTHQ-BS
Alternate Headquarters Command Facility [Military] (MCD)	AHCF
Alternate Headquarters United States Air Force (SAUO)	AFALT
Alternate Health Services	AHS
alternate hours (SAUS)	alt hor
Alternate Input Method [Computer science] (VERA)	AIM
Alternate Inspection Policy	AIP
Alternate Instruction (SAUS)	AI
Alternate Instruction Address Register [Computer science] (MHDI)	ALTINSAR
Alternate Interim Successor [Military] (NVT)	AIS
Alternate Joint Command Center (MCD)	AJCC
Alternate Joint Communications Center	AJCC
Alternate Joint Typhoon Warning Center (DNAB)	AJTWC
Alternate Joint War Room [Later, ANMCC] (CINC)	AJWR
Alternate Landing Site [NASA]	ALS
Alternate Launch and Recovery Surface (SAUS)	ALARS
Alternate Launch Officer [Air Force]	ALO
Alternate Launch Officer Console [Air Force]	ALOC
Alternate Launch Point System (SAUS)	ALPS
Alternate Launch Site (SAUS)	ALS
Alternate Liaison Officer	ALO
Alternate Library [Computer program] [NASA]	ALTLIB
Alternate Life Style	ALS
Alternate Lifestyle (SAUS)	ALT
Alternate Logistic Control Number (IUSS)	ALCN
Alternate Low Energy (CAAL)	ALE
Alternate Management Summary Report (MCD)	AMSR
Alternate Mark Inversion [Telecommunications] (IEEE)	AMI
Alternate Master Unit (MCD)	AMU
Alternate Media Center [New York University] [New York, NY] [Telecommunications]	AMC
Alternate Military Occupational Speciality (SAUS)	AMOS
Alternate Mission Equipment (MCD)	AME
Alternate Mode (CAAL)	AM
Alternate Monoaural Loudness Balance Test [Medicine] (DMAA)	AMLB
Alternate National Military Command Center [Formerly, AJWR] (AFM)	ANMCC
Alternate National Military Command Center Software Directorate (IUSS)	ANMCCSD
Alternate National Warning Center (SAUO)	ANWC
Alternate Net Control Officer [Navy] (NVT)	ANCO
Alternate Net Control Station (CET)	ANCS
Alternate [or Alternative] News Service (ADA)	ANS
alternate nights (SAUS)	alt noct
Alternate Nuclear Materials, secondary (SAUS)	ANM
Alternate Operating Base (ACAE)	AOB
Alternate Operational Support Center (SAUO)	AOSC

Alternate Operations Control Center [Air Force] (ACAE)	AOCC
Alternate Operator Service (SAUS)	AOS
Alternate Operator Service Provider [Telecommunications] (ITD)	AOSP
Alternate Path Reentry [Fujitsu Ltd.] [Computer science] (MCD)	APR
Alternate Payload Specialist (SAUS)	APS
Alternate Person On Line (SAUS)	APOL
Alternate Postal Delivery [NASDAQ symbol] (TTSB)	ALTD
Alternate Postal Delivery, Inc. [NASDAQ symbol] (SAG)	ALTD
Alternate Postal Delivery, Inc. [Associated Press] (SAG)	AltPosD
Alternate Print (SAUS)	AP
Alternate Proficiency Assessments	APA
Alternate Program (DNAB)	ALT PROG
Alternate Reconstitution Base (CCCA)	ARB
Alternate Record-Voice	ARV
Alternate Removal Systems [Environmental science] (COE)	ARS
Alternate Reproductive Behavior [Zoology]	ARB
Alternate Rod Insertion [Nuclear energy] (NRCH)	ARI
Alternate Route [Telecommunications] (TEL)	A/R
Alternate Route (SAUS)	A Route
Alternate Route Cancel [Telecommunications] (TEL)	ARC
Alternate Route Selection (SAUS)	ARS
Alternate Sector Table (SAUS)	AST
Alternate Source Council (MCD)	ASC
Alternate Source Development	ASD
Alternate Space Defense Operations Center (ACAE)	ASPADOC
Alternate Space Inversion (ACRL)	ASI
Alternate Space Surveillance Center (ACAE)	ASSC
Alternate Squadron Commander [Air Force]	ASC
Alternate Stability Augmentation System (SAUS)	ASAS
Alternate Supply Rate (MCD)	ASR
Alternate Supply Route	ASR
Alternate Tactical Air Control Center (SAUO)	ATACC
Alternate Tape Drive (SAUS)	ATD
Alternate Target (SAUS)	Alt T
Alternate Target Docking Adapter [NASA] (MCD)	ATDA
Alternate Target Point	ATP
Alternate Term Plan (SAUS)	ATP
Alternate Test Procedure [for aviation jet fuels] [Navy]	ATP
Alternate Thermal Protection System (MCD)	ATPS
Alternate Thermal Sight (ACAE)	ATS
Alternate Track Address (SAUS)	ATA
Alternate Training Assemby [Army] (ADDR)	ATA
Alternate Transient Program (SAUS)	ATP
Alternate Transoceanic Abort Landing (SAUS)	ATAL
Alternate Trunk Routing (SAUS)	ATR
Alternate Turbopump Development (SAUS)	ATD
Alternate Unit Codes (SAUS)	AUC
Alternate Uses [Personality research] [Psychology]	AU
Alternate Voice and Data Service (SAUS)	AVD Service
Alternate Voice Data	AVD
Alternate Volume Allocation (SAUS)	AVA
Alternate Weapon	AW
Alternate Weapon Attack (ACAE)	AWA
Alternate Weeks [Advertising term] (WDMC)	A/W
Alternate-Channel (SAUS)	Alt-Ch
Alternate-Day Treatment [Medicine]	ADT
Alternate-Fuel Vehicle (SAUS)	AFV
Alternate-Top-Bevel Teeth [Saw blades]	ATB
Alternating [Polymer] [Organic chemistry]	alt
Alternating (AAEL)	ALT
Alternating Conditional Expectation	ACE
Alternating Continuous Wave [Radio]	ACW
Alternating Current	A
Alternating Current	AC
Alternating Current (IDOE)	ac
Alternating Current Amplifier (SAUS)	ACA
Alternating Current Amplitude (SAUS)	ACA
Alternating Current Anode Voltage (SAUS)	ACAV
Alternating Current Circuit (SAUS)	ACC
Alternating Current Coil (SAUS)	ACC
Alternating Current Conductivity (SAUS)	ACC
Alternating Current Continuous Wave (SAUS)	ACCW
Alternating Current Control Voltage (SAUS)	ACCV
Alternating Current Discharge Plasma (ACAE)	ACDP
Alternating Current Discharge Tube (SAUS)	ACDT
Alternating Current Dump (SAUS)	ACD
Alternating Current Electrocoagulation [Chemical engineering]	ACE
Alternating Current Energy (SAUS)	ACE
Alternating Current Engineering (SAUS)	ACE
Alternating Current Fan-Out (SAUS)	ACFO
Alternating Current Field (SAUS)	ACF
Alternating Current Field Strength (SAUS)	ACFS
Alternating Current Flip-Flip (SAUS)	ACFF
Alternating Current Flip-Flop (IAA)	ACFF
Alternating Current Frequency Modulation (SAUS)	ACFM
Alternating Current Generator	ACG
Alternating Current Hum (SAUS)	ACH
Alternating Current Inductance (SAUS)	ACI
Alternating Current Induction (SAUS)	ACI
Alternating Current Inductivity (SAUS)	ACI
Alternating Current Input (MHDI)	ACI
Alternating Current Line (SAUS)	ACL
Alternating Current Loss (SAUS)	ACL
Alternating Current Mains (SAUS)	ACM
Alternating Current Meter (SAUS)	ACM

Alternating Current Motor (SAUS) ... ACM
Alternating Current Network ... ACNET
Alternating Current Normal Mode Rejection [*Electronics*] (IAA) ... ACNMR
Alternating Current Output (MHDI) ... ACO
Alternating Current Plasma Detector [*Spectrometry*] ... ACPD
Alternating Current Plasma Display Panel [*Electronics*] (IAA) ... ACPDP
Alternating Current Potential (SAUS) ... ACP
Alternating Current Power (SAUS) ... ACP
Alternating Current Probe (SAUS) ... ACP
Alternating Current Rectifier (SAUS) ... ACR
Alternating Current Relay [*Electronics*] (IAA) ... ACREL
Alternating Current Resistance (SAUS) ... ACR
Alternating Current Ringing (SAUS) ... ACR
Alternating Current Signal Generator ... AC-SG
Alternating Current Signalling System (SAUS) ... ACSS
Alternating Current Spark Plug (IAA) ... ACSP
Alternating Current Supply (SAUS) ... ACS
Alternating Current, Synchronous ... ACS
Alternating Current Synthesizer [*Exxon Corp.*] ... ACS
Alternating Current Test Volts (MSA) ... VACT
Alternating Current Testing Plant (SAUS) ... ACTP
Alternating Current Thin-film Electroluminescence (SAUS) ... ACTEL
Alternating Current Thin-Film Electroluminescence (MHDI) ... ACTEL
Alternating Current to Direct Current (SAUS) ... AC/DC
Alternating Current Transmission (SAUS) ... ACT
Alternating Current Vacuum Tube Voltmeter (IAA) ... ACVTVM
Alternating Current Voltage (SAUS) ... ACV
Alternating Current Volts (SAUS) ... A CV
Alternating Current Volts ... ACV
Alternating Current Winding (SAUS) ... ACW
Alternating Current Working Volts (MSA) ... VACW
Alternating Current/Direct Current (NTIO) ... AC/DC
Alternating Current/Direct Current Tube (SAUS) ... ACDCT
Alternating Current/Direct Current Valve (SAUS) ... ACDCV
Alternating Current-High Frequency (SAUS) ... AC-HF
Alternating Current-Low Frequency (SAUS) ... AC-LF
Alternating Current-Radio Frequency (SAUS) ... AC-RF
Alternating Current/Ripple (SAUS) ... AC/R
Alternating Days (SAUS) ... AD
Alternating Direction Implicit [*Algorithm*] ... ADI
Alternating Direction Iterative (PDAA) ... ADI
Alternating Double Filtration (SAUS) ... ADF
Alternating Exotropia [*Ophthalmology*] ... AXT
Alternating Field ... AF
Alternating Field Demagnetization ... AFD
Alternating Fixed and Flashing [*Lights*] ... ALTFFL
Alternating Fixed and Group Flashing (SAUO) ... Alt F Gp Fl
Alternating Fixed and Group Flashing [*Lights*] ... ALTFGPGL
Alternating, Fixed, and Group-Flashing [*Lights*] (DNAB) ... ALTFGFL
Alternating Flashing [*Lights*] ... ALTFL
Alternating Flashing (SAUS) ... Alt Fl
Alternating Flow ... AF
Alternating Frequency Rejection [*Automotive technology*] ... AFR
Alternating Gradient ... AG
Alternating Gradient Focusing ... AGF
Alternating Gradient Synchrotron (SAUS) ... AGS
Alternating Group Flashing (SAUO) ... Alt Gp Fl
Alternating Group Flashing (SAUO) ... Alt Gr Fl
Alternating Group Occulting [*Lights*] ... ALTGPOCC
Alternating Group Occulting (SAUO) ... Alt Gr Occ
Alternating Guidance Section ... AGS
Alternating Hamiltonian Path ... AHP
Alternating Hemiplegia Foundation (SAUO) ... AHF
Alternating Hemiplegia of Childhood [*Medicine*] ... AHC
Alternating Light [*Navigation signal*] ... Al
Alternating Light [*Navigation signal*] ... Alt
Alternating Light (SAUS) ... AltLt
Alternating Magnetic (IUSS) ... AM
Alternating Monocular Deprivation [*Optics*] ... AMD
Alternating Motion Rate ... AMR
Alternating Motion Reflex [*Neurology*] (DAVI) ... AMR
Alternating Motion Reflexes [*Medicine*] (BABM) ... AMR
Alternating Network (SAUS) ... AN
Alternating Occulting (SAUS) ... Alt Occ
Alternating Occulting [*Lights*] ... ALTOCC
Alternating Pressure Air Mattress [*for prevention of pressure sores*] ... APAM
Alternating Rate of Motion [*Neurophysiology*] (DAVI) ... ARM
Alternating Series (SAUS) ... AS
Alternating Sideband Note (SAUS) ... ASB
Alternating Voice and Data (SAUS) ... AVD
Alternating Voltage (SAUS) ... AV
Alternating-Current Control Unit (SAUS) ... A-C CU
Alternating-Current Current Pushing (SAUS) ... ACCP
Alternating-Current, Spark Plug (SAUS) ... ACSP
Alternating-Current Vacuum Tube Voltmeter (SAUS) ... AC VTVM
Alternation (SAUS) ... ALTN
Alternation Gradient Synchrotron (SAUS) ... AGS
Alternation Installation Requirements (IUSS) ... AIR
Alternation Note (SAUS) ... ALT NOT
Alternativa Revolucionaria del Pueblo [*Bolivia*] [*Political party*] (EY) ... ARP
Alternative (ROG) ... ALT
Alternative (BEE) ... alt
Alternative (SAUS) ... Alt
Alternative (IEEE) ... ALTN
Alternative (MSA) ... ALTNV
Alternative ... ALTRNTV
Alternative Access Vendor [*Telecommunications*] ... AAV
Alternative Age of Healing Association (EA) ... AAA
Alternative Agricultural Research and Commercialization Center ... AARC
Alternative Agricultural Research and Commercialization Center (SAUO) ... AARCC
Alternative Agricultural Research and Commercialization Corporation (SAUO) ... AARCCC
Alternative Analysis (PA) ... AA
Alternative and Innovative [*Wastewater treatment system*] (EEVL) ... A&I
Alternative Antenna Array (MCD) ... AAA
Alternative Automotive Power System Division (SAUO) ... AAPSD
Alternative Automotive Power Systems [*Environmental Protection Agency*] ... AAPS
Alternative Billing Service ... ABS
Alternative Binaural Loudness Balance (or Balancing) (SAUS) ... ABLB
Alternative Birth Crisis Coalition [*Defunct*] (EA) ... ABCC
Alternative Book Service [*Reference to an edition of the Anglican Book of Common Prayer*] (BARN) ... ASB
Alternative Broadcasting [*An association*] (EA) ... AB
Alternative Carrier Telecommunications Association (SAUO) ... ACRA
Alternative Carrier Telecommunications Association (EA) ... ACTA
Alternative Center for International Arts (EA) ... ACIA
Alternative Classrooms for the Academically Talented [*Education*] ... ACAT
Alternative Coal Mining Technologies (COE) ... ACMT
Alternative Coated Paper ... ACP
Alternative Command Centre (SAUS) ... ACC
Alternative Command Operations Center (ACAE) ... ACOC
Alternative Communities Movement [*British*] ... ACM
Alternative Community Telephone (SAUS) ... ACT
Alternative Complement Pathway [*Hematology*] ... ACP
Alternative Concentration Limits [*Environmental Protection Agency*] (EPA) ... ACL
Alternative Consumer Energy Society (SAUO) ... ACES
Alternative Control Strategies [*Environmental science*] (COE) ... ACS
Alternative Control Techniques (AAEL) ... ACT
Alternative Control Technology [*Environmental science*] ... ACT
Alternative County Government [*A publication*] (DLA) ... Alt County Gov't
Alternative Criminology Journal [*A publication*] ... Alt Criminol J
Alternative Curriculum Strategies [*Education*] (AIE) ... ACS
Alternative Defense Operations Control Center (ACAE) ... ADOCC
Alternative Defense Posture (DNAB) ... ADP
Alternative Delivery and Financing System [*Medicine*] (HCT) ... ADFS
Alternative Delivery Schedule Evaluator (MHDB) ... ADSE
Alternative Delivery Schedule Generator (CIST) ... ADSG
Alternative Delivery System [*Health care service*] ... ADS
Alternative Device (SAUS) ... ALTDEV
Alternative Dispute Resolution (WYGK) ... ADR
Alternative Economic Strategy ... AES
Alternative Education Project (EA) ... AEP
Alternative Energy ... AE
Alternative Energy Resources Organization (EA) ... AERO
Alternative Environmental Futures [*An association*] ... AEF
Alternative Family Project [*An association*] (EA) ... AFP
Alternative Fertility [*Demography*] ... AF
Alternative Fertility Proportion [*Demography*] ... AFP
Alternative Financing System [*Health care*] (HCT) ... AFS
Alternative Fluorocarbon Environmental Acceptability Study [*World Meteorological Organization*] ... AFEAS
Alternative Folklore Urban (SAUS) ... AFU
Alternative Force Generator (MCD) ... AFG
Alternative Forum [*An association*] (EAIO) ... AF
Alternative Frequencies (or Frequency) (SAUS) ... AF
Alternative Fuel Data Bank [*Bartlesville Energy Technology Center*] [*Database*] ... AFDB
Alternative Fuel Electronics [*Fuel systems*] [*Automotive engineering*] ... AFE
Alternative Fuel Vehicle ... AFV
Alternative Fuel Vehicle (SAUS) ... AHV
Alternative Fuels Development Unit [*La Porte, TX*] [*Department of Energy*] ... AFDU
Alternative Generator Model (DNAB) ... AGM
Alternative Health Care ... AHC
Alternative Health Care Systems Inc. (SAUO) ... AHCS
Alternative Health Care Systems, Inc. (SAUS) ... AHCS
Alternative Health Insurance Services [*An association*] (EA) ... AHIS
Alternative Health Plans [*Department of Health and Human Services*] (GFGA) ... AHP
Alternative Hypothesis (DAVI) ... H_1
Alternative in Higher Education (SAUO) ... AHE
Alternative Inertial Navigation System (SAUS) ... AINS
Alternative Information Center [*Israeli news organization*] ... AIC
Alternative Information Network (EA) ... AIN
Alternative Information Sources Project (SAUS) ... AISP
Alternative Intermediate Services for the Mentally Retarded ... AIS/MR
Alternative Internal Control Review (SAUS) ... AICR
Alternative Internet Resource ... AIR
Alternative Investment Market (WDAA) ... AIM
Alternative Justifiable Cost Method (SAUS) ... AJC Method
Alternative Land Uses and the Rural Economy [*Ministry of Agriculture*] [*British*] ... ALURE
Alternative Launch-Point System ... ALPS
Alternative Learning Program for High School Aged [*Education*] ... ALPHA
Alternative Lengthening of Telomeres [*Genetics*] ... ALT
Alternative Level of Care [*Medicine*] (MEDA) ... ALC
Alternative Lifestyle Checklist ... ALC
Alternative List [*Sweden*] [*Political party*] ... AL

Alternative Liste [*Alternative List*] [*Austria*] [*Political party*] .... AL
Alternative Liste Oesterreich [*Austrian Alternative List*] [*Political party*] (PPW) .... ALO
Alternative Living Manager's Association [*Defunct*] (EA) .... ALMA
Alternative Living Services [*AMEX symbol*] (SAG) .... ALI
Alternative Living Services [*Associated Press*] (SAG) .... AltLivng
Alternative Loan Program .... ALP
Alternative Local Exchange Carrier (CGWS) .... ALEC
Alternative Local Telephone Company (ECON) .... ALT
Alternative Mark Inversion Signal (NITA) .... AMI
Alternative Marriage and Relationship Council of the United States .... AMRCUS
Alternative Mating Technique [*Zoology*] .... AMT
Alternative Medecine Foundation (SAUO) .... AMF
Alternative Medical Association (EA) .... AMA
Alternative Medicine (MELL) .... AM
Alternative Method of Management (MHDB) .... AMM
Alternative Minimum Tax .... AMT
Alternative Minimum Taxable Income .... AMTI
Alternative Mode (SAUS) .... ALT
Alternative Mortgage Instrument .... AMI
Alternative Motor Fuels Act .... AMFA
Alternative Music Market .... AMM
Alternative Network Information Center (SAUO) .... ALTERNIC
Alternative Operational Concepts in Europe [*Military*] .... AOCEUR
Alternative Operator Services [*Telecommunications*] .... AOS
Alternative Patch (SAUS) .... AP
Alternative Performance Appraisal System (DOMA) .... APAS
Alternative Pink Pages. Australasian Plant Pathology (journ.) (SAUS) .... APP
Alternative Poland [*Defunct*] (EA) .... AP
Alternative Press Center (EA) .... APC
Alternative Press Centre, Toronto, ON, Canada [*Library symbol*] [*Library of Congress*] (LCLS) .... CaOTAP
Alternative Press Centre, Toronto, Ontario [*Library symbol*] [*National Library of Canada*] (NLC) .... OTAP
Alternative Press Index .... API
Alternative Press Index (journ.) (SAUS) .... API
Alternative Press Information Service (SAUS) .... APIS
Alternative Press Review [*A publication*] (BRI) .... Alt Pr R
Alternative Press Syndicate [*Defunct*] (EA) .... APS
Alternative Regulatory Option [*Environmental Protection Agency*] (GFGA) .... ARO
Alternative Release Procedure (SAUS) .... ARP
Alternative Release Procedures (MCD) .... ARP
Alternative Remedial Contract Strategy (EEVL) .... ARCS
Alternative Remedial Contracting Strategy (AAGC) .... ARCS
Alternative Remedial Contracting Systems [*Environmental Protection Agency*] .... ARCS
Alternative Reproduction Vehicle [*Medicine*] .... ARV
Alternative Research in Architecture, Resources, Art and Technology (SAUS) .... ARARAT
Alternative Resource Allocation Priorities [*Military*] .... ARAP
Alternative Resource Center (EA) .... ARC
Alternative Resources [*NASDAQ symbol*] (TTSB) .... ALRC
Alternative Resources Corp. [*NASDAQ symbol*] (SAG) .... ALRC
Alternative Resources Corp. [*Associated Press*] (SAG) .... AltResc
Alternative Risk Transfer [*Finance*] .... ART
Alternative Route to Ordained Service (DICI) .... ARTOS
Alternative Salient Features (SAUS) .... ASF
Alternative Salient Future (PDAA) .... ASF
Alternative Schedule of Reinforcement (DIPS) .... ALT
Alternative Service Book [*1980*] [*A publication*] (ODCC) .... ASB
Alternative Society [*British*] .... AS
Alternative Sources of Energy (EA) .... ASE
Alternative Space Defence Centre (SAUS) .... ASDC
Alternative Splicing Factor [*Genetics*] .... ASF
Alternative Subordinate War Headquarters (SAUS) .... ASWHQ
Alternative System Design Concept .... ASDC
Alternative System Exploration (MCD) .... ASE
Alternative Technologies and Approaches [*Military*] (RDA) .... ATA
Alternative Technology .... AT
Alternative Technology Association [*Australia*] .... ATA
Alternative Technology Information Group (EAIO) .... ATIG
Alternative Term Plan (IAA) .... ATP
Alternative Test Method (SAUS) .... ATM
Alternative to Amniocentesis [*Medicine*] .... ATA
Alternative to Dedicated Hospital Ship (CAAL) .... ADHOS
Alternative to the New York Times Committee (EA) .... ANYTC
Alternative Trade of Non-Traditional Products and Development in Latin America (SAUO) .... CANDELA
Alternative Treatment Technology Information Center [*Environmental Protection Agency*] (AEPA) .... ATTIC
Alternative Type Acceptance [*Model for interference measurement*] (NITA) .... ATA
Alternative Vote .... AV
Alternative War Headquarters (SAUS) .... AWHQ
Alternative Work Schedule (GFGA) .... AWS
Alternative-Based Language (SAUS) .... ABL
Alternatively Refined Carrageenan [*Food grade*] .... ARC
Alternatives for International Document Availability (TELE) .... AIDA
Alternatives for Learning through Educational Research and Technology (DICI) .... ALERT
Alternatives in Higher Education [*Program*] [*National Science Foundation*] .... AHE
Alternatives Loan Program [*Humane Society of the United States*] .... ALP
Alternatives to Abortion International (SAUO) .... AAI
Alternatives to Abortion International [*Later, AAI/WHEF*] (EA) .... AAI
Alternatives to Abortion International/Women's Health and Education Foundation (EA) .... AAI/WHEF
Alternatives to Slash-and-Burn (SAUS) .... ABS
Alternator (KSC) .... ALT
Alternator .... ALTNR
Alternator (MSA) .... ALTNTR
Alternator (SAUS) .... Alto
Alternator [*Automotive engineering*] .... ALTR
Alternator .... ALTRNTR
Alternator Currency (SAUS) .... AC
Alternator Research Package .... ARP
Alternator-Powered Electrically Heated Catalyst [*Automotive engineering*] .... APEHC
Alternis Diebus [*Alternate Days*] [*Pharmacy*] .... AD
Alternis Diebus [*Every Other Day*] [*Pharmacy*] .... ALT DIEB
Alternis Horis [*Every Other Hour*] [*Pharmacy*] .... ALTERN HOR
Alternis Horis [*Every Other Hour*] [*Pharmacy*] .... ALT HOR
Alternis Nocibus [*Every Other Night*] [*Pharmacy*] (BARN) .... alt noc
Alternis Nocte [*Every Other Night*] [*Pharmacy*] .... ALT NOCT
Altero Technology [*Vancouver Stock Exchange symbol*] .... ALK
Alterra Healthcare [*AMEX symbol*] (SG) .... ALI
Alters- und Hinterlassenen-Versicherung [*Old Age and Dependents Insurance*] [*State insurance company*] [*Liechtenstein*] (EY) .... AHV
Altertext Conversion System (DGA) .... ACS
Altertumswissenschaft (BJA) .... AW
Altes Testament [*Old Testament*] [*German*] .... AT
Altesse [*Highness*] [*French*] .... ALT
Altesse Imperiale [*Imperial Highness*] [*French*] .... AI
Altesse Royale [*Royal Highness*] [*French*] .... AR
Altesses [*Highnesses*] [*French*] .... AA
Altex Resources Ltd. [*Toronto Stock Exchange symbol*] .... AX
Altezza [*Highness*] [*Italian*] .... A
Althaea [*Rose of Sharon*] [*Pharmacology*] (ROG) .... ALTH
Althemer & Gray, Chicago, IL [*Library symbol*] [*Library of Congress*] (LCLS) .... ICAG
Althydusamband Islands [*Icelandic Federation of Labor*] .... ASI
Altimeter (NG) .... ALT
Altimeter (KSC) .... ALTM
Altimeter (ADWA) .... altm
Altimeter Check Location [*Aviation*] (FAAC) .... ACL
Altimeter Check Point (SAUS) .... ACP
Altimeter Control Equipment [*Aviation*] .... ACE
Altimeter Indicator (MCD) .... AI
Altimeter Setting (FAAC) .... ALSTG
Altimeter Setting (SAUS) .... AltSet
Altimeter Setting Indicator [*Aviation*] (FAAC) .... ASI
Altimeter Setting Region [*Aviation*] (AIA) .... ASR
Altimeter Setting Region [*Aviation*] .... ASRGN
Altimeter Station [*ITU designation*] (CET) .... ROA
Altimeter Transmitter Multiplier (DNAB) .... ATM
Altimeter Vertical Velocity Indicator [*NASA*] (MCD) .... AVVI
Altimeter/Radar Altimeter (SAUS) .... ALT/RA
Altimeter/Velocity Sensor Antenna .... A/VSA
Altimetry Data Fusion Center (SAUO) .... ADFC
Altimetry Research in Ocean Circulation (SAUS) .... TOPEX POSEIDON
Altimetry System Error [*Aviation*] (DA) .... ASE
Altintas [*Turkey*] [*Seismograph station code, US Geological Survey*] (SEIS) .... ALT
Altiranisches Woerterbuch [*A publication*] (BJA) .... AiWb
Altitude (AFM) .... ALT
Altitude (WA) .... alt
Altitude (WDAA) .... Alt
Altitude .... ALTTD
Altitude .... H
Altitude Alerting Unit (SAUS) .... AAU
Altitude and Rate-Indicating System (DNAB) .... ARIS
Altitude Barometric Switch [*Automotive engineering*] .... ABS
Altitude Command Indicator .... ACI
Altitude Compensation Induction System .... ACIS
Altitude Compensator [*Automotive engineering*] .... AC
Altitude Control (ACAE) .... A/C
Altitude Control Electronics .... ACE
Altitude Control Equipment (SAUS) .... ACE
Altitude Control System .... ACS
Altitude Control Test Facility .... ACTF
Altitude Controller Assembly (MCD) .... ACA
Altitude Controller Assembly (SAUS) .... ACA
Altitude Conversion Kit .... ACK
Altitude Coordinate Converter System (SAUS) .... ACCS
Altitude Deviation .... AD
Altitude Difference [*Navigation*] .... A
Altitude Difference Ranging (ACAE) .... ADR
Altitude Differential (SAUS) .... AD
Altitude Direction Indicator (AFM) .... ADI
Altitude Encoder Unit (MCD) .... AEU
Altitude Engine Control (AAG) .... AEC
Altitude Engine Control Panel (AAG) .... AECP
Altitude Error .... ALTE
Altitude Error (GAVI) .... HE
Altitude Gyro Accelerometer Package (SAUS) .... AGAP
Altitude Gyroscope Control Assembly [*Military*] (CAAL) .... AGCA
Altitude Heading Reference System (GAVI) .... AHRS
Altitude Hold Mode (GAVI) .... ALT HOLD
Altitude Identification Military System (MCD) .... AIMS
Altitude in Height Above Station .... QFE
Altitude Indicated Above Sea Level .... QNH
Altitude Indicating System (SAUS) .... AIS
Altitude Indication System .... AIS

Altitude Indicator [*Aviation*] (DA) .... AI
Altitude Indoctrination (MCD) .... AI
Altitude Instrument Flying (DA) .... AIF
Altitude Intercept (SAUS) .... A
Altitude Layer Surveillance Terminal Area Radar (SAUS) .... ALSTAR
Altitude Layer Surveillance Terminal Area RADAR .... ALSTAR
Altitude Manned Penetrator (MCD) .... AMP
Altitude Marking Radar (SAUS) .... AMR
Altitude Marking Range (KSC) .... AMR
Altitude Measurement System .... AMS
Altitude Proximity Sensor (MCD) .... APS
Altitude Radial (FAAC) .... ARAD
Altitude Rate [*Symbol*] (NASA) .... H
Altitude Rate Command .... ARC
Altitude Rate Command System (MCD) .... ARCS
Altitude Reconnaissance Probe (MUGU) .... ARP
Altitude Referenced Radiometer .... ARR
Altitude Report Status (SAA) .... ALRS
Altitude Reporting (DA) .... A/R
Altitude Reporting Mode of Secondary Radar [*FAA*] (TAG) .... MODE C
Altitude Reservation [*Air Force*] (AFM) .... ALTRV
Altitude Reservation Void for Aircraft Not Airborne By [*Aviation*] (FAAC) .... AVANA
Altitude Return (ACAE) .... AR
Altitude Select [*Aviation*] (PIPO) .... ASEL
Altitude Sensing System .... ASS
Altitude Sensing Unit [*Aviation*] (AIA) .... ASU
Altitude Sensor Bypass (MCD) .... ASB
Altitude Sounding Projectile (MUGU) .... ASP
Altitude Switch Assembly (SAUS) .... ASA
Altitude Test Facility (SAUS) .... ATF
Altitude Transmission Equipment (SAUS) .... ATE
Altitude Transmitting Equipment [*FAA*] (MSA) .... ALTE
Altitude Transmitting Equipment [*FAA*] .... ATE
Altitude Variation Rate and Displacement .... AVRAD
Altitude Velocity Chart .... AVC
Altitude Vertical Scale (SAUS) .... AVS
Altitude Vertical Velocity Computer (SAUS) .... AVVC
Altitude Warning Signal System (PDAA) .... AWSS
Altitude Warning System (MCD) .... AWS
Altitude Wind Tunnel .... AWT
Altitude/Depth (SAUS) .... A/D
Altitude-Vertical Velocity Indicator [*NASA*] (AFM) .... AVVI
Altman Information Systems, Inc. [*Information service or system*] (IID) .... AIS
Alto .... A
Alto .... a
Alto .... ALT
Alto Clarinet .... acl
Alto Comisionado de las Naciones Unidas para los Refugiados [*Office of the United Nations High Commissioner for Refugees*] [*Spanish*] (DUND) .... ACNUR
Alto Exploration [*Vancouver Stock Exchange symbol*] .... ANE
Alto Flute .... afl
Alto Palena [*Chile*] [*Airport symbol*] (AD) .... WAP
Alto Palena/Alto Palena [*Chile*] [*ICAO location identifier*] (ICLI) .... SCAP
Alto Parnaiba [*Brazil*] [*Airport symbol*] (AD) .... APY
Alto Rio Senguerr [*Argentina*] [*Airport symbol*] (OAG) .... ARR
Alto Rio Senguerr [*Argentina*] [*ICAO location identifier*] (ICLI) .... SAVR
Alto Rio Senguerr, AR (SAUO) .... ARR
Alto Saxophone .... asx
Alto Xylophone (SAUS) .... Alt Xyl
Altocumulus [*Cloud*] [*Meteorology*] .... AC
Altocumulus [*Cloud*] [*Meteorology*] (MUGU) .... ACU
Altocumulus [*Cloud*] [*Meteorology*] .... ALCU
Altocumulus Castellanus [*Cloud*] [*Meteorology*] .... ACC
Altocumulus Castellanus [*NWS*] (FAAC) .... ACCAS
Altocumulus Castellenas Cloud (WEAT) .... AcCast
Altocumulus Lenticularis Cloud (WEAT) .... AcLent
Altocumulus Standing Lenticular Cloud (WEAT) .... ACSI
Altoff High School, Belleville, IL [*Library symbol*] [*Library of Congress*] (LCLS) .... IBelHS
Altogether (ROG) .... ALTOGR
Altogether Builders, Labourers, and Constructional Workers Society [*A union*] [*British*] .... ABLCWS
Altogether Builders Labourers and Constructional Workers Society (SAUO) .... ABLCWS
Altogether Builders, Labourers and Constructional Workers Society (SAUS) .... ABLCWS
Alton & Southern (SAUO) .... A&S
Alton & Southern Railroad .... A & S
Alton and Southern Railroad (SAUO) .... ALT&S
Alton and Southern Railway Co. (SAUO) .... AL&S
[*The*] **Alton & Southern Railway Co.** [*AAR code*] .... ALS
[*The*] **Alton & Southern Railway Co.** .... ALT & S
Alton Community Unit 11, Alton, IL [*Library symbol*] [*Library of Congress*] (LCLS) .... IAlCU
Alton Downs [*Australia*] [*Airport symbol*] [*Obsolete*] (OAG) .... AWN
Alton, IL [*Location identifier*] [*FAA*] (FAAL) .... ALN
Alton, IL [*Location identifier*] [*FAA*] (FAAL) .... CVM
Alton, IL [*FM radio station call letters*] (BROA) .... KATZ-FM
Alton, IL [*FM radio station call letters*] .... KNJZ
Alton, IL [*AM radio station call letters*] .... WBGZ
Alton Memorial Hospital, Alton, IL [*Library symbol*] [*Library of Congress*] (LCLS) .... IAlH
Alton Mental Health Center, Development and Training Center, Staff Library, Alton, IL [*Library symbol*] [*Library of Congress*] (LCLS) .... IAlMH
Alton Public Library, Alton, IA [*Library symbol*] [*Library of Congress*] (LCLS) .... IaAltn
Altona Community Memorial Health Centre, Altona, MB, Canada [*Library symbol*] [*Library of Congress*] (LCLS) .... CaMACMH
Altona Community Memorial Health Centre, Manitoba [*Library symbol*] [*National Library of Canada*] (NLC) .... MACMH
Altona, Hamburg, Wandsbek (journ.) (SAUS) .... AHW
Altona, MB [*AM radio station call letters*] .... CFAM
Altona Medical Centre, Altona, MB, Canada [*Library symbol*] [*Library of Congress*] (LCLS) .... CaMAMC
Altona Medical Centre Library, Manitoba [*Library symbol*] [*National Library of Canada*] (NLC) .... MAMC
Altoona [*Pennsylvania*] .... ALT
Altoona [*Pennsylvania*] [*Airport symbol*] (OAG) .... AOO
Altoona Area Public Library, Altoona, PA [*OCLC symbol*] (OCLC) .... AOP
Altoona Area Public Library, Altoona, PA [*Library symbol*] [*Library of Congress*] (LCLS) .... PAlt
Altoona, PA [*Television station call letters*] .... WATM
Altoona, PA [*AM radio station call letters*] .... WFBG
Altoona, PA [*FM radio station call letters*] .... WFGY
Altoona, PA [*Television station call letters*] .... WKBS
Altoona, PA [*FM radio station call letters*] .... WPRR
Altoona, PA [*AM radio station call letters*] .... WRTA
Altoona, PA [*Television station call letters*] .... WTAJ
Altoona, PA [*AM radio station call letters*] .... WVAM
Altoona Public Library, Altoona, IA [*Library symbol*] [*Library of Congress*] (LCLS) .... IaAlto
Altoona, WI [*FM radio station call letters*] .... WISM
Altoona-Johnstown [*Diocesan abbreviation*] [*Pennsylvania*] (TOCD) .... ALT
Altoona-Martinsburg [*Pennsylvania*] [*Airport symbol*] (AD) .... AOO
Altorientalische Bilder zum Alten Testament [*A publication*] (BJA) .... AOBAT
Altos Computer Systems (NITA) .... ACS
Altos Hornos de Mexico ADS [*NYSE symbol*] (SG) .... IAM
Altos Hornos de Mexico SA de CV [*Associated Press*] (SAG) .... AltosHrn
Altos Hornos de Mexico SA de CV [*NYSE symbol*] (SAG) .... IAM
Altos Office Manager [*Altos Computer Systems*] .... AOM
Altostratus [*Also, AS*] [*Meteorology*] .... ALST
Altostratus [*Also, ALST*] [*Meteorology*] .... AS
Altostratus [*Cloud*] [*Meteorology*] (AIA) .... ASt
Altostratus and Altocumulus [*Meteorology*] .... ASAC
Altostratus Cloud (WEAT) .... As
Altostratus Opacus (SAUS) .... As op
Altpreussische Monatschrift (journ.) (SAUS) .... APM
Altris Software, Inc. [*Associated Press*] (SAG) .... Altris
Altris Software, Inc. [*NASDAQ symbol*] (SAG) .... ALTS
Altron, Inc. [*NASDAQ symbol*] (NQ) .... ALRN
Altron, Inc. [*Associated Press*] (SAG) .... Altron
altruism (SAUS) .... altru
altruist (SAUS) .... altru
altruistic (SAUS) .... altru
Altrusa International (EA) .... AI
Altrusa International (SAUO) .... AI
Altshuler, Aronov, Spivak oscillations (SAUS) .... AAS oscillations
Alturas, CA [*Location identifier*] [*FAA*] (FAAL) .... ARU
Alturas, CA [*FM radio station call letters*] (BROA) .... KALT-FM
Alturas, CA [*AM radio station call letters*] .... KCNO
Alturas, CA [*FM radio station call letters*] (RBYB) .... KCNO-FM
Alturas, CA [*AM radio station call letters*] (RBYB) .... KKFJ-AM
Alturas, CA [*FM radio station call letters*] .... KYAX
Altus [*Oklahoma*] [*Airport symbol*] (OAG) .... AXS
Altus Air Force Base [*Oklahoma*] [*ICAO location identifier*] (ICLI) .... KLTS
Altus Airlines [*ICAO designator*] (FAAC) .... AXS
Altus Junior College (SAUO) .... AJC
Altus Library, Altus, OK [*Library symbol*] [*Library of Congress*] (LCLS) .... OkAl
Altus, OK [*Location identifier*] [*FAA*] (FAAL) .... ALT
Altus, OK [*Location identifier*] [*FAA*] (FAAL) .... AXS
Altus, OK [*Location identifier*] [*FAA*] (FAAL) .... HVU
Altus, OK [*FM radio station call letters*] .... KEYB
Altus, OK [*FM radio station call letters*] .... KKVO
Altus, OK [*FM radio station call letters*] .... KRKZ
Altus, OK [*AM radio station call letters*] .... KWHW
Altus, OK [*Location identifier*] [*FAA*] (FAAL) .... LTS
Altyn Tagh Fault [*Geology*] .... ATF
Alufinance and Trade Ltd. (SAUO) .... Alufinance
Alula [*Somalia*] [*Airport symbol*] (OAG) .... ALU
Alula [*Somalia*] [*ICAO location identifier*] (ICLI) .... HCMA
Alum, Blood, and Charcoal [*A method of deodorizing by addition of a compound of these*] [*Medicine*] .... ABC
Alum, Blood and Charcoal (SAUS) .... ABC
Alum, Blood and Clay (SAUS) .... ABC
Alum, Blood, Clay Method [*Raw sewage treatment*] [*Organic chemistry*] (DAVI) .... ABC
Alum Co. Amer $3.75 Pfd [*AMEX symbol*] (TTSB) .... AAPr
Alum Precipitated [*Medicine*] .... AP
Alum Precipitated Pyridine [*Medicine*] (MAE) .... APP
Alum Precipitated Toxoid [*Medicine*] .... APT
Alumax, Inc. [*Associated Press*] (SAG) .... Alumax
Alumax, Inc. [*NYSE symbol*] (SAG) .... AMX
Alumina Ceramic Manufacturers Association (SAUO) .... ACM
Alumina Ceramic Manufacturers Association [*Defunct*] (EA) .... ACMA
Alumina Ceramic Test .... ACT
Alumina Trihydrate [*Inorganic chemistry*] .... ALTH
Alumina Trihydrate [*Inorganic chemistry*] .... ATH

Alumina-Zirconia-Silica [*Inorganic chemistry*] ... AZS
Aluminiosilicate Polyacrylate (SAUS) ... ASPA
Aluminium (SAUS) ... AL
Aluminium [*British*] (ADA) ... ALU
Aluminium Alloy (SAUS) ... ALALY
Aluminium Alloy Anodizing Wire (SAUS) ... AAA wire
Aluminium Alloy Conductor Steel Reinforced (SAUS) ... AACSR
Aluminium and Polyethylene (SAUS) ... ALPETH
Aluminium and Steel (SAUS) ... AS
Aluminium Bahrain (SAUO) ... ALBA
Aluminium, Brick and Glass Workers International Union (SAUO) ... ABGWIU
Aluminium Cable, Aluminium Reinforced (SAUS) ... ACAR
Aluminium Cable, Steel Reinforced (SAUS) ... ACSR
Aluminium Can Group [*Australia*] [*An association*] ... ACG
Aluminium Canada Ltd. (SAUO) ... ALCAN
Aluminium Casting (SAUS) ... ALC
Aluminium Chlorohydrate (SAUS) ... ACH
Aluminium Coatings Association [*British*] (DBA) ... ACA
Aluminium Coaxial Plug (SAUS) ... Al Coax PL
Aluminium Company of America (SAUO) ... AA
Aluminium Company of America (SAUO) ... ALCOA
Aluminium Company of Canada (SAUO) ... ALCAN
Aluminium Conductor, Steel Reinforced (SAUS) ... ACSR
Aluminium Conductors (SAUS) ... ALUCON
Aluminium Conductors (SAUO) ... Alucon
Aluminium Crown (SAUS) ... ALCr
Aluminium Diethyl Hydride (SAUS) ... ADEH
Aluminium Dihydroxyaminoacetate (SAUS) ... ADA
Aluminium Efficient Radiator (SAUS) ... AER
Aluminium Electrical Lead (SAUS) ... AEL
Aluminium Express Representative (SAUS) ... AER
Aluminium Extension Jacket (SAUS) ... AEJ
Aluminium Extruders Association (SAUO) ... AEA
Aluminium Fabricators' Association of Western Australia ... AAFAWA
Aluminium Federation ... AF
Aluminium Foil Conference (SAUO) ... AFCO
Aluminium Gallium Arsenide (SAUS) ... AlGaAs
Aluminium Indium Arsenide (SAUS) ... AlInAs
Aluminium Ion (SAUS) ... Al
Aluminium Manufacturing Company of Nigeria Ltd. (SAUO) ... ALUMACO
Aluminium Measuring Instrument (SAUS) ... AMI
Aluminium Oxide ... ALOX
Aluminium Plastic Tearoff (SAUS) ... APTO
Aluminium Powder Material (SAUS) ... APM
Aluminium Powder Metallurgy (SAUS) ... APM
Aluminium Production Commission (SAUO) ... AAPC
Aluminium Radiator Manufacturers Association [*British*] (DBA) ... ARMA
Aluminium Research Institute (SAUS) ... ARI
Aluminium Research Laboratories (SAUO) ... ALRL
Aluminium Resources Development Company (SAUO) ... ARDECO
Aluminium Rolled Products Manufacturers Association [*British*] (DBA) ... ARPMA
Aluminium Silicate Pigment (SAUS) ... ASP
Aluminium Silicon (SAUS) ... ALSI
Aluminium Stockholders' Association [*British*] ... ASA
Aluminium Submarine for Deep-Ocean Research [*Navy symbol*] [*British*] ... ALUMINAUT
Aluminium Suisse, SA [*Commercial firm*] ... AS
Aluminium Technical Information Service (SAUS) ... ATIS
Aluminium Trimethyl (SAUS) ... ATM
Aluminium Window Association [*British*] (DBA) ... AWA
Aluminium Window Industry Association of Victoria [*Australia*] ... AWIAV
Aluminium Wire & Cable Co., Ltd. (SAUO) ... AWCO
Aluminium-Coated Glass-Fibre (SAUS) ... ACGF
Aluminium-Free Inorganic Suspended Material (SAUS) ... AFISM
Aluminium-Jacketed (SAUS) ... ALJAK
Aluminium-Resin-Polyethylene-Aluminium-Polyethylene (SAUS) ... ARPAP
Aluminium-Sheat (SAUS) ... ALS
Aluminium-to-Copper (SAUS) ... AL-Cu
Aluminium-Zentrale eV ... AZ
Aluminocalcium Phosphorous Oxide [*Inorganic chemistry*] ... ALCAP
Aluminophosphate [*Inorganic chemistry*] ... ALPO
Aluminosilicate Polyacrylate [*Type of dental cement*] ... ASPA
Aluminum [*Chemical element*] ... Al
Aluminum [*Chemical symbol is Al*] ... ALUM
Aluminum ... Alum
Aluminum (VRA) ... alum
Aluminum [*Chemical symbol is Al*] ... ALUMN
Aluminum Alloy Constructor Steel Reinforced (IEEE) ... AACSR
Aluminum and Polyethylene [*Components of a type of telecommunications cable*] ... ALPETH
Aluminum and Steel [*Freight*] ... AS
Aluminum Anodizers Council (NTPA) ... AAC
Aluminum Antimonide (SAUS) ... AlSb
Aluminum Arsenide (SAUS) ... AlAs
Aluminum Association (EA) ... AA
Aluminum Association ... AlA
Aluminum Association Aluminum Standards and Data [*Information service or system*] (IID) ... AAASD
Aluminum Association, Inc. ... AA
Aluminum Association of Florida (SRA) ... AAF
Aluminum Beaker Oxidation Test [*Lubricant testing*] ... ABOT
Aluminum Biogeochemistry in Soils (SAUS) ... ALBIOS
Aluminum, Brick and Clay Workers International Union (SAUS) ... ABCWIU
Aluminum Brick and Clay Workers International Union (SAUO) ... ABCWIU
Aluminum, Brick, and Clay Workers International Union (EA) ... ABCWIU
Aluminum, Brick, and Glass Workers International Union ... ABG
Aluminum, Brick, and Glass Workers International Union ... ABGW
Aluminum, Brick, and Glass Workers International Union (EA) ... ABGWIU
Aluminum Building Products Credit Association [*Defunct*] ... ABPCA
Aluminum Cable Steel Reinforced ... ACSR
Aluminum Cable, Steel Reinforced (SAUS) ... ACSR
Aluminum Chlorohydrate [*Inorganic chemistry*] ... ACH
Aluminum Chlorohydroxyallantoinate [*Organic chemistry*] ... ALCA
Aluminum Co. of America [*NYSE symbol*] (SAG) ... AA
Aluminum Co. of America [*AMEX symbol*] (SAG) ... AAp
Aluminum Co. of America (EFIS) ... ACAP
Aluminum Co. of America [*Associated Press*] (SAG) ... Alcoa
Aluminum Co. of America, ALCOA Research Laboratories Library, New Kensington, PA [*Library symbol*] [*Library of Congress*] (LCLS) ... PNkA
Aluminum Co. of Canada Ltd. [*Toronto Stock Exchange symbol*] [*Vancouver Stock Exchange symbol*] ... ACC
Aluminum Co. of Canada Ltd. ... ALCAN
Aluminum Co. of Canada Ltd., Arvida, PQ, Canada [*Library symbol*] [*Library of Congress*] (LCLS) ... CaQAA
Aluminum Co. of Canada Ltd., Kingston, ON, Canada [*Library symbol*] [*Library of Congress*] (LCLS) ... CaOKAL
Aluminum Co. of Canada Ltd., Kingston, Ontario [*Library symbol*] [*National Library of Canada*] (NLC) ... OKAL
Aluminum Company of America [*Wall Street slang names: "Ack Ack" and "All American"*] [*NYSE symbol*] (SPSG) ... AA
Aluminum Company of America (SAUO) ... Ack-Ack
Aluminum Company of Colorado (SAUO) ... ALCO
Aluminum Conductor Alloy Reinforced (MCD) ... ACAR
Aluminum Conductor Steel Reinforced ... ACSR
Aluminum Conductor, Steel-einforced (SAUS) ... ACSR
Aluminum Corporation of America (SAUO) ... ALCOA
Aluminum Crown [*Dentistry*] ... AL CR
Aluminum Crown (SAUS) ... alcr
Aluminum Dihydroxyaminoacetate (SAUS) ... ADA
Aluminum Dihydroxyaminoacetate [*Also, ALGLYN*] [*Pharmacology*] ... ADA
Aluminum Efficient Radiator [*General Motors Corp.*] [*Automotive engineering*] ... AER
Aluminum Electrical Lead ... AEL
Aluminum Extension Jacket ... AEJ
Aluminum Extruders Association (DAC) ... AEA
Aluminum Extruders Council (EA) ... AEC
Aluminum Field Coil ... AFC
Aluminum Foil Container Manufacturers Association (EA) ... AFCMA
Aluminum Foil Container Manufacturers Association (SAUS) ... AFISM
Aluminum Foil Field Coil ... AFFC
Aluminum Four Barrel Carburetor [*Automotive engineering*] (DICI) ... AFB
Aluminum Four-Barrel [*Automotive term*] ... AFB
Aluminum Fracture Toughness Database [*Information service or system*] (IID) ... ALFRAC
Aluminum Gallium Arsenide (IEEE) ... AlGaAs
Aluminum Gallium Nitride (AAEL) ... A1GaN
Aluminum Gallium Nitride ... AiGaN
Aluminum Gallium Nitride (SAUS) ... AlGaN
Aluminum Glycinate [*Also, ADA*] [*Pharmacology*] ... ALGLYN
Aluminum Glycinate (SAUS) ... ALGLYN
aluminum hydroxide (SAUS) ... Al hydrox
Aluminum Hydroxide [*Antacid*] [*Pharmacology*] (DAVI) ... $Al(OH)_3$
Aluminum in Streams Study (SAUS) ... ALSS
Aluminum Intensive Vehicle [*Auto industry*] ... AIV
Aluminum Isopropoxide [*or Isopropylate*] [*Organic chemistry*] ... AIP
Aluminum Jacketed Coaxial Cable (SAUS) ... ALJAK
Aluminum Limited (SAUO) ... AL
Aluminum Linear Shaped Charge (PDAA) ... ALSC
Aluminum Manufacturers Credit Bureau [*Defunct*] (EA) ... AMCB
Aluminum Matting [*Military*] ... AM
Aluminum, Nickel, Cobalt [*Alloy*] ... ALNICO
Aluminum Oxide (AAEL) ... A1203
Aluminum oxide (SAUS) ... Al203
Aluminum Oxide (SAUS) ... Corundum
Aluminum Perchlorate (MCD) ... AP
Aluminum Phosphate Gel [*Medicine*] (MELL) ... APG
Aluminum Phosphide (SAUS) ... AIP
Aluminum Plasma Model (MCD) ... ALPLASMA
Aluminum Plastic Tearoff (SAUS) ... APTO
Aluminum Powder Metallurgy ... APM
Aluminum Powder Metallurgy Product ... APMP
Aluminum Recycling Association (EA) ... ARA
Aluminum Research Institute ... ARI
Aluminum Roofing Institute (SAUS) ... ARI
Aluminum Secretariat Ltd., Montreal, PQ, Canada [*Library symbol*] [*Library of Congress*] (LCLS) ... CaQMA
Aluminum Siding Association (SAUO) ... ASA
Aluminum Siding Association [*Later, AAMA*] (EA) ... ASA
Aluminum Silicate (SAUS) ... Andalusite
Aluminum Silicate Pigment ... ASP
Aluminum Silicon [*An alloy*] ... ALSI
Aluminum, Silicon, Calcium, Magnesium [*Geology*] ... ASCM
Aluminum Smelters Research Institute [*Later, ARA*] (EA) ... ASRI
Aluminum Smelting and Refining Co. (EFIS) ... ASARCO
Aluminum Structured Vehicle [*Automotive engineering*] ... ASV
Aluminum Structured Vehicle Technology [*Automotive engineering*] ... ASVT
Aluminum Sulphate Producers Association (SAUS) ... ASUPA
Aluminum Tartrate (DMAA) ... AIT
Aluminum Triethyl [*Organic chemistry*] ... ATE
Aluminum Trimethyl [*Organic chemistry*] ... ATM

Aluminum Tube Multi-Effect (PDAA) ... ATME

Aluminum Wares Association [*Later, CMA*] ... AWA

Aluminum Window and Door Manufacturers Association (SAUO) ... AWDMA

Aluminum Window Manufacturers Association [*Later, Architectural Aluminum Manufacturers Association*] ... AWMA

Aluminum Workers International Union [*Later, ABCWIU*] (EA) ... AWIU

Aluminum Workers International Union [*Later, ABCWIU*] ... AWU

Aluminum Workers Union (SAUO) ... AWU

Aluminum-Bronze (SAUS) ... ALB

Aluminum-Clad (MSA) ... ALCD

Aluminum(dihydroxy)allantoinate [*Organic chemistry*] ... ALDA

Aluminum-Free Inorganic Suspended Material ... AFISM

Aluminum-Oxide Electrolytic Capacitor (MUGU) ... ALOXCON

Aluminum-Polythene Laminate (SAUS) ... APL

Aluminurn Perchlorate (SAUS) ... AP

Alumna (NTIO) ... alum

Alumnae (ADWA) ... alum

Alumnae Advisory Center [*Later, CCP*] (EA) ... AAC

Alumni Association of Shriners Hospitals (EA) ... AASH

Alumni Association of the University of New England [*Australia*] ... AAUNE

Alumni Association. University of British Columbia. Chronicle (journ.) (SAUS) ... UBC Alumni Chronicle

Alumni Memorial Library, Orchard Lake, MI [*Library symbol*] [*Library of Congress*] (LCLS) ... MiOlA

Alumni Presidents Council of Independent Secondary Schools (SAUS) ... APCISS

Alumni Service Cooperative (SAUS) ... TASC

Alumni Without Library Schools ... AWOLS

Alumni Yalensia [*Alumni of Yale College*] [*Latin*] ... Alum Yalen

Alumnium Activation Clay Tool (SAUS) ... AACT

Alumnus (ROG) ... ALUM

Alum-Precipitated Protein [*Biochemistry*] (DAVI) ... APP

Alunite (SAUS) ... at

Alure Resource Corp. [*Vancouver Stock Exchange symbol*] ... ARU

Alushta [*Former USSR*] [*Seismograph station code, US Geological Survey*] [*Closed*] (SEIS) ... ALU

Alusuisse International N.V. (SAUO) ... ALINTER

Alusuisse Metals Inc. (SAUO) ... ALUMET

Aluta [*Leather*] [*Pharmacy*] (ROG) ... ALUT

Alva, OK [*Location identifier*] [*FAA*] (FAAL) ... AVK

Alva, OK [*AM radio station call letters*] ... KALV

Alva, OK [*FM radio station call letters*] ... KTTL

Alva, OK [*FM radio station call letters*] ... KXLS

Alveolar [*Gas*] [*Medicine*] ... A

Alveolar [*Anatomy*] ... alv

Alveolar Abscess [*Medicine*] (MELL) ... AA

Alveolar Capillary Membrane [*Medicine*] (MELL) ... ACM

Alveolar Carbon Dioxide Pressure [*in blood gases*] [*Medicine*] (DAVI) ... PA_{CO2}

Alveolar Cell Carcinoma [*Oncology*] (AAMN) ... ACC

Alveolar Crest [*Medicine*] (MELL) ... AC

Alveolar Dead-space Volume [*Medicine*] (DAVI) ... V_DA

Alveolar Duct (MAE) ... AV

Alveolar Echinococcis (DB) ... AE

Alveolar Gas (SAUS) ... A

Alveolar Gas Volume [*Medicine*] (DAVI) ... V_A

Alveolar Hemorrhage [*Medicine*] (MELL) ... AH

Alveolar Hypoventilation Syndrome [*Medicine*] (DMAA) ... AHS

Alveolar Lining Material [*Medicine*] (DAVI) ... ALM

Alveolar Macrophage [*Hematology*] ... AM

Alveolar Macrophages (SAUS) ... AM

Alveolar Mixing Efficiency [*Physiology*] ... AME

Alveolar Mucosa [*Medicine*] (DMAA) ... ALVM

Alveolar Mucosa (DB) ... AM

Alveolar Oxygen Pressure (WDAA) ... PAO2

Alveolar Pressure [*Medicine*] (DAVI) ... P_A

Alveolar Sac (MAE) ... AS

Alveolar Soft Part Sarcoma [*Oncology*] ... ASPS

Alveolar Tidal Volume [*Medicine*] (DAVI) ... V_TA

Alveolar Ventilation ... VA

Alveolar Ventilation per Minute [*Medicine*] (DAVI) ... V_A

Alveolar Ventilation Rate for Experimental Animal Species ... VAa

Alveolar Ventilation Rate for Human ... VAh

Alveolar Volume [*Clinical chemistry*] (AAMN) ... VA

Alveolar-Arterial [*Physiology*] (MAE) ... AA

alveolar-arterial (SAUS) ... aa

Alveolar-Arterial Carbon Dioxide Difference [*Biochemistry*] (DAVI) ... $(A-A)P\ CO_2$

Alveolar-Arterial Oxygen Difference [*Physiology*] ... $A-aDO_2$

Alveolar-Arterial Oxygen Gradient [*Biochemistry*] (DAVI) ... $A-AO_2$

Alveolar-Arterial Pressure Difference [*For A-aDO$_2$*] [*Medicine*] (DAVI) ... $P(A-a)O_2$

Alveolar-Capillary Membrane Permeability [*Medicine*] (DMAA) ... ACMP

Alveolar-Macrophage-Derived Growth Factor [*Biochemistry*] ... AMDGF

Alveolectomy [*Dentistry and maxillofacial surgery*] (DAVI) ... Alvx

Alveolectomy [*Medicine*] (DMAA) ... ALVX

Alverca [*Portugal*] [*ICAO location identifier*] (ICLI) ... LPAR

Alverno College (SAUO) ... AC

Alverno College, Milwaukee (SAUS) ... AC

Alverno College, Milwaukee, WI [*OCLC symbol*] (OCLC) ... GZA

Alverno College, Milwaukee, WI [*Library symbol*] [*Library of Congress*] (LCLS) ... WMA

Alverno College, Milwaukee, WI [*Library symbol*] [*Library of Congress*] (LCLS) ... WMAC

Alverthorpe Gallery, Rosenwald Collection, Jenkintown, PA [*Library symbol*] [*Library of Congress*] (LCLS) ... PJAIG

Alvey Research for Insurance Expert Systems (NITA) ... ARIES

Alvi Dejectiones [*Discharge from the Bowels*] [*Pharmacy*] ... ALV DEJECT

Alvin Ailey American Dance Center ... AAADC

Alvin Junior College, Alvin (SAUS) ... AJC

Alvin Junior College, Alvin, TX [*Library symbol*] [*Library of Congress*] (LCLS) ... TxAlvC

Alvin, Mid-Atlantic Ridge [*Oceanography*] ... AMAR

Alvin, TX [*FM radio station call letters*] ... KACC

Alvin, TX [*Television station call letters*] ... KHSH

Alvin, TX [*AM radio station call letters*] ... KTEK

Alvin W. Vogtle, Jr. Plant [*Nuclear energy*] (NRCH) ... AVP

Alvis Owners Club [*North Droitwich, Worcestershire, England*] (EAIO) ... AOC

Alvo Adstricta [*When the Bowels Are Constipated*] [*Pharmacy*] ... ALV ADST

Alvo Adstricta [*When the Bowels Are Constipated*] [*Pharmacy*] ... Alv Adstrict

Alvsbyn [*Sweden*] [*ICAO location identifier*] (ICLI) ... ESUV

Alvus [*Stomach*] [*Medicine*] (ROG) ... ALV

Always Accessible (SAUS) ... ALW-ACC

Always Accessible/Always Afloat (SAUS) ... AAAA

Always Afloat [*Ship's charter*] ... AA

Always Afloat Always Accessible (RIMS) ... AAAA

Always Causing Legal Unrest [*An association*] (EA) ... ACLU

Always On, Always Connected (SAUS) ... AOAC

Always On/Dynamic ISDN [*Integrated Services Digital Network*] [*Telecommunications*] ... AO/DI

Always Safely Afload (SAUS) ... ASA

Aly Aviation [*British*] [*ICAO designator*] (FAAC) ... AAV

Alyemda Democratic Yemen [*ICAO designator*] (AD) ... DY

Alyemda-Democratic Yemen Airlines [*ICAO designator*] (FAAC) ... DYA

Alyeska Air Service [*ICAO designator*] (FAAC) ... ALY

Alyn Corp. [*NASDAQ symbol*] (SAG) ... ALYN

Alyn Corp. [*Associated Press*] (SAG) ... AlynCp

ALZA Corp. [*Associated Press*] (SAG) ... ALZA

ALZA Corp. [*NYSE symbol*] (TTSB) ... AZA

Alzamento [*Raising, Lifting*] [*Music*] ... Alz

Alzheimer Disease and Associated Disorders (ADWA) ... ADAD

Alzheimer Group (SAUS) ... TAG

Alzheimer Senile Dementia [*Medicine*] (MELL) ... ASD

Alzheimer Society of Canada [*Societe Alzheimer du Canada*] (AC) ... ASC

Alzheimer Society of Oxford County (AC) ... ASOC

Alzheimer Support, Information, and Service Team (SAUO) ... ASIST

Alzheimer Support, Information and Service Team (SAUS) ... ASIST

Alzheimer Type Dementia [*Medicine*] ... ATD

Alzheimer Type Senile Dementia [*Medicine*] (MELL) ... ATSD

Alzheimer-Like Senile Dementia [*Medicine*] (DMAA) ... ALSD

Alzheimer's Amyloid Polypeptide [*Medicine*] (DB) ... AAP

Alzheimers Association [*Australia*] ... AA

Alzheimer's Dementia [*Medicine*] (MELL) ... AD

Alzheimers Disease (SAUS) ... AD

Alzheimer's Disease [*Medicine*] ... AD

Alzheimer's Disease [*Medicine*] (MELL) ... ALZ

Alzheimers Disease (SAUS) ... AZ

Alzheimer's Disease and Related Conditions [*Medicine*] ... ADRC

Alzheimer's Disease and Related Disorders Association (EA) ... ADRDA

Alzheimers Disease and Related Disorders Association (SAUS) ... ADRDA

Alzheimer's Disease Assessment Scale ... ADAS

Alzheimer's Disease Assessment Scale Cognitive Subscale ... ADAS-Cog

Alzheimers Disease Association of Maryland (SAUS) ... adam

Alzheimer's Disease Education Referral Center (BARN) ... ADERC

Alzheimer's Disease International (EA) ... ADI

Alzheimers Disease International (SAUS) ... ADI

Alzheimer's Disease Research ... ADR

Alzheimer's Disease Research Center [*Bronx, NY*] [*Department of Health and Human Services*] (GRD) ... ADRC

Alzheimer's Disease Society [*British*] ... ADS

Alzheimers Disease Society (SAUS) ... ADS

Alzheimer's Disease-Associated Protein [*Medicine*] ... ADAP

Alzheimer's Presenile Dementia [*Medicine*] (MELL) ... APSD

Alzhirskaia Kommunisticheskaia Partia [*Albanian Communist Party*] [*Political party*] ... AKP

Am Angefuehrten Orte [*At the Place Quoted*] [*German*] ... AAO

AM International [*AMEX symbol*] (TTSB) ... AM

AM International [*Associated Press*] (SAG) ... AM In

AM International [*Associated Press*] (SAG) ... AM Intl

AM International, Inc. [*Formerly, Addressograph-Multigraph Corp.*] [*AMEX symbol*] (SPSG) ... AM

AM Intl Wrrt [*AMEX symbol*] (TTSB) ... AM WS

A.M. MacArthur Primary School, Locust Valley, NY [*Library symbol*] [*Library of Congress*] (LCLS) ... NLvMP

Am Rhein [*on the River Rhine*] [*German*] (ODBW) ... a Rh

Ama [*Papua New Guinea*] [*Airport symbol*] (OAG) ... AMF

Ama Air Express [*ICAO designator*] (AD) ... YD

AMA Collection System (SAUS) ... AMACS

AMA International (SAUO) ... AAIM

AMA International (SAUO) ... AMAI

AMA On-Line CME Locator (SAUO) ... CME

AMA Recording Center (SAUO) ... AMARC

AMA Standard Entry (SAUS) ... AMASE

AMA Teleprocessing System (SAUS) ... AMATPS

AMA Transmitter (SAUS) ... AMAT

Amacrine Cell [*of the retina*] [*Optics*] ... AM

Amadeo [*Record label*] [*Austria, etc.*] ... Ama

Amadeus Global Travel Distrution SA [*Spain*] [*ICAO designator*] (FAAC) ... AGT

Amadeusair GmbH [*Austria*] [*ICAO designator*] (FAAC) ... AMU

Amador Central Railroad Co. [*AAR code*] ... AMC

Amador County Free Library, Jackson, CA [*Library symbol*] [*Library of Congress*] (LCLS) ... CJ

Amador Heritage Center, Almelund, MN [Library symbol] [Library of Congress] (LCLS) .... MnAlmA

Ama-Flyg [ICAO designator] (AD) .... VW

Amagansett Free Library, Amagansett, NY [Library symbol] [Library of Congress] (LCLS) .... NAma

Amagansett Historical Association, Amagansett, NY [Library symbol] [Library of Congress] (LCLS) .... NAmaHi

Amagat-Leduc Rule [Physics] .... ALR

Amahai [Indonesia] [Airport symbol] (OAG) .... AHI

Amahai [Indonesia] [ICAO location identifier] (ICLI) .... WAPA

AMA [American Management Association]/International [New York, NY] (EA) .... AMA/I

Amalagmated Society of Engineers, Machinists, Smiths, Millwrights, and Pattern Makers [A union] [British] .... ASEMSMP

Amalfi [Colombia] [Airport symbol] (AD) .... AFI

Amalgam (SAUS) .... Aaa

Amalgam (MELL) .... aaa

Amalgam [Dentistry] .... AM

Amalgam (SAUS) .... Amal

Amalgam (SAUS) .... Amlg

Amalgam [Metallurgy] .... AMLG

Amalgam (SAUS) .... amM

Amalgama [Amalgamation] [Pharmacy] (ROG) .... AAA

amalgamate (SAUS) .... amal

Amalgamate Paper Books [British] .... APB

Amalgamated (ADA) .... AMAL

Amalgamated (EY) .... AMALG

Amalgamated Association of Beamers, Twisters, and Drawers [A union] [British] (DCTA) .... AABTD

Amalgamated Association of Beamers, Twisters and Drawers (SAUO) .... AABTD

Amalgamated Association of Brass Founders, Turners, Fitters, and Coppersmiths [A union] [British] .... AABFTFC

Amalgamated Association of Card, Blowing and Ring Room Operatives (SAUO) .... AACBRRO

Amalgamated Association of Felt Hat Trimmers and Wool Formers [A union] [British] (DCTA) .... AAFHTWF

Amalgamated Association of Felt Hat Trimmers and Wool Formers [A union] [British] (DCTA) .... AFHTWF

Amalgamated Association of Iron, Steel and Tin Workers of America (SAUO) .... AAISTW

Amalgamated Association of Machine Workers [A union] [British] .... AAMW

Amalgamated Association of Operative Cotton Spinners (SAUO) .... AAOCS

Amalgamated Association of Operative Cotton Spinners and Twiners (SAUO) .... AAOCST

Amalgamated Association of Street and Electric Railway Employers of America (SAUO) .... AA of S & ERE of A

Amalgamated Association of Street, Electric Railway, and Motor Coach Employees of America [Later, ATU] .... SERMCE

Amalgamated Association of Wistful War Wives [World War II] .... AAWWW

Amalgamated Book Services [British] .... ABS

Amalgamated Carriage and Wagon Society [A union] [British] .... ACWS

Amalgamated Clothing and Textile Workers Union (EA) .... ACTWU

Amalgamated Clothing and Textile Workers Union of America (SAUO) .... ACTWUA

Amalgamated Clothing Workers (SAUO) .... ACW

Amalgamated Clothing Workers of America (SAUO) .... ACWA

Amalgamated Clothing Workers of America [Later, ACTWU] (EA) .... ACWA

Amalgamated Clothing Workers Union (SAUO) .... ACWU

Amalgamated Conservation Society (AC) .... ACS

Amalgamated Drillers and Hole Cutters Society [A union] [British] .... ADHCS

Amalgamated Engineering and Electrical Union (WA) .... AEEU

Amalgamated Engineering Union (SAUO) .... AEU

Amalgamated Engineering Union [United Kingdom] .... AEU

Amalgamated Engineering Union. Monthly Journal [A publication] .... Amal Engng Union Mon J

Amalgamated Film & Broadcasting Union (SAUO) .... AFBU

Amalgamated Film Studios (SAUO) .... AFS

Amalgamated Flying Saucer Clubs of America (EA) .... AFSCA

Amalgamated Footwear and Textile Workers' Union of Australia .... AFTWUA

Amalgamated Gas Accumulation [Stove designed by Gustaf Dalen in 1922] .... AGA

Amalgamated Hackle Pin Grinders Sick and Mutual Benefit Society [British] .... AHPGSMBS

Amalgamated Industrial Union of Packing Case Workers (SAUO) .... AIUPCW

Amalgamated Instrument Makers Society [A union] [British] .... AIMS

Amalgamated Lace Operatives of America .... ALO

Amalgamated Lace Operatives of America [Defunct] (EA) ...... ALOA

Amalgamated Lithographers of America [Later, GAIU] .... ALA

Amalgamated Lithographers of America (DGA) .... ALOA

Amalgamated Lithographers of America (SAUO) .... AL of A

Amalgamated Machine and General Labourers Union [British] .... AMGLU

Amalgamated Machine, Engine and Iron Grinders and Graziers Society (SAUO) .... AMEIGGS

Amalgamated Master Dairymen, Inc. (SAUO) .... AMD

Amalgamated Meat Cutters and Butcher Workmen of North America (SAUO) .... AMC&BW of NA

Amalgamated Meat Cutters and Butcher Workmen of North America [Later, UFCWIU] (EA) .... AMCBW

Amalgamated Meat Cutters and Butcher Workmen of North America [Later, UFCWIU] .... MCBW

Amalgamated Metal Corporation (SAUO) .... AMC

Amalgamated Metal Workers and Shipwrights' Union [Australia] .... AMSWU

Amalgamated Metalworkers and Shipwrights Union (SAUO) ..... AMWSU

Amalgamated Military and Technical Improvement Plan (DNAB) .... AMI

Amalgamated Military Technical (DNAB) .... AMT

Amalgamated Milk Vendors' Association of New South Wales [Australia] .... AMVANSW

Amalgamated Mining [Vancouver Stock Exchange symbol] .... AMA

Amalgamated Moulders and Kindred Industries Trade Union [British] .... AMKITU

Amalgamated Moulders and Kindred Industries Trade Union (SAUO) ..... AMKITU

Amalgamated Picture Frame Trade Union (SAUO) .... APFRU

Amalgamated Picture Frame Trade Union [British] .... APFTU

Amalgamated Power Engineering (ODBW) .... APE

Amalgamated Printers' Association (EA) .... APA

Amalgamated Printing Trades Employees' Union [Australia] (DGA) .... APTEU

Amalgamated Publishers, Inc. .... API

Amalgamated Publishers, Incorporated (SAUO) .... API

Amalgamated Scale, Beam, and Weighing Machine Makers Association [A union] [British] .... ASBWMMA

Amalgamated Sewing Machine, Cycle, and Tool Makers Association [A union] [British] .... ASMCTMA

Amalgamated Shipyard Helpers Association [A union] [British] .... ASHA

Amalgamated Slaters, Tilers and Roofing Operatives Society [British] (BI) .... ASTRO

Amalgamated Society of Anchorsmiths, Ship Tackle, and Shackle Makers [A union] [British] .... ASASTSM

Amalgamated Society of Ball Warpers (SAUO) .... ASBW

Amalgamated Society of Boilermakers, Shipwrights, Blacksmiths, and Structural Workers [A union] [British] (DCTA) .... ASBSBSW

Amalgamated Society of Boot and Shoe Makers and Repairers (SAUO) .... ASBSMR

Amalgamated Society of Brass Workers [A union] [British] ...... ASBW

Amalgamated Society of Brassworkers (SAUO) .... ASB

Amalgamated Society of Cane, Wicker and Perambulator Operatives (SAUO) .... ASCWPO

Amalgamated Society of Casters [A union] [British] .... ASC

Amalgamated Society of Coopers (SAUO) .... ASC

Amalgamated Society of Coremakers of Great Britain and Ireland [A union] .... ASCGBI

Amalgamated Society of Cricket Ball Makers (SAUO) .... ASCBM

Amalgamated Society of Engineers (SAUO) .... ASE

Amalgamated Society of Engineers [A union] [British] .... ASE

Amalgamated Society of Farriers and Blacksmiths (SAUO) .... ASFB

Amalgamated Society of General Tool Makers, Engineers, and Machinists [A union] [British] .... ASGTMEM

Amalgamated Society of Journeymen Felt Hatters (SAUO) ..... ASJFH

Amalgamated Society of Journeymen Felt Hatters and Allied Workers [A union] [British] (DCTA) .... ASJFHAW

Amalgamated Society of Leather Workers (SAUO) .... ASLW

Amalgamated Society of Lithographic Printers (SAUO) .... ASLP

Amalgamated Society of Lithographic Printers (DGA) .... ASLP

Amalgamated Society of Master Cloggers (SAUO) .... ASMC

Amalgamated Society of Metal Workers [A union] [British] ..... ASMW

Amalgamated Society of Operative Engineers [A union] [British] .... ASOE

Amalgamated Society of Operative Lace Makers and Auxiliary Workers (SAUO) .... ASOLMAW

Amalgamated Society of Plate and Machine Moulders [A union] [British] .... ASPMM

Amalgamated Society of Printers (SAUO) .... ASP

Amalgamated Society of Railway Servants (SAUO) .... ASRS

Amalgamated Society of Scale Beam and Weighing Machine Makers [A union] [British] .... ASSBWMM

Amalgamated Society of Shuttle Makers (SAUO) .... ASSM

Amalgamated Society of Shuttlemakers [A union] [British] ...... ASS

Amalgamated Society of Silk Twisters (SAUO) .... ASST

Amalgamated Society of Spring Makers, Tool Makers and Grinders (SAUO) .... ASSMTM&G

Amalgamated Society of Telegraph and Telephone Construction Men [A union] [British] .... ASTTCM

Amalgamated Society of Telephone Employees [A union] [British] .... ASTE

Amalgamated Society of Textile Workers and Kindred Trades [A union] [British] (DCTA) .... ASTWKT

Amalgamated Society of Textile Workers and Kindred Trades (SAUO) .... ASTWKT

Amalgamated Society of Tobacco Manufacturers [A union] [British] .... ASTM

Amalgamated Society of Vehicle Builders, Carpenters and Mechanics (SAUO) .... ASVBCM

Amalgamated Society of Wire Drawers and Kindred Workers (SAUO) .... ASWDKW

Amalgamated Society of Wire Drawers and Kindred Workers [A union] [British] (DCTA) .... ASWDKW

Amalgamated Society of Wood Workers [British] .... ASWW

Amalgamated Society of Woodcutting Machinists (SAUO) ..... ASWCM

Amalgamated Society of Woodcutting Machinists [British] (BI) .... ASWM

Amalgamated Society of Woodworkers [British] (BI) .... ASW

Amalgamated Society of Woodworkers (SAUO) .... ASWW

Amalgamated Software of North America, Inc. (SAUS) .... ASNA

Amalgamated Swimming Association (SAUO) .... ASA

Amalgamated Television Services (SAUO) .... ATS

Amalgamated Textile Warehousemen (SAUO) .... ATW

Amalgamated Textile Workers' Union [British] (DCTA) .... ATWU

Amalgamated Tin Mines of Nigeria .... ATMN

Amalgamated Transit Union (EA) .... ATU

Amalgamated Transit Unions (SAUO) .... ATU

Amalgamated Typefounders Trade Society (DGA) .... ATTS

Amalgamated Union of Asphalt Workers [British] (DCTA) ...... AUAW

Amalgamated Union of Asphalt Workers (SAUO) .... AUAW

Amalgamated Union of Building Trade Workers (SAUO) .... AUBTW

Amalgamated Union of Engineering and Foundry Workers (SAUO) .... AEF

Amalgamated Union of Engineering and Foundry Workers [British] .... AUEFW

Amalgamated Union of Engineering Workers [*British*] (DCTA) ... AUEW
Amalgamated Union of Engineering Workers - Constructional [*British*] (DCTA) ... AUEW(C)
Amalgamated Union of Engineering Workers - Engineering [*British*] (DCTA) ... AUEW(E)
Amalgamated Union of Engineering Workers - Foundry [*British*] (DCTA) ... AUEW(F)
Amalgamated Union of Engineering Workers - Technical and Supervisory [*British*] (DCTA) ... AUEW-TASS
Amalgamated Union of Foundry Workers [*British*] ... AUFW
Amalgamated Union of Foundry Workers (SAUO) ... AUFW
Amalgamated Union of Operative Bakers, Confectioners and Allied Workers (SAUO) ... AUOBCAW
Amalgamated Union of Public Employees [*Singapore*] ... AUPE
Amalgamated Union of Upholsterers (SAUO) ... AUU
Amalgamated Welded Boiler Makers Society [*A union*] [*British*] ... AWBMS
Amalgamated Wireless Australasia Computer Services (SAUS) ... AWACS
Amalgamated Wireless Australasia Computers Division Services (NITA) ... AWACS
Amalgamated Wireless Australasia Ltd. [*Telecommunications service*] ... AWA
Amalgamated Wireless Australasia Ltd. (SAUO) ... AWA
Amalgamated Wireless Valve Company (SAUO) ... AWV
Amalgamated Workers Union of New Zealand (SAUO) ... AVRUNZ
Amalgamation (SAUS) ... Aaa
Amalgamation (SAUS) ... Amal
Amalgamation of Left Political Organizations (SAUO) ... ALPO
Amalvius de Claris Aquis [*Flourished, 14th century*] [*Authority cited in pre-1607 legal work*] (DSA) ... Amal
Amalvius de Claris Aquis [*Flourished, 14th century*] [*Authority cited in pre-1607 legal work*] (DSA) ... Amalvis
Amami [*Japan*] [*ICAO location identifier*] (ICLI) ... RJKA
Amami O Shima [*Japan*] [*Airport symbol*] (OAG) ... ASJ
Amana Heritage Society, Middle Amana, IA [*Library symbol*] [*Library of Congress*] (LCLS) ... IaMidaHA
Amanab [*Papua New Guinea*] [*Airport symbol*] (OAG) ... AMU
Amanda Resources Ltd. [*Vancouver Stock Exchange symbol*] ... AAU
Amanita Phalloides (MELL) ... AP
Amanitinylazobenzoylglycylglycine (SAUS) ... ABGG
(Amanitinylazobenzoyl)glycylglycine ... ABGG
Amanu [*Tuamotu Archipelago*] [*Seismograph station code, US Geological Survey*] (SEIS) ... AMN
AMAP Assessment Report (SAUS) ... AAR
Amapa [*Brazil*] [*Airport symbol*] (AD) ... APA
Amapa [*Brazil*] [*ICAO location identifier*] (ICLI) ... SBAM
Amapala [*Honduras*] [*ICAO location identifier*] (ICLI) ... MHAM
AMARC Protocol Converter (SAUS) ... APC
AMARC [*Automatic Message Accounting Recording Center*] **Protocol Converter** (TEL) ... APC
Amarillo [*Texas*] [*Airport symbol*] (OAG) ... AMA
Amarillo Area Office (SAUO) ... AA
Amarillo Area Office (SAUO) ... AAO
Amarillo Biosciences, Inc. [*NASDAQ symbol*] (SAG) ... AMAR
Amarillo Biosciences, Inc. [*Associated Press*] (SAG) ... AmarBio
Amarillo Branch [*Military*] (SAA) ... AB
Amarillo College (SAUO) ... AC
Amarillo College, Amarillo, TX [*OCLC symbol*] (OCLC) ... ACC
Amarillo College, Amarillo, TX [*Library symbol*] [*Library of Congress*] (LCLS) ... TxAmC
Amarillo Grain Exchange (EA) ... AGE
Amarillo Public Library (SAUS) ... TAP
Amarillo Public Library, Amarillo, TX [*OCLC symbol*] (OCLC) ... TAP
Amarillo Public Library, Amarillo, TX [*Library symbol*] [*Library of Congress*] (LCLS) ... TxAm
Amarillo Technical Training Center (SAUO) ... ATTC
Amarillo, TX [*FM radio station call letters*] ... KACV
Amarillo, TX [*Television station call letters*] ... KACV-TV
Amarillo, TX [*FM radio station call letters*] ... KAEZ
Amarillo, TX [*Television station call letters*] ... KAMR
Amarillo, TX [*FM radio station call letters*] (RBYB) ... KAPU-FM
Amarillo, TX [*FM radio station call letters*] ... KATP
Amarillo, TX [*FM radio station call letters*] (BROA) ... KAVW-FM
Amarillo, TX [*FM radio station call letters*] ... KBUY-FM
Amarillo, TX [*Television station call letters*] ... KCIT
Amarillo, TX [*AM radio station call letters*] ... KDJW
Amarillo, TX [*Television station call letters*] ... KFDA
Amarillo, TX [*AM radio station call letters*] ... KGNC
Amarillo, TX [*FM radio station call letters*] ... KGNC-FM
Amarillo, TX [*AM radio station call letters*] ... KIXZ
Amarillo, TX [*FM radio station call letters*] ... KJRT
Amarillo, TX [*FM radio station call letters*] (RBYB) ... KLLR
Amarillo, TX [*FM radio station call letters*] ... KLMN
Amarillo, TX [*FM radio station call letters*] ... KMML
Amarillo, TX [*FM radio station call letters*] (BROA) ... KNSY-FM
Amarillo, TX [*FM radio station call letters*] (BROA) ... KPQZ-FM
Amarillo, TX [*AM radio station call letters*] ... KPUR
Amarillo, TX [*FM radio station call letters*] ... KPVY
Amarillo, TX [*FM radio station call letters*] ... KQAC
Amarillo, TX [*FM radio station call letters*] ... KQIZ
Amarillo, TX [*FM radio station call letters*] ... KRGN
Amarillo, TX [*AM radio station call letters*] (RBYB) ... KTNZ
Amarillo, TX [*Television station call letters*] ... KVII
Amarillo, TX [*FM radio station call letters*] ... KYFA
Amarillo, TX [*AM radio station call letters*] ... KZIP
Amarillo, TX [*Location identifier*] [*FAA*] (FAAL) ... TDW
Amarillo/Amarillo Air Terminal [*Texas*] [*ICAO location identifier*] (ICLI) ... KAMA
Amark Explorations Ltd. [*Vancouver Stock Exchange symbol*] ... AMK
Amaryllis Research Institute (EA) ... ARI
Amateur ... A
Amateur ... AMTR
Amateur All-Star Baseball [*An association*] (EA) ... AABI
Amateur Angling Society (SAUO) ... AAS
Amateur Artists Association of America [*Defunct*] (EA) ... AAAA
Amateur Arts Society (SAUS) ... RAAS
Amateur Astronomers Association [*Later, AAANY*] ... AAA
Amateur Astronomers Association, Brooklyn, NY [*Library symbol*] [*Library of Congress*] (LCLS) ... NBA
Amateur Astronomers Association, Brooklyn, NY [*Library symbol*] [*Library of Congress*] (LCLS) ... NBAA
Amateur Astronomers Association of New York [*Formerly, AAA*] (EA) ... AAANY
Amateur Astronomers Association of New York City [*Later, AAA*] (EA) ... AAANYC
Amateur Astronomers Incorporated (SAUO) ... AAI
Amateur Athletic Association (SAUO) ... AAA
Amateur Athletic Association [*British*] ... AAA
Amateur Athletic Association (SAUO) ... AAAssn
Amateur Athletic Association of America (SAUO) ... AAAA
Amateur Athletic Club ... AAC
Amateur Athletic Union (NTIO) ... AAU
Amateur Athletic Union of Canada (SAUO) ... AAU of C
Amateur Athletic Union of the United States (EA) ... AAU
Amateur Athletic Union of the United States (SAUO) ... AAUUS
Amateur Athletic Western Union (SAUO) ... AAWU
Amateur Athletics Union of Australia (SAUO) ... AAUA
Amateur Basket Ball Association (SAUO) ... ABBA
Amateur Basketball Association [*British*] (BI) ... ABBA
Amateur Basketball Association of Ireland (SAUO) ... ABAI
Amateur Basketball Association of Scotland (BI) ... ABAS
Amateur Basketball Association of the United States of America [*Later, USA Basketball*] (EA) ... ABAUSA
Amateur Beekeepers' Association of New South Wales [*Australia*] ... ABANSW
Amateur Beekeepers' Society of South Australia ... ABSSA
Amateur Bicycle League of America [*Later, USCF*] ... ABLA
Amateur Bicycle League of America (SAUO) ... ABLA
Amateur Book Collector (journ.) (SAUS) ... ABC
Amateur Boxing Association [*British*] ... ABA
Amateur Boxing Association of England (EAIO) ... ABAE
Amateur Canoe Association of Western Australia ... ACAWA
Amateur Cartoonist Extraordinary [*National Cartoonists' Society award*] ... ACE
Amateur Chamber Music Players (EA) ... ACMP
Amateur Cine World (journ.) (SAUS) ... ACW
Amateur Cinema League of America (SAUO) ... ACL
Amateur Computer Club (SAUO) ... ACC
Amateur Drama League [*Republic of Ireland*] (BI) ... ADL
Amateur Dramatic Club [*British*] ... ADC
Amateur Dramatic Club (SAUO) ... ADC
Amateur Dramatic Society [*Cambridge, England*] ... ADS
Amateur Entomologists' Society (EA) ... AES
Amateur Fencers League of America [*Later, USFA*] (EA) ... AFLA
Amateur Fencing Association (EAIO) ... AFA
Amateur Fencing Association (SAUO) ... AFA
Amateur Field Trial Clubs of America (EA) ... AFTCA
Amateur Fishermen's Association of the Northern Territory ... AFANT
Amateur Football Alliance [*British*] (BI) ... AFA
Amateur Football Association (SAUO) ... AFA
Amateur Football Club (SAUO) ... AFC
Amateur Golfers' Association of America (EA) ... AGA
Amateur Golfers' Association of America [*Defunct*] (EA) ... AGAA
Amateur Gymnastics Association (WDAA) ... AGA
Amateur Hockey Association of the United States (EA) ... AHAUS
Amateur Martial Association [*British*] (DBA) ... AMA
Amateur Microcomputer Teleprinting Over Radio (SAUS) ... AMTOR
Amateur Microprocessor Teleprinter Over Radio ... AMTOR
Amateur Motor Cycle Association [*British*] (DBA) ... AMCA
Amateur Music Association [*British*] (DBA) ... AMA
Amateur Organist Association International (EA) ... AOAI
Amateur Organists and Keyboard Association International (EA) ... AOKAI
Amateur Pistol Shooting Union of Australia ... APSU
Amateur Press Alliance [*Defunct*] (EA) ... APA
Amateur Press Association [*Generic term*] ... APA
Amateur Printers' Association (DGA) ... APA
Amateur Publishers' Association ... APA
Amateur Publishers' Association Magazine [*Generic term for one-person science-fiction fan magazine*] ... APAZINE
Amateur Radio Club (LAIN) ... ARC
Amateur Radio Direction Finding ... ARDF
Amateur Radio Emergency Association (SAUO) ... AREA
Amateur Radio Emergency Corps [*of ARPSC*] ... AREC
Amateur Radio Emergency Service ... ARES
Amateur Radio Emergency Services (SAUO) ... ARES
Amateur Radio League (SAA) ... ARL
Amateur Radio Mobile Society (SAUO) ... ARMS
Amateur Radio Monitor ... ARM
Amateur Radio Network (EA) ... AR-Net
Amateur Radio Observation Service (SAUS) ... AROS
Amateur Radio on the International Space Station ... ARISS
Amateur Radio Operator (SAUS) ... HAM
Amateur Radio Public Service Corps ... ARPSC
Amateur Radio Relay League (SAUS) ... ARRL
Amateur Radio Repeater Network (SAUS) ... ARRN
Amateur Radio Research and Development Corp. (IID) ... AMRAD

Amateur Radio Retailers Association (SAUO) .... ARRA
Amateur Radio Service (ECII) .... ARS
Amateur (Radio) Station [ITU designation] (CET) .... AR
Amateur Radio Station (IDOE) .... ARS
Amateur Radio Technical Abstracts .... ARTA
Amateur Radio Translater (or Translation) on Balloon (SAUS) .... ARTOB
Amateur Radio-Teletype Society (SAUO) .... ARTS
Amateur Riders Association [British] (DBA) .... ARA
Amateur Rocketeers of America .... ARA
Amateur Rose Breeders Association [British] (DBA) .... ARBA
Amateur Rowing Association [British] .... ARA
Amateur Rowing Association of Western Australia .... ARAWA
Amateur Scientist Research Organization (EA) .... ASRO
Amateur Skating Association of Canada (SAUO) .... ASAC
Amateur Skating Union of the United States (WGA) .... ASUUS
Amateur Skating Union of the United States of America (EA) .... ASU-USA
Amateur Softball Association of America (EA) .... ASA
Amateur Softball Association of America (SAUO) .... ASAA
Amateur Speedskating Union of the United States (EA) .... ASU-USA
Amateur Station [ITU designation] .... AT
Amateur Swimming Association .... ASA
Amateur Swimming Union of the Americas (SAUO) .... ASUA
Amateur Telescope Maker .... ATM
Amateur Telescope Making (SAUS) .... ATM
Amateur Teletype over Radio (SAUS) .... AMTOR
Amateur Television (MSA) .... ATV
Amateur Television Association (EA) .... ATA
Amateur Television Association (SAUO) .... ATA
Amateur Traffic Net [Radio] .... ATN
Amateur Trapshooting Association (SAUO) .... AMA
Amateur Trapshooting Association (SAUO) .... ATA
Amateur Trapshooting Association (EA) .... ATA
Amateur Trapshooting Association of America (SAUO) .... ATAA
Amateur Volleyball Association [British] (BI) .... AVA
Amateur Volume Control .... AVC
Amateur Yacht Research Society [Turnchapel, Plymouth, England]
  (EAIO) .... AYRS
Amatex Export Trade Association [Defunct] (EA) .... AETA
Amati Communications [NASDAQ symbol] (TTSB) .... AMTX
Amati Communications Corp. [Associated Press] (SAG) .... Amati
Amati Communications Corp. [NASDAQ symbol] (SAG) .... AMTX
Amatignak Island [Alaska] [Seismograph station code, US Geological Survey]
  [Closed] (SEIS) .... AMA
Amat.illo College (SAUS) .... AC
Amatol (SAUS) .... Am
Amatol [Materials] .... AM
Amatorius [of Plutarch] [Classical studies] (OCD) .... Amat
Amatsia [Israel] [Geomagnetic observatory code] .... AMT
Amaurosis Fugax [Medicine] (DMAA) .... AF
Amaurotic Familial Idiocy .... AFI
Amax Gold [Associated Press] (SAG) .... Amax
Amax Gold $3.75 SrB'Cv Pfd [NYSE symbol] (TTSB) .... AUPrB
Amax Gold, Inc. [Associated Press] (SAG) .... AmaxG
Amax Gold, Inc. [NYSE symbol] (SPSG) .... AU
Amax Gold, Inc. [Toronto Stock Exchange symbol] .... AXG
AMAX, Inc. [Formerly, Alumax, Inc., American Metal Climax, Inc.] [NYSE
  symbol] [Toronto Stock Exchange symbol] (SPSG) .... AMX
AMAX, Inc., Golden, CO [Library symbol] [Library of Congress] (LCLS) .... CoGA
Amazing Magic Pivot Swing [Training device for baseball batter's rear
  foot] .... AMPS
Amazon Basin Experiment (SAUO) .... LAMBADA
Amazon Bay [Papua New Guinea] [Airport symbol] (OAG) .... AZB
Amazon Biogeochemistry and Atmospheric Chemistry Experiment
  (SAUS) .... AMBIACE
Amazon Boundary Layer Experiment (MCD) .... ABLE
Amazon Ground Emissions (MCD) .... AGE
Amazon Petroleum Corp. [Vancouver Stock Exchange symbol] .... AMZ
Amazon River and Basin [MARC geographic area code] [Library of
  Congress] (LCCP) .... sa---
Amazon River and Basin (SAUS) .... sa
Amazonas Association of Dentists (SAUO) .... ADAM
Amazonas Heat Source Experiment (SAUS) .... AMAHSE
Amazon.com [NASDAQ symbol] (SG) .... AMZN
Amazonian Land Use Project (SAUS) .... AMUSE
AMB Financial [NASDAQ symbol] (TTSB) .... AMFC
AMB Financial Corp. [Associated Press] (SAG) .... AMBFinl
AMB Financial Corp. [NASDAQ symbol] (SAG) .... AMFC
AMB Property [NYSE symbol] (SG) .... AMB
Amba (SAUS) .... AW
Ambac Financial Group [NYSE symbol] (SG) .... ARK
AMBAC, Inc. [NYSE symbol] (SPSG) .... ABK
Ambac, Inc. [Associated Press] (SAG) .... Ambac
Ambac Industries, Inc. (SAUO) .... AB
Ambalavao [Madagascar] [ICAO location identifier] (ICLI) .... FMSA
Ambanc Corp. [Associated Press] (SAG) .... Ambanc
Ambanc Corp. [NASDAQ symbol] (SAG) .... AMBK
Ambanc Holding Co., Inc. [NASDAQ symbol] (SAG) .... AHCI
Ambanc Holding Co., Inc. [Associated Press] (SAG) .... AmbancH
Ambanja [Madagascar] [ICAO location identifier] (ICLI) .... FMNJ
Ambanja [Madagascar] [Airport symbol] (OAG) .... IVA
Ambar [Pakistan] [Seismograph station code, US Geological Survey] (SEIS) .... AMP
Ambar, Inc. [Associated Press] (SAG) .... Ambar
Ambar, Inc. [NASDAQ symbol] (SAG) .... AMBR
Ambassador (ADWA) .... amb
Ambassador .... AMB

Ambassador .... Ambass
Ambassador Airlines (SAUO) .... AA
Ambassador Airways Ltd. [British] [ICAO designator] (FAAC) .... AMY
Ambassador Apartments [NYSE symbol] [Formerly, Prime Residential]
  (SG) .... AAH
Ambassador Apartments, Inc. [Associated Press] (SAG) .... AmbssApt
Ambassador at Large .... AL
Ambassador Bridge (SAUS) .... Amb Brdg
Ambassador College (SAUO) .... Amb Col
Ambassador College, Big Sandy, TX [Library symbol] [Library of Congress]
  (LCLS) .... TxBsaA
Ambassador College Library, Pasadena, CA [Library symbol] [Library of
  Congress] (LCLS) .... CPAC
Ambassador College, Pasadena, CA [OCLC symbol] (OCLC) .... ACL
Ambassador College, Pasadena, CA [Library symbol] [Library of Congress]
  (LCLS) .... CPA
Ambassador Extraordinary (SAUS) .... Amb Ex
Ambassador Extraordinary and Plenipotentiary [Diplomacy] .... AE & P
Ambassador for Friendship (SAUO) .... AF
Ambassador Industries Ltd. [Vancouver Stock Exchange symbol] .... AMS
Ambassador of the United States .... AUS
Ambassador's Club [TWA's club for frequent flyers] (EA) .... AC
Ambassadors for Friendship (EA) .... AF
Ambassadors in Mission [Religious organization] [Canada] .... AIM
Ambassadors International, Inc. [Associated Press] (SAG) .... AmbIn
Ambassadors International, Inc. [NASDAQ symbol] (SAG) .... AMIE
Ambassadors Intl. [NASDAQ symbol] (TTSB) .... AMIE
Ambassadors of Mary (EA) .... AM
Ambassador's Secretary .... AMB SEC
Ambato [Ecuador] [ICAO location identifier] (ICLI) .... SEAM
Ambatomainty [Madagascar] [Airport symbol] (OAG) .... AMY
Ambatondrazaka [Madagascar] [ICAO location identifier] (ICLI) .... FMMZ
Ambatondrazaka [Madagascar] [Airport symbol] (OAG) .... WAM
Amber (AAG) .... A
Amber .... AM
Amber (MSA) .... AMB
Amber (VRA) .... amb
Amber (DAVI) .... AMBR
Amber Airways Ltd. [British] [ICAO designator] (FAAC) .... ABM
Amber Boron Nitride (PDAA) .... ABN
Amber Indicating Lamp (SAUS) .... AIL
Amber Indicating Light (SAUS) .... AIL
Amber Light (MSA) .... AL
Amber Light (IAA) .... ALT
Amber University, Garland, TX [Library symbol] [Library of Congress]
  (LCLS) .... TxGarA
Amberg [Germany] [ICAO location identifier] (ICLI) .... EDEA
Ambergate Exploration [Vancouver Stock Exchange symbol] .... AGQ
Amberhill Petroleum Ltd. [Vancouver Stock Exchange symbol] .... APT
Amberieu [France] [ICAO location identifier] (ICLI) .... LFXA
Amberley [Australia] [ICAO location identifier] (ICLI) .... ABAM
Amberley [New Zealand] [Later, EYR] [Geomagnetic observatory code] .... AML
Amberquest Resources Ltd. [Vancouver Stock Exchange symbol] .... AMB
Ambert-Le-Poyet [France] [ICAO location identifier] (ICLI) .... LFHT
AMBI, Inc. [NASDAQ symbol] (SAG) .... AMBI
Ambiance .... AMBNC
Ambient [Electronics] .... A
Ambient (KSC) .... AM
Ambient (MSA) .... AMB
Ambient Absolute Pressure (PDAA) .... AAP
Ambient Air Control Panel [Army] .... AACP
Ambient Air Cooling System [Military] .... AACS
Ambient Air Level [Toxicology] (LDT) .... AAL
Ambient Air Quality Standard (EG) .... AAQS
Ambient Air Ventilation Microclimate System [Army] (RDA) .... AVMCS
Ambient Air/Forced-Air-Cooled (SAUS) .... AA/FA
Ambient Background Sound Level (SAUS) .... ABSL
Ambient Brine (SAUS) .... AB
Ambient Cure Foam (SAUS) .... AC Foam
Ambient Multimedia Environmental Goals [Environmental Protection
  Agency] .... AMEG
Ambient Noise [Composite of sounds present at a given spot in the ocean]
  (NVT) .... AN
Ambient Noise and Data System [Pacific Missile Range] (MCD) .... ANADS
Ambient Noise Background .... ANB
Ambient Noise Background (SAUS) .... Are
Ambient Noise Buoy (SAUS) .... ANB
Ambient Noise Directionality Estimator (MCD) .... ANODE
Ambient Noise Directionality Estimator (SAUS) .... ANODi
Ambient Noise Index (CAAL) .... ANI
Ambient Noise Measurement (CAAL) .... ANM
Ambient Quality Assurance Data Base (SAUS) .... QAFILE
Ambient Quality Standard [Environmental science] (FFDE) .... AQS
Ambient Sea Noise Indication (SAUS) .... ASNI
Ambient Standards Branch (SAUO) .... ASB
Ambient Temperature .... AT
Ambient Temperature and Pressure, Dry [Medicine] .... ATPD
Ambient Temperature and Pressure, Saturated [Medicine] .... ATPS
Ambient Temperature Observer/Predictor (MCD) .... ATOP
Ambient Temperature Range .... ATR
Ambient Water Quality Criteria [Environmental Protection Agency]
  (AEPA) .... AWQC
Ambiguity [Used in correcting manuscripts, etc.] .... A
Ambiguity [or Ambiguous] (MCD) .... AMBIG
Ambiguity Eliminator [Electronics] .... AMBEL

Ambiguity Function Technique (GEOI) ... AFT
Ambiguity Reference Tone (MCD) ... ART
Ambiguity Resolver (SAUS) ... AR
Ambiguous [*Used in correcting manuscripts, etc.*] ... AMB
Ambiguous Genitalia Support Network (PAZ) ... AGSN
Ambilobe [*Madagascar*] [*Airport symbol*] (OAG) ... AMB
Ambilobe [*Madagascar*] [*ICAO location identifier*] (ICLI) ... FMNE
Ambio Special Report (SAUS) ... Ambio Spec Rep
Ambitendency [*Psychology*] ... A
Ambitious (DSUE) ... AMBI
Ambivalence (SAUS) ... AMBIV
ambivalent (SAUS) ... ambiv
Amble Resources Ltd. [*Vancouver Stock Exchange symbol*] ... ALU
Ambler [*Alaska*] [*Airport symbol*] (OAG) ... ABL
Ambler, AK [*Location identifier*] [*FAA*] (FAAL) ... AMF
Ambler, PA [*Location identifier*] [*FAA*] (FAAL) ... ING
Ambler's Reports, Chancery [*27 English Reprint*] [*A publication*] (DLA) ... Amb
Ambler's Reports, Chancery [*27 English Reprint*] [*A publication*] (DLA) ... Ambl
Ambleteuse [*France*] [*ICAO location identifier*] (ICLI) ... LFAA
Ambohijanahary [*Madagascar*] [*ICAO location identifier*] (ICLI) ... FMMJ
Amboin [*Papua New Guinea*] [*Airport symbol*] (OAG) ... AMG
Amboina [*Indonesia*] [*Seismograph station code, US Geological Survey*] (SEIS) ... AMO
Amboise/Dierre [*France*] [*ICAO location identifier*] (ICLI) ... LFEF
Ambon [*Indonesia*] [*Seismograph station code, US Geological Survey*] ... AAI
Ambon [*Indonesia*] [*Airport symbol*] (OAG) ... AMQ
Ambon Sector [*Indonesia*] [*ICAO location identifier*] (ICLI) ... WAPZ
Ambon/Pattimura [*Indonesia*] [*ICAO location identifier*] (ICLI) ... WAPP
Amboseli [*Kenya*] [*ICAO location identifier*] (ICLI) ... HKAM
Amboseli National Park (SAUS) ... Ambos
Ambra Oil & Gas Company (SAUO) ... AOGC
Ambridge, PA [*AM radio station call letters*] ... WMBA
Ambriz [*Angola*] [*ICAO location identifier*] (ICLI) ... FNAM
Ambrose Bierce (SAUS) ... A-B
ambrosia (SAUS) ... ambros
Ambrosian Library (SAUS) ... Amb Lib
Ambrosian Library (SAUS) ... Ambrosian
Ambrosius de Vignate [*Flourished, 15th century*] [*Authority cited in pre-1607 legal work*] (DSA) ... Amb de Vig
Ambrosius Opizonus [*Flourished, 15th century*] [*Authority cited in pre-1607 legal work*] (DSA) ... Ambr Opizo
Ambrotype (VRA) ... ATYP
Ambroziak Color Coordinate System (SAUS) ... ACCS
Ambulance (AFM) ... AMB
Ambulance ... AMBL
Ambulance and Medical Service Association of America [*Later, AAA*] (EA) ... AMSAA
Ambulance Association of America [*Later, AAA*] (EA) ... AAOA
Ambulance Association of America [*Later, AAA*] ... AA of A
Ambulance Association of America (SAUO) ... AA of A
Ambulance Association of Pennsylvania (SRA) ... AAP
Ambulance Car Company (SAUO) ... ACC
Ambulance Company (SAUO) ... AC
Ambulance Corps (ADA) ... AC
Ambulance Design Criteria [*National Highway Transportation Safety Administration*] ... ADC
Ambulance Driver ... AD
Ambulance Employees' Association of Tasmania [*Australia*] ... AEAT
Ambulance Employees' Association of Victoria [*Australia*] ... AEAV
Ambulance Exchange Point (SAUS) ... AEP
Ambulance Exchange Point [*Army*] (INF) ... AXP
Ambulance Loading Post [*Military*] ... ALP
Ambulance Manufacturers Association [*Later, TBEA*] (EA) ... AMA
Ambulance Manufacturers Division [*An association*] (EA) ... AMD
Ambulance Officer ... AO
Ambulance Plane [*Navy symbol*] ... VH
Ambulance Service Institute [*British*] (DBA) ... ASI
Ambulance Service Park (SAUO) ... Amb Serv Pk
Ambulance Station (WDAA) ... Amb Sta
Ambulance Superintendents' Association of Queensland [*Australia*] ... ASAQ
Ambulance Support Group (SAUO) ... ASG
Ambulance Train (SAUS) ... AT
Ambulances for Nicaragua (EA) ... AN
Ambulancias Insulares SA [*Spain*] [*ICAO designator*] (FAAC) ... AIM
ambulant (SAUS) ... ambt
Ambulate (SAUS) ... AMB
Ambulate with Assistance [*Medicine*] ... AWA
ambulating (SAUS) ... ambul
ambulation (SAUS) ... ambul
ambulatorily (SAUS) ... ambul
Ambulatory [*Medicine*] ... A
Ambulatory [*or Ambulation*] [*Also, AMBUL*] [*Medicine*] ... AMB
Ambulatory (MELL) ... amb
Ambulatory (AABC) ... AMBT
Ambulatory [*or Ambulation*] [*Also, AMB*] [*Medicine*] ... AMBUL
Ambulatory (VRA) ... ambul
Ambulatory (SAUS) ... Ambul
Ambulatory Blood Pressure Monitoring [*Medicine*] ... ABPM
Ambulatory Care [*Medicine*] (DAVI) ... A/C
Ambulatory Care - Sensitive Condition ... ACSC
Ambulatory Care Center (SAUS) ... ACC
Ambulatory Care Clinic [*or Center*] [*Medicine*] ... ACC
Ambulatory Care Clinic Effectiveness Systems Study (MELL) ... ACCESS
Ambulatory Care Facility (MELL) ... ACF
Ambulatory Care Groups (SAUO) ... ACG
Ambulatory Care Quality Improvement Program (ADWA) ... ACQIP
Ambulatory Care Research Facility [*Medicine*] (DMAA) ... ACRF
Ambulatory Care Unit (MELL) ... ACU
Ambulatory Care Utilization Review [*Insurance*] (WYGK) ... ACUR
Ambulatory Diagnostic Group [*Medicine*] (DMAA) ... ADG
Ambulatory Electrocardiogram (MCD) ... AECG
Ambulatory Health Care Information System ... AHCIS
Ambulatory Holter Monitoring [*Medicine*] (CPH) ... AHM
Ambulatory Information Management Association (SAUO) ... AIM
Ambulatory Medical Care (SAUS) ... AMC
Ambulatory Patient Group (ADWA) ... APG
Ambulatory Patient Groups (SAUO) ... APG
Ambulatory Payment Classification (SAUS) ... APC
Ambulatory Pediatric Association (EA) ... APA
Ambulatory Peritoneal Dialysis [*Medicine*] (CPH) ... APD
Ambulatory Procedure Unit (MELL) ... APU
Ambulatory Renal Monitoring [*Medicine*] ... ARM
Ambulatory Surgery Center (SAUS) ... ASC
Ambulatory Surgery Facility [*Health insurance*] (GHCT) ... ASF
Ambulatory Surgery Initiative [*Health insurance*] (GHCT) ... ASI
Ambulatory Surgery Management Society (SAUO) ... ASMS
Ambulatory Surgical Center [*Medicine*] ... ASC
Ambulatory Utilization Review ... AUR
Ambulatory Visit Group [*Patient classification*] [*Medicine*] (DAVI) ... AVG
Ambulatory Visit Groups (SAUO) ... AVG
Ambulong [*Philippines*] [*Seismograph station code, US Geological Survey*] [*Closed*] (SEIS) ... AMB
Ambunti [*Papua New Guinea*] [*Airport symbol*] (OAG) ... AUJ
Ambush ... AB
Ambush ... AMB
Ambush Communication Equipment [*Military*] ... ACE
Ambush Patrol ... AP
AMC Entertainment [*AMEX symbol*] (TTSB) ... AEN
AMC Entertainment, Inc. [*AMEX symbol*] (SPSG) ... AEN
AMC Entertainment, Inc. [*Associated Press*] (SAG) ... AMC
AMC Entertain't $1.75 Cv Pfd [*AMEX symbol*] (TTSB) ... AENPr
AMC [*Army Materiel Command*] **Logistics Program - Hardcore Automated** ... ALPHA
AMC Pacer Club (EA) ... AMCPC
AMC [*American Motors Corp.*] **Rambler Club** (EA) ... AMCRC
AMC Standard Installation Supply System (SAUS) ... DSISS
AMCA International Ltd., Ottawa, ON, Canada [*Library symbol*] [*Library of Congress*] (LCLS) ... CaOOAI
AMCA International Ltd., Ottawa, Ontario [*Library symbol*] [*National Library of Canada*] (NLC) ... OOAI
AMCA Resources Ltd. [*Vancouver Stock Exchange symbol*] ... AMC
Amcan Cyphermaster Ltd. [*Vancouver Stock Exchange symbol*] ... ACY
Amcast Industrial [*NYSE symbol*] (SPSG) ... AIZ
Amcast Industrial [*Associated Press*] (SAG) ... Amcast
AMCEL Propulsion Co. [*Later, Northrup Caroline Co.*] (KSC) ... APC
AMCEL Propulsion Co. (SAUO) ... APC
AMCEL Propulsion Co., Asheville (SAUS) ... APC
Amcel Propulsion Co., Asheville, NC [*Library symbol*] [*Library of Congress*] (LCLS) ... NcAAP
Amcel Propulsion Company (SAUO) ... APC
Amchem Products, Inc. (SAUO) ... Amchem
Amchitka [*Alaska*] [*Seismograph station code, US Geological Survey*] [*Closed*] (SEIS) ... AEB
Amchitka [*Alaska*] [*Seismograph station code, US Geological Survey*] [*Closed*] (SEIS) ... ANA
Amchitka [*Alaska*] [*Seismograph station code, US Geological Survey*] [*Closed*] (SEIS) ... ANB
Amchitka [*Alaska*] [*Seismograph station code, US Geological Survey*] [*Closed*] (SEIS) ... AND
Amchitka [*Alaska*] [*Seismograph station code, US Geological Survey*] [*Closed*] (SEIS) ... ASB
Amchitka [*Alaska*] [*Seismograph station code, US Geological Survey*] [*Closed*] (SEIS) ... ASC
Amchitka [*Alaska*] [*Seismograph station code, US Geological Survey*] [*Closed*] (SEIS) ... ASD
Amchitka [*Alaska*] [*Seismograph station code, US Geological Survey*] [*Closed*] (SEIS) ... AWA
Amchitka, AK [*Location identifier*] [*FAA*] (FAAL) ... AHT
Amchitka Central A [*Alaska*] [*Seismograph station code, US Geological Survey*] [*Closed*] (SEIS) ... ACA
Amchitka Central B [*Alaska*] [*Seismograph station code, US Geological Survey*] [*Closed*] (SEIS) ... ACB
Amchitka Central C [*Alaska*] [*Seismograph station code, US Geological Survey*] [*Closed*] (SEIS) ... ACC
Amchitka Central D [*Alaska*] [*Seismograph station code, US Geological Survey*] [*Closed*] (SEIS) ... ACD
Amchitka Central E [*Alaska*] [*Seismograph station code, US Geological Survey*] [*Closed*] (SEIS) ... ACE
Amchitka Central F [*Alaska*] [*Seismograph station code, US Geological Survey*] [*Closed*] (SEIS) ... ACF
Amchitka East [*Alaska*] [*Seismograph station code, US Geological Survey*] [*Closed*] (SEIS) ... AME
Amco Industrial Holdings Ltd. [*Toronto Stock Exchange symbol*] ... AMO
AMCOL International [*NYSE symbol*] ... ACO
Amcol International Corp. [*NASDAQ symbol*] (SAG) ... ACOL
Amcol International Corp. [*Associated Press*] (SAG) ... AMCOL
Amcol International Corp. [*Associated Press*] (SAG) ... Amcol Int
AMCOL Intl. [*NASDAQ symbol*] (TTSB) ... ACOL
AMCON Distributing [*Associated Press*] (SAG) ... AMCON
AMCON Distributing [*NASDAQ symbol*] (TTSB) ... DIST

Amcor Capital Ltd. [*Associated Press*] (SAG) .... Amcor
Amcor Limited ADR [*NASDAQ symbol*] (TTSB) .... AMCRY
Amcor Ltd. [*NASDAQ symbol*] (SAG) .... AMCP
Amcor Ltd. [*NASDAQ symbol*] (SAG) .... AMCR
Amcore Financial [*Associated Press*] (SAG) .... AmcorFn
Amcore Financial [*NASDAQ symbol*] (SAG) .... AMFI
Amcot, Inc. (EA) .... AI
Amdahl Corp. [*Associated Press*] (SAG) .... AMDHL
Amdahl Corp. [*AMEX symbol*] (SPSG) .... AMH
Amdahl Corporation (SAUO) .... Amdahl
Amdahl Diagnostics Assistance Center .... AMDAC
Amdahl Internally Developed Software .... AIDS
Amdahl Users Group (EA) .... AUG
Amdar [*Afghanistan*] [*ICAO location identifier*] (ICLI) .... OAAD
Amderma [*Former USSR*] [*Seismograph station code, US Geological Survey*] [*Closed*] (SEIS) .... AMD
AMDF [*Army Master Data File*] **Positive Improvement Program** (MCD) .... APIP
AMDF [*Army Master Data File*] **Reader Microfilm System** [*Formerly, AMDFRMS*] (AABC) .... ARMS
Amdocs Ltd. [*NYSE symbol*] (SG) .... DOX
Amdura Corp. [*Associated Press*] (SAG) .... Amdura
Amebiasis [*Medicine*] (DAVI) .... AMEBIA
Amebic Dysentery [*Medicine*] (MELL) .... AD
Amebic Meningoencephalitis [*Medicine*] (MELL) .... AME
Amebic Prevalence Rate (MAE) .... APR
AMECEA Pastoral Institute (SAUO) .... API
AMEDISYS, Inc. [*Associated Press*] (SAG) .... AMDSYS
AMEDISYS, Inc. [*NASDAQ symbol*] (SAG) .... AMED
Amegroid Society of America (EA) .... ASA
Ameican Medical Technologies, Inc. [*NASDAQ symbol*] (SAG) .... AMTI
Ameland [*Netherlands*] [*ICAO location identifier*] (ICLI) .... EHAL
Amelanotic Melanoma [*Medicine*] (DB) .... AM
Amelia Earhart Collectors Club (EA) .... AEC
Amelia Earhart Collectors Club (EA) .... AECC
Amelia Earhart Research Consortium (EA) .... AERC
Ameliasburgh Historical Society, Ontario [*Library symbol*] [*National Library of Canada*] (BIB) .... OAMHS
Amelioration (SAUS) .... AMELIOR
Amelioration .... AMLRTN
Amend .... AMD
Amend [*or Amendment*] (AFM) .... AMND
Amend Existing Orders Pertaining To .... AEOP
Amend Existing Orders Pertaining to (SAUS) .... AEOP
Amended (DLA) .... A
Amended (ADWA) .... amd
Amended Basis of Issue Plan [*DoD*] .... ABOIP
Amended Basis of Issue Plan, Feeder Data [*DoD*] .... ABOIPFD
Amended Clearance [*Aviation*] (FAAC) .... AMCL
Amended Operator and Maintenance Decision [*Army*] .... AOMD
Amended Program Decision Memoranda (SAUS) .... APDM
Amended Program Decision Memorandum [*Navy*] (NVT) .... APDM
Amended Route of Flight [*Aviation*] .... AMRF
Amended Shipping Instruction [*Military*] .... ASI
Amended Shipping Instrument (MCD) .... ASI
Amended Type Certificate (SAUS) .... ATC
Amendment .... AM
Amendment (AABC) .... AMDT
Amendment .... AMEND
Amendment .... AMENDT
Amendment List (SAUS) .... AL
Amendment Number (SAUS) .... Amd No
Amendment /Query [*Computer science*] (NITA) .... A/Q
Amendment Request [*Navy*] .... AR
Amendment to the Constitution (DLA) .... Const Amend
Amendment to the Constitution of the United States (DLA) .... ACUS
Amendment to the Constitution of the United States (DLA) .... Const US Amend
Amendment to the Final Qualitative and Quantitative Personnel Requirements Information (MCD) .... AFQQPRI
Amendments and Additions (DLA) .... A & A
Amendments and Additions (SAUS) .... A&A
Amendola [*Italy*] [*ICAO location identifier*] (ICLI) .... LIBA
Amenorrhea and Hirsutism [*Endocrinology*] (MAE) .... AH
Amenorrhea/Hyperprolactinemia [*Endocrinology*] .... A/H
Amer Acess Technologies [*NASDAQ symbol*] (SG) .... AATK
Amer Aircarriers Support [*NASDAQ symbol*] (SG) .... AIRS
Amer Axle & Manufacturing [*NYSE symbol*] (SG) .... AXL
Amer Bancorp Nevada [*NASDAQ symbol*] (TTSB) .... ABCN
Amer Bancorp Ohio [*NASDAQ symbol*] (TTSB) .... AMBC
Amer Bancshares [*NASDAQ symbol*] (TTSB) .... ABAN
Amer Bank, Conn [*AMEX symbol*] (TTSB) .... BKC
Amer Bank Note Holographics [*NYSE symbol*] (SG) .... ABH
Amer Bankers Insur Grp [*NYSE symbol*] (SG) .... ABI
Amer Bankers Insur Grp [*NASDAQ symbol*] (TTSB) .... ABIG
Amer Banknote [*NYSE symbol*] (TTSB) .... ABN
Amer Biltrite [*AMEX symbol*] (TTSB) .... ABL
AMER BINGO & GAMING [*NASDAQ symbol*] (TTSB) .... BNGO
Amer Bingo & Gaming Wrrt [*NASDAQ symbol*] (TTSB) .... BNGOW
Amer Biogenetic Sciences'A' [*NASDAQ symbol*] (TTSB) .... MABXA
Amer Body Armor & Equip [*AMEX symbol*] (TTSB) .... ABE
Amer Brands [*AMB*] (TTSB) .... AMEL
AMER BRANDS $2.67 CV Pfd [*NYSE symbol*] (TTSB) .... AMBPrA
Amer Buildings [*NASDAQ symbol*] (TTSB) .... ABCO
Amer Business Computers [*NASDAQ symbol*] (TTSB) .... ABCC
Amer Business Information [*NASDAQ symbol*] (TTSB) .... ABII
Amer Business Prod [*NYSE symbol*] (TTSB) .... ABP

Amer Capital Strategies [*NASDAQ symbol*] (SG) .... ACAS
Amer Casino Enterprises [*NASDAQ symbol*] (SG) .... ACES
Amer. Century Cal. Long Term Tax Free [*Mutual fund ticker symbol*] (SG) .... BCLTX
Amer. Century GNMA Fund [*Mutual fund ticker symbol*] (SG) .... BGNMX
Amer. Century Growth Fund [*Mutual fund ticker symbol*] (SG) .... TWCGX
Amer. Century Intermed.-Term Tax Free [*Mutual fund ticker symbol*] (SG) .... TWTIX
Amer. Century Long-Term Tax Free [*Mutual fund ticker symbol*] (SG) .... TWTLX
Amer. Century Select Fund [*Mutual fund ticker symbol*] (SG) .... TWCIX
Amer. Century Short Term Govt. [*Mutual fund ticker symbol*] (SG) .... TWUSX
Amer. Century Target 2000 Fund [*Mutual fund ticker symbol*] (SG) .... BTMTX
Amer. Century Target 2005 Fund [*Mutual fund ticker symbol*] (SG) .... BTFIX
Amer. Century Target 2010 Fund [*Mutual fund ticker symbol*] (SG) .... BTTNX
Amer. Century Target 2015 Fund [*Mutual fund ticker symbol*] (SG) .... BTFTX
Amer. Century Target 2020 Fund [*Mutual fund ticker symbol*] (SG) .... BTTTX
Amer. Century Ultra Fund [*Mutual fund ticker symbol*] (SG) .... TWCUX
Amer Claims Evaluation [*NASDAQ symbol*] (TTSB) .... AMCE
Amer Classic Voyages [*NASDAQ symbol*] (TTSB) .... AMCV
Amer Coin Merchandising [*NASDAQ symbol*] (TTSB) .... AMCN
Amer Communications Svcs [*NASDAQ symbol*] (TTSB) .... ACNS
Amer Community Properties Tr [*AMEX symbol*] (SG) .... APO
Amer Complex Care [*NASDAQ symbol*] (TTSB) .... ACCI
Amer Dental Technologies [*NASDAQ symbol*] (TTSB) .... ADLI
Amer Eagle Outfitters [*NASDAQ symbol*] (TTSB) .... AEOS
Amer Eco [*NASDAQ symbol*] (SG) .... ECGO
Amer Eco Corp. [*NASDAQ symbol*] (TTSB) .... ECGOF
Amer Ecology [*NASDAQ symbol*] (TTSB) .... ECOLE
Amer Educational Prd [*NASDAQ symbol*] (TTSB) .... AMEP
Amer Electric Pwr [*NYSE symbol*] (TTSB) .... AEP
Amer Exp 6.25% 'DECS' '96 [*NYSE symbol*] (TTSB) .... AXD
Amer Explor Cv Dep'C'Pfd [*AMEX symbol*] (TTSB) .... AXPrC
Amer Exploration(New) [*AMEX symbol*] (TTSB) .... AX
Amer Express [*NYSE symbol*] (TTSB) .... AXP
Amer Federal Bank [*NASDAQ symbol*] (TTSB) .... AMER
Amer Filtrona [*NASDAQ symbol*] (TTSB) .... AFIL
Amer Finl Group [*NYSE symbol*] (TTSB) .... AFG
Amer First Finl 1987-A Fd [*NASDAQ symbol*] (TTSB) .... AFFFZ
Amer First Prep Fd 2 L.P. [*AMEX symbol*] (TTSB) .... PF
Amer First Ptc/Pfd Eqty Mtg [*NASDAQ symbol*] (TTSB) .... AFPFZ
Amer First Tax Exempt Mtg 2 [*NASDAQ symbol*] (TTSB) .... ATAXZ
Amer First Tax Exempt Mtg L.P. [*NASDAQ symbol*] (TTSB) .... AFTXZ
Amer Freightways [*NASDAQ symbol*] (TTSB) .... AFWY
Amer Fuel [*NASDAQ symbol*] (TTSB) .... COAL
Amer Fuel Unit [*NASDAQ symbol*] (TTSB) .... COALU
Amer General [*NYSE symbol*] (TTSB) .... AGC
Amer Genl 7% Cv Pfd [*NYSE symbol*] (TTSB) .... AGCPrD
Amer Genl 8.125% 'MIPS' [*NYSE symbol*] (TTSB) .... AGCPrN
Amer Genl 8.45% 'MIPS' [*NYSE symbol*] (TTSB) .... AGCPrM
Amer Gen'l Del LLC 6% Cv'MIPS' [*NYSE symbol*] (TTSB) .... AGCPrC
Amer Greetings Cl'A' [*NYSE symbol*] (SG) .... AM
Amer. Growth Fund [*Mutual fund ticker symbol*] (SG) .... AMRGX
Amer Health Pro [*NYSE symbol*] (SG) .... AHE
Amer Healthcorp [*NASDAQ symbol*] (TTSB) .... AMHC
Amer Heritage Life [*NYSE symbol*] (SG) .... AHL
Amer Home Products [*NYSE symbol*] (SG) .... AHP
Amer Homestar [*NASDAQ symbol*] (TTSB) .... HSTR
Amer Industrial Prop [*NYSE symbol*] (TTSB) .... IND
Amer Ins Mtge Inv L.P. [*AMEX symbol*] (SG) .... AIA
Amer Ins Mtge Inv Ser 85 [*AMEX symbol*] (SG) .... AII
Amer Ins Mtge Inv Ser 86 [*AMEX symbol*] (SG) .... AIJ
Amer Ins Mtge Inv Ser 88 [*AMEX symbol*] (SG) .... AIK
Amer Intl. Group [*NYSE symbol*] (SG) .... AIG
Amer Intl. Petroleum [*NASDAQ symbol*] (TTSB) .... AIPN
Amer Israeli Paper Ord [*AMEX symbol*] (TTSB) .... AIP
Amer Italian Pasta'A' [*NYSE symbol*] (SG) .... PLB
Amer List [*AMEX symbol*] (TTSB) .... AMZ
Amer Locker Group [*NASDAQ symbol*] (TTSB) .... ALGI
Amer Media Cl'A' [*NYSE symbol*] (TTSB) .... ENQ
Amer Media Wrrt [*NYSE symbol*] (TTSB) .... ENQWS
Amer Medical Security Grp [*NYSE symbol*] (SG) .... AMZ
Amer Mgmt Systems [*NASDAQ symbol*] (SG) .... AMSY
Amer Mobile Satellite [*NASDAQ symbol*] (TTSB) .... SKYC
Amer Muni Term Trust [*NYSE symbol*] (TTSB) .... AXT
Amer Muni Term Trust II [*NYSE symbol*] (TTSB) .... BXT
Amer Natl Bancorp [*NASDAQ symbol*] (TTSB) .... ANBK
Amer Natl Can Group [*NYSE symbol*] (SG) .... CAN
Amer Natl Insur [*NASDAQ symbol*] (TTSB) .... ANAT
Amer Oilfield Divers [*NASDAQ symbol*] (TTSB) .... DIVE
Amer Oncology Res [*NASDAQ symbol*] (TTSB) .... AORI
Amer Opportunity Income [*NYSE symbol*] (TTSB) .... OIF
Amer Pac Bk Aumsville OR [*NASDAQ symbol*] (TTSB) .... AMPBA
Amer Pacific [*NASDAQ symbol*] (TTSB) .... APFC
Amer Paging [*AMEX symbol*] (TTSB) .... APP
Amer Physicians Svc Gr [*NASDAQ symbol*] (TTSB) .... AMPH
Amer Portable Telecom [*NASDAQ symbol*] (TTSB) .... APTI
Amer Power Conversion [*NASDAQ symbol*] (SG) .... APCC
Amer Precision Indus [*NYSE symbol*] (SG) .... APR
Amer President Cos. [*NYSE symbol*] (TTSB) .... APS
Amer Radio Systems'A' [*NASDAQ symbol*] (TTSB) .... AMRD
Amer Re Capital 8.50% 'QUIPS' [*NYSE symbol*] (TTSB) .... ARNPrA
Amer Re Corp. [*NYSE symbol*] (TTSB) .... ARN
Amer R.E. Ptnrs 5%'PIK'Pfd [*NYSE symbol*] (TTSB) .... ACPPr
Amer Real Estate Investment [*AMEX symbol*] (TTSB) .... REA
Amer Realty Tr SBI [*NYSE symbol*] (TTSB) .... ARB

Amer Recreation Ctrs [NASDAQ symbol] (TTSB) .... AMRC
Amer R.E.Ptnrs L.P. [NYSE symbol] (TTSB) .... ACP
Amer Res Del Wrrt [NASDAQ symbol] (TTSB) .... GASSW
Amer Residential Inv Trust [NYSE symbol] (SG) .... INV
Amer Resource [NASDAQ symbol] (TTSB) .... AREE
Amer Resources Del [NASDAQ symbol] (TTSB) .... GASS
Amer Restaurant Ptnrs'A' [AMEX symbol] (TTSB) .... RMC
Amer Retirement [NYSE symbol] (SG) .... ACR
Amer Rice [NASDAQ symbol] (TTSB) .... RICE
Amer Safety Closure [NASDAQ symbol] (TTSB) .... CLOS
Amer Safety Ins Grp [NYSE symbol] (SG) .... ASI
Amer Safety Razor [NASDAQ symbol] (TTSB) .... RAZR
Amer Science & Engr [AMEX symbol] (SG) .... ASE
Amer Sensors [NASDAQ symbol] (TTSB) .... SNIFF
Amer Service Group [NASDAQ symbol] (TTSB) .... ASGR
Amer Shared Hosp Sv [AMEX symbol] (TTSB) .... AMS
Amer Skiing [NYSE symbol] (SG) .... SKI
Amer Software'A' [NASDAQ symbol] (TTSB) .... AMSWA
Amer Standard [NYSE symbol] (TTSB) .... ASD
Amer States Financial [NYSE symbol] (TTSB) .... ASX
Amer States Water [NYSE symbol] (SG) .... AWR
Amer Stores [NYSE symbol] (TTSB) .... ASC
Amer Strategic Inc. Portfol III [NYSE symbol] (TTSB) .... CSP
Amer Strategic Inc. Portfolio [NYSE symbol] (TTSB) .... ASP
Amer Studios [NASDAQ symbol] (TTSB) .... AMST
Amer Superconductor [NASDAQ symbol] (TTSB) .... AMSC
Amer Techl Ceramics [AMEX symbol] (TTSB) .... AMK
Amer Telecasting [NASDAQ symbol] (TTSB) .... ATEL
Amer Tower'A' [NYSE symbol] (SG) .... AMT
Amer Toys [NASDAQ symbol] (TTSB) .... ATOY
Amer Travellers [NASDAQ symbol] (TTSB) .... ATVC
Amer United Global [NASDAQ symbol] (TTSB) .... AUGI
Amer Vanguard [NASDAQ symbol] (TTSB) .... AMGD
Amer Vanguard [AMEX symbol] (SG) .... AVD
Amer Wagering [NASDAQ symbol] (TTSB) .... BETM
Amer Waste Svcs'A' [NYSE symbol] (TTSB) .... AW
Amer Water Wks 5%Pref [NYSE symbol] (TTSB) .... AWKPrA
Amer Water Wks,5% Pfd [NYSE symbol] (TTSB) .... AWKPrB
Amer Water Works [NYSE symbol] (TTSB) .... AWK
Amer Woodmark [NASDAQ symbol] (TTSB) .... AMWD
Amerada Hess [NYSE symbol] (SG) .... AHC
Amerada Hess Corp. [NYSE symbol] [Toronto Stock Exchange symbol]
  (SPSG) .... AHC
Amerada Petroleum Corporation (SAUO) .... ARC
Amerada-Hess Corp. [Associated Press] (SAG) .... AmHes
Ameralia Inc. [NASDAQ symbol] (TTSB) .... AALA
Ameralia, Inc. [Associated Press] (SAG) .... Ameral
Amerasia Journal [A publication] (BRI) .... Amerasia J
Ameravia [Uruguay] [FAA designator] (FAAC) .... VAM
Amercian Express International (SAUO) .... AEI
Amercian League Championship .... ALC
AMERCO [NYSE symbol] (SAG) .... ACP
AMERCO [Associated Press] (SAG) .... AMERCO
AMERCO [NASDAQ symbol] (TTSB) .... AMOO
AMERCO [NYSE symbol] (SAG) .... AO
AMERCO [NASDAQ symbol] (SAG) .... UHAL
Amerco, Inc. [Associated Press] (SAG) .... Amerc
AMERCO Sr'A'Pfd [NYSE symbol] (TTSB) .... AOPrA
Ameren Corp. [NYSE symbol] (SG) .... AEE
Amerian College of Preventive Medicine (SAUO) .... ACPM
Ameriana Bancorp [Associated Press] (SAG) .... Ameriana
Ameriana Bancorp [Associated Press] (SAG) .... Amriana
Ameriana Bancorp [NASDAQ symbol] (SAG) .... ASBI
America (ROG) .... AM
America [A publication] (BRI) .... Am
America (ADWA) .... Ame
America (EBF) .... Amer
America [or American] .... AMER
America and Australia (SAUS) .... A&A
America and West Indies (SAUS) .... A&WI
America and West Indies [Obsolete] [British] .... AWI
America, Britain, Canada & Australia (SAUS) .... ABCA
America, Britain, Canada, Australia (ADA) .... ABCA
America, Britain, China, and Dutch East Indies [The ABCD Powers] [World
  War II] .... ABCD
America, Britain, China, Dutch East Indies (SAUS) .... ABCD
America Defense Society (SAA) .... ADS
America East (PSS) .... AE
America First (EA) .... AF
America First Apartment Investors LP [Associated Press] (SAG) .... AFstApt
America First Apartment Investors LP [NASDAQ symbol] (SAG) .... APRO
America First Committee .... AFC
America First Financial Fund 1987 [NASDAQ symbol] (NQ) .... AFFF
America First Financial Fund Ltd. [Associated Press] (SAG) .... AFFF
America First Mtg Investments [NYSE symbol] (SG) .... MFA
America First Part Preferred Equity Mortgage Fund Ltd. [Associated
  Press] (SAG) .... AmFPr
America First Preferred Equity Mortgage Ltd. [NASDAQ symbol] (NQ) .... AFPF
America First PREP [Preferred Real Estate Participation] Fund 2 Ltd.
  [Associated Press] (SAG) AFstP2
America First Tax Exempt Mortgage [NASDAQ symbol] (NQ) .... AFTX
America First Tax Exempt Mortgage Fund [Associated Press] (SAG) .... AFTxE
America First Tax Exempt Mortgage Fund [NASDAQ symbol] (NQ) .... ATAX
America: History and Life [ABC-Clio Information Services] [Database]
  [A publication] .... AHL

America: History and Life .... AmerH
America Israel Friendship League (EA) .... AIFL
America Online [NASDAQ symbol] (TTSB) .... AMER
America Online [Online Service] (PCM) .... AOL
America Online, Inc. [NASDAQ symbol] (SAG) .... AMER
America Online, Inc. [Associated Press] (SAG) .... AmerOn
America Online, Inc. (SAUO) .... AOL
America Outdoors (NTPA) .... AO
America Pop, Inc. (SAUO) .... HOST
America Realestate Investment Company (SAUO) .... ARICO
America Remembers (EA) .... AR
America Service Group, Inc. [Associated Press] (SAG) .... AmSvce
America Service Group, Inc. [NASDAQ symbol] (SAG) .... ASGR
America Sky Broadcasting .... ASkyB
America Society of Consulting Planners (SAUS) .... ASCP
America the Beautiful (WPI) .... ATB
America The Beautiful (SAUO) .... ATB
America the Beautiful Fund (EA) .... ABF
America Victory Force (EA) .... AVF
America West Airlines [ICAO designator] (FAAC) .... AWE
America West Airlines [ICAO designator] (AD) .... HP
America West Airlines 'B' [NYSE symbol] (TTSB) .... AWA
America West Airlines, Inc. [Associated Press] (SAG) .... AmWest
America West Airlines, Inc. [NYSE symbol] (SAG) .... AWA
America West Airlines Wrrt [NYSE symbol] (TTSB) .... AWA.WS
America West Holdings Corp. [Associated Press] (SAG) .... AWest
America West Holdings'B' [NYSE symbol] (SG) .... AWA
America-Australia Interaction Association (EA) .... AAIA
America-European Community Association (SAUO) .... AECA
America-India Dispensary [Pharmacology] (DAVI) .... AID
AmericaIntelligent Transportation Society of America [Formerly, IVHS
  America] .... ITS
America-Israel Council for Israeli-Palestinian Peace (EA) .... AICIPP
America-Israel Cultural Foundation (EA) .... AICF
America-Italy Society (EA) .... AIS
Americal Division [Army] (VNW) .... AMCAL
Americal Division Veterans Association (EA) .... ADVA
Americam Philatelist [A publication] .... Am Phil
America-Mideast Educational and Training Services [Acronym is now
  organization's official name] (EA) .... AMIDEAST
American .... A
American (EBF) .... Am
American (BARN) .... AME
American (EBF) .... Amer
American .... AMERCN
American Abolitionist Movement (EA) .... AAM
American Abstract Artists (EA) .... AAA
American Abstract Artists, New York (SAUO) .... AAA
American Academic Environments, Inc. .... AAE
American Academy (SAUO) .... AA
American Academy and Institute of Arts and Letters (EA) .... AAIAL
American Academy Facial, Plastic & Reconstructive Surgery
  (CMD) .... AAFP & RS
American Academy for Cerebral Palsy [Later, AACPDM] (EA) .... AACP
American Academy for Cerebral Palsy and Developmental Medicine
  (EA) .... AACPDM
American Academy for Child Psychiatry (SAUS) .... AACP
American Academy for Child Psychoanalysts (SAUO) .... AACP
American Academy for Health, Physical Education, and Recreation
  (DAVI) .... AAHPER
American Academy for Jewish Research (EA) .... AAJR
American Academy for Plastics Research in Dentistry [Later, Academy of
  Dental Materials - ADM] .... AAPRD
American Academy for Plastics Research in Dentistry (SAUO) .... AAPRD
American Academy for Professional Law Enforcement [Defunct] (EA) .... AAPLE
American Academy for Scientific Interrogation (SAUO) .... AASI
American Academy in Rome (EA) .... AAR
American Academy in Rome (SAUS) .... ACR
American Academy of Achievement (EA) .... AAA
American Academy of Actuaries [Washington, DC] (EA) .... AAA
American Academy of Actuaries (SAUO) .... AAC
American Academy of Addiction Psychiatry (NTPA) .... AAAP
American Academy of Addictionology (HCT) .... AAA
American Academy of Advertising [Charleston, SC] (EA) .... AAA
American Academy of Allergy [Later, AAAI] (EA) .... AAA
American Academy of Allergy and Immunology (EA) .... AAAI
American Academy of Allergy, Asthma and Immunology (SAUO) .... AAAAI
American Academy of Ambulatory Care Nursing (NTPA) .... AAACN
American Academy of Ambulatory Nursing Administration (EA) .... AAANA
American Academy of Anatomists (DAVI) .... AAA
American Academy of Anesthesiologists' Assistants (DAVI) .... AAAA
American Academy of Applied Dental Science (SAUO) .... AAADS
American Academy of Applied Nutrition [Later, ICAN] (EA) .... AAAN
American Academy of Art [Chicago, IL] .... AAA
American Academy of Arts and Letters [Later, AAIAL] (EA) .... AAA & L
American Academy of Arts and Letters [Later, AAIAL] (EA) .... AAAL
American Academy of Arts and Letters, New York, NY [Library symbol]
  [Library of Congress] (LCLS) .... NNAL
American Academy of Arts & Music (WDAA) .... AAAM
American Academy of Arts and Sciences (EA) .... AAA & S
American Academy of Arts and Sciences (EA) .... AAAS
American Academy of Arts and Sciences (SAUO) .... AAS
American Academy of Arts and Sciences, Boston, MA [Library symbol]
  [Library of Congress] (LCLS) .... MBA

American Academy of Arts and Sciences Memoirs (journ.) (SAUS) ... Amer Acad Arts&Sci Mem
American Academy of Asian Studies (EA) ... AAAS
American Academy of Audiology (NTPA) ... AAA
American Academy of Ballet ... AAB
American Academy of Behavioral Medicine (EA) ... AABM
American Academy of Child and Adolescent Psychiatry (EA) ... AACAP
American Academy of Child Psychiatry [*Later, AACAP*] (EA) ... AACP
American Academy of Child Psychiatry (SAUO) ... AACP
American Academy of Clinical Electroencephalographers (MELL) ... AACE
American Academy of Clinical Neurophysiology (NTPA) ... AACN
American Academy of Clinical Psychiatrists (EA) ... AACP
American Academy of Clinical Sexologists (NTPA) ... AACS
American Academy of Clinical Toxicology (EA) ... AACT
American Academy of Compensation Medicine [*Later, AALIM*] (EA) ... AACM
American Academy of Compensation Medicine (SAUO) ... AALIM
American Academy of Cosmetic Dentistry (NTPA) ... AACD
American Academy of Cosmetic Surgery (EA) ... AACS
American Academy of Craniomandibular Disorders (EA) ... AACD
American Academy of Criminalistics (EA) ... AAC
American Academy of Crisis Interveners (EA) ... AACI
American Academy of Crown and Bridge Prosthodontics (EA) ... AACBP
American Academy of Dental Electrosurgery (EA) ... AADE
American Academy of Dental Group Practice (EA) ... AADGP
American Academy of Dental Hygiene (SAUO) ... AADH
American Academy of Dental Medicine [*Later, AAOM*] (EA) ... AADM
American Academy of Dental Practice Administration (EA) ... AADPA
American Academy of Dental Prosthetics (DAVI) ... AADP
American Academy of Dental Radiology (EA) ... AADR
American Academy of Dental Schools (DAVI) ... AADS
American Academy of Dentists [*Defunct*] (EA) ... AAD
American Academy of Denture Prosthetics (SAUO) ... AADP
American Academy of Denturity (SAUO) ... AAD
American Academy of Dermatology (EA) ... AAD
American Academy of Dermatology and Syphilology (SAUO) ... AADS
American Academy of Diplomacy (EA) ... AAD
American Academy of Disability Evaluating Physicians (EA) ... AADEP
American Academy of Dramatic Arts (NTCM) ... AADA
American Academy of Emergency Medicine (NTPA) ... AAEM
American Academy of Emergency Physicians (SAUO) ... AAEM
American Academy of Emergency Physicians (SAUS) ... AAEP
American Academy of Environmental Engineers (EA) ... AAEE
American Academy of Environmental Medicine (EA) ... AAEM
American Academy of Environmental Medicine (SAUS) ... AAEM
American Academy of Equine Art (EA) ... AAEA
American Academy of Esthetic Dentistry (EA) ... AAED
American Academy of Facial Plastic and Reconstructive Surgery (EA) ... AAFPRS
American Academy of Facial, Plastic, and Reconstructive Surgery (SAUO) ... AAFRS
American Academy of Family Physicians [*Formerly, AAGP*] (EA) ... AAFP
American Academy of Family Physicians Foundation (SAUO) ... AAFPF
American Academy of Fixed Prosthodontics (NTPA) ... AAFP
American Academy of Forensic Psychology (EA) ... AAFP
American Academy of Forensic Sciences (EA) ... AAFS
American Academy of General Practice [*Later, AAFP*] (EA) ... AAGP
American Academy of Gnathologic Orthopedics (EA) ... AAGO
American Academy of Gold Foil Operators (EA) ... AAGFO
American Academy of Gynecologic Laparoscopists (DMAA) ... AAGI
American Academy of Head, Facial, and Neck Pain and TMJ [*Temporomandibular Joint*] **Orthopedics** (EA) ... AAHFNPTO
American Academy of Head, Neck, and Facial Pain (NTPA) ... AAHFNP
American Academy of Head, Neck and Facial Pain (EA) ... AAHNFP
American Academy of Health Administration (EA) ... AAHA
American Academy of Health & Fitness Professionals (SAUO) ... AAHFP
American Academy of Health Care Providers in the Addictive Disorders (NTPA) ... AAHCPAD
American Academy of Health Physics (NTPA) ... AAHP
American Academy of Healthcare Attorneys (NTPA) ... AAHA
American Academy of Home Care Physicians (NTPA) ... AAHCP
American Academy of Homeopathic Medicine (EA) ... AAHM
American Academy of Homiletics [*Later, AH*] ... AAH
American Academy of Hospice and Palliative Medicine (NTPA) ... AAHPM
American Academy of Hospital Attorneys (EA) ... AAHA
American Academy of Humor Columnists (DGA) ... AAHC
American Academy of Husband-Coached Childbirth (EA) ... AAHCC
American Academy of Implant Dentistry (EA) ... AAID
American Academy of Implant Dentures (SAUO) ... AAID
American Academy of Implant Prosthodontics (EA) ... AAIP
American Academy of Industrial Hygiene (EA) ... AAIH
American Academy of Insurance Medicine (NTPA) ... AAIM
American Academy of Judicial Education (DLA) ... AAJE
American Academy of Legal and Industrial Medicine (EA) ... AALIM
American Academy of Male Sexual Health (NTPA) ... AAMSH
American Academy of Matrimonial Lawyers (EA) ... AAML
American Academy of Matrimonial Lawyers. Journal [*A publication*] (DLA) ... Am Acad Matri Law J
American Academy of Maxillofacial Prosthetics (EA) ... AAMP
American Academy of Mechanics (EA) ... AAM
American Academy of Medical Acupuncture (NTPA) ... AAMA
American Academy of Medical Administrators (EA) ... AAMA
American Academy of Medical Administrators Research and Educational Foundation (EA) ... AAMA
American Academy of Medical Administrators Research and Educational Foundation (EA) ... AAMAREF
American Academy of Medical Directors [*American College of Physician Exec utives*] [*Absorbed by*] (EA) ... AAMD
American Academy of Medical Hypnoanalysts (EA) ... AAMH
American Academy of Medical Preventics [*Later, ACAM*] (EA) ... AAMP
American Academy of Medical-Legal Analysis (EA) ... AAMLA
American Academy of Medicine and Science (EA) ... AAMS
American Academy of Microbiology (EA) ... AAM
American Academy of Ministry (NTPA) ... AAM
American Academy of Natural Family Planning (EA) ... AANFP
American Academy of Neurological and Orthopaedic Surgeons (NTPA) ... AANOS
American Academy of Neurological Surgery (EA) ... AANS
American Academy of Neurology (EA) ... AAN
American Academy of Nurse Practitioners (NTPA) ... AANP
American Academy of Nursing (EA) ... AAN
American Academy of Nutrition (EA) ... AAN
American Academy of Occupational Medicine (EA) ... AAOM
American Academy of Ophthalmology (EA) ... AAO
American Academy of Ophthalmology and Otolaryngology (EA) ... AAOO
American Academy of Optometry (EA) ... AAO
American Academy of Optometry (SAUO) ... ACO
American Academy of Oral and Maxillofacial Pathology (NTPA) ... AAOMP
American Academy of Oral and Maxillofacial Radiology (NTPA) ... AAOMR
American Academy of Oral Medicine (EA) ... AAOM
American Academy of Oral Pathology (DMAA) ... AAOP
American Academy of Oral Roentgenology [*Later, AADR*] ... AAOR
American Academy of Organ (EA) ... AAO
American Academy of Orofacial Pain (NTPA) ... AAOP
American Academy of Orthodontics for the General Practitioner (EA) ... AAOGP
American Academy of Orthopaedic Surgeons (EA) ... AAOS
American Academy of Orthopaedic Surgeons (or Surgery) (SAUO) ... AAOS
American Academy of Orthotists and Prosthetists (EA) ... AAOP
American Academy of Osteopathy (EA) ... AAO
American Academy of Osteopathy Journal (SAUO) ... AAOJ
American Academy of Otolaryngologic Allergy (EA) ... AAOA
American Academy of Otolaryngology (DAVI) ... AAO
American Academy of Otolaryngology-Head and Neck Surgery (SAUO) ... AAO-HNS
American Academy of Pain Management (NTPA) ... AAPM
American Academy of Pain Medicine (EA) ... AAPM
American Academy of Pediatric Dentistry (EA) ... AAPD
American Academy of Pediatricians (PAZ) ... AAP
American Academy of Pediatrics (EA) ... AAP
American Academy of Pedicatrics Proficiency Testing (SAUO) ... AAP-PT
American Academy of Pedodontics [*Later, AAPD*] (EA) ... AAP
American Academy of Periodontology (EA) ... AAP
American Academy of Philately [*Later, APC*] (EA) ... AAP
American Academy of Physical Education (EA) ... AAPE
American Academy of Physical Medicine & Rehabilitation (SAUO) ... AAPM&R
American Academy of Physical Medicine and Rehabilitation (NTPA) ... AAPM&R
American Academy of Physical Medicine and Rehabilitation (EA) ... AAPMR
American Academy of Physical Therapy (SAUO) ... AAPT
American Academy of Physician Assistants (EA) ... AAPA
American Academy of Physiologic Dentistry (EA) ... AAPD
American Academy of Physiology Dentistry (SAUO) ... AAPD
American Academy of Plastic Surgeons (DAVI) ... AAPS
American Academy of Podiatric Administration (EA) ... AAPA
American Academy of Podiatric Practice Management (NTPA) ... AAPPM
American Academy of Podiatric Sports Medicine (EA) ... AAPSM
American Academy of Podiatry Administration (EA) ... AAPA
American Academy of Podiatry Administration (EA) ... AAPO
American Academy of Political and Social Science (EA) ... AAPSS
American Academy of Political and Social Science (DLA) ... Am Acad Pol & Soc Sci
American Academy of Political and Social Science. Annals [*A publication*] (BRI) ... AAPSS-A
American Academy of Political and Social Science. Annals (journ.) (SAUS) ... APSS
American Academy of Political and Social Sciences (SAUO) ... Am Acad Pol Soc Sci
American Academy of Procedural Coders (EA) ... AAPC
American Academy of Pro-Life Physicians (EA) ... AAPLP
American Academy of Psychiatrists in Alcoholism and Addictions (EA) ... AAPAA
American Academy of Psychiatry & Neurology (CMD) ... AAPN
American Academy of Psychiatry and the Law (EA) ... AAPL
American Academy of Psychiatry and the Law. Bulletin [*A publication*] (DLA) ... Am A Psych L Bull
American Academy of Psychoanalysis (EA) ... AAP
American Academy of Psychotherapists (EA) ... AAP
American Academy of Religion (EA) ... AAR
American Academy of Religion (SAUO) ... Am Acad Rel
American Academy of Research Historians of Medieval Spain (NTPA) ... AARHMS
American Academy of Restorative Dentistry (EA) ... AARD
American Academy of Safety Education (EA) ... AASE
American Academy of Sanitarians (EA) ... AAS
American Academy of Sanitary Engineers (SAUO) ... AASE
American Academy of Somnology (EA) ... AAS
American Academy of Spinal Surgeons (EA) ... AASS
American Academy of Sports Physicians (EA) ... AASP
American Academy of Stress Disorders (EA) ... AASD
American Academy of Teachers of Singing (EA) ... AATS
American Academy of the History of Dentistry (EA) ... AAHD
American Academy of Thermology (EA) ... AAT

American Academy of Transportation ... AAT
American Academy of Tropical Medicine (EA) ... AATM
American Academy of Tuberculosis Physicians (EA) ... AATP
American Academy of Underwater Sciences (SAUO) ... AUS
American Academy of Veterinary and Comparative Toxicology (EA) ... AAVCT
American Academy of Veterinary Dermatology (EA) ... AAVD
American Academy of Veterinary Disaster Medicine (GVA) ... AAVDM
American Academy of Veterinary Informatics (GVA) ... AAVI
American Academy of Veterinary Nutrition (EA) ... AAVN
American Academy of Veterinary Pharmacology and Therapeutics (EA) ... AAVPT
American Academy of Wine [*Defunct*] (EA) ... AAW
American Academy of Wound Management (NTPA) ... AAWM
American Academy on Mental Retardation (EA) ... AAMR
American Academy Oral and Maxillofacial Pathology (EA) ... AAOMP
American Access Technologies [*NASDAQ symbol*] ... AATK
American Accordion Musicological Society (EA) ... AAMS
American Accordionists' Association (EA) ... AAA
American Accounting Association [*Sarasota, FL*] (EA) ... AAA
American Accreditation Health Care Commission ... AAHC
American Accreditation Health Care Commission (ROAS) ... AAHCC
American Action Fund for Blind Children and Adults (EA) ... AAFBCA
American Acupuncture Association (EA) ... AAA
American Adjustable Rate Term Trust 1997 [*NYSE symbol*] (SPSG) ... CDJ
American Adoption Congress [*Later, NAAC*] (EA) ... AAC
American Adventure, Inc. (SAUS) ... GOAA
American Adventure Inc. (SAUO) ... GOAA
American Adventurers Association (DICI) ... AAA
American Advertising Federation [*Washington, DC*] (EA) ... AAF
American Aerobics Association (EA) ... AAA
American Aeronautic Forum (SAUO) ... AAF
American Aerospace Controls Inc. (SAUO) ... AAC
American Aerospace Industries Inc. (SAUO) ... AAI
American Affenpinscher Association (EA) ... AAA
American Affiliation of Visiting Nurses Associations and Services [*Later, VNAA*] (EA) ... AAVNA
American Afghan Action [*Later, FAAA*] (EA) ... AAA
American Afghan Education Fund (EA) ... AAEF
American Afro-Asian Educational Exchange [*Later, AAEE*] (EA) ... AAAEE
American Agents Association [*Indianapolis, IN*] (EA) ... AAA
American Aging Association (EA) ... AGE
American Agricultural Chemical Co. (SAUO) ... AHD
American Agricultural Economics Association (EA) ... AAEA
American Agricultural Economics Documentation Center [*Department of Agriculture*] (IID) ... AAEDC
American Agricultural Economics Documentation Center, Washington, DC [*OCLC symbol*] (OCLC) ... AGU
American Agricultural Editors' Association (EA) ... AAEA
American Agricultural Investment Management Company (SAUO) ... AAIMC
American Agricultural Law Association (EA) ... AALA
American Agricultural Marketing Association (EA) ... AAMA
American Agricultural News Service (SAUO) ... AANS
American Agriculture Movement (EA) ... AAM
American Agri-Women (EA) ... AAW
American Agri-Women Resource Center (EA) ... AAWRC
American Agronomists Corp. (SAUO) ... AAC
American Aid for Afghans (EA) ... AAF
American Aid for Afghans (EA) ... AAFA
American Aid Society for the West Indies (EA) ... AASWI
American Aid Society of Paris [*France*] (EA) ... AASP
American Aid to France (SAUO) ... AATF
American Aid to Ulster (EA) ... AATU
American Aid to Ulster (EA) ... AAU
American Air Corps (SAUO) ... AAC
American Air Defense Command (SAUS) ... AADC
American Air Export & Import Co. ... AAXICO
American Air Export and Import Company (SAUO) ... AAXICO
American Air Export & Import Company (SAUS) ... AAXICO
American Air Filter (SAUS) ... AAF
American Air Filter Co. (MHDB) ... AAF
American Air Filter Company (SAUO) ... AAF
American Air Force (SAUO) ... AAF
American Air Mail Society (EA) ... AAMS
American Air Raid Relief Committee (SAUO) ... AARRC
American Air Raid Relief Committee (SAUS) ... AARRC
American Air Services, Inc. [*ICAO designator*] (FAAC) ... EJM
American Air Transport (SAUS) ... AMAT
American Airforce [*World War II*] ... AAF
American Airlines, Inc. [*ICAO designator*] ... AA
American Airlines Inc. (SAUO) ... AA
American Airlines, Inc. [*Air carrier designation symbol*] (MCD) ... AAL
American Airlines, Inc. (SAUO) ... AMAIR
American Airlines, Inc. (SAUO) ... AMR
American Airlines Overseas Inc. (SAUO) ... AAO
American Airlines Technical Training Corp. ... AATTC
American Airlines Technical Training Corporation (SAUO) ... AATTC
American Airship Association (SAUO) ... AA
American Airship Association [*Later, Airship Association*] (EA) ... AAA
American Airways (SAUS) ... AA
American Albino Association (SAUO) ... AAA
American Albino Horse Club [*Later, WWWCRW*] (EA) ... AAHC
American Alfalfa Processors Association (EA) ... AAPA
American All Hobbies Association (SAUO) ... AAHA
American Allergy Association (EA) ... AAA
American Alliance Against Violence (EA) ... AAAV
American Alliance for Health, Physical Education and Recreation (SAUS) ... AAHPER
American Alliance for Health, Physical Education, Recreation, and Dance (EA) ... AAHPERD
American Alliance for Theatre & Education (NTPA) ... AATE
American Alliance for Theatre and Education (SAUO) ... CTAA
American Alligator Council [*Defunct*] (EA) ... AAC
American Alligator Farmers Association (EA) ... AAFA
American All-Terrain Vehicle Association (EA) ... AATVA
American Alpine Club (EA) ... AAC
American Alpine Club, New York, NY [*Library symbol*] [*Library of Congress*] (LCLS) ... NNAAI
American Alumni Council [*Later, Council for the Advancement and Support of Education*] (EA) ... AAC
American Amaryllis Society (EA) ... AAS
American Amaryllis Society (SAUO) ... AAS
American Amateur Baseball Congress (EA) ... AABC
American Amateur Inventors Club (EA) ... AAIC
American Amateur Karate Federation (EA) ... AAKF
American Amateur Press Association (EA) ... AAPA
American Amateur Racquetball Association (EA) ... AARA
American Ambulance and Field Service (SAUO) ... AAFS
American Ambulance and Rescue Association [*Defunct*] (EA) ... AARA
American Ambulance Association (EA) ... AAA
American Amputee Foundation (EA) ... AAF
American Amusement Machine Association (EA) ... AAMA
American Analgesia Society (MELL) ... AAS
American Ancient Order of Hibernians (SAUO) ... AAOH
American and Australian Line (SAUO) ... A&A
American and Australian Line [*Shipping*] (ROG) ... A & A
American & Australian Steamship Line (SAUO) ... A&ASL
American and British Commonwealth Association ... ABC
American and Canadian Connection for Efficient Securities Settlement [*Canada*] ... ACCESS
American and Common Market Club (EAIO) ... ACMC
American and Delaine-Merino Record Association (EA) ... AD-MRA
American and Delaine-Merino Record Association (SAUO) ... ADMRA
American and English Annotated Cases [*A publication*] (DLA) ... A & EAC
American and English Annotated Cases [*A publication*] (DLA) ... A & E Ann Cas
American and English Annotated Cases [*A publication*] (DLA) ... A & E Anno
American and English Annotated Cases [*A publication*] (DLA) ... A & E Cas
American and English Annotated Cases [*A publication*] (DLA) ... Am & Eng Ann Cas
American and English Annotated Cases [*A publication*] (DLA) ... Am-Eng Ann Cases
American and English Annotated Cases [*A publication*] (DLA) ... Ann Cas
American and English Corporation Cases [*United States*] [*A publication*] (DLA) ... A & ECC
American and English Corporation Cases [*United States*] [*A publication*] (DLA) ... A & E Cor Cases
American and English Corporation Cases [*A publication*] (DLA) ... A & E Corp Cas
American and English Corporation Cases [*A publication*] (DLA) ... Am & E Corp Cas
American and English Corporation Cases [*A publication*] (DLA) ... Am & Eng Corp Cas
American and English Corporation Cases [*A publication*] (DLA) ... Cor Cas
American and English Corporation Cases, New Series [*A publication*] (DLA) ... A & E Corp Cas NS
American and English Corporation Cases, New Series [*A publication*] (DLA) ... Am & E Corp Cas NS
American and English Decisions in Equity [*A publication*] (DLA) ... Am & E Eq D
American and English Decisions in Equity [*A publication*] (DLA) ... Am & Eng Dec Eq
American and English Decisions in Equity [*A publication*] (DLA) ... Am & Eng Eq D
American and English Encyclopedia of Law [*A publication*] (DLA) ... A & E Enc L
American and English Encyclopedia of Law [*A publication*] (DLA) ... A & E Ency
American and English Encyclopedia of Law [*A publication*] (DLA) ... Am & Eng Enc Law
American and English Encyclopedia of Law [*A publication*] (DLA) ... Am & Eng Ency Law
American and English Encyclopedia of Law [*A publication*] (DLA) ... Amer & Eng Enc Law
American and English Encyclopedia of Law [*A publication*] (DLA) ... Enc Law
American and English Encyclopedia of Law [*A publication*] (DLA) ... Ency Law
American and English Encyclopedia of Law and Practice [*A publication*] (DLA) ... A & E Enc
American and English Encyclopedia of Law and Practice [*A publication*] (DLA) ... A & E Enc L & Pr
American and English Encyclopedia of Law and Practice [*A publication*] (DLA) ... A & E Ency Law
American and English Encyclopedia of Law and Practice [*A publication*] (DLA) ... Am & Eng Enc Law & Pr
American and English Encyclopedia of Law and Practice [*A publication*] (DLA) ... Ency L & P
American and English Encyclopedia of Law. Supplement [*A publication*] (DLA) ... Am & Eng Enc Law Sup
American and English Patent Cases [*A publication*] (DLA) ... A & E Pat Cas
American and English Patent Cases [*A publication*] (DLA) ... Am & Eng Pat Cas
American and English Pleading and Practice [*A publication*] (DLA) ... A & EP & P
American and English Pleading and Practice [*A publication*] (DLA) ... A & EP & Pr
American and English Railroad Cases [*A publication*] (DLA) ... A & ERC
American and English Railroad Cases [*A publication*] (DLA) ... A & ER Cas
American and English Railroad Cases [*A publication*] (DLA) ... A & E RRC
American and English Railroad Cases (SAUS) ... A&ERRC

American and English Railroad Cases [*A publication*] (DLA) ... A & ERR Cas
American and English Railroad Cases [*A publication*] (DLA) ... Am & Eng R Cas
American and English Railroad Cases [*A publication*] (DLA) ... Am & Eng RR Ca
American and English Railroad Cases [*A publication*] (DLA) ... Am & Eng RR Cas
American and English Railroad Cases [*A publication*] (DLA) ... Am & Eng RR Cases
American and English Railroad Cases [*A publication*] (DLA) ... Am & ER Cas
American and English Railroad Cases, New Series [*A publication*] (DLA) ... A & ER Cas NS
American and English Railroad Cases, New Series [*A publication*] (DLA) ... A & ERR Cas (NS)
American and English Railroad Cases, New Series [*A publication*] (DLA) ... Am & Eng R Cas NS
American and English Railroad Cases, New Series [*A publication*] (DLA) ... Am & Eng Ry Cas NS
American and English Railroad Cases, New Series [*A publication*] (DLA) ... Am & ER Cas NS
American and English Railway Cases [*A publication*] (DLA) ... Am & Engl RC
American and English Railway Cases [*A publication*] (DLA) ... Am & Eng Ry Cas
American and Foreign Bible Society ... AFBS
American and Foreign Christian Union (EA) ... AFCU
American and Foreign Christian Union (SAUO) ... AFCU
American & Foreign Power Co., Inc. ... A & FP
American and Foreign Power Company (SAUO) ... A&FP
American & Foreign Power Company, Inc. (SAUO) ... AF
American and French Research on the Treasury of the French Language [*University of Chicago*] [*Research center*] (RCD) ... ARTFL
American and Indian (SAUS) ... Amerind
American and West Indies (SAUS) ... A&WI
American Angus Association (EA) ... AAA
American Animal Health Pharmaceutical Association [*Defunct*] ... AAHPhA
American Animal Hospital Association (EA) ... AAHA
American Animal Therapy Association (SAUO) ... AATA
American Annals of the Deaf (SAUS) ... AAD
American Annals of the Deaf (journ.) (SAUS) ... ANDFA
American Annotated Cases [*A publication*] (DLA) ... Am Ann Cas
American Annotated Cases [*A publication*] (DLA) ... Ann Cas
American Annotated Cases [*A publication*] (DLA) ... Anno Cases
American Annotated Cases (journ.) (SAUS) ... Anno Cases
American Annual (journ.) (SAUS) ... AmA
American Annuity Group [*Formerly, STI Group*] [*NYSE symbol*] (SPSG) ... AAG
American Annuity Group, Inc. [*Associated Press*] (SAG) ... AAnnuity
American Annuity Group, Inc. Capital Trust I [*Associated Press*] (SAG) ... AAnnu
American Anorexia Nervosa Association [*Later, AABA*] (EA) ... AANA
American Anorexia/Bulimia Association (EA) ... AABA
American Antarctic Association (EA) ... AAA
American Antarctic Mountaineering Expedition ... AAME
American Antarctic Ridge [*Lithospheric plate*] ... AAR
American Anthology [*A publication*] ... AA
American Anthropological Association (EA) ... AAA
American Anthropological Association Memoirs (SAUO) ... AAAM
American Anthropologist [*A publication*] (BRI) ... A Anth
American Antiquarian (journ.) (SAUS) ... Am Antiq
American Antiquarian Society (SAUO) ... AAS
American Antiquarian Society (EA) ... AAS
American Antiquarian Society (SAUO) ... AQM
American Antiquarian Society Library (SAUO) ... AASL
American Antiquarian Society Proceedings (GEAB) ... AASP
American Antiquarian Society, Proceedings (journ.) (SAUS) ... Am Antiq Soc Proc
American Antiquarian Society, Worcester (SAUS) ... AQM
American Antiquarian Society, Worcester, MA [*OCLC symbol*] (OCLC) ... AQM
American Antiquarian Society, Worcester, MA [*Library symbol*] [*Library of Congress*] (LCLS) ... MWA
American Antique Graphics Society (EA) ... AAGS
American Antiques and Crafts Society [*Defunct*] (EA) ... AACS
American Antiquity [*A publication*] (BRI) ... Am Ant
American Antiquity. Society for American Archaeology (journ.) (SAUS) ... SAA/AA
American Anti-Terrorism Institute [*Defunct*] (EA) ... AATI
American Anti-Vivisection Society (EA) ... AAVS
American Apartment Communities, Inc. [*Associated Press*] (SAG) ... AmApt
American Apitherapy Society (NTPA) ... AAS
American Apparel Contractors Association (EA) ... AACA
American Apparel Manufacturers Association (EA) ... AAMA
American Aquatech International [*Vancouver Stock Exchange symbol*] ... AAA
American Arab Relief Agency [*Defunct*] ... AARA
American Arabic Association ... AMARA
American Arabic Association (EA) ... AMERA
American Arbitration Association (SAUO) ... AA
American Arbitration Association (EA) ... AAA
American Arbitration Association, New York, NY [*Library symbol*] [*Library of Congress*] (LCLS) ... NNAAr
American Archery Council (EA) ... AAC
American Architect (journ.) (SAUS) ... Am Arch
American Architectural Foundation [*Later, AIAF*] ... AAF
American Architectural Manufacturers Association (EA) ... AAMA
American Archives Association (EA) ... ARA
American Archivist Quarterly [*A publication*] (BRI) ... A Arch
American Armament Corporation (SAUO) ... AAC
American Armwrestling Association (EA) ... AAA
American Army (DAS) ... AA
American Army (SAUO) ... AMA
American Art Association [*Predecessor of Parke-Bernet, New York*] ... AAA
American Art Pottery Association (EA) ... AAPA
American Art Therapy Association (EA) ... AATA
American Artist [*A publication*] (BRI) ... A Art
American Artists Professional League (EA) ... AAPL
American Artists Series ... AAS
American Arts Alliance (EA) ... AAA
American Arts and Crafts Alliance (EA) ... ARCA
American Arts Documentation Centre (EA) ... AMARTS
American Asronautical Society (SAUO) ... AAS
American Assembly (EA) ... AA
American Assembly for Men in Nursing (EA) ... AAMN
American Assembly of Collegiate Schools of Business (EA) ... AACSB
American Associated Rental Operators (SAUO) ... AARO
American Associates, Ben-Gurion University of the Negev (EA) ... AABGU
American Association [*Baseball league*] ... AA
American Association - Electronic Voice Phenomena (EA) ... AA-EVP
American Association af University Administrators (SAUS) ... AAUA
American Association Against Acronym Abuse (SAUO) ... AAAAA
American Association Against Addiction [*Defunct*] (EA) ... AAAA
American Association for Accreditation of Ambulatory Plastic Surgery Facilities (SAUO) ... AAAAPSF
American Association for Accreditation of Ambulatory Surgery Facilities (SAUO) ... AAAASF
American Association for Accreditation of Ambulatory Surgery Facilities (NTPA) ... AAAASF
American Association for Accreditation of Laboratory Animal Care (EA) ... AAALAC
American Association for Active Lifestyles and Fitness (NTPA) ... AAALF
American Association for Acupuncture and Oriental Medicine (EA) ... AAAOM
American Association for Adult and Continuing Education (EA) ... AAACE
American Association for Advance of Science (SAUO) ... AAAS
American Association for Aerosol Research (EA) ... AAAR
American Association for Affirmative Action (EA) ... AAAA
American Association for Agricultural Education (EA) ... AAAE
American Association for Animal Artists (SAUO) ... AAAA
American Association for Applied Linguistics (EA) ... AAAL
American Association for Artificial Intelligence (EA) ... AAAI
American Association for Artificial Internal Organs (SAUO) ... ASFAIO
American Association for Automotive Medicine (SAUO) ... AAAM
American Association for Automotive Medicine (DAVI) ... AAAM
American Association for Budget and Program Analysis (EA) ... AABPA
American Association for Cancer Education (EA) ... AACE
American Association for Cancer Research (EA) ... AACR
American Association for Career Education (EA) ... AACE
American Association for Child Care in Hospital (SAUO) ... AACCH
American Association for Child Psychiatry (SAUO) ... AACP
American Association for Chinese Studies (EA) ... AACS
American Association for Cleft Palate Rehabilitation [*Later, ACPA*] ... AACPR
American Association for Clinical Chemistry (HGEN) ... AACC
American Association for Clinical Histocompatibility Testing [*Later, ASHI*] (EA) ... AACHT
American Association for Clinical Immunology and Allergy (EA) ... AACIA
American Association for Collegiate Independent Study (SAUO) ... AACIS
American Association for Comprehensive Health Planning (SAUO) ... AACHP
American Association for Comprehensive Health Planning [*Later, AHPA*] ... AACHP
American Association for Conservation Information [*Later, ACI*] (EA) ... AACI
American Association for Conservation of Information (SAUS) ... AACI
American Association for Consumer Benefits (EA) ... AACB
American Association for Contamination Control [*Later, IES*] (EA) ... AACC
American Association for Continuity of Care (NTPA) ... AACC
American Association for Corporate Contributions [*Defunct*] (EA) ... AACC
American Association for Correctional Psychology (EA) ... AACP
American Association for Counseling (DIPS) ... AAC
American Association for Counseling and Development (EA) ... AACD
American Association for Crystal Growth (EA) ... AACG
American Association for Dental Research (EA) ... AADR
American Association for Employment in Education (NTPA) ... AAEE
American Association for Ethiopian Jews (EA) ... AAEJ
American Association for Fuel Cells (NTPA) ... AAFC
American Association for Functional Orthodontics (EA) ... AAFO
American Association for Geodetic Surveying (EA) ... AAGS
American Association for Hand Surgery (EA) ... AAHS
American Association for Health Education (NTPA) ... AAHE
American Association for Health, Physical Education, and Recreation (AEBS) ... AAHPEAR
American Association for Health, Physical Education and Recreation (SAUO) ... AAHPER
American Association for Higher Education (EA) ... AAHE
American Association for Hospital Planning [*Later, The Forum for Health Care Planning*] (EA) ... AAHP
American Association for Humanistic Psychology [*Later, AHP*] ... AAHP
American Association for Information Sciences (SAUO) ... AAIS
American Association for International Aging (EA) ... AAIA
American Association for International Conciliation (SAUO) ... AAIC
American Association for Italian Studies (BARN) ... AAIS
American Association for Jesuit Scientists (SAUS) ... AAJS
American Association for Jewish Education [*Later, JESNA*] (EA) ... AAJE
American Association for Justice (SAUO) ... AAJ
American Association for Labor Legislation (DMAA) ... AALL
American Association for Laboratory Accreditation (AAGC) ... A2LA
American Association for Laboratory Accreditation (EA) ... AALA
American Association for Laboratory Animal Science (EA) ... AALAS
American Association for Legal and Political Philosophy (EA) ... AALPP
American Association for Leisure and Recreation (EA) ... AALR
American Association for Marriage and Family Therapy (EA) ... AAMFT
American Association for Maternal and Child Health [*Defunct*] (EA) ... AAMCH

American Association for Maternal and Infant Health [*Later, AAMCH*] (EA) ... AAMIH
American Association for Medical Systems and Informatics [*Later, AMIA*] (EA) ... AAMSI
American Association for Medical Transcription (EA) ... AAMT
American Association for Middle East Studies [*Defunct*] (EA) ... AAMES
American Association for Museum Volunteers (EA) ... AAMV
American Association for Music Therapy (EA) ... AAMT
American Association for Nurses Practicing Independently (DAVI) ... AANPI
American Association for Paralegal Education (SAUO) ... AAFPE
American Association for Paralegal Education (EA) ... AAPE
American Association for Parapsychology (EA) ... AAP
American Association for Partial Hospitalization (EA) ... AAPH
American Association for Pediatric Ophthalmology and Strabismus (EA) ... AAPO & S
American Association for Pediatric Ophthalmology and Strabismus (SAUO) ... AAPO&S
American Association for Pediatric Ophthalmology and Strabismus (NTPA) ... AAPOS
American Association for Professional Law Enforcement (SAUS) ... AAPLE
American Association for Protecting Children (EA) ... AAPC
American Association for Public Information, Education and Research (AEBS) ... AAPIER
American Association for Public Information, Education and Research (SAUO) ... AAPIER
American Association for Public Opinion Research (EA) ... AAPOR
American Association for Rehabilitation Therapy [*Defunct*] (EA) ... AART
American Association for Respiratory Care (EA) ... AARC
American Association for Respiratory Therapy [*Later, AARC*] (EA) ... AART
American Association for Respiratory Therapy (SAUO) ... AART
American Association for Scientific Interrogation (SAUO) ... AASI
American Association for Small Dredging and Marine Construction Companies (SAUO) ... AASDMCC
American Association for Small Dredging and Marine Construction Companies (EA) ... AASDMCC
American Association for Social Psychiatry (EA) ... AASP
American Association for Social Security (EA) ... AASS
American Association for State and Local History (EA) ... AASLH
American Association for Study of Neoplastic Diseases (EA) ... AASND
American Association for Study of the United States in World Affairs (SAUS) ... USWA
American Association for Textile Technology (EA) ... AATT
American Association for the Abolition of Involuntary Mental Hospitalization [*Defunct*] ... AAIMH
American Association for the Advancement of Agnosticism (SAUO) ... AAAA
American Association for the Advancement of Atheism [*Later, AA*] (EA) ... AAAA
American Association for the Advancement of Criminology (SAUO) ... AAAAC
American Association for the Advancement of Health Education [*Medicine*] (DMAA) ... AAAHE
American Association for the Advancement of Science (SAUS) ... AAAS
American Association for the Advancement of Science - Herbicide Assessment Commission (SAUO) ... AAAS-HAC
American Association for the Advancement of Science Bulletins (SAUO) ... AAAS Bull
American Association for the Advancement of Science, Washington, DC [*Library symbol*] [*Library of Congress*] (LCLS) ... DAAAS
American Association for the Advancement of Slavic Studies (EA) ... AAASS
American Association for the Advancement of Tension Control [*Later, ISTC*] ... AAATC
American Association for the Advancement of the Humanities ... AAAH
American Association for the Comparative Study of Law (EA) ... AACSL
American Association for the Education of Severely/Profoundly Handicapped (EDAC) ... AAESPH
American Association for the Educational Service Agencies (EDAC) ... AAESA
American Association for the Gifted ... AAG
American Association for the History of Medicine [*University of Rochester Medical Center*] (EA) ... AAHM
American Association for the History of Nursing (EA) ... AAHN
American Association for the Improvement of Boxing (EA) ... AAIB
American Association for the International Commission of Jurists (EA) ... AAICJ
American Association for the Promotion of Science ... AAPS
American Association for the Promotion of Teaching Speech to the Deaf (WDAA) ... AAPTSD
American Association for the Study of Headache (EA) ... AASH
American Association for the Study of Liver Diseases (EA) ... AASLD
American Association for the Study of Neoplastic Diseases (SAUS) ... AASND
American Association for the Study of World Affairs (SAUO) ... AASWA
American Association for the Surgery of Trauma (EA) ... AAST
American Association for the United Nations [*Later, United Nations Association of the United States*] (EA) ... AAUN
American Association for the United Nations (SAUO) ... AAUN
American Association for Therapeutic Humor (EA) ... AATH
American Association for Thoracic Surgery (EA) ... AATS
American Association for Vital Records and Public Health Statistics [*Later, AVRHS*] (EA) ... AAVRPHS
American Association for Vital Records and Public Health Statistics (SAUO) ... AAVRPHS
American Association for Vocational Instructional Materials (EA) ... AAVIM
American Association for Women in Community Colleges (NTPA) ... AAWCC
American Association for Women Podiatrists (EA) ... AAWP
American Association for World Health (EA) ... AAWH
American Association for Zoological Nomenclature (EA) ... AAZN
American Association for/of Acupuncture and Oriental Medicine (SAUO) ... AAAOM
American Association for/of Applied Psychology (SAUO) ... AAAP
American Association for/of Correctional Psychology (SAUO) ... AACP
American Association for/of Geodetic Surveying (SAUO) ... AAGS
American Association for/of Geriatric Psychiatry (SAUO) ... AAGP
American Association for/of Gifted Children (SAUO) ... AAGC
American Association for/of Jesuit Scientists (SAUO) ... AAJS
American Association for/of Laboratory Animal Science (SAUO) ... AALAS
American Association for/of Women Radiologists (SAUO) ... AAWR
American Association for/or of Artificial Intelligence (SAUO) ... AAAI
American Association of Aardvark Aficionados (EA) ... AAAA
American Association of Academic Editors (EA) ... AAAE
American Association of Accompanists and Coaches (EA) ... AAAC
American Association of Acupuncture and Bio-Energetic Medicine (SAUO) ... AAABEM
American Association of Advanced Science (WPI) ... AAAS
American Association of Advertising Agencies [*New York, NY*] ... 4A's
American Association of Advertising Agencies (SAUO) ... A 4
American Association of Advertising Agencies [*New York, NY*] (EA) ... AAAA
American Association of Advertising Agencies, New York, NY [*Library symbol*] [*Library of Congress*] (LCLS) ... NNAdv
American Association of Agricultural College Editors [*Later, ACE*] (EA) ... AAACE
American Association of Agricultural Communicators of Tomorrow (EA) ... ACT
American Association of Agricultural Economics (SAUO) ... AAEA
American Association of AIDS [*Acquired Immune Deficiency Syndrome*] **Executives** (NTPA) ... AAAE
American Association of Aircraft Manufacturers (SAUO) ... AAAM
American Association of Aircraft Manufactures (SAUO) ... AAAM
American Association of Airport Executives (EA) ... AAAE
American Association of Aluminum Importers and Warehouse Distributors (SAUO) ... AAAIWD
American Association of Ambulatory Surgery Centers (NTPA) ... AAASC
American Association of Anatomists (EA) ... AAA
American Association of Applied and Preventive Psychology (DIPS) ... AAAPP
American Association of Applied Psychology [*Division of American Psychological Association*] ... AAAP
American Association of Architectural Bibliographers ... AAAB
American Association of Artificial Intelligence (SAUS) ... AAAI
American Association of Asphalt and Paving Technologists (SAUO) ... AAAPT
American Association of Attorney-Certified Public Accountants [*Mission Viejo, CA*] (EA) ... AAA-CPA
American Association of Audio Analgesia [*Defunct*] ... AAAA
American Association of Automatic Door Manufacturers ... AAADM
American Association of Avian Pathologists (EA) ... AAAP
American Association of Backgammon Clubs (EA) ... AABC
American Association of Baggage Traffic Managers [*Defunct*] (EA) ... AABTM
American Association of Bank Directors (NTPA) ... AABD
American Association of Behavioral and Social Sciences (SAUO) ... AABSS
American Association of Behavioral Therapists (EA) ... AABT
American Association of Behavioral Therapists (EA) ... BT
American Association of Bible Colleges (EA) ... AABC
American Association of Bicycle Importers (EA) ... AABI
American Association of Bioanalysts [*or Bioanalysis*] (DAVI) ... AAB
American Association of Biofeedback Clinicians [*Defunct*] (EA) ... AABC
American Association of Black Women Entrepreneurs [*Silver Spring, MD*] (EA) ... AABWE
American Association of Blacks in Energy (EA) ... AABE
American Association of Blood Banks (EA) ... AABB
American Association of Blood Banks (SAUO) ... Am Assn Blood
American Association of Book Publishers (SAUO) ... AABP
American Association of Book Wholesalers ... AABW
American Association of Botanic Gardens (SAUO) ... AABG
American Association of Botanical Gardens and Arboreta (or Arboretums) (SAUO) ... AABGA
American Association of Bovine Practitioners (EA) ... AABP
American Association of Breeders of Holsteiner Horses (EA) ... AABHH
American Association of Business Valuation Specialists (NTPA) ... AABVS
American Association of Cable TV Owners [*Inactive*] (EA) ... AACTO
American Association of Cable TV Owners (EA) ... AACTVO
American Association of Candy Technologists (EA) ... AACT
American Association of Cardiovascular and Pulmonary Rehabilitation (SAUO) ... AACPR
American Association of Cardiovascular and Pulmonary Rehabilitation (EA) ... AACVPR
American Association of Cat Enthusiasts (EA) ... AACE
American Association of Central Cancer Registries (SAUO) ... AACCR
American Association of Ceramic Industries (EA) ... AACI
American Association of Cereal Chemists (EA) ... AACC
American Association of Certified Allergists (EA) ... AACA
American Association of Certified Allied Health Personnel in Ophthalmology (EA) ... AACAHPO
American Association of Certified Allied Health Personnel in Ophthalmology (SAUO) ... AACAHPO
American Association of Certified Appraisers [*Cincinnati, OH*] (EA) ... AACA
American Association of Certified Orthopetists (SAUO) ... AACO
American Association of Certified Orthoptists (EA) ... AACO
American Association of Chairmen of Departments of Psychiatry (EA) ... AACDP
American Association of Chairs of Departments of Psychiatry (SAUO) ... AACDPA
American Association of Cheerleading Coaches and Advisors (SAUO) ... AACCA
American Association of Children's Residential Centers (12L) ... AACRC
American Association of Chiropractors (EA) ... AAC
American Association of Christian Schools (EA) ... AACS
American Association of Classified School Employees (EA) ... AACSE

American Association of Clinic Physicians and Surgeons [*Defunct*] (EA) ... AACPS
American Association of Clinical Chemistry (EA) ... AACC
American Association of Clinical Chemists (SAUO) ... AACC
American Association of Clinical Endocrinologists ... AACE
American Association of Clinical Psychologists (DIPS) ... AACP
American Association of Clinical Research (SAUO) ... AACR
American Association of Clinical Urologists (EA) ... AACU
American Association of College and University Business Officers [*Defunct*] ... AACUBO
American Association of College Baseball Coaches (EA) ... AACBC
American Association of College Business Officers (SAUO) ... AACBO
American Association of Colleges for Teacher Education (EA) ... AACTE
American Association of Colleges for/of Chiropody-Podiatry (SAUO) ... AACCP
American Association of Colleges of Chiropody-Podiatry ... AACCP
American Association of Colleges of Nursing (EA) ... AACN
American Association of Colleges of Osteopathic Medicine (EA) ... AACOM
American Association of Colleges of Osteopathic Medicine Applications Service (SAUO) ... AACOMAS
American Association of Colleges of Pharmacy (EA) ... AACP
American Association of Colleges of Pharmacy (SAUO) ... Am Assn Coll Pharm
American Association of Colleges of Podiatric Medicine (EA) ... AACPM
American Association of Colleges of Podiatric Medicine Application Service (SAUO) ... AACPMAS
American Association of Colleges of Podiatry [*Later, AACPM*] (EA) ... AACP
American Association of Collegiate Registrars and Admissions Officers (EA) ... AACRAO
American Association of Collegiate Registrars and Admissions Officers (SAUO) ... AACRAO
American Association of Collegiate Schools of Business (SAUO) ... AACSB
American Association of Commerce (or Commercial) Publications (SAUO) ... AACP
American Association of Commerce Publications [*Later, American Chamber of Commerce Executives Communications Council*] (EA) ... AACP
American Association of Commercial Colleges [*Later, United Business Schools Association*] (AEBS) ... AACC
American Association of Commodity Traders [*Defunct*] (EA) ... AACT
American Association of Community and Junior Colleges (EA) ... AACJC
American Association of Community Colleges (NFD) ... AACC
American Association of Community Mental Health Center Psychiatrists (SAUO) ... AACMHP
American Association of Community Psychiatrists (EA) ... AACP
American Association of Community Theatre (EA) ... AACT
American Association of Computer Professionals (EA) ... AACP
American Association of Concerned Engineers (EA) ... AACE
American Association of Conservators and Restorers (EA) ... AACR
American Association of Convention Planners [*Defunct*] (EA) ... AACP
American Association of Cooperative/Mutual Insurance Societies (NTPA) ... AAC/MIS
American Association of Correctional Facility Officers [*Later, IACO*] (EA) ... AACFO
American Association of Correctional Officers [*Later, IACO*] (EA) ... AACO
American Association of Correctional Training Personnel (EA) ... AACTP
American Association of Cosmetic Surgeons (SAUO) ... AACS
American Association of Cosmetology Schools (NTPA) ... AACS
American Association of Cost Engineers (EA) ... AACE
American Association of Councils of Medical Staffs [*Later, PDA*] (EA) ... CMS
American Association of Creamery Butter Manufacturers (SAUO) ... AACBM
American Association of Creamery Butter Manufactures (SAUO) ... AACBM
American Association of Creative Artists (EA) ... AACA
American Association of Credit Counselors [*Defunct*] (EA) ... AACC
American Association of Crimean Turks (EA) ... AACT
American Association of Criminology (AEBS) ... AAC
American Association of Critical Care Nurses (DAVI) ... AACCN
American Association of Critical-Care Nurses (SAUO) ... AACCN
American Association of Critical-Care Nurses ... AACN
American Association of Crop Insurers [*Washington, DC*] (EA) ... AACI
American Association of Dealers in Ancient, Oriental, and Primitive Art (EA) ... AADAOPA
American Association of Dental Consultants [*Bloomington, MN*] (EA) ... AADC
American Association of Dental Editors (EA) ... AADE
American Association of Dental Examiners (EA) ... AADE
American Association of Dental Schools (EA) ... AADS
American Association of Dental Schools Application Service (GAGS) ... AADSAS
American Association of Dental Victims (EA) ... AADV
American Association of Dermatology and Syphilology (SAUO) ... AADS
American Association of Diabetes Educators (EA) ... AADE
American Association of Directors of Psychiatric Residency Training (EA) ... AADPRT
American Association of Directors of Psychiatric Residency Training (SAUO) ... AADPRT
American Association of Disability Communicators [*Defunct*] (EA) ... AADC
American Association of Disabled Persons (EA) ... AADP
American Association of Doctors' Nurses (EA) ... AADN
American Association of Doctors Nurses (SAUS) ... AADN
American Association of Domain Names (VERA) ... AADN
American Association of Early Childhood Educators (NTPA) ... AAECE
American Association of Economic Entomologists (SAUO) ... AAEE
American Association of Electrical Engineers (SAUO) ... AAEE
American Association of Electrodiagnostic Medicine (EA) ... AAEM
American Association of Electromyography and Electrodiagnosis [*Later, AAEM*] (EA) ... AAEE
American Association of Electromyography and Electrodiagnostics (SAUO) ... AAEE
American Association of Electronic Reporters and Transcribers, Inc. ... AAERT
American Association of Elementary-Kindergarten-Nursery Educators (SAUO) ... AAEKNE
American Association of Elementary/Kindergarten/Nursery Educators [*Defunct*] ... AAE/K/N/E
American Association of Endodontists (EA) ... AAE
American Association of Engineering Societies (EA) ... AAES
American Association of Engineers [*Later, NSPE*] (EA) ... AAE
American Association of English Jewish Newspapers [*Later, AJPA*] (BJA) ... AAEJN
American Association of Enterprise Zones (NTPA) ... AAEZ
American Association of Entrepreneural Dentists (SAUO) ... AAED
American Association of Entrepreneurial Dentists (EA) ... AAED
American Association of Equine Practitioners (EA) ... AAEP
American Association of Equipment Lessors (EA) ... AAEL
American Association of Esthetics (EA) ... AAE
American Association of Evangelical Students [*Defunct*] (EA) ... AAES
American Association of Examiners and Administrators of Educational Personnel [*Later, American Association of School Personnel Administrators*] (AEBS) ... AAEAEP
American Association of Ex-Offenders in Criminal Justice (SAUO) ... AAEOCJ
American Association of Exporters and Importers [*New York, NY*] (EA) ... AAEI
American Association of Eye and Ear Hospitals (EA) ... AAEEH
American Association of Family and Consumer Sciences (PAZ) ... AAFCS
American Association of Family and Consumer Sciences (EA) ... AHEA
American Association of Family Businesses (NTPA) ... AAFB
American Association of Family Counselors and Mediators (DHP) ... AAFCM
American Association of Feed Control Officials (SAUO) ... AAFCO
American Association of Feed Exporters [*Defunct*] (EA) ... AAFE
American Association of Feed Microscopists (EA) ... AAFM
American Association of Feline Practitioners (EA) ... AAFP
American Association of Fighter Aces (SAUO) ... AAFA
American Association of Film Producers (BARN) ... AAFP
American Association of Financial Professionals [*Defunct*] (EA) ... AAFP
American Association of First Responders [*Later, National Association of First Aid Responders*] (EA) ... AAFAR
American Association of Fitness Directors in Business and Industry (EA) ... AAFDBI
American Association of Food Hygiene Veterinarians (GVA) ... AAFHV
American Association of Food Stamp Directors (EA) ... AAFSD
American Association of Foot Specialists [*Defunct*] (EA) ... AAFS
American Association of Foreign Medical Graduates [*Defunct*] (EA) ... AAFMG
American Association of Forms Executives (EA) ... AAFE
American Association of Foundations for Medical Care [*Later, AMCRA*] (EA) ... AAFMC
American Association of Franchisees and Dealers ... AAFD
American Association of Functional Orthodontists [*Later, American Association for Functional Orthodontics*] (EA) ... AAFO
American Association of Fund-Raising Counsel (EA) ... AAFRC
American Association of Fund-Raising Counsel, Inc. ... AAFRC
American Association of Fund-Raising Counsel, Inc., Trust for Philanthropy (NFD) ... AAFRC Trust for Philanthropy
American Association of Fund-Raising Counsel Trust for Philanthropy (EA) ... AAFRCTP
American Association of General Hospital Psychiatrists (SAUO) ... AAGHP
American Association of Genito-Urinary Surgeons (EA) ... AAGUS
American Association of Geodetic Surveying (SAUS) ... AAGS
American Association of Geographers (CARB) ... AAG
American Association of Gifted Children (SAUS) ... AAGC
American Association of Grain Inspection and Weighing Agencies (EA) ... AAGIWA
American Association of Gravity Field Energy [*Defunct*] (EA) ... AAGFE
American Association of Gynecological Laparoscopists (EA) ... AAGL
American Association of Handwriting Analysts (EA) ... AAHA
American Association of Health Data Systems [*Defunct*] (EA) ... AAHDS
American Association of Health Plans ... AAHP
American Association of Healthcare Consultants (EA) ... AAHC
American Association of Hides, Skins, and Leather Merchants [*Later, USHSLA*] ... AAHSLM
American Association of Hispanic CPA's [*Certified Public Accountants*] [*Houston, TX*] (EA) ... AAHCPA
American Association of Home-Based Businesses (NTPA) ... AAHBB
American Association of Homeopathic Pharmacists (EA) ... AAHP
American Association of Homes and Services for the Aging ... AAHSA
American Association of Homes for the Aging (EA) ... AAHA
American Association of Hospital Accountants [*Later, HFMA*] (EA) ... AAHA
American Association of Hospital Accountants (SAUO) ... Aging
American Association of Hospital Consultants [*Later, American Association of Healthcare Consultants*] (EA) ... AAHC
American Association of Hospital Dental Chiefs [*Later, AAHD*] ... AAHDC
American Association of Hospital Dentists [*Formerly, AAHDC*] (EA) ... AAHD
American Association of Hospital Podiatrists (EA) ... AAHP
American Association of Hospital Purchasing Agents (EA) ... AAHPA
American Association of Housing Educators (EA) ... AAHE
American Association of Immunologists (EA) ... AAI
American Association of Imported Car Dealers [*Defunct*] (EA) ... AAICD
American Association of Independent Architects ... AAIA
American Association of Independent News Distributors (EA) ... AAIND
American Association of Independent Publishers (NTCM) ... AAIP
American Association of Individual Investors [*Chicago, IL*] (EA) ... AAII
American Association of Individual Investors (SAUO) ... AAII
American Association of Industrial Dentists [*Defunct*] (EA) ... AAID
American Association of Industrial Editors [*Later, IABC*] (EA) ... AAIE
American Association of Industrial Engineers ... AAIE
American Association of Industrial Management [*Springfield, MA*] (EA) ... AAIM
American Association of Industrial Nurses [*Later, AAOHN*] (EA) ... AAIN

American Association of Industrial Physicians and Surgeons (SAUO) ...... AAIPS
American Association of Industrial Social Workers (EA) ...... AAISW
American Association of Industrial Veterinarians (EA) ...... AAIV
American Association of Inhalation Therapists [*Later, AART*] (EA) ...... AAIT
American Association of Inhalation Therapy (or Therapists) (SAUO) ...... AAIT
American Association of Instructors of the Blind [*Later, AEVH*] (EA) ...... AAIB
American Association of Insurance Management Consultants [*Houston, TX*] (EA) ...... AAIMCo
American Association of Insurance Management Consultants (SAUO) ...... AAIMCo
American Association of Insurance Services [*Bensenville, IL*] (EA) ...... AAIS
American Association of Integrated Healthcare Delivery Systems (SAUO) ...... AAIHDS
American Association of Inventors [*Defunct*] (EA) ...... AAI
American Association of Inventors ...... AAOI
American Association of Investigative Pathologists (HGEN) ...... AAIP
American Association of IV Therapy (EA) ...... AAIVT
American Association of Jesuit Scientists [*Defunct*] (EA) ...... AAJS
American Association of Journalism School Administrators (EA) ...... AAJSA
American Association of Judges (EA) ...... AAJ
American Association of Junior Colleges [*Later, AACJC*] (EA) ...... AAJC
American Association of Kidney Patients (EA) ...... AAKP
American Association of Laban Movement Analysts (EA) ...... AALMA
American Association of Laboratory Animal Science (SAUS) ...... AALAS
American Association of Land-Grant Colleges and State Universities (SAUO) ...... AALGCSU
American Association of Language Specialists (BARN) ...... AALS
[*The*] **American Association of Language Specialists** (EA) ...... TAALS
American Association of Law Libraries (EA) ...... AALL
American Association of Legal Nurse Consultants (NTPA) ...... AALNC
American Association of Library Trustees [*Later, ALTA*] ...... AALT
American Association of Limited Partners (EA) ...... AALP
American Association of Machinery Importers [*Defunct*] ...... AAMI
American Association of Managed Care Nurses ...... AAMCN
American Association of Managing General Agents [*Washington, DC*] (EA) ...... AAMGA
American Association of Marriage and Family Counselors [*Later, AAMFT*] ...... AAMFC
American Association of Marriage Counselors [*Later, AAMFT*] (EA) ...... AAMC
American Association of Meat Processors (EA) ...... AAMP
American Association of Media Specialists and Librarians [*Defunct*] (EA) ...... AAMSL
American Association of Medical Assistants (EA) ...... AAMA
American Association of Medical Clinics [*Later, AGPA*] (EA) ...... AAMC
American Association of Medical Colleges (DAVI) ...... AAMC
American Association of Medical Milk Commissioners (or Commissions) (SAUO) ...... AAMMC
American Association of Medical Record Administrators [*Formerly, American Association of Medical Record Librarians*] [*Also, AMRA*] (DAVI) ...... AAMRA
American Association of Medical Record Librarians [*Later, AMRA*] (EA) ...... AAMRL
American Association of Medical Review Officers (SAUO) ...... AAMRO
American Association of Medical Social Workers (SAUO) ...... AAMSW
American Association of Medical Social Workers [*Later, National Association of Social Workers*] (AEBS) ...... AAMSW
American Association of Medical Society Executives (EA) ...... AAMSE
American Association of Medical Writers (SAUO) ...... AAMW
American Association of Medico-Legal Consultants (EA) ...... AAMC
American Association of Medico-Physical Research (SAUO) ...... AAMPR
American Association of Mental Health Professionals in Corrections (EA) ...... AAMHPC
American Association of Meta-Science (EA) ...... AAMS
American Association of Microbiology (SAUO) ...... AAM
American Association of Microcomputer Investors [*Defunct*] (EA) ...... AAMI
American Association of Microprocessor Engineers ...... AAME
American Association of Minority Businesses (NTPA) ...... AAMB
American Association of Minority Enterprise Small Business Investment Companies [*Washington, DC*] (EA) ...... AAMESBIC
American Association of Motor Vehicle Administrators (EA) ...... AAMVA
American Association of Museums (EA) ...... AAM
American Association of Museums (SAUO) ...... AAMus
American Association of Music Festivals [*Defunct*] ...... AAMF
American Association of Naturopathic Physicians (EA) ...... AANP
American Association of Nephrology Nurses and Technicians [*Later, ANNA*] (EA) ...... AANNT
American Association of Neurological Surgeons (or Surgery) (SAUO) ...... AANS
American Association of Neuropathologists (DAVI) ...... AAN
American Association of Neuropathologists (EA) ...... AANP
American Association of Neuroscience (or Neurosurgical) Nurses (SAUO) ...... AANN
American Association of Neurosurgical Nurses [*Later, ABNN*] (EA) ...... AANN
American Association of Newspaper Representatives [*Later, NASA*] (EA) ...... AANR
American Association of Nurse Anesthetists (EA) ...... AANA
[*The*] **American Association of Nurse Attorneys** (EA) ...... AANA
[*The*] **American Association of Nurse Attorneys** (EA) ...... TAANA
American Association of Nurse Executives (SAUO) ...... AANE
American Association of Nurse-Midwives [*Later, ACNM*] ...... AANM
American Association of Nurserymen (EA) ...... AAN
American Association of Nurserymen, Inc. ...... AAN
American Association of Nursing Assistants (EA) ...... AANA
American Association of Nutritional Consultants (EA) ...... AANC
American Association of Obstetricians and Gynecologists [*Later, AGOS*] (EA) ...... AAOG
American Association of Obstetricians, Gynecologists and Abdominal Surgeons (SAUO) ...... AAOGAS
American Association of Occupational Health Nurses (EA) ...... AAOHN
American Association of Office Nurses (EA) ...... AAON
American Association of Oil Well Drilling Contractors (SAUS) ...... AAODC
American Association of Oilwell Drilling Contractors [*Later, IADC*] (EA) ...... AAODC
American Association of Ophthalmology [*Absorbed by American Academy of Ophthalmology - AAO*] ...... AAO
American Association of Oral & Maxillofacial Surgeons (SAUS) ...... AAOMS
American Association of Oral and Plastic Surgeons (SAUO) ...... AAOPS
American Association of Oral Biologists (SAUO) ...... AAOB
American Association of Oriental Medicine (NTPA) ...... AAOM
American Association of Orthodontists (EA) ...... AAO
American Association of Orthodontists Foundation (SAUO) ...... AAOF
American Association of Orthomolecular Medicine (EA) ...... AAOM
American Association of Orthopaedic Medicine (EA) ...... AAOM
American Association of Orthopedic Medicine (EA) ...... AAOrthMed
American Association of Orthoptic Technicians [*Later, AACO*] (EA) ...... AAOT
American Association of Orthoptic Technicians (SAUO) ...... AAOT
American Association of Osteopathic Colleges [*Later, AACOM*] (EA) ...... AAOC
American Association of Osteopathic Examiners (EA) ...... AAOE
American Association of Osteopathic Medical Examiners (EA) ...... AAOME
American Association of Osteopathic Specialists (EA) ...... AAOS
American Association of Owners and Breeders of Peruvian Paso Horses (EA) ...... AAOBPPH
American Association of Passenger Rate Men [*Defunct*] (EA) ...... AAPRM
American Association of Passenger Traffic Officers [*Defunct*] (EA) ...... AAPTO
American Association of Pastoral Counselors (EA) ...... AAPC
American Association of Pathologists (EA) ...... AAP
American Association of Pathologists and Bacteriologists (SAUO) ...... AAOPB
American Association of Pathologists and Bacteriologists (SAUO) ...... AAPB
American Association of Pathologists and Bacteriologists [*Later, AAP*] (EA) ...... AAPB
American Association of Pathologists' Assistants (EA) ...... AAPA
American Association of Pathologists Assistants (SAUS) ...... AAPA
American Association of Pediatrics (SAUO) ...... AAP
American Association of People with Disabilities (SAUO) ...... AAPD
American Association of Personal Financial Planners [*Defunct*] (EA) ...... AAPFP
American Association of Pesticide Control Officials (SAUO) ...... AAPCO
American Association of Petroleum Geologists (EA) ...... AAPG
American Association of Petroleum Geologists Bulletin (SAUO) ...... Am Assoc Pet Geol Bull
American Association of Petroleum Geologists Bulletin (SAUO) ...... Amer Assoc Pet Geol Bull
American Association of Petroleum Geologists, Energy Resources Library, Tulsa, OK [*Library symbol*] [*Library of Congress*] (LCLS) ...... OkTA
American Association of Petroleum Landmen (EA) ...... AAPL
American Association of Pharmaceutical Scientists (EA) ...... AAPS
American Association of Philosophy Teachers (EA) ...... AAPT
American Association of Phonetic Sciences (EA) ...... AAPS
American Association of Physical Anthropologists (EA) ...... AAPA
American Association of Physical Medicine and Rehabilitation (DAVI) ...... AAPMR
American Association of Physician Specialists (NTPA) ...... AAPS
American Association of Physician-Hospital Organization ...... AAPHO
American Association of Physicians and Surgeons (DAVI) ...... AAPS
American Association of Physicians' Assistants [*Defunct*] (EA) ...... AAPA
American Association of Physicians Assistants (SAUS) ...... AAPA
American Association of Physicians for Human Rights (EA) ...... AAPHR
American Association of Physicians Practicing the Transcendental Meditation Program [*Later, WMAFPH*] (EA) ...... AAPPTMP
American Association of Physicists in Medicine (EA) ...... AAPM
American Association of Physics Teachers (EA) ...... AAPT
American Association of Planned Parenthood Physicians [*Later, APPP*] (EA) ...... AAPPP
American Association of Planned Parenthood Physicians (SAUO) ...... AAPPP
American Association of Plastic Surgeons (EA) ...... AAPS
American Association of Podiatric Physicians and Surgeons (EA) ...... AAPPS
American Association of Poison Control Centers (EA) ...... AAPCC
American Association of Police Polygraphists (EA) ...... AAPP
American Association of Political Consultants (EA) ...... AAPC
American Association of Port Authorities (EA) ...... AAPA
American Association of Preferred Provider Organizations [*Alexandria, VA*] (EA) ...... AAPPO
American Association of Presidents of Independent Colleges and Universities (EA) ...... AAPICU
American Association of Private Railroad Car Owners (NTPA) ...... AAPCRO
American Association of Private Railroad Car Owners (EA) ...... AAPRCO
American Association of Pro Life Obstetricians and Gynecologists (EA) ...... AAPLOG
American Association of Professional Apiculturalists (QUAC) ...... AAPA
American Association of Professional Bridal Consultants (EA) ...... AAPBC
American Association of Professional Consultants [*Manchester, NH*] (EA) ...... AAPC
American Association of Professional Hypnologists [*Defunct*] (EA) ...... AAPH
American Association of Professional Hypnotherapists (EA) ...... AAPH
American Association of Professional Landmen (NTPA) ...... AAPL
American Association of Professional Standards Review Organizations [*Later, AMPRA*] (EA) ...... AAPSRO
American Association of Professors in Sanitary Engineering [*Later, AEEP*] ...... AAPSE
American Association of Professors of Yiddish (EA) ...... AAPY
American Association of Pro-Life Pediatricians (EA) ...... AAPLP
American Association of Psychiatric Administrators (EA) ...... AAPA

American Association of Psychiatric Clinics for Children [*Later, AAPSC*] (EA) .... AAPCC
American Association of Psychiatric Clinics for Children (SAUO) .... AAPCC
American Association of Psychiatric Services for Children (EA) .... AAPSC
American Association of Psychiatric Services for Children (SAUO) .... APSC
American Association of Psychiatric Social Workers (SAUO) .... AAPSW
American Association of Psychiatric Technicians .... AAPT
American Association of Psychiatrists (EA) .... AAP
American Association of Psychiatrists from India (EA) .... AAP
American Association of Psychiatrists in Alcoholism and Addictions (SAUO) .... AAPAA
American Association of Public Health Dentistry (EA) .... AAPHD
American Association of Public Health Dentists (DMAA) .... AAPHD
American Association of Public Health Dentists (or Dentistry) (SAUO) .... AAPHD
American Association of Public Health Physicians (EA) .... AAPHP
American Association of Public Health Veterinarians (GVA) .... AAPHV
American Association of Public Welfare Attorneys (EA) .... AAPWA
American Association of Public Welfare Information Systems Management (EA) .... AAPWISM
American Association of Public Welfare Information Systems Management (SAUO) .... AAPWISM
American Association of Publishers (SAUO) .... AAP
American Association of Publishers' electronic ordering system .... PUBNET
American Association of Rabbis (EA) .... AAR
American Association of Radio-Television News Analysts (SAUO) .... ARTNA
American Association of Radon Scientists and Technologists (EA) .... AARST
American Association of Railroad Superintendents (EA) .... AARS
American Association of Railroad Ticket Agents [*Defunct*] (EA) .... AARTA
American Association of Railway Surgeons [*Defunct*] (EA) .... AARS
American Association of Religious Therapists (EA) .... AART
American Association of Retired People (SAUO) .... AARP
American Association of Retired Persons (EA) .... AARP
American Association of Retired Persons (SAUO) .... AIM
American Association of Retired Persons, Washington, DC [*Library symbol*] [*Library of Congress*] (LCLS) .... DAARP
American Association of Retired Teachers (SAUO) .... AART
American Association of Retirement Communities (EA) .... AARC
American Association of School Administrators (SAUO) .... AAS
American Association of School Administrators (EA) .... AASA
American Association of School Librarians (EA) .... AASL
American Association of School Libraries (SAUO) .... AASL
American Association of School Personnel Administrators (EA) .... AASPA
American Association of Schools and Department of Journalism (SAUO) .... AASDJ
American Association of Schools and Departments of Journalism (EA) .... AASDJ
American Association of Schools of Religious Education [*Later, ATS*] (EA) .... AASRE
American Association of Schools of Religious Education (SAUO) .... AASRE
American Association of Scientific Workers (SAUO) .... AAScW
American Association of Scientific Workers (SAUO) .... AASW
American Association of Scientific Workers [*Later, USFSS*] (EA) .... AASW
American Association of Securities Representatives .... AASR
American Association of Senior Physicians (EA) .... AASP
American Association of Sex Educators and Counselors [*Later, AASECT*] (EA) .... AASEC
American Association of Sex Educators and Counselors (SAUO) .... AASEC
American Association of Sex Educators, Counselors and Therapists (SAUO) .... AASECT
American Association of Sex Educators, Counselors, and Therapists (EA) .... AASECT
American Association of Sheep and Goat Practitioners [*Later, AASRP*] (EA) .... AASGP
American Association of Sheep and Goat Practitioners (SAUO) .... AASP
American Association of Sheriff Posses and Riding Clubs (EA) .... AASPRC
American Association of Shotgunning [*Defunct*] (EA) .... AAS
American Association of Small Business [*Later, NSBU*] .... AASB
American Association of Small Business (SAUO) .... AASB
American Association of Small Cities (EA) .... AASC
American Association of Small Research Companies (EA) .... AASRC
American Association of Small Ruminant Practitioners (EA) .... AASRP
American Association of Soap and Glycerin Producers [*Later, SDA*] .... AAS & GP
American Association of Soap and Glycerin Producers (SAUO) .... AAS&GP
American Association of Social Directories (SAUO) .... AASD
American Association of Social Workers .... AASW
American Association of Special Educators [*Defunct*] (EA) .... AASE
American Association of Specialized Colleges (EA) .... AASC
American Association of Spinal Cord Injury Nurses (EA) .... AASCIN
American Association of Spinal Cord Injury Psychologists and Social Workers (NTPA) .... AASCIPSW
American Association of State Climatologists (EA) .... AASC
American Association of State Colleges and Universities (EA) .... AASCU
American Association of State Highway and Transportation Officials (EA) .... AASHTO
American Association of State Highway and Transportation Officials (GEOI) .... ASHTD
American Association of State Highway Officials [*Later, AASHTO*] (EA) .... AASHO
American Association of State Highway Officials (SAUO) .... AASHO
American Association of State Librarians (SAUO) .... AASL
American Association of State Libraries (SAUO) .... AASL
American Association of State Libraries [*Later, ASCLA*] .... AASL
American Association of State Libraries [*Later, ASCLA*] (EA) .... ASL
American Association of State Libraries (SAUO) .... ASL
American Association of State Library Agencies (SAUO) .... AASLA
American Association of State Psychology Boards (DHP) .... AASPB
American Association of State Social Work Boards (EA) .... AASSWB
American Association of Stomatologists (EA) .... AAS
American Association of Stratigraphic Palynologists (EA) .... AASP
American Association of Students of German [*Defunct*] (EA) .... AASG
American Association of Suicidology (EA) .... AAS
American Association of Sunday and Feature Editors (EA) .... AASFE
American Association of Surgeon's Assistants (EA) .... AASA
American Association of Surgeons Assistants (SAUS) .... AASA
American Association of Surgical Physician Assistants (NTPA) .... AASPA
American Association of Swine Practitioners (EA) .... AASP
American Association of Swiss Alpine Club Members [*Defunct*] (EA) .... AASACM
American Association of Teacher Educators in Agriculture [*Later, AAAE*] (EA) .... AATEA
American Association of Teacher Educators in Agriculture (SAUO) .... AATEA
American Association of Teachers of Arabic (EA) .... AATA
American Association of Teachers of Chinese Language and Culture [*Later, AACS*] (EA) .... AATCLC
American Association of Teachers of English as a Second Language .... AATESL
American Association of Teachers of Esperanto (EA) .... AATE
American Association of Teachers of French (EA) .... AATF
American Association of Teachers of German (EA) .... AATG
American Association of Teachers of Italian (EA) .... AATI
American Association of Teachers of Slavic and East European Languages [*Defunct*] (EA) .... AATSEEL
American Association of Teachers of Slavic and East European Languages Bulletin (SAUO) .... Aatseel Bull
American Association of Teachers of Slavic and East European Languages, Journal (SAUS) .... Aatseel Jour
American Association of Teachers of Slavic and Eastern European Languages (SAUS) .... AATSEEL
American Association of Teachers of Spanish and Portuguese (EA) .... AATSP
American Association of Teachers of Turkish (EA) .... AATT
American Association of Teaching Hospitals (SAUO) .... AATH
American Association of Temporary and Contract Employees (EA) .... AATCE
American Association of Testifying Physicians (EA) .... AATP
American Association of Textile Chemists and Colorists (EA) .... AATCC
American Association of the Deaf-Blind (EA) .... AADB
American Association of the Professions (EA) .... AAP
American Association of Theatre for Youth (EA) .... AATY
American Association of Theatre Organ Enthusiasts (SAUO) .... AATOE
American Association of Theological Schools [*Later, ATS*] (EA) .... AATS
American Association of Tissue Banks (EA) .... AATB
American Association of Trade and Industrial Instructors (NTPA) .... AATII
American Association of Trauma Specialists [*Defunct*] (EA) .... AATS
American Association of Traveling Passenger Agents [*Defunct*] .... AATPA
American Association of University Administrators (EA) .... AAUA
American Association of University Affiliated Programs for Persons with Developm (SAUS) .... AAUAPDD
American Association of University Affiliated Programs for Persons with Development (SAUO) .... AAUAPDD
American Association of University Affiliated Programs for Persons with Developmental Disabilities (EA) .... AAUAP
American Association of University Affiliated Programs for Persons with Developmental Disabilities [*Later, AAUAP*] (EA) .... AAUAPDD
American Association of University Affiliated Programs for the Developmentally Disabled [*Washington, DC*] .... AAUP
American Association of University Presses (SAUO) .... AAUP
American Association of University Professors (EA) .... AAUP
American Association of University Professors, Bulletin (journ.) (SAUS) .... AAUPB
American Association of University Professors Foundation (EA) .... AAUPF
American Association of University Professors of Italian (EDAC) .... AAUPI
American Association of University Professors of Urban Affairs and Environmental (SAUS) .... AAUP-UAES
American Association of University Professors of Urban Affairs and Environmental Sciences (SAUO) .... AAUP-UAES
American Association of University Professors of Urban Affairs and EnvironmentalSciences (EA) .... AAUP-UAES
American Association of University Students (EA) .... AAUS
American Association of University Supervisors and Coordinators (BARN) .... AAUSC
American Association of University Teachers of Insurance (SAUO) .... AAUTI
American Association of University Teachers of Insurance [*Later, ARIA*] .... AAUTI
American Association of University Women (EA) .... AAUW
American Association of University Women Educational Foundation (EA) .... AAUWEF
American Association of University Women Educational Foundation, Washington, DC [*Library symbol*] [*Library of Congress*] (LCLS) .... DAAUW
American Association of Utilization Management Nurses (NTPA) .... AAUMN
American Association of Variable Star Observers (EA) .... AAVSO
American Association of Veterinary Anatomists (EA) .... AAVA
American Association of Veterinary Bacteriologists [*Defunct*] (EA) .... AAVB
American Association of Veterinary Clinicians (NTPA) .... AAVC
American Association of Veterinary Immunologists (GVA) .... AAVI
American Association of Veterinary Laboratory Diagnosticians (EA) .... AAVLD
American Association of Veterinary Nutritionists (SAUS) .... AAVN
American Association of Veterinary Parasitologists (EA) .... AAVP
American Association of Veterinary Pathologists (SAUO) .... AAVP
American Association of Veterinary State Boards (EA) .... AAVSB
American Association of Vital Records and Organizations (SAUO) .... AAVRO
American Association of Volunteer Services Coordinators (SAUO) .... AAVSC

American Association of Volunteer Services Coordinators [*Later, AVA*] ... AAVSC
American Association of Wardens and Superintendents (SAUO) ... AAWS
American Association of Waterbed Manufacturers (SAUO) ... AAWM
American Association of Waterbed Manufacturers [*Later, WMA*] ... AAWM
American Association of Wildlife Veterinarians (EA) ... AAWV
American Association of Women (EA) ... AAW
American Association of Women Dentists (EA) ... AAWD
American Association of Women Emergency Physicians (NTPA) ... AAWEP
American Association of Women in Community and Junior Colleges (EA) ... AAWCJC
American Association of Women Ministers [*Later, IAWM*] (EA) ... AAWM
American Association of Women Ministers (SAUO) ... AAWM
American Association of Women Radiologists (EA) ... AAWR
American Association of Woodturners (EA) ... AAW
American Association of Workers for Children ... AAWC
American Association of Workers for the Blind [*Later, AER*] (EA) ... AAWB
American Association of Workers for the Blind (SAUO) ... AAWB
American Association of Working People ... AAWP
American Association of Yellow Pages Publishers [*Defunct*] (EA) ... AAYPP
American Association of Yiddish Professors (SAUO) ... AAYP
American Association of Youth Museums (EA) ... AAYM
American Association of Zoo Keepers (EA) ... AAZK
American Association of Zoo Veterinarians (EA) ... AAZV
American Association of Zoological Parks and Aquariums (EA) ... AAZPA
American Association of/on Suicidology (SAUO) ... AAS
American Association on Emeriti [*Later, NCE*] (EA) ... AAE
American Association on Mental Deficiencies (DHP) ... AMMD
American Association on Mental Deficiency [*Later, AAMR*] (EA) ... AAMD
American Association on Mental Retardation (EA) ... AAMR
American Association Stomatologists (NTPA) ... AAS
American Association-Electronic Voice Phenomena (SAUO) ... AA-EVP
American Associations for Vocational Instructional Materials (SAUS) ... AAVIM
American Associations of Spanish Speaking CPA's (EA) ... AASSCPA
American Astrionics, Inc. (SAUO) ... AAI
American Astronautical Federation [*Defunct*] (EA) ... AAF
American Astronautical Foundation (SAUO) ... AAF
American Astronautical Society (SAUO) ... AAS
American Astronautical Society (EA) ... AAS
American Astronomers Association (EA) ... AAA
American Astronomical Society (EA) ... AAS
American Astronomical Society (SAUO) ... AAS
American Astronomical Society, Tarzana, CA [*Library symbol*] [*Library of Congress*] (LCLS) ... CTarA
American Astrophysical Society (USDC) ... AAS
American Astro-Systems, Inc. (SAUO) ... AAS
American Atheist Addiction Recovery Groups (SAUO) ... AAARG
American Atheist Addiction Recovery Groups [*Later, MOM*] (EA) ... AAARG
American Atheist Center (SAUO) ... AAC
American Atheist Press (SAUO) ... AAP
American Atheist Women (EA) ... AAW
American Atheists (SAUO) ... AAs
American Athletic Association (SAUO) ... AAA
American Athletic Association for the Deaf (EA) ... AAAD
American Athletic Association of the Deaf (SAUS) ... AAAD
American Athletic Motivation Institute (SAUO) ... AAMI
American Athletic Trainers Association and Certification Board (EA) ... AATA
American Athletic Trainers Association and Certification Board (EA) ... AATACB
American Audio Institute ... AAI
American Auditory Society (EA) ... AAS
American Austin Bantam Club (SAUO) ... AABC
American Australian Association (EA) ... AAA
American Australian Bicentennial Foundation [*Defunct*] (EA) ... AABF
American Australian Business ... AAB
American Auto Laundry Association [*Later, ICA*] ... AALA
American Auto Racing Writers and Broadcasters Association (EA) ... AARWBA
American Autobahn Society (SAUO) ... AAS
American Autoduel Association (EA) ... AADA
American Autoimmune Related Diseases Association (SAUO) ... AARDA
American Automatic Control Council (EA) ... AACC
American Automatic Vending Corp. (EFIS) ... AAV
American Automatic Weapons Association (SAUO) ... AAWA
American Automatic Weapons Assoeiation (SAUS) ... AAWA
American Automobile Association (EA) ... AAA
American Automobile Labeling Act of 1992 ... AALA
American Automobile Manufacturers Association (SAUO) ... AAMA
American Automobile Touring Alliance (EA) ... AATA
American Automobile Touring Alliance (SAUO) ... AmerATA
American Automotive Association (SAUO) ... AAA
American Automotive Leasing Association (EA) ... AALA
American Aviation Historical Society (EA) ... AAHS
American Aviation Publications (SAUS) ... AAP
American Award Manufacturers Association [*Later, TDMA*] (EA) ... AAMA
American Bach Foundation (EA) ... ABF
American Back Society (SAUO) ... ABS
American Backgammon Players Association [*Defunct*] (EA) ... ABPA
American Backgammon Society ... ABS
American Bacteriological & Chemical Research Corp. (EFIS) ... ABC
American Badminton Association [*Later, USBA*] (EA) ... ABA
American Badminton Association (SAUO) ... ABA
American Bail Bondsman Association (EA) ... ABBA
American Bakers Association (EA) ... ABA
American Bakery and Confectionery Workers' International Union [*Later, BCTWIU*] ... ABCW
American Ballads and Folk Songs [*A publication*] ... ABF
American Ballads and Songs [*A publication*] ... ABS
American Ballet Competition (EA) ... ABC
American Ballet Ensemble (SAUS) ... ABE
American Ballet Theater ... ABT
American Ballet Theater (SAUO) ... ABT
American Bamboo Society (EA) ... ABS
American Bancorp [*NASDAQ symbol*] (NQ) ... AMBC
American Bancorp of Nevada [*NASDAQ symbol*] (SAG) ... ABCN
American Bancorp of Nevada [*Associated Press*] (SAG) ... ABcpNV
American Bancorp Ohio [*NASDAQ symbol*] (SAG) ... AMBC
American Bancorp Ohio [*Associated Press*] (SAG) ... AmBcp
American Bancshares, Inc. (FL) [*NASDAQ symbol*] (SAG) ... ABAN
American Bancshares, Inc. (FL) [*Associated Press*] (SAG) ... ABncFL
American Bandmasters Association (EA) ... ABA
American Bandstand Memory Club [*Later, 1950's American Bandstand Fan Club*] (EA) ... ABMC
American Banjo Fraternity (EA) ... ABF
American Bank Note (BARN) ... ABN
American Bank Note Co. (MHDW) ... ABNCO
American Bank Note Company (SAUS) ... ABN
American Bank Note Holographics, Inc. ... ABNH
American Bank Notes Development Corporation (AAGC) ... ABND
American Bank of Connecticut [*Associated Press*] (SAG) ... ABkCT
American Bank of Connecticut [*AMEX symbol*] (SPSG) ... BKC
American Banker [*A publication*] ... AB
American Bankers (EFIS) ... AMBANK
American Bankers Association [*Washington, DC*] (EA) ... ABA
American Bankers Association Computer Utilization Computer System (EBF) ... ABACUS
American Bankers Association, New York, NY [*Library symbol*] [*Library of Congress*] (LCLS) ... NNABA
American Bankers Insurance Group [*Associated Press*] (SAG) ... ABnkr
American Bankers Insurance Group, Inc. [*NASDAQ symbol*] (NQ) ... ABIG
American Banknote Corp. [*NYSE symbol*] (SAG) ... ABN
American Banknote Corp. [*Associated Press*] (SAG) ... AmBknt
American Bankruptcy [*A publication*] (DLA) ... Am Bankr
American Bankruptcy Institute (EA) ... ABI
American Bankruptcy, New Series [*A publication*] (DLA) ... Am Bankr NS
American Bankruptcy, New Series [*A publication*] (DLA) ... Am B (NS)
American Bankruptcy Register [*A publication*] (DLA) ... Am Bankr Reg
American Bankruptcy Reports [*A publication*] (DLA) ... ABR
American Bankruptcy Reports [*A publication*] (DLA) ... AB Rep
American Bankruptcy Reports [*A publication*] (DLA) ... Am Bank R
American Bankruptcy Reports [*A publication*] (DLA) ... Am Bankr R
American Bankruptcy Reports ... AMBANKRREP
American Bankruptcy Reports [*A publication*] (DLA) ... Am Bankruptcy Reps
American Bankruptcy Reports [*A publication*] (DLA) ... Am B'kc'y Rep
American Bankruptcy Reports [*A publication*] (DLA) ... Am BR
American Bankruptcy Reports, New Series [*A publication*] (DLA) ... ABRNS
American Bankruptcy Reports, New Series [*A publication*] (DLA) ... Am Bankr Rep NS
American Bankruptcy Reports, New Series [*A publication*] (DLA) ... Am Bankr R (NS)
American Bankruptcy Reports, New Series [*A publication*] (DLA) ... Am BR (NS)
American Bankruptcy Review [*A publication*] (DLA) ... AB Rev
American Bankruptcy Review [*A publication*] (DLA) ... Am Bank Rev
American Bankruptcy Review [*A publication*] (DLA) ... Am Bankr Rev
American Bantam Association (EA) ... ABA
American Baptist Association ... ABA
American Baptist Black Caucus (EA) ... ABBC
American Baptist Churches ... ABC
American Baptist Churches of Oregon (SRA) ... ABCO
American Baptist Convention (SAUO) ... ABC
American Baptist Education Association [*Defunct*] (EA) ... ABEA
American Baptist Extension Corp. ... ABEC
American Baptist Foreign Mission Society [*Congo - Leopoldville*] ... ABFMS
American Baptist Foreign Missionary Society (SAUO) ... ABFMS
American Baptist Historical Society (EA) ... ABHS
American Baptist Historical Society Library, Rochester, NY [*OCLC symbol*] (OCLC) ... RXP
American Baptist Historical Society, Rochester, NY [*Library symbol*] [*Library of Congress*] (LCLS) ... NRAB
American Baptist Home Mission Society [*Later, Board of National Ministries*] (EA) ... ABHMS
American Baptist Home Mission Society (SAUO) ... ABHMS
American Baptist Home Society (SAUO) ... ABHS
American Baptist Homes and Hospitals Association (EA) ... ABHHA
American Baptist Missionary Union [*Later, Board of International Ministries*] ... ABMU
American Baptist Missionary Union (SAUO) ... ABMU
American Baptist Publication Society (SAUO) ... ABPS
American Baptist Publication Society, Philadelphia, PA [*Library symbol*] [*Library of Congress*] [*Obsolete*] (LCLS) ... PPABP
American Baptist Publishing Society (BARN) ... ABPS
American Baptist Seminary of the West (SAUS) ... ABSW
American Baptist Seminary of the West, Berkeley, CA [*Library symbol*] [*Library of Congress*] (LCLS) ... CBGTU-B
American Baptist Theological Seminary, Nashville, TN [*Library symbol*] [*Library of Congress*] (LCLS) ... TNBT
American Baptist Women (EA) ... ABW
American Baptists Concerned (EA) ... ABC
American Bar Association (EA) ... ABA
American Bar Association (DLA) ... Am BA
American Bar Association Center for Professional Discipline (DLA) ... ABACPD

American Bar Association Center for Professional Responsibility (EA) .... ABACPR
American Bar Association. Comparative Law Bureau. Bulletin [*A publication*] (DLA) .... Bull Comp L
American Bar Association, Family Law Section, Mediation and Arbitration Committee [*Defunct*] (EA) .... ABAFLSMAC
American Bar Association. International and Comparative Law Section. Reports [*A publication*] (DLA) .... ABA Rep Int'l & Comp L Sec
American Bar Association Journal (SAUS) .... ABAJ
American Bar Association Model Business Corporation Act, Annotated [*A publication*] (DLA) .... Model Business Corp Act
American Bar Association Model Business Corporation Act, Annotated, Second Series [*A publication*] (DLA) .... Model Bus Corp Act Anno 2d
American Bar Association Model Procurement Code [*A publication*] (AAGC) .... ABA MPC
American Bar Association Reporter [*A publication*] (DLA) .... ABA Rep
American Bar Association Reports [*A publication*] (DLA) .... ABA Rep
American Bar Association Reports [*A publication*] (DLA) .... Am Bar Asso Rep
American Bar Association Representation of the Homeless Project (EA) .... ABARHP
American Bar Association Section of International Law and Practice (EA) .... ABASILP
American Bar Association. Section of Labor Relations Law (DLA) .... ABA Sec Lab Rel L
American Bar Association Special Committee on Dispute Resolution (EA) .... ABASCDR
American Bar Association Traffic Court Program (SAUO) .... ABA/TCP
American Bar Association Young Lawyers Division (EA) .... ABAYLD
American Bar Foundation (EA) .... ABF
American Bar Foundation, Chicago, IL [*Library symbol*] [*Library of Congress*] (LCLS) .... ICABF
American Bar Foundation Research Journal [*A publication*] (AAGC) .... Am B Found Res J
American Bar Foundation. Research Newsletter [*A publication*] (DLA) .... ABF Res Newsl
American Bar Foundation. Research Reporter [*A publication*] (DLA) .... ABF Research Reptr
American Bar Foundation. Research Reporter Journal [*A publication*] (DLA) .... ABF Research Reptr J
American Bar News [*A publication*] (DLA) .... Am B News
American Barefoot Club (EA) .... ABC
American Barred Plymouth Rock Bantam Club [*Defunct*] (EA) .... ABPRBC
American Barred Plymouth Rock Club [*Later, Plymouth Rock Fanciers Club*] (EA) .... ABPRC
American Barred Plymouth Rock Club (SAUO) .... ABPRC
American Barrick Resources Corp. [*LA Barrick Gold*] [*NYSE symbol*] [*Toronto Stock Exchange symbol*] (SPSG) .... ABX
American Bartenders' Association (EA) .... ABA
American Baseball Coaches Association (EA) .... ABCA
American Baseball Fans Association (EA) .... ABFA
American Bashkir Curly Registry (EA) .... ABCR
American Basketball Association [*Later, NBA*] [*League of professional basketball players*] (EA) .... ABA
American Bass Association (EA) .... ABA
American Battle Monument Commission (EBF) .... ABMC
American Battle Monuments Commission [*Independent government agency*] .... ABMC
American Battleship Association (EA) .... ABA
American Bay Horse Registry [*Defunct*] (EA) .... ABHR
American Beagle Club (EA) .... ABC
American Bearing Manufacturing Association (NTPA) .... ABMA
American Beauty Association (EA) .... ABA
American Bed and Breakfast Association (EA) .... ABBA
American Bee Breeders Association (EA) .... ABBA
American Bee Journal (SAUS) .... Amer Bee J
American Beefalo Association (EA) .... ABA
American Beefalo World Registry (EA) .... ABWR
American Beekeeping Federation (EA) .... ABF
American Beethoven Society (EA) .... ABS
American Begonia Society (EA) .... ABS
American Behavioural Scientist (journ.) (SAUS) .... ABS
American Behcet's Association (EA) .... ABA
American Behcet's Foundation (EA) .... ABA
American Belgian Blue Breeders Association (NTPA) .... ABBA
American Belgian Hare Club (EA) .... ABHC
American Belgian Malinois Club (EA) .... ABMC
American Belgian Tervuren Club (EA) .... ABTC
American Bell Association [*Later, ABAI*] (EA) .... ABA
American Bell Association (SAUO) .... ABA
American Bell Association International (SAUS) .... ABAI
American Bell Association International (EA) .... ABAI
American Bell, Inc. .... ABI
American Bell Incorporated (SAUO) .... ABI
American Bell International Incorporated (SAUO) .... ABII
American Bemberg Corporation (SAUO) .... ABC
American Benedictine Academy (EA) .... ABA
American Berkshire Association (EA) .... ABA
American Berlin Opera Foundation (EA) .... ABOF
American Best Corp. (EFIS) .... ABF
American Beverage Alcohol Association [*Defunct*] (EA) .... ABAA
American Beverage Institute .... ABI
American Beveren Club (EA) .... ABC
American Bible Society (EA) .... ABS
American Bible Society (SAUO) .... ABS

American Bible Society, New York, NY [*Library symbol*] [*Library of Congress*] (LCLS) .... NNAB
American Biblical Encyclopedia Society (EA) .... ABES
American Bibliographic Center-Clio Press (SAUS) .... Am Bibl
American Bibliographical Center .... ABC
American Bibliography of Slavic & East European Studies (SAUO) .... ABSEES
American Bicentennial Commemorative Society [*Defunct*] (EA) .... ABCS
American Bicycle Association (EA) .... ABA
American Bike Month Committee [*Defunct*] (EA) .... ABMC
American Bikers Aimed toward Education .... ABATE
American Bikeways Foundation [*Defunct*] (EA) .... ABF
American Bill of Rights Day Association [*Defunct*] (EA) .... ABRDA
American Billiard Association (EA) .... ABA
American Biltrite, Inc. [*AMEX symbol*] (SPSG) .... ABL
American Biltrite, Inc. [*Associated Press*] (SAG) .... AmBiltrt
American Binding Association (SAUO) .... ABA
American Bingo & Gambing Corp. [*NASDAQ symbol*] (SAG) .... BNGO
American Bingo & Gambling Corp. [*Associated Press*] (SAG) .... ABingo
American Biodynamics, Inc. [*Vancouver Stock Exchange symbol*] .... ACB
American Biogenetic Sciences, Inc. [*Associated Press*] (SAG) .... AmBiogn
American Biogenetic Sciences, Inc. [*NASDAQ symbol*] (SAG) .... MABX
American Biographical Institute Research Association (EA) .... ABIRA
American Biological Safety Association (NTPA) .... ABSA
American Biological Society (EA) .... ABS
American Biology Teacher (SAUS) .... Am Biol Teach
American Bionetics, Inc. .... ABN
American Biotechnology Laboratory [*A publication*] .... ABL
American Birding Association (EA) .... ABA
American Birth Control League .... ABCL
American Birth Control League (SAUO) .... ABCL
American Black (SAUS) .... Amer Blk
American Black and Tan Coonhound Association (EA) .... ABTCA
American Black Book Writers Association (EA) .... ABBWA
American Black Chiropractors Association (EA) .... ABCA
American Black Maine-Anjou Association (EA) .... ABMAA
American Blade Collectors (EA) .... ABC
American Blade Collectors Association (EA) .... ABCA
American Bladesmith Society (EA) .... ABS
American Blake Foundation (EA) .... ABF
American Blasting Association (SAUO) .... ABA
American Bleached Shellac Manufacturers Association (EA) .... ABSMA
American Blimp Corporation (SAUO) .... ABC
American Blind Bowling Association (EA) .... ABBA
American Blind Lawyers Association (EA) .... ABLA
American Blind Skiing Foundation (EA) .... ABSF
American Blonde d'Aquitaine Association (EA) .... ABAA
American Blood Commission (EA) .... ABC
American Blood Resources Association (EA) .... ABRA
American Bloodhound Club (EA) .... ABC
American Blue and White Rabbit Club (EA) .... ABWRC
American Blue Cheese Association [*Defunct*] (EA) .... ABCA
American Board Association (SAUO) .... ABA
American Board for Certification in Orthotics and Prosthetics (EA) .... ABC
American Board for Certification in Orthotics and Prosthetics (SAUO) .... ABCOP
American Board for Occupational Health Nurses (EA) .... ABOHN
American Board of Abdominal Surgeons (SAUS) .... ABAS
American Board of Abdominal Surgery (EA) .... ABAS
American Board of Allergy and Immunilogy (SAUO) .... ABAI
American Board of Allergy and Immunology (EA) .... ABAI
American Board of Anesthesia (CMD) .... ABA
American Board of Anesthesiology (EA) .... ABA
American Board of Applied Toxicology (DMAA) .... ABAT
American Board of Aviation Medicine (CMD) .... ABAvM
American Board of Bioanalysis (EA) .... ABB
American Board of Bio-Analysis [*No connection with ABB*] [*Defunct*] (EA) .... ABB-A
American Board of Bio-Analysis (SAUO) .... ABBA
American Board of Bionic Rehabilitative Psychology (EA) .... ABBRP
American Board of Bloodless Medicine and Surgery (EA) .... ABBMS
American Board of Blood-Transfusionless Medicine and Surgery (EA) .... ABBMS
American Board of Cardiovascular Perfusion (EA) .... ABCP
American Board of Catholic Missions (SAUO) .... ABCM
American Board of Certified and Registered Encephalographic Technicians and Tech (SAUS) .... ABCRETT
American Board of Certified and Registered Encephalographic Technicians and Technologists (EA) .... ABCRETT
American Board of Chelation Therapy (EA) .... ABCT
American Board of Clinical Biofeedback [*Defunct*] (EA) .... ABCB
American Board of Clinical Chemistry (EA) .... ABCC
American Board of Clinical Hypnosis (EA) .... ABCH
American Board of Clinical Immunology and Alergy (SAUS) .... ABCIA
American Board of Clinical Immunology and Allergy (EA) .... ABCIA
American Board of Clinical Neuropsychology (SAUO) .... ABCN
American Board of Colon and Rectal Surgery (EA) .... ABCRS
American Board of Commissioners for Foreign Missions [*Later, UCBWM*] .... ABCFM
American Board of Commissioners for Foreign Missions (SAUO) .... ABCFM
American Board of Commissioners for Foreign Missions, Boston, MA [*Library symbol*] [*Library of Congress*] (LCLS) .... MBACFM
American Board of Cosmetic Surgery (EA) .... ABCS
American Board of Criminal Lawyers (EA) .... ABCL
American Board of Criminalistics (EA) .... ABC
American Board of Dental Medicine and Surgery (EA) .... ABDMS
American Board of Dental Public Health (EA) .... ABDPH

American Board of Dermatology (EA) .... ABD
American Board of Disability Analysts (EA) .... ABDA
American Board of Education (SAUO) .... ABE
American Board of Emergency Medicine (EA) .... ABEM
American Board of Endocrinology & Metabolism (CMD) .... ABEM
American Board of Endodontics (EA) .... ABE
American Board of Environmental Medicine (EA) .... ABEM
American Board of Examiners (MELL) .... ABE
American Board of Examiners in Pastoral Counseling (EA) .... ABEPC
American Board of Examiners in Professional Psychology [Later, ABPP] .... ABEPP
American Board of Examiners in Professional Psychology (SAUO) .... ABEPP
American Board of Examiners in Psychological Hypnosis (SAUO) .... ABEPH
American Board of Examiners in Psychological Hypnosis [Later, ABPH] (EA) .... ABEPH
American Board of Examiners in Psychotherapy (EA) .... ABEP
American Board of Examiners in Speech Pathology and Audiology (SAUO) .... ABESPA
American Board of Examiners of Psychodrama Sociometry and Group Psychotherapy (SAUO) .... ABEPSGP
American Board of Examiners of Psychodrama, Sociometry, and Group Psychotherapy (EA) .... ABEPSGP
American Board of Examiners of Psychodrama, Sociometry and Group Psychotherapy (SAUS) .... ABEPSGP
American Board of Family Practice (EA) .... ABFP
American Board of Foreign Missions (SAUO) .... ABFM
American Board of Foreign Missions (SAUO) .... ABFM
American Board of Forensic Anthropology (EA) .... ABFA
American Board of Forensic Odontology (SAUO) .... ABFO
American Board of Forensic Psychiatry (EA) .... ABFP
American Board of Forensic Psychology (EA) .... ABFP
American Board of Forensic Toxicology (SAUO) .... ABFT
American Board of Funeral Service Education (EA) .... ABFSE
American Board of Genetic Counseling .... ABCG
American Board of Genetic Counseling (EA) .... ABMG
American Board of Hand Surgery (EA) .... ABHS
American Board of Health Physics (EA) .... ABHP
American Board of Homeopathic Medicine (EA) .... ABHM
American Board of Independent Medical Examiners (SAUO) .... ABIME
American Board of Industrial Hygiene (EA) .... ABIH
American Board of Industrial Medicine and Surgery (EA) .... ABIMS
American Board of Internal Medicine (EA) .... ABIM
American Board of Internal Medicine & Cardiology (CMD) .... ABIMC
American Board of International Missions (EA) .... ABIM
American Board of Laser Surgery (EA) .... ABLS
American Board of Managed Care Medicine (SAUO) .... ABMCM
American Board of Managed Care Nursing (SAUO) .... ABMCN
American Board of Master Educators (EA) .... ABME
American Board of Medical Genetics (EA) .... ABMG
American Board of Medical Hypnosis (CMD) .... ABMH
American Board of Medical Management (SAUO) .... ABMM
American Board of Medical Microbiology .... ABMM
American Board of Medical Oncology (CMD) .... ABMO
American Board of Medical Psychotherapists (EA) .... ABMP
American Board of Medical Psychotherapists and Psychodiagnosticians (EA) .... ABMPP
American Board of Medical Specialities (SAUO) .... AMS
American Board of Medical Specialties (EA) .... ABMS
American Board of Medical Toxicology (EA) .... ABMT
American Board of Medical-Legal Analysis in Medicine and Surgery (EA) .... ABMLAMS
American Board of Minor Brain Injury (SAUO) .... ABOMBI
American Board of Missions to the Jews (SAUO) .... ABMJ
American Board of Missions to the Jews [Later, CPM] (EA) .... ABMJ
American Board of National Missions (EA) .... ABNM
American Board of Neurological and Orthopaedic Medicine and Surgery (EA) .... ABNOMS
American Board of Neurological Microsurgery (EA) .... ABNM
American Board of Neurological Surgery (EA) .... ABNS
American Board of Neurological/Orthopaedic Laser Surgery (EA) .... ABNOLS
American Board of Neuroscience Nursing (EA) .... ABNN
American Board of Neurosurgery (CMD) .... ABNS
American Board of Nuclear Medicine (EA) .... ABNM
American Board of Nursing Specialties (SAUO) .... ABNS
American Board of Nutrition (EA) .... ABN
American Board of Obstetrics and Gynecology (EA) .... ABOG
American Board of Occupational Medicine (CMD) .... ABOM
American Board of Ophthalmology (EA) .... ABO
American Board of Opticianry [Later, NAO] (EA) .... ABO
American Board of Opticianry (SAUO) .... ABO
American Board of Optometry Certificate (SAUS) .... ABOC
American Board of Oral and Maxillofacial Surgery (EA) .... ABOMS
American Board of Oral Pathology (EA) .... ABOP
American Board of Oral Pathology [Later, ABOP] (EA) .... AMBOP
American Board of Oral Surgery [Later, ABOMS] (EA) .... ABOS
American Board of Oral Surgery (SAUO) .... ABOS
American Board of Orthodontics (EA) .... ABO
American Board of Orthopaedic Microneurosurgery (EA) .... ABOM
American Board of Orthopedic Surgery (EA) .... ABOS
American Board of Otolaryngology (EA) .... ABO
American Board of Pathology (EA) .... ABP
American Board of Pediatric Dentistry (EA) .... ABPD
American Board of Pediatric Dermatology (SAUO) .... ABPD
American Board of Pediatrics (EA) .... ABP
American Board of Pedodontics [Later, ABPD] (EA) .... ABP

American Board of Periodontology (EA) .... ABP
American Board of Physical Medicine and Rehabilitation (EA) .... ABPMR
American Board of Plastic Surgery (EA) .... ABPS
American Board of Podiatric Dermatology [Defunct] (EA) .... ABPD
American Board of Podiatric Orthopedics (EA) .... ABPO
American Board of Podiatric Orthopedics and Primary Medicine (EA) .... ABPOPPM
American Board of Podiatric Orthopedics and Primary Podiatric Medicine (NTPA) .... ABPOPPM
American Board of Podiatric Surgery (EA) .... ABPS
American Board of Post Anesthesia Nursing Certification (SAUS) .... ABPANC
American Board of PostAnesthesia Nursing Certification (EA) .... ABPANC
American Board of Preventive Medicine (EA) .... ABPM
American Board of Professional Disability Consultants (EA) .... ABPDC
American Board of Professional Liability Attorneys [Chicago, IL] (EA) .... ABPLA
American Board of Professional Psychology (EA) .... ABPP
American Board of Professional Psychology in Hypnosis (SAUO) .... ABPPH
American Board of Prosthodontics (EA) .... ABP
American Board of Psychiatry and Neurology (SAUO) .... A Bd P & N
American Board of Psychiatry and Neurology (EA) .... ABPN
American Board of Psychological Hypnosis (EA) .... ABPH
American Board of Quality Assurance and Utilization Review (EA) .... ABQAUR
American Board of Quality Assurance and Utilization Review Physicians [Later, ABQAUR] (EA) .... ABQAURP
American Board of Quality Assurance and Utilization Review Physicians (SAUS) .... ABQAURP
American Board of Radiology (EA) .... ABR
American Board of Registration of EEG and EP Technologists [Formerly, American Board of Registration of EEG Technologists] (EA) .... ABRET
American Board of Registration of EEG [Electroencephalographic] Technologists (EA) .... ABRET
American Board of Reproductive Endocrinology & Infertility (CMD) .... ABREI
American Board of Respiratory Medicine (CMD) .... ABRM
American Board of Ringside Medicine and Surgery (EA) .... ABRMS
American Board of Sexology (NTPA) .... ABS
American Board of Spinal Surgery (EA) .... ABSS
American Board of Surgery (EA) .... ABS
American Board of Surgery (SAUS) .... ABS
American Board of Surgery (SAUO) .... ABS
American Board of Surgery (SAUS) .... ABS
American Board of Thoracic Neurological Orthopaedic Medicine and Surgery (SAUS) .... ABTNOMS
American Board of Thoracic Neurological Orthopaedic Medicine and Surgery (EA) .... ABTNOMS
American Board of Thoracic Surgery (EA) .... ABTS
American Board of Toxicology (EA) .... ABT
American Board of Trade .... ABT
American Board of Transcultural Psychiatry (SAUO) .... ABTP
American Board of Trial Advocates (EA) .... ABOTA
American Board of Trial Advocates (EA) .... ABTA
American Board of Tropical Medicine [Inactive] (EA) .... ABTM
American Board of Urologic Allied Health Professionals (EA) .... ABUAHP
American Board of Urology (EA) .... ABU
American Board of Veterinary Practitioners (NTPA) .... ABVP
American Board of Veterinary Specialties [Formerly, Advisory Board on Veterinary Specialties] (EA) .... ABVS
American Board of Veterinary Toxicology (EA) .... ABVT
American Board of Vocational Experts (EA) .... ABVE
American Board on Clinical Hypnosis (SAUS) .... ABCH
American Board on Counseling Services [Later, IACS] (EA) .... ABCS
American Board Products Association [Later, AHA] (EA) .... ABPA
American Board Products Association (SAUO) .... ABPA
American Boarding Kennels Association (EA) .... ABKA
American Boards of Examiners in Speech Pathology and Audiology [Later, COPS] (EA) .... ABESPA
American Boardsailing Industries Association (EA) .... ABIA
American Boat and Yacht Council (EA) .... ABYC
American Boat Builders and Repairers Association (EA) .... ABBRA
American Boccaccio Association (EA) .... ABA
American Boccaccio Association (SAUO) .... ADA
American Boiler and Affiliated Industries (SAUO) .... ABAI
American Boiler Manufacturers Association (EA) .... ABMA
American Boiler Manufacturers Association and Affiliated Industries (SAUO) .... ABMA
American Boiler Manufacturers Association and Affiliated Industries (SAUO) .... ABMAAI
American Bonanza Society (EA) .... ABS
American Bonsai Society (EA) .... ABS
[The] American Book Award [Later, ABA] .... TABA
American Book Awards [Formerly, TABA] .... ABA
American Book Center for War Devastated Libraries (SAUO) .... ABC
American Book Co. (AEBS) .... ABC
American Book Collector (journ.) (SAUS) .... ABC
American Book Company (SAUO) .... Am Bk
American Book Council [Defunct] (EA) .... ABC
American Book Information Service (SAUO) .... ABIS
American Book Prices Current [A publication] .... ABPC
American Book Prices Current (SAUS) .... Am Bk Prices
American Book Producers Association (EA) .... ABPA
American Book Publishers Council [Later, AAP] .... ABPC
American Book Publishers Council (SAUO) .... ABPC
American Book Publishers Political Action Committee (EA) .... ABPPAC
American Book Publishing Record [A publication] .... ABPR
American Book Review [A publication] (BRI) .... ABR
American Book Trade Directory [A publication] .... ABTD

American Book-Prices Current [*A publication*] (DGA) ABC
American Booksellers Association (EA) ABA
American Booksellers Association (SAUO) Am Booksellers
American Border Fancy Canary Club (EA) ABFCC
American Border Leicester Association (NTPA) ABLA
American Bosch Arma Corp. (AAG) ABAC
American Bosch Arma Corp. (MCD) AMBAC
American Bosch Arma Corp. (AAG) ARMA
American Bosch Arma Corporation (SAUO) AB
American Bosch Arma Corporation (SAUO) ABA
American Bosch Arma Corporation (SAUO) ABAC
American Bosch Corp. (SAUO) BO
American Botanical Council (EA) ABC
American Bottled Water Association [*Later, IBWA*] (EA) ABWA
American Bottled Water Association (SAUO) ABWA
American Bottlers of Carbonated Beverages (SAUO) ABCB
American Bottlers of Carbonated Beverages [*Later, NSDA*] (EA) ABCB
American Bough of the International Society of Shropshires (EA) ABISS
American Bouvier de Flandres Club (SAUO) ABDFC
American Bouvier des Flandres Club (EA) ABDFC
American Bowhunters Association [*Defunct*] (EA) ABA
American Bowlers Association (SAUO) ABA
American Bowling Computer Service, Inc. (SAUO) ABCSI
American Bowling Congress (EA) ABC
American Boxer Club (EA) ABC
American Boxing Club (SAUO) ABC
American Boxwood Society (EA) ABS
American Boys Club in Defense of Errol Flynn [*Facetious organization*] ABCDEF
American Brachytherapy Society (SAUO) ABS
American Brahma Club (EA) ABC
American Brahman Breeders Association (EA) ABBA
American Brahmousin Council (NTPA) ABC
American Brain Tumor Association [*Formerly Association for Brain Tumor Research (AFBTR)*] (PAZ) ABTA
American Brake Shoe Co. (SAUO) ABK
American Bralers Association (EA) ABA
American Brands, Inc. (EFIS) ABCO
American Brands, Inc. [*Associated Press*] (SAG) ABrand
American Brands, Inc. [*Associated Press*] (SAG) ABrd
American Brands, Inc. [*NYSE symbol*] (SPSG) AMB
American Brass Company (SAUO) ABC
American Brazilian Association (SAUO) ABA
American Brazilian Association [*Later, Brazilian American Chamber of Commerce*] (EA) ABA
American Break Shoe (SAUS) ABS
American Breed Association (EA) ABA
American Breeder Service ABS
American Breweriana Association (EA) ABA
American Bridge Association (EA) ABA
American Bridge Teachers' Association (EA) ABTA
American Bridge Teachers Association (SAUO) ABTA
American Bridge, Tunnel and Turnpike Association (SAUO) ABTTA
American Bridge, Tunnel, and Turnpike Association [*Later, IBTTA*] (EA) ABTTA
American, British, and Canadian ABC
American, British, Australian [*Military*] ABA
American, British, Australien (SAUS) ABA
American British Cab Society (EA) ABCS
American, British, Canadian, and Australian Armies (SAUO) ABCA
American, British, Canadian, Australian (MHDB) ABCA
American British Canadian-Army Standarization Program (SAUS) ABC-ASP
American, British, Chinese & Dutch Allied Forces (SAUS) ABCD
American, British, Chinese, Dutch (Indies) (SAUO) ABCD
American, British, Dutch, Australian (ADA) ABDA
American, British, Dutch, Australian Air Operational Command (SAUO) ABDAIR
American, British, Dutch, Australian Army Operational Command (SAUO) ABDARM
American, British, Dutch, Australian Naval Operational Command (SAUO) ABDAFLOAT
American British Numismatic Society [*Defunct*] (EA) ABNS
American British-Canadian Airforces Standard (SAUS) ABC -AIR -STD
American Brittany Club (EA) ABC
American Brittle Bone Society [*Defunct*] (EA) ABBS
American Broadcasting Co. Contemporary Network (LAIN) ABC-C
American Broadcasting Co. Direction Network (LAIN) ABC-D
American Broadcasting Co. Entertainment Network (LAIN) ABC-E
American Broadcasting Co. FM Network (LAIN) ABC-F
American Broadcasting Co. Information Network (LAIN) ABC-I
American Broadcasting Co. Rock Radio Network (LAIN) ABC-R
American Broadcasting Co. Talkradio Network (LAIN) ABC-T
American Broadcasting Co. Television Satellite (NTCM) ABSAT
American Broadcasting Companies, Inc. [*Subsidiary of Capital Cities/ABC, Inc.*] ABC
American Broadcasting Company (SAUO) ABC
American Broadcasting Corporation (SAUO) ABC
American Broadcasting Network (SAUO) ABN
American Broadcasting Paramount (SAUS) ABP
American Broadcasting Station in Europe (SAUS) ABSiE
American Broadcasting Station in Europe [*OWI*] ABSIE
American Broadcasting System (IAA) ABS
American Broadcasting-Paramount Theatre, Inc. (SAUO) AB-PT
American Broadcasting-Paramount Theatres (SAUO) ABP
American Broadcasting-Paramount Theatres, Inc. (NTCM) AB-PT
American Broncho-Esophagological Association (EA) ABEA
American Broncho-Esophagological Association (EA) ABES
American Brown Leghorn Club (EA) ABLC
American Brunswick [*Record label*] AmB
American Brush Manufacturers Association (EA) ABMA
American Brussels Griffon Association (EA) ABGA
American Bryological and Lichenological Society (EA) ABLS
American Bryological Society [*Later, ABLS*] (EA) ABS
American Bryological Society (SAUO) ABS
American Buckskin Registry Association (EA) ABRA
American Buddhist Academy (EA) ABA
American Buddhist Association (EA) ABA
American Buddhist Movement (EA) ABM
American Budgerigar Society (EA) ABS
American Budgetel, Inc. [*Vancouver Stock Exchange symbol*] ABG
American Buff Plymouth Rock Club (EA) ABPRC
American Buff Wyandotte Club [*Defunct*] (EA) ABWC
American Buffalo Association (EA) ABA
American Bugatti Club (EA) ABC
American Building Contractors Association (EA) ABCA
American Building Maintenance (SAUO) ABM
American Building Maintenance Industries [*NYSE symbol*] (SPSG) ABM
American Buildings Co. (EFIS) ABC
American Buildings Co. [*NASDAQ symbol*] (SAG) ABCO
American Buildings Co. [*Associated Press*] (SAG) AmBldg
American Bulgarian League [*Defunct*] (EA) ABL
American Bullmastiff Association (EA) ABA
American Bum Association (SAUO) ABA
American Bureau for Medical Advancement in China (EA) ABMAC
American Bureau for Medical Aid to China (SAUO) ABMAC
American Bureau of Metal Statistics (EA) ABMS
American Bureau of Metal Statistics (SAUO) AMBS
American Bureau of Shipping AB
American Bureau of Shipping (EA) ABS
American Bureau of Shipping Anheuser-Busch, Inc. (SAUO) AB
American Bureau of Shipping (Hellas) (DS) ABH
American Bureau of Shipping Information Retrieval System (MSC) ABSORS
American Bureau of Shipping Worldwide Technical Services (MHDB) ABSTECH
American Burn Association (EA) ABA
American Bus Association (EA) ABA
American Business Association [*New York, NY*] (EA) ABA
American Business Cancer [*in name "ABC Research Foundation"*] ABC
American Business Cancer Research Foundation [*Later, ABFCR*] (EA) ABCRF
American Business Cancer Research Foundation (SAUO) ABCRF
American Business Card Club (EA) ABCC
American Business Collaboration for Quality Dependent Care ABC
American Business Communication Association [*Later, ABC*] ABCA
American Business Communication Association Unification of Engineering Standards (MHDB) ABCA/UES
American Business Communications Association (SAUO) ABCA
American Business Computers Corp. [*NASDAQ symbol*] (NQ) ABCC
American Business Computers Corp. [*Associated Press*] (SAG) ABsCpt
American Business Conference [*Washington, DC*] (EA) ABC
American Business Council, Malaysia (EA) ABC
American Business Council of Singapore (EA) ABCS
American Business Foundation for Cancer Research [*Defunct*] (EA) ABFCR
American Business History Collection [*Microfiche*] (IID) ABHC
American Business Information ABI
American Business Information, Inc. [*NASDAQ symbol*] (SAG) ABII
American Business Information, Inc. [*Associated Press*] (SAG) AmBusn
American Business Law Association (EA) ABLA
American Business Media Council [*Defunct*] (EA) ABMC
American Business Men's Research Foundation [*Later, ARIS*] (EA) ABMRF
American Business Mens Research Foundation (SAUS) ABMRF
American Business Network [*US Chamber of Commerce*] [*Washington, DC*] [*Cable-television system*] [*Telecommunications*] (TSSD) BIZNET
American Business Press [*Later, American Business Publishers*] ABP
American Business Press (SAUO) ABP
American Business Products, Inc. [*NYSE symbol*] (SPSG) ABP
American Business Products, Inc. [*Associated Press*] (SAG) ABusnP
American Business Products, Inc. [*Associated Press*] (SAG) ABusnPd
American Business Women's Association (EA) ABWA
American Business Writing Association [*Later, ABCA*] (EA) ABWA
American Business Writing Association (SAUO) ABWA
American Businessmen of Jeddah (EA) ABJ
American Businessmen's Club (EA) ABC
American Businessmen's Group of Riyadh (EA) ABGR
American Butter Institute (EA) ABI
American Buyers Federation (EA) ABF
American Buyers of Meeting and Incentive Travel (EA) ABMIT
American Cable and Radio (SAUS) AC&R
American Cable and Radio (SAUS) ACAR
American Cable & Radio Corp. AC & R
American Cable Network, Inc. (NTCM) ACN
American Cable Supply Corp. (SAUO) ACS
American Cadet Alliance (EA) ACA
American Camellia Society (EA) ACS
American Camillia Society (SAUO) ACS
American Camp and Hospital Service ACHS
American Campaign Medal [*Military decoration*] ACM
American Camping Association (EA) ACA
American Can Canada [*Toronto Stock Exchange symbol*] ACX
American Can Co. (CDAI) AC
American Can Co. (EFIS) ACC

American Can Co., Barrington, IL [*Library symbol*] [*Library of Congress*] (LCLS) .... IBarA
American Can Company (SAUO) .... AAC
American Can Company (SAUO) .... ACCo
American Can Company (SAUO) .... CANCO
American, Canadian, Australian, British Urban Game [*Computer-assisted simulation wargame*] [*Army*] (INF) .... ACABUG
American Canadian Caribbean Line (TRID) .... ACCL
American Canadian Systems, Inc. [*Vancouver Stock Exchange symbol*] .... ACW
American Canadian Systems, Inc (SAUS) .... ACW
American Canal Society (EA) .... ACS
American Cancer Society (EA) .... ACS
American Cancer Society, Inc. (SAUO) .... ACSI
American Cancer Society, New York, NY [*Library symbol*] [*Library of Congress*] (LCLS) .... NNACS
American Canine Sports Medicine Association (EA) .... ACSMA
American Cannabis Research Experiment (EA) .... ACRE
American Canoe Association (EA) .... ACA
American Canoe Manufacturers Union [*Defunct*] (EA) .... ACMU
American Canvas Institute .... ACI
American Capital Bond Fund, Inc. [*Associated Press*] (SAG) .... ACapBd
American Capital Bond Fund, Inc. [*NYSE symbol*] (SPSG) .... ACB
American Capital Convertible Securities, Inc. [*Associated Press*] (SAG) .... ACapCv
American Capital Convertible Securities, Inc. [*NYSE symbol*] (SPSG) .... ACS
American Capital Income Trust [*Associated Press*] (SAG) .... ACapIn
American Capital Income Trust [*NYSE symbol*] (SPSG) .... ACD
American Capon Producers Association (EA) .... ACPA
American Car and Foundry .... ACF
American Car and Foundry, Electronics .... ACFE
American Car and Foundry Industries .... ACFI
American Car & Foundry Industries Inc. (SAUO) .... ACF
American Car Buying Service .... ACS
American Car Rental Association (EA) .... ACRA
American Carbon Society (EA) .... ACS
American Cardiology Technologists Association [*Later, NSCPT*] (EA) .... ACTA
American Cardiology Technologists Association (SAUO) .... ACTA
American Cargo War Risk Reinsurance Exchange (EA) .... ACWRRE
American Cargo War Risk Reinsurance Exchange (SAUS) .... AVWRRE
American Carnation Society [*Defunct*] (EA) .... ACS
American Carnival Glass Association (EA) .... ACGA
American Carnivals Association (EA) .... ACA
American Carousel Society (EA) .... ACS
American Carpal Tunnel Syndrome Association (EA) .... ACTSA
American Carpet Institute [*Later, CRI*] (EA) .... ACI
American Carpet Institute (SAUO) .... ACI
American Cartographer [*A publication*] (GEOI) .... AC
American Cartographic Association (EA) .... ACA
American Casino Enterprises, Inc. [*NASDAQ symbol*] (NQ) .... ACES
American Casino Enterprises, Inc. [*Associated Press*] (SAG) .... AmCasn
American Cast Iron Pipe Company (SAUO) .... ACIPCO
American Cast Metals Association (EA) .... ACMA
American Casting Association (EA) .... ACA
American Casting Institute (SAUS) .... ACI
American Cat Association (EA) .... ACA
American Cat Fanciers Association (EA) .... ACFA
American Catalogue [*A bibliographic publication*] .... AmC
American Catfish Marketing Association (EA) .... ACMA
American Catholic Committee (EA) .... ACC
American Catholic Conference [*Defunct*] (EA) .... ACC
American Catholic Correctional Chaplains Association (SAUO) .... ACCA
American Catholic Correctional Chaplains Association (EA) .... ACCCA
American Catholic Esperanto Society (EA) .... ACES
American Catholic Historical Association (EA) .... ACHA
American Catholic Historical Researches (journ.) (SAUS) .... ACHR
American Catholic Historical Society (EA) .... ACHS
American Catholic Historical Society, Philadelphia, PA [*Library symbol*] [*Library of Congress*] (LCLS) .... PPACHi
American Catholic Philosophical Association (EA) .... ACPA
American Catholic Psychological Association [*Later, PIRI*] (EA) .... ACPA
American Catholic Psychological Association (SAUO) .... ACPA
American Catholic Quarterly Review (journ.) (SAUS) .... ACQR
American Catholic Sociological Society (SAUO) .... ACSS
American Catholic Sociological Society [*Later, ASR*] (EA) .... ACSS
American Catholic Theological Society (SAUO) .... ACTS
American Catholic Truth Society [*Defunct*] (EA) .... ACTS
American Catholic Union (EA) .... ACU
American Cause [*An association*] (EA) .... AC
American Cave Conservation Association (EA) .... ACCA
American Cavy Breeders Association (EA) .... ACBA
American CB Radio Association (EA) .... ACBRA
American Celiac Society [*Later, ACS/DSC*] (EA) .... ACS
American Celiac Society (SAUO) .... ACS
American Celiac Society/Dietary Support Coalition (EA) .... ACS/DSC
American Cement Alliance (EA) .... ACA
American Cement Corporation (SAUO) .... AAC
American Cement Trade Alliance [*Later, ACA*] (EA) .... ACTA
American Cement Trade Alliance (SAUS) .... ACTA
American Cemetery Association (EA) .... ACA
American Cemetery-Mortuary Council (EA) .... ACMC
American Center for Children and Media (SAUS) .... ACCM
American Center for Chinese Medical Sciences (EA) .... ACCMS
American Center for Design (EA) .... ACD
American Center for Homeopathy (EA) .... ACH
American Center for Immuno-Biology and Metabolism .... ACIBM
American Center for International Leadership (EA) .... ACIL
American Center for Law and Justice [*Located on Pat Robertson's estate*] [*Virginia Beach, VA*] (ECON) .... ACLJ
American Center for Oriental Research (SAUO) .... ACOR
American Center for Physics (SAUS) .... ACP
American Center for Social Awareness (ADWA) .... ACSA
American Center for Stanislavski Theater Art (SAUO) .... ACSTA
American Center for Stanislavski Theatre Art (EA) .... ACSTA
American Center for Students and Artists (EA) .... ACSA
American Center for the Alexander Technique (EA) .... ACAT
American Center for the Quality of Work Life (EA) .... ACQWL
American Center of Films for Children (EA) .... ACFC
American Center of Oriental Research .... ACOR
American Center of the Union Internationale de la Marionette (EA) .... UNIMA-USA
American Central European Dental Institute .... ACEDI
American Central NOTAM [*Notice to Airmen*] **Facility** [*Military*] .... ACNF
American Century Corp. (SAUO) .... AC-T
American Ceramic Society (EA) .... ACerS
American Ceramic Society (EA) .... ACS
American Ceramic Society Bulletin (SAUO) .... Amer Ceram Soc Bull
American Ceramic Society, Columbus, OH [*Library symbol*] [*Library of Congress*] (LCLS) .... OCoAC
American Ceramic Society, Inc. (SAUO) .... ACSI
American Certified Morticians Association [*Defunct*] (EA) .... ACMA
American Cetacean Society (EA) .... ACS
American Chain & Cable (SAUO) .... ACN
American Chain and Cable (SAUS) .... ACN
American Chain & Cable Co., Inc. (EFIS) .... ACCO
American Chain & Cable Company (SAUO) .... ACCO
American Chain Association (EA) .... ACA
American Chain of Warehouses (EA) .... ACW
American Chamber of Commerce (DCTA) .... ACC
American Chamber of Commerce (SAUS) .... AMCHAM
American Chamber of Commerce Executives (EA) .... ACCE
American Chamber of Commerce for Brazil-Sao Paulo (EA) .... AMCHAM-Sao Paulo
American Chamber of Commerce for Trade with Italy (SAUO) .... ACCI
American Chamber of Commerce in Argentina (EA) .... AmCham-Argentina
American Chamber of Commerce in Australia .... ACCA
American Chamber of Commerce in Australia .... AMCHAM
American Chamber of Commerce in Austria (EA) .... ACCA
American Chamber of Commerce in Belgium (EA) .... AMCHAM
American Chamber of Commerce in France (EA) .... ACCF
American Chamber of Commerce in Hong Kong (EA) .... AmCham HK
American Chamber of Commerce in Italy [*An association*] .... AmCham
American Chamber of Commerce in Japan (EA) .... ACCJ
American Chamber of Commerce in Japan (SAUO) .... ACCJJ
American Chamber of Commerce in Korea (EA) .... AMCHAM KOREA
American Chamber of Commerce in New Zealand (EA) .... AMCHAM
American Chamber of Commerce in Okinawa (EA) .... AMCHAM
American Chamber of Commerce in Republic of China (EA) .... ACC-ROC
American Chamber of Commerce in Thailand (EA) .... ACCT
American Chamber of Commerce in the Netherlands (EA) .... AMCHAM
American Chamber of Commerce of Bolivia (EA) .... ACCB
American Chamber of Commerce of El Salvador (EA) .... ACCES
American Chamber of Commerce of El Salvador (EA) .... AMCHAM EL SALVADOR
American Chamber of Commerce of Mexico (CROSS) .... AmCham
American Chamber of Commerce of Peru (EA) .... AMCHAM PERU
American Chamber of Commerce of the Philippines (EA) .... ACCP
American Chamber of Commerce Research Association (SAUS) .... ACCRA
American Chamber of Commerce Researchers Association (EA) .... ACCRA
American Chamber of Commerce-Egypt (EA) .... AMCHAM Egypt
American Chancery Digest [*A publication*] (DLA) .... Am Ch Dig
American Chaplain's Association (EA) .... ACA
American Chapter, International Real Estate Federation (EA) .... AC/IREF
American Chapter of the International Real Estate Federation (SAUO) .... AC/IREF
American Charbray Breeders Association (SAUO) .... ACBA
American Charbray Breeders Association [*Later, AICA*] (EA) .... ACBA
American Charter Enterprise Services Inc. (SAUO) .... ACES
American Checker Federation (EA) .... ACF
American Checkered Giant Club [*Later, ACGRC*] .... ACGC
American Checkered Giant Club (SAUO) .... ACGC
American Checkered Giant Rabbit Club (EA) .... ACGRC
American Cheerleader Association .... ACA
American Cheerleaders Association (SAUO) .... ACA
American Cheese (IIA) .... AC
American Cheese Society (EA) .... ACS
American Chemical Exchange .... ACE
American Chemical Paint Company (SAUO) .... ACP
American Chemical Society (SAUO) .... A Chem S
American Chemical Society (SAUO) .... AChS
American Chemical Society (EA) .... ACS
American Chemical Society (SAUO) .... Am Chem
American Chemical Society/ Division of Chemical Information (SAUO) .... ACS/DCI
American Chemical Society Monographs [*A publication*] (MEC) .... Am Chem Soc
American Chemical Society, Washington, DC [*Library symbol*] [*Library of Congress*] (LCLS) .... DACS
American Chemical Society/Division of Chemical Information (SAUS) .... ACS/DCI
American Chemical Society-Petroleum Research Fund (SAUO) .... ACS-PRF
American Chesapeake Club (EA) .... ACC
American Chess Academy [*Commercial firm*] (EA) .... ACA
American Chess Foundation (EA) .... ACF

American Chestnut Foundation (EA) ... ACF
American Cheviot Sheep Society (EA) ... ACSS
American Chianina Association (EA) ... ACA
American Child Care Services [*Defunct*] (EA) ... ACCS
American Child Custody Alliance (EA) ... ACCA
American Child Guidance Foundation [*Defunct*] (EA) ... ACGF
American Child Health Association (SAUO) ... ACHA
American Child (journ.) (SAUS) ... Am Child
American Childhood (journ.) (SAUS) ... Am Childhood
American Chinchilla Rabbit Breeders Association (EA) ... ACRBA
American Chinese Medical Society [*Later, CAMS*] (EA) ... ACMS
American Chinese Medical Society (SAUO) ... ACMS
American Chiropractic Association (EA) ... ACA
American Chiropractic Registry of Radiologic Technologists (EA) ... ACRRT
American Choral Directors (SAUO) ... ACD
American Choral Directors Association (EA) ... ACDA
American Choral Foundation (EA) ... ACF
American Christian Action Council [*Later, NCBBC*] (EA) ... ACAC
American Christian Association for Israel [*Later, American-Israel Cultural Foundation*] (EA) ... ACAI
American Christian Association for Israel (SAUO) ... ACAI
American Christian Committee for Refugees [*Post-World War II, Europe*] ... ACCR
American Christian League (SAUO) ... ACL
American Christian Palestine Committee [*Defunct*] ... ACPC
American Christian Television Service [*Cable-television system*] ... ACTS
American Christian Television System (SAUS) ... ACTS
American Christmas Crib Society [*Defunct*] (EA) ... ACCS
American Chronic Pain Association (EA) ... ACPA
American Church Building Fund Commission [*Later, Episcopal Church Building Fund*] (EA) ... ACBFC
American Church Building Fund Commission (SAUO) ... ACBFC
American Church Union (EA) ... ACU
American Cider and Vinegar Company (SAUO) ... ACVX
American Cimflex Corp. [*Pittsburgh, PA*] ... ACC
American Cinema Editors (EA) ... ACE
American Cinemastores [*NASDAQ symbol*] (SAG) ... ACSI
American Cinemastores [*Associated Press*] (SAG) ... AmCin
American Cinemastores [*Associated Press*] (SAG) ... AmCine
American Cinemastores Wrrt [*NASDAQ symbol*] (TTSB) ... ACSIW
American Circus Memorial Association (EA) ... ACMA
American Citizens [*Military*] (ADDR) ... AMCITS
American Citizens Abroad (EA) ... ACA
American Citizens and Lawmen Association (EA) ... ACLA
American Citizens Band Operators Association (EA) ... ACBOA
American Citizens Committee on Reducing Debt (EA) ... ACCORD
American Citizens Concerned for Life Education Fund/ACCL Communications Center [*Defunct*] (EA) ... ACCL
American Citizens for Honesty in Government [*Defunct*] (EA) ... ACHG
American Citizens for Justice [*An association*] (EA) ... ACJ
American Citizens for Political Action (EA) ... ACPA
American Citizens Together [*An association*] ... ACT
American Citizenship Center (EA) ... ACC
American City Bureau [*An association*] (EA) ... ACB
American City Planning Institute ... ACPI
American City Racing League [*Auto racing*] ... ACRC
American City Racing League [*Auto racing*] ... ACRL
American Civic Association (EA) ... ACA
American Civic Religion, Official Version (SAUS) ... ACROV
American Civil Aeronautics Board (SAUO) ... ACAB
[*The*] **American Civil Defense Association** (EA) ... TACDA
American Civil Law Journal [*A publication*] (DLA) ... ACLJ
American Civil Law Journal [*A publication*] (DLA) ... Am CLJ
American Civil Liberties Union (EA) ... ACLU
American Civil Liberties Union Foundation (EA) ... ACLUF
American Civil Liberties Union. Legislative Action Bulletin [*A publication*] (ILCA) ... ACLU Leg Act Bull
American Civil Liberties Union. Legislative Action Bulletin [*A publication*] (DLA) ... ACLU Leg Action Bull
American Civil War (SAUO) ... ACW
American Civil War Association (EA) ... ACWA
American Civil War Bulletin Board System [*Information service or system*] (IID) ... ACWBBS
American Civil War Bulletin Board System Information (SAUS) ... ACWBBS
American Civil War Round Table (EAIO) ... ACWRT
American Civil War Round Table, United Kingdom (SAUO) ... ACWRTUK
American Civilian Internee Information Bureau [*Army*] (AABC) ... ACIIB
American Civilian Internee Information Bureau (Branch) (GFGA) ... ACIIB(Br)
American Claims Evaluation, Inc. [*NASDAQ symbol*] (NQ) ... AMCE
American Claims Evaluators [*Associated Press*] (SAG) ... AClaim
American Classic Voyages, Inc. [*Associated Press*] (SAG) ... AClasVoy
American Classic Voyages, Inc. [*NASDAQ symbol*] (SAG) ... AMCV
American Classical Association (SAUO) ... ACA
American Classical League (EA) ... ACL
American Clean Water Association (EA) ... ACWA
American Cleaning Service (SAUO) ... ACS
American Cleft Palate Association (SAUO) ... ACPA
American Cleft Palate Association [*Later, ACPCA*] (EA) ... ACPA
American Cleft Palate-Craniofacial Association (EA) ... ACPA
American Cleft Palate-Craniofacial Association (EA) ... ACPCA
American Clinical and Climatological Association (EA) ... ACCA
American Clinical Laboratory Association (EA) ... ACLA
American Clinical Neurophysiological Society (NTPA) ... ACNS
American Clinical Neurophysiology Society [*Formerly, American Society of Electroencephalographic Technologists*] (EA) ... ASET
American Clipper Owners Club (EA) ... ACOC
American Cloak and Suit Manufacturers Association (SAUS) ... ACSMA
American Cloak and Suit Manufacturers Association (EA) ... ACSMA
American Club of Paris (EA) ... ACP
American Coal Ash Association (EA) ... ACAA
American Coal Enterprises, Inc. (SAUO) ... ACE
American Coal Foundation (EA) ... ACF
American Coal Sales Administration (SAUO) ... ACSA
American Coal Shipping, Inc. (SAUO) ... ACS
American Coalition for Abuse Awareness (EA) ... ACAA
American Coalition for Hispanic Americans (SAUO) ... ACHA
American Coalition for Life (EA) ... ACL
American Coalition for Traditional Values (EA) ... ACTV
American Coalition for Traffic Safety (EA) ... ACTS
American Coalition of Citizens with Disabilities [*Defunct*] (EA) ... ACCD
American Coalition of Patriotic Societies [*Defunct*] (EA) ... ACPS
American Coalition of Unregistered Churches (EA) ... ACUC
American Coalition on Trade Expansion with Canada (EA) ... ACTEC
American Coaster Enthusiasts (EA) ... ACE
American Cockatiel Society (EA) ... ACS
American Cocker Spaniel Club (EAIO) ... ACSC
American Cocoa Research Institute (EA) ... ACRI
American Coin Merchandising, Inc. [*NASDAQ symbol*] (SAG) ... AMCN
American Coin Merchandising, Inc. [*Associated Press*] (SAG) ... AmCoin
American Coke and Coal Chemicals Institute (SAUO) ... AC & CCI
American Coke and Coal Chemicals Institute (SAUS) ... AC&CCI
American Coke and Coal Chemicals Institute (EA) ... ACCCI
American Collection Association [*Orem, UT*] (EA) ... ACA
American Collectors Association [*Minneapolis, MN*] (EA) ... ACA
American Collectors of Infant Feeders (EA) ... ACIF
American College Admissions Advisory and Career Counseling Center (EA) ... ACAACCC
American College Admissions Advisory Center [*Later, ACAACCC*] (EA) ... ACAAC
American College Admissions Center [*Later, ACAAC*] ... ACAC
American College Admissions Centers (SAUO) ... ACAC
American College, Bryn Mawr, PA [*OCLC symbol*] (OCLC) ... AMC
American College Counseling Association (NTPA) ... ACCA
American College Dance Festival Association (EA) ... ACDFA
American College Dictionary (SAUS) ... ACD
American College for Advancement in Medicine (SAUO) ... ACAM
American College for Continuing Education (EA) ... ACCE
American College for the Applied Arts, Los Angeles, CA [*Library symbol*] [*Library of Congress*] (LCLS) ... CLACA
American College Health Association (EA) ... ACHA
American College in Rome (SAUO) ... ACR
American College of Addiction Treatment Administrators (EA) ... ACATA
American College of Advancement in Medicine (EA) ... ACAM
American College of Allergists (EA) ... ACA
American College of Allergy and Immunology (EA) ... ACAI
American College of Allergy, Asthma & Immunology (SAUO) ... ACAAI
American College of Allergy, Asthma, and Immunology (NTPA) ... ACAAI
American College of Allergy, Asthma, & Immunology (SAUS) ... ACAAI
American College of Anesthesiologists (EA) ... ACA
American College of Anesthetists (SAUO) ... ACAnes
American College of Angiology (EA) ... ACA
American College of Animal Laboratory Medicine (RDA) ... ACALM
American College of Aphothecaries (SAUS) ... ACA
American College of Apothecaries (EA) ... ACA
American College of Applied Arts, Atlanta, GA [*Library symbol*] [*Library of Congress*] (LCLS) ... GACA
American College of Bankruptcy (NTPA) ... ACB
American College of Cardiology (EA) ... ACC
American College of Cardiology Extended Learning (ADWA) ... ACCEL
American College of Cardiology Extended Study Services ... ACCESS
American College of Cardiovascular Administrators (EA) ... ACCA
American College of Chemosurgery (EA) ... ACC
American College of Chemosurgery (SAUO) ... ACMMSCO
American College of Chest Physicians (MELL) ... AACP
American College of Chest Physicians (EA) ... ACCP
American College of Childbirth Educators (NUJO) ... ACCE
American College of Chiropractic Consultants (SAUO) ... ACCC
American College of Chiropractic Orthopedists (EA) ... ACCO
American College of Clinic Administrators [*Defunct*] (EA) ... ACCA
American College of Clinic Managers [*Later, ACMGA*] (EA) ... ACCM
American College of Clinic Managers (SAUO) ... ACCM
American College of Clinical Hypnosis [*Defunct*] (EA) ... ACCH
American College of Clinical Pharmacology (EA) ... ACCP
American College of Clinical Pharmacy (EA) ... ACCP
American College of Computer Lawyers [*Defunct*] (EA) ... ACCL
American College of Counselors (EA) ... ACC
American College of Cryosurgery (EA) ... ACC
American College of Cryosurgery (EA) ... ACCRYO
American College of Dentists (EA) ... ACD
American College of Dentists Foundation (SAUO) ... ACDF
American College of Ecology [*Defunct*] (EA) ... ACE
American College of Emergency Physicians (EA) ... ACEP
American College of Epidemiology (EA) ... ACE
American College of Eye Surgeons (NTPA) ... ACES
American College of Foot and Ankle Orthopedics and Medicine (DMAA) ... ACFAO
American College of Foot and Ankle Orthopedics and Medicine (EA) ... ACFAOM
American College of Foot and Ankle Pediatrics (EA) ... ACFAP
American College of Foot and Ankle Surgeons (DMAA) ... ACFAS
American College of Foot Orthopedics (SAUS) ... ACFO
American College of Foot Orthopedists (EA) ... ACFO

American College of Foot Orthopedists (SAUO) .... ACOFO
American College of Foot Roentgenologists (SAUO) .... ACFR
American College of Foot Roentgenologists [*Later, American College of PodiatricRadiologists*] (EA) .... ACFR
American College of Foot Specialists [*Later, ACCE*] (EA) .... ACFS
American College of Foot Surgeons (EA) .... ACFS
American College of Forensic Examiners (NTPA) .... ACFE
American College of Forensic Psychiatry (NTPA) .... ACFP
American College of Gastroenterology (EA) .... ACG
American College of General Practice [*Later, ACM*] (EA) .... ACGP
American College of General Practice (SAUS) .... ACGP
American College of General Practitioners in Osteopathic Medicine and Surgery (SAUO) .... ACGP
American College of General Practitioners in Osteopathic Medicine and Surgery (EA) .... ACGPOMS
American College of General Practitioners in Osteopathic Medicine and Surgery (SAUS) .... ACGPOMS
American College of Health Care Administrators (EA) .... ACHCA
American College of Healthcare Executives (EA) .... ACHE
American College of Healthcare Information Administrators (NTPA) .... ACHIA
American College of Healthcare Marketing (NTPA) .... ACHM
American College of Heraldry (EA) .... ACH
American College of Home Health Administrators (NTPA) .... ACHHA
American College of Home Obstetrics (EA) .... ACHO
American College of Hospital Administrators [*Later, ACHE*] (EA) .... ACHA
American College of Integrated Delivery Systems (SAUO) .... ACIDS
American College of International Physicians (EA) .... ACIP
American College of Laboratory Animal Medicine (EA) .... ACLAM
American College of Legal Medicine (EA) .... ACLM
American College of Life Underwriters [*Later, The American College*] (EA) .... ACLU
American College of Life Underwriters (SAUO) .... ACLU
American College of Life Underwriters, Bryn Mawr, PA [*Library symbol*] [*Library of Congress*] (LCLS) .... PBmA
American College of Managed Care Administrators (NTPA) .... ACMCA
American College of Managed Care Medicine (SAUO) .... ACMCM
American College of Medical Genetics (HGEN) .... ACMG
American College of Medical Group Administrators (EA) .... ACMGA
American College of Medical Informatics (DMAA) .... ACMI
American College of Medical Physicists .... ACMP
American College of Medical Physics (NTPA) .... ACMP
American College of Medical Practice Executives (NTPA) .... ACMPE
American College of Medical Quality (NTPA) .... ACMQ
American College of Medical Technologists (EA) .... ACMT
American College of Medical Toxicology (NTPA) .... ACMT
American College of Medicine (EA) .... ACM
American College of Mental Health Administration (EA) .... ACMHA
American College of MOHS Micrographic Surgery and Cutaneous Oncology (EA) .... ACMMSCO
American College of Musicians (EA) .... ACM
American College of Neuropsychiatrists (EA) .... ACN
American College of Neuropsychiatrists (SAUO) .... ACNP
American College of Neuropsychopharmacology (EA) .... ACNP
American College of Neuropsycho-pharmacology (SAUS) .... ACNP
American College of Neuropsychopharmacology (SAUO) .... ACNPP
American College of Nuclear Medicine (EA) .... ACNM
American College of Nuclear Physicians (EA) .... ACNP
American College of Nurse Practitioners (SAUO) .... ACNP
American College of Nurse-Midwives (EA) .... ACNM
American College of Nursing Home Administrators [*Later, ACHCA*] .... ACNHA
American College of Nursing Home Administrators (SAUO) .... ACNHA
American College of Nutrition (EA) .... ACN
American College of Obstetricians and Gynecologists (EA) .... ACOG
American College of Occupational and Environmental Medicine (NTPA) .... ACOEM
American College of Occupational Medicine (MELL) .... ACOM
American College of Oncology Administrators (NTPA) .... ACOA
American College of Optometric Physicians (EA) .... ACOP
American College of Oral and Maxillofacial Surgeons (EA) .... ACOMS
American College of Orgonomy (EA) .... ACO
American College of Osteopathic Emergency Physicians (EA) .... ACOEP
American College of Osteopathic Family Physicians (NTPA) .... ACFP
American College of Osteopathic Hospital Administrators (SAUO) .... ACOHA
American College of Osteopathic Hospital Administrators [*Later, COHE*] (EA) .... ACOHA
American College of Osteopathic Internists (EA) .... ACOI
American College of Osteopathic Obstetricians and Gynecologists (EA) .... ACOOG
American College of Osteopathic Pain Management and Scleotherapy (NTPA) .... ACOPMS
American College of Osteopathic Pediatricians (EA) .... ACOP
American College of Osteopathic Surgeons (EA) .... ACOS
American College of Otorhinolaryngologists (EA) .... ACO
American College of Pain Medicine .... ACPM
American College of Pathologists (DAVI) .... ACP
American College of Pharmacists (EA) .... ACP
American College of Physician Executives (EA) .... ACPE
American College of Physician Inventors (NTPA) .... ACPI
American College of Physicians (EA) .... ACP
American College of Physicians Assistants [*Defunct*] (EA) .... ACPA
American College of Physicians-American Society of Internal Medicine .... ACP-ASIM
American College of Podiatric Radiologists (EA) .... ACPR
American College of Podopediatrics (EA) .... ACP
American College of Poultry Veterinarians .... ACPV

American College of Prehospital Medicine (SAUS) .... ACPM
American College of Prehospital Medicine (SAUO) .... ACPM
American College of Preventive Medicine (EA) .... ACPM
American College of Probate Counsel [*Later, ACTEC*] (EA) .... ACPC
American College of Probate Counsel (SAUO) .... ACPC
American College of Prosthodontists (EA) .... ACP
American College of Psychiatrists (EA) .... ACP
American College of Psychoanalysts (EA) .... ACPA
American College of Psychoanalysts (EA) .... ACPn
American College of Psychoanalysts (NTPA) .... ACPsa
American College of Radiation Oncology .... ACRO
American College of Radio Marketing (EA) .... ACRM
American College of Radiology (EA) .... ACR
American College of Radiology (SAUS) .... ARC
American College of Radiology, Reston, VA [*Library symbol*] [*Library of Congress*] (LCLS) .... ViReA
American College of Real Estate Consultants (SAUO) .... ACREC
American College of Real Estate Consultants [*Later, RECP*] (EA) .... ACREC
American College of Real Estate Lawyers (NTPA) .... ACREL
American College of Rheumatology (EA) .... ACR
American College of Sports Medicine (EA) .... ACSM
American College of Surgeons (EA) .... ACS
American College of Surgeons, Chicago, IL [*Library symbol*] [*Library of Congress*] (LCLS) .... ICAC
American College of Surgeons Committee on Trauma .... ACSCOT
American College of Switzerland .... ACS
American College of Switzerland (SAUO) .... acs
American College of Tax Counsel (NTPA) .... ACTC
American College of Theriogenologists (EA) .... ACT
American College of Toxicology (EA) .... ACT
American College of Trial Lawyers (EA) .... ACTL
American College of Trust and Estate Counsel (EA) .... ACTEC
American College of Utilization Review Physicians (EA) .... ACURP
American College of Veterinary Anesthesiologists (EA) .... ACVA
American College of Veterinary Dermatology (EA) .... ACVD
American College of Veterinary Internal Medicine (EA) .... ACVIM
American College of Veterinary Microbiologists (EA) .... ACVM
American College of Veterinary Ophthalmologists (EA) .... ACVO
American College of Veterinary Pathologists (EA) .... ACVP
American College of Veterinary Radiology (EA) .... ACVR
American College of Veterinary Surgeons (EA) .... ACVS
American College of Veterinary Toxicologists [*Later, AAVCT*] (EA) .... ACVT
American College of Veterinary Toxicologists (SAUS) .... ACVT
American College Personnel Accreditation (OICC) .... ACPC
American College Personnel Association (EA) .... ACPA
American College Public Relations Association [*Later, Council for the Advancement and Support of Education*] .... ACPRA
American College Public Relations Association (SAUO) .... ACPRA
American College Test (NTIO) .... ACT
American College Testing (SAUO) .... ACT
American College Testing Program (EA) .... ACT
American College Testing Program (DIPS) .... ACTP
American College Testing. Research Reports (journ.) (SAUS) .... Act Res Rep
American College Testing Service (HCT) .... ACTS
American College Theater Festival .... ACTF
American Collegians for Life .... ACL
American Collegiate Hockey Association (PSS) .... ACHA
American Collegiate Press .... ACP
American Collegiate Retailing Association (EA) .... ACRA
American Colon Therapy Association (EA) .... ACTA
American Colonization Society .... ACS
American Colonization Society (SAUO) .... ACS
American Color Association (EA) .... ACA
American Color Print Society (EA) .... ACPS
American Columbia [*Record label*] .... AmC
American Comedy Museum Association [*Defunct*] (EA) .... ACMA
American Comet Club - United Spoilers of America [*Later, MERCPAC*] (EA) .... ACC-USA
American Comics Grading (SAUS) .... ACG
American Command (SAUS) .... AMCO
American Commercial Arbitration Association (SAUO) .... ACAA
American Commercial Barge Lines, Inc. [*AAR code*] .... ACBL
American Commercial Collectors Association (EA) .... ACCA
American Commercial Lines, Inc. .... ACL
American Commercial Rabbit Association [*Defunct*] (EA) .... ACRA
American Commission for Protection and Salvage of Artistic and Historical Monuments in War Areas [*World War II*] [*Defunct*] .... ACPSAHMWA
American Commission for Protection and Salvage of Artistic and Historical Monuments in War Areas (SAUO) .... ACPSAHMWA
American Commission on Ministerial Training (EA) .... ACMT
American Commission on Stratigraphic Nomenclature (SAUS) .... ACSN
American Commission on Stratigraphic Nomenclature (SAUO) .... ACSN
American Commitee for Interoperable Systems (VERA) .... ACIS
American Committee for Aid to Poland (EA) .... ACAP
American Committee for Crystal Growth (SAUO) .... ACCG
American Committee for Cultural Freedom .... ACCF
American Committee for Democracy and Freedom in Greece (EA) .... ACDFG
American Committee for Flags of Necessity [*Later, FACS*] (EA) .... ACFN
American Committee for Flags of Necessity (EA) .... ACFN
American Committee for Human Rights (EA) .... ACHR
American Committee for International Conservation (EA) .... ACIC
American Committee for International Wild Life Protection [*Later, ACIC*] (EA) .... ACIWLP
American Committee for Interoperable Systems (SAUO) .... ACIS
American Committee for Irish Studies (AEBS) .... ACIS

American Committee for KEEP (EA) ... ACK
American Committee for Liberation [*Later, RFE/RL*] ... ACL
American Committee for Liberation (SAUO) ... ACL
American Committee for Liberation from Bolshevism (SAUO) ... ACLB
American Committee for Protection of Foreign Born (SAUO) ... ACPFB
American Committee for Rescue and Resettlement of Iraqi Jews (EA) ... AMCORR
American Committee for Shaare Zedek in Jerusalem (EA) ... ACSZJ
American Committee for South Asian Art [*Defunct*] [*Defunct*] (EA) ... ACSAA
American Committee for Struggle Against War (SAUO) ... ACSAW
American Committee for the Advancement of Torah Education in Israel [*Later, OTII*] (EA) ... ACATEI
American Committee for the Liberation of the Peoples of Russia (SAUO) ... ACLPR
American Committee for the National Sick Fund of Israel (EA) ... ACNSFI
American Committee for the Weizmann Institute of Science (EA) ... ACWIS
American Committee for Ulster Justice (EA) ... ACUJ
American Committee of OSE [*Defunct*] ... AMEROSE
American Committee of Slavists (EA) ... ACS
American Committee of the Slovak World Congress (EA) ... ACSWC
American Committee of United Europe ... ACUE
American Committee on Africa (SAUO) ... ACA
American Committee on Africa (EA) ... ACOA
American Committee on Arthropod-borne Viruses (SAUO) ... ACAV
American Committee on East-West Accord [*Later, ACUSSR*] (EA) ... ACEWA
American Committee on Italian Migration (EA) ... ACIM
American Committee on Japan (EA) ... ACJ
American Committee on Laboratory Animal Diseases (GVA) ... ACLAD
American Committee on the History of the Second World War (EA) ... ACHSWW
American Committee on US-Soviet Relations [*Defunct*] (EA) ... ACUSSR
American Committee to Advance the Study of Petroglyphs and Pictographs (EA) ... ACASPP
American Committee to Advance the Study of Petroglyphs and Pictographs (SAUO) ... ACASPP
American Commodities Exchange [*Business term*] (EBF) ... ACE
American Commodity Distribution Association (EA) ... ACDA
American Communication Services [*Evanston, IL*] [*Telecommunications*] (TSSD) ... ACS
American Communication Services, Inc. [*Evanston, IL*] (TSSD) ... ACSI
American Communication Services Incorporated (SAUO) ... ACSI
American Communications (SAUS) ... AMERICOM
American Communications Association ... ACA
American Communications Consultants, Inc. [*Telecommunications service*] (TSSD) ... ACC
American Communications Services, Inc. [*NASDAQ symbol*] (SAG) ... ACNS
American Communications Services, Inc. [*Associated Press*] (SAG) ... AComS
American Community Cultural Center Association (EA) ... ACCCA
American Community Gardening Association (EA) ... ACGA
American Community School (SAUO) ... ACS
American Community Schools [*In foreign countries*] ... ACS
American Community Survey (GEOI) ... ACS
American Community Theater Association (SAUO) ... ACTA
American Community Theatre Association (EA) ... ACTA
American Commuters Association ... ACA
American Comparative Literature Association (EA) ... ACLA
American Comparative Literature Association Newsletter (SAUO) ... ACLAN
American Compensation Association (EA) ... ACA
American Component Dealers Association (EA) ... ACDA
American Composers Alliance (EA) ... ACA
American Composers Orchestra ... ACO
American Computer Appraisal Service (MHDI) ... ACAS
American Computer Innovators (SAUO) ... ACI
American Computer Referal (SAUS) ... ACR
American Computer Referral (NITA) ... ACR
American Computer Science League (EA) ... ACSL
American Concert Choir [*Defunct*] (EA) ... ACC
American Concert Choir and Choral Foundation [*Later, ACF*] ... ACCCF
American Concert Choir and Choral Foundation (SAUO) ... ACCCF
American Concrete Agricultural Pipe Association [*Defunct*] ... ACAPA
American Concrete Institute (EA) ... ACI
American Concrete Institute, Detroit, MI [*Library symbol*] [*Library of Congress*] (LCLS) ... MiDACI
American Concrete Pavement Association (EA) ... ACPA
American Concrete Paving Association (SAUO) ... ACPA
American Concrete Pipe Association (SAUO) ... ACP
American Concrete Pipe Association (EA) ... ACPA
American Concrete Pressure Pipe Association (EA) ... ACPP
American Concrete Pressure Pipe Association (EA) ... ACPPA
American Concrete Pumping Association (EA) ... ACPA
American Conditions [*Insurance*] ... AC
American Confederation of Clinical Biochemistry (SAUO) ... Latin
American Conference for Irish Studies (EA) ... ACIS
American Conference Institute (AAGC) ... ACI
American Conference of Academic Deans (EA) ... ACAD
American Conference of Cantors (EA) ... ACC
American Conference of Gonvernmental Industrial Hygienists (SAUS) ... ACGIH
American Conference of Governmental Industrial Hygienists (EA) ... ACGIH
American Conference of Real Estate Investment Trusts [*Defunct*] (EA) ... ACREIT
American Conference of Therapeutic Psychiatric Selfhelp (SAUO) ... ACTPS
American Conference of Therapeutic Selfhelp/Selfhealth Social Action Clubs [*Defunct*] (EA) ... ACT
American Conference of Therapeutic Selfhelp/Selfhealth Social Action Clubs (SAUS) ... ACT
American Conferences of Crystal Growers (SAUO) ... ACCG
American Congregation of Jews from Austria (EA) ... ACJA
American Congregational Association (EA) ... ACA
American Congregational Association (SAUO) ... ACA
American Congregational Association, Boston, MA [*Library symbol*] [*Library of Congress*] (LCLS) ... MBC
American Congregational Union ... ACU
American Congress for Preventive Medicine (SAUS) ... ACPM
American Congress for/on Preventive Medicine (SAUO) ... ACPM
American Congress of Physical Medicine and Rehabilitation [*Later, ACRM*] (EA) ... ACPMR
American Congress of Physical Therapy (SAUO) ... ACPT
American Congress of Rehabilitation Medicine (EA) ... ACRM
American Congress of/on Surveying and Mapping (SAUO) ... ACSM
American Congress on Surveying and Mapping (EA) ... ACSM
American Congress on Surveying and Mapping Member societies (SAUS) ... ACSM
American Congressional Association (SAUO) ... ACA
American Conifer Society (EA) ... ACS
American Connemara Pony Society (EA) ... ACPS
American Conservation Association, Inc. (EPA) ... ACA
American Conservative Trust (EA) ... ACT
American Conservative Union (EA) ... ACU
American Conservative Union Education and Research Institute (EA) ... ACU-ERI
American Conservatives for Freedom (EA) ... ACF
American Conservatory of Music [*Chicago, IL*] ... ACM
American Conservatory of Music, Chicago, IL [*Library symbol*] [*Library of Congress*] (LCLS) ... ICACMu
American Conservatory of Music, Chicago, IL [*OCLC symbol*] (OCLC) ... IVI
American Conservatory Theater (SAUO) ... ACT
American Conservatory Theatre ... ACT
American Conservatory Theatre Foundation (EA) ... ACTF
American Consolidated Gold Corporation (SAUO) ... ACGC
American Constitutional and Civil Rights Union [*Defunct*] (EA) ... ACCRU
American Constitutional Association (SAUO) ... ACA
American Constitutional Law Foundation (EA) ... ACLF
American Constitutional League (SAUO) ... ACL
American Constitutional Rights Association (EA) ... ACRA
American Construction Council (SAUO) ... ACC
American Construction Inspectors Association (NTPA) ... ACIA
American Construction Owners Association [*Defunct*] (EA) ... ACOA
American Consul ... AMCON
American Consular Reporting Officer ... AMCONREPO
American Consulate General (CINC) ... AMCONGEN
American Consultants League (EA) ... ACL
American Consulting Engineers Council (EA) ... ACEC
American Consumer Alliance (EA) ... ACA
American Consumer Industries, Inc. (SAUO) ... ACA
American Consumer Products (EFIS) ... ACPI
American Consumers Association [*Chicago, IL*] (EA) ... ACA
American Contact Dermatitis Society (MELL) ... ACDS
American Contemplative Society [*Defunct*] (EA) ... ACS
American Continent (SAUS) ... Am Cont
American Continental Corp. ... ACC
American Contract Bridge League (EA) ... ACBL
American Contract Company (SAUO) ... ACC
American Control Conference (ACAE) ... ACC
American Coon Hunters Association (EA) ... ACHA
American Coordinated Medical Society (EA) ... ACMS
American Coordinating Committee for Equality in Sport and Society (EA) ... ACCESS
American Coordinating Committee for Equality in Sports and Society (SAUO) ... ACCESS
American Coordinating Committee on Corrosion (SAUO) ... ACCC
American Copper Council (EA) ... ACC
American Coptic Association (EA) ... ACA
American Copyright Council (EA) ... ACC
American Copyright Society [*Defunct*] (EA) ... ACS
American Cordage and Netting Manufacturers (EA) ... ACNM
American Cormo Sheep Association (EA) ... ACSA
American Corn Millers' Federation (EA) ... ACMF
American Corporate Counsel Association (EA) ... ACCA
American Corporate Counsel Institute [*Washington, DC*] (EA) ... ACCI
American Corporation Cases [*A publication*] (DLA) ... Amer Corp Cas
American Corporation Cases, by Withrow [*1868-87*] [*A publication*] (DLA) ... ACC
American Corporation Cases, by Withrow [*A publication*] (DLA) ... Am Corp Cas
American Correctional Association (EA) ... ACA
American Correctional Chaplains Association (EA) ... ACCA
American Correctional Food Service Association (EA) ... ACFSA
American Correctional Health Services Association (EA) ... ACHSA
American Corrective Therapy Association [*Later, AKA*] (EA) ... ACTA
American Corrective Therapy Association (SAUO) ... ACTA
American Corriedale Association (EA) ... ACA
American Cosmeticians Association (SAUO) ... ACA
American Cotswold Record Association (EA) ... ACRA
American Cottage Cheese Institute [*Later, ACDPI*] (EA) ... ACCI
American Cottage Cheese Institute (SAUO) ... ACCI
American Cotton Cooperative Association (EA) ... ACCA
American Cotton Exporters' Association (EA) ... ACEA
American Cotton Linter Association [*Defunct*] (EA) ... ACLA
American Cotton Manufacturers Institute [*Later, ATMI*] ... ACMI
American Cotton Shippers Association (EA) ... ACSA
American Cotton Waste Exchange [*Defunct*] (EA) ... ACWE
American Council for an Energy Efficient Economy (EA) ... ACEEE
American Council for Better Broadcasts (EA) ... ACBB
American Council for Capital Formation (EA) ... ACCF

American Council for Career Women [*New Orleans, LA*] (EA) ACCW
American Council for Collaboration in Education and Language Studies ACCELS
American Council for Collaboration in Education and Language Study (SAUO) ACCELS
American Council for Collaboration in Education and Language Study (SAUS) ACCELS
American Council for Competitive Telecommunications (SAUO) ACCT
American Council for Competitive Telecommunications [*Formerly, Ad Hoc Committee for Competitive Telecommunications*] (EA) ACCT
American Council for Construction Education (EA) ACCE
American Council for Coordinated Action [*Defunct*] (EA) ACCA
American Council for Drug Education (EA) ACDE
American Council for Elementary School Industrial Arts [*Later, TECC*] (EA) ACESIA
American Council for Emigrees in the Professions (SAUO) ACEP
American Council for Emigres in the Professions [*Defunct*] (EA) ACEP
American Council for Equal Compensation of Nazi Victims from Austria (SAUO) ACOA
American Council for Free Asia (EA) ACFA
American Council for Headache Education [*Medicine*] ACHE
American Council for Health Care Reform (EA) ACHCR
American Council for Healthful Living (EA) ACHL
American Council for International Studies (EA) ACIS
American Council for Judaism (EA) ACJ
American Council for Judaism, Inc. (SAUO) ACJ
American Council for Nationalities Service (EA) ACNS
American Council for Polish Culture (EA) ACPC
American Council for Private International Communication, Inc. (SAUS) ACPIC
American Council for Private International Communications (SAUS) ACPIC
American Council for Private International Communications, Inc. [*Proposed corporation to replace Radio Free Europe*] ACPIC
American Council for Romanians (EA) ACR
American Council for Soviet Relations (SAUO) ACSR
American Council for the Advancement of Human Rights (EA) ACAHR
American Council for the Arts (EA) ACA
American Council for the Arts in Education [*Defunct*] (EA) ACAE
American Council for the Blind (SAUO) ACB
American Council for Turfgrass [*Defunct*] (EA) ACT
American Council for University Planning and Academic Excellence (EA) ACUPAE
American Council for Voluntary International Action (SAUS) InterAction
American Council for Voluntary International Action (SAUO) INTERACTION
American Council for World Freedom (EA) ACWF
American Council of Applied Clinical Nutrition (EA) ACACN
American Council of Blind Government Employees (EA) ACBGE
American Council of Blind Lions (EA) ACBL
American Council of Certified Podiatric Physicians and Surgeons (SAUO) ACCPPS
American Council of Christian Churches (EA) ACCC
American Council of Christian Laymen [*Later, LCACCC*] (EA) ACCL
American Council of Christian Laymen (SAUO) ACCL
American Council of Commercial Laboratories (SAUO) ACCL
American Council of Commercial Laboratories [*Later, ACIL*] (KSC) ACCL
American Council of Executives in Religion [*Defunct*] (EA) ACER
American Council of Highway Advertisers (EA) ACHA
American Council of Human Rights [*Later, PHR*] (EA) ACHR
American Council of Human Rights (SAUO) ACHR
American Council of Hypnotist Examiners (EA) ACHE
American Council of Independent Laboratories (EA) ACIL
American Council of Industrial Arts State Association Officers [*Later, CTEA*] (EA) ACIASAO
American Council of Industrial Arts Supervisors (EA) ACIAS
American Council of Industrial Arts Teacher Education (SAUS) ACIATE
American Council of Learned Societies (EA) ACLS
American Council of Learned Societies Newsletter (SAUO) ACLSN
American Council of Learned Societies Newsletter (SAUO) ACLS Newsl
American Council of Life Insurance [*Washington, DC*] (EA) ACLI
American Council of Nanny Schools (EA) ACNS
American Council of Otolaryngology [*Later, ACO-HNS*] (EA) ACO
American Council of Otolaryngology (SAUO) ACO
American Council of Otolaryngology - Head and Neck Surgery [*Later, AAO-HNS*] (EA) ACO-HNS
American Council of Parent Cooperatives [*Later, PCPI*] (EA) ACPC
American Council of Parent Cooperatives (SAUO) ACPC
American Council of Polish Cultural Club (SAUO) ACPCC
American Council of Polish Cultural Clubs [*Later, ACPC*] (EA) ACPCC
American Council of Railroad Women (EA) ACRW
American Council of Spotted Asses (EA) ACSA
American Council of State Savings Supervisors (NTPA) ACSSS
American Council of Style and Design (SAUO) ACSD
American Council of Tax payers (SAUO) ACT
American Council of Taxpayers [*Formerly, COST*] (EA) ACT
American Council of Taxpayers (SAUS) ACT
American Council of Teachers of Russian (SAUO) ACRR
American Council of Teachers of Russian (EA) ACTR
American Council of Teachers of Uncommonly Taught Asian Language (SAUO) ACTUTAL
American Council of Teachers of Uncommonly Taught Asian Languages [*Defunct*] (EA) ACTUAL
American Council of the Blind (EA) ACB
American Council of the Blind Enterprises and Services (EA) ACBES
American Council of the Blind Federal Employees (EA) ACBFE
American Council of the Blind Parents [*Later, CFVI*] (EA) ACBP
American Council of the International Institute of Welding (EA) ACIIW
American Council of the Slovak World Congress [*Defunct*] (EA) ACSWC
American Council of Venture Clubs (EA) ACVC
American Council of Voluntary Agencies for Foreign Service [*Later, I/ACVIA*] (EA) ACVAFS
American Council of Women Chiropractors [*Later, Council of Women Chi ropractors*] (EA) ACWC
American Council of Women Chiropractors (SAUO) ACWC
American Council of Young Political Leaders (EA) ACYPL
American Council of/on Industrial Arts Teacher Education (SAUO) ACIATE
American Council of/on Pharmaceutical Education (SAUO) ACPE
American Council on Alcohol Problems (EA) ACAP
American Council on Alcoholism (EA) ACA
American Council on Capital Gains and Estate Taxation [*Later, ACCF*] [*Tax lobbying organization*] ACCGET
American Council on Chiropractic Physiotherapy [*Later, CCPT*] (EA) ACCP
American Council on Chiropractic Physiotherapy (SAUO) ACCP
American Council on Chiropractic Roentgenography (SAUO) ACCR
American Council on Chiropractic Roentgenology (SAUO) ACCR
American Council on Chiropractic Roentgenology [*Later, Council on Roentgenologyof the American Chiropractic Association*] (EA) ACCR
American Council on Consumer Interests (EA) ACCI
American Council on Cosmetology Education [*Defunct*] (EA) ACCE
American Council on Education (EA) ACE
American Council on Education for Journalism [*Later, ACEJMC*] (EA) ACEJ
American Council on Education for Journalism (SAUO) ACEJ
American Council on Education Registry Transcript System (SAUO) AARTS
American Council on Education Test (SAUO) ACE Test
American Council on Educational Simulation and Gaming ACESG
American Council on Exercise ACE
American Council on Exercise Hot Line (MELL) ACEHL
American Council on German Studies ACGS
American Council on Germany (EA) ACG
American Council on Gift Annuities (NFD) ACGA
American Council on Industrial Arts Teacher Education [*of the International Technology Education Association*] [*Later, CTTE*] (EA) ACIATE
American Council on Industrial Arts Teacher Education (SAUO) CTTE
American Council on International Personnel [*New York, NY*] (EA) ACIP
American Council on International Sports (EA) ACIS
American Council on Marijuana and Other Psychoactive Drugs [*Later, ACDE*] (EA) ACM
American Council on NATO [*Later, Atlantic Council of the United States*] ACN
American Council on North Atlantic Treaty Organization (SAUO) ACN
American Council on Pharmaceutical Education (EA) ACPE
American Council on Race Relations ACRR
American Council on Rural Special Education (SAUO) ACRES
American Council on Rural Special Education (EA) ACRSE
American Council on Rural Special Eduction ACRES
American Council on Schools and Colleges (EA) ACSC
American Council on Science and Health (EA) ACSH
American Council on the Environment (EA) ACE
American Council on the Middle East [*Defunct*] (EA) ACME
American Council on the Teaching of Foreign Languages (EA) ACTFL
American Council on Transplantation [*Defunct*] (EA) ACT
American Council to Improve Our Neighborhoods [*Later, NUC*] ACTION
American Council To Improve Our Neighborhoods (SAUO) ACTION
American Counseling Association (SAUO) ACA
American Counseling Association [*NACFT*] [*Absorbed by*] (EA) ACA
American Counseling Association of Missouri (SAUO) ACAM
American Counter-Trade Association (EA) ACA
American Country Life Association (EA) ACLA
American Court and Commercial Newspapers (EA) ACCN
American Craft [*A publication*] (BRI) Am Craft
American Craft Brewing International [*NASDAQ symbol*] (SAG) ABRE
American Craft Brewing International [*NASDAQ symbol*] (SAG) ABRW
American Craft Brewing International [*Associated Press*] (SAG) AmCraft
American Craft Brewing International [*Associated Press*] (SAG) AmCrft
American Craft Council (EA) ACC
American Craft Retailers Association (EA) ACRA
American Craftsmen's Council (BARN) ACC
American Cran Company (SAUO) AECO
American Cranberry Growers' Association [*Defunct*] (EA) ACGA
American Cranberry Growers Association (SAUS) ACGA
American Crane and Equipment Company (SAUO) ACECO
American Cream Draft Horse Association (EA) ACDHA
American Creativity Association (EA) ACA
American Cricket Growers Association [*Defunct*] (EA) ACGA
American Crime Fighters (EA) ACF
American Crime Writers League [*An association*] ACWL
American Criminal Justice Association [*A publication*] (DLA) ACJA
American Criminal Justice Association - Lambda Alpha Epsilon (EA) ACJA-LAE
American Criminal Justice Association-Lambda Alpha Epsilon (SAUO) ACJA-LAE
American Criminal Reports [*A publication*] (DLA) Am Cr
American Criminal Reports [*A publication*] (DLA) Am Cr R
American Criminal Reports, Edited by Hawley [*A publication*] (DLA) ACR
American Criminal Reports, Edited by Hawley [*A publication*] (DLA) Am Cr Rep
American Criminal Reports, Edited by Hawley [*A publication*] (DLA) Am Cr R (Hawley)
American Criminal Reports (journ.) (SAUS) ACR
American Criminal Trials (Chandler) [*A publication*] (DLA) Am Cr Tr
American Crisis Biographies (SAUS) ACB
American Croatian Academic Club [*Later, ACAS*] ACAC
American Croatian Academic Society [*Formerly, ACAC*] (EA) ACAS

American Croating Academic Club (SAUO) ... ACAC
American Crop Protection Association (NTPA) ... ACPA
American Crossbow Association (EA) ... ACA
American Crossbred Pony Registry (EA) ... ACPR
American Crossword Federation (EA) ... ACF
American Cryogenics Inc. (SAUS) ... ACI
American Cryogenics Incorporated (SAUO) ... ACI
American Cryonics Society (EA) ... ACS
American Cryptogram Association (EA) ... ACA
American Crystal Sugar (SAUS) ... ACS
American Crystal Sugar Co. (MHDW) ... ACS
American Crystallographic Association (EA) ... ACA
American Crystallographic Community ... ACC
American Crystallographic Society (SAUO) ... ACA
American Culinary Federation (EA) ... ACF
American Cultural Resources Association ... ACRA
American Cultural Society [*Defunct*] ... ACS
American Culture Association (EA) ... ACA
American Cultured Dairy Products Institute (EA) ... ACDPI
American Custard Glass Collectors (EA) ... ACGC
American Custom Gunmakers Guild (EA) ... ACGG
American Cut Glass Association (EA) ... ACGA
American Cutlery Manufacturers Association (EA) ... ACMA
American Cyanamid Co. (KSC) ... ACC
American Cyanamid Co. ... ACCO
American Cyanamid Co. (SAUS) ... ACY
American Cyanamid Co., Agricultural Division, Princeton, NJ [*Library symbol*] [*Library of Congress*] (LCLS) ... NjPA
American Cyanamid Co., Lederle Laboratories, Pearl River, NY [*Library symbol*] [*Library of Congress*] (LCLS) ... NPrA
American Cyanamid Co., Organic Chemicals Division, Bound Brook, NJ [*Library symbol*] [*Library of Congress*] (LCLS) ... NjBbA
American Cyanamid Co., Pigments Division, Piney River, VA [*Library symbol*] [*Library of Congress*] (LCLS) ... ViPrA
American Cyanamid Co., Pigments Divismon, Piney River (SAUS) ... ViPrA
American Cyanamid Co., Princeton, NJ [*OCLC symbol*] (OCLC) ... ACA
American Cyanamid Co., Stamford, CT [*Library symbol*] [*Library of Congress*] (LCLS) ... CtSA
American Cyanamid Company (SAUO) ... ACC
American Cyanamid Company (SAUO) ... ACCO
American Cyanamid Company (SAUO) ... ACY
American Cycling Union (EA) ... ACU
American Cyclopedia (SAUS) ... Am Cyc
American Cyphermaster Ltd. (SAUO) ... ACY
American Cystoscope Makers, Inc. (SAUO) ... ACMI
American Cystoscope Makers Incorporated (SAUO) ... ACMI
American Cytogenetics, Inc. (SAUO) ... ACYT
American Czech and Slovak Association (EA) ... ACSA
American Czechoslovak Society (EA) ... ACS
American Daffodil Society (EA) ... ADS
American Dahlia Society (EA) ... ADS
American Dairy Association (EA) ... ADA
American Dairy Association and Dairy Council (SRA) ... ADADC
American Dairy Association of Georgia and Alabama (SRA) ... ADAG
American Dairy Association of Virginia (SRA) ... ADAV
American Dairy Federation (SAUO) ... ADF
American Dairy Goat Association (EA) ... ADGA
American Dairy Goat Products Association (EA) ... ADGPA
American Dairy Products Institute (EA) ... ADPI
American Dairy Science Association (EA) ... ADSA
American Dairy Science Association (SAUS) ... ADSA
American Daleco Technologies, Inc. [*Vancouver Stock Exchange symbol*] ... AAD
American Dance Asylum ... ADA
American Dance Ensemble ... ADE
American Dance Festival [*Later, AADF*] (EA) ... ADF
American Dance Guild (EA) ... ADG
American Dance Machine ... ADM
American Dance Therapy Association (EA) ... ADTA
American Dart Association [*Defunct*] (EA) ... ADA
American Darts Organization (EA) ... ADO
American Data Processing Inc. (SAUO) ... ADP
American Data Processing, Inc. (SAUS) ... ADP
American Data Systems (SAUS) ... ADS
American Deaf Volleyball Association (EA) ... ADVA
American Deaf Volleyball Association (EA) ... ADVBA
American Deafness and Rehabilitation Association (EA) ... ADARA
American Decartelization Agency [*Post-World War II*] ... AMDAG
American Decca [*Record label*] ... AmD
American Decisions [*A publication*] (DLA) ... AD
American Decisions [*A publication*] (DLA) ... Am D
American Decisions [*A publication*] (DLA) ... Am Dec's
American Decisions [*A publication*] (DLA) ... Amer Dec
American Decisions, Select Cases [*San Francisco, CA*] [*A publication*] (DLA) ... Am Dec
American Deep Drawing Research Group (DICI) ... ADDRG
American Defenders [*Defunct*] (EA) ... AD
American Defenders Against Animal Mistreatment [*Inactive*] (EA) ... ADAM
American Defenders of Bataan and Corregidor (EA) ... ADBC
American Defense Foundation (EA) ... ADF
American Defense Institute (EA) ... ADI
American Defense Preparedness Association (EA) ... ADPA
American Defense Service Medal (BARN) ... ADSM
American Dehydrated Onion and Garlic Association (EA) ... ADOGA
American Dehydration Association (SAUO) ... ADA
American Dehydrators Association (SAUO) ... ADA
American Dehydrators Association [*Later, AAPA*] (EA) ... ADA
American Democratic Political Action Committee (EA) ... ADPAC
American Dental Assistants Association (SAUO) ... ADA
American Dental Assistants Association (EA) ... ADAA
American Dental Assistant's Program ... ADAP
American Dental Assistants Program (SAUS) ... ADAP
American Dental Association (EA) ... ADA
American Dental Association (SAUO) ... Am Dent
American Dental Association, Chicago, IL [*Library symbol*] [*Library of Congress*] (LCLS) ... ICADA
American Dental Association, Chicago, IL [*OCLC symbol*] (OCLC) ... JAA
American Dental Association Continuing Education Recognition Program (SAUO) ... ADA CERP
American Dental Association Health Foundation ... ADAHF
American Dental Association Specifications ... ADAS
American Dental Education Association (SAUO) ... ADEA
American Dental Equipment Company (SAUO) ... ADEC
American Dental Hygienists' Association (EA) ... ADHA
American Dental Hygienists Association (SAUS) ... ADHA
American Dental Institute [*Formerly, Dental Information*] (EA) ... DI
American Dental Interfraternity Council (EA) ... ADIC
American Dental LaserAm [*NASDAQ symbol*] (SAG) ... ADLI
American Dental LaserAm [*Associated Press*] (SAG) ... AmDentl
American Dental Library and Museum Association (SAUO) ... ADLMA
American Dental Service (SAUO) ... ADS
American Dental Society (SAUO) ... ADS
American Dental Society of Anesthesiology (EA) ... ADSA
American Dental Society of Europe (EA) ... ADSE
American Dental Technologies (EFIS) ... ADTEC
American Dental Trade Association (EA) ... ADTA
American Dentists for Foreign Service (EA) ... ADFS
American Denture Society ... ADS
American Depositary Receipt (SAUS) ... ADR
American Depositary Receipts ... ADRS
American Depositary Share (ECON) ... ADS
American Depository Receipts ... ADR
American Depot Unit (SAUS) ... ADU
American Dermatologic Society of Allergy and Immunology (EA) ... ADSAI
American Dermatological Association (EA) ... ADA
American Desalting Association (NTPA) ... ADA
American Deserters Committee, France (EA) ... ADC
American Desertes Committee (SAUO) ... ADC
American Design Bicentennial [*An association*] [*Defunct*] (EA) ... ADB
American Design Drafting Association (EA) ... ADDA
American Designers Institute (SAUS) ... ADI
American Development Corp (SAUS) ... ADCOR
American Devon Cattle Club [*Later, Devon Cattle Association*] (EA) ... ADCC
American Dexter Cattle Association (EA) ... ADCA
American Diabetes Association (EA) ... ADA
American Diagnostics Corp. ... AmD
American Dialect Dictionary (ACAE) ... ADD
American Dialect Society (EA) ... ADS
American Diamond Industry Association (EA) ... ADIA
American Diary Goat Association (SAUS) ... ADGA
American Die Casting Institute (EA) ... ADCI
American Die Casting Institute, Inc. ... ADCII
American Dietetic Association (EA) ... ADA
American Digest [*A publication*] (DLA) ... Am Dig
American Digest (Century Edition) [*A publication*] (DLA) ... Am Cent Dig
American Digest (Century Edition) [*A publication*] (DLA) ... Am Dig Cent Ed
American Digest (Decennial Edition) [*A publication*] (ILCA) ... Decen Dig
American Digest (Decennial Edition) (West) [*A publication*] (DLA) ... Am Dig Dec Ed
American Digest (Decennial Edition) (West) [*A publication*] (DLA) ... Am Dig Decen Ed
American Digest (Eighth Decennial Edition) (West) [*A publication*] (DLA) ... Am Dig Eighth Dec Ed
American Digest (Fifth Decennial Edition) (West) [*A publication*] (DLA) ... Am Dig Fifth Dec Ed
American Digest (Fourth Decennial Edition) (West) [*A publication*] (DLA) ... Am Dig Fourth Dec Ed
American Digest (Key Number Series) (West) [*A publication*] (DLA) ... Am Dig Key No Ser
American Digest (Second Decennial Edition) (West) [*A publication*] (DLA) ... Am Dig Secd Dec Ed
American Digest (Seventh Decennial Edition) (West) [*A publication*] (DLA) ... Am Dig Seventh Dec Ed
American Digest (Sixth Decennial Edition) (West) [*A publication*] (DLA) ... Am Dig Sixth Dec Ed
American Digest System, Decennial Digests [*A publication*] (DLA) ... Dec Dig
American Digest (Third Decennial Edition) (West) [*A publication*] (DLA) ... Am Dig Third Dec Ed
American Digestive Disease Society (EA) ... ADDS
American Digestive Health Foundation ... ADHF
American Digital Cartography ... ADC
American Digital Cartography Inc. (SAUO) ... ADC
American Dinner Theater Institute (SAUO) ... ADTI
American Dinner Theatre Institute (EA) ... ADTI
American Diopter and Decibel Society (EA) ... ADDS
American Directors Institute (EA) ... ADI
American Directory of Organized Labor [*A publication*] ... ADOL
American Disability Evaluation Research Institute [*Research center*] (RCD) ... ADERI
American Disabled for Accessible Public Transit (EA) ... ADAPT
American Disabled for Attendant Program Today [*An association*] (EA) ... ADAPT

American Disabled for Attendant Programs Today (ADWA) .... Adapt
American Disposal Services, Inc. [NASDAQ symbol] (SAG) .... ADSI
American Disposal Services, Inc. [Associated Press] (SAG) .... AmDisp
American Distilling Company (SAUO) .... ADC
American District Telegraph .... ADT
American Ditchley Foundation (EA) .... ADF
American Diversified Dog Society [Defunct] (EA) .... ADDS
American Divorce Association for Men .... ADAM
American Divorce Association of Men International (EA) .... ADAM
American Dock Company (SAUO) .... ADC
American Doctoral Dissertations [A publication] .... ADD
American Doctorial Dissertation (journ.) (SAUS) .... ADD
American Doctors (SAUS) .... Amdoc
American Doctors [Later, PCOS] (EA) .... AMDOC
American Doctors (SAUO) .... AMDOC
American Documentation Institute (SAUO) .... ADI
American Documentation Institute [Later, American Society for Information
  Science] .... ADI
American Documentation Institute (SAUO) .... Am Doc Inst
American Documentation (journ.) (SAUS) .... AD
American Dog Breeders Association [Defunct] (EA) .... ADBA
American Dog Feed Institute [Defunct] (EA) .... ADFI
American Dog Owners Association (EA) .... ADOA
American Dog Tick (MELL) .... ADT
American Dog Trainers Network (NTPA) .... ADTN
American Donkey and Mule Society (EA) .... ADMS
American Double Dutch League (EA) .... ADDL
American Dove Association (EA) .... ADA
American Down Association (EA) .... ADA
American Drag Racing Association [Commercial firm] (EA) .... ADRA
American Dredging Company (SAUO) .... ADCO
American Dressage Institute .... ADI
American Driver and Traffic Safety Education Association (EA) .... ADTSEA
American Driver Education Association [Later, ADTSEA] (EA) .... ADEA
American Driving Society (EA) .... ADS
American Drug Manufacturers (SAUO) .... ADM
American Drug Manufacturers' Association [Later, PMA] .... ADMA
American Druze Public Affairs Committee (EA) .... AD-PAC
American Druze Society (EA) .... ADS
American Dry Milk Institute [Later, ADPI] (EA) .... ADMI
American Dual Vest Fund, Inc. (SAUO) .... ADV
American Dutch Rabbit Club (EA) .... ADRC
American Duty Free [Freight] .... ADF
American Dyestuff Reporter (journ.) (SAUS) .... Amer Dyestuff Rep
American Eagle Group [Associated Press] (SAG) .... AEagIG
American Eagle Group [Associated Press] (SAG) .... AmEagl
American Eagle Group [NYSE symbol] (SAG) .... FLI
American Eagle Outfitters, Inc. [Associated Press] (SAG) .... AEagleO
American Eagle Outfitters, Inc. [NASDAQ symbol] (SAG) .... AEOS
American Eagle Petroleums Corp. [Toronto Stock Exchange symbol] .... AEO
American Ear Association for Research (EA) .... AEAR
American Eco Corp. [Associated Press] (SAG) .... AmerEco
American Eco Corp. [NASDAQ symbol] (SAG) .... ECGO
American Ecology Corp. [Associated Press] (SAG) .... AmEcol
American Ecology Corp. [NASDAQ symbol] (SAG) .... ECOL
American Ecology Services (EA) .... AES
American Economic Association (EA) .... AEA
American Economic Association Bulletin (journ.) (SAUS) .... Am Econ Assn Bul
American Economic Association Publications (journ.)
  (SAUS) .... Am Econ Assoc Pub
American Economic Council (EA) .... AEC
American Economic Development Council (EA) .... AEDC
American Economic Foundation (EA) .... AEF
American Economic Review (SAUS) .... Am Econ Rev
American Economic Review (journ.) (SAUS) .... AMER
American Economic Review, Papers and Proceedings (journ.)
  (SAUS) .... Am Econ R Papers&Proc
American Edge Collectors Association (EA) .... AECA
American Edition (DLA) .... Am Ed
American Editorial Association (SAUO) .... AEA
American Education Association (EA) .... AEA
American Education Coalition [Defunct] (EA) .... AEC
American Education Fellowship [Defunct] (AEBS) .... AEF
American Education Finance Association (EA) .... AEFA
American Education (journ.) (SAUS) .... AMED
American Education Week .... AEW
American Educational Computer Inc. (SAUO) .... AEDC
American Educational Computer, Inc. (SAUS) .... AEDC
American Educational Gender Information Service (EA) .... AEGIS
American Educational Products [NASDAQ symbol] (SAG) .... AMEP
American Educational Products, Inc. [Associated Press] (SAG) .... AmEduc
American Educational Publishers Institute [Later, AAP] .... AEPI
American Educational Research Association (EA) .... AERA
American Educational Research Journal [A publication] (DHP) .... AERJ
American Educational Society (EA) .... AES
American Educational Studies Association (EA) .... AESA
American Educational Television Network [Cable-television system] .... AETN
American Educational Theater Association (SAUO) .... AETA
American Educational Theatre Association [Later, ATA] (EA) .... AETA
American Egg Board (EA) .... AEB
American Egyptian Cooperation Foundation (EA) .... AECF
American Election Commission [Defunct] (EA) .... AEC
American Electric Co., Ltd. (EFIS) .... AMELCO
American Electric Power .... AEP
American Electric Power Co., Inc. [Associated Press] (SAG) .... AEIPw

American Electric Power Co., Inc. [NYSE symbol] (SAG) .... AEP
American Electric Power Co., Inc. Unified Dial Network (TEL) .... AUDINET
American Electric Power, Inc. (SAUO) .... AEP
American Electric Power Service (SAUO) .... AEPS
American Electric Power Service Corporation (SAUO) .... AEPSC
American Electric Power Service Corporation-Ohio Valley Electric
  Corporation (SAUO) .... AEP-OVEC
American Electric Railway Association (SAUO) .... AERA
American Electric Railway Engineering Association (SAUO) .... AEREA
American Electrical Association (SAUO) .... AEA
American Electrical Cases [A publication] (DLA) .... AEC
American Electrical Cases [A publication] (ILCA) .... Am El Ca
American Electrical Cases [A publication] (ILCA) .... Am Elec Ca
American Electrical Cases [A publication] (DLA) .... Am Elect Cas
American Electrical Cases [A publication] (ILCA) .... Am Electl Cas
American Electrical Cases [A publication] (DLA) .... Am Electr Cas
American Electrical Cases [A publication] (DLA) .... Amer Elec Ca
American Electro Chemical Society (SAUS) .... AECS
American Electro Metal Corporation (SAUO) .... AEMC
American Electro-Chemical Society (SAUO) .... AECS
American Electrochemical Society [Later, ECS] .... AES
American Electroencephalographic Society (EA) .... AEEGS
American Electroencephalographic Society (SAUO) .... AEES
American Electroencephalographic Society (EA) .... AES
American Electrology Association (EA) .... AEA
American Electrolysis Association (SAUO) .... AEA
American Electromechanical Society .... AES
American Electromedics Corporation (SAUO) .... AECO
American Electronic Co. (SAUO) .... AECO
American Electronic Components, Inc. [NASDAQ symbol] (SAG) .... AECI
American Electronic Components, Inc. [Associated Press] (SAG) .... AEICmp
American Electronic Laboratories (SAUS) .... AEL
American Electronic Laboratories, Inc. .... AEL
American Electronic Research Association (SAUO) .... AERA
American Electronical Society .... AES
American Electronics Association (EA) .... AEA
American Electronics Inc. (SAUO) .... AMELEX
American Electronics Laboratory (AAGC) .... AEL
American Electrophoresis Society (HGEN) .... AES
American Electroplaters & Surface Finishers Society [Association des
  Galvanoplastes d'Amerique] [Formerly, American Electroplaters Society]
  (AC) .... AESF
American Electroplaters' and Surface Finishers Society (EA) .... AESFS
American Electroplaters and Surface Finishers Society (SAUS) .... AESFS
American Electroplaters' and Surface Finishers Society Exposition
  (ITD) .... SUR/FIN
American Electroplaters and Surface Finishers Society Exposit²on
  (SAUS) .... SUR/FIN
American Electroplaters and Surface Finishers Society, Inc. (SAUS) .... AESF
American Electroplaters Society (SAUO) .... AEPS
American Electroplaters Society (SAUO) .... AES
American Electroplaters' Society (EA) .... AES
American Electroplating Society (SAUO) .... AES
American Electrotechnical Society (SAUO) .... AES
American Elsevier Publishing Co. (DGA) .... AEPCO
American Elsevier Publishing Company (SAUO) .... AEPCO
American Elsevier Publishing Company (SAUO) .... Am Elsevier
American Embassy (SAUO) .... AE
American Embassy .... AE
American Embassy (DNAB) .... AMEB
American Embassy (AFM) .... AMEMB
American Embassy (SAUO) .... AMEmb
American Embryo Transfer Association (EA) .... AETA
American Emergency Committee for Tibetan Refugees [Defunct] (EA) .... AECTR
American Emigrants' League (EA) .... AEL
American Emu Association (NTPA) .... AEA
American Encephalographic Society [Neurophysiology] (DAVI) .... AES
American Encyclopedic Dictionary [A publication] (DLA) .... Am Enc Dict
American Endocrine Society (DAVI) .... AES
American Endodontic Society (EA) .... AES
American Endurance Ride Conference (EA) .... AERC
American Energy Month [Defunct] (EA) .... AEM
American Energy Union (SAUO) .... AMEU
American Energy Week [Later, AEM] [An association] (EA) .... AEW
American Engine Rebuilders Association (SAUO) .... AERA
American Engineer (SAUS) .... Am Engr
American Engineering Association [Defunct] (EA) .... AEA
American Engineering Council .... AEC
American Engineering Model Society (EA) .... AEMS
American Engineering Standards Committee [Later, ANSI] .... AESC
American English (ADWA) .... AE
American English [Language] (WGA) .... AmE
American English (SAUS) .... Ameringlish
American English Spot Rabbit Club (EA) .... AESRC
American Enka Corp. .... ANK
American Enka Corp., Enka, NC [Library symbol] [Library of Congress]
  (LCLS) .... NcEnk
American Enterprise Association (SAUO) .... AEA
American Enterprise Association [Later, AEI] .... AEA
American Enterprise Institute (ACAE) .... AEI
American Enterprise Institute for Public Policy Research (EA) .... AEI
American Enterprise Institute for Public Policy Research (EA) .... AEIPPR
American Enterprise Institute for Public Policy Research (SAUO) .... AEIPRR
American Entomological Society (EA) .... AES
American Entrepreneurs Association [Defunct] (EA) .... AEA

American Entrepreneurs for Economic Growth (SAUS) .... AEEG
American Enuresis Foundation (SAUO) .... AEF
American Environmental Health Foundation (SAUO) .... AEHF
American Environmental Management Corp. (EFIS) .... AEMC
American Environmental Manufacturers Association (SAUO) .... AEMA
American Environments Company Inc. (SAUO) .... AE
American Ephemeris (SAUS) .... AE
American Epidemiological Society (EA) .... AES
American Epilepsy Society (EA) .... AES
American Equilibration Society (EA) .... AES
American Equine Association (EA) .... AEA
American Eskimo Association (EA) .... AEA
American Esquire [*Record label*] .... AmEsq
American Ethical Union (EA) .... AEU
American Ethnic Science Society (SAUO) .... AESS
American Ethnological Society (EA) .... AES
American Ethnologist [*A publication*] (BRI) .... Am Ethnol
American Ethnology Bureau [*British*] (DAS) .... AEB
American Eugenics Society [*Later, SSSB*] (EA) .... AES
American European Foundation [*Later, SFMJF*] (EA) .... AEF
American European Foundation (SAUO) .... AEF
American Euthanasia Foundation (EA) .... AEF
American Evaluation Association (EA) .... AEA
American Evangelical Lutheran Church (SAUO) .... AELC
American Excess Insurance Association [*East Hartford, CT*] (EA) .... AEIA
American Executives for Management Excellence [*An association*] (EA) .... AEME
American Exiles .... AMEX
American Exmoor Pony Registry (EA) .... AEPR
American Expeditionary Force [*World War I*] .... AEF
American Expeditionary Force (SAUO) .... AMEX
American Expeditionary Forces (SAUO) .... AEF
American Exploration Co. [*Associated Press*] (SAG) .... AExpl
American Exploration Co. [*AMEX symbol*] (SPSG) .... AX
American Exploration Co. [*AMEX symbol*] (SAG) .... AXpC
American Export Airlines .... AEA
American Export Industries Company (SAUO) .... AEX
American Export Isbrandtsen Lines [*Later, American Export Industries Co.*] .... AEIL
American Export Lines (SAUO) .... AMEX
American Export Lines, Inc. (SAUO) .... AEL
American Export Lines, Inc. (SAUO) .... AELI
American Export-Isbrandtsen Lines (SAUS) .... E
American Express (NTIO) .... AmEx
American Express Card [*Credit card*] .... AEC
American Express Co. (CDAI) .... AE
American Express Co. [*Associated Press*] (SAG) .... AExp
American Express Co. [*Associated Press*] (SAG) .... AExp 96
American Express Co. .... AMEX
American Express Co. .... AMEXCO
American Express Co. [*Associated Press*] (SAG) .... AmExp
American Express Co. (ADA) .... AX
American Express Co. [*NYSE symbol*] (SAG) .... AXD
American Express Co. [*NYSE symbol*] [*Toronto Stock Exchange symbol*] (SPSG) .... AXP
American Express Company (SAUO) .... AMEX
American Express Company (SAUO) .... AMEXCO
American Express Institute (SAUO) .... AEI
American Express Interactive [*Corporate travel computer site*] .... AXI
American Express International Banking Corporation (SAUO) .... AEIBC
American Express International Development Company (SAUO) .... AEIDC
American Express International Fund S.A. (SAUO) .... AEIFSA
American Express Line (SAUO) .... AEL
American Ex-Prisoners of War (EA) .... XPW
American Fabricating Institute of Technology [*Defunct*] (EA) .... AFIT
American Fabrics (journ.) (SAUS) .... AF
American Facsimile Association [*Later, IFAXA*] (EA) .... AFaxA
American Factory Trawler Association (NTPA) .... AFTA
American Fair Trade Council (SAUO) .... AFTC
American Fair Trade Council [*Sausalito, CA*] (EA) .... AMTC
American Falls District Library, American Falls, ID [*Library symbol*] [*Library of Congress*] (LCLS) .... IdAm
American Falls High School, American Falls, ID [*Library symbol*] [*Library of Congress*] (LCLS) .... IdAmHS
American Falls, ID [*FM radio station call letters*] (RBYB) .... KORR
American Falls, ID [*FM radio station call letters*] .... KOUU
American Family Association (EA) .... AFA
American Family Communiversity (EA) .... AFCO
American Family Farm and Ranch Association (EA) .... AFFRA
American Family Farm Foundation (EA) .... AFFF
American Family Foundation (EA) .... AFF
American Family Heritage Society [*Defunct*] (EA) .... AFHS
American Family Member .... AFM
American Family Physician (SAUS) .... AFP
American Family Physician [*A publication*] (MEC) .... Am Fam Phy
American Family Physician (journ.) (SAUS) .... Amer Fam Physician
American Family Publishers (SAUO) .... AFP
American Family Records Association (EA) .... AFRA
American Family Restaurants, Inc. [*Associated Press*] (SAG) .... AFamR
American Family Restaurants, Inc. [*AMEX symbol*] (SAG) .... FRI
American Family Society (EA) .... AFS
American Family Therapy Association (EA) .... AFTA
American Fan Association (EA) .... AFA
American Fan Collectors Association (EA) .... AFCA
American Fancy Rat and Mouse Association (EA) .... AFRMA
American Fans of Jon Pertwee (EA) .... AFOJP
American Far Eastern Society (EA) .... AFES
American Farm Bureau .... AFB
American Farm Bureau Federation (EA) .... AFBF
American Farm Bureau Research Foundation (EA) .... AFBRF
American Farm Economic Association [*Later, AAEA*] (EA) .... AFEA
American Farm Foundation [*Defunct*] (EA) .... AFF
American Farm Research Association [*Superseded by AFBRF*] (EA) .... AFRA
American Farm Research Association, Lafayette (SAUO) .... AFRA
American Farmer Labor Party (SAUO) .... AFLP
American Farmland Investment, Inc. (SAUO) .... AFI
American Farmland Trust (EA) .... AFT
American Farriers Association (EA) .... AFA
American Fashion Association (EA) .... AFA
American Fashion Home Sewing Council (SAUO) .... AFHSC
American Fashion Homesewing Council .... AFHSC
American Fastener and Closure Association [*Defunct*] (EA) .... AFCA
American Federal Bank [*NASDAQ symbol*] (CTT) .... AMFB
American Federal Communication Commission (SAUO) .... AFCC
American Federal Office of the Mercantile Marine (SAUO) .... AFOMM
American Federal Tax Reports [*Prentice-Hall, Inc.*] [*A publication*] (DLA) ...... AFTR
American Federal Tax Reports [*Prentice-Hall, Inc.*] [*A publication*] (DLA) .... Amer Fed Tax Rep
American Federal Tax Reports [*Prentice-Hall, Inc.*] [*A publication*] (DLA) .... Am Fed Tax R
American Federal Tax Reports (Prentice-Hall, Inc.) [*A publication*] (DLA) .... P-H Cas
American Federal Tax Reports, Second Series [*Prentice-Hall, Inc.*] [*A publication*] (DLA) AFTR2d
American Federal Tax Reports, Second Series [*Prentice-Hall, Inc.*] [*A publication*] (DLA) .... Am Fed Tax R 2d
American Federation for Aging Research (EA) .... AFAR
American Federation for Clinical Research (EA) .... AFCR
American Federation for Medical Research (NTPA) .... AFMR
American Federation for Polish Jews (SAUO) .... AFPJ
American Federation for the Blind (SAUO) .... AFB
American Federation for the Pueri Cantores (EA) .... AFPC
American Federation for/of Medical Research (SAUO) .... AFMR
American Federation of Arts (EA) .... AFA
American Federation of Astrologers (EA) .... AFA
American Federation of Aviculture (EA) .... AFA
American Federation of Catholic Workers for the Blind [*Later, CAPVI*] (EA) .... AFCWB
American Federation of Catholic Workers for the Blind and Visually Handicapped (SAUO) .... AFCWBVH
American Federation of Film Societies [*Defunct*] (EA) .... AFFS
American Federation of Foundrymen (SAUO) .... AFF
American Federation of Government Employees (EA) .... AFGE
American Federation of Grain Millers (EA) .... AFGM
American Federation of Guards (EA) .... AFG
American Federation of Home Health Agencies (EA) .... AFHHA
American Federation of Hosiery Workers [*Later, ACTWU*] .... AFHW
American Federation of Hosiery Workers (SAUO) .... AFHW
American Federation of Information Processing [*Formerly, AFIPS*] .... AFIP
American Federation of Information Processing Societies [*Later, AFIP*] (EA) .... AFIPS
American Federation of International Institutes [*Later, ACNS*] .... AFII
American Federation of Italian Evangelicals [*Later, AEIM*] (EA) .... AFIE
American Federation of Italian Evangelicals (SAUO) .... AFIE
American Federation of Jewish Fighters, Camp Inmates and Nazi Victims [*Defunct*] (EA) .... AFJFCINV
American Federation of Jews from Central Europe (EA) .... AFJCE
American Federation of Labor [*Later, AFL-CIO*] (GPO) .... AFL
American Federation of Labor (SAUO) .... AFL
American Federation of Labor (SAUO) .... AF of L
American Federation of Labor [*Later, AFL-CIO*] .... AF of L
American Federation of Labor and Congress of Industrial Organizations Library, Washington, DC [*Library symbol*] [*Library of Congress*] (LCLS) .... DAFL
American Federation of Labor-Congress of Industrial Organizations (SAUO) .... AFL-CIO
American Federation of Labor/Congress of Industrial Organizations (AL) .... AFL/CIO
American Federation of Medical Accreditation (EA) .... AFMA
American Federation of Medical Research (HGEN) .... AFMR
American Federation of Mineralogical Societies (EA) .... AFMS
American Federation of Musicians (SAUO) .... AFM
American Federation of Musicians of the United States and Canada [*Later, THFC*] (EA) .... AFM
American Federation of Musicians of the United States and Canada [*Later, THFC*] .... AFMUSC
American Federation of Negro Affairs (SAUO) .... AFNA
American Federation of New Zealand Rabbit Breeders (EA) .... AFNZRB
American Federation of Physicians and Dentists (SAUO) .... AFPD
American Federation of Police (EA) .... AFP
American Federation of Police and Concerned Citizens (NTPA) .... AFP&CC
American Federation of Polish Jews (EA) .... AFPJ
American Federation of Poultry Producers Associations [*Defunct*] (EA) .... AFPPA
American Federation of Priests .... AFP
American Federation of Radio Artists .... AFRA
American Federation of Retail Kosher Butchers (EA) .... AFRKB
American Federation of School Administrators (EA) .... AFSA
American Federation of School Administrators and Supervisors [*AFL-CIO*] .... AFSAS
American Federation of Scientists (SAUO) .... AFS

American Federation of Small Business [*Chicago, IL*] (EA) .... AFSB
American Federation of Small Business Organizations (SAUO) .... AFSBO
American Federation of Soroptimist Clubs [*Later, Soroptimist International of the Americas*] .... AFSC
American Federation of State, County, and Municipal Employees (EA) .... AFSCME
American Federation of State, County and Municipal Employees (SAUO) .... AFSCME
American Federation of State, County, and Municipal Employees .... SCME
American Federation of Teachers (SAUO) .... AFT
American Federation of Teachers in Virginia (SRA) .... AFTVA
American Federation of Technical Engineers (SAUO) .... AFTE
American Federation of Technical Engineers [*Later, International Federation of Professional and Technical Engineers*] (EA) .... AFTE
American Federation of Television and Radio Artists (EA) .... AFTRA
American Federation of the Physically Handicapped .... AFPH
American Federation of Violin and Bow Makers (EA) .... AFVBM
American Federation of World Citizens [*Later, Fellowship of World Citizens*] (EA) .... AFWC
American Feed Industry Association (EA) .... AFIA
American Feed Manufacturers Association [*Later, AFIA*] (EA) .... AFMA
American Feed Manufacturers Association (SAUO) .... Am Feed
American Feline Society (EA) .... AFS
American Female Impersonators Association (EA) .... AFIA
American Fence Association (NTPA) .... AFA
American Fern Society (EA) .... AFS
American Ferret Association (GVA) .... AFA
American Fertility Society (EA) .... AFS
American Fertility Society Classification of Endometriosis .... AFSCE
American Festival Ballet .... AFB
American Festival of Microtonal Music (EA) .... AFMM
American Fiber Institute .... AFI
American Fiber Manufacturers Association (EA) .... AFMA
American Fiber, Textile, Apparel Coalition (EA) .... AFTAC
American Fiberboard Association (NTPA) .... AFA
American Fibre Corp. [*Vancouver Stock Exchange symbol*] .... AFB
American Field Scholarship (SAUO) .... AFS
American Field Service [*Later, AFSIIP*] .... AFS
American Fighter Aces Association (EA) .... AFAA
American Fighter Aces Museum Foundation (EA) .... AFAMF
American Fighter Pilots Association (SAUO) .... AFPA
American Film and Video Association (EA) .... AFVA
American Film Export Association (EA) .... AFEA
American Film Institute (EA) .... AFI
American Film Institute Alumni Association Writers Workshop (EA) .... AFIAAWW
American Film Institute, Center for Advanced Film Studies, Beverly Hills, CA [*Library symbol*] [*Library of Congress*] (LCLS) .... CBevA
American Film Marketing Association (EA) .... AFMA
American Film Processor Corp. (EFIS) .... AFP
American Film Technologies, Inc. (SAUS) .... AFTI
American Film Technologies Incorporated (SAUO) .... AFTI
American Film Technology (EFIS) .... AFTI
American Film Theater .... AFT
American Filter Institute (SAUO) .... AFI
American Filtration and Separations Society (NTPA) .... AFS
American Filtrona Corp. .... AFC
American Filtrona Corp. [*NASDAQ symbol*] (NQ) .... AFIL
American Filtrona Corp. [*Associated Press*] (SAG) .... AFiltrn
American Finance Association (EA) .... AFA
American Finance Conference [*Later, NCFA*] (EA) .... AFC
American Finance System (SAUO) .... AFS
American Financial Group, Inc. [*NYSE symbol*] (SAG) .... AFG
American Financial Group, Inc. [*Associated Press*] (SAG) .... AFnclGp
American Financial Services Association [*Washington, DC*] (EA) .... AFSA
American Fine Arts Society (EA) .... AFAS
American Fine China Guild (EA) .... AFCG
American Fire Sprinkler Association (EA) .... AFSA
American Firearm Association (EA) .... AFA
American Firearms Industry [*A publication*] (EAAP) .... AFI
American Firewalking Association (EA) .... AFA
American First Committee (SAUO) .... AFC
American First Day Cover Foundation [*Defunct*] (EA) .... AFDCF
American First Day Cover Society (EA) .... AFDCS
American First PREP [*Preferred Real Estate Participation*] **Fund 2 Ltd.** [*AMEX symbol*] (SPSG) .... PF
American Fish Decoy Association (EA) .... AFDA
American Fish Farmers Federation [*Defunct*] (EA) .... AFFF
American Fisheries Advisory Committee .... AFAC
American Fisheries Protection Act .... AFPA
American Fisheries School (USDC) .... AFS
American Fisheries Society (EA) .... AFS
American Fisheries Society Symposium (SAUO) .... Am Fish Soc Symp
American Fishing Tackle Manufacturers Association (EA) .... AFTMA
American Fitness Association (EA) .... AFA
American Flag Association [*Defunct*] (EA) .... AFA
American Flag Committee (EA) .... AFC
American Flag Day Association (SAUO) .... AFDA
American Flag Institute [*Defunct*] (EA) .... AFI
American Flagship Available .... AFSA
American Fletcher National Bank (SAUO) .... AFNB
American Flight Echocardiograph (NAKS) .... AFE
American Flight Electrocardiograph (SAUS) .... AFE
American Flight Service Systems, Inc. [*ICAO designator*] (FAAC) .... XFS
American Flight Strips Association (EA) .... AFSA
American Flint Glass Workers (SAUO) .... AFGW
American Flint Glass Workers Union (EA) .... AFGWU
American Flint Glass Workers' Union of North America [*Later, AFGWU*] .... AFGW
American Flock Association (EA) .... AFA
American Floral Marketing Council (EA) .... AFMC
American Florists Association (EA) .... AFA
American Fluid Technology .... AFT
American Flux Measurement Network (SAUS) .... AMERIFLUX
American Flyers Airline (MCD) .... AFA
American Flywheel Systems [*Research center*] (ECON) .... AFS
American Folklife Center [*Library of Congress*] .... AFC
American Folklife Preservation Act [*1976*] .... AFPA
American Folklore Society (SAUO) .... AFLS
American Folklore Society (EA) .... AFS
American Food for Peace Council [*Defunct*] (EA) .... AFPC
American Food Manufacturers Association (SAUO) .... AFMA
American Foot and Ankle Society (SAUO) .... AFAS
American Foot Care Institute [*Defunct*] (EA) .... AFCI
American Foot Health Foundation (EA) .... AFHF
American Football Coaches Association (EA) .... AFCA
American Football Conference [*of NFL*] .... AFC
American Football League [*Reorganized as part of AFC and NFC*] (EA) .... AFL
American Footwear Industries Association [*Later, FIA*] .... AFIA
American Footwear Manufacturers' Association [*Later, FIA*] .... AFMA
American for Indian Opportunity (SAUO) .... AIO
American for Peace and Democracy in the Middle East (SAUO) .... APDME
American for Progressive Israel (SAUO) .... API
American Forage and Grassland Council [*Lexington, KY*] .... AFGC
American Forces Caribbean Network (SAUO) .... AFCN
American Forces in Action [*Military*] .... AFA
American Forces Information Council (DOMA) .... AFIC
American Forces Information Service [*DoD*] .... AFIS
American Forces Information Service [*DoD*] (AABC) .... AMFINFOS
American Forces Information System (EBF) .... AFIX
American Forces Italy (SAUO) .... AFI
American Forces Korea Network [*Military*] (GFGA) .... AFKN
American Forces Korean Network (SAUO) .... AFKN
American Forces Network (AABC) .... AFN
American Forces Network, Europe (AABC) .... AFNE
American Forces Network Television (SAUO) .... AFNTV
American Forces Press and Publications Service .... AFPPS
American Forces Press Service [*Formerly, AFNB*] .... AFPS
American [*formerly, Armed*] **Forces Radio and Television** [*DoD*] .... AFRT
American Forces Radio and Television Service [*Network of broadcast stations*] [*United States military*] [*Formerly, Armed Forces Radio Service*] (WDMC) .... AFRTS
American Forces Radio & Television Service (SAUS) .... AFRTS
American Forces Radio and Television Service-Los Angeles (SAUO) .... AFRTS-LA
American Forces Radio and Television Service-Programming Center [*See also AFIS*] [*DoD*] (WDMC) .... AFRTS-PC
American Forces Radio and Television Service-Worldwide (SAUO) .... AFRTS-W
American Forces Radio and Television-Bentwaters (SAUO) .... AFRT-B
American Forces Radio Station [*Vietnam*] (VNW) .... AFRS
American Forces Television (SAUO) .... AFTV
American Forces Thailand Network (SAUO) .... AFTN
American Forces Vietnam Network (SAUO) .... AFVN
American [*formerly, Armed*] **Forces Vietnam Network** .... AFVN
American Forces, Western Pacific (SAUO) .... AFWESPAC
American Foreign Insurance Association (EA) .... AFIA
American Foreign Law Association (EA) .... AFLA
American Foreign Law Association. Newsletter [*A publication*] (DLA) .... Am For L Ass'n Newsl
American Foreign Policy Institute [*Defunct*] (EA) .... AFPI
American Foreign Policy Institute - Europe (SAUO) .... AFPI
American Foreign Service Association (EA) .... AFSA
American Foreign Service Protective Association [*Washington, DC*] (EA) .... AFSPA
American Foreign Service Protective Association (SAUO) .... AFSPO
American Foreign Trade Definitions (SAUS) .... AFTD
American Forensic Association (EA) .... AFA
American Forensic Nurses (SAUO) .... AFN
American Forest Adventures [*Defunct*] (EA) .... AFA
American Forest & Paper Association (SAUO) .... AF&PA
American Forest and Paper Association (NTPA) .... AF&PA
American Forest and Paper Association (ECON) .... AFPA
American Forest Council (EA) .... AFC
American Forest Foundation (WPI) .... AFF
American Forest Institute [*Later, AFC*] .... AFI
American Forest Products Industries [*Later, AFC*] .... AFPI
American Forest Products Industries (SAUO) .... AFPI
American Forest Resources Alliance (WPI) .... AFRA
American Forestry Association (EA) .... AFA
American Forestry Association, Washington, DC [*Library symbol*] [*Library of Congress*] (LCLS) .... DAFA
American Forests [*A publication*] (BRI) .... AF
American Forests (journ.) (SAUS) .... Am For
American Forged Fitting and Flange Association [*Defunct*] (EA) .... AFFFA
American Formalwear Association [*Later, IFA*] (EA) .... AFA
American Forum: Education in a Global Age (SAUO) .... GPE
American Forum for Global Education (IID) .... AFGE
American Forum for Jewish-Christian Cooperation (EA) .... AFJCC
American Foster Care Resources (EA) .... AFCR
American Foulbrood [*Honeybee disease*] .... AFB
American Foundation for Aging Research (EA) .... AFAR

American Foundation for AIDS Research (SAUO) ... AFAIDSR
American Foundation for AIDS Research (EA) ... AFAR
American Foundation for AIDS Research [*New York, NY*] (EA) ... AmFAR
American Foundation for Aids Research (SAUO) ... AmFAR
American Foundation for AIDS Research (SAUS) ... AMFAR
American Foundation for Alternative Health Care [*Later, AFAHCRD*] (EA) ... AFAHC
American Foundation for Alternative Health Care, Research, and Development (EA) ... AFAHCRD
American Foundation for Continuing Education (EA) ... AFCE
American Foundation for Health (EA) ... AFH
American Foundation for Health Care Research and Development (SAUO) ... AFAHCRD
American Foundation for Homeopathy (EA) ... AFH
American Foundation for Homeopathy, Inc. (SAUO) ... AFH
American Foundation for Learning Disabilities ... AFLD
American Foundation for Management Research [*Later, AMA*] (EA) ... AFMR
American Foundation for Management Research (SAUO) ... AFMR
American Foundation for Management Research, Hamilton, NY [*Library symbol*] [*Library of Congress*] (LCLS) ... NHA
American Foundation for Management Research, Library, Hamilton, NY [*OCLC symbol*] (OCLC) ... ZUC
American Foundation for Maternal and Child Health (EA) ... AFMCH
American Foundation for Mental Hygiene ... AFMH
American Foundation for Negro Affairs (EA) ... AFNA
American Foundation for Overseas Blind [*Later, HKI*] (EA) ... AFOB
American Foundation for Pharmaceutical Education (EA) ... AFPE
American Foundation for Political Education ... AFPE
American Foundation for Psychoanalysis and Psychoanalysis in Groups (EA) ... AFPPG
American Foundation for Psychoanalysis and Psychoanalysis in Groups (SAUO) ... AFPPG
American Foundation for Resistance International (EA) ... AFRI
American Foundation for Studies in Government (SAUO) ... AFSG
American Foundation for Suicide Prevention (SAUO) ... AFSP
American Foundation for Surgery of the Hand (EA) ... AFSH
American Foundation for the Blind (EA) ... AFB
American Foundation for the Blind, New York, NY [*Library symbol*] [*Library of Congress*] (LCLS) ... NNAF
American Foundation for the Prevention of Venereal Disease (EA) ... AFPVD
American Foundation for the Science of Creative Intelligence (EA) ... AFSCI
American Foundation for the Study of Man (SAUO) ... AFSM
American Foundation for Tropical Medicine (EA) ... AFTM
American Foundation for Urologic Disease (EA) ... AFUD
American Foundation for Urologic Disease, Inc. ... AFUD
American Foundation for Urologic Diseases (SAUS) ... AFUD
American Foundation for Vision Awareness (EA) ... AFVA
American Foundation for World Youth Understanding (EA) ... AFWYU
American Foundation of Religion and Psychiatry [*Later, Institutes of Religion and Health*] (EA) ... AFRAP
American Foundation of Religion and Psychiatry (SAUO) ... AFRAP
American Foundation of Religion and Psychiatry [*Later, Institutes of Religion and Health*] ... AFRP
American Foundation of Traditional Chinese Medicine (EA) ... AFTCM
American Foundation on Automation and Employment [*Later, CNB-TV*] (EA) ... AFAE
American Foundrymen's Association [*Later, AFS*] ... AFA
American Foundrymens Association (SAUS) ... AFA
American Foundrymen's Society (EA) ... AFS
American Foundrymen's Society Archives and Museum, British Columbia Chapter, Delta, BC,Canada [*Library symbol*] [*Library of Congress*] (LCLS) ... CaBDEAF
American Foundrymen's Society, Des Plaines, IL [*Library symbol*] [*Library of Congress*] (LCLS) ... IDesA
American Fox Terrier Club (EA) ... AFTC
American Fox Trotting Horse Breed Association (EA) ... AFTHBA
American Foxhound Club (EA) ... AFC
American Fracture Association (EA) ... AFA
American Franchise Association (EA) ... AFA
American Franciscan Society for Vocations [*Later, FVC*] (EA) ... AFSV
American Fraternal Snowshoe Union (EA) ... AFSU
American Fraternal Union [*Ely, MN*] (EA) ... AFU
American Free Trade Club (SAUO) ... AFTC
American Freedom Association ... AFA
American Freedom Center (EA) ... AFC
American Freedom Coalition (EA) ... AFC
American Freedom from Hunger Foundation [*Later, MFM/FFH*] ... AFFHF
American Freedom from Hunger Foundation (SAUO) ... AFFHF
American Freedom of Residence Fund [*Defunct*] (EA) ... AFRF
American Freeman Association (EA) ... AFA
American Freightways Corp. [*NASDAQ symbol*] (NQ) ... AFWY
American Freightways Corp. [*Associated Press*] (SAG) ... AmFrght
American French (ADWA) ... AmerF
American Friends of Afghan Refugees (EA) ... AFAR
American Friends of Anne Frank Center (EA) ... AFAFC
American Friends of Beit Halochem (EA) ... AFBH
American Friends of Beth Hatefutsoth (EA) ... AFBH
American Friends of Boys Town of Jerusalem [*BTJFA*] [*Superseded by*] (EA) ... BTJ
American Friends of Cambridge University (EA) ... AFCU
American Friends of Chung-Ang University (EA) ... AFC-AU
American Friends of Covent Garden and the Royal Ballet (EA) ... AFCGRB
American Friends of Greece (EA) ... AFG
American Friends of Israel (EA) ... AFI
American Friends of Lafayette (EA) ... AFL
American Friends of Refugees [*Defunct*] ... AFR
American Friends of Religious Freedom in Israel [*Defunct*] (EAIO) ... AFRFI
American Friends of Romania (EA) ... AFRom
American Friends of Russian Freedom [*Later, AFR*] (EA) ... AFRF
American Friends of Scottish Opera (EA) ... AFSO
American Friends of Scottish War Blinded [*Defunct*] (EA) ... AFSWB
American Friends of Tel Aviv University (SAUO) ... AFTAU
American Friends of the Alliance Israelite Universelle (EA) ... AFAIU
American Friends of the Anti-Bolshevik Bloc of Nations (EA) ... AFABBN
American Friends of the Anti-Bolshevik Bloc of Nations (EA) ... AF-ABN
American Friends of the Association for Welfare of Soldiers in Israel (EA) ... AWSI
American Friends of the Australian National Gallery ... AFANG
American Friends of the Australian National Gallery Foundation (EA) ... AFANG
American Friends of the Captive Nations [*Defunct*] (EA) ... AFCN
American Friends of the Gutenberg Museum (EA) ... AFGM
American Friends of the Haifa Maritime Museum (EA) ... AFHMM
American Friends of the Hebrew University (EA) ... AFHU
American Friends of the Israel Museum (EA) ... AFIM
American Friends of the Jerusalem Institute for Talmudic Research (EA) ... AFJITR
American Friends of the Jerusalem Society for World Fellowship (EA) ... AFJSWF
American Friends of the Jewish Museum of Greece (EA) ... AFJMG
American Friends of the Middle East [*Later, AMIDEAST*] (EA) ... AFME
American Friends of the Paris Opera and Ballet (EA) ... AFPOB
American Friends of the Royal Shakespeare Theatre (EA) ... AFRST
American Friends of the Vatican Library (EA) ... AFVL
American Friends of Turkey (EA) ... AFOT
American Friends of Turkey (EA) ... AFT
American Friends of Vietnam (EA) ... AFV
American Friends Service Committee (EA) ... AFSC
American Friends Service Committee Inc. (SAUO) ... AFSC
American Frozen Food Institute (EA) ... AFFI
American Fuchsia Society (EA) ... AFS
American Fund for Alternatives to Animal Research (EA) ... AFAAR
American Fund for Czechoslovak Refugees (EA) ... AFCR
American Fund for Dental Education [*Later, AFDH*] (EA) ... AFDE
American Fund for Dental Health (EA) ... AFDH
American Fund for Free Jurists (EA) ... AFFJ
American Fund for Slovak Refugees [*Defunct*] (EA) ... AFSR
American Fund of Russian Freedom (SAUO) ... AFRF
American Funeral Directors and Embalmers Association (EA) ... AFDEA
American Fur Industry (EA) ... AFI
American Fur Liner Contractors Association (EA) ... AFLCA
American Fur Merchants Association (SAUS) ... AFMA
American Fur Resources Institute [*Defunct*] (EA) ... AFRI
American Furniture Manufacturers Association (EA) ... AFMA
American Gage Design (SAUO) ... AGD
American Gage Design Committee (SAUO) ... AGDC
American Galloway Breeders Association (SAUS) ... AGBA
American Galvanizers Association (EA) ... AGA
American Game Collectors Association (EA) ... AGCA
American Gaming Association (NTPA) ... AGA
American Gas Accumulator Company (SAUO) ... AGAC
American Gas and Electric Co. (SAUO) ... AGE
American Gas and Electric Services ... AGES
American Gas and Electric System (SAUS) ... AG&ES
American Gas Association (EA) ... AGA
American Gas Association (SAUO) ... AMGA
American Gas Association, Inc. (SAUO) ... AGA
American Gas Association Laboratories (SAUO) ... AGA
American Gas Association Laboratories ... AGAL
American Gas Association. Monthly (journ.) (SAUS) ... AGAMA
American Gas Association. Monthly (journ.) (SAUS) ... AGA Mon
American Gas Association Natural Gas Vehicle Coalition ... AGANGVC
American Gas Association, New York, NY [*Library symbol*] [*Library of Congress*] (LCLS) ... NNAG
American Gas Association. Operating Section. Proccedings (journ.) (SAUS) ... ACA Oper Sec Proc
American Gas Institute (SAUO) ... AGI
American Gasoline Dealers Association (EA) ... AGDA
American Gastroenterological Association (EA) ... AGA
American Gastroscopic Association (SAUO) ... AGA
American Gastroscopic Society (SAUO) ... AGS
American Gathering of Jewish Holocaust Survivors (EA) ... AGJHS
American Gauge Design Committee ... AGD
American Gauge Design Standard ... AGDS
American Gay Atheists (EA) ... AGA
American Gay/Lesbian Atheists (EA) ... AGLA
American Gear Manufacturers Association (EA) ... AGMA
American Gelbvieh Association (EA) ... AGA
American Gem and Mineral Suppliers Association (EA) ... AGMSA
American Gem Market System [*Information service or system*] (IID) ... AGMS
American Gem Society (EA) ... AGS
American Gem Trade Association (EA) ... AGTA
American Genealogical Research Institute ... AGRI
American Genealogical Resources in German Archives (SAUO) ... AGRIGA
American Genealogist [*A publication*] (BRI) ... Am Geneal
American General Bond Fund, Inc. (SAUO) ... AGB
American General Corp. [*Associated Press*] (SAG) ... AGenCp
American General Corp. Capital LLC [*Associated Press*] (SAG) ... AGC
American General Delaware LLC [*Associated Press*] (SAG) ... AGnDE
American General Hospitality Corp. [*Associated Press*] (SAG) ... AGnHosp
American General Hospitality Corp. [*NYSE symbol*] (SAG) ... AGT

American General Insurance Company (SAUO) .... AGC
American General Life Insurance Co. [*NYSE symbol*] (SPSG) .... AGC
American Genetic Association (EA) .... AGA
American Genetic Resources Alliance .... AGRA
American Geographical and Statistical Society (SAUO) .... AGSS
American Geographical and Statistical Society .... AGSS
American Geographical Institute .... AGI
American Geographical Society (EA) .... AGS
American Geographical Society (SAUO) .... AmerGS
American Geographical Society Bulletin (journ.) (SAUS) .... Am Geog Soc Bull
American Geographical Society, New York, NY [*Library symbol*] [*Library of Congress*] (LCLS) .... NNA
American Geographical Union (SAUO) .... AGU
American Geological Institute (EA) .... AGI
American Geological Institute (SAUO) .... Am Geol
American Geological Research Institute (SAUO) .... AGRI
American Geophysical Society (SAUO) .... AmerGS
American Geophysical Union (SAUO) .... Am Geophysical
American Geophysical Union (SAUS) .... Geophysical
American Geriatric Research Foundation [*Later, ARI*] .... AGRF
American Geriatrics Association (DAVI) .... AGA
American Geriatrics Society (EA) .... AGS
American Gesneria Society [*Later, GSI*] (EA) .... AGS
American GI Forum (OICC) .... AGIF
American Gioxinia Society (SAUS) .... AGS
American Girl Resources [*Vancouver Stock Exchange symbol*] .... AGA
American Glassware Association [*Defunct*] .... AGA
American Glovebox Society (EA) .... AGS
American Gloxinia and Gesneriad Society (EA) .... AGGS
American Gloxinia Society [*Later, AGGS*] (EA) .... AGS
American Glycerin Bomb (SAUS) .... AGB
American Go Association (EA) .... AGA
American Goat Society (EA) .... AGS
American Goiter Association [*Later, American Thyroid Association*] .... AGA
American Goiter Association (SAUO) .... AGA
American Gold Association [*Defunct*] (EA) .... AGA
American Gold Star Mothers (EA) .... AGSM
American Golden Cross (SAUS) .... AGC
American Golf Foundation (SAUO) .... AGF
American Golf Sponsors (EA) .... AGS
American Golf Sponsors Association (NTPA) .... AGSA
American Good Government Society [*Defunct*] (EA) .... AGGS
American Gotland Horse Association (EA) .... AGHA
American Gourd Society (EA) .... AGS
American Government Income Fund [*NYSE symbol*] (SPSG) .... AGF
American Government Income Fund [*Associated Press*] (SAG) .... AmGvl
American Government Income Portfolio, Inc. [*NYSE symbol*] (CTT) .... AAF
American Government Income Portfolio, Inc. [*Associated Press*] (SAG) .... AGIP
American Government Term Trust [*NYSE symbol*] (SPSG) .... AGT
American Government Term Trust [*Associated Press*] (SAG) .... AGTT
American Graduate School of International Management [*Formerly, Thunderbird Graduate School of International Management*] [*Glendale, AZ*] .... AGSIM
American Graduate School of International Management, Glendale, AZ [*Library symbol*] [*Library of Congress*] (LCLS) .... AzGAGS
American Grain Products Processing Institute [*Defunct*] (EA) .... AGPPI
American Grand Prix Association (EA) .... AGA
American Graniteware Association (EA) .... AGA
American Grape Growers Alliance for Fair Trade [*Defunct*] (EA) .... AGGAFT
American Graphological Society (EA) .... AGS
American Grassland Council [*Later, AFGC*] (EA) .... AGC
American Grassland Council (SAUO) .... AGC
American Graves Registration Command [*Military*] .... AGRC
American Graves Registration Command [*Military*] .... AGRCO
American Graves Registration Service [*Military*] .... AGRS
American Greek Exchange Society (EA) .... AGES
American Green Movement (EA) .... AGM
American Greenhouse Vegetable Growers Association (EA) .... AGVGA
American Greetings Corp. (EFIS) .... AG
American Greetings Corp. [*NASDAQ symbol*] (NQ) .... AGRE
American Greetings Corp. [*Associated Press*] (SAG) .... AGreet
American Greyhound Track Operators Association (EA) .... AGTOA
American Groomer's Guild (EA) .... AGG
American Grooming Shop Association (EA) .... AGSA
American Ground Flat Stock Association (EA) .... AGFSA
American Ground Water Trust (EA) .... AGWT
American Group of CPA Firms [*Lombard, IL*] (EA) .... TAG
American Group Practice (SAUO) .... AGPA
American Group Practice Association (EA) .... AGPA
American Group Practice Association of National Trade Groups for Wood and Proved Products Countries of the European Economic Community Agriculture (SAUS) .... AGPA
American Group Psychotherapy Association (EA) .... AGPA
American Guaranty Financial Corp. (EFIS) .... AGE
American Guernsey Association (EA) .... AGA
American Guernsey Cattle Club [*Later, AGA*] (EA) .... AGCC
American Guidance Service (DHP) .... AGS
American Guides Association [*Defunct*] (EA) .... AGA
American Guild for Infant Survival (EA) .... AGIS
American Guild of Animal Artists (EA) .... AGAA
American Guild of Authors and Composers (EA) .... AGAC
American Guild of English Handbell Ringers (EA) .... AGEHR
American Guild of Hypnotherapists (EA) .... AGH
American Guild of Luthiers (EA) .... AGL
American Guild of Music (EA) .... AGM
American Guild of Musical Artists (EA) .... AGMA
American Guild of Musical Artists Magazine [*A publication*] (EAAP) .... AGMAzine
American Guild of Organists (EA) .... AGO
American Guild of Patient Account Management (EA) .... AGPAM
American Guild of Variety Artists (EA) .... AGVA
American Gulf and West Indies (SAUS) .... AGWI
American Gulf West Indies Co. .... AGWI
American Gum Importers Laboratories (SAUO) .... AGIL
American Gun Dealers Association (EA) .... AGDA
American Guppy Association [*Later, IFGA*] (EA) .... AGA
American Guppy Association (SAUO) .... AGA
American Gynecological and Obstetrical Society (EA) .... AGOS
American Gynecological Society [*Later, AGOS*] (EA) .... AGS
American Habonim Association [*Later, Labor Zionist Alliance*] .... AHA
American Habonim Association (SAUO) .... AHA
American Hackney Horse Society (EA) .... AHHS
American Hair Loss Council (EA) .... AHLC
American Hair Replacement Association [*Inactive*] (EA) .... AHRA
American Hair Restoration .... AHR
American Half-Paso Association [*Defunct*] (EA) .... AHPA
American Hampshire Sheep Association (EA) .... AHSA
American Handwriting Analysis Foundation (EA) .... AHAF
American Hanoverian Society (EA) .... AHS
American Hardboard Association (EA) .... AHA
American Hardboard Association .... AHBA
American Hardware Corporation (SAUO) .... AHC
American Hardware Manufacturers Association (EA) .... AHMA
American Hardwood Association (WPI) .... AHA
American Hardwood Export Council (EA) .... AHEC
American Harlequin Rabbit Club (EA) .... AHRC
American Harp Society (EA) .... AHS
American Hazardous Waste Association (EA) .... AHWA
American Healing Association [*Defunct*] (EA) .... AHA
American Health (SAUS) .... AH
American Health and Beauty Aids Institute (EA) .... AHBAI
American Health and Temperance Association (EA) .... AHTA
American Health and Temperance Society (EA) .... AHTS
American Health Assistance Foundation (EA) .... AHAF
American Health Association (EA) .... AHA
American Health Care Advisory Association (EA) .... AHCAA
American Health Care Association (EA) .... AHCA
American Health Care Association Political Action Committee .... AHC-PAC
American Health Consultants [*Information service or system*] (IID) .... AHC
American Health Decisions (EA) .... AHD
American Health for Women [*A publication*] .... AHFW
American Health Foundation (EA) .... AHF
American Health Industries Institute (EA) .... AHII
American Health Information Management Association (NTPA) .... AHIMA
American Health Information Management Association [*Formerly, American Medical Records Association*] (EA) .... AMRA
American Health Institute (SAUO) .... AHI
American Health Magazine (SAUS) .... AHM
American Health Planning Association (EA) .... AHPA
American Health Professionals .... AHP
American Health Professions Institute (DAVI) .... AHPI
American Health Properties [*NYSE symbol*] (SPSG) .... AHE
American Health Properties [*NASDAQ symbol*] (SAG) .... AHEP
American Health Properties [*Associated Press*] (SAG) .... AHltPr
American Health Quality Association (SAUO) .... AHQA
American Health Security Act [*Medicine*] .... AHSA
American Health Services Corp. (SAUO) .... AHTS
American Healthcare Institute [*Later, AMHS Institute*] (EA) .... AHI
American Healthcare Management (SAUS) .... AHLTMG
American Healthcare Management, Inc. [*NYSE symbol*] (SPSG) .... AHI
American Healthcare Management, Inc. [*Associated Press*] (SAG) .... AHltMg
American Healthcare Management, Inc. (SAUS) .... QAHI
American Healthcare Radiology Administrators (EA) .... AHRA
American HealthChoice, Inc. [*NASDAQ symbol*] (SAG) .... AHIC
American HealthChoice, Inc. [*Associated Press*] (SAG) .... AHltCh
American Healthcorp [*NASDAQ symbol*] (SPSG) .... AMHC
American Healthcorp, Inc. [*Associated Press*] (SAG) .... AHlthcp
American Hearing Aid Association (SAUO) .... AHAA
American Hearing Impaired Hockey Association (EA) .... AHIHA
American Hearing Research Foundation (EA) .... AHRF
American Hearing Society [*Later, NAHSA*] (EA) .... AHS
American Hearing Society (SAUO) .... AHS
American Heart Association (EA) .... AHA
American Heart Association (SAUO) .... Am Heart
American Heart Association Council on Thrombosis (SAUO) .... AHACT
American Heart Association. Monograph (journ.) (SAUS) .... AHMOAH
American Heart Journal (SAUS) .... Amer Heart J
American Heartworm Society (EA) .... AHS
American Heating Association (SAUO) .... AHA
American Hebrew (BJA) .... AH
American Helicopter Association (SAUO) .... AHS
American Helicopter Company [*Air Force*] (MCD) .... AHC
American Helicopter Museum (SAUS) .... AHM
American Helicopter Society (EA) .... AHS
American Hellenic Alliance (EA) .... AHA
American Hellenic Congress [*Defunct*] (EA) .... AHC
American Hellenic Educational Progressive Association .... AHEPA
American Hellenic Institute (EA) .... AHI
American Hellenic Institute Public Affairs Committee (EA) .... AHIPAC
American Helvetia Philatelic Society (EA) .... AHPS
American Hemerocallis Society (EA) .... AHS

American Hemisphere Marine Agencies (SAUO) .... AHMA
American Hemochromatosis Society (SAUO) .... AHS
American Hepatic Foundation (EA) .... AHF
American Hepatitis Association (EA) .... AHA
American Hepatitis Association (SAUS) .... AHA
American Herb Association (EA) .... AHA
American Herbal Products Association (EA) .... AHPA
American Herbalists Guild (EA) .... AHG
American Hereford Association (EA) .... AHA
American Herens Association (EA) .... AHA
American Heritage [*A publication*] (BRI) .... AH
American Heritage Dictionary [*A publication*] .... AHD
American Heritage Foundation (EA) .... AHF
American Heritage Life Investment Corp. [*Associated Press*] (SAG) .... AHeritge
American Heritage Life Investment Corp. [*NYSE symbol*] (SPSG) .... AHL
American Heritage Publishing Company (SAUO) .... AHPC
American Heritage Society [*Defunct*] (EA) .... AHS
American Hibiscus Society (EA) .... AHS
American High-Density Gradient .... AHG
American Highland Cattle Association (NTPA) .... AHCA
American High-Speed Railway Corporation (SAUO) .... AHSRC
American Highway Sign Association (SAUO) .... AHSA
American Highway Users Alliance (NTPA) .... AHUA
American Highways and Byways [*A publication*] .... AHB
American Hiking Society (EA) .... AHS
American Himalayan Rabbit Association (EA) .... AHRA
American Hispanist (journ.) (SAUS) .... TAH
American Histadrut Cultural Exchange Institute [*Defunct*] (EA) .... AHCEI
American Historic and Cultural Society (EA) .... AHCS
American Historic Racing Motorcycle Association (EA) .... AHRMA
American Historical Association (EA) .... AHA
American Historical Association Reports (journ.) (SAUS) .... Am Hist Assn Rept
American Historical Philatelic Society [*Formerly, AHPS-CWPS*] (EA) .... AHPS
American Historical Philatelic Society - Civil War Philatelic Society [*Later, AHPS*] .... AHPS-CWPS
American Historical Print Collectors Society (EA) .... AHPCS
American Historical Record (journ.) (SAUS) .... Am Hist Rec
American Historical Register (journ.) (SAUS) .... Am Hist Reg
American Historical Review [*A publication*] (BRI) .... AHR
American Historical Society of Germans from Russia (EA) .... AHSGR
American History [*A publication*] (BRI) .... Am Hist
American History and Life (SAUS) .... AHL
American History Research Associates (SAUS) .... Am Hist Res
American Hitchhiker Association .... AHA
American Hobbit Association (EA) .... AHA
American Hobby Federation [*Defunct*] (EA) .... AHF
American Hockey Association (SAUO) .... AHA
American Hockey Coaches (SAUO) .... AHC
American Hockey Coaches Association (EA) .... AHCA
American Hockey League (EA) .... AHL
American Hoechst Corporation (SAUO) .... AHC
American Hoist & Derrick Co. (SAUO) .... AHO
American Holdings, Inc. [*NASDAQ symbol*] (SAG) .... HOLD
American Holistic Health Sciences Association [*Defunct*] (EA) .... AHHSA
American Holistic Medical Association (EA) .... AHMA
American Holistic Medical Foundation (EA) .... AHMF
American Holistic Medical Institute [*of the American Holistic Medical Association*] [*Formerly, BIA*] [*Later, AHMF*] (EA) .... AHMI
American Holistic Veterinary Medical Association (EA) .... AHVMA
American Holstein Horse Association (EA) .... AHHA
American Home Business Association [*Greenwich, CT*] (EA) .... AHBA
American Home Economics Association (EA) .... AHEA
American Home Industries Corporation (SAUO) .... AHIC
American Home (journ.) (SAUS) .... Am Home
American Home Laundry Manufacturers Association [*Later, AHAM*] (EA) .... AHLMA
American Home Lighting Institute (EA) .... AHLI
American Home Mission Society .... AHMS
American Home Mission Society (SAUO) .... AHMS
American Home Products Co. [*Associated Press*] (SAG) .... AHome
American Home Products Corp. (EFIS) .... AH
American Home Products Corp. [*Associated Press*] (SAG) .... AHme
American Home Products Corp. [*NYSE symbol*] (SPSG) .... AHP
American Home Products Corp. (SAUO) .... HPT
American Home Products Corp., Ayerst Medical Library, New York, NY [*Library symbol*] [*Library of Congress*] (LCLS) .... NNAy
American Home Satellite Association [*Defunct*] (EA) .... AHSA
American Home Security (SAUO) .... AHS
American Home Sewing and Craft Association (EA) .... AHSCA
American Home Sewing Association [*Later, AHSCA*] (EA) .... AHSA
American Home Sewing Council [*Later, AHSCA*] (EA) .... AHSC
American Homebrew Association (SAUO) .... AHA
American Homebrewers Association (EA) .... AHA
American Homeopathic Pharmacopoeia [*Last published in 1920*] .... AHP
American Homeowners Association [*Defunct*] (EA) .... AHA
American Homeowners Foundation (EA) .... AHF
American HomePatient Care [*NASDAQ symbol*] (SAG) .... AHOM
American HomePatient Care [*Associated Press*] (SAG) .... AHomPat
American Homestar Corp. [*Associated Press*] (SAG) .... AHomstr
American Homestar Corp. [*NASDAQ symbol*] (SAG) .... HSTR
American Hominological Association (EA) .... AHA
American Honey Institute [*Later, HICA*] (EA) .... AHI
American Honey Producers Association (EA) .... AHPA
American Hop Latent Virus [*Plant pathology*] .... AHLV
American Horizons [*Defunct*] (EA) .... AH
American Horse Council (EA) .... AHC
American Horse Protection Association (EA) .... AHPA
American Horse Publications (EA) .... AHP
American Horse Shows Association (EA) .... AHSA
American Horticultural Council [*Later, AHS*] .... AHC
American Horticultural Marketing Council (EA) .... AHMC
American Horticultural Society .... AHS
American Horticultural Therapy Association (NTPA) .... AHTA
American Hospital Association (EA) .... AHA
American Hospital Association (SAUO) .... AHospA
American Hospital Association, Chicago, IL [*Library symbol*] [*Library of Congress*] (LCLS) .... ICAH
American Hospital Association Library, Chicago, IL [*OCLC symbol*] (OCLC) .... IHD
American Hospital Corps .... AHC
American Hospital Formulary [*A publication*] .... AHF
American Hospital Formulary Service .... AHFS
American Hospital Formulary Service Drug Information (SAUO) .... AHFS DI
American Hospital Institute (SAUO) .... AHI
American Hospital Radiology Administrators (DAVI) .... AHRA
American Hospital Society .... AHS
American Hospital Supply (SAUS) .... AHS
American Hospital Supply Company (SAUO) .... AHSC
American Hospital Supply Corp. (EFIS) .... AHS
American Hospital Supply Corp., Evanston, IL [*Library symbol*] [*Library of Congress*] (LCLS) .... IEA
American Hospital Supply Corp., Evanston, IL [*Library symbol*] [*Library of Congress*] (LCLS) .... IEAH
American Hospital Supply Corp., Evanston, IL [*OCLC symbol*] (OCLC) .... JAU
American Hospital Video Network [*Satellite television system*] .... AHVN
American Host Foundation (EA) .... AHF
American Hosta Society (EA) .... AHS
American Hostage Committee [*Defunct*] (EA) .... AHC
American Hot Dip Galvanizers Association [*Later, AGA*] (EA) .... AHDGA
American Hot Rod Association (EA) .... AHRA
American Hot-Dip Galvanizers Association (SAUO) .... AHDGA
American Hotel & Motel Association (EA) .... AH & MA
American Hotel and Motel Association (TRID) .... AHMA
American Hotel and Motel Brokers [*Formerly, MBAA*] (EA) .... AHMB
American Hotel Association [*Later, AH & MA*] .... AHA
American Hotel Association (SAUO) .... AHA
American Hotel Trade Association Executives (EA) .... AHTAE
American Hound Association .... AHA
American Housing Guild (SAUO) .... AHG
American Housing Survey [*Department of Housing and Urban Development*] (GFGA) .... AHS
American Housing Survey-Metropolitan Sample [*Department of Housing and Urban Development*] (GFGA) .... AHS-MS
American Housing Survey-National Sample (SAUS) .... AHS-NS
American Hovercraft Association [*Superseded by HA*] (EA) .... AHA
American Hull Form (MARI) .... AHF
American Hull Insurance Syndicate [*New York, NY*] (EA) .... AHIS
American Humane Association (EA) .... AHA
American Humane Association Children's Division (EA) .... AHA
American Humane Association, Denver, CO [*Library symbol*] [*Library of Congress*] (LCLS) .... CoDAH
American Humane Education Society (EA) .... AHES
American Humane Society .... AHS
American Humanics (EA) .... AH
American Humanics Foundation [*Later, AH*] (EA) .... AHF
American Humanist Association (EA) .... AHA
American Humor Studies Association (EA) .... AHSA
American Hungarian Catholic Society [*Later, William Penn Association*] (EA) .... AHCS
American Hungarian Educators Association (SAUO) .... AHEA
American Hungarian Federation (EA) .... AHF
American Hungarian Folklore Centrum (EA) .... AHFC
American Hungarian Foundation (EA) .... AHF
American Hungarian Library and Historical Society (EA) .... AHLHS
American Hungarian Studies Foundation [*Later, AHF*] (EA) .... AHSF
American Hunter .... AH
American Hydrogen Association (EA) .... AHA
American Hyperlexia Association .... AHA
American Hypnodontic Society (EA) .... AHS
American Hypnosis Association (EA) .... AHA
American Hypnotherapy Association (SAUO) .... AHA
American Hypnotism Association (SAUO) .... AHA
American Hypnotists' Association (EA) .... AHA
American Iatrogenic Association (SAUO) .... AIA
American Imagery Association [*Defunct*] (EA) .... AIA
American Immigration and Citizenship Conference (EA) .... AICC
American Immigration Control Foundation (EA) .... AICF
American Immigration Lawyers Association (EA) .... AILA
American Imported Automobile Dealers Association (SAUO) .... AIADA
American Importers and Exporters Meat Products Group (NTPA) .... AIEMPG
American Importers Association (SAUO) .... AIA
American Importers Association [*Later, AAEI*] .... AIA
American Importers Meat Products Group (EA) .... AIMPG
American Incense Manufacturers Association (EA) .... AIMA
American Income Holding, Inc. [*NYSE symbol*] (SPSG) .... AIH
American Income Holdings, Inc. [*Associated Press*] (SAG) .... AmInc
American Indemnity Financial Corp. [*NASDAQ symbol*] (NQ) .... AIFC
American Indemnity Financial Corp. [*Associated Press*] (SAG) .... AIndF
American Independent Designers and Engineers Society .... AIDES
American Independent Designers Association (EA) .... AIDA

American Independent Oil Co. .... AMINOIL
American Independent Oil Company (SAUO) .... AMINOIL; Aminoil
American Independent Party .... AIP
American Independent Refiners Association (EA) .... AIRA
American Indian .... AI
American Indian .... AMERIND
American Indian (ADWA) .... AmerInd
American Indian .... AMIND
American Indian and Alaska Native .... AI/AN
American Indian and Alaska Native Mental Health Research. Monograph Series (SAUS) .... Am Indian Alsk Native Ment Health Res Monogr Ser
American Indian and Eskimo Cultural Foundation [*Defunct*] .... AIECF
American Indian Archaeological Institute (EA) .... AIAI
American Indian Arts Council (EA) .... AIAC
American Indian Assistance League (OICC) .... AIAL
American Indian Assistance League (SAUS) .... AL&L
American Indian Center (SAUO) .... AIC
American Indian Community House .... AICH
American Indian Community House [*An association*] .... ASO
American Indian Council of Architects and Engineers (EA) .... AICAE
American Indian Culture and Research Journal [*A publication*] (BRI) .... Am Ind CRJ
American Indian Culture Research Center (EA) .... AICRC
American Indian Development Association [*Defunct*] (EA) .... AIDA
American Indian Environmental Council (EA) .... AIEC
American Indian Environmental Office (AEPA) .... AIEO
American Indian Ethnohistorical Conference [*Later, American Society for Ethnohistory*] (EA) .... AIEC
American Indian Film Institute .... AIFI
American Indian Graduate Center (EA) .... AIGC
American Indian Health Care Association (EA) .... AIHCA
American Indian Heritage Foundation (EA) .... AIHF
American Indian Higher Education Consortium (EA) .... AIHEC
American Indian Higher Education Consortium (SAUO) .... IHEC
American Indian Historical Association (EA) .... AIHA
American Indian Historical Society [*Defunct*] (EA) .... AIHS
American Indian Horse Registry (EA) .... AIHR
American Indian Institute (EA) .... AII
American Indian Journal [*A publication*] (DLA) .... Am Ind J
American Indian Lands Environmental Support Project (GEOI) .... AILESP
American Indian Law Center (EA) .... AILC
American Indian Law Newsletter [*A publication*] (DLA) .... Am Ind L Newsl
American Indian Law Review [*A publication*] (DLA) .... Am Ind L Rev
American Indian Law Students Association [*Later, NALSA*] (EA) .... AILSA
American Indian Liberation Crusade (EA) .... AILC
American Indian Library Association (EA) .... AILA
American Indian Lore Association (EA) .... AILA
American Indian Medical Clinic (SAUO) .... AIMC
American Indian Movement (EA) .... AIM
American Indian Nurses Association (SAUO) .... AINA
American Indian Policy Review Commission .... AIPRC
American Indian Press Association [*Defunct*] (EA) .... AIPA
American Indian Projects Foundation [*Defunct*] (EA) .... AIPF
American Indian Quarterly (journ.) (SAUS) .... AIQ
American Indian Radio on Satellite (SAUS) .... AIROS
American Indian Radio on Satellite .... A/ROS
American Indian Refugees (EA) .... AIR
American Indian Registry for the Performing Arts (EA) .... AIRPA
American Indian Religious Freedom Act [*1978*] .... AIRFA
American Indian Research and Development [*An association*] (EA) .... AIRD
American Indian Research Center (OICC) .... AIRC
American Indian Reservation (GEOI) .... AIR
American Indian Scholarships [*Later, AIGC*] (EA) .... AIS
American Indian Science and Engineering Society (EA) .... AISES
American Indian Science Technology Education Consortium .... AISTEC
American Indian Sign Language (BYTE) .... AIS
American Indian Studies Center [*Research center*] (RCD) .... AISC
American Indian Travel Commission [*Defunct*] (EA) .... AITC
American Indian/Alaska Native Area (GEOI) .... AI/ANA
American Indian/Alaska Native Nurses Association (EA) .... AIANNA
American Indians (SAUS) .... Amerindians
American Indians for Sobriety (EA) .... AIS
American Indicator Digest Average [*American Stock Exchange*] .... AIDA
American Indonesian Chamber of Commerce (EA) .... AICC
American Indoor Soccer Association (EA) .... AISA
American Industrial Arts Association (EA) .... AIAA
American Industrial Arts Association (SAUO) .... Am Indus Arts
American Industrial Arts Student Association (SAUO) .... AIASA
American Industrial Arts Student Association [*Later, TSA*] (EA) .... AIASA
American Industrial Bankers Association [*Later, NCFA*] (EA) .... AIBA
American Industrial Development Council [*Later, AEDC*] (EA) .... AIDC
American Industrial Forum (SAUO) .... AIF
American Industrial Health Conference (SAUO) .... AIHC
American Industrial Health Council (EA) .... AIHC
American Industrial Heritage Project .... ATHP
American Industrial Hygiene Association (SAUO) .... AIHA
American Industrial Hygiene Association Journal (SAUS) .... Amer Ind Hyg Assoc J
American Industrial Hygiene Association Journal (SAUS) .... Am Ind Hyg Assoc J
American Industrial Hygiene Conference and Exposition (ADWA) .... AIHCE
American Industrial Music Association (EA) .... AIMA
American Industrial Properties [*Formerly, Trammell Crow Real Estate Investment*] [*NYSE symbol*] (SPSG) .... IND
American Industrial Properties Real Estate Investment Trust [*Associated Press*] (SAG) .... AIndPrp
American Industrial Radium and X-Ray Society (SAUO) .... AIRX
American Industrial Radium and X-Ray Society (SAUO) .... AIRXR
American Industrial Radium and X-Ray Society [*Later, ASNT*] .... AIRXRS
American Industrial Real Estate Association (EA) .... AIR
American Industrial Transport, Inc. .... AIT
American Industrial Transport Inc. (SAUO) .... AIT
American Industrial Writing Institute .... AIWI
American Industry and Labor for the Supersonic Transport (SAUO) .... AIL-SST
American Industry Foundation (SAUO) .... AIF
American Industry Government Emissions Research Consortium .... AIGER
American Indycar Series [*Auto racing*] .... AIS
American Information Exchange [*Information service or system*] (ECON) .... AMIX
American Information Network (EA) .... AIN
American Information Network Ltd. [*Information service or system*] (IID) .... AIN
American Information Retrieval Service [*Document delivery service*] (NITA) .... AIRS
American Information Services [*Information service or system*] (IID) .... AIS
American Information Technologies Corp. [*Telecommunications*] [*Chicago, IL*] .... AMERITECH
American Innerspring Manufacturers (EA) .... AIM
American Inns of Court Foundation (EA) .... AICF
American Insolvency Reports [*A publication*] (DLA) .... A Ins R
American Insolvency Reports [*A publication*] (DLA) .... Am Insolv Rep
American Insolvency Reports [*A publication*] (DLA) .... Am Ins Rep
American Institute .... AI
American Institute (SAUO) .... AI
American Institute - the Training School at Vineland [*Later, TTS*] (EA) .... AITSV
American Institute for a Free Labor Development (SAUO) .... AIFLD
American Institute for Aerological Research (MCD) .... AIAR
American Institute for Archaeological Research (EA) .... AIAR
American Institute for Cancer Research [*Research center*] (RCD) .... AICR
American Institute for Certified Public Accountants - Professional Standards (Commerce Clearing House) [*A publication*] (DLA) .... AICPA-Prof Stand (CCH)
American Institute for Character Education [*Later, CEI*] (EA) .... AICE
American Institute for Chartered Property Casualty Underwriters - Insurance Institute of America (NTPA) .... AICPCU/IIA
American Institute for Conservation of Historic and Artistic Works (EA) .... AIC
American Institute for Contemporary German Studies (EA) .... AICGS
American Institute for Decision Sciences (SAUO) .... AIDC
American Institute for Decision Sciences [*Later, DSI*] (EA) .... AIDS
American Institute for Design and Drafting [*Later, ADDA*] (EA) .... AIDD
American Institute for Economic Development (EA) .... AIED
American Institute for Economic Research [*Great Barrington, MA*] (EA) .... AIER
American Institute for Exploration (EA) .... AIFE
American Institute for Foreign Studies (or Study) (SAUO) .... AIFS
American Institute for Foreign Study (EA) .... AIFS
American Institute for Foreign Study Scholarship Foundation (EA) .... AIFSSF
American Institute for Foreign Trade .... AIFT
American Institute for Free Labor Development (EA) .... AIFLD
American Institute for Hollow Structural Sections (EA) .... AIHSS
American Institute for Human Engineering and Development (EA) .... AIHED
American Institute for Imported Steel (EA) .... AIIS
American Institute for International Steel (EA) .... AIIS
American Institute for Islamic Affairs (EA) .... AIIA
American Institute for Maghrib Studies (EA) .... AIMS
American Institute for Management .... AIM
American Institute for Marxist Studies [*Defunct*] (EA) .... AIMS
American Institute for Mathematical Statistics (SAUO) .... AIMS
American Institute For Medical and Biological Engineering (SAUO) .... AIMBE
American Institute for Mental Studies [*Later, AITSV*] (EA) .... AIMS
American Institute for Microminiaturization (SAUO) .... AIM
American Institute for Mining Engineers (SAUS) .... AIME
American Institute for Patristic and Byzantine Studies (EA) .... AIPBS
American Institute for Political Communication .... AIPC
American Institute for Professional Education (EA) .... AIPE
American Institute for Property and Liability Underwriters [*Malvern, PA*] (EA) .... AIPLU
American Institute for Psychoanalysis (SAUS) .... AIP
American Institute for Psychotherapy and Psychoanalysis (SAUO) .... AIPP
American Institute for Public Service (EA) .... AIPS
American Institute for Research and Education in Naturopathy (EA) .... AIREN
American Institute for Research in the Behavioral Sciences .... AIRBS
American Institute for Shippers' Associations (EA) .... AISA
American Institute for Teen AIDS Prevention (EA) .... AITAP
American Institute for the Medical Research of Trauma (EA) .... AIMRT
American Institute for the Prevention and Eradication of Dental Disease (SAUO) .... AIPEDD
American Institute for Verdi Studies (EA) .... AIVS
American Institute for/of Conservation of Historic and Artistic Works (SAUO) .... AIC
American Institute in Taiwan .... AIT
American Institute, Inc. (EA) .... AII
American Institute Incorporated (SAUO) .... AII
American Institute of Accountants (SAUO) .... AIA
American Institute of Actuaries (SAUO) .... AIA
American Institute of Aerological Research (SAUO) .... AIAR
American Institute of Aeronautics (SAUO) .... AIA
American Institute of Aeronautics and Astronautics (EA) .... AIAA
American Institute of Aeronautics and Astronautics, New York, NY [*Library symbol*] [*Library of Congress*] (LCLS) .... NNIA
American Institute of Aeronautics and Astronautics, Pacific Aerospace Library, Los Angeles, CA [*Library symbol*] [*Library of Congress*] (LCLS) .... CLIA

American Institute of Aeronautics and Astronautics, Technical Information Service, New York, NY [*Library symbol*] [*Library of Congress*] (LCLS) ... NNAIAA
American Institute of Aeronautics and Astronautics-Technical Information Serv (SAUS) ... AIAA-TIS
American Institute of Archaeology (SAUO) ... AIA
American Institute of Architects (EA) ... AIA
American Institute of Architects Foundation (EA) ... AIAF
American Institute of Architects in Kansas (SRA) ... AIAKS
American Institute of Architects Service Corp. [*Information service or system*] (IID) ... AIA/SC
American Institute of Architects, Washington, D.C. [*1867*] (NGC) ... AIA
American Institute of Architects, Washington, DC [*Library symbol*] [*Library of Congress*] (LCLS) ... DAIA
American Institute of Architecture Students (EA) ... AIAS
American Institute of Baking (EA) ... AIB
American Institute of Baking, Chicago, IL [*Library symbol*] [*Library of Congress*] (LCLS) ... ICAI
American Institute of Banking (EBF) ... AIB
American Institute of Biological Sciences (EA) ... AIBS
American Institute of Biomedical Climatology (NTPA) ... AIBC
American Institute of Bolt, Nut, and Rivet Manufacturers [*Later, Industrial Fasteners Institute*] ... AIBNRM
American Institute of Building Design (EA) ... AIBD
American Institute of Ceramic Engineers (SAUO) ... AICerE
American Institute of Ceramic Engineers (SAUS) ... AICerE
American Institute of Certified Planners (EA) ... AICP
American Institute of Certified Public Accountants [*New York, NY*] (EA) ... AICPA
American Institute of Certified Public Accountants, New York, NY [*Library symbol*] [*Library of Congress*] (LCLS) ... NNAIA
American Institute of Ceylonese Studies (EA) ... AICS
American Institute of Chefs [*Later, ACF*] ... AIC
American Institute of Chemical Engineering (SAUS) ... AIChE
American Institute of Chemical Engineers [*New York, NY*] ... AICE
American Institute of Chemical Engineers (EA) ... AIChE
American Institute of Chemical Engineers ... AICHE
American Institute of Chemists (EA) ... AIC
American Institute of Child Care Centers [*Defunct*] ... AICCC
American Institute of Child Life (SAUO) ... AICL
American Institute of Commemorative Art (EA) ... AICA
American Institute of Comparative Law and Legislation (SAUO) ... AICLL
American Institute of Computerized Accounting Professionals [*Defunct*] (EA) ... AICAP
American Institute of Constructors (EA) ... AIC
American Institute of Consulting Engineers [*Later, ACEC*] (EA) ... AICE
American Institute of Consulting Engineers (SAUO) ... AIConsE
American Institute of Cooperation [*Defunct*] (EA) ... AIC
American Institute of Criminology (SAUO) ... AIC
American Institute of Crop Ecology (EA) ... AICE
American Institute of Decorators (SAUO) ... AID
American Institute of Design and Drafting (SAUS) ... AIDD
American Institute of Discussion (SAUO) ... Am Inst Disc
American Institute of Driver Education (SAUO) ... AIDE
American Institute of Electrical and Electronics Engineers [*Also, IEEE*] (NTCM) ... AIEEE
American Institute of Electrical Engineers [*Later, IEEE*] ... AIEE
American Institute of Electrical Engineers (SAUO) ... AmerInstEE
American Institute of Electrical Engineers [*Later, IEEE*] ... AmInstEE
American Institute of Electrical Engineers. Proceedings (journ.) (SAUS) ... AIEE Proc
American Institute of Engineers ... AIE
American Institute of Esthetics (SAUO) ... AIE
American Institute of Family Relations ... AIFR
American Institute of Fellows in Free Enterprise [*Houston, DE*] (EA) ... FIFE
American Institute of Financial Brokers (EA) ... AIFB
American Institute of Fishery Research Biologists (EA) ... AIFRB
American Institute of Floral Designers (EA) ... AIFD
American Institute of Food Distribution (EA) ... AIFD
American Institute of France [*Defunct*] (EA) ... AIF
American Institute of Graphic Arts (EA) ... AIGA
American Institute of Group Counseling [*Defunct*] (EA) ... AIGC
American Institute of Homeopathy (EA) ... AIH
American Institute of Hydrology (EA) ... AIH
American Institute of Hypnotherapy ... AIH
American Institute of Indian Studies (EA) ... AIIS
American Institute of Indian Studies (SAUO) ... AILS
American Institute of Industrial Engineers [*Later, IIE*] (EA) ... AIIE
American Institute of Industrial Engineers. Detroit Chapier. Proceedings of the Annual Conference (journ.) (SAUS) ... AIDPA
American Institute of Interior Design (SAUS) ... AIID
American Institute of Interior Designers [*Later, ASID*] ... AID
American Institute of Interior Designers [*Later, ASID*] (AEBS) ... AIID
American Institute of Intermediate Coinage (SAUS) ... AIIC
American Institute of International Law (SAUO) ... AIIL
American Institute of Iranian Studies (EA) ... AIIS
American Institute of Islamic Studies (EA) ... AIIS
American Institute of Islamic Studies, Denver, CO [*Library symbol*] [*Library of Congress*] (LCLS) ... CoDAmI
American Institute of Kitchen Dealers ... AIKD
American Institute of Landscape Architects [*Later, ASLA*] (EA) ... AILA
American Institute of Laundering [*Later, IFI*] (EA) ... AIL
American Institute of Leisuretime (EA) ... AIL
American Institute of Maintenance (EA) ... AIM
American Institute of Man (SAUO) ... AIM
American Institute of Management [*Quincy, MA*] (EA) ... AIM
American Institute of Marine Development (SAUS) ... AIMD
American Institute of Marine Underwriters [*New York, NY*] (EA) ... AIMU
American Institute of Marine Underwriters (SAUO) ... AIU
American Institute of Maritime Services ... AIMS
American Institute of Marxist Studies (SAUS) ... AIMS
American Institute of Mathematical Statistics (SAUS) ... AIMS
American Institute of Mechanical Engineers (SAUO) ... AIME
American Institute of Mechanical Engineers (SAUO) ... AIMechE
American Institute of Medical and Biological Engineering ... AIMBE
American Institute of Medical Climatology (EA) ... AIMC
American Institute of Men's and Boys' Wear [*Later, MFA*] ... AIMBW
American Institute of Merchant Shipping [*Washington, DC*] (EA) ... AIMS
American Institute of Metallurgical, Mining and Petroleum Engineers (SAUO) ... AIME
American Institute of Mining and Metallurgical Engineers (NUCP) ... AIMME
American Institute of Mining and Metallurgy (SAUO) ... AIM&M
American Institute of Mining and Metallurgy (SAUS) ... AIM&M
American Institute of Mining Engineers (SAUS) ... AIME
American Institute of Mining, Metallurgical, and Petroleum Engineers (EA) ... AIME
American Institute of Mining, Metallurgical, and Petroleum Engineers (SAUO) ... AIMMPE
American Institute of Mortgage Brokers [*Washington, DC*] (EA) ... AIMB
American Institute of Musical Studies (EA) ... AIMS
American Institute of Nail and Tack Manufacturers (EA) ... AINTM
American Institute of Nautical Archaeology [*Later, INA*] (EA) ... AINA
American Institute of Nautical Archeology (SAUO) ... AINA
American Institute of Nutrition (EA) ... AIN
American Institute of Oral Biology (EA) ... AIOB
American Institute of Organbuilders (EA) ... AIO
American Institute of Pacific Relations [*Defunct*] ... AIPR
American Institute of Park Executives [*Later, APRS*] (EA) ... AIPE
American Institute of Parliamentarians (EA) ... AIP
American Institute of Pathologic Science [*Defunct*] (EA) ... AIPS
American Institute of Philanthropy (EA) ... AIP
American Institute of Physics (EA) ... AIP
American Institute of Physics. Information Program Newsletter (journ.) (SAUS) ... AIP Inf Progr Newsl
American Institute of Physics, New York, NY [*Library symbol*] [*Library of Congress*] (LCLS) ... NNAIP
American Institute of Planners [*Later, American Planning Association*] (EA) ... AIP
American Institute of Plant Engineers (EA) ... AIPE
American Institute of Polish Culture (EA) ... AIPC
American Institute of Pollution Prevention ... AIPP
American Institute of Professional Bookkeepers (NTPA) ... AIPB
American Institute of Professional Geologists (SAUS) ... AIFG
American Institute of Professional Geologists (EA) ... AIPG
American Institute of Psychoanalysis (SAUO) ... AIP
American Institute of Public Opinion (SAUO) ... AIPO
American Institute of Public Opinion [*Also, ARI*] (NTCM) ... AIPO
American Institute of Public Relations (SAUS) ... AIPR
American Institute of Radio Engineers [*Telecommunications*] [*An association*] (ECII) ... AIRE
American Institute of Real Estate Appraisers [*Later, AI*] (EA) ... AIREA
American Institute of Reciprocators [*Defunct*] (EA) ... AIR
American Institute of Refrigeration [*Defunct*] ... AIR
American Institute of Research (OICC) ... AIR
American Institute of Service Body Manufacturers (NTPA) ... AISBM
American Institute of Steel Construction (EA) ... AISC
American Institute of Steel Construction, Inc. (SAUO) ... AISC
American Institute of Stress (EA) ... AIS
American Institute of Supply Associations [*Later, ASA*] (EA) ... AISA
American Institute of Supply Associations (SAUO) ... AISA
American Institute of Tack Manufacturers (SAUS) ... AITM
American Institute of Tax Practice (EA) ... AITP
American Institute of Technical Illustrators Association [*Defunct*] (EA) ... AITIA
American Institute of Technology (MCD) ... AIT
American Institute of the City of New York (SAUS) ... AICNY
American Institute of the History of Pharmacy (EA) ... AIHP
American Institute of Timber Construction (EA) ... AITC
American Institute of Ultrasound in Medicine (EA) ... AIUM
American Institute of Ultrasound Medicine (MELL) ... AIUM
American Institute of Urban and Regional Affairs ... AIURA
American Institute of Vocal Pedagogy (EA) ... AIVP
American Institute of Weights and Measures [*Defunct*] (EA) ... AIWM
American Institute of Wholesale Plumbing and Heating Supply Associations (SAUO) ... AIWPHSA
American Institute of Wine and Food (EA) ... AIWF
American Institute on Problems of European Unity [*Later, AFPI*] (EA) ... AIPEU
American Institute on Problems of European Unity (SAUO) ... AIPEU
American Institute on Problems of European Unity (SAUS) ... AIPFU
American Institutes for Research [*Information service or system*] (IID) ... AIR
American Institutes for Research in the Behavioral Sciences (EA) ... AIR
American Institution in Thailand ... AIT
American Institution of Automobile Engineers (SAUO) ... AIAE
American Institutions Food Service Association (EA) ... AIFSA
American Instructors of the Deaf [*Also known as CAID*] (EA) ... AID
American Instrument Co. ... AMINCO
American Instruments Laboratory (SAUO) ... AIL
American Insulator Corporation (SAUO) ... AIC
American Insulator Corporation (SAUO) ... AICO
American Insurance Association [*New York, NY*] (EA) ... AIA
American Insurance Attorneys (NTPA) ... AIA
American Insurance Group [*Commercial firm*] ... AIG

American Insurance Services Group [*New York, NY*] (EA) .... AISG
American Insured Mortgage Investors - Series 85 Ltd. [*AMEX symbol*] (SPSG) .... AII
American Insured Mortgage Investors - Series 85 Ltd. [*Associated Press*] (SAG) .... AIM 85
American Insured Mortgage Investors - Series 86 Ltd. [*AMEX symbol*] (SPSG) .... AIJ
American Insured Mortgage Investors - Series 86 Ltd. [*Associated Press*] (SAG) .... AIM 86
American Insured Mortgage Investors - Series 88 Ltd. [*AMEX symbol*] (SPSG) .... AIK
American Insured Mortgage Investors 1988 [*Associated Press*] (SAG) .... AIM 88
American Insured Mortgage Investors Ltd. [*Associated Press*] (SAG) .... AIM 84
American Insured Mortgage Investors. Series 84 Ltd. [*AMEX symbol*] (SPSG) .... AIA
American Insurers Highway Safety Alliance (EA) .... AIHSA
American Intellectual Property Law Association (EA) .... AIPLA
American Interactive Media, Inc. [*Software manufacturer*] .... AIM
American Intercultural Student Exchange (EA) .... AISE
American Inter-Island, Inc. (SAUO) .... ITL
American International Academy [*Defunct*] (EA) .... AIA
American International Airways, Inc. [*ICAO designator*] (FAAC) .... AIT
American International Airways, Inc. [*FAA designator*] (FAAC) .... CKS
American International Assistance Service (SAUO) .... AIAS
American International Association for Economic and Social Development (SAUO) .... AIA
American International Association for Economic and Social Development [*Defunct*] (EA) .... AIA
American International Association for Economic and Social Development (SAUO) .... AIAESD
American International Assurance Co., Ltd. [*Commercial firm*] (ECON) .... AIA
American International Automobile Dealers Association (EA) .... AIADA
American International Automobile Dealers Association (SAUO) .... AIADS
American International Book Development Council (SAUO) .... AIBDC
American International Charolais Association (SAUO) .... AICA
American International Checkers Society (EA) .... AICS
American International College [*Springfield, MA*] .... AIC
American International College, Springfield, MA [*Library symbol*] [*Library of Congress*] (LCLS) .... MSAI
American International Communications Corp. [*Boulder, CO*] .... AIC
American International Corporation (SAUO) .... AMC
American International Data Search, Inc. [*Information service or system*] [*Defunct*] (IID) .... AIDSEARCH
American International Dragon Association (EA) .... AIDA
American International Exhibition for Travel (ITD) .... AIET
American International Freight Association .... AIFA
American International Group [*Associated Press*] (SAG) .... AmIntG
American International Group, Inc. [*NYSE symbol*] .... AIG
American International Health Alliance (SAUO) .... AIHA
American International Law Cases [*1783-1968*] [*A publication*] (DLA) .... AILC
American International Machigiana Society (SAUO) .... AIMS
American International Managers Society .... AIMS
American International Marchigiana Society (EA) .... AIMS
American International Media [*Joint venture of Philips International and PolyGram BV International*] .... AIM
American International Music Fund [*Defunct*] (EA) .... AIMF
American International Petroleum [*Associated Press*] (SAG) .... AmIntPt
American International Petroleum Corp. [*NASDAQ symbol*] (NQ) .... AIPN
American International Petroleum Corp. [*Associated Press*] (SAG) .... AmInPt
American International Pictures, Inc. .... AIP
American International Pictures Inc. (SAUO) .... AIP
American International Reinsurance Company (SAUO) .... AIRCO
American International Travel Service (IIA) .... AITS
American International Underwriters .... AIU
American Interplanetary Society (ACAE) .... AIS
American Interprofessional Institute [*Defunct*] (EA) .... AII
American Intersociety Board of Certification of Sanitarians (SAUO) .... AIBCS
American Intl. Pete Wrrt [*NASDAQ symbol*] (TTSB) .... AIPNW
American Intraocular Implant Society (SAUO) .... AIIS
American Intra-Ocular Implant Society [*Later, ASCRS*] (EA) .... AIOIS
American Inventors Association .... AIA
American Investment Company (SAUO) .... AIC
American Invitational Mathematics Examination [*Educational test*] .... AIME
American In-Vitro Allergy/ Immunology Society (SAUO) .... AIAIS
American Ionospheric Propagation Association .... AIPA
American Iraqui Shipping Company, Ltd. (SAUO) .... Am ISCL
American Ireland Fund (EA) .... AIF
American Iris Society (EA) .... AIS
American Irish Bicentennial Committee (EA) .... AIBC
American Irish Historical Society (EA) .... AIHS
American Irish Historical Society, New York, NY [*Library symbol*] [*Library of Congress*] (LCLS) .... NNAI
American Irish Political Education Committee (EA) .... PEC
American Irish Unity Committee (EA) .... AIUC
American Iron & Steel Engineers (SAUO) .... AISE
American Iron and Steel Institute (EA) .... AISI
American Iron and Steel Institute. Statistical Report [*A publication*] (EAAP) .... ASR
American Iron Ore Association (EA) .... AIOA
American Israel Numismatic Association (SAUO) .... AINA
American Israel Opera Foundation (EA) .... AIOF
American Israeli Civil Liberties Coalition (EA) .... AICLC
American Israeli Lighthouse (EA) .... AIL
American Israeli Paper Mills Ltd. [*AMEX symbol*] (SPSG) .... AIP
American Israeli Paper Mills Ltd. [*Associated Press*] (SAG) .... AIsrael
American Israeli Shipping (SAUO) .... AIS
American Israelite (BJA) .... AI
American Issues Forum [*American bicentennial project*] .... AIF
American Italian Congress (EA) .... AIC
American Italian Historical Association (EA) .... AIHA
American Ivy Society (EA) .... AIS
American Jail Association (EA) .... AJA
American Japanese Trade Committee (EA) .... AJTC
American Jazz Alliance [*Formerly, CJOA*] (EA) .... AJA
American Jazz Orchestra .... AJO
American Jersey Cattle Association (NTPA) .... AJCA
American Jersey Cattle Club (EA) .... AJCC
American Jesuit Missionary Association [*Later, JM*] (EA) .... AJMA
American Jewelry Marketing Association [*Defunct*] (EA) .... AJMA
American Jewish Alternatives to Zionism (EA) .... AJAZ
American Jewish Archives [*An association*] (EA) .... AJA
American Jewish Archives, Cincinnati, OH [*Library symbol*] [*Library of Congress*] (LCLS) .... OCAJA
American Jewish Archives (journ.) (SAUS) .... AJA
American Jewish Commission on the Holocaust (EA) .... AJCH
American Jewish Committee (EA) .... AJC
American Jewish Committee, New York, NY [*Library symbol*] [*Library of Congress*] (LCLS) .... NNAJ
American Jewish Committee (or Conference, or Congress) (SAUO) .... AJC
American Jewish Committee-Records Center (SAUO) .... AJC-RC
American Jewish Conference .... AJC
American Jewish Congress (EA) .... AJC
American Jewish Correctional Chaplains Association (EA) .... AJCCA
American Jewish Heritage Committee (EA) .... AJHC
American Jewish Historical Quarterly (journ.) (SAUS) .... AjHQ
American Jewish Historical Society (EA) .... AJHS
American Jewish Historical Society, Waltham, MA [*Library symbol*] [*Library of Congress*] (LCLS) .... MWalA
American Jewish History Center of the Jewish Theological Seminary [*Defunct*] (EA) .... AJHC
American Jewish Institute [*Later, JIB*] (EA) .... AJI
American Jewish Joint Distribution Committee (EA) .... AJJDC
American Jewish Joint Distribution Committee (EA) .... JDC
American Jewish Joint Distribution Committee Inc. (SAUO) .... AJDC
American Jewish Leadership Conference (EA) .... AJLC
American Jewish League Against Communism (EA) .... AJLAC
American Jewish League for Israel (EA) .... AJLI
American Jewish Periodical Center (EA) .... AJPC
American Jewish Periodical Center, Cincinnati, OH [*Library symbol*] [*Library of Congress*] (LCLS) .... OCAJ
American Jewish Philanthropic Fund (EA) .... AJPF
American Jewish Physicians' Committee [*Later, AFHU*] (EA) .... AJPC
American Jewish Physicians Committee (SAUS) .... AJPC
American Jewish Press Association (EA) .... AJPA
American Jewish Public Relations Society (EA) .... AJPRS
American Jewish Society for Service (EA) .... AJSS
American Jewish World Service (EA) .... AJWS
American Jews Against Ford (SAUO) .... AJAF
American Jews Opposed to Israeli Aggression (EA) .... AJOIA
American Jobs Abroad [*A publication*] .... AJA
American Joint Committee for Cancer Staging and End Results [*Oncology*] (DAVI) .... AJCCS & ER
American Joint Committee for Cancer Staging and End Results Reporting [*Later, AJCC*] (EA) .... AJC
American Joint Committee on Cancer (EA) .... AJCC
American Joint Committee on Cancer (SAUO) .... ASCE
American Joint Committee on Cancer Staging [*Oncology*] (DAVI) .... AJCCS
American Joint Distribution Committee .... AJDC
American Journal Law Review [*A publication*] (DLA) .... Am J L Rev
American Journal of Agricultural Economics (SAUS) .... Am J Agric Econ
American Journal of Alzheimers Care (journ.) (SAUS) .... AJAC
American Journal of Anatomy (journ.) (SAUS) .... AJA
American Journal of Anatomy (journ.) (SAUS) .... Amer J Anat
American Journal of Anesthesiology (SAUS) .... AJA
American Journal of Archaeology [*A publication*] (BRI) .... AJA
American Journal of Archaeology (journ.) (SAUS) .... AJAr
American Journal of Audiology (SAUS) .... AJA
American Journal of Botany (SAUS) .... Amer J Bot
American Journal of Botany (SAUS) .... Am J Bot
American Journal of Cardiology (SAUS) .... Amer J Cardiol
American Journal of Chinese Medicine (journ.) (SAUS) .... AJCM
American Journal of Chiropractic Medicine (SAUS) .... AJCM
American Journal of Clinical Hypnosis [*A publication*] .... AJCH
American Journal of Clinical Nutrition (journ.) (SAUS) .... AJCN
American Journal of Clinical Nutrition (journ.) (SAUS) .... Amer J Clin Nutr
American Journal of Clinical Oncology (journ.) (SAUS) .... AJCO
American Journal of Clinical Pathology (journ.) (SAUS) .... AJCP
American Journal of Clinical Pathology (journ.) (SAUS) .... Amer J Clin Pathol
American Journal of Comparative Law [*A publication*] .... AJCL
American Journal of Dentistry (SAUS) .... AJD
American Journal of Digestive Diseases (journ.) (SAUS) .... AJDDA
American Journal of Digestive Diseases (journ.) (SAUS) .... Amer J Dig Dis
American Journal of Diseases of Children (journ.) (SAUS) .... AJDC
American Journal of Diseases of Children (journ.) (SAUS) .... Am J Dis Child
American Journal of Economics and Sociology (SAUS) .... Am J Econ Sociol
American Journal of Economics and Sociology (journ.) (SAUS) .... AJES
American Journal of Economics and Sociology (journ.) (SAUS) .... AM J Econ
American Journal of Education [*A publication*] (BRI) .... AJE
American Journal of Education (journ.) (SAUS) .... Am J Educ
American Journal of Emergency Medicine (SAUS) .... AJEM

American Journal of Epidemiology. Johns Hopkins University, School of Hygiene. Baltimore (SAUS) .... JHU/AJE
American Journal of Epidemiology (journ.) (SAUS) .... AJE
American Journal of Epidemiology (journ.) (SAUS) .... Amer J Epidemiol
American Journal of Ethics &Medicine (SAUS) .... AJEM
American Journal of Forensic Psychiatry [*A publication*] (DLA) .... Am J For Psych
American Journal of Gastroenterology (journ.) (SAUS) .... AJG
American Journal of Gastroenterology (journ.) (SAUS) .... Amer J Gastroenterol
American Journal of Geriatric Psychiatry (SAUS) .... AJGP
American Journal of Health Behavior (SAUS) .... AJHB
American Journal of Health Communications (SAUS) .... AJHC
American Journal of Health Promotion (SAUS) .... AJHP
American Journal of Health-system Pharmacy (SAUS) .... AJHP
American Journal of Hematology (journ.) (SAUS) .... AJH
American Journal of Hospital Pharmacy (journ.) (SAUS) .... AJHP
American Journal of Hospital Pharmacy (journ.) (SAUS) .... Amer J Hosp Pharm
American Journal of Human Genetics (journ.) (SAUS) .... AJHG
American Journal of Human Genetics (journ.) (SAUS) .... Amer J Hum Genet
American Journal of Hygiene (journ.) (SAUS) .... AJH
American Journal of Hypertension (SAUS) .... AJH
American Journal of Industrial Medicine (journ.) (SAUS) .... AJIM
American Journal of Infection Control (journ.) (SAUS) .... AJIC
American Journal of Insanity (SAUS) .... AJI
American Journal of Integrated Healthcare (SAUS) .... AJIH
American Journal of International Law [*A publication*] .... AJIL
American Journal of International Law (SAUS) .... Am J Int Law
American Journal of International Law (journ.) (SAUS) .... Amer J Int Law
American Journal of Jurisprudence [*Lawyers Co-op*] [*A publication*] (AAGC) .... Am J Juris
American Journal of Kidney Diseases (SAUS) .... AJKD
American Journal of Law and Medicine (journ.) (SAUS) .... AJLM
American Journal of Managed Care [*A publication*] (MELL) .... AJMC
American Journal of Maternal/Child Health Nursing (SAUS) .... MCN
American Journal of Maternal/Child Nursing (SAUO) .... MCN
American Journal of Mathematics (journ.) (SAUS) .... AJM
American Journal of Mathematics (journ.) (SAUS) .... Amer J Math
American Journal of Medical Genetics (journ.) (SAUS) .... AJMG
American Journal of Medical Quality (SAUS) .... AJMQ
American Journal of Medical Technology (SAUS) .... AJMT
American Journal of Medical Technology (SAUS) .... Amer J Med Technol
American Journal of Medicine (journ.) (SAUS) .... AJM
American Journal of Medicine (journ.) (SAUS) .... Amer J Med
American Journal of Mental Deficiency (journ.) (SAUS) .... AJMD
American Journal of Mental Deficiency (journ.) (SAUS) .... Amer J Med Sci
American Journal of Mental Retardation (SAUS) .... AJMR
American Journal of Mental Sciences (SAUS) .... AJMS
American Journal of Neuroradiology [*A publication*] .... AJNR
American Journal of Nursing (IIA) .... AJN
American Journal of Nursing Co., New York, NY [*Library symbol*] [*Library of Congress*] (LCLS) .... NNAJN
American Journal of Obstetrics and Gynecology (journ.) (SAUS) .... AJOG
American Journal of Obstetrics and Gynecology (journ.) (SAUS) .... Amer J Obstet Gynecol
American Journal of Occupational Therapy (journ.) (SAUS) .... AJOT
American Journal of Ophthalmology (SAUS) .... AJO
American Journal of Opthalmology (SAUS) .... Amer J Opthalmol
American Journal of Optometry and Physiological Optics (journ.) (SAUS) .... AOP
American Journal of Optometry (journ.) (SAUS) .... AJO
American Journal of Optometry (journ.) (SAUS) .... Amer J Optom
American Journal of Orthodontics and Dentofacial Orthopedics (SAUS) .... AJO/DO
American Journal of Orthodontics (journ.) (SAUS) .... AJO
American Journal of Orthodontics (journ.) (SAUS) .... Amer J Orthodont
American Journal of Orthopedics (SAUS) .... Amer J Orthop
American Journal of Orthopsychiatry (journ.) (SAUS) .... AJOPs
American Journal of Orthopsychiatry (journ.) (SAUS) .... Amer J Orthopsychiat
American Journal of Otology (SAUS) .... AJO
American Journal of Pain Management (SAUS) .... AJPM
American Journal of Pathology (journ.) (SAUS) .... AJP
American Journal of Pathology (journ.) (SAUS) .... Amer J Pathol
American Journal of Pharmaceutical Education (SAUS) .... Amer J Pharm Educ
American Journal of Pharmacy and Sciences Supporting Public Health (SAUS) .... Amer J Pharm
American Journal of Pharmacy and Sciences Supporting Public Health (SAUS) .... APSHDH
American Journal of Pharmacy (journ.) (SAUS) .... AJP
American Journal of Philology [*A publication*] (BRI) .... AJP
American Journal of Physical Anthropology (journ.) (SAUS) .... AJPA
American Journal of Physical Anthropology (journ.) (SAUS) .... Amer J Phys Anthropol
American Journal of Physical Anthropology, New Series (SAUS) .... Am J Phys Anthrop ns
American Journal of Physical Medicine (SAUS) .... Amer J Phys Med
American Journal of Physics [*A publication*] (MEC) .... Am J Phys
American Journal of Physics (journ.) (SAUS) .... AJP
American Journal of Physics (journ.) (SAUS) .... AJPh
American Journal of Physiology (SAUS) .... AJP
American Journal of Physiology (SAUS) .... Amer J Physiol
American Journal of Physiology (SAUS) .... Am J Physiol
American Journal of Police Science [*A publication*] (DLA) .... Am J Police Sci
American Journal of Preventive Medicine (journ.) (SAUS) .... AJPM
American Journal of Psychiatry [*A publication*] .... AJP
American Journal of Psychiatry [*A publication*] (BRI) .... AJPsych
American Journal of Psychoanalysis (journ.) (SAUS) .... AJP
American Journal of Psychology [*A publication*] (BRI) .... A J Psy
American Journal of Psychotherapy (SAUS) .... AJP
American Journal of Psychotherapy (journ.) (SAUS) .... AJPst
American Journal of Public Health [*A publication*] (MELL) .... AJPH
American Journal of Public Health and the Nations Health (journ.) (SAUS) .... Amer J Public Health
American Journal of Public Health (journ.) (SAUS) .... Am J Pub Health
American Journal of Reproductive (SAUS) .... Am J Reprod Immunol
American Journal of Reproductive Immunology and Microbiology (SAUS) .... AJRIM
American Journal of Reproductive Immunology (journ.) (SAUS) .... AJRI
American Journal of Respiratory and Critical Care Medicine (SAUS) .... AJRCCM
American Journal of Respiratory Cell and Molecular Biology (SAUS) .... AJRCMB
American Journal of Roentgenology (journ.) (SAUS) .... AJR
American Journal of Roentgenology, Radium Therapie and Nuclear Medicine (journ.) (SAUS) .... Amer J Roentgenol Radium Th
American Journal of School Hygiene (journ.) (SAUS) .... Am J School Hygiene
American Journal of Semitic Language and Literatures (SAUS) .... AJSL
American Journal of Semitic Languages (SAUS) .... Am J Sem Lang
American Journal of Small Business (journ.) (SAUS) .... Jl Small Bus
American Journal of Sociology [*A publication*] (BRI) .... AJS
American Journal of Sociology [*A publication*] (DLA) .... Am Jour Soc
American Journal of Speech-Language Pathology (SAUS) .... AJSLP
American Journal of Sports Medicine [*A publication*] (MEC) .... Amer J Sports Med
American Journal of Sports Medicine (journ.) (SAUS) .... AJSM
American Journal of Surgery (journ.) (SAUS) .... AJS
American Journal of Surgery (journ.) (SAUS) .... Amer J Surg
American Journal of Surgical Pathology (journ.) (SAUS) .... AJSP
American Journal of Tax Policy [*A publication*] (DLA) .... Am J Tax Pol'y
American Journal of the Medical Sciences (journ.) (SAUS) .... AJMS
American Journal of the Medical Sciences (journ.) (SAUS) .... Amer J Med Sci
American Journal of Theology (journ.) (SAUS) .... AM J Theol
American Journal of Trial Advocacy [*A publication*] (DLA) .... Am J Trial Advoc
American Journal of Tropical Medicine and Hygiene (SAUS) .... Amer J Trop Med Hyg
American Journal of Veterinary Research (journ.) (SAUS) .... AJVR
American Journal of Veterinary Research (journ.) (SAUS) .... Amer J Vet Res
American Journal on Addictions (SAUS) .... AJA
American Journal on Mental Retardation [*A publication*] (BRI) .... AJMR
American Journalism Historians Association (NTPA) .... AJHA
American Journalism Review [*A publication*] [*Formerly, WJR Washington Journalism Review*] (WDMC) .... AJR
American Judges Association (EA) .... AJA
American Judicature Society (EA) .... AJS
American Judo Association (EA) .... AJA
American Junior Academy of Sciences .... AJAS
American Junior Bowling Congress (EA) .... AJBC
American Junior Brahman Association (EA) .... AJBA
American Junior Chianina Association (EA) .... AJCA
American Junior College of Puerto Rico, Bayamon, PR [*Library symbol*] [*Library of Congress*] (LCLS) .... PrBayA
American Junior College of Puerto Rico, Bayamon, PR [*OCLC symbol*] (OCLC) .... PRJ
American Junior Golf Association (EA) .... AJGA
American Junior Hereford Association (EA) .... AJHA
American Junior High School National Mathematics Exam .... AJHSNME
American Junior Paint Horse Association (EA) .... AJPHA
American Junior Polled Hereford Association [*Later, NJPHA*] (EA) .... AJPHA
American Junior Quarter Horse Association (EA) .... AJQHA
American Junior Red Cross .... AJRC
American Junior Rodeo Association .... AJRA
American Junior Shorthorn Association (EA) .... AJSA
American Junior Simmental Association [*Later, ASA*] (EA) .... AJSA
American Jurisprudence [*A publication*] (DLA) .... Am Jr
American Jurisprudence [*A publication*] (DLA) .... Am Jur
American Jurisprudence (journ.) (SAUS) .... AJ
American Jurisprudence Legal Forms [*A publication*] (DLA) .... Am Jur Legal Forms
American Jurisprudence Legal Forms, Annotated [*A publication*] (DLA) .... Am J Leg Forms Anno
American Jurisprudence Legal Forms, Annotated [*A publication*] (DLA) .... Am Jur Leg Forms Anno
American Jurisprudence Legal Forms, Second Series [*A publication*] (DLA) .... Am Jur Legal Forms 2d
American Jurisprudence Pleading and Practice Forms, Annotated [*A publication*] (DLA) .... Am J Pl & Pr Forms Anno
American Jurisprudence Pleading and Practice Forms, Annotated [*A publication*] (DLA) .... Am Jur Pl & Pr Forms
American Jurisprudence Pleading and Practice Forms, Revised Editions [*A publication*] (DLA) .... Am Jur Pl & Pr Forms (Rev Ed)
American Jurisprudence Proof of Facts [*A publication*] (DLA) .... Am J Proof of Facts
American Jurisprudence Proof of Facts [*A publication*] (DLA) .... Am Jur Proof of Facts
American Jurisprudence Proof of Facts [*A publication*] .... POF
American Jurisprudence Proof of Facts, Annotated [*A publication*] (DLA) .... Am Jur Proof of Facts Anno
American Jurisprudence, Second Series [*A publication*] (DLA) .... Am J 2d
American Jurisprudence, Second Series [*A publication*] (DLA) .... Am Jur 2d
American Jurisprudence Trials [*A publication*] (DLA) .... Am J Trials
American Jurisprudence Trials [*A publication*] (DLA) .... Am Jur Trials
American Jurist [*A publication*] (DLA) .... AJ
American Jurist [*A publication*] (DLA) .... Amer Jur
American Jurist [*A publication*] (DLA) .... Am Jr
American Jurist [*A publication*] (DLA) .... Am Jur
American Jurist [*A publication*] (DLA) .... Am Jurist

American Justice Federation [*An association*] .... AJF
American Justice Institute (EA) .... AJI
American Justinian Society of Jurist (SAUO) .... AJSJ
American Justinian Society of Jurists (SAUO) .... AJSJ
American Juvenile Arthritis Organization (EA) .... AJAO
American Karakul Fur Sheep Registry [*Later, AKSR*] (EA) .... AKFSR
American Karakul Sheep Registry (EA) .... AKSR
American Kennel Club (EA) .... AKC
American Kennel Club, New York, NY [*Library symbol*] [*Library of Congress*] (LCLS) .... NNAKC
American Kidney Fund (EA) .... AKF
American Killifish Association (EA) .... AKA
American Kinesiotherapy Association (EA) .... AKA
American Kinesiotherapy Association (NTPA) .... AKTA
American Kitefliers Association (EA) .... AKA
American Knit Glove Association (EA) .... AKGA
American Labor Arbitration Awards [*Prentice-Hall, Inc.*] [*A publication*] (DLA) .... ALAA
American Labor Arbitration Awards (Prentice-Hall, Inc.) [*A publication*] (DLA) .... Am Lab Arb Awards (P-H)
American Labor Arbitration Awards (Prentice-Hall, Inc.) [*A publication*] (DLA) .... P-H Am Lab Arb Awards
American Labor Arbitration Cases [*Prentice-Hall, Inc.*] [*A publication*] (DLA) .... Am Lab Arb Cas
American Labor Arbitration Services [*A publication*] (DLA) .... Am Lab Arb Serv
American Labor Cases [*Prentice-Hall, Inc.*] [*A publication*] (DLA) .... ALC
American Labor Cases [*Prentice-Hall, Inc.*] [*A publication*] (DLA) .... ALR
American Labor Cases [*Prentice-Hall, Inc.*] [*A publication*] (DLA) .... Am Lab Cas
American Labor Cases (Prentice-Hall, Inc.) [*A publication*] (DLA) .... P-H Am Lab Cas
American Labor Committee for Human Rights in Northern Ireland (EA) .... ALCHRNI
American Labor Education Center (EA) .... ALEC
American Labor Education Service [*Defunct*] .... ALES
American Labor Health Association [*Later, GHAA*] .... ALHA
American Labor Health Association (SAUO) .... ALHA
American Labor Legislation Review (journ.) (SAUS) .... Am Labor Leg R
American Labor Party .... ALP
American Lace Manufacturers Association .... ALMA
American Ladder Institute (EA) .... ALI
American LaMancha Club (EA) .... ALC
American Lamb Council (EA) .... ALC
American Laminators Association (EA) .... ALA
American Lancia Club (EA) .... ALC
American Land Alliance [*Defunct*] (EA) .... ALA
American Land Army (SAUO) .... ALA
American Land Development Association (EA) .... ALDA
American Land Forum [*Later, ALRA*] (EA) .... ALF
American Land Resource Association [*Defunct*] (EA) .... ALRA
American Land Rights Association (NTPA) .... ALRA
American Land Sailing Association (SAUO) .... ALSA
American Land Title Association (EA) .... ALTA
American Landrace Association (EA) .... ALA
American Landscape Architects (SAUO) .... ALA
American Landscape Horticulture Association (EA) .... ALHA
American Langshan Club (EA) .... ALC
American Language Academy (SAUO) .... ALA
American Language College Placement Test (DNAB) .... ALCPT
American Language Course [*Military*] (DNAB) .... ALC
American Laryngeal Papilloma Foundation (EA) .... ALPF
American Laryngological Association (EA) .... ALA
American Laryngological, Rhinological, and Otological Society (EA) .... ALROS
American Laryngological, Rhinological and Otological Society (SAUO) .... ALROS
American Laser Systems Inc. (SAUO) .... ALS
American Latvian Association in the United States (EA) .... ALA
American Lava Corporation (SAUO) .... ALCO
American Law Enforcement Officers Association (EA) .... ALEOA
American Law Firms for African Relief [*Defunct*] (EA) .... ALFAR
American Law Institute (EA) .... ALI
American Law Institute - American Bar Association Council of Legal Education Review [*A publication*] (DLA) .... ALI-ABA CLE Rev
American Law Institute - American Bar Association. Course Materials Journal [*A publication*] (DLA) .... ALI-ABA Course MJ
American Law Institute Federal Income Tax Project [*A publication*] (DLA) .... ALI Fed Income Tax Project
American Law Institute Model Land Development Code [*A publication*] (DLA) .... Model Land Dev Code
American Law Institute. Restatement of the Law [*A publication*] (DLA) .... Am Law Inst
American Law Institute. Restatement of the Law [*A publication*] (DLA) .... Am L Ins
American Law Institute. Restatement of the Law [*A publication*] (DLA) .... Am L Inst
American Law Magazine [*A publication*] (DLA) .... Am L Mag
American Law Network [*Telecommunications service*] (TSSD) .... ALN
American Law of Elections [*A publication*] (DLA) .... Am L Elec
American Law of Property [*A publication*] (DLA) .... Am Property
American Law of Veterans [*A publication*] (DLA) .... Am Vets
American Law Record [*Cincinnati*] [*A publication*] (DLA) .... AL Rec
American Law Record [*Cincinnati*] [*A publication*] (DLA) .... Am Law Rec
American Law Record [*Ohio*] [*A publication*] (DLA) .... Am L Rec
American Law Record (SAUS) .... Rec
American Law Record (Reprint) [*Ohio*] [*A publication*] (DLA) .... Am Law Rec
American Law Record (Reprint) [*Ohio*] [*A publication*] (DLA) .... Am Law Record
American Law Record (Reprint) (Ohio) [*A publication*] (DLA) .... Am L Rec (Ohio)
American Law Register [*A publication*] (DLA) .... ALR
American Law Register [*Philadelphia*] [*A publication*] (DLA) .... AL Reg
American Law Register [*Philadelphia*] [*A publication*] (DLA) .... Am Law Reg
American Law Register [*Philadelphia*] [*A publication*] (DLA) .... Am L Reg
American Law Register [*Philadelphia*] [*A publication*] (DLA) .... Law Reg
American Law Register (SAUS) .... NS Am Law Register
American Law Register and Review [*A publication*] (DLA) .... Am L Reg & Rev
American Law Register, New Series [*A publication*] (DLA) .... AL Reg (NS)
American Law Register, New Series [*A publication*] (ILCA) .... ALRNS
American Law Register, New Series [*A publication*] (DLA) .... Amer Law Reg (NS)
American Law Register, New Series [*A publication*] (DLA) .... Am Law Reg NS
American Law Register, New Series [*A publication*] (DLA) .... Am L Reg (NS)
American Law Register, Old Series [*A publication*] (DLA) .... AL Reg (OS)
American Law Register, Old Series [*A publication*] (DLA) .... Amer Law Reg (OS)
American Law Register, Old Series [*A publication*] (DLA) .... Am Law Reg OS
American Law Register, Old Series [*A publication*] (DLA) .... Am L Reg (OS)
American Law Register (Reprint) [*Ohio*] [*A publication*] (DLA) .... Am Law Reg (Old Ser)
American Law Register (Reprint) [*Ohio*] [*A publication*] (DLA) .... NS Am Law Register
American Law Reporter [*Davenport, IA*] [*A publication*] (DLA) .... AL Rep
American Law Reporter [*Davenport, IA*] [*A publication*] (DLA) .... Am L Rep
American Law Reports .... ALR
American Law Reports Annotated, 1st-5th Series [*Lawyers Co-op*] [*A publication*] (AAGC) .... ALR
American Law Reports, Annotated, Federal [*A publication*] (DLA) .... ALR Fed
American Law Reports, Annotated, Fourth Series [*A publication*] (DLA) .... ALR 4th
American Law Reports, Annotated, Second Series [*A publication*] (DLA) .... ALR 2d
American Law Reports, Annotated, Third Series [*A publication*] (DLA) .... ALR 3d
American Law Reports Later Case Service [*A publication*] (DLA) .... ALRLCS
American Law School Review [*A publication*] (DLA) .... Am Law S Rev
American Law School Review [*A publication*] (DLA) .... Am L School Rev
American Law School Review [*A publication*] (DLA) .... Am L Sch Rev
American Law School Review [*A publication*] (DLA) .... Am LS Rev
American Law Student Association [*Later, Law Student Division - American Bar Association*] (EA) .... ALSA
American Law Times [*A publication*] (DLA) .... ALT
American Law Times [*A publication*] (DLA) .... Am LT
American Law Times, Bankruptcy Reports [*A publication*] (DLA) .... ALT Bankr
American Law Times, Bankruptcy Reports [*A publication*] (DLA) .... AM LT Bankr
American Law Times, Bankruptcy Reports [*A publication*] (DLA) .... Am LT Bankr Rep
American Law Times, Bankruptcy Reports [*A publication*] (DLA) .... Bank Ct Rep
American Law Times, Bankruptcy Reports [*A publication*] (DLA) .... Bank Rep
American Law Times Reports [*A publication*] (DLA) .... ALTR
American Law Times Reports [*A publication*] (DLA) .... Am Law T Rep
American Law Times Reports [*A publication*] (DLA) .... Am LTR
American Law Times Reports [*A publication*] (DLA) .... Am LT Rep
American Law Times Reports, New Series [*United States*] [*A publication*] (DLA) .... ALTRNS
American Law Times Reports, New Series [*A publication*] (DLA) .... Am LTRNS
American Lawn Bowling Association (SAUO) .... ALBA
American Lawn Bowls Association (EA) .... ALBA
American Lawyers Association [*Later, TAG*] (EA) .... ALA
American Lawyers Auxiliary (EA) .... ALA
American Leadership Forum (EA) .... ALF
American Leading Cases [*A publication*] (DLA) .... ALC
American Leading Cases [*A publication*] (DLA) .... Amer Lea Cas
American Leading Cases [*A publication*] (DLA) .... Am LC
American Leading Cases [*A publication*] (DLA) .... Am L Cas
American Leading Cases [*A publication*] (DLA) .... Am Lead Cases
American Leading Cases [*A publication*] (DLA) .... Am Leading Cas
American Leading Cases, Edited by Hare and Wallace [*A publication*] (DLA) .... Am Lead Cas
American Leading Cases, Edited by Hare and Wallace [*A publication*] (DLA) .... Am Lead Cas (H & W)
American Leading Cases, Edited by Hare and Wallace [*A publication*] (DLA) .... Hare & Wallace Amer Leading Cases
American Leading Cases, Edited by Hare and Wallace [*A publication*] (DLA) .... Hare & Wallace Lead Cases (Am)
American Leading Cases, Edited by Hare and Wallace [*A publication*] (DLA) .... Hare & Wal LC
American Leading Cases, Edited by Hare and Wallace [*A publication*] (DLA) .... Lead Cas Am
American Leading Cases (Edition of 1871) [*A publication*] (DLA) .... Am Lead Ca (Ed of 1871)
American Leage for Peace and Democracy (SAUO) .... ALPD
American League [*Baseball*] .... A
American League [*Baseball*] .... AL
American League Against War and Fascism (SAUO) .... ALAWF
American League Championship Series [*Baseball*] .... ALCS
American League for Exports and Security Assistance [*Washington, DC*] (EA) .... ALESA
American League of Anglers (EA) .... ALA
American League of Anglers and Boaters (EA) .... ALAB
American League of Anglers, Inc. (SAUO) .... ALA
American League of Authors and Composers from Austria (SAUO) .... ALACA
American League of Automobilists (SAUO) .... ALA
American League of Financial Institutions [*Washington, DC*] (EA) .... ALFI
American League of Lobbyists (EA) .... ALL
American League of Professional Baseball Clubs (EA) .... ALPBC
American League to Abolish Capital Punishment [*Defunct*] (EA) .... ALACP
American Leather Belting Association [*Later, NIBA*] .... ALBA

American Leather Chemists Association (EA) ... ALCA
American Lebanese League (EA) ... ALL
American Lebanese Medical Association (EA) ... ALMA
American Lebanese Syrian Association Charities (EA) ... ALSAC
American Leduc Petroleums Ltd. [*Toronto Stock Exchange symbol*] ... ARL
American Legal Foundation [*WLF*] [*Absorbed by*] (EA) ... ALF
American Legal News [*A publication*] (DLA) ... Am Leg N
American Legal Studies Association (EA) ... ALSA
American Legation, United States Naval Attache (MUGU) ... ALUSNA
American Legation, United States Naval Liaison Officer ... ALUSLO
American Legation, United States Naval Liaison Officer (MCD) ... ALUSNLO
American Legation, United States Naval Observer ... ALUSNOB
American Legend (EA) ... AL
American Legend Cooperative (NTPA) ... ALC
American Legion (EA) ... AL
American Legion Auxiliary (EA) ... ALA
American Legion Auxiliary Juniors (SAUO) ... ALAJRS
American Legion Auxiliary Library, Cheyenne Wells, CO [*Library symbol*] [*Library of Congress*] (LCLS) ... CoChey
American Legion Baseball (EA) ... ALB
American Legion Convention (SAUO) ... ALC
American Legion, National Headquarters Library, Indianapolis, IN [*Library symbol*] [*Library of Congress*] (LCLS) ... InIAL
American Legion of Honor ... AL of H
American Legion Press Association [*Later, NALPA*] (EA) ... ALPA
American Legion Press Association (SAUO) ... ALPA
American Legion Transportation Post ... ALTP
American Legislative Exchange Council (EA) ... ALEC
American Legislator [*A publication*] (DLA) ... Am Leg
American Leprosy Mission (SAUO) ... ALM
American Leprosy Missions (EA) ... ALM
American Leprosy Missions (EA) ... ALMI
American Lessing Society [*Later, LS*] (EA) ... ALS
American Lessing Society (SAUO) ... ALS
American Lhasa Apso Club (EA) ... ALAC
American Liaison Office ... ALO
American Liberal Association (EA) ... ALA
American Liberation League ... ALL
American Liberty League (SAUO) ... ALL
American Librarians Agency (SAUS) ... Am Librarians
American Libraries [*Magazine*] (AL) ... AL
American Libraries [*A publication*] (BRI) ... A Lib
American Libraries (journ.) (SAUS) ... AmLibr
American Library and Educational Services Co. ... ALESCO
American Library and Educational Services Company (SAUO) ... ALESCO
American Library Association (EA) ... ALA
American Library Association Board of Education for Librarianship (SAUO) ... ALABEL
American Library Association, Booklist, Chicago, IL [*OCLC symbol*] (OCLC) ... JAB
American Library Association Bulletin (journ.) (SAUS) ... ALA Bull
American Library Association Chapter Relations Committee ... ALACRC
American Library Association, Chicago, IL [*Library symbol*] [*Library of Congress*] (LCLS) ... ICALA
American Library Association, Chicago, IL [*OCLC symbol*] (OCLC) ... IEH
American Library Association Information Science and Automation Division (NITA) ... ALA/ISAD
American Library Association Office for Library Personnel Resources (EA) ... ALAOLPR
American Library Association Washington Office Newsletter (SAUO) ... ALAWON
American Library Association-Information Science and Automation Division (SAUS) ... ALA-ISAD
American Library Association-Information Service and Automation Division (SAUO) ... ALA-ISAD
American Library Association's Electronic Information Service ... ALANET
American Library Association/Social Responsibilities Round Table/Gay and LesbianTask Force (EA) ... ALA/SRRT/GLTF
American Library Directory [*R. R. Bowker Co.*] [*Online database*] ... ALD
American Library for Education, Research, and Training ... ALERT
American Library History Round Table ... ALHRT
American Library in Paris ... ALP
American Library in Paris, Paris, France [*Library symbol*] [*Library of Congress*] (LCLS) ... FrPALP
American Library Society [*Defunct*] ... ALS
American Library Trustee Association (EA) ... ALTA
American Library Trustees Association (SAUO) ... ALTA
American Licensed Practical Nurses Association (EA) ... ALPNA
American Life Convention [*Later, ACLI*] ... ALC
American Life Education and Research Trust (EA) ... ALERT
American Life Federation (SAUO) ... ALF
American Life Foundation [*Press*] ... ALF
American Life Group, Inc. [*NYSE symbol*] (SAG) ... AGP
American Life Group, Inc. [*Associated Press*] (SAG) ... AmLife
American Life Holding Co. [*NASDAQ symbol*] (SAG) ... ALHC
American Life Holding Co. [*Associated Press*] (SAG) ... AmLfe
American Life Insurance Association [*Later, ACLI*] (EA) ... ALIA
American Life Insurance Co. [*Surinam*] (EY) ... ALICO
American Life Insurance Convention (SAUO) ... ALC
American Life League (EA) ... ALL
American Life Lobby (EA) ... ALL
American Lifesaving Emergency Response Team (EA) ... ALERT
American Lighting Association (EA) ... ALA
American Lighting Equipment Association (SAUO) ... ALEA
American Lightwave [*Vancouver Stock Exchange symbol*] ... AWV
American List Corp. [*Associated Press*] (SAG) ... AmList
American List Corp. [*AMEX symbol*] (SPSG) ... AMZ
American Liszt Society (EA) ... ALS
American Literary Anthology ... ALA
American Literary Magazine (journ.) (SAUS) ... Am Lit M
American Literary Society [*Defunct*] (EA) ... ALS
American Literary Translators Association (EA) ... ALTA
American Literature [*A publication*] (BRI) ... AL
American Lithotripsy Society (EA) ... ALS
American Lithuanian Catholic Federation Ateitis [*Later, LCFA*] (EA) ... ALCFA
American Lithuanian Engineers' and Architects' Association (EA) ... ALEAA
American Lithuanian Musicians Alliance (EA) ... ALMA
American Lithuanian Organist - Musicians Alliance [*Formerly, ALRCOA*] (EA) ... ALOMA
American Lithuanian Press and Radio Association ... ALPRA
American Lithuanian Press and Radio Association - Viltis (EA) ... ALPRA-V
American Lithuanian Roman Catholic Federation Ateitis (SAUO) ... ALRCFA
American Lithuanian Roman Catholic Organist Alliance [*Later, ALOMA*] (EA) ... ALRCOA
American Lithuanian Roman Catholic Organist Alliance (SAUO) ... ALRCOL
American Lithuanian Roman Catholic Women's Alliance [*Later, LCW*] (EA) ... ALRCWA
American Lithuanian Workers Literary Association (EA) ... ALWLA
American Littoral Society (EA) ... ALS
American Liver Foundation (EA) ... ALF
American Lives Endowment [*Defunct*] (EA) ... ALE
American Livestock Association (SAUO) ... ALA
American Loan Fund ... ALF
American Lobbyists Directory [*A publication*] ... ALD
American Lock Collectors Association (EA) ... ALCA
American Locker Group, Inc. [*NASDAQ symbol*] (NQ) ... ALGI
American Locker Group, Inc. [*Associated Press*] (SAG) ... AmLck
American Locomotive Company (SAUO) ... ALC
American Locomotive Company (SAUO) ... ALCO
American Logistics Association (EA) ... ALA
American Longevity Association (EA) ... ALA
American Loudspeaker Manufacturers Association (EA) ... ALMA
American Low Power Television Association [*Defunct*] (EA) ... ALPTA
American Luggage Dealers Association [*Later, ALDC*] (EA) ... ALDA
American Luggage Dealers Cooperative (EA) ... ALDC
American Lumber Standards ... ALS
American Lumber Standards Committee (EA) ... ALSC
American Lumen [*Record label*] ... AmLum
American Lunar Society (EA) ... ALS
American Lung Association (EA) ... ALA
[*The*] **American Lupus Society** (EA) ... TALS
American Lutheran Church (SAUO) ... ALC
American Lutheran Church [*Later, ELCA*] ... ALC
American Lutheran Church Men (EA) ... ALCM
American Lutheran Church Women [*Defunct*] (EA) ... ALCW
American Lutheran Conference (SAUO) ... ALConf
American Lutheran Education Association [*Later, ELEA*] (EA) ... ALEA
American Lutheran Evangelical Churches (SAUO) ... ALEC
American Lutheran Publicity Bureau (EA) ... ALPB
American Luxembourg Society (EA) ... ALS
American Lyceum Association (SAUS) ... TALA
American Lyme Disease Foundation (EA) ... ALDF
American Lyric Poems: from Colonial Times to the Present [*A publication*] ... AmLP
American Macaroni Export Institute (SAUS) ... AMEI
American Machine and Foundry (SAUS) ... AMF
American Machine & Foundry Co. (SAUO) ... AMF
American Machine Tool Distributors Association (EA) ... AMTDA
American Machine Tool Export Associates (EA) ... AMTEA
American Machinery Association ... AMA
American Machinist/Metalworking Manufacturing (journ.) (SAUS) ... Amer Mach/Metalwork Mfg
American Magazine of Art (journ.) (SAUS) ... AM M Art
American Magnetics Corp. (MHDW) ... AMMG
American Magnolia Society [*Later, TMS*] (EA) ... AMS
American Mail Line ... AML
American Mailorder Association (EA) ... AMOA
American Mail-Order Merchants Association (EA) ... AMMA
American Maine-Anjou Association (EA) ... AMAA
American Majority Party (EA) ... AMP
American Malacological Bulletin (SAUS) ... Am Malacol Bull
American Malacological Union (EA) ... AMU
American Malacological Union, Inc. Bulletin (SAUO) ... AMUBBK
American Malacological Union, Inc. Bulletin (journ.) (SAUS) ... AMUBBK
American Malacologists (SAUS) ... Am Malacologists
American Maltese Association (EA) ... AMA
American Malting Barley Association (EA) ... AMBA
American Managed Behavioral Healthcare Association (NTPA) ... AMBHA
American Managed Care and Review Association (EA) ... AMCRA
American Managed Care Pharmacy Association (EA) ... AMCPA
American Management Association [*New York, NY*] (EA) ... AMA
American Management Associations, New York, NY [*Library symbol*] [*Library of Congress*] (LCLS) ... NNAMA
American Management Institute (IIA) ... AMI
American Management Systems [*Associated Press*] (SAG) ... AMS
American Management Systems, Inc. [*Information service or system*] (IID) ... AMS
American Management Systems, Inc. [*NASDAQ symbol*] (NQ) ... AMSY
American Manchester Terrier Club (EA) ... AMTC
American Manganese Producers Association [*Defunct*] (EA) ... AMPA
American Manganese Steel Company (SAUO) ... AMSCO

American Manufacturing Company (SAUO) ... AMCO
American Map Company (SAUO) ... Am Map
American Map Service (SAUO) ... AMS
American Marine Hull Insurance Syndicate (SAUO) ... AMHIS
American Marine Insurance Clearing House (SAUO) ... AMICH
American Marine Insurance Clearinghouse [*New York, NY*] (EA) ... AMIC
American Marine Insurance Forum [*New York, NY*] (EA) ... AMIF
American Marine Insurance Syndicate (SAUO) ... AMIS
American Marine Insurance Syndicate for Insurance of Builder's Risks [*Defunct*] (EA) ... AMISIBR
American Marine Standards Committee (SAUO) ... AMSC
American Maritain Association (EA) ... AMA
American Maritime Association (EA) ... AMA
American Maritime Cases ... AMC
American Maritime Congress (NTPA) ... AMC
American Maritime Institute (SAUO) ... AMI
American Maritime Officers Service (EA) ... AMOS
American Market for International Program [*Telecommunications*] ... AMIP
American Market Selection [*Cigars*] ... AMS
American Marketing Association [*Chicago, IL*] (EA) ... AMA
American Marketing Service (SAUS) ... AMS
American Marksmanship Unit (SAUO) ... AMU
American Massage and Therapy Association (SAUS) ... AMTA
American Massage Therapy Association (EA) ... AMTA
American Match Council (NTPA) ... AMC
American Material Handling Society [*Later, IMMS*] (EA) ... AMHS
American Material Handling Society, Inc. (SAUO) ... AMHS
American Material Standard (SAUS) ... AMS
American Materials & Technologies Corp. (The) [*Associated Press*] (SAG) ... AmMatT
American Materials & Technologies Corp. (The) [*NASDAQ symbol*] (SAG) ... AMTK
American Mathematical Association of Two-Year Colleges (SAUS) ... AMATYC
American Mathematical Monthly [*A publication*] ... AMM
American Mathematical Monthly (journ.) (SAUS) ... AMMO
American Mathematical Society (SAUO) ... Am Math Soc
American Mathematical Society (EA) ... AMS
American Mathematical Society, Providence, RI [*Library symbol*] [*Library of Congress*] (LCLS) ... RPAM
American Mathematical Society TEX (SAUO) ... AMS-TEX
American Mathematics Competitions (SAUS) ... AMC
American Mathematics Project (EA) ... AMP
American Matthay Association (EA) ... AMA
American McAll Association (EA) ... AMA
American Mead Association [*Inactive*] (EA) ... AMA
American Measuring Instrument Company (SAUO) ... AMICO
American Measuring Tool Manufacturers Association [*Defunct*] (EA) ... AMTMA
American Meat Institute (EA) ... AMI
American Meat Institute Foundation (EA) ... AMIF
American Meat Science Association (EA) ... AMSA
American Mechanical Rights Agency ... AMRA
American Med Technologies [*NASDAQ symbol*] (TTSB) ... AMTI
American Medallic Sculpture Association (EA) ... AMSA
American Media, Inc. [*Formerly, Enquirer/Star Group*] [*Associated Press*] (SAG) ... Amdia
American Media, Inc. [*Formerly, Enquirer/Star Group*] [*Associated Press*] (SAG) ... AMedia
American Media, Inc. [*Formerly, Enquirer/Star Group*] [*NYSE symbol*] (SAG) ... ENQ
American Medical Acceleration Laboratory (SAUS) ... AMAL
American Medical Accreditation Program (SAUO) ... AMAP
American Medical Alert Corp. [*NASDAQ symbol*] (NQ) ... AMAC
American Medical Alert Corp. [*Associated Press*] (SAG) ... AMdAlt
American Medical Association (EA) ... AMA
American Medical Association Alliance (EA) ... AMAA
American Medical Association Auxiliary (EA) ... AMAA
American Medical Association/ California Medical Association (SAUO) ... AMA/CMA
American Medical Association, Chicago, IL [*Library symbol*] [*Library of Congress*] (LCLS) ... ICAM
American Medical Association Committee on Insurance and Prepayment Plans (SAUO) ... AMA-CIPP
American Medical Association, Division of Library and Archival Services, Chicago, IL [*OCLC symbol*] (OCLC) ... AMA
American Medical Association Drug Evaluation ... AMA-DE
American Medical Association Education and Research Foundation (EA) ... AMA-ERF
American Medical Association Education and Research Foundation (SAUO) ... AMAERF
American Medical Association Enterprise Information Base (SAUO) ... AMA EIB
American Medical Association Network (NITA) ... AMA/NET
American Medical Association Political Action Committee ... AMAPAC
American Medical Association, Washington Office, Washington, DC [*Library symbol*] [*Library of Congress*] (LCLS) ... DAMA
American Medical Association Womens Auxiliary (SAUS) ... AMAWA
American Medical Assurance Company (SAUO) ... AMACO
American Medical Athletic Association (EA) ... AMAA
American Medical Center at Denver (AAMN) ... AMCD
American Medical Center for Burma [*Defunct*] (EA) ... AMCB
American Medical Center, Medical Library, Denver, CO [*Library symbol*] [*Library of Congress*] (LCLS) ... CoDAMC-M
American Medical College Application Service ... AMCAS
American Medical College Association (SAUO) ... AMCA
American Medical Computer Center (SAUS) ... AMCC
American Medical Curling Association (EA) ... AMCA
American Medical Directors Association (EA) ... AMDA
American Medical Directory [*A publication*] (DHP) ... AMD
American Medical Division, American Near East Refugee Aid (EA) ... AMER
American Medical Education Foundation (SAUO) ... AMEF
American Medical Electroencephalographic Association (DAVI) ... AMEA
American Medical Electroencephalographic Association (EA) ... AMEEGA
American Medical Equestrian Association (EA) ... AMEA
American Medical Fly Fishing Association (EA) ... AMFFA
American Medical Golf Association (EA) ... AMGA
American Medical Group Association (NTPA) ... AMGA
American Medical Holdings (EFIS) ... AMI
American Medical Holdings, Inc. [*Associated Press*] (SAG) ... AMedH
American Medical Informatics Association (EA) ... AMIA
American Medical International (SAUO) ... AMI
American Medical International, Inc. (SAUS) ... AMI
American Medical International (journ.) (SAUS) ... AMI
American Medical Joggers Association [*Later, AMAA*] ... AMJA
American Medical Mission to Russia (SAUO) ... AMMR
American Medical News (SAUO) ... AMNews
American Medical Optics [*Commercial firm*] (DAVI) ... AMO
American Medical Optics Posterior Chamber [*Lens*] [*Ophthalmology*] (DAVI) ... AMO PC
American Medical Peer Review Association (EA) ... AMPRA
American Medical Peer Review Organization (SAUO) ... AMPRO
American Medical Political Action Committee (EA) ... AMPAC
American Medical Publishers' Association (EA) ... AMPA
American Medical Qualification [*British*] ... AMQ
American Medical Radio News (MELL) ... AMRN
American Medical Record Association (EA) ... AMRA
American Medical Records Association (SAUS) ... AMRA
American Medical Relief for Italy (SAUO) ... AMRI
American Medical Research Expedition to Mount Everest ... AMREE
American Medical Resources Foundation (DMAA) ... AMRF
American Medical Response [*Associated Press*] (SAG) ... AmMdRs
American Medical Response [*NYSE symbol*] (SPSG) ... EMT
American Medical Sailing and Yachting Association (SAUO) ... AMSYA
American Medical Security Group, Inc. ... AMS
American Medical Society for Sports Medicine (NTPA) ... AMSSM
American Medical Society on Alcoholism ... AMSA
American Medical Society on Alcoholism and Other Drug Dependencies [*Later, ASAM*] (EA) ... AMSAODD
American Medical Specialty Organization (SAUO) ... AMSO
American Medical Student Association (EA) ... AMSA
American Medical Support Flight Team [*Later, Operation Angel Plane*] (EA) ... AMSFT
American Medical Systems [*Commercial firm*] (DAVI) ... AMS
American Medical Systems, Inc., Minneapolis, MN [*Library symbol*] [*Library of Congress*] (LCLS) ... MnMAM
American Medical Technologies [*NASDAQ symbol*] (SAG) ... AMTI
American Medical Technologies, Inc. [*Associated Press*] (SAG) ... AmMdTc
American Medical Technologists (EA) ... AMT
American Medical Technology, Inc. [*Vancouver Stock Exchange symbol*] ... AMO
American Medical Television ... AMT
American Medical Tennis Association (EA) ... AMTA
American Medical Women's Association (EA) ... AMWA
American Medico-Legal Society (SAUO) ... AMLS
American Medicorp, Inc. (SAUO) ... Medicorp
American Medserve Corp. [*NASDAQ symbol*] (SAG) ... AMCI
American Medserve Corp. [*Associated Press*] (SAG) ... AmMdsv
American Megatrends, Inc. (SAUS) ... AMI
American Megatrends Incorporated (SAUO) ... AMI
American Melting Point ... AMP
American Men and Women of Science [*R. R. Bowker Co.*] [*Information service or system*] [*A publication*] (IID) ... AMWS
American Men and Women of Science [*Database*] [*R. R. Bowker Co.*] [*Information service or system*] (CRD) ... MWSC
American Men of Letters [*A publication*] ... AML
American Men of Science (SAUS) ... Amer Men Sci
American Mental Health Alliance (SAUO) ... AMHA
American Mental Health Counselors Association (EA) ... AMHCA
American Mental Health Foundation (EA) ... AMHF
American Mental Health Fund (EA) ... AMHF
American Merchandise Display Osaka [*Department of Commerce*] [*Japan*] (IMH) ... AMDO
American Merchant Marine (SAUO) ... AMM
American Merchant Marine Institute [*Later, AIMS*] (EA) ... AMMI
American Merchant Marine Institute, Inc. (SAUO) ... AMMI
American Merchant Marine Library Association (EA) ... AMMLA
American Merchant Marine Library Association, New York, NY [*Library symbol*] [*Library of Congress*] (LCLS) ... NNAMM
American Merchant Marine Veterans (EA) ... AMMV
American Merchant Marine Victory Medal (SAUS) ... AMMVM
American Messianic Fellowship (EA) ... AMF
American Metal Climax, Inc. [*Later, AMAX, Inc.*] ... AMAX
American Metal Climax, Inc. (SAUO) ... AMM
American Metal Climax, Inc. (SAUO) ... AMX
American Metal Detector Manufacturers Association (EA) ... AMDMA
American Metal Importers Association [*Defunct*] [*Defunct*] (EA) ... AMIA
American Metal Importes Association (SAUO) ... AMIA
American Metal Market forum (SAUS) ... AMM forum
American Metal Products (SAUS) ... APS
American Metal Products Co. (SAUO) ... APS
American Metal Repair Association [*Defunct*] ... AMRA
American Metal Stamping Association [*Later, PMA*] (EA) ... AMSA
American Metalcraft Corporation (SAUO) ... AMC

American Metalworking Technology for the European Community (SAA) ... AMTEC
American Metaphysical Association (EA) ... AMA
American Meteor Society (EA) ... AMS
American Meteorite Laboratory ... AML
American Meteorite Laboratory (SAUS) ... Am Meteorite
American Meteorological Observation Station (HGAA) ... AMOS
American Meteorological Society (SAUO) ... AmeS
American Meteorological Society [*Boston, MA*] ... AMS
American Meter Company (SAUO) ... AEM
American Metered Postage Society [*Defunct*] (EA) ... AMPS
American Methanol Institute ... AMI
American Mexican Claims Commission [*Terminated, 1947*] ... AMCC
American MGB Association (EA) ... AMGBA
American MGC Register (EA) ... AMGCR
American Micro Co., Kansas City, MO [*Library symbol*] [*Library of Congress*] (LCLS) ... AmCo
American Microchemical Society (EA) ... AMS
American Microfilm Association (SAUO) ... AMA
American Microfilm Information Society [*An association*] (ECII) ... AMFIS
American Microscopical Society (EA) ... AMS
American Microsystems Incorporated (SAUO) ... AMI
American Micro-Systems Incorporated/Metal Oxide Semiconductor (SAUO) ... AMI/MOS
American Microsystems International (SAUS) ... AMI
American Microwave, Inc. (SAUO) ... AMI
American Middle East Rehabilitation (EA) ... AMER
American Middle East Relief (SAUO) ... AMER
American Mideast Business Association (SAUO) ... AMBA
American Midland Naturalist (SAUS) ... Am Midl Nat
American Midwest Conference (PSS) ... AMWC
American Military Assistance Staff ... AMAS
American Military Assistance to Yugoslavia (SAUO) ... AMAY
American Military Association ... AMA
American Military Government ... AMG
American Military Government - Free Territory of Trieste (SAUO) ... AMG-FTT
American Military Industrial Complex ... AMERIMIC
American Military Institute (EA) ... AMI
American Military Insurance Association (SAUO) ... AMIA
American Military International Insurance Association (SAUO) ... AMILA
American Military Mission (SAUO) ... AMM
American Military Mission, Delhi [*World War II*] ... AMMDEL
American Military Mission to China [*World War II*] ... AMMISCA
American Military Music Association (EA) ... AMMA
American Military Police (SAUO) ... AMP
American Military Precision Flying Teams Association (EA) ... AMPFTA
American Military Retirees Association (EA) ... AMRA
American Military Society (EA) ... AMS
American Military Standard (SAUS) ... AMS
American Military University ... AMU
American Milk Goat Record Association [*Later, ADGA*] (EA) ... AMGRA
American Milking Devon Association (EA) ... AMDA
American Milking Shorthorn Junior Society (EA) ... AMSJS
American Milking Shorthorn Society (EA) ... AMSS
American Millinery Manufacturers Association [*Defunct*] ... AMMA
American Mime Theatre (EA) ... AMT
[*The*] **American Mime Theatre** (EA) ... TAMT
American Mineral Spirits (SAUS) ... AMS
American Mineral Spirits Company (SAUO) ... AMSCO
American Mineralogist (SAUS) ... Am Mineral
American Mineralogist (journ.) (SAUS) ... Amer Mineral
American Miniature Horse Association (EA) ... AMHA
American Miniature Horse Registry (EA) ... AMHR
American Miniature Racing Car Association ... AMRCA
American Miniature Schnauzer Club (EA) ... AMSC
American Mining Congress (EA) ... AMC
American Mining, Metallurgical, and Petroleum Engineers (SAUO) ... AMMPE
American Mining, Metallurgical and Petroleum Engineers (SAUS) ... AMMPE
American Ministerial Association (EA) ... AMA
American Minor Breeds Conservancy (EA) ... AMBC
American Miscellaneous Society (EA) ... AMSOC
American Mission for Aid to Greece ... AMAG
American Mission for Aid to Turkey ... AMAT
American Mission for Opening Churches (EA) ... AMOC
American Mission for Opening Closed Churches [*Later, AMOC*] (EA) ... AMOCC
American Mission in Korea ... AMIK
American Mission to Greece (SAUO) ... AMG
American Mission to Greeks [*Later, AMG International*] (EA) ... AMG
American Mission to the Chinese [*Later, American Mission to the Chinese and Asian*] (EA) ... AMC
American Mission to the Chinese (SAUO) ... AMC
American Mission to the Chinese and Asian [*Defunct*] (EA) ... AMCA
American Missionary Association ... AMA
American Missionary Fellowship (EA) ... AMF
American Mizrachi Women [*Formerly, MWOA*] (EA) ... AMW
American Mobile Satellite Corp. [*Associated Press*] (SAG) ... AmMbSat
American Mobile Satellite Corp. [*NASDAQ symbol*] (SAG) ... SKYC
American Mobile Telecommunications Association (NTPA) ... AMTA
American Mobilehome Association (EA) ... AMA
American Model Yachting Association (EA) ... AMYA
American Modern Dance Caucus (EA) ... AMDC
American Modified Golf Association (EA) ... AMGA
American Mohammedan Society [*Later, MM*] (EA) ... AMS
American Mold Builders Association (EA) ... AMBA
American Money Management Association [*Barrington, IL*] (EA) ... AMM
American Monitor Corp. (MCD) ... AMC
American Montessori Society (EA) ... AMS
American Monument Association (SAUO) ... AM
American Monument Association (EA) ... AMA
American Morab Horse Association (EA) ... AMHA
American Moral Reform Society (SAUO) ... AMRS
American Morgan Horse Association (EA) ... AMHA
American Morgan Horse Institute (EA) ... AMHI
American Mosquito Control Association (EA) ... AMCA
American Mosquito Extermination Society (SAUO) ... AMES
American Motel Association (EA) ... AMA
American Mothers Committee (EA) ... AMC
American Mothers, Inc. (EA) ... AMI
American Mothers of Korean Orphans (EA) ... AMKO
American Motility Society (EA) ... AMS
American Motion Picture Export Co. (EA) ... AMPEC
American Motion Picture Export Co./Africa [*Later, AMPEC*] [*An association*] (EA) ... AMPECA
American Motivational Association (EA) ... AMA
American Motor Company (SAUO) ... AMC
American Motor Hotel Association (EA) ... AMHA
American Motorcycle Association (SAUO) ... AMA
American Motorcycle Drag Racing Association [*of the National Hot Rod Association*] [*Later, NMRA*] (EA) ... AMDRA
American Motorcycle Heritage Foundation (EA) ... AMHF
American Motorcyclist Association (EA) ... AMA
American Motorcyclist Political Action Committee ... AMPAC
American Motors (SAUO) ... AM
American Motors (SAUO) ... Am Motors
American Motors (SAUS) ... AMO
American Motors Corp. ... AM
American Motors Corp. ... AMC
American Motors Corp. (SAUO) ... AMO
American Motors Corporation (SAUO) ... AMC
American Motors Owners Association (EA) ... AMO
American Motorsport International (EA) ... AMI
American Movement for World Government (EA) ... AMWG
American Movers Conference (EA) ... AMC
American Movers Institute (SAUO) ... AMI
American Movie Classics [*Cable-television network*] ... AMC
American Mule Association (EA) ... AMA
American Multi Cinema [*Third largest theatre chain in America*] ... AMC
American Municipal Association [*Later, NLC*] (EA) ... AMA
American Municipal Bond Assurance Corp. ... AMBAC
American Municipal Bond Assurance Corporation (SAUO) ... AMBAC
American Municipal Income Portfolio [*NYSE symbol*] (SPSG) ... XAA
American Municipal Income Portfolio, Inc. [*Associated Press*] (SAG) ... AMunInc
American Municipal Term Trust [*Associated Press*] (SAG) ... AmMuTr
American Municipal Term Trust [*NYSE symbol*] (SPSG) ... AXT
American Municipal Term Trust II [*Associated Press*] (SAG) ... AmMuT2
American Municipal Term Trust II [*NYSE symbol*] (SAG) ... BXT
American Municipal Term Trust III [*Associated Press*] (SAG) ... AmMuT3
American Municipal Term Trust III [*NYSE symbol*] (SPSG) ... CXT
American Munitions Maintenance & Inspection Consortium (SAUS) ... AMMICON
American Murray Grey Association (EA) ... AMGA
American Museum Novitates (SAUS) ... Am Mus Novit
American Museum Novitates (journ.) (SAUS) ... AMUNAL
American Museum of Atomic Energy (SAUO) ... AMAE
American Museum of Immigration (EA) ... AMI
American Museum of Magic (SAUO) ... Am Mus Mag
American Museum of Marine Archaeology ... AMMA
American Museum of Marine Archeology (SAUS) ... AMMA
American Museum of Natural History (SAUS) ... AMNH
American Museum of Natural History, New York, NY [*Library symbol*] [*Library of Congress*] (LCLS) ... NNM
American Museum of Natural History, New York, NY [*OCLC symbol*] (OCLC) ... YAM
American Museum of Photography (SAUO) ... AMP
American Museum of Safety (EA) ... AMS
American Museum of Social Anthropology (SAUO) ... AMSA
American Museum of the Moving Image [*New York City*] (ECON) ... AMMI
American Mushroom Institute (EA) ... AMI
American Music [*A publication*] (BRI) ... Am M
American Music Center (EA) ... AMC
American Music Conference (EA) ... AMC
American Music Festival Association (EA) ... AMFA
American Music Foundation (SAUO) ... AMF
American Music Scholarship Association (EA) ... AMSA
American Music Teacher [*A publication*] (BRI) ... Am MT
American Music Teacher (journ.) (SAUS) ... AMUTA
American Music Theater Festival ... AMTF
American Musical Instrument Society (EA) ... AMIS
American Musicians Union (EA) ... AMU
American Musicological Society (EA) ... AMS
American Musicological Society. Journal (journ.) (SAUS) ... AMSJ
American Muslim Council ... AMC
American Mustang and Burro Association (EA) ... AMBA
American Mustang Association (EA) ... AMA
American Mutual Alliance [*Insurance association*] [*Later, Alliance of American Insurers*] ... AMA
American Mutual Insurance Alliance (SAUO) ... AMIA
American Mutual Life Association (EA) ... AMLA
American Nail Producers Council ... ANPC
American Nail Producers Society (SAUO) ... ANPS
American Name Society (SAUO) ... ANA

American Name Society (EA) ... ANS
American Naprapathic Association (EA) ... ANA
American Narcolepsy Association (EA) ... ANA
American National Archives (DIT) ... ANA
American National Bancorp [*Associated Press*] (SAG) ... ANatBc
American National Bancorp [*NASDAQ symbol*] (SAG) ... ANBK
American National Bank and Trust Company (SAUO) ... ANB & TC
American National Cattle Women (EA) ... ANCW
American National Cattlemen's Association [*Later, NCA*] (EA) ... ANCA
American National Commission for the Accreditation of Colleges and Universities (EA) ... ANCACU
American National Committee for Homeless Armenians (SAUO) ... ANCHA
American National Committee to Aid Homeless Armenians (EA) ... ANCHA
American National Council for Health Education of the Public (EA) ... ANCHEP
American National Cowbelles [*Later, ANCW*] (EA) ... ANC
American National Cowbelles [*Later, ANCW*] (EA) ... ANCB
American National Dictionary for Information Processing (SAUS) ... ANDIP
American National Dictionary for Information Processing Systems [*A publication*] ... ANDIPS
American National Fine (SAUS) ... ANF
American National Form (SAUS) ... ANF
American National Fur Breeders Association (SAUS) ... ANFRA
American National Heritage Association (EA) ... ANHA
American National Holding Company (SAUO) ... ANHC
American National Insurance Co. [*NASDAQ symbol*] (NQ) ... ANAT
American National Insurance Co. ... ANI
American National Insurance Co. [*Associated Press*] (SAG) ... ANtIns
American National Insurance Company (SAUO) ... ANICO
American National Metric Council (EA) ... ANMC
American National Postal Employees Retirees Association (EA) ... ANPERA
American National Red Cross (SAUO) ... AMCROSS
American National Red Cross [*Later, ARC*] ... ANRC
American National Red Cross, Washington, DC [*Library symbol*] [*Library of Congress*] (LCLS) ... DARC
American National Resources Planning Board (SAUO) ... ANRPB
American National Savings Bank [*NASDAQ symbol*] (SAG) ... ANBK
American National Standard [*ANSI*] (MCD) ... ANS
American National Standard Character Set for Optical Character Recognition (MCD) ... ANSCS OCR
American National Standard Character Set for Optical Character Recognition (SAUS) ... ANSCSOCR
American National Standard Code for Information Interchange (SAUS) ... ANSCH
American National Standard Code for Information Interchange (MCD) ... ANSCII
American National Standard Code for Information Interchange (SAUO) ... ASCII
American National Standard for Bibliographic References (SAUS) ... ANSBR
American National Standard Institute (SAUS) ... ANSI
American National Standard Institute Common Business Oriented Language (SAUS) ... ANSCOBOL
American National Standard Labels (BUR) ... ANL
American National Standard Vocabulary for Information Processing ... ANSVIP
American National Standards Committee (SAUO) ... ANSC
American National Standards Institute (EA) ... ANSI
American National Standards (Institute) Committee [*Later, NISO*] ... ANSC
American National Standards Institute Committee on Pulp, Paper and Paperboard (SAUO) ... ANSIP3
American National Standards Institute, Inc. (SAUO) ... ANSI
American National Standards Institute, New York, NY [*Library symbol*] [*Library of Congress*] (LCLS) ... NNASA
American National Standards Institute/American Society for Quality Control (RDA) ... ANSI/ASQC
American National Taper Shank (SAUS) ... ANTS
American National Theater [*Kennedy Center for the Performing Arts*] ... ANT
American National Theater (or Theatre) and Academy (SAUO) ... ANTA
American Nationalities Council (EA) ... ANC
American Native Press Research Association [*Defunct*] (EA) ... ANPRA
American Natural Energy Corp. [*Associated Press*] (SAG) ... AmNtEn
American Natural Energy Corp. [*NASDAQ symbol*] (SAG) ... ANEC
American Natural Gas (SAUS) ... ANG
American Natural Gas Co. (SAUO) ... ANG
American Natural Hygiene Society (EA) ... ANHS
American Natural Resources (SAUS) ... ANR
American Natural Resources Co. (EFIS) ... ANR
American Natural Soda Ash Corp. (EA) ... ANSAC
American Naturalist (SAUS) ... Am Nat
American Naturalized Citizen Welfare Association [*Later, US Naturalized CitizenAssociation*] (EA) ... ANCWA
American Nature Association [*Defunct*] ... ANA
American Nature Study Society (EA) ... ANSS
American Naturopathic Association (NTPA) ... ANA
American Naturopathic Medical Association (EA) ... ANMA
American Navion Society (EA) ... ANS
American Navy (SAUO) ... AN
American Nazi Party (SAUO) ... ANP
American NAZI Party [*Later, NSWWP*] ... ANP
American Near East Refugee Aid (EA) ... ANERA
American Near East Relief Agency (SAUO) ... ANERA
American Needlepoint Guild (EA) ... ANG
American Negligence Cases [*A publication*] (DLA) ... Am Neg Ca
American Negligence Cases [*A publication*] (DLA) ... Am Neg Cas
American Negligence Cases [*A publication*] (DLA) ... Am Neg Cases
American Negligence Cases [*A publication*] (DLA) ... Am Negl Cas
American Negligence Cases [*A publication*] (DLA) ... ANC
American Negligence Digest [*A publication*] (DLA) ... Am Neg Dig
American Negligence Reports [*A publication*] (DLA) ... Am Negl R
American Negligence Reports [*A publication*] (DLA) ... Am Negl Rep
American Negligence Reports [*A publication*] (DLA) ... Am Neg Rep
American Negligence Reports, Current Series [*A publication*] (DLA) ... ANR
American Negro Academy (SAUO) ... ANA
American Negro Poetry [*A publication*] ... AmNP
American Nephrology Nurses Association (SAUS) ... ANNA
American Neturei Karta [*Friends of Jerusalem*] (EA) ... ANK
American Network Communications (SAUS) ... ANC
American Network, Inc. [*Portland, OR*] (TSSD) ... AMNET
American Network, Inc. (SAUS) ... ANWI
American Network, Incorporated (SAUO) ... ANWI
American Network of Community Options and Resources (NTPA) ... ANCOR
American Neurological Association (EA) ... ANA
American Neuromodulation Society (EA) ... ANS
American Neuropsychiatric Association (EA) ... ANA
American Neuropsychiatric Association (NTPA) ... ANPA
American Neurotology Society (EA) ... ANS
American Newcomen Society ... ANS
American News Company (SAUO) ... ANC
American News Service (SAUO) ... ANS
American News Women's Club (EA) ... ANWC
American Newspaper Association ... ANA
American Newspaper Guild [*Later, TNG*] (EA) ... ANG
American Newspaper Publishers Abstracting Technique ... ANPAT
American Newspaper Publishers Association (EA) ... ANPA
American Newspaper Publishers Association Foundation (EA) ... ANPAF
American Newspaper Publishers' Association Technical Exposition and Conference (ITD) ... ANPA/TEC
American Newspaper Publishers' Association/Research Institute (DGA) ... ANPA/RI
American Newspaper Publishers Association-Research Institute (SAUO) ... ANPA-RI
American Newspaper Representatives (SAUO) ... ANR
American Newspapers, 1821-1936 [*A bibliographic publication*] ... AN
American Nickel Collectors' Association (EA) ... ANCA
American Nitrox Divers Incorporated (SAUO) ... ANDI
American Nobel Anniversary Committee (EA) ... ANAC
American Nominalist Group (EA) ... ANG
American Normande Association (EA) ... ANA
American North Country Cheviot Sheep Association (EA) ... ANCCSA
American Norwich Society [*Defunct*] (EA) ... ANS
American Notary [*A publication*] (DLA) ... Am Notary
American Nouthetic Psychology Association (EA) ... ANPA
American Nuclear Corp. (SAUO) ... ANUC
American Nuclear Corporation (SAUO) ... ANC
American Nuclear Energy Council (EA) ... ANEC
American Nuclear Insurers [*Farmington, CT*] (EA) ... ANI
American Nuclear Science Corporation (SAUO) ... ANSC
American Nuclear Society (EA) ... ANS
American Nuclear Standards Institute ... ANSI
American Numismatic Association (EA) ... ANA
American Numismatic Association Certification Service ... ANACS
American Numismatic Association, Colorado Springs, CO [*Library symbol*] [*Library of Congress*] (LCLS) ... CoCAN
American Numismatic Exchange (SAUS) ... ANE
American Numismatic Society (EA) ... ANS
American Numismatic Society Museum Notes (journ.) (SAUS) ... ANSMusN
American Numismatic Society, New York, NY [*Library symbol*] [*Library of Congress*] (LCLS) ... NNAN
American Nursery Association (SAUO) ... ANA
American Nurses' Association (EA) ... ANA
American Nurses Association California (SAUO) ... ANAC
American Nurses' Association, Kansas City, MO [*Library symbol*] [*Library of Congress*] (LCLS) ... MoKA
American Nurses Association\California (SAUS) ... ANA\C
American Nurses Credentialing Center (SAUO) ... ANCC
American Nurses Foundation (SAUO) ... ANF
American Nurses in Business Association (NTPA) ... ANBA
American Nursing Assistante Association (SAUS) ... ANAA
American Nursing Assistants Association (SAUO) ... ANAA
American Nursing Assistant's Foundation (EA) ... ANCF
American Nursing Home Association [*Later, AHCA*] (EA) ... ANHA
American Nursing Informatics Association (SAUO) ... ANIA
American Nutrition Society (EA) ... ANS
American Nutritionists Association (EA) ... ANA
American Oat Association (NTPA) ... AOA
American Obesity Association (NTPA) ... AOA
American Observer, British Navy (SAUS) ... Am Obs BN
American Occupational Health Conference (SAUO) ... AOHC
American Occupational Medical Association (EA) ... AOMA
American Occupational Therapy Association (EA) ... AOTA
American Occupational Therapy Certification Board [*AOTA*] ... AOTCB
American Occupational Therapy Foundation (MEDA) ... AOTF
American Occupational Therapy Political Action Committee [*AOTA*] ... AOTPAC
American Oceanic Organization (EA) ... AOO
American Oceanographic and Meteorological Laboratory (SAUS) ... AOML
American Oceanographic Organization (GEOI) ... AOO
American Oceanology Association (SAUO) ... AOA
American Oceans Campaign [*An association*] (EA) ... AOC
American Office Supply Exporters Association [*Defunct*] (EA) ... AOSEA
American Oil and Gas Corporation (SAUS) ... AOG
American Oil Chemists Society (SAUS) ... AOCS
American Oil Chemists' Society (EA) ... AOCS
American Oil Co. [*Later, Amoco Oil Co.*] ... AMOCO
American Oil Co. [*Later, Amoco Oil Co.*], **Texas City, TX** [*Library symbol*] [*Library of Congress*] (LCLS) ... TxTA

American Oil Company (NTIO) .... Amoco
American Oilfield Divers, Inc. [*Associated Press*] (SAG) .... AmOilfDv
American Oilfield Divers, Inc. [*NASDAQ symbol*] (SAG) .... DIVE
American Oilseed Coalition (NTPA) .... AOC
American Old Time Fiddlers Association (EA) .... AOTFA
American Olympic Committee (SAUO) .... AOC
American Oncology Resources, Inc. [*Associated Press*] (SAG) .... AOncol
American Oncology Resources, Inc. [*NASDAQ symbol*] (SAG) .... AORI
American Online (SAUS) .... AO
American Ontoanalytic Association (EA) .... AOA
American Open University [*Computer science*] .... AOU
American Opera Society (SAUO) .... AOS
American Ophthalmological Color [*Chart*] .... AOC
American Ophthalmological Society (EA) .... AOS
American Opportunity Foundation [*Washington, DC*] (EA) .... AOF
American Opportunity Income [*NYSE symbol*] (SPSG) .... OIF
American Opportunity Income Fund, Inc. [*Associated Press*] (SAG) .... AOIF
American Opthalmological Color (SAUS) .... AOC
American Optical Company (SAUO) .... AOC
American Optical Corp. .... AO
American Optical Corp., Southbridge, MA [*Library symbol*] [*Library of Congress*] (LCLS) .... MSbrA
American Optical Differential Interference Contrast Microscope (SAUS) .... AODICV
American Optical Laser Welder/Driller (SAUS) .... AOLW/D
American Optometric Association (EA) .... AOA
American Optometric Foundation (EA) .... AOF
American Optometric Student Association (EA) .... AOSA
American Orchid Society (EA) .... AOS
American Order of Corpsmen and Combat Medics (EA) .... AOCCM
American Order of Pioneers (GEAB) .... AOP
American Order of Stationary Engineers (SAUO) .... AOSE
American Order of Stationary Engineers .... AOSE
American Order of the French Croix de Guerre (EA) .... AOFCG
American [*or Army*] **Ordnance Association** [*Later, ADPA*] (EA) .... AOA
American Ordnance Association (SAUO) .... AOA
American Ordnance Limited Liability Corporation .... AO LLC
American Orff-Schulwerk Association (EA) .... AOSA
American Organization for Rehabilitation through Training Federation (SAUO) .... AORTF
American Organization for the Education (SAUS) .... AOE
American Organization for the Education of the Hearing Impaired [*Later, IOEHI*] (EA) .... AOEHI
American Organization of Analytical Chemists (ABAC) .... AOAC
American Organization of Nurse Executives (EA) .... AONE
American Organization of Tour Operators to Israel [*Defunct*] (EA) .... AOTOI
American Oriental Bodywork Therapy Association (NTPA) .... AOBTA
American Oriental Society (EA) .... AOS
American Oriental Society Journal (SAUO) .... Amer Oriental Soc Jour
American Oriental Society Journal (SAUO) .... Am Oriental Soc J
American Ornithologists' Union (EA) .... AOU
American Orthodontic and Prosthetic Association (SAUO) .... AOPA
American Orthodontic Society (EA) .... AOS
American Orthopaedic Society for Sports Medicine (EA) .... AOSSM
American Orthopedic Association (EA) .... AOA
American Orthopedic Foot and Ankle Society (EA) .... AOFAS
American Orthopedic Foot Society [*Later, AOFAS*] (EA) .... AOFS
American Orthopsychiatric Association (EA) .... AOA
American Orthopsychiatric Association (SAUO) .... AOrPA
American Orthopsychiatric Association (EA) .... ORTHO
American Orthoptic Council (EA) .... AOC
American Orthoptic Journal (journ.) (SAUS) .... AOJTAW
American Orthotic and Prosthetic Association (EA) .... AOPA
American Osler Society (EA) .... AOS
American Osteopathic Academy of Addiction Medicine (NTPA) .... AOAAM
American Osteopathic Academy of Orthopedics (EA) .... AOAO
American Osteopathic Academy of Sclerotherapy (EA) .... AOAS
American Osteopathic Academy of Sports Medicine (EA) .... AOASM
American Osteopathic Association (EA) .... AOA
American Osteopathic Association, Chicago, IL [*Library symbol*] [*Library of Congress*] (LCLS) .... ICAO
American Osteopathic Board of Emergency Medicine (EA) .... AOBEM
American Osteopathic Board of Family Physicians (EA) .... AOBFP
American Osteopathic Board of General Practice (EA) .... AOBGP
American Osteopathic Board of Pediatrics (EA) .... AOBP
American Osteopathic College of Allergy and Immunology (EA) .... AOCAI
American Osteopathic College of Anesthesiologists (EA) .... AOCA
American Osteopathic College of Dermatology (EA) .... AOCD
American Osteopathic College of Nuclear Medicine [*Defunct*] (EA) .... AOCNM
American Osteopathic College of Pathologists (EA) .... AOCP
American Osteopathic College of Pathologists .... AOCPA
American Osteopathic College of Physical Medicine and Rehabilitation (SAUO) .... AOCPMR
American Osteopathic College of Preventive Medicine (EA) .... AOCPM
American Osteopathic College of Proctology (EA) .... AOCP
American Osteopathic College of Proctology .... AOCPR
American Osteopathic College of Proctology (EA) .... AOCPr
American Osteopathic College of Radiology (EA) .... AOCR
American Osteopathic College of Rehabilitation Medicine (EA) .... AOCRM
American Osteopathic College of Rheumatology (EA) .... AOCR
American Osteopathic Colleges of Ophthalmology and Otolaryngology, Head and Neck Surgery (SAUO) .... AOCOOHNS
American Osteopathic Foundation (SAUO) .... AOF
American Osteopathic Healthcare Association (EA) .... AOHA
American Osteopathic Historical Society [*Defunct*] (EA) .... AOHS
American Osteopathic Hospital Association (EA) .... AOHA
American Osteopathic Hospital Research and Education Foundation (EA) .... AOHREF
American Osteopathic Network [*American Osteopathic Association*] [*Information service or system*] (IID) .... AONET
American Osteopathic Network (SAUS) .... AONET
American Ostrich Association (EA) .... AOA
American Otological Society (EA) .... AOS
American Otological Society (SAUO) .... AOtS
American Otorhinolaryngologic Society for Plastic Surgery (SAUO) .... AOSPS
American Otorhinologic Society for Plastic Surgery [*Later, AAFPRS*] (EA) .... AOSPS
American Outboard Federation .... AOF
American Outpost in Great Britain (SAUS) .... AOGB
American Outreach Association (EA) .... AOA
American Overseas Airlines .... AOA
American Overseas Association [*Later, ARCOA*] (EA) .... AOA
American Overseas Book Company (SAUO) .... AOBC
American Overseas Campaign (SAUO) .... AOC
American Overseas Educators Organization [*Later, Association of Overseas Educators*] (AEBS) .... AOEO
American Overseas Finance Corporation (SAUO) .... AOFC
American Overseas Petroleum Limited (SAUO) .... Amoseas
American Oxford Down Record Association (SAUO) .... AODRA
American Oxford Down Record Association [*Later, AOSA*] (EA) .... AODRA
American Oxford Sheep Association (EA) .... AOSA
American Pacific Bank [*NASDAQ symbol*] (SAG) .... AMPB
American Pacific Bank [*Associated Press*] (SAG) .... APacBk
American Pacific Bank [*Vancouver Stock Exchange symbol*] .... APB
American Pacific Corp. [*Associated Press*] (SAG) .... AmPac
American Pacific Corp. (EFIS) .... AMPAC
American Pacific Corp. [*NASDAQ symbol*] (NQ) .... APFC
American Pacific Corporation (SAUO) .... APFC
American Pacific International (SAUS) .... APIC
American Pacific Minerals Ltd. [*Associated Press*] (SAG) .... APacMin
American Pacific Minerals Ltd. [*NASDAQ symbol*] (SAG) .... APML
American Package Express Carriers Association (EA) .... APECA
American Pad & Paper [*NYSE symbol*] (SAG) .... AGP
American Pad & Paper [*Associated Press*] (SAG) .... APadP
American Paging, Inc. [*Associated Press*] (SAG) .... AmerPag
American Paging, Inc. [*AMEX symbol*] (SAG) .... APP
American Pain Society (EA) .... APS
American Paint and Coatings Journal (journ.) (SAUS) .... APJ
American Paint Horse Association (EA) .... APHA
American Painting Contractor (journ.) (SAUS) .... APACB
American Palestine Committee [*Defunct*] (EA) .... APC
American Pancreatic Association (EA) .... APA
American Paper and Pulp Association [*Later, API*] .... APPA
American Paper and Pulp Mills Superintendents' Association (DGA) .... APPMSA
American Paper Co. .... AP
American Paper Exchange Club [*Later, PIR*] (EA) .... APEC
American Paper Industry (journ.) (SAUS) .... APPIB
American Paper Institute (EA) .... API
American Paper Institute. Food Additives Reference Manual (journ.) (SAUS) .... API Food Add Ref
American Paper Institute. Monthly Statistical Summary (journ.) (SAUS) .... API Statist Sum
American Paper Institute. Newsprint Division. Bulletin (journ.) (SAUS) .... API Newsprint Bull
American Paper Institute. Wood Pulp Statistics (journ.) (SAUS) .... API NVOW Pulp Statist
American Paper Machinery Association (EA) .... APMA
American Paralysis Association (EA) .... APA
American Paramedical Institute [*Hawaii*] .... API
American Paraplegia Society (EA) .... APS
American Parapsychological Research Foundation [*Later, AAP*] (EA) .... APRF
American Parents Committee (EA) .... APC
American Park and Recreation Society (EA) .... APRS
American Park Rangers Association (EA) .... APRA
American Parkinson Disease Association (EA) .... APDA
American Parkinsons Disease Association (SAUS) .... APDA
American Parquet Association [*Defunct*] (EA) .... APA
American Part-Blooded Horse Registry (EA) .... APB
American Part-Blooded Horse Registry (SAUO) .... APBHR
American Partridge Plymouth Rock Club (EA) .... APPRC
American Party (SAUO) .... AP
American Paso Fino Horse Association (EA) .... APFHA
American Patent (SAUS) .... AP
American Patent Law Association (SAUO) .... AIPLA
American Patent Law Association [*Later, AIPLA*] (EA) .... APLA
American Patent Law Association. Bulletin [*A publication*] (DLA) .... Am Pat LA Bull
American Patent Law Association. Bulletin [*A publication*] (DLA) .... Am Pat L Assoc Bull
American Pathology Foundation (EA) .... APF
American Patients Association (EA) .... APA
American Pawnbrokers Association (EA) .... APA
American Pax Association [*Later, PC-USA*] (EA) .... APA
American Payroll Association (EA) .... APA
American Peace Mobilization (SAUO) .... APM
American Peace Society (SAUO) .... Am Peace
American Peace Society (EA) .... APS
American Peace Test (EA) .... APT
American Peanut Product Manufacturers (NTPA) .... APPM
American Peanut Product Manufacturers, Incorporated (SAUO) .... APPMI

American Peanut Research and Education Association [*Later, APRES*] (EA) ... APREA
American Peanut Research and Education Society (EA) ... APRES
American Peanut Shellers Association (NTPA) ... APSA
American Peat Society (SAUO) ... APS
American Pedestrian Association (EA) ... APA
American Pediatric Gastroesophageal Reflux Association (EA) ... APGERA
American Pediatric Gastroesophageal Reflux Association (EA) ... APGRA
American Pediatric Gross Assessment Record ... APGAR
American Pediatric Society (SAUO) ... APdS
American Pediatric Society (EA) ... APS
American Pediatric Surgical Association (SAUS) ... APS
American Pediatric Surgical Association (EA) ... APSA
American Pediatric Surgical Nurses Association (SAUO) ... APSNA
American Pediatry Association (SAUO) ... APA
American Pel Products Manufacturers Association (SAUO) ... APPNM
American Penal Press Association (SAUO) ... APPA
American Pencil Collectors Society (EA) ... APCS
American Penstemon Society (EA) ... APS
American Peony Society (EA) ... APS
American People for American Prisoners (EA) ... APAP
American People/Link [*American Design and Communication*] [*Information service or system*] (IID) ... PLINK
American People's Mobilization [*Formerly, American Peace Mobilization*] [*World War II*] ... APM
American Peptide Society (SAUO) ... APS
American Performance Horse Association (EA) ... APHA
American Performing-Rights Society ... APRS
American Performing-Rigts Society (SAUO) ... APRS
American Personal and Guidance Association (SAUO) ... ARGA
American Personnel and Guidance Association [*Later, AACD*] (EA) ... APGA
American Peruvian Paso Horse Registry (EA) ... APPHR
American Pet Boarding Association (EA) ... APBA
American Pet Products Manufacturers Association (EA) ... APPMA
American Pet Society (EA) ... APS
American Petanque Association USA (EA) ... APA
American Petroleum (SAUO) ... AMPOL
American Petroleum Credit Association [*Minneapolis, MN*] (EA) ... APCA
American Petroleum Industries Committee (SAUO) ... APIC
American Petroleum Industry (EEVL) ... API
American Petroleum Institute (HEAS) ... API
American Petroleum Institute Degree (SAUS) ... API Degree
American Petroleum Institute. Medical Research Publications (journ.) (SAUS) ... API Med Res Publ
American Petroleum Institute Patents (NITA) ... APIPAT
American Petroleum Institute. Publication (journ.) (SAUS) ... API Publ
American Petroleum Institute Research (MCD) ... APIR
American Petroleum Institute Research Project ... APIRP
American Petroleum Institute, Washington, DC [*Library symbol*] [*Library of Congress*] (LCLS) ... DAPI
American Petroleum Refiners Association [*Later, AIRA*] (EA) ... APRA
American Pewter Guild (EA) ... APG
American Pharmaceutical Association ... APA
American Pharmaceutical Association (EA) ... APhA
American Pharmaceutical Association (SAUO) ... APKA
American Pharmaceutical Association, Washington, DC [*Library symbol*] [*Library of Congress*] (LCLS) ... DAPh
American Pharmaceutical Association-Academy of Pharmacy Practice and Management (EA) ... APPM
American Pharmaceutical Manufacturers Association (SAUO) ... APMA
American Pharmacists Association (MELL) ... APhA
American Pheasant and Waterfowl Society (SAUO) ... AP&WS
American Pheasant and Waterfowl Society (EA) ... AP & WS
American Pheasant and Waterfowl Society (SAUO) ... APW
American Pheasant Society (SAUO) ... APS
American Pheasant Society [*Later, AP & WS*] (EA) ... APS
American Phenolic Corporation (SAUO) ... AMPHENOL
American Philatelic Congress (EA) ... APC
American Philatelic Research Library (EA) ... APRL
American Philatelic Research Library, State College, PA [*Library symbol*] [*Library of Congress*] (LCLS) ... PStcA
American Philatelic Society (SAUO) ... Am Philatelic
American Philatelic Society (EA) ... APS
American Philatelic Society Writers Unit (EA) ... APSWU
American Philatelist [*A publication*] (BRI) ... Am Phil
American Philological Association (EA) ... APA
American Philosophical Association (EA) ... APA
American Philosophical Quarterly (journ.) (SAUS) ... APQ
American Philosophical Society (SAUO) ... Am Philos Soc
American Philosophical Society (EA) ... APS
American Philosophical Society, Philadelphia, PA [*Library symbol*] [*Library of Congress*] (LCLS) ... PPAmP
American Philosophical Society. Proceedings (journ.) (SAUS) ... APS
American Phoenix Group, Inc. [*Associated Press*] (SAG) ... AmPhoeG
American Phoenix Group, Inc. [*Associated Press*] (SAG) ... APhoe
American Phoenix Group, Inc. [*NASDAQ symbol*] (SAG) ... APHX
American Phonometer CIA (SAUS) ... APMCA
American Photocopy Equipment Company (SAUO) ... APECO
American Photoengravers Association (SAUO) ... APA
American Photo-Engravers Association (DGA) ... APEA
American Photograph Equipment Co. ... APECO
American Photographic Artisans Guild (EA) ... APAG
American Photographic Artists Guild (SAUO) ... APAG
American Photographic Book Publishing Co. ... AMPHOTO
American Photographic Historical Society (EA) ... APHS
American Photonics, Inc. [*Brookfield Center, CT*] (TSSD) ... API
American Photoplatemakers Association [*Later, IAP*] ... APA
American Physical Education Review (journ.) (SAUS) ... Am Phys Educ R
American Physical Fitness Research Institute [*Defunct*] (EA) ... APFRI
American Physical Society (SAUO) ... APhysS
American Physical Society (EA) ... APS
American Physical Therapy Association (EA) ... APTA
American Physical Therapy Association, Arkansas Chapter (SRA) ... ArPTA
American Physical Therapy Foundation (DMAA) ... APTF
American Physicians Art Association (EA) ... APAA
American Physicians Association of Computer Medicine (EA) ... APACM
American Physicians Fellowship for Medicine in Israel (EA) ... APF
American Physicians Fellowship for the Israel Medical Association (SAUO) ... APF
American Physicians Poetry Association (EA) ... APPA
American Physicians Service Group, Inc. [*NASDAQ symbol*] (NQ) ... AMPH
American Physicians Service Group, Inc. [*Associated Press*] (SAG) ... APhyG
American Physicists Association (SAUO) ... APA
American Physics Society (SAUO) ... APS
American Physiological Society (EA) ... APS
American Physiotherapy Association [*Later, APTA*] ... APA
American Phytopathological Society (EA) ... APS
American Phytopathological Society. Monograph (journ.) (SAUS) ... APYMAP
American Piedmontese Association (EA) ... APA
American Pigeon Racing Association (EA) ... APRA
American Pilots Association (SAUS) ... APA
American Pinto Horse Association (EA) ... APHA
American Pinzgauer Association (EA) ... APA
American Pioneer Inc. (SAUO) ... APIO
American Pioneer Line (SAUO) ... APL
American Pioneer Lines [*Steamship*] (MHDW) ... AP
American Pioneer Trails Association (EA) ... APTA
American Pipe Fittings Association (EA) ... APFA
American Pipe Institute (SAUO) ... API
American Pistol and Revolver Association [*Defunct*] (EA) ... APRA
American Pistol Institute (EA) ... API
American Place Theatre (EA) ... APT
American Plan [*Hotel room rate*] ... AP
American Plan Corp. (EFIS) ... APCO
American Planning and Civic Association (SAUO) ... APCA
American Planning Association (EAIO) ... APA
American Planning Civic Association [*Later, NUC*] (EA) ... APCA
American Plant Food Council (SAUO) ... APFC
American Plant Life Society (EA) ... APLS
American Plant Selections [*An association*] [*Defunct*] (EA) ... APS
American Plastics Association (SAUO) ... APA
American Plastics Council (NTPA) ... APC
American Plate Number Single Society (EA) ... APNSS
American Platform Tennis Association (EA) ... APTA
American Platinum, Inc. [*Vancouver Stock Exchange symbol*] ... AP
American Playwrights Theatre [*Defunct*] ... APT
American Pleader's Assistant [*A publication*] (DLA) ... Am Pl Ass
American Plum Line Pattern Virus [*Plant pathology*] ... APLPV
American Plywood Association (EA) ... APA
American Podiatric Circulatory Society (EA) ... APCS
American Podiatric Medical Association (EA) ... APMA
American Podiatric Medical Association Auxiliary (EA) ... APMAA
American Podiatric Medical Society (MELL) ... APMA
American Podiatric Medical Students Association (EA) ... APMA
American Podiatric Medical Students Association (EA) ... APMSA
American Podiatric Medical Writers Association (EA) ... APMWA
American Podiatry Association [*Later, APMA*] ... APA
American Podiatry Association (SAUO) ... APMA
American Podiatry Association Auxiliary [*Later, APMAA*] (EA) ... APAA
American Poems; a Contemporary Collection [*A publication*] ... AmPC
American Poetry [*A publication*] ... AmP
American Poetry [*A publication*] ... AmPo
American Poetry [*A publication*] ... AP
American Poetry [*A publication*] ... APA
American Poetry and Prose [*A publication*] ... AmPP
American Poetry Association (EA) ... APA
American Poetry League ... APL
American Poetry Review [*A publication*] (BRI) ... APR
American Poinsettia Society [*Defunct*] (EA) ... APS
American Point System [*Typography*] (DGA) ... APS
American Pointer Club (EA) ... APC
American Polar Society (EA) ... APS
American Polarity Therapy Association (NTPA) ... APTA
American Police Academy (EA) ... APA
American Police and Fire Foundation (SAUO) ... APFF
American Polish Rabbit Club (SAUO) ... APRC
American Polish War Relief [*Post-World War II*] ... APWR
American Political Item Collectors (SAUO) ... APIC
American Political Items Collectors (EA) ... APIC
American Political Science Association (SAUO) ... APS
American Political Science Association (EA) ... APSA
American Political Science Association. Quarterly [*A publication*] ... PS
American Political Science Review (SAUS) ... AMPSR
American Political Science Review [*A publication*] (BRI) ... APSR
American Political Science Review. American Political Science (SAUS) ... APSA/R
American Polled Hereford Association (EA) ... APHA
American Polled Shorthorn Society (EA) ... APSS
American Polygraph Association (EA) ... APA
American Polygraph Association members (SAUO) ... APAs

American Polypay Sheep Association (SAUO) ... APS
American Polypay Sheep Association (EA) ... APSA
American Pomeranian Club (EA) ... APC
American Pomological Society (EA) ... APS
American Poolplayers Association (EA) ... APA
American Popular Revolutionary Alliance [*Peru*] [*Political party*] ... APRA
American Porphyria Foundation (EA) ... APF
American Portland Cement Alliance (NTPA) ... APCA
American Portrait Society (EA) ... APS
American Portuguese Society (EA) ... APS
American Postal Chess League [*Defunct*] (EA) ... APCL
American Postal Chess Tournaments (EA) ... APCT
American Postal Service (SAUO) ... APS
American Postal Workers Union (EA) ... APWU
American Potash and Chemical (SAUS) ... APO
American Potash & Chemical Corp. (SAUO) ... APO
American Potash & Chemical Corp., Whittier, CA [*Library symbol*] [*Library of Congress*] (LCLS) ... CWhA
American Potash and Chemical Corporation (SAUO) ... APCC
American Potash Institute [*Later, PPI*] (EA) ... API
American Potato Journal (SAUS) ... Amer Potato J
American Poultry and Hatchery Federation [*Later, PEIA*] (EA) ... APHF
American Poultry Association (EA) ... APA
American Poultry Historical Society (EA) ... APHS
American Poultry International (EA) ... API
American Poultry United States of America (NTPA) ... APUSA
American Powder Metallurgy Institute (EA) ... APMI
American Power Boat (SAUS) ... APBA
American Power Boat Association (EA) ... APBA
American Power Committee [*Defunct*] (EA) ... APC
American Power Conference (SAUO) ... APC
American Power Conversion (SAUO) ... APC
American Power Conversion [*NASDAQ symbol*] (SAG) ... APCC
American Power Conversion [*Associated Press*] (SAG) ... APwrCnv
American Power Conversion Co. (PCM) ... APC
American Power Conversion Corp. (SAUO) ... APCC
American Power Drinkers Association ... APDA
American Power Jet Co. ... APJ
American Power Net Association [*Later, EFMCNTA*] (EA) ... APNA
American Practical Navigator (SAUS) ... APN
American Practice [*A publication*] (DLA) ... Am Pr
American Practice Reports [*Washington, DC*] [*A publication*] (DLA) ... Am Pr Rep
American Practice Reports, New Series [*A publication*] (DLA) ... Am Pr Rep NS
American Precision Industries (SAUS) ... APREC
American Precision Industries, Inc. (EFIS) ... API
American Precision Industries, Inc. [*NYSE symbol*] (SPSG) ... APR
American Precision Industries, Inc. [*Associated Press*] (SAG) ... APrec
American Precision Optics Manufacturers Association (EA) ... APOMA
American Premier Group [*NYSE symbol*] [*Formerly, American Premier Underwriters*] (SG) ... APZ
American Prepaid Legal Services Institute (EA) ... API
American Presbyterian Congo Mission ... APCM
American President Companies Ltd. ... APC
American President Companies Ltd. [*Associated Press*] (SAG) ... APresid
American President Companies Ltd. [*NYSE symbol*] (SPSG) ... APS
American President Line Unit (SAUO) ... APLU
American President Lines (SAUO) ... AP
American President Lines ... APL
American Press Association (SAUO) ... APA
American Press Institute (EA) ... API
American Preventive Medical Association (SAUO) ... APMA
American Pre-Veterinary Medical Association (GVA) ... APVMA
American Primrose Society (EA) ... APS
American Printed Fabrics Council (EA) ... APFC
American Printing History Association (EA) ... APHA
American Printing House for the Blind (EA) ... APH
American Printing House for the Blind ... APHB
American Printing House for the Blind Central Automated Resource List [*Information service or system*] (CRD) ... APH-CARL
American Printing Technologies (DGA) ... APT
American Prison Ministry [*An association*] (EA) ... APM
American Prisoner of War (AABC) ... APW
American Prisoner of War Information Bureau (AABC) ... APWIB
American Prisoners of War Information Bureau (SAUO) ... APWIB
American Private Line Services, Inc. [*Newton, MA*] [*Telecommunications*] (TSSD) ... APLS
American Pro Life Council (EA) ... APLC
American Probate, New Series [*A publication*] (DLA) ... Am Prob NS
American Probate Reports [*A publication*] (DLA) ... Am Prob
American Probate Reports [*A publication*] (DLA) ... Am Prob Rep
American Probate Reports [*A publication*] (DLA) ... Am Pro Rep
American Probation and Parole Association (EA) ... APPA
American Proctologic Society (SAUO) ... AprS
American Proctologic Society [*Later, ASCRS*] (EA) ... APS
American Produce Association (EA) ... APA
American Producers of Italian Type Cheese Association (EA) ... APITCA
American Production and Inventory Control Society (EA) ... APICS
American Production and Inventory Control Society Annual Conference Proceedings (SAUO) ... Amer Production and Inventory
American Production and Inventory Control Society, Annual Conference Proceedings (SAUS) ... Amer Production and Inventory
American Production Finishers Association (SAUO) ... APFA
American Productivity Center [*Houston, TX*] (EA) ... APC
American Productivity Management Association [*Skokie, IL*] (EA) ... APMA
American Professional Basketball Association [*Game*] [*Pronounced "ap-bah"*] ... APBA
American Professional Faceters Association [*Defunct*] (EA) ... APFA
American Professional Needlework Retailers (EA) ... APNR
American Professional Partnership for Lithuanian Education ... APPLE
American Professional Pet Distributors, Inc. [*An association*] (EA) ... APPDI
American Professional Practice Association (EA) ... APPA
American Professional Racquetball Organization (EA) ... APRO
American Professional Soccer League (NTPA) ... APSL
American Professional Society of the Deaf (EA) ... APSD
American Professional Society on the Abuse of Children ... Apsac
American Professional Society on the Abuse of Children (NTPA) ... APSAC
American Professional Surfing Association (SAUO) ... APS
American Professional Surfing Association (EA) ... APSA
American Professors for Peace in the Middle East [*Defunct*] (EA) ... APPME
American Program Bureau [*Lectures*] ... APB
American Programmers Guild ... APG
American Progress Foundation ... APF
American Property Corporation (SAUO) ... APC
American Prosecutors Research Institute (EA) ... APRI
American Prospect Research Association (EA) ... APRA
American Prosthetic Research Laboratory (DAVI) ... APRL
American Prosthodontic Society (EA) ... APS
American Prosthodontic Society (SAUS) ... APS
American Protective Association [*Late-19th-century organization opposed to so-called encroachments of the Catholic Church in the US*] ... APA
American Protective League (SAUO) ... APL
American Protestant Association ... APA
American Protestant Correctional Chaplains Association (EA) ... APCCA
American Protestant Defense League (EA) ... APDL
American Protestant Episcopal Mission (SAUO) ... APEM
American Protestant Health Association (EA) ... APHA
American Protestant Hospital Association (DAVI) ... APHA
American Protestant Society ... APS
American Protestants for Truth about Ireland (EA) ... APTI
American Protologic Society (SAUO) ... APS
American Psychiatric Association (EA) ... APA
American Psychiatric Nurses Association (EA) ... APNA
American Psychiatric Press, Inc. (SAUO) ... APPI
American Psychiatric Press, Inc (SAUS) ... APPI
American Psychical Institute ... API
American Psychoanalyst (SAUS) ... TAP
American Psychoanalytic Association (EA) ... APA
American Psychoanalytic Association (SAUO) ... APS
American Psychoanalytic Association (EA) ... APsaA
American Psychoanalytic Association (SAUS) ... ApsaA
American Psychoanalytic Association (SAUO) ... APsychoA
American Psychoanalytic Foundation (SAUO) ... APF
American Psycho-analytical Association (SAUS) ... APA
[*The*] **American Psycho/Info Exchange** [*Information service or system*] (IID) ... AMPIE
American Psycho/Info Exchange (SAUS) ... APIE
American Psychological Association (EA) ... APA
American Psychological Association - Division of Clinical Psychology (NTPA) ... APA/CP
American Psychological Association - Division of Psychotherapy (NTPA) ... APA-DP
American Psychological Association Division of Independent Practice (EA) ... APADIP
American Psychological Association-Project on Scientific Information Exchange in Psychology (SAUO) ... APA-PSIEP
American Psychological Foundation ... APF
American Psychological Practitioners Association (EA) ... APPA
American Psychological Society (DAVI) ... APS
American Psychologist (journ.) (SAUS) ... Am Psychologist
American Psychologists for Serial Action (SAUS) ... APS
American Psychologists for Social Action [*Later, PSA*] ... APSA
American Psychology-Law Society (EA) ... AP-LS
American Psychopathological Association ... APA
American Psychopathological Association (EA) ... APPA
American Psychopathological Association (SAUO) ... APsychpthA
American Psychosomatic Association (SAUO) ... APA
American Psychosomatic Society (EA) ... APS
American Psychosomatic Society (SAUO) ... APsychosomS
American Psychotherapy Association [*Inactive*] (EA) ... APA
American Public Cornmunications Council (SAUO) ... APCC
American Public Gas Association (EA) ... APGA
American Public Health Association (SAUO) ... Am Public Health
American Public Health Association (EA) ... APHA
American Public Health Association. Public Health Education. Section Newsletter (journ.) (SAUS) ... APHA
American Public Power Association (EA) ... APPA
American Public Radio ... APR
American Public Relations Association [*Later, PRSA*] ... APRA
American Public Television (SAUS) ... APT
American Public Transit Association (EA) ... APTA
American Public Transport Association (SAUO) ... APTA
American Public Utilities Bureau (SAUS) ... APUB
American Public Water Works Association (GEOI) ... APWWA
American Public Welfare Association (EA) ... APWA
American Public Works Association (EA) ... APWA
American Publicists Guild [*Defunct*] (EA) ... APG
American Publishing Co. [*NASDAQ symbol*] (SAG) ... AMPC
American Puerto-Rican Action League ... APAL
American Puffer Alliance [*An association*] (EA) ... APA

American Pulp and Paper Association (SAUO) .... APPA
American Pulp Association. Legislative Bulletin (journ.) (SAUS)...... APA Legisl Bull
American Pulpwood Association (EA) .... APA
American Puppet Arts Council [Defunct] .... APAC
American Purchasing Society (EA) .... APS
American Puritan Ethic .... APE
American Pyramid Resources, Inc. [Vancouver Stock Exchange symbol] .... APE
American Pyrotechnics Association (EA) .... APA
American Pyschologist (journ.) (SAUS) .... AP
American Quarter Horse Association (EA) .... AQHA
American Quarter Horse Racing Council (EA) .... AQHRC
American Quarter Pony Association (EA) .... AQPA
American Quarterly [A publication] (BRI) .... Am Q
American Quarterly (journ.) (SAUS) .... AQ
American Quasar Petro Co. (SAUO) .... AQAS
American Quaternary Association (EA) .... AMQUA
American Quick Printing Association [Defunct] (EA) .... AQPA
American Quicksilver Institute [Defunct] (EA) .... AQI
American Quilt Study Group (EA) .... AQSG
American Quilter's Society (EA) .... AQS
American Rabbit Breeders Association (EA) .... ARBA
American Rabbit Dealers Association (SAUO) .... ARDA
American Racing Drivers Club (SAUO) .... ARDC
American Racing Pigeon Union (EA) .... ARPU
American Racing Series .... ARS
American Rack Merchandisers Institute (SAUO) .... ARMI
American Radiator and Standard Sanitary (SAUS) .... AST
American Radiator & Standard Sanitary Corp. [Later, American Standard, Inc.] .... AMSTAN
American Radiator & Standard Sanitary Corp. [Later, American Standard, Inc.] .... ARSS
American Radio Associated (SAUO) .... ARA
American Radio Association (EA) .... ARA
American Radio Broadcasting Companies in Europe (SAUO) .... ARBIE
American Radio Co. of the Air [Radio program] .... ARC
American Radio Council [Later, PRO-IF] (EA) .... ARC
American Radio Forum (SAUO) .... ARF
American Radio Importers Association (EA) .... ARIA
American Radio Relay League (SAUO) .... Am Radio
American Radio Relay League (EA) .... ARRL
American Radio Relay League, Inc. (SAUO) .... ARRL
American Radio Systems Corp. [NASDAQ symbol] (SAG) .... AMRD
American Radio Systems Corp. [Associated Press] (SAG) .... ARadio
American Radio Telegraphists Association (SAUO) .... ARTA
American Radio Telephone System (TEL) .... ARTS
American Radiography Technologists (EA) .... ART
American Radiological Nurses Association (EA) .... ARNA
American Radium Society (EA) .... ARS
American Rafting Association [Defunct] (EA) .... ARA
American Railroad and Corporation Reports [A publication] (DLA).... Am R & Corp
American Railroad and Corporation Reports [A publication] (DLA) .... Am R & C Rep
American Railroad and Corporation Reports [A publication] (DLA) .... Am RR & C Rep
American Railroad Engineering Association (SAUO) .... AREA
American Railroad Foundation [Defunct] (EA) .... ARF
American Railway and Airline Supervisors Association (EA) .... RSA
American Railway Association [Later, AAR] .... ARA
American Railway Bridge and Building Association (SAUO) .... ARBA
American Railway Bridge and Building Association (EA) .... ARBBA
American Railway Car Export Association (EA) .... ARCEA
American Railway Car Institute (EA) .... ARCI
American Railway Cases [A publication] (DLA) .... Am Rail Cas
American Railway Cases [A publication] (DLA) .... Am Railw Cas
American Railway Cases [A publication] (DLA) .... Am R Ca
American Railway Cases [A publication] (DLA) .... Am RR Ca
American Railway Cases [A publication] (DLA) .... Am RR Cas
American Railway Cases [A publication] (DLA) .... Am Ry Ca
American Railway Cases [A publication] (DLA) .... Am Ry Cases
American Railway Cases [Legal] .... ARC
American Railway Development Association (EA) .... ARDA
American Railway Engineering Association (EA) .... AREA
American Railway Engineering Association Proceedings (SAUO) .... AREA Proc
American Railway Express (SAUS) .... ARE
American Railway Magazine Editors Association (SAUO) .... ARMEA
American Railway Magazine Editors Association [Later, Association of Railroad Editors] (EA) .... ARMEA
American Railway Master Mechanics' Association .... ARMMA
American Railway Reports [A publication] (DLA) .... Amer R'y Rep
American Railway Reports [A publication] (DLA) .... Am Rail R
American Railway Reports [A publication] (DLA) .... Am R Rep
American Railway Reports [A publication] (DLA) .... Am RR Rep
American Railway Reports [A publication] (DLA) .... Am Ry Rep
American Railway Reports [A publication] (DLA) .... ARR
American Railway Reports [A publication] (DLA) .... ARRR
American Railway Union .... ARU
American Rambouillet Sheep Breeders Association (EA) .... ARSBA
American Rape Prevention Association (EA) .... ARPA
American Rat, Mouse, and Hamster Society (EA) .... ARMHS
American Rationalist Association (SAUO) .... ARA
American Rationalist Federation (EA) .... ARF
American Rationalist (journ.) (SAUS) .... AR
American Rayon Institute [Defunct] .... ARI
American Re Corp. [Associated Press] (SAG) .... AmReCp
American Re Corp. Capital [Associated Press] (SAG) .... AmReC

American Re Corp. Capital [NYSE symbol] (SAG) .... ARN
American Reading Council [Defunct] (EA) .... ARC
American Real Estate and Urban Economics Association (EA) .... AREUEA
American Real Estate and Urban Economists Association (SAUO) .... AREUEA
American Real Estate Exchange .... AMREX
American Real Estate Investment Corp. [Associated Press] (SAG) .... AREInv
American Real Estate Investment Corp. [AMEX symbol] (SAG) .... REA
American Real Estate Partners Ltd. [Associated Press] (SAG) .... AREst
American Real Estate Partnership [NYSE symbol] (SPSG) .... ACP
American Real Estate Society (EA) .... ARES
American Realty and Petroleum Corp. (SAUO) .... AMREP
American Realty Corp. [NYSE symbol] (SPSG) .... ARN
American Realty Trust [Associated Press] (SAG) .... AmRlt
American Realty Trust SBI [NYSE symbol] (SPSG) .... ARB
American Reciprocal Insurers (SAUO) .... ARI
American Record Guide (journ.) (SAUS) .... Am Rec G
American Record Guide (journ.) (SAUS) .... AR
American Record Merchandisers and Distributors Association [Defunct] (EA) .... ARMADA
American Recorder (journ.) (SAUS) .... AR
American Recorder Society (EA) .... ARS
American Records Management Association (NITA) .... ARMA
American Records Society (SAUO) .... ARS
American Recovery Association (EA) .... ARA
American Recovery Association, Inc. (SAUO) .... ARA
American Recreation Centers, Inc. [NASDAQ symbol] (NQ) .... AMRC
American Recreation Centers, Inc. [Associated Press] (SAG) .... ARecr
American Recreation Co. Holdings [NASDAQ symbol] (SAG) .... AMRE
American Recreation Coalition (EA) .... ARC
American Recreation Society [Later, APRS] (EA) .... ARS
American Recreational Activities .... ARA
American Recreational Equipment Association (EA) .... AREA
American Recreational Golf Association (EA) .... ARGA
American Recreational Racket Sports Association (EA) .... ARRSA
American Recreational Vehicle Living Association [Defunct] (EA) .... ARVLA
American Red Brangus Association (EA) .... ARBA
American Red Cross .... AMCROSS
American Red Cross (SAUO) .... Am Red
American Red Cross (EA) .... ARC
American Red Cross (SAUO) .... ARX
American Red Cross Camp Club (SAUO) .... ARCCC
American Red Cross Children's Fund .... ARCCF
American Red Cross Childrens Fund (SAUS) .... ARCCF
American Red Cross Club (SAUO) .... ARCC
American Red Cross Nursing Services (SAUO) .... ARCNS
American Red Cross Overseas Association (EA) .... ARCOA
American Red Magen David for Israel [An association] .... ARMD
American Red Magen David for Israel (EA) .... ARMDI
American Red Poll Association (EA) .... ARPA
American Reference Books Annual [A publication] (BRI) .... ARBA
American Refineries Standard Dimension (SAUS) .... ARSD
American Refractories Institute (SAUO) .... ARI
American Refrigeration Transit Co. [AAR code] .... ART
American Refugee Committee .... ARC
American Regional Interprofessional Advisory Committee of World Federation for Mental Health (SAUO) .... IPAC
American Register of Architectural Antiquities (SAUS) .... ARAA
American Registered Inhalation Therapist [Academic degree] .... ARIT
American Registered Respiratory Therapist .... ARRT
American Registry for Internet Numbers (IGQR) .... ARIN
American Registry of Certified Professionals in Agronomy, Crops, and Soils (EA) .... ARCPACS
American Registry of Clinical Radiography Technologists (EA) .... ARCRT
American Registry of Diagnostic Medical Sonographers (EA) .... ARDMS
American Registry of Inhalation Therapists [Later, NBRT] (EA) .... ARIT
American Registry of Medical Assistants (EA) .... ARMA
American Registry of Pathologists .... ARP
American Registry of Pathology (EA) .... ARP
American Registry of Pathology (SAUO) .... AFIP/ARP
American Registry of Physical Therapists [Defunct] (EA) .... ARPT
American Registry of Professional Animal Scientists (SAUO) .... ARPAS
American Registry of Professional Entomologists (EA) .... ARPE
American Registry of Radiologic [or Radiology] Technologists (EA) .... ARRT
American Registry of X-ray Technicians (SAUO) .... ARXT
American Rehabilitation Association (MELL) .... ARA
American Rehabilitation Association [Formerly, National Association of Rehabilitation Facilities] (EA) .... NARF
American Rehabilitation Committee [FEGS] [Absorbed by] (EA) .... ARC
American Rehabilitation Counseling Association (EA) .... ARCA
American Rehabilitation Educational Network [Pittsburgh, PA] [Telecommunications service] (TSSD) .... AREN
American Rehabilitation Foundation [Later, SKI] (EA) .... ARF
American Rehabilitation Foundation Minneapolis, MN [Library symbol] [Library of Congress] (LCLS) .... MnMAR
American Reliance Group (EFIS) .... ARI
American Relief Administration Association (SAUO) .... ARAAssn
American Relief for France (SAUO) .... ARF
American Relief for Poland [Defunct] (EA) .... ARP
American Religious Zionist Organization (SAUO) .... ARZO
American Reloaders Association (EA) .... ARA
American Remount Association (EA) .... ARA
American Rental Association (EA) .... ARA
American Repair Service .... ARS
American Reperatory Ballet Company [Formerly, Princeton Ballet] .... ARBC
American Repertory Theatre .... ART

American Reports [*A publication*] (DLA) ... American Repts

American Reports [*A publication*] (DLA) ... Amer Rep

American Reports [*A publication*] (DLA) ... Amer Reports

American Reports [*A publication*] (DLA) ... Amer Reps

American Reports [*A publication*] (DLA) ... Am R

American Reports [*A publication*] (DLA) ... Am Rep

American Reports [*A publication*] (DLA) ... Am Reports

American Reports [*A publication*] (GFGA) ... Am Repts

American Reports [*A publication*] (DLA) ... AR

American Reports [*A publication*] (DLA) ... A Rep

American Reprossessors Association (SAUO) ... ARA

American Republics Area [*Department of State*] ... ARA

American Rescue Dog Association (EA) ... ARDA

American Rescue Workers (EA) ... ARW

American Research and Development (SAUO) ... ARD

American Research and Development Corporation (SAUO) ... ARDC

American Research Bureau ... ARB

American Research Center (SAUO) ... ARC

American Research Committee on Grounding (SAUS) ... ARCG

American Research Council (SAUO) ... Am Res

American Research Institute for Community Development (EA) ... ARICD

American Research Institute of Turkey [*University of Pennsylvania*] [*Research center*] (RCD) ... ARIT

American Research Merchandising Institute [*Later, NASM*] (EA) ... ARMI

American Reserve Mining Corp. [*Vancouver Stock Exchange symbol*] ... AMI

American Resettlement Foundation (SAUO) ... ARF

American Residential Services, Inc. [*Associated Press*] (SAG) ... AResidS

American Residential Services, Inc. [*NYSE symbol*] (SAG) ... ARS

American Resort and Residential Development Association (EA) ... ARRDA

American Resort Development Association (NTPA) ... ARDA

American Resource [*Vancouver Stock Exchange symbol*] ... AXE

American Resource Corp., Inc. [*Associated Press*] (SAG) ... AmResCp

American Resource Recovery Corporation (SAUO) ... ARRCO

American Resource Recovery Corporation Washington DC (SAUS) ... ARRCO

American Resources Corp, Inc. [*NASDAQ symbol*] (SAG) ... AREE

American Resources Group (EA) ... ARG

American Resources, Inc. [*Associated Press*] (SAG) ... AmResc

American Resources, Inc. [*Associated Press*] (SAG) ... AmRsc

American Resources, Inc. [*NASDAQ symbol*] (SAG) ... GASS

American Restaurant China Council (EA) ... ARCC

American Restaurant Partners Ltd. [*Associated Press*] (SAG) ... ARestr

American Restaurant Partners Ltd. [*AMEX symbol*] (SPSG) ... RMC

American Restitution Association (EA) ... ARA

American Retail Association Executives [*Defunct*] (EA) ... ARAE

American Retail Coal Association (EA) ... ARCA

American Retail Federation [*Later, NRF*] (EA) ... ARF

American Retail Federation (SAUO) ... ARF

American Retail Foundation (SAUO) ... ARF

American Retiree Association [*An association*] ... ARA

American Retreaders Association (EA) ... ARA

American Reuseable Textile Association (EA) ... ARTA

American Revenue Association (EA) ... ARA

American Review (journ.) (SAUS) ... AR

American Review of East-West Trade [*A publication*] (DLA) ... Amer Rev E-W Tr

American Review of Public Administration (SAUS) ... ARPA

American Review of Respiratory Diseases (journ.) (SAUS) ... Amer Rev Respirat Dis

American Review of Soviet and Eastern European Foreign Trade [*A publication*] (DLA) ... Sov & E Eur For Tr

American Review of Soviet and Eastern European Foreign Trade (journ.) (SAUS) ... Sov&E Eur For Tr

American Revised Version [*of the Bible*] ... ARV

American Revised Version [*of the Bible*], **Margin** ... ARVm

American Revoluting Round Table (SAUO) ... ARRT

American Revolution Bicentennial Administration [*Formerly, ARBC*] [*Disbanded, 1977*] ... ARBA

American Revolution Bicentennial Advisory Council [*American Revolution Bicentennial Administration*] ... ARBAC

American Revolution Bicentennial Board [*American Revolution Bicentennial Administration*] ... ARBB

American Revolution Bicentennial Commission [*Later, ARBA*] ... ARBC

American Revolution II Committee (EA) ... AR II

American Revolution Round Table (EA) ... ARRT

American Revolutionary Army (SAUO) ... ARA

American Reye's Syndrome Association [*Defunct*] (EA) ... ARSA

American Rheumatism Association [*Later, ACR*] (EA) ... ARA

American Rheumatism Association Medical Information System [*Information service or system*] (IID) ... ARAMIS

American Rhinologic Society (EA) ... ARS

American Rhododendron Society (EA) ... ARS

American Rice Growers Cooperative Association (SAUO) ... ARCA

American Rice Growers Cooperative Association [*Defunct*] (EA) ... ARGCA

American Rice, Inc. [*Associated Press*] (SAG) ... AmRice

American Rice, Inc. [*NASDAQ symbol*] (SAG) ... RICE

American Riding Association of Berlin [*Post-World War II*] ... ARAB

American Right of Way Association [*Later, IRWA*] (EA) ... ARWA

American Right of Way Association (SAUO) ... ARWA

American Right to Read [*Defunct*] (EA) ... ARR

American Risk and Insurance Association [*Orlando, FL*] (EA) ... ARIA

American River College, Sacramento, CA [*OCLC symbol*] (OCLC) ... ASR

American River College, Sacramento, CA [*Library symbol*] [*Library of Congress*] (LCLS) ... CSAR

American River Oil [*NASDAQ symbol*] (TTSB) ... AROC

American River Oil Co. [*Associated Press*] (SAG) ... AmRiverO

American River Oil Co. [*NASDAQ symbol*] (SAG) ... AROC

American River Touring Association ... ARTA

American Rivers (EA) ... AR

American Rivers Conservation Council [*Later, AR*] (EA) ... ARCC

American Road and Transportation Builders Association ... ARTB

American Road and Transportation Builders Association (EA) ... ARTBA

American Road Builders' Association [*Later, ARTBA*] ... ARBA

American Road Race of Champions ... ARRC

American Road Racing Association (EA) ... ARRA

American Robot Society (EA) ... ARS

American Rock Art Research Association (EA) ... ARARA

American Rock Garden Society (EA) ... ARGS

American Rock Mechanics Association (NTPA) ... ARMA

American Rocked Society Journal (SAUO) ... ARSJ

American Rocket Company (SAUO) ... AMROC

American Rocket, Incorporated (ACAE) ... AMROC

American Rocket Society [*Later, AIAA*] ... ARS

American Roentgen Ray Society (EA) ... ARRS

American Roentgen Society (SAUO) ... ARS

American Rolling Door Institute (NTPA) ... ARDI

American Rolling Mill Company (SAUO) ... Armco

American Romagnola Association (EA) ... ARA

American Romanian Academy of Arts and Sciences (EA) ... ARA

American Romanian Committee for Assistance to Refugees (EA) ... ARCAR

American Romanian Orthodox Youth (EA) ... AROY

American Romney Breeders Association (SAUO) ... ARBA

American Roque and Croquet Association [*Formerly, American Roque League*] (EA) ... ARL

American Roque League (EA) ... ARL

American Rose Council [*Defunct*] (EA) ... ARC

American Rose Foundation (EA) ... ARF

American Rose Society (EA) ... ARS

American Rottweiler Club (EA) ... ARC

American Rowing Association (EA) ... ARA

American Royal Association (EA) ... ARA

American RSROA [*Roller Skating Rink Operators Association of America*] **Roller Hockey Association** (EA) ... ARRHA

American RSROA Roller Hockey Association (SAUO) ... ARRHA

American Rubberband Duckpin Bowling Congress (EA) ... ARDBC

American Running and Fitness Association (EA) ... AR & FA

American Running & Fitness Association ... ARFA

American Rural Health Association (EA) ... ARHA

American Russian Aid Association (SAUO) ... ARAA

American Russian Institute, San Francisco, CA [*Library symbol*] [*Library of Congress*] (LCLS) ... CSfAR

American Sabbath Tract and Communications Council (EA) ... ASTCC

American Sabbath Tract Society [*Later, ASTCC*] (EA) ... ASTS

American Sabbath Tract Society (SAUO) ... ASTS

American Sable Rabbit Society (EA) ... ASRS

American Saddle Horse Breeders Association [*Later, ASHA*] (EA) ... ASHBA

American Saddle Horse Youth Club (EA) ... ASHYC

American Saddlebred Horse Association (EA) ... ASHA

American Saddlebred Pleasure Horse Association [*Later, ASHA*] (EA) ... ASPHA

American Safe Deposit Association (SAUO) ... ASDA

[*The*] **American Safe Deposit Association** (EA) ... TASDA

American Safety Belt Council (SAUO) ... ASBC

American Safety Council (EA) ... ASC

American Safety Equipment Corp. (EFIS) ... ASE

American Safety Razor Co. [*Associated Press*] (SAG) ... AmSafRz

American Safety Razor Co. [*NASDAQ symbol*] (SAG) ... RAZR

American Sail Training Association (EA) ... ASTA

American Sailing Association (EA) ... ASA

American Sailing Association Foundation (EA) ... ASF

American Sailing Council [*of the National Marine Manufacturers Association*] [*Chicago, IL*] ... ASC

American Sailing Foundation (EA) ... ASF

American Salers Association (EA) ... ASA

American Salers Junior Association (EA) ... ASJA

American Saluki Association (EA) ... ASA

American Salvage Pool Association (EA) ... ASPA

American Samoa ... AM SAM

American Samoa [*MARC country of publication code*] [*Library of Congress*] (LCCP) ... as

American Samoa [*Postal code*] [*ANSI two-letter standard code*] (CNC) ... AS

American Samoa (SAUS) ... ASA

American Samoa [*ANSI three-letter standard code*] (CNC) ... ASM

American Samoa [*MARC geographic area code*] [*Library of Congress*] (LCCP) ... poas-

American Samoa Administrative Code [*A publication*] (DLA) ... ASAC

American Samoa Code [*A publication*] (DLA) ... Am Samoa

American Samoa Code [*A publication*] (DLA) ... AS Code

American Samoa Code. Annotated [*A publication*] (DLA) ... Am Samoa Code Ann

American Samoa Commission (SAUO) ... ASC

American Sanitary Engineering Intersociety Board [*Later, AAEE*] (EA) ... ASEIB

American Satellite (MCD) ... AMSAT

American Satellite Company (SAUO) ... ASC

American Satellite Corporation (SAUO) ... ASC

American Satellite Television Alliance (EA) ... ASTA

American Satin Rabbit Breeders' Association (EA) ... ASRBA

American Saudi Roundtable (EA) ... ASR

American Savings and Loan Association (EA) ... ASLA

American Savings and Loan Bank (SAUO) ... AS&LB

American Savings and Loan Institute [*Later, IFE*] (EA) ... ASLI

American Savings and Loan League [*Later, ALFI*] (EA) ... ASLL

American Scantic Line (SAUO) ... ASL

American Scenic and Historic Preservation Society [*Defunct*] (EA) ... ASHPS

American Schizophrenia Association (EA) ... ASA
American Schizophrenia Foundation (SAUO) ... ASF
American Scholar [*A publication*] (BRI) ... AS
American Scholar (journ.) (SAUS) ... Amer Sch
American School Achievement Test [*Education*] (AEBS) ... ASAT
American School and Community Safety Association [*Later, The Safety Society*] ... ASCSA
American School Band Directors' Association (EA) ... ASBDA
American School Counselor Association (EA) ... ASCA
American School Food Service Association (EA) ... ASFSA
American School Health Association (EA) ... ASHA
American School in London ... ASL
[*The*] **American School in Switzerland** ... TASIS
American School Intelligence Test [*Education*] (AEBS) ... ASIT
American School of Classical Studies (SAUO) ... ASCS
American School of Classical Studies at Athens (SAUS) ... Am Sch Athens
American School of Classical Studies at Athens (SAUS) ... ASCSA
American School of Oriental Research (SAUS) ... ASOR
American School of Orthodontists (SAUO) ... ASO
American School of Technical Intelligence (SAUO) ... ASTI
American Schools and Colleges Association (SAUO) ... ASCA
American Schools and Hospitals Abroad [*Program*] [*Agency for International Development*] ... ASHA
American Schools Association (EA) ... ASA
American Schools, Iran (ACAE) ... ASI
American Schools of Oriental Research Bulletin (journ.) (SAUS) ... Am Sch Orient Res Bul
American Schooner Association (EA) ... ASA
American Science and Engineering (SAUO) ... Am Sci & Eng
American Science and Engineering (SAUS) ... AS&E
American Science and Engineering, Inc (SAUS) ... Am Sci&Eng
American Science & Engineering, Inc. [*Associated Press*] (SAG) ... ASciE
American Science & Engineering, Inc. [*AMEX symbol*] (SPSG) ... ASE
American Science and Engineering, Inc. (SAUO) ... ASE
American Science and Technology (ACAE) ... AS&T
American Science and Technology Corporation (ACAE) ... AS&TC
American Science Fiction Association (EA) ... ASFA
American Science Film Association (EA) ... ASFA
American Science Information Institute ... ASII
American Scientific Affiliation (EA) ... ASA
American Scientific Engineering (KSC) ... ASE
American Scientific Glassblowers Society (EA) ... ASGS
American Scientific Institute ... ASI
American Scientific Laboratories (AEBS) ... ASL
American Scientist [*A publication*] (MEC) ... Amer Scient
American Scientist [*A publication*] (BRI) ... Am Sci
American Scientist (SAUS) ... Am Sci
American Scientist (journ.) (SAUS) ... ASCENT
American Scotch Highland Breeders Association (SAUS) ... ASHBA
American Scottish Foundation (EA) ... ASF
American Scouting Traders Association (EA) ... ASTA
American Scripture Gift Mission [*Later, SGM/USA*] (EA) ... ASGM
American Sea Songs and Chanteys [*A publication*] ... AmSS
American Seafood Distributors Association (EA) ... ASDA
American Seafood Harvesters Association ... ASHA
American Seafood Retailers Association (EA) ... ASRA
American Sealyham Terrier Club (EA) ... ASTC
American Seamen's Friend Society [*Defunct*] (EA) ... ASFS
American Seat Belt Council [*Later, AORC*] (EA) ... ASBC
American Seating Co. (SAUO) ... AMZ
American Section, International Association for Philosophy of Law and Social Philosophy (SAUS) ... AMINTAPHIL
American Section of the International Solar Energy Society (SAUO) ... ASISES
American Section of the International Solar Energy Society (EA) ... AS of ISES
American Section of the Societe de Chimie Industrielle (EA) ... ASSCI
American Section-International Solar Energy Society (SAUO) ... AS-ISES
American Secular Union (SAUO) ... ASU
American Security Council (EA) ... ASC
American Security Council Education Foundation (SAUO) ... ASCEF
American Security Council Foundation (EA) ... ASCF
American Seed Research Foundation (EA) ... ASRF
American Seed Trade Association (EA) ... ASTA
American Segment Trainer [*NASA*] (SPST) ... AST
American Select Portfolio [*NYSE symbol*] (SPSG) ... SLA
American Select Portfolios, Inc. [*Associated Press*] (SAG) ... ASelPort
American Self-Protection Association ... ASP
American Self-Protection Association (EA) ... ASPA
American Selling Price ... ASP
American Selling Price System ... ASPS
American Semiconductor Corporation (SAUO) ... ASC
American Seminar Leaders Association (NTPA) ... ASLA
American Senior Citizens Association (EA) ... ASCA
American Seniors Housing Association (NTPA) ... ASHA
American Sensors, Inc. [*Associated Press*] (SAG) ... ASensrs
American Sensors, Inc. [*NASDAQ symbol*] (SAG) ... SNIF
American Sentic Association ... ASA
American Sephardi (BJA) ... ASe
American Sephardi Federation (EA) ... ASF
American Service Radio [*English-language broadcasting*] (VNW) ... ASR
American Service Veterans Association (EA) ... ASV
American Servicemen's Union (EA) ... ASU
American Sewing Guild (EA) ... ASG
American Sexual Freedom Movement (SAUO) ... ASFM
American Sexually Transmitted Diseases Association (NTPA) ... ASTDA
American Shakespeare Festival Theater and Academy (SAUO) ... ASFTA
American Share Coalition on Transplantation (SAUO) ... ASCOT
American Share Foundation (SAUO) ... ASF
American Shared Hospital Services [*AMEX symbol*] (SPSG) ... AMS
American Shared Hospital Services [*Associated Press*] (SAG) ... AmShrd
American Shark Association (EA) ... ASA
American Sheep Breeder and Wool Grower (journ.) (SAUS) ... Am Sheep B&W
American Sheep Industry Association (NTPA) ... ASI
American Sheep Industry Association (EA) ... ASIA
American Sheep Producers Council [*Later, ASIA*] (EA) ... ASPC
American Sheep Producers Council (SAUO) ... ASPC
American Shellfisheries Association ... ASA
American Shepherd Foundation (SAUO) ... ASF
American Shetland Pony Club (EA) ... ASPC
American Shetland Pony Club/American Miniature Horse Registry (NTPA) ... ASPC/AMHR
American Shetland Sheepdog Association (EA) ... ASSA
American Shiatsu Association (EA) ... ASA
American Shih Tzu Club (EA) ... ASTC
American Ship Building Company (SAUO) ... ABG
American Ship Building Company (SAUO) ... ASBCO
American Shipbuilding Association (NTPA) ... ASA
American Shipping Bureau (WDAA) ... ASB
American Shire Horse Association (EA) ... ASHA
American Shooting Sports Council ... ASSC
American Shore and Beach Association (SAUO) ... ASBA
American Shore and Beach Preservation Association (NOAA) ... ASBA
American Shore and Beach Preservation Association (EA) ... ASBPA
American Short Line Railroad Association (EA) ... ASLRA
American Short Line Railroads ... ASLR
American Shorthorn Association (EA) ... ASA
American Shorthorn Breeders Association [*Later, ASA*] ... ASBA
American Shortwave Listeners Club (EA) ... ASWLC
American Shoulder and Elbow Surgeons (EA) ... ASES
American Shrimp Canners and Processors Association [*Later, ASPA*] (EA) ... ASCPA
American Shrimp Canners Association [*Later, ASPA*] ... ASCA
American Shrimp Processors Association (EA) ... ASPA
American Shrimpboat Association [*Defunct*] (EA) ... ASA
American Shropshire Registry Association (EA) ... ASRA
American Shuffleboard Co. (EA) ... ASC
American Shuffleboard Leagues (EA) ... ASL
American Sighthound Field Association (EA) ... ASFA
American Sightseeing Association [*Later, ASI*] ... ASA
American Sightseeing International (EA) ... ASI
American Sign Language [*for the deaf*] ... AMESLAN
American Sign Language (NTIO) ... Ameslan
American Sign Language [*for the deaf*] ... ASL
American Silk Council [*Defunct*] (EA) ... ASC
American Silk Rayon Journal (journ.) (SAUS) ... Am Silk Rayon J
American Silkie Bantam Club (EA) ... ASBC
American Simmental Association (EA) ... ASA
American Simplified Keyboard [*Typewriter*] ... ASK
American Singers Club (EA) ... ASC
American Single Shot Rifle Association (EA) ... ASSRA
American Singles Golf Association (EA) ... ASGA
American Ski Association (EA) ... ASA
American Ski Federation (EA) ... ASF
American Ski Manufacturers' Association (EA) ... ASMA
American Ski Teachers Association of Natur Teknik (EA) ... ASTAN
American Skibob Association [*Later, USSBF*] (EA) ... ASBA
American Skin Association (NTPA) ... ASA
American Sleep Apnea Association (NTPA) ... ASAA
American Sleep Disorders Association (NTPA) ... ASDA
American Slovenian Catholic Union of the USA (EA) ... KSKJ
American Small and Rural Hospital Association (EA) ... ASRHA
American Small Businesses Association (EA) ... ASBA
American Small Center Cap (SAUS) ... ASCC
American Smelting & Refining (SAUO) ... AR
American Smelting & Refining Co. (IIA) ... AR
American Smelting & Refining Co., Research Department Library, South Plainfield,NJ [*Library symbol*] [*Library of Congress*] (LCLS) ... NjSopA
American Smelting & Refining Company (SAUO) ... AS&R
American Smoking Pipe Manufacturers Association [*Defunct*] (EA) ... ASPMA
American Snowmobile Association [*Defunct*] ... ASA
American Snowplowing Association [*Defunct*] (EA) ... ASA
American Snowshoe Union (SAUO) ... ASU
American Snowshoers Union (EA) ... ASU
American Soccer League ... ASL
American Social Communications Conference (EA) ... ASCC
American Social Health [*formerly, Hygiene*] **Association** (EA) ... ASHA
American Social Health Association (SAUO) ... ASHA
American Social Hygiene Association (SAUO) ... ASHA
American Social Science Association (SAUO) ... ASSA
American Societiy of Interventional and Therapeutic Neuroradiology (SAUS) ... ASITN
American Society for Abrasive Methods [*Later, AES*] (EA) ... ASAM
American Society for Abrasives [*Superseded by AES*] (EA) ... ASA
American Society for Adolescent Psychiatry (EA) ... ASAP
American Society for Adolescent Psychology (DAVI) ... ASAP
American Society for Advancement of Anesthesia in Dentistry (EA) ... ASAAD
American Society for Aerospace Education (SAUO) ... AEA
American Society for Aerospace Education (EA) ... ASAE
American Society for Aesthetic Plastic Surgery (EA) ... ASAPS
American Society for Aesthetics (EA) ... ASA
American Society For Aesthetics (SAUO) ... ASFE

American Society for African Culture (SAUO) .... ASAC
American Society for Amusement Park Security and Safety (EA) .... ASAPSS
American Society for Apheresis (EA) .... ASFA
American Society for Artificial Internal Organs (EA) .... ASAIO
American Society for Association Publishing (EA) .... ASAP
American Society for Automation in Pharmacy (EA) .... ASAP
American Society for Bariatric Obesity Surgery (HCT) .... ASBS
American Society for Bariatric Surgery (SAUO) .... ASBS
American Society for Biochemistry and Molecular Biology (SAUO) .... ASBC
American Society for Biochemistry and Molecular Biology (EA) .... ASBMB
American Society for Biotechnology (HGEN) .... ASB
American Society for Blood and Marrow Transplantation .... ASBMT
American Society for Bone and Mineral Research (EA) .... ASBMR
American Society for Cell Biology .... ACSB
American Society for Cell Biology (EA) .... ASCB
American Society for Church Architecture [*Later, IFRAA*] (EA) .... ASCA
American Society for Circumpolar Health (SAUO) .... ASCH
American Society for Clinical Evoked Potentials (EA) .... ASCEP
American Society for Clinical Investigation (EA) .... ASCI
American Society for Clinical Laboratory Science (NTPA) .... ASCLS
American Society for Clinical Nutrition (EA) .... ASCN
American Society for Clinical Pharmacology and Therapeutics (NTPA) .... ASCPT
American Society for Colposcopy and Cervical Pathology (EA) .... ASCCP
American Society for Concrete Construction (EA) .... ASCC
American Society for Conservation Archaeology (EA) .... ASCA
American Society for Crippled Children in Israel (EA) .... ASCCI
American Society for Cybernetics (EA) .... ASC
American Society for Cytotechnology (EA) .... ASCT
American Society for Deaf Children [*Defunct*] (EA) .... ASDC
American Society for Dental Aesthetics (EA) .... ASDA
American Society for Dermatologic Surgery (EA) .... ASDS
American Society for Eastern Arts .... ASEA
American Society for Ecological Education (SAUO) .... ASEE
American Society for Eighteenth-Century Studies (EA) .... ASECS
American Society for Engineering Education (EA) .... ASEE
American Society for Engineering Education, Computers in Education Division (SAUO) .... ASEE/COED
American Society for Engineering Education/Engineering Libraries Division .... ASEE/ELD
American Society for Engineering Management (EA) .... ASEM
American Society for Engineering Technology (SAUO) .... ASET
American Society for Enology and Viticulture (EA) .... ASEV
American Society for Environmental Education (EA) .... ASEE
American Society for Environmental History (EA) .... ASEH
American Society for Ethnohistory (EA) .... ASE
American Society for Experimental Pathology [*Later, AAP*] (EA) .... ASEP
American Society for Experimental Pathology (SAUO) .... ASEP
American Society for Experimental Stress Analysis (SAUO) .... ASESA
American Society for Friendship with Switzerland [*Later, ASA*] (EA) .... ASFS
American Society for Gastrointestinal Endoscopy (EA) .... ASGE
American Society for Genetics (DAVI) .... ASG
American Society for Geriatric Dentistry (EA) .... ASGD
American Society for German Literature of the 16th and 17th Centuries (SAUO) .... ASGLSSC
American Society for Head and Neck Surgery (EA) .... ASHNS
American Society for Health Care Marketing and Public Relations (EA) .... ASHCMPR
American Society for Healthcare Central Service Personel (SAUO) .... ASHCSP
American Society for Healthcare Central Service Personnel [*American Hospital Association*] (EA) .... ASHCSP
American Society for Healthcare Education and Training (SAUO) .... ASHET
American Society for Healthcare Education and Training - of the American Hospital Association (EA) .... ASHET
American Society for Healthcare Engineering (NTPA) .... ASHE
American Society for Healthcare Environmental Services (SAUO) .... ASHES
American Society for Healthcare Environmental Services of the American Hospital Association (EA) .... ASHES
American Society for Healthcare Food Service Administrators [*Formerly, American Society for Hospital Food Service Administrators*] (EA) .... ASHFSA
American Society for Healthcare Human Resources Administration (EA) .... ASHHRA
American Society for Healthcare Materials Management (NTPA) .... ASHMM
American Society for Healthcare Risk Management (EA) .... ASHRM
American Society for Heating and Ventilation (SAUO) .... ASFHV
American Society for Histocompatibility and Immunogenetics (EA) .... ASHI
American Society for Horticultural Science (EA) .... ASHS
American Society for Hospital Education and Training (SAUO) .... ASHET
American Society for Hospital Engineering (SAUO) .... ASHE
American Society for Hospital Engineering - of the American Hospital Association (EA) .... ASHE
American Society for Hospital Food Service Administrators (EA) .... ASHFSA
American Society for Hospital Marketing and Public Relations [*Later, ASHCMPR*] (EA) .... ASHMPR
American Society for Hospital Materials Management (EA) .... ASHMM
American Society for Hospital Personnel Administration [*Later, ASHHRA*] (EA) .... ASHPA
American Society for Hospital Planning .... ASHP
American Society for Hospital Purchasing and Materials Management [*Later, ASHMM*] (EA) .... ASHPMM
American Society for Industrial Security (EA) .... ASIS
American Society for Information Science [*Formerly, ADI*] (EA) .... ASIS
American Society for Information Science, Washington, DC [*Library symbol*] [*Library of Congress*] (LCLS) .... ASIS
American Society for Investigative Pathologists (HGEN) .... ASIP
American Society for Investigative Pathology (NTPA) .... ASIP
American Society for Jewish Music (EA) .... ASJM
American Society for Laser Medicine and Surgery (EA) .... ASLMS
American Society for Law Pharmacy (SAUS) .... ASPL
American Society for Legal History (EA) .... ASLH
American Society for Mass Spectrometry (EA) .... ASMS
American Society for Medical Technology (EA) .... ASMT
American Society for Metals (SAUO) .... Am Soc Metals
American Society for Metals [*Later, ASMI*] (EA) .... ASM
American Society for Metals Library, Metals Park, OH [*Library symbol*] [*Library of Congress*] (LCLS) .... OMpA
American Society for Metals Monographs (SAUO) .... ASMM
American Society for Metals-Europe (SAUO) .... ASM-Europe
American Society for Microbiology (EA) .... ASM
American Society for Missiology (SAUO) .... ASM
American Society for Mohs Surgery (SAUO) .... ASMS
American Society for Neo-Hellenic Studies (EA) .... ASNHS
American Society for Netherlands Philately (EA) .... ASNP
American Society for Neural Transplantation (SAUO) .... ASNT
American Society for Neurochemistry (EA) .... ASN
American Society for Nondestructive Testing (SAUO) .... ASNDT
American Society for Nondestructive Testing (EA) .... ASNT
American Society for Nursing Service Administrators [*Later, AONE*] (EA) .... ASNSA
American Society for Nutritional Sciences (NTPA) .... ASNS
American Society for Oceanography (SAUO) .... ASO
American Society for Oceanography [*Later, MTS*] (EA) .... ASO
American Society for Pain Relief, Research and Education (SAUO) .... ASPRRE
American Society for Pain Relief, Research and Education Net site (SAUO) .... ASPRREN
American Society for Parenteral and Enteral Nutrition (EA) .... ASPEN
American Society for Pediatric Neurosurgery (EA) .... ASPN
American Society for Performance Improvement [*Defunct*] (EA) .... ASPI
American Society for Personnel Administration [*Later, SHRM*] (EA) .... ASPA
American Society for Personnel Administration Accreditation Institute .... AAI
American Society for Personnel Administration International (EA) .... ASPA/I
American Society for Personnel Administrators (SAUO) .... ASPA
American Society for Pharmacology and Experimental Therapeutics (EA) .... ASPET
American Society for Pharmacy Law (EA) .... ASPL
American Society for Philatelic Pages and Panels (EA) .... ASPPP
American Society for Photobiology (EA) .... ASP
American Society for Photogrammetry and Remote Sensing (EA) .... ASPRS
American Society for Plasticulture (EA) .... ASP
American Society for Political and Legal Philosohy (SAUS) .... ASPLP
American Society for Portuguese Numismatics [*Defunct*] (EA) .... ASPN
American Society for Precision Engineering (NTPA) .... ASPE
American Society for Preventive Dentistry [*Defunct*] .... ASPD
American Society for Prophylaxis in Obstetrics (PAZ) .... ASPO/Lamaze
American Society for Psychical Research (EA) .... ASPR
American Society for Psychical Research, New York, NY [*Library symbol*] [*Library of Congress*] (LCLS) .... NNASP
American Society for Psychoprophylaxis in Obstetrics (EA) .... ASPO
American Society for Public Administration (EA) .... ASPA
American Society for Quality Control (EA) .... ASQC
American Society for Reconstructive Microsurgery (NTPA) .... ASRM
American Society for Reformation Research .... ASRR
American Society for Reproductive Medicine (PAZ) .... ASRM
American Society for Research in Psychosomatic Problems (SAUO) .... ASRPP
American Society for Russian Naval History (EA) .... ASRNH
American Society for Steel Treaters [*Later, ASM*] .... ASST
American Society for Steel Treating (SAUO) .... ASST
American Society for Steel Treating or Assistant (SAUO) .... ASST
American Society for Stereotactic and Functional Neurosurgery (EA) .... ASSFN
American Society for Surface Mining and Reclamation (EA) .... ASSMR
American Society for Surgery of the Hand (EA) .... ASSH
American Society for Technion-Israel Institute of Technology (EA) .... ASTIIT
American Society for Technion-Israel Institute of Technology (SAUO) .... ASTITT
American Society for Testing and Development (AAGC) .... ASTD
American Society for Testing and Materials [*Acronym is now organization's official name*] (EAIO) .... ASTM
American Society for Testing and Materials-Draft (SAUO) .... ASTM-D
American Society for Testing and Materials-Institute of Petroleum (SAUO) .... ASTM-IP
American Society for Testing Materials (GEOI) .... ASTM
American Society for the Abandonment of Acronyms (SAUO) .... ASAA
American Society for the Advancement of General Anesthesia in Dentistry (SAUO) .... ASAGAD
American Society for the Control of Cancer (MELL) .... ASCC
American Society for the Deaf (SAUO) .... ASD
American Society for the Defense of Tradition (SAUS) .... TFP
American Society for the Defense of Tradition, Family and Property (EA) .... TFP
American Society for the Hard of Hearing (SAUO) .... ASHH
American Society for the Perfection of Punctuation (SAUO) .... ASPP
American Society for the Preservation of Sacred, Patriotic and Operatic Music (SAUO) .... ASPSPOM
American Society for the Prevention of Crime [*Defunct*] (EA) .... ASPC
American Society for the Prevention of Cruelty to Animals (EA) .... ASPCA
American Society for the Prevention of Cruelty to Children (SAUO) .... ASPCC
American Society for the Promotion of Dentistry for Children (SAUO) .... ASPDC
American Society for the Protection of Nature in Israel (EA) .... ASPNI
American Society for the Republic of Panama (SAUO) .... ASRP
American Society for the Study of Allergy (SAUO) .... ASSA
American Society for the Study of Arteriosclerosis [*Later, CAAHA*] .... ASSA
American Society for the Study of Arthritis (SAUO) .... ASSArthr
American Society for the Study of Ideological Belief Systems (EA) .... ASSIBS

American Society for the Study of Orthodontics (EA) ASSO
American Society for the Study of Religion (EA) ASSR
American Society for the Study of Sterility [*Later, AFS*] (EA) ASSS
American Society for Theater Research (SAUS) ASTR
American Society for Therapeutic Radiology and Oncology (SAUO) ASTR
American Society for Therapeutic Radiology and Oncology (EA) ASTRO
American Society for Training and Development (EA) ASTD
American Society for Value Inquiry (EA) ASVI
American Society for X-Ray and Electron Diffraction (SAUO) ASXRED
American Society for Zero Defects [*Later, American Society for Performance Improvement*] ASZD
American Society for/of Cell Biology (SAUO) ASCB
American Society for/of Clinical Investigation (SAUO) ASCI
American Society for/of Clinical Nutrition (SAUO) ASCN
American Society for/of Concrete Construction (SAUO) ASCC
American Society for/of Hematology (SAUO) ASH
American Society for/of Horticultural Science (SAUO) ASHS
American Society for/of Human Genetics (SAUO) ASHG
American Society for/of Metals (SAUO) ASM
American Society for/of Microbiology (SAUO) ASM
American Society for/of Photogrammetry and Remote Sensing (SAUO) ASP
American Society for/of Public Administration (SAUO) ASPA
American Society for/of Quality Control (SAUO) ASQC
American Society for/of Reproductive Medicine (SAUO) ASRM
American Society for/of Theater or Theatre) Research (SAUO) ASTR
American Society in London (SAUO) ASL
American Society of Abdominal Surgeons (EA) ASAS
American Society of Abdominal Surgery (EA) ASAS
American Society of Access Professionals (EA) ASAP
American Society of Addiction Medicine (EA) ASAM
American Society of Adlerian Psychology (AEBS) ASAP
American Society of Adults with Pseudo-Obstruction ASAP
American Society of Advertising and Promotion, Inc. (NTCM) ASAP
American Society of Aeronautical Engineers [*Later, SAE*] (KSC) ASAE
American Society of Aerospace Pilots [*Defunct*] (EA) ASAP
American Society of African Culture [*Defunct*] (EA) AMSAC
American Society of African Culture (SAUO) Am Soc Afr Cult
American Society of Agricultural Appraisers (NTPA) ASAA
American Society of Agricultural Consultants (EA) ASAC
American Society of Agricultural Engineers (EA) ASAE
American Society of Agricultural Sciences (SAUO) ASAS
American Society of Agriculture (SAUO) ASAE
American Society of Agronomy (EA) ASA
American Society of Allied Health Professions (EA) ASAHP
American Society of Alternative Therapists (SAUO) ASAT
American Society of Ancient Instruments [*Defunct*] (EA) ASAI
American Society of Andrology (EA) ASA
American Society of Anesthesia Technologists and Technicians (SAUO) ASATT
American Society of Anesthesiologists (SAUO) ASA
American Society of Anesthesiologists (EA) ASA
American Society of Anesthesiologists (SAUO) ASAnes
American Society of Anesthesiologists, Park Ridge, IL [*Library symbol*] [*Library of Congress*] (LCLS) IParkA
American Society of Anesthesiologists Resident Component (SAUO) ASARC
American Society of Animal Production [*Later, ASAS*] ASAP
American Society of Animal Science (EA) ASAS
American Society of Anthropometric Medicine and Nutrition [*Defunct*] (EA) ASAMN
American Society of Appraisers [*Acronym also used as designation awarded to group's senior members*] [*Washington, DC*] (EA) ASA
American Society of Architectural Hardware Consultants [*Later, DHI*] (EA) ASAHC
American Society of Arms Collectors (EA) ASAC
American Society of Arms Collectors AS of AC
American Society of Artists (EA) ASA
American Society of Asset Managers (EA) ASAM
American Society of Association Executives (EA) ASAE
American Society of Association Historians (SAUO) ASAH
American Society of Auctioneers [*Defunct*] (EA) ASA
American Society of Automotive Engineers (SAUO) ASAE
American Society of Aviation Artists [*An association*] ASAA
American Society of Aviation Writers [*Later, IATJ*] (EA) ASAW
American Society of Bacteriologists (SAUO) ASB
American Society of Bacteriologists (BARN) ASB
American Society of Bacteriology (DAVI) ASB
American Society of Bakery Engineers (EA) ASBE
American Society of Bank Directors [*Arlington, VA*] (EA) ASBD
American Society of Bariatric Physicians (EA) ASBP
American Society of Bariatrics [*Later, ASBP*] ASB
American Society of Bariatrics (SAUO) ASB
American Society of Biochemists (SAUO) ASB
American Society of Biological Chemists [*Later, ASBMB*] (EA) ASBC
American Society of Biomechanics (SAUO) ASB
American Society of Biophysics and Cosmology (SAUO) ASBC
American Society of Body Engineers (EA) ASBE
American Society of Bookplate Collectors and Designers (DGA) ABCD
American Society of Bookplate Collectors and Designers (EA) ASBC & D
American Society of Breast Disease (NTPA) ASBD
American Society of Breast Disease [*Formerly, Society for the Study of Breast Disease*] (EA) SSBD
American Society of Brewing Chemists (EA) ASBC
American Society of Business Press Editors (EA) ASBPE
American Society of Camera Collectors (EA) ASCC
American Society of Cardiovascular Professionals. (SAUO) ASCP
American Society of Cardiovascular Professionals (SAUS) ASCP
American Society of Cardiovascular Professionals/Society for Cardiovascular Management (NTPA) ASCP
American Society of Cardiovascular Professionals/Society for Cardiovascular Management (EA) ASCP/SCM
American Society of Cartographers [*Defunct*] (EA) ASC
American Society of Cataract and Refractive Surgery (EA) ASCRS
American Society of Cataract & Refractive Surgery (SAUO) ASCRS
American Society of Certifed Engineering Technicians (SAUS) ASCET
American Society of Chartered Life Underwriters (SAUO) AmSoc CLU
American Society of Chartered Life Underwriters [*Later, ASCLU, ChFC*] (EA) ASCLU
American Society of Check Collectors (EA) ASCC
American Society of Chemical Engineers (SAUO) ASCE
American Society of Chemical Engineers (SAUO) ASCHE
American Society of Chemical Engineers (BARN) ASChE
American Society of Childbirth Educators [*Inactive*] (EA) ASCE
American Society of Chinese Medicine [*Inactive*] ASCM
American Society of Chiropodical Roentgenology ASCR
American Society of Christian Ethics [*Later, SCE*] ASCE
American Society of Church History (EA) ASCH
American Society of Church History. Papers (journ.) (SAUS) Am Soc Church Hist Papers
American Society of Cinematographers (EA) ASC
American Society of Civil Engineers (WDAA) AM SOC CE
American Society of Civil Engineers (SAUO) AmSocCE
American Society of Civil Engineers (EA) ASCE
American Society of Civil Engineers (SAUO) AS Civ E
American Society of Civil Engineers (SAUO) ASocCE
American Society of Civil Engineers and Architects (SAUO) ASCEA
American Society of Civil Engineers and Architects (WDAA) ASCEA
American Society of Civil Engineers. Environmental Engineering Division. Journal (journ.) (SAUS) Am Soc Civ Eng Environ Eng Div J
American Society of Civil Engineers. Proroceedings. Journal. Hydraulics Division (journ.) (SAUS) Am Soc Civ Eng Proc J Hydraul Div
American Society of Civil Engineers. Structural Division Journal. (journ.) (SAUS) Am Soc Civ E J Struct Div
American Society of Civil Engineers. Waterway, Port, Coastal and Ocean Division (journ.) (SAUS) Am Soc Civ E J Waterway Port Div
American Society of Clinic Radiologists (EA) ASCR
American Society of Clinical Genetics and Dysmorphology [*Later, BDCGS*] (EA) ASCGD
American Society of Clinical Hypnosis (EA) ASCH
American Society of Clinical Hypnosis-Education and Research Foundation (SAUO) ASCH-ERF
American Society of Clinical Laboratory Technicians (SAUO) ASCLT
American Society of Clinical Laboratory Technicians [*Later, ASMT*] ASCLT
American Society of Clinical Nutrition (SAUS) ASCN
American Society of Clinical Oncology (EA) ASCO
American Society of Clinical Pathologists (DMAA) ASCP
American Society of Clinical Pharmacology and Chemotherapy (DAVI) ASCPC
American Society of Clinical Psychopharmacology (EA) ASCP
American Society of CLU [*Chartered Life Underwriters*] **and ChFC** [*Chartered Financial Consultants*] [*Bryn Mawr, PA*] (EA) ASCLU & ChFC
American Society of Colon and Rectal Surgeons (EA) ASCRS
American Society of Comparative Law (NTPA) ASCL
American Society of Composers, Authors and Publishers (SAUO) ASCAP
American Society of Computer Dealers (EA) ASCD
American Society of Construction Inspectors (EA) ASCI
American Society of Consultant (or Consulting) Pharmacists (SAUO) ASCP
American Society of Consultant Pharmacists (EA) ASCP
American Society of Consulting Arborists (EA) ASCA
American Society of Consulting Chemists (SAUO) ASConsltgChem
American Society of Consulting Pharmacists (DMAA) ASCP
American Society of Consulting Planners (EA) ASCP
American Society of Contact Lens Specialists (SAUO) ASCLS
American Society of Contemporary Artists (EA) ASCA
American Society of Contemporary Medicine and Surgery (EA) ASCMS
American Society of Contemporary Ophthalmology (EA) ASCO
American Society of Corporate Historians, Archivists and Librarians (SAUO) ASCHAL
American Society of Corporate Secretaries [*New York, NY*] (EA) ASCS
American Society of Cosmetic Surgeons [*Later, AACS*] (EA) ASCS
American Society of Country Music (EA) ASCM
American Society of Crime Lab Directors (SAUO) ASCLD
American Society of Crime Laboratory Directors (EA) ASCLD
American Society of Criminology (EA) ASC
American Society of Critical Care Anesthesiolgists (SAUO) ASCCA
American Society of Cytology (EA) ASC
American Society of Cytopathology (NTPA) ASC
American Society of Cytopathology (MELL) ASCP
American Society of Danish Engineers (EA) ASDE
American Society of Dental Radiographers ASDR
American Society of Dental Surgeons (SAUO) ASDS
American Society of Dentist Anesthesiologists (SAUO) ASDA
American Society of Dentistry for Children (EA) ASDC
American Society of Dermatologic Surgery (SAUS) ASDS
American Society of Dermatological Retailers (EA) ASDR
American Society of Dermatopathology (EA) ASD
American Society of Dermatopathology (NTPA) ASDP
American Society of Dernmatological Retailers (SAUS) ASDR
American Society of Design Engineers (EA) ASDE
American Society of Directors of Volunteer Services (EA) ASDVS
American Society of Disk Jockeys [*Defunct*] (EA) ASDJ
American Society of Divorced Men (SAUO) ASDM

American Society of Dowsers (EA) .... ASD
American Society of Echocardiography (EA) .... ASE
American Society of Educators [Later, AAMSL] (EA) .... ASE
American Society of Electrical Engineers (NTCM) .... ASEE
American Society of Electroencephalographic Technologists (EA) .... ASET
American Society of Electro-Neurodiagnostic Technologists (EA) .... ASET
American Society of Electro-neurodiagnostic Technologists (SAUO) .... ASET
American Society of Electronics Engineers (SAUO) .... ASEE
American Society of Electroplated Plastics (EA) .... ASEP
American Society of Emergency Radiology (SAUO) .... ASER
American Society of Employers (SRA) .... ASE
American Society of Engineers .... ASE
American Society of Engineers and Architects .... ASEA
American Society of Enologists (EA) .... ASE
American Society of Exercise Physiologists (SAUO) .... ASEP
American Society of Extra-Corporal Technology (SAUO) .... AmSECT
American Society of Extra-Corporeal Technology (EA) .... AmSECT
American Society of Extra-Corporeal Technology [Medicine] (DAVI) .... ASECT
American Society of Facial Plastic Surgery (CMD) .... ASFPS
American Society of Farm Managers and Rural Appraisers (EA) .... ASFMRA
American Society of Forensic Odontology (EA) .... ASFO
American Society of Furniture Designers (EA) .... ASFD
American Society of Gas Engineers (EA) .... ASGE
American Society of Genealogists (EA) .... ASG
American Society of General Surgeons (SAUO) .... ASGS
American Society of Genetics (SAUO) .... ASG
American Society of Geolinguistics (EA) .... ASG
American Society of Golf Course Architects (EA) .... ASGCA
American Society of Greek and Latin Epigraphy (SAUO) .... ASGLE
American Society of Group Psychotherapy and Psychodrama (EA) .... ASGPP
American Society of Hand Therapists (EA) .... ASHT
American Society of Handicapped Physicians (EA) .... ASHP
American Society of Head and Neck Radiology (SAUO) .... ASHNR
American Society of Health Care Risk Managers (SAUO) .... ASHCRM
American Society of Health-System Pharmacists [Formerly, American Society of Hospital Pharmacists] .... ASHP
American Society of Heating and Air Conditioning Engineers (SAUO) .... ASHACE
American Society of Heating and Air-Conditioning Engineers [Later, ASHRAE] .... ASHAE
American Society of Heating and Ventilating Engineers .... ASHVE
American Society of Heating, Refrigerating and Air-Conditioning Engineers (SAUO) .... Am Soc HRAC Eng
American Society of Heating, Refrigerating and Air-Conditioning Engineers (SAUO) .... ASHRACE
American Society of Heating, Refrigerating and Air-Conditioning Engineers (MHDB) .... ASHRACE
American Society of Heating, Refrigerating, and Air-Conditioning Engineers (EA) .... ASHRAE
American Society of Heating, Refrigerating and Air-conditioning Engineers, Inc. (SAUS) .... Am Soc HRAC Eng
American Society of Heating, Refrigerating and Air-conditioning Engineers, Inc. (SAUS) .... ASHRAE
American Society of Hematology (EA) .... ASH
American Society of Highway Engineers (NTPA) .... ASHE
American Society of Home Inspectors (EA) .... ASHI
American Society of Hospice Care [Defunct] (EA) .... ASHC
American Society of Hospital Attorneys (EA) .... ASHA
American Society of Hospital Engineers (SAUO) .... ASHE
American Society of Hospital Pharmacists (EA) .... ASHP
American Society of Hospital Pharmacists Research and Education Foundation (EA) .... ASHPREF
American Society of Hospital Pharmacists Research and Education Foundation .... ASHPRF
American Society of Hospital-Based Emergency Air Medical Services (EA) .... ASHBEAMS
American Society of Human Genetics (EA) .... ASHG
American Society of Hypertension (EA) .... ASH
American Society of Ichthyologists and Herpetologists (EA) .... ASIH
American Society of Independent Business [Defunct] (EA) .... ASIB
American Society of Indexers (SAUO) .... Am Soc Indxrs
American Society of Indexers (EA) .... ASI
American Society of Indexers (SAUO) .... ASIs
American Society of Industrial Auctioneers (EA) .... ASIA
American Society of Industrial Designers [Later, IDSA] (EA) .... ASID
American Society of Industrial Medicine [Formerly, American Academy of Legal and Industrial Medicine] (EA) .... AALIM
American Society of Industrial Medicine (NTPA) .... ASIM
American Society of Industrial Security (SAUO) .... ASIS
American Society of Information and Data Processing (SAUO) .... ASIDP
American Society of Information Scientists (SAUO) .... ASIS
American Society of Insurance Management [Later, RIMS] (EA) .... ASIM
American Society of Interior Designers (EA) .... ASID
American Society of Internal Medicine (EA) .... ASIM
American Society of International Executives [Blue Bell, PA] (EA) .... ASIE
American Society of International Law (DLA) .... Am Soc Int L
American Society of International Law (EA) .... ASIL
American Society of International Law. Proceedings [A publication] (DLA) .... Am Soc'y Int'l Proc
American Society of Interpreters (EA) .... ASI
American Society of Interventional and Therapeutic Neuroradiology (SAUO) .... ASITN
American Society of Inventors (EA) .... ASI
American Society of Irrigation Consultants (EA) .... ASIC
American Society of Journalism School Administrators (SAUO) .... ASJA
American Society of Journalism School Administrators (EA) .... ASJSA

American Society of Journalists and Authors (EA) .... ASJA
American Society of Knitting Technologists (EA) .... ASKT
American Society of Laboratory Animal Practitioners (EA) .... ASLAP
American Society of Landscape Architects (EA) .... ASLA
American Society of Law and Medicine (EA) .... ASLM
American Society of Law Enforcement (SAUO) .... ASLE
American Society of Law Enforcement Trainers (EA) .... ASLET
American Society of Law, Medicine, and Ethics (NTPA) .... ASLME
American Society of Learned Societies on the Protection of Cultural Treasures inWar Areas [World War II] .... ASLSPCTWA
American Society of Legal History (SAUO) .... ASLH
American Society of Limnology and Oceanography (EA) .... ASLO
American Society of Lipo-Suction Surgery (NTPA) .... ASLSS
American Society of Local Officials [Defunct] (EA) .... ASLO
American Society of Lubricating (or Lubrication) Engineers (SAUO) .... ASLE
American Society of Lubrication Engineers (EA) .... ASLE
American Society of Lubrication Engineers (SAUO) .... ASLubE
American Society of Magazine Editors (EA) .... ASME
American Society of Magazine Photographers (EA) .... ASMP
American Society of Mammalogists (EA) .... ASM
American Society of Marine Artists (EA) .... ASMA
American Society of Master Dental Technologists (EA) .... ASMDT
American Society of Mature Catholics [Defunct] [Defunct] (EA) .... ASMC
American Society of Maxillofacial Surgeons (EA) .... ASMS
American Society of Mechanical Engineers (WDAA) .... Am Soc ME
American Society of Mechanical Engineers (SAUO) .... AmSocME
American Society of Mechanical Engineers (EA) .... ASME
American Society of Mechanical Engineers Auxiliary (EA) .... ASMEA
American Society of Media Photographers (NTPA) .... ASMP
American Society of Medical Missionaries .... ASMM
American Society of Medical Technologists (SAUO) .... ASMT
American Society of Mental Hospital Business Administrators [Later, AMHA] (EA) .... ASMHBA
American Society of Metal Definitions (SAUO) .... ASMD
American Society of Metals (SAUS) .... ASM
American Society of Microbiology (SAUS) .... ASM
American Society of Military Comptrollers (EA) .... ASMC
American Society of Military Insignia Collectors (EA) .... ASMIC
American Society of Military Insignia Collectors (SAUO) .... ASMIL
American Society of Miniature Painters (SAUO) .... ASMP
American Society of Missiology (EA) .... ASM
American Society of Motion Picture and Television Engineers [Formerly, ASMPE] .... ASMPTE
American Society of Motion Picture Engineers [Later, ASMPTE] .... ASMPE
American Society of Municipal Improvements (SAUO) .... ASMI
American Society of Music Arrangers (EA) .... ASMA
American Society of Music Arrangers and Composers (NTPA) .... ASMAC
American Society of Music Copyists (EA) .... ASMC
American Society of Naturalists (EA) .... ASN
American Society of Naval Architects and Marine Engineers (SAUO) .... ASNA&ME
American Society of Naval Engineers (EA) .... ASNE
American Society of Nephrology (EA) .... ASN
American Society of Neuroimaging (EA) .... ASN
American Society of Neuroradiology (EA) .... ASNR
American Society of Newspaper Editors (EA) .... ASNE
American Society of Notaries (SAUO) .... Am Soc Not
American Society of Notaries (EA) .... ASN
American Society of Nuclear Cardiology (NTPA) .... ASNC
American Society of Onomatologists [Defunct] (EA) .... ASO
American Society of Ophthalmic Administrators (EA) .... ASOA
American Society of Ophthalmic Plastic and Reconstructive Surgery (NTPA) .... ASOPRS
American Society of Ophthalmic Registered Nurses (EA) .... ASORN
American Society of Ophthalmologic and Otolaryngologic Allergy [Later, AAOA] (EA) .... ASOOA
American Society of Oral Surgeons [Later, AAOMS] (EA) .... ASOS
American Society of Orthodontists [Later, AAO] .... ASO
American Society of Outpatient Surgeons (EA) .... ASOS
American Society of Pain Management Nurses (NTPA) .... ASPMN
American Society of Papyrologists (EA) .... ASP
American Society of Paramedics (EA) .... ASPM
American Society of Parasitologists (EA) .... ASP
American Society of Parasitology (MELL) .... ASP
American Society of Payroll Management (NTPA) .... ASPM
American Society of Pediatric Hematology/Oncology (NTPA) .... ASPH/O
American Society of Pediatric Neuroradiologoy (SAUO) .... ASPNR
American Society of Pediatric Neurosurgeons (SAUO) .... ASPN
American Society of Pediatric Otolaryngology (SAUO) .... ASPO
American Society of Pension Actuaries (EA) .... ASPA
American Society of Perfumers [Defunct] (EA) .... ASP
American Society of Peri-Anesthesia Nurses (SAUO) .... ASPAN
American Society of Periodontists [Later, AAP] (EA) .... ASP
American Society of Peru (EAIO) .... AmSoc
American Society of Petroleum Operations Engineers (EA) .... ASPOE
American Society of Pharmacognosy (EA) .... ASP
American Society of Photobiology (SAUO) .... ASP
American Society of Photogrammetry [Later, ASPRS] (EA) .... ASP
American Society of Photographers (EA) .... ASP
American Society of Physician Analysts (EA) .... ASPA
American Society of Picture Professionals (EA) .... ASPP
American Society of Planning Officials [Later, American Planning Association] (EA) .... ASPO
American Society of Plant Physiologists (EA) .... ASPP
American Society of Plant Physiology (SAUO) .... ASPP

American Society of Plant Taxonomists (EA) ... ASPT
American Society of Plastic and Reconstructive Surgeons (EA) ... ASPRS
American Society of Plastic and Reconstructive Surgery (SAUO) ... ASPRS
American Society of Plastic and Reconstructive Surgical Nurses (EA) ... ASPRSN
American Society of Plastic Surgeons (SAUO) ... ASPS
American Society of Plumbing Engineers (EA) ... ASPE
American Society of Plumbing Officials (SAUO) ... ASPO
American Society of Podiatric Assistants [*Later, ASPMA*] (EA) ... ASPA
American Society of Podiatric Dermatology (EA) ... ASPD
American Society of Podiatric Medical Assistants (EA) ... ASPMA
American Society of Podiatric Medicine (EA) ... ASPM
American Society of Podiatry Executives (NTPA) ... ASPE
American Society of Polar Philatelists (EA) ... ASPP
American Society of Post-Anesthesia Nurses (EA) ... ASPAN
American Society of Practicing Architects ... ASPA
American Society of Precision Nailmakers [*Defunct*] ... ASPN
American Society of Pre-Dental Students (EA) ... ASPS
American Society of Preventive Oncology (EA) ... ASPO
American Society of Primatologists (EA) ... ASP
American Society of Professional and Executive Women [*Defunct*] (EA) ... ASPEW
American Society of Professional Appraisers (EA) ... ASPA
American Society of Professional Automobile Racing ... ASPAR
American Society of Professional Biologists [*Later, AIBS*] (EA) ... ASPB
American Society of Professional Draftsmen (SAUO) ... ASPD
American Society of Professional Draftsmen and Artists (EA) ... ASPDA
American Society of Professional Ecologists (EA) ... ASPE
American Society of Professional Engineers (SAUO) ... ASPE
American Society of Professional Estimators (EA) ... ASPE
American Society of Professional Salesmen (EA) ... ASPS
American Society of Psychical Research (SAUS) ... ASPR
American Society of Psychoanalytic Physicians (NTPA) ... ASPP
American Society of Psychoopthology of Expression (SAUO) ... ASPE
American Society of Psychosocial & Behavior Oncology/AIDS (SAUO) ... ASPBOA
American Society of Psychosomatic Dentistry and Medicine [*IPI*] [*Absorbed by*] (EA) ... ASPDM
American Society of Psychosomatic Dentistry and Medicine. Journal (journ.) (SAUS) ... JPDMB
American Society of Psycoanalytic Physicians (EA) ... ASPP
American Society of Public Administration (SAUS) ... ASPA
American Society of Pulp Export Associations (SAUO) ... ASPEA
American Society of Questioned Document Examiners (EA) ... ASQDE
American Society of Radiologic Technologists (EA) ... ASRT
American Society of Range Management [*Later, SRM*] (EA) ... ASRM
American Society of Real Estate Counselors (EA) ... ASREC
American Society of Refrigerating Engineers [*Later, ASHRAE*] ... ASRE
American Society of Regional Anesthesia (EA) ... ASRA
American Society of Retired Dentists (EA) ... ASRD
American Society of Rocketry ... ASR
American Society of Roommate Services (EA) ... ASRS
American Society of Russian Naval History (SAUO) ... ASRNH
American Society of Safety Engineers ... ASSA
American Society of Safety Engineers (EA) ... ASSE
American Society of Sanitary Engineering (SAUO) ... ASSanE
American Society of Sanitary Engineering (SAUO) ... ASSE
American Society of Sanitary Engineering (EA) ... ASSE
American Society of Sanitary Engineers (SAUO) ... ASSE
American Society of Scientific and Engineering Translators ... ASSET
American Society of Senior Wire Rope Engineers (EA) ... AS^{2}WRE
American Society of Senior Wire Rope Engineers ... ASSWRE
American Society of Sephardic Studies (EA) ... ASOSS
American Society of Spine Radiology (SAUO) ... ASSR
American Society of Sugar Beet Technologists (EA) ... ASSBT
American Society of Swedish Engineers (EA) ... ASSE
American Society of Tax Professionals (EA) ... ASTP
American Society of Teachers of Dancing (EA) ... ASTD
American Society of Technical Appraisers (SAUO) ... ASTA
American Society of Test Engineers (EA) ... ASTE
American Society of Testing and Materials (SAUS) ... ASTM
American Society of Testing Materials (WPI) ... ASTM
American Society of the French Legion of Honor (EA) ... ASFLH
American Society of the Greek Order of Saint Dennis of Zante (EA) ... ASGOSDZ
American Society of Theater Consultants (EA) ... ASTC
American Society of Theatre Research (SAUS) ... ASTR
American Society of Therapeutic Radiologists [*Later, ASTRO*] (EA) ... ASTR
American Society of Tool and Manufacturing Engineers (SAUO) ... Am Soc Tool and Mfg Eng
American Society of Tool and Manufacturing Engineers [*Later, SME*] (EA) ... ASTME
American Society of Tool Engineers [*Later, SME*] ... ASTE
American Society of Trade Movement (SAUO) ... ASTM
American Society of Traffic and Transportation (EA) ... ASTT
American Society of Training Directors (SAUO) ... ASTD
American Society of Transit Engineers (SAUO) ... ASTE
American Society of Transplant Physicians ... ASTP
American Society of Transplant Surgeons (EA) ... ASTS
American Society of Transportation and Logistics [*MTMC*] (TAG) ... AST&L
American Society of Transportation and Logistics (EA) ... ASTL
American Society of Travel Agencies (SAUO) ... ASTA
American Society of Travel Agents (EA) ... ASTA
American Society of Trial Consultants (EA) ... ASTC
American Society of Tropical Medicine (SAUO) ... ASTM
American Society of Tropical Medicine and Hygiene (EA) ... ASTMH
American Society of TV Cameramen (EA) ... ASTVC
American Society of Ultrasound Technical Specialists [*Later, SDMS*] (EA) ... ASUTS
American Society of University Composers (EA) ... ASUC
American Society of Utility Investors (EA) ... ASUI
American Society of Veterinary Ethology (EA) ... ASVE
American Society of Veterinary Ophthalmology (EA) ... ASVO
American Society of Veterinary Physiologists and Pharmacologists (EA) ... ASVPP
American Society of Wedding Professionals (EA) ... ASWP
American Society of Women Accountants (EA) ... ASWA
American Society of X-Ray Technicians (SAUO) ... ASXRT
American Society of X-Ray Technicians [*Later, ASRT*] ... ASXT
American Society of Zoologists (EA) ... ASZ
American Society on Aging (EA) ... ASA
American Society to Save Biharis and Other Minorities ... ASSB & OM
American Society to Save Biharis and Other Minorities (SAUO) ... ASSB&OM
American Sociological Association (EA) ... ASA
American Sociological Review (journ.) (SAUS) ... ASR
American Sociological Society (SAUO) ... Am Soc Soc
American Sociological Society (SAUO) ... ASOS
American Sociological Society (SAUO) ... ASS
American Sociometric Association [*Defunct*] (EA) ... ASA
American Sod Producers' Association (EA) ... ASPA
American Soda Foundain Company (SAUO) ... ASFCO
American Softball Association (SAUO) ... ASA
American Software [*NASDAQ symbol*] (SAG) ... AMSW
American Software, Inc. [*Associated Press*] (SAG) ... ASoft
American Software Users Group (EA) ... ASUG
American Soil Survey Association (SAUO) ... ASSA
American Sokol Educational and Physical Culture Organization (EA) ... ASO
American Sokol Educational and Physical Culture Organization ... SOK
American Solar Energy Association (EA) ... ASEA
American Solar Energy Society (EA) ... ASES
American Solar King Corp. (SAUO) ... AMSK
American Soldier ... AMSOL
American Solidarity Movement [*Defunct*] (EA) ... ASM
American Songbag [*A publication*] ... AS
American South African Line (SAUS) ... ASA
American Southdown Breeders' Association (EA) ... ASBA
American Southwest Conference (PSS) ... ASC
American Sovereignty Task Force (EA) ... ASTF
American Soy Bean Association (SAUO) ... ASBA
American Soybean Association (EA) ... ASA
American Soybean Institute [*Defunct*] (EA) ... ASI
American Spa and Health Resort Association (EA) ... ASHRA
American Space and Development Agency (NUCP) ... ASADA
American Space Foundation [*Defunct*] (EA) ... ASF
American Space Frontier Committee [*Defunct*] (EA) ... ASFC
American Space Institute (ACAE) ... ASI
American Spaniel Club (EA) ... ASC
American Spanish (ADWA) ... AmerSp
American Spanish Committee (EA) ... ASC
American Spanish Dance Theatre ... ASDT
American Spasmodic Torticollis Association (EA) ... ASTA
American Special Interest Group (ADWA) ... ASIG
[*The*] **American Specialty Surety Council** [*Later, ASA*] (EA) ... TASSC
American Specialty Toy Retailing Association (NTPA) ... ASTRA
American Specification Institute [*Defunct*] ... ASI
American Specifications Institute (SAUS) ... ASI
American Spectator [*A publication*] (BRI) ... Am Spect
American Spectator (SAUS) ... TAS
American Speech and Hearing Association (DAVI) ... ASHA
American Speech Correction Association (SAUO) ... ASCA
American Speech-Language-Hearing Association (EA) ... ASHA
American Speech-Language-Hearing Association (SAUO) ... ASLHA
American Speech-Language-Hearing Foundation ... ASLH
American Speed Association ... ASA
American Spelean Historical Association (EA) ... ASHA
American Spelean History Association (SAUO) ... ASHA
American Spice Trade Association (EA) ... ASTA
American Spide Trade Association (SAUO) ... ASTA
American Spinal Injury Association (EA) ... ASIA
American Spoon Collectors (EA) ... ASC
American Sport Fishing Association (NTPA) ... ASFA
American Sport Horse Registry [*Defunct*] (EA) ... ASHR
American Sport Touring Rider's Association (EA) ... ASTRA
American Sportfishing Association ... ASA
American Sports Education Institute (EA) ... ASEI
American Sports Medicine Association Board of Certification ... ASMA
American Sports Medicine Institute (SAUO) ... ASMI
American Sportscasters Association (EA) ... ASA
American Sportsman's Club [*Commercial firm*] (EA) ... ASC
American Sprint Car Association [*Auto racing*] ... ASCA
American Sprocket Chain Manufacturers Association [*Later, American Chain Association*] ... ASCMA
American Squadron of Aviation Historians (EA) ... ASAH
American Squid Marketing Association [*Defunct*] (EA) ... ASMA
American Stamp Club of Great Britain (EA) ... ASCGB
American Stamp Dealers Association (EA) ... ASDA
American Standard (WDAA) ... AMER STD
American Standard (SAUS) ... Amer Std
American Standard (SAUS) ... AM STD
American Standard ... AS
American Standard Acoustical Terminology (SAUS) ... ASAT

American Standard Building Code (IEEE) ... ASBC
American Standard Character Set (SAUS) ... ASCS
American Standard Chinchilla Association [*Later, ASCRA*] ... ASCA
American Standard Chinchilla Association (SAUO) ... ASCA
American Standard Chinchilla Rabbit Association (EA) ... ASCRA
American Standard Code (OA) ... ASC
American Standard Code for Information Exchange (SAUS) ... ASCII
American Standard Code for Information Interchange [*Pronounced "ask-ee"*] [*American National Standards Institute*] [*Computer science*] ... ASCII
American Standard Code for Information Interchange Keyboard (SAUS) ... ASCIIK
American Standard Code for Information Interexchange [*Telecommunications*] (OTD) ... ASCII
American Standard Companies, Inc. [*NYSE symbol*] (SAG) ... ASD
American Standard Cos., Inc. [*Associated Press*] (SAG) ... AmStd
American Standard Elevator Code ... ASEC
American Standard for Character Information Interchange (TELE) ... ASCII
American Standard, Inc. (SAUO) ... AST
American Standard Keyboard (SAUS) ... ASK
American Standard Language for Information Interchange ... ASCII
American Standard of Testing Materials ... ASTM
American Standard Pipe (SAUS) ... ASP
American Standard Practice for Industrial Lighting (IAA) ... ASPIL
American Standard Test Method (SAUS) ... ASTM
American Standard Thread (SAUS) ... ASThread
American Standard Version [*of the Bible, 1901*] ... ASV
American Standard Vocabulary for Information Processing (BUR) ... ASVIP
American Standard Wire Gage (SAUS) ... ASWG
American Standardbred Breeders Association (EA) ... ASBA
American Standards Association (SAUO) ... ANSA
American Standards Association [*Later, USASI, ANSI*] ... ASA
American Standards Committee for Information Interchange (ARMP) ... ASCII
American Standards for Testing of Materials (SAUO) ... ASTM
American Standards Group (ACAE) ... ASG
American Standards Institute (IAA) ... ASI
American Standards Test Manual ... ASTM
American Standards Testing Bureau Inc. (SAUO) ... ASTB
American State Papers [*A publication*] (DLA) ... Am State Papers
American State Papers [*A publication*] (DLA) ... Am St P
American State Papers [*A publication*] (DLA) ... Am St Papers
American State Reports [*A publication*] (DLA) ... American State Rep
American State Reports [*A publication*] (DLA) ... Amer State Reps
American State Reports [*A publication*] (DLA) ... Amer St Rep
American State Reports [*A publication*] (DLA) ... Am SR
American State Reports [*A publication*] (DLA) ... Am Sta Rep
American State Reports [*A publication*] (DLA) ... Am State Rep
American State Reports [*1886-1911*] [*A publication*] (DLA) ... Am St R
American State Reports [*A publication*] (DLA) ... Am St Rep
American State Reports [*A publication*] (DLA) ... Am St Reports
American State Reports [*A publication*] (DLA) ... ASR
American States Financial Corp. [*Associated Press*] (SAG) ... AmStFn
American States Financial Corp. [*NYSE symbol*] (SAG) ... ASX
American States Water [*NYSE symbol*] [*Formerly, Southern California Water*] ... AWR
American Statesmen [*A publication*] ... AS
American Statistical Association (EA) ... ASA
American Statistics Index [*Congressional Information Service, Inc.*] [*Bibliographic database*] [*A publication*] ... ASI
American Statistics Index (journ.) (SAUS) ... ASI
American Statistics Institute (SAUO) ... ASI
American Steam Ship Company (SAUO) ... ASSCO
American Steamship Traffic Executives Committee ... ASTEC
American Steel and Wire (SAUS) ... AS&W
American Steel and Wire Gage (SAUS) ... ASWG
American Steel and Wire Gauge ... AS & W
American Steel and Wire Gauge ... ASWG
American Steel Equipment (SAUS) ... ASE
American Steel Foundrymen's Association ... ASFA
American Steel Warehouse Association [*Later, SSCI*] ... ASWA
American Stereophonic Corporation (SAUO) ... ASCO
American Sterilizer Co. (SAUO) ... ASZ
American Sterilizer Company (SAUO) ... AMSCO
American Sternwheel Association (EA) ... ASA
American Stock Exchange [*New York, NY*] ... A
American Stock Exchange [*New York, NY*] (EA) ... AMEX
American Stock Exchange ... Amex
American Stock Exchange (SG) ... AS
American Stock Exchange (EA) ... ASE
American Stock Exchange Clearing Corp. ... ASECC
American Stock Exchange Guide [*Commerce Clearing House*] [*A publication*] (DLA) ... Am Stock Ex Guide
American Stock Exchange Option Display Book ... AODB
American Stock Yards Association (EA) ... ASYA
American Stockyards Association (SAUO) ... ASA
American Stomatological Association (DAVI) ... ASA
American Stone Importers Association (EA) ... ASIA
American Stop Smoking Intervention Study [*National Institutes of Health*] (EGAO) ... ASSIST
American Stores Co. [*Associated Press*] (SAG) ... AmStores
American Stores Co. [*NYSE symbol*] (SPSG) ... ASC
American Strategic Income Portfolio [*Associated Press*] (SAG) ... AmSIP
American Strategic Income Portfolio [*NYSE symbol*] (SAG) ... ASP
American Strategic Income Portfolio [*NYSE symbol*] (SPSG) ... CSP
American Strategic Income Portfolio II [*Associated Press*] (SAG) ... AmSIP2
American Strategic Income Portfolio II [*NYSE symbol*] (SAG) ... BSP
American Strategic Income Portfolio III [*Associated Press*] (SAG) ... AmSIP3
American Strategic Income Portfolio III [*NYSE symbol*] (SAG) ... CSP
American Street Machines [*Defunct*] (EA) ... ASM
American Street Railway Decisions [*A publication*] (DLA) ... Am St RD
American Street Railway Decisions [*A publication*] (DLA) ... Am St Ry Dec
American Street Railway Reports [*A publication*] (DLA) ... Am St Ry Rep
American String Teachers Association (EA) ... ASTA
American Striped Bass Society (EA) ... ASBS
American Studebaker Club ... ASC
American Student Association (EA) ... ASA
American Student Committee of the Occupational Therapy Association [*American Occupational Therapy Association*] ... ASCOTA
American Student Dental Association (EA) ... ASDA
American Student Health Association (SAUO) ... ASHA
American Student Information Service ... ASIS
American Student Media Association (EA) ... ASMA
American Student Union ... ASU
American Students Overseas Combined Action Forces (SAUO) ... ASOCAF
American Studies ... AMST
American Studies Association (EA) ... ASA
American Studies Centre [*University of Sydney*] [*Australia*] ... ASC
American Studies in Papyrology [*New Haven, CT*] [*A publication*] (BJA) ... AMStPapyr
American Studies International [*A publication*] (BRI) ... ASInt
American Studies (journ.) (SAUS) ... Am S
American Studies Library Group (SAUO) ... ASLG
American Studios, Inc. [*NASDAQ symbol*] (SAG) ... AMST
American Studios, Inc. [*Associated Press*] (SAG) ... AStudio
American Study Program for Educational and Cultural Training (EA) ... ASPECT
American Subacute Care Association ... ASCA
American Subcontractors Association (EA) ... ASA
American Sudden Infant Death Syndrome Institute (EA) ... ASIDSI
American Suffolk Horse Association (EA) ... ASHA
American Suffolk Sheep Society (EA) ... ASSS
American Sugar Alliance (EA) ... ASA
American Sugar Beet Industry Policy Committee [*Defunct*] (EA) ... ASBIPC
American Sugar Cane League (SAUO) ... ASCL
American Sugar Cane League of the USA (EA) ... ASCL
American Sugar Refining (SAUS) ... ASR
American Sugar Refining Co., Philadelphia, PA [*Library symbol*] [*Library of Congress*] [*Obsolete*] (LCLS) ... PPAmSR
American Sugarbeet Growers Association (EA) ... ASGA
American Suicide Fund [*An association*] ... ASF
American Sunbathing Association (EA) ... ASA
American Sunday School Union [*Later, AMF*] ... ASSU
American Sunday School Union, Philadelphia, PA [*Library symbol*] [*Library of Congress*] [*Obsolete*] (LCLS) ... PPAmS
American Sunroof Corp., Inc. ... ASC
American Supercharger Club and Owner's Association (EA) ... ASCOA
American Superconductor Corp. [*NASDAQ symbol*] (SPSG) ... AMSC
American Superconductor Corp. [*Associated Press*] (SAG) ... AmSupr
American Supplier Institute (EA) ... ASI
American Supply and Machinery Manufacturers (SAUO) ... ASMM
American Supply and Machinery Manufacturers Association (EA) ... ASMMA
American Supply Association (EA) ... ASA
American Surety Association (EA) ... ASA
American Surfing Association (EA) ... ASA
American Surgeon (journ.) (SAUS) ... Amer Surg
American Surgery Centers Corp. (SAUS) ... SRGY
American Surgical Association (EA) ... ASA
American Surgical Trade Association (EA) ... ASTA
American Survival Association [*Defunct*] (EA) ... ASA
American Swedish Historical Foundation and Museum (EA) ... ASHF
American Swedish Historical Foundation, Philadelphia, PA [*Library symbol*] [*Library of Congress*] (LCLS) ... PPAmSwM
American Swedish Institute (EA) ... ASI
American Swimming Coaches Association (EA) ... ASCA
American Swiss Foundation for Scientific Exchange (EA) ... ASFSE
American Symphony Orchestra ... ASO
American Symphony Orchestra League (EA) ... ASOL
American Synthetic Rubber Corp. ... ASRC
American Synthetic Rubber Corporation (SAUO) ... ASRC
American Syringomyelia Alliance Project (EA) ... ASAP
American Systems Incorporated (SAUO) ... ASI
American Tan Rabbit Specialty Club (EA) ... ATRSC
American Tang Soo Do Association [*Defunct*] (EA) ... ATSDA
American Tanker Rate Schedule (SAUS) ... ATRS
American Tanker Rate Scheme (SAUS) ... ATRS
American Tarantula Society [*Defunct*] (EA) ... ATS
American Tarentaise Association (EA) ... ATA
American Tarentaise Association (SAUO) ... ATA
American Tariff League [*Later, TRC*] ... ATL
American Tarpan Studbook Association (EA) ... ATSA
American Tax Policy Institute (EA) ... ATPI
American Tax Reduction Movement (EA) ... ATRM
American Tax Reform Project (EA) ... ATRP
American Tax Token Society (EA) ... ATTS
American Taxation Association (EA) ... ATA
American Taxicab Association [*Later, ITA*] (EA) ... ATA
American Taxicab Association (SAUO) ... ATA
American Taxpayers Association (SAUO) ... ATA
American Taxpayers Association (EA) ... ATA
American Taxpayers' Quarterly [*A publication*] (DLA) ... Am Tax Q
American Teachers Association [*Later, NEA*] (EA) ... ATA
American Teachers Association (SAUO) ... ATA

American Teachers' Series [*A publication*] ..... ATS
American Technical Ceramics [*AMEX symbol*] (SPSG) ..... AMK
American Technical Ceramics (SAUO) ..... ATC
American Technical Ceramics [*Associated Press*] (SAG) ..... ATechC
American Technical Education Association (EA) ..... ATEA
American Technical Publishers, Ltd. (SAUO) ..... ATP
American Technical Society (SAUO) ..... Am Technical
American Technical Society (SAUO) ..... Am Tech Soc
American Technical Society ..... ATS
American Technological University (MCD) ..... ATU
American Technology & Information, Inc. [*Vancouver Stock Exchange symbol*] ..... ATI
American Technology Institute (SAUO) ..... ATI
American Teilhard Association (EA) ..... ATA
American Teilhard Association for the Future of Man [*Later, ATA*] (EA) ..... ATAFM
American Teilhard de Chardin Association [*Later, ATAFM*] ..... ATCA
American Telco, Inc. [*Telecommunications service*] (TSSD) ..... ATI
American Telecasting, Inc. [*Associated Press*] (SAG) ..... AmTele
American Telecasting, Inc. [*NASDAQ symbol*] (SAG) ..... ATEL
American Telecommunications Corp. [*Vancouver Stock Exchange symbol*] ..... AMT
American Telecommunications Group (SAUO) ..... ATG
American Telegraph and Telephone Company (SAUS) ..... AT&T
American Telemarketing Association [*Deerfield, IL*] (EA) ..... ATA
American Telemedicine Association (SAUO) ..... ATA
American Telemedicine Association (SAUS) ..... ATA
American Telephone and Telegraph (SAUS) ..... Am Tel&Tel
American Telephone and Telegraph (SAUS) ..... AT&T
American Telephone and Telegraph (SAUO) ..... AT+T
American Telephone and Telegraph Co. (SAUO) ..... Am Tel & Tel
American Telephone & Telegraph Co. [*New York, NY*] ..... ATT
American Telephone & Telegraph Co. [*Wall Street slang name: "Telephone"*] [*NYSE symbol*] (SPSG) ..... T
American Telephone & Telegraph Co. Commission. Leaflets [*A publication*] (DLA) ..... AT & T Co Com L
American Telephone & Telegraph Co. Commission Telephone Cases [*A publication*] (DLA) ..... AT & T Co TC
American Telephone & Telegraph Co., Corporate Research Library, New York, NY [*Library symbol*] [*Library of Congress*] (LCLS) ..... NNAT
American Telephone & Telegraph Co. Information Systems (TEL) ..... ATTIS
American Telephone & Telegraph Co. Interexchange Carrier (TEL) ..... ATTIX
American Telephone & Telegraph Co. International (TEL) ..... ATTI
American Telephone & Telegraph Co., Long Lines, Bedminister, NJ [*OCLC symbol*] (OCLC) ..... ATT
American Telephone & Telegraph Co., Morristown Corporate Marketing Library, Morristown, NJ [*Library symbol*] [*Library of Congress*] (LCLS) ..... NjMoAT
American Telephone & Telegraph Co. Resource Center, Piscataway, NJ [*Library symbol*] [*Library of Congress*] (LCLS) ..... NjPwAT
American Telephone & Telegraph Co., Technical Process, Piscataway, NJ [*OCLC symbol*] (OCLC) ..... ATP
American Telephone & Telegraph Co. Technologies (TEL) ..... ATTT
American Telephone and Telegraph Communications (SAUS) ..... ATTCOM
American Telephone and Telegraph Company (SAUO) ..... ATTC
American Telephone and Telegraph Global Information Solutions (SAUS) ..... ATTGIS
American Telephone and Telegraph Information Systems (SAUS) ..... ATTIS
American Telephone Fundraisers Association (NFD) ..... ATFA
American Telephone Manufacturing Co. (WDAA) ..... ATMT
American Television & Communication Corp. (SAUO) ..... ATC
American Television & Communications Corp. [*Cable TV operator*] ..... ATC
American Television and Radio Artists (SAUO) ..... ATRA
American Television Incorporated (SAUO) ..... ATI
American Television Institute (SAUO) ..... ATI
American Television Society (NTCM) ..... ATS
American Temperance Society [*Later, AHTS*] (EA) ..... ATS
American Tennis Association (EA) ..... ATA
American Tennis Federation (EA) ..... ATF
American Tennis Industry Federation (EA) ..... ATIF
American Tentative Society ..... ATS
American Terms [*Business term*] ..... AT
American Testing & Engineering Corp. (EFIS) ..... ATEC
American Textbook Council (EA) ..... ATC
American Textbook Publishers Institute [*Later, AAP*] (EA) ..... ATPI
American Textile Industry (ABAC) ..... AMTEX
American Textile Machinery Association (EA) ..... ATMA
American Textile Machinery Exhibition - Yarn, Fiber, and Non-Woven ManufacturingProcesses (ITD) ..... ATME
American Textile Machinery Exhibition-International (SAUO) ..... ATME-I
American Textile Manufacturers Association (SAUO) ..... ATMA
American Textile Manufacturers Institute (EA) ..... ATMI
American Textile Manufacturing Institute (SAUO) ..... ATMI
American Textile Partnership ..... AMTEX
American Theater Campaign Medal (SAUS) ..... ATCM
American Theater (or Theatre) Critics Association (SAUO) ..... ATCA
American Theater Productions, Inc. ..... ATP
American Theater Wing (SAUO) ..... ATW
American Theatre [*A publication*] (BRI) ..... Am Theat
American Theatre Annual [*A publication*] ..... ATA
American Theatre Arts for Youth (EA) ..... TAFY
American Theatre Association (SAUO) ..... Am Theatre Assoc
American Theatre Association (SAUO) ..... ATA
American Theatre Association [*Defunct*] (EA) ..... ATA
American Theatre Organ Enthusiasts [*Later, ATOS*] ..... ATOE
American Theatre Organ Society (EA) ..... ATOS
American Theatre Society [*Commercial firm*] (EA) ..... ATS
American Theatre Wing (EA) ..... ATW
American Themis [*A publication*] (DLA) ..... Am Them
American Themis [*A publication*] (DLA) ..... Them
American Theological Library Association (EA) ..... ATLA
American Theological Library Association. Indexes ..... ATLAI
American Theological Library Association, Princeton, NJ [*OCLC symbol*] (OCLC) ..... ATL
American Theological Library Association, Yale University Divinity School, New Haven, CT [*Library symbol*] [*Library of Congress*] (LCLS) ..... ATLA
American Theological Society (SAUO) ..... ATS
American Theological Society - Midwest Division (EA) ..... ATS
American Therapeutic Association (EA) ..... ATA
American Therapeutic Recreation Association (EA) ..... ATRA
American Therapeutic Society [*Later, American Society for Clinical Pharmacologyand Therapeutics*] (EA) ..... ATS
American Thermographic Society [*Later, American Academy of Thermology*] (EA) ..... ATS
American Thesaurus of Slang ..... ATS
American Thoracic Society (EA) ..... ATS
American Three-Quarter Midget Racing Association [*Auto racing*] ..... ATQMRA
American Thyroid Association (EA) ..... ATA
American Thyroid Association (SAUO) ..... ATA
American Time Travel Society [*Defunct*] (EA) ..... ATTS
American Tin Trade Association (EA) ..... ATTA
American Tinnitus Association (EA) ..... ATA
American Tinnitus Association (SAUO) ..... ATA
American Title Association (SAUO) ..... ATA
American Title Association [*Later, ALTA*] ..... ATA
American Tobacco (SAUS) ..... AT
American Tobacco Co., Department of Research and Development, Hopewell, VA [*Library symbol*] [*Library of Congress*] (LCLS) ..... ViHopAT
American Tobacco Company (SAUO) ..... AT
American Tobacco Company (SAUO) ..... ATCo
American Tolkien Society (EA) ..... ATS
American Tool Companies, Inc. (EFIS) ..... ATC
American Topical Association (EA) ..... ATA
American Topical Association (SAUO) ..... ATA
American Torah Shelemah Committee (EA) ..... ATSC
American Tort Reform Association (EA) ..... ATRA
American Tour Managers Association [*Defunct*] (EA) ..... ATMA
American Tourist Association (SAUO) ..... ATA
American Towing Tank Conference (SAUO) ..... ATTC
American Toy Export Association (EA) ..... ATEA
American Toy Goat Association (EA) ..... ATGA
American Toy Institute (SAUS) ..... ATI
American Toy Retailers Association (EA) ..... ATRA
American Toys, Inc. [*Associated Press*] (SAG) ..... AmToys
American Toys, Inc. [*NASDAQ symbol*] (SAG) ..... ATOY
American Toys, Inc. [*Associated Press*] (SAG) ..... AToys
American Toys Non-Red Wrrt [*NASDAQ symbol*] (TTSB) ..... ATOYZ
American Toys Wrrt [*NASDAQ symbol*] (TTSB) ..... ATOYW
American Track [*National Railroad Passenger Corp.; formerly, Railpax*] ..... AMTRAK
American Track (NTIO) ..... Amtrak
American Tract Society (EA) ..... ATS
American Trade and Industrial Development ..... ATID
American Trade Association Executives [*Later, ASAE*] ..... ATAE
American Trade Association for British Woolens (EA) ..... ATABW
American Trade Association of British Woollens (SAUO) ..... ATABW
American Trade Consortium ..... ATC
American Trade Organization [*Commonwealth of Independent States*] ..... AMTORG
American Trade Union Council for Histadrut (EA) ..... ATUCH
American Trade Union Council for Histadruth (SAUO) ..... ATUCH
American Trade-Mark Cases (Cox) [*A publication*] (DLA) ..... Am T-M Cas
American Trade-Mark Cases (Cox) [*A publication*] (DLA) ..... Am Trade Mark Cas
American Traders Group (EA) ..... ATG
American Traffic Association ..... ATA
American Traffic Association (SAUO) ..... ATA
American Traffic Safety Council (SAUO) ..... ATSC
American Traffic Safety Services Association (EA) ..... ATSSA
American Traffic Services Association [*Later, ATSSA*] (EA) ..... ATSA
American Trails Foundation [*Defunct*] (EA) ..... ATF
American Train Dispatchers Association (EA) ..... ATDA
American Train Dispatchers Association ..... TDA
American Trainers Association (SAUO) ..... ATA
American Trainers Association (EA) ..... ATA
American Trakehner Association (EA) ..... ATA
American Tramp Shipowners Association (EA) ..... ATSA
American Trans Air (EFIS) ..... AMTRAN
American Trans Air (SAUS) ..... ATA
American Trans Air [*ICAO designator*] (AD) ..... TZ
American Trans Air, Inc. [*ICAO designator*] (FAAC) ..... AMT
American Trans Air, Inc. (SAUS) ..... TZ
American Transfer Printing Institute [*Later, ITPI*] (EA) ..... ATPI
American Transit Association [*Later, APTA*] (EA) ..... ATA
American Transit Association (SAUO) ..... ATA
American Transit Collectors' Association (EA) ..... ATCA
American Transit Engineering Association (SAUO) ..... ATEA
American Translation [*of the Bible*] ..... AT
American Translators Association (EA) ..... ATA
American Translators Association (SAUO) ..... ATA
American Transplant Association (EA) ..... ATA
American Transport Association (SAUO) ..... ATA
American Transport Association (SAUS) ..... ATA

American Transportation Advisory Council ... ATAC
American Transportation Bowling Association (EA) ... ATBA
American Transportation Corporation (SAUO) ... AMTRAN
American Trauma Society (SAUO) ... Amer Trauma Soc
American Trauma Society (EA) ... ATS
American Travel Association [*Later, ATI*] ... ATA
American Travel Association (SAUO) ... ATA
American Travel Inns (EA) ... ATI
American Travel Service (SAUO) ... ATS
American Travel Survey [*BTS*] (TAG) ... ATS
American Travellers Corp. [*Associated Press*] (SAG) ... ATravel
American Travellers Corp. [*NASDAQ symbol*] (NQ) ... ATVC
American Tree Association ... ATA
American Tree Association (SAUO) ... ATA
American Trial Lawyers Association (SAUO) ... ATLA
American Trial Lawyers Association. Journal [*A publication*] (DLA) ... ATLJ
American Trousers Institute (SAUS) ... ATI
American Trousers Institute Amtel Inc. (SAUO) ... ATI
American Truck Dealers (EA) ... ATD
American Truck Historical Society (EA) ... ATHS
American Truck Leasing Network, Inc. ... AMTRALEASE
American Truck Owners Association [*New York, NY*] (EA) ... ATOA
American Truck Stop Foundation (EA) ... ATSF
American Truck Stop Operators Association (EA) ... ATSOA
American Truckers Benevolent Association [*Defunct*] (EA) ... ATBA
American Trucking Association (SAUO) ... ATA
American Trucking Associations (EA) ... ATA
American Trudeau Society [*Later, American Thoracic Society*] ... ATS
American Tube Association/FMA (EA) ... ATA
American Tunaboat Association (EA) ... ATA
American Tunaboat Association (SAUO) ... ATA
American Tung Oil Association [*Defunct*] ... ATOA
American Turbine Corporation (SAUO) ... ATC
American Turkey Hunters Association [*Defunct*] (EA) ... ATHA
American Turners (EA) ... AT
American Turners [*An association*] ... TUR
American Turpentine Farmers Association Cooperative (EA) ... ATFAC
American Type Culture Collection (EA) ... ATCC
American Type Founders (DGA) ... ATF
American Type Founders, Inc. (SAUO) ... ATF
American Typecasting Fellowship (EA) ... ATF
American Underground-Construction Association (NTPA) ... AUA
American Underground-Space Association (EA) ... AUA
American Underground-Space Association (EA) ... AUSA
American Union of Men (EA) ... AUM
American Union of Students (EA) ... AUS
American Union of Swedish Singers (EA) ... AUSS
American Union Transport [*Steamship*] (MHDW) ... AUT
American Unit (SAUO) ... AU
American Unitarian Association ... AUA
American Unitarian Christian Association (EA) ... AUCA
American United Global, Inc. [*NASDAQ symbol*] (SAG) ... AUGI
American United Global, Inc. [*Associated Press*] (SAG) ... AUtdG
American United Global, Inc. [*Associated Press*] (SAG) ... AUtdGlb
American United Global Wrrt [*NASDAQ symbol*] (TTSB) ... AUGIW
American United Life (SAUO) ... AUL
American United Presbyterian Missions (SAUO) ... AUPM
American United Telecom (NITA) ... AUT
American United Telecommunications (SAUS) ... AUT
American Univac Users Association (SAUO) ... AUUA
American Universities Field Staff [*Later, UFSI-IWA*] (EA) ... AUFS
American Universities Field Staff - Institute of World Affairs [*Later, UFSI-IWA*] (EA) ... AUFS-IWA
American Universities Field Staff. Reports. Asia (journ.) (SAUS) ... Am Univ Field Staff Rep Asia
American Universities Field Staff. Reports. North America (journ.) (SAUS) ... Am Univ Field Staff Rep North Am
American Universities Field Staff. Reports Series [*A publication*] ... AUFS
American Universities Field Staff. Reports. South America (journ.) (SAUS) ... Am Univ Field Staff Rep South Am
American Universities Research Program (SAUO) ... AURP
[*The*] **American University** (GAGS) ... Amer U
American University [*Washington, DC*] ... AU
American University Cairo (SAUO) ... AUC
American University Club (SAUO) ... AUC
American University Hospital [*Lebanon*] ... AUH
American University in Paris, Paris, France [*Library symbol*] [*Library of Congress*] (LCLS) ... FrPAUP
American University Institute for Risk Analysis [*American University*] [*Research center*] (RCD) ... AURA
American University Intramural Law Review [*A publication*] (DLA) ... Am U Int L Rev
American University Intramural Law Review [*A publication*] (DLA) ... Am U Intra L Rev
American University Language Center (SAUO) ... AULC
American University Law Review [*A publication*] (DLA) ... Am U L
American University Law Review (SAUO) ... Am Univ Law Rev
American University Law Review (journ.) (SAUS) ... Am U L
American University Law Review (journ.) (SAUS) ... Am Univ L Rev
American University of Beirut [*Lebanon*] ... AUB
American University of Beirut (SAUO) ... AU of B
American University of Beirut, Beirut, Lebanon [*Library symbol*] [*Library of Congress*] (LCLS) ... LeBAU
American University of Beirut. Faculty of Agricultural Sciences. Publication (journ.) (SAUS) ... Am Univ Beirut Fac Agric Sci Publ
American University of Beirut Network (SAUO) ... AUBnet
American University of Cairo ... AUC
American University of Cairo (SAUO) ... AU of C
American University of Paris ... AUP
American University of the Caribbean ... AUC
American University Press Services, Inc. [*Information service or system*] (IID) ... AUPS
American University Publishers Group (SAUS) ... AUPG
American University Publishers Group Ltd. ... AUPG
American University Union (SAUO) ... AUU
American University, Washington College of Law, Washington, DC [*Library symbol*] [*Library of Congress*] (LCLS) ... DAU-L
American University, Washington, DC [*Library symbol*] [*Library of Congress*] (LCLS) ... DAU
American University, Washington, DC [*OCLC symbol*] (OCLC) ... EAU
American Urban and Regional Information Systems Association (EERA) ... URISA
American Urogynecologic Society (NTPA) ... AUGS
American Urogynecologic Society (EA) ... AUS
American Urologic Association Allied (SAUO) ... AUAA
American Urological Association (EA) ... AUA
American Urological Association Allied (EA) ... AUAA
American Used Computer Corporation (SAUO) ... AUCC
American Used Computer Corporation (SAUO) ... AUC Corporation
American Vaccine Corp. (SAUO) ... AMVX
American Vacuum Society (EA) ... AVS
American Values Center (EA) ... AVC
American Vanguard [*AMEX symbol*] ... AVD
American Vanguard Corp. [*NASDAQ symbol*] (NQ) ... AMGD
American Vanguard Corp. [*Associated Press*] (SAG) ... AVang
American Vaulting Association (EA) ... AVA
American Vecturist Association (EA) ... AVA
American Vegan Society (EA) ... AVS
American Vegetable Grower and Greenhouse Grower (journ.) (SAUS) ... Am Veg Grow Greenhouse Grow
American Vegetarian (EA) ... AV
American Vegetarian Party (SAUO) ... AVP
American Vegetarian Union [*Defunct*] (EA) ... AVU
American Veneer Package Association (EA) ... AVPA
American Venereal Disease Association (EA) ... AVDA
American Venereal Disease Association (SAUS) ... AVDA-1A
American Ventilation Association [*Defunct*] (EA) ... AVA
American Ventures [*Vancouver Stock Exchange symbol*] ... AVR
American Veteran (SAUS) ... AMVET
American Veterans (ADWA) ... AMVETS
American Veterans Alliance (EA) ... AVA
American Veterans Association - National Headquarters ... AVA
American Veterans of Israel (EA) ... AVI
American Veterans of World War II, Korea, and Vietnam (GPO) ... AMVETS
American Veterinary Chiropractic Association (GVA) ... AVCA
American Veterinary Dental College (GVA) ... AVDC
American Veterinary Dental Society (EA) ... AVDS
American Veterinary Distributors Association (EA) ... AVDA
American Veterinary Exhibitors' Association (EA) ... AVEA
American Veterinary Exhibitors Association (SAUO) ... AVEA
American Veterinary Holistic Medical Association [*Later, AHVMA*] (EA) ... AVHMA
American Veterinary Identification Device (SAUS) ... AVID
American Veterinary Lyme Disease Society ... AVLDS
American Veterinary Medical Association (EA) ... AVMA
American Veterinary Medical Association, Chicago, IL [*Library symbol*] [*Library of Congress*] (LCLS) ... ICAV
American Veterinary Medical Association. Journal (journ.) (SAUS) ... Am Vet Med Assn J
American Veterinary Medical Association. Proceedings (journ.) (SAUS) ... Am Vet Med Assn Proc
American Veterinary Medical Association. Scientific Proceedings of the Annual Meeting (journ.) (SAUS) ... Am Vet Med Assoc Sci Proc Annu Meet
American Veterinary Medical Foundation (GVA) ... AVMF
American Veterinary Neurology Association [*Defunct*] (EA) ... AVNA
American Veterinary Radiology Society [*Defunct*] (EA) ... AVRS
American Veterinary Review (journ.) (SAUS) ... Am Vet Rev
American Veterinary Society for Computer Medicine (EA) ... AVSCM
American Veterinary Society of Animal Behavior (EA) ... AVSAB
American Victims of Abortion (EA) ... AVA
American Video Association (EA) ... AVA
American Video Channels, Inc. [*New York, NY*] [*Telecommunications*] (TSSD) ... AVC
American Video Channels Inc. (SAUO) ... AVC
American Video Institute [*Rochester Institute of Technology*] [*Research center*] (RCD) ... AVI
American Video Teleconferencing Corp. [*Farmingdale, NY*] [*Telecommunications*] (TSSD) ... AVTC
American Videotext Services, Inc. [*Peekskill, NY*] [*Telecommunications*] (TSSD) ... AVS
American Videotext Services Inc. (SAUO) ... AVS
American Viennola [*Record label*] ... AmVien
American Viewcard Club (EA) ... AVC
American Viewpoint [*Later, ERC*] ... AV
American Vinegar Industry (journ.) (SAUS) ... Am Vinegar Ind
American Vineyard Foundation (EA) ... AVF
American Vintners Association (NTPA) ... AAV
American Viola Society (EA) ... AVS
American Virgin Islands (SAUS) ... AVI

American Viscose Co., Front Royal, VA [*Library symbol*] [*Library of Congress*] (LCLS) ... ViFroA
American Viscose Co., Roanoke, VA [*Library symbol*] [*Library of Congress*] (LCLS) ... ViRoA
American Viscose Company (ACAE) ... AVCO
American Viscose Corporation (SAUO) ... AVC
American Viscose Corporation (SAUO) ... AVISCO
American Vision Centers, Inc. (SAUO) ... AMVC
American Visionary Art Museum ... AVAM
American Visions [*A publication*] (BRI) ... Am Vis
American Viticultural Area Association (EA) ... AVAA
American Vocational Association (EA) ... AVA
American Vocational Education Personnel Development Association (EA) ... AVEPDA
American Vocational Education Research Association (EA) ... AVERA
American Vocational Information Association ... AVIA
American Vocational Journal (journ.) (SAUS) ... Am Voc J
American Voice Input/Output Society (EA) ... AVIOS
American Volksmarching Association (SAUO) ... AVA
American Volkssport Association (EA) ... AVA
American Volleyball Coaches Association (EA) ... AVCA
American Volunteer Group [*Flying Tigers*] [*World War II*] ... AVG
American Volunteer Group (SAUO) ... AVG
American Voter Coalition (SAUS) ... AVC
American Vox [*Record label*] ... AmVox
American Voyager Association (EA) ... AVA
American Wagering, Inc. [*Associated Press*] (SAG) ... AmWagr
American Wagering, Inc. [*NASDAQ symbol*] (SAG) ... BETM
American Waldensian Aid Society [*Later, AWS*] (EA) ... AWAS
American Waldensian Society (EA) ... AWS
American Waldension Aid Society (SAUO) ... AWAS
American Walking Horse Association (EA) ... AWHA
American Walking Pony Association (EA) ... AWPA
American Walnut Manufacturers Association [*Later, FHAWA*] (EA) ... AWMA
American War Dads (EA) ... AWD
American War Dads Auxiliary (SAUO) ... AWDA
American War Mothers (EA) ... AWM
American War Standards [*DoD*] ... AWS
American War Standards Committee (SAUO) ... AWSC
American Warehouse Association (NTPA) ... AWA
American Warehousemen's Association (EA) ... AWA
American Warmblood and Sport Horse Guild (EA) ... AW & SHG
American Warmblood Registry (EA) ... AWR
American Warmblood Society (EA) ... AWS
American Wash and Wear Institute ... AWWI
American Waste Services [*NYSE symbol*] (SPSG) ... AW
American Waste Services [*Associated Press*] (SAG) ... AWste
American Watch Association (EA) ... AWA
American Watch Workers Union ... AWWU
American Watchmakers Institute (EA) ... AWI
American Watchmakers-Clockmakers Institute ... AWI
American Water Color Society (SAUO) ... AWCS
American Water Color Society, New York [*1878, founded 1866 as American Society of Painters in Water Colors*] (NGC) ... AWCS
American Water Resources Association (EA) ... AWRA
American Water Resources Association. Proceedings Series (journ.) (SAUS) ... Am Water Resour Assoc Proc Ser
American Water Resources Association. Symposium. Proceedings (journ.) (SAUS) ... Am Water Resour Assoc Symp Proc
American Water Resources Association. Technical Publication Series. TPS85-1 (journ.) (SAUS) ... Am Water Resour Assoc Tech Publ Ser TPS-85-1
American Water Ski Association (EA) ... AWSA
American Water Ski Educational Foundation (EA) ... AWSEF
American Water Works [*Associated Press*] (SAG) ... AmWtr
American Water Works [*Associated Press*] (SAG) ... AWat
American Water Works Association (EA) ... AWWA
American Water Works Association (SAUO) ... JAWWAS
American Water Works Association. Annual Conference. Proceedings (journ.) (SAUS) ... Am Water Works Assoc Annu Conf Proc
American Water Works Association, Denver, CO [*Library symbol*] [*Library of Congress*] (LCLS) ... CoDAW
American Water Works Association. Disinfection Seminar. Proceedings (journ.) (SAUS) ... Am Water Works Assoc Disinfed Semin Proc
American Water Works Association. Jounal. Southeastern Section (journ.) (SAUS) ... Am Water Works Assoc Jour Southeastern Sec
American Water Works Association. Journal (journ.) (SAUS) ... Am Water Works Assn J
American Water Works Association. Journal (journ.) (SAUS) ... Am Water Works Assoc J
American Water Works Association. Ontario Section. Proceedings Annual Conference (journ.) (SAUS) ... Am Water Works Assoc Ont Sect Proc Annu Conf
American Water Works Association Research Foundation (EPA) ... AWWARF
American Water Works Association. Technology Conference Proceedings (journ.) (SAUS) ... Am Water Works Asoc Technol Conf Proc
American Water Works Co. (SAUO) ... AWK
American Water Works Co., Inc. [*NYSE symbol*] (SPSG) ... AWK
American Water Works Utility Council (COE) ... AWWUC
American Watercolor Society (EA) ... AWS
American Waterfowl Association ... AWA
American Watershed Council (EA) ... AWC
American Waterways Operators (EA) ... AWO
American Waterways Operators Incorporated (SAUO) ... AWOI
American Waterways Shipyard Conference (EA) ... AWSC
American Waterworks Association (SAUO) ... AWWA
American Wax Importers and Refiners Association (EA) ... AMERWAX
American Wax Importers and Refiners Association ... AWIRA
American Weather Service (SAUO) ... AWS
American Weight Lifting Association (EA) ... AWLA
American Welara Pony Society (EA) ... AWPS
American Welders Association (EA) ... AWA
American Welding (SAUO) ... AW
American Welding & Mfg. Co. (EFIS) ... AMWELD
American Welding Institute (EA) ... AWI
American Welding Society (EA) ... AWS
American Welding Society, Inc. ... AWS
American Welding Society. Journal (journ.) (SAUS) ... Am Weld Soc J
American Welding Society. Publication AWS A.58-76 (journ.) (SAUS) ... Am Weld Soc Publ AWS A58-76
American Welding Society. Publication (journ.) (SAUS) ... Am Weld Soc Publ
American West African Freight Conference (EA) ... AWAFC
American West Capital [*Vancouver Stock Exchange symbol*] ... ANW
American West Conference (PSS) ... AWC
American West Overseas Association (EA) ... AWOA
American Western Corp. (EFIS) ... AWC
American Westwater Technology Group Ltd. [*Vancouver Stock Exchange symbol*] ... AWW
American Wheat Striate Mosaic Virus [*Plant pathology*] ... AWSMV
American Wheelchair Bowling Association (EA) ... AWBA
American Whig Review (journ.) (SAUS) ... Am Whig R
American Whippet Club (EA) ... AWC
American White Cross [*Associated Press*] (SAG) ... AmWhite
American White Cross [*Associated Press*] (SAG) ... AmWhte
American White Cross [*NASDAQ symbol*] (SAG) ... AWCI
American Whitewater Affiliation (EA) ... AWA
American Whitewater Affiliation (SAUO) ... AWWA
American Wholesale Booksellers Association (EA) ... AWBA
American Wholesale Horticultural Dealers Association [*Later, HDA*] (EA) ... AWHDA
American Wholesale Marketers Association (NTPA) ... AWMA
American Wholesalers and Distributors Directory [*Pronounced "awed"*] [*A publication*] ... AWDD
American Wilderness Alliance [*Later, AW*] (EA) ... AWA
American Wildlands (EA) ... AW
American Wildlands Alliance (GNE) ... AWL
American Wildlife Foundation (SAUO) ... AWF
American Wind Energy Association (EA) ... AWEA
American Wind Energy Systems (SAUS) ... AWES
American Window Covering Manufacturers Association (EA) ... AWCMA
American Wine Association (EA) ... AWA
American Wine Society (EA) ... AWS
American Wire Association (SAUO) ... AWA
American Wire Cloth Institute (EA) ... AWCI
American Wire Gage (SAUS) ... AWG
American Wire Gauge [*Standard*] ... AWG
American Wire Producers Association ... AWP
American Wire Producers Association (EA) ... AWPA
American Wire Weavers Protective Association ... AWWPA
American Wit and Gags [*Book title*] ... AWAG
American Withe-Water Affiliation (SAUS) ... AWWA
American Woman above Ground [*Lifestyle classification*] ... AWAG
American Woman's Association [*Defunct*] (EA) ... AWA
American Woman's Economic Development Corp. (EA) ... AWED
American Woman's Society of Certified Public Accountants [*Chicago, IL*] (EA) ... AWSCPA
American Women Buyers Club (EA) ... AWBC
American Women Composers (EA) ... AWC
American Women in Radio and Television (EA) ... AWRT
American Women in Radio and Television (SAUS) ... AWRTV
American Women Playwrights Association (EA) ... AWPA
American Women's Association for Renewable Energy (EA) ... AWARE
American Women's Association of Rome [*Italy*] ... AWAR
American Women's Association of Saigon (VNW) ... AWAS
American Women's Clergy Association (EA) ... AWCA
American Women's Himalayan Expeditions ... AWHE
American Women's Hospital Reserve Corps [*British*] (DAS) ... AWHRC
American Women's Hospitals [*Later, AWHS*] ... AWH
American Women's Hospitals Service [*Formerly, AWH*] [*Later, AWHS/AMWA*] (EA) ... AWHS
American Women's Hospitals Service Committee of AMWA [*American Medical Women's Association*] (EA) ... AWHS/AMWA
American Women's Voluntary Services [*World War II*] (EA) ... AWVS
American Wood Chip Export Association (EA) ... AWCEA
American Wood Council (EA) ... AWC
American Wood Fabric Institute ... AWFI
American Wood Inspection Agency ... AWIA
American Wood Preservation Association (SAUO) ... AWPA
American Wood Preservers Association (SAUS) ... AWPA
American Wood Preservers Bureau [*Defunct*] (EA) ... AWPB
American Wood Preservers Institute (EA) ... AWPI
American Wood Window Institute (DAC) ... AWWI
American Wooden Money Guild (EA) ... AWMG
American Woodmark Corp. [*NASDAQ symbol*] (NQ) ... AMWD
American Woodmark Corp. [*Associated Press*] (SAG) ... AWood
American Wool Council (EA) ... AWC
American Word Processing Association (EA) ... AWPA
American Working Terrier Association (EA) ... AWTA
American World's Boxing Association (BARN) ... AWBA
American Wrestling Association (DAVI) ... AWA
American Wrestling Coaches and Officials Association [*Later, NWCA*] (EA) ... AWCOA

American Writers Theatre Foundation (EA) .... AWTF
American Yacht Club (SAUO) .... AYC
American Yachtsmen's Association [*Later, BOAT/US*] (EA) .... AYA
American Yankee Association (EA) .... AYA
American Yarn Spinners Association (EA) .... AYSA
American Y-Flyer Yacht Racing Association (EA) .... AYFYRA
American Yiddish (SAUS) .... Ameridish
American Yoga Association (EA) .... AYA
American Yorkshire Club (EA) .... AYC
American Yougoslav Claims Committee (SAUO) .... AYCC
American Youth Activities (SAUO) .... AYA
American Youth Center (SAUO) .... AYC
American Youth Congress .... AYC
American Youth for Democracy .... AYD
American Youth Foundation (EA) .... AYF
American Youth Hostels Association (SAUO) .... AYHA
American Youth Soccer Organization (EA) .... AYSO
American Youth Work Center (EA) .... AYWC
American Zellter, Inc. .... AZI
American Zinc Association (EA) .... AZA
American Zinc Institute [*Later, ZI*] (EA) .... AZI
American Zinc Institute, Inc. [*Later, ZI*] (MCD) .... AZII
American Zinc Institute, Inc. (SAUO) .... AZII
American Zionist (BJA) .... AZi
American Zionist Association (SAUO) .... AZA
American Zionist Council [*Later, AZF*] (EA) .... AZC
American Zionist Federation (EA) .... AZF
American Zionist Movement (EA) .... AZM
American Zionist Youth Council (EA) .... AZYC
American Zionist Youth Federation (SAUO) .... AZYF
American Zionist Youth Foundation (EA) .... AZYF
American Zombie Association [*Defunct*] (EA) .... AZA
American Zoo and Aquarium association (SAUO) .... AZA
American Zoologist (SAUS) .... Am Zool
American Zoologist (journ.) (SAUS) .... Amer Zool
Americana Gold & Diamond Holdings [*NASDAQ symbol*] (SAG) .... AGDM
Americana Gold & Diamond Holdings [*Associated Press*] (SAG) .... AmGold
Americana Gold&Diamond Hldgs [*NASDAQ symbol*] (TTSB) .... AGDM
Americana Hotels & Realty Corp. [*NYSE symbol*] (SPSG) .... AHR
Americana Hotels & Realty Corp. [*Associated Press*] (SAG) .... AmHotl
Americana Unit [*American Topical Association*] (EA) .... AU
Americanae Antiquarianae Societatis Socius [*Fellow of the American Antiquarian Society*] [*Latin*] .... AASS
Americanae Orientalis Societatis Socius [*Fellow of the American Oriental Society*] .... AOSS
American-African Affairs Association (EA) .... AAAA
American-Arab Affairs Council (EA) .... AAAC
American-Arab Anti-Discrimination Committee (EA) .... ADC
American-Arab Association for Commerce and Industry [*New York, NY*] (EA) .... AAACI
American-Arab Relations Committee (EA) .... AARC
American-ASEAN [*Association of South East Asian Nations*] **Trade Council** (EA) .... AATC
American-Asian Educational Exchange [*Defunct*] (EA) .... AAEE
American-Asians (SAUS) .... Amerasians
American-Australian Association (SAUO) .... AAA
American-Australian Studies Foundation .... AASF
American-Austrian Society (EA) .... A-AS
American-Born Chinese .... ABC
American-born Chinese (SAUS) .... AbC
American-British Conversation [*as ABC-1, a 1941 report that set forth Allied worldwide strategy*] [*World War II*] .... ABC
American-British Expeditionary Corps (SAUO) .... ABECO
American-British Forces [*World War II*] .... ABFOR
American-British Intelligence [*NATO*] (NATG) .... ABI
American-British Laboratory [*Harvard University*] .... ABL
American-British-Canadian (SAUS) .... ABC
American-British-Canadian Air Standardization Agreement (NG) .... ABCAIRSTD
American-British-Canadian Army Standardization Program .... ABC-ASP
American-British-Canadian Conference on Unification of Engineering Standards (SAUO) .... ABC
American-British-Canadian Navies Standard (SAUS) .... ABC-NAVY-STD
American-British-Canadian Standardization Program .... ABCSP
American-British-Canadian Stores Catalogue (DEN) .... ABCSC
American-British-Canadian-Army Standardization Program (SAUS) .... ABC-ASP
American-British-Canadian-Australian (SAUS) .... ABCA
American-British-Dutch-Australian (SAUS) .... ABDA
American-British-Dutch-Australian Air Operational Command [*1942*] .... ABDAIR
American-British-Dutch-Australian Army Operational Command [*1942*] .... ABDARM
American-British-Dutch-Australian Command (SAUS) .... ABDACOM
American-British-Dutch-Australian Naval Operational Command [*1942*] .... ABDAFLOAT
American-British-Dutch-Australian Supreme Command [*1942*] .... ABDACOM
American-Bulgarian League (SAUO) .... ABL
American-Byelorussian Cultural Relief Association (EA) .... ABCRA
American-Canada Trust Fund (SAUO) .... AMCA
American-Canadian Genealogical Society (EA) .... ACGS
American-Canadian Tour [*Auto racing*] .... ACT
American-Chilean Council (SAUO) .... ACC
American-European Express [*Railway*] .... AEE
American-European Line (SAUO) .... AEL
American-European Soda Ash Shipping Association (NTPA) .... AESSA
American-French Genealogical Society (EA) .... AFGS
American-German Review (journ.) (SAUS) .... AGR
American-Hawaiian Steamship Company (SAUO) .... AH
American-Hawaiian Line (SAUS) .... A-H
American-Hellenic Chamber of Commerce (EA) .... AHCC
American-Hellenic Educational Progressive Association (SAUO) .... AHEPA
American-Hungarian Federation (SAUO) .... AHF
American-Indonesian Friendship Association (SAUS) .... PPIA
American-International Reiki Association (SAUO) .... AIPA
American-International Charolais Association (EA) .... AICA
American-International Reiki Association (EA) .... AIRA
Americanism Education League (SAUO) .... AEL
Americanism Educational League [*Buena Park, CA*] (EA) .... AEL
Americanism Foundation [*Norwalk, OH*] (EA) .... AF
American-Israel Anti-Smoking Society (EA) .... AIASS
American-Israel Public Affairs Committee (SAUO) .... AIPAC
American-Israeli Political Action Committee .... AIPAC
American-Israeli Vocal Arts Foundation (SAUO) .... AIVAF
American-Isreal Chamber of Commerce and Industry (NTPA) .... AICCI
American-Italian Women of Achievement .... AMITA
American-Italy Society, Inc. .... AISI
Americanization (SAUS) .... A
Americanize (SAUS) .... A
Americanized Welsh Coal Charter (SAUS) .... Amwelsh Coal Charter
American-Korean Foundation [*Later, IHAP*] (EA) .... AKF
American-Mideast Business Association (EA) .... AMBA
American-Nepal Education Foundation (EA) .... ANEF
American-Netherlands Club of Rotterdam .... ANCOR
American-Oriental Lines (SAUO) .... AOL
American-Paraguayan Cultural Center [*Paraguay*] (EAIO) .... APCC
American-Polish National Relief for Poland (EA) .... APNRP
American-Portuguese Chamber of Commerce (SAUO) .... APCC
American-Portuguese Cultural Society (SAUO) .... APCS
American-Russian Aid Association (SAUO) .... ARAA
American-Russian Chamber of Commerce (SAUO) .... ARCC
American-Russian Institute (SAUO) .... ARI
American-Russian Institute for Cultural Relations (SAUO) .... ARICR
American-Russian Institute for Cultural Relations with the Soviet Union (SAUO) .... ARICRSU
American-Russian Research Society (SAUO) .... ARRS
Americans Against Abortion (EA) .... AAA
Americans Against Union Control of Government (EA) .... AAUCG
Americans by Choice (EA) .... ABC
Americans Combating Terrorism (SAUS) .... A CT
Americans Combatting Terrorism [*Commercial firm*] (EA) .... ACT
Americans Concerned about Corporate Power [*Defunct*] (EA) .... ACACP
Americans Concerned About Corporate Power (SAUO) .... ACACP
Americans Concerned about Southern Africa (EA) .... ACSA
Americans for a Common Sense Budget [*Inactive*] [*Defunct*] (EA) .... ACSB
Americans for a Music Library in Israel [*Defunct*] (EA) .... AMLI
Americans for a Non-Violent Society (EA) .... ANVIOS
Americans for a Safe Israel (EA) .... AFSI
Americans for a Sound AIDS [*Acquired Immune Deficiency Syndrome*] **Policy** (EA) .... ASAP
Americans for Better Care (EA) .... ABC
Americans for Budget Equity [*Defunct*] (EA) .... ABE
Americans for Children's Relief [*Defunct*] (EA) .... ACR
Americans for Common Sense [*Defunct*] (EA) .... ACS
Americans for Community Cooperation in Other Nations (AEBS) .... ACCION
Americans for Constitutional Action (EA) .... ACA
Americans for Constitutional Freedom [*Later, MC/ACF*] (EA) .... ACF
Americans for Constitutional Integrity [*An association*] (EA) .... ACI
Americans for Constitutional Training (SAUS) .... AC-T
Americans for Constitutional Training (EA) .... ACT
Americans for Customary Weight and Measure (EA) .... ACWM
Americans for Customary Weights and Measures (SAUO) .... ACWM
Americans for Death with Dignity [*An association*] (EA) .... ADD
Americans for Decency (EA) .... AFD
Americans for Democracy in Ukraine (EA) .... ADU
Americans for Democratic Action (EA) .... ADA
Americans for Due Process (EA) .... ADP
Americans for Economic Freedom (EA) .... AEF
Americans for Economic Reform (EA) .... AER
Americans for Educational Choice (EA) .... AEC
Americans for Effective Law Enforcement (EA) .... AELE
Americans for Energy Independence (SAUO) .... AEI
Americans for Energy Independence (EA) .... AFEI
Americans for Generational Equity (EA) .... AGE
Americans for God (EA) .... AFG
Americans for God (EA) .... AG
Americans for Historic Preservation (EA) .... AHP
Americans for Hope, Growth, & Opportunity .... AHGO
Americans for Human Rights and Social Justice (EA) .... AHRSJ
Americans for Human Rights in Ukraine (EA) .... AHRU
Americans for Immigration Control (EA) .... AIC
Americans for Indian Future and Traditions (SAUO) .... AIFT
Americans for Indian Opportunity (EA) .... AIO
Americans for International Aid (EA) .... AIA
Americans for Justice (SAUO) .... AJ
Americans for Justice in the Middle East [*Lebanon*] (EAIO) .... AJME
Americans for Justice on the Job [*Defunct*] (EA) .... AJJ
Americans for Life (EA) .... AFL
Americans for Medical Freedom [*Defunct*] (EA) .... AMF
Americans for Medical Progress (GVA) .... AMP
Americans for Medical Progress Educational Foundation (EA) .... AMPEF
Americans for Middle East Understanding (EA) .... AMEU
Americans for More Power Sources [*Defunct*] (EA) .... AMPS

Americans for Nonsmokers' Rights (EA) .... ANR
Americans for Nuclear Energy (EA) .... AFNE
Americans for Nuclear Energy (EA) .... ANE
Americans for Peace [Defunct] (EA) .... AFP
Americans for Peace (SAUO) .... AfP
Americans for Peace and Democracy in the Middle East (EA) .... APDME
Americans for Peace in the Americas (EA) .... APA
Americans for Peace Now [An association] (EA) .... APN
Americans for President Reagan's Foreign Policy [Defunct] (EA) .... APRFP
Americans for Progressive Israel (EA) .... API
Americans for Progressive Israel - Hashomer Hatzair (EA) .... API-HH
Americans for Rational Energy Alternatives (SAUO) .... AREA
Americans for Religious Liberty (EA) .... ARL
Americans for Responsible Government [Defunct] (EA) .... ARG
Americans for Safe and Competitive Trucking (EA) .... ASCT
Americans for Safe Food (GNE) .... ASF
Americans for Substance Abuse Prevention and Treatment (EA) .... ASAPT
Americans for Tax Reform (EA) .... ATR
Americans for Technology Leadership .... ATL
Americans for the Arts [An association] (NTPA) .... AA
Americans for the Competitive Enterprise System (SAUO) .... ACES
Americans for the Competitive Enterprise System [Later, ACEE] (EA) .... ACES
Americans for the Enforcement of Attorney Ethics .... AEAE
Americans for the Enforcement of Judicial Ethics .... AEJE
Americans for the Environment (EA) .... AFE
Americans for the National Interest [Defunct] (EA) .... ANI
Americans for the National Voter Initiative Amendment (EA) .... ANVIA
Americans for the Restitution and Righting of Old Wrongs [An association] .... ARROW
Americans for the Universality of UNESCO (EA) .... AUU
Americans for Undivided Israel USA (EA) .... AUIUSA
Americans in Israel Political Action Committee (EA) .... AMIPAC
Americans in Milan [An association] .... AIM
Americans in New Caledonia [Army's 23rd infantry; acronym used as name of division. Active in World War II, disbanded 1945; reactivated 1967-71] .... AMERICAL
Americans Mutually Interested in Giving Others a Start [Defunct] (EA) .... AMIGOS
Americans of European Ancestry [Psychometrics] .... AEA
Americans of Italian Descent (EA) .... AID
Americans of Japanese Ancestry [Psychometrics] .... AJA
Americans of Lebanese-Syrian Ancestry for America (SAUO) .... ALSAA
Americans United for a Smoke Free Society [Defunct] (EA) .... AUSFS
Americans United for God and Country (EA) .... AUGC
Americans United For Life (SAUO) .... AUFL
Americans United for Life (EA) .... AUL
Americans United for Life Legal Defense Fund (EA) .... AULLDF
Americans United for separation of church and state (SAUS) .... AU
Americans United for Separation of Church and State (EA) .... AUSCS
Americans United Research Foundation (EA) .... AURF
Americans United to Combat Fluoridation [Later, AUDF] (EA) .... AUCF
Americans United to Outlaw Fluoridation (EA) .... AUOF
Americans Want to Know [Defunct] (EA) .... AWK
Americans with Disabilities Act [An association] (EA) .... ADA
American/Saudi Business Roundtable (EA) .... ASBR
American-Scandinavian Foundation (EA) .... ASF
American-Scandinavian Foundation, New York, NY [Library symbol] [Library of Congress] (LCLS) .... NNASF
American-Serbian Cultural Association (EA) .... ASCA
American-South African Investment Co. Ltd. (SAUO) .... ASA
American-South African Line (SAUO) .... ASA
American-South African Study and Educational Trust .... ASSET
American-Southern Africa Chamber of Trade and Industry (EA) .... ASACOT
American-Southern Africa Chamber of Trade and Industry (NTPA) .... ASACTI
American-Southern Africa Council [Defunct] .... ASAC
American-Soviet Homestays (EA) .... ASH
American-Soviet Medical Society (SAUO) .... ASMS
American-Soviet Medical Society, New York, NY [Library symbol] [Library of Congress] [Obsolete] (LCLS) .... NNASovM
American-Soviet Textbook Study Project [An association] [Defunct] (EA) .... ASTSP
American-Swedish History Foundation (SAUO) .... ASHF
American-Swiss Association (EA) .... ASA
American-Swiss Foundation for Scientific Exchange (SAUO) .... ASFSE
American-Turkish Council (EA) .... ATC
American-Turkish Friendship Council .... ATFC
American-Turkish Society (EA) .... ATS
American-West African Line (SAUO) .... AWAL
Americares Foundation (EA) .... AF
Americas: A Quarterly Review of Inter-American Cultural History [A publication] (BRI) .... Ams
Americas: A Quarterly Review of Inter-American Cultural History (journ.) (SAUS) .... TAm
America's Blood Centers [An association] (NTPA) .... ABC
Americas Boychoir Federation (EA) .... ABF
America's Carriers Telecommunication Association .... ACTA
America's Carriers Telecommunication Association (SAUS) .... ACTA
America's Community Bankers [An association] (NTPA) .... ACB
America's Cup Organizing Committee .... ACOC
America's Ekiden Federation [Defunct] (EA) .... AEF
America's Foundation (EA) .... AF
America's Freedom Ride [Defunct] (EA) .... AFR
America's Funniest Home Videos [Television program] .... AFHV
Americas Funniest Home Videos (SAUS) .... AFHV
America's Future [New Rochelle, NY] (EA) .... AF

Americas Group (SAUO) .... AG
Americas Growth Fund, Inc. [NASDAQ symbol] (SAG) .... AGRO
[The] Americas Growth Fund, Inc. [Associated Press] (SAG) .... AmersGF
Americas Income Trust [Associated Press] (SAG) .... AmsInco
Americas Income Trust [NYSE symbol] (SPSG) .... XUS
Americas Inter-hemispheric Geobiosphere Organization (SAUS) .... AMIGO
America's Manifest Destiny [An association] .... AMD
America's Most Wanted [Television program] .... AMW
America's New Foundations [A publication] .... ANF
Americas Review: A Review of Hispanic Literature and Art of the USA [A publication] (BRI) .... Amer R
America's Small Business Political Action Committee [Defunct] (EA) .... ASBPAC
Americas Society (EA) .... AS
America's Society of Separated and Divorced Men (EA) .... ASDM
America's Sound Transportation Review Organization [AAR] [Defunct] .... ASTRO
Americas Textiles Reporter Bulletin (journ.) (SAUS) .... Textil Rep
America's Top 40 [Radio program] AT40
Americas UNIVAC [Universal Automatic Computer] Users Association [Formerly, USE, UUA] (EA) .... AUUA
Americas Ventures Associates (SAUS) .... TAVA
America's Victory Force [An association] (EA) .... AVF
Americas Watch (EA) .... AW
America/West Africa Conference [Shipping] .... AMWAC
Americium [Chemical element] .... Am
Americredit Corp. [NYSE symbol] (SAG) .... ACF
Americredit Corp. [Associated Press] (SAG) .... Amercrd
Americum (SAUS) .... Am
Americus [Georgia] [Seismograph station code, US Geological Survey] (SEIS) .... AMG
Americus, GA [Location identifier] [FAA] (FAAL) .... ACJ
Americus, GA [AM radio station call letters] .... WDEC
Americus, GA [FM radio station call letters] .... WDEC-FM
Americus, GA [AM radio station call letters] .... WISK
Americus, GA [FM radio station call letters] .... WISK-FM
AmeriData Technol [NYSE symbol] (TTSB) .... ADA
Ameridata Technologies, Inc. [Formerly, Sage Technologies] [NYSE symbol] (SAG) .... ADA
Ameridata Technologies, Inc. [Formerly, Sage Technologies] [Associated Press] (SAG) .... Ameridta
Amerifax Cattle Association (EA) .... ACA
Ameriflight, Inc. [ICAO designator] (FAAC) .... AMF
Amerigas Partners LP [Associated Press] (SAG) .... Amerigas
Amerigas Partners LP [Associated Press] (SAG) .... Amrigs
Amerigas Partners LP [NYSE symbol] (SAG) .... APU
Amerigon, Inc. [Associated Press] (SAG) .... Amerign
Amerigon, Inc. [NASDAQ symbol] (SAG) .... ARGN
Amerigon Inc.'A' [NASDAQ symbol] (TTSB) .... ARGNA
Amerihost Properties [NASDAQ symbol] (TTSB) .... HOST
Amerihost Properties, Inc. [Associated Press] (SAG) .... Amrhost
Amerihost Properties, Inc. [NASDAQ symbol] (NQ) .... HOST
Amerijet International [ICAO designator] (FAAC) .... AJT
Amerikanisch [American] [German] .... amerik
Amerikos Lietuviu Tautine Sajunga [National Lithuanian Society of America] (EA) .... ALTS
AmeriLink Corp. [NASDAQ symbol] (SAG) .... ALNK
AmeriLink Corp. [Associated Press] (SAG) .... AmrLink
Amerin Corp. [Associated Press] (SAG) .... Amerin
Amerin Corp. [NASDAQ symbol] (SAG) .... AMRN
Amerind Foundation (EA) .... AF
AmeriQuest Technol [NYSE symbol] (TTSB) .... AQS
Ameriquest Technology, Co. [Formerly, CMS Enhancements] [Associated Press] (SAG) .... AmeriqTc
Ameriquest Technology Co. [Formerly, CMS Enhancements] [NYSE symbol] (SAG) .... AQS
Amerisafe, Inc. [Associated Press] (SAG) .... Amrisfe
Amerisafe, Inc. [NYSE symbol] (SAG) .... ASF
AmeriSource Health Corp. [NYSE symbol] (SAG) .... AAS
AmeriSource Health Corp. [Associated Press] (SAG) .... AmeriSrc
AmeriSource Health Corp. [Associated Press] (SAG) .... AmriHlt
AmeriSource Health Corp. [NASDAQ symbol] (SAG) .... ASHC
AmeriSource Health'A' [NYSE symbol] (TTSB) .... AAS
Ameristar Casinos [NASDAQ symbol] (TTSB) .... ASCA
Ameristar Casinos, Inc. [Associated Press] (SAG) .... AmerCas
Ameristar Casinos, Inc. [NASDAQ symbol] (SAG) .... ASCA
Ameritech Corp. [NYSE symbol] (SPSG) .... AIT
Ameritech Corp. [Associated Press] (SAG) .... Ameritch
Ameritech Mobile Communications, Inc. [Schaumburg, IL] [Telecommunications] (TSSD) .... AMCI
Ameritech Mobile Communications Incorporated (SAUO) .... AMCI
Ameritech Network Management (ACRL) .... ANM
Ameritech Virtual Network (SAUS) .... AVN
Ameritel Management, Inc. [Vancouver Stock Exchange symbol] .... AEL
Ameritex Resources Ltd. [Vancouver Stock Exchange symbol] .... ATX
AmeriTrade Holding'A' [NASDAQ symbol] (SG) .... AMTD
AmeriVest Properties [AMEX symbol] (SG) .... AMV
AmeriVest Properties, Inc. [Associated Press] (SAG) .... AmriVst
AmeriVest Properties, Inc. [Associated Press] (SAG) .... AmrVst
AmeriVest Properties, Inc. [NASDAQ symbol] (SAG) .... AMVP
Ameriwood Indus Intl. [NASDAQ symbol] (TTSB) .... AWII
Ameriwood Industries International [Associated Press] (SAG) .... Ameriwd
Ameriwood Industries International Corp. [NASDAQ symbol] (SAG) .... AWII
Amerman's Reports [111-115 Pennsylvania] [A publication] (DLA) .... Amer
Ameroil Energy Corp. [Vancouver Stock Exchange symbol] .... ALN
Ameron, Inc. [Associated Press] (SAG) .... Ameron
Ameron, Inc. [NYSE symbol] (SPSG) .... AMN

Ameron, Inc. Corrosion Control Division, Brea, CA [*Library symbol*] [*Library of Congress*] (LCLS) .... CBreA
Ameron International [*NYSE symbol*] [*Formerly, Ameron, Inc.*] (SG) .... AMN
Ameron Intl. [*NYSE symbol*] (TTSB) .... AMN
Amersham [*England*] .... AMER
Amertool Services .... AS
AmerTranz Worldwide Holding Corp. [*Associated Press*] (SAG) .... AmTrnz
AmerTranz Worldwide Holding Corp. [*NASDAQ symbol*] (SAG) .... AMTZ
AmerTranz Worldwide Holding Corp. [*Associated Press*] (SAG) .... ATrnz
AmerUs Life Holdings'A' [*NYSE symbol*] (SG) .... AMH
Amery, WI [*Location identifier*] [*FAA*] (FAAL) .... AHH
Amery, WI [*AM radio station call letters*] .... WXCE
Ames Aeronautical Laboratory [*Air Force*] .... AAL
Ames Airborne Tracking Sunphotometer (ARMP) .... AATS
Ames Aircrew/Aircraft Integration Program [*NASA*] (RDA) A3I
Ames' Cases on Bills and Notes [*A publication*] (DLA) .... Ames Cas B & N
Ames' Cases on Partnership [*A publication*] (DLA) .... Ames Cas Par
Ames' Cases on Pleading [*A publication*] (DLA) .... Ames Cas Pl
Ames' Cases on Suretyship [*A publication*] (DLA) .... Ames Cas Sur
Ames' Cases on Trusts [*A publication*] (DLA) .... Ames Cas Trusts
Ames Cubic Precision Ranging System [*NASA*] .... ACPRS
Ames Daily Tribune, Ames, IA [*Library symbol*] [*Library of Congress*] (LCLS) .... IaAT
Ames Department Stores [*NASDAQ symbol*] (TTSB) .... AMES
Ames Department Stores [*Associated Press*] (SAG) .... Ames
Ames Department Stores [*Associated Press*] (SAG) .... Ames DS
Ames Department Stores, Inc. (SAUO) .... ADD
Ames Department Stores, Inc. [*NASDAQ symbol*] (SAG) .... AMES
Ames Dept Stores Wrrt 'C' [*NASDAQ symbol*] (TTSB) .... AMESW
Ames Dimensional Hypersonic Wind Tunnel (SAA) .... AHWT
Ames, IA [*Location identifier*] [*FAA*] (FAAL) .... AMW
Ames, IA [*AM radio station call letters*] .... KASI
Ames, IA [*FM radio station call letters*] .... KCCQ
Ames, IA [*FM radio station call letters*] .... KEZT
Ames, IA [*FM radio station call letters*] (BROA) .... KLTI-FM
Ames, IA [*Television station call letters*] (BROA) .... KPWB-TV
Ames, IA [*FM radio station call letters*] (RBYB) .... KURE-FM
Ames, IA [*FM radio station call letters*] .... KUSR
Ames, IA [*AM radio station call letters*] .... WOI
Ames, IA [*FM radio station call letters*] .... WOI-FM
Ames, IA [*Television station call letters*] .... WOI-TV
AMES Interactive Dynamic Display Editor (MCD) .... AIDDE
Ames Interactive Dynamic Display Editor (SAUS) .... AIDDE
Ames', Knowles', and Bradley's Reports [*8 Rhode Island*] [*A publication*] (DLA) .... Ames K & B
Ames Laboratory (SAUO) .... AL
Ames Laboratory .... AMES
Ames Laboratory (SAUO) .... AS
Ames Laboratory Research Reactor .... ALRR
Ames Life Sciences Directorate (DNAB) .... ALSD
Ames Prototype Hypersonic Free Flight Facility (KSC) .... APHFFF
Ames, Public Library, Ames IA [*Library symbol*] [*Library of Congress*] (LCLS) .... IaA
Ames' Reports [*1 Minnesota*] [*A publication*] (DLA) .... Ames
Ames' Reports [*4-7 Rhode Island*] [*A publication*] (DLA) .... Ames
Ames Research Center [*Moffett Field, CA*] [*NASA*] .... ARC
Ames Satellite Communications Facility (GEOI) .... ASCF
Ames Unitary Plan (SAA) .... AUP
Ames Unitary Wind Tunnel (SAA) .... AUWT
Amesbury Historical Society, Amesbury, MA [*Library symbol*] [*Library of Congress*] (LCLS) .... MAmHi
Amesbury Public Library, Amesbury, MA [*Library symbol*] [*Library of Congress*] (LCLS) .... MAm
Ames-Dryden Flight Research Facility [*NASA*] .... ADFRF
Ametek, Inc. [*NYSE symbol*] (SPSG) .... AME
Ametek, Inc. [*Associated Press*] (SAG) .... Ametek
Amethopterin [*Methotrexate*] [*Antineoplastic drug*] .... A
Amethopterin [*Methotrexate*] [*Also, A, M, MTX*] [*Antineoplastic drug*] (AAMN) .... AM
Amethopterin [*Methotrexate*] [*Antineoplastic drug*] (MAE) .... AMT
a-Methyl-p-Tyrosine (SAUS) .... AMT
Amethyst Color Enhancement .... ACE
Ametropia [*Ophthalmology*] .... AM
AMEV Securities, Inc. (SAUO) .... AMV
AMEX [*American Stock Exchange*] **Commodities Exchange** .... ACE
AMEX [*American Stock Exchange*] **Communications** [*Network*] .... AMCOM
AMEX [*American Stock Exchange*] **Computerized Order Display and Execution System** .... AMCODE
AMEX [*American Stock Exchange*] **Options Switching System** .... AMOS
AMF Apollo Sailing Class Association (EA) .... ASCA
AMF Bowling [*NYSE symbol*] (SG) .... PIN
AMF International [*Formerly, American Messianic Fellowhip*] (EA) .... AMF
AMF Sunfish Racing Class Association (EA) .... SRC
AMF Windflite Sailboard Class Association (EA) .... AMFWSCA
Amfed Financial, Inc. [*Associated Press*] (SAG) .... Amfed
Amfed Financial, Inc. [*NASDAQ symbol*] (SAG) .... AMFF
Amfion [*Record label*] [*Mexico*] .... Amf
AMFM, Inc. [*NYSE symbol*] (SG) .... AFM
Amfonelic Acid [*Biochemistry*] .... AFA
Amgen, Inc. [*Associated Press*] (SAG) .... Amgen
Amgen, Inc. [*NASDAQ symbol*] (NQ) .... AMGN
AMGOT Mail Service (SAUO) .... AMS
Amharic [*MARC language code*] [*Library of Congress*] (LCCP) .... amh
Amharic (SAUS) .... Amh
Amhawk Resources Corp. [*Vancouver Stock Exchange symbol*] .... AHK
Amherst College (SAUO) .... AC
Amherst College, Amherst, MA [*OCLC symbol*] (OCLC) .... AMH
Amherst College, Amherst, MA [*Library symbol*] [*Library of Congress*] (LCLS) .... MA
Amherst County Public Library, Amherst, VA [*Library symbol*] [*Library of Congress*] (LCLS) .... ViAm
Amherst Historical Society, Amherst, MA [*Library symbol*] [*Library of Congress*] (LCLS) .... MAHi
Amherst, MA [*FM radio station call letters*] .... WAMH
Amherst, MA [*FM radio station call letters*] .... WFCR
Amherst, MA [*FM radio station call letters*] .... WMUA
Amherst, MA [*FM radio station call letters*] .... WRNX
Amherst, MA [*AM radio station call letters*] .... WTTT
Amherst, NS [*AM radio station call letters*] .... CKDH
Amherst, NY [*AM radio station call letters*] .... WUFO
Amherst Papyri [*A publication*] (OCD) .... PAmh
Amherst Receiver Processor System (SAUS) .... ARPS
Amherst, VA [*AM radio station call letters*] .... WAMV
Amherst, VA [*FM radio station call letters*] .... WYYD
Amherstview Branch, Lennox and Addington County Public Library, Ontario [*Library symbol*] [*National Library of Canada*] (NLC) .... OALAC
AMI (Air Mercury International) [*Belgium*] [*ICAO designator*] (FAAC) .... MIA
Ami Frame Interface Development System [*Lotus Development Corp.*] (PCM) .... AFIDS
AMIA Internet Working Group (SAUO) .... AMIA-IWG
Amicable and Brotherly Society of Journeymen Millwrights [*A union*] [*British*] .... ABSJM
Amicable Settlement (SAUS) .... AS
Amicable Society of Coachmakers [*A union*] [*British*] .... ASC
Amici Thomae Mori [*Angers, France*] [*An association*] (EA) .... ATM
Amicus Curiae [*Friend of the Court*] [*Latin*] [*Legal term*] (ADA) .... AM CUR
Amide-Imide (SAUS) .... AI
Amidinophenylpyruvic Acid [*Organic chemistry*] .... APPA
Amidships (SAUS) .... Amids
Amiens/Glisy [*France*] [*ICAO location identifier*] (ICLI) .... LFAY
Amiga [*Record label*] [*Germany*] .... Ami
Amiga Restructured Extended Executor [*Computer Language*] (VERA) .... AREXX
Amigo Airways (SAUS) VLL
AMIGOS [*Access Method for Indexed Data Generalized for Operating System*] **Bibliographic Council** (EA) .... ABC
AMIGOS [*Access Method for Indexed Data Generalized for Operating System*] **Bibliographic Council, Dallas, TX** [*OCLC symbol*] (OCLC) IIC
AMIGOS [*Access Method for Indexed Data Generalized for Operating System*] **Bibliographic Council, Dallas, TX** [*OCLC symbol*] (OCLC) .... TPQ
AMIGOS [*Access Method for Indexed Data Generalized for Operating System*] **Bibliographic Council, Dallas, TX** [*OCLC symbol*] (OCLC) .... TPR
AMIGOS [*Access Method for Indexed Data Generalized for Operating System*] **Bibliographic Council, Dallas, TX** [*Library symbol*] [*Library of Congress*] (LCLS) .... TxDaABC
Amigos de Las Americas [*An association*] (EA) .... AMIGOS
Amika Rondo de Experantaj-Kolektantoj (SAUO) .... AREK
Amilcar Cabral International/Sal Island [*Cape Verde*] [*ICAO location identifier*] (ICLI) .... GVAC
Amilcar Register (EA) .... AR
Amiloride Inhibitable Lithium Transport [*Biochemistry*] (DAVI) .... AILT
Amilprilose Hydrocholoride (SAUS) .... AMILPRI
AMINCO American Instrument Co., Inc. (SAUO) .... AMINCO
Amine Precursor Uptake and Decarboxylation [*Cytology*] .... APUD
Amine Precursor Uptake and Decarboxylation Tumor [*Endocrinology*] (DAVI) .... APUD-Oma
Amine-Isobutyric Acid (SAUS) .... AIBA
Aminepenicillanic Acid (SAUS) .... APA
Amine-Terminated Butadiene/Acrylonitrile (ACAE) .... ATBN
Aminioallantoic Fluid (SAUS) .... AAF
Amino [*As substituent on nucleoside*] [*Biochemistry*] .... n
Amino Acid [*Biochemistry*] .... AA
Amino Acid Adenylate [*Also called adenomonophosphate*] [*Biochemistry*] (DAVI) .... AA-AMP
Amino Acid Analysis [*Biochemistry*] (DB) .... AAA
Amino Acid Decarboxylase [*An enzyme*] .... AADC
Amino Acid Formula [*Biochemistry*] .... AAF
Amino Acid Formula with Glutamate [*Biochemistry*] .... AAFG
Amino Acid Nitrogen [*Analytical biochemistry*] .... AAN
Amino Acid Oxidase [*An enzyme*] .... AAO
Amino Acid Racemization [*Dating process*] .... AAR
Amino Acid Razemization (SAUS) .... AAR
Amino Acid Replacement [*Medicine*] (MELL) .... AAR
Amino Acid Residue [*Biochemistry*] .... AA
Amino Acid Sequence [*Medicine*] (MELL) .... AASeq
Amino Acid, Unknown or Other [*Symbol*] [*Biochemistry*] X
Amino Acid-Activating Enzyme [*Biochemistry*] (MAE) .... AAAE
Amino Acids (SAUS) .... AMINOS
Amino Polycyclic Aromatic Hydrocarbon [*Environmental chemistry*] .... APAH
Aminoacetaldehyde Diethyl Acetal [*Organic chemistry*] .... AADEA
Aminoacetaldehyde Dimethyl Acetal [*Organic chemistry*] .... AADMA
Aminoacetone [*Organic chemistry*] .... AA
Aminoacetonitrile [*Organic chemistry*] .... AAN
Aminoacetylcatechol [*or Acetamidocatechol*] [*Biochemistry*] .... AAC
Aminoacyl (LDT) .... AA
Aminoadenosine Triacid Ester [*Biochemistry*] .... AATE
Aminoadipic Acid [*Organic chemistry*] .... AAA
Aminoadipic Acid [*Biochemistry*] .... Aad
(Aminoadipyl)cysteinylvaline Synthetase [*An enzyme*] .... ACVS
Amino(aminophenyl)benzamide [*Organic chemistry*] .... AAPBA
Aminoantipyrine (SAUS) .... AAP
AminoAzobenzene [*Organic chemistry*] .... AB

Aminobenzamide [*Organic chemistry*]	AB
Aminobenzamidine [*Biochemistry*]	ABD
Aminobenzoic Acid (MELL)	ABA
Aminobenzoic Acid [*Organic chemistry*]	ABOA
Aminobenzophenone [*Organic chemistry*]	AB
Aminobenzyloxy Methyl Cellulose Paper (DOG)	ABM Paper
Aminobiphenyl [*Biochemistry*] (OA)	ABP
Amino(bromo)(phenyl)pyrimidinone [*Antiherpes compound*]	ABPP
Aminobromophenylpyrimidinone (SAUS)	ABPP
Aminobutylethylisoluminol (SAUS)	ABEI
(Aminobutyl)ethylisoluminol [*Biochemistry*]	ABEI
Aminobutyraldehyde [*Organic chemistry*]	ABAL
Aminobutyric Acid [*Also, Abu*] [*Organic chemistry*]	ABA
Aminobutyric Acid (SAUS)	ABA
Aminobutyric Acid [*Also, ABA*] [*Biochemistry*]	Abu
Aminocaproic Acid [*Organic chemistry*]	ACA
Amino-Caproic Acid (SAUS)	ACA
Aminocaproic Acid [*Biochemistry*]	Acp
Aminocaprolactam [*Organic chemistry*]	ACL
Aminocarbonyl Reaction Product (DB)	ACRP
Aminocephalosporanic Acid [*Pharmacology*]	ACA
Aminocephalosporanic Acid (MELL)	ACSA
Aminochlorobenzophenone [*Organic chemistry*]	ACB
Amino(chloro)pentenedioic Acid [*Organic chemistry*]	ACPA
Amino(chloro)Pentenoic Acid [*Organic chemistry*]	ACP
Aminocyclopentane Carboxylic [*Acid*] (DMAA)	ACPC
Aminocyclopentanecarboxylic Acid (SAUS)	ACPC Acid
Amino(cyclopentyl)dicarboxylate [*Organic chemistry*]	ACPD
Aminocyclopropane-Carboxylic Acid [*Organic chemistry*]	ACC
Aminocyclopropanecarboxylicacid Oxidase [*An enzyme*]	ACCO
Aminodecephalosporanic Acid [*Biochemistry*]	ADCA
Aminodeoxyclavulanic Acid [*Organic chemistry*]	ADCA
Aminodihydroxytetrahydronaphthalene [*Organic chemistry*]	ADTN
Amino(dimethyl)dihydrobenzofuran [*Organic chemistry*]	ADD
Aminodiphenyl [*Organic chemistry*]	ADP
Aminoethoxyvinylglycine [*Organic chemistry*]	AVG
Aminoethyl (SAUS)	AE
Aminoethyl [*Biochemistry*]	Aet
Aminoethyl Benzene Sulfonyl Fluoride [*Organic chemistry*]	AEBSF
Aminoethyl Cellulose [*Organic chemistry*] (OA)	AEC
Aminoethyl Cysteine [*Biochemistry*] (OA)	AEC
Aminoethylaminopropylsilane	AEPS
Amino(ethyl)carbazole [*Organic chemistry*]	AEC
Aminoethylethanolamine [*Organic chemistry*]	AEEA
Aminoethylhomocysteine [*Biochemistry*]	AEHC
Aminoethylhomocysteine [*Biochemistry*] (OA)	AEOC
Aminoethylisothiuronium [*Radiology*]	AET
Aminoethyl(methyl)sulfone [*Biochemistry*]	AEMS
Aminoethylphosphonic Acid [*Organic chemistry*]	AEP
Aminoethylphosphonic Acid [*Organic chemistry*] (PDAA)	AEPA
Aminoethylphosphonic Acid (SAUS)	AEP Acid
Aminoethylpiperazine [*Organic chemistry*]	AEP
Amino(ethyl)propanediol [*Organic chemistry*]	AEPD
Aminoethylthioisourea Dihydrobromide (EDCT)	AET
Aminoethyltricosadiynamide [*Organic chemistry*]	AETDA
Aminofluorene [*Also, FA*] [*Carcinogen*]	AF
Amino-Form Bind Medium [*Analytical biochemistry*]	ABM
Amino-form Bind Medium (SAUS)	ABM
aminoglutethimide (SAUS)	agl
Aminoglutethimide [*Organic chemistry*] (MAE)	AGL
Aminoglutethimide [*Antineoplastic drug*] (CDI)	AGT
Aminoglycoside [*Endocrinology*] (DAVI)	AG
Aminoglycoside [*Medicine*] (MELL)	AGS
Aminoguanosine [*Biochemistry*]	AG
Aminohexaneic Acid (SAUS)	AHA
Aminohexanoic Acid [*Biochemistry*]	Ahx
Aminohippurate (MAE)	AH
aminohippurate (SAUS)	ah
Aminohydroxynaphthalenesulfonic Acid [*Organic chemistry*]	ANSA
Aminohydroxypropane Diphosphonate	APDP
Amino(hydroxy)propylidine [*Organic chemistry*]	APD
aminoimidazole carboxamide (SAUS)	aic
Aminoimidazole Ribonucleotide [*Biochemistry*]	AIR
Amino-Imidazole-Caboxamide Ribonucleotide (SAUS)	AICAR
Aminoimidazolecarboxamide [*Organic chemistry*]	AIC
Aminoimidazolecarboxamide [*Also, AICA*] [*Organic chemistry*]	AIC
Aminoimidazolecarboxamide [*Also, AIC*] [*Organic chemistry*]	AICA
Aminoimidazolecarboxamide (SAUS)	AICA
Amino-Imidazolecarboxamide Ribonucleotide (SAUS)	AICAR
Aminoimidazolecarboxamide Ribonucleotide [*Also, AICR*] [*Biochemistry*]	AICAR
Aminoimidazolecarboxamide Ribonucleotide [*Also, AICAR*] [*Biochemistry*]	AICR
Aminoimidazolecarboxylic Acid [*Organic chemistry*]	AICA
Amino-Imidazole-Carboxylic Acid (SAUS)	AICA
Aminoiodoacetamidovaleric Acid	AIAVA
Amino(iodoacetamido)valeric Acid [*Organic acid*]	AIAVA
(Amino)(Iodo)ketanserin [*Biochemistry*]	AMIK
Aminoisobutyrate (DMAA)	AIB
Amino-Isobutyric (SAUS)	AIB
aminoisobutyric acid (SAUS)	aib
Aminoisobutyric Acid [*Biochemistry*]	AIB
Aminoisobutyric Acid [*Biochemistry*] (AAMN)	AIBA
Amino-Isobutyric Acid (SAUS)	AIBA
Aminolaevulinate [*or Aminolaevulinic*] Acid [*Biochemistry*]	ALA

Aminolaevulinate Dehydratase [*Also, ALD*] [*An enzyme*]	ALAD
Aminolaevulinate Dehydratase [*Also, ALAD*] [*An enzyme*]	ALD
Aminolaevulinate Synthase [*An enzyme*]	ALAS
Aminolaevulinic Acid [*Biochemistry*]	AmLev
Aminolevulinic Acid Dehydrase (DB)	ALAD
Aminolevulinic Acid Synthetase (SAUS)	ALAS
Aminomalonic Acid [*Organic chemistry*]	AMA
Amino(mercapto)thiodiazole [*Organic chemistry*]	AMTD
Amino(mercopto)thiadiazole [*Organic chemistry*]	AMTD
Amino(methoxy)benzanilide [*Organic chemistry*]	AMBA
Aminomethyl Anthracene [*Organic chemistry*]	AMA
Aminomethyl Naphthalene [*Organic chemistry*]	AMN
Aminomethyl Phosphonic Acid [*Organic chemistry*]	AMPA
Aminomethylalizarindiacetic [*Organic chemistry*]	AMADAC
Amino-Methyl-Coumarin	AMC
Amino(methyl)coumarinacetate [*Organic chemistry*]	AMCA
Amino-Methyl-Cyclohexane Carboxylic Acid (SAUS)	AMCHA
Aminomethylcyclohexanecarboxylic Acid [*Pharmacology*] (AAMN)	AMCA
Aminomethylcyclohexanecarboxylic Acid [*Pharmacology*]	AMCHA
Aminomethyl(methyl)benzothiadiazinedioxide [*Biochemistry*]	AMBD
Amino(methyl)propanediol [*Organic chemistry*]	AMPD
Amino(methyl)propanol [*Organic chemistry*]	AMP
Aminomethyltrimethylpsoralen [*Cytology*]	AMT
Aminomethyltrioxsalen [*Organic chemistry*]	AMT
Aminomonophosphate [*Organic chemistry*] (DAVI)	AMP
Amino-naphthalene-trisulfonic Acid [*Organic chemistry*]	ANTS
Aminonaphtholsulfonic Acid [*Organic chemistry*]	ANSA
Amino-(nitro)cyclopentanecarboxylic Acid [*Organic chemistry*]	ANCPA
Aminonitrothiazole [*Biochemistry*] (DAVI)	ANT
Aminonucleoside (DMAA)	AMNS
Amino(octyl)guanidine [*Organic chemistry*]	AOG
Amino-Oligopeptidase [*An enzyme*]	AOP
Aminooxyacetic Acid [*Biochemistry*]	AOAA
Aminopenicillanic Acid [*Biochemistry*]	APA
Amino-Penicillanic Acid (SAUS)	APA
Aminopentanoic Acid [*An amino acid*]	APE
Aminopeptidase [*An enzyme*] (MAE)	AP
Aminopeptidase M (DB)	APM
Aminophenyl Disulfide [*Biochemistry*]	APDS
Aminophenylacetylene [*Organic chemistry*]	APA
Amino(phenyl)butanoic Acid [*Organic chemistry*]	APBA
Aminophenylmercuric Acid [*Organic chemistry*]	APMA
Aminophosphonobutyric Acid [*Organic chemistry*]	APB
Amino(phosphono)heptanoic Acid [*Organic chemistry*]	APH
Amino(phosphono)valerate [*Organic chemistry*]	APV
Amino(phosphono)valeric Acid [*An amino acid*]	APV
Aminophylline [*A drug*]	AM
aminophylline (SAUS)	aminoph
Aminophylline, Phenobarbital, Ephedrine [*Medicine*] (MAE)	APE
Aminopieroylglutamic Acid (SAUS)	APGA
Aminopimelic Acid [*An amino acid*]	APM
Aminopolystyrene (MELL)	APS
(Aminopropylamino)ethylthiophosphate [*Biochemistry*]	APAETP
Aminopropyldiethanolamine [*Organic chemistry*]	APDEA
Aminopropylisothiourea (SAUS)	APT
Aminopropyllisothiourea (SAUS)	APT
Aminopropyltrimethoxysilane (SAUS)	APTS
Aminopropylmorpholine [*Organic chemistry*]	APM
(Aminopropyl)triethoxysilane [*Organic chemistry*]	APTES
Aminopropyltrimethoxysilane [*Organic chemistry*]	APTMS
Aminopropyltrimethoxysilane [*Organic chemistry*]	APTS
Aminopterin [*Antineoplastic drug regimen*] (DAVI)	AMPT
Aminopterin [*Antiviral compound*]	AMT
Aminopteroylglutamic Acid [*Organic chemistry*]	APGA
Aminopurine [*Biochemistry*]	AP
Amino-Purine (SAUS)	AP
Aminopyrazolopyrimidine [*Biochemistry*]	APP
Aminopyrazolopyrimidine Ribonucleoside [*Biochemistry*]	APPR
Aminopyrene-trisulfonate [*Organic chemistry*]	APTS
Aminopyrine [*An antipyretic and anesthetic*]	AP
Aminopyrine Breath Test [*Medicine*] (MELL)	ABT
Aminopyrine Breath Test [*Clinical chemistry*]	APBT
Aminoquinoline [*Biochemistry*] (OA)	AQ
Aminoquinoline Oxide [*Biochemistry*] (OA)	AQO
Aminosalicyclic Acid [*Biochemistry*]	ASA
(Amino)selenadiazole [*Antiviral compound*]	ASD
Aminosultopride [*Biochemistry*]	AST
Aminothiazolineacetic Acid [*Biochemistry*]	ATAA
Aminotransferase [*An enzyme*]	AT
Aminotriazole [*Herbicide*] (MAE)	AT
Aminotriazole [*Herbicide*]	ATA
A-minus (SAUS)	A-
Amiodarone [*Coronary vasodilator*] [*Cardiology*]	AMIO
Amiodarone-Iodine-Induced Thyrotoxicosis [*Medicine*] (DMAA)	AIIT
Amiprophos Methyl	APM
Amir Mines Ltd. [*Toronto Stock Exchange symbol*]	AMM
Amiral Commandant le Groupe Anti-Sous-Marin [*Commander, Antisubmarine Force*] [*French*] (NATG)	ALGASM
Amiral Commandant les Porte-Avions [*Admiral, Aircraft Carriers*] [*French*] (NATG)	ALPA
Amiral Commandant l'Escadre [*Admiral, French Fleet*] (NATG)	ALESC
Amirante Islands (SAUS)	Amirantes
Amiri Flight-Bahrain [*ICAO designator*] (FAAC)	BAH
Amirican Society for Testing and Materials (EDCT)	ASTM

Amiridia, Genitourinary Abnormalities, and Mental Retardation [*Medicine*] (DMAA) ... AGR
Amis de la Terre [*Friends of the Earth*] [*Canada*] (EAIO) ... AT
Amisk Public Library, Alberta [*Library symbol*] [*National Library of Canada*] (NLC) ... AAMI
Amistad National Recreation Area (SAUS) ... ANRA
Amistad Recreation Area [*National Park Service designation*] ... AMIS
Amistad Research Center Library, New Orleans, LA [*Library symbol*] [*Library of Congress*] (LCLS) ... LNAC
Amistar Corp. [*Associated Press*] (SAG) ... Amistar
Amistar Corp. [*NASDAQ symbol*] (NQ) ... AMTA
AMISYS Managed Care Sys [*NASDAQ symbol*] (TTSB) ... AMCS
Amit Women (EA) ... AW
Amite, LA [*AM radio station call letters*] ... WABL
Amite, LA [*FM radio station call letters*] (BROA) ... WTGG-FM
Amitie Franco-Afghane [*French Afghan Friendship Committee*] ... AFRANE
Amities Belgo-Congolaises [*Belgian-Congolese Friendship Association*] ... ABC
Amitriptyline [*Also, AT*] [*Antidepressant compound*] ... AMI
Amitriptyline [*Also, AMI*] [*Antidepressant compound*] ... AT
Amity International (EAIO) ... AI
Amity Public Library, Amity, OR [*Library symbol*] [*Library of Congress*] (LCLS) ... OrAm
Amityville Junior High School, Amityville, NY [*Library symbol*] [*Library of Congress*] (LCLS) ... NAmiJH
Amityville Memorial High School, Amityville, NY [*Library symbol*] [*Library of Congress*] (LCLS) ... NAmiHS
Amityville Public Library, Amityville, NY [*Library symbol*] [*Library of Congress*] (LCLS) ... NAmi
Amkor Technology [*NASDAQ symbol*] (SG) ... AMKR
AML Communication, Inc. [*NASDAQ symbol*] (SAG) ... AMLJ
AML Communications [*NASDAQ symbol*] (TTSB) ... AMLJ
AML Communications, Inc. [*Associated Press*] (SAG) ... AML Com
AMLI Residential Properties [*NYSE symbol*] (SAG) ... AML
AMLI Residential Properties [*Associated Press*] (SAG) ... AMLI Rs
Amlikon [*Switzerland*] [*ICAO location identifier*] (ICLI) ... LSPA
Ammamonium (SAUS) ... AMM
Amman [*Jordan*] [*Airport symbol*] (OAG) ... AMM
Amman [*Jordan*] [*ICAO location identifier*] (ICLI) ... OJAC
Amman [*Jordan*] [*ICAO location identifier*] (ICLI) ... OJAF
Amman [*Jordan*] [*ICAO location identifier*] (ICLI) ... OJZZ
Amman World Trade Center [*Jordan*] (EAIO) ... AWTC
Ammanford [*District in Wales*] ... AMMAN
Amman/Marka [*Jordan*] [*ICAO location identifier*] (ICLI) ... OJAM
Amman/Queen Alia [*Jordan*] [*ICAO location identifier*] (ICLI) ... OJAI
Ammeter (MDG) ... A
Ammeter ... AM
Ammeter (ADWA) ... am
Ammeter ... AMM
Ammeter ... AMTR
Ammeter Switch (MSA) ... AS
Ammianus Marcellinus [*c. 330-395AD*] [*Classical studies*] (OCD) ... Amm Marc
Ammo War Reserve Level (CINC) ... AWRL
Ammonia (MAE) ... AMM
Ammonia ... AMMN
Ammonia ... ammon
Ammonia (MSA) ... AMNA
Ammonia (GNE) ... NH_3
Ammonia and Toluene (SAUS) ... AMATOL
Ammonia Blood Level [*Medicine*] (MELL) ... ABL
Ammonia Double-Alkali [*Organic chemistry*] (DICI) ... ADA
Ammonia Freeze Explosion [*Chemical engineering*] ... AFEX
Ammonia Oxidation Plant (MCD) ... AOP
Ammonia Service [*Military*] (DNAB) ... AS
Ammonia System (DS) ... AMM SYS
Ammonia System Operations [*NASA*] (NASA) ... ASO
Ammoniacal (SAUS) ... AMM
Ammoniacal Copper Arsenate [*Wood preservative*] ... ACA
Ammoniacal Copper Arsenite (OA) ... ACA
Ammoniacal Copper Quaternary ... ACQ
Ammoniacal Copper Zinc Arsenate [*Wood preservative*] ... ACZA
Ammonia-Fiber Explosion [*Agricultural engineering*] (PS) ... AFEX
Ammoniaque Synthetique et Derives [*Belgium*] ... ASED
ammoniated (SAUS) ... ammon
Ammoniated Mercury (MELL) ... AM
Ammoniated Mercury Ointment [*Medicine*] (MELL) ... AMO
Ammonite (SAUS) ... Ammon
Ammonium (SAUS) ... AMM
Ammonium Biflouride [*Inorganic chemistry*] ... ABF
Ammonium Chloride (SAUS) ... Amm Cl
Ammonium Chloride (SAUS) ... Sal Ammoniac
Ammonium Citrate [*Organic chemistry*] (OA) ... AC
Ammonium Dehydrogen Phosphate (SAUS) ... ADP
Ammonium Dideuterium phosphate (SAUS) ... AD
Ammonium Diethyldithiocarbamate [*Organic chemistry*] ... ADDC
Ammonium Dihydrogen Arsenate [*Inorganic chemistry*] ... ADA
Ammonium Dihydrogen Phosphate [*Inorganic chemistry*] ... ADP
Ammonium Dihydrogen Phosphate (IDOE) ... adp
Ammonium Dihydrogen Phosphate Crystal (MED) ... ADP crystal
Ammonium Dimolybdate [*Inorganic chemistry*] ... ADM
Ammonium Dinitramide [*Potential rocket fuel component*] [*Inorganic chemistry*] ... ADN
Ammonium Diuranate [*Inorganic chemistry*] ... ADU
Ammonium Heptamolybdate [*Inorganic chemistry*] ... AHM
Ammonium Hydrogen Sulfate [*Inorganic chemistry*] ... AHS
Ammonium Hydroxide (SAUS) ... Ammonia Water
Ammonium Isobutyrate (EDCT) ... AIB
Ammonium Lauryl Sulfate [*Organic chemistry*] ... ALS
Ammonium Metatungstate [*Inorganic chemistry*] ... AMT
Ammonium Metavanadate [*Inorganic chemistry*] ... AMV
Ammonium Molybdophosphate [*Inorganic chemistry*] ... AMP
Ammonium Nitrate [*Inorganic chemistry*] ... AN
Ammonium Nitrate and Fuel Oil [*Explosive*] ... ANFO
Ammonium Nitrate, Copper, Aluminum, and Plywood [*Proposed currency*] ... ANCAP
Ammonium Nitrate-Fuel Oil Explosives (EDCT) ... ANFOI
Ammonium Paratungstate [*Metallurgy*] ... APT
Ammonium Perchlorate [*Inorganic chemistry*] ... AP
Ammonium Perchlorate [*Inorganic chemistry*] ... APC
Ammonium Perchlorate (SAUS) ... NH4 ClO4
Ammonium Perchlorate Fuel (SAUS) ... AP fuel
Ammonium Persulfate [*Inorganic chemistry*] ... APS
Ammonium Polyphosphate [*Fertilizer*] ... APP
Ammonium Polysulfide [*Fertilizer*] ... APS
Ammonium Pyrrolidine Dithiocarbamate (SAUS) ... APDC
Ammonium Pyrrolidine-Dithio Carbonate (SAUS) ... APDC
Ammonium Pyrrolidinedithiocarbamate [*Also, APDTC*] [*Organic chemistry*] ... APDC
Ammonium Pyrrolidinedithiocarbamate [*Also, APDC*] [*Organic chemistry*] ... APDTC
Ammonium Sulfamate [*Inorganic chemistry*] ... AMS
Ammonium Sulfate-Nitrate [*Fertilizer*] ... ASN
Ammonium Thioglycolate ... ATG
Ammonium Thiosulfate [*Fertilizer*] ... ATS
Ammonium Uranyl Carbonate [*Inorganic chemistry*] ... AUC
Ammonium Uranyl Tricarbonate [*Inorganic chemistry*] ... AUT
Ammonium-Nitrate-Carbon (SAUS) ... ANC
Ammons Picture Vocabulary Test [*Speech and language therapy*] (DAVI) ... APVT
Ammunition (ADA) ... AM
Ammunition (KSC) ... AMM
Ammunition (AFM) ... AMMO
Ammunition (ADWA) ... ammo
Ammunition (SAUS) ... Ammu
Ammunition ... AMMUN
Ammunition ... AMN
Ammunition and Hazardous Materials Handling Review Board (MCD) ... AMHAZ
Ammunition Base Load (MCD) ... ABL
Ammunition Bearer [*Military*] (INF) ... AB
Ammunition Bearer [*Military*] (AABC) ... AMMOBR
Ammunition, Casualties, and Equipment (INF) ... ACE
Ammunition Clerk (SAUS) ... Am Clk
Ammunition Column (SAUS) ... AC
Ammunition Condition Report ... ACR
Ammunition Consolidated Stock Status Report ... ACSSR
Ammunition Container Assembly (SAUS) ... ACA
Ammunition Control Point (AFM) ... ACP
Ammunition Corporal (SAUS) ... AC
Ammunition Danger Area (SAUS) ... ADA
Ammunition Delivery System (SAUS) ... ADS
Ammunition Depot (SAUO) ... AD
Ammunition Disposition Request [*or Report*] ... ADR
Ammunition Distributing Point (SAUS) ... AMDP
Ammunition Distribution and Control (SAUS) ... AD&C
Ammunition Distribution and Control [*Military*] (NG) ... AD & C
Ammunition Distribution System ... ADS
Ammunition Dump (SAUO) ... AD
Ammunition Engineering Directorate [*Army*] (MCD) ... AED
Ammunition Examiner [*British and Canadian*] [*World War II*] ... AE
Ammunition Executive Office [*Military*] [*British*] ... AEO
Ammunition, Explosives, and Other Dangerous Articles ... AEDA
Ammunition Group - Picatinny Arsenal (MCD) ... AGPA
Ammunition Group-Picatinny Arsenal (SAUO) ... AGPA
Ammunition Handler (SAUS) ... ammo hand
Ammunition Handling Equipment ... AHE
Ammunition Handling System (MCD) ... AHS
Ammunition Hoist ... AMOHST
Ammunition Hoist Drive ... AMOHSTDR
Ammunition Identification Code ... AIC
Ammunition Initiatives Task Force (MCD) ... AITF
Ammunition Lighter [*Navy symbol*] (DNAB) ... YEN
Ammunition Lighter [*Navy symbol*] (DNAB) ... YWN
Ammunition Loading (SAA) ... A/L
Ammunition Loading Production Engineering Center [*Army*] ... ALPEC
Ammunition Loading System (MCD) ... ALS
Ammunition Logistics [*Army*] (RDA) ... AMMOLOG
Ammunition Lot Number ... ALN
Ammunition Maintenance Squadron (SAUO) ... AMS
Ammunition Peculiar Equipment (AABC) ... APE
Ammunition Performance Report [*Military*] (NVT) ... APR
Ammunition Point ... AP
Ammunition Pontoon [*Navy symbol*] (DNAB) ... YWN
Ammunition Post Processor [*Computer science*] [*Military*] ... APP
Ammunition Procurement and Supply Agency (SAUS) ... APS
Ammunition Procurement and Supply Agency [*Army*] ... APSA
Ammunition Rack ... AMMORK
Ammunition Railhead ... ARH
Ammunition Readiness Concept (MCD) ... ARC
Ammunition Records Clerk (SAUS) ... AMMO RCD CLK
Ammunition Refilling Point ... ARP
Ammunition Reliability Division [*Military*] ... ARD
Ammunition Reliability Evaluation Program (SAA) ... AREP

Ammunition Reliability Information Evolution System (MCD) .... ARIES
Ammunition Renovator (SAUS) .... AMMO RENOV
Ammunition Repair Workshop (NATG) .... ARW
Ammunition Reporting Management System [*Air Force*] (AFM) .... ARMS
Ammunition Resupply Projectile [*Military*] (RDA) .... ARP
Ammunition Section (SAUS) .... Am Sec
Ammunition Section Chief (SAUS) .... Ammo Sec ch
Ammunition Sergeant (SAUS) .... Am Sgt
ammunition ship (SAUS) .... AE
Ammunition Ship [*Navy symbol*] .... AE
Ammunition Ship .... AFD
Ammunition Ship (SAUS) .... AS
Ammunition Shipment Order [*Army*] .... AMSO
Ammunition Specialist (SAUS) .... ammo sp
Ammunition Specialist [*Military*] (GFGA) .... AS
Ammunition Stock Recording System .... ASRS
Ammunition Stockpile Reliability Program (MCD) .... ASRP
Ammunition Storage (SAUS) .... AS
Ammunition Storage Bay Terminal Box (ACAE) .... ASBTB
Ammunition Storage Facility [*Military*] .... ASF
Ammunition Storage Site (SAUS) .... AMSS
Ammunition Storage Sites (SAUS) .... ASS
Ammunition Store (SAUS) .... AS
Ammunition Stores Issue Ship .... ASIS
Ammunition Stores Management and Remote Set Fuzing (MCD) .... SM/RSF
Ammunition Subdepot [*United Kingdom*] (NATG) .... ASD
Ammunition Sub-Depot (SAUO) .... ASD
Ammunition Subpark (SAUS) .... Ammn Sub Pk
Ammunition Subpark (SAUS) .... AS/P
Ammunition Sub-Park [*British military*] (DMA) .... ASP
Ammunition Supply Authority (SAUO) .... AMSA
Ammunition Supply Depot .... ASD
Ammunition Supply Dump [*British*] [*World War II*] .... ASD
Ammunition Supply Installation [*Army*] (INF) .... ASI
Ammunition Supply Officer (AFM) .... ASO
Ammunition Supply Plan [*Army*] .... ASP
Ammunition Supply Point .... ASP
Ammunition Supply Squadron [*Air Force*] .... AMMISSq
Ammunition Supply Squadron [*Air Force*] .... ASUPS
Ammunition Supply Vehicle (SAUS) .... ASV
Ammunition Surveillance Information System (SAUS) .... ASIS
Ammunition Systems Reliability and Safety Division [*Picatinny Arsenal*] [*Army*] .... ASRSD
Ammunition Technical Office (SAUO) .... ATO
Ammunition Technical Officer [*Ireland*] .... ATO
Ammunition Technician [*British military*] (DMA) .... AT
Ammunition Technology Division [*Lake City Army Ammunition Plant*] [*Independence, MO*] .... ATD
Ammunition Torque (SAA) .... A/T
Ammunition, Toxic Material Open Space (SAUS) .... ATMOS
Ammunition Track (SAUS) .... AMTRAC
Ammunition Transfer Point [*or Pack*] (MCD) .... ATP
Ammunition Transport .... AKE
Ammunition War Reserve (CINC) .... AWR
Amnesic Shellfish Poisoning [*Medicine*] .... ASP
Amnesic-Dysnomic Aphasia [*Medicine*] (MELL) .... ADA
Amnesty International [*London, England*] (EAIO) .... AI
Amnesty International Canadian Section .... AICS
Amnesty International EC Representation [*Belgium*] (EAIO) .... AI-EC
Amnesty International in the United States of America (SAUO) .... AIUSA
Amnesty International Medical Group .... AIMG
Amnesty International Parliamentary Group .... AIPG
Amnesty International Publications (SAUO) .... AIP
Amnesty Review Board [*Terminated, 1976*] .... ARB
Amnex, Inc. [*Associated Press*] (SAG) .... Amnex
AMNEX, Inc. [*Formerly, NYCOM Information Services*] [*NASDAQ symbol*] (SPSG) .... AMXI
Amnio Acid Formula (SAUS) .... AAF
Amnioallantoic Fluid (SAUS) .... AAF
Amniocentesis [*Medicine*] (MELL) .... AC
Amniocentesis [*Obstetrics*] (DAVI) .... amnio
Amnion (MELL) .... A
Amnion (DMAA) .... Am
Amnionic Fluid Volume [*Obstetrics*] (DAVI) .... AFV
Amniotic Alphafetoprotein [*Obstetrics*] .... AFP
Amniotic Cavity [*Medicine*] (MELL) .... AC
Amniotic Deformity, Adhesion, Mutilation [*Syndrome*] [*Medicine*] (DMAA) .... ADAM
Amniotic Fluid [*Obstetrics*] .... AF
Amniotic Fluid Embolism [*Obstetrics*] .... AFE
Amniotic Fluid Glucose [*Obstetrics*] .... AFG
Amniotic Fluid Index [*Medicine*] (MELL) .... AFI
Amniotic Fluid SCan [*Medicine*] (MELL) .... AMN FS
Amnistie Internationale Section Canadienne [*Amnesty International Canadian Section*] .... AISC
Amnplitude-Modulation Double-Sideband Suppressed Carrier (SAUS) .... AMDSBSC
Amobarbital Elixir [*Medicine*] (MELL) .... ABE
amobarbital sodium (SAUS) .... amobarb
Amociation for Physical and System Mathematics (SAUS) .... APSM
AMOCO Canada Petroleum Co. Ltd., Calgary, AB, Canada [*Library symbol*] [*Library of Congress*] (LCLS) .... CaACAC
AMOCO Canada Petroleum Co. Ltd., Calgary, Alberta [*Library symbol*] [*National Library of Canada*] (NLC) .... ACAC
AMOCO Chemicals Customer Service System .... ACCESS
Amoco Chemicals Customer Service System (SAUO) .... ACCESS
AMOCO Corp. [*Associated Press*] (SAG) .... Amoco
Amoco Corp. [*NYSE symbol*] (TTSB) .... AN
Amoco Graphics System (SAUS) .... AGS
AMOCO Production Co., Library, Tulsa, OK [*OCLC symbol*] (OCLC) .... OUD
AMOCO Production Co., Research Center Geology Library, Tulsa, OK [*Library symbol*] [*Library of Congress*] (LCLS) .... OkTAm
Amoeba-Less Life Cycle (PDAA) .... ALC
Amoebic Prevalence Rate (SAUS) .... APR
Amoebocyte Lysate [*Biochemistry*] .... AL
Amol [*Iran*] [*ICAO location identifier*] (ICLI) .... OINA
Amold, CA [*FM radio station call letters*] .... KCFA
Amolds Geological Series (SAUS) .... AGS
Amon Carter Museum of Western Art (SAUO) .... ACMWA
Amon Carter Museum of Western Art, Fort Worth, TX [*Library symbol*] [*Library of Congress*] (LCLS) .... TxFACM
Amon G Carter Museum of Western Art (SAUO) .... AGCMWA
Among .... AMG
Among (SAUS) .... Amg
Among Others .... AO
Amongst (ROG) .... AMGST
Amonium Zingiber [*Ginger*] [*Pharmacology*] (ROG) .... AMON ZINGIB
Amook [*Alaska*] [*Airport symbol*] (OAG) .... AOS
AMOON Distributing [*NASDAQ symbol*] (SAG) .... DIST
Amora (BJA) .... A
Amored Cavalry Trainer (SAUS) .... ACT
Amored Cavalry Vehicle (SAUS) .... ACV
Amores [*of Ovid*] [*Classical studies*] (OCD) .... Am
Amorite Personal Names in the Mari Texts [*A publication*] (BJA) .... APNM
Amorphium Graphics Engine [*Computer science*] .... AGE
Amorphous (AAMN) .... AMOR
Amorphous [*Sediment*] [*Biochemistry*] (DAVI) .... AMORP
Amorphous .... amorph
Amorphous Calcium Phosphate (MELL) .... ACP
Amorphous, Hydrogenated Carbon (SAUS) .... AHC
Amorphous Hydrous Calcium Phosphate [*Inorganic chemistry*] .... ACP
Amorphous Inclusion [*Cytology*] .... AI
Amorphous Material [*Agronomy*] .... Am
Amorphous Material [*Clinical medicine*] .... A-MAT
Amorphous Polyalphaolefin [*Plastics technology*] .... APAO
Amorphous Polyamide [*Organic chemistry*] .... APA
Amorphous Polyethylene Terephthalate (SAUS) .... APET
Amorphous Polyolefin [*Organic chemistry*] .... APO
Amorphous Polypropylene [*Organic chemistry*] .... APP
Amorphous Semiconductor (PDAA) .... AS
Amorphous Silicon Drum (SAUS) .... ASI
Amorphous Sodium Aluminosilicate [*Inorganic chemistry*] .... ASAS
Amorphous Solid Water [*Materials science*] .... ASW
Amorphous Thin Film (PDAA) .... ATF
Amortization (ADWA) .... amort
amortization (SAUS) .... amort
Amortization and Partial Prepayment [*Business term*] .... APP
Amortized Cost (SAUS) .... AC
amortizement (SAUS) .... amort
amortizing (SAUS) .... amort
Amory, MS [*FM radio station call letters*] .... WAFM
Amory, MS [*AM radio station call letters*] .... WAMY
Amos [*Old Testament book*] .... Am
Amos [*California*] [*Seismograph station code, US Geological Survey*] (SEIS) .... AMS
Amos and Ferard on Fixtures [*A publication*] (DLA) .... A & F Fix
Amos and Ferard on Fixtures [*A publication*] (DLA) .... Am & Fer
Amos and Ferard on Fixtures [*A publication*] (DLA) .... Amos & F
Amos and Ferard on Fixtures [*A publication*] (DLA) .... Amos & F Fixt
Amos and Ferard on Fixtures [*A publication*] (DLA) .... Ferard Fixt
Amos' Fifty Years of the English Constitution [*A publication*] (DLA) .... Amos Fifty Years
Amos on an English Code [*A publication*] (DLA) .... Amos Eng Code
Amos on International Law [*A publication*] (DLA) .... Amos Int Law
Amos on Laws for Regulation of Vice [*A publication*] (DLA) .... Amos Reg Vice
Amos, PQ [*AM radio station call letters*] .... CHAD
Amos' Primer of the English Constitution [*A publication*] (DLA) .... Amos Engl Const
Amos' Science of Jurisprudence [*A publication*] (DLA) .... Amos Jur
Amotopo [*Surinam*] [*ICAO location identifier*] (ICLI) .... SMAM
Amougies [*Belgium*] [*ICAO location identifier*] (ICLI) .... EBAM
Amount (ROG) .... A
Amount .... AMNT
Amount (EBF) .... amt
Amount (AFM) .... AMT
Amount (SAUS) .... Amt
Amount Keyboard (SAUS) .... AK
Amount of Critical View (SAUS) .... ACV
Amount of Critical View .... ACV
Amount of Insulin Extracted from the Pancreas (SAUS) .... AIEP
Amount of Invested Mental Effort .... AIME
Amount of Semantic Information (SAUS) .... ASI
Amount of Substance [*Molecular quantity*] (MAE) .... ams
Amount of Substance [*Molecular quantity*] [*Symbol*] [*IUPAC*] .... n
Amount Received (SAUS) .... AMTRC
Amount Sign Code (SAUS) .... ASC
Amount Subject to Cash Discount (SAUS) .... AMSCD
Amount Tendered .... AT
Amount to be Excreted [*Medicine*] (MELL) .... ARE
Amount to Make the Property Operational [*Business term*] (EMRF) .... AMPO
Amoxicillin [*Medicine*] (DMAA) .... AMX

AMP Communications Outlet (SAUS) ... ACO
AMP Exploration & Mining Co. Ltd. [*Vancouver Stock Exchange symbol*] ... API
AMP, Inc. [*NYSE symbol*] (SPSG) ... AMP
AMP, Inc. [*FAA designator*] (FAAC) ... MMP
AMP, Inc., Harrisburg, PA [*Library symbol*] [*Library of Congress*] (LCLS) ... PHarA
Ampac Petroleum Resources, Inc. [*Vancouver Stock Exchange symbol*] ... AMP
Ampace Corp. [*Associated Press*] (SAG) ... Ampace
Ampace Corp. [*NASDAQ symbol*] (SAG) ... PACE
Ampal American Israel Corp. [*NASDAQ symbol*] (SAG) ... AMPL
Ampal-Amer Israel 6.50% Pfd [*NASDAQ symbol*] (TTSB) ... AMPLP
Ampal-Amer Israel Corp. [*AMEX symbol*] (SPSG) ... AIS
Ampal-Amer Israel'A' [*AMEX symbol*] (SG) ... AIS
Ampal-American Israel Corp. [*Associated Press*] (SAG) ... Ampal
Ampanihy [*Madagascar*] [*Airport symbol*] (OAG) ... AMP
Ampanihy [*Madagascar*] [*ICAO location identifier*] (ICLI) ... FMSY
Amparafaravola [*Malagasy*] [*Airport symbol*] (AD) ... AMF
Amparafaravola [*Madagascar*] [*ICAO location identifier*] (ICLI) ... FMMP
Ampco-Pittsburgh [*NYSE symbol*] (TTSB) ... AP
Ampco-Pittsburgh Corp. [*Associated Press*] (SAG) ... Ampco
Ampco-Pittsburgh Corp. [*NYSE symbol*] (SPSG) ... AP
Ampenan [*Indonesia*] [*Airport symbol*] (AD) ... AMI
amperage (SAUS) ... amp
Ampere [*Unit of electric current*] [*SI symbol*] ... A
Ampere [*or Amperage*] [*Unit of electric current*] (AFM) ... AMP
Ampere (DMAA) ... amp
Ampere [*Unit of electric current*] (ROG) ... C
Ampere Demand Meter (MSA) ... AD
Ampere Direct Current (MCD) ... ADC
Ampere Hour ... A H
Ampere Hour (IDOE) ... Ah
Ampere Hour (IDOE) ... amp-hr
Ampere Minute (IAA) ... AM
Ampere per Meter [*Unit of magnetic field strength*] ... A/M
Ampere per Meter (SAUS) ... A/m
Ampere Second ... As
Ampere Second (SAUS) ... AS
Ampere Turn Balance Detector (SAUS) ... ATB Detector
ampere turns per meter (SAUS) ... at/m
Ampere Turns per Motor (IAA) ... ATM
ampere turns per weber (SAUS) ... at/wb
Ampere, Volt, Ohm (IAA) ... AVO
Ampere-Hour (NTIO) ... ah
Ampere/Hour (MCD) ... A/HR
Ampere-Hour (MDG) ... AMP-HR
Ampere-Hour Capacity ... AHC
Ampere-Hour Meter ... AHM
Ampere-Hour Meter (WDAA) ... ahm
Ampere-Hour-Meter (SAUS) ... AHM
Amperemeter (IAA) ... A
Amperemeter (MAE) ... AM
Amperemeter (SAUS) ... Ammeter
Amperemeter Squared (SAUS) ... Amy
Amperemeter Switch (SAUS) ... AS
Amperes (KSC) ... AMPS
Amperes per Square Centimeter (IAA) ... ASC
Amperes per Square Foot ... ASF
Amperes per Square Inch ... APSI
Amperes per Square Inch [*Electrochemistry*] ... ASI
Amperes per Square Meter ... A/M^2
Amperes per Terminal ... A/T
Ampere-Seconds per Volt (IAA) ... ASV
Ampere-Turn [*Technical drawings*] ... A-T
Ampere-Turn (ADWA) ... At
Ampere-Turn per Meter (MCD) ... AT/M
Ampere-Volt-Ohm (SAUS) ... AVO
Amperometric [*Electromagnetics*] ... Amp
Ampex (SAUS) ... APX
Ampex Corp. [*Associated Press*] (SAG) ... Ampex
Ampex Corp. [*AMEX symbol*] (SAG) ... AXC
Ampex Corp., Redwood City, CA [*Library symbol*] [*Library of Congress*] (LCLS) ... CRcAm
Ampex Corp.'A' [*AMEX symbol*] (TTSB) ... AXC
Ampex Corporation (SAUO) ... APX
Ampex Digital Optics [*Telecommunications*] (WDMC) ... ADO
Ampex Disk Controller [*Computer science*] (IAA) ... ADC
Ampex, Inc. (SAUO) ... AM
Ampex Manufacturing Company (SAUO) ... APD
AMPEX [*Alexander M. Poniatoff, Excellence*] **Replacement Memory** (IAA) ... ARM
Ampex Semiconductor Memory (SAUS) ... ASM
Ampex to IBM Tape (SAUS) ... AMIT
Ampex-Time-Element-Compensator (SAUS) ... Amtec
Ampfing/Waldkraiburg [*Germany*] [*ICAO location identifier*] (ICLI) ... EDYA
Amphenol Corp. (SAA) ... AMP
Amphenol Corp. [*Associated Press*] (SAG) ... Amphnl
Amphenol Corp. [*NYSE symbol*] (SAG) ... APH
Amphenol Corp'A' [*NYSE symbol*] (TTSB) ... APH
Amphenol-Borg Electronics Corp. (MCD) ... ABEC
Amphenol-Borg Electronics Corporation (SAUO) ... ABEC
Amphetamine [*Also, AMT, amphet*] [*CNS stimulant*] ... A
Amphetamine [*Pharmacology*] (DAVI) ... AMP
Amphetamine [*Pharmacology*] (DAVI) ... AMPH
Amphetamine [*Also, A, AMT*] [*CNS stimulant*] ... amphet
Amphetamine [*Also, A, amphet*] [*CNS stimulant*] ... AMT
Amphetamine (SAUS) ... Amt
Amphetamine Sulfate [*Also callde Benzedrine*] [*Pharmacology*] (DAVI) ... A's
Amphiali [*Greece*] [*ICAO location identifier*] (ICLI) ... LGAM
amphiapomict (SAUS) ... AAPLE
Amphibian [*or Amphibious*] ... A
Amphibian [*Russian aircraft symbol*] ... E
Amphibian Boat Reconnaissance Aircraft ... ABR
Amphibian Command (SAUO) ... AC
Amphibian Imperial Forces ... AIF
Amphibian Papilla [*An auditory organ*] ... AP
Amphibian Reconnaissance [*Military*] ... AR
Amphibian Tank Escape Apparatus ... ATEA
Amphibian Technology Tested ... ATT
Amphibian [*or Amphibious*] **Tractor** [*or Truck*] ... AMTRAC
Amphibian [*or Amphibious*] **Tractor Battalion** [*or Truck*] ... AMTRACBN
Amphibians and Watercraft [*Army*] (RDA) ... AWC
Amphibians and Watercraft Product Manager [*Army*] (RDA) ... AWC-PM
Amphibious (AFM) ... AMPH
Amphibious ... AMPHBS
Amphibious ... AMPHIB
Amphibious [*JETDS*] ... K
Amphibious ... PHIB
Amphibious Air Traffic Control/Direct Altitude and Identity Readout [*Military*] (IUSS) ... AATC/DAIR
Amphibious and Watercraft (MCD) ... AWC
Amphibious, Armored Infantry Combat Vehicle (MCD) ... AAICV
Amphibious Armoured Vehicle (MILB) ... AAV
Amphibious Assault Bulk Fuel System [*Navy*] ... AABFS
Amphibious Assault Carrier [*or Ship*] **(Landing Helicopter Assault Ship)** [*Navy symbol*] ... LHA
Amphibious Assault Direction System (SAUS) ... AADS
Amphibious Assault Fire System (CAAL) ... AAFS
Amphibious Assault Fuel System [*Navy*] ... AAFS
Amphibious Assault Landing Craft [*Navy symbol*] ... AALC
Amphibious Assault Oceanographic Reconnaissance System [*Military*] (IUSS) ... AAORS
Amphibious Assault Ship [*Military*] ... LAA
Amphibious assault ship, helicopter (SAUS) ... LPH
Amphibious Assault Ship (Landing Platform, Helicopter) [*Navy symbol*] ... LPH
Amphibious Assault Vehicle (SAUS) ... AAV
Amphibious Auto Club of America (EA) ... AACA
Amphibious Bases, United Kingdom ... PHIBSUKAY
Amphibious Beach Unit [*Military*] ... ABU
Amphibious Car [*British*] ... AC
Amphibious Cargo Ship [*Navy symbol*] ... LKA
Amphibious Coastal Reconnaissance Ship [*Navy symbol*] ... LSSR
Amphibious Combat Group (SAUO) ... ACG
Amphibious Command (SAUS) ... Amph Comd
Amphibious Command and Control System (MCD) ... ACCS
Amphibious Command Car (NATG) ... ACC
Amphibious Command Information System [*Military*] (MUSM) ... ACIS
Amphibious Command Ship [*Formerly, AGC*] [*Navy symbol*] ... LCC
Amphibious Construction Battalion [*Also, PHIBCB*] ... ACB
Amphibious Construction Battalion [*Also, ACB*] (NVT) ... PHIBCB
Amphibious Control Center [*Military*] (IUSS) ... ACC
Amphibious Corps [*Marine Corps*] ... AC
Amphibious Corps [*Marine Corps*] ... PHIBCORPS
Amphibious Corps, Atlantic Fleet [*Marine Corps*] ... ACAF
Amphibious Corps Atlantic Fleet (SAUO) ... ACAF
Amphibious Corps, Pacific Fleet [*Marine Corps*] ... ACPF
Amphibious Corps, Pacific Fleet [*Marine Corps*] ... PHIBCORPAC
Amphibious Detachment ... PHIBDET
Amphibious Detachment, India ... PHIBDETIND
Amphibious Engineer Squadron (SAUO) ... Amph Engr Sqn
Amphibious Exercise [*Navy, Marine Corps*] ... AMPHIBEX
Amphibious Exercise [*NATO*] ... PHIBEX
Amphibious Fire Support Ship [*Navy symbol*] ... LFS
Amphibious Flagship Data System [*Military*] (NVT) ... AFDS
Amphibious Follow-on-Echelon [*Navy*] (MCD) ... AFOE
Amphibious Force (SAUS) ... AF
Amphibious Force, Atlantic (SAUO) ... AMPHFORLANT
Amphibious Force Flagship [*Later, LCC*] [*Navy symbol*] ... AGC
Amphibious Force Flagship (SAUS) ... AGC
Amphibious Force, Mediterranean (SAUO) ... AMPHFORMED
Amphibious Force, Pacific (SAUO) ... AMPHFORPAC
Amphibious Force Support Group (SAUO) ... AFSG
Amphibious Forces ... AMPHIBFOR
Amphibious Forces ... PHIBFOR
Amphibious Forces, Atlantic ... AMPHFORLANT
Amphibious Forces, Atlantic (MUGU) ... AMPHIBFORLANT
Amphibious Forces, Atlantic Fleet ... PHIBLANT
Amphibious Forces, Atlantic Fleet ... PHIBSLANT
Amphibious Forces, Central Pacific ... AMPHIBFORCENPAC
Amphibious Forces Command (SAUO) ... Amph Comd
Amphibious Forces Command (SAUS) ... PhibComd
Amphibious Forces, Europe ... PHIBEU
Amphibious Forces, Europe ... PHIBSEU
Amphibious Forces, Mediterranean ... AMPHFORMED
Amphibious Forces, Mediterranean (MUGU) ... AMPHIBFORMED
Amphibious Forces, Northwest African Waters ... PHIBNAW
Amphibious Forces Notes & Orders (SAUS) ... AFNO
Amphibious Forces Ordnance Material Mobile Instruction Unit [*Obsolete*] [*Navy*] ... AF(F)MMIU
Amphibious Forces, Pacific ... AMPHFORPAC
Amphibious Forces, Pacific (MUGU) ... AMPHIBFORPAC
Amphibious Forces, Pacific Fleet ... PHIBPAC
Amphibious Forces, Pacific Fleet ... PHIBSFORPAC

Amphibious Forces, Pacific Fleet	PHIBSPAC
Amphibious Forces Training Command, Atlantic Fleet (SAUS)	PhibsTraLant
Amphibious Forces Training Command, Pacific Fleet (SAUS)	PhibsTraPac
Amphibious Group (SAUO)	AMPHGR
Amphibious Group (SAUO)	Amphib Gru
Amphibious Group	PHIBGROUP
Amphibious Group	PHIBGRU
Amphibious Group Command [NATO] (NATG)	AGC
Amphibious [Warfare] Indoctrination (DOMA)	AMPHIBIND
Amphibious Infantry Combat Vehicle [Army] (ADDR)	AICV
Amphibious Infantry Support Vehicle	AISV
Amphibious Inhaul Device (PDAA)	AID
Amphibious Intelligence (DOMA)	AMPHIBINT
Amphibious Landing Exercise [Navy] (NVT)	PHIBLEX
Amphibious Logistics Support Ashore [Marine Corps] (MCD)	ALSA
Amphibious Logistics Systems [Navy]	ALS
Amphibious Maintenance Support Unit (DNAB)	AMSU
Amphibious Maintenance Support Unit, Atlantic (DNAB)	AMSULANT
Amphibious Maintenance Support Unit, Pacific (DNAB)	AMSUPAC
Amphibious Objective Area [Navy]	AOA
Amphibious Objective Studies (SAUS)	AOS
Amphibious Objective Study [Navy]	AOS
Amphibious Observation Regiment (SAUO)	AORegt
Amphibious Operating Area	AOA
Amphibious Operational Training Element	AOTE
Amphibious Operational Training Unit [Military] (DNAB)	AOTU
Amphibious Operations [Military] (IUSS)	AO
Amphibious Operations [Navy] (NVT)	PHIBOPS
Amphibious Operations (SAUS)	PhibOps
Amphibious Operations Officer [British military] (DMA)	AOO
Amphibious Pionier Erkundungsfahrzeug [Amphibious Engineer Reconnaissance Vehicle] [German] (MCD)	APE
Amphibious Planning (DOMA)	AMPHIBPLN
Amphibious Raid Exercise [Navy] (NVT)	PHIBRAIDEX
Amphibious Ready Group	ARG
Amphibious Ready Group-Special Landing Force (DNAB)	ARG-SLF
Amphibious Reconnaissance (SAUS)	Amphib Recon
Amphibious Reconnaissance Exercise [Navy] (NVT)	PHIBRECONEX
Amphibious Refresher Training [Navy] (CAAL)	PHIBREFTRA
Amphibious Refresher Training [Navy] (NVT)	PHIBRFT
Amphibious Refresher Training (SAUS)	PhibRfT
Amphibious Research Craft	ARC
Amphibious River Crossing Equipment [Military]	ARCE
Amphibious Schoolship [Navy] (NVT)	PHIBSS
Amphibious Ship, Dock	LSD
Amphibious Ship Shakedown Cruise [Navy] (NVT)	PHIBSKDN
Amphibious Ship, Tank	LST
Amphibious Squadron [Army]	PHIBRON
Amphibious Supply Platform [Army]	ASP
Amphibious Support Battalion [Military]	ASB
Amphibious Support Information System (NVT)	ASIS
Amphibious Tank (SAUS)	Amph Tk
Amphibious Tank (SAUS)	Amtank
Amphibious Tank [Military]	AMTANK
Amphibious Tank [Military]	AMTK
Amphibious Tank Crewman (SAUS)	Amph Tk Crm
Amphibious Tanker Terminal Facility [Navy]	ATTF
Amphibious Task Force [Navy] (NVT)	ATF
Amphibious Task Force [Navy] (NVT)	PHIBTF
Amphibious Task Group (SAUO)	ATG
Amphibious Task Group/Marine Amphibious Brigade (DNAB)	ATG/MAB
Amphibious Task Unit [Military] (DNAB)	ATU
Amphibious Track (SAUS)	Amph Trk
Amphibious Tractor (SAUS)	AMTRAC
Amphibious Tractor Exercise [Navy] (NVT)	TRACEX
Amphibious Training (SAUS)	Phibtra
Amphibious Training Base [Navy]	ATB
Amphibious Training Base [Navy]	PHIBTRABASE
Amphibious Training Base [Navy]	PHIBTRBASE
Amphibious Training Command, Atlantic (SAUS)	PhibTraLant
Amphibious Training Command Liaison Officer [Navy]	ATCLO
Amphibious Training Demonstrator	ADT
Amphibious Training Exercise [Navy] (NVT)	AMTREX
Amphibious Training Exercise [Navy] (NVT)	PHIBTRAEX
Amphibious Training Unit (SAUO)	Amphib Tra U
Amphibious Training Unit, Royal Marines [British]	ATURM
Amphibious transport (SAUS)	APA
Amphibious Transport [Navy ship symbol]	LPA
Amphibious Transport [Navy]	PHIBTRANS
Amphibious Transport Dock [Landing Platform, Dock] [Navy ship symbol]	LPD
Amphibious Transport Ship (SAUS)	ATS
Amphibious Transport (Small) [Navy ship symbol]	LPR
Amphibious Transport Submarine [Landing Platform, Submarine] [Navy ship symbol]	LPSS
Amphibious Transportation Group (SAUO)	AMPHTGP
Amphibious Trials & Testing Unit, Royal Marines (SAUS)	ATTURM
Amphibious Troops (SAUO)	AT
Amphibious Truck (SAUS)	Am Trk
Amphibious Truck, 2 1/2-ton Cargo	DUKW
Amphibious Warfare [Navy] (NVT)	AMW
Amphibious Warfare [British military] (DMA)	AW
Amphibious Warfare Branch [Navy] (DNAB)	AWB
Amphibious Warfare Communications [Navy] (MCD)	AWC
Amphibious Warfare Headquarters (SAUO)	AWHQ
Amphibious Warfare Headquarters (SAUS)	AWHQ

Amphibious Warfare Lift Capability [Navy] (MCD)	AMWL
Amphibious Warfare School (DNAB)	AWS
Amphibious Warfare ship (SAUS)	AW
Amphibious Warfare Squadron (SAUO)	AWS
Amphibious Warfare Training Center [Navy]	PHIBWARTRACEN
Amphibious Warfare Working Party (NATG)	AWWP
Amphibious Warping Tug [Navy symbol]	LWT
Amphibole (SAUS)	AM
Amphibole (SAUS)	Am
Amphibole [A mineral]	Amph
Amphicar Owners Club (EA)	AOC
amphigoric (SAUS)	amphig
amphigorical (SAUS)	amphig
amphigorist (SAUS)	amphig
amphigory (SAUS)	amphig
amphimict (SAUS)	amph
Amphion [Record label] [France]	Amph
Amphipathic Alpha Helix [Genetics]	AAH
Amphipathic Helix-Loop-Helix [Genetics]	A-HLH
Amphiphilic Flavin [Chemistry]	AF
Amphiregulin [Biochemistry]	AR
Amphitheater (VRA)	ampth
Amphitheatre (ROG)	AMPHI
Amphitruo [of Plautus] [Classical studies] (OCD)	Amph
Amphophil (SAUS)	A
Amphoric (SAUS)	AMPH
Amphoric [Sound] [Medicine] (DAVI)	amph
Amphotericin B [Antifungal agent]	AMB
Amphotericin B Lipid Complex [Antifungal]	ABLC
Amphotericin B Methyl Ester [A drug]	AME
Amphotrophic Murine Leukemia Virus [Medicine] (DMAA)	AmuLV
Ampicillin [Also, AM, AMP] [Antibacterial compound]	A
Ampicillin [Also, A, AMP] [Antibacterial compound]	AM
Ampicillin [Also, A, AM] [Antibacterial compound]	AMP
Ampicillin [Medicine] (MELL)	Amp
Amplicon, Inc. [NASDAQ symbol] (NQ)	AMPI
Amplicon, Inc. [Associated Press] (SAG)	Amplcn
Amplidyne [Electricity] (KSC)	ADYN
Amplidyne [Electricity] (SAA)	AMP
Amplidyne [Electricity]	AMPLDN
Amplidyne Generator [Electricity]	AMPLG
Amplidyne Motor Generator [Electricity]	AMPLMG
Amplification [Medicine] (DAVI)	amp
Amplification (COE)	AMPN
Amplification based on Stimulated Emission of Radiation (SAUS)	ASER
Amplification by Stimulated Emission of Radiation	ASER
Amplification Controlling Element [Genetics]	ACE
Amplification Factor	AF
Amplification Ratio (MCD)	AR
Amplification Refractory Mutation System [Biochemistry]	ARMS
Amplified (WDAA)	amp
Amplified	AMPLFD
Amplified Automatic Level Control [Air Force]	AALC
Amplified Failure or Unsatisfactory Report	AFUR
Amplified Failure or Unsatisfactory Report [Obsolete]	AMFUR
Amplified Fragment Length Polymorphism [Also, Ampli FLP] [Genetics]	AFLP
Amplified Fragment Length Polymorphism [Genetics]	AmpliFLP
Amplified Immunoradiometric Assay	AMIRA
Amplified Link Modulated (ACAE)	ALM
Amplified Output Voltage	AOV
Amplified Response Spectrum [Nuclear energy] (NRCH)	ARS
Amplified Spontaneous Emission (MCD)	ASE
Amplified Stimulated Emission (PDAA)	ASE
Amplified Substrate/Alkaline Phosphatase	AS/AP
Amplifier	A
Amplifier [JETDS nomenclature] [Military] (CET)	AM
Amplifier (KSC)	AMP
Amplifier [Electronic] (WDMC)	amp
Amplifier (AAG)	AMPL
Amplifier (IAA)	AR
Amplifier and Switch Assembly (MCD)	ASA
Amplifier Based on Stimulated Emission of Radiation (SAUS)	ASER
Amplifier Buffer Attenuator (MCD)	ABA
Amplifier Calibration (SAUS)	Amp Cal
Amplifier Control Cabinet [Military] (IUSS)	ACC
Amplifier Detector	AD
Amplifier Detector Assembly	ADA
Amplifier Discriminator [Instrumentation]	AD
Amplifier Dyne (SAUS)	AMPLIDYNE
Amplifier Input	AI
Amplifier Interface Group (IUSS)	AIG
Amplifier Open Loop Response	AOLR
Amplifier Oscillator, Radiofrequency	AORF
Amplifier Output [Computer science]	AO
Amplifier Output Stage	AOS
Amplifier Power Supply	APS
Amplifier Research (ACAE)	AR
Amplifier Subsystem (NASA)	AMS
Amplifier Under Test (SAUS)	AUT
Amplifier Unit (OA)	AU
Amplifier-Control Intercommunications (MCD)	ACI
Amplifier-Controlled Euphonic [Electronics] (IAA)	ACE
Amplifying Failure, Unsatisfactory or Removal Report (SAUS)	AMPFUR
Amplifying Relay Valve (SAUS)	AR Valve
Amplitron Amplifier (SAUS)	AMA

Amplitude [Physics]	A
Amplitude (DIPS)	a
Amplitude	AMP
Amplitude	AMPL
Amplitude (FAAC)	AMPLTD
Amplitude (MSA)	AMPTD
Amplitude Absorption Coefficient	AAC
Amplitude and Angle Modulation (SAUS)	AAM
Amplitude and Latency Instrument with Digital Output (SAUS)	ALIDO
Amplitude and Latency Measuring Instrument with Digital Output (MCD)	ALMIDO
Amplitude and Phase Extraction (SAUS)	APEX
Amplitude and Phase Keyed (or Keying) (SAUS)	APK
Amplitude and Phase Modulation (CCCA)	APM
Amplitude and Phase Shift Keyed (or Keying) (SAUS)	APSK
Amplitude and Risetime Compensation (or Compensator) (SAUS)	ARC
Amplitude Companded Single Sideband [Electronics]	ACSB
Amplitude Comparison Monopulse [Electronics] (IAA)	ACM
Amplitude Cross Modulation (SAUS)	CMA
Amplitude Degradation Test System (SAUS)	ADTS
Amplitude Demodulation (SAUS)	ADM
Amplitude Density Distribution Function (SAUS)	ADDF
Amplitude Detector (SAUS)	amp det
Amplitude Discriminator (SAUS)	AD
Amplitude Domain Multiple Access (SAUS)	ADMA
Amplitude Equalizer (ACAE)	A/EQ
Amplitude Frequency Distribution (SAUS)	AFD
Amplitude Gain Control	AGC
Amplitude Keyed	AK
Amplitude Limiter [Electronics] (OA)	AL
Amplitude Line Integration (IUSS)	ALI
Amplitude Miss Distance Acoustical Scoring System (MCD)	AMASS
Amplitude Modulated (PIPO)	AM
Amplitude Modulated Voice Frequency Telegraphy System (SAUS)	AM-VFT System
Amplitude Modulation (WDAA)	am
Amplitude Modulation [Electronics]	AM
Amplitude Modulation Continuous Wave (SAUS)	AMCW
Amplitude Modulation Data System (SAUS)	AMDS
Amplitude Modulation Distortion (SAUS)	AMD
Amplitude Modulation, Double Sideband [Electronics] (HGAA)	AM-DBS
Amplitude Modulation, Double Sideband [Electronics]	AMDSB
Amplitude Modulation, Double Sideband, Suppressed Carrier [Electronics] (CET)	AMDSB/SC
Amplitude Modulation Equivalent [Telecommunications] (TEL)	AME
Amplitude Modulation Generator	AMG
Amplitude Modulation Link Program	AMLP
Amplitude Modulation Noise (SAUS)	AM Noise
Amplitude Modulation On Pulse	AMOP
Amplitude Modulation, Single Sideband [Electronics]	AMSSB
Amplitude Modulation, Single Sideband, Suppressed Carrier [Electronics] (CET)	AMSSB/SC
Amplitude Modulation with Limiter (SAUS)	AML
Amplitude Modulation with Vestigial Sideband (SAUS)	AMVSB
Amplitude Modulation-Phase Modulation (SAUS)	AM-PM
Amplitude Modulation/Pulse Modulation (SAUS)	AM/PM
Amplitude Modulation-Reduced Carrier (SAUS)	AM RC
Amplitude Modulation-Suppressed Carrier (SAUS)	AM-SC
Amplitude Modulator (IDOE)	AM
Amplitude Noise Limiting	ANL
Amplitude of Accommodation [Ophthalmology]	AA
Amplitude Phase Conversion [Telecommunications] (OA)	APC
Amplitude Phase Extractor (SAUS)	APEX
Amplitude Phase Keyed [Telecommunications] (NITA)	APK
Amplitude Phase Modulation (SAUS)	APM
Amplitude Phase Shift Keying (MCD)	APK
Amplitude Phase-Keyed System (SAUS)	APK System
Amplitude Probability Distribution [Telecommunications]	APD
Amplitude Ratio Characteristic (PDAA)	ARC
Amplitude Ratio Detector (ACAE)	ARD
Amplitude Scale Factor (SAUS)	ASF
Amplitude Shift Keyed (or Keying) (SAUS)	ASK
Amplitude Shift Keying (SAUS)	ASK
Amplitude Spectral Density [Physics]	ASD
Amplitude Vibration Exciter Control (PDAA)	AVEC
Amplitude-Companded Single Sideband (DA)	ACSSB
Amplitude-Frequency Characteristic [Telecommunications] (OA)	AFC
Amplitude-Frequency Distortion	AFD
Amplitude-Frequency Modulation (SAUS)	AFM
Amplitude-Frequency Response [Telecommunications] (OA)	AFR
Amplitude-Modulated Link [Electronics]	AML
Amplitude-Modulated Peak Envelope Power (SAUS)	AMPEP
Amplitude-Modulated Transmitter [Electronics]	AMT
Amplitude-Modulation Noise Level (IDOE)	AMNL
Amplitudenmodulation, Faksimile (SAUS)	A4
Amplitudenmodulation/Pulsmodulation (SAUS)	AM/PM
Amplitudensieb (SAUS)	AS
Amplitudes/Hour	A/H
Amplitude-Weighted Mean Velocity (DMAA)	AWMV
Amplus [Large] [Pharmacy] (ROG)	AMP
Amplus [Large] [Pharmacy]	AMPL
Ampol Petroleum Limited (SAUO)	Ampol
Ampoule	AM
Ampower Instrument (SAUS)	APOW
Ampthill [England]	AMPT
Ampule [Pharmacy]	AMP
Ampule (DMAA)	amp
Ampulla [Ampule] [Pharmacy]	AMPUL
Ampulla of Anterior Semicircular Duct [Medicine] (MELL)	AASCD
Ampulla of Deferent Duct [Medicine] (MELL)	ADD
Ampulla of Lateral Semicircular Duct [Medicine] (MELL)	ALSCD
Ampulla of Posterior Semicircula Duct [Medicine] (MELL)	APSCD
Ampullary-Isthmic Junction [Anatomy]	AIJ
Amputation [Medicine]	AMP
Amputation (SAUS)	Amp
Amputee [Orthopedics and rehabilitation] (DAVI)	amp
Amputee Coalition of America (SAUO)	ACA
Amputee Shoe and Glove Exchange (EA)	ASGE
Amputee Sports Association [Defunct] (EA)	ASA
Amputee Sports Association of Australia	ASAA
Amputees' Association of Victoria [Australia]	AAV
Amputees for Training, Education and Rehabilitation (SAUO)	AFTER
Amputees in Motion (EA)	AIM
Amqui, PQ [AM radio station call letters]	CFVM
AMR American Eagle, Inc. [ICAO designator] (FAAC)	EGF
AMR Civic Association	ACA
AMR Combs, Inc. [AMR Services, Inc.] [ICAO designator] (FAAC)	XAM
AMR Corp. [NYSE symbol] (SPSG)	AMR
AMRAAM International Licensing Company (SAUO)	AILC
AMRAAM Producibility Enhancement Program (SAUS)	APREP
AMRE, Inc. [NYSE symbol] (SPSG)	AMM
AMRE, Inc. [Associated Press] (SAG)	Amre
Amrep Corp. [Associated Press] (SAG)	Amrep
AMREP Corp. [NYSE symbol] (SPSG)	AXR
AMRESCO Capital Tr [NASDAQ symbol] (SG)	AMCT
Amresco, Inc. [NASDAQ symbol] (SAG)	AMMB
Amresco, Inc. [Associated Press] (SAG)	Amresco
Amrinone [Cardiotonic]	AMR
Amrinone [Cardiotonic]	AR
Amrion, Inc. [NASDAQ symbol] (SAG)	AMRI
Amrion, Inc. [Associated Press] (SAG)	Amrion
Amritsar [India] [Airport symbol] (OAG)	ATQ
Amritsar [India] [ICAO location identifier] (ICLI)	VIAR
Amron Information Services (IID)	AIS
Amry's Acquisition Workforce	AAW
AMS Press, Inc., New York, NY [Library symbol] [Library of Congress] (LCLS)	AmS
AMSA, [Acridinylamine Methanesulphon-M-Aniside] Prednisone, and Chlorambucil [Antineoplastic drug regimen]	APC
AMSA, Prednisone and Chlorambucil (SAUS)	APC
AMSAA [Army Materiel Systems Analysis Agency] Evade Sustained Operations Performance Simulation (MCD)	AESOPS
AMSAA [Army Materiel Systems Analysis Agency] Missile End Game Simulation (MCD)	AMEGS
AMSAA [Army Materiel Systems Analysis Agency] Simulation Wargame (MCD)	AMSWAG
AMSAA [Army Materiel Systems Analysis Agency]/RARDE Combat Simulation [Royal Armament Research and Development Establishment] (MCD)	ARCS
Amsacrine [Also, M-AMSA] [Antineoplastic drug] (CDI)	AMSA
Amsacrine [Antineoplastic drug] [Also, AMSA] (CDI)	m-AMSA
Amsat-Oscar-B Satellite (SAUS)	A-O-B satellite
Amscan Holdings, Inc. [Associated Press] (SAG)	Amscan
Amscan Holdings, Inc. [NASDAQ symbol] (SAG)	AMSN
AMSCO International [Associated Press] (SAG)	Amsco
AMSCO International [NYSE symbol] (SPSG)	ASZ
Amsele [Sweden] [ICAO location identifier] (ICLI)	ESUA
Amserv Healthcare [NASDAQ symbol] (TTSB)	AMSR
AMSERV Healthcare, Inc. [Associated Press] (SAG)	Amserv
Amserv Healthcare, Inc. [NASDAQ symbol] (NQ)	AMSR
Amsha National Park (SAUS)	ANP
Amsler Grid (SAUS)	AG
AmSouth Bancorp [Associated Press] (SAG)	AmSouth
AmSouth Bancorp. [NYSE symbol] (SPSG)	ASO
Amstar American Petroleum [Vancouver Stock Exchange symbol]	AAP
Amstar Venture Corp. [Vancouver Stock Exchange symbol]	AMV
Amsted Industries, Inc. (SAUO)	AD
Amsterdam [Netherlands] [Airport symbol] (OAG)	AMS
Amsterdam (BARN)	Amst
Amsterdam [Netherlands] [ICAO location identifier] (ICLI)	EHAA
Amsterdam Center for Mathematics and Computer Sciences	ACM
Amsterdam Compiler Kit (SAUS)	ACK
Amsterdam Depository Company N.V. (SAUO)	ADC
Amsterdam Exchanges N.V. [Netherlands]	AEX
Amsterdam Free Library, Amsterdam, NY [Library symbol] [Library of Congress] (LCLS)	NAms
Amsterdam Institute of Finance	AIF
Amsterdam, NY [FM radio station call letters]	WBKK
Amsterdam, NY [AM radio station call letters]	WBUG
Amsterdam, NY [AM radio station call letters]	WCSS
Amsterdam, NY [Television station call letters]	WOCD
Amsterdam, NY [Television station call letters] (BROA)	WYPX
Amsterdam, Rotterdam, Antwerp	ARA
Amsterdam School for Executive Development in International Relations (SAUO)	ASEDIR
Amsterdam Stock Exchange (SG)	Am
Amsterdam Studies in the Theory and History of Linguistic Science (journ.) (SAUS)	SHL
Amsterdam Studies in the Theory and History of Linguistic Science. Series III. Studies in the History of Linguistic (journ.) (SAUS)	SHL-3

Amsterdam Studies in the Theory and History of Linguistic Science. Series V. Library and Information Sourees in Linguistics (journ.) (SAUS) .... LISL
Amsterdam Time (SAUS) .... AT
Amsterdam-Antwerpen-Rotterdam Area (RIMS) .... AARA
Amsterdam-Rotterdam Bank .... AMRO
Amsterdam-Rotterdam Bank [Netherlands] .... Amrobank
Amsterdam-Rotterdam-Antwerp-Gent Range (RIMS) .... ARAG
Amsterdam/Schiphol [Netherlands] [ICAO location identifier] (ICLI) .... EHAM
Amstrad Disc Operating System (SAUS) .... AMS-DOS
AmTec, Inc. [AMEX symbol] (SG) .... ATC
Amtech Corp. [NASDAQ symbol] (NQ) .... AMTC
Amtech Corp. [Associated Press] (SAG) .... AmtchCp
Amtech Sys Wrrt [NASDAQ symbol] (TTSB) .... ASYSW
Amtech Systems [Associated Press] (SAG) .... Amtch
Amtech Systems [NASDAQ symbol] (TTSB) .... ASYS
Amtech Systems, Inc. [Associated Press] (SAG) .... Amtech
Amtech Systems, Inc. [NASDAQ symbol] (NQ) .... ASYS
Am-Timan [Chad] [Airport symbol] (AD) .... AMC
Am-Timan [Chad] [ICAO location identifier] (ICLI) .... FTTN
Amtliches Verzeichnis der DATEX-Teilnehmer (SAUS) .... AdxVerz
Amtliches Verzeichnis der DATEX-Teilnehmer (SAUS) .... AVerzDX
Amtliches Verzeichnis der Ortsnetze (SAUS) .... AVON
AMTRAK Commuter Services Corp. [Later, CSC] .... ACSC
AMTRAK Commuter Services Corporation (SAUO) .... ACSC
Amtrak Historical Society (EA) .... AHS
AMTRAK Library, Washington, DC [OCLC symbol] (OCLC) .... ATK
AMTRAK Library, Washington, DC [Library symbol] [Library of Congress] (LCLS) .... DAmL
Amtran, Inc. [NASDAQ symbol] (SAG) .... AMTR
Amtran, Inc. [Associated Press] (SAG) .... Amtran
Amtrol, Inc. [NASDAQ symbol] (SAG) .... AMTL
Amtrol, Inc. [Associated Press] (SAG) .... Amtrol
AmTrust Capital [NASDAQ symbol] (TTSB) .... ATSB
AmTrust Capital Corp. [Associated Press] (SAG) .... AmTrst
AmTrust Capital Corp. [NASDAQ symbol] (SAG) .... ATSB
Amtsblatt [Official Gazette] [German] (DLA) .... ABL
Amtsgericht [Inferior Court] [German] .... AG
Amubri [Costa Rica] [ICAO location identifier] (ICLI) .... MRAM
Amulet Resources Corp. [Vancouver Stock Exchange symbol] .... AUO
Amur River and Basin [MARC geographic area code] [Library of Congress] (LCCP) .... aa---
Amuraviatrans [Former USSR] [FAA designator] (FAAC) .... AAX
Amusement .... AMUSE
Amusement and Music Operators Association (EA) .... AMOA
Amusement and Vending Machine Distributors Association (EA) .... AVMDA
Amusement Caterers' Association [British] (BI) .... ACA
Amusement Game Manufacturers Association [Later, AAMA] (EA) .... AGMA
Amusement Industry Manufacturers & Suppliers (SAUS) .... AIMS
Amusement Machine Operators' Association [Australia] .... AMOA
Amusement Park Club International [Defunct] (EA) .... APCI
Amusement Parks and Arcades [Public-performance tariff class] [British] .... AP
Amusement Trades Association [British] (BI) .... ATA
Amusement Trades Association (SAUO) .... ATA
Amusement Trades Exhibition (SAUO) .... ATE
Amusement Trades Exhibition International [British] (ITD) .... ATEI
Amusement with Prizes [Pinball machines] [British] .... AWP
AMVESCAP PLC ADS [NYSE symbol] (SG) .... AVZ
AmVestors Financial [Associated Press] (SAG) .... Amvst
AmVestors Financial Co. [NYSE symbol] (SAG) .... AMV
AmVestors Financial Co. [Associated Press] (SAG) .... AmvestF
AmVestors Finl [NYSE symbol] (TTSB) .... AMV
AmVestors Fin'l Wrrt [NASDAQ symbol] (TTSB) .... AMVWW
AMVETS Auxiliary (EA) .... AA
Amway Asia Pacific [NYSE symbol] (SPSG) .... AAP
Amway Asia Pacific [Associated Press] (SAG) .... AmwyAs
Amway Japan Ltd. [NYSE symbol] (SAG) .... AJL
Amway Japan Ltd. [Associated Press] (SAG) .... AmwyJ
Amway Japan LtduADS [NYSE symbol] (TTSB) .... AJL
Amwest Insur Group [AMEX symbol] (TTSB) .... AMW
Amwest Insurance Group, Inc. [AMEX symbol] (SPSG) .... AMW
Amwest Insurance Group, Inc. [Associated Press] (SAG) .... AMwest
AMX Corp. [Associated Press] (SAG) .... AMXCo
AMX Corp. [NASDAQ symbol] (SAG) .... AMXX
Amygdala Pars Lateralis [Neuroanatomy] .... APL
Amygdala Pars Medialis [Neuroanatomy] .... APM
Amygdaloid Complex (PDAA) .... AC
Amygdalus [Almond] [Pharmacology] (ROG) .... AMYGD
Amyl [Organic chemistry] .... Am
Amyl Acetate [Organic chemistry] .... AMA
Amyl Nitrate (SAUS) .... AMYL
Amyl Nitrate (SAUS) .... AMYS
Amyl Nitrite [Medicine] (MELL) .... AN
Amylas [An enzyme] (DAVI) .... AMY
Amylas Urine Spot [Test] [Gastroenterology] (DAVI) .... AMY-SP
Amylase [An enzyme] (MAE) .... AMS
Amylase [An enzyme] (DAVI) .... AMY
Amylase [An enzyme] (DAVI) .... AMYLAS
Amylase Clearance [Biochemistry] (DAVI) .... C_{am}
Amylase Inhibitor Activity [Food technology] .... AIA
Amylin Pharmaceuticals [NASDAQ symbol] (SPSG) .... AMLN
Amylin Pharmaceuticals, Inc. [Associated Press] (SAG) .... Amylin
Amyloglucosidase [An enzyme] .... AMG
Amyloid Beta Protein Precursor [Biochemistry] .... ABPP
Amyloid Enhancing Factor [Biochemistry] (DMAA) .... AEF
Amyloid of Immunoglobulin Origin [Medicine] .... AIO

Amyloid of Unknown Origin [Medicine] .... AUO
Amyloid Pack Core [Pathology] .... APC
Amyloid Precursor Protein .... APP
Amyloid Precursor Protein Secretase [Medicine] (DMAA) .... APPS
Amyloid Precursor-Like Protein [Medicine] (DMAA) .... APLP
Amyloid Protein [Biochemistry] .... AP
Amyloid Protein Precursor [Biochemistry] .... APP
Amyloid Substance [Medicine] .... AS
Amyloid-A-Degrading Protease [An enzyme] .... AADP
Amyloid-Associated [Protein] [Medicine] .... AA
Amyloid-Associated Protein [Biochemistry] (DAVI) .... AA
Amylopectinosis (MELL) .... AP
Amylopektin-1,6-glukosidase (SAUS) .... R-Enzym
Amyloplast Pressure Index [Botany] .... API
Amyloxycarbonyl (DB) .... AOC
Amyltrichlorosilane [Organic chemistry] .... AMTCS
Amyotrophic Cerebellar Hypoplasia [Medicine] (DMAA) .... ACH
Amyotrophic Lateral Sclerosis (SAUS) .... ALRTF
Amyotrophic Lateral Sclerosis [Medicine] .... ALS
Amyotrophic Lateral Sclerosis Association (EA) .... ALSA
Amyotrophic Lateral Sclerosis Society of America (EA) .... ALSSOA
Amyotrophic Lateral Sclerosis Society of Canada (SAUO) .... ALS
Amyotrophic Lateral Sclerosis Society of Canada .... ALSSOC
Amyotrophic Lateral Sclerosis/Parkinsonism-Dementia [Medicine] .... ALS/P-D
Amytal (SAUS) .... Amy
An Additional Programming Language (SAUS) .... AAPL
An Analytical Information Management System (SAUS) .... AAIMS
AN [Army-Navy] and MS Manual [Manufacturing Status] (AAG) .... AAMM
An Array Processing Language (SAUS) .... AAPL
An Automatic Test Control System (SAUS) .... AATCS
An Chomhairle Ealaion [Arts Council] (EAIO) .... ACE
An Comhairle Oiliuna (ACII) .... AnCO
An Commun Gaidhealach (SAUO) .... ACG
An Comunn Gaidhealach [The Highland Association] (EA) .... ACG
An Evolutionary System for On-line Processing (SAUS) .... AESOP
An Evolutionary System for Online Processing (SAUS) .... AESOP
An Existing Generalized Informnation Systerm (SAUS) .... AEGIS
An Experimental Structure for On-Line Planning (SAUS) .... AESOP
An Experimental Structure for Online Planning (SAUS) .... AESOP
An Extensible Programming Language (SAUS) .... AEPL
An Foras Forbartha [National Institute for Physical Planning and ConstructionResearch] [Ireland] [Research center] (IRC) .... AFF
An Foras Taluntais [Agricultural Institute] [Ireland] [Research center] (IRC) .... AFT
An Gluaiseacht Eireannach in Aghaidh Apartheid [Irish Anti-Apartheid Movement] (EAIO) .... AGEAA
An information service based on the Institute of Marine Engineers Library (SAUO) .... MARLIB
An integrated PC package from Datapoint (SAUS) .... DATALIBRIS
An International Initiative against Avoidable Disablement (SAUO) .... IMPACT
An Intersociety Liaison Committee on the Environment (SAUO) .... AISLE
An NOAA research program on hydrothermal activity in the oceans (SAUS) .... VENTS
An Oige [The Irish Youth Hostels Association] [Founded in 1931] .... O
An Old Bachelor [Pseudonym used by William Lloyd Garrison] [Acronym also facetiously translated as "Ass, Oaf, and Blockhead"] .... AOB
An Party Kenethlegek Kernow (EA) .... APKK
An Seni Respublica Gerenda Sit [of Plutarch] [Classical studies] (OCD) .... An Seni
Ana [Of Each] [Pharmacy] .... A
Ana [Of Each] [Pharmacy] .... AA
Ana G. Mendez Educational Foundation .... AGMEF
Ana Maria [Ecuador] [ICAO location identifier] (ICLI) .... SEAN
Ana Partes [Equal Parts] [Latin] .... aa
Anaa [French Polynesia] [ICAO location identifier] (ICLI) .... NTGA
ANAADIGICS Inc. [NASDAQ symbol] (TTSB) .... ANAD
Anabasis [of Xenophon] [Classical studies] (OCD) .... An
Anabasis [of Arrian] [Classical studies] (OCD) .... Anab
Anabolic Androgenic Steroids [Medicine] (MELL) .... AAS
Anabolism-Promoting Factor (MAE) .... APF
Anacapa Island [California] [Seismograph station code, US Geological Survey] (SEIS) .... AIC
Anacharsis [of Lucian] [Classical studies] (OCD) .... Anach
Anachronism .... ANAC
Anaco [Venezuela] [Airport symbol] (OAG) .... AAO
Anaco, Anzoategui [Venezuela] [ICAO location identifier] (ICLI) .... SVAN
Anacomp, Inc. [NYSE symbol] (SPSG) .... AAC
Anacomp, Inc. [Associated Press] (SAG) .... Anacmp
Anacomp, Inc. [Associated Press] (SAG) .... Ancmp
Anacomp, Inc. [NASDAQ symbol] (SAG) .... ANCO
Anaconda American Brass Co., Waterbury, CT [Library symbol] [Library of Congress] (LCLS) .... CtWAB
Anaconda Company (SAUO) .... A
Anaconda, MT [FM radio station call letters] .... KGLM
Anaconda Wire & Cable Co. (SAUO) .... AWC
Anacortes Public Library, Anacortes, WA [Library symbol] [Library of Congress] (LCLS) .... WaAn
Anacortes, WA [AM radio station call letters] .... KLKI
Anacostia Neighborhood Museum (SAUO) .... ANM
Anacreon [Greek poet, 527-488BC] [Classical studies] (OCD) .... Anac
Anacreon [Greek poet, 572-488BC] [Classical studies] (ROG) .... ANACR
Anada Marga Universal Relief Team (SAUO) .... AMURT
Anadarko, OK [AM radio station call letters] (BROA) .... KJON-AM
Anadarko, OK [AM radio station call letters] .... KRPT
Anadarko, OK [FM radio station call letters] .... KRPT-FM
Anadarko Petroleum [Associated Press] (SAG) .... Anadrk
Anadarko Petroleum [NYSE symbol] (SPSG) .... APC

Anadarko Petroleum Co. (SAUO) .... APC
Anadigics, Inc. [NASDAQ symbol] (SAG) .... ANAD
Anadigics, Inc. [Associated Press] (SAG) .... Anadigc
Anadromous Fish Conservation Act [1965] .... AFCA
Anaelectrodiabatic [Nuclear wave] .... AED
Anaerobe [Biochemistry] (DAVI) .... ANAERO
Anaerobic Attached-Film Expanded-Bed [For treating wastewater] .... AAFEB
Anaerobic Bacterial Flora [Microbiology] .... ABF
Anaerobic Broth Disk (PDAA) .... AnBD
Anaerobic Threshold .... AT
Anaerobic Upflow Fixed-Film Process [For treating wastewater] .... ANFLOW
Anaerobically Digested Municipal Sewage Solids [Culture medium] .... AD-MSS
Anaerobically Thioglycolate Broth Disk (PDAA) .... AnTBD
Anaesthesia [or Anaesthetic] (ADA) .... ANAES
Anaesthesia [or Anaesthetic] (ADA) .... ANAESTH
Anaesthesia and Critical Care Resources on the Internet (SAUS) .... ACCRI
Anaesthesia and Pharmacology with a Special Section on Professional Hazards (journ.) (SAUS) .... Anaesth Pharmacol Spec Sect Prof Hazards
Anaesthesia Literature Abstracting Retrieval Method [American Society of Anesthesiologists] (NITA) .... ALARM
Anaesthesia, Resuscitation and Intensive Therapy (journ.) (SAUS) .... Anaesth Resusc Intensive Ther
Anaesthesia Safety for All. Proceedings. World Congress of Anaesthesiologists (journ.) (SAUS) .... Anaesth Proc World Congr Anaesthesiol
Anaesthesiologist (SAUS) .... Anaesth
Anaesthesiology (SAUS) .... Anaesth
Anaesthesiology and Intensive Care Medicine (journ.) (SAUS) .... Anaesthesiol Intensive Care Med
Anaesthesiology and Intensive Care Medicine (journ.) (SAUS) ANIMD2
Anaesthesiology. Proceedings of the World Congress of Anaesthesiologists (journ.) (SAUS) .... Proc World Congr Anaesthesiol
Anaesthesiology. Proceedings of the World Congress of Anaesthesiology (journ.) (SAUS) .... Anaesthesiol Proc World Congr
Anaesthesist (journ.) (SAUS) .... Anaesth
Anaesthetic .... An
Anaesthetic Research Society (EAIO) .... ARS
Anaesthetics [Medical Officer designation] [British] .... A
Anaesthetist (ADA) .... ANAES
Anaesthetist (ADA) .... ANAESTH
Anagram (ADA) .... ANAG
anagram (SAUS) .... anag
anagramist (SAUS) .... anag
anagrams (SAUS) .... anag
Anagrapha Falcifera Nuclear Polyhedrosis .... AfNPV
Anaheim, CA [Location identifier] [FAA] (FAAL) .... ANA
Anaheim, CA [Television station call letters] .... KDOC
Anaheim, CA [FM radio station call letters] .... KEZY
Anaheim, CA [AM radio station call letters] .... KORG
Anaheim Public Library, Anaheim, CA [Library symbol] [Library of Congress] (LCLS) .... CAna
Anahuac, TX [Location identifier] [FAA] (FAAL) .... CBC
Anaihylactoid Purhura (SAUS) .... AP
Anair - Anich Airways [Croatia] [ICAO designator] (FAAC) .... ANH
Anaktuvuk Pass [Alaska] [Airport symbol] (OAG) .... AKP
Anal Fin Base [Fish anatomy] .... AFB
Anal Intraepithelial Neoplasia [Oncology] .... AIN
Anal Intrusion (SAUS) .... AI
Anal Pore .... AP
Anal Sphincter [Anatomy] .... AS
Anal Sphincter Muscle [Medicine] (MELL) .... ASM
Anal Transitional Zone [Medicine] (MELL) .... ATZ
Analabs, Inc. Research Notes (SAUO) .... Analabs Res Notes
Analabs, Inc.. Research Notes (journ.) (SAUS) .... Analabs Res Notes
Analalava [Madagascar] [ICAO location identifier] (ICLI) .... FMNL
Analalava [Madagascar] [Airport symbol] (OAG) .... HVA
Analcime [A zeolite] .... ANA
AN/ALE-47 Countermeasures Dispensing System (SAUS) .... CMDS
Analecia Orientalia (journ.) (SAUS) .... AOR
Analecta Bollandiana [A publication] (ODCC) .... Anal Boll
Analecta Hymnica Medii Aevi [A publication] (ODCC) .... AHMA
Analelectrodiabatic (SAUS) .... AED
Analgesic [Medicine] .... ANAL
Analgesic Abuse [Medicine] (MELL) .... AA
Analgesic Abuse Nephropathy [Medicine] (DAVI) .... AAN
Analgesic Dose .... AD
Analgesic-Associated Nephropathy [Medicine] .... AAN
Analog .... A
Analog (NASA) .... ANL
Analog (MSA) .... ANLG
Analog Alarm Section .... AAS
Analog Alignment Diskette (SAUS) .... AAD
Analog & Digital Monitoring Subsystem (SAUS) .... ADMS
Analog and Digital Monitoring System [Computer science] (MCD) .... ADMS
Analog & Digital Peripherals, Inc. (PCM) .... ADPI
Analog and Digital Systems (SAUS) .... ADS
Analog and Discrete Output (MCD) .... A & DO
Analog Antenna Positioner .... AAP
Analog Auto Pilot (SAUS) .... AAP
Analog Automatic Test Program Generation (ACAE) .... AATPG
Analog Circuit Analysis and Partitioning System [Computer science] .... ACAPS
Analog Circuit-Analysis by Time-Share System (SAUS) .... ANCIR/TS
Analog Command Module [Computer science] (NITA) .... ACM
Analog Computer (AAG) .... AC
Analog Computer .... ANACOM
Analog Computer Facility .... ACF

Analog Computer Subsystem .... ACSS
Analog Computer System .... ACS
Analog Computer Translator .... ACTRAN
Analog Concept Learning System (PDAA) .... ACLS
Analog Conditioning and Test System .... ACTS
Analog Control Technology [Computer science] .... ACT
Analog Data Acquisition Module .... ADAM
Analog Data Aquisition System .... ADAS
Analog Data Digitizer .... ADD
Analog Data Distributor and Control [Computer science] (KSC) .... ADDAC
Analog Data Equipment Switching System (ACAE) .... ADESS
Analog Data Handling Assembly (IAA) .... ADHA
Analog Data Handling System (AAG) .... ADHS
Analog Data Recorder Transcriber .... ADRT
Analog Data Recording Transcriber (SAUS) .... ADRT
Analog Data Reduction System (CAAL) .... ADAR
Analog Delay Unit .... ADU
Analog Device [Computer science] (IAA) .... AD
Analog Devices [NYSE symbol] (SAG) .... ADI
Analog Devices, Inc. .... ADI
Analog Devices, Inc. [Associated Press] (SAG) .... Analog
Analog Devices Incorporated (SAUO) .... ADI
Analog Digital/Digital Analog (RDA) .... AD/DA
Analog Display Indicator (MCD) .... ADI
Analog Display Services Interface [Interactive television technology] (PS) .... ADSI
Analog Display Unit .... ADU
Analog Divider [Electronics] (ECII) .... AD
Analog Drive Assembly (MCD) .... ADA
Analog Electronic Computer .... AEC
Analog Event Distribution System [Computer science] (MCD) .... AEDS
Analog Event Distributor [Computer science] (MCD) .... AED
Analog Event System [Computer science] (MCD) .... AES
Analog Expansion Bus [Computer science] (VERA) .... AEB
Analog Facility Terminal [Computer science] (TEL) .... AFT
Analog Factor Calibration Network .... AFCAN
Analog Filter Assembly (MCD) .... AFA
Analog Fly by Wire [Aviation] .... AFBW
Analog Function Control [Electronics] (ECII) .... AFC
Analog Function Generator .... AFG
Analog Ground Bus .... AGBUS
Analog Hardware Descriptive Language (ADWA) .... AHDL
Analog Hybrid (OA) .... AH
Analog Input .... AI
Analog Input [Electronics] (ECII) .... AIN
Analog Input Differential (MCD) .... AID
Analog Input Module [Computer science] .... AIM
Analog Input System .... AIS
Analog Input/Output Board [Computer science] (NITA) .... AIB
Analog Input/Output Board [Computer science] (NITA) .... AIO
Analog Input/Output Package [Computer science] .... AIOP
Analog Instrumentation Subsystem .... AIS
Analog Interface Unit (SAUS) .... AIU
Analog Interlock [Electronics] (ECII) .... AINL
Analog Junction (TEL) .... AJ
Analog Junction Module (TEL) .... AJM
Analog Line Driver [Computer science] (BUR) .... ALD
Analog Line Front End (SAUS) .... ALFE
Analog Line Termination Subsystem [Telecommunications] (TEL) .... ALTS
Analog Link [Telecommunications] (TEL) .... AL
Analog Loop [Computer science] (CIST) .... AL
Analog Loop-Back [Telecommunications] (TEL) .... AL
Analog Major Alarm (MCD) .... AMA
Analog Matched Filter .... AMF
Analog Mobile Phone System (PS) .... AMPS
Analog Module [Telecommunications] (TEL) .... AM
Analog Monitor Module [Computer science] .... AMM
Analog Monitor Unit (ACAE) .... AMU
Analog Monolithic [Electronics] (OA) .... AM
Analog Moving Window Detector (SAUS) .... AMW Detector
Analog Multiplexer Quantitizer [Computer science] (KSC) .... AMQ
Analog Multiplier Unit (ECII) .... AMU
Analog Number Identification [Electronics] (ECII) .... ANI
Analog Output [Computer science] (NASA) .... AO
Analog Output Differential [Computer science] (MCD) .... AOD
Analog Output Submodule (SAA) .... AOS
Analog Panel Meter (IEEE) .... APM
Analog Parameter Record (IAA) .... APR
Analog Phased Processing Loop Equipment [Computer science] (MHDB) .... APPLE
Analog Phase-Locked Loop (SAUS) .... APLL
Analog Pressure Transducer .... APT
Analog Private Line [Telecommunications] (ACRL) .... APL
Analog Process Variable Measurement [Process control] .... APVM
Analog Processing Electronics (ACAE) .... APE
Analog Processing Unit [Computer science] (NITA) .... APU
Analog Processor Interface Unit (ACAE) .... APIU
Analog Program Tape [Computer science] .... APT
Analog Programmable Microprocessor (ACAE) .... APUP
Analog Programming and Checking [Computer science] .... APACHE
Analog Quantum Computers .... AQC
Analog RADAR Absorber .... ARA
Analog RADAR Signal Processor (MCD) .... ARSP
Analog Random Access Memory [Computer science] (HGAA) .... ARAM
Analog Recording Dynamic Analyzer [Computer science] .... ARDA
Analog Recording System .... ARS

Analog Recurrent Neural Network [*Computer science*] ... ARNN
Analog Recursive Computer (IAA) ... ARC
Analog Remote Unit (MCD) ... ARU
Analog Response Conditioner (MCD) ... ARC
Analog Response Unit ... ARU
Analog Rod Position Indicator [*Electronics*] (IAA) ... ARPI
Analog Rotation Speed Control ... ARSC
Analog Schematic Translator for Algebraic Language (SAUS) ... ASRAL
Analog Schematic Translator to Algebraic Language [*Computer science*] (MHDB) ... ASTRAIL
Analog Schematic Translator to Algebraic Language [*Computer science*] (IEEE) ... ASTRAL
Analog Science Fiction and Fact [*A publication*] (BRI) ... Analog
Analog Select Keyboard [*Computer science*] (KSC) ... ASK
Analog Self-Checking Automatic Tester ... ASCAT
Analog Shift Register [*Computer science*] ... ASR
Analog signal (SAUS) ... A
Analog Signal Converter ... ASC
Analog Signal Correlator ... ASC
Analog Signal Processing (SAUS) ... ASP
Analog Signal to Discrete Time Interval Converter [*NASA*] ... ASDTIC
Analog Simulation System ... ASS
Analog Simulator (MHDB) ... ANSIM
Analog Simultaneous Voice/Data Technology (ITCA) ... ASVD
Analog Source Board (CIST) ... ASB
Analog Stimulus Unit ... ASU
Analog Strip Chart ... ASC
Analog Strip Chart Recorder ... ASCR
Analog Switching Subsystem [*Telecommunications*] (NITA) ... ASS
Analog System Assembly Pack ... ASAP
Analog Tape Recorder ... ATR
Analog Technology Company (SAUO) ... ATC
Analog Threshold Logic (SAUS) ... ATI
Analog Threshold Logic ... ATL
Analog to Digital Coding (ACAE) ... ADC
Analog to Digital Conversion [*Computer science*] ... ADC
Analog to Frequency Converter ... AFC
Analog to Pressure Converter ... APC
Analog to Time (MCD) ... A/T
Analog to Time to Digital [*Computer science*] ... ATD
Analog Tone Signal (MCD) ... ATS
Analog Translator [*Computer science*] ... ANATRAN
Analog Tree-Organized Multiplexer ... ATOM
Analog Tune in Progress (IAA) ... ATIP
Analog Video Bandwidth ... AVB
Analog Video Odd (ACAE) ... AVO
Analog Video Tape Recorder (MCD) ... AVTR
Analog-Analog-Digital (SAUS) ... AAD
Analog/Digital Adaptable Recorder Input/Output (SAUS) ... ADARIO
Analog-Digital Analysis Processing Techniques (ACAE) ... ADAPT
Analog-Digital Automatic Program (DNAB) ... ADAP
Analog-Digital Automatic Program Tester [*Computer science*] ... ADAPT
Analog-Digital Converter (SAUS) ... ADC
Analog/Digital Converter [*Computer science*] (IGQR) ... A/D converter
Analog-Digital Converter (NITA) ... ADCVR
Analog/Digital Input/Output (AAEL) ... ADIO
Analog-Digital Input/Output System [*Computer science*] ... ADIOS
Analog-Digital Integrating Translator [*Computer science*] ... ADIT
Analog-Digital Recorder [*Computer science*] ... ADR
Analog-Digital-Analog (IAA) ... ADA
Analog-Digital-Designer [*Trademark*] ... ADD
Analog-Digital-Digital (SAUS) ... ADD
Analog-Discrete Data Converter [*Computer science*] (MCD) ... ADDC
Analoger Anschluss an einer ISDN-Vermittlungsstelle (SAUS) ... ANIS
Analogic Corp. [*NASDAQ symbol*] (TTSB) ... ALOG
Analogic Corp. [*Associated Press*] (SAG) ... Anlogic
Analogical Circuit Technique (PDAA) ... ACT
Analog-In Single-Ended (MCD) ... AIS
Analogous (ADWA) ... anal
Analogous (SAUS) ... Anal
Analogous (MSA) ... ANLGS
Analogous Random Process (PDAA) ... ARP
Analog/Output (SAUS) ... A/O
Analog-to-Digital (AEBE) ... A2D
Analog-to-Digital (IDOE) ... a/d
Analog-to-Digital [*Converter*] [*Computer science*] (AFM) ... AD
Analog-to-Digital (SAUS) ... A/D
Analog-to-Digital [*Converter*] [*Computer science*] ... A-to-D
Analog-to-Digital Computer [*Computer science*] (MCD) ... ADC
Analog-to-Digital Computer (SAUS) ... ADCOM
Analog-to-Digital Conversion System [*Computer science*] ... ADIC
Analog-to-Digital Converter [*Computer science*] (MUGU) ... ADC
Analog-to-Digital Converter (IDOE) ... adc
Analog-to-Digital Converter [*Computer science*] ... ADCON
Analog-to-Digital Converter [*Computer science*] (DOM) ... A/D converter
Analog-to-Digital Data Converter [*Computer science*] (MCD) ... ADDC
Analog-to-Digital Data Recording System [*Computer science*] (IEEE) ... ADRS
Analog-to-Digital Data Reduction System for Oceanographic Research ... ADDRESOR
Analog-to-Digital Recorder (SAUS) ... A-D R
Analog-to-Digital Remastering of musical recordings (SAUS) ... ADRM
Analog-to-Digital-Analog Process and Testing System (SAUS) ... ADAPTS
Analog-to-Digital-Analog Recording (SAUS) ... ADAR
Analog-to-Digital-to-Analog Converter (IAA) ... ADAC
Analog-to-Pulse Duration ... APD
Analog-to-Pulse Width Converter ... A/PW
Analog-to-Pulse Width Converter (SAUS) ... APWC
Analog-to-Stochastic Converter (IAA) ... ASC
Analog-to-Time Module ... ATM
Analogue Aerial Positioner (SAUS) ... AAP
Analogue Autoland Improvement Programme (SAUS) ... AAIP
Analogue Code Encryption unit (SAUS) ... ACE
Analogue Expansion Bus (SAUS) ... AEB
Analogue Image Manipulation System (SAUS) ... AIMAS
Analogue Large Scale Integration (NITA) ... ALSI
Analogue Simple Data Interface set (SAUS) ... ASDI
Analogue Simulation of Competitive Operational Tactics [*Game*] ... ASCOT
Analogue Voice Terminal (SAUS) ... AVT
Analogue/Digital/Analogue Process and Test System (PDAA) ... ADAPTS
Analogy ... ANAL
Analogy, Inc. [*Associated Press*] (SAG) ... Analogy
Analogy Inc. [*NASDAQ symbol*] (TTSB) ... ANLG
Analysing Printer Base (SAUS) ... APB
Analysis (IAA) ... A
Analysis (AABC) ... ANAL
Analysis ... Anal
Analysis ... ANALYS
Analysis ... ANLY
Analysis (FAAC) ... ANLYS
Analysis - Forcast Transport and Diffusion [*Marine science*] (OSRA) ... AFTAD
Analysis Alarm [*Engineering*] ... AA
Analysis and Characterization of Oils, Fats and Fat Products (journ.) (SAUS) ... AOFFA4
Analysis and Computation Division [*National Range Operations Directorate*] [*White Sands Missile Range, NM*] ... ACD
Analysis and Control Element [*Army*] ... ACE
Analysis & Control Element (SAUS) ... ACE
Analysis and Digest of the Decisions of Sir George Jessel, by A. P Peter [*England*] [*A publication*] (DLA) ... Jes
Analysis and Digest of the Decisions of Sir George Jessel, by A. P. Peter [*England*] [*A publication*] (DLA) ... Peter
Analysis and Evaluation ... A & E
Analysis and Evaluation (SAUS) ... A&E
Analysis and Evaluation Branch (SAUS) ... AEB
Analysis and Evaluation Division [*Environmental Protection Agency*] (GFGA) ... AED
Analysis and Evaluation Staff [*Environmental Protection Agency*] (GFGA) ... AES
Analysis and Forecasting, Inc. [*Database producer*] (IID) ... A & F
Analysis and Forecasting Mode ... AFM
Analysis and Information Branch [*Climate Analysis Center*] [*National Weather Service*] ... AIB
Analysis and Pogram for Calculation of Optimum Propellant Performance for Liquid and Fluid (SAUS) ... APCOPPLSRF
Analysis and Prediction [*Program*] [*Marine science*] (OSRA) ... A&P
Analysis and Production (MCD) ... AAP
Analysis and Programming for Space Systems (SAUS) ... APSS
Analysis and Programming for Unmanned Satellites (SAUS) ... APUS
Analysis and Research of Methods for Management ... ARMM
Analysis and Simulation Tool for Resource Allocation (MCD) ... ASTRA
Analysis and Support Division [*Environmental Protection Agency*] (GFGA) ... ASD
Analysis & Technology [*NASDAQ symbol*] (TTSB) ... AATL
Analysis & Technology Inc. (SAUO) ... A&T
Analysis & Technology, Inc. [*NASDAQ symbol*] (NQ) ... AATI
Analysis & Technology, Inc. [*Associated Press*] (SAG) ... AnalyTc
Analysis and Transformation Unit (SAUS) ... ATU
Analysis Bar Charting (PDAA) ... ABC
Analysis by Synthesis (PDAA) ... AbS
Analysis Computer for Component Engineering Services (AAEL) ... ACCESS
Analysis Computer for Component Engineering Services Support (SAUS) ... ACCESS
Analysis Computer System ... ACS
Analysis Console (MCD) ... AC
Analysis Control Routine [*Computer science*] (OA) ... ACRT
Analysis Control Unit ... ACU
Analysis Coordination Element ... ACE
Analysis, Design, and Evaluation System (MCD) ... ADES
Analysis, Design and Evaluation System (SAUS) ... ADES
Analysis Division (ACII) ... AD
Analysis for Forces Objectives and Resources Determination (MCD) ... AFFORD
Analysis Group (SAUO) ... AG
Analysis Group for Regional Electricity Alternatives [*MIT Energy Laboratory Project*] ... AGREA
Analysis, Interpretation, Modelling and Synthesis (SAUS) ... AIMS
Analysis (journ.) (SAUS) ... ANLSCY
Analysis Mass Spectrometer (SAUS) ... AMS
Analysis of Accounts ... A/A
Analysis of Automatic Line Insulation Test [*Bell System*] ... ANALIT
Analysis of Capabilities, Opportunities, and Prospects ... ACOP
Analysis of Coping Style [*Test*] ... ACS
Analysis of Covariance ... ANCOVA
Analysis of Critical Actions Program (SAA) ... ACAP
Analysis of Dendroecological Variability and Natural Climates in Eurasia: the Last 10,000 Years (SAUS) ... ADVANCE-10K
Analysis of Digitized Seismic Signals [*Computer science*] ... ADSS
Analysis of Dynamical Systems Online [*Computer science*] (MHDI) ... ADSOL
Analysis of Intelligence (MCD) ... ANALIT
Analysis of Interconnected Decision Areas [*Business term*] (PDAA) ... AIDA
Analysis of Internal Management Systems ... AIMS
Analysis of Large Data Sets [*Computer science*] (MHDB) ... ALDS
Analysis of Large Plastic Incremental Deformation (MCD) ... ALPID

Analysis of Linear Electronic Circuits (MHDI) .... ALEC
Analysis of Local Oriented Edges [Cancer technology] .... ALOE
Analysis of Longwall Pillar Stability [Computer program] [US Bureau of
  Mines] .... ALPS
Analysis of Management Inventory Policy (SAUS) .... AMIP
Analysis of Means (PDAA) .... ANOM
Analysis of Military Organizational Effectiveness (MCD) ...... AMORE
Analysis of Mobility Platform [Military] (IUSS) .... AMP
Analysis of Multiple Source Obscurants on Realistic Battlefield
  (MCD) .... AMSORB
Analysis of Pacific Area Communications for Hardening to
  Electromagnetic Pulse (SAUS) .... APACHE
Analysis of Packing Methods for Ammunition Storage and Transportation
  (SAUS) .... APMAST
Analysis of Performance and Expense (SAUS) .... APEX
Analysis of Quantitative Data (SAUS) .... AQD
Analysis of Random Data [System documentation] [Oregon State
  University] .... ARAND
Analysis of Real-Time Systems / Data Base Oriented Systems
  (MHDI) .... ARTS/DB
Analysis of Real-Time Systems-Data Base-oriented (SAUS) ... ARTS-DB
Analysis of Recent Climate Change (SAUS) .... ARCC
Analysis of Records Obtained (SAUS) .... ARO
Analysis of Spare Parts Change (MCD) .... ASPC
Analysis of Tactical Single Channel Net Radios (MCD) .... ATACNET
Analysis of Variance .... ANOV
Analysis of Variance .... ANOVA
Analysis of Variance [Medicine] (DB) .... ANOVA(R)
Analysis of Variance (OA) .... AOV
Analysis Package (MHDI) .... ANAPAC
Analysis Processor (SAUS) .... AP
Analysis Production Persistency [LIMRA] .... APP
Analysis Program Linear Active Circuits (NASA) .... APLAC
Analysis, Refinement, and Extension of Nuclear Methodology
  [Military] .... ARENUM
Analysis, Requirements Determination, Design and Development, and
  Implementationand Evaluation (MHDB) .... ARDI
Analysis, Research, and Computation, Inc. (SAUO) .... ARC
Analysis System for Static and Dynamic Problems (MCD) .... ANSYS
Analysis Time .... AT
Analysis Virtual Machine (SAUS) .... AVM
Analysis/Architecture (SSD) .... A/A
Analysis-Forecast Transport and Diffusion (USDC) .... AFTAI
Analyst (DAVI) .... anal
Analyst .... ANLS
Analyst (AL) .... Anly
Analyst (TBD) .... Anlys
Analyst .... ANLYST
Analyst Capability .... ACAP
Analyst Console (SAUS) .... AC
Analyst [Information or Intelligence] Display and Exploitation System .... AIDES
Analyst Information Display and Exploitation System (SAUS) ..... AIDES
Analyst Intelligence Data System (MCD) .... AIDS
Analyst Intelligence Display and Exploitation System (SAUS) ... AIDES
Analyst Interpreter Interactive Display System (SAUS) .... AIIDS
Analyst (journ.) (SAUS) .... Anal
Analyst Watch on the Internet [Computer science] .... AWI
Analyst Workstations (SAUO) .... AWS
Analysts and Researchers (CIST) .... A&R
Analysts International Corp. [Associated Press] (SAG) ..... Analysts
Analysts International Corp. [NASDAQ symbol] (NQ) .... ANLY
Analysts International Corporation (SAUO) .... AIC
Analysts International Corporation (SAUS) .... ANLY
Analysts Intl. [NASDAQ symbol] (TTSB) .... ANLY
Analyst-to-Analyst Communications Service (MCD) .... ATACS
Analyst-to-Analyst Exchange Message Format (MCD) .... ANEX
Analytic (SAUS) .... ANAL
Analytic .... ANLYTC
Analytic Approximation Theory [Physics] (OA) .... AAT
Analytic [or Analytical] Chemist .... AC
Analytic Chemist (SAUS) .... AC
Analytic Computer Equipment (SAUS) .... ACE
Analytic Decisions Corp. [Information service or system] (IID) ..... ADC
Analytic Decisions Corporation (SAUO) .... ADC
Analytic Drag Control [Aviation] (NASA) .... ADC
Analytic Electron Microscope (or Microscopy) (SAUS) .... AEM
Analytic Element Method .... AEM
Analytic Ephemeris Generator .... AEG
Analytic Equation-of-State (SAUS) .... AEOS
Analytic Geometry Interpretive Language (SAUS) .... AGILE
Analytic Hierarchy Process .... AHP
Analytic Intelligence Test [Psychology] .... AIT
Analytic Language Manipulation System .... ALMS
Analytic Learning Disability Assessment [Child development test] ..... ALDA
Analytic Library Information Retrieval and Transfer (SAUS) ...... ALIRT
Analytic Methodology for System Evaluation and Control [Army] ..... AMSEC
Analytic Mission Reliability (MCD) .... AMR
Analytic Orbit Determination Program (MCD) .... ANODE
Analytic Orbit Deterrnination Program (SAUS) .... APC
Analytic Plotter Coordinagraph [Geoscience] .... APC
Analytic Processing Unit .... APU
Analytic Reaction (AAMN) .... AR
[The] Analytic Sciences Corp. .... TASC
Analytic Services (SAUS) .... ANSER
Analytic Services, Inc. .... ANSER

Analytic Solution to Queues (MHDI) .... ASQ
Analytic Subject Index (SAUS) .... ASI
Analytic Trouble Shooting (MHDB) .... ATS
Analytica Chimica Acta [A publication] .... ACA
Analytica Posteriora [of Aristotle] [Classical studies] (OCD) .... An Post
Analytica Priora [of Aristotle] [Classical studies] (OCD) .... An Pr
Analytical (ADWA) .... analyt
Analytical .... ANLYTCL
Analytical Abstract (SAUS) .... Anal Abstr
Analytical Abstracts Online [Royal Society of Chemistry] [Information service
  or system] (CRD) .... AA
Analytical Advances (journ.) (SAUS) .... Anal Adv
Analytical Aerial Triangulation (WDAA) .... AAT
analytical anatomy by the Braille method (SAUS) .... aaBm
Analytical and Computer Laboratory .... ACL
Analytical and Computer Latoratory (SAUO) .... ACL
Analytical and Quantitative Cytology and Histology (journ.) (SAUS) ...... AQCHED
Analytical Aspects of Environmental Chemistry (journ.)
  (SAUS) .... Anal Aspects Environ Chem
Analytical Assessments Corp. (MCD) .... AAC
Analytical Atomic Spectroscopy (journ.) (SAUS) ..... Anal At Spectrosc
Analytical Biochemise (journ.) (SAUS) .... ANBCA
Analytical Biochemistry [A publication] (MEC) .... Anal Biochem
Analytical Biochemistry (journ.) (SAUS) .... Anal Biochem
Analytical Biochemistry of Insects (journ.) (SAUS) ...... Anal Biochem Insects
Analytical Calibration Curve .... ACC
Analytical Calorimetry (journ.) (SAUS) ANACAD4
Analytical Cellular Pathology (SAUS) .... ACP
Analytical Chemisrty Laboratory (SAUO) .... ACL
Analytical Chemist (SAUS) .... AC
Analytical Chemistry (SAUS) .... Anal Chem
Analytical Chemistry [A publication] (MEC) .... Analyt Chem
Analytical Chemistry and Applied Spectroscopy (MUGU) ..... ACAS
Analytical Chemistry by Open Learning [A publication] .... ACOL
Analytical Chemistry Laboratory [Department of Energy] ..... ACL
Analytical Computer Program .... ACP
Analytical Condition Inspection [Air Force] (MCD) .... ACI
Analytical Condition Inspection Program [Air Force] (MCD) ..... ACIP
Analytical Control and Data (MHDB) .... ANACONDA
Analytical Data Interchange and Storage Standards (SAUS) ..... ADISS
Analytical Data Reflection (SAUS) .... ADR
Analytical Detection Methods for the Irradiation Treatment of Foods .... ADMIT
Analytical Determination of the Values of Information to Combat
  Effectiveness (PDAA) .... ADVICE
Analytical Determination of the Values of Information to Combat
  Effectiveness (SAUS) .... ADVICE
Analytical Development Corp. .... ADC
Analytical Electron Microscope [or Microscopy] (DAVI) .... AEM
Analytical Electron Microscopy .... AEM
Analytical Engineer (SAUS) .... Analyt Engr
Analytical Float Zone Experiment System (SAUS) .... AFZES
Analytical Function Generator (SAUS) .... AFG
Analytical Grade [Organic chemistry] .... AG
Analytical Graphics, Inc. (SAUO) .... AGI
Analytical Hierachy Process (SAUS) .... AHP
Analytical Imagery Matching System (SAUS) .... AIMS
Analytical Instruction Code (SAUS) .... AIC
Analytical Instruction Element (SAUS) .... AIE
Analytical Instruction Word (SAUS) .... AIW
Analytical Instrument Association (NTPA) .... AIA
Analytical Instrument Development (SAUS) .... AID
Analytical Instrument Development Inc. (SAUO) .... AID
Analytical Instrument Development, Inc. .... AID
Analytical Isoelectrofocusing Scanning Apparatus [Analytical chemistry] ..... AISA
Analytical Laboratory (NRCH) .... AL
Analytical Laboratory Managers Association (EA) .... ALMA
Analytical Laboratory Operations (ABAC) .... ALO
Analytical Letters [A publication] .... AL
Analytical Letters (journ.) (SAUS) .... ANALB
Analytical Letters (journ.) (SAUS) .... Anal Lett
Analytical Limits (NRCH) .... AL
Analytical Maintenance Program [Navy] (NVT) .... AMP
Analytical Method for System Evaluation and Control (SAUS) ...... AMSEC
Analytical Methodology Information Center [Environmental Protection
  Agency] .... AMIC
Analytical Methods Committee (SAUO) .... AMC
Analytical Methods, Inc. .... AMI
Analytical Methods/Inorganic .... AMI
Analytical Methods/Organic .... AMO
Analytical Methods/Partial .... AMP
Analytical Mode for Performing Logistic Evaluation (DNAB) ..... AMPLE
Analytical Nuclear Casualty Estimation Technique (PDAA) ...... ANCET
Analytical Photogrametric Positioning System (SAUS) ...... APPS
Analytical Photogrammetric Positioning System (MCD) ..... APPS
Analytical Photogrammetric Positioning System - II .... APPS II
Analytical Photogrammetric Processing System (MCD) ...... APPS
Analytical Photogrammetry Applications Consortium (SAUO) ..... APACE
Analytical Plotter (GEOI) .... AP
Analytical Procedures Subsystem (MCD) .... APS
Analytical Processing for Improved Composite (MCD) .... APIC
Analytical Processing Unit (SAUS) .... APU
Analytical Profile Index [Microbiology] .... API
Analytical Psychology .... AP
Analytical Psychology Club of New York (EA) .... APCNY
Analytical Quality Assurance (HEAS) .... AQUA

Analytical Quality Control Laboratory (IID)	AQCL
Analytical Quality Control Services (SAUS)	AQCS
Analytical Reagent [Chemistry]	AR
Analytical Reports Gathering and Updating System [Navy] (NG)	ARGUS
Analytical Research and Development Unit [British]	ARDU
Analytical Results Database	ARDB
Analytical Rework Program [Navy] (NG)	ARP
Analytical Satellite Orbit Predictor (MCD)	ASOP
Analytical Scanning Electron Microscope	ASEM
Analytical Services Progam	ASP
Analytical Solution of Groups [Thermodynamics]	ASOG
Analytical Spectral Devices (ARMP)	ASD
Analytical Spectral Devices, Inc. (SAUO)	ASD
Analytical Stereoplotter (DNAB)	AS
Analytical Studies of Surface Effects of Submerged Submarines [Navy] (DNAB)	ASSES
Analytical Studies of Surface Effects of Submerged Submarines [Navy]	ASSESS
Analytical Surveys [NASDAQ symbol] (TTSB)	ANLT
Analytical Surveys, Inc. [NASDAQ symbol] (NQ)	ANLT
Analytical Surveys, Inc. [Associated Press] (SAG)	AnlySur
Analytical Surveys Incorporated (SAUO)	ASI
Analytical Technology Applications Corp.	ATAC
Analytical Transient One-, Two-, and Three-Dimensional Model	AT123D
Analytical Transmission Electron Microscope	ATEM
Analytical Tree [Method used to analyze and design physical security for facilities] [Military] (RDA)	AT
Analytical Ultracentrifugation [Separation science]	AU
Analyze (MSA)	ANALY
Analyze Sample Pulse (SAUS)	ASP
Analyzed Reagent (SAUS)	ar
Analyzer	ANLYZ
Analyzer for FORTRAN [Formula Translation] Incremental Reengineering Methodology	AFFIRM
Analyzer Unit (CAAL)	AU
Analyzer/Classifier (IUSS)	A/C
Analyzer-Recorder-Controller	ARC
Anamilo Club of Detroit [Michigan] (EA)	ACD
Anamosa Eureka, Anamosa, IA [Library symbol] [Library of Congress] (LCLS)	IaAnaE
Anamosa, IA [AM radio station call letters]	KLEH
Anamosa Journal, Anamosa, IA [Library symbol] [Library of Congress] (LCLS)	IaAnaJ
Anamosa Public Library, Anamosa, IA [Library symbol] [Library of Congress] (LCLS)	IaAna
Ananda Marga (EA)	AM
Ananda Marga Universal Relief Team [India]	AMURT
Ananda Marga Women's Center [Australia]	AMWC
Ananeotiko Demokratiko Socialistiko Kinema [Democratic Socialist Reform Movement] [Cyprus] [Political party] (EY)	ADISOK
Anangel American Shipholdings Ltd. [Associated Press] (SAG)	Anangel
Anangel American Shipholdings Ltd. [NASDAQ symbol] (SAG)	ASIP
Anangel-Amer ShipHldgs ADS [NASDAQ symbol] (TTSB)	ASIPY
Anaphase-Promoting Complex [Cytology]	APC
Anaphylactoid Purpura [Medicine]	AP
Anaphylactoid Reaction [Immunology]	AR
Anaphylatoxin [Immunology]	AT
Anaphylaxis [Medicine]	A
Anaphylaxis [Medicine] (MELL)	APL
Anaplastic Anaemia [Medicine]	AA
Anaplastic Lymphoma Kinase [An enzyme]	ALK
Anapolis [Brazil] [Airport symbol] (AD)	APS
Anapolis (Base Aerea) [Brazil] [ICAO location identifier] (ICLI)	SBAN
Anar [Iran] [ICAO location identifier] (ICLI)	OIKE
[The] Anarchiad [American satirical epic poem, 1786-1787]	Anarch
Anarchist Association of the Americas [Defunct] (EA)	AAA
Anarchist Black Cross (SAUO)	ABC
Anarchist Federation [British]	AF
Anarchist Federation of Britain	AFB
Anarchist Red Cross	ARC
Anarchist-Communist Federation of North America [Canada]	ACFNA
ANARE Mapping and Geographic Information Committee (SAUO)	ANAREMAGIC
Anaren Microwave [NASDAQ symbol] (TTSB)	ANEN
Anaren Microwave, Inc. [Associated Press] (SAG)	Anaren
Anaren Microwave, Inc. [NASDAQ symbol] (NQ)	ANEN
Anastomosing Cell (SAUS)	AC
Anastomosis [Medicine] (MAE)	anast
Anastomosis Between Bile Duct and Jejunum [Medicine] (MELL)	ABJ
Anastomosis Group [Plant pathology]	AG
Anatech International Corp. [La Jolla, CA]	ANA
anathema (SAUS)	anath
anathematize (SAUS)	anath
Anatolian Fault Zone (SAUS)	AFZ
Anatom [Vanuatu] [ICAO location identifier] (ICLI)	NVVA
Anatomia, Histologia, Embryologia (journ.) (SAUS)	Anat Histol Embryol
Anatomic [Anatomy] (DAVI)	an
Anatomic Porous Replacement [Orthopedics] (DAVI)	APR
Anatomic Shunt Flow [Medicine] (DAVI)	Qsan
Anatomical (ADWA)	anat
Anatomical Dead Space (DAVI)	ADS
Anatomical Diffusion Factor [Physiology]	ADF
Anatomical Society of Great Britain and Ireland (DAVI)	ASGB
Anatomical Society of Great Britain and Ireland	ASGBI
Anatomical Society of Great Britain and Ireland (SAUO)	ASGBI

Anatomical Therapeutic Chemical Classification system for drugs (SAUO)	ATC Classification
Anatomical Transplant Association (SAUO)	ATA
Anatomical Transplant Association of California (SAUO)	ATAC
Anatomie [Anatomy] [German]	Anat
Anatomische Gesellschaft [Anatomical Society] [Germany] (EAIO)	AG
Anatomische Hefte (journ.) (SAUS)	AnH
Anatomist (SAUS)	Anat
Anatomy [or Anatomical]	ANAT
Anatomy (WDAA)	anat
Anatomy, Anthropology, Embryology and Histology (journ.) (SAUS)	Anat Anthropol Embryol Histol
Anatomy Covering Material (SAUS)	ACM
Anatomy Covering Memo (SAUS)	ACM
Anatuberculin, Pertragnani's Integral [Pharmacology] (DAVI)	AIP
Anatuberculina Diagnostica Petragnani [Petragnani Diagnostic Anatuberculin] [Medicine]	ADP
Anavatan Partisi [Motherland Parties] (EAIO)	AP
Anax Aviation [France] [ICAO designator] (FAAC)	ANX
ANB Corp. [Associated Press] (SAG)	ANB
ANB Corp. [NASDAQ symbol] (SAG)	ANBC
ANB Corp. [Associated Press] (SAG)	ANB Corp
Anbar Management Services Joint Index (journ.) (SAUS)	Anbar Mgmt Serv
Ancaster High and Vocational School, Ontario [Library symbol] [National Library of Canada] (NLC)	OAH
Ancenis [France] [ICAO location identifier] (ICLI)	LFFI
Ancestor	ANC
Ancestor Chart [Genealogy] (GEAB)	AC
Ancestry (GEAB)	anc
Ancestry Research Club (EA)	ARC
Anches [Reeds] [Music]	ANCH
Ancho Canyon (SAUS)	AC
Anchor (MSA)	AHR
Anchor	ANCHR
Anchor Bancorp (SPSG)	ABKR
Anchor Bancorp Wisc [NASDAQ symbol] (TTSB)	ABCW
Anchor Bancorp Wisconsin, Inc. [NASDAQ symbol] (SAG)	ABCW
Anchor Bancorp Wisconsin, Inc. [Associated Press] (SAG)	AncBWI
Anchor Bible Commentary [A publication] (BJA)	ABC
Anchor Bible Dictionary [A publication]	ABD
Anchor Block Foundation (EA)	ABF
Anchor Bolt [Technical drawings]	AB
Anchor Examined (SAUS)	E
Anchor Financial Corp. [NASDAQ symbol] (SAG)	AFSC
Anchor Financial Corp. [Associated Press] (SAG)	AnchFin
Anchor Gaming [Associated Press] (SAG)	AnchGm
Anchor Gaming [NASDAQ symbol] (SAG)	SLOT
Anchor Glass Container Corp. (SAUO)	ANC
Anchor Gold Corp. [Vancouver Stock Exchange symbol]	AHG
Anchor Handling (RIMS)	A/H
Anchor Handling Salvage Tug (DS)	AHST
Anchor Handling Tug (DS)	AHT
Anchor Handling Tug Supply Vessel (DS)	AHTS
Anchor Hocking Corp. (SAUO)	ARH
Anchor Light (SAUS)	ANLT
Anchor Line [Steamship] (MHDW)	A
Anchor Line Ltd. [Steamship] (MHDB)	ALL
Anchor Machine & Manufacturing Ltd. [Toronto Stock Exchange symbol]	AKC
Anchor Order (MSA)	AOR
Anchor Placement Equipment	APE
Anchor Tested (SAUS)	T
Anchor Volume Descriptor Pointer (SAUS)	AVPD
Anchor Windlass	AWNDLS
Anchorage [Alaska Methodist University] [Alaska] [Seismograph station code, US Geological Survey] [Closed] (SEIS)	AMU
Anchorage [Alaska] [Airport symbol] (OAG)	ANC
Anchorage [Maps and charts]	ANCH
Anchorage [Alaska] [ICAO location identifier] (ICLI)	PAZA
Anchorage, AK [Location identifier] [FAA] (FAAL)	CMQ
Anchorage, AK [Location identifier] [FAA] (FAAL)	EDF
Anchorage, AK [FM radio station call letters] (BROA)	KAFC-FM
Anchorage, AK [Television station call letters]	KAKM
Anchorage, AK [FM radio station call letters]	KASH
Anchorage, AK [FM radio station call letters]	KATB
Anchorage, AK [FM radio station call letters]	KBFX
Anchorage, AK [FM radio station call letters]	KBRJ
Anchorage, AK [AM radio station call letters]	KBYR
Anchorage, AK [Television station call letters]	KDMD
Anchorage, AK [FM radio station call letters]	KEAG
Anchorage, AK [AM radio station call letters]	KENI
Anchorage, AK [FM radio station call letters] (BROA)	KFAT-FM
Anchorage, AK [AM radio station call letters]	KFQD
Anchorage, AK [FM radio station call letters]	KGOT
Anchorage, AK [AM radio station call letters]	KHAR
Anchorage, AK [Television station call letters]	KIMO
Anchorage, AK [AM radio station call letters]	KKRO
Anchorage, AK [FM radio station call letters]	KLEF
Anchorage, AK [FM radio station call letters] (RBYB)	KMXS
Anchorage, AK [FM radio station call letters] (RBYB)	KNBA-FM
Anchorage, AK [FM radio station call letters]	KNIK
Anchorage, AK [FM radio station call letters]	KRUA
Anchorage, AK [FM radio station call letters]	KSKA
Anchorage, AK [Television station call letters]	KTBY
Anchorage, AK [Television station call letters]	KTUU-TV
Anchorage, AK [Television station call letters]	KTVA

Anchorage, AK [*AM radio station call letters*] (BROA) ... KTZN
Anchorage, AK [*FM radio station call letters*] ... KWHL
Anchorage, AK [*FM radio station call letters*] (RBYB) ... KWQJ-FM
Anchorage, AK [*AM radio station call letters*] ... KYAK
Anchorage, AK [*Television station call letters*] ... KYES
Anchorage, AK [*FM radio station call letters*] ... KYMG
Anchorage, AK [*Television station call letters*] ... KZXC
Anchorage, AK [*Location identifier*] [*FAA*] (FAAL) ... LHD
Anchorage, AK [*Location identifier*] [*FAA*] (FAAL) ... MRI
Anchorage, AK [*Location identifier*] [*FAA*] (FAAL) ... TGN
Anchorage, AK [*Location identifier*] [*FAA*] (FAAL) ... ZAN
Anchorage Community College, Anchorage, AK [*Library symbol*] [*Library of Congress*] (LCLS) ... AkAC
Anchorage Convention & Visitors Bureau (SAUO) ... ACVB
Anchorage Dependent Cell [*Culture technology*] ... ADC
Anchorage Family Investment Center (SAUO) ... AFIC
Anchorage Higher Education Consortium Library, Anchorage, AK [*Library symbol*] [*Library of Congress*] (LCLS) ... AkACon
Anchorage Museum of History and Art (SAUS) ... AMHA
Anchorage Neighborhood Housing Services (SAUO) ... ANHS
Anchorage Police Department (SAUO) ... APD
Anchorage Prohibited [*Nautical charts*] ... Anch Prohib
Anchorage School District, Library Resources, Anchorage, AK [*Library symbol*] [*Library of Congress*] (LCLS) ... AkAS
Anchorage Telephone Utility (SAUO) ... ATU
Anchorage/Elmendorf Air Force Base [*Alaska*] [*ICAO location identifier*] (ICLI) ... PAED
Anchorage/Ft. Richardson, AK [*Location identifier*] [*FAA*] (FAAL) ... CSR
Anchorage/International [*Alaska*] [*ICAO location identifier*] (ICLI) ... PANC
Anchorage/Merrill Field [*Alaska*] [*ICAO location identifier*] (ICLI) ... PAMR
Anchored ... ANCH
Anchored Catheter [*Medicine*] ... A/C
Anchored Cell Analysis and Sorting [*Cell culture*] ... ACAS
Anchored Filament ... ANCFIL
Anchored Filament ... ANF
Anchored Interplanetary Monitoring Platform ... AIMP
Anchored Polymerase Chain Reaction [*Genetics*] ... A-PCR
Anchored Radio Sonobuoy ... ARSB
Anchored Radio Sound Buoy (SAUS) ... ARSB
Anchored Radiosight ... ARS
Anchoring Fibril [*Anatomy*] ... AF
Anchorite ... A
Anchors and Chains Proved [*Shipping*] ... A & CP
Anchors and Chains Proved (SAUS) ... ACP
Ancien Testament [*Old Testament*] [*French*] ... AT
Anciens Moudjahidine et Victimes de la Guerre [*War Veterans and Victims*] [*Algeria*] ... AMVG
Ancient ... ANC
Ancient (VRA) ... anc
Ancient ... ANCNT
Ancient ... ANCT
Ancient Accepted Scottish Rite of Freemasonry, Northern Masonic Jurisdiction (SAUO) ... AASR-NMJ
Ancient American Rocket Pioneers (SAUS) ... AARP
Ancient and Accepted [*Freemasonry*] ... A and A
Ancient and Accepted Rite [*Freemasonry*] ... A and AR
Ancient and Accepted Scottish Rite [*Freemasonry*] (ROG) ... A & ASR
Ancient and Accepted Scottish Rite [*Freemasonry*] ... AASR
Ancient and Accepted Scottish Rite Masons (SAUO) ... AASRM
Ancient and Accepted Scottish Rite of Freemasonry, Southern Masonic Jurisdiction (SAUO) ... AASR-SMJ
Ancient and Honorable Artillery Co. of Massachusetts (EA) ... AHACM
Ancient and Honorable Artillery Company of Massachusetts (EA) ... A & HAC
Ancient and Honourable Guild of Town Criers (EAIO) ... AHGTC
Ancient and Illustrious Order Knights of Malta [*East Canton, OH*] (EA) ... AIOK of M
Ancient and Illustrous Order Knights of Malta (SAUO) ... AIOK of M
Ancient and Modern [*Hymns*] ... A and M
Ancient and Modern (SAUS) ... A&M
Ancient and Modern Palestine [*A publication*] (BJA) ... AMP
Ancient Arabic Order of Nobles of the Mystic Shrine (SAUS) ... AAONMS
Ancient Arabic Order of the Nobles of the Mystic Shrine (SAUO) ... AAONMS
Ancient Arts Fellowship [*Australia*] ... AAF
Ancient Astronaut Society (EA) ... AAS
Ancient Charters [*1692*] [*A publication*] (DLA) ... Anc Charters
Ancient Christian Writers [*A publication*] (ODCC) ... ACW
Ancient Christian Writers (journ.) (SAUS) ... ACW
Ancient Classics for English Readers [*A publication*] ... ACER
Ancient Conserved Region [*Genetics*] ... ACR
Ancient Dialogue upon the Exchequer [*A publication*] (DLA) ... Anc Dial Exch
Ancient Egypt Research Associates ... AERA
Ancient Egyptian Arabic Order Nobles of the Mystic Shrine (EA) ... AEAONMS
Ancient Egyptian Arabic Order Nobles of the Mystic Shrine (EA) ... NMS
Ancient Egyptian Order of Sciots (EA) ... AEOS
Ancient Egyptian Order of Sciots, Supreme Pyramid (SAUO) ... AEOS
Ancient English Christmas Carols [*A publication*] ... AnEC
Ancient Forest International [*An association*] ... AFI
Ancient Free and Accepted Masons [*Freemasonry*] ... AFAM
Ancient Free and Accepted Masons [*Freemasonry*] ... AF & AM
Ancient Freemasons ... AFM
Ancient Gneiss Complex [*Geology*] ... AGC
Ancient Greek (SAUS) ... Agreek
Ancient History Documents Research Center [*Macquarie University*] [*Australia*] ... AHDRC
Ancient Israel: Its Life and Institutions [*A publication*] (BJA) ... AncIsr
Ancient Mediterranean Research Association (EA) ... AMRA
Ancient Monuments Act [*Town planning*] [*British*] ... AM
Ancient Monuments Inspectorate (SAUO) ... AMI
Ancient Monuments Society (EAIO) ... AMS
Ancient Monuments Society. Transactions (journ.) (SAUS) ... T Anc Monum
Ancient Mystic Order of Bagmen of Bagdad Imperial Guild [*Roanoke, VA*] (EA) ... AMOB
Ancient Mystic Order of Samaritans (EA) ... AMOS
Ancient Mystical Order Rosae Crucis [*Rosicrucian Order*] (EA) ... AMORC
Ancient Near East (BJA) ... ANE
[*The*] **Ancient Near East in Pictures** [*A publication*] (BJA) ... ANEP
Ancient Near East in Pictures (journ.) (SAUS) ... ANEP
Ancient Near Eastern Texts Relating to the Old Testament [*A publication*] (BJA) ... ANET
Ancient Order of Druids ... AOD
Ancient Order of Druids (SAUO) ... D
Ancient Order of Foresters (SAUO) ... AOER
[*The*] **Ancient Order of Foresters** ... AOF
[*The*] **Ancient Order of Foresters** [*Freemasonry*] (ROG) ... FOREST
Ancient Order of Foresters of California [*Later, AOFPCJ*] (EA) ... AOFC
Ancient Order of Foresters of the Pacific Coast Jurisdiction [*Hilo, HI*] (EA) ... AOFPCJ
Ancient Order of Frothblowers [*British*] ... AOFB
Ancient Order of Frothblowers (SAUO) ... AOFB
Ancient Order of Hibernians in America (EA) ... AOH
Ancient Order of Maccabeans (BJA) ... AOM
Ancient Order of Shepherds ... AOS
Ancient Order of Shepherds (SAUO) ... AOS
Ancient Order of Shepherds (SAUO) ... AOSs
Ancient Order United Workmen [*Seattle, WA*] (EA) ... AOUW
Ancient Parish ... AP
Ancient Peoples and Places (journ.) (SAUS) ... APP
Ancient Petition ... AP
Ancient Philosophies for Modern Readers [*A publication*] ... APMR
Ancient Records of Assyria [*A publication*] (BJA) ... ARA
Ancient Records of Assyria and Babylonia [*A publication*] (BJA) ... ARAB
Ancient Records of Egypt [*A publication*] (BJA) ... ARE
Ancient World on Television (SAUS) ... AWOTV
Ancient York Mason [*Freemasonry*] ... AYM
Ancient York Masonry (SAUO) ... AYM
Ancilla College [*Formerly, Ancilla Domini College*] [*Donaldson, IN*] ... AC
Ancillae Sacri Cordis Jesu [*Handmaids of the Sacred Heart of Jesus*] [*Roman Catholic religious order*] ... ACJ
Ancillary (MCD) ... ANC
Ancillary (MCD) ... ANCIL
Ancillary Armament Equipment (DNAB) ... AAE
Ancillary Communications Services [*Australia*] ... ACS
Ancillary Composing Equipment (DGA) ... ACE
Ancillary Control Processor ... ACP
Ancillary Control Program (SAUS) ... ACP
Ancillary Data Service (SAUS) ... ADS
Ancillary Education Establishment ... AEE
Ancillary Equipment (SAUS) ... AE
Ancillary Services Review Program [*Health insurance*] (GHCT) ... ASRP
anclent (SAUS) ... anc
Ancom ATM International, Inc. [*Toronto Stock Exchange symbol*] ... ANY
Ancon [*Peru*] [*ICAO location identifier*] (ICLI) ... SPNO
Ancona [*Italy*] [*Airport symbol*] (OAG) ... AOI
Ancona/Falconara [*Italy*] [*ICAO location identifier*] (ICLI) ... LIPY
Ancor Communications [*Associated Press*] (SAG) ... AncorCm
Ancor Communicatons [*NASDAQ symbol*] (SAG) ... ANCR
Ancud [*Chile*] [*Airport symbol*] (AD) ... ZUD
Ancud/Pupelde [*Chile*] [*ICAO location identifier*] (ICLI) ... SCAC
And (ROG) ... A
, and Chassigny [*Egypt*] [*Pronounced "snick"*] [*Classification for a group of meteorites recovered from these sites*] [*French*] ... SNC
AND Circuit (SAUS) ... AC
And Elsewhere [*Mathematics*] ... ae
AND Extender (SAUS) ... AX
And Gate [*Logic element*] [*Computer science*] ... AG
AND Inverter (SAUS) ... AI
AND JEF - Parti Africain pour la Democratie et le Socialisme [*Senegal*] [*Political party*] (EY) ... AJ-PADS
AND Module (SAUS) ... AM
, and Nancy [*Dickerman*] [*Cook*] [*Democratic Party activists*] ... EMN
AND Operation (SAUS) ... AO
AND Operator (SAUS) ... AO
And Others ... AO
AND Power Inverter (SAUS) ... API
And So Forth [*Et cetera*] [*Latin*] (WDMC) ... etc
And So To Bed [*Commercial firm*] [*British*] ... ASTB
and Subassembly Facility [*or Refurbishment*] [*NASA*] (NASA) ... SRSF
And The Following [*A notation*] (WDMC) ... et seq
and the following (SAUS) ... et seq
and the following pages, sections, etc. (SAUS) ... ff
AND to Accumulator (SAUS) ... ANA
AND to Storage (SAUS) ... ANS
And Where Can I Get One (SAUS) ... AWCIGO
Andahuaylas [*Peru*] [*Airport symbol*] [*Obsolete*] (OAG) ... ANS
Andahuaylas [*Peru*] [*ICAO location identifier*] (ICLI) ... SPHY
Andalgala [*Argentina*] [*Seismograph station code, US Geological Survey*] [*Closed*] (SEIS) ... ANL
Andalusia, AL [*Location identifier*] [*FAA*] (FAAL) ... JUY
Andalusia, AL [*Location identifier*] [*FAA*] (FAAL) ... RIU
Andalusia, AL [*FM radio station call letters*] ... WAAO

Andalusia, AL [*AM radio station call letters*] ... WKYD
Andalusia, AL [*FM radio station call letters*] (RBYB) ... WSTF
Andalusia, AL [*FM radio station call letters*] (RBYB) ... WWSF
Andalusian Horse Registry (EA) ... AHR
Andalusite (SAUS) ... AD
Andalusite [*Mineralogy*] ... AND
Andaman and Nicobar Islands (SAUS) ... A&NI
Andaman Islands ... AND
Andamooka [*Australia*] [*Airport symbol*] (OAG) ... ADO
Andante [*Slow*] [*Music*] ... AND
Andante (ADWA) ... and
Andante [*Slow*] [*Music*] ... ANDTE
Andantino [*Slow*] [*Music*] ... ANDNO
Andantino [*Slow*] [*Music*] ... ANDO
Andapa [*Madagascar*] [*ICAO location identifier*] (ICLI) ... FMND
Andapa [*Madagascar*] [*Airport symbol*] (OAG) ... ZWA
Andataco, Inc. [*NASDAQ symbol*] [*Formerly, IPL Systems*] ... ANDA
Andaurex Resources, Inc. [*Vancouver Stock Exchange symbol*] ... AWX
Andco, Inc., Buffalo, NY [*Library symbol*] [*Library of Congress*] (LCLS) ... NBuAn
Andean Amazon Rivers Analysis and Monitoring Project (SAUS) ... AARAM
Andean Area [*MARC geographic area code*] [*Library of Congress*] (LCCP) ... sn---
Andean Commission of Jurists [*See also CAJ*] (EAIO) ... ACJ
Andean Common Market (EAIO) ... ANCOM
Andean Community-Colombia, Bolivia, Ecuador, Venezuela and Peru (SAUO) ... INEN
Andean Development Corp. [*NASDAQ symbol*] (SAG) ... ADCC
Andean Development Corp. [*Associated Press*] (SAG) ... Andean
Andean Development Corp. [*Associated Press*] (SAG) ... AndeanD
Andean Development Corporation (SAUO) ... IADC
Andean Federation for Pharmacy and Biochemistry (SAUO) ... FEDALFARBIO
Andean Group ... AG
Andean Nations Satellite Communications System (ACAE) ... ANSCS
Andean Pact Organization [*Chile, Peru, Bolivia, Ecuador, Colombia*] ... APO
Andean Potato Latent Virus [*Plant pathology*] ... APLV
Andean Potato Mottle Virus [*Plant pathology*] ... APMV
Andean Potato Mottle Virus (SAUS) ... ApNfV
Andean Report (journ.) (SAUS) ... Andean Rpt
Andean Reserve Fund (SAUO) ... AFR
Andean Reserve Fund (SAUO) ... ARF
Andean Trade Preference Act ... ATPA
Andelin Foundation for Education in Family Living (EA) ... AFEFL
Anden Community (SAUO) ... ANCOM
Andenes [*Norway*] [*Airport symbol*] (OAG) ... ANX
Andere [*Other*] [*German*] ... and
Andernos-Les-Bains [*France*] [*ICAO location identifier*] (ICLI) ... LFCD
Anders Gaan Leven [*Live Differently*] [*Belgium*] [*Political party*] (PPW) ... AGALEV
Anders Gaan Leven-Geweldloos, Rechtvaardig, Open Ecologisch Netwerk [*Belgium*] [*Political party*] (ECED) ... A-G
Andersen Air Force Base, Guam Island [*Mariana Islands*] [*ICAO location identifier*] (ICLI) ... PGUA
Andersen Group [*NASDAQ symbol*] (TTSB) ... ANDR
Andersen Group, Inc. [*NASDAQ symbol*] (NQ) ... ANDR
Andersen Group, Inc. [*Associated Press*] (SAG) ... AndrGr
Andersen Laboratories, Inc. ... AL
Andersen-Collingwood (SAUO) ... ANCO
Anderson [*South Carolina*] [*Airport symbol*] (OAG) ... AND
Anderson - Darling Test [*Statistics*] ... AD
Anderson Air Force Base Flightline ... AAFBF
Anderson Associates Ltd., Willowdale, Ontario [*Library symbol*] [*National Library of Canada*] (NLC) ... OWAA
Anderson Aviation, Inc. [*FAA designator*] (FAAC) ... ADX
Anderson, CA [*FM radio station call letters*] ... KEWB
Anderson Carnegie Public Library, Anderson, IN [*Library symbol*] [*Library of Congress*] (LCLS) ... InAnd
Anderson, Clayton and Co. (SAUO) ... AYL
Anderson, Clayton & Co., Foods Division Technical Library Dallas (SAUS) ... TxDaAC
Anderson, Clayton & Co., Foods Division Technical Library, Dallas, TX [*Library symbol*] [*Library of Congress*] (LCLS) ... TxDaAC
Anderson Clayton Foods [*of Anderson, Clayton & Co.*], **Richardson, TX** [*Library symbol*] [*Library of Congress*] (LCLS) ... TxRiA
Anderson Co. ... ANCO
Anderson College (SAUO) ... AC
Anderson College, Anderson, IN [*OCLC symbol*] (OCLC) ... INA
Anderson College, Anderson, IN [*Library symbol*] [*Library of Congress*] (LCLS) ... InAndC
Anderson College, Anderson, SC [*Library symbol*] [*Library of Congress*] (LCLS) ... ScAnC
Anderson College, Graduate School of Theology, Anderson, IN [*Library symbol*] [*Library of Congress*] (LCLS) ... InAcdC-T
Anderson College, Graduate School of Theology, Anderson, IN [*Library symbol*] [*Library of Congress*] (LCLS) ... InAndC-T
Anderson Company (SAUO) ... ANCO
Anderson County Library (SAUS) ... SAL
Anderson County Library (SAUS) ... ScAn
Anderson County Library, Anderson, SC [*OCLC symbol*] (OCLC) ... SAL
Anderson County Library, Anderson, SC [*Library symbol*] [*Library of Congress*] (LCLS) ... ScAn
Anderson Daily Bulletin, Anderson, IN [*Library symbol*] [*Library of Congress*] (LCLS) ... InAndB
Anderson Exploration [*Toronto Stock Exchange symbol*] (SG) ... AXL
Anderson Exploration Ltd. [*Toronto Stock Exchange symbol*] ... AXL
Anderson Galleries ... AG
Anderson, Greenwood & Co. (SAUO) ... AGCO
Anderson Herald, Anderson, IN [*Library symbol*] [*Library of Congress*] (LCLS) ... InAndH
Anderson Hospital for Cancer Research (SAUO) ... AHFCR
Anderson, IN [*Location identifier*] [*FAA*] (FAAL) ... AID
Anderson, IN [*FM radio station call letters*] (RBYB) ... WBSB-FM
Anderson, IN [*AM radio station call letters*] (BROA) ... WGNR
Anderson, IN [*AM radio station call letters*] ... WHBU
Anderson, IN [*AM radio station call letters*] ... WHUT
Anderson, IN [*FM radio station call letters*] ... WQME
Anderson, IN [*FM radio station call letters*] ... WXXP
Anderson Industries, Inc. (SAUO) ... ANDS
Anderson Junior College (SAUO) ... AJC
Anderson [*H. H.*] **Line** [*Steamship*] (MHDB) ... HHA
Anderson Localization. Proceedings. Taniguchi International Symposium (journ.) (SAUS) ... Anderson Localization Proc Taniguchi Int Symp
Anderson Model [*Physics*] ... AM
Anderson on Church Wardens [*A publication*] (DLA) ... And Ch W
Anderson Public Library, Anderson, IN [*OCLC symbol*] (OCLC) ... IAM
Anderson Reservoir [*California*] [*Seismograph station code, US Geological Survey*] (SEIS) ... ADR
Anderson, SC [*Location identifier*] [*FAA*] (FAAL) ... ELW
Anderson, SC [*AM radio station call letters*] ... WAIM
Anderson, SC [*AM radio station call letters*] ... WANS
Anderson, SC [*Television station call letters*] (RBYB) ... WFBC-TV
Anderson, SC [*FM radio station call letters*] ... WJMZ
Anderson, SC [*FM radio station call letters*] ... WROQ
Anderson-Brinkman-Morel State [*Superconductivity*] ... ABM
Anderson's Agricultural Decisions [*Scotland*] [*A publication*] (DLA) ... And Agr Dec
Anderson's Agriculture Cases [*England*] [*A publication*] (DLA) ... And
Anderson's English Common Pleas Reports [*1534-1605*] [*A publication*] (DLA) ... And
Anderson's Examination Questions and Answers [*A publication*] (DLA) ... And Q & A
Andersons Examination Questions and Answers (journ.) (SAUS) ... AndQ&A
Anderson's History of Commerce [*A publication*] (DLA) ... And Com
Andersons Inc. [*NASDAQ symbol*] (TTSB) ... ANDE
Anderson's Law Dictionary [*A publication*] (DLA) ... And Law Dict
Anderson's Reports, English Court of Common Pleas [*A publication*] (DLA) ... Ander (Eng)
Anderson's Reports, English Court of Common Pleas [*A publication*] (DLA) ... Anders
Anderson's Reports, English Court of Common Pleas [*A publication*] (DLA) ... Anderson
Anderson's Uniform Commercial Code [*A publication*] (DLA) ... Anderson UCC
Anderstorp [*Sweden*] [*ICAO location identifier*] (ICLI) ... ESMP
Andes Pact (SAUO) ... AP
Andhra Agricultural Journal (journ.) (SAUS) ... Andhra Agric J
Andhra Agricultural Journal (journ.) (SAUS) ... Andhra Agr J
Andhra Pradesh [*State in southeast India*] ... AP
Andhra Pradesh Ground Water Department. District Series (journ.) (SAUS) ... Andhra Pradesh Ground Water Dep Dist Ser
Andhra Pradesh Ground Water Department. Research Series (journ.) (SAUS) ... Andhra Pradesh Ground Water Dep Res Ser
Andhra Pradesh Industrial Development Corporation (SAUO) ... APIDC
Andhra Pradesh Mining Corporation (SAUO) ... APMC
Andhra Pradesh Small Scale Industrial Development Corporation (SAUO) ... APSSIDC
Andhra Pradesh State Financial Corporation (SAUO) ... APSFC
Andhra Pradesh State Road Transport Corporation (SAUO) ... APSTC
Andhra University (SAUO) ... And
Andimeshk [*Iran*] [*ICAO location identifier*] (ICLI) ... OIAN
Andizhan [*Former USSR*] [*Seismograph station code, US Geological Survey*] (SEIS) ... ANR
AND-JEF/Mouvement Revolutionnaire pour la Democratie Nouvelle [*AND-JEF/New Democratic Revolutionary Movement*] [*Senegal*] [*Political party*] ... AJ/MRDN
Andkhoi [*Afghanistan*] [*ICAO location identifier*] (ICLI) ... OAAK
Andocides [*Fifth century BC*] [*Classical studies*] (OCD) ... Andoc
Andong [*South Korea*] [*ICAO location identifier*] (ICLI) ... RKTA
And/Or (SAUS) ... AOR
And/Or ... A/OR
And-Or Amplifier (HGAA) ... AO AMPL
AND-OR Amplifier (SAUS) ... A-O-AMPL
AND-OR Delay (SAUS) ... AOD
AND-OR Extender (SAUS) ... AOX
AND/OR Graph (SAUS) ... AOG
And-Or Invert (IEEE) ... AOI
AND-OR Trigger (SAUS) ... AOT
Andoraq Resources Corp. [*Vancouver Stock Exchange symbol*] ... ARQ
AND-OR-Invert Gate (SAUS) ... AOI-Gate
Andorra [*ANSI two-letter standard code*] (CNC) ... AD
Andorra [*MARC country of publication code*] [*Library of Congress*] (LCCP) ... an
Andorra [*ANSI three-letter standard code*] (CNC) ... AND
Andorra [*MARC geographic area code*] [*Library of Congress*] (LCCP) ... e-an-
Andorran (ADWA) ... And
Andorran Philately Study Circle [*Defunct*] (EA) ... APSC
Andover Bancorp [*NASDAQ symbol*] (TTSB) ... ANDB
Andover Bancorp, Inc. [*NASDAQ symbol*] (NQ) ... ANDB
Andover Bancorp, Inc. [*Associated Press*] (SAG) ... AndvBc
Andover Controls Corp. (SAUO) ... ANDO
Andover Distributors Association (EA) ... ADA
Andover Historical Society, Andover, MA [*Library symbol*] [*Library of Congress*] (LCLS) ... MAnHi
Andover, KS [*FM radio station call letters*] (RBYB) ... KDGS

Andover, MA [*FM radio station call letters*] ... WPAA
Andover Newton Theological School [*Newton Center, MA*] ... ANTS
Andover Newton Theological School, Newton Center, MA [*OCLC symbol*] (OCLC) ... BAN
Andover Newton Theological School, Newton Center, MA [*Library symbol*] [*Library of Congress*] (LCLS) ... MNtcA
Andover Service Center [*IRS*] ... ANSC
Andover Togs, Inc. [*Associated Press*] (SAG) ... AndvTog
Andover Togs, Inc. [*NASDAQ symbol*] (NQ) ... ATOG
Andover Training Flight (SAUS) ... ATF
Andoya [*Norway*] [*ICAO location identifier*] (ICLI) ... ENAN
Andra Pradesh (SAUS) ... AP
Andradina [*Brazil*] [*Airport symbol*] (AD) ... ARD
Andravida [*Greece*] [*ICAO location identifier*] (ICLI) ... LGAD
Andre and Coquelin [*Often used as a pattern on clothes designed by Courreges, the initials represent the first names of the couturier and his wife*] ... AC
Andre Marsan & Associes, Inc., Montreal, PQ, Canada [*Library symbol*] [*Library of Congress*] (LCLS) ... CaQMAMA
Andrea Airlines SA [*Peru*] [*ICAO designator*] (FAAC) ... NDR
Andrea Electronics [*AMEX symbol*] (TTSB) ... AND
Andrea Electronics Corp. [*AMEX symbol*] (SPSG) ... AND
Andrea Electronics Corp. [*Associated Press*] (SAG) ... Andrea
Andrea McArdle Fan Club (EA) ... AMFC
Andrea Radio Corp. (SAUO) ... ANDREA
Andreafsky/St. Marys, AK [*Location identifier*] [*FAA*] (FAAL) ... SMA
Andreas Acconzaioco de Ravello [*Flourished, 1294-1300*] [*Authority cited in pre-1607 legal work*] (DSA) ... Andr Acza
Andreas Acconzaioco de Ravello [*Flourished, 1294-1300*] [*Authority cited in pre-1607 legal work*] (DSA) ... Andr Azaio
Andreas Acconzaioco de Ravello [*Flourished, 1294-1300*] [*Authority cited in pre-1607 legal work*] (DSA) ... Andr de Ra
Andreas Alciatus [*Deceased, 1550*] [*Authority cited in pre-1607 legal work*] (DSA) ... A Alciat
Andreas Alciatus [*Deceased, 1550*] [*Authority cited in pre-1607 legal work*] (DSA) ... Andr Alciat
Andreas Bonellus de Barulo [*Flourished, 1260-71*] [*Authority cited in pre-1607 legal work*] (DSA) ... A de Ba
Andreas Bonellus de Barulo [*Flourished, 1260-71*] [*Authority cited in pre-1607 legal work*] (DSA) ... An
Andreas Bonellus de Barulo [*Flourished, 1260-71*] [*Authority cited in pre-1607 legal work*] (DSA) ... And
Andreas Bonellus de Barulo [*Flourished, 1260-71*] [*Authority cited in pre-1607 legal work*] (DSA) ... And de Baro
Andreas Bonellus de Barulo [*Flourished, 1260-71*] [*Authority cited in pre-1607 legal work*] (DSA) ... Andr
Andreas Bonellus de Barulo [*Flourished, 1260-71*] [*Authority cited in pre-1607 legal work*] (DSA) ... Andr de Bar
Andreas Bonellus de Barulo [*Flourished, 1260-71*] [*Authority cited in pre-1607 legal work*] (DSA) ... Andre
Andreas de Capua [*Flourished, 1242-57*] [*Authority cited in pre-1607 legal work*] (DSA) ... An
Andreas de Capua [*Flourished, 1242-57*] [*Authority cited in pre-1607 legal work*] (DSA) ... And de Ca
Andreas de Capua [*Flourished, 1242-57*] [*Authority cited in pre-1607 legal work*] (DSA) ... Andr de Ca
Andreas de Capua [*Flourished, 1242-57*] [*Authority cited in pre-1607 legal work*] (DSA) ... Andr de Cap
Andreas de Isernia [*Deceased circa 1316*] [*Authority cited in pre-1607 legal work*] (DSA) ... An de Iser
Andreas de Isernia [*Deceased circa 1316*] [*Authority cited in pre-1607 legal work*] (DSA) ... Andr
Andreas de Isernia [*Deceased circa 1316*] [*Authority cited in pre-1607 legal work*] (DSA) ... Andr de Isern
Andreas de Isernia [*Deceased circa 1316*] [*Authority cited in pre-1607 legal work*] (DSA) ... Andre
Andreas Fachineus [*Deceased, 1622*] [*Authority cited in pre-1607 legal work*] (DSA) ... Andr Fachin
Andreas Pomates [*Authority cited in pre-1607 legal work*] (DSA) ... Andr Pomat
Andreas Tiraquellus [*Deceased, 1558*] [*Authority cited in pre-1607 legal work*] (DSA) ... Andr Tiraq
Andreas Tiraquellus [*Deceased, 1558*] [*Authority cited in pre-1607 legal work*] (DSA) ... And Tiraq
Andrei Sakharov Institute [*Later, FUWPH*] (EA) ... ASI
Andres Wines Ltd. [*Toronto Stock Exchange symbol*] [*Vancouver Stock Exchange symbol*] ... ADW
Andrew [*Stock market symbol*] ... ANDR
Andrew Bayne Memorial Library, Bellevue, PA [*Library symbol*] [*Library of Congress*] (LCLS) ... PBvu
Andrew College (SAUO) ... AC
Andrew College, Cuthbert, GA [*Library symbol*] [*Library of Congress*] (LCLS) ... GCuA
Andrew Corp. [*Associated Press*] (SAG) ... Andrew
Andrew Corp. [*NASDAQ symbol*] (NQ) ... ANDW
Andrew County Historical Society, Savannah, MO [*Library symbol*] [*Library of Congress*] (LCLS) ... MoSavHi
Andrew Development Environment Workbench [*Computer science*] (VERA) ... ADEW
Andrew File System [*Computer science*] (TNIG) ... AFS
Andrew Jackson [*US general and president, 1767-1845*] ... AJ
Andrew Jackson High School (SAUO) ... AJHS
Andrew Johnson National Historic Site (SAUS) ... AJNHS
Andrew Mail System (SAUS) ... AMS
Andrew Mail/Message System [*Unix*] (VERA) ... AMS
Andrew Message System (SAUS) ... AMS
Andrew Public Library, Alberta [*Library symbol*] [*National Library of Canada*] (NLC) ... AA
Andrew Public Library, Andrew, AB, Canada [*Library symbol*] [*Library of Congress*] (LCLS) ... CaAAn
Andrew R. Jennings Computing Center [*Case Western Reserve University*] [*Research center*] (RCD) ... ARJCC
Andrew Tool Kit [*Unix*] (VERA) ... ATK
Andrew Toolkit (SAUS) ... ATK
Andrew User Environment [*Unix*] (VERA) ... AUE
Andrew User Interface System [*Unix*] (VERA) ... AUIS
Andrew W. Breidenbach Environmental Research Center (AEPA) ... AWBERC
Andrew W. Mellon Foundation (SAUO) ... AWMF
Andrew W. Mellon Foundation, New York, NY [*Library symbol*] [*Library of Congress*] (LCLS) ... NNMel
Andrews Air Force Base [*Washington, DC*] ... AAFB
Andrews & McMeel [*Publisher*] ... A & M
Andrews and Stoney's Supreme Court of Judicature Acts [*A publication*] (DLA) ... And & Ston JA
Andrews and Stoneys Supreme Court of Judicature Acts (journ.) (SAUS) ... And&StonJA
Andrews Carnegie Library, Andrews, NC [*Library symbol*] [*Library of Congress*] (LCLS) ... NcAnd
Andrews' Digest of the Opinions of the Attorneys-General [*A publication*] (DLA) ... And Dig
Andrews' English King's Bench Reports [*95 English Reprint*] [*A publication*] (DLA) ... And
Andrews' English King's Bench Reports [*95 English Reprint*] [*A publication*] (DLA) ... Andr
Andrews' English King's Bench Reports [*95 English Reprint*] [*A publication*] (DLA) ... Andrews (Eng)
Andrews Federal Credit Union (SAUO) ... AFCU
Andrews' Manual of the United States Constitution [*A publication*] (DLA) ... And Man Const
Andrews, McMeel & Parker [*Later, A & M*] [*Publisher*] ... AM & P
Andrews on Criminal Law [*A publication*] (DLA) ... And Cr Law
Andrews on the Revenue Law [*A publication*] (DLA) ... And Rev Law
Andrews on the Revenue Law (journ.) (SAUS) ... And Rev Law
Andrews on United States Laws and Courts [*A publication*] (DLA) ... And L & Cts
Andrews on United States Laws and Courts (journ.) (SAUS) ... And L&Cts
Andrews' Precedents of Leases [*A publication*] (DLA) ... And Pr Lea
Andrews' Precedents of Mortgages [*A publication*] (DLA) ... And Pr Mort
Andrews Precedents of Mortgages (journ.) (SAUS) ... And Pr Mort
Andrews' Reports [*63-73 Connecticut*] [*A publication*] (DLA) ... And
Andrews, SC [*Location identifier*] [*FAA*] (FAAL) ... PHH
Andrews, SC [*FM radio station call letters*] ... WGTN
Andrews Sisters Fan Club (EA) ... ASFC
Andrews, TX [*Location identifier*] [*FAA*] (FAAL) ... ANR
Andrews, TX [*AM radio station call letters*] ... KACT
Andrews, TX [*FM radio station call letters*] ... KACT-FM
Andrews University (GAGS) ... Andrews U
Andrews University (SAUO) ... AU
Andrews University, Berrien Springs, MI [*OCLC symbol*] (OCLC) ... EXN
Andrews University, Berrien Springs, MI [*Library symbol*] [*Library of Congress*] (LCLS) ... MiBsA
Andrews University Press (SAUO) ... AUP
Andrews University. Seminary Studies (journ.) (SAUS) ... AndrUnSS
Andrews University. Seminary Studies (journ.) (SAUS) ... ANUSS
Andrews-Dallas Township Public Library, Andrews, IN [*Library symbol*] [*Library of Congress*] (LCLS) ... InAnw
Andrewsfield [*British*] [*ICAO location identifier*] (ICLI) ... EGSL
Andrews/Nelson/Whitehead [*Commercial firm*] ... A/N/W
Andria [*of Terence*] [*Classical studies*] (OCD) ... An
Andriamena [*Madagascar*] [*Airport symbol*] (OAG) ... WAD
Androecium [*Botany*] ... A
Androgen (MELL) ... A
Androgen [*Antineoplastic drug*] (DAVI) ... And
Androgen Binding Protein [*Endocrinology*] ... ABP
Androgen Insensitivity Syndrome [*Endocrinology*] ... AIS
Androgen Insensitivity Syndrome, Complete [*Medicine*] (MELL) ... AIS-C
Androgen Receptors [*Endocrinology*] ... AR
Androgen-Binding Fraction [*Medicine*] (MELL) ... ABF
Androgen-Binding Protein (SAUS) ... ABP
Androgen-Control Therapy [*Medicine*] (MELL) ... ACT
Androgen-Deprivation Therapy [*Medicine*] ... ADT
Androgenic Anabolic Agent [*Medicine*] (DMAA) ... AAA
Androgenic-Anabolic Steroid [*Medicine*] (MELL) ... AAS
Androgens and Antiandrogens. Papers Presented at the International Symposiurn en Androgens and Antiandrogens (journ.) (SAUS) ... Androgens Antiandrogens Pap Int Symp
Androgens in Normal and Pathological Conditions. Proceedings. Symposium en Steroid Hormones (journ.) (SAUS) ... Androgens Norm Pathol Cond Proc Symp Steroid Horm
androgyn (SAUS) ... androg
Androgyne (DHP) ... AN
Androgynous Peripheral Attachment System [*NASA*] (SPST) ... APAS
Andrologie (journ.) (SAUS) ... ANDLA
Andromache [*of Euripides*] [*Classical studies*] (OCD) ... Andr
Andromeda [*Constellation*] ... And
Andromeda [*Constellation*] ... Andr
Andromeda Galaxy (SAUS) ... M31
Andromeda Galaxy and Amplified Pixels Experiment (SAUS) ... AGAPE
Androne Resources Ltd. [*Vancouver Stock Exchange symbol*] ... AND
Andronicus Publishing Co., Inc., New York, NY [*Library symbol*] [*Library of Congress*] (LCLS) ... ApC
Andronicus Publishing Company, Inc. (SAUO) ... ApC

Androphy, White Collar Crime Cases (SAUS) ... WCC
Andros, Inc. [*Associated Press*] (SAG) ... Andros
Andros, Inc. [*NASDAQ symbol*] (NQ) ... ANDY
Andros Town [*Bahamas*] [*Airport symbol*] (OAG) ... ASD
Andros Town, Andros Island [*Bahamas*] [*ICAO location identifier*] (ICLI) ... MYAF
Androsta-1,4 Diene-3,17-Dione (SAUS) ... ADD
Androstanediene [*Biochemistry*] (DAVI) ... ADD
Androstanediene-Dione (BABM) ... ADD
Androstatrienedione [*Organic chemistry*] ... ATD
Androstenedione [*Endocrinology*] ... AD
Androstenoide (SAUS) ... AD
Androsterone [*Medicine*] (DMAA) ... A
Androsterone [*Pharmacology*] (DAVI) ... ANDRO
Androsterone [*Pharmacology*] (DAVI) ... ANDROS
Androsterone Sulfate [*Biochemistry*] (AAMN) ... AS
Andrulis Research Corp. ... ARC
Andrulis Tracker [*Military*] (CAAL) ... ANTRAC
Andrus Gerontological Information Center [*University of Southern California*] (IID) ... AGIC
Andrx Corp. [*NASDAQ symbol*] (SAG) ... ADRX
Andrx Corp. [*Associated Press*] (SAG) ... AndrxCp
Anduki/Seria [*Brunei*] [*ICAO location identifier*] (ICLI) ... WBAK
Andy Griffith Show Appreciation Society (EA) ... AGSAS
[*The*] **Andy Griffith Show Rerun Watchers Club** (EA) ... TAGSRWC
Andy Williams Fan Club (EA) ... AWFC
Andyne Computing [*NASDAQ symbol*] (TTSB) ... ADYNF
Andyne Computing Ltd. [*NASDAQ symbol*] (SAG) ... ADYN
Andyne Computing Ltd. [*Associated Press*] (SAG) ... Andyne
Anechoic (MSA) ... ANCH
Anechoic Acoustic Test Facility (MCD) ... AATF
Anechoic Water Tank ... AWT
Anegada [*Virgin Islands*] [*Seismograph station code, US Geological Survey*] (SEIS) ... ABV
A-negative (SAUS) ... A-
Aneityum [*Vanuata*] [*Airport symbol*] (OAG) ... AUY
Anekdote [*Anecdote*] [*German*] ... Anekd
Anemia of Chronic Disease [*Medicine*] (MELL) ... AOCD
Anemia-Inducing Factor [*Medicine*] (DB) ... AIF
Anemone [*Botany*] ... AN
Anencephaly of Spina Bifida (SAUS) ... ASB
Anencephaly Support Foundation (SAUO) ... ASF
Anergen, Inc. [*Associated Press*] (SAG) ... Anergen
Anergen, Inc. [*NASDAQ symbol*] (SPSG) ... ANRG
Aneroid (MSA) ... ANER
Anesta Corp. [*Associated Press*] (SAG) ... Anesta
Anesta Corp. [*NASDAQ symbol*] (SAG) ... NSTA
Anesthesia [*or Anesthetic*] [*Medicine*] (DAVI) ... AN
Anesthesia (SAUS) ... Ana
Anesthesia (SAUS) ... ANA
Anesthesia (MELL) ... Anes
Anesthesia (ADWA) ... anes
Anesthesia [*or Anesthetic*] [*Medicine*] ... ANESTH
Anesthesia ... ANSTHS
Anesthesia Abstracts (journ.) (SAUS) ... Anesth Abstr
Anesthesia Administration Assembly (SAUO) ... AAA
Anesthesia History Association (SAUO) ... AHA
Anesthesia Patient Safety Foundation (SAUO) ... APSF
Anesthesia Research Laboratories (or Laboratory) (SAUS) ... ARL
Anesthesia Standby [*Medicine*] ... ASB
anesthesiac (SAUS) ... ana
anesthesiologist (SAUS) ... anes
Anesthesiologist's Assistant [*Medicine*] (DAVI) ... AA
Anesthesiology [*Medical specialty*] (DHSM) ... AN
Anesthesiology (AABC) ... ANES
Anesthesiology ... ANESTHLGY
Anesthesiology ... ANSTHSLGY
Anesthesiology (journ.) (SAUS) ... Anesthesiol
Anesthesiology (journ.) (SAUS) ... ANFSA
Anesthetic [*Medicine*] ... A
Anesthetic Gas Standards ... AGS
Anesthetician (SAUS) ... Anes
Anesthetics (SAUS) ... Anes
Anethole Dithiolthione [*Biochemistry*] ... ADT
Anethum [*Dill Seed*] [*Pharmacology*] (ROG) ... ANETH
Aneurysm ... AN
Aneurysm of Ascending Aorta [*Cardiology*] (DMAA) ... AAA
Aneurysmal Bone Cyst [*Medicine*] (MELL) ... ABC
Anfang [*Beginning*] [*German*] ... Anf
Anfang Bedenk das Ende [*At the Beginning Consider the End*] [*Motto of Bruno II, Count of Mansfeld (1545-1615)*] [*German*] ... ABDE
Angavokely [*Madagascar*] [*Seismograph station code, US Geological Survey*] (SEIS) ... AVY
Angeborener Ausolsender Mechanismus [*Innate Release Mechanism*] [*Psychology*] ... AAM
Angeion Corp. [*Associated Press*] (SAG) ... Angeion
Angeion Corp. [*NASDAQ symbol*] (NQ) ... ANGN
Angel (ROG) ... A
Angel (SAUS) ... O
Angel Collectors Club of America (EA) ... ACCA
Angel Fire, NM [*FM radio station call letters*] ... KAFR
Angel Flight (EA) ... AnF
Angel Flight/Silverwings [*An association*] (EA) ... AnF/SW
Angel Island [*California*] [*Seismograph station code, US Geological Survey*] (SEIS) ... AGC
Angel, Jerald J., Los Angeles CA [*STAC*] ... AJJ
[*The*] **Angel Planes** [*An association*] (EA) ... AP
[*The*] **Angel Planes** (EA) ... TAP
Angel, Second Class [*Classification of angel Clarence Oddbody in 1947 film, "It's a Wonderful Life"*] ... AS2
Angele Fernande Daniel Family Organization (EA) ... AFDFO
Angelegenheit [*Affair*] [*German*] ... Angelegenh
Angeles Mortgage Investment Trust (SAUS) ... ANGMT
Angeles Mortgage Investors Trust (SAUS) ... ANM
Angeles Mortgage Partners [*Associated Press*] (SAG) ... AngMtg
Angeles Mortgage Partners [*AMEX symbol*] (SPSG) ... ANM
Angeles Mtge Inv Tr L.P. [*AMEX symbol*] (TTSB) ... ANM
Angeles Participating Mortgage Trust [*Associated Press*] (SAG) ... AngPar
Angeles Participating Mortgage Trust (SAUS) ... ANGPAR
Angeles Participating Mortgage Trust [*AMEX symbol*] (SPSG) ... APT
Angeles Participating Mortgage Trust Class A (SAUS) ... APT
Angeles Ptc Mtge'A'SBI [*AMEX symbol*] (TTSB) ... APT
Angelholm [*Sweden*] [*ICAO location identifier*] (ICLI) ... ESDB
Angelholm/Helsingbord [*Sweden*] [*Airport symbol*] (OAG) ... AGH
Angelic Warfare Confraternity [*Defunct*] (EA) ... AWC
Angelica Corp. [*NYSE symbol*] (SPSG) ... AGL
Angelica Corp. [*Associated Press*] (SAG) ... Angelic
Angelica Free Library, Angelica, NY [*Library symbol*] [*Library of Congress*] (LCLS) ... NAng
Angelina & Neches River Railroad Co. [*AAR code*] ... ANR
Angelina & Neches River Railroad Company (SAUO) ... ANR
Angelina College, Lufkin, TX [*Library symbol*] [*Library of Congress*] (LCLS) ... TxLufA
Angelina, Cotui [*Dominican Republic*] [*ICAO location identifier*] (ICLI) ... MDAN
Angelini Francesco [*Italy*] [*Research code symbol*] ... AF
Angell and Ames on Corporations [*A publication*] (DLA) ... A & A Corp
Angell and Ames on Corporations [*A publication*] (DLA) ... Ang & A Corp
Angell and Ames on Corporations [*A publication*] (DLA) ... Ang Corp
Angell and Durfee on Highways [*A publication*] (DLA) ... A & D High
Angell and Durfee on Highways [*A publication*] (DLA) ... Ang & D High
Angell and Durfee on Highways [*A publication*] (DLA) ... Ang High
Angell and Durfee on Highways [*A publication*] (DLA) ... Ang Highw
Angell and Durfee's Reports [*1 Rhode Island*] [*A publication*] (DLA) ... Ang
Angell and Durfee's Reports [*1 Rhode Island*] [*A publication*] (DLA) ... Ang & Dur
Angell on Adverse Enjoyment [*A publication*] (DLA) ... Ang Adv Enj
Angell on Assignment [*A publication*] (DLA) ... Ang Ass
Angell on Bank Tax [*A publication*] (DLA) ... Ang BT
Angell on Carriers [*A publication*] (DLA) ... Ang Car
Angell on Insurance [*A publication*] (DLA) ... Ang Ins
Angell on Limitation of Actions [*A publication*] (DLA) ... Ang Lim
Angell on Tide Waters [*A publication*] (DLA) ... Ang Tide Waters
Angell on Tide Waters [*A publication*] (DLA) ... Ang TW
Angell on Water Courses [*A publication*] (DLA) ... Ang Wat
Angell on Water Courses [*A publication*] (DLA) ... Ang Water Courses
Angell's Rhode Island Reports [*A publication*] (DLA) ... Ang
Angelman Syndrome [*Genetics*] ... AS
Angelman Syndrome Foundation (SAUO) ... ASF
Angelo State University (GAGS) ... Angelo St U
Angelo State University, San Angelo, TX [*Library symbol*] [*Library of Congress*] (LCLS) ... TxSalA
Angels Forever For Angels (SAUO) ... AFFA
Angel's Peak [*Nevada*] [*Seismograph station code, US Geological Survey*] (SEIS) ... APK
Angelus Carletus de Clavasio [*Deceased, 1492*] [*Authority cited in pre-1607 legal work*] (DSA) ... Angel de Clavas
Angelus de Gambilionibus de Aretio [*Flourished, 1422-51*] [*Authority cited in pre-1607 legal work*] (DSA) ... Ang
Angelus de Gambilionibus de Aretio [*Flourished, 1422-51*] [*Authority cited in pre-1607 legal work*] (DSA) ... Ang Are
Angelus de Gambilionibus de Aretio [*Flourished, 1422-51*] [*Authority cited in pre-1607 legal work*] (DSA) ... Ange
Angelus de Gambilionibus de Aretio [*Flourished, 1422-51*] [*Authority cited in pre-1607 legal work*] (DSA) ... Ange Aret
Angelus de Gambilionibus de Aretio [*Flourished, 1422-51*] [*Authority cited in pre-1607 legal work*] (DSA) ... Angel
Angelus de Periglis [*Deceased, 1446*] [*Authority cited in pre-1607 legal work*] (DSA) ... Ang de Perigl
Angelus de Ubaldis [*Deceased, 1407*] [*Authority cited in pre-1607 legal work*] (DSA) ... An
Angelus de Ubaldis [*Deceased, 1407*] [*Authority cited in pre-1607 legal work*] (DSA) ... Ang
Angelus de Ubaldis [*Deceased, 1407*] [*Authority cited in pre-1607 legal work*] (DSA) ... Ange
Angelus de Ubaldis de Perusio [*Deceased, 1407*] [*Authority cited in pre-1607 legal work*] (DSA) ... An de Peru
Angelus Domini [*Angel of the Lord*] [*Latin*] (BARN) ... AD
Anger Inventory [*Psychology*] (DHP) ... AI
Anger Rape (MELL) ... AR
Angers/Avrille [*France*] [*ICAO location identifier*] (ICLI) ... LFRA
Angestellter [*Clerk, Employee*] [*German*] ... Angest
Angestrebter Zielfunktionswert (SAUS) ... ZF Ziel
Angewandte Chemie Adlershof, Technologiepark Berlin-Adlershof (SAUS) ... ACA
Angewandte Chemie, International Edition in English [*A publication*] (MEC) ... Angew Chem Int Ed Engl
Angewandte Informatik (SAUS) ... AI
Angewandte Makromolekulare Chemie (journ.) (SAUS) ... ANMCB
Angewandte Parasitologie (journ.) (SAUS) ... Ang Paras
Angina Awareness Program (SAUS) ... AAP
Angina Pectoris [*Medicine*] ... AP
Angina Pectoris-Type Pain [*Medicine*] (MELL) ... APTP

Angina Threshold Heart Rate [*Cardiology*] (DAVI) ... ATHR
Angio Cardiographie (SAUS) ... ACG
Angioblastic Lymphadenopathy [*Medicine*] (MELL) ... ABL
Angiocardiogram [*Medicine*] (MELL) ... ACG
Angiocardiography [*Medicine*] ... ACG
Angiocatheter [*or Angiocatheterization*] [*Cardiology*] (DAVI) ... angio
Angiofollicular (Lymph Node) Hyperplasia [*Oncology*] ... AFH
Angiogenesis Factor [*Biochemistry*] ... AF
Angiogenesis Inhibitor [*Physiology*] ... AI
Angiogram [*Cardiology*] ... ANG
Angiogram (ADWA) ... ang
angiogram (SAUS) ... ang
Angiogram [*Cardiology*] ... angio
Angiographically Occult Intracranial Vascular Malformation [*Neurosurgery*] (DAVI) ... AOIVM
Angiography [*Cardiology*] (DAVI) ... angio
Angiography Occult Vascular Malformation [*Medicine*] (MELL) ... AOVM
Angioimmunoblastic Lymphadenopathy [*Medicine*] ... AIL
Angioimmunoblastic Lymphadenopathy with Dysproteinemia [*Medicine*] ... AILD
Angiologia (journ.) (SAUS) ... ANGOA
Angiology (SAUS) ... Angiol
Angiolymphoid Hyperplasia [*Medicine*] (MELL) ... ALH
Angio-Medical Corp. (SAUO) ... ANME
Angiomyolipoma [*Medicine*] (MELL) ... AML
Angio-Osteohypertrophy Syndrome [*Medicine*] (MELL) ... AOHS
Angioplasty, Transluminal, Percutaneous Coronary [*Medicine*] (MELL) ... ATPC
Angiotensin [*Biochemistry*] ... AII
Angiotensin [*Biochemistry*] ... ANG
Angiotensin [*Biochemistry*] ... AT
Angiotensin Converting Enzyme [*Biochemistry*] ... ACE
Angiotensin Converting Enzyme Inhibitor [*Biochemistry*] ... ATCEI
Angiotensin Generation Rate [*Biochemistry*] (MAE) ... Ang GR
Angiotensin I [*Biochemistry*] (MAE) ... AI
Angiotensin I Converting Enzyme (DMAA) ... AICE
Angiotensin Pressor Dose [*Medicine*] ... APD
Angiotensin Sensitivity Test [*Medicine*] ... AST
Angiotensin-Converting Enzyme Inhibitor [*Medicine*] (MELL) ... ACEI
Angiotensin-II-Ferritin [*Biochemistry*] ... ATF
Angiotensin-Like Substance [*Biochemistry*] (MAE) ... ALS
Angiotensinogen [*Biochemistry*] ... ATG
Angissoq [*Greenland*] [*ICAO location identifier*] (ICLI) ... BGAS
Angkatan Democratic Liberal Sabah [*Malaysia*] [*Political party*] (EY) ... Adil
Angkatan Keadilan Rakyat [*People's Justice Movement*] [*Malaysia*] [*Political party*] (EY) ... AKAR
Angkatan Perpaduan Ummah [*Muslim Unity Movement*] [*Malaysia*] [*Political party*] (EY) ... APU
Angkor Temple (SAUS) ... Angkor
Angle (SAUS) ... Ang
Angle (MSA) ... ANG
Angle ... ANGL
Angle ... L
Angle and Velocity Tracker (ACAE) ... A&VT
Angle at Leaf Base [*Botany*] ... BANG
Angle at Leaf Base [*Botany*] ... BANGLE
Angle at Tip of Leaf [*Botany*] ... TANGLE
Angle between Leaf Apex and Widest Point [*Botany*] ... AANG
Angle Bulkhead Jack ... ABHJ
Angle Bulkhead Jack ... ABJ
Angle Cell [*Military*] (IUSS) ... ANGCEL
Angle Closure Glaucoma [*Ophthalmology*] ... ACG
Angle Data Assembly ... ADA
Angle Data Recorder ... ADR
Angle Data Recorder (or Recording) (SAUS) ... ADR
Angle Data Subsystem ... ADS
Angle Deception Jamming ... ADJ
Angle Deception Jamming System ... ADJS
Angle Detector Parallel (SAUS) ... ADP
Angle Detector Sequential (SAUS) ... ADS
Angle Evaporated Vertical Channel Power MOSFET [*Metal-Oxide-Semiconductor Field-Effect Transistor*] (IAA) ... AEVMOST
Angle Frame (OA) ... AF
Angle Function (SAUS) ... ANGLFN
Angle Gate (ACAE) ... AG
Angle Gate Pull-Off (SAUS) ... AGPO
Angle Iron [*Freight*] ... AI
Angle Jamming System ... AJS
Angle Lap Edge Profilometry (SAUS) ... ALEP
Angle Lock ... AL
Angle Measurement Accuracy (ACAE) ... AMA
Angle Measuring Equipment ... AME
Angle Measuring Equipment, Correlation Tracking and Ranging ... AME/COTAR
Angle Memory (ACAE) ... AM
Angle Memory Initiate (ACAE) ... AMI
Angle, Meter (DAVI) ... AM
Angle Meter (SAUS) ... AM
Angle Neovascularization [*Opthalmology*] ... ANV
Angle of (SAUS) ... AO
Angle of Approach (SAUS) ... AAp
Angle of Arrival ... AOA
Angle of Attack [*Military*] (NG) ... A/A
Angle of Attack [*Aviation*] (PIPO) ... AGA
Angle of Attack (ACAE) ... AOA
Angle of Attack [*Military*] (WDAA) ... AoA
Angle of Attack Limiter (MCD) ... AAL
Angle of Attack Pitch right Ascension (SAUS) ... ALPHA
Angle of Attack Transmitter [*Military*] ... AOAT
Angle of Bank ... AOB
Angle of Beam ... AOB
Angle of Descent ... AOD
Angle of Downwash (SAUS) ... e
Angle of Elevation ... AE
Angle of Greatest Extension [*Orthopedics*] ... AGE
Angle of Greatest Flexion [*Orthopedics*] ... AGF
Angle of Incidence (SAUS) ... AOI
Angle of Incidence ... I
Angle of Inner Gimbal ... AIG
Angle of Lewis [*Medicine*] (MELL) ... AOL
Angle of Middle Gimbal (KSC) ... AMG
Angle of Reflection ... AOR
Angle of Sight (IAA) ... AS
Angle of Site ... AOS
Angle of Train ... AT
Angle of Yaw Indicator ... AYI
Angle on Jam (MCD) ... AOJ
Angle on Target ... AOT
Angle on the Bow [*Navy*] (NVT) ... AOB
Angle Order (IEEE) ... ANLOR
Angle Panel Jack ... APJ
Angle Plate (SAUS) ... AGPE
Angle Point ... AP
Angle Position Indicator ... API
Angle Position Memory (ACAE) ... APM
Angle Ranging (ACAE) ... AR
Angle Rate Bombing Set (DWSG) ... ARBS
Angle Rate Bombing System (SAUS) ... ARBS
Angle Rate Memory (ACAE) ... ARM
Angle Resolved [*Physics*] ... AR
Angle Resolved Ultraviolet Photoelectron (or Photoemission) Spectroscopy (SAUS) ... ARUPS
Angle Resolved XPS (SAUS) ... ARXPS
Angle Resolved X-Ray Photoelectron Spectroscopy (AAEL) ... ARXPS
Angle Resources Ltd. [*Vancouver Stock Exchange symbol*] ... AGU
Angle Shot [*Cinematography*] (NTCM) ... AS
Angle Side Angle [*Geometry*] (BARN) ... ASA
Angle Stop Valve [*Technical drawings*] ... ASV
Angle Template ... AT
Angle, Time, Range [*Computer science*] ... ATR
Angle Track on Target [*Military*] ... ATOT
Angle Tracker (MUGU) ... A/T
Angle Tracking Computer (MHDI) ... ATRAC
Angle Tracking System (SAUS) ... ATR
Angle Tracking System [*NASA*] ... ATS
Angle Versus Length [*Computer science*] ... AVL
Angle-American Cataloging Rules (SAUS) ... AACR
Angle-Angle-Side (SAUS) ... AAS
Angled (NTCM) ... A
Angled End [*Outdoor advertising*] (NTCM) ... AE
Angled Physical Contact (SAUS) ... APC
Angled Single [*Outdoor advertising*] (NTCM) ... AS
Angle-Dispersed Electron Spectroscopy (MCD) ... ADES
Angle-Dispersed Photoelectron Spectroscopy ... ADPES
Angle-Integrated Ultraviolet Photoelectron Spectroscopy ... AIUPS
Angle-of-Approach Indicator [*Aviation*] (AFM) ... AAI
Angle-of-Attack Indicator [*Military*] ... AAI
Angle-of-Attack Indicator [*Military*] ... AOAI
Angle-of-Attack Sensor [*Military*] (MCD) ... AOAS
Angle-Only Track ... AOT
Angleplied Laminate ... APL
Angler ... ANGLR
Angle-Resolved Electron Energy Loss Spectroscopy ... AREELS
Angle-Resolved Inverse Photoelectron Spectroscopy ... ARIPES
Angle-Resolved Photoelectron Spectroscopy ... ARPES
Angle-Resolved Photoemission (MCD) ... ARP
Angle-Resolved Photoemission Extended Fine Structure [*Analytical technique*] ... ARPEFS
Angle-Resolved Photo-Emission Spectroscopy (SAUS) ... ARPES
Angle-Resolved Scattering (AAEL) ... ARS
Angle-Resolved Ultraviolet Photoelectron Spectroscopy ... ARUPS
Anglers Association (SAUO) ... AA
Anglers' Co-Operative Association [*British*] (EAIO) ... ACA
Angler's Library [*A publication*] ... AL
Anglesey [*Welsh island and county*] (ROG) ... AGL
Anglesey [*Welsh island and county*] ... ANG
Anglesey Antiquarian Society [*British*] (DBA) ... AAS
Anglesey Antiquarian Society and Field Club (SAUO) ... AAS
Anglia and Prefect Owners' Club [*British*] (BI) ... APOC
Anglia Television (SAUO) ... ATV
Anglian Standing Conference (SAUO) ... ASC
Anglian Water Authority [*British*] (DCTA) ... AWA
Anglian Water Services Ltd. [*Commercial firm*] [*British*] (ECON) ... AW
Anglican ... A
Anglican ... ANG
Anglican ... ANGL
Anglican (ADWA) ... Angl
Anglican ... ANGLCN
Anglican Accredited Layworkers' Federation [*British*] ... AALF
Anglican and Eastern Churches Association [*British*] (EAIO) ... A & ECA
Anglican and Eastern Churches Association (SAUO) ... A and ECA
Anglican and Eastern Churches Association (SAUO) ... AECA
Anglican Association of Musicians (EA) ... AAM

Anglican Church Handbooks [*A publication*] ... ACH
Anglican Church House, Toronto, ON, Canada [*Library symbol*] [*Library of Congress*] (LCLS) ... CaOTCH
Anglican Church House, Toronto, Ontario [*Library symbol*] [*National Library of Canada*] (NLC) ... OTCH
Anglican Church of Canada ... ACC
Anglican Church of Canada, Archives, Toronto, ON, Canada [*Library symbol*] [*Library of Congress*] (LCLS) ... CaOTCHAr
Anglican Church of Canada Archives, Toronto, Ontario [*Library symbol*] [*National Library of Canada*] (NLC) ... OTCHAR
Anglican Church of Canada, British Columbia Provincial Synod, Archives, Vancouver, BC, Canada [*Library symbol*] [*Library of Congress*] (LCLS) ... CaBVaABSA
Anglican Church of Canada, Diocese of Algoma, Synod Office, Sault Ste. Marie, ON, Canada [*Library symbol*] [*Library of Congress*] (LCLS) ... CaOStMAAS
Anglican Church of Canada, Diocese of Brandon, Synod Office, Brandon, MB, Canada [*Library symbol*] [*Library of Congress*] (LCLS) ... CaMBABS
Anglican Church of Canada, Diocese of Caledonia, Synod Office, Victoria, BC, Canada [*Library symbol*] [*Library of Congress*] (LCLS) ... CaBPRACS
Anglican Church of Canada, Diocese of Fredericton, Archives, Fredericton, NB, Canada [*Library symbol*] [*Library of Congress*] (LCLS) ... CaNBFAFA
Anglican Church of Canada, Diocese of Keewatin, Synod Office, Kenora, ON, Canada [*Library symbol*] [*Library of Congress*] (LCLS) ... CaOKeAKS
Anglican Church of Canada, Diocese of Montreal, Archives, Montreal, PQ, Canada [*Library symbol*] [*Library of Congress*] (LCLS) ... CaQMADMA
Anglican Church of Canada, Diocese of Moosonee, Synod Office, Schumacher, ON, Canada [*Library symbol*] [*Library of Congress*] (LCLS) ... CaOSAMS
Anglican Church of Canada, Diocese of Nova Scotia, Synod Office, Halifax, NS, Canada [*Library symbol*] [*Library of Congress*] (LCLS) ... CaNSHANSS
Anglican Church of Canada, Diocese of Ontario, Synod Office, Kingston, ON, Canada [*Library symbol*] [*Library of Congress*] (LCLS) ... CaOKAOS
Anglican Church of Canada, Diocese of Ottawa, Archives, Ottawa, ON, Canada [*Library symbol*] [*Library of Congress*] (LCLS) ... CaOOAOA
Anglican Church of Canada, Diocese of Quebec, Synod Office, Quebec, PQ, Canada [*Library symbol*] [*Library of Congress*] (LCLS) ... CaQQAQS
Anglican Church of Canada, Diocese of Saskatchewan, Synod Office, Prince Albert,SK, Canada [*Library symbol*] [*Library of Congress*] (LCLS) ... CaSPAASS
Anglican Church of Canada, Ecclesiastical Province of British Columbia, Vancouver, BC, Canada [*Library symbol*] [*Library of Congress*] (LCLS) ... CaBVaABS
Anglican Church of Canada, St. George's Cathedral, Kingston, ON, Canada [*Library symbol*] [*Library of Congress*] (LCLS) ... CaOKASG
Anglican Communion ... AC
Anglican Communion Office [*British*] (EAIO) ... ACO
Anglican Community Services Council [*Australia*] ... ACSC
Anglican Consultative Council [*British*] (EAIO) ... ACC
Anglican Council of North America and the Caribbean ... ACNAC
Anglican Digest (SAUS) ... TAD
Anglican Episcopal Church (SAUO) ... AEC
Anglican Evangelical Group Movement (SAUO) ... AEGM
Anglican Evangelical Group Movement (BARN) ... AEGM
Anglican Fellowship of Prayer (EA) ... AFP
Anglican Information Office (SAUO) ... AIO
Anglican Men's Society in Australia ... AMSA
Anglican Messenger (journ.) (SAUS) ... ANGM
Anglican Pacifist Fellowship [*Oxford, England*] (EAIO) ... APF
Anglican Pacifist Fellowship (SAUO) ... APF
Anglican Renewal Ministries Australia (SAUO) ... ARMA
Anglican Review (journ.) (SAUS) ... Anglican R
Anglican Society (EA) ... AS
Anglican Theological College (SAUO) ... ACT
Anglican Truth Society (SAUO) ... ATS
Anglican Young People Association (SAUO) ... AYPA
Anglican Youth Movement [*Canada*] ... AYM
Anglican-Roman Catholic International Commission ... ARCIC-II
Anglice [*In English*] [*Latin*] ... ANGL
Angling ... A
Angling Club (SAUO) ... AC
Angling Society (SAUO) ... AS
Angling Trade Association (EAIO) ... ATA
Anglish-Yinglish (SAUS) ... Angl-Yingl
Anglistik [*Study of English language and literature*] [*German*] ... Angl
Anglo- (SAUS) ... Ang
Anglo Am Gold Inv ADR [*NASDAQ symbol*] (TTSB) ... AAGIY
Anglo Amer So Afr ADR [*NASDAQ symbol*] (TTSB) ... ANGLY
Anglo American Corp. of South Africa Ltd. [*NASDAQ symbol*] (NQ) ... ANGL
Anglo American Corp. of South Africa Ltd. [*Associated Press*] (SAG) ... AngSA
Anglo American Corporation Group (SAUO) ... AAC
Anglo American Gold [*Associated Press*] (SAG) ... AngAG
Anglo American Gold Investment Co. Ltd. [*NASDAQ symbol*] (NQ) ... AAGI
Anglo American Resources [*Vancouver Stock Exchange symbol*] ... AAM
Anglo Australian Resources ... AAR
Anglo Batarian Society. Proceedings (journ.) (SAUS) ... Anglo Bat Soc Proc
Anglo Canadian Mining Corp. [*Toronto Stock Exchange symbol*] [*Vancouver Stock Exchange symbol*] ... ANP
Anglo Cargo Ltd. [*British*] [*ICAO designator*] (FAAC) ... ANC
Anglo Dominion Gold Exploration Ltd. [*Toronto Stock Exchange symbol*] ... ADE
Anglo Norwegian (SAUS) ... Anglo-Nor
Anglo-Afghan (SAUS) ... Anglo-Afg
Anglo-African (SAUS) ... Anglo-Afr
Anglo-American ... AA
Anglo-American Air Force (DAS) ... AAAF
Anglo-American Air Forces (SAUO) ... AAAF
Anglo-American Associates (EA) ... AAA
Anglo-American Association (SAUO) ... AAA
Anglo-American Authority File of Authors ... AAAF
Anglo-American Blockade Commission (SAUO) ... AABC
Anglo-American Caribbean Commission (SAUO) ... AACC
Anglo-American Cataloging Rules (SAUS) ... AARC
Anglo-American Cataloguing Committee for Cartographic Materials (GEOI) ... AACCCM
Anglo-American Cataloguing Rules [*American Library Association*] [*A publication*] ... AACR
Anglo-American Cataloguing Rules, 2nd edition, 1998 revision [*A publication*] ... AACR2R
Anglo-American Cataloguing Rules, Second Edition [*American Library Association*] [*A publication*] ... AACR2
Anglo-American Code [*Cataloging*] (DIT) ... AAC
Anglo-American Committee [*World War II*] ... AAC
Anglo-American Corporation of Canada Ltd. (SAUO) ... AMCAN
Anglo-American Corporation of South Africa (SAUO) ... AACSA
Anglo-American Corporation of South Africa, Ltd. (SAUO) ... AAC
Anglo-American Council on Productivity [*British*] (DI) ... AACP
Anglo-American Families Association [*British*] (BI) ... AAFA
Anglo-American Food Committee [*World War II*] ... AAFC
Anglo-American Gold Investment Co. (SAUO) ... Amgold
Anglo-American Industrial Corporation Ltd. (SAUO) ... AMI
Anglo-American Industrial Newsletter (SAUS) ... AAIN
Anglo-American Information Bureau (SAUO) ... AAIB
Anglo-American Joint Chiefs of Staff ... AAJCS
Anglo-American Judicial Exchange (ILCA) ... AAJE
Anglo-American Press Association (SAUO) ... A-A PA
Anglo-American Press Association of Paris [*See also APAAP*] [*France*] (EA) ... AAPAP
Anglo-American Productivity Council (SAUO) ... AAPC
Anglo-American Properties Ltd. (SAUO) ... AMAPROP
Anglo-American Racers ... AAR
Anglo-American Rhodesian Development Corporation Ltd. (SAUO) ... Aardcor
Anglo-American Services Club (SAUO) ... AASC
Anglo-American Sporting Club ... AASC
Anglo-American Tourist Service Association (SAUO) ... AATA
Anglo-American Travel Service (SAUO) ... AATS
Anglo-American Treaty Association (SAUO) ... AATA
Anglo-American-Hellenic Bureau of Education [*Defunct*] ... AAHBE
Anglo-Antillean (SAUS) ... Anglo-Ant
Anglo-Arabian (SAUS) ... Anglo-Arab
Anglo-Arctic (SAUS) ... Anglo-Art
Anglo-Argentine (SAUS) ... Anglo-Arg
Anglo-Argentine Society (SAUO) ... AAS
Anglo-Australian (SAUS) ... Anglo-Aus
Anglo-Australian Observatory ... AAO
Anglo-Australian Telescope ... AAT
Anglo-Austrian (SAUS) ... Anglo-Aus
Anglo-Austrian Society (SAUO) ... AAS
Anglo-Bahaman (SAUS) ... Anglo-Bah
Anglo-Barbadian (SAUS) ... Anglo-Barb
Anglo-Basque (SAUS) ... Anglo-Bas
Anglo-Batavian Society (SAUO) ... ABS
Anglo-Belgian (SAUS) ... Anglo-Belg
Anglo-Belgian Society (DBA) ... ABS
Anglo-Belgian Union (SAUO) ... ABU
Anglo-Belizian (SAUS) ... Anglo-Bel
Anglo-Bhutanese (SAUS) ... Anglo-Bhu
Anglo-Bolivian (SAUS) ... Anglo-Bol
Anglo-Bomarc Mines [*Vancouver Stock Exchange symbol*] ... ANB
Anglo-Botswana (SAUS) ... Anglo-Bots
Anglo-Brazilian (SAUS) ... Anglo-Braz
Anglo-Brazilian Amazonian Climate Observational Study (SAUS) ... ABRACOS
Anglo-Brazilian Climate Observational Study (SAUS) ... ABRACOS
Anglo-Brazilian Information Service [*Information service or system*] (IID) ... ABIS
Anglo-Brazilian Society (SAUO) ... ABS
Anglo-Bulgarian (SAUS) ... Anglo-Bul
Anglo-Burman (SAUS) ... Anglo-Bur
Anglo-Buru-Indian (SAUS) ... Anglo-Bur
Anglo-Cameroonian (SAUS) ... Anglo-Cam
Anglo-Canadian Telephone Co. [*Toronto Stock Exchange symbol*] ... ACT
Anglo-Catalan (SAUS) ... Anglo-Cat
Anglo-Catholic (SAUS) ... Anglo-cath
Anglo-Catholic Congress (SAUO) ... ACC
Anglo-Central American (SAUS) ... Anglo-CA
Anglo-Ceylonese (SAUS) ... Anglo-Cey
Anglo-Chilean (SAUS) ... Anglo-Chil
Anglo-Chilean Society (EAIO) ... ACS
Anglo-Chinese (SAUS) ... Anglo-Chi
Anglo-Colombian (SAUS) ... Anglo-Col
Anglo-Continental Dental Society [*British*] ... ACDS
Anglo-Continental Educational Group (SAUO) ... ACEG
Anglo-Continental School of English, Bournemouth (SAUO) ... ACSE
Anglo-Continental Society [*British*] ... ACS
Anglo-Cuban (SAUS) ... Anglo-Cub
Anglo-Cypriot (SAUS) ... Anglo-Cyp
Anglo-Dahomean (SAUS) ... Anglo-Dah
Anglo-Danish (SAUS) ... Anglo-Dan
Anglo-Danish Society (SAUO) ... ADS
Anglo-Dutch (SAUS) ... Anglo-Du
Anglo-Dutch-United States ... ANDUS
Anglo-Ecuadorean (SAUS) ... Anglo-Ecu

Anglo-Egyptian (SAUS) ... Anglo-Egypt
Anglo-English (SAUS) ... Anglo-Eng
Anglo-Ethiopian (SAUS) ... Anglo-Ethio
Anglo-European Container Line (SAUO) ... AECL
Anglo-European Cultural Centre (SAUO) ... AECC
Anglo-Finnish (SAUS) ... Anglo-Fin
Anglo-Finnish Society (SAUO) ... AFS
Anglo-French [*Language, etc.*] ... AF
Anglo-French [*Language, etc.*] ... AFR
Anglo-French Exchange meeting (SAUS) ... AFEX
Anglo-French Offshore Surveys (SAUS) ... AFOS
Anglo-French Safety of Navigation Group (SAUO) ... AFSNG
Anglo-French Supply and Purchases [*World War II*] ... AFSP
Anglo-French Variable Geometry Fighter (SAUS) ... AFVG Fighter
Anglo-French Variable-Geometry [*Combat aircraft*] ... AFVG
Anglo-Frisian [*Language, etc.*] ... AF
Anglo-Gaelic (SAUS) ... Anglo-Gael
Anglo-Gambian (SAUS) ... Anglo-Gam
Anglo-German (SAUS) ... Anglo-Ger
Anglo-German Accommodation Training Areas Committee (SAUO) ... AGATAC
Anglo-German Association (SAUO) ... AGA
Anglo-German Club (SAUO) ... AGC
Anglo-German Exchange meeting (SAUS) ... AGEX
Anglo-German Fellowship (SAUO) ... AGF
Anglo-German Medical Review (journ.) (SAUS) ... Anglo-Ger MedRev
Anglo-German Variable Geometry [*Avaition*] (PDAA) ... AGVG
Anglo-German Variable-Geometry Aircraft (SAUS) ... AGVGA
Anglogold Ltd. ADS [*NYSE symbol*] (SG) ... AU
Anglo-Greek (SAUS) ... Anglo-Gr
Anglo-Guyanese (SAUS) ... Anglo-Guy
Anglo-Hellenic League (SAUO) ... AHL
Anglo-Honduran (SAUS) ... Anglo-Hond
Anglo-Hungarian (SAUS) ... Anglo-Hung
Anglo-Hungarian Society (SAUO) ... AHS
Anglo-Icelandic (SAUS) ... Anglo-Ice
Anglo-Indian [*Language, etc.*] ... AI
Anglo-Indian (BARN) ... A-Ind
Anglo-Indian (ADWA) ... Anglo-Ind
Anglo-Indonesian (SAUS) ... Anglo-Indo
Anglo-Iranian (SAUS) ... Anglo-Ir
Anglo-Iraqi (SAUS) ... Anglo-Ir
Anglo-Irish [*Language, etc.*] ... AI
Anglo-Irish (ADWA) ... Anglo-Ir
Anglo-Irish Agreement [*1985*] ... AIA
Anglo-Irish Beef Processors Ltd. [*Northern Ireland*] ... AIBP
Anglo-Irish Free Trade Agreement (SAUS) ... AIFTA
Anglo-Irish Free Trade Area [*British*] ... AIFTA
Anglo-Irish Free Trade Area Agreement (PDAA) ... AIFTAA
Anglo-Irish Intergovernmental Conference (SAUO) ... AIIC
Anglo-Irish Intergovernmental Council (SAUO) ... AIIC
Anglo-Israel Association [*British*] (BI) ... AIA
Anglo-Israel Friendship League (SAUO) ... AIFL
Anglo-Israeli (SAUS) ... Anglo-Isr
Anglo-Israelism [*or Anglo-Israelite*] ... AI
Anglo-Italian (SAUS) ... Anglo-Ital
Anglo-Italian Society (SAUO) ... AIS
Anglo-Italian Society [*British*] (DBA) ... AIS
Anglo-Ivorian Society [*British*] (DBA) ... AIS
Anglo-Jamaican (SAUS) ... Anglo-Jam
Anglo-Japanese (SAUS) ... Anglo-Jap
Anglo-Japanese Economic Institute [*British*] (EAIO) ... AJEI
Anglo-Jewish (SAUS) ... Anglo-Jew
Anglo-Jewish Association [*British*] ... AJA
Anglo-Jordanian (SAUS) ... Anglo-Jor
Anglo-Kenyan (SAUS) ... Anglo-Ken
Anglo-Kuwaiti (SAUS) ... Anglo-Kuw
Anglo-Latin [*Language, etc.*] ... AL
Anglo-Malawian (SAUS) ... Anglo-Mal
Anglo-Malaysian (SAUS) ... Anglo-Mal
Anglo-Malaysian Defence Agreement ... AMDA
Anglo-Maldivian (SAUS) ... Anglo-Mald
Anglo-Maltese (SAUS) ... Anglo-Mal
Anglo-Mexican (SAUS) ... Anglo-Mex
Anglo-Mongolian Society (EAIO) ... AMS
Anglo-Nepalese (SAUS) ... Anglo-Nep
Anglo-Netherlands Society (SAUO) ... ANS
Anglo-New Zealand (SAUS) ... Anglo-NZ
Anglo-Nigerian (SAUS) ... Anglo-Nig
Anglo-Norman [*Language, etc.*] ... AN
Anglo-Norman Text Society [*British*] ... ANTS
Anglo-Norse (SAUS) ... Anglo-N
Anglo-Oriental International Bank (SAUO) ... AOIB
Anglo-Pakistani (SAUS) ... Anglo-Pak
Anglo-Paraguayan (SAUS) ... Anglo-Para
Anglo-Persian (SAUS) ... Anglo-Per
Anglo-Persian Oil Company (SAUO) ... APOC
Anglo-Peruian (SAUS) ... Anglo-Per
Anglo-Polish (SAUS) ... Anglo-Pol
Anglo-Polish Catholic Association (SAUO) ... APCA
Anglo-Portuguese (SAUS) ... Anglo-Port
Anglo-Portuguese Society (SAUO) ... APS
Anglo-Rhodesian (SAUS) ... Anglo-Rho
Anglo-Rhodesian Society (EA) ... ARS
Anglo-Romanian (SAUS) ... Anglo-Rom
Anglo-Russian Co-Operative Society (SAUO) ... ARCOS
Anglo-Russian Trade Union Committee (SAUO) ... ARTUC
Anglo-Sanmoan (SAUS) ... Anglo-Sam
Anglo-Saxon [*MARC language code*] [*Library of Congress*] (LCCP) ... ang
Anglo-Saxon ... Ang-Sax
Anglo-Saxon (NTIO) ... AS
Anglo-Saxon [*Language, etc.*] (WA) ... AS
Anglo-Saxon Christian Patriot (EA) ... ASCP
Anglo-Saxon Chronicle ... ASC
Anglo-Saxon England (journ.) (SAUS) ... Anglo-Saxon Engl
Anglosaxon England (journ.) (SAUS) ... Angloux En
Anglo-Saxon Petroleum Company (SAUO) ... ASPC
Anglo-Saxon Protestant ... ASP
Anglo-Saxon Protestants (SAUO) ... ASPs
Anglo-Scandinavian Economic Committee (SAUS) ... UNISCAN
Anglo-Scandinavian Study of Early Thrombolysis ... ASSET
Anglo-Scottish (SAUS) ... Anglo-Scot
Anglo-Sierra Leonean (SAUS) ... Anglo-SL
Anglo-Somali (SAUS) ... Anglo-Som
Anglo-South African (SAUS) ... Anglo-SA
Anglo-South American (SAUS) ... Anglo-SA
Anglo-South American Bank (SAUO) ... ASA-Bank
Anglo-Soviet (SAUS) ... Anglo-Sov
Anglo-Soviet Committee (SAUO) ... ASC
Anglo-Soviet Co-operation on Agricultural Research (SAUO) ... ASCAR
Anglo-Soviet Joint Commission (SAUO) ... ASJC
Anglo-Soviet Pact (DAS) ... ASP
Anglo-Soviet Recognition Signals ... ASRS
Anglo-Soviet Trades Union Committee (SAUO) ... ASTUC
Anglo-Soviet Youth Friendship Alliance (SAUO) ... ASYFA
Anglo-Spanish (SAUS) ... Anglo-Span
Anglo-Spanish Quarterly Review (journ.) (SAUS) ... Anglo-Sp Q Rev
Anglo-Spanish Society (SAUO) ... ASS
Anglo-Sudanese (SAUS) ... Anglo-Sud
Anglo-Swedish (SAUS) ... Anglo-Swe
Anglo-Swedish Society (SAUO) ... ASS
Anglo-Swedish Travel Association (SAUO) ... ASTA
Anglo-Swiss (SAUS) ... Anglo-Swi
Anglo-Swiss Aluminium Co. Ltd. (SAUO) ... ANGLOSWISS
Anglo-Tanzanian (SAUS) ... Anglo-Tanz
Anglo-Tobagan (SAUS) ... Anglo-Tob
Anglo-Togolese (SAUS) ... Anglo-Togo
Anglo-Tongan (SAUS) ... Anglo-Ton
Anglo-Trinidadian (SAUS) ... Anglo-Trin
Anglo-Turkish (SAUS) ... Anglo-Turk
Anglo-Turkish Union (SAUO) ... ATU
Anglo-Ugandan (SAUS) ... Anglo-Ugan
Anglo-Uruguayan (SAUS) ... Anglo-Uru
Anglo-Venezuelan (SAUS) ... Anglo-Ven
Anglo-Vernacular ... AV
Anglo-Welsh (SAUS) ... Anglo-W
Anglo-Welsh Review (journ.) (SAUS) ... AngWWelsh
Anglo-Yemini (SAUS) ... Anglo-Yem
Anglo-Zambian (SAUS) ... Anglo-Zamb
Angmagssalik [*Greenland*] [*ICAO location identifier*] (ICLI) ... BGAM
Ango [*Zaire*] [*ICAO location identifier*] (ICLI) ... FZKO
Angoavia Angola [*FAA designator*] (FAAC) ... NGV
Angoche [*Mozambique*] [*ICAO location identifier*] (ICLI) ... FQAG
Angola [*ANSI three-letter standard code*] (CNC) ... AGO
Angola ... ANG
Angola (ADWA) ... Ang
Angola [*MARC country of publication code*] [*Library of Congress*] (LCCP) ... ao
Angola [*ANSI two-letter standard code*] (CNC) ... AO
Angola [*Aircraft nationality and registration mark*] (FAAC) ... D2
Angola [*MARC geographic area code*] [*Library of Congress*] (LCCP) ... f-ao-
Angola Air Charter Ltd. [*ICAO designator*] (FAAC) ... AAC
Angola Air Charter Ltd. [*ICAO designator*] (FAAC) ... AGO
Angola, IN [*Location identifier*] [*FAA*] (FAAL) ... ANQ
Angola, IN [*Location identifier*] [*FAA*] (FAAL) ... SJZ
Angola, IN [*FM radio station call letters*] ... WEAX
Angola, IN [*Television station call letters*] ... WINM
Angola, IN [*FM radio station call letters*] ... WLKI
Angola, LA [*FM radio station call letters*] ... KLSP
Angola Press (SAUO) ... ANGOP
Angolan Armed Forces (SAUO) ... FAA
Angolan Development Action (SAUO) ... AAD
Angolan Diamond Co. (SAUO) ... INDIAMA
Angolan Diamond Company (SAUS) ... INDIAMA
Angolan News Agency ... ANGOP
Angolan Provincial Humanitarian Coordinator (SAUO) ... APHC
Angolan Shipping Lines (SAUO) ... ANGONAVE
Angolia (VRA) ... Ang
Angoon [*Alaska*] [*Airport symbol*] (OAG) ... AGN
Angora [*Bolivia*] [*ICAO location identifier*] (ICLI) ... SLAN
Angora Goat and Mohair Journal (journ.) (SAUS) ... Angora Goat Mohair J
Angora Goat Record and Registry (EA) ... AGRR
Angoram [*Papua New Guinea*] [*Airport symbol*] (OAG) ... AGG
Angouleme/Brie-Champniers [*France*] [*ICAO location identifier*] (ICLI) ... LFBU
Angra Do Heroismo [*Azores*] [*Seismograph station code, US Geological Survey*] (SEIS) ... ADH
Angry Revengeful Frequent Fliers [*Aeronautics*] ... ARFF
Angry Young Man (BARN) ... AYM
Angst, Revolution, Titillation [*Art films*] ... ART
Angstrom [*Also, AU*] ... A
Angstrom (ADWA) ... angst
Angstrom Pyrheliometric Scale ... APS

Angstrom Unit (SAUS) ... A-1
Angstrom Unit [*Medicine*] (MELL) ... AU
Angstromeinheit [*Angstrom Unit*] [*German*] ... AE
Anguganak [*Papua New Guinea*] [*Airport symbol*] (OAG) ... AKG
Anguilla [*ANSI two-letter standard code*] (CNC) ... AI
Anguilla [*West Indies*] [*Airport symbol*] (OAG) ... AXA
Anguilla [*Leeward Islands*] [*Airport symbol*] (AD) ... AXA
Anguilla [*International civil aircraft marking*] (ODBW) ... VP-LA
Anguilla Democratic Party [*Political party*] (EY) ... ADP
Anguilla, MS [*Location identifier*] [*FAA*] (FAAL) ... RFK
Anguilla National Alliance (PPW) ... ANA
Anguilla People's Party [*Later, ADP*] [*Political party*] (PPW) ... APP
Anguilla Tourist Information and Reservation Office (EA) ... ATIRO
Anguilla Tourist Information Office [*Later, ATIRO*] (EA) ... ATIO
Angular ... ANLR
angular (SAUS) ... anlr
Angular Acceleration Susceptibility [*Orientation*] ... AAS
Angular Accelerometer [*NASA*] (MCD) ... AA
Angular Accelerometer Input Device (MCD) ... AAID
Angular Accelerometer Unit ... AAU
Angular Aperture (MCD) ... AA
Angular Baseline Corrector (SAUS) ... ABC
Angular Blocky Soil [*Agronomy*] ... ABK
Angular Correlation of Annihilation Radiation [*Spectroscopy*] ... ACAR
Angular Correlation of Positron Annihilation Radiation (SAUS) ... ACPAR
Angular Deformation (SAUS) ... d
Angular Dependence Model (ARMP) ... ADM
Angular Dependent Photoelectron Diffraction (PDAA) ... ADPD
Angular Dialing Unit (IAA) ... ADU
Angular Dialling Unit (SAUS) ... ADU
Angular Differentiating-Integrating Accelerometer ... ADA
Angular Display Unit (IAA) ... ADU
Angular Distribution Auger Microscopy ... ADAM
Angular Distribution Data Tape ... ADDT
Angular Distribution Pattern [*Surface analysis*] ... ADP
Angular impulse (SAUS) ... H
Angular Intensity Light Scattering [*Physics*] ... AILS
Angular Magnetic-Hydrodynamic Integrating Accelerometer ... AMIA
Angular Mapping Transformation [*Computer science*] ... AMT
Angular Measurement Accuracy ... AMA
Angular Measurement Precision (ACAE) ... AMP
Angular Moment (SAUS) ... ANGMOM
Angular Momentum ... AM
Angular Momentum [*Physics*] (BARN) ... J
Angular Momentum [*Symbol*] [*IUPAC*] ... L
Angular Momentum [*Symbol*] [*Physics*] ... M
Angular Momentum Wheel (KSC) ... AMW
Angular Motion Compensator ... AMC
Angular Motion Simulator (MCD) ... AMS
Angular Position Counter (SAA) ... APC
Angular Position Digitizer ... APD
Angular Position Sensor ... APS
Angular Position Transducer (SAUS) ... APT
Angular Rate Bombing System (MCD) ... ARBS
Angular Rate Matching Transfer Alignment (ACAE) ... ARMTA
Angular Rate Sensor ... ARS
Angular Second-Moment (SAUS) ... ASM
Angular Variable Differential Transformer (SAUS) ... AVDT
Angular Velocity (MCD) ... AV
Angular Velocity (BARN) ... W
angular V-shaped masonry joint (SAUS) ... V-joint
Angular Yaw Velocity (AAG) ... r
Angurugu Community Government Council [*Australia*] ... ACGC
Angus [*County in Scotland*] (ROG) ... AGS
Angus & Robertson [*Publisher*] [*Australia*] ... A & R
Angus Aviation Ltd. [*Canada*] [*ICAO designator*] (FAAC) ... AAZ
Angus Resources Ltd. [*Vancouver Stock Exchange symbol*] ... AGS
Angus Society of Australia ... ASA
Angus Telemanagement Group, Inc. [*Pickering, ON*] [*Information service or system*] [*Telecommunications*] (TSSD) ... ATMG
Angus Wildlife Review (journ.) (SAUS) ... Angus Wildl Rev
Angwin, CA [*FM radio station call letters*] ... KCDS
Angwin, CA [*FM radio station call letters*] (BROA) ... KNDL-FM
Anhang [*Appendix*] [*German*] (EG) ... ANH
Anharmonic Lattices, Structural Transitions and Melting (journ.) (SAUS) ... Anharmonic Lattices Struct Transitions Melting
Anharmonic Oscillator (SAUS) ... AHO
Anheuser-Busch Companies, Inc. [*Associated Press*] (SAG) ... Anheus
Anheuser-Busch Cos. [*NYSE symbol*] (TTSB) ... BUD
Anheuser-Busch, Inc. ... AB
Anheuser-Busch Inc. (SAUS) ... AB
Anheuser-Busch, Inc., Corporation Library, St. Louis, MO [*OCLC symbol*] (OCLC) ... ABS
Anheuser-Busch, Inc., St. Louis, MO [*Library symbol*] [*Library of Congress*] (LCLS) ... MoSAB
Anheuser-Busch Incorporated (SAUO) ... AB
Anholt [*Denmark*] [*ICAO location identifier*] (ICLI) ... EKAT
Anhwei Province [*China, Mainland*] [*MARC geographic area code*] [*Library of Congress*] (LCCP) ... a-cc-an
Anhydride (MSA) ... ANHYD
anhydritic (SAUS) ... anhic
Anhydrobis(beta-hydroxyethyl)biguanide [*Antiviral agent*] ... ABOB
Anhydroenneahepitol [*Organic chemistry*] ... AEH
Anhydroglucic (SAUS) ... AHG
Anhydroglucose [*Biochemistry*] ... AHG
Anhydroglucose Unit [*Biochemistry*] ... AGU
Anhydrotic Congenital Ectodermal Dysplasia [*Medicine*] (DMAA) ... ACED
Anhydrous ... AN
Anhydrous ... ANH
Anhydrous ... ANHY
Anhydrous ... ANHYD
Anhydrous (ADWA) ... anhyd
Anhydrous Hydrazine [*Rocket propellant*] ... AH
Anhydrous Hydrofluoric Acid (SAUS) ... AHF
Anhydrous Hydrogen Fluoride [*Inorganic chemistry*] ... AHF
Anhydrous Monocalcium Phosphate [*Inorganic chemistry*] ... AMCP
Anhydrous Sodium Metasilicate [*Inorganic chemistry*] ... ASM
Anhysteretic Remanent Magnetization ... ARM
Anhysteric Remanence (SAUS) ... ARM
Anhysteric Remanent Magnetization (SAUS) ... ARM
Aniak [*Alaska*] [*Airport symbol*] (OAG) ... ANI
Anicom, Inc. [*NASDAQ symbol*] (SAG) ... ANIC
Anicom, Inc. [*Associated Press*] (SAG) ... Anicom
Anie/Kolokope [*Togo*] [*ICAO location identifier*] (ICLI) ... DXKP
Anika Research [*NASDAQ symbol*] (TTSB) ... ANIK
Anika Research, Inc. [*NASDAQ symbol*] (SAG) ... ANIK
Anika Research, Inc. [*Associated Press*] (SAG) ... AnikaRs
Aniline [*Philately*] ... anil
Aniline (SAUS) ... Anil
Aniline Association (EA) ... AA
Aniline Blue-Lactophenol Medium [*Botany*] ... ABLP
Aniline Gentian Violet ... AGV
Aniline Hydrogen Phthalate (OA) ... AHP
Aniline Point (SAUS) ... AnPt
Aniline Point [*Measure of solvency*] ... AP
Aniline, Sulfur, and Formaldehyde [*Resin*] (AAMN) ... ASF
Aniline Sulphur and Formaldehyde (SAUS) ... ASF
Aniline-Furfuryl Alcohol-Hydrazine (SAA) ... A-FA-H
Anilinonaphthalenesulfonic Acid [*Also, ANSA*] [*Organic chemistry*] ... ANS
(Anilino)naphthalenesulfonic Acid [*Also, ANS*] [*Organic chemistry*] ... ANSA
(Anilinonaphthyl)maleimide [*Organic chemistry*] ... ANM
Anima Dulcis [*Sweet Soul*] [*Latin*] ... AD
Anima Quiescat in Christo [*May His, or Her, Soul Repose in Christ*] [*Latin*] ... AQIC
animadversion (SAUS) ... animad
Animal [*Psychology*] ... A
Animal ... AN
Animal ... ANI
Animal ... ANIM
Animal (WGA) ... ANL
Animal (SAUS) ... Anl
Animal ... ANML
Animal Air Transportation Association (EA) ... AATA
Animal Ambassadors International (SAUO) ... AAI
Animal and Plant Health Inspection Service ... APHI
Animal and Plant Health Inspection Service [*Department of Agriculture*] [*Also, an information service or system*] (IID) ... APHIS
Animal Behavior Abstracts (journ.) (SAUS) ... Anim Behav Abstr
Animal Behavior Monographs (journ.) (SAUS) ... ANBMAW
Animal Behavior Society (EA) ... ABS
Animal Behaviour (journ.) (SAUS) ... ANBEA
Animal Behaviour. Monographs (journ.) (SAUS) ... Anim Behav Monogr
Animal Birth Control (SAUS) ... ABC
Animal Breeding Abstracts (journ.) (SAUS) ... Anim Breed Abstr
Animal Breeding and Feeding (journ.) (SAUS) ... Anim Breed Feed
Animal Breeding and Genetics Research Organization (SAUO) ... ABGRO
Animal Breeding and Research Institute (SAUS) ... AB&RI
Animal Breeding (journ.) (SAUS) ... Anim Breed
Animal Breeding Research Organisation [*British*] ... ABRO
Animal Breeding Research Organisation (or Organization) (SAUO) ... ABRO
Animal Breeding Research Organization (SAUS) ... ABRO
Animal Care Panel (SAUO) ... ACP
Animal Care Panel [*Later, AALAS*] ... ACP
Animal Damage Control [*Department of Agriculture*] ... ADC
Animal Defence League of Canada (AC) ... ADLC
Animal Defence Society (SAUO) ... ADS
Animal Defense/Anti-Vivisection Society of BC (AC) ... ADAV
Animal Detail [*Rorschach*] [*Psychology*] ... Ad
Animal Disease and Parasite Research Division [*of ARS, Department of Agriculture*] ... ADP
Animal Disease and Parasite Research Division (SAUO) ... ADP
Animal Disease Eradication (SAUO) ... ADE
Animal Disease Eradication Division [*of ARS, Department of Agriculture*] ... ADE
Animal Disease Occurrence [*Database*] [*Commonwealth Agricultural Bureaux*] [*Information service or system*] (CRD) ... ADO
Animal Diseases Pathogenesis and Control Trust Fund (SAUO) ... ADPC
Animal Diseases Research Association [*Moredun Institute*] [*British*] (ARC) ... ADRA
Animal Diseases Research Institute [*Canada*] (IRC) ... ADRI
Animal Diseases Research Institute, Agriculture Canada [*Institut de Recherches Veterinaires, Agriculture Canada*] **Ottawa, Ontario** [*Library symbol*] [*National Library of Canada*] (NLC) ... OOAGA
Animal Diseases Research Institute (West), Agriculture Canada [*Institut de Recherches Veterinaires (Ouest), Agriculture Canada*] **Lethbridge, Alberta** [*Library symbol*] [*National Library of Canada*] (NLC) ... ALADR
Animal Drug Research Center [*Denver, CO*] [*Department of Health and Human Services*] (GRD) ... ADRC
Animal Educational League [*Defunct*] ... AEL
Animal Emergency Information System (SAUO) ... ANEMIS
Animal Enclosure Module (SAUS) ... AEM

Animal Ethics Committee (SAUO) ... AEC
Animal Feed and Tissue Residue Research Center [*Department of Health and Human Services*] (GRD) ... AFTRRC
Animal Feeding Stuffs (SAUS) ... AFS
Animal Genetic Resources (SAUS) ... AGR
Animal Genetic Resources (SAUS) ... AnGR
Animal Genetics (journ.) (SAUS) ... Anim Genet
Animal Guild of America (EA) ... AGA
Animal Health and Veterinary Group [*British*] (GVA) ... AHVG
Animal Health Board (SAUO) ... AHB
Animal Health Distributors Association [*British*] (DBA) ... AHDA
Animal Health Divisional Office (SAUS) ... AHDO
Animal Health Foundation (EA) ... AHF
Animal Health Institute (EA) ... AHI
Animal Health Insurance (SAUO) ... AHI
Animal Health (journ.) (SAUS) ... ANHEA4
Animal Health Laboratories (SAUO) ... AHL
Animal Health Office (SAUS) ... AHO
Animal Health Research Center (SAUS) ... AHRC
Animal Health Research Center, Entebbe (SAUO) ... AHRC
Animal Health Technician (SAUS) ... AHT
Animal Health Technologists Association of BC (AC) ... AHTA of BC
Animal Health Trust [*British*] (BI) ... AHT
Animal Health Yearbook (journ.) (SAUS) ... Anim Hlth Yb
Animal Health/Emerging Animal Disease (SAUO) ... AHEAD
Animal Husbandry (SAUS) ... AH
Animal Husbandry Division (SAUO) ... AHD
Animal Husbandry Research Division [*of ARS, Department of Agriculture*] ... AH
Animal Improvement Programs Laboratory [*Formerly, DHIA*] (EA) ... AIPL
Animal Improvement Programs Laboratory (SAUS) ... AIPL
Animal Industries Advisory Group (SAUO) ... AIAG
Animal Industries Division (SAUO) ... AID
Animal Industries Research Committee (SAUO) ... AIRC
Animal Industry Foundation (EA) ... AIF
Animal Inspection and Quarantine (SAUO) ... AIQ
Animal Inspection and Quarantine Division [*of ARS, Department of Agriculture*] ... AIQ
Animal Learning and Behavior (SAUS) ... Anim Learn Behav
Animal Legal Defense Fund (EA) ... ALDF
Animal Liberation (EA) ... AL
Animal Liberation Front (EA) ... ALF
Animal Medical Center (EA) ... AMC
Animal Medicinal Drug Use Clarification Act of 1994 ... AMDUCA
Animal Medicines Training and Regulatory Authority (GVA) ... AMTRA
Animal Models of Protecting Ischemic Myocardium [*Cardiology project*] ... AMPIM
Animal Nutrition Research Council (EA) ... ANRC
Animal Nutrition Research Council (SAUO) ... ANRD
Animal Parasitic Systems ... APS
Animal Pathology Laboratory, Food Production and Inspection Branch, Agriculture Canada , Saskatoon, Saskatchewan (SAUS) ... SSAGA
Animal Pathology Laboratory, Food Production and Inspection Branch, Agriculture Canada [*Laboratoire de Pathologie Veterinaire, Direction Generale de la Production et de l'Inspection des Aliments, Agriculture Canada*], **Richmond, BritishColumbia** [*Library symbol*] [*National Library of Canada*] (BIB) ... BRIAG
Animal Pathology Laboratory, Food Production and Inspection Branch, Agriculture Canada [*Laboratoire de Pathologie Veterinaire, Direction Generale de la Production et de l'Inspection des Aliments, Agriculture Canada*], **Saskatoon, Saskatchewan** [*Library symbol*] [*National Library of Canada*] (BIB) ... SSAGA
Animal Pharm World Animal Health News (journ.) (SAUS) ... APH
Animal Pituitary Gonadotrophin (DB) ... APG
Animal Placental Lactogen (DB) ... APL
Animal Political Action Committee (EA) ... ANPAC
Animal population ratio living in cool climate region (SAUS) ... A%C
Animal population ratio living in temperate climate region (SAUS) ... B%T
Animal population ratio living in warm climate region (SAUS) ... C%W
Animal Procedures Committee (GVA) ... APC
Animal Procurement Office [*Military*] ... APO
Animal Production (SAUS) ... Anim Prod
Animal Production and Health Commission for Asia [*Australia*] ... APHCA
Animal Production and Health Commission for Asia and the Pacific (SAUO) ... APHCA
Animal Production Committee (SAUO) ... APC
Animal Production (journ.) (SAUS) ... Animal Prod
Animal Protection Institute of America (EA) ... API
Animal Protection Institute of America (SAUO) ... APIA
Animal Protective Association (EA) ... APA
Animal Psi [*Parapsychology*] ... ANPSI
Animal Rescue League (SAUO) ... ARL
Animal Research and Development (SAUS) ... Anim Res Dev
Animal Research Centre [*Canada*] (ARC) ... ARC
Animal Research Committee ... ARC
Animal Research Facilities ... ARF
Animal Research Facility (SAUO) ... ARF
Animal Research Institute, Agriculture Canada [*Institut de Recherches Zootechniques, Agriculture Canada*] **Ottawa, Ontario** [*Library symbol*] [*National Library of Canada*] (NLC) ... OOAGAR
Animal Research Review Panel (SAUS) ... ARRP
Animal Resources Center [*University of Texas at Austin*] [*Research center*] (RCD) ... ARC
Animal Resources Centre (SAUO) ... ARC
Animal Resources Program [*Bethesda, MD*] [*Department of Health and Human Services*] (GRD) ... ARP
Animal Rights [*An association*] [*Australia*] ... AR
Animal Rights Coalition (EA) ... ARC
Animal Rights Information and Education Service (EA) ... ARIES
Animal Rights International (EA) ... ARI
Animal Rights Law Reporter [*A publication*] (DLA) ... Animal Rights L Rep
Animal Rights Law Reporter (journ.) (SAUS) ... AninW Rights L Rep
Animal Rights Mobilization (EA) ... ARM
Animal Rights Network (EA) ... ARN
Animal Rights Resource Site (SAUO) ... ARRS
Animal Service International (SAUO) ... ASI
Animal Test Certificate (GVA) ... ATC
Animal Transport [*Navy ship symbol*] [*Obsolete*] ... APA
Animal Transport [*British and Canadian*] [*World War II*] ... AT
Animal Transport Company (SAUO) ... ATC
Animal Transportation Association (EA) ... AATA
Animal Treatment Center (GVA) ... ATC
Animal Tub Sized (SAUS) ... ATS
Animal Tumor Research Facility [*Rochester University*] (PDAA) ... ATRE
Animal Tumor Research Facility (SAUO) ... ATRF
Animal Vegetable and Mineral (SAUS) ... AVM
Animal Virus Research Institute (SAUO) ... AVRI
Animal Virus Research Institute [*British*] (ARC) ... AVRI
Animal Welfare Advisory Committee (SAUO) ... AWAC
Animal Welfare Advisory Council (SAUO) ... AWAC
Animal Welfare Foundation (GVA) ... AWF
Animal Welfare Information Center [*Department of Agriculture*] [*Information service or system*] (IID) ... AWIC
Animal Welfare Institute (EA) ... AWI
Animal Welfare League (SAUO) ... AWL
Animal Welfare League of South Australia ... AWLSA
Animal Welfare Officer (SARE) ... AWO
Animal Welfare, Science, Ethics, and Law Veterinary Association (GVA) ... AWSELVA
Animal-Assisted Activities (SAUS) ... AAA
Animal-Assisted-Therapy (ADWA) ... AAT
Animal-Assisted-Therapy Teams (SAUO) ... AAT
Animal-Facilitated Therapy ... AFT
Animal-Protein Factor (SAUS) ... APF
Animals Defender and Anti-Vivisectionist (journ.) (SAUS) ... Anti-Viv
Animals without Frontiers-International (SAUO) ... AWF-International
Animal-Tub-Sized [*Paper*] ... ATS
Animal-Unit Month ... AUM
Animal-Vues (EA) ... AV
Animate (WGA) ... AN
Animated ... ANMTD
Animated Backlighted Burtek Trainer ... ABBT
Animated Biological Laboratories (SAUS) ... ABL
Animated Burtek Trainer ... ABT
Animated Computer Education ... ACE
Animated Cursor (SAUS) ... ANI
Animated Dissection of Anatomy for Medicine [*Interactive Multimedia Program*] ... ADAM
Animated Film Language (BUR) ... AFL
Animated Graphics System (WDMC) ... AGS
Animated Movie Language (BUR) ... AML
Animated Reconstruction of Telemetry ... ART
Animation [*Films, television, etc.*] ... ANIM
Animation Photo Transfer [*Animation technique developed by Disney Studio*] ... APT
Animation Producers' Association [*Defunct*] (EA) ... APA
Animato [*To be Performed in a lively Manner*] [*Italian*] [*Music*] (WDAA) ... anim
Animato [*Lively, Animated*] [*Music*] ... ANIMO
Animed, Inc. (SAUS) ... VETS
Animism (SAUS) ... Anim
Anina Resources, Inc. [*Vancouver Stock Exchange symbol*] ... ANI
Anina Resources, Incorporated (SAUO) ... ANI
Anion ... A
Anion Exchange Resin (DB) ... AER
Anion Exchanger 1 [*Biochemistry*] ... AE1
Anion Gap [*Medicine*] (DAVI) ... AG
Anion Selective Membrane (SAUS) ... ASM
Anion Vacancies (SAUS) ... AV
Anion Vacancy (IAA) ... AV
Anionic Neutrophil Activating Peptide (ADWA) ... ANAP
Anion-Responsive Electrode ... ARE
Anisakan [*Myanmar*] [*ICAO location identifier*] (ICLI) ... VBAS
Anisean [*Geology*] ... A
Anisidine Value [*Food science*] ... AnV
Anisocytosis [*Hematology*] (DAVI) ... ANIS
Anisocytosis [*Hematology*] ... aniso
Anisometropia [*Ophthalmology*] ... AN
Anisometropia (LDT) ... An
Anisometropia [*Ophthalmology*] ... Anisometr
anisotrop (SAUS) ... a
Anisotrophic Etch (SAUS) ... ATE
Anisotropic Constant (SAUS) ... AC
Anisotropic Hypernetted Chain [*Chemical physics*] ... AHNC
Anisotropic Magnetoresistance ... AMR
Anisotropic Remanent Magnetism (PDAA) ... ARM
Anisotropic Saturation Recovery [*NMR imaging*] ... ASR
Anisotropic Source Flux Iteration Technique (PDAA) ... ASFIT
Anisotropic Spin-Orbit (PDAA) ... ASO
Anisotropic Stress Effect (PDAA) ... ASE
Anisotropically Conductive Adhesive [*Electronics*] (AAEL) ... ACA
Anisotropically Conductive Silicone [*Rubber*] [*Robotics*] ... ACS

Anisotropy of Magnetic Susceptibility [*Geophysics*] ... AMS
Anisoyl [*As substituent on nucleoside*] [*Biochemistry*] ... an
Anisoylated-Plasminogen-Streptokinase Activator Complex [*Thrombolytic*] ... APSAC
Anistropy Telescope [*Instrumentation*] ... AT
Anisum [*Anise Seed*] [*Pharmacology*] (ROG) ... ANIS
Anisyl Acetone (SAUS) ... AA
Anisylacetone [*Organic chemistry*] ... AA
Anita Tribune, Anita, IA [*Library symbol*] [*Library of Congress*] (LCLS) ... IaAniT
Anitarmor Helicopter Troop (SAUO) ... AAHT
Anit-Intercontinental Ballistic Missile (SAUS) ... A-IBCM
Anit-Tank Battery (SAUO) ... ATkBty
Aniwa [*Vanuatu*] [*ICAO location identifier*] (ICLI) ... NVVB
Anixter International, Inc. [*Associated Press*] (SAG) ... Anixter
Anixter International, Inc. [*NYSE symbol*] (SAG) ... AXE
Anixter Intl. [*NYSE symbol*] (TTSB) ... AXE
Anjouan [*Comoro Islands*] [*Airport symbol*] (OAG) ... AJN
Anjouan/Ouani [*Comoros*] [*ICAO location identifier*] (ICLI) ... FMCV
Ankang [*China*] [*Airport symbol*] (OAG) ... AKA
Ankara [*Turkey*] [*Airport symbol*] (OAG) ... ANK
Ankara [*Turkey*] [*Seismograph station code, US Geological Survey*] (SEIS) ... ANK
Ankara [*Turkey*] [*ICAO location identifier*] (ICLI) ... LTAA
Ankara-Esenboga [*Turkey*] [*Airport symbol*] (OAG) ... ESB
Ankara/Esenboga [*Turkey*] [*ICAO location identifier*] (ICLI) ... LTAC
Ankara/Etimesgut [*Turkey*] [*ICAO location identifier*] (ICLI) ... LTAD
Ankara/Murted [*Turkey*] [*ICAO location identifier*] (ICLI) ... LTAE
Ankatan Udara Republik Indonesia ... AURI
Ankavandra [*Madagascar*] [*ICAO location identifier*] (ICLI) ... FMMK
Ankavandra [*Madagascar*] [*Airport symbol*] (OAG) ... JVA
Ankazoabo [*Madagascar*] [*ICAO location identifier*] (ICLI) ... FMSZ
Ankazoabo [*Madagascar*] [*Airport symbol*] (OAG) ... WAK
Anken Chemical & Film Corp. (SAUO) ... AKF
Ankeny, IA [*FM radio station call letters*] ... KJJY
Ankeny, IA [*FM radio station call letters*] ... KMXD
Ankeny, IA [*FM radio station call letters*] (BROA) ... KYSY-FM
Ankeny Press-Citizen, Ankeny, IA [*Library symbol*] [*Library of Congress*] (LCLS) ... IaAnkP
Anker Data Systems (IAA) ... ADS
Anker of the Association for the Abolition of Abused Abbreviations and Asinine Acronyms (SAUO) ... AAAAAAA
Ankina Breeders [*Inactive*] (EA) ... AB
Anklam [*Germany*] [*ICAO location identifier*] (ICLI) ... ETAM
Ankle (MAE) ... ank
ankle (SAUS) ... ank
Ankle Arm Index ... AAI
Ankle Clonus Test [*Medicine*] (MELL) ... ACT
Ankle Drop (MELL) ... AD
Ankle Jerk [*Neurology*] ... AJ
ankle jerk (SAUS) ... aj
Ankle Orthosis [*Medicine*] (MELL) ... AO
Ankle/Brachial Pressure Index ... A/B
Ankle/Brachial Pressure Index ... ABI
Ankle/Brachial Pressure Index ... ABPI
Ankle-Foot [*Orthosis*] [*Orthopedics*] (DAVI) ... A-F
Ankle-Foot Orthosis [*Orthopedics*] ... AFO
Ankle-Foot-Knee Orthosis [*Medicine*] (MELL) ... AFKO
Ankole-Watusi International Registry (EA) ... AWIR
Ankylosing Spondylitis [*Medicine*] ... AS
Ankylosing Spondylitis [*Medicine*] (DMAA) ... ASP
Ankylosing Spondylitis Association (EA) ... ASA
Anlichymotrypsin (SAUS) ... ACT
Anlinuclear Antibody (SAUS) ... ANA
ANLs Advanced Computing Research Facility (SAUS) ... ANL/ACRF
Anmerkung [*Note*] [*German*] ... ANM
Ann [*Myanmar*] [*ICAO location identifier*] (ICLI) ... VBAN
Ann Arbor (SAUS) ... AA
Ann Arbor [*Michigan*] [*Seismograph station code, US Geological Survey*] (SEIS) ... AAM
Ann Arbor [*Michigan*] ... A^2
Ann Arbor (SAUS) ... Ay
Ann Arbor Air Quality System (SAUS) ... AQSY
Ann Arbor AP-42 Program (SAUS) ... APGR
Ann Arbor Certification Information and Fuel Economy Data Base (SAUS) ... CIDB
Ann Arbor ECTD HD System (SAUS) ... ECHD
Ann Arbor Evaluation and Development Test System (SAUS) ... EDTS
Ann Arbor In-Use Test Data System (SAUS) ... IUTD
Ann Arbor Laboratory Computer System (SAUS) ... LCS
Ann Arbor, MI [*Location identifier*] [*FAA*] (FAAL) ... ARB
Ann Arbor, MI [*AM radio station call letters*] ... WAAM
Ann Arbor, MI [*Television station call letters*] ... WBSX
Ann Arbor, MI [*FM radio station call letters*] ... WCBN
Ann Arbor, MI [*FM radio station call letters*] ... WIQB
Ann Arbor, MI [*Television station call letters*] (BROA) ... WPXD
Ann Arbor, MI [*FM radio station call letters*] ... WQKL
Ann Arbor, MI [*AM radio station call letters*] ... WTKA
Ann Arbor, MI [*FM radio station call letters*] ... WUOM
Ann Arbor Public Library, Ann Arbor, MI [*Library symbol*] [*Library of Congress*] (LCLS) ... MiAa
Ann Arbor Railroad (SAUO) ... AARR
Ann Arbor Railroad Co. [*AAR code*] ... AA
Ann Arbor Railroad Company (SAUO) ... AA
Ann Arbor Railroad Company (SAUO) ... AARC
Ann Taylor Stores [*NYSE symbol*] (SPSG) ... ANN
Ann Taylor Stores [*Associated Press*] (SAG) ... AnnTayl
Anna [*Monetary unit*] [*India*] ... A
Anna [*Ohio*] [*Seismograph station code, US Geological Survey*] (SEIS) ... AN1
Anna [*Ohio*] [*Seismograph station code, US Geological Survey*] (SEIS) ... AN3
Anna, IL [*AM radio station call letters*] (BROA) ... WIBH
Anna, IL [*FM radio station call letters*] (BROA) ... WKIB-FM
Anna, IL [*AM radio station call letters*] ... WRAJ
Anna, IL [*FM radio station call letters*] ... WRAJ-FM
Anna Regina [*Queen Anne*] ... AR
Annaba [*Algeria*] [*Airport symbol*] (OAG) ... AAE
Annaba/El Mellah [*Algeria*] [*ICAO location identifier*] (ICLI) ... DABB
Annai [*Guyana*] [*Airport symbol*] (OAG) ... NAI
Annai [*Guyana*] [*ICAO location identifier*] (ICLI) ... SYAN
Annal (SAUS) ... Ann
Annales [*Annals*] [*Latin*] (GPO) ... ann
Annales [*of Tacitus*] [*Classical studies*] (OCD) ... Ann
Annales Africaines [*A publication*] (ILCA) ... AA
Annales de Chimie et de Physique [*A publication*] (MEC) ... Ann Chim Phys
Annales de Droit Commercial et Industriel Francais, Etranger, et International [*A publication*] (DLA) ... Ann Dr Com Ind Fr Etr
Annales de Droit Commercial Francais, Etranger, et International [*A publication*] (DLA) ... Ann Dr Com Fr Etr Int
Annales de Droit Economique [*A publication*] (DLA) ... Ann Econ
Annales de la Propriete Industrielle, Artistique, et Litteraire [*A publication*] (DLA) ... Ann de la Pro
Annales des Justices de Paix [*France*] [*A publication*] (ILCA) ... AJP
Annales des Justices de Paix [*France*] [*A publication*] (DLA) ... Ann JP
Annales Economiques [*A publication*] (DLA) ... Ann Econ
Annales. Faculte de Droit. Ecole Francaise de Droit de Beyrouth [*A publication*] (DLA) ... Ann Ec Fr Dr Beyrouth
Annales. Faculte de Droit et des Sciences Economiques [*Beyrouth, Lebanon*] [*A publication*] (DLA) ... Ann de la Fac de Droit et des Sci Econ (Beyrouth)
Annales. Faculte de Droit et des Sciences Economiques de Beyrouth. Faculte de Droit [*A publication*] (DLA) ... Ann Fac Beyrouth
Annales. Faculte de Droit et des Sciences Economiques de Lille, France [*A publication*] (DLA) ... Ann de la Fac de Droit et des Sci Econ de Lille
Annales. Faculte de Droit et des Sciences Economiques de Lyon [*A publication*] (DLA) ... Ann Fac Lyon
Annales Geophysicae. Atmospheres, Hydrospheres and Space Sciences (SAUS) ... Ann Geophys Atmos Hydrosph Space Sci
Annales Malgaches [*A publication*] (DLA) ... Ann Malg
Annales Parlementaires [*Belgium*] [*A publication*] (DLA) ... Ann Parl
Annales. Universite de Madagascar [*A publication*] (DLA) ... Ann Malg
Annali di Chimica [*A publication*] (MEC) ... Ann Chim
Annali di Diritto Internazionale [*Milan*] [*A publication*] (DLA) ... Ann Dir Int
Annali di Storia del Diritto [*A publication*] (ILCA) ... Ann St Dir
Annali. Facolta di Giurisprudenza. Universita di Bari [*A publication*] (DLA) ... Ann Fac Bari
Annali. Istituto di Corrispondenza Archeologica [*A publication*] (OCD) ... Ann Ist
Annali. Seminario Giuridico. Universita Catania [*A publication*] (ILCA) ... Ann Sem Giur Catania
Annali. Seminario Giuridico. Universita di Palermo [*A publication*] (ILCA) ... Ann Sem Giur
Annals ... ANN
Annals (ADWA) ... ann
Annals (SAUS) ... Ann
Annals (DAVI) ... Annls
Annals. Agricultural Experiment Station. Govemment General of Chosen (journ.) (SAUS) ... Ann Agric Exp Stn Gov Gen Chosen
Annals. American Academy of Political and Social Science (journ.) (SAUS) ... Ann Am Acad
Annals. American Academy of Political and Social Science (journ.) (SAUS) ... Ann Am Poli
Annals. American Academy of Political and Social Science (journ.) (SAUS) ... APS
Annals. American Conference of Governmental Industrial Hygienists (journ.) (SAUS) ... AnnAmConfGoylndHyg
Annals. Association of American Geographers (journ.) (SAUS) ... Ann As Am G
Annals Australia: Journal of Catholic Culture [*A publication*] (APTA) ... AA
Annals. Australian College of Dental Surgeons (journ.) (SAUS) ... Ann Aust Coll Dent Surg
Annals. Bhandarkar Oriental Research Institute (journ.) (SAUS) ... An Bhand Or Res Inst
Annals. Bhandarkar Oriental Research Institute (journ.) (SAUS) ... AunBhl
Annals. Chinese Society of International Law [*Taipei, Taiwan*] [*A publication*] (DLA) ... Chinese Soc'y Int'l L Annals
Annals for the American Academy of Political and Social Science (journ.) (SAUS) ... Ann Am Acad Pol Sci
Annals. Hitotsubashi Academy [*A publication*] (DLA) ... Ann Hitotsubashi Acad
Annals. Indian Academy of Medical Sciences (journ.) (SAUS) ... AIADAX
Annals. Kurashiki Central Hospital (journ.) (SAUS) ... KCBNAY
Annals. Medical Section. Polish Academy of Sciences (journ.) (SAUS) ... Ann Med Sect Pol Acad Sci
Annals. Missouri Botanical Garden (journ.) (SAUS) ... Ann MO Bot Gdn
Annals. National Academy of Medical Sciences (journ.) (SAUS) ... Ann Natl Acad Med Sci
Annals of Agriculture Science (journ.) (SAUS) ... Ann Agri Sci
Annals of Allergy, Asthma and Immunology (SAUS) ... Ann Allergy Asthma Immunol
Annals of Allergy (journ.) (SAUS) ... ANAEA3
Annals of Allergy (journ.) (SAUS) ... Ann Allergy
Annals of American Geographers (journ.) (SAUS) ... AAG
Annals of Anatomy (SAUS) ... Ann Anat
Annals of Applied Biology. Supplement (journ.) (SAUS) ... Arm Appl Biol Suppl
Annals of Arid Zone (journ.) (SAUS) ... ANA7BX
Annals of Arid Zone (journ.) (SAUS) ... Ann Arid Zone

Annals of Assurance Sciences. Proceedings of Reliability and Maintainability Conference (journ.) (SAUS) ... Ann Assur Sci Proc Reliab Maint Conf
Annals of Behavioral Medicine (journ.) (SAUS) ... Ann Behav Med
Annals of Biology (SAUS) ... Ann Biol
Annals of Bio-Medical Engineering (SAUS) ... ABME
Annals of Biomedical Engineering (SAUO) ... ABME
Annals of Botany (SAUS) ... Ann Bot
Annals of Botany (journ.) (SAUS) ... ANBOA
Annals of Collective Economy [*Later, Annals of Public and Co-Operative Economy*] [*A publication*] ... ACE
Annals of Congress [*A publication*] (DLA) ... Ann C
Annals of Congress [*A publication*] (DLA) ... Ann Cong
Annals of Fluid Dynamics (journ.) (SAUS) ... Ann Fluiddyn
Annals of Glaciology (SAUS) ... Ann Glaciol
Annals of Glaciology (journ.) (SAUS) ... ANGL
Annals of Human Biology (journ.) (SAUS) ... AHUBBJ
Annals of Human Genetics (journ.) (SAUS) ... ANHGAA
Annals of Improbable Research [*A publication*] ... AIR
Annals of Internal Medicine [*A publication*] (MELL) ... AIM
Annals of International Studies (journ.) (SAUS) ... Annals Internat Studies
Annals of Kentucky Natural History (journ.) (SAUS) ... Annals KY Nat History
Annals of Library Science (journ.) (SAUS) ... Annals Lib Sci
Annals of Life Insurance Medicine (journ.) (SAUS) ... Ann lafe Ins Med
Annals of Mathematics (journ.) (SAUS) ... Ann Math
Annals of Medical History (journ.) (SAUS) ... Ann Med Hist
Annals of Medicine (journ.) (SAUS) ... Ann Med
Annals of Neurology (journ.) (SAUS) ... Ann Neurol
Annals of Nuclear Energy (journ.) (SAUS) ... ANENDJ
Annals of Nutrition and Metabolism (journ.) (SAUS) ... Ann Nutr Metab
Annals of Ophthalmology and Otology (journ.) (SAUS) ... Ann Ophth Otol
Annals of Oriental Research (journ.) (SAUS) ... AOR
Annals of Oriental Research. University of Madras (journ.) (SAUS) ... Ann OR
Annals of Oto-Rino-Laryngologica Ibero-Americana (journ.) (SAUS) ... AOIAA
Annals of Philosophy [*A publication*] (BARN) ... AP
Annals of Physical Medicine (journ.) (SAUS) ... Ann Phys Med
Annals of Physical Medicine (journ.) (SAUS) ... APMDA6
Annals of Physics (journ.) (SAUS) ... Ann Phys
Annals of Physiological Anthropology (journ.) (SAUS) ... Anthropol
Annals of Physiological Anthropology (journ.) (SAUS) ... APANEE
Annals of Plastic Surgery (journ.) (SAUS) ... Ann Plast Surg
Annals of Probabilily (journ.) (SAUS) ... Anls Prob
Annals of Public and Cooperative Economy (journ.) (SAUS) ... APCE
Annals of Pure and Applied Logic (journ.) (SAUS) ... Ann Pur App
Annals of Science [*A publication*] (MEC) ... Ann Sci
Annals of Science [*A publication*] (BARN) ... AS
Annals of Science. Kanazawa University (journ.) (SAUS) ... KRSHB
Annals of Science. Kanazawa University. Part 2. Biology-Geology (journ.) (SAUS) ... Ann Sci Kanazawa Univ Part 2 Bio Geol
Annals of Science. Kanazawa University. Part 2. Biology-Geology (journ.) (SAUS) ... KDSRA2
Annals of Statistics (SAUS) ... Ann Stat
Annals of Statistics (journ.) (SAUS) ... Anls Stat
Annals of Surgery (journ.) (SAUS) ... Ann Surg
Annals of the American Academy of Political and Social Science [*A publication*] (AAGC) ... Annals
Annals of the Association of American Geographers (SAUO) ... AAAG
Annals of the Entomological Society of America (journ.) (SAUS) ... Ann Entomol Soc Amer
Annals of the ICRP (SAUS) ... Ann ICRP
Annals of the Kings of Assyria [*A publication*] (BJA) ... AKA
Annals of the Missouri Botanical Garden (SAUS) ... Ann Mo Bot Gard
Annals of the New York Academy of Sciences (journ.) (SAUS) ... Ann NY Acad Sci
Annals of the Propagation of the Faith (journ.) (SAUS) ... AP Faith
Annals of the Rheumatic Diseases (journ.) (SAUS) ... Ann Rheum Dis
Annals of the Royal College of Surgeons of England (SAUS) ... Ann R Coll Surg Engl
Annals of the South African Museum (SAUS) ... Ann S Afr Mus
Annals of Thoracic Surgery (journ.) (SAUS) ... Ann Thorac Surg
Annals of Tropical Medicine and Parasitology (journ.) (SAUS) ... Ann Trop Med Parasitol
Annals of Veterinary Research (journ.) (SAUS) ... Ann Vet Res
Annals of Western Medicine and Surgery. Los Angeles County Medical Association (journ.) (SAUS) ... Ann Western Med Surg
Annals of Wyoming (journ.) (SAUS) ... Ann Wyo
Annals of Zoology (SAUS) ... Ann Zool
Annals of Zoology (journ.) (SAUS) ... Ann Zool
Annals. Oklahoma Academy of Science (journ.) (SAUS) ... Ann Okla Acad Sci
Annals. Research Institute of Epidemiology and Microbiology (journ.) (SAUS) ... TNEMBJ
Annals. South Africa Museum [*A publication*] ... ASAM
Annals. Zimbabwe Geological Survey (journ.) (SAUS) ... Ann Zimbabwe Geol Surv
Annaly Mortgage Mgmt [*NYSE symbol*] (SG) ... NLY
Annaly's Lee Tempore Hardwicke [*7-10 George II, King's Bench*] [*1733-38*] [*A publication*] (DLA) ... Ann
Annamalai University. Agricultural Research Annual (journ.) (SAUS) ... Annamalai Univ Agric Res Annu
Annamalainagar [*India*] [*Geomagnetic observatory code*] ... ANN
Annament Control System (SAUS) ... ACS
Annamese (SAUS) ... An
Annandale Corp. (SAUO) ... ANNA
Annandale High School, Annandale, MN [*Library symbol*] [*Library of Congress*] (LCLS) ... MnAdH
Annandale Middle School, Annandale, MN [*Library symbol*] [*Library of Congress*] (LCLS) ... MnAdMS
Annandale Public Library, Annandale, MN [*Library symbol*] [*Library of Congress*] (LCLS) ... MnAd
Annapolis Bancshares [*NASDAQ symbol*] (TTSB) ... ANNB
Annapolis Bancshares, Inc. [*Associated Press*] (SAG) ... AnnapB
Annapolis Bancshares, Inc. [*NASDAQ symbol*] (SAG) ... ANNB
Annapolis Brass Quintet (SAUO) ... ABQ
Annapolis Division [*Maryland*] [*Navy*] (DNAB) ... ANNADIV
Annapolis Lymphoblast Globulin [*Biochemistry*] (MAH) ... ALG
Annapolis, MD [*Location identifier*] [*FAA*] (FAAL) ... ANP
Annapolis, MD [*AM radio station call letters*] ... WANN
Annapolis, MD [*AM radio station call letters*] (BROA) ... WBIS
Annapolis, MD [*FM radio station call letters*] ... WFSI
Annapolis, MD [*FM radio station call letters*] ... WHFS
Annapolis, MD [*Television station call letters*] ... WMPT
Annapolis, MD [*AM radio station call letters*] ... WNAV
Annapolis, MD [*AM radio station call letters*] ... WYRE
Annapolis Regiment (SAUO) ... A
Annapolis Regiment (SAUO) ... AnnRgt
Annapolis Region Community Arts Council (AC) ... ARCAC
Annapolis Science Center ... ASC
Annapolis Valley Regional Library, Annapolis Royal, NS [*Library symbol*] [*National Library of Canada*] (NLC) ... NSAR
Annapolis Valley Regional Library, Annapolis Royal, NS, Canada [*Library symbol*] [*Library of Congress*] (LCLS) ... CaNSAR
Annapurna Conservation Area Project [*Nepal*] ... ACAP
Anne Arundel Community College (SAUS) ... AACC
Anne Christy Fan Club (EA) ... ACFC
Anne Frank Center U.S.A. (EA) ... AFAFC
Anne Frank Fund [*Basel, Switzerland*] (EAIO) ... AFF
Anne Frank Institute of Philadelphia [*Formerly, NIH*] (EA) ... AFIP
Anne Frank Stichting [*Anne Frank Foundation*] [*Netherlands*] (EAIO) ... AFS
Anne Murray Fan Club (EA) ... AMFC
Anneal (KSC) ... ANL
Annealed (SAUS) ... Anld
Annealed (SAUS) ... Ann
Annealed ... ANN
Annealed Cast Iron (SAUS) ... ACI
Annealed Copper-covered Steel (SAUS) ... ACS
Annealed Copper-Covered Steel ... ACS
Annealed Proton Exchange (SAUS) ... APE
Annealing (ABBR) ... A
Annealing Point (MCD) ... AP
Annecy [*France*] [*Airport symbol*] (OAG) ... NCY
Annecy/Meythet [*France*] [*ICAO location identifier*] (ICLI) ... LFLP
Annee Courante [*Of the Current Year*] [*French*] ... AC
Annee de Lumiere [*Light Year*] [*French*] ... AL
Annee Mondiale du Refugie ... AMR
Annemasse [*France*] [*ICAO location identifier*] (ICLI) ... LFLI
Annenberg Research Institute for Judaic and Middle Eastern Studies, Philadelphia, PA [*Library symbol*] [*Library of Congress*] (LCLS) ... PPAnR
Annesley on Insurance [*A publication*] (DLA) ... Ann Ins
Annette Funicello Fan Club (EA) ... AFFC
Annette Island [*Alaska*] [*Airport symbol*] [*Obsolete*] (OAG) ... ANN
Annette Island [*Alaska*] [*ICAO location identifier*] (ICLI) ... PANT
Annex ... AN
Annex [*Commonly used*] (OPSA) ... ANEX
Annex ... ANN
Annex (SAUS) ... Ann
Annex [*Commonly used*] (OPSA) ... ANNX
Annex (AABC) ... ANX
Annex (SAUS) ... Anx
Annex to the Kyoto Protocol listing the GHGs and sector/source categories (SAUS) ... Annex A
Annex to the Kyoto Protocol listing the the quantified emission limitation or reduction commitment per Party (SAUO) ... Annex B
Annexure [*British and Canadian*] [*World War II*] ... annx
Annhurst College (SAUO) ... AC
Anni [*Years*] [*Latin*] (GPO) ... ann
Anni Caesar [*Era of the Caesars*] [*Latin*] (ROG) ... A CAES
Anni Currentis [*Of the Current Year*] [*Latin*] (ROG) ... AC
Anni Praesentis [*In the Present Year*] [*Latin*] ... ap
Annie Penn Hospital, Medical Library, Reidsville, NC [*Library symbol*] [*Library of Congress*] (LCLS) ... NcReH
Annie People (EA) ... AP
Annihilation Radiation [*Physics*] ... ACAR
Anniston [*Alabama*] [*Airport symbol*] (OAG) ... ANB
Anniston, AL [*Location identifier*] [*FAA*] (FAAL) ... RLI
Anniston, AL [*AM radio station call letters*] ... WANA
Anniston, AL [*AM radio station call letters*] ... WDNG
Anniston, AL [*FM radio station call letters*] (RBYB) ... WGRW-FM
Anniston, AL [*AM radio station call letters*] ... WHMA
Anniston, AL [*FM radio station call letters*] ... WHMA-FM
Anniston, AL [*Television station call letters*] ... WJSU
Anniston Army Depot (ACAE) ... AAD
Anniston Army Depot [*Alabama*] (AABC) ... ANAD
Anniston Museum of Natural History, Anniston, AL [*Library symbol*] [*Library of Congress*] (LCLS) ... AAnnM
Anniston Public Library, Anniston, AL [*Library symbol*] [*Library of Congress*] (LCLS) ... AAnn
anniversary (SAUS) ... aniv
Anniversary ... ANNIV
Anniversary ... Anniv
Anniversary (ADWA) ... anniv
Anno [*or Annus*] [*Year*] [*Latin*] ... A
Anno [*or Annus*] [*Year*] [*Latin*] ... AN

Anno [*Year*] [*Latin*] .... ANN
anno (SAUS) .... Ann
Anno Ab Urbe Condita [*In the Year from the Building of the City (Rome)*] [*Latin*] (ROG) .... ANAUC
Anno ante Christum [*In the Year before Christ*] [*Latin*] .... AAC
Anno ante Christum [*In the Year before Christ*] [*Latin*] (ROG) .... AN AC
Anno ante Christum Natum [*In the Year before the Birth of Christ*] [*Latin*] (DLA) .... AACN
Anno Christi [*In the Year of Christ*] [*Latin*] .... AC
Anno Christi [*In the Year of Christ*] [*Latin*] (ROG) .... AN C
Anno Christianis Aerae [*In the Year of the Christian Era*] [*Latin*] .... ACE
Anno Corrente [*In the Current Year*] [*Latin*] (ADA) .... AC
Anno Depositionis [*In the Year of the Deposit*] [*Freemasonry*] [*Latin*] .... A DEP
Anno Domini [*In the Year of Our Lord*] [*Latin*] (GPO) .... AD
Anno Domini [*In the Year of Our Lord*] [*Latin*] .... AN DO
Anno Futuro [*In the Next Year*] [*Latin*] .... AF
Anno Hebraico [*In the Hebrew Year*] [*Since 3761 BC*] [*Latin*] .... AH
Anno Hegirae [*In the Year of the Hegira*] [*The flight of Mohammed from Mecca*] [*AD 622*] [*Latin*] .... AH
Anno Humanae Salutis [*In the Year of Human Salvation*] [*Latin*] .... AHS
Anno Inventionis [*In the Year of the Discovery*] [*Latin*] .... AI
Anno Inventionis [*In the Year of the Discovery*] [*Freemasonry*] [*Latin*] .... A INV
Anno Lucis [*In the Year of Light*] [*Latin*] .... AL
Anno Mundi [*In the Year of the World*] [*Since 4004 BC*] [*Latin*] (GPO) .... AM
Anno Orbis Conditi [*In the Year of the Creation*] [*Latin*] .... AOC
Anno Ordinis [*In the Year of the Order*] [*Used by the Knights Templar*] [*Freemasonry*] (ROG) .... AO
Anno post Christum Natum [*In the Year after Christ Was Born*] [*Latin*] (ROG) .... APC
Anno post Christum Natum [*In the Year after Christ Was Born*] [*Latin*] .... APCN
Anno post Roman Conditam [*In the Year after the Building of Rome*] [*753 BC*] [*Latin*] .... APRC
Anno Regni [*In the Year of the Reign*] [*Latin*] .... AR
Anno Regni Regis [*or Reginae*] [*In the Year of the King's, or Queen's, Reign*] [*Latin*] .... ARR
Anno Regni Victoriae Regina Vicesimo Secundo (DLA) .... ARVR 22
Anno Reparatae Salutis [*In the Year of Our Redemption*] [*Latin*] .... ARS
Anno Salvatoris [*or Salutis*] [*In the Year of Salvation*] [*Latin*] .... AS
Anno Urbis [*In the Year of the City of Rome*] [*Latin*] .... AU
Anno Urbis Conditae [*In the Year from the Building of the City (Rome)*] [*753 BC*] [*Latin*] .... AUC
Anno Vixit [*He Lived (a given number of) Years*] [*Latin*] .... AV
Annored Gun System (SAUS) .... AGS
annotate (SAUS) .... anot
Annotate .... ANOT
Annotated (DLA) .... Ann
Annotated (DLA) .... Anno
Annotated .... ANNOT
Annotated (ADWA) .... annot
Annotated Bibliography. Animal/ Human Series. Commonwealth Bureau of Animal Health (journ.) (SAUS) .... Annot Bibliogr Anirn/Hum Ser Commonw Bur Anim Health
Annotated Bibliography. Commonwealth Bureau of Nutrition (journ.) (SAUS) .... Annot Bibliogr Commonw Bur Nutr
Annotated Bibliography. Commonwealth Bureau of Pastures and Field Crops (journ.) (SAUS) .... Annot Bibliogr Commonw Bur Pastures Field Crops
Annotated Bibliography of Medical Mycology (journ.) (SAUS) .... Annot Bibliogr Med Myc
Annotated Bibtiography. Commonwealth Bureau of Soils (journ.) (SAUS) .... Annot Bibliogr Commonw Bur Soils
Annotated Card Program .... AC
Annotated Card Program (SAUS) .... ACP
Annotated Code [*A publication*] (DLA) .... Ann Code
Annotated Code of Maryland [*A publication*] (DLA) .... MD Ann Code
Annotated Code of Maryland [*A publication*] (DLA) .... MD Code Ann
Annotated Law Reporter [*1932-35*] [*India*] [*A publication*] (DLA) .... Ann L Rep
Annotated Laws of Massachusetts [*A publication*] (DLA) .... Mass Ann Laws
Annotated Laws of Massachusetts (journ.) (SAUS) .... Mass Ann Laws
Annotated Legal Forms Magazine (journ.) (SAUS) .... Ann Leg Forms Mag
Annotated Manual of Statutes and Regulations [*of the Federal Home Loan Bank Board*] .... AMSR
Annotated Outline (SAUS) .... AO
Annotated Predicate Calculus (MCD) .... APC
Annotated Reference Manual (VERA) .... ARM
Annotated Revised Code of Washington (SAUO) .... ARCW
Annotated Statutes [*A publication*] (DLA) .... Ann St
Annotated Statutes of Indian Territory [*A publication*] (DLA) .... Ann St Ind T
Annotated Tax Cases [*England*] [*A publication*] (DLA) .... Ann Tax Cas
Annotated Tax Cases [*A publication*] .... ATC
annotation (SAUS) .... annot
Annotation Display Unit (SAUS) .... ADU
Annotations (SAUS) .... Ann
Annotations to Official Florida Statutes [*A publication*] (DLA) .... Fla Stat Anno
Annotator [*MARC relator code*] [*Library of Congress*] (LCCP) .... ann
Announce (AABC) .... ANN
Announce (SAUS) .... Ann
Announce (FAAC) .... ANNC
Announce Booth [*Soundproof room*] [*Television studio*] (NTCM) .... AB
Announced [*or Announcement of*] Flight Opportunity [*NASA*] (KSC) .... AFO
Announced Retransmission Random Access [*Computer science*] (VERA) .... ARRA
Announcement (SAUS) .... Anmt
Announcement (SAUS) .... Ann
Announcement and Order Sheet (SAA) .... AOS
Announcement Day [*Military*] (DNAB) .... A (Day)

Announcement Number (DNAB) .... ANN NO
Announcement of Flight Opportunities (or Opportunity) (SAUS) .... AFO
Announcement of Opportunity [*NASA*] (MCD) .... AO
Announcer (NTCM) .... ANN
Announcer (SAUS) .... Ann
Announcer .... ANNCR
Announcer (WDMC) .... anncr
Announcing (MSA) .... ANCG
Announcing (SAUS) .... Ancg
Annoyance Call Bureau [*Telephone-pest control*] .... ACB
Annoyance Index [*Aviation*] (OA) .... AI
Annoyance Level [*Aircraft noise*] .... ANL
Annuaire (BJA) .... Ann
Annuaire. Academie Theologique (S. Clement D'Ochride) [*A publication*] (BJA) .... AnClemOchr
Annuaire de Legislation Francaise [*A publication*] (DLA) .... Ann Leg Fr
Annuaire de Legislation Francaise et Etrangere [*A publication*] (DLA) .... Ann de Leg
Annuaire. Faculte de Droit de Skopje [*A publication*] (DLA) .... Annu de la Fac de Droit de Skopje
Annuaire Francais de Droit International [*A publication*] .... ANFRIDI
Annuaire Judiciaire. [*A publication*] (DLA) .... Ann Jud
Annual .... A
Annual (AABC) .... ANL
Annual .... ANN
Annual (EBF) .... Ann
Annual (ROG) .... ANNL
Annual Active Duty for Training [*Army*] .... ANACDUTRA
Annual Activities Summary (ABAC) .... AAS
Annual Advance Retainer Pay .... AARP
Annual Aircraft Movements .... AAM
Annual Allowable Cut (SAUS) .... AAC
Annual Allowance and Requirements Review [*Navy*] .... AARR
Annual Audit (SAUS) .... AA
Annual Authorizations Service [*of the Copyright Clearance Center*] .... AAS
Annual Automated Controls Survey [*of a ship*] (DS) .... AAS
Annual Average Daily Traffic [*on highways*] .... AADT
Annual Average Growth Rate (AAEL) .... AAGR
Annual Average Rate of Growth (SAUS) .... AARG
Annual Average Score (AABC) .... AAS
Annual Average Weekday Traffic [*TRB*] (TAG) .... AAWDT
Annual. Bar-Ilan University Studies in Judaica and Humanities (journ.) (SAUS) .... Ann Bar-Il
Annual Bibliography of English Language and Literature (journ.) (SAUS) .... Annu Bibliogr Engl Lang Lit
Annual Budget Authorization (AFM) .... ABA
Annual Cancer Statistics Review (SAUO) .... ACSR
Annual Capital Charge .... ACC
Annual Capital Expenditures Survey (SAUS) .... ACES
Annual Capital Grant [*Education*] (AIE) .... ACG
Annual Change Traffic .... ACT
Annual Computer Graphics Conference (SAUS) .... ACGC
Annual Conference (ADA) .... AC
Annual Conference of Trades Councils (SAUO) .... ACTC
Annual Conference on Engineering in Medicine and Biology (HGAA) .... ACEMB
Annual Conference Program Advisory Committee [*American Occupational Therapy Association*] .... ACPAC
Annual Confidential Report .... ACR
Annual Contracted Quantity (ADA) .... ACQ
Annual Contributions Contract [*Public housing development*] .... ACC
Annual Corrective Maintenance (CAAL) .... ACM
Annual Cost of Capital Recovery (SAUS) .... ACCR
Annual Cost of Ownership .... ACO
Annual Course Contribution .... ACC
Annual Crops Department of CIRAD (SAUO) .... CIRAD-CA
Annual Curriculum Review [*Education*] (AIE) .... ACR
Annual Customer Order [*Air Force*] (AFIT) .... ANCO
Annual Cycle Energy System [*Energy Research and Development Admininistration*] .... ACES
Annual Cycle of Readings from Torah and Prophets (BJA) .... AC
Annual Cycle Thermal Energy Storage (PDAA) .... ACTES
Annual Delegate Meeting [*British*] (DCTA) .... ADM
Annual Demographic Survey [*Bureau of the Census*] (GFGA) .... ADS
Annual Departmental Report by the Director of Agriculture and Fisheries (SAUS) .... Annu Dep Rep Dir Agric Fish
Annual Digest and Reports of Public International Law Cases [*A publication*] (DLA) .... AD
Annual Digest and Reports of Public International Law Cases [*A publication*] .... ADIL
Annual Digest and Reports of Public International Law Cases [*A publication*] (DLA) .... ADILR
Annual Digest and Reports of Public International Law Cases [*A publication*] (DLA) .... Ann Dig
Annual Digest and Reports of Public International Law Cases [*A publication*] (DLA) .... Ann Dig ILC
Annual Digest of International Law [*A publication*] .... ADIL
Annual Economic Report. South African Reserve Bank (journ.) (SAUS) .... S Afr AR
Annual Effective Dose Equivlent (ABAC) .... AEDE
Annual Effective Yield [*Finance*] .... AEY
Annual Efficiency Index [*Army*] .... AEI
Annual Engineering Plan (AFIT) .... AEP
Annual Estimated Usage .... AEU
Annual Execution Plan (RDA) .... AEP
Annual Field Training [*Army*] (AABC) .... AFT

Annual Financial Plan ... AFP
Annual Financial Target [*DoD*] ... AFT
Annual Fuel Utilization Efficiency [*Furnaces*] ... AFUE
Annual Funding Program [*Army*] ... AFP
Annual General Inspection [*Army*] ... AGI
Annual General Meeting ... AGM
Annual Goal [*Education*] ... AG
Annual Growth Rate ... AGR
Annual High School Mathematics Examination [*Educational test*] ... AHSME
Annual History Review (MCD) ... AHR
Annual Hospital Report [*Program of the Department of Health and Human Services*] ... AHR
Annual Housing Survey [*Department of Housing and Urban Development*] (GFGA) ... AHS
Annual Hull Survey (DS) ... AHS
Annual Implementation Plan [*Health Planning and Resource Development Act of 1974*] ... AIP
Annual Improvement Factor (MCD) ... AIF
Annual Improvement, Maintenance, and Support (MHDI) ... AIMS
Annual Improvement Maintenance and Support (SAUS) ... AIMS
Annual Inert Gas System Survey (DS) ... AIGSS
Annual Infrastructure Report (SAUS) ... AIR
Annual Inspection and Overhaul [*Nuclear energy*] (NRCH) ... AI & O
Annual Inspection and Overhaul (SAUS) ... AI&O
Annual Inspection Summary (MCD) ... AIS
Annual Installed Capital Cost (EEVL) ... AICC
Annual Integrated Assessment of Security Assistance [*Military*] (DOMA) ... AIASA
Annual international screening conference for the exchange of program ideas (SAUO) ... INPUT
Annual Law Register of the United States [*A publication*] (DLA) ... Ann L Reg US
Annual Law Register of the United States (journ.) (SAUS) ... Ann L R
Annual Law Review [*Australia*] [*A publication*] ... Ann Law Review
Annual Lease [*Business term*] (MHDB) ... AL
Annual Lease Value (SAUS) ... ALV
Annual Leave [*US Civil Service*] ... AL
Annual Legal Bibliography [*Harvard Law School Library*] [*A publication*] (DLA) ... Ann Leg Bibliog
Annual License Fee [*FCC*] (NTCM) ... ALF
Annual Life Unit (MCD) ... ALU
Annual Limit of Intake (MHDB) ... ALI
Annual Logistic Estimate (NATG) ... LOGEST
Annual Long Island Library Conference ... LILC
Annual Machinery Survey [*American Bureau of Shipping*] (DS) ... AMS
Annual Maintenance Grant [*British*] (DET) ... AMG
Annual Maintenance Manhours [*Military*] (AABC) ... AMMH
Annual Major Additions Rate (SAUS) ... AMAR
Annual Material Forecast [*Military*] (AFM) ... AMF
Annual Mean Precipitation (SAUS) ... AMP
Annual Mean Temperature (SAUS) ... AMT
Annual methane emission from enteric fermentation (SAUS) ... ACH4
Annual Military Inspection ... AMI
Annual Military Personnel Inspection ... AMPI
Annual National Information Retrieval Colloquium ... ANIRC
Annual National Information Retrieval Colloquium (CIST) ... ANRIC
Annual Natural Forest Cleared (SAUS) ... ANFC
Annual North Eastern Regional Antipollution Conference (SAUS) ... ANERAC
Annual Northeast Regional Antipollution Conference ... ANERAC
Annual. Notre Dame Estate Planning Institute (journ.) (SAUS) ... Ann Notre Dame Est Plan Inst
Annual of Animal Psychology (journ.) (SAUS) ... Ann Anim Ps
Annual of Psychoanalysis (journ.) (SAUS) ... APSACT
Annual of the American Schools of Oriental Research (journ.) (SAUS) ... AASOR
Annual of the British School at Athens (journ.) (SAUS) ... ABSA
Annual of Urdu Studies (journ.) (SAUS) ... ANUS
Annual Officer Billet Summary (DNAB) ... AOBS
Annual Operating & Maintenance (SAUS) ... AOM
Annual Operating Budget [*Army*] ... AOB
Annual Operating Hours (MCD) ... AOH
Annual Operating Plan (SAUS) ... AOP
Annual Operating Program [*Army*] ... AOP
Annual Operating Requirements ... AOR
Annual Ordinary Shareholders' Meeting [*Investment term*] ... AOSM
Annual Percentage Rate ... APR
Annual Percentage Yield ... APY
Annual Permanent Improvement Program (AAGC) ... APIP
Annual Personal Weapon Test (SAUS) ... APWT
Annual Plan ... AP
Annual Planning Estimate [*Navy*] (NVT) ... APE
Annual Planning Report ... APR
Annual Planning Report. District of Columbia (journ.) (SAUS) ... Ann Plan Rep DC
Annual Practice [*A publication*] (DLA) ... Ann Pr
Annual Practice [*A publication*] (DLA) ... AP
Annual Premium (MARI) ... AP
Annual Print Awards (DGA) ... APA
Annual Proceedings. Electron Microscopy Society of America (journ.) (SAUS) ... A Proc Electron Microsc Soc Am
Annual Proceedings. Gifu College of Pharmacy (journ.) (SAUS) ... A Proc Gifu Coll Pharm
Annual Proceedings. National Association of Railway Commissions [*A publication*] (DLA) ... Ann Proc Nat Asso R Coms
Annual Proceedings of the Gulf and Caribbean Fisheries Institute (SAUS) ... Annu Proc Gulf Caribb Fish Inst
Annual Proceedings. Phytochemical Society (journ.) (SAUS) ... APPHCZ
Annual Procurement Agreement (MCD) ... APA
Annual Production (SAUS) ... AP
Annual Program Objectives [*Navy*] (NG) ... APO
Annual Progress in Child Psychiatry and Child Development (journ.) (SAUS) ... APCCD
Annual Progress Report ... APR
Annual Progress Report Geological Survey.Western Australia (journ.) (SAUS) ... Ann Prog Rep Geol Surv West Austr
Annual Progress Report National Foundation for Cancer Research (journ.) (SAUS) ... Ann Prog Rep Nat Found Cancer Res
Annual Purdue Air Quality Conference. Proccedings (journ.) (SAUS) ... Ann Purdue Air Qual Conf Proc
Annual Qualifications Questionnaire [*Navy*] (NVT) ... AQQ
Annual Questionnaire ... AQ
Annual Rainfall, Australia (journ.) (SAUS) ... Ann Rainf Aust
Annual Rate ... AR
Annual Rate Plus Stock Dividend [*Investment term*] (DFIT) ... B
Annual Real Growth (IUSS) ... ARG
Annual Records of Tropical Systems (QUAC) ... ARTS
Annual Recurrence Interval (SAUS) ... ARI
Annual Reevaluation of Safe Areas (MCD) ... ARSA
Annual Refrigerated Machinery Survey [*of a vessel*] (DS) ... ARS
Annual Register [*London*] [*A publication*] (DLA) ... Ann Reg
Annual Register [*A publication*] ... AR
Annual Register, New Series [*A publication*] (DLA) ... Ann Reg NS
Annual Renewable Term [*Insurance*] ... ART
Annual Rent (SAUS) ... R
Annual Report (SAUS) ... Ann Rep
Annual Report [*A publication*] (DLA) ... Ann Rep
Annual Report (DNAB) ... ANNREPT
Annual Report (SAUS) ... Ann Rept
Annual Report ... ANREP
Annual Report ... AR
annual report (SAUS) ... Jber
Annual Report and Accounts. Anglian Water (SAUS) ... Annu Rep Acc Anglian Water
Annual Report and Accounts. Irish Sea Fisheries Board (SAUS) ... Annu Rep Acc Ir Sea Fish Board
Annual Report and Accounts. National Rivers Authority (SAUS) ... Annu Rep Acc Natl Rivers Auth
Annual Report and Accounts. Sea Fish Industry Authority (SAUS) ... Annu Rep Acc Sea Fish Ind Auth
Annual Report and Accounts. South West Water Authority (SAUS) ... Annu Rep Acc South West Water Auth
Annual Report and Accounts. Thames Water Authority (SAUS) ... Annu Rep Acc Thames Water Auth
Annual Report and Accounts. Yorkshire Water Authority (SAUS) ... Annu Rep Acc Yorks Water Auth
Annual Report and Financial Statements. Institute of Corn and Agricultural Merchants (journ.) (SAUS) ... Annu Rep Finan Statements Inst Corn Agy Merchants
Annual Report and Official Opinions of the Attorney General of Indiana [*A publication*] (DLA) ... Ann Rep & Op Ind Att'y Gen
Annual Report and Official Opinions of the Attorney General of Maryland [*A publication*] (DLA) ... Ann Rep & Op MD Att'y Gen
Annual Report. Atlantic Fisheries Restructuring Act (SAUS) ... Annu Rep Atl Fish Restructuring Act
Annual Report. Atlantic Salmon Federation (SAUO) ... Annu Rep Atl Salmon Fed
Annual Report. Australian Institute of Marine Science (SAUS) ... Annu Rep Aust Inst Mar Sci
Annual Report. Bermuda Biological Station for Research (SAUS) ... Annu Rep Bermud Biol Stn Res
Annual Report. Canada Institute for Scientific and Technical Information (SAUS) ... Annu Rep Can Inst Sci Tech Inf
Annual Report. Canada Water Act (SAUS) ... Annu Rep Can Water Act
Annual Report. Canadian Institute of Fisheries Technology (SAUS) ... Annu Rep Can Inst Fish Technol
Annual Report. Cancer Research Institute. Kanazawa University (journ.) (SAUS) ... KCRABB
Annual Report. Central Marine Fisheries Research Institute, Cochin (SAUS) ... Annu Rep Cent Mar Res Inst Cochin
Annual Report. Chesapeake Bay Foundation (SAUO) ... Annu Rep Chesapeake Bay Found
Annual Report. Chief Directorate Marine Development (SAUS) ... Annu Rep Chief Dir Mar Dev
Annual Report. Clyde River Purification Board (SAUS) ... Annu Rep Clyde River Purif Board
Annual Report Council (EA) ... ARC
Annual Report. Department of Fisheries (SAUS) ... Annu Rep Dep Fish
Annual Report. Department of Fisheries and Oceans (SAUS) ... Annu Rep Dep Fish Oceans
Annual Report. Department of Mines. New South Wales [*Australia*] [*A publication*] ... Ann Rept Dept Mines NSW
Annual Report. Durban Natural History Museum (SAUS) ... Annu Rep Durb Nat Hist Mus
Annual Report. Engineering Research Institute. Tokyo University (journ.) (SAUS) ... Annu Rep Eng Res Inst Tokyo Univ
Annual Report. Engineering Research Institute. University of Tokyo (journ.) (SAUS) ... Annu Rep Eng Res Inst Univ Tokyo
Annual Report. Entomological Society of Ontario (journ.) (SAUS) ... Annu Rep Entomol Sec Ont
Annual Report. Environment Canada (SAUS) ... Annu Rep Environ Can
Annual Report. Environmental Pollution Research Center. Fukui Prefecture (journ.) (SAUS) ... Annu Rep Environ Pollut Res Cent Fukui Prefect
Annual Report. Environmental Pollution Research Center of Ibaraki-Ken (journ.) (SAUS) ... Annu Rep Environ Pollut Res Cent Ibaraki-Ken

Annual Report. Environmental Research Laboratories, National Oceanic and Atmospheric Administration (SAUS) .... Annu Rep ERL/NOAA

Annual Report. Faculty of Education. Gunma University. Art and Technology Series (journ.) (SAUS) .... Annu Rep Fac Educ Gunma Univ Art Technol Ser

Annual Report. Faculty of Education. Gunma University. Art and Technology Series (journ.) (SAUS) GDKYA7

Annual Report. Faculty of Education. Gunma University. Art, Technology, Health and Physical Education and Science of Human Living Series (journ.) (SAUS) GDKKD2

Annual Report. Faculty of Education. Gunma University (journ.) (SAUS) .... Annu Rep Fac Educ Gunma Univ

Annual Report. Faculty of Education. Iwate University (journ.) (SAUS) .... Annu Rep Fac Educ Iwate Univ

Annual Report. Faculty of Education. University of Iwate (journ.) (SAUS) .... Annu Rep Fac Educ Univ Iwate

Annual Report. Farrners Union Grain Terminal Association (journ.) (SAUS) .... Annu Rep Farmers Union Grain Terminal Ass

Annual Report. Fish Marketing Organization, Hong Kong (SAUS) .... Annu Rep Fish Mark Organ Hong Kong

Annual Report. Fisheries and Aquaculture (SAUS) .... Annu Rep Fish Aquac

Annual Report. Fisheries Department (SAUS) .... Annu Rep Fish Dep

Annual Report. Fisheries Development Act. Department of Fisheries and Oceans (SAUS) .... Annu Rep Fish Dev Act Dep Fish Oceans

Annual Report. Fisheries Division (SAUS) .... Annu Rep Fish Div

Annual Report. Fisheries Prices Support Board Canada (SAUS) .... Annu Rep Fish Prices Support Board Can

Annual Report. Fishery Survey of India (SAUS) .... Annu Rep Fish Surv India

Annual Report. Florida University. Agricultural Experiment Station (journ.) (SAUS) .... Annu Rep Fla Univ Agr Exp Sta

Annual Report. Food Research Institute. Aichi Prefecture (journ.) (SAUS) .... Annu Rep Food Res Inst Aichi Prefect

Annual Report. Forth River Purification Board (SAUS) .... Annu Rep Forth River Purif Board

Annual Report. Freshwater Biological Association (SAUO) .... Annu Rep Freshw Biol Ass

Annual Report. Geological Survey. Federation of Nigeria (journ.) (SAUS) .... Annu Rep Geol Surv Fed Niger

Annual Report. Geological Survey of Malaysia (journ.) (SAUS) .... Annu Rep Geol Surv Malaysia

Annual Report. Geological Survey. Western Australia (journ.) (SAUS) .... Annu Rep Geol Surv West Aust

Annual Report. Great Barrier Reef Marine Park Authority (SAUS) .... Annu Rep Gt Barrier Reef Mar Park Auth

Annual Report. Great Lakes Fishery Commission (SAUS) .... Annu Rep GLFC

Annual Report. Highland River Purification Board (SAUS) .... Annu Rep Highl River Purif Board

Annual Report. Hokkaido Branch. Forestry and Forest Products Research Institute (journ.) (SAUS) .... Annu Rep Hokkaido Bor For For Prod Res Inst

Annual Report. Hokkaido Branch. Government Forest Experiment Station (journ.) (SAUS) .... Annu Rep Hokkaido Branch Gov For Exp Stn

Annual Report. Hokusei Gakuin Junior College (journ.) (SAUS) .... Annu Rep Hokusei Gakuin Jr Coll

Annual Report. Huntsman Marine Science Centre (SAUS) .... Annu Rep Huntsman Mar Sci Cent

Annual Report. Indiana Agricultural Experiment Station (journ.) (SAUS) .... Annu Rep Ind Agdc Exp Stn

Annual Report. Institute for Nuclear Study. University of Tokyo (journ.) (SAUS) .... Annu Rep Inst Nucl Stud Univ Tokyo

Annual Report. Institute for Virus Research. Kyoto University (journ.) (SAUS) .... Annu Rep Inst Virus Res Kyoto Univ

Annual Report. Institute of Food Microbiology. Chiba University (journ.) (SAUS) .... Annu Rep Inst Food Microbiol Chiba Univ

Annual Report. Institute of Landscape Ecology (SAUS) .... Annu Rep Inst Landsc Ecol

Annual Report. Institute of Marine Engineers (journ.) (SAUS) .... Annu Rep Inst Mar Eng

Annual Report. Institute of Oceanographic Sciences (SAUS) .... Annu Rep Inst Oceanogr Sci

Annual Report. Institute of Sciences and Technology. Meiji University (journ.) (SAUS) .... Annu Rep Inst Sci Technol Meiji Unir

Annual Report. Institute of Sociology (journ.) (SAUS) .... Annu Rep Inst Sociol

Annual Report. Inter-American Tropical Tuna Commission (SAUS) .... Annu Rep I-ATTC

Annual Report. International Association of Milk Sanitarians (journ.) (SAUS) .... Annu Rep Int Assoc Milk Sanit

Annual Report. International Crop Improvement Association (journ.) (SAUS) .... Annu Rep Int Crop Impr Ass

Annual Report. International North Pacific Fisheries Commission (SAUS) .... Annu Rep INPFC

Annual Report. International Pacific Halibut Commission (SAUS) .... Annu Rep IPHC

Annual Report. International Tin Research Council (journ.) (SAUS) .... Annu Rep Int Tin Res Counc

Annual Report. Iowa Cooperative Fish and Wildlife Research Unit (SAUS) .... Annu Rep Iowa Coop Fish Wildl Res Unit

Annual Report. Iranian Fisheries Research and Training Organization (SAUS) .... Annu Rep Iran Fish Res Train Organ

Annual Report. Itsuu Laboratory (journ.) (SAUS) .... Annu Rep Itsuu Lab

Annual Report. Japanese Association for Tuberculosis (journ.) (SAUS) .... Annu Rep Jpn Assoc Tuberc

Annual Report. Japanese Society for Tuberculosis (journ.) (SAUS) .... Annu Rep Jpn Soc Tuber

Annual Report. John Innes Horticultural Institution (journ.) (SAUS) .... Annu Rep John Innes Hortic Inst

Annual Report (journ.) (SAUS) .... Ann Rept

Annual Report. Kinki University. Atomic Energy Research Institute (journ.) (SAUS) .... KDGNBX

Annual Report. Kumamoto Livestock Experiment Station (journ.) (SAUS) .... Annu Rep Kumamoto Livest Exp Stn

Annual Report. Kyoritsu College of Pharmacy (journ.) (SAUS) .... Annu Rep Kyoritsu Coll Pharm

Annual Report. Kyoritsu College of Pharmacy (journ.) (SAUS) .... KYDKAJ

Annual Report. Laboratory of Algology (journ.) (SAUS) .... LKAAAN

Annual Report. Laboratory of Public Health. Hiroshirna Prefecture (journ.) (SAUS) .... Annu Rep Lab Public Health Hiroshima Prefect

Annual Report. Library Council of Philadelphia (journ.) (SAUS) .... Annu Rep Libr Counc Phila

Annual Report. MAFES. Mississippi Agricultural and Forestry Experiment Station (journ.) (SAUS) .... Annu Rep MAFES Miss Agric For Exp St

Annual Report. Marine Biological Association of the United Kingdom (SAUO) .... Annu Rep Mar Biol Assoc UK

Annual Report. Ministry of Agriculture and Fisheries (SAUS) .... Annu Rep Minist Agric Fish

Annual Report. Mississippi State University. Agricultural Experiment Station (journ.) (SAUS) .... Annu Rep Miss State Univ Agr Exp Sta

Annual Report. Murray-Darling Freshw. Research Centre (SAUS) .... Annu Rep Murray-Darling Freshw Res Cent

Annual Report. Natinal Oceanic and Atmospheric Administration, Environmental Reserach Laboratories, Pacific Marine Environmental Research Laboratory (SAUS) .... Annu Rep NOAA/ERL/PMEL

Annual Report. National Bureau of Fish Genetic Resources (SAUS) .... Annu Rep Natl Bur Fish Genet Resour

Annual Report. National Center for Atmospheric Research (SAUS) .... Annu Rep Natl Cent Atmos Res

Annual Report. National Institute for Freshwater Fisheries Research (SAUS) .... Annu Rep Natl Inst Freshw Fish Res

Annual Report. National Institute of Genetics (journ.) (SAUS) .... Annu Rep Natl Inst Genet

Annual Report. National Institute of Genetics (journ.) (SAUS) .... NIGAB

Annual Report. National Institute of Nutrition (journ.) (SAUS) .... Annu Rep Natl Inst Nutr

Annual Report. National Oceanic and Atmospheric Administration, Environmental Research Laboratories, Great Lakes Environmental Research Laboratory (SAUS) .... Annu Rep NOAA/ERL/GLEL

Annual Report. National Oceanographic Data Center (SAUS) .... Annu Rep NODC

Annual Report. National Veterinary Assay Laboratory (journ.) (SAUS) .... Annu Rep Natl Vet Assay Lab

Annual Report. Natural Products Research Institute. Seoul National University (journ.) (SAUS) .... STSODQ

Annual Report. Nebraska Grain Improvement Association (journ.) (SAUS) .... Annu Rep Nebr Grain Impr Ass

Annual Report. Nebraska Wheat Commission (journ.) (SAUS) .... Annu Rep Nebr Wheat Comm

Annual Report. Netherlands Institute for Sea Research (journ.) (SAUS) .... Annu Rep Neth Inst Sea Res

Annual Report. Netherlands Institute for the Law of the Sea (SAUS) .... Annu Rep Neth Inst Law Sea

Annual Report. New Mexico Agricultural Experiment Station (journ.) (SAUS) .... Annu Rep N Mex Agr Exp Sta

Annual Report. New York State Association of Dairy and Milk Inspectors (journ.) (SAUS) .... Annu Rep NY State Assoc Dairy Milk Insp

Annual Report. New York State Association of Milk and Food Sanitarians (journ.) (SAUS) .... Annu Rep NY State Assoc Milk Food Sanit

Annual Report. Nigeria Cocoa Research Institute (journ.) (SAUS) .... Annu Rep Nigeria Coma Res Inst

Annual Report. North East River Purification Board (SAUS) .... Annu Rep North East River Purif Board

Annual Report. North Pacific Anadromous Fish Commission (SAUS) .... Annu Rep North Pac Anadromous Fish Comm

Annual Report. North Pacific Marine Science Organization (SAUS) .... Annu Rep North Pac Mar Sci Organ

Annual Report. North South Wales Agriculture (SAUS) .... Annu Rep North South Wales Agric

Annual Report. North West Water Authority (SAUS) .... Annu Rep North West Water Auth

Annual Report. Northwest Atlantic Fisheries Organization (SAUS) .... Annu Rep NAFO

Annual Report. Nothumbrian Water (SAUS) .... Annu Rep Northumbr Water

Annual Report. Noto Marine Laboratory (journ.) (SAUS) .... Annu Rep Noto Mar Lab

Annual Report. Noto Marine Laboratory (journ.) (SAUS) .... KDRNBK

Annual Report of Catch and Effort Statistics and Fishing Grounds for the Korean Tuna Longline Fishery .... Annu Rep Catch Effort Stat Fish Grounds Korean Tuna Longline Fish

Annual Report of Chicago Natural History Museum (SAUS) .... Annu Rep Chicago Nat Hist Mus

Annual Report of Effort and Catch Statistics by area on Taiwan Demersal Fish Fisheries (SAUS) .... Annu Rep Effort Catch Stat Area Taiwan Demersal Fish Fish

Annual Report of Effort and Catch Statistics on Taiwan Distant Gill Net Fishery (SAUS) .... Annu Rep Effort Catch Stat Taiwan Distant Gill Net Fish

Annual Report of Japan Marine Science and Technology Center (SAUS) .... Annu Rep Jpn Mar Sci Technol Cent

Annual Report of Medicinal Chemistry [A publication] (MEC) .... Ann Rep Med Chem

Annual Report of Natural Science and Home Economics. Kinjo Gakuin College (journ.) (SAUS) .... Annu Rep Natur Sci Home Econ Kinio Gakuin Coll

Annual Report of Oceanographic Observations. National Fisheries Research and Development Agency (SAUS) .... Annu Rep Oceanogr Obs Natl Fish Res Dev Agency

Annual Report of the Attorney General of Florida [A publication] (DLA) .... Ann Rep Fla Att'y Gen

Annual Report of the Attorney General of South Carolina to the General Assembly [*A publication*] (DLA) ... Ann Rep SC Att'y Gen
Annual Report of the Board of Regents of the Smithsonian Institution (journ.) (SAUS) ... ARBRSI
Annual Report of the Director Department of Plant Biology (SAUS) ... Annu Rep Dir Dep Plant Biol
Annual Report of the Fishery Board for Scotland (SAUS) ... Annu Rep Fish Board Scotl
Annual Report of the Marine Mammal Commission (SAUS) ... Annu Rep Mar Mamm Comm
Annual Report of the National Institute of Oceanography (SAUS) ... Annu Rep Natl Inst Oceanogr
Annual Report of Transport Statistics (SAUS) ... ARTS
Annual Report. Ohio State Horticultural Society (journ.) (SAUS) ... Annu Rep Ohio State Hortic
Annual Report. Oklahoma Agricultural Experiment Station (journ.) (SAUS) ... Annu Rep Okla Agric Exp Stn
Annual Report on Carcinogens (SAUO) ... ARC
Annual Report on Geophysical Research in Norway (journ.) (SAUS) ... Annu Rep Geophys Res Norw
Annual Report on Mines. Nova Scotia Department of Mines (journ.) (SAUS) ... Annu Rep Mines NS Dep Mines
Annual Report on Research and Development. Department of Agriculture for Northern Ireland (SAUS) ... Annu Rep Res Dev Dep Agric North Irel
Annual Report on Stress (SAUS) ... AROS
Annual Report on the Department of Fisheries and the Cyprus Fisheries (SAUS) ... Annu Rep Dep Fish Cyprus Fish
Annual Report on Transport Statistics ... ARTS
Annual Report. Ontario Department of Mines (journ.) (SAUS) ... Annu Rep Ont Dep Mines
Annual Report. Oregon Horticultural Society (journ.) (SAUS) ... Annu Rep Oreg Hortic Soc
Annual Report. Oregon State Horticultural Society (journ.) (SAUS) ... Annu Rep Oreg State Hort Soc
Annual Report. Organization of the Petroleum Exporting Countries (journ.) (SAUS) ... AOPEC
Annual Report. Orient Hospital (journ.) (SAUS) ... Annu Rep Orient Hosp
Annual Report. Pacific Salmon Commission (SAUS) ... Annu Rep Pac Salmon Comm
Annual Report. Pacific States Marine Fisheries Commission (SAUS) ... Annu Rep Pac States Mar Fish Comm
Annual Report Producers Council ... ARPC
Annual Report Questionnaire (SAUS) ... ARQ
Annual Report. Royal Ontario Museum (SAUS) ... Annu Rep ROM
Annual Report. Sado Marine Biological Station. Niigata University (journ.) (SAUS) ... SRJKAK
Annual Report. Salmon Genetics Research Program (SAUS) ... Annu Rep Salm Genet Res Program
Annual Report. Salmon Research Agency of Ireland Inc. (SAUO) ... Annu Rep Salmon Res Agency Irel Inc
Annual Report. Sankyo Research Laboratories (journ.) (SAUS) ... SKKNAJ
Annual Report. Scottish Marine Biological Association (SAUO) ... Annu Rep Scott Mar Biol Ass
Annual Report. Scripps Institution of Oceanography (SAUS) ... Annu Rep Scripps Inst Oceanogr
Annual Report. Seychelles Fishing Authority (SAUS) ... Annu Rep Seychelles Fish Auth
Annual Report. Shionogi Research Laboratory (journ.) (SAUS) ... SKNEA7
Annual Report. Sir Alister Hardy Foundation for Ocean Science (SAUO) ... Annu Rep Sir Alister Hardy Found Ocean Sci
Annual Report. Southern California Coastal Water Research Project (SAUS) ... Annu Rep South Calif Coast Water Res Proj
Annual Report. Takeda Research Laboratories (journ.) (SAUS) ... TDKNAF
Annual Report to Shareholders [*Securities and Exchange Commission*] (IID) ... ARS
Annual Report to the Governor. Kansas Wheat Commission (journ.) (SAUS) ... Annu Rep Governor Kans Wheat Comm
Annual Report. Tobacco Research Institute. Taiwan Tobacco and Wine Monopoly Bureau (journ.) (SAUS) ... TSYICDE
Annual Report. Tohoku College of Pharmacy (journ.) (SAUS) ... TYDNAP
Annual Report. Tohoku College of Pharmacy (journ.) (SAUS) ... TYKNAQ
Annual Report. Worcester Art Museum (journ.) (SAUS) ... Arm Worc Art Mus
Annual Reporting Centre (SAUS) ... ARC
Annual Reports Abstracts (SAUS) ... ARA
Annual Reports. Faculty of Pharmaceutical Sciences. Tokushima University (journ.) (SAUS) ... Annu Rep Fac Pharm Sci Tokushima Univ
Annual Reports. Faculty of Pharmaceutical Sciences. Tokushima University (journ.) (SAUS) ... TDYKA8
Annual Reports in Inorganic and General Syntheses (journ.) (SAUS) ... Annu Rep Inorg Gen Synth
Annual Reports in Medicinal Chemistry (journ.) (SAUS) ... Annu Rep Med Chem
Annual Reports. Institute of Population Problems (journ.) (SAUS) ... Annu Rep Inst Popul Probl
Annual Reports. Institute of Population Problems (journ.) (SAUS) ... JMKWA2
Annual Reports. Kinki University Atomic Energy Research Institute (journ.) (SAUS) ... Annu Rep Kinki Univ At Energy Res Inst
Annual Reports. Natural Products Research Institute. Seoul National University (journ.) (SAUS) ... Annu Rep Nat Prod Res Inst Seoul Natl Univ
Annual Reports on Analytical Atomic Spectroscopy [*Later, JAAS*] [*A publication*] ... ARAAS
Annual Reports on Analytical Atomic Spectroscopy (journ.) (SAUS) ... ARAAS
Annual Reports on Analytical Atomic Spectroscopy (journ.) (SAUS) ... ARASC7
Annual Reports on Fermentation Processes (journ.) (SAUS) ... Annu Rep Ferment Process
Annual Reports on the Progress of Chemistry. Section A. Inorganic Chemistry (journ.) (SAUS) ... APCIC
Annual Reports. Research Reactor Institute. Kyoto University (journ.) (SAUS) ... KUAV
Annual Representative Meeting (SAUO) ... ARM
Annual Research Conference [*Bureau of the Census*] (GFGA) ... ARC
Annual Research Report. Kuwait Institute for Scientific Research (SAUS) ... Annu Res Rep Kuwait Inst Sci Res
Annual Research Reviews. Hypothalamic Releasing Factors (journ.) (SAUS) ... HRFADM
Annual Research Reviews. Oral Contraceptives (journ.) (SAUS) ... ORCODO
Annual Research Reviews. Physiological and Pathological Aspects of Prolactin Secretion (journ.) (SAUS) ... PPSED3
Annual Research Reviews. Prolactin (journ.) (SAUS) ... PROLDI
Annual Research Reviews. Prostaglandins and the Gut (journ.) (SAUS) ... Annu Res Rev Prostaglandins Gut
Annual Research Reviews. Proteins of Animal Cell Plasma Membranes (journ.) (SAUS) ... Annu Res Rev Proteins Anim Cell Plasma Membr
Annual Research Reviews. Reggulation of Growth Hormone Secretion (journ.) (SAUS) ... Annu Res Rev Regul Growth Horm Secretion
Annual Research Reviews. Renal Prostaglandins (journ.) (SAUS) ... Annu Res Rev Renal Prostaglandins
Annual Research Reviews. Renin (journ.) (SAUS) ... Annu Res Rev Renin
Annual Research Reviews Rheumatoid Arthritis and Related Conditions (journ.) (SAUS) ... Annu Res Rev Rheum Arthritis Relat Cond
Annual Research Reviews. Rheumatoid Arthritis and Related Conditions (journ.) (SAUS) ... RACND3
Annual Research Reviews. Somatostatin (journ.) (SAUS) ... Annu Res Rev Somatostatin
Annual Research Reviews. Somatostatin (journ.) (SAUS) ... SMTSDS
Annual Research Reviews. Sphingolipidoses and Allied Disorders (journ.) (SAUS) ... Annu Res Rev Sphi
Annual Research Reviews. Sphingolipidoses and Allied Disorders (journ.) (SAUS) ... SADID4
Annual Research Reviews. Substance P (journ.) (SAUS) ... Annu Res Rev Subst P
Annual Research Reviews. Substance P (journ.) (SAUS) ... SUBPDJ
Annual Research Reviews. Ultrastructural Pathology of Human Tumors (journ.) (SAUS) ... Annu Res Rev Ultrastruct Pathol Hum Tumors
Annual Research Reviews. Ultrastructural Pathology of Human Tumors (journ.) (SAUS) ... UPHTDE
Annual Research Reviews. Vitamin-Trace Mineral-Protein Interactions (journ.) (SAUS) ... Annu Res Rev Vitam Trace Miner Protein Interact
Annual Research Reviews. Vitamin-Trace Mineral-Protein Interactions (journ.) (SAUS) ... VTMIDB
Annual Research Task Summary ... ARTS
Annual Retail Trade Survey (SAUS) ... ARTS
Annual Return ... AR
Annual Return of Investment [*Business term*] ... AROI
Annual Review (NATG) ... AR
Annual Review and Information Symposium on the Technology of Training, Learning, and Education (SAUO) ... ARISTOTLE
Annual Review and Information Symposium on the Technology of Training, Learning,and Education [*DoD*] ... ARISTOTLE
Annual Review Committee [*NATO*] (NATG) ... ARC
Annual Review. Freshwater Fisheries Laboratory of Pitlochry (SAUS) ... Annu Rev Freshw Fish Lab Pitlochry
Annual Review. Great Lakes Fisheries Research Branch (SAUS) ... Annu Rev Gt Lakes Fish Res Branch
Annual Review in Automatic Programming (SAUS) ... ARAP
Annual Review of Anthropology (journ.) (SAUS) ... ARAPCW
Annual Review of Applied Linguistics (journ.) (SAUS) ... ARAL
Annual Review of Astronomy and Astrophysics (journ.) (SAUS) ... ARAA
Annual Review of Behavior Therapy Theory and Practice (journ.) (SAUS) ... Annu Rev Behav Ther Theory Pract
Annual Review of Biochemical and Allied Research in India (journ.) (SAUS) ... Annu Rev Biochem Allied Res India
Annual Review of Biochemistry [*A publication*] (MEC) ... Ann Rev Biochem
Annual Review of Biochemistry (journ.) (SAUS) ... Annu Rev Biochem
Annual Review of Biophysics and Bioengineering (journ.) (SAUS) ... Annu Rev Biophys Bioeng
Annual Review of Biophysics and Biophysical Chemistry (journ.) (SAUS) ... Annu Rev Biophys Biophys Chem
Annual Review of Cell Biology (journ.) (SAUS) ... Annu Rev Cell Biol
Annual Review of Chronopharmacology (journ.) (SAUS) ... Annu Rev Chronopharmacol
Annual Review of Earth and Planetary Science Letters (SAUS) ... Annu Rev Earth Planet Sci Lett
Annual Review of Earth and Planetary Sciences (journ.) (SAUS) ... Annu Rev Earth Planet Sci
Annual Review of Ecology and Systematics (journ.) (SAUS) ... Annu Rev Ecol Syst
Annual Review of Energy and the Environment (SAUS) ... Annu Rev Energy Environ
Annual Review of Energy (journ.) (SAUS) ... Annu Rev Energy
Annual Review of Entomology (journ.) (SAUS) ... Annu Rev Entomol
Annual Review of Fish Diseases (SAUS) ... Annu Rev Fish Dis
Annual Review of Fluid Mechanics (journ.) (SAUS) ... Annu Rev Fluid Mech
Annual Review of Food Technology (journ.) (SAUS) ... Annu Rev Food Technol
Annual Review of Genetics (journ.) (SAUS) ... Annu Rev Genet
Annual Review of Information Science and Technology [*A publication*] ... ARIST
Annual Review of International Affairs [*A publication*] (DLA) ... Ann Rev Int'l Aff
Annual Review of Medicine (journ.) (SAUS) ... Annu Rev Med
Annual Review of Microbiology (journ.) (SAUS) ... Annu Rev Microbiol
Annual Review of Nuclear and Particle Science (journ.) (SAUS) ... ANUSDC
Annual Review of Nursing Research (journ.) (SAUS) ... Annu Rev Nurs Res
Annual Review of Nutrition (journ.) (SAUS) ... Annu Rev Nutr

Annual Review of Ocean Affairs: Law and Policy, Main Documents (SAUS) .... Annu Rev Ocean Aff Law Policy Main Docs
Annual Review of Pharmacology (journ.) (SAUS) .... Annu Rev Pharmacol Pharmacol Toxicol
Annual Review of Photochemistry (journ.) (SAUS) .... Annu Rev Photochem
Annual Review of Phylopathology (journ.) (SAUS) .... APPYAG
Annual Review of Physical Chemistry [*A publication*] (MEC) .... Ann Rev Phys Chem
Annual Review of Physical Chemistry (journ.) (SAUS) .... Annu Rev Phys Chem
Annual Review of Physiology (journ.) (SAUS) .... Annu Rev Physiol
Annual Review of Phytopathology (journ.) (SAUS) .... Annu Rev Phytopathol
Annual Review of Phytopathology (journ.) (SAUS) .... APPYA
Annual Review of Plant Physiology and Plant Molecular Biology (SAUS) .... Annu Rev Plant Physiol Plant Mol Biol
Annual Review of Plant Physiology (journ.) (SAUS) .... Annu Rev Plant Physiol
Annual Review of Progress .... ARP
Annual Review of Psychology (journ.) (SAUS) .... Annu Rev Psychol
Annual Review of the Schizophrenic Syndrome (journ.) (SAUS) .... Annu Rev Schizophr Syndr
Annual Review of the Schizophrenic Syndrome (journ.) (SAUS) .... SZCSAV
Annual Review Questionnaire [*Military*] (AABC) .... ARQ
Annual Review Traveling Team [*NATO*] (NATG) .... ARTT
Annual Review Travelling Team (SAUO) .... ARTT
Annual Reviews (EA) .... AR
Annual Schedule of Circuit Estimates [*Telecommunications*] (NITA) .... ASCE
Annual Scientific Report (SAUS) .... ASR
Annual Service Order .... AnSO
Annual Service Practice [*Firings*] [*Military*] .... ASP
Annual Site Environmental Report (SAUS) .... ASER
Annual Summary of Fish and Marine Mammal Harvest Data for the Northwest Territories (SAUS) .... Annu Summ Fish Mar Mamm Harvest Data N W T
Annual Summary Report .... ASR
Annual Supply Inspection [*Military*] (NVT) .... ASI
Annual Support Cost (MCD) .... ASC
Annual Survey (DNAB) .... AS
Annual Survey of African Law [*A publication*] (DLA) .... Ann Surv Afr L
Annual Survey of African Law (journ.) (SAUS) .... Annu Surv of Afr L
Annual Survey of American Chemistry. National Research Council (journ.) (SAUS) .... Annu Surv Am Chem Nat Res Counc
Annual Survey of American Law [*A publication*] (DLA) .... Ann Surv Am
Annual Survey of American Law (journ.) (SAUS) .... Annu Surv of Amer L
Annual Survey of Australian Law [*A publication*] .... Ann Surv of Aust Law
Annual Survey of Australian Law [*A publication*] .... ASAL
Annual Survey of Banking Law [*A publication*] (DLA) .... Ann Surv Banking L
Annual Survey of Colleges [*The College Board*] [*Information service or system*] (CRD) .... ASC
Annual Survey of Colorado Law [*A publication*] (DLA) .... Ann Surv Colo L
Annual Survey of Communication Services (SAUS) .... ASCS
Annual Survey of Indian Law [*A publication*] (DLA) .... Ann Surv Ind L
Annual Survey of Indian Law (journ.) (SAUS) .... Annu Surv of Indian L
Annual Survey of Manufactures [*Department of Commerce*] [*Information service or system*] .... ASM
Annual Survey of Massachusetts Law [*A publication*] (DLA) .... Ann Survey
Annual Survey of Massachusetts Law [*A publication*] (ILCA) .... ASML
Annual Survey of South African Law [*A publication*] (DLA) .... Ann Surv S Afr L
Annual Survey of South African Law (journ.) (SAUS) .... Annu Surv of South Afr L
Annual Symposium. Eastern Pennsylvania Branch, American Society for Microbiology. Proceedings (journ.) (SAUS) .... Annu Symp East PA Branch Am Soc Microbiol Proc
Annual Symposium on Biomathematics and Computer Science in the Life Sciences. Abstracts (journ.) (SAUS) .... Annu Symp Biomath Comput Sci Life Sci Abstr
Annual Symposium on Biomathematics and Computer Science in the Life Sciences. Abstracts (journ.) (SAUS) .... SBCABE
Annual Symposium on Nursing Faculty Practice (journ.) (SAUS) .... Annu Symp Nurs Fac Pract
Annual System Operating Time (CAAL) .... ASOT
Annual System Practice (MCD) .... ASP
Annual Technical Conference [*Society of Plastics Engineers*] .... ANTEC
Annual Technical Conference. American Electroplaters Society (journ.) (SAUS) .... Annu Tech Conf Am Electroplat Soc
Annual Technical Conference Proceedings. Society of Vacuum Coaters (journ.) (SAUS) .... Annu Tech Conf Proc Soc Vac Coaters
Annual Technical Conference Transactions. American Scciety for Quality Control (journ.) (SAUS) .... Annu Tech Conf Trans Am Soc Qual Control
Annual Technical Progress Report .... ATPR
Annual to Decadal Variability in Climate in Europe (QUAC) .... ADVICE
Annual Tour .... AT
Annual Trade Survey (SAUS) .... ATS
Annual Training [*Military*] (AFM) .... AT
Annual Training Deployment (MCD) .... ATD
Annual Training Duty [*Marine Corps*] .... ATD
Annual Training Equipment Pools (AABC) .... ATEP
Annual Trauma Anesthesia and Critical Care Symposium and World Exposition (SAUO) .... ATACCS
Annual Value (ADA) .... AV
Annual Visiting Lecture Series. College of Pharmacy. University of Texas (journ.) (SAUS) .... Annu Visit fact Ser Coll Pharm Univ Tex
Annual Volume. Institute of Marine Engineers (journ.) (SAUS) .... Annu Vol Inst Mar Eng
Annual Wage Reporting [*Social Security Administration*] .... AWR
Annual Wage Survey (OICC) .... AWS
Annual Work Plan .... AWP
Annual Work Schedule .... AWS
Annual Worldwide Industry Review (IMH) .... AWIR
Annual Worth (SAUS) .... AW
Annual Yield [*Business term*] .... AY
annuale (SAUS) .... annu
Annuale Mediaevale (journ.) (SAUS) .... Ann Mediaev
Annualized Cost of Living Model .... ACOL
Annually (ROG) .... ANNLY
Annually (SAUS) .... Annu
Annuario di Statistiche Guidiziarie [*A publication*] (ILCA) .... Ann Stat Guid
Annuitant (ROG) .... ANNUIT
annuitant (SAUS) .... annuit
Annuity (EBF) .... Ann
Annuity (WDAA) .... ann
Annuity (DLA) .... ANNUI
Annuity .... ANNY
Annuity & Life Re [*NASDAQ symbol*] (SG) .... ALRE
Annular .... A
Annular .... ANLR
Annular Base Drag .... ABD
Annular Beam Oscillator (ADWA) .... ABO
Annular Bearing Engineers Committee (EA) .... ABEC
Annular Blast Fragmentation warhead (SAUS) .... ABF
Annular Core Pulse Reactor (SAUS) .... ACPR
Annular Core Pulsed Reactor .... ACPR
Annular Core Research Reactor [*Nuclear energy*] (NRCH) .... ACRR
Annular Expansion Column [*Chromatography*] .... A/E
Annular Fire Missile .... AFM
Annular Linear Induction Pump [*Nuclear energy*] (NRCH) .... ALIP
Annular Magnet (SAUS) .... AM
Annular Momentum Control Device [*NASA*] .... AMCD
Annular Phased-Array System [*Cardiology*] (DAVI) .... APAS
Annular Pressure Loss [*Well drilling technology*] .... APL
Annular Primary Combustor .... APC
Annular Proton Telescope .... APT
Annular Suspension and Pointing System (MCD) .... ASAP
Annular Suspension and Pointing System (SSD) .... ASPS
Annular Suspension Pointing (ACAE) .... ASP
Annular Turbojet Combustor .... ATC
Annular Turbojet Combustor .... ATJC
Annular Velocity (SAUS) .... AV
Annular Vortex Combustor [*Coal technology*] (PS) .... AVC
Annulment (DLA) .... ANNUL
Annulment (SAUS) .... Annul
Annulment of Certification .... AC
Annuloaortic Ectasia [*Medicine*] (DMAA) .... AAE
Annulospiral Nerve Ending [*Medicine*] (MELL) .... ASNE
Annulus Exhaust Gas Treatment System [*Nuclear energy*] (NRCH) .... AEGTS
Annulus Gas System [*Nuclear energy*] (NRCH) .... AGS
Annulus Vacuum Maintenance System [*Nuclear energy*] (NRCH) .... AVMS
Annulus-Pressure-Operated Tester (SAUS) .... APOT
Annum [*Year*] [*Latin*] (EES) .... a
Annunciation .... ANNUN
Annunciation [*or Annunciator*] (ROG) .... ANNUNC
Annunciation (SAUS) .... Annunc
Annunciator (NFPA) .... A
Annunciator [*Electronically controlled signal board*] (KSC) .... ANN
Annunciator .... ANNUN
Annunciator Bell (SAUS) .... ABE
Annunciator Buzzer (SAUS) .... ABU
Annunciator Control Assembly (MCD) .... ACA
Annunciator Control Unit [*Military*] (MCD) .... ACU
Annunciator Display Unit (MCD) .... ADU
Annunciator Horn (SAUS) .... AH
Annunciator Response Procedure [*Nuclear energy*] (NRCH) .... ARP
Annus [*Year*] [*Latin*] .... ANN
Annus Erat Augusti [*It Was in the Year of Augustus*] [*Coin inscription*] [*Latin*] (ROG) .... AEA
Annus Mirabilis [*The Wonderful Year (1666)*] [*Latin*] (GPO) .... AM
annus mirabilis (SAUS) .... a M
Annville-Cleona, PA [*AM radio station call letters*] .... WWSM
Anny Airways Communications System (SAUS) .... AACS
Annydrous (BARN) .... anhydr
Anococcygeal Nerve [*Medicine*] (MELL) .... ACN
Anodal Closing Contraction (SAUS) .... ACC
Anodal Closing Odor (SAUS) .... aco
Anodal Closing Odor [*Physiology*] .... ACO
Anodal Closing Odour (SAUS) .... ACO
Anodal Closing Picture [*Physiology*] .... ACP
Anodal Closing Sound [*Physiology*] .... ACS
Anodal Closure [*Physiology*] .... AC
Anodal Closure Clonus [*Physiology*] (MAE) .... ACCl
Anodal Closure Contraction [*Also, AnCC*] [*Physiology*] .... ACC
Anodal Closure Contraction [*Also, ACC*] [*Physiology*] .... AnCC
Anodal Closure Tetanus [*Physiology*] .... ACTe
Anodal Contraction [*Physiology*] .... AC
Anodal Deviation [*Physiology*] .... AD
Anodal Duration [*Physiology*] (MAE) .... AD
Anodal Duration Contraction [*Physiology*] .... ADC
Anodal Duration Tetanus [*Physiology*] (DMAA) .... ADTe
Anodal Duration Tetanus [*Physiology*] .... AnDTe
Anodal Opening [*Physiology*] .... AO
Anodal Opening Clonus [*Medicine*] (DMAA) .... ANOCL
Anodal Opening Clonus [*Medicine*] (DMAA) .... AOCl
Anodal Opening Clonus [*Physiology*] .... AOCL
Anodal Opening Contraction [*Also, AOC*] [*Physiology*] .... AnOC
Anodal Opening Contraction [*Also, AnOC*] [*Physiology*] .... AOC
Anodal Opening Odor [*Physiology*] .... AOO

Anodal Opening Picture [*Physiology*]	AOP
Anodal Opening Sound [*Physiology*]	AOS
Anodal Opening Tetanus [*Medicine*] (MAE)	AOTe
Anode [*Technical drawings*]	A
Anode (MSA)	AD
Anode	AN
Anode (LDT)	An
Anode Battery (SAUS)	AB
Anode Circuit	AC
Anode Current Efficiency [*Environmental science*]	ACE
Anode Excitation (MAE)	an ex
Anode Excitation (SAUS)	ANEX
Anode of Section One (SAUS)	aI
Anode of Section Two (SAUS)	aII
Anode Potential Stabilized (SAUS)	APS
Anode Reaction (SAUS)	AR
Anode Supply Voltage	ASV
Anode Tapping Point (IAA)	ATP
Anode Voltage (SAUS)	Va
Anode Voltage Drop	AVD
Anodic Behavior of Metals and Semiconductors Series (journ.) (SAUS)	Anodic Behav Met Semicond Ser
Anodic Electrolyte (SAUS)	anolyte
Anodic Iridium Oxide Film (PDAA)	AIROF
Anodic Layer (SAUS)	AL
Anodic Reaction (SAUS)	AR
Anodic Stripping Voltammetry [*Chemical analysis*]	ASV
Anodically Electrodeposited Iridium Oxide Film [*Electrochemistry*]	AEIROF
Anodically-formed Metal Oxide Semiconductor (SAUS)	AMOS
Anodize (SAUS)	Andz
Anodize (MSA)	ANDZ
Anodize (MSA)	ANOD
Anodize (SAUS)	Anod
Anodized Aluminum (VRA)	anod alum
Anodizing (SAUS)	ANDZNG
Anodyne [*Medicine*] (ROG)	ANO
Anodynum [*A Soothing Medicament*] [*Pharmacy*] (ROG)	ANODYN
Anoka Area Vocational Technical Institute, Anoka, MN [*Library symbol*] [*Library of Congress*] (LCLS)	MnAnVT
Anoka County Genealogical Society, Anoka, MN [*Library symbol*] [*Library of Congress*] (LCLS)	MnAnGS
Anoka County Historical Society, Anoka, MN [*Library symbol*] [*Library of Congress*] (LCLS)	MnAnHi
Anoka County Library, Minneapolis, MN [*Library symbol*] [*Library of Congress*] (LCLS)	MnMAC
Anoka, MN [*FM radio station call letters*]	KQQL
Anoka-Ramsey Community College, Anoka, MN [*Library symbol*] [*Library of Congress*] (LCLS)	MnAnA
Anolog Device Inc. (SAUS)	ADI
Anomalistic Observational Phenomena [*In study of UFO's*]	AOP
Anomalous Absorption (SAUS)	AA
Anomalous Atrioventricular Conduction [*Cardiology*]	AAVC
Anomalous Bundle Muscle [*Medicine*] (DB)	AMB
Anomalous Cirumflex [*Coronary Artery*] (DMAA)	ACx
Anomalous Cosmic Ray	ACR
Anomalous Diffraction Approximation (ARMP)	ADA
Anomalous Diffraction Theory (SAUS)	ADT
Anomalous Dispersion Spherical Array Target [*for increasing radio reflectivity*]	ADSAT
Anomalous Left Coronary Artery [*Cardiology*] (DMAA)	ALCA
Anomalous Left Coronary Artery from Pulmonary Artery (SAUS)	ALCAPA
Anomalous Magnetic Moment	AMM
Anomalous Pholovoltaic Effect (SAUS)	APVE
Anomalous Photovoltaic Effect (MCD)	APE
Anomalous Photovoltaic Effect (MCD)	APV
Anomalous Propagation [*Telecommunications*] [*Electronics*] (NVT)	ANAPROP
Anomalous Propagation [*Meteorology*] (WEAT)	ANAPROP
Anomalous Propagation [*Telecommunications*] [*Electronics*] (TEL)	AP
Anomalous Pulmonary Venous Drainage [*Medicine*] (DAVI)	APVD
Anomalous Retinal Correspondence [*Ophthalmology*]	ARC
Anomalous Scattering [*Crystallography*]	AS
Anomalous State of Knowledge [*Term used in artificial intelligence and concept experimentally used information systems*] (NITA)	ASK
Anomalous Winter Absorption (SAUS)	AWA
Anomalous X-Ray Pulsar [*Astronomy*]	AXP
Anomalously Enriched Element [*Environmental chemistry*]	AEE
Anomaly Dynamics Study [*NORPAX*]	ADS
Anomaly M0 (SAUS)	AM0
Anomaly Report (MCD)	AR
Anomaly Report Forms (ACAE)	ARF
Anomolous Skin Effect (PDAA)	ASE
Anonim Sirketi [*Corporation, Joint-Stock Company*]	AS
Anonima Lombarda Fabbrica Automobili	ALFA
Anonym Association against Acronym Abuse [*Slang*] (VERA)	AAAAA
Anonym Association Against Acronym Abuse (SAUO)	AAAAA
Anonyme (SAUS)	Anme
Anonymous	A
Anonymous (WGA)	AN
Anonymous	ANON
Anonymous (BEE)	Anon
Anonymous (VRA)	anon
Anonymous (SAUS)	NYM
Anonymous Arts Recovery Society (EA)	AARS
Anonymous Call Rejection (SAUS)	ACR
Anonymous Donor's Sperm [*Obstetrics*] (DAVI)	ADS

Anonymous Families History Project (EA)	AFHP
Anonymous FTP (SAUS)	AFTP
Anonymous Peer Refereeing	APR
Anonymous Reports at End of Benloe [*1661*] [*England*] [*A publication*] (DLA)	AB
Anonymous Reports at End of Benloe [*1661*] [*England*] [*A publication*] (DLA)	An
Anonymous Reports at End of Benloe [*1661*] [*England*] [*A publication*] (DLA)	An B
Anonymous Reports at End of Benloe (journ.) (SAUS)	An B
Anonymous Society (SAUS)	SA
Anonymous Society of Second Bananas (EA)	ASSB
Anopheles (MAE)	A
Anophthalmia (DMAA)	ANOP
Anordnung [*Direction, Instruction*] [*German*] (ILCA)	AnO
Anorectal Disorders [*Medicine*] (MELL)	ARD
Anorectal Dressing (MAE)	ARD
Anorectal Line [*Medicine*] (MELL)	ARL
Anorectal Sphincters [*Medicine*] (MELL)	ARS
Anorexia and Bulimia Nervosa Foundation of Victoria [*Australia*]	ABNFV
Anorexia & Bulimia Nervosa Foundation of Victoria (SAUO)	ABNFV
Anorexia Bulimia Nervosa Association (DBA)	ABNA
Anorexia Nervosa [*Medicine*]	AN
Anorexia Nervosa and Associated Disorders [*Later, ANAD-National Association of Anorexia Nervosa and Associated Disorders*] (EA)	ANAD
Anorexia Nervosa and Related Eating Disorders (EA)	ANRED
Anorexia Nervosa Inventory Self-Rating [*Medicine*] (MELL)	ANIS
Anorexia-Bulimia Syndrome [*Medicine*] (MELL)	ABS
Anorexic Family Aid and National Information Centre [*British*] (CB)	AFA
A-norprogesterone (SAUS)	A-np
A-Norprogesterone [*Medicine*] (MELL)	ANP
Anorthite [*CIPW classification*] [*Geology*]	an
Anorthosite-Norite-Troctolite suite of rock types (SAUS)	ANT
Anorthotiko Komma Ergazomenou Laou [*Progressive Party of the Working People*] [*Cyprus*] [*Political party*] (PPW)	AKEL
Anosmia and Hypogonadotropic Hypogonadism [*Syndrome*] [*Medicine*] (MELL)	AHH
Another	ANO
Another (GEAB)	ano
Another (ROG)	ANOR
Another (ROG)	ANR
Another Boring Book Bi-Monthly Rag [*Subtitle for the periodical Slightly Soiled*] [*British*] [*A publication*]	ABBBMR
Another Chicago Magazine [*A publication*] (BRI)	ACM
Another Copy (ROG)	AC
Another Debugger [*Computer science*] (BYTE)	adb
Another Mother for Peace [*Defunct*] (EA)	AMP
Another Ray Tracer (SAUS)	ART
Another Subject (SAUS)	AS
Another Three Letter Acronym (SAUS)	ATLA
Another World [*Television program title*]	AW
Another World Fan Club (EA)	AWFC
Another World Viewer Alliance (EA)	AWVA
Anovular Menstruation	AM
Anovulation [*Medicine*] (MELL)	AO
Anovulatory Persistent Proliferative Endometrium [*Medicine*]	APPEM
Anovulatory Syndrome [*Medicine*] (DMAA)	AS
Anoxic Encephalopathy [*Medicine*]	AE
Anoxic Limestone Drains	ALD
Anoxygenic Phototrophic Bacteria	APB
Anpu [*Republic of China*] [*Seismograph station code, US Geological Survey*] (SEIS)	ANP
ANQ: A Quarterly Journal of Short Articles, Notes, and Reviews [*A publication*] (BRI)	ANQ:QJ
Anruf-Variante (SAUS)	AVA
Ansaldo Signal [*Associated Press*] (SAG)	Ansaldo
Ansaldo Signal [*NASDAQ symbol*] (SAG)	ASIG
Ansan, Inc. [*Associated Press*] (SAG)	Ansan
Ansan, Inc. [*NASDAQ symbol*] (SAG)	ANSN
Ansan Inc. Unit [*NASDAQ symbol*] (TTSB)	ANSNU
Ansan Inc. Wrrt'A' [*NASDAQ symbol*] (TTSB)	ANSNW
Ansan Inc. Wrrt'B' [*NASDAQ symbol*] (TTSB)	ANSNZ
ANSA [*Agenzia Nazionale Stampa Associata*]'s Electronic Documentation Service [*ANSA Agency*] (IID)	DEA
Ansbach [*Germany*] [*ICAO location identifier*] (ICLI)	EDEB
Ansbacher Investment Management Ltd. (SAUO)	AIM
Ansbach/Petersdorf [*Germany*] [*ICAO location identifier*] (ICLI)	EDQF
Anschliessend [*Following, Subsequent*] [*German*]	anschl
Anschlussmodul (SAUS)	AM
Ansco Resources (BC) [*Vancouver Stock Exchange symbol*]	ANS
Anselmus de Baggio de Lucca [*Deceased, 1086*] [*Authority cited in pre-1607 legal work*] (DSA)	Ans
Anseriformes (SAUS)	Anseri
Ansett Airlines of Australia [*ICAO designator*] (FAAC)	AAA
Ansett Airlines of Australia [*ICAO designator*] (AD)	AN
Ansett Airlines of Australia	ANSETT
Ansett Airlines of New South Wales [*Australia*]	AANSW
Ansett Airlines of New South Wales [*Australia*] [*ICAO designator*] (FAAC)	NSW
Ansett Airlines of New South Wales [*ICAO designator*] (AD)	WX
Ansett Airlines of South Australia	AASA
Ansett Airlines of South Australia [*ICAO designator*] (AD)	GJ
Ansett Airways (SAUO)	AA
Ansett Airways	ANSETT
Ansett Australian National Airways (SAUS)	ANSETT ANA
Ansett Express [*Airport symbol*]	WX

Ansett New Zealand [Airline flight code] (ODBW) .... ZQ
Ansett Worldwide Aviation Services [Australia] .... AWAS
ANSI extended Latin alphabet coded character set for bibliographic use
  (SAUS) Z3947
ANSI SQL Standard Scalable and Portable (SAUS) AS3AP
Ansoft Corp. [Associated Press] (SAG) .... Ansoft
Ansoft Corp. [NASDAQ symbol] (SAG) .... ANST
Anson County Library, Wadesboro, NC [Library symbol] [Library of
  Congress] (LCLS) .... NcWad
Anson County Senior High School, Medial Center, Wadesboro, NC [Library
  symbol] [Library of Congress] (LCLS) .... NcWadAS
Anson on Contracts [A publication] (DLA) .... Ans Con
Anson on Contracts [A publication] (DLA) .... Anson Cont
Anson Technical College, Learning Resources Center, Polk Campus,
  Polkton (SAUS) .... NcPolA
Anson Technical College, Learning Resources Center, Polk Campus,
  Polkton, NC [Library symbol] [Library of Congress] (LCLS) .... NcPolA
Anson Technical Institute, Ansonville, NC [Library symbol] [Library of
  Congress] (LCLS) .... NcAnA
Anson, TX [FM radio station call letters] .... KKHR
Anson Unit [Of hydrolytic enzyme activity] .... AU
Ansongo [Mali] [ICAO location identifier] (ICLI) .... GAAO
Ansonia, CT [AM radio station call letters] .... WADS
Anstey's Guide to the English Law and Constitution [A publication]
  (DLA) .... Anst Eng Law
Anstey's Pleader's Guide [A publication] (DLA) .... Anst Pl Gui
Anstruther's English Exchequer Reports [145 English Reprint]
  [A publication] (DLA) .... Anst
Anstruther's English Exchequer Reports [145 English Reprint]
  [A publication] (DLA) .... Anstr
Anstruther's English Exchequer Reports [145 English Reprint]
  [A publication] (DLA) .... Anstr (Eng)
Ansul Chemical Company (SAUO) .... ACCX
Answer [In transcripts] .... A
Answer .... AN
Answer (AFM) .... ANS
Answer (WDMC) .... ans
Answer (ROG) .... ANSR
Answer Back Code (SAUS) .... ABC
Answer Center (SAUS) .... AC
Answer Complete [Telecommunications] (TEL) .... AC
Answer Construct .... AC
Answer in Sentence [Computer science] (MHDB) .... AIS
Answer Message (SAUS) .... ANM
Answer, No-Charge [Telecommunications] (TEL) .... ANN
Answer Only (TEL) .... AO
Answer Originate (IAA) .... AO
Answer Print (NTCM) .... AP
Answer Print, Optical (DOAD) .... APO
Answer Search Interface (MCD) .... ASI
Answer Seizure Point (SAUS) .... ASR
Answer Send and Receive [Telecommunications] (DGA) .... ASR
Answer Signal, Charge (SAUS) .... ANC
Answer Table (SAUS) .... AT
Answer Time Recorder (SAUS) .... ATR
Answer To Reset (SAUS) .... ATR
Answer Unit (IAA) .... AU
Answerable (ROG) .... ANSABLE
Answer-Back (SAUS) .... A/B
Answer-Back Code [Telecommunications] (TEL) .... ABC
Answer-Back Tone [Telecommunications] (HGAA) .... ABT
Answer-Back Unit (SAUS) .... ABU
Answer-Bid-Ratio (SAUS) .... ABR
answered (SAUS) .... ans
Answered (ROG) .... ANSD
Answering (SAUS) .... ANS
Answering (ROG) .... ANSG
Answering .... ANSWRNG
Answering Flag [Navy] [British] .... AN
Answering Machine Message (SAUS) .... ANM
Answering Machine Owner .... AMO
Answering, Recording and Dialling (SAUS) .... ARD
Answering Service (LAIN) .... AS
Answering Time Recorder [Telecommunications] (TEL) .... ATR
[The] Answering Voice [A publication] .... AV
Answer/Originate (SAUS) .... A/O
Answer-Return Query .... ARQ
Ansyl [Organic radical] .... Ans
ANSYS, Inc. [NASDAQ symbol] (SG) .... ANSS
Ansys, Inc. [Associated Press] (SAG) .... Ansys
Ant Guard Activity [Ecology] .... AA
Anta [Peru] [Airport symbol] (OAG) .... ATA
Antacid (MELL) .... AA
Anta/Comdte. FAP German Arias Grazziani [Peru] [ICAO location identifier]
  (ICLI) .... SPHZ
Antagonist (AAMN) .... ANTAG
Antagonist (MELL) .... antag
Antagonist Cimetidine [Ulcer medicine manufactured by SmithKline Beckman
  Corp.] .... TAGAMET
Antagonistic (DAVI) .... antag
Antagonistic (SAUS) .... Antag
Antair, SA de CV [Mexico] [FAA designator] (FAAC) .... TIR
Antalaha [Madagascar] [Airport symbol] (OAG) .... ANM
Antalaha [Madagascar] [ICAO location identifier] (ICLI) .... FMNH
Antalya [Turkey] [Airport symbol] (OAG) .... AYT

Antalya [Turkey] [ICAO location identifier] (ICLI) .... LTAI
Antananarivo [Madagascar] [ICAO location identifier] (ICLI) .... FMMD
Antananarivo [Madagascar] [ICAO location identifier] (ICLI) .... FMMM
Antananarivo [Madagascar] [Airport symbol] (OAG) .... TNR
Antananarivo/Arivonimamo [Madagascar] [ICAO location identifier] (ICLI) .... FMMA
Antananarivo/Ivato [Madagascar] [ICAO location identifier] (ICLI) .... FMMI
Antarctic .... A
Antarctic [Marguerite Bay] [Antarctica] [Seismograph station code, US
  Geological Survey] [Closed] (SEIS) .... ANC
Antarctic .... ANT
Antarctic .... Antarc
Antarctic [MARC geographic area code] [Library of Congress] (LCCP) .... t-----
Antarctic and other Ocean Environment (SAUS) .... ASOE
Antarctic Bedrock Mapping Project (SAUS) .... BEDMAP
Antarctic Bottom Water [Oceanography] .... AABW
Antarctic Bottom Water [Marine science] (OSRA) .... ABW
Antarctic Circle (ROG) .... AAC
Antarctic Circle .... Antarc Circ
Antarctic Circumpolar Current (SAUS) .... ACC
Antarctic Circumpolar Current [Oceanography] .... ACC
Antarctic Circumpolar Current .... ACC
Antarctic Circumpolar Current Levels from Altimetry and Island
  Measurement (SAUS) .... ACCLAIM
Antarctic Circumpolar Wave .... ACW
Antarctic Cold Reversal [Climatology] .... ACR
Antarctic Conservation Strategy (SAUS) .... ACS
Antarctic Current Experiment [Global Atmospheric Research Program]
  (USDC) .... ACE
Antarctic Data Management System (SAUS) .... ADMS
Antarctic Digital Database (SAUS) .... ADDB
Antarctic Divergence (SAUS) .... AD
Antarctic Environmental Implications of Mineral Exploration and
  Exploitation (SAUS) .... AEIMEE
Antarctic Expedition .... AE
Antarctic Fixed Station (SAUS) .... ANTARFIX
Antarctic Geodesy Symposium (SAUO) .... AGS
Antarctic Heritage Trust (SAUO) .... AHT
Antarctic Ice Drifting Buoy Programme (SAUS) .... AIDBP
Antarctic Ice Margin Evolution (SAUS) .... ANTIME
Antarctic Ice Thickness Measurement Programme (SAUS) .... AnITMP
Antarctic Ice Thickness Monitoring Project (SAUS) .... AnITMP
Antarctic Intermediate Water [Marine science] (OSRA) .... AAIW
Antarctic International Radiometric Survey (SAUS) .... AIRS
Antarctic Journal of the United States (SAUS) .... Antarctic JUS
Antarctic Lithospheric (SAUS) .... ANTALITH
Antarctic Marine Ecosystem Research at the Ice Edge Zone (SAUS) .... AMERIEZ
Antarctic Marine Ecosystem Research at the Ice-edge Zone (SAUS) ..... AMERIEZ
Antarctic Master Directory (SAUS) .... AMD
Antarctic Medal .... AntM
Antarctic Meteorite Bibliography [Lunar and Planetary Institute]
  [Database] .... AMB
Antarctic Meteorology Research Center .... AMRC
Antarctic Minerals Convention (SAUS) .... AMC
Antarctic Muon and Neutrino Detector Array [Astronomy] (ECON) .... AMANDA
Antarctic Names Committee of Australia (SAUS) .... ANCA
Antarctic Observation Team .... AOT
Antarctic Ocean (SAUS) .... Antarc O
Antarctic Offshore Acoustic Stratigraphy (SAUS) .... ANTOSTRAT
Antarctic Offshore Seismic Stratigraphy Project [Australia] .... ANTOSTRAT
Antarctic Operations [Military] (NVT) .... ANTOPS
Antarctic Operations .... Ant Ops
Antarctic Pack Ice Seals Programme (SAUS) .... APIS
Antarctic Peninsula (SAUS) .... Ant Pen
Antarctic Place Names Committee London (SAUS) .... APC
Antarctic Place-names Committee (SAUO) .... APC
Antarctic Plant Database (SAUS) .... APD
Antarctic Polar Front [Meteorology] .... APF
Antarctic Projects Office (ACAE) .... APO
Antarctic Reception Imagery for Environmental Studies .... ARIES
Antarctic Remote Sensing Aerial Photography and Mapping Information
  System (SAUS) .... ARAMIS
Antarctic Research (SAUS) .... ANTARES
Antarctic Research Advisory Council .... ARAC
Antarctic Research Book Series (SAUS) .... Antarct Res Book Ser
Antarctic Research Center (SAUO) .... ARC
Antarctic Research Program (SAUO) .... ARP
Antarctic Research Series (journ.) (SAUS) .... ANTRS
Antarctic Resesarch (SAUS) .... Antarct Res
Antarctic Science (SAUS) .... Antartct Sci
Antarctic Science (or Scientific) Advisory Committee (SAUO) .... ASAC
Antarctic Sciencific Advisory Committee (SAUS) .... ASAC
Antarctic Sea Ice Processes, Ecosystems and Climate (SAUS) .... ASPECT
Antarctic Sea Ice Thickness Project (SAUS) .... ASITP
Antarctic Search for Meteorites .... ANSMET
Antarctic Space Analog Program [NASA] .... ASAP
Antarctic Specially Protected Area (SAUS) .... ASPA
Antarctic Submillimeter Telescope and Remote Observatory (SAUS) .... ASTRO
Antarctic Support Activities .... ANTARCTICSUPPORT
Antarctic Support Associates (SAUS) .... ASA
Antarctic Support Association (SAUO) .... ASA
Antarctic Task Force .... ATF
Antarctic Treaty (SAUS) .... AT
Antarctic Treaty Consultative Parties (or Party) (SAUS) .... ATCP
Antarctic Treaty Consultative Party (SAUO) .... ATCP
Antarctic Treaty Meeting .... ATM

Antarctic Treaty Organization (ASF)	ATO
Antarctic Treaty Special Consultative Meeting (SAUS)	ATSCM
Antarctic Treaty System	ATS
Antarctic Water Mass (SAUS)	AAWM
Antarctic Wilderness Park (SAUS)	AWP
Antarctica (SAUO)	ANT
Antarctica (ADWA)	Ant
Antarctica (VRA)	Antar
Antarctca (BARN)	Antarc
Antarctica [ANSI two-letter standard code] (CNC)	AQ
Antarctica [ANSI three-letter standard code] (CNC)	ATA
Antarctica [MARC country of publication code] [Library of Congress] (LCCP)	ay
Antarctica [MARC geographic area code] [Library of Congress] (LCCP)	t-ay-
Antarctica Advisory Committee (SAUO)	AAC
Antarctica and Southern Oceans Coalition (EA)	ASOC
Antarctica Project (EA)	AP
[The] Antarctica Project [An association] (EAIO)	TAP
Antarctica Service Medal [Military decoration]	ASM
Antarctican Society (EA)	AS
Antares Oil Corp. (SAUO)	ANTS
Antares Resources [NASDAQ symbol] (TTSB)	ANTR
Antares Resources Corp. [Associated Press] (SAG)	Antares
Antares Resources Corp. [NASDAQ symbol] (SAG)	ANTR
Antartctic Record (SAUS)	Antarct Rec
Antartic Development Squadron (SAUS)	VXE
Ante [Before] [Latin]	A
Ante [Before] [Latin]	an
Ante Christum [Before Christ] [Latin]	AC
Ante Christum [Before Christ] [Latin]	A Ch
Ante Christum [Before Christ] [Latin]	AChr
Ante Christum Natum [Before Christ's Birth] [Latin]	AChrn
Ante Christum Natum [Before the Birth of Christ] [Latin]	ACN
Ante Cibum [Before Meals] [Pharmacy]	AC
Ante Diem [Before the Day] [Latin] (GPO)	ad
Ante Jentaculum [Before Breakfast] [Pharmacy]	ANT JENTAC
Ante Lucem [Before Daylight] [Latin]	Ant Luc
Ante Meridian [Before Noon] [Latin] (WA)	am
Ante Meridiem [Before Noon] [Latin] (GPO)	AM
Ante Nativitatem Christi [Before the Birth of Christ] [Latin] (ROG)	ANC
Ante Partum [Obstetrics]	AP
ante post (SAUS)	ap
Ante Prandium [Before Dinner] [Pharmacy]	ANT PRAND
Ante Prandium [Before Dinner] [Pharmacy]	AP
Antec Corp. [NASDAQ symbol] (SAG)	ANTC
Antec Corp. [Associated Press] (SAG)	Antec
Antecedent Index (NOAA)	AI
Antecedent Moisture Condition (ADWA)	AMC
Antecedent Precipitation Index	API
Ante-Communion	AC
Antecubital [Anatomy]	AC
Antedeluvian Order of Buffaloes (SAUO)	AOB
Antedeluvian Order of Buffaloes (SAUO)	AOBs
Antediluvian Knight [Old actor] (IIA)	AK
Antediluvian Order of Buffaloes [British]	AOB
Antegrade Scrotal Sclerotherapy [Medicine] (MELL)	ASST
Antelope Island [Utah] [Seismograph station code, US Geological Survey] (SEIS)	ANU
Antelope Resources [Vancouver Stock Exchange symbol]	ATF
Antelope Valey Junior College (SAUO)	AVJC
Antelope Valley College (SAUO)	AVC
Antelope Valley Junior College [Later, Antelope Valley College] [Lancaster, CA]	AVJC
Antelope Valley Junior College, Lancaster, CA [Library symbol] [Library of Congress] (LCLS)	CLAV
Antenatal [Medicine]	AN
Antenatal Care	ANC
Antenatal Clinic	ANC
Antenatal Diagnosis	AND
Ante-Nicene Christian Library [A publication] (ODCC)	ANCL
Antenna (IAA)	A
Antenna (AFM)	ANT
Antenna (IDOE)	ant
Antenna + Amplifier (SAUS)	Antennafier
Antenna + Converter (SAUS)	Antennaverter
Antenna + Radiofrequency Amplifier (SAUS)	Antennamplifier
Antenna + Transmitter (SAUS)	Antennamitter
Antenna Adjustable Current Distribution [Telecommunications] (OA)	AACD
Antenna and Transmitter Improvement Study	ATIS
Antenna Aperture	APR
Antenna Array (SAUS)	AA
Antenna Aspect Processor	AAP
Antenna Assembly (IAA)	AS
Antenna Base Spring	ABS
Antenna Beam-shape Factor (SAUS)	ABF
Antenna Bridge Structure (ACAE)	ABS
Antenna Contour Measuring Equipment	ACME
Antenna Control (ACAE)	AC
Antenna Control and Display Panel (MCD)	ACDP
Antenna Control Bay (SAUS)	ACB
Antenna Control Console	ACC
Antenna Control Display	ACD
Antenna Control Unit	ACU
Antenna Counterbalance Cylinder Assembly	ACCA
Antenna Coupler Receiver (MCD)	ACR
Antenna Coupling Regulator (IEEE)	ACR

Antenna Cross Talk	ACT
Antenna Current (IAA)	AC
Antenna Deployment Mechanism (ACAE)	ADM
Antenna Directive Gain	ADG
Antenna Dish Control	ADC
Antenna Driven (ACAE)	A/D
Antenna Dummy Load	ADL
Antenna Effective Height	AEH
Antenna Effective Length for Electric-Field Antennas (IEEE)	LE
Antenna Effective Length for Magnetic-Field Antennas (IEEE)	LEM
Antenna Effective Resistance	AER
Antenna Elevation Angle	AEA
Antenna Feed Horn	AFH
Antenna Feed System	AFS
Antenna Field Charge Kit	AFCK
Antenna Field Gain	AFG
Antenna for Communications	AFC
Antenna Group (SAUO)	AG
Antenna Group Interface Tube (SPST)	AGIT
Antenna Hoisting Adapter (ACAE)	AHA
Antenna Homing System	AHS
Antenna Impedance	AI
Antenna Impedance (SAUS)	ZA
Antenna Induced Modulation (ACAE)	AIM
Antenna Inductance (SAUS)	Ant Ind
Antenna Inductance Switch (SAUS)	Ant Ind Sw
Antenna Inductance Tuning (SAUS)	Ant Ind Tuning
Antenna Input (SAUS)	AI
Antenna Input Resistance	AIR
Antenna Interface Subsystem (CAAL)	AIS
Antenna Laboratory (MCD)	AL
Antenna Lightning Arrester	ALA
Antenna Loading Coil	ALC
Antenna Lobe for Variable Ionospheric Nimbus (IEEE)	ALVIN
Antenna Management (NASA)	AM
Antenna Mast Group [PATRIOT] [Army] (RDA)	AMG
Antenna Mast Groups (SAUO)	AMG
Antenna Mast Set (MCD)	AMS
Antenna Matching Unit	AMU
Antenna Measurement Techniques Association (EA)	AMTA
Antenna Measuring System (SAUS)	AMS
Antenna Module (ACAE)	AM
Antenna Noise Temperature	ANT
Antenna Ohmic Resistance	AOR
Antenna Pattern Analyzer	APA
Antenna Pattern Correction [for spacecraft data]	APC
Antenna Pattern Data System (ACAE)	APDS
Antenna Pattern Error Analysis	APEA
Antenna Pattern Measurement (SAUS)	APM
Antenna Pattern Measurement Test [Army] (AABC)	APMT
Antenna Pattern Recorder (SAUS)	APR
Antenna Pattern Test System [Army] (AABC)	APATS
Antenna Pointing Angle Change	APAC
Antenna Pointing Mechanism (ADWA)	APM
Antenna Pointing Subsystem	APS
Antenna Position Indicator	API
Antenna Position Programmer [Manned Space Flight Network]	APP
Antenna Position Recorder	APR
Antenna Positioner Group (ACAE)	APG
Antenna Positioner Mechanism (ACAE)	APM
Antenna Positioning Device	ANPOD
Antenna Positioning Electronics (ACAE)	APE
Antenna Positioning Mechanism	APM
Antenna Power Gain	APG
Antenna Radiation Pattern	ARP
Antenna Radiation Resistance	ARR
Antenna RADOME [RADAR Dome] Heater	ARH
Antenna Range Equipment	ARE
Antenna Receiver Group (SAUO)	ATG
Antenna Resistance (SAUS)	AR
Antenna Rotation Rate (NVT)	ARR
Antenna Scan (SAUS)	SCAN
Antenna Select Logic Unit [NASA] (NASA)	ASLU
Antenna Servo/Infrared (ACAE)	AS/IR
Antenna Signal Distribution System (ACAE)	ASDS
Antenna Signal Processing (SAUS)	ASP
Antenna Slave Data Equipment (IAA)	ASDE
Antenna Solar Panel Position (ACAE)	A/SPP
Antenna Solar Panel Positioner	ASPP
Antenna Steering Group	ASG
Antenna Subsystem (ADWA)	ANTS
Antenna Support Structure (SAUS)	ASS
Antenna Supports [JETDS nomenclature] [Military] (CET)	AB
Antenna Surface Contour Measurements (ACAE)	ASCM
Antenna Switching Matrix	ASM
Antenna System Readiness Monitor (MCD)	ASRM
Antenna Systems Laboratory [University of New Hampshire] (PDAA)	ASL
Antenna Test Bed (SPST)	ATB
Antenna Test Facility	ATF
Antenna Test Group [Army] (AABC)	ATG
Antenna Test Model	ATM
Antenna Test Station (SAUS)	ATS
Antenna to Antenna Compatibility Analysis Program (MCD)	ATACAP
Antenna Track (ACAE)	ATRK

Antenna Tracking Altitude, Azimuth and Range by Electronic Scan (SAUS) .... ANTAARES
Antenna Tracking Altitude, Azimuth, and Range by Electronic Scan (PDAA) .... ANTARES
Antenna Transmit Receive Module (ACAE) .... A/T/RM
Antenna Transmit-Receive (SAUS) .... ATR
Antenna Transmitter (SAUS) .... Antennamitter
Antenna Tuning Capacitor (IAA) .... ATC
Antenna Tuning Inductance (IAA) .... ATI
Antenna Tuning Inductance (SAUS) .... ati
Antenna Tuning Unit (MSA) .... ATU
Antenna Turn Around (ACAE) .... ATA
Antenna Turn Left (ACAE) .... ATL
Antenna Turn Right (ACAE) .... ATR
Antenna Turning Motor (IAA) .... ATM
Antenna Under Test (ACAE) .... AUT
Antenna with Reflector .... R
Antennapedia Complex [Gene cluster in fruit fly] ..... ANT-C
Antennapedia Complex (SAUS) .... Ant-C
Antenna-Receiver-Transmitter (IAA) .... ART
Antennas and Propagation (MCD) .... A/P
Antennas and Propagation Society (SAUO) .... APS
Antennas, Complex [JETDS nomenclature] [Military] (CET) .... AS
Antennas, Simple [JETDS nomenclature] [Military] (CET) .... AT
Antenna-Scatterer Analysis Program (SAUS) ...... ASAP
Antennule Length [of Crustacea] .... AL
Antennule Length to Total Body Length Ratio [of Crustacea] .... AL/TL
Anteparium Hemorrhage (SAUS) .... APH
Antepartum Hemorrhage [Medicine] .... APH
Anterior .... A
Anterior .... ANT
Anterior (MELL) .... ant
Anterior and Posterior (SAUS) .... A&P
Anterior and Posterior [Medicine] .... A & P
Anterior Aorta .... AA
Anterior Aortic Wall [Medicine] (DMAA) .... AAW
Anterior Auditory Field [Physiology] .... AAF
Anterior Axillary Line .... AAL
Anterior Axillary Line [Anatomy] (DAVI) ...... Ant Ax
Anterior Basal Body .... ABB
Anterior Bite Wing (SAUS) .... ABW
Anterior Born of Spinal Cord [Medicine] (MELL) .... AHSC
Anterior Bulbar Cell [Neurobiology] .... ABC
Anterior Burster [Neuron] .... AB
Anterior Byssus Retractor Muscle [Mollusk anatomy] .... ABRM
Anterior Cerebral Arteries (or Artery) (SAUS) .... ACA
Anterior Cerebral Artery [Anatomy] (AAMN) ... ACA
Anterior Cervical Cord Syndrome [Medicine] (MELL) .... ACCS
Anterior Cervical Diskectomy and Fusion [Medicine] (DAVI) .... ACDF
Anterior Cervical Fusion [Medicine] (MELL) ..... ACF
Anterior Cervical Plate [Medicine] (MELL) ...... ACP
Anterior Chamber [Ophthalmology] .... AC
Anterior Chamber Diameter [Ophthalmology] (DAVI) .... ACD
Anterior Chamber Intraocular Lens [Medicine] (MELL) .... AC-IOL
Anterior Chamber Intraocular Lens Implant (SAUS) .... ACIOL
Anterior Chamber Intraocular Lens Implantation [Medicine] (MELL) .... ACILI
Anterior Chamber Maintainer [Medicine] (MELL) .... ACM
Anterior Chamber of Eye (MELL) .... ACOE
Anterior Chamber Tube Shunt Encircling Band [Ophthalmology] (DAVI) .... ACTSEB
Anterior Chamber-Associated Immune Deviation [For study of foreign tissue grafts] .... ACAID
Anterior Chest Diameter .... ACD
Anterior Cingulate Cortex [Brain anatomy] ...... ACC
Anterior Clavicular Line (SAUS) .... ACL
Anterior Colporrhaphy [Gynecology] (CPH) .... AC
Anterior Commissure [Neuroanatomy] .... AC
Anterior Communicating Aneurysm (HGAA) ...... ACA
Anterior Communicating Artery (SAUS) .... ACoA
Anterior Connective [Anatomy] .... AC
Anterior Convex Side .... ACS
Anterior Coronary Artery (HGAA) .... ACA
Anterior Cortical [Anatomy] .... AC
Anterior Cranial Fossa [Medicine] (MELL) ...... ACF
Anterior Cruciate [Ligament] [Anatomy] (DAVI) .... AC
Anterior Cruciate [Medicine] (MELL) .... ACR
Anterior Cruciate Ligament [Anatomy] .... ACL
Anterior Cruciate Ligament Repair [Medicine] (MELL) .... ACLR
Anterior Deltoid [Myology] .... AD
Anterior Dendritic Field [Neurology] .... ADF
Anterior Descending Artery [Anatomy] (MAE) .... ADA
Anterior Descending Branch of Left Coronary Artery [Medicine] (MELL) .... ADBLCA
Anterior Diameter (SAUS) .... ANTD
Anterior Dorsolateral Scale (SAUS) .... ADLS
Anterior Dorsolateral Scale Count .... ADLS
Anterior Drawer Test (MELL) .... ADT
Anterior Ectosylvian Sulcus [Neuroanatomy] .... AES
Anterior Extreme Position [Medicine] .... AEP
Anterior Facial Height .... AFH
Anterior Faucial Pillar [Anatomy] (MAE) .... AFP
Anterior Fold from Typhlosole .... AFT
Anterior Fontanelle [Neonatology and pediatrics] (DAVI) .... AF
Anterior [Part of] Foot .... AF
Anterior Foot (SAUS) .... AF

Anterior Gray Column of Spinal Cord [Medicine] (MELL) .... AGCSP
Anterior Hyaloid Membrane [Ophthalmology] ... AHM
Anterior Hypothalamic Area .... AHA
Anterior Hypothalamic Nucleus [Brain anatomy] .... AH
Anterior Hypothalamic Preoptic (DB) .... AHPO
Anterior Hypothalamus [Medicine] (DB) .... AH
Anterior Hypothalamus, Preoptic Area [Brain anatomy] .... AHPOA
Anterior Inferior Cerebellar Artery [Anatomy] .... AICA
Anterior Inferior Communicating Artery [Anatomy] .... AICA
Anterior Inferior Iliac Spine [Medicine] (MELL) .... AIIS
Anterior Informal Vertebral Vein [Medicine] (DMAA) .... AIVV
Anterior Internal Cerebral Artery [Anatomy] (DAVI) .... AICA
Anterior Interosseous Nerve Syndrome [Medicine] (DMAA) .... AIS
Anterior Interpositus Nucleus [Anatomy] .... AIN
Anterior Ischemic Optic Neuropathy [Neurology and ophthalmology] (DAVI) .... AION
Anterior [Wall of] Kidney .... AK
Anterior Kidney (SAUS) .... AK
Anterior Knee Pain Syndrome [Medicine] (MELL) .... AKPS
Anterior Labrum Periosteum Shoulder Arthroscopic [Medicine] (MELL) ..... ALPSA
Anterior Lateral Dendrites [Neurology] .... ALD
Anterior Lateral Line Nerve [Fish anatomy] ...... ALLN
Anterior Lateral Myocardial Infarct [or Infarction] [Cardiology] .... ALMI
Anterior Lateral Nerve .... ALN
Anterior Latissimus Dorsi [Anatomy] .... ALD
Anterior Leaflet of Mitral Valve [Cardiology] (AAMN) .... ALMV
Anterior Lobe Hormone [Endocrinology] (MAE) .... ALH
Anterior Lobe of Hypophysis [Anatomy] (AAMN) .... ALH
Anterior Lobe of Pituitary [Gland] .... ALP
Anterior Longitudinal Ligament [Medicine] (MELL) .... ALL
Anterior Lymph Node [Medicine] (MAE) .... ALN
Anterior Mandibular Subapical Segmental Osteotomy [Medicine] (MELL) .... AMSSO
Anterior Median Nerve (SAUS) .... AMN
Anterior Middle Suprasylvian Association [Area of cat cortex] .... AMSA
Anterior Mitochondrion [Cytology] .... AM
Anterior Mitral Leaflet [Cardiology] .... AM
Anterior Mitral Leaflet [Cardiology] .... AML
Anterior Mitral Valve Leaflet [Cardiology] (AAMN) .... aMVL
Anterior Mitral Valve Leaflet [Medicine] (MELL) .... AMVL
Anterior Myocardial Infarction [Medicine] (DMAA) .... AMI
Anterior Nasal Discharge [Medicine] (DMAA) .... AND
Anterior Nasal Spine [Medicine] (DMAA) .... ANS
Anterior Neural Boundary Organizer .... ANB
Anterior Oblique (MAE) .... AO
Anterior Octaval Nucleus [Neuroanatomy] ..... AON
Anterior Osseous Ampulla [Medicine] (MELL) .... AOA
Anterior Papillary Muscle [Cardiology] (DAVI) .... APM
Anterior Pectoral Lymph Node [Medicine] (MELL) .... APLN
Anterior Pericardial Fluid (SAUS) .... APF
Anterior Pituitary [Endocrinology] .... ANT PIT
Anterior Pituitary [Endocrinology] .... AP
Anterior Pituitary Extract [Endocrinology] .... APE
Anterior Pituitary Gonadotrophin [Medicine] (MELL) .... APG
Anterior Pituitary Hormone [Endocrinology] .... APH
Anterior pituitary hormone; aphasia (SAUS) .... AOH
Anterior Pituitary Like Substance (SAUS) .... APL Substance
Anterior Pituitary Lobe [Anatomy] .... AL
Anterior Pituitary Reaction [Endocrinology] (AAMN) .... APR
Anterior Pituitary Resection [Medicine] (MAE) .... APR
Anterior Pituitary-Like [Endocrinology] .... APL
Anterior Portion - Medial Collateral Ligament [Anatomy] .... A-MCL
Anterior, Posterior and Lateral (SAUS) .... AP&Lat
Anterior Resection [Medicine] .... AR
Anterior Right Ventricular Wall [Cardiology] (DAVI) .... ARV
Anterior Sagittal Diameter [Medicine] (MEDA) .... ASD
Anterior Scalene Muscle [Medicine] (MELL) ..... ASM
Anterior Segmental Ocular Dysgenesis [Medicine] (DMAA) .... ASOD
Anterior Semicircular Canal [Medicine] (MELL) .... ASCC
Anterior Septal Artery [Anatomy] .... ASA
Anterior Sorting Area .... ASA
Anterior Spinothalamic Tract (DB) .... AST
Anterior Subapical Sliding Osteotomy [Medicine] (MELL) .... ASSO
Anterior Subcapsular Cataract [Ophthalmology] (DAVI) .... ASC
Anterior Superior Iliac Spine [Anatomy] .... ASIS
Anterior Superior Spine [Of ilium] [Anatomy] (DAVI) .... Ant Sup Spine
Anterior Superior Spine [Anatomy] .... ASS
Anterior Talofibular Ligament [Medicine] (MELL) .... ATFL
Anterior Tibial Compartment [Syndrome] [Medicine] (MELL) .... AT
Anterior Tibial Compartment Syndrome [Medicine] (DMAA) .... ATCS
Anterior Tibial (Muscle) [Anatomy] .... AT
Anterior Tibialis [Anatomy] .... ATB
Anterior Trabeculae Carneae [Heart anatomy] .... ATC
Anterior Tricuspid Valve Leaflet [Medicine] (MELL) .... ATVL
Anterior Tubercle of Atlas (MELL) .... ATA
Anterior Urethral Valve [Medicine] (DMAA) ..... AUV
Anterior Ventral (DB) .... AV
Anterior Ventral Microtubule [Anatomy] .... AVM
Anterior Ventral Neuron [Neurophysiology] .... AV
Anterior Visceral Endodermal .... AVE
Anterior Wall [Anatomy] .... AW
Anterior Wall Infarction [Cardiology] (MAE) .... AWI
Anterior Wall Myocardial Infarction [Cardiology] (MAE) .... AWMI
Anterior Wall of Aortic Root [Cardiology] (DMAA) .... AWAR
Anterior Wall Thickness [Anatomy] .... AWT

Anterior-Median [*Ophthalmology*] ... AM
Anterior-Posterior (SAUS) ... A-P
Anterior-Posterior and Lateral [*Chest x-ray*] (CPH) ... A-P & Lat
Anterior-Posterior Dual Energy Radiography [*Medicine*] (DMAA) ... APDER
Anterior-Posterior Lower Cervical [*Medicine*] (MELL) ... APLC
Anterograde Amnesia [*Medicine*] ... AA
Anterolateral Infarct [*Medicine*] (MELL) ... ALI
Anterolateral Pre-Olivary Nucleus [*Neuroanatomy*] ... ALPO
Anterolateral Rotatory [*or Rotational*] **Instability** [*Orthopedics*] ... ALRI
Anterolateral Sclerosis [*Neurology*] (DAVI) ... ALS
Anterolateral Wall Myocardial Infarction [*Cardiology*] ... ALWMI
Anteromeatal [*Anatomy*] (DAVI) ... AM
Anteromedial Puncture [*Medicine*] ... AMP
Anteromedial Rotatory Instability [*Medicine*] ... AMRI
Anteromedial-Anterolateral Rotatory Instability [*Medicine*] ... AM-ALRI
Anteroposterior [*Projection*] [*Radiology*] (DAVI) ... AP
Anteroposterior and Lateral [*X-ray views*] (AAMN) ... AP & L
Anteroposterior and Lateral (SAUS) ... AP&L
Anteroposterior and Lateral (SAUS) ... AP&Lat
Anteroposterior and Lateral [*X-ray views*] (AAMN) ... AP & Lat
Anteroposterior [*or Anterior-posterior*] **Diameter** [*Pelvic measurement*] [*Medicine*] ... A-PD
Anteroposterior Dianmeter (SAUS) ... APD
Anteropr Pillar of Fauces [*Medicine*] (MELL) ... APF
Anteroseptal Infarct [*Medicine*] (MELL) ... ASI
Anteroseptal Myocardial Infarct [*or Infarction*] [*Cardiology*] (MAE) ... ASMI
Anteroventral Cochlear Nucleus ... AVCN
Antero-Ventral Cochlear Nucleus (SAUS) ... AVCN
Anteroventral Periventricular [*Medicine*] (DB) ... AVPV
Anteroventral Portion of the Third Ventricle [*Neuroanatomy*] ... AV 3V
Anteversion [*Medicine*] ... AV
Anteverted, Anteflexed [*Medicine*] (MAE) ... AV/AF
anteverted/antetlexed (SAUS) ... av/af
Antex Data Systems (HGAA) ... ADS
Anthanthrene (SAUS) ... ANT
Anthelmintic [*Expelling Worms*] [*Medicine*] (ROG) ... ANTH
Anther [*Botany*] ... A
Anther [*Botany*] ... AN
Anther Primordium [*Botany*] ... AP
Anthes Industries, Inc. [*Toronto Stock Exchange symbol*] ... AII
Anthithsonian Institution (SAUS) ... AP
Anthium (SAUS) ... AP
Anthocyanin [*Fruit pigment*] ... ACN
Anthocyanin (SAUS) ... ACY
Anthocyanin Pigmented Juices [*Food technology*] ... API
Anthocyanin Pigmented Juices (SAUS) ... APJ
Anthologia Latina [*A publication*] (OCD) ... Anth Lat
Anthologia Lyrica Graeca [*A publication*] (OCD) ... Anth Lyr Graec
Anthologia Palatina [*Classical studies*] (OCD) ... Anth Pal
Anthologia Planudea [*Classical studies*] (OCD) ... Anth Plan
Anthologie [*Anthology*] [*German*] ... Anthol
Anthologie Sonore [*Record label*] [*France*] ... AS
Anthologize (SAUS) ... Anthol
Anthology ... ANTH
Anthology ... ANTHOL
Anthology (ADWA) ... anthol
Anthology (SAUS) ... Anthol
Anthology Film Archives (EA) ... AFA
Anthology Film Archives, New York, NY [*Library symbol*] [*Library of Congress*] (LCLS) ... NNAn
Anthology Film Archives, New York, NY [*Library symbol*] [*Library of Congress*] (LCLS) ... NNAnF
Anthology for Famous English and American Poetry [*A publication*] ... AnFE
Anthology for the Enjoyment of Poetry [*A publication*] ... AnEnPo
Anthology of Catholic Poets [*A publication*] ... ACP
Anthology of Commonwealth Verse [*A publication*] ... ACV
Anthology of Commonwealth Verse (journ.) (SAUS) ... ACV
Anthology of Contemporary Latin-American Poetry [*A publication*] ... AnCL
Anthology of English Verse [*A publication*] ... AEV
Anthology of French Poetry [*A publication*] ... AnFP
Anthology of German Poetry [*A publication*] ... AnGP
Anthology of German Poetry through the Nineteenth Century [*A publication*] ... AGP
Anthology of Irish Literature [*A publication*] ... AnIL
Anthology of Irish Verse [*A publication*] ... AnIV
Anthology of Light Verse [*A publication*] ... ALV
Anthology of Medieval Lyrics [*A publication*] ... AnML
Anthology of Medieval Lyrics (journ.) (SAUS) ... ANNM
Anthology of Mexican Poetry [*A publication*] ... AnMP
Anthology of Modern Poetry [*A publication*] ... AnMoPo
Anthology of New England Poets [*A publication*] ... AnNE
Anthology of New Zealand Verse [*A publication*] ... AnNZ
Anthology of Norwegian Lyrics [*A publication*] ... AnNoLy
Anthology of Old English Poetry [*A publication*] ... AnOE
Anthology of Spanish Poetry from Garsilaso to Garcia [*A publication*] ... AnSP
Anthology of Swedish Lyrics [*A publication*] ... AnSL
Anthology of World Poetry [*A publication*] ... AWP
Anthon Herald, Anthon, IA [*Library symbol*] [*Library of Congress*] (LCLS) ... IaAntH
Anthon Public Library, Anthon, IA [*Library symbol*] [*Library of Congress*] (LCLS) ... IaAnt
Anthon's Abridgment of Blackstone [*A publication*] (DLA) ... Anth Black
Anthon's Law Student [*A publication*] (DLA) ... Anth LS
Anthon's New Precedents of Declarations [*A publication*] (DLA) ... Anth Prec
Anthon's New York Nisi Prius Reports [*A publication*] (DLA) ... Anth
Anthon's New York Nisi Prius Reports [*A publication*] (DLA) ... Anth NP
Anthon's New York Nisi Prius Reports [*A publication*] (DLA) ... Anth NPR
Anthon's New York Nisi Prius Reports [*A publication*] (DLA) ... Anthon NP (NY)
Anthon's New York Nisi Prius Reports [*A publication*] (DLA) ... Anthon Rep
Anthon's New York Nisi Prius Reports [*A publication*] (DLA) ... Anthon's NP
Anthon's New York Nisi Prius Reports [*A publication*] (DLA) ... Anthon's Rep
Anthon's Nisi Prius Reports [*2nd ed.*] [*A publication*] (DLA) ... Anthon's NP (2d Ed)
Anthon's Study of Law [*A publication*] (DLA) ... Anth St
Anthony and Scovill Manufacturing Co. (SAUO) ... Ansco
Anthony Colin Bruce Chapman [*British auto industrialist and engineer, founder of Lotus Cars*] ... ACBC
Anthony Indus [*NYSE symbol*] (TTSB) ... ANT
Anthony Industries, Inc. [*NYSE symbol*] (SPSG) ... ANT
Anthony Industries, Inc. [*Associated Press*] (SAG) ... Anthony
Anthony, KS [*Location identifier*] [*FAA*] (FAAL) ... ANY
Anthony on Consolidation of Railroad Companies [*A publication*] (DLA) ... Anth RR Cons
Anthony Pape Memorial Law Library, Hamilton Law Association, Ontario [*Library symbol*] [*National Library of Canada*] (BIB) ... OHLA
Anthony Sharp and Rachael Ellison Family Organization (EA) ... ASREFO
Anthony, Smallhorn & Associates [*British*] ... AS & A
Anthony's Edition of Shephard's Touchstone [*A publication*] (DLA) ... Anth Shep
Anthophyllite (SAUS) ... AY
Anthracene Scintillation Dosimeter ... ASD
Anthracenecarboxylic Acid [*Organic chemistry*] ... AC
Anthracenecarboxylic Acid (SAUS) ... AC Acid
Anthracenedicarboxaldehyde [*Biochemistry*] ... ADC
Anthracite (ABBR) ... A
Anthracite Capital [*NYSE symbol*] (SG) ... AHR
Anthracite Industry Association (EA) ... AIA
Anthracite Information Bureau [*Defunct*] ... AIB
Anthracite Institute [*Absorbed by PCMA*] ... AI
Anthracite Railroads Historical Society (EA) ... ARHS
Anthrahydroquinone [*Organic chemistry*] ... AHQ
Anthrahydroquinone Disulfonate [*Organic chemistry*] ... AHDS
Anthranilamide [*Organic chemistry*] ... ATA
Anthranilate Synthase [*An enzyme*] ... AS
Anthranilate Synthase - Phosphoribosyl Transferase [*Enzyme complex*] ... AS-PRT
Anthranilate Synthetase (SAUS) ... AS
Anthranilic Acid [*Organic chemistry*] ... AA
Anthraquinone [*Organic chemistry*] ... AQ
Anthraquinone Disulfonate [*Organic chemistry*] ... AQDS
Anthraquinone Disulfonic Acid [*Organic chemistry*] ... ADA
Anthrax Antiserum [*Medicine*] ... AAS
anthrocosis (SAUS) ... anthroco
Anthropic Principle (SAUS) ... AP
Anthropogenic Climate Change [*Marine science*] (OSRA) ... ACC
Anthropogenic Climate Change (SAUS) ... CLIVAR-ACC
Anthropogenic Hydrocarbons ... AHC
Anthropogenic Sulfate Aerosol [*Meteorology*] ... ASA
Anthropogeography (SAUS) ... Anthro
Anthropological [*or Anthropology*] ... ANTHR
Anthropological (ADWA) ... anthrop
Anthropological (ADWA) ... anthropol
Anthropological ... ANTHROPOL
Anthropological Institute (BARN) ... AI
Anthropological Institute Journal (SAUS) ... Anthrop J
Anthropological Linguistics, a Publication of the Archives of the Languages of the World. Indiana University. Anthropology Department. Bloomington (journ.) (SAUS) ... IU/AL
Anthropological Papers. University of Alaska (journ.) (SAUS) ... APUA
Anthropological Research Center [*Memphis State University*] [*Research center*] (RCD) ... ARC
Anthropological Research Club (SAUO) ... ARC
Anthropological Research Council [*British*] ... ARC
Anthropological Review (journ.) (SAUS) ... Anthrop R
Anthropological Society (SAUO) ... AS
Anthropological Society of London (SAUO) ... ASL
Anthropological Society of New South Wales (SAUO) ... ASNSW
Anthropological Society of Queensland (SAUO) ... ASQ
Anthropological Society of Victoria (SAUO) ... ASV
Anthropological Society of Victoria (SAUO) ... A/SV
Anthropological Society of Victoria (SAUS) ... a/sv
Anthropological Society of Western Australia (SAUO) ... ASWA
Anthropologie [*Anthropology*] [*German*] ... Anthropol
Anthropology ... ANTH
Anthropology (ADWA) ... anthro
Anthropology (DD) ... Anthro
Anthropology ... ANTHRO
Anthropology ... ANTHROP
Anthropology (VRA) ... anthrop
Anthropology and Sociology Section [*Association of College and Research Libraries*] ... ANSS
Anthropology Case Materials Project [*National Science Foundation*] ... ACMP
Anthropology Film Center Foundation (EA) ... AFCF
Anthropology Film Institute [*Later, AFCF*] (EA) ... AFI
Anthropology of Development Programme [*McGill University*] [*Canada*] [*Research center*] (RCD) ... PAD
Anthropology Resource Center [*Defunct*] (EA) ... ARC
Anthropometric Survey [*Human figure simulation*] [*Army*] (RDA) ... ANSUR
Anthropometric Test Device [*Automotive safety*] ... ATD
Anthropometric Total Hip [*Medicine*] (MELL) ... ATH
Anthropomorphic Test Device [*MM*] (TAG) ... ATD
Anthropomorphic Test Dummy ... ATD
Anthropomorphism (SAUS) ... Anthro

anthropophagy (SAUS) .... anthro
Anthroposophical Society in America (EA) .... ASA
Anthroposophical Society in Australia, Victorian Branch .... ASA(VB)
Anthroposophical Society in Great Britain (EAIO) .... ASGB
Anthroposophical Society of America (SAUO) .... ASA
Anthroposophical Society of Great Britain (SAUO) .... ASGB
Anthroposphic Press (SAUS) .... Anthrnposophic
(Anthroyloxy)stearic Acid [Organic chemistry] .... AS
Anti + Aircraft (SAUS) .... AA
Anti + Chlorine (SAUS) .... Antichlor
Anti Aircraft Fire Control System (ACAE) .... AAFCS
Anti Ballistic Missile Treaty (ACAE) .... ABMT
Anti Blocking System (SAUS) .... ABS
Anti Body (SAUS) .... AB
Anti Curl System (SAUS) .... ACS
Anti Mast Armor Program (ACAE) .... AMAP
Anti Nuclear (SAUS) .... Antinuke
Anti Personnel Missile (SAUS) .... APM
Anti Racist Teacher Education Network (AIE) .... ARTEN
Anti Radiation Homing Projectile (ACAE) .... ARHP
Anti Radiation Projectiles (ACAE) .... ARP
Anti Shop Lifting Device (SAUS) .... ASLD
Anti Skinning Agent (SAUS) .... ASKA
Anti Submarine Data Analysis Center (ACAE) .... ASDAC
Anti Submarine Detection Investigation Committee (SAUS) .... ASDIC
Anti Submarine Warfare Tactical Decision Aid (ACAE) .... ASWTDA
Anti Submarine Weapon Electronic Prediction System (ACAE) .... ASWEPS
Anti Surface to Air Missile (ACAE) .... ANTSAM
Anti Tactical Radar (ACAE) .... ATR
Anti Tank Guided Rocket (ACAE) .... ATGR
Anti Tank Missile Study (ACAE) .... ATMS
Antiactin Antibody [Medicine] (DB) .... AAA
Anti-Aero (SAUS) .... AA
Anti-Afterburn Valve [Automotive engineering] .... AAV
Anti-AIDS drug (SAUS) .... AZT
Anti-Air Artillery Order of Battle (SAUS) .... AAAOB
Antiair Output .... AAO
Anti-Air Processing Program (SAA) .... AAP
Antiair Warfare .... AAW
Antiair Warfare Center .... AAWC
Anti-Air Warfare Center (SAUO) .... AAWC
Anti-Air Warfare Commander (SAUO) .... AAWC
Antiair Warfare Commander [or Coordinator] (NVT) .... AAWC
Antiair Warfare Coordinator (SAUS) .... AAWC
Antiair Warfare Exercise [Navy] (NG) .... AAWEX
Antiair Warfare Exercise in Port [Navy] (NVT) .... AAWEXINPT
Anti-Air Warfare Exercise in Port (SAUS) .... AAWEXINPT
Antiair Warfare Exercises in Port (SAUS) .... AAWEXINPT
Anti-Air Warfare On-Board Radar Simulator (SAUS) .... AAWOBRS
Antiair Warfare Readiness Assessment Training System (MCD) .... AAWRATS
Anti-Air Warfare Readiness Assessment Training System (SAUS) .... AAWRATS
Antiair Warfare Reporting [Navy] (NVT) .... AAW(R)
Antiair Warfare Support (NVT) .... AAWSUP
Antiair Warfare Systems [Navy] (MCD) .... AAWS
Anti-Air Warfare Systems (SAUS) .... AAWS
Antiair Warfare Training in Port [Navy] (NVT) .... AAWIPT
Anti-Air Warfare Training in Port (SAUS) .... AAWTIP
Antiair Weapon (SAA) .... AAW
Anti-Air Weapon Control System [Military] (IUSS) .... AAWCS
Antiaircraft [Officer's rating] [British Royal Navy] .... A
Antiaircraft [Army] .... AA
Antiaircraft (SAUS) .... A/A
Anti-Aircraft and Anti-Submarine (SAUS) .... AA and AS
Anti-Aircraft and Guided Missile (SAUS) .... AA&GM
Antiaircraft Armament .... AAA
Anti-Aircraft Armoured Truck [Military] (PDAA) .... AAAT
Antiaircraft Artillery (SAUS) .... AA
Antiaircraft Artillery (GPO) .... AAA
Anti-Aircraft Artillery (SAUS) .... Triple-A
Antiaircraft Artillery Airborne (SAUS) .... AA Abn
Anti-Aircraft Artillery and Guided Missile Center (SAUS) .... AAGMC
Anti-Aircraft Artillery and Guided Missile Equipment (SAUS) .... AAA&GM
Anti-Aircraft Artillery and Guided Missile School (SAUS) .... AAA&GM S
Antiaircraft Artillery Automatic Weapons (SAUS) .... AAA AW
Antiaircraft Artillery Automatic Weapons Battalion (SAUO) .... AAA AW Bn
Antiaircraft Artillery Automatic Weapons Battery (SAUS) .... AAA AQ Btry
Antiaircraft Artillery Automatic Weapons Battery (Self-Propelled) (SAUO) .... AAA AW Btry (SP)
Anti-aircraft Artillery Battery (SAUO) .... AAA Bty
Anti-Aircraft Artillery Battery (SAUS) .... AAA Bty
Antiaircraft Artillery Brigade (SAUO) .... AAA Brig
Anti-aircraft Artillery Brigade (SAUO) .... AABrig
Antiaircraft Artillery Command .... AAAC
Anti-Aircraft Artillery Fire Direction Center (SAUS) .... AAAFDC
Antiaircraft Artillery Group (SAUO) .... AAA Gp
Antiaircraft Artillery Gun Battalion (SAUO) .... AAA Gn Bn
Antiaircraft Artillery Gun Battery (SAUO) .... AAA Gn Bty
Anti-Aircraft Artillery Gun Battery (SAUS) .... AAA Gn Bty
Anti-Aircraft Artillery Gun Crewman (SAUS) .... AAA Gun Crm
Antiaircraft Artillery Information Service (SAUO) .... AAAIS
Antiaircraft Artillery Information [or Intelligence] Service .... AAAIS
Antiaircraft Artillery Information [or Intelligence] Service [Army] .... AAIS
Anti-Aircraft Artillery Integrated Fire Control (SAUS) .... AAA IFC
Antiaircraft Artillery Integrated Fire Control Platoon (SAUO) .... AAA IFC PL

Antiaircraft Artillery Integrated Fire Control Radar Equipment (SAUS) .... AAA IFC rdr eqp
Antiaircraft Artillery Intelligence Service (SAUO) .... AAAIS
Antiaircraft Artillery Intelligence Service (SAUO) .... AAIS
Anti-Aircraft Artillery Liaison Officer (SAUS) .... AAALO
Anti-Aircraft Artillery Light Machine Gun (SAUS) .... AAALMG
Anti-Aircraft Artillery Missile (SAUS) .... AAA Msl
Antiaircraft Artillery Missiles Battalion (SAUO) .... AAAMB
Antiaircraft Artillery Officer Candidate School (SAUO) .... AAAOCS
Anti-Aircraft Artillery Officer Candidate School (SAUS) .... AAAOCS
Antiaircraft Artillery Officer Candidate School (SAUS) .... AAOCS
Anti-Aircraft Artillery Officer Candidate School (SAUO) .... AAOCS
Anti-Aircraft Artillery Operation Center (SAUS) .... AAAOC
Anti-Aircraft Artillery Operations and Intelligence Specialist (SAUS) .... AAA Opns&Intel Sp
Antiaircraft Artillery Operations Center (SAUO) .... AAAOC
Anti-Aircraft Artillery Position (SAUS) .... AA Psn
Antiaircraft Artillery RADAR Crewman [Military] (IAA) .... AAARDRCRM
Antiaircraft Artillery Reception Center .... AAARC
Anti-Aircraft Artillery Reception Center .... AAARC
Antiaircraft Artillery Remote Control Repair Helper (SAUS) .... AAARC Rep Hlpr
Antiaircraft Artillery Remote Control Repair Inspector (SAUS) .... AAARC Rep Insp
Antiaircraft Artillery Remote Control Repairman (SAUS) .... AAARC Repm
Anti-Aircraft Artillery Remote-Controlled Aerial Target (SAUS) .... AAARCAT
Antiaircraft Artillery Remote-Controlled Aerial Target Detachment (SAUO) .... AAARCAT Det
Antiaircraft Artillery Remote-Controlled Aerial Target Detachment (SAUS) .... AARCAT Det
Anti-Aircraft Artillery Repair Foreman (SAUS) .... AAA Rep Fman
Antiaircraft Artillery Repair Helper (SAUS) .... AAA Rep Hlpr
Anti-Aircraft Artillery Repairman (SAUS) .... AAA Repm
Anti-Aircraft Artillery Replacement Training Center (SAUS) .... AAARTC
Antiaircraft Artillery Replacement Training Center (SAUO) .... AAARTC
Anti-Aircraft Artillery Searchlight (SAUS) .... AAA Slt
Anti-Aircraft Artillery Service Test Section (SAUO) .... AASTS
Anti-Aircraft Artillery Service Test Station (SAUS) .... AAASTS
Anti-Aircraft Artillery Training and Test Center (SAUS) .... AAT&TC
Antiaircraft Artillery Training Center (SAUO) .... AAATC
Anti-Aircraft Artillery Training Center (SAUS) .... AATRACEN
Antiaircraft Assistant (SAUS) .... AAA
Antiaircraft Assistant (SAA) .... AA-A
Antiaircraft Balloon [Obsolete] .... AA/B
Antiaircraft Battalion (SAUO) .... AA Bn
Anti-Aircraft Battalion (SAUS) .... AA Bn
Antiaircraft Battalion (or Battery) (SAUO) .... AAB
Anti-Aircraft Battery (SAUO) .... AABty
Anti-Aircraft Battery (SAUS) .... AA Bty
Antiaircraft Brigade (SAUO) .... AA Bde
Antiaircraft Cannon (KSC) .... AAC
Anti-Aircraft Cannon (SAUS) .... AAC
Anti-Aircraft Close Range Fire (SAUS) .... AACRF
Anti-Aircraft Command (SAUS) .... AAC
Anti-Aircraft Command (SAUS) .... AAC
Anti-Aircraft Command Centre (SAUS) .... AACC
Anti-Aircraft Command Post (SAUO) .... AACP
Antiaircraft Common [Projectile] .... AAC
Anti-Aircraft Control Station (MCD) .... AACS
Anti-Aircraft Control Station (SAUS) .... AACS
Anti-Aircraft Cooperation Flight (SAUS) .... AACF
Anti-Aircraft Co-Operation Unit [British military] (DMA) .... AACU
Anti-Aircraft Co-operative Unit (SAUO) .... AACU
Anti-Aircraft Corps [British military] (DMA) .... AAC
Antiaircraft Defence Commander [British] .... AADC
Anti-Aircraft Defence Headquarters (SAUO) .... AADefHq
Antiaircraft Defences [British] .... AAD
Anti-Aircraft Defences (SAUS) .... AAD
Anti-Aircraft Defended Area (SAUS) .... AADA
Anti-Aircraft Defended Point (SAUS) .... AADP
Antiaircraft Defended Point (MUGU) .... AADP
Antiaircraft Defense Area [NATO] .... AADA
Antiaircraft Defense Command (SAUO) .... AADC
Anti-Aircraft Defense Headquarters (SAUS) .... AA Def HQ
Anti-Aircraft Defense System (SAUS) .... AADS
Antiaircraft Defense System [Army] (AABC) .... AADS
Antiaircraft Director Center (MCD) .... AADC
Anti-Aircraft Division (SAUO) .... AAD
Anti-Aircraft Experimental Section [British military] (DMA) .... AAES
Anti-Aircraft Fire (SAUS) .... AAF
Antiaircraft Fire Control .... AAFC
Antiaircraft Guided Missile (AAG) .... AAGM
Antiaircraft Guided Missile Center (SAA) .... AAGMC
Anti-Aircraft Guided Missile School (SAA) .... AAGMS
Antiaircraft Guided Missile Site (SAUO) .... AAGMS
Anti-Aircraft Guided Missile Site (SAUS) .... AAGMS
Anti-Aircraft Guided Missile Station (SAUS) .... AAGMS
Antiaircraft Guided Missile Station (SAUO) .... AAGMS
Antiaircraft Guided Missile System (NG) .... AAGMS
Anti-Aircraft Guided Missile System (SAUS) .... AAGMS
Anti-Aircraft Gun Station (SAUS) .... AAG Stn
Antiaircraft Gun-Laying (DEN) .... AAGL
Anti-Aircraft Gunnery Range (SAUO) .... AAGR
Antiaircraft Hostile Battery (SAUO) .... AAHB
Anti-Aircraft Hostile Battery (SAUS) .... AAHB
Anti-Aircraft Information System (SAUS) .... AAIS
Antiaircraft Liaison Officer (SAA) .... AALO

Antiaircraft Light Cruiser [*Navy symbol*]	CLAA
Antiaircraft Light Machine Gun	AALMG
Anti-Aircraft Light Machine Gun (SAUS)	AAL Mg
Anti-Aircraft Long-Range Fire (SAUS)	AALRF
Antiaircraft Machine Gun [*Army*]	AAMG
Anti-Aircraft Machine Gunner (SAUS)	AA Mach Gnr
Antiaircraft Missile (KSC)	AAM
Antiaircraft Missile Battalion [*Marine Corps*]	AAMSBN
Antiaircraft Observation Post	AAOP
Anti-Aircraft Observation Post	AAOP
Anti-Aircraft Officer (SAUS)	AAO
Antiaircraft Officer (IIA)	AAO
Antiaircraft Operations Center [*Air Force*]	AAOC
Anti-Aircraft Operations Room (MCD)	AAOR
Anti-Aircraft, Practice (SAUS)	AAP
Antiaircraft Regiment (SAUO)	AA Regt
Antiarmor Regional Command (MCD)	AARC
Anti-Aircraft Regional Command (SAUS)	AARC
Anti-Aircraft Replacement Training Center (SAUS)	AARTC
Antiaircraft Replacement Training Center (SAUO)	AARTC
Anti-Aircraft Rocket Gun (SAUS)	Z-Gun
Antiaircraft Searchlight	AASL
Antiaircraft Searchlight Battalion (SAUO)	AA Sl Bn
Anti-Aircraft Searchlight Station (SAUS)	AASLS
Anti-Aircraft Sector (SAUS)	AA Sec
Antiaircraft Self-Destroying	AASD
Anti-Aircraft Service (SAUO)	AAS
Antiaircraft Signal Company (SAUO)	AASC
Anti-Aircraft Smoke Shell (SAUS)	AAS Sh
Anti-Aircraft Station (SAUS)	AASTA
Antiaircraft Station	AASTA
Anti-Aircraft Switch (SAUS)	ASW
Antiaircraft Talker (SAA)	AAT
Antiaircraft Tank (IAA)	AAT
Anti-Aircraft Technician (MCD)	AAT
Anti-Aircraft Throw-Off Firing (SAUS)	AATOF
Antiaircraft Training and Test Center [*Navy*]	AAT & TC
Antiaircraft Training Center [*Navy*]	AATC
Antiaircraft Training Center [*Navy*]	AATRACEN
Anti-Aircraft Training Center (SAUS)	AATRACEN
Anti-Aircraft Training System (SAUS)	AATS
Antiaircraft Troops (SAUO)	AA Tps
Anti-Aircraft Troops (SAUS)	AA tps
Anti-Aircraft Unit (SAUS)	AAU
Antiaircraft Volunteer	AAV
Antiaircraft-Defended Area (SAUO)	AADA
Anti-alpha-staphylolysin [*Immunology*]	ASTA
Anti-Antimissile Missile	AAM
Anti-Antimissile Missile (IAA)	AAMM
Anti-Apartheid Movement [*South Africa*] [*Political party*] (EA)	AAM
Anti-Apartheids Beweging Nederland [*Anti-Apartheid Movement*] [*South Africa*] [*Political party*] (EAIO)	AABN
Antiarmor Capabilities Study (MCD)	AACS
Anti-Armor Capabilities Study (SAUS)	AACS
Antiarmor Cluster Munition (MCD)	ACM
Antiarmor Fuze	AAF
Antiarmor Kill Zone [*Military*] (INF)	AKZ
Antiarmor Missile System - Heavy [*Army*] (INF)	AMS-H
Anti-Armor System Company (SAUS)	TAASCO
Anti-armor Threat Warning System (SAUS)	ATWS
Anti-Armor Vehicle Evaluation (SAUS)	ARMVAL
Anti-Armor Weapon Systems-Medium [*Military*] (MUSM)	AAWS-M
Anti-Armor Weapons (SAUS)	AAWs
Anti-Armor Weapons System-Heavy (SAUS)	AAWS-H
Anti-Armour Helicopter [*Military*] (PDAA)	AAH
Anti-Arteriosclerosis Polysaccharide Factor [*Medicine*] (DMAA)	AAPF
Anti-Axial Compression/Liquid Chromatography	AC/LC
Anti-Backfire Valve [*Automotive engineering*]	ABFV
Antibacklash Gear	ABG
Antibacklash Gear	ABLG
Antibacterial Activity [*Medicine*] (MAE)	ABA
Antibacterial Agent (MELL)	ABA
Antiballistic Missile [*Air Force*]	ABM
Antiballistic Missile Early Warning System [*Air Force*]	ABMEWS
Antiballistic-Missile Missile [*Air Force*] (AFM)	ABMM
Antibasement Membrane Antibody [*Medicine*] (MELL)	AMA
Anti-Beevers-Ross [*Beta-alumina crystallography*]	aBR
Antibiot Chem Topics in Antibiotic Chemistry (journ.) (SAUS)	Top
Antibiotic (MELL)	AB
Antibiotic [*Pharmacology*] (DAVI)	ATB
Antibiotic Concentrate [*Medicine*] (DMAA)	AC
Antibiotic Medicine and Clinical Therapy (SAUS)	AM&CT
Antibiotic Ointment (MELL)	ABO
Antibiotic Removal Device [*Pharmacology*] (DAVI)	ARD
Antibiotic Sensitivity Test [*Medicine*] (MELL)	AST
Antibiotic-Acquired Pseudomembranous Colitis (DAVI)	AAPC
Antibiotic-Associated Colitis [*Medicine*]	AAC
Antibiotic-Associated Diarrhea [*Medicine*] (MELL)	AAD
Antibiotic-Associated Pseudomembranous Colitis [*Medicine*] (DMAA)	AAC
Antibiotic-Associated Pseudomembranous Colitis [*Medicine*]	AAPMC
Antibiotic-Resistant Bacteria [*Medicine*] (MELL)	ARB
Antibiotic-Resistant Tuberculosis [*Medicine*] (MELL)	ART
Antibiotics [*Pharmacology*] (DAVI)	ABx
Antibiotics in Animal Feeds (DICI)	AAF
Anti-Blacklash Gear (SAUS)	ABLG
Antiblocking System (IAA)	ABS
Anti-Boat-Obstacle (SAUS)	ABO
Antibodies [*Immunochemistry*] (DAVI)	ABO
Antibodies to Cardiac Myosin [*Immunology*] (DAVI)	AM
Antibodies to Hepatitis C Virus (SAUS)	Anti-HCV
Antibodies to Murine Cardiac Myosin [*Immunology*] (DAVI)	AMM
Antibodies to Nuclear Antigen [*Immunology*]	ANA
Antibody [*Also, aby*] [*Immunology*]	Ab
Antibody [*Medicine*] (DMAA)	ab
Antibody [*Immunology*]	AB
Antibody [*Also, Ab*] [*Immunology*]	aby
Antibody [*Biochemistry*] (DAVI)	ANTI
Antibody Activity [*Immunology*]	AA
Antibody Against Panel (SAUS)	ABAP
Antibody Deficiency Syndrome [*Immunology*] (MAE)	ADS
Antibody Hepatitis-Associated Antigen [*Immunology*] (MAE)	anti-HAA
Antibody Mediated Cell Dependent Immune Lympholysis [*Immunology*]	ABCIL
Antibody Mediated Immunity (SAUS)	AbMI
Antibody Nitrogen (DMAA)	AbN
Antibody Positive	ab+
Antibody Smooth Muscle-Ribonucleoprotein [*Genetics*] (DAVI)	anti-SM/RNP
Antibody Thyroglobulin [*Immunology*]	TGA
Antibody to Deoxyribonucleic Acid Test [*Rheumatology*] (DAVI)	anti-DNA
Antibody to Extractable Nuclear Antigen Test [*Rheumatology*] (DAVI)	anti-ENA
Antibody to Hepatitis A Virus [*Medicine*] (MEDA)	anti-HAV
Antibody to Hepatitis B Core Antigen [*Medicine*] (MEDA)	anti-HBc
Antibody to Hepatitis B Surface Antigen [*Immunology*] (DAVI)	anti-HB5Ag
Antibody to Hepatitis B Surface Antigen [*Medicine*] (MEDA)	anti-HBs
Antibody Unit	ABU
Antibody-Against-Panel [*Immunology*] (AAMN)	AbAP
Antibody-Antigen Complex Nephritis [*Medicine*] (MELL)	AACN
Antibody-Coated Bacteria [*Medicine*] (MELL)	ABB
Antibody-Coated Bacteria [*Immunology*]	ACB
Antibody-Coated Grid Technique [*Medicine*] (DMAA)	ACGT
Antibody-Containing Cell [*Immunology*]	ACC
Antibody-Dependent Cell Cytotoxicity [*Medicine*] (MELL)	ADCC
Antibody-Dependent Cell-Mediated Cytotoxicity [*Immunology*]	ADCC
Antibody-Dependent Cell-Mediated Cytotoxicity [*Immunology*]	ADCMC
Antibody-Dependent Cellular Cell-Mediated [*Medicine*] (DB)	ADCC
Antibody-Dependent Cellular Cytotoxicity (DOG)	ADCC
Antibody-Dependent Enhancement [*of viral infection*]	ADE
Antibody-Dependent Lymphocyte-Mediated Cytotoxicity [*Clinical chemistry*]	ADLC
Antibody-Dependent Lymphocyte-mediated Cytotoxicity (SAUS)	ADLC
Antibody-Dependent Macrophage-Mediated Cytotoxicity [*Clinical chemistry*]	ADMC
Antibody-Directed Enzyme Prodrug Therapy [*Oncology*]	ADEPT
Antibody-Forming [*Immunology*] (MAE)	AF
Antibody-Forming Cell [*Immunology*]	AFC
Antibody-Induced Cell-Mediated Cytotoxicity [*Medicine*] (PDAA)	AICC
Antibody-Induced Cell-mediated Cytotoxicity (SAUS)	AICC
Antibody-mediated Cell-dependent Immune Lympholysis (SAUS)	ABCIL
Antibody-Negative Mice with Latent Infection [*Immunology*]	ANLI
Antibody-Producing Cell [*Medicine*] (DMAA)	ABPC
Antibody-Secreting Cells [*Immunology*]	ASC
Antibody-to-Surface Antigen (DB)	ASA
Antibonding Molecular Orbital (DB)	ABMO
Anti-Bonding Molecular Orbital (SAUS)	ABMO
Anti-Bureaucracy Special Interest Group [*Mensa*] (EA)	ABSIG
Anti-Bursa Serum (SAUS)	ABS
Anti-Camout Ribbed Bit [*Screwdriving tool*]	ACR
Anticancer Drug Design (SAUS)	Anticancer Drug Des
Anti-Cancer Foundation of the Universities of South Australia	ACFUSA
Anticar Melt (SAUS)	ACT
Anticar Theft [*Campaign or Committee*]	ACT
Anti-Cardiolipin Antibodies (SAUS)	ACA
Anticardiolipin Antibody [*Immunochemistry*]	ACA
Anticarrier Warfare (MCD)	ACW
Anti-Catholic League (EA)	ACL
Anti-Caucasian Scale (SAUS)	A-C Scale
Anticenter	AC
Anti-Center (or Centre) (SAUS)	AC
Anticentromere Antibody [*Immunology*]	ACA
Antichaff Circuit (IEEE)	ANTC
Anti-Char	AC
Anti-Char a Effet Dirige (SAUS)	ACED
Anti-Char Rapide Autopropulse [*French antitank weapon system*]	ACRA
Antichloristic (SAUS)	Antichlor
Antichymotrypsin [*Biochemistry*]	ACT
Anticipate (FAAC)	ANCPT
Anticipate (AABC)	ANTCP
Anticipate Discharge Tomorrow [*Medicine*] (DAVI)	ADS
Anticipate Discharge Tomorrow (MELL)	ADT
Anticipated (WGA)	ANT
Anticipated Answer (SAUS)	AA
Anticipated Card Release Date (SAUS)	ACRD
Anticipated Data Transmission Date (SAUS)	ADTD
Anticipated Engine Not Operationally Ready Supply [*Military*] (AFIT)	AENORS
Anticipated Freight [*Commerce*] (BARN)	ant frt
Anticipated Freight	Ant Frt
Anticipated Level of Business	ALB
Anticipated Life Scan (SAUS)	ALS
Anticipated Life Span [*Statistics*] (DAVI)	ALS
Anticipated Net Mission Capable Supply (SAUS)	ANMCS
Anticipated Not Mission Capable, Supply [*Military*] (NVT)	ANMCS

Anticipated Not Operationally Ready, Maintenance (NVT) ... ANORM
Anticipated Not Operationally Ready-Supply (SAUS) ... ANORS
Anticipated Operational Occurrence [*Nuclear energy*] (NRCH) ... AOO
Anticipated Time of Discharge (MELL) ... ATD
Anticipated Transient Operating Guideline [*Nuclear energy*] (NRCH) ... ATOG
Anticipated Transient without Scram [*Physics*] ... ATWS
Anticipated Vacancy [*Civil Service*] ... AV
Anticipation Span (SAUS) ... A Span
Anticipations Point (ACAE) ... AP
Anticipatory Account (ABAC) ... AA
Anticipatory Avoidance [*Medicine*] ... AA
Anticipatory Goal Response [*Medicine*] ... AGR
Anticipatory Modification (SAUS) ... AM
Anticipatory Nausea and Vomiting [*Medicine*] ... ANV
Anticipatory Reactor Trips (NRCH) ... ART
Anticipatory Response (SAUS) ... AR
Anticipatory Vomiting [*Medicine*] (MELL) ... AV
Anticircling Run [*Navy*] (NG) ... ACR
Anti-Circular Run (SAUS) ... ACR
anticlimax (SAUS) ... anticli
anticlinal (SAUS) ... anticli
anticline (SAUS) ... anticli
anticlinorium (SAUS) ... anticli
Anticlockwise ... A
Anticlockwise ... ACW
Anti-Clockwise (SAUS) ... ACW
Anticlonus Index [*Neurology*] [*Medicine*] (DAVI) ... ACI
Anticlutter (NATG) ... AC
Anti-Clutter (SAUS) ... ac
Anticoagulant [*or Anticoagulation*] ... AC
Anticoagulant [*or Anticoagulation*] (AAMN) ... ANTICOAG
Anticoagulant Citrate Dextrose [*Hematology*] ... ACD
Anticoagulant Therapy [*Medicine*] ... ACT
Anticoagulant-Related Bleeding [*Medicine*] (MELL) ... ARB
Anticoagulants in the Secondary Prevention of Events in Coronary Thrombosis ... ASPECT
Anticodon Stem-Loop Analog [*Genetics*] ... ASL
Anticoincidence Counter (OA) ... AC
Anticoincidence Detection System ... ADS
Anticollagen Antibody [*Immunology*] ... ACA
Anti-Collision Light System [*or Subsystem*] (MCD) ... ALS
Anticomet Tail (IAA) ... ACT
Anti-Comet Tail Gun [*Television*] (WDMC) ... ACT
Anticomintern Pact (SAUO) ... ACP
Anti-Comintern Pact ... ACP
Anti-Common Market League [*British*] (BI) ... ACML
Anti-Communications Threat (SAUS) ... ACT
Anti-Communism International (EAIO) ... ACI
Anti-Communist (ADA) ... A-C
Anti-Communist Advisory Committee (EA) ... ACAC
Anti-Communist Committee (EA) ... ACC
Anti-Communist Confederation of Polish Freedom Fighters in USA (EA) ... ACCPFF
Anti-Communist International (EA) ... ACI
Anti-Communist League of America (EA) ... ACLA
Anticommunist League of America (SAUO) ... ACLA
Anti-Communist Society [*Belize*] (PD) ... ACS
Anticomplement Activity [*Medicine*] (DMAA) ... ACA
Anticomplement Immunofluorescence Test [*Immunochemistry*] ... ACIF
Anticomplement Immunofluorescence Test (SAUS) ... ACIF Test
Anticomplementary [*Immunology*] ... AC
Anti-Compromise Emergency Destruct (SAUS) ... ACED
Anticompromise Emergency Destruction (MCD) ... ACED
Anticompromise Technique ... ACT
Anti-Concorde Project (EA) ... A-CP
Anti-Concrete (SAUS) ... AC
Anti-Constipating Regimen (SAUS) ... ACR
Anticonstipation Regimen [*Medicine*] ... ACR
Anticonvulsant Medication [*Medicine*] (MELL) ... ACM
Anti-Corrosion Methods and Materials (SAUS) ... Anti-CorrosMethods Mater
Anti-Corrosive (SAUS) ... AC
anticorrosive (SAUS) ... ac
Anticorrosive ... AC
Anti-Corruption Agency ... ACA
Anti-Counterfeit Action Group [*Australia*] ... ACAG
Anticountermeasures Trainer ... ACTER
Anti-Countermeasures Trainer (SAUS) ... ACTER
Anti-Crime (LAIN) ... AC
Anti-Crime Foundation (SAUO) ... ACF
Anticrime Unit ... ACU
Anti-Cronyism Movement [*Philippines*] ... ACRONYM
Anticruise Missile (MCD) ... ACM
Anti-Cruise Missile (SAUS) ... ACM
Anticrystallizing Rubber (SAUS) ... AC-Rubber
Anti-Curl System [*Intellifax*] [*Brother Industries USA, Inc.*] [*Telecommunications*] ... ACS
Anticyclone on Jupiter (SAUS) ... Great Red Spot
Anticyclonic [*Meteorology*] (BARN) ... ACYC
Anticytoplasmic Antibody [*Medicine*] (DMAA) ... ACA
Anti-Defamation League (EA) ... ADL
Anti-Defamation League of B'nai B'rith (EA) ... ADL
Anti-Defamation League of B'nai B'rith, New York, NY [*Library symbol*] [*Library of Congress*] (LCLS) ... NNAD
Anti-Deficiency Act (AAGC) ... ADA
Antideoxyribonuclease [*Medicine*] (DMAA) ... ADN
Antidepressant (MELL) ... AD
Antidetonation Injection ... ADI
Antidiarrhea [*Medicine*] ... AD
Anti-Diesel Device [*Automotive engineering*] ... ADV
Anti-Digit Dialing League (EA) ... ADDL
Antidigoxigenin-Tetrarhodamin-Isothiocyanat (SAUS) ... TRITC
Anti-Discrimination Act [*Australia*] ... ADA
Anti-Discrimination Association (SAUO) ... ADA
Antidisestablishmentarianism (SAUS) ... Antidis
Anti-Disturbance (MCD) ... AD
Antidiuretic Hormone [*Vasopressin*] [*Endocrinology*] ... ADH
Antidiuretic Substance ... ADS
Antidiuretisches Prinzip (SAUS) ... ADP
Antidotum [*Antidote*] [*Latin*] ... Antid
Anti-Drainback Valve [*Automotive engineering*] ... ADV
Antidromic Potential [*Medicine*] (DMAA) ... AP
Anti-Drug Coalition [*Later, NADC*] (EA) ... ADC
Anti-Drug Network (DOMA) ... ADNET
Anti-Dumping [*International trade*] (GFGA) ... AD
Anti-Dumping Authority ... ADA
Anti-Dumping Tribunal [*Canada*] ... ADT
Anti-Dumping/Countervailing Duties (SAUS) ... AD/CV
Anti-Embolic Stockings [*Medicine*] (DMAA) ... AES
Antiembolitic [*Medicine*] (MELL) ... AE
Anti-Enemy-Backing-Up Society (SAUO) ... AEBUS
Antient [*Archaic variation of "ancient"*] (ROG) ... ANT
Antiepileptic Drug ... AED
Anti-Estrogen Binding Site [*Biochemistry*] ... AEBS
Antiestrogen Therapy [*Medicine*] (MELL) ... AET
Antietam National Battlefield Site ... ANTI
Antiexposure Flight Suit ... AEFS
Anti-Fading Compensation (SAUS) ... AFC
Antifaschistischer Kampf Kaiserslautern [*Kaiserslautern Antifascist Struggle*] [*Germany*] (PD) ... AKK
Anti-Fascist Organization [*Later, AFPFL*] [*Burma*] [*World War II*] ... AFO
Anti-Fascist People's Freedom League [*Formerly, AFO*] [*Burma*] [*World War II*] ... AFPFL
Antifatty Liver [*Medicine*] ... AFL
Anti-Ferro-Electric (SAUS) ... AFE
Antiferroelectric (SAUS) ... AFE
Antiferroelectric ... AFLC
Antiferromagnet [*Physics*] ... AFM
Antiferromagnetic ... AF
Anti-Ferromagnetic Resonance (or Resonator) (SAUS) ... AFMR
Antiferromagnetism (SAUS) ... AFM
Antifibrilysine (SAUS) ... AFL
Antifibrinogen [*Hematology*] (DAVI) ... A-F
Antifibrinolysin [*Medicine*] (MELL) ... AFL
Antifibrinolysine (SAUS) ... AFL
Antifibroblast Serum (DB) ... AFS
Antifibrolysin (SAUS) ... AFL
Anti-Flood Valve (MCD) ... AFV
Anti-Fluoridation Association of Victoria [*Australia*] ... AFAV
Anti-Foam (SAUS) ... AF
Anti-Fouling Paint (DNAB) ... AF
Anti-Fratricide Identification Device [*Military*] (DOMA) ... AFID
Antifreeze Glycoprotein [*Biochemistry*] ... AFGP
Antifreeze Polypeptide [*Biochemistry*] ... AFP
Antifreeze Protein ... AFP
Antifreeze protein (SAUS) ... AFT
Anti-Friction [*Lubricants*] ... AF
Antifriction Bearing ... AFB
Anti-Friction Bearing Distributors Association [*Later, BSA*] (EA) ... AFBDA
Antifriction Bearing Manufacturers Association (SAUO) ... AFBMA
Antifriction Metal ... AFM
Antifriction Metal (SAUS) ... afm
Anti-Frogman Grenade (SAUS) ... AFG
Anti-G [*Gravity*] **Straining Maneuver** (DOMA) ... AGSM
Anti-Gammaglobulin Factor [*Medicine*] (MELL) ... AGF
Antigas [*Military*] ... AG
Antigas Gangrene Serum [*Medicine*] ... AGGS
Anti-Gas Instructor [*British military*] (DMA) ... A/GI
Antigas Officer (SAUS) ... AGO
Anti-Gas School (SAUO) ... AGS
Antigas Training (SAUS) ... A/GT
Antigen [*Also, a, Ag*] [*Immunology*] ... A
Antigen [*Also, A, a*] [*Immunology*] ... Ag
Antigen (DB) ... AG
Antigen (LDT) ... An
Antigen Binding Fragments (MELL) ... FAB
Antigen Detection Test [*Clinical chemistry*] ... ADT
Antigen E ... AgE
Antigen Fixation Test [*Medicine*] (MELL) ... AFT
Antigen Processing Cell [*Medicine*] (TAD) ... APC
Antigen Receptor [*Medicine*] (MELL) ... AR
Antigen Receptor Response Element [*Immunology*] ... ARRE
Antigen Recognition Activation Motif [*Immunology*] ... ARAM
Antigen Recognition Site [*Genetics*] ... ARS
Antigen Virulence Antigen (SAUS) ... VI
Antigen-Against-Panel (DB) ... AGAP
Antigen-Antibody [*Complex*] [*Immunology*] ... Ag-AB
Antigen-Antibody Complex [*Medicine*] (MELL) ... AAC
Antigen-Antibody Crossed Electrophoresis [*Biochemistry*] (DAVI) ... AACE
Antigen-Antibody Reaction [*Medicine*] (MELL) ... AAR
Antigen-Antiglobulin Reaction [*Immunology*] (MAE) ... AAR

Antigen-Binding [*Immunology*]	AB
Antigen-Binding Capacity [*Immunology*]	ABC
Antigen-Binding Cell [*Medicine*] (MELL)	ABC
Antigen-Binding Cells (SAUS)	ABCs
Antigen-Binding Fragment [*Immunology*]	Fab
Antigen-Binding Lymphocyte [*Immunology*] (AAMN)	ABL
Antigen-Carrier Lipid [*Immunology*]	ACL
Antigenic Determinant [*Medicine*]	AD
Antigenic Determinant [*Medicine*] (MELL)	AGD
Antigenic Modulation [*Medicine*] (MELL)	AGM
Antigen-Independent Determinants [*Medicine*] (MELL)	AID
Antigen-Inducing Unit [*Medicine*] (DMAA)	AIU
Antigen-Neutralizing Capacity (DB)	ANC
Antigen-Presenting Cell [*Immunology*]	APC
Antigen-Presenting Liposome [*Immunochemistry*]	APL
Antigen-Reactive Cell [*Immunology*]	ARC
Antigenreceptor Homology [*Immunochemistry*]	ARH
Antigens (SAUS)	Ags
Antigen-Specific Electrophoretic Cell Separation [*Medicine*] (MELL)	ASECS
Antigen-Specific Suppressor Cells [*Medicine*] (MELL)	ASSC
Anti-Gentilism (SAUS)	AG
Antigen-Transporting Cell [*Immunology*]	ATC
Antiglare, Antireflective, Antistatic [*Cathode ray tube treatment*] (PCM)	AGRAS
Antigliadin Antibodies [*Immunology*]	AGA
Antiglobin Consumption Test (SAUS)	AGCT
Antiglobulin [*Clinical chemistry*]	AG
Antiglobulin Test [*Hematology*]	AGT
Antiglomerular Antibody (DB)	AGA
Antiglomerular Basement Antibody Test	AGBM
Antiglomerular Basement Membrane [*Antibodies*] [*Cardiology*] (DAVI)	anti-GMB
Antiglomerular Basement Membrane Antibody (SAUS)	AGBM
Antigo Public Library, Antigo, WI [*Library symbol*] [*Library of Congress*] (LCLS)	WAn
Antigo, WI [*Location identifier*] [*FAA*] (FAAL)	AIG
Antigo, WI [*FM radio station call letters*] (BROA)	WACD-FM
Antigo, WI [*AM radio station call letters*]	WATK
Antigo, WI [*Television station call letters*] (BROA)	WAZW
Antigo, WI [*FM radio station call letters*]	WRLO
Antigone [*of Sophocles*] [*Classical studies*] (OCD)	Ant
Antigonish, NS [*Television station call letters*]	CJCB-2
Antigonish, NS [*AM radio station call letters*]	CJFX
Antigravity	AG
Antigravity Suit [*NASA*] (MCD)	AGS
Antigravity Suit [*Air Force clothing for supersonic flight*]	G (Suit)
Antigua [*Antigua*] [*Seismograph station code, US Geological Survey*] (SEIS)	ANG
Antigua (ROG)	ANT
Antigua (ROG)	ANTIG
Antigua [*IYRU nationality code*] [*Airport symbol*]	ANU
Antigua [*MARC country of publication code*] [*Library of Congress*] (LCCP)	aq
Antigua [*Antigua*] [*Seismograph station code, US Geological Survey*] [*Closed*] (SEIS)	AWI
Antigua [*MARC geographic area code*] [*Library of Congress*] (LCCP)	nwaq-
Antigua [*International civil aircraft marking*] (ODBW)	V2
Antigua and Barbuda (SAUS)	A&B
Antigua and Barbuda (MILB)	AB
Antigua and Barbuda Airways International Ltd. [*ICAO designator*] (FAAC)	ABI
Antigua and Barbuda Broadcasting Service (EY)	ABBS
Antigua Base Command (SAUO)	ABC
Antigua Caribbean Liberation Movement [*Political party*] (EAIO)	ACLM
Antigua Labour Party [*Political party*] (PPW)	ALP
Antigua, Leeward Islands (SAUO)	ANU
Antigua Tourist Information Center (SAUO)	ATIC
Antigua-Barbuda [*ANSI two-letter standard code*] (CNC)	AG
Antigua-Barbuda [*ANSI three-letter standard code*] (CNC)	ATG
Antihaemolytic Factor (SAUS)	AHF
Antihaemophilic Factor (SAUS)	AHF
Antihaemophilic Globulin (SAUS)	AHG
Antihaemophytic Factor (SAUS)	AHF
Antihalation	AH
Antihalation Undercoat [*Photography*] (OA)	AHU
Anti-Heart Antibody [*Medicine*] (DMAA)	AHA
Anti-Helicopter Device	AHD
Anti-Helicopter Mine [*Military*]	AHM
Anti-Hemagglutinating Unit (SAUS)	AHAU
Antihemolytic Factor (DB)	AHF
Antihemolytic Globulin (DB)	AHG
Antihemophilic Factor [*Factor VIII*] [*Also, AHG, PTF, TPC*] [*Hematology*]	AHF
Anti-Hemophilic Factor (SAUS)	AHF
Antihemophilic Globulin [*Factor VIII*] [*Hematology*]	AGH
Antihemophilic Globulin [*Factor VIII*] [*Also, AHF, PTF, TPC*] [*Hematology*]	AHG
Anti-Hemophilic Globulin (SAUS)	AHG
Antihernophin (SAUS)	AHG
Anti-Hispanic Scale (SAUS)	A-H Scale
Antihistone Antibody [*Medicine*] (DMAA)	AHA
Antihuman Gamma-Globulin (DB)	AHGG
Antihuman Globulin [*Consumption test*] [*Medicine*]	AHG
Antihuman Lymphocyte Globulin [*Medicine*] (DMAA)	AHLG
Antihuman Lymphocyte Serum [*Immunochemistry*] (MAE)	AHLS
Antihuman Lymphocytic [*Globulin*] (DB)	AL
Antihuman Thymocyte Gamma Globulin [*Immunochemistry*]	AHTGG
Antihuman Thymocyte Globulin [*Medicine*] (DAVI)	ATG
Antihuman Thymocytic Globulin [*Clinical chemistry*] (MAE)	AHTG
Antihuman Thymocytic Plasma [*Clinical chemistry*] (MAE)	AHTP
Antihuman Thymus Serum (DMAA)	AHTS
Antihunt [*Circuit*] [*Electronics*]	AH
Anti-Hunt Device (SAUS)	AH Device
Antihyaluronidase [*Clinical chemistry*]	AH
Antihyaluronidase [*Bacteriology*] (DAVI)	AHI
Antihyaluronidase Titer [*Clinical chemistry*] (MAE)	AHT
Antihypertensive and Lipid-Lowering Heart Attack Trial [*Clinical trial*]	ALLHAT
Antihypertensive Drug [*Medicine*]	AHD
Antihypertensive Neural Renomedullary Liquid	ANRL
Antihypertensive Neutral Renomedullary Lipids [*Cardiology*] (DAVI)	ANRL
Antihypertensive Polar Renomedullary Lipid (DB)	APRL
Anti-Ice (PIPO)	A/I
Anti-Ice/De-Ice System [*or Subsystem*] (MCD)	ADS
Anti-ice/De-ice System (SAUS)	ADS
Anti-Icing [*Technical drawings*]	AI
Anti-Icing Additive (NATG)	AIA
Anti-Icing Fluid [*Aviation*] (DA)	AAF
Anti-Icing System [*Aircraft*]	AIS
Anti_Immunoglobulin [*Medicine*] (DMAA)	AIG
Anti-Immunoglobulin	AIG
Anti-Immunoglobulin Antibodies (DOG)	AIA
Anti-Inflammatory Corticoid [*Pharmacology*] (DAVI)	AC
Anti-Inflammatory Drug [*Pharmacology*] (DAVI)	AID
Anti-Inflammatory Nonsteroidal [*Agent or drug*] [*Pharmacology*] (DAVI)	AINS
Anti-Inflammatory Protein (PDAA)	AIP
Anti-Inflation Act [*Canada*]	AIA
Anti-Inflation Appeal Tribunal [*Canada*]	AIAT
Anti-Inflation Board	AIB
Anti-Injunction Act of 1932 (WYGK)	AIA
Anti-Insulin Antibody [*Medicine*] (MELL)	AIA
Anti-Insulin Antibody [*Endocrinology*] (DAVI)	AI-Ab
Anti-Insulin Receptor Antibody [*Medicine*] (DMAA)	AIRA
Anti-Insulin Serum [*Biochemistry*] (MAE)	AIS
Anti-Intercontinental Ballistic Missile	AICBM
Anti-Intermediate Range Ballistic Missile	AIRBM
Anti-Internment League (SAUO)	AIL
Anti-Intrusion Alarm	AIA
Anti-Intrusion Alarm Set	AIAS
Anti-Intrusion Defence Barriers (SAUS)	AIDB
Anti-Invasion Factor [*In bone resorption*]	AIF
Anti-Invasion Mine	AIM
Anti-Jackknife System [*Automotive engineering*]	AJS
Anti-Jam (SAUS)	A/J
Anti-Jam Control Modem [*Military*] (DOMA)	AJCM
Antijam Display	AJD
Antijam Equipment	AJE
Antijam Frequency	AJF
Antijam Frequency Hopper	AJFH
Antijam Hopper	AJH
Anti-Jam Hopper (SAUS)	AJH
Anti-Jam Manpack Antenna (SAUS)	AJMA
Antijam Manpack Antenna (MCD)	AJMA
Anti-Jam Modem	AJM
Anti-Jam Modem Controller [*Computer science*] (LAIN)	AJM/C
Antijam MODEM [*Modulate, Demodulate*], Very-Low Frequency (CAAL)	VERDIN
Antijam Operator (CET)	AJO
Antijam Synthesizer	AJS
Antijamming [*RADAR*]	AJ
Anti-Jamming, Anti-Interference (SAUS)	AJAI
Antijamming Blackout	AJBO
Antijamming Improvements (AABC)	AJI
Antijamming/Anti-Interference (CET)	AJ/AI
Anti-Jamming/Anti-Interference (SAUS)	AJ/AI
Anti-Japanese Union (SAUO)	AJU
Anti-Killer Organization of Expatriates (SAUO)	AKOE
Anti-Knock Index [*Automotive industry*]	AKI
AntiLASER Beam Coating	ALBC
Antilla [*Cuba*] [*ICAO location identifier*] (ICLI)	MUAT
Antillaanse Luchtvaart Maatschappij [*Airline*] [*Netherlands Antilles*]	ALM
Antillana de Nevegacion Aerea SA [*Dominican Republic*] [*ICAO designator*] (FAAC)	SUN
Antillea West Indian Federation (SAUO)	Ant
Antillean (SAUS)	Ant
Antilles (SAUS)	Ant
Antilles (VRA)	L Anti
Antilles Air Boats (MHDB)	AD
Antilles Air Boats, Inc. (SAUO)	AD
Antilles Air Boats Incorporated (SAUO)	AABI
Antilles Command, United States Army Caribbean	ANTCOMDUSARCARIB
Antilles Current (SAUS)	Ant Cur
Antilles Research Program [*Yale University*]	ARP
Antilles Resources Ltd. [*Vancouver Stock Exchange symbol*]	ARY
Antillliaanse Luchtvaart Maatschappij [*Netherlands*] [*ICAO designator*] (FAAC)	ALM
Antilock Brake [*Automotive engineering*]	ALB
Antilock Brake Control Module [*Automotive engineering*]	ABCM
Antilock Braking System [*Automotive engineering*]	ABS
Anti-Lock Braking System (SAUS)	ALBS
Anti-Locust Research Centre [*Later, Centre for Overseas Pest Research*] [*British*] (MCD)	ALRC
antilog (SAUS)	ant
Antilog [*Mathematics*] (BARN)	illog
Antilogarithm	antilog
Antilogarithm	ANTILOG
Antilogarithmic Function	ANLG
Antilogarithmic Function (SAUS)	ANLG Function
Antilymphocyte Antibody [*Medicine*] (DMAA)	AL-Ab

Antilymphocyte [*or Antilymphocytic*] **Globulin** [*Immunology*] ... ALG
Antilymphocyte Globulin (SAUS) ... ALG
Antilymphocyte Plasma [*Immunology*] (MAE) ... ALP
Antilymphocyte [*or Antilympholytic*] **Serum** [*Immunology*] ... ALS
Antilymphocyte Serum (SAUS) ... ALS
Anti-Lymphocyte Stimulator (SAUS) ... ALS
Antilymphocytic Globulin (SAUS) ... ALG
Antilymphocytic Serum (SAUS) ... ALS
Antilyphocyte Serum (SAUS) ... ALS
Antimacrophage Globulin (MAE) ... AMG
Antimacrophage Serum (MAE) ... AMS
Antimagnetic (SAUS) ... Antimag
Anti-Malaria Campaign (SAUO) ... AMC
Antimalarial Agent ... AMA
Antimalignant Antibody Test [*Medicine*] (MELL) ... AMAT
Antimassed Armor Strike Weapon System (MCD) ... AASWS
Anti-Material (SAUS) ... AM
Antimateriel [*Munitions*] ... AM
Antimateriel Incendiary ... AMI
Anti-Materiel Incendiary Submunition (SAUS) ... AMIS
Antimateriel Warhead ... AMW
Antimateriel Warhead ... AMWH
antimatter (SAUS) ... antimat
Antimatter Decelerator ... AD
Antimechanized (SAUS) ... AMECD
Antimechanized [*Army*] (AABC) ... AMECZ
Anti-Metric Society of America [*An association*] ... AMSA
Antimicrobial Agent [*Medicine*] (MELL) ... AMA
Antimicrobial Agent Associated Colitis [*Medicine*] ... AAAC
Antimicrobial Agent-Associated Colitis [*Medicine*] (DAVI) ... AAC
Antimicrobial Agents and Chemotherapy ... AAC
Antimicrobial Removal Device ... ARD
Antimicrobial Susceptibility Test [*Medicine*] (MELL) ... AMST
Antimicrobial Therapy [*Medicine*] (MELL) ... AMT
Antimicrosomal Antibody [*Clinical chemistry*] ... AMcA
Antimilitarismus Information (SAUO) ... AMI
Anti-Mine Countermeasure (MCD) ... AMCM
Anti-Mine Sweeping Explosive Float (SAUS) ... AMSEF
Anti-Mines (SAUS) ... AM
Antimissile Array RADAR ... AMAR
Anti-Missile Defence (SAUS) ... AMD
Anti-Missile Discarding Sabot (SAUS) ... AMDS
Anti-Missile Infra-Red (SAUS) ... AMIR
Antimissile Missile [*Air Force*] ... AMM
Antimissile Missile and Space Defense Office ... AMMSDO
Antimissile Missile Test Range [*Military*] ... AMMTR
Anti-Missile Research Advisory Council ... AMRAC
Anti-Missile Surface-to-Air Missile (SAUS) ... AMSAM
Antimissile Surface-to-Air Missile (SAUS) ... ANSAM
Antimissile Warfare ... AMW
Antimisting Kerosene [*Aviation*] ... AMK
Anti-Misting Kerosene (SAUS) ... AMK
Antimitochondral Antibody [*Immunology*] ... AMA
Antimonium [*Antimony*] [*Symbol is Sb*] [*Chemical element*] (ROG) ... ANT
Antimonium [*Antimony*] [*Symbol is Sb*] [*Chemical element*] (ROG) ... ANTIM
Antimony [*Chemical element*] (DOG) ... Sb
Antimony Sodium Dimercaptosuccinate [*Stibocaptate*] (BABM) ... TWSb/6
Antimony Sulfide-Oxysulfide (SAUS) ... ASOS
Antimony Tin Oxide (IAA) ... ATO
Antimony Trisisooctyl Mercaptoacetate (GNE) ... ATOM
Antimony Trisulfide Oxysulfide ... ASOS
Antimony-125 (SAUS) ... Sb-125
Antimorphine Dose (SAUS) ... AMD
Antimotor Torpedo Boat [*Navy*] ... AMTB
Antimotorboat ... AMB
Anti-mouse Lymphocyte Serum (SAUS) ... ALS
Antimouse Lymphocyte Serum [*Immunology*] (MAE) ... AMLS
Anti-Muellerian Hormone [*Also, MIS*] [*Embryology*] [*Biochemistry*] ... AMH
Anti-Mullerian Hormone [*Medicine*] (MELL) ... AMH
Anti-Multipath Equipment (SAUS) ... AME
Antimultipath Equipment ... AME
Antimuscle Factor [*Immunology*] ... AMF
Antimycin (DAVI) ... Ant
Antimycin A (DMAA) ... AntA
Antimycobacterial Agent [*Medicine*] (MELL) ... AMBA
Antimyosin Antibody [*Medicine*] (DMAA) ... AMA
Anti-Narcotics Office (SAUO) ... ANO
Anti-Navire Supersonique (SAUS) ... ANS
Anti-Nazi Boycott Committee (SAUO) ... ANBC
Anti-Negro Scale (SAUS) ... A-N Scale
Antineoplastic Agent [*Medicine*] (MELL) ... ANA
Antineoplastic Urinary Protein ... ANUP
Antineuraminidase (DB) ... AN
Antineutrophil Cytoplasmic Antibodies (SAUS) ... ANCA
Antineutrophil Cytoplasmic Antibody [*Medicine*] (MELL) ... ANA
Antineutrophil Cytoplasmic Antibody [*Immunology*] ... ANCA
Antineutrophilic Serum [*Hematology*] (DAVI) ... ANS
Antinicotinyl Adenine Dinucleotidase (MELL) ... ANADase
Antinode (SAUS) ... AN
[*The*] **Antinoe Papyrus of Theocritus** [*Classical studies*] (OCD) ... PAntin
Antinoopolis Papyri [*A publication*] (OCD) ... PAntinoop
Antinuclear Antibodies (or Antibody) (SAUS) ... ANA
Antinuclear Antibody [*Medicine*] (DMAA) ... A
Antinuclear Antibody [*Immunology*] ... ANA
Antinuclear Antibody [*Medicine*] (DMAA) ... ANuA
Antinuclear Antibody Fluid [*Medicine*] (DAVI) ... ANA-FL
Anti-Nuclear Campaign [*British*] ... ANC
Antinuclear Factor [*Immunology*] ... ANF
Anti-Nuclear Factor (SAUS) ... ANF
Antinuclear Fluorescent [*Medicine*] (MELL) ... ANFF
Anti-Nuclear Force (DNAB) ... ANF
Anti-Nuclear Group Representing York (NRCH) ... ANGRY
Antinuclear Submarine Warfare [*Navy*] ... ANSW
Antinucleolar Antibodies [*Immunology*] (AAMN) ... ANoA
Anti-Obesity Drug (MELL) ... AOD
Antioch College (SAUO) ... AC
Antioch College, Yellow Springs (SAUS) ... ANC
Antioch College, Yellow Springs, OH [*OCLC symbol*] (OCLC) ... ANC
Antioch College, Yellow Springs, OH [*Library symbol*] [*Library of Congress*] (LCLS) ... OYesA
Antioch Program for Interracial Education [*Antioch College*] (EA) ... APIE
Antioch Review [*A publication*] (BRI) ... Ant R
Antioch Review (journ.) (SAUS) ... AR
Antioptimal and Right (SAUS) ... A and R
Antioptimal and Wright (SAUS) ... A and W
Anti-Oriental Scale (SAUS) ... A-O Scale
Anti-ovarian Antibody (SAUS) ... AVA
Antiovarian Antibody (ADWA) ... AVA
Anti-Ovarian Antibody [*Medicine*] ... AVA
Anti-Ovotransferrin [*Biochemistry*] ... AOT
Anti-Oxidant (SAUS) ... AO
Antioxidant (MELL) ... AO
Antioxidant Activity [*Food technology*] ... AA
Anti-Papal Association (SAUO) ... APA
Anti-Parachutist Corps (SAUO) ... APC
Antiparasitic (SAUS) ... Antip
Antiparietal Antibody ... APA
Antiparietal Cell Antibody (SAUS) ... APCA
Antiparietat Antibody (SAUS) ... APA
Antiparkinsonian [*Medicine*] (MEDA) ... APK
Antiparkinsonian Drugs (SAUS) ... APdrugs
Antiparticle (SAUS) ... Antip
Anti-Partition League (SAUO) ... APL
Antipathetic (SAUS) ... Antip
Antiperinuclear Factor [*Medicine*] (MELL) ... APF
Antiperiodic (SAUS) ... antip
Antiperiplanar [*Chemistry*] ... ap
Antipernicious Anemia Factor [*Also, APAF, EF, LLD*] [*Hematology*] (AAMN) ... APA
Antipernicious Anemia Factor [*Also, APA, EF, LLD*] [*Hematology*] ... APAF
Antipernicious Anemia Principle [*Hematology*] (IIA) ... AAP
Anti-Personal Bomb (SAUS) ... APB
Antipersonnel [*Projectile*] ... AP
Antipersonnel [*Projectile*] ... APER
Antipersonnel [*Projectile*] (AABC) ... APERS
Antipersonnel Antimaterial [*Weaponry*] (MCD) ... APAM
Antipersonnel Bomb ... APB
Antipersonnel Improved Conventional Munitions [*Army*] (ADDR) ... APICM
Anti-Personnel Improved Conventional Munitions (SAUS) ... APICM
Anti-Personnel Land-Mine (MILB) ... APL
Anti-Personnel Mine [*Military*] (MUSM) ... APM
Antipersonnel Obstacle Breaching System [*Marine Corps*] (INF) ... APOBS
Antipersonnel Projectile ... APP
Anti-Personnel, Tracer (SAUS) ... APERS-T
Anti-Personnel Weapon (SAUS) ... APW
Antiperspirant (MELL) ... AP
Antiperspirants and Deodorants (MELL) ... A & D
Antiphase Boundaries [*Mineralogy*] ... APB
Anti-Phase Boundary (SAUS) ... APB
Anti-Phase Boundary Energy (PDAA) ... APBE
Antiphase Domains [*Mineralogy*] ... APD
Antiphlogistic-Corticoid [*Medicine*] (AAMN) ... AC
Antiphlogistic-Corticoid [*Medicine*] (MAE) ... APC
Antiphlogistic-Corticoid Conditioning Effect [*Medicine*] ... A-CC
Antiphon ... ANT
Antiphonale Sacrosanctae Romanae Ecclesiae ... AR
Anti-Phopholipid Antibody [*Medicine*] ... APA
Antiphospholipid Antibody [*Medicine*] (DMAA) ... APAB
Antiphospholipid Antibody [*Medicine*] (MELL) ... APLA
Antiphospholipid Syndrome (ADWA) ... APLS
Antiphospholipid Syndrome ... APS
Antiphospholyrosine (SAUS) ... APT
Antiphosphotyrosine [*Biochemistry*] ... APT
Antiplasmin [*Hematology*] ... AP
Antiplatelet Antibody [*Medicine*] (MELL) ... APAb
Antiplatelet Drug Therapy [*Medicine*] (MELL) ... APDT
Antiplatelet Plasma (DB) ... APP
Antiplatelet Therapy [*Medicine*] (MELL) ... APT
Anti-Plugging Relay (SAUS) ... APR
Anti-Poaching Unit (BARN) ... APU
antipodal (SAUS) ... antip
Antipodal Propagation Phenomena ... APP
Antipode (SAUS) ... Antip
Antipollutant (SAUS) ... Antipol
Anti-Pollution Transfer and Storage System (SAUS) ... APTS System
Antipolo [*Philippines*] [*Later, MUT*] [*Geomagnetic observatory code*] ... ANO
Anti-Poverty (SAUS) ... Antip
Antiprostaglandin Antiserum [*Immunology*] ... APS
Antiprotein Accumulator (DAVI) ... AA
Antiproton (SAUS) ... Antip

Antiproton Accumulator [*Particle physics*] ... AA
Antiproton Collector [*Particle physics*] ... ACOL
AntiProton Experiments ... APEX
Anti-Pseudomonas Human Plasma [*Immunology*] (MAE) ... APHP
antipsychotic (SAUS) ... antip
Antipsychotic Drug ... APD
antipyretic (SAUS) ... antip
Antipyrine (SAUS) ... Antip
Antipyrine [*Analgesic*] (AAMN) ... AP
Antipyrine Test [*Medicine*] (MELL) ... APT
Antipyrylbenzoquinoneimine [*Organic chemistry*] ... ABQI
Antiqua Tourist Information Center (SAUS) ... ATIC Aerospace Technical Intel
Antiquarian [*or Antiquities*] ... ANTIQ
Antiquarian (ADWA) ... antiq
Antiquarian Book and Collectibles Information Systems (IID) ... ABACIS
Antiquarian Booksellers Association [*International*] ... ABA
Antiquarian Booksellers Association of America (SAUO) ... AABA
Antiquarian Booksellers Association of America (EA) ... ABAA
Antiquarian Booksellers Association of Canada ... ABAC
Antiquarian Booksellers Association of Japan (SAUO) ... ABAJ
Antiquarian Booksellers' Center (EA) ... ABC
Antiquarian Horological Society (EA) ... AHS
Antiquarian Horological Society (SAUO) ... AHS
Antiquarian Horological Society. Monograph (journ.) (SAUS) ... AHSM
Antiquarian House, Plymouth, MA [*Library symbol*] [*Library of Congress*] (LCLS) ... MPIA
Antiquarian Society (SAUO) ... AS
Antiquarian Society of Edinburgh (SAUO) ... ASE
Antiquarian Society of London (SAUO) ... ASL
Antiquarian Trade List Annual [*A publication*] ... ATLA
Antiquaries' Journal [*A publication*] (WDAA) ... ANJ
Antiquaries Journal [*A publication*] (BRI) ... Antiq J
Antiquaries Journal [*A publication*] (OCD) ... Ant Journ
Antiquariorum Regiae Societatis Socius [*Fellow of the Royal Society of Antiquaries*] [*Latin*] ... ARSS
Antiquary (GEAB) ... ant
Antique [*Bookbinding*] (ROG) ... ANTIQ
Antique (VRA) ... antq
Antique ... ANTQ
Antique Airplane Association (EA) ... AAA
Antique and Amusement Photographers International (NTPA) ... AAPI
Antique and Art Glass Salt Shaker Collectors Society (EA) ... AAGSSCS
Antique and Classic Boat Society (EA) ... ACBS
Antique and Historial Glass Foundation (SAUO) ... AHGF
Antique Appraisal Association of America (EA) ... AAAA
Antique Auto Racing Association (EA) ... AARA
Antique Automobile Club of America (EA) ... AACA
Antique Automobile Coalition [*Legislative lobbying group*] ... AAC
Antique Bicycle Club of America (EA) ... ABCA
Antique Boat and Yacht Club (EA) ... ABYC
Antique Boat Society (EA) ... ABS
Antique Bottle Collectors Association [*Defunct*] ... ABCA
Antique Bowie Knife Association (EA) ... ABKA
Antique Collectors' Club [*British*] (DBA) ... ACC
Antique Comb Collectors Club (EA) ... ACCC
Antique Doorknob Collectors of America (EA) ... ADCA
Antique Engine and Thresher Association (EA) ... AETA
Antique Engine, Tractor, and Toy Association (EA) ... AETTA
Antique Laid [*Paper*] (ADA) ... ANTLD
Antique Latin (ADA) ... ANTLAT
Antique Latin (SAUS) ... Ant Lat
Antique Motorcycle Club of America (EA) ... AMCA
Antique Old Style [*Paper*] (ADA) ... ANTOS
Antique Phonograph Collectors Club (EA) ... APCC
Antique Powercraft Historical Society [*Defunct*] (EA) ... APHS
Antique Radio Club of America (EA) ... ARCA
Antique Radio Guild of America ... ARGA
Antique Snowmobile Club of America (EA) ... ASCOA
Antique Souvenir Collectors (EA) ... ASC
[*The*] **Antique Stove Association** (EA) ... TASA
Antique Stove Information Clearinghouse (EA) ... ASIC
Antique Studebaker Club (EA) ... ASC
Antique Telephone Collectors Association [*Later, TCI*] (EA) ... ATCA
Antique Toy Collectors of America (EA) ... ATCA
Antique Trade Weekly, Dubuque, IA [*Library symbol*] [*Library of Congress*] (LCLS) ... IaDuAn
Antique Truck Club of America (EA) ... ATCA
Antique Wireless Association (EA) ... AWA
Antique Wove [*Paper*] (ADA) ... ANTWO
Antiques & Collecting Magazine [*A publication*] (BRI) ... Ant & CM
Antiques Dealers' Association of America (EA) ... ADA
Antiques Fairs Organisers Association [*British*] (DBA) ... AFOA
Antiques Publications (SAUS) ... Antiques
Antiquitates Judaicae [*Jewish Antiquities*] [*of Josephus*] [*Classical studies*] (OCD) ... AJ
Antiquitates Judaicae [*Jewish Antiquities*] [*of Josephus*] [*Classical studies*] (BJA) ... Ant
Antiquitates Romanae [*of Dionysius Halicarnassensis*] [*Classical studies*] (OCD) ... Ant Rom
Antiquite Classique [*A publication*] (OCD) ... Ant Class
Antiquities ... ANT
Antiquities (SAUS) ... Ant
Antiquities (GEAB) ... antiq
Antiquities Act of 1906 (COE) ... AA
Antiquity (ADWA) ... ant
Antiquity and Survival (SAUS) ... Antsurv
Antiquo [*I Oppose*] [*Used by Romans to signify a negative vote*] [*Latin*] ... A
Antirabies Serum [*Medicine*] ... ARS
antirachitic (SAUS) ... vit D
Anti-Racketeering (SAUS) ... AR
Antiracketeering ... AR
AntiRADAR (NATG) ... AR
Anti-Radar Drone (SAUS) ... ARD
Anti-Radar Futur (SAUS) ... ARF
Anti-Radar Guidance Sensor (SAUS) ... ARGS
Anti-Radar Homing (SAUS) ... ARH
Anti-Radar Longue Portee (SAUS) ... ARLP
AntiRADAR Missile ... ARM
Anti-Radar missile Matra (SAUS) ... ARMAT
AntiRADAR Surveillance and Target Acquisition System ... ASTAS
Anti-Radiation Countermeasures (SAUS) ... ARCM
Anti-Radiation Homer (SAUS) ... ARH
Anti-Radiation Homing / Infrared [*Military*] (PDAA) ... ARH/IR
Anti-Radiation Homing and Warning System [*Military*] (DNAB) ... ARHAWS
Antiradiation Missile ... ARM
Anti-Radiation Missile Decoy (SAUS) ... ARM-D
Anti-Radiation Missile Defense, Lightweight Objective (SAUS) ... ARMADILLO
Anti-Radiation Projectile (SAUS) ... ARP
Antiradiation Projectile ... ARP
Antiradiation Projectile Simulation (MCD) ... ARPSIM
Antiradiation Weapon System (NVT) ... ARWS
Anti-Radio Missile (SAUS) ... ARM
Anti-Rape Task Force (SAUS) ... ARTF
Antirat Neutrophil Serum [*Medicine*] (DMAA) ... ANS
Antirat Thymocyte Serum [*Medicine*] (DMAA) ... ATS
Antirattler [*Automotive engineering*] ... A/RATLR
Antireceptor Antibody [*Immunology*] ... ARA
Antirecession Fiscal Assistance ... ARFA
Antireflection ... AR
Anti-Reflection (SAUS) ... AR
Antireflection Coated Metal-Oxide Semiconductor (MCD) ... AMOS
Antireflection Coating (EDCT) ... ARC
Antireflective, Antiglare [*Cathode ray tube treatment*] (PCM) ... ARAG
Antireflective, Antistatic [*Cathode ray tube treatment*] (PCM) ... ARAS
Antireflective Coating (AAEL) ... ARC
Anti-Reflux Drugs (MELL) ... ARD
Anti-Rejection Drug [*Medicine*] (MELL) ... ARD
Anti-Repeat Relay (SAUS) ... ARR
Anti-Repression Resource Team (EA) ... ARRT
Anti-Reset Windup (SAUS) ... arw
Anti-Resonance Isolation System (SAUS) ... ARIS
Antiresonant Frequency (SAUS) ... f
Anti-Resonant Reflecting Optical Waveguide (SAUS) ... ARROW
Antireticular Cytotoxic Serum ... ACS
Antireticulo-Endothelial Serum [*Medicine*] (DMAA) ... ARES
Antiretroviral Drug [*Medicine*] (MELL) ... ARVD
Antiretroviral Therapy [*Medicine*] (MELL) ... ARVT
Antireversionary [*Method of exhaust control*] [*Automotive engineering*] ... AR
Anti-Revolutionaire Partij - Evangelische Volkspartij [*Antirevolutionary Party*] [*Netherlands*] [*Political party*] (PPW) ... ARP
Antiribonucleoprotein [*Genetics*] (DAVI) ... anti-RNP
Antiribosomal Antibody [*Medicine*] (MELL) ... ARA
Antiriot Laws ... ARL
Anti-Roll Bar ... ARB
Anti-Saccade Oculomotor Delayed Response [*Neurobiology*] ... AS-OUR
Anti-Saloon League (SAUO) ... ASL
Anti-Satellite [*Weaponry*] [*Military*] (MUSM) ... ASAT
Antisatellite (SAUS) ... ASAT
Antisatellite Command and Control Center (ACAE) ... ACCC
Anti-Satellite Engagement Model [*Military*] ... ASEM
Antisatellite Satellite ... ASAT
Anti-Satellite Technique (SAUS) ... SAT
Anti-Satellite Weapon (WDAA) ... ASAT
Anti-Satellite Weapon (IAA) ... ASW
Antisatellite Weapons (SAUS) ... ASATs
Anti-Saturation Inverter (SAUS) ... ASI
Antisaturation Inverter ... ASI
Antiself Homing [*System*] [*Torpedo safety device*] [*Navy*] ... ASH
anti-Semitic (SAUS) ... anti-Sem
Antisense Orientation ... AS
Antisense RNA [*Ribonucleic Acid*] [*Genetics*] (DOG) ... asRNA
Antiseparation Tailored Contour (MCD) ... ATC
Antiseptic (MSA) ... ANTSPT
antiseptic (SAUS) ... as
Antiseptic Biological Suppository [*Medicine*] (IIA) ... ABS
Antiseptics and Disinfectants (MELL) ... A & D
Antiserum [*Immunology*] ... AS
Antiserum to Somatostatin (DB) ... AS
Antiserum/Horse [*Medicine*] (DMAA) ... AS/Ho
Anti-Shark Research Association (SAUO) ... ASRA
Anti-Shelter Submunition (SAUS) ... ASS
Anti-Shine-Dalgarno (SAUS) ... ASD
Antiship Capable Missile (NVT) ... ASCM
Antiship Cruise Missile ... ASCM
Anti-Ship Cruise Missile (SAUS) ... ASCM
Anti-Ship Euro-Missile (SAUS) ... ASEM
Antiship Missile (NVT) ... ASM
Antiship Missile Defense ... ASMD
Anti-Ship Missile Defense (SAUS) ... ASMD
Anti-Ship Missile Defense / Electronic Warfare (PDAA) ... ASMD/EW

Antiship Missile Defense Missile System (MCD)	ASMDMS
Antiship Missile Target (MCD)	ASMT
Antiship Phoenix	ASP
Anti-Ship Supersonic Missile (SAUS)	ASSM
Anti-Ship Surveillance & Targeting (SAUS)	ASST
Antiship Surveillance and Targeting [Navy] (NVT)	ASST
Antiship Torpedo (IEEE)	ASTOR
Anti-Ship Torpedo (SAUS)	ASTOR
Antiship Torpedo Defense [or Device] (MCD)	ASTD
Antiship Underwater Warfare (MCD)	ASUW
Anti-Ship Variant radar (SAUS)	ASV
Anti-Shipping Campaign Model (MCD)	ASCAM
Anti-Shipping Missile (SAUS)	ASM
Anti-Shock Body (SAUS)	ASB
Antishock Body	ASB
Antishock Therapy (MELL)	AST
Antisidetone [Telecommunications] (TEL)	AST
Antisiphon Valve (DB)	ASV
Anti-Siphonage Pipe (SAUS)	ASP
Antiskid Braking System [General Motors Corp.]	ABS
Antiskywave Antenna (NTCM)	ASWA
Antislack Device	ASD
Anti-Slavery and Aborigines Protection Society (SAUO)	ASAPS
Anti-Slavery International [England] (EAIO)	ASI
Anti-Slavery Society for the Protection of Human Rights (SAUO)	ASS
Anti-Slavery Society for the Protection of Human Rights (EA)	ASSPHR
Anti-Slip Differential [Automotive engineering]	ASD
Anti-Slip Regulation [Automotive engineering]	ASR
Anti-Smith [Antibody] [Hematology] (DAVI)	anti-Sm
anti-Smith (SAUS)	Sm
Anti-Smooth Muscle Antibody (SAUS)	ASMA
Antismooth Muscle Antibody [Immunology]	ASMA
Antisnake Venom [Medicine]	ASV
Anti-Snake Venom (SAUS)	A-S V
Antisocial Personality [Psychology]	ASP
Antisocial Personality Disorder [Psychology] (WDAA)	APD
Antisocial Personality Disorder (MELL)	ASPD
Anti-Socialist and Anti-Communist Union (SAUO)	ASACU
Anti-Socialist Party (ADA)	ANTI-SOC
Antisolar (KSC)	A-SOL
Antispasticity Index [Neurology] (DAVI)	ASTI
Antisperm Antibody [Medicine] (MELL)	As
Anti-Sperm Antibody [Medicine]	ASA
Antispleen Globulin [Medicine] (DMAA)	ASPG
Anti-Spoofing [Jamming resistance feature on global positioning satellites] (SSD)	A-S
Anti-Spoofing (GEOI)	AS
Anti-Spoofing on GPS Transmissions (SAUS)	AS
Antisqueak [Automotive engineering]	A/SQK
Anti-Standoff Jammer [Defense system] (MCD)	ASOJ
Antistaphylosin-Test (SAUS)	AStT
Anti-Static Additive (SAUS)	ASA
Antistatic Additive	ASA
Anti-Static Agent (SAUS)	ASA
Anti-Static Compound (SAUS)	ASC
Antistatic Compound	ASC
Anti-Static Computer (SAUS)	ASCOM
antisterility vitamin (SAUS)	vit E
Anti-Stoke Stimulated Raman Scattering [Spectrometry] (MCD)	ASRS
Antistrategic Submarine Warfare (SAUS)	ASSW
Antistreptococcal Hyaluronidase [Medicine] (DMAA)	ASH
Antistreptococcal Polysaccharide Test [Medicine] (DMAA)	ASPAT
Antistreptokinase [Immunology]	ASK
Antistreptokinase Titer (DB)	AST
Antistreptolysin [Immunology] (MAE)	AS
Antistreptolysin [Immunology]	ASL
Antistreptolysin [Immunology] (DHSM)	ASTO
Antistreptolysin Factor (PDAA)	ASF
Anti-Streptolysin Reaction [Medicine] (DMAA)	ASR
Antistreptolysin Test [Medicine] (DMAA)	ASLT
Antistreptolysin Test [Medicine] (MELL)	AST
Antistreptolysin Titer (SAUS)	ASL-Titer
Antistreptolysin Titer (SAUS)	ASO Titer
Antistreptolysine (DB)	AST
Anti-Streptolysine Reaction (SAUS)	ASR
Anti-Streptolysine Test (SAUS)	AST
Antistreptolysin-O [Also, ASO] [Clinical chemistry]	ASLO
Antistreptolysin-O [Also, ASLO] [Clinical chemistry]	ASO
Antistreptolysin-O Titer [Clinical chemistry] (AAMN)	ASOT
Antistreptozyme (DMAA)	ASTZ
Antistreptozyme Test [Clinical chemistry]	ASTZ
Antisubmarine	AS
Antisubmarine [Designation for all US military aircraft]	S
Antisubmarine Air Control [Navy] (MCD)	ASAC
Antisubmarine Attack Plotter [Navy]	ASAP
Antisubmarine Attack Teacher	ASAT
Antisubmarine Attack Teacher Training Unit	ASATTU
Antisubmarine Classification Analysis Test	ASCAT
Antisubmarine Classification and Analysis Center [Navy]	ASCAC
Antisubmarine Classification and Analysis Center/Tactical Support Center (DNAB)	ASCAC/TSC
Antisubmarine Combat Activity Center (DNAB)	ASCAC
Antisubmarine Commander (SAUS)	ASCO
Antisubmarine Composite Engineering Squadron	ACES
Antisubmarine Contact Analysis Center (SAUO)	ASCAC

Anti-Submarine Contact Analysis Center (SAUS)	ASCAC
Antisubmarine Contact Analysis Team (SAUO)	ASCAT
Antisubmarine Contact Evaluation System [Navy] (MCD)	ASCES
Anti-Submarine Course (SAUS)	A/S Cse
Antisubmarine Defence (or Defense) Group (SAUO)	ASDG
Antisubmarine Defense (SAUS)	AntiSubDef
Antisubmarine Defense Force, Atlantic Fleet (SAUO)	AntiSubDefLant
Antisubmarine Defense Force, Atlantic Fleet (SAUO)	ASDEFORLANT
Antisubmarine Defense Force, Pacific Fleet (SAUO)	AntiSubDefPac
Antisubmarine Defense Forces, Atlantic [Obsolete] [Navy]	ASDEFORLANT
Antisubmarine Defense Forces, Pacific [Obsolete] [Navy]	ASDEFORPAC
Antisubmarine Defense Group	ASDG
Anti-Submarine Depth Indicating Control (SAUS)	Asdic
Antisubmarine Detection Investigation Committee [A group in World War I that gave rise to the device that bore its name in World War II]	ASDIC
Anti-Submarine Detector Indicator (WDAA)	ASDIC
Antisubmarine Development Detachment [Atlantic Fleet] [Norfolk, VA]	ASDD
Antisubmarine Development Detachment [Navy] (DNAB)	ASDEVDET
Antisubmarine Development Detachment, Atlantic Fleet [Navy]	ASDEVLANT
Anti-Submarine Division [British military] (DMA)	ASD
Anti-Submarine Establishment [Navy] [British]	ASE
Anti-Submarine Establishment (SAUO)	ASE
Anti-Submarine Establishment (SAUS)	ASE
Antisubmarine Experimental Establishment	A/SEE
Antisubmarine Fighter Squadron [Navy]	ANTISUBFITRON
Antisubmarine Fighter Squadron [Navy]	VSF
Antisubmarine Fixed Defenses Officer [Navy]	A/SFDO
Antisubmarine Frigate (SAUS)	ASF
Antisubmarine Helicopter (NATG)	HPS
Antisubmarine Launched Ballistic Missile	ASLBM
Antisubmarine Patrol	ASP
Antisubmarine Projector (SAUS)	A/SP
Antisubmarine Rocket [Navy]	ASROC
Antisubmarine Rocket Computer [Navy] (IAA)	ASROC
Antisubmarine Rocket (Extended Range) (DNAB)	ASROC(ERA)
Antisubmarine School (SAUO)	A/S Sch
Antisubmarine Squadron (SAUO)	AntiSubRon
Antisubmarine Submarine [Navy symbol]	SSK
Antisubmarine Systems Project Office [Navy]	ASPO
Antisubmarine Tactical Data System (DNAB)	ASTDS
Antisubmarine Technical Evaluation Center [Navy]	ASTEC
Antisubmarine Terrier Missile [Navy]	ASTER
Anti-Submarine Terrier Missile (SAUS)	ASTER Missile
Antisubmarine Test Requirement Outline	ASTRO
Antisubmarine Torpedo (MSA)	ASTOR
Antisubmarine Torpedo Ordnance Rocket (MCD)	ASTOR
Anti-Submarine Training Indicator [Military] (PDAA)	ASTI
Antisubmarine Training Indicator (SAUS)	ASTI
Antisubmarine War Division [British]	A/SWD
Antisubmarine Warfare	ASW
Anti-Submarine Warfare Advisory Committee (SAUO)	ASWAC
Antisubmarine Warfare Air Control Ship (NVT)	ASWACS
Antisubmarine Warfare Airborne Simulation Program [Navy] (CAAL)	ASWASP
Anti-Submarine Warfare Analysis Centre (SAUS)	ASWAC
Anti-Submarine Warfare and Antiair Warfare	ASW/AAW
Anti-Submarine Warfare Area System (SAUS)	ASWAS
Antisubmarine Warfare Automated Detection Prediction System (MCD)	ADEPS
Antisubmarine Warfare Barrier Submarine Patrol Area [Navy] (NVT)	SUBPA
Antisubmarine Warfare Barrier Submarine Patrol Zone [Navy] (NVT)	SUBPZ
Antisubmarine Warfare Barrier Surface Patrol Area [Navy] (NVT)	SURFPA
Antisubmarine Warfare Barrier Surface Patrol Ship [Navy] (NVT)	SURF
Antisubmarine Warfare Barrier Surface Patrol Zone [Navy] (NVT)	SURFPZ
Antisubmarine Warfare Barriers [Military]	ASWB
Antisubmarine Warfare Center [NATO] (NATG)	ASWC
Antisubmarine Warfare Centers Command and Control System [Navy] (CAAL)	ASWCCCS
Antisubmarine Warfare Combat System Integration [Navy] (CAAL)	ASWCSI
Antisubmarine Warfare Command and Control Centers System (MCD)	ASWCCS
Antisubmarine Warfare Command and Control System (SAUS)	ASWCCS
Anti-Submarine Warfare Command, Control, and Communications Systems [Military] (IUSS)	ASWCCS
Antisubmarine Warfare Commander [Navy] (NVT)	ASWC
Antisubmarine Warfare Communications (DNAB)	ASCOMM
Antisubmarine Warfare Communications Detachment (DNAB)	ASCOMMDET
Antisubmarine Warfare Control System [Navy] (CAAL)	ASWCS
Anti-Submarine Warfare Data System (SAUS)	ASWDS
Antisubmarine Warfare Electronic Countermeasures System (MCD)	ASWEC
Antisubmarine Warfare Environmental Prediction Services (SAUS)	ASWEPS
Antisubmarine Warfare Exercise (NVT)	ASWEX
Antisubmarine Warfare Fighter Squadron (DNAB)	ASWFITRON
Antisubmarine Warfare Fire Control Officer [Navy] (CAAL)	ASWFCO
Antisubmarine Warfare Force [Atlantic Fleet] [Norfolk, VA]	ASW
Antisubmarine Warfare Force, Sixth Fleet [Navy]	ASWFORSIXTHF
Antisubmarine Warfare Group	ASWGRU
Antisubmarine Warfare Improved Localization System (NVT)	ASWILS
Antisubmarine Warfare Information Exchange System [or Subsystem] [Navy] (NVT)	ASWIXS
Antisubmarine Warfare In-Port Training (SAUS)	ASWIPT
Antisubmarine Warfare Installations [NATO] (NATG)	ASWI
Antisubmarine Warfare Integrated Combat System [Navy] (MCD)	ASWICS
Antisubmarine Warfare Laboratory [Military]	ASWL
Antisubmarine Warfare Missile [Navy] (CAAL)	ASWM
Anti-Submarine Warfare Module [Military] (IUSS)	ASWM

Antisubmarine Warfare Officer [*Navy*] (CAAL) ... ASWO
Antisubmarine Warfare Operational Research Group [*World War II*] ... ASWORG
Antisubmarine Warfare Operations Centers [*Navy*] (NVT) ... ASWOC
Anti-Submarine Warfare Operations Center-Tape Operation Systems [*Military*] (IUSS) ... ATOS
Antisubmarine Warfare Operations Controller [*Navy*] (CAAL) ... ASWOC
Antisubmarine Warfare Operations Patrol (NVT) ... ASWPTL
Anti-Submarine Warfare Operations Patrol (SAUO) ... ASWPTL
Anti-Submarine Warfare Operations Research Group (SAUO) ... ASWORG
Anti-Submarine Warfare Opposed Transit (SAUS) ... ASWOT
Antisubmarine Warfare Program (SAUO) ... AWP
Antisubmarine Warfare Program System [*Navy*] (GFGA) ... ASWEPS
Antisubmarine Warfare Programs [*Navy*] (MCD) ... AWP
Antisubmarine Warfare Project Office [*Navy*] ... ASWPO
Antisubmarine Warfare RADAR (IIA) ... ASWR
Antisubmarine Warfare Research Center [*NATO*] (NATG) ... ASWRC
Anti-Submarine Warfare Research Center (SAUO) ... ASWRC
Antisubmarine Warfare Research Center [*NATO*] ... ASWRECEN
Anti-Submarine Warfare School [*Military*] (IUSS) ... ASWS
Antisubmarine Warfare Schoolship [*Navy*] (NVT) ... ASWSS
Antisubmarine Warfare Ship Command and Control System (NVT) ... ASWSCCS
Anti-Submarine Warfare Special Projects Office (SAUO) ... ASWSPO
Antisubmarine Warfare Standoff Weapon ... ASW/SOW
Anti-Submarine Warfare Standoff Weapon (SAUS) ... ASWSOW
Anti-Submarine Warfare Surveillance System [*Military*] (IUSS) ... ARIADNE
Antisubmarine Warfare Systems [*Navy*] ... ASWS
Antisubmarine Warfare Systems Analysis Group [*Navy*] ... ASWSAG
Anti-Submarine Warfare Systems Project [*Military*] (IUSS) ... ASWSP
Antisubmarine Warfare Systems Project Office [*Washington, DC*] [*Navy*] ... ASWR
Antisubmarine Warfare Systems Project Office [*Navy*] ... ASWSPO
Antisubmarine Warfare Systems Project Office [*Navy*] (DNAB) ... ASWSYSPROJOFC
Antisubmarine Warfare Tactical Data System [*Navy*] (NVT) ... ASWTDS
Antisubmarine Warfare Tactical Navigation System [*Navy*] (NG) ... ASWTNS
Antisubmarine Warfare Tactical School ... ASWTACSCOL
Anti-Submarine Warfare Tactical Support Center [*Military*] (IUSS) ... ASTAC
Antisubmarine Warfare Target Vehicle (MCD) ... ASWTV
Anti-Submarine Warfare Technical Center (SAUO) ... ASW Tech Cen
Antisubmarine Warfare Technical Center (SAUS) ... ASWTechCen
Antisubmarine Warfare Test Requirement Outline (MCD) ... ASWTRO
Anti-Submarine Warfare Trainer (SAUS) ... ASWT
Antisubmarine Warfare Training Center [*Navy*] ... ASWTC
Antisubmarine Warfare Training Center [*Navy*] ... ASWTRACEN
Antisubmarine Warfare Training in Port [*Navy*] (NVT) ... ASWIPT
Anti-Submarine Warfare Training Unit (SAUO) ... ASWTU
Antisubmarine Warfare Unit [*Navy*] ... ASWU
Anti-Submarine Warfare/Search and Rescue [*Military*] (IUSS) ... ASW/SAR
Antisubmarine Warfare/Underwater Warfare ... ASW/UW
Antisubmarine Warning - Long Range (NATG) ... ASW-LR
Antisubmarine Warning - Short Range (NATG) ... ASW-SR
Antisubmarine Weapon (NATG) ... ASW
Antisubmarine Weapons Environmental Prediction Service [*Navy*] ... ASWEPS
Anti-Submarine Wire-Guided Weapon [*British military*] (DMA) ... ASWGW
Anti-Submarine Work (SAUS) ... ASW
Antisulfanilic Acid [*Biochemistry*] (DAVI) ... anti-S
Antisurface [*Military*] (NVT) ... A/S
Antisurface (SAUS) ... AS
Antisurface Boat ... ASB
Anti-Surface Euromissile Consortium (PDAA) ... ASEM
Anti-Surface Missile Defence (SAUS) ... ASMD
Antisurface Raiders Exercise [*NATO*] (NATG) ... RAIDEX
Antisurface Ship Missile [*NATO*] (MCD) ... ASSM
Antisurface Ship Surveillance and Targeting (MCD) ... ASST
Antisurface Ship Warfare (MCD) ... ASSW
Anti-Surface Ship Warfare (SAUS) ... ASSW
Antisurface Ship Warfare [*Navy*] (CAAL) ... ASU
Antisurface Vessel [*Navy*] ... ASV
Anti-Surface Vessel Warfare (SAUS) ... ASVW
Antisurface Warfare [*Navy*] ... ASUW
Antisurface Warfare Commander [*Navy*] ... ASUWC
Anti-Surface Warfare Commander (SAUS) ... ASUWC
Antisurface Weapons Exchange and Reaction Simulation (MCD) ... ANSWERS
Antisymmetric [*Chemistry*] ... a
Antisymmetric Filter (SAUS) ... AFL
Antisymmetrized Geminal Power [*Chemical physics*] ... AGP
Antisyphilitic Treatment [*Medicine*] ... AST
Antitactical Ballistic Missile (MCD) ... ATB
Antitactical Ballistic Missile ... ATBM
Antitactical Missile ... ATM
Anti-Tactical Patriot (SAUS) ... ATP
Antitampering and Fuel-Switching Information System (SAUS) ... TAMPER
Antitampering Program [*Environmental science*] (COE) ... ATP
Antitank [*Also, ATk*] ... AT
Antitank [*Also, AT*] (NATG) ... ATk
Antitank Air Defense System ... ATADS
Anti-Tank Aircraft Rocket (SAUS) ... ATAR
Antitank Assault Air Defense (MCD) ... ATAAD
Antitank Assault Weapon [*Army*] ... ATAW
Anti-Tank Ballistic Missile (SAUS) ... ATB Missile
Antitank Battalion [*Marine Corps*] ... ATBN
Antitank Battery [*Military*] ... ATB
Anti-Tank Battery (SAUO) ... ATB
Antitank Grenade Launcher (AABC) ... ATGL
Anti-Tank Guided Air Rocket (SAUS) ... ATGAR
Antitank Guided Aircraft Rocket (SAUS) ... ATGAR
Anti-Tank Guided Weapon System (SAUS) ... ATGWS
Anti-Tank Gun (SAUS) ... ATG
Antitank Gun [*Military*] ... ATG
Antitank Gun (SAUS) ... ATGn
Antitank Helicopter (MCD) ... ATH
Anti-Tank Influence Sensor (SAUS) ... ATIS
Antitank LASER-Assisted System [*British*] ... ATLAS
Antitank Mine (SAUS) ... ATM
Anti-Tank Mine-Dispensing System (SAUS) ... ATMDS
Antitank Missile [*Army*] ... ATM
Antitank Missile System (ACAE) ... AMS
Antitank Missile Test (MCD) ... ATMT
Antitank Nonmetallic (SAUS) ... ATNM
Antitank Regiment [*Military*] ... ATR
Anti-Tank Regiment (SAUO) ... ATR
Anti-Tank Regiment, Royal Artillery (SAUO) ... ATkRegtRA
Antitank Rifle (SAUS) ... A/TK R
Anti-Tank Rocket Launcher (SAUS) ... ATRL
Antitank Rocket Launcher Imagery Interpretation (AABC) ... ATRL
Antitank Target System [*Military*] (INF) ... ATTS
Anti-Tank Troup (SAUO) ... ATTp
Antitank Weapon (NATG) ... ATW
Antitank Weapons Effect Signature Simulator [*Army*] (INF) ... ATWESS
Antitank/Antivehicle (MCD) ... AT/AV
Antitank/Assault/Air Defense System (MCD) ... ATAADS
Anti-Tank-Guided Missile (SAUS) ... ATGM
Antitension Line (MAE) ... ATL
Antiterrain Avoidance RADAR System (MCD) ... ATARS
Antiterritorial Land Mine (MCD) ... ATLAM
Antiterrorism [*Measure*] [*DoD*] ... AT
Anti-Terrorism Assistance Program [*FAA*] (TAG) ... ATAP
Anti-Terrorism Coordinating Committee (DOMA) ... ATCC
Antiterrorism Instructor Qualification Course (COE) ... AIQC
Antiterrorism Operations and Intelligence Cell [*Army*] ... ATOIC
Anti-Terrorismo ETA [*Anti-ETA Terrorism*] [*Spanish*] (PPE) ... ATE
Anti-Terrorist (MUSM) ... Aterr
Anti-Terrorist Alert Center [*Navy*] (LAIN) ... ATAC
Anti-Terrorist Liberation Group [*Undercover anti-Basque terrorist interior-ministry network*] [*Acronym is based on foreign phrase*] [*Spain*] (ECON) ... GAL
Anti-Terrorist Union (SAUO) ... ATU
Anti-Tetanic Serum (SAUS) ... ATS
Antitetanus Serum [*Medicine*] ... ATS
Antitetanus Therapy [*Medicine*] (MELL) ... ATT
Antitetanus Toxoid [*Medicine*] (MELL) ... ATT
Anti-Tetany Substance 10 [*Same as DHT, Dihydrotachysterol*] [*Pharmacology*] ... AT-10
Anti-Theater Ballistic Missile (SAUS) ... ATBM
Antithrombin [*Hematology*] ... AT
Antithrombin Activity [*Medicine*] (MELL) ... ATA
Antithrombocyte Globulin [*Immunology*] (MAE) ... ATG
Antithrombotics in the Prevention of Reocclusion in Coronary Thrombolysis [*Cardiology study*] ... APRICOT
Anti-Thrust Law (SAUS) ... ATL
Antithymocyte Gamma-Globulin [*Immunology*] ... ATGAM
Antithymocyte Globulin [*Immunochemistry*] ... ATG
Antithymocyte Serum [*Immunochemistry*] ... ATS
Anti-Thymocyte Serum (SAUS) ... ATS
Antithymozytenglobulin (SAUS) ... ATG
Anti-Thymus Serum (SAUS) ... ATS
Antithyroglobulin [*Immunochemistry*] (MAE) ... ATG
Antithyroglobulin Antibody [*Immunochemistry*] ... ATA
Anti-Thyroid Antibody (SAUS) ... ATA
Antithyroid Drug (AAMN) ... ATD
Antithyroid Peroxidase Antibody [*Medicine*] (MELL) ... APAb
Antithyroid Plasma Membrane Antibody [*Medicine*] (DMAA) ... ATMA
Antitorpedo [*Navy*] ... AT
Antitorpedo (MSA) ... ATORP
Antitorpedo (SAUS) ... Atorp
Anti-Torpedo Air-launched Acoustic Countermeasures (SAUS) ... ATAAC
Anti-Torpedo Craft [*British military*] (DMA) ... ATC
Antitorque Pedal ... ATP
Anti-Torque Pedal (SAUS) ... ATP
Anti-Torture Research [*Copenhagen, Denmark*] [*An association*] (EAIO) ... ATR
Anti-Torture Research Team (SAUO) ... ATR
Antitoxin (MSA) ... ANTOX
Antitoxin Botulism Equine Trivalent [*Biochemistry*] (DAVI) ... ABE
Antitoxin Titer [*Medicine*] (MELL) ... ATT
Antitoxin Unit [*Immunology*] ... AU
Antitoxineinheit [*Antitoxin Unit*] [*German*] ... AE
Anti-Toxoplasma Antibody [*Immunology*] (MAE) ... ATA
Anti-Tracking Control (SAUS) ... ATRC
Antitransmit-Receive (SAUS) ... ATR
Anti-Transmit-Receive ... ATR
Anti-Transmit/Receive Switch (SAUS) ... Anti-TR-switch
Anti-Transmit-Receive Tube ... ATRT
Anti-Transmit-Receive Tube (MED) ... ATR tube
Anti-Transmitter-Receiver (or Receiving) (SAUS) ... ATR
Anti-Transmitting/Receiving Switch (SAUS) ... Anti-TR-switch
Anti-Trust (LAIN) ... AT
Anti-trust and Consumer Protection Division (SAUO) ... ACPD
Antitrust and Monopoly Subcommittee [*US Senate*] ... A & M
Antitrust Bulletin (AAGC) ... Antitrust Bull
Antitrust Bulletin (journ.) (SAUS) ... ANB
Antitrust Law ... ATL

Antitrust Law and Trade Regulations Report [*Bureau of National Affairs*] [*A publication*] (ILCA) ... Antitrust L & Trade Reg Rep

Antitrust Procedural Improvements Act of 1980 ... APIA

Antitrypsin [*Biochemistry*] ... AT

Antitrypsin Deficiency [*Medicine*] (MELL) ... ATD

Antitumour Serum (SAUS) ... ATUS

Anti-U-Boat Warfare [*British*] [*World War II*] ... AU

Antiunderwater Warfare [*Navy*] (CINC) ... AUW

Antivaccinial Immunoglobulin [*Medicine*] (PDAA) ... AVIG

Antivehicle [*Munitions*] ... AV

Antivehicle Device [*Air Force*] (MCD) ... AVD

Antivehicle Land Mine ... AVLM

Antivehicle Mine ... AVM

Anti-Vehicle Munition (SAUS) ... AV Munition

Antivenin Institute of America (SAUS) ... AIA

Anti-Vermin [*Battle dress*] [*British and Canadian*] [*World War II*] ... A/V

Antivibration Joint ... AVJ

Antiviral Antibody [*Medicine*] (MELL) ... AVA

Antiviral Chemistry & Chemotherapy [*A publication*] (MEC) ... Antiviral Chem & Chemother

Antiviral Chemotherapy [*Medicine*] (MELL) ... AVCT

Antiviral Factor ... AVF

Antiviral Protein [*Immunology*] ... AVP

Antiviral Research (journ.) (SAUS) ... AR

Antivirus [*Computer science*] ... AV

Anti-Virus Emergency Response Team [*McAfee*] [*Computer science*] ... AVERT

Antivirus Product [*Computer science*] ... AVP

Anti-Virus Toolkit for Windows [*Dr. Solomon's Software, Inc.*] ... AVTK

Anti-Vivisection League (SAUO) ... AVL

Anti-Vivisection League (SAUS) ... AVL

Anti-Vivisection Party [*British*] ... AV

Anti-Vivisection Society [*VIL*] [*Absorbed by*] (EA) ... AVS

Anti-Vivisection Society (SAUO) ... AVS

Antivoice-Operated Transmission (CET) ... ANTIVOX

Antivoice-Operated Transmission (SAUS) ... antivox

Anti-Wear (SAUS) ... AW

Antiwear ... AW

Anti-Whole Rabbit Serum [*Immunology*] ... AWRS

Antiyeast Factor [*Medicine*] ... AYF

Anti-Yeast Factor (SAUS) ... AYF

Antler (VRA) ... atlr

Antlers, OK [*Location identifier*] [*FAA*] (FAAL) ... AEE

Antlia [*Constellation*] ... Ant

Antlia [*Constellation*] ... Antl

Anto-Disturbance [*Device*] [*Military*] (MUSM) ... AD

Antofagasta [*Chile*] [*Airport symbol*] (OAG) ... ANF

Antofagasta [*Chile*] [*Seismograph station code, US Geological Survey*] (SEIS) ... ANT

Antofagasta (SAUS) ... Antf

Antofagasta (SAUS) ... Anto

Antofagasta [*Chile*] [*ICAO location identifier*] (ICLI) ... SCFZ

Antofagasta & Bolivia Railroad Co. (MHDB) ... A & B

Antofagasta and Bolivia Railway Co. (MHDB) ... A & BRC

Antofagasta/Internacional Cerro Moreno [*Chile*] [*ICAO location identifier*] (ICLI) ... SCFA

Antoko Demokraty Kristiana Malagasy [*Malagasy Christian Democratic Party*] (AF) ... ADKM

Antokon'ny Kongresin'ny Fahaleovantenan'i Madagasikara [*Congress Party for Malagasy Independence*] [*Political party*] (AF) ... AKFM

Antoky ny Revolosiona Malagasy [*Vanguard of the Malagasy Revolution*] (PPW) ... AREMA

Anton Breini Center for Tropical Health and Medicine [*James Cook University*] [*Australia*] ... ABCTHM

Anton Chico, NM [*Location identifier*] [*FAA*] (FAAL) ... ACH

Antoniani Benedictini Armeni [*Mechitarists*] ... ABA

Antonine Sisters (TOCD) ... RA

Antonio Castro (GEOI) ... AC

Antonio Castro (GEOI) ... CA

Antonio Enes [*Mozambique*] [*Airport symbol*] (AD) ... ANO

Antonius [*of Plutarch*] [*Classical studies*] (OCD) ... Ant

Antonius Albergati [*Deceased, 1634*] [*Authority cited in pre-1607 legal work*] (DSA) ... An Albg

Antonius Augustinus [*Deceased, 1586*] [*Authority cited in pre-1607 legal work*] (DSA) ... AA

Antonius Augustinus [*Deceased, 1586*] [*Authority cited in pre-1607 legal work*] (DSA) ... A August

Antonius Augustinus [*Deceased, 1586*] [*Authority cited in pre-1607 legal work*] (DSA) ... Ant Aug

Antonius Augustinus [*Deceased, 1586*] [*Authority cited in pre-1607 legal work*] (DSA) ... Ant August

Antonius Boidus [*Flourished, 16th century*] [*Authority cited in pre-1607 legal work*] (DSA) ... Ant Boid

Antonius Burgos [*Deceased, 1525*] [*Authority cited in pre-1607 legal work*] (DSA) ... Anton Burg

Antonius Corsettus [*Flourished, 15th century*] [*Authority cited in pre-1607 legal work*] (DSA) ... Ant Corse

Antonius de Butrio [*Deceased, 1408*] [*Authority cited in pre-1607 legal work*] (DSA) ... An

Antonius de Butrio [*Deceased, 1408*] [*Authority cited in pre-1607 legal work*] (DSA) ... An de Bu

Antonius de Butrio [*Deceased, 1408*] [*Authority cited in pre-1607 legal work*] (DSA) ... Ant de But

Antonius de Butrio [*Deceased, 1408*] [*Authority cited in pre-1607 legal work*] (DSA) ... Anto

Antonius de Butrio [*Deceased, 1408*] [*Authority cited in pre-1607 legal work*] (DSA) ... Anto de But

Antonius de Rosellis [*Deceased, 1466*] [*Authority cited in pre-1607 legal work*] (DSA) ... Ant de Rosell

Antonius de Rosellis [*Deceased, 1466*] [*Authority cited in pre-1607 legal work*] (DSA) ... Ant Rosel

Antonius de Tremolis [*Flourished, 16th century*] [*Authority cited in pre-1607 legal work*] (DSA) ... Anto de Trem

Antonius Faber [*Deceased, 1624*] [*Authority cited in pre-1607 legal work*] (DSA) ... Ant Fab

Antonius Faber [*Deceased, 1624*] [*Authority cited in pre-1607 legal work*] (DSA) ... Anto Fab

Antonius Faber [*Deceased, 1624*] [*Authority cited in pre-1607 legal work*] (DSA) ... Anton Fab

Antonius Gabrielius (Romanus) [*Deceased, 1555*] [*Authority cited in pre-1607 legal work*] (DSA) ... Ant Gab Rom

Antonius Gabrielius (Romanus) [*Deceased, 1555*] [*Authority cited in pre-1607 legal work*] (DSA) ... Anton Gabr

Antonius Gabrielius (Romanus) [*Deceased, 1555*] [*Authority cited in pre-1607 legal work*] (DSA) ... Anton Gabr Roman

Antonius Gomez [*Flourished, l6th century*] [*Authority cited in pre-1607 legal work*] (DSA) ... An Go

Antonius Guibertus Costanus [*Flourished, 16th century*] [*Authority cited in pre-1607 legal work*] (DSA) ... Anton Costan

Antonius Nicellus [*Flourished, 15th century*] [*Authority cited in pre-1607 legal work*] (DSA) ... Anto Nice

Antonius Nicenus [*Authority cited in pre-1607 legal work*] (DSA) ... Anto Nice

Antonov [*Former USSR*] [*ICAO aircraft manufacturer identifier*] (ICAO) ... AN

Antonov Design Bureau [*Former USSR*] [*ICAO designator*] (FAAC) ... ADB

Antony and Cleopatra [*Shakespearean drama*] (BARN) ... A & C

Antony and Cleopatra (SAUS) ... A&C

Antony and Cleopatra [*Shakespearean work*] ... Ant

Antony and Cleopatra [*Shakespearean drama*] (BARN) ... Ant & Cl

Antony Resources [*Vancouver Stock Exchange symbol*] ... AYI

Antonym ... ANT

antonym (WDAA) ... ant

Antonym (ADA) ... ANTON

Antrag Transportgenehmigung (SAUS) ... AT

Antral Ethmoidal Sphenoidectomy [*Otorhinolaryngology*] (DAVI) ... AES

Antral Vascular Ectasia [*Medicine*] (MELL) ... AVE

Antrim [*County in Ireland*] (ROG) ... ANT

Antrim (SAUS) ... Antr

Antrim Mountains of Northern Ireland (SAUS) ... Antrims

Antrum [*Maxillary sinus*] [*Otorhinolaryngology*] (DAVI) ... A

Antrum-Corpus Boundary [*Anatomy*] ... ACB

Ants, Mice, and Gophers [*Electromagnetic antipest device*] ... AMIGO

Antsalova [*Madagascar*] [*ICAO location identifier*] (ICLI) ... FMMG

Antsalova [*Madagascar*] [*Airport symbol*] (OAG) ... WAQ

Antsirabe [*Madagascar*] [*ICAO location identifier*] (ICLI) ... FMME

Antsiranana/Arrachart [*Madagascar*] [*ICAO location identifier*] (ICLI) ... FMNA

Antsohihy [*Madagascar*] [*Airport symbol*] (OAG) ... WAI

Antsohihy/Ambalabe [*Madagascar*] [*ICAO location identifier*] (ICLI) ... FMNW

Antu Telescope (SAUS) ... Antu

Antur Teifi [*Teifi Valley Business Centre*] [*British*] ... AT

Anturane Reinfarction Trial (DB) ... ART

Antwerp [*Belgium*] [*Airport symbol*] (OAG) ... ANR

Antwerp (SAUS) ... Anr

Antwerp (SAUS) ... Ant

Antwerp to Hamburg (SAUS) ... A/H

Antwerp-Anvers [*Belgium*] [*ICAO location identifier*] (ICLI) ... EBAW

Antwerp/Hamburg [*Range of ports between and including these two cities*] [*Shipping*] (DS) ... A/H

Antwerp-Hamburg Range (RIMS) ... ANTHAM

Antwerp-Rotterdam (SAUS) ... A/R

Antwerp-Rotterdam-Amsterdam (SAUS) ... A/R/A

Antwerp-Rotterdam-Amsterdam-Zeebrugge (SAUS) ... ARAZ

Anual Review of Information Science and Technology (SAUS) ... ARIST

Anuario de Prehistoria Madrilena (journ.) (SAUS) ... APM

Anuario Espanol e Hispano-Americano [*A publication*] ... AEHA

Anuhco, Inc. [*AMEX symbol*] (SPSG) ... ANU

Anuhco, Inc. [*Associated Press*] (SAG) ... Anuhco

Anuradhapura [*Ceylon*] [*Airport symbol*] (AD) ... ADP

Anuradhapura [*Sri Lanka*] [*ICAO location identifier*] (ICLI) ... VCCA

Anus ... A

Anuvrat Vishva Bharati [*Anuvrat Global Organization*] [*India*] (EAIO) ... ANUVIBHA

Anvil Cirrus Cloud (SAUS) ... Ci

Anvil Cirrus Parameterization (SAUS) ... ACP

Anvil Mountain [*Alaska*] [*Seismograph station code, US Geological Survey*] (SEIS) ... ANV

Anvil Stratus (ARMP) ... AS

Anwendungssystem (SAUS) ... AS

Anworth Mortgage Asset [*AMEX symbol*] (SG) ... ANH

Anxiety (SAUS) ... ANX

Anxiety [*Psychology*] (DAVI) ... anx

Anxiety Adjective Check List [*Psychology*] ... AACL

Anxiety and Dyspnea (MELL) ... A & D

Anxiety Disorders Association of America (EA) ... ADAA

Anxiety Disorders Education Program ... ADEP

Anxiety Index [*Psychology*] ... AI

Anxiety Management Training [*Psychology*] (DHP) ... AMT

Anxiety Neurosis [*Medicine*] (MELL) ... AN

Anxiety Neurosis [*Psychology*] (DAVI) ... anx Neur

Anxiety Reaction [*Psychology*] (DAVI) ... anx reac

Anxiety Reaction, Intense (SAUS) ... ARI

Anxiety Reaction, Mild (SAUS) ... ARM

Anxiety Scale for the Blind [*Psychology*] ... ASB
Anxiety Scale Questionnaire [*Psychology*] ... ASQ
Anxiety Score [*Psychology*] ... AS
Anxiety Sign [*Psychology*] ... AxS
Anxiety State [*Psychology*] ... AS
Anxiety Status Inventory [*Medicine*] [*Medicine*] (DMAA) ... ASI
Anxiety Symptom Checklist [*Psychology*] (DHP) ... ASCL
Anxiety Tension State [*Psychology*] ... ATS
Anxiety Tension State (SAUS) ... ATS
Any (ADWA) ... AY
Any Acceptable ... A/A
Any Boy Can [*Program*] [*Defunct*] (EA) ... ABC
Any Credible Evidence [*Environmental science*] (EPAT) ... ACE
Any Day Now (ADWA) ... ADN
Any Desired Thing [*Notation in a placebo prescription*] [*Medicine*] ... ADT
Any Desired Thing (SAUS) ... ADT
Any Good Brand (SAUS) ... agb
Any Good Brand ... AGB
Any Interest Date (EBF) ... AID
Any Modulation Link (ACAE) ... AML
Any Old Time [*Journalism*] (WDMC) ... AOT
Any One Accident [*Insurance*] (AIA) ... AOA
Any One Accident (MARI) ... aoa
Any One Accident [*Insurance*] (AIA) ... AOAcc
Any One Aircraft [*Insurance*] (AIA) ... AOA
Any One Bottom [*Marine insurance*] (DS) ... AOB
Any One Bottom (MARI) ... aob
Any One Event (MARI) ... aoe
Any One Location [*Marine insurance*] (DS) ... AOLOC
Any One Loss [*Insurance*] (AIA) ... AOL
Any One Loss (MARI) ... aol
Any One Occurrence (MARI) ... aoo
Any One Occurrence [*Insurance*] (AIA) ... AOOcc
Any One Person [*Insurance*] (AIA) ... AOP
Any One Steamer [*Marine insurance*] (DS) ... AOS
Any One Vessel [*Marine insurance*] (DS) ... AOV
Any One Vessel (MARI) ... aov
Any One Voyage (MARI) ... aovov
Any Other Business (WDAA) ... aob
Any Other Business (ADA) ... AOB
Any Other Color (WDAA) ... AOC
Any Other Competent Business (ODBW) ... AOCB
Any Other Variety (WDAA) ... AOV
Any Quantity ... AQ
Any Quantity ... AQAN
Any Reliable Brand [*Pharmacology*] ... ARB
Any Safe Port in the World (RIMS) ... ASPW
Any Service/Any Port (SAUS) ... ASAP
Any Solid Color Other than Black [*Refers to cocker spaniels*] (IIA) ... ASCOB
Any Tape Search [*Computer program*] (KSC) ... ANTS
Any Time Day/Night Sundays and Holidays Included (RIMS) ... ATDNSHINC
Any Will Provider (ADWA) ... AWP
Any Willing Provider [*Insurance*] ... AWP
Anybody but Carter [*1976 presidential campaign*] ... ABC
Anybody but McGovern [*1972 presidential campaign*] ... ABM
Anybody but Wallace [*Political slogan referring to Alabama governor George Wallace*] ... ABW
Anyone (IAA) ... AY
Anyone for Tennis (WDAA) ... AFT
Anything (ADWA) ... AYG
Anything Invented Anywhere [*As opposed to NIH, Not Invented Here, an acronym indicating refusal to accept foreign technology*] ... AIA
Any-to-Come [*Type of wager where any cash forthcoming from earlier bets finances further bets*] [*British*] ... ATC
ANZ Exch Pfd Tr [*NYSE symbol*] (SG) ... ANU Pr
Anza-Borrego Desert State Park (SAUS) ... ABDSP
Anzac Community School, Fort McMurray, Alberta [*Library symbol*] [*National Library of Canada*] (BIB) ... AFMAS
ANZAC [*Australia-New Zealand Army Corps*] **Day Commemoration Committee, Queensland** ... ADCCQ
Anzar Road [*California*] [*Seismograph station code, US Geological Survey*] (SEIS) ... ANZ
Anzeiger [*or Anzeigen*] [*German*] (OCD) ... Anz
ANZHES [*Australian and New Zealand History of Education Society*] **Journal** [*A publication*] ... ANZHES Jl
ANZUS Council (SAUS) ... ANZUS
A.O. Tatneft ADS [*NYSE symbol*] (SG) ... TNT
AOAC International Journal (SAUS) ... AOAC Int J
AOCS Monograph (journ.) (SAUS) ... AOMOD
Aoetylene Reduction Assay (SAUS) ... ARA
Aoinori (SAUS) ... AOM
AOL [*America Online*] **Instant Messenger** [*Computer science*] ... AIM
AOM-Minerve, SA [*France*] [*FAA designator*] (FAAC) ... AOM
Aomori [*Japan*] [*Airport symbol*] (OAG) ... AOJ
Aomori [*Japan*] [*Seismograph station code, US Geological Survey*] (SEIS) ... AOM
Aomori [*Japan*] [*ICAO location identifier*] (ICLI) ... RJSA
Aomori Journal of Medicine (journ.) (SAUS) ... AOPA Med
Aomori Outpost [*Japan*] [*Seismograph station code, US Geological Survey*] (SEIS) ... AOMJ
Aon Corp. [*NYSE symbol*] (SPSG) ... AOC
Aon Corp. [*Associated Press*] (SAG) ... Aon
Aon Corp. [*Associated Press*] (SAG) ... Aon Cp
Aon Cp 6.25% Cv Ex Pfd [*NYSE symbol*] (TTSB) ... AOCPrB
Aon Cp 8% Perpetual Pfd [*NYSE symbol*] (TTSB) ... AOCPrA
Aonde Vamos (BJA) ... AV
Aontas Fiontair Agus Spoirt [*Association for Adventure Sports*] [*British*] (EAIO) ... AFAS
Aontas Vaimheolochta na hEireann [*Speleological Union of Ireland*] (EAIO) ... AVE
A-Operator (SAUS) ... AO
Aorist (ADWA) ... aor
Aorist [*Grammar*] (ROG) ... AOR
Aoritic Valve Defect [*Medicine*] (MELL) ... AVD
aorta (SAUS) ... ao
Aorta [*Cardiology*] (AAMN) ... Ao
Aorta (ADWA) ... AO
Aortacoronary Bypass Graft [*Cardiology*] ... ACBG
Aorta-Iliac [*Cardiology*] (DAVI) ... ao-il
Aortenstenose (SAUS) ... AS
Aortenton (SAUS) ... A1/A2
Aortic Aneurysm [*Cardiology*] (DAVI) ... AA
Aortic Arch [*Medicine*] (MELL) ... AA
Aortic Arch Syndrome [*Medicine*] ... AAS
Aortic Artery [*Gradient*] [*Cardiology*] (DAVI) ... A-A
Aortic Blood Flow [*Medicine*] (DMAA) ... ABF
Aortic Blood Pressure (MELL) ... AoBC
Aortic Closure [*Cardiology*] ... AC
Aortic Counterpulsation [*Medicine*] (MELL) ... ACP
Aortic Cross Clamping [*Cardiology*] ... ACC
Aortic Depressor Nerve [*Medicine*] (DB) ... ADN
Aortic Dissection [*Medicine*] (MELL) ... AD
Aortic Ejection Sound [*Medicine*] (MELL) ... AES
Aortic First Heart Sound [*Cardiology*] ... A_1
Aortic Flow [*Cardiology*] ... AF
Aortic Incompetence [*or Insufficiency*] [*Medicine*] ... AI
Aortic Insufficiency [*Medicine*] (DB) ... AI
Aortic Insufficiency [*Cardiology*] (DAVI) ... AInsuf
Aortic Plexus [*Anatomy*] ... AP
Aortic Posterior Wall [*Cardiology*] (DMAA) ... AoPW
Aortic Pressure [*Medicine*] ... AoP
Aortic Pressure [*Medicine*] ... AP
Aortic Regurgitation [*Medicine*] (MEDA) ... AOR REGURG
Aortic Regurgitation [*Medicine*] (CPH) ... aort regurg
Aortic Regurgitation [*Medicine*] ... AR
Aortic Root [*Cardiology*] ... AR
Aortic Root Replacement [*Medicine*] (DMAA) ... ARR
Aortic Sac [*Cardiology*] (DAVI) ... AS
Aortic Second Heart Sound [*Cardiology*] ... A_2
Aortic Second Sound (SAUS) ... Ay
Aortic Smooth Muscle Cells [*Medicine*] (DB) ... ASMC
Aortic Stenosis [*Medicine*] (MEDA) ... AORT STEN
Aortic Stenosis [*Medicine*] (MELL) ... AoSt
Aortic Stenosis [*Medicine*] ... AS
Aortic Stenosis [*Cardiology*] (DAVI) ... A Sten
Aortic Stenosis and Aortic Insufficiency Murmurs [*Cardiology*] (MAE) ... ASAI
Aortic Systolic Pressure [*Medicine*] (DB) ... ASP
Aortic Trileaflet Valve [*Medicine*] (MELL) ... ATLV
Aortic Valve [*Medicine*] (MELL) ... AoV
Aortic Valve [*Cardiology*] ... AV
Aortic Valve Closure [*Medicine*] ... AOC
Aortic Valve Cusp Separation [*On echocardiogram*] [*Cardiology*] (DAVI) ... AVSC
Aortic Valve Disease [*Cardiology*] ... AVD
Aortic Valve Echophonocardiogram [*Cardiology*] ... AVE
Aortic Valve Opening [*Cardiology*] ... AO
Aortic Valve Partial Closure [*Medicine*] (MELL) ... AVPC
Aortic Valve Prolapse [*Medicine*] (MELL) ... AVP
Aortic Valve Replacement [*Cardiology*] ... AVR
Aortic Valve Stenosis [*Cardiology*] (DMAA) ... AVS
Aortic Valve Stroke Volume [*Cardiology*] ... AVSV
Aortic Valved Graft Prosthesis [*Medicine*] (MELL) ... AVGP
Aortic Valvuloplasty [*Medicine*] (MELL) ... AVP
Aorticincompetence (SAUS) ... AI
Aorticopulmonary (ADWA) ... AP
Aorticopulmonary Septal Defect [*Medicine*] (DMAA) ... APSD
Aortic-Pressure Pulse (SAUS) ... AOP
Aortic-Valve Atresia [*Medicine*] (MELL) ... AVA
Aortic-Valve Cusp [*Medicine*] (MELL) ... AVC
Aortic-Valve Incompetence [*Medicine*] (MELL) ... AVI
Aortic-Valve Insufficiency [*Medicine*] (MELL) ... AVI
Aortobifemoral [*Medicine*] (DMAA) ... ABF
Aortocoronary Bypass [*Cardiology*] ... ACB
Aortocoronary Bypass Graft Surgery [*Cardiology*] (CPH) ... ACBGS
Aortocoronary Bypass Surgery [*Cardiology*] (CPH) ... ACBS
Aortocoronary Bypass Surgery [*Medicine*] (MELL) ... ACBYS
Aortocoronary Graft [*Cardiology*] (DMAA) ... ACG
Aortocoronary Saphenous Vein [*Cardiology*] (MAE) ... ACSV
Aortocoronary Saphenous Vein Bypass [*Cardiology*] (AAMN) ... ACB
Aortocoronary saphenous vein Bypass (SAUS) ... ACB
Aorto-Coronary Venous Bypass (SAUS) ... ACVB
Aortocoronary Venous Bypass [*Cardiology*] (DMAA) ... ACVB
Aortocranial Occlusive Vascular Disease [*Medicine*] (MELL) ... ACOV
Aortoenteric Fistula [*Medicine*] (MELL) ... AEF
Aorto-Femoral Bypass [*Medicine*] ... AFB
Aortofemoral Bypass Graft [*Cardiology*] (DMAA) ... AFBG
Aorto-Iliac Occlusive Disease [*Medicine*] ... AIOD
Aortopulmonar (SAUS) ... AP
Aortopulmonary [*Cardiology*] ... AP
Aortopulmonary Shunt [*Medicine*] (MELL) ... APS
Aortorenography [*Medicine*] (MELL) ... ARG
Aorto-Right Ventricle (SAUS) ... Ao-RV
Aortovenography [*Medicine*] (MELL) ... AVG

Aortoventriculoplasty (MELL) ... AVP
Aos-Oideachas Naisiunta Tri Aontu Saorlach [*National Association of Adult Education*] (EAIO) ... AONTAS
Aosta [*Italy*] [*ICAO location identifier*] (ICLI) ... LIMW
Aoulef [*Algeria*] [*ICAO location identifier*] (ICLI) ... DAAF
Aoulef [*Algeria*] [*Airport symbol*] (AD) ... WAE
AOUON [*All of Us or None*] **Archive** [*An association*] (EA) ... AA
APA Internacional [*Dominican Republic*] [*ICAO designator*] (FAAC) ... APY
APA Optics [*NASDAQ symbol*] (TTSB) ... APAT
APA Optics, Inc. [*Associated Press*] (SAG) ... APA
APA Optics, Inc. [*Blaine, MN*] [*NASDAQ symbol*] (NQ) ... APAT
APAC Customer Services [*NASDAQ symbol*] (SG) ... APAC
APAC TeleServices [*NASDAQ symbol*] (TTSB) ... APAC
APAC TeleServices, Inc. [*NASDAQ symbol*] (SAG) ... APAC
APAC TeleServices, Inc. [*Associated Press*] (SAG) ... APACT
Apache [*MARC language code*] [*Library of Congress*] (LCCP) ... apa
APACHE [*Active Thermal Protection for Avionics Crew and Heat-Sensitve Equipment*] **Action Team** [*Army*] ... AAT
Apache Attack Helicopter [*Military*] (RDA) ... AAH
Apache, Black Hawk, and Chinook Self-Deployments [*Military*] ... ABCD
Apache Corp. [*NYSE symbol*] (SPSG) ... APA
Apache Corp. [*Associated Press*] (SAG) ... Apache
Apache Energy & Mining Co. (SAUO) ... APEM
Apache Helicopter [*Anti-armor attack helicopter*] ... AH
Apache Junction, AZ [*FM radio station call letters*] ... KVVA-FM
Apache Medical Systems, Inc. [*NASDAQ symbol*] (SAG) ... AMSI
Apache Medical Systems, Inc. [*Associated Press*] (SAG) ... ApcheM
Apache Petroleum (SAUS) ... APP
Apache Railway Co. (SAUO) ... APA
[*The*] **Apache Railway Co.** [*AAR code*] ... APA
APACHE [*Active Thermal Protection for Avionics Crew and Heat-Sensitive Equipment*] **Readiness Improvement Program** [*Army*] ... ARIP
Apachito [*Race of maize*] ... APA
APACM Energy and Particle Monitors (SAUS) ... AEPM
Apalachee Community Mental Health Services, Inc., Tallahassee, FL [*Library symbol*] [*Library of Congress*] (LCLS) ... FTaA
Apalachicola, FL [*Location identifier*] [*FAA*] (FAAL) ... AAF
Apalachicola, FL [*Location identifier*] [*FAA*] (FAAL) ... AQQ
Apalachicola, FL [*FM radio station call letters*] ... WOYS
Apalachicola, FL [*FM radio station call letters*] (RBYB) ... WXGJ-FM
Apalachicola Northern Railroad Co. [*AAR code*] ... AN
Aparent Molar Quantity (SAUS) ... AMQ
Aparri, Cagayan [*Philippines*] [*ICAO location identifier*] (ICLI) ... RPUA
Apartamento ... APT
Apartment [*Classified advertising*] (ADA) ... APART
Apartment ... APT
Apartment (VRA) ... apt
Apartment (TBD) ... Apt
Apartment and Office Building Association [*of Metro Washington, DC*] (SRA) ... AOBA
Apartment Association of Indiana (SRA) ... AAI
Apartment Association of New Mexico (SRA) ... AANM
Apartment House Addressing Program [*US Postal Service*] ... AHAP
Apartment Investment & Management Co. [*NYSE symbol*] (SAG) ... AIV
Apartment Investment & Management Co. [*Associated Press*] (SAG) ... AptInv
Apartment Investment & Mgmt'A' [*NYSE symbol*] (TTSB) ... AIV
Apartment Owners and Managers Association of America (EA) ... AOMA
Apartment Owners and Managers Association of America (SAUO) ... AOMAA
Apartment/Commercial (SAUS) ... A/C
Apartments ... APTS
Apataki [*French Polynesia*] [*Airport symbol*] (OAG) ... APK
Apataki [*French Polynesia*] [*ICAO location identifier*] (ICLI) ... NTGD
Apatite [*CIPW classification*] [*Geology*] ... ap
Apatite Subgroup [*Apatite, fluorite, calcite, pyrite, iron*] [*CIPW classification*] [*Geology*] ... A
Apatity [*Former USSR*] [*Seismograph station code, US Geological Survey*] (SEIS) ... APA
APCE [*Automated Product Control Environment*] **Interface Set** (SSD) ... AIS
APCHE [*Automatic Program Checkout Equipment*] **Relay Box** ... ARB
Apco Argentina [*NASDAQ symbol*] (SAG) ... APAG
Apco Argentina [*NASDAQ symbol*] (TTSB) ... APAGF
Apco Argentina, Inc. [*Associated Press*] (SAG) ... Apco
APE [*Automatic Processing Equipment*] **Control Facility** ... ACF
APEA [*Australian Petroleum Exploration Association*] **Journal** [*A publication*] ... APEA JI
Apeal Cases in the United States (journ.) (SAUS) ... App Cas
Apeiranthos Of Naxos [*Greece*] [*Seismograph station code, US Geological Survey*] (SEIS) ... APE
Apel. Notation of Polyphonic Music [*A publication*] ... ApNPM
Apellation (SAUS) ... Apell
Apentina [*Surinam*] [*ICAO location identifier*] (ICLI) ... SMPT
Aperient [*Pharmacy*] (ROG) ... APE
Aperient [*Pharmacy*] (ROG) ... APER
Aperiodic Stochastic Resonance [*Model of neurophysiological reactions*] ... ASR
Apert's Disease [*Medicine*] (MELL) ... AD
Aperture ... AP
Aperture ... APER
Aperture (ADWA) ... aper
Aperture (MSA) ... APERT
Aperture Card (MSA) ... APTC
Aperture Card Raster Image Scanner [*Versatec Co.*] (NITA) ... ACRIS
Aperture Card Raster Input Scanner (SAUS) ... ACRIS
Aperture Card Remote Imaging System (SAUS) ... ACRIS
Aperture Current [*Medicine*] (DMAA) ... APC
Aperture Current Setting [*In Coulter counter*] [*Microbiology*] ... ACS
Aperture Direct Read-Out ... ADR
Aperture Distribution and Maintenance [*System*] ... ADAM
Aperture Door (NAKS) ... AD
Aperture File Protocol [*Computer science*] ... AFP
Aperture Lip ... APL
Aperture Plate Character Generator ... APCG
Aperture Plate Character Generator (SAUS) ... APCG/16
Aperture Processed Imagers (ACAE) ... API
Aperture Relay Experiment Definition (MCD) ... ARED
Aperture Stop (ACAE) ... AS
Aperture Uncertainty Time (ACAE) ... AUT
Aperture Value [*Photography*] ... AV
Apertus Technologies [*NASDAQ symbol*] (TTSB) ... APTS
Apertus Technologies, Inc. [*Associated Press*] (SAG) ... Apertus
Apertus Technologies, Inc. [*NASDAQ symbol*] (SPSG) ... APTS
apethic (SAUS) ... aph
Apex (SAUS) ... Ap
Apex [*Medicine*] (DMAA) ... Ap
Apex Air Cargo [*ICAO designator*] (FAAC) ... APX
Apex Beat [*Medicine*] ... AB
Apex Cardiogram [*Medicine*] ... ACG
Apex Cardiogram [*Medicine*] ... APCG
Apex Clubs of Australia ... ACA
Apex Energy Corp. [*Vancouver Stock Exchange symbol*] ... APG
Apex Global Information Services [*Computer science*] ... AGIS
Apex Global Internet Service [*Computer science*] ... AGIS
Apex Global Internet Services ... AGIS
Apex, Inc. [*NASDAQ symbol*] (SG) ... APEX
Apex Mortgage Capital [*NYSE symbol*] (SG) ... AXM
Apex Muni Fund [*NYSE symbol*] (TTSB) ... APX
Apex Municipal Fund, Inc. [*Associated Press*] (SAG) ... Apex
Apex Municipal Fund, Inc. [*NYSE symbol*] (SPSG) ... APX
APEX PC Solutions [*Stock market symbol*] ... APEX
Apex Silver Mines [*AMEX symbol*] (SG) ... SIL
Apexcardiogram (SAUS) ... ACG
Apexcardiography [*Medicine*] (MELL) ... ACG
Aphakic Bullous Keratopathy [*Medicine*] (MELL) ... ABK
Aphanizomenon Flos-Aquae [*Blue green algae*] ... AFA
Aphasia [*Medicine*] (DMAA) ... Aph
Aphasia (SAUS) ... APH
Aphasia, Agnosia, Apraxia, Agraphia, Alexia [*Medicine*] (MEDA) ... AAAAA
Aphasia Diagnostic Profiles [*Test*] (TMMY) ... ADP
Aphasia Language Performance Scale [*Speech and language therapy*] (DAVI) ... ALPS
aphelion (SAUS) ... aph
Aphetic (BARN) ... aph
aphetic (SAUS) ... aphet
Aphetized (ADWA) ... aphet
Aphorism ... APH
Aphoxide [*Also, TEPA*] [*Mutagen*] ... APO
Aphrodisiac [*Medicine*] (ROG) ... APHRO
Aphthous Ulcer [*Medicine*] (MELL) ... AU
Aphton Corp. [*NASDAQ symbol*] (SPSG) ... APHT
Aphton Corp. [*Associated Press*] (SAG) ... Aphton
API [*American Petroleum Institute*] **Literature** [*New York, NY*] [*Bibliographic database*] ... APILIT
Apia [*Samoa Islands*] [*Seismograph station code, US Geological Survey*] (SEIS) ... API
Apia [*Samoa Islands*] [*Airport symbol*] (OAG) ... APW
Apia [*Western Samoa*] [*ICAO location identifier*] (ICLI) ... NSAP
Apiary Circular. British Columbia Department of Agriculture (journ.) (SAUS) ... Apiary Circ BC Dep Agric
Apiary Inspectors of America (EA) ... AIA
Apical (DAVI) ... A
Apical Beat [*Medicine*] (MELL) ... AB
Apical Cell [*Botany*] ... AC
Apical Ectodermal Ridge [*Embryology, genetics*] ... AER
Apical Impulse [*Medicine*] (AAMN) ... AI
Apical Meristem [*Botany*] ... AP
Apical Pulse [*Medicine*] ... AP
Apical Rate [*Medicine*] ... AR
Apical Sensory Region (SAUS) ... ASR
Apical Vacuoles (SAUS) ... AV
Apical/Radial [*Pulse*] [*Medicine*] ... A/R
Apiculture ... APIC
Apiculture in Western Australia (journ.) (SAUS) ... Apic W Aust
Apiculture Newsletter. Plant Industry Division. Alberta Department of Agriculture (journ.) (SAUS) ... Apic Newsl Pl Ind Div Alberta Dep Agric
APIJ. Australian Planning Institute. Journal (journ.) (SAUS) ... APIJ
APIU Common Communications Enhanced Software Segment (SAUS) ... ACCESS
APL Ltd. [*NYSE symbol*] [*Formerly, American President Companies*] (SG) ... APL
APL [*Applied Physics Laboratory*] **Management Planning and Engineering Resource Evaluation** [*Navy*] ... AMPERE
Aplasia Cutis Congenita [*Medicine*] (MEDA) ... ACC
Aplastic Anemia [*Medicine*] (DMAA) ... AA
Aplastic Anemia Foundation of America (EA) ... AAFA
APLE Prototype Experiment (SAUS) ... APEX
Aplington Legion Memorial Library, Aplington, IA [*Library symbol*] [*Library of Congress*] (LCLS) ... IaAp
A-plus (SAUS) ... A+
Apnea and Bradycardia [*Medicine*] (MELL) ... A & B
Apnea, Bradycardia, Cyanosis [*Medicine*] (MAE) ... ABC
Apnea During Sleep (MELL) ... ADS
Apnea of Infancy [*Also, AOP (Apnea of Prematurity)*] (PAZ) ... AOI

Apnea of Prematurity [*Also, AOI (Apnea of Infancy)*] (PAZ) ... AOP
Apnea-Bradycardia [*Spells*] [*Medicine*] (DAVI) ... AB
Apnea-Plus-Hypopnea Index [*Medicine*] (DMAA) ... AHI
Apneustic Center [*Brain anatomy*] ... APC
Apnoic Diffusion Oxygenation [*Medicine*] (MELL) ... ADO
APO. The Australian Post Office Magazine (journ.) (SAUS) ... APO
APOC Reconciliation (SAUS) ... APOC-REC
Apocalypse (BJA) ... Ap
Apocalypse (VRA) ... apcys
Apocalypse ... Apoc
Apocalypse of Abraham (BJA) ... ApocAbr
Apocalypse of Abraham (SAUS) ... AporAbr
Apocalypse of Baruch (SAUS) ... APOCBAR
Apocalypse of Baruch [*Apocalyptic book*] ... APOC BAR
Apocalypse of Elijah (BJA) ... ApocElij
Apocalypse of Moses (BJA) ... ApocMos
Apocalypse of Peter (BJA) ... ApocPet
Apocalyptic (BJA) ... Apoc
Apocalyptic Literature (journ.) (SAUS) ... ApLit
Apocatypse of Peter (SAUS) ... ApoPet
Apochromatic [*Photography*] ... APO
Apocolocyntosis [*of Seneca the Younger*] [*Classical studies*] (OCD) ... Apocol
Apocrine Gland [*Medicine*] (MELL) ... AG
Apocrine Sweat Gland [*Medicine*] (MELL) ... ASG
Apocrypha (BJA) ... Apcr
Apocrypha (BJA) ... Apoc
Apocrypha (ROG) ... APOCH
Apocrypha (VRA) ... apocph
Apocrypha ... APOCR
[*The*] **Apocrypha and Pseudepigrapha of the Old Testament** [*A publication*] (BJA) ... APOT
Apocrypha and Pseudepigrapha of the Old Testament (journ.) (SAUS) ... APOT
[*The*] **Apocryphal Literature: A Brief Introduction** [*1945*] [*A publication*] (BJA) ... TAL
[*The*] **Apocryphal New Testament** [*A publication*] (BJA) ... ANT
Apocryphon (SAUS) ... Apn
Apoenzyme [*Clinical chemistry*] (MAE) ... AE
Apoenzyme (ADWA) ... apo
Apoenzyme Reactivation Immunoassay System [*Clinical chemistry*] ... ARIS
Apogam (SAUS) ... Ap
Apogee ... APG
Apogee ... APO
Apogee (GEOI) ... Apo
Apogee ... APOG
Apogee Altitude (NASA) ... HA
Apogee and Maneuvering Stage [*Space flight*] ... AMS
Apogee and Perigee (SAUS) ... A&P
Apogee Boost Motor [*Aerospace*] (MCD) ... ABM
Apogee Enterprises [*NASDAQ symbol*] (TTSB) ... APOG
Apogee Enterprises, Inc. [*NASDAQ symbol*] (NQ) ... APOG
Apogee Enterprises, Inc. [*Associated Press*] (SAG) ... ApogEn
Apogee, Inc. [*NASDAQ symbol*] (SAG) ... APGG
Apogee, Inc. [*Associated Press*] (SAG) ... Apogee
Apogee Injection Module [*NASA*] ... AIM
Apogee Intercept Defense (MCD) ... AID
Apogee Kick [*NASA*] (KSC) ... AK
Apogee Kick Motor [*NASA*] (KSC) ... AKM
Apogee Kick Motor Capture Device (SAUS) ... ACD
Apogee Motor Assembly with Paired Satellites [*NASA*] ... AMAPS
Apogee Motor Fire [*Aerospace*] ... AMF
Apogee Motor Firing (ACAE) ... AMF
Apogee Motor Firing Attitude (ACAE) ... AMFA
Apogee Motor Igniter [*NASA*] ... AMI
Apogee Motor Timer [*NASA*] ... AMT
Apogee Robotics, Inc. (SAUO) ... APGE
Apogee Structured Query Language [*Computer science*] ... ASQL
Apogee Technology, Inc. (SAUO) ... APGG
Apogee-Perigee Injection System (PDAA) ... APIS
Apolipoprotein [*Biochemistry*] ... Apo
Apolipoprotein A [*Biochemistry*] ... ApoA
Apolipoprotein B (DB) ... apoB
Apolipoprotein C [*Biochemistry*] ... ApoC
Apolipoprotein E (MELL) ... ALPE
Apolipoprotein E [*Biochemistry*] ... ApoE
Apolipoprotein-B [*Biochemistry*] (ECON) ... APOB
Apolipoprotein-E (ADWA) ... apo-E
Apolle Program Office (SAUS) ... APO
Apollo [*A publication*] (BRI) ... Apo
Apollo Abort System [*NASA*] (IAA) ... AAS
Apollo Access Arm [*NASA*] (KSC) ... AAA
Apollo Airlines [*Greece*] [*FAA designator*] (FAAC) ... AOA
Apollo Airlines [*ICAO designator*] (AD) ... ID
Apollo Airways, Inc. D/B/A Pacific Coast Airlines (SAUS) ... SNC
Apollo Applications [*NASA*] ... AA
Apollo Applications Program [*NASA*] ... AAP
Apollo Applications Program Office [*NASA*] (MCD) ... AAPO
Apollo Applications Test Requirements [*NASA*] (MCD) ... AATR
Apollo Bioenvironmental Information System (PDAA) ... ABIS
Apollo Command and Service Module [*NASA*] (IAA) ... ACSM
Apollo Command [*or Communications*] **System** [*NASA*] ... ACS
Apollo Command Systems (SAUS) ... ACS
Apollo Communications System (SAUS) ... ACS
Apollo Computer Address Matrix [*NASA*] ... ACAM
Apollo Computer Incorporated (SAUO) ... APCI
Apollo Contractor Information Center [*NASA*] (KSC) ... ACIC
Apollo Crew Systems Branch [*NASA*] (KSC) ... ACSB
Apollo Data Bank [*NASA*] (MCD) ... ADB
Apollo Data [*or Document*] **Descriptions Standards** [*NASA*] (MCD) ... ADDS
Apollo Data Descriptions Standards (SAUS) ... ADDS
Apollo Data Manager [*NASA*] (KSC) ... ADM
Apollo Development [*NASA*] (KSC) ... AD
Apollo Display Console [*NASA*] ... ADC
Apollo Docking Test Device [*NASA*] ... ADTD
Apollo Document Descriptions Standards (SAUS) ... ADDS
Apollo Document Distribution Requirements Index [*NASA*] (KSC) ... ADDRI
Apollo Document Index [*NASA*] (KSC) ... ADI
Apollo Document Preparation Standards [*Handbook*] [*NASA*] (KSC) ... ADPS
Apollo Documentation Administration Instruction [*NASA*] (KSC) ... ADAI
Apollo Documentation Description Standards (SAUS) ... ADDS
Apollo Documentation List [*NASA*] (MCD) ... ADL
Apollo Dynamic Programs [*NASA*] (KSC) ... ADP
Apollo Earth-Orbiting Station [*NASA*] ... AES
Apollo Engineering [*NASA*] (SAA) ... AE
Apollo Engineering and Technology Index [*NASA*] (KSC) ... AETI
Apollo Engineering Bulletin [*NASA*] (SAA) ... AEB
Apollo Engineering Development Board (SAUO) ... AEDB
Apollo Engineering Documentation Board [*NASA*] (MCD) ... AEDB
Apollo Environmental Control System [*NASA*] (IAA) ... AECS
Apollo Experiment Pallet [*NASA*] ... AEP
Apollo Experiment Support [*NASA*] ... AES
Apollo Extension Program [*NASA*] ... AEP
Apollo Extension System [*NASA*] ... AES
Apollo Extension System / Apollo Logistics Support System / Lunar Exploration System for Apollo [*NASA*] (SAA) ... AES/ALSS/LESA
Apollo Flight Control [*NASA*] (MCD) ... AFC
Apollo Follow-On Missions [*NASA*] (SAA) ... AFM
Apollo Group, Inc. [*NASDAQ symbol*] (SAG) ... APOL
Apollo Group, Inc. [*Associated Press*] (SAG) ... ApolloG
Apollo Group'A' [*NASDAQ symbol*] (TTSB) ... APOL
Apollo Grp.-Univ. Phoenix Online [*NASDAQ symbol*] ... VOPX
Apollo Guidance and Navigation Industrial Support [*NASA*] ... AGNIS
Apollo Guidance and Navigation Information [*NASA*] ... AGANI
Apollo Guidance Computer [*NASA*] ... AGC
Apollo Guidance Equipment [*NASA*] (KSC) ... AGE
Apollo Guidance Ground Display [*NASA*] (MCD) ... AGGD
Apollo Implementing Instructions [*NASA*] (KSC) ... AII
Apollo Initiator Resistance Measuring Equipment [*NASA*] (NASA) ... AIRME
Apollo Instrumentation Ship (SAUS) ... AIS
Apollo Instrumentation Ships [*NASA*] (MCD) ... AIS
Apollo Intermediate Chart [*NASA*] (MCD) ... AIC
Apollo Launch Data System [*NASA*] ... ALDS
Apollo Launch Operation Panel [*NASA*] (KSC) ... ALOP
Apollo Launch Operations Committee [*NASA*] (KSC) ... ALOC
Apollo Launch Trajectory Data System [*NASA*] (KSC) ... ALTDS
Apollo Launch Trajectory System (SAUS) ... ALTDS
Apollo Light-Flash Moving-Emulsion Detector [*NASA*] ... ALFMED
Apollo Logistic Support System [*NASA*] ... ALSS
Apollo Logistic Support System / Lunar Explorations System for Apollo [*NASA*] (SAA) ... ALSS/LESA
Apollo Lunar Excursion Module Sensors [*NASA*] ... ALEMS
Apollo Lunar Exploration Mission [*NASA*] ... ALEM
Apollo Lunar Hand Tool [*NASA*] ... ALHT
Apollo Lunar Hand Tool Carrier [*NASA*] ... ALHTC
Apollo Lunar Landing System [*NASA*] (SAA) ... ALLS
Apollo Lunar Logistic Support [*NASA*] ... ALLS
Apollo Lunar Module [*NASA*] ... ALM
Apollo Lunar Orbit [*NASA*] ... ALO
Apollo Lunar Orbital Science [*NASA*] (KSC) ... ALOS
Apollo Lunar Polar Orbiter [*NASA*] ... ALPO
Apollo Lunar Radioisotopic Heater [*NASA*] (MCD) ... ALRH
Apollo Lunar Sample Return Container [*NASA*] ... ALSRC
Apollo Lunar Sounder Experiment [*NASA*] ... ALSE
Apollo Lunar Surfac Experiment (SAUS) ... ALSE
Apollo Lunar Surface Close-up Camera (SAUS) ... ALSCC
Apollo Lunar Surface Closeup Camera [*Apollo 11*] [*NASA*] ... ALSCC
Apollo Lunar Surface Drill [*NASA*] ... ALSD
Apollo Lunar Surface Experimental (or Experiments) Package (SAUS) ... ALSEP
Apollo Lunar Surface Experiments Package [*NASA*] ... ALSEP
Apollo Master Measurements Program [*NASA*] (KSC) ... AMMP
Apollo Mission Planning Task Force [*NASA*] (KSC) ... AMPTF
Apollo Mission Programs [*NASA*] (KSC) ... AMP
Apollo Mission Simulator [*NASA*] ... AMS
Apollo Navigation Working Group [*NASA*] (MCD) ... ANWG
Apollo Network [*NASA*] (KSC) ... ANW
Apollo Network Simulations [*NASA*] (KSC) ... ANS
Apollo Operations Director [*NASA*] (SAA) ... AOD
Apollo Operations Handbook [*NASA*] ... AOH
Apollo Orbital Research Laboratory [*NASA*] ... AORL
Apollo Orbiting Laboratory Module [*NASA*] ... AOLM
Apollo Owners Register (EA) ... AOR
Apollo, PA [*AM radio station call letters*] ... WAVL
Apollo Pad Test [*NASA*] (KSC) ... APT
Apollo Part Task Trainer [*NASA*] (KSC) ... APTT
Apollo Parts Information Center [*NASA*] (MCD) ... APIC
Apollo Parts Task Trainer (SAUS) ... APTT
Apollo Payload Exploration [*NASA*] ... APPLE
Apollo Personnel Identification [*or Investigation*] **Program** [*NASA*] (KSC) ... APIP
Apollo Personnel Identification Program (SAUS) ... APIP
Apollo Personnel Investigation Program (SAUS) ... APIP
Apollo Preflight Operations Procedures [*NASA*] (KSC) ... APOP

Apollo Problem Bulletin [*NASA*] ... APB
Apollo Program [*NASA*] ... AP
Apollo Program Control Center [*NASA*] (KSC) ... APCC
Apollo Program Control Room [*NASA*] (KSC) ... APCR
Apollo Program Definition Phase [*NASA*] (KSC) ... APDP
Apollo Program Directive [*NASA*] (KSC) ... APD
Apollo Program Logic Network [*NASA*] (KSC) ... APLN
Apollo Program Office [*NASA*] (KSC) ... APO
Apollo Program Requirements [*NASA*] (KSC) ... APR
Apollo Program Specifications [*NASA*] (KSC) ... APS
Apollo Project Office (SAUS) ... APO
Apollo Propellant Gauging System [*NASA*] (KSC) ... APGS
Apollo Propulsion Analysis Program [*NASA*] ... APAP
Apollo Propulsion Development Facility (SAUS) ... APDF
Apollo Qualification [*NASA*] (KSC) ... AQ
Apollo Range Instrumentation Aircraft [*NASA*] ... ARIA
Apollo Reentry Communications Blackout Working Group [*NASA*] ... ACBWG
Apollo Reentry Ship [*NASA*] ... ARS
Apollo Reliability Engineering [*NASA*] (KSC) ... ARE
Apollo Reliability Engineering Electronics [*NASA*] (KSC) ... AREE
Apollo Requirements Manual [*NASA*] (KSC) ... ARM
Apollo Saturn (SAUS) ... AS
Apollo Service Module [*NASA*] (MCD) ... ASM
Apollo Ship's Operational Readiness Force [*NASA*] ... ASORF
Apollo Signal Definition Document [*NASA*] (KSC) ... ASDD
Apollo Simple Penetrometer [*NASA*] ... ASP
Apollo Simulated Remote Site [*NASA*] (KSC) ... ASRS
Apollo Simulation Checkout and Training System [*NASA*] ... ASCATS
Apollo Site Selection Board [*NASA*] (KSC) ... ASSB
Apollo Soyuz Test Mission (ACAE) ... ASTM
Apollo Space Program (SAUS) ... ASP
Apollo Spacecraft Development Test Plan [*NASA*] (KSC) ... ASDTP
Apollo Spacecraft Hardware Utilization Request [*NASA*] ... ASHUR
Apollo Spacecraft Parts and Materials Information Services [*NASA*] (KSC) ... ASPMIS
Apollo Spacecraft Program Office (SAUS) ... ASPO
Apollo Spacecraft Project [*NASA*] (IAA) ... ASP
Apollo Spacecraft Project Office [*NASA*] ... ASPO
Apollo Special Task Team [*NASA*] ... ASTT
Apollo Standard Detonator [*NASA*] ... ASD
Apollo Standard Initiator [*NASA*] ... ASI
Apollo Supplemental Procedural Information [*NASA*] (KSC) ... ASPI
Apollo Support Department [*NASA*] (KSC) ... ASD
Apollo Surface Lunar Experiments Package (SAUS) ... ASLEP
Apollo Systems Manual [*A publication*] (MCD) ... ASM
Apollo Systems Test [*NASA*] (IAA) ... AST
Apollo Technical Documentation Distribution List [*NASA*] (KSC) ... ATDDL
Apollo Telemetry Aircraft Project [*NASA*] ... ATAP
Apollo Telescope Mount [*NASA*] ... ATM
Apollo Telescope Mount - Deployed [*NASA*] (MCD) ... ATM-D
Apollo Telescope Mount - Stowed [*NASA*] (MCD) ... ATM-S
Apollo Telescope Mount Console [*NASA*] ... ATMC(O)
Apollo Telescope Mount Deployment Assembly [*NASA*] ... ATMDA
Apollo Telescope Mount Digital Computer [*NASA*] ... ATMDC
Apollo Telescope Orientation Mount Program [*NASA*] (MCD) ... ATOM
Apollo Test and Operations (SAUS) ... AT&O
Apollo Test Box [*NASA*] (SAA) ... ATB
Apollo Test Integration Working Groups [*NASA*] (KSC) ... ATIWG
Apollo Test Operations [*NASA*] (KSC) ... ATO
Apollo Test Requirements [*NASA*] (KSC) ... ATR
Apollo Test Unsatisfactory Report [*NASA*] (IAA) ... ATUR
Apollo Time Conditioner [*NASA*] ... ATC
Apollo Trajectory Decision Logic Prototype [*NASA*] ... ATDLP
Apollo Unified S-Band Circuit Margin [*Program*] [*NASA*] ... AUSBCM
Apollo User Group (SAUS) ... AUG
Apollo Validation Test [*NASA*] (KSC) ... AVT
Apollo Vehicle Systems Section [*NASA*] (KSC) ... AVSS
Apollo Wind-Tunnel Testing Program [*NASA*] ... AWTTP
Apollo XI Collector Society [*Defunct*] (EA) ... AXICS
Apollodorus [*Second century BC*] [*Classical studies*] (OCD) ... Apollod
Apollo/GOSS [*Ground Operations Support System*] **Navigation Qualifications** [*NASA*] ... AGNQ
Apollonius Rhodius [*Third century BC*] [*Classical studies*] (OCD) ... Ap Rhod
Apollo-Saturn [*NASA*] (MCD) ... AS
Apollo-Soyuz Docking Module [*NASA*] ... ASDM
Apollo-Soyuz Test Program (or Project) (SAUO) ... ASTP
Apollo-Soyuz Test Project [*NASA/USSR*] ... ASTP
Apolo [*Bolivia*] [*ICAO location identifier*] (ICLI) ... SLAP
apologete (SAUS) ... apol
apologetics (SAUS) ... apol
Apologeticus [*of Tertullian*] [*Classical studies*] (OCD) ... Apol
Apologia [*of Plato*] [*Classical studies*] (OCD) ... Ap
Apologia [*of Apuleius*] [*Classical studies*] (OCD) ... Apol
Apologia Socratis [*of Xenophon*] [*Classical studies*] (OCD) ... Ap
apologise (SAUS) ... apol
apologize (SAUS) ... apol
apology (SAUS) ... apol
Apomict [*Biology*] (BARN) ... apm
Apomorphine (MELL) ... AM
Apomorphine [*Neurochemistry, pharmacology*] ... APO
Apophthegmata [*of Julian*] [*Classical studies*] (OCD) ... Apophth
Apophysitis Calcanei (DB) ... AC
Apopka, FL [*AM radio station call letters*] (BROA) ... WHIM
Apopka, FL [*AM radio station call letters*] ... WTLN
Apopka, FL [*FM radio station call letters*] ... WTLN-FM
Apoprotein [*Biochemistry*] ... Apo
Apoptosis Signal-Regulating Kinase [*Cytology*] ... ASK
Apoptosis-Inducing Factor [*Cytology*] ... AIF
A-positive (SAUS) ... A+
Apostilb [*Unit of luminance*] ... Asb
Apostle [*Church calendars*] ... A
Apostle ... AP
Apostle (VRA) ... ap
Apostle (ADWA) ... Ap
Apostle and Evangelist [*Church calendars*] ... AE
Apostle and Martyr [*Church calendars*] (ROG) ... A & M
Apostle, Evangelist, and Martyr [*Church calendars*] (ROG) ... AE & M
Apostle Islands, Lake Superior (SAUS) ... Apostles
Apostles ... APP
Apostles of the Sacred Heart of Jesus [*Roman Catholic women's religious order*] ... ASCJ
Apostleship of Prayer (EA) ... AP
Apostleship of the Sea [*See also AM*] [*Vatican City, Vatican City State*] (EAIO) ... AOS
Apostleship of the Sea in the United States (EA) ... AOSUS
Apostleship of the Sea in the United States (EA) ... ASUS
Apostolate ... APSTLT
Apostolate for Family Consecration (EA) ... AFC
Apostolate of Christ the Worker ... ACW
Apostolate to Hungarians [*Diocesan abbreviation*] [*District of Columbia*] (TOCD) ... ATH
Apostolatus Maris [*Apostleship of the Sea - AOS*] (EA) ... AM
Apostolic ... A
Apostolic (BJA) ... Ap
Apostolic (SAUS) ... APO
Apostolic (BJA) ... apost
Apostolic ... APSTLC
Apostolic Anti-Communist Alliance [*Spain*] ... AAA
Apostolic Church ... AC
Apostolica Sedes [*Apostolic See*] [*Latin*] [*Reference to the papacy*] (BARN) ... Ap Sed
Apostolicam Actuositatem [*Decree on the Apostolate of the Laity*] [*Vatican II document*] ... AA
Apostrophe ... APOS
Apoteri [*Guyana*] [*ICAO location identifier*] (ICLI) ... SYAP
Apothecaries (SAUS) ... ap
apothecaries (SAUS) ... apoth
Apothecaries Company (SAUO) ... AC
Apothecaries' Ounce (WDAA) ... OZ AP
Apothecaries Ounce (SAUS) ... oz ap
Apothecaries Ounce (BARN) ... oz apoth
Apothecaries' Pound (BARN) ... lb ap
Apothecaries' Weight (BARN) ... ap wt
Apothecary (ADWA) ... ap
Apothecary (WGA) ... AP
Apothecary ... APOTH
Apovincaminic Acid [*Biochemistry*] ... AVA
Apoyeque [*Nicaragua*] [*Seismograph station code, US Geological Survey*] (SEIS) ... APY
Apoyos a Servicios a la Comercializaciãn Agropecuaria (SAUO) ... ASERCA
Appal Pwr,7.40% Pfd [*NYSE symbol*] (TTSB) ... AEWPrC
Appalachia Education Laboratory (SAUO) ... AEL
Appalachia Educational Laboratory [*Department of Education*] [*Charleston, WV*] ... AEL
Appalachia Science in the Public Interest [*An association*] ... ASPI
Appalachian (FAAC) ... APLCN
Appalachian Airport Safety Improvement Program (SAUS) ... AASIP
Appalachian Area [*MARC geographic area code*] [*Library of Congress*] (LCCP) ... n-usa-
Appalachian Bible Institute, Bradley, WV [*Library symbol*] [*Library of Congress*] (LCLS) ... WvBrA
Appalachian Center for Occupational Safety and Health (SAUO) ... ACOSH
Appalachian Community Service Network [*Cable-television system*] ... ACSN
Appalachian Consortium (EA) ... AC
Appalachian Cooperative Economics Network ... AceNET
Appalachian Development Highway System ... ADHS
Appalachian Educational Laboratory, Inc., Charleston, WV [*Library symbol*] [*Library of Congress*] (LCLS) ... WvCAE
Appalachian Electric Power Company (SAUO) ... AEPC
Appalachian Environmental Laboratory [*University of Maryland Center for Environmental and Estuarine Studies*] [*Research center*] (RCD) ... AEL
Appalachian Finance Association [*Later, Eastern Finance Association*] (EA) ... APFA
Appalachian Finance Association (SAUO) ... APFA
Appalachian Flying Service, Inc. [*ICAO designator*] (FAAC) ... APL
Appalachian Forum [*An association*] (EA) ... AF
Appalachian Geological Society (SAUO) ... AGS
Appalachian Geological Society. Bulletin (journ.) (SAUS) ... Appalachian Geol Soc Bull
Appalachian Hall Medical Library, Asheville, NC [*Library symbol*] [*Library of Congress*] (LCLS) ... NcAAH
Appalachian Hardwood Manufacturers (SAUO) ... AHM
Appalachian Hardwood Manufacturers, Inc. (EA) ... AHMI
Appalachian Helicopter Pilots Association (SAUO) ... AHPA
Appalachian Integrated Pest Management (SAUS) ... AIPM
Appalachian Laboratory for Occupational Respiratory Diseases ... ALFORD
Appalachian Laboratory for Occupational Safety and Health [*Department of Health and Human Services*] (GFGA) ... ALOSH
Appalachian Land Stabilization and Conservation Program ... ALSCP
Appalachian Mountain Club (EA) ... AMC

Appalachian Mountains	AM
Appalachian National Park Association (SAUO)	ANPA
Appalachian News Service (journ.) (SAUS)	Appl News
Appalachian Oil & Gas Company, Inc. (SAUS)	AOGI
Appalachian Oil & Gas Company, Incorporated (SAUO)	AOGI
Appalachian Power Co. [NYSE symbol] (SPSG)	AEW
Appalachian Power Co. [NYSE symbol] (SAG)	APJ
Appalachian Power Co. [Associated Press] (SAG)	ApPw
Appalachian Power Company (SAUO)	APC
Appalachian Regional Commission [Washington, DC]	ARC
Appalachian Regional Development Act of 1965	ARDA
Appalachian Regional Library, North Wilkesboro, NC [Library symbol] [Library of Congress] (LCLS)	NcNwA
Appalachian Resources Company (SAUO)	ARC
Appalachian Soil and Water Conservation Research Laboratory [Beckley, WV] [Department of Agriculture] (GRD)	ASWCRL
Appalachian State Teachers College [Later, ASU] [North Carolina]	ASTC
Appalachian State University (GAGS)	Appal St U
Appalachian State University [Boone, NC]	ASU
Appalachian State University, Boone, NC [Library symbol] [Library of Congress] (LCLS)	NcBoA
Appalachian State University, Boone, NC [OCLC symbol] (OCLC)	NJB
Appalachian Trail	AT
Appalachian Trail Conference (EA)	ATC
Appalachian Ultradeep Core Hole [Project of seismic profiling]	ADCOH
Appalachian Volunteers (SAUO)	AV
Appalachian Volunteers, Inc. (EA)	AVI
Appaloosa Color Breeders Association (EA)	ACBA
Appaloosa Horse Club (EA)	AHC
Appaloosa Horse Club (EA)	ApHC
Appaloosa Horse Club of Canada (AC)	ApHCC
Appaloosa Sport Horse Association (EA)	ApSHA
Apparate (SAUS)	Ap
Apparatus (MUGU)	APAR
Apparatus (KSC)	APP
Apparatus (WDAA)	app
Apparatus (AFM)	APPAR
Apparatus	APPRTS
Apparatus	APTUS
Apparatus (SAUS)	Aptus
Apparatus Carrier Telephone [British military] (DMA)	ACT
Apparatus Drawings Project (SAUS)	ADP
Apparatus for Pore Examination [Geophysics]	APEX
Apparatus Mounted in Plastic	AMPLAS
Apparatus Mounted in Plastic (SAUS)	AMPLAs
Apparatus Repair - Strategy Evaluation Guidelines [Telecommunications] (TEL)	AREG
Apparatus Slide-In Unit [Computer science] (NITA)	ASU
Apparel (SAUS)	App
Apparel	APPRL
Apparel Agents' Association of Queensland [Australia]	AAAQ
Apparel Agents' Association of Victoria [Australia]	AAAV
Apparel Agents' Association of Western Australia	AAAWA
Apparel and Fashion Industry's Association [British] (BI)	AFIA
Apparel Business Control [System] [Computer science]	ABC
Apparel Guild (EA)	AG
Apparel Importers' Association of Australia	AIAA
Apparel Industries Inter-Association Committee [Defunct] (EA)	AIIC
Apparel Industry Committee on Imports (EA)	AICI
Apparel Manufacturers Association (EA)	AMA
Apparel Manufacturing Executives Association (EA)	AMEA
Apparel Manufacturing Technology Center [Research center] (RCD)	AMTC
Apparel Performance Level Standards [Pronounced "apples"]	APLS
Apparel Research Foundation [Defunct]	ARF
Apparel World (journ.) (SAUS)	App World
Apparel-Computer Integrated Manufacturing Center [Research center] (RCD)	A-CIM
Apparent (ADA)	AP
Apparent (MELL)	app
Apparent	APPAR
Apparent (ADWA)	appar
Apparent (MSA)	APRNT
Apparent (SAUS)	Aprnt
Apparent Activation Energy	AAE
Apparent Body Orientation (PDAA)	ABO
Apparent Bulk Density	ABD
Apparent Candle Power	ACP
Apparent Consumption (SAUS)	APC
Apparent Depth of Compensation [Geology]	ADC
Apparent Digestible Energy [Nutrition]	ADE
Apparent Elastic Thickness [Geoscience]	AET
Apparent Fault (SAUS)	AF
Apparent Free Testosterone Concentration [Clinical chemistry]	AFTC
Apparent Half-Life (DMAA)	AHL
Apparent Impedance (SAUS)	AI
Apparent International (journ.) (SAUS)	Apparel Int
Apparent Life-Threatening Agent [Medicine] (DB)	ALTA
Apparent Life-Threatening Episode [Medicine]	ALTE
Apparent Metabolisable Energy	AME
Apparent Mineralocorticoid Excess [Medicine]	AME
Apparent Net Transfer Rate (MAE)	ANTR
Apparent Norepinephrine Secretion Rate [Medicine] (DMAA)	ANESR
Apparent Oxygen Utilization	AOU
Apparent Polar Wander [Paleomagnetism]	APW
Apparent Polar Wander Path [Paleomagnetism]	APWP

Apparent Power [Symbol] (DEN)	S
Apparent Sidereal Time (PDAA)	AST
Apparent Solar Time (PDAA)	AST
Apparent Time (ADA)	AT
Apparent Time (SAUS)	At
Apparent Time at Ship (DS)	ATS
Apparent Total Nitroso Compound [Organic chemistry]	ATNC
Apparent Volume of Distribution [Clinical chemistry]	AVD
Apparent Watt [Electricity] (IAA)	AW
Apparently	APP
Apparently (ADWA)	app
Apparently (BEE)	appar
Apparently, the term is a registered trademark licensed to L-Soft international, Inc. (SAUO)	LISTSERV
Appeal (ADA)	APP
Appeal	APPL
Appeal and Error [Legal term] (DLA)	A & E
Appeal and Error (SAUS)	A&E
Appeal and Marathon Republic, Albert City, IA [Library symbol] [Library of Congress] (LCLS)	IaAIcAM
Appeal Cases [Canada] [A publication] (DLA)	AC
Appeal Cases [A publication] (DLA)	App
Appeal Cases, District of Columbia [A publication] (DLA)	ADC
Appeal Cases, District of Columbia [1-74] [A publication] (DLA)	App Cas
Appeal Cases, District of Columbia [1-74] [A publication] (DLA)	App Cas (DC)
Appeal Cases, District of Columbia [A publication] (DLA)	App DC
Appeal Cases, English Law Reports [1875-90] [A publication] (DLA)	App Cas
Appeal Cases, English Law Reports, Second Series [A publication] (DLA)	App Cas 2d
Appeal Cases in the United States [A publication] (DLA)	App Cas
Appeal Cases (journ.) (SAUS)	App
Appeal Cases of the Different States [A publication] (DLA)	App Cas
Appeal Cases of the Different States (journ.) (SAUS)	App Cas
Appeal Court [Legal] [British] (ROG)	AC
Appeal Court (SAUO)	AC
Appeal Court Reports [Ceylon] [A publication] (DLA)	ACR
Appeal Court Reports, New Zealand [A publication] (DLA)	App Ct Rep
Appeal Court Reports, New Zealand (journ.) (SAUS)	App Ct Rep
Appeal Denied (DLA)	app den
Appeal Dismissed (DLA)	app dism
Appeal Dismissed (SAUS)	APP DISM
Appeal Examiner (SAUS)	App Exam
Appeal [or Appeals] Examiner (DLA)	App Exam
Appeal Examining Officer (SAUS)	AEO
Appeal of Conscience Foundation (EA)	ACF
Appeal, Plain Facts, Personalities, Local Angle, Action, Uniqueness (or Universality), Significance, Energy (SAUS)	APPLAUSE
Appeal Referee (DLA)	App Ref
Appeal Reports, New Zealand [A publication] (DLA)	App NZ
Appeal Reports, New Zealand [A publication] (DLA)	App RNZ
Appeal Reports, New Zealand, Second Series [A publication] (DLA)	App NZ 2d
Appeal Reports, Upper Canada [1846-66] [A publication] (DLA)	AR
Appeal Reports, Upper Canada (journ.) (SAUS)	AR
Appeal Tribunal (DLA)	App Trib
Appeal Tribunal (DLA)	AT
Appeals (AAGC)	App
Appeals and Long-Form Experiment (SAUS)	ALFE
Appeals Council [Social Security Administration] (OICC)	AC
Appeals Court Electronic Service (SAUO)	ACES
Appeals Examining Office [CSC]	AEO
Appeals from Fisheries Commission [1861-93] [Ireland] [A publication] (DLA)	App Fish Com
Appeals from Fisheries Commission (journ.) (SAUS)	App Fish Com
Appeals Notes [A publication] (DLA)	AN
Appeals Relating to Tax on Servants [1781] [England] [A publication] (DLA)	App Tax Serv
Appeals Review Board [Formerly, BAR] [Civil Service Commission]	ARB
Appear (FAAC)	APPR
Appearance [In urinalysis] [Biochemistry] (DAVI)	APEAR
Appearance (MSA)	APP
Appearance (ROG)	APPCE
Appearance Energy [Surface ionization]	AE
Appearance, Mood, Sensorium, Intelligence, and Thought Processes [Mental status examination] [Medicine] (DAVI)	AMSIT
Appearance Potential [Physics]	AP
Appearance Potential Spectroscopy [Physics]	APS
Appearance Station (SAA)	APS
Appeared (ROG)	APPD
Appeared (GEAB)	apprd
Appears (SAUS)	APP
Appelate Court (SAUO)	AC
Appelbo [Sweden] [Seismograph station code, US Geological Survey] (SEIS)	APP
Appellant [Legal shorthand] (LWAP)	APPANT
Appellant (WDAA)	APPL
Appellant (SAUS)	Appl
Appellants (SAUS)	Appts
Appellants (ROG)	APPTS
Appellate [Legal term] (DLA)	APP
Appellate (AAGC)	App
Appellate Court (DLA)	AC
Appellate Court (BARN)	App Ct
Appellate Court Administration Review (journ.) (SAUS)	App Court Ad Rev
Appellate Court Records and Data System (SAUO)	ACORDS
Appellate Court Reports [A publication] (AAGC)	Ill App Illinois

Appellate Department (DLA) ... App Dep't
Appellate Department of the Superior Court, California (ILCA) ... App Dept Super Ct
Appellate Division [*Legal term*] ... AD
Appellate Division (DLA) ... App Div
Appellate Division (SAUS) ... APP Div
Appellate Division Reports [*Massachusetts*] [*A publication*] (DLA) ... ADR
Appellate Jurisdiction Act of 1876 [*39, 40 Victoria, c. 59*] (DLA) ... App Jur Act 1876
Appellation d'Origine Controlle [*Official place name for wine*] ... AOC
Appellation d'Origine Vin de Qualite Superieure [*Trademark for Vintage Wine of Superior Quality*] ... AOVDQS
Appellee [*Legal shorthand*] (LWAP) ... APPLEE
Append [*or Appendix*] (AFM) ... APP
Append (SAUS) ... App
Appendage ... APPEN
Appendectomy [*Medicine*] ... AP
Appendectomy [*Medicine*] (AAMN) ... APPY
Appendectomy [*Medicine*] (DMAA) ... appy
Appended (SAUS) ... App
Appendiceal Carcinoids [*Medicine*] (MELL) ... AC
Appendices of Proceedings of the Scottish Land Court [*A publication*] (DLA) ... SL Co
Appendices of Proceedings of the Scottish Land Court [*A publication*] (DLA) ... SL Co R
Appendices on Provisional Nomenclature Symbols, Terminology and Conventions. International Union of Pute and Applied Chemistry (journ.) (SAUS) ... Append Provis Nomencl Symb Terminol Conv IUPAC
Appendices to the Report of the Scottish Land Court [*A publication*] (DLA) ... Sc La Rep Ap
Appendices to the Report of the Scottish Land Court [*A publication*] (DLA) ... Sc La Rep App
Appendicitis [*Medicine*] (DAVI) ... AP
Appendix [*Anatomy*] (DAVI) ... AP
Appendix (AAGC) ... App
Appendix (WDAA) ... app
Appendix (SAUS) ... APP
Appendix (DLA) ... Append
Appendix (KSC) ... APPX
Appendix [*Medicine*] (DMAA) ... appx
Appendix (ADWA) ... apx
Appendix (WGA) ... APX
Appendix to 11 Peters, United States Reports [*A publication*] (DLA) ... Bald App
Appendix to Breese's Reports [*Illinois*] [*A publication*] (DLA) ... Ap Bre
Appendix to Breese's Reports [*Illinois*] [*A publication*] (DLA) ... Appx Bre
Appendix to Tidd's Practice [*A publication*] (DLA) ... Tidd App
Appendix to Tidds Practice (journ.) (SAUS) ... Tidd App
Appendix to Volume 10 of Hare's Vice-Chancellor's Reports [*England*] [*A publication*] (DLA) ... Ha App
Appendixes (DLA) ... apps
Appendixes (SAUS) ... Apps
Appenweiler [*Germany*] [*ICAO location identifier*] (ICLI) ... EDZU
Apperception (SAUS) ... App
Appetite (SAUS) ... App
Appetizer (SAUS) ... App
Appian [*Second century AD*] [*Classical studies*] (OCD) ... App
Appian Technology Inc. (SAUO) ... APPN
Appied Graphics Technologies, Inc. [*Associated Press*] (SAG) ... AppGrph
APPITA. Journal of the Australian and New Zealand Pulp and Paper Industry Technical Association (journ.) (SAUS) ... APPITA
Applanation [*Ophthalmology*] ... APPLAN
Applanation tonometry (SAUS) ... A
Applanation tonometry (SAUS) ... Ap
Applanation Tonometry [*Ophthalmology*] ... AT
Applantus [*Flattened*] [*Latin*] (MAE) ... applan
Apple [*Philately*] ... ap
Apple and Pear Development Council (SAUO) ... APDC
Apple and Pear Disease Workers (EA) ... APDW
Apple and Pear Growers Association (SAUO) ... APGA
Apple and Pear Growers' Association of South Australia ... APGASA
Apple Assistance Center (SAUO) ... AAC
Apple Attachment Unit Interface (SAUS) ... AAUI
Apple AUI [*Attachment Unit Interface*] (CDE) ... AAUI
Apple Bulletin Board System [*Pronounced "abbies"*] ... ABBS
Apple Business Systems (VERA) ... ABS
Apple Chlorotic Leafspot Virus [*Plant pathology*] ... ACLV
Apple Classroom of Tomorrow ... ACOT
Apple Classrooms of Tomorrow (SAUS) ... ACOT
Apple Communications Framework (VERA) ... ACF
Apple Communications Protocol Card (VERA) ... ACPC
Apple Computer [*NASDAQ symbol*] (TTSB) ... AAPL
Apple Computer, Inc. [*NASDAQ symbol*] (NQ) ... AAPL
Apple Computer Inc. (SAUS) ... AAPL
Apple Computer, Inc. [*Associated Press*] (SAG) ... AppleC
Apple Computer Incorporated (SAUO) ... AAPL
Apple Desktop Bus [*Computer science*] ... ADB
Apple Desktop Bus Microcontroller [*Computer processor*] ... ADBM
Apple Developer Association (SAUS) ... APDA
Apple Distribution Center (VERA) ... ADC
Apple Document Mangagement And Conrol System (SAUS) ... ADMACS
Apple Event Interprocess Messaging Protocol (VERA) ... AEIMP
Apple Event Terminology Extension (VERA) ... AETE
Apple Event User Terminology (VERA) ... AEUT
Apple Events (VERA) ... AE
Apple Events Object Model (VERA) ... AEOM
Apple File Exchange [*Computer science*] ... AFE
Apple File Protocol (SAUS) ... AFP
Apple Growers Association (SAUO) ... AGA
Apple II Digital Image Processing System (SAUS) ... A/DIPS
Apple Image Processing Educator (SAUS) ... AIPE
Apple [*Computer*] **Infected Disk Syndrome** (NHD) ... AIDS
Apple, Intel, Motorola (SAUS) ... AIM
Apple Interactive Media Toolkit (SAUS) ... AIMT
Apple Internet Mail Server (VERA) ... AIMS
Apple Leafspot Virus (SAUS) ... ALV
Apple Library for Object Embedding (SAUS) ... ALOE
Apple Macintosh computer (SAUS) ... Mac
Apple Macintosh Computer (SAUS) ... MAC
Apple Management Association (EA) ... AMA
Apple Media Tool (VERA) ... AMT
Apple Media Tool Programming Environment (VERA) ... AMTPE
Apple Memory-mapped I/O Controller (SAUS) ... AMIC
Apple Mosaic Virus (SAUS) ... APMV
Apple Mosaic Virus ... ApMV
Apple Network Managers Association (VERA) ... ANMA
Apple Octopus Fan Club (EA) ... AOFC
Apple Octopus Now [*An association*] (EA) ... AOFC
Apple Open Collaboration Environment [*Computer science*] (PCM) ... AOCE
Apple Orthodontix'A' [*AMEX symbol*] (SG) ... AOI
Apple Peel Syndrome [*Medicine*] (MELL) ... APS
Apple Preferred Format [*Computer science*] ... APF
Apple Print Recognizer [*Handwriting recognition system*] (IDAI) ... APR
Apple Processors Association (EA) ... APA
Apple Programmers and Developers Association (DOM) ... APDA
Apple QuickTime [*Computer science*] ... mov
Apple Real Time Architecture (SAUS) ... ARTA
Apple Remote Access [*Apple Computer, Inc.*] (PCM) ... ARA
Apple Ring Spot Virus (SAUS) ... ARSV
Apple Scar Skin Viroid [*Plant pathology*] ... ASSVd
Apple Session Protocol (SAUS) ... ASP
Apple Shared Library Manager [*Computer science*] ... ASLM
Apple Sound Chip [*Apple Computer, Inc.*] (BYTE) ... ASC
Apple South [*NASDAQ symbol*] (SPSG) ... APSO
Apple South, Inc. [*Associated Press*] (SAG) ... ApplSou
Apple Stem Grooving Virus [*Plant pathology*] ... ASGV
Apple Stem Groving Virus (SAUS) ... SGV
Apple Talk Filing Protocol (SAUS) ... AFP
Apple Talk Remote Access (SAUS) ... ARA
Apple Terminal Services (VERA) ... ATS
Apple Text Services for Unicode Imaging (SAUS) ... ATSUI
Apple Transaction Protocol (SAUS) ... ATP
Apple University Consortium ... AUC
Apple UNIX [*Computer science*] (ACRL) ... AUX
Apple User Group Europe (VERA) ... AUGE
Apple Valley [*California*] [*Airport symbol*] [*Obsolete*] (OAG) ... APV
Apple Valley, CA [*AM radio station call letters*] (RBYB) ... KIXW
Apple Valley, CA [*AM radio station call letters*] (RBYB) ... KWRN
Apple Valley, CA [*FM radio station call letters*] ... KZXY-FM
Apple Workgroup Server (VERA) ... AWS
Apple-Based Bulletin Board Service [*Computer science*] (CIST) ... ABBS
Applebee's International, Inc. [*NASDAQ symbol*] (NQ) ... APPB
Applebees International, Inc. (SAUS) ... APPB
Applebee's International, Inc. [*Associated Press*] (SAG) ... Applebee
Applebee's Intl. [*NASDAQ symbol*] (TTSB) ... APPB
Appleby College, Oakville, ON, Canada [*Library symbol*] [*Library of Congress*] (LCLS) ... CaOOakA
Appleby College, Oakville, Ontario [*Library symbol*] [*National Library of Canada*] (NLC) ... OOAKA
Appled (SAUS) ... APPL
Apple/IBM/Motorola (CDE) ... AIM
Applejack ... AJ
Applejack and Benedictine (SAUS) ... A&B
Apples [*Phonetic alphabet*] [*Royal Navy*] [*World War I*] (DSUE) ... A
Apple's Kin [*An association*] [*Defunct*] (EA) ... AK
Apples Unix-Variante (SAUS) ... A/UX
Applesauce, Bananas, Cereal [*Diet*] (MEDA) ... ABC
Appletalk Address Resolution Protocol [*Computer science*] (VERA) ... AARP
AppleTalk Control Protocol (VERA) ... ATCP
AppleTalk Data Stream Protocol [*Apple Computer, Inc.*] (PCM) ... ADSP
Appletalk Data Stream Protocol (SAUS) ... ADSP
AppleTalk Echo Protocol [*Apple Computer, Inc.*] (PCM) ... AEP
AppleTalk File Protocol (SAUS) ... AFP
AppleTalk Filing Protocol [*Apple Computer, Inc.*] (BYTE) ... AFP
AppleTalk Link Access Protocol [*Apple Computer, Inc.*] (BYTE) ... ALAP
Appletalk Local Talk Link Access Protocol (SAUS) ... ALAP
AppleTalk Phase 2 (VERA) ... ATP2
AppleTalk Print Service [*Apple Computer, Inc.*] (PCM) ... ATPS
Appletalk Remote Access [*Apple Computer Inc.*] ... ARA
Appletalk Remote Access Protocol [*Apple Computer Inc.*] ... ARAP
Appletalk Remote Network Server (VERA) ... ARNS
AppleTalk Session Protocol [*Apple Computer, Inc.*] (BYTE) ... ASP
AppleTalk Transaction Protocol [*Apple Computer, Inc.*] ... ATP
Appletalk Transaction Protocol (SAUS) ... ATP
AppleTalk Update Routing Protocol [*Apple Computer, Inc.*] (CIST) ... AURP
Apple-Talk Update-Based Routing Protocol [*Computer science*] ... AURP
Appleton [*Wisconsin*] [*Airport symbol*] (OAG) ... ATW
Appleton Elementary School, Grand Junction, CO [*Library symbol*] [*Library of Congress*] (LCLS) ... CoGjAE
Appleton Memorial Hospital, Appleton, WI [*Library symbol*] [*Library of Congress*] (LCLS) ... WAM

Appleton, MN [*FM radio station call letters*] (RBYB)	KNCM-FM
Appleton, MN [*FM radio station call letters*]	KRSU
Appleton, MN [*Television station call letters*]	KWCM
Appleton Municipal Hospital, Appleton, MN [*Library symbol*] [*Library of Congress*] (LCLS)	MnApH
Appleton, OH [*Location identifier*] [*FAA*] (FAAL)	APE
Appleton Post Crescent, Appleton, WI [*Library symbol*] [*Library of Congress*] (LCLS)	WAPC
Appleton Public Library (SAUS)	WA
Appleton Public Library, Appleton, MN [*Library symbol*] [*Library of Congress*] (LCLS)	MnAp
Appleton Public Library, Appleton, WI [*Library symbol*] [*Library of Congress*] (LCLS)	WA
Appleton Public Library, Appleton, WI [*Library symbol*] [*Library of Congress*] (LCLS)	WAPL
Appleton Public Library, Appleton, WI [*OCLC symbol*] (OCLC)	WIQ
Appleton Public Schools, Appleton, MN [*Library symbol*] [*Library of Congress*] (LCLS)	MnApPS
Appleton, WI [*Location identifier*] [*FAA*] (FAAL)	FXV
Appleton, WI [*Television station call letters*] (RBYB)	WACY
Appleton, WI [*FM radio station call letters*]	WAPL
Appleton, WI [*FM radio station call letters*] (RBYB)	WEMI
Appleton, WI [*FM radio station call letters*]	WLFM
Appleton, WI [*AM radio station call letters*]	WRJQ
Appleton-Century-Crofts [*Publisher*]	ACC
Appleton-Century-Crofts (SAUS)	A-C-C
Appleton-Century-Crofts Medical (SAUS)	ACCM P-H
Appleton's Reports [*19, 20 Maine*]	App
Appleton's Reports [*19, 20 Maine*] [*A publication*] (DLA)	Appleton
Appletons Rules of Evidence [*A publication*] (DLA)	App Ev
Appletons Rules of Evidence(journ.) (SAUS)	App Ev
Appletree Companies [*Associated Press*] (SAG)	Appltree
Appletree Companies [*NASDAQ symbol*] (SAG)	ATRE
Applewoods, Inc. [*Associated Press*] (SAG)	Aplewds
Applewoods, Inc. [*NASDAQ symbol*] (SAG)	APWD
Appliance	APPL
Appliance (SAUS)	Appl
Appliance	APPLNC
Appliance Computer (SAUS)	AC
Appliance Leakage Current Interrupter (BARN)	ALCI
Appliance Manufacturer (journ.) (SAUS)	Appliance Manuf
Appliance Manufacturer (journ.) (SAUS)	Appl Mfr
Appliance Parts Distributors Association (EA)	APDA
Appliance Parts Jobbers Association [*Later, APDA*]	APJA
Appliance, Range, Adjust [*Computer science*]	ARGA
Appliance Recycling Centers of America [*Associated Press*] (SAG)	AplRecy
Appliance Recycling Centers of America (PS)	ARCA
Appliance Recycling Centers of America [*NASDAQ symbol*] (SAG)	ARCI
Appliance Recycling Ctrs Amer [*NASDAQ symbol*] (TTSB)	ABCI
Appliance Testing Laboratories (SAUO)	ATL
Appliance Wiring Material	AWM
Appliances (ADWA)	appl
Appliances [*Classified advertising*]	APPL
Applicability Code	APCOD
Applicable (AFM)	APPL
Applicable (SAUS)	Appl
Applicable Approved Accounting Standard	AAAS
Applicable Document Contractual Record [*Military*]	ADCR
Applicable Federal Rate (SAUS)	AFR
Applicable High-Yield Discount Obligation [*Finance*]	AHYDO
Applicable or Relevant and Appropriate Requirement [*Environmental science*]	ARAR
Applicable or Relevant and Appropriate Requirements [*Environmental science*] (COE)	ARARS
Applicable, Revelant, or Appropriate Requirements (ADWA)	ARARs
Applicandus [*To Be Applied*] [*Pharmacy*]	APPLICAND
Applicant [*or Application*] (DNAB)	APPL
Applicant Data System [*Department of Labor*]	ADS
Applicant File Search [*US Employment Service*] [*Department of Labor*]	AFS
Applicant Holding Office [*Employment*]	AHO
Applicant Information Service [*Institute of International Education*] (AEBS)	AIS
Applicant Master File [*State Employee Security Agency*] (OICC)	AMF
Applicant Outreach Program [*Department of Labor*]	AOP
Applicant Qualification Test [*Navy*]	AQT
Applicant Tracking System [*Human resources*] (WYGK)	ATS
Application [*Computer science*]	app
Application	APP
Application (EBF)	appin
Application	APPLCTN
Application	APPLN
Application	APPLON
Application and Industry (SAUS)	AI
Application and Resource Control (SAUS)	A&RC
Application and Resource Control (NASA)	A & RC
Application Association (SAUO)	AA
Application Based Network Services (SAUO)	ABNS
Application Binary Interface [*Computer science*] (BYTE)	ABI
Application Block (MSA)	AB
Application Builder Class [*Computer science*]	ABC
Application Builder Editor [*Computer science*]	ABE
Application Channel Interface (TEL)	ACHI
Application Code (CDE)	app code
Application Configuration Access Protocol (SAUS)	ACAP
Application Configurator	APCO
Application Connectivity Link (SAUS)	ACL
Application Context (SAUS)	AC
Application Control [*or Controller*] [*Computer science*] (NASA)	AC
Application Control (SAUS)	APCTL
Application Control and Teleprocessing System (MHDI)	ACTS
Application Control Architecture [*Computer science*]	ACA
Application Control Architecture Service [*Computer science*]	ACAS
Application Control Block [*Computer science*] (NITA)	ACB
Application Control Block Generation [*Computer science*] (MHDI)	ACBGEN
Application Control Center	ACC
Application Control Code (SAUS)	ACC
Application Control Language [*Computer science*] (BUR)	ACL
Application Control Language [*Computer science*] (MHDI)	ACOL
Application Control Management System (MCD)	ACMS
Application Control Operating System [*Computer science*] (CIST)	ACOS
Application Control Service Element (ACII)	ACSE
Application Control Service Element (ACII)	ASCE
Application Control Structure (SAUS)	ACS
Application Controller (SAUS)	AC
Application Creation Made Easy [*Watcom International Corp.*] [*Computer science*] (PCM)	ACME
Application Data Interchange [*Telecommunications*] (OSI)	ADI
Application Data Management (IAA)	ADM
Application Data Management Services (MCD)	ADMS
Application Data Material Readiness List [*DoD*]	ADMRL
Application Data Type [*Computer science*] (VERA)	ADT
Application Date [*Bell System*] (TEL)	APP
Application Dedicated Terminal [*Computer science*] (IAA)	ADT
Application Definition File (SAUS)	ADF
Application Description Manual (SAUS)	ADM
Application Design Service [*IBM Corp.*]	ADS
Application Development Classes (SAUS)	ADC
Application Development Facility [*IBM Corp.*] [*Computer science*]	ADF
Application Development Interface Guidelines (AAEL)	ADIG
Application Development Solutions (SAUS)	ADS
Application Development System/Online [*Computer science*] (HGAA)	ADS/O
Application Development Systems [*Computer science*]	ADS
Application Development Task Group [*Navy*]	ADTG
Application Development Tools [*Computer science*] (VERA)	ADT
Application Development Workbench [*Sterling Software, Atlanta, GA*] (CDE)	ADW
Application Development/Cycle [*Computer science*]	AD/Cycle
Application Documentation (SAUS)	AD
Application Enabling Interface [*IBM Corp*] (VERA)	AEI
Application Engineering	AE
Application Engineering [*Computer science*] (VERA)	APE
Application Entity (SAUS)	AE
Application Environment (SAUS)	AE
Application Environment Specification (SAUS)	AES
Application Evaluation Matrix (SAUS)	AEM
Application Execution (SAUS)	AE
Application Execution Environment [*Computer science*] (VERA)	AXE
Application Executive [*Software interface for Integrated Modular Avionics*] [*Computer science*]	APEX
Application Explorer Bus (SAUS)	AE BUS
Application Explorer Mission [*NASA*]	AEM
Application Fit Analysis	AFA
Application for Certiorari Denied [*Legal term*] (DLA)	CD
Application for Federal Assistance (OICC)	AFA
Application for Federal Assistance and Assurances (OICC)	AFAA
Application for Federal Student Aid (GFGA)	AFSA
Application for Mandamus Granted in Part [*Legal term*] (DLA)	MGP
Application for New Stock Item	ANSI
Application for Passport for Self and/or Dependents Accordance BUPERS Manual [*Navy*]	PLYPASSPORT
Application for Review Decisions [*A publication*] (DLA)	ARD
Application for State School Aid	ASSA
Application for Writ of Error Dismissed by Agreement of Parties [*Legal term*] (DLA)	DAP
Application for Writ of Error Dismissed for Want of Jurisdiction [*Legal term*] (DLA)	D
Application for Writ of Error Dismissed, Judgment Correct [*Legal term*] (DLA)	DJC
Application for Writ of Error Granted [*Legal term*] (DLA)	G
Application for Writ of Mandamus Dismissed for Want of Jurisdiction [*Legal term*] (DLA)	MD
Application for Writ of Mandamus Refused [*Legal term*] (DLA)	MR
Application for Writ of Mandamus Refused in Part [*Legal term*] (DLA)	MRP
Application Foundation Classes [*Microsoft Corp.*] [*Computer science*]	AFC
Application Framework Definition (AAEL)	AFD
Application Frameworx [*Microsoft Corp.*]	AFX
Application Function Routine (SAUS)	AFR
Application Functions Module [*Computer science*]	AFM
Application Identification (ADWA)	APID
Application Information System (SAUS)	AIS
Application Integrated Architecture (SAUS)	AIA
Application Integrated Module (SAUS)	AIM
Application Integration Architecture [*Computer science*] (VERA)	AIA
Application Integration Module [*Telecommunications*] (TSSD)	AIM
Application Integration Services (SAUS)	AIS
Application Interface Engine [*Computer science*]	AIE
Application Kit (SAUS)	AK
Application Language Interface Conversion and Extension (SAUS)	ALICE
Application Language Liberator (MCD)	ALL
Application Launching and Embedding [*Computer science*]	ALE
Application Layer (SAUS)	AL

Application Layer Structure [*Telecommunications*] (OSI) ... ALS
Application Library File [*Computer science*] ... ALF
Application Limiting Constituent [*Environmental science*] (COE) ... ALC
Application Link Enabling [*Computer science*] (VERA) ... ALE
Application Load List (SAUS) ... ALL
Application Loadable Module (SAUS) ... ALM
Application Logic Element (AAEL) ... ALE
Application Macro Language (PCM) ... AML
Application Macro Library (SAUS) ... AML
Application Management Services (SAUS) ... AMS
Application Management System (SAUS) ... AMS
Application Mapping Service (SAUS) ... AMS
Application Message Handler (SAUS) ... AMH
Application Module Library [*IBM Corp.*] ... AML
Application Module Processing Routine (SAUS) ... AMPR
Application of Autonomous Passive Classification (MCD) ... AAPC
Application of Chemical Engineering to the Treatment of Sewage and Industrial Liquid Effluents. Symposium (journ.) (SAUS) ... Appl Chem Eng Treat Sewage Ind Liq Effluents Symp
Application of Computers to Manufacturing Engineering ... ACME
Application of Filters to Demand Forecasting (MCD) ... APOFDF
Application of Herbicides in Oil Crops Plantings (journ.) (SAUS) ... Appl Herbic Oil Crops Plant
Application of High Magnetic Fields in Semiconductor Physics. Lectures Presented at the International Conference (journ.) (SAUS) ... Appl High Mag Fields Semicond Phys Lect Int Conf
Application of Integrated Modules (SAUS) ... AIM
Application of Isotope Techniques in Hydrology and Hydraulics (journ.) (SAUS) ... Appl Isol Tech Hydrol Hydraul
Application of Modern Technology to International Development (SAUO) ... AMTID
Application of Neutral Networks for Industry in Europe (SAUO) ... ANNIE
Application of Radar Ballistic Ammunition Testing (ACAE) ... ARBAT
Application of RADAR to Ballistic Acceptance Testing [*of ammunition*] (MCD) ... ARBAT
Application of Radar to Ballistic Acceptance Testing (SAUS) ... ARBAT
Application of Remote Manipulators in Space [*Robot*] [*NASA*] ... ARMS
Application of Science and Technology to Rural Areas [*An association*] ... ASTRA
Application of Solar Energy. Proceedings of the Southeastern Conference on Application of Solar Energy (journ.) (SAUS) ... Appl Sol Energ Proc Southeast Conf
Application of Space Techniques Relating to Aviation [*International Civil Aviation Organization*] ... ASTRA
Application of Space Techniques Relating to Aviation Panel (SAUO) ... ASTRAP
Application Operating Environment [*AT&T*] (VERA) ... AOE
Application Operating Environment (SAUS) ... AOE
Application Oriented Language [*Computer science*] (BUR) ... AOL
Application Package for Chemical Engineers (SAUS) ... APACHE
Application Performance Test System [*Computer science*] ... APTS
Application Portability Profile (SAUS) ... APP
Application Process [*Telecommunications*] (OSI) ... AP
Application Process Invocation [*Telecommunications*] (OSI) ... API
Application Process [*or Program*] **(Structure)** [*Telecommunications*] (TEL) ... AP(S)
Application Process Subsystem [*Telecommunications*] (TEL) ... APS
Application Processor (SAUS) ... AP
Application Program [*Computer science*] (BUR) ... AP
Application Program Evaluator Tool [*Computer science*] (MHDB) ... APET
Application Program Generating and Executive System (SAUS) ... APGES
Application Program Generator [*Computer science*] ... APG
Application Program Interface [*Telecommunications*] (OSI) ... API
Application Program Interface Association (BTTJ) ... APIA
Application Program Preparation Utility (MHDI) ... APPU
Application Program Title (SAUS) ... APT
Application Program to Program Converter [*IBM Corp*] (VERA) ... APPC
Application Program to Transaction Manager [*Computer science*] (VERA) ... APTM
Application Program Unit (SAUS) ... APU
Application Programm Library (SAUS) ... APL
Application Programmer Interface (SAUS) ... API
Application Programmers Reference Manual (SAUS) ... APRM
Application Programmers Toolkit (SAUS) ... APT
Application Programming Interface [*Telecommunications*] (ACRL) ... API
Application Protocol (SAUS) ... APC
Application Protocol Data Unit [*Telecommunications*] (OSI) ... APDU
Application Quality Assurance [*Automotive engineering*] [*3M Co.*] ... AQA
Application Reference Manual (IAA) ... ARM
Application Replacement Factor ... ARF
Application Requirements Document (SAUS) ... ARD
Application Resource Unit (SAUS) ... ARU
Application Review (IAA) ... AR
Application Routine (SAUS) ... AR
Application Service Element [*Telecommunications*] (OSI) ... ASE
Application Service Provider (SAUS) ... APS
Application Service Provider ... ASP
Application Software Incorporated (SAUO) ... ASI
Application Software Module (MCD) ... ASM
Application Specific Coding Flag (NTCM) ... ASCF
Application Specific Digital Signal Processor (SAUS) ... ASDSP
Application Specific Execution Unit (SAUS) ... AXU
Application Specific Instruction (SAUS) ... ASI
Application Specific Integrated System (SAUS) ... ASIS
Application Specific Memory (SAUS) ... ASM
Application Specific Microwave Integrated Circuit (ACAE) ... ASMMIC
Application Specific semiconductor Chip (SAUS) ... ASIC
Application Specific Standard Part (CDE) ... ASSP
Application Specific Standard Product (AAEL) ... ASSP
Application Support Environment [*Computer science*] (CIST) ... ASE
Application Support System (IAA) ... APPS
Application Swapping Extensions [*Computer science*] (PCM) ... ASE
Application System (ADA) ... AS
Application System Generator ... ASG
Application System/400 [*IBM minicomputer series*] (CDE) ... AS/400
Application Systems Developer [*Army*] ... ASD
Application Technology Satellite (SAUS) ... ATS
Application Terminal Unit [*Telecommunications*] (TEL) ... ATU
Application Transaction Language (SAUS) ... ATL
Application Transaction Program (ACRL) ... ATP
Application Transaction Protocol (SAUS) ... ATP
Application Transfer Study [*IBM problem solving process*] ... ATS
Application Transfer Teams [*IBM Corp.*] ... ATT
Application Under Test (SAUS) ... AUT
Application Visualization System [*Computer science*] (BTTJ) ... AVS
Application Whatnot (SAUS) ... AW
Application-Adaptable Database System (SAUS) ... APAD System
Application/Adjunct Processor (SAUS) ... AP
Application-by-Forms (HGAA) ... ABF
Application-Entity [*Telecommunications*] (OSI) ... AE
Application-Entity Invocation [*Telecommunications*] (OSI) ... AEI
Applications (SAUS) ... Aplns
Applications (SAUS) ... Apps
Applications Access Point (VERA) ... AAP
Applications Analysis Report (EEVL) ... AAR
Applications and Industry (MCD) ... AI
Applications Configuration Management Board [*NASA*] (NASA) ... ACMB
Applications Data Base (SAUS) ... ADB
Applications Database [*Environmental Protection Agency*] (GFGA) ... ADB
Applications Development Environment [*Computer science*] ... ADE
Applications Development Language [*Computer science*] (CIST) ... ADL
Applications Developmental Data System (SAUS) ... ADDS
Applications Environment System ... AES
Applications Experience ... AEXP
Applications Explorer [*NASA*] ... AE
Applications Explorer Mission (SAUO) ... AEM
Applications for Certification (SAUS) ... CERTAPPL
Applications in Design Automation Committee (SAUS) ... ADAC
Applications In Mathematics for High Schools ... AIM-HI
Applications Information Processing System (MCD) ... AIPS
Applications Integration Architecture (SAUS) ... AIA
Applications Interface (IUSS) ... AIF
Applications Interface Device (SAUS) ... AID
Applications Interface Message Set ... AIMS
Applications Management [*Computer science*] ... AM
Applications Management System [*Computer application*] (PCM) ... AMS
Applications Network Software (IUSS) ... ANS
Applications Notice (SAUS) ... AN
Applications of Broadband Communication (SAUO) ... ABC
Applications of Commercial Oxygen to Water and Wastewater Systems (journ.) (SAUS) ... Appl Commer Oxygen Water Wastewater Syst
Applications of Cost-Saving Concepts through Equipment and System Salvage (SAUS) ... ACCESS
Applications of Cryogenic Technology (journ.) (SAUS) ... Appl Cryog Technol
Applications of Electronic Structure Theory (journ.) (SAUS) ... Appl Electron Struct Theory
Applications of Meteorology Programme (SAUS) ... AMP
Applications of Moessbauer Spectroscopy (journ.) (SAUS) ... Appl Moessbauer Spectrosc
Applications of Space Technology Panel to Requirements of Civil Aviation [*ICAO*] (DA) ... ASTRA
Applications of Surface Science (journ.) (SAUS) ... Appl Surf Sci
Applications of the Newer Techniques of Analysis (journ.) (SAUS) ... Appl Newer Tech Anal
Applications Portability Profile [*Computer science*] (BARN) ... APP
Applications Process Identification (NAKS) ... APID
Applications Processor (IEEE) ... AP
Applications Program Environment (SAUS) ... API
Applications Program Integration Board [*NASA*] ... APIB
Applications Programming Language (SAUS) ... APL
Applications Reference Index (SAUS) ... ARI
Applications Research and Defense Fund (DNAB) ... ARDF
Applications Research Corp. ... ARC
Applications Server [*Computer science*] ... APPS
Applications Software [*Computer science*] ... ASW
Applications Software Kit (SAUS) ... ASK
Applications System Verification and Transfer (SAUS) ... ASVT
Applications Systems Verification and Transfer (MCD) ... ASVT
Applications Systems Verification Test [*NASA*] ... ASVT
Applications Technology Satellite [*Communications satellite*] [*NASA*] ... ATS
Applications Technology Satellite Operations Control Center [*NASA*] ... ATSOCC
Applications Terminal Language [*Computer science*] (MHDB) ... ATL
Applications Vertical Test Program [*Communication Satellite program*] ... AVT
Application-Specific Image Processor [*Computer science*] (CIST) ... ASIP
Application-Specific Integrated Circuit [*Electronics*] ... ASIC
Application-Specific Power Conditioning (CIST) ... ASPC
Application-Specific-Integrated Chip (ADWA) ... ASTC
Applicative Language Idealized Computing Engine [*Imperial College*] [*British*] ... ALICE
Applicator ... APPLCTR
Applicatur [*Let It Be Applied*] [*Pharmacy*] (ROG) ... APPLIC

Applicatur [*Let It Be Applied*] [*Pharmacy*] ... APPLICAT
Applicon Graphic-System (SAUS) ... AGS
Applied (MSA) ... APLD
Applied ... APP
Applied (WDAA) ... app
Applied (VRA) ... appl
Applied ... APPL
Applied ... APPLD
Applied Acoustics (journ.) (SAUS) ... Appl Acoust
Applied Agricultural Research Inc. (SAUO) ... AAR
Applied Agricultural Research, Inc. [*Research center*] (RCD) ... AAR
Applied Agricultural Research (journ.) (SAUS) ... Appl Agric Res
Applied Analysis Spectral Analytical Process (SAUS) ... AASAP
Applied Analytical Industries [*NASDAQ symbol*] (SG) ... AAII
Applied Analytical Industries, Inc. [*NASDAQ symbol*] (SAG) ... AAII
Applied Analytical Industries, Inc. [*Associated Press*] (SAG) ... AppAnl
Applied and Environmental Microbiology (SAUS) ... AEM
Applied and Fundamental Aspects of Plant Cell Tissue and Organ Culture (journ.) (SAUS) ... Appl Fundam Aspects Plant Cell Tissue Organ Cult
Applied and Theorotical Electrophoresis (journ.) (SAUS) ... Appl Theor Electrophor
Applied Animal Behaviour Science (journ.) (SAUS) ... Appl Anim Behav Sci
Applied Anthropology (journ.) (SAUS) ... Appl Antbrop
Applied Ballistics Department (SAUO) ... ABD
Applied Behavior Analysis [*Psychology*] ... ABA
Applied Behaviour Analysis (SAUS) ... ABA
Applied Biochemistry and Bioengineering (journ.) (SAUS) ... Appl Biochem Bioeng
Applied Biochemistry and Biotechnology (SAUS) ... ABAB
Applied Biological Science (SAUS) ... Appl Biol Sci
Applied Biometrics [*NASDAQ symbol*] (TTSB) ... ABIO
Applied Biometrics, Inc. [*NASDAQ symbol*] (NQ) ... ABIO
Applied Biometrics, Inc. [*Associated Press*] (SAG) ... ApBiomet
Applied Bioscience [*NASDAQ symbol*] (TTSB) ... APBI
Applied Bioscience International [*Associated Press*] (SAG) ... ABiosci
Applied Bioscience International, Inc. [*NASDAQ symbol*] (NQ) ... APBI
Applied Biosystems, Inc. ... AB
Applied Biosystems Inc. (SAUO) ... AB
Applied Biosystems, Inc. (HGEN) ... ABI
Applied Biosystems, Inc. (EFIS) ... ABIO
Applied Biotreatment Association (SAUO) ... ABTA
Applied Business Technology Corp. ... ABT
Applied Business Telecommunications [*San Ramon, CA*] [*Information service or system*] [*Telecommunications*] (TSSD) ... ABC
Applied Carbon Technology [*NASDAQ symbol*] (TTSB) ... ACTYF
Applied Cardiology (journ.) (SAUS) ... Appl Cardiol
Applied Catalysis (journ.) (SAUS) ... APC
Applied Catalysis (journ.) (SAUS) ... Appl Catal
Applied Cellular Technology [*NASDAQ symbol*] (SAG) ... ACTC
Applied Cellular Technology [*Associated Press*] (SAG) ... AplCell
Applied Chemistry (SAUS) ... App Chem
Applied Chemistry at Protein Interfaces. Symposium (journ.) (SAUS) ... Appl Chem Protein Interfaces Symp
Applied Circuit Technology (SAUS) ... ACRT
Applied Climate Research Unit (SAUS) ... ACRU
Applied Color Systems, Inc. (SAUS) ... ACS
Applied Color Systems Inc. (SAUO) ... ACS
Applied Combinatorial Analysis (SAUS) ... ACA
Applied Communication Research, Inc. [*Information service or system*] (IID) ... ACR
Applied Communications Research Inc. (SAUO) ... ACR
Applied Communications Research, Inc. (SAUS) ... ACR
Applied Communications Systems Center [*AT & T*] ... ACSC
Applied Computational Electromagnetics Society ... ACES
Applied Computer Research [*Information service or system*] (IID) ... ACR
Applied Computer Research Institute [*La Trobe University*] [*Australia*] ... ACRI
Applied Computer Science (IAA) ... ACS
Applied Computer Sciences (SAUS) ... ACS
Applied Computer Solution ... ACS
Applied Computer Tech [*NASDAQ symbol*] (TTSB) ... ACTI
Applied Computer Tech Wrrt [*NASDAQ symbol*] (TTSB) ... ACTIW
Applied Computer Techniques (TEL) ... ACT
Applied Computer Techniques Limited (SAUS) ... ACT
Applied Computer Technology, Inc. [*NASDAQ symbol*] (SAG) ... ACTI
Applied Computer Technology, Inc. [*Associated Press*] (SAG) ... ApdCmp
Applied Computer Technology, Inc. [*Associated Press*] (SAG) ... ApdCptr
Applied Computerized Telephony (SAUS) ... ACT
Applied Cost for Work Performed (SSD) ... ACWP
Applied Data Communication [*Computer science*] (IAA) ... ADC
Applied Data Communications Inc. (SAUO) ... ADCC
Applied Data Research [*Commercial firm*] (NITA) ... ADR
Applied Data Research, Inc. [*Princeton, NJ*] (TSSD) ... ADR
Applied Decision Analysis ... ADA
Applied Decision Systems [*Information service or system*] (IID) ... ADS
Applied Demographic Research Group [*Database producer*] (IID) ... ADRG
Applied Diagnostic Techniques (AAEL) ... ADT
Applied Digital Access [*NASDAQ symbol*] (SAG) ... ADAX
Applied Digital Access [*Associated Press*] (SAG) ... ApdDgtl
Applied Digital Data Systems [*Commercial firm*] (NITA) ... ADDS
Applied Digital Data Systems, Inc. (SAUO) ... ADDS
Applied Digital Solutions [*NASDAQ symbol*] (SG) ... ADSX
Applied Drilling Technology (SAUS) ... ADT
Applied Dynamics (IAA) ... AD
Applied Dynamics International ... ADI
Applied Dynamics Ltd. (SAUS) ... AD
Applied Ecology Abstracts (SAUS) ... Appl Ecol Abstr
Applied Economic Research and Information Centre [*Conference Board of Canada*] [*Ottawa, ON*] ... AERIC
Applied Electrical Phenomena (journ.) (SAUS) ... Appl Electr Phenom
Applied Electro Mechanics Inc. (SAUO) ... AEM
Applied Electronics Annual (journ.) (SAUS) ... Appl El Ann
Applied Energy, Inc. [*Vancouver Stock Exchange symbol*] ... AEG
Applied Energy (journ.) (SAUS) ... Appl Energy
Applied Energy Services [*Commercial firm*] (ECON) ... AES
Applied Engineering Products [*Connecticut*] (ACAE) ... AEP
Applied Entomology ... AE
Applied Entomology Group [*Natick Labs, MA*] [*Army*] ... AE
Applied Extrasensory Projection [*Psychology*] (DAVI) ... AESP
Applied Extrusion Tech [*NASDAQ symbol*] (TTSB) ... AETC
Applied Extrusion Technologies [*NASDAQ symbol*] (SPSG) ... AETC
Applied Extrusion Technologies [*Associated Press*] (SAG) ... ApdExtr
Applied Fisheries Laboratory (SAUO) ... AFL
Applied General System Theory (SAUS) ... AGST
Applied Genetics News (journ.) (SAUS) ... AGN
Applied Geochemistry (SAUS) ... Appl Geochem
Applied Geography and Development (SAUS) ... Appl Geogr Dev
Applied Geomechanics (journ.) (SAUS) ... App Geomech
Applied Geosystems (EFIS) ... AGS
Applied Graphics Tech [*NASDAQ symbol*] (SG) ... AGTX
Applied Graphics Technologies, Inc. [*NASDAQ symbol*] (SAG) ... AGTX
Applied Graphics Technology (SAUS) ... AGT
Applied Health Physics Ind. (SAUO) ... AHP
Applied Hydraulics (journ.) (SAUS) ... Appl Hydraul
Applied Imagery Pattern Recognition ... AIPR
Applied Imaging Corp. [*NASDAQ symbol*] (SAG) ... AICX
Applied Imaging Corp. [*Associated Press*] (SAG) ... ApplImg
Applied Immune Sciences, Inc. [*NASDAQ symbol*] (SAG) ... AISX
Applied Immune Sciences, Inc. [*Associated Press*] (SAG) ... ApdImu
Applied Immunoenzymometric Assay [*Clinical chemistry*] ... AIMEA
Applied Indus Technologies [*NYSE symbol*] (SG) ... APZ
Applied Industrial Technology [*Associated Press*] (SAG) ... ApldIndIT
Applied Industrial Technology [*NYSE symbol*] (SAG) ... APZ
Applied Informatics (SAUS) ... AI
Applied Information and Data Management Systems Section [*Battelle Memorial Institute*] [*Information service or system*] (IID) ... AIDMS
Applied Information and Documentation [*Database producer*] (IID) ... AID
Applied Information Development Inc. (SAUO) ... AID
Applied Information Development, Inc. (SAUS) ... AID
Applied Information Management Sciences, Inc. (SAUS) ... AIMS
Applied Information Management System [*Computer science*] (DIT) ... AIMS
Applied Information Resources [*Research center*] (RCD) ... AIR
Applied Information Sciences (VERA) ... AIS
Applied Information Systems (VERA) ... AIS
Applied Information Technologies Corporation (SAUO) ... AITIC
Applied Information Technologies Research Center [*Information service or system*] (IID) ... AITRC
Applied Innovation [*NASDAQ symbol*] (TTSB) ... AINN
Applied Innovation, Inc. [*NASDAQ symbol*] (SAG) ... AINN
Applied Innovation, Inc. [*Associated Press*] (SAG) ... ApIInov
Applied Intelligence Group, Inc. [*Associated Press*] (SAG) ... AppGrp
Applied Intelligence Group, Inc. [*Associated Press*] (SAG) ... ApplGrp
Applied Intelligence Group, Inc. [*NASDAQ symbol*] (SAG) ... IQIQ
Applied Journalism ... AJ
Applied Knowledge Test [*Vocational guidance test*] ... AKT
Applied Laboratory Method (OA) ... ALM
Applied Language Technology ... ALTech
Applied LASER Projects Staff ... ALPS
Applied Logics Comprehensive Computing (SAUS) ... AL/COM
Applied Magnetics [*NYSE symbol*] (SAG) ... APM
Applied Magnetics Corp. (SAUO) ... APM
Applied Magnetics Corp. [*Associated Press*] (SAG) ... ApplMg
Applied Manufacturing Research and Process Development ... AMRPD
Applied Mapping Inc. (SAUS) ... AMI
Applied Mapping Incorporated (SAUO) ... AMI
Applied Marine Research Laboratory [*Old Dominion University*] [*Research center*] (RCD) ... AMRL
Applied Materials [*NASDAQ symbol*] (TTSB) ... AMAT
Applied Materials [*Associated Press*] (SAG) ... ApldMat
Applied Materials, Inc. [*NASDAQ symbol*] (NQ) ... AMAT
Applied Materials, Inc. ... AMI
Applied Mathematic Series (SAUS) ... AMS
Applied Mathematical Panel (SAUO) ... AMP
Applied Mathematics and Computation (journ.) (SAUS) ... APMCC5
Applied Mathematics & Statistics Laboratory (SAUS) ... AMSL
Applied Mathematics and Statistics Laboratory [*Stanford University*] (MCD) ... AMSL
Applied Mathematics Group [*Brown University*] (MCD) ... AMG
Applied Mathematics Institute [*University of Delaware*] [*Research center*] (RCD) ... AMI
Applied Mathematics Laboratory ... AML
Applied Mathematics Notes (journ.) (SAUS) ... Appl Math Notes
Applied Mathematics Panel [*DoD*] ... AMP
Applied Mathematics Series ... AMS
Applied Mathematics Series (journ.) (SAUS) ... App Math Ser
Applied Measurement Systems Inc. (SAUO) ... AMSI
Applied Mechanics (SAUS) ... APM
Applied Mechanics Division [*American Society of Mechanical Engineers*] ... AMD
Applied Mechanics Engineer [*Academic degree*] ... App ME
Applied Mechanics Research Laboratory (SAUO) ... AMRL
Applied Mechanics Reviews (journ.) (SAUS) ... AMR
Applied Mechanics Symposia Series (journ.) (SAUS) ... Appl Mech Symp Ser

Applied Meteorology, Inc. (EFIS) .... AMI
Applied Meteorology Unit (SAUS) .... AMU
Applied Micro Circuits [*NASDAQ symbol*] (SG) .... AMCC
Applied Micro Circuits Corporation (SAUO) .... AMCC
Applied Microbiology [*NASDAQ symbol*] (TTSB) .... AMBI
Applied Microbiology and Biotechnology (journ.)
 (SAUS) .... Appl Microbiol Biotechnol
Applied Microbiology Group [*Natick Laboratories*] [*Army*] (RDA) .... AMG
Applied Microbiology, Inc. [*NASDAQ symbol*] (SAG) .... AMBI
Applied Microbiology, Inc. [*Associated Press*] (SAG) .... ApdM
Applied Microbiology, Inc. [*Associated Press*] (SAG) .... ApdMicr
Applied Microbiology, Inc. (SAUO) .... APLY
Applied Microbiology Wrrt [*NASDAQ symbol*] (TTSB) .... AMBIW
Applied Microsystems [*NASDAQ symbol*] (TTSB) .... APMC
Applied Microsystems Corp. [*NASDAQ symbol*] (SAG) .... APMC
Applied Microsystems Corp. [*Associated Press*] (SAG) .... ApMicro
Applied Microwave Laboratory (SAUS) .... AML
Applied Microwave Laboratory, Inc. (SAUO) .... AML
Applied Mineral Sciences (DD) .... AppMinSci
Applied Mineralogy. Technische Mineralogie (journ.) (SAUS) .... Appl Mineral
Applied Naturalist Guild [*Defunct*] .... ANG
Applied Nuclear Radiochemistry (journ.) (SAUS) .... Appl Nucl Radiochem
Applied Nucleonics Company, Inc. (SAUO) .... ANCO
Applied Numerical Mathematics (journ.) (SAUS) .... Appl Num M
Applied Nursing Research (SAUS) .... ANR
Applied Nutrition (journ.) (SAUS) .... Appl Nutr
Applied Nutrition Programme (SAUO) .... ANP
Applied Ocean Research (journ.) (SAUS) .... Appl Ocean Res
Applied Optics, Inc. (SAUO) .... APOP
Applied Optics. Supplement (journ.) (SAUS) .... Appl Opt Suppl
Applied Ornithology (journ.) (SAUS) .... Appl Ornithol
Applied Parallel Programming Language Experiment [*Computer science*]
 (MCD) .... APPLE
Applied Pathology (journ.) (SAUS) .... Appl Pathol
Applied Pathology (journ.) (SAUS) .... APTHDM
Applied Peripheral System (IAA) .... APS
Applied Peripheral Systems, Inc. (SAUS) .... APS
Applied Philosophy (journ.) (SAUS) .... Applied Phil
Applied Physicist (SAUS) .... Appl Phys
Applied Physics (IEEE) .... AP
Applied Physics and Engineering (journ.) (SAUS) .... Appl Phys Eng
Applied Physics and Materials Laboratory [*Princeton University*] .... APML
Applied Physics Branch [*Air Proving Ground Center*] .... APB
Applied Physics Corporation (SAUO) .... APC
Applied Physics (journ.) (SAUS) .... Aphyc
Applied Physics Laboratory [*Johns Hopkins University*] .... APL
Applied Physics Laboratory. Johns Hopkins University. Special Report
 (journ.) (SAUS) .... APLJHUSR
Applied Physics Laboratory/ University of Washington (SAUO) .... APL/UW
Applied Physics Laboratory/Johns Hopkins University .... APL/JHU
Applied Physics. Part B. Photophysics and Laser Chemistry (journ.)
 (SAUS) .... APPCC
Applied Physics Quarterly (journ.) (SAUS) .... Appl Phys Q
Applied Physics Research Section .... APRS
Applied Physics Staff (SAA) .... APS
Applied Plant Ecology Research Unit (SAUS) .... APERU
Applied Plastics (journ.) (SAUS) .... Appl Plast
Applied Polymer Symposia (journ.) (SAUS) .... Appl Polym Symp
Applied Potential Tomography [*Medicine*] .... APT
Applied Power A [*NYSE symbol*] (SAG) .... APW
Applied Power CI'A' [*NYSE symbol*] (TTSB) .... APW
Applied Power, Inc. [*Associated Press*] (SAG) .... ApldPw
Applied Power, Inc. [*NYSE symbol*] (SPSG) .... APW
Applied Power Inc. (SAUO) .... APWR
Applied Psycholinguistics (journ.) (SAUS) .... Appl Psycholinguist
Applied Psycholinguistics (journ.) (SAUS) .... APPSDZ
Applied Psychological Measurement (journ.) (SAUS) .... APMEDC
Applied Psychological Services (KSC) .... APS
Applied Psychology Corporation (SAUO) .... APC
Applied Psychology Monographs (journ.) (SAUS) .... Appl Psych Monogr
Applied Psychology Panel [*of NDRC*] [*World War II*] .... APP
Applied Psychology Research Unit (SAA) .... APRU
Applied Psychology Unit .... APU
Applied Quaternary Studies (QUAC) .... AQR
Applied Radiation Corporation (SAUO) .... ARCO
Applied Radiology and Nuclear Medicine (journ.) (SAUS) .... Appl Radiol Nud Med
Applied Rangeland Ecology Program (SAUS) .... AREP
Applied Remote Sensing Program (MCD) .... ARSP
Applied Research .... APPRES
Applied Research [*of ASRA*] [*National Science Foundation*] .... AR
Applied Research and Design Center [*Research center*] (RCD) .... ARDC
Applied Research and Development Company (SAUO) .... ARDCO
Applied Research Associates (SAUO) .... ARA
Applied Research Corp. .... ARC
Applied Research Corporation (SAUO) .... ARC
Applied Research Ethics National Association (EA) .... ARENA
Applied Research in Mental Retardation (journ.) (SAUS) .... Appl Res Ment Retard
Applied Research, Incorporated (ACAE) .... ARI
Applied Research Laboratories [*Commercial firm*] .... ARL
Applied Research Laboratories. University of Texas at Austin (SAUO) .... ARLUT
Applied Research Laboratory [*Johns Hopkins University, University of Texas
 at Austin, Pennsylvania State University*] [*Research center*] .... ARL
Applied Research Laboratory/University of Texas (IUSS) .... ARL/UT
Applied Research Management .... ARM
Applied Research Objective .... ARO

Applied Research of Australia (SAUO) .... ARA
Applied Research of Cambridge [*British*] (NITA) .... ARC
Applied Research: Operation Weather Analysis [*Navy*] .... AROWA
Applied Research Planning Document (SAUS) .... ARPD
Applied Research Program .... ARPO
Applied Research Programme (SAUO) .... ARP
Applied Resource Image Exploitation System (SAUS) .... ARIES
Applied Science .... AS
Applied Science and Research Applications [*Program*] [*Supersedes RANN*]
 [*National Science Foundation*] .... ASRA
Applied Science & Tech [*NASDAQ symbol*] (TTSB) .... ASTX
Applied Science & Tech Wrrt [*NASDAQ symbol*] (TTSB) .... ASTXW
Applied Science & Technology, Inc. [*Associated Press*] (SAG) .... ApdSci
Applied Science & Technology, Inc. [*NASDAQ symbol*] (SAG) .... ASTX
Applied Science Associates .... ASA
Applied Science Associates, Incorporated (ACAE) .... ASAL
Applied Science Corp. (MCD) .... ASC
Applied Science Corporation (SAUO) .... ASC
Applied Science Corporation of Princeton (SAUO) .... ASCOP
Applied Science Division [*GAO*] (AAGC) .... ASD
Applied Science Laboratories (SAUS) .... ASL
Applied Science Laboratory .... ASL
Applied Science Technologist [*Canada*] (ASC) .... AScT
Applied Science Technologists & Technicians of British Columbia
 [*Formerly, Society of Engineering Technologists of BC*] (AC) .... ASTTBC
Applied Science through Research and Engineering .... ASTRE
Applied Sciences and Development (journ.) (SAUS) .... Appl Sci Dev
Applied Scientific Research Corporation of Thailand (SAUO) .... ASRCT
Applied Scientific Research Corporation of Thailand. Annual Report
 (journ.) (SAUS) .... Appl Sci Res Corp Thail Annu Rep
Applied Scientist (PGP) .... App Sc
Applied Signal Technology [*NASDAQ symbol*] (TTSB) .... APSG
Applied Signal Technology, Inc. [*Associated Press*] (SAG) .... ApldSig
Applied Signal Technology, Inc. [*NASDAQ symbol*] (SAG) .... APSG
Applied Simulation and Modelling (SAUS) .... ASM
Applied Social Science Index and Abstracts (SAUS) .... ASSIA
Applied Social Sciences Index and Abstracts [*Information service or
 system*] (IID) .... ASSIA
Applied Software Development Center (EFIS) .... ASDC
Applied Software Technology [*Computer science*] (HGAA) .... ASTEC
Applied Soil Ecology (SAUS) .... Appl Soil Ecol
Applied Solar Energy Corp. (SAUS) .... SOLR
Applied Solar Energy (journ.) (SAUS) .... Appl Sol Energy
Applied Solid State Science (journ.) (SAUS) .... Appl Solid State Sci
Applied Space Resources .... ASR
Applied Space Technology-Regional Advancement (SAUS) .... ASTRA
Applied Statistics (journ.) (SAUS) .... APS
Applied Statistics Training Institute .... ASTI
Applied Superconductivity Conference, Inc. (MCD) .... ASC
Applied Superconductivity Research Center [*University of Wisconsin -
 Madison*] [*Research center*] (RCD) .... ASC
Applied System Development Evaluation Center (SAUS) .... ASDEC
Applied System Technology .... AST
Applied Systems and Personnel (BUR) .... ASAP
Applied Systems Knowledge Ltd. [*British*] (NITA) .... ASK
Applied Systems Unit (SAUS) .... ASU
Applied Technology Advanced Computer .... ATAC
Applied Technology Associates (SAUO) .... ATA
Applied Technology Associates (SAUS) .... ATA
Applied Technology Council (EA) .... ATC
Applied Technology Gasification [*Coal*] .... ATGAS
Applied Technology Laboratory [*Army*] (GRD) .... ATL
Applied Technology Satellite (SAUS) .... ATS
Applied Theory Corp. [*NASDAQ symbol*] .... ATHY
Applied Therapeutics (journ.) .... Appl Ther
Applied to Previous Charge [*Business term*] .... APC
Applied Urbanetics, Inc. [*Information service or system*] (IID) .... AUI
Applied Videotex Systems, Inc. [*Telecommunications service*] (TSSD) .... AVS
Applied Viewdata Systems (SAUS) .... AVS
Applied Voice Technology [*Telecommunications service*] (TSSD) .... AVT
Applied Voice Technology [*NASDAQ symbol*] (TTSB) .... AVTC
Applied Voice Technology, Inc. [*Associated Press*] (SAG) .... ApdVoice
Applied Voice Technology, Inc. [*NASDAQ symbol*] (SAG) .... AVTC
Applique .... A
Applique (VRA) .... apliq
Applique (MSA) .... APLQ
Applique .... APPLQ
Applique Armor Kit (SAUS) .... AAK
Applix, Inc. [*NASDAQ symbol*] (SAG) .... APLX
Applix, Inc. [*Associated Press*] (SAG) .... Applix
Apply Fixture (AAG) .... APFX
Apply Force [*Industrial engineering*] .... AF
Apply Pressure [*Industrial engineering*] .... AP
Apply Template (MCD) .... AT
Apply/Develop Track Specific Equipment Model (AAEL) .... ATDSEM
APPN Implementers (or Implementors) Workshop (SAUS) .... APNT
Appoint (FAAC) .... APNT
Appoint (ADWA) .... appt
Appoint (AABC) .... APT
Appointed .... APP
Appointed (WDAA) .... app
Appointed .... APPNTD
Appointed (WDAA) .... apptd
Appointed .... APPTD
Appointed Factory Doctor (PDAA) .... AFD

Appointing Order .... AO
Appointment (SAUS) .... APP
Appointment .... APPMT
Appointment (ADWA) .... appmt
Appointment (WGA) .... APPNT
Appointment (AFM) .... APPT
Appointment [*Medicine*] (DMAA) .... appt
Appointment (ROG) .... APPTNT
Appointment (ROG) .... APPTT
Appointment and Promotion Advisory Committee [*UN Food and Agriculture Organization*] .... APAC
Appointment Not Kept [*Medicine*] (WDAA) .... ANK
Appointment of Agents - Excise [*Revenue Canada - Customs and Excise*] [*Information service or system*] (CRD) .... AAE
Appointment Recommended (NOAA) .... APRMD
Appointment, Registration, Information System and Evaluation (SAUS) .... ARISE
Appointment Will Be Regarded as Having Terminated upon This Date .... POINTERM
Appointments and Honours (SAUS) .... APH
Appointments Register .... AR
Appointments Review Group (SAUO) .... ARG
Appollo High School, St. Cloud, MN [*Library symbol*] [*Library of Congress*] (LCLS) .... MnStclA
Appomattox Court House National Historic Park .... APCO
Appomattox Court House National Historical Park (SAUS) .... ACHNHP
Appomattox Regional Library, Hopewell, VA [*Library symbol*] [*Library of Congress*] (LCLS) .... ViHop
Appomattox, VA [*FM radio station call letters*] .... WLDJ
Appomattox, VA [*FM radio station call letters*] .... WTTX-FM
Appomattox, VA [*AM radio station call letters*] (RBYB) .... WWAR
Apportioned Effort (MCD) .... AE
Apportionment of Close Companies' Income [*Business term*] (NITA) .... ACCI
Appositive (WDAA) .... APPOS
Appraisal .... APPRSL
Appraisal & Valuation Consultants Ltd. [*British*] .... AVC
Appraisal, Evaluation and Sectoral Studies (SAUS) .... AESS
Appraisal Institute (EA) .... AI
Appraisal Institute of Canada .... AIC
Appraisal Journal (journ.) (SAUS) .... APJ
Appraisal Management Center (SAUS) .... AMC
Appraisal Management System (SAUS) .... AMS
Appraisal of Language Disturbance [*Test*] .... ALD
Appraisal of the Navy RDT & E [*Research, Development, Test, and Evaluation*] **Program** .... ANREP
Appraisal: Science Books for Young People [*A publication*] (BRI) .... ASBYP
Appraisals, Evaluation, and Sectoral Study .... AESS
Appraised (WGA) .... APP
Appraisement (ROG) .... APPRAIST
Appraiser .... APPRSER
Appraisers Association of America (EA) .... AAA
Appraisor .... APPRSOR
Appreciate [*Wire service abbreviation*] (WDMC) .... APC
Appreciate [*Wire service abbreviation*] (WDMC) .... apc
Appreciate .... Apc
Appreciation .... app
Appreciation (SAUS) .... APPR
Appreciation Index [*Television ratings*] [*British*] .... AI
Appreciation of Capital, Protection, Income [*Finance*] .... API
Apprehend (AABC) .... APP
Apprehend (AFM) .... APPR
Apprehended Violence Order [*A publication*] .... AVO
Apprehension (SAUS) .... Appr
Apprentice .... APP
Apprentice (WDAA) .... app
Apprentice (ROG) .... APPRCE
Apprentice .... APPRENT
Apprentice .... APPRNTC
Apprentice (AFM) .... APR
Apprentice Boys of Derry (SAUO) .... ABD
Apprentice Seaman .... AS
Apprentice Training Incentive .... ATI
Apprentices Free Library, Philadelphia (SAUS) .... PPAp
Apprentices' Free Library, Philadelphia, PA [*Library symbol*] [*Library of Congress*] [*Obsolete*] (LCLS) .... PPAp
Apprentices National Insurance [*British*] .... ANI
Apprentices Union [*British*] .... AU
Apprenticeship (AABC) .... APPR
Apprenticeship and Training Conference [*Bureau of Apprenticeship and Training*] [*Department of Labor*] .... ATC
Apprenticeship and Training Representative [*Bureau of Apprenticeship and Training*] [*Department of Labor*] .... ATR
Apprenticeship Committee [*Department of Labor*] .... AC
Apprenticeship Information Center [*Department of Labor*] .... AIC
Apprenticeship News [*A publication*] .... Apprent News
Apprenticeship News (journ.) (SAUS) .... Apprent News
Apprenticeship Outreach Program [*Bureau of Apprenticeship and Training*] (OICC) .... AOP
Apprenticeship Program (DD) .... AP
Apprenticeship, Referral, and Outreach for Women [*An association*] [*Defunct*] (EA) .... AROW
Appretur Zeitung (journ.) (SAUS) .... Appretur Ztg
Approach (WDAA) .... A
Approach [*Database terminology*] (NITA) .... AP
Approach .... APCH
Approach .... APP
Approach (MSA) .... APRCH
Approach Aid [*Aviation*] (IAA) .... AA
Approach and Departure Control [*Aviation*] (FAAC) .... AADC
Approach and Landing [*Aviation*] (NASA) .... A & L
Approach and Landing (SAUS) .... A&L
Approach & Landing [*MTMC*] (TAG) .... AL
Approach and Landing Flight Test [*Aviation*] (MCD) .... ALFT
Approach and Landing Guidance System (SAUS) .... ALGS
Approach and Landing Procedures Simulator [*Aviation*] (MCD) .... ALPS
Approach and Landing Simulator [*Aviation*] .... ALS
Approach and Landing Test [*Aviation*] (MCD) .... ALT
Approach and Landing Test Requirement [*NASA*] (NASA) .... ALTR
Approach Astrophysics Payload [*NASA*] .... AAP
Approach Astrophysics Payload [*NASA*] (MCD) .... APP
Approach by Concept [*Information retrieval*] .... ABC
Approach By Concept (SAUS) .... ABC
Approach Chart .... AC
Approach Control [*Aviation*] .... A/C
Approach Control [*Aviation*] .... APC
Approach Control [*FAA*] .... APCON
Approach Control [*Aviation*] (AFM) .... APPCON
Approach Control Center (MCD) .... ACC
Approach Control Function [*Aviation*] (AIA) .... APF
Approach Control Office [*Aviation code*] .... APP
Approach Control Office [*ICAO designator*] (ICDA) .... ZA
Approach Control Office [*FAA designator*] (FAAC) .... ZAZ
Approach Control RADAR [*Aviation*] .... ACR
Approach Control Radar (SAUS) .... ACR
Approach Control RADAR (DA) .... APP-R
Approach Coupler (SAUS) .... AC
Approach Deterioration Parameter (MCD) .... ADP
Approach End Barrier Engagement (MCD) .... AEBE
Approach End Runway [*Aviation*] (FAAC) .... AER
Approach Flash-Lighting System (SAUS) .... AFLS
Approach, Horizon Indicator [*Aviation*] (PDAA) .... AHI
Approach Indexer .... APEXER
Approach (journ.) (SAUS) .... APP
Approach Landing Autopilot System (SAUS) .... ALAS
Approach Landing Autopilot System [*or Subsystem*] [*Aviation*] (MCD) .... ALAS
Approach Landing System [*Aviation*] (MCD) .... ALS
Approach Light Contact Height .... ALCH
Approach Light Facility (PDAA) .... ALF
Approach Light System [*Aviation*] .... ALS
Approach Light System with Sequenced Flashing Lights in ILS CAT-I Configuration [*FAA*] (TAG) .... ALSF-I
Approach Light System with Sequenced Flashing Lights in ILS CAT-II Modification [*FAA*] (TAG) .... ALSF-II
Approach Lighting [*Aviation*] (DA) .... A
Approach Lighting System [*Aviation*] (PIPO) .... ALS
Approach Lighting System Improvement Program [*FAA*] (TAG) .... ALSIP
Approach Lighting System with Sequenced Flashers [*Aviation*] .... ALSF
Approach Lighting System With Sequenced Flashing Lights [*FAA*] (TAG) .... ALSF
Approach Lights [*Aviation*] (AIA) .... AP
Approach, Naval Aviation Safety Review [*A publication*] .... ANAR
Approach Path Alignment Panel [*Aviation*] (FAAC) .... APAP
Approach Path Control System [*NASA*] (MCD) .... APCS
Approach Positive Control .... APC
Approach Power Compensator [*NASA*] .... APC
Approach Power Compensator System [*NASA*] .... APCS
Approach Power Control (SAUS) .... APC
Approach Power Control Set (NG) .... APCS
Approach Progress Display (SAUS) .... APD
Approach Radar Controller (SAUS) .... ARC
Approach Reference Speed (SAUS) .... VREF
Approach Resources, Inc. [*Vancouver Stock Exchange symbol*] .... APH
Approach Surveillance Radar (SAUS) .... ASR
Approach Time (SAUS) .... AT
Approach to Command and Control Implementation and Design (SAA) .... ACCID
Approach to Distributed Processing Transaction [*Computer science*] (MHDB) .... ADOPT
Approach to Systematic Planning and Evaluation of Clinical Trials [*Medicine*] (DB) .... ASPECT
Approach/Approach Mode (GAVI) .... APPR
Approach/Departure [*Aviation*] (DNAB) .... APP/DEP
Approacher .... APPRCHR
Approaches (NATG) .... AP
Approaches [*Maps and charts*] .... Apprs
Approaches (SAUS) .... APPRS
Approaches to Behavior Change Inventory (EDAC) .... ABC
Approaches to the Cell Biology of Neurons (journ.) (SAUS) .... Approaches Cell Biol Neurons
Approaching (SAUS) .... APCC
Approaching .... APCHG
Approaching Lactate Dehydrogenase [*LD*] **1:2 Flip** [*Cardiology*] (DAVI) .... APPR
Approach/Landing .... A/L
Approach/Landing Thrust Reverser programme (SAUS) .... ALTR
Approbation .... APPRO
Appropriale Technology Ltd. (SAUO) .... APTEC
Appropriate (DMAA) .... approp
Appropriate (AABC) .... APROP
Appropriate Authority [*Office of Censorship*] [*World War II*] .... AA
Appropriate Disability (MELL) .... AD
Appropriate Duty [*Air Force*] (AFM) .... APDY
Appropriate for Gestational Age [*Medicine*] .... AGA

Appropriate Health Resources and Technologies Action Group [*London, England*] ... AHRTAG
Appropriate Home Energy Cooperative [*Canada*] ... AHEC
Appropriate Labor Organization (OICC) ... ALO
Appropriate Military Systems Guide (SAUS) ... AMSG
Appropriate National Authorities [*NATO*] (NATG) ... ANA
Appropriate Superior Authority [*British military*] (DMA) ... ASA
Appropriate Technology ... AT
Appropriate Technology - United Kingdom Unit [*ITDG*] [*British*] ... AT-UK
Appropriate Technology for Developing Countries (SAUO) ... ATOL
Appropriate Technology for Health Information System (SAUO) ... ATHIS
Appropriate Technology in the Third World [*G. V. Olsen Associates*] [*Information service or system*] (CRD) ... AT3
Appropriate Technology Information Service [*International Council of Scientific Unions*] ... ATIS
Appropriate Technology International (EA) ... ATI
Appropriate Technology (journ.) (SAUS) ... Approp Technol
Appropriate Technology Ltd. [*British*] (IRUK) ... APTEC
Appropriate Technology Project [*Maintained by the Volunteers in Asia*] ... ATP
Appropriate Technology Transfer for Rural Areas [*National Center for Appropriate Technology*] (GNE) ... ATTRA
Appropriate Use Policies (or Policy) (SAUS) ... AUP
Appropriated (ROG) ... APP
Appropriated Funds ... AF
Appropriated Funds (AABC) ... APF
Appropriateness Evaluation Protocol [*Medicine*] (MEDA) ... AEP
Appropriating Property in Possession of Common Carrier [*FBI standardized term*] ... APIPOCC
Appropriation ... APPN
Appropriation ... APPROP
Appropriation Account Data [*Business term*] ... AAD
Appropriation Accounts and Data Processing Division [*Ministry of Agriculture, Fisheries, and Food*] [*British*] ... AA & DPD
Appropriation Accounts and Data Processing Division (SAUO) ... AA&DPD
Appropriation and Budget Account Code ... ABAC
Appropriation and Budget Activity [*Army*] (AABC) ... ABA
Appropriation and Expense (AFIT) ... AAE
Appropriation and Expense (AFM) ... A & E
Appropriation and Expense (SAUS) ... A&E
Appropriation Purchases Account ... APA
Appropriation Transfer Account (AFM) ... ATA
Appropriations and Allocations (OICC) ... AA
Approval (ADA) ... APP
Approval (AFM) ... APPR
Approval ... APPRO
Approval (WDAA) ... appro
Approval (ROG) ... APPVAL
Approval (MSA) ... APPVL
Approval (KSC) ... APRVL
Approval ... APVL
Approval for Full Production [*Navy*] (DOMA) ... AFP
Approval for Service Use [*Military*] (NVT) ... ASU
Approval in Principle (NRCH) ... AIP
Approval MILSTRIP [*Military Standard Requisition and Issue Procedures*] **Change Letter** [*DoD*] ... AMCL
Approval Request [*Military*] (DNAB) ... APREQ
Approval Requests [*Military*] (AABC) ... APREQS
Approval to Build Prototype [*Automotive project management*] ... ABP
Approval to Start Production [*Automotive project management*] ... ASP
Approvals Committee for Terminal Equipment (SAUO) ... ACTE
Approve ... APPRV
Approve (MSA) ... APPV
Approve (KSC) ... APRV
Approve ... APV
Approved ... A
Approved (WDAA) ... app
Approved (CTAS) ... APP
Approved (MARI) ... Appd
Approved (EBF) ... appd
Approved (KSC) ... APPD
Approved (DAVI) ... APPROV
Approved (ILCA) ... apprvd
Approved (MSA) ... APVD
Approved (EBF) ... OK
Approved and Removed ... A & R
Approved and Removed (SAUS) ... A&R
Approved As Amended (SAUS) ... AAA
Approved Auto Repair [*American Automobile Association*] ... AAR
Approved Basic Stock Level of Ammunition (MCD) ... ABSLA
approved by the United States Coast Guard (SAUS) ... USCG-approved
Approved Capital Costs [*Canada*] ... ACC
Approved Carriage List (HEAS) ... ACL
Approved Code of Practice (DS) ... ACOP
Approved Conference Rate and Interconference Agreement [*of Steamship Lines in the Foreign Commerce of the United States*] ... ACRA
Approved Consumer Information ... ACI
Approved Cult ... AC
Approved Data Element (AFM) ... ADE
Approved Deferred Share Trust (ODBW) ... ADST
Approved Departure Time (MCD) ... ADT
Approved Deposit Fund (ADA) ... ADF
Approved Dosimetry Service (HEAS) ... ADS
Approved Driving Instructor [*British*] (DBQ) ... ADI
Approved Drug Product [*Medicine*] (DMAA) ... ADP
Approved Engineering Test Laboratories (SAUO) ... AETL
Approved Engineering Test Laboratory [*Military*] (CAAL) ... AETL
Approved Equivalent Parts List ... AEPL
Approved Fastener Substitution List (MCD) ... AFSL
Approved Financial Plan (SAUS) ... AFP
Approved Flight Manual [*FAA*] [*A publication*] (MCD) ... AFM
Approved for Limited Production (MCD) ... ALP
Approved for Operational Use (IUSS) ... AOU
Approved for Release ... AR
Approved Force Acquisition Objective [*Army*] (AABC) ... AFAO
Approved Force Budget Objective [*Army*] (AABC) ... AFBO
Approved Force Gross Requirement [*Army*] (AABC) ... AFGR
Approved Force Inventory Objective [*Military*] ... AFIC
Approved Force Inventory Objective [*Army*] (AABC) ... AFIO
Approved Force Investment Level Requirement (AFIT) ... AFILR
Approved Force Retention Stock [*Air Force*] (AFIT) ... AFRS
Approved Force War Reserve (SAUS) ... AFWR
Approved Funding Plan (SAUS) ... AFP
Approved Funding Program (SAUS) ... AFP
Approved Health Plan [*Medicine*] ... AHP
Approved Item Name ... AIN
Approved Item Name Reclassification Program [*DoD*] (AFIT) ... AINRP
Approved MAPAD [*Military Assistance Program Address File*] **Change Letter** (AAGC) ... AMCL
Approved Marine Devices Company (SAUO) ... AMD
Approved Market [*Business term*] ... AM
Approved Material Substitution List ... AMSL
Approved Materials List [*NASA*] ... AML
Approved Modernization Maintenance Program (AFM) ... AMMP
Approved Modification and Maintenance Program (ACAE) ... AMMP
Approved Operating Budget [*Army*] (AABC) ... AOB
Approved Parts and Vendors List (ACAE) ... APVL
Approved Parts List ... APL
Approved Parts, Materials, and Processes List (ACAE) ... APMPL
Approved Prescription Services Ltd. [*British*] ... APS
Approved Processes List (ACAE) ... APL
Approved Production Inspection System [*Manufacturing*] (MCD) ... APIS
Approved Quality Assurance ... AQA
Approved Quality Level (SAUS) ... AQL
Approved Regulations for Transportable Pressure Receptacles (HEAS) ... ARTPR
Approved Research Institute ... ARI
Approved Source List (SAA) ... ASL
Approved Spare Parts List (MCD) ... ASPL
Approved Species - Specfic Protocol [*Marine science*] (OSRA) ... ASSP
Approved Species-Specific Protocol (USDC) ... ASSP
Approved Study Structure ... ASS
Approved Supplier Tab List ... ASTL
Approved Suppliers' List (DNAB) ... ASL
Approved System Requirement ... ASR
Approved Tank Requirements (HEAS) ... ATR
Approved Tank Wagon ... ATW
Approved Test Officer ... ATO
Approved to British Standard [*British Standards Institution*] ... ABS
Approved Training Center (GVA) ... ATC
Approved Training Organisation [*Manpower Services Commission*] (AIE) ... ATO
Approved Type Certificate [*Governmental airworthiness certification for planes*] ... ATC
Approved Vendors List ... AVL
Approving Authority ... AA
Approvisionnements et Services Canada [*Supply and Services Canada - SSC*] ... ASC
Approximate [*Rate*] [*Value of the English pound*] ... A
Approximate ... APP
Approximate (WDAA) ... app
Approximate (ADWA) ... appr
Approximate (ADA) ... APPR
Approximate (EY) ... APPROX
Approximate (ADWA) ... approx
Approximate ... APPRX
Approximate (VRA) ... appx
Approximate (AFM) ... APRX
Approximate Absolute [*Temperature*] ... AA
Approximate Calculation (SAUS) ... AC
Approximate Computation (SAUS) ... AC
Approximate Cubic Search [*Mathematics*] ... ACS
Approximate Degrees of Freedom [*Statistics*] ... ADF
Approximate Digestibility ... AD
Approximate Exposure Time ... AET
Approximate Inertial Manifold (SAUS) ... AIM
Approximate Lethal Concentration [*Medicine*] (DMAA) ... ALC
Approximate Lethal Dose ... ALD
Approximate Pore Diameter (SAUS) ... APD
Approximate Quadratic Search [*Mathematics*] ... AQS
Approximate Ray Tracing [*Of seismic waves*] ... ART
Approximate Theoretical Error Variance (MHDB) ... ATEV
Approximate Vertical Profile (CTAS) ... AVP
Approximated (SAUS) ... APPROX
Approximately (WDAA) ... APPROX
Approximately (GEAB) ... approx
Approximately (DEN) ... APRXLY
Approximately (WDMC) ... apx
Approximating (SAUS) ... APPROX
Approximation (DAVI) ... APPROX
Approximation Calculus (SAUS) ... AC
Approximation to English ... ATE

Appurtenances (SAUS) .... APPUR
Appurtenances (ROG) .... APPURTS
AppWare Loadable Module [Computer science] (PCM) .... ALM
Appware Loadable Module (SAUS) .... ALM
Apraxia [Neurology] (DAVI) .... aprax
Apraxia Battery for Adults (TES) .... ABA
Apres Jesus-Christ [After Christ] [French] .... AP JC
Apres Livraison [After Delivery of Goods] [French] .... AL
Apria Healthcare Group, Inc. [NYSE symbol] (SAG) .... AHG
Apria Healthcare Group, Inc. [NASDAQ symbol] (SAG) .... APRA
Apria Healthcare Group, Inc. [Associated Press] (SAG) .... Apria
Apricot Producers of California (EA) .... APC
Apricot Ring Pox Virus (SAUS) .... ARPV
April .... A
April .... AP
April .... APL
April (ADWA) .... Apl
April (ADWA) .... Apr
April (AFM) .... APR
April 19 Movement (SAUO) M-19
April and October [Denotes semiannual payments of interest or dividends in
    these months] [Business term] .... A & O
April Computing Executive [Commercial firm] [British] .... ACE
April Fan Club (EA) .... AFC
April Fools Day (SAUS) .... AFD
April Fools Joke (SAUS) .... AFJ
April, July, October, and January [Denotes quarterly payments of interest or
    dividends in these months] [Business term] .... AJOJ
Aprobarbital [Pharmacology] (DAVI) .... APRO
Aprobarbital Elixir [Medicine] (MELL) .... ABE
Aprogenex, Inc. [AMEX symbol] (SPSG) .... APG
Aprogenex, Inc. [Associated Press] (SAG) .... Aprognx
Apron [Aviation] .... APN
Apron Lighting (SAUS) .... ALI
Aprovecho Institute (EA) .... AI
APS Holding 'A' [NASDAQ symbol] (TTSB) .... APSI
APS Holding Corp. [Associated Press] (SAG) .... APS Hld
APS Holding Corp. [NASDAQ symbol] (SAG) .... APSI
APSDEP Information Network [Islamabad, Pakistan] [Information service or
    system] (IID) .... APSDIN
APT Satellite Hldg Ltd ADS [NYSE symbol] (SG) .... ATS
APT Satellite Holdings Ltd. [NYSE symbol] (SAG) .... ATS
Aptargroup, Inc. [Associated Press] (SAG) .... Aptar
AptarGroup Inc. [NYSE symbol] (TTSB) .... ATR
Aptian (SAUS) .... Apt
Aptitude (AABC) .... APT
Aptitude Area .... AA
Aptitude Area .... APTA
Aptitude Assessment Battery Programming [Computer science] (IEEE) ...... AABP
Aptitude Based Career Decision Test (TES) .... ABCD
Aptitude for and Sensitivity to Music-Junior Form [1982] (TES) ...... ASMJ
Aptitude for and Sensitivity to Music-Senior Form [1982] (TES) ...... ASMS
Aptitude Index .... AI
Aptitude Index Battery [LIMRA] .... AIB
Aptitude Interest Inventory [Test] (TMMY) .... ABCD
Aptitude Interest Inventory (TMMY) .... Aii
Aptitude Interest Measurement (DHP) .... AIM
Aptitude Strategies (PDAA) .... APSTRAT
Aptitude Test .... AT
Aptitude Test Battery [Educational test] .... ATB
Aptitude Test for Adults [Psychoeducational test] .... AA
Aptitude Test for Programmer Personnel (SAUS) .... ATPP
Aptitude Test for School Beginners [Child development test] .... ASB
Aptitude-Treatment Interactions [Education] .... ATI
Apt/Saint-Christol [France] [ICAO location identifier] (ICLI) .... LFXI
Apud [In the Work Of] [Latin] (EES) .... ap
Apud [At, In the Works Of, According To] [Latin] .... AP
Apud Bonifacium [Latin] (DSA) .... Ap Bon
Apud Bonifacium [Latin] (DSA) .... Bon
Apud Gregorium [Latin] (DSA) .... Ap Greg
Apud Justinianum [Latin] (DLA) .... Ap Just
Apud Justinianum [Latin] (DLA) .... Ap Justin
Apuleius (SAUS) .... APU
Apuleius [Second century AD] [Classical studies] (OCD) .... Apul
Apus [Constellation] .... Aps
Apus (SAUS) .... APS
Aputiteq [Greenland] [ICAO location identifier] (ICLI) .... BGAT
Aqaba [Jordan] [Airport symbol] (OAG) .... AQJ
Aqaba [Jordan] [ICAO location identifier] (ICLI) .... OJAQ
Aqua [Water] [Latin] .... A
Aqua [Water] [Pharmacy] .... AQ
Aqua (DB) .... Aq
Aqua 1 Beverage [Vancouver Stock Exchange symbol] .... AQB
Aqua Ad [Add Water] [Latin] (MELL) .... aq ad
Aqua Alliance'A' [AMEX symbol] (SG) .... AAI
Aqua Ammoniae [Ammoniated Water] [Pharmacy] (ROG) ...... AQ AMMON
Aqua Anethi [Dill Water] [Pharmacy] (ROG) .... AQ ANETH
Aqua Anisi [Anise Water] [Pharmacy] (ROG) .... AQ ANIS
Aqua Astricta [Frozen Water] [Pharmacy] (ROG) .... AQ ASTR
Aqua Bulliens [Boiling Water] [Pharmacy] .... AQ BULL
Aqua Bulliens [Boiling Water] [Latin] (MELL) .... aq bull
Aqua Bulliens [Boiling Water] [Pharmacy] (ROG) .... AQ BULLIENS
Aqua Calida [Hot Water] [Pharmacy] .... AQ CAL
Aqua Calida [Hot Water] [Latin] (MELL) .... aq cal
Aqua Calida [Hot Water] [Pharmacy] (ROG) .... AQ CALID

Aqua Care Sys Wrrt'A' [NASDAQ symbol] (TTSB) .... AQCRW
Aqua Care Sys Wrrt'B' [NASDAQ symbol] (TTSB) .... AOCRZ
Aqua Care Systems [NASDAQ symbol] (SAG) .... AQCR
Aqua Care Systems [Commercial firm] [Associated Press] (SAG) ...... AquaC
Aqua Care Systems [Commercial firm] [Associated Press] (SAG) ...... AquaCre
Aqua Care Systems [Commercial firm] [Associated Press] (SAG) ...... AquC
Aqua Cinnamoni [Cinnamon Water] [Pharmacy] (ROG) .... AQ CINNAM
Aqua Communis [Tap Water] [Pharmacy] .... AQ COM
Aqua Communis [Tap water] [Pharmacology] (DAVI) .... aq comm
Aqua Destillata [Distilled Water] [Pharmacy] .... AQ DEST
Aqua Europa - European Federation for Water Treatment [British]
    (EAIO) .... AEEFWT
Aqua Fervens [Warm Water] [Pharmacy] .... AQ FERV
Aqua Fluviatilis [River Water] [Pharmacy] (ROG) .... AQ FLUV
Aqua Fontis [Spring Water] [Pharmacy] (ROG) .... AQ FONT
Aqua Fortis [Sulphuric Acid] [Pharmacy] (ROG) .... AQ FORT
Aqua Frigida [Cold Water] [Pharmacy] .... AQ FRIG
Aqua Frigida [Cold Water] [Pharmacy] (ROG) .... AQ FRIGID
Aqua Gelida [Cold Water] [Pharmacy] .... AQ GEL
Aqua Lung Dealers Association [Defunct] (EA) .... ALDA
Aqua Marina [Sea Water] [Pharmacy] (ROG) .... AQ MAR
Aqua Mentha [Mint Water] [Pharmacy] (ROG) .... AQ MENTH
Aqua Mentha Piperitae [Peppermint Water] [Pharmacy] (ROG) ...... AQ MENTH PIP
Aqua Nivalis [Snow Water] [Pharmacy] (ROG) .... AQ NIV
Aqua Pimentae [Allspice Water] [Pharmacy] (ROG) .... AQ PIMENT
Aqua Pluvialis [or Pluviatilis] [Rain Water] [Pharmacy] (ROG) ...... AQ PLUV
Aqua Pura [Pure Water] [Pharmacy] (ROG) .... AQ PUR
Aqua Rosa [Rose Water] [Pharmacy] (ROG) .... AQ ROS
Aqua Ruta [Rue Water] [Pharmacy] (ROG) .... AQ RUT
Aqua Sciences International, Inc. (SAUO) .... AQSI
Aqua Soda [Soda Water] [Pharmacy] (ROG) .... AQ SOD
Aqua Tepida [Lukewarm Water] [Pharmacy] .... AQ TEP
Aqua Tepida [Lukewarm Water] [Pharmacy] (ROG) .... AQ TEPID
Aqua Terra (journ.) (SAUS) .... AQTEAH
Aqua-Cat Catamaran Sailing Association (EA) .... ACSA
Aquacultural Engineering (SAUS) .... Aquac Eng
Aquacultural Engineering Society (NTPA) .... AES
aquaculture (SAUS) .... aquacult
Aquaculture (SAUS) .... Aquaculture
Aquaculture and Fisheries Management (journ.) (SAUS) ...... Aquacult Fish Manage
Aquaculture Development and Coordination Programme (SAUS) ...... ADCP
Aquaculture Development and Coordination Programme. Report
    (SAUS) .... Aquac Dev Coord Programme Rep
Aquaculture Europe (SAUS) .... Aquac Eur
Aquaculture Information Center [Department of Agriculture] [Information
    service or system] (IID) .... AIC
Aquaculture Information System (SAUS) .... AQUIS
Aquaculture (journ.) (SAUS) .... AQCLAL
Aquaculture Magazine (SAUS) .... Aquac Mag
Aquaculture Magazine (journ.) (SAUS) .... Aquaculture Mag
Aquaculture News (SAUS) .... Aquac News
Aquaculture Nutrition (SAUS) .... Aquac Nutr
Aquaculture Products Technology (SAUS) .... AQUA
Aquaculture Research (SAUS) .... Aquac Res
Aquaculture Research Center [Texas A & M University] [Research center]
    (RCD) .... ARC
Aquaculture Situation and Outlook Report (SAUS) ...... Aquac Situat Outlook Rep
Aquada, PR [Television station call letters] .... WQHA
Aquadag [Graphite coating] (NTCM) .... DAG
aquadag (SAUS) .... dag
Aquagenic Pruritus [Medicine] .... AP
Aquagenix, Inc. [Associated Press] (SAG) .... Aqgnx
Aquagenix, Inc. [Associated Press] (SAG) .... Aquagnx
Aquagenix, Inc. [NASDAQ symbol] (SAG) .... AQUX
Aquagenix Inc. Wrrt [NASDAQ symbol] (TTSB) .... AQUXW
Aquair Luftfahrt GmbH [Germany] [ICAO designator] (FAAC) ...... AQU
Aqualine Abstracts (journ.) (SAUS) .... Aqualine Abstr
Aquamarine [Philately] .... Aqua
Aquanatural Co. [NASDAQ symbol] (TTSB) .... AQQA
Aquanautics Corp. (SAUO) .... AQNT
Aquaplanning Risk Indicator for Landings (SAUS) .... APRIL
Aquarama and Fairmount Park Aquarium (SAUS) .... AFPA
aquaria (SAUS) .... aqua
Aquarian Digest International [A publication] .... ADI
Aquarian Research Foundation (EA) .... ARF
Aquarien Magazin (journ.) (SAUS) .... Aquarien Mag
Aquarien Terrarien (journ.) (SAUS) .... AQTEBI
Aquarion Co. [Associated Press] (SAG) .... Aquarn
Aquarion Co. [NYSE symbol] (SPSG) .... WTR
Aquarist and Pondkeeper (SAUS) .... Aquar Pondkeep
Aquarium Journal (journ.) (SAUS) .... AQJOAV
Aquarium Journal (journ.) (SAUS) .... Aquarium J
Aquarius [Constellation] .... Aqar
Aquarius [Constellation] .... Aqr
Aquarius (ADWA) .... AQR
Aquarius [Constellation] .... AQU
Aquarius Resources Ltd. [Vancouver Stock Exchange symbol] .... AQR
Aquarius Resources Ltd. (SAUO) .... AQRLF
Aquarius Seafarms [Vancouver Stock Exchange symbol] .... AQS
Aquarius Systems International (SAUO) .... ASI
Aqua-Sol, Inc. (SAUO) .... AQSLU
Aquatic .... AQUA
Aquatic (SAUS) .... Aqua
Aquatic Airlines [ICAO designator] (AD) .... VZ
Aquatic Based Recreation Survey [Environmental Protection Agency] ...... ABRS

Aquatic Biological Laboratory (SAUS) ... ABL
Aquatic Biology Abstracts (journ.) (SAUS) ... Ab
Aquatic Botany(journ.) (SAUS) ... AQBODS
Aquatic Conservation (SAUS) ... Aquat Conserv
Aquatic Ecosystem Health and Management Society (SAUO) ... AEHMS
Aquatic Ecosystem Objectives Committee [*Great Lakes Science Advisory Board*] [*Canada*] ... AEOC
Aquatic Ecosystem Restoration Foundation ... AERF
Aquatic Ecosystem Simulator (SAUS) ... AEcoS
Aquatic Effects Research Program (AUEG) ... AERP
Aquatic Environment Monitoring Report. Directorate of Fisheries Research (SAUS) ... Aquat Environ Monit Rep Dir Fish Res
Aquatic Environment Protection. Analytical methods. Directorate of Fisheries Research (SAUS) ... Aquat Environ Prot Anal Methods Dir Fish Res
Aquatic Environmental Protection (SAUS) ... AEP
Aquatic Environments Ltd., Calgary, AB, Canada [*Library symbol*] [*Library of Congress*] (LCLS) ... CaACAqE
Aquatic Environments Ltd., Calgary, Alberta [*Library symbol*] [*National Library of Canada*] (NLC) ... ACAQE
Aquatic Exercise Association (EA) ... AEA
Aquatic Federation of Canada ... AFC
Aquatic Geochemistry (SAUS) ... Aquat Geochem
Aquatic Information Retrieval (GNE) ... ACQUIRE
Aquatic Information Retrieval Database [*Chemical Information Systems, Inc.*] [*Information service or system*] ... AQUIRE
Aquatic Living Resources (SAUS) ... Aquat Living Resour
Aquatic Mammals (SAUS) ... Aquat Mamm
Aquatic Mammals (journ.) (SAUS) ... AQMAD7
Aquatic Mammals (journ.) (SAUS) ... Aquat Mamm
Aquatic Microbial Ecology (SAUS) ... Aquat Microb Ecol
Aquatic Microbiological Ecology. Proccedings (journ.) (SAUS) ... Aquat Microbiol Ecol Proc
Aquatic Nuisance Prevention and Control Act (COE) ... ANPCA
Aquatic Nuisance Species [*Oceanography*] ... ANS
Aquatic Nuisance Species Program [*Environmental science*] (COE) ... ANSP
Aquatic Nuisance Species Task Force [*Environmental science*] (COE) ... ANSTF
Aquatic Plant ... AP
Aquatic Plant Control Research Program [*Army Corps of Engineers Waterways Experiment Station*] (MSC) ... APCRP
Aquatic Plant Management Society (EA) ... APMS
Aquatic Plant Resource and Operations Online System ... APROPOS
Aquatic Plants Control Program (SAUS) ... APCP
Aquatic Processes and Effects Group [*Army*] ... APEG
Aquatic Research Board (SAUO) ... AQUREB
Aquatic Research Institute (EA) ... ARI
Aquatic Resource Division [*Environmental Protection Agency*] (GFGA) ... ARD
Aquatic Science and Fisheries Information Service (SAUS) ... ASFIS
Aquatic Science Information Retrieval Center (SAUS) ... ASIRC
Aquatic Sciences an Fisheries Information System (SAUO) ... ASFIS
Aquatic Sciences and Fisheries Abstracts ... AquaScl
Aquatic Sciences and Fisheries Abstracts (SAUS) ... Aquat Sci Fish Abstr
Aquatic Sciences and Fisheries Abstracts [*Database producer*] (NITA) ... ASFA
Aquatic Sciences and Fisheries Abstracts (journ.) (SAUS) ... Aqua Sci&Fish Abstr
Aquatic Sciences and Fisheries Abstracts (journ.) (SAUS) ... ASFA
Aquatic Sciences and Fisheries Abstracts. Part I. Biological Sciences and Living Resources (journ.) (SAUS) ... Aquat Sci Fish Abst Part I
Aquatic Sciences and Fisheries Abstracts. Part II. Ocean Technology, Policy and Non-Living Resources (journ.) (SAUS) ... Aquat Sci Fish Abst Part II
Aquatic Sciences and Fisheries Information System [*Food and Agriculture Organization*] [*United Nations*] (IID) ... ASFIS
Aquatic Sciences Information Retrieval Center [*University of Rhode Island*] ... ASIRC
Aquatic Sciences (journ.) (SAUS) ... Aquat Sci
Aquatic Systems, Inc. (EFIS) ... ASI
Aquatic Toxicity ... AQTX
Aquatic Toxicity [*Environmental science*] ... AT
Aquatic Toxicology (journ.) (SAUS) ... AQTOD
Aquatic Weed Control Society. Proceedings (journ.) (SAUS) ... Aquat Weed Control Soc Proc
Aquatic Weeds in South East Asia. Proceedings of a Regional Seminar on Noxious Aquatic Vegetation (journ.) (SAUS) ... Aquat Weeds South East Asia Proc Reg Semin Noxious Aquat Veg
AquaticBotany (journ.) (SAUS) ... AquatBot
Aquatint (VRA) ... aqut
Aquative Sciences and Fisheries Abstracts (SAUS) ... ASFIS Abstracts
Aqueduct (VRA) ... aqdt
Aqueous [*Medicine*] (DMAA) ... A
Aqueous ... AQ
Aqueous (MELL) ... aq
Aqueous (AAMN) ... AQU
Aqueous Extraction Process ... AEP
Aqueous Film Forming Foam (SAUS) ... AFFF
Aqueous Film-Forming Foam [*Firefighting chemical for ships*] ... AFFF
Aqueous Flare Response [*Physiology*] ... AFR
Aqueous Homogeneous Critical Facility (SAUS) ... AHCF
Aqueous Homogeneous Reactor ... AHR
Aqueous Humor [*Anatomy*] (CPH) ... AH
Aqueous Makeup [*Room*] [*Nuclear energy*] (NRCH) ... AMU
Aqueous Potassium Carbonate (MUSM) ... APC
Aqueous Powder Suspension [*For coating plastics*] ... APS
Aqueous Procaine Penicillin G [*Antibiotic*] ... APPG
Aqueous Recycle Technologies (SAUS) ... ART
Aqueous Solubility Database [*Chemical Information Systems, Inc.*] [*Information service or system*] (CRD) ... SOLUB
Aqueous Solution ... AS
Aqueous Suspension ... AS
Aqueous to Organic [*Ratio*] ... A/O
Aqueous Vasopressin (DB) ... AVP
Aquidauana [*Brazil*] [*Airport symbol*] (AD) ... AQU
Aquifer Storage and Recovery [*Water supply technology*] ... ASR
Aquifer Test Solver ... AQTESOLV
Aquifer Test Toolbox [*Computer science*] ... ATT
Aquifer Thermal Energy Storage ... ATES
Aquila [*Constellation*] ... Aqil
Aquila [*Constellation*] ... Aql
Aquila [*Italy*] [*Seismograph station code, US Geological Survey*] (SEIS) ... AQU
Aquila Air, Inc. [*FAA designator*] (FAAC) ... CNH
Aquila Air, Inc. [*ICAO designator*] (FAAC) ... PCY
Aquila Air Ltd. [*Canada*] [*ICAO designator*] (FAAC) ... AQL
Aquila Airways, Ltd. (SAUO) ... AQ
Aquila Airways Ltd. ... AQU
Aquila Biopharmaceuticals, Inc. [*NASDAQ symbol*] (SAG) ... AQLA
Aquila Biopharmaceuticals, Inc. [*Associated Press*] (SAG) ... AquilaB
Aquila Gas Pipeline [*NYSE symbol*] (SPSG) ... AQP
Aquila Gas Pipeline Corp. [*Associated Press*] (SAG) ... AquilaG
Aquila's Greek Translation of the Bible [*A publication*] (BJA) ... Aq
Aquileia Nostra [*Publication*] (SAUS) ... Aquil Nost
Aquinas College (SAUO) ... AC
Aquinas College, Grand Rapids, MI [*OCLC symbol*] (OCLC) ... EXQ
Aquinas College, Grand Rapids, MI [*Library symbol*] [*Library of Congress*] (LCLS) ... MiGrA
Aquinas High School, Augusta, GA [*Library symbol*] [*Library of Congress*] (LCLS) ... GAuAH
Aquinas Institute, Dubuque, IA [*Library symbol*] [*Library of Congress*] (LCLS) ... IaDuA
Aquinas Institute Library, Rochester, NY [*OCLC symbol*] (OCLC) ... RVO
Aquinas Junior College, Nashville, TN [*Library symbol*] [*Library of Congress*] (LCLS) ... TNAC
Aquire (SAUS) ... ACQ
Aquisition and Security Division (SAUS) ... ASD
Aquisition Point (SAUS) ... AP
Aquisition Policy (SAUS) ... AP
Ara Appaloosa and Foundation Breeders International (EA) ... AAFBI
ARA Historical Foundation, ARA Industries, Philadelphia, PA [*Closed*] [*Library symbol*] [*Library of Congress*] (LCLS) ... PPARA
Arab [*or Arabic*] (BJA) ... A
Arab Agricultural Aviation [*Egypt*] [*ICAO designator*] (FAAC) ... AGC
Arab Air Cargo [*Jordan*] [*ICAO designator*] (FAAC) ... AWF
Arab Air Carriers Organization (EAIO) ... AACO
Arab Airways Association, Ltd. (SAUO) ... AAA
Arab Airways Jerusalem Ltd. (SAUO) ... AAJ
Arab Airways (Jerusalem) Ltd. ... AAJ
Arab, AL [*FM radio station call letters*] (BROA) ... WAFN-FM
Arab, AL [*FM radio station call letters*] ... WCRQ
Arab, AL [*AM radio station call letters*] ... WRAB
Arab Amateur Athletic Federation [*See also CAA*] (EAIO) ... AAAF
Arab American Democratic Federation (EA) ... AADF
Arab American Institute (EA) ... AAI
Arab American Leadership Council (EA) ... ALC
Arab American Medical Association (EA) ... AAMA
Arab American Republican Federation [*Defunct*] (EA) ... AARF
Arab American Vehicles Co. (SAUO) ... AAV
Arab Authority for Agricultural Investment and Development [*Khartoum, Sudan*] (EAIO) ... AAAID
Arab Bank Corporation (SAUO) ... ABC
Arab Bank for Economic Development in Africa (SAUO) ... ABAD
Arab Bank for Economic Development in Africa ... ABEDA
Arab Bankers' Association ... ABA
Arab British Engine Co. (SAUO) ... ABECO
Arab British Helicopters Co. (SAUO) ... ABH
Arab Canadian Association of the Atlantic Provinces (AC) ... ACAAP
Arab Center for the Studies of Arid Zones and Dry Lands (SAUS) ... ACSAD
Arab Center for the Study of Arid Zones and Dry Lands [*of the League of Arab States*] [*Syria*] [*Research center*] (IRC) ... ACSAD
Arab Center (or Centre) for Studies of Arid Zones and Dry Lands (SAUO) ... ACSAD
Arab Centre for the Studies of Arid Zones and Dry Lands (SAUO) ... ACSAZADL
Arab Common Market [*United Arab Republic, Iraq, Jordan, Kuwait, and Syria*] ... ACM
Arab Communications Satellite (SAUS) ... Arabsat
Arab Communications Satellite System (SAUS) ... ARCOMSAT System
Arab Communications Satellite System (SAUS) ... ARMCOMSAT
Arab Communist Party [*Political party*] ... ACP
Arab Co-Operation Council (ECON) ... ACC
Arab Cooperation Council (SAUO) ... ACC
Arab Cooperative Federation (SAUO) ... ACF
Arab Deterrent Force [*Palestine*] (PD) ... ADF
Arab Development Bank (EBF) ... ADB
Arab Economic and Social Council (SAUO) ... AFSC
Arab Electronic Company (SAUO) ... AEC
Arab Energy. Prospects to 2000 (journ.) (SAUS) ... Arab EaW
Arab Federation for Food Industries (EA) ... AFFI
Arab Federation for Technical Education [*Baghdad, Iraq*] (EAIO) ... AFTE
Arab Federation for the Organs of the Deaf [*Damascus, Syria*] (EAIO) ... AFOD
Arab Federation for/of Engineering Industries (SAUO) ... AFEI
Arab Federation of Chemical Fertilizer Producers (SAUO) ... AFCEFP
Arab Federation of Chemical Fertilizer Producers (EA) ... AFCFP
Arab Federation of Petroleum, Mines and Chemical Workers (SAUO) ... AFPMCW
Arab Federation Social Workers (SAUO) ... AFSW

Arab Film and Television Center News (journ.) (SAUS) ..... Arab F&TV
Arab Fund for Economic and Social Development ..... AFESD
Arab Fund for Economic and Social Development (SAUO) ..... AFESO
Arab Fund for Economic & Social Development (SAUS) ..... AFSED
Arab Fund for Technical Assistance to Arab and African Countries ..... AFTA
Arab Gulf Co-operation Council (SAUS) ..... GCC
Arab Gulf Journal (journ.) (SAUS) ..... Arab Gulf J
Arab Gulf Journal of Scientific Research (journ.) (SAUS) ..... Arab Gulf J Sci Res
Arab Gulf Program for UN Development Organisations (SAUS) ..... AGFUND
Arab Gulf States Information Documentation Center [*Information service or system*] (IID) ..... AGSIDC
Arab Gulf States Information Documentation Center [*Information service or system*] (IID) ..... GSIDC
Arab Higher Committee of Palestine (SAUO) ..... AHCP
Arab Historians Association (EAIO) ..... ARABHA
Arab Horse Society (EAIO) ..... AHS
Arab Industrial Development Organization (SAUS) A1DO
Arab Industrial Development Organization (EA) ..... AIDO
Arab Industrial Information Bank (SAUO) ..... ARIFO
Arab Industrialization Organization (SAUO) ..... AIO
Arab Information Bank [*Information service or system*] (IID) ..... AIB
Arab Information Center (SAUS) ..... AIC
Arab Information Center, Arab League Office, Washington, DC [*Library symbol*] [*Library of Congress*] (LCLS) ..... DArl
Arab Information System Network (SAUO) ..... ARISNET
Arab International Aviation Co. (SAUO) ..... KK
Arab Inter-Parliamentary Union [*Syrian Arab Republic*] (EAIO) ..... AIPU
Arab Inter-Parliamentary Union (SAUO) ..... Arab AIPU
Arab Journal of Mathematics (journ.) (SAUS) ..... Arab J Math
Arab Journal of Nuclear Sciences and Applications (journ.) (SAUS) ..... Arab J Nucl Sci Appl
Arab Latin American Bank ..... ARLABANK
Arab Lawyers Union [*See also UAA*] [*Cairo, Egypt*] (EAIO) ..... ALU
Arab League ..... AL
Arab League (SAUO) ..... AL
Arab League Documentation and Information Centre (SAUO) ..... ALDOC
Arab League Educational, Cultural and Scientific Organization (SAUO) ..... ALECSO
Arab League Educational, Cultural, and Scientific Organization [*Tunisia*] ..... ALECSO
Arab League Educational, Cultural and Scientific Organization (SAUO) ..... ALESCO
Arab League Educational, Cultural and Scientific Organization (SAUO) ..... ALESCSO
Arab Liberation Army ..... ALA
Arab Liberation Front ..... ALF
Arab Maghreb Union [*Morocco, Algeria, Mauritania, Tunisia, and Libya*] ..... AMU
Arab Malaysian Development Bank ..... AMDB
Arab Maritime Transport Academy (SAUO) ..... AMTA
Arab Military Industrialisation Organisation (SAUO) ..... AMIO
Arab Military Industrialization Organization (SAUS) ..... AMIO
Arab Mining Journal (journ.) (SAUS) ..... Arab Min J
Arab Monetary Fund ..... AMF
Arab National Bank (SAUS) ..... A
Arab Network of America (BARN) ..... ANA
Arab Network of Documentation Centres on Communication Research and Policies (SAUO) ..... Arab COMNET
Arab News [*A publication*] ..... ARN
Arab News Agency ..... ANA
Arab Oil and Economic Review [*A publication*] ..... AOER
Arab Organization for Agricultural Development (EAIO) ..... AOAD
Arab Organization for Standardization (SAUO) ..... ASO
Arab Organization for Standardization and Metrology (EAIO) ..... ASMO
Arab Organization for Standardization and Metrology (SAUO) ..... ASRY
Arab Organization for/of Administrative Sciences (SAUO) ..... AOAS
Arab Organization of Administrative Sciences (EAIO) ..... AOAS
Arab Organization of Administrative Services (SAUO) ..... AOAS
Arab Organization of Petroleum Exporting Countries (SAUS) ..... AOP
Arab Organization of Petroleum Exporting Countries ..... AOPEC
Arab Passenger Airline Reservation System (SAUS) ..... APARS
Arab Petroleum Investment Corporation (SAUO) ..... APIC
Arab Petroleum Investments Corp. (ECON) ..... APICORP
Arab Petroleum Pipelines Company (SAUS) ..... SUMED
Arab Petroleum Training Institute [*Defunct*] (EA) ..... APTI
Arab Physical Soctety (SAUS) ..... ARPS
Arab Political and Cultural Organization [*Iran*] (PD) ..... APCO
Arab Postal Union ..... APU
Arab Public Relations Society (SAUO) ..... APRS
Arab Regional Branch of the International Council of/on Archives (SAUO) ..... ARBICA
Arab Regional Telecommunications Institute (SAUO) ..... ARTI
Arab Relief Agency ..... ARA
Arab Report & Record [*A publication*] ..... ARR
Arab Republic of Egypt ..... ARE
Arab Republic of Egypt (SAUS) ..... Egypt
Arab Republic of Egypt Telephone Organization (SAUS) ..... ARETO
Arab Republic of National Telephone Organization (ACRL) ..... ARENTO
Arab Research Center for Injuries (SAUO) ..... ARCI
Arab Research Centre [*British*] (CB) ..... ARC
Arab Revolution News Agency ..... ARNA
Arab Revolutionary Army (SAUO) ..... ARA
Arab Roads Association [*Cairo, Egypt*] (EAIO) ..... ARA
Arab Satellite Communications Organization [*Saudi Arabia*] [*Telecommunications*] ..... ARABSAT
Arab Satellite Communications Organization [*League of Arab States*] [*Riyadh, Saudi Arabia*] (EAIO) ..... ASCO
Arab Satellite Telecommunications Organisation (SAUO) ..... ASTO
Arab scam (SAUS) ..... Abscam
Arab Socialist Party [*Egypt*] [*Political party*] (PPW) ..... ASP
Arab Socialist Party [*Syria*] [*Political party*] (PPW) ..... ASP
Arab Socialist Renaissance Party [*Syria*] ..... ASRP
Arab Socialist Union [*Syria*] [*Political party*] (PPW) ..... ASU
Arab Society of Certified Accountants (SAUO) ..... ASC
Arab Sports Confederation [*Saudi Arabia*] (EAIO) ..... ASC
Arab States [*MARC geographic area code*] [*Library of Congress*] (LCCP) ..... ma---
Arab States Broadcasting Union ..... ASBU
Arab States Centre of Educational Planning and Administration (SAUO) ..... ASCATEP
Arab States Regional Centre for Functional Literacy in Rural Areas (SAUO) ..... ASFEC
Arab Sugar Federation [*Khartoum, Sudan*] (EAIO) ..... ASF
Arab Telecommunications Union (EA) ..... ATU
Arab Towns Organization [*Safat, Kuwait*] (EAIO) ..... ATO
Arab Tunisian Bank ..... ATB
Arab Union for Cement and Building Materials [*See also UACMC*] (EAIO) ..... AUCBM
Arab Union for/of Pharmaceutical Manufacturers and Medical Appliance Manufacturers (SAUO) ..... AUPAM
Arab Union of the Producers, Transporters and Distributors of Electricity (SAUO) ..... AUPTDE
Arab University Library Association (SAUO) ..... AULA
Arab Urban Development Institute (EA) ..... AUDI
Arab Wings Co. [*Jordan*] [*ICAO designator*] (FAAC) ..... AWS
Arab Wings Co. (SAUS) ..... SI
Arab Women's Council (EA) ..... AWC
Arab World and Islamic Resources and School Services (EA) ..... AWAIR
Arab World (journ.) (SAUS) ..... ArabW
Arab Youth Federation (SAUO) ..... AYF
Arab-American Media Society (EA) ..... AAMS
Arab-American Media Society (EA) ..... AMS
Arab-American Press Guild (EA) ..... AAPG
Arab-British Chamber of Commerce (SAUS) ..... A-B CC
Arab-Burundi Bank SARL (EY) ..... ABB
Arabesque [*Embossed*] [*Bookbinding*] (ROG) ..... ARA
Arabesque (VRA) ..... arbsq
Arabesque Resources Ltd. [*Vancouver Stock Exchange symbol*] ..... AAR
Arabia (VRA) ..... Arab
Arabia [*ICAO designator*] (AD) ..... RZ
Arabian (ADWA) ..... Arab
Arabian ..... ARBN
Arabian Bank Trade [*Saudi Arabia*] ..... ABT
Arabian Bulk Trade [*Saudi Arabia*] [*Commercial firm*] ..... ABT
Arabian Communication Satellite ..... ARCOMSAT
Arabian Communication Satellite (SAUS) ..... ARCOM Satellite
Arabian Exhibition Management WLL [*Manama, Bahrain*] ..... AEM
Arabian General Investment Corporation (SAUO) ..... AGICO
Arabian Horse Club Registry of America [*Later, AHR*] ..... AHCRA
Arabian Horse Owners Foundation (EA) ..... AHOF
Arabian Horse Registry of America (EA) ..... AHR
Arabian Horse Registry of America (NTPA) ..... AHRA
Arabian Horse Trust (EA) ..... AHT
Arabian Jockey Club (EA) ..... AJC
Arabian Oil Company (SAUO) ..... AOC
Arabian Peninsula [*MARC geographic area code*] [*Library of Congress*] (LCCP) ..... ar---
Arabian Petroleum Congress (SAUO) ..... APC
Arabian Sea and Area [*MARC geographic area code*] [*Library of Congress*] (LCCP) ..... au---
Arabian Shield Dev [*NASDAQ symbol*] (TTSB) ..... ARSD
Arabian Shield Development Co. [*Associated Press*] (SAG) ..... ArabSh
Arabian Shield Development Co. [*NASDAQ symbol*] (NQ) ..... ARSD
Arabian Sport Horse Association (EA) ..... ASHA
Arabian-American Oil Company (SAUO) ..... ARAMCO
Arabian-Nubian Shield [*Geology*] ..... ANS
Arabic ..... AR
Arabic (BEE) ..... Ar
Arabic [*MARC language code*] [*Library of Congress*] (LCCP) ..... ara
Arabic [*Language, etc.*] ..... ARA
Arabic (NTIO) ..... Arab
Arabic Sciences and Philosophy [*A publication*] ..... ASP
Arabic Socialist Union (SAUS) ..... ASU
Arabidopsis Information Service ..... AIS
Arabinofuranosyladenine [*or Adenine Arabinoside*] [*Also, Vira-A*] [*Antiviral compound*] ..... ara-A
Arabinofuranosyladenine (SAUS) ..... Ara-A
Arabinofuranosylfluorocytosine (SAUS) ..... Am-FC
Arabinofuranosylfluorocytosine [*Also, FCA*] [*Antineoplastic drug*] ..... ara-FC
Arabinofuranosylthymine (SAUS) ..... Am-T
Arabinofuranosylthymine [*Biochemistry*] ..... ara-T
Arabinogalactan Protein [*Biochemistry*] ..... AGP
Arabinose [*One-letter symbol; see Ara*] [*A sugar*] ..... a
Arabinose [*Also, a*] [*A sugar*] ..... Ara
Arabinose (DMAA) ..... ara
arabinose (SAUS) ..... Ara
Arabinose Binding Protein [*Biochemistry*] ..... ABP
Arabinoside ..... Ar
Arabinosyl Hypoxanthine [*Medicine*] (MELL) ..... ARA-Hx
Arabinosylazacytidine [*Biochemistry*] ..... AAC
Arabinosylhypoxanthine (SAUS) ..... Am-H

Arabinosylhypoxanthine [*Biochemistry*] ... ara-H
Arabinosylmercaptopurine [*Antineoplastic drug*] ... ara-MP
Arabinosylmereaptopurine (SAUS) ... Am-MP
Arabis Mosaic Virus [*Plant pathology*] ... ARMV
Arabische Wirtschaftsgemeinschaft (SAUO) ... AWG
Arab-Jewish Women's Dialogue for Peace [*Defunct*] (EA) ... AJWDFP
, ara-C , Prednisone [*Vincristine*] [*Cytarabine*] [*Antineoplastic drug regimen*] ... ROAP
, ara-C , Prednisone, Bleomycin [*Vincristine*] [*Cytarabine*] [*Antineoplastic drug regimen*] ... HOAP-BLEO
Aracaju [*Brazil*] [*Airport symbol*] (OAG) ... AJU
Aracaju/Santa Maria [*Brazil*] [*ICAO location identifier*] (ICLI) ... SBAR
Aracatuba [*Brazil*] [*Airport symbol*] (OAG) ... ARU
Aracatuba [*Brazil*] [*ICAO location identifier*] (ICLI) ... SBAU
Aracca Petroleum Corp. (SAUO) ... ARAC
Arachidonate-Insensitive Platelet (DB) ... AIP
Arachidonate-Sensitive Platelet (DB) ... ASP
Arachidonic Acid [*Biochemistry*] ... AA
Arachidonic Linoleic Acid Ratio [*Clinical chemistry*] ... ALR
Arachnoid Cyst of the Middle Fossa [*Medicine*] (DMAA) ... ACMF
Arachnology ... ARACH
Aracruz Celulose SA [*NYSE symbol*] (SPSG) ... ARA
Aracruz Celulose SA [*Associated Press*] (SAG) ... Aracruz
Aracruz Celulose SA [*Associated Press*] (SAG) ... Aracrz
Aracruz Celulose S.A. ADS [*NYSE symbol*] (TTSB) ... ARA
Aracytidine [*Cytarabine*] [*Also, CA, CAR*] [*Antineoplastic drug*] ... ara-C
Aracytidine, Hydroxyurea [*Antineoplastic drug regimen*] ... ara-C-HU
Aracytidine, Hydroxyurea (SAUS) ... Ara-C-HU
Arad [*Romania*] [*Airport symbol*] (OAG) ... ARW
Arad [*Romania*] [*ICAO location identifier*] (ICLI) ... LRAR
Aradigm Corp. [*Associated Press*] (SAG) ... Aradigm
Aradigm Corp. [*NASDAQ symbol*] (SAG) ... ARDM
Aragarcas [*Brazil*] [*Airport symbol*] (OAG) ... ARS
Aragip [*Papua New Guinea*] [*Airport symbol*] (OAG) ... ARP
Araguacema [*Brazil*] [*Airport symbol*] (AD) ... AGX
Araguaina [*Brazil*] [*Airport symbol*] (OAG) ... AUX
Arajuno [*Ecuador*] [*ICAO location identifier*] (ICLI) ... SEAR
Arak [*Iran*] [*ICAO location identifier*] (ICLI) ... OIHR
Arakan Independence Organization [*Myanmar*] [*Political party*] ... AIO
Arakan Liberation Army [*Myanmar*] [*Political party*] (EY) ... ALA
Arakan Liberation Party [*Myanmar*] [*Political party*] ... ALP
Arakawa-Schubert (SAUS) ... A-S
Arakhin [*or Arakin*] (BJA) ... Ar
Arakis Capital [*Vancouver Stock Exchange symbol*] ... AKS
Arakis Energy [*NASDAQ symbol*] (TTSB) ... AKSEF
Arakis Energy Corp. [*NASDAQ symbol*] (SAG) ... AKSE
Arakis Energy Corp. [*Associated Press*] (SAG) ... Arakis
Aral [*Kazakhstan*] [*FAA designator*] (FAAC) ... AZD
Aral Sea (SAUS) ... Aral
Aralsk [*Former USSR*] [*ICAO location identifier*] (ICLI) ... UATA
Aram Public Library, Delavan, WI [*Library symbol*] [*Library of Congress*] (LCLS) ... WDA
Aramac [*Australia*] [*Airport symbol*] (OAG) ... AXC
Aramaeische Papyri aus Elephantine [*A publication*] (BJA) ... APE
Aramaic [*Language, etc.*] ... A
Aramaic [*Language, etc.*] (ROG) ... AR
Aramaic (ADWA) ... Ar
Aramaic (ADWA) ... Aram
Aramaic [*Language, etc.*] ... ARAM
Aramaic [*MARC language code*] [*Library of Congress*] (LCCP) ... arc
[*The*] **Aramaic of the Old Testament** [*A publication*] (BJA) ... AOT
Aramaic Papyri Discovered at Assuan [*A publication*] (BJA) ... AP
Aramco Services Co., Corporate Information Center, Houston, TX [*Library symbol*] [*Library of Congress*] (LCLS) ... TxHAS
Aramed, Inc. Gensia Pharmaceuticals [*NASDAQ symbol*] (SAG) ... ARAM
Aramed Incorporated Gensia Pharmaceuticals [*Associated Press*] (SAG) ... Aramed
Aramex International Ltd. [*NASDAQ symbol*] (SAG) ... ARMX
Aramex International Ltd. [*Associated Press*] (SAG) ... ArmxIntl
Aramid Fibre Reinforced Plastic (SAUS) ... AFRP
Aramid Reinforced Aluminum Laminate (MCD) ... ARALL
Aramis en Rames Automatisees de Modules Independants dans les Stations [*Arrangement in Automated Trains of Independent Modules in Stations*] [*France*] ... ARAMMIS
Aran Energy Ltd. [*NASDAQ symbol*] (SAG) ... ARAN
Aran Energy Ltd. [*Associated Press*] (SAG) ... AranEgy
Arandis [*Namibia*] [*ICAO location identifier*] (ICLI) ... FAAR
Araneta Journal of Agriculture (journ.) (SAUS) ... Araneta J Agric
Araneta Research Journal (journ.) (SAUS) ... Amneta Res J
Aranjuez [*Costa Rica*] [*ICAO location identifier*] (ICLI) ... MRAJ
Aransas National Wildlife Refuge near Rockport, Texas (SAUS) ... Aransas
Aranuka [*Kiribati*] [*Airport symbol*] (OAG) ... AAK
Aranuka [*Kiribati*] [*ICAO location identifier*] (ICLI) ... NGUK
Arapaho [*MARC language code*] [*Library of Congress*] (LCCP) ... arp
Arapahoe Community College, Littleton, CO [*Library symbol*] [*Library of Congress*] (LCLS) ... CoLiAJ
Arapahoe Community College, Littleton, CO [*OCLC symbol*] (OCLC) ... DVZ
Arapahoe County Evaluation Center, Englewood, CO [*Library symbol*] [*Library of Congress*] (LCLS) ... CoEnE
Arapahoe County School District 6, Littleton, CO [*Library symbol*] [*Library of Congress*] (LCLS) ... CoLiSD
Arapahoe Mining [*Vancouver Stock Exchange symbol*] ... ATH
Arapahoe Regional Library District, Littleton, CO [*Library symbol*] [*Library of Congress*] (LCLS) ... CoLiA
Arapicos [*Ecuador*] [*ICAO location identifier*] (ICLI) ... SEAP
Arapuni [*New Zealand*] [*Seismograph station code, US Geological Survey*] [*Closed*] (SEIS) ... ARA
Arar [*Saudi Arabia*] [*ICAO location identifier*] (ICLI) ... OERR
Arar [*Saudi Arabia*] [*Airport symbol*] (OAG) ... RAE
Araracuara [*Colombia*] [*Airport symbol*] (OAG) ... ACR
Araraquara [*Brazil*] [*Airport symbol*] [*Obsolete*] (OAG) ... AQA
Ararat [*Australia*] [*Airport symbol*] [*Obsolete*] (OAG) ... ARY
Aratea [*of Germanicus*] [*Classical studies*] (OCD) ... Arat
Aratica [*French Polynesia*] [*ICAO location identifier*] (ICLI) ... NTGR
Arator Society [*Defunct*] (EA) ... AS
Aratus [*of Plutarch*] [*Classical studies*] (OCD) ... Arat
Arauca [*Colombia*] [*Airport symbol*] (OAG) ... AUC
Araucanian [*MARC language code*] [*Library of Congress*] (LCCP) ... arn
Arauca/Santiago Perez [*Colombia*] [*ICAO location identifier*] (ICLI) ... SKUC
Aravco Ltd. [*British*] [*ICAO designator*] (FAAC) ... ARV
Arawa [*Papua New Guinea*] [*Airport symbol*] (OAG) ... RAW
Arawak [*MARC language code*] [*Library of Congress*] (LCCP) ... arw
Arawak Airlines (OAG) ... LK
Arax Airlines Ltd. [*Nigeria*] [*ICAO designator*] (FAAC) ... RXA
Araxa [*Brazil*] [*Airport symbol*] (OAG) ... AAX
Araxos [*Greece*] [*ICAO location identifier*] (ICLI) ... LGRX
Aray Qualification Battery (SAUS) ... AQB
Arba Minch [*Ethiopia*] [*ICAO location identifier*] (ICLI) ... HAAM
Arba Mintch [*Ethiopia*] [*Airport symbol*] (AD) ... AMH
Arba Sicula [*Sicilian Dawn*] (EA) ... AS
Arbat Interactive Multi-user System (SAUS) ... AIMS
Arbed Cockerill Process (SAUS) ... AC Process
Arbeidernes Kommunistiske Parti [*Workers' Communist Party*] [*Norway*] [*Political party*] (PPE) ... AKP
Arbeidernes Kommunistparti (Marxist-Leninistene) [*Workers Communist Party (Marxist-Leninist)*] [*Norway*] [*Political party*] ... AKP (M-L)
Arbeit und Sitte in Palaestina [*A publication*] (BJA) ... AS
Arbeit und Sitte in Palaestina [*A publication*] (BJA) ... AuS
Arbeitgeber [*Employer*] [*German*] ... Arbeitg
Arbeits Gemeinschaft der Offentlichrechtlichen Rundfunk Anstalten der Bundesrepublik Deutschland [*Broadcasting organization*] ... ARD
Arbeitseinheit [*Work Unit*] [*German*] ... AE
Arbeitsgemeinschaft [*Study Group*] [*German*] ... Arbeitsgem
Arbeitsgemeinschaft Alpenlaender [*Working Group of Alpine Regions*] (EAIO) ... ARGE ALP
Arbeitsgemeinschaft der Bibliotheken und Dokumentationsstellen der Osteuropa-, Sudosteuropa und DDR-Forschung [*Association of Libraries and Documentation Centres for the Study of Eastern Europe, South-Eastern Europe and the German Democratic Republic*] (PDAA) ... ABDOSD
Arbeitsgemeinschaft der Grossfochungseinrichtungen [*The Association of National Research Centers of the Federal Republic of Germany*] [*Computer science*] (TNIG) ... AGFNET
Arbeitsgemeinschaft der Verbande der Europaischen Schloss- und Beschlagindustrie [*European Federation of Associations of Lock and Builders' Hardware Manufacturers*] (EAIO) ... ARGE
Arbeitsgemeinschaft Europaeischer Chorverbaende [*Federation of European Choirs*] [*Utrecht, Netherlands*] (EAIO) ... AGEC
Arbeitsgemeinschaft Europaeischer Chorverbaende [*European Choral Association - ECA*] (EA) ... EUROCHOR
Arbeitsgemeinschaft fuer Osteosynthesefragen North America (GVA) ... AONA
Arbeitsgemeinschaft fuer Osteosynthesefragen-Association for the Study of Internal Fixation (GVA) ... AO/ASIF
Arbeitsgericht [*Labor Court*] [*German*] ... AG
Arbeitsgericht [*Labor Court*] [*German*] (DLA) ... Arb G
Arbeitsgerichtsgesetz [*Law on labor courts*] [*German*] (ILCA) ... Arb GG
Arbeitsgruppe fuer Menschenrechte [*Germany*] ... AFM
Arbeitskraft ... AK
Arbeitsschutz und Arbeitsmedizin [*Industrial Safety and Medicine*] [*German*] ... A & A
Arbeitsschutzinformationssystem [*Information System for Occupational Safety and Health*] [*West Germany*] (IID) ... ASIS
Arbeitsverwendungsfaehig [*Fit for labor duty only*] [*German military - World War II*] ... AV
Arbejdsloshedsstatistikkens Bruger-Bank [*Danmarks Statistik*] [*Denmark*] [*Information service or system*] (CRD) ... ABBA
Arberia Airlines [*Albania*] [*FAA designator*] (FAAC) ... ABE
Arberia Airways [*Albania*] [*FAA designator*] (FAAC) ... ABW
Arbet International Ltd. [*Hungary*] [*ICAO designator*] (FAAC) ... RBE
Arbetarnas och Smabrukarnas Socialdemokratiska Foerbund [*Social Democratic League of Workers and Smallholders*] [*Finland*] [*Political party*] (PPE) ... ASSF
Arbetarpartiet Kommunisterna [*Communist Workers' Party*] [*Sweden*] (PPE) ... APK
Arbetsmarknadsstyrelsen [*National Labor Market Board*] [*Sweden*] ... AMS
Arbiter (ADA) ... ARB
Arbitrage Networks ... ArbiNet
Arbitrage Pricing Theory [*Finance*] ... APT
Arbitrageur [*Stock exchange term*] ... Arb
Arbitrageur [*Business term*] ... arb
Arbitrageur [*Stock exchange term*] (ODBW) ... ARB
Arbitrarily Primed Polymerase Chain Reaction [*Genetics*] ... APPCR
Arbitrary (MSA) ... ARB
Arbitrary (SAUS) ... Arb
Arbitrary ... ARBRY
Arbitrary Access (SAUS) ... AA
Arbitrary Correction To Hit (SAUS) ... ACTH
Arbitrary Correction to Hit [*Gunnery term*] [*Navy*] ... ACTH
Arbitrary Degree of Freedom (MCD) ... ADOF
Arbitrary Device Handler (SAUS) ... ADH
Arbitrary Diode Function Generator (SAUS) ... ADFG

Arbitrary Evolution Index (DMAA) ... AEI
Arbitrary Function Generator (MUGU) ... AFG
Arbitrary Lagrangian-Eulerian (SAUS) ... ALE
Arbitrary Parameter (SAUS) ... AP
Arbitrary Precision Approximating Algorithm (SAUS) ... APA Algorithm
Arbitrary Precision Multiplication (SAUS) ... APM
Arbitrary Sequence Computer (SAUS) ... ASC
Arbitrary Unit [Medicine] (MELL) ... AU
Arbitrary Value (SAUS) ... AV
Arbitrary Waveform Generation (SAUS) ... AWG
Arbitrary Waveform Generator [Electronics] ... AWG
Arbitrated Access Timer [Telecommunications] (OSI) ... AAT
Arbitrated Loop (SAUS) ... AL
Arbitrating Test-and-Set (SAUS) ... ATS
Arbitration (DLA) ... Arb
Arbitration (AAGC) ... ARB
Arbitration (DLA) ... Arbitr
Arbitration (ADA) ... ARBITRN
Arbitration (ROG) ... ARBRON
Arbitration (WGA) ... ARBTRN
Arbitration and Award [Legal term] (DLA) ... ARB & A
Arbitration and Mediation Center (SAUO) ... AMC
Arbitration & Mediation Institute of Canada Inc. [Institut d'Arbitrage et de Mediation du Canada Inc.] [Formerly, Arbitrators' Institute of Canada] (AC) ... AMIC
Arbitration & Mediation Institute of Saskatchewan Inc. (AC) ... AMIS
Arbitration as an Alternative (DICI) ... AAA
Arbitration Court of Trade Unions (SAUO) ... ACTU
Arbitration Journal (AAGC) ... Arb J
Arbitration Journal (journ.) (SAUS) ... ARB
Arbitration Law: A Digest of Court Decisions [A publication] (DLA) ... Arb L Dig
Arbitrator (DLA) ... Arb
Arbitrator (ROG) ... ARBR
Arbitrator (ROG) ... ARBROR
Arbitron Information on Demand [Marketing service] (DOAD) ... AID
Arbitron Radio Summary Data [Arbitron Ratings Co.] [Information service or system] ... ARB
Arbitron's Information on Demand [Arbitron Co.] [Information service or system] (NTCM) ... AID
Arboga [Sweden] [ICAO location identifier] (ICLI) ... ESQO
Arbois [France] [ICAO location identifier] (ICLI) ... LFGD
Arboletas [Colombia] [Airport symbol] (OAG) ... ARO
Arbor Drugs [Associated Press] (SAG) ... ArborD
Arbor Drugs [NASDAQ symbol] (TTSB) ... ARBR
Arbor Drugs, Inc. [NASDAQ symbol] (NQ) ... ARBR
Arbor Health Care Co. [NASDAQ symbol] (SAG) ... AHCC
Arbor Health Care Co. [Associated Press] (SAG) ... ArborHl
Arbor (journ.) (SAUS) ... Arb
Arbor Press (SAUS) ... ARB Press
Arbor Property Tr [NYSE symbol] (TTSB) ... ABR
Arbor Property Trust Co. [Formerly, EQK Green Acres Trust] [NYSE symbol] (SAG) ... ABR
Arbor Property Trust Co. [Formerly, EQK Green Acres Trust] [Associated Press] (SAG) ... ArborPT
Arbor Resources, Inc. [Vancouver Stock Exchange symbol] ... AOR
Arbor Software [NASDAQ symbol] (TTSB) ... ARSW
Arbor Software Corp. [Associated Press] (SAG) ... ArborSft
Arbor Software Corp. [NASDAQ symbol] (SAG) ... ARSW
Arboreal Pollen (QUAC) ... AP
Arborescent Pollen (SAUS) ... AP
Arboricultural Association (EA) ... AA
Arboricultural Journal (SAUS) ... Arboric J
Arboriculture (SAUS) ... Arbor
Arboriculture ... ARBOR
Arbovirus Disease [Medicine] (MELL) ... AVD
Arbovirus Infection [Medicine] (MELL) ... AI
Arbovirus Infection [Medicine] (MELL) ... AVI
Arbra [Sweden] [ICAO location identifier] (ICLI) ... ESUB
Arbuckle National Recreation Area (SAUS) ... ANRA
Arbuscular Mycorrhizal Fungi [Botany] ... AMF
Arbuthnot's Select Criminal Cases [Madras] [A publication] (DLA) ... Arbuth
Arc (ABBR) ... A
Arc (SAUS) ... a
Arc Brazing ... AB
ARC Cap Wrrt'A' [NASDAQ symbol] (TTSB) ... ARCCW
ARC Cap Wrrt'B' [NASDAQ symbol] (TTSB) ... ARCCZ
ARC Capital [Associated Press] (SAG) ... ARC
ARC Capital [NASDAQ symbol] (SAG) ... ARCC
ARC Capital [Associated Press] (SAG) ... ARCCap
ARC Capital [NASDAQ symbol] (SAG) ... ARCO
ARC Capital CI'A' [NASDAQ symbol] (TTSB) ... ARCCA
Arc Consistency (SAUS) ... AC
Arc Cosecant (ADWA) ... arc csc
arc cosine (SAUS) ... arcos
Arc Current Time Simulator ... ACTS
Arc Cutting [Welding] ... AC
Arc Data Monitor [Welding] [Automotive engineering] ... ADM
Arc Detector Unit ... ADU
ARC Digital (or Digitized) Raster Graphics (SAUS) ... ADRG
Arc Digitized Raster Graphics (GEOI) ... ADRG
Arc Drop Voltage ... ADV
Arc Facilities Manager (GEOI) ... ArcFM
Arc Gas Heater ... AGH
Arc Heater Housing ... AHH
Arc Heating Device ... AHD

ARC International Corp. [Associated Press] (SAG) ... ARC
ARC International Corp. [AMEX symbol] (SPSG) ... ATV
ARC Intl. [AMEX symbol] (TTSB) ... ATV
Arc Jet ... AJ
Arc Lamp Assembly ... ALA
Arc Lamp Igniter ... ALI
Arc LASER Light ... ALL
Arc LASER Light Pump ... ALLP
ARC Macro Language (SAUS) ... AML
Arc Melting Furnace ... AMF
Arc Plasma Spray Technique (SAUS) ... APS Technique
Arc Resistance Tester ... ART
Arc Secant (ADWA) ... arc sec
Arc Sine (ADWA) ... arc sin
arc sine (SAUS) ... arsin
Arc Spraying [Welding] ... ASP
Arc Tangent (ADWA) ... arc tan
arc tangent ... atan
Arc Tangent Mechanism ... ATM
Arc Vacuum Cast ... AVC
Arc View Marine Spill Analysis System (GEOI) ... AWMSAS
ARC [Agricultural Research Council] Weed Research Organization [Research center] [British] (IRC) ... WRO
Arc Weld (KSC) ... ARC/W
Arc Welding ... AW
Arc Welding Machine ... AWM
Arc Xenon Lamp ... AXL
Arca Aerovias Colombians Ltda. [Colombia] [ICAO designator] (FAAC) ... AKC
Arcachon/La Teste De Buch [France] [ICAO location identifier] (ICLI) ... LFCH
Arcade (WDAA) ... A
Arcade (WDAA) ... AR
Arcade [Commonly used] (OPSA) ... ARC
Arcade (ADWA) ... Arc
Arcade [Commonly used] (OPSA) ... ARCADE
Arcade & Allica Railroad Corp. (SAUS) ... ARA
Arcade & Attica Railroad Corp. (IIA) ... A & A
Arcade & Attica Railroad Corp. [AAR code] ... ARA
Arcade Game (SAUS) ... AG
Arcadia, CA [FM radio station call letters] (RBYB) ... KLYY-FM
Arcadia, CA [FM radio station call letters] ... KMAX
Arcadia College (SAUO) ... AC
Arcadia Financial Ltd. [NYSE symbol] (SG) ... AAC
Arcadia, FL [AM radio station call letters] ... WKGF
Arcadia, FL [FM radio station call letters] ... WKGF-FM
Arcadia, FL [FM radio station call letters] (RBYB) ... WWRZ-FM
Arcadia Public Library, Arcadia, CA [Library symbol] [Library of Congress] (LCLS) ... CAr
Arcadian Corp. [NYSE symbol] (SAG) ... ACA
Arcadian Corp. Mand Cv Pfd [NYSE symbol] (TTSB) ... ACAPrA
Arcadian Partners Ltd. [Associated Press] (SAG) ... Arcadn
Arcana Workshops [Teaches philosophy of Alice A. Bailey toward human relations] (EA) ... AW
Arcane Order [Defunct] (EA) ... AO
Arcansas National Wildlife Refuge (SAUS) ... ANWR
ARCAS [Atlantic Research Corporation Atmospheric Sounding Missile] Piggyback Emulsion Experiment (MUGU) ... APEX
Arcata [California] [Seismograph station code, US Geological Survey] (SEIS) ... ARC
[The] Arcata & Mad River Rail Road Co. [AAR code] ... AMR
Arcata and Mad River Rail Road Co. (SAUO) ... AMR
Arcata, CA [Television station call letters] ... KAEF
Arcata, CA [AM radio station call letters] ... KATA
Arcata, CA [FM radio station call letters] ... KHSU
Arcata, CA [FM ràdio station call letters] ... KXGO
Arcata Microfilm Corp., Winston-Salem, NC [Library symbol] [Library of Congress] (LCLS) ... AmC
Arcata Public Library, Arcata, CA [Library symbol] [Library of Congress] (LCLS) ... CArc
Arcata-Eureka [California] [Airport symbol] (AD) ... ACV
Arcato [With the Bow] [Music] ... ARC
Arcato [With the Bow] [Music] (ROG) ... ARCO
Arcavacata [Italy] [Seismograph station code, US Geological Survey] (SEIS) ... ACI
arccosecant (SAUS) ... arccsc
arccosine (SAUS) ... arccos
arccotangent (SAUS) ... arccot
Arch (SAUS) ... Arc
Arch (VRA) ... arh
Arch Chemicals [NYSE symbol] (SG) ... ARJ
Arch Coal [NYSE symbol] (SG) ... ACI
Arch Communications Group [NASDAQ symbol] (SPSG) ... APGR
Arch Communications Group, Inc. [Associated Press] (SAG) ... ArchCm
Arch Development Corp. [Vancouver Stock Exchange symbol] ... ARV
Arch of Aorta [Medicine] (MELL) ... AOA
Arch Petroleum [Associated Press] (SAG) ... ArchPet
Arch Petroleum, Inc. [NASDAQ symbol] (NQ) ... ARCH
Archaeologia Aeliana [A publication] (OCD) ... Arch Ael
Archaeologiae Christianae Doctor [Doctor of Christian Archeology] ... ACD
Archaeological (SAUS) ... Archaeol
Archaeological Conservancy (EA) ... AC
Archaeological Data Archive Project (SAUS) ... ADAP
Archaeological Fieldwork Opportunities Bulletin [A publication] ... AFOB
Archaeological Information and Documentation Services (SAUS) ... AIDOS
Archaeological Institute of Great Britain and Ireland (SAUS) ... AIGBI
Archaeological Institute of Great Britain and Ireland (SAUO) ... AIGBI
Archaeological Journal [A publication] (WDAA) ... AJ

Archaeological Journal [A publication] (OCD) ... Arch Journ
Archaeological Reports [A publication] (OCD) ... Arch Rep
Archaeological Reports (journ.) (SAUS) ... AR
Archaeological Research, Environment Canada [Recherches Archeologiques, Environnement Canada] **Ottawa, Ontario** [Library symbol] [National Library of Canada] (NLC) ... OOEAB
Archaeological Resource Centre (SAUO) ... ARC
Archaeological Resources Management Service [Ball State Univesity] [Research center] (RCD) ... ARMS
Archaeological Resources Protection Act ... ARPA
Archaeological Sites Data Base [Tucson] [Information service or system] (IID) ... AZSITE
Archaeological Society of Alberta (AC) ... ASA
Archaeological Society of British Columbia (AC) ... ASBC
Archaeological Survey Association of Southern California, La Verne, CA [Library symbol] [Library of Congress] (LCLS) ... CLavA
Archaeological Survey of Alberta [Canada] (QUAC) ... ASA
Archaeological Survey of Alberta. Occasional Papers (journ.) (SAUS) ... OPAAER
Archaeological Survey of Canada (QUAC) ... ASC
Archaeologiral Report (journ.) (SAUS) ... AR
Archaeologischer Anzeiger in Jahrbuch des [Kaiserlichen] **Deutschen Archaeologischen Instituts** [A publication] (OCD) ... Arch Anz
Archaeologist (SAUS) ... Archaeol
Archaeology [or Archaeologist] ... ARCHAE
Archaeology ... ARCHAEOL
Archaeology (SAUS) ... Archaeol
Archaeology (VRA) ... archeo
Archaeology Abroad (EAIO) ... AA
Archaeology and the Religion of Israel [A publication] (BJA) ... ARI
Archaeology. Archaeological Institute of America (journ.) (SAUS) ... AIA/A
[The] **Archaeology of Palestine** [A publication] (BJA) ... AP
[The] **Archaeology of Palestine and the Bible** [A publication] (BJA) ... APB
Archaeology Research Program [Southern Methodist University] [Research center] (RCD) ... ARP
Archaeology Section (SAUO) ... AS
Archaeology Subsection Office, Prairie Region Library, Parks Canada [Recherches Archeologiques, Bibliotheque de la Region des Pres, Parcs Canada] **Winnipeg, Manitoba** [Library symbol] [National Library of Canada] (NLC) ... MWPCPA
Archaeus Project (EA) ... AP
Archaic ... ARCH
Archaic (WDAA) ... arch
Archaism (ADWA) ... arch
Archaism ... ARCH
Archana Airways Ltd. [India] [FAA designator] (FAAC) ... ACY
Archangelos [Greece] [Seismograph station code, US Geological Survey] (SEIS) ... ARG
Archangelos [Greece] [Seismograph station code, US Geological Survey] (SEIS) ... RHD
Archangelsk Airlines [Former USSR] [FAA designator] (FAAC) ... AUL
Archbishop ... AABP
Archbishop (ROG) ... AB
Archbishop (ADWA) ... ABP
Archbishop (WDAA) ... abp
Archbishop ... ABSHP
Archbishop (ADA) ... Arch
Archbishop ... ARCHBP
Archbishop (WDAA) ... Archbp
Archbishop Carroll High School, Radnor, PA [Library symbol] [Library of Congress] (LCLS) ... PRaCHS
Archbishop of Canterbury's Certificate in Church Music [British] (DBQ) ... ACertCM
Archbishop of Canterburys Diploma in Church Music (SAUS) ... ACDCM
Archbishop of Canterbury's Diploma in Church Music [British] ... ADCM
Archbishop of Canterbury's Doctorate in Music [British] (DBQ) ... DMusCantuar
Archbishop Oscar Arnulfo Romero Relief Fund (EA) ... AOARRF
Archbold. Indictments, with Forms [1916] [A publication] (DLA) ... Arch Forms
Archbold. Justice of the Peace [7th ed.] [1859] [A publication] (DLA) ... Arch JP
Archbold. Law of Landlord and Tenant [3rd ed.] [1864] [A publication] (DLA) ... Arch L & T
Archbold. Lunacy Laws [5th ed.] [1915] [A publication] (DLA) ... Arch Lun
Archbold. Municipal Corporations Act [1836] [A publication] (DLA) ... Arch Mun Corp
Archbold, OH [FM radio station call letters] ... WBCY
Archbold, OH [FM radio station call letters] (BROA) ... WBCY-FM
Archbold, OH [FM radio station call letters] ... WMTR
Archbold on Baines' Acts on Criminal Justice [A publication] (DLA) ... Arch Baines' Act
Archbold on Bankruptcy [1825-56] [A publication] (DLA) ... Arch Bank
Archbold. Practice of the Court of Common Pleas [1829] [A publication] (DLA) ... Arch PCP
Archbold's Abridgment of Poor Law Cases [1842-58] [A publication] (DLA) ... Arch PL Cas
Archbold's Bankrupt Law [A publication] (DLA) ... Arch BL
Archbold's Civil Pleading [A publication] (DLA) ... Archb Civil Pl
Archbold's Civil Pleading and Evidence [A publication] (ILCA) ... Archb Civ Pl
Archbold's Civil Pleading and Evidence [A publication] (DLA) ... Arch Civ Pl
Archbold's Criminal Law [A publication] (DLA) ... Arch Cr L
Archbold's Criminal Pleading [A publication] (DLA) ... Archb Crim Pl
Archbold's Criminal Pleading [A publication] (DLA) ... Arch Cr Pl
Archbold's Criminal Practice [A publication] (DLA) ... Arch Cr Prac
Archbold's Criminal Procedure [A publication] (DLA) ... Arch Cr Proc
Archbold's Edition of Blackstone's Commentaries [A publication] (DLA) ... Arch Black
Archbold's Forms in King's Bench and Common Pleas [A publication] (DLA) ... Arch KB Forms
Archbold's Forms of Indictment [A publication] (DLA) ... Arch Forms Ind
Archbold's King's Bench Practice [A publication] (DLA) ... Arch KB Pr
Archbold's Landlord and Tenant [A publication] (DLA) ... Archb Landl & Ten
Archbold's Law of Arbitration and Award [A publication] (DLA) ... Arch Arb
Archbold's Law of Nisi Prius [A publication] (DLA) ... Archb NP
Archbold's Law of Nisi Prius [A publication] (DLA) ... Arch NP
Archbold's Law of Partnership [A publication] (DLA) ... Arch Part
Archbold's New Common Law Practice [A publication] (DLA) ... Arch CL Pr
Archbold's New Practice [A publication] (DLA) ... Archb New Pr
Archbold's New Practice [A publication] (DLA) ... Archb N Prac
Archbold's New Practice in Poor Law Removals and Appeals [A publication] (DLA) ... Arch PL Pr
Archbold's Pleading and Evidence in Criminal Cases [A publication] (DLA) ... Archb Cr Prac & Pl
Archbold's Pleading and Evidence in Criminal Cases [A publication] (DLA) ... Arch Cr
Archbold's Pleading and Evidence in Criminal Cases [A publication] (DLA) ... Arch Cr Law
Archbold's Pleas of the Crown [A publication] (DLA) ... Arch PC
Archbold's Poor Law [1840-1930] [A publication] (DLA) ... Arch PL
Archbold's Poor Law Cases [1842-58] [A publication] (DLA) ... APL Cas
Archbold's Poor Law Cases [1842-58] [A publication] (DLA) ... Arch PLC
Archbold's Practice [A publication] (DLA) ... Archb Pr
Archbold's Practice, by Chitty [A publication] (DLA) ... Arch P Ch
Archbold's Practice, by Cholty [A publication] (DLA) ... Arch Pr Ch
Archbold's Practice in Judges Chambers [A publication] (DLA) ... Arch Pr JC
Archbold's Practice in Quarter Sessions [A publication] (DLA) ... Arch Pr QS
Archbold's Practice in the Common Pleas [A publication] (DLA) ... Arch CP
Archbold's Practice in the Common Pleas [A publication] (DLA) ... Arch Pr CP
Archbold's Practice in the King's Bench [A publication] (DLA) ... Archb Pr KB
Archbold's Practice in the King's Bench [A publication] (DLA) ... Arch PKB
Archbold's Practice in the Queen's Bench [A publication] (DLA) ... Arch QB
Archbold's Summary of Laws of England [A publication] (DLA) ... Arch Sum
Arch-Chancellor ... AC
Archconfraternity of Christian Mothers (EA) ... ACM
Archconfraternity of Perpetual Adoration [Defunct] (EA) ... APA
Archconfraternity of Prayer for Israel (EA) ... API
Archconfraternity of the Holy Ghost (EA) ... AHG
Archdeacon ... ADCON
Archdeacon ... ADN
Archdeacon (ROG) ... ARCH
Archdeacon [or Archdeaconry] ... ARCHD
Archdeacon (WDAA) ... Archd
Archdeacon Nares [Pseudonym used by Robert Nares] ... AN
Archdeaconry ... AD
Archdeanery ... Achdny
Archdiocesan (ABBR) ... ADIOCN
Archdiocesan Development Fund [Catholic] ... ADF
Archdiocese (ABBR) ... ADIOC
Archdiocese (ADA) ... ARCHDIOC
Archduke ... AD
Archduke (WDAA) ... ARCH
Archduke ... ARCHD
Archduke (WDAA) ... Archd
Arche (journ.) (SAUS) ... Ar
Arc-Heated Materials Jet [Langley Research Center] ... AHMJ
Archelaus Smith Museum, Centreville (Shelburne Co.), Nova Scotia [Library symbol] [National Library of Canada] (NLC) ... NSCAS
Archelaus Smith Museum, Shelburne County, NS, Canada [Library symbol] [Library of Congress] (LCLS) ... CaNSCeAS
Archenemy (ABBR) ... AENM
Archeological (SAUS) ... archeo
Archeological ... ARCHEOL
Archeological and Historic Preservation Act (BCP) ... AHPA
Archeological Excavation (SAUS) ... Digs
Archeological Institute of America (SAUS) ... AIA
Archeological Research Laboratory [Texas A & M University] [Research center] (RCD) ... ARL
Archeological Resources Protection Act [1979] ... ARPA
Archeologist (SAUS) ... Archeo
Archeology (BJA) ... Arch
Archeology (BEE) ... Archeol
Archeology and Ecology [Coined by Paolo Soleri, Italian-born architect] ... ARCHOLOGY
Archeology Section (EA) ... AS
Archeozoic (SAUS) ... Archeoz
Archer and Hogue. Reports [2 Florida] [A publication] (DLA) ... Archer & H
Archer Communications, Inc. (SAUS) ... QSNDF
Archer Daniels Midland (SAUS) ... ADM
Archer Daniels Midland [Associated Press] (SAG) ... ArchDan
Archer Elementary School, Freeport, NY [Library symbol] [Library of Congress] (LCLS) ... NFreeAE
Archer International Developments Ltd. [Vancouver Stock Exchange symbol] ... ADV
Archer-Daniels-Midland [NYSE symbol] (SG) ... ADM
Archer-Daniels-Midland Co. [NYSE symbol] (SPSG) ... ADM
Archer-Daniels-Midland Co. [Associated Press] (SAG) ... ArchDn
Archer-Daniels-Midland Company (SAUO) ... ADM
Archers Association of Nova Scotia (AC) ... AANS
Archer's Reports [2 Florida] [A publication] (DLA) ... Archer
Archery ... ARCH
Archery ... ARCHRY
Archery Association of Australia ... AAA

Archery Association of Europe (SAUO) ... AAE
Archery Manufacturers and Dealers Association [*Later, AMO*] (EA) ... AMADA
Archery Manufacturers and Merchants Organization (NTPA) ... AMO
Archery Manufacturers Association [*Later, AMO*] ... AMA
Archery Manufacturers Organization (EA) ... AMO
Archery Range and Retailers Organization (EA) ... ARRO
Archery Society of Tasmania [*Australia*] ... AST
Arches National Monument ... ARCH
Archeus Project (SAUO) ... AP
Archeveche de Rimouski, Quebec [*Library symbol*] [*National Library of Canada*] (NLC) ... QRA
Archeveche de Sherbrooke, Sherbrooke, PQ, Canada [*Library symbol*] [*Library of Congress*] (LCLS) ... CaQSherA
Archibald. Country Solicitor's Practice in the Queen's Bench [*1881*] [*A publication*] (DLA) ... Arch CS Pr
Archibald Foundation, Regina, Saskatchewan [*Library symbol*] [*National Library of Canada*] (NLC) ... SRAF
Archibald Foundation, Regina, SK, Canada [*Library symbol*] [*Library of Congress*] (LCLS) ... CaSRAF
Archibald Library, Caronport, Saskatchewan [*Library symbol*] [*National Library of Canada*] (NLC) ... SCA
Archibald Library, Caronport, SK, Canada [*Library symbol*] [*Library of Congress*] (LCLS) ... CaSCA
Archibald on Practice of Judges' Chambers [*A publication*] (DLA) ... Arch JC Pr
Archidiaconal [*Ecclesiastical*] (ROG) ... ARCHIDIAC
Archidiaconus [*Authority cited in pre-1607 legal work*] (DSA) ... Ar
Archidiaconus [*Authority cited in pre-1607 legal work*] (DSA) ... Arch
Archidiaconus [*Authority cited in pre-1607 legal work*] (DSA) ... Archi
Archidiaconus [*Authority cited in pre-1607 legal work*] (DSA) ... Archid
Archidiaconus [*Authority cited in pre-1607 legal work*] (DSA) ... Archidi
Archidiaconus [*Authority cited in pre-1607 legal work*] (DSA) ... Ard
Archie Campbell Fan Club [*Defunct*] (EA) ... ACFC
Archie Frazer-Nash [*British auto industrialist and founder of AFN Cars*] ... AFN
Archie Phinny Hall (SAUS) ... PHI
Archignac [*France*] [*Seismograph station code, US Geological Survey*] (SEIS) ... ARH
Archilochus [*Seventh century BC*] [*Classical studies*] (OCD) ... Archil
archipela (SAUS) ... arch
Archipelago [*Maps and charts*] ... ARCH
Archipelago (WDAA) ... arch
archipelago (SAUS) ... archip
Archipelago Mundi [*An international association*] (EA) ... AM
Architect ... A
Architect [*or Architecture*] ... ARCH
Architect (SAUS) ... Arch
Architect ... ARCHT
Architect (VRA) ... archt
Architect and Engineer (SAUS) ... A&E
Architect Building (SAUS) ... AB
Architect Member of the Inc. Association of Architects and Surveyors (SAUS) ... AL&A
Architect Member of the Incorporated Association of Architects and Surveyors [*British*] (DI) ... AIAA
Architect Member of the Incorporated Association of Architects and Surveyors (SAUO) ... AL&A
Architect of the Capitol [*US*] ... AC
Architect of the Capitol [*US*] ... AOC
Architect/Engineer (COE) ... A/E
Architect-Engineer (SAUS) ... A-E
Architect-Engineer-Manager [*Plan*] ... AEM
Architect-Engineers - Spanish Bases ... AESB
Architect-Engineers Liaison Commission ... AELC
Architect-in-Training (OA) ... AIT
Architects (SAUS) ... Arch
Architects and Designers (SAUS) ... A&D
Architects and Designers [*Building*] [*New York City*] ... A & D
Architects and Engineers ... A & E
Architects and Planners in Support of Nicaragua (EA) ... APSN
Architects and Surveyors Institute (EAIO) ... ASI
Architect's Associate [*Army research program*] (RDA) ... AA
Architects Association of New Brunswick [*Association des Architectes du Nouveau-Brunswick*] (AC) ... AANB
Architects Association of Prince Edward Island (AC) ... AAPEI
Architects' Benevolent Society [*British*] (BI) ... ABS
Architects' Board of Western Australia ... ABWA
Architects Central Constructional Engineering Surveying Service (SAUO) ... ACCESS
Architects' Central Constructional Engineering Surveying Service [*British*] (NITA) ... ACCESS
[*The*] **Architects Collaborative** [*Design firm*] ... TAC
Architects, Construction and Consulting Engineers, Specialist Service (MHDB) ... ACCESS
Architects Council of Europe (DAC) ... ACE
Architects Emergency Committee (SAUO) ... AEC
Architects for Social Responsibility (EA) ... ASR
Architects in Industry Group (SAUO) ... AIG
Architects, Interior Designers, Landscape Designers [*British*] ... AIDLD
Architects Job Costing [*ICS*] [*Software package*] (NCC) ... ARCOS
Architects Journal (journ.) (SAUS) ... AJ
Architects' Law Reports [*British*] [*A publication*] (DLA) ... Architects' LR
Architects' Law Reports [*British*] ... ARCHLR
Architects, Professional Engineers, Land Surveyors Council on Registration (SAUO) ... APELSCOR
Architects' Registration Council [*British*] ... ARC
Architects Renewal Committee in Harlem [*Defunct*] ... ARCH
Architects/Designers/Planners for Social Responsibility (EA) ... ADPSR
Architectural (AL) ... Arch
Architectural ... ARCHL
Architectural (SAUS) ... Archtl
Architectural Acoustics Society (EA) ... AAS
Architectural Aluminium Fabricators Association (SAUO) ... AAFA
Architectural Aluminum Association (DAC) ... AAA
Architectural Aluminum Manufacturers Association (MHDB) ... AAMA
Architectural and Engineering (AFIT) ... AAE
Architectural and Engineering [*Also, A-E*] (AFM) ... A & E
Architectural and Engineering (SAUS) ... A&E
Architectural and Engineering [*Also, A & E*] (KSC) ... A-E
Architectural and Engineering Construction (BYTE) ... AEC
Architectural and Industrial Maintenance [*Coatings*] ... AIM
Architectural and Mechanical (SAUS) ... A&M
Architectural and Planning Information Service (SAUO) ... APIS
Architectural and Transportation Barriers Compliance [*Board*] (AAGC) ... ATBC
Architectural and Transportation Barriers Compliance Board [*Office of Human Development Services*] [*Washington, DC*] ... A & TBCB
Architectural and Transportation Barriers Compliance Board (ADWA) ... ACCESS
Architectural and Transportation Barriers Compliance Board [*Office of Human Development Services*] [*Washington, DC*] ... ATBCB
Architectural Anodizers Council (EA) ... AAC
Architectural Association [*British*] (EA) ... AA
Architectural Association (SAUO) ... AA
Architectural Association Diploma (SAUO) ... AA Dip
Architectural Association Incorporated (SAUO) ... AAI
Architectural Association of Ireland (SLS) ... AAI
Architectural Association Quarterly (SAUO) ... AAQ
Architectural Association School of Architecture (SAUO) ... AASA
Architectural Barriers ... A/B
Architectural Barriers Act of 1968 (WYGK) ... ABA
Architectural Barriers Committee (EA) ... ABC
Architectural Block Diagram Language ... ABL
Architectural Block-diagram Language (SAUS) ... ABL
Architectural Cladding Association [*British*] (DBA) ... ACA
Architectural Control Document (SSD) ... ACD
Architectural Design Study (SAUS) ... ADS
Architectural Engineer (SAUS) ... AE
Architectural Engineer ... Arch E
Architectural Engineer ... Ar E
Architectural Engineering (OICC) ... A/E
Architectural Engineering Construction (SAUS) ... AEC
Architectural Engineering Firm (IAA) ... AEF
Architectural Engineering Service Corporation (SAUS) ... AESC
Architectural Engineering System (SAUS) ... AES
Architectural Fabric Structures Institute (EA) ... AFSI
Architectural Heritage Foundation (EA) ... AHF
Architectural Heritage Year [*1975*] [*British*] (DI) ... AHY
Architectural History Foundation (EA) ... AHF
Architectural Implications of Mission (ACAE) ... AIM
Architectural Information System (SAUS) ... ARCHISYST
Architectural Institute of British Columbia [*1914*] [*Canada*] (NGC) ... AIBC
Architectural Institute of Japan (SAUO) ... AIJ
Architectural Interaction Design System ... AIDS
Architectural Inventory Group [*Association of Canadian Archivists*] ... AIG
Architectural League (SAUO) ... AL
Architectural League (SAUS) ... AL
Architectural League (SAUO) ... ArchLg
Architectural League of New York (EA) ... AL
Architectural League of New York [*Later, AL*] (EA) ... ALNY
Architectural Metal Craftsmen's Association [*British*] (BI) ... AMCA
Architectural Millworkers of Ontario (AC) ... AMO
Architectural Periodicals Index [*Royal Institute of British Architects*] [*Information service or system*] (IID) ... API
Architectural Photographers Association [*Defunct*] (EA) ... APA
Architectural Precast Association (EA) ... APA
Architectural Precast Association (SAUS) ... APA
Architectural Projected Window [*Technical drawings*] ... APW
Architectural Psychology Newsletter [*British*] ... AP
Architectural Record Books (SAUS) ... Arch Rec Bks
Architectural Science Series (SAUS) ... ASS
Architectural Secretaries Association [*Later, SAA*] (EA) ... ASA
Architectural Show (SAUS) ... TAS
Architectural Society of Liverpool (SAUO) ... ASL
Architectural Space Laboratory (SAUO) ... ASL
Architectural Spray Coaters Association (EA) ... ASCA
Architectural Students Association (SAUO) ... ArchSA
Architectural Terra-Cotta [*Technical drawings*] (DAC) ... ATC
Architectural Woodwork Institute (EA) ... AWI
Architectural Woodwork Manufacturers Association of Canada (AC) ... AWMAC
Architecture ... AR
Architecture ... ARCH
Architecture (VRA) ... arch
Architecture (AL) ... Arch
Architecture (ADWA) ... archit
Architecture ... ARCHIT
Architecture and Building Aids Computer Unit of Stratclyde (SAUO) ... ABACUS
Architecture and Building Aids Computer Unit, Strathclyde University (PDAA) ... ABACUS
Architecture and Engineering (AAGC) ... A&E
Architecture and Engineering Performance Information Center [*University of Maryland*] [*College Park*] [*Information service or system*] (IID) ... AEPIC
Architecture and Fine Arts Library, University of Manitoba, Winnipeg, Manitoba [*Library symbol*] [*National Library of Canada*] (NLC) ... MWUAF

Architecture and Planning Research Laboratory [*University of Michigan*] [*Research center*] (RCD) .... APRL
Architecture and Technical Centre (SAUO) .... ATC
Architecture Bulletin [*A publication*] .... AB
Architecture Central Constructional Engineering Surveying Service (SAUO) .... ACCESS
Architecture Characterization Template (SAUS) .... ACT
Architecture Description Document (SPST) .... ADD
Architecture Description Language [*Computer science*] (CSR) .... ADL
Architecture Design, Analysis and Planning Tool (SAUS) .... ADAPT
Architecture Design and Assessment System [*Software package*] .... ADAS
Architecture Development and Assessment System (SAUS) .... ADAS
Architecture, Engineering and Construction (SAUS) .... AEC
Architecture Extended (SAUS) .... AX
Architecture for Reliable Managed Storage [*Cheyenne*] (VERA) .... ARMS
Architecture for Virtual Interfaces for Applications (SAUS) .... AVIA
Architecture for Voice, Video and Integrated Data (SAUS) .... AVVID
Architecture Implementation Review (SAUS) .... AIR
Architecture Management Group (SAUO) .... AMG
Architecture Methodology Working Group (SAUO) .... AMWG
Architecture Neutral Distributation Format (SAUS) .... ANDF
Architecture Neutral Distributed Format (CDE) .... ANDF
Architecture New York [*A publication*] .... ANY
Architecture of Integrated Information Systems (SAUS) .... ARIS
Architecture Research Unit (SAUO) .... ARU
Architecture Review Board (VERA) .... ARB
Architecture Summary Design (SAUS) .... ASD
Architecture Technology Corp. [*Minneapolis, MN*] [*Information service or system*] [*Telecommunications*] (TSSD) .... ATC
Architecture to an Interactive Migration System (SAUS) .... AIMS
Architecture to Logic Equation Realization Technique (SAUS) .... ALERT
Architecture/Engineering (SAUS) .... A/E
Architecture-Neutral Distribution Format (SAUS) .... ANDF
Architectures (SAUS) .... ARCH
Architectures for Heterogeneous European Distributed Databases .... ARCHEDDA
Architrave (VRA) .... archtr
Archiv der Geschichter der Naturwissenschaften und Technik [*A publication*] (MEC) .... Arch Gesch Naturwiss Technik
Archiv des Kreises Asch, Fernleihe, Bayern, Federal Republic of Germany [*Library symbol*] [*Library of Congress*] (LCLS) .... GyBaA
Archiv des Oeffentlichen Rechts [*A publication*] (ILCA) .... Arch Off R
Archiv foer Retsvidenskaben og dens Anvendelse [*Denmark*] [*A publication*] (ILCA) .... AfR
Archiv fuer die Civilistische Praxis [*A publication*] (ILCA) .... ACP
Archiv fuer die Zivilistische Praxis [*A publication*] (ILCA) .... Arch Ziv Pr
Archiv fuer die Zivilistische Praxis [*A publication*] (ILCA) .... AZP
Archiv fuer Papyrusforschung [*A publication*] (OCD) .... Arch Pap
Archiv fuer Rechts und Sozialphilosophie [*A publication*] (ILCA) .... Arch R Soz Phil
archival (SAUS) .... archi
Archival and Manuscripts Control [*USMARC format*] [*Computer science*] .... AMC
Archival Association of Atlantic Canada .... AAAC
Archival Climatic History Survey (SAUS) .... ARCHISS
Archival Management and Storage System (SAUS) .... AMASS
Archival Micrographics, Midland Park, NJ [*Library symbol*] [*Library of Congress*] (LCLS) .... ArcM
Archival Records Management System (SAUS) .... ARM System
Archival Research Catalog [*A publication*] .... ARC
Archival Security Program [*An association*] [*Defunct*] (EA) .... ASP
Archivaria [*A publication*] (BRI) .... Archiv
Archive (MSA) .... ARCH
Archive (VRA) .... archv
Archive .... ARCHV
Archive (AL) .... Archv
Archive 1 Data Analyzer (SAUS) .... AIDA
Archive and Operations System (ACAE) .... AOS
Archive and Record Cataloguing and Indexing by Computer (SAUS) .... ARCAIC
Archive and Records Centre [*Geneva, Switzerland*] [*United Nations*] (ECON) .... ARC
Archive and Retrieval Subsystem (NAKS) .... ARS
Archive Device (SAUS) .... AD
Archive for History of Exact Sciences [*A publication*] .... AHES
Archive for History of Exact Sciences (journ.) (SAUS) .... Arch Hist Exact Sci
Archive for the History of Exact Science [*A publication*] (MEC) .... Arch Neerl Sci Exactes Nat
Archive for the History of Quantum Physics (SAUS) .... AHQP
Archive of Fishery and Marine Research (SAUS) .... Arch Fish Mar Res
Archive Preservation Programme and Retrieval by Automated Techniques [*Computer science*] .... APPARAT
Archive Press (SAUS) .... Archive
Archived file format (SAUS) .... ZIP
Archives (SAUS) .... ARCH
Archives Acadiennes, Universite de Moncton, New Brunswick [*Library symbol*] [*National Library of Canada*] (NLC) .... NBMOUA
Archives and General Library, College of Cape Breton, Sydney, Nova Scotia [*Library symbol*] [*National Library of Canada*] (NLC) .... NSSXA
Archives and Manuscripts [*A publication*] .... Arch Ms
Archives and Manuscripts [*A publication*] .... Archs Man
Archives and Manuscripts (journ.) (SAUS) .... A&M
Archives and Record Cataloging and Indexing by Computer (MHDB) .... ARCAIC
Archives and Special Collections Department, University of New Brunswick, Fredericton, New Brunswick [*Library symbol*] [*National Library of Canada*] (NLC) .... NBFUA
Archives and Special Collections Division, McMaster University, Hamilton, Ontario [*Library symbol*] [*National Library of Canada*] (NLC) .... OHMA
Archives and Special Collections, Simon Fraser University, Burnaby, British Col umbia [*Library symbol*] [*National Library of Canada*] (NLC) .... BVASA
Archives and surveillance (SAUS) .... FAS
Archives, Archdiocese of Kingston, Catholic Church, Ontario [*Library symbol*] [*National Library of Canada*] (NLC) .... OKCAA
Archives, Archdiocese of Vancouver, Catholic Church, British Columbia [*Library symbol*] [*National Library of Canada*] (NLC) .... BVACAA
Archives Association of British Columbia (AC) .... AABC
Archives Association of Ontario [*L'Association des Archives de l'Ontario*] (AC) .... AAO
Archives Authority of New South Wales (SAUO) .... AANSW
Archives, Brandon University, Manitoba [*Library symbol*] [*National Library of Canada*] (BIB) .... MBCA
Archives, British Columbia Conference, United Church, Vancouver, British Columbia [*Library symbol*] [*National Library of Canada*] (NLC) .... BVAUBCA
Archives, British Columbia Provincial Synod, Anglican Church of Canada, Vancouver, British Columbia [*Library symbol*] [*National Library of Canada*] (NLC) .... BVAABSA
Archives, City of Etobicoke, Ontario [*Library symbol*] [*National Library of Canada*] (BIB) .... OEA
Archives, Dalhousie University, Halifax, Nova Scotia [*Library symbol*] [*National Library of Canada*] (BIB) .... NSHDA
Archives de la Chancellerie, L'Archeveche de Montreal, Quebec [*Library symbol*] [*National Library of Canada*] (NLC) .... QMAA
Archives de la Chancellerie, Montreal, PQ, Canada [*Library symbol*] [*Library of Congress*] (LCLS) .... CaQMAA
Archives de la Compagnie de Jesus, Province du Canada - Francais, Saint-Jerome, Quebec, Quebec [*Library symbol*] [*National Library of Canada*] (NLC) .... QQACJ
Archives de la Congregation de Notre-Dame, Montreal, PQ, Canada [*Library symbol*] [*Library of Congress*] (LCLS) .... CaQMACN
Archives de la Congregation de Notre-Dame, Montreal, Quebec [*Library symbol*] [*National Library of Canada*] (NLC) .... QMACN
Archives de la Congregation de Sainte-Croix, Montreal, PQ, Canada [*Library symbol*] [*Library of Congress*] (LCLS) .... CaQMCSCA
Archives de la Congregation de Sainte-Croix, Montreal, Quebec [*Library symbol*] [*National Library of Canada*] (NLC) .... QMCSCA
Archives de l'Archeveche de Quebec, Quebec [*Library symbol*] [*National Library of Canada*] (NLC) .... QQAA
Archives de l'Archeveche de Quebec, Quebec, PQ, Canada [*Library symbol*] [*Library of Congress*] (LCLS) .... CaQQAA
Archives de Philosophie du Droit [*A publication*] (ILCA) .... APD
Archives des Augustines du Monastere de l'Hopital General de Quebec, Quebec [*Library symbol*] [*National Library of Canada*] (NLC) .... QQMAGA
Archives des Augustines du Monastere de l'Hopital General de Quebec, Quebec, PQ,Canada [*Library symbol*] [*Library of Congress*] (LCLS) .... CaQQMAGA
Archives des Clercs de Saint-Viateur, Province de Montreal, Outremont, PQ, Canada [*Library symbol*] [*Library of Congress*] (LCLS) .... CaQMCSVA
Archives des Clercs de Saint-Viateur, Province de Montreal, Outremont, Quebec [*Library symbol*] [*National Library of Canada*] (NLC) .... QMCSVA
Archives des Franciscains, Montreal, PQ, Canada [*Library symbol*] [*Library of Congress*] (LCLS) .... CaQMFRA
Archives des Franciscains, Montreal, Quebec [*Library symbol*] [*National Library of Canada*] (NLC) .... QMFRA
Archives des Freres de Saint-Gabriel, Montreal, PQ, Canada [*Library symbol*] [*Library of Congress*] (LCLS) .... CaQMFSGA
Archives des Freres de Saint-Gabriel, Montreal, Quebec [*Library symbol*] [*National Library of Canada*] (NLC) .... QMFSGA
Archives des Freres des Ecoles Chretiennes, Ville de Laval, Quebec [*Library symbol*] [*National Library of Canada*] (NLC) .... QLFECA
Archives des Freres Maristes, Iberville, PQ, Canada [*Library symbol*] [*Library of Congress*] (LCLS) .... CaQIFMA
Archives des Freres Maristes, Iberville, Quebec [*Library symbol*] [*National Library of Canada*] (NLC) .... QIFMA
Archives des Murasu [*A publication*] (BJA) .... AM
Archives des Peres Eudistes, Charlesbourg, PQ, Canada [*Library symbol*] [*Library of Congress*] (LCLS) .... CaQQPEA
Archives des Peres Eudistes, Charlesbourg, Quebec [*Library symbol*] [*National Library of Canada*] (NLC) .... QQPEA
Archives des Religieuses Hospitalieres de Saint-Joseph, Montreal, PQ, Canada [*Library symbol*] [*Library of Congress*] (LCLS) .... CaQMRSJA
Archives des Religieuses Hospitalieres de Saint-Joseph, Montreal, Quebec [*Library symbol*] [*National Library of Canada*] (NLC) .... QMRSJA
Archives des Soeurs de la Charite de Quebec, Quebec, Quebec [*Library symbol*] [*National Library of Canada*] (NLC) .... QQSCA
Archives des Soeurs de la Charite d'Ottawa, Ontario [*Library symbol*] [*National Library of Canada*] (NLC) .... OOSCA
Archives des Soeurs de la Charite d'Ottawa, Ottawa, ON, Canada [*Library symbol*] [*Library of Congress*] (LCLS) .... CaOOSCA
Archives des Soeurs de Sainte-Anne, Lachine, Quebec [*Library symbol*] [*National Library of Canada*] (NLC) .... QLSAA
Archives des Ursulines, Trois-Rivieres, PQ, Canada [*Library symbol*] [*Library of Congress*] (LCLS) .... CaQTUrA
Archives des Ursulines, Trois-Rivieres, Quebec [*Library symbol*] [*National Library of Canada*] (NLC) .... QTURA
Archives Deschatelets (Oblats de Marie-Immaculee), Ottawa, Ontario [*Library symbol*] [*National Library of Canada*] (NLC) .... OOADE
Archives Deschatelets [*Oblates de Marie-Immaculee*], **Ottawa, ON, Canad a** [*Library symbol*] [*Library of Congress*] (LCLS) .... CaOOAD
Archives d'Histoire Doctrinale et Litteraire du Moyen Age [*A publication*] (ODCC) .... AHDLMA
Archives, Diocese of Fredericton, Anglican Church of Canada, New Brunswick [*Library symbol*] [*National Library of Canada*] (NLC) .... NBFAFA

Archives, Diocese of Montreal, Anglican Church of Canada, Quebec [*Library symbol*] [*National Library of Canada*] (NLC) .... QMADMA
Archives, Diocese of Ottawa, Anglican Church of Canada, Ontario [*Library symbol*] [*National Library of Canada*] (NLC) .... OOAOA
Archives, Diocese of Yarmouth, Catholic Church, Nova Scotia [*Library symbol*] [*National Library of Canada*] (NLC) .... NSYCDA
Archives du Monastere des Augustines, Quebec, PQ, Canada [*Library symbol*] [*Library of Congress*] (LCLS) .... CaQQMAA
Archives du Monastere des Augustines, Quebec, Quebec [*Library symbol*] [*National Library of Canada*] (NLC) .... QQMAA
Archives du Monastere des Ursulines de Merici, Quebec, PQ, Canada [*Library symbol*] [*Library of Congress*] (LCLS) .... CaQQUA
Archives du Monastere des Ursulines de Merici, Quebec, Quebec [*Library symbol*] [*National Library of Canada*] (NLC) .... QQUA
Archives du Monastere Notre-Dame-Des-Anges, Quebec, PQ, Canada [*Library symbol*] [*Library of Congress*] (LCLS) .... CaQQAND
Archives du Monastere Notre-Dame-Des-Anges, Quebec, Quebec [*Library symbol*] [*National Library of Canada*] (NLC) .... QQAND
Archives du Seminaire de Quebec, Quebec, PQ, Canada [*Library symbol*] [*Library of Congress*] (LCLS) .... CaQQAS
Archives du Seminaire de Quebec, Quebec, Quebec [*Library symbol*] [*National Library of Canada*] (NLC) .... QQAS
Archives du Seminaire de Saint-Sulpice, Montreal, PQ, Canada [*Library symbol*] [*Library of Congress*] (LCLS) .... CaQMAS
Archives du Seminaire de Saint-Sulpice, Montreal, Quebec [*Library symbol*] [*National Library of Canada*] (NLC) .... QMAS
Archives et Documents. Micro-Edition (SAUS) .... Arch Doc Micro-ed
Archives Generales des Soeurs Grises, Montreal, Quebec [*Library symbol*] [*National Library of Canada*] (NLC) .... QMSGA
Archives Historiques, Universite du Quebec, Trois-Rivieres, Quebec [*Library symbol*] [*National Library of Canada*] (NLC) .... QTUAH
Archives Jean Piaget, Geneve, Switzerland [*Library symbol*] [*Library of Congress*] (LCLS) .... SzGPAr
Archives, Manuscripts, and Special Collections [*Research Libraries Group project*] (IT) .... AMSC
Archives, Maritime Conference, United Church of Canada Halifax, Nova Scotia [*Library symbol*] [*National Conference of Commissioners on Uniform State Laws*] (BIB) .... NSHMCA
Archives Nationales du Film, de la Television, et de l'Enregistrement Sonore [*National Film, Television, and Sound Archives*] [*NFTSA*] [*Canada*] .... ANFTES
Archives Nationales du Quebec, Quebec [*Library symbol*] [*National Library of Canada*] (NLC) .... QQA
Archives Nationales du Quebec, Rimouski, Quebec [*Library symbol*] [*National Library of Canada*] (BIB) .... QRAN
Archives Nationales du Quebec, Trois-Rivieres, PQ, Canada [*Library symbol*] [*Library of Congress*] (LCLS) .... CaQTA
Archives Nationales du Quebec, Trois-Rivieres, Quebec [*Library symbol*] [*National Library of Canada*] (NLC) .... QTA
Archives of Acoustics (journ.) (SAUS) .... ARACC
Archives of American Art (EA) .... AAA
Archives of Andrology (SAUS) .... Arch Androl
Archives of Andrology (journ.) (SAUS) .... ARANDR
Archives of Biochemistry and Biophysics (SAUO) .... ABB
Archives of Biochemistry and Biophysics (journ.) (SAUS) .... Arch Biochem Biophys
Archives of Biochemistry and Biophysics (journ.) (SAUS) .... ArchBiochemBiophys
Archives of Dermatological Research (SAUS) .... Arch Dermatol Res
Archives of Dermatology (journ.) (SAUS) .... ArchDermatol
Archives of Environmental Health (SAUS) .... AEH
Archives of Environmental Health (SAUS) .... Arch Environ Health
Archives of General Psychatry (journ.) (SAUS) .... AGP
Archives of General Psychatry (journ.) (SAUS) .... Arch Gen Psychat
Archives of Gynecology snd Obstetrics (SAUS) .... Arch Gynecol Obstet
Archives of Immunology and Experimental Therapy (journ.) (SAUS) .... Arch Immunol Exp Ther
Archives of Interamerican Rheumatology (journ.) (SAUS) .... AIARA
Archives of Interamerican Rheumatology (journ.) (SAUS) .... AIR
Archives of Internal Medicine [*A publication*] (MELL) .... AIM
Archives of Internal Medicine (journ.) (SAUS) .... Arch Intern Med
Archives of Lithuanian Folklore of the Institute of Lithuanian Literature and Folklore (SAUS) .... LTR
Archives of Natural History (journ.) (SAUS) .... ANHIDJ
Archives of Neurology and Psychatry (journ.) (SAUS) .... ANP
Archives of Neurology and Psychatry-Chicago (journ.) (SAUS) .... ANPC
Archives of Neurology and Psychatry-London (journ.) (SAUS) .... ANPL
Archives of Neurology (journ.) (SAUS) .... Arch Neurol
Archives of Ontario, Toronto, Ontario [*Library symbol*] [*National Library of Canada*] (NLC) .... OTAR
Archives of Opthalmology (journ.) (SAUS) .... Arch Opthalmol
Archives of Oral Biology (journ.) (SAUS) .... Arch Oral Biol
Archives of Orthopaedic and Trauma Surgery (SAUS) .... Arch Orthop Trauma Surg
Archives of Otolaryngology and Head and Neck Surgery (journ.) (SAUS) .... AONSEJ
Archives of Otolaryngology (journ.) (SAUS) .... Arch Otolaryngol
Archives of Otolaryngology-Head and Neck Surgery (SAUS) .... Arch Otolaryngol Head Neck Surg
Archives of Pathology and Laboratory Medicine (journ.) (SAUS) .... APLMAS
Archives of Pathology (journ.) (SAUS) .... Arch Pathol
Archives of Physics, Medicine and Rehabilitation (journ.) (SAUS) .... APMHAI
Archives of Podiatric Medicine and Foot Surgery (journ.) (SAUS) .... APMSDK
Archives of Psychiatric Nursing (SAUO) .... APN
Archives of Social History (SAUS) .... Archives Soc Hist
Archives of Surgery (journ.) (SAUS) .... Arch Surg
Archives of the Canadian Rockies, Banff, AB, Canada [*Library symbol*] [*Library of Congress*] (LCLS) .... CaABA
Archives of the Canadian Rockies, Banff, Alberta [*Library symbol*] [*National Library of Canada*] (NLC) .... ABA
Archives of the Ecclesiastical Province of British Columbia, Vancouver, BC, Canada [*Library symbol*] [*Library of Congress*] (LCLS) .... CaBVaRE
Archives of the Ecclesiastical Province of British Columbia, Vancouver, British Columbia [*Library symbol*] [*National Library of Canada*] (NLC) .... BVARE
Archives of the Leo Baeck Institute (SAUO) .... LBIA
Archives of the Miramichi Historical Society, Newcastle, New Brunswick [*Library symbol*] [*National Library of Canada*] (NLC) .... NBNAM
Archives of the Moravian Church, Bethlehem, PA [*Library symbol*] [*Library of Congress*] (LCLS) .... PBMCA
Archives of Virology (SAUS) .... Arch Virol
Archives of Yad Washem [*A publication*] (BJA) .... AYW
Archives Office (ADA) .... AO
Archives Online System (SAUS) .... ARCHON System
Archives Providence, Montreal, PQ, Canada [*Library symbol*] [*Library of Congress*] (LCLS) .... CaQMPRA
Archives Providence, Montreal, Quebec [*Library symbol*] [*National Library of Canada*] (NLC) .... QMPRA
Archives Provinciales des Capucins, Montreal, PQ, Canada [*Library symbol*] [*Library of Congress*] (LCLS) .... CaQMArC
Archives Provinciales des Capucins, Montreal, Quebec [*Library symbol*] [*National Library of Canada*] (NLC) .... QMARC
Archives Provinciales des Clercs de Saint-Viateur, Joliette, Quebec [*Library symbol*] [*National Library of Canada*] (NLC) .... QJCSVA
Archives Publiques du Canada [*Public Archives of Canada - PAC*] .... APC
Archives, Queen's University, Kingston, Ontario [*Library symbol*] [*National Library of Canada*] (NLC) .... OKQAR
Archives, Region of Peel, Brampton, Ontario [*Library symbol*] [*National Library of Canada*] (BIB) .... OBRAPA
Archives, St. Paul University [*Archives, Universite St-Paul*] **Ottawa, Ontario** [*Library symbol*] [*National Library of Canada*] (NLC) .... OOSUA
Archives, Unitarian Church of Vancouver, British Columbia [*Library symbol*] [*National Library of Canada*] (NLC) .... BVAUCA
Archives, Universite d'Ottawa [*Archives, University of Ottawa*], **Ontario** [*Library symbol*] [*National Library of Canada*] (BIB) .... OOUA
Archiving Utility [*Computer science*] .... arc
Archiving Utility [*Computer science*] .... zip
Archivio Dati e Programmi per le Scienze Sociali [*Data and Program Archive for the Social Sciences*] [*University of Milan*] [*Italy*] [*Information service or system*] (IID) .... ADPSS
Archivio Dati Italiani di Geologia [*Italian Geological Data Archive*] [*National Research Council*] [*Database*] (IID) .... ADIGE
Archivio dei Libri Italiani, su Calcolatore Elettronica [*Editrice Bibliografica*] [*Italian*] [*Information service or system*] (CRD) .... ALICE
archivist (SAUS) .... archi
Archivists and Librarians in the History of the Health Sciences (NTPA) .... ALHHS
Archivo del Libertador, Caracas, Venezuela [*Library symbol*] [*Library of Congress*] (LCLS) .... VeCAL
Archivo General de Indias [*Archives of the Indies*], **Seville, Spain** [*Library symbol*] [*Library of Congress*] (LCLS) .... SpSAG
Archivolt (VRA) .... arvlt
Archivum Franciscanum Historicum [*A publication*] (ODCC) .... AFH
Archivum Linguisticum [*A publication*] (BARN) .... ALing
Arch-Loop-Whorl [*Basis of Galton's System of Fingerprint Classifications*] .... ALW
Archonist Club (EA) .... AC
Archonist Club (EA) .... ARCLUB
Archons of Colophon (EA) .... AC
Archstone Communities Tr. [*NYSE symbol*] [*Formerly, Security Cap. Pacific Tr.*] .... ASN
Arch-Treasurer .... AT
Archuleta County Public Library, Pagosa Springs, CO [*Library symbol*] [*Library of Congress*] (LCLS) .... CoPs
Archuleta County Public Library, Pagosa Springs, CO [*Library symbol*] [*Library of Congress*] (LCLS) .... CoPsC
Arcing (MSA) .... ARNG
Arc-Jet Wind Tunnel .... AWT
Arclic Institute of North America. Technical Paper (journ.) (SAUS) .... AIAT-TP
ARCNET Trade Association (EA) .... ATA
Arcnet User Group (SAUO) .... AUG
ARCNET User Group (SAUS) .... AUG
ARCO Chemical [*NYSE symbol*] (TTSB) .... RCM
ARCO Chemical Co. [*Associated Press*] (SAG) .... ARCOCh
ARCO Chemical Co. [*NYSE symbol*] (SPSG) .... RCM
ARCO Chemical Co., Channelview, TX [*Library symbol*] [*Library of Congress*] (LCLS) .... TxCvS
ARCO Exploration and Technology Co. .... AETC
ARCO Nuclear Co. (SAUO) .... ARCO
ARCO-Alaska, Inc., Anchorage, AK [*Library symbol*] [*Library of Congress*] (LCLS) .... AkAArA
Arcola Community Unit School District, Arcola, IL [*Library symbol*] [*Library of Congress*] (LCLS) .... IArcSD
Arcola, IL [*FM radio station call letters*] (RBYB) .... WKJR
Arcola, IL [*FM radio station call letters*] (BROA) .... WXET-FM
Arcola Public Library, Arcola, IL [*Library symbol*] [*Library of Congress*] (LCLS) .... IArc
Arcola, TX [*Location identifier*] [*FAA*] (FAAL) .... AXH
Arcola, TX [*Location identifier*] [*FAA*] (FAAL) .... SYG
Arc-Plasma Spraying [*Magnetic film*] .... APS
ARCS Data and Management System (SAUS) .... ADaM
ARCS Meteorological Instruments (SAUS) .... SMET
arcsecant (SAUS) .... arcsec

Arcseconds ... ARCSEC
arcsine (SAUS) ... arcsin
ArcSys, Inc. [*NASDAQ symbol*] (SAG) ... ARCS
ArcSys, Inc. [*Associated Press*] (SAG) ... ArcSys
arctangent (SAUS) ... arctan
Arctco, Inc. [*NASDAQ symbol*] (SAG) ... ACAT
Arctco, Inc. [*Associated Press*] (SAG) ... Arctco
Arctec Canada Ltd., Calgary, Alberta [*Library symbol*] [*National Library of Canada*] (NLC) ... ACARC
Arctec Canada Ltd., Kanata, ON, Canada [*Library symbol*] [*Library of Congress*] (LCLS) ... CaOKanA
Arctec Canada Ltd., Kanata, Ontario [*Library symbol*] [*National Library of Canada*] (NLC) ... OKANA
Arctec, Inc., Columbia, MD [*Library symbol*] [*Library of Congress*] (LCLS) ... MdCoA
Arctec Ltd., Calgary, AB, Canada [*Library symbol*] [*Library of Congress*] (LCLS) ... CaACARC
Arctic [*Air mass*] [*Meteorological symbol*] ... A
Arctic [*Iceland*] [*ICAO designator*] (FAAC) ... AEB
Arctic (WDAA) ... ARC
Arctic ... Arct
Arctic (SAUS) ... Arctic
Arctic Aeromedical Laboratory [*Later, AMRL*] [*Fort Wainwright, AK*] [*Air Force*] (KSC) ... AAL
Arctic Aeromedical Laboratory [*Later, AMRL*] [*Air Force*] ... AAML
Arctic Aeromedical (or Aerospace) Laboratory (SAUO) ... AAL
Arctic Aerospace Laboratory (SAUS) ... AAL
Arctic and Alpine Research (SAUS) ... Arct Alp Res
Arctic and Alpine Research (journ.) (SAUS) ... ARAR
Arctic and Antarctic Research Institute (SAUO) ... AANII
Arctic and Antarctic Research Institute (SAUO) ... AANTI
Arctic and Antarctic Research Institute [*Russian Federation*] [*Marine science*] (OSRA) ... AARI
Arctic and Antarctic Scientific Research Institute ... AASRI
Arctic and Marine Oil Spill Program [*Environment Canada*] ... AMOP
Arctic Anthropology (journ.) (SAUS) ... ARANBP
Arctic Approach Limitation (AFM) ... AAL
Arctic Archipelago (SAUS) ... Arc Arch
Arctic Atmospheric Radiation and Cloud Station (ARMP) ... A-ARCS
Arctic Bay, NT [*ICAO location identifier*] (ICLI) ... CYAB
Arctic Bibliography [*A publication*] ... AB
Arctic Bibliography (journ.) (SAUS) ... AB
Arctic Biological Station, Fisheries and Oceans Canada [*Station Biologique del'Arctique, Peches et Oceans Canada*] **Ste-Anne-De-Bellevue, Quebec** [*Library symbol*] [*National Library of Canada*] (NLC) ... QMFR
Arctic Bottom Water (MUSM) ... ABW
Arctic Boundary Layer Expedition (SAUS) ... ABLE
Arctic Cat [*NASDAQ symbol*] [*Formerly, Arctco, Inc.*] (SG) ... ACAT
Arctic Circle ... AC
Arctic Circle Service, Inc. [*ICAO designator*] (FAAC) ... CIR
Arctic Climate System (SAUS) ... ACSYS
Arctic Climate System Study (ECON) ... ACSYS
Arctic Climate Systems Study (SAUO) ... ACSYS
Arctic Coastal Zone Management. Newsletter (journ.) (SAUS) ... ACZMN
Arctic College, Iqaluit, Northwest Territories [*Library symbol*] [*National Library of Canada*] (BIB) ... NWIAC
Arctic Communication Satellite (IAA) ... ARCOM
Arctic Construction and Frost Effects Laboratory [*Army*] (PDAA) ... ACEFEL
Arctic Construction and Frost Effects Laboratory [*Boston, MA*] [*Army*] ... ACFEL
Arctic Control Area [*Aviation*] (FAAC) ... ACA
Arctic Current (SAUS) ... Arc Cur
Arctic Drift Barge ... ADB
Arctic Drift Station ... ADS
Arctic Drilling System ... ADS
Arctic Enterprises Incorporated (SAUO) ... AEI
Arctic Environment Data Directory (SAUS) ... AEDD
Arctic Environment Information and Data Center (SAUS) ... AEIDC
Arctic Environmental Buoy System (NOAA) ... AEB
Arctic Environmental Engineering Laboratory [*University of Alaska*] ... AEEL
Arctic Environmental Field Station [*Environmental Protection Agency*] (GFGA) ... AEFS
Arctic Environmental Information and Data Center [*University of Alaska, Fairbanks*] [*Research center*] (IID) ... AEIDC
Arctic Environmental Information and Data Center (SAUS) ... AEIDC
Arctic Environmental Research Laboratory [*Environmental Protection Agency*] (NOAA) ... AERL
Arctic Environmental System in Global Change and its Impact to East Asia (SAUS) ... AESEA
Arctic Forward Area Refueling Equipment (DWSG) ... AFARE
Arctic Fuel Dispensing Equipment (MCD) ... AFDE
Arctic Gas and Aerosol Sampling Program [*Marine science*] (OSRA) ... AGASP
Arctic Gas Profile (journ.) (SAUS) ... AGP
Arctic Global Change Program Office (SAUO) ... AGCPO
Arctic Goose Habitat Working Group ... AGHWG
Arctic Health Research Laboratory [*HEW*] ... AHRL
Arctic Health Services Research Center [*HEW*] ... AHSRC
Arctic Ice Dynamics Joint Experiment [*National Science Foundation - Canada*] ... AIDJEX
Arctic Ice Monitoring System (SAUS) ... AIMS
Arctic Ice Thickness Project (CARB) ... AITP
Arctic Icebreaker Coordinating Committee (SAUO) ... AICC
Arctic Ice-Ocean-Atmosphere Interactions (SAUS) ... ARICE
Arctic Indigenous Peoples Secretariat (SAUO) ... IPS
Arctic Institute ... AI
Arctic Institute of America (SAUO) ... AIA
Arctic Institute of North America (SAUO) ... ACNA
Arctic Institute of North America (EA) ... AINA
Arctic Institute of North America. Annual Report (journ.) (SAUS) ... AIANAT
Arctic Institute of North America, Calgary, AB, Canada [*Library symbol*] [*Library of Congress*] (LCLS) ... CaACAI
Arctic Institute of North America, Montreal, PQ, Canada [*Library symbol*] [*Library of Congress*] [*Obsolete*] (LCLS) ... CaQMAI
Arctic Institute of North America. Special Publication (journ.) (SAUS) ... AIASAA
Arctic Institute of North America, University of Calgary, Alberta [*Library symbol*] [*National Library of Canada*] (NLC) ... ACUAI
Arctic International Wildlife Range Society (EA) ... AIWRS
Arctic Interplanetary Scintillation Experiment (or Project) (SAUO) ... IPS
Arctic Islands Pipeline Program [*Canada*] ... AIPP
Arctic Lands and Shelves: Key Assessments (SAUS) ... ALASKA
Arctic Leads Dynamics Experiment (SAUO) ... LEADEX
Arctic Logistics Information Access Service (QUAC) ... ALIAS
Arctic Long-Term Environmental Research Transects program (SAUO) ... ALERT
Arctic Marine Engineering Geological Expedition (SAUO) ... AMEGE
Arctic Marine Engineering Geological Expeditions (SAUO) ... AMIGE
Arctic Marine Freighters (SAUO) ... AMF
Arctic Marine Locomotive [*An icebreaker used in oil exploration in the Arctic*] ... AML
Arctic Marine Oil Gas Reconnaissance (SAUS) ... AMNGR
Arctic Marine Oil Program (SAUS) ... AMOP
Arctic Marine Pipelaying System ... AMPS
Arctic Marine Science (SAUO) ... AMS
Arctic Meteorology Photographic Probe ... AMPP
Arctic Military Environmental Cooperation (SAUO) ... AMEC
Arctic Missions [*Later, IM*] (EA) ... AM
Arctic Mobile Drilling Structure (PDAA) ... AMDS
Arctic Monitoring and Assessment Program (ARMP) ... AMAP
Arctic National Wildlife Refuge [*Alaska*] ... ANWR
Arctic National Wildlife Reserve (SAUO) ... ANWR
Arctic Natural Wildlife Refuge in Alaska (SAUS) ... ANWR
Arctic Ocean ... ARC
Arctic Ocean (SAUS) ... Arc O
Arctic Ocean and Region [*MARC geographic area code*] [*Library of Congress*] (LCCP) ... r----
Arctic Ocean Buoy (SAUS) ... AOB
Arctic Ocean Command (SAUO) ... Arc O
Arctic Ocean Environment Simulator ... AOES
Arctic Ocean Grand Challenge (SAUS) ... AOGC
Arctic Ocean Radiative Fluxes [*Data set*] (OSRA) ... AORF
Arctic Ocean Science Board (OSRA) ... AOSB
Arctic Ocean Variability Project (SAUS) ... AOVP
Arctic Offshore Program [*National Science Foundation*] (GFGA) ... AOP
Arctic Operations [*Military*] (NVT) ... ARCOPS
Arctic Oscillation ... AO
Arctic Paleo-River Discharge (SAUS) ... APARD
Arctic Petroleum Operators' Association [*Canada*] ... APOA
Arctic Polynya Experiment [*Marine science*] (OSRA) ... APEX
Arctic Radiation and Chemistry (SAUS) ... ARC
Arctic Radiation and Turbulence Interaction Study (SAUS) ... ARTIST
Arctic Red Resources [*Vancouver Stock Exchange symbol*] ... ARP
Arctic Regional Climate simulation (SAUS) ... ARCsym
Arctic Regional Climate System Model (ARMP) ... ARCSYM
Arctic Remote Autonomous Measurement Platform (SAUS) ... ARAMP
Arctic Research and Policy Act of 1984 ... ARPA
Arctic Research Center (SAUO) ... ARC
Arctic Research Commission (SAUO) ... ARC
Arctic Research Consortium of the United States ... ARCUS
Arctic Research Directors Committee [*Canada*] ... ARDC
Arctic Research in Environmental Acoustics [*Navy*] (MSC) ... AREA
Arctic Research Laboratory [*Point Barrow, AK*] [*Army*] ... ARL
Arctic Research Laboratory Ice Station (SAUO) ... ARLIS
Arctic Research Laboratory Island [*A floating ice island in the Arctic Ocean*] [*Navy*] ... ARLIS
Arctic Research Vessel ... ARV
Arctic Runoff Database (SAUS) ... ARDB
Arctic Science and Technology Information System [*Arctic Institute of North America*] [*University of Calgary*] [*Information service or system*] (IID) ... ASTIS
Arctic Slope Native Association ... ASNA
Arctic Small Tool Tradition [*Archeology*] ... ASTt
Arctic Small Tool tradition (SAUS) ... ASTt
Arctic Stratus Cloud (ARMP) ... ASC
Arctic Submarine Laboratory [*Navy*] (MSC) ... ASL
Arctic Subsurface Surveillance System (SAUS) ... ARCSSS
Arctic Surface Effects Vehicle [*Navy*] ... ASEV
Arctic Survey Boat [*Coast Guard*] (DNAB) ... ASB
Arctic Survival Instructor [*British military*] (DMA) ... ASI
Arctic Sustainable Development Initiative (SAUO) ... ASDI
Arctic System Science [*Program*] [*Marine science*] (OSRA) ... ARCSS
Arctic Tent Stake Driver (MCD) ... ATSD
Arctic Test Branch [*Army*] (MCD) ... ATB
Arctic Test Center [*Army*] ... ATC
Arctic Vessel and Marine Research Institute [*National Research Council of Canada*] [*Later, Institute of Marine Dynamics*] [*Research center*] (RCD) ... AVMRI
Arctic Village [*Alaska*] [*Airport symbol*] (OAG) ... ARC
Arctic Warfare Training [*British military*] (DMA) ... AWT
Arctic Wildlife Refuge (SAUS) ... AWR
Arctic Wings and Rotors Ltd. [*Canada*] [*FAA designator*] (FAAC) ... AWR
Arctic Winter Games International Committee [*Formerly, Arctic Winter Games Corporation*] (AC) ... AWGIC
Arctic Working Group [*University of Toronto*] [*Research center*] (RCD) ... AWG

Arctica (SAUO) ART
arctic-alpine (SAUS) aa
Arctic/Atlantic/Atmospheric Boundary Layer Experiment (SAUS) ABLE-2B
Arctic-Desert-Tropic Information Center [*Air University*] [*Maxwell Air Force Base, AL*] ADTIC
Arcuate [*Brain anatomy*] AR
Arcuate Hypothalamus [*Medicine*] (DB) AH
Arcuate Nucleus [*In the medulla oblongata*] AN
Arcuate Nucleus [*Neuroanatomy*] ARC
Arcuate-Median Eminence [*Anatomy*] A-ME
arcus (SAUS) arc
Arcus-Air-Logistic GmbH [*Germany*] [*ICAO designator*] (FAAC) AZE
ArcView Marine Spill Analysis System (SAUS) AWMSAS
arcweld (SAUS) arc/w
Ardakan-E-Fars [*Iran*] [*ICAO location identifier*] (ICLI) OISC
Ardakan-E-Yazd [*Iran*] [*ICAO location identifier*] (ICLI) OIYA
Ardeer Double Cartridge Test [*Sensitivity to propagation test of an explosive*] ADC
Arden Branch, Frontenac County Library, Ontario [*Library symbol*] [*National Library of Canada*] (BIB) OAFC
Arden Group Cl'A' [*NASDAQ symbol*] (TTSB) ARDNA
Arden Group, Inc. [*Associated Press*] (SAG) Arden
Arden Group, Inc. [*NASDAQ symbol*] (NQ) ARDN
Arden Hill Hospital Medical Library, Goshen, NY [*Library symbol*] [*Library of Congress*] (LCLS) NGosA
Arden Industrial Products [*NASDAQ symbol*] (SAG) AFAS
Arden Industrial Products [*Associated Press*] (SAG) ArdenPd
Arden Realty [*NYSE symbol*] (SG) ARI
Arden Realty, Inc. [*Associated Press*] (SAG) ArdenRlt
Arden Realty, Inc. [*NYSE symbol*] (SAG) ARI
Ardent (DSUE) ARD
ARDENT Software [*NASDAQ symbol*] [*Formerly, VMARK Software*] (SG) ARDT
Ardestan [*Iran*] [*ICAO location identifier*] (ICLI) OIFD
Ardito [*Ardently*] [*Music*] (ROG) ARD
Ardito [*Ardently*] [*Music*] Ardo
Ardleigh [*England*] ARDL
Ardmore [*Oklahoma*] [*Airport symbol*] [*Obsolete*] (OAG) ADM
Ardmore [*Oklahoma*] [*Airport symbol*] [*Obsolete*] (OAG) AHD
Ardmore [*New Zealand*] [*Airport symbol*] (OAG) AMZ
Ardmore [*Oklahoma*] [*ICAO location identifier*] (ICLI) KADM
Ardmore [*New Zealand*] [*ICAO location identifier*] (ICLI) NZAR
Ardmore Industrial Air Park (SAUS) AIAP
Ardmore Industrial Air Park (SAUS) NArd
Ardmore, OK [*Location identifier*] [*FAA*] (FAAL) AIW
Ardmore, OK [*Location identifier*] [*FAA*] (FAAL) AUV
Ardmore, OK [*FM radio station call letters*] (RBYB) KACO-FM
Ardmore, OK [*FM radio station call letters*] KKAJ-FM
Ardmore, OK [*FM radio station call letters*] (BROA) KLCU-FM
Ardmore, OK [*FM radio station call letters*] (RBYB) KRXZ
Ardmore, OK [*AM radio station call letters*] (RBYB) KVSO
Ardmore, TN [*AM radio station call letters*] WSLV
Ardsley House Publ., Inc. (SAUO) ISBN 0-912675
Ardsley Public Library (SAUS) Ardsley
Ardsley Public Library, Ardsley, NY [*Library symbol*] [*Library of Congress*] (LCLS) NArd
Arduously (ABBR) ADUY
Are [*Also, a*] [*A unit of area in the metric system*] A
ARE Reconfigurable IR Scanner Equipment (SAUS) ARISE
Are You [*Communication*] RU
Are You OK? [*Internet language*] [*Computer science*] RUOK
Are You Still There? (SAUS) AYST
Are You There [*Online dialogue*] (IGQR) AYT
Are You There? [*Computer science*] (DOM) ENQ?
Area (IDOE) a
Area A
Area AR
Area Advisory Group [*British Overseas Trade Board*] (DS) AAG
Area Agencies on Aging (MELL) AAA
Area Agencies on Aging Association of Michigan (SRA) AAAAM
Area Agency on Aging (DHSM) AAA
Area Air Defense Commander [*Military*] AADC
Area Air Defense System (MCD) AADS
Area Airports Checked (FAAC) ARAC
Area Airspace Management Authority (SAUO) AAMA
Area Alarm Sum (ECII) AAS
Area Altitude Requirement (SAA) AR
Area Analysis Intelligence Agency (SAUO) AAIA
Area Approach Control Center (DOMA) AACC
Area Approach Control Centre AACC
Area Assembly Control Group (SAUO) AACG
Area Audit Office (ACAE) AAO
Area Bancshares [*NASDAQ symbol*] (TTSB) AREA
Area Bancshares Corp. [*NASDAQ symbol*] (SAG) AREA
Area Bancshares Corp. [*Associated Press*] (SAG) AreaBnc
Area Bombing (SAUS) AB
Area Business Databank [*Information Access Co.*] [*Belmont, CA*] [*Information service or system*] (IID) ABD
Area Capability Training (SAUS) ACT
Area Chart A
Area Chemist Contractors' Committee [*National Health Service*] [*British*] (DI) ACCC
Area Child Protection Committee [*British*] (DET) ACPC
Area Clearance Officer (MUGU) ACO
Area Club Management [*Military*] ACM
Area Code AC
Area Combined Headquarters [*World War II*] (DMA) ACH
Area Combined Headquarters [*World War II*] ACHQ
Area Combined Movements Center [*Army*] (AABC) ACMC
Area Command Information Exchange System (MCD) ARCIXS
Area Command Post (FAAC) ACP
Area Commander [*British military*] (DMA) AC
Area Commanders' Meeting [*NATO*] (NATG) ARCOMET
Area Commanders Operations Report AREAOPREP
Area Common User System (SAUS) ACUS
Area Communication Controller (SAUS) AAC
Area Communication Controller (VERA) ACC
Area Communication Operations Center (SAUS) ACOC
Area Communications Control Function [*Defense Communications System*] (DNAB) ACCF
Area Communications Electronics Capabilities [*Environmental science*] (COE) ACAPS
Area Communications Operations Center [*Telecommunications*] (TEL) ACOC
Area Communications Terminal Subsystem [*Ground Communications Facility, NASA*] ACTS
Area Community Physician (SAUS) ACP
Area Composition Machine (DGA) ACM
Area Composition Terminal (DGA) ACT
Area Computing Facilities (CET) ACF
Area Computing Facilities (or Facility) (SAUS) ACF
Area Computing Facility (SAUO) ACF
Area Concept Papers [*Military*] ACP
Area Confinement Facility [*Military*] (AABC) ACF
Area Consultative Committee ACC
Area Control Center (DA) ACC
Area Control Center [*ICAO designator*] (ICDA) ZR
Area Control Centre [*FAA designator*] (FAAC) ZRZ
Area Control Computer (SAUS) ACC
Area Control Computer Complex [*FAA*] (TAG) ACCC
Area Control Error (OA) ACE
Area Control Facility [*FAA*] (TAG) ACF
Area Control Operation Center (CCCA) ACOC
Area Control Operations Center (SAUO) ACOC
Area Control Room [*Environmental science*] (COE) ACR
Area Controller (SAUS) AC
Area Control-RADAR (DA) ACC-R
Area Cooperative Educational Service (SAUO) ACES
Area Cooperative Educational Services [*Information service or system*] ACES
Area Coordinating Paper ACP
Area Coordination Center ACC
Area Coordination Group [*Air Force*] (AABC) ACG
Area Coordination Group [*Air Force*] (AFM) ACGp
Area Coordination Review ACR
Area Coordination Subgroup [*Air Force*] (AFM) ACSG
Area Coordination Subgroup [*Air Force*] (AFM) ACSGp
Area Coordination Subgroup [*Air Force*] ACSGRP
Area Coordination to Command Designated in Appropriate Instructions (MCD) AREACORD
Area Coordinator (DEMM) AC
Area Correlation Tracker [*Air Force*] ACT
Area Council for Economic Education (EA) ACEE
Area Coverage AC
Area Coverage File (MCD) ACF
Area Cutover Manager (DNAB) ACOM
Area Damage Control (MCD) ADC
Area Damage Control Center [*Army*] ADCC
Area Damage Control Center [*Army*] ADCOC
Area Damage Control Party [*Army*] ADCOP
Area Data Center ADC
Area Data Center (or Centre) (SAUS) ADC
Area Data Distribution System [*Army*] (ADDR) ADDS
Area, Date, Subject (SAUS) ADS
Area Dean [*Church of England in Australia*] AD
Area Defense Anti-Missile Missile (SAUS) ADAMM
Area Defense Counsel [*Military*] ADC
Area Defense Homing Interceptor ADHI
Area Defense Missile ADM
Area Denial Anti-personnel Munition (SAUS) ADAM
Area Denial Artillery Munition (AABC) ADAM
Area Denial Munition (MCD) ADM
Area Denial Visual Indication Security Equipment (MCD) ADVISE
Area Denial Weapon (SAUS) ADW
Area Dental Laboratory [*Military*] ADL
Area Dental Officer (SAUS) ADO
Area Dental Visual Identification Security Equipment (SAUS) ADVISE
Area Detection System [*Military*] (LAIN) ADS
Area Diastolic Pressure [*Cardiology*] (DAVI) ADP
Area Director (HEAS) AD
Area Discriminator [*SAGE*] AD
Area Distribution Officers [*Military*] [*British*] [*World War II*] ADOS
Area Distribution Panel ADP
Area Division Multiple Access [*Computer science*] (VERA) ADMA
Area Drain [*Technical drawings*] AD
Area Edcuation Agency (SAUS) AEA
Area Education Agency (OICC) AEA
Area Education Officer [*Military*] [*British*] AEO
Area Education Officer (SAUO) AEO
Area Electricity Board (SAUO) AEB
Area Electronic Supervisor AES
Area Engineering Officer [*Army Corps of Engineers*] (AAG) AEO
Area Engineering Officer (SAUO) AEO

Area Entertainments Officer (SAUS) ... A Ent O
Area Entertainments Officer (SAUO) ... AEO
Area Equipment Compounds [*Military*] (AABC) ... AEC
Area Executive (HEAS) ... AE
Area Exploration Battalion (SAUO) ... AEB
Area Fire Armor System ... AFAS
Area Flag Officer (SAUS) ... AFO
Area Forecast [*Aviation*] ... ARFOR
Area Forecast Center [*Meteorology*] (BARN) ... AFC
Area Forecast Center (or Centre) (SAUS) ... AFC
Area Forecast in Metric Unit [*Meteorology*] (BARN) ... ARMET
Area Forecast System (SAUS) ... AFS
Area Frequency Coordinator (MUGU) ... AFC
Area Frequency Response Characteristic (PDAA) ... AFRC
Area Fuel Consumption Allocation [*Environmental Protection Agency*] (GFGA) ... AFCA
Area Full Value (ECII) ... AFV
Area Full Value Display (ECII) ... AFVD
Area Headquarters (NATG) ... AHQ
Area Health Authority ... AHA
Area Health Authority Full Time [*Chiropody*] [*British*] ... AHF
Area Health Authority (Teaching) [*British*] ... AHA(T)
Area Health Education Activity (DMAA) ... AHEA
Area Health Education Center [*Veterans Administration*] (DHSM) ... AHEC
Area Health Education Officer [*National Health Service*] [*British*] (DI) ... AHEO
Area Hyperbolic Sine (SAUS) ... arsh
Area Hyperbolic Tangent (SAUS) ... arth
Area II Library Services Authority [*Library network*] ... ALSA 2
Area Imaging Device (MCD) ... AID
Area Inertial Navigation System (SAUS) ... AINS
Area Inspector [*British railroad term*] ... AI
Area Intelligence Office (SAUO) ... AIO
Area Interdiction Mine [*Air Force*] (MCD) ... AIM
Area Intrusion Detection System (MCD) ... AIDS
Area Joint Blood Program Office (COE) ... AJBPO
Area Junction [*Telecommunications*] (OA) ... AJ
Area L AHEC Library, Rocky Mount, NC [*Library symbol*] [*Library of Congress*] (LCLS) ... NcRmHE
Area Learning Resource Center ... ALRC
Area Letter of Acceptance [*Department of Housing and Urban Development*] (GFGA) ... ALA
Area Library Services Authority [*Indiana*] ... ALSA
Area Local Control Panel (NRCH) ... ALCP
Area Location of Hazardous Atmospheres [*Environmental science*] (COE) ... ALOHA
Area Logistics Center (SAUO) ... ALC
Area Logistics Command ... ALC
Area Mail Processing [*US Postal Service*] ... AMP
Area Mail Processing Center [*US Postal Service*] ... AMPC
Area Maintenance Facility ... AMF
Area Maintenance Office (CIST) ... AMO
Area Maintenance Supply Facility [*Army*] (AABC) ... AMSF
Area Maintenance Support Activity (AABC) ... AMSA
Area Maintenance Support Facility (ACAE) ... AMSF
Area Manager (SAUO) ... AM
Area Manpower Instructional Development Systems ... AMIDS
Area Manpower Review [*Department of Labor*] ... AMR
Area Medical Laboratory [*Military*] (AABC) ... AML
Area Medical Officer (SAUS) ... AMO
Area Meteorological Coordinator (SAUS) ... AMC
Area Microwave Assembly [*Ground Communications Facility, NASA*] ... AMWA
Area Milk Officer (SAUS) ... AMO
Area Minimum Altitude [*Aviation*] (FAAC) ... AMA
Area Monitoring Office [*Military*] (DNAB) ... AMO
Area Moving Target Indicator [*NASA*] (KSC) ... AMTI
Area Multiplexer (CAAL) ... AM
Area Museums Service for South-Eastern England (SAUO) ... AMSSEE
Area Music Shop (SAUS) ... AMS
Area Naval Commander [*NATO*] (NATG) ... ANC
Area Navigation ... ANAV
Area Navigation (PIAV) ... Rnav
Area Navigation ... RNAV
Area Normalization with Response Factors (CIST) ... ANRF
Area Notice (FAAC) ... ARNOT
Area of Cardiac Disease (MEDA) ... ACD
Area of Cardiac Dullness [*Cardiology*] (DAVI) ... ACD
Area of Concentration (RDA) ... AOC
Area of Concern (MCD) ... AOC
Area of Contamination (SAUS) ... AOC
Area of Critical Environmental Concern [*Bureau of Land Management designation*] ... ACEC
Area of Display (SAUS) ... AOD
Area of Dominant Influence [*Mapmaking*] [*Telecommunications*] ... ADI
Area of Emphasis (SPST) ... AOE
Area of Intense Aerial Activity [*Aviation*] (PIAV) ... AIAA
Area of Intense Air Activity (DA) ... AIAA
Area of Interest (AABC) ... AOI
Area of Mutual Visibility [*Aviation*] (PDAA) ... AMV
Area of Operation [*Military*] (VNW) ... AO
Area of Operations [*Military*] (AABC) ... AO
Area of Outstanding Natural Beauty [*Great Britain*] ... AONB
Area of Positive Control [*FAA*] ... APC
Area of Possible Incompatibility [*Military*] (DNAB) ... API
Area of Potential Effects [*Environmental science*] (COE) ... APE
Area of Prime Responsibility (SAUS) ... AOPR
Area of Probability (NVT) ... AOP
Area of Projection (SAUS) ... AOP
Area of Resolution ... AR
Area of Responsibility (MCD) ... AOR
Area of Responsibility Centre [*Aviation*] ... ARC
Area of Safe Operation ... ASO
Area of Savanna (SAUS) ... AS
Area of Savanna Burned annually (SAUS) ... ASB
Area of Significant Conservation Value (SAUS) ... ASCV
Area of Special Tourist Interest (SAUS) ... ASTI
Area of Strategic Value [*Military*] ... ASV
Area of Substantial Unemployment [*CETA*] [*Department of Labor*] ... ASU
Area of Uncertainty (CAAL) ... AOU
Area of Uncertainty Factor ... AOUF
Area Office ... AO
Area Office Director [*OFCCP*] (AAGC) ... AOD
Area Operations Center (SAUO) ... AOC
Area Operations Office [*Employment and Training Administration*] (OICC) ... AOO
Area Passive Dosimeter (MCD) ... APD
Area Patrol Officer (SAUS) ... APO
Area Petroleum Management Office (SAUO) ... APMO
Area Petroleum Office [*or Officer*] ... APO
Area Pharmaceutical Officer (SAUS) ... APhO
Area Planning ... AP
Area Planning Council [*Department of Education*] (OICC) ... APC
Area Planning Report ... APR
Area Planning-Action Councils ... APAC
Area Positive Control (SAUS) ... APC
Area Postal Directory [*Army*] (AFIT) ... APD
Area Postrema (DB) ... AP
Area Precipitation Measurement Equipment ... APME
Area Precipitation Measurement Indicator (IEEE) ... APMI
Area Production Urgency Committee ... APUC
Area Protect Feature (SAUS) ... APF
Area Public Works Officer (SAUS) ... AREAPWOFC
Area RADAR Prediction Analysis (PDAA) ... ARPA
Area Radiation Monitor (NRCH) ... ARM
Area Radiological Monitoring System (NRCH) ... ARMS
Area Railway Transport Officer [*British military*] (DMA) ... ARTO
Area Real Estate Office ... AREO
Area Records Officer (MCD) ... ARO
Area Recruiting Concept Special Test Army Reserve ... ARCSTAR
Area Redesignation [*Environmental Protection Agency*] ... AR
Area Redevelopment Act ... ARA
Area Redevelopment Administration [*Terminated, 1965; functions transferred to Economic Development Administration*] [*Department of Commerce*] ... ARA
Area Redevelopment Program ... ARP
Area Reference Resource Center [*Library network*] ... ARRC
Area Reintegration and Development Center (SAUO) ... ARDC
Area Reprogramming Capability (ACAE) ... ARC
Area Requirements and Product Status [*Military*] (DNAB) ... ARAPS
Area Resident Officer-in-Charge of Construction (DNAB) ... AROICC
Area Resource Center [*Library network*] ... ARC
Area Resource File [*Public Health Service*] [*Information service or system*] (IID) ... ARF
Area Resource File System [*Department of Health and Human Services*] (GFGA) ... ARFS
Area Responsibilities Transfer (SAA) ... ART
Area Resupply ... ARS
Area Re-Supply (SAUS) ... ARS
Area Safety Officer ... ASO
Area Sales Manager (DS) ... ASM
Area Sample (SAUS) ... AS
Area Sampling Frames ... ASF
Area Scale Temperature Display ... ASTD
Area Scanning Alarm ... ASA
Area Search Program ... ASP
Area Section of the Automobile Association (SAUO) ... ASAA
Area Security [*Military*] (MUSM) ... AS
Area Security Coordination Center ... ASCC
Area Security Information Center ... ASIC
Area Security Office (SAUO) ... ASO
Area Security Surveillance System (SAA) ... ASSS
Area Service Command (SAUO) ... ASCOM
Area Service Command (SAUS) ... ASCom
Area Service Unit ... ASU
Area Settlement Plan (TRID) ... ASP
Area Signal Center [*Army*] (AABC) ... ASIGCEN
Area Signal Conditioner (MCD) ... ASC
Area Source [*Environmental Protection Agency*] (GFGA) ... AS
Area Source Category [*Environmental Protection Agency*] (GFGA) ... ASC
Area Spatial Filtering (MCD) ... ASF
Area Specialist Officer (SAUS) ... ASO
Area Specialist Program [*Air Force training program*] ... ASP
Area Specialist Team [*Army*] ... AST
Area Specialized Division [*Army*] (MCD) ... AS
Area Stores Module (NITA) ... ASM
Area Supervisor (FAAC) ... ARSUP
Area Supervisor [*Bureau of Apprenticeship and Training*] [*Department of Labor*] ... AS
Area Supply and Maintenance Facility (MCD) ... ASMF
Area Supply Officer [*Army*] ... ASO
Area Supply Support Activity [*Army*] (AFIT) ... ASSA
Area Supply Support Plan [*Military*] (DNAB) ... ASSP
Area Support and Coordination Committee [*Military*] (VNW) ... ASCC

Area Support Command (SAUO)	ASCOM
Area Support Group [Military] (AABC)	ASG
Area Support Group (SAUO)	ASGP
Area Support Group Kaiserslautern (SAUO)	ASGK
Area Surveillance	AS
Area Surveillance Control System (IEEE)	ASCS
Area Surveillance RADAR	ASR
Area Systems Coordinating Document (ACAE)	ASCOD
Area Systolic Pressure (MAE)	ASP
Area Test Equipment	ATE
Area Traffic Commissioner (SAUS)	ATC
Area Traffic Officer	ATO
Area Training Center [Environmental Protection Agency] (GFGA)	ATC
Area Training Director [Red Cross]	TD
Area Transport & Movements Officer (SAUO)	ATMO
Area Transportation Authority (SAUO)	ATA
Area Under Curve (DB)	AUC
Area under Plasma Concentration Curve [Hematology]	AUC
Area Under the Curve [Medicine] (DMAA)	AUC
Area under the Disease Progress Curve [Botany]	AUDPC
Area Utilization Office [GSA]	AUO
Area Ventralis of Tsai [Of the brain] [Neurology] (DAVI)	AVT
Area VI Library Services Authority [Library network]	ALSA 6
Area Wage and Classification Office	AWCO
Area Wage Survey (OICC)	AWS
Area Weapon Forward (MCD)	AF
Area Weapon Left (MCD)	AL
Area Weapon Right (MCD)	AR
Area Weapon Subsystem (ACAE)	AWS
Area Weapon Verify (MCD)	AV
Area Weapons Effect Simulator (SAUS)	AWES
Area Weighted Average Resolution [Photography]	AWAR
Area Weighted Average T-Number (IEEE)	AWAT
Area Wide Library Network (SAUS)	AWLNET
Area Working Standard (SAUS)	AWS
Area Working Standards (SAUS)	AWS
Area Youth Office [British]	AYO
Area-by-Area-Allocation [Marketing] (DOAD)	ABA
Area-Denial munition (SAUS)	AD
Area-Dominant Military Aircraft	ADMA
Areal Hypolimnetic Oxygen Deficit [Hydrobiology]	AHOD
Areal Power Density (SAUS)	APD
Area-Oriented Depots [Military] (RDA)	AOD
Area-Oriented Distribution [DoD]	AOD
Area/Point Search System (CAAL)	APSS
Areas of Change Questionnaire	ACQ
Areas of Critical State Concern (PA)	ACSC
Areas of Deeper Convection (PDAA)	ADC
Areas of Development International Conference and Exhibition [British] (ITD)	AD 2000
Areas Requiring Corrective Action [Department of Emergency Management] (DEMM)	ARCA
Areas Source Program [Environmental Protection Agency]	ASP
areasinus (SAUS)	arsinh
areatangens (SAUS)	artanh
Areawide Planning Organization [Department of Housing and Urban Development] (GFGA)	APO
Arecaidine Propargyl Ester [Biochemistry]	APE
Arecibo [Puerto Rico] [Seismograph station code, US Geological Survey] (SEIS)	APR
Arecibo [Diocesan abbreviation] [Puerto Rico] (TOCD)	ARE
Arecibo (SAUS)	ArE
Arecibo Initiative with Dynamics of the Atmosphere (SAUS)	AIDA
Arecibo Ionospheric Observatory [Later, National Astronomy and Ionospheric Observatory] [Puerto Rico]	AIO
Arecibo, PR [Location identifier] [FAA] (FAAL)	ABO
Arecibo, PR [Television station call letters]	WCCV
Arecibo, PR [AM radio station call letters]	WCMN
Arecibo, PR [FM radio station call letters]	WCMN-FM
Arecibo, PR [Television station call letters]	WMEI
Arecibo, PR [AM radio station call letters]	WMIA
Arecibo, PR [AM radio station call letters]	WNIK
Arecibo, PR [FM radio station call letters]	WNIK-FM
Arecibo Radio Telescope (SAUS)	Arecibo
A-Register 1-Bit (SAUS)	A Reg 1
A-Register 8-Bit (SAUS)	A Reg 8
A-Register A-Bit (SAUS)	ARAB
A-Register A-Bit (SAUS)	A Reg A
A-Register B-Bit (SAUS)	ARBB
A-Register B-Bit (SAUS)	A Reg B
A-Register B-Bit (SAUS)	A Reg BB
A-Register C-Bit (SAUS)	ARCB
A-Register C-Bit (SAUS)	A Reg CB
A-Register Eight Bit (SAUS)	A Reg 8 B
A-Register Four Bit (SAUS)	A Reg 4 B
A-Register One Bit (SAUS)	A Reg 1 B
A-Register Two Bit (SAUS)	A Reg 2 B
A-Register Word Mark (SAUS)	A Reg Wd Mk
A-Register Word Mark (SAUS)	ARWM
Areito (journ.) (SAUS)	AR
Arel Comm & Software [NASDAQ symbol] (TTSB)	ARLCF
Arel Comm & Software Wrrt'A' [NASDAQ symbol] (TTSB)	ARLWF
Arel Communications & Software Ltd. [Associated Press] (SAG)	Arel C
Arel Communications & Software Ltd. [Associated Press] (SAG)	ArelCom
Arel Communications & Software Ltd. [NASDAQ symbol] (SAG)	ARLC

Arel Communications & Software Ltd. [NASDAQ symbol] (SAG)	ARLW
Arena	ARN
Arena (journ.) (SAUS)	Ar
Arena Magazine [A publication] (BRI)	Arena
Arena Managers Association [Defunct] (EA)	AMA
Arena Managers Association, Inc. [Defunct]	AMAI
Arena Meetings, Conventions and Exhibitions Proprietary Ltd.	AMCE
Areole Trace (SAUS)	AT
Arequipa [Peru] [Airport symbol] (OAG)	AQP
Arequipa [Peru] [Seismograph station code, US Geological Survey] (SEIS)	ARE
Arequipa/Rodriguez Ballon [Peru] [ICAO location identifier] (ICLI)	SPQU
Arerugi. Japanese Journal of Allergology (SAUS)	Arerugi
Arethusa Off-Shore Ltd. [Associated Press] (SAG)	Arethusa
Arethusa Off-Shore Ltd. [NASDAQ symbol] (SAG)	ARTH
Arezzo [Italy] [ICAO location identifier] (ICLI)	LIQB
Arfendazam [Biochemistry]	ARF
Argcen Holdings [Vancouver Stock Exchange symbol]	AGN
Argent [Money] [French]	A
Argent [Heraldry]	A
Argent [Heraldry]	ARG
Argent (ADWA)	arg
Argent Bank [Associated Press] (SAG)	ArgentB
Argenta Systems [Vancouver Stock Exchange symbol]	AEA
Argentaffin [Cytology]	AN
Argentan [France] [ICAO location identifier] (ICLI)	LFAJ
Argentaria Banco Hipotecario ADS [NYSE symbol] (SG)	AGR
ArgentBank [NASDAQ symbol] (TTSB)	ARGT
Argentex Resource Exploration Corp. [Vancouver Stock Exchange symbol]	AXR
Argentia, NF [FM radio station call letters]	CFOZ
Argentia, NF [Television station call letters] (RBYB)	CJOM
Argentin (SAUS)	Argen
Argentina [IYRU nationality code] (IYR)	A
Argentina [MARC country of publication code] [Library of Congress] (LCCP)	ag
Argentina [ANSI two-letter standard code] (CNC)	AR
Argentina [ANSI three-letter standard code] (CNC)	ARG
Argentina (VRA)	Arg
Argentina (SAUS)	RA
Argentina [MARC geographic area code] [Library of Congress] (LCCP)	s-ag-
Argentina Association of Nuclear Technology (NUCP)	AANT
Argentina, Brazil, Chile	ABC
Argentina, Brazil, Chile, and Peru (IIA)	ABCP
Argentina, Chile, Paraguay, Uruguay (SAUS)	Southern Cone
Argentina Fund [NYSE symbol] (SPSG)	AF
Argentina Fund [Associated Press] (SAG)	ArgentFd
Argentina-American Chamber of Commerce (NTPA)	AACC
Argentina-Brazil bilateral nuclear safeguards agency (SAUO)	ABACE
Argentine (SAUS)	Argen
Argentine (SAUS)	RA
Argentine Accreditation Body (SAUS)	OAA
Argentine and Uruguayan Joint Technical Commission for the Maritime Front (SAUS)	CTM-FM
Argentine Angel [Record label]	ArgA
Argentine Anticommunist Alliance [Political party] (LAIN)	AAA
Argentine Banking Corporation (SAUO)	ABC
Argentine Centre of Engineering (SAUO)	CAI
Argentine Columbia [Record label]	ArgC
Argentine Commission for Human Rights (EA)	ACHR
Argentine Decca [Record label]	ArgD
Argentine Industrial Production Institute (SAUO)	IAPI
Argentine Industrial Union (BUAC)	UIA
Argentine Information Service Center (EA)	AISC
Argentine Interplanetary Association	AIA
Argentine Island [Antarctica] [Seismograph station code, US Geological Survey] (SEIS)	AIA
Argentine London [Record label]	ArgLon
Argentine Oceanographic Data Centre (SAUO)	AODC
Argentine Odeon [Record label]	ArgOd
Argentine Parlophone [Record label]	ArgP
Argentine Pathe [Record label]	ArgPat
Argentine Victor [Record label]	ArgV
Argentinean (ADWA)	Arg
Argentinia, Brazil, Chile (SAUS)	ABC
Argentinian Communist Party [Political party]	AKP
Argentinian Hemorrhagic Fever [Medicine] (DMAA)	AHF
Argentinian Oceanographic Data Centre (SAUS)	CEADO
Argentinien [Argentina] [German]	Argent
Argenton-Sur-Creuse [France] [ICAO location identifier] (ICLI)	LFEG
Argentum [Silver] [Chemical element]	AR
Argentum [Silver] [Numismatics]	AR
Argentum [Silver]	ARG
Arges [Romania] [Seismograph station code, US Geological Survey] (SEIS)	ARR
Argillite (VRA)	argil
Argilnyl (SAUS)	R
Arginase [An enzyme]	AS
Arginase Deficiency [Medicine] (MELL)	AD
Arginine [Also, R] [An amino acid]	Arg
Arginine [Also, R] [An amino acid] (DOG)	arg
Arginine (DB)	ARG
Arginine [One-letter symbol; see Arg]	R
Arginine Decarboxylase [An enzyme]	ADC
Arginine, Glutamate, alpha-Ketoglutarate Oxalacetate	AGKO
Arginine Insulin Tolerance Test [Endocrinology] (MAE)	AITT
Arginine Maturity Index [For prediction of peanut harvest date]	AMI
Arginine Phosphate (MELL)	ArgP

Arginine Rich Motif [*Biochemistry*] ... ARM
Arginine Tolerance Test [*Endocrinology*] ... ATT
Arginine Vascotocin (SAUS) ... AVT
Arginine Vasopressin [*Antidiuretic hormone*] ... AVP
Arginine Vasotocin [*Endocrinology*] ... AVT
Arginine-Vasopressin (DMAA) ... ARVP
Argininosuccinate [*Biochemistry*] (DAVI) ... ASA
Argininosuccinate Lyase [*Also, ASL*] [*An enzyme*] ... AL
Argininosuccinate Lyase [*Also, AL*] [*An enzyme*] ... ASL
Argininosuccinate Synthetase [*An enzyme*] ... AS
Argininosuccinate Synthetase [*An enzyme*] (AAMN) ... ASAS
Argininosuccinate Synthetase [*An enzyme*] ... ASS
Argininosuccinate Synthetase Pseudogene (DMAA) ... ASSP
Argininosuccinic Acid (MAE) ... ASA
Arginino-Succinic Acid (SAUS) ... ASA
Arginio-Succinic Acid (SAUS) ... ASA
Arginosuccinic Acid Lyase (DMAA) ... ASAL
Argles' French Law of Bills of Exchange [*A publication*] (DLA) ... Arg Bills Ex
Argo [*Constellation*] ... ARG
Argo Development Corp. [*Vancouver Stock Exchange symbol*] ... ARG
Argo Navis [*Constellation*] (WDAA) ... Arg
Argo, SA [*Dominican Republic*] [*ICAO designator*] (ICDA) ... DI
Argo SA [*Dominican Republic*] [*ICAO designator*] (FAAC) ... RGO
ARGO Systems, Inc., Sunnyvale, CA [*OCLC symbol*] (OCLC) ... ASI
Argon [*Chemical symbol is Ar*] [*Chemical element*] ... A
Argon [*Preferred form, but also see A*] [*Chemical element*] ... Ar
Argon Beam Coagulator (MELL) ... ABC
Argon Gas LASER ... AGL
Argon Glow Lamp ... AGL
Argon Ion LASER ... AIL
Argon Ionization Detector [*Medicine*] (DMAA) ... AID
Argon LASER Discharge Tube ... ALDT
Argon LASER Lining ... ALL
Argon Laser Photocoagulation [*Medicine*] (MELL) ... ALPC
Argon LASER Trabeculoplasty [*Ophthalmology*] (DAVI) ... ALT
Argon Laser Trabeculoplasty [*Medicine*] (MELL) ... ALTP
Argon Oxygen Refining (DNAB) ... AOR
Argon Purge Cart [*Nuclear energy*] (NRCH) ... APC
Argonaut Group [*NASDAQ symbol*] (SG) ... AGII
Argonaut Group, Inc. [*NASDAQ symbol*] (NQ) ... AGII
Argonaut Group, Inc. [*Associated Press*] (SAG) ... ArgoGp
Argonaut Resources Ltd. [*Vancouver Stock Exchange symbol*] ... AGP
Argonautica [*of Apollonius Rhodius*] [*Classical studies*] (OCD) ... Argon
Argone Code Center Exchange and Storage System (SAUS) ... ACCESS
Argonex International Ltd. [*Vancouver Stock Exchange symbol*] ... AXI
Argonne Advanced Research Reactor ... AARR
Argonne Advanced Research Reactor (NRCH) ... A^{2R2}
Argonne Area Office (SAUO) ... AR
Argonne Boiling Reactor Experiment (SAUS) ... ARBOR Experiment
Argonne Boiling Reactor Facility (SAUS) ... ARBOR Facility
Argonne Boiling Water Reactor (NRCH) ... ARBOR
Argonne Boundary Layer Experiment (ARMP) ... ABLE
Argonne Cancer Research Hospital [*Illinois*] ... ACRH
Argonne Cancer Research Hospitel (SAUO) ... ACRH
Argonne Code Center [*Department of Energy*] (IID) ... ACC
Argonne Code Center Exchange and Storage System (MHDB) ... ACCESS
Argonne Computer-Aided Diffraction Equipment ... ARCADE
Argonne Dispersion Code (MCD) ... ARDISC
Argonne Fast Source Reactor ... AFSR
Argonne High Flux Reactor (SAUS) ... AHFR
Argonne Institute of Nuclear Science and Engineering [*AEC*] ... AINSE
Argonne Interactive Display ... AID
Argonne Low-Power Reactor [*Obsolete*] ... ALPR
Argonne Microprocessor ... AMP
Argonne Multichannel Stored Program Analyzer (SAUS) ... ARMSPAN
Argonne Natioanl Laboratory-West (SAUO) ... ANL-W
Argonne National Laboratory [*Argonne, IL*] [*Department of Energy*] (GRD) ... ANL
Argonne National Laboratory (SAUO) ... M-ANL
Argonne National Laboratory Accelerator Division (SAUO) ... ANLAD
Argonne National Laboratory, Accelerator Division (SAUS) ... ANLAD
Argonne National Laboratory, Argonne, IL [*OCLC symbol*] (OCLC) ... ANL
Argonne National Laboratory, Argonne, IL [*Library symbol*] [*Library of Congress*] (LCLS) ... IArg
Argonne National Laboratory, Argonne-West Technical Library, Idaho Falls, ID [*Library symbol*] [*Library of Congress*] (LCLS) ... IdIfAL
Argonne National Laboratory Division of Environmental Impact Studies ... ANL/ES
Argonne National Laboratory Energy and Environmental Systems Division ... ANL/EES
Argonne National Laboratory. Energy and Environmental Systems Division. Report ANL/CNSV (journ.) (SAUS) ... ANLSD
Argonne National Laboratory Engineering and Technology Division [*Illinois*] ... ANL/ETD
Argonne National Laboratory, Idaho Division (SAUS) ... ANLID
Argonne National Laboratory Illinois Site (AAGC) ... AIS
Argonne National Laboratory-East [*Argonne, IL*] (GAAI) ... ANL-E
Argonne National Laboratory-West [*Idaho Falls, ID*] (GAAI) ... ANL-W
Argonne Nuclear Assembly for University Training ... ARGONAUT
Argonne Reactor Computation (IEEE) ... ARC
Argonne Reactor Physics [*AEC*] (PDAA) ... ARP
Argonne Remote Manipulator ... ARM
Argonne Reviews (journ.) (SAUS) ... Argonne Rev
Argonne Tandem Linear Accelerator System ... ATLAS
Argonne Tandem/LINAC Accelerator System [*Department of Energy*] ... ATLAS
Argonne Thermal Source Reactor ... ATSR
Argonne Unified Safeguards (SAUS) ... ARGUS
Argonne Universities Association ... AUA
Argonne Version of Institute Digital Automatic Computer (SAUS) ... AVIDAC
Argon-Oxygen Decarburization [*Steelmaking*] ... AOD
Argonz del Castillo Syndrome [*Medicine*] (DMAA) ... ADCS
ARGOS Data Acquisition Platform (SAUS) ... ADAP
ARGOS Data Collection and Location System (SAUS) ... ARGOS+
Argos Data Collection and Location System [*France*] (EOSA) ... ARGOS
ARGOS Data Collection and Position Location System (SAUS) ... ARGOS
ARGOS Processing Centre (SAUS) ... APC
Argos Public Library, Argos, IN [*Library symbol*] [*Library of Congress*] (LCLS) ... InAr
Argos Tribune, Argos, IN [*Library symbol*] [*Library of Congress*] (LCLS) ... InArT
ARGOS/Data Collection System (SAUS) ... DCS
Argostolion [*Greece*] [*Airport symbol*] (OAG) ... EFL
Argosy [*A publication*] (ROG) ... ARG
Argosy Airways [*Canada*] [*ICAO designator*] (FAAC) ... ARY
Argosy Gaming [*NYSE symbol*] (SG) ... AGY
Argosy Gaming [*NASDAQ symbol*] (TTSB) ... ARGY
Argosy Gaming Co. [*NYSE symbol*] (SAG) ... AGY
Argosy Gaming Co. [*Associated Press*] (SAG) ... Argosy
Argosy Gaming Co. [*NASDAQ symbol*] (SAG) ... ARGY
Argosy Mining Corp. Ltd. [*Toronto Stock Exchange symbol*] ... AGY
Argosy-Antiquarian Limited (SAUS) ... Argosy
Argrel Resources Ltd. [*Formerly, Sundance Gold Ltd.*] [*Vancouver Stock Exchange symbol*] ... AGL
Argument (OCD) ... ARG
Argument + Programming (SAUS) ... AP
Argument Association (SAUO) ... AA
Argument Byte (SAUS) ... AB
Argument Pointer (RALS) ... AP
Argument Programming (MSA) ... AP
argumentation (SAUS) ... arg
argumentative (SAUS) ... arg
Argumentator (SAUS) ... Arg
Argumento [*By an argument drawn from such a law*] [*Latin*] ... ARG
argumentum ad verecundiam (SAUS) ... Argh
argus (SAUS) ... arg
Argus Communications Protocol (SAUS) ... ACP
Argus Corp. Ltd. [*Toronto Stock Exchange symbol*] ... AR
Argus Open Numerical Environments [*Computer science*] ... Argus ONE
Argus Press Group [*British*] ... APG
Argus Printing & Publishing Co., Butler, NJ [*Library symbol*] [*Library of Congress*] (LCLS) ... NjButA
Argus Shuttle Pallet Satellite (SAUS) ... Argus SPAS
Argus Telescope (SAUS) ... Argus
Argyl Light Infantry (SAUO) ... ALI
Argyle Community Library, Port Loring, Ontario [*Library symbol*] [*National Library of Canada*] (NLC) ... OPLAC
Argyle, NY [*FM radio station call letters*] (BROA) ... WNGN-FM
Argyle Robertson Pupil (SAUS) ... ARP
Argyle School, Argyle, MN [*Library symbol*] [*Library of Congress*] (LCLS) ... MnArS
Argyle Television 'A' [*NASDAQ symbol*] (TTSB) ... ARGL
Argyle Television, Inc. [*NASDAQ symbol*] (SAG) ... ARGL
Argyle Television, Inc. [*Associated Press*] (SAG) ... ArgyleT
Argyle Ventures [*Vancouver Stock Exchange symbol*] ... AGV
Argyll [*County in Scotland*] ... ARG
Argyll and Sutherland Highlanders (SAUO) ... AA&SH
Argyll and Sutherland Highlanders [*Military unit*] [*British*] ... A & SH
Argyll Energy Corp. [*Toronto Stock Exchange symbol*] ... AYE
Argyll Light Infantry [*Military unit*] [*British*] ... ALI
Argyll Light Infantry (SAUO) ... ALI
Argyll Robertson Pupil [*Ophthalmology*] (MAE) ... AR
Argyllshire [*County in Scotland*] ... ARGYL
Argyllshire (SAUS) ... Argyll
Argyllshire [*County in Scotland*] (ROG) ... ARGYLLS
Argyre Plamitia [*A filamentary mark on Mars*] ... AP
Argyrophil ... AL
Argyrophil, Fluorescent, Granulated [*Cells*] [*Anatomy*] ... AFG
Arhus/Kirstinesminde [*Denmark*] [*ICAO location identifier*] (ICLI) ... EKKM
ARI Network Services [*NASDAQ symbol*] (SPSG) ... ARIS
ARI Network Services, Inc. [*Associated Press*] (SAG) ... ARI Net
ARIA [*Apollo Range Instrumentation Aircraft*] **Operations Control Center** [*NASA*] ... AOCC
ARIA [*Advanced Range Instrumentation Aircraft*] **Phased Array Telemetry System** [*Air Force*] ... APATS
ARIA Phased Array Telemetry System (SAUS) ... APATS
Ariad Pharmaceutical, Inc. [*NASDAQ symbol*] (SAG) ... ARIA
ARIAD Pharmaceuticals [*NASDAQ symbol*] (TTSB) ... ARIA
Ariad Pharmaceuticals, Inc. [*Associated Press*] (SAG) ... Ariad
Ariad Pharmaceuticals, Inc. [*Associated Press*] (SAG) ... AriadP
ARIAD Pharmaceuticals Wrrt [*NASDAQ symbol*] (TTSB) ... ARIAW
Ariana Afghan Airlines [*Afganistan*] [*ICAO designator*] (FAAC) ... AFG
Ariana Afghan Airlines (SAUS) ... ARIANA
Ariana Afghan Airlines [*ICAO designator*] (AD) ... FG
Ariana Afghan Airlines (SAUS) ... ZZ
Ariana-Afghan Airlines (SAUO) ... Ariana
Ariane Passenger Experiments (ACAE) ... APEX
ARIANE [*Artificial Satellite*] **Passenger Payload Experiment** (PDAA) ... APPLE
Ariane Passenger Payload Experiment (SAUS) ... APPLE
Ariane Structure for Auxiliary payloads (SAUS) ... ASAP
Ariane Technology Experiment Platform (SAUS) ... ARTEP
Ariane Transfer Vehicle (SAUS) ... ATV
Arianespace SA, Paris (SAUS) ... AE
Ariba, Inc. [*NASDAQ symbol*] (SG) ... ARBA

Aribinda [*Burkina Faso*] [*ICAO location identifier*] (ICLI) ... DHOY
Arica [*Chile*] [*Airport symbol*] (OAG) ... ARI
Arica [*Chile*] [*Seismograph station code, US Geological Survey*] (SEIS) ... ARI
Arica Institute (EA) ... AI
Arica/Internacional Chacalluta [*Chile*] [*ICAO location identifier*] (ICLI) ... SCAR
Aricana Resources [*Vancouver Stock Exchange symbol*] ... ANO
Aricraft Radio Instrument (SAUS) ... ARI
Arid and Semi-Arid Lands (SAUS) ... ASAL
Arid Climate, Adaptation and Cultural Innovation in Africa (SAUS) ... ACACIA
Arid Climate, Adaptation, and Cultural Innovation in Africa (QUAC) ... ACACIA
Arid Integrated Demonstration (ABAC) ... arid ID
Arid Land Ecology [*AEC project*] ... ALE
Arid Lands Agricultural Development [*Program*] [*Later, ICARDA*] [*Middle East*] ... ALAD
Arid Lands Ecology ... ARE
Arid Lands Ecology Reserve ... ALE
Arid Lands Environment Centre [*Australia*] ... ALEC
Arid Lands Information Center [*University of Arizona*] [*Tucson*] ... ALIC
Arid Lands Information System [*University of Arizona*] [*Tucson*] (IID) ... ALIS
Arid Lands Newsletter (SAUS) ... ALN
Arid Zone Research Institute (SAUS) ... AZRI
Arida [*Japan*] [*Seismograph station code, US Geological Survey*] (SEIS) ... ARD
Ariel Appreciation Fund [*Mutual fund ticker symbol*] (SG) ... CAAPX
Ariel Corp. [*NASDAQ symbol*] (SAG) ... ADSP
Ariel Corp. [*Associated Press*] (SAG) ... Ariel
Ariel Corp. [*Associated Press*] (SAG) ... ArielCp
Ariel Corp. Unit 2000 [*NASDAQ symbol*] (TTSB) ... ADSPU
Ariel Corp. Wrrt [*NASDAQ symbol*] (TTSB) ... ADSPW
Ariel Growth Fund [*Mutual fund ticker symbol*] (SG) ... ARGFX
Ariel Owners Motorcycle Club (SAUS) ... AOMC
Ariel Resources [*TS Symbol*] (TTSB) ... AU
Ariel Resources Ltd. [*Vancouver Stock Exchange symbol*] ... ALL
Ariely Advertising Ltd. [*Associated Press*] (SAG) ... Ariely
Ariely Advertising Ltd. [*NASDAQ symbol*] (SAG) ... RELE
Ariely Advertising Ltd [*NASDAQ symbol*] (TTSB) ... RELEF
Aries [*Constellation*] ... Ari
Aries (NTIO) ... ARI
Aries [*Constellation*] ... Arie
Aries Air Cargo International [*Air carrier designation symbol*] ... AACX
Aries Resources [*Vancouver Stock Exchange symbol*] ... AIE
Aril Society International (EA) ... ASI
ARINC [*Aeronautical Radio, Inc.*] **Communications Addressing and Reporting System** (USDC) ... ACARS
ARINC Communications Addressing and Reporting System (SAUS) ... ACARS
ARINC [*Aeronautical Radio Inc.*] **Communications Addressing and Reporting Systems** [*Marine science*] (OSRA) ... ACARS
ARINC [*Aeronautical Radio Incorporated*] **Communications and Address Reporting System** [*Digital communications system used primarily for aircraft-to-airline messages*] (GAVI) ... ACARS
ARINC Communications and Relay System (SAUS) ... ACARS
ARINC (Corp.) Communications Addressing and Reporting System (SAUO) ... ACARS
Arion Resources, Inc. [*Vancouver Stock Exchange symbol*] ... AIO
Arion Systems, Inc. ... ASI
Ariprandus [*Flourished, 12th century*] [*Authority cited in pre-1607 legal work*] (DSA) ... Ar
Ariprandus [*Flourished, 12th century*] [*Authority cited in pre-1607 legal work*] (DSA) ... Ari
Ariprandus [*Flourished, 12th century*] [*Authority cited in pre-1607 legal work*] (DSA) ... Arip
Ariprandus [*Flourished, 12th century*] [*Authority cited in pre-1607 legal work*] (DSA) ... Aripnd
Ariprandus [*Flourished, 12th century*] [*Authority cited in pre-1607 legal work*] (DSA) ... Arp
Ariprandus [*Flourished, 12th century*] [*Authority cited in pre-1607 legal work*] (DSA) ... Arpn
Arising Anew [*Latin*] (EES) ... de novo
Arista Investors Corp. [*NASDAQ symbol*] (NQ) ... ARIN
Arista Investors Corp. [*Associated Press*] (SAG) ... AristIn
Arista Invs Corp. [*NASDAQ symbol*] (TTSB) ... ARINA
Arista Manufacturing Systems (SAUS) ... AMS
Aristo International [*NASDAQ symbol*] (TTSB) ... ATSP
Aristo International Corp. [*Associated Press*] (SAG) ... AristoIn
Aristo International Corp. [*NASDAQ symbol*] (SAG) ... ATSP
Aristocrat (DSUE) ... ARISTO
Aristocrat (ADWA) ... aristo
Aristocrat ... ARSTCRT
Aristophanes [*Greek playwright, c. 445-380BC*] [*Classical studies*] (OCD) ... Ar
Aristophanes [*Greek playwright, c. 445-380BC*] [*Classical studies*] (ROG) ... ARIST
Aristos Foundation (EA) ... AF
Aristos Guild (EA) ... AG
Aristotelian Society [*British*] (EAIO) ... AS
Aristotelian Society (SAUO) ... AS
Aristotle [*Greek philosopher, 384-322BC*] [*Classical studies*] (ROG) ... ARIST
Aristotle Corp. [*Associated Press*] (SAG) ... Aristotle
Aristotle Corp. [*NASDAQ symbol*] (SPSG) ... ARTL
Aristotle's Nicomachean Ethics [*A publication*] (DLA) ... Eth Nic
Aristoxenus [*Fourth century BC*] [*Classical studies*] (OCD) ... Aristox
Arithmetic (IAA) ... A
Arithmetic (DNAB) ... ARI
Arithmetic [*Flowchart*] ... ARITH
Arithmetic (NTIO) ... arith
Arithmetic Age [*Education*] (BARN) ... Ar A
Arithmetic and Control Processor ... ACP
Arithmetic and Control Unit (BUR) ... ACU
Arithmetic and Controls (IAA) ... AAC
Arithmetic and Controls (SAA) ... A & C
Arithmetic and Controls (SAUS) ... A&C
Arithmetic and Controls (SAUS) ... Append
Arithmetic and Logic Box (SAUS) ... ALB
Arithmetic and Logic Circuit (SAUS) ... ALC
Arithmetic and Logic Circuits (VERA) ... ALC
Arithmetic and Logic Unit [*Computer science*] ... A & LU
Arithmetic and Register (SAUS) ... A&R
Arithmetic Array Identification (or Identifier) (SAUS) ... AAID
Arithmetic Assignment Statement (SAUS) ... AAS
Arithmetic Assignment Statement ... AAS
Arithmetic Assignment Statement (SAUS) ... AAS
Arithmetic Average ... AA
Arithmetic Bit (SAUS) ... AB
Arithmetic Building Element [*Computer science*] ... ABE
Arithmetic Bus [*Computer science*] (IAA) ... AB
Arithmetic Checker In Bus (SAUS) ... ACIB
Arithmetic Checker Out Bus (SAUS) ... ACOB
Arithmetic, Coding, Information, and Digit Symbols [*Psychometrics*] ... ACID
Arithmetic, Coding, Information and Digit Symbols (SAUS) ... ACID Symbols
Arithmetic Computation (SAUS) ... AC
Arithmetic Computation Module (SAUS) ... ACM
Arithmetic Computation Test [*Military*] ... AC
Arithmetic Computer ... ACU
Arithmetic Control (SAUS) ... AC
Arithmetic Data Word (SAUS) ... ADW
Arithmetic Design System (SAUS) ... ADS
Arithmetic Device ... AD
Arithmetic Element (BUR) ... AE
Arithmetic Element (SAUS) ... Arith Elem
Arithmetic Element Output Register (SAUS) ... AEOR
Arithmetic Element Program ... ARELEM
Arithmetic Elements (SAUS) ... AEs
Arithmetic Expression (IEEE) ... AE
Arithmetic Factor Register (SAUS) ... AFR
Arithmetic Factor Register [*Computer science*] ... D
Arithmetic Flag (SAUS) ... AF
Arithmetic Flag Aspect Factor (MHDI) ... AF
Arithmetic Function Designator ... AFD
Arithmetic Function Identifier ... AFID
Arithmetic IF Statement (SAUS) ... AIS
Arithmetic Input Left [*Computer science*] (MHDI) ... AIL
Arithmetic Input Right [*Computer science*] (MHDI) ... AIR
Arithmetic Logic and Control Unit [*Computer science*] ... ALCU
Arithmetic Logic Processor ... ALP
Arithmetic Logic Register Stack [*Computer science*] (MHDI) ... ALRS
Arithmetic Logic Section [*Computer science*] ... ALS
Arithmetic Logic Unit [*Computer science*] ... ALU
Arithmetic Logic Unit (SAUS) ... Arith Log U
Arithmetic Logic Unit for Control (SAUS) ... ALUTROL
Arithmetic Mask Register (SAUS) ... AMR
Arithmetic Mean [*Statistics*] (DCTA) ... AM
Arithmetic Mean [*Statistics*] ... X
Arithmetic Notation (SAUS) ... AN
Arithmetic Operation (SAUS) ... AO
Arithmetic Operator (SAUS) ... AO
Arithmetic Organ (SAUS) ... AO
Arithmetic Organ (SAUS) ... Arith Org
Arithmetic Output Control Unit ... AOCU
Arithmetic Output Data [*Computer science*] ... AOD
Arithmetic Output Unit ... AOU
Arithmetic Problem (SAUS) ... AP
Arithmetic Processing Accelerator (VERA) ... APA
Arithmetic Processing Module (SAUS) ... APM
Arithmetic Processing Unit [*Computer science*] ... APU
Arithmetic Processor ... AP
Arithmetic Processor Queue (IAA) ... APQ
Arithmetic Proficiency Training Program [*Computer-assisted training program*] ... APTP
Arithmetic Progression ... AP
Arithmetic Project [*National Science Foundation*] ... AP
Arithmetic Quotient (BARN) ... Ar Q
Arithmetic Reading Test [*Military*] ... ART
Arithmetic Reasoning Test ... ART
Arithmetic Reconstruction Technique (SAUS) ... ART
Arithmetic Register (ACAE) ... A
Arithmetic Register ... AR
Arithmetic Section (SAUS) ... AS
Arithmetic Series Weight Function (PDAA) ... ASWF
Arithmetic Series Weight Vector (SAUS) ... ASWV
Arithmetic Shift Left [*Computer science*] ... ASL
Arithmetic Shift Right [*Computer science*] ... ASR
Arithmetic Simple Variable ... ASV
Arithmetic Statement Function ... ASF
Arithmetic Subroutine (SAUS) ... AS
Arithmetic Technique (SAUS) ... AT
Arithmetic Underachievers [*Education*] ... AUA
Arithmetic Unit [*Computer science*] ... ARITHU
Arithmetic Unit [*Computer science*] ... AU
Arithmetic Unit Program Control Unit (ACAE) ... AUPCU
Arithmetic Verb (SAUS) ... AV
Arithmetical (SAUS) ... Arith
Arithmetical Administrator (SAUO) ... AA
Arithmetical Algorithm (SAUS) ... AA

Arithmetical Association (SAUO) .... AA
Arithmetical Average (SAUS) .... AA
Arithmetical Fixed Point Operation (SAUS) .... AFPO
Arithmetical Function (SAUS) .... AF
Arithmetical Instruction (SAUS) .... AI
Arithmetical Item (SAUS) .... AI
Arithmetical Progression (SAUS) .... AP
Arithmetical Unit [*Computer science*] (NITA) .... ARU
arithmetician (SAUS) .... arith
Arivaca Silver Mines Ltd. [*Vancouver Stock Exchange symbol*] .... AVC
Arizako Mines Ltd. [*Vancouver Stock Exchange symbol*] .... AZK
Arizona .... ARI
Arizona (AFM) .... ARIZ
Arizona (SAUO) .... Ariz
Arizona (ADWA) .... Ariz
Arizona [*Postal code*] .... AZ
Arizona [*MARC country of publication code*] [*Library of Congress*] (LCCP) .... azu
Arizona [*MARC geographic area code*] [*Library of Congress*] (LCCP) .... n-us-az
Arizona Academy of Family Physicians (SRA) .... AzAFP
Arizona Administrative Code [*A publication*] (AAGC) .... Ariz Admin Code
Arizona Administrative Digest [*A publication*] (DLA) .... Ariz Admin Dig
Arizona Administrative Register [*A publication*] (AAGC) .... Ariz Admin Reg
Arizona Air [*Aviation Services West, Inc.*] [*ICAO designator*] (FAAC) .... AAE
Arizona Air National Guard (MUSM) .... AZANG
Arizona Airways, Inc. [*ICAO designator*] (FAAC) .... AZY
Arizona Appeals Reports [*A publication*] (DLA) .... Ariz App
Arizona Archaeological and Historical Society (SAUO) .... AAHS
Arizona Articulation Proficiency Scale [*Speech and language therapy*] (DAVI) .... AAPS
Arizona Association for Economic Development (SRA) .... AAED
Arizona Association for Home Care (SRA) .... AAHC
Arizona Association of Chiropractic (SRA) .... AAC
Arizona Association of Counties (SRA) .... AACo
Arizona Association of Health Underwriters (SRA) .... AzAHU
Arizona Association of Homes and Housing for the Aging (SRA) .... AzAHA
Arizona Association of Industries (SRA) .... AAI
Arizona Association of Life Underwriters (SRA) .... AALU
Arizona Association of Medical Products Suppliers (SRA) .... AAMPS
Arizona Association of Mortgage Brokers (SRA) .... AAMB
Arizona Association of Realtors (SRA) .... AAR
Arizona Association of School Business Officials (SRA) .... AASBO
Arizona Association of School Psychologists (SRA) .... AASP
Arizona Automatic Fire Alarm Association (SRA) .... AAFAA
Arizona Automobile Dealers Association (SRA) .... AADA
Arizona Automotive Recyclers Association (SRA) .... AARA
Arizona Automotive Trade Organization (SRA) .... AzAUTO
Arizona Bankers Association (SRA) .... ABA
Arizona Basic Assessment and Curriculum Utilization System (EDAC) .... ABACUS
Arizona Beef Council (SRA) .... ABC
Arizona Broadcasters Association (SRA) .... ABA
Arizona Builders Alliance (SRA) .... ABA
Arizona Bureau of Geology and Mineral Technology [*University of Arizona*] [*Research center*] (RCD) .... ABGMT
Arizona Business Association (SRA) .... ABA
Arizona Cable Telecommunications Association (SRA) .... ACTA
Arizona Cactus and Succulent Research (EA) .... ACSR
Arizona Cardinals [*National Football League*] [*1994-present*] (NFLA) .... Ari
Arizona Cattlemen's Association (SRA) .... ACA
Arizona Center for the Blind and Visually Impaired (SAUO) .... ACBVI
Arizona City, AZ [*FM radio station call letters*] .... KONZ
Arizona Civil Liberties Union (SAUO) .... ACLU
Arizona Clearing House Association (SRA) .... ACHA
Arizona Community College Athletic Conference (PSS) .... ACCAC
Arizona Concrete Contractors Association (SRA) .... ACCA
Arizona Conference (PSS) .... AZC
Arizona Congress of Parents and Teachers (SAUO) .... ACPT
Arizona Constitution [*A publication*] (DLA) .... Ariz Const
Arizona Construction Industry Association (SRA) .... ACIA
Arizona Consulting Engineers Association (SRA) .... ACEA
Arizona Cotton Growers Association (SRA) .... ACGA
Arizona Council of Engineering and Scientific Associations (SAUO) .... ACESA
Arizona Court of Appeals Reports [*A publication*] (DLA) .... AZ A
Arizona Credit Union League (SRA) .... ACUL
Arizona Crop Improvement Association (SRA) .... ACIA
Arizona Crop Protection Association (SRA) .... ACPA
Arizona Dance Theatre .... ADT
Arizona Data Accessing Programming and Training (SAUS) .... ADAPT
Arizona Dental Association (SAUO) .... AzDA
Arizona Department of Library Archives, Tempe, AZ [*OCLC symbol*] (OCLC) .... AZP
Arizona Department of Transportation (GEOI) .... ADOT
Arizona Department of Water Resources (GEOI) .... ADWR
Arizona Desert Bighorn Sheep Society (SRA) .... ADBSS
Arizona Dietetics Association (SRA) .... AZDA
Arizona Education Association (SRA) .... AEA
Arizona Employers Council (SRA) .... AEC
Arizona Energy Management Council (SRA) .... AEMC
Arizona Farm Bureau Federation (SRA) .... AFBF
Arizona Federation of Teacher Unions (SAUO) .... AFTU
Arizona Financial Services Association (SRA) .... AFSA
Arizona Funeral Directors Association (SRA) .... AFDA
Arizona Geographic Information Council (GEOI) .... AGIC
Arizona Golden Pacific [*Vancouver Stock Exchange symbol*] .... AZA
Arizona Golf Association (SRA) .... AGA
Arizona Health Care Association (SRA) .... AHCA
Arizona Heat Pump Council (SRA) .... AHPC
Arizona Highway Department - Environment Planning Division (SAUO) .... AZHD-EPD
Arizona Highway Users Conference (SRA) .... AzHUC
Arizona Highways (journ.) (SAUS) .... Ariz H
Arizona Historical Foundation (SAUO) .... Ariz Hist Found
Arizona Historical Foundation, Arizona State University, Tempe, AZ [*Library symbol*] [*Library of Congress*] (LCLS) .... AzTeS-Hi
Arizona Historical Society, Tucson, AZ [*Library symbol*] [*Library of Congress*] (LCLS) .... AzTP
Arizona Hospital Association (SRA) .... ArHA
Arizona Hotel and Motel Association (SRA) .... AzHMA
Arizona Independent Auto Dealers Association (SRA) .... AIADA
Arizona Information Dissemination for Educators (SAUO) .... AIDE
Arizona Instrument [*NASDAQ symbol*] (TTSB) .... AZIC
Arizona Instrument Corp. [*Associated Press*] (SAG) .... ArizInst
Arizona Instrument Corp. [*NASDAQ symbol*] (SAG) .... AZIC
Arizona International Campus [*University of Arizona*] .... AIC
Arizona Jewelers Association (SRA) .... AJA
Arizona Job College (SAUO) .... AJC
Arizona Job Colleges [*An association*] [*Defunct*] (EA) .... AJC
Arizona Jojoba Growers Association (EA) .... AJGA
Arizona Jojoba, Inc. [*Vancouver Stock Exchange symbol*] .... AJJ
Arizona Land Income Corp. [*Associated Press*] (SAG) .... ArizLd
Arizona Land Income Corp. [*AMEX symbol*] (SPSG) .... AZL
Arizona Land Income'A' [*AMEX symbol*] (TTSB) .... AZL
Arizona Land Use Experiment (SAUS) .... ALUE
Arizona Landscape Contractors Association (SRA) .... ALCA
Arizona Library Association (SRA) .... AzLA
Arizona Licensed Beverage Association (SRA) .... ALBA
Arizona Long Term Care Gerontology Center [*University of Arizona*] [*Research center*] (RCD) .... ALTCGC
Arizona Macintosh Users Group .... AMUG
Arizona Mapping Advisory Council (GEOI) .... AzMAP
Arizona Masonry Guild (SRA) .... AMG
Arizona Medical Association (SRA) .... ArMA
Arizona Medical Center, University of Arizona, Tucson, AZ [*Library symbol*] [*Library of Congress*] (LCLS) .... AzTAM
Arizona Mining Association (SRA) .... AMA
Arizona Mobile Housing Association (SRA) .... AMHA
Arizona Mortgage Bankers Association (SRA) .... AMBA
Arizona Motor Tariff Bureau Inc., AZ (SAUO) .... AZB
Arizona Motor Tariff Bureau, Inc., Phoenix AZ [*STAC*] .... AZB
Arizona Motor Transport Association (SRA) .... AMTA
Arizona Multihousing Association (SRA) .... AMA
Arizona Music Educators Association (SAUO) .... AMEA
Arizona Newspapers Association (SRA) .... ANA
Arizona Nuclear Power Project (SAUO) .... ANPP
Arizona Nursery Association (SRA) .... ANA
Arizona Nurses Association (SRA) .... AzNA
Arizona Official Compilation of Administrative Rules and Regulations [*A publication*] (DLA) .... Ariz Admin Comp
Arizona Official Compilation of Administrative Rules and Regulations [*A publication*] (DLA) .... Ariz Admin Comp R
Arizona On-Line Users Group (SAUO) .... AOLUG
Arizona Optometric Association (SRA) .... AzOA
Arizona Osteopathic Medical Association (SRA) .... AOMA
Arizona Pacific Airways [*Arizona Flight School, Inc.*] [*ICAO designator*] (FAAC) .... AZP
Arizona Parks and Recreation Association (SRA) .... APRA
Arizona Pedagocical Computer (SAUS) .... APE Computer
Arizona Personnel and Guidance Association (SAUO) .... APGA
Arizona Pest Control Association (SRA) .... APCA
Arizona Pharmaceutical Association (SAUO) .... APA
Arizona Pharmacy Association (SRA) .... APA
Arizona Photopolarimeter Telescope (SAUS) .... APT
Arizona Physical Therapy Association (SRA) .... AzPTA
Arizona Pioneer Historical Society (SAUO) .... APHS
Arizona Planning Association (SRA) .... APA
Arizona Poison and Drug Information Center .... APDIC
Arizona Pork Council (SRA) .... APC
Arizona Professional Photographers Association (SRA) .... APPA
Arizona Promotional Products Association (SRA) .... AZPPA
Arizona Psychiatric Society (SRA) .... APS
Arizona Pub SvAdj Rt Q Pfd [*NYSE symbol*] (TTSB) .... ARPPrQ
Arizona Pub Svc 10%'MIDS' [*NYSE symbol*] (TTSB) .... AZD
Arizona Pub Svc $1.8125 Pfd [*NYSE symbol*] (TTSB) .... ARPPrW
Arizona Public Service [*Associated Press*] (SAG) .... AriP
Arizona Public Service Co. (SAUO) .... AZP
Arizona Public Service Company (SAUO) .... APS
Arizona Public Services [*NYSE symbol*] (SPSG) .... ARP
Arizona Public Services Co. [*NYSE symbol*] (SAG) .... AZD
Arizona Regional Ecological Test Site [*Department of the Interior*] .... ARETS
Arizona Regional Library for the Blind and Physically Handicapped, Phoenix, AZ [*Library symbol*] [*Library of Congress*] (LCLS) .... Az-BPH
Arizona Research Information Center [*Information service or system*] (IID) .... ARIC
Arizona Resources Information System (GEOI) .... ARIS
Arizona Restaurant Association (SRA) .... ARA
Arizona Retailers Association (SRA) .... ARA
Arizona Revised Statutes [*A publication*] (DLA) .... Ariz Rev Stat
Arizona Revised Statutes [*A publication*] (DLA) .... Ariz Rev State
Arizona Revised Statutes [*A publication*] (DLA) .... ARS
Arizona Revised Statutes, Annotated [*A publication*] (DLA) .... Ariz Rev Stat Ann

Arizona Road Dust [*Environmental chemistry*] ... AZRD
Arizona Rock Products Association (SRA) ... ARPA
Arizona Roofing Contractors Association (SRA) ... ARCA
Arizona School Administrators Association (SRA) ... ASA
Arizona School Boards Association (SRA) ... ASBA
Arizona Self-Insurers Association (SRA) ... ASIA
Arizona Session Laws [*A publication*] (DLA) ... Ariz Sess Laws
Arizona Sign Association (SRA) ... ASA
Arizona Silver Corp. [*Vancouver Stock Exchange symbol*] ... ARZ
Arizona Silver Corp. [*Vancouver Stock Exchange symbol*] ... ASC
Arizona Small Business Association (SRA) ... ASBA
Arizona Small Utilities Association (SRA) ... ASUA
Arizona Society of Association Executives (SRA) ... AzSAE
Arizona Society of Health System Pharmicists (SRA) ... AzSHP
Arizona Society of Practicing Accountants (SRA) ... ASPA
Arizona Society of Professional Engineers (SRA) ... ASPE
Arizona Software Association (SRA) ... ASA
Arizona Sports Network [*Cable TV programming service*] ... ASN
Arizona Star Resource Corp. [*Vancouver Stock Exchange symbol*] ... AZS
Arizona State College ... ASC
Arizona State Dental Association (SRA) ... ASDA
Arizona State Electronics Association (SRA) ... ASEA
Arizona State Law Journal [*A publication*] (DLA) ... Ariz State LJ
Arizona State Library Association (SAUO) ... ASLA
Arizona State Medical Association (SAUO) ... ASMA
Arizona State Museum [*University of Arizona*] [*Research center*] (RCD) ... ASM
Arizona State Prison (SAUO) ... ASP
Arizona State Prison Library, Florence, AZ [*Library symbol*] [*Library of Congress*] (LCLS) ... AzFIP
Arizona State University (GAGS) ... Ariz St U
Arizona State University [*Arizona*] [*Seismograph station code, US Geological Survey*] (SEIS) ... ASU
Arizona State University Center for Latin American Studies (SAUO) ... ASU Lat Am St
Arizona State University, College of Educational Technology and Library Science,Tempe, AZ [*OCLC symbol*] (OCLC) ... ASE
Arizona State University, College of Law Library, Tempe, AZ [*OCLC symbol*] (OCLC) ... AZC
Arizona State University, College of Law, Tempe, AZ [*Library symbol*] [*Library of Congress*] (LCLS) ... AzTeS-L
Arizona State University, Tempe, AZ [*OCLC symbol*] (OCLC) ... AZS
Arizona State University, Tempe, AZ [*Library symbol*] [*Library of Congress*] (LCLS) ... AzTeS
Arizona Statistical Repetitive Analog Computer ... ASTRAC
Arizona Stock Exchange ... AZX
Arizona Territory [*Obsolete*] (ROG) ... AT
Arizona Thoroughbred Breeders Association (SRA) ... ATBA
Arizona Tire and Service Dealers Association (SRA) ... ATSDA
Arizona Trade-Off Model [*State of Arizona and Department of Commerce project to resolve conflicts between economic and environmental goals*] ... ATOM
Arizona Transportation and Traffic Institute (SAUO) ... ATTI
Arizona Transportation Research Center [*Arizona State University*] [*Research center*] (RCD) ... ATRC
Arizona Travel Industry Association (SRA) ... ATIA
Arizona Travel Parks Association (SRA) ... ATPA
Arizona Trial Lawyers Association (SRA) ... AzTLA
Arizona Vegetation Resource Inventory (GEOI) ... AVRI
Arizona Veterinary Medical Association (SRA) ... AzVMA
Arizona Vocational Association (SRA) ... AzVA
Arizona Water Information System (SAUS) ... AWIS
Arizona Water Quality Association (SRA) ... AWQA
Arizona Water Well Association (SRA) ... AzWWA
Arizona Western College (SAUO) ... AWC
Arizona Western College, Yuma, AZ [*OCLC symbol*] (OCLC) ... AZY
Arizona Western College, Yuma, AZ [*Library symbol*] [*Library of Congress*] (LCLS) ... AzYAW
Arizona Wholesale Beer and Liquor Association (SRA) ... AWBLA
Arizona Wool Producers Association (SRA) ... AWPA
Arizona-Nogales [*Mexico*] [*Airport symbol*] (AD) ... NOG
Arizonian (SAUS) ... Ariz
Ark Energy Ltd. [*Vancouver Stock Exchange symbol*] ... ARK
Ark Restaurants [*NASDAQ symbol*] (SAG) ... ARKR
Ark Restaurants [*Associated Press*] (SAG) ... ArkRst
Arkadelphia, AR [*Location identifier*] [*FAA*] (FAAL) ... ADF
Arkadelphia, AR [*FM radio station call letters*] ... KDEL
Arkadelphia, AR [*Television station call letters*] ... KETG
Arkadelphia, AR [*FM radio station call letters*] ... KSWH
Arkadelphia, AR [*AM radio station call letters*] ... KVRC
Arkansas [*Postal code*] ... AR
Arkansas (AFM) ... ARK
Arkansas (BEE) ... Ark
Arkansas (SAUO) ... Ark
Arkansas [*MARC country of publication code*] [*Library of Congress*] (LCCP) ... aru
Arkansas [*MARC geographic area code*] [*Library of Congress*] (LCCP) ... n-us-ar
Arkansas Academy of Science (SAUO) ... AAS
Arkansas Aging Foundation (SRA) ... AAF
Arkansas Agricultural Aviation Association (SRA) ... AAAA
Arkansas Air National Guard (ACAE) ... ARANG
Arkansas & Louisiana Missouri Railway Co. [*AAR code*] ... ALM
Arkansas and Louisiana Missouri Railway Company (SAUO) ... ALM; A&LM
Arkansas & Louisiana-Missouri (SAUS) ... A&LM
Arkansas & Ozarks Railway [*AAR code*] ... AO
Arkansas Appellate Reports [*A publication*] (DLA) ... Ark App
Arkansas Appellate Reports [*A publication*] (DLA) ... Ark App Rep
Arkansas Arts Center, Little Rock, AR [*OCLC symbol*] (OCLC) ... AKA
Arkansas Arts Center, Little Rock, AR [*Library symbol*] [*Library of Congress*] (LCLS) ... ArLA
Arkansas Association of Bank Holding Companies (SRA) ... AABHC
Arkansas Association of Conservation Districts (SRA) ... AACD
Arkansas Association of Educational Administrators (SRA) ... AAEA
Arkansas Association of Oriental Medicine (SRA) ... AAOM
Arkansas Association of Registered Land Surveyors (GEOI) ... AARLS
Arkansas Association of School Administrators (SRA) ... AASA
Arkansas Association of Secondary School Principals (SRA) ... AASSP
Arkansas Automobile Dealers Association (SRA) ... AADA
Arkansas Bar Association (SRA) ... ABA
Arkansas Bar Association. Proceedings [*A publication*] (DLA) ... Ark BA
Arkansas Basin Red River Forecast Center (ARMP) ... ABRFC
Arkansas Best [*NASDAQ symbol*] (TTSB) ... ABFS
Arkansas Best $2.875 'A 'Pfd [*NASDAQ symbol*] (TTSB) ... ABFSP
Arkansas Best Corp. [*NASDAQ symbol*] (SAG) ... ABFS
Arkansas Best Corp. [*Associated Press*] (SAG) ... ArkBest
Arkansas Best Corp. [*Associated Press*] (SAG) ... ArkBst
Arkansas Broadcasters Association (SRA) ... ABA
Arkansas Cancer Research Center [*Little Rock*] ... ACRC
Arkansas Chiropractic Association (SRA) ... ACA
Arkansas City, KS [*FM radio station call letters*] (BROA) ... KAXR-FM
Arkansas City, KS [*FM radio station call letters*] (BROA) ... KLPQ-FM
Arkansas City, KS [*AM radio station call letters*] ... KSOK
Arkansas City, KS [*FM radio station call letters*] ... KYQQ
Arkansas Code Annotated [*A publication*] (AAGC) ... Ark Code Ann
Arkansas College [*Batesville*] ... AC
Arkansas College, Batesville, AR [*Library symbol*] [*Library of Congress*] (LCLS) ... ArBaA
Arkansas Community Bankers (TBD) ... ACB
Arkansas Constitution [*A publication*] (DLA) ... Ark Const
Arkansas Corporation Commission Report [*A publication*] (DLA) ... Ark CC
Arkansas Council of Independent Colleges and Universities (SAUO) ... ACICU
Arkansas County Quality Deer Association ... ACQDA
Arkansas Credit Union League (SRA) ... ACUL
Arkansas Criminal Justice Highway Safety Information System (SAUS) ... ACJHSIS
Arkansas Crop Protection Association (SRA) ... ACPA
Arkansas Democrat, Little Rock, AR [*Library symbol*] [*Library of Congress*] (LCLS) ... ArLAD
Arkansas Department of Health (SAUO) ... ADH
Arkansas Department of Pollution Control and Ecology (SAUO) ... ADPCE
Arkansas Department of Public Utilities Report [*A publication*] (DLA) ... Ark PU
Arkansas Education Association (SRA) ... AEA
Arkansas Electric Cooperatives (SRA) ... AEC
Arkansas Environmental Federation (SRA) ... AEF
Arkansas Farm Bureau Federation (SRA) ... AFBF
Arkansas Farmers Union (SRA) ... AFU
Arkansas Forestry Association (SRA) ... AFA
Arkansas Foundation of Associated Colleges (SAUO) ... AFAC
Arkansas Gazette (journ.) (SAUS) ... AG
Arkansas Geological Commission (GEOI) ... AGC
Arkansas Health Care Association (SRA) ... AHCA
Arkansas Historical Quarterly (journ.) (SAUS) ... AHQ
Arkansas History Commission, Department of Archives and History, Little Rock, AR [*Library symbol*] [*Library of Congress*] (LCLS) ... Ar-Hi
Arkansas Home Builders Association (SRA) ... AHBA
Arkansas Hospital Association (SRA) ... AHA
Arkansas Hospitality Association (SRA) ... AHA
Arkansas Independent Automobile Dealers Association (SRA) ... AIADA
Arkansas Industrial Development Commission (SAUO) ... AIDC
Arkansas Inspection and Rating Bureau (SAUO) ... AIRB
Arkansas Intercollegiate Conference (PSS) ... AIC
Arkansas Law Journal [*A publication*] (DLA) ... Ark LJ
Arkansas League of Savings Institutions (SRA) ... ALSI
Arkansas Library Association (SAUO) ... ALA
Arkansas Library Commission, Little Rock (SAUS) ... AR
Arkansas Library Commission, Little Rock, AR [*OCLC symbol*] (OCLC) ... AKF
Arkansas Library Commission, Little Rock, AR [*Library symbol*] [*Library of Congress*] (LCLS) ... Ar
Arkansas Livestock Show Association (SRA) ... ALSA
Arkansas Louisiana Gas Co. (IIA) ... AKG
Arkansas, Louisiana, Oklahoma, Texas (SAUS) ... South Central States
Arkansas Manufactured Housing Association (SRA) ... AMHA
Arkansas Medical Society (SRA) ... AMS
Arkansas Motor Carriers Association (SRA) ... AMCA
Arkansas Municipal League (SRA) ... AML
Arkansas Municipal Police Association (SRA) ... AMPA
Arkansas Music Educators Association (SAUO) ... AMEA
Arkansas Music Operators Association (SRA) ... AMOA
Arkansas National Guard (SAUO) ... ArkNG
Arkansas National Wildlife Refuge (SAUS) ... ANWR
Arkansas Nuclear One (NRCH) ... ANO
Arkansas Nurserymen's Association (SRA) ... ANA
Arkansas Nurses Association (SRA) ... ArNA
Arkansas Oil Marketers Association (SRA) ... AOMA
Arkansas Optometric Association (SRA) ... AOA
Arkansas Osteopathic Medical Association (SRA) ... AOMA
Arkansas Personnel and Guidance Association (SAUO) ... APGA
Arkansas Petroleum Council (SRA) ... APC
Arkansas Pharmaceutical Association (SAUO) ... APA
Arkansas Pharmacists Association (SRA) ... APA
Arkansas Polytechnic College (SAUO) ... APC
Arkansas Polytechnic College [*Later, Arkansas Technical University*] ... APC

Arkansas Polytechnic College [*Later, Arkansas Technical University*], Russellville, AR [*Library symbol*] [*Library of Congress*] (LCLS) .... ArRuA
Arkansas Pork Producers Association (SRA) .... APPA
Arkansas Post National Monument .... ARPO
Arkansas Poultry Federation (SRA) .... APF
Arkansas Poultry Improvement Association (SAUO) .... APIA
Arkansas Power & Light [*NYSE symbol*] (SAG) .... AKP
Arkansas Power & Light (SAUO) .... AP&L
Arkansas Power and Light Co. (IIA) .... AKP
Arkansas Power & Light Co. [*Associated Press*] (SAG) .... ArkPL
Arkansas Press Association (SRA) .... APA
Arkansas Propane Gas Association (SRA) .... APGA
Arkansas Public Policy Information System (SAUS) .... APPIS
Arkansas Railroad Association (SRA) .... ARA
Arkansas Ready Mixed Concrete Association (SRA) .... ARMCA
Arkansas Realtors Association (SRA) .... ARA
Arkansas Register [*A publication*] (DLA) .... Ark Admin Reg
Arkansas Register [*A publication*] (AAGC) .... Ark Reg
Arkansas Reports [*A publication*] (DLA) .... Ak
Arkansas Reports [*A publication*] (DLA) .... Ark R
Arkansas Reports [*A publication*] (DLA) .... Ark Rep
Arkansas Reports [*A publication*] (DLA) .... Ark's
Arkansas Research Test Station .... ARTS
Arkansas Resource Management Information System (GEOI) .... ARMIS
Arkansas River Valley Regional Library, Dardanelle, AR [*Library symbol*] [*Library of Congress*] (LCLS) .... ArDar
Arkansas River Valley Regional Library, Dardanelle, AR [*OCLC symbol*] (OCLC) .... AVR
Arkansas School Boards Association (SRA) .... ASBA
Arkansas Sheriffs' Association (SRA) .... ASA
Arkansas Society of Association Executives (SRA) .... ASAE
Arkansas Society of Professional Engineers (SRA) .... ASPE
Arkansas Society of Professional Surveyors (GEOI) .... ASPS
Arkansas Soft Drink Association (SRA) .... ASDA
Arkansas State Association of Life Underwriters (SRA) .... ASALU
Arkansas State Chamber of Commerce (SRA) .... ASCC
Arkansas State College [*Later, ASU*] .... ASC
Arkansas State Dental Association (SRA) .... ASDA
Arkansas State Employees Association (SRA) .... ASEA
Arkansas State Library, Little Rock, AR [*OCLC symbol*] (OCLC) .... AST
Arkansas State Police Association (SRA) .... ASPA
Arkansas State Teachers College [*Later, University of Central Arkansas*] .... ASTC
Arkansas State University (GAGS) .... Ark St U
Arkansas State University [*Beebe*] .... ASU
Arkansas State University Library, State University, AR [*OCLC symbol*] (OCLC) .... ASU
Arkansas State University, State University, AR [*Library symbol*] [*Library of Congress*] (LCLS) .... ArStC
Arkansas Statutes [*A publication*] (DLA) .... Ark Stats
Arkansas Statutes, Annotated [*A publication*] (DLA) .... Ark Stat Ann
Arkansas Supreme Court Library, Little Rock, AR [*Library symbol*] [*Library of Congress*] (LCLS) .... Ar-SC
Arkansas Supreme Court Reports [*A publication*] (DLA) .... Ark
Arkansas Technical University, Russellville, AR [*OCLC symbol*] (OCLC) .... AKP
Arkansas Telephone Association (SRA) .... ATA
Arkansas Transit Association (SRA) .... ATA
Arkansas Trial Lawyers Association (SRA) .... ATLA
Arkansas Valley Regional Library Service System [*Library network*] .... AVRLSS
Arkansas Veterinary Medical Association (SRA) .... AVMA
Arkansas Vocational Association (SRA) .... ArVA
Arkansas Water Resources Research Center [*University of Arkansas*] [*Research center*] (RCD) .... AWRRC
[*The*] Arkansas Western Railway Co. [*AAR code*] .... ARW
[*The*] Arkansas Western Railway Co. (IIA) .... AW
Arkansas Western Railway Company (SAUO) .... ARW
Arkansas White-Red Basins Interagency Committee (SAUO) .... AWRBIAC
Arkansas-Louisiana Gas Company (SAUO) .... ARKLA
Arkansas-Red Basin River Forecast Center (SAUS) .... ABRFC
Arkhangelsk [*Former USSR*] [*Geomagnetic observatory code*] .... ARK
Arkhangelsk 2 Aviation Division [*Former USSR*] [*FAA designator*] (FAAC) .... OAO
Arkia Israel Inland Airlines [*ICAO designator*] (FAAC) .... AIZ
Arkia-Israel Inland Airlines [*ICAO designator*] (AD) .... IZ
Arkib Negara [*National Archives of Malaysia*], Federal Government Building, Kuala Lumpur, Malaysia [*Library symbol*] [*Library of Congress*] (LCLS) .... MlyKA
Ark-La-Tex Genealogical Association (EA) .... ALTGA
Ark-La-Tex Industries [*Vancouver Stock Exchange symbol*] .... AKL
Arkley's Justiciary Reports [*Scotland*] [*A publication*] (DLA) .... Ark
Arkley's Justiciary Reports [*Scotland*] [*A publication*] (DLA) .... Ark Just
Arkley's Justiciary Reports [*Scotland*] [*A publication*] (DLA) .... Arkl
Arkley's Justiciary Reports [*Scotland*] [*A publication*] (DLA) .... Arkley
Arlans Department Stores Inc. (SAUO) .... AAD
Arlen Communications, Inc. [*Bethesda, MD*] [*Information service or system*] [*Telecommunications*] (TSSD) .... ACI
Arlen Realty & Development Corp. (SAUO) .... ARE
Arli [*Burkina Faso*] [*ICAO location identifier*] (ICLI) .... DHER
Arlin J. Brown Information Center (EA) .... AJBIC
Arlin Test of Formal Reasoning [*Intelligence test*] .... ATFR
Arlington [*Diocesan abbreviation*] [*Virginia*] (TOCD) .... ARL
Arlington Annex (SAUO) .... AA
Arlington Annex [*Navy*] .... AA
Arlington Annex [*Navy*] (DNAB) .... ARLAN
Arlington Annex [*Navy*] (DNAB) .... ARLEX
Arlington Baptist Junior College, Arlington, TX [*Library symbol*] [*Library of Congress*] (LCLS) .... TxArB

Arlington College, Arlington, CA [*Library symbol*] [*Library of Congress*] (LCLS) .... CArlA
Arlington County Department of Libraries, Arlington, VA [*OCLC symbol*] (OCLC) .... VIA
Arlington County Department of Libraries, Arlington, VA [*Library symbol*] [*Library of Congress*] (LCLS) .... ViAr
Arlington County Department of Libraries, Aurora Hills Branch, Arlington, VA [*Library symbol*] [*Library of Congress*] (LCLS) .... ViAr-A
Arlington County Department of Libraries, Cherrydale Branch, Arlington, VA [*Library symbol*] [*Library of Congress*] (LCLS) .... ViAr-Ch
Arlington County Department of Libraries, Clarendon Branch, Arlington, VA [*Library symbol*] [*Library of Congress*] (LCLS) .... ViAr-Cl
Arlington County Department of Libraries, Fairlington Branch, Arlington, VA [*Library symbol*] [*Library of Congress*] (LCLS) .... ViAr-F
Arlington County Department of Libraries, Glencarlyn Branch, Arlington, VA [*Library symbol*] [*Library of Congress*] (LCLS) .... ViAr-G
Arlington County Department of Libraries, Westover Branch, Arlington, VA [*Library symbol*] [*Library of Congress*] (LCLS) .... ViAr-W
Arlington Development Center, Arlington, TN [*Library symbol*] [*Library of Congress*] (LCLS) .... TArDC
Arlington Hall Station [*Virginia*] [*Army*] (AABC) .... AHS
Arlington Heights, IL [*Location identifier*] [*FAA*] (FAAL) .... JLH
Arlington Heights, IL [*FM radio station call letters*] .... WCBR
Arlington Heights Public Library, Arlington Heights, IL [*Library symbol*] [*Library of Congress*] (LCLS) .... IArlh
Arlington Inventory Management System (SAUS) .... AIMS
Arlington Memorial Amphitheater Commission [*Abolished 1960, functions transferred to Department of Defense*] .... AMAC
Arlington Military Cemetery (SAUO) .... ANC
Arlington National Cemetery .... ANC
Arlington Naval Annex (MCD) .... ANA
Arlington, NY [*FM radio station call letters*] .... WDSP
Arlington Public Library, Arlington, IA [*Library symbol*] [*Library of Congress*] (LCLS) .... IaArl
Arlington Public Library, Arlington, OR [*Library symbol*] [*Library of Congress*] (LCLS) .... OrAr
Arlington Public Library, Arlington, SD [*Library symbol*] [*Library of Congress*] (LCLS) .... SdAr
Arlington Public Library, Genealogy Department, Arlington, TX [*Library symbol*] [*Library of Congress*] (LCLS) .... TxAr-G
Arlington State College [*Texas*] .... ASC
Arlington, TN [*Location identifier*] [*FAA*] (FAAL) .... LHC
Arlington, TX [*FM radio station call letters*] (RBYB) .... KEWS-FM
Arlington, TX [*TV station call letters*] (RBYB) .... KINZ-TV
Arlington, TX [*Television station call letters*] (BROA) .... KPXD
Arlington, TX [*FM radio station call letters*] .... KSNN
Arlington, TX [*Television station call letters*] .... KTXA
Arlington, TX [*FM radio station call letters*] (BROA) .... KWRD-FM
Arlington, VA [*AM radio station call letters*] .... WABS
Arlington, VA [*FM radio station call letters*] .... WAVA
Arlington, VA [*AM radio station call letters*] .... WMZQ
Arlington, VA [*Television station call letters*] .... WTMW
Arlington, VA [*AM radio station call letters*] (RBYB) .... WZHF-AM
Arlington, WA [*Location identifier*] [*FAA*] (FAAL) .... AWO
Arlit [*Niger*] [*ICAO location identifier*] (ICLI) .... DRZL
Arlit [*Niger*] [*Airport symbol*] (OAG) .... RLT
ARL:UT Automated Information System Security Plan (SAUS) .... AISSP
Arm (IAA) .... A
Arm and Hammer [*Brand of soda*] .... A & H
Arm and Hammer (SAUS) .... A&H
Arm, Chest, Hip Index (SAUS) .... ACH-Index
Arm Circumference .... AC
Arm Data Archive .... DA
Arm Enhanced Shortwave Experiment (SAUS) .... ARESE
ARM Experiment Center (SAUS) .... AEC
Arm Experiment Center (SAUS) .... EC
Arm External Data Center (SAUS) .... XDC
ARM Financial Group [*AMEX symbol*] (SPSG) .... ARM
ARM Financial Group [*Associated Press*] (SAG) .... ARM F
ARM Financial Grp'A' [*NYSE symbol*] (SG) .... ARM
ARM Fin'l 9.50% Pfd [*AMEX symbol*] (TTSB) .... ARMPr
Arm Girth, Chest Depth, and Hip Width [*Anatomical index*] .... ACH
Arm Girth, Chest Depth, Hip Width Index (SAUS) .... ACH-Index
ARM Holdings ADS [*NASDAQ symbol*] (SG) .... ARMHY
ARM Information Architecture (SAUS) .... AIA
Arm Length .... AL
Arm Length Index .... ALI
Arm Length Order .... ALO
Arm Lock Magnet .... ALM
Arm Management Team (SAUS) .... AMT
Arm Multiple Antenna Profiler (SAUS) .... MAPR
Arm Muscle Circumference .... AMC
ARM Ocean Working Group (SAUO) .... AWOG
Arm Ocean Working Group (SAUS) .... AWOG
Arm Range of Motion [*Medicine*] (DHP) .... AROM
Arm Retracting Strut [*Nuclear energy*] (AAG) .... AR-RET-ST
Arm Tropical Pacific Experiment (SAUS) .... ATPEX
Arm Width .... AW
Arm Width Index .... AWI
Armada Free Public Library, Armada, MI [*Library symbol*] [*Library of Congress*] (LCLS) .... MiArm
Armada Gold & Mining [*Vancouver Stock Exchange symbol*] .... ARM
Armadillo .... ARMDLL
Armadillo Breeders Association [*Defunct*] (EA) .... ABA
Armageddon Project [*Later, AAAP*] (EA) .... AP

Armagh [*County in Ireland*] (ROG) ... AR
Armagh [*County in Ireland*] (WGA) ... ARM
Armak Chemicals, Saskatoon, Saskatchewan [*Library symbol*] [*National Library of Canada*] (NLC) ... SSAC
Armak Chemicals, Saskatoon, SK, Canada [*Library symbol*] [*Library of Congress*] (LCLS) ... CaSSAC
Armak Co., McCook, IL [*Library symbol*] [*Library of Congress*] (LCLS) ... IMccA
Armament ... A
Armament (SAA) ... AR
Armament ... ARM
Armament (AFM) ... ARMT
Armament and Ammunition (SAUS) ... AA&A
Armament and Avionics Planning Guidance (MCD) ... AAPG
Armament and Chemical Acquisition and Logistics Agency [*Army*] (INF) ... ACALA
Armament and Combal Vehicle Center (SAUS) ... ACVC
Armament and Combat Vehicle Center (MCD) ... ACVC
Armament and Combat Vehicle Center (SAUO) ... ACVS
Armament and Disarmament Information Unit [*British*] ... ADIU
Armament and Electronic Maintenance Squadron [*Air Force*] ... A & EMSq
Armament and Electronic Maintenance Squadron (SAUS) ... A&EMSq
Armament and Electronics (AFIT) ... AAE
Armament and Electronics [*Air Force*] ... A & E
Armament and Electronics (SAUS) ... A&E
Armament and Electronics [*Air Force*] (IAA) ... ARMEL
Armament and Electronics Laboratory ... AEL
Armament and Electronics Maintenance Squadron (SAUS) ... AANDEMAINTSQ
Armament and Electronics Test Laboratory [*NATO*] ... AETL
Armament and Fire Control (MCD) ... A & FC
Armament and Fire Control (SAUS) ... A&FC
Armament and Flight Control System (SAA) ... AFCS
Armament and Fuel Coordinator (MCD) ... AFC
Armament and Instrument Experiment Unit (SAUS) ... AIEU
Armament and Supply Officer (SAUS) ... ASO
Armament Artificer [*British and Canadian*] [*World War II*] ... AA
Armament Auxiliaries Test Set (MCD) ... AATS
Armament Boresight Line ... ABL
Armament Command (SAUS) ... AC
Armament Command [*Army*] (AABC) ... ARMCOM
Armament Concepts Office [*Army*] (RDA) ... ACO
Armament Control ... AC
Armament Control Agency (SAUS) ... ACA
Armament Control and Delivery System (MCD) ... ARCADS
Armament Control and Display Panel (PDAA) ... ACDP
Armament Control & Display Panel (SAUS) ... ACDP
Armament Control & Monitoring System (SAUS) ... ACMS
Armament Control Computer (MCD) ... ACC
Armament Control Console (ACAE) ... ACC
Armament Control Indicator (SAUS) ... ACI
Armament Control Indicator Set (DWSG) ... ACIS
Armament Control Panel ... ACP
Armament Control Processor Set (CAAL) ... ACPS
Armament Control Relay Panel (MCD) ... ACRP
Armament Control System [*Air Force*] ... ACS
Armament Control System Checkout [*Air Force*] (SAA) ... ACSC
Armament Control Test Set (ACAE) ... ACTS
Armament Control Unit (DNAB) ... ACU
Armament Data Line [*Military*] (NVT) ... ADL
Armament Datum Line (MCD) ... ADL
Armament Delivery Analysis Programming System (PDAA) ... ADAPS
Armament Delivery Point (SAUS) ... ADP
Armament Depot [*Military*] [*British*] ... AD
Armament Development and Test Center [*Eglin Air Force Base, FL*] (MCD) ... ADTC
Armament Development Center [*Army*] ... ADC
Armament Development, Enfield ... ADEN
Armament Development, Enfield/Direction Etude Fabrication [*Military*] (MCD) ... ADEN/DEFA
Armament Development Laboratory (ACAE) ... ADL
Armament Development Technical Report ... AD-TR
Armament Directors Conference (SAUS) ... ADC
Armament Division [*Air Force Systems Command*] [*Eglin Air Force Base, FL*] ... AD
Armament Division, Deputy for Engineering [*Eglin Air Force Base, FL*] ... AD/EN
Armament Electronic Maintenance Squadron ... AEMS
Armament Engineering Directorate [*Dover, NJ*] [*Army*] (GRD) ... AED
Armament Enhancement Initiative [*DoD*] ... AEI
Armament Flight Control System (SAUS) ... AFCS
Armament Handling Equipment (MCD) ... AHE
Armament Interface Unit (SAUS) ... AIU
Armament Logistics Center (SAUO) ... ALC
Armament Logistics Command [*Army*] (PDAA) ... ALC
Armament Maintenance Management Information Center [*Navy*] (NG) ... AMMIC
Armament Maintenance Training System (SAUS) ... AMTS
Armament Manufacturing Corporation (SAUO) ... ARMSCOR
Armament Material Bulletin (NG) ... AMB
Armament Material Change (NG) ... AMC
Armament Material Readiness Command ... AMRECOM
Armament Materiel Readiness Command (SAUO) ... ARRCOM
Armament Mode Selection Logic (ACAE) ... AMSL
Armament Modification Committee (SAUO) ... ArmMC
Armament Monitor and Control (CAAL) ... AMAC
Armament Munitions and Chemical Command [*Army*] (ACAE) ... AMCOM
Armament, Munitions, and Chemical Command Regulation [*Military*] ... AMCCOMR
Armament Practice Camp [*British military*] (DMA) ... APC
Armament Practice Station [*British military*] (DMA) ... APS
Armament Ready Legend (ACAE) ... ARL
Armament Recording Program [*Military*] ... ARP
Armament Release Panel (DNAB) ... ARP
Armament Research and Development Center [*Army*] (RDA) ... ARDC
Armament Research and Development Command [*Army*] (ACAE) ... ARADCOM
Armament Research and Development Command (MCD) ... ARDCOM
Armament Research and Development Command (SAUO) ... ARRADCOM
Armament Research and Development Establishment [*British*] (MCD) ... ARDE
Armament Research and Development Establishment, Canada (SAUO) ... ARDEC
Armament Research Department (SAUO) ... ARD
Armament Research Development [*British*] (MCD) ... ARD
Armament Research, Development, and Engineering Center [*Picatinny Arsenal*] [*Dover, NJ*] [*Army*] (RDA) ... ARDEC
Armament Retooling and Manufacturing Support Initiative [*1993*] ... ARMS
Armament School (SAUO) ... ASch
Armament School (SAUS) ... A Sch
Armament Sergeant Major [*British*] ... ASM
Armament Signal Data Converter (SAUS) ... ASDC
Armament Station Control Unit ... ASCU
Armament Stores Issuing Ship [*Navy*] ... ASIS
Armament Supplies (SAUS) ... AS
Armament Supply Department [*Navy*] [*British*] ... ASD
Armament Supply Officer [*British Navy slang*] [*World War II*] (DSUE) ... ARSO
Armament Supply Officer [*Navy*] [*British*] (DMA) ... ASO
Armament System Test Environment (MCD) ... ASTE
Armament System Test Set (MCD) ... ASTS
Armament Systems Control Unit (MCD) ... ASCU
Armament Systems Personnel Research Laboratory [*Lowry Air Force Base, CO*] ... ASPRL
Armament Systems Section [*Air Force*] ... ASS
Armament Technical Manual (SAA) ... ATM
Armament Technology and Procurement Group (ACAE) ... ATPG
Armament Technology Division [*Air Force*] (MCD) ... ATL
Armament Technology Laboratory [*Air Force*] ... ATL
Armament Test ... AT
Armament Test Center [*Military*] ... ATC
Armament Test Division (SAUO) ... ATD
Armament Test Preparation Facility ... ATPF
Armament Test Set (ACAE) ... ATS
Armament Training Camp [*Military*] (OA) ... ATC
Armament Training Station [*Military*] (OA) ... ATS
Armament/Munitions Requirements, Acquisition and Development Committee [*Military*] [*Washington, DC*] ... AMRAD
Armaments and Electronics (SAUS) ... A & E
Armaments Command [*Formerly, Munitions Command*] [*Rock Island, IL*] [*Army*] ... AC
Armaments Committee (SAUO) ... AC
Armaments Control Agency [*Western European Union*] (NATG) ... ACA
Armaments Cooperation Steering Committee ... ACSC
Armaments Depot (SAUO) ... AD
Armaments Design Department [*Ministry of Supply*] [*British*] [*World War II*] ... ADD
Armaments Design Establishment (SAUS) ... ADE
Armaments, Munitions, and Chemical Command (SAUO) ... AMCCOM
Armaments Planning Questionnaire (SAUS) ... APQ
Armaments Research Department [*Ministry of Supply*] [*British*] ... ARD
Armaments Standardization and Interoperability [*NATO*] (NATG) ... ASI
Armani Exchange (ECON) ... A/X
Armanient Practice Station (SAUS) ... APS
Armanino Foods Distinction [*NASDAQ symbol*] (TTSB) ... ARMF
Armanino Foods of Distinction, Inc. [*Associated Press*] (SAG) ... Arman
Armanino Foods of Distinction, Inc. [*NASDAQ symbol*] (SAG) ... ARMF
Arm-Ankle Indices [*Cardiology*] (DAVI) ... AAI
Armata Revoluzione Nucleare [*Armed Revolutionary Nucleus*] [*Italy*] ... ARN
Armatron International, Inc. [*Associated Press*] (SAG) ... Armtrn
Armatron International, Inc. [*AMEX symbol*] (SPSG) ... ART
Armature (IAA) ... A
Armature (KSC) ... ARM
Armature ... ARMA
Armature (VRA) ... armt
Armature ... ARMTR
Armature ... armtr
Armature Acceleration (IAA) ... ARMACCEL
Armature Acceleration (SAUS) ... ARM ACCEL
Armature Accelerator ... AA
Armature Knockoff (SAUS) ... AK
Armature Shunt [*Electromagnetism*] (IAA) ... ARMSH
Armature Shunt [*Electromagnetism*] ... ARMSHT
Armature Shunt [*Electromagnetism*] (IAA) ... AS
Armature Shunt [*Electromagnetism*] ... ASH
Armature Winding [*Wiring*] (DNAB) ... AW
Armbro Enterprises, Inc. [*Toronto Stock Exchange symbol*] ... ARE
Armchair Detective [*A publication*] (BRI) ... Arm Det
Arm/Chest Height [*Medicine*] (DB) ... ACH
Arm-Chest-Height (SAUS) ... ACH
Arm/Chest/Hip [*Medicine*] (DB) ... ACH
Armco $3.625 Cv A Pfd [*NYSE symbol*] (TTSB) ... ASPrB
Armco $4.50 Cv B Pfd [*NYSE symbol*] (TTSB) ... ASPrA
Armco, Inc. [*Formerly, Armco Steel Corp.*] [*Associated Press*] (SAG) ... Armc
Armco, Inc. [*Formerly, Armco Steel Corp.*] [*Associated Press*] (SAG) ... Armco
Armco, Inc. [*Formerly, Armco Steel Corp.*] [*NYSE symbol*] (SPSG) ... AS
Armco, Inc., Advanced Materials Division, Research Library, Baltimore, MD [*Library symbol*] [*Library of Congress*] (LCLS) ... MdBAS

Armco, Inc., Research Center, Technical Library, Middletown, OH [*Library symbol*] [*Library of Congress*] (LCLS) ... OMidAR
Armco Inc,$2.10 Cv Pfd [*NYSE symbol*] (TTSB) ... ASPr
Armco Steel Corp. (SAUO) ... AS
Arm/Destruct (KSC) ... A/D
Arm-Disarm [*Military*] (IUSS) ... A-D
Armed (CINC) ... ARMD
Armed Advanced Scout Helicopter (AABC) ... ARMEDASH
Armed Aircraft Qualification ... AAQ
Armed Boarding Vessel ... ABV
Armed Career Criminal Act of 1984 ... ACCA
Armed City Partisans (SAUO) ... ACP
Armed Combat Youth [*Government of South Vietnam training program*] (VNW) ... ACY
Armed Escort Operations (ACAE) ... AEO
Armed Experimental [*British military*] (DMA) ... AE
Armed for Anti-Personnel Attack (MILB) ... AP
Armed Force Journal (SAUS) ... AFJ
Armed Forces ... AF
Armed Forces Acquisition Document (NASA) ... AFAD
Armed Forces Act ... AFA
Armed Forces Air Intelligence Training Center ... AFAITC
Armed Forces Americas ... AA
Armed Forces and Society [*A publication*] (BRI) ... Arm F & S
Armed Forces Assistance to Korea [*Military*] ... AFAK
Armed Forces Benefit and Aid Association (EA) ... AFBAA
Armed Forces Benefit Association ... AFBA
Armed Forces Benefit Association ... AFRBA
Armed Forces Broadcasters Association (EA) ... AFBA
Armed Forces Central Medical Registry [*School of Aerospace Medicine*] (PDAA) ... AFCMR
Armed Forces Chemical Association [*Later, ADPA*] (EA) ... AFCA
Armed Forces Chemical Association (SAUO) ... AFCE
Armed Forces Christian Fellowship ... AFCF
Armed Forces Civilian Instructors Association (EA) ... AFCIA
Armed Forces Combat Bulletin ... AFCB
Armed Forces Committee (SAUO) ... AFC
Armed Forces Communication Association (SAUO) ... AFCA
Armed Forces Communications and Electronics Association (EA) ... AFCEA
Armed Forces Communications Association [*Later, AFCEA*] (MCD) ... AFCA
Armed Forces Council ... AFC
Armed Forces Courier Service ... AFCOS
Armed Forces Courier Service ... ARFCOS
Armed Forces Courier Service (ACAE) ... ARFOCS
Armed Forces Courier Station (AFM) ... ARFCOSTA
Armed Forces Cycling Association ... AFCA
Armed Forces Day ... AFD
Armed Forces Dental Benefit Association (SAUO) ... AFDBA
Armed Forces Dental Officers Association (EA) ... AFDOA
Armed Forces Development Board ... AFDB
Armed Forces Disciplinary Control Board ... AFDCB
Armed Forces Division (SAUO) ... AFD
Armed Forces DNA Identification Laboratory (SAUO) ... AFDIL
Armed Forces Enlisted Personnel Benefit Association [*Later, MBA*] ... AFEPBA
Armed Forces Epidemiological Board [*Washington, DC*] ... AFEB
Armed Forces Europe ... AE
Armed Forces European Network (SAUO) ... AFEN
Armed Forces Examining and Induction Stations ... AFEIS
Armed Forces Examining Station ... AFES
Armed Forces Examining Stations and Armed Forces Induction Stations (SAUO) ... AFEIS
Armed Forces Exchange (SAUS) ... AFEX
Armed Forces Exchange Service (DNAB) ... AFES
Armed Forces Expeditionary Medal [*Military decoration*] (AFM) ... AFEM
Armed Forces Explosive Ordnance Disposal Facilities (SAUO) ... AFEODF
Armed Forces Financial Advisory Services [*British*] ... AFFAS
Armed Forces for the Liberation of Cabinda [*Angola*] (PD) ... FALC
Armed Forces Headquarters (SAUO) ... AFHQ
Armed Forces Headquarters (SAUS) ... HQUNTAC
Armed Forces Health Profession Scholarship Program ... AFHPSP
Armed Forces Hostess Association (EA) ... AFHA
Armed Forces Identification Review Board [*US Total Army Personnel Agency*] (EGAO) ... AFIRB
Armed Forces in Germany and Austria (SAUO) ... AFGA
Armed Forces Induction Station ... AFIS
Armed Forces Industrial College (SAUO) ... AFIC
Armed Forces Information and Education (MCD) ... AFIE
Armed Forces Information and Education Center (SAA) ... AFIEC
Armed Forces Information and Education Division ... AFIED
Armed Forces Information Film (AFM) ... AFIF
Armed Forces Information Program ... AFIP
Armed Forces Information School ... AFIS
Armed Forces Information Service [*DoD*] ... AFIS
Armed Forces Information System (SAUS) ... AFIS
Armed Forces Institute ... AFI
Armed Forces Institute of Pathology [*DoD*] (DNAB) ... AFINSPATH
Armed Forces Institute of Pathology [*DoD*] (EA) ... AFIP
Armed Forces Institute of Pathology/American Registry of Pathology (SAUS) ... AFIP/ARP
Armed Forces Institute of Patholology (SAUO) ... AFIP/ARP
Armed Forces Institute of Technology ... AFIT
Armed Forces Insurance ... AFI
Armed Forces Intelligence Training Center ... AFITC
Armed Forces Language Program ... AFLP
Armed Forces Leave Act of 1946 ... AFLA
Armed Forces Liaison Representative [*Red Cross*] ... AFLR
Armed Forces Librarians Round Table [*American Library Association*] ... AFLRT
Armed Forces Librarians Section [*Public Library Association*] ... AFLS
Armed Forces Libraries Round Table (AL) ... AFLRT
Armed Forces Mail Call [*Defunct*] (EA) ... AFMC
Armed Forces Management (AABC) ... AFM
Armed Forces Management Association [*Later, ADPA*] (EA) ... AFMA
Armed Forces Management Association (SAUO) ... AFMA
Armed Forces Marketing Council (EA) ... AFMC
Armed Forces Master Records [*Solicited phonograph records, and money to buy records, for the armed forces*] [*See also RFOFM*] [*World War II*] ... AFMR
Armed Forces Medical Aid Association (SAUO) ... AFMAA
Armed Forces Medical Intelligence Center [*Fort Detrick*] [*Frederick, MD*] ... AFMIC
Armed Forces Medical Library [*Later, National Library of Medicine, 1956*] ... AFML
Armed Forces Medical Procurement Agency ... AFMPA
Armed Forces Medical Publication Agency (SAUS) ... AFMPA
Armed Forces Medical Services (SAUO) ... AFMS
Armed Forces Menu Service Committee (AABC) ... AFMSC
Armed Forces, Middle Pacific (SAUO) ... AFMIDPAC
Armed Forces Military Report [*DoD*] ... AFMR
Armed Forces Movement [*Portugal*] ... AFM
Armed Forces National Research Council [*National Academy of Sciences*] ... AFNRC
Armed Forces Network [*TV-radio*] (DOMA) ... AFN
Armed Forces Network, Europe (SAUO) ... AFNE
Armed Forces Network, Iceland (SAUO) ... AFNI
Armed Forces Network, Island (SAUS) ... AFNI
Armed Forces News Bureau [*Later, AFPS*] ... AFNB
Armed Forces of Haiti (SAUO) ... FA&H
Armed Forces of Malaysia (SAUO) ... AFM
Armed Forces of the Philippines (MUSM) ... AFP
Armed Forces of the Republic of Korea (CINC) ... AFK
Armed Forces of the Unites States (SAUO) ... AFUS
Armed Forces of Zaire (SAUO) ... FAZ
Armed Forces Optometric Society (EA) ... AFOS
Armed Forces Pacific (SAUO) ... AFPAC
Armed Forces Pacific ... AP
Armed Forces Pest Control Board [*Washington, DC*] ... AFPCB
Armed Forces Pest Management Board (RDA) ... AFPMB
Armed Forces Philippine Network (SAUO) ... AFPN
Armed Forces Philippines Supply Center (CINC) ... AFPSC
Armed Forces Police ... AFP
Armed Forces Police Department [*or Detachment*] ... AFPD
Armed Forces Police Detachment (SAUO) ... AFPD
Armed Forces Policy Council ... AFPC
Armed Forces Post Office ... APO
Armed Forces Press Service (SAUO) ... AFPS
Armed Forces Procurement Regulation ... AFPR
Armed Forces Product Evaluation Committee (AABC) ... AFPEC
Armed Forces Production Distribution Service (DNAB) ... AFPDS
Armed Forces Production Resources Agency (MUGU) ... APRA
Armed Forces Professional Entertainment Office ... AFPEO
Armed Forces Provisional Ruling Council [*Gambia*] [*Political party*] ... AFPRC
Armed Forces Publication (COE) ... AFP
Armed Forces Qualification Test ... AFQT
Armed Forces Qualification Test, Verbal Arithmetic Subtest ... AFQTVA
Armed Forces Radio (ADA) ... AFR
Armed Forces Radio and Television (SAUO) ... AFRT
Armed Forces Radio and Television Network (SAUS) ... AFRTN
Armed Forces Radio and Television Service (SAUO) ... AFRTVS
Armed Forces Radio and Television Service-Broadcast Center (GFGA) ... AFRTS-BC
Armed Forces Radio and Television Service-Washington (SAUO) ... AFRTS-W
Armed Forces Radio Service [*United States military*] [*Established during World War II*] [*Later, Armed Forces Radio and Television Service*] (WDMC) ... AFRS
Armed Forces Radio Television Service (SAUS) ... AFRTS
Armed Forces Radiobiological (or Radiobiology) Research Institute (SAUO) ... AFRRI
Armed Forces Radiobiology Institute ... AFFRI
Armed Forces Radiobiology Research Institute ... AFRADBIORSCHINST
Armed Forces Radiobiology Research Institute [*Bethesda, MD*] [*DoD*] ... AFRRI
Armed Forces Radiobiology Research Institute, Bethesda, MD [*OCLC symbol*] (OCLC) ... AFR
Armed Forces Radiological Research Center (COE) ... AFRRC
Armed Forces Radio-Television [*Cable-television system*] ... AFRTS
Armed Forces Readiness Command (MCD) ... AFREDCOM
Armed Forces Recipe Service Committee (AABC) ... AFRSC
Armed Forces Recreation Center ... AFRC
Armed Forces Recruiting Stations [*DoD*] ... AFRS
Armed Forces Relief and Benefit Association (EA) ... AFRBA
Armed Forces Reporting Unit [*Red Cross*] ... AFRU
Armed Forces Research Institute of Medical Sciences [*Bangkok - collaboration of Thailand and United States*] ... AFRIMS
Armed Forces Reserve Act (SAUS) ... AFRA
Armed Forces Reserve Act of 1952, as Amended ... AFRA
Armed Forces Reserve Center (AABC) ... AFRC
Armed Forces Reserve Medal [*Military decoration*] ... AFRESM
Armed Forces Reserve Medal [*Military decoration*] ... AFRM
Armed Forces Retirement Home ... AFRH
Armed Forces Revolutionary Council [*Ghana*] (PPW) ... AFRC
Armed Forces Screen Reports ... AFSR
Armed Forces Security Agency [*Obsolete*] ... AFSA
Armed Forces Security Agency [*Obsolete*] ... AFSAG
Armed Forces Security Agency Council [*Abolished, 1952*] ... AFSAC

Armed Forces Security Agency Council Intelligence Requirements Committee [*Obsolete*] .... AFSAC/IRC
Armed Forces Special Weapons Agency .... AFSWA
Armed Forces Special Weapons Project [*Later, DASA*] .... AFSWP
Armed Forces Sports Committee (EA) .... AFSC
Armed Forces Staff College .... AFSC
Armed Forces Staff College (SAUO) .... AFSTAFFCOL
Armed Forces Stamp Exchange Club (EA) .... AFSEC
Armed Forces Supply Control Center [*DoD*] .... AFSCC
Armed Forces Supply Support Center [*Merged with Defense Logistics Services Center*] .... AFSSC
Armed Forces Surplus Property Bidders Registration and Sales Information Office (SAUO) .... AFSPBRSIO
Armed Forces Technical Information Agency (NATG) .... AFTIA
Armed Forces Television (SAUO) .... AFTV
Armed Forces Television Service (NTCM) .... AFTS
Armed Forces Vietnam Network (SAUO) .... AFVN
Armed Forces Vocational Testing Group [*Randolph Air Force Base, TX*] (AFM) .... AFVTG
Armed Forces Women's Selection Test .... AFWST
Armed Forces Womens Selection Test (SAUS) .... AFWST
Armed Forces Writers League [*Later, NAGC*] (EA) .... AFWL
Armed Guard .... AG
Armed Guard (MUGU) .... ARMGRD
Armed Guard (SAUS) .... Armgrd
Armed Guard Center .... AGC
Armed Guard Center Training School [*Obsolete*] .... AGCTS
Armed Guard Inspection Officer .... AGIO
Armed Guard Inspection Service .... AGIS
Armed Guard Inspection System (SAUS) .... AGIS
Armed Guard School .... AGS
Armed Islamic Group [*Anti-government faction*] [*Algeria*] [*Acronym is based on foreign phrase*] (ECON) .... GIA
Armed Merchand Cruiser (SAUS) .... AMC
Armed Merchant Cruiser [*Obsolete*] [*Navy*] [*British*] .... AMC
Armed Merchant Cruiser [*Navy symbol*] XCL
Armed Nuclear Bombardment Satellite .... ANBS
Armed Proletarian Nuclei [*Italy*] .... NAP
Armed Propaganda Team [*Military*] .... APT
Armed Public Security Force (CINC) .... APSF
Armed RECCE [*Reconnaissance*] [*Military*] (VNW) .... AR
Armed Reconnaissance (MUGU) .... A/R
Armed Reconnaissance (SAUS) .... AR
Armed Resistance Movement (EA) .... ARM
Armed Resistance Unit (EA) .... ARU
Armed Revolutionary Movement [*Puerto Rico*] .... ARM
Armed Robbery (SAUS) .... AR
Armed Scout Mission [*Military*] (DOMA) .... ASM
Armed Serviced Papers (SAUS) .... ASP
Armed Services .... AS
Armed Services - Civilian Interest Survey [*Test*] .... ASCVIS
Armed Services Biomedical Research and Evaluation Management Committee .... ASBREM
Armed Services Biomedical Research Evaluation and Management (RDA) .... ASBREM
Armed Services Biomedical Research, Evaluation & Management committee (SAUS) .... ASBREM
Armed Services Blood Program Office (DOMA) .... ASBPO
Armed Services Board of Contract Appeal (SAUO) .... ASBA
Armed Services Board of Contract Appeals .... ASBCA
Armed Services Bulletin .... ASB
Armed Services Commissary Store Regulations (DNAB) .... ASCSR
Armed Services Committee (SAUO) .... AS
Armed Services Committee [*US Senate*] (AAG) .... ASC
Armed Services Community Housing Office (SAUO) .... ASCHO
Armed Services Court Lawyers Association [*Now BCALA*] (AAGC) .... ASCTLA
Armed Services Documents Intelligence Center [*DoD*] .... ASDIC
Armed Services Edition [*Publishing*] [*World War II*] .... ASE
Armed Services Education Conference (SAUO) .... ASEC
Armed Services Electro Standards Agency (SAUO) .... ASESA
Armed Services Electron Tube Committee .... ASETC
Armed Services Electro-Standards Agency [*Later, DESC*] .... ASESA
Armed Services Electro-Standards Agency (SAUS) .... ASESA
Armed Services Exchange Regulation [*DoD*] .... ASER
Armed Services Explosive Ordnance Disposal Coordinating Group .... ASEODCG
Armed Services Explosives Safety Board [*Army*] .... ASESB
Armed Services Explosives Safety Board [*Army*] (AABC) .... ASESBD
Armed Services Graves Registration Office [*Later, AFIRB*] .... ASGRO
Armed Services Industrial Readiness Council .... ASIRC
Armed Services Medical Material Coordination Committee (CINC) .... ASMMCC
Armed Services Medical Procurement Agency [*Later, Medical Material Directorate*] .... ASMPA
Armed Services Medical Regulating Office (DOMA) .... ASMRO
Armed Services Mutual Benefit Association (SAUO) .... ASMBA
Armed Services Papers .... ASP
Armed Services Patent Advisory Board [*DoD*] .... ASPAB
Armed Services Personnel Interrogation Center (AFM) .... ASPIC
Armed Services Petroleum Agency .... ASPA
Armed Services Petroleum Board .... ASPB
Armed Services Petroleum Purchasing Agency .... ASPPA
Armed Services Police (SAUO) .... ASP
Armed Services Pricing Manual [*A publication*] (AAGC) .... ASPM
Armed Services Procurement Act .... ASPA
Armed Services Procurement Manual (MCD) .... ASPM
Armed Services Procurement Medal .... ASPM
Armed Services Procurement Office (SAUS) .... ASPO
Armed Services Procurement Planning Office (SAUO) .... ASPPO
Armed Services Procurement Planning Officer .... ASPPO
Armed Services Procurement Regulation [*Later, DAR*] .... ASPR
Armed Services Procurement Regulation Manual (AABC) .... ASPRM
Armed Services Procurement Regulation Supplement (AABC) .... ASPRS
Armed Services Procurement Regulation Supplement .... ASPS
Armed Services Procurement Regulations .... ASPERS
Armed Services Procurement Regulations (SAUO) .... ASPR
Armed Services Product Planning Officer (SAUO) .... ASPPO
Armed Services Production Planning Officer (MCD) .... ASPPO
Armed Services Renegotiation Board [*Later, RB*] .... ASRB
Armed Services Research Specialists Committee .... ASRSC
Armed Services Technical Information Agency [*Later, Defense Documentation Center*] .... ASTIA
Armed Services Technical Information Agency Bulletin [*A publication*] (DNAB) .... ASTIAB
Armed Services Textile and Apparel Procurement Agency (DNAB) .... ASTAPA
Armed Services Vocational Aptitude Battery [*Tests*] .... ASVAB
Armed Services Whole Blood Processing Laboratory (AABC) .... ASWBPL
Armed Services Young Men's Christian Association [*Military*] .... ASYMCA
Armed Strike Reconnaissance (AABC) .... ASR
Armed Surface Reconnaissance [*Navy*] (DOMA) .... ASR
Armed Tactical Fighter [*General Dynamics Corp.*] (ECON) .... ATF
Armed White Male (ECON) .... AWM
Armedia/El Elden [*Colombia*] [*ICAO location identifier*] (ICLI) .... SKAP
Armee de Liberation Nationale [*National Liberation Army*] [*Guadeloupe*] [*Political party*] (PD) .... ALN
Armee de Liberation Nationale [*National Liberation Army*] [*Algeria*] [*Political party*] (AF) .... ALN
Armee de Liberation Nationale de l'Angola [*Angolan Army of National Liberation*] .... ALNA
Armee de Liberation Nationale Kamerounaise [*Cameroonese National Liberation Army*] .... ALNK
Armee de Liberation Nationale Kamerunaise [*Cameroonian Army of National Liberation*] (AF) .... ALNK
Armee Korps [*Army Corps*] [*German*] .... AK
Armee Nationale Congolaise [*Congolese National Army*] .... ANC
Armee Populaire Nationale [*National People's Army*] [*Congo*] (AF) .... APN
Armee-Munitionslager [*Army ammunition depot*] [*German military - World War II*] .... AML
Armeestab (SAUS) .... A Stab
Armenia [*Internet country code*] .... AM
Armenia (VRA) .... Arm
Armenia .... ARM
Armenia [*Colombia*] [*Airport symbol*] (OAG) .... AXM
Armenian [*MARC language code*] [*Library of Congress*] (LCCP) .... arm
Armenian (ADWA) .... Arm
Armenian (BJA) .... Armen
Armenian Alumni Association .... AAA
Armenian Artistic Union (SAUO) .... AAU
Armenian Assembly Charitable Trust (EA) .... AACT
Armenian Assembly of America, Student Affairs Division (EA) .... AAASAD
Armenian Assembly Student Services [*Later, AAASAD*] (EA) .... AASS
Armenian Catholic Exarchate [*Diocesan abbreviation*] [*Pennsylvania*] (TOCD) .... ARM
Armenian Church Youth Organization of America (EA) .... ACYOA
Armenian Educational Foundation (EA) .... AEF
Armenian Express Canada [*Vancouver Stock Exchange symbol*] .... APN
Armenian Film Foundation (EA) .... AFF
Armenian General Benevolent Union (EA) .... AGBU
Armenian General Benevolent Union of America [*Later, AGBU*] (EA) .... AGBUA
Armenian International Airlines [*ICAO designator*] (FAAC) .... RME
Armenian Literary Society (EA) .... ALS
Armenian Missionary Association of America (EA) .... AMAA
Armenian National Army [*Guerrilla force*] [*Former USSR*] (ECON) .... ANA
Armenian National Committee (EA) .... ANC
Armenian National Council of America (EA) .... ANCA
Armenian National Education Committee (EA) .... ANEC
Armenian National Federation (AC) .... ANF
Armenian Numismatic Society (EA) .... ANS
Armenian Pan-National Movement [*Political party*] (EY) .... APM
Armenian Pan-National Movement (SAUO) .... ARNM
Armenian Progressive League of America (EA) .... APLA
Armenian Relief Society [*Later, ARSNA*] (EA) .... ARS
Armenian Relief Society of North America (EA) .... ARSNA
Armenian Revolutionary Federation [*Political party*] (EY) .... ARF
Armenian Revolutionary Federation (SAUO) .... ARF
Armenian Revolutionary Federation of America [*Later, ARF*] (EA) .... ARFA
Armenian Rugs Society (EA) .... ARS
Armenian Secret Army for the Liberation of Armenia [*Turkey*] (PD) .... ASALA
Armenian Secret Army of the Liberation for Armenia (SAUO) .... ASALA
Armenian Secret Liberation Army .... ASLA
Armenian Soviet Socialist Republic [*MARC country of publication code*] [*Library of Congress*] (LCCP) .... air
Armenian Soviet Socialist Republic .... ArmSSR
Armenian Soviet Socialist Republic (SAUO) .... ASSR
Armenian Soviet Socialist Republic [*MARC geographic area code*] [*Library of Congress*] (LCCP) .... e-ur-ai
Armenian Students Association of America (EA) .... ASA
Armenian Students Association of America (EA) .... ASAA
Armenian Women's Welfare Association (EA) .... AWWA
Armenian Youth Federation - Youth Organization of the ARF (EA) .... AYF-YOARF
Armenian Youth Federation of America - Youth Organization of the ARF [*Armenian Revolutionary Federation of America*] (EA) .... AYF

Armenian Youth Foundation of America (SAUO) ... AYF
Armeno Resources, Inc. [*Vancouver Stock Exchange symbol*] ... ARO
Arm/Fire Device (MCD) ... AFD
ARM-FIRE Water Vapor Experiment (SAUS) ... AFWEX
Arm/Firing Mechanism (MCD) ... A/FM
Armidale [*Australia*] [*Airport symbol*] (OAG) ... ARM
Armidale City and Dumarasq Shire War Memorial Library, Armidale, NSW, Australia [*Library symbol*] [*Library of Congress*] (LCLS) ... AuAr
Armidale Historical Society. Journal [*A publication*] ... Arm Hist Soc J
Armidale Newspaper Co. Ltd., Armidale, NSW, Australia [*Library symbol*] [*Library of Congress*] (LCLS) ... AuArA
armiert (SAUS) ... arm
Armijo, NM [*FM radio station call letters*] (RBYB) ... KNKT
Armillaria mellea [*A fungus*] ... AM
Arming (MSA) ... ARM
Arming and Fusing (AFM) ... A & F
Arming and Fusing Device ... AFD
Arming and Fusing (or Fuzing) (SAUS) ... A&F
Arming and Fusing System (MSA) ... AFS
Arming Decision Device (MUGU) ... ADD
Arming Device ... ARMDEV
Arming Device Assemblies [*Army*] (MCD) ... ADA
Arming, Fuzing and Firing (SAUS) ... AF&F
Arming, Safing, and Initiating (SAA) ... AS & I
Arming System Tester (MCD) ... AST
Arming Unit Distribution Box [*Army*] (MCD) ... AUDB
Arming Wire [*Bombs*] ... AW
Armingford [*England*] ... ARMINGF
Armistice and Post-War Committee [*British*] [*World War II*] ... APW
Armistice Terms and Civil Administration [*British*] [*World War II*] ... ACA
Armitage Academy Library, Kenosha, WI [*Library symbol*] [*Library of Congress*] (LCLS) ... WKenA
ARMMS [*Automated Reliability and Maintenance Management System*] **Control Executive System** [*NASA*] ... ACES
Armor All Products [*NASDAQ symbol*] (TTSB) ... ARMR
Armor All Products Corp. [*Associated Press*] (SAG) ... Armor
Armor All Products Corp. [*NASDAQ symbol*] (NQ) ... ARMR
Armor and Arms Club (EA) ... AAC
Armor and Engineer Board [*Army*] (PDAA) ... ARENBD
Armor, Armament, and Ammunition ... AA & A
Armor, Armament and Ammunition (SAUS) ... AA&A
Armor, Artillery, and Engineers Aptitude Area [*Army*] ... AE
Armor Board (MCD) ... AB
Armor Board (SAUO) ... AB
Armor Combat Operations Model Support [*TCATA*] (RDA) ... ARCOMS
Armor Development Corp. [*Vancouver Stock Exchange symbol*] ... ADP
Armor Enhancement Initiative [*Army*] ... AEI
Armor Full Crew Research Simulator Center-Laboratory (SAUS) ... AFCIS-L
Armor Grating [*Technical drawings*] ... AG
Armor Holdings [*AMEX symbol*] [*Formerly, American Body Armor & Equipment*] (SG) ... ABE
Armor Holdings [*NYSE symbol*] (SG) ... AH
Armor Holdings, Inc. [*AMEX symbol*] (SAG) ... ABE
Armor Holdings, Inc. [*Associated Press*] (SAG) ... ArmorH
Armor Human Research Unit (SAUO) ... AHRU
Armor Information Management System-Logistics ... ARIMS-LOG
Armor Machine Gun (MCD) ... AMG
Armor Management Information System - Logistics ... ARMIS-LOG
Armor Plate (MUGU) ... A/PL
Armor Plate (KSC) ... ARM-PL
Armor Protection Program (SAUS) ... APP
Armor Qualification Number (SAUS) ... AQN
Armor Remoted Target System (RDA) ... ARETS
Armor School [*Army*] (MCD) ... AS
Armor Support Battalion (MCD) ... ASB
Armor Systems Program Review (MCD) ... ASPR
Armor Target Mechanism [*Army*] ... ATM
Armor Training Devices (RDA) ... ATD
Armoral Tutle Public Library, New Plymouth, ID [*Library symbol*] [*Library of Congress*] (LCLS) ... IdNpm
Armored (ADA) ... A
Armored (CINC) ... ARM
Armored (AFM) ... ARMD
Armored (MILB) ... armd
Armored ... ARMRD
Armored Ambulance ... AA
Armored and Combat Vehicle Materiel Center (SAUO) ... ACVMC
Armored and Mechanized Unit Air Defense [*Army*] ... ARMAD
Armored Anti-Aircraft System (SAUS) ... AAAS
Armored Artillery Resupply Vehicle (MCD) ... AARV
Armored Box Launcher [*Shipboard launching system*] ... ABL
Armored Cable ... AC
Armored Cannon Vehicle (MCD) ... ACV
Armored Cavalry Assault Vehicle ... ACAV
Armored Cavalry Cannon Vehicle (MCD) ... ACCV
Armored Cavalry Enlisted Reserve (SAUO) ... ACER
Armored Cavalry Platoon (SAUO) ... ACP
Armored Cavalry Regiment ... ACR
Armored Cavalry Regiment ... Armd Cav Regt
Armored Cavalry Towing Vehicle (SAUS) ... ACTV
Armored Cavalry Trainer [*Army*] (AABC) ... ACT
Armored Cavalry Troop (SAUO) ... ACT
Armored Cavalry Vehicle ... ACV
Armored Cavalry's Veterans of Vietnam and Cambodia ... ACVVC
Armored Column Cover (MCD) ... ACC
Armored Combat Command (SAUS) ... ACC
Armored Combat Earthmover [*Army*] ... ACE
Armored Combat Equipment (DOMA) ... ACE
Armored Combat Logistics Support Vehicle [*Army*] ... ACLSV
Armored Combat Logistics Support Vehicle Family ... ACLSVF
Armored Combat Vehicle ... ACV
Armored Combat Vehicle Material Center (MCD) ... ACVMC
Armored Combat Vehicle Technology (RDA) ... ACVT
Armored Combat Vehicle Technology Program ... ACVTP
Armored Command and Reconnaissance Vehicle [*Former USSR*] (AABC) ... ACRV
Armored Command Post [*Army*] (RDA) ... ACP
Armored Command Vehicle [*Army*] ... ACV
Armored Crashworthy Crew Set (MCD) ... ACCS
Armored Crew Seat ... ACS
Armored Cruiser [*Navy symbol*] [*Obsolete*] ... ACR
Armored Division [*Military*] (MCD) ... AD
Armored Division [*Army*] ... ARMD
Armored Division Equivalent [*Military*] ... ADE
Armored Engineer Battalion (SAUO) ... AEB
Armored Engineer Vehicle (MCD) ... AEV
Armored Family of Vehicles [*Military*] (RDA) ... AFV
Armored Field Artillery Battalion (SAUO) ... AFA Bn
Armored Fighting Vehicle [*Marine Corps*] ... AFV
Armored Force Vehicle ... AFV
Armored Forward Area Rearm Vehicle (MCD) ... AFARV
Armored Forward Area Resupply Vehicle (MCD) ... AFARV
Armored Gun System [*Army*] (MUSM) ... AGS
Armored Gun System, Armament [*Army*] (RDA) ... AGS ARMT
Armored Infantry Battalion ... AIB
Armored Infantry Combat Vehicle ... AICV
Armored Infantry Fighting Vehicle (NATG) ... AIFV
Armored Infantry Vehicle (MSA) ... AIV
Armored Maintenance Vehicle ... AMV
Armored Maintenance Vehicle (SAUS) ... ANW
Armored Personnel Carrier [*Military*] ... APC
Armored Personnel Carrier/Qualification Course [*Army*] ... APC/QC
Armored Personnel Vehicle [*Military*] (IAA) ... APV
Armored Reconnaissance ... AR
Armored Reconnaissance Airborne Assault Vehicle (AABC) ... ARAAV
Armored Reconnaissance All-Purpose Fighting Team (SAUO) ... ARAFT
Armored Reconnaissance Battalion (SAUO) ... ARB
Armored Reconnaissance Carrier (MCD) ... ARC
Armored Reconnaissance Scout Vehicle [*Army*] (AABC) ... ARSV
Armored Reconnaissance Scout Vehicle [*Army*] (RDA) ... RSV
Armored Reconnaissance Scout Vehicle - Task Force (MCD) ... ARSV-TF
Armored Reconnaissance Vehicle (MCD) ... ARV
Armored Recovery Vehicle ... ARV
Armored Replacement Training Center (SAUO) ... ARTC
Armored Rifle Battalion ... ARB
Armored Security Vehicle [*Army*] ... ASV
Armored Support Patrol Boat [*Military*] ... ASPB
Armored Support Vehicle (MCD) ... ASV
Armored Systems Integration [*Army*] (RDA) ... ASI
Armored Systems Modernization [*Formerly, Heavy Forces Modernization Program*] [*Army*] (RDA) ... ASM
Armored Systems Modernization - Future [*Formerly, Heavy Forces Modernization Program*] [*Army*] (RDA) ... ASM-F
Armored Systems Modernization programme (SAUS) ... ASM
Armored Tank Cannon [*Army*] ... ATAC
Armored Training Devices [*Army*] (RDA) ... ARD
Armored Transport Vehicle (NATG) ... ATV
Armored Transportation Institute (EA) ... ATI
Armored Troop Carrier [*Army*] ... ATC
Armored Troop Carrier (Helicopter) [*Army*] (SAA) ... ATC (H)
Armored, Universal Engineer Tractor ... AUET
Armored Utility Vehicle ... AUV
Armored Vehicle (MCD) ... AV
Armored Vehicle General Purpose [*General Motors armored car*] [*Canada*] ... AVGP
Armored Vehicle Launched [*Military*] (MCD) ... AVL
Armored Vehicle Launched Bridge [*Military*] (INF) ... AVLB
Armored Vehicle Technology Associates [*Army*] (RDA) ... AVTA
Armored-Infantry-Mechanized (AABC) ... AIM
Armorer (AABC) ... ARMR
Armorer (SAUS) ... Armr
Armorer Sergeant (SAUS) ... Armr Sergt
Armorial and Heraldry Society of Australasia ... AHSA
Armorican ... ARM
Armor-Piercing [*Ammunition*] ... AP
Armor-Piercing Capped [*Ammunition*] ... APC
Armor-Piercing, Carbide, Ballistic Cap [*Ammunition*] (NATG) ... APCBC
Armor-Piercing Carbide Ballistic Cap (SAUS) ... APCBC
Armor-Piercing Discarding Sabot [*Ammunition*] (NATG) ... APDS
Armor-Piercing Discarding Sabot, Fin-Stabilized [*Ammunition*] (MCD) ... APDSFS
Armor-Piercing Discarding Sabot with Tracer [*Ammunition*] (AABC) ... APDS-T
Armor-Piercing Fin Stabilized Discarding Sabot [*Ammunition*] (MCD) ... APFSDS
Armor-Piercing Fin Stabilized Discarding Sabot with Tracer [*Ammunition*] (INF) ... APFSDS-T
Armor-Piercing High Explosive [*Ammunition*] ... APHE
Armor-Piercing High Explosive Weaponry [*Army*] (VNW) ... APHE
Armor-Piercing Incendiary [*Ammunition*] ... API
Armor-Piercing Incendiary Tracer [*Ammunition*] ... APIT
Armor-Piercing Infantry Light-Arm System [*Ammunition*] ... APILAS
Armor-Piercing Reduced (Caliber) [*Ammunition*] ... APCR

Armor-Piercing Sabot [*Ammunition*] (SAA) .... APS
Armor-Piercing with Tracer [*Ammunition*] .... APT
Armor-Piercing-Capped, Ballistic-Capped [*Ammunition*] (MSA) .... APCBC
Armor-Piercing-Capped Incendiary [*Ammunition*] .... APCI
Armor-Piercing-Capped Incendiary with Tracer [*Ammunition*] .... APCIT
Armor-Piercing-Capped with Tracer [*Ammunition*] .... APCT
Armorplate (SAUS) .... A/PL
Armory .... ARMRY
Armour & Co., Chicago, IL [*Library symbol*] [*Library of Congress*] [*Obsolete*] (LCLS) .... ICArmour
Armour & Company (SAUO) .... AM
Armour Pharmaceutical Co. [*Research code symbol*] .... AB
Armour Pharmaceutical Co. [*Research code symbol*] .... P
Armour Piercing - Hard Core (PDAA) .... AP-HC
Armour Piercing, Composite, Non-Rigid (SAUS) .... APCNR
Armour Piercing, Composite, Rigid (SAUS) .... APCR
Armour Piercing, Explosive (SAUS) .... APE
Armour Piercing, High Explosive & Incendiary (SAUS) .... APEI
Armour Piercing, Super Velocity (SAUS) .... APSV
Armour Public Library, Armour, SD [*Library symbol*] [*Library of Congress*] (LCLS) .... SdArm
Armour. Queen's Bench and County Court Reports Tempore Wood [*Manitoba*] [*A publication*] (DLA) .... Manitoba
Armour Remote Target System (SAUS) .... ARETS
Armour Research Center Library, Scottsdale, AZ [*Library symbol*] [*Library of Congress*] (LCLS) .... AzSArm
Armour Research Center, Scottsdale, AZ [*OCLC symbol*] (OCLC) .... AZR
Armour Research Foundation [*Later, IITRI*] .... ARF
Armour Research Foundation Reactor .... ARR
Armour Tenderometer (SAUS) .... AT
Armoured Automobile Detachment (SAUO) .... AAD
Armoured Boarding Steamer [*British military*] (DMA) .... ABS
Armoured Box Launcher (SAUS) .... ABL
Armoured Brigade (SAUO) .... AB
Armoured Brigade (SAUO) .... A Bde
Armoured Brigade (SAUO) .... Armd Bde
Armoured Brigade (SAUO) .... Armd Brig
Armoured Cannon Vehicle (SAUS) .... ACV
Armoured Car [*Military*] [*British*] .... AC
Armoured Car Company (SAUO) .... ACC
Armoured Car Company (SAUO) .... ACCoy
Armoured Car Division (SAUO) .... ACD
Armoured Car Section, Royal Naval Air Service [*British military*] (DMA) .... ACSRNAS
Armoured Cavalry (SAUO) .... AC
Armoured Cavalry (SAUO) .... A/C
Armoured Cavalry (SAUO) .... A Cav
Armoured Cavalry Vehicle (SAUS) .... ACV
Armoured Combat Logistics Support Vehicle (SAUS) .... ACLSV
Armoured Combat Logistics Support Vehicle Family (SAUS) .... ACLSVF
Armoured Combat Vehicle, Tracked (SAUS) .... ACVT
Armoured Combat Vehicle Weapon System [*Military*] (PDAA) .... ACVWS
Armoured Control Vehicle [*Military*] .... ACV
Armoured Delivery Regiment (SAUS) .... ADR
Armoured Delivery Squadron (SAUS) .... ADS
Armoured Division (SAUS) .... AD
Armoured Division (SAUO) .... ADiv
Armoured Division Ordnance Field Park (SAUO) .... ADOFP
Armoured Engineer Squadron (SAUO) .... Armd Eng Sqn
Armoured Field Artillery (SAUO) .... AFA
Armoured Field Artillery Battalion (SAUO) .... Armd FA Bn
Armoured Fire Support Vehicle (SAUS) .... AFSV
Armoured Infantry Training & Advisory Team (SAUS) .... AITAT
Armoured Landmine Clearing Vehicle (SAUS) .... ALCV
Armoured Launching Turret (SAUS) .... ALT
Armoured Mine Clearing Vehicle [*Military*] .... AMCV
Armoured Mortar System (SAUS) .... AMS
Armoured Motor Battery [*British military*] (DMA) .... AMB
Armoured Observation Post [*British and Canadian*] [*World War II*] .... AOP
Armoured Patrol Unit (SAUS) .... APU
Armoured Patrol Vehicle (SAUS) .... APV
Armoured Recovery Vehicle (SAUS) .... ARV
Armoured Regiment (SAUO) .... AR
Armoured Regiment (SAUO) .... A Rgt
Armoured Reinforcement Unit (SAUO) .... ARU
Armoured Repair & Recovery Vehicle (SAUS) .... ARRV
Armoured Repair Vehicle (SAUS) .... ARV
Armoured Replacement Group [*British and Canadian*] [*World War II*] .... ARG
Armoured Resupply Maintenance System (SAUS) .... ARMS
Armoured Scout Reconnaissance Vehicle [*Military*] (PDAA) .... ASRV
Armoured Tank Destroyer [*Military*] (PDAA) .... ATD
Armoured Tractor [*British*] .... AT
Armoured Train [*British*] .... AT
Armoured Transport Squadron (SAUO) .... ATS
Armoured Trials & Development Unit (SAUO) .... ATDU
Armoured Vehicle Bridge Launcher [*Military*] (PDAA) .... AVBL
Armoured Vehicle Driving Simulators (SAUS) .... AVDS
Armoured Vehicle, General Purpose (SAUS) .... AVGP
Armoured Vehicle, Heavy (SAUS) .... AVH
Armoured Vehicle, Light (SAUS) .... AVL
Armoured Vehicle, Medium (SAUS) .... AVM
Armoured Vehicle Multiple Rocket Launcher (SAUS) .... AVMRL
Armoured Vehicle, Reconnaissance [*British military*] (DMA) .... AVR
Armoured Vehicle, Royal Engineers [*British and Canadian*] [*World War II*] .... AVRE
Armoured Vehicle-Launched Bridge (SAUS) .... AVLB
Armourer Quartermaster Sergeant [*British*] .... AQMS
Armourer Shop (SAUO) .... AS
Armour-Piercing, Capped, Tracer (SAUS) .... APC-T
Armour-Piercing, Capped, Tracer, Base Fuze (SAUS) .... APCT-BF
Armour-Piercing Composite Rigid [*British military*] (DMA) .... APCR
Armour-Piercing, Enhanced Performance (SAUS) .... APEP
Armour-Piercing, Fragmentation Incendiary, Discarding Sabot (SAUS) .... APFIDS
Armour-Piercing, Hard Core, Incendiary (SAUS) .... APHCI
Armour-Piercing, High Capacity (SAUS) .... APHC
Armour-Piercing, High Explosive, Incendiary (SAUS) .... APHEI
Armour-Piercing, High Explosive, Self-Destroying (SAUS) .... APHE-SD
Armour-Piercing, Incendiary, Hard Core (SAUS) .... APIHC
Armour-Piercing Secondary Effects [*British military*] (DMA) .... APSE
Armour-Piercing, Secondary Effect-Tracer (SAUS) .... APSE-T
Armpit [*Medicine*] (DHSM) .... AX
Arms and Ammunition Division [*Army*] .... AAD
Arms & Armor (VRA) .... ar/arm
Arms & Armour Press [*Publisher*] [*British*] .... A & AP
Arms and Armour Society (EA) .... AAS
Arms and Militaria Collectors' Association of New South Wales [*Australia*] .... AMCNSW
Arms and Services on Duty with Air Force .... ASWAF
Arms and Services with the Army Air Forces .... ASWAAF
Arms Basic Trainig Unit (SAUO) .... ABTU
Arms Basic Training Unit (SAUS) .... ABTU
Arms Control and Disarmament [*A publication*] .... ACD
Arms Control and Disarmament Act [*1961*] .... ACDA
[*United States*] **Arms Control and Disarmament Agency** (USGC) .... ACDA
Arms Control and Disarmament Agency (AAGC) .... USACD
Arms Control and Disarmament Agency Military and Economic Affairs Bureau [*Washington, DC*] .... ACDA/MEA
Arms Control and Disarmament Agency Weapons Evaluation and Control Bureau [*Washington, DC*] .... ACDA/WEC
Arms Control and Disarmament Agency Weapons Evaluation and Control Bureau Field Operations Division [*Washington, DC*] .... ACDA/WEC/FO
Arms Control and Disarmament Research Unit [*British*] .... ACDRU
Arms Control and Foreign Policy Caucus (EA) .... ACFPC
Arms Control Association (EA) .... ACA
Arms Control Associations (SAUO) .... ACAs
Arms Control Computer Network [*Defunct*] (EA) .... ACCN
Arms Control Education Project [*Defunct*] (EA) .... ACEP
Arms Control Impact Statement (MCD) .... ACIS
Arms Control Obserevation Satellite (SAUS) .... ACOS
Arms Control Observation Satellite .... ACOS
Arms Control Proposal [*Military*] (IUSS) .... ACP
Arms Control Simulation (SAA) .... ACSIM
Arms Control Technical Information and Analysis Center [*Department of State*] .... ACTIAC
Arms Control Technical Information and Analysis Center (or Centre) (SAUS) .... ACTIAC
Arms Control through Defense (SAUS) .... ACD
Arms Control Verification Committee [*Pronounced "acey-veecee"*] .... ACVC
Arms Corporation of the Philippines (SAUO) .... ARMSCOR
Arms Export Control Act .... AECA
Arms Export Control Board .... AECB
ARMS Firms Users Association (SAUO) .... AFUA
Arms Material (AABC) .... AM
Arms Memorandum .... AM
ARMS [*Action Research into Multiple Sclerosis*] **of America** (EA) .... AA
Arms of Precision (SAUS) .... A of P
Arms Transfer Management Group .... ATMG
Arm/Safe (SAA) .... A/S
ARMS/FIRMS Users Association (EA) .... AFUA
Armstrong Aerospace Medical Research Laboratory (SAUO) .... AAMRL
Armstrong Air, Inc. [*Canada*] [*ICAO designator*] (FAAC) .... ARQ
Armstrong Aldren Collins [*Lunar mineral named after three astronauts*] .... ARMALCOLITE
Armstrong Association of Philadelphia, Philadelphia, PA [*Library symbol*] [*Library of Congress*] [*Obsolete*] (LCLS) .... PPArmA
Armstrong Browning Library [*Baylor University*] [*Research center*] (RCD) .... ABL
Armstrong College (SAUO) .... AC
Armstrong Community Library, Ontario [*Library symbol*] [*National Library of Canada*] (NLC) .... OARMS
Armstrong. Contested Election Cases [*New York*] [*A publication*] (DLA) .... Arms Con El
Armstrong Cork Company (SAUO) .... ACK
Armstrong Journal, Armstrong, IA [*Library symbol*] [*Library of Congress*] (LCLS) .... IaArmJ
Armstrong, Macartney, and Ogle's Irish Nisi Prius Reports [*A publication*] (DLA) .... AM & O
Armstrong, Macartney, and Ogle's Irish Nisi Prius Reports [*A publication*] (DLA) .... Arm & O
Armstrong, Macartney, and Ogle's Irish Nisi Prius Reports [*A publication*] (DLA) .... Arm Mac & Og
Armstrong, Macartney, and Ogle's Irish Nisi Prius Reports [*A publication*] (DLA) .... Arm M & O
Armstrong, Macartney, and Ogle's Irish Nisi Prius Reports [*A publication*] (DLA) .... Arms Mac & Og
Armstrong, Macartney, and Ogle's Irish Nisi Prius Reports [*A publication*] (DLA) .... Arms M & O
Armstrong, Macartney, and Ogle's Irish Nisi Prius Reports [*A publication*] (DLA) .... Armstrong M & O (Ir)
Armstrong Monitoring Corp. (SAUO) .... AMC
Armstrong, ON [*ICAO location identifier*] (ICLI) .... CYYW

Armstrong, Parkside, Coventry (SAUO) ... A
Armstrong Public Library, Armstrong, ON, Canada [*Library symbol*] [*Library of Congress*] (LCLS) ... CaOARMS
Armstrong Rubber Co. (EFIS) ... ARCO
Armstrong Rubber Company (SAUO) ... ARM
Armstrong Siddeley Car Club [*Australia*] ... ASCC
Armstrong Siddeley Owners Club (EA) ... ASOC
Armstrong State College (GAGS) ... Armstrong St C
Armstrong State College, Savannah, GA [*OCLC symbol*] (OCLC) ... GAC
Armstrong State College, Savannah, GA [*Library symbol*] [*Library of Congress*] (LCLS) ... GSA
Armstrong University (GAGS) ... Armstrong U
Armstrong World Ind 7.45% 'QUIBS' [*NYSE symbol*] (SG) ... AKK
Armstrong World Indus [*NYSE symbol*] (TTSB) ... ACK
Armstrong World Industries, Inc. [*Formerly, Armstrong Cork Co.*] [*NYSE symbol*] (SPSG) ... ACK
Armstrong World Industries, Inc. [*Formerly, Armstrong Cork Co.*] [*Associated Press*] (SAG) ... ArmWI
Armstrong's Breach of Privilege Cases, New York [*A publication*] (DLA) ... Arms Br P Cas
Armstrong's Cases of Contested Elections, New York [*A publication*] (DLA) ... Arms Elect Cas
Armstrong's Disease [*Medicine*] (MELL) ... AD
Armstrong's Limerick Trials [*Ireland*] [*A publication*] (DLA) ... Arms Tr
Armstrong's New York Contested Elections [*A publication*] (DLA) ... Arms Con Elec
Armstrong-Spallumcheen Museum and Archives Society, Armstrong, British Columbia [*Library symbol*] [*National Library of Canada*] (NLC) ... BARS
Armstrong-Whitworth Sperry Gyroscope (IAA) ... AWSG
Armstrong-Withworth (SAUS) ... AW
Armstrong-Withworth and Sperry Gyroscope (SAUS) ... AWSG
Armx Excess Property (SAUS) ... AES
Army ... A
Army ... AR
Army (SAUS) ... R
Army - Navy Retractor [*Surgery*] (DAVI) ... A/N
Army Achievement Medal (INF) ... AAM
Army Achievement Medal [*Military decoration*] ... ARAM
Army Acquisition Corps (RDA) ... AAC
Army Acquisition Corps Management Office (RDA) ... AACMO
Army Acquisition Corps Program (INF) ... AACP
Army Acquisition Executive ... AAE
Army Acquisition Executive Support Agency (RDA) ... AAESA
Army Acquisition Information System (AAGC) ... AAIS
Army Acquisition Objective ... AAO
Army Acquisition Pollution Prevention Support Office ... AAPSO
Army Acquisition Program Executive Review System [*Army*] ... AAPERS
Army Acquisition Workforce ... AAW
Army Acquisition Workforce Management Information System (RDA) ... AAWMIS
Army Act (ILCA) ... AA
Army Adaptation Inventory ... AAI
Army Administration Center, Fort Benjamin Harrison (AABC) ... ADMINCEN
Army Administrative Unit (SAUO) ... AAU
Army Advanced Marksmanship Unit ... AAMU
Army Advanced Materiel Concepts Agency (PDAA) ... AAMCA
Army Adviser Discharge Affairs [*British and Canadian*] [*World War II*] ... AADA
Army Advisory Group, China ... AGC
Army Advisory Group on Energy ... AAGE
Army Aerial Reconnaissance System ... AARS
Army Aerobiology and Evaluation Laboratory (SAUS) ... ARMY AEL
Army Aeromedical Research Laboratory (RDA) ... AARL
Army Aeronautical Activity at Ames (ACAE) ... AAAA
Army Aeronautical Depot Maintenance Center [*AMC-ASMC*] ... ARADMAC
Army Aeronautical Research Center (SAUS) ... AARC
Army Aeronautical Research Center [*Ames Research Center*] ... AARL
Army Aeronautical Service Office (ACAE) ... AASO
Army After Next ... AAN
Army Agent (SAUS) ... AR AGT
Army Aid Corps (SAUO) ... AAC
Army Air Base (MCD) ... AAB
Army Air Corps [*British*] [*ICAO designator*] (FAAC) ... AAC
Army Air Corps (SAUO) ... AAC
Army Air Corps (SAUS) ... ALE
Army Air Corps Centre [*British military*] (DMA) ... AACC
Army Air Corps Enlisted Pilots Association (SAUO) ... AACEPA
Army Air Cushioned Vehicle (VNW) ... ACV
Army Air Defense ... AAD
Army Air Defense Area ... AADA
Army Air Defense Artillery Board ... AADAB
Army Air Defense Board (KSC) ... AADB
Army Air Defense Command [*or Commander*] [*Later, AADCOM*] ... AADC
Army Air Defense Command [*or Commander*] [*Formerly, AADC, ARADCOM*] (AABC) ... AADCOM
Army Air Defense Command [*or Commander*] [*Later, AADCOM*] ... ARADCOM
Army Air Defense Command (ACAE) ... ARDCOM
Army Air Defense Command and Control (MCD) ... AADC2
Army Air Defense Command Post ... AADCP
Army Air Defense Control and Coordination System (AABC) ... AADCCS
Army Air Defense Control Artillery Panel (SAUO) ... AADCAP
Army Air Defense Information Service ... AADIS
Army Air Defense Information System (SAUS) ... AADIS
Army Air Defense Operations Office [*or Officer*] ... AADOO
Army Air Defense School (KSC) ... AADS
Army Air Defense School ... ARADSCH
Army Air Defense Site ... AADS
Army Air Defense Staff (MCD) ... AADS
Army Air Defense System [*Formerly, FABMDS*] ... AADS
Army Air Defense Unit (SAUO) ... AADU
Army Air Force Base Unit (SAUO) ... AAFBU
Army Air Force Basic Training Center (SAUO) ... AAFBTC
Army Air Force Board ... AAFB
Army Air Force Bombardier School (SAUO) ... AAFBS
Army Air Force Bulletin [*A publication*] (MCD) ... AAFB
Army Air Force Central Flying Training Command ... AAFCFTC
Army Air Force Central Technical Training Command ... AAFCTTC
Army Air Force Classification Center ... AAFCC
Army Air Force Clemency and Parole Board ... AAFCPB
Army Air Force Eastern Flying Training Command ... AAFEFTC
Army Air Force Eastern Technical Training Command ... AAFETTC
Army Air Force Flying Training Detachment ... AAFFTD
Army Air Force Headquarters, Mediterranean Theatre of Operations (SAUO) ... AAFMTO
Army Air Force Intelligence Report (MCD) ... AAFIR
Army Air Force Manual [*A publication*] (MCD) ... AAFM
Army Air Force, Mediterranean Theater of Operations (SAUS) ... AAFMTO
Army Air Force Nontechnical Intelligence Report (MCD) ... AAFNTIR
Army Air Force Officer-in-Charge ... AAFOIC
Army Air Force Technical Intelligence Report (MCD) ... AAFTIR
Army Air Force Technical Order (MCD) ... AAFTO
Army Air Force Translation (MCD) ... AAFT
Army Air Force Weather Service Bulletin (MCD) ... AAFWSB
Army Air Force Weather Service Manual [*A publication*] (MCD) ... AAFWSM
Army Air Forces ... AAF
Army Air Forces Aid Society [*World War II*] ... AAFAS
Army Air Forces Air Adjutant General [*World War II*] ... AFMAG
Army Air Forces Anti-Submarine Command (SAUS) ... AFSUB
Army Air Forces Assistant Secretary of War for Air [*World War II*] ... AFSWA
Army Air Forces Base Unit ... AAFBU
Army Air Forces Basic Training Center ... AAFBTC
Army Air Forces Bombardier School ... AAFBS
Army Air Forces Center ... AAFC
Army Air Forces Central Flying Training Command (SAUS) ... AAFCFTC
Army Air Forces Chief of the Air Staff [*World War II*] ... AFCAS
Army Air Forces Commanding General [*World War II*] ... AFACG
Army Air Forces Deputy Chiefs of Air Staff [*World War II*] ... AFIAS
Army Air Forces Engineer Command ... AAFEC
Army Air Forces Engineering Command (SAUS) ... AAFEC
Army Air Forces Gunnery School ... AAFGS
Army Air Forces Intelligence School ... AAFIS
Army Air Forces Material Center (SAUO) ... AAFMC
Army Air Forces Military Personnel [*World War II*] ... AFPMP
Army Air Forces Navigation School ... AAFNS
Army Air Forces, Pacific Ocean Areas ... AAFPOA
Army Air Forces, Pacific Ocean Areas (Administrative) ... AAFPOA (ADMIN)
Army Air Forces Pilot School ... AAFPS
Army Air Forces Pre-Flight School (SAUO) ... AAFPFS
Army Air Forces Pre-Flight School (Pilot) ... AAFPFS(P)
Army Air Forces Requirements Division [*World War II*] ... AFREQ
Army Air Forces School of Applied Tactics [*World War II*] ... AAFSAT
Army Air Forces School of Applied Tactics, Orlando (SAUO) ... AAFSAT
Army Air Forces Service Command ... AAFSC
Army Air Forces Southeast Training Command [*World War II*] ... AAFSETC
Army Air Forces Standard (SAUS) ... AAF STD
Army Air Forces Tactical Center [*World War II*] ... AAFTAC
Army Air Forces Tactical Center, Orlando (SAUO) ... AAFTAC
Army Air Forces Technical School [*World War II*] ... AAFTS
Army Air Forces Technical Training Command [*World War II*] ... AAFTTC
Army Air Forces Technical Training School (SAUO) ... AAFTTS
Army Air Forces Training Aids Division [*World War II*] ... AAFTAD
Army Air Forces Training Center (SAUS) ... AAFTC
Army Air Forces Training Center, Orlando (SAUO) ... AAFTC
Army Air Forces Training Command [*World War II*] ... AAFTC
Army Air Forces Training Detachment (SAUO) ... AAFTD
Army Air Forces Troop Information and Education (SAUS) ... AAFTI&E
Army Air Forces Western Flying Training Command [*World War II*] ... AAFWFTC
Army Air Forces Western Technical Training Command [*World War II*] ... AAFWTTC
Army Air Ground System (SAUS) ... AAGS
Army Air Liaison Officer (SAUS) ... AALO
Army Air Material Command (SAUO) ... AAMC
Army Air Mobility Research and Development Laboratories [*Army*] ... AAMRDL
Army Air Mobility Research and Development Laboratory (SAUO) ... AAMRDL
Army Air Movement Support Unit (MCD) ... AAMSU
Army Air Operations (MCD) ... AA
Army Air Personnel (SAUS) ... AAP
Army Air Reconnaissance for Damage Assessment in the Continental (SAUS) ... AARDC
Army Air Reconnaissance for Damage Assessment in the Continental United States (AABC) ... AARDAC
Army Air Service ... AAS
Army Air Support Control [*British and Canadian*] [*World War II*] ... A AIR SC
Army Air Traffic Control and Navigation System (MCD) ... AATCAN
Army Air Traffic Control and Navigation System (SAUS) ... AATCAN System
Army Air Traffic Coordinating Office (AABC) ... AATCO
Army Air Traffic Regulation and Identification ... AATRI
Army Air Traffic Regulation and Identification System (AFM) ... AATRIS
Army Air Training Center (SAUS) ... AATC
Army Air Transport and Development Centre (SAUS) ... AATDC
Army Air Transport Command (SAUO) ... AATC

Army Air Transport Organization	AATO
Army Air Transport Training and Development Centre (SAUO)	AATC
Army Air Transport Training & Development Centre (SAUS)	AATDC
Army Air Transport Training and Development Centre [England]	AATDC
Army Air Transport Training and Development Centre (SAUO)	AATTDC
Army Air Warning Net (SAUO)	AAWN
Army Airborne Command and Control (SAUO)	AACC
Army Airborne Electronics and Special Warfare Board	AAESWB
Army Aircraft (AABC)	AACFT
Army Aircraft Avionics Study (MCD)	A3S
Army Aircraft Maintenance (AABC)	AAM
Army Aircraft Maintenance Shop (AABC)	AAMS
Army Aircraft Maintenance Training Assistance Program (SAUO)	AAMTAP
Army Aircraft Radio Laboratory (IAA)	AARL
Army Aircraft Repair Ship	AARS
Army Aircraft Requirements Review Board (SAUO)	AARRB
Army Aircraft Requirements Review Committee	AARRC
Army Airfield	AAF
Army Airforce Training Command Orchestra (WDAA)	AAFTCO
Army Airspace Command & Control (SAUS)	A2C2
Army Airspace Command and Control (SAUS)	A/C/C
Army Airspace Command and Control (DOMA)	A²C²
Army Airways Communication System (SAUO)	AACS
Army Airways Communications System	AACS
Army Amateur Radio System	AARS
Army Ambulance Service (SAUO)	AAmbServ
Army Ambulance Service (SAUO)	AAS
Army Ammunition Command (SAUO)	AAC
Army Ammunition in Thailand (MCD)	AIT
Army Ammunition Plant (AABC)	AAP
Army Ammunition Reporting Service (SAUS)	TAARS
[The] Army Ammunition Reporting System (AABC)	TAARS
Army Analysis of Intelligence	AAI
Army and Air Force (SAUO)	AAF
Army and Air Force Act [British military] (DMA)	A & AFA
Army and Air Force Air Intelligence School [British]	AAFAIS
Army and Air Force Air Intelligence School (SAUO)	AAFAIS
Army and Air Force Base	AAFB
Army and Air Force Central Welfare Fund (SAUO)	AAFCWF
Army and Air Force Civilian Welfare Fund	AAFCWF
Army and Air Force Exchange and Motion Picture Service	AAFEMPS
Army and Air Force Exchange and Motion Picture Service Board of Directors [DoD]	AAFBD
Army and Air Force Exchange and Motion Picture Services Board of Directors (SAUO)	AAFBD
Army and Air Force Exchange Service	AAFES
Army and Air Force Exchange Service	A & AFES
Army and Air Force Exchange Service (SAUS)	A&AFES
Army and Air Force Exchange Service Board of Directors (ACAE)	AAFBD
Army and Air Force Intelligence Staff (SAUO)	AAFIS
Army and Air Force Intelligence Staff [British]	AAFIS
Army and Air Force Motion Picture Service	AAFMPS
Army and Air Force Motion Picture Service-Europe (SAUO)	AAFMPS-E
Army and Air Force Mutual Aid Association (EA)	AAFMAA
Army and Air Force Pilot School (SAUO)	AAFPS
Army and Air Force Postal Service	AAFPS
Army and Air Force Wage Board	AAFWB
Army and Air Forces Technical Training Center (SAUS)	AAFTTC
Army and Ammunition Division (SAUO)	AAD
Army and Navy (SAUO)	A&N
Army and Navy	A & N
Army and Navy	AN
Army and Navy Air Service Association (SAUO)	ANASA
Army and Navy Civil Committee on Aircraft (SAUO)	ANC
Army and Navy Club (SAUO)	A&NC
Army and Navy Club, Washington, DC [Library symbol] [Library of Congress] (LCLS)	DAN
Army and Navy Life [New York] [A publication] (ROG)	A & NL
Army and Navy Medical Procurement Office (SAUO)	ANMPO
Army and Navy Munitions Board [British] (DAS)	A & NB
Army and Navy Munitions Board (SAUS)	A&NB
Army and Navy Munitions Board (SAUO)	ANMB
Army and Navy Staff College [Redesignated National War College, 1946]	ANSC
Army and Navy Staff College [See ANSC]	ANSCOL
Army and Navy Stores (SAUO)	ANS
Army and Navy Stores (SAUS)	ANS
Army and Navy Union (SAUO)	ANU
Army and Navy Union of the United States (SAUO)	ANUUS
Army and Navy Union, USA (EA)	ANU
Army Antiaircraft Command (SAUO)	AAAC
Army Antiaircraft Command (SAUO)	AAACOM
Army Anti-Aircraft Command (SAUS)	AAACOM
Army Antiaircraft Command, Colorado Springs (SAUO)	ARAACOM
Army Antiaircraft Guided Missile Center (SAUO)	AAGMC
Army Apprentices College (SAUO)	AAC
Army Apprentices College (SAUO)	AA Coll
Army Apprenticeship Program	AAP
Army Appropriation Account (SAUS)	AAA
Army Area Analysis Intelligence Agency (SAA)	AAIA
Army Area Calibration Facilities (MCD)	AACF
Army Area Communications [System] (IAA)	AACOM
Army Area Communications System (MCD)	AACOMS
Army Area Representative	AAR
Army Area Signal Center (AABC)	AASC
Army Area Signal System (IAA)	AASS
Army Area Supply Center (SAUO)	AASC
Army Armament, Material, and Chemical Command (SAUO)	AMCCOM
Army Armament Materiel Readiness Command	ARRCOM
Army Armament Research and Development Center [or Command] Technical Support Directorate [Dover, NJ]	ARTSD
Army Armament Research & Development Command (SAUS)	AARADCOM
Army Armament Research and Development Command [Dover, NJ] (MCD)	ARRADCOM
Army Armament Research and Development Command Chemical Systems Laboratory	ARCSL
Army Armament Research and Development Command Product Assurance Directorate	ARPAD
Army Armament Research Ballistic Research Laboratory [Aberdeen Proving Ground, MD] (MCD)	ARBRL
Army Armament Research Development Command (SAUO)	AARADCOM
Army Armor Board (MCD)	A-ARM
Army Armor School (AAG)	AAMS
Army Artificial Heart Pump (SAUS)	AAHP
Army Artillery and Missile Center [Fort Sill, OK] (MCD)	AAMC
Army Artillery and Missile School	AAMS
Army Artillery Board (AAG)	AAB
Army Artillery Board (MCD)	A-ART
Army Artillery Group (AABC)	AAG
Army Artillery Headquarters (SAUO)	AAHQ
Army Aspirin (VNW)	APC
Army Assault Team	AAT
Army Atomic Weapon Systems Safety Committee (SAUS)	AAWSSC
Army Atomic Weapons Systems Safety Committee [Later, DNA] (AABC)	AAWSSC
Army Atomic Weapons Systems Safety Committee (SAUO)	AAWSSC
Army Attache	ARMA
Army Attache System	AAS
Army AttachS System (SAUS)	AAS
Army Attrition Rates Committee (NATG)	AARC
Army Audio Visual Agency (SAUS)	AAVA
Army Audio-Visual Agency (PDAA)	AAVA
Army Audiovisual Center	AAC
Army Audit Agency	AAA
Army Authority for Major Commands to Disseminate Information and Take Appropriate Action	ACTCOM
Army Authorization Document System (SAUS)	TAADS
Army Auto Plan and Progress Evaluation System	AAPPES
[The] Army Automated Budget System	TAABS
Army Automated Environmental Management Information System	AAEMIS
Army Automated Library and Information Support System (SAUS)	AALIS System
[The] Army Automated Logistic Data System	TAALODS
Army Automation and Communication Steering Committee	AACSC
Army Automation Command Operating Budget (AAGC)	AACOB
Army Automation Command Operating Budget Estimate	AACOBE
Army Automation Communications System (AAGC)	AACOMS
Army Automation Directorate (SAUO)	AAD
Army Automation Directorate [Formerly, DMIS] (MCD)	AAD
Army Automation Master Plan	AAMAP
Army Automation Memorandum Budget	AAMB
Army Automation Planning, Programming, and Evaluation System (MCD)	AAPES
Army Automation Planning, Programming, and Evaluation System	AAPPES
Army Automation Planning, Programming and Evaluation System (SAUS)	AAPPES
Army Automation Program	AAP
Army Automation Program Budget Guidance	AAPBG
Army Automation Security Program	AASP
Army Automation Steering Committee	AASC
Army Aviation (AABC)	AAVN
Army Aviation and Missile Command	AMCOM
Army Aviation & Surface Command (SAUS)	AVSCOM
Army Aviation Association of America (EA)	AAAA
Army Aviation Board	AAB
Army Aviation Center (SAUO)	AAC
Army Aviation Centre [British] (BI)	AAvnC
Army Aviation Centre, Middle Wallop, near Stockbridge (SAUO)	AAvnC
Army Aviation Combat Center (SAUO)	AACC
Army Aviation Control Center	AACC
Army Aviation Decontamination Station (DOMA)	AADS
Army Aviation Depot Maintenance Center (MCD)	AADMC
Army Aviation Development Plan (MCD)	AADP
Army Aviation Element (AABC)	AAE
Army Aviation Employment Conference	AVNEC
Army Aviation Engineering Flight Activity	AAEFA
Army Aviation Engineers	AAE
Army Aviation Flight Activity (SAUO)	AAFA
Army Aviation Flight Information Detachment (SAUO)	AAFID
Army Aviation Maintenance Support Activity	AAMSA
Army Aviation Material Laboratories (SAUO)	AVLABS
Army Aviation Materiel Command	AAMC
Army Aviation Materiel Laboratory (MCD)	AAML
Army Aviation Medical Officer's Badge [Military decoration]	AR Av MO Bad
Army Aviation Medical Officers Badge (SAUS)	AR Av MO Bad
Army Aviation Mission Area Analysis	AAMAA
Army Aviation Mobile Technical Assistance Program (SAUO)	AAMTAP
Army Aviation Modernization Plan (MCD)	AAMP
Army Aviation Operating Detachment	AAOD
Army Aviation (or Aviator) Badge (SAUS)	Av Bad

Army Aviation Personnel Requirements of Sustained Operations Study (MCD) .... AAPRSO
Army Aviation Planning Manual (AABC) .... AAPM
Army Aviation Program Review (MCD) .... AAPR
Army Aviation Regiment (SAUO) .... AAR
Army Aviation Research and Development Activity (SAUO) ...... AVRADA
Army Aviation Research and Development Command [Fort Monmouth, NJ] (MCD) .... AVRADCOM
Army Aviation Research and Development Objectives Program (SAUO) .... AARDOP
Army Aviation School (SAUO) .... AAS
Army Aviation Support Element (AABC) .... AASE
Army Aviation Support Facility (MCD) .... AASF
Army Aviation System Support Center (SAUO) ...... AASSC
Army Aviation Systems Test Activity (SAUO) ...... AASTA
Army Aviation Systems Test Activity [Also, USAASTA] ...... AASTA
Army Aviation Test Activity (SAUO) .... AATA
Army Aviation Test Board .... AATB
Army Aviation Test Command [ATEC] .... AATC
Army Aviation Unit Training Command (MCD) ...... AAUTC
Army Aviator (AABC) .... ARAV
Army Aviator Badge [Military decoration] ...... AR Av Bad
Army Aviator Badge [Military decoration] ...... AVBAD
Army Avionics Program .... AAP
Army Background Experiment .... ABE
Army Bacteriological Warfare Laboratory (SAUO) ...... ABWL
Army Ballistic Missile Agency [Redstone Arsenal, AL] ...... ABMA
Army Ballistic Missile Division (ACAE) .... ABMD
Army Ballistic Research (SAUS) .... ABR
Army Ballistic Research Laboratories (SAUO) ...... ABRL
Army Ballistic Research Laboratory (SAA) .... ABRL
Army Base Information Transfer System (MCD) ...... ARBITS
Army Base Supply Depot (SAUS) .... ABSD
Army Baseline Electric Laser (ACAE) .... ABEL
Army Basic Training Unit [British military] (DMA) ...... ABTU
Army Battle Command System (RDA) .... ABCS
Army Battle Command Systems [Army] .... ABCS
Army Battle Damage Repair (GFGA) .... ABDR
Army Battlefield Interface Concept (MCD) .... ABIC
Army Bearer Corps (SAUO) .... AB
Army Benevolent Fund (SAUO) .... AbF
Army Benevolent Fund [British] .... ABF
Army Biological Laboratory .... ABL
Army Biological Warfare Research Center .... ABWRC
Army Blood Transfusion Service (SAUO) .... ABTS
Army Board for Correction of Military Records ...... ABCMR
Army Board of Contract Appeals (AAGC) .... ABCA
Army Board of Review for Eliminations .... ABRE
Army Book [British and Canadian] [World War II] ...... AB
Army Broadcasting Service (GFGA) .... ABS
Army Budget Directive .... ABD
Army Budget Office .... ABO
Army Bureau of Current Affairs [To encourage British soldiers to think and talk about what they were fighting for] [World War II] ...... ABCA
Army Cadet College (SAUO) .... ACC
Army Cadet Force [Military unit] [British] .... ACF
Army Cadet Force Association [British military] (DMA) ...... ACFA
Army Calibration System .... ACS
Army Camouflage School (SAUO) .... ACS
Army Canteen Service (SAUO) .... ACS
Army Capabilities Plan .... ACP
Army Career and Alumni Program (INF) .... ACAP
Army Career Education System .... ACES
Army Career Group .... ACGP
Army Careers Information Office (SAUO) .... ACIO
Army, Caribbean (SAUO) .... ARCARIB
Army Cataloguing Authority (SAUO) .... ACA
Army Catering Corps (SAUO) .... ACC
Army Catering Corps [British] .... ACC
Army Catering Corps Association (SAUO) ...... ACC Association
Army Catering Corps Training Centre (SAUO) ...... ACCTC
Army Cavalry Scout Experiment (MCD) .... ARCAVEX
Army [Forces US] Central [Command] (DOMA) ...... ARCENT
Army Central Budget Office .... ACBO
Army Central Intelligence Service (SAUO) .... ACIS
Army Central Logistics Data Bank (AABC) .... ACLDB
Army Central Logistics Data-Bank (SAUS) .... ACLDB
Army Central Service Point .... ACSP
Army Central Welfare Fund .... ACWF
Army Certificate of Education (SAUS) .... ACE
Army Chaplains Department [British military] (DMA) ...... ACD
Army Chemical Center .... ACC
Army Chemical Center (SAUO) .... ACMIC
Army Chemical Center (SAUO) .... A Cml C
Army Chemical Center .... ACMLC
Army Chemical Center Procurement Agency .... ACCPA
Army Chemical Corps (SAUO) .... ACC
Army Chemical Corps Medical Laboratories (KSC) ...... ACCML
Army Chemical Research and Development Laboratory (SAUS) ...... ACRDL
Army Chemical Research and Development Labs (MCD) ...... ACRDL
Army Chemical Supply Point (SAUO) .... ACSP
Army Chemical Typewriter (SAUS) .... ACT
Army Chemical Warfare Laboratory .... ACWL
Army Chief of Research and Development (SAA) ...... ACRD
Army Chief of Staff (AAGC) .... CSA

Army Chief of Staff for Communications Electronics (SAUS) ...... ACSCE
Army Chief of Support Services .... ACSS
Army Child Advocacy Program (MCD) .... ACAP
Army Circular [British military] (DMA) .... AC
Army Civil Services' Union [Singapore] .... ACSU
Army Civilian Career Evaluation System .... ACCES
Army Civilian Personnel System .... ACPERS
Army Civilian Training, Education, and Development System ...... ACTEDS
Army Civilian Training, Education and Development System (SAUS) ...... ACTEDS
Army Class Management Activity (SAUS) .... ACMA
Army Class Manager Activity (AABC) .... ACMA
Army Classification Battery [Military tests] .... ACB
Army Classification Evaluation Board .... ACEB
Army Clerical Speed Test .... ACST
Army Close Support (SAUS) .... ARCLOS
Army Clothing and Equipment Board (MCD) .... ACEB
Army Clothing and Textile Material Center (SAUO) ...... ACTMC
Army Clothing, Textile and Material Center (SAUS) ...... ACTMC
Army Clothing, Textile, and Materiel Center .... ACTMC
Army Club Fund .... ACF
Army Coastal Engineering Research Center .... ACERC
Army Coating and Chemical Laboratory (MCD) ...... ACCL
Army Cohesion and Stability Program .... ARCOST
Army Cohesion Study (MCD) .... ARCOST
Army College Fund .... ACF
Army Combat Artist Program .... ACAP
Army Combat Development Committee [British] ...... ACDC
Army Combat Development Experimental Center (AAG) ...... ACDEC
Army Combat Development Experimentation Center (SAUS) ...... ACDEC
Army Combat Development Experimentation Command (SAUO) ...... ACDC
Army Combat Developments Command .... ACDC
Army Combat Engineers (CINC) .... ACE
Army Combat Identification System (SAUS) .... ACIS
Army Combat Identification Systems .... ACIS
Army Combat Operations Vietnam (AABC) .... ARCOV
Army Combat Surveillance Agency (ACAE) .... ACSA
Army Combat Surveillance Office (SAUO) .... AMCSOF
[The] Army Combined Arms Weapons System ...... TACAWS
Army Comforts Fund (SAUO) .... ACF
Army Command and Administration Communication Agency (NATG) ...... ACACA
Army Command and Administrative Network (SAUO) ...... ARCAN
Army Command and Control Communications Network (MCD) ...... ARCCNET
Army Command and Control Communications Network (MCD) ...... ARCONET
Army Command and Control Management Information System ...... ACCMIS
Army Command and Control Master Plan AC2MP
Army Command and Control Network (AABC) .... ACCNET
Army Command and Control Network (MCD) .... ARCNET
Army Command and Control Study (MCD) .... ACCS
Army Command and Control System (MCD) AC2S
Army Command and Control System (RDA) .... ACCS
Army Command and Control System Engineering Implementation Plan .... ASEIP
Army Command and General Staff College .... ARCGSC
Army Command and General Staff School .... ACGSC
Army Command and General Staff School (SAUS) ...... ACGSS
Army Command & Staff Course (SAUS) .... ACSC
Army Command Center (SAUO) .... ACC
Army Command Control Master Plan (CCCA) .... ACCMP
Army Command Management System .... ACMS
Army [Forces] Command Post .... ARCP
Army Commanders' Conference .... ACC
Army Commanders Conference (SAUS) .... ACC
Army Commanders Initiatives Program (RDA) .... ARCIP
Army Commanding Service .... ACS
Army Commendation Medal (MUSM) .... ACM
Army Commendation Medal [Military decoration] ...... ARCM
Army Commendation Medal [Military decoration] ...... ARCOM
Army Commercial Vehicle Code (AABC) .... ACVC
Army Commissary Automation System (GFGA) ...... ACAS
Army Commissary Computer Entry Store System (AABC) ...... ACCESS
Army Common Operating Environment (RDA) .... ACOE
Army Communication Operations Center Agency ...... ACOCA
Army Communication Service Division (SAUS) .... ACSD
Army Communications - Service Division .... ACSD
Army Communications Administrative Network [Domestic and overseas integrated system of fixed radio, wire, cable, and associated communications facilities] ...... ACAN
Army Communications and Control System (ROAS) ...... ACCS
Army Communications and Electronic Command ...... ACEC
Army Communications and Electronics Management Information System (SAUS) ...... ACEMIS
Army Communications and Equipment Coordination (SAUS) ...... AC&EC
Army Communications and Equipment Coordination ...... AC & EC
Army Communications Board .... ACB
Army Communications Command [Fort Huachuca, AZ] ...... ACC
Army Communications Command Advanced Concepts Office [Fort Huachuca, AZ] ...... ACC-ACO
Army Communications Division .... ACD
Army Communications Electronics School (MCD) ...... ACES
Army Communications Equipment Support (MCD) ...... ACES
Army Communications Objectives Measurement Survey [or System] (GFGA) ...... ACOMS
Army Communications Service (SAUO) .... ACS
Army Communications Systems (SAUS) .... ACUS
Army Communications Systems Agency (SAUO) ...... ACSA
Army Communicative Systems [Provisional] (RDA) ...... ACS

Army Communicative Technology (RDA) ... ACT
Army Communicative Technology Office ... ACTO
Army Communities of Excellence ... ACOE
Army Community Health Nursing [*Army*] ... ACHN
Army Community Service ... ACS
Army Community Services (SAUS) ... ACS
Army Community Services/Child Support Services (SAUO) ... ACS/CSS
Army Competitive Category (RDA) ... ACC
Army Component Command (CINC) ... ACC
Army Comptroller (SAUS) ... A Compt
Army Computer Capabilities Online Repository and Disseminator (PDAA) ... ACCORD
Army Computer Systems Command [*Also, CSC*] ... ACSC
Army Computer Systems Command (SAUO) ... ACSC
Army Computer-Aided Acquisition and Logistics Support ... ACALS
Army COMSEC [*Communications Security*] **Central Office of Record** (AABC) ... ACCOR
Army COMSEC [*Communications Security*] **Commodity, Logistical, and Accounting Information Management System** (AABC) ... ACCLAIMS
Army Concept Development Program (SAUO) ... ACDP
Army Concept Team in Vietnam ... ACTIV
Army Concepts Analysis Agency ... ACAA
Army Consideration of Tactical Air Support ... ACTAS
Army Container-Oriented Distribution System (SAUS) ... ACODS
Army Container-Oriented Distribution Systems ... ACODS
Army Continuing Education System ... ACES
Army Continuing Educations System (SAUO) ... ACES
Army Continuing Evaluation Services ... ACES
Army Contract Adjustment Board ... ACAB
Army Contract Adjustment Region (MCD) ... ACAR
Army Contract Appeals Panel ... ACAP
Army Control Program Directive ... ACPD
Army Controllership Program ... ACP
Army Controlling Education Service ... ACES
Army Co-Operation [*British military*] (DMA) ... AC
Army Cooperation Command [*British*] ... ACC
Army Cooperation Command (SAUO) ... ACC
Army Co-operation Squadron (SAUO) ... ACSqn
Army Co-Operation Squadron [*British and Canadian*] [*World War II*] ... AC Sqn
Army Corporate Data Base (SAUO) ... ACDB
Army Corporate Database (GFGA) ... ACDB
Army Corps ... AC
Army Corps (SAUO) ... AC
Army Corps Commander (SAUS) ... ACC
Army Corps Depot (SAUS) ... ACD
Army Corps of Engineers (SAUO) ... ACDB
Army Corps of Engineers ... ACE
Army Corps of Engineers (COE) ... ACOE
Army Corps of Engineers (SAUS) ... CGUSACE
Army Corps of Engineers (AAGC) ... COE
Army Corps of Engineers (SAUO) ... CORPS
Army Corps of Engineers (AAGC) ... ENG
Army Corps of Engineers Claims and Appeals Board (AAGC) ... ENG C&A
Army Corps of Engineers, Office of the Chief Engineer (AAGC) ... ACE-OCE
Army Corps of Engineers Socioeconomic Information System [*Information service or system*] (IID) ... ACESIS
Army Corps of Engineers/Naval Facilities Engineering Command ... CE/NAVFAC
Army Correspondence Course Program ... ACCP
Army Cost Analysis Information and Data System (MCD) ... ARCAIDS
Army Cost Analysis Paper ... ACAP
Army Cost Position ... ACP
Army Cost Reduction Program (AABC) ... ACRP
Army Council (ADA) ... AC
Army Council (SAUO) ... AC
Army Council Command (SAUO) ... ACC
Army Council Form (SAUO) ... ACF
Army Council Instruction [*World War II*] ... ACI
Army Council of Review Boards ... ACRB
Army Council Secretariat (SAUO) ... ACS
[*The*] **Army Counter-Air Weapons System** ... TACAWS
Army Countermine Mobility Equipment System (MCD) ... ACMES
Army Crisis Action System ... ACAS
Army Criteria Tracking System ... ACTS
Army Customer Order Control System ... ACOCS
Army Customer Order Program ... ACOP
Army Cycling (or Cyclist) Corps (SAUO) ... ACC
Army Cycling Union (SAUO) ... ACU
Army Damage Assessment System (AABC) ... ARMDAS
Army Data Dictionary (RDA) ... ADD
Army Data Distribution System ... ADDS
Army Data Field Systems Command (SAUO) ... ADFSC
Army Data Processing System (SAUS) ... ADPS
Army Data Retrieval Engineering System (MCD) ... ADRES
Army Data Retrieval System (NITA) ... ADRES
Army Data Services and Administrative Systems Command (ACAE) ... ADSC
Army Data Validation and Netting Capabilities Establishment ... ADVANCE
Army Decision Support System ... ADSS
Army Defense Acquisition Regulation [*Superseded by AFARS in 1984*] (AAGC) ... ADAR
Army Defense Acquisition Regulation Supplement (AABC) ... ADARS
Army Defense Ammunition Center and School (SAUO) ... ADACS
Army Defense Combined Arms Tactical Trainer (SAUS) ... ADCATT
Army DEIS [*Defense Energy Information System*] **Data Entry System** ... ADDS
Army Density Report ... ADR
Army Density Report, United States Army Reserve ... ADRUSAR
Army Dental Care System (SAUO) ... ADCS
Army Dental Corps [*British*] ... AD
Army Dental Corps [*British*] ... ADC
Army Dental Laboratory (SAUO) ... ADL
Army Dental Service ... ADS
Army Department [*British*] (RDA) ... AD
Army Department Establishments [*British*] ... ADE
Army Dependents' Assurance Trust [*British*] (DI) ... ADAT
Army Dependents Assurance Trust (SAUS) ... ADAT
Army Deployment Reporting System (AABC) ... ADEPREP
Army Deployment Reporting System (SAUS) ... ADEPREP System
Army Depot (AABC) ... AD
Army Depot Automatic Diagnostic System (RDA) ... ADADS
Army Depot of Supplies (or Supply) (SAUO) ... AD of S
Army Depot of Supply (SAUO) ... ADOS
Army Depot Operations Management (MCD) ... ADOM
Army Depot Police [*British military*] (DMA) ... ADP
Army Development and Acquisition of Threat Simulators ... ADATS
Army Development and Employment Agency [*Fort Lewis, WA*] ... ADE
Army Development and Employment Agency [*Fort Lewis, WA*] (INF) ... ADEA
Army Development Reporting System (SAUS) ... ADEPREP System
Army Development Test Command ... ADTC
Army Digital Avionics System (MCD) ... ADAS
Army Digitalization Office ... ADO
Army Digitization Office (SAUO) ... ADO
Army Disability Rating Review Board (AABC) ... ADRRB
Army Disability Review Beard (SAUS) ... ADRB
Army Disability Review Board ... ADRB
Army Discharge Review Board ... ADRB
Army Dispensary (ACAE) ... AD
Army Distaff Foundation (EA) ... ADF
Army Distinguished Service Cross (SAUS) ... ADSC
Army Distinguished Service Medal (SAUS) ... ADSM
Army Distribution Objective (MCD) ... ADO
Army Dollar Resource Allocation ... ADRA
Army Driver (SAUS) ... AD
Army Drug and Alcohol Technical Activity (ACAE) ... ADATA
Army Education ... AE
Army Education and Welfare Services (SAUO) ... AEWS
Army Education Center ... AEC
Army Education Information System (MCD) ... AREIS
Army Education Requirement System (DOMA) ... AERS
Army Education Review Board ... AERB
Army Education Scheme (SAUS) ... AES
Army Educational Corps [*Later, RAEC*] [*British*] ... AEC
Army Educational Department (SAUO) ... AE
Army Educational Requirements Board ... AERB
Army Electronic Command (SAUS) ... AECOM
Army Electronic Proving Ground ... AEPG
Army Electronic Proving Ground (IIA) ... AREPG
Army Electronic Warfare and Intelligence Board ... AEWIB
Army Electronic Warfare Board (MCD) ... AEWB
Army Electronic Warfare Information System ... AEWIS
Army Electronic Warfare Intelligence Committees (SAUO) ... AEWIC
Army Electronic Warfare Policy Committee (IAA) ... AEWPC
Army Electronics Command ... AEC
Army Electronics Command (MUGU) ... AECOM
Army Electronics Command (SAUO) ... ECOM
Army Electronics Laboratories (KSC) ... AEL
Army Electronics Logistics Research Office (KSC) ... AELRO
Army Electronics Material Support Agency ... AEMSA
Army Electronics Proving Ground (SAUS) ... AEPG
Army Electronics Research and Development Activity [*White Sands Missile Range, NM*] ... AERDA
Army Electronics Research and Development Command (SAUO) ... AERDC
Army Electronics Research and Development Laboratory (AABC) ... AERDL
Army Electronics Research and Development Laboratry (SAUO) ... AERDL
Army EMC Agency (SAUS) ... AEMCE
Army Emergency Relief (EA) ... AER
Army Emergency Reserve [*British*] ... AER
Army Energy Office ... AEO
Army Engineer Center (SAA) ... AEC
Army Engineer District, Far East ... FED
Army Engineer Geodesy, Intelligence and Mapping Research and Development Agency (SAUO) ... AEGIMRDA
Army Engineer Geodesy, Intelligence and Mapping Research and Development Agency. (SAUS) ... AEGIMRDA
Army Engineer Reactors Group [*Fort Belvoir, VA*] ... AERG
Army Engineer Regiment (SAUO) ... AER
Army Engineer Research and Development Laboratories [*Fort Belvoir, VA*] ... AERDL
Army Engineer School (SAUO) ... AES
Army Engineer Topographic Laboratories (RDA) ... AETL
Army Engineer Waterway Experiment Station (SAUO) ... AEWES
Army Engineer Waterways Experiment Station [*Vicksburg, MS*] ... AEWES
Army Engineers Waterways Experiment Station (SAUS) ... AEWES
Army Enlisted Education Review Board (MCD) ... AEERB
Army Entertainment Scholarships and Awards Program (AABC) ... AESAP
Army Entrance Examination (SAUS) ... AEE
Army Environment Health Laboratory (SAUO) ... AEHL
Army Environmental Center [*Aberdeen Proving Ground, MD*] (RDA) ... AEC
Army Environmental Health Agency ... AEHA
Army Environmental Health Laboratory ... AEHL
Army Environmental Hygiene Agency ... AEHA
Army Equipment Authorizations Review Center (AABC) ... AEARC

Army Equipment Board (SAUO)	AEB
Army Equipment Engineering Establishment	AEEE
Army Equipment Policy [British military] (DMA)	AEP
Army Equipment Policy Committee (AAG)	AEPC
[The] Army Equipment Record System [Later, TAMMS]	TAERS
Army Equipment Status Report	AESR
Army Equipment Status Reporting System (AABC)	AESRS
Army Establishment Committee (SAUO)	AEC
Army Excess Property (AABC)	AES
Army Exchange Central Purchasing Office (SAUO)	AECPO
Army Exchange Service [Centralized the control of PX's in US] [World War II]	AES
Army Executives for Software Program [Army Materiel Command] (RDA)	ARES
Army Exhibit Unit	AEU
Army Experimental Flight Activity (MCD)	AEFA
Army Experimentation Campaign Plan	AECP
Army Extension Course Program (AABC)	AECP
Army Extension Training (GFGA)	AET
Army Extension Training Information System	AETIS
Army Extension Training System	AETS
Army Facilities Components System (AABC)	AFCS
Army Facilities Energy Program (MCD)	AFEP
Army Family Action Planning	AFAP
Army Family Housing	AFH
Army Family Term Building	AFTB
Army Federal Acquisition Regulations Supplement	AFARS
Army Field Artillery Brigade (SAUO)	AFA Bde
Army Field Artillery Combat Effectiveness Model (MCD)	AFACE
Army Field Artillery School	AFAS
Army Field Artillery Tactical Data System (SAUS)	AFATDS
Army Field Assistance and Technology	AFAST
Army Field Code (SAUS)	AFC
Army Field Command (SAUS)	AFC
Army Field Commands	AFC
Army Field Depot (SAUO)	AFD
Army Field Feeding System (INF)	AFFS
Army Field Forces	AFF
Army Field Forces Board	AFFB
Army Field Headquarters	AFHQ
Army Field Park Squadron (SAUO)	AFPS
Army Field Regiment, Royal Artillery (SAUO)	A Fd Rgt RA
Army Field Stock Control System (AABC)	AFSCS
Army Field Workshop	AFW
Army Field Workshop (SAUO)	AFW
Army Film and Photographic Section [British military] (DMA)	AFPS
Army Film and Photographic Unit [British military] (DMA)	AFPU
Army Finance and Accounting Center (MCD)	AFAC
Army Finance Association [Defunct] (EA)	AFA
Army Finance Center	AFC
Army Financial Stock Summary Analysis	AFSSA
Army Fire Service	AFS
Army Fire Service (SAUO)	AFS
Army Fire Support Center (SAUS)	AFSC
Army Five-Year Force Structure and Financial Plan (SAUO)	AFYSFP
Army Fixed Wing Aptitude Battery (AABC)	AFWAB
Army Flight Activity	AFA
Army Flight Operations Center (SAUO)	AFOC
Army Flight Operations Facility (SAUO)	AFOF
Army Flying Corps [British] (AIA)	AFC
Army Flying Time Report (MCD)	AFTR
Army Food Management Information System (GFGA)	AFMIS
Army Food Service Energy Management (AABC)	AFSEM
Army Food Supply (SAUS)	AFS
Army Force	AF
Army Force, Atlantic (SAUS)	ARLANT
Army Force Development Plan	AFDP
Army Force Guidance	AFG
Army Force Integration Study	AFIS
Army Force Modernization Coordination Office	AFMCO
Army Force Planning Cost Handbook	AFPCH
Army Force Planning Data and Assumptions (AABC)	AFPDA
Army Force Program	AFP
Army Force Status Reporting System (AABC)	ARFORSTAT
Army Force/Materiel Cost Methodology Improvement Project	ACMIP
Army Forces [Element of a joint task force]	ARFOR
Army Forces Atlantic (MCD)	ARLANT
Army Forces, Central Command (SAUS)	ARCENT
Army Forces Command (SAUS)	FORSCOM
Army Forces Far East	AFFE
Army Forces, Middle Pacific (SAUS)	AFMIDPAC
Army Forces Readiness Command (MCD)	ARRED
Army Forces, Western Pacific (SAUO)	AFWESPAC
Army Forces-Alaska (SAUO)	ARFOR-AK
Army Form	AF
Army Forwarding Officer [British]	AFO
Army Fuels and Lubricants Laboratory	AFLL
Army Fuels and Lubricants Research Laboratory	AFLRL
Army Functional Component System	AFCS
[The] Army Functional Files System	TAFFS
[The] Army Functional Files Test System (MCD)	TAFFTS
Army Fuze Program (MCD)	AFP
Army Garrison (ACAE)	AG
Army Gas Dynamic LASER (MCD)	A-GDL
Army Gas Dynamic Laser (SAUS)	A-GDL
Army Gas-Cooled Reactor System (SAA)	AGCRS

Army Gas-Cooled Reactor Systems Program	AGCRSP
Army Gateway Program (SAUS)	AGP
Army General & Administrative Instructions (SAUS)	AGAI
Army General Classification Test [Measurement of intelligence]	AGCT
Army General Council	AGC
Army General Education Development Center (SAUS)	AGES
Army General Equipment Command	AGEC
Army General Orders (SAUS)	AGO
Army General Staff	AGS
Army General Staff Civilian Personnel Office (SAUO)	AGSCPO
Army General Supplies Commodity Center	AGSCC
Army Global Command and Control System [Army]	AGCCS
Army Good Conduct Medal	AGCM
Army Good Conduct Medal	AGCMDL
Army Graves Registration Service (SAUO)	AGRS
Army Ground Forces	AGF
Army Ground Pool [for officers]	AGP
Army Ground Transportable Emitter Location Identification System	AGTELIS
Army Group (NATG)	AG
Army Group (SAUO)	AGp
Army Group Effects Department	AGED
Army Group Headquarters	AGH
Army Group Photo Interpretation Unit (SAUO)	AGPIU
Army Group Royal Artillery [British]	AGRA
Army Group, Royal Engineers [British and Canadian] [World War II]	AGRE
Army Guard School (SAUS)	AGS
Army Guard Ship (SAUS)	AGS
Army Guidance	AG
Army Gun Air Defense Systems (RDA)	ARGADS
Army Gunner Training (MCD)	AGT
Army Handicapped Employe of the Year (RDA)	AHEY
Army Headquarters	AHQ
Army Headquarters Transport Division (SAUO)	AHTD
Army Health Clinic (ACAE)	AHC
Army Health Nurse (AABC)	AHN
Army Helicopter [British military] (DMA)	AH
Army Helicopter Improvement Program	AHIP
Army Heliport (AABC)	AHP
Army Help for Education and Development	AHEAD
Army High Frequency Electronic Warfare System (SAUS)	AHFEWS
Army High Performance Computing Research Center [University of Minnesota] [Research center] (RCD)	AHPCRC
Army High School Completion Program (MCD)	AHSCP
Army High-Performance Computing Research (RDA)	AHPCRC
Army Historical Foundation (EA)	AHF
Army Hospital	AH
Army Hospital Corps	AHC
Army Hospital Corps (SAUO)	AHC
Army Housing Committee (AABC)	ARHOC
Army Human Engineering Laboratory (MCD)	AHEL
Army Human Factors Research Advisory Committee	AHFRAC
Army Human Factors Research and Development Committee (AABC)	AHFRDC
Army Imagery Intelligence Corps	AIIC
Army in Burma Reserve of Officers [British military] (DMA)	ABRO
Army in Europe	AE
Army in India Reserve of Officers (SAUO)	AIRO
Army in the Field (MCD)	AITF
Army in the Field Containers System Study (MCD)	AFCSS
Army Individual Test (SAUS)	AIT
Army Industrial Center (SAUS)	ARMIC
Army Industrial College	AIC
Army Industrial Engineering Activity (AAGC)	EA
Army Industrial Fund	AIF
Army Industrial Preparedness Program	AIPP
Army Industrial School (SAUO)	AIS
Army Infantry Board (RDA)	AIB
Army Infantry Board (MCD)	A-INF
Army Infantry School (KSC)	AIS
Army In-Flight Data Transmission System (MCD)	AIDATS
Army Information and Data System Command (SAUO)	AI&DSC
Army Information and Data Systems Command (ACAE)	AIDSC
Army Information and Data Systems Command	AIDSCOM
Army Information Architecture	AIA
Army Information Data Systems Command (SAUO)	AIDSCOM
Army Information Digest	AID
Army Information Engineering (GFGA)	AIE
Army Information Engineering Command (SAUS)	AISEC
Army Information Management System	AIMS
Army Information Processing Center (CIST)	AIPC
Army Information Processing Standards (MCD)	AIPS
Army Information Program	AIP
Army Information Radio Service (MCD)	AIRS
Army Information Systems (RDA)	AIS
Army Information Systems / Information Systems Management Activity (RDA)	AIS/ISMA
Army Information Systems Command	AISC
Army INFOSEC Resource Program (SAUS)	ISSRP
Army Insecticide Measuring System (RDA)	AIMS
Army Inspector General (MCD)	AIG
Army Installation (SAUS)	AIN
Army Installation File (SAUO)	AIF
Army Installation Management	AIM
Army Installation Management Course	AIMC
Army Installations Planning Committee (AABC)	AIPC

Army Institute for Professional Development (MCD) .... AIPD
Army Institute for Research in Management Information, Communications, and Computer Science (SAUO) .... AIRMICS
Army Institute of Administration (MCD) .... AIA
Army Institute of Advanced Studies .... AIAS
Army Institute of Dental Research (RDA) .... AIDR
Army Institute of Research (SAUO) .... AIR
Army Institute of Surgical Research (RDA) .... AISR
Army Instructor Cadre Interceptor Transporter / Loader Operations Maintenance Course .... AICITLOM
Army Instructor Cadre Interceptor Transporter Loader Operations [*Course*] .... AICITLO
Army Integrated Decision Equipment .... AIMS
Army Integrated Meteorological Systems (NOAA) .... AIM
Army Integrated Meteorological Systems .... AIMS
Army Integrated Microfilm System .... AIMS
Army Integrated Publishing and Printing Service (SAUO) .... AIPPS
Army Intelligence .... AI
Army Intelligence Agency .... AIA
Army Intelligence and Security (SAUO) .... AI & S
Army Intelligence and Security .... AIS
Army Intelligence and Security Command (ACAE) .... AISC
Army Intelligence and Threat Analysis Center (SAUS) .... AIAIT
Army Intelligence & Threat Analysis Center (SAUS) .... AIAIT
Army Intelligence Center .... AIC
Army Intelligence Center and School (MCD) .... AICS
Army Intelligence Department [*British*] .... AID
Army Intelligence Interpreter .... AII
Army Intelligence Master Plan (SAUS) .... AIMP
Army Intelligence Network [*Guatemala*] (BUAC) G-2
Army Intelligence Officer (SAUS) .... AIO
Army Intelligence Reserve .... AIR
Army Intelligence School .... AIS
Army Intelligence School, Fort Devens (MCD) .... AISD
Army Intelligence Survey [*ITAC*] (MCD) .... AIS
Army Intelligence Translator .... AIT
Army Intelligence Unit [*Panama*] (BUAC) G-2
Army Intelligence/Electronic Warfare Reorganization Overwatch Committee (SAUO) .... AIEWROC
Army Intelligence/Electronic Warfare Reorganization Overwatch Committee (MCD) .... AIEWROC
Army Intercontinental Ballistic Missile (SAUS) .... A-ICBM
Army Internal Control Program (RDA) .... AICP
Army Interoperability Network (RDA) .... AIN
Army Interpretation Platoon (SAUO) .... AIP
Army Inventory Control Point .... AICP
Army Inventory Data Systems .... AIDS
Army Inventory Objective (AABC) .... AIO
Army Investigational Drug Review Board (AABC) .... AIDRB
Army Job Activities Questionnaire .... AJAQ
Army Job Questionnaire .... AJQ
Army Key Management System .... AKMS
Army Kinema Corporation (SAUO) .... AKC
Army Kinematograph Corp. [*British military*] (DMA) .... AKC
Army Laboratory of the Year Award (RDA) .... ALYA
Army Land Forces .... ALANF
Army Language Aptitude Test [*Later, DLAT*] .... ALAT
Army Language Bureau (SAUO) .... ALB
[*The*] **Army Language School** .... TALS
Army LASER Target Designator System .... ALTDS
Army Laser Weapon Simulation (ACAE) .... ALWSIM
Army Launch Area .... ALA
Army Lawyer [*A publication*] (AAGC) .... Army Law
Army Legal Aid Department (SAUO) .... ALAD
Army Legal Corps [*British military*] (DMA) .... ALC
Army Legal Services (SAUO) .... ALS
Army Lessons Learned Management Information System (INF) .... ALLMIS
Army Liaison Element (MCD) .... ALE
Army Liaison Officer (MCD) .... ARMLO
Army Library .... ALIB
Army Library Automated Systems (IID) .... ALAS
Army Life Cycle Cost Analysis Model (MCD) .... ALCCAM
Army Life Cycle Cost Model (MCD) .... ALCCM
Army Life-Support Power Source System (MCD) .... ALPSS
Army Limited War Laboratory .... ALWL
Army Linguist Personnel Study .... ALPS
Army List [*British military*] (DMA) .... AL
Army Logistic Development Committee [*British*] (RDA) .... ALDC
Army Logistic Management Integrated Data System (SAUS) .... ALMIDS
Army Logistic Operations Center (SAUO) .... ALOC
Army Logistical Control Center (SAUO) .... ALCC
Army Logistician (journ.) (SAUS) .... ALOG
Army Logistics Assessment .... ALA
Army Logistics Center .... ALC
Army Logistics Command (SAUO) .... ALC
Army Logistics Command Japan (CINC) .... ALCJ
Army Logistics Data Base and Access System .... ALDBAS
Army Logistics Data Center .... ALDC
Army Logistics Evaluation Agency (MCD) .... ARLEA
Army Logistics Management College [*Fort Lee, VA*] .... ALMC
Army Logistics Management Integrated Data Systems (AABC) .... ALMIDS
Army Logistics Management Systems Activity .... ALMSA
Army Logistics Manpower Office [*Merged with Operations Personnel Office*] .... ALMO
Army Logistics Objectives Program .... ALOP
Army Logistics Policy Council (AABC) .... ALPC
Army Logistics Readiness Evaluation System .... ALRES
Army Logistics Research and Development .... ALRD
Army Logistics Specialty Committee (MCD) .... ALSC
Army Logistics Study Program .... ALSP
Army Long Range Capabilities Plan (SAUS) .... ALRCP
Army Long-Range Appraisal .... ALRA
Army Long-Range Planning Guidance .... ALRPG
Army Long-Range Technological Forecast (AABC) .... ALRTF
Army Long-Range Training Plan (RDA) .... ALRTP
Army Low-Speed Air Research Tasks .... ALART
Army Main Optical Site (ACAE) .... AMOS
Army Maintenance and Supply Procedures [*or Publications*] (NATG) .... AMSP
Army Maintenance Board .... AMB
Army Maintenance Command (SAUO) .... AMC
Army Maintenance Management (MCD) .... AMM
Army Maintenance Management Center .... AMMC
Army Maintenance Management System (MCD) .... AMMS
[*The*] **Army Maintenance Management System** [*Formerly, TAERS*] (AABC) .... TAMMS
Army Maintenance Support Activity (SAUO) .... AMSA
Army Maintenance Training and Evaluation Simulation System (MCD) .... AMTESS
Army Management Engineering College (RDA) .... AMEC
Army Management Engineering Training Agency (RDA) .... AMETA
Army Management Fund .... AMF
Army Management Headquarters Activity (MCD) .... AMHA
Army Management Information Program (AABC) .... AMIP
Army Management Information System .... AMIS
Army Management Information Systems Course .... AMISC
Army Management Intern Program (RDA) .... AMIP
Army Management Milestone System .... AMMS
Army Management School (KSC) .... AMS
Army Management Staff College (RDA) .... AMSC
Army Management Structure .... AMS
Army Management Structure Code .... AMSCO
Army Management System .... AMS
Army Management System - Korea .... AMS-K
Army Management Systems Support Agency (ACAE) .... AMSSA
Army Maneuver Support Command (SAUO) .... AMSCOM
Army Manpower and Personnel Requirements Process (ACAE) .... ARMPREP
Army Manpower Cost System (RDA) .... AMCOS
Army Manpower Resources Research and Development Center (SAUO) .... AMRRDC
Army Manual .... AM
Army Map Service [*Later, Defense Mapping Agency Topographic Center*] [*Washington, DC*] .... AMS
Army Map Service-Geographical Section-General Staff (SAUO) .... AMS-GSGS
Army Marine Products (SAUO) .... AMP
Army Marksmanship Training Unit [*CONARC*] (AABC) .... AMKTU
Army Marksmanship Training Unit [*CONARC*] (INF) .... AMTU
Army Marksmanship Unit .... AMU
Army Master Data File (AABC) .... AMDF
Army Master Data File Reader Microfilm System [*Later, ARMS*] (AABC) .... AMDFRMS
Army Master Data File Retrieval Microform System .... ARMS
Army Master Force Development Plan (MCD) .... AMFDP
Army Master Study Program (AABC) .... AMSP
Army Material Acquisition Reorganization Committee (MCD) .... AMARC
Army Material Command - Subordinate Weapons (SAUO) .... AMSWE
Army Material Command Automated Logistics Management Systems Agency (SAUO) .... AMCALMSA
Army Material Command Circular (MCD) .... AMCC
Army Material Command-Subordinate Weapons-Test, Measurement and Diagnostic Equipment (SAUO) .... AMSWE-TMDE
Army Material (or Materiel) Command (SAUO) .... AMC
Army Material Systems Analysis Activity (SAUS) .... AMSAA
Army Material Systems Analysis Agency (SAUO) .... AMSAA
Army Material Test Evaluation Directorate (ACAE) .... ARMTE
Army Material Test Laboratory (SAUS) .... AMTL
Army Materials and Mechanics Research Center [*Watertown, MA*] .... AMMRC
Army Materials Research Agency [*Later, AMMRC*] [*Watertown, MA*] .... AMRA
Army Materials Research Reactor .... AMRR
Army Materials Technology Laboratory [*Watertown, MA*] .... AMTL
Army Materiel Acquisition Guidance .... AMAG
Army Materiel Acquisition Review Committee [*Terminated, 1974*] .... AMARC
Army Materiel Command [*Formerly, DARCOM*] [*Alexandria, VA*] .... AMC
Army Materiel Command Administrative Data Center .... AMCADC
Army Materiel Command, Alexandria (SAUO) .... AMCA
Army Materiel Command Announcement Distribution System (RDA) .... AMCADS
Army Materiel Command Automated Logistics Management Systems Agency (AABC) .... AMCALMSA
Army Materiel Command Automated Logistics Management Systems Agency (SAUS) .... AMCALMSA
Army Materiel Command Board [*Aberdeen Proving Ground, MD*] (MCD) .... AMCB
Army Materiel Command Catalog Data Office (AABC) .... AMCCDO
Army Materiel Command Data Center .... AMCDC
Army Materiel Command Depot Data Center .... AMCDDC
Army Materiel Command Deputy Chief of Staff for Chemical and Nuclear Matters .... AMCCN
Army Materiel Command Deputy Chief of Staff for Developments Engineering and Acquisition .... AMCDE
Army Materiel Command Facilities and Services Center (AABC) .... AMCFASC
Army Materiel Command Field Assistance for Science and Technology Program (RDA) .... AMC-FAST

Army Materiel Command Field Office (RDA) .... AMCFO
Army Materiel Command Field Safety Agency (AABC) .... AMCFSA
Army Materiel Command General Order .... AMCGO
Army Materiel Command Information Center .... AMCIC
Army Materiel Command Inspector General, Western Inspection
    Activity .... AMCIGW
Army Materiel Command Installation Division .... AMCID
Army Materiel Command Installations and Service Agency (AABC) .... AMCI & SA
Army Materiel Command Installations and Service Agency (SAUO) ..... AMCI&SA
Army Materiel Command International Logistics Directorate (MCD) .... AMCIL
Army Materiel Command Logistic Data Center (AABC) .... AMCLDC
Army Materiel Command Logistics Systems Support Agency
    (AABC) .... AMCLSSA
Army Materiel Command Materiel Requirements Directorate (MCD) .... AMCMR
Army Materiel Command Memorandum .... AMCM
Army Materiel Command Missile Field Office (SAUO) .... AMCMFO
Army Materiel Command Mission Area Manager .... AMAM
Army Materiel Command Packaging, Storage, and Containerization Center
    [Tobyhanna, PA] .... AMCPSCC
Army Materiel Command Packaging, Storage and Containerization Center
    (SAUO) .... AMCPSCC
Army Materiel Command Pamphlet (MCD) .... AMCP
Army Materiel Command Procurement and Production Directorate .... AMCPP
Army Materiel Command Procurement Instructions .... AMCPI
Army Materiel Command Regulations .... AMCR
Army Materiel Command Research and Development .... AMCRD
Army Materiel Command Support Activity .... AMCSA
Army Materiel Command Technical Committee .... AMCTC
Army Materiel Command-Logistics Support Agency (SAUS) .... AMC-LOGSA
Army Materiel Development and Readiness Command [Now AMC]
    (AAGC) .... DARCOM
Army Materiel Education and Training Activity [School of Engineering at Red
    River Army Depot] [Texarkana, TX] (RDA) .... AMETA
Army Materiel Plan (AABC) .... AMP
Army Materiel Plan Modernization .... AMPMOD
Army Materiel Status Committees (AABC) .... ARMATSC
Army Materiel Supply Command (SAUS) .... AMSC
Army Materiel Systems Analysis Activity [or Agency] [Aberdeen Proving
    Ground, MD] (MCD) .... AMSAA
Army Materiel Test and Evaluation Directorate [White Sands Missile Range,
    NM] .... ARMTE
Army Mathematics Research Center [Madison, Wisconsin] .... AMRC
Army Mathematics Steering Committee .... AMSC
Army Mechanical Transport School (SAUO) .... AMTS
Army Medical Advisory Board (SAUO) .... AMAB
Army Medical Advisory Board (SAUS) .... AMAB
Army Medical Biochemical Research Laboratory (SAUO) .... AMBRL
Army Medical Bioengineering Research and Development Laboratory
    (RDA) .... AMBRDL
Army Medical Center .... AMC
Army Medical Corps (SAUO) .... AMC
Army Medical Corps/Dental Corps .... AMED/DC
Army Medical Department .... AMD
Army Medical Department (SAUS) .... AMED
Army Medical Department (AABC) .... AMEDD
Army Medical Department .... ARMED
Army Medical Department Center and School .... AMEDDC&S
Army Medical Department Property Accounting System (AABC) .... AMEDDPAS
Army Medical Equipment Depot (SAUO) .... AMED
Army Medical Intelligence and Information Agency (MCD) .... AMIIA
Army Medical Laboratory (SAUO) .... A Med Lab
Army Medical Library [Became Armed Forces Medical Library, 1952; later,
    NLM] .... AML
Army Medical Material Maintenance Center, Europe (SAUO) .... AMMCE
Army Medical Materiel Agency (SAUO) .... AMMA
Army Medical Nutrition Laboratory (MCD) .... AMNL
Army Medical Officer (SAUS) .... AMO
Army Medical Regulating Office (SAUO) .... AMRO
Army Medical Research and Development Command .... AMRDC
Army Medical Research and Nutrition Laboratory (DAVI) .... AMRL
Army Medical Research and Nutrition Laboratory .... AMRNL
Army Medical Research Institute of Chemical Defense (RDA) .... AMRICD
Army Medical Research Institute of Infectious Diseases (RDA) .... AMRIID
Army Medical Research Laboratory .... AMRL
Army Medical Research Laboratory, Alaska (RDA) .... AMRLA
Army Medical Science .... AMEDS
Army Medical Service .... AMEDS
Army Medical Service [British] .... AMS
Army Medical Service Graduate School .... AMSGS
Army Medical Service Research and Development Command .... AMSRDC
Army Medical Service School [Later, Medical Field Service School] .... AMSS
Army Medical Services (SAUS) .... AMS
Army Medical Specialist Corps (SAUO) .... AMCS
Army Medical Specialist Corps .... AMSC
Army Medical Specialists Corps (SAUO) .... AMSC
Army Medical Staff .... AMS
Army Medical Supply Control Officer .... AMSCO
Army Medical Supply Support Activity .... AMSSA
Army Medical Unit .... AMU
Army Medical Working Party (SAUO) .... AMWP
Army Member, Inter-American Defense Board (AABC) .... AMIADB
Army Methods of Instruction Centre [British military] (DMA) .... AMIC
Army Metrology and Calibration Center .... AMCC
Army Metrology and Calibration Center Metrology Development and
    Engineering Division .... AMCC-MM

Army Military Assistance Program (SAUO) .... AMAP
Army Military Clothing Sales Store (DOMA) .... AMCSS
Army Military Damage Assessment System (ACAE) .... AMDAS
Army Military Damage Data Element List (ACAE) .... AMDEL
Army Military Intelligence Battalion (MCD) .... AMIB
Army Military Police Operations Agency (ACAE) .... AMPOA
Army Military Review Boards Agency (ACAE) .... AMRBA
Army Mine Planter .... AMP
Army Mine Planter Service .... AMPS
Army Missile and Rockets Directorate .... AMRD
Army Missile and Rockets Division - NATO Supply Center .... AMRD-NASC
Army Missile and Rockets Division-NATO Supply Centre Ch‡teauroux
    (SAUO) .... AMRD-NASCC
Army Missile Command .... AMC
Army Missile Command .... AMICOM
Army Missile Command (MUGU) .... ARMSLC
Army Missile Defense Command (AABC) .... AMDC
Army Missile Development Center (MCD) .... AMDC
Army Missile Laboratory (RDA) .... AML
Army Missile Research and Development Command (MCD) .... AMRDC
Army Missile Test and Evaluation Directorate (SAUO) .... AMTED
Army Missile Test Center [White Sands Missile Range, NM] .... AMTC
Army Missile Transport System (SAUS) .... AMTRANS
Army Missile Transport Systems (KSC) .... AMTRANS
Army Mobile Missile Operation .... AMMO
Army Mobility Command .... AMC
Army Mobility Command .... AMOCOM
Army Mobility Equipment Center (SAA) .... AMEC
Army Mobility Equipment Research and Development Center
    (MCD) .... AMERADC
Army Mobility Model (RDA) .... AMM
Army Mobility Research and Development Center .... AMRDC
Army Mobility Research Center .... AMRC
Army Mobility Support Center .... AMSC
Army Mobilization and Operations Planning System .... AMOPS
Army Mobilization Capabilities Study .... AMCS
Army Mobilization Operations System (COE) .... AMOPS
Army Mobilization Planning and Programming Directive (AABC) .... AMPPD
Army Mobilization Planning and Programming Guidance Document
    (AABC) .... AMPPGD
Army Mobilization Program Directive .... AMPD
Army Model Improvement Program (RDA) .... AMIP
Army Model Improvement Program Management Office (RDA) .... AMMO
Army Modeling and Simulation Office .... AMSO
Army Modernization Information Memorandum (RDA) .... AMIM
Army Modernization Manual (SAUS) .... AMM
Army Modernization Plan (RDA) .... AMP
Army Modernization Training .... AMT
Army Modernization Training Automation System .... AMTAS
Army Molecular Sieve Oxygen Generator (RDA) .... AMSOG
Army Morale Support Fund (AABC) .... AMSF
Army Mortar Program (RDA) .... ARMOP
Army Mortar Requirements Study .... AMOR
Army Motion Picture Service .... AMPS
Army Mounteering Association [British military] (DMA) .... AMA
Army Multibus Avionics Multi-Process (MCD) .... AMAMP
Army Multiple Engagement Model (ACAE) .... AMEM
Army Munition Command .... AMUCOM
Army Munitions Command [Later merged with Army Weapons Command] .... AMC
Army Munitions Command [Later merged with Army Weapons
    Command] .... AMUCOM
Army Munitions Command [Later merged with Army Weapons
    Command] .... AMUNC
Army Mutual Aid Association [Later, AAFMAA] (EA) .... AMAA
Army Natick Laboratories (SAUS) .... ANL
Army Natick Laboratory .... ANL
Army National Guard .... ANG
Army National Guard .... ARNG
Army National Guard Bureau (BCP) .... NGB
Army National Guard Management Information System (GFGA) .... ARNGMIS
Army National Guard of the United States .... ARNGUS
Army National Guard Troop Structure Program .... ARNG-TSP
Army Native Hospital Corps [British military] (DMA) .... ANHC
Army Nautic Laboratory (SAUO) .... ANL
Army Navy Aeronautical Design (ACAE) .... ANAL
Army, Navy and Air Force Comforts Association (SAUO) .... ANACA
Army, Navy & Air Force Veterans in Canada [Les Anciens Combattants de
    l'Armee, de la Marine et des Forces Aeriennes au Canada] (AC) .... ANAVETS
Army Navy Integrated Presentation .... ANIP
Army, Navy, NASA Air Force (SAUO) .... ANNA
Army, Navy, NASA, Air Force Geodetic Satellite .... ANNA
Army, Navy, NASA, and Air Force (ACAE) .... ANNA
Army Navy Performance Number (SAUS) .... ANPN
Army Navy-Air Force Journal (journ.) (SAUS) .... ANAFJ
Army Navy/Airborne Radio Communications (SAUS) .... AN/ARC
Army Navy/Fixed Communications Cabinet (MCD) .... AN/FCC
Army Navy/Fixed Satellite Communication (MCD) .... AN/FSC
Army Net Assessment, Central Europe .... ANACE
Army Net Assessment, Central Europe (SAUS) .... ANACF
Army Network Station .... ANS
Army News Features .... ANF
Army News Service .... ANS
Army News Service .... ARNEWS
Army Newspaper Service .... ANS
Army Newspaper Unit (SAUO) .... ANU

Army Non-Destructive Readout (SAUS) ... ANDRO
Army Nozzle Technology Program (MCD) ... ANTP
Army Nuclear Agency (ACAE) ... ANA
Army Nuclear, Biological and Chemical Information System (SAUS) ... ANBACIS
Army Nuclear Data System [*Study*] (AABC) ... ANUDS
Army Nuclear Defense Laboratory (MCD) ... ANDL
Army Nuclear Power Program ... ANPP
Army Nuclear Weapon Coordination Group ... ANWCG
Army Nuclear Weapons Stockpile Reliability Program ... ANWSRP
Army Nuclear Weapons Surety Group (ACAE) ... ANWSG
Army Number (SAUS) ... AN
Army Nurse Corps ... ANC
Army Nursing Service [*British*] ... ANS
Army Nursing Service (SAUO) ... ANS
Army Observation Plane (SAUS) ... AOP
Army Observation Post [*British military*] (DMA) ... AOP
Army Occupational Survey Program [*Formerly, MODB*] ... AOSP
Army of Excellence [*Military program*] (INF) ... AOE
Army of Lamers [*Computer hacker terminology*] ... AOL
Army of Northern Virginia [*Civil War*] ... ANV
Army of Occupation Medal [*Military decoration*] ... AOM
Army of Occupation Medal [*Military decoration*] ... OCCMDL
Army of Occupation of Germany Medal [*Military decoration*] ... AOGM
Army of Occupation of Germany Medal [*Military decoration*] ... OCCGERMDL
Army of Tennessee (SAUO) ... AoT
Army of Tennessee, CSA [*An association*] (EA) ... AT
Army of the Cumberland (SAUO) ... AoC
Army of the Ohio (SAUO) ... AoO
Army of the Potomac (SAUO) ... AoP
Army of the Republic of North Vietnam (NTIO) ... ARVN
Army of the Republic of Serbian Krajina (SAUS) ... ARSK
Army of the Republic of Vietnam [*Also, ARVN*] [*South Vietnam*] ... ARVIN
Army of the Republic of Vietnam [*Also, ARVIN*] [*South Vietnam*] [*Defunct*] ... ARVN
Army of the Republic of Vietnam Sea, Air, and Land Team (VNW) ... ARVN SEAL
Army of the Serbian Republic (SAUS) ... ASR
Army of the Tennessee (SAUO) ... AotT
Army of the United States (SAUS) ... AUS
Army of the United States Medical Corps (SAUO) ... AUSMC
Army of Tripura People's Liberation Organization [*India*] (PD) ... ATPLO
Army of Virginia (SAUO) ... AoV
Army of Yugoslavia (SAUS) ... YA
Army Officer Basic Course [*Army*] (RDA) ... AOBC
Army Officers Art Society (SAUO) ... AOAS
Army Officers Candidate School (SAUS) ... AOCS
Army Officers Emergency Reserve (SAUO) ... AOER
Army Oil Analysis Program (MCD) ... AOAP
Army Operating Availability Data ... AOAD
Army Operational Research ... AOR
Army Operational Research Establishment [*British*] ... AORE
Army Operational Research Group [*British*] ... AORG
Army Operational Test Command ... AOTC
Army Operations Center (SAUO) ... AOC
[*The*] **Army Operations Center** ... AOC
[*The*] **Army Operations Center** ... TAOC
[*The*] **Army Operations Center System** ... TARMOCS
Army Operations Research Symposia (RDA) ... AORS
Army Operations Research Symposium (SAUO) ... AORS
Army Optical Station ... AOS
Army Order [*British*] ... AO
Army Ordnance Ammunition Command [*Merged with Munitions Command*] ... AOAC
Army Ordnance Arsenal District (SAUO) ... AOAD
Army Ordnance Association (SAUO) ... AOA
Army Ordnance Ballistic Missile Office ... AOBMO
Army Ordnance Combat Equipment Office ... AOCEO
Army Ordnance Corps [*Later, RAOC*] [*British*] ... AOC
Army Ordnance Corps (SAUO) ... AOC
Army Ordnance Department [*British*] ... AOD
Army Ordnance Depot (SAUO) ... AOD
Army Ordnance District (SAUO) ... AOD
Army Ordnance Guided Missile School (MCD) ... AOGMS
Army Ordnance Missile Center (MCD) ... AOMC
Army Ordnance Missile Command [*Later, Missile Command*] [*Redstone Arsenal, AL*] ... AOMC
Army Ordnance Missile Support Agency ... AOMSA
Army Ordnance Missile Support Center (NATG) ... AOMSC
Army Ordnance Society (SAUO) ... AOS
Army Ordnance Stores (SAUO) ... AOS
Army Ordnance Stores [*British*] ... AOS
Army Ordnance Submarine Mine Laboratory (KSC) ... AOSML
Army Ordnance Weapons Command ... AOWC
Army Ordnance Workshop [*British military*] (DMA) ... AOW
Army Ordnance Workshop Services (SAUO) ... AOWS
Army Ordnance-Birmingham District (SAUO) ... AO-BIRMDis
Army Ordnance-Boston District (SAUO) ... AO-BOSTDis
Army Ordnance-Chicago District (SAUO) ... AO-CHIDis
Army Ordnance-Cleveland District (SAUO) ... AO-CLEVDis
Army Ordnance-Los Angeles District (SAUO) ... AO-LADis
Army Ordnance-New York District (SAUO) ... AO-NYDis
Army Ordnance-Philadelphia District (SAUO) ... AO-PHILDis
Army Ordnance-St Louis District (SAUO) ... AO-STLDis
Army Ordnance-St. Louis District (SAUS) ... AO-STLDis
Army Orientation Training (MCD) ... AOT
Army Outward Bound School [*British military*] (DMA) ... AOBS
Army Pacific (CINC) ... ARPAC
Army Package Power Reactor ... APPR
Army Packaging Board (AABC) ... APB
Army Panel (SAUS) ... AP
Army Parachute Association [*British military*] (DMA) ... APA
Army Parachute Team ... APT
Army Part Number (MCD) ... APN
Army Pay Corps [*Later, RAPC*] [*British*] ... APC
Army Pay Department [*British*] ... APD
Army Pay Ledger Unit (SAUS) ... APLU
Army Pay Office (SAUO) ... APO
Army Pay Officer (SAUS) ... APO
Army Pay Tables (SAUS) ... APT
Army Pearl Harbor Board [*World War II*] ... APHB
Army Pensions ... AP
Army Pensions Office (SAUO) ... APO
Army Performance-Oriented Review and Standards Program ... APORS
Army Performance-Oriented Reviews and Standards ... APORS
Army Personnel Attached to the Air Force for Duty ... ARWAF
Army Personnel Letter (AABC) ... APL
Army Personnel Newsletter (SAUS) ... APNL
Army Personnel Research Committee (MCD) ... APRC
Army Personnel Research Establishment [*British*] ... APRE
Army Personnel Research Office [*Washington, DC*] ... APRO
Army Personnel Research Service ... APRS
Army Personnel System Committee ... APSC
Army Petroleum Center ... APC
Army Photo Center (SAUO) ... APC
Army Photo Interpretation Center ... APIC
Army Photo Interpretation Detachment ... APID
Army Photo Interpretation Unit (NATG) ... APIU
Army Photographic Intelligence Service (SAUO) ... APIS
Army Photographic Interpretation Section [*British*] ... APIS
Army Photographic Interpretation Unit (SAUO) ... APIU
Army Physical Disability Activity (MCD) ... APDA
Army Physical Disability Appeal Board ... APDAB
Army Physical Evaluation Board ... APEB
Army Physical Fitness Program ... APFP
Army Physical Fitness Test (INF) ... APFT
Army Physical Fitness Training (ADDR) ... APFT
Army Physical Readiness Test (INF) ... APRT
Army Physical Review Council ... APRC
Army Physical Training Corps [*British*] ... APTC
Army Physical Training Staff [*British military*] (DMA) ... APTS
Army Physiological Research Establishment [*British*] ... ARPE
Army Pictorial Center ... APC
Army Pictorial Division ... APD
Army Pictorial Service ... APS
Army Pigeon Service (SAUO) ... APS
Army Pilot School ... APS
[*The*] **Army Plan** ... TAP
[*The*] **Army Plan for Equipment Records** ... TAPER
Army Planning and Programming Guidance Memorandum (MCD) ... APPGM
Army Planning Group ... APG
Army Plant Representative Office (AAGC) ... ARPRO
Army Plant Representative's Offices ... APRO
Army Point of Contact (AABC) ... APOC
Army Pointing and Tracking (ACAE) ... APT
Army Polar Research and Development Center (SAUO) ... APRDC
Army Police Coordinating Committee (SAUO) ... APCC
Army Policy Council ... APC
Army Pollution Abatement Program (MCD) ... APAP
Army Port and Service Command ... AP & SC
Army Port and Service Command (SAUO) ... AP&SC
Army Port and Service Command (SAUS) ... AP&SC
[*The*] **Army Portion of Force Status and Identify Report** [*Force Status Report*] (AABC) ... TAPFOR
Army Post Office ... APO
Army Post Office Corps [*British military*] (DMA) ... APOC
Army Postal Clerk (AABC) ... APC
Army Postal Group, Europe (SAUO) ... APGE
Army Postal Service ... APS
Army Postal Service Agency (AFM) ... ARPSA
Army Postal Unit ... APU
Army Power Package Reactor (SAUS) ... APPR
Army Power Procurement Office ... APPO
Army Power Procurement Officer Representative (MCD) ... APPOR
Army Precommission Extension Course (AABC) ... APCEC
Army Premilinary Evaluation (SAUS) ... APE
Army Prepositioned Stocks ... APS
Army Primary Standards Laboratory ... APSL
Army Printing and Stationery Service (SAUO) ... APSS
Army Printing and Stationery Services [*British*] ... APSS
Army Procurement Appropriation ... APA
Army Procurement Appropriation Reporting System ... APARS
Army Procurement District ... APD
Army Procurement Procedure ... APP
Army Procurement Regulation [*or Requirement*] ... APR
Army Procurement Research Office ... APRO
Army Procurement-Sharpe General Depot (SAUS) ... APSGD
Army Program for Individual Training ... ARPRINT
Army Program Memorandum (AABC) ... APM
Army Projects Management Department (SAA) ... APM
Army Promotion List (AABC) ... APL
Army Propulsion Laboratory and Center (KSC) ... APLC

Army Prosthetics Research Laboratory .... APRL
Army Proving Ground (SAUO) .... APG
Army Proving Grounds .... APG
Army Provisioning Process Course [*DoD*] (RDA) .... APPC
Army Provost Marshal (SAUS) .... APM
Army Psychological Warfare Department (SAUO) .... APWD
Army Psychological Warfare Division (SAUO) .... APWD
Army Pulse Radiation Directorate (PDAA) .... APRD
Army Pulse Radiation Facility [*Aberdeen Proving Ground, MD*] .... APRF
Army Pulse Radiation Facility (SAUS) .... ARPF
Army Pulse Radiation Facility Reactor [*Nuclear energy*] (OA) .... APRFR
Army Pulsed Experimental Research Assembly .... APRA
Army Pulsed Reactor Assembly (SAUS) .... APRA
Army Pulsed Reactor Facility (SAUS) .... APRF
Army Qualification Battery [*of tests*] .... AQB
Army Qualification Battery of Tests (SAUS) .... AQB of Tests
Army Quartermaster Corps [*Merged with Supply and Maintenance Command*] .... AQMC
Army Quartermaster Research and Engineering Command (MCD) .... AQREC
Army Radar Approach Control (SAUO) .... ARAC
Army RADAR Approach Control Facility (FAAC) .... ARAC
Army Radar Gun Air Defense System (ACAE) .... ARGADS
Army Radiation Laboratory .... ARL
Army Radio Code .... ARC
Army Radio Code Aptitude Test (IAA) .... ARCAT
Army Radio Code Aptitude Test .... ARCT
Army Radio Code Test (SAUS) .... ARCT
Army Radio Engineered Network (SAUS) .... AREN
Army Radio School [*British military*] (DMA) .... ARS
Army Radio School (SAUO) .... ARS
Army Radio Station (IAA) .... ARS
Army Ration Credit System (AABC) .... ARCS
Army Reactor Area (SAA) .... ARA
Army Reactor Experimental Area .... AREA
Army Reactor Systems Health and Safety Review Committee (AABC) .... ARCHS
Army Reactors Branch (SAA) .... ARB
Army Reader Microfilm System (SAUS) .... ARMS
Army Readiness and Mobilization Regions (MCD) .... ARMR
Army Readiness Evaluation System (MCD) .... ARES
Army Readiness Management [*or Measurement*] **System** (MCD) .... ARMS
Army Readiness Region (AABC) .... ARR
Army Readiness Region .... ARRED
Army Readiness Training and Evaluation Plan (SAUS) .... ARTEP
Army Ready Material (SAUS) .... ARM
Army Rearming Base (SAUS) .... APB
Army Rearming Base .... ARB
Army Receiving-Valve (IAA) .... AR
Army Receiving-Valve (SAUS) .... ar
Army Reception Group, Europe (SAUO) .... ARGE
Army Recorder Experimental Area (SAUS) .... AREA
Army Records Society (EAIO) .... ARS
Army Recreational Service (SAUO) .... ARS
Army Recruiting and Accession Data System (GFGA) .... ARADS
Army Recruiting Support Center (ACAE) .... ARSC
Army Regional Threat .... ART
Army Registry of Physical Therapists .... ARPT
Army Registry of Special Educational Materials (AABC) .... ARSEM
Army Regulation .... AR
Army Regulations Supplement [*A publication*] (AAGC) .... ARS
Army Relief Society [*AER*] [*Absorbed by*] (EA) .... ARS
Army Remount Department (SAUO) .... ARD
Army Renegotiation Division [*of ASRB*] .... ARD
Army Requirements and Management Board .... ARMB
Army Requirements Control Office (AABC) .... ARCO
Army Requirements Development Plan (AABC) .... ARDP
Army Requirements for Space Technologies (MCD) .... ARST
Army Requirements for Tactical Communications (AABC) .... ARTACOM
Army Research and Development [*Later, R, D & A*] [*A publication*] (SAA) .... ARD
Army Research and Development Bulletin [*A publication*] (RDA) .... ARAB
Army Research and Development Command .... ARDC
Army Research and Development Group (MCD) .... ARDG
Army Research and Development Group (Europe) .... ARDG(E)
Army Research and Development Group (Far East) .... ARDG(FE)
Army Research and Development Information System (CIST) .... ARDIS
Army Research and Development Information System Office (SAUO) .... ARDISO
Army Research and Development Information Systems Office (RDA) .... ARDISO
Army Research and Development Test and Evaluation Information Systems .... ARDIS
Army Research Associates Program (DOMA) .... ARAP
Army Research Command (SAUS) .... ARCom
Army Research Consortium (RDA) .... ARC
[*The*] **Army Research Council** .... TARC
Army Research Council (SAUS) .... TARC
Army Research, Development, and Acquisition .... ARDAA
Army Research, Development, and Acquisition .... ARDAC
Army Research Institute (RDA) .... ARI
Army Research Institute for Environmental Medicine .... ARIEM
Army Research Institute for the Behavioral and Social Sciences [*Alexandria, VA*] .... ARI
Army Research Institute for the Behavioral and Social Sciences (SAUO) .... ARIBBS
Army Research Institute of Environmental Medicine (SAUO) .... ARIEM
Army Research Laboratory (RDA) .... ARL
Army Research Office [*Research Triangle Park, NC*] .... ARO
Army Research Office - Durham .... ARO-D
Army Research Office - Europe .... ARO-E
Army Research Office - Far East (AABC) .... ARO-FE
Army Research Office - Japan .... ARO-J
Army Research Office/University Research Initiative (RDA) .... ARO/URI
Army Research Plan .... ARP
Army Research Task Summary .... ARTS
Army Reserve [*Formerly, ERC, ORC*] .... AR
Army Reserve (SAUO) .... AR
Army Reserve and Reserve Officers Training Corps Affairs .... ARROTCA
Army Reserve Association .... ARA
Army Reserve Association .... AResA
Army Reserve Civilian Acquired Skills Program (MCD) .... ARCASP
Army Reserve Command .... ARCOM
Army Reserve Command (MCD) .... ARRCOM
Army Reserve Components (MCD) .... ARC
Army Reserve Components Achievement Medal [*Military decoration*] (AABC) .... ARCAM
Army Reserve Components Overseas Training Ribbon [*Military decoration*] (GFGA) .... ARCOTR
Army Reserve Forces Policy Committee (SAUO) .... ARFPC
Army Reserve Forces Policy Council (MCD) .... ARFPC
Army Reserve Officers Training Corps (AEE) .... AROTC
Army Reserve Personnel Center [*St. Louis, MO*] (INF) .... ARPERCEN
Army Reserve Personnel Command .... ARPERSCOM
Army Reserve Readiness Training Center [*Fort McCoy, WI*] (INF) .... ARRTC
Army Reserve Recruiting Unit .... ARRU
Army Reserve Review Committee .... ARRC
Army Reserve Technician .... ART
Army Resettlement Employment Liaison Cell (SAUO) .... ARELC
Army Resident Training (MCD) .... ART
Army Resource Management Advisory and Assessment Program .... ARMAAP
Army Resources Management Institute (SAUO) .... ARMI
Army Restricted Operations Zones (SAUO) .... AROZ
Army Retail Requirements .... ARR
Army Retiring Board .... ARB
Army Review Boards Agency .... ARBA
Army Rifle Association (SAUO) .... ARA
Army Rifle Association [*British military*] (DMA) .... ARA
Army River Mine System (ACAE) .... ARMS
Army Rocket and Guided Missile Agency [*Redstone Arsenal, AL*] .... ARGMA
Army Rocket Transportation System (MCD) .... ARTP
Army Rotary Wing Aptitude Battery (AABC) .... ARWAB
Army Routine Order .... ARO
Army Saddle Club Association (SAUO) .... ASCA
Army Safety Management Information System (MCD) .... ASMIS
Army Satellite Communications project (SAUO) .... ASCOM
Army Satellite Tracking Center .... AST
Army Satellite Tracking Center (IAA) .... ASTC
Army Scaling & Codification Authority (SAUS) .... ASCA
Army School of Ammunition (SAUO) .... ASA
Army School of Cookery (SAUO) .... ASC
Army School of Cookery (SAUS) .... ASC
Army School of Education (SAUO) .... ASchof Educt
Army School of Education (SAUO) .... ASE
Army School of Education [*British*] .... ASE
Army School of Education and Depot [*British*] (BI) .... ASED
Army School of Hygiene (SAUO) .... ASH
Army School of Mechanical Transport (SAUO) .... ASMT
Army School of Physical Training (SAUO) .... ASPT
Army School of Physical Training [*British*] .... ASPT
Army School of the Air (SAUO) .... ASOA
Army School on Instructional Technolgy (SAUO) .... ASIT
Army School on Instructional Technology [*British*] .... ASI
Army Schools Department [*British military*] (DMA) .... ASD
Army Science and Technology Master Plan (RDA) .... ASTMP
Army Science and Technology Working Group .... ASTWG
Army Science Board [*Formerly, ASAP*] (RDA) .... ASB
Army Scientific Advisory Panel [*Later, ASB*] .... ASAP
Army Scientific Advisory Panel (SAUO) .... ASAP
[*The*] **Army Scientific Advisory Panel** .... TASAP
Army Scientific and Technical Information Program (DIT) .... ASTIP
Army Scientific Assistance Program (RDA) .... ASAP
Army Scripture Reader [*British military*] (DMA) .... ASR
Army Seal of Approval .... ASA
Army Secure Operating System .... ASOS
Army Security .... AS
Army Security Agency [*Later, INSCOM*] [*Arlington, VA*] .... ASA
Army Security Agency, Europe (SAUO) .... ASAE
Army Security Agency, Pacific (CINC) .... ASAPAC
Army Security Agency School [*Merged with Defense Security Agency School*] .... ASAS
Army Security Assistance Coordinating Group .... ASACG
[*The*] **Army Security Assistance Program Study Group** .... TASAPS
Army Security Review Board .... ASRB
Army Security Service (SAUO) .... ASA
Army Security Vetting Unit (SAUO) .... ASVU
Army Security Vetting Unit (SAUS) .... ASVU
Army Selection Centre [*British*] .... ASC
Army Selective Aerial Rocket (MCD) .... ASAR
Army Serial Number .... ASN
Army Service [*British*] (ROG) .... AS
Army Service Area (SAUS) .... ASA
Army Service Command (SAUO) .... ASC
Army Service Command .... ASCOM

Army Service Corps [*Initialism also facetiously translated during World War I as "Ally Sloper's Cavalry," Ally Sloper being a comic-paper buffoon*] [*Later, RASC*] [*British*] .... ASC
Army Service Corps (SAUO) .... ASC
Army Service Forces [*Formerly, SOS*] .... ASF
Army Service Forces Training Center .... ASFTC
Army Service Forces Training Center Unit .... ASFTCU
Army Service Number .... ASN
Army Service Reserve [*British*] (ROG) .... ASR
Army Service Ribbon [*Military decoration*] .... ASR
Army Service Squadron [*Corresponds to Navy's CASU*] .... ASSERON
Army Shipping Document (SAUO) .... ASD
Army Signal Association .... ASA
Army Signal Corps [*Later, CEC*] .... ASC
Army Signal Corps, Communications Security Service (MUGU) .... ASCCSS
Army Signal Intelligence Agency .... ASIA
Army Signal Material Support Agency (SAUS) .... ASMA
Army Signal Material [*or Missile*] **Support Agency** .... ASMSA
Army Signal Material Support Agency (SAUO) .... ASMSA
Army Signal Officer (SAUS) .... ASO
Army Signal Radio Propagation Agency .... ASRPA
Army Signal Research and Development Laboratory .... ASRDL
Army Signal School (MCD) .... ASIGSCH
Army Signal School [*British*] .... ASS
Army Signal Squadron (IAA) .... ASS
[*The*] **Army Signal Supply Agency** (MCD) .... ASSA
Army Signal Supply Agency (SAUO) .... ASSA
[*The*] **Army Signal Supply Agency** .... TASSA
Army Signal Support Agency .... ASSA
Army Signals (SAUS) .... A Sigs
Army Simulation Strategic Planning Office (SAUS) .... DAMO-ZS
Army Ski Association [*British military*] (DMA) .... ASA
Army Small Arms Experimental Station (SAUO) .... ASAES
Army Small Arms Program .... ARSAP
Army Small Arms Requirements Simulation [*Battle model*] (MCD) .... ASARS
Army Small Arms Requirements Studies (MCD) .... ASARS
Army Small Computers Program .... ASCP
Army Snow and Mountain Warfare School (SAUO) .... ASMWS
Army Snow, Ice and Permafrost Research Establishment (SAUO) .... ASIPRE
Army Space [*Command*] .... ARSPAC
Army Space Command (SAUO) .... ARSPACE
Army Space Council (SAUO) .... ASC
Army Space Exploitation Demonstration Program [*Army*] .... ASEDP
Army Space Initiatives Study .... ASIS
Army Space Office (SAUO) .... ASO
Army Space Operations Center .... ARSPOC
Army Space Program Office (MCD) .... ASPO
Army Space Study Group (SAUO) .... ASSG
Army Space Technology and Research Office (RDA) .... ASTRO
Army Special Award for Accomplishment (RDA) .... ASAA
Army Special Operation Forces Command, Control, Communications, Computers, Intelligences, Psychological Operations, and Civil Affairs System (RDA) .... ARSOF C4I PYSOP and CA
Army Special Operation Task Force .... ARSOTF
Army Special Operations Command (DOMA) .... ARSOC
Army Special Operations Command Network (SAUS) .... ASOCNet
Army Special Operations Force [*Army*] .... ASOF
Army Special Operations Forces (GFGA) .... ARSOF
Army Special Operations Forces Task Force (DOMA) .... ARSOFTF
Army Special Operations Pictorial Detachment (SAUO) .... ASOP-D
Army Special Operations Pictorial Detachment .... ASOPD
Army Special Staff .... ASS
Army Special Training Program (SAUS) .... ASTP
Army Special Warfare Center .... ASWC
Army Special Weapons Depot .... ASWD
Army Specialist Corps [*Functions transferred to Officer Procurement Service*] .... ASC
Army Specialized Training .... AST
Army Specialized Training Division .... ASTD
Army Specialized Training Program [*World War II*] .... ASTP
Army Specialized Training Reserve Program .... ASTRP
Army Specialized Training Reserve Program (SAUO) .... ASTRP
Army Specialized Training Unit .... ASTU
Army Spectrometric Oil Analysis Program (AABC) .... ASOAP
Army Spectrum Management Steering Committee (MCD) .... ASMSC
Army Sports Control Board [*British*] .... ASCB
[*The*] **Army Staff** (AABC) .... ARSTAF
Army Staff (SAUS) .... ARSTAF
Army Staff .... AS
[*The*] **Army Staff** .... TAS
Army Staff Automated Administrative Support System (MCD) .... ARSTADS
Army Staff College (DOMA) .... ASC
Army Staff Council .... ASC
Army Staff Counsel (AAGC) .... ASC
Army Staging Area Command (SAUO) .... ARSAC
Army Standard Family (SAUS) .... ASF
Army Standard Group Order of Battle System (MCD) .... ASGOBS
Army Standard Information Management System .... ASIMS
Army Standard Program Languages .... ASPL
Army Standardization Program .... ASP
Army Standards Electronic Mail Host (SAUS) .... ASEMH
Army Standards Laboratory .... ASL
Army Standing Operating Procedure (SAUS) .... ASOP
Army Stationing and Installation Plan (AABC) .... ASIP
Army Status Report (AABC) .... ASR

Army Stock Funbd (SAUS) .... ASF
Army Stock Fund .... ASF
Army Stock Fund/Non-Stock Fund .... ASF/NSF
Army Strategic and Tactical Reorganization Objective .... ASTRO
Army Strategic Appraisal .... ASA
Army Strategic Capabilities Plan .... ASCP
Army Strategic Command and Control Systems (MCD) .... ASTRACCS
Army Strategic Communications Command .... ASCC
Army Strategic Defense Command [*Huntsville, AL*] .... ASDC
Army Strategic Mobility Plan (SAUS) .... ASMP
Army Strategic Objectives Plan .... ASOP
Army Strategic Plan [*A document*] .... ASP
Army Strategy and Tactics Analysis (SAUS) .... ASTA
Army Streamlined Acquisition Process [*or Program*] (RDA) .... ASAP
Army Strike Command (SAUO) .... ARSTRAC
Army Student Nurse Program (AABC) .... ASNP
Army Student Nurse Program Identification Badge (GFGA) .... ASNPIDBAD
Army Student Nurse Program Identification Badge (AABC) .... ASNPIdentBad
[*The*] **Army Studies Program** (AABC) .... TASP
Army Study Advisory Committee .... ASAC
Army Study Documentation and Information Retrieval System [*Later, ALAS*] .... ASDIRS
[*The*] **Army Study System** .... TASS
Army Subject Schedule (AABC) .... ASUBJSCD
Army Subordinate Command Management Information System [*Formerly, CARMOCS*] (AABC) .... ASMIS
Army Subsistence Center .... ASC
Army Subsistence Supply Center [*Merged with Defense Subsistence Supply Center*] .... ASSC
Army Suggestions Awards Committee (SAUO) .... ASAC
Army Summary Jurisdiction Regulations [*British military*] (DMA) .... ASJR
Army Supply and Maintenance Command (SAUS) .... AS&MC
Army Supply and Maintenance Command .... ASMC
Army Supply and Maintenance Command (MUGU) .... ASMCOM
[*The*] **Army Supply and Maintenance System** (AABC) .... TASAMS
Army Supply Base (SAUS) .... ASB
Army Supply Point (SAUO) .... ASP
Army Supply Program .... ASP
Army Support Center (AABC) .... ASPTC
Army Support Engineering (ACAE) .... ASE
Army Support Jamming programme (SAUS) .... ASJ
Army Surgeon General .... ASG
Army Survey Establishment (SAUO) .... ASE
Army Survival Measures Plan (AABC) .... ASMP
Army Switched Data and Secure Voice Network .... ASD & SVN
Army Switched Data and Secure Voice Network .... ASDSVN
Army System Engineering Office (RDA) .... ASEO
Army System for Standardized Intelligence Support Terminals (MCD) .... ASSIST
Army System Management .... ASM
Army Systems Acquisition Review Council .... ASARC
Army Systems Acquisition Review Council Independent Evaluation Team (MCD) .... ASARC IET
Army Systems Command (SAUO) .... ASCOM
Army Systems Coordinating Documents .... ASCOD
Army Systems Development and Acquisition Priorities (MCD) .... ASDAP
Army Tactical Air Control Center (SAUO) .... ATACC
Army Tactical Air Control System/ Tactical Air Defense Systems Advisory Group (SAUO) .... ATTAG
Army Tactical Airspace Regulation System (MCD) .... ATARS
Army Tactical Area Communications System (SAUS) .... ATACS
Army Tactical Area Communications System .... ATACS
Army Tactical Command (NVT) .... ATC
Army Tactical Command and Control System (ROAS) .... ATCCS
Army Tactical Command and Control System (SAUS) .... ATCOS
Army Tactical Command and Control/Information System (MCD) .... ATACCIS
Army Tactical Communication System Simulator (MCD) .... ATCSS
Army Tactical Communications Management System (SAUS) .... ATACMS
Army Tactical Communications System (COE) .... ATACS
Army Tactical Data Link .... ATDL
Army Tactical Data Systems (AABC) .... ARTADS
Army Tactical Data Test (SAUS) .... ARTDT
Army Tactical Digital Image Generator (SAUS) .... ATACDIG
Army Tactical Frequency Engineering System .... ATFES
Army Tactical Information Distribution System (ACAE) .... ATIDS
Army Tactical Intelligence Agency Blueprint (MCD) .... ATIB
Army Tactical Intelligence Committee (MCD) .... ATIC
Army Tactical Intelligence Concept (MCD) .... ATIC
Army Tactical, Logistical, and Air Simulation (MCD) .... ATLAS
Army Tactical Missile System (MCD) .... ATACM
Army Tactical Missile System (RDA) .... ATACMS
Army Tactical Missile System Block II (RDA) .... ATACMS BLK II
Army Tactical Missile System-Brilliant Anti-Armor Submunition (RDA) .... ATACMS-BAT
Army Tactical Mobility Requirements Board (SAUO) .... ATMRB
Army Tactical Multichannel Communications System (MCD) .... ATMCS
Army Tactical Operational Control (SAUS) .... ARTOC
Army Tactical Operations Center (SAUO) .... ARTOC
Army Tactical Operations Center (CCCA) .... ATOC
Army Tactical Operations Center (or Central) (SAUS) .... ARTOC
Army Tactical Requirements for Infrared Systems (MCD) .... ATAIRS
Army Tactical Requirements for National Reconnaissance (MCD) .... ATRN
Army Tank and Automotive Command (SAUO) .... ATAC
Army Tank Automotive Center (SAUO) .... ATAC
Army Tank Battalion (SAUO) .... ATB
Army Tank Brigade (SAUO) .... ATB

Army Tank Brigade (SAUO) ... ATBde
Army Tank Brigade (SAUO) ... ATkBde
Army Tank Contractor ... ATC
Army Tank Office (RDA) ... ATO
Army Tank Plant ... ATP
Army Tank Program (MCD) ... ATP
Army Tank-Automotive Center [*or Command*] [*Warren, MI*] ... ATAC
Army Technical Architecture [*Military*] ... ATA
Army Technical Group (SAUO) ... ATG
Army Technical Libraries and Information Systems (SAUS) ... ATLIS
Army Technical Library Improvement Studies ... ATLIS
Army Technical School [*British military*] (DMA) ... ATS
Army Technical Service Corps ... ATSC
Army Technology-Base Master Plan (SAUS) ... ATBMP
Army Telecommunications Automation Program (SAUO) ... ATCAP
Army Telecommunications Center Automatic Programming (MCD) ... ATCAP
Army Telecommunications Combat Theater and General Support [*5 Year Plan*] (MCD) ... ATCOGS
Army Telecommunications System (GFGA) ... ATS
Army Telegraph [*Stamp surcharge*] [*British*] (ROG) ... AT
Army Telephone Book (SAUS) ... ATB
Army Temperance Association (SAUO) ... ATA
Army Terminal Command ... ATC
Army Terrain Information [*or Intelligence*] **System** (MCD) ... ARTINS
Army Terrain Information System (SAUS) ... ARTINS
Army Terrain Requirements Data Base ... ATRDB
Army Territorial Service (SAUO) ... ATS
Army Test and Evaluation Command [*AMC*] ... ATEC
Army Test and Evaluation Command [*AMC*] (MUGU) ... ATECOM
Army Test and Evaluation Seminar ... ATES
Army Test Technology Office ... ATTO
Army Theater Missile [*Air*] **Defense Element** [*Army*] ... ATMDE
Army Theater Missile Defense Project Office (SAUS) ... ATMDPO
Army Theatre Arts Association [*Defunct*] (EA) ... ATAA
Army Times (journ.) (SAUS) ... AT
Army TMDE Modernization (RDA) ... ATM
Army Topographic Command [*Formerly, Army Map Service*] ... ATC
Army Topographic Command (SAUO) ... ATC
Army Topographic Service (SAUO) ... JATOP
Army Topographic Station (AABC) ... ATS
Army Topographic Support Establishment (SAUO) ... ATSE
Army Training and Evaluation Program (AABC) ... ARTEP
Army Training Battle Simulation System (MCD) ... ARTBASS
Army Training Battle Simulation System ... ARTBSS
Army Training Board ... ATB
Army Training Center ... ATC
Army Training Circular (SAUS) ... ATC
Army Training Command (SAUO) ... ATC
Army Training Corps (SAUO) ... ATC
Army Training Device Agency [*Orlando, FL*] (AABC) ... ATDA
Army Training Diagnostic Program (SAUS) ... ATDP
Army Training Effectiveness and Simulation System (MCD) ... AMTESS
Army Training Extension Course Program ... ATECP
Army Training Film ... ATF
Army Training Instruction (SAUS) ... ATI
Army Training Memorandum [*British*] ... ATM
Army Training Plan (MCD) ... ATP
Army Training Program ... ATP
[*The*] **Army Training Requirements and Resource System** ... ATARRS
Army Training Requirements and Resources System ... ATRRS
Army Training Station (SAUO) ... ATS
Army Training Study ... ARTS
Army Training Support Center [*Fort Eustis, VA*] ... ATSC
Army Training Target System (MCD) ... ATTS
Army Training Test ... ATT
Army Transition to War Measure (SAUS) ... ATWM
Army Transport [*British military*] (DMA) ... AT
Army Transport Boat (SAUS) ... ATB
Army Transport Service [*Later, Military Sea Transportation Service, then Military Sealift Command*] [*Obsolete*] ... ATS
Army Transport Service (SAUO) ... ATS
Army Transport Service Quartermaster Corps (SAUO) ... ATSQMC
Army Transport Service Quartermaster Corps [*Obsolete*] ... ATSQMC
Army Transportation Association ... ATA
Army Transportation Association (SAUO) ... ATA
Army Transportation Board (MCD) ... ATB
Army Transportation Command (IUSS) ... ATC
Army Transportation Corps ... ATC
Army Transportation Engineering Agency (SAUO) ... ATEA
Army Transportation Materiel Command (SAUO) ... ATMC
Army Transportation Plan in Support of the Army Strategic Capabilities Plan (AABC) ... ATP-ASCP
Army Transportation Research Command ... ATRC
Army Transportation Supply and Maintenance Command (SAUO) ... ATSMC
Army Transportation Unit (SAUO) ... ATU
Army Troop Test (ACAE) ... ATT
Army Troops (SAUO) ... AT
Army Troops (SAUS) ... AT
Army troops (SAUO) ... Atps
Army Troops [*British and Canadian*] [*World War II*] ... A Tps
Army Tropic Test Center (MCD) ... ATTC
Army Type Classification Code ... ATCC
Army Uniform Data Inquiry Technique ... AUDIT
Army Unit ... AU
Army Unit for United States Air Force (SAUO) ... AUFUSAF
Army Unit Resiliancy Analysis [*Computer science*] (RDA) ... AURA
Army Unit Standard Manpower Information System (SAUS) ... AUSMIS
Army Universal Gun (SAUS) ... AUG
Army User Equipment (MCD) ... AUE
Army Validation Program ... AVP
Army Veterinary and Remount Services [*British*] ... AVR
Army Veterinary and Remount Services [*British military*] (DMA) ... AVRS
Army Veterinary Corps [*Facetious translation during World War I "All Very Cushy"*] [*Later, RAVC*] [*British*] ... AVC
Army Veterinary Corps (SAUO) ... AVC
Army Veterinary Department (SAUO) ... AVD
Army Veterinary Department [*British*] ... AVD
Army Veterinary Service [*British*] (DAS) ... AVS
Army Victualling Department [*British*] ... AVD
Army Victualling Department (SAUO) ... AVD
Army Vietnam ... ARV
Army Vocational Training Centre (SAUO) ... AVTC
Army Vocational Training Centre (SAUS) ... AVTC
Army Volunteer Reserve (SAUO) ... AVR
Army Volunteer Reserve [*British*] ... AVR
Army Volunteer Reserves (SAUS) ... AVR
Army Volunteers Corps [*British*] ... AVC
Army War College (MCD) ... ARWARCOL
Army War College ... ARWC
Army War College (SAUO) ... ArWC
Army War College (SAUO) ... AWC
Army War College ... AWC
Army War College Correspondence Studies (MCD) ... AWCCS
Army War College Corresponding Studies Course (INF) ... AWCCSC
Army War Room (AABC) ... AWR
Army War Room Information System ... AWRIS
Army Warfighting Experiments ... AWE
Army Warranty Program ... AWP
Army Wartime Asset Distribution Study ... AWADS
Army Waterways Experiment Station (SAUO) ... AWES
Army Waterways Experimental Station (SAUS) ... AWES
Army Weapons and Mobilty Command (SAUO) ... AWMC
Army Weapons Command [*AMC*] ... AWC
Army Weapons Command [*AMC*] (MCD) ... AWECOM
Army Weather Service (NATG) ... AWS
Army Welfare Committee (SAUO) ... AWC
Army Welfare Office (SAUO) ... AWO
Army Welfare Officer [*British*] ... AWO
Army Welfare Services [*British*] ... AWS
Army Wholesale Logistic System (AABC) ... AWLOG
Army Wholesale Logistic System (SAUS) ... AWLOGS
Army Wide (SAUS) ... AW
Army Wireless Officer [*Obsolete*] (IAA) ... AWO
Army with Navy [*Personnel*] ... ARNA
Army (Wives) Senior Assistance Program ... ASAP
Army Women's Services Officers School [*British military*] (DMA) ... AWSOS
Army Work Study Group ... AWSG
Army Work Study Organisation (SAUO) ... AWSO
Army Working Capital Fund-Supply Management Army ... AWCF-SMA
Army World Wide Military Command and Control System (SAUS) ... WWMCCS
Army Worldwide Military Command and Control Information Systems (RDA) ... AWWMCCS
Army WWMCCS [*Worldwide Military Command and Control System*] **Information System** (GFGA) ... AWIS
Army WWMCCS Information System (SAUS) ... AWIS
Army Year of Values Scales ... AYVS
Army Youth Team [*British*] ... AYT
Army-Air Force Center for Low-Intensity Conflict [*Langley Air Force Base, VA*] (INF) ... A-AF CLIC
Army-Air Force Civilian Welfare Fund (ACAE) ... A-AFCWF
Army/Air Force Motion Picture Service ... AAFM
Army/Air Force Post Office (AAGC) ... APO
Army/American Council on Education (INF) ... ACE
Army/American Council on Education Registry Transcript System (INF) ... AARTS
Army-Armament Research Development and Engineering Center (SAUO) ... ARDEC
Army/Industry Material Information Liaison Office (ACAE) ... AMILO
Army/Industry Materiel Information Liaison Office [*or Officer*] ... AIMILO
Army/Navy (ACAE) ... A/N
Army-Navy Anticorrosion Compound ... ANC
Army-Navy Civil Aeronautics Committee (SAUO) ... ANC
Army-Navy Communications Intelligence Board [*Later, STANCIB*] ... ANCIB
Army-Navy Communications Intelligence Coordinating Committee [*Later, ANCIB*] ... ANCICC
Army-Navy Communications Production Expediting Agency ... ANCPEA
Army-Navy Country Club ... ANCC
Army-Navy Design (SAUS) ... AND
Army-Navy Design Standards ... AND
Army-Navy Electronic and Electrical Standards Agency (SAUO) ... ANEESA
Army-Navy Electronics Evaluation Group (SAUO) ... ANEEG
Army-Navy Electronics Production Agency ... ANEPA
Army-Navy Fuel (SAUS) ... ANF
Army-Navy Ground Radio Communications ... AN/GRC
Army-Navy Instrumentation Program ... ANIP
Army-Navy Joint Specifications Board ... ANJSB
Army-Navy Joint Type Ordnance ... AN
Army-Navy Liquidation Commission [*World War II*] ... ANLC
Army-Navy Munitions Board [*Later, Munitions Board*] ... ANMB
Army/Navy Number ... A/N

Army-Navy Petroleum Board ANPB
Army-Navy Petroleum Pool, Pacific Coast (SAUO) ANPPC
Army-Navy Petroleum Pool, Pacific Coast ANPPPC
Army-Navy Radio Frequency Cable Coordination Committee (SAUO) ANRFCCC
Army-Navy Safety Board (SAUO) ANSB
Army-Navy Shipping Information Agency ANSIA
Army-Navy Vehicular Radio Communications (SAUS) ANFVRC
Army-Navy Vehicular Radio Communications AN/VRC
Army-Navy-Air Force (MCD) ANA
Army-Navy-Air Force ANAF
Army-Navy-Air Force Times Alliance [*A publication*] ANAFTA
Army-Navy-British ANB
Army-Navy-British Standard (SAA) ANBS
Army-Navy-Civil (MSA) ANC
Army-Navy-Commerce ANC
Army-Navy-Commercial (SAUS) ANC
Army-Navy-Industry (MCD) ANI
Armys Airborne Fire-Support System (SAUS) AAFSS
Armys Automated Logistic Data System (SAUS) TAALODS
Army's Electronic Environmental Test Facility [*Military*] (IAA) AEETF
Army's Five-Year Defense Program AFYDP
Army's Incentive Awards Program (RDA) AIAP
Army's Mobility Opportunity Development Program AMOD
Armys Program for Individual Training (SAUS) APRINT
Army's Requirement to Own and Operate Watercraft (MCD) ARROW
Armys Robotic Resupply Vehicle (SAUS) ROBARV
Armys Special Operations Unit (SAUS) D-2
Armys Study Program (SAUS) TASP
Army/Tactical Group Headquarters (SAUO) Army/Tac Gp HQ
Army-Wide AW
Army-Wide Doctrinal and Training Literature Program ADTLP
Army-wide Doctrinal and Training Literature Program (SAUS) ADTLP
Army-Wide Library Council (RDA) ALC
Army-Wide Signature Program (MCD) AWSP
Army-Wide Training and Doctrinal Literature Program ATDLP
Armywide Training Literature ATL
Army-Wide Training Literature Program (AABC) ATLP
Army-wide Training Literature Program (SAUO) ATLP
Army-Wide Training Support (AABC) AWTS
Army-Wide Training Support System AWTSS
Arnada Resources [*Vancouver Stock Exchange symbol*] AAN
Arnbruck [*Germany*] [*ICAO location identifier*] (ICLI) EDYB
Arnenorrhea/Hyperprolactinernia (SAUS) A/H
Arner Medical Alert [*NASDAQ symbol*] (TTSB) AMAC
Arnerican Holistic Nurses Association (SAUO) AHNA
Arnhem Resources, Inc. [*Vancouver Stock Exchange symbol*] AHR
Arnold Air Development Center [*Air Force*] AADC
Arnold Air Society (EA) AAS
Arnold and Hodges' English Bail Court Reports [*A publication*] (DLA) Arn & HBC
Arnold and Hodges' English Bail Court Reports [*A publication*] (DLA) Arn & Hod BC
Arnold and Hodges' English Practice Cases [*A publication*] (DLA) Arn & Hod PC
Arnold and Hodges' English Practice Cases [*A publication*] (DLA) Arn & Hod Pr Cas
Arnold and Hodges' English Queen's Bench Reports [*1840-41*] [*A publication*] (DLA) A & H
Arnold and Hodges' English Queen's Bench Reports [*1840-41*] [*A publication*] (DLA) Arn & H
Arnold and Hodges' English Queen's Bench Reports [*1840-41*] [*A publication*] (DLA) Arn & Hod
Arnold and Hodges' English Queen's Bench Reports [*1840-41*] [*A publication*] (DLA) Arnold & H
Arnold Arboretum of Harvard University (SAUO) A
Arnold, CA [*FM radio station call letters*] KBYN
Arnold Constable Corporation (SAUO) ACT
Arnold Cook Braille and Talking Book Library [*Australia*] ACBTBL
Arnold Engineering Development Center [*Arnold Air Force Base, TN*] AEDC
Arnold Engineering Development Center (SAUS) AEDC
Arnold Engineering Development Center, Arnold Air Force Station, TN [*OCLC symbol*] (OCLC) TAF
Arnold Gregory Memorial Hospital, Albion, NY [*Library symbol*] [*Library of Congress*] (LCLS) NAlbiH
Arnold Indus [*NASDAQ symbol*] (TTSB) AIND
Arnold Industries, Inc. [*NASDAQ symbol*] (NQ) AIND
Arnold Industries, Inc. [*Associated Press*] (SAG) Arnold
Arnold, MO [*FM radio station call letters*] KCWA
Arnold Palmer Golf Co. (The) [*Associated Press*] (SAG) APalmer
Arnold Palmer Golf Co. (The) [*NASDAQ symbol*] (SAG) APGC
Arnold. Public Meetings and Political Societies [*1833*] [*A publication*] (DLA) Arn Pub M
Arnold. Public Meetings and Political Societies [*1833*] [*A publication*] (DLA) Arn Pub Meet
Arnold Ranch [*California*] [*Seismograph station code, US Geological Survey*] (SEIS) ARN
Arnold Schoenberg Institute [*University of Southern California*] [*Research center*] (RCD) ASI
Arnold Schoenberg Institute, Los Angeles, CA [*Library symbol*] [*Library of Congress*] (LCLS) CLAS
Arnold Transit Co. [*Later, ATCO*] [*AAR code*] ATC
Arnold Transit Co. [*Formerly, ATC*] [*AAR code*] ATCO
Arnold Transit Company (SAUO) ATC
Arnold Transit Company (SAUO) ATCO
Arnold, White & Durkee, Houston, TX [*Library symbol*] [*Library of Congress*] (LCLS) TxHAWD
Arnold-Chiari [*Syndrome*] [*Medicine*] (DB) AC
Arnold-Chiari Malformation [*Medicine*] ACM
Arnoldia Zimbabwe (SAUS) Arnoldia Zimb
Arnolds Cove Public Library, Arnolds Cove, NF, Canada [*Library symbol*] [*Library of Congress*] (LCLS) CaNfAC
Arnolds Cove Public Library, Newfoundland [*Library symbol*] [*National Library of Canada*] (NLC) NFAC
Arnold's Election Cases [*England*] [*A publication*] (DLA) Arn El Cas
Arnold's English Common Pleas Reports [*1838-39*] [*A publication*] (DLA) Arn
Arnold's English Common Pleas Reports [*1838-39*] [*A publication*] (DLA) Arnold
Arnold's Geological Series AGS
Arnold's Municipal Corporations [*A publication*] (DLA) Arn Mun Cor
Arnolt-Bristol Owners Club [*Later, ABR*] (EA) ABOC
Arnolt-Bristol Registry (EA) ABR
Arnot's Criminal Cases [*1536-1784*] [*Scotland*] [*A publication*] (DLA) Arnot Cr C
Arnot's Criminal Trials [*1536-1784*] [*Scotland*] [*A publication*] (DLA) Arn
Arnould on Marine Insurance [*A publication*] (DLA) Arn
Arnould on Marine Insurance [*A publication*] (DLA) Arn Ins
Arnprior, ON [*AM radio station call letters*] CHVR-2
Arnprior Public Library, Arnprior, ON, Canada [*Library symbol*] [*Library of Congress*] (LCLS) CaOARB
Arnprior Public Library, Ontario [*Library symbol*] [*National Library of Canada*] (NLC) OAR
Arnsberg [*Germany*] [*ICAO location identifier*] (ICLI) EDLA
ARO, Inc., AEDC Library, Arnold Air Force Station, TN [*Library symbol*] [*Library of Congress*] (LCLS) TArnA
Aromate and Aliphate (SAUS) ARAL
Aromatic [*Chemistry*] ar
Aromatic (MSA) AROM
Aromatic Amine Terminated Butadiene/Acrylonitrile [*Organic chemistry*] AATBN
Aromatic Amino Acid Decarboxylase [*Also, AADC*] [*An enzyme*] AAAD
Aromatic Amino Acid Decarboxylase [*Also, AAAD*] [*An enzyme*] AADC
Aromatic Amino Acids [*Biochemistry*] AAA
Aromatic Hydrocarbon Hydroxylase [*An enzyme*] AHH
Aromatic Polyamide (SAUS) AP
Aromatic Red Cedar Closet Lining Manufacturers Association (EA) ARCCLMA
Aromatic Solvent-Induced Shift [*Physical chemistry*] ASIS
Aromatic Weathering Ratio [*Ecology*] (DAVI) AWR
Aromatica [*Essence*] [*Chemistry*] (ROG) AROMAT
Aromatics [*Organic chemistry*] Aro
Aromatics Hydrogenation [*Fuel technology*] AHYD
Arona [*New Guinea*] [*Airport symbol*] (AD) AON
Aronex Pharmaceuticals [*NASDAQ symbol*] (TTSB) ARNX
Aronex Pharmaceuticals, Inc. [*NASDAQ symbol*] (SAG) ARNX
Aronex Pharmaceuticals, Inc. [*Associated Press*] (SAG) AronexPh
Aronex Pharmaceuticals, Inc. [*Associated Press*] (SAG) AronxPh
Aroostook Aviation, Inc. [*FAA designator*] (FAAC) PXX
Aroostook Health Information and Resource Consortium (SAUS) AHIRC
Aroostook State Teachers College [*Merged with University of Maine*] ASTC
Aroostook Valley Railroad Co. [*AAR code*] AVL
Arorae [*Kiribati*] [*Airport symbol*] (OAG) AIS
Arorae [*Kiribati*] [*ICAO location identifier*] (ICLI) NGTR
Around (FAAC) ARND
Around the Clock [*Medicine*] ATC
around the clock (SAUS) atc
Around the World (TRID) ATW
Around-the-clock keyword-based electronic news service (SAUS) X-PRESS
Arousal A
Arousal Mechanism [*Medicine*] AM
Arousal Seeking Tendency Scale [*Test*] (TMMY) MAST
ARPA Calibration Satellite (MCD) ACS
ARPA [*Advanced Research Projects Agency*] **Maui Optical Station** (MUGU) AMOS
ARPA Maui Optical Station (SAUS) AMOS
ARPA [*Advanced Research Projects Agency*] **Measurements RADAR** [*Raytheon*] AMRAD
ARPA [*Advanced Research Projects Agency*] **Network Terminal System** ANTS
Arpad Academy of Hungarian Scientists, Writers, and Artists Abroad (EA) AAHSWAA
Arpad Federation (EA) AF
ARPA [*Advanced Research Projects Agency*]**/Lincoln C-Band Observable RADAR** [*Army*] (AABC) ALCOR
ARPANET Reference Model (SAUS) ARM
Arpeggio [*Music*] ARP
Arpeggio [*Record label*] [*Italy*] Arp
Arpeggio [*Music*] ARPO
ARPS Data Analysis System (SAUS) ADAS
ArQule, Inc. [*NASDAQ symbol*] (SAG) ARQL
ArQule, Inc. [*Associated Press*] (SAG) ArQule
Arracacha Virus A [*Plant pathology*] AVA
Arracacha Virus B [*Plant pathology*] AVB
Ar-Rajhi Banking & Investment Co. [*Saudi Arabia*] (EY) ARABIC
Arrange (AABC) ARNG
Arrange (ROG) ARRE
Arranged ARR
Arranged (ADWA) arr
Arranged ARRD
Arranged Total Loss [*Insurance*] ARRTL
Arranged Total Loss (MARI) Arr Tl
Arranged Total Loss [*Insurance*] (AIA) ATL
Arrangement (SAUS) AR

Arrangement (SAUS) .... Argmt
Arrangement (WDAA) .... arr
Arrangement [*Music*] .... ARR
Arrangement (DLA) .... Arrang
Arrangement .... ARRANGT
Arrangement (ROG) .... ARRGT
Arrangement (EBF) .... arrgt
Arranger [*MARC relator code*] [*Library of Congress*] (LCCP) .... arr
Arras/Roclincourt [*France*] [*ICAO location identifier*] (ICLI) .... LFQD
Array (NASA) .... ARR
Array Bending (SSD) .... AB
Array Calculation (SAUS) .... AC
Array Computing Element (ACAE) .... ACE
Array Configuration Utility [*Computer science*] .... ACU
Array Declaration (SAUS) .... AD
Array Declarator Subscript (SAUS) .... ADS
Array Descriptor (SAUS) .... AD
Array Drive Electronics (ADWA) .... ADE
Array Element Study .... AES
Array Element Successor Function (SAUS) .... AESF
Array Expression (SAUS) .... AE
Array Factor (SAUS) .... AF
Array Gain (IUSS) .... AG
Array Identifier (SAUS) .... AI
Array Interconnection Logic [*Computer science*] .... AIL
Array Interface Unit [*Computer science*] (CAAL) .... AIU
Array List (SAUS) .... AL
Array Logic and Storage (SAUS) .... ALAS
Array Machine Language [*Computer science*] .... AML
Array Motion Sensor .... AMS
Array of Building Blocks (MHDI) .... ABB
Array of Low Energy X ray Imaging Sensors (SAUS) .... ALEXIS
Array of Low Energy X-Ray Imaging Sensors (ADWA) .... ALEXIS
Array Out Counter (SAUS) .... AOC
Array Position Message (IUSS) .... APM
Array Processing Instruction Set [*Computer science*] (MSA) ..... APIS
[*An*] Array Processing Language [*Programming language*] ...... AAPL
Array Processing System (SAUS) .... APS
Array Processor [*Computer science*] (BUR) .... AP
Array Processor Access Method [*Computer science*] (BUR) .... APAM
Array Processor Assembly Language [*Computer science*] .... APAL
Array Processor Formula Translation (SAUS) .... AP FORTRAN
Array Processor Software [*Computer science*] (IEEE) .... APS
Array Processor Subroutine Package [*Computer science*] (BUR) .. APSP
Array Processor System (SAUS) .... APS
Array Radar (SAUS) .... Arr Rad
Array Reduction Analysis Circuit (MHDB) .... ARAC
Array Segment (SAUS) .... AS
Array Signal Processing (MCD) .... ASP
Array Structure Experiment Package [*Computer science*] (IAA) .. ASEP
Array Transform Processor .... ATP
Array Variable (SAUS) .... AV
Arrays, Inc. (SAUO) .... ARAY
Array-Scaling (SAUS) .... AS
Array/Vector (SAUS) .... AV
Arrears in Pay [*Military*] .... ARSIP
Arrecife [*Canary Islands*] [*Airport symbol*] (OAG) .... ACE
Arrecife/Lanzarote [*Canary Islands*] [*ICAO location identifier*] (ICLI) .. GCRR
Arrendamiento de Aviones Jets, SA [*Mexico*] [*FAA designator*] (FAAC) ...... JTS
Arrest (FAAC) .... ARST
Arrest after Arrival [*Medicine*] (DMAA) .... AAA
Arrest Temperature (SAUS) .... AT
Arrested Carrier Landing (SAUS) .... TRAP
Arrested Relaxation [*Molecular dynamics*] .... AR
Arrester [*Electricity*] (IAA) .... AR
Arrester [*Electricity*] (KSC) .... ARR
Arrester [*Electricity*] .... ARSR
Arresting .... ARG
Arresting Gear [*Aviation*] .... A-G
Arresting Gear Officer [*Military*] (MCD) .... AGO
Arresting Gear Tester .... AGT
Arret de la Chambre Civile de la Cour de Cassation [*Decision of the Court of Appeal, Civil Division*] [*French*] (ILCA) .... Cass Civ
Arret de la Chambre Civile de la Cour de Cassation [*Decision of the Court of Appeal, Civil Division*] [*French*] (ILCA) Civ
Arret de la Chambre Criminelle de la Cour de Cassation [*Decision of the Court of Appeal, Criminal Division*] [*French*] (ILCA) .. Cass Crim
Arret de la Chambre Criminelle de la Cour de Cassation [*Decision of the Court of Appeal, Criminal Division*] [*French*] (ILCA) ..... Crim
Arret de la Chambre des Requetes de la Cour de Cassation [*Decision of the Court of Appeal, Chamber of Requests*] [*French*] (ILCA) ...... Cass Req
Arret de la Cour de Cassation [*Decision of the Court of Appeal*] [*Belgium*] (ILCA) .... Cass
Arret de la Cour de Cassation Toutes Chambres Reunies [*Decision of the Full Court of the Court of Appeal*] [*French*] (ILCA) ..... Ch Reun
Arret de la Section Commerciale de la Cour de Cassation [*Decision of the Commercial Section of the Court of Appeal*] [*French*] (ILCA) ..... Cas Com
Arret de la Section Sociale de la Cour de Cassation [*Decision of the Social Security and Labor Division of the Court of Appeal*] [*French*] (ILCA) ..... Cass Soc
Arrete [*Decision, Ordinance, By-law*] [*French*] .... AR
Arrete [*Decision, Order*] [*French*] (ILCA) .... Arr
Arrhenatherum Blue Dwarf Virus [*Plant pathology*] .... ABDV
Arrhythmia [*Medicine*] (MELL) .... ARRHTH
Arrhythmia [*Cardiology*] (DAVI) .... Arry
Arrhythmia Research Technology [*AMEX symbol*] (SPSG) .... HRT

Arrhythmia Research Technology, Inc. [*Associated Press*] (SAG) ..... Arhyth
Arrhythmogenic Dose of Epinephrine [*Medicine*] .... ADE
Arrhythmogenic Right Ventricular Dysplasia [*Medicine*] (MELL) .. ARVD
Arrhythmogenic Right Ventricular Dysplasia [*Cardiology*] (DMAA) .. ARVI
Arrhythmogenic Ventricular Activity [*Medicine*] (MELL) .... AVA
Arrian [*Second century AD*] [*Classical studies*] (OCD) .... Arr
Arricaccato (VRA) .... arric
Arrick, Douglas B., Denver CO [*STAC*] .... ARK
Arriflex [*Camera*] [*Named for manufacturers Arnold and Richter*] .. ARRI
Arrington [*England*] .... ARR
Arris Pharmaceutical [*NASDAQ symbol*] (TTSB) .... ARRS
Arris Pharmaceutical Corp. [*Associated Press*] (SAG) .... ArrisPh
Arris Pharmaceutical Corp. [*NASDAQ symbol*] (SAG) .... ARRS
Arrival .... AR
Arrival (ADWA) .... ar
Arrival (EBF) .... arr
Arrival [*or Arrive*] .... ARR
Arrival Aircraft Interval [*FAA*] (TAG) .... AAI
Arrival Aircraft Interval [*Aviation*] (FAAC) .... AAITVL
Arrival Airfield Control Group [*Military*] (AABC) .... AACG
Arrival and Assembly Area [*Marine Corps*] (DOMA) .... AAA
Arrival and Assembly Operations Element [*Navy*] (ANA) ...... AAOE
Arrival and Assembly Operations Group [*Navy*] (ANA) .... AAOG
Arrival and Assembly Support Party [*Navy*] (ANA) .... AASP
Arrival and Return [*Shipping*] .... AR
Arrival Angle [*Army*] .... AA
Arrival Approved (SAUS) .... AA
Arrival Date (DOMA) .... ARRDATE
Arrival Delay [*Air Traffic Control*] (FAAC) .... ADLY
Arrival First Sea Pilot Station (RIMS) .... AFSPS
Arrival Further Proceed Immediately and Report [*Navy*] .. ARPROIMREP
Arrival Further Proceed Port in which Activity Designated May Be [*Navy*] .... ARPROPORICH
Arrival Locator .... AL
Arrival Message [*Aviation code*] .... ARR
Arrival Notice [*Shipping*] .... AN
Arrival Notice (EBF) .... an
Arrival Notice (SAUS) .... arrn
Arrival of Goods (WDMC) .... AOG
Arrival Pilot Station (RIMS) .... APS
Arrival Report [*Navy*] .... ARREP
Arrival Report [*Navy*] (NVT) .... ARRIVEDREP
Arrival Report Commanding Officer that Vessel Duty [*Navy*] .. ARREPCOVES
Arrival Report Immediate Superior in Command [*Navy*] .. ARREPISIC
Arrival Report Will be Filed With [*Aviation*] (FAAC) .... FIRIV
Arrival Sequencing Program [*FAA*] (TAG) .... ASP
Arrival Time (AABC) .... AT
Arrival Time [*Aviation*] .... PX In
Arrival Time Distribution [*Chemical physics*] .... ATD
Arrival Unknown [*Aviation*] .... ARUNK
Arrival/Departure (CTAS) .... A/D
Arrival/Departure Airfield Control Group (DOMA) .... A/DACG
Arrive (ADA) .... A
arrive (SAUS) .... A
Arrive (WDAA) .... ar
Arrive (WGA) .... ARV
Arrived (EBF) .... arr
Arrived .... ARRD
Arrived Notification Form [*British*] (DCTA) .... ANF
Arrived Report (SAUS) .... ARRIVEDREP
Arrived Unannounced (SAUS) .... ARRUNA
Arrived within Continental Limits of United States (SAUS) .... ARRUS
Arrived Within Continental Limits of US [*Navy*] .... ARRUS
Arrives (SAUS) .... ARR
Arriving (SAUS) .... ARR
ARRL [*American Radio Relay League*] Foundation (EA) .... ARRLF
Arrny Parachute Association (SAUO) .... APA
Arrocillo Amarillo [*Race of maize*] [*Mexico*] .... A-A
Arrow .... ARW
Arrow Airways, Inc. [*ICAO designator*] (FAAC) .... APW
Arrow Airways, Inc. (SAUO) .... JW
Arrow Automotive Industries, Inc. [*AMEX symbol*] (SPSG) ..... AI
Arrow Automotive Industries, Inc. [*Associated Press*] (SAG) .. ArrowA
Arrow Aviation Ltd. [*Canada*] [*ICAO designator*] (FAAC) ...... ARO
Arrow Bank Corp. [*NASDAQ symbol*] (NQ) .... AROW
Arrow Bank Corp. [*Associated Press*] (SAG) .... ArowFn
Arrow Continuation Experiment (SAUS) .... ACE
Arrow Continuation Experiments (SAUS) .... ACES
Arrow Diagramming Method (MCD) .... ADM
Arrow Electronics [*NYSE symbol*] (TTSB) .... ARW
Arrow Electronics, Inc. [*Associated Press*] (SAG) .... ArowE
Arrow Electronics, Inc. [*NYSE symbol*] (SPSG) .... ARW
Arrow Financial [*NASDAQ symbol*] (TTSB) .... AROW
Arrow International [*NASDAQ symbol*] (TTSB) .... ARRO
Arrow International, Inc. [*Associated Press*] (SAG) .... ArowInt
Arrow International, Inc. [*NASDAQ symbol*] (SAG) .... ARRO
Arrow of Light [*Boy Scouts of America*] .... AOL
Arrow Point Communications [*NASDAQ symbol*] (SG) .... ARPT
Arrow Transportation [*NASDAQ symbol*] (TTSB) .... ARRW
Arrow Transportation Co. [*Associated Press*] (SAG) .... ArrowTrn
Arrow Transportation Co. [*NASDAQ symbol*] (SAG) .... ARRW
Arrowfield Resources [*Vancouver Stock Exchange symbol*] ..... ARW
Arrow-Hart & Hegeman Electric Co. (SAUO) .... A-H
Arrow-Hart & Hegeman Electric Company (SAUS) .... A-H
Arrowhead (SAUS) .... AhD

Arrowhead [*Military decoration*] (AABC) ... Ahd
Arrowhead Airways [*ICAO designator*] (FAAC) ... ARH
Arrowhead Athletic Conference (PSS) ... AAC
Arrowhead Energy Corporation (SAUO) ... AHEC
Arrowhead Library System [*Library network*] ... ALS
Arrowhead Library System, Janesville Public Library, Janesville, WI [*OCLC symbol*] (OCLC) ... WIJ
Arrowhead Library System, Virginia, MN [*Library symbol*] [*Library of Congress*] (LCLS) ... MnVA
Arrowhead National Wildlife Refuge (SAUS) ... ANWR
Arrowhead Professional Libraries Association [*Library network*] ... APLA
Arrowhead Resources Ltd. [*Vancouver Stock Exchange symbol*] ... AWR
Arrow-Magnolia International, Inc. [*Associated Press*] (SAG) ... ArrowM
Arrow-Magnolia International, Inc. [*NASDAQ symbol*] (SAG) ... ARWM
Arrows Ltd. [*British*] [*ICAO designator*] (FAAC) ... ARW
Arrowwood Municipal Library, Alberta [*Library symbol*] [*National Library of Canada*] (NLC) ... AARM
Arroyo Grande, CA [*AM radio station call letters*] ... KKAL
Ars Aequi; Juridisch Studentenblad [*Netherlands*] (ILCA) ... AAe
Ars Amatoria [*of Ovid*] [*Classical studies*] (OCD) ... Ars Am
Ars Electronica Center (SAUO) ... AEC
Ars Orientalis: The Arts of Islam and the East [*A publication*] ... AO
Ars Poetica [*of Horace*] [*Classical studies*] (OCD) ... Ars P
Ars Rhetorica [*of Dionysius Halicarnassensis*] [*Classical studies*] (OCD) ... Rhet
ARS [*American Rocket Society*] **Structures and Materials Committee** ... ASTMC
ARS Structures and Materials Committee (SAUO) ... ASTMC
Arsanilic Acid [*Organic chemistry*] ... ARS
'Arse over Kettle [*Head over heels*] [*Slang*] [*British*] (DSUE) ... AK
'Arse over Top [*Head over Heels*] [*Bowdlerized version*] (ADA) ... AOT
Arsenal (AABC) ... ARS
Arsenal (MCD) ... ARSL
Arsenal (SAUS) ... ARsl
Arsenal ... ARSNL
Arsenal Exchange Model (MCD) ... AEM
Arsenal Family and Children's Center [*Research center*] (RCD) ... AFCC
Arsenal Management Information System ... ARMIS
Arsenal Operations Directorate [*Rock Island Arsenal*] [*Army*] ... AOD
arsenal operations division (SAUO) ... AOD
Arsendinus de Forlivio [*Authority cited in pre-1607 legal work*] (DSA) ... Ar
Arsendinus de Forlivio [*Authority cited in pre-1607 legal work*] (DSA) ... Ar de For
Arsenic [*Chemical element*] (DAVI) ... ARSEN
Arsenic [*Chemical element*] ... As
Arsenic (SAUS) ... AS
Arsenic Atmosphere Czochralski [*System for growing crystals*] ... AAC
Arsenic Silicate Glass (SAUS) ... ASG
Arsenical Tough Pitch (SAUS) ... ATP
Arsenious chloride (SAUS) ... BR
Arsenophyrite (SAUS) ... ar
Arsenosilicate Glass (SAUS) ... AsSG
Arshan [*Former USSR*] [*Seismograph station code, US Geological Survey*] (SEIS) ... ARS
Arsine [*Inorganic chemistry*] ... ARS
Arsine (AAEL) ... AsH3
Arsine [*Medicine*] (ADDR) ... SA
Arso [*Indonesia*] [*ICAO location identifier*] (ICLI) ... WAJA
Arson [*Criminology*] (LAIN) ... ARS
Arson and Explosion Squad (SAUS) ... A&ES
Arson and Explosion Squadron (SAUO) ... A&ES
Arson Information Management System [*Developed by National Fire Administration*] [*Emmitsburg, MD*] ... AIMS
Arson Task Force Assistance Program ... ATFAP
Arsphenamine [*Antisyphilitic compound*] (MAE) ... AR
Arsphenamine [*Antisyphilitic compound*] ... ARS
Art (ADA) ... A
Art Advisory Committee ... AAC
Art Against Apartheid (SAUO) ... AAA
Art and Antique Dealers League of America (EA) ... AADLA
Art and Archaeology (journ.) (SAUS) ... AaA
Art and Archaeology, Washington (journ.) (SAUS) ... A&AW
Art and Archeology (journ.) (SAUS) ... A&A
Art and Architecture Thesaurus (TELE) ... AAT
Art and Architecture Thesaurus Program, Bennington College, Bennington, VT [*Library symbol*] [*Library of Congress*] (LCLS) ... AatP
Art and Australia [*A publication*] ... Art Aust
Art and Craft Materials Institute (EA) ... ACMI
Art and Design Advisory Council (SAUO) ... ADAC
Art and Mechanical [*Graphics*] (NTCM) ... A & M
Art and Mechanical [*Graphic arts*] (WDMC) ... AM
Art and Requirements of Command (MCD) ... ARC
Art and Text [*A publication*] ... Art & T
Art and the Law [*A publication*] (DLA) ... Art & Law
Art Bulletin [*A publication*] (WDAA) ... AB
Art Bulletin [*A publication*] (BRI) ... Art Bull
Art Center College of Design, Los Angeles, CA [*Library symbol*] [*Library of Congress*] (LCLS) ... CLArt
Art Center School ... ACS
Art Circle Public Library, Crossville, TN [*Library symbol*] [*Library of Congress*] (LCLS) ... TCrA
Art Class Teacher's Certificate [*British*] ... ACTC
Art Class Teachers Certificate (SAUS) ... ACTC
Art Collecting Point (SAUO) ... ACP
Art Collectors Club of America (EA) ... ACCA
Art Commission of New York City (SAUO) ... ACNYC
Art Complete (MCD) ... AC
Art Dealers Association of America (SAUO) ... AD
Art Dealers Association of America (SAUO) ... ADAA
Art Dealers Association of America (EA) ... ADAA
Art Deco ... AD
Art Deco Societies of America (EA) ... ADSA
Art Design Architecture and Media [*Project*] [*British*] (TELE) ... ADAM
Art Digest (journ.) (SAUS) ... AD
Art Direction [*A publication*] (BRI) ... Art Dir
Art Director [*Films, television, etc.*] ... AD
Art Directors Annual [*A publication*] ... ADA
Art Directors Annual (journ.) (SAUS) ... ADA
Art Directors Club (EA) ... ADC
Art Directors Club (SAUO) ... ADC
Art Directors Club of Los Angeles (SAUO) ... ADLA
Art Directors Club of Montreal [*1950*] [*Canada*] (NGC) ... ADCM
Art Directors Club of Toronto [*1947*] [*Canada*] (NGC) ... ADCT
Art Directors Club, Toronto (SAUO) ... ADCT
Art Dreco Institute (EA) ... ADI
Art Education Society of New South Wales [*Australia*] ... AESNW
Art Exhibition Bureau (SAUO) ... AEB
Art Exhibitions Australia ... AEA
Art Exhibitions Bureau ... AEB
Art For All ... AFA
Art for World Friendship (AEBS) ... AWF
Art Galleries Association [*British*] (DBA) ... AGA
Art Gallery ... AG
Art Gallery, Mount Saint Vincent University, Halifax, Nova Scotia [*Library symbol*] [*National Library of Canada*] (NLC) ... NSHVA
Art Gallery of Cobourg, Cobourg, ON, Canada [*Library symbol*] [*Library of Congress*] (LCLS) ... CaOCoA
Art Gallery of Cobourg, Ontario [*Library symbol*] [*National Library of Canada*] (NLC) ... OCOA
Art Gallery of Greater Victoria, Victoria, BC, Canada [*Library symbol*] [*Library of Congress*] (LCLS) ... CaBViA
Art Gallery of Greater Victoria, Victoria, British Columbia [*Library symbol*] [*National Library of Canada*] (NLC) ... BVIA
Art Gallery of Hamilton, Hamilton, ON, Canada [*Library symbol*] [*Library of Congress*] (LCLS) ... CaOHAG
Art Gallery of Hamilton, Ontario [*Library symbol*] [*National Library of Canada*] (NLC) ... OHAG
Art Gallery of Nova Scotia, Halifax, Nova Scotia [*Library symbol*] [*National Library of Canada*] (NLC) ... NSHAG
Art Gallery of Nova Scotia, Halifax, NS, Canada [*Library symbol*] [*Library of Congress*] (LCLS) ... CaNSHAG
Art Gallery of Ontario [*UTLAS symbol*] ... AGO
Art Gallery of Ontario, Audiovisual Library, Toronto, ON, Canada [*Library symbol*] [*Library of Congress*] (LCLS) ... CaOTAGAV
Art Gallery of Ontario, Toronto, ON, Canada [*Library symbol*] [*Library of Congress*] (LCLS) ... CaOTAG
Art Gallery of Ontario, Toronto, Ontario [*Library symbol*] [*National Library of Canada*] (NLC) ... OTAG
Art Gallery of South Australia ... AGSA
Art Gallery of Toronto (SAUO) ... AGT
Art Gallery of Windsor, Ontario [*Library symbol*] [*National Library of Canada*] (NLC) ... OWAG
Art Gallery of Windsor, Windsor, ON, Canada [*Library symbol*] [*Library of Congress*] (LCLS) ... CaOWAG
Art Glass Suppliers Association (EA) ... AGSA
Art Hazards Information Center (EA) ... AHIC
Art, Historical and Scientific Association (SAUS) ... AHSA
Art History and Archaeology (SAUS) ... AHA
Art in America [*A publication*] (BRI) ... Art Am
Art Index ... ArtI
Art Information Center (EA) ... AIC
Art Institute of Chicago ... AIC
Art Institute of Chicago, Chicago, IL [*Library symbol*] [*Library of Congress*] (LCLS) ... ICA
Art Institute of Fort Lauderdale, Fort Lauderdale, FL [*Library symbol*] [*Library of Congress*] (LCLS) ... FFIAI
Art Institute of Light (EA) ... AIL
Art Journal [*A publication*] (BRI) ... Art J
Art Leather [*Abbreviation of artificial*] [*Visual material*] (WDMC) ... art
Art Libraries Society [*British*] (BI) ... ARLIS
Art Libraries Society of North America (SAUO) ... ARLIS/NA
Art Libraries Society/North America (SAUO) ... ARLIS/NA
Art Master's Certificate ... AMC
Art Master's Teaching Certificate [*British*] ... AMTC
Art Material Club [*Later, AMMA*] (EA) ... AMC
Art Material Club (SAUO) ... AMC
Art Material Manufacturers Association [*Defunct*] (EA) ... AMMA
Art Metalware Manufacturers' Association [*British*] (DBA) ... AMMA
Art Museum Association of America (EA) ... AMAA
Art Museum Development Association (NFD) ... AMDA
Art Museum of Princeton University, Princeton, NJ [*Library symbol*] [*Library of Congress*] (LCLS) ... NjP-A
Art Museum of South Texas, Corpus Christi, TX [*Library symbol*] [*Library of Congress*] (LCLS) ... TxCcMST
Art Patrons Association of America (EA) ... APAA
Art Reference Libraries of Ohio (SAUO) ... ARLO
Art Research Libraries of Ohio [*Library network*] ... ARLO
Art Resources in Collaboration (EA) ... ARC
Art Self-Concept Inventory (EDAC) ... ASCI
Art Services Grants [*British*] ... ASG
Art Services International (SAUO) ... ASI
Art Society of New South Wales (SAUO) ... ASNSW
Art Students' League of New York (EA) ... ASLNY

Art Teacher's Certificate [*British*] — ATC
Art Teachers Certificate (SAUS) — ATC
Art Teachers Diploma (SAUS) — ATD
Art Teacher's Diploma [*British*] — ATD
Art Teacher's Diploma [*British*] — ATDip
Art Therapist, Registered — ATR
Art Velum [*Abbreviation of artificial*] [*Visual material*] (WDMC) — art
Art Vocabulary [*Test*] (TES) — AV
Art Workers Coalition (SAUO) — AWC
Art Workers Guild (EAIO) — AWG
Arta [*Djibouti*] [*Seismograph station code, US Geological Survey*] [*Closed*] (SEIS) — ART
Arta Group [*NYSE symbol*] (TTSB) — ATA
Arta Observatory [*Djibouti*] (SEIS) — ARO
Artac [*Spain*] [*FAA designator*] (FAAC) — AVS
ARTADS Requirements Coordinating Committee — ARCC
Artagraph Reproduction Technology [*NASDAQ symbol*] (SAG) — XARO
Artbibliographies Modern [*Database*] [*Clio Press Ltd.*] [*Information service or system*] (CRD) — ABM
ARTCC Maintenance Control Center [*FAA*] (TAG) — AMCC
Artem-Avia [*Ukraine*] [*FAA designator*] (FAAC) — ABA
artenoventricular node (SAUS) — av node
ARTEP Mission Training Plan (SAUS) — AMTP
ARTEP [*Army Training and Evaluation Program*] **Mission Training Plan** (INF) — AMTP
Arteria [*Artery*] [*Latin*] — A
Arteria Basilaris Thrombose [*Medicine*] (DB) — ABT
Arteria/Deep Venous (SAUS) — A/DV
arterial (SAUS) — art
Arterial [*Medicine*] (MELL) — ART
Arterial Blood [*Medicine*] (MAE) — a
Arterial Blood Gas [*Medicine*] — ABG
Arterial Blood Pressure [*Medicine*] — ABP
Arterial Blood Sampler [*Medicine*] (DB) — ABS
Arterial Cannulation Support [*Cardiology*] (DAVI) — ACS
Arterial Carbon Dioxide Pressure (SAUS) — PaCO2
Arterial Carbon Dioxide Pressure, Tension [*Medicine*] (MAE) — $Paco_2$
Arterial Deep Venous (SAUS) — ADV
Arterial Diagnostic Unit [*Medicine*] (DB) — ADU
Arterial Diastolic Hypertension [*Medicine*] (MELL) — ADH
Arterial Filter (DB) — AF
Arterial Flow Rate — AFR
Arterial Gas Embolism — AGE
Arterial Hypertension [*Medicine*] — AH
Arterial in the Blood Phase [*Medicine*] (DAVI) — A
Arterial Insufficiency of the Lower Extremities [*Medicine*] — AILE
Arterial Mean (MELL) — AM
Arterial Occlusive Disease [*Medicine*] — AOD
Arterial Oxygen Pressure (MAE) — PAO_2
Arterial Oxygen Pressure (WDAA) — PAO2
Arterial Oxygen Saturation (SAUS) — SaO2
Arterial Oxygen Saturation [*Medicine*] (DAVI) — SO_2
Arterial Partial Pressure of Oxygen [*Medicine*] (DAVI) — PaO_2
Arterial pH [*Hydrogen ion concentration*] [*Medicine*] (DAVI) — PHA
Arterial Premature Beat [*Cardiology*] — APB
Arterial Premature Contraction [*Cardiology*] — APC
Arterial Presssure [*Medicine*] (DHSM) — AP
Arterial Pressure Index [*Medicine*] (MELL) — API
Arterial Pulse Wave Transducer — APWT
Arterial Road (SAUS) — ARd
Arterial Smooth Muscle Cell [*Medicine*] (MELL) — ASMC
arterial to Alveolar oxygen ratio (SAUS) — a/A
Arterial Vascular Engineering [*NASDAQ symbol*] (TTSB) — AVEI
Arterial Vascular Engineering, Inc. [*Associated Press*] (SAG) — ArtVasc
Arterial Vascular Engineering, Inc. [*NASDAQ symbol*] (SAG) — AVEI
Arterialized Capillary Blood [*Medicine*] (AAMN) — ACB
Arterial/Venous [*Ratio in fundi*] [*Ophthalmology*] (DAVI) — A:V
Arteries [*Medicine*] (DMAA) — AA
Arteries (ADWA) — aa
arteries (SAUS) — aa
Arterio Venous Filstula (SAUS) — AVF
Arteriocoronarer Bypass (SAUS) — ACB
Arterio/Deep Venous [*Medicine*] — A/DV
Arteriofemoral Bypass Graft [*Medicine*] — AFBG
Arteriolar [*Medicine*] (DAVI) — A
Arteriolar Nephrosclerosis [*Medicine*] (MELL) — ANS
Arteriole/Veinule ratio (SAUS) — A/V
Arteriolonephrosclerosis [*Urology*] — ANS
Arteriosclerosis [*Medicine*] — AS
Arteriosclerosis [*or Arteriosclerotic*] [*Medicine*] — ASC
Arteriosclerosis [*Cardiology*] (DAVI) — ASCL
Arteriosclerosis [*Medicine*] (MAE) — ATS
Arteriosclerosis Obliterans [*Medicine*] — ASO
Arteriosclerosis Obliterans [*Cardiology*] (DAVI) — ASOblit
Arteriosclerosis, Thrombosis and Vascular Biology (SAUS) — ATVB
Arteriosclerosis, Thrombosis, and Vascular Biology: Journal of the American Heart Association (SAUO) — ATVB
arteriosclerosistic (SAUS) — asc
Arteriosclerotic Brain Syndrome [*Cardiology and neurology*] (DAVI) — ASBS
Arteriosclerotic Cardiovascular Disease (ADWA) — ACVD
Arteriosclerotic Cardiovascular Disease [*Cardiology*] — ASCVD
Arteriosclerotic Cardiovascular Renal Disease [*Medicine*] (DAVI) — ACVRD
Arteriosclerotic Cardiovascular Renal Disease [*Medicine*] (DAVI) — ASCVRD
Arteriosclerotic Coronary Artery Disease [*Cardiology*] (MAE) — ASCAD
Arteriosclerotic Dementia [*Medicine*] (MELL) — ASD
Arteriosclerotic Heart Disease [*Cardiology*] — AHD
Arteriosclerotic Heart Disease [*Cardiology*] — ASHD
Arteriosclerotic Nephritis [*Medicine*] (DMAA) — ASN
Arteriosclerotic Occlusive Disease [*Medicine*] (MELL) — AOD
Arteriosclerotic Peripheral Vascular Disease [*Medicine*] (MEDA) — ASPVD
Arteriosclerotic Peripheral Vascular Occlusive Disease (SAUS) — APVOD
Arteriosclerotic Renal Vascular Disease [*Medicine*] — ARVD
Arteriosclerotic Vascular [*or Vessel*] **Disease** [*Cardiology*] (DAVI) — ASVD
Arterio/Superficial Venous [*Medicine*] (MAE) — A/SV
Arteriosuperficial Venous (SAUS) — A-S V
Arteriovenous [*Medicine*] — AV
Arteriovenous Anastomosis [*Medicine*] — AVA
Arteriovenous Fistula [*Medicine*] — AVF
Arteriovenous Internal Mammary [*Fistula*] [*Cardiology*] (DAVI) — A-V IMA
Arteriovenous Malformation [*Medicine*] (CPH) — ARM
Arteriovenous Malformation [*Medicine*] — AVM
ArterioVenous Malformation (SAUS) — AVM
Arteriovenous Malformation (MELL) — AVMF
Arteriovenous Oxygen Content Difference [*Medicine*] (DAVI) — $C(a\text{-}v)O_2$
Arteriovenous Oxygen Difference [*Medicine*] (MAE) — $A\text{-}VO_2$
Arteriovenous Oxygen Differnce [*Biochemistry*] (DAVI) — $AV\ DO_2$
Arteriovenous Oxygen Saturation Difference [*Medicine*] (DMAA) — AVDO
Arteriovenous Shunt [*Cardiology*] — AVS
Arteriovenous Shunt (ADWA) — A-V Shunt
Artery [*or Arterial*] — ART
Artery — ARTRY
Artery and Nerve [*Cardiology*] (DAVI) — A/N
Artesia, MS [*FM radio station call letters*] — WQNN
Artesia, MS [*FM radio station call letters*] (RBYB) — WSMS-FM
Artesia, NM [*Location identifier*] [*FAA*] (FAAL) — ATS
Artesia, NM [*AM radio station call letters*] — KSVP
Artesia, NM [*FM radio station call letters*] — KTZA
Artesia Public Library, Artesia, NM [*OCLC symbol*] (OCLC) — ANM
Artesia Public Library, Artesia, NM [*Library symbol*] [*Library of Congress*] (LCLS) — NmAr
Artesia Public Library, Artesia, NM [*Library symbol*] [*Library of Congress*] (LCLS) — NmArP
Artesian Resources Corp. [*Associated Press*] (SAG) — ArtesRes
Artesian Resources Corp. [*NASDAQ symbol*] (SAG) — ARTN
Artesian Resources'A' [*NASDAQ symbol*] (TTSB) — ARTNA
Artesian Well Lease (SAUS) — AWL
Artesyn Technologies [*NASDAQ symbol*] [*Formerly, Computer Products*] — ATSN
Arther Young (SAUS) — AY
Arthmetic Ratio (BARN) — Ar R
Arthritic (SAUS) — ARTH
Arthritic Dose [*Medicine*] (BABM) — AD
Arthritis (DMAA) — arth
Arthritis and Musculoskeletal and Skin Diseases Database [*National Arthritis and Musculoskeletal and Skin Diseases Information Clearinghouse*] [*Information service or system*] (CRD) — AMS
Arthritis and Rheumatic Disease [*Medicine*] (DAVI) — ARD
Arthritis and Rheumatic Diseases Abstracts [*A publication*] — ARD
Arthritis and Rheumatic Diseases Abstracts (SAUS) — ARD Abstracts
Arthritis and Rheumatism Branch — ARB
Arthritis and Rheumatism Council (SAUO) — ARC
Arthritis and Rheumatism Council for Research [*British*] (IRUK) — ARC
Arthritis and Rheumatism Council for Research (SAUO) — ARCR
Arthritis and Rheumatism Council for Research in Great Britain and the Commonwealth (SAUO) — ARC
Arthritis and Rheumatism Foundation [*Later, Arthritis Foundation*] — ARF
Arthritis and Rheumatism (journ.) (SAUS) — Arthritis Rheum
Arthritis Care [*An association*] (EAIO) — AC
Arthritis Care Association [*British*] — ACA
Arthritis Foundation (EA) — AF
Arthritis Foundation of Australia (Australian Capital Territory) — AFA(ACT)
Arthritis Foundation of Australia, Queensland — AFAQ
Arthritis Foundation of New South Wales [*Australia*] — AFNSW
Arthritis Foundation of South Australia — AFSA
Arthritis Foundation of Tasmania [*Australia*] — AFT
Arthritis Foundation of Victoria [*Australia*] — AFV
Arthritis Foundation of Western Australia — AFWA
Arthritis Health Professions Association (EA) — AHPA
Arthritis Impact Measurement Scales [*Medicine*] — AIMS
Arthritis Information Clearinghouse [*Public Health Service*] (EA) — AIC
Arthritis Pain Formula [*Medicine*] (DB) — APF
Arthritis Rehabilitation Center (EA) — ARC
Arthritis Society, Winnipeg, Manitoba [*Library symbol*] [*National Library of Canada*] (NLC) — MWAS
Arthritis Society, Winnipeg, MB, Canada [*Library symbol*] [*Library of Congress*] (LCLS) — CaMWAS
Arthritis Syphilitica Deformans [*Medicine*] (DB) — ASD
Arthritis-Dermatitis Syndrome [*Medicine*] (MELL) — ADSD
ArthroCare Corp. [*NASDAQ symbol*] (TTSB) — ARTC
ArthroCare Corp. [*Associated Press*] (SAG) — ArthroC
Arthrodentosteodysplasia [*Medicine*] (DMAA) — ADOD
Arthrogryposis Association (EA) — AA
Arthrogryposis Multiplex Congenita [*Medicine*] (MEDA) — AMC
Arthroper Oblong Acetabular Cup [*Medicine*] (MELL) — AOAC
Arthropoda (SAUS) — Arth
Arthropod-Borne [*Also, ARBOR*] [*Virology*] — ARBO
Arthropod-Borne [*Also, ARBO*] [*Virology*] — ARBOR
Arthropod-Borne Animal Diseases Research Laboratory [*Department of Agriculture*] (GRD) — ABADRL
Arthropod-Borne Virus [*Medicine*] (DMAA) — ABV
Arthropods of La Selva [*Costa Rica*] — ALAS

Arthroscopically-Assisted Reduction and Internal Fixation [*Medicine*] (MELL) ... ARIF
Arthroscopie Belge - Belgische Arthroscopie. Belgian Arthroscopy Association (SAUO) ... ABA
Arthroscopy [*Orthopedics*] (DAVI) ... arthro
Arthroscopy Association of North America (EA) ... AANA
Arthrotomy & Arthroscopy [*Medicine*] (MELL) ... A&A
Arthur Adaptation of the Leiter International Performance Scale [*Psychology*] ... AALIPS
Arthur Andersen & Co., Carolinas Central Library, Charlotte, NC [*Library symbol*] [*Library of Congress*] (LCLS) ... NcCA
Arthur Anderson & Co., Portland, OR [*Library symbol*] [*Library of Congress*] (LCLS) ... OrPAA
Arthur Brown's Compendious View of the Civil Law [*A publication*] (DLA) ... Bro (A) CL
Arthur Community School District, Arthur, IL [*Library symbol*] [*Library of Congress*] (LCLS) ... IArtSD
Arthur D. Little [*Commercial firm*] (NITA) ... ADL
Arthur D. Little Inc. (SAUO) ... ADL
Arthur D. Little, Inc. (SAUO) ... ADL
Arthur D. Little, Inc. [*Cambridge, MA*] [*Research code symbol*] ... ADL
Arthur D. Little, Inc. ... ALI
Arthur D. Little, Inc. [*Research code symbol*] ... NSC
Arthur D. Little, Inc., Cambridge, MA [*OCLC symbol*] (OCLC) ... ADL
Arthur D. Little, Inc., Cambridge, MA [*Library symbol*] [*Library of Congress*] (LCLS) ... MCA
Arthur D. Little, Inc., Cambridge, MA [*Library symbol*] [*Library of Congress*] (LCLS) ... MCAL
Arthur D. Little Research Institute (SAUO) ... ADLRI
Arthur Daniels Midland ... ADM
Arthur District High School, Arthur, ON, Canada [*Library symbol*] [*Library of Congress*] (LCLS) ... CaOAtD
Arthur District High School, Arthur, Ontario [*Library symbol*] [*National Library of Canada*] (NLC) ... OARD
Arthur G. McKee & Co. (SAUO) ... MKE
Arthur G. McKee & Co., Cleveland, OH [*Library symbol*] [*Library of Congress*] (LCLS) ... OCIAM
Arthur Johnson Memorial Library, Raton, NM [*OCLC symbol*] (OCLC) ... AJM
Arthur Johnson Memorial Library, Raton, NM [*Library symbol*] [*Library of Congress*] (LCLS) ... NmRa
Arthur Kill Correctional Facility (SAUO) ... AKCF
Arthur Machen Society [*Defunct*] (EA) ... AMS
Arthur, ND [*FM radio station call letters*] ... KCQV
Arthur, ND [*FM radio station call letters*] (BROA) ... KOCL-FM
Arthur Public Library, Arthur, IL [*Library symbol*] [*Library of Congress*] (LCLS) ... IArt
[*The*] **Arthur Ransome Society** [*British*] (EAIO) ... TARS
Arthur Vining Davis Corp. ... ARVIDA
Arthur Young & Company (SAUO) ... AYC
Arthurian Resources Ltd. [*Vancouver Stock Exchange symbol*] ... ATU
Arthurs Pass National Park (SAUS) ... APNP
Arthur's Town [*Bahamas*] [*Airport symbol*] (OAG) ... ATC
Arthur's Town, Eleuthera Island [*Bahamas*] [*ICAO location identifier*] (ICLI) ... MYCA
Arti [*Former USSR*] [*Seismograph station code, US Geological Survey*] (SEIS) ... ARU
Artial Septal Defect (SAUS) ... ASD
Artibus Asiae [*A publication*] ... Art Asiae
Artic Aerospace Laboratory [*Air Force*] ... AAL
Artic Lidar Observatory for Middle Atmospheric Research (SAUS) ... ALOMAR
Artic Military Environmental Cooperation [*U.S., Russia, and Norway study of radioactive waves*] ... AMEC
Artical Meristem (SAUS) ... AP
Artichoke Advisory Board (EA) ... AAB
Artichoke Italian Latent Virus [*Plant pathology*] ... AILV
Artichoke Mottled Crinkle Virus [*Plant pathology*] ... AMCV
Artichoke Vein Banding Virus [*Plant pathology*] ... AVBV
Artichoke Yellow Ringspot Virus [*Plant pathology*] ... AYRV
Article ... A
Article (AFM) ... ART
Article (NTIO) ... art
Article (WDAA) ... Art
Article 19 - International Centre Against Censorship [*British*] (EAIO) ... A19
Article 19 - International Centre on Censorship (EAIO) ... ICC
Article Delivery Over Network Information Systems (SAUS) ... ADONIS
Article Number Association (EAIO) ... ANA
Article Numbering Association [*Retailing*] [*British*] (NITA) ... ANA
Article Numbering Association of Ireland (EAIO) ... ANAI
Article Procurement with Online Local Ordering [*Document delivery system*] [*Telecommunications*] ... APOLLO
Article Type [*Database terminology*] (NITA) ... AT
Articled Clerk [*1867-68*] [*A publication*] (DLA) ... Artic Cl
Articled Clerk and Debater [*1866*] [*A publication*] (DLA) ... Artic Cl Deb
Articled Clerks' Journal and Examiner [*1879-81*] [*A publication*] (DLA) ... Artic Cl J Exam
Articles (SAUS) ... Arts
Articles for the Government of the Navy [*Obsolete*] ... AGN
Articles of Association (WDAA) ... AoA
Articles of War ... AOW
Articles of War ... AW
Articular Capsule [*Medicine*] (MELL) ... AC
Articular Cartilage [*Medicine*] (MELL) ... AC
Articular Chondrocalcinosis (DB) ... ACC
Articular Disc (SAUS) ... AD
Articular Disk (MELL) ... AD
Articular Layer (SAUS) ... AL
Articular Tubercle (SAUS) ... AT
Articulare [*Craniometric point*] ... AR
Articulated (DCTA) ... A
Articulated [*or Articulation*] (ADA) ... ART
Articulated ... ARTCLD
Articulated (SAUS) ... ARTIC
Articulated Computer Hierarchy (SAUS) ... ARCH
Articulated Computing Hierarchy [*British*] ... ARCH
Articulated Dump Truck [*Caterpillar Tractor Co.*] ... ADT
Articulated Flexible Appendage Subroutine (ACAE) ... AFAS
Articulated Instructional Media (SAA) ... AIM
Articulated Leg Platform [*Drilling technology*] ... ALP
Articulated Linear Thrust Engine [*Submarine technology*] ... ALTEN
Articulated Mirror System [*Astronomy*] ... AMS
Articulated Requirements Transaction System [*NASA*] ... ARTS
Articulated Subject Index (NITA) ... ASI
Articulated Total Body (MCD) ... ATB
Articulated Vehicle Dynamic Simulation Model (SAUS) ... AVDS Model
Articulated Vehicle Dynamic Simulator (PDAA) ... AVDS
Articulated-Frame Mechanical-Drive Vehicle [*Automotive engineering*] ... AMV
Articulating Dolly [*Trailer engineering*] ... A (Dolly)
Articulating Portable Foot Restraints ... APFR
Articulation (SAUS) ... ART
Articulation ... ARTIC
Articulation Control Subsystem [*NASA*] ... ARTC
Articulation Index ... AI
Articulation Loss of Consonants [*Audiology*] ... ALcons
Articulation Score [*Percentage of words correctly understood over a radio channel perturbed by interference*] [*Telecommunications*] ... AS
Articulation Screening Assessment [*Speech development test*] ... ASA
Articuli Cleri [*Articles of the Clergy*] [*Latin*] (DLA) ... Artic Cleri
Articuli Super Chartas [*Articles upon the Charters*] [*Latin*] (DLA) ... Artic Sup Chart
Articulos Industriales SA (SAUO) ... AISA
Articulotrochanteric Distance (PDAA) ... ATD
Artifact (SAUS) ... Art
Artifical Gravity Structure (SAUS) ... AGS
Artificer ... ART
Artificer (ADA) ... ARTIF
Artificer and Mechanical Staff Association (SAUO) ... AMSA
Artificer Candidate Course (SAUS) ... ACC
Artificer Candidate Induction Training (SAUS) ... ACIT
Artificer Diver [*British military*] (DMA) ... AD
Artificer Engineer (SAUS) ... Art E
Artificer Quartermaster Sergeant [*British*] ... AQMS
Artificer Sergeant Major [*British*] ... ASM
Artificial ... ARFL
Artificial (WDAA) ... art
Artificial (TEL) ... ART
Artificial (MSA) ... ARTF
Artificial ... ARTIF
Artificial (VRA) ... artif
Artificial ... ARTIFCL
Artificial Aerial (DEN) ... AA
Artificial Aquifer Data Collection System (SAUS) ... AQUIFR
Artificial Beta Cells [*Biochemistry*] (DAVI) ... ABC
Artificial Breeding Box ... ABB
Artificial Breeding Center, Victoria [*Australia*] ... ABCV
Artificial Cable Kit (SAUS) ... ACK
Artificial Cells, Blood Substitutes and Immobilization Biotechnology (SAUS) ... Artif Cells Blood Substit Immobil Biotechnol
Artificial Cerebrospinal Fluid [*Medicine*] ... ACSF
Artificial Circus Movement Tachycardia [*Medicine*] (DMAA) ... ACMT
Artificial Cloud Nucleation [*Rainmaking*] ... ACN
Artificial Compression Method ... ACM
Artificial Delay Line (IAA) ... ADL
Artificial Earth Pulse (SAUS) ... AEP
Artificial Earth Research and Orbiting Satellite (NATG) ... AEROS
Artificial Earth Satellite [*NASA*] ... AES
Artificial Earth Satellite Observation Program [*Navy*] ... AESOP
Artificial Endocrine Pancreas [*Medicine*] ... AEP
Artificial Erythrocyte [*Hematology*] ... AE
Artificial Flower Manufacturers' Association of Great Britain (BI) ... AFMA
Artificial Flower Manufacturers Board of Trade [*Defunct*] (EA) ... AFMBT
Artificial Gravity (NASA) ... AG
Artificial Heart [*Medicine*] ... AH
Artificial Heart Energy System ... AHES
Artificial Hip Joint (DMAA) ... AHJ
Artificial Horizon (MCD) ... AH
Artificial Horizon Indicator [*Aerospace*] (MCD) ... AHI
Artificial Illumination Center (SAUS) ... AIC
Artificial Illumination Centre (SAUO) ... AIC
Artificial Insemination [*Medicine*] ... AI
Artificial Insemination [*Medicine*] (HGAA) ... art insem
Artificial Insemination [*From George Orwell's novel, "1984"*] ... ARTSEM
Artificial Insemination by Donor [*Medicine*] ... AID
Artificial Insemination by Husband [*Medicine*] ... AIH
Artificial Insemination Centre [*Australia*] ... AIC
Artificial Insemination Centre (SAUO) ... AIC
Artificial Insemination Centre (SAUS) ... AI Centre
Artificial Insemination Homologous (SAUS) ... AIH
Artificial Insemination, Homologous [*Medicine*] (MAE) ... AIH
Artificial Insemination of Surrogate Mother [*Medicine*] (MELL) ... AISM
Artificial Intelligence [*Computer science*] ... AI
Artificial Intelligence (COE) ... AIR

Artificial Intelligence Advisory Committee (AUEG) .... AIAC
Artificial Intelligence and Expert System .... AL/ES
Artificial Intelligence and Robotics (SAUS) .... AI&R
Artificial Intelligence and Simulation of Behaviour (SAUO) .... AISB
Artificial Intelligence Applications Institute [British] .... AIAI
Artificial Intelligence Center (VERA) .... AIC
Artificial Intelligence Corporation (SAUO) .... AIC
Artificial Intelligence Diagnostics (ACAE) .... AID
Artificial Intelligence Expert System .... AIES
Artificial Intelligence for Engineering Design, Analysis, and Manufacturing
  [A publication] .... AI EDAM
Artificial Intelligence for Engineering Design, Analysis and Manufacturing
  (journ.) (SAUS) .... AI EDAM
Artificial Intelligence Group [MIT] .... AIG
Artificial Intelligence in Design (SAUS) .... AID
Artificial Intelligence in Medicine .... AIM
Artificial Intelligence in Real-Time Control [Symposium] (VERA) .... AIRTC
Artificial Intelligence Job Performance Aid [Army] .... AIJPA
Artificial Intelligence Knowledge Representation [Computer science]
  (NITA) .... AIKR
Artificial Intelligence Laboratory [Massachusetts Institute of Technology]
  [Research center] (RCD) .... AIL
Artificial Intelligence Module Test Bed (SAUS) .... AIMTB
Artificial Intelligence Project Office (SSD) .... AIPO
Artificial Intelligence Research [Computer science] (DAVI) .... AIR
Artificial Intelligence Research in Environmental Science (SAUS) .... AIRES
Artificial Intelligence Research Support [Program] [Computer science] .... AIRS
Artificial Intelligence Robot [Sony Corp.] .... AIBO
Artificial Intelligence Situation Assessment Focus (ACAE) .... AISAF
Artificial Intelligence Special Interest Group (SAUO) .... AISIG
Artificial Intelligence/Expert Systems (SAUS) .... AI/ES
Artificial Intelligence-Transaction Security Ltd. [British] (NITA) ...... AI-TSL
Artificial Interference to Transmission or Reception [Broadcasting] .... QRM
Artificial Interstitial Fluid (SAUS) .... AIF
Artificial Ionization Mirror (SAUS) .... AIM
Artificial Language (SAUS) .... AL
Artificial Life [Computer science] .... AL
Artificial Life Interactive Video Environment (SAUS) .... ALIVE
Artificial Limb (HGAA) .... AFL
Artificial Limb and Appliance Centre [British] .... ALAC
Artificial Line [Electricity] (OA) .... AL
Artificial Luminance [Theory proposed by James Clerk Maxwell in 1864] .... ALC
Artificial Luminous Cloud .... ALC
Artificial Lung-Expanding Compound [Medicine] (DB) .... ALEC
Artificial Methods Analyst (MCD) .... ARMAN
Artificial Neural Network (IDAI) .... ANN
Artificial Neural System .... ANS
Artificial Neural Vision Learning System (ACAE) .... ANVIL
Artificial Neuron .... ARTRON
Artificial Nutrition and Hydration [Medicine] .... ANH
artificial pacemaker ventricular rhythm (SAUS) .... apivr
Artificial Pacemaker-Induced Ventricular Rhythm [Medicine] (DMAA) .... APIVR
Artificial Personality .... AP
Artificial Pilot Phased Array (SAUS) .... APPA
Artificial Pneumothorax [Medicine] .... AP
Artificial Pneumothorax [Medicine] .... APN
Artificial Pond Water .... APW
Artificial Pond Water with additional Saccharose (SAUS) .... APWS
Artificial Programming Language (SAUS) .... APL
Artificial Pupil (SAA) .... AP
Artificial Respiration [Medicine] .... AR
Artificial Resynthesis Technology [Mechanical mouth used in dental
  research] .... ART
Artificial Rupture of Bag of Water [Medicine] (MELL) .... ARBOW
Artificial Rupture of Membrane [Medicine] (CPH) .... AROM
Artificial Rupture of Membranes [Medicine] .... ARM
Artificial Satellite .... AS
Artificial Satellite Time and Radio Orbit (MCD) .... ASTRO
Artificial Seawater .... ASW
Artificial Site Tuff [Geology] .... AST
Artificial Sweetener .... AS
Artificial Sweetner (MELL) .... ASW
Artificial Tears (SAUS) .... AT
Artificial Time History [Nuclear energy] (NRCH) .... ATH
Artificial Top Component [Virology] .... ATC
Artificial Traffic Equipment [Telecommunications] (NITA) .... ATE
Artificial Transmission Line .... ATL
Artificial Vagina [Veterinary science] (OA) .... AV
Artificial White Light .... AWL
Artificially Fed .... AF
Artificially Induced Aurora .... AIA
Artificially Intelligent Computer Performer .... AICP
Artificially Intelligent Devices and Techniques (NITA) .... ADAT
Artificially Random Self-Motivated (MHDI) .... ARASEM
Artificially Sweetened (HGAA) .... asw
Artigas [Uruguay] [Airport symbol] (OAG) .... ATI
Artigas/Aeropuerto Deptal [Uruguay] [ICAO location identifier] (ICLI) .... SUAG
Artikelen [Articles] [Dutch] (ILCA) .... artt
Artikkel-Indeks Database [Norwegian Center for Informatics] [Information
  service or system] .... AID
Artikkel-Indeks Tidsskrifter [Norwegian Center for Informatics] [Database] .... AITI
Artillerie [Artillery] [German] .... ArtI
Artilleriefuehrer [Division artillery commander] [German military - World War
  II] .... AF
Artillery .... A

Artillery .... ART
Artillery (ADWA) .... art
Artillery .... ARTIL
Artillery (SAUS) .... Artil
Artillery .... ARTILL
Artillery .... ARTLY
Artillery (AFM) .... ARTY
Artillery (MILB) .... arty
Artillery (CINC) .... AT
Artillery Air Observer (DNAB) .... AAO
Artillery Ammunition and Rocket Development Laboratory [Army]
  (MCD) .... AARDL
Artillery Ammunition Development Laboratory (SAUO) .... AADL
Artillery Ammunition Distributing Point (SAUS) .... Arty Am DP
Artillery Ammunition Rocket Development Laboratory (SAUS) .... AARDL
Artillery and Guided Missile School (SAUO) .... AGMS
Artillery and Missile School [Army] (MCD) .... AMS
Artillery & Mortar Fire Control Training Simulator (SAUS) .... AMFCTS
Artillery Ballistic Meteorological System (MCD) .... ABMS
Artillery Barge [Navy symbol] [Obsolete] .... APB
Artillery Battery Computer Support system (SAUS) .... ABACUS
artillery brigade (SAUO) .... arty Bde
Artillery Brigade (SAUO) .... Arty Brig
Artillery Clerk (SAUS) .... AC
Artillery College (SAUO) .... AC
Artillery Combat Observer Vehicle Simulator (SAUS) .... ACOVS
Artillery Command Reconnaissance Vehicle [Former USSR] .... ACRV
Artillery Communication Aural Protection System (SAUS) .... ACAPS
Artillery Computer System .... ACS
Artillery Computer Unit (SAUS) .... ACU
Artillery Concepts Test System (SAUS) .... ACTS
Artillery Control Console [British] .... ACC
Artillery Controller (NATG) .... AC
Artillery Controller (SAUS) .... AC
Artillery Corps (SAUO) .... AC
Artillery Counterfire Information [Army] (ADDR) .... ACIF
Artillery Delivered Antipersonnel Munition (SAUS) .... ADAM
Artillery Delivered Antipersonnel Munitions (MCD) .... ADAM
Artillery Delivered Expendable Jammer (SAUS) .... AD/XJAM
Artillery Destruction Program .... ADP
Artillery Destruction Programs (SAUS) .... ADPs
Artillery Direct Fire Trainer (AABC) .... ADFT
Artillery Division [Military] (MCD) .... AD
Artillery Engagement (SAUS) .... Arty engmt
Artillery Engagement Simulation System (MCD) .... ARES
Artillery Equipment School [British] (DAS) .... AES
Artillery Equipment School (SAUO) .... AES
Artillery Exercise (SAUO) .... ARTEX
Artillery Fire Control (SAUS) .... Arty FC
Artillery Fire Control System (SAUS) .... AFCS
Artillery Fire Control System (ACAE) .... FARCO
Artillery Fire Control Training Simulator (SAUS) .... AFCTS
Artillery Fire Data Computer (PDAA) .... AFDC
Artillery Fire Support Center (SAUS) .... AFSC
Artillery Flash Ranging [Army] (AABC) .... AFR
Artillery Forces Simulation Model (MCD) .... AFSM
Artillery Forward Observer .... AFO
Artillery Ground Burst Simulator (MCD) .... AGBS
Artillery Hunting Radar (SAUS) .... ARTHUR
Artillery Intelligence Officer [Army] .... AIO
Artillery Intelligence School (SAUS) .... AIS
Artillery Liaison Office [or Officer] (DNAB) .... ARTYLO
Artillery Liaison Officer (SAUS) .... Arty Ln O
Artillery Line Communications Equipment (SAUS) .... ALICE
Artillery Location Acoustic System (MCD) .... ALAS
Artillery Meteorological (SAUS) .... ARTYMEY
Artillery Meteorological System (SAUS) .... AMETS
Artillery Meteorological System (NATG) .... AMETS
Artillery Meteorological System (SAUS) .... AMS
Artillery Meteorological Team [Army] (ADDR) .... ARTYMET
Artillery, Mortars, Cruise Missiles, Antiradiation Missiles [Military] .... ARM
Artillery Observation (SAUS) .... AO
Artillery Observation Post [British military] (DMA) .... AOP
Artillery Observation Vehicle (SAUS) .... AOV
Artillery Observation Vehicle (SAUS) .... VOA
Artillery Officer (SAUS) .... AO
Artillery Park (SAUO) .... Arty Pk
Artillery Preparation (SAUS) .... Arty prepn
Artillery Preparation Fire (SAUS) .... APF
Artillery Procedures Working Party (SAUO) .... APWP
Artillery Re-arm Module (SAUS) .... ARM
Artillery Reconnaissance (SAUS) .... Arty R
Artillery Reconnaissance [British and Canadian] [World War II] .... arty R
Artillery Registration/Adjustment System [ARRADCOM] (MCD) .... ARADS
Artillery Registration/Adjustment System [ARRADCOM] (MCD) .... ARAS
Artillery Repair Truck [British] .... ART
Artillery Resources Ltd. [Vancouver Stock Exchange symbol] .... ARY
Artillery Saturation Rocket System [Army] .... ASTROS
Artillery School (SAUO) .... ArtS
Artillery School (SAUO) .... Arty Sch
Artillery School (SAUS) .... TAS
Artillery School Antiaircraft and Guided Missile Branch (SAUO) .... ASAAGMB
Artillery Siege Train Traction Engine [British] .... ASTTE
Artillery Spotting Division [Air Force] .... ASD
Artillery Supply Truck [British] .... AST

Artillery Survey vehicle (SAUS) .... AT-ST
Artillery Systems Cooperation Activities (SAUS) .... ASCA
Artillery Systems Research Programme (SAUS) .... ASRP
Artillery Tactical Automated Fire System (SAUS) .... ATAFS
Artillery Tactical Terminal .... ATT
Artillery Target Intelligence (MCD) .... ATI
Artillery Target Location Vehicle (SAUS) .... ATLV
Artillery Test Board [Army] .... ATB
Artillery Towing Light Auxiliary System [Army] (MCD) .... ATLAS
Artillery Tractor [British] .... AT
Artillery Training (SAUS) .... AT
Artillery Vehicle Park (SAUO) .... AVP
Artillery Volunteer Corps .... AVC
Artillery Volunteer Corps [British] .... AVC
Artillery Volunteers (SAUO) .... AV
Artillery Volunteers [Military] (WDAA) .... AV
Artillery Weapons Data Transmission System (MCD) .... AWDATS
Artillery-Delivered Antipersonnel Mine (RDA) .... ADAM
Artillery-Delivered Antitank Mine (MCD) .... ADATM
Artillery-Delivered Anti-Tank Mine (SAUS) .... ADATM
Artillery-Delivered Expendable Jammer [Army] .... ADEXJAM
Artillery-Delivered Multipurpose Submunition (AABC) .... ARDEMS
Artillery-Fired Atomic Projectile .... AFAP
Artillery-Launched Television System (PDAA) .... ALTEL
Artillery-Locating RADAR .... ALR
Artillery/Ordnance (MCD) .... AO
Artina Resources Ltd. [Vancouver Stock Exchange symbol] .... ARS
ARTINS [Army Terrain Information System] Requirements Coordination Committee (RDA) .... ARCC
Artisan (SAUS) .... Art
Artisan .... ARTSN
Artisan Quartermaster Sergeant [British] .... AQMS
Artisan Works Co. [British and Canadian] [World War II] .... art wks coy
artisan works company (SAUO) .... art wks coy
Artisans Order of Mutual Protection [Philadelphia, PA] (EA) .... AOMP
Artisoft, Inc. [Associated Press] (SAG) .... Artsft
Artisoft, Inc. [NASDAQ symbol] (SPSG) .... ASFT
Artisoft LAN [Linked Access Network] Interface Chip for Ethernet [Artisoft, Inc.] [Computer science] (PCM) .... ALICE
Artist [MARC relator code] [Library of Congress] (LCCP) .... art
Artist .... ART
Artist [Record label] .... Atst
Artist and Repertoire (WDMC) .... A & R
Artist and Repertory Man (SAUS) .... A&R Man
Artist Blacksmith Association of North America (EA) .... ABANA
Artist Direct [Record label] .... AD
Artist in Residence (BARN) .... AIR
Artistic (SAUS) .... art
Artistic .... ARTSTC
Artistic Crafts Series of Technical Handbooks [A publication] .... ACSTH
Artistic Greetings [NASDAQ symbol] (TTSB) .... ARTG
Artistic Greetings, Inc. [NASDAQ symbol] (NQ) .... ARTG
Artistic Greetings, Inc. [Associated Press] (SAG) .... ArtistG
Artistic License (EA) .... AL
Artistic Roller Skating Federation (EA) .... ARSF
Artist-Owned Label [Music] .... AOL
Artistry (SAUS) .... art
Artistry .... ARTSTRY
Artistry [Record label] .... Asty
Artists and Athletes Against Apartheid (EA) .... AAAA
Artists and Repertory (ADWA) .... A and R
Artists and Repertory (SAUS) .... AR
Artists Civil Rights Assistance Fund [Defunct] .... ACRAF
Artist's Collection (VRA) .... artist coll
Artists Confronting AIDS [An association] (EA) .... ACA
Artist's Diploma (PGP) .... AD
Artist's Diploma (PGP) .... ADP
Artists Equity Association [Later, NAEA] (EA) .... AEA
Artists Equity Fund [of the National Artists Equity Association] (EA) .... AEF
Artists' Fellowship (EA) .... AF
Artists for Nuclear Disarmament [Defunct] (EA) .... AND
Artists for Survival/Artists for Mideast Peace (EA) .... AFS/AFMEP
Artists' General Benevolent Institution [British] .... AGBI
Artists Guild .... AG
Artists' Guild of Australia .... AGA
Artists Guild of Chicago [Defunct] (EA) .... AGC
Artists Guild of New York (SAUO) .... AG
Artists Guild of New York (EA) .... AGNY
Artists in Bark Association of Australia .... AIBAA
Artists in Christian Testimony (EA) .... ACT
Artists in Christian Testimony (SAUS) .... AC-T
Artists in Stained Glass [Canada] .... AISG
Artists in the Schools Program (EDAC) .... AIS
Artists' Legal Advice Services (AC) .... ALAS
Artists of Chelsea (SAUO) .... AOC
Artist's Proof .... AP
Artist's Proof (ADA) .... ART PF
Artists' Representatives Association [Defunct] (EA) .... ARA
Artists Rights Association [Defunct] .... ARA
Artists' Service Bureau (NTCM) .... ASB
Artists Space (EA) .... AS
Artists Technical Research Institute (EA) .... ATRI
Artists United Against Apartheid (EA) .... AUAA
Artium Baccalaureate [Bachelor of Arts] .... AB
Artium Elegantiam Doctor [Doctor of Fine Arts] .... AED

Artium Liberalium Magister [Master of the Liberal Arts] .... ALM
Artium Magister [Master of Arts] .... AM
Artium Magister [Master of Arts] in Social Work (IIA) .... AMSW
Artlantic Offshore Fish and Lobster Association (USDC) .... AOFLA
ARTnews [A publication] (BRI) .... Art N
Artra Group, Inc. [Associated Press] (SAG) .... Artra
Artra Group, Inc. [NYSE symbol] (SPSG) .... ATA
Arts Action Australia [An association] .... AAA
Arts and Architecture (journ.) (SAUS) .... A&A
Arts and Business Council (EA) .... ABC
Arts and Crafts Exhibition Society (SAUO) .... ACES
Arts and Crafts Movement [c. 1860-1920] .... A & C
Arts and Crafts Society of New South Wales [Australia] .... ACSNSW
Arts and Crafts Society of Victoria [Australia] .... ACSV
Arts and Entertainment (ADWA) .... A&E
Arts and Entertainment Channel (SAUS) .... A&E
Arts & Entertainment Network [Cable-television system] .... A & E
Arts and Entertainment Network (SAUS) .... A&E Network
Arts & Entertainment Training Council (WDAA) .... AETC
Arts and Humanities .... AH
Arts and Humanities Data Service [British] (TELE) .... AHDS
Arts and Industry (SAUS) .... A&I
Arts and Letters Club, Toronto [1908] [Canada] (NGC) .... ALCT
Arts and Letters Club, Toronto, ON, Canada [Library symbol] [Library of Congress] (LCLS) .... CaOTAL
Arts and Letters Club, Toronto, Ontario [Library symbol] [National Library of Canada] (NLC) .... OTAL
Arts and Sciences .... A & S
Arts Anonymous (EA) .... AA
Arts Asiatiques (journ.) (SAUS) .... Ar As
Arts Baccalaureate (SAUS) .... AB
Arts Bachelor in Library Science (SAUS) .... ABLS
Arts, Bachelor of (PROS) .... AB
Arts Centre Group (EAIO) .... ACG
Arts Council (EAIO) .... AC
Arts Council (SAUO) .... AC
Arts Council of America (SAUO) .... ACA
Arts Council of Australia .... ACA
Arts Council of Great Britain (EAIO) .... AC
Arts Council of Great Britain .... ACGB
Arts Council of Northern Ireland (WDAA) .... ACNI
Arts Council of Wales (WDAA) .... ACW
Arts Councils of America [Later, American Council for the Arts] .... ACA
Arts Create Excellent Schools [Program] .... ACES
Arts Development Association [British] (DBA) .... ADA
Arts Documentation Service [Australian Council Library] [Information service or system] .... ARTS
[The] Arts, Education, and Americans (EA) .... AEA
Arts, Education, and Americans (SAUO) .... AEA
Arts Education for a Multicultural Society (AIE) .... AEMS
Arts et Metiers [Arts and Crafts] [French] .... A et M
Arts for a New Nicaragua (EA) .... ANN
Arts for Everyone [An association] (WDAA) A4E
Arts Foundation for Research in the Afro-American Creative Arts (SAUO) .... FRAC
Arts in Danger [An association] [British] (DI) .... AID
Arts International (EA) .... AI
Arts Law Australia [A publication] .... ALA
Arts Management Training Initiative, Scotland (AIE) .... AMTIS
Arts of the Church [A publication] .... AC
Arts Recognition and Talent Search [National Foundation for Advancement in the Arts] .... ARTS
Arts Society of Tasmania (SAUO) .... AST
Arts Training New South Wales [An association] [Australia] .... ATN
Art's Way Manufacturing Co. [Associated Press] (SAG) .... ArtWay
Art's Way Manufacturing Co., Inc. [NASDAQ symbol] (NQ) .... ARTW
Art's Way Mfg [NASDAQ symbol] (TTSB) .... ARTW
Arturo Rodriguez Martinez [Mexico] [FAA designator] (FAAC) .... MTI
Arturo Toscanini (SAUO) .... ATS
Arturo Toscanini Society (EA) .... ATS
Artwork (WDMC) .... art
Artwork (WDMC) .... A/W
Artwork Delivery System (SAUS) .... ADS
Artwork-Interactive Design System (SAUS) .... AIDS
Artwork-Interactive Design System (MCD) .... AIDS
Arua [Uganda] [Airport symbol] (AD) .... AAU
Arua [Uganda] [ICAO location identifier] (ICLI) .... HUAR
Arua [Uganda] [Airport symbol] (OAG) .... RUA
Aruada, CO [AM radio station call letters] .... KQXI
Aruba [ANSI three-letter standard code] (CNC) .... ABW
Aruba [Netherlands Antilles] [Airport symbol] .... AUA
Aruba [ANSI two-letter standard code] (CNC) .... AW
Aruba [Aircraft nationality and registration mark] (FAAC) P4
Aruba, Bonaire, and Curacao [Islands] .... ABC
Aruba, Bonaire, and Curacao Islands (NTIO) .... ABC Islands
Arubaanse Volks Partij [Aruban People's Party] [Netherlands Antilles] [Political party] (PPW) .... AVP
Arubair [Aruba] [ICAO designator] (FAAC) .... ARB
Aruban Florin [Monetary unit] (ODBW) .... Af
Arum Pin [Medicine] (MELL) .... AP
Arunachal People's Conference [India] [Political party] (PPW) .... APC
Arundell on the Law of Mines [A publication] (DLA) .... Arun Mines
Arusha [Tanzania] [Airport symbol] (AD) .... ARY
Arusha [Tanzania] [ICAO location identifier] (ICLI) .... HTAR
Arusha National Park (SAUS) .... ANP

Arussi Liberation Army [Ethiopia] (AF) ... ALA
Arutua [French Polynesia] [ICAO location identifier] (ICLI) ... NTGU
ARV Assisted Living [NASDAQ symbol] (TTSB) ... ARVI
ARV Assisted Living [AMEX symbol] (SG) ... SRS
ARV Assisted Living, Inc. [NASDAQ symbol] (SAG) ... ARVI
ARV Assisted Living, Inc. [Associated Press] (SAG) ... ARVLiv
Arvada, CO [AM radio station call letters] (BROA) ... KAYK-AM
Arvada Public Library, Arvada, CO [Library symbol] [Library of Congress] (LCLS) ... CoAr
Arvika [Sweden] [ICAO location identifier] (ICLI) ... ESKV
Arvin, CA [FM radio station call letters] (BROA) ... KBDS-FM
Arvin Industries [NYSE symbol] (SAG) ... ARV
Arvin Industries, Inc. [Associated Press] (SAG) ... Arvin
Arwick International Resources Ltd. [Vancouver Stock Exchange symbol] ... AWK
Aryepiglottic [Medicine] (DAVI) ... AE
Aryl [Chemistry] ... Ar
Aryl Hydrocarbon Hydroxylase [An enzyme] ... AHH
Aryl Hydrocarbon Receptor [Biochemistry] ... AHR
Aryl Hydrocarbon Receptor-Interacting Protein ... AIP
Arylated Poly(phenylene Sulfide) [Organic chemistry] ... APPS
Arylene Isopropylidene Polymers [Organic chemistry] ... AIP
Arylhydrocarbon-Receptor Nuclear Translocator [Genetics] ... ARNT
Arylhydroxamic(acyltransferase) [An enzyme] ... AHAT
Arylhydroxamicacyltransferase (SAUS) ... AHAT
Arylsulfatase A (DMAA) ... ARSA
Arylsulfatase C (DMAA) ... ARSC
Arylsulfatase-A (MAE) ... ASA
Aryt Inds Ltd [NASDAQ symbol] (TTSB) ... ARYTF
Aryt Industries Ltd. [Associated Press] (SAG) ... ArytInd
Aryt Optronics Industries Ltd. [NASDAQ symbol] ... ARYT
Arzaero [Azerbaijan] [FAA designator] (FAAC) ... AZO
Arzan International Ltd. [Associated Press] (SAG) ... ArzanInt
Arzan International Ltd. [NASDAQ symbol] (SAG) ... ARZN
Arzan International Ltd. [NASDAQ symbol] (SAG) ... ARZW
Arzan Intl(1991) Ltd [NASDAQ symbol] (TTSB) ... ARZNF
Arzan Intl(1991) Wrrt [NASDAQ symbol] (TTSB) ... ARZWF
Arzana [United Arab Emirates] [ICAO location identifier] (ICLI) ... OMAR
As a Matter of Fact [Online dialog] ... AAMOF
AS Agriculture Bulletin. University of Alberta (journ.) (SAUS) ... AGBA
As Amended By [Army] ... AABY
As Ammended By (SAUS) ... AABY
A.S. Beck Shoe Corp. (SAUO) ... BEK
As Before ... AB
As Before (SAUS) ... AB
As Built Baseline (ACAE) ... ABB
As Built Hardware Reporting System (NAKS) ... ABHRS
As Design Changes Occur (MCD) ... ADCO
As Drawn (MSA) ... AD
A/S Eksportcinans 8.70% Pfd [NYSE symbol] (TTSB) ... EKPPr
A/S Eksportfinans [Export Finance] [NYSE symbol] (SPSG) ... EKP
A/S Eksportfinans [Export Finance] Capital Securities [Associated Press] (SAG) ... Eksprt
As Expeditiously as Practicable (COE) ... AEAP
As Far as I Can Recall (ADWA) ... AFAICR
As Far As I Can See [Online dialog] ... AFAICS
As Far as I Can Tell (ADWA) ... AFAICT
As Far As I Know [Internet language] [Computer science] ... AFAIK
As Far As I Know [Online dialog] ... AFAIR
As Far As I Know Today [Online dialog] ... AFAIKT
As Far as I Recall (ADWA) ... AFAIR
As Far As I Recall (SAUS) ... AFAIR
As Far As I Understand It (SAUS) ... AFAIUI
As Found (WDAA) ... A/F
As Generated (MCD) ... ASGEN
As Good As ... AGA
As I Mentioned Before (SAUS) ... AIMB
As I Said Before (SAUS) ... AISB
As I Understand It (SAUS) ... AIUI
As Interest May Accrue (SAUS) ... AIMA
As Interest May Appear [Insurance] ... AIMA
As It Was (or Were) (SAUS) ... AIW
As Late as Possible (PCM) ... ALAP
As Late as Reasonably Achievable (ADWA) ... ALARA
As Low as Possible [or Practical] (NRCH) ... ALAP
As Low As Practical (SAUS) ... ALAP
As Low as Reasonably Achievable [Radiation exposure] [Nuclear Regulatory Commission] ... ALARA
As Low as Reasonably Practicable [Radiation exposure] [Nuclear Regulatory Commission] ... ALARP
As Low as Technically Achievable (NUCP) ... ALATA
As Low as Technically and Economically Praticable (ABAC) ... ALATE
AS Lufttransport [Norway] [ICAO designator] (FAAC) ... LTR
As Manifested By [Medicine] (MELL) ... AMB
As Many As Possible (SAUS) ... AMAP
AS Morefly [Norway] [ICAO designator] (FAAC) ... MOR
As Much As Possible [Medicine] ... AMAP
As Needed (NRCH) ... A/N
AS Norving [Norway] [ICAO designator] (FAAC) ... NOR
As Often As Possible (DAVI) ... AOAP
As per List ... APL
As per List (MARI) ... apl
As Per List (SAUS) ... APL
As Planned Paris List (SAUS) ... APPL
As Planned Parts List (MCD) ... APPL
As Prescribed (AFM) ... AP

As Purchased ... AP
As Quickly As Possible (SAUS) ... AQAP
As Quoted [Business term] ... AQ
As Received ... AR
As Required (AFM) ... AR
As Required (MCD) ... ASR
As Required (ACAE) ... ASREQ
As Rolled [Technical drawings] (DAC) ... AR
As Soon As Possible [Internet language] [Computer science] ... ASAP
As Soon As Possible [Pronounced a-sap] (WDMC) ... asap
As Soon as Possible ... ASP
As Stated ... AS
As The Subject Says [Internet language] [Computer science] ... ATSS
As the World Turns [A television program] ... ATWT
As the World Turns Fan Club (EA) ... ATWTFC
As Their Respective Interests May Appear [Legal term] (ADA) ... ATRIMA
As Tolerated [Medicine] (CPH) ... as tol
As Tolerated (SAUS) ... AS TOL
As Trustee For [Banking] ... ATF
As We Informed You (SAUS) ... AWIY
As Well As (SAUS) ... AWA
As You Like It [Shakespearean work] ... AYL
As You Like It [Shakespearean drama] (BARN) ... AYLI
ASA [Former USSR] [ICAO designator] (FAAC) ... SPB
ASA, Air Starline, AG [Switzerland] [ICAO designator] (FAAC) ... ACR
ASA Holdings, Inc. [Associated Press] (SAG) ... ASA Hold
ASA Holdings, Inc. [NASDAQ symbol] (SAG) ... ASAI
ASA International Ltd. [NASDAQ symbol] (NQ) ... ASAA
ASA International Ltd. [Associated Press] (SAG) ... ASA Int
Asa Lafitte Stark Family Association [Defunct] (EA) ... ALSFA
ASA Ltd. [Formerly, American-South African Investment Co. Ltd.] [NYSE symbol] (SPSG) ... ASA
ASA Ltd. [Formerly, American-South African Investment Co. Ltd.] [Associated Press] (SAG) ... ASA Ltd
Asab [United Arab Emirates] [ICAO location identifier] (ICLI) ... OMAC
Asad Abad [Iran] [ICAO location identifier] (ICLI) ... OIHB
Asahi Brand Research (SAUS) ... ABR
Asahi Broadcasting Company (SAUO) ... ABC
Asahi Chemical Exchange Process [Nuclear energy] (NUCP) ... ACEP
Asahi New Cast [Metal fabrication] ... ANC
Asahi Technical Information System (SAUS) ... ATIS
Asahi Television News (SAUO) ... ATENE
ASAHI/America [NASDAQ symbol] (SG) ... ASAM
Asahi/America, Inc. [Associated Press] (SAG) ... AsahiAm
Asahi/America, inc. [NASDAQ symbol] (SAG) ... ASAM
Asahikawa [Japan] [Airport symbol] (OAG) ... AKJ
Asahikawa [Japan] [Seismograph station code, US Geological Survey] (SEIS) ... ASA
Asahikawa [Japan] [ICAO location identifier] (ICLI) ... RJCA
Asahikawa [Japan] [ICAO location identifier] (ICLI) ... RJEC
ASAM Patient Placement Criteria (SAUO) ... ASAM PPC
Asama [Japan] [Seismograph station code, US Geological Survey] (SEIS) ... ASM
Asamblea Majorera [Spain] [Political party] (EY) ... AM
Asamblea Nicaraguense de Unidad Democratica [Nicaraguan Assembly Democratic Unity] (PD) ... Anude
Asamera Minerals Ltd. [Toronto Stock Exchange symbol] ... AUA
Asante Technologies, Inc. [Associated Press] (SAG) ... Asante
Asante Technologies, Inc. [NASDAQ symbol] (SAG) ... ASNT
Asanteman Association (EA) ... AA
Asantle Technologies [NASDAQ symbol] (TTSB) ... ASNT
ASAP Air, Inc. (SAUS) ... SAP
ASAP and Computer Interface Unit ... ACIU
ASAP Interface Unit ... AIU
ASARCO, Inc. [Formerly, American Smelting & Refining Co.] [NYSE symbol] (SPSG) ... AR
ASARCO, Inc. [Formerly, American Smelting & Refining Co.] [Associated Press] (SAG) ... Asarco
Asarhaddon (BJA) ... Asarh
ASARS Deployable Processing Station (SAUS) ... ADPS
ASARS Exploitation Cell (SAUS) ... AEC
ASAS Data Recording and Summary System (SAUS) ... ADARS
ASAS Operator ID (SAUS) ... ASID
ASAS Program Office (SAUS) ... APO
Asatru Alliance (EA) ... AA
Asatru Free Assembly [Later, AA] (EA) ... AFA
Asau [Western Samoa] [ICAO location identifier] (ICLI) ... NSAU
ASB Financial [NASDAQ symbol] (TTSB) ... ASBR
ASB Financial Corp. [Associated Press] (SAG) ... ASB Fn
ASB Financial Corp. [NASDAQ symbol] (SAG) ... ASBP
Asbestos (MSA) ... A
Asbestos (KSC) ... ASB
Asbestos (VRA) ... asb
Asbestos ... ASBSTS
Asbestos Action Program [Environmental Protection Agency] (GFGA) ... AAP
Asbestos & Danville [AAR code] ... ASDA
Asbestos and Danville [Railroad] (MHDB) ... ASDE
Asbestos and Small Business Ombudsman [Environmental Protection Agency] ... ASBO
Asbestos Association (SAUO) ... AA
Asbestos Bodies ... AB's
Asbestos Body (DAVI) ... AB
Asbestos Cement [Technical drawings] ... AC
Asbestos Cement Board ... ACB
Asbestos Cement Manufacturers Association [British] (BI) ... ACMA
Asbestos Cement Product Producers Association (NTPA) ... ACPPA

Asbestos Cement Sheet (ADA) ACS
Asbestos Claims Council (EA) ACC
Asbestos Cloth Neck (OA) ACN
Asbestos Compensation Coalition (EA) ACC
Asbestos Containing Construction Material (ACAE) ACCM
Asbestos Containing Material ACM
Asbestos Contractor Tracking System [*Environmental Protection Agency*] (ERG) ACTS
Asbestos Coordinator (SAUO) AC
Asbestos Corp. Ltd. [*Toronto Stock Exchange symbol*] AB
Asbestos Hazard Emergency Response Act (SAUO) AHERA
Asbestos Hazard Emergency Response Act of 1986 AHERA
Asbestos Hill [*Canada*] [*Airport symbol*] [*Obsolete*] (OAG) YAF
Asbestos in Schools Hazard Abatement Act (SAUO) ASHAA
Asbestos in Schools Hazard Abatement Automated Information System (SAUS) ASHAAIS
Asbestos in Schools Tracking System (SAUS) ASTS
Asbestos Industries of America (EFIS) AIA
Asbestos Information Association [*Environmental science*] (COE) AIA
Asbestos Information Association/North America (EA) AIA/NA
Asbestos Information Centre (SAUS) AIC
Asbestos Information Centre Ltd. [*British*] (CB) AIC
Asbestos Information Committee (SAUO) AIC
Asbestos Information System (SAUS) AIS
Asbestos Inspection and Management Plan Assistance Program [*Environmental Protection Agency*] AIMPAP
Asbestos Institute (EA) AI
Asbestos Insulated Wire AIW
Asbestos Insulation Board (HEAS) AIB
Asbestos International Association [*British*] (EAIO) AIA
Asbestos Licensing Principal Inspector (HEAS) ALPI
Asbestos Licensing Regulations (HEAS) ASLIC
Asbestos Licensing Unit (HEAS) ALU
Asbestos Litigation Group (EA) ALG
Asbestos Lung Disease ALD
Asbestos Medical Surveillance Program [*Military*] (DNAB) AMSP
Asbestos Mill Board [*Technical drawings*] AMB
Asbestos Millboard (SAUS) AMB
Asbestos Pipe Producers Association (SAUO) APPA
Asbestos, PQ [*AM radio station call letters*] CJAN
Asbestos Related Illness ARI
Asbestos Removal and Treatment Contractors' Association [*Australia*] ARTCA
Asbestos Removal Contractors Association (EAIO) ARCA
Asbestos Rock (SAUS) Azrock
Asbestos Roof Shingles [*Technical drawings*] ARS
Asbestos Safety Equipment Manufacturer's Association (HEAS) ASEMA
Asbestos School Hazard Abatement Act (GFGA) ASHAA
Asbestos School Hazard Abatement Reauthorization Act [*Environmental Protection Agency*] (AEPA) ASHARA
Asbestos School Hazards Abatement Reauthorization Act (MEC) ASHARA
Asbestos Shingles AS
Asbestos Technical Institute (SAUO) ATI
Asbestos Textile Institute (EA) ATI
Asbestos Victims of America (EA) AVA
Asbestos Working Group (SAUO) AWG
Asbestos-Cement Board [*Technical drawings*] ACB
Asbestos-Cement Pressure [*Construction*] (DICI) ACP
Asbestos-Cement Products Association [*Defunct*] (EA) A-CPA
Asbestos-Containing Building Material (ERG) ACBM
Asbestos-Containing Waste Material (EPAT) ACWM
Asbestos-Covered Frame Building (GEOI) ASBCI
Asbestos-Covered frame building (SAUS) ASB CL
Asbestos-Covered Metal [*Technical drawings*] ACM
Asbestosis Research Council [*British*] ARC
As-Built Configuration File (MCD) ABCF
As-Built Configuration Lists ABCL
As-Built Configuration Record (NASA) ABCR
Asbury College (SAUS) AC
Asbury College, Wilmore, KY [*OCLC symbol*] (OCLC) KWW
Asbury College, Wilmore, KY [*Library symbol*] [*Library of Congress*] (LCLS) KyWA
Asbury, IA [*FM radio station call letters*] KIKR
Asbury, MO [*FM radio station call letters*] KWXD
Asbury Park Free Public Library, Asbury Park, NJ [*Library symbol*] [*Library of Congress*] (LCLS) NjAs
Asbury Park, NJ [*AM radio station call letters*] (BROA) WADB
Asbury Park, NJ [*AM radio station call letters*] WJLK
Asbury Park, NJ [*FM radio station call letters*] WJLK-FM
Asbury Park Press, Asbury Park, NJ [*Library symbol*] [*Library of Congress*] (LCLS) NjAsP
Asbury Park/Monmouth County [*New Jersey*] [*Airport symbol*] (OAG) ARX
Asbury Theological Seminary, Wilmore (SAUS) KyWAT12
Asbury Theological Seminary, Wilmore, KY [*OCLC symbol*] (OCLC) KAT
Asbury Theological Seminary, Wilmore, KY [*Library symbol*] [*Library of Congress*] (LCLS) KyWAT
ascarid (SAUS) asc
Ascazubi [*Ecuador*] [*ICAO location identifier*] (ICLI) SEAS
Ascencion De Guarayos [*Bolivia*] [*ICAO location identifier*] (ICLI) SLAS
Ascend (SAUS) ASC
Ascend Communications [*NASDAQ symbol*] (TTSB) ASND
Ascend Communications, Inc. [*Associated Press*] (SAG) Ascend
Ascend Communications, Inc. [*NASDAQ symbol*] (SAG) ASND
Ascend Inverse Multiplexing [*Computer science*] (VERA) AIM
Ascend Tunnel Management Protocol (SAUS) ATMP
Ascendance Submission (SAUS) AS
Ascendance-Submission [*Psychology*] AS
Ascendant (WDAA) Asc
ascendens (SAUS) asc
Ascending (ADWA) asc
Ascending ASC
Ascending (SAUS) ASDNG
Ascending Activating System (DIPS) AAS
Ascending and Descending (MAE) A & D
Ascending and Descending (SAUS) A&D
Ascending Aorta [*Anatomy*] AA
Ascending Aorta [*Medicine*] (DB) AS
Ascending Aorta Synchronized Pulsation [*Medicine*] (DB) AASP
Ascending Aortic Pressure [*Medicine*] (STED) Pao
Ascending Horizon Crossing Time (OA) AHCT
Ascending Neuron [*Neurology*] AN
Ascending Order Arrangement (MHDB) AOA
Ascending Pharyngeal System [*Anatomy*] APS
Ascending Reticular Activating (or Activation) System (SAUS) ARAS
Ascensio Recta [*Right Ascension*] [*Latin*] ar
Ascension [*Bolivia*] [*Airport symbol*] [*Obsolete*] (OAG) ASC
Ascension (SAUS) Ascen
Ascension Island [*Internet country code*] AC
Ascension Island (ACAE) ACN
Ascension Island [*MARC geographic area code*] [*Library of Congress*] (LCCP) lsai-
Ascension Island Station [*NASA*] (SAA) AIS
Ascension Island Tracking Station [*NASA*] (NASA) ACN
Ascension of Isaiah (BJA) Ascls
Ascension Parish Library, Donaldsonville, LA [*Library symbol*] [*Library of Congress*] (LCLS) LDA
Ascension Poetry Reading Series (EA) APRS
Ascent AS
Ascent (MCD) ASC
Ascent Air Data System (NASA) AADS
Ascent Closed Loop (MCD) ACL
Ascent Descent Director (PDAA) ADD
Ascent Engine Arming Assembly [*NASA*] (KSC) AEAA
Ascent Engine Latching Device [*NASA*] (KSC) AELD
Ascent Entertainment Group, Inc. [*Associated Press*] (SAG) AscentEnt
Ascent Entertainment Group, Inc. [*NASDAQ symbol*] (SAG) GOAL
Ascent Entertainment Grp [*NASDAQ symbol*] (TTSB) GOAL
Ascent Flight Systems Integration Group [*NASA*] (NASA) AFSIG
Ascent Guidance and Control System [*NASA*] (KSC) AGS
Ascent Particle Monitor (SAUS) APM
Ascent Phase AP
Ascent Propulsion System [*NASA*] APS
Ascent Stage [*NASA*] (MCD) AS
Ascent Thrust Vector Control [*or Controller*] [*NASA*] (MCD) ATVC
Ascent Thrust Vector Control Driver [*NASA*] (MCD) ATVCD
Ascent Thrust Vector Controller (SAUS) ATVC
Ascent/Abort (MCD) ASC/ABT
Ascertain (GEAB) ascert
Aschaffenburg [*Germany*] [*ICAO location identifier*] (ICLI) EDEC
Aschaffenburg-Grossostheim [*Germany*] [*ICAO location identifier*] (ICLI) EDFC
Ascheim-Zondek Test [*Medicine*] AZT
Aschheim-Zondek [*Pregnancy*] **Test** [*Medicine*] (AAMN) AZ
ASCII Block Terminal Services (SAUS) ABTS
ASCII COBOL [*Computer science*] ACOB
ASCII COBOL Data Manipulation Language-Preprocessor [*Computer science*] ADMLP
ASCII Front Panel (SAUS) AFP
ASCII [*American Standard Code for Information Interchange*] **Message Definition Table** (NITA) AMDT
ASCII String, Zero Terminated (SAUS) ASCIIZ
ASCII Terminal Controller (SAUS) ATC
ASCII text (SAUS) ASC
ASCII To Binary (SAUS) ATOB
Ascites [*Medicine*] (MELL) A
Ascites Hepatoma [*Medicine*] AH
Ascites-Plasma Ratio [*Medicine*] (MAE) A/P
Ascitic Fluid (MAE) Ascit Fl
Ascitic Tumor Fluid (DB) ATF
ASCLA [*Association of Specialized and Cooperative Library Agencies*] **Libraries Serving Special Populations Section** ASCLA LSSPS
ASCLA LSSPS [*Association of Specialized and Cooperative Library Agencies - Libraries Serving Special Populations Section*] **Academic Librarians Assisting the Disabled Discussion Group** ASCLA LSSPS ALAD
ASCLA LSSPS [*Association of Specialized and Cooperative Library Agencies - Libraries Serving Special Populations Section*] **Bibliotherapy Forum** ASCLA LSSPS BF
ASCLA LSSPS [*Association of Specialized and Cooperative Library Agencies - Libraries Serving Special Populations Section*] **Health Care Libraries Forum** ASCLA LSSPS HCLF
ASCLA LSSPS [*Association of Specialized and Cooperative Library Agencies - Libraries Serving Special Populations Section*] **Library Service to Developmentally Disabled Persons Membership Activity Group** ASCLA LSSPS LSDDP MAG
ASCLA LSSPS [*Association of Specialized and Cooperative Library Agencies - Libraries Serving Special Populations Section*] **Library Service to Prisoners Forum** ASCLA LSSPS LSPF
ASCLA LSSPS [*Association of Specialized and Cooperative Library Agencies - Libraries Serving Special Populations Section*] **Library Service to the Blind andPhysically Handicapped Forum** ASCLA LSSPS LSBPHF

ASCLA LSSPS [*Association of Specialized and Cooperative Library Agencies - Libraries Serving Special Populations Section*] **Library Service to the Deaf Forum** ... ASCLA LSSPS LSDF
ASCLA LSSPS [*Association of Specialized and Cooperative Library Agencies - Libraries Serving Special Populations Section*] **Library Service to the Impaired Elderly Forum** ... ASCLA LSSPS LSIEF
ASCLA [*Association of Specialized and Cooperative Library Agencies*] **Multitype Library Networks and Cooperatives Section** ... ASCLA Multi-LINCS
ASCLA [*Association of Specialized and Cooperative Library Agencies*] **State Library Agency Section** ... ASCLA SLAS
Asclepius [*of Apuleius*] [*Classical studies*] (OCD) ... Asclep
Ascochinga [*Argentina*] [*ICAO location identifier*] (ICLI) ... SACN
Ascom City [*South Korea*] [*ICAO location identifier*] (ICLI) ... RKSA
Ascom Hasler AG (SAUS) ... XHA
Ascona [*Switzerland*] [*ICAO location identifier*] (ICLI) ... LSZD
Ascor Flyservice AS [*Norway*] [*ICAO designator*] (FAAC) ... NOC
Ascorbic Acid [*Vitamin C*] [*Biochemistry*] ... AA
Ascorbic Acid [*Also called vitamin C*] (DAVI) ... ASC
Ascorbic Acid [*Vitamin C*] (DAVI) ... C
Ascorbic Acid (SAUS) ... vit C
Ascorbic Acid Factor [*Biochemistry*] ... AAF
Ascorbic Acid Oxidase (SAUS) ... AAO
Ascorbic Free Radical [*Biochemistry*] ... AFR
Ascorbyl Dipalmitate [*Organic chemistry*] ... ADP
Ascot Investment Corp. [*Toronto Stock Exchange symbol*] [*Vancouver Stock Exchange symbol*] ... AIP
Ascot Resources Ltd. [*Vancouver Stock Exchange symbol*] ... AOT
Ascriptum [*Ascribed To*] [*Latin*] (MAE) ... ascr
ASD (Production and Logistics) (DOMA) ... ASD(P & L)
ASDC Journal of Dentistry for Children (SAUS) ... ASDC J Dent Child
ASE Test Ltd. [*Associated Press*] (SAG) ... ASE Tst
ASE Test Ltd. [*NASDAQ symbol*] (SAG) ... ASTS
ASE Test Ltd. [*NASDAQ symbol*] (SG) ... ASTSF
ASE [*National Institute for Automotive Service Excellence*] **Test Registration Booklet** [*A publication*] (EAAP) ... R/B
ASEA AB [*NASDAQ symbol*] (NQ) ... ASEA
Asea Brown Boveri [*Swedish-Swiss manufacturing company*] (ECON) ... ABB
ASEA Brown Boveri AB (SAUO) ... ABB
Asea Brown Boveri AG, Mannheim (SAUS) ... ABB
ASEA Brown Boveri, Inc., Montreal, Quebec (SAUS) ... QMASBB
ASEA [*Allmaenna Svenska Elektriska Aktiebolaget*] **Brown Boveri, Inc., Montreal, Quebec** [*Library symbol*] [*National Library of Canada*] (BIB) ... QMASBB
ASEAN [*Association of South East Asian Nations*] **- Australia Business Council** ... ASEAN-ABC
ASEAN [*Association of Southeast Asian Nations*] **- Australia Consultative Meeting** ... AACM
ASEAN [*Association of South East Asian Nations*] **- United States Business Council** [*Bangkok, Thailand*] (EAIO) ... AUSBC
ASEAN [*Association of South East Asian Nations*] **Association for Planning and Housing** (EAIO) ... AAPH
ASEAN Association for Planning and Housing (SAUO) ... AAPH
ASEAN [*Association of South East Asian Nations*] **Association of Museums** (EAIO) ... ASEANAM
ASEAN Association of Radiologists (SAUO) ... AAR
ASEAN Bankers Association (SAUO) ... ABA
ASEAN [*Association of South East Asian Nations*] **Bankers Association** [*Singapore, Singapore*] (EAIO) ... ABA
ASEAN Banking Council (SAUO) ... ABS
ASEAN Brussels Committee (SAUO) ... ABC
ASEAN Chamber of Commerce and Industry (SAUO) ... ACCI
ASEAN Chamber of Commerce and Industry (SAUO) ... Asean-CCI
ASEAN Confederation of Employers (SAUO) ... ACE
ASEAN Confederation on Women Organizations (SAUO) ... ACWO
ASEAN Cooperative Association (SAUO) ... ACO
ASEAN Council for Higher Education in Environment (SAUO) ... ACHEE
ASEAN Council of Teachers (SAUO) ... ACT
ASEAN Council on Petroleum (SAUO) ... ASCOPE
ASEAN [*Association of South East Asian Nations*] **Council on Petroleum** [*Indonesia*] ... ASCOPE
ASEAN Experts Group on the Environment (SAUO) ... AEGE
ASEAN Federation for Psychatric and Mental Health (SAUO) ... AFPMH
ASEAN Federation of Automotive Associations (SAUO) ... AFAA
ASEAN [*Association of South East Asian Nations*] **Federation of Cement Manu facturers** [*Indonesia*] (EAIO) ... AFCM
ASEAN Federation of Cement Manufacturers (SAUO) ... AFCM-ASEAN-CCI
ASEAN Federation of Endocrine Societies (SAUO) ... AFES
ASEAN Federation of Engineering Organizations (SAUO) ... AFEO
ASEAN Federation of Food Processing Industries (SAUO) ... AFFPI-ASEAN-CCI
ASEAN Federation of Mining Associations (SAUO) ... AFMA
Asean Finance Corporation (SAUO) ... AFC
ASEAN Food Journal (SAUS) ... ASEAN Food J
ASEAN Food Security Reserve Board (SAUO) ... AFSRB
ASEAN [*Association of South East Asian Nations*] **Free Trade Area** (ECON) ... AFTA
ASEAN Hotel and Restaurant Association (SAUO) ... AHRA
ASEAN Institute for Physics (SAUO) ... ASEANIP
ASEAN Insurance Council (SAUO) ... AIC
ASEAN Inter-Parliamentary Organization (SAUO) ... AIPO
ASEAN Iron and Steel Industry Federation (SAUO) ... AISIF
ASEAN [*Association of South East Asian Nations*] **Japan Development Fund** ... AJDF
ASEAN Law Association (SAUO) ... ALA
ASEAN Ministerial Meeting (SAUO) ... AMM
ASEAN Motion Picture Producers Association (SAUO) ... AMPPA
ASEAN National Police Chiefs Conference (SAUO) ... ASANAPOL
ASEAN Population Coordination Unit (SAUO) ... APCU
ASEAN Professional Association on Food and Agriculture (SAUO) ... APAFA
ASEAN [*Association of Southeast Asian Nations*] **Regional Forum** (ECON) ... ARF
ASEAN Regional Specialized Meteorological Centre (SAUO) ... ARSMC
ASEAN Senior Environment Officers (SAUS) ... ASOEM
ASEAN [*Association of South-East Asian Nations*] **Specialized Meteorological Centre** [*Marine science*] (OSRA) ... ASMC
ASEAN Standing Committee (SAUO) ... ASC
ASEAN Subregion Environment Program (SAUS) ... ASEP
ASEAN Timber Technology Center (SAUO) ... ATTC
ASEAN Tourism Information Centre (SAUO) ... ATIC
ASEAN Training Centre for Primary Health Care Development (SAUO) ... ATC/PHC
ASEAN Travel Association (SAUO) ... ASEANTA
ASEAN University Sports Council (SAUO) ... AUSC
ASEAN Valuers Association (SAUO) ... AVA
ASEAN [*Association of South East Asian Nations*] **Valuers Association** [*Kuala Lumpur, Malaysia*] (EAIO) ... AVA
ASEAN-Australian Economic Cooperation Program (SAUO) ... AAECP
ASEAN-EEC Joint Cooperation Committee (SAUO) ... ASEAN-EEC JCC
Aseco Corp. [*NASDAQ symbol*] (SAG) ... ASEC
Aseco Corp. [*Associated Press*] (SAG) ... Aseco
Aseki [*Papua New Guinea*] [*Airport symbol*] [*Obsolete*] (OAG) ... AEK
Asele [*Sweden*] [*ICAO location identifier*] (ICLI) ... ESUS
Aseptic Bone Necrosis [*Medicine*] ... ABN
Aseptic Epiphyseal Necrosis [*Medicine*] (DMAA) ... AEN
Aseptic Fluid Transfer System [*NASA*] ... AFTS
Aseptic Food Processing System ... AFPS
Aseptic Maintenance by Pressurization [*NASA*] ... AMP
Aseptic Meningitis [*Medicine*] ... AM
Aseptic Meningitis Syndrome [*Medicine*] (MELL) ... AMS
Aseptic Necrosis [*Medicine*] ... AN
Aseptic Packaging Council (EA) ... APC
Aseptically Packaged Liquids (SAUS) ... Aseptics
Aserradero [*Nicaragua*] [*Seismograph station code, US Geological Survey*] (SEIS) ... ASE
asexualization (SAUS) ... asex
ASFE [*Association of Soil and Foundation Engineers*]**/Association of Engineering Firms Practicing in the Geosciences** (EA) ... ASFEAEFPG
ASG Industries, Inc. [*Formerly, American St. Gobain*] ... ASG
Ash Fall (SAUS) ... AF
Ash Fusion Temperature [*Coal industry*] ... AFT
Ash Grove, MO [*FM radio station call letters*] (RBYB) ... KQMO-FM
Ash Grove, MO [*FM radio station call letters*] ... KZPD
Ash Lighter [*Navy symbol*] ... YA
Ash Trap (EEVL) ... AT
Ashanti Goldfields Co. Ltd. [*Associated Press*] (SAG) ... Ashanti
Ashanti Goldfields Co. Ltd. [*NYSE symbol*] (SAG) ... ASL
Ashanti Goldfields Ltd GDS [*NYSE symbol*] (TTSB) ... ASL
Ashbrooke-Pembleton-Ffrench [*Mythical British family appearing in "Announcements" column of Times of London*] ... A-P-F
Ashburn, GA [*FM radio station call letters*] ... WFFM
Ashburner. Principles of Equity [*2nd ed.*] [*1933*] [*A publication*] (DLA) ... Ashb
Ashburton Oil Ltd. [*Vancouver Stock Exchange symbol*] ... ASB
Ashbury College (SAUO) ... AC
Ashbury College, Ottawa, ON, Canada [*Library symbol*] [*Library of Congress*] (LCLS) ... CaOOASH
Ashbury College, Ottawa, Ontario [*Library symbol*] [*National Library of Canada*] (NLC) ... OOASH
Ashby Public School, Ashby, MN [*Library symbol*] [*Library of Congress*] (LCLS) ... MnAshS
Ashcroft, BC [*ICAO location identifier*] (ICLI) ... CYZA
Ashcroft Museum, British Columbia [*Library symbol*] [*National Library of Canada*] (NLC) ... BASM
Ashdown, AR [*FM radio station call letters*] ... KARQ
Ashdown, AR [*FM radio station call letters*] ... KHSP
Ashdown, AR [*FM radio station call letters*] (BROA) ... KOWS-FM
Ashe County Public Library, West Jefferson, NC [*Library symbol*] [*Library of Congress*] (LCLS) ... NcWj
Asheboro, NC [*Location identifier*] [*FAA*] (FAAL) ... CQJ
Asheboro, NC [*FM radio station call letters*] ... WKRR
Asheboro, NC [*AM radio station call letters*] ... WKXR
Asheboro, NC [*FM radio station call letters*] (RBYB) ... WPER
Asheboro, NC [*FM radio station call letters*] (BROA) ... WWMO-FM
Asheboro, NC [*AM radio station call letters*] ... WZOO
Ashendon [*England*] ... ASH
Ashe's Tables to the Year Books, Coke's Reports, or Dyer's Reports [*A publication*] (DLA) ... Ashe
Asheville [*North Carolina*] [*Airport symbol*] (OAG) ... AVL
Asheville, NC [*Location identifier*] [*FAA*] (FAAL) ... BRA
Asheville, NC [*Location identifier*] [*FAA*] (FAAL) ... IMO
Asheville, NC [*Location identifier*] [*FAA*] (FAAL) ... SUG
Asheville, NC [*Television station call letters*] ... WASV
Asheville, NC [*FM radio station call letters*] ... WCQS
Asheville, NC [*Television station call letters*] ... WHNS
Asheville, NC [*AM radio station call letters*] ... WISE
Asheville, NC [*AM radio station call letters*] ... WKJV
Asheville, NC [*FM radio station call letters*] ... WKSF
Asheville, NC [*FM radio station call letters*] ... WLFA
Asheville, NC [*Television station call letters*] ... WLOS
Asheville, NC [*AM radio station call letters*] ... WSKY
Asheville, NC [*Television station call letters*] ... WUNF
Asheville, NC [*AM radio station call letters*] ... WWNC

Asheville-Buncombe Technical Institute, Asheville, NC [Library symbol] [Library of Congress] (LCLS) .... NcAAB
Asheville-Henderson [North Carolina] [Airport symbol] (AD) .... AVL
Ashford Press Publishing [British] .... APP
Ash-Free Dry Mass [Analytical chemistry] .... AFDM
Ash-Free Dry Weight [DMAA] .... AFDW
Ashiya [Japan] [ICAO location identifier] (ICLI) .... RJFA
Ashizuri [Japan] [Seismograph station code, US Geological Survey] (SEIS) ..... ASZ
Ashkenazic [Jews from Central or Eastern Europe] (BJA) .... Ashken
Ashkezar [Iran] [ICAO location identifier] (ICLI) .... OIYZ
Ashkhabad [Former USSR] [Airport symbol] (OAG) .... ASB
Ashkhabad [Former USSR] [Seismograph station code, US Geological Survey] (SEIS) .... ASH
Ashland [Wisconsin] [Airport symbol] [Obsolete] (OAG) .... ASX
Ashland Chemical Co., Research Library, Columbus, OH [OCLC symbol] (OCLC) .... ASO
Ashland City, TN [AM radio station call letters] .... WQSV
Ashland Coal [NYSE symbol] (SPSG) .... ACI
Ashland Coal, Inc. [Associated Press] (SAG) .... AsCoal
Ashland College (SAUO) .... AC
Ashland College, Ashland, OH [OCLC symbol] (OCLC) .... ASC
Ashland College, Ashland, OH [Library symbol] [Library of Congress] (LCLS) .... OAsC
Ashland Community College [Ashland, KY] .... ACC
Ashland Inc. [NYSE symbol] (TTSB) .... ASH
Ashland, Inc. [Formerly, Ashland Oil] [Associated Press] (SAG) .... Ashland
Ashland, Inc. [Associated Press] (SAG) .... AshInd
Ashland Inc. $3.125 Cv Pfd [NYSE symbol] (TTSB) .... ASHPr
Ashland, KY [Location identifier] [FAA] (FAAL) .... AJY
Ashland, KY [AM radio station call letters] .... WCMI
Ashland, KY [FM radio station call letters] (RBYB) .... WDGG
Ashland, KY [Television station call letters] .... WKAS
Ashland, KY [Television station call letters] .... WTSF
Ashland, MA [AM radio station call letters] (BROA) .... WRPT
Ashland, MO [FM radio station call letters] .... KBXR
Ashland, OH [Location identifier] [FAA] (FAAL) .... AAU
Ashland, OH [AM radio station call letters] .... WNCO
Ashland, OH [FM radio station call letters] .... WNCO-FM
Ashland, OH [FM radio station call letters] .... WRDL
Ashland Oil and Refining Company (SAUO) .... Ashland
Ashland Oil Canada Ltd., Calgary, AB, Canada [Library symbol] [Library of Congress] (LCLS) .... CaACAO
Ashland Oil, Inc. (SAUO) .... ASH
Ashland, OR [AM radio station call letters] .... KCMX
Ashland, OR [FM radio station call letters] .... KCMX-FM
Ashland, OR [FM radio station call letters] (RBYB) .... KKJJ-FM
Ashland, OR [FM radio station call letters] .... KSMF
Ashland, OR [FM radio station call letters] .... KSOR
Ashland, OR [FM radio station call letters] (RBYB) .... KSRG
Ashland Public Library, Ashland, KY [Library symbol] [Library of Congress] (LCLS) .... KyA
Ashland Public Library, Ashland, MA [Library symbol] [Library of Congress] (LCLS) .... MAsl
Ashland State General Hospital, Ashland, PA [OCLC symbol] (OCLC) .... PHZ
Ashland Theological Seminary, Ashland, OH [Library symbol] [Library of Congress] (LCLS) .... OAsT
Ashland, VA [Location identifier] [FAA] (FAAL) .... LJK
Ashland, VA [Location identifier] [FAA] (FAAL) .... OFP
Ashland, VA [Television station call letters] .... WAWB
Ashland, VA [AM radio station call letters] (BROA) .... WHAN
Ashland, VA [AM radio station call letters] .... WPES
Ashland, VA [Television station call letters] (BROA) .... WUPV
Ashland, VA [FM radio station call letters] .... WYFJ
Ashland, WI [Location identifier] [FAA] (FAAL) .... ENY
Ashland, WI [AM radio station call letters] .... WATW
Ashland, WI [FM radio station call letters] .... WBSZ
Ashland, WI [FM radio station call letters] .... WJJH
Ashland-Lineville, AL [FM radio station call letters] .... WASZ
Ashley Community Consolidated District 15, Ashley, IL [Library symbol] [Library of Congress] (LCLS) .... IAsyCD
Ashley, Drew and Northern Railroad Company (SAUO) .... AD&N
Ashley, Drew & Northern Railway Co. [AAR code] .... ADN
Ashley, MI [FM radio station call letters] .... WJSZ
Ashley, ND [Location identifier] [FAA] (FAAL) .... ASY
Ashley Public Library, Ashley, IL [Library symbol] [Library of Congress] (LCLS) .... IAsy
Ashmead's Pennsylvania Reports [1808-41] [A publication] (DLA) .... Ash
Ashmead's Pennsylvania Reports [1808-41] [A publication] (DLA) .... Ashm
Ashmead's Pennsylvania Reports [1808-41] [A publication] (DLA) .... Ashmead
Ashmead's Pennsylvania Reports [1808-41] [A publication] (DLA).... Ashmead (PA)
Ashmead's Pennsylvania Reports [1808-41] [A publication] (DLA) .... Ashmead's Penn Rep
Ashmead's Pennsylvania Reports [1808-41] [A publication] (DLA) .... Ashm (PA)
Ashmolean Museum (SAUO) .... Ash Mus
Ashmolean Natural History Society of Oxfordshire (SAUO) .... ANHSO
Ashmont, AB [Television station call letters] CFRN-4
Ashmont Public Library, Alberta [Library symbol] [National Library of Canada] (NLC) .... AAS
Ashmont Public Library, Ashmont, AB, Canada [Library symbol] [Library of Congress] (LCLS) .... CaAAs
Ashmore and Cartier Islands [at (Australia) used in records cataloged after January 1978] [MARC country of publication code] [Library of Congress] (LCCP) .... ac
Ashmore and Cartier Islands [MARC geographic area code] [Library of Congress] (LCCP) .... u-ac-

Ashmore/Cartier Reef (SAUS) .... ACR
Ashoka Society [Later, Ashoka: Innovators for the Public] (EA) .... AS
Ashore Coordinated ASW [Antisubmarine Warfare] Training [Navy] (DOMA) .... ACAT
Ashore Navigation Center [Military] (IUSS) .... ANC
ASHP Resident Matching Program (SAUS) .... RMP
Ashpit [British] (ROG) .... AP
Ashridge Centre for Transport Management [Ashridge Management College] [British] (CB) .... ACTM
Ashtabula County District Library, Ashtabula, OH [Library symbol] [Library of Congress] (LCLS) .... OAsht
Ashtabula, OH [AM radio station call letters] .... WFUN
Ashtabula, OH [FM radio station call letters] .... WREO
Ashtech Office Suite for Survey (GEOI) .... AOSS
Ashton Public Library, Ashton, ID [Library symbol] [Library of Congress] (LCLS) .... IdAs
Ashton Tech Group [NASDAQ symbol] (TTSB) .... ASTN
Ashton Tech Group Wrrt [NASDAQ symbol] (TTSB) .... ASTNW
Ashton Technology Group, Inc. (The) [Associated Press] (SAG) .... AshtnT
Ashton Technology Group, Inc. (The) [NASDAQ symbol] (SAG) .... ASTN
Ashton-Potter America [Printer of U.S. postage stamps] (BARN) .... APA
Ashton's Reports [9-12 Opinions of the United States Attorneys General] [A publication] (DLA) .... Ashton
Ashton-Tate Corp. (SAUS) .... TATE
Ashton-Under-Lyne Public Library, Ashton-Under-Lyne, United Kingdom (SAUS) .... UK AUL
Ashton-Under-Lyne Public Library, Ashton-Under-Lyne, United Kingdom [Library symbol] [Library of Congress] (LCLS) .... UkAul
Ashuganj Fertilizer and Chemical Company Ltd. (SAUS) .... AFCC
Ashurst's Manuscript Reports, Printed in Volume 2, Chitty [A publication] (DLA) .... Ashurst
Ashurst's Manuscript Reports, Printed in Volume 2, Chitty [A publication] (DLA) .... Ashurst MS
Ashurst's Paper Books, Lincoln's Inn Library [A publication] (DLA) .... APB
Ashurst's Paper Books, Lincoln's Inn Library [A publication] (DLA) .... Ashurst
Ashurst's Paper Books, Lincoln's Inn Library [A publication] (DLA)..... Ashurst MS
Ashworth, Inc. [NASDAQ symbol] (SAG) .... ASHW
Ashworth, Inc. [Associated Press] (SAG) .... Ashwrth
ASI Solutions [Stock market symbol] .... ASIS
Asia [MARC geographic area code] [Library of Congress] (LCCP) .... a----
Asia .... AS
Asia (VRA) .... As
Asia Aero Survey & Consulting Engineers, Inc. [Korea] [ICAO designator] (FAAC) .... KAA
Asia and Near East (SAUO) .... ANE
Asia and Oceania Society for Comparative Endocrinology (SAUO) .... AOSCE
Asia and Oceania Workshop (SAUO) .... AOW
Asia and Pacific Commission on Agricultural Statistics (SAUO) .... APCAS
Asia and Pacific Maritime Cooperation Centre (SAUO) .... APMC
Asia and Pacific Plant Protection Commission [Formerly, Plant Protection Committeefor the Southeast Asia and Pacific Region] (SAUO) .... APPPC
Asia and Pacific Special Interest Group [Australian Library and Information Association] .... APSIG
Asia and South Pacific Area Council (SAUO) .... ASPAC
Asia Baptist Graduate Theological Seminary (SAUO) .... ABGTS
Asia, Central [MARC geographic area code] [Library of Congress] (LCCP) ...... ac---
Asia Crime Prevention Foundation (EAIO) .... ACPF
Asia Data Research, Inc. [Database producer] (IID) .... ADR
Asia Dive Exhibition and Conference (SAUS) .... ADEC
Asia, East [MARC geographic area code] [Library of Congress] (LCCP) .... ae---
Asia Education Foundation .... AEF
Asia Electronic Conference (SAUO) .... AEC
[The] Asia Foundation (EA) .... TAF
Asia Foundation, Women Development Center (SAUO) .... AFWDC
Asia Global Crossing "A" [NASDAQ symbol] .... AGCX
Asia House [An association] (EA) .... AH
Asia Info Holdings [NASDAQ symbol] (SG) .... ASIA
Asia Library Services, Auburn, NY [Library symbol] [Library of Congress] (LCLS) .... AIS
Asia Minor (VRA) .... As Min
Asia Monitor Resources Center (SAUO) .... AMRC
Asia Network for Industrial Technology Information and Extension [Singapore] (BUAC) .... TECHNO-NET
Asia Network for Industrial Technology Information and Extension TECNI-BERIA (SAUS) .... TECHNO-NET
Asia Oceanian Congress of Perinatology (SAUO) .... AOCP
Asia Pac Resources Intl'A' [NYSE symbol] (TTSB) .... ARH
Asia Pacific Academy of Ophthalmology (SAUO) .... APAO
Asia Pacific Air Cargo PTE Ltd. [Singapore] [ICAO designator] (FAAC) .... APK
Asia Pacific Association of Japan .... APAJ
Asia Pacific Broadcasting Union (EAIO) .... ABU
Asia Pacific Business Association .... APBA
Asia Pacific Capital Corp. [Vancouver Stock Exchange symbol] .... APP
Asia Pacific Center (SAUO) .... APC
Asia Pacific Center for Justice and Peace (EA) .... APCJP
Asia Pacific Christian Mission .... APCM
Asia Pacific Development Information Programme .... APDIP
Asia Pacific Distribution [Australia] [ICAO designator] (FAAC) .... APD
Asia Pacific Economic Community (SAUO) .... APEC
Asia Pacific Economic Cooperation [Forum] .... APEC
Asia Pacific Economic Cooperation Council .... APECC
Asia Pacific Economic Group .... APEG
Asia Pacific Energy Studies Consortium (SAUO) .... APESC
Asia Pacific Forum (SAUO) .... APF

Asia Pacific Foundation of Canada [*Fondation Asie Pacifique du Canada*] (AC) .... APFC
Asia Pacific Foundation of Canada, Information Services, Vancouver, BC, Canada [*Library symbol*] [*Library of Congress*] (LCLS) .... CaBVaAP
Asia Pacific Fund [*NYSE symbol*] (SPSG) .... APB
Asia Pacific Fund [*Associated Press*] (SAG) .... AsiaPc
Asia Pacific Group (SAUO) .... APG
Asia Pacific Network Information Center (or Centre) (SAUO) .... APNIC
Asia Pacific Physics Teachers and Education Association (SAUO) .... APPTEA
Asia Pacific Real Estate Federation (SAUO) .... APREF
Asia Pacific Research Unit (SAUO) .... APRU
Asia Pacific Resources International Holdings Ltd. [*NYSE symbol*] (SAG) .... ARH
Asia Pacific Resources International Holdings Ltd. [*Associated Press*] (SAG) .... AsiaPR
Asia Pacific Resources Ltd. [*NASDAQ symbol*] (SAG) .... APQC
Asia Pacific Resources Ltd [*NASDAQ symbol*] (TTSB) .... APQCF
Asia Pacific Resources Ltd. [*Associated Press*] (SAG) .... AsiaPac
Asia Pacific Telecommunications (SAUS) .... APT
Asia Pacific Wire & Cable [*NYSE symbol*] (SG) .... AWC
Asia Pacific Wire & Cable Corp. Ltd. [*Associated Press*] (SAG) .... AsiaPWi
Asia Pacific Wire & Cable Corp. Ltd. [*NYSE symbol*] (SAG) .... AWC
ASIA Project, Los Angeles, CA [*Library symbol*] [*Library of Congress*] (LCLS) .... CLASIA
Asia Pulp & Paper ADS [*NYSE symbol*] (TTSB) .... PAP
Asia Pulp and Paper Co. Ltd. [*Associated Press*] (SAG) .... AsiaPlp
Asia Pulp and Paper Co. Ltd. [*NYSE symbol*] (SAG) .... PAP
Asia Research Bulletin (journ.) (SAUS) .... ANC
Asia Research Centre (SAUO) .... ARC
Asia Research News Analysis Team (SAUO) .... ARNAT
Asia Resource Center (EA) .... ARC
Asia Satellite Telecom ADS [*NYSE symbol*] (SG) .... SAT
Asia Satellite Telecommunications Holdings Ltd. [*Associated Press*] (SAG) .... AsiaSat
Asia Satellite Telecommunications Holdings Ltd. [*NYSE symbol*] (SAG) .... SAT
Asia Service Airlines [*Kazakhstan*] [*FAA designator*] (FAAC) .... ASQ
Asia Society (EA) .... AS
Asia Society (SAUS) .... TAS
Asia, Southeastern [*MARC geographic area code*] [*Library of Congress*] (LCCP) .... as---
Asia, Southwestern [*MARC geographic area code*] [*Library of Congress*] (LCCP) .... aw---
Asia Teachers Association (SAUO) .... ATA
Asia Theological Association (SAUO) .... ATA
Asia Tigers Fund [*Associated Press*] (SAG) .... AsiaTigr
Asia Tigers Fund [*NYSE symbol*] (SPSG) .... GRR
Asia Watch (SAUO) .... AsW
Asia Watch Committee (EA) .... AsW
Asiaamerica Holdings [*Vancouver Stock Exchange symbol*] .... AAK
Asia-Europe Meeting .... ASEM
Asialoglycoprotein [*Biochemistry*] .... ASG
Asialoglycoprotein Receptor [*Biochemistry*] .... ASGPR
Asialo-Orosomucoid [*Liver metabolism*] .... ASOr
Asiamerica Equities Ltd. [*Vancouver Stock Exchange symbol*] .... AEQ
Asian (ADWA) .... As
Asian, African, and Middle Eastern Section [*ACRL*] (AL) .... AAMES
Asian Agricultural Journalists and Writers Association [*Jakarta, Indonesia*] (EAIO) .... AAJWA
Asian Agriculture, Agrotechnology and Agribusiness Exhibition and Conference (SAUS) .... AGASIA
Asian Alliance of Appropriate Technology Practitioners (SAUO) .... AAAIP
Asian Alliance of Appropriate Technology Practitioners (EA) .... AAATP
Asian Alliance of Appropriate Technology Practitioners (SAUO) .... AATP
Asian Amateur Swimming Federation [*Dhaka, Bangladesh*] (EAIO) .... AASF
Asian Amedas Network (SAUS) .... AAN
Asian American Arts Alliance (EA) .... AAAA
Asian American Caucus for Disarmament (EA) .... AACD
Asian American Certified Public Accountants (EA) .... AACPA
Asian American Free Labor Institute (EA) .... AAFLI
Asian American Health Initiative (SAUO) .... AAHI
Asian American Journalists Association (EA) .... AAJA
Asian American Law Students Association (SAUO) .... AALSA
Asian American Legal Defense and Education Fund (EA) .... AALDEF
Asian American Librarians Association [*Defunct*] (EA) .... AALA
Asian American Librarians Caucus (EA) .... AALC
[*The*] Asian American Magazine [*A publication*] .... ASIAM
Asian American Manufacturers Association (EA) .... AAMA
Asian American Psychological Association (EA) .... AAPA
Asian American Voters Coalition (EA) .... AAVC
Asian Americans (SAUS) .... AAs
Asian Americans Information Directory [*A publication*] .... AAID
Asian and African American Materials [*Association for Library Collections and Technical Services*] .... AAM
Asian & African Materials [*ALCTS*] (AL) .... AAM
Asian and African Section [*Association of College and Research Libraries*] .... AAS
Asian and Pacific Skill Development Programme (SAUO) .... APSDEP
Asian and Pacific Americans for Nuclear Awareness (EA) .... APANA
Asian and Pacific Centre for Tansfer of Technology (SAUO) .... APCTT
Asian and Pacific Centre for Transfer of Technology [*India*] (EAIO) .... APCTT
Asian and Pacific Coconut Community [*Jakarta, Indonesia*] (EAIO) .... APCC
Asian and Pacific Council (SAUO) .... ASPAC
Asian and Pacific Council Food and Fertilizer Technology Center (SAUO) .... APCFFT
Asian and Pacific Development Center (or Centre) (SAUO) .... APDC
Asian and Pacific Energy Planning Network [*of the Asian and Pacific Development Centre*] (EAIO) .... APENPLAN

Asian and Pacific Information Network on Medicinal and Aromatic Plants [*UNESCO*] [*United Nations*] (DUND) .... APINMAP
Asian and Pacific Islander (ADWA) .... API
Asian and Pacific Parliamentary Union (SAUS) .... APPU
Asian and Pacific Professional Language and Education Services (SAUS) .... APPLES
Asian and Pacific Professional Language and Education Services [*Defunct*] (EA) .... APPLES
Asian and Pacific Regional Agricultural (or Agriculture) Credit Association (SAUO) .... APRACA
Asian and Pacific Regional Organization of the International Federation of Commercial, Clerical, Professional and Technical Employees (SAUO) .... APRO-FIET
Asian and Pacific Skill Development Information Network [*ILO*] [*United Nations*] (DUND) .... APSDIN
Asian and Pacific Statistical Institute (SAUO) .... APSI
Asian Association of Agricultural Colleges and Universities [*Philippines*] .... AAACU
Asian Association of Agricultural Engineers (SAUO) .... AAAE
Asian Association of Agronomical Centres and Universities (SAUO) .... AAACU
Asian Association of Convention and Visitor Bureaus (EA) .... AACVB
Asian Association of Insurance Commissioners (EAIO) .... AAIC
Asian Association of Management Organisations [*Kuala Lumpur, Malaysia*] .... AAMO
Asian Association of Occupational Health (EA) .... AAOH
Asian Association of Social Science Research Councils (SAUO) .... AASSREC
Asian Association of Track and Field Statisticians (SAUO) .... AATES
Asian Association of Track and Field Statisticians (SAUO) .... AATFS
Asian Association on Remote Sensing (GEOI) .... AARS
Asian Automotive and Accessories Exhibition .... AAAE
Asian Banking Council (SAUO) .... ABC
Asian Baptist Fellowship (SAUO) .... ABF
Asian Basketball Confederation (EA) .... ABC
Asian Benevolent Corps (EA) .... ABC
Asian Billiards Confederation (SAUO) .... ABC
Asian Broadcasters Conference (SAUO) .... ABC
Asian Broadcasting Conference (NTCM) .... ABC
Asian Bureau Australia Newsletter [*A publication*] .... ABAN
Asian Business Contact Center (SAUO) .... ABCC
Asian Business League [*Later, ABL-SF*] (EA) .... ABL
Asian Business League (SAUS) .... ABL
Asian Business League of San Francisco [*California*] (EA) .... ABL-SF
Asian Canadian Resources Ltd. [*Vancouver Stock Exchange symbol*] .... ANC
Asian Center for Organization, Research and Development (SAUO) .... ACODR
Asian Center for Organization, Research and Development (SAUO) .... ACORD
Asian Center for South and Southeast Asian Studies (SAUS) .... Ctr S&SE
Asian Center for the Progress of Peoples [*Hong Kong*] (EAIO) .... ACPP
Asian Center (or Centre) of Educational Innovation for Development (SAUO) .... ACEID
Asian Centre for Agricultural Machinery (SAUO) .... ACAM
Asian Centre for Comparative Education (SAUO) .... ACCET
Asian Centre for Development Administration (SAUO) .... ACDA
Asian Centre for Population and Community Development (SAUO) .... ACPD
Asian Centre for Tax Administration and Research (SAUO) .... ACTAR
Asian Centre for Training and Research in Social Welfare and Development (SAUO) .... ACTRSWD
Asian Centre of Agricultural Machinery (SAUS) .... ACAM
Asian Christian Association [*Taiwan*] (EAIO) .... ACA
Asian Christian Male (ADWA) .... ACM
Asian CineVision [*Later, ACV*] [*An association*] (EA) .... AC
Asian CineVision (EA) .... ACV
Asian Clearing Union .... ACU
Asian Club Federation (EAIO) .... ACF
Asian Coalition for Housing Rights (SAUO) .... ACHR
Asian Coalition of Human Rights Organizations (SAUO) .... ACHRO
Asian Coconut Community (SAUO) .... ACC
Asian Coconut Community [*Later, APCC*] .... ACC
Asian Committee for Standardization of Physical Fitness Tests [*Obu-Shi, Japan*] (EAIO) .... ACSPFT
Asian Communist [*Later, B Group*] [*Division of National Security Agency*] .... ACOM
Asian Comparative Law Review [*A publication*] (DLA) .... Asian Comp L Rev
Asian Confederation of Credit Unions [*of the World Council of Credit Unions*] [*Bangkok, Thailand*] (EAIO) .... ACCU
Asian Confederation of Physical Therapy (EAIO) .... ACPT
Asian Conference of/on Religion and Peace (SAUO) .... ACRP
Asian Conference on Industrialization (SAUO) .... ACI
Asian Conference on Religion and Peace [*Singapore, Singapore*] (EAIO) .... ACRP
Asian Conference on Remote Sensing (GEOI) .... ACRS
Asian Council of Peace Research (SAUO) .... ACPR
Asian Council of Securities Analysts (SAUO) .... ASAC
Asian Cropping Systems Network (SAUO) .... ACSN
Asian Cultural Centre for UNESCO .... ACCU
Asian Cultural Council (EA) .... ACC
Asian Cultural Exchange Foundation (EA) .... ACEF
Asian Cultural Forum on Development - USA [*Defunct*] (EA) .... ACFOD-USA
Asian Currency Unit .... ACU
Asian Developing Bank (SAUO) .... ADB
Asian Development Bank (GNE) .... ADB
Asian Development Bank (EY) .... AsDB
Asian Development Center (SAUO) .... ADC
Asian Development Center (SAUO) .... ADC
Asian Development Fund [*Asian Development Bank*] .... ADF
Asian Development Fund (SAUO) .... ASDF
Asian Dust Input to the Oceanic System [*Research project*] .... ADIOS
Asian EDIFACT Board (SAUO) .... ASEB

Asian Electronics Union (SAUS) .... AEU
Asian Federation for the Mentally Retarded [*Singapore*] (EAIO) .... AFMR
Asian Federation of Employees in Public Service (SAUO) .... ASIAFEDOP
Asian Federation of Library Associations [*Japan*] .... AFLA
Asian Federation of Obstetrics and Gynaecology (PDAA) .... AFOG
Asian Federation on Mental Retardation (SAUO) .... AFMR
Asian Female (MELL) .... AF
Asian Finance and Investment Corporation (SAUO) .... AFIC
Asian Finance/Investment Corp. [*Proposed*] (ECON) .... AFIC
Asian Fisheries Science (SAUS) .... Asian Fish Sci
Asian Fisheries Society [*Marine science*] (OSRA) .... AFS
Asian Folklore Studies Group [*Later, ISA*] (EA) .... AFSG
Asian Folklore Studies (journ.) (SAUS) .... AFS
Asian Football Confederation (EAIO) .... AFC
Asian Free Trade Association (SAUO) .... AFTA
Asian Free Trade Zone (SAUO) .... AFTZ
Asian Geotechnical Engineering Information Center [*Information service or system*] (IID) .... AGE
Asian Geotechnology Engineering Database [*Asian Institute of Technology*] [*Information service or system*] (CRD) .... AGE
Asian Hockey Federation (SAUO) .... AHF
Asian Indian Chamber of Commerce (EA) .... AICC
Asian Industrial Development Council (SAUO) .... AIDC
Asian influenza virus (SAUS) .... Ay
Asian Information Centre (SAUS) .... AIC
Asian Infrastructure Consortia Program [*Australia*] .... AICP
Asian Insitute of Christian Communication (SAUO) .... AICC
Asian Institute for Development Communication and Management (SAUO) .... AIDCOM
Asian Institute for Economic Development and Planning .... AIEDP
Asian Institute of Management [*Philippines*] .... AIM
Asian Institute of Metalurgics (SAUO) .... AIM
Asian Institute of Technology [*Bangkok, Thailand*] (MCD) .... AIT
Asian Institute of Technology Alumni Association [*Thailand*] (EAIO) .... AITAA
Asian International Acceptances and Capital Ltd. (SAUO) .... Asiac
Asian International Chemical and Process Engineering and Contracting Show and Conference .... CHEMASIA
Asian International Hardware Exposition .... AIHEX
Asian Inter-Network Interconnection Initiative (SAUO) AI3
Asian Inter-Parliamentary Organisation (SAUO) .... AIPO
Asian ISDN User Forum (SAUS) .... AIUF
Asian Journal of Modern Medicine (journ.) (SAUS) .... AJMM
Asian Law Caucus (SAUO) .... ALC
Asian Law Centre [*University of Melbourne*] [*Australia*] .... ALC
Asian Law Collective (SAUO) .... ALC
Asian Literature Division (SAUO) .... ALD
Asian Literature Division - of MLA [*Modern Language Association of America*] (EA) .... ALD
Asian Lutheran Coordination and Information Board (SAUO) .... ALCIB
Asian Male (MELL) .... AM
Asian Manpower Skill Development Program [*United Nations*] .... AMSDEP
Asian Marine Biology (SAUS) .... Asian Mar Biol
Asian Mass Communication Research and Information Centre [*Singapore*] (EAIO) .... AMIC
Asian Media Coalition [*Inactive*] (EA) .... AMC
Asian, Middle-Aged Female (MELL) .... AMF
Asian Monetary Union (SAUO) .... AMU
Asian Monetary Unit .... AMU
Asian Music (journ.) (SAUS) .... AMus
Asian Music Rostrum (SAUO) .... AMR
Asian Network for Biological Sciences (SAUO) .... ANBS
Asian Network for Industrial Technology and Extension (SAUS) .... TECHNONET
Asian Network for Industrial Technology Information and Extension (BUAC) .... TECH-NOSET-ASIA
Asian Network of Biological Sciences (CARB) .... ANBS
Asian NGO Coalition for Agrarian Reform and Rural Development (SAUO) .... ANGOC
Asian NGO Coalition for Agrarian Reform and Rural Development (SAUO) .... ANGOLO
Asian NonGovernmental Organizations Coalition for Agrarian Reform and Rural Development [*Philippines*] (EAIO) .... ANGOC
Asian Nongovernmental Organizations Coalition for Agrarian Reform and Rural Development (SAUS) .... ANGOC
Asian Oceanic Computing Industry Organization (SAUO) .... ASCIO
Asian Oceanic Postal Union [*Later, APPU*] [*China, Korea, Philippines, Thailand*] .... AOPU
Asian Organisation (or Organization) of Supreme Audit Institutions (SAUO) .... ASOSAI
Asian Pacific Alliance for Creative Equality .... APACE
Asian Pacific American Heritage Council (EA) .... APAHC
Asian Pacific Anti-Communist League (SAUO) .... APACL
Asian Pacific Center for Theoretical Physics [*Institute, based in Seoul, Korea*] .... APCTP
Asian Pacific Confederation of Chemical Engineering (EAIO) .... APCChE
Asian Pacific Conference on Arts Education (SAUO) .... ASPACAE
Asian Pacific Cooperation of Chemical Engineering (SAUS) .... APCCE
Asian Pacific Council (SAUS) .... ASPAC
Asian Pacific Dental Federation/Asian Pacific Regional Organisation (EAIO) .... APDF/APRO
Asian Pacific Dental Students' Association [*Singapore, Singapore*] (EAIO) .... APDSA
Asian Pacific Economic Community (SAUS) .... APEC
Asian Pacific Energy Planning Network (SAUO) .... APENPLAN
Asian Pacific Federation of Personnel Management Associations (SAUO) .... APFPMA
Asian Pacific Federation of UNESCO Clubs and Associations (SAUO) .... APFUCA
Asian Pacific Law and Tax Review [*A publication*] .... APLTR
Asian Pacific Materials and Corrosion Association .... APMCA
Asian Pacific Weed Science Society (SAUO) .... APWS
Asian Pacific Weed Science Society (EA) .... APWSS
Asian Pacific Youth Forum (EA) .... APYF
Asian Pacific Youth Freedom League [*Tokyo, Japan*] (EAIO) .... APYFL
Asian Parasite Control Organization [*Japan*] (EAIO) .... APCO
Asian Parliamentarians Union (SAUO) .... APU
Asian Partnership for Human Development (SAUO) .... APHD
Asian Patent Attorneys Association (EA) .... APAA
Asian Peoples Anti-Communist League (SAUS) .... APACL
Asian Pest Control (SAUO) .... APESCO
Asian Philosophical Studies (journ.) (SAUS) .... APHS
Asian Polilical Scientists Group in USA (SAUS) .... APSGUSA
Asian Productivity Organisation (or Organization) (SAUO) .... APO
Asian Productivity Organization [*Japan*] (EAIO) .... APO
Asian Professional Female (ADWA) .... APF
Asian Profiles [*Database*] [*SRG International Ltd.*] [*Information service or system*] (CRD) .... APR
Asian Program for Education Innovation for Development .... APEID
Asian Program for the Advancement of Training and Studies (SAUO) .... APATS
Asian Racing Conference .... ARC
Asian Recycling Association (EAIO) .... ARA
Asian Regional Association for Voluntary Sterilization (SAUO) .... ARAVS
Asian Regional Forum (SAUO) .... ARF
Asian Regional Medical Student Association (SAUO) .... ARMSA
Asian Regional Organization .... ARO
Asian Regional Organization - International Confederation of Free Trade Unions .... ARO-ICFTU
Asian Regional Remote Sensing Training Centre (GEOI) .... ARRSTC
Asian Regional Trade Development Organisation (SAUO) .... ARTDO
Asian Regional Training and Development Organization .... ARTDO
Asian Reinsurance Corporation (SAUO) .... Asian Re
Asian Reinsurance Corporation (SAUO) .... ASIANRE
Asian Reinsurance Pool (SAUO) .... ARP
Asian Religio-Cultural Forum on Development .... ARCFOD
Asian Research Center (SAUO) .... ARC
Asian Research Service (SAUO) .... ARS
Asian Reserve Bank (SAUO) .... ARB
Asian Review (journ.) (SAUS) .... AR
Asian Rice Biotechnology Network (SAUO) .... ARBN
Asian Rice Farming Systems Network (SAUO) .... ARFSN
Asian Rice Trade Fund (SAUO) .... ARTF
Asian Rural Insitute-Rural Leaders Training Center (SAUO) .... ARI
Asian Science Communicators' Organization [*International Council of Scientific Unions*] .... ASCO
Asian Scientific and Technological Information Network (EAIO) .... ASTINFO
Asian Securities Analysts Council [*See also CAAF*] [*Japan*] (EAIO) .... ASAC
Asian Socialist Conference .... ASC
Asian Society for Comparative Education (SAUO) .... ASCE
Asian Society for Manpower Development (SAUO) .... ASMD
Asian Society of Wales (SAUO) .... ASW
Asian South Pacific Bureau of Adult Education (SAUO) .... ASPBAE
Asian Standards Advisory Committee (HEAS) .... ASAC
Asian Standards Committee (SAUO) .... ASCO
Asian Statistical Institute .... ASI
Asian Student Press Bureau (SAUO) .... ASPB
Asian Students Association (SAUO) .... ASA
Asian Students' Association [*Kowloon, Hong Kong*] (EAIO) .... ASA
Asian Studies Association of Australia .... ASAA
Asian Studies Association of Australia. Review [*A publication*] .... ASAA Rev
Asian Studies Centre [*St. Antony's College*] [*British*] (CB) .... ASC
Asian Studies Council [*Australia*] .... ASC
Asian Studies in America (SAUO) .... ASIA
Asian Surgical Association (EAIO) .... ASA
Asian Symposium on Medicinal Plants, Spices and other Natural Products (SAUO) .... ASOMPS
Asian Technology Information Program (SAUS) .... ATIP
Asian Test Symposium (SAUS) .... ATS
Asian Track and Field Coaches Association [*India*] (EAIO) .... ATFCA
Asian Trade Expansion Programme (SAUO) .... ATEP
Asian Union of Family Organizations (SAUO) .... AUFO
Asian University [*EDUCATSS*] [*UTLAS symbol*] .... AUT
Asian Vegetable Research and Development Center (EA) .... AVRDC
Asian Vegetable Research and Development Center (or Centre) (SAUO) .... AVRDC
Asian Yachting Federation (SAUO) .... AYF
Asian Youth and Population Coalition (SAUO) .... AYPC
Asiana Airlines [*South Korea*] [*ICAO designator*] (FAAC) .... AAR
Asian-African (SAUS) .... A-A
Asian-American Almanac [*A publication*] .... AAA
Asian-American Christian Fellowship .... AACF
Asian-American Donor Program (NUJO) .... AADP
Asian-American Free Labor Institute (SAUO) .... AAFLI
Asian-American Women's Political Caucus (EA) .... AAWPC
Asian-Australasian Society of Neurological Surgeons [*Kowloon, Hong Kong*] (EAIO) .... AASNS
Asian-Australian Monsoon Implementation Plan (SAUS) .... AAMIP
Asian-Indian Women in America (EA) .... AIWA
Asian-Japan Development Corporation (SAUO) .... AJDC
Asian-Japan Forum (SAUO) .... AJF
Asian-New Zealand Development Consultants (SAUO) .... ANZDEC
Asian-New Zealand Development Corporation (SAUO) .... ANZDEC
Asian-Oceanian Computing Industry Organization (SAUS) .... ASOCIO

Asia-North America Eastbound Rate Agreement [*Shipping*] ... Anera
Asian/Pacific American ... APA
Asian/Pacific American Librarians Association (EA) ... APALA
Asian-Pacific Association for the Study of the Liver ... AsPASL
Asian-Pacific Association of LASER Medical Surgery ... AsPALMS
Asian-Pacific Dental Federation (SAUS) ... APDF
Asian-Pacific Global Environmental Research Network (SAUO) ... APGERN
Asian-Pacific Integrated Model (SAUS) ... AIM
Asian-Pacific Parliamentary Union ... APPU
Asian-Pacific Postal Union [*Manila, Philippines*] (EAIO) ... APPU
Asian-Pacific Section [*International Union of Local Authorities*] [*Australia*] ... ASPAC
Asian-Pacific Section - IPRS [*International Confederation for Plastic and Reconstructive Surgery*] [*Singapore*] (EAIO) ... APS-IPRS
Asian-Pacific Society for Digestive Endoscopy ... AsPCDE
Asian-Pacific Society of Cardiology (EA) ... APSC
Asian-Pacific Society of Cardiology ... AsPSC
Asian-Pacific Society of Nephrology ... AsPSN
Asian-Pacific Society of Paediatric Gastroenterology and Nutrition ... AsPSPGN
Asian-Pacific Tax and Investment Research Centre [*Singapore*] (EA) ... APTIRC
Asian-Pacific Union of Karatedo Organizations (SAUO) ... APUKO
Asian-Pacific-American Advocates of California (SAUO) ... APAAC
Asia-Oceania Clinical Oncology Association ... AsOCOA
Asia-Oceania Electronic Messaging Association [*Japan*] (DDC) ... AOEMA
Asia-Oceania Federation of Nuclear Medicine ... AsOFNM
Asia-Oceania Workshop [*Computer science*] (TNIG) ... AOW
Asia-Pacific Academy of Ophthalmology [*Tokyo, Japan*] (EAIO) ... APAO
Asia-Pacific Association for Agricultural Education ... APAAE
Asia-Pacific Aviation Medicine Association ... AsPAvMA
Asia-Pacific Broadcasting Union (SAUO) ... ABU
[*Annual*] **Asia-Pacific Conference** ... ASPAC
Asia-Pacific Council of American Chambers of Commerce (EA) ... APCAC
Asia-Pacific Council of American Chambers of Commerce (SAUS) ... APCACC
Asia-Pacific Fellowship ... APF
Asia-Pacific Finance Corporation (SAUO) ... APCOR
Asia-Pacific Fishery Commission (SAUS) ... APFIC
Asia-Pacific Forestry Commission [*UN Food and Agriculture Organization*] ... APFC
Asia-Pacific Information Network in Social Sciences ... APINESS
Asia-Pacific Information Network in Social Sciences (SAUS) ... APINFSS
Asia-Pacific Institute for Broadcasting Development (EAIO) ... AIBD
Asia-Pacific Institute for Broadcasting Development (SAUO) ... AIBO
Asia/Pacific Market Analysis [*MMS International*] [*Information service or system*] (CRD) ... APMA
Asia-Pacific Network (ARMP) ... APN
Asia-Pacific News Agencies (SAUO) ... APNA
Asia-Pacific News Network ... ANN
Asia-Pacific People's Environment Network [*Penang, Malaysia*] (EAIO) ... APPEN
Asia-Pacific Peoples Environment Network (SAUO) ... APPEN
Asia-Pacific Petroleum Conference ... APPEC
Asia-Pacific Population Information Network (SAUO) ... Asia-Pacific POPIN
Asia-Pacific Railway Co-operation Group (SAUO) ... APRCG
Asia-Pacific Regional Operations Centre [*Taiwan*] ... APROC
Asia-Pacific Resources [*Vancouver Stock Exchange symbol*] ... APQ
Asia-Pacific Socialist Organization [*Political party*] [*Tokyo, Japan*] (EAIO) ... APSO
Asia-Pacific Society for Impotence Research ... AsPSIR
Asia-Pacific Technology Information System [*ESCAP*] [*United Nations*] (DUND) ... APTIS
Asia-Pacific Telecommunity [*Thailand*] [*Telecommunications*] ... APT
Asia-Pacific Television News Exchange (SAUO) ... Aisavision
Asiatic (SAUS) ... As
Asiatic Fleet (SAUO) ... AF
Asiatic Fleet [*Obsolete*] [*Navy*] ... AF
Asiatic Parrot Society of America (EA) ... APSA
Asiatic Petroleum Company (SAUO) ... APC
Asiatic Quarterly (journ.) (SAUS) ... AQ
Asiatic Quarterly Review (journ.) (SAUS) ... AQR
Asiatic Society (SAUO) ... AS
Asiatic Society of Bengal (SAUO) ... ASB
Asiatic Society of Bombay (SAUO) ... ASB
Asiatic Society of Japan (SAUO) ... ASJ
Asiatic Steam Navigation Company (SAUO) ... ASN
Asiatic-Pacific Campaign Medal [*Military decoration*] ... APCM
Asiatic-Pacific Meater of War (SAUS) ... APTW
Asiatic-Pacific Theater (SAUS) ... As Pac Th
Asiatic-Pacific Theater of War ... APTW
Asican Confederation of Credit Unions (SAUO) ... ACCU
Asinaria [*of Plautus*] [*Classical studies*] (OCD) ... Asin
Asio-African Management of CIOS (SAUO) ... AAMOCIOS
ASIST: A Structured Addictions Assessment Interview for Selecting Treatment (TMMY) ... ASIST
Asistencia Reciproca Petrolera Estatal Latinoamericana [*Mutual Assistance of the Latin American Government Oil Companies*] (EAIO) ... ARPEL
Asitka Resources Corp. [*Vancouver Stock Exchange symbol*] ... ATK
Ask a Friend to Explain Reconstruction [*An association*] (EA) ... AFTER
ASK Information Search, Anchorage, AK [*Library symbol*] [*Library of Congress*] (LCLS) ... AkAAS
ASK Jeeves [*NASDAQ symbol*] (SG) ... ASKJ
Ask, Praise, Encourage, Advise, Check (SAUS) ... APEAC
Askania (SAUS) ... ASK
Askania Cine-Theodolite Opticaltracking Range (SAUS) ... ACTOR
Askania Cine-Theodolite Optical-Tracking Range ... ACTOR
Askania Optical Tracker ... AOT
Askania Theodolite Camera (MUGU) ... ASK
Asked ... A
Asked Price (SG) ... A
Askew Redundancy Check-Track (SAUS) ... ARCT
asking (SAUS) ... askg
Asking [*Automotive advertising*] ... ASKNG
Asking Price ... AP
Aslib Economics and Business Information Group (NITA) ... AEBIG
ASLIB Electronics Group (SAUS) ... AEG
Aslib Social Sciences Information Group (SAUO) ... ASSIG
ASM [*American Society for Metals*] **Foundation for Education and Research** [*ASM International*] ... ASMFER
ASM International (SAUO) ... ASM
ASM [*American Society for Metals*] **International** (EA) ... ASMI
ASM International NV [*Associated Press*] (SAG) ... ASM Intl
ASM Intl. N.V. [*NASDAQ symbol*] (SG) ... ASMI
ASM Lithography Holding NV [*NASDAQ symbol*] (SAG) ... ASML
ASM Lithography Holding NV [*Associated Press*] (SAG) ... ASM Lit
ASM Lithography Holding NV [*Associated Press*] (SAG) ... ASM Litho
ASM Litography Hldg NV [*NASDAQ symbol*] (TTSB) ... ASMILF
Asmar [*Afghanistan*] [*ICAO location identifier*] (ICLI) ... OAAS
Asmara [*Ethiopia*] [*Airport symbol*] (AD) ... ASM
Asmara App [*Ethiopia*] [*ICAO location identifier*] (ICLI) ... HAAS
Asmara/Yohannes IV [*Ethiopia*] [*ICAO location identifier*] (ICLI) ... HAAY
ASME [*American Society of Mechanical Engineers*] **International Gas Turbine Institute** (EA) ... ASMEIGTI
Asmonean (BJA) ... AS
Asnchronous Response Mode [*Computer science*] (VERA) ... ARM
Asnuntuck Community College, Learning Resources Center, Enfield, CT [*Library symbol*] [*Library of Congress*] (LCLS) ... CtEnA
Aso [*Japan*] [*Seismograph station code, US Geological Survey*] [*Closed*] (SEIS) ... ASO
Asociacián de Industrias Pl sticas (SAUO) ... ASIPLA
Asociacián Interamericana de Jueces des Menores (SAUO) ... AIJM
Asociacián Nacional de Criadores de Ganado Porcino (SAUO) ... ANCRIGAP
Asociacion [*Association*] [*Spanish*] ... ASOC
Asociacion Argentina de Tecnologia Nuclear (NUCP) ... AATN
Asociacion Argentino-Norteamericana para el Avance de la Ciencia, Technologia, yCultura [*Argentine-North American Association for the Advancement of Science, Technology, and Culture*] (EA) ... ANACITEC
Asociacion Bancaria de Panama (EY) ... ABP
Asociacion Centroamericana de Armadores [*Central American Association of Shipowners*] [*Guatemala, Guatemala*] (EAIO) ... ACAMAR
Asociacion Chilena de Empresas de Turismo [*Chile*] (EY) ... ACHET
Asociacion Cristiana de Jovenes [*Young Men's Christian Association*] (EAIO) ... ACJ
Asociacion de Bancos e Instituciones Financieras de Bolivia (EY) ... ASOBAN
Asociacion de Empresas Estatales de Telecomunicaciones del Acuerdo Subregional Andino [*Association of State Telecommunication Undertakings of the Andean Sub regional Agreement*] [*Ecuador*] (EAIO) ... ASETA
Asociacion de Familiares de Uruguayos Desaparecidos [*France*] ... AFUDE
Asociacion de Ferias Internacionales de America [*Association of International Trade Fairs of America*] (EAIO) ... AFIDA
Asociacion de Industriales Latinoamericanos [*Latin American Industrialists Association - LAIA*] [*Uruguay*] ... AILA
Asociacion de Linguistica y Filologia de America Latina ... ALFAL
Asociacion de Tecnicos de Informatica [*Association of Spanish Information Technology Professionals*] [*Spain*] (DDC) ... ATI
Asociacion de Universidades del Caribe [*Association of Caribbean Universities and Research Institutes*] (EAIO) ... AUC
Asociacion de Universidades del Caribe [*Association of Caribbean Universities and Research Institutes*] (EA) ... UNICA
Asociacion del Congreso Panamericano de Ferrocarriles [*Pan American Railway Congress Association*] (EAIO) ... ACPF
Asociacion Europea de Libre Intercambio (SAUO) ... AELI
Asociacion Filatelica de Filipinas [*Philatelic Association of the Philippines*] (EA) ... AFF
Asociacion Guatemalteca de Agentes de Viajes [*Guatemalan Association of Travel Agents*] (EY) ... AGAV
Asociacion Guatemalteca Pro Naciones Unidas [*Guatemala*] (EAIO) ... AGNU
Asociacion Hispanoamericana de Centros Investigacion y Empresas de Telecomunicaciones (SAUO) ... AHCIET
Asociacion Iberoamericana de Camaras de Comercio [*Ibero-American Association of Chambers of Commerce - IAACC*] [*Bogota, Colombia*] (EAIO) ... AICO
Asociacion Interamericana de Bibliotecarios y Documentalistas Agricolas [*Inter-American Association of Agricultural Librarians and Documentalists*] (EAIO) ... AIBDA
Asociacion Interamericana de Contabilidad [*Interamerican Accounting Association - IAA*] [*Mexico City, Mexico*] (EAIO) ... AIC
Asociacion Interamericana de Gastroenterologia [*Interamerican Association of Gastroenterology*] [*Guatemala*] ... AIGE
Asociacion Interamericana de Hombres de Empresa [*Inter-American Businessmen's Association*] ... AIHE
Asociacion Interamericana de Ingeniera Sanitaria [*Inter-American Assocation of Sanitary and Environmental Engineering*] (EA) ... AIDIS
Asociacion Interamericana de la Propiedad Industrial [*Inter-American Association of Industrial Property - IAAIP*] (EAIO) ... ASIPI
Asociacion Interamericana de Radiodifusion [*Inter-American Association of Broadcasters - IAAB*] [*Montevideo, Uruguay*] (EA) ... AIR
Asociacion Interamericana pro Democracia y Libertad [*Interamerican Association for Democracy and Freedom*] ... AIDL
Asociacion Internacional de Beisbol Amateur [*International Association of Amateur Baseball*] (EA) ... AINBA
Asociacion Internacional de Derecho de Aguas [*International Association for Water Law - IAWL*] [*Spain*] (EAIO) ... AIDA
Asociacion Internacional de Escritores Policiacos [*International Association of Crime Writers*] (EAIO) ... AIEP

Asociacion Internacional de Estructuras Laminares y Espaciales [*International Association for Shell and Spatial Structures*] .... AIEL
Asociacion Internacional de Estudio Integral del Deporte [*International Association of Sport Research*] .... AIEID
Asociacion Internacional de Fomento [*International Development Association*] .... AIF
Asociacion Internacional de Hispanistas [*International Association of Hispanists*] [*Aalst, Belgium*] (EA) .... AIH
Asociacion Internacional de Investigacion para la Paz [*International Peace Research Association*] (EAIO) .... AIIP
Asociacion Internacional de Mercadotecnia Social [*Social Marketing International Association - SMIA*] [*Defunct*] [*Mexico*] (EAIO) .... AIMS
Asociacion Internacional de Planificacion Familiar [*Social Marketing International Association - SMIA*] (EAIO) .... AIPF
Asociacion Internacional de Radiodifusion [*International Association of Broadcasting - IAB*] (EAIO) .... AIR
Asociacion Internacional para el Progreso de la Ensenanza y de la Investigacion de la Propiedad Intelectual [*International Association for the Advancement of Teaching and Research in Intellectual Property*] (EAIO) .... ATRIP
Asociacion Latinoamericana de Administracion Publica .... ALAP
Asociacion Latinoamericana de Agentes de Carga Aerea y Transporte [*Latin American Association of Freight and Transport Agents - LAFTA*] (EA) .... ALACAT
Asociacion Latinoamericana de Analisis y Modificacion del Comportamiento [*Latin American Association of Behavior Analysis and Modification*] (EAIO) .... ALAMOC
Asociacion Latinoamericana de Archivos [*Latin American Association of Archives - LAAA*] (EAIO) .... ALA
Asociacion Latinoamericana de Armadores [*Latin American Shipowners' Association*] (EAIO) .... ALAMAR
Asociacion Latinoamericana de Ciencias Fisiologicas [*Latin American Association of Physiological Sciences*] [*ICSU*] (EAIO) .... ALACF
Asociacion Latinoamericana de Derecho Aeronautico y Espacial .... ALADA
Asociacion Latinoamericana de Derecho Constitucional [*Latin American Constitutional Law Association - LACLA*] (EAIO) .... ALDC
Asociacion Latinoamericana de Editores en Geociencias .... ALEGEO
Asociacion Latinoamericana de Educacion Agricola Superior .... ALEAS
Asociacion Latinoamericana de Escuelas de Bibliotecologia y Ciencias de la Informacion .... ALEBCI
Asociacion Latinoamericana de Estudios Afroasiaticos [*Latin American Association for Afro-Asian Studies - LAAAAS*] (EAIO) .... ALADAA
Asociacion Latinoamericana de Facultades y Escuelas de Medicina de America Latina [*Latin American Association of Medical Schools and Faculties - LAAMSF*] [*Quito, Ecuador*] (EAIO) .... ALAFEM
Asociacion Latinoamericana de Ferrocarriles [*Latin American Railways Association - LARA*] [*Argentina*] .... ALAF
Asociacion Latinoamericana de Industrias Farmaceuticas [*Latin American Association of Pharmaceutical Industries - LAAPI*] (EAIO) .... ALIFAR
Asociacion Latinoamericana de Instituciones Financieras de Desarrollo [*Latin American Association of Development Financing Institutions*] [*Lima, Peru*] (EAIO) .... ALIDE
Asociacion Latinoamericana de Libre Comercio [*Also, LAFTA*] [*Latin American Free Trade Association*] .... ALALC
Asociacion Latinoamericana de Politica Cientifica y Tecnologica [*Latin American Association for Science and Technology*] [*Mexico*] (EAIO) .... ALPCyT
Asociacion Latinoamericana de Produccion Animal .... ALPA
Asociacion Latinoamericana de Psicologia Social [*Latin American Association for Social Psychology - LAASP*] (EAIO) .... ALPS
Asociacion Latinoamericana de Sociologia Rural [*Latin American Rural Sociological Association - LARSA*] (EAIO) .... ALASRU
Asociacion Latinoamericana para el Desarrollo y la Integracion de la Mujer [*Latin American Association for the Development and Integration of Women - LAADIW*] [*Santiago, Chile*] (EAIO) .... ALADIM
Asociacion Latinoamericana y del Caribe de Mundazas Internacionales [*Latin American and Caribbean International Moving*] [*Panama*] (EAIO) .... ALCMI
Asociacion Mexicana de Administradoras de Fondos para el Retiro (SAUO) .... AMAFORE
Asociacion Mexicana de Bibliotecarios, Asociacion Civil [*Spanish*] .... AMBAC
Asociacion Mexicana de Medicos Veterinarios Especialistas en Pequenas Especies [*Mexican Small Animal Veterinary Association*] (GVA) .... AMMVEPE
Asociacion Mexicana para las Naciones Unidas [*United Nations Association of Mexico*] (EAIO) .... AMNU
Asociacion Mundial de Veterinarios Higienistas de los Alimentos [*World Association of Veterinary Food-Hygienists - WAVFH*] [*Berlin, Federal Republic of Germany*] (EAIO) .... AMVHA
Asociacion Mundial Veterinaria de Avicola [*World Veterinary Poultry Association - WVPA*] [*Huntingdon, Cambridgeshire, England*] (EAIO) .... AMVA
Asociacion Mundial Veterinaria de Pequenos Animales [*World Small Animal Veterinary Association - WSAVA*] [*Hatfield, Hertfordshire, England*] (EAIO) .... AMVPA
Asociacion Nacional Campesina Pro-Tierra [*National Peasant Association for Land*] [*Guatemala*] [*Political party*] .... ANC
Asociacion Nacional de Universidades e Institutos de Ensenanza Superior [*The Mexican Association of Universities and Public Institutes of Higher Education*] (CROSS) .... ANUIES
Asociacion Nacional pro Personas Mayores [*National Association for Hispanic Elderly*] (EA) .... ANPPM
Asociacion Nicaraguense de Agencias de Viajes (EY) .... ANAVIT
Asociacion Panamena de Agencias de Viajes y Turismo (EY) .... APAVIT
Asociacion Panamericana de Instituciones de Credito Educativo [*Pan American Association of Educational Credit Institutions - PAAECI*] (EAIO) .... APICE
Asociacion Panamericana de Oftalmologia [*Panamerican Association of Ophthalmology*] [*Washington, DC*] .... APO
Asociacion para el Progreso de Honduras [*Association for the Progress of Honduras*] [*Political party*] .... APROH
Asociacion Petroquimica Latinoamericana [*Argentina*] (EAIO) .... APLA
Asociacion pro Derechos Humanos de Espana [*Spanish Human Rights Association*] .... APDH
Asociacion pro Derechos Humanos de Espana [*Spanish Human Rights Association*] (EAIO) .... APDHE
Asociacion pro Zarzuela en America (EA) .... APZA
Asociacion Protestante de Cooperacion para el Desarrollo en Alemania (SAUS) .... EZE
Asociacion Universal de Federalistas Mundiales [*World Association of World Federalists*] .... AUFM
Asociacion Universitaria Interamericana [*Interamerican University Association*] [*Spanish*] .... AUI
Asocial Personality .... ASP
Asociation de Juventud Rebelde [*Association of Rebel Youth*] .... AJR
Asociation for the Introduction of New Biological Nomenclature (SAUO) .... AINBN
Association of Learned and Professional Society Publishers (SAUO) .... ALPSP
Association of Records Managers and Administrators, Inc. (SAUO) .... ARMA
Asociatiunea Reuniunilor Femeilor Ortodoxe Romane-Americane [*Association of Romanian-American Orthodox Ladies Auxiliaries*] .... ARFORA
Asocio de Esperantistoj en Pollando (SAUO) .... AEP
Asocio Nederlanda de Scienculoy Esperantistaj (SAUO) .... ANSE
Asocio por la Enkondukode Nova Biologia Nomenklaturo (SAUO) .... AINBN
As-Of Date (AFM) .... AOD
Asolute Henry (SAUS) .... abhenry
Asom Gana Parishad [*Assam People's Council*] [*India*] [*Political party*] (FEA) .... AGP
Asorptivity/Emissivity Ratio (SAUS) .... A/E Ratio
Asosa [*Ethiopia*] [*Airport symbol*] (OAG) .... ASO
Asosan [*Japan*] [*Seismograph station code, US Geological Survey*] (SEIS) .... ASJ
Asotin County Library, Clarkston, WA [*Library symbol*] [*Library of Congress*] (LCLS) .... WaCl
Asotin, WA [*AM radio station call letters*] .... KCLK
Asparaginase [*Medicine*] (MELL) .... ASP
Asparaginase (DB) .... Asp
Asparaginase, Vincreistine, Doxorubicin, Prednisone [*Antineoplastic drug*] (CDI) .... AVDP
Asparagine [*One-letter symbol; see Asn*] .... A
Asparagine [*Also, Asp(NH_2), N*] [*An amino acid*] .... Asn
Asparagine (DB) .... ASN
Asparagine [*Also, N*] [*An amino acid*] (DOG) .... asn
Asparagine (BARN) .... Asp N
Asparagine [*Also, Asn, N*] [*An amino acid*] .... Asp(NH_2)
Asparagine [*Biochemistry*] (DAVI) .... N
Asparagine-Rich Protein (DB) .... ARP
Asparaginyl (SAUS) .... N
Asparagus Club (EA) .... AC
Asparagus Stunt Virus [*Plant pathology*] .... ASV
Asparagus Virus .... AV
Asparagus Virus II [*Plant pathology*] .... AVII
Asparate ¤-Semialdehyde (SAUS) .... ASA
Aspartame [*Sweetening agent*] .... APM
Aspartame Committee of the International Food Information Council (EA) .... ACIFIC
Aspartame Consumer Safety Network (ADWA) .... ACSN
aspartate (DOG) .... asp
Aspartate (DB) .... ASP
Aspartate Aminotransaminase [*Liver enzyme*] [*Medicine*] (TAD) .... AST
Aspartate Aminotransferase [*Also, ASAT, AST, GOT*] [*An enzyme*] .... AAT
Aspartate Aminotransferase [*Also, AAT, AST, GOT*] [*An enzyme*] .... ASAT
Aspartate Aminotransferase [*Medicine*] (MELL) .... ASPAT
Aspartate Aminotransferase [*Also, AAT, ASAT, GOT*] [*An enzyme*] .... AST
Aspartate Aminotransferase [*An enzyme*] (DAVI) .... GOT
Aspartate ¤-Semialdehyde (SAUS) .... ASA
Aspartate Carbamoyl Transferase (SAUS) .... ACT
Aspartate Transaminase .... AST
Aspartate Transcarbamylase [*Also, ATCase*] [*An enzyme*] .... ATC
Aspartate Transcarbamylase [*Also, ATC*] [*An enzyme*] .... ATCase
Aspartic Acid [*Also, D*] [*An amino acid*] .... Asp
Aspartic Acid [*or Asparagine*] [*Also, B*] [*An amino acid*] .... Asx
Aspartic Acid (DB) .... ASX
Aspartic Acid [*or Asparagine*] [*Also, Asx*] [*An amino acid*] [*Symbol*] .... B
Aspartic Acid [*One-letter symbol; see Asp*] .... D
Aspartocin [*Endocrinology*] .... AT
Aspartyl Naphthylamide (MAE) .... ANA
Aspartyl-Hydroxamic Acid (MAE) .... AHA
Aspect (ROG) .... ASP
Aspect Angle Radiation Code (MCD) .... AARAD
Aspect Camera (SAUS) .... AC
Aspect Card (SAUS) .... AC
Aspect Cutoff (ACAE) .... ACO
Aspect Determination Subsystem (SAUS) .... ADS
Aspect Determination System (SAUS) .... ADS
Aspect Development [*NASDAQ symbol*] (TTSB) .... ASDV
Aspect Development [*Associated Press*] (SAG) .... AspctDv
Aspect Factor (PDAA) .... AF
Aspect Medical Systems [*NASDAQ symbol*] (SG) .... ASPM
Aspect Ratio .... AR
Aspect Ratio Dependent Etching [*Microlithography*] .... ARDE
Aspect Ratio Enhancement (MCD) .... ARE
Aspect Telecommunications [*Associated Press*] (SAG) .... AspctTel
Aspect Telecommunications [*NASDAQ symbol*] (TTSB) .... ASPT
Aspect Telecommunications Corp. [*Associated Press*] (SAG) .... AspctTl

Aspect Telecommunications Corp. [*NASDAQ symbol*] (SAG) ... ASPT
Aspect-Ratio-Dependent Etching (SAUS) ... ARDE
Aspects of Gymnastics and Independent Learning Experience (AIE) ... AGILE
Aspects of Plant Sciences (journ.) (SAUS) ... APLSDF
Aspen [*Colorado*] [*Airport symbol*] (OAG) ... ASE
aspen (SAUS) ... asp
Aspen Airways [*ICAO designator*] (AD) ... AP
Aspen Airways [*Air carrier designation symbol*] ... APN
Aspen Airways (SAUS) ... PX
Aspen Bancshares [*NASDAQ symbol*] (TTSB) ... ASBK
Aspen Bankshares, Inc. [*NASDAQ symbol*] (SAG) ... ASBK
Aspen Bankshares, Inc. [*Associated Press*] (SAG) ... AspenB
Aspen, CO [*Location identifier*] [*FAA*] (FAAL) ... BUK
Aspen, CO [*FM radio station call letters*] ... KAJX
Aspen, CO [*AM radio station call letters*] ... KRKE
Aspen, CO [*FM radio station call letters*] ... KSPN
Aspen, CO [*Location identifier*] [*FAA*] (FAAL) ... PKN
Aspen, CO [*Location identifier*] [*FAA*] (FAAL) ... RDY
Aspen, CO [*Location identifier*] [*FAA*] (FAAL) ... RNE
Aspen Exploration Corp. [*Vancouver Stock Exchange symbol*] ... ASP
Aspen Imaging International [*NASDAQ symbol*] (NQ) ... ARIB
Aspen Imaging International, Inc. [*Associated Press*] (SAG) ... AspnIm
Aspen Institute (SAUO) ... AI
Aspen Institute for Humanistic Studies (EA) ... AIHS
Aspen Institute of the Humanities (SAUO) ... AIH
Aspen Institute Program on Communications and Society (NTCM) ... AIPCS
Aspen Law Center, Aspen, CO [*Library symbol*] [*Library of Congress*] (LCLS) ... CoAsL
Aspen Leaf Inc. (SAUS) ... TREE
Aspen Technology [*NASDAQ symbol*] (TTSB) ... AZPN
Aspen Technology, Inc. [*Associated Press*] (SAG) ... AspenTc
Aspen Technology, Inc. [*NASDAQ symbol*] (SAG) ... AZPN
Aspencade Motorcyclists Convention (EA) ... ASP/MC
Aspendale ISCCP Regional Experiment (SAUS) ... ASPIRE
Asperger Syndrome Education Network (SAUO) ... ASPEN
Asperger's Syndrome [*Medicine*] ... AS
Aspergillosis [*A fungal disease*] (DAVI) ... ASPER
Aspergillus Asthma ... AA
Aspergillus Flavus (DB) ... AFL
Aspergillus fumigatus [*A fungus*] ... Af
Aspergillus niger [*Factor*] ... AN
Asphalt ... ASP
Asphalt (KSC) ... ASPH
Asphalt (SAUS) ... Asph
Asphalt ... ASPHLT
Asphalt (SAUS) ... At
Asphalt Ageing Index (SAUS) ... AAI
Asphalt and Vinyl Asbestos Tile Institute (SAUO) ... AVATI
Asphalt and Vinyl Asbestos Tile Institute [*Later, RFCI*] (EA) ... AVATI
Asphalt Cement (SAUS) ... AC
Asphalt Coking Technology ... ASCOT
Asphalt Composition (KSC) ... AC
Asphalt Concrete [*FHWA*] (TAG) ... AC
Asphalt Contractors Association of Florida (SRA) ... ACAF
Asphalt Disc (WDAA) ... A/D
Asphalt Employees Protection Society [*A union*] [*British*] ... AEPS
Asphalt Emulsion Manufacturers Association (EA) ... AEMA
Asphalt Institute (EA) ... AI
Asphalt Macadam (SAUS) ... Asph Mac
Asphalt Pavement Association of Indiana (SRA) ... APAI
Asphalt Paving Association of Iowa (SRA) ... APAI
Asphalt Paving Association of Washington (SRA) ... APAW
Asphalt Recycling and Reclaiming Association (EA) ... ARRA
Asphalt Residual Treatment [*Petroleum refining*] ... ART
Asphalt Roads Association [*British*] (BI) ... ARA
Asphalt Roof Shingles [*Technical drawings*] ... ASPHRS
Asphalt Roofing Industry Bureau [*Later, ARMA*] (EA) ... ARIB
Asphalt Roofing Manufacturers Association ... ARM
Asphalt Roofing Manufacturers Association (EA) ... ARMA
Asphalt Rubber Producers Group (EA) ... ARPG
Asphalt Runway (SAUS) ... ASPH
Asphalt Surface Course (DAC) ... ASC
Asphalt Tile [*Technical drawings*] ... AT
Asphalt Tile Institute (SAUS) ... ATI
Asphalt Treated Base [*FHWA*] (TAG) ... ATB
Asphaltenic Bottom Cracking [*Hydrocarbon processing*] ... ABC
Asphaltic (SAUS) ... At
Asphaltic Concrete ... AC
Asphaltic Concrete Pavement ... ACP
Asphalt-Plank Floor (MSA) ... ASPHPF
Asphalt-Plastic-Asphalt-Chip (PDAA) ... APAC
Asphalt-Tile Base [*Technical drawings*] ... ATB
Asphalt-Tile Floor [*Technical drawings*] ... ATF
Aspheronics Inc. (SAUO) ... Aspheronics
Asphodel Township Public Library, Westwood, Ontario [*Library symbol*] [*National Library of Canada*] (BIB) ... OWEST
Asphyxiant (SAUS) ... Asphyx
Asphyxiated (SAUS) ... Asphyx
Asphyxiating Thoracic Dystrophy [*Medicine*] ... ATD
Aspinall's Maritime Law Cases [*1871-1940*] [*England*] [*A publication*] (DLA) ... Asp
Aspinall's Maritime Law Cases [*1871-1940*] [*England*] [*A publication*] (DLA) ... Asp Cas
Aspinall's Maritime Law Cases [*1871-1940*] [*England*] [*A publication*] (DLA) ... Aspin
Aspinall's Maritime Law Cases [*1871-1940*] [*England*] [*A publication*] (DLA) ... Asp Mar Law Cas
Aspinall's Maritime Law Cases [*1871-1940*] [*England*] [*A publication*] (DLA) ... Asp Mar L Cas (Eng)
Aspinall's Maritime Law Cases [*1871-1940*] [*England*] [*A publication*] (DLA) ... Asp MC
Aspinall's Maritime Law Cases [*1871-1940*] [*A publication*] (DLA) ... Asp MCL
Aspinall's Maritime Law Cases [*1871-1940*] [*England*] [*A publication*] (DLA) ... Asp MLC
Aspinall's Maritime Law Cases [*1871-1940*] [*A publication*] (DLA) ... Asp Rep
Aspira of America (EA) ... AOA
Aspiration [*Medicine*] (MELL) ... ASP
Aspiration Biopsy [*Medicine*] (MELL) ... AB
Aspiration Biopsy Cytology [*Medicine*] ... ABC
Aspiration Biopsy Syringe [*Medicine*] (MELL) ... ABS
Aspiration Percutaneus Lumber Dickectomy [*Medicine*] ... APLD
Aspiration Pneumonia [*Medicine*] (MELL) ... AP
Aspirator (NASA) ... ASP
Aspirator (MSA) ... ASPRTR
Aspirator Air System [*Automotive engineering*] ... AAS
Aspirator-Assisted Vacuum System [*Automotive engineering*] ... AAVS
Aspirin, Caffeine, Phenacetin [*Medicine*] (AAMN) ... ACP
Aspirin Compound [*Pharmacology*] (DAVI) ... APC
Aspirin Foundation of America (EA) ... AFA
Aspirin Myocardial Infarction Study [*Medicine*] ... AMIS
Aspirin, Phenacetin, Caffeine [*Medicine*] (DHSM) ... APC
Aspirin, Phenacetin, Caffeine with Codeine [*Medicine*] (MAE) ... APC-C
Aspirin Tolerance Time [*Medicine*] (DMAA) ... ATT
Aspirin-Induced Asthma [*Medicine*] ... AIA
Aspirin-Sensitive Asthma [*Medicine*] (DB) ... ASA
Aspiryl Chlonde (SAUS) ... ACI
Aspiryl Chloride [*Organic chemistry*] (MAH) ... ACI
ASPP [*Atmospheric and Space Plasma Physics*] **Sortie Laboratory** [*NASA*] (NASA) ... ASPSL
ASPP Sortie Laboratory (SAUS) ... ASPSL
Aspres-Sur-Buech [*France*] [*ICAO location identifier*] (ICLI) ... LFNJ
ASR Investments [*AMEX symbol*] (TTSB) ... ASR
ASR Investments Corp. [*Formerly, American Southwest Mortgage Investment Co.*] [*Associated Press*] (SAG) ... ASR
ASR Investments Corp. [*Associated Press*] (SAG) ... ASR Inv
A-S-R Products Corp. (SAUO) ... A-S-R
ASRA Journal (SAUS) ... ASRA J
ASRL-RTP Northeast Regional Oxidant Study (SAUS) ... NEROS
ASRL-RTP Regional Air Pollution Study (SAUS) ... RAPS
ASROC [*Antisubmarine Rocket*] **Missile Assembly** ... AMA
ASROC [*Antisubmarine Rocket*] **Splashpoint Telemetry System** [*Navy*] ... ASTS
Asrtonomical Great Circle (SAUS) ... AGC
As-Run Procedure [*Military*] (MCD) ... ARP
Assab [*Ethiopia*] [*Airport symbol*] (OAG) ... ASA
Assab [*Ethiopia*] [*ICAO location identifier*] (ICLI) ... HASB
Assafoetida [*Pharmacy*] (ROG) ... ASSAFOET
Assam Agricultural University (SAUO) ... AAU
Assam Bengal Railway (SAUO) ... AB
Assam Carbon Black (SAUS) ... ACB
Assam, India (ILCA) ... Ass Ind
Assam Valley Light Horse [*British military*] (DMA) ... AVLH
Assamese [*MARC language code*] [*Library of Congress*] (LCCP) ... asm
Assassination (ROG) ... ASS
Assassination (ROG) ... ASSAS
Assassination Archives and Research Center (EA) ... AARC
Assassination Information Bureau [*An association*] (EA) ... AIB
Assateage Island National Seashore (SAUS) ... AINS
Assateague Island National Seashore [*National Park Service designation*] ... ASIS
Assault [*FBI standardized term*] ... A
Assault (AFM) ... ASLT
Assault (MILB) ... aslt
Assault Airlift Control Officer ... AACO
Assault Amphibian Vehicle [*Military*] ... AAV
Assault Amphibian Vehicle, Personnel (SAUS) ... AAVP
Assault Amphibian Vehicle, Recovery (SAUS) ... AAVR
Assault Amphibious Battalion (DNAB) ... ASLTPHIBBN
Assault & Battery [*Legal term*] (WDAA) ... AAB
Assault and Battery ... A & B
Assault and Battery (SAUS) ... A&B
Assault and Battery [*Legal term*] (DLA) ... ASSLT & B
Assault and Battery with Intent to Kill ... ABWIK
Assault and Robbery (SAUS) ... A&R
Assault Ballistic Rocket System (SAUS) ... ABRS
Assault Battalion Task Force (MCD) ... ABTF
Assault Breaker (MCD) ... AB
Assault Combat Battalion (SAUO) ... ACB
Assault Combat Group (SAUO) ... ACG
Assault Command Post Vehicle (SAUS) ... ACPV
Assault Craft Division (DNAB) ... ACDIV
Assault Craft Unit (NVT) ... ACU
Assault Crisis Center ... ACC
Assault Data System (DNAB) ... ADS
Assault Day (SAUS) ... A-day
Assault Echelon (NVT) ... AE
Assault Engineer [*British military*] (DMA) ... AE
Assault Engineer Regiment (SAUO) ... AER
Assault Fire Command Console [*Army*] ... AFCC
Assault Fire Command Post (SAUS) ... AFCC
Assault Fire Console (ACAE) ... AFC
Assault Fire Platoon (ACAE) ... AFP

Assault Fire Platoon Plus (SAUS) .... AFP+
Assault Fire Unit [*Army*] .... AFU
Assault Follow-On Echelon [*Marine Corps*] (MCD) .... AFOE
Assault Follow-on Echelon (SAUS) .... AFOE
Assault Gun (MCD) .... AG
Assault Gun (AABC) .... ASLTG
Assault Gun Battalion (INF) .... AGB
Assault Gun Battalion (SAUS) AGB-53
Assault Gun System vehicle (SAUS) .... AGS
Assault Gun Vehicle (SAUS) .... AGV
Assault Helicopter Aircraft Carrier [*Navy symbol*] [*Obsolete*] .... CVHA
Assault Helicopter Battalion [*Military*] .... AHB
Assault Helicopter Company [*Army*] (AABC) .... AHC
Assault Helicopter Company [*Air Force*] (AFM) .... AHCo
Assault Helicopter Support Company [*Air Force*] (AFM) .... AHSCo
Assault Hospital Ship [*Navy symbol*] (VNW) .... LPH
Assault Landing Area (SAUS) .... ALA
Assault Landing Craft (SAUS) .... ALCt
Assault Landing Zone (AFM) .... ALZ
Assault Occasioning Actual Bodily Harm [*Criminology*] .... AOABH
Assault Occasioning Grievous Bodily Harm [*Criminology*] .... AOGBH
Assault on Illiteracy Program (EA) .... AIP
Assault on Illiteracy Program (EA) .... AOIP
Assault Operations Room (SAUS) .... AOR
Assault Regiment Royal Engineers [*British military*] (DMA) .... ARRE
Assault Rifle (SAUS) .... AR
Assault Squadron [*British military*] (DMA) .... AS
Assault Supply Officer (SAUS) .... ASO
Assault Support Helicopter [*Military*] .... ASH
Assault Support Helicopter Company [*Army*] (VNW) .... ASHC
Assault Support Patrol Boat (DNAB) .... ASP
Assault Support Patrol Boat [*Navy symbol*] .... ASPB
Assault to Kill [*FBI standardized term*] .... A to K
Assault Unit (SAUO) .... AU
Assault Vehicle, Royal Engineers [*British*] .... AVRE
Assault with Deadly Weapon .... ADW
Assaulting Federal Officer [*FBI standardized term*] .... AFO
Assay Ton .... AT
Asselin, Benoit, Boucher, Ducharme & Lapointe, Inc., Montreal, PQ, Canada [*Library symbol*] [*Library of Congress*] (LCLS) .... CaQMABB
Assemblage (VRA) .... asmblg
Assemble (AABC) .... ASBL
Assemble (SAUS) .... ASM
Assemble (IAA) .... ASMBL
Assemble (SAUS) .... ASSBL
Assemble (MSA) .... ASSEM
Assemble .... ASSMBL
Assemble and Checkout (MCD) .... A/C
Assemble and Recycle (SAA) .... A & R
Assemble and Test .... A & T
Assemble and Test (SAUS) .... A&T
Assemble and Test (SAUS) .... A and T
Assemble and Weld (SAUS) .... ASM/W
Assemble Complete (SAUS) .... ASM/C
Assembled .... ASMBD
Assembled Air-Launched Weapon .... AALW
Assembled Electronic Component .... AEC
Assemblee de l'Atlantique Nord [*North Atlantic Assembly*] [*Brussels, Belgium*] (EAIO) .... AAN
Assemblee des Franco-Americains/Association of Franco-Americans (EA) .... AFA
Assemblee des Gestionnaires de Reseaux Electriques Municipalises et Cooperatives [*Assembly of Managers of Municipal and Cooperative Electrical Systems*] [*Canada*] .... AGREMC
Assemblee des Nations Captives d'Europe [*Assembly of Captive European Nations*] .... ANCE
Assemblee des Premieres Nations (AC) .... APN
Assemblee des Regions d'Europe [*Later, AER*] (EAIO) .... ARE
Assemblee Generale des Federations Internationales Sportives [*General Assembly of International Sports Federations*] .... AGFIS
Assemblee Generale du Contentieux, Conseil d'Etat [*France*] (ILCA) .... Ass
Assemblee Generale Permanente des Comites Nationaux Olympiques [*Permanent General Assembly of National Olympic Committees*] .... AGP-CNO
Assemblee Internationale des Parlementaires de Langue Francaise (AC) .... AIPLF
Assemblee Mondiale de la Jeunesse [*World Assembly of Youth*] .... AMJ
Assemblee Mondiale des Petites et Moyennes Entreprises [*World Assembly of Small and Medium Enterprises - WASME*] [*See also AMEPM*] [*New Delhi,India*] (EAIO) .... AMPME
Assemblee Nationale Des Franco-Americains [*National Association of Franco-Americans*] .... AFA
Assemblee Parlementaire Europeenne .... APE
Assemblee Populaire Communale [*People's Communal Assembly*] [*Algeria*] (AF) .... APC
Assemblee Populaire Nationale [*Haiti*] [*Political party*] (EY) .... APN
Assemble/Load [*Computer science*] .... A/L
Assembler [*Computer science*] (IAA) .... AS
Assembler [*Computer science*] .... ASM
Assembler (MHDB) .... asmblr
Assembler (NITA) .... ASS
Assembler [*Computer science*] .... ASSM
Assembler .... ASSMBLR
Assembler (SAUS) .... ASSR
Assembler and Process Executive (SAUS) .... APEX
Assembler Card Deck (SAUS) .... ACD
Assembler Code (SAUS) .... AC
Assembler Control System (SAUS) .... ACS
Assembler Deck (SAUS) .... AD
Assembler Generating System (SAUS) .... ASM/GEN System
Assembler Instruction (SAUS) .... AI
Assembler Language [*Computer science*] (CIST) .... AL
Assembler Language (SAUS) .... ASM
Assembler Language [*Computer science*] (CMD) .... ASS
Assembler Language for MULTICS .... ALM
Assembler Unit [*Computer science*] (IAA) .... AU
Assembler-Editor (SAUS) .... ASMEDIT
Assembler-Text Editor (SAUS) .... ATE
Assemblies (SAUS) .... ASS
Assemblies, Components, Spare Parts, and Materials [*NATO*] (NATG) .... ACSM
Assemblies, Components, Spare-parts and Materials (SAUS) .... ACSM
Assemblies of God (ADA) .... AOG
Assemblies of God Graduate School, Springfield, MO [*OCLC symbol*] (OCLC) .... MOG
Assemblies of God Graduate School, Springfield, MO [*Library symbol*] [*Library of Congress*] (LCLS) .... MoSpA
Assembling [*FBI standardized term*] .... ASMB
Assembly (IAA) .... A
Assembly (AFM) .... ASBLY
Assembly (WGA) .... ASM
Assembly (ADWA) .... asm
Assembly .... ASMBLY
Assembly .... ASS
Assembly (AAMN) .... ASSBY
Assembly (DLA) .... Assem
Assembly (ADWA) .... assem
assembly (SAUO) .... assem
assembly (SAUO) .... assy
Assembly (ADWA) .... assy
Assembly .... ASSY
Assembly (DNAB) .... AY
Assembly Aid [*Tool*] (AAG) .... ASAD
Assembly Anchorage Headquarters (SAUS) .... AAHQ
Assembly and Checkout [*Minuteman*] [*Military*] (AFIT) .... AAC
Assembly and Checkout [*Minuteman*] [*Military*] (AFIT) .... A & CO
Assembly and Checkout (SAUS) .... AAO
Assembly and Disassembly (IAA) .... AAD
Assembly and Disassembly (SAUS) .... A&D
Assembly and Equipment (IAA) .... AAE
Assembly and Equipment (SAA) .... A & E
Assembly and Equipment (SAUS) .... A&E
Assembly and Erection (SAUS) .... AAE
Assembly and Erection (SAUS) .... A&E
Assembly and Erection (SAA) .... A & E
Assembly and Fabrication .... AF
Assembly and Installation (SAUS) .... A&I
Assembly and Maintenance (IAA) .... AAM
Assembly and Maintenance (KSC) .... A & M
Assembly and Maintenance (SAUS) .... A&M
Assembly and Operations Plan .... AOP
Assembly and Refurbishment Facility (SAUS) .... ARF
Assembly and Repair .... A & R
Assembly and Repair (IAA) .... AAR
Assembly and Rework Operation .... ARO
Assembly and Structure Test .... AST
Assembly and Test (SAUS) .... A&T
Assembly and Test (IAA) .... AAT
Assembly and Test [*Aerospace*] (AAG) .... A/T
Assembly and Test Area [*NASA*] (KSC) .... ATA
Assembly and Test Pit [*Nuclear energy*] (NRCH) .... A & TP
Assembly and Test Pit [*Nuclear energy*] (IAA) .... AATP
Assembly and Verification (SAUS) .... A&V
Assembly and Verification Review (SSD) .... AVR
Assembly Area .... AA
Assembly Area (IAA) .... ASSA
Assembly Area Command .... AAC
Assembly Bill [*in state legislatures*] .... AB
Assembly Breakdown List .... ABL
Assembly Complete (SAUS) .... AC
Assembly Concept for Construction of Erectable Space Structures [*Space shuttle experiment*] [*NASA*] .... ACCESS
Assembly Configuration and Integration Panel (NAKS) .... ACIP
Assembly Constitutional Amendment (SAUS) .... ACA
Assembly Contingency Radio Frequency Group (SPST) .... ACRFG
Assembly Control System [*IBM Corp.*] (BUR) .... ACS
Assembly Coordination Advice (MCD) .... ACA
Assembly Cost System (SAUS) .... ACS
Assembly Decay Indicator .... ADI
Assembly Department Shortage List .... ADSL
Assembly Detail Purchased Parts (AAG) .... ADPP
Assembly District .... AD
Assembly Drawing .... AD
Assembly Engineering Instruction (SAUS) .... AEI
Assembly Facility Tool (MCD) .... AFT
Assembly Fixture (MCD) .... AF
Assembly Fixture [*Tool*] (AAG) .... ASFX
Assembly Fixture Accessory (MCD) .... AFA
Assembly for Behavioral and Social Sciences [*National Research Council*] .... ABASS
Assembly for Behavioural and Social Sciences (SAUS) .... ABASS
Assembly, Handling and Shipping Equipment (SAUS) .... AHSE

Assembly History Tag	AHT
Assembly Identification Number (NG)	AIN
Assembly Implementation Requirements Document [*NASA*] (SPST)	AIRD
Assembly Inactive File (SAUS)	AIF
Assembly Inspection Record (SAA)	AIR
Assembly Inspection Report (SAUS)	AIR
Assembly Inspection Test (SAUS)	AIT
Assembly Instruction Device (DNAB)	AID
Assembly Instruction Mnemonics [*Computer science*]	AIM
Assembly Integration and Test	AI & T
Assembly, Integration, and Test (ADWA)	AIT
Assembly Jig	AJ
Assembly Joint Resolution [*Congress*]	AJR
Assembly Language [*Computer science*]	AL
Assembly Language Coding [*Computer science*]	ALC
Assembly Language Compiler (SAUS)	ALC
Assembly Language Preprocessor [*Computer science*] (IEEE)	ALP
Assembly Language Processing (SAUS)	ALP
Assembly Language Program [*Computer science*]	ALP
Assembly Language Translator [*Xerox Corp.*]	ALTRAN
Assembly Layout [*Computer science*] (MHDB)	ASLO
Assembly Line Communications Link [*General Motors computerized automotive production*]	ALCL
Assembly Line Diagnostic Link [*Automotive engineering*]	ALDL
Assembly Line Effectiveness Center	ALEC
Assembly Line Planning System (MHDB)	ALPS
Assembly Line Shortages Log	ALSL
Assembly Line Test and Selective Enforcement Audit Data (SAUS)	ALT-SEA
Assembly List Shortage Log (AAG)	ALSL
Assembly Machine Fixture (MCD)	AMF
Assembly, Maintenance, and Servicing (SSD)	AMS
Assembly Management Operating System (MCD)	AMOS
Assembly Manufacturing Payroll System (MHDB)	AMPS
Assembly Manufacturing Payrolls System (SAUS)	AMPS
Assembly Manufacturing Planning Record (SAUS)	AMPR
Assembly Manufacturing Process Record (SAUS)	AMPR
Assembly Micro Library (SAUS)	AML
Assembly No Operation (SAUS)	ANOP
Assembly of Baptist Union (SAUO)	ABU
Assembly of Captive European Nations (EA)	ACEN
Assembly of Episcopal Hospitals and Chaplains (EA)	AEHC
Assembly of European Regions [*Later, AER*] (EAIO)	ARE
Assembly of First Nations [*Canadian Indian organization*]	AFN
Assembly of First Nations, Ottawa, Ontario [*Library symbol*] [*National Library of Canada*] (NLC)	OOAFN
Assembly of Free Spirit Baptist Churches (EA)	AFSBC
Assembly of God in Australia	AOGA
Assembly of Governmental Employees [*Defunct*] (EA)	AGE
Assembly of Hospital Schools of Nursing (EA)	AHSN
Assembly of Librarians of the Americas [*Defunct*] (EA)	ALA
Assembly of Librarians of the Americas [*Defunct*]	ALOA
Assembly of Mathematical and Physical Sciences [*National Research Council*]	AMPS
Assembly of National Postsecondary Educational Organizations (EDAC)	ANPEO
Assembly of National Tourist Office Representatives in New York [*Defunct*] (EA)	ANTOR
Assembly of Parties [*INTELSAT*]	AP
Assembly of State Conferences [*American Association of University Professors*] (EDAC)	ASC
Assembly of Station by EVA Methods (SAUS)	ASEM
Assembly of Surgical Group Practice Administrators (ADWA)	ASGPA
Assembly of the Librarians of the Americas (SAUS)	ALA
Assembly of Turkish American Associations (EA)	ATAA
Assembly Operation and Inspection Report	AOIR
Assembly Operations Record	AOR
Assembly Order	AO
Assembly Order Control Number	AOCN
Assembly Outline	AO
Assembly Outline Tooling	AOT
Assembly Over-Ships Records	AO-SR
Assembly Page Change Notice (SAA)	APCN
Assembly Page Listing (SAA)	APL
Assembly Page Maintenance (SAA)	APM
Assembly Part List	APL
Assembly Position (SAUS)	Ass P
Assembly Process Flow Chart (IAA)	APFC
Assembly Production Order [*Manufacturing*] (AAG)	APO
Assembly Program Listing (ACAE)	APL
Assembly Programming Language [*Computer science*]	APL
Assembly Programming System [*Computer science*] (IEEE)	APS
Assembly Quality Record	AQR
Assembly Routine (SAUS)	AR
Assembly Science and Technology Advisory Council (SAUO)	ASTAC
Assembly Sequence Record Sheet	ASRS
Assembly Sequence Record Sheet-Work Sheet (SAUS)	ASRSWS
Assembly Shortage Control (MCD)	ASC
Assembly Statement (SAUS)	AS
Assembly Status Tracking System (SAUS)	ASTS
Assembly System	AS
Assembly System for Central Processor [*Computer science*]	ASCENT
Assembly System for Peripheral Processors [*Computer science*]	ASPER
Assembly Telling (SAA)	AT
Assembly, Test, and Launch Operations (ACAE)	ATLO
Assembly, Test & Subsystem Support (SAUS)	AT&SS
Assembly, Test, and System Support	AT & SS
Assembly Test Program (IAA)	ATP
Assembly Test Record (IAA)	ATR
Assembly Test Recording System	ATRS
Assembly Text Chip [*Computer science*]	ATC
Assembly Time Standard Estimating Sheet (MCD)	ATSES
Assembly Tool (AAG)	ASTO
Assembly Tracking and Management System (MCD)	ATMS
Assembly Truss and Structure (SSD)	ATS
Assembly Type Supply Directive [*Military*] (AFIT)	ATSD
Assembly Under Test (SAUS)	AUT
Assembly Week (MCD)	AW
Assembly Work Authorization Document (NAKS)	AWAD
Assembly Work in Process (SAUS)	AWIP
Assembly Work Schedule Order	AWSO
Assembly Workstand [*NASA*] (NASA)	AW
Assembly/Disassembly	A/D
Assembly/Disassembly Facility	A/D
Assembly-Integration-Verification (ADWA)	AIV
Assembly-Line Preventive Maintenance [*Automotive engineering*]	ALPM
Assented [*Investment term*]	A
Assented [*Investment term*]	ASD
Assented [*Securities*]	ASST
Assented (WGA)	ASSTD
Assented [*Economics*]	AST
Assented [*Investment term*]	ASTD
Assented (EBF)	Astd
Assented Security [*Investment term*]	AS
Assertive Behavior Inventory Tool [*Psychology*] (DMAA)	ABIT
Assertive Sentence Title [*Report writing*]	AST
Assertiveness Training (WGA)	AT
Assessable Stock [*Investment term*]	AS
Assessed (WGA)	ASSD
Assessed Annual Value [*Accounting*] (ADA)	AAV
Assessed Tax Case (DLA)	ATC
Assessed Taxes (Decisions of Judges) [*A publication*] (DLA)	Ass Tax
Assessing Semantic Skills Through Everyday Themes (TES)	ASSET
Assessing Severity: Age of Patient, Systems Involved, State of Disease, Complications, Response to Therapy [*Medicine*] (MEDA)	AS-SCORE
Assessing the Cognitivie Consequences of Computer Environments for Learning Project (EDAC)	ACCCEL
Assessment [*Medicine*]	A
Assessment	ASMNT
Assessment	ASMT
Assessment (KSC)	ASSESMT
Assessment (EBF)	Assmet
Assessment [*Business term*]	ASSMT
Assessment	ASST
Assessment	AST
Assessment Adjustment Pass [*Psychiatry*] (DAVI)	AAP
Assessment and Career Development Centre [*Australia*]	ACDC
Assessment and Coordination Branch, Environmental Protection Service, Environment Canada [*Direction de l'Evaluation et de la Coordination, Service de la Protection de l'Environnement, Environnement Canada*] Yellowknife, Northwest Territories [*Library symbol*] [*National Library of Canada*] (NLC)	NWYEEP
Assessment and Evaluation [*Educational Resources Information Center (ERIC) Clearinghouse*] [*The Catholic University of America*] (PAZ)	TM
Assessment and Information Services Center [*National Oceanic and Atmospheric Administration*] [*Information service or system*] (IID)	AISC
Assessment and Plans [*Medicine*]	AP
Assessment and Remediation of Contaminated Sediments [*Environmental science*]	ARCS
Assessment and Training for Employment (AIE)	ATE
[*Kaufman*] Assessment Battery for Children [*Diagnostic assessment test*] (PAZ)	ABC
Assessment Biological and Chemical [*Warfare*] (NATG)	ABC
Assessment Center [*Business term*]	AC
Assessment for Community Care Services [*Health Care Financing Administration*]	ACCESS
Assessment Guidance Centre [*British*]	AGC
Assessment, Improvement, and Monitoring System [*School milk programs*]	AIMS
Assessment, Improvement and Monitoring System (SAUS)	AIMS
Assessment Inventory for Management (TMMY)	AIM
Assessment Models in Support of Hazzard Assessment Handbook (SAUS)	AMSHAH
Assessment of Basic Competencies [*Child development test*]	ABC
Assessment of Career Decision Making [*Vocational guidance test*]	ACDM
Assessment of Chemical Health Inventory [*Test*] (TMMY)	ACHI
Assessment of Children's Language Comprehension [*Education*]	ACLC
Assessment of Cognitive Skills	ACS
Assessment of Combat Effectiveness [*Army*] (AABC)	ACE
Assessment of Effectiveness of Geologic Isolation Systems (SAUS)	AEGIS
Assessment of Environmental Effects (SAUO)	AEE
Assessment of Fluency in School-Age Children [*Speech evaluation test*]	AFSC
Assessment of Instructional Terms (EDAC)	AIT
Assessment of Intelligibility of Dysarthric Speech [*Speech and language therapy*] (DAVI)	AIDS
Assessment of Interpersonal Relations (TMMY)	AIR
Assessment of Language and Reading Maturity Test (EDAC)	ALARM
Assessment of Language Proficiency of Bilingual Persons Project (EDAC)	ALPBP
Assessment of Living Skills and Resources (TMMY)	ALSAR
Assessment of Long-Range Fleet Architecture [*Military*] (IUSS)	ALFA

Assessment of Motor and Process Skills [*Occupational therapy*] .... AMPS
Assessment of Performance Unit [*Education*] [*British*] .... APU
Assessment of Prior Learning .... APL
Assessment of Productivity & Recruitment in Subarctic Ecosystems (SAUS) .... APRISE
Assessment of Risk for Release [*Medicine*] (MELL) .... ARR
Assessment of Safety Significant Events Team [*IAEA*] (NUCP) .... ASSET
Assessment of Sea Bases Air Platform Project (SAUO) .... ASBAPP
Assessment of Skills in Computation [*Mathematics test*] .... ASC
Assessment of Stationery Target Acquisition Techniques programme (SAUS) .... ASTAT
Assessment of Survivability Against LASER Threat (MCD) .... ASALT
Assessment of the Provision of Part Time Training [*Education*] (AIE) .... APPT
Assessment of Theater Warfare [*Model*] (MCD) .... ATWAR
Assessment Paid [*Billing*] .... AP
Assessment Paid .... Apd
Assessment, Plan, Implementation, and Evaluation [*Medicine*] (DMAA) .... APIE
Assessment Policy Committee [*National Assessment of Educational Progress*] (EDAC) .... APC
Assessment Quality Report (MCD) .... AQR
Assessment Report (SAUS) .... ASSESSREP
Assessment, Review, and Treatment [*Medicine*] (MELL) .... ART
Assessment Statute Expiration Date [*IRS*] .... ASED
Assessment Subgroup [*NATO*] (NATG) .... ASG
Assessment Tools for the Evaluation of Risk [*Environmental Protection Agency*] (AEPA) .... ASTER
Assessment Unit (WDAA) .... AU
Assessments for Integration into Mainstream Settings .... AIMS
Assessor (GEAB) .... asr
Assessor [*Assistant, Assessor*] [*German*] .... Ass
Assessor of Archdeaconry [*Ecclesiastical*] (ROG) .... ASSER
Assessors Association of Pennsylvania (SRA) .... AAP
Assessor's Data Exchange [*A publication*] (EAAP) .... ADE
Asset .... ASST
Asset and Liability Management Committee (EBF) .... ALCO
Asset [*or Availability*] Balance File [*Military*] (AABC) .... ABF
Asset Capitalization Program [*Air Force*] (DOMA) .... ACP
Asset Control System [*or Subsystem*] [*Army*] (AABC) .... ACS
Asset Control Techniques [*TRW, Inc.*] .... ACT
Asset Depreciation Range [*IRS*] .... ADR
Asset Depreciation Range System (EBF) .... ADR
Asset Depreciation Range System [*Accounting*] .... ADRS
Asset Depreciation Ranges (SAUS) .... ADRs
Asset Investors Corp. [*NYSE symbol*] (SPSG) .... AIC
Asset Investors Corp. [*Associated Press*] (SAG) .... AsetInv
Asset Management (EBF) .... AM
Asset Management Account .... AMA
Asset Management Performance (HGAA) .... AMP
Asset Master Balance File [*Military*] (AABC) .... AMBF
Asset Position .... AP
Asset Protection Trust .... APT
Asset Record Performance Quota (SAUS) .... ARPQ
Asset Record Quota Points (SAUS) .... ARQP
Asset Report Request .... ARR
Asset Requirements Depot Maintenance Data (MCD) .... ARDMA
Asset Share Value [*Insurance*] .... ASV
Asset Source for Software Engineering Technology .... ASSET
Asset Source for Software Engineering Technology programme (SAUS) .... ASSET
Asset Status Cards .... ASC
Asset Support Request .... ASR
Asset Type [*Database terminology*] (NITA) .... AT
Asset Utilization (EBF) .... AU
Asset Utilization Factor (SAUS) .... AUF
Asset Value (WDAA) .... AV
Asset-Backed Security [*Finance*] .... ABS
Asset-Liability Committee [*Banking*] .... ALCO
Asset/Liability Management [*Banking*] .... ALM
Asset/Locating (LAIN) .... AL
Assets Accounting [*Business term*] .... AA
Assets and Depreciation [*Accounting*] .... A/D
Assets and Expenditures Survey (SAUS) .... AES
Assets and Liabilities (SAUS) .... AL
Assets Availability Code (MCD) .... AAC
Assets Less Than (NITA) .... AL
Assets Management Reporting System (ACAE) .... AMRS
Assets Management System .... AMS
Assets Repriced Before Liabilities [*Business term*] (MHDB) .... ARBL
Assets Valuation Standards Committee (SAUO) .... AVSC
Assia Regis David [*A publication*] (DLA) .... Ass Reg Da
Assication of Exhibition Organisers (SAUO) .... AEO
Assicurazioni Generali [*General Assurance*] [*Commercial firm*] [*Italy*] .... AG
Assiginack Public Library, Manitowaning, Ontario [*Library symbol*] [*National Library of Canada*] (NLC) .... OMAS
Assign (AABC) .... ASG
Assign (AFM) .... ASGN
Assign .... ASSN
Assign and Display Switch Initialization [*Environmental science*] (COE) .... ASI
Assign Buffer (SAUS) .... ASGBFR
Assign Fixed Directory (COE) .... AFD
Assign Missile RADAR (CAAL) .... AMR
Assign Secondary Traffic Channels [*Environmental science*] (COE) .... AST
Assign Symbolic Device (IAA) .... ASD
Assign Thresholds [*Environmental science*] (COE) .... ATH
Assign Traffic Metering [*Environmental science*] (COE) .... ATM

Assign Variable Location (COE) .... AVL
Assign Volume (IAA) .... ASVOL
Assign Zone Restriction [*Environmental science*] (COE) .... AZR
Assignable Square Feet .... ASF
Assignation (DSUE) .... ASSIG
Assigned (ADWA) .... asg
Assigned (GEAB) .... asgd
Assigned (AABC) .... ASGD
Assigned .... ASGED
Assigned (DLA) .... Assd
Assigned (BARN) .... assnd
Assigned Activity Standardization Office [*Air Force*] (AFIT) .... AASO
Assigned Altitude Deviation [*Aviation*] (DA) .... AAD
Assigned Board Member (SAUS) .... ABM
Assigned Contractor (SAA) .... AC
Assigned Night Answer [*Telecommunications*] (TEL) .... ANA
Assigned Personnel (SAUS) .... AP
Assigned Procurement Responsibility (AAG) .... APR
Assigned Protection Factor (SARE) .... APF
Assigned Rating [*Sailing*] .... AR
Assigned Responsible Agency [*DoD*] .... ARA
Assigned Service Contractor .... ASC
Assigned Slot Release (MHDI) .... ASR
Assignee [*MARC relator code*] [*Library of Congress*] (LCCP) .... asg
Assignee [*Legal shorthand*] (LWAP) .... ASGEE
Assignee .... ASSGN
Assignee Name [*Database terminology*] (NITA) .... AN
Assigning Range (SAUS) .... AR
Assignment [*FCC*] (NTCM) .... A
Assignment .... ASGMT
Assignment (WDMC) .... asgmt
Assignment (SAUS) .... ASGN
Assignment (IAA) .... ASSG
Assignment (ROG) .... ASSGT
Assignment .... ASSIGT
Assignment (ROG) .... ASSMT
Assignment (ROG) .... ASST
Assignment Action Number (AFM) .... AAN
Assignment and Status Chart .... A & S
Assignment Control and Tracking System [*Computer science*] .... ACTS
Assignment Control Authority [*Military*] (NVT) .... ACA
Assignment Control Number [*Army*] .... ACN
Assignment Control Trainee (MCD) .... ACT
Assignment Date [*Telecommunications*] (TEL) .... AD
Assignment Eligibility and Availability [*Military*] (AABC) .... AEA
Assignment Instructions .... AI
Assignment Instructions Remain Firm [*Army*] .... AIRF
Assignment Instructions Were Furnished Your Command [*Military*] .... AIFURC
Assignment Instructions Will Include MOS [*Military Occupational Specialty*]within Army Career Group (AABC) .... AIMOSACGP
Assignment Management Planning System (SAUS) .... AMPS
Assignment Memorandum [*Army*] (AABC) .... AM
Assignment of Beneficial Interest (SAUS) .... ABI
Assignment of Claims Act [*1940*] (OICC) .... ACA
Assignment of (Construction) Permit [*FCC*] (NTCM) .... AP
Assignment of (Construction) Permit and License [*FCC*] (NTCM) .... APL
Assignment of License [*FCC*] (NTCM) .... AL
Assignment of Mortgage [*Business term*] (EMRF) .... A/M
Assignment Oriented Training .... AOT
Assignment Phase (SAUS) .... AP
Assignment Problem (SAUS) .... AP
Assignment Routine (SAUS) .... AR
Assignment Selection Date [*Military*] (AFM) .... ASD
Assignment Source Point (SAUS) .... ASP
Assignment Statement (SAUS) .... AS
Assignment Symbol (SAUS) .... AS
Assignment Tracking System (SAUS) .... ATS
Assignments for Benefits of Creditors [*A publication*] (DLA) .... Assign for Crs
Assignor [*Legal shorthand*] (LWAP) .... ASGOR
Assigns (ROG) .... ASS
Assigns (ROG) .... ASSNS
Assigns (ROG) .... ASSS
Assimilable Organic Carbon [*Environmental chemistry*] .... AOC
Assimilated .... ASSIM
Assimilated (ADWA) .... assim
Assimilation and Fractional Crystallization [*Geology*] .... AFC
Assimilation Efficiency .... AE
Assimilation Regulatory Protein [*Medicine*] (DMAA) .... ARP
Assimilations Per Second (SAUS) .... APS
Assimilative Mapping of the Ionospheric Electrodynamics (SAUS) .... AMIE
Assimilatory Quotient .... AQ
Assinado [*Signed*] [*Portuguese*] [*Business term*] .... a
Assiniboine Community College, Brandon, Manitoba [*Library symbol*] [*National Library of Canada*] (NLC) .... MBAC
Assiniboine Community College, Brandon, MB, Canada [*Library symbol*] [*Library of Congress*] (LCLS) .... CaMBAC
Assiniboine Park Zoo (SAUS) .... APZ
Assiniboine South School Division No. 3, Winnipeg, Manitoba [*Library symbol*] [*National Library of Canada*] (NLC) .... MWASD
Assisi Bird Campaign (SAUS) .... ABC
Assist [*Sports*] .... A
Assist [*Health care*] .... A
Assist Card International (EA) .... ACI
Assist Control (DAVI) .... AC
Assist for Telecommunications Program and Control (IAA) .... ATPC

Assist Order ... AO
Assist Ship's Force Funds [*Navy*] (NVT) ... ASF
Assist with Bath (MELL) ... AcB
Assist Work Authorization ... AWA
Assistaant Secretary of Defense/Public Affairs (SAUS) ... ASD/PA
Assistance [*or Assist*] (DAVI) ... ASST
Assistance (MSA) ... ASSTN
Assistance ... ASSTNCE
Assistance Aeroportuaire de l'Aeroport de Paris [*France*] [*ICAO designator*] (ICDA) ... XJ
Assistance Aeroportuaire de l'Aeroport de Paris [*France*] [*FAA designator*] (FAAC) ... XJA
Assistance and Command Evaluation (ACAE) ... ACE
Assistance and Independence for the Disabled [*British*] ... AID
Assistance and Instructions (MCD) ... AI
Assistance aux Createurs d'Entreprises du Nord-Ouest Europeen [*Multinational organization*] (EAIO) ... ACENOE
Assistance Board (SAUO) ... AB
Assistance Disputes (SAUS) ... ADTRACS
Assistance Dogs International (EA) ... ADI
Assistance Dogs of America [*An association*] (EA) ... ADAI
Assistance for Disabled Students in Post-Secondary Education [*Australia*] ... ADSPSE
Assistance for the Blind ... AB
Assistance in Divorce [*British*] (DI) ... AID
Assistance in Ministries (EA) ... AIM
Assistance Information and Data Acquisition Center [*Navy*] ... AIDAC
Assistance Line (SAUS) ... AL
Assistance Medicale a l'Afrique Centrale [*Medical Assistance to Central Africa*] [*Belgium*] (AF) ... AMAC
Assistance Medicale Internationale [*International Medical Assistance*] [*Canada*] ... AMI
Assistance Militaire Technique [*Military Technical Assistance*] [*Niger*] (AF) ... AMT
Assistance Payments [*Social Security Administration*] ... AP
Assistance Payments Administration [*Later, Office of Family Assistance*] [*Social Security Administration*] ... APA
Assistance Technique de l'Organisation des Nations Unies ... ATONU
Assistance-in-Kind [*Funds*] ... AIK
Assistant [*Military*] ... A
Assistant ... ASS
Assistant ... ASSIST
Assistant (EY) ... ASST
Assistant (PHSD) ... Asst
Assistant (WDMC) ... asst
Assistant (SAUS) ... Ast
Assistant [*Navy*] ... AST
Assistant Adjutant ... AA
Assistant Adjutant and Quartermaster-General [*British*] ... AA & QMG
Assistant Adjutant-General [*Military*] ... AAG
Assistant Administrator (GFGA) ... AA
Assistant Air Attache [*British*] ... AAA
Assistant Air Attache (SAUS) ... AAIRA
Assistant Air AttachS (SAUS) ... AAA
Assistant Air Force Postal Clerk (AFM) ... AAFPC
Assistant Air Provost Marshal (SAUS) ... A/APM
Assistant Airport Traffic Controller (IAA) ... AAPTC
Assistant Airway Traffic Controller (IAA) ... AAWTC
Assistant and Deputy Director of Naval Recruiting [*British*] ... ADDNR
Assistant and Deputy Director of Naval Recruiting (SAUO) ... ADDNR
Assistant Area Commander (SAUS) ... AAC
Assistant [*US*] **Army Military Attache** (CINC) ... AARMA
Assistant Associate Director for Public and Intergovernmental Affairs (SAUO) ... AADPA
Assistant Attorney General (SAUO) ... AAG
Assistant Auditor Freight Accounts [*Business term*] ... AAFA
Assistant Barrister [*British*] (ROG) ... AB
Assistant Base Operations Manager [*NASA*] (KSC) ... ABOM
Assistant Battalion Officer-of-the-Watch (DNAB) ... ABOOW
Assistant Beach Commander (SAUS) ... ABC
Assistant Beach Master [*British*] ... ABM
Assistant Cameraman ... AC
Assistant Camp Commandant [*British*] ... ACC
Assistant Captain [*Worn on assistant captains' uniforms*] [*Hockey*] ... A
Assistant Captain of Transportation (SAUS) ... ACOTP
Assistant Casework Supervisor [*Red Cross*] ... ACWS
Assistant Cashier [*Banking*] ... AC
Assistant Cashier (MHDB) ... Asst Cash
Assistant Catering Accountant [*British military*] (DMA) ... ACA
Assistant Censor (SAUS) ... AC
Assistant Chaplain General (SAUS) ... ACG
Assistant Chaplain General (SAUO) ... ACG
Assistant Chaplain-General [*British*] ... ACG
Assistant Chief and Director (SAUS) ... Asst Chf&Dir
Assistant Chief, Bureau of Aeronautics (SAUS) ... Asst Chf BuAer
Assistant Chief, Bureau of Supplies and Accounts (SAUS) ... AsstChfBuS and A
Assistant Chief, Chemical Warfare Service ... ACCWS
Assistant Chief Fire Officer [*British*] ... ACFO
Assistant Chief for Accounting and Disbursing (SAUS) ... Asst Chf for Acctg&Disb
Assistant Chief for Research ... ACR
Assistant Chief Inspecting Officer (HEAS) ... ACIO
Assistant Chief Medical Director ... ACMD
Assistant Chief Observer [*Navy*] (NVT) ... ACHOBS
Assistant Chief of Air Staff [*Army*] [*British*] ... ACAS
Assistant Chief of Air Staff (SAUS) ... AC/AS
Assistant Chief of Air Staff [*Army*] [*British*] ... AC of AS
Assistant Chief of Air Staff (Intelligence) [*Army*] [*British*] ... ACAS(I)
Assistant Chief of Air Staff (Operations) [*Army*] [*British*] ... ACAS(O)
Assistant Chief of Air Staff (Policy) [*Army*] [*British*] ... ACAS(P)
Assistant Chief of Air Staff (Technical) [*Army*] [*British*] ... ACAS(T)
Assistant Chief of Air Staff (Technical Requirements) [*Army*] [*British*] ... ACAS(TR)
Assistant Chief of Defence Staff [*British*] [*Australia*] (NATG) ... ACDS
Assistant Chief of Defense Staff (SAUO) ... ACDS
Assistant Chief of Engineers [*Military*] ... ACE
Assistant Chief of Fleet Support [*Navy*] [*British*] ... ACFS
Assistant Chief of Intelligence (SAUO) ... ACOF INTEL
Assistant Chief of Logistics (SAUO) ... ACofLOG
Assistant Chief of Mission [*Foreign Service*] ... ACM
Assistant Chief of Mission Operations [*NASA*] ... ACMO
Assistant Chief of Naval Operations ... ACNO
Assistant Chief of Naval Operations (SAUS) ... Asst Chf Nav Op
Assistant Chief of Naval Operations (Communications)/Director, Naval Communications (DNAB) ... ACNO(COMM)/DNC
Assistant Chief of Naval Operations for Communications and Cryptology (IAA) ... ACNOCOMM
Assistant Chief of Naval Operations for Communications and Cryptology (SAUS) ... ACNOCOMM
Assistant Chief of Naval Operations (Transportation) ... ACNOT
Assistant Chief of Naval Operations-Transportation (SAUO) ... ACNOT
Assistant Chief of Naval Personnel (SAUO) ... ACNP
Assistant Chief of Naval Technical Services (SAUO) ... ACNTS
Assistant Chief of Ordnance (SAUO) ... AC of ORD
Assistant Chief of Ordnance (SAUS) ... AC of Ord
Assistant Chief of Organisation and Training (SAUO) ... AC of O&T
Assistant Chief of Personnel and Administration (SAUO) ... AC of P&A
Assistant Chief of Staff (SAUO) ... A
Assistant Chief of Staff (SAUO) ... AC of S
Assistant Chief of Staff [*Army*] ... ACofS
Assistant Chief of Staff (MCD) ... ACOFS
Assistant Chief of Staff ... ACOS
Assistant Chief of Staff ... ACS
Assistant Chief of Staff (SAUO) ... AC/S
Assistant Chief of Staff (SAUS) ... Asst C/S
Assistant Chief of Staff, Air Force ... AC/SAF
Assistant Chief of Staff for Automation and Communications [*Military*] (AABC) ... ACSAC
Assistant Chief of Staff for Command and Control Information Management ... ACSCCIM
Assistant Chief of Staff for Command and Control Information Management (SAUS) ... ACSCCIM
Assistant Chief of Staff for Communications - Electronics [*Army*] (AABC) ... ACSC-E
Assistant Chief of Staff for Communications and Electronics (SAUO) ... ASCE-E
Assistant Chief of Staff for Communications-Electronics (SAUS) ... ACSC-E
Assistant Chief of Staff for Force Development [*Army*] ... ACSFOR
Assistant Chief of Staff for Information Management [*Army*] ... ACSIM
Assistant Chief of Staff for Information Management-Command, Control, Communications, and Computers [*Military*] (GFGA) ... ACSIM-C4
Assistant Chief of Staff for Intelligence [*Washington, DC*] [*Army*] ... ACSI
Assistant Chief of Staff for Intelligence (SAUO) ... ACSINT
Assistant Chief of Staff for Operations (ACAE) ... ACSO
Assistant Chief of Staff for Research and Development (ACAE) ... ACRD
Assistant Chief of Staff for Reserve Components [*Army*] ... ACSRC
Assistant Chief of Staff for Studies and Analysis [*Air Force*] ... CSA
Assistant Chief of Staff, Installations (SAUO) ... ACSI
Assistant Chief of Staff, Intelligence (NATG) ... ACINTEL
Assistant Chief of Staff, Intelligence [*Air Force*] (MCD) ... AFIN
Assistant Chief of Staff, Intelligence, Automatic (SAUS) ... ACSI-MATIC
Assistant Chief of Staff, Logistics (NATG) ... ACLOG
Assistant Chief of Staff, Organization and Training Division (NATG) ... ACOT
Assistant Chief of Staff, Plans and Policy Division (NATG) ... ACPANDP
Assistant Chief of Staff, Programs Division (NATG) ... ACPROG
Assistant Chief of Staff, Studies and Analysis [*Air Force*] (MCD) ... ACS/S & A
Assistant Chief of Staff, Studies and Analysis (SAUO) ... ACS/S&A
Assistant Chief of Staff War Plans Division (SAUS) ... ACOFS WPD
Assistant Chief of Supplies [*British military*] (DMA) ... ACS
Assistant Chief of the General Staff [*Military*] [*British*] ... ACGS
Assistant Chief of the General Staff (Operational Requirements) [*British*] (RDA) ... ACGS(OR)
Assistant Chief of the Imperial General Staff [*British*] ... ACIGS
Assistant Chief of the Naval Staff [*British*] ... ACNS
Assistant Chief of the Naval Staff (Air) [*British*] ... ACNS(A)
Assistant Chief of Transportation [*Army*] ... AC of T
Assistant Chief of United States Airstaff (SAUS) ... ACUSA
Assistant Chief Officer (WDAA) ... AC
Assistant Chief Patrol Inspector [*Immigration and Naturalization Service*] ... ACPI
Assistant Chief Quartermaster (SAUO) ... ACQM
Assistant Chief Signal Officer (SAUS) ... ACSig O
Assistant Chief Statistician ... ACS
Assistant Chief Surgeon (SAUS) ... Asst CS
Assistant Chief-of-Staff, Organization & Training (SAUS) ... ACOT
Assistant Civil Engineer Adviser [*Military*] [*British*] ... ACEA
Assistant Clerk [*Navy*] [*British*] (ROG) ... AC
Assistant Clerks Association [*A union*] [*British*] ... ACA
Assistant Combat Cargo Officer, Well Deck (CAAL) ... ACCOW
Assistant Combat Information Center Officer (MUGU) ... ACICO
Assistant Command Director [*Military*] (MCD) ... ACD
Assistant Command Duty Officer [*Military*] (MCD) ... ACDO
Assistant Command Post Operator (SAUS) ... ACPO
Assistant Commandant [*Army/Marine Corps*] ... AC

Assistant Commandant [*Coast Guard*] .... CA
Assistant Commandant of the [*US*] Marine Corp (DOMA) .... DOMA
Assistant Commander, Royal Engineers (SAUS) .... Asst C RE
Assistant Commissary General (SAUO) .... ACG
Assistant Commissary General .... ACG
Assistant Commissary-General (SAUO) .... AssCom-Gen
Assistant Commissary-General (SAUO) .... AsstCommGen
Assistant Commissioner .... AC
Assistant Commissioner of the Metropolitan Police [*British*] (DAS) .... ACMP
Assistant Comptroller for Budget (SAUS) .... ACBUD
Assistant Comptroller for Finance (SAUS) .... ACFIN
Assistant Comptroller of the Army for Finance and Accounting ...... ACOA(F & A)
Assistant Controller (DCTA) .... AC
Assistant Controller of Stores Department (SAUO) .... ACSD
Assistant Controller of the Navy [*British*] .... AC of N
Assistant Controller, Personnel and Logistics [*Navy*] [*British*] .... ACPL
Assistant Controller, Research and Development [*Admiralty*]
  [*British*] .... AC(R & D)
Assistant Cook [*British military*] (DMA) .... ACK
Assistant Counterbattery Officer (SAUS) .... ACBO
Assistant Countermortar Officer (SAUS) .... ACMO
Assistant County Advisory Officer (SAUS) .... ACAO
Assistant County Architect [*British*] .... ACA
Assistant Cub Master [*Scouting*] .... ACM
Assistant Customs Officer .... ACO
Assistant Data Recording System Analyst (MUGU) .... ADRSA
Assistant Defence Advisor [*British military*] (DMA) .... ADA
Assistant Defense Counsel .... ADC
Assistant Deputy Chief of Naval Material (MCD) .... ADCNM
Assistant Deputy Chief of Naval Operations (DNAB) .... ADCNO
Assistant Deputy Chief of Naval Operations (Civilian Personnel/Equal
  Employment Opportunity) (DNAB) .... ADCNO(CP/EEO)
Assistant Deputy Chief of Staff for Combat Developments [*Army*] .... ADCSCD
Assistant Deputy Chief of Staff for Logistics [*Army*] .... ADCSLOG
Assistant Deputy Chief of Staff for Logistics for Security Assistance
  [*Military*] .... ADCSLOG-SA
Assistant Deputy Chief of Staff for Operations and Plans [*Military*] ...... ADCSOPS
Assistant Deputy Chief of Staff for Operations and Plans (Joint Affairs)
  [*Military*] .... ADCSOPS (JA)
Assistant Deputy Chief of Staff for Operations, Plans, Command, Control,
  Communications and Computers (SAUO) ADCSOPS-C4
Assistant Deputy Chief of Staff for Research, Development, and
  Acquisition [*Military*] .... ADCSRDA
Assistant Deputy Chief of Staff for Research, Development and
  Acquisition (SAUS) .... ADCSRDA
Assistant Deputy Chief of Staff, in Test and Evaluation [*Army*] .... ADCSTE
Assistant Deputy Judge Advocate General [*Military*] [*British*] .... ADJAG
Assistant Deputy Judge Advocate General (SAUO) .... ADJAG
Assistant Deputy Military Governor [*US Military Government, Germany*] .... ADMG
Assistant Deputy Minister [*Canada*] .... ADM
Assistant Deputy Postmaster-General [*Canada*] .... ADPMG
Assistant Deputy Registrar General [*Canada*] .... ADRG
Assistant Director .... AD
Assistant Director Army Dental Service (SAUO) .... ADADS
Assistant Director, Army Postal Services [*British military*] (DMA) .... ADPS
Assistant Director Army Veterinary and Remount Services (SAUO) ..... ADAV&RS
Assistant Director, Auxiliary Territorial Service [*British military*] (DMA) ..... ADATS
Assistant Director, Curatorial .... ADC
Assistant Director Electrical & Mechanical Engineers (SAUS) .... ADEME
Assistant Director Electrical and Mechanical Engineers (SAUO) .... ADEME
Assistant Director, Flight Operations [*NASA*] (KSC) .... ADFO
Assistant Director for Education [*Vietnam*] .... ADEDU
Assistant Director for Legal and Legislative Affairs [*National Security A
gency*] [*Obsolete*] .... ADLA
Assistant Director for Plans and Resources [*National Security Agency*]
  [*Obsolete*] .... ADPR
Assistant Director for Plans and Resources (SAUS) .... ADPR
Assistant Director for Policy and Liaison [*National Security Agency*]
  [*Obsolete*] .... ADPL
Assistant Director for Training [*National Security Agency*] .... ADT
Assistant Director, Lightweight Anti-Submarine Weapons (SAUS) .... AD/LASW
Assistant Director of Accident Prevention (SAUO) .... ADPA
Assistant Director of Administrative Planning (SAUO) .... ADAP
Assistant Director of Administrative Planning [*Military*] [*British*] .... ADAP
Assistant Director of Army Contracts (SAUO) .... ADAC
Assistant Director of Army Health [*British*] .... ADAH
Assistant Director of Army Postal Services (SAUO) .... ADAPS
Assistant Director of Army Psychatry (SAUS) .... ADAP
Assistant Director of Army Psychiatry (SAUO) .... ADAP
Assistant Director of Army Psychiatry [*British*] .... ADAP
Assistant Director of Army Telegraph (SAUO) .... ADAT
Assistant Director of Army Welfare Services (SAUO) .... ADAWS
Assistant Director of Army Welfare Services [*British*] .... ADAWS
Assistant Director of Artillery [*British*] .... ADA
Assistant Director of Auxiliary Territorial Service (SAUO) .... ADATAS
Assistant Director of Auxiliary Territorial Service (SAUS) .... ADATS
Assistant Director of Ceremonies [*Freemasonry*] .... ADC
Assistant Director of Contracts [*Military*] [*British*] .... ADC
Assistant Director of Dental Services .... ADDS
Assistant Director of Dockyards (SAUO) .... AD of D
Assistant Director of Expense Accounts [*Navy*] [*British*] .... ADEA
Assistant Director of Fortification and Works .... ADFW
Assistant Director of Fortifications and Works [*Military*] [*British*] .... ADFW
Assistant Director of Guided Missiles (SAUO) .... ADGM
Assistant Director of Hygiene [*Military*] [*British*] .... ADH

Assistant Director of Hygiene and Pathology (SAUO) .... ADHP
Assistant Director of Intelligence [*British military*] (DMA) .... ADI
Assistant Director of Intelligence, Department K [*Air Ministry*] [*British*] ...... ADI(K)
Assistant Director of Labour (SAUO) .... ADL
Assistant Director of Light Railways [*British military*] (DMA) .... ADLR
Assistant Director of Manning Department (SAUO) .... ADMD
Assistant Director of Mechanical Engineering [*British military*] (DMA) .... ADME
Assistant Director of Medical Services .... ADMS
Assistant Director of Medical Services (SAUO) .... ADMS
Assistant Director of Military Transport (SAUO) .... ADMT
Assistant Director of Mobilization Department (SAUO) .... ADMD
Assistant Director of Naval Accounts (SAUO) .... ADNA
Assistant Director of Naval Accounts [*British*] .... ADNA
Assistant Director of Naval Construction [*British*] .... ADNC
Assistant Director of Naval Construction (SAUO) .... ADNC
Assistant Director of Naval Equipment (SAUO) .... ADNE
Assistant Director of Naval Equipment (SAUS) .... ADNE
Assistant Director of Naval Intelligence (SAUO) .... ADNI
Assistant Director of Naval Intelligence [*British*] .... ADNI
Assistant Director of Naval Ordnance (SAUO) .... ADNO
Assistant Director of Naval Ordnance (SAUS) .... ADNO
Assistant Director of Nursing (BARN) .... ADN
Assistant Director of Nursing (NUJO) .... ADON
Assistant Director of Operations Division [*British military*] (DMA) .... ADOD
Assistant Director of Ordnance Factories [*Ministry of Supply*] [*British*] [*World
  War II*] .... ADOF
Assistant Director of Ordnance Factories (SAUO) .... ADOF
Assistant Director of Ordnance Service .... ADOS
Assistant Director of Ordnance Services (SAUO) .... ADOS
Assistant Director of Ordnance Services [*British*] .... ADOS
Assistant Director of Pathology [*Military*] [*British*] .... ADP
Assistant Director of Pathology (SAUO) .... ADP
Assistant Director of Personnel Services (SAUO) .... ADPS
Assistant Director of Physical Training and Sports (SAUO) .... ADPTS
Assistant Director of Physical Training and Sports (SAUS) .... ADPTS
Assistant Director of Plans Division (SAUO) .... AD of P
Assistant Director of Port (SAUO) .... ADP
Assistant Director of Port (SAUS) .... ADP
Assistant Director of Postal Services (SAUO) .... ADPS
Assistant Director of Prevention of Accident (SAUS) .... ADPA
Assistant Director of Printing and Stationary Services (SAUO) .... ADPSS
Assistant Director of Psychiatry [*British*] (DAVI) .... ADAP
Assistant Director of Public Relation (SAUO) .... ADPR
Assistant Director of Public Relations [*Military*] [*British*] .... ADPR
Assistant Director of Public Relations (SAUS) .... ADPR
Assistant Director of Railway Transport [*British military*] (DMA) .... ADRT
Assistant Director of Railways (SAUO) .... AD Ry
Assistant Director of Remounts (SAUO) .... ADR
Assistant Director of Remounts (SAUS) .... ADR
Assistant Director of Salvage (SAUO) .... AD Salv
Assistant Director of Sea Transport (SAUO) .... AD of ST
Assistant Director of Sea Transport (SAUO) .... ADST
Assistant Director of Signals (SAUO) .... ADSigs
Assistant Director of Signals (IAA) .... ADSIGS
Assistant Director of Signals (SAUS) .... Ad Sigs
Assistant Director of Supplies and Transport (SAUO) .... AD of S&T
Assistant Director of Supplies and Transport [*Military*] [*British*] .... ADS & T
Assistant Director of Supplies and Transport (SAUO) .... ADSAT
Assistant Director of Survey (SAUO) .... ADS
Assistant Director of Survey (SAUO) .... AD Svy
Assistant Director of the Army Budget .... ADAB
Assistant Director of the Army Budget (Financial Systems
  Management) .... ADAB (FSM)
Assistant Director of the Meteorological Office (SAUS) .... ADMO
Assistant Director of Torpedoes [*Navy*] [*British*] .... ADT
Assistant Director of Training (SAUO) .... ADTng
Assistant Director of Training (SAUS) .... ADTng
Assistant Director of Transport (SAUO) .... AD of T
Assistant Director of Transport (SAUO) .... ADT
Assistant Director of Transport (SAUO) .... ADTn
Assistant Director of Transportation [*British military*] (DMA) .... ADTn
Assistant Director of Transportation .... ADTr
Assistant Director of Veterinary and Remount Services [*British military*]
  (DMA) .... ADVRS
Assistant Director of Veterinary Services [*Military*] [*British*] .... ADVS
Assistant Director of Veterinary Services (SAUO) .... ADVS
Assistant Director of Warlike Stores (SAUO) .... ADWS
Assistant Director of Warlike Stores (SAUS) .... ADWS
Assistant Director of Works (SAUO) .... AD of W
Assistant Director of Works (SAUO) .... ADW
Assistant Director of Works, Electrical and Mechanical [*Military*]
  [*British*] .... ADWE & M
Assistant Director of Works, Electrical and Mechanical (SAUS) .... ADWE&M
Assistant Director Research and Development Navy (SAUO) .... AD/RDN
Assistant Director-General [*British*] .... ADG
Assistant Director-General, Army Veterinary Services (SAUO) .... ADGAVS
Assistant Director-General of Medical Services [*Military*] [*British*] .... ADGMS
Assistant Director-General of Transportation [*British military*] (DMA) .... ADGT
Assistant District Attorney .... ADA
Assistant District Commission (MCD) .... ADC
Assistant District Manager (DCTA) .... ADM
Assistant District Officer (SAUS) .... ADO
Assistant District Postmaster [*British*] (DCTA) .... ADP
Assistant Division Chief (SAUS) .... ADC
Assistant Division Commander (SAUO) .... ADC

Assistant Division Commander [*Military*] ... ADC
Assistant Division Commander for Maneuver [*Military*] (INF) ... ADC(M)
Assistant Division Communications Electronics Officer [*Military*] (AABC) ... ADCEO
Assistant Division Engineer [*Army*] (AABC) ... ADE
Assistant Division Supply Officer [*Army*] ... ADSO
Assistant Divisional Officer (WDAA) ... ADO
Assistant Driller (or Drilling) (SAUS) ... AD
Assistant Editor [*Publishing*] ... AE
Assistant Education Officer (SAUO) ... AEO
Assistant Embarkation, Supply and Stores Officer (SAUS) ... AESSO
Assistant Engineer ... AE
Assistant Equipment Officer (SAUO) ... AEO
Assistant Executive Engineer [*British*] (DCTA) ... AEE
Assistant Experimental Officer [*Ministry of Agriculture, Fisheries, and Food*] [*Also, AExO, AXO*] [*British*] ... AEO
Assistant Experimental Officer (SAUO) ... AEO
Assistant Experimental Officer [*Ministry of Agriculture, Fisheries, and Food*] [*Also, AEO, AXO*] [*British*] ... AExO
Assistant Experimental Officer [*Ministry of Agriculture, Fisheries, and Food*] [*Also, AEO, AExO*] [*British*] ... AXO
Assistant Field Director [*Red Cross*] ... AFD
Assistant Fighter Director Office [*Navy*] ... AFDO
Assistant Fire Support Coordinator [*Military*] (AABC) ... AFSCOORD
Assistant Firemaster [*British*] ... AFMR
Assistant Firemaster (WDAA) ... AFmr
Assistant Fleet Liaison Officer (SAUS) ... Asst Flt Liaison Off
Assistant Flight Director [*NASA*] (KSC) ... AFD
Assistant Flight Dynamics Officer [*NASA*] ... AFDO
Assistant Flying Instructor (DA) ... AFI
Assistant for Atomic Energy (SAUS) ... AFOAT
Assistant for Development Planning [*Air Force*] ... AFDAP
Assistant for Engineering Co-ordination (SAUS) ... A Eng Co-ord
Assistant for Logistics Planning (SAUS) ... ALP
Assistant for Materiel Program Control [*Air Force*] ... AFMPC
Assistant for Service Requirements (SAUS) ... ASR
Assistant for Standardization (SAUS) ... A Stand
Assistant for Women Personnel (SAUO) ... AWP
Assistant Freight Agent ... AFA
Assistant Freight Claim Agent ... AFCA
Assistant Freight Traffic Manager ... AFTM
Assistant Garrison Engineer (SAUS) ... AGE
Assistant General Freight Agent ... AGFA
Assistant General Manager [*AEC*] ... AGM
Assistant General Manager for Administration [*AEC*] ... AGMA
Assistant General Manager for International Activities [*AEC*] ... AGMIA
Assistant General Manager for Military Applications (SAUS) ... AGMMA
Assistant General Manager for Operations [*AEC*] ... AGMO
Assistant General Manager for Plans and Production [*AEC*] ... AGMPP
Assistant General Manager for Research and Development [*AEC*] ... AGMRD
Assistant General Secretary (DCTA) ... AGS
Assistant Governor (WDAA) ... AG
Assistant Grand Director of Ceremonies [*Freemasonry*] ... AGDC
Assistant Grand Sojourner [*Freemasonry*] ... AGS
Assistant Gunner/Driver [*Military*] (INF) ... AG/DR
Assistant Head Nurse (AAMN) ... AHN
Assistant Head of Section (DCTA) ... AHS
Assistant Head Postmaster (DCTA) ... AHP
Assistant House Physician ... AHP
Assistant House Surgeon ... AHS
Assistant in Nursing ... AIN
Assistant in Private Practice [*Chiropody*] [*British*] ... P
Assistant Industrial Manager [*of Naval District*] (MUGU) ... AIM
Assistant Industrial Manager [*of Naval District*] (MUGU) ... ASTINDMAN
Assistant Information Officer (DCTA) ... AIO
Assistant Inspector (DCTA) ... AI
Assistant Inspector Armourer [*British and Canadian*] [*World War II*] ... AIA
Assistant Inspector General [*Military*] ... AIG
Assistant Inspector General for Auditing (DNAB) ... AIG(A)
Assistant Inspector, Navy Material (SAUS) ... AINM
Assistant Inspector of Naval Materiel ... AINM
Assistant Inspector of Naval Materiel ... AINSMAT
Assistant Inspector of Naval Ordnance ... AINO
Assistant Inspector of Physical Training [*Military*] [*British*] ... AIPT
Assistant Inspector-General, Royal Irish Constabulary (ROG) ... AIGRIC
Assistant Instructor ... AI
Assistant Instructor in Gunnery [*British military*] (DMA) ... AIG
Assistant Instrumentation Operations Coordination (KSC) ... AIOC
Assistant Judge Advocate General [*Army*] ... AJAG
[*The*] **Assistant Judge Advocate General** [*Army*] (AABC) ... TAJAG
Assistant Judge Advocate General for Civil Law [*Army*] (AABC) ... AJAG/CIV
Assistant Judge Advocate General for Military Law [*Army*] (AABC) ... AJAG/MIL
Assistant Laboratory Director ... ALD
Assistant Language Teacher ... ALT
Assistant Librarian (SAUS) ... Asst Lib
Assistant Loan Officer [*Banking*] (TBD) ... ALO
Assistant Local Director (DCTA) ... ALD
Assistant Major-General [*Military*] [*British*] (ROG) ... AM-G
Assistant Major-General (SAUS) ... AMG
Assistant Manager ... AM
Assistant Manager of Facility Transition (ABAC) ... AMF
Assistant Marshal of the Diplomatic Corps [*British*] ... AMDC
Assistant Master-General of Ordnance [*British*] ... AMGO
Assistant Master-General of Ordnance (SAUO) ... AMGO
Assistant Masters and Mistresses Association (EAIO) ... AMMA
Assistant Masters Association (SAUO) ... AMA
Assistant Masters in Secondary School, Inc. (SAUO) ... AMSS
Assistant Mathematician (SAUS) ... TAM
Assistant Medical Officer ... AMO
Assistant Military Landing Officer [*British and Canadian*] [*World War II*] ... AMLO
Assistant Military Secretary [*British*] ... AMS
Assistant Missile Flight Safety Officer (MUGU) ... AMFSO
Assistant Naval Attache [*British*] ... ANA
Assistant Naval Liaison Officer (SAUS) ... ANLO
Assistant Naval Science Instructor (DNAB) ... ANSI
Assistant Naval Stores Officer ... ANSO
Assistant Navy Mail Clerk ... ANMC
Assistant Network Controller [*NASA*] (KSC) ... ANC
Assistant Network Operations Manager [*NASA*] (KSC) ... ANOM
Assistant Nurse Manager (NUJO) ... ANM
Assistant of Staff (SAUS) ... AC of S
Assistant Officer in Charge [*DoD*] ... AOIC
Assistant Operations Director [*Air Force/Army*] (MCD) ... AOD
Assistant Ordnance Mechanical Engineer [*British military*] (DMA) ... AOME
Assistant Parachute Jump Instructor [*British military*] (DMA) ... APJI
Assistant Patrol Leader (DI) ... APL
Assistant Paymaster ... AP
Assistant Paymaster [*Marine Corps*] ... APM
Assistant Polaris Systems Officer [*British military*] (DMA) ... APSO
Assistant Poor Law Commissioner [*British*] (ROG) ... APLC
Assistant Postmaster General (SAUO) ... APMG
Assistant Principal ... AP
Assistant Principal (SAUS) ... A/Prin
Assistant Principal Chaplain [*British*] (ADA) ... APC
Assistant Private Secretary to the First Sea Lord [*Navy*] [*British*] ... APSFSL
Assistant Professor of Military Science (SAUS) ... APMS
Assistant Program Manager (IUSS) ... APM
Assistant Program Manager, Logistics (SAUO) ... APML
Assistant Project Engineer ... APE
Assistant Project Manager [*NASA*] (NASA) ... APM
Assistant Project Manager for Business Administration ... APMBA
Assistant Project Manager for Logistics (SAUS) ... APMI
Assistant Project Manager for Logistics ... APML
Assistant Project Officer ... APO
Assistant Provost Marshal [*Facetious translation: "A Permanent Malingerer"*] ... APM
Assistant Provost-Marshall (SAUO) ... APM
Assistant Public Works Officer ... APWO
Assistant Quartermaster ... AQM
Assistant Quartermaster General for Administration (SAUS) ... ASST QMG ADM
Assistant Quartermaster General for Operations (SAUO) ... ASST QMG OPS
Assistant Quartermaster-General [*Military*] ... AQMG
Assistant Regional Administrator [*Environmental Protection Agency*] (GFGA) ... ARA
Assistant Regional Commissioner [*IRS*] ... ARC
Assistant Regional Commissioner Disability Insurance [*Social Security Administration*] (OICC) ... ARCDI
Assistant Regional Manager ... ARM
Assistant Regional Security Officer [*Foreign service*] ... ARSO
Assistant Regional Technical Adviser (SAUS) ... ARTA
Assistant Registrar (ROG) ... AR
Assistant Representative (SAUS) ... Asst Rep
Assistant Research Officer [*Ministry of Agriculture, Fisheries, and Food*] [*British*] ... ARO
Assistant Resident (SAUS) ... AR
Assistant Scientific Officer (HEAS) ... ASO
Assistant Scoutmaster [*Boy Scouts of America*] ... ASM
Assistant Secretary ... AS
Assistant Secretary, Controller [*Admiralty*] [*British*] ... AS(C)
Assistant Secretary for Administration and Management [*Department of Labor*] ... ASAM
Assistant Secretary for Congressional and Intergovernmental Affairs (SAUO) ... CP
Assistant Secretary for Conservation and Renewable Energy ... ASCRE
Assistant Secretary for Defense Programs ... ASDP
Assistant Secretary for Defense Programs (SAUO) ... DP-1
Assistant Secretary for Employment and Training [*Department of Labor*] ... ASET
Assistant Secretary for Employment Standards [*Department of Labor*] ... ASES
Assistant Secretary for Energy Technology (SAUO) ... ASET
Assistant Secretary for Environment, Safety, and Health ... ASESH
Assistant Secretary for Environment, Safety, and Health (SAUS) ... EH
Assistant Secretary for Fossil Energy ... ASFE
Assistant Secretary for Fossil Energy (SAUO) ... FE
Assistant Secretary for Health [*HEW*] ... ASH
Assistant Secretary for International Affairs and Energy Emergencies ... ASIAEE
Assistant Secretary for International Affairs and Energy Emergencies (SAUS) ... ASIE
Assistant Secretary for International Affairs and Energy Emergencies (SAUO) ... IE
Assistant Secretary for Labor-Management Relations [*Department of Labor*] ... ASLMR
Assistant Secretary for Nuclear Energy ... ASNE
Assistant Secretary for Occupational Safety and Health [*Department of Labor*] ... ASOSH
Assistant Secretary for Personnel Administration [*U.S. Department of Health and Human Services*] ... ASPER
Assistant Secretary for Planning and Evaluation [*Department of Health and Human Services*] ... ASPE
Assistant Secretary for Planning and Evaluation. U. S. Department of Health and Human Services (SAUO) ... ASPE

Assistant Secretary for Policy Evaluation and Research [*Department of Labor*] ... ASPER
Assistant Secretary for Policy, Safety and Environment (SAUO) ... ASPE
Assistant Secretary for the Environment (SAUO) ... ASEV
Assistant Secretary General (NATG) ... ASG
Assistant Secretary General (NATG) ... ASYG
Assistant Secretary General for Air Navigation [*ICAO*] ... ASGAN
Assistant Secretary General for Infrastructure, Logistics, and Council Operations [*NATO*] ... ASG ILCO
Assistant Secretary General Staff (SAUS) ... ASGS
Assistant Secretary of Air Navigation (SAUS) ... ASGAN
Assistant Secretary of Defense ... ASD
Assistant Secretary of Defense (ACAE) ... ASOD
Assistant Secretary of Defense (DNAB) ... ASSTSECDEF
Assistant Secretary of Defense (Administration) (AABC) ... ASD (A)
Assistant Secretary of Defense (Civil Defense) ... ASD (CD)
Assistant Secretary of Defense (Communications, Command-Control, and Intelligence) (AABC) ... ASD(C3I)
Assistant Secretary of Defense (Comptroller) ... ASD (C)
Assistant Secretary of Defense (Comptroller) (DNAB) ... ASSTSECDEF(COMPT)
Assistant Secretary of Defense for Acquisition and Logistics ... ASD(A & L)
Assistant Secretary of Defense for Economic Security (RDA) ... ASD(ES)
Assistant Secretary of Defense (Force Management and Personnel) (DOMA) ... ASD(FM & P)
Assistant Secretary of Defense (Health Affairs) (AABC) ... ASD(HA)
Assistant Secretary of Defense (Health Affairs) (DNAB) ... ASSTSECDEF(HELAFF)
Assistant Secretary of Defense (Health and Environment) ... ASD (H & E)
Assistant Secretary of Defense (Health and Medical) ... ASD/H & M
Assistant Secretary of Defense (Installations and Logistics) ... ASD (I & L)
Assistant Secretary of Defense/ Installations & Logistics (SAUS) ... ASD/I&L
Assistant Secretary of Defense (Intelligence) ... ASD (I)
Assistant Secretary of Defense (Intelligence) (DNAB) ... ASSTSECDEF(INTEL)
Assistant Secretary of Defense (International Security Affairs) (DNAB) ... ASSTSECDEF(INTSECAFF)
Assistant Secretary of Defense (Legislative Affairs) (DOMA) ... ASD(LA)
Assistant Secretary of Defense (Manpower) ... ASD (M)
Assistant Secretary of Defense (Manpower and Reserve Affairs) [*Later, ASD (MRA & L)*] (AABC) ... ASD (M & RA)
Assistant Secretary of Defense (Manpower, Personnel, and Reserves) ... ASD/MP & R
Assistant Secretary of Defense (Manpower, Reserve Affairs, and Logistics) [*Formerly, ASD (M & RA)*] ... ASD (MRA & L)
Assistant Secretary of Defense (Manpower, Reserve Affairs, and Logistics) (DNAB) ... ASSTSECDEF(MPRRESAFFLOG)
Assistant Secretary of Defense (Program Analysis and Evaluation) (AABC) ... ASD (PA & E)
Assistant Secretary of Defense (Properties and Installations) ... ASD/P & I
Assistant Secretary of Defense (Public Affairs) ... ASD (PA)
Assistant Secretary of Defense (Public Affairs) (DNAB) ... ASSTSECDEF(PUBAFF)
Assistant Secretary of Defense (Research and Development) ... ASD/R & D
Assistant Secretary of Defense (Research and Engineering) ... ASD/R & E
Assistant Secretary of Defense (Reserve Affairs) [*DoD*] (GFGA) ... ASD(RA)
Assistant Secretary of Defense (Supply and Logistics) ... ASD/S & L
Assistant Secretary of Defense (Systems Analysis) (AABC) ... ASD (SA)
Assistant Secretary of Defense (Telecommunications) ... ASD (T)
Assistant Secretary of Defense/Health and Medical (SAUS) ... ASD/H&M
Assistant Secretary of Defense/International Security Affairs (SAUS) ... ASD/ISA
Assistant Secretary of Defense/Manpower, Personnel and Reserves (SAUS) ... ASD/MP&R
Assistant Secretary of Defense/System Analysis (SAUS) ... ASD/SA
Assistant Secretary of State (DAS) ... ASS
Assistant Secretary of State (SAUO) ... ASS
Assistant Secretary of State for Economic Affairs (SAUO) ... ASSEA
Assistant Secretary of the Air Force (MCD) ... ASAF
Assistant Secretary of the Air Force ... ASOFAF
Assistant Secretary of the Air Force (SAUO) ... AS of AF
Assistant Secretary of the Air Force (SAUO) ... AstSecAF
Assistant Secretary of the Air Force ... ASTSECAF
Assistant Secretary of the Air Force (SAUS) ... SAFMP
Assistant Secretary of the Air Force (Acquisition) (DOMA) ... ASAF(A)
Assistant Secretary of the Air Force (Financial Management) ... ASAF(FM)
Assistant Secretary of the Air Force for Acquisition (AAGC) ... SAF/AQ
Assistant Secretary of the Air Force (Manpower and Personnel) ... SAFMP
Assistant Secretary of the Air Force (Manpower, Reserve Affairs and Installations Logistics) ... ASAF (MRA & 1L)
Assistant Secretary of the Air Force (Materiel) ... ASAFMA
Assistant Secretary of the Air Force (Research and Development) ... SAFRD
Assistant Secretary of the Air Force (Research, Development, and Acquisition) (MCD) ... ASAF(RD & A)
Assistant Secretary of the Air Force (Research, Development, and Logistics) (MCD) ... ASAF(RDL)
Assistant Secretary of the Air Force (Research, Development, and Logistics) ... SAF/AL
Assistant Secretary of the Army ... ASA
Assistant Secretary of the Army ... AS of A
Assistant Secretary of the Army (SAUO) ... ASOFA
[*The*] **Assistant Secretary of the Army** ... TASA
Assistant Secretary of the Army (Acquisition) ... ASA(A)
Assistant Secretary of the Army (Civil Works) ... ASA(CW)
Assistant Secretary of the Army (Financial Management) ... ASA (FM)
Assistant Secretary of the Army for Acquisition, Logistics and Technology ... ASAALT
Assistant Secretary of the Army for Acquistion, Logistics, and Technology ... ASAALT
Assistant Secretary of the Army for Installations, Logistics and Environment ... ASA(ILE)
Assistant Secretary of the Army for Installations, Logistics, and Financial Management (MCD) ... IL & FM
Assistant Secretary of the Army for Installations, Logistics and Financial Management (SAUO) ... IL&FM
Assistant Secretary of the Army for Research, Development and Acquisition (SAUS) ... SARDA
Assistant Secretary of the Army (Installations and Logistics) ... ASA (I & L)
Assistant Secretary of the Army (Installations, Logistics, and Financial Management) (AABC) ... ASA(IL & FM)
Assistant Secretary of the Army (Manpower and Reserve Affairs) (AABC) ... ASA (M & RA)
Assistant Secretary of the Army, Materiel (SAA) ... ASAMAT
Assistant Secretary of the Army (Research and Development) ... ASA (R & D)
Assistant Secretary of the Army (Research, Development, and Acquisition) ... ASA(RDA)
Assistant Secretary of the General Staff ... ASGS
Assistant Secretary of the Navy ... ASN
Assistant Secretary of the Navy ... ASTSECNAV
Assistant Secretary of the Navy (SAUO) ... AstSecNav
Assistant Secretary of the Navy, Financial Management (SAUS) ... ASN F/M
Assistant Secretary of the Navy (Financial Management) ... ASN (FM)
Assistant Secretary of the Navy (Financial Management) (DNAB) ... ASSTSECNAVFINMGMT
Assistant Secretary of the Navy, Financial Management (SAUO) ... ASTSECNAVFIN
Assistant Secretary of the Navy for Air ... ASTSECNAVAIR
Assistant Secretary of the Navy for Material (SAUO) ... ASTSECNAVMAT
Assistant Secretary of the Navy for Materiel (SAUS) ... ASTSECNAVMAT
Assistant Secretary of the Navy for Personnel (SAUO) ... ASTSECNAVPERS
Assistant Secretary of the Navy (Installation and Logistics) ... ASN(I & L)
Assistant Secretary of the Navy (Installation and Logistics) (DNAB) ... ASSTSECNAVINSTLOG
Assistant Secretary of the Navy (Installation and Logistics) ... ASTSECNAVINSLOG
Assistant Secretary of the Navy, Installations and Logistics (SAUO) ... ASN I/L
Assistant Secretary of the Navy Installations and Logistics (SAUS) ... ASN I/L
Assistant Secretary of the Navy (Manpower and Reserve Affairs) (MCD) ... ASN(M & RA)
Assistant Secretary of the Navy (Manpower and Reserve Affairs) (DNAB) ... ASSTSECNAVMPRESAFF
Assistant Secretary of the Navy (Research and Development) ... ASN(R & D)
Assistant Secretary of the Navy, Research and Development (SAUO) ... ASN R/D
Assistant Secretary of the Navy (Research and Development) (DNAB) ... ASN(RES)
Assistant Secretary of the Navy (Research and Development) (DNAB) ... ASSTSECNAVRES
Assistant Secretary of the Navy (Research and Development) ... ASTSECNAVRESDEV
Assistant Secretary of the Navy (Research, Development, and Acquisition) (DOMA) ... ASN(RD & A)
Assistant Secretary of the Navy (Research, Engineering, and Systems) (DNAB) ... ASN(RE & S)
Assistant Secretary of the Navy (Research, Engineering, and Systems) (DNAB) ... ASSTSECNAVRESENGSYS
Assistant Secretary of the Navy (Shipbuilding and Logistics) (MCD) ... ASN(S & L)
Assistant Secretary of the Navy (Shipbuilding and Logistics) (DNAB) ... ASSTSECNAVSHIPLOG
Assistant Secretary of War (SAUO) ... AsstSecWar
Assistant Secretary of War ... ASW
Assistant Secretary of War for Air (SAUO) ... AFSWA
Assistant Secretary of War for Air [*World War II*] ... ASWA
Assistant Secretary of War of Air (SAUS) ... ASWA
Assistant Secretary's Office [*Navy*] ... ASO
Assistant Section Officer [*Air Force*] [*British*] ... ASO
Assistant Sector Controller [*Aviation*] (DA) ... ASC
Assistant Sector Programming Leader (SAA) ... ASPL
Assistant Sector System Training Leader (SAA) ... ASSTL
Assistant Senior Naval Officer Landing [*British and Canadian*] [*World War II*] ... ASNOL
Assistant Senior Naval Officer, Landing (SAUS) ... ASNOL
Assistant Service Manager [*Automobile sales*] ... ASM
Assistant Solicitor-General (DAS) ... ASG
Assistant Special Agent in Charge ... ASAIC
Assistant Squad Leader (SAUS) ... ASL
Assistant Staff Duty Officer (CINC) ... ASDO
Assistant Staff Judge Advocate [*Air Force*] ... ASJA
Assistant Staff Meteorologist [*NASA*] (KSC) ... ASM
Assistant Stage Manager ... ASM
Assistant State Director ... ASD
Assistant Station Master [*British*] (ADA) ... ASM
Assistant Steward [*British military*] (DMA) ... ASTD
Assistant Stores Accountant [*British military*] (DMA) ... ASA
Assistant Superintendent (DCTA) ... A/SUPT
Assistant Superintendent, Range Operations [*NASA*] (KSC) ... ASRO
Assistant Superintendents of Police (SAUO) ... ASP
Assistant Supervisor of Shipbuilding [*Navy*] ... ASOS
Assistant Supply Officer-in-Chief (SAUO) ... ASOC
Assistant Surgeon (DAS) ... AS
Assistant Surgeon [*Department of Health and Human Services*] (GFGA) ... Asst Surg
Assistant Surgeon General (DAS) ... ASG
Assistant Tactical Officer [*Navy*] (CAAL) ... ATACO

Assistant Test Chief ... ATC
Assistant Test Conductor ... ATC
Assistant Test Director ... ATD
Assistant to the Deputy Military Governor (SAUO) ... ADMG
Assistant to the Secretary of Defense (DOMA) ... ATSD
Assistant to the Secretary of Defense (Atomic Energy) ... ATSD (AE)
Assistant to the Secretary of Defense (Intelligence Oversight) (DOMA) ... ATSD(IO)
Assistant to the Secretary of Defense (Intelligence Policy) (DOMA) ... ATSD(IP)
Assistant to the Secretary of Defense (Review and Oversight) ... ATSD(R & O)
Assistant to the Secretary of the Army (SAUS) ... ASA
Assistant to the Surgeon General (SAUS) ... A Surg G
Assistant Town Clerk [*British*] ... ATC
Assistant Traffic Manager ... ATM
Assistant Traffic Supervisor (DCTA) ... ATS
Assistant Transmission Controller ... ATC
Assistant Trial Counsel ... ATC
Assistant Trust Officer [*Banking*] (TBD) ... ATO
Assistant Under Secretary of State (SAUS) ... AUS
Assistant Under-Secretary (ADA) ... AUS
Assistant Under-Secretary, General [*Air Ministry*] [*British*] ... AUS(G)
Assistant Under-Secretary of State (DAS) ... AUSS
Assistant United States Attorney (EPA) ... AUSA
Assistant Veterans Employment Representative [*Department of Labor*] ... AVER
Assistant Vice Chancellor (DLA) ... AVCH
Assistant Vice Chief of Staff ... AVCS
Assistant Vice Chief of Staff, Army [*Later, AVCSA*] (AABC) ... AVC of SA
Assistant Vice Chief of Staff, Army [*Formerly, AVC of SA*] (AABC) ... AVCSA
Assistant Vice Director for Estimates (MCD) ... DE
Assistant Vice President ... AVP
Assistant Weapons Control Officer ... AWCO
Assistant Writer [*British military*] (DMA) ... AWTR
Assistant Yard Master [*Railroads*] [*British*] ... AYM
Assistant-Commissary-General [*British*] ... Ass Com Gen
Assist-Control (SAUS) ... AC
Assist-Control Mechanical Ventilation [*Medicine*] ... ACMV
Assist-Control Mode Ventilation (MELL) ... ACMV
Assisted (ADWA) ... asstd
Assisted Control (MEDA) ... AC
Assisted Health Insurance Plan ... AHIP
Assisted Home-Ownership Program [*Canada*] ... AHOP
Assisted Hydrothermal Oxidation [*Of hazardous wastes*] ... AHO
Assisted Living Concepts [*AMEX symbol*] (TTSB) ... ALF
Assisted Living Concepts, Inc. [*AMEX symbol*] (SAG) ... ALF
Assisted Living Concepts, Inc. [*Associated Press*] (SAG) ... AstLiving
Assisted Living Facilities Association of America ... ALFAA
Assisted Living Federation of America ... ALFA
Assisted Maintenance Period [*British military*] (DMA) ... AMP
Assisted Mechanical Ventilation [*Medicine*] (DAVI) ... AMV
Assisted Mechanical Ventilator [*Medicine*] (MELL) ... AMV
Assisted Places Committee [*Education*] [*British*] ... APC
Assisted Places Scheme (AIE) ... APS
Assisted Prison Visit (WDAA) ... APV
Assisted Prison Visits Unit (WDAA) ... APVU
Assisted Rental Program [*Canada*] ... ARP
Assisted Reproductive Technologies (SAUS) ... ART
Assisted Reproductive Technology [*Medicine*] (MELL) ... ART
Assisted Reproductive Technology Services [*Medicine*] (MELL) ... ARTS
Assisted Resonance (NTCM) ... AR
Assisted Respiration [*Medicine*] (MELL) ... AR
Assisted Search for Knowledge (SAUS) ... ASK
Assisted Spontaneous Breathing [*Medicine*] (MELL) ... ASB
Assisted Spontaneous Ventilation [*Medicine*] (MELL) ... ASV
Assisted Takeoff [*British aviation and rocket term*] ... ATO
Assisted Takeoff and Landing (ACAE) ... ATOL
Assisted Takeoff System ... ATOS
Assisted-Draught Crossflow Tower (PDAA) ... ADCT
Assisted-Living Facility [*Health care*] ... ALF
Assistent [*Assistant*] [*German*] ... Assist
Assistenz (SAUS) ... Assist
Assisting ... ASSTG
Assisting in Deployment of Energy Practices and Technologies Program (SAUO) ... ADEPT
Assisting Organization (ACAE) ... AO
Assisting Women to Advance through Resources and Encouragement Project (EDAC) ... AWARE
Assisting Work Center ... AWC
Assistive Device Center [*Research center*] (RCD) ... ADC
Assistive Listening Device (WYGK) ... ALD
Assistive Listening Devices (PAZ) ... ALDs
Assistive Reproductive Technology (SAUS) ... ART
Assistive Technology ... AT
Assistive Technology Resource Alliance (ADWA) ... ATRA
Assiut [*Egypt*] [*Airport symbol*] (AD) ... ATZ
Assize Rolls [*British*] ... ASS
Assizes of Jerusalem [*A publication*] (DLA) ... Ass Jerus
Asso and Manuel's Institutes of Spanish Civil Law [*A publication*] (DLA) ... Asso & Man
Assoc Estates Rlty 9.75% Dep Pfd [*NYSE symbol*] (TTSB) ... AECPrA
Assocation of Canadian Industrial Designers (SAUO) ... ACID
Assocation of Canadian University Teachers of French (SAUS) ... ACUTF
Assocation of Universities for Research in Astronomy (SAUO) ... AURA
Associacao Brasileira de Buiatria [*Brazilian Veterinary Cattle Association*] (GVA) ... ABB
Associacao Brasileira de Imprensa [*Brazilian Press Association*] ... ABI
Associacao Brasileira de Veterinarios de Animais Selvagens [*Brazilian Small Animal Veterinary Association*] (GVA) ... ABRAVAS
Associacao Brasileiro dos Colectionadores de Discos [*Record label*] [*Brazil*] ... ABCD
Associacao Catolica Interamericana de Filosofia (EAIO) ... ACIF
Associacao Civica Angolana [*Political party*] (EY) ... ACA
Associacao Internacional de Missoes dos Israelitas [*International Board of Jewish Missions*] (EAIO) ... AIMI
Associacao Latino-Americana de Direito Agrario ... ALADA
Associacao Social Democrata Independente [*Independent Social Democrat Association*] [*Portugal*] [*Political party*] (PPE) ... ASDI
Associacao Universitaria Interamericana [*Interamerican University Association*] [*Portuguese*] ... AUI
Associacion Latino Americana para la Promocion de l'Habitat la Arquitectura y elUrbanismo [*Latin American Association for the Promotion of the Habitat, Architecture and Town Planning*] [*Ecuador*] (PDAA) ... ALAHUA
Associacion Mexicana Automovilistica (GEOI) ... AMA
Associate [*In an academic degree*] ... A
Associate ... ASSO
Associate [*or Association*] (AFM) ... ASSOC
Associate (EBF) ... assoc
Associate (CMD) ... Assoc
Associate Administrator [*NASA*] ... AA
Associate Administrator for Airway Facilities (CTAS) ... AFF
Associate Administrator for Information Systems [*Social and Rehabilitation Service, HEW*] ... AAIS
Associate Administrator for Management [*Social and Rehabilitation Service, HEW*] ... AA/M
Associate Administrator for Manned Space Flight [*NASA*] (KSC) ... AA/MSF
Associate Administrator for Minority Small Business and Capital Ownership Development (AAGC) ... AA/MSB&COD
Associate Administrator for NAS Development [*FAA*] (TAG) ... AND
Associate Administrator for Space Flight [*NASA*] (MCD) ... AASF
Associate Advisor ... AA
Associate Aide (SAUS) ... ATA
Associate, American College of Physicians (CMD) ... AACP
Associate, American College of Surgeons (CMD) ... AACS
Associate and Advisory Committee to the Special Committee on Electronic Data Ret (SAUS) ... AACSCEDR
Associate Chief Medical Director (DMAA) ... ACMD
Associate Citizens for Responsible Education [*Group opposing sex education in schools*] ... ACRE
Associate Client Program [*Business International Corp.*] [*Information service or system*] (IID) ... ACP
Associate, College of Violinists ... ACV
Associate Collegiate Players ... ACP
Associate Commissioner for Health Affairs [*U.S. Department of Health and Human Services*] ... ACHA
Associate Commissioner for Legislative Affairs [*U.S. Department of Health and Human Services*] ... ACLA
Associate Commissioner for Office of Management [*U.S. Food and Drug Administration*] ... ACOM
Associate Commissioner for Planning and Evaluation [*U.S. Food and Drug Administration*] ... ACPE
Associate Commissioner for Public Affairs [*U.S. Food and Drug Administration*] ... ACPA
Associate Commissioner for Regulatory Affairs [*U.S. Food and Drug Administration*] ... ACRA
Associate Committee of Geodesy and Geophysics [*Canada*] ... ACGG
Associate Committee on Aerodynamics [*National Research Council*] [*Canada*] ... ACOA
Associate Committee on Air Cushion Technology [*Canada*] (HGAA) ... ACACT
Associate Committee on Air-Cushion Technology (SAUO) ... ACACT
Associate Committee on Aviation Medical Research [*Canada*] ... ACAMR
Associate Committee on Geo-Technical Research [*Canada*] (HGAA) ... ACGR
Associate Committee on Soil and Snow Mechanics (SAUO) ... ACSSM
Associate Committee on the National Building Code [*National Research Council Canada*] ... ACNBC
Associate Committee on Tribology (SAUO) ... ACOT
Associate Computer Professional ... ACP
Associate Content Retrieval Network (SAUS) ... ACORN
Associate Contractor ... AC
Associate Contractor (SAA) ... ACR
Associate Contractor (ACAE) ... ASCON
Associate Contractor Agreement (MCD) ... ACA
Associate Contractor Program Manager [*NASA*] (NASA) ... ACPM
Associate Contractor Projects Office [*NASA*] (NASA) ... ACPO
Associate Creative Director [*Advertising*] (WDMC) ... ACD
Associate Credit Executive [*Society of Certified Consumer Credit Executives*] [*Designation awarded by*] ... ACE
Associate Credit Executive (SAUS) ... ACE
Associate Degree ... AD
Associate Degree Competition Program (SAUO) ... ADCP
Associate Degree Completion Program [*Navy*] (NG) ... ADCOP
Associate Degree in Nursing ... ADN
Associate Degree in Science (SAUO) ... ADS
Associate Deputy Director for Operations/Military Affairs ... ADDO/MA
Associate Diploma ... AssocDip
Associate Diploma Built Environment Technician ... AssocDipBltEnvir
Associate Diploma in Aboriginal Community Management and Development ... AssocDipAbComMgt & Dev
Associate Diploma in Aboriginal Health ... AssocDipAbHlth
Associate Diploma in Aboriginal Health and Community Development ... AssocDipAHCD
Associate Diploma in Aboriginal Studies ... ADipAborStud

Associate Diploma in Aboriginal Studies ... AssocDipAbStudies
Associate Diploma in Accounting ... AssocDipAcctg
Associate Diploma in Administration ... AssocDipAdmin
Associate Diploma in Advertising ... AssocDipAdvrt
Associate Diploma in Agricultural Production ... AssocDipAgProd
Associate Diploma in Agricultural Services ... AssocDipAgServs
Associate Diploma in Agriculture ... AssocDipAg
Associate Diploma in Agriculture ... AssocDipAgr
Associate Diploma in Applied Biology ... AssocDipAppBiol
Associate Diploma in Applied Science ... AssocDipAppSc
Associate Diploma in Applied Science (Agriculture) ... AssocDipAppSci(Ag)
Associate Diploma in Applied Science (Animal Science) ... AssocDipAppSci(AnimalSc)
Associate Diploma in Applied Science (Animal Technology) ... AssocDipAppSci(AnimalTech)
Associate Diploma in Applied Science (Grain Management) ... AssocDipAppSci(GrainMgmt)
Associate Diploma in Architectural Drafting ... AssocDipArchDraft
Associate Diploma in Architectural Technology ... AssocDipArchTech
Associate Diploma in Arts (ADA) ... ADipA
Associate Diploma in Arts ... AssocDipArts
Associate Diploma in Arts (Applied Photography) ... AssocDipArts(AppPhotog)
Associate Diploma in Arts (Commercial Art) ... AssocDipArts(ComArt)
Associate Diploma in Asian Studies ... AssocDipAsianSt
Associate Diploma in Biological Science (Animal Technology) ... AssocDipBiolSc(AnimalTech)
Associate Diploma in Building Construction ... AssocDipBuildCons
Associate Diploma in Business ... AssocDipBus
Associate Diploma in Cartography (ADA) ... AssocDipCart
Associate Diploma in Civil Engineering ... AssocDipCivEng
Associate Diploma in Clinical Laboratory Techniques ... AssocDipClinLabTech
Associate Diploma in Clinical Nursing Studies (Gerontology) ... AssocDipClinNursStud(Gerontol)
Associate Diploma in Community Health Nursing ... AssocDipCHN
Associate Diploma in Computer Applications ... AssocDipCompAppl
Associate Diploma in Computing ... ADC
Associate Diploma in Diversional Therapy ... AssocDipDT
Associate Diploma in Education ... AssocDipEd
Associate Diploma in Electrical Engineering ... AssocDipElecEng
Associate Diploma in Fine Arts ... ADipFA
Associate Diploma in Forestry ... AssDipFor
Associate Diploma in Forestry ... AssocDipFor
Associate Diploma in Furniture Technology ... AssocDipFurnTechnology
Associate Diploma in Geology ... ADipGeol
Associate Diploma in Horse Management ... AssocDipHorseMgmt
Associate Diploma in Horticulture ... AssocDipHort
Associate Diploma in Human Studies ... AssocDipHumanSt
Associate Diploma in International Trade ... AssocDipIntTrade
Associate Diploma in Legal Practice ... AssocDipLegPrac
Associate Diploma in Library Studies ... ADipLibStud
Associate Diploma in Local and Applied History ... AssocDipLoc&AppHist
Associate Diploma in Marketing ... AssocDipMktg
Associate Diploma in Marketing and Japanese ... AssocDipMktgJap
Associate Diploma in Mechanical Engineering ... ADipME
Associate Diploma in Mechanical Engineering ... AssocDipMechEng
Associate Diploma in Medical Laboratory Technology ... AssocDipMedLabTech
Associate Diploma in Music ... AssocDipMus
Associate Diploma in Nurse Education ... AssocDipNursEd
Associate Diploma in Nursing Studies ... AssocDipNursStudies
Associate Diploma in Occupational Health and Safety ... AssocDipOccHlth&Saft
Associate Diploma in Office Administration ... AssocDipOffAdmin
Associate Diploma in Photography ... ADipPhot
Associate Diploma in Physiotherapy ... ADipPhysio
Associate Diploma in Political Studies ... AssocDipPolSt
Associate Diploma in Professional Writing ... ADipProWri
Associate Diploma in Recreation ... ADipRec
Associate Diploma in Recreation ... AssocDipRec
Associate Diploma in Rehabilitation Counselling ... AssocDipRc
Associate Diploma in Science ... AssocDipSc
Associate Diploma in Science (Animal Science) ... AssocDipSc(AnimalScience)
Associate Diploma in Science (Systems Agriculture) ... AssocDipSc(SystemsAg)
Associate Diploma in Security Management ... AssocDipSecMgt
Associate Diploma in Small Business Management ... AssocDipSmallBusMgt
Associate Diploma in Social Welfare ... ADipSocWel
Associate Diploma in Social Work ... ADipSW
Associate Diploma in Sports Science ... AssocDipSptSc
Associate Diploma in Surveying and Mapping ... AssocDipSurvMap
Associate Diploma in Training and Development ... AssocDipTrainDev
Associate Diploma in Valuation ... ADipVal
Associate Diploma of Mining and Mineral Technology ... AssocDipMMT
Associate Diploma of Modern Languages ... AssocDipModLang
Associate Diploma of Social Science ... AssocDipSocSc
Associate Diploma of Surveying ... AssocDipSurv
Associate Director ... AD
Associate Director for Operations (SAUS) ... ADO
Associate Directorate for Design [*Kennedy Space Center*] [*NASA*] (NASA) ... DD
Associate Directorate for Facilities and Systems Management [*Kennedy Space Center*] [*NASA*] (NASA) ... DF
Associate Directorate for LPS [*Launch Processing System*] **Development** [*Kennedy Space Center*] [*NASA*] (NASA) ... DL
Associate Editor [*Publishing*] ... AE
Associate Enforcement Counsel [*Environmental Protection Agency*] (GFGA) ... AEC
Associate Engineer (SAUS) ... Assoc Engr
Associate Engraver [*British*] (ROG) ... AE
Associate Engraver, Royal Academy [*British*] ... AERA
Associate, Faculty Occupational Medicine (CMD) ... AFOM
Associate Fellow (ADA) ... AF
Associate Fellow, American College of Cardiology (CMD) ... AFACC
Associate Fellow, College of Chest Physicians (CMD) ... AFCCP
Associate Fellow of American College of Allergists (DHSM) ... AFACAL
Associate Fellow of the American Institute of Aeronautics and Astronautics [*Formerly, AFIAS*] ... AFAIAA
Associate Fellow of the American Institute of Aeronautics and Astronautics (SAUS) ... AFAIAA
Associate Fellow of the British Interplanetary Society (DI) ... AFBIS
Associate Fellow of the British Psychological Society ... AFBPS
Associate Fellow of the Canadian Aeronautic and Space Institute (DD) ... AFCASI
Associate Fellow of the Canadian Aeronautical Institute ... AFCAI
Associate Fellow of the Catering Institute of Australia ... AFCIA
Associate Fellow of the Institute of Aeronautical Sciences (SAUS) ... AFIAeS
Associate Fellow of the Institute of Aeronautical Sciences [*Later, AFAIAA*] ... AFIAS
Associate Fellow of the Institute of Civil Defence [*British*] ... AFICD
Associate Fellow of the Institute of Industrial Managers [*British*] ... AFIIM
Associate Fellow of the Institute of Mathematics and its Applications (SAUS) ... AFIMA
Associate Fellow of the Institute of Petroleum [*British*] ... AF Inst Pet
Associate Fellow of the Institute of the Aerospace Sciences (SAUS) ... AFIAS
Associate Fellow of the Royal Aeronautical Society [*British*] ... AFR Ae S
Associate Fellow of the Royal Aeronautical Society [*British*] ... AFRAS
Associate Fellow of the Society of Electronic and Radio Technicians (SAUO) ... AFSERT
Associate Fellow of the Society of Licensed Aircraft Engineers and Technologists (SAUO) ... AFSLAET
Associate Fellowship of Youth Development [*British*] (DBQ) ... FYDA
Associate for Radiation Research [*British*] ... ARR
Associate for Reform of Latin Teaching [*British*] ... ARLT
Associate for Religious Education for Teachers and Lecturers [*British*] ... ARETL
Associate for Research in Ophthalmology (DMAA) ... ARO
Associate General Counsel (COE) ... AGC
Associate General Counsels (SAUO) ... AGC
Associate in Accountancy of the University of Queensland (SAUO) ... AAUQ
Associate in Accounting ... AA
Associate in Administration ... A Adm
Associate in Administration (SAUS) ... AAdm
Associate in Aeronautical Engineering ... A Ae E
Associate in Agriculture ... A Agri
Associate in Agriculture (NADA) ... AAgric
Associate in Air-Conditioning and Refrigeration Technology ... AA-C & Ref Tech
Associate in Air-Conditioning and Refrigeration Technology (SAUS) ... AA-C&Ref Tech
Associate in Applied Arts ... AAA
Associate in Applied Science ... AAS
Associate in Architecture ... A Arch
Associate in Architecture of the Sydney Technical College (SAUS) ... AASTC
Associate in Architecture-Sydney Technical College (SAUS) ... AASTC
Associate in Arts ... AA
Associate in Arts (ROG) ... AIA
Associate in Arts in Agriculture ... AA Ag
Associate in Arts in Arts and Science ... AAA & S
Associate in Arts in Business ... AAB
Associate in Arts in Business ... AA Bus
Associate in Arts in Fine Arts ... AAFA
Associate in Arts in Home Economics ... AAHE
Associate in Arts in Judaic Studies (BJA) ... AAJS
Associate in Arts in Law Enforcement ... AALE
Associate in Arts in Liberal Arts ... AALA
Associate in Arts in Music ... AAMus
Associate in Arts in Nursing ... AAN
Associate in Arts in Terminal Education ... AA Ter Ed
Associate in Automotive Technology ... AA Tech
Associate in Aviation Technology ... A Av Tech
Associate in Business ... AB
Associate in Business Administration ... ABA
Associate in Business Administration ... ABus
Associate in Business Management ... ABM
Associate in Business Management ... ASBM
Associate in Business Science ... ABS
Associate in Business Technology ... ABT
Associate in Chemistry ... A Chem
Associate in Claims [*Insurance*] ... AIC
Associate in Commerce ... AC
Associate in Commerce ... A Com
Associate in Commercial Arts ... ACA
Associate in Commercial Development (SAUS) ... AC Ed
Associate in Commercial Education ... AC Ed
Associate in Commercial Science ... ACS
Associate in Criminal Justice ... ACJ
Associate in Customer Service [*Canada*] (DD) ... ACS
Associate in Diesel Technology ... A Dies Tech
Associate in Drafting and Design ... A Dr & Dgn
Associate in Drafting and Design (SAUS) ... A Dr&Dgn
Associate in Education ... AE
Associate in Education ... A Ed
Associate in Education (SAUO) ... AED
Associate in Electrical Technology (IAA) ... AELECTECH
Associate in Electrical Technology ... AET
Associate in Electronics (SAUS) ... AE

Associate in Electronics Technology (IAA) .... AELECTRTECHN
Associate in Elementary Education .... A El Ed
Associate in Engineering .... AE
Associate in Engineering .... AEE
Associate in Engineering .... A Eng
Associate in Engineering .... A Engr
Associate in Engineering .... ASE
Associate in Engineering Administration .... AEA
Associate in Engineering Electronics .... A Eng Elect
Associate in Engineering Technology .... AET
Associate in Engineering Technology (WGA) .... ASET
Associate in English .... A En
Associate in Fine Arts .... AFA
Associate in Fine Arts in Art .... AFA Art
Associate in Fine Arts in Dance .... AFA Dance
Associate in Fine Arts in Drama .... AFA Drama
Associate in Fine Arts in Music .... AFA Mus
Associate in Fuel Technology and Chemical Engineering (SAUS) .... AFCE
Associate in General Education .... AGE
Associate in General Education .... AGEd
Associate in General Education .... A in G Ed
Associate in General Studies .... AGS
Associate in Glass Technology (SAUS) .... AGT
Associate in Home Economics .... AHE
Associate in Home Economics .... AH Ec
Associate in Industrial Education .... AI Ed
Associate in Industrial Education (SAUS) .... AI Ed
Associate in Industrial Management .... AIM
Associate in Industrial Management .... ASIM
Associate in Journalism .... AJ
Associate in Letters .... A Litt
Associate in Letters, Arts and Sciences (SAUS) .... ALAS
Associate in Liberal Arts .... ALA
Associate in Literature .... A Lit
Associate in Local Government Administration (ADA) .... ALGA
Associate in Management [*Insurance*] .... AIM
Associate in Marine Insurance Management .... AMIM
Associate in Mechanical Technology .... AMT
Associate in Medical Technology .... AMT
Associate in Metallurgy [*British*] .... A Met
Associate in Metallurgy (SAUS) .... Assoc Met
Associate in Minerals Technology (SAUS) .... AMinisTech
Associate in Music .... AMus
Associate in Music, London College of Music [*British*] (WDAA) .... A Mus LCM
Associate in Music of the London College of Music (ROG) .... A MUS LCM
Associate in Music of the London Col-lege of Music (SAUS) .... A Mus LCM
Associate in Music of Trinity College of Music, London [*British*] (DBQ) .... AMusTCL
Associate in Nursing .... AN
Associate in Nursing .... ASN
Associate in Nursing Science (DAVI) .... ANS
Associate in Nursing Science .... ASN
Associate in Philosophy .... A Ph
Associate in Physical Education .... AP Ed
Associate in Practical Arts .... APA
Associate in Public Administration .... APA
Associate in Public Service Technology .... APST
Associate in Recreation Leadership .... ARL
Associate in Religion .... A Rel
Associate in Religious Arts .... ARA
Associate in Religious Education .... ARE
Associate in Retailing .... AR
Associate in Risk Management [*Canada*] (DD) .... ARM
Associate in Science .... AS
Associate in Science .... ASc
Associate in Science .... Assoc Sc
Associate in Science (SAUS) .... Assoc Sci
Associate in Science Education .... ASEd
Associate in Science in Basic Engineering .... ASBE
Associate in Science in Business .... ASB
Associate in Science in Commerce .... ASC
Associate in Science in Electronic Engineering (IAA) .... ASEE
Associate in Science in Electronic Engineering Technology .... ASEET
Associate in Science in Engineering .... ASE
Associate in Science in Medical Secretarial .... ASMS
Associate in Science in Recreation Leadership .... ASRL
Associate in Science in Secretarial Studies .... ASSS
Associate in Secretarial Administration .... ASA
Associate in Secretarial Science .... A Se S
Associate in Secretarial Science .... A Se Sc
Associate in Secretarial Science .... ASS
Associate in Secretarial Science .... SSA
Associate in Secretarial Studies .... ASS
Associate in Specialized Business .... ASB
Associate in Technical Affairs (SAUS) .... ATA
Associate in Technical Arts .... ATA
Associate in Technical Education .... ATE
Associate in Technology .... AT
Associate in Technology (NADA) .... ATECH
Associate in Technology (SAUS) .... ATech
Associate in the Technology of Surface Coatings [*British*] (DBQ) .... ATSC
Associate in Theology .... A Th
Associate in Theology (ADA) .... ThA
Associate in Therapy .... ATh
Associate in Underwriting [*Insurance*] .... AIU
Associate in Wildlife Technology .... AWT
Associate Infantry Officer Career Course [*Army*] .... AIOCC
Associate, Institute of Hospital Administrators [*or Administration*] (DAVI) .... AHA
Associate Insurance Broker (DD) .... AIB
Associate Insurance Data Manager .... AIDM
Associate, International College of Surgeons (CMD) .... AICS
Associate Jewelers [*Defunct*] (EA) .... AJ
Associate Justice [*US Supreme Court*] .... AJ
Associate Learning from Relative Environmental Data (SAUS) .... ALFRED
Associate List Searcher (SAUS) .... ALS
Associate List Selection (or Selector) (SAUS) .... ALS
Associate Logistics Executive Development Course .... ALEDC
Associate Managing Editor (WDMC) .... AME
Associate Manufacturers of Veterinary and Agricultural Products (SAUS) .... AMVAP
Associate Member .... AM
Associate Member (SAUS) .... AsMem
Associate Member, Canadian Academy of Allergy (CMD) .... AMCAA
Associate Member, College of General Practice of Canada (CMD) .... AMCGP
Associate Member of Engineering Institute of Canada .... AMEIC
Associate Member of Institute of Accredited Public Accountants .... APA
Associate Member of Institution of Aeronautical Engineers [*British*] .... AMI Ae E
Associate Member of the American Institute of Electrical Engineers (SAUS) .... AMAmIEE
Associate Member of the American Society of Civil Engineers .... AM Am Soc CE
Associate Member of the American Society of Mechanical Engineers .... AMASME
Associate Member of the Association of Business Executives [*British*] (DCTA) .... AMABE
Associate Member of the Association of Cost and Industrial Accountants (SAUO) .... AMCIA
Associate Member of the Association of Medical Secretaries, Practice Administrators, and Receptionists [*British*] (DBQ) .... AAMS
Associate Member of the Association of Supervisory and Executive Engineers [*British*] (DBQ) .... AMASEE
Associate Member of the Australian Association of Neurologists .... AMAAN
Associate Member of the Australian Institution of Engineers (SAUS) .... AMIE Aust
Associate Member of the British Arts Association (DBQ) .... AMBA
Associate Member of the British Association of Chemists (SAUO) .... AMBAC
Associate Member of the British Computer Society (DBQ) .... AMBCS
Associate Member of the British Institute of Management .... AMBIM
Associate Member of the British Institution of Radio Engineers [*Later, AMIERE*] .... AM Brit IRE
Associate Member of the Chartered Institute of Transport [*British*] (DI) .... AMCIT
Associate Member of the Commonwealth Institute of Accountants [*British*] (ODBW) .... AICA
Associate Member of the Construction Surveyor's Institute [*British*] (DBQ) .... AMCSI
Associate Member of the Corporation of Insurance Brokers [*British*] (DI) .... AMCIB
Associate Member of the Engineering Institute of Canada (SAUS) .... AMEIC
Associate Member of the Fundraising Institute-Australia, Inc. (NFD) .... AMFIA
Associate Member of the Guild of Cleaners and Launderers [*British*] (DBQ) .... AGCL
Associate Member of the Highway and Traffic Technicians' Association [*British*] (DBQ) .... AMHTTA
Associate Member of the Hotel and Catering Institute (SAUS) .... AMHCI
Associate Member of the Inc. Advertising Managers Association (SAUS) .... AMIAMA
Associate Member of the Industrial Transport Association (SAUO) .... AMITA
Associate Member of the Institute of Aeronautical Engineers [*British*] (DI) .... AMIAE
Associate Member of the Institute of Almoners (SAUS) .... AMIA
Associate Member of the Institute of Asphalt Technology [*British*] (DBQ) .... AMIAT
Associate Member of the Institute of Automobile Engineers [*British*] (ROG) .... AMIAE
Associate Member of the Institute of Automotive Engineer Assessors [*British*] (DBQ) .... AMInstAEA
Associate Member of the Institute of Automotive Engineers (SAUS) .... AMIAE
Associate Member of the Institute of Biology [*British*] (DI) .... AIBiol
Associate Member of the Institute of British Foundrymen (SAUS) .... AMIBritF
Associate Member of the Institute of Building (SAUS) .... AMIOB
Associate Member of the Institute of Business and Technical Management [*British*] (DBQ) .... AMInstBTM
Associate Member of the Institute of Clerks of Works [*British*] (DI) .... AMICW
Associate Member of the Institute of Commercial Management [*British*] (DCTA) .... AM Inst CM
Associate Member of the Institute of Credit Management [*British*] (DBQ) .... MICM
Associate Member of the Institute of Electronics [*British*] .... AM Inst E
Associate Member of the Institute of Employment Consultants [*British*] (DBQ) .... AECI
Associate Member of the Institute of Export [*British*] .... AMIEx
Associate Member of the Institute of Fuel [*British*] .... AMIF
Associate Member of the Institute of Fuel [*British*] .... AM Inst F
Associate Member of the Institute of Gas Engineers [*British*] (ROG) .... AM INST GE
Associate Member of the Institute of Gas Engineers (SAUS) .... Assoc M Inst Gas E
Associate Member of the Institute of Housing (SAUS) .... AMIH
Associate Member of the Institute of Management Specialists [*British*] (DBQ) .... AMIMS

Associate Member of the Institute of Manufacturing [*British*] (DBQ) .... AMIManf
Associate Member of the Institute of Marine Engineers [*British*] .... AMI Mar E
Associate Member of the Institute of Marine Engineers [*British*] (DS) ...... AMIME
Associate Member of the Institute of Materials Handling [*British*] (DBQ) .... AMIMH
Associate Member of the Institute of Medical and Biological Illustration [*British*] (DBQ) .... AIMBI
Associate Member of the Institute of Metallurgists [*British*] (DBQ) .... AMIM
Associate Member of the Institute of Naval Engineers (SAUS) .... AMINE
Associate Member of the Institute of Park Administration (SAUS) .... AMIPA
Associate Member of the Institute of Plant Engineers [*British*] .... AMI Plant E
Associate Member of the Institute of Practitioners in Advertising [*British*] (DI) .... AMIPA
Associate Member of the Institute of Printing (DGA) .... AMIOP
Associate Member of the Institute of Printing Management (DGA) ..... AMI PTG M
Associate Member of the Institute of Printing Management (SAUS) ...... AMIPtgM
Associate Member of the Institute of Production Control [*British*] (DBQ) .... AMIPC
Associate Member of the Institute of Public Cleansing [*British*] (DI) ..... AMInstPC
Associate Member of the Institute of Quality Assurance (ODBW) .... AMIQM
Associate Member of the Institute of Quarrying [*British*] (DBQ) .... AMIQ
Associate Member of the Institute of Radio and Electronic Engineers (Australia) .... AMIREE (Aust)
Associate Member of the Institute of Refrigeration [*British*] .... AMInstR
Associate Member of the Institute of Road Transport Engineers [*British*] (DBQ) .... AMIRTE
Associate Member of the Institute of Structural Engineers [*British*].... AMIStruct E
Associate Member of the Institute of Structural Engineers (SAUS) .... AMI Struct E
Associate Member of the Institute of Supervisory Management [*British*] (DBQ) .... AMISM
Associate Member of the Institute of Technical Engineers (SAUS) ...... AMI Tec E
Associate Member of the Institute of the Motor Industry [*British*] .... AMIMI
Associate Member of the Institute of Training and Development [*British*] (DBQ) .... AMITD
Associate Member of the Institute of Transport [*British*] (EY) .... AMInstT
Associate Member of the Institute of Transport (SAUS) .... AM Inst T
Associate Member of the Institute of Transport (SAUS) .... AMIT
Associate Member of the Institute of Transport Administration [*British*] (DCTA) .... AM Inst TA
Associate Member of the Institute of Water Engineers [*British*] .... AMI Water E
Associate Member of the Institute of Water Pollution Control [*British*] (DBQ) .... AMIWPC
Associate Member of the Institute of Welding [*British*] .... AM Inst W
Associate Member of the Institute of Welding [*British*] .... AMIW
Associate Member of the Institute of Wood Science [*British*] (DBQ) .... AIWSc
Associate Member of the Institute of Work Study Practitioners [*British*] .... AIWSP
Associate Member of the Institution of Aeronautical Engineers (SAUS) .... AMIAeE
Associate Member of the Institution of Aeronautical Engineers [*British*] .... AssocMIAeE
Associate Member of the Institution of Agricultural Engineers [*British*] .... AMIAgrE
Associate Member of the Institution of Analysts & Programmers (SAUS) .... AMIAP
Associate Member of the Institution of Body Engineers [*British*] (DBQ) .... AMBEI
Associate Member of the Institution of British Engineers .... AMInstBE
Associate Member of the Institution of British Engineers (SAUS) .... AM Inst BE
Associate Member of the Institution of Chemical Engineers [*British*] .... AMI Chem E
Associate Member of the Institution of Chemical Engineers (SAUS) .... AM Inst Chem E
Associate Member of the Institution of Civil Engineers [*Later, MICE*] [*British*] .... AMICE
Associate Member of the Institution of Civil Engineers [*British*] (EY)..... AMInstCE
Associate Member of the Institution of Civil Engineers (SAUS) .... Assoc MICE
Associate (Member) of the Institution of Civil Engineers [*British*] .... Assoc (M) Inst CE
Associate Member of the Institution of Civil Engineers of Ireland (SAUS) .... AMICEI
Associate Member of the Institution of Corrosion Science and Technology [*British*] (DBQ) .... AMICorrST
Associate Member of the Institution of Electrical and Electronics Incorporated Engineers [*British*] (DBQ) .... AMIElecIE
Associate Member of the Institution of Electrical Engineers [*Later, MIEE*] [*British*] (EY) .... AMIEE
Associate Member of the Institution of Electronic and Radio Engineers (SAUS) .... AMIERE
Associate Member of the Institution of Engineering Designers [*British*] .... AMIED
Associate Member of the Institution of Engineering Inspection (SAUS) ..... AMIEI
Associate Member of the Institution of Engineers, India (SAUS) .... AMIE Ind
Associate Member of the Institution of Fire Engineers (SAUS) .... AMI Fire E
Associate Member of the Institution of Fire Engineers [*British*] .... AMIFireE
Associate Member of the Institution of Gas Engineers [*British*] .... AMIGasE
Associate Member of the Institution of Heating and Ventilating Engineers (SAUS) .... AMIHVE
Associate Member of the Institution of Highway Engineers [*British*] (DBQ) .... AMIHT
Associate Member of the Institution of Highway Engineers [*British*] ..... AMInstHE
Associate Member of the Institution of Locomotive Engineers [*British*] .... AMILocoE
Associate Member of the Institution of Locomotive Engineers (SAUS) .... AMI Loco E
Associate Member of the Institution of Mechanical and General Technician Engineers [*British*] (DBQ) .... AMIMGTechE
Associate Member of the Institution of Mechanical Engineers [*Later, MIMechE*] [*British*] (EY) .... AMIMechE
Associate Member of the Institution of Mechanical Engineers (SAUS) .... AMI Mech E
Associate Member of the Institution of Mining and Metallurgy [*British*].... AMIMM
Associate Member of the Institution of Mining Engineers [*British*] .... AMIME
Associate Member of the Institution of Mining Engineers [*British*] (EY) .... AMIMinE
Associate Member of the Institution of Municipal and County Engineers (SAUS) .... AM Inst M&Cy E
Associate Member of the Institution of Municipal Engineers (SAUS) .... AMIMunE
Associate Member of the Institution of Municipal Engineers [*British*] .... AMI Mun E
Associate Member of the Institution of Naval Architects [*British*] .... AMINA
Associate Member of the Institution of Nuclear Engineers (SAUS) .... AMINucE
Associate Member of the Institution of Occupational Safety and Health [*British*] (DCTA) .... AMIOSH
Associate Member of the Institution of Plant Engineers (SAUS) .... AMIPlantE
Associate Member of the Institution of Production Engineers [*British*] ..... AMIPE
Associate Member of the Institution of Production Engineers [*British*] (DBQ) .... AMI-ProdE
Associate Member of the Institution of Public Health Engineers (SAUS) .... AMIPHE
Associate Member of the Institution of Radio Engineers (SAUS) .... AMIRE
Associate Member of the Institution of Sales Management [*British*] (DI) .... AMInstSM
Associate Member of the Institution of Transport Engineers (SAUS) .... AMInstTE
Associate Member of the Institution of Water Engineers (SAUS) .... AMIWE
Associate Member of the Institution of Water Engineers and Scientists [*British*] (DI) .... AMIWES
Associate Member of the Institution of Works and Highways Technician Engineers [*British*] (DBQ) .... AMIWHTE
Associate Member of the Institution of Works Managers [*British*] .... AMIWM
Associate Member of the International Institute of Arts and Letters (SAUS) .... AIAL
Associate Member of the International Institute of Social Economics [*British*] (DBQ) .... AMIISE
Associate Member of the Iron and Steel Institute (SAUS) .... AMISI
Associate Member of the Master Photographers Association [*British*] (DBQ) .... AMPA
Associate Member of the National Institute of Engineering (SAUS) .... AMN Inst E
Associate Member of the Nautical Institute [*British*] .... AMNI
Associate Member of the New Zealand Institution of Engineers (SAUS) .... AMNZIE
Associate Member of the Pensions Management Institute [*British*] (DBQ) .... APMI
Associate Member of the Royal Institution of Naval Architects [*British*] .... AMRINA
Associate Member of the Royal School of Church Music [*British*] .... ARSCM
Associate Member of the Royal Society of Health [*Formerly, ARSH*] [*British*] .... AMRSH
Associate Member of the Royal Television Society (SAUO) .... AMRTS
Associate Member of the Society of Cardiological Technicians [*British*] (DBQ) .... ASCT
Associate Member of the Society of Certified Professionals [*British*] (DBQ) .... AMSCP
Associate Member of the Society of Commercial Teachers [*British*] (DBQ) .... ASCT
Associate Member of the Society of Electronic and Radio Technicians (SAUO) .... AMSERT
Associate Member of the Society of Engineers (SAUO) .... AMSE
Associate Member of the Society of Engineers, Inc. [*British*] (DBQ) .... AMSE
Associate Member of the Society of Hearing Aid Audiologists [*British*] (DI) .... AMSHAA
Associate Member of the Society of Licensed Aircraft Engineers and Technologists (SAUO) .... AMSLAET
Associate Member of the South Wales Institute of Engineers (SAUS)..... AMSWIE
Associate Member of the Technology Institute (SAUS) .... AM Tech I
Associate Member of the Television Society (SAUO) .... AMTS
Associate Member of the Town Planning Institute [*British*] (EY) .... AMTPI
Associate Member of the Womens Engineering Society (SAUS) .... AMWES
Associate Memory Processor (SAUS) .... AMP
Associate Mercantile Market (DICI) .... AMM
Associate Missionaries of the Assumption (EA) .... AMA
Associate, National Academician .... ANA
Associate National Academician (SAUS) .... ANA
Associate Normal Form (SAUS) .... ANF
Associate of Accountants' and Executives' Corp. of Canada .... AAE
Associate of American Guild of Organists .... AAGO
Associate of Arts in Agriculture (SAUS) .... AA Ag
Associate of Association of Certified and Corporate Accountants [*British*] .... AACCA
Associate of British Theatre Technicians .... ABTT
Associate of Canadian Institute of Chemistry .... ACIC
Associate of City & Guilds of London (SAUS) .... ACGL
Associate of Fire Loss Adjusters (SAUS) .... AFLA
Associate of Heriot-Watt College, Edinburgh (SAUS) .... AHWC
Associate of Heriot-Watt College, Edinburgh .... AH-WC
Associate of Incorporated Secretaries Association .... AISA
Associate of Institute of Marketing [*Canada*] (ASC) .... ACInstM
Associate of Institution of Electrical Engineers (SAUS) .... AIEE
Associate of Iron and Steel Institute (SAUS) .... AISI
Associate of King's College [*London*] .... AKC

Associate of King's College London .... AKCL
Associate of Manchester College of Technology [*British*] .... AMCT
Associate of Music (SAUS) .... A Mus
Associate of Music University of Adelaide (SAUO) .... AMUA
Associate of New Era Academy of Dance [*British*] .... ANEA
Associate of Public Health Association .... APHA
Associate of Queen's College [*London*] .... AQC
Associate of Queens College (SAUS) .... AQC
Associate of Registered Interior Designers of Ontario [*Canada*] (ASC) .... ARDIO
Associate of Speech and Drama, Australia .... ASDA
Associate of the Alberta Society of Artists [*Canada*] (ASC) .... AASA
Associate of the Ambulance Service Institute [*British*] (DBQ) .... AASI
Associate of the American Antiquarian Society (SAUO) .... AAAS
Associate of the American Institute of Electrical Engineers .... AAIEE
Associate of the American Institute of Mining and Metallurgical Engineers .... AAIMME
Associate of the American Institute of Mining and Metallurgical Engineers (SAUS) .... AAIMME
Associate of the American Institute of Physics .... AAIP
Associate of the American Society of Mechanical Engineers .... AASME
Associate of the Association of Certified and Corporate Accountants (SAUO) .... AACCA
Associate of the Association of Computer Professionals [*British*] (DBQ) .... AACP
Associate of the Association of Cost Accountants (ADA) .... AACA
Associate of the Association of Health Care Information and Medical Record Officers [*British*] (DBQ) .... AMR
Associate of the Association of International Accountants [*British*] .... AAIA
Associate of the Association of Psychiatric Social Workers (SAUO) .... AAPSW
Associate of the Association of Public Health Inspectors (SAUO) .... AAPHI
Associate of the Auctioneers Institute (SAUO) .... AAI
Associate of the Australian Chemistry Institute (SAUS) .... AACI
Associate of the Australian College of Health .... AHA
Associate of the Australian Institute of Food Science and Technology .... AAIFScT
Associate of the Australian Psychological Society .... AAPS
Associate of the Bandsmans College of Music (SAUS) .... ABCM
Associate of the Bankers Institute of Australasia (SAUS) .... ABIA
Associate of the Benesh Institute of Choreology [*British*] (DBQ) .... AIChor
Associate of the Birmingham and Midland Institute School of Music [*British*] .... ABSM
Associate of the Birmingham School of Music (SAUS) .... ABSM
Associate of the Bookkeepers Institute (SAUS) .... ABI
Associate of the Boot and Shoe Institution (SAUS) .... ABSI
Associate of the Brandsmen's College of Music (WDAA) .... ABCM
Associate of the British Association of Accountants and Auditors (BARN) .... ABAA
Associate of the British Ballet Organisation .... ABBO
Associate of the British Ballet Organisation (or Organization) (SAUS) .... ABBO
Associate of the British Display Society (DBQ) .... ABDS
Associate of the British Hypnotherapy Association (DBQ) .... ABHA
Associate of the British Institute of Certified Carpenters .... ABICC
Associate of the British Institute of Interior Design (DBQ) .... ABID
Associate of the British Institute of Professional Photography (DBQ) .... ABIPP
Associate of the British Institution of Radio Engineers .... Assoc Brit IRE
Associate of the British Interplanetary Society (IAA) .... ABIS
Associate of the British Psychological Society .... AB Ps S
Associate of the British Psychological Society (SAUO) .... ABPSS
Associate of the British Society of Commerce .... ABSC
Associate of the British Society of Master Glass Painters (SAUO) .... ABSMGP
Associate of the Building Societies [*Institute*] [*British*] [*German*] (BARN) .... ABS
Associate of the Building Societies Institute (SAUS) .... ABS
Associate of the Camborne School of Mines [*British*] .... ACSM
Associate of the Canadian Bankers Association (DD) .... ACBA
Associate of the Canadian College of Oeganists (SAUS) .... ACCO
Associate of the Canadian College of Organists .... ACCO
Associate of the Canadian Public Relations Society, Inc. (ASC) .... AccSCRP
Associate of the Casualty Actuarial Society [*Designation awarded by Casualty Actuarial Society*] .... ACAS
Associate of the Chartered Association of Certified Accountants (WDAA) .... ACCA
Associate of the Chartered Auctioneers' and Estate Agents' Institute [*British*] .... AAI
Associate of the Chartered Building Societies Institute [*British*] (DBQ) .... ACBSI
Associate of the Chartered Institute of Arbitrators [*British*] (DBQ) .... ACIArb
Associate of the Chartered Institute of Loss Adjustors [*Insurance*] .... ACILA
Associate of the Chartered Institute of Secretaries [*Later, Institute of Chartered Secretaries and Administrators*] [*British*] (EY) .... ACIS
Associate of the Chartered Insurance Institute [*British*] (EY) .... ACII
Associate of the Chartered Land Agents' Society [*British*] .... ALAS
Associate of the City and Guilds of London Institute [*British*] .... ACGI
Associate of the Clothing Institute (SAUS) .... ACI
Associate of the College of Craft Education [*British*] (DI) .... ACCEd
Associate of the College of Engineering [*British*] (ROG) .... ACE
Associate of the College of Handicraft (SAUS) .... A Coll H
Associate of the College of Preceptors [*British*] .... ACP
Associate of the College of Technology [*British*] .... ACT
Associate of the College of Violinists (SAUS) .... ACV
Associate of the Commerce Institute (SAUS) .... ACI
Associate of the Confederation of Professional Management [*British*] (DBQ) .... ACPM
Associate of the Cooperation of Certified Secretaries (SAUS) .... ACCS
Associate of the Corporation of Insurance Agents (ODBW) .... ACIA
Associate of the Corporation of Insurance Brokers [*Canada*] (DD) .... ACIB
Associate of the Corporation of Registered Accountants (SAUO) .... ACRA
Associate of the Corporation of Secretaries [*Associate of the Corp. of Certified Secretaries*] [*Acronym is based on former name,*] [*British*] (DI) .... ACCS
Associate of the Drama Board (Education) [*British*] (DI) .... ADB(Ed)
Associate of the Drama Board (Special) [*British*] (DI) .... ADB(S)
Associate of the Educational Institute of Scotland .... AEIS
Associate of the Experimental Station Laboratory Association (SAUO) .... AESLA
Associate of the Faculty of Actuaries [*British*] .... AFA
Associate of the Faculty of Architects and Surveyors [*British*] .... AFAS
Associate of the Faculty of Architects and Surveyors [*British*] (DBQ) .... AFS
Associate of the Faculty of Astrological Studies [*British*] .... AFAS
Associate of the Faculty of Auditors (SAUS) .... AFA
Associate of the Faculty of Commerce and Industry [*British*] (DBQ) .... AFCI
Associate of the Faculty of Insurance (SAUS) .... AFI
Associate of the Faculty of Physiatrics [*British*] .... AFPhys
Associate of the Faculty of Teachers in Commerce [*British*] (DBQ) .... AFTCom
Associate of the Farriers Company of London (SAUO) .... AFCL
Associate of the Federal Institute of Accountants [*Australia*] (ODBW) .... AFIA
Associate of the Geological Society [*British*] (DBQ) .... AMIGeol
Associate of the Greek Institute [*British*] (DI) .... AGI
Associate of the Guilhall School of Music (SAUS) .... AGSM
Associate of the Hotel, Catering and Institutional Management Association (SAUS) .... AHCIMA
Associate of the Imperial College of Tropical Agriculture [*British*] .... AICTA
Associate of the Imperial Society of Teachers of Dancing [*British*] (DBQ) .... AISTD
Associate of the Incorporated Association of Architects and Surveyours (SAUO) .... AIAS
Associate of the Incorporated British Institute of Certified Carpenters (SAUS) .... AIBIC
Associate of the Incorporated British Institute of Certified Carpenters (SAUO) .... AIBICC
Associate of the Incorporated British Institute oficertified Carpenters (SAUO) .... AIBIC
Associate of the Incorporated Guild of Church Musicians [*British*] .... AIGCM
Associate of the Incorporated Society of Auctioneers and Landed Property Agents [*British*] .... AALPA
Associate of the Incorporated Society of Organ Builders [*British*] (DBQ) .... AISOB
Associate of the Incorporated Society of Valuers and Auctioneers [*British*] (DBQ) .... ASVA
Associate of the Indian Institute of Architects (SAUS) .... AIIA
Associate of the Institute of Accountants, New Zealand (SAUS) .... AIANZ
Associate of the Institute of Actuaries [*British*] .... AIA
Associate of the Institute of Administrative Accounting and Data Processing [*British*] (DCTA) .... AAAI
Associate of the Institute of Administrative Management [*British*] (DCTA) .... A Inst AM
Associate of the Institute of Animal Technicians [*British*] (DI) .... AIAT
Associate of the Institute of Arbitrators [*British*] .... AI Arb
Associate of the Institute of Arbitrators Australia .... AIArbA
Associate of the Institute of Architects (SAUS) .... AIA
Associate of the Institute of Arts and Letters (SAUS) .... AIAL
Associate of the Institute of Automobile Engineers [*British*] (MCD) .... AIAE
Associate of the Institute of Automotive Engineer Assessors [*British*] (DBQ) .... AssocInstAEA
Associate of the Institute of Automotive Engineer Assessors (Body Division) [*British*] (DBQ) .... AssocInstAEA (Body Dvn)
Associate of the Institute of Bankers [*British*] (EY) .... AIB
Associate of the Institute of Bankers in Scotland (DBQ) .... AIB(Scot)
Associate of the Institute of Baths Management (SAUS) .... AIBM
Associate of the Institute of British Bakers (DBQ) .... AInstBB
Associate of the Institute of British Decorators .... AIBD
Associate of the Institute of British Photographers .... AIBP
Associate of the Institute of Builders [*British*] .... AIOB
Associate of the Institute of Building Estimators (SAUS) .... AIBE
Associate of the Institute of Building Societies (SAUS) .... AIBS
Associate of the Institute of Burial and Cremation Administration [*British*] (DBQ) .... AInstBCA
Associate of the Institute of Canadian Bankers (DD) .... AICB
Associate of the Institute of Carpenters [*British*] (DBQ) .... AIOC
Associate of the Institute of Ceramics (SAUS) .... AICeram
Associate of the Institute of Certificated Grocers [*British*] .... AGI
Associate of the Institute of certified Grocers (SAUO) .... AGI
Associate of the Institute of certified Grocers (SAUO) .... AIG
Associate of the institute of Chartered Accountants (SAUO) .... ACA
Associate of the Institute of Chartered Accountants [*British*] (EY) .... ACA
Associate of the Institute of Chartered Shipbrokers [*British*] .... AICS
Associate of the Institute of Chemistry [*Later, ARIC*] [*British*] .... AIC
Associate of the Institute of Chiropodists [*British*] (DBQ) .... ACh
Associate of the Institute of Civil Engineers [*British*] .... AICE
Associate of the Institute of Clerks of Works [*British*] (DI) .... AICW
Associate of the Institute of Commerce [*British*] (DCTA) .... ACI
Associate of the Institute of Commerce (SAUO) .... AIC
Associate of the Institute of Company Accountants [*British*] .... AIAC
Associate of the Institute of Company Accountants (SAUO) .... AICA
Associate of the Institute of Cost and Management Accountants [*British*] .... ACMA
Associate of the Institute of Cost and Works Accountants [*British*] .... ACWA
Associate of the Institute of Data Processing (SAUS) .... AIDP
Associate of the Institute of Data Processing Management [*British*] (DCTA) .... AIDPM
Associate of the Institute of Electrical Engineers [*British*] .... AIEE
Associate of the Institute of Electrical Engineers of Canada (DD) .... AIEE
Associate of the Institute of Executive Engineers (SAUS) .... A Inst ExE
Associate of the Institute of Executives and Managers [*British*] (DBQ) .... AIEM

Associate of the Institute of Explosives Engineers [British] (DBQ) ... AIExpE
Associate of the Institute of Factory Managers [British] (DI) ... AIFM
Associate of the Institute of Fire Engineers (SAUS) ... AI Fire E
Associate of the Institute of Food Science and Technology [British] (DBQ) ... AIFST
Associate of the Institute of Freight Forwarders [British] (DBQ) ... AInstFF
Associate of the Institute of Freight Trades Association (DS) ... AIFTA
Associate of the Institute of General Managers (SAUS) ... AIGM
Associate of the Institute of Health Service Administrators [British] (DCTA) ... AHA
Associate of the Institute of Hospital Almoners [British] ... AIHA
Associate of the Institute of Housing (SAUS) ... AIHsg
Associate of the Institute of Incorporated Photographers [British] (DI) ... AIIP
Associate of the Institute of Incorporated Practitioners in Advertising (DGA) ... AIPA
Associate of the Institute of Incorporated Technologists [British] (DI) ... AIITech
Associate of the Institute of Information Scientists (SAUS) ... AIInfSc
Associate of the Institute of Land Agents [British] (DI) ... AILA
Associate of the Institute of Landscape Architects [British] ... AILA
Associate of the Institute of Leisure and Amenity Management [British] (DBQ) ... AILAM
Associate of the Institute of Linguists [British] ... AIL
Associate of the Institute of Local Government Administrators [British] (DI) ... AILGA
Associate of the Institute of Management Services [British] (DBQ) ... AMS
Associate of the Institute of Marine Engineers [British] [Australia] ... AI Mar E
Associate of the Institute of Marine Engineers [British] ... AIME
Associate of the Institute of Market Officers [British] (DI) ... AInstMO
Associate of the Institute of Market Officers (SAUS) ... A Inst MO
Associate of the Institute of Marketing [British] (DCTA) ... A Inst M
Associate of the Institute of Marketing and Sales Management [British] ... A Inst MSM
Associate of the Institute of Mechanical Engineers ... AIME
Associate of the Institute of Medical Laboratory Sciences [British] (DBQ) ... AIMLS
Associate of the Institute of Mining and Metallurgy [British] ... Assoc Inst MM
Associate of the Institute of Mining Engineers ... AIME
Associate of the Institute of Mining Engineers (SAUS) ... Assoc I Min E
Associate of the Institute of Municipal Building Management [British] (DBQ) ... AIMBM
Associate of the Institute of Municipal Entertainment (SAUS) ... AIME
Associate of the Institute of Municipal Treasurers and Accountants [British] ... AIMTA
Associate of the Institute of Municipal Treasures and Accountants (SAUS) ... AIMTA
Associate of the Institute of Musical Instrument Technicians (SAUS) ... AIMIT
Associate of the Institute of Musical Instrument Technology [British] (DBQ) ... AIMIT
Associate of the Institute of Naval Architects ... AINA
Associate of the Institute of Naval Architects (SAUS) ... Assoc INA
Associate of the Institute of Occupational Safety and Health (HEAS) ... AIOSH
Associate of the Institute of Park Administration (SAUS) ... A Inst PA
Associate of the Institute of Patentees and Inventors [British] (EY) ... AInstPI
Associate of the Institute of Personnel Management (ADA) ... AIPM
Associate of the Institute of Personnel Management of Australia ... AIMPA
Associate of the Institute of Petroleum [British] (DI) ... AInstPet
Associate of the Institute of Physicians [British] ... AIP
Associate of the Institute of Physics (ADA) ... AIP
Associate of the Institute of Physics and the Physical Society [British] (EY) ... AInstP
Associate of the Institute of Plumbing [British] (DBQ) ... AIP
Associate of the Institute of Printing (DGA) ... ASSOC IOP
Associate of the Institute of Purchasing and Supply [British] (DCTA) ... A Inst PS
Associate of the Institute of Qualified Private Secretaries [British] (DI) ... AIQPS
Associate of the Institute of Quantity Surveyors [British] ... AIQS
Associate of the Institute of Quarrying (SAUS) ... AIQ
Associate of the Institute of Road Transport Engineers (DBQ) ... AIRTE
Associate of the Institute of Sales and Marketing Management [British] (DBQ) ... AInstSMM
Associate of the Institute of Sales Technology and Management [British] (DBQ) ... AISTM
Associate of the Institute of Secretaries Association (SAUO) ... AISA
Associate of the Institute of Shipping and Forwarded Agents (SAUO) ... ASF
Associate of the Institute of Shipping and Forwarding Agents (ODBW) ... ASF
Associate of the Institute of Statisticians [Later, MIS] [British] ... AIS
Associate of the Institute of Structural Engineers [British] ... AI Struct E
Associate of the Institute of Taxation [British] (DBQ) ... ATII
Associate of the Institute of the Motor Industry (SAUS) ... AIMI
Associate of the Institute of Trading Standards Administration [British] (DBQ) ... AITSA
Associate of the Institute of Transport (SAUS) ... Assoc Inst T
Associate of the Institute of Transport Administration [British] (DBQ) ... AInstTA
Associate of the Institute of Weights and Measures Administration (SAUS) ... AIWMA
Associate of the Institution of Agricultural Engineers [British] (DBQ) ... AIAgrE
Associate of the Institution of Analysts and Programmers [British] (DBQ) ... AMIAP
Associate of the Institution of Business Agents [British] (DBQ) ... AIBA
Associate of the Institution of Certified Public Accountants [British] ... ACPA
Associate of the Institution of Civil Engineers (SAUS) ... AInstCE
Associate of the Institution of Commercial Engineers (SAUS) ... AICE
Associate of the Institution of Electrical and Electronics Incorporated Engineers [British] (DBQ) ... AssociateIElecIE
Associate of the Institution of Electrical Engineers [British] ... Assoc IEE
Associate of the Institution of Electronic and Radio Engineers [British] ... AIERE
Associate of the Institution of Fire Engineers (SAUS) ... AIFE
Associate of the Institution of Fire Engineers [British] ... AIFireE
Associate of the Institution of Heating and Ventilating Engineers (SAUS) ... AIHVE
Associate of the Institution of Highway Engineers (SAUS) ... A Inst HE
Associate of the Institution of Industrial Managers [British] (DCTA) ... AIIM
Associate of the Institution of Linguists (SAUO) ... AIL
Associate of the Institution of Locomotive Engineers [British] ... AI Loco E
Associate of the Institution of Mechanical Engineers [British] ... AI Mech E
Associate of the Institution of Mechanical Engineers [British] ... AIMEE
Associate of the Institution of Mechanical Engineers [British] ... Assoc I Min E
Associate of the Institution of Metallurgists [British] ... AIM
Associate of the Institution of Mining and Metallurgy [British] ... AIMM
Associate of the Institution of Mining Engineers (SAUS) ... AIMinE
Associate of the Institution of Naval Architects [British] ... Assoc INA
Associate of the Institution of Production Engineers [British] ... AIPE
Associate of the Institution of Public Health Engineers (SAUS) ... AIPHE
Associate of the Institution of Public Health Engineers [British] (DBQ) ... AssocIPHE
Associate of the Institution of Sanitary Engineers (SAUS) ... AI San E
Associate of the Institution of Structural Engineers (SAUS) ... AI Struct E
Associate of the Institution of the Rubber Industry (SAUS) ... AIRI
Associate of the Institution of Water Engineers (SAUS) ... AIWE
Associate of the Institution of Works and Highways Technician Engineers (SAUS) ... AIWHTE
Associate of the Insurance Institute of America ... AIIA
Associate of the Insurance Institute of Canada ... AIIC
Associate of the International Association of Book-Keepers (DCTA) ... AIAB
Associate of the International Association of Bookkeepers (SAUO) ... AIAB
Associate of the International Council of Psychologists ... AICP
Associate of the International Dance Teachers' Association [British] (DBQ) ... AIDTA
Associate of the International Faculty of Arts (SAUS) ... AIFA
Associate of the International Institute of Arts and Letters [British] (DI) ... AIIAL
Associate of the International Institute of Arts and Letters (SAUS) ... AIISL
Associate of the International Institute of Sports Therapy [British] (DBQ) ... AISTC
Associate of the Iron and Steel Institute [British] ... AssocISI
Associate of the Landscape Institute [British] (DBQ) ... ALI
Associate of the Library Association [British] (EY) ... ALA
Associate of the Library Association of Australia ... ALAA
Associate of the Linean Society (SAUS) ... ALS
Associate of the Linnean Society (SAUO) ... ALS
Associate of the London Academy of Music (SAUS) ... ALAM
Associate of the London and Counties Society of Physiologists [British] (DBQ) ... LSCP(Assoc)
Associate of the London Association of Certified and Corporate Accountants [British] (EY) ... ALAA
Associate of the London College of Divinity [British] ... ALCD
Associate of the London College of Music [British] ... ALCM
Associate of the Manchester College of Science and Technology (SAUS) ... AMCST
Associate of the Mathematical Association (SAUO) ... AMA
Associate of the Museums Association [British] (EY) ... AMA
Associate of the National Academy (SAUS) ... ANA
Associate of the National Academy of Design ... ANA
Associate of the National Academy of Design, New York (NGC) ... ANA
Associate of the National Association of Estate Agents [British] (DBQ) ... ANAEA
Associate of the National College of Rubber Technology [British] (DI) ... ANCRT
Associate of the National Institute of Hardware [British] (DBQ) ... ANIH
Associate of the New Zealand Institute of Architects (SAUS) ... ANZIA
Associate of the New Zealand Institute of Chemistry ... ANZIC
Associate of the New Zealand Institute of Chemists (SAUS) ... ANZIC
Associate of the New Zealand Library Association (SAUO) ... ANZLA
Associate of the Non-Destructive Testing Society [British] ... ANDTS
Associate of the Normal School of Science ... ANSS
Associate of the Northeast Coast Institution of Engineers and Shipbuilders [British] ... ANECInst
Associate of the Northeast Coast Institution of Engineers and Shipbuilders (SAUS) ... ANECInst
Associate of the Otago School of Mines (SAUS) ... AOSM
Associate of the Pharmaceutical Society [British] ... APS
Associate of the Philosophical Society (SAUO) ... APS
Associate of the Philosophical Society of Great Britain (SAUO) ... APSGB
Associate of the Photographic Society of America (SAUO) ... APSA
Associate of the Plastics and Rubber Institute (ODBW) ... APRI
Associate of the Plastics Institute [British] ... API
Associate of the Psychological Society of Ireland ... APsSI
Associate of the Psychologiral Society of Ireland (SAUO) ... APsS1
Associate of the Public Accountants of New Zealand (SAUS) ... APANZ
Associate of the Rating and Valuation Association [British] (DBQ) ... ARVA
Associate of the Retail Management Institute of Australia ... ARMIA
Associate of the Royal Academy [British] ... ARA
Associate of the Royal Academy of Dancing [British] ... ARAD
Associate of the Royal Academy of Literature (SAUS) ... ARAL
Associate of the Royal Academy of Music [British] ... ARAM
Associate of the Royal Aeronautical Society [British] ... ARAeS
Associate of the Royal Aeronautical Society (SAUO) ... AR Ae S
Associate of the Royal Aeronautical Society (SAUO) ... ARAS
Associate of the Royal Aeronautical Society and Institution (SAUO) ... ARAeSI
Associate of the Royal Agricultural College [British] (BARN) ... ARAC
Associate of the Royal Agricultural Society (SAUO) ... ARAS
Associate of the Royal Astronomical Society [British] ... ARAS
Associate of the Royal Birmingham Society of Artists [British] (DI) ... ARBSA
Associate of the Royal British Colonial Society of Artists ... ARBC

Associate of the Royal Cambrian Academy [*British*] .... ARCA
Associate of the Royal Cambrian Academy [*British*] .... ARCamA
Associate of the Royal Canadian Academy .... ARCA
Associate of the Royal Canadian Academy of Arts (NGC) .... ARCA
Associate of the Royal Canadian College of Organists .... ARCCO
Associate of the Royal College of Advanced Technology [*British*] .... Assoc RCATS
Associate of the Royal College of Art [*British*] (EY) .... ARCA
Associate of the Royal College of Arts (SAUS) .... ARCA
Associate of the Royal College of Dancing [*British*] .... ARCD
Associate of the Royal College of Music [*British*] (EY) .... ARCM
Associate of the Royal College of Organists [*British*] (EY) .... ARCO
Associate of the Royal College of Organists (Choir-Training Diploma) [*British*] .... ARCO(CHM)
Associate of the Royal College of Psychiatrists [*British*] (DI) .... ARCPsych
Associate of the Royal College of Science [*British*] (EY) .... ARCS
Associate of the Royal College of Science [*British*] .... ARCSc
Associate of the Royal College of Science and Technology (SAUS) .... ARCST
Associate of the Royal College of Science and Technology, Glasgow [*Later, ARTC*] [*Scotland*] .... ARCST
Associate of the Royal College of Surgeons [*British*] (ROG) .... ARCS
Associate of the Royal College of Veterinary Surgeons [*British*] .... ARCVS
Associate of the Royal Colonial Institute [*British*] .... ARCI
Associate of the Royal Conservatory of Music of Toronto .... ARCT
Associate of the Royal Drawing Society [*British*] .... ARDS
Associate of the Royal Hibernian Academy [*British*] .... ARHA
Associate of the Royal Incorporation of Architects in Scotland .... ARIAS
Associate of the Royal Institute of British Architects .... ARIBA
Associate of the Royal Institute of Chemistry [*Formerly, AIC*] [*British*] .... ARIC
Associate of the Royal Institute of Public Health and Hygiene [*British*] .... ARIPHH
Associate of the Royal Institution of Chartered Surveyors [*Formerly, PASI*] [*British*] .... ARICS
Associate of the Royal Institution of Naval Architects [*British*] (DI) .... ARINA
Associate of the Royal Institution of Naval Architects [*British*] .... AssocRINA
Associate of the Royal Manchester College of Music (SAUS) .... ARMCM
Associate of the Royal Red Cross [*British*] .... ARRC
Associate of the Royal Sanitary Institute [*British*] (ROG) .... ARSANI
Associate of the Royal Sanitary Institute (SAUS) .... AR San I
Associate of the Royal Sanitary Institute [*British*] .... ARSI
Associate of the Royal School of Art (SAUS) .... ARSA
Associate of the Royal School of Mines [*British*] (EY) .... ARSM
Associate of the Royal Scottish Academy .... ARSA
Associate of the Royal Scottish Society of [*Painting*] **in Water Colours** (BARN) .... ARSW
Associate of the Royal Society for the Promotion of Health (SAUO) .... ARSH
Associate of the Royal Society for the Promotion of Health [*British*] (DAVI) .... ARSPH
Associate of the Royal Society for the Promotion of the Health (SAUO) .... ARSPH
Associate of the Royal Society of Antiquaries [*British*] .... ARSA
Associate of the Royal Society of Arts [*British*] (EY) .... ARSA
Associate of the Royal Society of British Artists .... ARBA
Associate of the Royal Society of British Sculptors .... ARBS
Associate of the Royal Society of Chemistry [*British*] (DAVI) .... ARSC
Associate of the Royal Society of Health [*Later, AMRSH*] [*British*] .... ARSH
Associate of the Royal Society of Literature [*British*] .... ARSL
Associate of the Royal Society of Miniature Painters [*British*] .... ARMS
Associate of the Royal Society of Miniature Painters, Sculptors and Gravers (SAUS) .... ARMS
Associate of the Royal Society of Musicians [*British*] .... ARSM
Associate of the Royal Society of Painter-Etchers and Engravers [*British*] .... ARE
Associate of the Royal Society of Painters in Water Colours [*British*] .... ARWS
Associate of the Royal Society of Sciences [*British*] (ROG) .... ARSSC
Associate of the Royal Technical College, Glasgow [*Formerly, ARCST*] .... ARTC
Associate of the Royal Technical College (Salford) [*British*] .... ARTC(S)
Associate of the Royal Victoria Institute of Architects [*British*] .... ARVIA
Associate of the Royal Water-Colour Society [*British*] (ROG) .... ARWS
Associate of the Royal West of England Academy .... ARWA
Associate of the Society of Actuaries [*Society of Actuaries*] [*Designation awarded by*] .... ASA
Associate of the Society of Art Masters [*British*] .... ASAM
Associate of the Society of Chiropodists [*British*] .... AChS
Associate of the Society of Chiropodists (SAUS) .... A Ch S
Associate of the Society of Commercial Accountants [*British*] .... A Comm A
Associate of the Society of Company and Commercial Accountants [*British*] (DCTA) .... ASCA
Associate of the Society of Dyers and Colourists [*British*] (DBQ) .... ASDC
Associate of the Society of Engineers (SAUO) .... ASE
Associate of the Society of Health and Beauty Therapists [*British*] (DBQ) .... ASBTh
Associate of the Society of Incorporated Accountants and Auditors [*British*] .... ASAA
Associate of the Society of Industrial Artists (Education) [*British*] .... ASIA(Ed)
Associate of the Society of Instrument Technology (SAUO) .... ASIT
Associate of the Society of Investment Analysts [*British*] (DBQ) .... ASIA
Associate of the Society of Licensed Aircraft Engineers and Technologists [*British*] (DBQ) .... AssocSLAET
Associate of the Society of Non-Destructive Examination (SAUO) .... ASNDE
Associate of the Society of Surveying Technicians [*British*] (DBQ) .... AMSST
Associate of the Society of the Chiropodists (SAUO) .... ACHS
Associate of the Society of Typographic Designers (DGA) .... ASTD
Associate of the Society of Valuers and Auctioneers (SAUO) .... ASVA
Associate of the South African Institute of Mechanical Engineers .... ASAI Mech E
Associate of the South African Library Association (SAUO) .... ASALA
Associate of the Swimming Teachers' Association [*British*] (DBQ) .... ASTA
Associate of the Textile Institute [*British*] .... ATI
Associate of the Tonic Solfa College (WDAA) .... ATSC
Associate of the Toronto Conservatory of Music .... ATCM
Associate of the Welding Institute [*British*] (DBQ) .... AWeldI
Associate of Theological Study [*British*] .... ATS
Associate of Trinity College, London (SAUS) .... ATCL
Associate of Trinity College of Music, London [*British*] .... ATCL
Associate of Victory College of Music (SAUS) .... AVCM
Associate of Youth Development [*British*] (DBQ) .... AYD
Associate Presbyterian (IIA) .... AP
Associate Principle for Addition (SAUS) .... APA
Associate Processor/Associative Processor Controller (SAUS) .... AP/APC
Associate Producer .... AP
Associate Professor (ADA) .... Aspro
Associate Program Manager (CTAS) .... APM
Associate Program Manager for Contracting (CTAS) .... APMC
Associate Program Manager for General Counsel (CTAS) .... APMGC
Associate Program Manager for Logistics (CTAS) .... APML
Associate Program Manager for Operations (CTAS) .... APMO
Associate Program Manager for Procedures (CTAS) .... APMP
Associate Program Manager for Quality (CTAS) .... APMQ
Associate Program Manager for Requirements (CTAS) .... APMR
Associate Program Manager for System Engineering (CTAS) .... APMSE
Associate Program Manager for Test (CTAS) .... APMT
Associate Pulmonary Technologist [*Academic degree*] .... A-Put
Associate Regional Administrator .... ARA
Associate, Royal Manchester College of Music [*British*] (ROG) .... ARMCM
Associate Safety Professional [*Board of Certified Safety Professionals*] [*Designation awarded by*] .... ASP
Associate Scottish Hospital Bureau of Management (DAVI) .... ASHBM
Associate Surveyor Member of the Incorperated Association of Architects and Surveyors (SAUO) .... AIAS
Associate Technical Aide (SAUO) .... ATA
Associate Technical Aide .... ATA
Associate Technical Director for Engineering and Test [*Army*] (RDA) .... ATDE/T
Associate Technical Project Officer .... ATPO
Associate, Trinity College of Music [*Canadian*] .... ATCM
Associated .... ASSD
Associated (EY) .... ASSOCD
Associated .... ASSTD
Associated Accounting Firms International [*Washington, DC*] (EA) .... AAFI
Associated Actors and Artistes of America (EA) .... 4A's
Associated Actors and Artistes of America (EA) .... AAAA
Associated Actors and Artists of America (SAUO) .... AAA
Associated Actors and Artists of America (SAUO) .... AAAA
Associated Aero Science Laboratories (SAA) .... AASL
Associated Aero-Science Laboratories (SAUO) .... AASL
Associated African and Malagasy States (SAUO) .... AAMS
Associated African States and Madagascar (MHDB) .... AAASM
Associated African States, Madagascar and Mauritius [*Later, Association of African, Caribean and Pacific States*] (PDAA) .... AASMM
Associated African States, Madagascar and Mauritius (SAUO) .... AASMM
Associated Agents of America (EA) .... AAA
Associated Air Balance Council (SAUO) .... AABB
Associated Air Balance Council (EA) .... AABC
Associated Airlines [*ICAO designator*] (AD) CV
Associated Amusement Machine Operators of New York (SAUO) .... AAMONY
Associated Anesthetists of the United States of America (SAUO) .... AAUS
Associated Antique Dealers of America (EA) .... AADA
Associated Array Processor (SAUS) .... AAP
Associated Asian Securities (SAUO) .... AAA
Associated Audio Archives Committee (SAUS) .... AAA Committee
Associated Australasian Banks in London .... AABL
Associated Australian Banks of London (SAUO) .... AABL
Associated Australian Stock Exchanges (SAUS) .... AASE
Associated Aviation Underwriters .... AAU
Associated Baby Carriage Dealers (EA) .... ABCD
Associated Banc-Corp [*NASDAQ symbol*] (NQ) .... ASBC
Associated Banc-Corp. [*Associated Press*] (SAG) .... AsdBnc
Associated Banks of Europe (SAUO) .... Abecor
[*The*] **Associated Banks of Europe Corp.** (IID) .... ABECOR
Associated Banks of Europe Corp. (ODBW) .... ABERCOR
Associated Beer Distributors of Illinois (SRA) .... ABDI
Associated Biomedic Systems Inc. (SAUO) .... ABS
Associated Biomedic Systems, Inc. .... ABS
Associated Birdkeepers and Traders [*Australia*] .... ABKT
Associated Blacksmiths, Forge, and Smithy Workers Society [*A union*] [*British*] .... ABFSWS
Associated Blacksmiths Forge and Smithy Workers Society (SAUO) .... ABFSWS
Associated Blacksmiths, Forge and Smithy Workers Society (SAUS) .... ABFSWS
Associated Blacksmiths of Scotland [*A union*] .... ABS
Associated Board of the Royal Schools of Music [*British*] (BI) .... ABRSM
Associated Boards of the Royal Schools of Music (SAUO) .... ABRSM
Associated Body of Church Schoolmasters [*A union*] [*British*] .... ABCS
Associated Bodywork and Massage Professionals (EA) .... ABMP
Associated Book Publishers [*Subsidiary of International Thomson Organisation*] .... ABP
Associated Booksellers (SAUO) .... AB
Associated Booksellers (SAUO) .... Assoc Bk
Associated Booksellers of Great Britain and Ireland (SAUO) .... ABGBI
Associated Booksellers of Great Britain and Ireland (DGA) .... ABGBI

Associated Booksellers of Great Britian (SAUO) .... BGB
Associated Borrowers Endorsement [British] .... ABE
Associated Bottlers Company (SAUO) .... ABC
Associated Bread Manufacturers of Australia and New Zealand .... ABMANZ
Associated Brewing Company (SAUO) .... ABW
Associated British Cables (SAUO) .... ABCAL
Associated British Cinemas .... ABC
Associated British Cinemas Ltd. (SAUO) .... ABC
Associated British Combustion, Ltd. (SAUO) .... ABC
Associated British Film Company (SAUO) .... AB
Associated British Foods (SAUO) .... AbF
Associated British Foods [Commercial firm] .... ABF
Associated British Machine Tool Makers Ltd. (SAUO) .... ABMTM
Associated British Maltsters Ltd. (SAUO) .... ABM
Associated British Oil Engines (SAUO) .... ABOE
Associated British Picture Corporation (SAUO) .... ABC
Associated British Picture Corporation (SAUO) .... ABPC
Associated British Picture Distributors (SAUO) .... ABPD
Associated British Ports (DS) .... ABP
Associated Broadcast News [Cable-television system] ..... ABN
Associated Broadcasting Company (SAUO) .... ABC
Associated Brotherhood of Iron and Steel Workers (SAUO) .... ABISW
Associated Builders and Contractors (EA) .... ABC
Associated Builders and Owners of Greater New York (SRA) .... ABOGNY
Associated Building Material Distributors of America (EA) .... ABM
Associated Building Material Distributors of America (EA) .... ABMDA
Associated Bulbgrowers of Holland (SAUO) .... ABGH
Associated Business Papers (NTCM) .... ABP
Associated Business Papers Association (SAUO) .... ABPA
Associated Business Publications (SAUO) .... ABP
Associated Business Writers of America (EA) .... ABWA
Associated California Loggers (SRA) .... ACL
Associated Carpenters and Joiners Society of Scotland [A union] .... ACJSS
Associated Carters Society of Scotland [A union] .... ACSS
Associated Central West Africa Lines (SAUO) .... CEWAL
Associated Chain Drug Stores (EA) .... ACDS
Associated Chambers of Manufacturers of Australia (SAUO) .... ACMA
Associated Chemical Companies (SAUO) .... ACC
Associated Chinese Chambers of Commerce and Industry (SAUO) .... ACCCI
Associated Chip Chandlers (SAUS) .... ASC
Associated Chiropodists of America (ACA) .... ACA
[The] Associated Christian Colleges of Oregon [Library network] .... ACCO
Associated Christian Colleges of Oregon (SAUS) .... ACCO
Associated Church Press (EA) .... ACP
[The] Associated Clubs (EA) .... AC
Associated Coffee Industries of America (SAUO) .... ACIA
Associated Collection Agencies [Colorado] (SRA) .... ACA
Associated Collectors of El Salvador (EA) .... ACES
Associated College Libraries of Central Pennsylvania [Library network] .... ACLCP
Associated Colleges of Indiana (SAUO) .... ACI
Associated Colleges of the Chicago Area .... ACCA
Associated Colleges of the Midwest (EA) .... ACM
Associated Colleges of the Midwest, Periodical Bank, Chicago, IL [Library symbol] [Library of Congress] (LCLS) .... ICACM
Associated Colleges of Upper New York .... ACUNY
Associated Collegiate Press (EA) .... ACP
Associated Collegiate Press, National Scholastic Press Association (NTPA) .... ACP/NSPA
Associated Commercial Vehicles, Ltd. (SAUO) .... ACV
Associated Committee of Friends on Indian Affairs (EA) .... ACFIA
Associated Communications Corp. .... ACC
Associated Community Theaters (SAUO) .... ACT
Associated Computer Consultants (SAUS) .... ACC
Associated Computer System (MHDI) .... ACS
Associated Concrete Contractors of Michigan (SRA) ..... ACCM
Associated Construction Distributors International (EA) .... ACD
Associated Construction Distributors, International (EA) .... ACDI
Associated Construction Publications (EA) .... ACP
Associated Container Transportation .... ACT
Associated Container Transportation Ltd. (SAUO) .... ACT
Associated Container Transportation New Zealand (SAUO) .... ACTNZ
Associated Contractor Orginated Change (SAUS) .... ACOC
Associated Contractor Originated Change (AAG) .... ACOC
Associated Control Channel (CGWS) .... ACCH
Associated Cooperage Industries of America (EA) .... ACIA
Associated Corpuscular Emission .... ACE
Associated Correspondents New Service (SAUO) .... ACNS
Associated Correspondents News Service .... ACNS
Associated Corset and Brassiere Manufacturers (EA) .... ACBM
Associated Corset and Brassiere Manufacturers Association (NTPA) .... ACBMA
Associated Councils for Social Engineering (SAUO) ...... ACSE
Associated Councils of the Arts (SAUO) .... ACA
Associated Councils of the Arts [Later, American Council for the Arts] .... ACA
Associated Councils of the Arts (SAUO) .... Assoc Coun Arts
Associated Counseling Services (SAUO) .... ACS
Associated Country Women of the World [British] .... ACWW
Associated Court and Commercial Newspapers (DGA) ..... ACCN
Associated Credit Bureau of New Zealand (SAUO) .... ACBNZ
Associated Credit Bureaus [Houston, TX] (EA) .... ACB
Associated Credit Bureaus (SAUO) .... ACBs
Associated Credit Bureaus of America (SAUO) .... ACB of A
[The] Associated Daimler Co. [British] (DCTA) .... ADC
Associated Dairies [Commercial firm] [British] .... ASDA
Associated Dairies (WDAA) .... Asda
Associated Dairies Supermarket (SAUS) .... Asda Supermarket

Associated Day Care Centers .... ADCC
Associated Deliveries Limited [British] .... ADL
Associated Deliveries, Ltd., London E. 15 (SAUO) ...... ADL
Associated Designers of Canada (AC) .... ADC
Associated Disbursing Officer [Military] (DNAB) .... ADO
Associated Driving Schools of Australia .... ADSA
Associated Drug and Chemical Industries of Missouri .... ADACIOM
Associated Dry Goods Corp. (SAUO) .... DG
Associated Electrical Industries [British] .... AEI
Associated Electrical Industries of Great Britain Ltd. (SAUO) .... AEI
Associated Employers of Montana (SRA) .... AEM
Associated Engineering, Limited (SAUO) .... AEL
Associated Engineering Services [Canada] .... AESL
Associated Engineering Services Ltd., Vancouver, BC, Canada [Library symbol] [Library of Congress] (LCLS) .... CaBVaAE
Associated Engineering Services Ltd., Vancouver, British Columbia [Library symbol] [National Library of Canada] (NLC) .... BVAAE
Associated Enterprises, Inc. (TSSD) .... AEI
Associated Equipment Company (SAUO) .... AEC
Associated Equipment Dealers (SAUO) .... AED
Associated Equipment Distributors (EA) .... AED
Associated Equipment Distributors of Arizona (SRA) .... AEDA
Associated Equipment Distributors' Research and Services Operation .... AED/R & S
Associated Estates Realty [NYSE symbol] (SPSG) .... AEC
Associated Estates Realty [Associated Press] (SAG) .... AsdEst
Associated Estates Realty [Associated Press] (SAG) .... AsdEstat
Associated European Consultants (SAUO) .... ACE
Associated European Management Publishers (SAUS) .... AEMP
Associated Examining Board [British] .... AEB
Associated Exhibitors Inc. (SAUO) .... Assoc
Associated Factory Mutual Fire Insurance Companies [Later, FMS] (EA) .... AFMFIC
Associated Fantasy Publishers .... AFP
Associated Federated Hotels (SAUO) .... AFH
Associated Feed Manufacturers (SAUO) .... AFM
Associated Film Distribution (BARN) .... AFD
Associated Fishing Tackle Manufacturers (SAUO) ...... AFTM
Associated Foam Manufacturers (EA) .... AFM
Associated Food Dealers of Michigan (SRA) .... AFD
Associated Fraternities of America .... AFA
Associated Fraternity of Iron Forgers [A union] [British] .... AFIF
Associated Fresh Foods [British] .... AFF
Associated Funeral Directors, International (NTPA) .... AFDI
Associated Funeral Directors Service (EA) .... AFDS
Associated Funeral Directors Service International (EA) .... AFDSI
Associated Fur Manufacturers (EA) .... AFM
Associated Gas Distributors .... AGD
Associated General Contractors (SAUO) .... AGC
Associated General Contractors of America (EA) .... AGC
Associated General Contractors of America .... AGCA
Associated General Contractors of America, Inc. (SAUO) .... AGCA
Associated General Contractors of California (AAGC) .... AGCC
Associated Geographers of America .... AGA
Associated Glass and Pottery Manufacturers (EA) ...... AGPM
Associated Gospel Churches of Canada (AC) .... AGO
Associated Granite Craftsmen's Guild (EA) .... AGCG
Associated Granite Craftsmens Guild (SAUS) .... AGCG
Associated Grantmakers of Massachusetts (SRA) .... AGM
Associated Ground Equipment (CINC) .... AGE
[The] Associated Group, Inc. [NASDAQ symbol] (SAG) .... AGRP
Associated Group, Inc. (The) [Associated Press] (SAG) .... AscdGp
Associated Harvard Clubs (SAUO) .... AHC
Associated Health Foundation (EA) .... AHF
Associated Health Services (SAUS) .... AHS
Associated Heat Services [Energy management contractor] [British] .... AHS
Associated Hosts, Inc. (SAUO) .... AHST
Associated Humane Societies (EA) .... AHS
Associated Humber Lines [Steamship] (MHDB) .... AHL
Associated Independent Colleges of Kansas (SAUO) ..... AICK
Associated Independent Dairies of America (SAUO) ..... AIDA
Associated Independent Distributors [Later, IDA] (EA) .... AID
Associated Independent Electrical Contractors of America [Later, IEC] (EA) .... AIECA
Associated Industrial Photographic Dealers (SAUO) .... AIPA
Associated Industrial Photographic Dealers [Defunct] .... AIPD
Associated Industries of Florida (SRA) .... AIF
Associated Industries of Kentucky (SRA) .... AIK
Associated Industries of Massachusetts (SRA) .... AIM
Associated Industries of Missouri (SRA) .... AIM
Associated Industries of the Inland Northwest (SRA) ... AIIN
Associated Industries of Vermont (SRA) .... AIV
Associated Information Managers (EA) .... AIM
Associated In-Group Donors .... AID
Associated Iron Moulders of Scotland [A union] .... AIMS
Associated Iron, Steel, and Brass Dressers of Scotland (SAUO) .... AISBDS
Associated Japan-America Societies of the United States (EA) .... AJAS
Associated Klans of America (SAUO) .... AKA
Associated Knowledge Systems [Imperial Chemical Industries Ltd.] [Information service or system] (IID) .... AKS
Associated Koi Clubs of America (EA) .... AKCA
Associated Laboratories (EA) .... AL
Associated Landscape Contractors of America (EA) ..... ALCA
Associated Landscape Contractors of Colorado (SRA) ... ALCC
Associated Landscape Contractors of Massachusetts (SRA) .... ALCM

Associated Law Societies of Wales (SAUO) .... ALSW
Associated Legislative Rabbinate of America (EA) .... ALRA
Associated Levant Lines (SAUS) .... SAL
Associated Licensed Detectives of New York State (SRA) .... ALDONYS
Associated Locksmiths of America .... ALA
Associated Locksmiths of America (EA) .... ALOA
Associated Logic Parallel System (BUR) .... ALPS
Associated Long Distance Interstate Message (SAUS) .... ALDI Message
Associated Long-Distance Interstate Message [Telecommunications]
    (TEL) .... ALDI
Associated Lutheran Charities [Later, Lutheran Social Welfare Conference of
    America] (EA) .... ALC
Associated Lutheran Charities (SAUO) .... ALC
Associated Mail and Parcel Centers (EA) .... AMPC
Associated Maintenance Module [Telecommunications] (TEL) .... AMM
Associated Male Choruses of America (SAUO) .... AMCA
Associated Male Choruses of America (EA) .... AMC of A
Associated Manitoba Arts Festivals, Inc. (AC) .... AMAF
Associated Manufacturers of Domestic Electric Cookers (SAUO) ..... AMDEC
Associated Manufacturers of Domestic Electric Cookers (SAUS) ..... AMDEC
Associated Manufacturers of Domestic Electrical Appliances (SAUS) .... AMDEA
Associated Manufacturers of Electric Wiring Accessories (SAUO) ...... AMEWA
Associated Manufacturers of Veterinary and Agricultural Products
    (SAUO) .... AMVAP
Associated Manufacturing and Design [Alexandria, Virginia] (ABAC) ..... AMD
Associated Marine Officers Association of the Philippines .... AMOAP
Associated Mariners' Society [A union] [British] .... AMS
Associated Master Barbers and Beauticians of America [Later, HI/AMBBA]
    (EA) .... AMBBA
Associated Master Plumbers and Domestic Engineers (SAUO) .... AMP
Associated Medical Care Plans (SAUS) .... AMCP
Associated Member (SAUS) .... AM
Associated Member of the Institution of Civil Engineers (SAUS) .... Assoc MICE
Associated Memory Equipment .... AME
Associated Merchandising Corp. .... AMC
Associated Merchandising Corporation (SAUO) .... AMC
Associated Metal Workers Society [A union] [British] .... AMWS
Associated Metal Workers Union [British] .... AMWU
Associated Metalworkers' Union [British] (DCTA) .... AMU
Associated Microfilming Service, Inc., Mountain Lakes, NJ [Library symbol]
    [Library of Congress] (LCLS) .... AssM
Associated Midwestern Universities (SAUS) .... AMU
Associated Midwestern Universities, Inc. .... AMU
Associated Migrant Opportunity Services .... AMOS
Associated Milk Producers (SAUO) .... AMPI
Associated Milk Producers, Inc. .... AMPI
Associated Milk Producers/Southern Region [Texas] (SRA) .... AMP/S
Associated Millinery Men (EA) .... AMM
Associated Minicomputer Dealers Association (SAUS) .... AMDA
Associated Minority Contractors of America (EA) .... AMC
Associated Missile Product Company (SAUO) .... AMPCO
Associated Missile Products Corporation (SAUO) .... AMPCO
[The] Associated Missions (EA) .... TAM
Associated Motion Picture Advertisers (EA) .... AMPA
Associated Motor Carriers Tariff Bureau (SAUO) .... AMC
Associated Motor Carriers Tariff Bureau (EA) .... AMCTB
Associated Motor Carriers Tariff Bureau, Saint Paul MN [STAC] ..... AMC
Associated Multiplier Agency Liaison Group [Australia] .... AMALG
Associated Municipal Electrical Engineers (SAUO) .... AMEE
Associated Music Publishers (NTCM) .... AMP
Associated Music Publishers [Musical slang] .... AMPS
Associated Music Publishers, Inc. (SAUO) .... AMP
Associated Music Publishers, Incorporated (SAUO) .... AMPI
Associated Musicians of Greater New York (SAUO) .... AMGNY
Associated Name [MARC relator code] [Library of Congress] (LCCP) ..... asn
Associated Natural Gas Corp. (SAUS) .... NGA
Associated Negro Press (IIA) .... ANP
Associated Networks for European Research [EC] (ECED) .... RARE
Associated New York State Food Processors (SRA) .... ANYSFP
Associated Newsagents Co-operative Ltd. (SAUO) .... ANCOL
Associated Newspaper Holdings [British] .... ANH
Associated Newspapers Ltd., London, United Kingdom [Library symbol]
    [Library of Congress] (LCLS) .... UkLA
Associated Newspapers of Ceylon Ltd. (SAUO) .... ANC
Associated Nuclear Services [British] (IRUK) .... ANS
Associated Number (SAUS) .... AN
Associated Nursery Guides Emphatically Lacking in Leisure ...... ANGELL
Associated of Correctors of the Press [Later, NGA] (DGA) .... ACP
Associated Offices of Primary Responsibility (SAUS) .... AOPR
Associated Offices Technical Committee (SAUO) .... AOTC
Associated Offices Technical Committee (HEAS) .... AOTC
Associated Oklahoma Trucking Association (SRA) .... AMCO
Associated Oregon Industries (SRA) .... AOI
Associated Oregon Loggers (SRA) .... AOL
Associated Organizations for Professionals in Education (SAUS) ..... AOP
Associated Organizations for Professionals in Education [Defunct] (EA)... AOPE
Associated Organizations for Teacher Education [Later, AOPE] .... AOTE
Associated Overseas Countries (SAUO) .... AOC
Associated Overseas Countries and Territories (DS) .... AOCT
Associated Overseas Countries of the European Economic Community ... AOC
Associated Owners and Developers (NTPA) .... AOD
Associated Paper Industries [British] .... API
Associated Parishes (EA) .... AP
Associated Patternmakers of Scotland [A union] .... APS
Associated Pennsylvania Constructors (SRA) .... APC

Associated Period [Medicine] (DAVI) .... AP
Associated Person [Stock exchange term] .... AP
Associated Petroleum Industries of Michigan (SRA) .... APIM
Associated Petroleum Industries of Pennsylvania (SRA) .... API-PA
Associated Pharmacologists and Toxicologists (EPA) .... APT
Associated Photographers International (EA) .... API
Associated Pimiento Canners [Defunct] (EA) .... APC
Associated Pipe Organ Builders of America (EA) .... APOBA
Associated Police Communications Officers (SAUO) .... APCO
Associated Porcupine Mines Ltd. [Toronto Stock Exchange symbol] ..... APC
Associated Portland Cement Manufacturers Ltd. (SAUO) .... APCM
Associated Portland Cement Manufacturers of Great Britain ..... APCM
Associated Portland Cement Manufactures (SAUO) .... APC
Associated Pot and Kettle Clubs of America [Later, IPKC] (EA) ..... APKCA
Associated Poultry and Egg Industries [Defunct] (EA) .... APEI
Associated Presbyterian [British] (ROG) .... AP
Associated Pre-Service (SAUS) .... APS
Associated Press [News agency and wire service] (EA) .... AP
Associated Press Broadcasters (EA) .... APB
Associated Press Broadcasters Association [Later, APB] (EA) ...... APBA
Associated Press Managing Editors (EA) .... APME
Associated Press Managing Editors (SAUO) .... APME
Associated Press Managing Editors Association (DGA) .... APMEA
Associated Press of America (SAUO) .... Assopress
Associated Press of Australia (SAUO) .... APA
Associated Press of India (SAUO) .... API
Associated Press of Pakistan .... APP
Associated Press Radio .... APR
Associated Press Radio Network (NTCM) .... APRN
Associated Press Radio-Television Association [Later, APB] .... APRTA
Associated Press Service .... APS
Associated Press Sports Editors [Defunct] (EA) .... APSE
Associated Press Television .... APTV
Associated Products of America (SAUO) .... APA
Associated Professional Massage Therapists and Bodyworkers [Later,
    ABMP] (EA) .... APMT
Associated Provincial Law Societies (SAUO) .... APLS
Associated Public School Systems .... APSS
Associated Public-Safety Communications Officers (EA) .... APCO
Associated Publishers (EA) .... AP
Associated Publishers Amsterdam (SAUO) .... APA
Associated Pulp and Paper Mills (DGA) .... APPM
Associated Purchasing Publications .... APP
Associated Radio and Television Servicemen (SAUO) .... ARTS
Associated Radio Navigation (SAUS) .... ARN
Associated Rare Breeds of New England [Defunct] (EA) .... ARBNE
[The] Associated Readers of Tarot International (EA) .... TAROT
Associated Recovery Routines [IBM] (CIST) .... ARR
Associated Rediffusion [Television] .... AR
Associated Rediffusion Ltd. (SAUO) .... AR
Associated Reformed Presbyterian .... ARP
Associated Regional Accounting Firms [Atlanta, GA] (EA) .... ARAF
Associated Reinforcing Bar Producers (EA) .... ARBP
Associated Retail Bakers of America [Later, Retail Bakers of America]
    (EA) .... ARBA
Associated Retail Confectioners of North America [Later, RCI] (EA) .... ARC
Associated Retail Confectioners of the United States [Later, RCI] ...... ARCUS
Associated Risk Managers International [Austin, TX] (EA) .... ARMI
Associated Risk Managers of New York State (SRA) .... ARMNY
Associated Risk Managers of Ohio (SRA) .... ARM/OH
Associated Rocky Mountain Universities [AEC] .... ARMU
Associated Roller Rink Operators of Wisconsin (SRA) .... ARROW
Associated Roofing Contractors of Maryland (SRA) .... ARCOM
Associated Sandblasting Contractors (EA) .... ASC
Associated Scholastic Society (SAUO) .... ASS
Associated School Boards of South Dakota (SRA) .... ASBSD
Associated Schools of Construction (EA) .... ASC
Associated Schools Project in Education for International Cooperation and
    Peace [UNESCO] [Paris, France] (EAIO) .... ASPEICP
Associated Schools Projets (SAUO) .... ASP
Associated Scientific and Technical Societies (SAUO) .... AS&TS
Associated Scottish Life Officer (SAUO) .... ASLO
Associated Scottish Life Offices (EAIO) .... ASLO
Associated Seattle Prostitutes (SAUO) .... ASP
Associated Seed Growers (SAUS) .... ASGROW
Associated Seed Growers, Inc. (SAUO) .... ASGROW
Associated Semiconductor Manufacturers (SAUO) .... ASM
Associated Service Organization .... ASO
Associated Services for the Blind (EA) .... ASB
Associated Sheep, Police and Army Dog Society (SAUO) .... ASPADS
Associated Sheet Metal/Roofing Contractors, Connecticut Chapter
    (SRA) .... ASMRCC
Associated Ship Chandlers (SAUO) .... ASC
Associated Skin Divers (SAUO) .... ASD
Associated Societies for the Care of Women and Children (SAUO) ..... ASCWC
Associated Society of Locomotive Engineers and Firemen [British]
    (ODBW) .... Aslef
Associated Society of Locomotive Engineers and Firemen [A union]
    [British] (DCTA) .... ASLEF
Associated Society of Moulders [A union] [British] .... ASM
Associated Society of Moulders (SAUO) .... ASM
Associated Society of Range Stove and Ornamental Workers [A union]
    [British] .... ASRSOW
Associated Sociologists Society (SAUO) .... ASS
Associated Specialty Contractors (EA) .... ASC

Associated Spring Cooporation (SAUO) .... ASCO
Associated Spring Corporation (SAUO) .... ASC
Associated States of Indochina (NATG) .... ASIC
Associated Steamships (SAUO) .... AS
Associated Steamships Proprietary Limited (SAUO) .... ASPL
Associated Stenotypists of America (SAUO) .... ASA
Associated Stenotypists of America [Later, NSRA] (EA) .... ASA
Associated Student Body (SAUO) .... ASB
Associated Students of Kansas (SAUO) .... ASK
Associated Students of the University of California .... ASUC
Associated Students Promoting Individual Rights for Everyone .... ASPIRE
Associated Subcontractors of Massachusetts (SRA) .... ASM
Associated Support Items of Equipment (MCD) .... ASIOE
Associated Surplus Dealers (EA) .... ASD
Associated Surplus Dealers and Associated Merchandise Dealers Trade
   Show (ITD) .... ASD/AMD
Associated Swedish Steel AB (SAUO) .... ASSAB
Associated Talmud Torahs [A publication] (BJA) .... ATT
Associated Technical Services, Inc. [Glen Ridge, NJ] [Information service or
   system] .... ATS
Associated Technical Services, Inc., Glen Ridge, NJ [Library symbol] [Library
   of Congress] (LCLS) .... NjGlriA
Associated Technology Co. [Information service or system] (IID) .... ATC
Associated Tele Vision (SAUS) .... ATV
Associated Telemanagement, Inc. [Newburyport, MA] [Telecommunications]
   (TSSD) .... ATI
Associated Telephone Answering Exchanges [Formerly, ATE] (EA) .... ATAE
Associated Telephone Answering Exchanges (SAUO) .... ATAE
Associated Telephone Exchanges [Later, ATAE] .... ATE
Associated Television Ltd. [British independent, commercial television
   company] .... ATV
Associated Testing Laboratories (SAUS) .... ATL
Associated Theatre Properties (SAUO) .... ATP
Associated Third Class Mail Users [Later, TCMA] (EA) .... ATCMU
Associated Tie Manufacturers of Australia .... ATMA
Associated Tobacco Manufacturers [Defunct] (EA) .... ATM
Associated Traffic Clubs of America [Later, TCI] (EA) .... ATC
Associated Traffic Clubs of America (SAUO) .... ATCA
Associated Training Specialist (SAA) .... ATS
Associated Transport, Inc. (SAUO) .... ATP
Associated Truck Lines (SAUO) .... ATL
Associated Trustee Savings Banks of New Zealand (SAUO) .... ATSBNZ
[The] Associated Turtles [Defunct] (EA) .... TAT
Associated Two-Year Schools in Construction [Defunct] (EA) A2YSC
Associated Underground Contractors (SRA) .... AUC
Associated Unions of America [Later, OPEIU] (EA) .... AUA
Associated Universities (SAUO) .... AU
Associated Universities for Toxicology Research and Education [Research
   center] (RCD) .... AUTRE
Associated Universities, Inc. (EA) .... AUI
Associated Universities Incorporated (SAUO) .... AUI
Associated University Bureaus of Business and Economic Research [Later,
   AUBER] .... AUBBER
Associated Utility Contractors of Maryland (SRA) .... AUCM
Associated Veterinary Laboratories [Defunct] (EA) .... AVL
Associated Video Dealers of America (SAUO) .... ACDA
Associated Video Dealers of America [Defunct] (EA) .... AVDA
Associated Water Colour Painters, Toronto [1912] [Canada] (NGC) .... AWCP
Associated Western Universities (SAUO) .... AWU
Associated Western Universities [Salt Lake City, UT] [Department of
   Energy] .... AWU
Associated Western Universities-Northwest (ABAC) .... AWUNW
Associated Wire Rope Fabricators (EA) .... AWRF
associated with (SAUS) .... assoc w
Associated with Brokers [London Stock Exchange] .... AB
Associated with Dual Capacity Firms [London Stock Exchange] .... AD
Associated with Jobbers [London Stock Exchange] .... AJ
Associated Women of the American Farm Bureau Federation (SAUO) .... AWAFBF
Associated Workers' Union [Philippines] .... AWU
Associated Writing Programs (EA) .... AWP
Associates (VRA) .... assoc
Associates (SAUS) .... Assoc
Associates (BEE) .... assocs
Associates and Advisory Committee to the Special Committee on
   Electronic Data Retrieval (MCD) .... AACSCEDR
Associates Catalog Librarians, Richmond, VA [Library symbol] [Library of
   Congress] (LCLS) .... ViRACL
Associates First Capital Corp. [NYSE symbol] (SAG) .... AFS
Associates First Capital Corp. [Associated Press] (SAG) .... AscFCap
Associates First Captial'A' [NYSE symbol] (TTSB) .... AFS
Associates for Radio Astronomy .... ARA
Associates for Religion and Intellectual Life (EA) .... ARIL
Associates for Research into the Science of Enjoyment .... ARISE
Associates in Rural Development (SAUO) .... ARD
Associates Investment Company (SAUO) .... ATS
Associates of Clinical Pharmacology (EA) .... ACP
Associates of Elvis Presley Fan Clubs (EA) .... AEPFC
Associates of the Graymoor Ecumenical Institute [Defunct] (EA) .... AGEI
Associateship of Loughborough University of Technology [British]
   (DBQ) .... ALUT
Associateship of the London School of Polymer Technology [British]
   (DBQ) .... ALSPT
Associateship of the Manchester College of Technology [British] .... AssocMCT
Associateship of the University of Manchester Institute of Science and
   Technology [British] (DI) .... AUMIST

Associateship, Royal Conservatory of Ontario [Canada] (CPGU) .... ARCT
Associatin of British Brush Machinery Manufacturers (MHDB) .... ABBMM
Associatin of Tarot & Associated Psychic Services (WDAA) .... ATTAPS
Association .... A
Association (SAUO) .... Asn
Association (SAUO) .... Ass
Association .... ASS
Association (GEOI) .... Ass
Association (EY) .... ASSCN
Association .... ASSN
Association (ODBW) .... assn
Association (PROS) .... Assn
Association (MELL) .... Assoc
Association (NTIO) .... assoc
association (SAUO) .... assoc
Association (SAUS) .... ASSOC
association (SAUO) .... assocn
Association .... ASSOCN
Association Actuarielle Internationale [International Actuarial Association -
   IAA] [Brussels, Belgium] (EAIO) .... AAI
Association Adjustment Inventory [Psychology] .... AAI
Association Africaine de Cartographie [African Association of Cartography]
   (EAIO) .... AAC
Association Agency of Korean Newspapers (SAUO) .... HAPDONG
Association Algerienne des Transports Automobiles [Algerian Automobile
   Transport Association] [Algeria] .... ATA
Association Belge pour le Developpement Pacifique de l'Energie Atomique
   [Belgium Association for the Peaceful Development of Atomic Energy]
   (NUCP) .... ADEA
Association Belgo-Americaine [Later, American-Belgian Association] (EA) ..... ABA
Association Belgo-Congolaise du Textile [Belgo-Congolese Textile
   Association] [Zaire] .... ABCT
Association Beton Quebec (AC) .... ABQ
Association Botanique du Canada (AC) .... ABC
Association Canadienne Contre la Tuberculose et les Maladies
   Respiratoires [Canadian Association Against Tuberculosis and Respiratory
   Diseases] .... ACTMR
Association Canadienne d'Administrateurs de Recherche Universitaire
   [Canadian Association of University Research Administrators -
   CAURA] .... ACARU
Association Canadienne d'Archaeologie [Canadian Archaeological
   Association - CAA] .... ACA
Association Canadienne d'Assistance Juridique, d'Information et de
   Recherche desHandicapes [Canadian Legal Advocacy Information and
   Research Association of the Disabled] .... CAJIR
Association Canadienne d'Athletisme [Canadian Athletics Association] .... ACA
Association Canadienne de Badminton [Canadian Badminton Association] .... ACB
Association Canadienne de Cinema-Television [Canada] .... ACC-T
Association Canadienne de Cross (AC) .... ACC
Association Canadienne de Direction D'Artists (AC) .... ACDA
Association Canadienne de Documentation Professionnelle (AC) .... ACADOP
Association Canadienne de Fabricants d'Armoires de Cuisine (AC) .... ACAC
Association Canadienne de Financement et de Location (AC) .... ACFL
Association Canadienne de Football Amateur [Canadian Association of
   Amateur Football] .... ACFA
Association Canadienne de Gestion des Achats [Purchasing Management
   Association of Canada - PMAC] .... ACGA
Association Canadienne de Hockey Amateur [Canadian Amateur Hockey
   Association - CAHA] .... ACHA
Association Canadienne de la Construction [Canadian Construction
   Association] .... ACC
Association Canadienne de la Courtepointe (AC) .... ACC
Association Canadienne de la Gestion du Personnel des Services Publics
   [Canadian Association of Public Service Personnel Management] .... ACGPSP
Association Canadienne de la Presse Syndicale [Canadian Syndicated Press
   Association] .... ACPS
Association Canadienne de la Recherche Operationnelle [Canadian
   Association of Operational Research] .... ACRO
Association Canadienne de l'Acoustique [Canadian Acoustics
   Association] .... ACA
Association Canadienne de l'Ataxie de Friedreich [Canadian Association of
   Friedreich's Ataxia] .... ACAF
Association Canadienne de l'Electricite (AC) .... ACE
Association Canadienne de l'Enseignement a Distance [Canadian
   Association for Distance Education - CADE] .... ACED
Association Canadienne de l'Habitation et du Developpement Urbain
   [Canadian Association of Housing and Urban Development] .... ACHDU
Association Canadienne de l'Immeuble [Canadian Real Estate Association -
   CREA] .... ACI
Association Canadienne de l'Imprimerie (EAIO) .... ACI
Association Canadienne de l'Industrie du Bois (AC) .... ACIB
Association Canadienne de l'Informatique [Canadian Information Processing
   Society - CIPS] .... ACI
Association Canadienne de Linguistique Appliquee [Canadian Association of
   Applied Linguistics - CAAL] .... ACLA
Association Canadienne de Litterature Comparee [Canadian Comparative
   Literature Association - CCLA] .... ACLC
Association Canadienne de Maisons Mobiles [Canadian Association of
   Mobile Homes] .... ACMM
Association Canadienne de Nage Synchronisee Amateur [Canadian
   Association of Amateur Synchronized Swimmers] .... ACNSA
Association Canadienne de Normalisation [Canadian Association of
   Standardization] .... ACNOR
Association Canadienne de Patinage Artistique [Canada] .... ACPA

Association Canadienne de Philosophie [*Canadian Philosophical Association - CPA*] ... ACP
Association Canadienne de Recherche en Evaluation Nondestructifs (AC) ... ACREND
Association Canadienne de Recherche et d'Education pour la Paix [*Canadian Peace Research and Education Association - CPREA*] ... ACREP
Association Canadienne de Recherches Sociales Appliquees [*Canadian Association of Applied Social Research - CAASR*] ... ACRSA
Association Canadienne de Sante Publique (AC) ... ACSP
Association Canadienne de Science Politique [*Canadian Political Science Association - CPSA*] ... ACSP
Association Canadienne de Semiotique [*Canadian Semiotic Association - CSA*] ... ACS
Association Canadienne de Sociologie et d'Anthropologie [*Canadian Sociology and Anthropology Association - CSAA*] ... ACSA
Association Canadienne de Softball Amateur [*Canadian Association of Amateur Softball*] ... ACSA
Association Canadienne de Technologie Avancee [*Canadian Association of Advanced Technology*] ... ACTA
Association Canadienne de Therapie Animale [*Canadian Animal Therapy Association*] ... ACTA
Association Canadienne de Traitement d'Images et Reconnaissance des Formes [*Canada*] ... ACTIRF
Association Canadienne de Vexillologie (AC) ... CFA
Association Canadienne de Vol a Voile [*Canada*] ... ACVV
Association Canadienne d'Economique [*Canadian Economics Association - CEA*] ... ACE
Association Canadienne d'Education [*Canadian Education Association - CEA*] ... ACE
Association Canadienne d'Education de Langue Francaise (AC) ... ACELF
Association Canadienne d'Entraineurs de Badminton [*Canadian Association of Badminton Coaches*] ... ACEB
Association Canadienne des Adjoints Juridiques (AC) ... ACAJ
Association Canadienne des Administrateurs et des Administratrices Scolaires (AC) ... ACAS
Association Canadienne des Administrateurs Scolaires [*Canadian Association of Academic Administrators*] ... ACAS
Association Canadienne des Arbitres de Badminton [*Canadian Association of Badminton Referees*] ... ACAB
Association Canadienne des Bibliothecaires de Langue Francaise [*Later, ASTED*] ... ACBLF
Association Canadienne des Bibliotheques [*Canadian Library Association - CLA*] ... ACB
Association Canadienne des Bibliotheques de Droit [*Canadian Association of Law Libraries - CALL*] ... ACBD
Association Canadienne des Bibliotheques Musicales [*Canadian Association of Music Libraries*] ... ACBM
Association Canadienne des BibliothSques de Droit (SAUO) ... ACBD
Association Canadienne des Boursiers Rhodes [*Canadian Association of Rhodes Scholars - CARS*] ... ACBR
Association Canadienne des Cadres en Informatique [*Canadian Association of Information Officials*] ... ACFOR
Association Canadienne des Centres de Vie Autonome (AC) ... ACCVA
Association Canadienne des Chefs de Pompiers [*Canadian Association of Fire Chiefs*] ... ACCP
Association Canadienne des Chercheurs en Education [*Canadian Educational Researchers Association - CERA*] ... ACCE
Association Canadienne des Chirurgiens Generaux [*Canadian Association of General Surgeons - CAGS*] ... ACCG
Association Canadienne des Cinq Quilles [*Formerly, Canadian Bowling Congress*] (AC) ... L'ACSQ
Association Canadienne des Communications [*Canadian Communication Association - CCA*] ... ACC
Association Canadienne des Communications entre l'Homme et l'Ordinateur [*Canadian Association of Communications between Man and Computers*] ... ACCHO
Association Canadienne des Courtiers en Valeurs Mobilieres [*Investment Dealers' Association of Canada - IDA*] ... ACCOVAM
Association Canadienne des Dessinateurs Editoriaux (AC) ... ACDE
Association Canadienne des Detaillants en Quincaillerie (AC) ... ACDQ
Association Canadienne des Dietetistes [*Canadian Association of Dietitians*] ... ACD
Association Canadienne des Eaux Potables et Usees (AC) ... ACEPU
Association Canadienne des Ecoles de Bibliothecaires [*Canadian Association of Library Schools*] ... ACEB
Association Canadienne des Ecoles de Traduction ... ACET
Association Canadienne des Ecoles du Service Social [*Canadian Association of Schools of Social Work - CASSW*] ... ACESS
Association Canadienne des Ecoles Universitaires de Musique [*Canadian Association of University Schools of Music - CAUSM*] ... ACEUM
Association Canadienne des Ecoles Universitaires de Nursing [*Canadian Association of University Schools of Nursing - CAUSN*] ... ACEUN
Association Canadienne des Editeurs de Musique [*Canadian Music Publishers Association - CMPA*] ... ACEM
Association Canadienne des Editeurs de Quotidiens [*Canadian Association of Newspaper Editors*] ... ACEQ
Association Canadienne des Educateurs de Musique [*Canadian Music Educators' Association*] ... CAEM
Association Canadienne des Employes de Telephone [*Canadian Telephone Employees' Association - CTEA*] ... ACET
Association Canadienne des Employes du Transport Aerien [*Canadian Air Line Employees' Association - CALEA*] ... ACETA
Association Canadienne des Enseignants Noirs [*Canadian Association of Black Teachers*] ... ACEN
Association Canadienne des Entraineurs [*Canadian Association of Coaches*] ... ACE
Association Canadienne des Entrepreneurs en Couverture [*Canadian Association of Bedding Entrepreneurs*] ... ACEC
Association Canadienne des Entreprises de Telecommunications [*Canadian Association of Telecommunication Businesses*] ... ACET
Association Canadienne des Etudes Africaines [*Canadian Association of African Studies*] (EAIO) ... ACEA
Association Canadienne des Etudes Asiatiques [*Canadian Asian Studies Association - CASA*] ... ACEA
Association Canadienne des Etudes Avancees (AC) ... ACDEA
Association Canadienne des Etudes Cinematographiques [*Canadian Association of Film Studies*] ... ACEC
Association Canadienne des Etudes Ecossaises [*Canadian Association for Scottish Studies - CASS*] ... ACEE
Association Canadienne des Etudes Finno-Ougriennes [*Finno-Ugrian Studies Association - FUSAC*] ... ACEFO
Association Canadienne des Etudes Hongroises [*Canadian Association of Hungarian Studies - CAHS*] ... ACEH
Association Canadienne des Etudes Latino-Americaines [*Canadian Association of Latin American Studies - CALAS*] ... ACELA
Association Canadienne des Etudes Latino-Americaines et Caraibes [*Canadian Association of Latin American and Caribbean Studies*] ... ACELAC
Association Canadienne des Etudes Patristiques [*Canadian Society of Patristic Studies - CSPS*] ... ACEP
Association Canadienne des Etudes Prospectives [*Canadian Association for Future Studies - CAFS*] ... ACEP
Association Canadienne des Fabricants de Panneaux de Particules (AC) ... ACFPP
Association Canadienne des Fabricants de Tuyaux de Beton (AC) ... ACTB
Association Canadienne des Femmes Arabes (AC) ... ACFA
Association Canadienne des Femmes en Radio et Television (AC) ... ACFR
Association Canadienne des Fondements de l'Education (AC) ... ACFE
Association Canadienne des Geographes [*Canadian Association of Geographers*] ... ACG
Association Canadienne des Gerants de la Redaction [*Canadian Association of Editorial Directors*] ... ACGR
Association Canadienne des Hispanistes [*Canadian Association of Hispanists - CAH*] ... ACH
Association Canadienne des Humanites [*Humanities Association of Canada - HAC*] ... ACH
Association Canadienne des Implantes Intraoculaires [*Canadian Implant Association*] (EAIO) ... ACII
Association Canadienne des Infirmieres et Infirmiers en Sante du Travail [*Formerly, National Association of Occupation Health Nurses*] (AC) ... ACIIST
Association Canadienne des Infirmieres et Infirmiers Pediatriques (AC) ... ACIIP
Association Canadienne des Laboratoires d'Analyse Environmenmentale (AC) ... ACLAE
Association Canadienne des Laboratoires d'Essais [*Canadian Testing Association*] (AC) ... ACLE
Association Canadienne des Maitres de Poste et Adjoints [*Canadian Postmasters and Assistants Association - CPAA*] ... ACMPA
Association Canadienne des Manufacturiers de Fenetres et Portes [*Canadian Association of Window and Door Manufacturers*] ... ACMFP
Association Canadienne des Manufacturiers de Maconnerie en Beton (AC) ... ACMMB
Association Canadienne des Manufacturiers de Palettes et Contenants [*Canadian Wood Pallet and Container Association*] (EAIO) ... ACMPC
Association Canadienne des Optometristes [*Canadian Association of Optometrists*] ... ACO
Association Canadienne des Orchestres de Jeunes [*Canadian Association of Youth Orchestras - CAYO*] ... ACOJ
Association Canadienne des Paiements (AC) ... ACP
Association Canadienne des Palynologues (QUAC) ... ACP
Association canadienne des Palynologues (SAUO) ... ACP
Association Canadienne des Patineurs Professionnels [*Canadian Association of Professional Skaters*] ... ACPP
Association Canadienne des Periodiques Catholiques [*Canadian Association of Catholic Periodicals*] ... ACPC
Association Canadienne des Physiciens et Physiciennes (AC) ... ACP
Association Canadienne des Pigistes de l'Edition [*Canada*] ... ACPE
Association Canadienne des Presidents de Departements d'Anglais [*Canadian Association of Chairmen of English Departments - CACE*] ... ACPDA
Association Canadienne des Producteurs de Films d'Animation [*Canada*] ... ACPFA
Association Canadienne des Professeures et Professeurs d'Universite (AC) ... ACPPU
Association Canadienne des Professeurs de Comptabilite [*Canadian Association of Professors of Accounting*] ... ACPC
Association Canadienne des Professeurs de Droit [*Canadian Association of Law Teachers - CALT*] ... ACPD
Association Canadienne des Professeurs de Langue Seconde (AC) ... ACPLS
Association Canadienne des Professeurs de Redaction Technique et Scientifique [*Canadian Association of Teachers of Technical Writing - CATTW*] ... ACPRTS
Association Canadienne des Professeurs d'Immersion (AC) ... ACPI
Association Canadienne des Professeurs d'Universite [*Canadian Association of University Professors*] ... ACPU
Association Canadienne des Quotidiens (AC) ... ACQ
Association Canadienne des Radiodiffuseurs (AC) ... ACR
Association Canadienne des Redacteurs Agricoles de Langue Francaise (AC) ... ACRA
Association Canadienne des Regulateurs des Vols [*Canadian Air Line Dispatchers' Association - CALDA*] ... ACRV

Association Canadienne des Relations Industrielles [*Canadian Industrial Relations Association - CIRA*] .... ACRI

Association Canadienne des Resources Hydriques [*Canadian Water Resources Association*] (EAIO) .... ACRH

Association Canadienne des Responsables de l'Habitation et de l'Urbainisme [*Canada*] .... ACRHU

Association Canadienne des Restaurateurs Professionnels [*Canadian Association of Professional Conservators - CAPC*] .... ACRP

Association Canadienne des Sciences de l'Information [*Canadian Association for Information Science*] .... ACSI

Association Canadienne des Sciences Geodesiques et Cartographiques [*Canadian Institute of Surveying and Mapping*] (EAIO) .... ACSGC

Association Canadienne des Sciences Regionales [*Canadian Regional Science Association - CRSA*] .... ACSR

Association Canadienne des Sciences Sportives [*Canadian Association of Sports Sciences*] .... ACSS

Association Canadienne des Slavistes [*Canadian Association of Slavists - CAS*] .... ACS

Association Canadienne des Societes d'Investissement en Capital de Risque .... ACSICR

Association Canadienne des Sociologues et Anthropologues de Langue Francaise [*Canadian Association of French-Language Sociologists and Anthropologists*] .... ACSALF

Association Canadienne des Soins Palliatifs (AC) .... ACSP

Association Canadienne des Techniciens en Radiation Medicale [*Canadian Association of Medical Radiation Technologists*] (EAIO) .... ACTRM

Association Canadienne des Techniciens et Technologistes en Sante Animale (AC) .... ACTTSA

Association Canadienne des Techniques de l'Asphalte [*Canadian Technical AsphaltAssociation*] (EAIO) .... ACTA

Association Canadienne des Travailleurs Sociaux [*Canadian Association of Social Workers - CASW*] .... ACTS

Association Canadienne des Utilisateurs SAS (AC) .... ACUS

Association Canadienne des Veterans du Hockey [*Canadian Association of Hockey Veterans*] .... ACVH

Association Canadienne des Veterinaires [*Canadian Veterinary Medical Association*] (EAIO) .... ACV

Association Canadienne d'Etudes Fiscales (AC) .... ACEF

Association Canadienne d'Exportation [*Canadian Export Association*] .... ACE

Association Canadienne d'Habitation et de Renovation Urbaine (AC) .... ACHRU

Association Canadienne d'Hygiene Publique [*Canadian Association of Public Health*] .... ACHP

Association Canadienne d'Orthopedie (AC) .... ACO

Association Canadienne Droit et Societe [*Canadian Law and Society Association - CLSA*] .... ACDS

Association Canadienne du Canotage Recreatif [*Canadian Association of Recreational Boating*] .... ACCR

Association Canadienne du Commerce des Semences (AC) .... ACCS

Association Canadienne du Contreplaque de Bois (AC) .... ACCBD

Association Canadienne du Controle du Trafic Aerien [*Canadian Air Traffic Control Association - CATCA*] .... ACCTA

Association Canadienne du Droit de l'Environnement [*Canadian Association of Environmental Law*] .... ACDE

Association Canadienne du Genie Eolien [*Canada*] .... ACGE

Association Canadienne du Marketing Direct (AC) .... ACMD

Association Canadienne du Personnel Administratif Universitaire [*Canadian Association of University Administration Personnel*] .... ACPAU

Association Canadienne d'Urbanisme [*Canadian City Planning Association*] .... ACU

Association Canadienne Fournisseurs Bibliotheque [*Canadian Association of Library Suppliers*] .... ACFB

Association Canadienne Linguistique [*Canadian Linguistic Association - CLA*] .... ACL

Association Canadienne pour la Formation des Enseignants (AC) .... ACFE

Association Canadienne pour la Gestion de la Production et let Stocks [*Also, APICS Region VIII*] (AC) .... ACGPS

Association Canadienne pour la Recherche en Economie de Sante [*Canadian Health Economics Research Association - CHERA*] .... ACRES

Association Canadienne pour la Recherche en Economie Familiale [*Canadian Association for Research in Home Economics - CARHE*] .... ACREF

Association Canadienne pour la Technologie des Animaux de Laboratoire [*Canadian Association for Laboratory Animals Technology*] .... ACTA

Association Canadienne pour l'Avancement de la Litterature de Jeunesse [*Canadian Association for the Advancement of Children's Literature*] .... ACALJ

Association Canadienne pour l'Avancement des Etudes Neerlandaises [*Canadian Association for the Advancement of Netherlandic Studies - CAANS*] .... ACAEN

Association Canadienne pour le Droit a l'Avortement [*Canadian Abortion Rights Action League - CARAL*] .... ACDA

Association Canadienne pour le Soustitrage (AC) .... ACST

Association Canadienne pour les Deficients Mentaux [*Canadian Association for the Mentally Retarded*] .... ACDM

Association Canadienne pour les Etudes du Folklore [*Canadian Folklore Studies Association*] .... ACEF

Association Canadienne pour les Etudes en Cooperation [*Canadian Association for Studies in Cooperation - CASC*] .... ACEC

Association Canadienne pour les Etudes Rurales [*Canadian Association of Rural Studies - CARS*] .... ACER

Association Canadienne pour les Etudes sur les Femmes [*Canadian Women's Studies Association - CWSA*] .... ACEF

Association Canadienne pour les Nations Unies (SAUO) .... ACNU

Association Canadienne pour les Nations-Unies [*United Nations Association in Canada*] (EAIO) .... ACNU

Association Canadienne pour les Structures et Materiaux Composites (AC) .... ACSMAC

Association Canadienne pour l'Etude de la Litterature et des Langues du Commonwealth [*Canadian Association for Commonwealth Literature and Language Studies - CACLALS*] .... ACELLC

Association Canadienne pour l'Etude de l'Administration Scolaire [*Canadian Association for the Study of Academic Administration*] .... ACEAS

Association Canadienne pour l'Etude de l'Education des Adultes [*Canadian Association for the Study of Adult Education - CASAE*] .... ACEEA

Association Canadienne pour l'Integration Communautarie [*Canadian Association for Community Living*] (EAIO) .... ACIC

Association Canadienne-Francaise de l'Alberta (AC) .... ACFA

Association Canadienne-Francaise de l'Ontario (AC) .... ACFO

Association Canadienne-Francaise pour l'Avancement des Sciences .... ACFAS

Association Canado-Americaine (EA) .... ACA

Association Candienne de la Formation Professionelle (AC) .... ACFP

Association Candienne de Television par Cable [*Formerly, National Community Antenna Television Association of Canada*] (AC) .... ACTC

Association Candienne sur la Qualite de l'Eau [*Also, Canadian National Committee of the Internation Association on Water Quality*] [*Formerly, Canadian Association on Water Pollution Research & Control*] (AC) .... ACQE

Association Catholique Canadienne de la Sante [*Canadian-Catholic Health Association*] .... ACCS

Association Catholique de la Jeunesse Canadienne-Francaise [*Catholic Association of Francophone Youth*] [*Canada*] .... ACJC

Association Catholique des Etudes Bibliques au Canada [*Catholic Association of Bible Studies in Canada*] .... ACEBAC

Association Catholique Internationale des Oeuvres de Protection de la Jeune Fille [*Later, ACISJF*] .... ACIOPJF

Association Catholique Internationale des Services de la Jeunesse Feminine [*International Catholic Society for Girls*] [*Geneva, Switzerland*] (EAIO) .... ACISJF

Association Cerification Comite European de Normalisation (OSI) .... CENCER

Association Chiropratique Canadienne [*Canadian Chiropractic Association*] .... ACC

Association Cinematographique Professionnelle de Conciliation et d'Arbitrage (EAIO) .... ACPCA

Association Congolaise pour les Nations Unies [*United Nations Association of the Congo*] (EAIO) .... ACNU

Association Control Server Element (SAUO) .... ACSE

Association Control Service Element (SAUO) .... ACSC

Association Control Service Element [*Telecommunications*] (OSI) .... ACSE

Association Control Service Entity (SAUO) .... ACSE

Association Cooperative de Productions Audio-Visuelles (AC) .... ACPAV

Association Cooperative d'Economie Familiale - Montreal (Nord) (AC) .... ACEF du Nord

Association Cooperative Feminine du Quebec (AC) .... ACFQ

Association County Commissioners of Georgia (SRA) .... ACCG

Association Culturelle et Touristique des Cantons [*Cultural and Tourist Association of Cantons*] [*Canada*] .... ACTC

Association Culturelle Franco-Manitobaine (AC) .... ACFM

Association Culturelle Internationale: Reliance [*Leucate, France*] (EAIO) .... ACIR

Association d'Amitie et de Solidarite Franco-Algerienne [*Franco-Algerian Friendship and Solidarity Association*] .... AASFA

Association Danse au Canada [*Dance Association of Canada*] .... ADAC

Association de Climatologie du Quebec (AC) .... ACLIQ

Association de Comites Nationaux Olympiques d'Afrique [*Association of National Olympic Committees of Africa - ANOCA*] (EA) .... ACNOA

Association de Consultants Internationaux en Droits de l'Homme [*Association of International Consultants on Human Rights*] [*Geneva, Switzerland*] (EAIO) .... CID

Association de Coureurs Internationaux en Multicoques Oceaniques [*Association of International Competitors on Oceanic Multihulls*] (EAIO) .... ACIMO

Association de Gestion Internationale Collective des Oeuvres Audiovisuelles [*Association for the International Collective Management of Audiovisual Works*] [*Geneva, Switzerland*] (EAIO) .... AGICOA

Association de Gestion Portuaire de l'Afrique de l'Est et de l'Afrique Australe [*Port Management Association of Eastern and Southern Africa - PMAESA*] (EAIO) .... AGPAEA

Association de Golf du Quebec (AC) .... AGQ

Association de la Construction de l'Outaouais [*Outaouais Construction Association*] (AC) .... ACO

Association de la Construction du Quebec [*Construction Association of Quebec*] (AC) .... ACQ

Association de la Jeunesse Rurale du Quebec (AC) .... AJRQ

Association de la Librairie Ancienne du Canada [*Association of Antique Bookstores of Canada*] .... ALAC

Association de la Paralysie Cerebrale du Quebec [*Quebec Cerebral Palsy Association*] (AC) .... APCQI

Association de la Presse Anglo-Americaine de Paris [*Anglo-American Press Association of Paris*] (EAIO) .... APAAP

Association de la Presse Eurafricaine [*Eurafrican Press Association*] [*Belgium*] .... APEA

Association de la Presse Sportive du Quebec (AC) .... APSQ

Association de la Recherche en Communication du Quebec (AC) .... ARCQ

Association de la Securite Industrielle du Canada [*Industrial Security Association of Canada*] .... ASIC

Association de l'Evangelisation des Enfants (AC) .... AEF

Association de l'Huile a Chauffage du Quebec (AC) .... AHCQ

Association de l'Industrie de la Fonte de Fromage de la CEE [*Association of the Processed Cheese Industry of the European Economic Community*] .... ASSIFONTE

Association de l'Industrie de l'Aluminium du Quebec (AC) .... AIAQ

Association de l'Industrie des Fruits et Legumes au Vinaigre, en Saumure, a l'Huile et des Produits Similaires des CE [*Association of the Industry of Fruit and Vegetables in Vinegar, Brine, Oil and Similar Products of the EC*] (ECED) .... AIFLV

Association de l'Industrie des Just et Nectars de Fruits et de Legumes de la CEE [*Association of the Industry of Juices and Nectars from Fruits and Vegetables of the EEC*] (ECED) ... AIJN
Association de l'Industrie Laitiere de la CE [*European Community Dairy Trade Association*] [*Belgium*] (EAIO) ... ASSILEC
Association de l'Industrie Touristique du Canada [*Travel (later, Tourism) Industry Association of Canada - TIAC*] ... AITC
Association de Manutention du Quebec (AC) ... AMQ
Association de Placement Universitaire et Collegial [*University and College Placement Association*] [*Canada*] ... APUC
Association de Planification Fiscale et Financiere (AC) ... APFF
Association de Prevention des Accidents dans l'Industrie Forestiere [*Forest Products Accident Prevention Association*] [*Canada*] ... APAIF
Association de Psychologie du Travail de Langue Francaise [*French-Language Association of Work Psychology*] (EAIO) ... APTLF
Association de Psychologie Scientifique de Langue Francaise [*French-Language Association of Scientific Psychology*] (EAIO) ... APSLF
Association de Recherche et d'Exploitation de Diamant et de l'Or [*Guinea*] [*ICAO designator*] (FAAC) ... GIN
Association de Recherches Theatrales au Canada (AC) ... ARTC
Association de Recyclage du Polystyrene du Canada (AC) ... ARPC
Association de Reseaux Informatique en Systeme Totalement et Tres Elabore [*Association of Information Networks in a Completely Open and Very Elaborate System*] [*France*] [*Computer science*] (TNIG) ... ARISTOTE
Association de Sante et Securite des Industries de la Foret du Quebec [*Quebec Logging Health & Safety Association Inc.*] (AC) ... ASSIFQ
Association de Sante et Securite des Pates et Papiers du Quebec Inc. [*Quebec Pulp & Paper Health & Safety Association Inc.*] (AC) ... ASSPPQ
Association de Ski Nautique du Canada [*Canadian Water Ski Association*] ... ASNC
Association de Textiles des Cantons de l'Est (AC) ... ATCE
Association d'Economie Familiale du Quebec (AC) ... AEFQ
Association d'Economie Politique [*Political Economic Association*] [*Canada*] ... AEP
Association d'Education Prescolaire du Quebec (AC) ... AEPQ
Association Democratique des Femmes du Maroc [*Morocco*] ... ADFM
Association Democratique des Francais de l'Etranger [*Democratic Association of French Citizens Abroad*] (PPW) ... ADFE
Association d'Entraide pour les Agoraphobes (AC) ... ADEPA
Association des Administrateurs de Recherches Universitaires du Quebec (AC) ... ADARUQ
Association des Administrateurs du Personnel de la Fonction Publique [*Association of Personnel Administrators of Public Functions*] [*Canada*] ... AAP
Association des Agences de Publicite du Quebec [*Association of Quebec Advertising Agencies*] (AC) ... AAPQ
Association des Agents de Voyages du Quebec (AC) ... ACTA-Quebec
Association des Amenagistes Regionaux du Quebec (AC) ... AARQ
Association des Amidonneries de Cereales de la CEE [*EC*] (ECED) ... AAC
Association des Amidonneries de Mais de la CEE [*Association of the Maize Starch Industries of the European Economic Community*] ... AAM
Association des Amis de Maurice Zundel [*Paris, France*] (EAIO) ... AAMZ
Association des Amis du Musee International des Hussards [*Association of Friends of the International Museum of the Hussars*] [*France*] (EAIO) ... AAMIH
Association des Anciens Fonctionnaires Internationaux [*Association of Former International Civil Servants - AFICS*] [*Geneva, Switzerland*] (EA) ... AAFI
Association des Animateurs et Animatrices de Pastorale de la Sante du Quebec (AC) ... AAAPSQ
Association des Architectes en Pratique Privee du Quebec (AC) ... AAPPQ
Association des Architectes Paysagistes du Quebec (AC) ... AAPQ
Association des Archivistes du Quebec (AC) ... AAQ
Association des Armateurs Canadiens [*Formerly, Dominion Marine Association*] (AC) ... AAC
Association des Artisans du Film Canadien (AC) ... AAFC
Association des Artisans Glaciers et des Fabricants de Mix pour Glace des Pays de la CEE [*Association of Home-Made Ice-Cream and Ice-Mix Manufacturers in the European Economic Community*] ... ASSOGLACE
Association des Artistes Non Figuratifs de Montreal [*1956-61*] [*Canada*] (NGC) ... AANFM
Association des Arts Graphiques du Quebec, Inc. (AC) ... AAGQ
Association des Arts Plastiques, Montreal [*1955*] [*Canada*] (NGC) ... AAP
Association des Assureurs Cooperatifs Europeens [*Association of European Cooperative Insurers - AECI*] [*Brussels, Belgium*] (EAIO) ... AACE
Association des Assureurs-Vie du Canada [*Association of Life Insurers of Canada*] ... AAVC
Association des Auditeurs et Anciens Auditeurs de l'Academie [*Association of Attenders and Alumni of the Hague Academy of International Law*] (EAIO) ... AAA
Association des Auteurs des Cantons de l'Est [*Association of Writers of Cantons of the East*] [*Canada*] ... AACE
Association des Auxiliaires Familiales et Sociales du Quebec (AC) ... AAFSQ
Association des Banques Centrales Africaines [*Association of African Central Banks*] (EAIO) ... ABCA
Association des Banquiers Canadiens [*Canadian Bankers Association*] ... ABC
Association des Bibliothecaires du Quebec (AC) ... ABQ
Association des Bibliothecaires Parlementaires au Canada [*Association of Parliamentary Librarians of Canada*] ... ABPAC
Association des Bibliothecaires Professionel du Nouveau-Brunswick (AC) ... ABPNB
Association des Bibliotheques de la Sante Affiliee a l'Universite de Montreal (AC) ... ABSAUM
Association des Bibliotheques de la Sante du Canada [*Canadian Association of Health Libraries*] ... ABSC
Association des Bibliotheques de Recherche du Canada [*Canadian Association of Research Libraries*] (EAIO) ... ABRC
Association des Bibliotheques des Provinces de l'Atlantique [*Atlantic Provinces Association of Libraries*] [*Canada*] ... ABPA
Association des Bibliotheques Publiques de l'Estrie (AC) ... ABIPE
Association des Bureaux de Congres du Quebec (AC) ... ABCQ
Association des Bureaux de l'Information des Universites [*Association of University Information Bureaus*] [*Canada*] ... ABUIC
Association des Cablodistributeurs du Quebec Inc. (AC) ... ACQ
Association des Cadres des Colleges du Quebec (AC) ... ACCQ
Association des Cadres d'Institutions Culturelles (AC) ... ACIC
Association des Cadres Intermediaires de la Sante et des Services Sociaux du Quebec (AC) ... ACISSSQ
Association des Cadres Intermediaires des Affaires Sociales (AC) ... ACIAS
Association des Camps du Canada (AC) ... ACC
Association des Cartotheques et des Archives Cartographiques du Canada [*Association of Canadian Map Libraries and Archives*] (EAIO) ... ACACC
Association des Centres de Ski de Fond du Quebec (AC) ... ACSFQ
Association des Centres Hospitaliers et Centres d'Accueil Prives du Quebec (AC) ... ACHAB
Association des Chantiers Maritimes Canadiens [*Association of Canadian Maritime Shipyards*] ... ACMC
Association des Chefs de Service d'Incendie du Quebec [*Quebec Fire Chief Association*] (AC) ... ACSIQ
Association des Chimistes de l'Industrie Textile [*Association of Chemists of the Textile Industry*] (EAIO) ... ACIT
Association des Citoyens de Culture Francaise d'Amerique [*American Association of Citizens of French Culture*] [*Canada*] ... ACCFA
Association des Classes Moyennes Africaines [*African Middle Classes Association*] ... ACMAF
Association des Collaboratrices et Partenaires en Affaires (AC) ... ACPA
Association des Comites Nationaux Olympiques [*Association of National Olympic Committees - ANOC*] [*Paris, France*] (EAIO) ... ACNO
Association des Comites Nationaux Olympiques d'Europe [*Association of the European National Olympic Committees - ENOC*] [*Brussels, Belgium*] (EAIO) ... ACNOE
Association des Commissaires Industriels du Quebec (AC) ... ACIQ
Association des Communicateurs Municipaux du Quebec (AC) ... ACMQ
Association des Communicateurs Scientifiques du Quebec (AC) ... ACSQ
Association des Conseillers en Environnement du Quebec (AC) ... ACEQ
Association des Conseillers et Conseilleres Scolaires Francophones du Nouveau-Brunswick (AC) ... ACCSFNB
Association des Conseils Sub-Aquatiques Canadiens [*Association of Canadian Underwater Councils*] ... ASCS
Association des Consommateurs du Canada [*Consumers' Association of Canada - CAC*] ... ACC
Association des Consommateurs du Quebec (AC) ... ACQ
Association des Constructeurs de Machines a Coudre de la CEE [*Association of Sewing Machine Manufacturers of the EEC*] ... ASCOMACE
Association des Constructeurs de Routes et Grands Travaux du Quebec [*Quebec Road Builders & Heavy Construction Association*] (AC) ... ACRGTQ
Association des Constructeurs Europeens d'Automobiles [*Association of European Car Manufacturers*] [*EC*] (ECED) ... ACEA
Association des Constructeurs Europeens de Systemes d'Alarme Incendie et Vol [*Association of European Manufacturers of Fire and Intruder Alarm Systems*] (EAIO) ... EURALARM
Association des Cooperatives d'Epargne et de Credit d'Afrique [*African Confederation of Cooperative Savings and Credit Associations - ACCOSCA*] [*Nairobi, Kenya*] (EAIO) ... ACECA
Association des Coordonnateurs de Congres des Universites et des Colleges du Canada (AC) ... ACCUCC
Association des Courtiers d'Assurances de la Province de Quebec [*Insurance Brokers Association of Quebec*] (AC) ... ACAPQ
Association des Createurs et Intervenants de la Bande Dessinee (AC) ... ACIBD
Association des Denturologistes du Quebec (AC) ... ADQ
Association des Dermatologistes du Quebec [*Association of Dermatologists of Quebec*] (AC) ... ADQ
Association des Designers Industriels du Quebec (AC) ... ADIQ
Association des Detaillants de Materiaux de Construction du Quebec [*Quebec Building Materials Dealers Association*] (AC) ... ADMACQ
Association des Detaillants en Alimentation du Quebec [*Quebec Food Retailers Association*] (AC) ... ADA
Association des Directeurs d'Agence-Vie de Montreal (AC) ... ADAM
Association des Directeurs de Departements de Sante Communautaire [*Association of Public Health Department Directors*] [*Canada*] ... ADDSC
Association des Directeurs de Departements d'Etudes Francaises des Universites et Colleges du Canada [*Association of Directors of Departments of French Studies of Canadian Universities and Colleges*] ... ADEFUCC
Association des Directeurs de Recherche Industrielle du Quebec (AC) ... ADRIQ
Association des Directeurs d'Ecole de Montreal (AC) ... ADEM
Association des Directeurs des Centres Europeens des Plastiques [*Association of Directors of European Centres for Plastics*] (EAIO) ... ADICEP
Association des Directeurs Generaux des Commissions Scolaires du Quebec (AC) ... ADIGECS
Association des Distributeurs Aux Services Alimentaires du Quebec (AC) ... ADSAQ
Association des Distributeurs Exclusifs de Livres en Langue Francaise [*Association of Exclusive Distributors of French-Language Books*] [*Canada*] ... ADELF
Association des Distributeurs Independants de Produits Petroliers (AC) ... ADIP
Association des Ecoles Internationales ... AEI
Association des Economistes, Sociologues, et Statisticiens [*Economists', Sociologists', and Statisticians' Association ESSA*] [*Canada*] ... AESS
Association des Ecrivains de Langue Francaise [*Association of French-Language Writers*] (EAIO) ... ADELF

Association des Editeurs Canadiens [*Association of Canadian Editors*] .... AEC
Association des Eglises Evangelique (AC) .... AEE
Association des Electrolystes du Quebec (AC) .... AEQ
Association des Employes du Conseil de Recherches [*Research Council Employees' Association - RCEA*] [*Canada*] .... AECR
Association des Employes du Trafic [*Association of Traffic Employees*] [*Canada*] .... AET
Association des Employes d'Universites et de Colleges [*Association of University and College Employees - AUCE*] [*Canada*] .... AEUC
Association des Enducteurs, Calandreurs et Fabricants de Revetements de Sols Plastiques de la CEE [*Association of Coated Fabrics, Plastic Films and Plastic and Synthetic Floor Coverings of the European Economic Community*] (PDAA) .... AEC
Association des Enseignantes et des Enseignants Franco-Ontariens [*Franco-Ontarien Teachers' Association*] (AC) .... AEFO
Association des Enseignants de la Construction et du Meuble du Quebec (AC) .... AECMQ
Association des Enseignants des Metiers du Vetement du Quebec (AC) .... AEMVQ
Association des Enseignants du CO, division B (SAUS) .... AECOB
Association des Enseignants en Imprimerie du Quebec (AC) .... AEIQ
Association des Enseignants en Refrigeration et Climatisation du Quebec (AC) .... AERCQ
Association des Entomologistes Amateurs du Quebec (AC) .... AEAQ
Association des Entrepreneurs de Services en Environnement du Quebec (AC) .... AESEQ
Association des Entrepreneurs en Construction du Quebec (AC) .... AECQ
Association des Entrepreneurs en Couture du Quebec (AC) .... AECQ
Association des Entrepreneurs en Isolation de la Province du Quebec (AC) .... AIQ
Association des Etablissements Multiplicateurs de Semences Fourrageres des Communautes Europeennes [*Association of Forage Seed Breeders of the European Community*] [*Brussels, Belgium*] .... AMUFOC
Association des Etudes Canadiennes [*Association for Canadian Studies - ACS*] .... AEC
Association des Etudes de l'Europe Centrale et de l'Europe de l'Est du Canada [*Central and East European Studies Association of Canada - CEESAC*] .... AEECEEC
Association des Etudiants et Etudiantes en Medecine de l'Universite de Montreal (AC) .... AEMUM
Association des Etudiants Musulmans Nord-Africains [*North African Muslim Students Association*] (AF) .... AEMNA
Association des Etudiants Tchadiens en France [*Association of Chadian Students in France*] [*Chad*] (AF) .... AETF
Association des Evangeliques d'Afrique et Madagascar [*Association of Evangelicals of Africa and Madagascar*] (EAIO) .... AEAM
Association des Fabricants de Cafe Soluble des Pays de la CEE [*Association of Soluble Coffee Manufacturers of the Countries of the European Economic Community*] .... AFCASOLE
Association des Fabricants de Glucose de la CEE [*Association of the Glucose Producers in the European Economic Community*] .... AFG
Association des Fabricants de Laits de Conserve des Pays de la CEE [*Association of Powdered Milk Manufacturers of the EEC*] .... ASFALEC
Association des Fabricants de Material Agricole du Quebec (AC) .... AFMAQ
Association des Fabricants d'Engrais du Quebec (AC) .... AFEQ
Association des Fabricants et Distributeurs de l'Industrie de la Cuisine du Quebec (AC) .... AFDICQ
Association des Fabricants Europeens d'Appareils de Controle [*European Control Manufacturers Association*] (EAIO) .... AFECOGAZ
Association des Fabricants Europeens d'Appareils de Controle et de Regulation [*European Control Device Manufacturers' Association*] [*EC*] (ECED) .... AFECOR
Association des Fabricants Europeens de Chauffe-Bains et Chauffe-Eau Instantaneset de Chaudieres Murales au Gaz [*Association of European Manufacturers of Instantaneous Gas Water Heaters and Wall-Hung Boilers*] (EA) .... AFECI
Association des Fabricants Europeens de Rubans Auto-Adhesifs [*Association of European Manufacturers of Self-Adhesive Tapes - AEMSAT*] (EAIO) .... AFERA
Association des Fabricants Europeens d'Emulsifants Alimentaires [*Association of European Manufacturers of Food Emulsifiers*] (EAIO) .... EFEMA
Association des Fabricants Europeens d'Equipements Ferroviaires [*Association of European Railway Equipment Manufacturers*] (EAIO) .... AFEDEF
Association des Facultes de Medecine du Canada [*Association of Medical Faculties of Canada*] .... AFMC
Association des Facultes de Pharmacie du Canada [*Association of Faculties of Pharmacy of Canada*] .... AFPC
Association des Facultes Dentaires du Canada [*Association of Dentistry Faculties in Canada*] .... AFDC
Association des Familles Paguin [*Association of the Paguin Family*] [*Canada*] .... AFP
Association des Federations Africaines de Basketball Amateur [*African Association of Basketball Federations*] [*Egypt*] .... AFABA
Association des Femmes Africaines pour la Recherche sur le Developpement [*Association of African Women for Research and Development - AAWORD*] (EAIO) .... AFARD
Association des Femmes Collaboratrices [*Association of Feminine Collectives*] [*Canada*] .... ADFC
Association des Femmes d'Affaires du Quebec (AC) .... AFAQ
Association des Fermieres de l'Ontario (AC) .... AFO
Association des Firmes-Conseils en Technologie de l'Information de Quebec (AC) .... AFTIQ
Association des Fournisseurs d'Hotels et Restaurants Inc. (AC) .... AFHR
Association des Gens d'Affaires Haitiens de Montreal [*Haitian Businessmen's Association of Montreal*] (AC) .... AGAHM
Association des Grandes Entreprises de Distribution de Belgique [*Trade organization*] [*Belgium*] (EY) .... AGED
Association des Graveurs du Quebec [*1971, CGQ from 1978, CQE from 1984*] [*Canada*] (NGC) .... AGQ
Association des Groupements de Negoce Interieur du Bois et des Produits Derives dans les Pays de la CEE [*Association of National Trade Groups for Wood and Derived Products in Countries of the European Economic Community*] .... AGNIB
Association des Groupes d'Astronomes Amateurs [*Association of Amateur Astronomy Groups*] [*Canada*] .... AGAA
Association des Hommes d'Affaires et Professionnels du Quebec (AC) .... AHAPQ
Association des Hopitaux Catholiques du Canada [*Association of Catholic Hospitals of Canada*] .... AHCC
Association des Hopitaux du Canada [*Association of Hospitals of Canada*] .... AHC
Association des Hopitaux du Quebec [*Quebec Hospital Association*] (AC) .... AHQ
Association des Industries de Cidre et Vins de Fruits de la CE [*Belgium*] (EAIO) .... AICVF-CE
Association des Industries de Glaces Alimentaires de la CEE [*Association of the Ice Cream Industries of the European Economic Community*] .... EUROGLACES
Association des Industries de la Chocolaterie, Biscuiterie-Biscotterie et Confiserie de la CEE [*Association of the Chocolate, Biscuit and Confectionery Industries of the EEC*] (ECED) .... CAOBISCO
Association des Industries des Aliments Dietetiques de la CEE [*Association of Dietetic Foods Industries of the European Economic Community*] .... IDACE
Association des Industries des Carrieres [*Federations of Quarrying Industries*] [*Belgium*] (EY) .... AIC
Association des Industries des Cidres et Vins de Fruits de la CEE [*Association of the Cider and Fruit Wine Industries of the EEC*] (ECED) ..... AICV
Association des Industries des Fruits et Legumes Deshydrates de la CEE [*European Organization of the Dehydrated Fruit and Vegetable Industries*] [*EC*] (ECED) .... AIFLD
Association des Industries des Fruits et Legumes Deshydrates de la CEE [*European Organization of the Dehydrated Fruit and Vegetable Industries*] (EAIO) .... AJFLD
Association des Industries du Jute Europeennes [*Association of European Jute Industries*] .... AIJE
Association des Industries Margarinieres des Pays de la CEE [*Association of Margarine Industries of the EEC Countries*] [*Belgium*] .... IMACE
Association des Infirmieres Canadiennes [*Canadian Nurses' Association - CNA*] .... AIC
Association des Infirmieres et Infirmiers du Canada (EAIO) .... AIIC
Association des Infirmieres et Infirmiers en Sante du Travail du Quebec (AC) .... AIISTQ
Association des Ingenieurs Municipaux du Quebec [*Association of Quebec Municipal Engineers*] (AC) .... AIMQ
Association des Ingenieurs-Conseils du Canada [*Association of Canadian Engineer-Councils*] .... AICC
Association des Ingenieurs-Conseils du Quebec [*Consulting Engineers of Quebec*] (AC) .... AICQ
Association des Institutions de Niveaux Prescolaire et Elementaire du Quebec (AC) .... AIPEQ
Association des Institutions d'Enseignement Secondaire (AC) .... AIES
Association des Instituts de Theologie du Moyen-Orient [*Association of Theological Institutes in the Middle East - ATIME*] (EAIO) .... AITME
Association des Instituts d'Etudes Europeennes [*Association of Institutes for European Studies*] .... AIEE
Association des Intermediaires en Assurance de Personnes du Quebec (AC) .... AIAPQ
Association des Intervenants en Toxicomanie du Quebec (AC) .... AITQ
Association des Jeunes Juristes Africains [*France*] .... AJJAF
Association des Journalistes Independants du Quebec [*Quebec Association of Independent Journalists*] (AC) .... AJIQ
Association des Journaux Regionaux du Quebec (AC) .... AJRQ
Association des Juifs Anciens Resistants [*Association of Jews in the Resistance*] [*Acronym is pseudonym of writer Romain Gary*] .... AJAR
Association des Juristes d'Expression Francaise de l'Ontario (AC) .... AJEFO
Association des Libraires du Quebec (AC) .... ALQ
Association des Litteratures Canadiennes et Quebecoises [*Association for Canadian and Quebec Literatures - ACQL*] .... ALCQ
Association des Maitres Couvreurs du Quebec [*Quebec Master Roofers Association*] (AC) .... AMCQ
Association des Malentendants Canadiens (AC) .... AMEC
Association des Manoeuvres Interprovinciaux [*Interprovincial Labourers Association*] (AC) .... AMI
Association des Manufacturiers de Bois de Sciage du Quebec [*Quebec Lumber Manufacturers Association*] (AC) .... AMBSQ
Association des Manufacturiers de Maconnerie de Beton (AC) .... AMMB
Association des Manufacturiers de Produits Alimentaires du Quebec [*Quebec Food Processors Association*] (AC) .... AMPAQ
Association des Marchands de Bois en Gros du Quebec [*Quebec Wholesale Lumber Association*] (AC) .... AMBQ
Association des MBA du Quebec (AC) .... AMBAQ
Association des Medecins Biochimistes du Canada (AC) .... AMBC
Association des Medecins de Langue Francaise [*Canada*] (EAIO) .... AMLF
Association des Medecins Haitiens a l'Etranger [*Association of Haitian Physicains Abroad*] (EA) .... AMHE
Association des Medecins Psychiatres du Quebec [*Quebec Psychiatrists' Association*] (AC) .... AMPQ
Association des Media et de la Technologie en Education au Canada [*Association for Media and Technology in Education in Canada - AMTEC*] .... AMTE
Association des Medias Ecrits Communautaires du Quebec (AC) .... AMECQ
Association des Microbiologistes du Quebec (AC) .... AMQ

Association des Mines d'Aminante du Quebec (AC) .... AMAQ
Association des Municipalities du Nouveau-Brunswick (AC) .... AMNB
Association des Myopathes de Tunisie (SAUS) .... AMT
Association des Numismates Francophones du Canada (AC) .... ANFC
Association des Obtenteurs de Pommes de Terre du Marche Commun [*Association of Certified Seed Potato Suppliers of the Common Market*] .... ASSOPOMAC
Association des Optometristes du Quebec (AC) .... AOQ
Association des Orchestres de Jeunes du Canada [*Canadian Association of Youth Orchestras*] .... AOJC
Association des Organisations Nationales de la Boulangerie et de la Patisserie de la CE [*Association of National Organizations in the Bakery and Confectionery Trade in the European Community*] [*Belgium*] (EAIO) .... AONBP-CE
Association des Organisations Nationales d'Entreprises de Peche de la CEE [*Association of National Organizations of Fishing Enterprises in the European Economic Community*] .... EUROPECHE
Association des Organisations Professionnelles du Commerce des Sucres pour les Pays de la Communaute Economique Europeenne [*Association of Sugar Trade Organizations for the European Economic Community Countries*] [*Belgium*] .... ASSUC
Association des Parents Catholiques du Quebec (AC) .... APCQ
Association des Parents Francophones de la Colombie-Britannique (AC) .... APFCB
Association des Parlementaires du Commonwealth [*Commonwealth Parliamentary Association*] [*Canada*] .... APC
Association des Pays Exportateurs de Mineral de Fer [*Association of Iron Ore Exporting Countries*] [*Switzerland*] (EAIO) .... APEF
Association des Peres Gais de Montreal Inc. [*Gay Fathers of Montreal Inc.*] (AC) .... APGM
Association des Pharmaciens des Etablissements de Sante du Quebec (AC) .... APES
Association des Physiciens et Ingenieurs Biomedicaux du Quebec (AC) .... APIBQ
Association des Policiers Provinciaux du Quebec [*Quebec Provincial Police Association*] (AC) .... APPQ
Association des Presses Universitaires Canadiennes [*Association of Canadian University Presses - ACUP*] .... APUC
Association des Producteurs de Films et Television du Quebec (AC) .... APFTQ
Association des Producteurs de Theatre Professionnel (AC) .... APTP
Association des Producteurs d'Isoglucose de la CE [*Association of the Producers of Isoglucose of the European Community*] [*Common Market*] .... API
Association des Producteurs Europeens d'Azote [*European Association of Nitrogen Manufacturers*] (EAIO) .... APEA
Association des Professeurs d'Allemand des Universites Canadiennes [*Canadian Association of University Teachers of German - CAUTG*] .... APAUC
Association des Professeurs d'Anglais des Universites Canadiennes [*Association of Canadian University Teachers of English - ACUTE*] .... APAUC
Association des Professeurs de Francais des Universites Canadiennes [*Association of Canadian University Teachers of French*] .... APFUC
Association des Professeurs de Francais des Universites et Colleges Canadiens [*Association of Canadian University and College Teachers of French - ACUCTF*] .... APFUCC
Association des Professeurs de Francais des Universites et Colleges Canadiens (SAUO) .... APFUCC
Association des Professeurs de Francais en Afrique [*Association of French Teachers in Africa - AFTA*] [*Khartoum, Sudan*] (EAIO) .... APFA
Association des Professeurs de Sciences du Quebec (AC) .... APSQ
Association des Professeurs Franco-Americains [*Defunct*] (EA) .... APFA
Association des Professionnels du Chauffage (AC) .... APC
Association des Professionnels en Exposition du Quebec (AC) .... APEQ
Association des Proprietaires d'Autobus du Quebec (AC) .... APAQ
Association des Proprietaires de Camions-Remorques Independants du Quebec Inc. (AC) .... APCRIQ
Association des Proprietaires de Machinerie Lourde du Quebec Inc. (AC) .... APMLQ
Association des Proprietaires du Quebec Inc. (AC) .... APQ
Association des Prospecteurs du Quebec [*Quebec Prospectors Association*] (AC) .... APQ
Association des Psychiatres du Canada [*Canadian Psychiatric Association*] (EAIO) .... APC
Association des Psychologues de l'Ocean Indien (EAIO) .... APsyOI
Association des Psychologues du Quebec [*Quebec Psychological Association*] (AC) .... APQ
Association des Radiodiffuseurs Communautaires du Quebec (AC) .... ARCQ
Association des Redacteurs de Devis du Canada [*Specification Writers Association of Canada*] .... ARDC
Association des Registraires d'Universites et de Colleges du Canada [*Association of Registrars of the Universities and Colleges of Canada*] .... ARUCC
Association des Religieuses Enseignantes du Quebec (AC) .... AREQ
Association des Residences d'Accueil du Quebec (AC) .... ARAQ
Association des Responsables des Bibliotheques [*Centres de Documentation Universitaires et Recherche d'Expression Francaise au Canada*] (AC) .... ABCDEF-Canada
Association des Ressortissants du Haut et du Moyen Congo [*Association of Natives of the Upper and Middle Congo*] .... ASSORECO
Association des Restaurateurs du Quebec [*Quebec Restaurant Association*] (AC) .... ARQ
Association des Restauratrices-Cuisinieres (EA) .... ARC
Association des Routes et Transports du Canada [*Roads and Transportation Association of Canada*] .... ARTC
Association des Scientifiques, Ingenieurs, et Techniciens du Canada [*Association of the Scientific, Engineering, and Technological Community of Canada*] .... ASITC
Association des Sculpteurs du Quebec [*1961, CSQ from 1978*] [*Canada*] (NGC) .... ASQ
Association des Secretaires et Tresoriers Municipaux de l'Ontario (AC) .... ASTMO
Association des Services aux Etudiants des Colleges et Universites du Canada [*Canadian Association of College and University Student Services*] .... ASECUC
Association des Services d'Aide aux Jeunes Entrepreneurs du Quebec (AC) .... ASAJEQ
Association des Services de Rehabilitation Sociale du Quebec Inc. [*Association of Social Rehabilitation Agencies of Quebec Inc.*] (AC) .... ASRSQ
Association des Services Geologiques Africains [*Association of African Geological Surveys - AAGS*] [*ICSU*] (EAIO) .... ASGA
Association des Sexologues du Quebec (AC) .... ASQ
Association des Societes Nationales, Europeennes, et Mediterraneennes de Gastroenterologie [*Association of National, European, and Mediterranean Societies of Gastroenterology*] (EAIO) .... ASNEMGE
Association des Specialistes de la Mesure en Education [*Association of Specialists in Educational Measures*] [*Canada*] .... ASME
Association des Statisticiens de l'Athletisme [*Association of Track and Field Statisticians*] (EAIO) .... ASA
Association des Syndicats de Cheminots Canadiens [*Canadian Railway Labour Association - CRLA*] .... ASCC
Association des Techniciens Congolais des Telecommunications [*Association of Congolese Telecommunications Technicians*] [*Zaire*] .... ATCT
Association des Techniciens en Sante Animal du Quebec (AC) .... ATSAQ
Association des Technologistes Agricoles [*Association of Agricultural Technologists*] [*Canada*] .... ATA
Association des Technologistes Agro-Alimentaires [*Association of Subsistence Agriculture Technologists*] [*Canada*] .... ATA
Association des Traducteurs Anglophones du Quebec [*Association of Anglophone Translators of Quebec*] .... ATAQ
Association des Traducteurs et Traductrices Litteraires du Canada [*Literary Translators Association of Canada*] (EAIO) .... ATTLC
Association des Traducteurs Litteraires [*Literary Translators' Association*] [*Canada*] .... ATL
Association des Transitaires Internationaux Canadiens, inc. (AC) .... ATIC
Association des Transporteurs Aeriens de la Zone Franc [*Association of Air Transporters of the Franc Zone*] (AF) .... ATAF
Association des Transports du Canada [*Transportation Association of Canada*] (EAIO) .... ATC
Association des Tremblay d'Amerique [*Tremblay (Family) Association of America*] [*Canada*] .... ATA
Association des Universitaires d'Europe .... AUE
Association des Universites Africaines [*Association of African Universities - AAU*] (EAIO) .... AUA
Association des Universites Partiellement ou Entierement de Langue Francaise [*Association of Wholly or Partially French Language Universities*] [*Montreal, PQ*] (EA) .... AUPELF
Association d'Etudes Baha'ies [*Association for Baha'i Studies*] (EAIO) .... AEB
Association d'Etudes Linguistiques Interculturelles Africaines [*Canada*] .... AELIA
Association d'Etudes Politiques Transeuropeennes [*Trans European Policy Studies Association - TEPSA*] (EA) .... ADEPT
Association d'Histoire du Theatre du Canada [*Association for Canadian Theatre History - ACTH*] .... AHTC
Association d'Ileostomie & Colostomie de Montreal [*Colostomy Association of Montreal*] (AC) .... AICM
Association d'Instituts Europeens de Conjoncture Economique [*Association of European Conjuncture Institutes*] (EAIO) .... AIECE
Association du Camionnage du Quebec, Inc. [*Quebec Trucking Association Inc.*] (AC) .... ACQ
Association du Commerce et de l'Industrie du Cafe dans la CEE [*Association for the Coffee Trade and Industry in the EEC*] .... ACICAFE
Association du Disque et de l'Industrie du Spectacle Quebecoise [*Quebec Association of the Record and Entertainment Industry*] [*Canada*] .... ADISQ
Association du Droit de Retransmission Canadien (AC) .... ADRC
Association du Negoce des Grains Oleagineux, Huiles, et Graisses Animales et Vegetales et Leurs Derives de la CEE [*Trade Association for Oilseeds, Oil, Vegetable and Animal Fats, and Their Derivatives of the European Economic Community*] .... ANGO
Association du Patrimoine d'Aylmer (AC) .... APA
Association du Personnel de Geneve OMS [*Geneva Staff Association World Health Organization*] [*Switzerland*] (EAIO) .... APGOMS
Association du Personnel Navigant des Lignes Aeriennes Canadiennes [*Canadian Air Line Flight Attendants' Association - CALFA*] .... APENAC
Association du Peuple pour l'Unite et l'Action [*Algeria*] [*Political party*] (EY) .... APUA
Association du Quebec pour Enfants avec Problemes Auditifs (AC) .... AQEPA
Association du Quebec pour l'Integration Sociale [*Quebec Association for Community Living*] (AC) .... AQIS
Association du Traite Atlantique [*Atlantic Treaty Association*] (EAIO) .... ATA
Association Educative et Culturelle Canada Egypte (AC) .... AECCE
Association Europea de Profesores de Espanol (AIE) .... AEPE
Association Europeene de Saint Vladimir (EAIO) .... AESV
Association Europeene des Decafeineurs [*European Association of Decaffeinators*] [*France*] (EAIO) .... AED
Association Europeene des Enseignants Dentaires [*European Association of Teachers of Dentistry*] (PDAA) .... AEED
Association Europeenne d'Athletisme [*European Athletic Association - EAA*] (EA) .... AEA
Association Europeenne de Ceramique [*European Ceramic Association*] [*France*] .... AEC
Association Europeenne de la Boyauderie [*European Natural Sausage Casings Association - ENSCA*] (EA) .... AEB

Association Europeenne de Laboratoires de Teledetection [*European Association of Remote Sensing Laboratories - EARSEL*] (EA) .... AELT
Association Europeenne de l'Asphalte [*European Mastic Asphalt Association - EMAA*] (EAIO) .... AEA
Association Europeenne de Libre-Echange [*European Free Trade Association - EFTA*] [*Geneva, Switzerland*] .... AELE
Association Europeenne de Radiologie [*European Association of Radiology - EAR*] (EA) .... AER
Association Europeenne de Vente par Correspondance [*European Mail Order Traders' Association*] [*Belgium*] (ECED) .... AEVPC
Association Europeenne des Assures de l'Industrie [*European Association of Industrial Insurers*] [*Brussels, Belgium*] (EAIO) .... AEAI
Association Europeenne des Audioprothesistes [*European Association of Hearing Aid Dispensers*] (EAIO) .... AEA
Association Europeenne des Centres d'Audiophonologie [*European Association of Audiophonological Centres - EAAC*] (EAIO) .... AECA
Association Europeenne des Centres Nationaux de Productivite [*European Association for National Productivity Centers - EANPC*] (EAIO) .... AECNP
Association Europeenne des Conservatoires [*European Association of Conservatories - EAC*] (EAIO) .... AEC
Association Europeenne des Conservatoires, Academies de Musique, et Musikhochschulen [*European Association of Music Conservatories, Academies, and High Schools*] (EAIO) .... AECAH
Association Europeenne des Constructeurs de Materiel Aerospatial [*European Association of Aerospace Manufacturers*] (EAIO) .... AECMA
Association Europeenne des Contribuables [*European Taxpayers Association - ETA*] (EA) .... AEC
Association Europeenne des Directeurs de Bureaux de Concerts et Spectacles [*European Association of Directors of the Bureau of Concerts and Events*] [*France*] (EAIO) .... AEDBCS
Association Europeenne des Directeurs d'Hopitaux [*Later, EAHM*] (EA) .... AEDH
Association Europeenne des Ecoles et Colleges d'Optometre [*European Association of Schools and Colleges of Optometry - EASCO*] (EA) .... AESCO
Association Europeenne des Editeurs d'Annuaires [*European Association of Directory Publishers - EADP*] (EA) .... AEEA
Association Europeenne des Exploitations Frigorifiques [*European Association of Refrigeration Enterprises*] [*Common Market*] [*Belgium*] .... AEEF
Association Europeenne des Fabricants de Blocs de Mousse Souple de Polyurethane [*European Association of Flexible Foam Block Manufacturers*] (EAIO) .... EUROPUR
Association Europeenne des Festivals [*European Association of Festivals*] [*Switzerland*] (EAIO) .... AEF
Association Europeenne des Festivals de Musique [*European Association of Music Festivals - EAMF*] (EAIO) .... AEFM
Association Europeenne des Gaz de Petrole Liquefies [*European Liquefied Petroleum Gas Association - ELPGA*] (EAIO) .... AEGPL
Association Europeenne des Graveurs et des Flexographes [*European Association of Engravers and Flexographers*] (EAIO) .... AEGRAFLEX
Association Europeenne des Industries de l'Habillement [*European Association of Clothing Industries*] (EA) .... AEIH
Association Europeenne des Industries de Produits de Marque [*European Association of Industries of Branded Products*] (EAIO) .... AIM
Association Europeenne des Institutions d'Amenagement Rural [*European Association of Country Planning Institutions*] (EAIO) .... AEIAR
Association Europeenne des Marches aux Bestiaux [*European Association of Livestock Markets - EALM*] [*Brussels, Belgium*] (EAIO) .... AEMB
Association Europeenne des Metaux [*European Association of Metals*] [*Belgium*] (EAIO) .... AEM
Association Europeenne des Musees de l'Histoire des Sciences Medicales [*European Association of Museums of the History of Medical Sciences - EAMHMS*] (EAIO) .... AEMHSM
Association Europeenne des Officiers Professionnels de Sapeurs-Pompiers [*European Association of Professional Fire Brigade Officers - EAPFBO*] (EAIO) .... AE
Association Europeenne des Organisations Nationales des Commercants Detaillants en Textiles [*European Association of National Organizations of Textile Manufacturers*] .... AEDT
Association Europeenne des Photographes Professionnels [*European Association of Professional Photographers*] .... EUROPHOT
Association Europeenne des Producteurs d'Acides Gras [*European Association of Fatty Acid Producing Companies*] (EAIO) .... APAG
Association Europeenne des Reserves Naturelles Libres [*European Association for Free Nature Reserves*] [*Inactive*] (EAIO) .... EUREL
Association Europeenne des Specialites Pharmaceutiques Grand Public [*European Proprietary Association*] (EA) .... AESGP
Association Europeenne des Vehicules Electriques Routiers [*European Electric Road Vehicle Association*] (EAIO) .... AVERE
Association Europeenne d'Etudes Chinoises [*European Association of Chinese Studies - EACS*] (EAIO) .... AEDEC
Association Europeenne du Commerce en Gros des Viandes [*European Association Wholesale Trade in Meat*] [*EC*] (ECED) .... AECGV
Association Europeenne du Laser [*European Laser Association - ELA*] (EA) .... AEL
Association Europeenne du Moulinage [*European Throwsters Association - ETA*] (EA) .... AEM
Association Europeenne l'Anodisation [*European Anodisers' Association*] (EA) .... EURAS
Association Europeenne pour la Cooperation [*European Association for Cooperation*] .... AEC
Association Europeenne pour l'Echange de la Litterature Technique dans le Domaine de la Siderurgie [*European Association for the Exchange of Technical Literature in the Field of Ferrous Metallurgy - EAETLFFM*] (EAIO) .... ASELT
Association Europeenne pour l'Etude de la Population [*European Association for Population Studies - EAPS*] (EAIO) .... AEEP
Association Europeenne pour l'Etude de l'Alimentation et Developpement de l'Enfant [*European Association of Nutrition and Child Development*] (EAIO) .... ADE
Association Europeenne pour l'Etude du Diabete [*European Association for the Study of Diabetes - EASD*] (EAIO) .... AEED
Association Europeenne Rubans, Tresses, Tissus Elastiques [*European Ribbon, Braid, and Elastic Material Association*] .... AERTEL
Association Europeenne Thyroide [*European Thyroid Association - ETA*] (EAIO) .... AET
Association Executives Human Rights Caucus (EA) .... AEHRC
Association Executives of North Carolina (SRA) .... AENC
Association Feeling Truth and Living It .... AFTLI
Association Feminine d'Education et d'Action Sociale [*Women's Association of Education and Social Action*] [*Canada*] .... AFEAS
Association Football Club [*British*] (DI) .... AFC
Association Football Club (SAUO) .... AFC
Association for a Competitive Data Processing Industry (SAUO) .... ACDPI
Association for a National Recycling Policy (EA) .... ANRP
Association for a Progressive Reform of Judaism (SAUO) .... APRJ
Association for a World Language (EA) .... AWL
Association for Academic Surgery (EA) .... AAS
Association for Academic Surgery (SAUO) .... ASC
Association for Academic Travel Abroad (SAUO) .... AATA
Association for Academic Travel Abroad (SAUO) .... ATA
Association for Academic Travel Abroad (EA) .... ATA
Association for Accounting Marketing (NTPA) .... AAM
Association for Administration of Volunteer Services [*Later, AVA*] (EA) .... AAVS
Association for Adult Continuing Education [*British*] .... AACE
Association for Adult Development and Aging (EA) .... AADA
Association for Adult Education (AIE) .... AAE
Association for Advanced Life Underwriting [*Washington, DC*] (EA) .... AALU
Association for Advanced Training in Behavioral Sciences (SAUO) .... AATBS
Association for Advancement of Blind and Retarded (EA) .... AABR
Association for Advancement of Blind Children [*Later, AABR*] (EA) .... AABC
Association for Advancement of Maternity Care [*British*] (DBA) .... AAMC
Association for Advancement of Modelling and Simulation Techniques in Enterprises [*France*] (EAIO) .... AMSE
Association for Advancement of Modelling and Simulation Techniques in Enterprises (SAUO) .... AMSTE
Association for Advancement of Psychoanalysis (SAUO) .... AAP
Association for Advancement of Psychoanalysis (of the Karen Horney Psychoanalytic Institute and Center) (EA) .... AAP
Association for Advancement of Psychology (EA) .... AAP
Association for Affiliated College and University Offices [*Later, ACUO*] (EA) .... AACUO
Association for African and Malagasy Economic Cooperation and Development (SAUO) .... AAMECD
Association for Agricultural Education Staffs [*British*] (DBA) .... AAES
Association for All Speech Impaired Children (EAIO) .... AFASIC
Association for Ambulatory Behavorial Healthcare (NTPA) .... AABH
Association for Ambulatory Pediatric Services (SAUO) .... AAPS
Association for Ambulatory Pediatric Services [*Later, APA*] (EA) .... AAPS
Association for Anesthesiologists' Assistants Training Program (DAVI) .... AAATP
Association for Applied Community Researchers (NTPA) .... ACCRA
Association for Applied Hypnosis (EAIO) .... AAH
Association for Applied Interactive Multimedia (VERA) .... AAIM
Association for Applied Poetry (EA) .... AAP
Association for Applied Psychoanalysis (EA) .... AAP
Association for Applied Psychophysiology and Biofeedback (EA) .... AAPB
Association for Applied Solar Energy [*Later, International Solar Energy Society*] .... AASE
Association for Applied Solar Energy (SAUO) .... AASE
Association for Applied Solar Energy (SAUO) .... AFASE
Association for Applied Solar Energy [*Later, International Solar Energy Society*] .... AFASE
Association for Archery in Schools (EAIO) .... AAS
Association for Archery School (SAUO) .... AAS
Association for Arid Lands Studies (EA) .... AALS
Association for Armenian Information Professionals (EA) .... AAIP
Association for Asian Studies (EA) .... AAS
Association for Asian Studies, Committee on American Library Resources on the Far East, Center for Research Libraries, Chicago, IL [*Library symbol*] [*Library of Congress*] (LCLS) .... CALRFE
Association for Assesment in Counseling (NTPA) .... AAC
Association for Assessment and Accreditation of Laboratory Animal Care International (NTPA) .... AAALAC
Association for Assessment and Accreditation of Laboratory Animal Care International (SAUO) .... AAALAC
Association for Astrological Networking (EA) .... AFAN
Association for Astrological Psychology (EA) .... AAP
Association for Astronomy Education [*British*] (DBA) .... AAE
Association for Australian Rural Nurses .... AARN
Association for Automated Reasoning (EA) .... AAR
Association for Baha'i Studies (EAIO) .... ABS
Association for Balance of Political Power (EA) .... BOP
Association for Beautiful Colorado Roads (SAUO) .... ABCR
Association for Behavior Analysis (EA) .... ABA
Association for Behavioral Sciences and Medical Education (SAUS) .... ABSAME
Association for Behaviorial Sciences and Medical Education (EA) .... ABSAME
Association for Behaviour Analysis (SAUO) .... ABA
Association for Biology Laboratory Education (EA) .... ABLE
Association for Biomedical Research (EA) .... ABR
Association for Birth Psychology (EA) .... ABP
Association for Brain Tumor Research (EA) .... ABTR

Association for Brain Tumor Research (EA) .... AFBTR
Association for Bridge Construction and Design (EA) .... ABCD
Association for Bright Children [*Societe pour Enfants Doues et Surdoues*] [*Ontario*] (AC) .... ABC
Association for Bright Children [*Canada*] .... CBA
Association for British Music (EAIO) .... ABM
Association for Broadcast Engineenng Standards (SAUS) .... ABES
Association for Broadcast Engineering Standards [*Defunct*] (EA) .... ABES
Association for Business Communication [*Urbana, IL*] (EA) .... ABC
Association for Business Simulation and Experiential Learning [*Tulsa, OK*] (EA) .... ABSEL
Association for Business Sponsorship of the Arts [*British*] (EAIO) .... ABSA
Association for Business Sponsorships of the Arts (SAUO) .... ABSA
Association for Business Stimulation and Experiential Learning (SAUS) .... ABSEL
Association for Canada Educational Resources (AC) .... ACER
Association for Canadian and Quebec Literatures .... ACQL
Association for Canadian Registered Safety Professionals [*Association des Professionnels en Securite Agrees du Canada*] (AC) .... ACRSP
Association for Canadian Studies [*See also AEC*] .... ACS
Association for Canadian Studies in the United States (EA) .... ACSUS
Association for Canadian Theatre History .... ACTH
Association for Canadian Theatre Research (AC) .... ACTR
Association for Central Asian Studies (EA) .... ACAS
Association for Chemoreception Sciences (EA) .... AChemS
Association for Child & Adolescent Psychiatric Nurses (SAUO) .... ACAPN
Association for Child Psychiatrists (DAVI) .... ACP
Association for Child Psychoanalysis (EA) .... ACP
Association for Child Psychology and Psychiatry [*British*] .... ACPP
Association for Childbirth at Home, International (EA) .... ACHI
Association for Childhood Education International .... ACE
Association for Childhood Education International (EA) .... ACEI
Association for Childhood Education International of Western New York (SAUO) .... ACEI-WNY
Association for Children and Adults with Learning Disabilities [*Later, LDA*] (EA) .... ACALD
Association for Children for Enforcement of Support (EA) .... ACES
Association for Children with Down Syndrome (EA) .... ACDS
Association for Children with Language, Speech and Hearing Impairments of Namibia (SAUO) .... CLaSH
Association for Children with Learning Disabilities [*Later, LDA*] (EA) .... ACLD
Association for Children with Learning Disabilities (SAUO) .... ACLD
Association for Children with Retarded Mental Development (SAUO) .... ACRMD
Association for Children with Retarded Mental Development (EA) .... A/CRMD
Association for Children with Russell-Silver Syndrome (EA) .... ACRSS
Association for Christian Ethics [*Vatican*] (EA) .... ACE
Association for Christian Schools [*Defunct*] (EA) .... ACS
Association for Christian Training and Service (EA) .... ACTS
Association for Citizens with Special Needs [*Australia*] .... ACSN
Association for Classical Music [*Later, MA*] (EA) .... ACM
Association for Classical Music [*Later, MA*] (EA) .... AFCM
Association for Clinical Data Management (SAUO) .... ACDM
Association for Clinical Pastoral Education (EA) .... ACPE
Association for Clinical Theological Training and Care [*British*] (EAIO) .... ACTTCL
Association for Clinical Theological Training and Care (SAUO) .... CTA
Association for College and University Religious Affairs (NTPA) .... ACURA
Association for Colleges [*British*] (DET) .... AFC
Association for Common European Nursing Diagnosis, Interventions and Outcomes (SAUO) .... ACENDIO
Association for Commonwealth Language and Literature Studies (SAUO) .... ACLALS
Association for Commonwealth Literature and Language Studies (SAUO) .... ACLAIS
Association for Commonwealth Literature and Language Studies (EAIO) .... ACLALS
Association for Commonwealth Literature and Languages Studies .... ACLLS
Association for Communication Administration (EA) .... ACA
Association for Communications and Technology (SAUO) .... ACT
Association for Communist Unity [*Australia*] .... ACU
Association for Community Based Education (EA) .... ACBE
Association for Community Based Educational Institutions [*Later, ACBE*] (EA) .... ACBEI
Association for Community Based Educational Institutions (SAUO) .... ACBEI
Association for Community Design (EA) .... ACD
Association for Community Education (SAUO) .... ACE
Association for Community Living (SRA) .... ACL
Association for Community Organizations for Refaring Now .... ACORN
Association for Commuter Transportation (EA) .... ACT
Association for Comparative Economic Studies [*Notre Dame, IN*] (EA) .... ACES
Association for Comparative Economics [*Later, ACES*] .... ACE
Association for Comparative Economics (SAUO) .... ACE
Association for Composite Tanks (EA) .... ACT
Association for Comprehensive Neurotherapy (SAUO) .... ACN
Association for Computational Liguistics (SAUO) .... ACL
Association for Computational Linguistics (EA) .... ACL
Association for Computer Aided Architectural Design Research In Asia (SAUO) .... CAADRIA
Association for Computer Art and Design Education [*Defunct*] (EA) .... ACADE
Association for Computer Assisted Learning (AIE) .... ACAL
Association for Computer Operations Management (EA) .... ACOM
Association for Computer Operations Management (NTPA) .... AFCOM
Association for Computer Operations Managers (SAUO) .... AFCOM
Association for Computer-Aided Design in Architecture (SAUO) .... ACADIA
Association for Computer-Assisted Text Analysis (SAUO) .... ACATA
Association for Computer-Based Systems for Career Information (OICC) .... ACSCI
Association for Computers and Information Technology in Teaching (AIE) .... ACITT
Association for Computers and the Humanities (EA) .... ACH
Association for Computers and/in the Humanities (SAUO) .... ACH
Association for Computing and Information Sciences (SAUO) .... ACIS
Association for Computing Machinery - Special Interest Group on Automata and Computerability Theory (SAUO) .... ACM-SIGACT
Association for Computing Machinery Journal (SAUS) .... Assn Comp Mach J
Association for Computing Machinery-German Association for Applied Mathematics (SAUO) .... ACM-GAMM
Association for Computing Machinery-Special Interest Group on Architecture of Computer Systems (SAUO) .... ACM-SIGARCH
Association for Computing Machinery-Special Interest Group on Artificial Intel (SAUS) .... ACM-SIGART
Association for Computing Machinery-Special Interest Group on Artificial Intelligence (SAUO) .... ACM-SIGART
Association for Computing Machinery-Special Interest Group on Automata and Communication (SAUS) .... ACM-SIGACT
Association for Computing Machinery-Special Interest Group on Biomedical Computer (SAUS) .... ACM-SIGBIO
Association for Computing Machinery-Special Interest Group on Biomedical Computing (SAUO) .... ACM-SIGBIO
Association for Computing Machinery-Special Interest Group on Business Data Processing (SAUO) .... ACM-SIGBDP
Association for Computing Machinery-Special Interest Group on Computer Graphic (SAUS) .... ACM-SIGGRAPH
Association for Computing Machinery-Special Interest Group on Computer Personal Research (SAUO) .... ACM-SIGCPR
Association for Computing Machinery-Special Interest Group on Computer Science (SAUS) .... ACM-SIGCSE
Association for Computing Machinery-Special Interest Group on Computer Science Education (SAUO) .... ACM-SIGCSE
Association for Computing Machinery-Special Interest Group on Computer Systems (SAUS) .... ACM-SIGCOSIM
Association for Computing Machinery-Special Interest Group on Computer Systems Installation Management (SAUO) .... ACM-SIGCOSIM
Association for Computing Machinery-Special Interest Group on Computer Uses in Education (SAUO) .... ACM-SIGCUE
Association for Computing Machinery-Special Interest Group on Computer Uses in Engineering (SAUS) .... ACM-SIGCUE
Association for Computing Machinery-Special Interest Group on Computer-Assisted Instruction (SAUO) .... ACM-SIBCAI
Association for Computing Machinery-Special Interest Group on Computer-Assisted Instruction (SAUO) .... ACM-SIGCAI
Association for Computing Machinery-Special Interest Group on Computerized Retrieval Services (SAUO) .... ACM-SIGCRS
Association for Computing Machinery-Special Interest Group on Computers and Society (SAUO) .... ACM-SIGCAS
Association for Computing Machinery-Special Interest Group on Computers and the Public Health (SAUO) .... ACM-SIGCAPH
Association for Computing Machinery-Special Interest Group on Design Automation (SAUO) .... ACM-SIGDA
Association for Computing Machinery-Special Interest Group on Documentation (SAUO) .... ACM-SIGDOC
Association for Computing Machinery-Special Interest Group on Information Publishing (SAUO) .... ACM-SIGIP
Association for Computing Machinery-Special Interest Group on Information Retrieval (SAUO) .... ACM-SIGIR
Association for Computing Machinery-Special Interest Group on Language Analysis and Studies in Humanities (SAUS) .... ACM-SIGLASH
Association for Computing Machinery-Special Interest Group on Language Analysis and Studies in the Humanities (SAUO) .... ACM-SIGLASH
Association for Computing Machinery-Special Interest Group on Management of Data (SAUO) .... ACM-SIGMOD
Association for Computing Machinery-Special Interest Group on Mathematical Programming (SAUO) .... ACM-SIGMAP
Association for Computing Machinery-Special Interest Group on Measurement (SAUS) .... ACM-SIGME
Association for Computing Machinery-Special Interest Group on Measurement and Environment (SAUO) .... ACM-SIGME
Association for Computing Machinery-Special Interest Group on Microprogramming (SAUO) .... ACM-SIGMICRO
Association for Computing Machinery-Special Interest Group on Minicomputers (SAUO) .... ACM-SIGMINI
Association for Computing Machinery-Special Interest Group on Mini-computers (SAUS) .... ACM-SIGMINI
Association for Computing Machinery-Special Interest Group on Operating System (SAUO) .... ACM-SIGOPS
Association for Computing Machinery-Special Interest Group on Programming Languages (SAUO) .... ACM-SIGPLAN
Association for Computing Machinery-Special Interest Group on Programming Languages (SAUS) .... ACM-SIGPLAN
Association for Computing Machinery-Special Interest Group on Simulation (SAUO) .... ACM-SIGSIM
Association for Computing Machinery-Special Interest Group on Social and Behavioural Science Computing (SAUO) .... ACM-SIGSOC
Association for Computing Machinery-Special Interest Group on Symbolic and Algbraic Manipulation (SAUO) .... ACM-SIGSAM
Association for Computing Machinery-Special Interest Group on Symbolic and Algebraic Manipulation (SAUS) .... ACM-SIGSAM
Association for Computing Machinery-Special Interest Group on University Computer Centers (SAUO) .... ACM-SIGUCC

Association for Computing Machinery-Special Interest Group on User Online Interaction (SAUO) ... ACM-SIGUOL
Association for Computing Machinery-Standards Committee (SAUS) ... ACM-SC
Association for Computing Machinery-Technical Standards Committee [*New York, NY*] (DDC) ... ACM-TSC
Association for Conflict Resolution [*Defunct*] (EA) ... ACR
Association for Conservation Information (EA) ... ACI
Association for Constitutional Democracy in Liberia (EA) ... ACDL
Association for Construction of a Pavilion in Commemoration of General MacArthur (SAUO) ... ACPCGM
Association for Consumer Research (EA) ... ACR
Association for Consumer Research (SAUO) ... Assn Consumer Res
Association for Continuing Education (EA) ... ACE
Association for Continuing Higher Education (EA) ... ACHE
Association for Continuing Professional Education [*Formerly, AFSTE*] (EA) ... ACPE
Association for Convention Marketing Executives (NTPA) ... ACME
Association for Convention Operations Management (EA) ... ACOM
Association for Cooperation in Banana Research in the Caribbean and Tropical America [*Guadeloupe, French West Indies*] (EAIO) ... ACORBAT
Association for Cooperation in Banana Research in the Caribbean and Tropical America (SAUS) ... ACORBAT
Association for Cooperation in Engineering [*Defunct*] ... ACE
Association for Co-Ordinated Rural Development [*Government body*] [*British*] ... ACCORD
Association for Corporate Growth [*Deerfield, IL*] (EA) ... ACG
Association for Corporate Growth and Diversification [*Later, ACG*] (EA) ... ACGD
Association for Corporate Growth and Diversification (SAUO) ... ACGD
Association for Correctional Research and Information Management (EA) ... ACRIM
Association for Correctional Research and Statistics (OICC) ... ACRS
Association for Counselor Education and Supervision (EA) ... ACES
Association for Counselors and Educators in Government (NTPA) ... ACEG
Association for Couples in Marriage Enrichment (EA) ... ACME
Association for Creative Change in Religious and Other Social Systems (SAUO) ... ACC
Association for Creative Change within Religious and Other Social Systems (EA) ... ACC
Association for Cultural Exchange ... ACE
Association for Cultural Exchange (EA) ... CULTUREX
Association for Cultural Interchange (EA) ... ACI
Association for Cultural, Technical and Educational Cooperation (SAUO) ... ACTEC
Association for Dance Movement Therapy (EAIO) ... ADMT
Association for Data Processing and Computer Management (NITA) ... ADPCM
Association for Database Services (COBU) ... ADSET
Association for Death Education and Counseling (EA) ... ADEC
Association for Dental Prothesis (SAUO) ... ADP
Association for Denture Prosthesis (EAIO) ... ADP
Association for Development and Cooperation Austria (SAUO) ... ADC
Association for Development of Computer-based Instructional Systems (SAUO) ... ACDIS
Association for Development of Computer-Based Instructional Systems (EA) ... ADCIS
Association for Development of Instructional Systems [*Later, ADCIS*] [*Western Washington University*] [*Bellingham, WA*] (BUR) ... ADIS
Association for Direct Instruction (EA) ... ADI
Association for Documentary Editing (EA) ... ADE
Association for Dressings and Sauces (EA) ... ADS
Association for Economic Assistance e.V. (SAUO) ... AEA
Association for Education and Cultural Advancement [*South Africa*] ... ASECA
Association for Education and Rehabilitation of the Blind and Visually Impaired (EA) ... AER
Association for Education and Rehabilitation of the Blind and Visually Impaired (SAUO) ... AER
Association for Education by Radio (SAUO) ... AER
Association for Education by Radio-Television [*Defunct*] (AEBS) ... AERT
Association for Education in Citizenship (SAUO) ... AEC
Association for Education in International Business [*Later, AIB*] (EA) ... AEIB
Association for Education in International Business (SAUS) ... AEIB
Association for Education in Journalism [*Later, AEJMC*] (EA) ... AEJ
Association for Education in Journalism and Mass Communication (EA) ... AEJMC
Association for Education in/on International Business (SAUO) ... AEIB
Association for Education of the Visually Handicapped [*Later, AER*] (EA) ... AEVH
Association for Educational and Training Technology (EAIO) ... AETT
Association for Educational Communications and Technology (NTCM) ... ACET
Association for Educational Communications and Technology [*Washington, DC*] ... AECT
Association for Educational Communications and Technology (SAUS) ... AECT
Association for Educational Communications and Technology (SAUO) ... Assn Ed Comm Tech
Association for Educational Data Processing ... AEDP
Association for Educational Data Systems (EA) ... AEDS
Association for Educational Development (EA) ... AED
Association for Electric Home Appliances (SAUO) ... AEHA
Association for Electronic Data Systems [*Database producer*] (ECII) ... AEDS
Association for Electronics Manufacturing of the Society of Manufacturing Engineers (EA) ... AEM/SME
Association for Employee Health and Fitness (EA) ... AEHF
Association for Energy Systems, Operations, and Programming (ABAC) ... AESOP
Association for Engineering Graphics and Imaging Systems (NTPA) ... AEGIS
Association for Enterprise Integration (SAUO) ... AFEI
Association for Enterprise Opportunity (NTPA) ... AEO
Association for Environmental and Outdoor Education (EA) ... AEOE
Association for Environmental Archaeology (QUAC) ... AEA
Association for Environmental Education (AUEG) ... AEE
Association for Environmental Education (New South Wales) [*Australia*] ... AEE(NSW)
Association for Equine Sports Medicine (EA) ... AESM
Association for European Airlines (SAUS) ... AEA
Association for Evolutionary Economics [*Lincoln, NE*] (EA) ... AFEE
Association for Experiential Education (EA) ... AEE
Association for Experimental Education (SAUO) ... AeE
Association for Facilities Engineering (NTPA) ... AFE
Association for Faculty in the Medical Humanities (EA) ... AFMH
Association for Fair Play for Children in Scotland (EAIO) ... AFPCS
Association for Family Living [*Defunct*] (EA) ... AFL
Association for Family Welfare (SAUO) ... AFW
Association for Federal Information Resources Management (EA) ... AFFIRM
Association for Field Archaeology [*Defunct*] (EA) ... AFFA
Association for Field Services in Teacher Education [*Later, ACPE*] ... AFSTE
Association for Field Services in Teacher Education (SAUO) ... AFSTE
Association for Financial and Debt Instrument Professionals (NTPA) ... AFDIP
Association for Finishing Processes of the Society of Manufacturing Engineers (EAIO) ... AFP/SME
Association for Font Information Interchange (VERA) ... AFII
Association for Food Self-Sufficiency (EAIO) ... AFS
Association for Food Service Management [*Later, SFM*] (EA) ... AFSM
Association for Gay and Lesbian Issues in Counseling [*Later, AGLBIC*] (EA) ... AGLIC
Association for Gay, Lesbian, and Bisexual Issues in Counseling (EA) ... AGLBIC
Association for General and Liberal Studies (EA) ... AGLS
Association for Geographic Information [*London, England*] (GEOI) ... AGI
Association for Geoscientists for International Development (SAUS) ... AGID
Association for Gerontology in Higher Education (EA) ... AGHE
Association for Gifted and Talented Students (EA) ... AGTS
Association for Glycogen Sterage Disease (SAUS) ... AGSD
Association for Gnotobiotics (EA) ... AG
Association for Government Assisted Housing [*Defunct*] (EA) ... AGAH
Association for Governmental Leasing and Finance [*Washington, DC*] (EA) ... AGLF
[*The*] **Association for Graduate Education and Research** ... TAGER
Association for Graduate Education and Research (SAUS) ... TAGER
Association for Graphic Arts Training (NTPA) ... AGAT
Association for Gravestone Studies (EA) ... AGS
Association for Group Psychoanalysis and Process (EA) ... AGPP
Association for Handicapped Student Services Programs in Post-Secondary Education (DHP) ... AHSSPPE
Association for Health Records [*Later, AHQ*] (EA) ... AHR
Association for Health Services Research (EA) ... AHSR
Association for Healthcare Philanthropy ... AHP
Association for Healthcare Philanthropy Foundation (NFD) ... AHP Foundation
Association for Healthcare Quality [*Defunct*] (EA) ... AHQ
Association for High Speed Photography [*British*] (BI) ... AHSP
Association for Higher Education [*of the NEA*] [*Later, AAHE*] (EA) ... AHE
Association for Higher Education, Dallas, TX [*OCLC symbol*] (OCLC) ... IUC
Association for Hispanic Handicapped of New Jersey (EA) ... AHH
Association for Holistic Health [*Defunct*] (EA) ... AHH
Association for Holistic Living (EA) ... AHL
Association for Hospital Medical Education (EA) ... AHME
Association for Hospital Medical Education. Journal (journ.) (SAUS) ... AHME J
Association for Human Emergence [*Defunct*] (EA) ... AHE
Association for Human Rights (EA) ... AHR
Association for Humane Abortion (SAUO) ... AHA
Association for Humanist Sociology (EA) ... AHS
Association for Humanistic Education (EA) ... AHE
Association for Humanistic Education and Development (EA) ... AHEAD
Association for Humanistic Psychology (EA) ... AHP
Association for Humanistic Psychology in Britain (EAIO) ... AHPB
Association for Humanistic Studies (SAUO) ... AHS
Association for Immigration Reform (SAUO) ... AIR
Association for Improvement in the Maternity Services (SAUO) ... AIMS
Association for Improvements in the Maternity Services (EAIO) ... AIMS
Association for Improving Moral Standards [*British*] (BI) ... AIMS
Association for Improving the Condition of the Poor (SAUO) ... AICP
Association for Independent Disabled Self-Sufficiency [*British*] ... AIDS
Association for Indiana Media Educators (SRA) ... AIME
Association for Individually Guided Education (EA) ... AIGE
Association for Industrial Archaeology (SAUO) ... AIA
Association for Industrial Development and Economic Cooperation (SAUS) ... AIDEC
Association for Infant Massage (EA) ... AIM
Association for Informal Logic and Critical Thinking (EA) ... AILACT
Association for Informatics in Medicine (SAUO) ... AIMS
Association for Information and Image Management (EA) ... AIIM
Association for Information Management [*Aslib*] (NITA) ... AIM
Association for Information Management (WA) ... ASLIB
Association for Information Systems (DDC) ... AIS
Association for Information Systems Professionals (SAUO) ... AISP
Association for Informational Media and Equipment (EA) ... AIME
Association for Innovation in Higher Education [*Defunct*] (EA) ... AIHE
Association for Innovative Marketing (EA) ... AIM
Association for Institutional Research (EA) ... AIR
Association for Integrated Manufacturing Technology [*Later, NCS/AIMTECH*] (EA) ... AIMT

Association for Integrated Manufacturing Technology (SAUO) .... AIMT
Association for Integrated Manufacturing Technology [*Later, NCS/AIMTECH*] (EAAP) .... AIM Tech
Association for Integrative Medicine (SAUO) .... AIM
Association for Integrative Studies (EA) .... AIS
Association for Intelligent Systems Technology (EA) .... AIST
Association for Interactive Media (NTPA) .... AIM
Association for Intercollegiate Athletics for Women (EA) .... AIAW
Association for International Agricultural and Extension Education (EA) .... AIAEE
Association for International Agriculture and Rural Development (EA) .... AIARD
Association for International Cancer Research (EAIO) .... AICR
Association for International Children and Youth (EA) .... AICY
Association for International Cotton Emblem [*Brussels, Belgium*] (EAIO) .... AFICE
Association for International Development [*Defunct*] (EA) .... AID
Association for International Medical Study [*Defunct*] (EA) .... AIMS
Association for International Practical Training (EA) .... AIPT
Association for International Technical Promotion .... AITEP
Association for International Youth Work (SAUO) .... AIYW
Association for Internet Service Providers (VERA) .... AISP
Association for Investment Management and Research (EA) .... AIMR
Association for Jewish Studies (EA) .... AJS
Association for Jewish Youth [*British*] .... AJY
Association for Korean Studies (EA) .... AKS
Association for Laboratory Automation .... ALA
Association for Latin American Studies [*Defunct*] .... ALAS
Association for Latin Liturgy (EA) .... ALL
Association for Legal Justice [*Northern Ireland*] .... ALJ
Association for Liberal Education [*British*] .... ALE
Association for Library and Information Science Education (EA) .... ALISE
Association for Library Automation Research Communications (EA) .... LARC
Association for Library Collections and Technical Services .... ALCTS
Association for Library Collections & Technical Services Acquisitions Section .... ALCTSAS
Association for Library Collections & Technical Services Collection Management &Development Section .... ALCTSCMDS
Association for Library Collections & Technical Services Preservation & Refor- matting Section .... ALCTSPARS
Association for Library Information [*Duquesne University Library*] [*Information service or system*] (IID) .... AFLI
Association for Library Information, Pittsburgh, PA [*OCLC symbol*] (OCLC) .... AFL
Association for Library Service to Children (EA) .... ALSC
Association for Literary and Linguistic Computing [*University College of North Wales*] [*Gwynedd*] (EA) .... ALLC
Association for Literary and Linguistic Computing Bulletin (SAUO) .... ALLCB
Association for Literary and Linguistic Computing Journal (SAUS) .... ALLCJ
Association for Living Historical Farms and Agricultural Museums (EA) .... ALHFAM
Association for Local Telecommunications Services .... ALTS
Association for Loss Prevention and Security (EA) .... ALPS
Association for Low Flow Anaesthesia (SAUO) .... ALFA
Association for Machine Translation and Computational Linguistics [*Later, Association for Computational Linguistics*] (EA) .... AMTCL
Association for Macular Diseases (EA) .... AMD
Association for Maintained Girls' Schools (AIE) .... AMGS
Association for Management Excellence [*Later, AAIM*] (EA) .... AME
Association for Manufacturing Excellence (EA) .... AME
Association for Manufacturing Technology (EA) .... AMT
Association for Maternal and Child Health and Crippled Children's Programs (EA) .... AMCHCCP
Association for Maternal and Child Health Programs (SAUO) .... AMCHP
Association for Measurement and Evaluation in Counseling and Development (SAUO) .... AMECD
Association for Measurement and Evaluation in Counseling and Development (EA) .... AMECD
Association for Measurement and Evaluation in Guidance [*Later, AMECD*] (EA) .... AMEG
Association for Mechanical Translation and Computation Linguistics (NITA) .... AMTC
Association for Media and Technology in Education (SAUO) .... AMTEC
Association for Media and Technology in Education in Canada [*See also AMTE*] .... AMTEC
Association for Media Psychology (EA) .... AMP
Association for Media Psychology (SAUO) .... AMPS
Association for Media-based Continuing Education for Engineers (SAUO) .... AMCEE
Association for Media-Based Continuing Education for Engineers (EA) .... AMCEE
Association for Medical Deans in Europe (SAUO) .... AMDF
Association for Medical Education and Research in Substance Abuse (SAUS) .... AMERSA
Association for Medical Education in Europe [*Scotland*] .... AMEE
Association for Medical Education in the Eastern Mediterranean Region [*United Arab Emirates*] (EAIO) .... AMEEMR
Association for Medical Education in the Western Pacific (SAUO) .... AMEWP
Association for Medical Physics Technology [*British*] .... AMPT
Association for Men in Psychology .... AMP
Association for Mental Health Affiliation with Israel (EA) .... AMHAI
Association for Methodology and Documentation in Psychiatry (DB) .... AMDP
Association for Methodology in Psychiatry (DB) .... AMP
Association for Mexican Cave Studies (EA) .... AMCS
Association for Middle-Income Housing [*Later, MMHA*] (EA) .... AMIH
Association for Model Aviation (SAUO) .... AMA
Association for Molecular Pathology (EA) .... AMP
Association for Moral and Social Hygiene (SAUO) .... AMSH
Association for Moral and Social Hygiene [*British*] (BI) .... AMSH
Association for Multicultural Counseling and Development (EA) .... AMCD
Association for Multi-Image (EA) .... AMI
Association for Multi-Media International (NTPA) .... AMI
Association for Native Develop-ment in the Performing and Visual Arts (SAUO) .... ANDPVA
Association for Native Development in the Performing and Visual Arts [*Canada*] .... ANDPVA
Association for Neuro-Linguistic Programming (COBU) .... ANLP
Association for Non-White Concerns in Personnel and Guidance (EA) .... ANWC
Association for Nordic Transplant and Dialysis Personnel (EAIO) .... NORDIATRANS
Association for Nuclear Development and Research in Electrical Engineering (SAUO) .... ANDREE
Association for Parents of Addicts [*British*] (BI) .... APA
Association for Parents of Children with Juvenile Chronic Arthritis (SAUO) .... KOURIR
Association for Participation in Development (SAUO) .... APD
Association for Past-Life Research and Therapy (EA) .... APRT
Association for Pediatric Education in Europe (PDAA) .... APEE
Association for Pediatric Therapists (EA) .... APT
Association for People with Arthritis [*Defunct*] (EA) .... APA
Association for Petroleum and Explosives Administration [*British*] .... APEA
Association for Philosophy of the Unconscious (EA) .... APU
Association for Physical and Mental Rehabilitation [*Later, ACTA*] (EA) .... APMR
Association for Physical and System Mathematics (EA) .... APSM
Association for Planning and Regional Reconstruction (SAUO) .... APRR
Association for Play Therapy (NTPA) .... APT
Association for Poetry Therapy [*Later, NAPT*] (EA) .... APT
Association for Politics and the Life Sciences (EA) .... APLS
Association for Population/Family Planning Libraries and Information Centers - International [*Also, an information service or system*] (IID) .... APLIC
Association for Population/Family Planning Libraries and Information Centers, International (EA) .... APLIC-Intl
Association for Practical and Professional Ethics (EA) .... APPE
Association for Practical Theology (EA) .... APT
Association for Practitionen in Infection Control (SAUS) .... APIC
Association for Practitioners of Infection Control (MELL) .... API
Association for Precision Graphics [*Defunct*] (EA) .... APG
Association for Pre-School Education of Deaf Children .... APSEDC
Association for Preservation Technology [*Later, APTI*] (EA) .... APT
Association for Prevention of Disabilities (EAIO) .... APD
Association for Productive Teaching (AEBS) .... APT
Association for Professional Broadcasting Education [*Later, Broadcast EducationAssociation*] (EA) .... APBE
Association for Professional Education for Ministry [*Later, APT*] (EA) .... APEM
Association for Professional Environmental Auditing in Nova Scotia [*Formerly, Association for Professional Environmental Auditors*] (AC) .... APEA
Association for Professionals in Infection Control and Epidemiology, Inc. (SAUO) .... APIC
Association for Programmed Learning (SAUO) .... APL
Association for Programmed Learning and Educational Technology .... APLET
Association for Progressive Communications .... APC
Association for Progressive Education (EA) .... AFPE
Association for Promoting Christian Knowledge [*Church of Ireland*] .... APCK
Association for Promoting Retreats [*British*] (BI) .... APR
Association for Promoting the Reform of Convocation [*British*] .... APRC
Association for Promoting the Unity of Christiandom (SAUO) .... APUC
Association for Promoting Unity of Christendom .... APUC
Association for Protection of Fur-Bearing Animals [*Canada*] .... APFA
Association for Protection of Jewish Immigrants (GEAB) .... APJI
Association for Psychoanalytic and Psychosomatic Medicine (SAUO) .... APPM
Association for Psychoanalytic Medicine (EA) .... APM
Association for Psychological Type (EA) .... APT
Association for Psychotheatrics [*Defunct*] (EA) .... AP
Association for Public Broadcasting (EA) .... APB
Association for Public Health Statistics and Information Systems (NTPA) .... AVRHS
Association for Public Justice (EA) .... APJ
Association for Public Justice Education Fund [*Later, CPJ*] (EA) .... APJEF
Association for Public Policy Analysis and Management (EA) .... APPAM
Association for Puerto Rican-Hispanic Culture (EA) .... APRHC
Association for Quality and Participation (EA) .... AQP
Association for Quality Circles (SAUO) .... AQP
Association for Radiation Research [*British*] (NRCH) .... ARR
Association for Rational Emotive Therapists (COBU) .... ARET
Association for Rational Environmental Alternatives [*Defunct*] (EA) .... AREA
Association for Realistic Philosophy [*Defunct*] (EA) .... ARP
Association for Recognizing the Life of Stillborns (EA) .... ARLS
Association for Recorded Sound Collections (EA) .... ARSC
Association for Recreation and Cultural Activities with People in Detention [*Canada*] .... ARCAD
Association for Recurrent Education [*British*] .... ARE
Association for Regulatory Reform (EA) .... ARR
Association for Relatives of the Mentally, Emotionally, and Nervously Disturbed [*British*] (BI) .... AMEND
Association for Religious and Value Issues in Counseling (EA) .... ARVIC
Association for Religious Education .... ARE
Association for Repetitive Motion Syndromes (EA) .... ARMS
Association for Research, Administration, Professional Councils and Societies (SAUO) .... ARAPCS
Association for Research and Enlightenment (EA) .... ARE
Association for Research and Enlightenment, Virginia Beach, VA [*Library symbol*] [*Library of Congress*] (LCLS) .... ViVbRE

Association for Research and Environmental Aid Ltd. (SAUO) .... AREA
Association for Research in Cosmecology (EA) .... ARC
Association for Research in Growth Relationship (SAUS) .... ARGR
Association for Research in Growth Relationships [*Defunct*] (EA) .... ARGR
Association for Research in Nervous and Mental Disease (EA) .... ARNMD
Association for Research in Ophthalmology [*Later, ARVO*] (EA) .... ARO
Association for Research in Otolaryngology (NTPA) .... ARO
Association for Research in Parodentosis (SAUO) .... ARPA
Association for Research in Vision and Ophthalmology (EA) .... ARVO
Association for Research into Restricted Growth [*British*] .... ARRG
Association for Research into the Folklore of Imagination [*French*] (ECON) .... ARFI
Association for Research into the Science of Enjoyment (WDAA) .... ARISE
Association for Research Libraries (SAUS) .... ARL
Association for Research of Childhood Cancer (EA) .... AROCC
Association for Research on Nonprofit Organizations and Voluntary Action (EA) .... ARNOVA
Association for Research on Periodontal Diseases (SAUO) .... ARPA
Association for Residential Care [*British*] (EAIO) .... ARC
Association for Responsible Communication (SAUO) .... ARC
Association for Responsible Dissent (EA) .... ARD
Association for Restriction of Radio and Television Commercials [*Defunct*] (EA) .... ARRTVC
Association for Restriction of TV Commercials [*Later, ARRTVC*] (EA) .... ARTVC
Association for Retarded Children (DAVI) .... ARC
Association for Retarded Citizens (EA) .... ARC
Association for Retarded Citizens/Georgia (SAUO) .... ARC/Georgia
Association for Retired Persons Over 50 (WDAA) ARPO50
Association for Rural Mental Health [*Later, NARMH*] (EA) .... ARMH
Association for Safe International Road Travel (EA) .... ASIRT
Association for Sane Psychiatric Practices (EA) .... ASPP
Association for School, College, and University Staffing (EA) .... ASCUS
Association for Schools of Public Health in the European Region (SAUS) .... ASPHER
Association for Science Education [*British*] (DEN) .... ASE
Association for Science Education (SAUO) .... ASE
Association for Science (or Scientific) Cooperation in Asia (SAUO) .... ASCA
Association for Science, Technology and Innovation (SAUO) .... ASTI
Association for Scientific Journals (EA) .... ASJ
Association for Scottish Literary Studies [*Aberdeen, Scotland*] (EAIO) .... ASLS
Association for Seismological Cooperation in the Western Pacific and South-East Asia (SAUO) .... ASCWP
Association for Service Management .... AFSM
Association for Services Management International (EA) .... ASMI
Association for Short Term Psychotherapy (EA) .... ASTP
Association for Sickle Cell Anemia [*Defunct*] .... ASCA
Association for Singles (EA) .... AS
Association for Small Business Advancement [*Defunct*] (EA) .... ASBA
Association for Social and Moral Hygiene (SAUO) .... ASMH
Association for Social Anthropology in Oceania (EA) .... ASAO
Association for Social Design [*Later, BRI*] (EA) .... ASD
Association for Social Economics (EA) .... ASE
Association for Social Knowledge (SAUO) .... ASK
Association for Social Work Education in Africa [*See also AESA*] (EAIO) .... ASWEA
Association for Software Protection (EA) .... ASP
Association for Software Testing and Evaluation [*Defunct*] (EA) .... ASTE
Association for Special Education [*British*] (BI) .... ASE
Association for Special Education [*British*] .... ASPE
Association for Special Education Technology .... ASET
Association for Specialists in Group Work (EA) .... ASGW
Association for Spina Bifida and Hydrocephalus (SAUS) .... ASBAH
Association for Spina Bifida and Hydrocephalus [*Australia*] [*British*] (IRUK) .... ASBAH
Association for Spina Bifida and Hydrocephalus (SAUO) .... ASBAH
Association for Spiritual Awareness (EA) .... AFSA
Association for Spiritual, Ethical, and Religious Values in Counseling (NTPA) .... ASERVIC
Association for Stammerers (EAIO) .... AFS
Association for Stamp Exhibitions [*Defunct*] .... ASE
Association for Strengthening Agricultural Research in Eastern and Central Africa (ECON) .... ASERCA
Association for Strengthening of Agricultural Research in East and Central Africa (SAUO) .... ASARECA
Association for Student Counsellors (AIE) .... ASC
Association for Student Teaching [*Later, ATE*] (EA) .... AST
Association for Student Training (SAUO) .... AST
Association for Studies in the Conservation of Historic Buildings [*British*] .... ASCHB
Association for Study of Internal Fixation (DMAA) .... ASIF
Association for Study of Karma (EA) .... ASK
Association for Supervision and Curriculum Development (EA) .... ASCD
Association for Suppliers of Printing and Publishing Technologies (SAUO) .... ASPPT
Association for Suppliers of Printing and Publishing Technologies (SAUS) .... NPES
Association for Surgical Education (EA) .... ASE
Association for Symbolic Logic (EA) .... ASL
Association for Systematics Collections [*Taxonomy*] .... ASC
Association for Systems Management (EA) .... ASM
Association for Teacher Education in Europe [*Belgium*] (EAIO) .... ATEE
Association for Teaching Aids in Mathematics (SAUO) .... ATAM
Association for Teaching Psychology (SAUO) .... ATPsych
Association for Technical Education on Schools (SAUO) .... ATES
Association for Technology in Music Instruction (EA) .... ATMI
Association for Tele-Education in Canada (AC) .... ATEC
Association for the Abolition of Abused Abbreviations and Asinine Acronyms (SAUO) .... AAAAAA
Association for the Abolition of Round Fish Bowls (SAUO) .... AARFB
Association for the Accreditation of Human Research Protection Programs (SAUO) .... AAHRPP
Association for the Advancement of Aeronautical Research [*France*] .... AAAR
Association for the Advancement of Aging Research [*Defunct*] (EA) .... AAAR
Association for the Advancement of Agricultural Sciences in/of Africa (SAUO) .... AAASA
Association for the Advancement of Applied Sport Psychology (NTPA) .... AAASP
Association for the Advancement of Appropriate Technologies for Developing Count (SAUS) .... AAATDC
Association for the Advancement of Appropriate Technology (or Technologies) for Developing Countries (SAUO) .... AAATDC
Association for the Advancement of Assistive Technology in Europe (SAUO) .... AAATE
Association for the Advancement of Automotive Medicine (EA) .... AAAM
Association for the Advancement of Baltic Studies (EA) .... AABS
Association for the Advancement of British Biotechnology (EAIO) .... AABB
Association for the Advancement of Central Asian Research (EA) .... AACAR
Association for the Advancement of Civil Rights [*Gibraltar*] [*Political party*] (PPE) .... AACR
Association for the Advancement of Civil Rights (SAUO) .... AACR
Association for the Advancement of Computing in Education .... AACE
Association for the Advancement of Creative Musicians (EA) .... AACM
Association for the Advancement of Dutch-American Studies (EA) .... AADAS
Association for the Advancement of Family Stability [*Later, AFCO*] .... AAFS
Association for the Advancement of Health Care Managers [*Defunct*] (EA) .... AAHCM
Association for the Advancement of Health Education (EA) .... AAHE
Association for the Advancement of Instruction about Alcohol and Narcotics [*Defunct*] .... AAIAN
Association for the Advancement of International Education (EA) .... AAIE
Association for the Advancement of Invention and Innovation [*Patent lobby*] [*Defunct*] .... AAII
Association for the Advancement of Invention and Innovation (SAUO) .... AAII
Association for the Advancement of Medical Education [*Defunct*] (EA) .... AAME
Association for the Advancement of Medical Instrumentation (EA) .... AAMI
Association for the Advancement of Ophthalmology [*Defunct*] (EA) .... AAO
Association for the Advancement of Philosophy and Psychiatry (SAUO) .... ABPP
Association for the Advancement of Policy, Research, and Development in the Third World (EA) .... AAPRDTW
Association for the Advancement of Private Health (SAUO) .... AAPH
Association for the Advancement of Psychoanalysis (NTPA) .... AAP
Association for the Advancement of Psychology (NTPA) .... AAP
Association for the Advancement of Psychotherapy (EA) .... AAP
Association for the Advancement of Psychotherapy (SAUO) .... AAPT
Association for the Advancement of Released Convicts (SAUO) .... AARC
Association for the Advancement of Research in Multiple Sclerosis (SAUO) .... AARMS
Association for the Advancement of Scandinavian Studies in Canada GG2 [*See also AAESC*] .... AASSC
Association for the Advancement of Science (SAUO) .... AAS
Association for the Advancement of Science in Canada .... AASC
Association for the Advancement of Sports Potential (EA) .... AASP
Association for the Advancement of Teacher Education in Music (AIE) .... AATEM
Association for the Advancement of the Science and Technology of Documentation (SAUO) .... AASTD
Association for the Advancement of Wound Care (NTPA) .... AAWC
Association for the Aid of Crippled Children [*Later, Foundation for Child Development*] (EA) .... AACC
Association for the Alleviation of Asinine Abbreviations and Absurd Acronyms [*Satirical nonassociation*] .... AAAAAA
Association for the Alleviation of Asinine Abbreviations and Absurd Acronyms (SAUO) .... AAAAAA
Association for the American Dance Festival (EA) .... AADF
[*The*] **Association for the Anthropological Study of Play** (EA) .... TAASP
Association for the Bedouin Culture Museum (SAUO) .... ABCM
Association for the Behavioral Sciences and Medical Education (SAUS) .... ABSAME
Association for the Behavioral Treatment of Sexual Abusers (EA) .... ABTSA
Association for the Benefit of Non-contrast Employees (SAUO) .... ABNE
Association for the Bibliography of History (EA) .... ABH
Association for the Blind [*Australia*] .... AFTB
Association for the Blind of Western Australia .... AFTBWA
Association for the Blind, Queensland [*Australia*] .... AFTBQ
Association for the Care of Asthma (EA) .... ACA
Association for the Care of Children in Hospitals (SAUO) .... ACCH
Association for the Care of Children's Health (EA) .... ACCH
Association for the Care of Childrens Health (SAUS) .... ACCH
Association for the Conservation of Energy [*British*] (IRUK) .... ACE
Association for the Coordination of University Religious Affairs (EA) .... ACURA
Association for the Cure of Cancer of the Prostate .... CaP CURE
Association for the Defense of Djibouti Human Rights and Liberties .... ADDHL
Association for the Development of Collective Action in the Field of Permanent Education in Europe (SAUO) .... ACEPE
Association for the Development of Fertilizers Industry in Latin America (SAUO) .... ADIFAL
Association for the Development of Further Professional Training in the Foundry and Related Industries (SAUO) .... FOPBRPIC
Association for the Development of Human Potential (EA) .... ADHP

Association for the Development of Religions (or Religious) Information Systems (SAUO) ... ADRIS
Association for the Development of Religious Information Systems (EA) ... ADRIS
Association for the Development of Social Therapy [*Defunct*] (EA) ... ADST
[*The*] **Association for the Education and Welfare of the Visually Handicapped** [*British*] ... AEWVH
Association for the Education and Welfare of the Visually Handicapped (SAUO) ... AEWVR
Association for the Education of Teachers in Science (EA) ... AETS
Association for the Encouragement of Correct Punctuation, Spelling, and Usage inPublic Communications (EA) ... AECPSUPC
Association for the Evaluation of the Elementary School (AEBS) ... AEES
Association for the Exchange of Students for Technical Experience (SAUO) ... AESTE
Association for the Export of Canadian Books [*Association pour l'Exportation du Livre Canadien*] (AC) ... AECB
Association for the Final Advance of Scripture Translation (SAUO) ... FAST
Association for the Free Distribution of the Scriptures [*British*] ... AFDS
[*The*] **Association for the Gifted** (EA) ... TAG
Association for the Help of Retarded Children (SAUO) ... AHRC
Association for the History of Chiropractic (EA) ... AHC
Association for the Ice Cream Industries of the EEC (SAUO) ... EUROGLACES
Association for the Improvement of Community College Teaching [*Defunct*] (EA) ... AICCT
Association for the Improvement of Geometrical Teaching (SAUO) ... AIGT
Association for the Improvement of the Mississippi River (EA) ... AIMR
Association for the Instrumentation Control and Automation Industry in the United Kingdom (BUAC) ... GAMBICA
Association for the Integration of Management [*New York, NY*] (EA) ... AIM
Association for the International Collective Management of Audiovisual Works (SAUO) ... AGICOA
Association for the Introduction of New Biological Nomenclature [*Belgium*] (EAIO) ... AINBN
Association for the Legal Right to Abortion (Western Australia) ... ALRA(WA)
Association for the Liberation of Ukraine [*Defunct*] (EA) ... ALU
Association for the Locked-In Syndrome (SAUO) ... ALIS
Association for the Management of Organization Design (NTPA) ... AMOD
Association for the Monetary Union of Europe ... AMUE
Association for the Neurologically Disabled of Canada (AC) ... AND
Association for the Preservation and Preventation of the Arts (SAUO) ... APPA
Association for the Preservation of Anti-Psychiatric Artifacts [*Defunct*] (EA) ... APAPA
Association for the Preservation of Political Americana (EA) ... APPA
Association for the Preservation of Rural Life [*British*] (BI) ... APRL
Association for the Preservation of Rural Scotland (BI) ... APRS
Association for the Preservation of the Auction Market [*Defunct*] (EA) ... APAM
Association for the Preservation of Virginia Antiquities (SAUO) ... APV
Association for the Preservation of Virginia Antiquities (EA) ... APVA
Association for the Prevention of Accidents (SAUO) ... APA
Association for the Prevention of Addiction (SAUO) ... APA
Association for the Prevention of Thefts in Shops [*British*] ... APTS
Association for the Professional Treatment of Offenders [*Defunct*] (EA) ... APTO
Association for the Promotion & Advancement of Science Education (AC) ... APASE
Association for the Promotion of African Community Initiatives (EAIO) ... APACI
Association for the Promotion of Humor in International Affairs (EA) ... APHIA
Association for the Promotion of Inter-African Trade (SAUO) ... APIAT
Association for the Promotion of Space Activities in Europe (SAUO) ... C
Association for the Promotion of the International Circulation of the Press [*Distipress*] ... APICP
Association for the Propagation of the Faith (SAUO) ... APF
Association for the Propogation of the Faith (SAUO) ... APF
Association for the Protection of Evolution [*British*] ... APE
Association for the Protection of Fur-Bearing Animals (EAIO) ... APFBA
Association for the Protection of Patients and Staff (SAUO) ... APPS
Association for the Protection of Rural Australia ... APRA
Association for the Protection of Rural Scotland [*British*] ... APRS
Association for the Protection of Rural Scotland (SAUO) ... APRS
Association for the Protection of the Adirondacks (EA) ... APA
Association for the Psychiatric Study of Adolescents (SAUO) ... APS
Association for the Psychiatric Study of Adolescents [*British*] ... APSA
Association for the Psychophysiological Study of Sleep [*Later, Sleep Research Society - SRS*] ... APSS
Association for the Psychophysiological Study of Sleep Association (journ.) (SAUS) ... APSS
Association for the Reduction of Aircraft Noise (EA) ... ARAN
Association for the Reform of the Latin Teaching (SAUO) ... ARLT
Association for the Rehabilitation of the Brain Injured (AC) ... ARBI
Association for the Rights of Catholics in the Church (EA) ... ARCC
Association for the Scientific Study of Anomalous Phenomena ... ASSAP
Association for the Severely Handicapped (SAUS) ... TASH
Association for the Sexually Harassed (EA) ... ASH
Association for the Sociological Study of Jewry (EA) ... ASSJ
Association for the Sociology of Religion (EA) ... ASR
Association for the Study and Advancement of Supportive Values (EA) ... ASASV
Association for the Study and Application of the Method of Ilizarov (SAUO) ... ASAMI
Association for the Study of Abortion [*Later, NAF*] ... ASA
Association for the Study of Abortion. Newsletter [*A publication*] (DLA) ... ASA Newsl
Association for the Study of Afro-American Life and History (SAUO) ... ASAALH
Association for the Study of Afro-American Life and History (EA) ... ASALH
Association for the Study of Animal Behavior ... ASAB
Association for the Study of Animal Behavior (SAUS) ... Assn Study Anim Behav
Association for the Study of Animal Behaviour (SAUO) ... Assn Study Anim Behav
Association for the Study of Canadian Radio and Television [*Pronounced "Askrat"*] [*See also AERTC*] ... ASCRT
Association for the Study of Classical African Civilizations (EA) ... ASCAC
Association for the Study of Dada and Surrealism (EA) ... ASDS
Association for the Study of Dreams (EA) ... ASD
Association for the Study of Food and Society (EA) ... ASFS
Association for the Study of Higher Education (EA) ... ASHE
Association for the Study of Human Infertility (SAUO) ... ASH
Association for the Study of Human Infertility (DAVI) ... ASHI
Association for the Study of Internal Secretions (SAUO) ... ASIS
Association for the Study of International Development [*See also AEDI*] [*Canada*] ... ASID
Association for the Study of Jewish Languages [*Haifa, Israel*] (EAIO) ... ASJL
Association for the Study of Literature and Alchemy (EA) ... ASLA
Association for the Study of Literature and Environment ... ASLE
Association for the Study of Literature and the Environment (QUAC) ... ASLE
Association for the Study of Man-Environment Relations (EA) ... ASMER
Association for the Study of Medical Education ... ASME
Association for the Study of Negro Life and History [*Later, Association for theStudy of Afro-American Life and History*] (EA) ... ASNLH
Association for the Study of Obesity (EAIO) ... ASO
Association for the Study of Primary Education (AIE) ... ASPE
Association for the Study of Snow and Ice (SAUO) ... ASSI
Association for the Study of Soviet-Type Economies [*Later, ACES*] (EA) ... ASTE
Association for the Study of the Grants Economy (EA) ... ASGE
Association for the Study of the Nationalities-USSR and East Europe (SAUO) ... ASN
Association for the Study of the World Refugee Problem [*Vaduz, Liechtenstein*] (EAIO) ... AWR
Association for the Support and Diffusion of Art (EA) ... ASDA
Association for the Teaching of Psychology [*British*] ... ATP
Association for the Teaching of the Social Sciences (SAUO) ... ATSS
Association for the Therapeutic Education [*British*] ... ATE
Association for the Understanding of Man (SAUO) ... Assn Under Man
Association for the Understanding of Man (EA) ... AUM
Association for the United Nations in Russia (EAIO) ... UNAR
Association for the World University (EA) ... AWU
Association for Theatre and Disability (EA) ... ATD
Association for Theatre in Higher Education (EA) ... ATHE
Association for Theological Education in South East Asia (EAIO) ... ATESEA
Association for Theological Education in the Near East [*Later, ATIME*] ... ATENE
Association for Totally Dependent Persons of South Australia ... TDPSA
Association for Trade with America (SAUO) ... ATA
Association for Transarmament Studies [*Later, CBDA*] (EA) ... ATS
Association for Transpersonal Psychology (EA) ... ATP
Association for Transportation Law, Logistics, and Policy (NTPA) ... ATLLP
Association for Tropical Biology (EA) ... ATB
Association for Uncertainty in Artificial Intelligence (VERA) ... AUAI
Association for Union Democracy (EA) ... AUD
Association for University Business and Economic Research [*University, AL*] (EA) ... AUBER
Association for Unmanned Vehicle Systems (EA) ... AUVS
Association for Vertical Market Computing [*Defunct*] (EA) ... AVMC
Association for Veterinary Clinical Pharmacology and Therapeutics (GVA) ... AVCPT
Association for Veterinary Informatics (GVA) ... AVI
Association for Vital Records and Health Statistics (EA) ... AVRHS
Association for Voluntary Action in Europe [*See also AVE*] (EAIO) ... AVAE
Association for Voluntary action in Europe (SAUO) ... AVE
Association for Voluntary Sterilization (SAUO) ... AVS
Association for Voluntary Sterilization, Inc. [*New York, NY*] [*Research center*] ... AVS
Association for Voluntary Sterilization, Inc., International Project, New York, NY [*Library symbol*] [*Library of Congress*] (LCLS) ... NNAVS
Association for Voluntary Surgical Contraception (EA) ... AVSC
Association for Volunteer Administration (EA) ... AVA
Association for Woman in Computing (SAUS) ... AWC
Association for Women Geoscientists (EA) ... AWG
Association for Women in Communications (NTPA) ... AWC
Association for Women in Computing (EA) ... AWC
Association for Women in Development (EA) ... AWD
Association for Women in Development (EA) ... AWID
Association for Women in Mathematics (EA) ... AWM
Association for Women in Psychology (EA) ... AWP
Association for Women in Science (EA) ... AWIS
Association for Women in Science and Engineering [*British*] ... AWiSE
Association for Women in Sports Media (EA) ... AWSM
Association for Women Veterinarians (EA) ... AWV
Association for Women's Active Return to Education [*Defunct*] ... AWARE
Association for Women's AIDS [*Acquired Immune Deficiency Syndrome*] **Research and Education** ... AWARE
Association for Workplace Democracy [*Defunct*] (EA) ... AWD
Association for Worksite Health Promotion (NTPA) ... AWHP
Association for World Education (EA) ... AWE
Association for World Evangelism (EA) ... AWE
Association for World Peace [*Founded in 1951*] [*Defunct*] [*British*] ... AWP
Association for World Travel Exchange (EA) ... AWTE
Association for World Travel Service (SAUO) ... AWTS
Association Forestiere Canadienne [*Canadian Forestry Association*] (EAIO) ... AFC
Association Forestiere de la Vallee du St-Maurice Inc. (AC) ... AFVSM
Association Forestiere de l'Abitibi-Temiscamingue, Inc. (AC) ... AFAT

Association Forestiere Quebecoise Inc. [*Quebec Forestry Association Inc.*] (AC) .... AFQ
Association Forestiere Saguenay-Lac St-Jean Inc. (AC) .... AFSL
Association for/of American Schools in South America (SAUO) .... AASSA
Association for/of Applied Psychoanalysis (SAUO) .... AAP
Association for/of Computing Machinery (SAUO) .... ACM
Association for/of Death Education and Counseling (SAUO) .... ADEC
Association for/of Educational Data Systems (SAUO) .... AEDS
Association for/of Electronic Data Systems (SAUO) .... AEDS
Association for/of European Airlines (SAUO) .... AEA
Association for/of General and Liberal Studies (SAUO) .... AGLS
Association for/of Geoscientists for International Development (SAUO) ..... AGID
Association for/of International Health Researches (SAUO) .... AIHR
Association for/of Jewish Studies (SAUO) .... AJS
Association for/of Medical Deans in Europe (SAUO) .... AMDE
Association for/of Medical Education and Research in Substance Abuse (SAUO) ..... AMERSA
Association for/of Medical Schools in Africa (SAUO) .... AMSA
Association for/of Poetry Therapy (SAUO) .... APT
Association for/of Population-Family Planning Libraries and Information Centers International (SAUO) .... APLIC
Association for/of Radiation Research (SAUO) .... ARR
Association for/of Schools of Public Health in the European Region (SAUO) ..... ASPHER
Association for/of Symbolic Logic (SAUO) .... ASL
Association for/of Tropical Biology (SAUO) .... ATB
Association for/of Unmanned Vehicle Systems (SAUO) .... AUVS
Association for/of Voluntary Surgical Contraception (SAUO) ...... AVSC
Association for/of Women in Science (SAUO) .... AWIS
Association Francaise de Calcul [*French*] (CIST) .... AFCAL
Association Francaise De Lutte Contre La Mucoviscidose [*French Cystic Fibrosis Association*] .... AFLM
Association Francaise de Normalisation [*French Association for Standardization*] [*Database producer*] (IID) .... AFNOR
Association Francaise de Terminologie [*French Association of Terminology*] [*Canada*] .... AFTERM
Association Francaise des Documentalistes et des Bibliothecaires Specialises (NITA) .... AFDBS
Association Francaise des Entreprises pour l'Environnement [*French Environmentalist Association*] .... AFEE
Association Francaise des Etudes Canadiennes [*French Association of Canadian Studies*] .... AFEC
Association Francaise d'Experts de la Cooperation Technique Internationale [*French Association of Experts Assigned to International Technical Cooperation*] (AF) .... AFECTI
Association Francaise pour la Cybernetique Economique et Technique [*French Association for Economic and Technical Cybernetics*] ..... AFCET
Association Francaise pour l'Accueil des Travailleurs Africains et Malgaches [*French Association for the Reception of African and Malagasy Workers*] (AF) .... AFTAM
Association Francaise pour l'Etude des Eaux [*French Water Study Association*] [*Paris*] [*Information service or system*] (IID) ..... AFEE
Association France-Etats-Unis [*France-United States Association*] (EA) .... AFEU
Association Francophone d'Amitie et de Liaison (EA) .... AFAL
Association Francophone de Spectrometrie de Masse de Solides [*French-Speaking Association of Solids Mass Spectrometry*] (EAIO) ..... AFSMAS
Association Francophone d'Education Comparee [*French-Speaking Comparative Education Association - FSCEA*] (EAIO) .... AFEC
Association Francophone Internationale des Directeurs d'Etablissements Scolaires [*International Association of French-Speaking Directors of Educational Institutions*] [*Anjou, PQ*] .... AFIDES
Association Francophone Internationale des Groupes d'Animation de la Paraplegie [*International French-Speaking Association of Paraplegic Therapy Groups*] [*Brie-Comte-Robert, France*] (EAIO) .... AFIGAP
Association Franco-Yukonnaise (AC) .... AFY
Association Generale des Eleves et Etudiants du Dahomey en France [*General Association of Dahomean Pupils and Students in France*] [*Dahomey*] .... AGEED
Association Generale des Etudiants Reunionnais en Metropole [*General Association of Reunionese Students in France*] (AF) ...... AGERM
Association Generale des Federations Internationales de Sports [*General Association of International Sports Federations - GAISF*] (EA) ...... AGFIS
Association Generale des Hygienistes et Techniciens Municipaux [*General Association of Municipal Health and Technical Experts*] (EAIO) ..... AGHTM
Association Geologique Carpatho-Balkanique [*Carpathian Balkan Geological Association - CBGA*] (EA) .... AGCB
Association Graph (SAUO) .... AG
Association Guineenne des Editeurs de la Presse Independente [*Press association*] [*Guinea*] (EY) .... AGEPI
Association Health Plan .... AHP
Association Henri Capitant (EA) .... AHC
Association in Occupational Studies [*Associate degree*] (PAZ) ..... AOS
Association in Scotland to Research into Astronautics (EAIO) ..... ASTRA
Association in Solidarity with Guatemala (EA) .... ASOGUA
Association Information Recherche (SAUS) .... AIR
Association Institute (EA) .... AI
Association Intercontinentale du Mais Hybride .... INTERHYBRID
Association Internationale Contre la Torture [*International Association Against Torture*] [*Milan, Italy*] (EAIO) .... AICT
Association Internationale Contre la Violence dans le Sport [*International Association for Non-Violent Sport - IANVS*] [*Monte Carlo, Monaco*] (EAIO) .... AICVS
Association Internationale Contre le Bruit [*International Association Against Noise*] [*ICSU*] (EAIO) .... AICB

Association Internationale d'Allergologie [*International Association of Allergology*] .... AIA
Association Internationale de Bibliophile [*International Association of Bibliophiles - IAB*] [*Paris, France*] (EAIO) .... AIB
Association Internationale de Boxe Amateur [*International Amateur Boxing Association*] (EA) .... AIBA
Association Internationale de Bryozoologie [*International Bryozoology Association - IBA*] [*Paris, France*] (EAIO) .... AIB
Association Internationale de Chimie Cerealiere [*International Association for Cereal Chemistry*] [*Also, ICC*] .... AICC
Association Internationale de Chimie Cerealiere [*International Association for Cereal Chemistry*] [*Also, AICC*] ICC
Association Internationale de Cybernetique [*International Association for Cybernetics - IAC*] (EAIO) .... AIC
Association Internationale de Defense des Artistes [*International Association for the Defence of Artists*] (EAIO) .... AIDA
Association Internationale de Defense des Artistes [*International Associationfor the Defense of Artists*] - USA (EA) .... AIDA-USA
Association Internationale de Developpement et d'Action Communautaires [*International Association for Community Development*] [*Marcinelle, Belgium*] (EAIO) .... AIDAC
Association Internationale de Droit Constitutionnel [*International Association of Constitutional Law - IACL*] (EAIO) .... AIDC
Association Internationale de Droit des Assurances [*International Association for Insurance Law*] [*Belgium*] (EAIO) .... AIDA
Association Internationale de Droit Penal [*International Association of Penal Law*] .... AIDP
Association Internationale de Geodesie [*International Association of Geodesy*] .... AIG
Association Internationale de Geologie de l'Ingenieur [*International Association of Engineering Geology*] .... AIGI
Association Internationale de Geomagnetisme et d'Aeronomie [*International Association of Geomagnetism and Aeronomy*] .... AIGA
Association Internationale de Grands Magasins [*International Association of Department Stores - IADS*] (EAIO) .... AIGM
Association Internationale de la Boulangerie Industrielle [*International Association of the Bread Industry*] (EAIO) .... AIBI
Association Internationale de la Couleur [*International Color Association*] [*Soesterberg, Netherlands*] (EA) .... AIC
Association Internationale de la Distribution [*International Association of Distribution*] [*Belgium*] (EAIO) .... AIDA
Association Internationale de la Distribution des Produits Alimentaires et des Produits de Grande Consommation [*International Association for the Distribution of Food Products and General Consumer Goods*] (EAIO) ..... AIDA
Association Internationale de la Fonction Publique [*Avignon, France*] (EAIO) .... AIFP
Association Internationale de la Gestion du Personnel [*International Association of Personnel Administration*] [*Canada*] .... AIGP
Association Internationale de la Meunerie [*International Milling Association - IMA*] (EAIO) .... AIM
Association Internationale de la Mutualite [*International Association for Mutual Assistance*] [*Switzerland*] (EAIO) .... AIM
Association Internationale de la Presse Echiqueenne [*International Association of Chess Press*] [*Kerteminde, Denmark*] (EAIO) ..... AIPE
Association Internationale de la Presse Sportive [*International Sport Press Association*] (EAIO) .... AIPS
Association Internationale de la Psychologie Adlerienne [*International Association of Adlerian Psychology*] .... AIPA
Association Internationale de la Savonnerie et de la Detergence [*International Association of the Soap and Detergent Industry*] (EAIO) ..... AIS
Association Internationale de la Science du Sol [*International Society of Soil Science - ISSS*] (EAIO) .... AISS
Association Internationale de la Securite Sociale [*International Social Security Association*] .... AISS
Association Internationale de la Soie [*International Silk Association - ISA*] (EAIO) .... AIS
Association Internationale de la Teinture et de l'Impression Textiles [*International Association of Textile Dyers and Printers*] (EAIO) ..... AITIT
Association Internationale de l'Etancheite [*International Waterproofing Association - IWA*] (EAIO) .... AIE
Association Internationale de l'Industrie des Bouillions et Potages [*International Association of the Manufacture of Soups and Broths*] (EAIO) .... AIIBP
Association Internationale de l'Industrie des Engrais [*International Fertilizer Industry Association - IFA*] (EAIO) .... IFA
Association Internationale de Linguistique Appliquee [*International Association of Applied Linguistics*] (EA) .... AILA
Association Internationale de Litterature Comparee [*International Comparative Literature Association*] .... AILC
Association Internationale de Medecine et de Biologie de l'Environnement [*International Association of Medicine and Biology of Environment - IAMBE*] [*France*] (EAIO) .... AIMBE
Association Internationale de Medecine Traditionnelle Chinoise [*International Association of Traditional Chinese Medicine*] [*Canada*] ..... AIMTC
Association Internationale de Musees de Transports [*International Association of Transport Museums - IATM*] (EAIO) .... AIMT
Association Internationale de Mycologie [*International Mycological Association*] (EAIO) .... AIM
Association Internationale de Numerotation des Articles [*International Article Numbering Association*] (EAIO) .... EAN
Association Internationale de Paleontologie Humaine (EAIO) ..... AIPH
Association Internationale de Palynologie Africaine [*International Association of African Palynology*] (QUAC) .... AIPA
Association Internationale de Papyrologues [*International Association of Papyrologists*] (EAIO) .... AIP

Association Internationale de Pedagogie Experimentale de Langue Francaise [*International Association of Experimental French Language Education*] [*Canada*] ... AIPELF
Association Internationale de Pediatrie [*International Pediatric Association - IPA*] [*Paris, France*] (EAIO) ... AIP
Association Internationale de Philosophie du Droit et de Philosophie Sociale [*See also IAPLSP*] ... AIPDPS
Association Internationale de Photobiologie [*International Photobiology Association*] [*Epalinges, Switzerland*] (EA) ... AIP
Association Internationale de Presse pour l'Etude des Problemes d'Outre-Mer [*International Press Association for Studying Overseas Problems*] ... AIPEPO
Association Internationale de Prophylaxie de la Cecite [*International Association for the Prevention of Blindness*] ... AIPC
Association Internationale de Psychologie Appliquee [*International Association of Applied Psychology*] ... AIPA
Association Internationale de Relations Professionnelles [*International Industrial Relations Association - IIRA*] (EAIO) ... AIRP
Association Internationale de Science Politique [*International Political Science Association - IPSA*] [*Canada*] ... AISP
Association Internationale de Sociologie [*International Sociological Association - ISA*] (EAIO) ... AIS
Association Internationale de Standardisation Biologique [*International Association of Biological Standardization - IABS*] (EAIO) ... AISB
Association Internationale de Terminologie [*International Association of Terminology*] [*Quebec, PQ*] (EAIO) ... TERMIA
Association Internationale de Volcanologie [*International Association of Volcanology*] ... AIV
Association Internationale d'Epigraphie Grecque et Latine [*International Association for Greek and Latin Epigraphy*] (EAIO) ... AIEGL
Association Internationale d'Epigraphie Latine [*International Association for Latin Epigraphy*] ... AIEL
Association Internationale des Aeroports Civils [*International Civil Airports Association - ICAA*] (EAIO) ... AIAC
Association Internationale des Approvisionneurs de Navires [*British*] (EAIO) ... AIAN
Association Internationale des Arbitres de Water Polo [*International Association of Water Polo Referees - IAWPR*] (EAIO) ... AIA
Association Internationale des Arts Plastiques [*International Association of Art - IAA*] (EAIO) ... AIAP
Association Internationale des Assureurs Contre la Grele [*International Association of Hail Insurers*] ... AIAG
Association Internationale des Automobile Clubs Reconnus [*International Automobile Federation*] ... AIACR
Association Internationale des Bibliotheques, Archives, et Centres de Documentation Musicaux [*International Association of Music Libraries, Archives, and Documentation Centres - IAML*] (EAIO) ... AIBM
Association Internationale des Charites [*International Association of Charities - IAC*] (EAIO) ... AIC
Association Internationale des Charites de St. Vincent De Paul [*International Association of Charities of St. Vincent De Paul*] (EAIO) ... AIC
Association Internationale des Circuits Permanents [*Circuits International*] [*Germany*] (EAIO) ... AICP
Association Internationale des Constructeurs de Materiel Aerospatial [*International Association of Aerospace Equipment Manufacturers*] ... AICMA
Association Internationale des Constructeurs de Materiel Roulant [*International Association of Rolling Stock Builders - IARSB*] (EAIO) ... AICMR
Association Internationale des Cordeliers [*International Songwriters' Association - ISA*] (EAIO) ... AIC
Association Internationale des Critiques d'Art [*International Association of Art Critics*] (EAIO) ... AICA
Association Internationale des Critiques de Theatre [*International Association of Theatre Critics*] ... AICT
Association Internationale des Critiques Litteraires [*International Association of Literary Critics*] (EAIO) ... AICL
Association Internationale des Debardeurs [*International Longshoremen's Association - ILA*] [*Canada*] ... AID
Association Internationale des Demographes de Langue Francaise (EAIO) ... AIDELF
Association Internationale des Diffuseurs d'Oeuvres d'Art Originales [*International Association of Original Art Diffusors - IAOAD*] (EAIO) ... AIDOAO
Association Internationale des Distributions d'Eau ... AIDE
Association Internationale des Docteurs (Lettres et Sciences Humaines) de l'Universite de Paris et des Autres Universites de France [*International Association of Doctors (Letters and Liberal Studies) of the University of Paris and Other Universities of France*] [*Canada*] ... AIDLUPA
Association Internationale des Documentalistes et Techniciens de l'Information [*International Association of Documentalists and Information Officers*] ... AID
Association Internationale des Documentaristes [*International Association of Documentary Filmmakers*] ... AID
Association Internationale des Ecoles de Service Social [*International Association of Schools of Social Work - IASSW*] (EA) ... AIESS
Association Internationale des Ecoles de Voile [*International Sailing Schools Association*] [*France*] (EAIO) ... ISSA
Association Internationale des Ecoles des Sciences de l'Information [*International Association of Information Sciences Schools*] [*Canada*] (EAIO) ... AIESI
Association Internationale des Ecoles Privees Europeennes ... AIEPE
Association Internationale des Ecoles Superieures d'Education Physique [*International Association for Physical Education in Higher Education*] (EAIO) ... AIESEP
Association Internationale des Editeurs de Catalogues de Timbres-Poste [*International Association of Publishers of Postage Stamp Catalogues*] (EA) ... ASCAT
Association Internationale des Educateurs de Jeunes Inadaptes [*International Association of Workers for Troubled Children and Youth*] (EAIO) ... AIEJI
Association Internationale des Entreprises d'Equipement Electrique [*International Association of Electrical Contractors - IAEC*] (EAIO) ... AIE
Association Internationale des Etudes Byzantines [*International Association for Byzantine Studies - IABS*] (EAIO) ... AIEB
Association Internationale des Etudes de l'Asie du Sud-Est [*Paris, France*] (EAIO) ... AIEAS
Association Internationale des Etudes et Recherches sur l'Information [*International Association of Mass Communications Research*] ... AIERI
Association Internationale des Etudes Francaises [*Paris, France*] (EAIO) ... AIEF
Association Internationale des Etudiants Dentaires [*International Association of Dental Students - IADS*] [*British*] (EA) ... AIED
Association Internationale des Etudiants en Agriculture [*International Association of Agriculture Students - IAAS*] (EAIO) ... AIEA
Association Internationale des Etudiants en Sciences Economiques et Commerciales [*International Association of Students in Economics and Commerce*] [*Brussels, Belgium*] (EAIO) ... AIESEC
Association Internationale des Femmes d'Affaires Noires [*Black Business Women - International - BBWI*] [*France*] (EAIO) ... AIFAN
Association Internationale des Femmes Medecins [*Medical Women's International Association - MWIA*] [*Germany*] (EAIO) ... AIFM
Association Internationale des Hautes Juridictions Administratives [*International Association of Supreme Administrative Jurisdictions*] (EAIO) ... AIHJA
Association Internationale des Hydrogeologues [*International Association of Hydrogeologists - IAH*] ... AIH
Association Internationale des Interets Radio-Maritimes ... AIIRM
Association Internationale des Interpretes de Conference [*International Association of Conference Interpreters*] (EAIO) ... AIIC
Association Internationale des Jeunes Avocats [*Young Lawyers' International Association*] (EAIO) ... AIJA
Association Internationale des Journalistes de la Presse Feminine et Familiale [*International Association of Women and Home Page Journalists - IAWHPJ*] (EAIO) ... AIJPF
Association Internationale des Journalistes Philateliques [*International Association of Philatelic Journalists*] [*Germany*] ... AIJP
Association Internationale des Juges des Enfants ... AIJE
Association Internationale des Juristes Democrates [*International Association of Democratic Lawyers*] ... AIJD
Association Internationale des Lotteries d'Etat [*International Association of State Lotteries*] [*Canada*] (EAIO) ... AILE
Association Internationale des Magistrats de la Jeunesse [*International Association of Youth Magistrates*] ... AIJE
Association Internationale des Maires et Responsables des Capitales et Metropoles Partiellement ou Entierement Francophones [*International Association of Mayors Responsible for Capital Cities or Metropolises Partially or Entirely French-Speaking*] (EA) ... AIMF
Association Internationale des Maires Francophones - Bureau a Quebec (AC) ... AIMF
Association Internationale des Metiers et Enseignements d'Art [*International Association for Crafts and the Teaching of Art*] ... AIMEA
Association Internationale des Musees d'Agriculture [*International Association of Agricultural Museums*] (EAIO) ... AIMA
Association Internationale des Navigants de Langue Francaise (EAIO) ... AINLF
Association Internationale des Numismates Professionnels [*International Association of Professional Numismatists - IAPN*] [*Switzerland*] (EAIO) ... AINP
Association Internationale des Organisateurs de Courses Cyclistes [*International Association of Organizers of Cycle Competitions*] [*France*] (EAIO) ... AIOCC
Association Internationale des Palais des Congres [*International Association of Congress Centers*] [*Zagreb, Yugoslavia*] (EA) ... AIPC
Association Internationale des Parlementaires de Langue Francaise [*International Association of French-Speaking Parliamentarians*] (EAIO) ... AIPLF
Association Internationale des Ponts et Charpentes [*International Association of Bridges and Construction*] [*Switzerland*] ... AIPC
Association Internationale des Ports [*International Association of Ports and Harbors - IAPH*] [*Tokyo, Japan*] (EAIO) ... AIP
Association Internationale des Presses Universitaires de Langue Francaise [*International Association of French Language University Presses*] [*Canada*] [*Defunct*] ... AIPULF
Association Internationale des Producteurs de l'Horticulture [*International Association of Horticultural Producers*] [*Netherlands*] ... AIPH
Association Internationale des Professeurs de Philosophie [*International Association of Teachers of Philosophy*] (EAIO) ... AIPPh
Association Internationale des Sciences de l'Education [*International Association for the Advancement of Educational Research*] ... AISE
Association Internationale des Sciences Economiques [*International Economic Association - IEA*] [*Paris, France*] (EAIO) ... AISE
Association Internationale des Sciences Juridiques [*International Association of Legal Science - IALS*] (EAIO) ... AISJ
Association Internationale des Secretaires Professionnelles [*International Association of Professional Secretaries*] [*Canada*] ... AISP
Association Internationale des Selectionneurs pour la Protection des Obtentions Vegetales [*International Association of Plant Breeders for the Protection of Plant Varieties - IAPBPPV*] (EAIO) ... ASSINSEL
Association Internationale des Skal Clubs [*International Association of Skal Clubs*] (EAIO) ... AISC
Association Internationale des Societes d'Assurance Mutuelle [*International Association of Mutual Insurance Companies*] [*Paris, France*] (EAIO) ... AISAM
Association Internationale des Sociologues de Langue Francaise [*International Association of French Language Sociologists*] (EAIO) ... AISLF
Association Internationale des Statisticiens d'Enquetes [*International Association of Survey Statisticians*] (EAIO) ... AISE

Association Internationale des Traducteurs de Conference [*International Association of Conference Translators*] (EAIO) ... AITC

Association Internationale des Travailleurs [*International Association of Workers*] [*France*] ... AIT

Association Internationale des Travaux en Souterrain - International Tunneling Association [*Bron, France*] (EA) ... AITES-ITA

Association Internationale des Universites [*International Association of Universities - IAU*] (EAIO) ... AIU

Association Internationale des Universites du Troisieme Age [*International Association of Universities of the Third Age*] (EAIO) ... AIUTA

Association Internationale des Urbanistes [*International Society of City and Regional Planners - ISOCARP*] (EAIO) ... AIU

Association Internationale des Usagers d'Embranchements Particuliers [*International Association of Users of Private Sidings*] ... AIEP

Association Internationale des Utilisateurs de Files de Fibres Artificielles et Synthetiques [*International Association of Users of Yarn of Man-Made Fibers*] ... AIUFFAS

Association Internationale des Villes d'Avenir [*International Association of Cities of the Future*] (EA) ... AIVA

Association Internationale des Villes Francophones des Congres [*International Association of French-Speaking Congress Towns - IAFCT*] (EAIO) ... AIVFC

Association Internationale d'Etude des Civilisations Mediterraneennes [*International Association of Studies on Mediterranean Civilizations*] (EAIO) ... AIECM

Association Internationale d'Etudes du Sud-Est Europeen [*International Association of South-East European Studies - IASEES*] (EAIO) ... AIESEE

Association Internationale d'Etudes Patristiques [*International Association for Patristic Studies*] (EAIO) ... AIEP

Association Internationale d'Etudes pour la Protection des Investissements ... ADPI

Association Internationale d'Eutonie Gerda Alexander [*International Association for Gerda Alexander Eutony*] [*Switzerland*] (EAIO) ... AIEGA

Association Internationale d'Experts Scientifiques du Tourisme [*International Association of Scientific Experts in Tourism*] (EAIO) ... AIEST

Association Internationale d'Histoire Contemporaine de l'Europe [*International Association for Contemporary History of Europe*] [*Defunct*] (EAIO) ... AIHCE

Association Internationale d'Hotellerie [*International Hotel Association - IHA*] (EAIO) ... AIH

Association Internationale d'Hydrologie Scientifique ... AIH

Association Internationale d'Information et de Documentation en Administration Publique [*International Association for Information and Documentation in Public Administration*] (EAIO) ... AIIDAP

Association Internationale d'Information Scolaire, Universitaire, et Professionelle [*International Association for Educational and Vocational Information - IAEVI*] (EAIO) ... AIISUP

Association Internationale d'Irradiation Industrielle [*Association of International Industrial Irradiation*] (EAIO) ... AIII

Association Internationale: Donnees pour le Developpement [*Data for Development International Association - DFD*] (EA) ... DD

Association Internationale d'Orientation Professionnelle ... AIOP

Association Internationale d'Orientation Scolaire et Professionnelle [*International Association for Educational and Vocational Guidance - IAEVG*] (EAIO) ... AIOSP

Association Internationale du Cinema Scientifique [*International Scientific Film Association*] ... AICS

Association Internationale du Congres des Chemins de Fer [*International Railway Congress Association - IRCA*] (EAIO) ... AICCF

Association Internationale du Droit Nucleaire [*International Nuclear Law Association - INLA*] (EA) ... AIDN

Association Internationale du Film d'Animation [*International Animated Film Association*] (EAIO) ... ASIFA

Association Internationale du Mohair [*International Mohair Association*] (EAIO) ... AIM

Association Internationale du Nouvel Objet Visuel [*International Association for New Visual Objects*] [*Paris, France*] (EAIO) ... INOV

Association Internationale du Registre des Bateaux du Rhin [*International Association of the Rhine Ships Register*] ... AIRBR

Association Internationale du Theatre Amateur [*International Amateur Theatre Association - IATA*] (EAIO) ... AITA

Association Internationale du Theatre pour l'Enfance et de la Jeunesse [*International Association of Theatre for Children and Youth*] (EAIO) ... ASSITEJ

Association Internationale Francophone des Aines [*Canada*] (EAIO) ... AIFA

Association Internationale Futuribles [*Futuribles International*] (EAIO) ... AIF

Association Internationale Permanente des Congres de la Route [*Permanent International Association of Road Congresses - PIARC*] (EAIO) ... AIPCR

Association Internationale pour la Defense des Langues et Cultures Menacees [*International Association for the Defence of Threatened Languages and Cultures*] (EAIO) ... AIDLCM

Association Internationale pour la Lecture (EAIO) ... AIL

Association Internationale pour la Mobilisation de la Creativite [*International Association for the Mobilization of Creativity*] [*Canada*] (EAIO) ... AIMC

Association Internationale pour la Prevention du Suicide [*International Association for Suicide Prevention*] ... AIPS

Association Internationale pour la Protection de la Propriete Industrielle [*International Association for the Protection of Industrial Property*] [*Zurich, Switzerland*] (EA) ... AIPPI

Association Internationale pour la Recherche et la Diffusion des Methodes Audio-Visuelles et Structuro-Globales [*International Association for Research and Diffusion of Audio-Visual and Structural-Global Methods*] (EA) ... AIMAV

Association Internationale pour la Recherche Medicale et les Echanges Culturels [*International Association for Medical Research and Cultural Exchange*] [*Paris, France*] (EAIO) ... AIRMEC

Association Internationale pour la Securite Aerienne [*International Air Safety Association*] ... AISA

Association Internationale pour le Calcul Analogique [*International Association for Analogue Computation*] [*Later, IMACS*] ... AICA

Association Internationale pour le Calcul Analogique [*International Association for Analogue Computation*] [*Later, IMACS*] ... ASICA

Association Internationale pour le Developpement des Bibliotheques en Afrique [*International Association for the Development of Libraries in Africa*] ... AIDBA

Association Internationale pour le Developpement des Universites Internationaleset Mondiales [*International Association for the Development of International and World Universities - IADIWU*] [*Aulnay-Sous-Bois, France*] (EAIO) ... AIDUIM

Association Internationale pour le Developpement des Universites Internationaleset Mondiales [*International Association for the Development of International and World Universities - IADIWU*] ... AIDUM

Association Internationale pour le Developpement en Afrique des Sciences Humaines Appliquees [*International Association for the Development of Applied Human Sciences in Africa*] (AF) ... AIDASA

Association Internationale pour le Progres Social ... AIPS

Association Internationale pour le Sport des Aveugles [*International Blind Sports Association - IBSA*] [*Farsta, Sweden*] (EAIO) ... AISA

Association Internationale pour l'Education Integrative [*International Association for Integrative Education - IAIE*] (EAIO) ... AIEI

Association Internationale pour les Etudes Sanskrites [*France*] (EAIO) ... AIES

Association Internationale pour les Recherches au Bas Fourneau d'Ougree ... AIRBO

Association Internationale pour les Residus Solides et le Nettoiement des Vil les [*International Solid Wastes and Public Cleansing Association*] [*INTAPUC and IRGRD*] [*Formed by a merger of*] [*Denmark*] (EAIO) ... ISWA

Association Internationale pour les Voiles Minces [*en Beton*] [*International Association for Shell Structures*] ... AIVM

Association Internationale pour l'Etude de la Mosaique Antique [*International Association for the Study of Ancient Mosaics*] ... AIEMA

Association Internationale pour l'Etude de l'Economie de l'Assurance [*Switzerland*] (EAIO) ... AIEEA

Association Internationale pour l'Etude des Argiles [*International Association for the Study of Clays*] (EAIO) ... AIPEA

Association Internationale pour l'Etude du Foie [*International Association for the Study of the Liver*] (EAIO) ... AIEF

Association Internationale pour l'Etude du Quaternaire [*International Association for the Study of the Quaternary*] [*Canada*] (EAIO) ... AIEQ

Association Internationale pour l'Evaluation du Rendement Scolaire [*International Association for the Valuation of Educational Achievement*] (EAIO) ... AIERS

Association Internationale pour l'Histoire du Verre [*International Association for the History of Glass*] (EAIO) ... AIHV

Association Internationale pour l'Oceanographie Biologique [*International Association of Biological Oceanography - IABO*] (EAIO) ... AIOB

Association Internationale Urbanisme et Commerce [*International Association for Town Planning and Distribution*] (EAIO) ... URBANICOM

Association Internationale Veterinaire de Production Animale [*International Veterinary Association for Animal Production - IVAAP*] [*Brussels, Belgium*] (EAIO) ... AIVPA

Association Interrogation Register (SAUO) ... AIR

Association Jeunesse Fransaskoise [*Canada*] ... AJF

Association Litteraire et Artistique Internationale [*International Literary and Artistic Association*] ... ALAI

Association Lyrique Internationale [*Toulouse, France*] (EAIO) ... ALI

Association Management Centre (AC) ... AMC

Association Marketing Roundtable (EA) ... AMR

Association Mathematique du Quebec (AC) ... AMQ

Association Media Independents Ltd. [*British*] (DBA) ... AMI

Association Medicale Canadienne [*Canadian Medical Association - CMA*] ... AMC

Association Medicale du Quebec (AC) ... AMQ

Association Medicale Franco-Americaine (EA) ... AMFA

Association Medicale Internationale pour l'Etudes des Conditions de Vie et de Sante [*International Medical Association for the Study of Living Conditions and Health*] [*Sofia, Bulgaria*] (EAIO) ... AMIEV

Association Medicale Mondiale [*World Medical Association - WMA*] [*Ferney-Voltaire, France*] ... AMM

Association Member of the Plastics and Rubber Institute [*British*] (DBQ) ... AMPRI

Association Miniere du Quebec (AC) ... AMQ

Association Mondiale de Hockey [*World Hockey Association - WHA*] [*Canada*] ... AMH

Association Mondiale de Lutte Contre la Faim [*World Association for the Struggle Against Hunger*] ... ASCOFAM

Association Mondiale de Prospective Sociale [*World Social Prospects Study Association*] [*Geneva, Switzerland*] (EAIO) ... AMPS

Association Mondiale de Zootechnie [*World Association for Animal Production*] ... AMZ

Association Mondiale des Amis de l'Enfance [*World Association of Children's Friends*] [*Monaco*] (EAIO) ... AMADE

Association Mondiale des Arts Divinatoires [*Divinatory Arts World Association - DAWA*] [*Rillieux-La-Pape, France*] (EAIO) ... AMAD

Association Mondiale des Federalistes Mondiaux [*World Association of World Federalists - WAWF*] (EA) ... AMFM

Association Mondiale des Guides et des Eclaireuses [*World Association of Girl Guides and Girl Scouts - WAGGGS*] [*London, England*] (EAIO) ... AMGE

Association Mondiale des Inventeurs [*World Association of Inventors and Researchers*] (EAIO) ... AMINA

Association Mondiale des Medecins Francophones [*Ottawa, ON*] (EAIO) .... AMMF
Association Mondiale des Sciences de l'Education [*World Association for Educational Research - WAER*] (EAIO) .... AMSE
Association Mondiale des Travailleurs Scientifiques [*Scientific Workers World Association*] (NATG) .... AMTS
Association Mondiale des Veterinaires Microbiologistes, Immunologistes, et Specialistes des Maladies Infectieuses [*World Association of Veterinary Microbiologists, Immunologists, and Specialists in Infectious Diseases - WAVMI*] [*Maisons-Alfort, France*] (EAIO) .... AMVMI
Association Mondiale pour l'Ecole Instrument de Paix [*World Association for the School as an Instrument of Peace*] [*Geneva, Switzerland*] (EAIO) .... EIP
Association Mondiale pour l'Energie Non-Polluante [*Planetary Association for Clean Energy - PACE*] .... AMEN
Association Mondiale Veterinaire [*World Veterinary Association - WVA*] [*Madrid, Spain*] (EAIO) .... AMV
Association Montessori International - USA (EA) .... AMI-USA
Association Montessori Internationale [*International Montessori Association*] [*Amsterdam, Netherlands*] (EAIO) .... AMI
Association Multinationale des Producteurs et Revendeurs d'Electricite-Documentation [*Multinational Association of Producers and Retailers of Electricity-Documentation*] [*Electricity Supply Board*] [*Information service or system*] (IID) .... AMPEREDOC
Association Museums New Brunswick [*Association des Musees du Nouveau-Brunswick*] (AC) .... AMNB
Association Nationale d'Aide aux Handicapes [*National Association of Aids to Handicapped Persons*] [*Canada*] .... ANAH
Association Nationale de la Recherche Technique [*National Association of Technical Research - NATR*] [*France*] [*Information service or system*] (IID) .... ANRT
Association Nationale de Recherche sur les Technologies de Telecommunications [*Research organization advocating open systems*] [*France*] (DDC) .... ANRTT
Association Nationale des Anciens Detenus et Internes Resistants [*National Association of Former Resistance Prisoners and Internees*] [*Algeria*] (AF) .... ANADIR
Association Nationale des Anciens Moudjahidine et Mutiles de Guerre [*National Association of War Veterans and War Wounded*] [*Algeria*] .... ANAMMG
Association Nationale des Camionneurs Artisans (AC) .... ANCAI
Association Nationale des Distributeurs de Tabac et de Confiserie (AC) .... ANDTC
Association Nationale des Editeurs de Livres (AC) .... ANEL
Association Nationale des Forblantiers et Couvreurs, Section Locale 2020 [*National Association of Tinsmiths & Tilers, Local 2020*] (AC) .... ANFC
Association Nationale des Telespectateurs [*National Association of Telespectators*] [*Canada*] .... ANT
Association Nationale d'Etudes pour la Documentation Automatique [*National Association for Studies in Automatic Documentation*] [*French*] (NITA) .... ANEDA
Association Nationale pour l'Infographie [*National Computer Graphics Association of Canada*] .... ANI
Association Newspaper Classified Advertising Managers (SAUO) .... ANCAM
Association Nordique des Etudes Canadiennes [*Nordic Association for Canadian Studies*] .... ANEC
Association Nucleaire Canadienne [*Canadian Nuclear Association - CNA*] .... ANC
Association of Abrasive Blastcleaners and Protective Coaters, Queensland [*Australia*] .... AABPC(Qld)
Association of Academic Health Centers (EA) .... AAHC
Association of Academic Health Centers (NTPA) .... AHC
Association of Academic Health Sciences Libraries (SAUO) .... AAHSL
Association of Academic Health Sciences Library Directors (EA) .... AAHSLD
Association of Academic Physiatrists (EA) .... AAP
Association of Academic Psychiatry (SAUO) .... AAP
Association of Academies of Science (SAUO) .... AAS
Association of Academies of Science [*Later, NAAS*] .... AAS
Association of Accommodation and Welfare Officers [*British*] (DBA) .... AAWO
Association of Accounting Administrators [*Commercial firm*] [*Washington, DC*] (EA) .... AAA
Association of Accounting Technicians (EAIO) .... AAT
Association of Accredited Advertising Agencies of New Zealand (SAUO) .... AAAANZ
Association of Accredited Medical Laboratory Schools [*Later, NAHCS*] (EA) .... AAMLS
Association of Accredited Practitioners in Advertising (DGA) .... AAPA
Association of Administrative Assistants [*Association des Adjoints Administratifs*] (AC) .... AAA
Association of Administrative Assistants and Secretaries to United States Senators (EA) .... AAASUSS
Association of Administrators of the Interstate Compact on the Placement of Children (EA) .... AAICPC
Association of Adult Education (SAUO) .... AOR
Association of Advanced Rabbinical and Talmudic Schools (EA) .... AARTS
Association of Adventist Forums (EA) .... AAF
Association of Advertisers in Ireland Ltd. (SAUO) .... AAI
Association of Advertising Film Companies .... AAFC
Association of Advertising Lawyers [*Defunct*] (EA) .... AAL
Association of Advertising Men and Women [*Later, Advertising and Marketing Association*] (EA) .... AAMW
Association of Advisers, Craft, Design, and Technology [*British*] (DBA) .... AACDT
Association of Advisers on Education in International Religious Congregations (SAUO) .... EDUC International
Association of Advisers (or Advisors) in Design and Technical Studies (SAUO) .... AADTS
Association of Advisors in Design and Technical Studies [*British*] .... AADTS
Association of Aerial Surveyors Australia .... AASA
Association of Aerial Surveyors, Australia Inc (SAUO) .... AASA
Association of African Airlines .... AAFRA
Association of African American People's Legal Council (EA) .... AAPLC
Association of African Central Banks [*Dakar, Senegal*] .... AACB
Association of African Development Finance Institutions (MHDB) .... AADFI
Association of African Finance and Development Institutions (SAUO) .... AAFDI
Association of African Geological Surveys [*See also ASGA*] (EAIO) .... AAGS
Association of African Industrial Technology Organizations (SAUO) .... AAITC
Association of African Industrial Technology Organizations .... AAITO
Association of African Maritime Training Institutes (SAUO) .... AAMT
Association of African National Shipping Lines (SAUO) .... ANSL
Association of African Physicians in North America (EA) .... AAPNA
Association of African Sports Confederations [*See also UCSA*] [*Yaounde, Cameroon*] (EAIO) .... AASC
Association of African Studies Programs (EA) .... AASP
Association of African Trade Promoting (or Promotion) Organizations (SAUO) .... AATPO
Association of African Trade Promotion Organizations [*Tangier, Morocco*] (EAIO) .... AATPO
Association of African Universities (EAIO) .... AAU
Association of African Women for Research and Development (EAIO) .... AAWORD
Association of African Women for Research and Development (SAUO) .... AA-WORD
Association of African-American Education (SAUO) .... AAAE
Association of African-American Women Business Owners (NTPA) .... AAAWBO
Association of Agricultrual Computer Companies (EA) .... AACC
Association of Agricultural Computer Companies (SAUO) .... AACC
Association of Agricultural Education Staffs [*British*] .... AAES
Association of Agriculture (SAUO) .... AA
Association of Air Force Missileers (EA) .... AAFM
Association of Air Medical Services (NTPA) .... AAMS
Association of Air Pollution Control Equipment Manufacturers (SAUO) .... AAPCEM
Association of Air Transport Unions [*Defunct*] (EA) .... AATU
Association of Airborne Ranger Companies of the Korean War (EA) .... AARCKW
Association of Aircraft Brokers (SAUO) .... AAB
Association of Airline Companies of the EEC (SAUO) .... ACE
Association of Alaska Housing Authorities (SAUO) .... AAHA
Association of Alaska School Boards (SRA) .... AASB
Association of Alcohol/Addictions Programs in Washington State (SRA) .... AAP
Association of Allergists for Mycological Investigation (SAUO) .... AAMI
Association of Allergists for Mycological Investigations [*Defunct*] (EA) .... AAMI
Association of Allied Health Professionals Ontario [*Association des Professionnels Unis de la Sante, Ontario*] (AC) .... AAHP-O
Association of Alternate Postal Systems (EA) .... AAPS
Association of Alternative Newsweeklies .... AAN
Association of Amateur Magicians [*Defunct*] (EA) .... AAM
Association of Ambulatory Behavior Healthcare (SAUO) .... AABH
Association of American Air Travel Clubs [*Defunct*] (EA) .... AAATC
Association of American and Canadian Importers of Green Olives [*Later, Green Olive Trade Association*] (EA) .... AACIGO
Association of American Battery Manufacturers [*Later, BCI*] (EA) .... AABM
Association of American Battery Manufacturers, Inc. .... AABM
Association of American Boards of Examiners in Veterinary Medicine [*Later, AAVSB*] (EA) .... AABEVM
Association of American Cancer Institutes (EA) .... AACI
Association of American Chambers of Commerce in Latin America (EA) .... AACCLA
Association of American Choruses [*Later, Drinker Library of Choral Music*] (EA) .... AAC
Association of American CIRP [*College Internationale pour l'Etude Scientifique des Techniques de Production Mechanique*] **Industrial Sponsors** (EA) .... AACIS
Association of American Colleges (EA) .... AAC
Association of American Colleges and Universities (NTPA) .... AAC&U
Association of American Colleges Arts Program (SAUO) .... AACAP
Association of American Collegiate Literary Societies (EA) .... AACLS
Association of American Correspondents in London [*England*] (EA) .... AACL
[*The*] **Association of American Cultures** (EA) .... TAAC
Association of American Dance Companies [*Defunct*] (EA) .... AADC
Association of American Dentists .... AAD
Association of American Editorial Cartoonists (EA) .... AAEC
Association of American Engineering Societies (SAUO) .... AAES
Association of American Feed Control Officials (EA) .... AAFCO
Association of American Fertilizer Control Officials [*Later, AAPFCO*] (EA) .... AAFCO
Association of American Foreign Service Women (EA) .... AAFSW
Association of American Geographers (EA) .... AAG
Association of American Geographers (SAUO) .... AAG
Association of American Geographers Annals [*A publication*] (BRI) .... AAAGA
Association of American Historic Inns (EA) .... AAHI
Association of American Indian Affairs (SAUO) .... AAIA
Association of American Indian and Alaska Native Social Workers [*Later, NISWA*] (EA) .... AAIANSW
Association of American Indian Physicians (EA) .... AAIP
Association of American Indian Social Workers [*Later, NISWA*] (EA) .... AAISW
Association of American Jurists (EA) .... AAJ
Association of American Law Schools (EA) .... AALS
Association of American Library Schools (BARN) .... AAIS
Association of American Library Schools (SAUO) .... AALS
Association of American Medical Book Publishers [*Later, AMPA*] (EA) .... AAMBP
Association of American Medical Colleges (EA) .... AAMC
Association of American Military Uniform Collectors (EA) .... AAMUC
Association of American Motorcycle Road Racers [*Defunct*] (EA) .... AAMRR

Association of American Pesticide Control Officials (EA) .... AAPCO
Association of American Pesticide Control Officials (or Officers) (SAUS) .... AAPCO
Association of American Pesticides Control Officers (SAUO) .... AAPCO
Association of American Physicians (EA) .... AAP
Association of American Physicians and Surgeons (EA) .... AAPS
Association of American Plant Food Control Officials (EA) .... AAPFCO
Association of American Playing Card Manufacturers [*Defunct*] (EA) .... AAPCM
Association of American Publishers (EA) .... AAP
Association of American Publishers Political Action Commitee (EA) .... AAP/PAC
Association of American Publishers/Professional and Scholarly Publishing Division (SAUO) .... AAP/PSP
Association of American Railroad Dining Car Officers (EA) .... AARDCO
Association of American Railroads (EA) .... AAR
Association of American Railroads/ Bureau of Explosives (SAUS) .... AAR/BOE
Association of American Railroads, Economics and Finance Department Library, Washington, DC [*Library symbol*] [*Library of Congress*] (LCLS) .... DBRE
Association of American Railroads Operating Transportation Division (SAUO) .... AAROTD
Association of American Railroads/Bureau of Explosives (SAUO) .... AAR/BOE
Association of American Rhodes Scholars .... AAR
Association of American Rhodes Scholars (EA) .... AARS
Association of American Rod and Gun Clubs (SAUO) .... AARGC
Association of American Rod and Gun Clubs, Europe (EA) .... AARGCE
Association of American Schools in South America (EA) .... AASSA
Association of American Seed Control Officials (EA) .... AASCO
Association of American Ship Owners (EA) .... AASO
Association of American Soap and Glycerine Producers (SAUO) .... AASGP
Association of American State Boards of Examiners in Veterinary Medicine (SAUO) .... AASBEVM
Association of American State Boards of Examiners in Veterinary Medicine [*Later, AAVSB*] (EA) .... AASBEVM
Association of American State Geologists [*Defunct*] (EA) .... AASG
Association of American Steel Manufacturers .... AASM
[*The*] **Association of American Sword Collectors** (EA) .... TAASC
Association of American Universities (EA) .... AAU
Association of American University Presses (EA) .... AAUP
Association of American Veterinary Medical Colleges (EA) .... AAVMC
Association of American Vintners (EA) .... AAV
Association of American Volunteer Physicians (EA) .... AAVP
Association of American Weather Observers (EA) .... AAWO
Association of American Wives of Europeans (EA) .... AAWE
Association of American Women Dentists (SAUO) .... AAWD
Association of American Wood Pulp Importers (EA) .... AAWPI
Association of American Youth of Ukrainian Descent (EA) .... ODUM
Association of American-Chinese Professionals (EA) .... AACP
Association of Americans and Canadians for Aliyah [*Later, North American AliyahMovement*] .... AACA
Association of Americans and Canadians in Israel (EA) .... AACI
Association of Americans Resident Overseas (EA) .... AARO
Association of Americas Public Television Stations (SAUS) .... AAPTS
Association of America's Public Television Stations (NTPA) .... APTS
Association of Amusement Park Proprietors (SAUO) .... AAPP
Association of Anaesthetists (SAUO) .... AA
Association of Anaesthetists (DAVI) .... AA
Association of Analytical Chemists, Inc. .... AAC
Association of Analytical Chemists, Inc. (EA) .... ANACHEM
Association of Ancient Historians (EA) .... AAH
Association of Anglican Musicians (EA) .... AAM
Association of Apex Clubs of Australia .... AACA
Association of Apollo-Soyuz Test Project Philatelists (EA) .... A-ASTP-P
Association of Appliance and Home Entertainment Distributors [*Defunct*] (EA) .... AAHED
Association of Applied Biologists [*Midlothian, Scotland*] (EA) .... AAB
Association of Applied Insect Ecologists (EA) .... AAIE
Association of Applied Psychoanalysis (SAUS) .... AAP
Association of Applied Psychologists (DIPS) .... AAP
Association of Arab Engineers (SAUO) .... AAE
Association of Arab Institutes and Centres for Economic and Social Development Research (SAUO) .... AICARDES
Association of Arab Universities [*Amman, Jordan*] (EAIO) .... AARU
Association of Arab-American University Graduates (EA) .... AAUG
Association of Architects and Surveyors (SAUO) .... AAS
Association of Architects, Engineers, Surveyors and Draughtsmen of Australia (SAUS) .... AAESDA
Association of Architects, Surveyors, and Technical Assistants (SAUO) .... AASTA
Association of Architectural Hardware Manufacturers (EA) .... AAHM
Association of Architectural Librarians (EA) .... AAL
Association of Architectural Technologists of Ontario (AC) .... AATO
Association of Area Business Publications (EA) .... AABP
Association of Area Medical Officers [*British*] .... AAMO
Association of Arizona Food Banks (SRA) .... AAFB
Association of Arkansas Counties (SRA) .... AAC
Association of Art Historians [*British*] (EAIO) .... AAH
Association of Art Institutions [*British*] .... AAI
Association of Art Museum Directors (EA) .... AAMD
Association of Artist-Run Galleries (EA) .... AARG
Association of Arts Administration Educators (EA) .... AAAE
Association of Arts Centres in Scotland [*British*] .... AACS
Association of Asbestos Cement Pipe Producers (EA) .... AACPP
Association of Asian Indians in America (EA) .... AAIA
Association of Asian Open Universities (SAUO) .... AAOU
Association of Asian Pacific Community Health Organizations (SAUO) .... AAPCHO
Association of Asian Social Science Research Councils [*New Delhi, India*] .... AASSREC
Association of Asian-American Chambers of Commerce [*Washington, DC*] (EA) .... AAACC
Association of Asian/Pacific American Artists (EA) .... AAPAA
Association of Asphalt Paving Technologists (EA) .... AAPT
Association of Assistant Librarians .... AAL
Association of Assistant Mistresses in Secondary Schools (SAUO) .... AAMSS
Association of Assistant Mistresses, Inc. [*British*] .... AAMI
Association of Astronomy Educators .... AAE
Association of Atlantic Universities [*Association des Universites de l'Atlantique*] (AC) .... AAU
Association of Atlantic Universities/ Blackwell North America (SAUS) .... AAU/BNA
Association of Atlantic Universities/Blackwell North America [*Project*] [*Information service or system*] (IID) .... AAU/BNA
Association of Atlantic University Business Officers (SAUO) .... AAUBO
Association of Attenders and Alumni of The Hague Academy of International Law (EA) .... AAAHAIL
Association of Auctioneers and Landed Property Agents (SAUO) .... AALPA
Association of Audio-Visual Technicians (EA) .... AAVT
Association of Australian Investigators .... AAI
Association of Australian Marine Port and Marine Authorities Inc. (SAUS) .... AAPMA
Association of Australian Port and Marine Authorities Inc. (SAUO) .... AAPMA
Association of Australian Rural Nurses (SAUO) .... AARN
Association of Australian Teachers of English (SAUO) .... AATE
Association of Australian University Presses .... AAUP
Association of Authorized Public Accountants [*British*] (DBA) .... AAPA
Association of Authors Agents (SAUS) .... AAA
Association of Authors Representatives (SAUS) .... AAR
Association of Authors' Representatives (NTPA) .... AAR
Association of Auto and Truck Recyclers (SAUO) .... AATR
Association of Auto and Truck Recyclers [*Later, ADRA*] (EA) .... AATR
Association of Autoelectrical Technicians Ltd. [*British*] (BI) .... AET
Association of Auto-Electrical Technicians Ltd. (SAUO) .... AET
Association of Automotive Aftermarket Distributors (EA) .... AAAD
Association of Average Adjusters of the United States [*New York, NY*] (EA) .... AAA
Association of Average Adjusters of the United States .... AAAUS
Association of Avian Veterinarians (EA) .... AAV
Association of Avian Veterinarias (SAUO) .... AAV
Association of Aviation and Space Museums [*Defunct*] (EA) .... AASM
Association of Aviation Engine Manufacturers (SAUO) .... ASSAD
Association of Aviation Maintenance Organizations (EAIO) .... AMOSA
Association of Aviation Psychologists (EA) .... AAP
Association of Balloon and Airship Constructors (EA) .... ABAC
Association of Ballrooms [*British*] (EAIO) .... ABL
Association of Bank Holding Companies [*Washington, DC*] (EA) .... ABHC
Association of Bank Travel Bureaus [*Defunct*] (EA) .... ABTB
Association of Banking Teachers [*British*] (DBA) .... ABT
Association of Bankrupts (EAIO) .... AB
Association of Banks in Singapore (SAUO) .... ABS
Association of Banyan Users International (VERA) .... ABUI
Association of Baptist Chaplains (EA) .... ABC
Association of Baptist Churches of the Australian Capital Territory .... ABCACT
Association of Baptist Homes and Hospitals [*Later, ABHHA*] (EA) .... ABHH
Association of Baptist Homes and Hospitals (SAUO) .... ABHH
Association of Baptist Professors of Religion .... ABPR
Association of Baptists for World Evangelism (EA) .... ABWE
Association of Battery Recyclers (NTPA) .... ABR
Association of Battlefords Realtors (AC) .... BREB
Association of Bay Area Governments [*California*] (GEOI) .... ABAG
Association of Beauty Teachers [*British*] .... ABT
Association of Bedding and Furniture Law Officials (EA) .... ABFLO
Association of Bee Appliance Manufacturers (SAUO) .... ABAM
Association of Behavioral Healthcare Management (SAUO) .... ABHM
Association of Bendectin Children [*Later, ABDC*] (EA) .... ABC
Association of Better Business Bureaus [*Later, CBBB*] .... ABBB
Association of Better Business Bureaus (SAUO) .... ABBB
Association of Better Computer Dealers (SAUO) .... ABCD
Association of Better Computer Dealers [*Later, ABCD: The Microcomputer IndustryAssociation*] (EA) .... ABCD
Association of Beverage Container Recyclers (EA) .... ABCR
Association of Bibliographic Agencies of Britain, Australia, Canada, and the United States (ADA) .... ABACUS
Association of Bibliophiles (SAUO) .... AIB
Association of Biological Collections Appraisers (EA) .... ABCA
Association of Biomedical Communication Directors (EA) .... ABCD
Association of Biomolecular Resource Facilities (HGEN) .... ABRF
Association of Biotechnology Companies (EA) .... ABC
Association of Birmingham Clearing Banks (SAUO) .... ABCB
Association of Birth Defect Children (EA) .... ABDC
Association of Bituminous Contractors (EA) .... ABC
Association of Black Admissions and Financial Aid Officers of the Ivy League andSister Schools (EA) .... ABAFAOILSS
Association of Black Anthropologists (EA) .... ABA
Association of Black Cardiologists (EA) .... ABC
Association of Black Catholics Against Abortion (EA) .... ABC
Association of Black CPA [*Certified Public Accountant*] **Firms** [*Defunct*] (EA) .... ABCPAF
Association of Black Foundation Executives (EA) .... ABFE
Association of Black Motion Picture and Television Producers (EA) .... ABMPTP

Association of Black Nursing Faculty in Higher Education (EA) ... ABNF
Association of Black Psychologists (EA) ... ABP
Association of Black Psychologists (EA) ... ABPsi
Association of Black Sociologists (EA) ... ABS
Association of Black Storytellers (EA) ... ABS
Association of Black Women Entrepreneurs (NTPA) ... ABWE
Association of Black Women Historians (EA) ... ABWH
Association of Black Women in Higher Education (EA) ... ABWHE
Association of Blauvelt Descendants (EA) ... ABD
Association of Blind and Partially Sighted Teachers and Students [*British*] ... ABPSTS
Association of Blind and Partially-Sighted Teachers and Students [*British*] ... ABAPSTAS
Association of Blind and Partially-Sights Teachers and Students (SAUO) ... ABAPSTAS
Association of Blind Chartered Physiotherapists (EA) ... ABCP
Association of Blind Chartered Physiotherapists (SAUO) ... ATBCP
Association of Blind Citizens of New South Wales [*Australia*] ... ABCNSW
Association of Blind Piano Tuners [*British*] (BI) ... ABPT
Association of Blood Donor Recruiters [*Defunct*] (EA) ... ABDR
Association of Board Makers [*British*] (DBA) ... ABM
Association of Boards of Certification (EA) ... ABC
Association of Boiler Setters, Chimney and Furnace Constructors [*British*] (BI) ... ABSC
Association of Bone and Joint Surgeons (EA) ... ABJS
Association of Book Publishers of British Columbia (AC) ... ABPBC
Association of Book Travelers (EA) ... ABT
Association of Borderlands Scholars (NTPA) ... ABS
Association of Bottled Beer Collectors (EAIO) ... ABBC
Association of Boys and Girls Clubs Professionals (EA) ... ABGCP
Association of Boys and Students Clothing Manufacturers (EA) ... ABSCM
Association of Brass and Bronze Ingot Manufacturers (EA) ... ABBIM
Association of Breastfeeding Mothers (EAIO) ... ABM
Association of Brethren Caregivers (EA) ... ABC
Association of Brewers (SAUO) ... AB
Association of Brewers [*Later, AOB*] (EA) ... AB
Association of Brewers (EA) ... AOB
Association of Bridal Consultants (EA) ... ABC
Association of British Abattoir Owners (SAUO) ... ABAO
Association of British Adoption and Fostering Agencies (DI) ... ABAFA
Association of British Aero Clubs (BI) ... ABAC
Association of British Aero Clubs and Centres (SAUO) ... ABAC
Association of British and International Hairdressers and Hairdressing Schools (DBA) ... ABIH
Association of British Aviation Consultants (DA) ... ABAC
Association of British Brush Machinery Manufacturer.s (SAUS) ... ABBMM
Association of British Certification Bodies (SAUO) ... ABCB
Association of British Chambers of Commerce (SAUO) ... ABBCC
Association of British Chambers of Commerce ... ABCC
Association of British Chemical Manufacturers (SAUO) ... ABCM
Association of British Chemical Manufacturers (BARN) ... ABCM
Association of British Climatologists (EAIO) ... ABC
Association of British Columbia Archivists (SAUO) ... ABCA
Association of British Columbia Grape Growers (AC) ... ABCGG
Association of British Columbia Libraries (SAUO) ... ABCL
Association of British Columbia Professional Foresters (AC) ... ABCPF
Association of British Conference Organisers (BI) ... ABCO
Association of British Correspondence Colleges (EAIO) ... ABCC
Association of British Correspondence Colleges (SAUO) ... ABCC
Association of British Counties (DBA) ... ABC
Association of British Creditors of Russia (SAUO) ... ABCR
Association of British Dental Surgery Assistants ... ABDSA
Association of British Detectives (DI) ... ABD
Association of British Directory Publishers (EAIO) ... ABDP
Association of British Dispensing Opticians (DBA) ... ABDO
Association of British Dogs' Homes (GVA) ... ABDH
Association of British Editors (EAIO) ... ABE
Association of British Factors ... ABF
Association of British Factors and Discounters (EAIO) ... ABFD
Association of British Foam Laminators (BI) ... ABFL
Association of British Generating Set Manufacturers (MHDB) ... ABGSM
Association of British Geodesists ... ABG
Association of British Hairdressers (SAUO) ... ABH
Association of British Hairdressers and Hairdressing Schools ... ABH
Association of British Hardware Manufacturers (SAUO) ... ABHM
Association of British Healthcare Industries (COBU) ... ABHI
Association of British Hispanists ... ABH
Association of British Independent Oil Exploration Companies ... BRINDEX
Association of British Industries (SAUO) ... ABOI
Association of British Insecticide Manufacturers (DI) ... ABIM
Association of British Insurers (EAIO) ... ABI
Association of British Introduction Agencies (EAIO) ... ABIA
Association of British Investigators (EAIO) ... ABI
Association of British Launderers and Cleaners (DI) ... ABLC
Association of British Launderers and Cleaners (SAUO) ... ABLC
Association of British Library and Information Science Schools ... ABLISS
Association of British Library and Information Studies Schools (DBA) ... ABLISS
Association of British Library Schools ... ABLS
Association of British Malaya (SAUO) ... ABM
Association of British Manufacturers of Agricultural Chemicals (BI) ... ABMAC
Association of British Manufacturers of Printers' Machinery (DI) ... ABMPM
Association of British Marketing Research Companies (DBA) ... ABMRC
Association of British Meat Processors (DBA) ... ABMP
Association of British Mining Equipment Companies (EAIO) ... ABMEC
Association of British Mining Equipment Exporters (MHDB) ... ABMEX
Association of British Neurologists ... ABN
Association of British Oceanic Industries (DS) ... ABOI
Association of British Oceanic (or Oceanological) Industries (SAUO) ... ABOI
Association of British Offshore Industries (DBA) ... ABOI
Association of British Orchestras (DBA) ... ABO
Association of British Organic and Compound Fertilisers Ltd. (BI) ... ABOCF
Association of British Organic Fertilisers (SAUO) ... ABOF
Association of British Orientalists ... ABO
Association of British Packing Contractors (BI) ... ABPC
Association of British Paediatric Nurses ... ABPN
Association of British Pewter Craftsmen ... ABPC
Association of British Pharmaceutical Industry (SAUS) ... ABPI
Association of British Picture Restorers ... ABPR
Association of British Plywood and Veneer Manufacturers (BI) ... ABPVM
Association of British Plywood and Veneer Manufacturers (SAUO) ... ABPVM
Association of British Professional Conference Organisers (COBU) ... ABPCO
Association of British Reclaimed Rubber Manufacturers (BI) ... ABRRM
Association of British Riding Schools (BI) ... ABRS
Association of British Riding Schools (SAUO) ... ABRS
Association of British Roofing Felt Manufacturers Ltd. (SAUO) ... ABRFM
Association of British Roofing Felt Manufacturers Ltd. (BI) ... ABRFM
Association of British Rose Producers (SAUO) ... ABRP
Association of British Sailmakers (DBA) ... ABS
Association of British Science Writers ... ABSW
Association of British Secretaries in America ... ABSA
Association of British Solid Fuel Appliance Manufacturers (DBA) ... ABSAM
Association of British Sound Reinforcement Engineers (WDAA) ... ABSRE
Association of British Spectroscopists (DBA) ... ABS
Association of British Steriliser Manufacturers (EAIO) ... ABSM
Association of British Steriliser (or Sterilizer) Manufacturers (SAUO) ... ABSM
Association of British Theatre Technicians, London W.1 (SAUO) ... ABTT
Association of British Theological and Philosophical Libraries ... ABTAPL
Association of British Theological and Philosophical Libraries (SAUO) ... ABTPL
Association of British Transport Museums ... ABTM
Association of British Travel Agents ... ABTA
Association of British Tree Surgeons and Arborists (DI) ... ABTSA
Association of British Veterinary Acupuncture (DBA) ... ABVA
Association of British Wild Animal Keepers (DBA) ... ABWAK
Association of British Yacht Agents (SAUO) ... ABYA
Association of British Yacht Agents (BI) ... ABYA
Association of British Zoologists (BI) ... ABZ
Association of British Zoologists (SAUO) ... Assn Brit Zool
Association of Broadcasting Journalists (SAUO) ... ABJ
Association of Broadcasting Staff [*A union*] [*British*] (DCTA) ... ABS
Association of Brokers and Yacht Agents [*British*] (DBA) ... ABYA
Association of Bronze and Brass Founders [*British*] (BI) ... ABBF
Association of Builders' Hardware Manufacturers (EAIO) ... ABHM
Association of Building Centres [*British*] (BI) ... ABC
Association of Building Component Manufacturers (EAIO) ... ABCM
Association of Building Contractors of Quebec (AC) ... ABCQ
Association of Building Services Agencies (COBU) ... ABSA
Association of Building Technicians [*A union*] [*British*] ... ABT
Association of Burglary Insurance Surveyors [*British*] (DI) ... ABIS
Association of Burglary Insurance Surveyors-Australia (SAUO) ... ABISA
Association of Burroughs Computer Users (SAUO) ... ABCU
Association of Business Administration Studies [*British*] (EAIO) ... ABAS
Association of Business Advertising Agencies [*British*] (DBA) ... ABAA
Association of Business and Administrative Computing (MHDB) ... ABAC
Association of Business and Industry [*Iowa*] (SRA) ... ABI
Association of Business and Professional Women in Construction (EA) ... ABPWC
Association of Business Centres [*British*] (DBA) ... ABC
Association of Business Executives [*British*] (DBA) ... ABE
Association of Business Form Manufacturers (SAUO) ... ABFM
Association of Business Forms Manufacturers [*Defunct*] (EA) ... ABFM
Association of Business Officers of Preparatory Schools (EA) ... ABOPS
Association of Business Product Manufacturers (EA) ... ABPM
Association of Business Publishers (EA) ... ABP
Association of Business Schools (COBU) ... ABS
Association of Button Merchants (EAIO) ... ABM
Association of Buying Offices [*Defunct*] (EA) ... ABO
Association of Byelorussian American Veterans in America (EA) ... ZBAV
Association of C and C++ Users (SAUO) ... ACCU
Association of Cable Television Suppliers (EA) ... ACTS
Association of California Community College Administrators (SAUO) ... ACCCA
Association of California Enhanced Telemessaging Services (SRA) ... ACETS
Association of California Hospital Districts (SRA) ... ACHD
Association of California Hospitals (SAUO) ... ACH
Association of California Insurance Companies (SRA) ... ACIC
Association of California Life Insurance Companies (SRA) ... ACLIC
Association of California School Administrators (SRA) ... ACSA
Association of California State Attorneys (SRA) ... ACSA
Association of California State College Professors (SAUO) ... ACSCP
Association of California Surety Companies (SRA) ... ACSC
Association of California Water Agencies (SRA) ... ACWA
Association of Cambodian Survivors of America (EA) ... ACSA
Association of Cambridge University Assistants (SAUO) ... ACUA
Association of Camp Nurses (EA) ... ACN
Association of Camps Farthest Out (EA) ... CFO
Association of Canadian Teaching Hospitals (AC) ... ACTH
Association of Canadian Advertisers, Inc. (WDMC) ... ACA
Association of Canadian Alumni Administrators (NFD) ... ACAA
Association of Canadian Archivists ... ACA
Association of Canadian Bible Colleges (AC) ... ACBC

Association of Canadian Biscuit Manufacturers [*Association Canadienne des Manufacturiers de Biscuits*] (AC) .... ACBM
Association of Canadian Choral Conductors [*Association des Chefs des Choeurs Canadiens*] .... ACCC
Association of Canadian College and University Teachers of French .... ACCUTF
Association of Canadian Commercial Testing Laboratories and Consultants .... ACCTLC
Association of Canadian Community Colleges [*Association des Colleges Communautaires du Canada*] .... ACCC
Association of Canadian Courts Administrators (AC) .... ACCA
Association of Canadian Distillers [*Association des Distallateurs Canadiens*] (AC) .... ACD
Association of Canadian Editorial Cartoonists (AC) .... ACEC
Association of Canadian Faculties of Dentistry .... ACFD
Association of Canadian Faculties of Environmental Studies (SAUO) .... ACFES
Association of Canadian Film Craftspeople (AC) .... ACFC
Association of Canadian Financial Corporations (AC) .... ACFC
Association of Canadian Fire Marshals (SAUO) .... ACFM
Association of Canadian Fire Marshals and Fire Commissioners (SAUO) .... ACFMFC
Association of Canadian Fire Marshals & Fire Commissioners [*L'Association Canadienne des Directeurs et Commissaires des Incendies*] (AC) .... ACFM-FC
Association of Canadian Industrial Designers .... ACID
Association of Canadian Interpreters .... ACI
Association of Canadian Land Surveyors (GEOI) .... ACLS
Association of Canadian Law Teachers .... ACLT
Association of Canadian Manufacturers (BARN) .... ACM
Association of Canadian Map Libraries (GEOI) .... ACML
Association of Canadian Map Libraries and Archives (EAIO) .... ACMLA
Association of Canadian Medical Colleges (AC) .... ACMC
Association of Canadian Mountain Guides [*Association des Guides de Montagne Canadiens*] (AC) .... ACMG
Association of Canadian Orchestras .... ACO
Association of Canadian Pension Management .... ACPM
Association of Canadian Publishers .... ACP
Association of Canadian Television and Radio Artists .... ACTRA
Association of Canadian Underwater Councils .... ACUC
Association of Canadian Universities for Northern Studies .... ACUNS
Association of Canadian University and College Teachers of French .... ACUCTF
Association of Canadian University Information Bureaus [*See also ABUIC*] .... ACUIB
Association of Canadian University Presses .... ACUP
Association of Canadian University Teachers of English .... ACUTE
Association of Canadian University Teachers of French .... ACUTF
Association of Canadian Venture Capital Companies .... ACVCC
Association of Canadian Women Composers .... ACWC
Association of Cancer Online Resources (SAUO) .... ACOR
Association of Car Fleet Operators [*British*] (DBA) .... ACFO
Association of Career Teachers [*British*] .... ACT
Association of Career Training Schools [*Defunct*] (EA) .... ACTS
Association of Caribbean Historians [*Nassau, Bahamas*] (EAIO) .... ACH
Association of Caribbean Studies (EA) .... ACS
Association of Caribbean Universities and Research Institutes (SAUS)..... UNICA
Association of Caribbean University and Research Institute Libraries..... ACURIL
Association of Caribbean University and Research Institute Libraries (SAUO) .... ACURIL
Association of Caribbean University and Research Libraries (SAUO) ...... ACURL
Association of Carpathian Region Universities (SAUO) .... ACRU
Association of Cartonboard Makers [*British*] (DBA) .... ACBM
Association of Casing Importers (SAUO) .... ASCIM
Association of Casing Importers Ltd. [*British*] (BI) .... ASCIM
Association of Casualty Accountants and Statisticians [*Later, SIA*] .... ACAS
Association of Casualty Accountants and Statisticians (SAUO) .... ACAS
Association of Casualty and Surety Companies (SAUO) .... ACSC
Association of Casualty and Surety Companies [*Later, AIA*] (EA) .... ACSC
Association of Casualty and Surety Executives (SAUO) .... ACSE
Association of Casualty Care Personnel [*Canada*] .... ACCP
Association of Catholic Colleges and Universities (EA) .... ACCU
Association of Catholic Diocesan Archivists (EA) .... ACDA
Association of Catholic School Principals [*Australia*] .... ACSP
Association of Catholic Teachers [*Defunct*] .... ACT
Association of Catholic Trade Unionists (EA) .... ACTU
Association of Catholic TV and Radio Syndicators (EA) .... ACTRS
Association of CCTV [*Closed Circuit Television*] Surveyors (EAIO) .... ACCTVS
Association of Celebrity Personal Assistants (NTPA) .... ACPA
Association of Centers of Medieval and Renaissance Studies [*Later, CARA*] (EA) .... ACOMARS
Association of Central American Departments of Medicine (SAUO) .... ACAFAM
Association of Centres of Excellence in Foreign Language Training (COBU) .... ACCENT
Association of Cereal Food Manufacturers (EAIO) .... ACFM
Association of Cereal Research (SAUO) .... AGF
Association of Certification Bodies [*British*] (DBA) .... ACB
Association of Certified Accountants (EAIO) .... ACA
Association of Certified and Chartered Accountants (SAUO) .... ACCA
Association of Certified and Corporate Accountants (SAUO) .... ACCA
Association of Certified and Corporate Accountants [*British*] .... ACCA
Association of Certified Fraud Examiners (NTPA) .... ACFE
Association of Certified Liquidators (EA) .... ACL
Association of Certified Professional Secretaries (NTPA) .... ACPS
Association of Certified Public Accountant Examiners (SAUO) .... ACPAE
Association of Certified Public Accountant Examiners [*Later, NASBA*] (EA) .... ACPAE
Association of Certified Servers (EA) .... ACS

Association of Certified Social Workers .... ACSW
Association of Certified Survey Technicians and Technologists of Ontario [*Canada*] (GEOI) .... ACSTTO
Association of Chairmen of Departments of Mechanics (EA) .... ACDM
Association of Chambers of Automobile Manufacturers of the Andean Group (SAUO) .... CAFANDINA
Association of Chambers of Commerce (SAUO) .... ACC
Association of Chambers of Commerce (SAUO) .... ASSOCOM
Association of Chambers of Commerce of Ireland (DI) .... ACCI
Association of Charity Officers (EAIO) .... ACO
Association of Chart and Technical Analysts [*British*] .... ACTA
Association of Charter Trustees [*British*] .... ACT
Association of Charter Trustees and Urban Parish Councils [*British*] (DBA) .... ACT & UPC
Association of Chartered Accountants (SAUO) .... ACA
Association of Chartered Accountants in the United States (EA) .... ACAUS
Association of Chartered Accountants Students Societies (SAUO) .... ACASS
Association of Chartered Industrial Designers of Ontario (AC) .... ACIDO
Association of Chartered Physiotherapists in Animal Therapy (GVA) .... ACPAT
Association of Chartered Physiotherapists in Sports Medicine (EAIO) .... ACPSM
Association of Chemical and Allied Employees (SAUS) .... AC&AE
Association of Chemical and Allied Employers (SAUO) .... AC&AE
Association of Chemical Industry of Texas (SRA) .... ACIT
Association of Chief Administrators of Health Authorities [*British*] .... ACAHA
Association of Chief Ambulance Officers [*British*] (DBA) .... ACAO
Association of Chief Architects of Scottish Local Authorities (EAIO) ..... ACASLA
Association of Chief Business Officials (SAUO) .... ACBO
Association of Chief Education Officers [*British*] (BI) .... ACEO
Association of Chief Education Social Workers [*British*] (DBA) .... ACESW
Association of Chief Executives of National Voluntary Organisations (COBU) .... ACENVO
Association of Chief Officers of Police (SAUO) .... ACOP
Association of Chief Officers of Police [*British*] (DI) .... ACOP
Association of Chief Officers of Probation [*British*] (DBA) .... ACOP
Association of Chief Police Officers [*British*] .... ACPO
Association of Chief Police Officers of England, Wales and Northern Ireland (SAUO) .... ACPOEWNI
Association of Chief State School Audio-Visual Officers [*Defunct*] (EA) .... ACSSAVO
Association of Chief Technical Officers (EAIO) .... ACTO
Association of Child Advocates (EA) .... ACA
Association of Child and Adolescent Psychiatric Nurses .... ACAPN
Association of Child Care Centers in New South Wales [*Australia*] ...... ACCCNSW
Association of Child Care Officers [*British*] (DI) .... ACCO
Association of Child Psychotherapists (EAIO) .... ACP
Association of Children's Officers [*British*] (DI) .... ACO
Association of Children's Prosthetic-Orthotic Clinics (EA) .... ACPOC
Association of Childrens Prosthetic-Orthotic Clinics (SAUS) .... ACPOC
Association of Chinese and American Engineers .... ACAE
Association of Chinese from Indochina [*Later, SEAC*] (EA) .... ACI
Association of Chiropodists (NADA) .... NAC
Association of Chiropractic Colleges (EA) .... ACC
Association of Choral Conductors (EA) .... ACC
Association of Christian Centres in Europe (SAUO) .... ACCE
Association of Christian Church Educators (EA) .... ACCE
Association of Christian Institutions for Social Concern in Asia (SAUO) .... ACISCA
Association of Christian Lay Centres in Africa (SAUO) .... ACLCA
Association of Christian Librarians (EA) .... ACL
Association of Christian Schools International (EA) .... ACSI
Association of Christian Teachers [*British*] (EAIO) .... ACT
Association of Christian Thinkers (WDAA) .... ACT
Association of Christian Universities and Colleges in Asia (EA) .... ACUCA
Association of Christians in Local Broadcasting [*British*] .... ACLB
Association of Church Missions Committees (EA) .... ACMC
Association of Cinema and Video Laboratories (EA) .... ACVL
Association of Cinema Laboratories [*Later, ACVL*] (EA) .... ACL
Association of Cinema Laboratories (SAUO) .... ACL
Association of Cinema Technicians (SAUO) .... ACT
Association of Cinematograph and Television Technicians (SAUS) .... ACTT
Association of Cinematograph, Television and Allied Technicians (SAUO) .... ACTATA
Association of Cinematograph, Television and Allied Technicians (SAUO) .... ACTT
Association of Cinematograph, Television, and Allied Technicians [*Canada*] .... ACTT
Association of Cinematograph, Television and allied Technicians (SAUS) .... ACTT
Association of Circus Proprietors of Great Britain (BI) .... ACP
Association of Civil Defence and Emergency Planning Officers [*British*] (DBA) .... ACDEPO
Association of Civil Service Temporary Clerks and Writers [*A union*] [*British*] .... ACSTCW
Association of Civilian Technicians (EA) .... ACT
Association of Civilian Technicians .... CTA
Association of Civilian Widows of Australia .... ACWA
Association of Clandestine Radio Enthusiasts (EA) .... ACE
Association of Classroom Teachers [*Defunct*] .... ACT
Association of Clerical, Technical, and Supervisory Staffs [*British*] (DCTA) .... ACTS
Association of Clerical, Technical and Supervisory Staffs (SAUO) .... ACTS
Association of Clerks and Stewards in Mental Hospitals [*A union*] [*British*] .... ACSMH
Association of Clerks and Stewards of Mental Hospitals (SAUO) .... ACSMH
Association of Clinical Biochemists [*British*] .... ACB

Association of Clinical Biochemists (SAUO) ... Assn Clin Biochem
Association of Clinical Pathologists (SAUO) ... ACP
Association of Clinical Pathologists ... ACP
Association of Clinical Research [*British*] (DBA) ... ACR
Association of Clinical Research for the Pharmaceutical Industry (SAUO) ... ACRPI
Association of Clinical Research Pharmaceutical Industries [*British*] (DBA) ... ACRPI
Association of Clinical Research Professionals (SAUO) ... ACRP
Association of Clinical Scientists (EA) ... ACS
Association of Clinical Scientists (NTPA) ... Ass Clin Sci
Association of Clinicians for the Underserved (SAUO) ... ACU
Association of Coffee Mill Enthusiasts (EA) ... ACME
Association of Coffee Producing Countries ... ACPC
Association of College Administration Professionals (NTPA) ... ACAP
Association of College Admissions Counselors (SAUO) ... ACAC
Association of College Admissions Counselors [*Later, NACAC*] (EA) ... ACAC
Association of College and Research Libraries [*American Library Association*] (EA) ... ACRL
Association of College & Research Libraries Acquisitions Section ... ACRLAS
Association of College & Research Libraries African American Studies Librarians Section ... ACRLAASLS
Association of College & Research Libraries Asian, African, & Middle Eastern Section ... ACRLAAMES
Association of College & Research Libraries Digital Libraries Section ... ACRLDLS
Association of College & Research Libraries Instruction Section ... ACRLIS
Association of College & Research Libraries Library Public Relations Council ... ACRLLPRC
Association of College and University Auditors [*Madison, WI*] (EA) ... ACUA
Association of College and University Broadcasting Stations (NTCM) ... ACUBS
Association of College and University Business Officers (NFD) ... ACUBO
Association of College and University Concert Managers (SAUO) ... ACUCM
Association of College and University Concert Managers [*Later, ACUCAA*] ... ACUCM
Association of College and University Housing Officers [*Later, ACUHO-I*] (EA) ... ACUHO
Association of College and University Housing Officers (SAUO) ... ACUHO
Association of College and University Housing Officers - International (EA) ... ACUHO-I
Association of College and University Housing Officers-International (SAUO) ... ACUHO-I
Association of College and University Museums and Galleries (EA) ... ACUMG
Association of College and University Offices (EA) ... ACUO
Association of College and University Printers (EA) ... ACUP
Association of College and University Telecommunications Administrators (EA) ... ACUTA
Association of College and University Telecommunications Administrators (SAUS) ... ACUTA
Association of College Auxiliary Services [*Later, NACAS*] (EA) ... ACAS
Association of College Auxiliary Services (SAUO) ... ACAS
Association of College Educators: Deaf and Hard of Hearing (NTPA) ... ACE-DHH
Association of College Honor Societies (EA) ... ACHS
Association of College Management [*British*] (DBA) ... ACM
Association of College Professors of Textiles and Clothing (EA) ... ACPTC
Association of College Registrars [*British*] ... ACR
Association of College Registrars and Administrators [*British*] ... ACRA
Association of College Unions [*Later, ACU-I*] (EA) ... ACU
Association of College Unions (SAUO) ... ACU
Association of College Unions-International (NTPA) ... ACUI
Association of College, University and Community Arts Administrators (SAUO) ... ACUCAA
Association of College, University, and Community Arts Administrators [*Later, APAP*] (EA) ... ACUCAA
Association of Colleges and Secondary Schools (SAUO) ... ACSC
Association of Colleges and Secondary Schools (SAUO) ... ACSS
Association of Colleges and Secondary Schools [*Later, SACS*] (EA) ... ACSS
Association of Colleges and Secondary Schools for Negroes [*Later, ACSS*] ... ACSSN
Association of Colleges and Universities for International Intercultural Studies (SAUO) ... ACUIIS
Association of Colleges and Universities for International-Intercultural Studies [*Defunct*] (EA) ... ACUIIS
Association of Colleges and Universities of the State of New York (SAUO) ... ACUSNY
Association of Colleges for Further and Higher Education [*British*] (EAIO) ... ACFHE
Association of Colleges Implementing the Diploma of Higher Education [*British*] ... ACID
Association of Colleges of Applied Arts & Technology of Ontario [*Association des Colleges d'Arts Appliquees et de Technologie de l'Ontario*] (AC) ... ACAATO
Association of Colleges of Podiatry (SAUO) ... AACP
Association of Collegiale Schools of Planning (SAUO) ... ACSP
Association of Collegiate Alumnae (SAUO) ... ACA
Association of Collegiate Business Schools and Programs (NTPA) ... ACBSP
Association of Collegiate Entrepreneurs (EA) ... ACE
Association of Collegiate Schools of Architecture (EA) ... ACSA
Association of Collegiate Schools of Nursing [*Later, NLN*] ... ACSN
Association of Collegiate Schools of Nursing (SAUO) ... ACSN
Association of Collegiate Schools of Planning (EA) ... ACSP
Association of Colored Railway Trainmen and Locomotive Firemen (SAUO) ... ACRTLF
Association of Combined Youth Clubs [*British*] (DBA) ... ACYC
[*The*] **Association of Comedy Artists** (EA) ... TACA
Association of Comics Enthusiasts (EAIO) ... ACE
Association of Commerce and Industry (EA) ... ACI
Association of Commerce and Industry of New Mexico (SRA) ... ACI-NM
Association of Commercial Diving Educators (EA) ... ACDE
Association of Commercial Finance Attorneys (EA) ... ACFA
Association of Commercial Finance Companies of New York [*Later, NCFA*] (EA) ... ACFC
Association of Commercial Mail Receiving Agencies [*Defunct*] (EA) ... ACMRA
Association of Commercial Records Centers (EA) ... ACRC
Association of Commissioned Officers (USDC) ... ACO
Association of Commodity Exchange Firms [*Later, Futures Industry Association*] (EA) ... ACEF
Association of Commodity Exchange Firms (SAUO) ... ACEF
Association of Commonwealth Archivists and Records Managers (EAIO) ... ACARM
Association of Commonwealth Students [*British*] (BI) ... ACS
Association of Commonwealth Universities [*British*] (EAIO) ... ACU
Association of Commonwealth Universities (SAUO) ... ACU
Association of Communication Engineers [*Charlotte, NC*] (TSSD) ... ACE
Association of Communications Technicians (EA) ... ACT
Association of Community Arts Agencies of Kansas (SRA) ... ACAAK
Association of Community Cancer Centers (EA) ... ACCC
Association of Community College Facilities (SAUO) ... ACCF
Association of Community College Trustees (EA) ... ACCT
Association of Community Colleges for Excellence in Systems and Services [*Consortium*] ... ACCESS
Association of Community Colleges for Excellence in Systems and Services (SAUO) ... ACCESS
Association of Community Health Councils (SAUO) ... ACHIC
Association of Community Health Nursing Educators (NTPA) ... ACHNE
Association of Community Home Schools [*British*] ... ACHS
Association of Community Information Centres in Ontario (AC) ... ACICO
Association of Community Mental Health Centers of Kansas (SRA) ... ACMHCK
Association of Community Organizations for Reform Now (EA) ... ACORN
Association of Community Radio Broadcasters (SAUO) ... AMARC
Association of Community Technical Aid Centres (SAUO) ... ACRAC
Association of Community Technical Aid Centres (EAIO) ... ACTAC
Association of Community Travel Clubs (EA) ... ACTC
Association of Community Tribal Schools (EA) ... ACTS
Association of Community Workers [*British*] ... ACW
Association of Commuter Airlines [*Later, NATA*] ... ACA
Association of Commuter Airlines (SAUO) ... ACA
Association of Compact Disk Publishers (EA) ... ACDP
Association of Company Registration Agents [*British*] (DBA) ... ACRA
Association of Comparative Haematology [*British*] (DBA) ... ACH
Association of Competition Car Manufacturers (SAUO) ... ACCM
Association of Competitive Telecommunications Suppliers (AC) ... ACTS
Association of Computer and CD-ROM Users (SAUO) ... ACCU
Association of Computer Consultants (EA) ... ACC
Association of Computer Educators (SAUO) ... ACE
Association of Computer Manufacturers (SAUO) ... ACM
Association of Computer Professionals (EA) ... ACP
Association of Computer Professionals Australia (SAUO) ... ACPA
Association of Computer Programmers and Analysts (EA) ... ACPA
Association of Computer Retailers (EA) ... ACR
Association of Computer Time-Sharing Users ... ACTSU
Association of Computer Training Professionals (NTPA) ... ACTP
Association of Computer Units in Colleges and Institutions of Higher Education (SAUO) ... ACUCHE
Association of Computer User Groups (SAUO) ... ACUG
Association of Computer Users (EA) ... ACU
Association of Computing Machinery Geographic Information Systems (GEOI) ... ACMGIS
Association of Computing Machinery Special Interest Group on Graphics (GEOI) ... ACM-SIGGRAPH
Association of Concentrated and Powdered Milk Manufacturers (SAUO) ... ACPMME
Association of Concentrated and Powdered Milk Manufacturers of the EEC (EAIO) ... ACPMME
Association of Concern for Ultimate Reality and Meaning (EA) ... ACURM
Association of Concern for Ultimate Reality & Meaning (AC) ... URAM
Association of Concerned African Scholars (EA) ... ACAS
Association of Concert Bands (EA) ... ACB
Association of Concert Bands of America [*Later, ACB*] (EA) ... ACBA
Association of Condominium Managers of Ontario (AC) ... ACMO
Association of Conference and Events Directors-International (EA) ... ACED-I
Association of Conference Executives (COBU) ... ACE
Association of Connecticut Career Schools (SRA) ... ACCS
Association of Connecticut Fairs (SRA) ... ACF
Association of Conservation Engineers (EA) ... ACE
Association of Conservation Officers (EAIO) ... ACO
Association of Conservative Clubs [*British*] (DBA) ... ACC
Association of Conservative Clubs (SAUO) ... ACC
Association of Construction Inspectors (SAUO) ... ACI
Association of Consultant Architects (EAIO) ... ACA
Association of Consultant (or Consulting) Architects (SAUO) ... ACA
Association of Consultant (or Consulting) Engineers of New Zealand (SAUO) ... ACENZ
Association of Consultant Quantity Surveyors (MHDI) ... ACQS
Association of Consultant Surveyors (SAUO) ... ACS
Association of Consulting Actuaries (EAIO) ... ACA
Association of Consulting Architects Australia ... ACAA
Association of Consulting Chemists and Chemical Engineers (EA) ... ACC & CE
Association of Consulting Chemists and Chemical Engineers (NTPA) ... ACCCE
Association of Consulting Chemists and Chemical Engineers (SAUO) ... ACCE

Association of Consulting Engineers [*British*] (DI) ... ACE
Association of Consulting Engineers of Alberta (AC) ... CEA
Association of Consulting Engineers of Canada ... ACEC
Association of Consulting Engineers of Great Britain ... ACE
Association of Consulting Engineers of Great Britain ... ACEGB
Association of Consulting Engineers of Ireland (EAIO) ... ACEI
Association of Consulting Engineers of Manitoba (AC) ... ACEM
Association of Consulting Engineers of Ontario (AC) ... CEO
Association of Consulting Engineers of Saskatchewan (AC) ... ACES
Association of Consulting Engineers of the Yukon (AC) ... CEY
Association of Consulting Engineers-Australia (SAUO) ... ACEA
Association of Consulting Englneers of Ireland (SAUS) ... ACEI
Association of Consulting Foresters (SAUO) ... ACF
Association of Consulting Foresters (EA) ... ACF
Association of Consulting Foresters of Australia ... ACFA
Association of Consulting Management Engineers (EA) ... ACME
Association of Consulting Science and Technology (COBU) ... ACST
Association of Consulting Scientists (COBU) ... ACS
Association of Consulting Structural Engineers of New South Wales [*Australia*] ... ACSENSW
Association of Consulting Surveyors Australia Inc (SAUO) ... ACSA
Association of Consumer Health Information Specialists (SAUO) ... ACHIS
Association of Consumers and Taxpayers [*Political Group*] [*New Zealand*] ... ACT
Association of Contact Lens Manufacturers [*British*] (DBA) ... ACLM
Association of Contact Lens Manufacturers Ltd. (SAUO) ... ACLM
Association of Contact Lens Practitioners (SAUO) ... ACLP
Association of Contact Lens Practitioners [*British*] (BI) ... ACLP
Association of Container Reconditioners ... NABADA
Association of Contemplative Sisters (EA) ... ACS
Association of Contemporary Historians (EA) ... ACH
Association of Continuing Dental Education (SAUO) ... ACDE
Association of Continuing Legal Education Administrators (EA) ... ACLEA
Association of Control Manufacturers (BUAC) ... TACMA
Association of Cooperative Banks of the EC [*Economy Community*] [*Belgium*] (EAIO) ... ACB-EC
Association of Cooperative Educators (EA) ... ACE
Association of Cooperative Library Organizations [*Later, ASCLA*] ... ACLO
Association of Cooperative Library Organizations (SAUO) ... ACLO
Association of Cooperative Retailers-Owned Wholesalers of Europe (EAIO) ... ACROWE
Association of Cord and String Manufacturers of the European Economic Community (SAUO) ... COMICORD
Association of Corporate Travel Executives (EA) ... ACTE
Association of Corporate Treasurers (EAIO) ... ACT
[*The*] **Association of Corporate Trustees** [*British*] (EAIO) ... TACT
Association of Correctional Administrators ... ACA
Association of Correctional Psychologists ... ACP
Association of Correctors of the Press (BARN) ... ACP
Association of Correspondence School Teachers (AEBS) ... ACST
Association of Corrugated Papermakers [*British*] (BI) ... ACPM
Association of Cosmetologists [*Later, ACH*] (EA) ... AC
Association of Cosmetologists and Hairdressers (EA) ... ACH
Association of Cost and Executive Accountants [*British*] (EAIO) ... ACEA
Association of Cost Engineers [*British*] (DBA) ... ACE
Association of Cotton Textile Merchants of New York (SAUO) ... ACTM
Association of Cotton Textile Merchants of New York [*Later, ATMI*] (EA) ... ACTM
Association of Cotton Textile Merchants of New York (SAUO) ... ACTMNY
Association of Cotton Yarn Distributors (SAUO) ... ACYD
Association of Cotton Yarn Distributors [*Later, AYD*] ... ACYD
Association of Council Secretaries [*Later, NAES*] (EA) ... ACS
Association of Council Secretaries (SAUO) ... ACS
Association of Country Entertainers (EA) ... ACE
Association of Country Greyhound Clubs [*Australia*] ... ACGC
Association of County Archivists [*British*] (DBA) ... ACA
Association of County Chief Executives [*British*] (EAIO) ... ACCE
Association of County Commissioners of Oklahoma (SRA) ... ACCO
Association of County Commissions of Alabama (SRA) ... ACCA
Association of County Councils (SAUO) ... ACC
Association of County Councils [*British*] ... ACC
Association of County Public Health Officers [*British*] ... AssCPHO's
Association of County Supplies Officers [*British*] (DBA) ... ACSO
Association of Coupon Processors (EA) ... ACP
Association of Coupon Professionals (NTPA) ... ACP
Association of Crafts and Creative Industries (EA) ... ACCI
Association of Crane Makers [*British*] (BI) ... ACM
Association of Credit Counselors (SAUO) ... AACC
Association of Credit Union League Executives (EA) ... ACULE
Association of Cricket Statisticians (EAIO) ... ACS
Association of Cricket Umpires (EAIO) ... ACU
Association of Crossroads Care Attendant Schemes (EAIO) ... ACCAS
Association of Cuban Architects in Exile (EA) ... ACAE
Association of Cultural Advancement through Visual Art [*British*] (DBA) ... ACAVA
Association of Cultural Exchange (SAUO) ... ACE
Association of Cultural Executives [*Canada*] ... ACE
Association of Customers' Brokers [*Later, AIB*] (EA) ... ACB
Association of Cutlers and Scalers (SAUO) ... ACS
Association of Cycle Exhibitors [*Later, NABEA*] (EA) ... ACE
Association of Cycle Traders (EAIO) ... ACT
Association of CycleTraders (SAUO) ... ACT
Association of Cytogenelic Technologists (SAUO) ... ACT
Association of Cytogenetic Technologists (EA) ... ACT
Association of Dabatase Producers (SAUO) ... ADP
Association of Dairymen's Assistants [*A union*] [*British*] ... ADA
Association of Dandyroll and Mould Makers (DGA) ... ADMM
Association of Dandyroll and Mould Makers (SAUO) ... AdMM
Association of Dandyroll and Mould Makers (SAUO) ... ADR&MM
Association of Danish Research Libraries (SAUS) ... SDF
Association of Dark Leaf Tobacco Dealers and Exporters (EA) ... ADLTDE
Association of Data Center Owners and Managers (CIST) ... ADCOM
Association of Data Communications Users [*Defunct*] (EA) ... ADCU
Association of Data Processing Employees (SAUO) ... ADPE
Association of Data Processing Librarians (SAUO) ... ADPL
Association of Data Processing Service Organizations [*Later, CSSIA*] [*US and Canada*] (EA) ... ADAPSO
Association of Data Processing Service Organizations [*Includes American and Canadian companies*] [*Later, ADAPSO - The Computer Software and Services Industry Association*] (EA) ... ADPSO
Association of Data Processing Service Organizations Panels ... ADAPSP
Association of Data Terminal Distributers (SAUO) ... ADTC
Association of Data Terminal Distributers (or Distributors) (SAUS) ... ADTD
Association of Data Terminal Distributors ... ADTD
Association of Database Producers (IID) ... ADP
Association of Day Care Operators of Ontario (AC) ... ADCO
Association of Deans of American Colleges of Veterinary Medicine [*Later, Association of American Veterinary Medical Colleges*] (AEBS) ... ADACVM
Association of Deans of American Veterinary Colleges (SAUO) ... ADAVC
Association of Defense Counselors (EA) ... ADC
Association of Defense Trial Attorneys (EA) ... ADTA
Association of Defensive Spray Manufacturers (NTPA) ... ADSM
Association of Delaware Hospitals (SRA) ... ADH
Association of Dental Hospitals (SAUS) ... ADH
Association of Dental Hospitals of Great Britain and Northern Ireland (BI) ... ADH
Association of Dental Implant Auxiliaries & Practice Management (SAUO) ... ADIA&PM
Association of Dental Manufacturers and Traders (SAUS) ... ADMT
Association of Department Heads of Catering [*British*] (DBA) ... ADHOC
Association of Departments of English (EA) ... ADE
Association of Departments of Foreign Languages (EA) ... ADFL
Association of Desk and Derrick Clubs (EA) ... ADDC
Association of Desk and Derrick Clubs of North America (SAUO) ... ADDC
Association of Destination Management Executives (NTPA) ... ADME
Association of Detergent Zeolite Producers (SAUS) ... ZEODET
Association of Development Financing Institutions in Asia and the Pacific (SAUO) ... ADFIAF
Association of Development Financing Institutions in Asia and the Pacific [*Manila, Philippines*] (EA) ... ADFIAP
Association of Development Institutes for the Pacific and Asia ... ADIPA
Association of Development Research and Training Institutes of Asia and the Pacific (SAUO) ... ADIPA
Association of Diesel Specialists (EA) ... ADS
Association of Direct Labour Organisations [*British*] ... ADLO
Association of Direct Labour Organizations (SAUO) ... ADLO
Association of Direct Marketing Agencies [*Defunct*] (EA) ... ADMA
Association of Directors and Producers [*British*] ... ADP
Association of Directors of Education (AIE) ... ADE
Association of Directors of Education in Scotland (SAUO) ... ADES
Association of Directors of Education, Scotland (DI) ... ADES
Association of Directors of Recreation, Leisure, and Tourism [*British*] (DBA) ... ADRLT
Association of Directors of Social Services (EAIO) ... ADSS
Association of Directors of Social Work (EAIO) ... ADSW
Association of Directory Marketing (NTPA) ... ADM
Association of Directory Publishers (NTPA) ... ADP
Association of Disabled Professionals (EAIO) ... ADP
Association of Disciples for Meotogical Discussion (SAUO) ... ADTC
Association of Disciples for Theological Discussion (EA) ... ADTD
Association of Dispensing Opticians [*British*] (DBQ) ... ADO
Association of Distributors of Advertising Material (EAIO) ... ADAM
Association of Distributors to the Self-Service and Coin-operated Laundry and Allied Trades (SAUO) ... ADSCAT
Association of District Council Surveyors (SAUO) ... ADCS
Association of District Council Treasurers [*British*] ... ADCT
Association of District Councils [*British*] ... ADC
Association of District Councils (SAUO) ... ADC
Association of District Secretaries [*British*] ... ADS
Association of Diving Contractors (EA) ... ADC
Association of Drainage Authorities (SAUO) ... AD
Association of Drainage Authorities [*British*] (DCTA) ... ADA
Association [*or Associate*] **of Drama Boards** [*British*] ... ADB
Association of Drilled Shaft Contractors (EA) ... ADSC
Association of Drinkwatchers International [*Defunct*] (EA) ... DW
Association of Driver Educators for the Disabled (EA) ... ADED
Association of Drug Referral Centers [*Australia*] ... ADRC
Association of Drum Manufacturers [*British*] (DBA) ... ADM
Association of Dry Battery Manufacturers (SAUO) ... ADBM
Association of Dutch Language Teachers (SAUO) ... ADULT
Association of DX [*Distance*] **Reporters** (EA) ... ADXR
Association of Early Childhood Educators, Ontario (AC) ... AECEO
Association of Earth Science Editors (GEOI) ... AESE
Association of Economic Entomologists (SAUO) ... AEE
Association of Economic Poisons Control Officials (SAUO) ... AEPCO
Association of Ecosystem Research Centers (EA) ... AERC
Association of Edison Illuminating Companies (EA) ... AEIC
Association of Editorial Businesses (EA) ... AEB
Association of Editors in the South East Asian Region (SAUO) ... EDITEAST
Association of Education by Radio-Television Journal (SAUS) ... AERTJ
Association of Education Committees [*British*] ... AEC

Association of Education Committees (SAUO) .... AEC
Association of Education Officers [British] .... AEO
Association of Educational Advisers Scotland (DBA) .... AEAS
Association of Educational Communication and Technology (SAUS) .... AECT
Association of Educational Data-Systems (SAUS) .... AEDS
Association of Educational Negotiators (SAUO) .... AEN
Association of Educational Negotiators [Later, NAEN] (EA) ..... AEN
Association of Educational Psychologists [British] .... AEP
Association of Educational Research Officers of Ontario [Association Ontarienne des Agents de Recherche en Education] (AC) .... AERO
Association of Educational Sororities (SAUO) .... AES
Association of Educators in Radiological Sciences (SAUO) ..... AERS
Association of Educators of Gifted Children (SAUO) .... AEGC
Association of Educators of Homebound and Hospitalized Children [Later, DPH] (EA) .... AEHHC
Association of Electric Companies of Texas (SRA) .... AECT
Association of Electrical Contractors Ireland (EAIO) .... AECI
Association of Electrical Housecraft Advisers (SAUO) .... AEHA
Association of Electrical Industries (SAUS) .... AEI
Association of Electrical Industries, Ltd. (SAUO) .... AEI
Association of Electrical Machinery Trades (EAIO) .... AEMT
Association of Electrical Station Engineers (SAUO) .... AESE
Association of Electrical Wiremen [A union] [British] .... AEW
Association of Electronic Cottagers [Defunct] (EA) .... AEC
Association of Electronic Data Systems (SAUS) .... AEDS
Association of Electronic Distributors (EA) .... AED
Association of Electronic Guard Manufacturers [British] ..... AEGM
Association of Electronic Manufacturers [Later, EIA] (EA) .... AEM
Association of Electronic Manufacturers, Eastern Division (EA) .... AEM-ED
Association of Electronic Manufacturers Eastern Division (SAUO) .... AEM-ED
Association of Electronic Parts and Equipment Manufacturers [Later, EIA] .... AEPEM
Association of Electronic Parts and Equipment Manufacturers (SAUO) ..... EPEM
Association of Electronic Reserve Officers (SAUO) .... AERO
Association of Electronics Distributors (SAUS) .... AED
Association of Embroiderers and Pleaters (SAUO) .... AEP
Association of Embroiderers and Pleaters [British] (BI) ...... AEP
Association of Emergency Medical Technicians [British] (DBA) .... AEMT
Association of Emergency Physicians (SAUO) .... AEP
Association of Employees Supporting Education Services [Canada] .... AESES
Association of Energy Engineers (EA) .... AEE
Association of Energy Service Companies (NTPA) .... AESC
Association of Energy Services Professionals (NTPA) .... AESP
Association of Engineering and Shipbuilding Draughtsmen (SAUO) .... AESD
Association of Engineering Distributors [British] (BI) .... AED
Association of Engineering Employees of Oregon (SRA) .... AEE
Association of Engineering Firms Practicing in the Geosciences (SAUO) ...... ASFE
Association of Engineering Geologists (EA) .... AEG
Association of Engineering Societies (SAUO) .... AES
Association of Engineering Technicians & Technologists of Newfoundland (AC) .... AETTN
Association of Engineers and Scientists (Independent) .... AES(I)
Association of Engineers and Scientists of the Bureau of Naval Weapons (SAUO) .... AESBNW
Association of Engineers and Scientists of the Bureau of Weapons (SAUS) .... AESBOW
Association of English Singers and Speakers [British] (DBA) ... AES & S
Association of Enrolled Agents [Later, NAEA] (EA) .... AEA
Association of Enterprises of the Chemical Industry of Portugal (SAUO) .... APEIPQ
Association of Entertainers (EA) .... AE
Association of Entertainment Industry Computer Professionals (EA) .... AEICP
Association of Environmental and Outdoor Education (SAUO) .... AEOE
Association of Environmental and Resource Economists (EA) .... AERE
Association of Environmental Authorities (SRA) .... AEA
Association of Environmental Conscious Builders [British] (DBA) .... AECB
Association of Environmental Engineering Professors (EA) ..... AEEP
Association of Environmental Laboratories (SAUO) .... AEL
Association of Environmental Scientists and Administrators [Defunct] (EA) .... AESA
Association of Episcopal Colleges (EA) .... AEC
Association of Episcopal Conferences for English-Speaking West Africa (SAUO) .... AECEWA
Association of Episcopal Conferences of Anglophone West Africa (EAIO) .... AECAWA
Association of Equipment Distributors (MHDB) .... AED
Association of Equipment Lessors [Later, AAEL] .... AEL
Association of Escort/Interpreters (EA) .... AEI
Association of Essex Philatelic Societies (SAUO) .... AEPS
Association of Established Civil Servants (SAUO) .... AECS
Association of Ethnic Broadcasters and Coordinators of New South Wales [Australia] .... AEBCNSW
Association of European Aeronautical and Astronautical Students (PDAA) .... EUROAVIA
Association of European Airlines (EAIO) .... AEA
Association of European Battery Manufacturers (EA) .... EUROBAT
Association of European Candle Manufacturers (EA) .... AECM
Association of European Chemical Coastal Tanker Owners (SAUO) .... ECCTO
Association of European Conjuncture Institutes (EA) .... AECI
Association of European Conjuncture Institutes (SAUO) .... AIECE
Association of European Co-operative Insurers (SAUO) .... AECI
Association of European Cooperative Insurers [Brussels, Belgium] (EAIO) .... AECI
Association of European Correspondence Schools (EA) .... AECS

Association of European Express Carriers (DA) .... AEEC
Association of European Federations of Agro-Engineers [EC] (ECED) .... AEFA
Association of European Federations of Agro-engineers (SAUO) .... AEFA
Association of European Geological Societies (SAUO) .... AFGS
Association of European Jute Industries .... AEJI
Association of European Machine Tool Merchants [Berkhamsted, Hertfordshire, England] (EAIO) .... AEMTM
Association of European Manufacturers of Fire and Intruder Alarm Systems (SAUO) .... EURALARM
Association of European Manufacturers of Self-Adhesive Tapes (EA) .... AEMSAT
Association of European Manufacturers of Storage Gas-Waterheaters (SAUO) .... ACCUGAZ
Association of European Metal Sink Manufacturers (EAIO) ..... AEMSM
Association of European Psychiatrists (SAUO) .... AEP
Association of European Research Networks (TELE) .... AERN
Association of European Schools and/of Planning (SAUO) ..... AESOP
Association of European Steel Producers (PDAA) .... EUROFER
Association of European Universities (SAUO) .... CRE
Association of Europeans for Safety in Ordnance & Propellants (WDAA) .... AESOP
Association of Evangelical Lutheran Churches .... AELC
Association of Evangelical Professors of Missions (EA) .... AEPM
Association of Evangelical Relief and Development Organizations (DICI) .... AERDO
Association of Evangelicals for Italian Missions (EA) .... AEIM
Association of Executive Recruiting Consultants [Later, AESC] (EA) .... AERC
Association of Executive Search Consultants (EA) .... AESC
Association of Exhibition Organisers [British] (DBA) .... AEO
Association of Exhibitors and Conference Managers Ltd. (SAUO) .... AECM
Association of Existential Psychology and Psychiatry [Defunct] (EA) .... AEPP
Association of Exploration Geochemists [ICSU] (EAIO) .... AEG
Association of Export Subscription Newsagents (DGA) .... AESN
Association of Faculty Clubs International (NTPA) .... AFCI
Association of Fair Housing Committee (SAUO) .... AFHC
Association of Fair Housing Committees [Defunct] .... AFHC
Association of Family and Conciliation Courts (EA) .... AFCC
Association of Family Case Workers (SAUO) .... AFCW
Association of Family Case-Workers [British] (BI) .... AFCW
Association of Family Farmers (EA) .... AFF
Association of Family Practice Administrators (EA) .... AFPA
Association of Family Practice Residency Directors (EA) ..... AFPRD
Association of Family Therapy [British] (DBA) .... AFT
Association of Fancy Box Makers [A union] [British] .... AFBM
Association of Farmer FAO and WFP Staff Members (SAUO) .... FFOA
Association of Farmworker Opportunity Programs (EA) .... AFOP
Association of Fashion Advertising and Editorial Photographers (EAIO) .... AFAEP
Association of Fashion, Advertising and Editorial Photographers (SAUO) .... AFAEP
Association of Fashion and Image Consultants (EA) .... AFIC
Association of Fatty Acid Distillers [British] (BI) .... AFAD
Association of Federal Appraisers [Later, Association of Governmental Appraisers] .... AFA
Association of Federal Appraisers (SAUO) .... AFA
Association of Federal Architects .... AFA
Association of Federal Communications Consulting Engineers (NITA) ...... AFCC
Association of Federal Communications Consulting Engineers (EA) .... AFCCE
Association of Federal Computer Users [Defunct] (EA) .... AFCU
Association of Federal Fiscal Technicians (EA) .... AFFT
Association of Federal Government Employees (SAUO) .... AFGE
Association of Federal Investigators (EA) .... AFI
Association of Federal Photographers [Defunct] (EA) .... AFP
Association of Federal Safety and Health Professionals [Defunct] (EA) ...... AFSHP
Association of Federal, State, County and Municipal Employees (SAUO) .... AFSCME
Association of Federal Technology Transfer Executives (SAUO) AFT2E
Association of Federal Woman's Award Recipients [Defunct] (EA) .... AFWAR
Association of Feminine Collectives [Canada] .... AFC
Association of Field Ornithologists (EA) .... AFO
Association of Field Service Managers [Later, ASMI] (EA) ..... AFSM
Association of Field Service Managers (CIST) .... ASFM
Association of Field Service Managers, International [Later, ASMI] (EA) .... AFSMI
Association of Film Commissioners (EA) .... AFC
Association of Film Commissioners International (NTPA) ...... AFCI
Association of Film Laboratory Employers (SAUO) .... AFLE
Association of Finance and Insurance Professionals (NTPA) ... AFIP
Association of Financial Services Holding Companies (NTPA) ... AFSHC
Association of Finishing Processes of the Society of Manufacturing Engineers (SAUO) .... AFP/SME
Association of Finnish Electric Industries .... AFEI
Association of Fire Loss Adjustors (SAUO) .... AFLA
Association of Firearm and Tool Mark Examiners (EA) .... AFTE
Association of First Class Mailers .... AFCM
Association of First Division Civil Servants [British] .... AFDCS
Association of First Division Civil Servants (SAUO) .... AFDCS
Association of Fish Canners [British] (DBA) .... AFC
Association of Fish Meal Manufacturers [British] (DBA) ...... AFMM
Association of Fleet Maintenance Supervisors (SAUO) .... AFMS
Association of Flight Attendants (EA) .... AFA
Association of Flight Training Organizations [British] (DBA) ... AFTO
Association of Flock Processors [Defunct] (EA) .... AFP
Association of Floor Constructors (SAUO) .... AFC
Association of Flooring Contractors (SAUO) .... AFC

Association of Flooring Contractors [British] (BI) .... AFC
Association of Florida Community Developers (SRA) .... AFCD
Association of Fluorocarbon Consumers and Manufacturers
[Australia] .... AFCAM
Association of Folding Furniture Manufacturers [British] (BI) .... AFFM
Association of Food and Drug Officials (SAUO) .... AFADO
Association of Food and Drug Officials (EA) .... AFDO
Association of Food and Drug Officials of the United States [Later, AFDO]
(EA) .... AFDOUS
Association of Food Distributors [Later, AFI] (EA) .... AFD
Association of Food Industries (EA) .... AFI
Association of Food Journalists (NTPA) .... AFJ
Association of Food Marketing Agencies in Asia and the Pacfic
(SAUO) .... AFMA
Association of Food Marketing Agencies in Asia and the Pacific (EA) .... AFMA
Association of Football Players and Trainers Union (SAUO) .... AFPTU
Association of Football Statisticians [British] (DBA) .... AFS
Association of Footwear Distributors [Defunct] (EA) .... AFD
Association of Foreign Investors in US Real Estate (EA) .... AFIRE
Association of Foreign Trade Representatives (EA) .... AFTR
Association of Foremen and Supervisors [Australia] .... AFS
Association of Foremen Iron Founders [A union] [British] .... AFIF
Association of Forensic Document Examiners (EA) .... AFDE
Association of Forest Service Employees for Environmental Ethics
(EA) .... AFSEEE
Association of Former Agents of the United States Secret Service
(SAUO) .... AFAUSSS
Association of Former FAO and WFP Staff Members (SAUO) .... FFOA Rome
Association of Former Intelligence Officers (EA) .... AFIO
Association of Former International Civil Servants in Chile
(SAUO) .... AFICS Santiago
Association of Former International Civil Servants-Geneva
(SAUO) .... AAFI-AFICS Geneva
Association of Former International Civil Servants-Geneva
(SAUO) .... AAFIAFICS Geneval
Association of Former International Civil Servants-New York
(SAUO) .... AFICS New York
Association of Former Members of Congress [Formerly, FMC] (EA) .... AFMC
Association of Former Secretaries of Health (SAUO) .... AFSH
Association of Former Secretaries of the Department of Health, Education
and Welfare (SAUO) .... AFSHEW
Association of Former Senate Aides (EA) .... AFSA
Association of Former Students of the College of Europe (EAIO) .... AFSCE
Association of Former Trainees of the European Communities (SAUO) .... ADEK
Association of Former United Nations Personnel in and of India
(SAUO) .... AFUNPI Bangalore
Association of Franchised Distributors of Electronic Components
[British] .... AFDEC
Association of Fraternity Advisors (EA) .... AFA
Association of Free Community Papers (NTPA) .... AFCP
Association of Free French in the US (EA) .... AFFUS
Association of Free Lutheran Congregation and Seminary Headquarters,
Minneapolis, MN [Library symbol] [Library of Congress] (LCLS) .... MnMFL
Association of Free Lutheran Congregations .... AFLC
Association of Free Magazines (DGA) .... AFM
Association of Free Magazines and Periodicals [British] (EAIO) .... AFMP
Association of Free Methodist Educational Institutions (EA) .... AFMEI
Association of Free Newspapers [British] (EAIO) .... AFN
Association of Free Trade Unions [Former USSR] .... AFTU
Association of Freestanding Radiation Oncology Centers (EA) .... AFROC
Association of French Host Centers [Paris] [Information service or system]
(IID) .... ACSF
Association of French Language Epidemiologists (EAIO) .... AFLE
Association of French Mechanical Industries (EA) .... AFMI
Association of French Teachers in Africa [See also AFPA] [Khartoum,
Sudan] (EAIO) .... AFTA
Association of French Telephone, Telegraph and Related Telematia
Industries (SAUS) SI3T
Association of French-Language Leprologists [Paris, France] (EAIO) .... AFLL
Association of French-Speaking Dieticians (SAUO) .... ADLF
Association of Frozen Food Producers (SAUO) .... AFFP
Association of Fund Raisers and Direct Sellers (EA) .... AFRDS
Association of Fund Raising Professionals of British Columbia
[Canada] .... AFRP BC
Association of Fundamental Institutions of Religious Education .... AFIRE
Association of Fund-Raising Directors (SAUO) .... AFRD
Association of Future Brokers and Dealers (SAUO) .... AFBD
Association of Futures Brokers and Dealers (EAIO) .... AFBD
Association of Futures Investment [British] (DBA) .... AFI
Association of Gardening and Hardware Wholesalers [British] (DBA) .... AGHW
Association of Gaugers and Appraisers Ltd. [British] (BI) .... AGA
Association of Gay and Lesbian Psychiatrists (EA) .... AGLP
Association of Gay Psychologists [Later, ALGP] (EA) .... AGP
Association of Genealogists and Record Agents [British] (EAIO) .... AGRA
Association of General and Liberal Studies (SAUS) .... AGLS
Association of General Heating and Domestic Engineer Assistants [A
union] [British] .... AGHDEA
Association of General Merchandise Chains [NMRI] [Absorbed by]
(EA) .... AGMC
Association of General Practitioner Community Hospitals [British]
(EAIO) .... AGPCH
Association of General Practitioner Community Hospitals (SAUS) .... AGPCH
Association of General States of Students from Europe (SAUO) .... GSSE
Association of Genetic Technologists (NTPA) .... ACT
Association of Genetic Technologists (SAUO) .... AGT

Association of Geography Teachers of Ireland (AIE) .... AGTI
Association of Geology Teachers (SAUO) .... AGT
Association of Geoscientists for International Development [Bangkok,
Thailand] (EAIO) .... AGID
Association of German Broadcasters (EA) .... AGB
Association of German Chambers of Industry and Commerce (EA) .... AGCIC
Association of German Language Authors in America [Defunct] (EA) .... AGLAA
Association of Gifted-Creative Children (EA) .... AGCC
Association of Girl Scout Executive Staff (EA) .... AGSES
Association of Girl Scout Professional Workers [Later, AGSES] (EA) .... AGSPW
Association of Glass Container Manufacturers (SAUO) .... AGCM
Association of Golf Club Secretaries (EAIO) .... AGCS
Association of Golf Writers (EAIO) .... AGW
Association of Good Motorists [British] (BI) .... AGM
Association of Governing Boards (NFD) .... AGB
Association of Governing Boards of Universities and Colleges (EA) .... AGB
Association of Governing Boards of Universities and Colleges
(SAUO) .... AGBUC
Association of Governing Bodies of Girls Public Schools (SAUO) .... GBGSA
Association of Governing Bodies of Public Schools (SAUO) .... AGBPS
Association of Governing Bodies of Public Schools (SAUO) .... GBA
Association of Government Accountants [Arlington, VA] (EA) .... AGA
Association of Government Auditors (AAGC) .... AGA
Association of Government Bodies of Public Schools (SAUO) .... GBA
Association of Government Marketing Assistance Specialists (EA) .... AGMAS
Association of Government Supervisors and Radio Officers [British] .... AGSRO
Association of Governmental Appraisers [American Society of Appraiser]
[Absorbed by] (EA) .... AGA
Association of Graduate Careers Advisory Service (SAUO) .... AGCAS
Association of Graduate Careers Advisory Services [British] (DBA) .... AGCAS
Association of Graduate Liberal Studies Programs (EA) .... AGLSP
Association of Graduate Recruiters [British] (DBA) .... AGR
Association of Graduate Schools in Association of American Universities
(SAUO) .... AGS
Association of Graduate Schools in Association of American Universities
(NTPA) .... AGSAAU
Association of Graduates of the United States Air Force Academy (EA) .... AOG
Association of Graphic Arts Consultants (EA) .... AGAC
Association of Graphic Communications (SRA) .... AGC
Association of Graphic Designers (DGA) .... AGD
Association of Great Lakes Outdoor Writers (SRA) .... AGLOW
Association of Greek Plastic Boat Manufacturers (SAUS) .... SEKAPLAS
Association of Green Crop Driers [British] (BI) .... AGCD
Association of Grey Board Makers [British] (DBA) .... AGBM
Association of Ground Investigation Specialists [British] (DBA) .... AGIS
Association of Ground Water Scientists and Engineers (EA) .... AGWSE
Association of Group Travel Executives (EA) .... AGTE
Association of Growers of the New Varieties of Hops (SAUO) .... AGNVH
Association of Gut Processors [British] (BI) .... AGP
Association of Gypsy Organizations [British] (DBA) .... AGO
Association of Halfway House Alcoholism Programs of North America
(EA) .... AHHAP
Association of Handicapped Artists (EA) .... AHA
Association of Handicapped Student Service Programs in Postsecondary
Education (SAUS) .... AHSSPPE
Association of Head and Neck Oncologists of Great Britain .... AHNO
Association of Head Mistresses, Inc. [British] .... AHMI
Association of Head Mistresses, Inc. (SAUS) .... AUMI
Association of Head Mistresses, Incorporated (SAUO) .... AUMI
Association of Head Postmasters (SAUO) .... AHP
Association of Headmasters (SAUO) .... AHM
Association of Headmistresses [British] (DI) .... AH
Association of Headmistresses [British] (BI) .... AHM
Association of Headmistresses (SAUO) .... AHM
Association of Headmistresses of Preparatory Schools [British] .... AHMPS
Association of Headmistresses of Preparatory Schools [British] (BI) .... AHPS
Association of Heads of Girls Boarding Schools [British] .... AHGBS
Association of Heads of Independent and Direct Grant Girls Schools
[British] .... AHIDGS
Association of Heads of Independent Schools [British] .... AHIS
Association of Heads of Independent Schools .... ANIS
Association of Heads of Outdoor Education Centres [British] (DBA) .... AHOEC
Association of Heads of Polytechnic Student Services [British] (AIE) .... AHOPSS
Association of Heads of Recognised Independent Schools, Gillingham
(SAUO) .... AHRIS
Association of Heads of Surveying (SAUO) .... AHDS
Association of Health and Pleasure Resorts (SAUO) .... AHPR
Association of Health Care Information and Medical Records Officers
(SAUO) .... AMRO
Association of Health Care Information and Medical Records Officers
(EAIO) .... AMRO
Association of Health Facility Licensure and Certification Directors
(SAUO) .... AHFLCD
Association of Health Facility Survey Agencies (NTPA) .... AHFSA
Association of Health Insurance Agents (NTPA) .... AHIA
Association of Health Management Organizations in Michigan (SRA) .... AHMOM
Association of Health Occupations Teacher Educators (EA) .... AHOTE
Association of Health Professionals [Australia] .... AHP
Association of Health Service Personnel Managers (SAUO) .... AHSPM
Association of Health Service Treasurers [British] .... AHST
Association of Healthcare Internal Auditors (NTPA) .... AHIA
Association of Hebrew Catholics (EA) .... AHC
Association of Heritage Approved Specialists [An association] (EAIO) .... AHAS
Association of High Medicare Hospitals (EA) .... AHMH
Association of High Tech Distributors (SAUO) .... AHID

Association of High Tech Distributors (EA) .... AHTD
Association of High Technology Distribution (NTPA) .... AHTD
Association of Higher Education and Disabilities .... AHEAD
Association of Higher Education Facilities Officers (SAUO) .... APPA
Association of Higher Educational Institutions Concerned with Home Economics [British] (DBA) .... AHEIHE
Association of Highway Officials of the North Atlantic States (SAUO) .... AHONAS
Association of Highway Steel Transporters (EA) .... AHST
Association of Highway Technicians (SAUO) .... AHT
Association of Hillei-Jewish Campus Professionals (SAUO) .... AHJCP
Association of Hillel/Jewish Campus Professionals (EA) .... AHJCP
Association of Hispanic Aris (SAUO) .... AHA
Association of Hispanic Arts (EA) .... AHA
Association of Hispanists [British] .... AH
Association of Hispanists of Great Britain and Ireland (AIE) .... ABH
Association of H.M. Inspectors of Taxes (SAUO) .... AIT
Association of Holocaust Organizations (EA) .... AHO
Association of Home Appliance Manufacturers (EA) .... AHAM
Association of Home Study Schools (SAUO) .... AEM
Association of Home Study Schools [Later, ACTS] (EA) .... AHSS
Association of Hongkong Air Freight Agents (SAUO) .... AHAFA
Association of Hospital and Institution Libraries [of ALA] [Later, ASCLA] .... AHIL
Association of Hospital and Institution Libraries Quarterly (journ.) (SAUS) .... AHILQ
Association of Hospital and Welfare Administrators [British] (BI) .... AHWA
Association of Hospital Directors of Medical Education [Later, AHME] (EA) .... AHDME
Association of Hospital Health and Fitness (EA) .... AHHF
Association of Hospital Management Committees .... AHMC
Association of Hospital Pharmacists of Victoria [Australia] .... AHPV
Association of Hospital Security Administrators .... AHSA
Association of Hospital Television Networks (EA) .... AHTN
Association of Hotel Booking Agents [British] (BI) .... AHBA
Association of Hotels and Restaurants of Great Britain (SAUO) .... AHRGB
Association of House Democratic Press Assistants (EA) .... AHDPA
Association of Household Distributors [British] (EAIO) .... AHD
Association of Housing Aid [British] (DBA) .... AHA
Association of Human Resource Systems Professionals (EA) .... HRSP
Association of Human Resources Management and Organizational Behavior [Later, AM] (EA) .... HRMOB
Association of Human Services in Alberta (AC) .... AHSA
Association of Humanistic Psychology Practitioners (EAIO) .... AHPP
Association of Humanistic Rabbis (EA) .... AHR
Association of Hungarian Students in North America [Defunct] (EA) .... AHS
Association of Hydraulic Equipment Manufacturers .... AHEM
Association of Ice Monitoring Contractors of Canada (SAUS) .... AIMCC
Association of Idaho Cities (SRA) .... AIC
Association of Illinois Electric Cooperatives (SRA) .... AIEC
Association of Illinois Middle-Level Schools (SRA) .... AIMS
Association of Illustrators [British] (DBA) .... AOL
Association of Image Consultants (EA) .... AIC
Association of Image Consultants International (NTPA) .... AICI
Association of Imaging Manufacturers (VERA) .... AIM
Association of Imaging Manufacturers/Shared Resource Control Facility (SAUO) .... AIMSRCF
Association of Imaging Service Bureaus (VERA) .... AISB
Association of Immigration and Nationality Lawyers [Later, AILA] (EA) .... AINL
Association of Immigration Attorneys (EA) .... AIA
Association of Importers and Producers of Admixtures [Belgium] (EAIO) .... AIPA
Association of Importers-Manufacturers for Muzzleloading (NTPA) .... AIM
Association of Importers-Manufacturers for Muzzleloading (EA) .... AIMM
Association of Incentive Marketing (NTPA) .... AIM
Association of Incorporated Managers and Administrators [British] (EAIO) .... AIMA
Association of Indepedent Liberal Arts Colleges for Teacher Education (EDAC) .... AILACTE
Association of Independent Business (SAUO) .... AIB
Association of Independent Businesses (EAIO) .... AIB
Association of Independent California Colleges and Universities (SRA) .... AICCU
Association of Independent Camps (EA) .... AIC
Association of Independent Church Schools (AC) .... AICS
Association of Independent Cinemas [British] .... AIC
Association of Independent Clinical Research Contractors [British] (DBA) .... AICRC
Association of Independent Colleges and Schools (EA) .... AICS
Association of Independent Colleges and Universities in Massachusetts (SAUO) .... AICUM
Association of Independent Colleges and Universities of Michigan (SAUO) .... AICUM
Association of Independent Colleges and Universities of Nebraska (SAUO) .... AICUN
Association of Independent Colleges and Universities of Ohio (SAUO) .... AICUO
Association of Independent Colleges of Art and Design (NTPA) .... AICAD
Association of Independent Colleges of Music (EA) .... AICM
Association of Independent Commercial Editors (NTCM) .... AICE
Association of Independent Commercial Producers [New York, NY] (EA) .... AICP
Association of Independent Composers and Performers (EA) .... AICP
Association of Independent Computer Specialists (EAIO) .... AICS
Association of Independent Conservators of Music (SAUO) .... AICM
Association of Independent Consultants (AC) .... AIC
Association of Independent Contract Research Organisations [British] .... AICRO
Association of Independent Copy Machine Dealers and Manufacturers (EA) .... AICMDM
Association of Independent Corrugated Converters (EA) .... AICC
Association of Independent Crop Consultants [British] (DBA) .... AICC
Association of Independent Electricity Producers [British] (DBA) .... AIEP
Association of Independent Hospitals (SAUO) .... AIH
Association of Independent Hospitals and Kindred Organisations [British] (BI) .... AIH
Association of Independent Information Professionals (EA) .... AIIP
Association of Independent Investment Managers [Formerly, National Micrographics Association] (EAIO) .... AIIM
Association of Independent Kentucky Colleges and Universities (SRA) .... AIKCU
Association of Independent Living Centers in New York (SRA) .... AILCNY
Association of Independent Mailing Equipment Dealers (EA) .... AIMED
Association of Independent Maryland Schools (EDAC) .... AIMS
Association of Independent Medical Equipment Suppliers (EA) .... AIMES
Association of Independent Merchant Stockists (DGA) .... AIMS
Association of Independent Metropolitan Stations (NTCM) .... AIMS
Association of Independent Microdealers [Later, CMC] (EA) .... AIM
Association of Independent Motor Stores [British] (DBA) .... AIMS
Association of Independent Museums [British] (EAIO) .... AIM
Association of Independent Music Publishers (EA) .... AIMP
Association of Independent Optical Wholesalers [Later, OLA] .... AIOW
Association of Independent Optical Wholesalers (SAUO) .... AIOW
Association of Independent Producers [British] .... AIP
Association of Independent Radio Contractors [British] .... AIRC
Association of Independent Railways [British] (DBA) .... AIR
Association of Independent Research and Technology Organizations [British] (DBA) .... AIRTO
Association of Independent Research Institutes (EA) .... AIRI
Association of Independent Schools & Colleges in Alberta (AC) .... AISCA
Association of Independent Schools of New South Wales [Australia] .... AISNSW
Association of Independent Schools of Queensland [Australia] .... AISQ
Association of Independent Schools of the Australian Capital Territory .... AISACT
Association of Independent Schools of Western Australia .... AISWA
Association of Independent Software Companies [Later, ADAPSO] (EA) .... AISC
Association of Independent Television Stations (SAUO) .... AITVS
Association of Independent Television Stations (EA) .... INTV
Association of Independent Television Stations, Inc. (NTCM) .... AITS
Association of Independent Tour Operators [British] (DBA) .... AITO
Association of Independent Trust Companies (NTPA) .... AITCo
Association of Independent Video and Filmmakers (EA) .... AIVF
Association of Independents in Radio (SAUO) .... AIR
Association of Indian Engineering Industry (SAUO) .... AIEI
Association of Indian Muslims (EA) .... AIM
Association of Indian Muslims of America .... AIM
Association of Indians in America (EA) .... AIA
Association of Industrial Advertisers [Later, B/PAA] (EA) .... AIA
Association of Industrial Archaeology (EAIO) .... AIA
Association of Industrial Colleges and Schools (OICC) .... AICS
Association of Industrial Filter and Separator Manufacturers [British] (DBA) .... AIFSM
Association of Industrial Medical Officers [British] (BI) .... AIMO
Association of Industrial Metallizers, Coaters and Laminators (SAUS) .... AIMCAL
Association of Industrial Real Estate Brokers (NTPA) .... AIREB
Association of Industrial Road Safety Officers [British] (DBA) .... AIRSO
Association of Industrial Scientists (SAUO) .... AIS
Association of Industrial Scientists (SAUO) .... ASI
Association of Industrial Scientists [affiliated with] Marine Engineers Beneficial Association [A union] .... AIS-MEBA
Association of Industrial Scientists-Marine Engineers Beneficial Association (SAUO) .... AIS-MEBA
Association of Industrial Truck Trainers [British] (DBA) .... AITT
Association of Industrialised Building Component Manufacturers Ltd. (SAUO) .... AIBCM
Association of Industrialized Building Component Manufacturers Ltd. [British] (BI) .... AIBCM
Association of Industry Manufacturers Representatives (EA) .... AIM/R
Association of Information and Dissemination Centers (SAUO) .... AIDC
Association of Information and Dissemination Centers (MHDB) .... ASDIC
Association of Information and Dissemination Centers (EA) .... ASIDIC
Association of Information and Dissemination Centres (SAUO) .... AIDS
Association of Information Management (SAUO) .... AIM
Association of Information Managers (NITA) .... AIM
Association of Information Managers for Financial Institutions [Defunct] (EA) .... AIM
Association of Information Officers in the Pharmacentical Industry (SAUS) .... AIOPI
Association of Information Systems Professionals [Defunct] (EA) .... AISP
Association of Information Technology Professionals .... AITP
Association of Informed Senior Citizens [Defunct] (EA) .... AISC
Association of Inplant Managers (DGA) .... AIM
Association of Insolvency Accountants [Chicago, IL] (EA) .... AIA
Association of Inspectors, Advisers, and Consultants for Religious Education (AIE) .... AREIAC
Association of Inspectors of Taxes [British] .... AIT
Association of Institute and School of Education In-Service Tutors [British] .... AISEIT
Association of Institute and School of Education In-Service Tutors (SAUO) .... AJSEJT
Association of Institute for Research and Development in the Indian Ocean (SAUO) .... ARDOI
Association of Institutes of Automobile Engineers (SAUO) .... AIAE
Association of Institutional Distributors [Later, FOOD] (EA) .... AID
Association of Insulin-Dependent Diabetics [Defunct] (EA) .... AIDD
Association of Insurance Advertisers [Defunct] (EA) .... AIA
Association of Insurance and Risk Managers in Industry and Commerce (SAUO) .... AIRMIC

Association of Insurance Attorneys [*Later, ADTA*] (EA) ... AIA
Association of Insurance Brokers Ltd. [*British*] (BI) ... AIB
Association of Insurance Committee Officers (SAUO) ... AICO
Association of Insurance Managers in Industry and Commerce [*British*] (BI) ... AIMC
Association of Insurance Managers in Industry and Commerce (SAUO) ... AIMIC
Association of Insurance Teachers [*British*] (DBA) ... AIT
Association of Intelligence Officers in the Department of Overseas Trade (SAUO) ... AIODOT
Association of Interior Decor Specialists [*Later, ASCR*] ... AIDS
Association of Internal Management Consultants [*East Bloomfield, NY*] (EA) ... AIMC
Association of International Accountants [*British*] (EAIO) ... AIA
Association of International Accountants Ltd. (SAUO) ... AIA
Association of International Advertising Agencies (EA) ... AIAA
Association of International Automobile Manufacturers (EA) ... AIAM
Association of International Automobile Manufacturers (SAUS) ... AI&M
Association of International Automobile Manufacturers (SAUO) ... AL&M
Association of International Automobile Manufacturers of Canada [*Association des Fabricants Internationaux d'Automobiles du Canada*] (AC) ... AIAMC
Association of International Bond Dealers [*Zurich, Switzerland*] (EAIO) ... AIBD
Association of International Bond Dealers Quotation [*Stock exchange term*] ... AIBDQ
Association of International Bond Dyers Quotation (SAUO) ... AIBDQ
Association of International Border Agencies (EA) ... AIBA
Association of International Colleges and Universities (EA) ... AICU
Association of International Courier and Express Services (EAIO) ... AICES
Association of International Education Administrators (EA) ... AIEA
Association of International Health Researchers (EA) ... AIHR
Association of International Healthcare Recruiters and Employers (NTPA) ... AIHRE
Association of International Industrial Irradiation (SAUO) ... AIII
Association of International Industrial Irradiation (SAUO) ... AIII
Association of International Institute of Arts and Letters ... AIAL
Association of International Insurance Agents [*Later, Intersure*] (EA) ... AIIA
Association of International Insurance Agents (SAUO) ... AIIA
Association of International Irradiation (SAUO) ... AIII
Association of International Libraries (TELE) ... AIL
Association of International Libraries/North America ... AIL/NA
Association of International Marathons and Road Races (SAUO) ... AIMR
Association of International Marathons and Road Races [*New Zealand*] (EAIO) ... AIMS
Association of International Marketing (EAIO) ... AEME
Association of International Marketing [*British*] (EAIO) ... AIM
Association of International Meeting Planners (EA) ... AIMP
Association of International Photography Art Dealers (EA) ... AIPAD
Association of International Publishers Representatives (SAUO) ... AIPR
Association of International Relations Clubs (EA) ... AIRC
Association of International Schools in Africa (EA) ... AISA
Association of International Workcamps for Peace (SAUO) ... AIWCP
Association of Interns and Medical Students (SAUO) ... AIMES
Association of Interpreters and Translators of South Australia ... AITSA
Association of Interpretive Naturalists [*Later, NAI*] (EA) ... AIN
Association of Interracial Marriages ... AIM
Association of Interstate Commerce Commission Practitioners (EA) ... AICCP
Association of Interstate Motor Carriers (SAUO) ... AIC
Association of Interstate Motor Carriers [*Defunct*] ... AIMC
Association of Interstate Motor Carriers, Newark NJ [*STAC*] ... AIC
Association of Investment Brokers [*New York, NY*] (EA) ... AIB
Association of Investment Clubs (SAUO) ... AIC
Association of Investment Managment Sales Executives (NTPA) ... AIMSE
Association of Investment Trust Companies (ODBW) ... AITC
Association of Investment Trusts [*British*] (BI) ... AIT
Association of Invoice Factors [*British*] (DBA) ... AIF
Association of Iowa Fairs (SRA) ... AIF
Association of Iowa Merchants (SRA) ... AIM
Association of Irish Launderers and Cleaners (SAUO) ... AILC
Association of Irish Musical Societies (EAIO) ... AIMS
Association of Iron and Steel (SAUO) ... AIS
Association of Iron and Steel Engineers (EA) ... AISE
Association of Iron Ore Exporting Countries ... AIOEC
Association of Iron-ore Exporting Countries (SAUO) ... APEF
Association of Island Marine Laboratories of the Caribbean (EA) ... AIMLC
Association of Italian Bankers (SAUO) ... ABI
Association of Italian Families and Friends of Handicapped Children [*Australia*] ... HANDITAL
Association of Jamaican Trusts (United Kingdom) [*British*] ... AJT(UK)
Association of Japanese Business Studies (VERA) ... AJBS
Association of Japanese Geographers (SAUO) ... AJG
Association of Japanese Residing in Japan (SAUO) ... AJRJ
Association of Jensen Owners (EA) ... AJO
Association of Jesuit Colleges and Universities (EA) ... AJCU
Association of Jewish Antiboverty Workers (SAUO) ... AJAPW
Association of Jewish Anti-Poverty Workers [*Superseded by ECJF*] ... AJAPW
Association of Jewish Book Publishers (EA) ... AJBP
Association of Jewish Center Professionals (NTPA) ... AJCP
Association of Jewish Center Workers (EA) ... AJCW
Association of Jewish Chaplains of the Armed Forces (EA) ... AJCAF
Association of Jewish Community Relations Workers (EA) ... AJCRW
Association of Jewish Day Schools [*Association des Ecoles Juives*] (AC) ... AJDS
Association of Jewish Ex-Service Men and Women (SAUO) ... AJEX
Association of Jewish Family and Children's Agencies (EA) ... AJFCA
Association of Jewish Family, Children's Agency Professionals (EA) ... NACHES
Association of Jewish Genealogical Societies (EA) ... AJGS
Association of Jewish Libraries (EA) ... AJL
Association of Jewish Refugees in Great Britain ... AJR
Association of Jewish Sponsored Camps (EA) ... AJSC
Association of Jewish Women's Organisations [*British*] (DI) ... AJWO
Association of Journalists Against Extremism [*British*] (DI) ... AJAX
Association of Junior Leagues (EA) ... AJL
Association of Junior Leagues International (NTPA) ... AJLI
Association of Jute Spinners and Manufacturers [*British*] (DBA) ... AJSM
Association of Jute Spinners and Manufacturers (SAUO) ... AJSM
Association of Juvenile Compact Administrators (SAUO) ... AJCA
Association of Kew Gardeners in America [*Defunct*] (EA) ... AKGA
Association of Kinsmen Clubs (EA) ... KIN
Association of Knitted Fabrics Manufacturers (EA) ... AKFM
Association of Korean University Press (SAUO) ... AKUP
Association of Korean University Presses ... AKUP
Association of Labor and Management Administrators and Consultants on Alcoholism (SAUO) ... ALMACA
Association of Labor Management Administrators and Consultants (SAUO) ... ALMAC
Association of Labor Mediation Agencies [*Later, ALRA*] (EA) ... ALMA
Association of Labor Relations Agencies (EA) ... ALRA
Association of Labor-Management Administrators and Consultants on Alcoholism (EA) ... ALMACA
Association of Ladies of Charity of the United States (EA) ... ALCUS
Association of Land and Property Owners ... ALPO
Association of Land Grant Colleges and Universities [*Later, NASULGC*] ... ALGCU
Association of Land-Grant Colleges and Universities (SAUO) ... ALGU
Association of Language Learning [*British*] (DBA) ... ALL
Association of Late-Deafened Adults (EA) ... ALDA
Association of Latvian Academic Societies [*Defunct*] (EA) ... ALAS
Association of Law Costs Draftsmen [*British*] (DBA) ... ALCD
[*The*] **Association of Law Teachers** [*British*] ... ALT
Association of Lawyers for the Defence of the Unborn (EAIO) ... ALDU
Association of Leadership Educators (EA) ... ALE
Association of Learned Societies in Social Sciences [*British*] (DBA) ... ALSISS
Association of Learning Disabled Adults [*Defunct*] (EA) ... ALDA
Association of Lecturers in Accountancy (SAUO) ... ALA
Association of Lecturers in Accountancy [*British*] ... ALIA
Association of Lecturers in Accountancy (SAUO) ... ALJA
Association of Lecturers in Colleges of Education in Scotland ... ALCES
Association of Lecturers in Scottish Central Institutions (AIE) ... ALSCI
Association of Legal Administrators (EA) ... ALA
Association of Legal Aid Attorneys of the City of New York (EA) ... ALAA
Association of Legal Aid Lawyers (SAUO) ... ALAL
Association of Legal Secretaries [*British*] (DBA) ... ALS
Association of Lesbian and Gay Psychologists (EA) ... ALGP
Association of Liberal Councillors (SAUO) ... ALC
Association of Liberal Trade Unionists (SAUO) ... ALTU
Association of Liberal Trade Unionists [*British*] (DI) ... ALTU
Association of Libertarian Feminists (EA) ... ALF
Association of Librarians in the History of the Health Sciences (EA) ... ALHHS
Association of Libraries of Judaica and Hebraica (SAUO) ... ALJH
Association of Libraries of Judaica and Hebraica in Europe ... ALJH
Association of Library and Information Professionals (SAUS) ... SKIP
Association of Library Magazines of America (DGA) ... ALMA
Association of Licensed Aircraft Engineers [*A union*] [*British*] ... ALAE
Association of Licensed Automobile Manufacturers ... ALAM
Association of Licensed Clubs of Western Australia ... ALCWA
Association of Licensed Trade Relief Agencies [*British*] (DBA) ... ALTRA
Association of Life Agency Officers [*Later, LIMRA*] ... ALAO
Association of Life Insurance Counsel (EA) ... ALIC
Association of Life Insurance Medical Directors (SAUO) ... ALIMD
Association of Life Insurance Medical Directors of America (EA) ... ALIMDA
Association of Life Underwriters of South Dakota (SRA) ... ALU
Association of Lifting Tackle Manufacturers (SAUO) ... ALTM
Association of Light Alloy Refiners and Smelters Ltd. [*British*] (BI) ... ALAR
Association of Lightweight Aggregate Manufacturers (SAUO) ... ALAM
Association of Liquidpaperboard Carton Manufacturers ... ALCM
Association of Literary Magazines of America [*Later, CCLM*] (EA) ... ALMA
Association of Literary Scholars and Critics (NTPA) ... ALSC
Association of Lithuanian Foresters in Exile [*Defunct*] (EA) ... LMSI
Association of Lithuanian Workers (EA) ... ALW
Association of Litigation Support Managers [*Australia*] ... ALSM
Association of Little Presses (DGA) ... ALP
Association of Little Theatre Groups [*Australia*] ... ALTG
Association of Living Historical Farms and Agricultural Museum (SAUS) ... ALHFAM
Association of Lloyd's Members [*British insurers' organization*] (ECON) ... ALM
Association of Loading and Elevating Equipment Manufacturers [*British*] (EAIO) ... ALEM
Association of Loading Equipment Manufacturers (CIST) ... ALEM
Association of Local Air Pollution Control Officers [*Environmental Protection Agency*] (ERG) ... ALAPO
Association of Local Air Pollution Control Officials (EA) ... ALAPCO
Association of Local Authority Chief Executives [*British*] (DBA) ... ALACE
Association of Local Authority Valuers and Estate Surveyors (SAUO) ... ALAVES
Association of Local Government Clerks (SAUO) ... ALGC
Association of Local Government Engineers and Surveyors [*British*] (DI) ... ALGES
Association of Local Government Finance Officers (SAUO) ... ALGFO
Association of Local Government Financial Officers [*British*] (DI) ... ALGFO
Association of Local Housing Finance Agencies (EA) ... ALHFA
Association of Local Official Health Agencies (AC) ... ALOHA
Association of Local Telecommunications Services (NTPA) ... ALTS

Association of Local Television Stations (SAUO) ... ALTV
Association of Local Television Stations (NTPA) ... ILTV
Association of Local Television Stations, Inc. ... ALTV
Association of Local Transport Airlines [*Defunct*] (EA) ... ALTA
Association of London Authorities (HEAS) ... ALA
Association of London Borough Engineers and Surveyors [*British*] (BI) ... ALBES
Association of London Chief Librarians ... ALCL
Association of London Computer Clubs (NITA) ... ALCC
Association of London Graduates and Students (SAUO) ... ALGS
Association of London Housing Estates [*British*] (DI) ... ALHE
Association of London Master Tailors (SAUO) ... ALMT
Association of London Theatre Press Representatives (SAUO) ... ALTPR
Association of Long Distance Telephone Companies (EA) ... ALTEL
Association of Long-distance Telephone Companies (SAUO) ... ALTEL
Association of Los Alamos Scientists (SAUO) ... ALAS
Association of Louisiana Electric Cooperatives (SRA) ... ALEC
Association of Lunar and Planetary Observers (EA) ... ALPO
Association of Lutheran College Faculties (EA) ... ALCF
Association of Lutheran Men (EA) ... ALM
Association of Lutheran Secondary Schools (EA) ... ALSS
Association of Machinery and Equipment Appraisers (EA) ... AMEA
Association of Magisterial Officers [*British*] (DBA) ... AMO
Association of Mail Order Publishers (DGA) ... AMOP
Association of Major Charitable Associations ... AMCO
Association of Major City Building Officials (EA) ... AMCBO
Association of Major Power Consumers in Ontario (AC) ... AMPCO
Association of Major Power Consumers of Ontario (SAUO) ... AMPCO
Association of Major Symphony Orchestra Volunteers (EA) ... AMSO
Association of Makers of Packaging Papers [*British*] (DBA) ... AMPP
Association of Makers of Printing and Writing Papers (DGA) ... AMPW
Association of Makers of Printings and Writings [*British*] (DBA) ... AMPW
Association of Makers of Soft Tissue Papers [*British*] (DBA) ... AMSTP
Association of Malt Products Manufacturers [*British*] (BI) ... AMPM
Association of Managed Care Dentists (SAUO) ... AMCD
Association of Managed Care Providers (SAUO) ... AMCP
Association of Managed Healthcare Organizations (NTPA) ... AMHO
Association of Management (EA) ... AM
Association of Management (NTPA) ... AoM
Association of Management Analysts in State and Local Government (EA) ... AMASLG
Association of Management Analysts in State and Local Government (EA) ... MASLIG
Association of Management and Business Education (AIE) ... AMBE
Association of Management & International Association of Management (NTPA) ... AoM/IAoM
Association of Management and Professional Staffs [*British*] (DBA) ... AMPS
Association of Management Consultants (EA) ... AMC
Association of Management Education and Development [*British*] (DBA) ... AMED
Association of Management Education Centres [*British*] ... AMEC
Association of Management in Public Health [*Later, AAHA*] (EA) ... AMPH
Association of Managerial Electrical Executives [*British*] (BI) ... AMEE
Association of Managerial Electrical Executives (SAUO) ... AMEE
Association of Managers, Carders and Overlookers (SAUO) ... AMCO
Association of Managers in Magnetic Resonance Laboratories (SAUO) ... AMMRL
Association of Manipulative Medicine [*British*] (BI) ... AMM
Association of Manitoba Museums (AC) ... AMM
Association of Manpower Franchise Owners (EA) ... AMFO
Association of Manufacturers Allied to the Electrical and Electronic Industry (SAUO) ... AMA
Association of Manufacturers and Exporters of Concentrated and Unconcentrated Soft Drinks [*British*] (BI) ... AMECUSD
Association of Manufacturers and Suppliers for the Graphic Arts (DGA) ... AMSGA
Association of Manufacturers and Suppliers for the Graphic Arts (SAUO) ... AMSGA
Association of Manufacturers of Animal-Derived Food Enzymes [*EC*] (ECED) ... AMAFE
Association of Manufacturers of Chilled Car Wheels (SAUO) ... AMCCW
Association of Manufacturers of Confectionery and Chocolate (EA) ... AMCC
Association of Manufacturers of Domestic Electric Appliances [*British*] (DI) ... AMDEA
Association of Manufacturers of Small Switch and Fuse Gear (SAUO) ... AMSSFG
Association of Manufacturers of Woodworking Machinery (SAUO) ... AMWM
Association of Map Memorabilia Collectors (EA) ... AMMC
Association of Marian Helpers (SAUO) ... AMG
Association of Marian Helpers (EA) ... AMH
Association of Marine and General Engineers [*A union*] [*British*] ... AMGE
Association of Marine Catering and Supply [*British*] (DBA) ... AMCS
Association of Marine Engine Manufacturers (EA) ... AMEM
Association of Marine Engineering Schools [*Liverpool, Merseyside, England*] (EAIO) ... AMES
Association of Marine Engineering Schools (SAUO) ... AMES
Association of Marine Laboratories of the Caribbean (EAIO) ... AMLC
Association of Marine Traders [*British*] (BI) ... AMT
Association of Marine Underwriters (SAUO) ... AMU
Association of Marine Underwriters of British Columbia (AC) ... AMUBC
Association of Marine Underwriters of the United States (EA) ... AMUUS
Association of Marine Undewaters of the United States (SAUS) ... AMUUS
Association of Maritime Transport Users in the Central American Isthmus [*Guatemala*] (EAIO) ... USARIOS
Association of Maritime Transport Users in the Central American Isthmus [*Guatemala, Guatemala*] (EAIO) ... USUARIOI
Association of Market Survey Organisations [*British*] ... AMSO
Association of Marriage Enrichment [*British*] (DBA) ... AME
Association of Married Women (EA) ... AMW
Association of Marshall Scholars (EA) ... AMS
Association of Mary Immaculate (EA) ... AIM
Association of Maryland Pilots (SRA) ... AMP
Association of Massachusetts Homes and Services for the Aging (SRA) ... AMHSA
Association of Massage Therapists [*Australia*] ... AMT
Association of Master Hypnotists (EA) ... AMH
Association of Master Lightermen and Barge Owners [*British*] (BI) ... AML
Association of Master Lightermen and Barge Owners (SAUO) ... AMLBO
Association of Master of Business Administration (SAUO) ... AMBA
Association of Master of Business Administration Executives (NTPA) ... AMBA
Association of Master of Business Administration Executives [*New York, NY*] (EA) ... AMBAE
Association of Master Upholsterers [*British*] (BI) ... AMU
Association of Masters of Business Administration Executives (SAUO) ... AMBAE
Association of Maternal and Child Health Programs (NTPA) ... AMCHP
Association of Mature Canadians (AC) ... AMC
Association of Maximum Service Telecasters ... AMST
Association of Maximum Service Telecasters (EA) ... MST
Association of Maximum Service Telecasters, Inc. (SAUO) ... AMST
Association of Meat Inspectors [*British*] ... AMI
Association of Meat Inspectors (SAUO) ... AMJ
Association of Media Companies (WDAA) ... AMCO
Association of Media Producers [*ICIA*] [*Absorbed by*] (EA) ... AMP
Association of Media Sales Executives [*British*] (BI) ... AMSE
Association of Medical Advertising Agencies (EA) ... AMAA
Association of Medical Advisers in the Pharmaceutical Industry (SAUO) ... AMAPI
Association of Medical Deans in Europe (EAIO) ... AMDE
Association of Medical Diagnostic Manufactures (NTPA) ... AMDM
Association of Medical Education and Research in Substance Abuse (EA) ... AMERSA
Association of Medical Expenses Insurers (COBU) ... AMEI
Association of Medical Group Psychoanalysts (EA) ... AMGP
Association of Medical Illustrators (EA) ... AMI
Association of Medical Record Consultants [*Defunct*] (EA) ... AMRC
Association of Medical Record Officers [*British*] (BI) ... AMRO
Association of Medical Record Officers, Brighton (SAUO) ... AMRO
Association of Medical Rehabilitation Administrators (EA) ... AMRA
Association of Medical Rehabilitation Directors and Coordinators [*Later, AMRA*] (EA) ... AMRDC
Association of Medical Research Charities [*British*] ... AMRC
Association of Medical School Pediatric Department Chairmen (EA) ... AMSPDC
Association of Medical Secretaries [*British*] (BI) ... AMS
Association of Medical Secretaries, Practice Administrators and Receptionists (SAUO) ... AMSPAR
Association of Medical Superintendents of Mental Hospitals [*Later, AAPA*] (EA) ... AMSMH
Association of Medical Technologists [*British*] (DBA) ... AMT
Association of Medical Women in Western Australia ... AMWWA
Association of Meeting Professionals (NTPA) ... AMPs
Association of Members and Friends of the Historic Southern Tenant Farmers Union [*Defunct*] (EA) ... AMFHSTFU
Association of Members of Boards of Visitors [*British*] (DI) ... AMBOV
Association of Members of Boards of Visitors (WDAA) ... Ambov
Association of Membership and Marketing Executives (NTPA) ... AME
Association of Membership Executives (EA) ... AME
Association of Memoirists and Family Historians (EA) ... AMFH
Association of Men's Belt Manufacturers [*BA*] [*Absorbed by*] (EA) ... AMBM
Association of Mental Health Administrators (EA) ... AMHA
Association of Mental Health Clergy (EA) ... AMHC
Association of Mental Health Librarians (EA) ... AMHL
Association of Mental Health Practitioners with Disabilities [*Defunct*] (EA) ... AMHPD
Association of Mental Health Specialties (EA) ... AMHS
Association of Mental Hospital Chaplains (SAUO) ... AMHC
Association of Mercy Colleges (EA) ... AMC
Association of Messenger Services ... AMS
Association of Metal Sprayers [*British*] (EAIO) ... AMS
Association of Methodist Historical Societies [*Later, General Commission on Archives and History of the United Methodist Church*] (EA) ... AMHS
Association of Methodist Historical Societies (SAUO) ... AMHS
Association of Metropolitan Borough Engineers and Surveyors (SAUO) ... AMBES
Association of Metropolitan Authorities [*British*] ... AMA
Association of Metropolitan Chief Librarians [*London*] ... AMCL
Association of Metropolitan District Chief Librarians [*British*] ... AMDCL
Association of Metropolitan District Education and Children's Librarians [*British*] (DBA) ... AMDECL
Association of Metropolitan Sewage Agencies (SAUS) ... AMSA
Association of Metropolitan Sewer Agencies (SAUO) ... AMSA
Association of Metropolitan Sewerage Agencies (EA) ... AMSA
Association of Metropolitan Water Agencies (EA) ... AMWA
Association of Mexican-American Educators (OICC) ... AMAE
Association of Mezzanine Manufacturers (NTPA) ... AMM
Association of Microbial Food Enzyme Producers (EA) ... AMFEP
Association of Microbial Food Enzyme Producers within Western Europe (SAUO) ... AMFEP
Association of Microbiological Diagnostic Manufacturers (EA) ... AMDM

Association of Mideast Colleges (PSS) ... AMC
Association of Midwest Fish and Game Commissioners [*Later, AMFWA*] ... AMFGC
Association of Midwest Fish and Wildlife Agencies (EA) ... AMFWA
Association of Midwest Fish and Wildlife Commissioners [*Later, AMFWA*] (EA) ... AMFWC
Association of Midwest Game and Fish Commissioners (SAUO) ... AMGFC
Association of Migrants from Turkey [*Australia*] ... AMFT
Association of Military Banks of America [*Bethesda, MD*] (EA) ... AMBA
Association of Military Chefs Europe (SAUO) ... AMCE
Association of Military Colleges and Schools of the United States (NTPA) ... AMCSUS
Association of Military Dental Surgeons ... AMDS
Association of Military Surgeons (SAUO) ... AMS
Association of Military Surgeons of the United States (RDA) ... AMS
Association of Military Surgeons of the United States (EA) ... AMSUS
Association of Mill and Elevator Mutual Insurance Companies (EA) ... AMEMIC
Association of Miniature Engine Manufacturers [*British*] (DBA) ... AMEM
Association of Minicomputer Users (EA) ... AMU
Association of Mining and Exploration Companies Inc. (SAUO) ... AMEC
Association of Mining, Electrical, and Mechanical Engineers [*British*] (DI) ... AMEME
Association of Minnesota Counties (SRA) ... AMC
Association of Minority Health Professions Schools (EA) ... AMHPS
Association of Missile and Rocket Industries ... AMRI
Association of Missouri Electric Cooperatives (SRA) ... AMEC
Association of Model Agents [*British*] (DBA) ... AMA
Association of Motion Picture Producers [*Later, AMPTP*] (EA) ... AMPP
Association of Motion Pictures and Television Producers (SAUS) ... AMPTP
Association of Motor Racing Circuit Owners [*British*] (DBA) ... AMRCO
Association of Motor Vehicle Training Agents [*British*] (DBA) ... AMVTA
Association of Motorists Protection Services (SAUO) ... AMPS
Association of Movie Image Archivists (NTPA) ... AMIA
Association of Multiracial Playgroups ... AMP
Association of Municipal Administrators, Nova Scotia (AC) ... AMANS
Association of Municipal Authorities [*British*] (DCTA) ... AMA
Association of Municipal Clerks & Treasurers of Ontario (AC) ... AMCTO
Association of Municipal Corporations (SAUO) ... AMC
Association of Municipal Corporationss [*British*] ... AMC
Association of Municipal Employers (SAUO) ... AME
Association of Municipal Engineers (SAUO) ... AME
Association of Municipal Recycling Coordinators (AC) ... AMRC
Association of Municipalities of Ontario (AC) ... AMO
Association of Museum Stores (EA) ... AMS
Association of Music Personnel in Public Radio (SAUO) ... AMPPR
Association of Music Video Broadcasters [*Defunct*] (EA) ... AMVB
Association of Musical Instrument Industries [*British*] (BI) ... AMII
Association of Muslim Scientists and Engineers (EA) ... AMSE
Association of Muslim Social Scientists (EA) ... AMSS
Association of Mutual Fire Insurance Engineers [*Later, ILCA*] ... AMFIE
Association of Mutual Fund Plan Sponsors [*Later, ICI*] (EA) ... AMFPS
Association of Mutual Insurance Engineers [*Later, ILCA*] (EA) ... AMIE
Association of Mutual Insurance Engineers (SAUO) ... AMIE
Association of Name Plate Manufacturers (SAUO) ... ANPM
Association of National Advertisers (SAUO) ... ANA
Association of National Advertisers (EA) ... ANA
Association of National Grasslands (EA) ... ANG
Association of National Health Service Corps Scholarship Recipients [*Defunct*] (EA) ... ANHSCSR
Association of National Health Service Corps Scholarship Recipients (SAUO) ... ANHSCSR
Association of National Health Service Officers [*British*] ... ANHSO
Association of National Health Service Supplies Officers [*British*] (DBA) ... ANHSSO
Association of National Non-Profil Artists Centres (SAUS) ... ANNPAC
Association of National Non-Profit Artists' Centres [*Canada*] ... ANNPAC
Association of National Olympic Committees [*See also ACNO*] [*Paris, France*] (EAIO) ... ANOC
Association of National Olympic Committees of Africa (EA) ... ANOCA
Association of National Organizations in the Bakery and Confectionery Trade in the EC [*European Community*] [*Belgium*] (EAIO) ... ANOBCT-EC
Association of National Organizations of Fishing Enterprises of the EEC (SAUO) ... EURO-PECHE
Association of National Park Officers [*British*] ... ANPO
Association of National Trade Groups of Wood and Derived Products in the EEC [*European Economic Community*] **Countries** [*Denmark*] (EAIO) ... ANTGWDPEC
Association of Natural Resource Enforcement Trainers (EA) ... ANRET
Association of Natural Rubber Producing Countries [*Kuala Lumpur, Malaysia*] (EAIO) ... ANRPC
Association of Naturopathic Physicians of British Columbia (AC) ... ANPBC
Association of Naval Aviation (EA) ... ANA
Association of Naval ROTC [*Reserve Officers' Training Corps*] **Colleges and Universities** (NTPA) ... ANROTCCU
Association of Naval Weapons, Engineers, and Scientists [*Later, ASE*] ... ANWES
Association of Navigation Schools (SAUO) ... ANS
Association of Navy Safety Professionals [*Defunct*] (EA) ... ANSP
Association of Nebraska Community Action Agencies (SRA) ... ANCAA
Association of Negro Press Photographers ... ANPP
Association of Neighbourhood Councils [*British*] ... ANC
Association of Neighbourhood Houses of Greater Vancouver (AC) ... ANH
Association of Nepalese Cottage and Small (SAUO) ... ANCSI
Association of Neuro-Metabolic Disorders (EA) ... ANMD
Association of Neuroscience Departments and Programs (SAUO) ... ANDP
Association of Neurosurgical Physician Assistants (SAUO) ... ANSPA
Association of Neutron Radiographers (SAUO) ... ANR
Association of New Brunswick Land Surveyors [*Association des Arpenteurs-Geometres du Nouveau-Brunswick*] (AC) ... ANBLS
Association of New Jersey Environmental Commissions (SRA) ... ANJEC
Association of New York Libraries for Technical Services (SAUO) ... ANYLTS
Association of Newfoundland & Labrador Archivists [*L'Association des Archivistes de Terre-Neuve et de Labrador*] (AC) ... ANLA
Association of Newspaper Classified Advertising Managers (EA) ... ANCAM
Association of Nicaraguan Municipalities (SAUO) ... AMUNIC
Association of Nigerians Abroad ... ANA
Association of Noise Consultants [*British*] ... ANC
Association of Nonsmokers' Rights [*British*] (DBA) ... ANSR
Association of Nordic Aeroclubs (EA) ... ANA
Association of Nordic Paper Historians [*See also FNPH*] [*Sweden*] (EAIO) ... NPH
Association of Nordic War and UN Military Veterans (SAUO) ... ANWUNMV
Association of North American Directory Publishers (EA) ... ANADP
Association of North American Missions (EA) ... ANAM
Association of North American Paleontological Societies (SAUO) ... ANAPS
Association of North American Radio Clubs (EA) ... ANARC
Association of North Dakota Geographers (SAUO) ... ANDG
Association of Northwest Steelheaders (EA) ... ANWS
Association of Norwalk School Administration ... ANSA
Association of Norwegian Students Abroad (SAUO) ... ANSA
Association of Nova Scotia Hairdressers (AC) ... ANSH
Association of Nuclear Instrument Manufacturers [*Later, SAMA*] ... ANIM
Association of Nurse Administrators [*British*] (DBA) ... ANA
Association of Nursery Training Colleges [*British*] ... ANTC
Association of Nurses Aides (SAUO) ... AGAE
Association of Nurses Endorsing Transplantation (EA) ... ANET
Association of Nurses in AIDS [*Acquired Immune Deficiency Syndrome*] **Care** (EA) ... ANAC
Association of Nurses of Prince Edward Island (AC) ... ANPEI
Association of Nursing Directors & Supervisors of Ontario Official Health Agencies (AC) ... ANDSOOHA
Association of Nursing Religious [*British*] (DBA) ... ANR
Association of Obedience Clubs and Judges (EA) ... AOCJ
Association of Occupational and Environmental Clinics (NTPA) ... AOEC
Association of Occupational Health Professionals (NTPA) ... AOHP
Association of Occupational Therapists [*British*] (BI) ... AOT
Association of Occupational Therapists in Mental Health (SAUO) ... AOTMH
Association of Occupational Therapists of Manitoba [*Association des Ergotherapeutes du Manitoba*] (AC) ... AOTM
Association of Officers of Taxes (SAUO) ... AOT
Association of Officers of the Ministry of Labour (SAUO) ... AOML
Association of Officers of the Supreme Court (SAUO) ... AOSC
Association of Official Agricultural Chemists (DAVI) ... AOAC
Association of Official Analytical Chemists (EA) ... AOAC
Association of Official Analytical Chemists - Europe [*Bennekom, Netherlands*] (EAIO) ... AOAC Europe
Association of Official Architects [*British*] ... AOA
Association of Official Racing Chemists (EA) ... AORC
Association of Official Seed Analysts (EA) ... AOSA
Association of Official Seed Certifying Agencies (EA) ... AOSCA
Association of Official Shortland Writers (SAUO) ... AOSW
Association of Offshore Diving Contractors [*British*] (DBA) ... AODC
Association of Ohio Children's Hospitals (SRA) ... AOCH
Association of Ohio Life Insurance Companies (SRA) ... AOLIC
Association of Ohio Longrifle Collectors (EA) ... AOLRC
Association of Ohio Philanthropic Homes and Housing for the Aging (SRA) ... AOPHA
Association of Oil Pipe Lines (SAUO) ... AOP
Association of Oil Pipe Lines (EA) ... AOPL
Association of Oilwell Servicing Contractors (EA) ... AOSC
Association of Oklahoma General Contractors (SRA) ... AOGC
Association of Old Crows (EAIO) ... AOC
Association of Old Crows (SAUO) ... AOCs
Association of Oldetime Barbell and Strongmen (EA) ... AOBS
Association of Oncology Social Work (NTPA) ... AOSW
Association of Online Professionals ... AOP
Association of Ontario Health Centres [*Association des Centres de Sante de l'Ontario*] (AC) ... AOHC
Association of Ontario Land Surveyors [*Canada*] (GEOI) ... AOLS
Association of Ontario Midwives [*Association des Sages-Femmes de l'Ontario*] [*Formerly, Ontario Association of Midwives*] (AC) ... AOM
Association of Ontario Road Superintendents (AC) ... AORS
Association of Operating Room Nurses (EA) ... AORN
Association of Operating Room Nurses, Denver, CO [*Library symbol*] [*Library of Congress*] (LCLS) ... CoDORN
Association of Operating Room Technicians [*Later, AST*] (EA) ... AORT
Association of Operating Room Techniques (SAUO) ... AORT
Association of Operative Millers (EA) ... AOM
Association of Optical Practitioners [*British*] (BI) ... AOP
Association of Optical Practitioners (SAUO) ... AOP
Association of Optical Workers and Spectacle Frame Makers [*A union*] [*British*] ... AOWSFM
Association of Optometric Educators (EA) ... AOE
Association of Optometrists [*British*] (DBA) ... AOP
Association of Oregon Community Development Organizations (SRA) ... AOCDO
Association of Oregon Counties (SRA) ... AOC
Association of Organ Procurement Organizations (NTPA) ... AOPO
Association of Organised Trades (SAUO) ... AOT
Association of Organisers of Music, Scotland ... AOMS
Association of Organisers of Physical Education (SAUO) ... AOP

Association of Organisers of Physical Education in Scotland (SAUO) ..... AOPES
Association of Organisers of Physical Education, Scotland (SAUS) .... AOP
Association of Organisers of Physical Education, Scotland .... AOPES
Association of Orthodox Jewish Scientists (EA) .... AOJS
Association of Orthodox Jewish Teachers (EA) .... AOJT
Association of Orthodox Jews in Communications (EA) .... AOJC
Association of Orthopaedic Chairmen (EA) .... AOC
Association of Osteopathic Directors and Medical Educators (SAUO) ..... AODME
Association of Osteopathic Publications [*Defunct*] .... AOP
Association of Osteopathic State Executive Directors (EA) .... AOSED
Association of Otolaryngology Administrators (EA) .... AOA
Association of Our Lady of Salvation [*Defunct*] .... AOLS
Association of Outplacement Consulting Firms (EA) .... AOCF
Association of Outplacement Consulting Firms International (NTPA) .... AOCFI
Association of Overseas Educators [*Defunct*] (EA) .... AOE
Association of Pacific Coast Geographers (SAUO) .... APCG
Association of Pacific Fisheries (SAUO) .... APF
Association of Pacific Fisheries [*Later, PSPA*] (EA) .... APF
Association of Package Tour Travellers [*British*] (DBA) .... APTT
Association of Paediatric Anaesthetists of Great Britain and Ireland [*Birmingham, England*] (EAIO) .... APA
Association of Paid Circulation Publications (EA) .... APCP
Association of Painting Craft Teachers [*British*] .... APCT
Association of Painting Craft Teachers (SAUO) .... APCT
Association of Pakistani Physicians (EA) .... APP
Association of Pakistani Physicians (EA) .... APPNA
Association of Palm Oil Importers [*British*] (DBA) .... APOI
Association of Paper Distributors (DGA) .... APD
Association of Parents of Vaccine-Damaged Children (SAUO) .... APVDC
Association of Parents Paying Child Support (EA) .... APPCS
Association of Parliamentary Librarians in Canada .... APLIC
Association of Parliamentary Librarians of Australasia .... APLA
Association of Paroling Authorities (NTPA) .... APAI
Association of Paroling Authorities International (EA) .... APA
Association of Parti-Colored Arabians .... APA
Association of Part-Time Professionals (EA) .... AP-TP
Association of Passenger Transport Executives and Managers [*British*] (DCTA) .... APTEM
Association of Pastoral Care of the Mentally Ill [*British*] (DBA) .... APCMI
Association of Pathology Chairmen (EA) .... APC
Association of Pathology Chairs [*Formerly, Association of Pathology Chairmen*] (EA) .... APC
Association of Patternmakers and Allied Craftsmen [*A union*] [*British*] (DCTA) .... APAC
Association of Payment Clearance Services (WDAA) .... APCS
Association of Payment Clearing Services [*British*] (DBA) .... APACS
Association of PC User Groups (SAUS) .... APCUG
Association of Pediatric Oncology Nurses (EA) .... APON
Association of Pediatric Oncology Social Workers (EA) .... APOSW
Association of Pediatric Program Directors (NTPA) .... APPD
Association of Pediatric Societies of the Southeast Asian Region (EA) .... APSSEAR
Association of Pennsylvania State College and University Faculties (SRA) .... APSCUF
Association of Pension Lawyers [*British*] (DBA) .... APL
Association of Pensioneer Trustees [*British*] (DBA) .... APT
Association of Pensioners & Injured Workmen of Ontario (AC) .... APIO
Association of People for Practical Life Education (SAUO) .... APPLE
Association of Performing Arts Presenters (EA) .... APAP
Association of Performing Arts Presenters (NTPA) .... ARTSP
Association of perioperative Registered Nurses (SAUO) .... AORN
Association of Permanent Building Societies of Queensland (SAUO) .... APBSQ
Association of Personal Assistants and Secretaries [*Leamington Spa, Warwickshire, England*] [*Defunct*] (EAIO) .... APAS
Association of Personal Computer User Groups (PCM) .... APCUG
Association of Personal Injury Lawyers .... APIL
Association of Personnel Agencies of New York .... APANY
Association of Pet Behavior Counsellors (GVA) .... APBC
Association of Petrochemical Producers in Europe (ECON) .... APPE
Association of Petroleum Exploration Agencies (SAUO) .... APEA
Association of Petroleum Geologists (IID) .... AAPG
Association of Petroleum Writers (EA) .... APW
Association of Pharmaceutical Employers (SAUO) .... APE
Association of Pharmaceutical Importers [*British*] (DBA) .... API
Association of Philippine Coconut Desiccators .... APCD
Association of Philippine Coconut Desiccators Ceduna (SAUO) .... APCDC
Association of Philippine Physicians in America (EA) .... APPA
Association of Philippine Practicing Physicians in America [*Later, APPA*] (EA) .... APPPA
Association of Philippine-American Women (EA) .... APAW
Association of Philosophical Journals Editors (SAUO) .... APJE
Association of Philosophy Journal Editors (EA) .... APJE
Association of Photo Sensitizers (EA) .... APS
Association of Photographers (SAUO) .... AOP
Association of Photographic Importers and Distributors (EA) .... APID
Association of Photographic Laboratories [*British*] (DBA) .... APL
Association of Physical Education and Sport for Girls and Women (SAUO) .... APESGW
Association of Physical Fitness Centers (EA) .... APFC
Association of Physical Oceanographers (SAUO) .... APO
Association of Physical Oceanography (SAUO) .... APO
Association of Physical Plant Administrators (SARE) .... APPA
Association of Physical Plant Administrators of Universities and Colleges (SAUO) .... APPA
Association of Physical Plant Administrators of Universities and Colleges (SAUO) .... APPAUC
Association of Physician Assistant Programs (EA) .... APAP
Association of Physician Assistants in Obstetrics and Gynecology (SAUO) .... APAOG
Association of Physicians Assistants in Cardio-Vascular Surgery (SAUS) .... APACVS
Association of Physicians in Industry (SAUO) .... API
Association of Piano Class Teachers [*British*] (BI) .... APCT
Association of Planned Parenthood Physicians (SAUO) .... APPP
Association of Planned Parenthood Professionals [*Later, ARHP*] (EA) .... APPP
Association of Plant Breeders of the European Economic Community (SAUO) .... COMASSO
Association of Plastic Cable Makers [*British*] (BI) .... APCM
Association of Plastic Raw Material Distributors [*Defunct*] (EA) .... APRMD
Association of Plastics Manufacturers in Europe (EA) .... APME
Association of Plastics Sciences (SAUO) .... APS
Association of Plastics Societies (SAUO) .... APS
Association of Playing Fields Officers and Landscape Managers [*British*] (DBA) .... APFO & LM
Association of Pleasure Craft Operators [*British*] (BI) .... APCO
Association of Podiatrists in Federal Service [*Later, FSPMA*] (EA) .... APFS
Association of Point-of-Sale-Advertising (SAUO) .... APS
Association of Point-of-Sale-Advertising [*British*] .... APSA
Association of Police Surgeons of Great Britain .... APSGB
Association of Polish Geomorphologists (QUAC) .... APG
Association of Polish Translator and Interpreters (SAUO) .... ATIP
Association of Polish Women in the United States (EA) .... APWUS
Association of Polish Women of the United States (SAUO) .... APWUS
Association of Political Risk Analysts [*Later, CIBRM*] (EA) .... APRA
Association of Polysomnographic Technologists (EA) .... APT
Association of Polytechnic Teachers [*British*] .... APT
Association of Port Authorities .... APA
Association of Port Authorities (SAUO) .... APA
Association of Port Authotities (SAUS) .... APA
Association of Post Production Companies [*British*] (DBA) .... APPCo
Association of Postal Officials of Canada .... APOC
Association of Postal Supervising Officers (SAUO) .... APSO
Association of Postdoctoral Programs in Clinical Neuropsychology (SAUO) .... APPCN
Association of Postgraduate Physician Assistant Programs (SAUO) .... APPAP
Association of Poultry Processors and Poultry Import- and Export-Trade in the EEC Countries (EAIO) .... AVEC
Association of Poultry Slaughterhouse Operators (EA) .... APSO
Association of Practicing Accountants .... APA
Association of Practicing Certified Public Accountants (SRA) .... APCPA
Association of Presbyterian Colleges and Universities (EA) .... APCU
Association of Preserved Milk Manufacturers of the EEC [*European Economic Community*] [*France*] (EAIO) .... APMM-EEC
Association of Principals of Colleges [*British*] .... APC
Association of Principals of Colleges for Adult Education [*British*] .... APCAE
Association of Principals of Technical Institutions [*British*] .... APTI
Association of Principals, Wardens, and Advisers of University Women Students [*British*] (AIE) .... APWA
Association of Printing Machinery Importers (DGA) .... APMI
Association of Printing Technologists [*Later, IOP*] (DGA) .... APT
Association of Private Camps [*Later, AIC*] (EA) .... APC
Association of Private Client Investment Managers and Stockbrokers (ODBW) .... APCIMS
Association of Private Colleges and Universities in Georgia (SRA) .... APCUG
Association of Private Enterprise Education (EA) .... APEE
Association of Private Hospitals (EA) .... APH
Association of Private Hospitals (SAUO) .... APH
Association of Private Investors [*British*] (DBA) .... API
Association of Private Libraries (EA) .... APL
Association of Private Mortgage Professionals (NTPA) .... APMP
Association of Private Office Personnel Agencies .... APOPA
Association of Private Pension and Welfare Plans (EA) .... APPWP
Association of Private Postal Systems [*Later, AAPS*] (EA) .... APPS
Association of Private Traders [*British*] (BI) .... APT
Association of Private Weather Related Companies (EA) .... APWRC
Association of Privately Owned Seventh-Day Adventist Services and Industries (EA) .... ASI
Association of Producers of Isoglucose of the EEC (SAUO) .... API
Association of Producing Artists .... APA
Association of Productivity Specialists (EA) .... APS
Association of Professional and Executive Staff [*British*] .... APEX
Association of Professional Architects (SAUO) .... APA
Association of Professional Ball Players of America (EA) .... APBPA
Association of Professional Baseball Physicians (EA) .... APBP
Association of Professional Boardsailing Centres [*British*] (DBA) .... APBC
Association of Professional Bridge Players (EA) .... APBP
Association of Professional Collectors .... APC
Association of Professional Color Laboratories (EA) .... APCL
Association of Professional Communication Consultants (NTPA) .... APCC
Association of Professional Composers [*British*] (DBA) .... APC
Association of Professional Computer Consultants [*Canada*] (EAIO) .... APCC
Association of Professional Conservatories of Music (EA) .... APCM
Association of Professional Design Firms (EA) .... APDF
Association of Professional Directors of YMCAs [*Young Mens' Christian Associations*] in the United States (NTPA) .... APDYMCA
Association of Professional Energy Managers (EA) .... APEM
Association of Professional Engineers (SAUO) .... APE
Association of Professional Engineers (SAUS) .... APEA

Association of Professional Engineers & Geoscientists of British Columbia (AC) ... APEG BC
Association of Professional Engineers & Geoscientists of Newfoundland [*Formerly, Association of Professional Engineers of Newfoundland*] (AC) ... APEGN
Association of Professional Engineers, Geologists, and Geophysicists of Alberta [*Canada*] (DD) ... APEGGA
Association of Professional Engineers, Geologists and Geophysicists of Alberta (SAUO) ... APEGGA
Association of Professional Engineers, Geologists & Geophysicists of the Northwest Territories (AC) ... NAPEGG
Association of Professional Engineers of Manitoba (AC) ... APEM
Association of Professional Engineers of New Brunswick (AC) ... APENB
Association of Professional Engineers of Nova Scotia (AC) ... APENS
Association of Professional Engineers of Prince Edward Island (AC) ... APEPEI
Association of Professional Engineers of Saskatchewan (AC) ... APES
Association of Professional Engineers, Scientists, and Managers, Australia ... APESMA
Association of Professional, Executive, Clerical and Computer Staff (SAUO) ... APEX
Association of Professional Foresters (EAIO) ... APF
Association of Professional Genealogists (EA) ... APG
Association of Professional Geological Scientists [*Later, AIPG*] (EA) ... APGS
Association of Professional Hygienists (SARE) ... APIH
Association of Professional Insurance Women [*Acronym is now organization's official name*] (EA) ... APIW
Association of Professional Investigative Photographers (NTPA) ... APIP
Association of Professional Landscape Designers (EA) ... APLD
Association of Professional Librarians of New Brunswick (AC) ... APLNB
Association of Professional Material Handling Consultants (EA) ... APMHC
Association of Professional Music Therapists [*British*] (DBA) ... APMT
Association of Professional Organizations (SAUO) ... APO
Association of Professional Photogrammetrists (EA) ... APP
Association of Professional Piercers ... APP
Association of Professional Placement Agencies & Consultants [*Association de Placement en Personnel Agences et Conseillers*] (AC) ... APPAC
Association of Professional Police Investigators (EA) ... APPI
Association of Professional Recording Studios (SAUO) ... APRS
Association of Professional Recording Studios Ltd. [*British*] (BI) ... APRS
Association of Professional Researchers for Advancement (NTPA) ... APRA
Association of Professional Schools of International Affairs (EA) ... APSIA
Association of Professional Schools of Music (SAUO) ... APSM
Association of Professional Sleep Societies (EA) ... APSS
Association of Professional Staff (SAUO) ... APS
Association of Professional Student Services Personnel [*Association du Personnel Professionnel des Services aux Etudiants*] (AC) ... APSSP
Association of Professional Team Physicians (SAUS) ... PTP
Association of Professional Video Distributors [*British*] (DBA) ... APVD
Association of Professional Vocal Ensembles [*Later, Chorus America*] (EA) ... APVE
Association of Professional Writing Consultants (EA) ... APWC
Association of Professions (SAUO) ... AP
Association of Professions for the Mentally Handicapped [*British*] ... APMH
Association of Professors and Researchers in Religious Education (EA) ... APRRE
Association of Professors of Cardiology (EA) ... APC
Association of Professors of Gynecology and Obstetrics (EA) ... APGO
Association of Professors of Medicine (EA) ... APM
Association of Professors of Mission (EA) ... APM
Association of Professors of Modern Languages in Technological Universities (AIE) ... APMLTU
Association of Profiles Consultants (EA) ... APC
Association of Program Directors in Internal Medicine (EA) ... APDIM
Association of Program Directors in Radiology (SAUO) ... APDR
Association of Program Directors in Surgery (NTPA) ... APDS
Association of Programmed Learning [*London, England*] (MCD) ... APL
Association of Progressive Rental Organizations (EA) ... APRO
Association of Proposal Management Professionals ... APMP
Association of Protestant Development (SAUO) ... APRODEV
Association of Protestant Faiths (SAUO) ... APF
Association of Psychiatric Outpatient Centers of America [*Psychiatric Out patient Centers of America*] [*Acronym is based on former name,*] (EA) ... POCA
Association of Psychiatric Social Workers [*British*] (BI) ... APSW
Association of Psychiatrists in Training (SAUO) ... APIT
Association of Psychiatrists in Training (SAUO) ... APJT
Association of Psychological Counselling and Training [*British*] (DBA) ... APCT
Association of Psychology Internship Centers (EA) ... APIC
Association of Psychology Postdoctoral and Internship Centers (NTPA) ... APPIC
Association of Public Address Engineers [*British*] (BI) ... APAE
Association of Public Analysts [*British*] ... APA
Association of Public Analysts (SAUO) ... APA
Association of Public and Private Labor Employees ... APPLE
Association of Public Authority Surveyors [*Australia*] ... APAS
Association of Public Broadcasting Stations of New York (SRA) ... APBSNY
Association of Public Cooperations (SAUO) ... APC
Association of Public Corporations [*Miami, FL*] (EA) ... APC
Association of Public Data Users (SAUO) ... ADPU
Association of Public Data Users (EA) ... APDU
Association of Public Health Inspectors ... APHI
Association of Public Lighting Engineers [*British*] (BI) ... APLE
Association of Public Radio Stations [*Later, NPR*] (EA) ... APRS
Association of Public Service Administrative Staff [*British*] (DBA) ... APSAS
Association of Public Service Financial Administrators [*Association des Gestionnaires Financiers de la Fonction Publique*] (AC) ... APSFA
Association of Public Television Stations (SAUO) ... APTS
Association of Public Wharfingers of the Port of London (SAUO) ... APWPL
Association of Public Works Officials (SAUO) ... APWO
Association of Publication Production Managers (EA) ... APPM
Association of Publicly Traded Cornpanies (SAUO) ... APTC
Association of Publicly Traded Investment Funds [*Defunct*] (EA) ... APTIF
Association of Public-Safety Communications Officials-International (NTPA) ... APCO Internat'l
Association of Publishers ... AAP
Association of Publishers' Educational Representatives [*British*] ... APER
Association of Publishers Educational Representatives (SAUO) ... APERL
Association of Publishers of European Legal and Economic Works (SAUO) ... EUROLIBRI
Association of Publishers Representatives [*Later, NAPR*] (EA) ... APR
Association of Puddlers and Forgemen of Great Britain (SAUO) ... APF
Association of Pulp Consumers, Inc. [*Later, American Paper Institute*] (EA) ... APC
Association of Pulp Consumers, Inc. ... APCI
Association of Pulp Consumers, Incorporated (SAUO) ... APCI
Association of Qualified Curative Hypnotherapists [*British*] (DBA) ... AQCH
Association of Qualitative Research Practitioners (COBU) ... AQRP
Association of Quality Management Consultants [*British*] (DBA) ... AQMC
Association of Racing Commissioners International (EA) ... ARCI
Association of Racquetsports Manufacturers and Suppliers [*Inactive*] (EA) ... ARMS
Association of Radical Midwives [*British*] (DBA) ... ARM
Association of Radio and Electrical Engineers [*A union*] [*British*] ... AREE
Association of Radio and Television Employees of Canada ... ARTEC
Association of Radio Battery Manufacturers (SAUO) ... ARBM
Association of Radio Broadcasters (BARN) ... ARB
Association of Radio News Analysts [*Later, ARTNA*] ... ARNA
Association of Radio Reading Services (EA) ... ARRS
Association of Radio-Television News Analysts (SAUO) ... ARNA
Association of Radio-Television News Analysts [*Defunct*] (EA) ... ARTNA
Association of Railroad Advertising and Marketing (EA) ... ARAM
Association of Railroad Advertising Managers (SAUO) ... ARAM
Association of Railroad Editors [*Formerly, ARMEA*] (EA) ... ARE
Association of Railway Communicators (EA) ... ARC
Association of Railway Museums (EA) ... ARM
Association of Railway Preservation Societies (SAUO) ... ARPS
Association of Railway Preservation Societies Ltd. [*British*] ... ARPS
Association of Railway Superintendents of Bridges and Buildings (SAUO) ... ARSBB
Association of Railway Trainmen and Locomotive Firemen (EA) ... ARTLF
Association of Railway Trainmen and Locomotive Firemen ... RTLF
Association of Rain Apparel Contractors (EA) ... ARAC
Association of Real Estate License Law Officials (NTPA) ... ARELLO
Association of Real Estate Syndicators (EA) ... ARES
Association of Real Estate Women (NTPA) ... AREW
Association of Reclaimed Textile Processors [*British*] (DBA) ... ARTP
Association of Recognised English Language Schools [*British*] ... ARELS
Association of Recognised English Language Services (SAUO) ... ARELS
Association of Recognition Business Schools [*British*] (DBA) ... ARBS
Association of Record Librarians of North America (SAUO) ... ARLNA
Association of Records Executives and Administrators [*Later, ARMA*] (EA) ... AREA
Association of Records Managers and Administrators (EA) ... ARMA
Association of Recovering Motorcyclists (EA) ... ARM
Association of Reform Zionists of America (EA) ... ARZA
Association of Refrigerant and Desuperheating Manufacturing (EA) ... ARDM
Association of Regional Religious Communicators (EA) ... ARRC
Association of Registered Bank Holding Companies [*Later, ABHC*] (EA) ... ARBHC
Association of Registered Child Care Centers of Western Australia ... ARCCCWA
Association of Registered Driving Instructors [*British*] (BI) ... ARDI
Association of Registered Interior Designers of New Brunswick [*Association des Designers d'Interieur Immatricules du Nouveau-Brunswick*] (AC) ... IDNB
Association of Registered Interior Designers of Ontario [*Formerly, Interior Designers of Ontario*] (AC) ... ARIDO
Association of Registered Nurses of Newfoundland (AC) ... ARNN
Association of Registered Professional Foresters of New Brunswick [*Association des Forestiers Agrees du Nouveau-Brunswick*] (AC) ... ARPFNB
Association of Registrars of the Universities and Colleges of Canada ... ARUCC
Association of Regular Army Sergeants (EA) ... ARAS
Association of Regulatory and Clinical Scientists ... ARCS
Association of Rehabilitation Centers [*Later, NARF*] (EA) ... ARC
Association of Rehabilitation Facilities (SAUO) ... ARF
Association of Rehabilitation Ltd. ... AOR
Association of Rehabilitation Nurses (EA) ... ARN
Association of Rehabilitation Programs in Computer Technology (NTPA) ... ARPCT
Association of Rehabilitation Programs in Data Processing (EA) ... ARPDP
Association of Religion and Applied Behavioral Science (SAUO) ... ARABAS
Association of Religion and Applied Behavioral Science [*Later, ACC*] (EA) ... ARABS
Association of Relocation Agents [*British*] (DBA) ... ARA
Association of Renault and Chrysler for Automotive Development (SAUO) ... ARCAD
Association of Repeal Abortion Laws (SAUO) ... ARAL
Association of Reporters of Judicial Decisions (NTPA) ... ARJD
Association of Representatives of Old Pupils' Societies [*British*] ... AROPS
Association of Representatives of Professional Athletes (EA) ... ARPA

Association of Reproduction Materials Manufacturers (EA) .... ARMM
Association of Reproductive Health Professionals (EA) .... ARHP
Association of Reptilian & Amphibian Veterinarians (GVA) .... ARAV
Association of Research Directors (EA) .... ARD
Association of Research Libraries Collection Analysis Project .... ARLCAP
Association of Researchers in Construction Management (SAUO) .... ARCOM
Association of Researchers in Voluntary Action and Community Involvement (SAUO) .... ARVAC
Association of Reserve City Bankers (EA) .... ARCB
Association of Reserve Officers of the US Public Health Service [*Defunct*] (EA) .... AROUSPHS
Association of Reserves for Improving Social Economics (AC) .... ARISE
Association of Residential Care Homes of New Jersey (SRA) .... ARCH
Association of Residential Communities [*British*] (DBA) .... ARC
Association of Residential Letting Agents [*British*] (DBA) .... ARLA
Association of Residential Resources in Minnesota (SRA) .... ARRM
Association of Residents in Radiation Oncology (SAUO) .... ARRO
Association of Resort Publicity Officers [*British*] (BI) .... ARPO
Association of Retail Candy Shops .... ARCS
Association of Retail Confectioners (SAUO) .... ARC
Association of Retail Corn Dealers (SAUO) .... ARCD
Association of Retail Management Information Systems (SAUO) .... ARMIS
Association of Retail Marketing Services (NTPA) .... ARMS
Association of Retail Travel Agents (EA) .... ARTA
Association of Retailer-Owned Wholesalers in Foodstuff (SAUO) .... AROW
Association of Retailer-Owned Wholesalers in Foodstuffs [*Later, ACROWE*] (EAIO) .... AROWF
Association of Retarded Citizens of Anchorage (SAUO) .... ARCA
Association of Retired Americans (EA) .... ARA
Association of Retired Intelligence Officers (SAUO) .... ARIO
Association of Retired Members of the Armed Forces (SAUO) .... ARMAF
Association of Retired Naval Officers (SAUO) .... ARNO
Association of Retired Naval Officers [*British military*] (DMA) .... ARNO
Association of Retired Persons International [*Later, IARP*] .... ARP
Association of Retired United Nations Officals in Mexico (SAUO) .... AFPNU Mexico DF
Association of Retired United Nations Officials in Mexico (SAUO) .... AFPNU
Association of Rheumatology Health Professionals (NTPA) .... ARHP
Association of Rhode Island Health Sciences Librarians [*Library network*] .... ARIHSL
Association of Rhodesian and Nyasaland Industries .... ARNI
Association of River Authorities [*British*] (BI) .... ARA
Association of Road Racing Athletes (EA) .... ARRA
Association of Road Racing Clubs [*British*] (DBA) .... ARRC
Association of Road Surface Dressing Contractors [*British*] (BI) .... ARSD
Association of Road Traffic Sign Makers [*British*] (EAIO) .... ARTSM
Association of Roentgenological Organizations (SAUO) .... ARO
Association of Romanian Catholics of America (EA) .... ARCA
Association of Romanian-American Orthodox Ladies Auxiliaries (EA) .... ARAOLA
Association of Rooflight Manufacturers [*British*] (DBA) .... ARM
Association of Rotational Molders (EA) .... ARM
Association of Rotational Moulders (SAUO) .... ARM
Association of Round Tables in Central Africa .... ARTCA
Association of Rover Clubs (EAIO) .... ARC
Association of Rural District Council Surveyors [*British*] (BI) .... ARDCS
Association of Russian Imperial Medical Officers [*Defunct*] (EA) .... ARIMO
Association of Russian Imperial Naval Officers in America (EA) .... ARINOA
Association of Russian War Invalids of First World War (SAUO) .... ARWI
Association of Russian War Invalids of World War II (EA) .... ARWI
Association of Russian-American Scholars in the United States of America (SAUO) .... ARASUSA
Association of Sacred Heart Schools [*Australia*] .... ASHS
Association of Safety Council Executives (EA) .... ASCE
Association of Sales Administration Managers (EA) .... ASAM
Association of Sales Professionals (COBU) .... ASP
Association of Sanitary Protection Manufacturers [*British*] (DBA) .... ASPM
Association of Sanitary Towel Manufacturers (SAUO) .... ASTM
Association of School Based Administrators and Supervisors (NTPA) .... ASBAS
Association of School Business Officials International (EA) .... ASBO
Association of School Business Officials of the United States and Canada (SAUO) .... ASBO
Association of School Natural History Societies [*British*] .... ASNHS
Association of Schools and Colleges of Optometry (EA) .... ASCO
Association of Schools of Allied Health Professions (SAUO) .... ASAHP
Association of Schools of Journalism and Mass Communication (EA) .... ASJMC
Association of Schools of Public Health (EA) .... ASPH
Association of Schools of Public Health in the European Region (EAIO) .... ASPHER
Association of Science and Technology Centers (SAUO) .... ASTC
Association of Science Education (SAUO) .... ASE
Association of Science Fiction, Fantasy and Horror Films (SAUO) .... ASFFHF
Association of Science Museum Directors (EA) .... ASMD
Association of Science-Technology Centers (EA) .... ASTC
Association of Science-Technology Centers .... ASTEC
Association of Scientific Information Dissemination Centers (NITA) .... ASIDIC
Association of Scientific, Technical, and Managerial Staffs [*British*] .... ASTMS
Association of Scientific Workers [*British*] .... AScW
Association of Scientific Workers (SAUO) .... A Sc W
Association of Scientific Workers (SAUO) .... ASW
Association of Scientific Workers of South Africa (SAUO) .... AScWSA
Association of Scientific Writers (SAUO) .... ASW
Association of Scientists and Engineers of the Naval Sea Systems Command (SAUO) .... ASE
Association of Scientists and Engineers of the Naval Sea Systems Command (EA) .... ASE
Association of Scientists and Professional Engineering Personnel .... ASPEP
Association of Scottish Climbing Clubs (BI) .... ASCC
Association of Scottish Games and Festivals (EA) .... ASGF
Association of Scottish Local Health Councils [*British*] .... ASLHC
Association of Scottish Motoring Writers (SAUS) .... SMW
Association of Screen Magazine Publishers [*Defunct*] .... ASMP
Association of Sea and Air Ports Health Authority [*British*] .... ASAPHA
Association of Sea Fisheries Committees of England and Wales (DCTA) .... ASFC
Association of Sea Grant Program Institutes [*Marine science*] (OSRA) .... ASGPI
Association of Sea Training Organisations [*British*] (DBA) .... ASTO
Association of Seafood Importers (EA) .... ASI
Association of Sealant Applicators [*British*] (DBA) .... ASA
Association of Search and Selection Consultants [*British*] (DBA) .... ASSC
Association of Seattle Prostitutes (SAUO) .... ASP
Association of Second Class Mail Publishers (EA) .... ASCMP
Association of Secondary Teachers, Ireland (BI) .... ASTI
Association of Secretaries General of Parliaments (EA) .... ASGP
Association of Secretaries in Asia (SAUO) .... ASA
Association of Securities and Exchange Commission Alumni (EA) .... ASECA
Association of Self Employment Developers of Ontario (AC) .... ASEDO
Association of Self-Employed People (SAUO) .... ASEP
Association of Seminary Professors in the Practical Fields [*Later, APT*] (EA) .... ASPPF
Association of Semi-Rotary Wing Pump Manufacturers (MHDB) .... ASRWPM
Association of Senior Citizens Clubs (SAUO) .... ASC
Association of Senior Engineers [*NAVSHIPS*] .... ASE
Association of Senior Engineers of the Bureau of Ships [*Later, ASE*] (EA) .... ASEBS
Association of Senior Members (SAUO) .... ASM
Association of Service and Computer Dealers International (NTPA) .... ASCDI
Association of Seventh Day Pentecostal Assemblies (EA) .... ASDPA
Association of Seventh-Day Adventist Educators (EA) .... ASDAE
Association of Seventh-Day Adventist Engineers and Architects (EA) .... AEA
Association of Seventh-Day Adventist Librarians (EA) .... ASDAL
Association of Sexual and Marital Therapists [*British*] (DBA) .... ASMT
Association of Shareware Professionals (SAUS) .... ASP
Association of Shareware Professionals [*Canada*] .... ASP
Association of Shareware Professionals (SAUS) .... ASP
Association of Shell Boilermakers [*British*] (DBA) .... ASB
Association of Ship Brokers and Agents (SAUO) .... ASBA
Association of Ship Brokers and Agents - USA (EA) .... ASBA
Association of Ships' Compositions Manufacturers [*British*] (BI) .... ASCM
Association of Shopfront Section Manufacturers [*British*] (BI) .... ASSM
Association of Shopfront Section Manufacturers (SAUO) .... ASSM
Association of Short Circuit Testing Authorities (SAUO) .... ASCTA
Association of Short-Circuit Testing Authorities, Inc. [*British*] (BI) .... ASTA
Association of Show and Agricultural Organisations [*British*] .... ASAO
Association of SIDS [*Sudden Infant Death Syndrome*] **Program Professionals** (EA) .... ASPP
Association of Sixth Form Colleges [*British*] (DET) .... APVIC
Association of Ski Schools in Great Britain .... ASSGB
Association of Ski Schools of/in Great Britain (SAUO) .... ASSGB
Association of Sleep Disorders Centers (EA) .... ASDC
Association of Small Business Development Centers [*Washington, DC*] (EA) .... ASBDC
Association of Small Computer Users [*Later, ACU*] (EA) .... ASCU
Association of Small Computer Users [*Later, ACU*] (CSR) .... ASCUE
Association of Small Computer Users in Education (NITA) .... ASCUE
Association of Small Computers in Education (SAUO) .... ASCUE
Association of Small Island States (SAUO) .... AOSIS
Association of Small Island States (SAUO) .... ASIS
Association of Small Public Libraries of Ontario (AC) .... ASPLO
Association of Smoked Fish Processors (EA) .... ASFP
Association of Social and Behavioral Scientists (EA) .... ASBS
Association of Social Anthropologists of the Commonwealth [*British*] (EAIO) .... ASA
Association of Social Research Organisation (SAUO) .... ASRO
Association of Social Research Organisations [*British*] .... ASRO
Association of Social Science Teachers [*Later, ASBS*] (EA) .... ASST
Association of Social Services Directors (WDAA) .... ASSD
Association of Social Workers (SAUO) .... ASW
Association of Social Workers [*British*] (BI) .... ASW
Association of Societies for Growing Australian Plants .... ASGAP
Association of Software Brokers (EA) .... ASB
Association of Soil and Foundation Engineers [*Later, ASFE/The Association of Engineering Firms Practicing in the Geosciences*] (EA) .... ASFE
Association of Soil Conservation Officer Trainees .... ASCOT
Association of Solid Woven Belting Manufacturers [*British*] (BI) .... ASWB
Association of Sorbitol Producers in the European Community (EAIO) .... ASPEC
Association of Sorbitol Producers within the EC (SAUO) .... ASPEC
Association of Sound and Communication Engineers (SAUO) .... ASCE
Association of South Asian Archaeologists in Western Europe (EAIO) .... ASAAWE
Association of South Carolina Life Insurance Companies (SRA) .... ASCLIC
Association of South Central Oklahoma Governments (SAUO) .... ASCOG
Association of South East Asia (SAUO) .... ASEA
Association of South East Asian Nations: Indonesia-Singapore [*Submarine cable*] [*Telecommunications*] .... ASEANIS
Association of South East Asian Nations: Philippines-Singapore [*Submarine cable*] [*Telecommunications*] (TEL) .... ASEANPS
Association of South East Field Naturalists Societies .... ASEFNS
Association of South Pacific Airlines .... ASPA

Association of South Pacific Environmental Institutions ASPEI
Association of South Polar Research (SAUO) ASPR
Association of South-East Asia (SAUO) ASA
Association of Southeast Asian Institutions of Higher Learning [*Bangkok, Thailand*] ASAIHL
Association of South-East Asian Marine Scientists [*Marine science*] (OSRA) ASEAMS
Association of Southeast Asian Nations (DOMA) ASEAN
Association of South-East Asian Nations (SAUO) ASEAN
Association of South-East Asian States ASAS
Association of Southeast Asian Studies in the (United Kingdom) ASEAS(UK)
Association of Southeast Asian University Students ASEAUS
Association of Southeastern Railroads (SAUO) ASR
Association of Southeastern Research Libraries [*Library network*] ASERL
Association of Southern Agricultural Workers [*Later, SAAS*] ASAW
Association of Southern Baptist Campus Ministers (EA) ASBCM
Association of Southern Baptist Colleges and Schools (EA) ASBCS
Association of Space Explorers [*Later, ASE-USA*] (EA) ASE
Association of Space Explorers - USA (EAIO) ASE-USA
Association of Speakers Clubs [*British*] (DBA) ASC
Association of Special Education Administrators in Queensland [*Australia*] ASEAQ
Association of Special Events Professionals (SRA) ASEP
Association of Special Libraries and Documentation Centres (SAUO) ASLIC
Association of Special Libraries and Information Bureaux [*Association for Information Management*] [*British*] (AIE) ASLIB
Association of Special Libraries and Information Bureaux [*Acronym is now organization's official name*] Aslib
Association of Special Libraries and Information Services (SAUO) ASLIS
Association of Special Libraries in the Philippines (SAUS) ASLP
Association of Special Libraries of the Philippines ASLP
Association of Special Libraries Proceedings (journ.) (SAUS) ASLIB Proc
Association of Specialists in Cleaning and Restoration (EA) ASCR
Association of Specialists in Cleaning and Restoration (SAUO) ASCR International
Association of Specialists in Cleaning and Restoration International (NTPA) ASCRI
Association of Specialized and Cooperative Library Agencies (EA) ASCLA
Association of Specialized & Cooperative Library Agencies Chief Officers of State Library Agencies ASCLACOSLA
Association of Specialized & Cooperative Library Agencies Library Service to People with Visual & Physical Disabilities Forum ASCLALSPVPDF
Association of Specialized & Cooperative Library Agencies Library Service to Prisoners Forum ASCLALSPF
Association of Specialized Film Exhibitors [*Defunct*] (EA) ASFE
Association of Specialized Film Producers (SAUO) ASFP
Association of Specialized Film Producers (SAUO) ASPF
Association of Specialty Cut Flower Growers (NTPA) ASCFG
Association of Spectacle Makers [*Australia*] ASM
Association of Sports Information Directors (EA) ASID
Association of Sports Medicine of the Balkans (SAUO) ASMB
Association of Sports Museums and Halls of Fame [*Later, IASMHF*] (EA) ASMHF
Association of Sprocket Chain Manufacturers [*Defunct*] ASCM
Association of Sri-Lankans in America (EA) ASIA
Association of Staff Physician Recruiters (SAUO) ASPR
Association of Standards Laboratories ASL
Association of State and Inter-state Water Pollution Control Administrators (SAUO) ASIWCPA
Association of State and Interstate Water Pollution Control Administrators (SAUO) ASIWPCA
Association of State and Provincial Psychology Boards (NTPA) ASPPB
Association of State and Provincial Safety Coordinators [*Later, ASPSO*] (EA) ASPSC
Association of State and Provincial Safety Officials [*Formerly, ASPSC*] (EA) ASPSO
Association of State and Public Health Laboratory Directors (SAUO) ASTPHLD
Association of State and Territorial Chronic Disease Program Directors (SAUO) ASTCDPD
Association of State and Territorial Dental Directors (EA) ASTDD
Association of State and Territorial Directors of Health Promotion and Public Health Education (SAUO) ASTDHPPHE
Association of State and Territorial Directors of Local Health Services (SAUO) ASTDLHS
Association of State and Territorial Directors of Nursing (EA) ASTDN
Association of State and Territorial Directors of Public Health Education (NTPA) ASTDPHE
Association of State and Territorial Directors of Public Health Nursing (SAUO) ASTDPHN
Association of State and Territorial Epidemiologists (SAUO) ASTE
Association of State and Territorial Health Officers (SAUS) ASTHO
Association of State and Territorial Health Officials (EA) ASTHO
Association of State and Territorial Nutrition Directors ASTND
Association of State and Territorial Public Health Laboratory Directors (EA) ASTPHLD
Association of State and Territorial Public Health Nutrition Directors [*Defunct*] (EA) ASTPHND
Association of State and Territorial Public Health Nutrition Directors (SAUO) ASTPHND
Association of State and Territorial Solid Waste Management Officials (SAUO) ASTSWMO
Association of State Colleges and Universities [*Later, AASCU*] ASCU
Association of State Colleges and Universities Forestry Research Organizations (SAUO) ASCUFRO
Association of State Correctional Administrators (EA) ASCA
Association of State Dam Safety Officials (EA) ASDSO
Association of State Democratic Chairs (EA) ASDC
Association of State Drinking Water Administrators (SAUS) ASDWA
Association of State Employees in Management (SRA) ASEM
Association of State Floodplain Managers ASFM
Association of State Floodplain Managers (EA) ASFPM
Association of State Foresters [*Later, NASF*] ASF
Association of State Juvenile Justice Administrators [*NAJCA*] [*Absorbed by*] (EA) ASJJA
Association of State Labor Relations Agencies (EA) ASLRA
Association of State Library Agencies [*Formerly, Association of State Libraries*] [*Later, ASCLA*] ASLA
Association of State Maternal and Child Health and Crippled Children's Directors[*Later, AMCHCCP*] (EA) ASMCHCCD
Association of State Mediation Agencies [*Later, ALRA*] ASMA
Association of State Medical Officers [*Western Australia*] ASMO
Association of State Planning and Development Agencies [*Later, NASDA*] (EA) ASPDA
Association of State Public Health Veterinarians [*Later, NASPHV*] (EA) ASPHV
Association of State Supervisors of Mathematics (EA) ASSM
Association of State Telecommuni-cation Undertakings of the Andean Sub-regional Agreement (SAUO) ASETA
Association of State Trading Organizations of Developing Countries (SAUO) ASTRO
Association of State Universities and Land-Grant Colleges (EA) ASULGC
Association of State Veterinary Officers (GVA) ASVO
Association of State Wetland Managers (EA) ASWM
Association of Statisticians of American Religious Bodies (EA) ASARB
Association of Steel Conduit Manufacturers (SAUO) ASCM
Association of Steel Distributors (EA) ASD
Association of Steel Drum Manufacturers [*British*] (BI) ASDM
Association of Sterilizer and Disinfector Equipment Manufacturers [*British*] (EAIO) ASDEM
Association of Stock Exchange Firms [*Later, SIA*] (EA) ASEF
Association of Strategic Planning Consultants (EA) ASPC
Association of Street Lighting Contractors [*British*] (DBA) ASLC
Association of Street Lighting Erection Contractors [*British*] (BI) ASLEC
Association of String Class Teachers [*British*] (BI) ASCT
Association of Structural Draftsmen of America (EA) ASDA
Association of Structural Fire Protection Contractors and Manufacturers Ltd. [*British*] (DBA) ASFPCM
Association of Stud Sheep Breeders of Australia ASSBA
Association of Student and Professional Italian-Americans (EA) ASPI
Association of Student Chapters, American Institute of Architects ASC/AIA
Association of Student Chapters, American Institute of Architects (SAUO) ASCAIA
Association of Student Councils [*Canada*] AOSC
Association of Student Counselling [*British*] (DBA) ASC
Association of Student Governments ASG
Association of Student International Law Societies (EA) ASILS
Association of students of the European Management Programme (SAUO) EMP
Association of Students of the Radiologic Sciences (SAUO) ASRS
Association of Study Curriculum [*British*] (DBA) ASC
Association of Subscription Agents [*British*] (DBA) ASA
Association of Subspecialty Professors (SAUO) ASP
Association of Sugar Producers of Puerto Rico [*Defunct*] (EA) ASPPR
Association of Summer Olympic International Federations (SAUO) ASOIF
Association of Summer Session Deans and Directors (SAUO) ASSDD
Association of Summer Session Deans and Directors [*Later, AUSS*] (EA) ASSDD
Association of Summer Villages of Alberta (AC) ASVA
Association of Sun Tanning Organisations [*British*] (DBA) ASTO
Association of Superannuation and Pension Funds (SAUO) ASPF
Association of Supervising Electrical Engineers (SAUO) ASEE
Association of Supervisors in Purchasing and Supply [*British*] (DBQ) ASPS
Association of Supervisors of Sorting Assistants (SAUO) ASSA
Association of Supervisory and Administrative School Personnel (NTPA) ASASP
Association of Supervisory and Executive Engineers [*A union*] [*British*] ASEE
Association of Supervisory Public Health Inspectors (Ontario) (AC) ASPHIO
Association of Supervisory Staff Executives and Technicians (SAUO) ASSET
Association of Suppliers to Airlines, Airports, and Shipping [*British*] (DBA) ASAAS
Association of Suppliers to the Furniture Industries Show [*Wood Work Industrial Exhibition*] (TSPED) AFSI
Association of Suppliers to the Furniture Industry [*British*] (EAIO) ASFI
Association of Supportive Care Homes ASCH
Association of Surf Angling Clubs (EA) ASAC
Association of Surfing Professionals (EA) ASP
Association of Surgeons in Training [*British*] (DBA) ASIT
Association of Surgeons of Great Britain and Ireland (BI) AS
Association of Surgeons of South East Asia (EAIO) ASSEA
Association of Surgical Technologists (EA) AST
Association of Swimming Pool Contractors [*British*] (BI) ASPC
Association of Swimming Therapy [*British*] AST
Association of Symbolic Logic (SAUS) ASL
Association of Synthetic Yarn Manufacturers (EA) ASYM
Association of System 2000 Users for Technical Exchange ASTUTE
Association of Systematics Collections (SAUO) ASC
Association of Systems Management (SAUO) ASM
Association of Talent Agents (EA) ATA
Association of Tar Distillers (SAUO) ATD
Association of Tasmanian Forum Clubs [*Australia*] ATFC

Association of Tax Consultants (EA) ... ATC
Association of Teacher Educators (SAUO) ... Assn Tchr Ed
Association of Teacher Educators (EA) ... ATE
Association of Teacher Training Colleges and Departments of Education [*British*] (DI) ... ATTCDE
Association of Teachers and Lecturers [*British*] (DET) ... ATL
Association of Teachers in Colleges and Departments of Education [*British*] ... ATCDE
Association of Teachers in Colleges and Departments of Education (AIE) ... ATCODE
Association of Teachers in Independent Schools in New York City and Vicinity (EA) ... ATIS
Association of Teachers in Independent Schools in New York City and Vicinity (EA) ... ATISNYCV
Association of Teachers in Independent Schools of New York City and Vicinity (SAUO) ... ATIS
Association of Teachers in Penal Establishments [*British*] ... ATPE
Association of Teachers in Sixth Form and Tertiary Colleges [*British*] (AIE) ... ATVIC
Association of Teachers in Technical Institutes (SAUO) ... ATTI
Association of Teachers in Technical Institutions [*British*] ... ATTI
Association of Teachers of Domestic Science [*British*] (BI) ... ATDS
Association of Teachers of Dramatic Science [*British*] ... ATDS
Association of Teachers of Electrical Engineering [*British*] ... ATEE
Association of Teachers of English as a Foreign Language (SAUO) ... ATEFL
Association of Teachers of English as a Second Language (EA) ... ATESL
Association of Teachers of English in Quebec (AC) ... ATEQ
Association of Teachers of English of Quebec (SAUO) ... ATEQ
Association of Teachers of English to Pupils from Overseas (SAUO) ... ATEPO
Association of Teachers of Foundry and Allied Subjects (SAUO) ... ATFAS
Association of Teachers of French (AIE) ... ATF
Association of Teachers of Geology [*British*] ... ATG
Association of Teachers of German [*British*] ... ATG
Association of Teachers of German [*British*] ... ATGER
Association of Teachers of Italian [*British*] ... ATI
Association of Teachers of Japanese (EA) ... ATJ
Association of Teachers of Language in Negro Colleges (SAUO) ... ATLNC
Association of Teachers of Latin American Studies (EA) ... ATLAS
Association of Teachers of Lipreading to Adults [*British*] (DBA) ... ATLA
Association of Teachers of Management [*British*] ... ATM
Association of Teachers of Maternal and Child Health (EA) ... ATMCH
Association of Teachers of Mathematics [*Derby, England*] (EAIO) ... ATM
Association of Teachers of Mathematics (SAUO) ... ATM
Association of Teachers of Preventive Medicine (EA) ... ATPM
Association of Teachers of Printing and Allied Subjects [*British*] ... ATPAS
Association of Teachers of Russian [*British*] ... ATR
Association of Teachers of Russian (SAUO) ... ATR
Association of Teachers of Social Studies [*British*] ... ATSS
Association of Teachers of Spanish and Portuguese [*British*] ... ATSP
Association of Teachers of Technical Writing (EA) ... ATTW
Association of Teaching Aids in Mathematics (SAUO) ... ATM
Association of Technical and Supervisory Professionals (EA) ... ATSP
Association of Technical Artists [*Later, IG*] ... ATA
Association of Technical Artists (SAUO) ... ATA
Association of Technical Institutions (EY) ... ATI
Association of Technical Personnel in Ophthalmology (NTPA) ... ATPO
Association of Technical Professionals [*Defunct*] (EA) ... ATP
Association of Technical Studies Advisers [*British*] ... ATSA
Association of Technical Writers and Editors (SAUO) ... ATWE
Association of Technicians in Financing and Accounting (CIST) ... ATEA
Association of Technicians in Financing and Accounting (SAUO) ... ATFA
Association of Telegraph and Radio-telegraph Operators (SAUO) ... ARTG
Association of Telemedicine Service Providers (SAUO) ... ATSP
Association of Telemessaging Services International (EA) ... ATSI
Association of Telephone Answering Exchanges (SAUO) ... ATAE
Association of Telephone Answering Services (EA) ... ATAS
Association of Telephone Information and Entertainment Providers [*British*] ... ATIEP
Association of Telephone Messaging Suppliers [*Defunct*] (EA) ... ATMS
Association of Temporary and Interim Executive Services (COBU) ... ATIES
Association of Temporary Office Services ... ATOS
Association of Temporary Personnel Contractors ... ATPC
Association of Tennis Professionals [*Defunct*] (EA) ... ATP
Association of Tequila Producers (EA) ... ATP
Association of Test Publishers (NTPA) ... ATP
Association of Texas Colleges and Universities (SRA) ... ATCU
Association of Texas Graduate Schools (SRA) ... ATGS
Association of Texas Professional Educators (SRA) ... ATPE
Association of Texas Soil and Water Conservation Districts (SRA) ... ATSWCD
Association of Thalidomide-Damaged Children ... ATDC
Association of Thames Motor Boat Clubs (SAUO) ... ATMBC
Association of the Baltic National Parks (SAUO) ... ABNP
Association of the Bar of the City of New York. Committee on Amendment of the Law. Bulletin [*A publication*] (DLA) ... CAL Bull
Association of the Bar of the City of New York, New York, NY [*Library symbol*] [*Library of Congress*] (LCLS) ... NNB
Association of the Boot and Shoe Industry (SAUO) ... ABSI
Association of the Brazilian Computer and Peripherals Industries (SAUO) ... ABICOMP
Association of the British Pharmaceutical Industry ... ABPI
Association of the Chemical Profession of Ontario (AC) ... ACPO
Association of the Cider and Fruit Wine Industry of the EC [*Economic Community*] [*Belgium*] (EAIO) ... ACFWI-EC
Association of the Confectionery Industries of the EEC (SAUO) ... CAOBISCO
Association of the Customs Bar (SAUO) ... ACB
Association of the Customs Bar [*Later, CITBA*] (EA) ... ACB
Association of the Directors of Medical Student Education in Psychiatry (SAUS) ... ADMSEP
Association of the Electricity Supply Industry of East Asia and the Western Pacific (SAUO) ... AESIEAP
Association of the Episcopal Conferences of the Congo, of the Central African Republic and of Chad (SAUO) ... ACECCT
Association of the European Economic Community and the Associated African and Malagasy States (SAUO) ... EEC-AAMS
Association of the European Host Operators Group (SAUO) ... EHOG
Association of the European Independent Informatics Industry (PDAA) ... EIII
Association of the European Independent Informatics (or Information) Industry (SAUS) ... EIII
Association of the European National Olympic Committees (SAUO) ... AENOC
Association of the European National Olympic Committees [*See also ACNOE*] [*Brussels, Belgium*] (EAIO) ... ENOC
Association of the Free French in the United States (SAUO) ... AFFUS
Association of the German Nobility in North America (EA) ... DAGNA
Association of the Glucose Producers in the EEC (SAUO) ... AFG
Association of the Graphic Arts (EA) ... AGA
Association of the Health Occupations Teacher Educators (SAUO) ... AHOTE
Association of the Hungarian Librarians (SAUO) ... MKE
Association of the Institute for Certification of Computer Professionals (SAUO) ... AICCP
Association of the Institute of Asphalt Technology [*British*] (DBQ) ... AIAT
Association of the international Christian Youth Exchange in Europe (SAUO) ... AICYE
Association of the International Christian Youth Exchange in Europe (EAIO) ... AICYEE
Association of the International Christian Youth Exchange in Eurpoe (SAUO) ... AICYE
Association of the International Winter Sports Federations [*Switzerland*] (EAIO) ... AIWF
Association of the International Winter Sports Federations [*Berne, Switzerland*] (EAIO) ... AIWSF
Association of the IOC Recognized International Sports Federations [*Seoul, Republic of Korea*] (EAIO) ... ARISF
Association of the Junior Leagues of America [*Later, AJL*] (EA) ... AJLA
Association of the Margarine Industry of the EEC Countries (SAUO) ... IMACE
Association of the Otago School of Mines (SAUO) ... AOSM
Association of the Processed Cheese Industry (SAUO) ... ASSIFONTE
Association of the Royal Red Cross (SAUO) ... ARRC
[*The*] **Association of the Scientific, Engineering, and Technological Community of Canada** ... SCITEC
Association of the Scientific Engineering and Technological Community of Canada (SAUS) ... SCITEC
Association of the Sons of Poland (EA) ... SSP
Association of the State Oil Corporations of Latin America (SAUO) ... ARPEL
Association of the United States Army (EA) ... AUSA
Association of the Wall and Ceiling Industries - International (EA) ... AWCI
Association of the Wholesale Licensed Trade of Northern Ireland (BI) ... AWLTNI
Association of Theaters of Emilia and Romagna [*Ballet company*] ... ATER
Association of Theatre Benefit Agents [*Defunct*] (EA) ... ATBA
Association of Theatre Screen Advertising Companies [*Defunct*] ... ATSAC
Association of Theatrical Press Agents and Managers (EA) ... ATPAM
Association of Theological Insitutes in the Middle East (SAUO) ... ATIME
Association of Theological Institutes in the Middle East (EAIO) ... ATIME
Association of Theological Schools (EA) ... ATS
Association of Theological Schools in the United States and Canada (PGP) ... ATS
Association of Third World Affairs (EA) ... ATWA
Association of Third World Studies (EA) ... ATWS
Association of Thrift Holding Companies [*Washington, DC*] (EA) ... ATHC
Association of Tile, Terrazzo, Marble Contractors and Affiliates [*Later, NTCA*] (EA) ... ATTMCA
Association of Time-Sharing Users [*Later, ACU*] (EA) ... ATSU
Association of Time-Sharing Users (SAUO) ... ATSU
Association of Tin Producing Countries [*Australia*] ... ATPC
Association of Toilet Paper Manufacturers [*British*] (BI) ... ATPM
Association of Tongue Depressors (EA) ... ATD
Association of Touring and Producing Managers (SAUO) ... ATPM
Association of Touring and Production Managers [*British*] (BI) ... ATPM
Association of Toy and Fancy Goods Factors [*British*] (BI) ... ATFGF
Association of Track and Field Statisticians [*British*] (EAIO) ... ATFS
Association of Track and Structure Suppliers [*Later, REMSA*] (EA) ... ATSS
Association of Track and Structure Suppliers (SAUO) ... ATSS
Association of Trading Standards Officers [*British*] (DBA) ... ATSO
Association of Trailer Manufacturers [*British*] (DBA) ... ATM
Association of Training and Employment Professionals (EA) ... ATEP
Association of Translation Companies [*British*] (DBA) ... ATC
Association of Translators & Interpreters of Ontario [*Association des Traducteurs et Interpretes de l'Ontario*] (AC) ... ATIO
Association of Translators and Interpreters of Ontario (SAUO) ... ATIO
Association of Translators & Interpreters of Saskatchewan [*Association des Traducteurs et Interpretes de la Saskatchewan*] (AC) ... ATIS
Association of Transport Advisers of Japan (SAUO) ... ATAJ
Association of Transport Coordinating Officers (DCTA) ... ATCC
Association of Transport Co-ordinating Officers [*British*] (DBA) ... ATCO
Association of Transportation Practitioners (EA) ... ATP
Association of Transportation Security Officers (SAUO) ... ATSO
Association of Travel and Tourist Agents (SAUO) ... ATTA
Association of Travel Marketing Executives (EA) ... ATME
Association of Trial Behavior Consultants [*Later, ASTC*] (EA) ... ATBC
Association of Trial Lawyers of America (EA) ... ATLA

Association of Trial Lawyers of America. Newsletter [A publication] (DLA) .... Ass'n Trial Law Am Newsl
Association of Tutors [British] .... AOT
Association of Tutors (SAUO) .... AOT
Association of Tutors in Adult Education [British] .... ATAE
Association of Ukrainian Sports Clubs in North America (EA) .... AUSC-NA
Association of Ukrainians in Great Britain Ltd. (BI) .... AUGB
Association of Ukrainians in Tasmania [Australia] .... AUT
Association of Umbrella Manufacturers and Suppliers [Defunct] (EA) .... AUM
Association of Unclaimed Property Administrators [Later, NAUPA] .... AUPA
Association of Underwater Contractors (SAUO) .... AUC
Association of Unit Trust Managers [British] (BI) .... AUTM
Association of United Contractors of America [Defunct] (EA) .... AUCOA
Association of United Kingdom Media Librarians (DBA) .... AUKML
Association of United Kingdom Oil Independents .... AUKOI
Association of United States Members of the International Institute of
  Space Law (SAUO) .... AUSMIISL
Association of United States Night Vision Manufacturers (EA) .... ANVM
Association of United States Night Vision Manufacturers (EA) .... AUSNVM
Association of United States University Directors of International
  Agricultural Programs (SAUO) .... AUSUDIAP
Association of United Ukrainian Canadians (AC) .... AUUC
Association of Unity Churches (EA) .... AUC
Association of Universities and Colleges in/of Canada (SAUO) .... AUCC
Association of Universities and Colleges of Canada [Association des
  Universites et Colleges du Canada] .... AUCC
Association of Universities and Colleges of Canada, Ottawa, ON, Canada
  [Library symbol] [Library of Congress] (LCLS) .... CaOOCU
Association of Universities and Colleges of Canada [Association des
  Universites et Colleges du Canada], Ottawa, Ontario [Library symbol]
  [National Library of Canada] (NLC) .... OOCU
Association of Universities of the British Commonwealth .... AUBC
Association of University Affiliated Facilities [Later, AAUAP] (EA) .... AUAF
Association of University Affiliated Facilities (SAUO) .... AUAF
Association of University and College Counseling Center Directors
  (EA) .... AUCCCD
Association of University and College Employees [See also AEUC]
  [Canada] .... AUCE
Association of University Anesthesiologists (EA) .... AUA
Association of University Anesthetists (EA) .... AUA
Association of University Architects (EA) .... AUA
Association of University Chemical Education Tutors (SAUO) .... AUCET
Association of University Clinical Academic Staff [British] ..... AUCAS
Association of University Environmental Health/Sciences Centers
  (EA) .... AUEHSC
Association of University Evening Colleges [Later, ACHE] (EA) .... AUEC
Association of University Fisheries and Wildlife Program Administrators
  (EA) .... AUFWPA
Association of University Forestry Schools of Canada [Association des
  Ecoles Forestieres Universitaires du Canada] (AC) .... AUFSC
Association of University Interior Designers (EA) .... AUID
Association of University Professors (French) [British] .... AUP(Fr)
Association of University Professors of Ophthalmology (EA) .... AUPO
Association of University Programs in Health Administration (EA) .... AUPHA
Association of University Programs in Hospital Administration
  (SAUS) .... AUPHA
Association of University Programs in Occupational Health and Safety
  (EA) .... AUPOHS
Association of University Radiation Protection Officers [British] .... AURPO
Association of University Radiologists (EA) .... AUR
Association of University Related Research Parks (EA) .... AURRP
Association of University Staff of Promote Inter-University Cooperation in
  Europe (SAUO) .... AUSPICE
Association of University Summer Sessions (EA) .... AUSS
Association of University Teachers [A union] [British] .... AUT
Association of University Teachers in Accounting [British] ..... AUTA
Association of University Teachers in/of Accounting (SAUO) ...... AUTA
Association of University Teachers of Economics (SAUO) .... AUTE
Association of University Teachers of Scotland (SAUO) .... AUTS
Association of University Technology Managers (AAGC) .... AUTM
Association of University Women Teachers (SAUO) .... AUWT
Association of Unmanned Vehicle Systems (SAUS) .... AUVS
Association of Uptown Converters (EA) .... AUC
Association of Urban Universities [Defunct] (EA) .... AUU
Association of US Chess Journalists [Later, CJA] (EA) .... AUSCJ
Association of Used Tyre Merchants [British] (BI) .... AUTM
Association of Users of Research Agencies [British] (DBA) ...... AURA
Association of Vacuum Equipment Manufacturers (EA) .... AVEM
Association of Valuers of Licensed Property [British] (DBA) ..... AVLP
Association of Vascular and Interventional Radiographers (SAUO) ..... AVIR
Association of Vegetarian Dietitians and Nutrition Educators (EA) ..... VEGEDINE
Association of Vehicle Recovery Operators [British] (DBA) ...... AVRO
Association of Venture Capital Clubs [Defunct] (EA) .... AVCC
Association of Venture Founders [Defunct] (EA) .... AVF
Association of Vermiculite Exfoliators Ltd. [British] (BI) ..... AVE
Association of Vermont Independent Colleges (SRA) .... AVIC
Association of Veterinarians for Animal Rights (GVA) .... AVAR
Association of Veterinarians in Industry (GVA) .... AVI
Association of Veterinary Anaesthetists [British] .... AVA
Association of Veterinary Anaesthetists of Great Britain and Ireland
  (SAUO) .... AVA
Association of Veterinary Consultants (GVA) .... AVC
Association of Veterinary Inspectors (SAUO) .... AVI
Association of Veterinary Inspectors .... AVI
Association of Veterinary Students of Great Britain and Ireland (BI) ...... AVS

Association of Veterinary Surgeons Practicing in Northern Ireland
  (GVA) .... AVSPNI
Association of Veterinary Teachers and Research Workers (GVA) .... AVT&RW
Association of Veterinary Teachers and Research Workers (SAUO) .... AVTRW
Association of Veterinary Teachers and Research Workers [British] ...... AVTRW
Association of Vice-Principals in Colleges [British] .... AVPC
Association of Victorian Greyhound Clubs [Australia] .... AVGC
Association of Viewdata Information Providers (EA) .... AVIP
Association of View-data Information Providers (SAUO) .... AVIP
Association of Village Council Presidents Regional Housing Authority
  (SAUO) .... AVCP
Association of Virginia Colleges (SAUO) .... AVC
Association of Vision (or Visual) Science Librarians (SAUO) ..... AVSL
Association of Vision Science Librarians (SAUS) .... AVSL
Association of Visual Communications (SAUO) .... AVC
Association of Visual Communications (or Communicators) (SAUS) ..... AVC
Association of Visual Communicators (EA) .... AVC
Association of Visual Language Interpreters of Canada (SAUO) ..... AVLIC
Association of Visual Merchandise Representatives (EA) .... AVMR
Association of Visual Science Librarians (EA) .... AVSL
Association of Vitamin Chemists (EA) .... AVC
Association of Volleyball Professionals (EA) .... AVP
Association of Voluntary Action Scholars [Later, ARNOVA] (EA) ..... AVAS
Association of Voluntary Action Scholars (SAUO) .... AVAS
Association of Voluntary Agencies on Narcotics Treatment .... AVANT
Association of Voluntary Aided Secondary Schools [British] ..... AVASS
Association of Voluntary Emergency Radio Teams (SAUO) .... AVERT
Association of Voluntary Groups [Republic of Ireland] (BI) ..... AVG
Association of Voluntary/Independent Schools [British] (DBA) .... AVIS
Association of Volunteer Bureaus [Later, NVC] (EA) .... AVB
Association of Volunteer Bureaus of America (SAUO) .... AVBA
Association of Waldorf Schools of North America (EA) .... AWSNA
Association of Wall and Ceiling Contractors of Queensland
  [Australia] .... AWCCQ
Association of Wall and Ceiling Contractors of Victoria [Australia] .... AWCCV
Association of Wall and Ceiling Contractors of Western Australia .... AWCCWA
Association of Washington Business (SRA) .... AWB
Association of Washington Cities (SRA) .... AWC
Association of Washington Housing Authorities (SAUO) .... AWHA
Association of Washington School Principals (SRA) .... AWSP
Association of Waste Hazardous Materials Transporters .... AWHMT
Association of Water Officers [British] (DBA) .... AWO
Association of Water Technologies (NTPA) .... AWT
Association of Water Transportation Accounting Officers [New York, NY]
  (EA) .... AWTAO
Association of Waterloo Groups [British] (DI) .... AWG
Association of Waterworks Officers [British] (BI) .... AWO
Association of Webbing Load Restraint Equipment Manufacturers [British]
  (DBA) .... AWLREM
Association of Welding Distributors [British] (DBA) .... AWD
Association of Welsh Local Authorities (SAUO) .... AWLA
Association of West European Shipbuilders [London, England] (EAIO) ...... AWES
Association of Western Hospitals [Later, HCF] .... AWH
Association of Western Hospitals (SAUO) .... AWH
Association of Western Pulp and Paper Workers (EA) .... AWPPW
Association of Western Pulp and Paper Workers .... WPPW
Association of Western Railways (SAUO) .... AWR
Association of Western Railways [Later, WRA] .... AWR
Association of White House Press Secretaries (SAUO) .... AWHPS
Association of Wholesale and Manufacturing Opticians (SAUO) ..... AWMO
Association of Wholesale Electrical Bulk Buyers [British] (DBA) ..... AWEBB
Association of Wholesale Woollen Merchants Ltd. [British] (BI) ..... AWWM
Association of Wholly or Partially French Language Universities
  (SAUO) .... AUPELF
Association of Wind Teachers [British] .... AWT
Association of Winery Suppliers (EA) .... AWS
Association of Wireless and Cable Telegraphists (SAUO) .... AWCT
Association of Wisconsin Cleaning Contractors (SRA) .... AWCC
Association of Wisconsin School Administrators (SRA) .... AWSA
Association of Women Broadcasters .... AWB
Association of Women Clerks and Secretaries (SAUO) .... AWCS
Association of Women Deans and Counselors (DHP) .... AWDC
Association of Women Executives [Canada] .... AWE
Association of Women Gemologists [Defunct] (EA) .... AWG
Association of Women Highway Safety Leaders .... AWHSL
Association of Women in Architecture [Defunct] (EA) .... AWA
Association of Women in Natural Foods (EA) .... AWIN
Association of Women in Public Relations [British] (DBA) ...... AWPR
Association of Women in Science and Engineering (COE) .... AWISE
Association of Women in the Metal Industries (NTPA) .... AWMI
Association of Women Launderers [British] (BI) .... AWL
Association of Women Launderers and Cleaners (SAUO) .... AWLC
Association of Women Lawyers (SAUO) .... AWL
Association of Women Mathematicians (SAUO) .... AWM
Association of Women of the Motion Picture Industry (SAUO) ..... AWMPI
Association of Women Science Teachers (SAUO) .... AWST
Association of Women Soil Scientists (EA) .... AWSS
Association of Women Surgeons (EA) .... AWS
Association of Women Tax Clerks [A union] [British] .... AWTC
Association of Women Welders [A union] [British] .... AWW
Association of Women Workers in the Bedstead Trade [A union]
  [British] .... AWWBT
Association of Women's Forum Clubs of Australia .... AWFCA
Association of Women's Music and Culture (NTPA) .... AWMAC
Association of Woodworking and Furnishings Suppliers (NTPA) ..... AWFS

Association of Workers for Maladjusted Children (SAUO) .... AMWC
Association of Workers for Maladjusted Children (SAUO) .... AWMC
Association of Workers for Maladjusted Children [*British*] .... AWMC
Association of Workshop Way Consultants (EA) .... AWWC
Association of World Citizens (EA) .... AWC
Association of World Colleges and Universities [*Later, AWE*] .... AWCU
Association of World Trade Chamber Executives (EA) .... AWTCE
Association of Wyoming Insurance Agents (SRA) .... AWIA
Association of X-Ray Equipment Manufacturers [*British*] (DBA) .... AXrEM
Association of Yarn Distributors (EA) .... AYD
Association of Yougoslav Jews in the U.S.A. (SAUO) .... AYJUSA
Association of Young Children in Europe (SAUO) .... AYCE
Association of Young Computer Enthusiasts (AIE) .... AYCF
Association of Young Irish Archaeologists (SAUO) .... AYJA
Association of Young Launderers and Cleaners (SAUO) .... AYLC
Association of Youth Museums (NTPA) .... AYM
Association of Yukon Communities [*Formerly, Association of Yukon Municipalities*] (AC) .... AYC
Association Olympique Canadienne [*Canadian Olympic Association - COA*] .... AOC
Association on Broadcasting Standards [*Later, Association for Broadcast Engineering Standards*] .... ABS
Association on Broadcasting Standards (SAUO) .... ABS
Association on Handicapped Student Service Programs in a Postsecondary Education (SAUS) .... AHSSPPE
Association on Handicapped Student Service Programs in Postsecondary Education (EA) .... AHSSPPE
Association on Higher Education and Disability (SAUO) .... AHEAD
Association on Japanese Textile Imports [*Defunct*] (EA) .... AJTI
Association on Programs for Female Offenders (EA) .... APFO
Association on/of International Libraries (SAUO) .... AIL
Association Package Sequence Number (MCD) .... APSN
Association Parallel Processor (SAUO) .... APP
Association Paritaire pour la Sante et la Securite du Travail - Affaires Municipales (AC) .... APSAM
Association Paritaire pour le Sante et le Securite du Travail - Mines (AC) .... APSM
Association Parlementaire Europe-Afrique [*Eur-African Parliamentary Association*] .... APEA
Association Period (MAE) .... AP
Association Petroliere pour la Conservation de l'Environnement Canadien [*Petroleum Association for Conservation of the Canadian Environment*] .... APCE
Association Pharmaceutique Canadienne [*Canadian Pharmaceutical Association*] (EAIO) .... APhC
Association Phonetique Internationale [*International Phonetic Association*] .... API
Association Pointer (SAUO) .... APTR
Association pour la Conservation et la Reproduction Photographique de la Presse,Paris, France [*Library symbol*] [*Library of Congress*] (LCLS) .... ACRPP
Association pour la Cooperation Islamique [*Senegal*] (EY) .... ACIS
Association pour la maladie de Charcot-Marie-Tooth (SAUS) .... CMT France
Association pour la Maladie de Charcot-Marie-Tooth (SAUO) .... CMT France
Association pour la Prevention de la Contamination Atmospherique (AC) .... APCA
Association pour la Promotion des Initiatives Communautaires Africaines [*Association for the Promotion of African Community Initiatives - APACI*] (EAIO) .... APICA
Association pour la Promotion Industrie - Agriculture [*Association for the Promotion of Industry - Agriculture*] (EAIO) .... APIA
Association pour la Promotion Industrie-Agriculture (SAUO) .... APIA
Association pour la Promotion Sociale de la Masse [*Association for the Social Betterment of the Masses*] [*Burundi and Rwanda*] (AF) .... APROSOMA
Association pour la Protection des Automobilistes [*Canada*] .... APA
Association pour la Protection des Interets des Consommateurs [*Association for the Protection of Consumer Interests*] [*Canada*] .... APIC
Association pour la Recherche dans l'Industrie Siderurgique Canadienne (AC) .... ARISC
Association pour la Recherche en Tourisme [*Travel Research Association*] [*Canada*] .... ART
Association pour la Recherche et le Developpement en Informatique Chimique [*Association for Research and Development of Chemical Informatics*] [*Information service or system*] (IID) .... ARDIC
Association pour la Reduction des Depenses Publiques [*Association for the Reduction of Public Spending*] (AC) .... ARDP
Association pour la Sante et la Securite du Travail, Secteur Affaires Sociales [*Association for the Health and Safety of Labour, Social Affairs Sector*] [*Canada*] .... ASSTSAS
Association pour la Sante et la Securite du Travail, Secteur Affaires Sociales, Centre de Documentation, Montreal, PQ, Canada [*Library symbol*] [*Library of Congress*] (LCLS) .... CaQMASSAS
Association pour la Sante Publique du Quebec [*Quebec Public Health Association*] (AC) .... ASPQ
Association pour la Solidarite Franco-Algerienne [*Association for Franco-Algerian Solidarity*] [*French*] (AF) .... ASFA
Association pour l'Anthropologie Physique au Canada [*Association for Physical Anthropology in Canada*] .... AAPC
Association pour l'Avancement de la Micro-Informatique [*Association for the Advancement of Micro-Information*] [*Canada*] .... AMIQ
Association pour l'Avancement des Etudes Scandinaves au Canada [*Association for the Advancement of Scandinavian Studies in Canada - AASSC*] .... AAESC
Association pour l'Avancement des Sciences et des Techniques de la Documentation [*Acronym is now organization's official name*] .... ASTED
Association pour l'Avancement en Afrique des Sciences de l'Agriculture [*Association for the Advancement of Agricultural Sciences in Africa*] [*Addis Ababa, Ethiopia*] .... AAASA
Association pour le Developpement de la Riziculture en Afrique de l'Ouest [*West Africa Rice Development Association - WARDA*] (EAIO) .... ADRAO
Association pour le Developpement de l'Administration de l'Education [*Association for the Development of Educational Administration*] [*Canada*] .... ADAE
Association pour le Developpement de l'Audiovisuel et de la Technologie en Education [*Canada*] .... ADATE
Association pour le Developpement de l'Enseignement Technique d'Outre-Mer [*Association for the Development of Overseas Technical Education*] [*French*] (AF) .... ADETOM
Association pour le Developpement des Oeuvres Sociales d'Outre-Mer [*Association for the Development of Social Welfare Projects Overseas*] [*French*] (AF) .... ADOSOM
Association pour le Developpement du Tourisme International [*Louveciennes, France*] (EAIO) .... ADTI
Association pour le Rayonnement de l'Opera de Paris [*France*] .... AROP
Association pour le Retablissement des Institutions et Oeuvres Israelites en France (EA) .... ARIF
Association pour le Socialisme au Gabon [*Political party*] (EY) .... APSG
Association pour le Volontariat a l'Acte Gratuit en Europe [*Association for Voluntary Action in Europe - AVAE*] (EAIO) .... AVE
Association pour l'Education Interculturelle du Quebec [*Quebec Association for Intercultural Education*] (AC) .... APEIQ
Association pour l'Education Permanente dan les Universites du Canada (AC) .... AEPUC
Association pour l'Enseignement Medical en Europe [*Association for Medical Education in Europe - AMEE*] (EA) .... AEME
Association pour l'Enseignement Social en Afrique [*Association for Social Work Education in Africa - ASWEA*] (EAIO) .... AESA
Association pour les Etudes sur la Radio-Television Canadienne [*Association for the Study of Canadian Radio and Television - ASCRT*] .... AERTC
Association pour les Recherches sur les Parodontopathies [*International Association for Research in Paradentosis*] .... ARPA
Association pour l'Etude des Etats Proches de la Mort [*International Association for Near-Death Studies*] (EAIO) .... AEEPM
Association pour l'Etude des Langues Juives [*Association for the Study of Jewish Languages*] (EAIO) .... AELJ
Association pour l'Etude des Problemes d'Outre-Mer [*Association for the Study of Overseas Problems*] [*French*] (AF) .... AEPOM
Association pour l'Etude du Developpement International [*Association for the Study of International Development ASID*] [*Canada*] .... AEDI
Association pour l'Etude Taxonomique de la Flore d'Afrique Tropicale [*Association for the Taxonomic Study of Tropical African Flora*] [*French*] (AF) .... AETFAT
Association pour l'Histoire de la Science et de la Technologies au Canada (AC) .... AHSTC
Association pour l'Union Monetaire de l'Europe [*Association for the Monetary Union of Europe*] [*France*] (EAIO) .... AUME
Association Proessionnelle des Informaticiens et Informaticiennes du Quebec [*Association for Information Technology Professionals in Quebec*] [*Canada*] (DDC) .... APIIQ
Association Professionals International (SAUO) .... API
Association Professionnelle Catholique des Voyageurs de Commerce du Canada [*Catholic Professional Association of Commercial Representatives of Canada*] .... APCV
Association Professionnelle de Mesure en Education [*Professional Association of Educational Measures*] [*Canada*] .... APME
Association Professionnelle des Aides Pedagegiques Individuels (SAUO) .... APAPI
Association Professionnelle des Aides Pedagogiques Individuels [*Professional Association of Individual Educational Assistants*] [*Canada*] .... APAPI
Association Professionnelle des Criminologues du Quebec (AC) .... APCQ
Association Professionnelle des Enseignants de Technologie du Quebec (AC) .... APETQ
Association Professionnelle des Enseignants et Enseignantes en Commerce (AC) .... APEC
Association Professionnelle des Geographes du Quebec (AC) .... APGQ
Association Professionnelle des Infirmieres et Infirmiers Cadres du Quebec (AC) .... APIICQ
Association Professionnelle des Ingenieurs du Gouvernement du Quebec [*Association of Professional Engineers of the Government of Quebec*] (AC) .... APIGQ
Association Professionnelle des Meuniers du Quebec [*Quebec Feed Manufacturer's Association*] (AC) .... APMQ
Association Professionnelle des Nettoyeurs et Buandiers du Quebec (AC) .... APNB
Association Professionnelle des Pharmaciens Salaries du Quebec (AC) .... APPSQ
Association Professionnelle des Techniciens en Documentation du Quebec (AC) .... APTDQ
Association Professionnelle des Technologues Diplomes en Electrophysiologie Medicale (AC) .... APTDEPM
Association Professionnelle Internationale des Medicins [*International Professional Association of Physicians*] .... APIM
Association Provinciale des Constructeurs d'Habitations du Quebec Inc. [*Provincial Home Builders Association of Quebec Inc.*] (AC) .... APCHQ
Association Provinciale des Parents Fransaskois [*Fransaskois Parents Association*] (AC) .... APPF
Association Quebec Solaire (AC) .... AQS
Association Quebec-France (AC) .... AQF
Association Quebecoise de Canoe-Kayak de Vitesse (AC) .... AQCKV
Association Quebecoise de la Fibrose Kystique [*Quebec Cystic Fibrosis Association*] (AC) .... AGFK
Association Quebecoise de la Qualite (AC) .... AQQ

Association Quebecoise de l'Industrie de la Peche [*Quebec Fish Processor Association*] (AC) AQIP
Association Quebecoise de l'Industrie de la Peinture (AC) AQIP
Association Quebecoise de l'Industrie du Nautisme [*Quebec Marine Trades Association*] (AC) AQIN
Association Quebecoise de Loisir pour Personnes Handicapees [*Quebec Leisure Association for Handicapped Persons*] (AC) AQLPH
Association Quebecoise de Lutte Contre la Pollution Atmospherique (AC) AQLPA
Association Quebecoise de Pedagogie Collegiale (AC) AQPC
Association Quebecoise des Archivistes Medicales (AC) AQAM
Association Quebecoise des Auteurs Dramatiques (AC) AQAD
Association Quebecoise des Consommateurs Industriels d'Electricite (AC) AQCIE
Association Quebecoise des Critiques de Cinema (AC) AQCC
Association Quebecoise des Critiques de Theatre (AC) AQCT
Association Quebecoise des Directeurs et Directrices du Loisir Municipal (AC) AQDLM
Association Quebecoise des Ecoles de Francais (AC) AQEFT
Association Quebecoise des Editeurs de Magazines (AC) AQEM
Association Quebecoise des Educateurs du Primaire (AC) AQEP
Association Quebecoise des Enseignants de Francais Langue Seconde [*Quebec Association of Teachers of French as a Second Language*] (AC) AQUEFLS
Association Quebecoise des Enterprises Adaptees (AC) AQEA
Association Quebecoise des Fabricants de l'Industrie Medicale (AC) AQFIM
Association Quebecoise des Marionnettistes (AC) AQM
Association Quebecoise des Organismes de Co-operation Internationale [*Canada*] (CROSS) AQOCI
Association Quebecoise des Personnes de Petite Taille (AC) AQPPT
Association Quebecoise des Presses Universitaires (AC) AQPU
Association Quebecoise des Professeurs de Francais (AC) AQPF
Association Quebecoise des Professionnels de la Philatelie (AC) AQPP
Association Quebecoise des Realisateurs et Realisatrices de Cinema et de Television (AC) AQRRCT
Association Quebecoise des Soins Palliatifs (AC) AQSP
Association Quebecoise des Sports en Fauteuil Roulants (AC) AQSFR
Association Quebecoise des Techniques de l'Eau [*Canada*] (ASF) AQTE
Association Quebecoise des Transporteurs Aeriens (AC) AQTA
Association Quebecoise des Utilisateurs de l'Ordinateur au Primaire et au Secondaire (AC) AQUOPS
Association Quebecoise d'Etudes Americaines (AC) AQEA
Association Quebecoise d'Information Scolaire et Professionnelle (AC) AQISEP
Association Quebecoise d'Interpretation du Patrimoine (AC) AQIP
Association Quebecoise du Personnel de Direction des Ecoles (AC) AQPDE
Association Quebecoise du Personnes de Direction des Ecoles (AC) AQPPT
Association Quebecoise du Propane (AC) AQP
Association Quebecoise du Theatre Amateur Inc. (AC) AQTA
Association Quebecoise du Transport et des Routes Inc. (AC) AQTR
Association Quebecoise Plaidoyer-Victimes (AC) PV
Association Quebecoise pour la Defense des Droits des Retraites et des Pre-Retraites (AC) AQDR
Association Quebecoise pour la Maitrise de l'Energie (AC) AQME
Association Quebecoise pour le Patrimoine Industriel (AC) AQPI
Association Quebecoise pour les Troubles d'Apprentissage (AC) AQETA
Association Quebecoise pour les Troubles d'Apprentissage (AC) LDAQ
Association Referral Information Service ARIS
Association Regionale Caraibeenne des Infirmieres [*Martinique*] (EAIO) ARCI
Association Resource Institute [*Commercial firm*] (EA) ARI
Association Reunion Departement Francais [*Association for Reunion as a French Department*] [*Political party*] (PPW) ARDF
Association Science (SAUO) Assoc S
Association Scientifique de l'Industrie Europeenne du Talc [*Scientific Association of European Talc Industry*] (EAIO) EUROTALC
Association Scientifique et Technique pour la Recherche en Informatique Documentaire [*Scientific and Technical Association for Research in Documentary Information*] [*Belgium*] [*Information service or system*] ASTRID
Association Scientifique Europeenne pour la Prevision Economique a Moyen et LongTerme [*European Scientific Association for Medium and Long-Term Economic Forecasts*] ASEPELT
Association Scientifique Internationale du Cafe [*International Scientific Association of Coffee*] (EAIO) ASIC
Association Sectorielle de Fabrication d'Equipement de Transport et de Machines,St.-Leonard, Quebec [*Library symbol*] [*National Library of Canada*] (NLC) OSLEAS
Association Sectorielle, Fabrication d'Equipement de Transport et de Machines (AC) ASFETM
Association Social-Democrate du Cameroun [*Political party*] (EY) ASDC
Association Stomatologique Internationale [*International Stomatological Association*] ASI
Association Storage (or Storing) Processor (SAUS) ASP
Association Suisse des Experts-comptables (SAUO) ASE
Association Suisse d'Usagers de Telecommunications [*Swiss Association of Telecommunications Users*] [*Zurich*] (TSSD) ASUT
Association Technique de l'Importation Charbonniere (EA) ATIC
Association Technique de l'Industrie des Liants Hydrauliques [*Technical Association for the Hydraulic Binders Industry*] (IID) ATILH
Association Technique du Tourisme [*Tourism Technique Association*] [*Canada*] ATT
Association Technique Internationale des Bois Tropicaux [*International Technical Tropical Timber Association*] (EAIO) ATIBT
Association to Advance Ethical Hypnosis (EA) AAEH
Association to Aid Refugees (SAUO) AAR
Association to Aid the Sexual and Personal Relationships of People with a Disability (BUAC) SPOD
Association to Combat Huntington's Chorea [*British*] (EAIO) ACHC
Association to Remind Husbands to Remember Birthdays and Anniversaries (SAUO) ATRHTRBA
Association to Remind Husbands to Remember Birthdays and Anniversaries [*Probably mythical*] ATRHTRBAA
Association to Repeal Abortion Laws (EA) ARAL
Association to Repeat Abortion Laws (SAUS) ARAL
Association to Resource Co-Operative Housing [*Australia*] ATRCH
Association to Unite the Democracies (EA) AUD
Association Touristique Regionale de la Monteregie (AC) ATRM
Association Tunesienne des Radio Amateurs (SAUS) ASTRA
Association Typographique Internationale [*International Typographic Association*] ATYPI
Association Universelle d'Aviculture Scientifique [*World's Poultry Science Association - WPSA*] (EAIO) AVI
Association Universitaire Canadienne d'Etudes Nordiques [*Association of Canadian Universities for Northern Studies*] AUCEN
Association Universitaire Interamericaine [*Interamerican University Association*] [*France*] AUI
Association Universitaire pour le Developpement de l'Enseignement et de la Culture en Afrique et a Madagascar [*University Association for the Development of Teaching and Culture in Africa and Madagascar*] [*Paris, France*] (AF) AUDECAM
Association Value [*Psychometrics*] AV
Association Vocanologique Europeenne [*European Volcanological Association*] [*Paris, France*] (EAIO) LAVE
Association Zen Internationale [*International Zen Association - IZA*] (EAIO) AZI
Associational Fluency [*Personality research*] [*Psychology*] AF
Associationi on Golf Merchandisers (NTPA) AGM
Associations Canadienne pour l'Education Pastorale (AC) ACEP
Associations Council of the National Association of Manufacturers (EA) ACNAM
Associations des Industries du Poisson de la CEE [*Association of the Fish Industries of the European Economic Community*] AIPCEE
Associations for Community Design (NTPA) ACD
Associations of Lesbian, Gay and Bisexual Psychologies in Europe (SAUO) ALGBP
Associations of Service Providers Implementing IDEA Reforms in Education ASPIIRE
Associations' Publications in Print [*Database*] [*R. R. Bowker Co.*] [*Information service or system*] (CRD) APIP
Associations Touristiques Regionales Associees du Quebec [*Quebec Regional Tourist Associations Inc.*] (AC) ATRAQ
Association-Sensation [*Psychology*] (BARN) AS
Association-Storing Processor (SAUO) ACP
Association-Storing Processor [*Computer science*] ASP
Associative (SAUS) ASSOC
Associative Array Processor (MCD) AAP
Associative Buffer (SAUS) ASSB
Associative Communication Multiplexer ACM
Associative Computer Device ACD
Associative Content Addressable Memory (SAUS) ACA Memory
Associative Content Retrieval Network [*A. D. Little, Inc.*] [*Information service or system*] ACORN
Associative Content Retrieval Network (SAUO) ACORN
Associative Crosspoint Processor (MHDI) AXP
Associative File Processor (SAUS) AFP
Associative Film Memory (SAUS) AFM
Associative Film Store (SAUS) AFS
Associative Index Method AIM
Associative Information Processing Unit (PDAA) AIPU
Associative Interactive Dictionary [*for databases*] [*National Library of Medicine*] AID
Associative Ionization AI
Associative Law (SAUS) AL
Associative Learning from Relative Environmental Data ALFRED
Associative Light Searcher (SAA) ALS
Associative Linear Array Processor [*Computer science*] ALAP
Associative List Selection ALS
Associative List Selection (or Selector) (SAUS) ALS
Associative Logic Parallel System (SAUS) ALPS
Associative Logic Processor System (SAUS) ALPS
Associative Memory [*Computer science*] AM
Associative Memory Address [*Computer science*] AMA
Associative Memory and Parallel Processing Language (SAUS) AMPPL
Associative Memory Array [*Computer science*] AMA
Associative Memory Computer [*Computer science*] AMC
Associative Memory Data (SAUS) AMD
Associative Memory Device [*Computer science*] (DIT) AMD
Associative Memory Organizing System AMOS
Associative Memory, Parallel Processing Language (SAUS) AMPPL
Associative Memory Processor [*Computer science*] (BUR) AMP
Associative Memory System [*Computer science*] (DIT) AMS
Associative Memory with Ordered Retrieval (SAUS) AMOR
Associative Output Control Unit [*Computer science*] AOCU
Associative Output Unit [*Computer science*] AOU
Associative Parallel Processor [*Computer science*] APP
Associative Principle for Addition [*Mathematics*] APA
Associative Principle for Multiplication [*Mathematics*] APM
Associative Processing Element (MCD) APE
Associative Processor [*Computer science*] (BUR) AP
Associative Processor [*Computer science*] (MCD) ASPRO
Associative Processor Computer System APCS

Associative Processor Control [*Computer science*] ... APC
Associative Processor Microelectronic Element ... APME
Associative Processor Programming Language Evaluation ... APPLE
Associative Processor with Integrated Logic (SAUS) ... APRIL
Associative Programming Language [*Computer science*] (BUR) ... APL
Associative Push Down Memory [*Computer science*] (MHDB) ... APDM
Associative Read-Only Memories (SAUS) ... AROMs
Associative Read-Only Memory [*Computer science*] (IAA) ... AROM
Associative Register [*Computer science*] ... AR
Associative Registers for Generalized User Switching [*Computer typesetting system*] ... ARGUS
Associative Storing Processor (SAUS) ... ASP
Associative String Processor (MCD) ... ASP
Associative Structure Computer (BUR) ... ASC
Associative Structures Package (BUR) ... ASP
Associative Surface Ionization [*Organic chemistry*] ... ASI
Associative Thin-Film Memory (SAUS) ... ATFM
Associative Visual Cortex [*Anatomy*] ... AVC
Associative-Capacitive Read-Only Memory (SAUS) ... ACROM
Associative-Data Structure Package (SAUS) ... ASP
Associaton for Responsible Communication (AC) ... ARC
Associaton of College & Research Libraries English & American Literature Setion ... ACRLEALS
Associaton of Commissioned Officers [*Marine science*] (OSRA) ... ACO
Associazione degli Industriali delle Conserve Animali [*Meat Products Manufacturers Association*] [*Italy*] (EY) ... AICA
Associazione Generale Italiana dello Spettacolo [*General Italian Entertainments Association*] [*Italy*] (EY) ... AGIS
Associazione Informatici Professionisti [*Association of Information Technology Professionals*] [*Italy*] (DDC) ... AIP
Associazione Internazionale dei Professori d'Italiano [*International Association of Teachers of Italian*] (EAIO) ... AIPI
Associazione Internazionale di Archeologia Classica [*International Association for Classical Archaeology - IACA*] (EAIO) ... AIAC
Associazione Internazionale Mosaicisti Contemporanei [*International Association of Contemporary Mosaicists*] (EAIO) ... AIMC
Associazione Internazionale per gli Studi di Lingua e Letteratura Italiane [*International Association for the Study of the Italian Language and Literature - IASILL*] (EAIO) ... AISLLI
Associazione Italiana dei Fornitori e Distributori di Informazione Telematica [*Italian Association for the Production and Distribution of Online Information*] [*Rome*] [*Information service or system*] (IID) ... AFDIT
Associazione Italiana della Communicazione Interattiva [*Organization for multimedia professionals*] [*Italy*] (DDC) ... INTERACTA
Associazione Italiana di Studi Canadesi [*Italian Association of Canadian Studies*] ... AISC
Associazione Italiana Industriali Prodotti Alimentari [*Food manufacturers association*] [*Italy*] (EY) ... AIIPA
Associazione Italiana Manufatture Ombrelli [*Umbrella manufacturers association*] [*Italy*] (EY) ... AIMO
Associazione Italiana Manufatturieri Pelli-Cuoio e Succedanei [*Leather and Imitation Skins Association*] [*Italy*] (EY) ... AIMPES
Associazione Italiana Pellicceria [*Furriers association*] [*Italy*] (EY) ... AIP
Associazione Italiana per il Calcolo Automatico [*Italian Association for Automatic Data Processing*] ... AICA
Associazione Italiana per la Documentazione Avanzata [*Italian Association forAdvanced Documentation*] [*Information service or system*] (IID) ... AIDA
Associazione Italiana per la Documentazione e l'Informazione [*Italian Association for Documentation and Information*] (NITA) ... AIDI
Associazione Italiana Telerilevamento (SAUS) ... AIT
Associazione la Nostra Famiglia [*Ponte Lambro, Italy*] (EAIO) ... ANF
Associazione Nazionale Ex-Deportati Politici nei Campi Nazisti [*National Association of Political Ex-Deportees of the Nazi Camps*] [*Italy*] [*Political party*] (EAIO) ... ANED
Associazione Nazionalista Italiana [*Italian Nationalist Association*] [*Political party*] (PPE) ... ANI
Associes Benevoles Qualifies au Service des Jeunes (AC) ... ABQSJ
Associometrics Data Management System (IEEE) ... ADAM
Associometrics Remote Terminal Inquiry Control System (IEEE) ... ARTIC
Associometrics Remote Terminal Inquiry Control System (SAUS) ... ARTIC System
Associu di Patrioti Corsi [*Association of Corsican Patriots*] [*France*] [*Political party*] (PPE) ... APC
Assort (MSA) ... ASRT
Assort ... ASST
Assorted (ROG) ... ASSD
Assorted ... ASSTD
Assorted (EBF) ... Asstd
Assortment ... ASMT
Assortment (SAUS) ... Asmt
Assortment (SAUS) ... Ass
Assortment (EBF) ... Assmet
Assortment [*Business term*] ... ASSMT
Assortment ... AT
Assosa [*Ethiopia*] [*ICAO location identifier*] (ICLI) ... HASO
Assumed ... ASD
Assumed (FAAC) ... ASMD
Assumed (EBF) ... Asmd
Assumed Average Terrain Elevation (OTD) ... AATE
Assumed Binary Point (SAUS) ... ABP
Assumed Decimal Point (SAUS) ... ADP
Assumed Investment Return [*Business term*] (DICI) ... AIR
Assumed Latitude [*Navigation*] ... AL
Assumed Leading Bit (SAUS) ... ALB
Assumed Mean ... AM
Assumed Position [*Navigation*] ... AP
Assumpsit [*Legal shorthand*] (LWAP) ... ASSPT
Assumption ... ASSMPTN
Assumption Based System [*Logic system*] (IDAI) ... ABS
Assumption College (SAUO) ... AC
Assumption College (GAGS) ... Assump C
Assumption College, Worcester, MA [*OCLC symbol*] (OCLC) ... AZM
Assumption College, Worcester, MA [*Library symbol*] [*Library of Congress*] (LCLS) ... MWAC
Assumption Commercial College (SAUO) ... ACC
Assumption Guild (EA) ... AG
Assumption High School, East St. Louis, IL [*Library symbol*] [*Library of Congress*] (LCLS) ... IEsAHS
Assumption of Control (SAUS) ... AOC
Assumption of Control Message [*Aviation*] ... AOC
Assumption of Moses [*Apocalyptic book*] ... ASMP M
Assumption of Moses (Pseudepigrapha) (BJA) ... AssMos
Assumption Parish Library, Napoleonville (SAUS) ... LNBpA
Assumption Parish Library, Napoleonville, LA [*Library symbol*] [*Library of Congress*] (LCLS) ... LNapA
Assumption University (SAUO) ... AU
Assumption University of Windsor (SAUO) ... Assum
Assumption-Based Truth Maintenance System [*Philosophy*] ... ATMS
Assumptionists (TOCD) ... AA
Assumptionists (TOCD) ... aaa
Assurance [*Insurance*] [*French*] (ILCA) ... Ass
Assurance [*Insurance*] [*French*] ... Assce
Assurance ... ASSNCE
Assurance ... Assur
Assurance ... ASSURNC
Assurance and Stabilization Trends for Reliability by Analysis of Lots (MHDI) ... ASTRAIL
Assurance and Stabilization Trends for Reliability by Analysis of Lots (SAUS) ... ASTRAL
Assurance Control Economics System (MUGU) ... ACES
Assurance Engineering [*or Effectiveness*] **Division** [*Military*] (DNAB) ... AED
Assurance Engineering Field Facility (DNAB) ... AEFF
Assurance Engineering Office (SAUO) ... AEO
Assurance Management Office (SAUO) ... AMO
Assurance Medical Society [*British*] ... AMS
Assurance Problem ... AP
Assurance sur la Vie [*Life Insurance*] [*French*] ... ASLV
Assurances Generales de France ... AGF
Assurbanipal [*King of ancient Assyria*] (BJA) ... Assurb
Assure ... ASSUR
Assure Compelitive Transportation (SAUS) ... ACT
Assure Competitive Transportation [*Truckers' lobby*] ... ACT
Assure Contre l'Incendie [*Insured Against Fire*] [*French*] ... ACI
Assured (ROG) ... ASSD
Assured (SAUS) ... Assd
Assured Crew Rescue System (SAUO) ... ACRV
Assured Crew Return Capability (NAKS) ... ACRC
Assured Crew Return Vehicle [*Aerospace*] ... ACRV
Assured Depot Task ... ADT
Assured Destruction [*Capability*] [*of missiles*] ... AD
Assured Destruction Force [*Military*] ... ADF
Assured Field Shop Task ... AFST
Assured Information Systems, Inc. (SAUS) ... AIS
Assured Intermediate Task (MCD) ... AIT
Assured Shuttle Availability (SAUS) ... ASA
Assurex International (EA) ... AI
Assyria ... ASS
Assyria ... ASSYR
Assyrian (ADWA) ... Assyr
Assyrian and Babylonian Letters Belonging to the Kouyunjik Collection(s) of the British Museum [*A publication*] (BJA) ... ABL
Assyrian and Babylonian Religious Texts [*A publication*] (BJA) ... ABRT
Assyrian Australian Association ... AAA
Assyrian Medical Texts [*A publication*] (BJA) ... AMT
Assyrian Personal Names [*A publication*] (BJA) ... APN
Assyrische Rechtsurkunden [*A publication*] (BJA) ... ARu
Assyro-Babylonian (SAUS) ... Assyr Babyl
AST Research [*NASDAQ symbol*] (TTSB) ... ASTA
AST Research, Inc. [*Associated Press*] (SAG) ... AST
AST Research, Inc. [*NASDAQ symbol*] (NQ) ... ASTA
Asta Funding, Inc. [*NASDAQ symbol*] (SAG) ... ASFI
Asta Funding, Inc. [*Associated Press*] (SAG) ... AstaFd
Asta Werke AG [*Germany*] [*Research code symbol*] ... A
Asta Werke AG [*Germany*] [*Research code symbol*] ... P
Astable (MSA) ... ASTB
Astable Blocking Oscillator ... ABO
Astable Circuit (SAUS) ... AC
Astable Multivibrator ... AMV
Astara [*Iran*] [*ICAO location identifier*] (ICLI) ... OIGA
Astarte: Journal of Arctic Biology (SAUS) ... Astarte: J Arctic Biol
Astatine [*Chemical element*] ... At
AST-Computer founded by Albert Wong, Safi Qureshey and Tom Yuen (SAUS) ... AST Computer
Astea International, Inc. [*Associated Press*] (SAG) ... Astea
Astea International, Inc. [*NASDAQ symbol*] (SAG) ... ATEA
Astea Intl. [*NASDAQ symbol*] (TTSB) ... ATEA
Astec Industries [*NASDAQ symbol*] (TTSB) ... ASTE
Astec Industries, Inc. [*NASDAQ symbol*] (NQ) ... ASTE
Astec Industries, Inc. [*Associated Press*] (SAG) ... Astec
Astemizole [*Medicine*] (MELL) ... AMZ

Astemizole [Pharmacology]	AST
Aster Growth with Aster [Ecology]	AA
Aster Growth with Brown Sedge [Ecology]	AB
ASTER Steering Committee (SAUS)	ASC
Aster Yellow Virus (MELL)	AYV
Aster Yellows [A plant disease]	AY
Asterisk Placement Executive (SAUO)	APE
Asterism (DGA)	ASTM
Astern	ASTN
Astern Flag [Navy] [British]	AT
Asteroid Belt Probe	ABP
Asteroid Detection System	ADS
Asteroid Meteoroid Detector	AMD
Asteroid Negation System	ANS
Asterriquinone [Antineoplastic drug]	ARQ
Asthenopia [Ophthalmology] [Medicine]	ASTH
asthenosphere (SAUS)	astheno
Asthma and Allergic Disease Center [Department of Health and Human Services] (GRD)	AADC
Asthma and Allergy Foundation of America (PAZ)	AAFA
Asthma and Allergy Foundation of America (EA)	A & AFA
Asthma and Allergy Information and Research (SAUO)	AAIR
Asthma and Dyspnea (MELL)	A & D
Asthma Care Association of America [Defunct] (EA)	ACAA
Asthma Care Training (MEDA)	ACT
Asthma Research Council [British]	ARC
Asthma Research Council (SAUO)	ARC
Asthma Rhinitis [Immunology]	AR
Asthma Society of Canada [Societe Canadienne de l'Asthme] (AC)	ASC
Asthmatic Bronchitis [Medicine] (ADA)	AB
Asthmatic Children's Foundation of New York (EA)	ACFNY
Asthmatic Childrens Foundation of New York (SAUS)	ACFNY
ASTIA Document (SAUS)	AD
ASTIA [Armed Services Technical Information Agency] Document	AD
ASTIA [Armed Services Technical Information Agency] Report Bibliography (MCD)	ARB
ASTIA Report Bibliography (SAUS)	ARB
Astig against the rule Astigmatism (SAUS)	ATR
astigmanzer (SAUS)	astig
astigmatic (SAUS)	astig
Astigmatic Keratotomy (SAUS)	AK
Astigmatic Spectral Line	ASL
Astigmatism [Also, Ast] [Ophthalmology]	As
Astigmatism (SAUS)	AS
Astigmatism (SAUS)	AST
Astigmatism [Also, As] [Ophthalmology]	Ast
Astigmatism [Electronics]	ASTIG
Astigmatism [Ophthalmology] (DAVI)	Astigm
Astigmatism (SAUS)	Astigm
Astigmatism, Hypermetropic [Also, AsH] [Ophthalmology]	AH
Astigmatism, Hypermetropic [Also, AH] [Ophthalmology]	AsH
Astigmatism, Myopic [Also, AsM] [Ophthalmology]	AM
Astigmatism, Myopic [Also, AM] [Ophthalmology]	AsM
Astigmatism with Myopia Predominating (SAUS)	AMH
Astigmatizer (SAUS)	ASTIG
Astigmatoscope (or Astigmatoscopy) (SAUS)	ASTIG
Astigmia (SAUS)	ASTIG
Astigmometer (SAUS)	ASTIG
Astigmoscope (SAUS)	ASTIG
ASTM Spec. Tech. Publ (SAUS)	ASTM Spec Tech Publ
ASTM Standardization News (journ.) (SAUS)	STDNA
Aston Campus Communicatins for Europe and Ninety-Two	ACCENT
Aston Dark Space [Physics]	ADS
Aston Martin Owners Club (EA)	AMOC
Aston Martin Racing [British]	AMR
Aston Resources Ltd. [Vancouver Stock Exchange symbol]	ASU
Aston Whole Number [Chemistry]	AWN
Aston's Entries [1673] [A publication] (DLA)	Ast Ent
Astor Home for Children, Rhinebeck, NY [Library symbol] [Library of Congress] (LCLS)	NRhbA
Astor Library, Astoria, OR [Library symbol] [Library of Congress] (LCLS)	OrAst
Astoria [Oregon] [Airport symbol] [Obsolete] (OAG)	AST
Astoria Financial [NASDAQ symbol] (SAG)	ASFC
Astoria Financial [Associated Press] (SAG)	AstoriaF
Astoria, OR [AM radio station call letters]	KAST
Astoria, OR [FM radio station call letters]	KAST-FM
Astoria, OR [AM radio station call letters] (BROA)	KCHT
Astoria, OR [FM radio station call letters]	KMUN
Astoria, OR [AM radio station call letters]	KVAS
Astoria, OR [FM radio station call letters] (BROA)	KZNX-FM
Astoria, OR [Location identifier] [FAA] (FAAL)	NMW
Astoria, OR [Location identifier] [FAA] (FAAL)	PEN
Astorville Branch, East Ferris Township Public Library, Ontario (SAUS)	OAEFI
Astorville Branch, East Ferris Township Public Library, Ontario [Library symbol] [National Library of Canada] (NLC)	OAEFT
Astqa Funding [NASDAQ symbol] (TTSB)	ASFI
AST/Quadram/Ashton-Tate Enhanced Memory Specification [Quadram] [Norcross, GA] [Computer science]	AQA EMS
Astra AB [NYSE symbol] (SAG)	A
Astra AB [NYSE symbol] (SAG)	AAB
Astra AB [Associated Press] (SAG)	AstraA
Astra AB [Associated Press] (SAG)	AstraB
Astra AB'A'ADS [NYSE symbol] (TTSB)	A
Astra AB'B' ADS [NYSE symbol] (TTSB)	AAB
ASTRA Compania Argentina [BA Symbol] (TTSB)	AST.BA

ASTRA Digital Radio (SAUS)	ADR
Astra Pharmaceuticals Canada Ltd., Mississauga, Ontario [Library symbol] [National Library of Canada] (NLC)	OMAPC
Astragal (SAUS)	a
Astragal (MSA)	A
A-Strain Spontaneous Leukemia [Type of cell line]	ASL
Astrakhan [Former USSR] [FAA designator] (FAAC)	ASZ
Astral Aviation, Inc. d/b/a Skyway Airlines [FAA designator] (FAAC)	SYX
Astral Bellevue Pathe, Inc. [Toronto Stock Exchange symbol]	ACM
AstraZeneca ADR [NYSE symbol] (SG)	AZN
A-Streptococci Polysaccharide Antibody Titer [Medicine] (MELL)	ASPAT
Astrida [Rwanda] [Seismograph station code, US Geological Survey] [Closed] (SEIS)	AST
Astringedent Topical Hemostatic Solution [Medicine] (MELL)	ATHS
Astro Air International, Inc. [Philippines] [ICAO designator] (FAAC)	AAP
Astro Communication Laboratory (SAUS)	ACL
Astro Communications System [NASA] (KSC)	ACS
Astro Digital Doppler Speedometer (SAUS)	ADDS
Astro Electronic Gimballess Inertial System (SAUS)	AEGIS
Astro Guidance Digital Computer (IEEE)	AGDIC
Astro Inertial Guidance Equipment (SAUS)	AIGE
Astro Launch Circuit [NASA] (KSC)	ALC
Astro Musical Research (EA)	AMR
Astro Research Corp. (KSC)	ARC
Astro Research Corporation (SAUO)	ARC
ASTRO Satellite Operations Center (MCD)	ASOC
Astro Sciences Corp. [NASDAQ symbol] (SAG)	AOSC
Astro Sciences Corp. [Associated Press] (SAG)	AstroSci
Astro Star Tracker (NAKS)	AST
Astro Systems Research Laboratory (SAA)	ASRL
astrobiological (SAUS)	astrobio
astrobiologist (SAUS)	astrobio
Astrochronological Relatives (SAUS)	Astrochronics
Astrocyte-Conditioned Medium [Analytical biochemistry]	ACM
Astrocytoma [Medicine] (MELL)	Astro
Astrodata Data Acquisition and Control (SAUS)	ADAC
Astrodigital Doppler Speedometer [Electronics]	ADDS
Astrodome Stadium, Houston (SAUS)	Astrodome
Astrodynamical Report (SAA)	AR
Astro-Electronics Division [RCA]	AED
Astro-Electronics Division-RCA (SAUO)	AED-RCA
Astro-Eugenics (SAUS)	A-E
astrogenealogy (SAUS)	astrogen
Astro-Geodetic Geoid Data Station Spacing and Distribution (SAA)	AGGDSSD
Astrogeodetic World Datum	AWD
Astrogeological (SAUS)	astrog
astrogeologist (SAUS)	astrog
astrogeology (SAUS)	astrog
Astrogeology of Celestial Bodies (SAUS)	ASTROGEO
Astrogeophysical Transmission Network [Air Force's Air Weather Service Teletypewriter circuit]	ATN
Astrograph Mean Time [Navigation]	AMT
astrolabe (SAUS)	astro
Astrologer (SAUS)	Astrol
Astrologers' Guild of America (EA)	AGA
Astrologers International [Defunct] (EA)	AI
Astrological (ADWA)	astrol
Astrological (SAUS)	astrol
Astrological Association (EAIO)	AA
Astrology (SAUS)	AST
Astrology [or Astrologer]	ASTROL
Astrology (NTIO)	astrol
Astrology Encyclopedia [A publication]	AE
Astrology Information Centre (AC)	AIC
Astromechanics Research Division (SAA)	ARD
Astro-Med [NASDAQ symbol] (TTSB)	ALOT
Astro-Med, Inc. [NASDAQ symbol] (NQ)	ALOT
Astro-Med, Inc. [Associated Press] (SAG)	AstroM
Astromedicine (SAUS)	ASTROMED
Astrometric Interferometry Mission [to determine locations of stars] (ECON)	AIM
Astrometric Telescope (SAUS)	AT
Astrometric Telescope Facility (SSD)	ATF
Astrometry (SAUS)	Astro
Astromical Unit (SAUS)	AU
Astronaut Activities Office [NASA] (KSC)	AAO
Astronaut Communications (MCD)	ASTROCOM
Astronaut Control Console [NASA]	ACC
Astronaut Control Panel [NASA] (NASA)	ACP
Astronaut Crew Rescue Vehicle [NASA]	ACRV
Astronaut Crew Return Vehicle (SAUS)	ACRV
Astronaut Life Support Assembly [NASA]	ALSA
Astronaut Life Support Equipment [NASA] (MCD)	ALSE
Astronaut Maneuvering Equipment [NASA] (MCD)	AME
Astronaut Maneuvering Research Vehicle [NASA]	AMRV
Astronaut Maneuvering Unit [Gemini] [NASA]	AMU
Astronaut Memorial Foundation (NAKS)	AMF
Astronaut Operations Requirement Document [NASA] (KSC)	AORD
Astronaut Positioning Mechanism [NASA] (SPST)	APM
Astronaut Positioning System (SAUS)	APS
Astronaut Preference Kit [NASA]	APK
Astronaut Preference Test [NASA] (NASA)	APT
Astronaut Rescue Air Pack [NASA] (KSC)	ARAP
Astronaut Stabilizer Maneuvering Unit (SAUS)	ASMU
Astronaut Survival Kit [NASA]	ASK

Astronaut Work Station [*NASA*] ... AWS
Astronaut-Actuated Abort [*NASA*] (MCD) ... AAA
Astronautic ... ASTRNTC
Astronautica Acta (journ.) (SAUS) ... AA
Astronautical (MSA) ... ASNAUT
Astronautical ... ASTRO
Astronautical Activities Office (SAUO) ... AAO
Astronautical Defensive-Offensive System ... ADOS
Astronautical Monkey (SAUS) ... Astromonk
Astronautical Research and Development Agency (SAA) ... ARDA
Astronautical Research Laboratory (SAA) ... ARL
Astronautical Society of Canada ... ASC
Astronautics (DD) ... Astro
Astronautics (ADWA) ... astronaut
Astronautics and Aeronautics (journ.) (SAUS) ... A/A
Astronautics and Aeronautics (journ.) (SAUS) ... Astronaut Aeronaut
Astronautics and Space (KSC) ... ASTROSPACE
Astronautics Notice (AAG) ... AN
Astronautics Standard Practice (AAG) ... ASP
Astronautics Support Center ... ASC
Astronautics Test Procedures (AAG) ... ATP
Astronauts' Wives Club ... AWC
Astronavigation (NATG) ... AN
Astronic (SAUS) ... ASTN
Astronics Corp. [*Associated Press*] (SAG) ... Astron
Astronics Corp. [*NASDAQ symbol*] (NQ) ... ATRO
Astronomer [*or Astronomy*] ... ASTRON
Astronomer (ADWA) ... astron
Astronomiae Professor Greshamii [*Professor of Astronomy at Gresham College, London*] ... APG
Astronomic (AABC) ... ASTN
Astronomic Journal (SAUS) ... AJ
Astronomical ... Astro
Astronomical and Astrophysical Society of America (SAUO) ... AASA
Astronomical and Space Techniques for Research on the Atmosphere [*National Science Foundation project*] ... ASTRA
Astronomical, Atmospheric, Earth, and Ocean Sciences [*National Science Foundation*] (GRD) ... AAEO
Astronomical Constant ... AC
Astronomical Data Center (ACAE) ... ADC
Astronomical, Earth and Ocean Sciences (SAUO) ... AEOS
Astronomical Explorer Satellite ... AES
Astronomical Great Circle (SAUS) ... AGC
Astronomical Great Circle Course ... ACC
Astronomical Guidance System for Air Navigation (OA) ... AGSAN
Astronomical Image Processing System ... AIPS
Astronomical Information Processing System [*Computer program*] ... AIPS
Astronomical Instrument Markup Language (RALS) ... AIML
Astronomical Journal [*A publication*] ... AJ
Astronomical League (EA) ... AL
Astronomical Netherlands Satellite ... ANS
Astronomical Observation Template (ADWA) ... AOT
Astronomical Observatory ... AO
Astronomical Observatory of Cordoba (SAUS) ... MAS
Astronomical Observatory Satellite (KSC) ... AOS
Astronomical Position Line (SAUS) ... APL
Astronomical Radio Interferometric Earth Survey [*or Surveying*] [*NASA*] ... ARIES
Astronomical Radio Interferometric Earth Surveying (SAUS) ... ARIES
Astronomical Roentgen Observatory (SAUS) ... ASRO
Astronomical Satellite (SAUS) ... ANS
Astronomical Society of Edinburgh (SAUO) ... ASE
Astronomical Society of India (SAUO) ... ASI
Astronomical Society of New South Wales (SAUO) ... ASNSW
Astronomical Society of South Africa (SAUO) ... ASSA
Astronomical Society of South Australia (SAUO) ... ASSA
Astronomical Society of the Atlantic ... ASA
Astronomical Society of the Pacific (SAUO) ... ASP
Astronomical Society of the Pacific (EA) ... ASP
Astronomical Society of Victoria (SAUO) ... ASV
Astronomical Society of Victoria (SAUO) ... A/SV
Astronomical Society of Victoria (SAUS) ... a/sv
Astronomical Space Telescope Research Assembly (SAUS) ... Astra
Astronomical Studies of Extrasolar Planetary Systems [*NASA*] ... ASEPS
Astronomical Telescope Orientation Mount [*NASA*] ... ATOM
Astronomical Time ... AT
Astronomical Time Switch ... ATS
Astronomical Unit [*Equal to average distance from earth to sun*] ... AU
astronomically (SAUS) ... astron
Astronomische Einheit [*Astronomical Unit*] [*German*] ... AE
Astronomy (ROG) ... AS
Astronomy (NASA) ... AST
Astronomy ... ASTR
Astronomy (WDAA) ... astr
Astronomy [*A publication*] (BRI) ... Astron
Astronomy and Astrophysics ... A&A
Astronomy and Astrophysics (SAUS) ... Astrophys
Astronomy Department Library, Nanjing University (SAUS) ... NU
Astronomy Information Service [*Space Telescope Science Institute*] [*Information service or system*] (IID) ... ASTIS
Astronomy Institute Potsdam ... AIP
Astronomy Library, University of Toronto (SAUS) ... UTor
Astronomy Missions Board [*NASA*] ... AMB
Astronomy Payload (SAUS) ... Astro
Astronomy Space and Radio Board [*Science and Engineering Research Council*] (PDAA) ... ASR
Astronomy, Space and Radio Division (SAUO) ... ASRD
Astronomy Spacelab Payloads [*NASA*] (MCD) ... ASP
Astronomy Study Unit [*American Topical Association*] (EA) ... ASU
Astronomy Technology Centre [*British*] ... ATC
Astronomy Unit [*Later, ASU*] [*American Topical Association*] (EA) ... AU
Astronomy with a Neutrino Telescope and Abyss environmental Research (SAUS) ... ANTARES
Astronomy Working Group (SAUO) ... AWG
Astronomy/Mathematic/Statistics Library (SAUS) ... MATH
Astronuclear Laboratory [*Westinghouse Electric Corp.*] (MCD) ... AL
Astrophysical (SAUS) ... Astrophys
Astrophysical Data Program [*NASA*] ... ADP
Astrophysical Data System (SAUS) ... ADS
Astrophysical Journal [*A publication*] ... ApJ
Astrophysical Journal, Supplement Series (SAUS) ... Astrophys J Suppl Ser
Astrophysical Journal. Supplement Series (journ.) (SAUS) ... APJSA
Astrophysical Letters (journ.) (SAUS) ... Astrophys Lett
Astrophysical Observatory [*Smithsonian Museum*] ... APO
Astrophysical Observatory (SAUS) ... Astro Obsv
Astrophysical Observatory, Potsdam (SAUS) ... AOP
Astrophysical, Planetary, and Atmospheric Sciences ... APAS
Astrophysical Research Consortium ... ARC
Astrophysics Data Facility (SAUS) ... ADF
Astrophysics Data System [*NASA*] ... ADS
Astrophysics Data System-5 (SAUS) ... ADS
Astrophysics Payload [*NASA*] (MCD) ... APP
Astrophysics Research Unit (SAUO) ... ARU
Astrophysics Transient Explorer ... ATREX
Astropower Laboratory [*Douglas Aircraft Corp.*] (MCD) ... AL
Astro-Psychology Institute (EA) ... API
Astro-Science Corporation (SAUO) ... ASC
Astro-Space Lab, Inc. (MCD) ... ASL
Astrosurveillance Science Laboratory ... ASL
Astrosystems, Inc. [*NASDAQ symbol*] (NQ) ... ASTR
Astrosystems, Inc. [*Associated Press*] (SAG) ... Astrosy
Astrotech International Corp. [*AMEX symbol*] (SPSG) ... AIX
Astrotech International Corp. [*Associated Press*] (SAG) ... Astrotc
Astrotech Intl. [*AMEX symbol*] (TTSB) ... AIX
Astruxius [*Authority cited in pre-1607 legal work*] (DSA) ... Astrux
Asuka Spacecraft (SAUS) ... ASCA
Asuncion [*Paraguay*] [*Airport symbol*] (OAG) ... ASU
Asuncion [*Paraguay*] [*ICAO location identifier*] (ICLI) ... SGFA
Asuncion/Presidente General Stroessner [*Paraguay*] [*ICAO location identifier*] (ICLI) ... SGAS
ASV, Inc. [*NASDAQ symbol*] (SAG) ... ASVI
ASV, Inc. [*Associated Press*] (SAG) ... ASV Inc
ASW [*Antisubmarine Warfare*] **Acoustic Deception Device** (MCD) ... ADDS
ASW Combat System (SAUS) ... ASWCS
ASW [*Antisubmarine Warfare*] **Coordinator** (MCD) ... ASWC
ASW [*Antisubmarine Warfare*] **Formatted Message Reporting System** ... AFMRS
ASW [*Antisubmarine Warfare*]**, Gun, and Missile Escort Ship** [*Navy symbol*] ... DX/DXG
ASW [*Antisubmarine Warfare*] **Module** [*Navy*] ... ASWM
ASW [*Antisubmarine Warfare*] **Submarine System Evaluation Technique** ... ASSET
ASW [*Antisubmarine Warfare*] **Support Aircraft Carrier** [*Navy symbol*] ... CVS
ASW [*Antisubmarine Warfare*] **Tactical Center Systems** [*Data or Support*] (MCD) ... ASTACS
ASW Torpedo Rocket (SAUS) ... ASTOR
ASW [*Antisubmarine Warfare*] **Torpedo-Carrying Helicopter** (MCD) ... ATCH
ASW Track Management System (SAUS) ... ATMS
Aswan [*Egypt*] [*Airport symbol*] (OAG) ... ASW
Aswan [*Egypt*] [*ICAO location identifier*] (ICLI) ... HESN
ASWE Serial Highway (SAUS) ... ASH
ASWEPS Submarine Ocean (SAUS) ... ASODDS
ASWEPS [*Antisubmarine Warfare Environmental Prediction Service*] **Submarine Oceanographic Digital Data System** ... ASODDS
Asychronous Line Module (SAUS) ... ALM
Asychronous Time Division Multiplexing (SAUS) ... ATDM
Asylum ... ASY
Asylum ... ASYL
Asymetric Mult-Processing (SAUS) ... AMP
Asymmetric ... A
Asymmetric [*Chemistry*] ... as
Asymmetric (MSA) ... ASYM
Asymmetric (ADWA) ... asym
Asymmetric Aminohydroxylation [*Organic chemistry*] ... AA
Asymmetric and Planar Structural Analysis (SAUS) ... APSA
Asymmetric Balance [*Marine science*] (OSRA) ... AB
Asymmetric Data Exchange ... ADX
Asymmetric Digital Subscriber Line [*Telecommunications*] ... ADSL
Asymmetric Digital Subscriber Line Forum (DDC) ... ADSI
Asymmetric Digital Subscriber Loop (WDAA) ... ADSL
Asymmetric Dihydroxylation [*Organic chemistry*] ... AD
Asymmetric Double Cantilever Beam (SAUS) ... ADCB
Asymmetric Epoxidation [*Organic chemistry*] ... AE
Asymmetric Hindquarters Syndrome (SAUS) ... AHQS
Asymmetric Illumination Contrast [*Microscopy*] ... AIC
Asymmetric Maximum Likelihood [*Statistics*] ... AML
Asymmetric Multiplier (SAUS) ... AM
Asymmetric Multiprocessing [*Computer science*] (PCM) ... AMP
Asymmetric Multiprocessing (CDE) ... ASMP
Asymmetric Multiprocessing System [*IBM Corp.*] ... AMS
Asymmetric Multiprocessing System [*Electronics*] (ECII) ... ASP
Asymmetric Resonant Cavity [*Physics*] ... ARC
Asymmetric [*or Asymmetrical*] **Septal Hypertrophy** [*Medicine*] ... ASH

Asymmetric Sideband (SAUS) ... ASB
Asymmetric Silicon Controlled Rectifier [*Electronics*] (TEL) ... ASCR
Asymmetric Stress Analysis of Axisymmetric Solids [*Computer program*] ... ASAAS
Asymmetrical [*Chemistry*] (BARN) ... U
Asymmetrical Coplanar Waveguide (SAUS) ... ACPW
Asymmetrical Digital Single Line (DMAA) ... ADSL
Asymmetrical Digital Subscriber Line (SAUS) ... ADSL
Asymmetrical Digital Subscriber Loop (SAUS) ... ADSL
Asymmetrical Septal Hypertrophy (SAUS) ... ASH
Asymmetrical Sideband ... ASB
Asymmetrical Silicon Controlled Rectifier (SAUS) ... ASCR
Asymmetrical Tonic Neck Reflex ... ATNR
Asymmetry, Border, Color, and Diameter [*Rule*] [*Dermatology*] ... ABCD
Asymmetry, Border, Colour and Diameter (SAUS) ... ABCD
Asymmetry Factor [*Mathematics*] ... AF
Asympotically Admissible Linear Unbiased Estimator (SAUS) ... AALUE
Asymptomatic [*Medicine*] (MELL) ... ANS
Asymptomatic (MELL) ... ASX
Asymptomatic [*Medicine*] (MEDA) ... Asx
Asymptomatic Bacteriuria [*Medicine*] (DMAA) ... ABU
Asymptomatic Bacteriuria [*Medicine*] (PDAA) ... ASB
Asymptomatic Bacteriuria [*Medicine*] (DB) ... ASC
Asymptomatic Carotid Bruit [*Medicine*] (DMAA) ... ACB
Asymptomatic Rhegmatogenous Retinal Detachments [*Medicine*] (MELL) ... ARRD
Asymptomatic Urinary Abnormalities [*Medicine*] (MELL) ... AUA
Asymptomatic Urinary Tract Infection [*Medicine*] (MELL) ... AUTI
Asymptomatic Variance ... AVAR
Asymptote [*Mathematics*] ... ASYMP
Asymptotic Conical Dipole (PDAA) ... ACD
Asymptotic Giant Branch [*Astronomy*] ... AGB
Asymptotic Relative Efficiency [*Statistics*] ... ARE
Asymptotic Stability with Probability One (SAUS) ... ASWP 1
Asymptotic Standard Error [*Statistics*] ... ASE
Asymptotic Temporary Threshold Shift (PDAA) ... ATTS
Asymptotic Threshold Shift [*Hearing*] ... ATS
Asymptotic Waveform Evaluation (AAEL) ... AWE
Asymptotically Admissible Linear Unbiased Estimator [*Statistics*] ... AALUE
Asymptotically Best Linear Estimate (PDAA) ... ABLE
Asymptotically Best Linear Unbiased Estimator [*Statistics*] ... ABLUE
Asymptotically Most Powerful Rank Test [*Statistics*] ... AMPRT
Asymptotically Pointwise Optimal (DNAB) ... APO
Asynchron Transfer (SAUS) ... ATF
Asynchronous ... A
Asynchronous (MSA) ... ASYN
Asynchronous ... ASYNC
Asynchronous ... ASYNCH
Asynchronous Adapter (SAUS) ... ASA
Asynchronous Address Communications Systems ... AACS
Asynchronous Balanced Mode [*Computer science*] ... ABM
Asynchronous Balanced Mode Extended [*Telecommunications*] (OSI) ... ABME
Asynchronous Bipolar Pulse Length Modulation [*Electronics*] (IAA) ... ABPLM
Asynchronous Bipolar Pulse Length Modulation (or Modulator) (SAUS) ... ABPLM
Asynchronous Channel Multiplexer (IUSS) ... ACM
Asynchronous Circuit Design Language [*Computer science*] (PDAA) ... ACDL
Asynchronous Communication (SAUS) ... ASYNC
Asynchronous Communication Adapter [*Computer science*] (IAA) ... ACA
Asynchronous Communication Channel Multiplexer (IUSS) ... ACCM
Asynchronous Communication Control Module (MHDI) ... ACM
Asynchronous Communication Control Program (SAUS) ... ASCOM
Asynchronous Communication Device Interface (SAUS) ... ACDI
Asynchronous Communication Element (MHDB) ... ACE
Asynchronous Communication Interface Adapter (SAUS) ... ACIA
Asynchronous Communication Procedure (BUR) ... ASC
Asynchronous Communication Server (SAUS) ... ACS
Asynchronous Communication Subsystem (SAUS) ... ACS
Asynchronous Communications Adapter (SAUS) ... ACA
Asynchronous Communications Base [*Computer science*] (CIST) ... ACB
Asynchronous Communications Control ... ACC
Asynchronous Communications Control Attachment ... ACCA
Asynchronous Communications Control Module (SAUS) ... ACCM
Asynchronous Communications Device Interface [*Computer science*] (VERA) ... ACDI
Asynchronous Communications Facility (SAUO) ... ACF
Asynchronous Communications Interface [*Computer science*] (HGAA) ... ACI
Asynchronous Communications Interface Adapter [*Computer science*] (MDG) ... ACIA
Asynchronous Communications Server [*Computer science*] (IT) ... ACS
Asynchronous Computer (SAUS) ... AC
Asynchronous Computer Conferencing ... ACC
Asynchronous Data Channel (MCD) ... ADC
Asynchronous Data Communications Channel ... ADCC
Asynchronous Data Communications Controller (SAUS) ... ADCC
Asynchronous Data Link Control (SAUS) ... ADLC
Asynchronous Data Modem (SAUS) ... ADM
Asynchronous Data Mover Facility (SAUS) ... ADMF
Asynchronous Data Multiplexer Synchronizer ... ADMS
Asynchronous Data Transceiver ... ADT
Asynchronous Data Transfer [*Transmission technique*] (CDE) ... ADT
Asynchronous Data Unit [*AT&T*] (CIST) ... ADU
Asynchronous DataLink Control [*IBM Corp.*] ... ADLC
Asynchronous Digital Combiner (MCD) ... ADC
Asynchronous Digital Subscriber Loop [*Computer science*] ... ADSL
Asynchronous Disconnected Mode ... ADM
Asynchronous Element (SAUS) ... ACE
Asynchronous Event Notification (CIST) ... AEN
Asynchronous Exit Routine (SAUS) ... AER
Asynchronous Exit Routine (SAUS) ... AXR
Asynchronous Framing Technique [*Computer science*] ... AFT
Asynchronous Input/Output [*Computer science*] (VERA) ... AIO
Asynchronous Interface Module (SAUS) ... AIM
Asynchronous Learning Network (SAUS) ... ALN
Asynchronous Limited Distance (SAUS) ... ALD
Asynchronous Line Control Unit [*Telecommunications*] ... ALCU
Asynchronous Line Driver [*Prentice Corp.*] ... ALD
Asynchronous Line Group (SAUO) ... ALG
Asynchronous Line Interface [*Telecommunications*] ... ALI
Asynchronous Line Multiplexer [*Telecommunications*] ... ALM
Asynchronous Line Pairs (SAUS) ... ALP
Asynchronous Line Terminator (SAUS) ... ASYLT
Asynchronous Line Unit [*Telecommunications*] ... ALU
Asynchronous Look-Ahead Simulator (IEEE) ... ALAS
Asynchronous Mode (SAUS) ... AM
Asynchronous MODEM ... AM
Asynchronous Multiline Communications Coupler [*Telecommunications*] (NITA) ... AMLCC
Asynchronous Multiline Controller [*Telecommunications*] ... AMLC
Asynchronous Multiplexer Adapter (SAUS) ... AMA
Asynchronous Multiprocessing (SAUS) ... AMP
Asynchronous Operation (SAUS) ... AO
Asynchronous Overlay Supervisor (SAUS) ... AOS
Asynchronous Packet Assembler/ Disassembler (SAUS) ... APAD
Asynchronous Procedure Call (RALS) ... APC
Asynchronous Processing Unit [*Computer science*] (NITA) ... APU
Asynchronous Protocol Specification (VERA) ... APS
Asynchronous Pulse Length Modulation [*Electronics*] (IAA) ... APLM
Asynchronous Quenching (SAUS) ... AQ
Asynchronous Remote Takeover Server [*Computer science*] (VERA) ... ARTS
Asynchronous Remote Takeover Terminal [*Computer science*] (VERA) ... ARTT
Asynchronous Repeater (SAUS) ... AR
Asynchronous Response Mode [*Computer science*] ... ARM
Asynchronous Ripple Adder (SAUS) ... ARA
Asynchronous SCSI Interface (SAUS) ... ASI
Asynchronous Sender/Reader (ACAE) ... ASR
Asynchronous Sequential Machine (SAUS) ... ASM
Asynchronous Serial Interface [*Telecommunications*] (NITA) ... ASI
Asynchronous Single Sideband [*Electronics*] (IAA) ... ASSB
Asynchronous State Machine (IEEE) ... ASM
Asynchronous Synchronous Programmable Interface [*Computer science*] ... ASPI
Asynchronous Synchronous Transmitter Receiver [*Electronics*] (IAA) ... ASTR
Asynchronous System Trap (SAUS) ... AST
Asynchronous Task Group (SAUO) ... ATG
Asynchronous Task Storage [*NASA*] (NASA) ... ATS
Asynchronous Terminal Adapter [*Telecommunications*] ... ATA
Asynchronous Terminal Concentrator [*Telecommunications*] (TSSD) ... ATC
Asynchronous Terminal Controller (SAUS) ... ATC
Asynchronous Terminal Emulation [*Computer science*] (VERA) ... ATE
Asynchronous Time Diversity Device (MCD) ... ATDD
Asynchronous Time Division [*Telecommunications*] ... ATD
Asynchronous Time Division Multiple Access [*Computer science*] (VERA) ... ATDMA
Asynchronous Time Division Multiplexer (SAUS) ... ATDM
Asynchronous Time Division Multiplexing [*Telecommunications*] ... ATDM
Asynchronous Time Multiplexing (IAA) ... ATM
Asynchronous Time-Division Multiplex Method (SAUS) ... ATDM Method
Asynchronous Time-Division Multiplexing [*Computer science*] (IAA) ... ARDM
Asynchronous Traction Motor (PDAA) ... ATM
Asynchronous Transfer (SAUS) ... ATF
Asynchronous Transfer Mode [*Computer science*] ... ATM
Asynchronous Transfer Mode Adaptation Layer [*Computer science*] (DDC) ... AAL
Asynchronous Transfer Mode Data Exchange Interface (SAUS) ... ATM-DXI
Asynchronous Transfer Mode/Address Resolution Protocol (SAUS) ... ATMARP
Asynchronous Transfer Mode-Oriented Multimedia Information System (SAUS) ... ATOMIS
Asynchronous Transmission (DDC) ... AT
Asynchronous Transmission Mode (AEBE) ... ATM
Asynchronous Unit Delay [*Computer science*] (IAA) ... AUD
Asynchronous/Synchronous (SAUS) ... A/S
Asynchronous-Synchronous Adapter (SAUS) ... ASA
Asynchronous-to-Synchronous Transmission Adapter (SAUS) ... ASTA
Asyst Technologies [*Commercial firm*] [*Associated Press*] (SAG) ... AsystTch
Asyst Technologies [*NASDAQ symbol*] (SAG) ... ASYT
Asyut [*Egypt*] [*ICAO location identifier*] (ICLI) ... HEAT
At ... A
At [*An altitude*] (GAVI) ... AT
At a Discount ... AAD
At a distance (SAUS) ... distal
At a Later Date ... ALD
At All Times [*Medicine*] (MELL) ... AAT
At All Times (PIPO) ... AATM
At and Maintain [*Aviation*] (FAAC) ... ATAM
AT & T Aviation Group [*ICAO designator*] (FAAC) ... XAT
AT & T Capital Corp. [*Associated Press*] (SAG) ... ATT Cap
AT & T Capital Corp. (SPSG) ... TCC
AT & T College and University System [*Bedminster, NJ*] [*Telecommunications service*] (TSSD) ... ACUS

AT & T Communications [*Telecommunications*] (TSSD) ATTCOM
AT & T Information Systems [*Telecommunications*] ATIS
AT & T Information Systems [*Telecommunications*] (TSSD) ATTIS
AT & T Philips Telecommunications APT
AT & T Stock Fund [*Equity Income Fund*] [*AMEX symbol*] (SPSG) ATF
AT & T Stock Fund (Equity Income Fund) [*Associated Press*] (SAG) ATT Fd
AT & T Technologies, Inc., Winston-Salem, NC [*Library symbol*] [*Library of Congress*] (LCLS) NcWsAT-R
AT & T Transfer System [*Telecommunications*] ATS
AT & Technologies, Inc., Winston-Salem, NC [*Library symbol*] [*Library of Congress*] (LCLS) NcWsAT
AT Attachment (SAUS) ATA
AT Attachment Packet Interface (SAUS) ATAPI
AT [*Advanced Technology*] **Attachment Packet Interface** (CDE) ATAPI
At Bat [*Baseball*] AB
At Bed Side [*Medicine*] ABS
AT Bus Attachment (SAUS) ATA
At Earliest Convenience [*Medicine*] (AAMN) AEC
At Entertainment, Inc. [*NASDAQ symbol*] (SG) ATEN
At Fault (DI) af
At Gage Marks (SAA) AGM
At Gestational Age [*Medicine*] (DAVI) AGA
At Home AH
At Home Corp.'A' [*NASDAQ symbol*] (SG) ATHM
At Home Series [*Baseball*] AHS
AT Line Solution Assay (SAUS) ALSAS
At My Command (SAUS) AMC
At No Expense to the Government ANEXGOVT
At Occupation [*An underwriting designation for an occupational accident*] [*Insurance*] AO
At or Above [*Aviation*] AOA
At or After (FAAC) AOAF
At or Before (FAAC) AOBF
At or Below [*Aviation*] AOB
At or Below [*Constrained Altitude*] (GAVI) B
At Own Risk [*Medicine*] (BARN) AOR
AT Plastics [*AMEX symbol*] (TTSB) ATJ
AT Plastics, Inc. [*AMEX symbol*] (SAG) ATJ
AT Plastics, Inc. [*Associated Press*] (SAG) AT Plas
At Present (SAUS) At Pres
At Reactor Storage [*Nuclear energy*] (NUCP) ARS
At Risk (MAE) AR
At Risk Period (MAE) ARP
At Risk Provision (DICI) ARP
At Same Time AST
At Sea Tactical Exercises [*Military*] (IUSS) ASTE
At Sight (ADWA) A/S
At Sight AS
At Sight (EBF) as
AT Tactical Interface Modem (SAUS) ATTIM
At the Center of Things [*Slang*] ACT
At the Market [*Market order*] [*Stock exchange term*] ATM
At The Moment (SAUS) ATM
At the Opening [*Investment term*] ATO
At the Rate Of (MUGU) A/R
At The Same Time (SAUS) ATST
At the Suit Of ATS
At the Time of Bombing [*Radiation Effects Research Foundation, Japan*] ATB
At the Umbilicus [*Obstetrics*] (DAVI) U/
At This Time (SAUS) ATT
At This Time ATTM
At Time or Place (SAUS) ATP
At Your Option (SAUS) ATYROPT
At Your Own Risk (SAUS) AYOR
At Your Service AYS
ATA Packet Interface (SAUS) ATAPI
Ata-Aerocondor Transportes Aereos Ltda. [*Portugal*] [*ICAO designator*] (FAAC) ARD
Atacama Large Millimeter (SAUS) ALMA
Atacama Large Millimeter Array ALMA
Atacames [*Ecuador*] [*ICAO location identifier*] (ICLI) SEAT
ATACMS Enhanced (SAUS) ATACMS EN
ATACMS Extended Range (SAUS) ATACMS ER
Atactic Polypropylene [*Organic chemistry*] APP
Atakpame/Akpaka [*Togo*] [*ICAO location identifier*] (ICLI) DXAK
Atalanta Sosnoff Capital Corp. [*Associated Press*] (SAG) AtalSos
Atalanta Sosnoff Capital Corp. [*NYSE symbol*] (SPSG) ATL
Atalanta/Sosnoff Capital [*NYSE symbol*] (SG) ATL
Atambua/Haliwen [*Indonesia*] [*ICAO location identifier*] (ICLI) WRKA
Atanasoff-Berry Computer [*Early computer*] ABC
AT&T Canada'B' [*NASDAQ symbol*] (SG) ATTC
AT&T Capital [*NYSE symbol*] (TTSB) TCC
AT&T Capital 8.125% 'PINES' [*NYSE symbol*] (SG) NCF
AT&T Capital 8.25% 'PINES' [*NYSE symbol*] (SG) NCD
AT&T Capital Corp. [*NYSE symbol*] (SAG) TOC
AT&T Communications (SAUS) ATTCOM
AT&T Corp. [*NYSE symbol*] (TTSB) T
AT&T Corp-Wireless Grp. [*NYSE symbol*] (SG) AWE
AT&T Global Information Solutions [*Dayton, OH*] [*Formerly, NCR Corp.*] (CDE) AT&T GIS
AT&T Global Network Services (SAUS) AGNS
AT&T Information Systems (SAUS) ATTIS
AT&T Interexchange Carrier (SAUS) ATTIX
AT&T International (SAUS) ATTI
AT&T Netware Connect Services (VERA) ANCS
AT&T Novell Telephone Services (VERA) ANTS
AT&T Optimized Materials Simulator (SAUS) ATOMS
AT&T Philips Telecommunications (SAUS) APT
AT&T Technologies (SAUS) ATTT
AT&T Technologies Inc., Legal Library, Greensboro, NC [*Library symbol*] [*Library of Congress*] (LCLS) NcGAT
AT&T Technologies Inc., Technical Library, Burlington, NC [*Library symbol*] [*Library of Congress*] (LCLS) NcBurAT
Ataq [*People's Democratic Republic of Yemen*] [*ICAO location identifier*] (ICLI) ODAT
Atar [*Djibouti*] [*Seismograph station code, US Geological Survey*] (SEIS) ATA
Atar [*Mauritania*] [*Airport symbol*] (OAG) ATR
Atar [*Mauritania*] [*ICAO location identifier*] (ICLI) GQPA
Atari Competence Center (VERA) ACC
Atari Computer System Interface (SAUS) ACSI
Atari Corp. [*Associated Press*] (SAG) Atari
Atari Corp. [*AMEX symbol*] (SPSG) ATC
Atari Hard-Disk Controller (SAUS) AHDC
ATARI Inc. Warner Communication Inc. (SAUO) ATARI
Atari Message and Information System (SAUS) AMIS
Atari Users Association (EA) AUA
Atari-Version American Standard Code for Information Interchange [*Character code*] ATASCII
Atascadero, CA [*FM radio station call letters*] KIQO
Atascadero State Hospital, Atascadero, CA [*Library symbol*] [*Library of Congress*] (LCLS) CAtaH
Atauro [*East Timor*] [*ICAO location identifier*] (ICLI) WPAT
atavism (SAUS) atav
atavist (SAUS) atav
Ataxia Telangiectasia [*Genetic disease*] AT
Ataxia Telangiectasia Mutated [*Medicine*] ATM
Ataxia-Deafness-Retardation [*Syndrome*] (MELL) ADR
Ataxic Nystagmus [*Medicine*] (MELL) AN
Atbara [*Sudan*] [*Airport symbol*] (OAG) ATB
Atbara [*Sudan*] [*ICAO location identifier*] (ICLI) HSAT
ATC Communications [*NASDAQ symbol*] (TTSB) ATCT
ATC Communications, Inc. [*Associated Press*] (SAG) ATC Com
ATC Communications, Inc. [*NASDAQ symbol*] (SAG) ATCT
ATC Environmental [*NASDAQ symbol*] (TTSB) ATCE
ATC Environmental, Inc. [*NASDAQ symbol*] (NQ) ATCE
ATC Environmental, Inc. [*Associated Press*] (SAG) ATC EnC
ATC Environmental, Inc. [*Associated Press*] (SAG) ATC Env
ATC Environmental Wrrt 'C' [*NASDAQ symbol*] (TTSB) ATCEL
ATC Group Services, Inc. [*Associated Press*] (SAG) ATC Grp
ATC Group Services, Inc. [*NASDAQ symbol*] (SAG) ATCS
ATC Group Srvices, Inc. [*Associated Press*] (SAG) ATC GrpC
ATC [*Air Training Command*] **Operations Center** ATC OPSCEN
ATC [*Air Traffic Control*] **Systems Command Center** [*Marine science*] (OSRA) ATCSCC
ATC Systems Command Center (SAUS) ATCSCC
ATC [*Air Traffic Control*] **Systems Command Center** (USDC) ATCSCO
ATCCS Common Operating System (SAUS) ACOS
ATCCS Experimentation Site (SAUS) AES
ATCCS [*Army Tactical Command and Control System*] **Test Bed** ATB
Atcheson's Election Cases [*England*] [*A publication*] (DLA) Atch EC
Atchinson, Topeka, & Santa Fe Railway Co. ASTF
Atchison Casting [*NASDAQ symbol*] (TTSB) ACCX
Atchison Casting [*NYSE symbol*] (SG) FDY
Atchison Casting Corp. [*NASDAQ symbol*] (SAG) ACCX
Atchison Casting Corp. [*Associated Press*] (SAG) AtchCst
Atchison Casting Corp. [*NYSE symbol*] (SAG) FDY
Atchison. English Navigation and Trade Reports [*A publication*] (DLA) Atch
Atchison, KS [*Location identifier*] [*FAA*] (FAAL) JNL
Atchison, KS [*AM radio station call letters*] (RBYB) KAIR-AM
Atchison, KS [*AM radio station call letters*] KERE
Atchison, Topeka & Santa Fe (SAUS) Santa Fe
[*The*] **Atchison, Topeka & Santa Fe Railway Co.** [*Also known as Santa Fe*] AT & SF
[*The*] **Atchison, Topeka & Santa Fe Railway Co.** [*Also known as Sante Fe*] AT & SFR
[*The*] **Atchison, Topeka & Santa Fe Railway Co.** [*Also known as Santa Fe*] [*AAR code*] ATSF
[*The*] **Atchison, Topeka & Santa Fe Railway Co. - DF Loaders** [*AAR code*] SFRB
[*The*] **Atchison, Topeka & Santa Fe Railway Co. - Refrigerator Cars** [*AAR code*] SFRD
Atco Ltd. [*Toronto Stock Exchange symbol*] ACO
At-Completion Variance (SAUS) ACV
At-Depth Test Facility (SAUO) ADTF
Atdvanced Technology Group (SAUO) ATG
ATE Computer (MCD) ATC
ATE Management Service Co., Inc., Cincinnati, OH [*OCLC symbol*] (OCLC) ATE
Ateba Mines, Inc. [*Toronto Stock Exchange symbol*] ABA
ATEC Group [*NASDAQ symbol*] (TTSB) ATEC
ATEC Group, Inc. [*NASDAQ symbol*] (SAG) ATEC
ATEC Group, Inc. [*Associated Press*] (SAG) ATEC Gp
ATEC Group Wrrt [*NASDAQ symbol*] (TTSB) ATECW
Ateista Tutmonda Esperanto-Organizo (SAUO) ATEO
Ateitis Association of Lithuanian Catholic Intellectuals (EA) AALCI
Atelier de Modelisation de l'Architecture des Plantes [*Software manufacturer*] [*Paris, France*] AMAP
Atelier de Production et Creation [*French fashion label*] APC
Atelier Parisien d'Urbanisme [*Paris Office of Urbanization*] [*France*] [*Information service or system*] (IID) APUR

Ateliers de Constructions Electriques de Charleroi [*Telecommunications equipment manufacturers*] [*Belgium*] (NITA) .... ACEC

Ateliers de Gestion Integree des Ressources Limitees [*Canada*] .... AGIR

Ateliers d'Ingenierie Dominion, Lachine, Quebec [*Library symbol*] [*National Library of Canada*] (NLC) .... QLAID

Ateliers et Chantiers de Bretagne [*France*] (NUCP) .... ACB

Ateliers et Chantiers de l'Afrique Equatoriale [*Equatorial Africa Shipyards*] [*Gabon*] .... ACAE

Ateneo de Manila University, Manila, Philippines [*Library symbol*] [*Library of Congress*] (LCLS) .... PiMA

Ateneo Law Journal [*A publication*] (DLA) .... Ateneo LJ

Atex Commercial Users Group (EA) .... ACUG

Atex Newspaper Users Group (EA) .... ANUG

ATFM Information Message (SAUS) .... AIM

ATFM Notification Message (SAUS) .... ANM

Athabasca, AB [*AM radio station call letters*] .... CKBA

Athabasca Public Library, Alberta [*Library symbol*] [*National Library of Canada*] (NLC) .... AATH

Athabasca Public Library, Athabasca, AB, Canada [*Library symbol*] [*Library of Congress*] (LCLS) .... CaAAth

Athabasca University, Alberta [*Library symbol*] [*National Library of Canada*] (NLC) .... AEAU

Athabasca University, Edmonton, AB, Canada [*Library symbol*] [*Library of Congress*] (LCLS) .... CaAEAU

Athabasca University Library [*UTLAS symbol*] .... AUL

Athabasca University Students' Association (AC) .... AUSA

Athabaska Airways Ltd. [*Canada*] [*ICAO designator*] (FAAC) .... ABS

Athabaska Delta Community School, Fort Chipewyan, Alberta [*Library symbol*] [*National Library of Canada*] (BIB) .... AFCAS

Athabaska Gold [*Vancouver Stock Exchange symbol*] .... AHB

Athapascan [*MARC language code*] [*Library of Congress*] (LCCP) .... ath

Atharan Hazari [*Pakistan*] [*Airport symbol*] (AD) .... ARH

atheism (SAUS) .... ath

Atheist Agnostic Christians for the Truth (EA) .... AACT

Atheist Association (EA) .... AA

Atheist Foundation of Australia .... AFA

Atheist Student Union (SAUO) .... ASU

Atheists United (EA) .... AU

Athena Gold Corp. [*Vancouver Stock Exchange symbol*] .... AGC

Athena Neurosciences [*NASDAQ symbol*] (SPSG) .... ATHN

Athena Neurosciences, Inc. [*Associated Press*] (SAG) .... Athena

Athenaeum of Ohio (SAUS) .... TAO

Athenaeum of Ohio, Eugene H. Maly Library, Cincinnati, OH [*Library symbol*] [*Library of Congress*] (LCLS) .... OCAO

Athenaeum of Ohio, Norwood, OH [*OCLC symbol*] (OCLC) .... ATO

Athenaeum of Ohio, Norwood, OH [*Library symbol*] [*Library of Congress*] (LCLS) .... ONowdM

Athenaeum of Philadelphia (EA) .... PAT

Athenaeum of Philadelphia, Philadelphia, PA [*OCLC symbol*] (OCLC) .... PAT

Athenaeum of Philadelphia, Philadelphia, PA [*Library symbol*] [*Library of Congress*] (LCLS) .... PPA

Athenaeus [*First century AD*] [*Classical studies*] (OCD) .... Ath

Athenagence [*News agency*] [*Greece*] (EY) .... ANA

Athenian (SAUS) .... Athen

Athenian Institute of Anthropos (SAUO) .... AIA

[*The*] Athenian Tribute Lists [*A publication*] (OCD) .... ATL

Athenium (SAUS) .... Ath

Athens [*Georgia*] [*Airport symbol*] (OAG) .... AHN

Athens [*Greece*] [*Airport symbol*] (OAG) .... ATH

Athens Air [*Greece*] [*ICAO designator*] (FAAC) .... THN

Athens, AL [*AM radio station call letters*] .... WKAC

Athens, AL [*AM radio station call letters*] .... WVNN

Athens, AL [*FM radio station call letters*] .... WZYP

Athens Are Technical Institute, Athens, GA [*Library symbol*] [*Library of Congress*] (LCLS) .... GAtT

Athens Centre of Ekistics (SAUO) .... ACE

Athens College (SAUO) .... AC

Athens College, Athens, GA [*Library symbol*] [*Library of Congress*] (LCLS) .... AAthC

Athens Community Hospital, Athens, TN [*Library symbol*] [*Library of Congress*] (LCLS) .... TACH

Athens Environmental Research Laboratory [*Athens, GA*] [*Environmental Protection Agency*] (GRD) .... ERL/ATH

Athens, GA [*FM radio station call letters*] .... WALR

Athens, GA [*AM radio station call letters*] .... WGAU

Athens, GA [*Television station call letters*] .... WGTV

Athens, GA [*FM radio station call letters*] .... WMSL

Athens, GA [*FM radio station call letters*] .... WNGC

Athens, GA [*Television station call letters*] .... WNGM

Athens, GA [*AM radio station call letters*] .... WRFC

Athens, GA [*FM radio station call letters*] .... WUGA

Athens, GA [*FM radio station call letters*] .... WUOG

Athens, GA [*FM radio station call letters*] (RBYB) .... WXAG

Athens News Agency [*Greece*] .... ANA

Athens Observatory [*Greece*] [*Seismograph station code, US Geological Survey*] (SEIS) .... ATH

Athens, OH [*AM radio station call letters*] .... WATH

Athens, OH [*FM radio station call letters*] (BROA) .... WJKW-FM

Athens, OH [*AM radio station call letters*] .... WOUB

Athens, OH [*FM radio station call letters*] .... WOUB-FM

Athens, OH [*Television station call letters*] .... WOUB-TV

Athens, OH [*FM radio station call letters*] .... WXTQ

Athens Regional Library, Athens, GA [*Library symbol*] [*Library of Congress*] (LCLS) .... GAt

Athens Regional Library, Athens, GA [*Library symbol*] [*Library of Congress*] (LCLS) .... GAtL

Athens Symphony Orchestra (SAUO) .... ASO

Athens, TN [*Location identifier*] [*FAA*] (FAAL) .... MMI

Athens, TN [*FM radio station call letters*] .... WJSQ

Athens, TN [*AM radio station call letters*] .... WLAR

Athens, TN [*AM radio station call letters*] .... WYXI

Athens Township Library, Athens, MI [*Library symbol*] [*Library of Congress*] (LCLS) .... MiAAth

Athens, TX [*Location identifier*] [*FAA*] (FAAL) .... AHX

Athens, TX [*Location identifier*] [*FAA*] (FAAL) .... CSZ

Athens, TX [*AM radio station call letters*] .... KLVQ

Athens, TX [*Location identifier*] [*FAA*] (FAAL) .... LIQ

Athens University [*Greece*] [*Seismograph station code, US Geological Survey*] (SEIS) .... ATU

Athens/Albany, OH [*Location identifier*] [*FAA*] (FAAL) .... UNI

atheological (SAUS) .... atheol

atheologist (SAUS) .... atheol

atheology (SAUS) .... atheol

Atherectomy Imaging Device [*Medicine*] .... AID

Atherley on Marriage Settlements [*A publication*] (DLA) .... Ath Mar Set

Atheroembolism [*Medicine*] (MELL) .... AE

Atherogenic Index [*By ultracentrifugation*] [*Cardiology*] (DAVI) .... AI

Atherogenic Index (SAUS) .... AI

Atherosclerosis [*Medicine*] (MAE) .... AS

Atherosclerosis [*Medicine*] .... ATHSC

atherosclerosis (SAUS) .... athsc

Atherosclerosis [*Cardiology*] (DAVI) .... ATS

Atherosclerosis Risk in Communities Study [*Department of Health and Human Services*] (GFGA) .... ARIC

Atherosclerotic Brain Infarction [*Medicine*] (CPH) .... ABI

Atherosclerotic Cardiovascular Disease [*Medicine*] (MAE) .... ASCVD

Atherosclerotic Coronary Artery Disease (SAUS) .... ASCVD

Atherosclerotic Coronary Heart Disease [*Medicine*] (MELL) .... ACHD

Atherosclerotic Heart Disease [*Cardiology*] (DAVI) .... AHD

Atherosclerotic Heart Disease [*Medicine*] (MELL) .... ASHD

Atherosclerotic Plaque [*Medicine*] (MELL) .... AP

Atherosclerotic Plaque [*Medicine*] (MELL) .... ASP

Atherothrombotic Brain Infarction [*Medicine*] (DAVI) .... ABI

Atherton, CA [*FM radio station call letters*] .... KCEA

Atherton Tools Interface Specification (SAUS) .... ATIS

Athey Products [*NASDAQ symbol*] (TTSB) .... ATPC

Athey Products Corp. [*Associated Press*] (SAG) .... Athey

Athey Products Corp. [*NASDAQ symbol*] (NQ) .... ATPC

Athinai [*Greece*] [*ICAO location identifier*] (ICLI) .... LGAC

Athinai [*Greece*] [*ICAO location identifier*] (ICLI) .... LGAT

Athinai [*Greece*] [*ICAO location identifier*] (ICLI) .... LGGG

Athinaikon Praktoreion Eidiseon [*Athens News Agency*] [*Greece*] .... APE

Athlete (ADWA) .... athl

Athlete Assistance Program [*See also PAA*] [*Canada*] .... AAP

Athlete Information Bureau [*Canada*] .... AIB

Athletes' Advisory Council [*See also CCA*] [*Canada*] .... AAC

Athletes for a Better Education .... AthBE

Athletes in Action (SAUO) .... AiA

Athletes United for Peace (EA) .... AUP

Athletic (ADA) .... A

Athletic (MUGU) .... ATH

Athletic (ADWA) .... ath

Athletic .... ATHL

Athletic Association .... AA

Athletic Association (SAUO) .... AA

Athletic Association of Western Universities (BARN) .... AAWU

Athletic Clothing Manufacturers' Association [*British*] (BI) .... ACMA

Athletic Club [*Usually in combination with proper noun, as, DAC, Detroit Athletic Club*] .... AC

Athletic Conference of American College Women [*Later, ARFCW*] .... ACACW

Athletic Conference of American College Women (SAUO) .... ACACW

Athletic Director .... AD

Athletic Equipment Managers Association (EA) .... AEMA

Athletic Footwear Association (EA) .... AFA

Athletic Footwear Council [*Later, AFA*] (EA) .... AFC

Athletic Goods Manufacturers Association [*Later, SGMA*] (EA) .... AGMA

Athletic Goods Team Distributors (EA) .... AGTD

Athletic Institute (EA) .... AI

Athletic Motivation Inventory [*Test*] (TES) .... AMI

Athletic Training Council (SAUO) .... ATC

[*The*] Athletics Congress [*Track*] [*An association*] .... TAC

[*The*] Athletics Congress/USA (EA) .... TAC/USA

[*The*] Athletics Congress/USA Trust Fund .... TACTRUST

Athletics New Brunswick [*Athletisme du Nouveau-Brunswick*] (AC) .... ANB

Athlone Industries, Inc. (SAUO) .... ATH

Athlone Resources Ltd. [*Vancouver Stock Exchange symbol*] .... AT

Athmospheric Temperature (SAUS) .... TO

Athol, MA [*AM radio station call letters*] .... WCAT

Athol, MA [*FM radio station call letters*] (BROA) .... WCAT-FM

Athrotomy [*Orthopedics*] (DAVI) .... arthr

Athwartships .... ATH

Athwartships Reference Axis .... ASRA

Ati [*Chad*] [*Airport symbol*] (AD) .... ATV

Ati [*Chad*] [*ICAO location identifier*] (ICLI) .... FTTI

ATI Multimedia Channel [*Computer science*] .... AMC

Atico [*Peru*] [*Seismograph station code, US Geological Survey*] (SEIS) .... ATI

Atico [*Peru*] [*ICAO location identifier*] (ICLI) .... SPOY

Atico Financial Corp. (IIA) .... ATF

Atigaru Point, AK [*Location identifier*] [*FAA*] (FAAL) .... AUJ

Atikameg-Sovereign School, Alberta [*Library symbol*] [*National Library of Canada*] (BIB) ... AATS
Atikokan [*Canada*] [*Airport symbol*] (OAG) ... YIB
Atikokan Centennial Museum, Ontario [*Library symbol*] [*National Library of Canada*] (BIB) ... OATM
Atikokan High School, Atikokan, ON, Canada [*Library symbol*] [*Library of Congress*] (LCLS) ... CaOAtH
Atikokan High School, Ontario [*Library symbol*] [*National Library of Canada*] (NLC) ... OATH
Atikokan, ON [*AM radio station call letters*] ... CKDR-6
Atikokan, ON [*ICAO location identifier*] (ICLI) ... CYIB
Atikokan Public Library, Ontario [*Library symbol*] [*National Library of Canada*] (NLC) ... OAT
Atirro [*Costa Rica*] [*ICAO location identifier*] (ICLI) ... MRAR
Atiu [*Cook Islands*] [*Airport symbol*] (OAG) ... AIU
Atiu [*Cook Islands*] [*ICAO location identifier*] (ICLI) ... NCAT
Atkasuk Village, AK [*Location identifier*] [*FAA*] (FAAL) ... ATK
Atkins, AR [*FM radio station call letters*] (BROA) ... KBHY-FM
Atkins Research & Development [*W.S. Atkins Group Ltd.*] [*Research center*] [*British*] ... AR & D
Atkins Stress Analysis System [*Atkins Research & Development*] [*Software package*] (NCC) ... ASAS
Atkins Structural Analysis System (MCD) ... ASAS
Atkinson [*Guy F.*] **Co. of California** [*Associated Press*] (SAG) ... Atkinsn
Atkinson [*Guy F.*] **Co. of California** [*NASDAQ symbol*] (NQ) ... ATKN
Atkinson Elementary School, Houston, TX [*Library symbol*] [*Library of Congress*] (LCLS) ... TxHAE
Atkinson (Guy F.)Calif [*NASDAQ symbol*] (TTSB) ... ATKN
Atkinson on Conveyancing [*A publication*] (DLA) ... Atk Con
Atkinson on Marketable Titles [*A publication*] (DLA) ... Atk Titles
Atkinson on Sheriffs [*A publication*] (DLA) ... Atk Sher
Atkinson's Chancery Practice [*A publication*] (DLA) ... Atk Ch Pr
Atkinson's Law of Solicitors' Liens [*1905*] [*A publication*] (DLA) ... Atkinson
Atkinson's Quarter Sessions Records [*Yorkshire, England*] [*A publication*] (DLA) ... Atk
Atkyn's English Chancery Reports [*1736-55*] [*A publication*] (DLA) ... Atk
Atkyn's Parliamentary Tracts [*A publication*] (DLA) ... Atk PT
Atlanta [*Iceland*] [*ICAO designator*] (FAAC) ... ABD
Atlanta [*Georgia*] [*Seismograph station code, US Geological Survey*] (SEIS) ... ATL
Atlanta (SAUS) ... Atl
Atlanta [*Branch in the Federal Reserve regional banking system*] (BARN) ... F
Atlanta [*Georgia*] [*ICAO location identifier*] (ICLI) ... KRTL
Atlanta Aerospace Rescue and Recovery Center [*Air Force*] ... AARRC
Atlanta & Saint Andrews Bay Railway Co. [*AAR code*] ... ASAB
Atlanta & West Point Rail Road Co. ... A & WP
Atlanta & West Point Rail Road Co. [*AAR code*] ... AWP
Atlanta & West Point Railroad Co. (SAUO) ... A&WP
Atlanta Area School for the Deaf (SAUO) ... AASD
Atlanta Army Depot [*Georgia*] (AABC) ... ATAD
Atlanta Art Institute, Atlanta, GA [*Library symbol*] [*Library of Congress*] (LCLS) ... GAAI
Atlanta, Birmingham and Atlantic Railway (SAUO) ... AB&AR
Atlanta, Birmingham and Coast (SAUS) ... AB&C
Atlanta, Birmingham & Coast Railroad Co. ... AB & C
Atlanta, Birmingham and Coast Railroad Company (SAUO) ... AB&C
Atlanta, Birmingham & Coast Railroad/Company (SAUO) ... AB&CRC
Atlanta, Birmingham & Coast Railroad/Company (SAUO) ... AB&CRR
Atlanta Cancer Surveillance Center [*Emory University*] [*Research center*] (RCD) ... ACSC
Atlanta Centennial Olympic Games ... ACOG
Atlanta Chamber of Commerce, Atlanta, GA [*Library symbol*] [*Library of Congress*] (LCLS) ... GACC
Atlanta College of Art Library, Atlanta, GA [*OCLC symbol*] (OCLC) ... GAA
Atlanta Committee for the Olympic Games ... ACOG
Atlanta Constitution (SAUS) ... AC
Atlanta Contract Management District (SAUS) ... ATCMD
Atlanta Corp. (EFIS) ... ATCO
Atlanta [*Georgia*] **De Kalb/Peachtree Airport** [*Airport symbol*] [*Obsolete*] (OAG) ... PDK
Atlanta Falcons [*National Football League*] [*1966-present*] (NFLA) ... Atl
Atlanta Flames Fan Club (EA) ... AFFC
Atlanta, GA [*Location identifier*] [*FAA*] (FAAL) ... AFA
Atlanta, GA [*Location identifier*] [*FAA*] (FAAL) ... BRU
Atlanta, GA [*Location identifier*] [*FAA*] (FAAL) ... FSQ
Atlanta, GA [*Location identifier*] [*FAA*] (FAAL) ... FTY
Atlanta, GA [*Location identifier*] [*FAA*] (FAAL) ... FUN
Atlanta, GA [*Location identifier*] [*FAA*] (FAAL) ... HZK
Atlanta, GA [*Location identifier*] [*FAA*] (FAAL) ... LYN
Atlanta, GA [*Location identifier*] [*FAA*] (FAAL) ... RHX
Atlanta, GA [*Location identifier*] [*FAA*] (FAAL) ... SZJ
Atlanta, GA [*FM radio station call letters*] ... WABE
Atlanta, GA [*AM radio station call letters*] ... WAEC
Atlanta, GA [*AM radio station call letters*] ... WAFS
Atlanta, GA [*Television station call letters*] ... WAGA
Atlanta, GA [*Television station call letters*] (BROA) ... WAGA-DT
Atlanta, GA [*AM radio station call letters*] (RBYB) ... WALR
Atlanta, GA [*AM radio station call letters*] ... WAOK
Atlanta, GA [*Television station call letters*] ... WATC
Atlanta, GA [*Television station call letters*] ... WATL
Atlanta, GA [*AM radio station call letters*] (BROA) ... WAZJ
Atlanta, GA [*FM radio station call letters*] ... WCLK
Atlanta, GA [*AM radio station call letters*] (BROA) ... WDWD-AM
Atlanta, GA [*AM radio station call letters*] ... WGKA
Atlanta, GA [*Television station call letters*] ... WGNX
Atlanta, GA [*Television station call letters*] (BROA) ... WGNX-DT
Atlanta, GA [*AM radio station call letters*] ... WGST
Atlanta, GA [*AM radio station call letters*] ... WGUN
Atlanta, GA [*AM radio station call letters*] ... WKHX
Atlanta, GA [*FM radio station call letters*] ... WKLS
Atlanta, GA [*AM radio station call letters*] ... WNIV
Atlanta, GA [*FM radio station call letters*] ... WNNX
Atlanta, GA [*Television station call letters*] ... WPBA
Atlanta, GA [*FM radio station call letters*] ... WPCH
Atlanta, GA [*AM radio station call letters*] ... WQXI
Atlanta, GA [*FM radio station call letters*] ... WRAS
Atlanta, GA [*FM radio station call letters*] ... WREK
Atlanta, GA [*FM radio station call letters*] ... WRFG
Atlanta, GA [*AM radio station call letters*] ... WSB
Atlanta, GA [*Television station call letters*] (BROA) ... WSB-DT
Atlanta, GA [*FM radio station call letters*] ... WSB-FM
Atlanta, GA [*Television station call letters*] ... WSB-TV
Atlanta, GA [*Television station call letters*] ... WTBS
Atlanta, GA [*TV station call letters*] (RBYB) ... WUPA-TV
Atlanta, GA [*FM radio station call letters*] ... WVEE
Atlanta, GA [*Television station call letters*] ... WVEU
Atlanta, GA [*Television station call letters*] ... WXIA
Atlanta, GA [*Television station call letters*] (BROA) ... WXIA-DT
Atlanta, GA [*AM radio station call letters*] ... WYZE
Atlanta, GA [*FM radio station call letters*] ... WZGC
Atlanta, GA [*Location identifier*] [*FAA*] (FAAL) ... ZTL
Atlanta Gas & Light Co. [*NYSE symbol*] (SPSG) ... ATG
Atlanta Gas & Light Co. [*Associated Press*] (SAG) ... AtlGas
Atlanta Gas & Light Co. [*Associated Press*] (SAG) ... AtlGs
Atlanta Gas Lt 7.70% Dep Pfd [*NYSE symbol*] (TTSB) ... ATGPr
Atlanta General Depot (SAUO) ... AGD
Atlanta Gold Corp. [*Vancouver Stock Exchange symbol*] [*Toronto Stock Exchange symbol*] ... AAG
Atlanta, Hampton [*Georgia*] [*ICAO location identifier*] (ICLI) ... KZTL
Atlanta Hartsfield International Airport (SAUS) ... ATL
Atlanta Historical Society, Atlanta, GA [*Library symbol*] [*Library of Congress*] (LCLS) ... GAHi
Atlanta Housing Authority ... AHA
Atlanta, IL [*FM radio station call letters*] (BROA) ... WMNW-FM
Atlanta Information Services, Decatur (SAUS) ... GDAIS
Atlanta Information Services, Decatur, GA [*Library symbol*] [*Library of Congress*] (LCLS) ... GDAIS
Atlanta Journal-Constitution ... AJC
Atlanta Junior College, Atlanta, GA [*Library symbol*] [*Library of Congress*] (LCLS) ... GAJ
Atlanta Linux Enthusiasts (VERA) ... ALE
Atlanta, MI [*FM radio station call letters*] ... WAIR
Atlanta Motor Speedway ... AMS
Atlanta Public Library, Atlanta, GA [*Library symbol*] [*Library of Congress*] (LCLS) ... GA
Atlanta Public Library, Atlanta, GA [*OCLC symbol*] (OCLC) ... GAP
Atlanta Public Schools, Professional Library, Atlanta, GA [*Library symbol*] [*Library of Congress*] (LCLS) ... GAP
Atlanta Region Metropolitan Planning Commission (SAUO) ... ARMPC
Atlanta School of Art, Atlanta, GA [*Library symbol*] [*Library of Congress*] (LCLS) ... GAA
Atlanta Service Center [*IRS*] ... ATSC
Atlanta Skylark Club, Inc. (SAUS) ... SLK
[*The*] **Atlanta, Stone Mountain & Lithonia Railway Co.** [*AAR code*] ... ASML
Atlanta, Stone Mountain & Lithonia Railway Company (SAUO) ... ASML
Atlanta Street Railroad ... A ST
Atlanta Support Office (SAUO) ... AT
Atlanta Symphony Orchestra (SAUO) ... ASO
AtLANta Technologies, Inc. [*Atlanta, GA*] [*Telecommunications service*] (TSSD) ... ATI
Atlanta, TX [*Location identifier*] [*FAA*] (FAAL) ... ATA
Atlanta, TX [*AM radio station call letters*] ... KALT
Atlanta, TX [*FM radio station call letters*] ... KPYN
Atlanta University (SAUO) ... AU
Atlanta University, Atlanta, GA [*Library symbol*] [*Library of Congress*] (LCLS) ... GAU
Atlanta University Center, Atlanta, GA [*OCLC symbol*] (OCLC) ... AUU
Atlanta-International, GA (SAUO) ... ATL
Atlantair Ltd. [*Canada*] [*ICAO designator*] (FAAC) ... ATB
Atlanta/Sosnoff [*NYSE symbol*] (TTSB) ... ATL
Atlanta/The William B. Hartsfield Atlanta International [*Georgia*] [*ICAO location identifier*] (ICLI) ... KATL
Atlanten (SAUS) ... LANt
Atlantic [*Ocean*] (ABBR) ... A
Atlantic [*Record label*] ... Atl
Atlantic ... ATL
Atlantic ... LANT
Atlantic 10 Conference (PSS) ... A-10
Atlantic Aero, Inc. [*ICAO designator*] (FAAC) ... MDC
Atlantic Aerospace Rescue and Recovery Center (SAUO) ... AARC
Atlantic Aerospace Rescue and Recovery Center (SAUO) ... AARRC
Atlantic Air BVI Ltd. [*British*] [*ICAO designator*] (FAAC) ... BLB
Atlantic Air Rescue Center (SAUO) ... AARC
Atlantic Airborne Early Warning [*Military*] ... AAEW
Atlantic Airline Ltd. [*Gambia*] [*FAA designator*] (FAAC) ... AWA
Atlantic Airways, PF (Faroe Islands) [*Denmark*] [*ICAO designator*] (FAAC) ... FLI
Atlantic Alliance for Maritime Heritage Conservation (EA) ... AAMHC
Atlantic American [*NASDAQ symbol*] (TTSB) ... AAME
Atlantic American Corp. [*NASDAQ symbol*] (NQ) ... AAME
Atlantic American Corp. [*Associated Press*] (SAG) ... AtlAm
Atlantic Amphibious Force [*Navy*] ... AAF

Atlantic Amphibious Ready Group (MCD) ... AARG
Atlantic & East Carolina Railway Co. [*AAR code*] ... AEC
Atlantic and East Carolina Railway Co. (SAUO) ... AEC
Atlantic and East Carolina Railway Company (SAUO) ... A&EC
Atlantic & Great Western Railroad ... A & GW
Atlantic and Gulf American Flag Berth Operators ... AGAFBO
Atlantic and Pacific Railroad Company (SAUO) ... APR
Atlantic & Pacific Tea Company (SAUO) ... A&P
Atlantic & Pacific Travel International (SAUO) ... A&P
Atlantic & St. Lawrence Railroad ... A & StL
Atlantic and West Indies ... A & WI
Atlantic and West Indies (SAUS) ... A&WI
Atlantic & Western [*Railroad*] (MHDB) ... A & W
Atlantic & Western (SAUO) ... A&W
Atlantic & Western Railway Co. (IIA) ... A & W
Atlantic & Western Railway Co. [*AAR code*] ... ATW
Atlantic & Yadkin Railroad (IIA) ... A & Y
Atlantic Antisubmarine Warfare Communication Net (NVT) ... AMANET
Atlantic Area [*Services to the Armed Forces*] [*Red Cross*] ... AA
Atlantic Area (SAUO) ... LANT
Atlantic Art Institute ... AAI
Atlantic Association of Broadcasters (AC) ... AAB
Atlantic Association of Teacher Educators [*Canada*] ... AATE
Atlantic Association of Young Political Leaders (EA) ... AAYPL
Atlantic Avenue School, Lynbrook, NY [*Library symbol*] [*Library of Congress*] (LCLS) ... NLynAE
Atlantic Aviation Services (SAA) ... AAS
Atlantic Ballistic Missile Range ... ABMR
Atlantic Bank & Trust [*NASDAQ symbol*] (TTSB) ... ATLB
Atlantic Bank and Trust Co. [*NASDAQ symbol*] (SAG) ... ATLB
Atlantic Bank and Trust Co. [*Associated Press*] (SAG) ... AtlBkTC
Atlantic Barrier Patrol [*Eastern seaward extension of the DEW Line*] [*Obsolete*] ... BARLANT
Atlantic Base Section ... ABS
Atlantic Beach (SAUS) ... AB
Atlantic Beach, FL [*FM radio station call letters*] ... WFYV
Atlantic Beach, FL [*AM radio station call letters*] ... WNCM
Atlantic Beach, FL [*AM radio station call letters*] (BROA) ... WQOP-AM
Atlantic Beach, SC [*AM radio station call letters*] (BROA) ... WMIR-AM
Atlantic Beach, SC [*AM radio station call letters*] ... WMIW
Atlantic Beach, SC [*FM radio station call letters*] (BROA) ... WSEA-FM
Atlantic Beverage [*NASDAQ symbol*] (TTSB) ... ABEV
Atlantic Beverage Corp. [*NASDAQ symbol*] (SAG) ... ABEV
Atlantic Beverage Corp. [*Associated Press*] (SAG) ... AtlBev
Atlantic Books Today [*A publication*] (BRI) ... Atl BT
Atlantic Booster Test (KSC) ... ABT
Atlantic Building Supply Dealers Association (AC) ... ABSDA
Atlantic Canada Airborne Sensing (SAUS) ... ACAS
Atlantic Canada Opportunities Agency ... ACOA
Atlantic Canada Society for Human Resource Development ... ACSHRD
Atlantic Canada Teacher (journ.) (SAUS) ... ACT
Atlantic Capital Corporation (SAUO) ... ACC
Atlantic Capital I [*NYSE symbol*] (SAG) ... ATE
Atlantic Capital I [*Associated Press*] (SAG) ... AtlCap
Atlantic, Caribbean, and Pacific Countries Association of Canadian Publishers (SAUO) ... ACPCACP
Atlantic Centennial Olympic Properties ... ACOP
Atlantic Center for the Environment (EA) ... ACE
Atlantic Charter ... AC
Atlantic Christian College [*Wilson, NC*] ... ACC
Atlantic Christian College, Wilson, NC [*Library symbol*] [*Library of Congress*] (LCLS) ... NcWilA
Atlantic Circulation and Climate Experiment [*Marine science*] (OSRA) ... ACCE
Atlantic City [*New Jersey*] [*Airport symbol*] (OAG) ... ACY
Atlantic City [*New Jersey*] [*Airport symbol*] (OAG) ... AIY
Atlantic City & Shore Railroad ... AC & S
Atlantic City Electric Co. (SAUO) ... ACE
Atlantic City Electric Company (SAUO) ... ATE
Atlantic City Free Public Library, Atlantic City, NJ [*OCLC symbol*] (OCLC) ... ACP
Atlantic City Free Public Library, Atlantic City, NJ [*Library symbol*] [*Library of Congress*] (LCLS) ... NjAc
Atlantic City Municipal Airport (SAUO) ... ACY
Atlantic City, NJ [*Location identifier*] [*FAA*] (FAAL) ... PVO
Atlantic City, NJ [*Television station call letters*] ... WACI
Atlantic City, NJ [*FM radio station call letters*] (BROA) ... WAJM-FM
Atlantic City, NJ [*FM radio station call letters*] ... WAYV
Atlantic City, NJ [*AM radio station call letters*] ... WFPG
Atlantic City, NJ [*FM radio station call letters*] ... WFPG-FM
Atlantic City, NJ [*AM radio station call letters*] (BROA) ... WGYM-AM
Atlantic City, NJ [*FM radio station call letters*] ... WMGM
Atlantic City, NJ [*AM radio station call letters*] ... WMID
Atlantic City, NJ [*FM radio station call letters*] ... WNJN
Atlantic City, NJ [*FM radio station call letters*] (BROA) ... WPUR-FM
Atlantic City, NJ [*AM radio station call letters*] ... WUSS
Atlantic City, NJ [*Television station call letters*] ... WWAC
Atlantic City Radio Regulations (SAUS) ... ACRR
Atlantic City Remodelers Exposition [*Remodeling Contractors Association*] (TSPED) ... ACRE
Atlantic City Reporter, Atlantic City, NJ [*Library symbol*] [*Library of Congress*] (LCLS) ... NjAcR
Atlantic City Table of Frequency Allocations (SAUS) ... ACTFA
Atlantic City to the Atlantic Highlands (SAUS) ... North Jersey Coast
Atlantic City/Atlantic City [*New Jersey*] [*ICAO location identifier*] (ICLI) ... KACY
Atlantic Climate Change ... ACC
Atlantic Climate Change Program [*Marine science*] (OSRA) ... ACCP
Atlantic Coast Air Service ... ACAS
Atlantic Coast Airlines [*NASDAQ symbol*] (TTSB) ... ACAI
Atlantic Coast Airlines [*Westair Airlines, Inc.*] [*ICAO designator*] (FAAC) ... BLR
Atlantic Coast Airlines Hldgs [*NASDAQ symbol*] (SG) ... ACAI
Atlantic Coast Airlines, Inc. [*NASDAQ symbol*] (SAG) ... ACAI
Atlantic Coast Airlines, Inc. [*Associated Press*] (SAG) ... AtlCstAir
Atlantic Coast Conference (EA) ... ACC
Atlantic Coast Copper Corp. Ltd. [*Toronto Stock Exchange symbol*] ... ATC
Atlantic Coast Football League ... ACFL
Atlantic Coast Line R. R. [*AAR code*] ... ACL
Atlantic Coast Line R. R. ... ACLRR
Atlantic Coast Line Railroad (SAUO) ... ACL
Atlantic Coast Line Railroad (SAUO) ... ACLRR
Atlantic Coast Line Railroad Co. (SAUO) ... AX
Atlantic Command [*Military*] ... ACOM
Atlantic Command [*Navy*] ... LANTCOM
Atlantic Command Defense Analysis Center (SAUO) ... LANTDAC
Atlantic Command Deployable Intelligence System (SAUS) ... LANTDIS
Atlantic Command Inspector General (DNAB) ... LANTCOMINSGEN
Atlantic Command Intelligence Operating Procedures (MCD) ... ACIOP
Atlantic Command Military Blood Program Office (DNAB) ... LANTCOMMBPO
Atlantic Command Operational Control Center (SAUO) ... LCOCC
Atlantic Command Operations Support Facility (DNAB) ... LANTCOMOPSUPPFAC
Atlantic Commander Operational Control Center (SAUS) ... ACOCC
Atlantic [*Fleet*] **Commander Operational Control Center** [*Navy*] ... ACOCC
Atlantic [*Fleet*] **Commander Operational Control Center** [*Navy*] ... LANTCOMOPCONCEN
Atlantic [*Fleet*] **Commander Operational Control Center** [*Navy*] ... LCOCC
Atlantic Commodities Purchasing Service (SAUO) ... ATCOPS
Atlantic Communication and Technical Workers Union (SAUO) ... AC&TWU
Atlantic Communication and Technical Workers Union ... AC & TWU
Atlantic Community College, Mays Landing, NJ [*OCLC symbol*] (OCLC) ... ANJ
Atlantic Community College, Mays Landing, NJ [*Library symbol*] [*Library of Congress*] (LCLS) ... NjMIAC
Atlantic Community Development Group for Latin America [*Joint US-European private investment company*] ... ADELA
Atlantic Community Newspapers Association (AC) ... ACNA
Atlantic Community Quarterly [*A publication*] (DLA) ... Atl Comm Q
Atlantic Computer Microfilm Corporation (SAUS) ... ATCOM
Atlantic Conference of CPAs, Inc. (SAUO) ... ACCPA
Atlantic Congress ... AC
Atlantic Container Line [*British*] ... ACL
Atlantic Container Line, Ltd. (SAUO) ... ACL
Atlantic Co-Operator, Antigonish, Nova Scotia [*Library symbol*] [*National Library of Canada*] (NLC) ... NSAAC
Atlantic Co-Operator, Antigonish, NS, Canada [*Library symbol*] [*Library of Congress*] (LCLS) ... CaNSAAC
Atlantic Council (SAUO) ... AC
Atlantic Council [*Later, ACUS*] [*NATO*] (NATG) ... AC
Atlantic Council of Canada (EAIO) ... ACC
Atlantic Council of the United States (EA) ... ACUS
Atlantic County Advertiser, Northfield, NJ [*Library symbol*] [*Library of Congress*] (LCLS) ... NjNoA
Atlantic County Clerk, Atlantic City, NJ [*Library symbol*] [*Library of Congress*] (LCLS) ... NjAcCoC
Atlantic County Clerk, Mays Landing, NJ [*Library symbol*] [*Library of Congress*] (LCLS) ... NjMICoC
Atlantic County Library, Mays Landing, NJ [*Library symbol*] [*Library of Congress*] (LCLS) ... NjMIA
Atlantic County Record, Mays Landing, NJ [*Library symbol*] [*Library of Congress*] (LCLS) ... NjMIR
Atlantic Dairy Council (AC) ... ADC
Atlantic Data Coverage ... ADC
Atlantic Database for Exchange Processes at the Deep Sea Floor (SAUS) ... ADEPD
Atlantic Daylight Time ... ADT
Atlantic Deeper Waterways Association (EA) ... ADWA
Atlantic Defense Identification Zone (SAUS) ... ADIZ
Atlantic Development Board (SAUO) ... ADB
Atlantic Development Council Canada ... ADCC
Atlantic Development Group for Latin America (SAUO) ... ADELA
Atlantic Division, Military Air Transport Service (SAUO) ... ATLDMATS
Atlantic Division Naval Facilities Engineering Command ... LANTNAVFACENGCOM
Atlantic Division Transport Control Center [*Military*] ... ATCC
Atlantic Economic Society (EA) ... AES
Atlantic Education Association [*Canada*] ... AEA
Atlantic Educational Research Council [*Canada*] ... AERC
Atlantic Energy [*Vancouver Stock Exchange symbol*] ... ACG
Atlantic Energy [*NYSE symbol*] (SPSG) ... ATE
Atlantic Energy, Inc. [*Associated Press*] (SAG) ... AtlEnrg
Atlantic Environmental Group [*National Marine Fisheries Service*] ... AEG
Atlantic Episcopal Assembly (AC) ... AEA
Atlantic Estuarine Fisheries Center [*National Oceanic and Atmospheric Administration*] (MSC) ... AEFC
Atlantic Estuarine Research Society (EA) ... AERS
Atlantic Estuarine Society ... AES
Atlantic Ferry Organization [*Based in Canada under Ministry of Aircraft Production*] [*British*] [*World War II*] ... ATFERO
Atlantic Ferry Service [*World War II*] ... AFS
Atlantic Ferry Service (SAUO) ... AFS
[*The*] **Atlantic Fertilizer Institute** (AC) ... AFI
Atlantic Filmmakers' Co-Operative (AC) ... AFCOOP
Atlantic Fleet (SAUO) ... AF
Atlantic Fleet ... LANTFLT

Atlantic Fleet Amphibious Force [*Navy*] ... AFAF
Atlantic Fleet Amphibious Ready Group (MCD) ... ARG
Atlantic Fleet Antisubmarine Warfare Tactical School [*Navy*] ... LANTFLEASWTACSCOL
Atlantic Fleet Antisubmarine Warfare Tactical School (SAUS) ... LANTFLEASWTASCOL
Atlantic Fleet Audio-Visual Center [*Navy*] (DNAB) ... AFAVC
Atlantic Fleet Chief of Naval Reserve Representative (DNAB) ... LANTREPCNAVRES
Atlantic Fleet Combat Camera Group [*Obsolete*] ... AFCCG
Atlantic Fleet Headquarters Support Activity [*Navy*] (DNAB) ... LANTFLTHEDSUPPACT
Atlantic Fleet Material Control Office (SAUS) ... LANFLTMATCONOFF
Atlantic Fleet Material Control Office [*Navy*] (DNAB) ... LANTFLTMATCONOFF
Atlantic Fleet Mobile Photographic Group (SAUO) ... AFMPG
Atlantic Fleet Naval Forces Intelligence Collection Manual (MCD) ... AFNFICM
Atlantic Fleet Naval Forces Intelligence Collection Manual ... ANFICM
Atlantic Fleet Organization ... AFO
Atlantic Fleet Polaris Material Office (SAUO) ... AFPMO
Atlantic Fleet Propulsion Examining Board [*Navy*] (DNAB) ... LANTFLTPEB
Atlantic Fleet Range Support Facility [*Navy*] (DNAB) ... AFRSF
Atlantic Fleet Signals Security Operations Center [*Navy*] (DNAB) ... LANTSOC
Atlantic Fleet Training Support Facilities ... LANTFLTRANSUPPFAC
Atlantic Fleet Weapons Range [*Later, AFRSF*] [*Navy*] ... AFWR
Atlantic Fleet Weapons Range [*Later, AFRSF*] [*Navy*] ... LANTFLTWPNRAN
Atlantic Fleet Weapons Training Facility [*Navy*] ... AFWTF
Atlantic Fleet Weapons Training Facility [*Navy*] (DNAB) ... LANTFLTWPNTRAFAC
Atlantic Fleet Worldwide Military Command Control System [*Navy*] (DNAB) ... LANTWWMCCS
Atlantic Forward Area Support Team [*Military*] (DNAB) ... LANTFAST
Atlantic Free Trade Area ... AFTA
Atlantic Frontier Environmental Network ... AFEN
Atlantic Gas Research Exchange (MHDB) ... AGRE
Atlantic Generating Station [*Nuclear energy*] (NRCH) ... AGS
Atlantic Geology (SAUS) ... Atl Geol
Atlantic Geoscience Association ... AGS
Atlantic Geoscience Centre (SAUO) ... AGC
Atlantic Gulf Airlines, Inc. [*ICAO designator*] (FAAC) ... AGF
Atlantic, Gulf and West Indiens Steamship Lines (SAUO) ... AGWI
Atlantic Gulf Communities Corp. [*NASDAQ symbol*] (SAG) ... AGLF
Atlantic Gulf Communities Corp. [*Associated Press*] (SAG) ... AtlGulf
Atlantic, Gulf, West Indies [*Marine insurance*] (ODBW) ... AGWI
Atlantic Highlands Public Library Association, Atlantic Highlands, NJ [*Library symbol*] [*Library of Congress*] (LCLS) ... NjAt
Atlantic, IA [*Location identifier*] [*FAA*] (FAAL) ... AIO
Atlantic, IA [*AM radio station call letters*] ... KJAN
Atlantic, IA [*FM radio station call letters*] ... KXKT
Atlantic Independent Film & Video Association (AC) ... AIFVA
Atlantic Independent Union ... AIU
Atlantic Information Center for Teachers (SAUO) ... AICT
Atlantic Information Center (or Centre) for Teachers (SAUS) ... AICT
Atlantic Institute for Defence Study (SAUO) ... AIDS
Atlantic Institute for International Affairs [*France*] (EA) ... AIIA
Atlantic Institute of Education, Halifax, NS, Canada [*Library symbol*] [*Library of Congress*] (LCLS) ... CaNSHAI
Atlantic Institution, Correctional Service Canada [*Etablissement Atlantique, Service Correctionnel Canada*], **Renous, New Brunswick** [*Library symbol*] [*National Library of Canada*] (BIB) ... NBRCA
Atlantic Instruments & Electronics (SAUO) ... AIE
Atlantic Intelligence Center [*Navy*] ... AIC
Atlantic Intelligence Center (SAUS) ... LANTINCEN
Atlantic Intelligence Center [*Navy*] ... LANTINTCEN
Atlantic International Air and Surface Search and Rescue Seminar (PDAA) ... LANTSAR
Atlantic International Marketing Committee [*Maryland, Virginia, North Carolina, and South Carolina*] ... AIM
Atlantic Intracoastal Waterway (SAUS) ... AIW
Atlantic Island Air [*Iceland*] [*ICAO designator*] (FAAC) ... TRG
Atlantic Isopycnic Model ... AIM
Atlantic Lottery Corp. [*Societe des Loteries de l'Atlantique*], **Moncton, New Brunswick** [*Library symbol*] [*National Library of Canada*] (NLC) ... NBMOAL
Atlantic Margin Coring Project ... AMCOR
Atlantic Marine Center [*National Oceanic and Atmospheric Administration*] ... AMC
Atlantic Marine Oceanographic Laboratory (SAUS) ... AMOL
Atlantic Merchant Shipping Instructions ... AMSI
Atlantic Meteorology Experiment (SAUS) ... AMEX
Atlantic Missile Range [*Later, Eastern Test Range*] ... AMR
Atlantic Missile Range Integrated Telemetry (ACAE) ... AMR/IT
Atlantic Missile Range [*later, Eastern Test Range*] **Operations** ... AMRO
Atlantic Missile Range [*later, Eastern Test Range*] **Operations Office** ... AMROO
Atlantic Missile Range Operations Office (SAUO) ... AMROO
Atlantic Missile Range [*Later, Eastern Test Range*] **Telemetry Submodule** (SAA) ... AMRTS
Atlantic Missile Range Telemetry Submodule (SAUS) ... AMRTS
Atlantic Missile Test Range (KSC) ... AMTR
Atlantic Monthly [*A publication*] (BRI) ... Atl
Atlantic Monthly (journ.) (SAUS) ... AM
Atlantic Monthly Press ... AMP
Atlantic Motorcycle Competition Riders' Association (AC) ... AMCRA
Atlantic Naval Intelligence Summary (MCD) ... LNIS
Atlantic, NC [*FM radio station call letters*] ... WTKF
Atlantic News-Telegraph, Atlantic, IA [*Library symbol*] [*Library of Congress*] (LCLS) ... IaAtNT
Atlantic Nuclear Force [*NATO*] ... ANF
Atlantic Nutritional Association (EA) ... ANA
Atlantic Ocean ... AT
Atlantic Ocean ... AtlO
Atlantic Ocean (SAUS) ... Atl O
Atlantic Ocean (SAA) ... ATO
Atlantic Ocean [*MARC geographic area code*] [*Library of Congress*] (LCCP) ... l----
Atlantic Ocean Air Traffic Control [*NATO*] (NATG) ... AOATC
Atlantic Ocean Area ... AOA
Atlantic Ocean Recovery Area [*NASA*] ... AORA
Atlantic Ocean Region [*INTELSAT*] ... AOR
Atlantic Ocean Ship [*INTELSAT*] ... AOS
Atlantic Oceanographic and Meteorological Laboratory [*Miami, FL*] [*National Oceanic and Atmospheric Administration*] ... AOML
Atlantic Oceanographic Group (SAUO) ... AOG
Atlantic Oceanographic Laboratories [*of Environmental Science Services Administration*] ... AOL
Atlantic Oceanographic Laboratories (or Laboratory) (SAUO) ... AOL
Atlantic Oceanographic (or Oceanography) Laboratories (SAUS) ... AOL
Atlantic Offshore Fish and Lobster Association (OSRA) ... AOFLA
Atlantic Offshore Fishermen's Association (EA) ... AOFA
Atlantic Offshore Fishermens Association (SAUS) ... AOFA
Atlantic Offshore Lobstermen's Association (SRA) ... AOLA
Atlantic Operating Area [*Military*] (DNAB) ... AOA
Atlantic Operations Supply Facilities (MCD) ... LANTOPS
Atlantic Operations Supply Facilities ... LANTOPSSUPFAC
Atlantic Outer Continental Shelf ... AOCS
Atlantic Packet Satelite Network (SAUS) ... SATNET
Atlantic Passenger Steamship Conference (SAUO) ... APSC
Atlantic Pharmaceuticals [*NASDAQ symbol*] (TTSB) ... ATLC
Atlantic Pharmaceuticals, Inc. [*Associated Press*] (SAG) ... AtlPharm
Atlantic Pharmaceuticals, Inc. [*Associated Press*] (SAG) ... AtlPhr
Atlantic Pharmaceuticals,Inc. [*NASDAQ symbol*] (SAG) ... ATLC
Atlantic Pharma'l Units 2000 [*NASDAQ symbol*] (TTSB) ... ATLCU
Atlantic Pharm'l Wrrt 2000 [*NASDAQ symbol*] (TTSB) ... ATLCW
Atlantic Pilotage Authority ... APA
Atlantic Political Advisory Group [*NATO*] ... APAG
Atlantic Premium Brands [*AMEX symbol*] (SG) ... ABR
Atlantic Professional Boatman's Association [*Defunct*] (EA) ... APBA
Atlantic Province Reports [*Information service or system*] [*A publication*] (DLA) ... Atl PR
Atlantic Province Reports [*Information service or system*] [*A publication*] (DLA) ... Atl Prov
Atlantic Province Reports (journ.) (SAUS) ... APR
Atlantic Provinces Art Gallery Association [*Canada*] ... APAGA
Atlantic Provinces Association of Landscape Architects (AC) ... APALA
Atlantic Provinces Association of Learning Materials and Education Representatives (SAUO) ... APALMER
Atlantic Provinces Association of Learning Materials and Education Representatives [*Canada*] ... APALMER
Atlantic Provinces Council on the Sciences (AC) ... APCS
Atlantic Provinces Economic Council ... APEC
Atlantic Provinces Library Association (AC) ... APLA
Atlantic Provinces Library Association. Bulletin (journ.) (SAUS) ... APLA Bull
Atlantic Provinces Linguistic Association [*Canada*] ... APLA
Atlantic Provinces Numismatic Association [*Canada*] ... APNA
Atlantic Provinces Power Development Act [*Canada*] ... APPDA
Atlantic Provinces Resource Centre for the Visually Impaired, Halifax, Nova Scotia (SAUS) ... NSHAVI
[*The*] **Atlantic Provinces Resource Centre for the Visually-Impaired, Hal ifax, NS, anada** [*Library symbol*] [*Library of Congress*] (LCLS) ... CaNSHAVI
[*The*] **Atlantic Provinces Resource Centre for the Visually-Impaired, Halifax, Nova Scotia** [*Library symbol*] [*National Library of Canada*] (NLC) ... NSHAVI
Atlantic Provinces Trucking Association [*Canada*] ... APTA
Atlantic Public Library, Atlantic, IA [*Library symbol*] [*Library of Congress*] (LCLS) ... IaAt
Atlantic Public Library, Atlantic, IA [*Library symbol*] [*Library of Congress*] (LCLS) ... IaAtL
Atlantic Publishers Association (AC) ... APA
Atlantic Quarterly (journ.) (SAUS) ... AQ
Atlantic Range Instrumentation Ship ... ARIS
Atlantic Readiness Exercise (MCD) ... LANTREADEX
Atlantic Realty Trust [*NASDAQ symbol*] (TTSB) ... ATLRS
Atlantic Realty Trust SBI [*NASDAQ symbol*] (SAG) ... ATLR
Atlantic Realty Trust SBI [*Associated Press*] (SAG) ... AtlReal
Atlantic Records (SAUS) ... AR
Atlantic Refining Co., Philadelphia, PA [*Library symbol*] [*Library of Congress*] (LCLS) ... PPAtR
Atlantic Refining Company (SAUO) ... AFI
Atlantic Refining Company of Germany GmbH (SAUO) ... ARC
Atlantic Region, Atmospheric Environment Service, Environment Canada [*Bureau Regional de l'Atlantique, Service de l'Environnement Atmospherique, Environnement Canada*] **Halifax, Nova Scotia** [*Library symbol*] [*National Library of Canada*] (NLC) ... NSHW
Atlantic Region Canadian University Press (SAUO) ... ARCUP
Atlantic Regional Laboratory (SAUO) ... ARL
Atlantic Regional Laboratory, National Research Council [*Laboratoire Regionalde l'Atlantique, Conseil National de Recherches du Canada*] **Halifax, Nova Sco tia** [*Library symbol*] [*National Library of Canada*] (NLC) ... NSHM
Atlantic Regional Library, Parks Canada [*Bibliotheque Regionale de l'Atlantique, Parcs Canada*] **Halifax, Nova Scotia** [*Library symbol*] [*National Library of Canada*] (NLC) ... NSHIAP
Atlantic Regional Library, Public Works Canada [*Bibliotheque Regionale de l'Atlantique, Travaux Publics Canada*] **Halifax, Nova Scotia** [*Library symbol*] [*National Library of Canada*] (NLC) ... NSHPW

Atlantic Regional Library, Transport Canada [*Bibliotheque Regionale de l'Atlantique, Transports Canada*], **Moncton, New Brunswick** [*Library symbol*] [*National Library of Canada*] (NLC) .... NBMOTAR
Atlantic Regional Panel (SAUS) .... ARP
Atlantic Remote Sensing Land Ocean Experiment (MCD) .... ARSLOE
Atlantic Reporter [*A publication*] (DLA) .... A
Atlantic Reporter [*A publication*] (DLA) .... AR
Atlantic Reporter [*A publication*] (DLA) .... A Rep
Atlantic Reporter [*A publication*] (DLA) .... At
Atlantic Reporter [*A publication*] (BARN) .... Atl
Atlantic Reporter [*A publication*] (DLA) .... Atl R
Atlantic Reporter [*A publication*] (DLA) .... Atl Rep
Atlantic Reporter [*A publication*] (DLA) .... Atl Repr
Atlantic Reporter [*A publication*] (DLA) .... At Rep
Atlantic Reporter, Second Series [*West*] [*A publication*] (AAGC) A2d
Atlantic Reporter, Second Series (West) [*A publication*] (DLA) .... Atl 2d
Atlantic Representative for Commander Naval Surface Reserve Force (DNAB) .... LANTREPCOMNAVSURFRES
Atlantic Research Automatic Position Telemetering (SAUS) .... ARAPT
Atlantic Research Center (KSC) .... ARC
Atlantic Research Centre for Mental Retardation [*Dalhousie University*] [*Canada*] [*Research center*] (RCD) .... ARCMR
Atlantic Research Corporation (SAUO) .... ARC
Atlantic Research Corporation (SAUO) .... ATRC
Atlantic Research Corporation Atmospheric Sounding [*Missile*] (MUGU) .... ARCAS
Atlantic Research Laboratories [*National Research Council of Canada*] (MCD) .... ARL
Atlantic Research Marketing Systems Inc. (SAUO) .... ARMS
Atlantic Reserve Fleet (SAUS) .... LantResFlt
Atlantic Reserve Fleet .... LANTRESFLT
Atlantic Rich $3 Cv Pref [*NYSE symbol*] (TTSB) .... ARCPrA
Atlantic Rich 9% Exch Nts'97 [*NYSE symbol*] (TTSB) .... LYX
Atlantic Rich$2.80 Cv Pref [*NYSE symbol*] (TTSB) .... ARCPrC
Atlantic Richfield [*NYSE symbol*] (TTSB) .... ABC
Atlantic Richfield [*NYSE symbol*] (SG) .... ARC
Atlantic Richfield Canada, Ltd. (SAUO) .... ARCAN
Atlantic Richfield Co. [*NYSE symbol*] (SPSG) .... ARC
Atlantic Richfield Co. .... ARCO
Atlantic Richfield Co. [*Associated Press*] (SAG) .... AtlRc
Atlantic Richfield Co. [*Associated Press*] (SAG) .... AtlRich
Atlantic Richfield Co. [*Associated Press*] (SAG) AtlRich97
Atlantic Richfield Co. [*NYSE symbol*] (SAG) .... LYX
Atlantic Richfield Co. [*ICAO designator*] (FAAC) .... NRS
Atlantic Richfield Co., Geoscience Library, Dallas, TX [*OCLC symbol*] (OCLC) .... ATR
Atlantic Richfield Co., Geoscience Library, Dallas, TX [*Library symbol*] [*Library of Congress*] (LCLS) .... TxDaAR-G
Atlantic Richfield Co., R and D Library, Dallas (SAUS) .... TxDaAR-R
Atlantic Richfield Co., R and D Library, Dallas, TX [*OCLC symbol*] (OCLC) .... ATC
Atlantic Richfield Co., R and D Library, Dallas, TX [*Library symbol*] [*Library of Congress*] (LCLS) .... TxDaAR-R
Atlantic Richfield Co., Technical Library, Dallas, TX [*Library symbol*] [*Library of Congress*] (LCLS) .... TxDaAR-T
Atlantic Richfield Company (SAUO) .... ARC
Atlantic Richfield Company (SAUO) .... ARCO
Atlantic Richfield Hanford Co. (MCD) .... ARH
Atlantic Richfield Hanford Co., Richland, WA [*Library symbol*] [*Library of Congress*] (LCLS) .... WaRiAR
Atlantic Richfield Hanford Company (SAUO) .... ARHCO
Atlantic Route [*Aviation*] (FAAC) .... AR
Atlantic Salmon Association (EA) .... ASA
Atlantic Salmon Convention Act of 1982 .... ASCA
Atlantic Salmon Federation (EA) .... ASF
Atlantic Salmon Journal (SAUS) .... Atl Salmon J
Atlantic Salmon Research Treaty (SAUS) .... ASRT
Atlantic Salt Fish Commission (SAUO) .... ASFC
Atlantic Satellite Network [*Cable-television system*] .... ASN
Atlantic School of Theology [*Canada*] .... AST
Atlantic School of Theology, Halifax, Nova Scotia [*Library symbol*] [*National Library of Canada*] (NLC) .... NSHPH
Atlantic School of Theology, Halifax, NS, Canada [*Library symbol*] [*Library of Congress*] (LCLS) .... CaNSHPH
Atlantic Sea Run Salmon Commission (EA) .... ASRSC
Atlantic Seaboard Circuit [*Horse racing*] .... ASC
Atlantic Semiconductor (IAA) .... AS
Atlantic Shopping Centres Ltd. [*Toronto Stock Exchange symbol*] .... ATS
Atlantic Site 1 (GAAI) .... ATL 1
Atlantic Site 2 (GAAI) .... ATL 2
Atlantic, SL [*Spain*] [*FAA designator*] (FAAC) .... RCU
Atlantic Slope Project (SAUS) .... ASP
Atlantic So'east Air [*NASDAQ symbol*] (TTSB) .... ASAI
Atlantic Southeast [*ICAO designator*] (AD) .... EV
Atlantic Southeast Airlines .... ASA
Atlantic Southeast Airlines (SAUO) .... ASEX
Atlantic Southeast Airlines [*Associated Press*] (SAG) .... AtlSeAir
Atlantic Southeast Airlines, Inc. .... ASA
Atlantic Southeast Airlines, Inc. [*NASDAQ symbol*] (NQ) .... ASAI
Atlantic Southeast Airlines, Inc. [*ICAO designator*] (FAAC) .... ASE
Atlantic Southeast Airlines, Inc. [*Air carrier designation symbol*] .... ASEX
Atlantic Squadron .... ATRON
Atlantic Standard Time .... AST
Atlantic Standard Time .... AT
Atlantic Standard Time .... ATST

Atlantic States Marine Fisheries Commission (EA) .... ASMFC
Atlantic States Marine Fisheries Commission (or Committee) (SAUO) .... ASMFC
Atlantic States Marine Fisheries Compact (COE) .... ASMFC
Atlantic Steam Navigation (MHDW) .... ASN
Atlantic Steam Navigation Company (SAUO) .... ASNC
Atlantic Stratocummulus Translator Experiment (SAUS) .... ASTEX
Atlantic Stratocumulus Transition Experiment [*Meteorology*] .... ASTEX
Atlantic Stratocumulus Transition Experiment/Marine Aerosol and Gas Exchange (SAUS) .... ASTEX/MAGE
Atlantic Systems Conference [*Navy/NATO*] (MCD) .... ASC
Atlantic Tankers Limited (SAUO) .... ATL
Atlantic Tele-Network [*AMEX symbol*] (SG) .... ANK
Atlantic Tele-Network [*NASDAQ symbol*] (SPSG) .... ATNI
Atlantic Tele-Network, Inc. [*Associated Press*] (SAG) .... AtlTele
Atlantic Telephone & Telegraph .... AT&T
Atlantic Test Site (SAA) .... ATS
Atlantic Time (SAUS) .... At
Atlantic to the Urals [*Conventional forces in Europe treaty zone*] .... ATTU
Atlantic Tracking Range [*NASA*] .... ATR
Atlantic Tracking Ship [*NASA*] (KSC) .... ATS
Atlantic Trade Experiment (SAUS) .... ATEX
Atlantic Trade Study .... ATS
Atlantic Tradewind [*or Tropical*] Experiment [*National Science Foundation*] .... ATEX
Atlantic Tradewind Experiment (SAUO) .... ATEX
Atlantic Transport Company (SAUO) .... ATCo
Atlantic Transportation Terminal Command [*Army*] .... ATTC
Atlantic Treaty Association (EA) .... ATA
Atlantic Treaty Association (SAUO) .... ATA
Atlantic Treaty Education Committee [*NATO*] (NATG) .... ATEC
Atlantic Tropical Experiment (SAUO) .... ATEX
Atlantic Tropical Oceanic Lower Layer [*National Oceanic and Atmospheric Administration*] .... ATOLL
Atlantic Tuna Convention Act of 1975 .... ATCA
Atlantic Undersea (or Underwater) Test Evaluation Center (SAUS) .... AUTEC
Atlantic Undersea Test and Evaluation Center [*Acronym also used to refer to device for detection, amplification, and transmission of undersea noise*] [*Navy*] .... AUTEC
Atlantic Undersea Test and Evaluation Center (SAUO) .... AUTEC
Atlantic Union (SAUO) .... AU
Atlantic Union (DAS) .... AU
Atlantic Union College [*South Lancaster, MA*] .... AUC
Atlantic Union College, South Lancaster, MA [*Library symbol*] [*Library of Congress*] (LCLS) .... MSIA
Atlantic Union Oil (SAUO) .... AUO
Atlantic Unit (SAUO) .... ANTU
Atlantic Universities Athletic Association [*Association Sportive Interuniversitaire de l'Atlantique*] (AC) .... AUAA
Atlantic Varnish & Paint Co., Richmond, VA [*Library symbol*] [*Library of Congress*] (LCLS) .... ViRAV
Atlantic Visitors Association (SAUO) .... AVA
Atlantic Waterfowl Council (EA) .... AWC
Atlantic Wind Test Site, Tignish, Prince Edward Island [*Library symbol*] [*National Library of Canada*] (NLC) .... PTAWT
Atlantic Women's College Conference (PSS) .... AWCC
Atlantic World Airways, Inc. [*ICAO designator*] (FAAC) .... BJK
Atlantic Yacht Club (SAUO) .... AYC
Atlantic-Gulf Coastwise Steamship Freight Bureau .... AGCSB
Atlantic-Gulf Coastwise Steamship Freight Bureau, Elizabeth NJ [*STAC*] .... AGC
Atlantic-Pacific Interoceanic Canal Study Commission (SAUO) .... APICSC
Atlantis [*ICAO designator*] (AD) .... SG
Atlantis Airlines [*ICAO designator*] (FAAC) .... AAO
Atlantis Airlines [*ICAO designator*] (AD) .... MP
Atlantis Commodities Purchasing Service .... ATCOPS
Atlantis Enterprise [*Vancouver Stock Exchange symbol*] .... ATE
Atlantis Group, Inc. [*AMEX symbol*] (SPSG) .... AGH
Atlantis Group, Inc. [*NASDAQ symbol*] (SAG) .... ATLA
Atlantis Group, Inc. [*Associated Press*] (SAG) .... AtlantisG
Atlantis Plastics [*AMEX symbol*] (SG) .... AGH
Atlantis Plastics, Inc. [*Formerly, Atlantis Group*] [*AMEX symbol*] (SAG) .... AGH
Atlantis Plastics, Inc. [*Associated Press*] (SAG) .... Atlantis
Atlantis Research Centre (EA) .... ARC
Atlantis Research Group (EA) .... ARG
Atlantis Resources Ltd. [*Toronto Stock Exchange symbol*] .... AIN
Atlantis Tank Landing Craft .... ATL
Atlantis Transportation Services Ltd. [*Canada*] [*ICAO designator*] (FAAC) .... ATE
Atlantische Passatwind Experiment [*Atlantic Tradewind Experiment*] [*US, England, Germany*] (MSC) .... APEX
Atlantoaxial Cervical Spine Arthritis [*Medicine*] (MELL) .... AACSA
Atlantoaxial Joint [*Medicine*] (MELL) .... AAJ
Atlantoaxial Rotatory Subluxation [*Medicine*] (MELL) .... AARS
Atlantoaxial Subluxation (PDAA) .... AAS
Atlantodens Interval [*Neurosurgery and orthopedics*] (DAVI) .... ADI
Atlantology (SAUS) .... Atlantol
Atlanto-occipital Ligament [*Medicine*] (MELL) .... AOL
Atlant-Soyuz [*Former USSR*] [*FAA designator*] (FAAC) .... AYZ
Atlant-SV [*Ukraine*] [*FAA designator*] (FAAC) .... ATG
Atlas (MELL) .... A
Atlas (SAUS) .... AT
Atlas (ROG) .... ATL
Atlas .... ATLS
Atlas Agena [*NASA*] .... AA
Atlas Air [*NASDAQ symbol*] (TTSB) .... ATLS
Atlas Air [*NYSE symbol*] (SG) .... CGO
Atlas Air, Inc. [*Associated Press*] (SAG) .... AtlasAir

Atlas Air, Inc. [*NASDAQ symbol*] (SAG) .... ATLS
Atlas Air, Inc. [*Associated Press*] (SAG) .... AtlsAir
Atlas Air, Inc. [*ICAO designator*] (FAAC) .... GTI
Atlas Airlines [*ICAO designator*] (FAAC) .... ATR
Atlas Aviation Simera (Pty) Ltd. [*South Africa*] [*FAA designator*] (FAAC) .... SMA
Atlas [*Abbreviated Test Language for Avionics Systems*] **Basic Language** [*Computer science*] .... ABL
Atlas Basic Language [*Computer science*] (ECII) .... ATL
Atlas Biomedical Literature System .... ABLS
ATLAS Block Structure (MCD) .... ABS
Atlas Chemical Industries (SAUS) .... ACI
Atlas Chemical Industries, Inc. (SAUO) .... ACI
Atlas Chemical Industries, Inc. [*Research code symbol*] .... AT
Atlas Chemical Industries, Inc., Wilmington, DE [*Library symbol*] [*Library of Congress*] (LCLS) .... DeWAt
Atlas Commercial Language [*Computer science*] (BUR) .... ACL
ATLAS Composing Terminal (SAUS) .... ACT
Atlas Computer Laboratory (SAUO) .... ACL
Atlas Configuration Control Board [*Aerospace*] (AAG) .... ACCB
Atlas Corp. [*Associated Press*] (SAG) .... Atlas
Atlas Corp. [*NYSE symbol*] (SPSG) .... AZ
Atlas Corp. Wrrt [*AMEX symbol*] (TTSB) .... AZ.WS
ATLAS Crew Procedures Laboratory [*NASA*] (MCD) .... ACPL
Atlas Crew Procedures Laboratory (SAUS) .... ACPL
Atlas Economic Research Foundation (EA) .... AERF
Atlas Educational Center (EA) .... AEC
Atlas Explorer [*Computer geography tutorial*] (PCM) .... AE
Atlas Folio (SAUS) .... Atlas Fol
Atlas Gemini [*NASA*] (KSC) .... AG
Atlas General Survey Program (IEEE) .... AGSP
Atlas Historique du Canada [*Historical Atlas of Canada*] [*Project*] .... AHC
Atlas Intercontinental Ballistic Misile (SAUS) .... Atlas ICBM-65
Atlas LISP [*Library and Information Software Packaging*] **Algebraic Manipulator** (PDAA) .... ALAM
Atlas Microfilming Service, Pennsauken, NJ [*Library symbol*] [*Library of Congress*] (LCLS) .... AtMcS
Atlas Mountain Region [*MARC geographic area code*] [*Library of Congress*] (LCCP) .... fa---
Atlas Mountains of Algeria and Morocco (SAUS) .... Atlas
Atlas of Australian Resources [*A publication*] .... AAR
Atlas [*Missile*] **Operational Data Summary** .... AODS
Atlas Operational Data Summary (SAUS) .... AODS
Atlas Pacific Limited [*All Symbol*] (TTSB) .... ATP
Atlas Pacific Ltd. [*NASDAQ symbol*] (SAG) .... APCF
Atlas Pacific Ltd. [*Associated Press*] (SAG) .... AtlasPac
Atlas Pipeline Ptnrs. LP [*AMEX symbol*] (SG) .... APL
Atlas Port Surveillance System (SAUS) .... APSS
Atlas Powder Company (SAUO) .... APC
Atlas Propulsion Information Notice (SAUS) APIN-3
Atlas Reliability Group .... ARG
Atlas Short Range Air Defence (SAUS) .... ASRAD
Atlas Weapon System (SAUS) .... AWS
Atlas Yellowknife Resources Ltd. [*Toronto Stock Exchange symbol*] .... AY
Atlas-Agena D (SAUS) .... AAD
Atlas-Centaur (SAUS) .... AC
Atlas-Centaur [*Missile*] .... A-C
Atlin Historical Museum, British Columbia [*Library symbol*] [*National Library of Canada*] (NLC) .... BATM
ATM Adaptation Layer (SAUS) .... AAL
ATM Address Resolution Protocol (SAUS) .... ATMARP
ATM Channel/Data Service Unit (SAUS) .... ATM CSU/DSU
ATM Circuit Steering Management Information Base (SAUS) .... ACSMIB
ATM Crossconnect (SAUS) .... ATM-CC
ATM Data Service Unit (SAUS) .... ADSU
ATM Electrical Power System (SAUS) .... AEPS
ATM [*Apollo Telescope Mount*] **Electrical Power System** [*NASA*] .... AEPS
ATM End System Address (SAUS) .... AESA
ATM [*Apollo Telescope Mount*] **Experiments Officer** [*NASA*] .... AEO
ATM Forum (SAUS) .... AF
ATM Interface Port Module (SAUS) .... APIM
ATM Interface Processor (SAUS) .... AIP
ATM Inverse Multiplexer (SAUS) .... AIM
ATM Line Interface (SAUS) .... ALI
ATM Management Interface (SAUS) .... AMI
ATM MIB. IETF-defined Management Information Base (SAUS) .... AToMMIB
ATM Multiplexer/Demultiplexer (SAUS) .... AMDM
ATM Navigation and Timing Summary (SAUS) .... ANTS
ATM [*Apollo Telescope Mount*] **Navigation and Timing Summary** [*NASA*] .... ANTS
ATM Research Consortium (SAUS) .... ARC
ATM Switched Virtual Circuit (SAUS) .... SVC
ATM Terminating Equipment (SAUS) .... ATE
ATM User-to-User (SAUS) .... AUU
Atmautluak [*Alaska*] [*Airport symbol*] (OAG) .... ATT
ATMDC [*Apollo Telescope Mount Digital Computer*] **Software Control Officer** [*NASA*] .... ASCO
Atmel Corp. [*Associated Press*] (SAG) .... Atmel
Atmel Corp. [*NASDAQ symbol*] (SPSG) .... ATML
ATMI, Inc. [*NASDAQ symbol*] (SG) .... ATMI
ATMI, Inc. [*NASDAQ symbol*] [*Formerly, Advanced Technology Materials*] (SG) .... ATMID
Atmore, AL [*AM radio station call letters*] .... WASG
Atmore, AL [*FM radio station call letters*] .... WDWG
Atmore, AL [*AM radio station call letters*] .... WGYJ
Atmore, AL [*AM radio station call letters*] (BROA) .... WPHG-AM
Atmore, AL [*FM radio station call letters*] .... WYDH
Atmos Energy Corp. [*Associated Press*] (SAG) .... ATMOS
Atmos Energy Corp. [*NYSE symbol*] (SPSG) .... ATO
Atmosphere (ABBR) .... A
Atmosphere (ADWA) .... at
Atmosphere (ADWA) .... atm
Atmosphere .... ATM
Atmosphere (KSC) .... ATMOS
Atmosphere (VRA) .... atmos
Atmosphere Absolute (ADWA) .... ata
Atmosphere, Absolute .... ATA
Atmosphere Absolute (SAUS) .... Atm Abs
Atmosphere and Land Surface Processes (OSRA) .... ALSP
Atmosphere and Space .... AS
Atmosphere Boundary Layer Facility (MCD) .... ABLF
Atmosphere Climate Study [*National Science Foundation*] (MSC) .... ACS
Atmosphere Control System [*NASA*] (KSC) .... ACS
Atmosphere Defense Initiative (LAIN) .... ADF
Atmosphere Ecosystem Gas Interchange Study (SAUS) .... AEGIS
Atmosphere Exchange System (SAUS) .... AES
Atmosphere Explorer B [*Satellite*] [*NASA*] .... AE-B
Atmosphere Explorer E [*Satellite*] [*NASA*] .... AE-E
Atmosphere General Circuiation Experiment (SAUS) .... AGCE
Atmosphere, Ionosphere and Magnetosphere (SAUS) .... AIM
Atmosphere Launched Boost Intercept System (SAUS) .... ALBIS
Atmosphere, Magnetosphere, and Plasmas in Space [*Space shuttle payload*] [*NASA*] .... AMPS
Atmosphere, Normal (MAE) .... An
Atmosphere, Normal (SAUS) .... an
Atmosphere Normale Internationale [*International Normal Atmosphere*] .... ANI
Atmosphere Particulate Radioactivity Detector (IEEE) .... APRD
Atmosphere Radiation and Cloud Station (ARMP) .... ARCS
Atmosphere Radiation Monitor (IEEE) .... ARM
Atmosphere Reactants Supply Subsystem .... ARSS
Atmosphere Reactants Supply Subsystem Group (MCD) .... ARSSG
Atmosphere Reactants Supply System (SAUS) .... ARSS
Atmosphere Revitalization Section [*or System*] [*NASA*] .... ARS
Atmosphere Revitalization System (SAUS) .... ARS
Atmosphere Sensing and Maintenance System [*NASA*] (KSC) .... ASMS
Atmosphere Spectroscopy Applications (CARB) .... ASA
Atmosphere Standard (SAUS) .... As
Atmosphere, Standard [*Unit of pressure*] .... atm
Atmosphere Storage and Control Section (SAUS) .... ASCS
Atmosphere, Technical [*Unit of pressure*] .... at
Atmosphere Transport Model Evaluation Study (OSRA) .... ATMES
Atmosphere-Ocean (CARB) .... AO
Atmosphere-Ocean (SAUS) .... Atmos-Ocean
Atmosphere/Ocean Chemistry Experiment [*Marine science*] (OSRA) .... AEROCE
Atmosphere-Ocean General Circulation Model [*Climatology*] .... AOGCM
Atmosphere-Ocean System (SAUS) .... Atmos-Ocean Syst
Atmospheres Absolute (SAUS) .... ATA
Atmospheres absolute (SAUS) .... Atm ab
Atmospheres absolute over Sea level (SAUS) .... ATS
Atmosphere-Sounding Projectile (SAUS) .... ASP
Atmosphere-Surface Turbulent Exchange Research (SAUS) .... ASTER
Atmospheric .... ATMO
Atmospheric (ADWA) .... atmos
Atmospheric (SAUS) .... ATMOS
Atmospheric Aerosols and Optics Data Library (RDA) .... AAODL
Atmospheric Analysis and Prediction [*National Center for Atmospheric Research*] .... AAP
Atmospheric and Environmental Research (EOSA) .... AER
Atmospheric and Ocean Sciences Program (OSRA) .... AOSP
Atmospheric and Oceanic Information Proeessing System (SAUS) .... AOIPS
Atmospheric and Oceanic Physics (journ.) (SAUS) .... Atmos Oceanic Phys
Atmospheric and Oceanographic Image Processing System (GEOI) .... AOIPS
Atmospheric and Oceanographic Information Processing System [*Satellite image enhancing system*] (MCD) .... AOIPS
Atmospheric and Oceanographic Satellite (SAUS) .... ATMOS
Atmospheric and Space Physics (SAUS) .... AP
Atmospheric and Space Plasma Physics [*NASA*] (NASA) .... ASPP
Atmospheric Angular Momentum [*Geophysics*] .... AAM
Atmospheric Applications (MCD) .... AA
Atmospheric Attenuation of Sound (MCD) .... ATMAT
Atmospheric Boundary Layer [*Marine science*] (OSRA) .... ABL
Atmospheric Boundary Layer Experiment [*National Oceanic and Atmospheric Administration*] .... ABLE
Atmospheric Burst Locator (MCD) .... ABL
Atmospheric Camp (SAUS) .... ATM
Atmospheric Center of Data Working Group (SAUO) .... ACDWG
Atmospheric Change (IAA) .... ATMCHG
Atmospheric Changes (SAUS) .... Atm Chgs
Atmospheric Chemical Transformations (SAUS) .... ACT
Atmospheric Chemical Transport Model (CARB) .... ACTM
Atmospheric Chemistry Division (SAUS) .... ACD
Atmospheric Chemistry Model (SAUS) .... ACHEM
Atmospheric Chemistry Modelling Support Unit .... ACMSU
Atmospheric Chemistry of Aerosols (SAUS) .... ACA
Atmospheric Chemistry of Transient Species (SAUS) .... ACTS
Atmospheric Chemistry Program (SAUS) .... ACP
Atmospheric Chemistry Studies in the Oceanic Environment .... ACSOE
Atmospheric Circulation in Relation to Oscillations of Sea-Ice and Salinity (SAUS) .... ACROSS
Atmospheric Cloud Physics Laboratory [*Spacelab*] [*NASA*] .... ACPL
Atmospheric Collection Equipment [*Marine science*] (OSRA) .... ACE
Atmospheric Compensation Satellite (SAUS) .... ATCOS

Atmospheric Composition Payload Group [*NASA*] (SSD) .... ACG
Atmospheric Composition Satellite [*NASA*] .... ATCOS
Atmospheric Containment Atmosphere Dilution (PDAA) .... ACAD
Atmospheric Contamination Potential .... ACP
Atmospheric Control Experimentation .... ACE
Atmospheric Convergence Line .... ACL
Atmospheric Corrosion Resistant (SAUS) .... ACR
Atmospheric Data Acquisition System (SAUS) .... ADAS
Atmospheric Deposition Monitoring Program [*Environmental Protection Agency*] .... ADMN
Atmospheric Devices Laboratory [*Cambridge, MA*] (AAG) .... ADL
Atmospheric Diffusion Measuring System .... ADMS
Atmospheric Diffusion of Beryllium Program [*NASA*] (KSC) .... ADOBE
Atmospheric Dispersion of Radionuclides (SAUS) .... AIRDOS-EPA
Atmospheric Distributed Data System (ACAE) .... ADDS
Atmospheric Diving Suit [*Deep sea diving*] .... ADS
Atmospheric Diving System .... ADS
Atmospheric Dump Valves [*Nuclear energy*] (NRCH) .... ADV
Atmospheric Dynamic Payload Group [*NASA*] (SSD) .... ADG
Atmospheric Dynamics and Fluxes in the Mediterranean Sea (SAUS) .... DYFAMED
Atmospheric Dynamics Program [*National Oceanic and Atmospheric Administration*] .... ADP
Atmospheric Effect Correction System (SAUS) .... AECS
Atmospheric Effects of Stratospheric Aircraft (SAUS) .... AESA
Atmospheric Electric Detection System (KSC) .... AEDS
Atmospheric Electrical Hazards Protection (ACAE) .... AHEP
Atmospheric Electricity Hazards Protection .... AEHP
Atmospheric Electromagnetic Pulse .... AEMP
Atmospheric Emissions Photometric Imaging [*Plasma physics*] .... AEPI
Atmospheric Emitted Radiance Instrument (SAUS) .... AERI
Atmospheric Emitted Radiance Interferometer (ARMP) .... AERI
Atmospheric Emitted Radiance Interferometer-extended Resolution (SAUS) .... AERI-X
Atmospheric Entry .... AE
Atmospheric Environment (journ.) (SAUS) .... Atmos Environ
Atmospheric Environment Service [*Canada*] .... AES
Atmospheric Environment Service, Environment Canada [*Service de l'Environnement Atmospherique, Environnement Canada*] **Dorval, Quebec** [*Library symbol*] [*National Library of Canada*] (NLC) .... QMEA
Atmospheric Environment Service, Environment Canada [*Service de l'Environnement Atmospherique, Environnement Canada*] **Downsview, Ontario** [*Library symbol*] [*National Library of Canada*] (NLC) .... OTM
Atmospheric Environment Service, Environment Canada [*Service de l'Environnement Atmospherique, Environnement Canada*] **Edmonton, Alberta** [*Library symbol*] [*National Library of Canada*] (NLC) .... AEEAE
Atmospheric Environment Service, Environment Canada [*Service de l'Environnement Atmospherique, Environnement Canada*] **Vancouver, British Columbia** [*Library symbol*] [*National Library of Canada*] (NLC) .... BVAEAE
Atmospheric Environment Service, Environment Canada [*Service de l'Environnement Atmospherique, Environnement Canada*] **Ville St-Laurent, Quebec** [*Library symbol*] [*National Library of Canada*] (NLC) .... QVSLEA
Atmospheric Environment Service (ODIT Ontario Weather Centre), Environment Canada [*Service de l'Environnement Atmospherique (Centre Meteorologique de l'Ontario), Environnement Canada*] **Toronto, Ontario** [*Library symbol*] [*National Library of Canada*] (NLC) .... OTEAOW
Atmospheric Environmental Research, Inc. (ARMP) .... AER
Atmospheric Exchange System (NAKS) .... AES
Atmospheric Experiment on Orographic flows, Leewaves, Upslope Snowstorms (SAUS) .... AEOLUS
Atmospheric Experimental Branch (SAUS) .... SGG
Atmospheric Explorer [*Satellite*] [*NASA*] .... AE
Atmospheric Explorer Mission (GEOI) .... AEM
Atmospheric Explorer Missions (ACAE) .... AEM
Atmospheric Fleet Support (SAUS) .... AERO
Atmospheric Flight .... AF
Atmospheric Flight Test (NASA) .... AFT
Atmospheric Fluidized Bed [*Chemical engineering*] .... AFB
Atmospheric Fluidized Bed Coal [*Energy technology*] .... AFBC
Atmospheric Fluidized-Bed Combustion [*Fuel technology*] .... AFBC
Atmospheric Forcings for the Mid-Atlantic Bight [*Oceanography*] (MSC) .... AFMAB
Atmospheric Gas Measurements Section (SAUS) .... AGM
Atmospheric Gas Oil [*Petroleum technology*] .... AGO
Atmospheric General Circulation Model (CARB) .... ACCM
Atmospheric General Circulation Model [*Meteorology*] .... AGCM
Atmospheric Global Climate Model (SAUS) .... AGCM
Atmospheric Head (AAG) .... H
Atmospheric Infrared Attenuation Coefficient .... AIRAC
Atmospheric Infrared Attenuation Coefficient (journ.) (SAUS) .... AIRAC
Atmospheric Infrared Sounder (SSD) .... AIRS
Atmospheric Infrared-Advanced Microwave Sounding Unit (SAUS) .... AIRS-AMSU
Atmospheric Integrated Research Monitoring Network (SAUO) .... AIRMON
Atmospheric Kinetics Project (SAUS) .... AKP
Atmospheric Laboratory for Applications and Science [*Satellite mission*] .... ALAS
Atmospheric Laboratory for Applications and Science [*NASA*] (OSRA) .... ATLAS
Atmospheric Laser Doppler Instrument (SAUS) .... ALADIN
Atmospheric Layer and Density Distribution of Ions and Neutrals [*Rocket*] [*NASA*] .... ALADDIN
Atmospheric LIDAR [*LASER Infrared RADAR*] (SSD) .... ATLID
Atmospheric Lidar (SAUS) .... ATLID
Atmospheric Lidar Experiment in Space (SAUS) .... ALEXIS
Atmospheric Lifetime Experiment [*Environmental science*] .... ALE
Atmospheric Lifetime Experiment Station [*Adrigole, Ireland*] .... ALE
Atmospheric Lifetime Experiment/Global Atmospheric Gases Experiment (SAUS) .... AGAGE
Atmospheric Lifetime Experiment/Global Atmospheric Gases Experiment (SAUS) .... ALE/GAGE
Atmospheric Light Detection and Ranging Facility [*Los Alamos, NM*] [*Los Alamos National Laboratory*] [*Department of Energy*] (GRD) .... LIDAR
Atmospheric Lyman Alpha Emissions (GEOI) .... ALAE
Atmospheric Lyman Alpha Experiment (NAKS) .... ALAE
Atmospheric, Magnetospheric and Plasma Studies (SAUS) .... AMPS
Atmospheric Magnetospheric Plasma System (NASA) .... AMPS
Atmospheric Maneuvering Reentry Vehicle (IEEE) .... AMRV
Atmospheric Mass Balance of Industrially Emitted and Natural Sulfur [*Environmental Protection Agency*] (GFGA) .... AMBIENS
Atmospheric Mesoscale Campaigns (QUAC) .... AMC
Atmospheric Meteorological Probe (SAUS) .... AMP
Atmospheric Model Intercomparison Project (SAUS) .... AMIP
Atmospheric Model Intercomparison Project (USDC) .... AMIP
Atmospheric Moisture Intercomparison Study (SAUS) .... ATMIS-II
Atmospheric Monitor Oxygen Analyzer (IEEE) .... AMOA
Atmospheric Monitor System (IEEE) .... AMS
Atmospheric Nutrient Input to Coastal Areas [*Project*] (OSRA) .... ANICA
Atmospheric Observation Bell (PDAA) .... AOB
Atmospheric Observation Panel for Climate (SAUS) .... AOPC
Atmospheric Observations Satellite (SAUS) .... ATMOS
Atmospheric Odd Nitrogen species project (SAUS) .... AON
Atmospheric or Remote Manipulator System [*Deep-sea diving*] .... ARMS
Atmospheric Particle Monitor (SAUS) .... APM
Atmospheric Passivation Module (SAUS) .... APM
Atmospheric Physical and Chemical Monitor .... APACM
Atmospheric Physics and Chemistry Laboratory (SAUO) .... APCL
Atmospheric Physics and Chemistry Monitor (SAUS) .... APACM
Atmospheric Physics Programme [*International Council of Scientific Unions*] .... APP
Atmospheric Pollution Sensor .... APS
Atmospheric Pressure .... AP
Atmospheric Pressure (IAA) .... ATMPR
Atmospheric Pressure and Ambient Temperature .... APAT
Atmospheric Pressure and Composition Control (NASA) .... APCC
Atmospheric Pressure at Aerodrome Elevation (SAUS) .... QFE
Atmospheric Pressure Chemical Ionization .... APCI
Atmospheric Pressure Chemical Vapor Deposition [*Photovoltaic energy systems*] .... APCVD
Atmospheric Pressure Converted to Mean Sea Level E levation [*Aviation code*] (AIA) .... QFF
Atmospheric Pressure Ion Evaporation .... APIE
Atmospheric Pressure Ionization [*Physics*] .... API
Atmospheric Pressure Ionization Mass Spectroscopy (AAEL) .... APIMS
Atmospheric Pressure Mass Spectroscopy (ACAE) .... APM
Atmospheric Pressure Plasma Sprayed [*Thermal barrier coating*] .... APPS
Atmospheric Pressure Sensor .... APS
Atmospheric Pressure Supply System [*or Subsystem*] [*NASA*] (NASA) .... APSS
Atmospheric Profile Record (ACAE) .... APR
Atmospheric Protection System (SAUS) .... APS
Atmospheric Quality and Modification [*National Center for Atmospheric Research*] .... AQM
Atmospheric Quality Division (SAUS) .... AQD
Atmospheric Quarterly and Modification (SAUS) .... AQM
Atmospheric Radiation Analysis (SAUS) .... ARA
Atmospheric Radiation and Cloud Station (SAUO) .... ARCS
Atmospheric Radiation Measurement Program [*Department of Energy*] (ECON) .... ARM
Atmospheric Radiation Measurement Satellite (CARB) .... ARMSAT
Atmospheric Radiation Measurement-Clouds and Radiation Testband (SAUS) .... ARM-CART
Atmospheric Radiation Monitoring (SAUS) .... ARM
Atmospheric Radiation Working Group (SAUO) .... ARWG
Atmospheric Radiative Heating (ARMP) .... ARH
Atmospheric Radio Noise .... ARN
Atmospheric Radio Wave .... ARW
Atmospheric Reentry Materials and Structural Evaluation Facility (MCD) .... ARMSEF
Atmospheric Release Advisory Capability [*Energy Research and Development Administration*] .... ARAC
Atmospheric Rendezvous Space Logistics [*NASA*] (MCD) .... ARSL
Atmospheric Research (SAUS) .... Atmos Res
Atmospheric Research and Environment Program [*Marine science*] (OSRA) .... AREP
Atmospheric Research and Exposure Assessment Laboratory [*Environmental Protection Agency*] .... AREAL
Atmospheric Research and Remote Sensing Plane [*Marine science*] (OSRA) .... ARAT
Atmospheric Research Equipment .... ARE
Atmospheric Research Information Exchange Study (SAUS) .... ARIES
Atmospheric Research Program Staff [*Environmental Protection Agency*] (GFGA) .... ARPS
Atmospheric Resid Desulfurization [*Petroleum technology*] .... ARDS
Atmospheric Residue Hydrodesulfurization [*Petroleum technology*] .... ARHDS
Atmospheric Revitalization (MCD) .... AR
Atmospheric Revitalization Pressure Control System (MCD) .... ARPCS
Atmospheric Roving Manipulator System (PDAA) .... ARMS
Atmospheric Science .... AS
Atmospheric Science Facility [*NASA*] (NASA) .... ASF
Atmospheric Science Paper [*A publication*] (MEC) .... Atmos Sci
Atmospheric Sciences Center (SAUO) .... ASC

Atmospheric Sciences Laboratory [*Army Laboratory Command*] [*White Sands Missile Range, NM*] ... ASL
Atmospheric Sciences Modeling Division [*Air Resources Laboratory*] (USDC) ... ASMD
Atmospheric Sciences Research Center [*State University of New York*] [*Research center*] ... ASRC
Atmospheric Sciences Research Laboratory [*Research Triangle Park, NC*] [*Environmental Protection Agency*] (GRD) ... ASRL
Atmospheric Simulation Facility (MCD) ... ASF
Atmospheric Sound Refraction ... ASR
Atmospheric Sound-Focusing Gain ... ASFG
Atmospheric Sounding, Central Evaluation and Test Support (SAUS) ... ASCENT
Atmospheric Sounding Projectile (SAUS) ... ASP
Atmospheric Stablization Framework (SAUS) ... ASF
Atmospheric Storage and Control Section [*Spacelab*] [*NASA*] ... ASCS
Atmospheric Structure Instrument (ACAE) ... ASI
Atmospheric Structure Investigation/Meteorology Experiment [*Planetary science*] ... ASI/MET
Atmospheric Structure Satellite (SAA) ... ASS
Atmospheric Studies in Complex Terrain (PDAA) ... ASCOT
Atmospheric Surface Layer [*Marine science*] (OSRA) ... ASL
Atmospheric Surveillance and Warning (ACAE) ... ASW
Atmospheric Surveillance Technology (MCD) ... AST
Atmospheric Tactical Warning (MCD) ... ATW
Atmospheric Technology Division (SAUS) ... ATD
Atmospheric Thermonuclear Weapons Testing ... ATWT
Atmospheric Trace Molecules Observed by Spectroscopy ... ATMOS
Atmospheric Trace Spectroscopy (ARMP) ... ATMOS
Atmospheric Transmission Factor (CARB) ... ATF
Atmospheric Transmission Measurement Equipment ... ATME
Atmospheric Transport and Dispersion [*Model*] [*Marine science*] (OSRA) ... ATAD
Atmospheric Transport Model (SAUS) ... ATM
Atmospheric Transport Model Evaluation Study (SAUS) ... ATMES
Atmospheric Turbulence and Diffusion Division [*Air Resources Laboratory*] (USDC) ... ATDD
Atmospheric Turbulence and Diffusion Laboratory [*Oak Ridge, Tennessee*] ... ATDL
Atmospheric Turbulence Measuring Set (MCD) ... ATMS
Atmospheric Utility Signatures-Predictions and Experiments (SAUS) ... AUSPEX
Atmospheric Variability Experiment [*NASA*] ... AVE
Atmospheric Vehicle Detection ... AVD
Atmospheric Vertical Profiling System (SAUS) ... AVAPS
Atmospheric Wind Velocity ... AWV
Atmospheric Winds Aloft ... AWA
Atmospheric X-Ray Imaging Spectrometer (MCD) ... AXIS
Atmospherics [*NWS*] (FAAC) ... SFERICS
ATM-Service Access Point (SAUS) ... ATM-SAP
Atna Resources Ltd. [*Vancouver Stock Exchange symbol*] ... ATN
Atoka, OK [*AM radio station call letters*] ... KEOR
Atoka, OK [*FM radio station call letters*] ... KHKC
Atoll Commander [*In Pacific operations*] [*World War II*] ... ATCOM
Atoll Research Bulletin (SAUS) ... Atoll Res Bull
Atolls and Guyots Detailed Planning Group (SAUO) ... A&G-DPG
Atom [*or Atomic*] ... A
Atom Bomb ... A (Bomb)
Atom Development Administration (SAUS) ... ADA
Atom Fluorescence for Chemical Analysis (SAUS) ... AFCA
Atom Inelastic Scattering (SAUS) ... AIS
Atom Parts per Million (MCD) ... APPM
Atom Probe Field Ion Microscopy (SAUS) ... APFIM
Atom Transfer Radical Polymerization [*Chemistry*] ... ATRP
Atom-Absorptions-Spektroskopie (SAUS) ... AAS
Atomarity, Consistency, Isolation, Durability (SAUS) ... ACID
Atomatic Data Switching System (SAUS) ... ADSS
Atomatic Typewriter (SAUS) ... AT
Atomedic Research Center (EA) ... ARC
Atomic ... AT
Atomic ... ATMC
Atomic Absorption [*Chemical analysis*] ... AA
Atomic Absorption Coefficient ... AAC
Atomic Absorption Flame Spectrometer ... AAFS
Atomic Absorption Newletter (journ.) (SAUS) ... At Absorption Newslett
Atomic Absorption Spectrometer [*or Spectrophotometer or Spectroscopy*] ... AAS
Atomic Absorption Spectrometer (or Spectroscopy) (SAUS) ... AAS
Atomic absorption Spectroscopy (SAUS) ... AS
Atomic Age (IAA) ... AA
Atomic Air Raid Precaution (IAA) ... AARP
Atomic Air Raid Precautions (SAUS) ... AARP
Atomic and Molecular Data (SAUS) ... AMD
Atomic and Molecular Physical Data Program [*American Society for Testing and Materials*] (IID) ... AMD
Atomic and Molecular Processes Information Center [*ORNL*] ... AMPIC
Atomic and Plasma Physics Laboratory (SAUO) ... APP
Atomic and Space Development Authority (SAUO) ... ASDA
Atomic, Bacteriological & Chemical (SAUS) ... ABC
Atomic Bargain Analysis Report (CINC) ... ATBAN
Atomic Beam Method ... ABM
Atomic, Biological, and Chemical [*as, ABC Officer, ABC Warfare*] [*Obsolete*] ... ABC
Atomic, Biological and Chemical Washdown (SAUS) ... ABC Washdown
Atomic, Biological, Chemical, and Damage Control ... ABCD
Atomic, Biological, Chemical, and Radiological [*Warfare*] (NATG) ... ABCR
Atomic, Biological, Chemical and Radiological (SAUS) ... ABCR
Atomic, Biological, Chemical Warfare ... ABCW
Atomic Bomb (ODBW) ... A-bomb

Atomic Bomb Casualty Commission (SAUO) ... ABCC
Atomic Bomb Casualty Commission [*Later, RERF*] ... ABCC
Atomic Bomb Casualty Commission, Seattle, WA [*Library symbol*] [*Library of Congress*] (LCLS) ... WaSAB
Atomic Central Heating and Power Plant (SAUO) ... ACHPP
Atomic Cesium Beam MASER ... ACBM
Atomic Cesium Beam Maser (SAUS) ... ACBM
Atomic Collision Cross Sections Information Center [*ORNL*] ... ACCSIC
Atomic Commitment Protocol (SAUS) ... ACP
Atomic Coordinating Office (Washington, DC) [*British Defense Staff*] ... ACO(W)
Atomic Coordination Office [*British*] ... ACO
Atomic Damage Template [*Military drafting*] ... ADT
Atomic Datapool (SAUS) ... ADP
Atomic Defence (or Defense) (SAUS) ... AD
Atomic Defence (or Defense) (SAUS) ... Atomdef
Atomic Defense ... ATOMDEF
Atomic Defense and Space Group [*Westinghouse Electric Corp.*] (MCD) ... ADSG
Atomic Defense Engineering (MUGU) ... ADE
Atomic Defense Support Agency ... ADSA
Atomic Delivery Unit (SAUO) ... ADU
Atomic Demolition Munition ... ADM
Atomic Demolition Munition (SAUS) ... ATM
Atomic Development Administration (SAUS) ... ADA
Atomic Development Authority (SAUO) ... AD
Atomic Development Authority [*Proposed by Bernard Baruch to exercise control over those aspects of atomic energy inimical to global security; never organized*] ... ADA
Atomic Device [*Military*] ... ATOMDEV
Atomic Device (SAUS) ... Atomdev
Atomic Drive (AAG) ... AD
Atomic Drive ... A-DRV
Atomic Electric Project (SAUO) ... AEP
Atomic Emission ... AE
Atomic Emission Detector [*Instrumentation*] ... AED
Atomic Emission Monitoring (SAUS) ... AEM
Atomic Emission Spectroscopy ... AES
Atomic Energy (ADA) ... AE
Atomic Energy Act [*1954*] ... AEA
Atomic Energy Advisory Committee (SAUO) ... AEAC
Atomic Energy Authority [*British*] ... AEA
Atomic Energy Board (SAUO) ... AEB
Atomic Energy Bureau [*Korea*] (NUCP) ... AEB
Atomic Energy Bureau [*Japan*] (NUCP) ... AEB
Atomic Energy Bureau of Science and Technics Agency [*Japan*] ... AEBSTA
Atomic Energy Centre - Lahore (MCD) ... AECL
Atomic Energy Centre Dacca (SAUO) ... AECD
Atomic Energy Centre Lahore (SAUO) ... AECL
Atomic Energy Commission [*Functions divided, 1975, between Nuclear Regulatory Commission and Energy Research and Development Administration*] ... AEC
Atomic Energy Commission - Armed Forces Special Weapons Project Technical Publication (MCD) ... AEC-AFSWP-TP
Atomic Energy Commission - Defense Atomic Support Agency Technical Publication (MCD) ... AEC-DASA-TP
Atomic Energy Commission - Defense Nuclear Agency Technical Publication (MCD) ... AEC-DNA-TP
Atomic Energy Commission Board of Contract Appeals [*Replaced by the Energy Research and Development Administration Board of Contract Appeals in 1975*] (AAGC) ... AECBCA
Atomic Energy Commission Classified (SAUS) ... AECC
Atomic Energy Commission /Commission for Conventional Armaments (SAUO) ... AEC/CCA
Atomic Energy Commission Declassified (SAUS) ... AECD
Atomic Energy Commission Declassified Report (NUCP) ... AECD
Atomic Energy Commission Document (SAUS) ... AECD
Atomic Energy Commission Manual ... AECM
Atomic Energy Commission of Canada (SAUO) ... AECC
Atomic Energy Commission of Iran (SAUO) ... AECI
Atomic Energy Commission Procurement Regulations [*Obsolete*] ... AECPR
Atomic Energy Commission. Reports [*A publication*] (DLA) ... AEC
Atomic Energy Commission Unclassified Report (NUCP) ... AECU
Atomic Energy Commission, Upton, New York (SAUS) ... AEC-UN
Atomic Energy Commission-Aiken, South Carolina (SAUO) ... AEC-ASC
Atomic Energy Commission-Albuquerque New Mexico (SAUO) ... AEC-ANM
Atomic Energy Commission-Albuquerque, New Mexico (SAUS) ... AEC-ANM
Atomic Energy Commission-Albuquerque Operations Office (SAUO) ... AEC-A
Atomic Energy Commission-Argonne, Illinois (SAUO) ... AEC-AI
Atomic Energy Commission-Berkeley, California (SAUO) ... AEC-BC
Atomic Energy Commission-Canoga Park, California (SAUO) ... AEC-CC
Atomic Energy Commission-Defense Atomic Support Agency Technical Publication (SAUS) ... AEC-DASA-TP
Atomic Energy Commission-Defense Nuclear Agency Technical Publication (SAUS) ... AEC-DNA-TP
Atomic Energy Commission-Department of Defense (SAUO) ... AEC-DD
Atomic Energy Commission-Fernal Office Area (SAUO) ... AEC-FOA
Atomic Energy Commission-Fernal Office Area, Cincinnati, Ohio (SAUS) ... AEC-FOA
Atomic Energy Commission-Hanford, Washington (SAUO) ... AEC-HW
Atomic Energy Commission-Idaho Falls, Idaho (SAUO) ... AEC-II
Atomic Energy Commission-Las Vegas, Nevada (SAUO) ... AEC-LN
Atomic Energy Commission-Lockland Aircraft Reactors Operations, Cincinnati (SAUS) ... AEC-LOC
Atomic Energy Commission-Lockland Aircraft Reactors Operations, Cincinnati, Ohio (SAUO) ... AEC-LOC

Atomic Energy Commission-National Aeronautics and Space Administration (SAUS) .... AEC-NASA
Atomic Energy Commission-New York Operations Office (SAUO) .... AEC-NY
Atomic Energy Commission-Oak Ridge Operations Office (SAUO) .... AEC-OR
Atomic Energy Commission-Oak Ridge, Tennessee (SAUO) .... AEC-OT
Atomic Energy Commission-Pittsburgh Naval Reactors Operations Office (SAUS) .... AEC-PR
Atomic Energy Commission-Pittsburgh, Pennsylvania (SAUO) .... AEC-PP
Atomic Energy Commission-Richland, Washington (SAUO) .... AEC-RW
Atomic Energy Commission/Technical Information Center (MCD) .... AEC/TIC
Atomic Energy Commission-Upton, NY (SAUO) .... AEC-UN
Atomic Energy Committee (SAUO) .... AEC
Atomic Energy Control Board [Canada] .... AECB
Atomic Energy Control Board, Ottawa, ON, Canada [Library symbol] [Library of Congress] (LCLS) .... CaOOAECB
Atomic Energy Control Board [Commission de Controle de l'Energie Atomique]Ottawa, Ontario [Library symbol] [National Library of Canada] (NLC) .... OOAECB
Atomic Energy Corporation [South Africa] [Research center] .... AEC
Atomic Energy Council (SAUO) .... AEC
Atomic Energy Detection System [Nuclear energy] .... AEDS
Atomic Energy Division (SAUO) .... AED
Atomic Energy Establishment [British] .... AEE
Atomic Energy Establishment [Libya] (NUCP) .... AEE
Atomic Energy Establishment, [Trombay, India] (NUCP) .... AEET
Atomic Energy Establishment (SAUO) .... AEEW
Atomic Energy Establishment Bombay (SAUS) .... AEEB
Atomic Energy Establishment, Winfrith [England] .... AEEW
Atomic Energy Establishment-Winfrith Heath (SAUS) .... AEEW
Atomic Energy Executive (SAUO) .... AEX
Atomic Energy in Australia (journ.) (SAUS) .... At Energy Aust
Atomic Energy Labor Management Relations Panel .... AELMRP
Atomic Energy Laboratory, Santa Fe (SAUO) .... AE-SF
Atomic Energy Law Journal [A publication] (DLA) .... AELJ
Atomic Energy Law Journal [A publication] (AAGC) .... Atom Energy LJ
Atomic Energy Law Reporter (Commerce Clearing House) [A publication] (DLA) .... Atom En L Rep CCH
Atomic Energy Law Reporter (Commerce Clearing House) [A publication] (DLA) .... CCH Atom En L Rep
Atomic Energy Level .... AEL
Atomic Energy Levels Data Center .... AELDC
Atomic Energy of Canada, Chalk River, ON, Canada [Library symbol] [Library of Congress] (LCLS) .... CaOCkA
Atomic Energy of Canada [L'Energie Atomique du Canada] Chalk River, Ontario [Library symbol] [National Library of Canada] (NLC) .... OCKA
Atomic Energy of Canada Chemical Co., Ottawa, ON, Canada [Library symbol] [Library of Congress] (LCLS) .... CaOOAEC
Atomic Energy of Canada Limited (SAUO) .... AECL
Atomic Energy of Canada Ltd. .... AECL
Atomic Energy of Canada, Ltd. (SAUS) .... AECL
Atomic Energy of Canada Ltd. Library [UTLAS symbol] .... ATM
Atomic Energy of Canada Ltd., Research Co., Ottawa, ON, Canada [Library symbol] [Library of Congress] (LCLS) .... CaOOAER
Atomic Energy of Canada, Montreal, PQ, Canada [Library symbol] [Library of Congress] (LCLS) .... CaQMAEC
Atomic Energy of Canada [L'Energie Atomique du Canada] Montreal, Quebec [Library symbol] [National Library of Canada] (NLC) .... QMAEC
Atomic Energy of Canada, Ottawa, ON, Canada [Library symbol] [Library of Congress] (LCLS) .... CaOOAE
Atomic Energy of Canada Research Company (SAUO) .... AERC
Atomic Energy of Canada, Toronto, ON, Canada [Library symbol] [Library of Congress] (LCLS) .... CaOTAE
Atomic Energy of Canada [L'Energie Atomique du Canada] Toronto, Ontario [Library symbol] [National Library of Canada] .... OTAE
Atomic Energy of Canada, Whiteshell Nuclear Research Establishment, Pinawa, MB, Canada [Library symbol] [Library of Congress] (LCLS) ...... CaMPW
Atomic Energy Organisation [Iran] (NUCP) .... AEO
Atomic Energy Organisation of Iran (SAUS) .... AEOI
Atomic Energy Organization (SAUO) .... AEO
Atomic Energy Plant Safety Committee (SAUS) .... AEPSC
Atomic Energy Project .... AEP
Atomic Energy Project, Chalk River (SAUO) .... AEPC
Atomic Energy Regulatory Board [India] .... AERB
Atomic Energy Research Department [NASA] (KSC) .... AERD
Atomic Energy Research Establishment [of United Kingdom Atomic Energy Authority] .... AERE
Atomic Energy Research Establishment (SAUO) .... HAR
Atomic Energy Research Establishment, Didcot, Oxfordshire, United Kingdom [Library symbol] [Library of Congress] (LCLS) .... UkHA
Atomic Energy Research Institute (SAUO) .... AERI
Atomic Energy Review (journ.) (SAUS) .... AER
Atomic Energy Review (journ.) (SAUS) .... At Energy Rev
Atomic Energy Safety Bureau (SAUO) .... AESB
Atomic Energy Security Branch (SAUO) .... AESB
Atomic Energy Society of Japan (NUCP) .... AESJ
Atomic Energy Technical Unit (SAUO) .... AETU
Atomic Establishment Trombay (SAUO) .... AEET
Atomic Explosion .... ATXPL
Atomic Fluid Cell (OA) .... AFC
Atomic Fluorescence .... AF
Atomic Fluorescence Spectroscopy .... AFS
Atomic Force Microscope (or Microscopy) (SAUS) .... AFM
Atomic Force Microscopy [Chemistry] (MEC) .... AFM
Atomic Forum (IEEE) .... AF
Atomic Frequency Standard .... AFS

Atomic Fuel Corp. [Japan] .... AFC
Atomic Fuel Corporation (SAUO) .... AFC
Atomic Ground Intercept (MCD) .... ATGIN
Atomic Heat (SAUS) .... at ht
Atomic Hydrogen Weld .... AT/W
Atomic Incident Control Plan .... AICP
Atomic Industrial Forum [Later, USCEA] (EA) .... AIF
Atomic Industrial Forum, Inc. (SAUO) .... AFI
Atomic Industrial Forum, Inc. (SAUO) .... AIF
Atomic Industrial Health Forum, Inc. (SAUO) .... AIF
Atomic Industry Research Institute (SAUO) .... AIRI
Atomic International - Combustion Engineering .... AI-CE
Atomic International Forum (SAUS) .... AIF
Atomic International Time (SAUS) .... AIT
Atomic Layer Deposition (AAEL) .... ALD
Atomic Layer Epitaxy [Physical chemistry] .... ALE
Atomic Layer-by-Layer Molecular Beam Epitaxy .... ALL-MBE
Atomic Line Filter (SAUS) .... ALF
Atomic Line Molecular Spectroscopy .... ALMS
Atomic Magneto-Optic Resonance Spectrometry .... AMORS
Atomic Mass (IIA) .... ATM
Atomic Mass Number .... AMN
Atomic Mass Spectrometry (SAUS) .... AMS
Atomic Mass Unit .... AMU
Atomic Mass Unit (ABAC) .... amu
Atomic Migration .... AM
Atomic, Molecular, and Optical .... AMO
Atomic, Molecular, and Optical Physics .... AMO
Atomic Molecular Process Information Center (SAUS) .... AMPIC
Atomic Nuclear Forum (SAUO) .... ANF
Atomic Number .... AN
Atomic Number .... ATNO
Atomic Number (SAUS) .... At No
Atomic Number (WDAA) .... at no
Atomic Number [Symbol] .... Z
Atomic Orbital .... AO
Atomic Orbital with Angular Momentum Quantum Number 3 [Symbol] (DAVI) .... f
Atomic Ordnance Cataloging Office .... AOCO
Atomic Ordnance Platoon (NG) .... AOP
Atomic Organic Matter (DB) .... AOM
Atomic Oxygen Resistance Monitor (SAUS) .... AORM
Atomic Packing Factor (IEEE) .... APF
Atomic per Cent (SAUS) .... at-%
Atomic Photoelectric Effect .... APE
Atomic Physics Consortium at Oak Ridge .... APCOR
Atomic Post-Strike Analysis Report .... ATPOS
Atomic Power Company (SAUO) .... APC
Atomic Power Construction Ltd. .... APC
Atomic Power Construction Ltd. .... APCL
Atomic Power Constructions Ltd. (SAUO) .... APC
Atomic Power Development Associates, Inc. .... APDA
Atomic Power Development Association (SAUO) .... APDE
Atomic Power Equipment Department (SAA) .... APED
Atomic Power Group [Nuclear energy] (NUCP) .... APG
Atomic Power Plant (SAUO) .... APP
Atomic Power Station (NRCH) .... APS
Atomic Powered .... AP
Atomic Powered (SAUS) .... A-Powered
Atomic Products Division (SAUS) .... APD
Atomic Reactor and Fuel Development Corporation (SAUO) .... ARFDC
Atomic Reactor in Space (MUGU) .... ARIS
Atomic Research and Development Authority [Nuclear Regulatory Commission] (GFGA) .... ARDA
Atomic Resolution Analytical Electron Microscope (or Microscopy) (SAUS) .... ARAEM
Atomic Resolution Microscope .... ARM
Atomic Resonance Absorption Spectroscopy [Physics] .... ARAS
Atomic Resonance Filter Optical Receiver Module (MCD) .... ARFORM
Atomic Resonance Optical Filter (MCD) .... AROF
Atomic Safeguards (or Safety) and Licensing Appeal Board (SAUO) .... ASLAB
Atomic Safety and Licensing Appeal Board (NRCH) .... ASLAB
Atomic Safety and Licensing Appeal Panel [Nuclear Regulatory Commission] .... ASLAP
Atomic Safety and Licensing Board [Nuclear Regulatory Commission] .... ASLB
Atomic Safety and Licensing Board Panel (SAUO) .... ASLAP
Atomic Safety and Licensing Board Panel [Nuclear Regulatory Commission] .... ASLBP
Atomic Safety Licensing Board (SAUS) .... ASLB
Atomic Safety Line (IAA) .... ASL
Atomic Scattering Factor .... ASF
Atomic Sciences Committee (SAUO) .... ASC
Atomic Scientists' Association [Great Britain] .... ASA
Atomic Scientists News (journ.) (SAUS) .... ASN
Atomic Security Agency [Army] .... ASA
Atomic Shell of 98 Electrons per Shell (BARN) .... Q
Atomic Solution Diffusion .... ASD
Atomic Solvation Parameter [Physical chemistry] .... ASP
Atomic Space and Development Authority [Nuclear energy] (NRCH) .... ASADA
Atomic Space and Development Authority [Nuclear energy] .... ASDA
Atomic Spin Orbital (IAA) .... ASO
Atomic Standing Operating Procedures (NATG) .... ASOP
Atomic Standing Operation Procedures (SAUS) .... ASOP
Atomic Status Report (SAUS) .... ATOMSTATREP
Atomic Status Report (NATG) .... ATOMSTATSREP

Atomic Strike (SAUS) .... AS
Atomic Strike Evaluation Center .... ASTREC
Atomic Strike Net (AABC) .... ASN
Atomic Strike Plan (AFM) .... ASP
Atomic Strike Plan Control Group Alternate (AABC) .... ASPCGA
Atomic Strike Recording [*Air Force*] .... ASR
Atomic Strike Recording System [*Air Force*] .... ASTREC
Atomic Strike Recording System (SAUS) .... ASTREC System
Atomic Submarine (SAUS) .... A-Sub
Atomic Support Command (SAUS) .... ASC
Atomic Time .... AT
Atomic Time Unit .... ATU
Atomic Torpedo [*Military*] .... ATORP
Atomic Transition Probabilities Data Center .... ATPDC
Atomic Units (MCD) .... AU
Atomic Value (ADA) .... AV
Atomic Vapor LASER Isotope Separation (NUCP) .... ALVIS
Atomic Vapor LASER Isotope Separation .... AVLIS
Atomic Volume (DNAB) .... AT VOL
Atomic Warfare .... AW
Atomic Weapon Detection, Recognition & Estimation of Yield (SAUS) .... AWDREY
Atomic Weapon Retrofilt Order (SAUS) .... AWRO
Atomic Weapons (SAUS) .... ATOM WONS
Atomic Weapons (SAUS) .... ATOM WPNS
Atomic Weapons Detection, Recognition and Yield (SAUS) .... AWDREY
Atomic Weapons Electrical Assembler (SAUS) .... ATOM WPNS ELEC ASSR
Atomic Weapons Mechanical Assembler (SAUS) .... ATOM WPNS MECH ASSR
Atomic Weapons Nuclear Assembler (SAUS) .... ATOM WPNS NUC ASSR
Atomic Weapons Research Establishment (SAUO) .... AWRE
Atomic Weapons Research Establishment [*British Ministry of Defense*] [*Research center*] .... AWRE
Atomic Weapons Special Transport (DNAB) .... AWST
Atomic Weapons Support Command (SAUO) .... AWSCOM
Atomic Weapons Tests Safety Committee (SAUS) .... AWTSC
Atomic Weapons Training Group [*DASA*] .... AWTG
Atomic Weight .... A
Atomic Weight .... ATWT
Atomic Weight (WDAA) .... at wt
Atomic Weight .... AW
Atomic Weight (IAA) .... AWT
Atomic Weight Unit .... AWU
Atomic-Beam Magnetic Resonance (SAUS) .... ABMR
Atomicity, Consistency, Isolation, and Durability .... ACID
Atomicity, Consistency, Isolation, and Durability Test (DOM) .... ACID test
Atomicity, Consistency, Isolation, Durability (SAUS) .... ACID
Atomicity Controller .... AC
Atomic/Nuclear Energy Study Group (EA) .... ANESG
Atomic/Nuclear Energy Study Group (SAUO) .... ANFSG
Atomics International (NRCH) .... AI
Atomics International, Canoga Park, CA [*Library symbol*] [*Library of Congress*] (LCLS) .... CCpA
Atomics International Division (SAUO) .... AI
Atomics International Division .... AID
Atomics International Evaluated Nuclear Data Files (KSC) .... AIENDF
Atomics International Prototype Fast Reactor (SAUS) .... AIPFR
Atomic-Type Field Army (SAA) .... ATFA
Atomic-Weapon-Carrying Tactical Aircraft (SAUS) .... AWCTA
Atomization Energy [*Chemistry*] (MEC) .... AE
Atomized Suspension Technique .... AST
Atomizer, Source, Inductively (SAUS) .... ASIA
Atomizing .... ATMG
Atoms in Molecules (SAUS) .... AIM
Atomspheric Cloud Physics Laboratory (SAUO) .... ACPL
Atonement .... Aton
Atonement Seminary of the Holy Ghost, Washington, DC [*Library symbol*] [*Library of Congress*] (LCLS) .... DAtS
Atonic Sclerotic Muscle Dystrophy [*Medicine*] (DB) .... ASMD
Atopic Dermatitis [*Medicine*] (DB) .... AD
Atopic Dermatitis [*Medicine*] .... AT
Atopic Respiratory Disease [*Medicine*] (DB) .... ARD
ATP [*Adenosine Triphosphate*]**-Binding Cassette** [*Biochemistry*] .... ABC
Atqasuk [*Alaska*] [*Airport symbol*] (OAG) .... ATK
A-Track Initiator (SAA) .... ATI
Atraumatic [*Medicine*] (DAVI) .... AT
Atraumatic Normocephalic [*Medicine*] .... ATNC
Atresia [*Medicine*] .... ATR
Atria Communities, Inc. [*NASDAQ symbol*] (SAG) .... ATRC
Atria Communities, Inc. [*Associated Press*] (SAG) .... AtriaCo
Atria Software [*NASDAQ symbol*] (TTSB) .... ATSW
Atria Software, Inc. [*Associated Press*] (SAG) .... AtriaSft
Atria Software, Inc. [*NASDAQ symbol*] (SAG) .... ATSW
Atria/Carotid/Ventricular [*Anatomy*] .... ACV
Atrial [*Cardiology*] (DAVI) .... AT
Atrial [*Cardiology*] (DAVI) .... atr
atrial (SAUS) .... atrl
Atrial Bolus Dynamic Computer Tomography [*Cardiology*] (DAVI) .... ABDCT
Atrial Diastolic Gallop [*Cardiology*] (MAE) .... ADG
Atrial Ectopic Tachycardia [*Medicine*] .... AET
Atrial Ectopy [*Cardiology*] .... AT-ECT
Atrial Effective Refractory Period (DB) .... AERP
Atrial Emptying Index [*Medicine*] (DMAA) .... AEI
Atrial Fibrillation [*Cardiology*] .... AF
Atrial Fibrillation [*Cardiology*] .... AFIB
Atrial Fibrillation [*Medicine*] (DB) .... AFib
Atrial Fibrillation [*Cardiology*] .... AT FIB
Atrial Fibrillation [*Cardiology*] (MAE) .... atr fib
Atrial Fibrillation and/or Flutter [*Cardiology*] (DAVI) .... AF/F
Atrial Filling Fraction [*Cardiology*] .... AFF
Atrial Filling Index [*Medicine*] (MELL) .... AFI
Atrial Filling Pressure [*Cardiology*] (DAVI) .... AFP
Atrial Filling Rate [*Cardiology*] .... AFR
Atrial Flutter [*Cardiology*] .... Af
Atrial Flutter (SAUS) .... AF
Atrial Flutter [*Cardiology*] (MAE) .... AFL
Atrial Gallop [*Cardiology*] .... AG
Atrial His-Bundle [*Cardiology*] .... AH
Atrial Inhibited Pacemaker [*Cardiology*] (DMAA) .... AAI
Atrial Insufficiency [*Cardiology*] (AAMN) .... AI
Atrial Myxoma [*Medicine*] (DAVI) .... AM
Atrial Natriuretic Factor [*Biochemistry*] .... ANF
Atrial Natriuretic Peptide [*Biochemistry*] .... ANP
Atrial Overdrive Stimulation Rate [*Cardiology*] (DMAA) .... AST
Atrial Pacing (DB) .... AP
Atrial Pore Field [*Botany*] .... APF
Atrial [*or Auricular*] **Premature Beat** [*Cardiology*] (DAVI) .... APB
Atrial Premature Beat (SAUS) .... APB
Atrial Premature Beats [*Cardiology*] .... APB
Atrial Premature Contraction [*Cardiology*] .... APC
Atrial Premature Contractions (SAUS) .... APC
Atrial Premature Depolarization [*Cardiology*] .... APD
Atrial Rate [*Cardiology*] .... AR
Atrial Septal Defect [*Cardiology*] .... ASD
Atrial Septal Heart Defect [*Medicine*] (MELL) .... ASHD
Atrial Stenosis [*Cardiology*] (AAMN) .... AS
Atrial Synchronous Ventricular Inhibited Pacemaker [*Cardiology*] .... ASVIP
Atrial Tachycardia [*Medicine*] (DB) .... AT
Atrial Tachycardia with Block [*Cardiology*] (AAMN) .... ATB
Atrial Vascular Relaxant Substance [*Biochemistry*] .... AVRS
Atrialelectrogram [*Cardiology*] .... AEG
Atriocarotid [*Medicine*] .... AC
Atrion Corp. [*NASDAQ symbol*] (TTSB) .... ATRI
Atrion Corp. [*Associated Press*] (SAG) .... Atrion
Atriopeptin [*Biochemistry*] .... AP
Atriopeptin-Like Immunoreactive [*Neurons*] (DB) .... APIr
Atrioseptal Heart Disease [*Cardiology*] (DMAA) .... ASHD
Atriovenous (SAUS) .... AV
Atrioventriclar Nodal Tachycardia [*Medicine*] (MELL) .... AVNT
Atrioventricular [*Cardiology*] .... AV
Atrioventricular Block [*Cardiology*] (DMAA) .... AVB
Atrioventricular Canal [*Cardiology*] .... AVC
Atrioventricular Canal Defect [*Also called endocardial cushion defect*] [*Cardiology*] (DAVI) .... AVCD
Atrioventricular Conduction System [*Cardiology*] .... AVCS
Atrioventricular Dissociation [*Medicine*] (DB) .... AVD
Atrioventricular Heart Block [*Cardiology*] (DAVI) .... AVHB
Atrioventricular Junction [*Medicine*] (DMAA) .... AVJ
Atrioventricular Junctional Arrhythmia [*Medicine*] (MELL) .... AVJA
Atrioventricular Junctional Tachycardia [*Medicine*] (MELL) .... AVJT
Atrioventricular Nodal Reentry [*Cardiology*] .... AVNR
Atrioventricular Node [*Cardiology*] .... AVN
Atrioventricular Node Dysfunction [*Medicine*] (DMAA) .... AVND
Atrioventricular Node Functional Refractory Period [*Medicine*] (DB) .... AVNFRP
Atrioventricular Opening (SAUS) .... AO
Atrioventricular Reciprocating Tachycardia [*Medicine*] (MELL) .... AVRT
Atrioventricular Reentrant Tachycardia [*Cardiology*] (DMAA) .... AVRT
Atrioventricular Refractory Period [*Cardiology*] (MAE) .... AVRP
Atrioventricular Septal Defect [*Cardiology*] (DMAA) .... AVSD
Atrioventricular Sequential Pacing [*Medicine*] (MELL) .... AVSP
Atrioventricular Valve Opening (DAVI) .... AO
Atrioventricular Valves (SAUS) .... AV Valves
Atrium [*Medicine*] (DMAA) .... A
Atrium Pace [*Cardiology*] .... AP
atriventricular (SAUS) .... a-v
Atrix International [*NASDAQ symbol*] (TTSB) .... ATXI
Atrix International, Inc. [*Associated Press*] (SAG) .... AtrixInt
Atrix International, Inc. [*NASDAQ symbol*] (SAG) .... ATXI
Atrix Laboratories .... ATRIX
Atrix Laboratories [*NASDAQ symbol*] (TTSB) .... ATRX
Atrix Laboratories, Inc. [*Associated Press*] (SAG) .... AtrixL
Atrix Laboratories, Inc. [*NASDAQ symbol*] (SAG) .... ATRX
Atrodynamic and Propulsion Test Unit (SAUS) .... APTU
Atrophic Rhinitis [*Medicine*] (DMAA) .... AR
Atrophy (MAE) .... atr
Atrophy, Fasciculation, Tremor, Rigidity (SAUS) .... AFTR
Atropine (MAE) .... A
Atropine [*Medicine*] (MELL) .... ATR
Atropine 1% (SAUS) A1
Atropine Coma Therapy [*Medicine*] (DB) .... ACT
Atropine Retinoscopy (SAUS) .... ARNS
atropine sulfate (SAUS) .... atr sulf
Atropine Sulfate (MELL) .... ATS
Atropine Sulphate (DB) .... AS
Atropine-Like Psycho-Chemical Substance (PDAA) .... APS
Atroxin-Defibrinated Plasma [*Clinical chemistry*] .... ADFP
Atruvera [*Former USSR*] [*FAA designator*] (FAAC) .... AUV
ATS Aircharter Ltd. [*British*] [*ICAO designator*] (FAAC) .... AVT
ATS Med Inc. Wrrt [*NASDAQ symbol*] (TTSB) .... ATSIW
ATS Medical [*NASDAQ symbol*] (TTSB) .... ATSI
ATS Medical, Inc. [*NASDAQ symbol*] (SAG) .... ATSI

ATS Medical, Inc. [*Associated Press*] (SAG) .... ATS M
ATS Medical, Inc. [*Associated Press*] (SAG) .... ATS Med
ATS Route Network (SAUS) .... ARN
At-Sea Calibration Procedure .... ASCAP
ATS-Servicii de Transport Aerian [*Italy*] [*ICAO designator*] (FAAC) .... ROS
Atsugi [*Japan*] [*ICAO location identifier*] (ICLI) .... RJTA
Atsugi Technical Center (SAUS) .... ATC
Attach [*or Attachment*] (AFM) .... ATCH
Attach (ADWA) .... atch
Attach (KSC) .... ATT
Attach Center [*Military*] (IUSS) .... AC
Attach on Morning Report the Following Named EM [*Enlisted Man*] Who Has Been Authorized to Report to Your Station upon Expiration of Leave. Retain Him/Her Pending Further Instructions (AABC) .... ATCHEMPI
Attach Points Only (MCD) .... APO
Attach-Detach Kit .... ADK
Attache (ATT)
Attache Support Message (MCD) .... ASM
Attached .... ATCHD
Attached (EBF) .... Atchd
Attached (EBF) .... Att
Attached (WDMC) .... att
Attached [*Classified advertising*] .... ATTCH
Attached Applications Processor .... AAP
Attached FORTRAN Processor [*Burroughs Corp.*] [*Computer science*] (BUR) .... AFP
Attached Gingiva [*Medicine*] (DMAA) .... AG
Attached Inflatable Decelerator [*Aerodynamics*] .... AID
Attached Inflatable Detector .... AID
Attached Payload (SAUS) .... AP
Attached Payload Accommodations Equipment (SSD) .... APAE
Attached Payload and Associated Equipment (SSD) .... AP & AE
Attached Payload Module (SAUS) .... APM
Attached Pressurized Module [*European Space Agency*] .... APM
Attached Processor [*Computer science*] (BUR) .... AP
Attached Processor for Speech [*IBM Corp.*] (NITA) .... APS
Attached Processor System [*Telecommunications*] (TEL) .... APS
Attached Proton Test (SAUS) .... APT
Attached Resource Computer (MHDB) .... ARC
Attached Resource Computer Network .... ARCnet
Attached Resource Computing Network (DDC) .... ARCnet
Attached Resources Computer Network [*Microcomputer LAN*] [*Datapoint Corp.*] (NITA) .... ARCNET
Attached Resupply Carrier [*NASA*] (SPST) .... ARCA
Attached Support Processor [*Computer science*] .... ASP
Attached Support Program (SAUS) .... ASP
Attached to Other Correspondence [*Business term*] .... AOC
Attached to Other Correspondence [*Business term*] .... A to OC
Attached Trailer Towed Vehicle Weight [*Automotive engineering*] .... ATVW
Attached Training Vessel [*Navy*] .... ATV
Attached Unassigned (SAUS) .... A/U
Attached Unit Interface (SAUS) .... AUI
Attached Virtual Processor [*Computer science*] (NITA) .... AVP
Attachie [*British Columbia*] [*Seismograph station code, US Geological Survey*] [*Closed*] (SEIS) .... ATC
Attaching (SAUS) .... Atch
Attachment (SAUS) .... Atchmt
Attachment (MUGU) .... ATCHMT
Attachment [*Telecommunications*] (TEL) .... ATT
Attachment (ADWA) .... att
Attachment .... ATTACHT
Attachment Disorder [*Medicine*] .... AD
Attachment Plaque .... AP
Attachment Point [*Genetics*] (DOG) .... ap
Attachment Unit (MCD) .... AU
Attachment Unit Interface [*Computer science*] (PCM) .... AUI
Attachment Universal Interface (SAUS) .... AUI
Attack [*Designation for all US military aircraft*] .... A
Attack [*Men's lacrosse position*] .... A
Attack (DNAB) .... ATAK
Attack (MSA) .... ATCK
Attack (AABC) .... ATK
Attack .... ATTK
Attack Air Mobility System [*Army*] .... AAMS
Attack Aircraft Carrier (MCD) .... AAC
Attack Aircraft Carrier [*Navy symbol*] .... CVA
Attack Aircraft Carrier (Nuclear Propulsion) [*Navy symbol*] .... CVAN
Attack and Release (SAUS) .... AR
Attack Assessment [*Military*] .... AA
Attack Assessment Probe (ACAE) .... AAP
Attack Assessment Radar (ACAE) .... AARAD
Attack Assessment System (MCD) .... AAS
Attack Aviation (SAUS) .... Atk Avn
Attack Cargo Ship [*Navy symbol*] .... AKA
Attack Cargo Ship [*Navy symbol*] .... LKA
Attack Carrier Air Wing [*Navy*] .... ATKCARAIRWING
Attack Carrier Air Wing [*Navy symbol*] .... CVW
Attack Carrier Striking Force .... ACSF
Attack Center .... AC
Attack Center Display .... ACD
Attack Center Indicator Panel .... ACIP
Attack Center Panel .... ACP
Attack Center Switchboard .... ACS
Attack Characterization (MCD) .... AC
Attack Class Patrol Boat [*Navy*] .... ACPB

Attack Console .... AC
Attack Control Concept .... ACC
Attack Control Console .... ACC
Attack Cut Out [*Military*] (NG) .... ACO
Attack Cut-Out (SAUS) .... ACO
Attack Director [*Military*] (MCD) .... AD
Attack Display Group (MCD) .... ADG
Attack Evaluation Model (MCD) .... AEM
Attack Experimental [*Air Force*] (MCD) .... AX
Attack Formation (SAUS) .... atk formn
Attack Geometry Display (DNAB) .... AGD
Attack Group (IUSS) .... AG
Attack Group Commander [*Military*] (IUSS) .... AGC
Attack Guidance Matrix [*Military*] (INF) .... AGM
Attack Heading Slot (SAA) .... AHS
Attack Heavy (DNAB) .... AH
Attack Helicopter (CINC) .... AH
Attack Helicopter [*MTMC*] (TAG) .... ATK HEL
Attack Helicopter Armament Control System (ACAE) .... AHACS
Attack Helicopter Battalion .... AHB
Attack Helicopter Battalion [*Army*] (ADDR) .... ATKHB
Attack Helicopter Company [*Military*] .... AHC
Attack Helicopter Company [*Military*] (AABC) .... ATKHC
Attack Helicopter Instrument Test (MCD) .... AHIT
Attack Helicopter Interface Unit (MCD) .... AIU
Attack Helicopter Operations (CAAL) .... AHO
Attack Helicopter Operations and Analysis Group .... AHOAG
Attack Helicopter Organization [*Military*] .... ATHELO
Attack Helicopter Self Test (MCD) .... AHST
Attack Helicopter Support (MCD) .... AHS
Attack Helicopter Team .... AHT
Attack Information Center (AFM) .... AIC
Attack Jet .... AJ
Attack Laydown Model (ACAE) .... ALM
Attack Laydown Model (ACAE) .... ATM
Attack Light Torpedo (SAUS) .... ALT
Attack Mine Squadron (SAUO) .... AtakMinRon
Attack Operations (SAUS) .... AO
Attack Plan (MCD) .... AP
Attack Plot (SAUS) .... ATP
Attack Plotter (NVT) .... AP
Attack Radar Set (ACAE) .... ARS
Attack Reference Point .... ARP
Attack Response Evaluation (MCD) .... ARE
Attack Response Exercise (MCD) .... ARE
Attack Response Mission-Oriented Reasoner (SAUS) .... ARMOR
Attack Squadron [*Navy*] (MUGU) .... ATKRON
attack squadron (SAUO) .... ATKRON
Attack Squadron [*Symbol*] (MCD) .... VA
Attack Squadron Detachment [*Navy*] (DNAB) .... ATKRONDET
Attack Submarine Team Trainer (SAUS) .... ASTT
Attack Surveillance Committee [*Army*] (AABC) .... ATKSC
Attack Surveillance Coverage [*Army*] (AABC) .... ATKSC
Attack, Sustain, Release [*Electronic musical instruments*] .... ASR
Attack Teacher .... A/T
Attack Transport [*Later, LPA*] [*Navy symbol*] .... APA
Attack Warning (ACAE) .... AW
Attack Warning Processing and Display System (MCD) .... AWPDS
Attack Warning System [*Civil Defense*] .... AWS
Attack Warning/Attack Assessment (ACAE) .... AW/AA
Attack Working Group [*Military*] .... AWG
Attack/Decay/Sustain/Release [*Audio programming parameters*] .... ADSR
Attacking Hardened Air Bases [*Air Force*] (PDAA) .... AHAB
Attain (ROG) .... ATTN
Attained Competency Level .... ACL
Attainment Area (EEVL) .... AA
Attainment Quotient .... AQ
Attainment Target (WDAA) .... AT
Attala, AL [*FM radio station call letters*] .... WKXX
Attawapiskat [*Canada*] [*Airport symbol*] (OAG) .... YAT
Attawapiskat Band Library, Attawapiskat, ON, Canada [*Library symbol*] [*Library of Congress*] (LCLS) .... CaOAttB
Attawapiskat Band Library, Ontario [*Library symbol*] [*National Library of Canada*] (BIB) .... OAB
Attachment Unit Interface (SAUS) .... AUI
Attempt (FAAC) .... ATMT
Attempt Break and Enter [*Criminology*] .... AB & E
Attempt per Circuit per Hour (SAUS) .... ACH
Attempt to Contact (FAAC) .... ATMTC
Attempt to Locate (FAAC) .... ALCT
Attempt to Locate .... ATL
Attempt to Steal from Motor Vehicle [*Criminology*] .... ASFMV
Attempted [*FBI standardized term*] .... ATT
Attempted Corporate Integration of Dividends [*Economics*] .... ACID
Attempts .... ATT
Attempts per Circuit per Hour [*Telecommunications*] (TEL) .... ACH
Attend (ROG) .... ATTD
Attendance [*Sports*] .... A
Attendance (ROG) .... ATTCE
Attendance and Labor System (MCD) .... ATLAS
Attendance Record (SAUS) .... AR
Attendant [*Telecommunications*] (TEL) .... AD
Attendant (MUGU) .... ATDNT
Attendant .... ATDT
Attendant (MSA) .... ATT

Attendant (AL) .... Atten
Attendant (AABC) .... ATTND
Attendant (SAUS) .... Attnd
Attendant .... ATTNDNT
Attendant Care Evaluation .... ACE
Attendant Care Scheme .... ACS
Attendant Control of Facilities [*Western Electric Co.*] .... ACOF
Attendant Recall (SAUS) .... ARC
Attended Pay Station [*Attended Public Telephone*] (TEL) .... APS
Attended Public Telephone [*Telecommunications*] (TEL) .... ATT
Attended Resource Computer [*Datapoint Corp.*] (NITA) .... ARC
Attending .... ATT
Attending .... ATTG
Attending .... ATTNG
Attending Physician (SAUS) .... ATP
Attending Physician Work Station (DMAA) .... APWS
Attending Physician's Statement .... APS
Attending's Admission Notes [*Medicine*] (DMAA) .... AAN
Attente [*Leave on*] [*Knitting term*] [*French*] (BARN) .... ATSDR
Attention [*Electronics*] .... AT
Attention .... ATN
Attention .... ATT
Attention (EBF) .... Att
Attention (WDMC) .... att
Attention .... ATTEN
Attention (AFM) .... ATTN
Attention (ODBW) .... attn
Attention and Information Processing (SAUS) .... AIP
Attention Command (SAUS) .... AC
Attention Control Training .... ACT
Attention Deficit and Distractability Disorder with Hyperactivity [*Medicine*] (DAVI) .... ADDD/H
Attention Deficit Disorder [*Psychology*] .... ADD
Attention Deficit Disorder Association (SAUO) .... ADDA
Attention Deficit Disorder Behavior Rating Scales [*Test*] (TMMY) .... ADDBRS
Attention Deficit Disorder with Hyperactivity [*Medicine*] .... ADD-HA
Attention Deficit Disorder with Hyperactivity [*Psychology*] (DAVI) .... ADD W H
Attention Deficit Disorder-Residual Type .... ADD-RT
Attention Deficit Hyperactivity Disorder [*Medicine*] .... ADHD
Attention Deficit Information Network (EA) .... ADIN
Attention Dial Pulse [*Telecommunications*] (VERA) .... ATDP
Attention Dial Tone [*Computer science*] (DOM) .... ATDT
Attention Director (MCD) .... ATTNDIR
Attention Display [*Communications device*] .... AD
Attention Getting [*by the hearing-impaired*] .... AG
Attention Handling (SAUS) .... AH
Attention Hang Up [*Telecommunications*] (VERA) .... ATH
Attention Identification (SAUS) .... AID
Attention Identification Character (SAUS) .... AI Character
Attention Identifier (SAUS) .... AID
Attention Inquiry (SAUS) .... ATTNINQ
Attention, Interest, Desire, Conviction, Action, and Satisfaction [*Sales*] (WDMC) .... AIDCAS
Attention Interrupt Drive (SAUS) .... AID
Attention Interrupt Request (SAUS) .... AIR
Attention Interruption (SAUS) .... AI
Attention Invited (MCD) .... ATTNINV
Attention Key (SAUS) .... AK
Attention Operating Characteristic [*Psychometrics*] .... AOC
Attention Routine (SAUS) .... AR
Attention To File (SAUS) .... ATF
Attention-Deficit Disorder Association (EA) .... ADDA
Attention-Deficit Disorder with Hyperactivity (DIPS) .... ADDH
Attention-Deficit Hyperactivity Disorder (DIPS) .... AHD
Attention-Interest-Desire-Action [*Formula*] [*Marketing*] .... AIDA
Attentuation (SAUS) .... ATT
Attentuation Equivalent Nettiness (SAUS) .... AEN
Attenuated (AAEL) .... ATT
Attenuated RADAR Monitor .... ARM
Attenuated Total Reflectance [*Instrumentation*] .... ATR
Attenuated Total Reflectance Fourier Transform Infrared Spectroscopy (SAUS) .... ATR-FTIR
Attenuated Total Reflectance (or Reflection) (SAUS) .... ATR
Attenuation (IAA) .... A
Attenuation (DEN) .... AT
Attenuation [*Instrumentation*] .... ATT
Attenuation Characteristics (SAUS) .... AC
Attenuation Distortion Equivalent (SAUS) .... ADE
Attenuation Efficiency Score (PDAA) .... AES
Attenuation Equalizer (IAA) .... AE
Attenuation Equivalent Nettiness (SAUS) .... AEN
Attenuation Factor (SAUS) .... AF
Attenuation Index .... AI
Attenuation Reaction .... AR
Attenuation to Crosstalk Radio (VERA) .... ACR
Attenuator (KSC) .... ATTEN
Attenuator .... ATTN
Attenuator Pad (SAUS) .... AP
Attenuator-Thermoelement Voltmeter .... ATVM
Attestation .... ATTESTN
Attestation (SAUS) .... Attestn
Attesting (ROG) .... ATTESTG
At-the-Knee Amputation (VNW) .... AK Amp
At-the-Money [*Options*] [*Investment term*] (NUMA) .... ATM
Atti della Accademia di Scienze morali e politiche della Societ nazionale di Scienze, Lettere ed Arti di Napoli (SAUS) .... AAN
Atti della Settimana Biblica [*A publication*] (BJA) .... AtSetBib
Atti Parlamentari [*Parliamentary Acts*] [*Italian*] (ILCA) .... Atti Parl
Attic [*Greek dialect*] (ROG) .... ATT
Attic (SAUS) .... Att
Attic .... ATTC
Attica [*New York*] [*Seismograph station code, US Geological Survey*] [*Closed*] (SEIS) .... ATT
Attica (SAUS) .... Att
Attica Daily Ledger Tribune, Attica, IN [*Library symbol*] [*Library of Congress*] (LCLS) .... InAttLT
Attica Friendly Oracle, Attica, IN [*Library symbol*] [*Library of Congress*] (LCLS) .... InAttFO
Attica, IN [*FM radio station call letters*] .... WGBD
Attica, NY [*FM radio station call letters*] .... WBTF
Attica, NY [*FM radio station call letters*] (BROA) .... WXOX-FM
Attica Public Library, Attica, IN [*Library symbol*] [*Library of Congress*] (LCLS) .... InAtt
Atticus [*of Nepos*] [*Classical studies*] (OCD) .... Att
Attimeter (SAUS) .... Alt
Attitude .... ATT
Attitude (KSC) .... ATTD
Attitude .... ATTTD
Attitude Acquisition Technique .... AAT
Attitude and Antenna Control System [*NASA*] (MCD) .... AACS
Attitude and Articulation Control Subsystem [*NASA*] .... AACS
Attitude and Heading Reference System (SAUS) .... AHRS
Attitude and Orbit Control (ACAE) .... AOC
Attitude and Orbit Control Electronics [*Aerospace*] (NASA) .... AOCE
Attitude and Orbit Control Measurement System (ADWA) .... AOCMS
Attitude and Orbit Control System [*or Subsystem*] (MCD) .... AOCS
Attitude and Pointing (SAUS) .... A&P
Attitude and Pointing (MCD) .... AP
Attitude and Pointing Control System [*NASA*] (MHDW) .... APC
Attitude and Pointing Control System [*NASA*] (KSC) .... APCS
Attitude and Pointing Control System [*NASA*] .... APS
Attitude and Rate Indicating System .... ARIS
Attitude and Reaction Control (ACAE) .... A&RC
Attitude and Spin Control Subsystem [*NASA*] .... ASCS
Attitude and Translation Control Assembly [*Aviation*] (MCD) .... ATCA
Attitude and Translation Control Electronics .... ATCE
Attitude and Translation Control System (MCD) .... ATCS
Attitude and Translation Control Unit .... ATCU
Attitude Angle Transducer .... AAT
Attitude Anomaly Detector (ADWA) .... AAD
Attitude Axis Emergency Control [*Aerospace*] (MCD) .... AAEC
Attitude Calibration Module [*NASA*] (SPST) .... ACM
Attitude Command System (IEEE) .... ACS
Attitude Configuration System (SSD) .... ACS
Attitude Control [*System*] [*Aerospace*] .... AC
Attitude Control (IDOE) .... ac
Attitude Control and Determination Subsystem (MCD) .... ACDS
Attitude Control and Maneuver Rate [*Aerospace*] .... ACMR
Attitude Control and Maneuvering Electronics [*Aerospace*] (MCD) .... ACME
Attitude Control and Maneuvering Electronics System [*Aerospace*] (MCD) .... ACMES
Attitude, Control, and Stabilization [*NASA*] (SPST) .... AC&S
Attitude Control and Stabilization [*NASA*] (KSC) .... ACS
Attitude Control and Translation System [*Aerospace*] (MCD) .... ACTS
Attitude Control and Translation System/Propulsion [*Aerospace*] .... ACTS/PROP
Attitude Control and Translation System/Stabilization and Control Electronics [*Aerospace*] .... ACTS/SCE
Attitude Control and Translation System/Stabilization and Control Electronics (SAUS) .... ACTS/SCE
Attitude Control Assembly (SAUS) .... ACA
Attitude Control, Command, and Telemetry Program (ACAE) .... ACCTP
Attitude Control Development [*Aerospace*] (SSD) .... ACD
Attitude Control Document (SSD) .... ACD
Attitude Control Electronics [*Aerospace*] .... ACE
Attitude Control Indicator [*Aerospace*] (IAA) .... ACI
Attitude Control Jet [*Aerospace*] .... ACJ
Attitude Control Motor (ACAE) .... ACM
Attitude Control Processor (ACAE) .... ACP
Attitude Control Propulsion Motor [*Aerospace*] .... ACPM
Attitude Control Propulsion Subsystem (SAUS) .... ACPS
Attitude Control Propulsion System [*or Subsystem*] [*NASA*] .... ACPS
Attitude Control Subsystem (SAUS) .... ACS
Attitude Control System [*or Subsystem*] [*Aerospace*] .... ACS
Attitude Control Torquing Device [*Aerospace*] .... ACTD
Attitude Control Unit (ADWA) .... ACU
Attitude Controller Assembly [*NASA*] (KSC) .... ACA
Attitude Controls Indicator (SAUS) .... ACI
Attitude Coordinate Converter System (AAG) .... ACCS
Attitude Data Processor (ACAE) .... ADP
Attitude Determination and Control (ACAE) .... ADAC
Attitude Determination and Control Software [*Orbital satellites*] .... ADACS
Attitude Determination and Control Subsystem (ADWA) .... ADACS
Attitude Determination and Control Subsystem (ACAE) .... ADCS
Attitude Determination and Control System (MCD) .... ADACS
Attitude Determination Device [*Military*] .... ADD
Attitude Direction Indicator [*Aerospace*] .... ADI
Attitude Director Converter (ACAE) .... ADC
Attitude Director Indicator (PIPO) .... ADI
Attitude Director Indicator System (PDAA) .... ADIS

Attitude Displacement Sensor (SAUS)	ADS
Attitude Display Group (SAUO)	ADG
Attitude Display Indicator [Aerospace] (MCD)	ADI
Attitude Display System (MCD)	ADS
Attitude Engine Control (SAUS)	AEC
Attitude, Genes, Exercise, Investigate New Challenges, Nutrition, Get Rid of Stress and Smoking	AGEING
Attitude Ground Support System (MCD)	AGSS
Attitude Gyro (MCD)	AG
Attitude Gyro Accelerometer Assembly (MCD)	AGAA
Attitude Gyro Accelerometer Package (KSC)	AGAP
Attitude Gyro Assembly (MCD)	AGA
Attitude Gyro Coupling Unit (KSC)	AGCU
Attitude Heading Gyroscope System	AHGS
Attitude Heading Reference Unit	AHRU
Attitude Hold (MCD)	AH
Attitude Hold Pitch [Axis]	AHP
Attitude Hold Roll [Axis] (NASA)	AHR
Attitude Horizon Sensor (IIA)	AHS
Attitude Indicating System (MCD)	AIS
Attitude Indicator [NASA] (KSC)	AI
Attitude Indicator Measurement System (SAUS)	AIMS
Attitude Maneuvering System (SAA)	AMS
Attitude Matchup Update (SAUS)	AMU
Attitude Measurement Sensor (GEOI)	AMS
Attitude Monitor Switching Unit (MCD)	AMSU
Attitude Nutation Control Electronics (NASA)	ANCE
Attitude Pointing Mechanism Electronics (ADWA)	APME
Attitude Processor (NASA)	AP
Attitude Processor procurement, support and transportation (SAUS)	AP
Attitude Propulsion Subsystem	APS
Attitude Pulse Digitizer (ACAE)	APD
Attitude Reaction Wheel	ARW
Attitude Reference Assembly (MCD)	ARA
Attitude Reference Bombing Computer (MCD)	ARBC
Attitude Reference Bombing Computer Set [or System] (MCD)	ARBCS
Attitude Reference Program [NASA]	ATTREF
Attitude Reference System (KSC)	ARS
Attitude Reference Unit	ARU
Attitude Sensing and Control System (SAUS)	ASCS
Attitude Sensor Digitizer (ACAE)	ASD
Attitude Sensor Package (NAKS)	ASP
Attitude Sensor Parachute Staging Unit (MCD)	ASPSU
Attitude Set [Aerospace] (MCD)	AS
Attitude Set and Gimbal Position Display [NASA] (KSC)	AS/GPD
Attitude Set and Gimbal Position Indicator [NASA]	AS/GPI
Attitude Set Control Panel [Aerospace] (NASA)	ASCP
Attitude Stabilization and Control System (MCD)	ASCS
Attitude, Steering, Turn, Rate, Azimuth (SAUS)	ASTRA
Attitude Sun Sensor (ACAE)	ATSS
Attitude Thrustor System	ATS
Attitude toward Caring for the Dying Scale	ACD
Attitude Toward Disabled Persons Scale (DIPS)	ATDPS
Attitude toward School Questionnaire [Test]	ASQ
Attitude Transfer System (MCD)	ATS
Attitude Transmitting Equipment (SAUS)	ATE
Attitude Vapor Crystal Growth (SSD)	AVCG
Attitude, Velocity & Control (SAUS)	AVC
Attitude-Interest Analysis Test [Psychology]	AIAT
Attitude-Referenced Radiometer Study [NASA]	ARRS
Attitude-Related Disorder [Medicine] (MELL)	ARD
Attitudes, Interests, and Opinions	AIO
Attitudes, Interests, and Opinions of Individuals [Psychographics] (WDMC)	AIO Inventory
Attitudes Toward Blindness Questionnaire [Psychology] (EDAC)	ATBQ
Attitudes toward Disabled Persons [Psychology]	ATDP
Attitudes Toward Educational Research Scale [Psychology] (EDAC)	ATERS
Attitudes Toward Feminist Issues Scales [Psychology] (EDAC)	ATFI
Attitudes Toward Handicapped Individuals Scale [Psychology] (EDAC)	ATHI
Attitudes toward Industrialization [Psychology]	ATI
Attitudes Toward Mainstreaming Scale [Psychology] (EDAC)	ATMS
Attitudes toward Parental Control of Children [Psychology]	ATPCC
Attitudes Toward Parental Control of Children (SAUS)	ATPCC
Attitudes Toward Sex Roles Instrument [Psychology] (EDAC)	ATSR
Attitudes Toward Women Scale [Psychology] (DHP)	AWS
Attitudinal Information Data System (NVT)	AIDS
Attiyeh Foundation (EA)	AF
Attleboro, MA [AM radio station call letters]	WARA
Attleboro, MA [AM radio station call letters] (BROA)	WJYT
Attleboro Public Library, Attleboro, MA [Library symbol] [Library of Congress] (LCLS)	MAtt
Atto [A prefix meaning divided by 10 to the 18th power] [SI symbol]	a
Atto [Act] [Italian]	A
attoampere (SAUS)	aA
Attofarad (IDOE)	aF
Attohenry (IDOE)	aH
attohenry (SAUS)	aH
Attopeu [Laos] [ICAO location identifier] (ICLI)	VLAP
Attorney (WGA)	AT
Attorney	ATT
Attorney (EBF)	Att
Attorney (WDAA)	att
Attorney (PHSD)	Atty
Attorney (SAUS)	Atty
Attorney (EBF)	atty
Attorney (AFM)	ATTY
Attorney and Client (SAUS)	Atty&C
Attorney General	AG
Attorney General (AAGC)	Ag
Attorney General (WDAA)	Att Gen
Attorney General (ADA)	ATTGEN
Attorney General (WGA)	Atty Gen
Attorney General Letter Opinions (SAUO)	AGLO
Attorney General of England (ROG)	AGE
Attorney General of Ontario, Crown Law Office, Toronto, ON, Canada [Library symbol] [Library of Congress] (LCLS)	CaOTAGC
Attorney General of the Duchy of Lancaster (ILCA)	AGDL
Attorney General of the Queen's Troop [Military] [British] (ROG)	AGQT
Attorney General's Annual Report [A publication] (DLA)	Att'y Gen Ann Rep
Attorney General's Decisions [A publication] (DLA)	AG Dec
Attorney General's Department (ADA)	AGD
Attorney Generals Department (SAUS)	AGs
Attorney General's Law Journal [A publication] (DLA)	Att'y Gen LJ
Attorney General's Ministry [Canada]	AGM
Attorney Generals Opinion (SAUS)	AGO
Attorney General's Opinions [A publication] (DLA)	AG
Attorney General's Opinions [A publication] (DLA)	Atty Gen Op
Attorney General's Opinions [A publication] (DLA)	Atty Gen Op NY
Attorneys, Certified Public Accountants, and Enrolled Agents [In "Operation ACE," IRS investigation of these occupations as sources of income tax evasion]	ACE
Attorneys for Animal Rights (EA)	AFAR
Attorneys Generals Reports (SAUS)	Rep Atty Gen
[The] Attorneys Group (EA)	TAG
Attotesla (ADWA)	aT
attovolt (SAUS)	aV
attowatt (SAUS)	aW
Attractions Bars Cabarets Dancings (SAUO)	ABCD
Attractive (ADWA)	attr
attractive (SAUS)	attr
Attraktiv und Preiswert [Attractive and Priced Right] [West German grocery products brand]	A & P
Attributable Number (MELL)	AN
Attributable Risk (MELL)	AR
Attribute	A
Attribute	ATR
Attribute	ATTRIB
Attribute Configuration File (SAUS)	ACF
Attribute Distributed Tree (MHDI)	ADT
Attribute Grammer (SAUS)	AG
Attribute ID (SAUS)	ATID
Attribute Information Table (SAUS)	AIT
Attribute Level Number (SAUS)	ALN
Attribute Mark Count (SAUS)	AMC
Attribute Requirement Inventory	ARI
Attribute Value (MHDI)	ATRVAL
Attribute Value Time (SAUS)	AVT
Attributed (VRA)	attr
attributed (SAUS)	attrd
Attributed	ATTRIB
Attributes List (SAUS)	ALIST
Attribute-Treatment Interaction	ATI
Attribution (WDAA)	attrib
attributive (SAUS)	attrib
Attributively (ADWA)	attrib
Attrition (SAUS)	Attrit
Attrition and Modification Work Order	AMWO
Attrition and Pregnancy [Reasons for high turnover rate among women employees]	A and P
Attrition Reserve	AR
Attrition, Utilization, and Loss Rate (AFM)	AULR
Attrition, Utilization and Loss Rate (SAUS)	AULR
Attu, AK [Location identifier] [FAA] (FAAL)	ATU
Atuminum, Nickel, Copper (SAUS)	ALNICO
Atuona [Marquesas Islands] [Airport symbol] (OAG)	AUQ
ATV [All-Terrian Vehicle] Safety Institute (EA)	ASI
Atwater, CA [FM radio station call letters]	KVRQ
Atwater Kent Museum, Philadelphia, PA [Library symbol] [Library of Congress] (LCLS)	PPAK
Atwater Library, Montreal, PQ, Canada [Library symbol] [Library of Congress] (LCLS)	CaQMMI
Atwater Library [Formerly, Mechanics Institute Library] Montreal, Quebec [Library symbol] [National Library of Canada] (NLC)	QMMI
Atwater Library of the Mechanics' Institute of Montreal [UTLAS symbol]	ATW
Atwater, NM [FM radio station call letters]	KYRS
Atwater Public Library, Atwater, MN [Library symbol] [Library of Congress] (LCLS)	MnAt
Atwater-Grove City Junior High School, Grove City, MN [Library symbol] [Library of Congress] (LCLS)	MnGcJH
Atwater-Grove City Public Schools, Atwater, MN [Library symbol] [Library of Congress] (LCLS)	MnAtPS
Atwater's Reports [1 Minnesota] [A publication] (DLA)	Atw
Atwater's Reports [1 Minnesota] [A publication] (DLA)	Atwater
Atwood, KS [Location identifier] [FAA] (FAAL)	ADT
Atwood Oceanics [NYSE symbol] (SG)	ATW
Atwood Oceanics [NASDAQ symbol] (TTSB)	ATWD
Atwood Oceanics, Inc. [NASDAQ symbol] (NQ)	ATWD
Atwood Oceanics, Inc. [Associated Press] (SAG)	AtwdOc
Atwood, TN [FM radio station call letters] (BROA)	WTKB-FM

ATWS [*Anticipated Transient without Scram*] **Mitigating System Actuation Circuitry** [*Nuclear energy*] (NRCH) .... AMSAC
ATWS [*Anticipated Transient without Scram*] **Rod Injection System** [*Nuclear energy*] (NRCH) .... ARI
Atypical Acid-Fast Bacilli [*Microbiology*] .... AAFB
Atypical Alzheimer's Disease [*Medicine*] (MELL) .... AAD
Atypical Antibody Titer [*Medicine*] (MELL) .... AAT
Atypical Chest Pain [*Medicine*] .... ACP
Atypical Chronic Myeloid Leukemia [*Medicine*] (DMAA) .... ACMI
Atypical Facial Pain [*Medicine*] (MELL) .... AFP
Atypical Glandular Cells of Undetermined Significance [*Gynecology*] .... AGUS
Atypical Legionella-Like Organism .... ALLO
Atypical Lymphocyte [*Hematology*] (DAVI) .... A-LYM
Atypical Lymphocytes (DAVI) .... ATL
Atypical Lymphoepitheloid Cell Proliferation [*Medicine*] .... ALEP
Atypical Lymphoid Hyperplasia [*Medicine*] .... ALH
Atypical Measles Syndrome [*Medicine*] .... AMS
Atypical Mole Syndrome .... AMS
Atypical Mycobacteriosis [*Medicine*] (MELL) .... aM
Atypical Odontalgia [*Dental pain that has no apparent organic cause*] .... AO
Atypical Orofacial Pain [*Medicine*] (MELL) .... AOFP
Atypical Squamous Cells of Undetermined Significance [*Medicine*] .... ASCUS
Atypical Transformation Zone [*Gynecology*] (DAVI) .... ATZ
Atypical Ventricular Tachycardia [*Cardiology*] (DAVI) .... AVT
Au Bon Pain [*NASDAQ symbol*] (SPSG) .... ABPC
Au Bon Pain, Inc. [*Associated Press*] (SAG) .... AuBon
Au Bon Pain'A' [*NASDAQ symbol*] (TTSB) .... ABPCA
Au Resources Ltd. [*Vancouver Stock Exchange symbol*] .... AUE
Au Tau [*Hong Kong*] [*Later, HKO*] [*Geomagnetic observatory code*] .... AUT
Aua [*Papua New Guinea*] [*Airport symbol*] (OAG) .... AUI
Au¤erirdische Lebensform (SAUS) .... ALF
Au¤erparlamentarische Opposition (SAUS) .... APO
Aubenas [*France*] [*Airport symbol*] (OAG) .... OBS
Aubenas-Vals-Lanas [*France*] [*ICAO location identifier*] (ICLI) .... LFHO
Auberger [*Blood group*] .... Au
Auberry, CA [*FM radio station call letters*] (RBYB) .... KLBN
Aubeville [*Congo*] [*ICAO location identifier*] (ICLI) .... FCBU
Aubigny-Sur-Nere [*France*] [*ICAO location identifier*] (ICLI) .... LFEH
Auburn [*Nebraska*] [*Seismograph station code, US Geological Survey*] (SEIS) .... ABN
Auburn [*New York*] [*Airport symbol*] (AD) .... SSN
Auburn, AL [*AM radio station call letters*] .... WAUD
Auburn, AL [*FM radio station call letters*] .... WEGL
Auburn, AL [*FM radio station call letters*] .... WKKR
Auburn, CA [*Location identifier*] [*FAA*] (FAAL) .... AUN
Auburn, CA [*AM radio station call letters*] .... KAHI
Auburn, CA [*FM radio station call letters*] .... KHYL
Auburn, CA [*AM radio station call letters*] (BROA) .... KSMH
Auburn Community College [*New York*] .... ACC
Auburn Dam [*California*] [*Seismograph station code, US Geological Survey*] (SEIS) .... ADC
Auburn Enterprise, Auburn, IA [*Library symbol*] [*Library of Congress*] (LCLS) .... IaAubE
Auburn Evening Star, Auburn, IN [*Library symbol*] [*Library of Congress*] (LCLS) .... InAubS
Auburn High School, Rockford, IL [*Library symbol*] [*Library of Congress*] (LCLS) .... IRoAH
Auburn Hills, MI [*FM radio station call letters*] .... WAHS
Auburn, IN [*FM radio station call letters*] (RBYB) .... WGLL
Auburn, IN [*AM radio station call letters*] .... WIFF
Auburn, ME [*FM radio station call letters*] .... WKZS
Auburn, ME [*FM radio station call letters*] (BROA) .... WMWX-FM
Auburn Memorial Hospital, Learning Resources Center, Auburn, NY [*Library symbol*] [*Library of Congress*] (LCLS) .... NAuMH
Auburn National [*NASDAQ symbol*] (SAG) .... AUBN
Auburn National [*Associated Press*] (SAG) .... AubNB
Auburn Natl Bancorp [*NASDAQ symbol*] (TTSB) .... AUBN
Auburn, NE [*FM radio station call letters*] (RBYB) .... KNCY-FM
Auburn, NY [*AM radio station call letters*] .... WAUB
Auburn, NY [*FM radio station call letters*] .... WDWN
Auburn, NY [*FM radio station call letters*] (BROA) .... WHCD-FM
Auburn, NY [*AM radio station call letters*] (BROA) .... WKGJ
Auburn, NY [*AM radio station call letters*] .... WMBO
Auburn, NY [*FM radio station call letters*] .... WPCX
Auburn Public Library, Auburn, IA [*Library symbol*] [*Library of Congress*] (LCLS) .... IaAub
Auburn Public Library, Auburn, IL [*Library symbol*] [*Library of Congress*] (LCLS) .... IAub
Auburn Public Library, Auburn, ME [*Library symbol*] [*Library of Congress*] (LCLS) .... MeAu
Auburn Public Library, Auburn, ME [*Library symbol*] [*Library of Congress*] (LCLS) .... MeAub
Auburn Public Library, Auburn, WA [*Library symbol*] [*Library of Congress*] (LCLS) .... WaAu
Auburn Research Foundation (KSC) .... ARF
Auburn Theological Seminary, Auburn, NY [*Library symbol*] [*Library of Congress*] [*Obsolete*] (LCLS) .... NAuT
Auburn University [*Alabama*] .... AU
Auburn University (GAGS) .... Auburn U
Auburn University, Archives, Auburn, AL [*Library symbol*] [*Library of Congress*] (LCLS) .... AAP-A
Auburn University at Montgomery (GAGS) .... Auburn U (Montgomery)
Auburn University at Montgomery, Montgomery, AL [*OCLC symbol*] (OCLC) .... AAM

Auburn University at Montgomery, Montgomery, AL [*Library symbol*] [*Library of Congress*] (LCLS) .... AMU
Auburn University, Auburn, AL [*OCLC symbol*] (OCLC) .... AAA
Auburn University, Auburn, AL [*Library symbol*] [*Library of Congress*] (LCLS) .... AAP
Auburn, WA [*AM radio station call letters*] .... KBSG
Auburn, WA [*FM radio station call letters*] .... KGRG
Auburn-Cord-Duesenberg Club (EA) .... ACDC
Auburndale, FL [*AM radio station call letters*] .... WTWB
Auburndale, WI [*AM radio station call letters*] .... WLBL
Auburn-Lewiston [*Maine*] [*Airport symbol*] (AD) .... LEW
Auburn/Lewiston, ME [*Location identifier*] [*FAA*] (FAAL) .... LEW
Auburn/Lewiston, ME [*Location identifier*] [*FAA*] (FAAL) .... PDS
Auburn/Opelika [*Alabama*] [*Airport symbol*] (OAG) .... AUO
Auburn-Placer County Library, Auburn, CA [*OCLC symbol*] (OCLC) .... APR
Auburn-Placer County Library, Auburn, CA [*Library symbol*] [*Library of Congress*] (LCLS) .... CAuP
Auchinleck's Manuscript Cases, Scotch Court of Session [*A publication*] (DLA) .... Auch
Auchinoon [*Scotland*] [*Seismograph station code, US Geological Survey*] (SEIS) .... EAU
Auch/Lamothe [*France*] [*ICAO location identifier*] (ICLI) .... LFDH
Aucilla River Prehistory Project (SAUO) .... ARPP
Aucilla River Prehistory Project, Florida (SAUS) .... ARPP
Auckland [*New Zealand*] [*Seismograph station code, US Geological Survey*] (SEIS) .... AUC
Auckland [*New Zealand*] [*ICAO location identifier*] (ICLI) .... NZAK
Auckland [*New Zealand*] [*ICAO location identifier*] (ICLI) .... NZAQ
Auckland [*New Zealand*] [*ICAO location identifier*] (ICLI) .... NZZA
Auckland [*New Zealand*] [*ICAO location identifier*] (ICLI) .... NZZO
Auckland Astronomical Society (SAUO) .... AAS
Auckland City Art Gallery (SAUO) .... ACAG
Auckland Commercial and Technical Information Service [*New Zealand*] (CIST) .... ACTIS
Auckland Explorations Ltd. [*Vancouver Stock Exchange symbol*] .... AUK
Auckland Industrial Development Division (SAUO) .... AIDD
Auckland Industrial Development Laboratory (SAUO) .... AIDL
Auckland Islands (SAUS) .... Aucklands
Auckland Mounted Rifles (SAUO) .... AuckMtdRif
Auckland Nuclear Accessory Co. (SAUO) .... ANAC
Auckland Regional Authority (SAUO) .... ARA
Auckland Regional Rescue Helicopter Trust [*New Zealand*] [*FAA designator*] (FAAC) .... WPR
Auckland Science Teachers Association (SAUO) .... ASTA
Auckland University, Auckland, New Zealand [*Library symbol*] [*Library of Congress*] (LCLS) .... NzAU
Auckland University College (SAUO) .... AUC
Auckland/International [*New Zealand*] [*ICAO location identifier*] (ICLI) .... NZAA
Auction (ROG) .... AUCN
Auction .... AUCT
Auction Marketing Institute (NTPA) .... AMI
Auction Preferred Stock [*Investment term*] (DFIT) .... APS
Auction Register and Law Chronicle [*A publication*] (DLA) .... Auct Reg & L Chron
Auction Transfer Authority .... ATA
Auctioneer .... AUCTNR
Auctioneering .... ACTNRG
Auctioneering .... AUCTNRG
Auctioneers and Estate Agents Institute (SAUO) .... AEAI
Auctioneers and Valuers' Association of Western Australia .... AVAWA
Auctioneers and Valuers of Western Australia [*An association*] .... AVWA
Auctioneers Association of Canada .... AA of C
Auction-Market Preferred Stock .... AMPS
Auctores Antiquissimi [*Classical studies*] .... AA
Auctores Varii (SAUS) .... AAVV
Auctoris [*One that Gives Increase; an Originator*] [*Latin*] .... auct
Auctorum [*Of Authors*] [*Biology, taxonomy*] .... auct
Audeli Air Express [*Spain*] [*ICAO designator*] (FAAC) .... ADI
Audemars Piguet [*Trademark for line of watches*] (ECON) .... AP
Audi Air, Inc. [*ICAO designator*] (FAAC) .... AUD
Audi International Motor Car Club (EA) .... AIMCC
Audi Space Frame [*Concept car*] [*Automotive engineering*] .... ASF
audibility (SAUS) .... aud
audible (SAUS) .... aud
Audible (WGA) .... AUD
Audible Alarm (IAA) .... AA
Audible and Visual Indicator (SAUS) .... A&V
Audible Current Meter [*Electronics*] (DICI) .... ACM
Audible Doppler Enhancer [*Telecommunications*] (TEL) .... ADE
Audible Manufacturing Training Aid (SAUS) .... AMATA
Audible Rumble Loudness Level [*Stereo*] .... ARLL
Audible Signal (SAUS) .... AS
Audible Signal Devices [*JETDS nomenclature*] [*Military*] (CET) .... BZ
Audible User Interface [*Computer science*] (VERA) .... AUI
Audible Warning (SAUS) .... A-W
Audibly Instructed Manufacturing Operations [*Military*] .... AIMO
Audichron Recorded Information System (SAUS) .... ARIS
Audience (ADWA) .... aud
Audience Development Committee (EA) .... AUDELCO
Audience Interest Factor .... AIF
Audience Measurement by Market for Outdoor (NTCM) .... AMMO
Audience Participation Unit (WDAA) .... APU
Audience Reaction Assessment [*Television ratings*] [*British*] .... AURA
Audience Reaction Indicator (IIA) .... ARI
Audience Research (NTCM) .... AR
Audience Research Analysis (SAUS) .... ARA

Audience Research Bureau (IIA)	ARB
Audience Research Bureau (SAUO)	ARB
Audience Research Institute [*Also, AIPO*] (NTCM)	ARI
Audience Studies, Inc. [*Television program testing system*]	ASI
Audience Studies Incorporated (SAUO)	ASI
Audiences (WDMC)	auds
Audimeter/Diary System [*A. C. Nielson Co.*] (NTCM)	A/D
Audio (WDMC)	A
Audio (WDMC)	a
Audio [*or Audible or Audiology*] (MSA)	AUD
Audio Alarm Module [*Automotive engineering*]	AAM
Audio and Electroacoustics [*IEEE*]	AU
Audio and Power Connectors [*JETDS nomenclature*] [*Military*] (CET)	U
Audio Applications Programming Interface (SAUS)	AAPI
Audio Archives [*Record label*]	AudA
Audio Automatic Switch (CCCA)	AAS
Audio Bandpass Filter	ABF
Audio Bandpass Filter	ABPF
Audio Bandwidth	AB
Audio Book Club (SG)	KLB
Audio Capture and Playback Adapter (PCM)	ACPA
Audio Cartridge (WDMC)	ACR
Audio Cascading Style Sheets (SAUS)	ACSS
Audio Cassette Interface (SAUS)	ACI
Audio Cassette Recorder (IDOE)	acr
Audio Cassette Recorder (RDA)	ACR
Audio Cassette Recording (IDOE)	acr
Audio Center [*Command and Service Module*] [*NASA*]	AC
Audio Center - Receiver (KSC)	ACRC
Audio Center - Receiver (KSC)	ACRV
Audio Center - Transmitter (KSC)	ACTM
Audio Center Equipment (SAA)	ACP
Audio Center (or Centre) Module (SAUS)	ACM
Audio Center (or Centre) Receiver (SAUS)	ACRC
Audio Center (or Centre) Receiver (SAUS)	ACRV
Audio Center (or Centre) Transmitter (SAUS)	ACTM
Audio Central Control Unit (NASA)	ACCU
Audio CODEC 97 (SAUS)	AC97
Audio Collectors [*Record label*]	AudC
Audio Commercial Message Repeating Unit [*Device delivering a recorded commercial from cigarette vending machines*]	ACMRU
Audio Communications Controller (ROAS)	ACC
Audio Communications System	ACS
Audio Compression Manager (SAUS)	ACM
Audio Compression-3 (SAUS)	AC3
Audio Conducted Susceptibility (IAA)	ACS
Audio Control Center	ACC
Audio Control Panel (NASA)	ACP
Audio Data Communication [*Computer science*] (IAA)	ADC
Audio Data Sequence [*Telecommunications*] (NTCM)	ADSQ
Audio Decade Oscillator (SAUS)	ADO
Audio Decode Oscillator	ADO
Audio Devices (SAUS)	AUDEV
Audio Distribution Amplifier	ADA
Audio Distribution System (NASA)	ADS
Audio Dynamics Corporation (SAUO)	ADC
Audio End Instrument (MCD)	AEI
Audio Engineering Society (EA)	AES
Audio Engineering Society/ European Broadcast Union (SAUO)	AES/EBU
Audio Enhanced Computer Aided Learning (AIE)	AECAL
Audio Equipment (IAA)	AUDEQUIP
Audio Equipment (SAUS)	audequip
Audio Fidelity (NTCM)	AF
Audio File [*Computer science*] (IGQR)	AU file
Audio Flat Panel [*Speaker system*]	AFP
Audio Follow Video [*Tape editing*] (NTCM)	AFV
Audio Freight Claims (SAUS)	AFC
Audio Frequency [*Data transmission*]	AF
Audio Frequency (ABAC)	af
Audio Frequency Amplifier	AFA
Audio Frequency Apparatus	AFA
Audio Frequency Change	AFC
Audio Frequency Choke	AFC
Audio Frequency Coder	AFC
Audio Frequency Coder (or Coding) (SAUS)	AFC
Audio Frequency Interference	AFI
Audio Frequency Line Transformer (SAUS)	AFLT
Audio Frequency Magnetotelluric	AMT
Audio Frequency Modulation	AFM
Audio Frequency Shift (IEEE)	AFS
Audio Frequency Shift Key	AFSK
Audio Frequency Shift Keying (NITA)	AFSK
Audio Frequency Transformer	AFT
Audio Function Generator (MCD)	AFG
Audio High Density	AHD
Audio Home Recording Act of 1992	AHRA
Audio Information Exchange (SAUS)	AUDIX
Audio Input Frequency Tolerance	AIFT
Audio Input Level	AIL
Audio Institutional Membership [*Telecommunications*]	AIM
Audio Integrating System (DA)	AIS
Audio Interchange File Format [*Computer science*] (BTTJ)	AIFF
Audio Interchange Format	AIF
Audio Interface Format	AIFF
Audio Interface Unit (SAUS)	AIU
Audio Junction Box (MCD)	AJB
Audio King [*NASDAQ symbol*] (TTSB)	AUDK
Audio King, Inc. [*NASDAQ symbol*] (SAG)	AUDK
Audio King, Inc. [*Associated Press*] (SAG)	AudKng
Audio Level Meter	ALM
Audio Library Services of Northwestern Ontario, Lakehead University, Thunder Bay, Ontario [*Library symbol*] [*National Library of Canada*] (NLC)	OTBLA
Audio Lingual Education Press (KSC)	ALEP
Audio Lingual Method (SAUS)	ALM
Audio Load Compensator (MCD)	ALC
Audio Manufacturers Group (SAUO)	AMG
Audio Media Integration Standard [*Telecommunications*] (BARN)	AMIS
Audio Message Interchange Specification (SAUS)	AMIS
Audio Message Interface Standard (VERA)	AMIS
Audio MODEM Riser (SAUS)	AMR
Audio Modulation (SAUS)	AM
Audio Monitoring System (SAUS)	AMS
Audio News Release (WDMC)	ANR
Audio Notch Filter (SAUS)	ANF
Audio Operator (NTCM)	AO
Audio Oscillator	AO
Audio Peak Clipping Amplifier	APCA
Audio Playback Unit	APU
Audio Precision Series One Analyzer [*CD-sound quality test*] (PCM)	APSO
Audio Publishers Association [*Defunct*] (EA)	APA
Audio RAM (SAUS)	ARAM
Audio Rarities [*Record label*]	AudR
Audio Receive Only (NTCM)	ARO
Audio Recording Rights Coalition [*Defunct*] (EA)	ARRC
Audio Renaissance Tapes [*Los Angeles, CA*]	ART
Audio Reply (IEEE)	AUDREY
Audio Response	AR
Audio Response Control (BUR)	ARC
Audio Response Interface System (PDAA)	ARIS
Audio Response System	ARS
Audio Response Time-Shared System [*Computer science*] (MHDB)	ARTS
Audio Response Unit	ARU
Audio Ringing Codec Filter (SAUS)	ARCOFI
Audio Sensitivity	AS
Audio Signal (IAA)	AUDSNL
Audio Signal (SAUS)	audsnl
Audio Signal Processor (SAUS)	ASP
Audio Signal-to-Noise (SAUS)	AS/N
Audio Stream Handler (PCM)	ADSH
Audio Stream Input Output (SAUS)	ASIO
Audio Subsystem (SAUS)	ADS
Audio Support Equipment	ASE
Audio Switch Assembly [*Ground Communications Facility, NASA*]	ASWA
Audio Switching Matrix (IUSS)	ASM
Audio Tape (SAUS)	AT
Audio Tape Cassette Player Set	ATCPS
Audio Tape Recording	ATR
Audio Techniques and Evaluation Laboratory [*NASA*]	ATEL
Audio Teleconference Network [*Acadia University*] [*Wolfville, NS*] (TSSD)	ATN
Audio Teleconference (or Teleconferencing) (SAUS)	ATC
Audio Terminal Unit (NASA)	ATU
Audio Test Set (NITA)	ATS
Audio Thermal Unit (MCD)	ATU
Audio Tone Decoder	ATD
Audio Video (WDMC)	AV
Audio Video and Multimedia Services (SAUS)	AVMMS
Audio Video Interleave [*Computer science*]	AVI
Audio Video Market Place [*A publication*]	AVMP
Audio Video Review Digest [*A publication*]	AVRD
Audio Visual Association [*British*] (DBA)	AVA
Audio Visual Authoring [*Computer programming language*] (PCM)	AVA
Audio Visual Computer Display (SAUS)	AVCD
Audio Visual Connection (SAUS)	AVC
Audio Visual Drive (CDE)	AV drive
Audio Visual Innovations [*Computer science*]	AVI
Audio Visual Instructional Division (SAUO)	AVID
Audio Visual Interleaved [*Computer science*] (PCM)	AVI
Audio, Visual, Kinesthetic, and Oral [*Teaching techniques*] (EA)	AVKO
Audio Visual Library, University of Toronto [*UTLAS symbol*]	AVL
Audio Visual Service (ACAE)	AVS
Audio Visual Superimposed Electrocardiogram Presentation (SAUS)	AVSEP
Audio Voice Exchange	AVX
Audio Warning Amplifier (AAG)	AWA
Audio Wave Analyzer	AWA
Audio Waveform Amplifier and Converter [*Apple*] (VERA)	AWAC
Audio-Acitve Language Laboratory (SAUO)	AALAB
Audiobook Service to the Handicapped, British Columbia Library Services Branch, Burnaby [*Library symbol*] [*National Library of Canada*] (NLC)	BBLA
Audio-CD	CD-A
Audio-Connecting Equipment (SAUS)	ACE
Audio/Digital Systems [*Telecommunications service*] (TSSD)	A/DS
Audio-Follow-Video (SAUS)	AFV
Audiofrequency (SAUS)	AF
Audiofrequency (SAUS)	Audio
Audiofrequency Control [*Electronics*] (ECII)	AFC
Audio-Frequency Electromagnetic Noise (SAUS)	AFMAG
Audiofrequency Magnetic Fields [*Prospecting technique*]	AFMAG
Audio-Frequency Reactor (SAUS)	AFR
Audio-Frequency Signal Generator (SAUS)	AF SIG GEN

audiogenic (SAUS)	audio
Audiogenic Seizure [Medicine] (DB)	AGS
Audiogenic Seizure [Neurophysiology]	AS
Audiographic Conferencing (SAUS)	AGC
Audiographic Learning Facilities (or Facility) (SAUS)	ALF
Audiographic Teleconference	AGT
Audiographics Terminal (SAUS)	AGT
Audio-Lingual Language Programming (SAUS)	ALLP
Audiolingual Language Programming [Computer science]	ALLP
Audiologic Assessment [Medicine] (MELL)	AA
Audiological Society of Australia	ASA
audiologist (SAUS)	audiol
Audiologist	AUDLGST
Audiology	AUDLGY
Audiology and Speech Pathology (DAVI)	AUSPE
Audiometer Telephone Interface [for the hearing-impaired]	ATI
audiometrist (SAUS)	audiom
Audiometry (SAUS)	AUD
audiometry (SAUS)	audio
Audiometry Sweep Test	AST
Audio-Monitored Talk Amplifier (DNAB)	AMTA
audion (SAUS)	au
Audion (SAUS)	Au
Audio-Only	AO
Audiophile [Record label]	Aphe
Audiophile (SAUS)	Audio
Audioprothesis	AUDIOPR
Audio-Selectronic (SAUS)	ASC
Audiosonometry (IAA)	ASM
Audio-Tactile Display (PDAA)	ATD
Audiotape Recorder (WDMC)	ATR
[The] Audiotex Group [Princeton, NJ] [Telecommunications service] (TSSD)	TAG
Audio-Video Interactive	AVI
Audio/Video Interface (RALS)	AVI
Audio-Video Interleaved [Computer science]	AVI
Audio-Video Kernel (SAUS)	AVK
Audio/Video Recording System (SAUS)	AVRS
Audio-Video Recording System [Air Force]	AVRS
Audio-Video Subsystem Software (SAUS)	AVSS
Audiovisual (SAUS)	AUD
Audiovisual (SAUS)	A/V
Audio-Visual (IDOE)	a/v
Audiovisual	AV
Audio-Visual Aids Committee [British]	AVAC
Audio-Visual and Cartographic Archives division (SAUS)	AVCA
Audio-Visual and Cartographic Archives Division [National Archives of Canada] (GEOI)	AVCA
Audio/Visual Annunciator (SAUS)	AVA
Audiovisual Annunciator	AVA
Audio-Visual Center (SAUO)	AVC
Audiovisual, Computer, and Communication Office Automation	AVCCOA
Audiovisual Conference of Medical and Allied Sciences (SAUO)	ACMAS
Audio-Visual Connection (PCM)	AVC
Audio-Visual Copyright Society, Ltd. (SAUO)	AVCS
Audio-Visual Credit Interchange [Defunct] (EA)	AVCI
Audiovisual Display Unit	AVDU
Audio-Visual Display Unit	AVDU
Audiovisual Distribution System (MCD)	AVDS
Audio-Visual Division [Environmental Protection Agency] (GFGA)	AVD
Audiovisual Education Committee (SAUO)	AVEC-IFOS
Audiovisual Education in Neurosurgery	AVENS
Audio-Visual Group (SAUO)	AVG
Audiovisual Information System	AVIS
Audio-Visual Institute (SAUO)	AVI
Audio-Visual Instruction Department (SAUS)	AVID
Audiovisual Instructional Media Services Group (SAUO)	AIMS Group
Audio-Visual Instructional Technology [Military] (AABC)	AVIT
Audio-Visual Instructional Technology (SAUS)	AVIT
Audio-Visual Integrated Trainer (PDAA)	AVIT
Audio/Visual Interleave [Windows] [Computer science]	avi
Audiovisual Kit [Army]	AVK
Audio-Visual Language Association [British]	AVLA
Audio-Visual Learning Objectives Catalog (SAUS)	AVLOC
Audiovisual Liaison Officer [Army]	AVLO
Audiovisual Library, Art Gallery of Ontario, Toronto, Ontario [Library symbol] [National Library of Canada] (NLC)	OTAGAV
Audio-Visual Library, University of Toronto, Ontario [Library symbol] [National Library of Canada] (NLC)	OTUAV
Audiovisual Machine Readable Catalogue [A database] [British Library Automated Dissemination of Information] (NITA)	AVMARC
Audio-Visual Machine Readable Cataloguing (SAUS)	AVMARC
Audio-Visual Management Association (EA)	AVMA
Audio-Visual MARC file (SAUS)	AVMARC
Audio-Visual Modulator (SAUS)	AVM
Audiovisual Modulator	AVM
Audio/Visual Object (GEOI)	AVO
Audiovisual Online	AVLINE
Audiovisual Recording and Presentation (SAUS)	AVRP
Audiovisual Recording System (SAUS)	AVRS
Audio-Visual Research Association (SAUO)	AVRA
Audio-Visual Section (SAUS)	AVS
Audio-Visual Service Specific Convergence Sublayer	AVSSCS
Audio-Visual Squadron [Air Force]	AVS
Audiovisual Squadron [Air Force]	AVSq
Audiovisual Support Center [Army] (AABC)	AVSC

Audio-Visual Support Center (SAUO)	AVSC
Audiovisual System of Communication (SAUO)	ASC
Audio-Visual Terminal	AVT
Audio-Visual Tracking of Aircraft (SAUS)	AVISTA
Audiovisual Tutorial (SAUS)	AVT
AudioVisuals Online (SAUO)	AVLINE
Audiovisuals On-Line [National Library of Medicine] [Rockville Pike, MD] [Database]	AVLINE
Audiovisual-Tutorial [Instruction] [Media System Corp.]	AVT
Audiovisual/Visual Information (COE)	AV/VI
Audiovisuelle Integration (SAUS)	AVI
Audiovox Cl'A' [AMEX symbol] (TTSB)	VOX
Audiovox Corp. [Associated Press] (SAG)	Audvox
Audiovox Corp. [AMEX symbol] (SAG)	VOX
Audiovox Corp. Class A (SAUS)	VOX
Audit [or Audited]	A
Audit	AU
Audit [or Auditor] (AFM)	AUD
Audit (EBF)	Aud
Audit (ODBW)	aud
Audit	AUDT
Audit Agency	AA
Audit and Accounting Guides (SAUS)	AAG
Audit and Management Consulting Division [United Nations] (ECON)	AMCD
Audit Base Inventory System [IRS]	ABIS
Audit Basic Learning Examination (MCD)	ABLE
Audit Bureau of Circulations (EA)	ABC
Audit Bureau of Marketing Services (DOAD)	ABMS
Audit Bureau of Verification Services (SAUS)	ABVS
Audit Central Control Network (MCD)	ACCN
Audit Command Language	ACL
Audit Compliance (MCD)	AC
Audit, Control, and Evaluation (PDAA)	ACE
Audit, Control and Evaluation (SAUS)	ACE
Audit Control Point	ACP
Audit Discrepancy Report (NRCH)	ADR
Audit Entry [Accounting, finance] (BUR)	AE
Audit Entry Language [Burroughs Corp.]	AEL
Audit Error List	AEL
Audit Finding Report (SAUS)	AFR
Audit Information Management System [Department of the Treasury]	AIMS
Audit Information Management-Systems File [IRS]	AIMF
Audit Integrated Reporting System [IRS]	AIRS
Audit Inventory Team (SAUS)	AIT
Audit Item Disposition (MCD)	AID
Audit Liaison Division (AAGC)	OAL
Audit Management Information Reporting System (SAUS)	AMIR System
Audit Operations Staff [Environmental Protection Agency] (GFGA)	AOS
Audit Organization (DNAB)	AO
Audit Procedure Studies (SAUS)	APS
Audit Program Generator (SAUS)	APG
Audit Programs Division (AAGC)	OPD
Audit Reports Handbook [IRS]	ARH
Audit Technical Time Report [IRS]	ATTR
Audit Tracking and Control System (SAUS)	ATCS
Audit Trail	AT
Audit Trail Report [Military]	AUDITRPT
Audita Querela [A publication] (DLA)	Aud Q
Auditable Internal Control Systems (SAUS)	AUDICS
Auditing	ADTNG
Auditing (TBD)	Aud
Auditing Interpretations (SAUS)	AUI
Auditing Order Error	AOE
Auditing Practices Board [British] (ECON)	APB
Auditing Practices Committee [British]	APC
Auditing Standards Board	ASB
Auditing Standards Division Statements of Position (SAUS)	AUD-SOP
Auditing Standards Executive Committee (SAUO)	AUDSEC
Auditing Standards Executive Committee (EBF)	AudSEC
audition (SAUS)	aud
Auditor (EBF)	Aud
Auditor (ADWA)	aud
Auditor (MSA)	AUDTR
Auditor Camerae [Auditor of the Papal Treasury]	AC
Auditor Freight Accounts	AFA
Auditor Freight Claims	AFC
Auditor Freight Overcharge Claim	AFOC
Auditor Freight Receipts	AFR
Auditor Freight Traffic	AFT
Auditor General [Military]	AG
Auditor General of Canada (SAUO)	AGCan
Auditor General of the Navy	AUDGENAV
Auditor General of the Navy (DNAB)	AUDGENNAV
Auditor General's Department [Air Force]	AGD
Auditor General's Office	AGO
Auditor General's Report [Canada] [Information service or system] (IID)	AGR
Auditor of Receipts	AR
Auditor of Revenue	AR
Auditor of Traffic Accounts	ATA
Auditor Overcharge Claims	AOC
Auditorium	ADTRM
Auditorium (SAUS)	Aud
Auditorium (DAC)	AUD
Auditorium (VRA)	audit
Auditorium and Training Facility [NASA] (NASA)	ATF

Auditoriums (WDMC) .... auds
Auditory (ABBR) .... A
Auditory (DAVI) .... aud
Auditory and Kinesthetic Sensation [*Medicine*] (DB) .... AKS
Auditory Apperception Test [*Psychology*] .... AAT
Auditory Attending Task (SAUS) .... AAT
Auditory Brain Response [*Neurology*] (DAVI) .... ABR
Auditory Brainstem Evoked Response [*Medicine*] (DMAA) .... ABER
Auditory Brainstem Evoked Response [*Medicine*] (MELL) .... ABR
Auditory Brainstem Implant [*Hearing technology*] .... ABI
Auditory Brainstem Response [*Neurophysiology*] .... ABR
Auditory Brain-Stem-Evoked Potential [*Neurology*] (DAVI) .... ABEP
Auditory Continuous Performance Test (TMMY) .... ACPT
Auditory Cortex [*Neurology*] .... AC
Auditory Discrimination in Depth [*Program*] [*Education*] .... ADD
Auditory Discrimination Test [*"Wepman"*] [*Education*] .... ADT
Auditory Gross Error .... AGE
Auditory Induction .... AI
Auditory Information Display .... AID
Auditory Input Task [*Computer science*] .... AUDIT
Auditory Integrated Training .... AIT
Auditory Integration Training .... AIT
Auditory Integrative Abilities Test .... AIAT
Auditory Interneuron [*Neurology*] .... AIN
Auditory, Kinesthetic, Tactile Approach [*Teaching method*] .... AKT
Auditory Memory Span [*Psychometrics*] .... AMS
Auditory Nerve Activating Substance [*Physiology*] .... ANAS
Auditory Performance [*Medicine*] (MELL) .... AP
Auditory Processing Disorder .... APD
Auditory Prosthesis [*Medicine*] (MELL) .... AP
Auditory Selective Attention Test (TMMY) .... ASAT
Auditory Sensation Area .... ASA
Auditory Vocal Automatic [*Test*] [*Medicine*] (DB) .... AVA
Auditory Vocal Sequencing [*Medicine*] (DMAA) .... AVS
Auditory-Evoked Magnetic Field [*Neurophysiology*] .... AEF
Auditory-Evoked Potential [*Neurophysiology*] .... AEP
Auditory-Evoked Response [*Neurophysiology*] .... AER
Auditory-Flutter Fusion (PDAA) .... AFF
Auditory-Flutter Fusion Threshold (PDAA) .... AFFT
Auditory-Visual (DAVI) .... AV
Audits & Surveys Worldwide [*AMEX symbol*] (TTSB) .... ASW
Audits & Surveys Worldwide, Inc. [*AMEX symbol*] (SAG) .... ASW
Audits & Surveys Worldwide, Inc. [*Associated Press*] (SAG) .... AudSurv
Audits of Certain Nonprofit Organizations (SAUO) .... ACNO
Audits of Data Quality [*Environmental science*] (EPAT) .... ADQ
Audits of Great Britain .... AGB
Audits of Great Britain, Ltd. (SAUO) .... AGB
Audits of State and Local Governmental Units (SAUO) .... ASLGU
Audit Polycystic Kidney Disease [*Medicine*] (CPH) .... ADPKD
Audre Recognition Systems, Inc. [*Vancouver Stock Exchange symbol*] .... ADY
Audrey Resources, Inc. [*Toronto Stock Exchange symbol*] .... AUY
Audubon [*A publication*] (BRI) .... Aud
Audubon Artists (EA) .... AA
Audubon County Courthouse, Audubon, IA [*Library symbol*] [*Library of Congress*] (LCLS) .... IaAuCoC
Audubon County Journal, Exira, IA [*Library symbol*] [*Library of Congress*] (LCLS) .... IaExJ
Audubon, IA [*Location identifier*] [*FAA*] (FAAL) .... ADU
Audubon, IA [*FM radio station call letters*] (RBYB) .... KSOM
Audubon National Wildlife Refuge (SAUS) .... ANWR
Audubon Naturalist Society of the Central Atlantic States (SAUO) .... ANS
Audubon News-Advocate, Audubon, IA [*Library symbol*] [*Library of Congress*] (LCLS) .... IaAuNA
Audubon Public Library, Audubon, IA [*Library symbol*] [*Library of Congress*] (LCLS) .... IaAu
Audubon Public School, Audubon, MN [*Library symbol*] [*Library of Congress*] (LCLS) .... MnAudS
Audubon Regional Library, Clinton, LA [*Library symbol*] [*Library of Congress*] (LCLS) LCli
Audubon Shrine and Wildlife Sanctuary (COE) .... ASWS
Audubon Society of Rhode Island, Providence, RI [*Library symbol*] [*Library of Congress*] (LCLS) .... RPAS
Audubon Yacht Club (SAUO) .... AYC
Auer Bodies [*Medicine*] .... AB
Auerbach Information Management System (SAUS) .... AIMS
Auerbach Power Index (NITA) .... API
Auerbach's Plexus [*Medicine*] (MELL) .... AP
Auf Bestellung [*On Order*] [*German*] (ILCA) .... aB
Auffuehrung [*Performance*] [*German*] .... Auff
Aufgabe [*Task*] [*German*] .... Aufg
Aufklaerungsgruppe [*Air Forces Reconnaissance Unit*] [*German military - World War II*] .... AG
Auflage [*Edition*] [*German*] .... AUFL
Aufsatz [*Essay*] [*German*] .... Aufs
Aufschlagzuender ohne Verzoegerung [*Nondelay fuze*] [*German military - World War II*] .... AZOV
Aufsichtsrat [*Supervisory Board*] [*German*] .... AR
Auftrag [*Order*] [*German*] .... Auftr
Aufzeichnung [*Note*] [*German*] .... Aufz
Augat, Inc. [*NYSE symbol*] (SPSG) .... AUG
Augat, Inc. [*Associated Press*] (SAG) .... Augat
Augdome Corp. [*Vancouver Stock Exchange symbol*] .... AUG
Augenklinik und Poliklinik (SAUS) .... UAK
Augenwirtschaftsgesetz (SAUS) .... AWG
Auger and Elevator Manufacturers Council (EA) .... AEMC
Auger Electron (AAEL) .... AE
Auger Electron Analysis .... AEA
Auger Electron Appearance Potential Spectroscopy .... AEAPS
Auger Electron Spectrometry [*or Spectroscopy*] .... AES
Auger Electron Spectroscopy (SAUS) .... AES
Auger Emission Spectroscopy (SAUS) .... AES
Auger Hole (SAUS) .... AH
Auger Photoelectron Coincidence Spectroscopy (SAUS) .... APECS
Auger Spectroscopy (SAUS) .... AS
Augere [*Increase*] [*Pharmacy*] .... AUG
Aughey Spark Chamber .... ASC
Augite (SAUS) .... au
Augmenied Human Intellegence (SAUS) .... AHI
Augment (MSA) .... AGMT
Augment (AABC) .... AUG
Augment Docking Target Adapter (SAUS) .... ADTA
Augment Thermally Electric Propulsion (SAUS) .... ATEP
Augmentation [*Music*] .... A
Augmentation .... AGN
Augmentation [*Music*] .... Aug
Augmentation [*Music*] .... Augm
Augmentation Concentration [*Biochemistry*] .... AC
Augmentation Mammaplasty [*Medicine*] (MELL) .... AM
Augmentation Reaction (SAUS) .... AR
Augmentation Reliability (MCD) .... AR
Augmentation Research Center [*Stanford Research Institute*] .... ARC
Augmentation Reserve Force (SAUO) .... ARF
Augmentation Stabilization Equipment .... ASE
Augmentation System .... AS
Augmentation System Test Bed (SAUO) .... ASTB
Augmentative (ADWA) .... aug
Augmentative (ADWA) .... augm
Augmentative .... AUGM
Augmentative and Alternative Communication [*A publication*] .... AAC
Augmented Air Jet .... AAJ
Augmented Assault Fire Units [*Army*] (AABC) .... AAFU
Augmented Ballast Expulsion (SAUS) .... ABE
Augmented Bibliographic Citation (ADA) .... ABC
Augmented Built-In Test .... AMBIT
Augmented Catalytic Thruster (MCD) .... ACT
Augmented Contact Support Set [*TOW*] .... ACSS
Augmented Content-Addressed Memory .... ACAM
Augmented Data Manipulation (or Manipulator) (SAUS) .... ADM
Augmented Deflector Exhaust Nozzle [*Aviation*] .... ADEN
Augmented Direct Support Unit (SAUO) .... ADSU
Augmented Energy Management (MCD) .... AEM
Augmented Export Schema (SAUS) .... AES
Augmented Final Fade (SAA) .... AF
Augmented Finite State Machine [*Computer science*] .... AFSM
Augmented Fire Support Terminal (SAUS) .... AFST
Augmented Histamine Test [*Medicine*] (MAE) .... AHT
Augmented Human Intellect (KSC) .... AHI
Augmented Ignition Delay Sensor (CAAL) .... AIDS
Augmented Index and Digest [*Information Retrieval Ltd.*] [*British*] (NITA) .... AID
Augmented Insulin Tolerance Test (SAUS) .... AITT
Augmented Landing Site (NAKS) .... ALC
Augmented Logistics Support (MCD) .... ALS
Augmented Lunar Module (MCD) .... ALM
Augmented Lunar Payload Module .... ALPM
Augmented Materials Production (ABAC) .... AMP
Augmented Off-Gas System [*Nuclear energy*] (NRCH) .... AOG
Augmented Phase Wave [*Thermodynamics*] .... APW
Augmented Plane Wave .... APW
Augmented Predictive Analyzer [*Computer science*] (DIT) .... APA
Augmented Programming Training [*Computer science*] (IEEE) .... APT
Augmented Proportional Navigation (SAUS) .... APN
Augmented RCMAT (SAUS) .... ARCMAT
Augmented Reentry Test (IAA) .... ART
Augmented Relational Intelligence Analysis System (SAUS) .... ARIAS
Augmented Roman (ADA) .... AR
Augmented Roman Alphabet (DGA) .... ARA
Augmented Satellite Launch Vehicle [*India*] .... ASLV
Augmented Spark Igniter [*NASA*] .... ASI
Augmented Spherical Wave (AAEL) .... ASW
Augmented Support (ACAE) .... AS
Augmented Support Period [*or Plan*] .... ASP
Augmented Support Plan (SAUS) .... ASP
Augmented Support Unit (SAUO) .... ASU
Augmented Surveyor [*NASA*] (MCD) .... AS
Augmented Synoptic Oceanographic Data Acquisition System [*Navy*] (MSC) .... ASODAS
Augmented System Igniter (SAUS) .... ASI
Augmented System Ignition [*NASA*] (KSC) .... ASI
Augmented Target Docking Adapter [*Gemini*] [*NASA*] .... ATDA
Augmented Target Screener (or Screening) Subsystem (SAUS) .... ATSS
Augmented Target Screening Subsystem (MCD) .... ATSS
Augmented Telemetry .... ATM
Augmented Test Set, Guided Missile System (ACAE) .... ATSGMS
Augmented Thermally Electric Propulsion .... ATEP
Augmented Thrust Propulsion .... ATP
Augmented Transition (WDAA) .... AT
Augmented Transition Network [*Language analysis*] .... ATN
Augmented Transition Tree (MCD) .... ATT
Augmented V Lead, Left Arm [*Electrocardiogram*] [*Medicine*] .... AVL
Augmented V Lead, Left Leg [*Electrocardiogram*] [*Medicine*] .... AVF

Augmented V Lead, Right Arm [Electrocardiogram] [Medicine] ...... AVR
Augmented Visual Carrier Aircraft Recovery System (MCD) ...... AVCARS
augmented Voltage Left arm (SAUS) ...... aVL
augmented Voltage left Foot (SAUS) ...... aVF
augmented Voltage Right arm (SAUS) ...... aVR
Augmenter Wing Jet STOL [Short Takeoff and Landing] Research Aircraft ...... AWJSRA
Augmenting Unit [Navy] ...... AUGU
Augmentor Fuel Flow Test Unit (MCD) ...... AFFTU
Augmentor of Liver Regeneration [Biochemistry] ...... ALR
Augmentor Wing (SAUS) ...... AW
Augmentor Wing Research Aircraft [Aviation] (MCD) ...... AWRA
Augmentor-Wing [Aviation] ...... AW
Augmitto Explorations Ltd. [Toronto Stock Exchange symbol] ...... AU
Augsburg College and Seminary, Minneapolis, MN [Library symbol] [Library of Congress] (LCLS) ...... MnMA
Augsburg College, Minneapolis, MN [OCLC symbol] (OCLC) ...... MNA
Augsburg Hospital [Germany] [ICAO location identifier] (ICLI) ...... EDII
Augsburg Transmission Upgrade (MCD) ...... ATU
Augsburg/Gablingen [Germany] [ICAO location identifier] (ICLI) ...... EDOX
Augsburg/Muehlhausen [Germany] [ICAO location identifier] (ICLI) ...... EDMA
August (CDAI) ...... A
August ...... AG
August (ADWA) ...... Ag
August ...... AU
August (EY) ...... AUG
August (BEE) ...... Aug
August (ROG) ...... AUGT
August 15 and February 15 [Denotes interest payable on these dates] [Business term] ...... A & F 15
August and February [Denotes semiannual payments of interest or dividends in these months] [Business term] ...... A & F
August Derleth Society (EA) ...... ADS
August, November, February, and May [Denotes quarterly payments of interest or dividends in these months] [Business term] ...... ANFM
Augusta [Georgia] [Airport symbol] ...... AGS
Augusta [Maine] [Airport symbol] (OAG) ...... AUG
Augusta [Maine] [ICAO location identifier] (ICLI) ...... KAUG
Augusta Airways [ICAO designator] (AD) ...... BH
Augusta & Summerville Railroad Co. [AAR code] ...... AUS
Augusta, AR [FM radio station call letters] ...... KABK
Augusta Area Committee for Health Information Resources [Library network] ...... AACHIR
Augusta Chronicle-Herald, Augusta, GA [Library symbol] [Library of Congress] (LCLS) ...... GAuACH
Augusta College (SAUO) ...... AC
Augusta College (GAGS) ...... Augusta C
Augusta College, Augusta, GA [Library symbol] [Library of Congress] (LCLS) ...... GAuA
Augusta College, Augusta, GA [OCLC symbol] (OCLC) ...... GJG
Augusta, GA [Location identifier] [FAA] (FAAL) ...... DNL
Augusta, GA [Location identifier] [FAA] (FAAL) ...... EMR
Augusta, GA [Location identifier] [FAA] (FAAL) ...... MZX
Augusta, GA [FM radio station call letters] ...... WACG
Augusta, GA [Television station call letters] ...... WAGT
Augusta, GA [AM radio station call letters] (BROA) ...... WAWX-AM
Augusta, GA [AM radio station call letters] ...... WBBQ
Augusta, GA [FM radio station call letters] ...... WBBQ-FM
Augusta, GA [FM radio station call letters] ...... WEKL
Augusta, GA [AM radio station call letters] ...... WFAM
Augusta, GA [FM radio station call letters] ...... WFXA
Augusta, GA [Television station call letters] ...... WFXG
Augusta, GA [AM radio station call letters] ...... WGAC
Augusta, GA [Television station call letters] ...... WJBF
Augusta, GA [AM radio station call letters] ...... WKIM
Augusta, GA [FM radio station call letters] ...... WLPE
Augusta, GA [AM radio station call letters] ...... WRDW
Augusta, GA [Television station call letters] ...... WRDW-TV
Augusta, GA [AM radio station call letters] ...... WTHB
Augusta, GA [FM radio station call letters] ...... WZNY
Augusta Huiell Seaman Society [Defunct] (EA) ...... AHSS
Augusta, IL [FM radio station call letters] (RBYB) ...... WAHI-FM
Augusta, KS [FM radio station call letters] ...... KLLS
Augusta, ME [Location identifier] [FAA] (FAAL) ...... CCM
Augusta, ME [Television station call letters] ...... WCBB
Augusta, ME [AM radio station call letters] (RBYB) ...... WEZW
Augusta, ME [FM radio station call letters] ...... WKCG
Augusta, ME [AM radio station call letters] ...... WMDR
Augusta, ME [FM radio station call letters] ...... WMME-FM
Augusta Mental Health Institute, Augusta, ME [Library symbol] [Library of Congress] (LCLS) ...... MeAM
Augusta Mental Health Institute, Augusta, ME [OCLC symbol] (OCLC) ...... MEZ
Augusta Public Library (SAUO) ...... APL
Augusta Railroad Co. [AAR code] ...... AUG
Augusta Railroad Company (SAUO) ...... AUG
Augusta Technical Institute, Augusta, GA [Library symbol] [Library of Congress] (LCLS) ...... GAuT
Augusta Township Public Library, Brockville, Ontario [Library symbol] [National Library of Canada] (NLC) ...... OBAT
Augusta Warshaw Advertising Library, New York, NY [Library symbol] [Library of Congress] (LCLS) ...... NNAA
Augustan Prose Sample [Machine readable selection of English prose] (NITA) ...... APS
Augustan Reprint Society (EA) ...... ARS
Augustan Society (EA) ...... AS

Augustana College (SAUO) ...... AC
Augustana College (GAGS) ...... Augustana C
Augustana College, Rock Island, IL [OCLC symbol] (OCLC) ...... ICY
Augustana College, Rock Island, IL [Library symbol] [Library of Congress] (LCLS) ...... IRA
Augustana College, Sioux Falls, SD [OCLC symbol] (OCLC) ...... SDA
Augustana College, Sioux Falls, SD [Library symbol] [Library of Congress] (LCLS) ...... SdSifA
Augustana Historical Society (EA) ...... AHS
Augustana Hochschule Bibliothek, Neuendettelsau, Federal Republic of Germany [Library symbol] [Library of Congress] (LCLS) ...... GyNeA
Augustana Institute Bulletin (journ.) (SAUS) ...... AIB
Augustana Luther League [Later, ILLL] ...... ALL
Augustana Swedish Institute [Later, AHS] ...... ASI
Augusta-Richmond County Library, Augusta, GA [Library symbol] [Library of Congress] (LCLS) ...... GAu
Augusta-Richmond County Library, Augusta, GA [Library symbol] [Library of Congress] (LCLS) ...... GAuCL
Augusta-Ross Township District Library (McKay Library), Augusta, MI [Library symbol] [Library of Congress] (LCLS) ...... MiAu
Auguste Reymond, SA ...... ARSA
Augustine [Deceased, 430] [Authority cited in pre-1607 legal work] (DSA) ...... Ag
Augustine [354-430AD] [Classical studies] (OCD) ...... August
Augustine Island [Alaska] [Seismograph station code, US Geological Survey] (SEIS) ...... AGI
Augustine Island [Alaska] [Seismograph station code, US Geological Survey] (SEIS) ...... AUF
Augustine Island [Alaska] [Seismograph station code, US Geological Survey] (SEIS) ...... AUI
Augustine Island [Alaska] [Seismograph station code, US Geological Survey] (SEIS) ...... AUM
Augustines de la Misericorde de Jesus [Religious order] [Canada] ...... AMJ
Augustinian Educational Association [Defunct] (EA) ...... AEA
Augustinian Historical Institute, Villanova University, Villanova, PA [Library symbol] [Library of Congress] (LCLS) ...... PVAHI
Augustinian Nuns of Contemplative Life (TOCD) ...... OSA
Augustinian Recollect Fathers (SAUO) ...... AR
Augustinian Recollect Sisters [An association] [Australia] ...... AR
Augustinian Recollect Sisters (TOCD) ...... OAR
Augustinian Secondary Educational Association (EA) ...... ASEA
Augustinian Sisters of Our Lady of Consolation (TOCD) ...... OSA
Augustiniani Assumptionis [Assumptionists] [Roman Catholic men's religious order] ...... AA
[The] Augustinians (TOCD) ...... osa
[The] Augustinians (TOCD) ...... OSA
Augustinus Berous [Deceased, 1554] [Authority cited in pre-1607 legal work] (DSA) ...... Aug Bero
Augustinus Berous [Deceased, 1554] [Authority cited in pre-1607 legal work] (DSA) ...... Augu
Augustus Downs [Australia] [Airport symbol] [Obsolete] (OAG) ...... AUD
Augustus Resources Ltd. [Vancouver Stock Exchange symbol] ...... AST
AUI Peace Language International (EA) ...... APLI
AUI Peace Language International (SAUO) ...... aPLI
Aujeszky's Disease [Medicine] (MELL) ...... AD
Aujeszky's Disease Virus [Medicine] (DB) ...... ADV
Aujourd'hui [Today] [French] ...... AUJ
Auke Bay Coastal Fisheries Research Center [National Oceanic and Atmospheric Administration] (PDAA) ...... ABCFRC
Auke Bay Fisheries Laboratory (SAUO) ...... ABFL
Auki [Solomon Islands] [Airport symbol] (OAG) ...... AKS
Auki [Solomon Islands] [Seismograph station code, US Geological Survey] (SEIS) ...... AUK
Ault & Wiborg (DGA) ...... A & W
Ault, Inc. [NASDAQ symbol] (NQ) ...... AULT
Ault Public Library, Ault, CO [Library symbol] [Library of Congress] (LCLS) ...... CoAul
Aulus Caius Decimus [Coin inscription] (ROG) ...... ACD
Aumentado [Enlarged] [Spanish] (BARN) ...... aum
Aunes [French Ells] ...... AU
AU-Pakistan Post and Telegraph Union (SAUS) ...... APPTU
A-Upper (SAUS) ...... AU'
Aupracondylar Knee-Ankle[Orthosis] [Orthopedics] (DAVI) ...... SKA
Aupraorbita Artery [Anatomy] (DAVI) ...... SOA
Aur [Marshall Islands] [Airport symbol] (OAG) ...... AUL
AUR Resources, Inc. [Toronto Stock Exchange symbol] ...... AUR
Aura Systems, Inc. [NASDAQ symbol] (NQ) ...... AURA
Aura Systems, Inc. [Associated Press] (SAG) ...... AuraSy
Aurakhmat [Former USSR] [Seismograph station code, US Geological Survey] [Closed] (SEIS) ...... AUR
Aural ...... AUR
Aural Aided Acquisition Signal (ACAE) ...... AAAS
Aural and Visual Code (SAUS) ...... AVC
Aural Bearing Generator ...... ABG
Aural Cascading Style Sheets (SAUS) ...... ACSS
Aural Comprehension Course (DNAB) ...... ACC
Aural Perception Heterodyne Exciter [Inter-Technology Exchange Ltd.] [Psychoacoustics] ...... APHEX
Aural Style Sheet (SAUS) ...... ASS
Aural Training (SAUS) ...... au tr
Aural Transducer (SAUS) ...... AT
Aural Warning Logic Unit (MCD) ...... AWLU
Aural Warning System [Aviation] (PIPO) ...... AWS
Aurally Coded English [in The ACE Spelling Dictionary] [British] ...... ACE
Auramine-O [A biological stain] ...... AO
Aurangabad [India] [Airport symbol] (OAG) ...... IXU

Aurangabad [*India*] [*ICAO location identifier*] (ICLI) ... VAAU
Auranofin [*An organogold*] ... AF
Auranteum [*Orange (Rind)*] [*Pharmacy*] (ROG) ... AURANT
Aurelia Public Library, Aurelia, IA [*Library symbol*] [*Library of Congress*] (LCLS) ... IaAur
Aurelia Sentinel, Aurelia, IA [*Library symbol*] [*Library of Congress*] (LCLS) ... IaAurS
Aurelian [*of Scriptores Historiae Augustae*] [*Classical studies*] (OCD) ... Aurel
Aurelio y Gustavo Pompa Estrella [*Mexico*] [*FAA designator*] (FAAC) ... POM
Aurelius Corbulus [*Flourished, 16th century*] [*Authority cited in pre-1607 legal work*] (DSA) ... Aurel Corbul
Aures Unitas [*Both Ears*] [*Latin*] ... AU
Aurex Resources, Inc. [*Vancouver Stock Exchange symbol*] ... ARX
Aurich [*Germany*] [*ICAO location identifier*] (ICLI) ... EDZR
auricle (SAUS) ... aur
Auricular [*or Auricle*] [*Also, AUR*] [*Medicine*] ... A
Auricular [*or Auricle*] [*Also, A*] [*Medicine*] ... AUR
Auricular [*Cardiology*] (DAVI) ... auric
Auricular Chondritis [*Medicine*] (MELL) ... AC
Auricular Fibrillation [*Medicine*] ... AF
Auricular Fibrillation [*Medicine*] (MAE) ... aur fib
Auricular Premature Beat [*Medicine*] (MAE) ... APB
Auriculocarotid [*Medicine*] (MAE) ... AC
auriculocarotid (SAUS) ... ac
Auriculo-Osteodysplasia [*Medicine*] ... AOD
Auriculotemporal Nerve [*Medicine*] (MELL) ... ATN
Auriculoventricular [*Medicine*] ... AV
Auriculoventricular Valve Opening [*Medicine*] (DB) ... AO
Auriga [*Constellation*] ... Aur
Auriga [*Constellation*] ... Auri
Aurignacian (VRA) ... Aurig
Aurigny Air Services [*ICAO designator*] (AD) ... GR
Aurigny Air Services Ltd. [*British*] [*ICAO designator*] (FAAC) ... AUR
Aurillac [*France*] [*Airport symbol*] [*Obsolete*] (OAG) ... AUR
Aurillac [*France*] [*ICAO location identifier*] (ICLI) ... LFLW
Aurinarium [*Ear Cone*] [*Medicine*] ... AURIN
Aurintricarboxylic Acid (MAE) ... ATA
Auris [*Ear*] [*Latin*] ... A
Auris [*Ear*] [*Latin*] ... AUR
Auris Dextra [*Right Ear*] [*Latin*] ... AD
Auris Dextra [*Right Ear*] [*Otorhinolaryngology*] (DAVI) ... Aurd
Auris Laeva [*Left Ear*] [*Medicine*] ... AL
Auris Sinistra [*Left Ear*] [*Latin*] ... AS
Auris Sinistra [*Left Ear*] [*Otorhinolaryngology*] (DAVI) ... Aurs
Auris Uterque [*Each Ear*] [*Latin*] ... AU
Auristillae [*Ear Drops*] [*Pharmacy*] ... AURIST
Auristillae [*Ear Drops*] [*Pharmacy*] ... AURISTILL
Aurizon Mines Ltd. [*Toronto Stock Exchange symbol*] [*Vancouver Stock Exchange symbol*] ... ARZ
Aurogin Resources [*Vancouver Stock Exchange symbol*] ... AUQ
Auromatic Production Recording (SAUS) ... APR
Auropalpebral Reflex [*Response to sound*] ... APR
Aurora Air Service, Inc. (SAUO) ... ARA
Aurora Borealis ... AURBO
Aurora, Canadian Forces Base, Greenwood, Nova Scotia [*Library symbol*] [*National Library of Canada*] (NLC) ... NSGCFA
Aurora, CO [*AM radio station call letters*] ... KEZW
Aurora, CO [*AM radio station call letters*] (RBYB) ... KMXA-AM
Aurora, CO [*AM radio station call letters*] ... KYBG
Aurora College (SAUO) ... AC
Aurora College, Aurora, IL [*Library symbol*] [*Library of Congress*] (LCLS) ... IAurC
Aurora College, Aurora, IL [*OCLC symbol*] (OCLC) ... ICA
Aurora Electronics [*AMEX symbol*] (TTSB) ... AUR
Aurora Electronics Co., Inc. [*Formerly, BSN Corp.*] [*AMEX symbol*] (SPSG) ... AUR
Aurora Electronics Co., Inc. [*Formerly, BSN Corp.*] [*Associated Press*] (SAG) ... AurorEl
Aurora, Elgin & Fox River (SAUS) ... AEFR
Aurora, Elgin & Fox River Electric R. R. [*AAR code*] ... AEFR
Aurora, Elgin & Fox River Electric Railroad (SAUO) ... AEFR
Aurora Environmental, Inc. [*NASDAQ symbol*] (NQ) ... AURE
Aurora Foods [*NYSE symbol*] (SG) ... AOR
Aurora Foundation (EA) ... AF
Aurora High School PRECIS Project [*UTLAS symbol*] ... AUE
Aurora High School PRECIS Project [*UTLAS symbol*] ... AUR
Aurora High School, PRECIS Project, Aurora, ON, Canada [*Library symbol*] [*Library of Congress*] (LCLS) ... CaOAuHS
Aurora Historical Society, Aurora, ON, Canada [*Library symbol*] [*Library of Congress*] (LCLS) ... CaOAuH
Aurora Historical Society, Ontario [*Library symbol*] [*National Library of Canada*] (NLC) ... OAUH
Aurora, IL [*Location identifier*] [*FAA*] (FAAL) ... ARR
Aurora, IL [*AM radio station call letters*] ... WBIG
Aurora, IL [*Television station call letters*] ... WEHS
Aurora, IL [*AM radio station call letters*] ... WKKD
Aurora, IL [*FM radio station call letters*] ... WKKD-FM
Aurora, IL [*FM radio station call letters*] ... WYSY
Aurora, IN [*FM radio station call letters*] ... WSCH
Aurora Memorial Park (SAUS) ... AMP
Aurora, MO [*FM radio station call letters*] ... KGMY
Aurora, MO [*AM radio station call letters*] ... KSWM
Aurora Museum, Aurora, ON, Canada [*Library symbol*] [*Library of Congress*] (LCLS) ... CaOAUM
Aurora Museum, Ontario [*Library symbol*] [*National Library of Canada*] (BIB) ... OAUM
Aurora, NC [*Location identifier*] [*FAA*] (FAAL) ... AUR
Aurora, NC [*FM radio station call letters*] (BROA) ... WFPF-FM
Aurora, NE [*Location identifier*] [*FAA*] (FAAL) ... AUH
Aurora, NE [*FM radio station call letters*] ... KLRB
Aurora, OR [*Location identifier*] [*FAA*] (FAAL) ... HBU
Aurora Public Library, Aurora, CO [*Library symbol*] [*Library of Congress*] (LCLS) ... CoAur
Aurora Public Library, Aurora, CO [*OCLC symbol*] (OCLC) ... COB
Aurora Public Library, Aurora, IL [*Library symbol*] [*Library of Congress*] (LCLS) ... IAur
Aurora Public Library, Aurora, IN [*Library symbol*] [*Library of Congress*] (LCLS) ... InAur
Aurora Public Library, Aurora, MN [*Library symbol*] [*Library of Congress*] (LCLS) ... MnAur
Aurora Public Library, Aurora, ON, Canada [*Library symbol*] [*Library of Congress*] (LCLS) ... CaOAu
Aurora Public Library, Ontario [*Library symbol*] [*National Library of Canada*] (NLC) ... OAU
Aurora Pump (SAUS) ... AP
Aurora Scientific Academies (EA) ... ASA
Auroral Absorption Index (CET) ... Ka
Auroral Atmospheric Radiance Code (SAUS) ... AARC
Auroral Electrojet [*Index*] ... AE
Auroral Hydrogen Line ... AHL
Auroral Hydrogen Line Emission ... AHLE
Auroral Imaging Observatory (CARB) ... AURIO
Auroral Imaging Remote Sensor (SAUS) ... AIRS
Auroral Ionospheric Mapper (SAUS) ... AIM
Auroral Kilometric Radiation [*Planetary science*] ... AKR
Auroral Large Imaging System ... ALIS
Auroral Multiscale Midex (SAUS) ... AMM
Auroral Photography Experiment (SAUS) ... APE
Auroral Time [*Geophysics*] ... AT
Auroral/Ionospheric Remote Sensor (SAUS) ... AIRS
Aurtex, Inc. [*NASDAQ symbol*] (SAG) ... AURT
Aurtex, Inc. [*Associated Press*] (SAG) ... Aurtex
Aurukun Mission [*Australia*] [*Airport symbol*] (OAG) ... AUU
Aurum [*Gold*] [*Chemical element*] ... Au
Aurum [*Gold*] [*Latin*] ... AUR
Aurum [*Gold*] [*Numismatics*] ... AV
Aurum Software, Inc. [*NASDAQ symbol*] (SAG) ... AURM
Aurum Software, Inc. [*Associated Press*] (SAG) ... AurmSft
Aus Alter und Neuer Zeit [*Illustrated Addition to Israelitisches Familienblatt, Hamburg*] [*A publication*] (BJA) ... AAUNZ
aus einer fremden Nachricht zitieren (SAUS) ... Quoten
Aus-Air [*Australia*] [*ICAO designator*] (FAAC) ... AUZ
Ausbildung [*Education*] [*German*] ... Ausb
Ausbildung der Ausbilder (SAUS) ... AdA
Auscultation [*Medicine*] (AAMN) ... AUS
Auscultation [*Medicine*] (AAMN) ... AUSC
Auscultation (SAUS) ... Ausc
Auscultation [*Medicine*] (AAMN) ... AUSCUL
Auscultation and Palpation [*Medicine*] (AAMN) ... A & P
Auscultation and Palpation (SAUS) ... A&P
Auscultation and Percussion (SAUS) ... A&P
Auscultation and Percussion [*Medicine*] ... A & P
Auscultation and Percussion (SAUS) ... A and P
Auscultation and Percussion (SAUS) ... A-P
Ausfrech-Melcher-Grossapach [*Mercedes-Benz cars*] [*High-performance parts supplier*] ... AMG
Ausfuehrungsanweisung [*Regulatory Instructions*] [*German*] (DLA) ... AA
Ausfuehrungsgesetz zur Burgerlichen Gesetzbuch [*Implementing law to the civil code*] [*German*] (ILCA) ... AGBGB
Ausgabe [*Edition*] [*German*] ... AUSG
Ausgabestelle [*Distribution Point*] [*German military - World War II*] ... A
Ausgleichrechnung (SAUS) ... AR
Ausgleichsleistungs-Gesetz (SAUS) ... AusglLeistG
Auskunftstelle (SAUS) ... Ausk-St
Auslandumzugskosten-Verordnung (SAUS) ... AUV
AUSLANG [*Australian Supply Language*] **Dictionary of Item Names** [*A publication*] ... ADIN
Ausonius [*Fourth century AD*] [*Classical studies*] (OCD) ... Auson
Auspex Gold Ltd. [*Vancouver Stock Exchange symbol*] ... APJ
Auspex Systems [*NASDAQ symbol*] (TTSB) ... ASPX
Auspex Systems, Inc. [*NASDAQ symbol*] (SAG) ... ASPX
Auspex Systems, Inc. [*Associated Press*] (SAG) ... Auspex
Auspuff-Turbolaeder [*Exhaust turbocharger*] [*German*] [*Automotive engineering*] ... ATL
Ausschu¤ Terminologie (SAUS) ... AT
Ausserdem [*Furthermore*] [*German*] ... ausserd
Ausstellung [*Exhibition*] [*German*] ... Ausst
Ausstellungs-Tegung fuer Chemisches Apparatewesen [*Triennial international chemical engineering exhibition*] ... ACHEMA
Austalian National Commission for UNESCO (SAUS) ... ANC UNESCO
Austalia-New Zealand-United Kingdom Intergovernmental Agreement On Climate Change (SAUS) ... ANZUK
Aust&N.ZealandBk9.125%Pfd [*NYSE symbol*] (TTSB) ... ANZPr
Austasia Aquaculture (SAUS) ... Austasia Aquac
Austast-Synchron-Signal (MCD) ... AS-SIGNAL
Austell, GA [*AM radio station call letters*] ... WAOS
Austempered Ductile Iron [*Metallurgy*] ... ADI
Austen Riggs Center, Inc., Stockbridge, MA [*Library symbol*] [*Library of Congress*] (LCLS) ... MStocA
Austenite (IAA) ... A
Austenite and Ferrite [*Manufacturing materials*] (IAA) ... AAF

austenitic (SAUS) ... austen
Austere Airborne Ranging and Sighting System (MCD) ... AARSS
Austere Heads-Up Display [*Aviation*] (MCD) ... AHUD
Austere Surface-to-Air Missile System ... ASAMS
Austere Tank Retrofittable Optronic System (SAUS) ... ATREOS
Austere Version (MCD) ... AV
Austerity ... AU
Austin [*Nevada*] [*Airport symbol*] [*Obsolete*] (OAG) ... ASQ
Austin [*Minnesota*] [*Airport symbol*] (AD) ... AUM
Austin [*Texas*] [*Seismograph station code, US Geological Survey*] [*Closed*] (SEIS) ... AUS
Austin Airways [*ICAO designator*] (AD) ... UH
Austin & Pickersgill Ltd. (SAUO) ... A&P
Austin Area Vocational-Technology Institute, Austin, MN [*OCLC symbol*] (OCLC) ... AVT
Austin College (SAUO) ... AC
Austin College, Sherman, TX [*OCLC symbol*] (OCLC) ... IAU
Austin College, Sherman, TX [*Library symbol*] [*Library of Congress*] (LCLS) ... TxShA
Austin Community College (SAUS) ... ACO
Austin Community College, Austin, MN [*OCLC symbol*] (OCLC) ... ACO
Austin Community College, Austin, TX [*OCLC symbol*] (OCLC) ... TAC
Austin Community College, Austin, TX [*Library symbol*] [*Library of Congress*] (LCLS) ... TxAuCC
Austin Concept Vehicle ... ACV
Austin Data Recorder [*Military*] (SAA) ... ADR
Austin Healy Club (SAUO) ... AHC
Austin, IN [*FM radio station call letters*] ... WJAA
Austin, IN [*FM radio station call letters*] (RBYB) ... WJCP-FM
Austin, IN [*FM radio station call letters*] ... WJLR
Austin Junior College [*Later, Austin Community College*] [*Minnesota*] ... AJC
Austin, MN [*Location identifier*] [*FAA*] (FAAL) ... AUM
Austin, MN [*Television station call letters*] ... KAAL
Austin, MN [*AM radio station call letters*] ... KAUS
Austin, MN [*FM radio station call letters*] ... KAUS-FM
Austin, MN [*FM radio station call letters*] ... KMSK
Austin, MN [*AM radio station call letters*] ... KNFX
Austin, MN [*Television station call letters*] ... KSMQ
Austin Moore Prosthesis [*Medicine*] (DAVI) ... AM Pros
Austin, Nichols & Company, Inc. (SAUO) ... ANO
Austin Peay State College [*Later, Austin Peay State University*] [*Tennessee*] ... APSC
Austin Peay State University [*Tennessee*] ... APSU
Austin Peay State University (GAGS) ... Aus Peay St U
Austin Peay State University, Clarksville, TN [*Library symbol*] [*Library of Congress*] (LCLS) ... TCIA
Austin Peay State University, Clarksville, TN [*OCLC symbol*] (OCLC) ... TPA
Austin Presbyterian Theological Seminary, Austin, TX [*Library symbol*] [*Library of Congress*] (LCLS) ... TxAuP
Austin Public Library (SAUS) ... TxAu
Austin Public Library, Austin, MN [*Library symbol*] [*Library of Congress*] (LCLS) ... MnAu
Austin Public Library, Austin, TX [*Library symbol*] [*Library of Congress*] (LCLS) ... TxAu
Austin Public Library, Austin, TX [*OCLC symbol*] (OCLC) ... TXG
Austin Public Library, Austin-Travis County Collection, Austin, TX [*Library symbol*] [*Library of Congress*] (LCLS) ... TxAu-AT
Austin Public Schools Media, Austin, MN [*OCLC symbol*] (OCLC) ... APS
Austin Public Schools Media, Austin, MN [*Library symbol*] [*Library of Congress*] (LCLS) ... MnAuPS
Austin Resources, Inc. [*Vancouver Stock Exchange symbol*] ... AUS
Austin Rover [*British-built automobile*] ... AR
Austin Rover Cars of North America, Inc. ... ARCONA
Austin Rover Group Ltd. ... ARG
Austin Rover Japan ... ARJ
Austin Service Center [*IRS*] ... AUSC
Austin Seven Clubs Association (EAIO) ... A7CA
Austin State Hospital, Austin, TX [*Library symbol*] [*Library of Congress*] (LCLS) ... TxAuSHos
Austin State Junior College, Austin, MN [*Library symbol*] [*Library of Congress*] (LCLS) ... MnAuS
Austin Ten Drivers Club [*High Wycombe, Buckinghamshire, England*] (EAIO) ... ATDC
Austin Trumbull Radio [*Air transport radio prior to April 15, 1967*] (MCD) ... ATR
Austin, TX [*Location identifier*] [*FAA*] (FAAL) ... BSM
Austin, TX [*Location identifier*] [*FAA*] (FAAL) ... EBL
Austin, TX [*Location identifier*] [*FAA*] (FAAL) ... GFQ
Austin, TX [*FM radio station call letters*] ... KASE
Austin, TX [*FM radio station call letters*] ... KAZI
Austin, TX [*Television station call letters*] (RBYB) ... KEYE-TV
Austin, TX [*AM radio station call letters*] ... KFON
Austin, TX [*FM radio station call letters*] ... KKMJ
Austin, TX [*AM radio station call letters*] ... KLBJ
Austin, TX [*FM radio station call letters*] ... KLBJ-FM
Austin, TX [*Television station call letters*] ... KLRU
Austin, TX [*Television station call letters*] (BROA) ... KLRU-DT
Austin, TX [*FM radio station call letters*] ... KMFA
Austin, TX [*Television station call letters*] ... KNVA
Austin, TX [*FM radio station call letters*] ... KPEZ
Austin, TX [*Television station call letters*] ... KTBC
Austin, TX [*FM radio station call letters*] ... KUT
Austin, TX [*AM radio station call letters*] ... KVET
Austin, TX [*FM radio station call letters*] ... KVET-FM
Austin, TX [*FM radio station call letters*] ... KVRX
Austin, TX [*Television station call letters*] ... KVUE
Austin, TX [*Television station call letters*] ... KXAN
Austin, TX [*Location identifier*] [*FAA*] (FAAL) ... MMR
Austin Vocational Technical Institute, Austin, MN [*Library symbol*] [*Library of Congress*] (LCLS) ... MnAuV
Austin/Bergstrom Air Force Base [*Texas*] [*ICAO location identifier*] (ICLI) ... KBSM
Austin-Crothersville News, Austin, IN [*Library symbol*] [*Library of Congress*] (LCLS) ... InAusN
Austin-Healey Club of America (EA) ... AHCA
Austin-Healey Sports and Touring Club (EA) ... AHSTC
Austin-Moore [*Prosthesis*] [*Medicine*] ... A-M
Austin-Moore Prosthesis [*Medicine*] ... A-MP
Austin-Moore Prosthesis [*Medicine*] (DMAA) ... A-M Pr
Austin/Robert Mueller Municipal [*Texas*] [*ICAO location identifier*] (ICLI) ... KAUS
Austin's Appeal Reports [*Ceylon*] [*A publication*] (ILCA) ... Aus Rep
Austin's Ceylon Reports [*A publication*] (DLA) ... Austin (Ceylon)
Austin's English County Court Cases [*1867-69*] [*A publication*] (DLA) ... Aust
Austin's English County Court Reports [*A publication*] (DLA) ... Austin CC
Austin's International [*NASDAQ symbol*] (TTSB) ... AUST
Austin's International, Inc. [*Associated Press*] (SAG) ... AustInt
Austin's Kandran Appeals [*Ceylon*] [*A publication*] (DLA) ... Aust KA
Austin's Lectures on Jurisprudence [*A publication*] (DLA) ... Aust Jr
Austin's Lectures on Jurisprudence [*A publication*] (ILCA) ... Aust Jur
Austin's Lectures on Jurisprudence, Abridged [*A publication*] (DLA) ... Aust Jur Abr
Austin's Reports [*Ceylon*] [*A publication*] (DLA) ... Austin
Austins Steak & Saloon, Inc. [*Associated Press*] (SAG) ... Austins
Austins Steak & Saloon, Inc. [*NASDAQ symbol*] (SAG) ... STAK
Austins Steaks & Saloon [*NASDAQ symbol*] (TTSB) ... STAK
Austra Resources Corp. [*Vancouver Stock Exchange symbol*] ... ARC
Austrain Institute Library, New York, NY [*Library symbol*] [*Library of Congress*] (LCLS) ... NNAIL
Austral Islands of Polynesia (SAUS) ... Australs
Austral Lineas Aereas [*Airline*] [*Argentina*] (EY) ... ALA
Austral Lineas Aereas [*ICAO designator*] (AD) ... AU
Austral Lineas Aereas [*Argentina*] [*ICAO designator*] (FAAC) ... AUT
Australasia (ADA) ... A'ASIA
Australasia (SAUS) ... Alasia
Australasia (BARN) ... AUSTL
Australasia (SAUS) ... Austral
Australasia (ADA) ... AUSTSIA
Australasia [*MARC geographic area code*] [*Library of Congress*] (LCCP) ... u----
Australasia and South East Asia Network [*Computer science*] (TNIG) ... AUSEAnet
Australasian (ADA) ... A'ASIAN
Australasian (ROG) ... AUSTRAL
Australasian (SAUS) ... Australas
Australasian (ADA) ... AUSTSN
Australasian Academy of Broadcast Arts and Sciences ... AABAS
Australasian Advisory Committee on Land Information (SAUO) ... AACLI
Australasian Antarctic Expedition (SAUS) ... AAE
Australasian Association for Logic ... AAL
Australasian Association for the History, Philosophy and Social Studies of Science (SAUO) ... AAHPSSS
Australasian Association of Clinical Biochemists (SAUO) ... AACB
Australasian Association of Secretaries and Managers ... AASM
Australasian Association of University Teachers of Accountancy (SAUO) ... AAUTA
Australasian Bulletin of Medical Physics and Biophysics (SAUS) ... Australas Bull Med Phy Bio
Australasian Business Conditions Bulletin [*A publication*] ... Aust Bus Cond Bull
Australasian Catholic Record [*A publication*] ... Australas Cath Rec
Australasian College for Emergency Medicine (SAUO) ... ACEM
Australasian College of Nutritional & Environmental Medicine (SAUO) ... ACNEM
Australasian College of Physical Scientists and Engineers in Medicine ... ACPSEM
Australasian College of Physical Scientists in Medicine (SAUO) ... ACPSM
Australasian Communications Law Association (SAUO) ... ACLA
Australasian Computer Graphics Association (SAUO) ... ACGA
Australasian Conference of Assessment and Certification Agencies ... ACACA
Australasian Conference on Chemical Engineering (SAUO) ... CHEMECA
Australasian Corrosion Association (EAIO) ... ACA
Australasian Corrosion Association (SAUO) ... ACA
Australasian Corrosion Association. Preprinted Papers of the Annual Conference (journ.) (SAUS) ... Prepr Pap Annu Conf Australas Corros Assoc
Australasian Corrosion Centre (SAUS) ... ACC
Australasian Corrosion Engineering (journ.) (SAUS) ... Australas Corros Eng
Australasian Data Exchange Centre (GEOI) ... AUSDEC
Australasian Drama Studies ... Aus Drama St
Australasian Drug Information Service (SAUS) ... ADIS
Australasian Drug Information Services ... ADIS
Australasian Electrical Times [*A publication*] ... Aust Elec Times
Australasian Engineer [*A publication*] ... Aust Eng
Australasian Engineer (journ.) (SAUS) ... Australas Eng
Australasian Faculty of Occupational Medicine (SAUO) ... AFOM
Australasian Faculty of Public Health Medicine (SAUS) ... AFPHM
Australasian Federation for Medical and Veterinary Mycology (SAUO) ... AFMVM
Australasian Genetic Support Group Association ... AGSA
Australasian Institute of Chartered Accountants ... AICA
Australasian Institute of Fundraising ... AIF
[*The*] **Australasian Institute of Fundraising** ... TAIF
Australasian Institute of Mining and Metallurgy (SAUO) ... AI of M&M
Australasian Institute of Mining and Metallurgy (SAUS) ... AI of M&M
Australasian Insurance and Banking Record [*A publication*] ... Australas Insur Banking Rec
Australasian Insurance Journal [*A publication*] ... Australas Insur J
Australasian Journal of Philosophy [*A publication*] (APTA) ... AJP

Australasian Journal of Philosophy [*A publication*] ..... Aus J Phil
Australasian Labour Federation (SAUO) ..... ALF
Australasian Land Information Management Group (SAUO) ..... ALIMG
Australasian Law Students Association ..... ALSA
Australasian Medical Index [*A publication*] ..... AMI
Australasian Official Journal of Patents, Trade Marks and Designs (journ.) (SAUS) ..... AOJPTMD
Australasian Oil and Gas Review (journ.) (SAUS) ..... AOGRDE
Australasian Performing Right Association. Journal (journ.) (SAUS) ..... APRAJ
Australasian Pharmaceutical Science Association (SAUO) ..... APSA
Australasian Photo Review [*A publication*] ..... Aust Photo Rev
Australasian Photo Review (journ.) (SAUS) ..... APR
Australasian Physical & Engineering Sciences in Medicine (SAUS) ..... APESM
Australasian Plant Pathology Society (SAUO) ..... APPS
Australasian Political Studies Association (SAUO) ..... APSA
Australasian Porcelain Art Teachers [*An association*] ..... APAT
Australasian Presentation and Multi-Media Association ..... APMMA
Australasian Public Libraries and Information Services [*A publication*] ..... APLIS
Australasian Radiology (journ.) (SAUS) ..... Australas Radiol
Australasian Regional Association of Zoological Parks and Aquaria ..... ARAZP
Australasian Regional Association of Zoological Parks and Aquaria (GVA) ..... ARAZPA
Australasian Register of Agricultural Consultants ..... ARAC
Australasian Religion Index [*A publication*] (APTA) ..... ARI
Australasian Schoolmaster and Literary Review [*A publication*] ..... Australas Schoolmaster
Australasian Seabird Group (EA) ..... ASG
Australasian Sketcher [*A publication*] ..... AS
Australasian Smaller Companies Trust ..... ASCT
Australasian Society for HIV [*Human Immunodeficiency Virus*] **Medicine** ..... ASHM
Australasian Society for HIV Medicine (SAUO) ..... ASHM
Australasian Society for the Study of Animal Behaviour ..... ASSAB
Australasian Society of Animal Production (SAUO) ..... ASAP
Australasian Society of Clinical & Experimental Pharmacologists & Toxicologists (SAUO) ..... ASCEPT
Australasian Society of Engineers ..... ASE
Australasian Spatial Data Exchange Centre (SAUO) ..... AUSDEC
Australasian Species Management Plan ..... ASMP
Australasian Study of Parliament Group ..... ASPG
Australasian Subterranean Clover and Alternative Legumes Improvement Program (SAUO) ..... ASCALIP
Australasian Typographical Journal [*A publication*] ..... ATJ
Australasian Universities Language and Literature Association (EAIO) ..... AULLA
Australasian Urban and Regional Information Systems Association (GEOI) ..... AURISA
Australasian Urban and Regional Information Systems Association Inc. (SAUO) ..... AURISA
Australasian Wildlife Management Society (SAUO) ..... AWMS
Australasians in Property in London ..... AIPIL
Australasien Conference on the Mechanics of Structures and Materials (SAUO) ..... ACMS
Australasisan Universities Modern Language Association (SAUO) ..... AUMLA
Australia ..... AS
Australia (SAUS) ..... Astrl
Australia [*MARC country of publication code*] [*Library of Congress*] (LCCP) ..... at
Australia (SAUS) ..... Atl
Australia [*ANSI two-letter standard code*] (CNC) ..... AU
Australia [*ANSI three-letter standard code*] (CNC) ..... AUS
Australia (ADWA) ..... Aus
Australia (ADWA) ..... Aust
Australia (ADWA) ..... Austl
Australia ..... AUSTL
Australia ..... AUSTR
Australia (VRA) ..... Austr
Australia (NTIO) ..... Austral
Australia ..... AUSTRAL
Australia [*IYRU nationality code*] (IYR) ..... KA
Australia [*MARC geographic area code*] [*Library of Congress*] (LCCP) ..... u-at-
Australia - Papua New Guinea [*Submarine cable*] [*Telecommunications*] ..... APNG
Australia 1938 Bulletin [*A publication*] ..... A 1938 B
Australia. Aeronautical Research Labo-ratories. Materials Note (journ.) (SAUS) ..... Mater Note Aust Aeronaut Res Lab
Australia. Aeronautical Research Laboratories. Materials Report (journ.) (SAUS) ..... Mater Rep Aust Aeronaut Res lb
Australia. Aeronautical Research Laboratories. Metallurgy Report (journ.) (SAUS) ..... Metall Rep Aeronaut Res Lab Aust
Australia. Aeronautical Research Laboratories Metallurgy Technical Memorandum (journ.) (SAUS) ..... Metall Tech Memo Aust Aeronaut Res Lab
Australia. Aeronautical Research Laboratories. Structures and Materials Report (journ.) (SAUS) ..... Struct Mater Rep Aust Aeronaut Res Lab
Australia. Aeronautical Research Laboratories Structures Note (journ.) (SAUS) ..... Struct Note Aust Aeronaut Res Lab
Australia. Aeronautical Research Laboratories Structures Report (journ.) (SAUS) ..... Struct Rep Aust Aeronaut Res Lab
Australia Ag (SAUS) ..... Au-Ag
Australia Air Publications [*A publication*] ..... AAP
Australia and New Zealand (SAUS) ..... Antipodes
Australia and New Zealand Army Corps (ADWA) ..... Anzac
Australia & New Zealand Bank [*NYSE symbol*] (SPSG) ..... ANZ
Australia and New Zealand Bank (SAUO) ..... ANZ Bank
Australia & New Zealand Banking Group [*Associated Press*] (SAG) ..... AusNZ
Australia & New Zealand Banking Group [*Associated Press*] (SAG) ..... AustNZ
Australia & New Zealand Corps (SAUS) ..... ANZAC
Australia and New Zealand Emigrants and Families Association (SAUO) ..... ANZEFA
Australia and New Zealand Exploration Company (SAUO) ..... ANZECO
Australia and New Zealand Funds Management [*Banking*] ..... ANZFM
Australia and New Zealand Passenger Conference (SAUO) ..... ANZPC
Australia and New Zealand Professional Photographers Association (SAUO) ..... ANZPPA
Australia and New Zealand Society for Theological Study (SAUO) ..... ANZSTS
Australia and New Zealand Society for Theologyical Study (SAUS) ..... ANZSTS
Australia and New Zealand Trade Advisory Committee [*British Overseas Trade Board*] (DS) ..... ANZTAC
Australia & N.Z. Bk ADS [*NYSE symbol*] (TTSB) ..... ANZ
Australia and South Pacific External Studies Association (SAUO) ..... ASPESA
Australia Antigen [*Immunology*] (DAVI) ..... AA
Australia Antigen [*Immunology*] ..... Au
Australia Antigen [*Immunology*] (MAE) ..... Au Ag
Australia Antigen (DB) ..... AuAg
Australia Antigen [*Medicine*] (MAH) ..... Au(l)
Australia Antigen Radioimmunoassay [*Immunology*] (AAMN) ..... AAR
Australia Asia Airlines [*Air carrier designation symbol*] ..... AAA
Australia Asia Airlines Ltd. [*ICAO designator*] (FAAC) ..... AAU
Australia. Australian Radiation Laboratory. Technical Report Series ARL/TR (journ.) (SAUS) ..... Tech Rep Ser ARL/TR Aust Radiat Lab
Australia Braford Society ..... ABS
Australia Canada Association (ADA) ..... ACA
Australia, Canada, New Zealand, United Kingdom, United States (SAUO) ..... AUCANNZUKUS
Australia, Canada, United Kingdom, United States (ADA) ..... AUCANUKUS
Australia, Canada, United Kingdom, United States (ACAE) ..... AUSCANUCUS
Australia, Canada, United Kingdom, United States (MCD) ..... AUSCANUKUS
Australia, China, Hong Kong, Indonesia, Japan, Malaysia, New Zealand, Philippines, Singapore, South Korea, Taiwan, Thail (SAUS) ..... Pacific Basin Countries
Australia. Commonwealth Bureau of Census and Statistics. Queensland Office. Bulletin (journ.) (SAUS) ..... Q Census&Statistics Bul
Australia. Commonwealth Bureau of Census and Statistics. South Australian Office. Bulletin (journ.) (SAUS) ..... SA Ceasus&Statistics Bul
Australia. Commonwealth Scientifc and Industrial Research Organisation. Marine Laboratories. Report (journ.) (SAUS) ..... RCMLDR
Australia. Commonwealth Scientific and Industrial Organisation. Division of Fisheries and Oceanography. Fisheries Synopsis (journ.) (SAUS) AOFSA9
Australia. Commonwealth Scientific and Industrial Research Organisation. Division of Food Preservation. Technical Paper (journ.) (SAUS) ..... AOFPAY
Australia. Commonwealth Scientific and Industrial Research Organisation. Division of Land Research and Regional Survey. Technical Paper (journ.) (SAUS) ..... AOLPAU
Australia. Commonwealth Scientific and Industrial Research Organisation. Division of Meteorological Physics. Technical Paper (journ.) (SAUS) ..... AOMPAZ
Australia. Commonwealth Scientific and Industrial Research Organisation. Division of Plant Industry. Annual Report (journ.) (SAUS) ..... AOP
Australia. Commonwealth Scientific and Industrial Research Organisation. Division of Plant Industry. Field Station Record (journ.) (SAUS) ..... AOIRAL
Australia. Commonwealth Scientific and Industrial Research Organisation. Division of Plant Industry. Technical Paper (journ.) (SAUS) ..... APIPAM
Australia. Commonwealth Scientific and Industrial Research Organisation. Division of Tropical Crops and Pastures Tropical Agronomy Technical Memorandum (SAUS) ..... Trop Agron Tech Memo Aust CSIRO Div Trop Crops Pastures
Australia. Commonwealth Scientific and Industrial Research Organisation. National Measurement Laboratory. Technical Pape (SAUS) ..... Natl Meas Lab Tech Pap CSIRO Anst
Australia Commonwealth Scientific and Industrial Research Organisation. National Standards Laboratory. Technical Paper (SAUS) ..... Natl Stand Lab Tech Pap CSIRO Aust
Australia Container Services (SAUO) ..... ACS
Australia Council Press Clips [*Database*] ..... ACP
Australia. Defence Standards Laboratories. Technical Note (journ.) (SAUS) ..... Tech Note Def Stand Lab Aust
Australia. Department of Foreign Affairs. Treaty Series [*A publication*] ..... Aust DFA Treaty Series
Australia. Department of Supply. Aeronautical Research Laboratories. Structures and Materials Note (journ.) (SAUS) ..... Struct Mater Note Aust Aeronaut Res Lab
Australia Esperanto-Ascoio (SAUO) ..... AEA
Australia Europe Container Service (SAUO) ..... AECS
Australia Fan Club (EA) ..... AFC
Australia First [*Political party*] ..... AF
Australia France Technical Exchange (SAUS) ..... AFTEX
Australia Hepatitis-Associated Antigen [*Immunology*] (MAE) ..... AUHAA
Australia in Print [*Book distributor*] ..... AIP
Australia Institute of Mining and Metallurgy (SAUO) ..... AusIMM
Australia. Institute of Science and Industry. Bulletin [*A publication*] ..... Inst Sci & Indust Bull
Australia International Defence Equipment Exhibition ..... AIDEX
Australia Kangaroo Club [*Defunct*] (EA) ..... AKC
Australia. Materials Research Laboratories. Technical Note (journ.) (SAUS) ..... Tech Note Mater Res Lab Aust
Australia National University (SAUS) ..... ANU
Australia, New Zealand and Malaysia (SAUS) ..... ANZAM
Australia, New Zealand, and Malaysia [*Defense pact*] (BARN) ..... ANZAM
Australia, New Zealand, and the United States [*Signatories to the Tripartite Security Treaty of 1951*] ..... ANZUS
Australia, New Zealand, and United Kingdom ..... ANZUK
Australia, New Zealand and United Kingdom. Military alliance (SAUO) ..... ANZUK
Australia New Zealand Land Information Council (GEOI) ..... ANZLIC

Australia, New Zealand, United States (SAUS) ANZUS
Australia, New Zealand, US [*Pacific Council*] (EBF) ANZUS
Australia. Radio Propagation Committee. Ionospheric Bulletin [*A publication*] ARPC Ionospheric Bull
Australia School Library Association ASLA
Australia Serum Hepatitis [*Medicine*] (DMAA) AuS
Australia Serum Hepatitis [*Antigen*] [*Immunology*] (MAE) AuSH
Australia Standard White [*Variety of wheat*] ASW
Australia Straits Container Line (SAUO) ASCL
Australia, Tasmania, New Zealand and islands of Melanesia (SAUS) Australasian
Australia Telescope (SAUS) AT
Australia Telescope Compact Array ATCA
Australia Telescope National Facility ATNF
Australia Television International ATVI
Australia-Brazil Chamber of Commerce ABCC
Australia-Britain Society ABS
Australia-British Trade Association ABTA
Australia-China Business Co-Operation Committee ACBCC
Australia-China Business Cooperation Committee (SAUO) ACBCC
Australia-China Business Council ACBC
Australia-China Chamber of Commerce ACCC
Australia-China Friendship Society ACFS
Australia.Commonwealth Scientific and Industrial Research Organisation. Groundwater Research. Technical Paper (journ.) (SAUS) GRTPEP
Australia/East India Outward Shipping Conference (SAUS) EASTINDIACON
Australia-France Technological Exchange Scheme AFTEX
Australia-India Chamber of Commerce AICC
Australia-Indonesia Business Council AIBC
Australia-Indonesia Youth Exchange Program AIYEP
Australia-Israel Chamber of Commerce and Industry AICCI
Australia-Japan International Finance (SAUO) AJIF
Australia-Japan Research Centre [*Australian National University*] AJRC
Australia-Korea Chamber of Commerce and Industry AKCCI
Australia-Korea Foundation AKF
Australia-Malaysia Chamber of Commerce AMCC
Australian A
Australian (SAUS) As
Australian AUST
Australian (BEE) Aust
Australian (SAUS) Austral
Australian - French Metals Corporation (SAUO) AFMECO
Australian Abalone Producers' Association AAPA
Australian Aboriginal Studies [*A publication*] Aus Ab St
Australian Academic and Research Libraries [*A publication*] Aust Acad Res Libs
Australian Academic and Research Libraries (journ.) (SAUS) Austr Acad Res Libr
Australian Academic and Research Network (SAUO) AARNET
Australian Academic and Research Network [*Computer science*] (TNIG) AARNet
Australian Academy of Anatomy AAA
Australian Academy of Art AAA
Australian Academy of Cricket AAC
Australian Academy of Optometry AAO
Australian Academy of Paediatrics AAP
Australian Academy of Science (SAUO) AAS
Australian Academy of Technological Science and Engineering (SAUO) AATSE
Australian Academy of the Humanities (SAUO) AAH
Australian Accountancy Student [*A publication*] Aust Account Student
Australian Accountant [*A publication*] Aust Acctnt
Australian Accounting Standard Committee (SAUO) AASC
Australian Acoustic Society (SAUO) AAS
Australian Acoustical Society (SAUO) AAS
Australian Administrative Law Bulletin [*A publication*] AALB
Australian Administrative Law Bulletin [*A publication*] AAL Bull
Australian Administrative Law Bulletin [*A publication*] ADL Bull
Australian Advanced Air Traffic Services (GAVI) AAATS
Australian Advanced Air Traffic System (SAUS) TAATS
Australian Advisory Council on Bibliographical Services (SAUO) AACOBS
Australian Aerial Agricultural Association (SAUO) AAAA
Australian Aero Club (SAUO) AAC
Australian Aerobatic Club AAC
Australian Aeronautical Academy AAA
Australian Affiliation of Herpetological Societies AAHS
Australian Agricultural Economics Society (SAUO) AAES
Australian Agricultural Machinery Manufacturers' Association AAMMA
Australian Air Freight Forwarding Association (SAUO) AAFFA
Australian Air International AAI
Australian Air League New South Wales Boys Group AALNSWBG
Australian Air League Victorian Group AALVG
Australian Air Pilots Mutual Benefit Fund AAPMBF
Australian Air Services (SAUO) AAS
Australian Aircraft Consortium (LAIN) AAC
Australian Airline Flight Engineers Association (SAUO) AAFEA
Australian Airlines AA
Australian Airlines [*ICAO designator*] (FAAC) AUS
Australian Airlines [*Airline flight code*] (ODBW) TN
Australian Alps of New South Wales and Victoria (SAUS) Aust Alps
Australian Alt Society (SAUO) AAS
Australian Amateur Football Council AAFC
Australian Amateur Ice Racing Council AAIRC
Australian Amateur Water Polo Association AAWPA
Australian American Education Foundation (SAUS) AAEF
Australian and New Zealand Association for Canadian Studies ANZACS
Australian and New Zealand Association for Medical Education (SAUO) ANZAME
Australian & New Zealand Association for the Advancement of Science (WDAA) ANZAAS
Australian and New Zealand College of Anaesthetists (SAUO) ANZCA
Australian and New Zealand Commentary on Halsbury's Laws of England [*A publication*] ANZC Hals
Australian and New Zealand Conveyancing Report [*A publication*] ACR
Australian and New Zealand Council for the Care of Animals in Research and Teaching (SAUO) ANZCCART
Australian and New Zealand Environment and Conservation Council ANZECC
Australian and New Zealand Environment Council (SAUO) ANZEC
Australian and New Zealand Environmental Report (journ.) (SAUS) ANV
Australian and New Zealand Equal Opportunity Law and Practice [*A publication*] AEOP
Australian and New Zealand Federation of Animal Societies ANZFAS
Australian and New Zealand Graduates Association of Malaysia (SAUO) ANZGAM
Australian and New Zealand Income Tax Reports [*A publication*] (DLA) ANZITR
Australian and New Zealand Insurance Reporter [*A publication*] AIN
Australian and New Zealand Journal of Criminology [*A publication*] ANZJ of Crim
Australian and New Zealand Journal of Criminology [*A publication*] Aust & NZJ Crim
Australian and New Zealand Journal of Criminology [*A publication*] Aust NZ Jl Criminol
Australian and New Zealand Journal of Medicine (SAUS) Aust NZJ Med
Australian and New Zealand Journal of Obstetrics and Gynaecology (SAUS) Aust NZJ Obstet Gynaecol
Australian and New Zealand Journal of Ophthalmology (SAUS) Aust N Z J Ophthalmol
Australian and New Zealand Journal of Psychiatry (SAUS) Aust N Z J Psychiatry
Australian and New Zealand Journal of Sociology [*A publication*] Aust NZ Jl Sociol
Australian and New Zealand Journal of Surgery [*A publication*] Aust NZ Jl Surgery
Australian and New Zealand Journal of Surgery (SAUS) Aust NZJ Surg
Australian and New Zealand Merchants' and Shippers' Association (DS) ANZMSA
Australian and New Zealand Physicist [*A publication*] Aust & NZ Phys
Australian and New Zealand Pulp and Paper (SAUS) APPITA
Australian and Pacific Regional Agricultural Credit Association (SAUO) APRACA
Australian Animal Disease Information System (SAUS) ANADIS
Australian Animal Health Council (GVA) AAHC
Australian Animal Health Laboratory AAHL
Australian Animal Protection Society AAPS
Australian Annual Digest [*A publication*] (DLA) Austl AD
Australian Antarctic Expedition [*1911-14*] AAE
Australian Antarctic Territory AAT
Australian Antarctic Territory (SAUO) ANT
Australian Anthropological Journal (journ.) (SAUS) AAJ
Australian Anti-Apartheid Movement [*An association*] AAM
Australian antigen (SAUS) Au virus
Australian Apple & Pear Corporation (SAUO) AA&PC
Australian Apple and Pear Growers' Association AAPGA
Australian Apple and Pear Shippers' Association AAPSA
Australian Appliance Association AAA
Australian Architectural Periodicals Index (ADA) AAPI
Australian Archives Electronic Research Project AAERP
Australian Argos Regional Processing Center of Melbourne (SAUS) AURPC
Australian Armed Forces Radio AAFR
Australian Army AA
Australian Army Educational Corps (SAUO) AAEC
Australian Army Medical Womens Service (SAUS) AAMWS
Australian Army Order (SAUS) AAO
Australian Army Ordnance Depot (SAUO) AAOD
Australian Army Pay Corps (SAUO) AAPC
Australian Army Psychology Corps (SAUO) AAPC
Australian Army Tactical Command Control System (ACAE) AUSTACCS
Australian Army Training Team, Vietnam (VNW) AATTV
Australian Army Training Team, Vietnam (VNW) AATTVV
Australian Aromatherapists' Association AAA
Australian Art Index [*Database*] AART
Australian Art Index [*Australian National Gallery Library*] [*Database*] (ADA) AARTI
Australian Asian Association AAA
Australian Associated Press Party Ltd. AAP
Australian Associated Press Proprietary Ltd. (SAUO) AAP
Australian Associated Stock Exchanges (ADA) AASE
Australian Association Against Painful Experiments on Animals AAAPEA
Australian Association for Armed Neutrality AAAN
Australian Association for Deserted Children AADC
Australian Association for Engineering Education AAEE
Australian Association for Environmental Education AAEE
Australian Association for Predetermined Titme Standards and Research (SAUS) AAPTSR
Australian Association for Quality and Participation AAQP
Australian Association for the History and Philosophy of Science (SAUO) AAHPS
Australian Association for the Study of Religions (SAUO) AASR
Australian Association of Bush Regenerators AABR
Australian Association of Business Publication (SAUO) AABP
Australian Association of Cattle Veterinarians AACV

Australian Association of Ceramic Tile Merchants	AACTM
Australian Association of Chief Information Officers	AACIO
Australian Association of Community Language Services	AACLS
Australian Association of Consulting Planners	AACP
Australian Association of Farm Management Consultants	AAFMC
Australian Association of Film and Video Libraries	AAFVL
Australian Association of Gerontology (SAUO)	AAG
Australian Association of Independent Businesses Ltd.	AAIB
Australian Association of Infant Mental Health (SAUO)	AAIMHI
Australian Association of Mental Health	AAMH
Australian Association of Musical Instrument Makers	AAMIM
Australian Association of Nematologists	AAN
Australian Association of Neurologists (SAUO)	AAN
Australian Association of Occupational Therapists (SAUO)	AAOT
Australian Association of Pathology Practices	AAPP
Australian Association of Philanthropy	AAP
Australian Association of Police Citizens' Youth Clubs	AAPCYC
Australian Association of Prisoner Support Organizations	AAPSO
Australian Association of Psychology and Philosophy (SAUO)	AAPP
Australian Association of Rural Fire Authorities	AARFA
Australian Association of Taxation and Management Accountants	AATMA
Australian Association of University Teachers of Accounting	AAUTA
Australian Association of Veterans' Athletic Clubs	AAVAC
Australian Association of Veterinary Conservation Biologists (GVA)	AAVCB
Australian Athletics Union (SAUO)	AAU
Australian Atomic Energy Commission (NUCP)	AAEC
Australian Audio-Visual Reference Book [A publication] (APTA)	AAVRB
Australian Automobile Association (SAUO)	AAA
Australian Automotive Manufacturers' Association	AAMA
Australian Aviation Underwriters' Pool	AAUP
Australian Avocado Growers' Association	AAGF
Australian Ayrshire Breeders' Association	AABA
Australian Babji Joga Sangam [An association]	ABJS
Australian Ballet	AB
Australian Ballet School	ABS
Australian Banana Growers' Council	ABGC
Australian Banana Growers Council (SAUO)	ABGC
Australian Bank Ltd.	ABL
Australian Bank of Commerce	ABC
Australian Bank Officials Association (SAUO)	ABOA
Australian Bankers Association (SAUO)	ABA
Australian Banking Institute of New Zealand (SAUO)	ABINZ
Australian Baptist [A publication] (APTA)	AB
Australian Bar Review [A publication]	Aust Bar Rev
Australian Barefoot Association	ABA
Australian Barley Marketing Federation	ABMF
Australian Bartenders' Guild	ABG
Australian Baseball League	ABL
Australian Bat Lyssavirus	ABL
Australian Baton Twirling Association	ABTA
Australian Beef Promotion Committee	ABPC
Australian Biathlon Association Victoria	ABAV
Australian Bibliographic Network [National Library of Australia] [Information service or system] (IID)	ABN
Australian Bicentennial Authority	ABA
Australian Bicycle Motocross Association	ABMXA
Australian Billiards and Snooker Council	ABSC
Australian Biographical and Genealogical Record [A publication] (ADA)	ABGR
Australian Biological Resources Advisory Committee	ABRAC
Australian Biological Resources Study Advisory Committee (or Council) (SAUO)	ABRSAC
Australian Biotechnology Association (HGEN)	ABA
Australian Bird and Bat Banding Scheme (SAUS)	ABBBS
Australian Bird Count	ABC
Australian Birthright Movement [An association]	ABM
Australian Blind Sports Federation	ABSF
Australian Bloodhorse Breeders Association	ABBA
Australian Board of Mineral Resources (SAUO)	ABMR
Australian Board of Missions (SAUO)	ABM
Australian Board of Translators	ABT
Australian Boating [A publication]	AB
Australian Bone Marrow Transplant Foundation	ABMTF
Australian Book Heritage Resources Project	ABHR
Australian Book Review [A publication] (BRI)	Aust Bk R
Australian Book Trade Advisory Comittee (SAUO)	ABTAC
Australian Book Trade Directory [A publication] (APTA)	ABTD
Australian Boot Trade Employees' Federation	ABTEF
Australian Borrowers' Association	ABA
Australian Bowling Federation	ABF
Australian Bowls Board	ABB
Australian Boxing Federation	ABF
Australian Boys' Choir	ABC
Australian Brangus Cattle Association	ABCA
Australian Breeding Center	ABC
Australian Bridge [A publication]	AB
Australian Bridge Federation	ABF
Australian Brigade (SAUO)	Aust Bde
Australian British Chamber of Commerce (DBA)	ABCC
Australian British Trade Association, Sydney (SAUO)	ABTA
Australian Broadcasting Co.	ABC
Australian Broadcasting Commission-television (SAUS)	ABC-tv
Australian Broadcasting Corporation Senior Executives' Association	ABCSOA
Australian Brown Swiss and Braunvieh Association	ABSBA
Australian Brushmakers' Union	ABU
Australian Builder [A publication]	Aust Build

Australian Builder and Land Advertiser [A publication]	AB & LA
Australian Builders' Laborers Federated Union of Workers	ABLFUW
Australian Building Cost Database	ABCD
Australian Building Research Congress. Proceedings (journ.) (SAUS)	Proc Aust Bldg Res Congr
Australian Bulletin of Labour [A publication]	Aust BL
Australian +Bureau of Agricultural and Resource Economics (IID)	ABARE
Australian Bureau of Agricultural (or Agriculture) and Resource Economics (SAUO)	ABARE
Australian Bureau of Animal Health	ABAH
Australian Bureau of Criminal Intelligence	ABCI
Australian Bureau of Meteorology [Marine science] (OSRA)	ABOM
Australian Bureau of Resource Science (SAUO)	ABRS
Australian Bureau of Statistics (GEOI)	ABS
Australian Bureau of Statistics Database	ABSDATA
Australian Business and Estate Planning Reporter [A publication]	AEB
Australian Business Brief [A publication]	Aust Bus Brief
Australian Business Brief and Hansard Service [Australian Chamber of Commerce] [Information service or system] [Defunct] (IID)	BBHS
Australian Business Communications Directory [A publication]	ABCD
Australian Business Directory [A publication]	ABD
Australian Business Forms Association	ABFA
Australian Business Index [Database] [Computer science] (CIST)	ABIX
Australian Business Law Review [A publication]	ABLR
Australian Business Law Review [A publication]	Aust Bus Law Rev
Australian Business Law Review [A publication]	Aust Bus Rev
Australian Business Lawyer [A publication]	Aust Bus Lawyer
Australian Business Monthly [A publication]	ABM
Australian Buying Advisory Service (SAUO)	ABAS
Australian Cable and Subscription Communications Association	ACSCA
Australian Calisthenics Federation	ACF
Australian Camellia Research Society	ACRS
Australian Cancer Patients Federation (SAUS)	ACPF
Australian Cane Farmers' Association	ACFA
Australian Cane Growers Association (SAUO)	ACGA
Australian Cane Growers Council (SAUO)	ACGC
Australian Canned Fruits Board (SAUO)	ACFB
Australian Canvas and Synthetic Products Association	ACSPA
Australian Capital Territory (PPW)	ACT
Australian Capital Territory Amateur Weightlifting Association	ACTAWA
Australian Capital Territory Association for the Teaching of English	ACTATE
Australian Capital Territory Athletics [An association]	ACTA
Australian Capital Territory Basketball	ACTB
Australian Capital Territory Bridge Association	ACTBA
Australian Capital Territory Continence Promotion Group	ACTCPG
Australian Capital Territory Council of Cultural Societies	ACTCCS
Australian Capital Territory Credit Union Association Cooperative	ACTCUAC
Australian Capital territory Division of General Practice (SAUO)	ACtdGP
Australian Capital territory Division of General Practice (SAUS)	ACTDGP
Australian Capital Territory Education Information Network	ACTEIN
Australian Capital Territory Geographical Society	ACTGS
Australian Capital Territory Geography Teachers' Association	ACTGTA
Australian Capital Territory Hockey Association	ACTHA
Australian Capital Territory Injury Surveillance and Prevention Project	ACTISPP
Australian Capital Territory Institute of Technical and Further Education	ACTITFE
Australian Capital Territory Land Information Council (SAUO)	ACTLIC
Australian Capital Territory Lieder Society	ACTLS
Australian Capital Territory Marching Association	ACTMA
Australian Capital Territory Master Joiners' Association	ACTMJA
Australian Capital Territory Nurses' Board	ACTNB
Australian Capital Territory Parks and Conservation Service (SAUO)	ACTP&CS
Australian Capital Territory Parks and Conservation Service (SAUO)	ACTPCS
Australian Capital Territory Pistol Association	ACTPA
Australian Capital Territory Racing Club	ACTRC
Australian Capital Territory Recycling Campaign	ARC
Australian Capital Territory. Reports (journ.) (SAUS)	ACTR
Australian Capital Territory Smallbore Rifle Club	ACTSRC
Australian Capital Territory Soccer Federation	ACTSF
Australian Capital Territory Softball Association	ACTSA
Australian Capital Territory Sport and Recreational Fishing Council	ACTSRFC
Australian Capital Territory Totalizater Agency Board (SAUS)	ACTTAB
Australian Capital Territory Touch Association	ACTTA
Australian Capitol [Record label]	ACap
Australian Cardiacs' Association	ACA
Australian Carpet Wool Council	ACWC
Australian Carpetmaster Sheepbreeders' Association	ACSA
Australian Casemix Bulletin [A publication]	ACB
Australian Casemix Clinical Committee (SAUS)	ACCC
Australian Cashmere Growers' Association (SAUO)	ACGA
Australian Catholic Bishops' Conference	ACBC
Australian Catholic Health Care Association	ACHCA
Australian Catholic Historical Society. Journal (journ.) (SAUS)	JACHS
Australian Catholic Theological Association	ACTA
Australian Catholic University Aquinas Campus	ACU Aq
Australian Catholic University Castle Hill Campus	ACU CH
Australian Catholic University Christ Campus	ACU Christ
Australian Catholic University Mackillop Campus	ACU MacK
Australian Catholic University McAuley Campus	ACU McA
Australian Catholic University Mercy Campus	ACU Mercy
Australian Catholic University Mount St. Mary Campus	ACU MSM
Australian Catholic University Signadou Campus	ACU Sign
Australian Cattle Dog Club of America (EA)	ACDCA

Australian Cattle Dog Society of New South Wales ... ACDSNSW
Australian Centennial Roads Development (SAUS) ... ACRD
Australian Center for Leadership Research and Development ... ACLRD
Australian Centre for Advanced Risk and Reliability Engineering ... ACARRE
Australian Centre for Egyptology ... ACE
Australian Centre for Environmental Law (SAUS) ... ACEL
Australian Centre for Remote Sensing ... ACRES
Australian Centre for Research in Library and Information Science (SAUS) ... ACRiLIS
Australian Centre for UFO Studies ... ACUFOS
Australian Centre for Water Quality Research (SAUS) ... ACWQR
Australian Cerebral Palsy Sports Federation ... ACPSF
Australian Chamber Music Society ... ACMS
Australian Chamber of Commerce and Industry (SAUO) ... ACCI
Australian Chamber of Fruit and Vegetable Industries ... ACFVI
Australian Chamber of Manufacturers (SAUO) ... ACM
Australian Chemical Engineering (journ.) (SAUS) ... Aust Chem Eng
Australian Chemical Industry Council ... ACIA
Australian Chemical Institute (SAUS) ... ACI
Australian Chemical (or Chemistry) Institute (SAUO) ... ACI
Australian Chemical Processing and Engineering (journ.) (SAUS) ... ACPE
Australian Chemical Processing and Engineering (journ.) (SAUS) ... Aust Chem Process Eng
Australian Chemical Trauma Alliance (SAUO) ... ACTA
Australian Chemistry Institute (SAUS) ... ACI
Australian Cherry Growers' Federation ... ACGF
Australian Chicken Growers' Council ... ACGC
Australian Chicken Meat Federation ... ACMF
Australian Child and Family Welfare [*A publication*] ... Aust Child Family Welf
Australian Children's Foundation ... ACF
Australian Children's Television Committee. Newsletter [*A publication*] ... Aust Children TV Com Newsl
Australian Childrens Television Foundation ... ACTVF
Australian Chinese Community Association of New South Wales ... ACCANSW
Australian Choral Directors (SAUO) ... ACD
Australian Choreographic Ensemble ... ACE
Australian Christian [*A publication*] (APTA) ... AC
Australian Christian Endeavour Union (SAUO) ... ACEU
Australian Christian Endevour Union (SAUO) ... ACE
Australian Christian Party [*Political party*] ... ACP
Australian Church Union (SAUO) ... ACU
Australian Cinema Advertising Council ... ACAC
Australian Citrus Exporters' Association ... ACEA
Australian Citrus Growers Association (SAUO) ... ACGA
Australian Citrus Growers Federation (SAUS) ... ACGF
Australian Citrus Industry Council ... ACIC
Australian Citrus Processors' Association ... ACPA
Australian Civil Affairs Unit (VNW) ... ACAU
Australian Civil Aviation Authority, Flying Unit [*ICAO designator*] (FAAC) ... ADA
Australian Civil Engineering and Construction [*A publication*] ... Aust Civil Engng Constr
Australian Civil Engineering (journ.) (SAUS) ... Aust Civ Eng
Australian Civil Police ... AUSTCIVPOL
Australian Clay Minerals Conference. Proceedings (journ.) (SAUS) ... Proc Aust Clay Miner Conf
Australian Clay Pipe Manufacturers' Association ... ACPMA
Australian Clay Target Association ... ACTA
Australian Clearing House for Library and Information Science (SAUS) ... ACHLIS
Australian Clearinghouse for Publications in Recreation Sport and Tourism (SAUS) ... ACHPIRST
Australian Co. Secretary's Business Law Manual [*A publication*] ... LABL
Australian Co. Secretary's Letter [*A publication*] ... ACSL
Australian Coal Association Research (SAUO) ... ACAR
Australian Coal Corporation (SAUO) ... ACCOR
Australian Coal Exporters Association (SAUS) ... ACEA
Australian Coal Industries Research Laboratories (SAUO) ... ACIRL
Australian Coal Marketing and Technology Council ... ACMTC
Australian Coal Trade and Technology Committee ... ACTTC
Australian Coalition of Young People ... ACYP
Australian Coastal Atlas (SAUS) ... ACA
Australian Code for the Transportation of Dangerous Goods by Road and Rail (SAUS) ... ADG
Australian Code of Residential Design and Construction (SAUS) ... ACRDC
Australian Coffee Growers Association ... ACGA
Australian College of Education. Queensland Chapter. Newsletter [*A publication*] ... Newsl Aust Coll Ed Qd
Australian College of Herbal Medicine (SAUO) ... ACoHM
Australian College of Metaphysical Studies ... ACMS
Australian College of Midwives ... ACM
Australian College of Obstetricians and Gynaecologists (SAUO) ... ACOG
Australian College of Paediatrics (SAUO) ... ACP
Australian College of Travel and Hospitality ... ACTH
Australian Colleges and Universities Staff Association ... ACUSA
Australian Comic Collector (journ.) (SAUS) ... TACC
Australian Commercial and Economics Teachers Association (SAUS) ... ACETA
Australian Commercial Law Association ... ACLA
Australian Commission for the Future ... ACF
Australian Commission on Advanced Education (SAUO) ... ACAE
Australian Committee for Coding Rural Accounts (SAUO) ... ACCRA
Australian Committee for Earth Resources Satellites (SAUS) ... ACERTS
Australian Committee for the World Climate Research Programme (SAUO) ... ACWCRP
Australian Committee of Directors of Principals (SAUO) ... ACDP
Australian Committee on Africa ... ACA
Australian Committee on Data Processing (SAUO) ... ACDP
Australian Commodities [*Database*] ... AUSTCOM
Australian Commonwealth Military Forces (SAUO) ... ACMF
Australian Commonwealth Scientific and Industrial Research Organization (SAUO) ... ACSIRO
Australian Communication Satellite (SAUS) ... AUST DOMSAT
Australian Communications Industry Forum (SAUO) ... ACIF
Australian Community Languages and Cultural Program ... ACLCP
Australian Community Theatre ... ACT
Australian Companies Legislation [*A publication*] ... ACL
Australian Companion Animal Health Foundation (GVA) ... ACAHF
Australian Company Law and Practice [*A publication*] ... ACP
Australian Company Number (TBD) ... ACN
Australian Company Secretarys Letter (SAUS) ... ACSL
Australian Company Secretary's Practice Manual [*A publication*] ... LSEC
Australian Computer Bulletin (journ.) (SAUS) ... ACB
Australian Computer Bulletin (journ.) (SAUS) ... Aust Comput Bull
Australian Computer Emergency Response Team (SAUS) ... AUSCERT
Australian Computer Equipment Manufacturers' Association ... ACEMA
Australian Computer Equipment Suppliers Association (SAUO) ... ACESA
Australian Computer Science (SAUO) ... ACS
Australian Computer Science Network (SAUO) ... ACSnet
Australian Computer Society-Software Industries Association (SAUO) ... ACS-SIA
Australian Computer-Aided Design Systems ... ACADS
Australian Conference on Nuclear Techniques of Analysis. Proceedings (journ.) (SAUS) ... Proc Aust Conf Nucl Tech Anal
Australian Conference on Nuclear Techniques of Analysis Summary of Proceedings (journ.) (SAUS) ... Summ Proc Aust Conf Nucl Tech Anal
Australian Consolidated Industries Computer Service (SAUS) ... ACICS
Australian Consolidated Industries Ltd. (SAUO) ... ACI
Australian Consolidated Minerals (SAUO) ... ACM
Australian Construction Industry Law Letter [*A publication*] ... ACILL
Australian Construction Law Newsletter [*A publication*] ... ACLN
Australian Construction Law Reporter [*A publication*] ... Aust Con LR
Australian Consulate-General, Australian Reference Library, New York, NY [*Library symbol*] [*Library of Congress*] (LCLS) ... NNAUR
Australian Consultants (SAUO) ... AUSTCON
Australian Consumer Sales and Credit Law Cases [*A publication*] ... ACSCC
Australian Consumers' Association (ODBW) ... ACA
Australian Contemporary Music Ensemble (SAUO) ... ACME
Australian Contract Bridge League (SAUO) ... ACBL
Australian Conveyancer and Solicitors' Journal [*A publication*] (DLA) ... Austl Convey & Sol J
Australian Conveyor Manufacturers Association ... ACMA
Australian Corporate Affairs Commission (SAUO) ... ACAC
Australian Corporate Law [*Database*] ... ACLID
Australian Corporate Law Data-Base (SAUS) ... ACLDB
Australian Corporation Law Bulletin [*A publication*] ... ACLB
Australian Corporations and Securities Reports [*A publication*] ... ACSR
Australian Corps Troops Ammunition Column (SAUO) ... Aust CT Amn Col
Australian Cotton Foundation ... ACF
Australian Cotton Growers' Research Association ... ACGRA
Australian Cotton Growers Research Association (SAUO) ... ACGRA
Australian Cotton Textile Industries Ltd (SAUO) ... ACTIL
Australian Council for Aeronautics ... ACA
Australian Council for Aeronautics. Report [*A publication*] ... Aust Council Aeronautics Rept
Australian Council for Care of Animals in Research and Teaching (SAUO) ... ACCART
Australian Council for Children's Films and Television ... ACCFTV
Australian Council for Educational Research (WDAA) ... ACER
Australian Council for Educational Research, Hawthorn, V, Australia [*Library symbol*] [*Library of Congress*] (LCLS) ... AuHaA
Australian Council for Health, Physical Education and Recreation (SAUO) ... ACHPER
Australian Council for Private Education and Training ... ACPET
Australian Council for Responsible Nutrition Inc. (SAUO) ... ACRN
Australian Council for Teaching Foreign Languages ... ACTFL
Australian Council for the Care of Animals in Research and Teaching ... ACCART
Australian Council of Alcohol and Other Drug Associations ... ACAODA
Australian Council of Churches ... ACOC
Australian Council of Egg Producers ... ACEP
Australian Council of Employers' Federations ... ACEF
Australian Council of Independent Business Schools ... ACIBS
Australian Council of Manufacturing Associates ... ACMA
Australian Council of Marriage Counselling ... ACMC
Australian Council of Recyclers ... ACR
Australian Council of Rural Youth ... ACRY
Australian Council of Social Service ... ACSS
Australian Council of Social Services (SAUO) ... ACSS
Australian Council of Solaried and Professional Associations (SAUS) ... ACSPA
Australian Council of Trade Unions (WDAA) ... ACTU
Australian Council of Wool Exporters (SAUO) ... ACWE
Australian Counter-Disaster College (SAUO) ... ACDC
Australian Country Music Awards ... ACMA
Australian Country Party [*Political party*] (BARN) ... ACP
Australian Country Party [*Political party*] ... AustCP
Australian Courier and Taxi Truck Operators' Association ... ACTTOA
Australian Cranio-Facial Foundation ... ACFF
Australian Credit Unions Magazine [*A publication*] ... Aust Credit Unions Mag
Australian Cricket Association ... ACA
Australian Crime Prevention Council. Quarterly Journal [*A publication*] ... ACPCQJ

Australian Criminal Lawyers' Association	ACLA
Australian Croatian Association	ACA
Australian Croquet Association	ACA
Australian Cruiser (DMA)	AC
Australian Cultural Center Association	ACCA
Australian Curling Association	ACA
Australian Current (SAUS)	Aust Cur
Australian Current Case Annotator [A publication]	ACCA
Australian Current Law Articles [A publication]	ACL AT
Australian Current Law Review [A publication] (DLA)	Austl Current L Rev
Australian Customer Service Association	ACSA
Australian Customs Notice [A publication]	ACN
Australian Customs Service Surveillance Program (SAUO)	COASTWATCH
Australian Cystic Fibrosis Association (SAUO)	ACFA
Australian Cystic Fibrosis Associations Federation	ACFAF
Australian Czech Association of New South Wales	ACANSW
Australian Dairy Development Council (SAUO)	ADDC
Australian Dairy Farmers Federation (SAUO)	ADFF
Australian Dairy Foods Advisory Bureau	ADFAB
Australian Dairy Industry Council (SAUO)	ADIC
Australian Dairy Products Federation	ADPF
Australian Dairy Products Standards Organization	ADPSO
Australian Dairy Traders' Federation	ADTF
Australian Dance Foundation	ADF
Australian Dance Theatre [Adelaide]	ADT
Australian Database Development Association (CIST)	ADDA
Australian Database Development Association Database	ADDABASE
Australian De Facto Relationships Law [A publication]	ADR
Australian Deaf Sports Federation	ADSF
Australian Deer Breeders Federation (SAUS)	ADBF
Australian Deer Farmers' Federation	ADFF
Australian Deerstalkers' Federation	ADF
Australian Defence Board (SAUO)	ADB
Australian Defence Force (ADA)	ADF
Australian Defence Force Academy (SAUO)	AFDA
Australian Defence Forces (SAUS)	ADF
Australian Defence Industries Ltd. (SAUO)	ADI
Australian Defence Representative (SAUO)	ADR
Australian Defence Science and Technology Information Service (SAUO)	ADSATIS
Australian Defense Data Dictionary (ACAE)	ADDD
Australian Defense Force Warfare Center [Military]	ADFWC
Australian Defense Formatted Message System [Military]	ADFORMS
Australian Defense Science and Technology Information Service (SAUS)	ADSATIS
Australian Defense Scientific Service (SAUS)	ADSS
Australian Democratic Labor Party [Political party] (PPW)	ADLP
Australian Democratic Party [Political party] (PPW)	ADP
Australian Democrats [Political party] (EAIO)	AD
Australian Dental Association (SAUO)	AD
Australian Dental Association (SAUO)	ADA
Australian Dental Journal (SAUS)	ADJ
Australian Dental Journal (SAUS)	Aust Dent J
Australian Dental Research Foundation (SAUO)	ADRF
Australian Dental Research Fund	ADRF
Australian Department of Foreign Affairs (SAUO)	ADFA
Australian Department of Health and Family Services (SAUO)	HFS
Australian Department of Primary Industry Regulations for the Carriage of Chille (SAUS)	DPI regulations
Australian Department of Tourism and Recreation (SAUO)	ADTR
Australian Design Council	ADC
Australian Design Rule [Automotive technology]	ADR
Australian Diabetes Foundation	ADF
Australian Diabetic Council (SAUO)	ADC
Australian Diagnosis Related Groups (SAUO)	AN-DRG
Australian Dictionary of Acronyms and Abbreviations (SAUS)	ADA
Australian Dictionary of Acronyms and Abbreviations [A publication]	ADAA
Australian Die Casting Association	ADCA
Australian Digest [A publication]	ADA
Australian Digest [A publication] (DLA)	Austl D
Australian Digest (journ.) (SAUS)	AD
Australian Digest, Second Edition [A publication] (DLA)	Aust D 2d
Australian Directory of Music Organizations (SAUS)	ADMO
Australian Directory of Vocational Education and Training [A publication]	ADVET
Australian Disabilities Review [A publication]	ADR
Australian Disabled Skiers' Federation	ADSF
Australian Disabled Students Union (SAUS)	ADSU
Australian Dispute Resolution Journal [A publication]	ADRJ
Australian Diving Association	ADA
Australian Dollar (SAUO)	AD
Australian Dollar [Monetary unit]	AUD
Australian Down Syndrome Association	ADSA
Australian Drama Studies Association	ADSA
Australian Dried Fruits Association (SAUO)	ADFA
Australian Driver Trainers' Association	ADTA
Australian Driving Society	ADS
Australian Drug and Alcohol Foundation	ADAF
Australian Drug Database	ADDB
Australian Drug Database (Law Enforcement Component)	ADDBLEC
Australian Duty Free Operators' Association	ADFOA
Australian Early Childhood Education Association	AECEA
Australian Early Holden Association	AEHA
Australian Earth Sciences Information System [Database on AUSINET] (NITA)	AESI
Australian Eastern Daylight Saving Time (ADA)	AEDST
Australian Economic Indicators [A publication]	AEI
Australian Economic Papers [A publication]	Aust Econ P
Australian Economic Review [A publication]	Aust Econ R
Australian Education directory [A publication]	AED
Australian Education Directory (SAUS)	AED
Australian Education Researcher [A publication]	Aus Ed Res
Australian Education Researcher [A publication]	Aust Ed Res
Australian Education Review [A publication]	Aust Ed Rev
Australian Educational Allowance Fund	AEAF
Australian Educational Secretariat (SAUO)	AES
Australian Egg Marketing Council	AEMC
Australian Electric Transport Association (South Australia)	AETM(SA)
Australian Electrical & Electronic Manufacturers Association Ltd. (SAUO)	AEEMA
Australian Electrical Manufacturers Association (SAUO)	AEMA
Australian Electrical World (journ.) (SAUS)	Aust Electr World
Australian Electronic Government Information Service (SAUO)	AEGIS
Australian Electronic Journal of Nursing Education (SAUO)	AEJNE
Australian Electronics Consumer Industry Association (SAUO)	AECIA
Australian Electronics Engineering (journ.) (SAUS)	Aust Electron Eng
Australian Elizabethan Theater Trust (SAUO)	AETT
Australian Embassy, Washington, DC [Library symbol] [Library of Congress] (LCLS)	DAusE
Australian Employee Survey Group	AESG
Australian Employers' Federation	AEF
Australian Employment Law Guide [A publication]	AEM
Australian Employment Legislation [A publication]	AEL
Australian Energy Commission (SAUO)	AEC
Australian Energy Commission (SAUS)	AEC
Australian Energy Management News [A publication]	AEMN
Australian Energy Research, Development and Demonstration Projects (SAUS)	AERDDP
Australian Energy Research Laboratory	AERL
Australian Engineers (SAUS)	AE
Australian Environment Management Export Corporation Ltd. (SAUS)	AUSTEMEX
Australian Environmental Law News [A publication]	AELN
Australian Environmental On-line Service (SAUO)	AEOS
Australian Environmental Statistics Project (SAUS)	AESOP
Australian Equestrian Trade Association	AETA
Australian Equine Research Foundation	AERF
Australian Equine Veterinary Association	AEVA
Australian Ethnic Democrats [Political party]	AED
Australian Ethnic Democrats [An association]	AUSED
Australian European Finance Corporation	AEFC
Australian Executive Service Overseas Program Ltd. (SAUO)	AESOP
Australian Export Commodity Classification	AECC
Australian Export Statistics [Database]	AEEC
Australian Fabian Society	AFS
Australian Factors' Guild	AFG
Australian Faculty Directory [A publication]	AFD
Australian Family and Society Abstracts (SAUO)	FAMI
Australian Family Association	AFA
Australian Family Law Bulletin [A publication]	AFLB
Australian Family Law Guide [A publication]	AFAM
Australian Family Lawyer [A publication]	AFL
Australian Family Research Bulletin [A publication] (ADA)	AFRB
Australian Family Studies Database	AFAM
Australian Fast Delivery Processor (SAUS)	AFDP
Australian Federal Police [A publication]	Aust Fed Police
Australian Federal Tax Reporter [A publication]	FTR
Australian Federated Union of Locomotive Engineers (SAUO)	AFULE
Australian Federation of Air Freight Forwarders	AFAFF
Australian Federation of Airline Pilots (SAUO)	AFAP
Australian Federation of Consumer Organisations (SAUO)	AFCO
Australian Federation of Credit Unions	AFCU
Australian Federation of Homeopaths	AFH
Australian Federation of Pipe Band Associations	AFPBA
Australian Federation of Police Unions (SAUO)	AFPU
Australian Federation of Right to Life Associations	AFRTLA
Australian Federation of the Women's International Zionist Organization	AFWIZO
Australian Federation of Timber Merchants' Associations	AFTMA
Australian Federation of Travel Agents (BARN)	AFTA
Australian Feeds Information Centre [Database]	AFIC
Australian Fencing Federation	AFF
Australian Fertilizer Manufacturers' Committee	AFMC
Australian Festival [Record label]	AFest
Australian Festival of Life	AFL
Australian Fibreboard Container Manufacturers Association (SAUO)	AFCMA
Australian Fiducial Network (SAUS)	AFN
Australian Film Corp.	AFC
Australian Film Finance Corp.	AFFC
Australian Film Institute Distribution	AFID
Australian Film Making Association	AFMA
Australian Finance Availability Guide [A publication]	AFIN
Australian Financial Futures Market	AFFM
Australian Financial Review [A publication]	Fin Rev
Australian Financial Review Information Service (SAUS)	AFRIS
Australian Financial Review Property Review [A publication] (ADA)	FRPR
Australian Firms Information System	AFIS
Australian Fish Health Reference Laboratory	AFHRL
Australian Fisheries (SAUS)	Aust Fish
Australian Fisheries [A publication]	Aust Fisheries

Australian Fisheries Service [*Marine science*] (OSRA) .... AFS
Australian Fisheries Zone Information Service (SAUO) .... AFZIS
Australian Fishing Zone Authority .... AFZA
Australian Flour Export Promotion Committee .... AFEPC
Australian Flute Association .... AFA
Australian Flux Measurement Network (SAUS) .... OZFLUX
Australian Flying Corps (SAUO) .... AFC
Australian Folk Music Associates .... AFMA
Australian Folklore Association .... AFA
Australian Folkloric Dance Company [*An association*] .... AFDC
Australian Foodservice Manufacturers' Association .... AFMA
Australian Football Coaches Association .... AFCA
Australian Foreign Affairs Record [*A publication*] .... Aust For Aff Rec
Australian Foreign Trade Office .... AFTO
Australian Forest Grower [*A publication*] .... Aust Forest Grower
Australian Forest Research (SAUS) .... Aust For Res
Australian Fossil Mammal Site (SAUS) .... AFMS
Australian Foundation for Alcoholism (SAUO) .... AFA
Australian Foundation for Alcoholism and Drug Dependence (SAUO) .... AFADD
Australian Foundation for the Disabled .... AFD
Australian Foundation for the Peoples of the South Pacific .... AFPSP
Australian Freedom from Hunger Campaign .... AFHC
Australian Fresh Juice and Cordial Manufacturers' Association .... AFJCMA
Australian Fresh Juice Association .... AFJA
Australian Friendly Societies' Association .... AFSA
Australian Friesian Sahiwal [*Cattle terminology*] .... AFS
Australian Fringe Benefits Tax Guide for Employers [*A publication*] .... AFB
Australian Fruit Growers [*An association*] .... AFG
Australian Futsal Federation .... AFF
Australian Garden History Society .... AGHS
Australian Garlic Association .... AGA
Australian Garrison Artillery (SAUO) .... AGA
Australian Garrison Royal Artillery (SAUO) .... AGRA
Australian Gas Light (SAUO) .... AGL
Australian Genealogical Computer Index (SAUS) .... AGCI
Australian General Electric Company (SAUO) .... AGE
Australian General Hospital (SAUO) .... AGH
Australian Genome Research Facility .... AGAP
Australian Geographer [*A publication*] .... Aus Geo
Australian Geographic (SAUS) .... Aust Geogr
Australian Geographic Data Base (SAUS) .... AGDB
Australian Geographic Society (SAUS) .... AGS
Australian Geographical Studies [*A publication*] .... AGS
Australian Geographical Studies [*A publication*] .... Aus G Stud
Australian Geography Teachers Association (SAUO) .... AGTA
Australian Geological Survey Organisation [*Formerly, BMR - Bureau of Mineral Resources*] .... AGSO
Australian Geological Survey Organisation (or Organization) (SAUO) .... AGSO
Australian Geomechanics Journal (SAUS) .... Aust Geomech J
Australian Geriatrics' Society .... AGS
Australian Glass Workers' Union .... AGWU
Australian Global Ocean Observing System (SAUS) .... AGOOS
Australian GNSS Coordinating Group (SAUO) .... AGCG
Australian Gold [*Vancouver Stock Exchange symbol*] .... AZG
Australian Golf Course Superintendents' Association .... AGCSA
Australian Govemment Student Assistance Fund (SAUS) .... AGSAF
Australian Government Acronyms And Abbreviations (SAUS) .... AGAAA
Australian Government Analytical Laboratories (SAUO) .... AGAL
Australian Government Offsets Program (SAUS) .... AGOP
Australian Government Photographic Service (SAUO) .... AUSPIC
Australian Government Scheme of Educational Allowances (SAUS) .... AUSTUDY
Australian Government Solicitors' Office .... AGSO
Australian Graduate of the School of Management (ODBW) .... AGSM
Australian Grain Exporters' Association .... AGEA
Australian Grape Exporters' Committee .... AGEC
Australian Greeting Card Association .... AGCA
Australian Gruen Party [*Political party*] .... AGP
Australian Guild of Music and Speech .... AGMS
Australian Guild of Screen Composers .... AGSC
Australian Guitar Journal [*A publication*] (APTA) .... AGJ
Australian Hairdressers, Wigmakers, and Hairworkers Employees Federation .... AHWHEF
Australian Handball Council .... AHC
Australian Handball Federation .... AHF
Australian Hard Wheat [*Agriculture*] .... AHW
Australian Hardwood Quality Council .... AHQC
Australian Harness Racing Council .... AHRC
Australian Hayward Kiwifruit Growers Association .... AHKGA
Australian Health Ethics Committee .... AHEC
Australian Health Insurance Program (SAUO) .... AHIP
Australian Health Professionals Association .... AHPA
Australian Health Services .... AHS
Australian Health Services Commission .... AHSC
Australian Hepatitis Antigen [*Biochemistry*] (DAVI) .... AHA
Australian Heraldic Archival Record .... AHAR
Australian Heritage Award .... AHA
Australian Herpetological Society (SAUO) .... AHS
Australian Hides, Skins, and Leather Exports Association .... AHSLEA
Australian High Commission (SAUO) .... AUSHC
Australian Historic Records Register [*Database*] .... AHRR
Australian Historical Association Bulletin (SAUO) .... AHAB
Australian Historical Bibliography [*A publication*] .... Aust Hist Bibl
Australian Historical Geography [*A publication*] .... AHG
Australian Historical Statistics [*A publication*] .... AHS
Australian Historical Studies [*A publication*] (APTA) .... AHS
Australian Historical Studies [*A publication*] .... Aust Hist Stud
Australian Historical Studies (journ.) (SAUS) .... AHS
Australian Home Owners' Club .... AHOC
Australian Horticultural Corporation (SAUO) .... AHC
Australian Horticultural Correspondence School .... AHCS
Australian Horticultural Export Council .... AHEC
Australian Horticultural Exporters Association .... AHEA
Australian Horticultural Growers Council (SAUS) .... AHGC
Australian Horticultural Trades Exhibition .... AHTE
Australian Horticulture Corporation (SAUO) .... AHC
Australian Hotels Association (WDAA) .... AHA
Australian Housing Industry Development Council .... AHIDC
Australian Hungarian Association of Western Australia .... AHAWA
Australian Imagery Organisation (SAUO) .... AIO
Australian Immigration Research Center .... AIRC
Australian Income Tax Guide [*A publication*] .... AITG
Australian Income Tax Guide [*A publication*] .... ITG
Australian Income Tax Legislation [*A publication*] .... ATL
Australian Income Tax Reports [*A publication*] (DLA) .... ITR
Australian Income Tax Rulings [*A publication*] .... ATRU
Australian Independent Publishers Association (SAUO) .... AIPA
Australian Indonesian Association of Victoria [*Australia*] .... AIAV
Australian Indonesian Ministerial Meeting (SAUO) .... AIMM
Australian Indoor Bias Bowls Council .... AIBBC
Australian Indoor Cricket Federation .... AICF
Australian Indoor Soccer Federation .... AISF
Australian Industrial and Intellectual Property [*A publication*] .... ALEC
Australian Industrial Development Laboratories (SAUO) .... AIDL
Australian Industrial Participation (ACAE) .... AIP
Australian Industrial Refractories (SAUS) .... AIR
Australian Industrial Relations Bureau (SAUO) .... AIRB
Australian Industrial Research Directory (journ.) (SAUS) .... AIRD
Australian Industrial Safety, Health, and Welfare [*A publication*] .... ASH
Australian Industrial Safety, Health, and Welfare Cases [*A publication*] .... AISHWC
Australian Industrial Union of Academic Staff .... AIUAS
Australian Industries Development Association. Bulletin [*A publication*] .... Bull Aust Ind Devt Ass
Australian Industries Development Corporation (SAUS) .... AIDC
Australian Industries (or Industry) Development Corporation (SAUO) .... AIDC
Australian Information Network (NITA) .... AUSINET
Australian Information Service (SAUO) .... AIS
Australian Infrastructure Fund .... AIF
Australian Insolvency Bulletin [*A publication*] .... AIB
Australian Insolvency Bulletin (journ.) (SAUS) .... AIB
Australian Insolvency Management Practice [*A publication*] .... AISP
Australian Institute for International Understanding .... AIIU
Australian Institute for NonDestructive Testing (SAUO) .... AINDT
Australian Institute for Rational Emotive Therapy .... AIRET
Australian Institute For Suicide Research And Prevention (SAUO) .... AISRAP
Australian Institute For Suicide Research and Prevention (SAUS) .... AISRAP
Australian Institute of Aboriginal Studies. Newsletter (journ.) (SAUS) .... AIAS News
Australian Institute of Agricultural (or Agriculture) and Science (SAUS) .... AIAS
Australian Institute of Agricultural Science (SAUO) AJA5
Australian Institute of Archaeology .... AIA
Australian Institute of Bankers .... AIB
Australian Institute of Cartographers .... AIC
Australian Institute of Cartographers (Queensland) .... AIC(Q)
Australian Institute of Consultant Valuers .... AICV
Australian Institute of Cost Accountants (SAUO) .... CAA
Australian Institute of Criminology (SAUO) .... AIC
Australian Institute of Engineering Associates Ltd. (SAUO) .... AIEAL
Australian Institute of Fuel (SAUO) .... AIF
Australian Institute of Graphic Art Management (SAUO) .... AIGAM
Australian Institute of Higher Energy Physics .... AUSHEP
Australian Institute of Homeopathy .... AIH
Australian Institute of Incorporated Accountants (SAUO) .... AHA
Australian Institute of International Affairs (SAUO) .... AIIA
Australian Institute of Jewish Affairs .... AIJA
Australian Institute of Loss Adjusters .... AILA
Australian Institute of Marine Science .... AIMS
Australian Institute of Marine Studies (SAUO) .... AIMS
Australian Institute of Materials Management .... AIMM
Australian Institute of Medical and Biological Illustrators (SAUO) .... AIMBI
Australian Institute of Medical Laboratory Technology (SAUO) .... AIMLT
Australian Institute of Medical Scientists .... AIMS
Australian Institute of Metal Finishing (SAUS) .... AIMF
Australian Institute of Mining and Metallurgy (NUCP) .... AIMM
Australian Institute of Mining and Metallurgy (SAUS) .... AUSIMM
Australian Institute of Mining Engineers (SAUO) .... AIME
Australian Institute of Navigation (SAUO) .... AIN
Australian Institute of Parapsychological Research .... AIPR
Australian Institute of Petroleum Ltd. (SAUO) .... AIP
Australian Institute of Physics, NSW Branch (SAUS) .... NSWAIP
Australian Institute of Political Science (SAUO) .... AIPS
Australian Institute of Purchasing and Supply Management .... AIPSM
Australian Institute of Radio and Television .... AIRT
Australian Institute of Radio Engineers (SAUS) .... AIRE
Australian Institute of Radiography (EAIO) .... AIR
Australian Institute of Radiography (SAUO) .... AIR
Australian Institute of Refrigeration, Air Conditioning and Heating (SAUO) .... AIRAH
Australian Institute of Refrigeration, Air-Conditioning and Heating (SAUS) .... AIRAH

Australian Institute of Sales and Marketing Executives	AISME
Australian Institute of Science Technology (SAUO)	AIST
Australian Institute of Surgical and Dental Technicians	AISDT
Australian Institute of Systems Analysis (SAUO)	AISA
Australian Institute of Tourism Officers	AITO
Australian Institute of Travel (SAUO)	AIT
Australian Institute of Travel and Tourism	AITT
Australian Int. Development Assistance Bureau (SAUS)	AIDAB
Australian Integrative Medicine Association (SAUO)	AIMA
Australian Intellectual Disabilities Research Foundation	AIDRF
Australian Intellectual Property Cases [A publication]	AIP
Australian Intellectual Property Cases [A publication]	AIPC
Australian Intellectual Property Law Bulletin [A publication]	AIPLB
Australian Interactive Multimedia Industry Association	AIMIA
Australian International Development Aid Bureau (SAUO)	AIDAB
Australian International Development Assistance Bureau	AIDAB
Australian International Gravitational Observatory (SAUS)	AIGO
Australian International Hotel School	AIHS
Australian International Law News [A publication]	AILN
Australian International Law Review [A publication]	AILR
Australian International Pilots' Industrial Organisation	AIPIO
Australian International Tax Agreements [A publication]	AIX
Australian International Technology Exhibition	AITE
Australian International UFO [Unidentified Flying Object] Research	AIUFOR
Australian Internationals (EA)	AI
Australian Intra-Venous League (SAUO)	AIVL
Australian Inventory of Chemical Substances	AICS
Australian Investment Planning Guide [A publication]	AVST
Australian Investor [A publication] (ADA)	AI
Australian Irish Dancing Association	AIDA
Australian Irish Welfare Bureau	AIWB
Australian Iron and Steel (SAUO)	AIS
Australian Jaycees	AJ
Australian Jersey Breeders' Association	AJBA
Australian Jockey (SAUO)	AJC
Australian Joint Citrus Exporters [An association]	AJCE
Australian Joint Council for Operational Research (SAUO)	AJCOR
Australian Joint Lamb and Sheepmeat Promotion Committee	AJLSPC
Australian Journal for Health, Physical Education, and Recreation [A publication]	AJHPER
Australian Journal. Institute of Transport [A publication]	Aust J Inst Transp
Australian Journal of Advanced Education [A publication]	Aust J Adv Ed
Australian Journal of Advanced Nursing [A publication] (APTA)	AJAN
Australian Journal of Agricultural Research (SAUS)	Aust J Agric Res
[The] Australian Journal of Anthropology [A publication]	TAJA
Australian Journal of Applied Science (journ.) (SAUS)	AJAS
Australian Journal of Biological Sciences (SAUS)	Aust J Biol Sci
Australian Journal of Botany (SAUS)	AJAZ
Australian Journal of Botany (SAUS)	Aust J Bot
Australian Journal of Chemistry (SAUS)	Aust J Chem
Australian Journal of Dairy Technology (journ.) (SAUS)	AJDT
Australian Journal of Dermatology (SAUS)	Aust J Dermatol
Australian Journal of Earth Sciences (SAUS)	Aust J Earth Sci
Australian Journal of Ecology [A publication]	AJ Ecol
Australian Journal of Ecology (SAUS)	Aust J Ecol
Australian Journal of Ecology (journ.) (SAUS)	AJ Ecol
Australian Journal of Education [A publication]	AJ Ed
Australian Journal of Educational Technology [A publication]	AJET
Australian Journal of Experimental Agriculture [A publication]	AJEA
Australian Journal of Experimental Agriculture and Animal Husbandry (SAUS)	Aust J Exp Agric Anim Hus
Australian Journal of Experimental Biology and Medical Science (SAUS)	Aust J Exp Biol Med Sci
Australian Journal of Experimental Biology and Medical Science [A publication]	Aust J Exper Biol & Med Sci
Australian Journal of Family Law [A publication]	AJFL
Australian Journal of Forensic Sciences [A publication]	Aust J Foren Sci
Australian Journal of French Studies (journ.) (SAUS)	AJFH
Australian Journal of Health, Physical Education, and Recreation [A publication]	Aust J Hlth Phys Ed Rec
Australian Journal of Higher Education (journ.) (SAUS)	AJHE
Australian Journal of Holistic Nursing [A publication]	AJOHN
Australian Journal of Instrumentation and Control (SAUS)	Aust J Instrum Contr
Australian Journal of Labour Law [A publication]	AJLL
Australian Journal of Labour Law (journ.) (SAUS)	AJLL
Australian Journal of Law and Society [A publication]	Aust JLS
Australian Journal of Law and Society [A publication] (DLA)	Austl JL Soc'y
Australian Journal of Law and Society (journ.) (SAUS)	AJLS
Australian Journal of Linguistics [A publication]	AJL
Australian Journal of Linguistics [A publication]	Aus J Lin
Australian Journal of Liturgy [A publication] (APTA)	AJL
Australian Journal of Management [A publication]	AJM
Australian Journal of Management [A publication]	Aust J Mgmt
Australian Journal of Management (journ.) (SAUS)	AJM
Australian Journal of Marine and Freshwater Research (SAUS)	Aust J Mar Freshw Res
Australian Journal of Medical Technology (SAUS)	Aust J Med Technol
Australian Journal of Mental Health Nursing (SAUS)	AJMHN
Australian Journal of Mining [A publication]	AJM
Australian Journal of Music Education (journ.) (SAUS)	AJME
Australian Journal of Ophthalmology (journ.) (SAUS)	AJO
Australian Journal of Pharmaceutical Sciences (journ.) (SAUS)	AJPS
Australian Journal of Pharmacy [A publication]	AJP
Australian Journal of Physics, Astrophysical Supplement (SAUS)	Aust J Phys Astrophys Supp
Australian Journal of Physics (journ.) (SAUS)	Aust J Phys
Australian Journal of Plant Physiology (journ.) (SAUS)	AJPP
Australian Journal of Psychology and Philosophy [A publication]	Aust J Psych & Phil
Australian Journal of Psychology (journ.) (SAUS)	AJP
Australian Journal of Public Administration [A publication]	Aust J Publ Admin
Australian Journal of Public Administration (journ.) (SAUS)	AJPA
Australian Journal of Reading (journ.) (SAUS)	AJR
Australian Journal of Scientific Research (journ.) (SAUS)	AJSR
Australian Journal of Sex, Marriage, and Family [A publication] (APTA)	AJSMF
Australian Journal of Social Issues [A publication]	AJ Soc Is
Australian Journal of Social Issues [A publication]	Aust Jnl of Social Issues
Australian Journal of Social Issues [A publication]	Aust J Soc Is
Australian Journal of Social Issues (journ.) (SAUS)	AJSI
Australian Journal of Special Education [A publication]	Aust J Spec Ed
Australian Journal of Teacher Education [A publication]	Aust J Teach Ed
Australian Journal of Zoology (SAUS)	AJZO
Australian Journal of Zoology (SAUS)	Aust J Zool
Australian Journalism Review [A publication] (APTA)	AJR
Australian Journalist [A publication]	AJ
Australian Journalist [A publication]	J
Australian Journalists Association (WDAA)	AJA
Australian Ju Jitsu Association	AJJA
Australian Junior Chamber of Commerce	AJCC
Australian Junior Rugby Football Union	AJRFU
Australian Jurist [A publication] (DLA)	Austl Jr
Australian Jurist Reports [A publication] (ILCA)	Aust Jur R
Australian Karate Federation	AKF
Australian Kelpie Club of New South Wales	AKCNSW
Australian Kendo Federation	AKF
Australian Key Center in Land Information Studies	AKCLIS
Australian Key Centre in Land Information Studies (SAUO)	AKCLIS
Australian Kite Association	AKA
Australian Kiwifruit Growers' Association	AKGA
Australian Korea Business Council	AKBC
Australian Korfball Association	AKA
Australian Labour Advisory Council (SAUO)	ALAC
Australian Labour Party [Political party] (PPW)	ALP
Australian Lace Guild	ALG
Australian Land Development Association (SAUO)	ALDA
Australian Land Transport Development Program	ALTD
Australian Landcare Council (SAUO)	ALC
Australian LANDSAT [Land Satellite] Station	ALS
Australian Landsat Station (SAUS)	ALS
Australian Laser Disk Information Services (SAUS)	ALDIS
Australian Law Journal Reports (SAUS)	ALJR
Australian Law Reports [A publication] (DLA)	Austl LR
Australian Law Times [A publication] (DLA)	Austl L Times
Australian Lawyer [A publication] (DLA)	Austl Law
Australian Lead/Zinc Development Association	ALZDA
Australian League of Ex-Servicemen and Women	ALESW
Australian Leather and Suede Clothing Association	ALSCA
Australian Leather Research Association (SAUO)	ALRA
Australian Leave and Holidays Practice Manual [A publication]	ALVE
Australian Lecture Foundation	ALF
Australian Left Review [A publication]	Aus L Rev
Australian Left Review [A publication]	Aust Left R
Australian Left Review [A publication]	Aust Left Rev
Australian Legal Aid (SAUO)	ALA
Australian Legal Monthly Digest [A publication] (DLA)	Austl LMD
Australian Leisure Index [Information service or system] [A publication]	ALI
Australian Liberal Party (SAUO)	ALP
Australian Liberation Front [Political party]	ALF
Australian Libraries: the Essential Directory [A publication]	ALED
Australian Library and Information Association	ALIA
Australian Library and Information Professionals [A publication]	ALIP
Australian Library Fair	ALF
Australian Library Journal (journ.) (SAUS)	ALJ
Australian Library Journal (journ.) (SAUS)	Aust Libr J
Australian Library News [A publication]	Aust Libr News
Australian Library News (journ.) (SAUS)	ALN
Australian Library-Based Information System [National Library of Australia] (NITA)	ALBIS
Australian Light Horse (SAUO)	ALH
Australian Lighthouse Association	ALA
Australian Limousin Breeders' Society	ALBS
Australian Literary Awards and Fellowships [A publication]	ALAF
Australian Literary Society (SAUO)	ALS
Australian Literary Studies (journ.) (SAUS)	ALS
Australian Literature [A database] (NITA)	ALIT
Australian Literature Index [A publication]	ALI
Australian Lithuanian Catholic Federation	ALCF
Australian Lithuanian Community	ALC
Australian Livestock Exporters' Association	ALEA
Australian Loan Council	ALC
Australian Local Government Training Board (SAUS)	ALGTB-2
Australian Logic Teachers' Association	ALTA
Australian Lutheran World Service	ALWS
Australian Lychee Growers' Association	ALGA
Australian Macadamia Growers' Society	AMGS
Australian Macadamia Manufacturers' Association	AMMA
Australian Macadamia Society	AMS
Australian Machine Readable Cataloguing Record Service [National Library of Australia] (NITA)	AMRS
Australian Major Energy Statistics [Database]	AMES

Australian Malaysian Singaporean Association .... AMSA
Australian Malaysian Society .... AMS
Australian Mammal Society (GVA) .... AMS
Australian Management College Mount Eliza Association .... AMCMEA
Australian Management Industrial Association .... AMIA
Australian Manager [*A publication*] .... Aust Mger
Australian Manufacturing Production Commodity Classification .... AMPCC
Australian Map Circle Inc. (SAUO) .... AMC
Australian Map Grid (GEOI) .... AMG
Australian Map Industry Association (SAUS) .... AMIA
Australian Marathon Swimming Federation .... AMSF
Australian MARC [*Machine readable catalogue*] (NITA) .... AUSMARC
Australian MARC [*Machine Readable Catalogue*] **Distribution Service** (NITA) .... AMDS
Australian Marching Association .... AMA
Australian Marine Data Information Service .... AMDIS
Australian Marine Force (SAUO) .... AMF
Australian Marine Industries and Sciences Council (SAUO) .... AMISC
Australian Marine Oil Spill Centre (SAUO) .... AMOSC
Australian Marine Science and Technologies Advisory Council (SAUS) .... AMSTAC
Australian Marine Science and Technologies Advisory Council (or Committee) (SAUO) .... AMSTAC
Australian Marine Science Bulletin (SAUS) .... Aust Mar Sci Bull
Australian Marine Sciences Association .... AMSA
Australian Maritime Engineering Cooperative Reseach Centre (SAUO) .... AMECRC
Australian Maritime Historical Society (SAUO) .... AMHS
Australian Maritime Safety Authority .... AMSA
Australian Market Basket Survey .... AMB
Australian Master Tax Guide Updater [*A publication*] .... MTGU
Australian Mathematical Society (SAUO) .... AMS
Australian Mathematics Olympiad Committee .... AMOC
Australian Meat & Livestock Research & Development Corporation (SAUS) .... AMLRDC
Australian Meatworks Federal Council .... AMFC
Australian Mechanical Copyright Owners Society (SAUO) .... AMCOS
Australian Media Contacts [*A publication*] (ADA) .... AMC
Australian Medical Acupuncture College (SAUO) .... AMAC
Australian Medical Acupuncture Society (SAUO) .... AMAS
Australian Medical Informatics Association (VERA) .... AMIA
Australian Medical Service (SAUO) .... AMS
Australian Medical Writers Association (SAUO) .... AMWA
Australian Merchant Vessel [*Shipping*] (ADA) .... AMV
Australian Merchant Vessel (SAUS) .... AW
Australian Meteorological and Oceanographic Society .... AMOS
Australian Meteorological Magazine [*A publication*] .... AMM
Australian Micrographic Congress (SAUS) .... AMC
Australian Migration Consultants' Association .... AMCA
Australian Migration Office (SAUO) .... AMO
Australian Military Medical Association (SAUO) .... AMMA
Australian Militia (SAUO) .... AM
Australian Militia Force (SAUO) .... AMF
Australian Milk Vendors' Council .... AMVC
Australian Milking Zebu Breed [*Agriculture*] .... AMZB
Australian Mineral Industry (journ.) (SAUS) .... Aust Miner Ind
Australian Mineral Industry (or Industries) Research Association (SAUO) .... AMIRA
Australian Mineral Ventures (SAUS) .... ANW
Australian Minesweeper [*A publication*] .... AMS
Australian Minesweeping and Surveillance System (SAUS) .... AMASS
Australian Mining & Smelting Company Limited (SAUO) .... AM&S
Australian Mining Industrial (or Industry) Council (SAUO) .... AMIC
Australian Mining Industry Research Association (SAUS) .... AMIRA
Australian Mining Standard [*A publication*] .... Aust Mining Stand
Australian Ministry [*A publication*] (APTA) .... AM
Australian Modern Pentathlon Union .... AMPU
Australian Modular Optical Remote Sensor (SAUS) .... AMORS
Australian Mohair Breeders' Association .... AMBA
Australian Molasses Pool [*An association*] .... AMP
Australian Monopoly Association .... AMA
Australian Monthly Magazine [*A publication*] .... Aust Mon Mag
Australian Monthly Newspapers and Periodicals Association (SAUO) .... AMN&PA
Australian Monthly Newspapers and Periodicals Association .... AMNPA
Australian Motor Industries (SAUO) .... AMI
Australian Motor Sports & Automobiles (journ.) (SAUS) .... AMS
Australian Motor Vehicle Standards Committee (SAUO) .... AMVSC
Australian Motorcycle Trailriders' Association .... AMTRA
Australian Mountain Bike Association .... AMBA
Australian Multiexperimental Assessment of SIR-B radar (SAUS) .... AMAS
Australian Museum Society .... AMS
Australian Musical Association (SAUO) .... AMA
Australian Musicians' Guild .... AMG
Australian Mutual Providence Society (SAUO) .... AMp
Australian Nashi Growers' Association .... ANGA
Australian National Advisory Committee for UNESCO Information Circular (journ.) (SAUS) .... UNESCO Inf Circ
Australian National Airlines Commission (SAUO) .... ANAS
Australian National Airlines Conimission (SAUS) .... ANAC
Australian National Airways .... ANA
Australian National Antarctic Research Establishment (CARB) .... ANARE
Australian National Antarctic Research Expeditions (GEOI) .... ANARE
Australian National Antarctic Research Expeditions communications Satellite (SAUS) .... ANARESAT
Australian National Antarctic Research Organisation (SAUS) .... ANARE
Australian National Antarctic Research Satellite .... ANARESAT
Australian National Association for Mental Health. Newsletter [*A publication*] .... Newsl Aust Natn Ass Ment Hlth
Australian National Average Fuel Consumption (SAUS) .... ANAFC
Australian National Botanic Gardens Herbarium (SAUS) .... CBG
Australian National Capital Dancers [*An association*] .... ANCD
Australian National Centre in HIV Social Research (SAUS) .... NCHSR
Australian National Commission for UNESCO (SAUO) .... ANC UNESCO
Australian National Committee for the United Nations (SAUO) .... ANCUN
Australian National Committee for/on Antarctic Research (SAUO) .... ANCAR
Australian National Committee of the International Dairy Federation .... ANCIDF
Australian National Committee, World Energy Council .... ANCWEC
Australian National Copyright Information Centre (SAUS) .... ANCIC
Australian National Council of Women (SAUO) .... ANCW
Australian National Council on AIDS and Related Diseases (SAUO) .... ANCARD
Australian National Dictionary [*A publication*] .... AND
Australian National Discase Eradication Campaign (SAUS) .... ANDEC
Australian National Eisteddfod Society .... ANES
Australian National Energy Advisory Committee (SAUO) .... ANEAC
Australian National Field Days .... ANFD
Australian National Field Days Committee .... ANFDC
Australian National Film School (WDAA) .... ANFS
Australian National Flower Show Organising Committee .... ANFSOC
Australian National Formulary .... ANF
Australian National Four Wheel Drive Council .... ANFWDC
Australian National Gallery (SAUO) .... ANG
Australian National Genomic Info. Service (HGEN) .... ANGIS
Australian National Heart Foundation (SAUO) .... ANHF
Australian National Herbarium (SAUO) .... CANB
Australian National Herbarium, Atherton (SAUS) .... QRS
Australian National Herbarium Specimen Information Register (SAUS) .... ANHSIR
Australian National Highway (SAUS) .... ANH
Australian National Historic Site (SAUS) .... ANHF
Australian National Hotels (SAUO) .... ANH
Australian National Humanities and Arts Library (SAUO) .... ANHAL
Australian National Industries (SAUS) .... ANI
Australian National Kennel Council .... ANKC
Australian National Kung Fu Federation .... ANKFF
Australian National Line (SAUO) .... ANLINE
Australian National Maritime Association Inc. (SAUO) .... ANMA
Australian National Opinion Polls (SAUS) .... ANOP
Australian National Parks Council (SAUS) .... ANPC
Australian National Party [*Political party*] .... ANP
Australian National Publicity Association (SAUO) .... ANPA
Australian National Review [*A publication*] .... Aust National Rev
Australian National Review [*A publication*] .... Aust Natn Rev
Australian National Social Sciences Library (SAUO) .... ANSSL
Australian National Socialist Party (SAUO) .... ANSP
Australian National Sportfishing Association (EAIO) .... ANSA
Australian National Standards Institute (SAUO) .... ANSI
Australian National Standards Laboratory (SAUO) .... ANSL
Australian National Times (SAUS) .... ANT
Australian National University .... ANU
Australian National University, Canberra, ACT, Australia [*Library symbol*] [*Library of Congress*] (LCLS) .... AuCU
Australian National University, Canberra, ACT, Australia [*Library symbol*] [*Library of Congress*] (LCLS) .... AuU
Australian National University. Historical Journal (journ.) (SAUS) .... ANUHJ
Australian National University Library and Information Service .... ANULIS
Australian National University Library Automated Systems (SAUO) .... ANULAS
Australian National University Meta Language (VERA) .... ANUML
Australian National University. News (journ.) (SAUS) .... ANU News
Australian National University. Social Science Monograph (journ.) (SAUS) .... ANUSSM
Australian National University Staff Association .... ANUSA
Australian National University Zoology Department (SAUO) .... ANUZ
Australian National Wildlife Collection (SAUS) .... ANWC
Australian National Word Festival .... ANWF
Australian Native Dog Training Society of New South Wales [*Australia*] .... ANDTSNSW
Australian Naval and Military Expeditionary Force (SAUS) .... AN&MEF
Australian Naval Reserve .... ANR
Australian Netherlands Chamber of Commerce .... ANCC
Australian Neurological Research Institute .... ANRI
Australian Neutron Beam Users' Group .... ANBUG
Australian New Guinea (SAUO) .... ANG
Australian, New Zealand, African [*Radio network*] .... ANZA
Australian New Zealand Scientific Exploration Society (SAUO) .... ANZSES
Australian Newspaper Council (SAUO) .... ANC
Australian Newspaper Guild (SAUO) .... ANG
Australian Newsprint Mills Limited (SAUS) .... ANM
Australian NGO Environment Network (SAUS) .... ANEN
Australian Nixa [*Record label*] .... ANix
Australian Noise Exposure Index .... ANEI
Australian Northern Territory (SAUS) .... ANT
Australian Nuclear Science and Technology Organisation (SAUS) .... ANSTRO
Australian Nuclear Science and Technology Organisation (or Organization) (SAUO) .... ANSTO
Australian Nuclear Science and Technology Organization (SAUS) .... ANSTO
Australian Nuffied Farming Scholars' Association .... ANFSA
Australian Numerical Meteorology Research Center (SAUS) .... ANMRC
Australian Nurses' Journal [*A publication*] (APTA) .... ANJ
Australian Nursing Homes and Extended Care Association .... ANHECA

Australian Nutgrowers' Council	ANC
Australian Oceanographic Data Center (or Centre) (SAUS)	AODC
Australian Oceanographic Data Centre	AODC
Australian Officer (SAUO)	AO
Australian Official Journal of Patents, Trade Marks and Designs (journ.) (SAUS)	AOJP
Australian Oil and Gas (SAUO)	AOG
Australian Oil Refining (SAUO)	AOR
Australian Oilseed Crushers' Association	AOCA
Australian Oilseeds Federation	AOF
Australian Olympic Federation (SAUO)	AOER
Australian Onion Association	AOA
Australian Optical Fibre Research Pty Ltd. (SAUO)	AOFR
Australian Options Market (NUMA)	AOM
Australian Orchidee Foundation (SAUS)	AOF
Australian Ordnance Council	AOC
Australian Organisations Coordinating Committee for Overseas Students (SAUO)	AOCCOS
Australian Organizations Industrial Policy	AOIP
Australian Origin Nuclear Material (SAUS)	AONM
Australian Ornithologists Union (SAUO)	AOU
Australian Orthopaedic Foot and Ankle Society (SAUO)	AOFAS
Australian Osteopathic Association	AOA
Australian Outlook [A publication]	Aus Outl
Australian Outward Bound Foundation	AOBF
Australian Overseas Construction Council	AOCC
Australian Overseas Disaster Relief Organization (SAUO)	AODRO
Australian Overseas Smelting (SAUO)	AOS
Australian Overseas Telecommunications Corporation (SAUO)	AOTC
Australian Overseas Trading Corporation (SAUO)	AOTA
Australian Overseas Transport Association (SAUO)	AOTA
Australian Owned Companies Association	AOCA
Australian Ownership & Control of Information (SAUS)	AOCI
Australian Pacific Economic Cooperation Committee	AUSPECC
Australian Packet Switching Service [Telecommunications] (NITA)	AUSTPAC
Australian Packet Switching Service (SAUS)	AUSTPAC Service
Australian PaintBall Players' Association	APBPA
Australian Paper Manufacturers (SAUO)	APM
Australian Paper Manufacturers Federation (SAUO)	APMF
Australian Paper Mills (SAUO)	APM
Australian Parliamentary Paper [A publication]	Aust Parl Paper
Australian Particleboard Research Institute	APRI
Australian Patent (SAUS)	AUST P
Australian Payments Clearing Association	APCA
Australian Payroll Tax Manual [A publication]	APY
Australian Peace Education and Research Association (SAUO)	APERA
Australian Peak Shippers' Association	APSA
Australian People for Health, Education and Development Abroad (SAUO)	APHEDA
Australian Perendale Association	APA
Australian Performing Right Association (SAUO)	APRA
Australian Periodicals in Print [A publication] (APTA)	APIP
Australian Permanent Building Society (SAUO)	APBS
Australian Permanent Force (SAUO)	APF
Australian Personal Computer (journ.) (SAUS)	APC
Australian Personnel Management (journ.) (SAUS)	APM
Australian Pesticides Analytical Committee	APAC
Australian Pet Industry Joint Advisory Council	APIJAC
Australian Petanque Federation	APF
Australian Petroleum Industry Research Association	APIRA
Australian Petroleum Institute	API
Australian Petroleum Production and Exploration Association Limited (SAUO)	APPEA
Australian Physicist (journ.) (SAUS)	Aust Phys
Australian Picture Framers' Association	APFA
Australian Pig Artificial Breeding Association	APABA
Australian Pig Breeders' Association	APBA
Australian Pig Breeders' Society	APBS
Australian Pioneers' Club	APC
Australian Pistacio Growers' Association	APGA
Australian Plaiters and Whipmakers' Association	APWA
Australian Planning Institute. Journal (journ.) (SAUS)	API Journal
Australian Plant Pathology Society (SAUS)	APPS
Australian Plant Specialists Group (SAUO)	APSG
Australian Plastic Modellers' Association	APMA
Australian Pocket Oxford Dictionary (journ.) (SAUS)	APOD
Australian Podiatry Association	APA
Australian Podiatry Council	APC
Australian Police Journal [A publication]	A Pol J
Australian Police Journal [A publication]	Aust Pol J
Australian Police Ministers' Council, Senior Officers' Group	APMCSOG
Australian Political Register [Australian Consolidated Press] [Database]	APOL
Australian Political Studies Association (SAUO)	APSA
Australian Poll Dorset Association	APDA
Australian Poll Hereford Association	APHA
Australian Polo Council	APC
Australian Pony Club Council	APCC
Australian Population Association	APA
Australian Population Research Institute	APRU
Australian Porcelain Decorators' Association	APDA
Australian Pork Producers Federation (SAUO)	APPF
Australian Port Authorities Association (SAUO)	APAA
Australian Postal Commission (SAUO)	AUPOSTCOM
Australian Potato Industry Council	APIC
Australian Powerlifting Federation	APF

Australian Presbyterian Life [A publication]	Aust Presb Life
Australian Pre-School Quarterly [A publication]	Aust Presch Q
Australian Preservation and Conservation Abroad Group	APACA
Australian Primary Producers Union (WDAA)	APPU
Australian Product Liability Association	APLA
Australian Product Liability Reporter [A publication]	APLR
Australian Product Number Association	APNA
Australian Productivity Action [A publication]	Aust Prod Action
Australian Products First [An association]	APF
Australian Professional Interpreting Society (SAUO)	APIS
Australian Professional Rodeo Association	APRA
Australian Professional Society on Alcohol & other Drugs (SAUO)	APSAD
Australian Professional Triathletes Association	APTA
Australian Property Law Bulletin [A publication]	APLB
Australian Property News [A publication] (ADA)	APN
Australian Prosthodontic Society	APS
Australian Protea Growers' Association	APGA
Australian Provincial Insurance (SAUO)	APA
Australian Proving Ground (SAUO)	APG
Australian Psychoanalytical Society	APS
Australian Psychologist [A publication]	Aus Psych
Australian Psychologists Press [A publication]	APP
Australian Psychology and Hypnotherapy Association	APHA
Australian Public Affairs Information Service	AusPAIS
Australian Public Affairs Information Service (journ.) (SAUS)	APAIS
Australian Public Library Issues [A publication]	Aust Publ Libr Issues
Australian Public Opinion Polls (SAUO)	APOP
Australian Public Risk Insurance Management Association	APRIMA
Australian Public Sector and Broadcasting Union	APSBU
Australian Public Service Benevolent Society Inc.	APSBSI
Australian Public Service Board (SAUO)	APSB
Australian Publishers' Bureau	APB
Australian Pulp and Paper Industry Technical Association. Proceedings (journ.) (SAUS)	APPITA Piroc
Australian Pulp and Paper Institute [Monash University] [Australia]	APPI
Australian Quadriplegic Association (SAUO)	AQA
Australian Quarterly (journ.) (SAUS)	AQ
Australian Quaternary Data Archive (SAUO)	AQUADATA
Australian Queen Bee Breeders' Association	AQBBA
Australian Queensland Fever (DAVI)	QuF
Australian Quilters' Association	AQA
Australian Racing and Breeding Stables (SAUO)	ARABS
Australian Radiation Laboratory (CARB)	ARL
Australian Radio DX Club (SAUO)	ARDXC
Australian Radio Propagation Committee (SAUO)	ARPC
Australian Radio Technical Sevices and Patents (SAUS)	ARTS&P
Australian Railway and Locomotive Historical Society (SAUO)	ARLHS
Australian Railway Union (SAUO)	ARU
Australian Railways Industry Commission	ARIC
Australian Railways Research and Development Organisation (SAUS)	ARRDO
Australian Rainfall and Runoff [Meteorology]	ARR
Australian Rare or Threatened (SAUS)	AROT
Australian Records Management Association	ARMA
Australian Recreation and Sport Fishing Confederation (SAUO)	ARSFC
Australian Red Cross Society (SAUO)	ARC
Australian Red Cross Society (SAUO)	ARCS
Australian Red Poll Cattle Breeders' Association	ARPCBA
Australian Red Poll Society	ARPS
Australian Refined Diagnosis Related Groups (SAUO)	AR-DRG
Australian Region of the International Plant Propagators' Society	ARIPPS
Australian Register of Therapeutic Goods	ARTG
Australian Registrars Committee	ARC
Australian Religion Studies Review [A publication] (APTA)	ARSR
Australian Remote Sensing Conference (GEOI)	ARSC
Australian Renderers' Association	ARA
Australian Reptile Park (SAUS)	ARP
Australian Research Council	ARC
Australian Resources and Environment Assessment (SAUO)	AREA
Australian Resources Quarterly [A publication]	ARQ
Australian Retinitis Pigmentosa Association	ARPA
Australian Review [A publication]	Aust R
Australian Review Council	ARC
Australian Rights Movement	ARM
Australian Road Index [Australian Road Research Board] (NITA)	ARi
Australian Road Research Board	AARB
Australian Road Research Board. Proceedings (journ.) (SAUS)	Aust Road Res Bd Proc
Australian Road Research (journ.) (SAUS)	Aust Road Res
Australian Romney Association	ARA
Australian Rope and Cordage Workers' Union	ARCWU
Australian Rotary Health Research Fund	ARHRF
Australian Rough Riders Association (SAUO)	ARRA
Australian Rowing Council	ARC
Australian Royal Air Force (SAUO)	ARAF
Australian Rules Football League of Sydney	ARFLS
Australian Rural Publishers' Association	ARPA
Australian Rural Research in Progress [Database]	ARRIP
Australian Rural Youth	ARY
Australian Safety News (SAUS)	Austr Safety News
Australian Safety News [A publication]	Aust Saf N
Australian Sahiwal Society	ASS
Australian Sales Tax Cases [Australia]	ASTC
Australian Salvadorian Association	ASA
Australian Satellite [Telecommunications] (NITA)	AUSSAT
Australian Scholarly Newsletter [A publication]	ASN

Australian School Catalogue Information Service (ADA) .... ASCIS
Australian School Cataloguing Information Service (SAUS) .... ASCIS
Australian School Librarian [*A publication*] .... Aust School Libn
Australian School of Health and Beauty .... ASHB
Australian School of Hypnotherapy .... ASH
Australian Schools' Cricket Council .... ASCC
Australian Schools' Rugby Football Union .... ASRFU
Australian Schools Sports Council .... ASSC
Australian Science Advisory Committee .... ASAC
Australian Science and Technology Council (SAUO) .... ASTC
Australian Science and Technology Council .... ASTEC
Australian Science and Technology Counsellor Network .... ASTCON
Australian Science Network (SAUO) .... ASN
Australian Science Teachers Association (SAUO) .... ASTA
Australian Science Teachers Journal (SAUS) .... Aust Sci Teach J
Australian Scientific Research Liaison [*British*] .... ASRL
Australian Scrabble Players' Association .... ASPA
Australian Screen Directors' Association .... ASDA
Australian Second Language Proficiency Ratings [*Ingram and Wylie*] (TES) .... ASLPR
Australian Secret Intelligence Organization (LAIN) .... ASIO
Australian Security and Intelligence Organisation (SAUO) .... ASIO
Australian Security Industry Association .... ASIA
Australian Security Industry Association Ltd. (SAUO) .... ASIAL
Australian Security Intelligence Service (SAUO) .... ASIS
Australian Security Organisation (SAUO) .... ASO
Australian Security Service (SAUO) .... ASS
Australian Seed Industry Advisory Council .... ASIAC
Australian Seismological Center .... ASC
Australian Seismological Centre (SAUO) .... ASC
Australian Sentencing Digest [*A publication*] .... ASD
Australian Sentencing Judgements Bulletin [*A publication*] .... ASJB
Australian Serials in Print [*A publication*] .... ASIP
Australian Shareholders Association (SAUO) .... ASA
Australian Sheep and Wool Information Service [*Database*] .... ASWIS
Australian Sheep Breeders Association (SAUO) .... ASBA
Australian Sheepbreeders Association (SAUO) .... ASA
Australian Shiatsu College .... ASC
Australian Shipbuilders' Association .... ASA
Australian Shipbuilding Industries (SAUO) .... ASI
Australian Shipping Board (SAUO) .... ASB
Australian Shipping Officers Association (SAUO) .... ASOA
Australian Shooters Party [*Political party*] .... ASP
Australian Silky Terrier Club .... ASTC
Australian Skeptics, Inc. [*An association*] .... ASI
Australian Ski Areas Association .... ASAA
Australian Small Animal Veterinary Association (GVA) .... ASAVA
Australian Small Business Awards .... ASBA
Australian Small-Bore and Air Rifle Association .... ASARA
Australian Social Security Cases [*A publication*] .... ASSC
Australian Social Security Guide [*A publication*] .... ASS
Australian Social Welfare [*A publication*] .... Aust Soc Welf
Australian Social Welfare Impact [*A publication*] .... Aust Soc Welf Impact
Australian Social Work [*A publication*] .... Aus Soc W
Australian Social Work [*A publication*] .... Aust Soc Work
Australian Socialist Party (SAUO) .... ASP
Australian Society [*A publication*] (ADA) .... AS
Australian Society [*A publication*] .... Aus Soc
Australian Society [*A publication*] (APTA) .... Aust Soc
Australian Society for Animal Production (SAUS) .... ASAP
Australian Society for Classical Studies .... ASCS
Australian Society for Intercountry Aid (Children) .... ASIAC
Australian Society for Microbiology (SAUO) .... ASM
Australian Society for Sports History .... ASSH
Australian Society for/of Animal Production (SAUO) .... ASAP
Australian Society of Accountants (ODBW) .... ASA
Australian Society of Anaesthesists (SAUO) .... ASA
Australian Society of Anaesthetists (SAUS) .... ASA
Australian Society of Animal Production (SAUO) .... ASAP
Australian Society of Association Executives .... ASAE
Australian Society of Authors (SAUO) .... ASA
Australian Society of Calligraphers .... ASC
Australian Society of Clinical and Experimental Pharmacologists (SAUO) .... ASCEP
Australian Society of Dairy Technology. Technical Publication (journ.) (SAUS) .... Tech Publ Aust Soc Dairy Technol
Australian Society of Endodontology (SAUO) .... ASE
Australian Society of Engineers (SAUO) .... ASE
Australian Society of Engineers .... ASOE
Australian Society of Herpetologists, Inc. (SAUO) .... ASH
Australian Society of Horticultural Science .... ASHS
Australian Society of Infectious Diseases .... ASID
Australian Society of New York [*Later, Australia-New Zealand Society of New York*] (EA) .... AS of NY
Australian Society of New York (SAUO) .... AS of NY
Australian Society of Plant Physiologists (SAUO) .... ASPP
Australian Society of Prosthodontists (SAUO) .... ASP
Australian Society of Real Estate Agents and Valuers .... ASREAV
Australian Society of Rheology .... ASR
Australian Society of Soil Science (SAUO) .... ASSS
Australian Society of Soil Science (SAUO) .... ASSSI
Australian Society of Sport Administrators .... ASSA
Australian Society of Sugar Cane Technologists. Proceedings of the Conference (journ.) (SAUS) .... Proc Conf Aust Soc Sugar Cane Technol
Australian Society of Travel Writers .... ASTW
Australian Sociological Association .... ASA
Australian Softwood Producers' Council .... ASPC
Australian Sogetsu Teachers' Association .... ASTA
Australian Soil and Plant Analysis Council .... ASPAC
Australian Songwriters' Association .... ASA
Australian Spatial data Infrastructure (SAUS) .... ASDI
Australian Special Air Service Regiment (SAUS) .... SASR
Australian Special Air Services (VNW) .... ASAS
Australian Special Libraries [*A publication*] .... ASL
Australian Special Libraries News (journ.) (SAUS) .... Aust Spec Libr News
Australian Speedway Media Association .... ASMA
Australian Sponsored Training Scholarships (SAUS) .... ASTAS
Australian Sport Aviation Confederation .... ASAC
Australian Sport Climbing Federation .... ASCF
Australian Sport Index [*Database*] .... AUSPORT
Australian Sporting Goods Association .... ASGA
Australian Sports Acrobatic Federation .... ASAF
Australian Sports and Economics Institute .... ASEI
Australian Sports Science Council .... ASSC
Australian Staff Corps (SAUO) .... ASC
Australian Stamp Duties [*A publication*] .... ASTM
Australian Standard Diagnostic Techniques (SAUO) .... ASDT
Australian Standard Industry Classification (SAUS) .... ASIC
Australian Standard Research Classification .... ASRC
Australian Standard White [*Wheat*] (ADA) .... ASW
Australian Standard White-Noodles (SAUO) .... ASWN
Australian Standards (SAUS) .... AS
Australian State Family Law Legislation [*A publication*] .... ASFL
Australian Statistics [*Database*] .... AUSSTATS
Australian Steel Association .... ASA
Australian Stevedoring Supervisors' Association .... ASSA
Australian Stock Exchange .... ASX
Australian Stock Exchange (SG) .... Au
Australian Stock Exchange Derivatives (NUMA) .... ASXD
Australian Stock Exchange Indices [*Database*] [*Sydney Stock Exchange*] [*Information service or system*] (CRD) .... ASE
Australian Stock Exchange Indices [*Database*] [*Sydney Stock Exchange*] [*Information service or system*] .... ASEINDEX
Australian Stock Exchanges Share Prices [*Database*] .... AUSTOCK
Australian Stock Horse Society .... ASHS
Australian Street Machine Federation .... ASMF
Australian String Teachers' Association .... ASTA
Australian Student Christian Movement (SAUO) .... ASCM
Australian Studies Association .... ASA
Australian Studies Resources [*Database*] .... AUST STUDY
Australian Studies Schools Project .... ASSP
Australian Submarine Corporation (SAUO) .... ASC
Australian Sunflower Association .... ASA
Australian Superfine Wool Growers' Association .... ASWGA
Australian Surface Ship Towed Array Surveillance System (SAUS) .... ASSTASS
Australian Surfers' Association .... ASA
Australian Surfriders' Association .... ASA
Australian Survey Office (GEOI) .... ASO
Australian Surveying and Land Information Group (GEOI) .... AUSLIG
Australian Swimming [*An association*] .... AS
Australian Synchronised Swimming .... ASS
Australian Synchrotron Beam Users' Group .... ASBUG
Australian Table Grape Growers' Association .... ATGGA
Australian Table Tennis Association .... ATTA
Australian Tax Decisions [*A publication*] (DLA) .... Austr Tax
Australian Tax Monitor [*A publication*] .... ATM
Australian Tax Planning Report (journ.) (SAUS) .... APX
Australian Taxation Office (SAUS) .... Aust Telecomm Res
Australian Taxation Office Practice [*A publication*] .... ATOP
Australian Taxpayers Association (SAUO) .... ATA
Australian Teacher [*A publication*] .... Aust Teacher
Australian Teachers Federation (SAUO) .... ATF
Australian Teachers of Media [*An association*] .... ATM
Australian Technical Publications (SAUS) .... ATP
Australian Technology Export Committee .... ATEC
Australian Telecommunication Standardization Committee (ACRL) .... ATSC
Australian Telecommunications Authority (SAUS) .... ATA
Australian Telecommunications Commission (SAUO) .... AUTELCOM
Australian Telecommunications Research (SAUS) .... ATR
Australian Television Network .... ATN
Australian Terms (SAUS) .... AusT
Australian Terrier Club of America (EA) .... ATCA
Australian Territory (EERA) .... TER
Australian Tertiary Institutions Consulting Companies Association (SAUO) .... ATICCA
Australian Textile, Clothing, and Footwear Industry Training Council.......... ATCFITC
Australian Tibet Council .... ATC
Australian Timber Importers Federation (SAUO) .... ATIF
Australian Timber Industry Stabilization Conference .... AUSTIS
Australian Timber Producers Council (SAUO) .... ATPC
Australian Timber Research Institute .... ATRI
Australian Tin Producers' Association .... ATPA
Australian Tin Producers' Council .... ATPC
Australian Tire Manufacturers' Association .... ATMA
Australian Tomato Processors' Association .... ATPA
Australian Toolmakers Association (SAUO) .... ATA
Australian Torts Reporter [*A publication*] .... ATOR
Australian Torts Reports [*A publication*] .... Aust Torts Reports
Australian Touch Association .... ATA
Australian Tourism Commission .... ATCO

Australian Tourism Exchange	ATE
Australian Tourism Industry Association	ATIA
Australian Tourism Research Institute	ATRI
Australian Toy Association	ATA
Australian Toy Library Association	ATLA
Australian Trade Commission (EA)	ATC
Australian Trade Commission	AUSTRADE
Australian Trade Practices Reporter. Cases and Decisions Digest [A publication]	ATPR (Digest)
Australian Trade Practices Reporter. Commission Decisions [A publication]	ATPR (Com)
Australian Training Information Network (SAUS)	TRAIN
Australian Transcontinental Airways	ATA
Australian Translators Association (SAUO)	ATA
Australian Transplant Sports Association	ATSA
Australian Transport (journ.) (SAUS)	Aust Transp
Australian Transport Literature Informatin System [Database on AUSINET] (NITA)	ATLS
Australian Transputer Centre (SAUS)	ATC
Australian Trifolium Genetic Resource Centre (SAUO)	ATGRC
Australian Tropical Research Foundation	AUSTROP
Australian Trust for Conservation Volunteers	ATFCV
Australian Tug-of-War Association	ATOWA
Australian Tuna Boat Owners' Association	ATBOA
Australian Tuna Boat Owners Association (SAUO)	ATBOA
Australian Tuna Canners Association (SAUS)	ATCA
Australian Turkey Federation	ATF
Australian Turkish Islamic Federation	ATIF
Australian Tyre Dealers' Association	ATDA
Australian Underground Construction and Tunnelling Association	AUCTA
Australian Underwater Hockey Association	AUHA
Australian Underwriters Federation (SAUO)	AUF
Australian Uniform Building Regulations Coordinating Council (SAUO)	AUBRCC
Australian United Corp. (SAUO)	AUC
Australian United Fresh Fruit and Vegetable Association	AUFFVA
Australian United Press	AUP
Australian United Press, Ltd. (SAUO)	AUP
Australian Universities Academic Research Network (SAUS)	AARNET
Australian Universities Commission (WDAA)	AUC
Australian Universities Language and Literature Association Journal (SAUS)	AULLAJ
Australian Universities Modern Language Association (SAUS)	AUMLA
Australian Universities Sports Federation	AUSF
Australian Unlisted Securities Quotation System	AUSQS
Australian Uranium Producers Forum (SAUO)	AUPF
Australian Urban and Regional Information Systems Association Inc. (SAUO)	AURISA
Australian Utility Truck (SAUS)	UTE
Australian Valuation Office (SAUO)	AVO
Australian Vegetable Growers' Federation	AVGF
Australian Vegetarian Society	AVS
Australian Veterans and Defence Services Council [Also, AVADSC]	AVDSC
Australian Veterans and Defense Services Council [Also, AVDSC]	AVADSC
Australian Veterinary (SAUS)	Aust Vet J
Australian Veterinary and Chemicals Association (SAUO)	AVCA
Australian Veterinary Association (GVA)	AVA
Australian Veterinary Emergency Plan	AUSVETPLAN
Australian Vice-Chancellors Committee (SAUS)	AVCC
Australian Vietnam War Veterans' Trust	AVWVT
Australian Visual Copyright Society	AVCS
Australian Vocational Training System	AVTS
Australian Volleyball Association	AVA
Australian Waste Management Association	AWMA
Australian Water Research Advisory Council (SAUS)	AWRAC
Australian Water Ski Association	AWSKA
Australian Waterbird Association	AWA
Australian Weightlifting Federation	AWF
Australian Welding Journal (SAUS)	Aust Weld J
Australian Wheat Starch Producers' Association	AWSPA
Australian Wheatgrowers Federation (SAUO)	AWF
Australian Wheelchair Athletes [An association]	AWA
Australian Wheelchair Sports Federation	AWSF
Australian White [Cattle]	AW
Australian Wholesale Softgoods Federation (SAUO)	AWSF
Australian Wide Array of Geomagnetic Stations	AWA
Australian Wide Array of Geomagnetic Stations	AWAGS
Australian Wildlife Protection Council	AWPC
Australian Wind Energy Association (SAUO)	AWEA
Australian Window Roller Shutter Association	AWRSA
Australian Windscreen Association	AWA
Australian Wine and Brandy Producers' Association	AWBPA
Australian Wine Foundation	AWF
Australian Winemakers' Forum	AWF
Australian Winter Storm Experiment (SAUS)	AWSE
Australian Wire Industry (SAUO)	AWI
Australian Women's Book Review [A publication]	AWBR
Australian Women's Bowling Council	AWBC
Australian Women's Tennis Association	AWTA
Australian Women's Vigoro Association	AWVA
Australian Wood Panels Association	AWPA
Australian Wool and Meat Producers Federation (SAUO)	AWMPF
Australian Wool Bureau	AWB
Australian Wool Industries (SAUO)	AWI
Australian Wool Industry Conference (SAUO)	AWIC
Australian Wool Processors' Council	AWPC
Australian Wool Realization Agency (SAUO)	AWRA
Australian Wool Realization Commission (SAUO)	AWRC
Australian Wool Selling Brokers Employers' Federation	AWSBEF
Australian Woolgrowers and Graziers Council (SAUO)	AWGC
Australian Worker [A publication]	AW
Australian Worker's Compensation Case Digests [A publication]	AWCCD
Australian Workers' Compensation Guide [A publication]	AWK
Australian Workman [A publication]	AW
Australian Wrestling Union	AWU
Australian Writers and Editors' Guide [A publication]	AWEG
Australian X.25 public packet-switched data service operated by Telecom (SAUS)	AUSTPAC
Australian Yearbook of International Law [A publication] (DLA)	Aust Y Int L
Australian Youth Hotels Association (SAUO)	AYHA
Australian Youth Initiatives Grant	AYIG
Australian Youth Policy Action Coalition (SAUO)	AYPAC
Australian Yugoslav Welfare Society	AYWS
Australian Zebu Association	AZA
Australian Zoologist (SAUS)	Aust Zool
Australiana Society	AS
Australian-American Education Foundation (SAUO)	AAEF
Australian-American Engineering Corporation (SAUO)	AAEC
Australian-Antarctic Discordance [Geology]	AAD
Australian-Arab Association	AAA
Australian-Arab Chamber of Commerce and Industry	AACCI
Australian-Asian Society of Queensland	AASQ
Australian-British Trade Association. Bulletin [A publication]	ABTA Bull
Australian-British-Dutch-American (SAUS)	ABDA
Australia-New Zealand Association [Also, The ANZA Club] (AC)	ANZA
Australia-New Zealand Business Council	ANZBC
Australia-New Zealand Closer Economic Relations (SAUO)	CER
Australia-New Zealand Closer Economic Relations Agreement (SAUO)	ANZCER
Australia-New Zealand Closer Economic Relations Trade Agreement (BARN)	ANZCERTA
Australia-New Zealand Direct Line	ANZDL
Australia-New Zealand Studies Centre [Pennsylvania State University]	ANZSC
Australia-New Zealand-Canada (SAUO)	ANZCAN
Australian-German Welfare Society	AGWS
Australian-Greek Welfare Society	AGWS
Australian-Indian Society	AIS
Australian-Italian Association (SAUO)	AIA
Australian-Japan Foundation (SAUO)	AJF
Australian-New Zealand Army Corps (VNW)	ANZAC
Australian/new Zealand EDIFACT Board (SAUO)	AZEB
Australian-New Zealand Society of New York (EA)	A-NZSNY
Australian-New Zealand-United States security Treaty (SAUS)	ANZUS
Australians Against Further Immigration [An association]	AAFI
Australians against Further Immigration [Political party]	AFI
Australians Against Further Immigration Party [An association]	AAFIP
Australians for Reconciliation [An association]	AFR
Australian-Spanish Co-operative Development (SAUS)	ASCOD
Australian-United States Ministerial Talks [Conference]	AUSMIN
Australian/Victorian Biathlon Association	AVBA
Australia-Papua New Guinea Education and Training Scheme (SAUO)	APETS
Australia-Papua New Guinea Friendship Association	APNGFA
Australia's Heritage [A publication]	Aust Her
Australia's Independent Optometrists [An association]	AIO
Australia's Indigenous Peoples Party [Political party]	AIP
Australia's International Engineering Exhibition	AIEE
Australia's Library, Information and Archives Services: an Encyclopaedia of Practice and Practitioners [A publication]	ALIAS
Australias Long-term Ecological Research & Monitoring Program (SAUS)	ALTERM
Australia's Strategic Planning in the Nineties [An association]	ASP90
Australia-Taiwan Business Council	ATBC
Australia-Thailand Association	ATA
Australia-Thailand Business Council	ATBC
Australia/West India Outward Shipping Conference (SAUS)	WESTINDIACON
Australia/West Pakistan Outward Shipping Conference (SAUS)	WESTPACON
Australia-Wide Funeral Information [Database]	AFIN
Austrgian Pipeline Industry Association (SAUO)	APIA
Austria	A
Austria [ANSI two-letter standard code] (CNC)	AT
Austria [MARC country of publication code] [Library of Congress] (LCCP)	au
Austria	AU
Austria	AUS
Austria (SAUS)	Aus
Austria	AUST
Austria (VRA)	Aust
Austria [ANSI three-letter standard code] (CNC)	AUT
Austria [MARC geographic area code] [Library of Congress] (LCCP)	e-au-
Austria [International civil aircraft marking] (ODBW)	OE
Austria, Bohemia, Bosnia, Croatia, Moravia, Bukovina, Transylvania, Galicia, Hungary (SAUS)	Austro-Hungarian Empire
Austria Erit In Orbe Ultima [Austria Will Be The Last in the World] [Variation of 15th-century inscription]	AEIOU
Austria Esperantista Federacio (SAUS)	AEF
Austria Fund [Associated Press] (SAG)	Austr
Austria Fund [NYSE symbol] (SPSG)	OST
Austria Microsystems International (NITA)	AMI
Austria Philatelic Society of New York (EA)	APSNY
Austria Press Agentur (SAUS)	APA
Austria Presse Agentur [Press agency] [Austria]	APA

Austria (Republic) SIGNs [*NYSE symbol*] (TTSB) ... SPJ
Austria [*Republic of*] **Stock Index Growth Notes** [*Associated Press*] (SAG) ... AustStk
Austria [*Republic of*] **Stock Index Growth Notes** [*NYSE symbol*] (SPSG) ... SPJ
Austria Stock Index Growth Notes (SAUS) ... SPJ
Austriae Est Imperare Orbi Universo [*It Is Given to Austria to Rule the Whole World*] [*Variation of 15th-century inscription*] ... AEIOU
Australian Computer Emergency Response Team (SAUO) ... AUSCERT
Austrian Academic Computer Network (SAUO) ... ACOnet
Austrian Air [*ICAO designator*] (AD) ... SO
Austrian Air Ambulance [*ICAO designator*] (FAAC) ... OAF
Austrian Air Services [*ICAO designator*] (FAAC) ... AAS
Austrian Air Services [*Austria*] [*ICAO designator*] (ICDA) ... SO
Austrian Airlines [*ICAO designator*] (FAAC) ... AUA
Austrian Airlines [*ICAO designator*] (AD) ... OS
Austrian Airtransport [*ICAO designator*] (FAAC) ... AAT
Austrian Airtransport (SAUS) ... OB
Austrian Airways [*Oesterreichische Luftverkehrs AG*] ... AUA
Austrian Art Service (SAUS) ... AAS
Austrian Atomic Energy Group (SAUO) ... AUSTRIATOM
Austrian CCITT Comittee (SAUO) ... ACC
Austrian Communist Party [*Political party*] ... AKP
Austrian Cooperative Research (SAUS) ... ACR
Austrian Cultural Institute (EA) ... ACI
Austrian Documentation Centre for Media and Communication Research [*Information service or system*] (IID) ... ADMAC
Austrian Documentation Centre for Media and Comunication Research (SAUS) ... ADMACR
Austrian Forum [*Defunct*] (EA) ... AF
Austrian Institute [*Later, ACI*] (EA) ... AI
Austrian Institute (SAUS) ... AI
Austrian Institute for Peace Research and Peace Education (SAUO) ... APRI
Austrian Microsystems, Inc. (SAUS) ... AMI
Austrian Microsystems Incorporated (SAUO) ... AMI
Austrian National Tourist Office (EA) ... ANTO
Austrian Non-Governmental Organization (SAUS) ... AUS-NGO
Austrian Press and Information Service (EA) ... APIS
Austrian RADAR Site Analysis ... ARSA
Austrian Schilling [*Monetary unit*] ... AS
Austrian Society of Acupuncture and Auricular Therapy [*Multinational organization*] (EAIO) ... ASAAT
Austrian Telefunken [*Record label*] ... AusT
Austrian Trade Commission (EA) ... ATC
Austrian Trade Union Federation ... ATUF
Austrian Traded Index (NUMA) ... ATX
Austrian-Spanish Co-Operative Development (SAUS) ... ASCOD
Austria's Empire Is Obviously Upset [*Variation of 15th-century inscription*] ... AEIOU
Austria's Empire Is Overall Universal [*Variation of 15th-century inscription*] ... AEIOU
Austro-Daimler Motoren AG [*Automobile manufacturer*] ... ADM
Austroton [*Austria, Germany, etc.*] [*Record label*] ... Attn
Auswaertiges [*Nonresident*] [*German*] ... Ausw
Auswaertiges Amt [*Foreign Ministry*] [*German*] ... AA
Auswaschung [*Erosion*] [*German*] ... Auswasch
Auteroposterior [*Medicine*] (DHP) ... AP
Authentic ... A
Authentic ... AUTH
Authentic (WDMC) ... auth
Authentic (AABC) ... AUTHEN
Authentic (VRA) ... authn
Authentic Fitness [*NYSE symbol*] (TTSB) ... ASM
Authentic Fitness Corp. [*NYSE symbol*] (SPSG) ... ASM
Authentic Fitness Corp. [*Associated Press*] (SAG) ... AuthFit
Authentic Reproduction of an Independent Earth Satellite ... ARIES
authenticate (SAUS) ... auth
Authenticated Firewall Traversal (VERA) ... AFT
Authenticated Post Office Protocol (SAUS) ... APOP
Authentication (AFM) ... AUTHN
Authentication, Authorizing, Accounting (SAUS) ... AAA
Authentication Center (CGWS) ... AC
Authentication Center (CGWS) ... AuC
Authentication Center ... AUC
Authentication Centre (SAUO) ... AUC
Authentication Header [*Computer science*] ... AH
Authentication Maneuver [*Aviation*] (FAAC) ... ATM
Authentication Request (ADWA) ... ARq
Authentication Response (ADWA) ... ARs
Authentication Server (SAUS) ... AS
Authentication Service (VERA) ... AS
Authenticator Organization (MCD) ... AO
Authenticis Pandectis [*Latin*] (DSA) ... Aut Pand
Authenticity (SAUS) ... Auth
Authenticity Verification (SAUS) ... AV
Authenticum [*A publication*] (DSA) ... A
Authenticum [*A publication*] (DSA) ... Aut
Authenticum [*A publication*] (DSA) ... Authen
Author ... A
Author [*Online database field identifier*] [*Computer science*] ... AU
Author [*Editing notation*] (WDMC) ... Au
Author [*Editing notation*] (WDMC) ... au
Author [*Online database field identifier*] [*Computer science*] ... AUT
Author ... AUTH
Author (VRA) ... auth
Author and Keyword in Context ... AKWIC
Author and Keywords in Alphabetical Sequence (ADA) ... AKWAS
Author Catalogue (ROG) ... AC
Author Comfort Index [*Publishing*] ... ACI
Author Earn-Out [*Publishing*] ... AEO
Author Index ... AUTDEX
Author of "Southern Harmony" [*Initials singer Billy Walker put after his name*] ... ASH
Author Organization Source [*Database terminology*] (NITA) ... AOS
Author Title Subject (SAUS) ... ATS
Authoring of Instructional Materials ... AIM
Authorised Computer Distributors (NITA) ... ACD
Authorised Dealer Bank Bill Rate [*Australia*] [*Finance*] ... ADBBR
Authorised Futures and Options Funds [*British*] (NUMA) ... AFOF
Authorised Unregistered Vehicle Inspection Station [*Australia*] ... AUVIS
Authorised Validation Agencies [*British*] (DET) ... AVA
Authoritative Data Producer (SAUS) ... ADP
Authoritative Data Source (SAUS) ... ADS
Authority ... ATHRTY
Authority ... AUT
Authority (AFM) ... AUTH
Authority (ADWA) ... auth
Authority ... AUTHY
Authority and Format Identifier [*Telecommunications*] (OSI) ... AFI
Authority and Format Indicator (SAUS) ... AFI
Authority Committee on Co-ordination of Nuclear Waste (SAUO) ... ACCNW
Authority Coordinating the Transport of Inland Continental Europe [*NATO*] ... ACTICE
Authority Directing Arrest or Confinement [*Military*] ... ADA
Authority for Expenditure ... AFE
Authority for Intellectually Handicapped Persons [*Western Australia*] ... AIHP
Authority for Issue Indicator (AFIT) ... AI
Authority for Material Substitution (MCD) ... AMS
Authority for Purchase ... AFP
Authority for Removal of Accepted Spacecraft Installations (MCD) ... AFROASI
Authority for the Coordination of Inland Transport in Southern Europe [*NATO*] ... ACTISUD
Authority for Tooling Expenditures ... AFTE
Authority for Uniform Specification of Meat and Livestock [*Australia*] ... AUSMEAT
Authority for Uniform Specifications Meat and Livestock (SAUO) ... AUS-MEAT
Authority Frame Identifier (SAUS) ... AFI
Authority Granted (NOAA) ... AUGRA
Authority Granted [*Army*] ... AUTHGR
Authority Granted [*Military*] (NVT) ... AUTHGRA
Authority Granted to Execute Acceptance and Oath of Office for ___ ... AUTHEXANDO
Authority Health and Safety Branch (SAUO) ... AHSB
Authority Health and Safety Division, Warrington, Lancashire (SAUO) ... AHSD
Authority Is Requested (NOAA) ... AUREQ
Authority Is Requested to Inter [*the remains of*] [*Army*] (AABC) ... ARI
Authority Record [*Database terminology*] (NITA) ... AR
Authority Revocation List (SAUS) ... ARL
Authority Safety and Reliability Directorate (SAUO) ... ASRD
Authority Sequence Number [*Online bibliographies*] ... ASN
Authority Supervising the Aerodome [*FAA designator*] (FAAC) ... YDY
Authority Supervising the Aerodrome [*ICAO designator*] (ICDA) ... YD
Authority to Participate Card ... ATP
Authority to Pay [*or Purchase*] ... A/P
Authority to Proceed (MCD) ... ATP
Authority to Prospect (ADA) ... A to P
Authority, Worldliness, and Power ... AW & P
Authorization [*or Authorized*] (EY) ... AUTH
Authorization (SAUS) ... Auth
Authorization Accounting Activity (SAUO) ... AAA
Authorization and Access Control (VERA) ... AAC
Authorization and Consent (OICC) ... AC
Authorization and Resource Table (SAUS) ... ART
Authorization Control Facility [*Computer access security software*] (NITA) ... ACF
Authorization for Disposal of Overhead Supplies (MCD) ... ADOS
Authorization for Interceptor Operations (MCD) ... AFIO
Authorization for Local Purchase ... ALP
Authorization for Program Development [*NASA*] (NASA) ... AFPD
Authorization for Sale of Salvage Material ... ASSM
Authorization for Temporary Admission [*Customs*] ... ATA
Authorization of Special Types General Order [*British*] (DCTA) ... ASTGO
Authorization of Transfer Material (SAUS) ... ATTM
Authorization Response ... AUTHR
Authorization Source Code (SAA) ... ASC
Authorization to Copy [*Computer science*] (ODBW) ... ATC
Authorization to Purchase [*Food stamp card*] [*Department of Agriculture*] ... ATP
Authorization To Recruit (SAUS) ... ATR
Authorization to Transfer Material ... ATTM
Authorization under Consideration (DCTA) ... AC
Authorizations Subsystem [*Military*] ... AS
Authorized (WDMC) ... auth
Authorized (ROG) ... AUTHD
Authorized Abbreviation (MCD) ... AUTHAB
Authorized About ... AUTHAB
Authorized Absence (DAVI) ... AA
Authorized Academic Training Program (VERA) ... AATP
Authorized Accounting Activity [*DoD*] ... AAA
Authorized Acquisition Objective [*Army*] (AABC) ... AAO
Authorized Active Inventory (MCD) ... AAI
Authorized Allowance ... AA
Authorized Allowance List (MCD) ... AAL

Authorized Auto-CAD Dealer (SAUS) AAD

Authorized Bond Allotment (MCD) ABA

Authorized Break of Inspection (SAUS) ABI

Authorized Code Number (AFM) ACN

Authorized Commanders Atomic Air Defense (CINC) ACAAD

Authorized Computer Distributors (SAUS) ACD

Authorized Configuration List (ACAE) ACL

Authorized Consumption List [*Military*] (AABC) ACL

Authorized Contracting Officer (SAA) ACO

Authorized Control Material Order (AAGC) ACM

Authorized Controlled Material Order [*Military*] (AFIT) ACMO

Authorized Controller Material ACM

Authorized Data Chain (AFM) ADC

Authorized Data Consumer (SAUS) ADC

Authorized Data Distributor (HGAA) ADD

Authorized Data Element ADE

Authorized Data Item Description Manual [*A publication*] (MCD) ADM

Authorized Data Link (ACAE) ADL

Authorized Data List [*DoD*] ADL

Authorized Dental Allowance List [*Military*] (DNAB) ADAL

Authorized Depot Stockage List [*Army*] ADSL

Authorized Derivative Classifier (SAUS) ADC

Authorized Development Deviation (IUSS) ADD

Authorized Direct Expenditure Plan (SAA) ADEP

Authorized Distributor (SAUS) AD

Authorized Equipment and Stores (SAUS) AE&S

Authorized Equipment Listing (AABC) AEL

Authorized in Accordance with Bureau of Naval Personnel Manual ABPM

Authorized in Bureau of Naval Personnel Manual AUTHBUPERSMAN

Authorized "In Excess" AIE

Authorized Industrial Control Distributor (SAUS) AICD

Authorized Industrial Distributor (SAUS) AID

Authorized Inspector AI

Authorized Item Identification Data Collaborator Code AIIDC

Authorized Item Identification Data Receiver Code AIIDR

Authorized Item Identification Data Submitter Code AIIDS

Authorized Landing Area (ADA) ALA

Authorized Leave with pay (SAUS) AL

Authorized Level of Organization (AABC) ALO

Authorized Linux Education Center (SAUS) ALEC

Authorized Medical Allowance List (CAAL) AMAL

Authorized Medical Examiner (DA) AME

Authorized Military Occupational Specialty Code (AABC) AMOSC

Authorized Newsagents Association of Queensland [*Australia*] (BUAC) QUANA

Authorized Notice of Change ANOC

Authorized Nuclear Inspector (NRCH) ANI

Authorized Order AO

Authorized Ordering Agency (MCD) AOA

Authorized Organizational Stockage List (SAUS) AOSL

Authorized Organizational Storage List [*Army*] AOSL

Authorized Part Number APN

Authorized Parts Substitution List APSL

Authorized Pick-Up [*Trucking terminology*] APU

Authorized Possession Limits [*Nuclear energy*] (NRCH) APL

Authorized Price List APL

Authorized Procurement Information Requirements Description [*NASA*] (NASA) APIRD

Authorized Procurement Information Requirements List [*NASA*] (NASA) APIRL

Authorized Program Analysis Report [*Computer science*] (IBMDP) APAR

Authorized Program Facility [*Computer science*] (BUR) APF

Authorized Program File [*Computer science*] (PCM) APF

Authorized Protective Connecting Module (MHDB) APCM

Authorized Repair Unaccomplished at Base [*Military*] (AFIT) ARUB

Authorized Replacement Parts List (IUSS) ARPL

Authorized Retention Level [*Military*] (AABC) ARL

Authorized Review Officer ARO

Authorized Revisit Above-Mentioned Places and Vary Itinerary as Necessary REVAR

Authorized Rotational Retention [*Navy*] RORET

Authorized Selling Representative [*Marketing*] (WDMC) ASR

Authorized Service Center (SAUS) ASC

Authorized Service Provider [*Sun*] (VERA) ASP

Authorized Shortages and Discrepancies (KSC) ASAD

Authorized Signature Card (MCD) ASC

Authorized Solution Provider [*Intel*] ASP

Authorized Standard Version [*of the Bible*] [*A publication*] ASV

Authorized Stock Level (CINC) ASL

Authorized Stockage Level [*Army*] ASL

Authorized Stockage List [*Army*] ASL

Authorized Support Center (SAUO) ASC

Authorized Terminal Strength ATS

Authorized to Delay [*Number of Days*]**, Any Portion of Which May Be Taken inCONUS** [*Navy*] DELINUS

Authorized to Delay [*Number of Days*]**, Any Portion of Which May Be Taken Prior to or after Arrival in United States** [*Navy*] DELREPARUS

Authorized to Delay [*Number of Days*]**, Any Portion of Which May Be Taken Prior to or after Departure** [*Navy*] DELPARTURE

Authorized to Delay [*Number of Days*]**, in Reporting** [*Navy*] DELREP

Authorized to Delay [*Number of Days*]**, in Reporting, Any Portion of Which May Be Taken Prior to or after Reporting at Temporary Duty Station** [*Navy*] DELREPANY

Authorized to Delay [*Number of Days*]**, in Reporting, Keep New Station Advised Address** [*Navy*] DELREPVAN

Authorized to Delay [*Number of Days*]**, in Reporting, to Count as GraduationLeave** [*Navy*] DELREPGRAD

Authorized to Proceed On or About [*Date*] [*Military*] AUTHPROBOUT

Authorized to Travel [*Military*] (DNAB) AUTHTRAV

Authorized Training and Education Center (VERA) ATEC

Authorized Training Associate Program [*Novell, Inc.*] ATA

Authorized User (DCTA) AU

Authorized User Key [*Computer science*] (ITCA) AUK

Authorized Validating Agency (AIE) AVA

Authorized Version [*or King James Version of the Bible, 1611*] (ROG) AUTH

Authorized Version (ADWA) Auth Ver

Authorized Version [*or King James Version of the Bible, 1611*] AV

Authorized Walk-In [*Patient*] [*Medicine*] (DAVI) AWI

Author-Publisher Network (WDAA) A-PN

Author's Alteration (ADWA) aa

Author's Alteration [*Publishing*] AA

Authors and Artists for Young Adults [*A publication*] AAYA

Authors' and Printers' Dictionary [*A publication*] (DGA) APD

Authors and Publishers Lending Right Association Committee (SAUS) APLA

Authors at Auction [*A publication*] AAA

Author's Correction [*Publishing*] AC

Authors Correction (SAUS) AC

Authors Guild (EA) AG

Authors Guild of the Authors League of America (EA) AGALA

Authors Institute of America (EA) AIA

Authors League of America (EA) ALA

Authors' Lending and Copyright Society [*British*] ALCS

Authors Lending and Copyright Society Ltd. (SAUO) ALCS

Authors' Lending Royalty ALR

Authors' Licensing and Collecting Society [*British*] (DBA) ALCS

Author's Licensing and Correcting Society [*British*] ALCS

Author's Proof [*Publishing*] AP

Author's Proof [*Publishing*] (WDMC) ap

Authors' Registry AR

Author's Resource Kit [*Asymetrix Co.*] [*Computer software*] (PCM) ARK

Author's Standard Pre-Press Interface Code [*Mark-up code for word processing/typesetter interface*] (NITA) ASPIC

Authors' Symbolic Pre-Press Interfacing Codes (DGA) ASPIC

Author's Time [*Publishing*] AT

Autism Association [*Australia*] AA

Autism Genetic Resources Exchange AGRE

Autism National Committee AutCom

Autism Network International (EA) ANI

Autism Research Institute ARI

Autism Screening Instrument for Educational Planning ASIEP

Autism Services Center (EA) ASC

Autism Services Center [*Formerly, National Autism Hotline*] (EA) NAH

Autism Society Canada ASC

Autism Society Nova Scotia [*Formerly, Nova Scotia Society for Autistic Children*] (AC) ASNS

Autism Society of America (EA) ASA

Autistic Children's Association of Queensland [*Australia*] ACAQ

Autistic Children's Association of South Australia ACASA

Autistic Citizens' Residential and Resources Society of Victoria [*Australia*] ACRRSV

Autistic Spectrum AS

Autistic Spectrum Disorder ASD

Autistics and Cousins AC

Auto Acquisition [*RADAR*] AA

Auto Alert Force Exercise Schedule (SAUO) AAFES

Auto Alliance International [*Joint manufacturing venture of Ford Motor Co. and Mazda*] AAI

Auto and Truck Recyclers Association of New Hampshire (SRA) ATRANH

Auto and Truck Recyclers of Illinois (SRA) ATRI

Auto Answer (CDE) AA

Auto Backlight Control [*Photography*] ABC

Auto Beacon (KSC) AB

Auto Bill Calling (SAUS) ABC

Auto Bit Error Rate Test (ACAE) ABERT

Auto Body Computer [*Software*] [*Automotive Computer Group*] [*Automotive engineering*] ABC

Auto Body Repair and Painting ABRP

Auto Body Representatives Council (EA) ABRC

Auto Bracketing Control [*Photography*] ABC

Auto Call Originator (SAUS) ACO

Auto Camping Club (SAUO) ACC

Auto Camping Club Ltd. [*British*] (BI) ACC

Auto Car Guard ACG

Auto Carriers Ltd. (SAUO) AC

Auto Chek Centres [*Vancouver Stock Exchange symbol*] ACN

Auto Club Europa (SAUS) ACE

Auto Collision Repair Association ACRA

Auto Dealers Traffic Safety Council [*HUF*] [*Absorbed by*] (EA) ADTSC

Auto Defense Ordinance (CINC) ADO

Auto Diesels Edghill HML Ltd. (SAUO) ADEHML

Auto Directional Antenna ADA

Auto Dismantlers Association of Southern California (SAUO) ADASC

Auto Document Format (SAUS) ADF

Auto Engineering Society/European Broadcasting Union (SAUO) AESEBU

Auto Enthusiasts International [*Defunct*] (EA) AEI

Auto Enthusiats International (SAUO) AEI

Auto Exhaust Testing AET

Auto Exposure Bracketing [*Photography*] AEB

Auto Exposure Lock [*Photography*] AEL

Auto Force Generator [*Military*] (DOMA) AFG

Auto Glass Industry Committee for Highway Safety [*Later, AGIC*]
(EA) .... AGICHS
Auto Glass Industry Council (EA) .... AGIC
Auto, Head and Drive (SAUS) .... AHD
Auto Headway Control [*Mitsubishi*] [*Automotive engineering*] .... AHC
Auto Hold Fire (KSC) .... AHF
Auto house (SAUS) .... A
Auto House (GEOI) .... A
Auto Ignition Point [*Environmental science*] (COE) ...... AIP
Auto in basement (SAUS) .... A IN B
Auto in Basement (GEOI) .... A IN B
Auto Industries Highway Safety Committee [*Later, DSMC*] (EA) .... AIHSC
Auto Industry Highway Safety Committee (SAUS) .... AIHSC
Auto Insert Notification (SAUS) .... AIN
Auto Insurance Plans Services Office [*A rule and rate-making association*] .... AIPSO
Auto Internacional Association (EA) .... AIA
Auto Marine Electric Ltd. [*Vancouver Stock Exchange symbol*] ..... AUM
Auto Part (NRCH) .... AP
Auto Parts Advisory Committee [*US Committee designed to combat the trade deficit with Japan*] (ECON) .... APAC
Auto Pilot (ACAE) .... AP
Auto Pilot System (SAUS) .... APS
Auto Power Reserve (SAUS) .... APR
Auto Radar Plotting Aid (SAUS) .... ARPA
Auto Radiogram (SAUO) .... ARG
Auto Read Reallocation [*Computer science*] .... ARRE
Auto Regressive Moving Average with Integration (AAEL) .... ARIMA
Auto Sequential (NRCH) .... AS
Auto Shop Tester (ACAE) .... AST
Auto Squad (SAUO) .... AS
Auto Steel Partnership Program [*Industry manufacturing standards*] .... ASPP
Auto Stop Latch (SAUS) .... ASL
Auto Target Acquisition by Observation Integration (ACAE) ...... ATABOI
Auto Terrain Avoidance (SAUS) .... ATA
Auto Test in Elementary Programming and Operation (SAUS) ..... ATEPO
Auto Theft Prevention Authority .... ATPA
Auto Tracking Scan System [*for television video quality*] [*Sony Corp.*] .... ATSS
Auto Transport de l'Ouest [*Western Auto Transport*] [*Madagascar*] .... ATO
Auto Trol Technology Corp. [*Associated Press*] (SAG) ...... AutTrT
Auto Wake Up (SAUS) .... AWU
Auto Workers Action Caucus (EA) .... AWAC
Autoadaptive Inventory Management System (SAUS) .... AIMS
Auto-Alerting (IUSS) .... AA
Auto-Alignment Angle Sensor (ACAE) .... AAS
Autoallergic Myositis [*Dermatology*] .... AM
Autoanalyzer .... AA
Autoantibodies to Human Thyroglobulin [*Endocrinology*] (DAVI) .... AHT
Autoantibodies to Nuclear Antigens (MCD) .... ANA
Autoantibody [*Panel*] [*Biochemistry*] (DAVI) .... AUTOAB
Auto/Axial Compression [*Chromatography*] .... AC
Auto/Axial Compression/Liquid Chromatography ..... AC/LC
Autoband Welder (SAUS) .... ABW
AutoBaud Rate [*Detect*] (CDE) .... ABR
Autobiographically Consequential Experiences .... ACE
Autobody and Paint Association of Hawaii (SRA) .... ABPAH
Autobody Craftsman Association (SRA) .... ACA
Autobody Filler Manufacturers Association [*ASEMC*] [*Absorbed by*]
(EA) .... AFMA
Autobody Supply and Equipment Manufacturers Council [*Defunct*]
(EA) .... ASEMC
AutoBond Acceptance [*AMEX symbol*] (SG) .... ABD
AutoBond Acceptance Corp. [*NASDAQ symbol*] (SAG) ..... ABND
AutoBond Acceptance Corp. [*Associated Press*] (SAG) ..... AtoBond
Autobond Welder .... ABW
autobytel.com, Inc. [*NASDAQ symbol*] (SG) .... ABTL
AutoCAD Data Extension (GEOI) .... ADE
AutoCAD Developers Group Europe (SAUO) .... ADGE
AutoCAD [*Computer-Aided Design*] Development System (PCM) .... ADS
Autocad Device Interface [*Computer science*] (VERA) ..... ADI
AutoCAD [*Computer-Aided Design*] Sequel Extension [*Computer science*] ..... ASE
AutoCAD [*Computer-Aided Design*] SQL Extension [*Structured Query Language*] (PCM) .... ASE
Autocad Visualization Extension (SAUS) .... AVE
Autocad Windows Extension [*Computer science*] (VERA) ..... AWE
Autocads Digital Exchange Format (SAUS) .... DXF
Auto-Call-Telex (SAUS) .... ACT
Autocam Corp. [*NASDAQ symbol*] (SAG) .... ACAM
Autocam Corp. [*Associated Press*] (SAG) .... Autocam
Autocarrier [*Predecessor of British auto maker, AC Cars*] ...... AC
Autocheck (SAUS) .... AC
Autochrome (VRA) .... ATCH
Auto-Cite [*VERALEX, Inc.*] [*Information service or system*] (CRD) .... AC
Autoclave (SAUS) .... Clave
Autoclave Building Products Association (SAUO) ..... ABPA
Autoclave Engineers, Inc. .... AE
Autoclaved Aerated Concrete .... AAC
Autoclaved Aerated Concrete Products Association [*British*] (DBA) .... AACPA
Autoclaved Cellular Concrete (SAUS) .... ACC
Autocode List Processing (SAUS) .... ALP
Autocoder (SAUS) .... AC
Autocoder (SAUS) .... AU
Autocoder to COBOL Translator (SAUS) .... ACT
Autocoder-to-COBOL Conversion Aid Program [*IBM Corp.*] [*Computer science*] .... ACCAP

Autocoder-to-COBOL Translating Service [*Computer science*] (IEEE) .... ACTRAN
Autocollimator .... AC
Autocontext [*Freight-forwarding company*] [*British*] ...... AC
Autocorrelation (SAUS) .... Autocorrel
Auto-Correlation Function (SAUS) .... ACF
Autocorrelation Function [*Statistics*] .... ACF
Autocorrelation Histogram [*Statistics*] .... ACH
Autocorrelation Method (SAUS) .... AUTOC Method
Autocorrelation Sequence (SAUS) .... ACS
Auto-Correlation-Average Magnitude Difference Function (SAUS) .... AC-AMDF
Autocorrelator Photon Spectroscopy .... APS
Autocostruzioni Societa per Azione [*Automobile manufacturing company*]
[*Italy*] .... ASA
Autocovariance Function (SAUS) .... ACVF
Autocovariance Generating Function [*Statistics*] ..... ACGF
Autocrine Differentiation-Inhibiting Factor [*Biochemistry*] .... ADIF
Autocrine Mobility Factor [*Oncology*] .... AMF
Autocycle Union [*British*] .... ACU
Autocycle Union (SAUO) .... ACU
Auto-Dairy Engineers, Ltd. (SAUO) .... ADE
Autodecoder (IAA) .... AC
Autodesk Development System [*Computer science*] (PCM) ..... ADS
Autodesk Device Interface (SAUS) .... ADI
Autodesk, Inc. [*Sausalito, CA*] [*NASDAQ symbol*] (NQ) ..... ACAD
Autodesk, Inc. [*NASDAQ symbol*] (SAG) .... ADSK
Autodesk, Inc. [*Associated Press*] (SAG) .... Autodesk
Auto-Dialed Remote Message Players [*Telecommunications*] .... ADRMPS
Auto-Dialled Remote Message Players (SAUS) .... ADRMPS
Auto-Diesel Technician Program [*Association of Independent Colleges and Schools specialization code*] .... AD
AUTODIN Communication Operations Center (SAUO) ..... ACOC
AUTODIN Coordination Station (CET) .... ADCS
AUTODIN CRT for Secure Reserve Force (MCD) ..... RESFOR
AUTODIN Data Identification Number (SAUS) .... DIN
AUTODIN Digital Subscriber Terminal (AABC) .... ADST
AUTODIN Enhancement Program [*Computer science*] (MCD) ..... AEP
AUTODIN Facility (MCD) .... AUTOFAC
AUTODIN Interface Control Unit (MCD) .... AICU
AUTODIN Interface Device (SAUS) .... AID
AUTODIN Interface in a Multiprogramming Environment (SAUS) .... AIME
AUTODIN Mail Server (SAUS) .... AMS
AUTODIN Memory/Memory Control Replacement Program (MCD) ..... M/MCRP
AUTODIN Multimedia Terminal (NVT) .... AMT
AUTODIN Station Maintenance Console (AABC) ..... ASMC
AUTODIN Switch Upgrade Project (MCD) .... ASUP
AUTODIN Switching Center .... ASC
AUTODIN Upgrade Program (MCD) .... AUP
AUTODIN/AUTOVON Interface (CET) .... AAI
AUTODIN-to-DISN Interface (SAUS) .... ADI
Autodyne Detection and Ranging .... AUDAR
Autodyne Detection And Ranging (SAUS) .... AUDAR
Autoerotic Asphyxiation [*Medicine*] .... AEA
Auto-Fiche (MCD) .... AF
Autofocus [*Cameras*] .... AF
Auto-Focus 35mm-camera (SAUS) AF35m
Autofocus RADAR Projector .... ARP
Autofocus Requirements Analysis and Technique Evaluation (ACAE) ..... ARATE
Auto-Free Ottawa (AC) .... AFO
Auto-Free Zone [*TRB*] (TAG) .... AFZ
Autogen (SAUS) .... aut
Autogenetically-Controlled Cesium Electro-Nuclear Thrust System
(MCD) .... ACCENT
Autogenetically-Controlled Cesium Electro-Nuclear Thrust System
(SAUS) .... ACCENT System
Autogenic Feedback Training (MCD) .... AFT
Autogenic Feedback Training Experiment (NAKS) .... AFTE
Autogenic Training [*Influencing the body through autosuggestion*] .... AT
Autogenous Ignition Temperature (DNAB) .... AIT
Autogenous Saphenous Vein (Graft) [*Surgery*] .... ASV
Autograph .... AUT
Autograph .... AUTOG
Autograph Card Signed [*Manuscript descriptions*] .... ACS
Autograph Chapter of the American First Day Cover Society [*Defunct*]
(EA) .... ACAFDCS
Autograph Document [*Manuscript descriptions*] .... AD
Autograph Document Signed [*Manuscript descriptions*] ..... ADS
Autograph Letter [*Manuscript descriptions*] .... AL
Autograph Letter Signed [*Manuscript descriptions*] .... ALS
Autograph Letter Signed [*Manuscript description*] (ODBW) ..... als
Autograph Manuscript Signed [*Manuscript descriptions*] ..... AMSS
Autograph Note (BARN) .... AN
Autograph Note Signal (SAUS) .... ANS
Autograph Note Signed [*Manuscript descriptions*] .... ANS
Autograph Poem Signed [*Manuscript descriptions*] (ADA) ..... APS
Autograph Postcard Signed [*Manuscript descriptions*] ..... APS
Autographa Californica Multiply-embedded Nuclear Polyhedrosis Virus
(SAUS) .... ACMNPV
Autographa Californica Multipnucleocapsid Nuclear Polyhedrosis Virus
[*Entomology*] .... ACMNPV
Autographa Californica Nuclear Polyhedrosis Virus ..... AcNPV
Autographa Californica Nuclear Polyhedrosis Virus (SAUS) ..... ACNPV
Autographed (SAUS) .... Autog
Autographed Manuscript [*Manuscript description*] (WGA) ..... AMS
Autographed Presentation Copy .... APC
Autographic Theme Extraction [*System*] .... ATE

Auto-Graphics Interactive Library Exchange [*Auto-Graphics, Inc.*] [*Information service or system*] (IID) .... AGILE
Autographics International (EA) .... AI
Autogyro Helicopter (SAUS) .... Gyrocopter
Auto-Igniting Propellant (SAA) .... AIP
Autoignition Temperature .... AIT
Auto-Ignition Temperature (SAUS) .... AIT
Autoimmune Chronic Active Hepatitis [*Medicine*] .... ACAH
Autoimmune Collagen Vascular Disease [*Medicine*] (CPH) .... A-CVD
Autoimmune Complement Fixation [*Immunochemistry*] .... AICF
Autoimmune Deficiency [*or Disease*] [*Immunology*] .... AID
Autoimmune Encephalomyelitis [*Hematology*] .... AE
Auto-Immune Haemolytic Disease (SAUS) .... AHD
Autoimmune Haemolytic Disease (SAUS) .... AHD
Autoimmune Hemolytic Anemia [*Hematology*] .... AHA
Autoimmune Hemolytic Anemia [*Medicine*] (MELL) .... AIH
Autoimmune Hemolytic Anemia [*Hematology*] .... AIHA
Autoimmune Hemolytic Disease [*Medicine*] .... AHD
Autoimmune, Inc. [*NASDAQ symbol*] (SAG) .... AIMM
Autoimmune, Inc. [*Associated Press*] (SAG) .... Autoimu
Autoimmune Oophoritis [*Medicine*] .... AO
Autoimmune Polyendocrinopathy-Candidiasis-Ectodermal Dystrophy [*Medicine*] (MELL) .... APECED
Autoimmune Progesterone Dermatitis [*Medicine*] (DMAA) .... APD
Autoimmune Thyroid Disease [*Endocrinology*] .... AITD
Autoimmune Thyroid Disease (DAVI) .... ATD
Autoimmune-Related Diseases Association .... AARDA
Autoinfection [*Medicine*] (MELL) .... AI
AutoInfo, Inc. [*NASDAQ symbol*] (SPSG) .... AUTO
AutoInfo, Inc. [*Associated Press*] (SAG) .... AutoInf
Auto-Initiate Manual-Confirm (CAAL) .... AIMC
Auto-Instructional Device (AEBS) .... AID
Auto-Instructional Media for Library Orientation [*Colorado University Library*] (NITA) .... AIMLO
Auto-Interactive Design [*Combines operator-executed and automatic features*] [*Computer science*] .... AID
AUTOLAND [*Automatic Landing*] (NASA) .... A/L
AUTOLAND [*Automatic Landing*] **Flight Tests** [*NASA*] (MCD) .... AFL
Autoland Flight Tests (SAUS) .... AFL
AUTOLAND [*Automatic Landing*] **Rollout** [*NASA*] (MCD) .... A/R
Autoleather Guild (EA) .... AG
AutoLend Group, Inc. [*Associated Press*] (SAG) .... AutoL
AutoLend Group, Inc. [*Associated Press*] (SAG) .... AutoLend
Autolend Group, Inc. [*NASDAQ symbol*] (SAG) .... CARS
Autoliv, Inc. [*NYSE symbol*] (SG) .... ALV
Auto-lock Channel Tuning (SAUS) .... ACT
Autolock Channel Tuning (SAUS) .... ACT
Auto-Lock Channel Tuning [*Television technology*] .... ACT
Autologic Information International, Inc. [*NASDAQ symbol*] (SAG) .... AIII
Autologic Information International, Inc. [*Associated Press*] (SAG) .... Autolog
Autologic Paginating and Photoimaging System [*Typography*] (DGA) .... APPS
Autologous Blood and Marrow Transplant Registry (ADWA) .... ABMTR
Autologous Blood Transfusion [*Medicine*] (DMAA) .... ABT
Autologous Bone Marrow Transpantation [*Medicine*] (DMAA) .... ABMI
Autologous Bone Marrow Transplant [*Medicine*] .... ABMT
Autologous Bone Marrow Transplantation (ADWA) .... ABMT
Autologous Bone-Marrow Transplantation [*Medicine*] (PDAA) .... ABMS
Autologous Chrondrocyte Implantation [*Medicine*] (MELL) .... ACI
Autologous Mixed Lymphocyte Reaction [*Immunochemistry*] .... AMLR
Autologous Peripheral Blood Stem Cell Transplantation [*Medicine*] .... ABSCT
Autologous Rosette-Forming Cell [*s*] [*Immunology*] .... ARFC
Autologous Tumor Extract (DB) .... ATE
Autologuous Immune Complex Disease [*Medicine*] (MELL) .... AICD
Autologus Blood & Marrow Transplant Registry (SAUO) .... ABMTR
Autolymphocyte Therapy [*Oncology*] .... ALT
Autolysed Yeast Protein [*Biochemistry*] (DAVI) .... AYP
Autolyzed Mouse Brain (SAUS) .... AMB
Auto-Magnetic Plasma-Filled Ion Diode (MCD) .... AMPFION
Auto-Manual Bridge Control [*Telecommunications*] (TEL) .... AMB
Auto-Manual Center [*Telecommunications*] (TEL) .... AMC
Auto-Manual Switching Unit [*Telecommunications*] (DCTA) .... AMSU
Automate Picture Taking (SAUS) .... APT
Automatech Graphics Corp. [*Information service or system*] (IID) .... AGC
Automatech Graphics Corporation (SAUO) .... AGC
Automated (SAUS) .... AUTD
Automated .... AUTOM
Automated Accounting System (BUR) .... AAS
Automated Acoustic Detection System (MCD) .... AADS
Automated Adaptive Flight Training System (MCD) .... AAFTS
Automated Agency Accounting .... AAA
Automated Air Facilities Intelligence File [*Naval Oceanographic Office*] .... AAFIF
Automated Air Facility Information File [*Defense Mapping Agency*] (MCD) .... AAFIF
Automated Air Information Production System (MCD) .... AAIPS
Automated Air Load Planning System [*Developed for the Army by SRI International*] .... AALPS
Automated Aircraft Reporting (ACAE) .... AAR
Automated Aircraft Reporting System (ADWA) .... AARS
Automated Aircrew Escape System (MCD) .... AAES
Automated Airframe Assembly Program (SAUS) .... AAAP
Automated Airlift Analysis [*MTMC*] (TAG) .... AAA
Automated Airload Planning System .... AALP
Automated Ambulatory Medical Record System [*Medicine*] (DMAA) .... AAMRS
Automated Amino Acid Analysis [*Food technology*] .... AAA
Automated Analysis Equipment (SAUS) .... AAE
Automated Analyst Aides (ACAE) .... AAA
Automated Analytical Electrophoresis Apparatus (SAUS) .... AAEA
Automated Analytical Electrophoresis Facility [*NASA*] (MCD) .... AAEF
Automated Antenna Alignment System (ACAE) .... AAAS
Automated Armed Forces Examining and Entrance Station .... AFEES
Automated Armed Forces Examining and Entrance Station System (MCD) .... AAFEESS
Automated Assessment Signal Processor .... AASP
Automated Assessment Tool (MCD) .... AAT
Automated Astronomic Positioning Device [*Defense Mapping Agency*] (MCD) .... AAPD
Automated Astronomic Positioning System [*Defense Mapping Agency*] .... AAPS
Automated Attendance Accounting System [*Jet Propulsion Laboratory, NASA*] .... AAAS
Automated Attendance Reporting System (MCD) .... AARS
Automated Attendant Exchange (SAUS) .... AAX
Automated Attitude Hold [*Manned maneuvering unit*] [*Aerospace*] (NASA) .... AAH
Automated Auger Microprobe .... A^2M
Automated Auger Microprobe (SAUS) .... AyM
Automated Azimuth Measuring System (MCD) .... AAMS
Automated Banking .... AB
Automated Batch Manufacturing System [*Computer science*] (MHDI) .... ABMS
Automated [*or Automatic*] **Batch Mixing** [*Computer science*] .... ABM
Automated Batch Mixing (SAUS) .... ABM
Automated Batch Weighing .... ABW
Automated Batch Weighting (SAUS) .... ABW
Automated Battlefield Interface Concept [*Army*] .... ABIC
Automated Beacon Removal (SAUS) .... ABR
Automated Behavioral Intelligence (MCD) .... ABI
Automated Bibliography .... AB
Automated Bidirectional Reflectance Measurement System (SAUS) .... ABRAMS
Automated Bill Payment System [*Computer science*] (CIST) .... ABPS
Automated Bioassay System (MCD) .... ABS
Automated Biological and Chemical Data [*System*] .... ABCD
Automated Biological Laboratory [*NASA*] .... ABL
Automated Biology Library (SAUS) .... ABL
Automated Bit Access Test System (SAUS) .... ABATS
Automated Block Diagramming (SAUS) .... ABD
Automated Blood Inventory Information System (PDAA) .... ABIIS
Automated Bond System [*Investment term*] (DFIT) .... ABS
Automated Book Request System [*Computer science*] .... ABRS
Automated Booster Assembly Checkout System (SAUS) .... ABACS
Automated Breathing Metabolic Simulator [*Medicine*] (PDAA) .... ABMS
Automated Broker Interface [*Customs Service*] (GFGA) .... ABI
Automated Budget Interactive Data Environment System (ACAE) .... ABIDES
Automated Budget System .... AUTOBUS
Automated Bulk Items List System (MCD) .... ABILS
Automated Business Mail Processing System [*Computer science*] (MHDI) .... ABMPS
Automated Calibrated Control System (SAUS) .... ACCS
Automated Calibration Procedure .... ACP
Automated Calibration Temperature Activated [*Electronic balance*] .... ACTA
Automated Call Distribution (SAUS) .... ACD
Automated Call Distribution (or Distributor) (SAUS) .... ACD
Automated Calling Card Service (ROAS) .... ACCS
Automated Camera Effects System .... ACES
Automated Car Identification [*Railroads*] .... ACI
Automated Career Management Information System .... ACMIS
Automated Career Management System .... ACMS
Automated Cargo Clearance and Enforcement Processing Technique [*US Customs Service*] .... ACCEPT
Automated Cargo Document System .... ACDS
Automated Cargo Release and Operations Service System (SAUS) .... ACROSS
Automated Carrier Landing System [*Military*] .... ACLS
Automated Carrier Landing Systems Project [*Military*] .... ACLSP
Automated Cartographic Drafting and Photogrammetric System (HGAA) .... ACDPS
Automated Cartographic, Drafting and Photogrammetric System (SAUS) .... ACDPS
Automated Cartographic Information Center [*University of Minnesota Library*] (GEOI) .... ACIC
Automated Cartographic Systems (GEOI) .... ACS
Automated Cartography System (SAUS) .... ACS
Automated Cartridge System (SAUS) .... ACS
Automated Catalog of Computer Equipment and Software Systems [*Army*] (NITA) .... ACCESS
Automated Cell-Injection System .... AIS
Automated Census Mapping System (GEOI) .... ACMS
Automated Central Tumor Registry (SAUO) .... ACTUR
Automated Centralized Operations and Maintenance Centers (SAUO) .... ACOM
Automated Chart Display (SAUS) .... ACD
Automated Chart Production System (GEOI) .... ACAPS
Automated Chemical Analysis for Process Solutions (SAUS) .... ACAPS
Automated Chemical Analysis for Process Solutions System [*Hughes Aircraft Co.*] (ECON) .... ACAPS
Automated Chemical Inventory System (SAUS) .... ACIS
Automated Chemistry Program [*Computer science*] .... ACP
Automated Circuit Card Etching Layout [*Computer science*] .... ACCEL
Automated Circuit Card Lay-Out and Implementation [*Computer science*] (PDAA) .... ACCLAIM
Automated Circuit Card Layout and Implementation (SAUS) .... ACCLAIM
Automated Circuit Etching Layout System (SAUS) .... ACCELS
Automated Circulation and Enquiry System [*University of Aberdeen*] [*British*] (CIST) .... ACES
Automated Circulation Control System [*Library management*] .... ACCS

Automated Circulation System [*Computer science*] ... ACS
Automated Claims Information System [*Air Force*] (DNAB) ... ACIS
Automated Classification of Medical Entities [*National Center for Health Statistics*] (GFGA) ... ACME
Automated Classified Document Control System ... ACDCS
Automated Classified Material Accountability System ... ACMAS
Automated Clearinghouse [*Banking*] ... ACH
Automated Clinical Evaluation System [*Medicine*] (DB) ... ACES
Automated Cloud Observation System (MCD) ... ACOS
Automated Coagulation Laboratory ... ACL
Automated Code Evaluation System ... ACES
Automated Coder of Report Narrative [*Computer science*] (DIT) ... ACORN
Automated Coin Toll Service (SAUS) ... ACTS
Automated Collection Management System ... ACOMS
Automated Collision Notification (SAUS) ... ACN
Automated Color Separation System (PDAA) ... ACSS
Automated Combat Mission Folder System (MCD) ... ACMFS
Automated Combustor [*Computer code*] ... AUTOCOM
Automated Command and Control Evaluation System (ACAE) ... ACCES
Automated Command and Control Executive Support System (ACAE) ... ACCESS
Automated Command and Control Executive Support System (ACAE) ... ACESS
Automated Command and Control Information System (ACAE) ... ACCIS
Automated Command and Control Message Processing System [*Military*] (IUSS) ... ACCMPS
Automated Command and Control System (MCD) ... ACCS
Automated Command Center (ACAE) ... ACC
Automated Command Control Executive Support System [*Air Force*] (DOMA) ... ACCESS
Automated Command Response Verification (MCD) ... ACRV
Automated Commercial System [*US Customs Service computerized system*] ... ACS
Automated Commitment Tracking System [*Nuclear energy*] (NRCH) ... ACTS
Automated Communications and Control System [*Navy*] (MCD) ... ACCS
Automated Communications and Electronics Management Information System [*Army*] ... ACEMIS
Automated Communications and Electronics Management Information System (SAUS) ... ACEMIS
Automated Communications and Message Processing System [*Army*] (RDA) ... ACAMPS
Automated Communications and Message Processing System [*Army*] (MCD) ... ACMPS
Automated Communications Electronic Service System (SAUS) ... ACCESS
Automated Communications Processor (SAUS) ... ACP
Automated Communications Publications (AFIT) ... ACP
Automated Communications Set (BUR) ... ACS
Automated Communications System (PCM) ... ACS
Automated Component Trading System ... ACTS
Automated Computer Assisted Test (ACAE) ... ACAT
Automated Computer Communications Electronic Service System (SAUS) ... ACCESS
Automated Computer Controlled Editing Sound System ... ACCESS
Automated Computer Program ... ACP
Automated Computer Science Education ... ACSED
Automated Computer Science Education System ... ACSES
Automated Computer Time Service (ACAE) ... ACTS
Automated Computer-assisted EW System (SAUS) ... ACEWS
Automated Computerized Axial Tomography [*Radiology*] (DAVI) ... ACAT
Automated Computerized Axial Tomography (MELL) ... ACATI
Automated Computerized Tomography [*Radiology*] (DAVI) ... ACT
Automated Computerized Transverse [*Axial scanner*] [*Radiology*] (DAVI) ... ACTH
Automated Computing Engine (PDAA) ... ACE
Automated CONARC Command Echelon Standard Systems (MCD) ... ACCESS
Automated Configuration Management System [*NASA*] (NASA) ... ACMS
Automated Configuration Status Accounting System [*Navy*] ... ACSAS
Automated Configuration Tracking System (MCD) ... ACTS
Automated Confirmation Transaction (EBF) ... ACT
Automated Contingency Support Capability (AFM) ... ACSC
Automated Contingency Support System ... ACSS
Automated Contingency Translator [*Computer science*] ... ACT
Automated Continuity Tester (SAUS) ... ACT
Automated Continuous Acceptance of Propellants (MCD) ... AUTOCAP
Automated Contract Specification System ... ACSS
Automated Control and Checking of Electrical Systems Support (MCD) ... ACCESS
Automated Control and Distribution of Trainees [*Army*] (MCD) ... ACT
Automated Control and Landing System [*Aerospace*] ... ACLS
Automated Control Function (SAUS) ... ACF
Automated Control of a Document Management System [*Computer science*] (DIT) ... ACDMS
Automated Control System (SAUS) ... ACS
Automated Conversion Routine (SAUS) ... ACORN
Automated Corporate Planning Tool (SAUS) ... ACPT
Automated Cost Estimates ... ACE
Automated Cost Estimates (or Estimating) (SAUS) ... ACE
Automated Cost Model ... ACM
Automated Costing and Planning System (DNAB) ... ACAPS
Automated Credit Authorization Subsystem (SAUS) ... ACASS
Automated Credit Enquiry [*British*] [*Information service or system*] (IID) ... ACE
Automated Cross-Section Analysis Program [*Computer science*] ... ACSAP
Automated Culture System ... ACUSYST
Automated Custom Terminal System ... ACTS
Automated Data Acquisition and Control System (MCD) ... ADACS
Automated Data Acquisition and Transfer System (SAUS) ... ADATS
Automated Data Acquisition System [*GCA Corp.*] ... ADAS
Automated Data Analysis and Planning Technique (SAUS) ... ADAPT
Automated Data Analysis and Presentation Techniques (MCD) ... ADAPT
Automated Data Analysis using Pattern-recognition Techniques (SAUS) ... ADAPT
Automated Data and Telecommunications Service [*Later, Office of Information andResources Management*] ... ADTS
Automated Data and Telecommunications Service (SAUO) ... ADTS
Automated Data and Telecomunications Service (SAUO) ... ADATS
Automated Data Collection [*Computer science*] (BTTJ) ... ADC
Automated Data Collection and Location System (SAUS) ... ADCLS
Automated Data Editing and Switching System (SAUS) ... ADESS
Automated Data Entry Measurement System [*Computer science*] (IAA) ... ADEMS
Automated Data Entry System [*Computer science*] (IAA) ... ADES
Automated Data Exchange (SAUS) ... ADE
Automated Data Input Terminal [*Computer science*] (VERA) ... AUDIT
Automated Data Interchange Systems Panel [*Computer science*] (MHDB) ... ADIP
Automated Data Interchange Systems Panel (SAUO) ... ADISP
Automated Data Management (IAA) ... ADM
Automated Data Management Information System ... ADMIS
Automated Data Network System [*Army*] ... ADNS
Automated Data on Instruction Technology (SAUS) ... ADIT
Automated Data on Instructional Technology ... ADIT
Automated Data Preparation by Electronic Photocomposition (MCD) ... ADPEP
Automated Data Preparation Evaluation Program (MCD) ... ADPEP
Automated Data Processing [*FAA*] (TAG) ... ADP
Automated Data Processing (SAUS) ... AQL
Automated Data Processing and Communications Service (MHDI) ... ADPACS
Automated Data Processing Equipment (CTAS) ... ADPE
Automated Data Processing Liaison Office (SAUS) ... ADPLO
Automated Data Processing Standardization Working Group (IUSS) ... ADPSWG
Automated Data Processing Standards Policy Group (IUSS) ... ASPG
Automated Data Processing System (SAUS) ... ADPS
Automated Data Processing System Security Enhancement Program (GFGA) ... ADPSSEP
Automated Data Processing Telecommunications (MCD) ... ADP-T
Automated Data Reports Submission System ... ADRSS
Automated Data Retrieval and Operations Involving Timeseries (SAUS) ... ADROIT
Automated Data Retrieval System (NRCH) ... ADRS
Automated Data Retrieval Technical System [*Computer science*] (CIST) ... ADARTS
Automated Data Service (SAUS) ... ADS
Automated Data Sheet (SAUS) ... ADS
Automated Data Subsystem (AABC) ... ADSS
Automated Data System Development Plan [*Military*] (MCD) ... ADSDP
Automated Data System-Development Plan (IUSS) ... ADDS-DP
Automated Data Systems Analysis Technique (SAUS) ... AUTOSATE
Automated Data Systems Manual [*Military*] (GFGA) ... ADSM
Automated Data Unit Movement (AABC) ... ADUM
Automated Data Wiring ... ADW
Automated Debugging Environment [*Applied Data Research, Inc.*] ... ADE
Automated Declassification System (MCD) ... ADS
Automated Defense Information Network (SAUS) ... AUTODIN
Automated Deferred Discrepancy File ... ADDF
Automated Demand Resolution [*FAA*] (TAG) ... ADR
Automated Deposition of Advanced Materials [*Materials technology*] ... ADAM
Automated Depot Maintenance ... ADM
Automated Design and Documentation (SAA) ... ADD
Automated Design and Manufacturing (SAA) ... ADAM
Automated Design and Packaging Service (CIST) ... ADAPS
Automated Design Engineering [*Telecommunications*] (TEL) ... ADE
Automated Design Facility (MCD) ... ADF
Automated Design of Damage Resistant Structures (MCD) ... ADDRESS
Automated Design System (MCD) ... ADS
Automated Detection/Computer Assisted Classification (ACAE) ... AD/CAC
Automated Detection/Computer-Aided Classification (IUSS) ... AD/CAC
Automated Diagnostic System (SAUS) ... ADS
Automated Diagram Drafting (SAA) ... ADD
Automated Dialler and Recorded Message Player (SAUS) ... ADRMP
Automated Dictionary Support System [*Army*] (RDA) ... ADSS
Automated Differential Agglutination (PDAA) ... ADA
Automated Differential Cell Counter [*Medicine*] (DB) ... ADCC
Automated Digital Aerial (or Antenna) Measurement System (SAUS) ... ADAM System
Automated Digital Antenna Measurement (SAUS) ... ADAM
Automated Digital Data System ... ADDS
Automated Digital Design System [*Raytheon Co.*] ... ADDS
Automated Digital Interior Communications (MCD) ... ADIC
Automated Digital Terminal System (SAUS) ... ADTS
Automated Digital Weather Communications Program [*Air Force*] (AFM) ... ADWCP
Automated Digital Weather Switch (SAUS) ... ADWS
Automated Digitized Document Storage, Retrieval and Transmission System (SAUS) ... ADDSRTS
Automated Digitized Document Storage, Retrieval and Transmission System [*Computer science*] (MHDB) ... ADDSRTS
Automated Direct Entry Packaging Technique ... ADEPT
Automated Direct Labor Reporting (MCD) ... ADLR
Automated Direct-Entry Packaging Technique (SAUS) ... ADEPT
Automated Directional Solidification Furnace [*Materials processing*] ... ADSF
Automated Directives System (SAUO) ... ADS
Automated Disk Library [*Computer science*] (CIST) ... ADL
Automated Dispatch System [*Telecommunications*] ... ADS
Automated Dispensing Analyzer (PDAA) ... ADA
Automated Display Language (SAUS) ... ADL

Automated Dithionate Test (AAMN) ...... ADT
Automated Dividend Reinvested (EBF) ...... ADR
Automated Document Analysis (SAUS) ...... ADA
Automated Document Composer (SAUS) ...... ADC
Automated Document Control and Retrieval System [Computer science] (GFGA) ...... ADCAR
Automated Document Control Register Management Group (SAUO) ..... ADCRMG
Automated Document Control System [Computer science] (MCD) ...... ADCS
Automated Document Delivery Over Networked Information Service (NITA) ...... ADONIS
Automated Document Management Information Network (NITA) ...... ADMIN
Automated Document Management System (SAUS) ...... ADMS
Automated Document Management Systems (DGA) ...... ADMS
Automated Document Ordering System (SAUS) ...... ADOS
Automated Document Request Service (SAUO) ...... ADRS
Automated Documentation (IAA) ...... AUTODOC
Automated Documentation Development and Maintenance [FAA] (TAG) ...... ADDM
Automated Documentation Systems [Computer science] ...... ADS
Automated Drafting and Digitizing Machine [Computer science] (RDA) ...... ADDM
Automated Drafting and Manufacturing System (ACAE) ...... ADAM
Automated Drafting Equipment (SAUS) ...... ADE
Automated Drafting Language (SAUS) ...... ADL
Automated Drafting Machine ...... ADM
Automated Drafting Services (SAUS) ...... ADS
Automated Drafting System ...... ADS
Automated Draughting Equipment (SAUS) ...... ADE
Automated Drawing Parts List (MCD) ...... ADPL
Automated Drawing Parts List System (MCD) ...... ADPLS
Automated Dredging and Disposal System [U.S. Army Corps of Engineers] ...... ADDAMS
Automated Drug Identification ...... AUDRI
Automated Duplicating System (SAUS) ...... ADS
Automated Durability Road ...... ADR
Automated Dutch union catalogue for periodicals (SAUO) ...... IBL
Automated Dynamic Analysis of Mechanical Systems [Mechanical Dynamics, Inc.] [Automotive engineering] ...... ADAMS
Automated Dynamic Digital Test System (SAUS) ...... AUDDITS
Automated EAM Processing and Dissemination System (MCD) ...... AEPDS
Automated Economic Analysis System (SAUO) ...... EASY
Automated Edge Match System (MCD) ...... AEMS
Automated Educational Services On-Line Processing (MCD) ...... AESOP
Automated Educational Services Online Processing (SAUS) ...... AESOP
Automated Electrified Monorail Product Section - Material Handling Institute (NTPA) ...... AEMPS/MHI
Automated Electrocardiograph Interpretive System [Veterans Administration] ...... AECGIS
Automated Electronic Maintenance Training (MCD) ...... AEMT
Automated Electrophoresis Microscope System (MCD) ...... AEMS
Automated Eligibility Verification System (MEDA) ...... AEVS
Automated Endoscopic System for Optimal Positioning [Medicine] ...... AESOP
Automated Engineering and Scientific Optimization Program [NASA] ...... AESOP
Automated Engineering Design [Programming language] [1960] [Computer science] ...... AED
Automated Engineering Design Circuit Analysis Program (MHDB) ...... AEDCAP
Automated Engineering Design of Networks [Computer science] (IAA) ...... AEDNET
Automated Engineering Document Preparation System (MCD) ...... AEDPS
Automated Engineering Documentation Preparation System (SAUS) ...... AEDPS
Automated En-Route Air Traffic Control [Proposed] [FAA] ...... AERA
Automated Environmental Control System (MCD) ...... AECS
Automated Environmental Prediction (CAAL) ...... AEP
Automated Environmental Prediction System (MCD) ...... AEPS
Automated Equipment Control System (AAEL) ...... AECS
Automated Equipment Identification (BTTJ) ...... AEI
Automated Equipment Interface (AAEL) ...... AEI
Automated Execution [FAA] (TAG) ...... AEX
Automated External Defibrillator ...... AED
Automated External Defibrillator-Pacemaker [Cardiology] ...... AEDP
Automated Fare Collection ...... AFC
Automated Fault Tree Analyzer (MCD) ...... AFTA
Automated Feature Extraction System (SAUS) ...... AFES
Automated Fiber Winner System ...... AFWS
Automated Field Evaluation and Test System (MCD) ...... AUTO-FETS
Automated Field Fire ...... AFF
Automated Field Interview System ...... AFIS
Automated Filter Photometer (SAUS) ...... AFP
Automated Financial Improvement Program [Navy] (GFGA) ...... AFIP
Automated Financial Information System [Computer science] (MHDI) ...... AFIS
Automated Fingerprint Identification System [NEC Corp.] ...... AFIS
Automated Fingerprint Image Reporting and Match (SAUS) ...... AFIRM
Automated Fire Support Artillery (MCD) ...... AFSA
Automated Flaw Detector ...... AFD
Automated Flight Information Service [ICAO designator] (FAAC) ...... FISA
Automated Flight Service Station [FAA] (TAG) ...... AFSS
Automated Flight Test Data System (MCD) ...... AFTDS
Automated Flight Training System (SAUS) ...... AFTS
Automated Flow Technology ...... AFT
Automated Forces [Air Force] (RDA) ...... AFOR
Automated Format Recognition (SAUS) ...... AFR
Automated Forward Area Alerting RADAR [Army] ...... AFAAR
Automated Frequency Assignment System [Telecommunications] ...... AFAS
Automated Frequency Deconfliction [Telecommunications] (LAIN) ...... AFD
Automated Fuels Service Stations (SAUO) ...... AFSS
Automated Funds Transfer (EBF) ...... AFT

Automated Funds Transfer System [Computer science] (CIST) ...... AFTS
Automated General Experimental Device [Animal performance testing] ...... AGED
Automated Generic Case Analysis Program (MCD) ...... AGCAP
Automated Genetic Analyzer [Instrumentation] ...... AGA
Automated Geographic Information System (GEOI) ...... AGIS
Automated Geomagnetic Airborne Survey System [Aviation] (PDAA) ...... AGASS
Automated Grants Documentation System (SAUS) ...... AGDS
Automated Graphic System (SAUS) ...... AGS
Automated Graphic Technology (SAUS) ...... AGT
Automated Graphics Application Program (MCD) ...... AGAP
Automated Graphics Digitizing System (GEOI) ...... AGDS
Automated Ground Engine Test System (MCD) ...... AGETS
Automated Ground Network System ...... AGNS
Automated Ground Operations Scheduling System [Also, AUTO-GOSS] (MCD) ...... AGOSS
Automated Ground Operations Scheduling System [Also, AGOSS] (MCD) ...... AUTO-GOSS
Automated Ground Tactical Emitter Location System (SAUS) ...... AGTELS
Automated Group Learning (PDAA) ...... AGL
Automated Guideway Transit [TRB] (TAG) ...... AGT
Automated Gun Laying (Turret) Training [British military] (DMA) ...... AGL(T)TRG
Automated Gyro Test Set ...... AGTS
Automated Health Research Information System (ADWA) ...... AHRIS
Automated High Accuracy Comparator (SAUS) ...... AHAC
Automated Highway Systems [FHWA] (TAG) ...... AHS
Automated Historical Data Base ...... AHDB
Automated Hospital Data Management System [Medicine] (DMAA) ...... AHDMS
Automated Hospital Information System [Veterans Administration] (IID) ...... AHIS
Automated Ice Information System for Arctic (SAUS) ...... AIISA
Automated Identification Division System [FBI] ...... AIDS
Automated Identification System [FBI] ...... AIS
Automated Image Analysis [Instrumentation] ...... AIA
Automated Image Data Extraction System (MCD) ...... AIDES
Automated Image Device Evaluator [Electronics] ...... AIDE
Automated Image Makeready (SAUS) ...... AIM
Automated Image Retrieval (SAUS) ...... AIR
Automated Image Retrieval System (ACAE) ...... AIRS
Automated Imagery Processing (PDAA) ...... AIP
Automated Imaging Association (EA) ...... AIA
Automated Imaging System (DGA) ...... AIS
Automated Immunochemistry System ...... AutoICS
Automated Immunoephelometric Assay (SAUS) ...... AINA
Automated Immunonephelometric Assay [Medicine] (DMAA) ...... AINA
Automated Immunoprecipitin [System] [Clinical chemistry] ...... AIP
Automated Immunoprecipitin System (SAUS) ...... AIP System
Automated Implementation Plan ...... AIP
Automated Import Inspection System [Department of Agriculture] (GFGA) ...... AIIS
Automated Incendiary Submunition (MCD) ...... AMIS
Automated Index (SAUS) ...... AI
Automated Indicator System (MCD) ...... AIS
Automated Industrial Control System [Computer science] (MHDB) ...... AICS
Automated Industrial Drilling (MHDI) ...... AID
Automated Industrial Management System ...... AIMS
Automated Information and Documentation System (SAUS) ...... AIDS
Automated Information and Management System (BUR) ...... AIMS
Automated Information and Management Systems (MCD) ...... AIMES
Automated Information and Reservation Combined Operations Network (SAUS) ...... AIRCON
Automated Information and Reservation Computer Operated Network ...... AIRCON
Automated Information and Reservation Computer Oriented Network (SAUS) ...... AIRCON
Automated Information Data System ...... AIDS
Automated Information Dictionary (ACAE) ...... AID
Automated Information Directory Update System (PDAA) ...... AIDUS
Automated Information Display System (SAUS) ...... AIDS
Automated Information Dissemination System (NITA) ...... AIDS
Automated Information Distribution System (ACAE) ...... AIDS
Automated Information Management (NASA) ...... AIM
Automated Information Proccuring Request (SAUS) ...... AIPR
Automated Information Processing [Computer science] (MCD) ...... AIP
Automated Information Processing Request (MCD) ...... AIPR
Automated Information Processing Resources (SAUS) ...... AIPR
Automated Information Processing System (SAUS) ...... AIPS
Automated Information Reference Systems (SAUS) ...... AIRS
Automated Information Reference Systems, Inc. [Information service or system] (IID) ...... AIRS
Automated Information Resource System (SAUS) ...... AIRES
Automated Information Security (ADWA) ...... AIS
Automated Information Security Policy Review Team (SAUO) ...... AISPRT
Automated Information System ...... AIS
Automated Information Systems Acquisition Review Council (SAUO) ..... AISARC
Automated Information Systems Review Council (SAUO) ...... AISRC
Automated Information Systems Security Officer (SAUO) ...... AISSO
Automated Information Systems Security Program ...... AISSP
Automated Information Transfer [FAA] (TAG) ...... AIT
Automated Information Transfer System [Department of Commerce] [Database] ...... AITS
Automated Input and Document Update Service [International Data Corp.] ...... AIDUS
Automated Inspection of Data ...... AIDA
Automated Installation and Diagnostic Services (SAUS) ...... AIDS
Automated Installation File (MCD) ...... AIF
Automated Installation Intelligence File (COE) ...... AIF
Automated Installation Intelligence File ...... AIIF

Automated Instruction (DNAB) .... AI
Automated Instruction Fetch Unit [*Computer science*] (MHDI) .... AIFU
Automated Instructional Management System [*Army*] .... AIMS
Automated Instructional Materials Services [*Developed by the System Development Corp.*] (IID) .... AIMS
Automated Instructional Materials-handling System (SAUS) .... AIMS
Automated Instrumentation System .... AIS
Automated Insurance Rating Services, Inc. (SAUS) .... AIRS
Automated Insurance Service .... AIS
Automated Integrated Data System (SAUS) .... AIDS
Automated Integrated Debugging System (MCD) .... AIDS
Automated Integrated Design and Engineering (SAUS) .... AIDE
Automated Integrated Design Engineering (IEEE) .... AIDE
Automated Integrated Director Equipment (SAUS) .... AIDE
Automated Integrated Dynamic Avionics Tester (SAUS) .... AIDAT
Automated Integrated Language (IUSS) .... AIL
Automated Integrated Language System Identification Number (IUSS) .... AILSIN
Automated Integrated Manufacturing (MCD) .... AIM
automated integrated radar control for air traffic (SAUS) .... aircat
Automated Integrative Design Engineering (NITA) .... AIDE
Automated Intelligence Correlation (SAUS) .... AIC
Automated Intelligence Data System [*Air Force*] .... AIDS
Automated Intelligence File [*Military*] (AABC) .... AIF
Automated Intelligence Processing System (MCD) .... AIPS
Automated Intelligent Cruise Control [*FHWA*] (TAG) .... AICC
Automated Intelligent Microscope .... AIM
Automated Interaction Detector (AUEG) .... AID
Automated Interactive Design and Evaluation System (SAUS) .... AIDES
Automated Interactive Simulation Model (ACAE) .... AISIM
Automated Interactive Simulation Model (ACAE) .... AISM
Automated Interchange of Information (ACAE) .... AITI
Automated International Flight Service Station [*FAA*] (TAG) .... AIFSS
Automated Interpretation System of Chest Roentgenograms (SAUS) .... AISCR
Automated Interrogation Routine (SAUS) .... AIR
Automated Inventory Control System (SAUS) .... AICS
Automated Inventory Distribution System .... AIDS
Automated Inventory Management Evaluation System (IEEE) .... AIMES
Automated Jail Information System .... AJIS
Automated Job Control (SAUO) .... AJCON
Automated Joint Application Development [*Computer science*] (BTTJ) .... AJAD
Automated Juvenile Law Archive [*National Center for Juvenile Justice*] [*Information service or system*] (CRD) .... AJLA
Automated Keyed Continuous Wave (DNAB) .... ACW
Automated Labor and Attendance Subsystem (SAA) .... ALAS
Automated Laboratory Diagnostic Instrument .... ALADIN
Automated Lamellar Kerotaplasty [*Medicine*] .... ALK
Automated Land and Minerals Records System [*Department of the Interior*] (GFGA) .... ALMRS
Automated Land Information System (GEOI) .... ALIS
Automated Land Titles System (ADA) .... ALTS
Automated Lands Project (GEOI) .... ALP
Automated Language Processing (NITA) .... ALP
Automated Language Processing Systems [*Electronic translation of foreign languages*] [*Commercial firm*] (NITA) .... ALPS
Automated Language Processing Systems, Inc. (MHDW) .... AILP
Automated Language Processing Systems Ltd. (SAUO) .... ALPS
Automated Large Experiment [*NASA*] .... ALE
Automated Large Panel Display (CCCA) .... ALPD
Automated LASER Seeker Performance Evaluation System (MHDI) .... ALSPEC
Automated LASER Seeker Performance Evaluation System (MCD) .... ALSPES
Automated Law Enforcement Communications System (SAUS) .... ALECS
Automated Law Enforcement Reporting Technique (SAUS) .... ALERT
Automated Law Enforcement Response Team (DICI) .... ALERT
Automated Layout Design Program [*IBM Corp.*] .... ALDEP
Automated Learning Process .... ALP
Automated Leave and Pay System [*Military*] (DNAB) .... ALPS
Automated Legal Research (SAUS) .... ALR
Automated Legal Text Entry and Revision System (SAUS) .... ALTER System
Automated Letter Preparation System (SAUS) .... ALPS
Automated Library Acquisitions System [*Suggested name for the Library of Congress computer system*] .... ALAS
Automated Library Expandable Program, Hebrew University of Jerusalem [*Israel*] [*Information service or system*] (IID) .... ALEPH
Automated Library, Information Control and Exchange (SAUS) .... ALICE
Automated Library Information Service (SAUS) .... ALIS
Automated Library Information System [*National Technological Library of Denmark*] [*Lyngby*] (IID) .... ALIS
Automated Library Information System [*Dataphase Systems, Inc.*] (IID) .... ALIS
Automated Library Issue Document (NVT) .... ALID
Automated Library Management System (SAUS) .... ALMS
Automated Library Processing Services [*System Development Corp.*] (IID) .... ALPS
Automated Library Processing System (SAUS) .... ALPS
Automated Library Program [*Computer science*] (DIT) .... ALP
Automated Library System [*Foundation for Library Research, Inc.*] [*Information service or system*] (IID) .... ALS
Automated library system marketed by SLS Ltd (SAUS) .... LIBERTAS
Automated library system-Universal Real-time Information Control Administration (SAUS) .... URICA
Automated Library Technical Services [*Program*] [*Los Angeles Public Library*] .... ALTS
Automated Light Survey .... ALS
Automated Lightning Detection and Reporting System (SAUS) .... ALDARS
Automated Line Record Update [*Telecommunications*] (TEL) .... ALRU
Automated Line Replaceable Unit Tracking System (NAKS) .... ALRUTS
Automated Lines of Communications and Target System (MCD) .... ALCATS
Automated Linguistic Extraction and Retrieval Technique .... ALERT
Automated Linguistic Fieldworker [*Computer science*] (DIT) .... AUTOLING
Automated Linguistics (SAUS) .... AUTOLING
Automated Liquid Sampler [*Instrumentation*] .... ALS
Automated List Service (SAUS) .... ALS
Automated Literature Alerting System [*Computer science*] (DIT) .... ALAS
Automated Literature Processing, Handling and Analysis (SAUS) .... ALPHA
Automated Litigation Support [*Department of Justice*] (GFGA) .... ALS
Automated Living User Intervention Anarchy [*Computer science*] .... ALUIA
Automated Loading of Features and Assemblies (SAUS) .... ALFA
Automated Loans System [*Library science*] .... ALS
Automated Local Evaluations in Real Time [*National Oceanic and Atmospheric Administration*] .... ALERT
Automated Location and Data Netting System (ACAE) .... ALADNS
Automated Location of Isolation and Continuity Error [*Module*] [*Raytheon Co.*] .... ALICE
Automated Location of Isolation and Continuity Errors (SAUS) .... ALICE
Automated Logic Design (SAUS) .... ALD
Automated Logic Diagram [*Computer science*] (IBMDP) .... ALD
Automated Logic Implementation [*Computer science*] (IEEE) .... ALI
Automated Logic Mapping System (PDAA) .... ALMS
Automated Logic Matrix System (SAUS) .... ALMS
Automated Logistics Data Processing System .... ALDPS
Automated Logistics Management and Inventory Control System (MCD) .... ALMICS
Automated Logistics Management System (SSD) .... ALMS
Automated Logistics Management Systems Activity (SAUS) .... ALMSA
Automated Logistics Management Systems Agency [*DoD*] .... ALMSA
Automated Logistics Planning System (MCD) .... ALPS
Automated Logistics System for Tracking, Analysis, and Reporting .... ALSTAR
Automated Logistics Systems Review (MCD) .... ALSR
Automated Low flying Flight planning Enquiry & System (SAUS) .... ALFENS
Automated Low flying Flight planning Entry & System (SAUS) .... ALFENS
Automated Low-Cost Weather Observation System (MCD) .... ALWOS
Automated Maintenance Control and Records System (MCD) .... AMCARS
Automated Maintenance Data Base (SAUS) .... AMDB
Automated Maintenance Data Exchange (MCD) .... AMDEX
Automated Maintenance Depot .... AMD
Automated Maintenance Information System (MCD) .... AMIS
Automated Maintenance Performance and Engineering Reliability Evaluation System (SAUS) .... AMPERES
Automated Maintenance Support Tool (CIST) .... AMST
Automated Management and Reporting System [*Department of Housing and Urban Development*] (GFGA) .... AMRS
Automated Management Information Center (SSD) .... AMIC
Automated Management Information Civil Users System [*Department of Justice*] (GFGA) .... AMICUS
Automated Management Information System (DIT) .... AMIS
Automated Management of Document Access (SAUS) .... AMANDA
Automated Management Reports (BUR) .... AMR
Automated Management System (ACAE) .... AMS
Automated Manifest System (DA) .... AMS
Automated Manpower Data Department of the Navy Reports (MCD) .... AMDAR
Automated Manpower Management Information System .... AMMIS
Automated Manufacturing Cell (SAUS) .... AMC
Automated Manufacturing Planning (SAUS) .... AMP
Automated Manufacturing Research Facility [*Gaithersburg, MD*] [*Department of Commerce*] (GRD) .... AMRF
Automated Manufacturing Technology (SAUS) .... AMT
Automated Map Information File [*DoD*] (PDAA) .... AMIF
Automated Mapping [*Cartography*] .... AM
Automated Mapping Facilities Management (SAUS) .... AM/FM
Automated Mapping System (GEOI) .... AMS
Automated Mapping/Facilities Management (SAUO) .... AM/FM
Automated Mapping/Facility Management [*Computer science*] .... AMFM
Automated Maritime Telecommunications Systems (OTD) .... AMTS
Automated Mask Inspection System (PDAA) .... AMIS
Automated Material Handling (VERA) .... AMH
Automated Material Management System (ACAE) .... AMMS
Automated Material Parts Request System (MCD) .... AMPRS
Automated Material Processing System [*Computer science*] .... AMPS
Automated Material System (SAA) .... AMS
Automated Material System (MCD) .... AUTOMAT
Automated Materials Handling (CIST) .... AMH
Automated Materials Handling System [*Computer science*] .... AMHS
Automated Materials Handling Systems Association [*British*] (DBA) .... AMHSA
Automated Materials Ordering System (SAUS) .... AMOS
Automated Materiel System (SAUS) .... AMS
Automated Mathematics Program (SAUS) .... AMP
Automated Measurement Corporation (SAUO) .... AMC
Automated Measurement Evaluator and Director System (MHDB) .... AMEDS
Automated Measurement of Lineups [*A. C. Nielsen Co.*] (WDMC) .... AMOL
Automated Mechanical Transmission [*Automotive engineering*] .... AMT
Automated Media Information (SAUS) .... AMI
Automated Media Management System (CIST) .... AMMA
Automated Medical Examination System (PDAA) .... AMES
Automated Medical History .... AMH
Automated Medical Record System (AAMN) .... AMRS
Automated MEDICARE Log (MEDA) .... AML
Automated Merchandise Processing System [*US Customs Service*] .... AMPS
Automated Merchant Vessel Emergency Rescue (SAUS) .... AMVER
Automated Merchant Vessel Emergency Rescue Network (SAUS) .... AMVER Network
Automated [*formerly, Atlantic*] **Merchant Vessel Report** [*Coast Guard*] .... AMVER

Automated [formerly, Atlantic] Merchant Vessel Report System [Coast Guard] ..... AMVERS
Automated Message Handler (COE) ..... AMH
Automated Message Handling System ..... AMHS
Automated Message Management System (MCD) ..... AMMS
Automated Message Processing Dissemination System (MCD) ..... AMPDS
Automated Message Processing Equipment (IUSS) ..... AMPE
Automated Message Processing Exchange (SAUS) ..... AMPE
Automated Message Processing Exchange System [Military] (GFGA) ..... AMPES
Automated Message Processing System (SAUS) ..... AMPS
Automated Message Recording (SAUS) ..... AMR
Automated Messaging and Directory Assistance (SAUS) ..... AMANDA
Automated Meteorological and Terminal Information Service (SAUS) ..... AMATIS
Automated Meteorological Observing System (SAUS) ..... AMOS
Automated Meteorological Station (AUEG) ..... AMS
Automated Meteorological Terminal Information Service (SAUS) ..... AMATIS
Automated Methane Instrument Evaluation (SAUS) ..... AMIE
Automated Microbial Metabolism Laboratory [NASA] ..... AMML
Automated Microbial Systems (MCD) ..... AMS
Automated Microfiche Terminal (PDAA) ..... AMT
Automated Microfilm Aperture Card Updating System [Army] ..... AMACUS
Automated Microfilm Storage and Retrieval [Army] (IID) ..... AMSR
Automated Microform Storage and Retrieval [Computer science] (MHDI) ..... AMSO
Automated Microhemagglutination Assay for Antibodies to Treponema pallidum [Serology] ..... AMHA-TP
Automated Military Construction Progress Reporting System (GFGA) ..... AMPRS
Automated Military Justice Analysis and Management System ..... AMJAMS
Automated Military Medical Outpatient System (SAUO) ..... AMOS
Automated Military Outpatient System (RDA) ..... AMOS
Automated Military Outpatient System Specialist (MCD) ..... AMOSIST
Automated Minefield System (MCD) ..... AMS
Automated Minerals Information System [Bureau of Mines] [Database] ..... AMIS
Automated Mission Planning (SAUS) ..... AMP
Automated Mission Planning Society (SAUO) ..... AMPS
Automated Mission Planning System (SAUS) ..... AMPS
Automated Mixed Traffic Transit (PDAA) ..... AMTT
Automated Mobile EW System (SAUS) ..... AMEWS
Automated Modification Analyzer [Computer science] ..... AMA
Automated Modular Preplanner Programming System (MCD) ..... AMPPS
Automated Molding Plant [Manufacturing] ..... AMP
Automated Mooney Decay [Chemical engineering] ..... AMD
Automated Mortgage Management Information Network [Computer science] (MHDI) ..... AMMINET
Automated Multimedia Exchange [Communications] [Army] (MCD) ..... AMME
Automated Multi-Media Exchange (SAUS) ..... AMME
Automated Multi-Media Switch (PDAA) ..... AMMS
Automated Multi-Media Terminal (SAUS) ..... AMMT
Automated Multiparameter Analyzer for Cells ..... AMAC
Automated Multiphasic Health Testing ..... AMHT
Automated Multiphasic Health Testing and Services (KSC) ..... AMHTS
Automated Multiphasic Screening [Medicine] (MAH) ..... AMS
Automated Multiple Development [Chromatography] ..... AMD
Automated Multistage Substructuring (MCD) ..... AMSS
Automated Multitest Laboratory ..... AML
Automated Mutual-Assistance Vessel Resue System (SAUS) ..... AMVER
Automated Nautical Chart Index File [System] [DoD] ..... ANCIF
Automated Nautical Charting System (ADWA) ..... ANCS
Automated Nautical Charting System (USDC) ..... ANCS-II
Automated Naval Architecture (PDAA) ..... ANA
Automated NBC Information System (SAUS) ..... ANBCIS
Automated Near-Term Improvement (MCD) ..... ANTI
Automated Nephelometric Immunoassay [Medicine] (DMAA) ..... ANIA
Automated Network Analyzer [Computer science] (CIST) ..... ANA
Automated Network Control Center [Military] (DOMA) ..... ANCC
Automated Network Schedule with Evaluation of Resources (MCD) ..... ANSWER
Automated News Clipping, Indexing and Retrieval System (SAUS) ..... ANCIRS
Automated Newspaper Delivery System (PDAA) ..... ANDS
Automated Nikkei News Editing and Composing System (SAUS) ..... ANNECS
Automated Non-Destructive Inspector [Robotics] (PS) ..... ANDI
Automated Notices to Mariners System ..... ANMS
Automated Nuclear, Biological, and Chemical Information System [Military] (DOMA) ..... ANBACIS
Automated Office AG (SAUS) ..... AOAG
Automated Office Battery [Selection and career development test] ..... AOB
Automated Office Support System [Department of Energy] ..... AOSS
Automated Office System (HGAA) ..... AOS
Automated Offset Unit [Air Force] ..... AOU
Automated Onboard Gravimeter ..... AOG
Automated Operations Extension Facility [IBM] (CIST) ..... AOEF
Automated Optical Inspection ..... AOI
Automated Optical Navigation (MCD) ..... AON
Automated (or Automatic) Clearing House (SAUO) ..... ACH
Automated (or Automatic) Geophysical Observatory (SAUS) ..... AGO
Automated (or Automatic) Secure Voice Communications system (SAUS) ..... AUTOSEVOCOM
Automated Orbit Control System (MCD) ..... AOCS
Automated Order Writing Process (MCD) ..... AOWP
Automated Order Writing Program (SAUS) ..... AOWP
Automated Order Writing System (MCD) ..... AOWS
Automated Outgoing Interface (SAUS) ..... AOI
Automated Overseas Employment Referral Program ..... AOERP
Automated Package Test System (IUSS) ..... APTS
Automated Packaging Code [Army] (MCD) ..... APC
Automated Packaging Planning System (MCD) ..... APPS
Automated Packet Recognition/Translation (SAUS) ..... APART

Automated Parking Lot Control (MCD) ..... APLC
Automated Parking Support System [Vehicle storage] ..... AUTOPASS
Automated Parking System ..... APS
Automated Password Generator (SAUS) ..... APG
Automated Patching System (SAUS) ..... APS
Automated Patent Searching [Computer science] ..... APS
Automated Patent System ..... APS
Automated Patient Evacuation System (SAUS) ..... APES
Automated Payload Processing Facility [NASA] (NASA) ..... APPF
Automated Payment and Deposit [Banking] ..... APD
Automated Payroll, Cost, and Personnel System [Defense Supply Agency] ..... APCAPS
Automated PEMA [Procurement of Equipment and Munition Appropriations] Bud get System [Military] (AABC) ..... APBS
Automated People Mover [MOCD] [TXDOT] (TAG) ..... APM
Automated Percutaneous Discectomy [Spinal surgery] ..... APD
Automated Percutaneous Lumbar Diskectomy [Medicine] (MELL) ..... APLD
Automated Performance Measurement (MCD) ..... APM
Automated Performance Measurement System [FAA] (TAG) ..... APMS
Automated Peritoneal Dialysis [Medicine] ..... APD
Automated Personnel Accounting, Cost, Historical Estimating System [Army] ..... APACHES
Automated Personnel Data System (ACAE) ..... APDS
Automated Personnel Information Exchange (DNAB) ..... APIX
Automated Personnel Procurement System (ACAE) ..... APPS
Automated Personnel System (SAUS) ..... APS
Automated Phase and Amplitude Data Acquisition System (SAUS) ..... APADAS
Automated Photogrammetric Positioning System (DNAB) ..... APPS
Automated Pilot Aptitude Measurement System (MCD) ..... APAMS
Automated Pit Trading [Developed by London International Financial Futures Exchange] [Stock exchange term] ..... APT
Automated Planning and Execution (SAUS) ..... APEX
Automated Planning Fabrication Outline (MCD) ..... APFO
Automated Plat Design (SAUS) ..... APD
Automated Plate Measuring [for Spectrography] ..... APM
Automated Point of Sale System (SAUS) ..... APOSS
Automated Postal Directory Service (SAUO) ..... APDS
Automated Powder Diffractometer ..... APD
Automated Power System Management (ACAE) ..... APSM
Automated Prediction Analysis Technique (ACAE) ..... APAT
Automated Procedures for Engineering Consultants. (SAUS) ..... APEC
Automated Procedures for Engineering Consultants, Inc. ..... APEC
Automated Process Control System (SAUS) ..... APCS
Automated Process Generator (SAUS) ..... APG
Automated Process Information File [Library of Congress] ..... APIF
Automated Process Interrupt System (SAUS) ..... APIS
Automated Process Line System (SAUS) ..... APLS
Automated Process Planning System (PDAA) ..... AUTOPROS
Automated Processing Center (WDAA) ..... APC
Automated Processing Method (SAUS) ..... APM
Automated Processing of Medical English (SAUS) ..... APME
Automated Procurement and Production Scheduling and Management System [Army] ..... APPSMS
Automated Procurement Documentation System [Environmental Protection Agency] (GFGA) ..... APDS
Automated Procurement Planning, Execution, and Control ..... APEX
[The] Automated Procurement Planning System ..... TAPPS
Automated Procurement Request System (SAUS) ..... APRS
Automated Product Control Environment (SSD) ..... APCE
Automated Product Development Framework ..... APDF
Automated Production and Control [Industrial engineering] ..... APC
Automated Production Control (SAUS) ..... APC
Automated Production Equipment Corp. (SAUO) ..... APE
Automated Production Protocol (SAUS) ..... APC
Automated Production System (SAUS) ..... APS
Automated Productivity Services (MCD) ..... APS
Automated Program Debugging System (MCD) ..... APD
Automated Program for Aerospace-Vehicle Synthesis ..... APAS
Automated Program Management information System (SAUS) ..... APMS
Automated Program Search [Tape recorder feature] ..... AMPS
Automated Program Support System [Computer science] ..... APSS
Automated Program Testing Facility (MHDI) ..... APTF
Automated Program to Project AIT [Advanced Individual Training] Training Spaces [DoD] ..... APPATS
Automated Programmable Assembly System [Computer science] ..... APAS
Automated Programming, Budgeting, and Operational Evaluation [Army] ..... AUTOPROBE
Automated Programming Language (SAUS) ..... APL
Automated Programming of Lathes (SAUS) ..... AUTOPOL
Automated Programming of Machine Tools (SAUS) ..... AUTOPROMPT
Automated Project Control System (NAKS) ..... APCS
Automated Project Management Information System [Computer science] ..... APMIS
Automated Projective Drawing [GMW Computers Ltd.] [Software package] (NCC) ..... AUTOPROD
Automated Pronunciation Instructor ..... API
Automated Proofreading and Formatting: OCR/ICR in Reconversion Catalogues (SAUS) ..... APFORC
Automated Propeller Optical Measurement System ..... APOMS
Automated Publication Preparation System [Army] (MCD) ..... APPS
Automated Publications Maintenance System (DNAB) ..... APMS
Automated Punch Requisition (SAUS) ..... APR
Automated Purchase and Payment System [United Nations] (DUND) ..... APPS
Automated Quality of Care Evaluation Support System [Military] ..... AQCESS
Automated Quotation System (IAA) ..... AQS

Automated Radar Controlled Terminal System (SAUS)	ARCTS
Automated RADAR Measurement System (MCD)	ARMS
Automated Radar Monitor (SAUS)	ARM
Automated RADAR Monitor System	ARM
Automated Radar Terminal System [*FAA*] (TAG)	ARTS
Automated Radar Terminal System (SAUS)	Arts
Automated Radar Terrain Follow/Terrain Avoidance (ACAE)	ARTF/TA
Automated RADAR Tracking System (MCD)	ARTS
Automated Radioimmunoassay	AR
Automated Radioimmunoassay [*Immunology*] (DAVI)	ARIA
Automated Radiotheodolite [*Marine science*] (OSRA)	ARC
Automated Radioxenon Sampler/Analyzer [*Chemistry*]	ARSA
Automated Range Management System (MCD)	ARMS
Automated Reactor Inspection System [*Nuclear energy*] (NRCH)	ARIS
Automated Readability Index (MCD)	ARI
Automated Reading Aid for the Physically Handicapped	ARAPH
Automated Reading Aid for the Physically Handicapped (SAUS)	ARA-PH
Automated Ready-Supply Stores System (DNAB)	ARSSS
Automated Reagin [*Serology*]	AR
Automated Reagin Test [*Serology*]	ART
Automated Real-Time Imaging System	ARIS
Automated Realtime Investment Exchange Limited (SAUS)	ARIEL
Automated Real-Time Investments Exchange [*NASDAQ trading computer*]	ARIEL
Automated Real-Time Investments Exchange Limited, London (SAUO)	ARIEL
Automated Real-time Mapping System [*Navigation systems*]	ARMS
Automated Real-Time Radiography Inspection System	ARTRIS
Automated Reasoning Assistant (IAA)	AURA
Automated Reasoning Tool (MCD)	ART
Automated Records Control System	ARCS
Automated Records Management System [*Computer science*] (HGAA)	ARMS
Automated Reference Service [*Ohio State University Libraries*] (OLDSS)	ARS
Automated Regional Justice Information System (SAUS)	ARJIS
Automated Registration, Indexing, and Enquiries System [*Computer science*]	ARIES
Automated Regression Tester [*Computer science*] (ITCA)	ART
Automated Reiter Protein Complement - Fixation Test (PDAA)	ARPCFT
Automated Reliability and Maintainability Measurement System (SAUS)	ARMMS
Automated Reliability and Maintenance Management [*or Measurement*] System [*Navy*] (NG)	ARMMS
Automated Reliability Assessment Program [*FAA*]	ARAP
Automated Reliability, Availability and Maintainability Standard (SAUS)	ARAMS
Automated Reliability Estimation Program [*Computer science*]	ARIES
Automated Reliability Interactive Estimation System (SAUS)	ARIES
Automated Remediation Assessment Methodology (ABAC)	ARAM
Automated Remote Network Evaluation (SAUS)	ARNE
Automated Remote Recognition and Tracking System	ARRTS
Automated Remote Tracking Station (MCD)	ARTS
Automated Rendezvous and Docking System (SAUO)	AR&D
Automated Rent Cellections (SAUS)	ARC
Automated Rent Collections	ARC
Automated Repair Service Bureau (TEL)	ARSB
Automated Repeat Request (SAUS)	ARQ
Automated Reporting and Management Information System [*Federal Communications Commission*] (GFGA)	ARMIS
Automated Reporting, Tracking, and Evaluation Management Information System (SSD)	ARTEMIS
Automated Reports Control Handling (MCD)	ARCH
Automated Reproduction and Collating System (MCD)	ARCS
Automated Request Transmission (MHDB)	ART
Automated Request Transmission by Telephone (PDAA)	ARTTel
Automated Requirement Computation System Initial Provisioning [*Army*]	ARCSIP
Automated Requirements Allocation Data (MCD)	ARAD
Automated Requirements Development System (MCD)	ARDS
Automated Requirements Management System (SAUS)	ARMS
Automated Requirements Traceability System (SSD)	ARTS
Automated Research Facility [*National Bureau of Standards*] (NITA)	AMRF
Automated Resolution from Century to Honeywell (SAUS)	ARCH
Automated Resource for Chemical Hazard Incident Evaluation [*Environmental science*] (COE)	ARCHIE
Automated Resource Management System (MCD)	ARMS
Automated Resource Planning and Analysis System (MCD)	ARPAS
Automated Resource Tracking System (NAKS)	ARTS
Automated Resources Management System (SAUS)	ARMS
Automated Response to Query	ARQ
Automated Responsive Environment (BUR)	ARE
Automated Retail Outlet System (MCD)	AUTOROS
Automated Retirement and Integrated Extraction System (SAUS)	ARIES
Automated Retrieval Mail Service (SAUS)	ARMS
Automated Retrieval of Text from Europes Multinational Information Service (SAUS)	ARTEMIS
Automated Retrieval System (SAUS)	ARS
Automated Retroactive Minimal Moderation (SAUS)	ARMM
Automated Revenue Collection System [*Business term*] (MHDW)	ARCS
Automated Ring Code Search (DIT)	ARCS
Automated Ring Code System (SAUS)	ARCS
Automated Roadside Safety Inspection [*FHWA*] (TAG)	ARSI
Automated Rotary Dipping Apparatus (SAUS)	ARDA
Automated Route Management (DEN)	ARM
Automated Route Manager (SAUS)	ARM
Automated Runbook/Library System	ARLS
Automated Safety Officer	ASO

Automated Scanning Low Energy Electron Probe (SAUS)	ASLEEP
Automated Schedule Information System	ASIS
Automated Schedule Procedures	ASP
Automated Sciences Group (SAUO)	ASG
Automated Screen Trading [*Business term*]	AST
Automated Seat Reservation System [*Aviation*]	ASRS
Automated Seavan Shipment Planning System [*MTMC*] (TAG)	ASSP
Automated Security Clearance Approval System (SAUS)	ASCAS
Automated Security Enhancement Tool	ASET
Automated Security Holdings ADS [*NYSE symbol*] (SPSG)	ASI
Automated Security Holdings Ltd. [*Associated Press*] (SAG)	AutSec
Automated Seismic Processor [*Earthquake analyzer*]	ASP
Automated Seismological Observation System [*Marine science*] (OSRA)	ASOS
Automated Send Receive (AAEL)	ASR
Automated Sequential Trace Enrichment of Dialysate	ASTED
Automated Service Center	ASC
Automated Service Center	AUTOSERVCEN
Automated Service Center (SAUS)	AUTOSERVCen
Automated Shareholder Record System (SAUS)	ASRS
Automated Shareholder Records System (MCD)	ASRS
Automated Shell Theory for Rotating Structures [*NASA*]	ASTROS
Automated Ship Classification System (MCD)	ASCS
Automated Ship Data Library (IEEE)	ASDL
Automated Ship Location and Attitude Measuring System	ASLAMS
Automated Shipboard Aerological program (SAUS)	ASAP
Automated Shipboard Aerological Programme (SAUS)	ASAP
Automated Shipboard Forecasting System	ASFS
Automated Signal Excess Prediction (MCD)	ASEP
Automated Single Area Field Scanner [*Department of Agricultural Meteorology, University of Nebraska*]	ASAFS
Automated Small Purchase System [*DoD*]	ASPS
Automated Sneak Program (SAUS)	ASP
Automated Soft Lander [*Aerospace*] (MCD)	ASL
Automated Software Distribution (SAUS)	ASD
Automated Software Evaluation System	ASES
Automated Software Quality (SAUS)	ASQ
Automated Software Reporting System (SAUS)	ASRS
Automated Software System Used for Reliability Evaluation	ASSURE
Automated Software Trouble Report	ASTR
Automated Space Management (SAUS)	ASM
Automated Space Production Experimenters Network [*Robotics*]	ASPEN
Automated Spares Simulation Estimating Technique [*The Boeing Co.*]	ASSET
Automated Special Security Information System Terminal (SAUS)	ASSIST
Automated Specifications [*Computer science*] (DIT)	AUTOSPEC
Automated Speech Recognition (ACAE)	ASR
Automated Speech Technology (MCD)	AST
Automated Speed Enforcement	ASE
Automated Speed Enforcement Device	ASED
Automated Spooling Priority [*Computer science*]	ASP
Automated Staff Message Processing System	ASMPS
Automated Station Test and Monitor (ACAE)	ASTAAM
Automated Statistical Analysis Program	ASAP
Automated Statistical Analysis Technique (DNAB)	ASAT
Automated Status Board	ASB
Automated Status Board (DNAB)	ASTAB
Automated Status Board	ASTABS
Automated Stock Transfer System (MCD)	ASTS
Automated Storage Control System (MCD)	ASCS
Automated Storage, Kitting, and Retrieval Systems [*Tandem Computers*] [*Navy*]	ASKARS
Automated Storage Management (SAUS)	ASM
Automated Storage/Retrieval [*Computer science*]	AS/R
Automated Storage/Retrieval System (SAUS)	AS/RS
Automated Structural Design [*NASA*]	ASD
Automated Structural Optimization Program [*Air Force*]	ASOP
Automated Submarine Frame [*Navy*]	ASF
Automated Summary Tables (SAUS)	AST
Automated Support Requirements System (NAKS)	ASRS
Automated Support System for Army Unit Logistics Training	ASSAULT
Automated Surface Observation System [*Aviation*] (PIPO)	ASOS
Automated Surface Observing System [*Meteorology*] (FAAC)	ASOS
Automated Surface Perspectives (SAUS)	ASPEX
Automated Switched Communications Network (MCD)	ASCON
Automated System (ACRL)	AS
Automated System Character (SAUS)	ASC
Automated System Charter (IAA)	ASC
Automated System Design Methodology (ACAE)	ASDM
Automated System for Composing, Revising, Illustrating and Phototype-setting (SAUS)	AUTOSCRIPT
Automated System for Production Management (IAA)	ASPM
Automated System for Sequential Extraction and Tabulation (NVT)	ASSET
Automated System for Storing and Subsequently Selecting Information [*Developed by ICI, Inc.*]	ASSASSIN
Automated System for the Control of Atmospheric Sampling [*Marine science*] (MSC)	ASCAS
Automated System for Thesaurus Updating, Testing and Editing (SAUS)	ASTUTE
Automated System for Transport Intelligence (SAUS)	ASTI
Automated System for Transported (or Transportation, or Transporting) Data (SAUS)	AUTOSTRAD
Automated System for Transportation Data [*Military*]	AUTOSTRAD
Automated System for Transportation Intelligence [*Army*] (RDA)	ASTI
Automated System Initialisation (or Initialization) (SAUS)	ASI
Automated System of Legal Information (SAUS)	ASLI
Automated System Performance Analysis (SAUS)	ASPA

Automated Systems Analysis Technique (SAUS)	AUTOSATE
Automated Systems and Services Branch [NTIS]	AS & SB
Automated Systems and Services Branch (SAUO)	AS&SB
Automated Systems and Software Engineering Technology (MCD)	ASSET
Automated Systems Army Commissaries (AABC)	ASAC
Automated Systems Design Methodology (SAUS)	ASDM
Automated Systems Development Group (SAUO)	ASDG
Automated Systems Management System (MCD)	ASMS
Automated Systems Operations (SAUS)	ASO
Automated Systems Program Office (SAUO)	ASPO
Automated Systems Service Request [Computer science] (CIST)	ASSR
Automated System-Trust Real-Time Accounting (SAUS)	ASTRA
Automated Tactical Aircraft Launch and Recovery System (SAUS)	ATALARS
Automated Tactical Environmental System	ATES
Automated Tactical Environmental System (MCD)	ATESS
Automated Tactical Fusion Division	ATFD
Automated Tactical Information Display System (IUSS)	ATIDS
Automated Tactical Information System (IUSS)	ATIS
Automated Tactical Intelligence (ACAE)	ATI
Automated Tactical Target Graphic	ATTG
Automated Tape Label Assignment System (MCD)	ATLAS
Automated Tape Lay-up System (SAUS)	ATLAS
Automated Tape Library (SAUS)	ATL
Automated Target Detection (SAUS)	ATD
Automated Target Recognition [Military]	ATR
Automated Tariff Filing and Information System [Washington, DC] (EGAO)	ATFI
Automated Technical Control [System] [Honeywell, Inc.] [Army] (RDA)	ATC
Automated Technical Control [System] [Honeywell, Inc.] [Army]	ATEC
Automated Technical Information (MCD)	ATI
Automated Technical Information Support	ATIS
Automated Technical Library Information System (SAUS)	ATLIS
Automated Technical Manual (IUSS)	ATM
Automated Technical Order Maintenance Sequences [or Systems] [The Boeing Co.] (MCD)	ATOMS
Automated Technical Order Maintenance Systems (SAUS)	ATOMS
Automated Technical Order System [Air Force] (MCD)	ATOS
Automated Technical Systems (GEOI)	ATS
Automated Technique for Spacecraft Monitoring [NASA]	ATSM
Automated Telecommunications Center (MCD)	ATC
Automated Telecommunications Center	ATCC
Automated Telecommunications System [Army] (ADDR)	ATS
Automated Telecommunications Systems Center (SAUO)	ATSC
Automated Telecommunications Systems Directorate (SAUS)	SK
Automated Telemetry System (SAUS)	ATS
Automated Telephone Answering System (SAUS)	ATAS
Automated Telephone Line Address System (SAUS)	Atlas
Automated [or Automatic] Teller Machine (ADA)	AT
Automated [or Automatic] Teller Machine [Banking]	ATM
Automated Terminal Station (SAUS)	ATS
Automated Terminal Weather Dissemination Display System (MCD)	ATWDDS
Automated Terrain Information System	ARTINS
Automated Test Data Base Management System [Army]	ATDBMS
Automated Test Data Generator [Computer science]	ATDG
Automated Test Equipment	ATE
Automated Test Network (SAUS)	ATN
Automated Test Pattern Generation (SAUS)	ATPG
Automated Test Plan (BUR)	ATP
Automated Test Procedure (SAUS)	ATP
Automated Test Validation	ATV
Automated Test-Case Guidance [Computer science]	ATG
Automated Testing Analyzer [Computer science]	ATA
Automated Testing and Load Analysis System (SAUS)	ATLAS
Automated Testing Equipment (SAUS)	ATE
Automated Testing Procedure (SAUS)	ATP
Automated Text Message Handling System (IUSS)	ATMHS
Automated Text System (SAUS)	ATS
Automated Ticket and Boarding Pass [Travel industry]	ATB
Automated Ticket and Fare Determination System [Travel industry] (TRID)	ATFDS
Automated Ticket Dispenser	ATD
Automated Timber Sale Accounting (WPI)	ATSA
Automated Time and Attendance Procedures (MHDB)	ATAP
Automated Time Standards (MCD)	ATS
Automated Titling System (SAUS)	ATS
Automated TMA for Tactical Commanders (SAUS)	ATTAC
Automated Toll Collection (PA)	ATC
Automated Tracking and Monitoring System	ATAMS
Automated Traction Control (SAUS)	ATC
Automated Trade System (NUMA)	ATS
Automated Trading System [NYSE computer]	ATS
Automated Traffic Advisory and Resolution Service [Collision-avoidance system] [Aviation]	ATARS
Automated Traffic Engineering and Management Information System (SAUS)	ATEMIS
Automated Traffic Overload Protection (DNAB)	ATOP
Automated Traffic Surveillance and Control [Automotive engineering]	ATSAC
Automated Train Operation by Minicomputer [Computer science] (PDAA)	ATOMIC
Automated Transfer Service (EBF)	ATS
Automated Transfer Vehicle [Space technology]	ATV
Automated Transponder Navigation System (PDAA)	AUTRANAV
Automated Transponder Navigation System (SAUS)	AUTRANAVS
Automated Transportation Management System (ABAC)	ATMS
Automated Travel Agents Reservation	ATAR

Automated Travel Agents Reservation Systems (PDAA)	ATARS
Automated Trouble Reporting System (SAUS)	ATRS
Automated Trunk Measurement System (SAUS)	ATMS
Automated Ultrasonic Flaw Imaging System (ACAE)	AUFIS
Automated Ultrasonic Scanner (MCD)	AUS
Automated Unit Equipment List	AUEL
Automated Unit Placement Model	AUPM
Automated Unit Reference Sheets (MCD)	AURS
Automated Unit Test (SAUS)	AUT
Automated Universal Array (MCD)	AUA
Automated Urease-Chromous Method [Analytical chemistry]	AUCM
Automated Vacuum	AVAC
Automated Vacuum-Assisted Collection System [Disney World trash disposal system]	AVAC
Automated Vehicle Diagnostic System (SAUS)	AVDS
Automated Vendor Selection System (NRCH)	AVSS
Automated Verification System [Computer science] (MCD)	AVS
Automated Vibration Diagnostic System (MCD)	AVID
Automated Video Maintenance Information (MCD)	AVMI
Automated Video Target Scoring System	AVTSS
Automated Viscoelastic Grain Structural Analysis Program (MCD)	AVGSAP
Automated Vision Association [Later, AIA] (EA)	AVA
Automated Visual Sensitivity Tester	AVST
Automated Vocabulary Control [Subsystem of PLIS] [Computer science]	AVOCON
Automated Voice Annunciator Systems [FTA] (TAG)	AVAS
Automated Voice Response System [DoD]	AVRS
Automated Voice Switching System (IUSS)	AVSS
Automated Volt Left [Medicine] (DMAA)	aVL
Automated Voltammetric Electrode [Electrochemistry]	AVE
Automated Want and Warrant System [Data processing system used in police work]	AWWS
Automated Warehouse System (ACAE)	AWS
Automated Weapon System Trainer (ACAE)	AWST
Automated Weapons Test Analysis System	AWTAS
Automated Weather Acquisition and Retrieval Data System [Marine science] (OSRA)	AWARDS
Automated Weather Advisory Station (GAVI)	AWAS
Automated Weather Data Network [National Climate Program Office]	AWDN
Automated Weather Distribution System (MCD)	AWDS
Automated Weather Information Processing System	AWIPS
Automated Weather Information System (ACAE)	AWIS
Automated Weather Information Systems (SAUS)	AWIS
Automated Weather Network [Air Force]	AWN
Automated Weather Network Coordinating Station [Air Force]	AWNCS
Automated Weather Network Management Center [Military]	AWNMC
Automated Weather Observing Station [FAA] (TAG)	AWOS
Automated Weather Observing System (SAUS)	AWOS
Automated Weather Station (ARMP)	AWS
Automated Wire Data System	AWDS
Automated Wire List [NASA] (NASA)	AWL
Automated Wiring System (MCD)	AWS
Automated Work Authorization System (MCD)	AWAS
Automated Work Request (NVT)	AWR
Automated Worthless Document Index	AWDI
Automated Wreck and Obstruction Information System [National Oceanic and Atmospheric Administration] [Information service or system] (IID)	AWOIS
Automated X-Ray Orientation System (MCD)	AXROS
Automated-Systems Engineering Design (SAUS)	AED
Automatic (IAA)	A
Automatic (IAA)	AU
Automatic	AUT
Automatic	AUTM
Automatic (AFM)	AUTO
Automatic	AUTOMTC
Automatic 4-Speed Heavy Duty Transmission [Automotive engineering]	A4HD
Automatic 4-Speed Light Duty Transmission [Automotive engineering]	A4LD
Automatic Abort-Sensing System [NASA]	AASS
Automatic Abstract (SAUS)	AUTOBSTRACT
Automatic Abstracting (SAUS)	AA
Automatic Accounting Machine (SAUS)	AAM
Automatic Acquisition (SAUS)	AA
Automatic Action (SAUS)	Automation
Automatic Activation Analysis System (SAUS)	AAAS
Automatic Adaption Data	AUTOMAD
Automatic Adaptive Equalization [Telecommunications]	AAE
Automatic Address Modification (SAUS)	AAM
Automatic Address Recognition System [or Subsystem] [Computer science]	AARS
Automatic Address Selector (SAUS)	AAS
Automatic Address Substitution (SAUS)	AAS
Automatic Addressing System [Computer science]	AAS
Automatic Adjusted Suspension (SAUS)	AAS
Automatic Aerial Timer (SAUS)	AAT
Automatic Aimpoint Selection and Maintenance (MCD)	AUASAM
Automatic Aimpoint Selection and Maintenance (DNAB)	AUASM
Automatic Air Data Calibration System [Aerospace]	AADCS
Automatic Air Defense Information System (SAUO)	AADIS
Automatic Air Traffic Control [System] [IEEE]	AATC
Automatic Aircraft Diagnostic System	AADS
Automatic Aircraft Intercept Control System	AAICS
Automatic Aircraft Vectoring Control System [Air Force]	AAVCS
Automatic Aircraft Vectoring System [Air Force] (MUGU)	AAVS
Automatic Air-Valving Surface Effects Device [Army] (MCD)	AAVSED
Automatic Alarm (SAUS)	AUTOALARM

Automatic Alignment (SAUS) AUTOLIGN
Automatic Alternate Voice Data (SAUS) AAVD
Automatic Alternate Voice/Data [*Computer science*] AAVD
Automatic Alternative Routing [*Telecommunications*] (TEL) AAR
Automatic Alternative Voice/Data (SAUS) AAVD
Automatic Altitude Reporting System (SAUS) AARS
Automatic Altitude Trim System [*for helicopters*] (NG) AATS
Automatic Amplitude Control (CET) AAC
Automatic and Dynamic Monitor with Immediate Relocation (SAUS) ADMIREL
Automatic and Dynamic Monitor with Immediate Relocation, Allocation and Loading (SAUS) ADMIRAL
Automatic and Dynamic Monitor with Immediate Relocation, Allocation, and Loading (IEEE) ADMIRAL
Automatic Anechoic Chamber Test System [*Navy*] (MCD) AACTS
Automatic Announcement Subsystem [*Telecommunications*] (TEL) AAS
Automatic Answer [*Telecommunications*] (TEL) AA
Automatic Answer Trunk [*Computer science*] (IAA) AAT
Automatic Answering (DDC) AUTO-answer
Automatic Answering Equipment [*Telecommunications*] (IAA) AAE
Automatic Answering Unit [*Telecommunications*] (TEL) AAU
Automatic Antenna Matching & Tuning Unit (SAUS) AAMTU
Automatic Antenna Timer AAT
Automatic Antenna Tuning Unit (SAUS) AATU
Automatic Anti-Aircraft (SAUS) AAA
Automatic Antijam Circuit (CET) AAJAC
Automatic Antitheft System [*Electronic lock*] AATS
Automatic Anti-Theft System (SAUS) AATS
Automatic Aperture Control AAC
Automatic Applications Development System [*Computer science*] (CIST) AADS
Automatic Approach (ACAE) AA
Automatic Approach Control [*Aviation*] (AAG) AAC
Automatic Approach Control Coupler [*or Complex*] [*Aviation*] (MCD) AACC
Automatic Approach to Hover (SAUS) AATH
Automatic Approach/Autoland (SAUS) AA/AL
Automatic Approach/AUTOLAND (NASA) AA/AL
Automatic Approval (SAUS) AA
Automatic Armor Cluster Munition AACM
Automatic Array Scaling (SAUS) AAS
Automatic Assemble Editing (NTCM) AAE
Automatic Atrial Tachycardia [*Medicine*] (MELL) AAT
Automatic Attack Warning System (AFM) AAWS
Automatic Attitude Hold (SAUS) ATH
Automatic Auto-Collimator (SAUS) AAC
Automatic Aviation Weather Service (SAUS) AAWS
Automatic Azimuth Laying Theodolite (KSC) AALT
Automatic Back Bias [*RADAR*] ABB
Automatic Back Bias (SAUS) abb
Automatic Background Control (SAUS) ABC
Automatic Backlight Compensation [*Photography*] ABLC
Automatic Backup and Recovery [*Computer science*] (IAA) ABR
Automatic Backup Restore [*Computer science*] (CIST) ABR
Automatic Backup Shutdown (SAUS) ABS
Automatic Backup Shutdown of Safety Computer (SAUS) ABS-SC
Automatic Backup Shutdown of the Safety Computer [*Environmental science*] (COE) ABS-SC
Automatic Band Rate (IEEE) ABR
Automatic Bandwidth Control ABC
Automatic Bandwidth Control (MSA) ABWC
Automatic Bar and Chucking (SAUS) ABS
Automatic Bar Checker ABC
Automatic Barrier Crossing, Locally Monitored (HEAS) ABCL
Automatic Base Communication Systems (PDAA) ABCS
Automatic Baseband Monitor (PDAA) ABBM
Automatic Bass Compensation [*Radio*] ABC
Automatic Bass Compensation (IDOE) abc
Automatic Bass Compensation [*Radio*] (MSA) ABSC
Automatic Bass Control ABC
Automatic Batch Mixing (SAUS) ABM
Automatic Battery Test ABT
Automatic Beam Control (IAA) ABC
Automatic Beam Current Stabilizing (IAA) ABS
Automatic Beam Forming [*Military*] (IUSS) ABF
Automatic Beam-current Stabilization (SAUS) ABS
Automatic Beam-current Stabilizing System (SAUS) ABS System
Automatic Bearing Instrumentation (IUSS) ABI
Automatic Bending Center (SAUS) ABC
Automatic Bias Compensation ABC
Automatic Bias Compensation (MSA) ABCP
Automatic Bias Control ABC
Automatic Bias Control (IDOE) abc
Automatic Bibliographic Services (SAUS) ABS
Automatic Bill Calling (SAUS) ABC
Automatic Bill Calling [*Later, MCCS*] [*Telecommunications*] ABC
Automatic Billing Machine (SAUS) ABM
Automatic Binary Computer (ADA) ABC
Automatic Binary Data Link [*Computer science*] (CET) ABDL
Automatic Bird Feeder (SAUS) AUTOBIRD
Automatic Bit Access Test System [*Computer science*] (VERA) ABATS
Automatic BIT [*Binary Digit*] **Error Rate Test** [*Computer science*] (MCD) ABERT
Automatic Bit Rate ABR
Automatic Black Level (SAUS) ABL
Automatic Black Signal [*TRB*] (TAG) ABS
Automatic Blade Control (SAUS) ABC
Automatic Blank Character (SAUS) ABC
Automatic Blip Counter ABC
Automatic Blip Counter System ABCS
Automatic Blip-Scan Counter ABSC
Automatic Blip-Scan Counter System ABSCS
Automatic Block Controller (MCD) ABC
Automatic Block End (SAUS) ABE
Automatic Block Transfer (SAUS) ABT
Automatic Block Transport (SAUS) ABT
Automatic, Block-schematic Advanced Control User-oriented System (SAUS) ABACUS
Automatic, Block-Schematic Advanced Control User-Oriented System (PDAA) ABACUS
Automatic Blow Down (IEEE) AB
Automatic Blowdown (SAUS) AB
Automatic Bobbin Handling (SAUS) ABH
Automatic Boiling-Column Reactor ABC
Automatic Bomb Sight (SAUS) ABS
Automatic Boost Control (SAUS) ABC
Automatic Bootstrap Loader [*Computer science*] ABL
Automatic Braking System (MCD) ABS
Automatic Braking Technology [*Rollerblade, Inc.*] (PS) ABT
Automatic Branch Control (IAA) ABC
Automatic Bridge Control [*Navy*] (MCD) ABC
Automatic Brightness Compensation (IDOE) abc
Automatic Brightness Control (IDOE) abc
Automatic Brightness Control [*Telecommunications*] (TEL) ABC
Automatic Broadcast (BARN) ABCST
Automatic Broadcast Control System (SAUS) ABCS
Automatic Broadcasting Control System [*Japan*] ABCS
Automatic Built in Self Test [*IBM Corp*] (VERA) ABIST
Automatic Built-In Self-Test (SAUS) ABIST
Automatic Bulk Tape Degausser ABTD
Automatic Bus Terminal [*Computer science*] (MCD) ABT
Automatic Bus Transfer (NVT) ABT
Automatic Cable Equalization (SAUS) ACE
Automatic Cable Pair Identification [*Computer science*] (IAA) ACPI
Automatic Cable Tester ACT
Automatic Calculator (SAUS) AC
Automatic Calibration and Equalization ACE
Automatic Call Director [*Telecommunications*] ACD
Automatic Call Disposition Analyzer (SAUS) ACDA
Automatic Call Distributing system (SAUS) ACD
Automatic Call Distribution [*Switching system*] [*Telecommunications*] ACD
Automatic Call Distribution Unit [*Computer science*] (DDC) ACDunit
Automatic Call Distributor [*Datapoint Corp.*] (NITA) ACD
Automatic Call Distributor - Electronic Switching System [*Telecommunications*] (TEL) ACD-ESS
Automatic Call Number Identification [*Telecommunications*] (IAA) ACNI
Automatic Call Originate (or Origination, or Originator) (SAUS) ACO
Automatic Call Origination [*Telecommunications*] ACO
Automatic Call Recorder (SAUS) ACR
Automatic Call Recording [*Telecommunications*] (CMD) ACR
Automatic Call Recording Equipment [*Telecommunications*] ACRE
Automatic Call Selector (SAUS) ACS
Automatic Call Unit (SAUS) ACU
Automatic Call [*or Calling*] **Unit** [*Telecommunications*] (TEL) ACU
Automatic Called Number Identification (SAUS) ACNI
Automatic Calling and Answering Unit [*Telecommunications*] (OA) ACAU
Automatic Calling Card Service [*Telecommunications*] (TEL) ACCS
Automatic Calling Encoder (SAUS) ACE
Automatic Calling Equipment [*Telecommunications*] (BUR) ACE
Automatic Calling Unit Adapter (CIST) ACUA
Automatic Calling Unit Interface [*Telecommunications*] (IEEE) ACUI
Automatic Calling Unit Terminator (SAUS) ACUT
Automatic Camera Control (SAUS) ACC
Automatic Cancellation (CAAL) ACNX
Automatic Cancellation of Exended Targets (SAUS) ACET
Automatic Cancellation of Extended Targets (AABC) ACET
Automatic Cannon Technology (MCD) ACT
Automatic Canteen Company of America (SAUO) AUM
Automatic Capacitance Testing (SAUS) ACT
Automatic Capacitor Tester ACT
Automatic Car Wash Association (SAUO) ACWA
Automatic Car Wash Association International [*Later, ICA*] ACWA
Automatic Car Wash Association International (SAUO) ACWAI
Automatic Card Control Entrance Security System [*Computer science*] ACCESS
Automatic Card Ejection (SAUS) ACE
Automatic Card Feeding (SAUS) ACF
Automatic Card Identification ACI
Automatic Card Reader ACR
Automatic Carriage Return ACR
Automatic Carrier Control [*Telecommunications*] (TEL) ACC
Automatic Carrier Landing System [*Military*] ACL
Automatic Carrier Landing System [*FAA*] (TAG) ACLS
Automatic Cartographic System ACS
Automatic Cartridge Handler (SAUS) ACH
Automatic Cartridge Handler (SAUS) Auto Ctdg Hdl
Automatic Cartridge Loader (SAUS) ACL
Automatic Cartridge, Pistol [*Military*] (VNW) ACP
Automatic Case Control System ACCS
Automatic Cassette Recorder (SAUS) ACR
Automatic Cat Feeder (SAUS) AUTOCAT
Automatic Caution Guard (SAUS) ACG
Automatic Celestial Navigation (SAUS) acn

Automatic Celestial Navigation [Air Force]	ACN
Automatic Central Communications Electronic Switching System	ACCESS
Automatic Centralized Data Processing (SAUS)	ACDP
Automatic Centrifugal Timing Apparatus (SAUS)	ACTA
Automatic Centrifugal Tinning Apparatus	ACTA
Automatic Channel and Time [Toshiba Corp.] [Programmable television set]	ACT
Automatic Channel Programming (SAUS)	ACP
Automatic Channel Selection (SAUS)	ACS
Automatic Character Generation (SAUS)	ACG
Automatic Character Reader (SAUS)	ACR
Automatic Character Recognition (SAUS)	ACR
Automatic Characterization and Extraction System (ACAE)	ACES
Automatic Chart Display (SAUS)	ACD
Automatic Charting (SAUS)	AUTOCHART
Automatic Check (SAUS)	AC
Automatic Check Personalization (DGA)	ACP
Automatic Check Value (SAUS)	AUTO CV
Automatic Check Valve (MSA)	AUTO CV
Automatic Checking and Control for Electrical Systems Support (SAUS)	ACCESS
Automatic Checkout (BUR)	AC
Automatic Checkout and Control System	ACCS
Automatic Checkout and Evaluation System [Air Force]	ACES
Automatic Checkout and Readiness Equipment	ACRE
Automatic Checkout and Recording Equipment	ACORN
Automatic Checkout and Recording Equipments (SAUS)	ACORN
Automatic Checkout and Recording Network (SAUS)	ACORN
Automatic Checkout Equipment	ACE
Automatic Checkout Equipment	ACOE
Automatic Checkout Equipment Sequencer (NASA)	ACES
Automatic Checkout Set (AAG)	ACOS
Automatic Checkout System [NASA] (AAG)	ACHS
Automatic Checkout System [NASA]	ACS
Automatic Checkout Technician [or Technique] (MCD)	ACT
Automatic Checkout Techniques (SAUS)	ACT
Automatic Checkout Test Equipment (AAG)	ACTE
Automatic Chemical Agent Alarm [Military] (RDA)	ACAA
Automatic Chemical Agent Alarm [Military] (RDA)	ACADA
Automatic Chemical Agent Alarm System (MCD)	ACAAS
Automatic Chemical Agent Detector Alarm (SAUS)	ACADA
Automatic Chemical Biological Warning System	ACBWS
Automatic Chemical Reaction System	ACRS
Automatic Chemical Sprinklers (SAUS)	ACS
Automatic Cheque Sorter (SAUS)	ACS
Automatic Chinese Message Switching System (SAUS)	ACMES System
Automatic Chroma Circuit (SAUS)	ACC
Automatic Chroma Control (SAUS)	ACC
Automatic Chrominance Control (IDOE)	acc
Automatic Chrominance Control (DEN)	ACC
Automatic Circuit Analysis (ACAE)	ACA
Automatic Circuit Analysis Program	ACAP
Automatic Circuit Analyzer	ACA
Automatic Circuit Assurance Feature (CET)	ACAF
Automatic Circuit Board Card Tester	ACBCT
Automatic Circuit Board Tester	ACBT
Automatic Circuit Design (SAUS)	ACID
Automatic Circuit Exchange	ACE
Automatic Circuit Exchange (MSA)	ACKTX
Automatic Circuit Quality Monitoring (PDAA)	ACOM
Automatic Circuit Quality Monitoring (MHDI)	ACQM
Automatic Circuit Tester	ACT
Automatic Claiming and Cancelling (SAUS)	ACC
Automatic Class Selection (SAUS)	ACS
Automatic Classification (SAUS)	AUTOCLASS
Automatic Classification and Interpretation of Data (BUR)	ACID
Automatic Clearing (SAUS)	AC
Automatic Client Update [Computer science] (VERA)	ACU
Automatic Climate Control [Automotive engineering]	ACC
Automatic Climate Station (SAUS)	ACS
Automatic Climatological Recording Equipment [Meteorology] (PDAA)	ACRE
Automatic Clinical Analyzer [Medicine] (MAE)	ACA
Automatic Clock (SAUS)	AK
Automatic Closed Transition Transfer Switch	ACTTS
Automatic Closing Device (DAC)	ACD
Automatic Closure and Interlock [Nuclear energy] (NRCH)	ACI
Automatic Cloud Cover Assessment by EOSAT (SAUS)	ACCA-E
Automatic Clutch and Throttle System [Automotive powertrain]	ACTS
Automatic Clutch System [Powertrain] [Automotive engineering]	ACS
Automatic Clutter Eliminator [FAA]	ACE
Automatic Clutter Eliminator (MSA)	ACLE
Automatic Clutter Mapper (or Mapping) (SAUS)	ACM
Automatic Clutter Mapping (ACAE)	ACL
Automatic Coating Machine	ACM
Automatic Code Generator	ACG
Automatic Code Machine (SAUS)	ACOM
Automatic Code Translation [Computer science]	ACT
Automatic Code Translation (or Translator) (SAUS)	ACT
Automatic Code Translator (NITA)	ACT
Automatic Coder of Report Narrative (SAUS)	ACORN
Automatic Coding Machine [Computer science] (CET)	ACOM
Automatic Coding System [Computer science] (IAA)	ACS
Automatic Coin Telephone Service	ACTS
Automatic Collision Avoidance System (SAUS)	ACAS
Automatic Color Compensation (IDOE)	acc
Automatic Color Control	ACC
Automatic Color Killer [Video recording]	ACK
Automatic Color-Scanned Device (MCD)	ACSD
Automatic Colt Pistol (DICI)	ACP
Automatic Combat Intelligence Center (MCD)	ACIC
Automatic Combat System Checklist (SAUS)	ACSCL
Automatic Combustion Control	ACC
Automatic Combustion Control and Feedwater Control (DNAB)	ACC/FWC
Automatic Combustion Control Unmanned (PDAA)	ACCU
Automatic Combustion-Control Unmanned	ACCU
Automatic Command Processing (SAUS)	ACP
Automatic Command to Line of Sight [Military] [British]	ACLOS
Automatic Communication Management System (SAUS)	ACMS
Automatic Communication Relay (NVT)	AUTOCAT
Automatic Communications Addressing and Reporting System [FAA] (TAG)	ACARS
Automatic Communications and Reporting System (SAUS)	ACARS
Automatic Communications EW System (SAUS)	ACEWS
Automatic Communications Monitor (CCCA)	ACM
Automatic Communications Program (DWSG)	ACP
Automatic Compilation Equipment	ACE
Automatic Component Assembly System (SAUS)	ACAS
Automatic Component Ordering (SAUS)	ACORD
Automatic Component Tester	ACT
Automatic Comprehensive Display System [Computer science]	ACDS
Automatic Compression - Release	ACR
Automatic Compression - Release Device	ACRD
Automatic Compression Regulator (IEEE)	ACR
Automatic Computed Air Release Point (SAUS)	AUTO CARP
Automatic Computer	AC
Automatic Computer (IDOE)	ac
Automatic Computer Calculation of Optical Systems (MCD)	ACCOS
Automatic Computer Controlled Electronic Scanning System (SAUS)	ACCESS
Automatic Computer Display System (SAUS)	ACDS
Automatic Computer Evaluation (BUR)	ACE
Automatic Computer, Ministry of Supply [British] (DEN)	AMOS
Automatic Computer Telex Services	ACTS
Automatic Computer Telex System (SAUS)	ACTS
Automatic Computer Voltage Stabilizer (MHDI)	ACVS
Automatic Computer-controlled Dispensing System (SAUS)	ACDS
Automatic Computer-Controlled Electronic Scanning Set (SAUS)	ACCESS
Automatic Computer-Controlled Electronic Scanning System [National Institute of Standards and Technology]	ACCESS
Automatic Computerized Solvent Litholysis (MELL)	ACSL
Automatic Computerized Transverse Axial [Computer X-ray system]	ACTA
Automatic Computing Engine [Early computer] [National Physical Laboratory]	ACE
Automatic Computing Equipment (IAA)	ACE
Automatic Computing Transfer Oscillator (IEEE)	ACTO
Automatic Conditional Release (WDAA)	ACR
Automatic Conference Arranger (CET)	ACA
Automatic Configuration Management Tool	ACMT
Automatic Console Control (SAUS)	ACC
Automatic Contact Evaluation Plotter (SAUS)	ACEP
Automatic Continuity Equipment	ACE
Automatic Continuity Verifiers (SAUS)	ACVS
Automatic Continuous Air Monitoring System (MCD)	ACAMS
Automatic Continuous Evaporation	ACE
Automatic Continuous Function Generation [Computer science]	ACFG
Automatic Continuous Function Generation (or Generator) (SAUS)	ACFG
Automatic Contour (SAUS)	AUTOCON
Automatic Contour Digitizer	ACD
Automatic Contrast Control	ACC
Automatic Contrast Selection (SAUS)	ASC
Automatic Control	AC
Automatic Control Center [Purdue University]	ACC
Automatic Control Certified (DCTA)	ACC
Automatic Control Certified for Unattended Engine Room (DS)	ACCU
Automatic Control Certified for Unattended Engine Room - Open Seas (DS)	ACCU-OS
Automatic Control Console (NASA)	ACC
Automatic Control Distribution (IAA)	ACD
Automatic Control Equipment	ACE
Automatic Control Evaluation Simulator [Spaceflight training machine]	ACES
Automatic Control Features (NRCH)	ACF
Automatic Control Gear (SAUS)	ACG
Automatic Control Instrumentation	ACI
Automatic Control Module	ACM
Automatic Control of Air Transmissions (NATG)	AUTOCAT
Automatic Control of Execution (SAUS)	ACE
Automatic Control of Training Unit (IAA)	ACTU
Automatic Control Operations Center (DNAB)	ACOC
Automatic Control System	ACS
Automatic Control Unit (IAA)	ACU
Automatic Controlled Exposure	ACE
Automatic Controlled Instrument Landing (NASA)	ACIL
Automatic Controller (SAUS)	AC
Automatic Cop Feeder (SAUS)	ACF
Automatic Cop Feeder (PDAA)	ACF
Automatic Corps [Communications System] [General Electric Co.]	AutoKo
Automatic Correction of Multiple Errors (SAUS)	ACME
Automatic Correlation Guidance	ACG
Automatic Coulometric Titration (PDAA)	ACT
Automatic Counter System	ACS
Automatic Countermeasures Dispensing System (PDAA)	ACDS

Automatic Coupling [*Music*] .... Auto
Automatic Course Control [*Air Force*] .... ACC
Automatic Course Keeping (IAA) .... ACK
Automatic CPU Overheating Prevention System (SAUS) .... ACOPS
Automatic Crane Control Storage System .... ACCESS
Automatic Crash-Program Systems (SAUS) .... ACPS
Automatic Credit Transfer (CDAI) .... ACT
Automatic Cross-Connection Equipment [*Computer science*] .... ACE
Automatic Cross-referencing and Indexing Document Generation (SAUS) .... ACID Generation
Automatic Cross-referencing and Indexing Document Generator (SAUS) .... ACID Generator
Automatic Crystal Resistivity Indexing Tester (SAUS) .... ACRIT
Automatic Current Limiting (SAUS) .... ACL
Automatic Cutout [*Valve*] [*Aviation*] (AIA) .... ACO
Automatic Daily System Operability Test .... ADSOT
Automatic Damage Template (SAUS) .... ADT
Automatic Damper Arm (KSC) .... ADA
Automatic Damper Manufacturers Association [*Defunct*] (EA) .... ADMA
Automatic Damping Control [*Automotive suspensions*] .... ADC
Automatic Data Accumulation and Transfer .... ADAT
Automatic Data Acquisition [*Programming language named for Augusta Ada Byron*] .... ADA
Automatic Data Acquisition and Computer Complex [*Air Force*] .... ADACC
Automatic Data Acquisition and Computer Complex (SAUS) .... ADACX
Automatic Data Acquisition and Computer Complex [*Computer science*] (MHDB) .... ADAEX
Automatic Data Acquisition and Control System (SAUS) .... ADACS
Automatic Data Acquisition & Processing (SAUS) .... ADAPS
Automatic Data Acquisition and Processing for Transportation System (SAUS) .... ADAPTS
Automatic Data Acquisition and Processing Techniques [*Army*] (RDA) .... ADAPT
Automatic Data Acquisition Module (SAUS) .... ADAM
Automatic Data Acquisition System (SAUS) .... ADAS
Automatic Data Aids (MCD) .... ADA
Automatic Data Analysis System (SAUS) .... ADAS
Automatic Data and Select Program (KSC) .... ADASP
Automatic Data Automatic Correction (SAUS) .... ADAC
Automatic Data Capture (VERA) .... ADC
Automatic Data Center (ECII) .... ADC
Automatic Data Channel (SAUS) .... ADC
Automatic Data Coding (SAUS) .... ADC
Automatic Data Collection and Analysis System [*Fort Huachuca, AZ*] [*United States Army Electronic Proving Ground*] (GRD) .... ADCAS
Automatic Data Collection Association (SAUO) .... ADCA
Automatic Data Collection System (RDA) .... ADCS
Automatic Data Collector [*National Weather Service*] .... ADC
Automatic Data Computer (or Computing) (SAUS) .... ADC
Automatic Data Computing [*Computer science*] (IAA) .... ADC
Automatic Data Correction and Transfer (SAUS) .... ADCAT
Automatic Data Correlation System (MCD) .... ADCS
Automatic Data Descriptor .... ADD
Automatic Data Digitizing System [*Air Force*] .... ADDS
Automatic Data Distribution System [*Army*] (AABC) .... ADDS
Automatic Data Encoding (SAUS) .... ADE
Automatic Data Entry [*Air Force*] .... ADE
Automatic Data Entry Unit .... ADEU
Automatic Data Evaluation .... ADE
Automatic Data Exchange .... ADX
Automatic Data Extraction Routine (CAAL) .... ADER
Automatic Data Extractor and Plotting Table .... ADEPT
Automatic Data Field Systems Command [*Fort Belvoir, VA*] [*Army*] .... ADFSC
Automatic Data Handling [*Computer science*] .... ADH
Automatic Data Input (SAUS) .... ADI
Automatic Data Input Terminal (SAUS) .... AUDIT
Automatic Data Interchange System [*International Civil Aviation Organization*] .... ADIS
Automatic Data Interchange System (SAUS) .... ADIS
Automatic Data Link [*Computer science*] .... ADL
Automatic Data Link Plotting System .... ADLIPS
Automatic Data Logger (PDAA) .... ADL
Automatic Data Material Requirements List .... ADMRL
Automatic Data Monitoring System (ACAE) .... ADMS
Automatic Data Network .... ADN
Automatic Data Plotter .... ADP
Automatic Data Plotter (or Plotting) (SAUS) .... ADP
Automatic Data Proc [*NYSE symbol*] (TTSB) .... AUD
Automatic Data Proceising Systems and Equipment (SAUS) .... ADPSE
Automatic Data Procesing System Security Officer (SAUS) .... ADPSSO
Automatic Data Processing .... ADP
Automatic Data Processing (IDOE) .... adp
Automatic Data Processing [*Associated Press*] (SAG) .... AutoDt
Automatic Data Processing 3 (SAUS) ADat-P3
Automatic Data Processing and Telecommunications Management (SAUS) .... ADP/TM
Automatic Data Processing Budget (DNAB) .... ADPBUD
Automatic Data Processing Budget Control Totals .... ADPBCT
Automatic Data Processing by Equipment Systems .... ADPES
Automatic Data Processing Center .... ADPC
Automatic Data Processing Center (or Centre) (SAUS) .... ADPC
Automatic Data Processing Centre (SAUO) .... ADPC
Automatic Data Processing Engineering .... ADPE
Automatic Data Processing Equipment .... ADPE
Automatic Data Processing Equipment Selection Office [*Navy*] .... ADPESO
Automatic Data Processing Equipment Services (SAUO) .... ADPES
Automatic Data Processing Equipment/ System (SAUS) .... ADPE/S
Automatic Data Processing Equipment/Data System (AAGC) .... ADPE/DS
Automatic Data Processing Field Branch [*BUPERS*] .... ADPFB
Automatic Data Processing, Inc. [*Trademark for data processing services*] .... ADP
Automatic Data Processing Inc. (SAUO) .... ADP
Automatic Data Processing, Inc. [*NYSE symbol*] (SPSG) .... AUD
Automatic Data Processing, Inc. [*Associated Press*] (SAG) .... AutoDta
Automatic Data Processing International Program (SAUO) .... ADPIP
Automatic Data Processing Liaison Officer [*Military*] (MCD) .... ADPLO
Automatic Data Processing Machine .... ADPM
Automatic Data Processing Management Information System (AABC) .... ADPMIS
Automatic Data Processing Modification Order .... ADPMO
Automatic Data Processing Operations (SAUS) .... ADPO
Automatic Data Processing Plan (ACAE) .... ADPP
Automatic Data Processing Planning and Development Branch [*BUPERS*] .... ADPP & DB
Automatic Data Processing Production Branch [*BUPERS*] .... ADPPB
Automatic Data Processing Program Reporting System [*Military*] (MCD) .... ADPPRS
Automatic Data Processing Programming and Processing Branch [*BUPERS*] .... ADPP & PB
Automatic Data Processing Requirements Office [*Jet Propulsion Laboratory, NASA*] .... ADPRO
Automatic Data Processing Resource Estimating Procedures .... ADPREP
Automatic Data Processing Resource Estimating Procedures .... ADREP
Automatic Data Processing Security [*Military*] (MCD) .... ADPS
Automatic Data Processing Selection Office [*Military*] (MCD) .... ADPSO
Automatic Data Processing Service Center [*Service of the US military*] (AABC) .... ADPSC
Automatic Data Processing Services .... ADPS
Automatic Data Processing Standards Policy Group (CCCA) .... ASPG
Automatic Data Processing Subsystem (SAUS) .... ADPS
Automatic Data Processing System [*or Subsystem*] .... ADPS
Automatic Data Processing System Security Officer (MCD) .... ADPSSO
Automatic Data Processing Systems and Equipment (GFGA) .... ADPSE
Automatic Data Processing Systems Development (SAUS) .... ADPSD
Automatic Data Processing Tactical Operation System (DNAB) .... ADPTOS
Automatic Data Processing Training Center [*Military*] (MCD) .... ADPTC
Automatic Data Processing Unit (IAA) .... ADPU
Automatic Data Processor (SAUS) .... ADP
Automatic Data Range Changer (SAUS) .... ADRC
Automatic Data Rate Changer .... ADRC
Automatic Data Rate Detection (or Detector) (SAUS) .... ADRD
Automatic Data Recorder (SAUS) .... ADR
Automatic Data Recording (SAUS) .... ADR
Automatic Data Relay .... ADR
Automatic Data Reporting System (NATG) .... ADRS
Automatic Data Retrieval (SAUS) .... ADR
Automatic Data Routing Group (AAG) .... ADRG
Automatic Data Service Center .... ADSC
Automatic Data Service Center (or Centre) (SAUO) .... ADSC
Automatic Data Set Editing Program [*NASA*] (KSC) .... ADSEP
Automatic Data Surveillance (SAUS) .... ADS
Automatic Data Switching System [*Deep Space Network*] .... ADSS
Automatic Data System [*Computer science*] .... ADS
Automatic Data System Uniform Practices (SAUS) .... ADSU
Automatic Data System Uniform Practices [*A programming language*] .... ADSUP
Automatic Data System within the Army in the Field .... ADSAF
Automatic Data Systems Analysis Technique (SAUS) .... AUTOSATE
Automatic Data Test System [*Bell System*] .... ADTS
Automatic Data Transfer System (MCD) .... ADTS
Automatic Data Transition (CCCA) .... ADT
Automatic Data Translator [*or Transmitter*] .... ADT
Automatic Data Transmission (or Transmitter) (SAUS) .... ADT
Automatic Data Unit .... ADU
Automatic Data-Processing Intelligence Network (SAUO) .... ADPRIN
Automatic Day/Night Optical Tracker (SAUS) .... ARDNOT
Automatic Day/Night Optronic Tracker System (SAUS) .... ADNOTS
Automatic Dead Reckoning Instrument Systems [*Navigation*] [*Canada*] .... ADRIS
Automatic Dead-Reckoning Instrument [*Aviation*] (PDAA) .... ADRI
Automatic Debit Transfer [*Banking*] .... ADT
Automatic Debiting and Electronic Payment for Transport [*Automotive engineering*] (ECON) .... ADEPT
Automatic Decentral Data Acquisition (SAUS) .... ADDA
Automatic Decisions Optimizing Predicted Estimates .... ADOPE
Automatic Defense Operation Center .... ADOC
Automatic Defense System (MCD) .... ADS
Automatic Degaussing (IAA) .... ADG
Automatic De-Gaussing (SAUS) .... ADG
Automatic Degaussing System (DWSG) .... ADS
Automatic Degreasing Machine .... ADM
Automatic Delection Procedure (SAUS) .... ADP
Automatic Deletion Procedure (DNAB) .... ADP
Automatic Demolition Munition (SAUS) .... ADM
Automatic Dependence Surveillance System [*International Civil Aviation Organisation*] .... ADS
Automatic Dependent Surveillance [*FAA*] (TAG) .... ADS
Automatic Dependent Surveillance Unit [*ICAO designator*] (FAAC) .... ADSU
Automatic Dependent Surveillance-Broadcast (SAUS) .... ADS-B
Automatic Depositor [*Banking*] (BUR) .... AD
Automatic Depot Inertial Navigation Test System (SAUS) .... ADINTS
Automatic Depressurization System [*Nuclear energy*] (NRCH) .... ADS
Automatic Depth Control (MCD) .... ADC
Automatic Depth Keeping (IAA) .... ADK
Automatic Depth/Deployed Moored Sweep (MCD) .... ADDMS

Automatic Derivation of Invariants (MCD) ... ADI
Automatic Design Engineering (SAUS) ... ADE
Automatic Design Optimization Techniques (MCD) ... ADOPT
Automatic Destruct Program (MUGU) ... ADP
Automatic Detection [*Air Force*] ... AD
Automatic Detection and Integrated Tracking (MCD) ... ADIT
Automatic Detection and Tracking (MCD) ... ADT
Automatic Detection Mark (NVT) ... ADM
Automatic Detection/Automatic Classification [*Antisubmarine warfare*] (MCD) ... AD/AC
Automatic Development System (MCD) ... ADS
Automatic Deviation Control (MCD) ... ADC
Automatic Device for Mechanical Order Selection ... ADMOS
Automatic Diagnosis Automatic Correction (SAUS) ... ADAC
Automatic Diagnostic and Recovery (SAUS) ... ADR
Automatic Diagnostic Input/Output System [*Computer science*] ... ADIOS
Automatic Diagnostic Maintenance Information Retrieval [*Computer science*] (IAA) ... ADMIR
Automatic Diagnostic Maintenance Information Retrieval System [*Computer science*] (MCD) ... ADMIRE
Automatic Dial Order Wire [*Military*] (NVT) ... ADOW
Automatic Dialer with Recorded Message Player [*Telecommunications*] ... ADRMP
Automatic Dialing (DDC) ... Auto-dial
Automatic Dialing Alarm System (PDAA) ... ADAS
Automatic Dialing and Indicating Equipment [*Telecommunications*] (IAA) ... ADIE
Automatic Dialing Unit [*Telecommunications*] ... ADU
Automatic Dialing Unit (IDOE) ... adu
Automatic Dialogue Replacement ... ADR
Automatic Dial-Out (NITA) ... ADO
Automatic Dictionary (SAUS) ... AD
Automatic Dictionary Look-up (SAUS) ... DICAUTOM
Automatic Die Positioner [*Electronics*] (EECA) ... ADP
Automatic Diffemic Identification of Speakers [*University of Bonn*] ... ADIS
Automatic Digit Recognition (SAUS) ... AUDREC
Automatic Digit Recognition ... AUDREY
Automatic Digit Recognizing (SAUS) ... ADR
Automatic Digital Aerial Measurement (SAUS) ... ADAM
Automatic Digital Assembly Test Equipment (MCD) ... ADATE
Automatic Digital Calculator [*Computer science*] (ADA) ... ADC
Automatic Digital Circuit Switch (SAUS) ... ADCS
Automatic Digital Computer (SAUS) ... ADC
Automatic Digital Data Acquisition and Recording [*Computer science*] ... ADDAR
Automatic Digital Data Assembly System [*Computer science*] ... ADDAS
Automatic Digital Depth (IAA) ... ADD
Automatic Digital Design System (SAUS) ... ADDS
Automatic Digital Display (SAUS) ... ADD
Automatic Digital Encoding System [*Computer science*] ... ADES
Automatic Digital Exchange [*Telecommunications*] (ODBW) ... ADX
Automatic Digital Information Network (ACAE) ... AUTODIN
Automatic Digital Input/Output System [*Computer science*] ... ADIOS
Automatic Digital Message Switch Equipment (MCD) ... ADMSE
Automatic Digital Message Switcher (or Switching) (SAUS) ... ADMS
Automatic Digital Message Switching Center [*AUTODIN*] ... ADMSC
Automatic Digital Microphotometer (SAUS) ... ADM
Automatic Digital Network [*DoD*] ... AUTODIN
Automatic Digital Network - Evolutionary Modernization [*Military*] (DNAB) ... AUTODIN EMOD
Automatic Digital Network - Integrated Circuits Communications Data Processor [*Military*] (DNAB) ... AUTODIN ICCDP
Automatic Digital Online Information System (SAUS) ... ADONIS
Automatic Digital Online Instrumentation (or Instruments) System (SAUS) ... ADONIS
Automatic Digital Optical Tracker [*Army*] (AABC) ... ADOT
Automatic Digital Processor (MCD) ... ADP
Automatic Digital Recording and Control ... ADRAC
Automatic Digital Switch ... ADS
Automatic Digital Switching Center (IEEE) ... ADSC
Automatic Digital Test (ACAE) ... ADIT
Automatic Digital Test Unit ... ADTU
Automatic Digital Tracking Analyzer Computer (SAUS) ... ADTAC
Automatic Digital Weather Switch [*Air Force*] (AFM) ... ADWS
Automatic Digital-Data-Error Recorder [*Computer science*] ... ADDER
Automatic Digitizing of Interpretation Overlay System (SAUS) ... ADIOS
Automatic Diode Function Generator (ACAE) ... ADFG
Automatic Direct Access Management (SAUS) ... ADAM
Automatic Direct Access to Information with the On-Line UDC [*Universal Decimal Classification*] **System** [*American Institute of Physics*] [*Information retrieval*] ... AUDACIOUS
Automatic Direct Analog Computer (BUR) ... ADAC
Automatic Direct Current Level Amplifier (SAUS) ... ADCLAMPLIFIER
Automatic Direct Distance Dialing System (SAUS) ... ADDDC
Automatic Direct Reader (or Reading) (SAUS) ... ADR
Automatic Direct-Distance Dialing System [*Telecommunications*] (IEEE) ... ADDDS
Automatic Direction Finder [*Military*] ... ADF
Automatic Direction Finder, Remote Control (AAG) ... ADFR
Automatic Direction Finding Approach (SAA) ... ADFA
Automatic Direction Finding Approach ... ADFAP
Automatic Direction Finding equipment (SAUS) ... ADF
Automatic Direction Finding System ... ADFS
Automatic Direction Indication (SAUS) ... ADI
Automatic Direction Indicator (SAUS) ... adi
Automatic Direction Indicator (AFM) ... ADI
Automatic Dish Detergent ... ADD
Automatic Dishwasher Compound (EDCT) ... ADWC
Automatic Disk Allocation System [*Computer science*] (CIST) ... ADAS
Automatic Dispatch System [*Nuclear energy*] (NRCH) ... ADS
Automatic Dispatching Stick Repeater ... ADSP
Automatic Display [*Computer science*] ... AD
Automatic Display and Plotting System (BUR) ... ADAPS
Automatic Display Call Indicator (SAUS) ... ADCI
Automatic Display Finder [*Computer science*] (NASA) ... ADF
Automatic Display Mode [*Computer science*] (BUR) ... ADM
Automatic Display Plotting System (MCD) ... ADPS
Automatic Display Switching Oscilloscope ... ADSO
Automatic Distance and Angle Measurement ... ADAM
Automatic Distortion Reduction (IAA) ... ADR
Automatic Distribution of Documents [*DoD*] ... ADD
Automatic Distribution of Microfiche ... ADM
Automatic Distribution System (SAUS) ... ADS
Automatic Divide (SAUS) ... AD
Automatic Dividend Reinvestment [*Investment term*] ... ADR
Automatic Document Abstracting Method (NITA) ... ADAM
Automatic Document Analysis (DIT) ... ADA
Automatic Document Detection (SAUS) ... ADD
Automatic Document Distribution (MCD) ... ADD
Automatic Document Feeder [*For copying machines*] ... ADF
Automatic Document Online Information System [*Document delivery system*] [*Association of European Publishers*] (NITA) ... ADONIS
Automatic Document Request (AIE) ... ADRS
Automatic Document Request Service [*or System*] ... ADRS
Automatic Document Request System (SAUS) ... ADRS
Automatic Document Storage and Retrieval [*Computer science*] ... ADSTAR
Automatic Document Storage and Retrieval System [*Computer science*] ... ADSTARS
Automatic Document Version Improving System for Easy Revising (SAUS) ... ADVISER
Automatic Documentation (SAUS) ... AUTODOC
Automatic Documentation and Mathematical Linguistics (journ.) (SAUS) ... Autom Doc Math Linguist
Automatic Documentation in Action (SAUO) ... ADIA
Automatic Documentation Section (SAUS) ... DOCA
Automatic Documenting System (SAUS) ... ADS
Automatic Dog Feeder (SAUS) ... AUTODOG
Automatic Door Isolating Cock [*British railroad term*] ... DIC
Automatic Door Seal [*Technical drawings*] ... ADS
Automatic Door Seal (SAUS) ... ADS
Automatic Drafting Equipment (IEEE) ... ADE
Automatic Drafting Language (SAUS) ... ADL
Automatic Drafting Machine (DIT) ... ADMA
Automatic Drag-Limiting System (SAUS) ... ADLS
Automatic Drawing Device (DIT) ... ADD
Automatic Drawing Equipment (SAUS) ... ADE
Automatic Drift Control (AFM) ... ADC
Automatic Drip Coffee [*Brand name*] ... ADC
Automatic Drive Control (IAA) ... ADC
Automatic Drive Maintenance (SAUS) ... ADM
Automatic Drivetrain Management [*Automotive engineering*] ... ADM
Automatic Drought Monitoring Integrative Technique (SAUS) ... ADMIT
Automatic Duplicator Printer (SAUS) ... ADP
Automatic Dynamic Analysis Measurement (SAUS) ... ADAM
Automatic Dynamic Analyzer (SAUS) ... ADA
Automatic Dynamic Digital Test System (MHDB) ... AUDDIT
Automatic Dynamic Digital Test System (SAUS) ... AUDDIT System
Automatic Dynamic Evaluation by Programmed (or Programming) Testing (SAUS) ... ADEPT
Automatic Dynamic Evaluation by Programmed Organizations ... ADEPO
Automatic Dynamic Evaluation by Programmed Test ... ADEPT
Automatic Dynamic Incremental Nonlinear Analysis (MCD) ... ADINA
Automatic Dynamic Response Analyzer (PDAA) ... ADRA
Automatic Earnings Recomputation Operation [*Social Security*] ... AERO
Automatic Editing Control (SAUS) ... AEC
Automatic Electric (MCD) ... AE
Automatic Electric Energy Management System [*Aviation*] (OA) ... AEEMS
Automatic Electrical Inspection (SAUS) ... AEI
Automatic Electrical Instruction (SAUS) ... AEI
Automatic Electrode Changer (or Changing) (SAUS) ... AEC
Automatic Electronic Exchange (SAUS) ... AEX
Automatic Electronic Intelligence Emitter Location System (IUSS) ... AEELS
Automatic Electronic Production (IAA) ... AEP
Automatic Electronic Range Instrumentation System (MCD) ... AERIS
Automatic Electronic Ranging Information System (SAUS) ... AERIS
Automatic Electronic Switching Center ... AESC
Automatic Electronic Switching System ... AESRS
Automatic Electronic Switching System (MCD) ... AESS
Automatic Electronic Voice Switch (RDA) ... AEVS
Automatic Emergency Broadcast Alert [*Telecommunications*] (IAA) ... AEBA
Automatic Emergency Broadcast Alerting (SAUS) ... AEBA
Automatic Emission Spectroscopy (MCD) ... AES
Automatic Emulation Management [*Brother*] (VERA) ... AEM
Automatic Emulation Switching [*Lexmark*] (VERA) ... AES
Automatic End of Block (SAUS) ... AEB
Automatic End Point ... AEP
Automatic Energy Control (SAUS) ... AEC
Automatic Engine Control [*Heavy-duty diesel engines*] ... AEC
Automatic Engine Data Acquisition Test System (SAUS) ... AEDATS
Automatic Envelope Compression (SAUS) ... AEC
Automatic Environment Monitoring (BUR) ... AEM
Automatic Equalization/Analyzation System ... AEAS

Automatic Equipment Corp. (EFIS)	AEC
Automatic Equipment Identification (SAUS)	AEI
Automatic Error Analysis	AEA
Automatic Error Correction (SAUS)	AEC
Automatic Error Interrogation [*Telecommunications*] (OA)	AEI
Automatic Error Request Equipment [*Aviation*]	ARQ
Automatic Evaporation Control System (SAUS)	AECS
Automatic Exchange Equipment (SAUS)	AXE
Automatic Exchange Tester (CIST)	AET
Automatic Exciter Control	AEC
Automatic Execute Batch (CDE)	AUTOEXEC BAT
Automatic Execution (SAUS)	AUTOEXEC
Automatic Experimental Monitoring (IUSS)	AEM
Automatic Explosion/Fire Sensing & Suppression system (SAUS)	AEFSS
Automatic Exposure Camera	AE
Automatic Exposure Control [*In reprographic systems*]	AEC
Automatic Exposure Control Technique	AECT
Automatic External Defibrillator (PDAA)	AED
Automatic External Standard [*or Standardization*] [*Radioactivity measurement*]	AES
Automatic Extracting Program	AEP
Automatic Extraction System [*Computer science*] (MHDI)	AES
Automatic Facilities Control Subsystem (IUSS)	AFCS
Automatic Facilities Test System (SAUS)	AFACTS
Automatic Fall-Back (SAUS)	AFB
Automatic False Alarm (SAUS)	AFA
Automatic False Alarm Rate	AFAR
Automatic Fare Collection [*TRB*] (TAG)	AFC
Automatic Fare Collection System	AFCS
Automatic Fast Demagnetization	AFD
Automatic Fast Feed (NITA)	AFF
Automatic Fault Detection (or Detector) (SAUS)	AFDET
Automatic Fault Isolation	AFI
Automatic Fault Isolation Test	AFIT
Automatic Fault Location	AFL
Automatic Fault Simulator	AFS
Automatic Fault-Finding and Maintenance (SAA)	AFM
Automatic Feature Extraction System (MCD)	AFES
Automatic Feature Negotiation [*Computer science*]	AFN
Automatic Feed Hopper (SAUS)	AFH
Automatic Feed Punch (SAUS)	AFP
Automatic Feedback Control (SAUS)	AFC
Automatic Feeding Device (SAUS)	AFD
Automatic Feeding Form (SAUS)	AFF
Automatic Fidelity Control	AFC
Automatic Field Analog Computer	AFAC
Automatic Field Assistant (MCD)	AFA
Automatic Field Control (MHDB)	AFC
Automatic Field Recognition	AFR
Automatic Field/Format Recognition [*Computer science*] (NITA)	AFR
Automatic File Control and Documentation (SAUS)	AFCAD
Automatic File Distribution [*Computer science*] [*Telecommunications*]	AFD
Automatic Film Data Collection System (MCD)	AFDCS
Automatic Filter (ADA)	AF
Automatic Fine Cull Machine (MHDB)	AFCM
Automatic Fine Tuning	AFT
Automatic Fingerprint Verification Computer System	AFVCS
Automatic Fire Alarm (WDAA)	AFA
Automatic Fire Alarm Association (EA)	AFAA
Automatic Fire & Explosion Detection & Suppression System (SAUS)	AFEDDS
Automatic Fire Control	AFC
Automatic Fire Control System (AAG)	AFCS
Automatic Fire Detection (or Detector) (SAUS)	AFD
Automatic Fire Extinguisher (MCD)	AFE
Automatic Fire Extinguishing System (ACAE)	AFES
Automatic Fire Overheat Logic Test System (SAUS)	AFOLTS
Automatic Firearms Identification System [*Jet Propulsion Laboratory, NASA*]	AFIDS
Automatic Firing Sequencer	AFS
Automatic Five Speed [*DOE*] (TAG)	A5
Automatic Flatness Control (SAUS)	AFC
Automatic Flexible Test Station	AFTS
Automatic Flight Control	AFC
Automatic Flight Control and Augmentation System (DA)	AFCAS
Automatic Flight Control Augmentation System (SAUS)	AFCAS
Automatic Flight Control Equipment	AFCE
Automatic Flight Control Panel (MCD)	AFCP
Automatic Flight Control System [*Aerospace*]	AFCS
Automatic Flight Control System Control Panel (MCD)	AFCSCP
Automatic Flight Director System (MCD)	AFDS
Automatic Flight Guidance System (SAUS)	AFGS
Automatic Flight Inspection (DA)	AFIS
Automatic Flight Management	AFM
Automatic Flight Management System (SAUS)	AFMS
Automatic Flight Operation Center [*Army*] (RDA)	AFOC
Automatic Flight Path Control System [*Aviation*] (PDAA)	AFPCS
Automatic Flight Planning and Monitoring	AFPAM
Automatic Flight Stabilization and Control System (SAA)	AFSC
Automatic Flight System [*Aviation*] (AIA)	AFS
Automatic Flight Termination	AFT
Automatic Flight Weather Advisory (SAUS)	AFWA
Automatic Floating Point (SAUS)	AFP
Automatic Flow Control	AFC
Automatic Flow Controller	AFC
Automatic Flow Process Analysis (IEEE)	AFPA
Automatic Flowcharting	AUTOFLOW
Automatic Flue Closing Device (HEAS)	AFCD
Automatic Fluorescent Penetrant Processing Facility (MCD)	AFPPF
Automatic Flushing Cistern (SAUS)	AFC
Automatic Focusing [*Photography*]	AF
Automatic Focusing Random Scene Tracker (MCD)	AFRST
Automatic Follower (or Following) (SAUS)	AF
Automatic Following [*RADAR*]	AF
Automatic Following Control	AFC
Automatic Font Change [*Computer science*] (VERA)	AFC
Automatic Force Adjustment Data System (SAUS)	AFADS
Automatic Format Recognition [*Computer science*] (ADA)	AFR
Automatic Formation Drone Control (MCD)	AFDC
Automatic Four Speed [*DOE*] (TAG)	A4
Automatic Frame Scan Control (PDAA)	AFSC
Automatic Frequency Assignment Model [*Telecommunications*]	AFAM
Automatic Frequency Control [*Electronics*]	AFC
Automatic Frequency Control Intermediate Frequency (SAUS)	AFCIF
Automatic Frequency Follower	AFF
Automatic Frequency Follower (or Following) (SAUS)	AFF
Automatic Frequency Ratio Control (SAUS)	AFRC
Automatic Frequency Ratio Controller (MHDB)	AFRC
Automatic Frequency Scanning/Channel Selecting (SAUS)	SELSCAN
Automatic Frequency Selection (SAUS)	AFS
Automatic Frequency Shift Keying (SAUS)	AFSK
Automatic Frequency Stabilization	AFS
Automatic Frequency Tone Shift (NVT)	AFTS
Automatic Frequency Tuner	AFT
Automatic Frequency-Assignment Model (SAUS)	AFAM
Automatic Frequency/Phase-Controlled [*Loop*] (IEEE)	AF/PC
Automatic Front Feed (ECII)	AFF
Automatic Fuel Cutoff [*NASA*] (KSC)	AFCO
Automatic Function Generator (HGAA)	AFG
Automatic Functional Test and Evaluation Routine [*Raytheon Co.*]	AFTER
Automatic Fund Allocation (SAUS)	AFA
Automatic Funds Transfer	AFT
Automatic Fuze Radiograph Inspection Device (PDAA)	AFRID
Automatic Gain Adjusting Amplifier [*Telecommunications*]	AGAA
Automatic Gain Adjusting Amplifier [*Telecommunications*] (TEL)	AGAMP
Automatic Gain and Frequency Control (SAUS)	AGFC
Automatic Gain and Frequency Response (SAUS)	AGFR
Automatic Gain Calibration Program	AGCP
Automatic Gain Control [*Electronics*]	AGC
Automatic Gain Control Effects (SAUS)	AGC Effects
Automatic Gain Control/Constant False Alarm Rate	AGC/CFAR
Automatic Gain Controlling (SAUS)	AGC-ING
Automatic Gain Correction (SAUS)	AGC
Automatic Gain Ranging Amplifier (MCD)	AGRA
Automatic Gain Stabilization (or Stabilizer) (SAUS)	AGS
Automatic Gang Punch (SAUS)	AGP
Automatic Gas Analyzer [*Nuclear energy*] (NRCH)	AGA
Automatic Gauge	AG
Automatic Gauge Control [*or Controller*]	AGC
Automatic Generation (ACAE)	ACTGEN
Automatic Generation and Retrieval of Information on Chemical Components (SAUS)	AGRICC
Automatic Generation Control (ACII)	AGC
Automatic Generation of Requests [*Computer science*] (DIT)	AUTOQEST
Automatic Gimbaled-Antenna Vectoring Equipment [*Air Force*]	AGAVE
Automatic Government Source Inspection (EDDS)	AGSI
Automatic Governing Valve Control [*Nuclear energy*] (NRCH)	AGVC
Automatic Graphic Digitizing System (SAUS)	AGDS
Automatic Gravity Gradient	AGGD
Automatic Grenade Launcher (SAUS)	AGL
Automatic Grenade Launcher (SAUS)	AGS
Automatic Ground Checkout System (KSC)	AGCS
Automatic Ground Computer System (KSC)	AGCS
Automatic Ground Control Station (KSC)	AGCS
Automatic Ground Control System Computer (KSC)	AGCSC
Automatic Ground Effect Augmentation System (MCD)	AGEAS
Automatic Ground Environment Computer (SAUS)	AGEC
Automatic Ground Equipment	AGE
Automatic Ground Position Indicator [*Military*]	AGPI
Automatic Ground Spoiler - Rejected Takeoff (MCD)	AGS-RTO
Automatic Ground Transportable Emitter Location and Identification System [*Army*]	AGTELIS
Automatic Ground Unit	AGU
Automatic Ground-Controlled Approach [*RADAR*]	AGCA
Automatic Ground-Controlled Intercept (MCD)	AGCI
Automatic Ground-Controlled Landing	AGCL
Automatic Ground-to-Air Communications System	AGACS
Automatic Grouping System [*Hospital records*] (DHSM)	AUTOGRP
Automatic Guard Receiver Terminals [*Navy*] (MCD)	AGRT
Automatic Guidance and Control System	AGCS
Automatic Guidance Electronics	AGE
Automatic Guidance Programming (NATG)	AGP
Automatic Guided Flight (MUGU)	AGF
Automatic Guided Vehicle [*Robotic manufacturing equipment*]	AGV
Automatic Guided Vehicle System [*Robotics*]	AGVS
Automatic Guided Vehicle Systems (EA)	AGVS
Automatic Guideway Transit (SAUS)	AGT
Automatic Gun Layer (SAUS)	AGL
Automatic Gun Laying System (SEAS)	AGLS
Automatic Gun Positioning System	AGPS
Automatic Gunfire Control System (DNAB)	AGFCS

Automatic Gun-Laying (DEN) ... AGL
Automatic Gun-Laying Turrets [World War II] [British] ... AGLT
Automatic Half Barrier ... AHB
Automatic Hand (SAUS) ... AUTOHAND
Automatic Handwriting Reader (SAUS) ... AHR
Automatic Heading Reference System ... AHRS
Automatic Headway Control ... AHC
Automatic Helicopter Approach System [Army] ... AHAS
Automatic High Accuracy Comparator (SAUS) ... AHAC
Automatic High Speed Plot (SAUS) ... AHSP
Automatic High-Voltage Regulator (SAUS) ... AHVR
Automatic Highway System (SAUS) ... AHS
Automatic Hold Fire (SAUS) ... AHF
Automatic Hydrologic Observing System [National Weather Service] ... AHOS
Automatic Hydrologic Radio Reporting Network (DNAB) ... AHRRN
Automatic Identification (SAUS) ... AI
Automatic Identification [Computer science] ... Auto ID
Automatic Identification Manufacturers (EA) ... AIM
Automatic Identification Outward Dialing (SAUS) ... AIOD
Automatic Identification System (SAUO) ... AIS
Automatic Identification Technology [Army] (RDA) ... AIT
Automatic Identified Outward Dialing [Telecommunications] ... AIOD
Automatic Idle Speed [Automotive engineering] ... AIS
Automatic Illustrated Documentation System [Information International, Inc.] ... AIDS
Automatic Image Density Control [Photocopying toning technique] (NITA) ... AIDC
Automatic Image Matching System (SAUS) ... AIMS
Automatic Image Refinement [Computer science] (VERA) ... AIR
Automatic Image Retrieval System (MCD) ... AIRS
Automatic Image Screening ... AIS
Automatic Imagery Interpretation ... AII
Automatic Implantable Cardiovascular Defibrillator [Unit] [Cardiology] (DAVI) ... AICD
Automatic Implantable Cardioverter-Defibrillator [Cardiology] ... AICD
Automatic Implantable Defibrillator [Cardiology] ... AID
Automatic Inboard Vent-tank (SAUS) ... AIV
Automatic Incident Action [Environmental science] (COE) ... AIA
Automatic Incident Actuation System (SAUS) ... AIAS
Automatic Incident Detector (DI) ... AID
Automatic Indexing and Proofreading System ... AIPS
Automatic Indexing and Retrieval (SAUS) ... AIR
Automatic Indexing of Documents (SAUS) ... AID
Automatic Indication of Range (SAUS) ... AIR
Automatic Industrial Drilling (SAUS) ... AID
Automatic Industrial Management System (SAUS) ... AIMS
Automatic Industries Holdings [Associated Press] (SAG) ... AutoInd
Automatic Inercept System (SAUS) ... AIS
Automatic Inflation Module ... AIM
Automatic In-Flight Data System (SAUS) ... AIDS
Automatic In-Flight Insertion (NG) ... AIFI
Automatic Information Acquisition (SAUS) ... AIA
Automatic Information Center (SAUS) ... AIC
Automatic Information Display System (SAUS) ... AIDS
Automatic Information Distribution [Computer science] (MHDI) ... AID
Automatic Information Processing (SAUS) ... AIP
Automatic Information Reduction (SAUS) ... AIR
Automatic Information Retrieval System [Information service or system] (BUR) ... AIRS
Automatic Information Station [or System] (BUR) ... AIST
Automatic Information Test [Military] ... AIT
Automatic Informational Station (SAUS) ... AIST
Automatic Infrared Diagnostic System (ACAE) ... AIDS
Automatic Infra-red Test & Inspection System (SAUS) ... AITIS
Automatic Initial Distribution (DNAB) ... AID
Automatic Initiation Circuit (IEEE) ... AIC
Automatic Inlet Control System (NG) ... AICS
Automatic Inline Device Evaluator ... AIDE
Automatic In-process Microcircuit Evaluation (SAUS) ... AIME
Automatic In-Process Microcircuit Evaluation (MCD) ... AIME
Automatic Input [Computer science] (BUR) ... AI
Automatic Input Processing [Computer science] (MCD) ... AIP
Automatic Inspection and Diagnostic Equipment (ACAE) ... AIDE
Automatic Inspection Data Accumulator (SAUS) ... AIDA
Automatic Inspection Device for Explosive Charge Shell (AABC) ... AIDECS
Automatic Inspection, Diagnostic, and Prognosis System (ACAE) ... AIMDAPS
Automatic Inspection, Diagnostic, and Prognostic [System] [Army] ... AIDAP
Automatic Inspection, Diagnostic, and Prognostic System [Army] ... AIDAPS
Automatic Inspection of Data (SAUS) ... AIDA
Automatic Installation and Diagnostic Service (VERA) ... AIDS
Automatic Instrument Landing Approach System [Aviation] ... AILAS
Automatic Instrument Landing System (FAAC) ... AILS
Automatic Instrument Low Approach System (ACAE) ... AILAS
Automatic Instrument Low-Approach (SAUS) ... AILAS
Automatic Instrumented Decision Equipment (SAUS) ... AIDE
Automatic Instrumented Diving Assembly ... AIDA
Automatic Integrated Circuit Tester ... AICT
Automatic Integrated Container Handling (PDAA) ... AICH
Automatic Integrated Debugging System [Computer science] (BUR) ... AIDS
Automatic Integrated Diagnostic and Prognostic Subsystem (ACAE) ... AIDAPS
Automatic Integrated Dynamic Avionics Tester ... AIDAT
Automatic Integrated Telephone System [Telecommunications] (OA) ... AITS
Automatic Integrating Fluctation Meter ... AIFM
Automatic Intelligent Material Location and Identification System (SAUS) ... AIMLIS
Automatic Interaction Detection [or Detector] [Computer science] ... AID

Automatic Interactive Computer Control (MCD) ... AICC
Automatic Interactive Debug System (ACAE) ... AIDS
Automatic Interactive Debugging System (SAUS) ... AIDS
Automatic Intercept Bureau [Telecommunications] (TEL) ... AIB
Automatic Intercept Center [Bell System] ... AIC
Automatic Intercept Center (or Centre) (SAUS) ... AIC
Automatic Intercept Communications Controller (ROAS) ... AICC
Automatic Intercept Switch (SAUS) ... AIS
Automatic Intercept System [Bell System] ... AIS
Automatic Intercity Station [Telecommunications] (OA) ... AIS
Automatic Intercity Telephone Exchange [Telecommunications] (OA) ... AITE
Automatic Intercom Switching System ... AISS
Automatic Interface Management [Brother] (VERA) ... AIM
Automatic Interference Limiter [Automotive sound systems] ... AIL
Automatic Interference Measurement System (MCD) ... AIMS
Automatic Intermediate Station (MCD) ... AIS
Automatic Internal Diagnosis (SAUS) ... AID
Automatic Interrogation Distortion [Telecommunications] (OA) ... AID
Automatic Interrogation Routine (SAUS) ... AIR
Automatic Interrupter (or Interruption) (SAUS) ... AI
Automatic Intersection Control System ... AICS
Automatic Intruder Detector Alarm [Military] [British] ... AIDA
Automatic Inventory Dispatching System (SAUS) ... AIDS
Automatic Invoicing Machine (SAUS) ... AIM
Automatic Iris Control (PDAA) ... AIC
Automatic Item Correction (SAUS) ... AIC
Automatic "J" Relay (MCD) ... AJR
Automatic Jamming Avoidance Circuitry (AABC) ... AJAC
Automatic Job Recovery (SAUS) ... AJR
Automatic Job-stream Generator (SAUS) ... AJG
Automatic Junction Analyzer and Recorder (SAUS) ... AJAR
Automatic Key Distribution ... AKD
Automatic Key Distribution Center (IUSS) ... AKDC
Automatic Key Management (CIST) ... AKM
Automatic Keying Unit (SAUS) ... AKU
Automatic Kinetic Enzyme System (PDAA) ... AKES
Automatic Label Exchange ... ALEX
Automatic Labor Exchange (SAUS) ... ALEX
Automatic Laboratory Techniques Exhibition (SAUO) ... ALTEX
Automatic Landing [NASA] (NASA) ... AUTOLAND
Automatic Landing Autopilot Subsystem (NASA) ... ALAS
Automatic Landing Control (SAA) ... ALC
Automatic Landing Instrument Control Equipment (SAUS) ... ALICE
Automatic Landing Mode (ACAE) ... ALM
Automatic Landing Positioning System ... ALPS
Automatic Landing System ... ALS
Automatic Language Data Processing ... ALDP
Automatic Language Identification (MCD) ... ALI
Automatic Language Processing Advisory Committee [National Research Council] ... ALPAC
Automatic Language Translation (SAUS) ... ALT
Automatic LASER Encoder ... ALE
Automatic Laser Inspection Measurement System (SAUS) ... ALIMS
Automatic LASER Instrumentation Measuring System (MCD) ... ALIMS
Automatic Laser Target Classification (ACAE) ... ALTC
Automatic LASER Test Set [Hughes Aircraft Co.] ... ALTS
Automatic Launch Control (ACAE) ... ALC
Automatic Launch Control System (DNAB) ... ALCS
Automatic Launching of Expendables (SAUS) ... ALEX
Automatic Laundering Instrument Control Equipment (SAUS) ... ALICE
Automatic Law Enforcement Response Time (SAUS) ... ALERT II
Automatic Layshaft Transmission [Automotive engineering] ... ALT
Automatic Lead Former ... ALF
Automatic Lean (SAUS) ... AUTO LEAN
Automatic Lector Position Handwriting Machine (SAUS) ... ALPHA Machine
Automatic Ledger Feet Attachment (SAUS) ... ALFA
Automatic Letter Facer ... ALF
Automatic Letter Facer (or Facing) (SAUS) ... ALF
Automatic Level and Slope Control (CIST) ... ALSC
Automatic Level Camera (SAUS) ... ALC
Automatic Level Control (IDOE) ... alc
Automatic Level Control [Camera] [Aviation] ... ALC
Automatic Level Control Assembly (MCD) ... ALCA
Automatic Level Controller (SAUS) ... ALC
Automatic Level Recorder ... ALR
Automatic Level Setting ... ALS
Automatic Leveling Seat [Automotive engineering] ... ALS
Automatic License Plate (ACAE) ... ALP
Automatic License Plate Scanning ... ALPS
Automatic License Revocation ... ALR
Automatic Life Testing and Recording of Electronic Components [Canada] ... ALTREC
Automatic Light Aircraft Readiness Monitor ... ALARM
Automatic Light Block (SAUS) ... ALB
Automatic Light Control (KSC) ... ALC
Automatic Lightning Detection System [To aid in the prevention of forest fires] ... ALDS
Automatic Line Buildout [Bell Laboratories] ... ALBO
Automatic Line Build-Out ... ALBO
Automatic Line Device Store (SAUS) ... ALDS
Automatic Line Equalization (CIST) ... ALE
Automatic Line Fault Analysis (MHDB) ... ALFA
Automatic Line Feed [Telecommunications] ... ALF
Automatic Line Insulation Test [or Tester] [Bell System] ... ALIT
Automatic Line Integration (NVT) ... ALI

Automatic Line Record Update (SAUS) .... ALRU
Automatic Line Selection (SAUS) .... ALS
Automatic Line Supervision (SAUS) .... ALS
Automatic Line Test and Administrative System [*Taiwan International Standard Electronics Ltd., a subsidiary of ITT*] (NITA) .... ALTA
Automatic Line Test and Administrative System (SAUS) .... ALTA System
Automatic Line Test Set [*Telecommunications*] (TEL) .... ALTS
Automatic Line Testing [*Telecommunications*] (TEL) .... ALT
Automatic Line Tracing and Programming Equipment (SAUS) .... ALTAPE
Automatic Line Tracking (SAUS) .... ALT
Automatic Linear Positioning System .... ALPS
Automatic Linear Temperature Programmer .... ALTP
Automatic Linguistic Extraction and Retrieval Technique (SAUS) .... ALERT
Automatic Link Establishment (DOMA) .... ALE
Automatic Link Intelligence (SAUS) .... ALI
Automatic Link Quality Analysis (SAUS) .... ALQA
Automatic Link Setup (SAUS) .... ALIS
Automatic Liquid Agent Detector (AABC) .... ALAD
Automatic Liquid Nitrogen Transfer System .... ALNTS
Automatic List Classification and Profile Production .... ALCAPP
Automatic Listing and Flowcharting Reorganized into an Elementary Dictionary (SAUS) .... ALFRED
Automatic Literature Distribution System (SAUS) .... ALDS
Automatic Load Alleviation System (MCD) .... ALAS
Automatic Load and Drive Control (SAUS) .... ALDC
Automatic Load Control .... ALC
Automatic Load Regulator .... ALR
Automatic Load-dependent Brake (SAUS) .... ALB
Automatic Loading (SAUS) .... AUTOLOAD
Automatic Local Frequency Control .... ALFC
Automatic Location Identification [*Street crime locator*] .... ALI
Automatic Loc-Bottom [*Packaging*] .... ALB
Automatic Locking Circuit (SAUS) .... ALC
Automatic Locking Differential .... ALD
Automatic Lock-On (MCD) .... ALO
Automatic Lockup Four Speed [*DOE*] (TAG) L4
Automatic Log and Restart Mechanism (SAUS) .... ALARM
Automatic Logging Electronic Reporting and Telemetering System [*Maintains surveillance over petroleum wells and pipelines*] .... ALERT
Automatic Logic Design Generator (SAUS) .... ALDG
Automatic Logic Diagram (SAUS) .... ALD
Automatic Logic Implementation (SAUS) .... ALI
Automatic Logic Network Analyzer (SAUS) .... ALNA
Automatic Logic Tester (SAUS) .... ALT
Automatic Logic Testing and Recording Equipment .... ALTARE
Automatic Logical Equipment Readiness Tester .... ALERT
Automatic Logical Translation and Information Retrieval [*Computer science*] (DIT) .... ALTAIR
Automatic Logician Evaluation Readiness Tester (SAUS) .... ALERT
Automatic Login Executor (SAUS) .... ALEX
Automatic Louver Damper (OA) .... ALD
Automatic Low Altitude Bombing System (SAUS) .... AUTOLABS
Automatic Low Data Processing System (SAUS) .... ALDPS
Automatic Low Data Rate Input (SAUS) .... ALDRI
Automatic Low-Altitude Bombing System (MCD) .... AUTOLABS
Automatic Low-Frequency Gain-Limiting Circuit (RDA) .... ALFGL
Automatic Low-Frequency Gain-Limiting Circuit (SAUS) .... ALFGL Circuit
Automatic Lubrication System .... ALS
Automatic Machine Loading .... AML
Automatic Machining Program .... AUTOMAP
Automatic Magazine Loader (or Loading) (SAUS) .... AML
Automatic Magazine Loading .... AML
Automatic Magnetic Data Acquisition System (MCD) .... AMDAS
Automatic Magnetic Guidance .... AMG
Automatic Magnetic Tape Dissemination [*Defense Documentation Center*] .... AMTD
Automatic Magnetic Tape Distribution [*Program*] .... AMTD
Automatic Maintenance Management System (SAUS) .... AMMS
Automatic Maintenance Monitor (SAUS) .... AM&M
Automatic Maintenance Monitor .... AMM
Automatic Make Ready .... AMR
Automatic Malfunction Analysis (KSC) .... AMA
Automatic Management Switch [*Communication Devices, Inc.*] .... AMS
Automatic Maneuvering Attack System [*Air Force*] .... AMAS
Automatic Maneuvering Control (DNAB) .... AMC
Automatic Manifold Pressure Regulator [*Aviation*] .... AMPR
Automatic Manoeuvring Device System (SAUS) .... AMDS
Automatic Manual Switch (SAUS) .... AM Switch
Automatic Manufacturing Test Equipment (ACAE) .... AUTOMATE
Automatic Map Display (MCD) .... AMD
Automatic Map Reader (or Reading) (SAUS) .... AMR
Automatic Mapping and Planning System [*Environmental Protection Agency*] (ERG) .... AMPS
Automatic Margin Test Unit (SAUS) .... AMTU
Automatic Marking System (SAUS) .... AMS
Automatic Masking Data-generation for Electron-beam-exposure System (SAUS) .... AMDES
Automatic Master Sequence Selector .... AMSS
Automatic Mathematical Analysis and Symbolic Translation [*Computer science*] .... AUTOMAST
Automatic Mathematical Analysis and Symbolic Translation (or Translator) (SAUS) .... AUTOMAST
Automatic Mathematical Translation (or Translator) (SAUS) .... AMTRAN
Automatic Mathematical Translator [*Programming language*] [*1970*] .... AMTRAN
Automatic Measurement (SAUS) .... AUT MEAS

Automatic Measurement and Analysis (SAUS) .... AMANDA
Automatic Measurement and Compensation System (SAUS) .... AMCS
Automatic Measuring, Computing, and Sorting .... AMECOS
Automatic Memory Allocation [*Computer science*] (BUR) .... AMA
Automatic Merchandising Association of Florida (SRA) .... AMAF
Automatic Message Accounting [*Bell Laboratories*] [*Telecommunications*] .... AMA
Automatic Message Accounting / Magnetic Tape Recording [*Computer science*] (MHDB) .... AMA/MTR
Automatic Message Accounting Collecting System [*Telecommunications*] (TEL) .... AMACS
Automatic Message Accounting Recording Center [*Telecommunications*] (TEL) .... AMARC
Automatic Message Accounting Recording System [*Bell System*] .... AMARS
Automatic Message Accounting Standard Entry (SAUS) .... AMASE
Automatic Message Accounting System (MCD) .... AMAS
Automatic Message Accounting Tele-Processing System (SAUS) .... AMATPS
Automatic Message Accounting Transmitter (SAUS) .... AMAT
Automatic Message Accounting-Magnetic Tape Recording (SAUS) .... AMA-MTR
Automatic Message Address Routing System (AABC) .... AMARS
Automatic Message and Mail Sorting System (SAUS) .... AMMSS
Automatic Message Counting .... AMC
Automatic Message Display (SAUS) .... AMD
Automatic Message Distribution System (CET) .... AMDS
Automatic Message Entry System [*Computer science*] (MCD) .... AMES
Automatic Message Exchange (SAUS) .... AME
Automatic Message Exchange .... AMX
Automatic Message Exchange (SAUS) .... AUTOMEX
Automatic Message Exchange Service .... AUTOMEX
Automatic Message Exchange Service (SAUS) .... AUTOMEX Service
Automatic Message Handler (SAUS) .... AMH
Automatic Message Processing Center .... AMPC
Automatic Message Processing Equipment (CCCA) .... AMPE
Automatic Message Processing System [*USAERDL*] .... AMPS
Automatic Message Processor (MCD) .... AMP
Automatic Message Recording .... AMR
Automatic Message Registering .... AMR
Automatic Message Routeing and Distribution (SAUS) .... AMRAD
Automatic Message Routing (BUR) .... AMR
Automatic Message Routing Device .... AMRD
Automatic Message Switching (SAUS) .... AMS
Automatic Message Switching Center (NOAA) .... AMSC
Automatic Meteorological Correction [*A missile guidance technique*] .... AUTOMET
Automatic Meteorological Correction (SAUS) .... AUTOMET Correction
Automatic Meteorological Data Acquisition and Processing System (MCD) .... AMDAPS
Automatic Meteorological Data and Reporting (SAUS) .... AMDAR
Automatic Meteorological Observation [*or Observing*] Station [*or System*] .... AMOS
Automatic Meteorological Observation System (SAUS) .... AMOS
Automatic Meteorological, Oceanographic, (and Radiation) Station .... AMO(R)S
Automatic Meteorological Oceanographic Buoy [*Marine science*] (MSC) .... AMOB
Automatic Meteorological Sensors System (SAUS) .... AMSS
Automatic Meteorological System (RDA) .... AMS
Automatic Meteorological System - Artillery (MCD) .... AMS-A
Automatic Meter Reading .... AMR
Automatic Meter Reading Association (EA) .... AMRA
Automatic Meterological Observation Station (SAUO) .... AMOS
Automatic Methods and Times (CIST) .... AUTOMAT
Automatic Microfiche Editor .... AME
Automatic Microfilm Information System .... AMFIS
Automatic Microscope Electronic Data Accumulator (MHDB) .... AMEDA
Automatic Miss Distance Indicator .... AMDI
Automatic Missile Detection Radar (SAUS) .... AMDR
Automatic Mission Control .... AMC
Automatic Mixture Control .... AMC
Automatic Mobile Aerostation (SAUO) .... AMAS
Automatic Mobile Director and Reporting System (SAUS) .... AMDRS
Automatic Mobile Public Telephone System (SAUS) .... AMPTS
Automatic Modal Tuning and Analysis System (NASA) .... AMTAS
Automatic Mode Status (CAAL) .... AMS
Automatic Model Generator (SAUS) .... AMG
Automatic Model Linking (AAEL) .... AML
Automatic Modulation Control (DEN) .... AMC
Automatic Modulation Limiter (or Limiting) (SAUS) .... AML
Automatic Modulation Limiting [*Electronics*] (MED) .... AML
Automatic Module for Industrial Control Analysis .... AMICA
Automatic Module Production Tester (SAUS) .... AMPT
Automatic Monitor of Yarn (SAUS) .... AMY
Automatic Monitoring (CET) .... AM
Automatic Monitoring Circuit [*Telecommunications*] (OA) .... AMC
Automatic Monitoring Equipment .... AME
Automatic Monitoring System [*Aviation*] .... AMS
Automatic Moon Tracking .... AMT
Automatic Motion Control System (MCD) .... AMCS
Automatic Motion Inhibit [*Nuclear energy*] (NRCH) .... AMI
Automatic Motor Tester .... AMT
Automatic Moving Target Indicator (MSA) .... AMTI
Automatic Multiaddress Segregation System (MCD) .... AMASS
Automatic Multiaddress Segregation System (SAUS) .... AMSS
Automatic Multiloop Optimal Approach Controller [*Navy*] .... AMOAC
Automatic Multimode Mass Spectrometry .... AMMS
Automatic Multiparameter Semiconductor Test Set .... AMSTS
Automatic Multi-Pattern (SAUS) .... AMP
Automatic Multipattern Metering [*Photography*] .... AMP
Automatic Multiple Blade Damper (OA) .... AMBD

Automatic Multiple-Parameter Collection Processing System [*Air Force*] (MCD)	AMCAPS
Automatic Multiplying Punch (SAUS)	AMP
Automatic Multi-Program Selection [*Photography*] [*Minolta Corp.*]	AMPS
Automatic Multispectral Image Compaction Algorithm (SAUS)	AMICA
Automatic Music Scan (SAUS)	AMS
Automatic Music Sensor (SAUS)	AMS
Automatic Musical Instrument Collectors Association (EA)	AMICA
Automatic Musical Instrument Collectors Association International (EA)	AMICA
Automatic Nautical Charting (ACAE)	ANC
Automatic Navigation and Data Acquisition System	ANDAS
Automatic Navigation Computer for Land and Amphibious Vehicles	ANCLAV
Automatic Navigation Kit (MCD)	ANK
Automatic Navigation System	ANS
Automatic Nesting Program [*Kongsberg Vaapenfabrikk*] [*Software package*] (NCC)	AUTONEST
Automatic Nesting Program (SAUS)	AUTONEST Program
Automatic Net Radio Interfacing (SAUS)	ANRI
Automatic Network (SAUS)	AUTONET
Automatic Network Analyzer	ANA
Automatic Network Dialing [*Telecommunications*] (TEL)	AND
Automatic Network Display	AUTONET
Automatic Network Display (SAUS)	AUTONET Display
Automatic Network for Indirect Transmission (SAUS)	ANIT
Automatic Network Management System (SAUS)	ANMS
Automatic Network Routing [*Telecommunications*] (ACRL)	ANR
Automatic Neural Networks (SAUS)	ANN
Automatic New Line (SAUS)	ANL
Automatic Night Tracking (ACAE)	ANT
Automatic Nitrogen Transfer System	ANTS
Automatic Noise Figure Indicator (MCD)	ANFI
Automatic Noise Levelling (SAUS)	ANL
Automatic Noise Limited (or Limiter, or Limiting) (SAUS)	ANL
Automatic Noise Limiter [*Electronics*]	ANL
Automatic Noise Reduction Circuit [*Electronics*]	ANRC
Automatic Noise Reduction System (SAUS)	ANRS
Automatic Noise-Landing (DNAB)	ANL
Automatic Null Steering/Surveillance Array System (MCD)	ANSAS
Automatic Number Analysis (NITA)	ANA
Automatic Number Announcer [*Telecommunications*] (TEL)	ANA
Automatic Number Forwarding (SAUS)	ANF
Automatic Number Identification [*Telecommunications*]	ANI
Automatic Number Identification Failure [*Telecommunications*] (TEL)	ANF
Automatic Number Identifier (SAUS)	ANI
Automatic Observer	AO
Automatic Observing Station (PIPO)	AUTOB
Automatic Open Crossing Locally Monitored (HEAS)	AOCL
Automatic Open Crossing, Remotely Monitored (HEAS)	AOCR
Automatic Operating and Scheduling Program [*Computer science*]	AOSP
Automatic Operating System [*IBM Corp.*]	AUTOPSY
Automatic Operation Control	AOC
Automatic Operations Panel	AOP
Automatic Optical Bench [*Hughes Aircraft Co.*]	AOB
Automatic Optical Inspection (SAUS)	AOI
Automatic Orbiting Operations System (SAUS)	AOOSY
Automatic Outgoing Intertoll Trunk-test (SAUS)	AOIT
Automatic Outgoing Message Processor System (NVT)	AOMPS
Automatic Outgoing Trunk Test [*Bell System*]	AOTT
Automatic Output Control	AOC
Automatic Overdrive	AOD
Automatic Overdrive Transaxle [*Automotive engineering*]	AXOD
Automatic Overload (IAA)	AUTOOVLD
Automatic Overload (SAUS)	AUTO OVLD
Automatic Overload Circuit	AOC
Automatic Overload Circuit (MSA)	AOVC
Automatic Overload Control (IEEE)	AOC
Automatic Page Composition (DGA)	APC
Automatic Page Positioning (SAUS)	APP
Automatic Page Search [*Imtec Co.*] [*Information retrieval*] (NITA)	APS
Automatic Pagination (VERA)	AP
Automatic Paging Optimizer (SAUS)	APO
Automatic Paralleling Relay (MCD)	APR
Automatic Particle Size Analyzer (SAUS)	APS
Automatic Particle Size Analyzer (OA)	APSA
Automatic Parts Handler	APH
Automatic Parts Testing (IAA)	APT
Automatic Passbook Reader (BUR)	APR
Automatic Passbook Recording (SAUS)	APR
Automatic Passenger Counter [*FTA*] (TAG)	APC
Automatic Passenger Counting	APC
Automatic Patching System (IEEE)	APS
Automatic Patching Verification (SAUS)	APV
Automatic Pattern Recognition	APR
Automatic Payroll Deposit Plan (DNAB)	APDP
Automatic Performance Analysis (ACAE)	APAS
Automatic Performance Analysis System	APAS
Automatic Performance Control	APC
Automatic Performance Reserve	APR
Automatic Performance Review [*Aerospace*]	APR
Automatic Peripheral Control (SAUS)	APC
Automatic Permanent Magneticfield Compensator (SAUS)	APMC
Automatic Permanent Magnetic-Field Compensator (PDAA)	APMC
Automatic Personal Accident [*Insurance*] (AIA)	Auto PA
Automatic Personal Identification Code [*IBM Corp.*]	AUTOPIC
Automatic Personal (or Personnel) Identification Code (SAUS)	AUTOPIC
Automatic Personnel Locator	APL
Automatic Pet Feeder (SAUS)	AUTOPET
Automatic Phase and Amplitude Data System (MCD)	APADAS
Automatic Phase and Frequency Control (SAUS)	APFC
Automatic Phase Control [*Telecommunications*] (TEL)	APC
Automatic Phase Control	apc
Automatic Phase Lock	APL
Automatic Phase Shifter	APS
Automatic Phase Synchronization	APS
Automatic Phased-Locked Loop (PDAA)	APLL
Automatic Phase-Locked Loop [*Electronics*] (IAA)	APLL
Automatic Phono-Cardiac Analyzer (SAA)	APCA
Automatic Photoelectric Telescope (SAUS)	APT
Automatic Photographic Analysis	APA
Automatic Photomapping Equipment (SAUS)	APE
Automatic Photometric Telescope (SAUS)	APT
Automatic Picture Control (IDOE)	APC
Automatic Picture Replacement (SAUS)	APR
Automatic Picture Setting (SAUS)	APS
Automatic Picture Taking (IEEE)	APT
Automatic Picture Transmission [*NASA*]	APT
Automatic Picture Transmission Ground System (NOAA)	APTGS
Automatic Picture Transmission Receiver (SAUS)	APTR
Automatic Picture Transmission Subsystem (SAUS)	APTS
Automatic Picture Transmission System [*or Subsystem*] [*NASA*]	APTS
Automatic Pilot (MCD)	A/P
Automatic Pilot (SAUS)	Autopilot
Automatic Pilot System	APS
Automatic Pistol (SAUS)	AP
Automatic Pistol	AUTOP
Automatic Pitch Control	APC
Automatic Placement and Routing (SAUS)	APAR
Automatic Planetary Station [*Astronomy*]	APS
Automatic Planning and Technology (SAUS)	APT
Automatic Plate Loading (SAUS)	APL
Automatic Plate Modulation (SAUS)	APM
Automatic Plate Processor	APP
Automatic Plotter (SAUS)	AUTOPLOT
Automatic Plotting Routine (ADA)	AUTOPLOT
Automatic Plugging Meter (PDAA)	APM
Automatic Point Marking, Measuring, and Recording Instrument	APMMRI
Automatic Point Marking, Measuring and Recording Instrument (SAUS)	APMMRI
Automatic Point of Sale System (IAA)	APOSS
Automatic Point Positioning System (MCD)	APPS
Automatic Point Transfer Instrument (MCD)	APTI
Automatic Polarity Indication (IAA)	AUTPOL
Automatic Polling [*Computer science*] (EECA)	AUTOPOLL
Automatic Position Control (SAUS)	APC
Automatic Position Planning	APP
Automatic Position Reference Monitor (IEEE)	APRM
Automatic Position Reference System	APRS
Automatic Position Report System (SAUS)	APRS
Automatic Position Select (SAUS)	APS
Automatic Position Telemetering	APT
Automatic Position Telemetering (or Telemetry) (SAUS)	APT
Automatic Positioning and Control (SAUS)	APAC
Automatic Positioning Equipment	APE
Automatic Positioning of Telemetering Aerial (or Antenna) (SAUS)	APOTA
Automatic Positioning Telemetering Antenna	APOTA
Automatic Potential Control (MHDI)	APC
Automatic Power Boom Lowering (HEAS)	APBL
Automatic Power Compensator (ACAE)	APC
Automatic Power Control (NTCM)	APC
Automatic Power Factor Control System (SAUS)	APFCS
Automatic Power Input Controller	APIC
Automatic Power Off (CIST)	APO
Automatic Power Plant Checker	APPC
Automatic Power Protection	APP
Automatic Power Reserve [*Aeronautics*]	APR
Automatic Precipitation Gauge (NOAA)	APG
Automatic Predictive Maintenance (MHDI)	APM
Automatic Premium Loan [*Insurance*]	APL
Automatic Press Feed	APF
Automatic Pressure Conveyor	APC
Automatic Pressure Relief [*Nuclear energy*] (NRCH)	APR
Automatic Pressure Relief System [*Military*] (CAAL)	APRS
Automatic Print Transfer Instrument (SAUS)	APTI
Automatic Printed Circuit Board Routing with Intermediate Control of the Tracking (MHDB)	APRICOT
Automatic Printing Line Selection (SAUS)	APLS
Automatic Printing Machine (SAUS)	APM
Automatic Priority Group [*Fujitsu Ltd.*] [*Japan*] (MCD)	APG
Automatic Priority Interrupt [*Computer science*]	API
Automatic Priority Processing (SAUS)	APP
Automatic Private Branch Exchange (SAUS)	APBX
Automatic Problem Verification (ACAE)	APV
Automatic Process Control (SAUS)	APC
Automatic Process Line System (SAUS)	APLS
Automatic Processing and Recording (NITA)	APAR
Automatic Processing System (MCD)	APS
Automatic Procurement Capability System	AUTOPROC
Automatic Procurement Documentation Systems (SAUS)	APDS
Automatic Production Line	APL

Automatic Production Record System ... APRS
Automatic Production Recording ... APR
Automatic Production Registering (SAUS) ... APR
Automatic Production Test Equipment (DNAB) ... APTE
Automatic Program Analysis Report [*Computer science*] (BUR) ... APAR
Automatic Program Finding [*Electronics*] ... APF
Automatic Program Loading Unit [*Computer science*] ... APLU
Automatic Program Selection [*Automobile accessory*] ... APS
Automatic Program System [*Computer science*] ... APS
Automatic Program Unit, High-Speed [*Component of ADIS*] ... APUHS
Automatic Program Unit, Low-Speed [*Component of ADIS*] ... APULS
Automatic Programing Information Centre, London (SAUO) ... APIC
Automatic Programmable Assembly System (SAUS) ... APAS
Automatic Programmable Film Reader (SAUS) ... APFR
Automatic Programmed Checkout Equipment ... APCHE
Automatic Programmed Test Input (NASA) ... APTI
Automatic Programmed Test Input (SAUS) ... AUI
Automatic Programmed Tooling (SAUS) ... APT
Automatic Programmed Tools (SAUS) ... APT
Automatic Programmer and Data System [*Air Force*] ... APADS
Automatic Programmer and Test System [*Army*] ... APATS
Automatic Programmer and Test System [*Army*] (MCD) ... APTS
Automatic Programming [*Computer science*] ... AP
Automatic Programming [*Computer science*] ... AUTO PROG
Automatic Programming (SAUS) ... AUTOPROG
Automatic Programming and Data System (SAUS) ... APADS
Automatic Programming and Recording [*Computer science*] ... APAR
Automatic Programming and Recording [*Computer science*] (MCD) ... APR
Automatic Programming and Scaling of Equations (SAUS) ... APSE
Automatic Programming Checkout Equipment (SAUS) ... APCHE
Automatic Programming for Positioning System (DNAB) ... AUTOPROPS
Automatic Programming for Positioning Systems (SAUS) ... AUTOPROPS
Automatic Programming for Tools (SAUS) ... APT
Automatic Programming Including Technology (SAUS) ... AUTOPIT
Automatic Programming Information Center (or Centre) (SAUS) ... APIC
Automatic Programming Instruction [*Computer science*] ... API
Automatic Programming Language [*Computer science*] (CMD) ... APL
Automatic Programming Loading Unit (ACAE) ... APLU
Automatic Programming Machine [*Computer science*] ... APM
Automatic Programming National Information Center (or Centre) (SAUS) ... APNIC
Automatic Programming of Lathes (PDAA) ... AUTOPOL
Automatic Programming of Machine Tools (SAUS) ... AUTOPROMPT
Automatic Programming of Machine Tools [*IBM Corp.*] ... AUTOPROMT
Automatic Programming of Tools (SAUS) ... APT
Automatic Programming System (SAUS) ... APS
Automatic Programming System Extended [*Computer science*] (IAA) ... APX
Automatic Programmed Technique (SAUS) ... APT
Automatic Programming Technologies for Avionics Software (ACAE) ... APTAS
Automatic Programming Testing System (SAUS) ... APTS
Automatic Programming Tool [*Computer science*] (NITA) ... APT
Automatic Progression Testing (TEL) ... APT
Automatic Progressive Register Sender Tester (SAUS) ... APRST
Automatic Proof of Delivery ... AUTOPOD
Automatic Propulsion Control System (DNAB) ... APS
Automatic Protection Switch (SAUS) ... APS
Automatic Protection Switching [*Telecommunications*] (ACRL) ... APS
Automatic Protocol Analysis System (SAUS) ... APAS
Automatic Provisioning System [*Military*] (CAAL) ... APS
Automatic Pulse Measurement System (SAUS) ... APMS
Automatic Pulse-Analyzer (DNAB) ... APA
Automatic Punching Card Recording (SAUS) ... APCR
Automatic Punching of Cards (SAUS) ... APC
Automatic Quench Calibration [*or Correction*] ... AQC
Automatic Quench Compensation [*Beckman Instruments, Inc.*] [*Instrumentation*] ... AQC
Automatic Quench Correction (SAUS) ... AQC
Automatic Query Formulation (SAUS) ... AQF
Automatic RADAR Beacon ... ARB
Automatic RADAR Beacon Sequencer ... ARBS
Automatic RADAR Chain Acquisition System [*Air Force*] ... ARCAS
Automatic RADAR Control and Data Equipment ... ARCADE
Automatic RADAR Data Measuring Equipment ... ARDME
Automatic RADAR Distance Measuring Equipment (MSA) ... ARDME
Automatic RADAR Pattern Recognition (MCD) ... ARPR
Automatic RADAR Plotting Aids ... ARPA
Automatic Radar Plotting Disc [*Navy*] ... ARPD
Automatic RADAR Plotting System [*Collision avoidance aid*] ... ARPS
Automatic RADAR Reconnaissance Exploitation System ... ARRES
Automatic Radar Target Identification (ACAE) ... ARTI
Automatic Radar Tracking (ACAE) ... ART
Automatic Radar Traffic Control System (SAUS) ... ARTS
Automatic Radial Centering [*Aviation*] (PIPO) ... ARC
Automatic Radiating Tester ... ART
Automatic Radiation Monitoring System (MCD) ... ARMS
Automatic Radio Control (ECII) ... ARC
Automatic Radio Information [*System which relays traffic information through car radios*] ... ARI
Automatic Radio Location Beacon (PDAA) ... ARLB
Automatic Radio Manufacturing Co., Inc. ... AR
Automatic Radio Meteorological Measurements and Survey (IAA) ... ARMS
Automatic Radiotheodolite [*Meteorology*] ... ART
Automatic RAM Control (SAUS) ... ARC
Automatic Random Access Transport ... ARAT
Automatic Range Compensating [*Firearms*] ... ARC
Automatic Range Control ... ARC
Automatic Range Detection and Measuring Equipment ... ARDME
Automatic Range Detector and Measuring Equipment (SAUS) ... ARDME
Automatic Range Only ... ARO
Automatic Range Testing, Reporting and Control (SAUS) ... ARTRAC
Automatic Range Tracker [*or Tracking*] ... ART
Automatic Range Tracking Unit [*Military*] ... ARTU
Automatic Range Unit ... ARU
Automatic Ranging Telescope [*Weaponry*] (INF) ... ART
Automatic Rate Changer ... ARC
Automatic Rate Control ... ARC
Automatic Ratio Control (SAUS) ... ARC
Automatic Reaction Control (ACAE) ... ARC
Automatic Reader (SAUS) ... AR
Automatic Reading of Characters (SAUS) ... ARC
Automatic Reasoning Tool (MCD) ... ART
Automatic Receiving and Measuring System (MCD) ... ARMS
Automatic Reception Control (SAUS) ... ARC
Automatic Recirculation Valve [*Engineering*] ... ARC
Automatic Reclosing (SAUS) ... AUTO RECL
Automatic Reclosing (IAA) ... AUTORECL
Automatic Recognition of Continuous Speech (SAUS) ... ARCS
Automatic Reconfigurable Modular Multicompressor System (SAUS) ... ARMMS
Automatic Record Analysis Language [*Computer science*] ... ARAL
Automatic Record Evaluation ... ARE
Automatic Record Evaluation System ... ARES
Automatic Record Level (IAA) ... ARL
Automatic Recorder of Deformation (SAUS) ... ARD
Automatic Recording and Reduction Facility ... ARRF
Automatic Recording Infrared Spectrometer ... ARIS
Automatic Recording Inverted Echo Sounder (SAUS) ... AIRES
Automatic Recording Spectrometer ... ARS
Automatic Recovery Computer (SAUS) ... ARC
Automatic Recovery of Remotely piloted Aircraft (SAUS) ... AURORA
Automatic Recovery Option [*NCR Corp.*] (NITA) ... ARO
Automatic Recovery Process (MCD) ... ARP
Automatic Recovery System ... ARS
Automatic Reel Mounting ... ARM
Automatic Reentry Flight Dynamics Simulator [*NASA*] (NASA) ... ARFDS
Automatic Reference System (MCD) ... ARS
Automatic Reference System/Sequential Launch Adapter ... ARS/SLA
Automatic Regulation and Electronic Protection ... AREP
Automatic Relative Plotter (IAA) ... ARP
Automatic Relay Calculator [*Early computer*] [*Birkbeck College*] [*British*] (MCD) ... ARC
Automatic Relay Computer (IAA) ... ARC
Automatic Relay Computer (SAUS) ... Arc
Automatic Relay of Digital Information (SAUS) ... ARDI
Automatic Release Data (AAGC) ... ARD
Automatic Release Date [*Military*] (AABC) ... ARD
Automatic Reliability and Maintainability Measurement System (ACAE) ... ARMMS
Automatic Reliability Mathematical Model (DNAB) ... ARMM
Automatic Reliability Mathematical Model (CIST) ... ARMMS
Automatic Remote Cassette Handler (NTCM) ... ARCH
Automatic Remote Control (DEN) ... ARC
Automatic Remote Data Terminal (IAA) ... ARDT
Automatic Remote Geomagnetic Observatory System (SAUS) ... ARGOS
Automatic Remote Manned System (MCD) ... ARMS
Automatic Remote Terminal Information System ... ARTIS
Automatic Repeat Request [*Computer science*] (MCD) ... ARQ
Automatic Repeat Request (SAUS) ... ARR
Automatic Repeat Request Mode Counter [*Computer science*] (IAA) ... ARMC
Automatic Repetition Requested (SAUS) ... ARQ
Automatic Report Feature (SAUS) ... ARF
Automatic Reporting Feature (MCD) ... ARF
Automatic Reporting Maintenance System (MCD) ... ARMS
Automatic Reporting Post [*Air defense*] [*NATO*] (NATG) ... ARP
Automatic Reporting System (IUSS) ... ARS
Automatic Reporting Telephone [*Telecommunications*] (TEL) ... ART
Automatic Request [*Computer science*] (DOM) ... ARQ
Automatic Request for Correction (NITA) ... ARQ
Automatic Request Transmission by Telephone (TELE) ... ARTTel
Automatic Request-Repeat (COE) ... ARQ
Automatic Requirements Engineering Systems (MCD) ... ARES
Automatic Rerouting [*Telecommunications*] (TEL) ... ARR
Automatic Reseau Measuring Equipment (MCD) ... ARME
Automatic Reservation and Communication (IAA) ... ARCO
Automatic Reserve Ripcord Release [*for a parachute*] (RDA) ... AR3
Automatic Reset Counter ... ARC
Automatic Resistance Test Set ... ARTS
Automatic Resolution Control (SAUS) ... ARC
Automatic Resolution Selection Control (NITA) ... ARSC
Automatic Response Tape System (SAUS) ... ARTS
Automatic Response Tuning System (SAUS) ... ARTS
Automatic Responsivity Control (MCD) ... ARC
Automatic Restart (SAUS) ... AR
Automatic Restart Switch (ACAE) ... ARS
Automatic Resupply (NVT) ... AR
Automatic Resupply and Buildup Time [*Air Force*] (AFIT) ... AIRBUT
Automatic Resupply Logistics System (AFM) ... ARLS
Automatic Retailers of America (MCD) ... ARA
Automatic Retailers of America, Inc. (SAUO) ... ARA
Automatic Retransmission Exchange [*ITT World Communications, Inc.*] [*Secaucus, NJ*] (TSSD) ... ARX

Automatic Retransmission Queue [*Computer science*] (HGAA) .... ARQ
Automatic Retransmission Request for Correction [*Computer science*] (NTCM) .... ARQ
Automatic Retrieval of Information Electronically (SAUS) .... ARIEL
Automatic Retrival of Test through European Multipurpose Information Services (SAUS) .... ARTEMIS
Automatic Return Fire [*ARPA*] .... ARF
Automatic Return Item List (MCD) .... ARIL
Automatic Return Items (AABC) .... ARI
Automatic Return Items List (SAUS) .... ARIL
Automatic Return to Search (ACAE) .... ARTS
Automatic Revenue Collection (SAUS) .... ARC
Automatic Rich (SAUS) .... AUTO RICH
Automatic Ride Control Suspension [*Automotive engineering*] .... ARC
Automatic Rifle [*or Rifleman*] [*DoD*] .... AR
Automatic Rifleman (SAUS) .... AR
Automatic Rifleman (SAUS) .... Autorif
Automatic Ring Down (SAUS) .... ARD
Automatic Road Analyzer [*FHWA*] (TAG) .... ARAN
Automatic Rocket Impact Predictor .... ARIP
Automatic Room Identification (SAUS) .... ARI
Automatic Route Advancement (MCD) .... ARA
Automatic Route Control System [*Truck-delivery computer system*] .... ARCS
Automatic Route Selection [*Also, MERS*] [*Bell System*] [*Telecommunications*] .... ARS
Automatic Routine Generating and Updating System [*Compiler*] [*Computer science*] .... ARGUS
Automatic Routing Character (SAUS) .... ARC
Automatic Rubber Tensile Tester (PDAA) .... ARTT
Automatic Rudder Control (MUGU) .... ARCON
Automatic Safe Load Indicator (HEAS) .... ASLI
Automatic Safety Monitor [*PUR*] (PS) .... ASM
Automatic Sample Preparation Extraction Column [*Chromatography*] .... ASPEC
Automatic Sample Processor (KSC) .... ASP
Automatic Sample Processor and Injector .... ASPI
Automatic Sampling Injector .... ASI
Automatic Satellite / Computer Aid to Navigation [*Computer science*] (PDAA) .... AUTOSCAN
Automatic Saturation Control (ACAE) .... ASC
Automatic Scan Counter .... ASC
Automatic Scan Counter System .... ASCS
Automatic Scan Tracking [*Videotape head*] (NTCM) .... AST
Automatic Scanner (SAUS) .... AUTOSCAN
Automatic Scanning Control Unit .... ASCU
Automatic Scanning Correlator .... AUSCOR
Automatic Scanning Unit Out of Service (FAAC) .... SCANO
Automatic Scanning Unit Returned to Service (FAAC) .... SCAOK
Automatic Schedule Procedure .... ASP
Automatic Schedule Processor (SAUS) .... ASP
Automatic Scheduling and Operating Program (BUR) .... ASOP
Automatic Scheduling Message (GFGA) .... ASM
Automatic Scheduling Procedure (SAUS) .... ASP
Automatic Scheduling with Time-Integrated Resource Allocation .... ASTRA
Automatic Science Citation Alerting (IEEE) .... ASCA
Automatic Scoring Electronic Target (SAUS) .... ASET
Automatic Screw Works Apparatenfabriek N.V. (SAUO) .... ASW
Automatic SDI [*Selective Dissemination of Information*] [*British Library Automated Information Service*] (NITA) .... AUTOSD
Automatic Search Jammer (SAUS) .... ASJ
Automatic Seat Reservation System (SAUS) .... ASRS
Automatic Secondary Allocation (SAUS) .... ASA
Automatic Secure Voice Communications (CAAL) .... ASVC
Automatic Secure Voice Communications (ACAE) .... AUTOSEV
Automatic Secure Voice Communications .... AUTOSEVCOM
Automatic Secure Voice Communications (ACAE) .... AUTOSEVOCO
Automatic Secure Voice Communications Network .... AUTOSEVOCON
Automatic Secure Voice Communications Network, Phase II (IUSS) .... AUTOSEVCOMII
Automatic Selection of Any Channel (IAA) .... ASAC
Automatic Selection of Digital Electronic Computers .... ASDEC
Automatic Selective Control (SAUS) .... ASC
Automatic Selective Dissemination of Information .... ASDI
Automatic Selectivity Control (DEN) .... ASC
Automatic Self Allocating Processors (SAUS) .... ASAP
Automatic Self Verification (SAUS) .... ASV
Automatic, Self-Powered (SAUS) .... ASP
Automatic Self-Powered Cannon (MCD) .... ASP
Automatic Sending and Receiving (SAUS) .... ASR
Automatic Send/Receive [*Computer science*] (DDC) .... ASR
Automatic Send/Receive Teletypewriter [*or Terminal*] [*Communications equipment*] .... AS/R
Automatic Send-Receive Terminal (SAUS) .... ASR Terminal
Automatic Sensitivity Control [*Aviation*] .... ASC
Automatic Separation Assurance System (SAUS) .... ASA System
Automatic Sequence (SAUS) .... AUTO SEQ
Automatic Sequence Control [*Computer science*] (EECA) .... ASC
Automatic Sequence Controlled Calculator [*First all-automatic calculating machine*] .... ASCC
Automatic Sequence Enable .... ASE
Automatic Sequence Execution and Processor (MCD) .... ASEP
Automatic Sequence Register (NTCM) .... ASR
Automatic Server Restart [*Computer science*] (VERA) .... ASR
Automatic Service Panel (SAUS) .... ASP
Automatic Services and Products .... ASP
Automatic Servo Plotter .... ASP
Automatic Shaft Position Data Encoder (SAUS) .... ASPDE
Automatic Sheet Feeder .... ASF
Automatic Shift Keying (HGAA) .... ASK
Automatic Ship Identification .... ASI
Automatic Shipboard Aerological Program (SAUS) .... ASAP
Automatic Shipboard Checkout and Readiness Equipment (MCD) .... ASCORE
Automatic Shipboard Launch Aircraft Data System .... ASLADS
Automatic Ship's Heading Measurement System (DNAB) .... ASHMS
Automatic Shop Tester (OA) .... AST
Automatic Shorebased Acceptance Checkout Equipment (PDAA) .... AutoSACE
Automatic Shot Dispensing Pump .... ASDP
Automatic Shutdown [*Automotive engineering*] .... ASD
Automatic Shutoff (AAEL) .... ASO
Automatic Shuttle Valve .... ASV
Automatic Signal Excess Prediction System [*Military*] (CAAL) .... ASEPS
Automatic Signal Filtration [*Electronics*] (IAA) .... ASF
Automatic Signal Finding (SAUS) .... ASF
Automatic Signal Processing Unit (MCD) .... ASPU
Automatic Signal Recognition Unit (IAA) .... ASRU
Automatic Signature Verification System .... ASVS
Automatic Skin [*NASA*] (KSC) .... AS
Automatic Skip Driver [*Computer science*] .... ASD
Automatic Sky Quality Assessment (MCD) .... ASQA
Automatic Slack Adjuster [*Truck brakes*] .... ASA
Automatic Solution Crystal Growth [*Materials processing*] .... ASCG
Automatic SONAR Readout .... ASR
Automatic Sorting, Testing, Recording Analysis .... ASTRA
Automatic Space Management .... ASM
Automatic Space Plasma Experiment with a Rotating Analyser [*Instrumentation*] .... ASPERA
Automatic Spacing Pause System (SAUS) .... ASPS
Automatic Spares Analysis Technique .... ASAT
Automatic Sparrow Operational Test Systems (MCD) .... ASOTS
Automatic Speaker Verification (SAUS) .... ASV
Automatic Specimen Positioning .... ASP
Automatic Specimen Positioning System .... ASPS
Automatic Speckle Cancellation Techniques (PDAA) .... ASPECT
Automatic Spectrum Analyzer (MHDB) .... ASA
Automatic Spectrum Display and Signal Recognition System (IEEE) .... ASDSRS
Automatic Speech Exchange System [*Voice messaging*] .... ASPEN
Automatic Speech Recognition .... ASR
Automatic Speech Recognition (or Recognizer) (SAUS) .... ASR
Automatic Speed Control Device .... ASCD
Automatic Spooling with Asynchronous Processing [*Computer science*] (PDAA) .... ASAP
Automatic Spray Gun .... ASG
Automatic Sprinkler [*Technical drawings*] .... AS
Automatic Sprinkler Riser [*Technical drawings*] .... ASR
Automatic Sprinklers (GEOI) .... AS
Automatic Stability Control System [*Bavarian Motor Works*] [*Automotive engineering*] .... ASC
Automatic Stability Regulation [*Automotive engineering*] .... ASR
Automatic Stabilization and Control System (SAUS) .... AS&CS
Automatic Stabilization and Control System .... ASCS
Automatic Stabilization Equipment .... ASE
Automatic Stabilization System .... ASS
Automatic Standard Magnetic Observatory .... ASMO
Automatic Standard Magnetic Observatory - Remote .... ASMOR
Automatic Start (SAUS) .... Auto Str
Automatic Starter .... ASt
Automatic Starter .... AUTOSTRT
Automatic Starting .... AUTOSTRTG
Automatic Start-Up System [*Reactor*] .... ASS
Automatic Statewide Auto Theft Inquiry System (SAUS) .... AUTO-STATIS
Automatic Station Identification Device .... ASID
Automatic Station Keeping System .... ASKS
Automatic Station Selection (SAUS) .... ASS
Automatic Status Board Subsystem (MCD) .... ASTABS
Automatic Steam-Temperature Control .... ASTC
Automatic Steel Products (SAUS) .... ASP
Automatic Steerable Null Antenna Processor .... ASNAP
Automatic Steering Antenna .... ASA
Automatic Stellar Tracking, Recognition and Orientation Computer (SAUS) .... ASTROC
Automatic Step Regulator .... ASR
Automatic Stereo Broadcast Scanner (IAA) .... AUTOSCAN
Automatic Stereo Level (SAUS) .... ASL
Automatic Stereo Recording Amplifier .... ASRA
Automatic Stiffening (MSA) .... AUTOSTIF
Automatic Stop and Check Valve (AAG) .... AUTO S & CV
Automatic Stop and Check Valve (SAUS) .... AUTO S&CV
Automatic Stop Announcement .... ASA
Automatic Storage and Retrieval (SAUS) .... ASR
Automatic Storage Evaluator Test System (SAUS) .... ASETS
Automatic Store and Forward .... ASF
Automatic Storm Observation Service [*AFCRL*] .... ASOS
Automatic Strength Regulation (IAA) .... ASR
Automatic Strobe Tracking (CET) .... ASTRA
Automatic Structure Analysis of Mass Spectra .... ASAMS
Automatic Subject Citation Alert (CIST) .... ASCA
Automatic Submarine Control [*Navy*] (MCD) .... ASC
Automatic Submerged Arc Welding Process (NUCP) .... ASAW
Automatic Substrate Tinner Inline (SAUS) .... AUSTIN
Automatic Support Equipment [*Military*] .... ASE
Automatic Support Systems Symposium (SAUO) .... ASSC

Automatic Support Systems Symposium for Advanced Maintainability (SAUS) .... ASSAM
Automatic Surface Observing System (ARMP) .... ASOS
Automatic Surveillance Receiver (MCD) .... ASR
Automatic Sustainer Cut-Off (SAUS) .... ASCO
Automatic Switched Communications Network (SAUS) .... ASCON
Automatic Switching [*Telecommunications*] (OA) .... AS
Automatic Switching (SAUS) .... AUTSWITCH
Automatic Switching and Networking System (ACAE) .... ASNS
Automatic Switching and Processing [*Command Communications, Inc.*] [*Telecommunications*] (PCM) .... ASAP
Automatic Switching Center (or Centre) (SAUS) .... ASC
Automatic Switching Control (SAUS) .... ASC
Automatic Switching Panel .... ASP
Automatic Switching Unit [*Telecommunications*] .... ASU
Automatic Synchronized Control (DEN) .... ASC
Automatic Synchronized Discriminator (DEN) .... ASD
Automatic Synchronizer .... AS
Automatic Synchronizer (SAUS) .... Synchro
Automatic Synthesis Program .... ASP
Automatic System Checkout Program .... ASCP
Automatic System Control .... ASC
Automatic System for Kinematic Analysis (SAUS) .... ASKA
Automatic System for Performance Evaluation of the Network (VERA) .... ASPEN
Automatic System for Positioning Tools .... AUTOSPOT
Automatic System for Selection of Receiver and Transmitter [*Computer science*] (MHDB) .... ASSORT
Automatic System Installation (VERA) .... ASI
Automatic System of Secondary Index Selection Technique (SAUS) .... ASSIST
Automatic System Procedure (SAUS) .... ASP
Automatic System Recovery (SAUS) .... ASR
Automatic System Self-Test (SAUS) .... ASSLT
Automatic System Self-Test [*Aviation*] (MCD) .... ASST
Automatic System Trouble Analysis [*Computer science*] (MHDB) .... ASTA
Automatic Systems Analysis (KSC) .... ASA
Automatic Systems for Kinematic Analysis [*NASA*] (NASA) .... ASKA
Automatic Systems Management and Control [*Aviation*] (OA) .... ASMC
Automatic Systems Pressure Alarm (PDAA) .... ASPA
Automatic Systems Test Unit .... ASTU
Automatic Tabulating, Listing, and Sorting System [*Software*] .... ATLAS
Automatic Tabulating, Listing and Sorting System (SAUS) .... ATLAS System
Automatic Tactical Air Control Center (MCD) .... ATACC
Automatic TAEM [*Terminal Area Energy Management*] [*NASA*] (NASA) .... AT
Automatic Takeoff Thrust Control System (IEEE) .... ATTCS
Automatic Tally and Sort (PDAA) .... ATS
Automatic Tank Target System [*Military*] (INF) .... ATTS
Automatic Tap-Changing (SAUS) .... ATC
Automatic Tape Degausser .... ATD
Automatic Tape Delete (SAUS) .... ATD
Automatic Tape Dispenser (SAUS) .... ATD
Automatic Tape Handler (IAA) .... ATH
Automatic Tape Load Audit System .... ATLAS
Automatic Tape Reader (DNAB) .... ATR
Automatic Tape Winder (IAA) .... ATW
Automatic Target Acquisition (MCD) .... ATA
Automatic Target Acquisition & Tracking System (SAUS) .... ATATS
Automatic Target Acquisition, Detection (MCD) .... ATAD
Automatic Target Acquisition Logic (ACAE) .... ATAL
Automatic Target and Battery Evaluation [*Military*] .... ATABE
Automatic Target Assignment and Battery Evaluation (SAUS) .... ATABE
Automatic Target Counting .... ATC
Automatic Target Cueing (ACAE) .... ATC
Automatic Target Designation .... ATAD
Automatic Target Designation .... ATD
Automatic Target Detection (MCD) .... ATD
Automatic Target Detection & Tracking (SAUS) .... ATDT
Automatic Target Detector (ACAE) .... ATD
Automatic Target Evaluator and Weapon Assignor .... ATEWA
Automatic Target Finder (IAA) .... ATF
Automatic Target Follow .... ATF
Automatic Target Follower (SAUS) .... ATF
Automatic Target Hand Off Controller (ACAE) .... ATHOC
Automatic Target Handoff Computer (MCD) .... ATHOC
Automatic Target Handoff System (DOMA) .... ATAH
Automatic Target Handover (SAUS) .... ATH
Automatic Target Handover System [*Army*] .... ATHS
Automatic Target Handover System/Avionics Integration .... ATHS/AI
Automatic Target Identification .... ATI
Automatic Target Recognition .... ATR
Automatic Target Recognition Analysis .... AUTRAN
Automatic Target Recognition and Reporting (ACAE) .... ATRR
Automatic Target Recognition Device .... ATRD
Automatic Target Recognition, Identification, and Detection .... ATRID
Automatic Target Recognition module (SAUS) ATR1
Automatic Target Recognizer (SAUS) .... ATR
Automatic Target Scoring Systems (MCD) .... ATSS
Automatic Target Selection File (CINC) .... ATSF
Automatic Target Tracking (MCD) .... ATT
Automatic Target Voltage Control (ACAE) .... ATVC
Automatic Teaching Device .... ATD
Automatic Technical Control (SAUS) .... ATEC
Automatic Technical Control (SAUS) .... AYEC
Automatic Technical Reliability Assessment of PATRIOT [*Phased Array Tracking to Intercept of Target*] .... ATRAP
Automatic Techniques for Selection and Identification of Targets [*Army/Air Force*] (MCD) .... ATSIT
Automatic Telecommunications Program (IUSS) .... ATP
Automatic Telecommunications Switching System .... ATSS
Automatic Telecommunications Switching System - Data Services [*Computer science*] (MHDI) .... ATSS-D
Automatic Telecommunications System Security Manager [*Military*] (GFGA) .... ATSSM
Automatic Telegram Transmission with Computers [*Telecommunications*] (TEL) .... ATECO
Automatic Telegraph Equipment for Stockholm Telegraph Office (SAUS) .... ATESTO
Automatic Telegraph Message Switching System (PDAA) .... ATMSS
Automatic Telegraph Subsystem [*Navy*] [*British*] (MCD) .... ATSS
Automatic Telemetry Decommutation System .... ATDS
Automatic Telemetry System .... ATS
Automatic Telemetry Tracking Antenna System (MCD) .... ATTRAS
Automatic Telemetry Tracking Receiving Antenna .... ATTRA
Automatic Telemetry Tracking System [*NASA*] .... ATTS
Automatic Telephone (IAA) .... AT
Automatic Telephone and Electric Co., Ltd. (SAUO) .... ATE
Automatic Telephone Call (IAA) .... ATC
Automatic Telephone Call Distribution (PDAA) .... ACTD
Automatic Telephone Company (SAUO) .... ATC
Automatic Telephone Exchange (NITA) .... ATE
Automatic Telephone Set .... ATS
Automatic Telephone Switching System (NITA) .... ATSS
Automatic Telephone Using Radio [*Telecommunications service*] (TEL) .... ATUR
Automatic Teleprinter Exchange Service [*of Western Union Corp.*] .... TEX
Automatic Teletypewriter Exchange Service [*of Western Union*] .... TELEX
Automatic TELEX Exchange [*Telecommunications*] (TEL) .... ATX
Automatic Teller Machine Deposit (SAUS) .... ATM/D
Automatic Telling [*Banking*] (IAA) .... ATL
Automatic Temperature Compensation .... ATC
Automatic Temperature Control .... ATC
Automatic Temporary Roof Support [*Mining industry*] .... ATRS
Automatic Terminal Approach System (MCD) .... ATAS
Automatic Terminal Information Service [*Aviation*] (AFM) .... ATIS
Automatic Terminal Recognition [*Computer science*] (VERA) .... ATR
Automatic Terminal System [*NASA*] (NASA) .... ATS
Automatic Terrain Avoidance [*Air Force*] .... ATA
Automatic Terrain Avoidance System [*Military*] .... ATAS
Automatic Terrain Following [*Military*] (MCD) .... ATF
Automatic Terrain Following/Automatic Terrain Avoidance [*Military*] .... ATF/ATA
Automatic Terrain Recognition and Identification Device (PDAA) .... ATRID
Automatic Terrain Recognition and Navigation (SAUS) .... ATRAN
Automatic Terrain Recognition and Navigation Guidance System .... ATRAN
Automatic Terrain Recognition Navigation (MED) .... atran
Automatic Terrain-Following RADAR [*Military*] .... ATFR
Automatic Test .... AT
Automatic Test Analysis System .... ATAS
Automatic Test and Checkout Equipment (AFM) .... ATCE
Automatic Test and Evaluation .... ATE
Automatic Test Application Language (SAUS) .... ATAL
Automatic Test Break and Access [*Telecommunications*] (TEL) .... ATBA
[*An*] Automatic Test Control System (MCD) .... AATCS
Automatic Test Control System [*Air Force*] .... ATCS
Automatic Test Equipment Association (SAUO) .... ATEA
Automatic Test Equipment Complex (MCD) .... ATEC
Automatic Test Equipment Compute [*or Computer*] .... ATC
Automatic Test Equipment Conference and Exposition (SAUS) .... ATEX
Automatic Test Equipment for Internal Combustion Engines (MCD) .... ATE/ICE
Automatic Test Equipment Language Standardization (MCD) .... ATLAS
Automatic Test Equipment Materiel Manager .... ATEMM
Automatic Test Equipment, Missile (MCD) .... ATEM
Automatic Test Equipment Software Support Environment [*Computer science*] .... ATESSE
Automatic Test Equipment Support Center [*Army*] .... ATESC
Automatic Test Formatter (NITA) .... ATF
Automatic Test Generation .... ATG
Automatic Test Generation Facility (MHDI) .... ATGF
Automatic Test Generator .... ATG
Automatic Test Grading .... ATG
Automatic Test Guide .... ATG
Automatic Test Inhibit (SAUS) .... ATI
Automatic Test Language for All Systems [*DoD*] .... ATLAS
Automatic Test Line .... ATL
Automatic Test Message Handling (MCD) .... ATMH
Automatic Test Pattern [*or Program*] Generation (MCD) .... ATPG
Automatic Test Pattern Generation (or Generator) (SAUS) .... ATPG
Automatic Test Scoring .... ATS
Automatic Test Set [*Support*] [*Military*] (DOMA) .... ATSE
Automatic Test Station (SAUO) .... ATS
Automatic Test Support Systems (RDA) .... ATSS
Automatic Test System .... ATS
Automatic Test System Jet Engine Accessories .... ATSJEA
Automatic Test Vector Generation (CIST) .... ATVG
Automatic Testing Committee (AAGC) .... ATC
Automatic Testing Equipment (SAUS) .... ATE
Automatic Testing, Evaluation and Reporting (SAUS) .... ATER
Automatic Testing Multiple Operating System (MCD) .... ATMOS
Automatic Testing Operating and Maintenance (SAUS) .... ATOM
Automatic Text Formatter .... ATF
Automatic Text Processing (SAUS) .... ATP
Automatic Thin-Layer Analytical System .... ATLAS

Automatic Threat Countering (SAUS)	ATC
Automatic Threat Detection System [Aviation] (DA)	ATD
Automatic Three Speed [DOE] (TAG)	A3
Automatic Three-Axis Stabilization	ATAS
Automatic Three-Dimensional Electronics Scanning Array (IAA)	ATDESA
Automatic Three-Dimensional Electronics Scanning Array (MUGU)	ATHESA
Automatic Threshold Adjust (SAUS)	ATA
Automatic Threshold Circuit (MCD)	ATC
Automatic Threshold Control (ACAE)	ATC
Automatic Threshold Variation	ATV
Automatic Throttle Control (SAA)	ATC
Automatic Throttle/Speed Control System (MCD)	ATS
Automatic through Center [Telecommunications] (OA)	ATC
Automatic through Junction [Telecommunications] (OA)	ATJ
Automatic Thrust Vector Control [NASA]	ATVC
Automatic Ticket Vendor (SAUS)	ATV
Automatic Ticket Vendors (ADA)	ATV
Automatic Ticketing	AT
Automatic Time Control (SAUS)	ATC
Automatic Time Element Compensator (SAA)	AMTEC
Automatic Time Interval Measurement System [Air Force]	ATIMS
Automatic Timing and Controls, Inc. (SAUO)	ATC
Automatic Timing Control (SAUS)	ATC
Automatic Timing Corrector	ATC
Automatic Timing Device [Diesel engines]	ATD
Automatic Tint Control [Electronics] (IAA)	ATC
Automatic Toll Ticketing (TEL)	ATT
Automatic Tone Control	ATC
Automatic Tone Correction	ATC
Automatic Toning Machine [Color printing technology]	ATM
Automatic Tool Changer	ATC
Automatic Tool Setting Unit (SAUS)	ATSU
Automatic Topographic Mapper	ATOM
Automatic Torque Biasing Differential [Automotive engineering]	ATBD
Automatic Total Last Card (SAUS)	ATLC
Automatic TOW Infantry Depot Equipment (ACAE)	A-TIDE
Automatic Track Acquisition	ATA
Automatic Track Finding [System] [Video technology]	ATF
Automatic Track Following (SAUS)	ATF
Automatic Track Initiation	ATI
Automatic Track Transfer (ACAE)	ATT
Automatic Tracking (IAA)	AT
Automatic Tracking Antenna	ATA
Automatic Tracking Antenna System	ATAS
Automatic Tracking Control (MSA)	ATC
Automatic Tracking Feature (NVT)	ATF
Automatic Tracking LASER Illumination System (MCD)	ATLIS
Automatic Tracking Razor Action [The Gillette Co.]	ATRA
Automatic Tracking System (ABAC)	ATS
Automatic Tracking Telemetry Receiving Antenna (SAUS)	ATTRA
Automatic Tracking Telemetry Receiving System (DNAB)	ATTRS
Automatic Tracking Unit	ATU
Automatic Track-while-Scan [Radar]	ATWS
Automatic Traction Control [Automotive engineering]	ATC
Automatic Traffic Advisory and Resolution Service (SAUO)	ATARS
Automatic Traffic Control	ATC
Automatic Traffic Engineering and Management Information System (MHDI)	ATEMIS
Automatic Traffic Information System (ACAE)	ATIS
Automatic Traffic Recorder [Telecommunications] (NITA)	ATR
Automatic Traffic Recording and Analysis Complex (IAA)	AUTRAX
Automatic Traffic Usage Recording System (TEL)	ATURS
Automatic Traffic-Flow Control (MHDB)	ATFC
Automatic Train Control	ATC
Automatic Train Operation (BARN)	ATO
Automatic Train Protection [TRB] (TAG)	ATP
Automatic Train Stop (SAA)	ATS
Automatic Train Supervision (BARN)	ATS
Automatic Trains, Protection, Operation and Supervision (SAUS)	AUTOPOS
Automatic Transaxle	ATX
Automatic Transfer of Savings [Banking]	ATS
Automatic Transfer Service [Banking]	ATS
Automatic Transfer Switch	ATS
Automatic Transfer Switches [Standby electrical power systems]	ATS
Automatic Transformer (IEEE)	AXFMR
Automatic Transient Detection System (MCD)	ATDS
Automatic Transistor Card Analyzer (SAUS)	ATCA
Automatic Transistor Test Equipment	ATTE
Automatic Translation	AT
Automatic Translation	AUTOTRAN
Automatic Translation [Computer science] (CIST)	AUTRAN
Automatic Translation Aiding System (SAUS)	ATLAS
Automatic Transmission [Automotive engineering]	A/T
Automatic Transmission [Automotive engineering]	A/TRANS
Automatic Transmission	ATX
Automatic Transmission	AUTO
Automatic Transmission	Auto
Automatic Transmission (SAUS)	AX
Automatic Transmission Control (SAUS)	ATC
Automatic Transmission Control Unit [Automotive engineering]	ATCU
Automatic Transmission Fluid	ATF
Automatic Transmission Fluids (SAUS)	ATF
Automatic Transmission Measuring Equipment [Telecommunications] (TEL)	ATME
Automatic Transmission Measuring System [Terminated]	ATMS
Automatic Transmission of Mail [Early electronic mail system]	ATOM
Automatic Transmission of Telegrams by (or with) Computer (SAUS)	ATECO
Automatic Transmission Rebuilders Association (EA)	ATRA
Automatic Transmission System [Telecommunications] (NTCM)	ATS
Automatic Transmission Test and Control [Telecommunications] (TEL)	ATTC
Automatic Transmission Testing Equipment (SAUS)	ATTE
Automatic Transmission With Overdrive (SAUS)	AT W/OD
Automatic Transmitter	AT
Automatic Transmitter Identification System [Citizens band radio]	ATIS
Automatic Transportation, Protection, Operation and Supervision (SAUS)	AUTOPOS
Automatic Transportation Research Investigation Program (PDAA)	AUTO-TRIP
Automatic Trim System (PDAA)	ATS
Automatic Trouble Analysis (TEL)	ATA
Automatic Truck Control (SAUS)	ATC
Automatic Trunk Measuring System [Bell System]	ATMS
Automatic Trunk Office [Telecommunications] (OA)	ATO
Automatic Trunk Routiner (MCD)	ATR
Automatic Trunk Synchronizer [Telecommunications] (TEL)	ATS
Automatic Trunk Testing and Transmission Measuring Equipment (SAUS)	ATTM Equipment
Automatic Tuned Circuit Adjustment [Telecommunications] (OA)	ATCA
Automatic Tuned Circuit Adjustment Amplitude [Telecommunications] (OA)	ATCAA
Automatic Tuning (IAA)	ATTUN
Automatic Tuning (IAA)	AUTTUN
Automatic Tuning Control	ATC
Automatic Tuning Device	ATD
Automatic Tuning System	ATS
Automatic Turbidity Compensation Hemoglobin Test	ATC
Automatic Turbine Tester (NRCH)	ATT
Automatic Turret Lathe	ATL
Automatic Type Placement System	ATPS
Automatic Typewriter (IAA)	AT
Automatic Unattended Detection Inspection Transmitter [Raytheon Co.]	AUDIT
Automatic Unconditional Release [Legal term] (WDAA)	AUR
Automatic Unit for National Taxation and Insurance (MHDB)	AUNTIE
Automatic Unit Record Store (SAUS)	AURS
Automatic Universal Translator	AUNT
Automatic Unmanned Weather Station	AUWS
Automatic Update Transaction System [DoD]	AUTS
Automatic Utility Translator (IEEE)	AUTRAN
Automatic Vacuum Deposition System (IAA)	AVDS
Automatic Valve Control (IEEE)	AVC
Automatic Vapor Crystal Growth [Materials processing]	AVCG
Automatic Variable Character Compensation (DGA)	AVCC
Automatic Variable Orifice [Steam trap of Agontz Corp.]	AVO
Automatic Vehicle Classification [Automotive engineering]	AVC
Automatic Vehicle Identification [Automotive engineering]	AVI
Automatic Vehicle Locating (SAUS)	AVL
Automatic Vehicle Location (IEEE)	AVL
Automatic Vehicle Location System (DA)	AVLS
Automatic Vehicle Monitoring [Antihijack device]	AVM
Automatic Vehicle Monitoring System [Army] (MCD)	AVMS
Automatic Vending Association of Britain (EAIO)	AVAB
Automatic Vending Machine Association [British] (BI)	AVMA
Automatic Vent Control (IEEE)	AVC
Automatic Verification, Evaluation, and Readiness Tester	AVERT
Automatic Verifier (SAUS)	AUTOVERIFIER
Automatic Vertical Door (SAUS)	AVD
Automatic Vertical Electrophoresis System [Instrumentation]	AVES
Automatic VFR [Visual Flight Rules] Advisory Service [Aviation] (OA)	AVAS
Automatic Vibration Control	AVC
Automatic Vibration Exciter Control	AVEC
Automatic Video Noise Leveling [or Limiting]	AVNL
Automatic Video Noise Levelling	AVNL
Automatic Video Noise Limiter (or Limiting) (SAUS)	AVNL
Automatic Video Scoring System [Army] (INF)	AVSS
Automatic Video Tracker	AVT
Automatic Vision Testing (NITA)	AVT
Automatic Visual Inspection System [NASA]	AVIS
Automatic Vocal Transaction Analysis (IAA)	AVTA
Automatic Vocal Transaction Analysis (or Analyzer) (SAUS)	AVTA
Automatic Voice Advice (SAUS)	AVA
Automatic Voice Alarm (SAUS)	AVA
Automatic Voice Alerting Device (DA)	AVAD
Automatic Voice Alerting System	AVAD
Automatic Voice Answering [Computer-generated recording unit for telephone directory assistance]	AVA
Automatic Voice Data (MCD)	AVD
Automatic Voice Link Observation	AVOLO
Automatic Voice Network [DoD]	AUTOVON
Automatic Voice Recognition (NITA)	AVR
Automatic Voice Relay	AVR
Automatic Voice Response [Telephone] (WDMC)	AVR
Automatic Voice Switching Network (AFIT)	AVSN
Automatic Voice System (SAUS)	ADS
Automatic Voltage Clamp (SAUS)	AVC
Automatic Voltage Control (NATG)	AVC
Automatic Voltage Digitizer	AVD
Automatic Voltage Margin (SAUS)	AVM
Automatic Voltage Regulation (or Regulator) (SAUS)	AVR
Automatic Voltage Regulator	AVR
Automatic Volume [Electronics] (ECII)	AV

Automatic Volume Control [*Telecommunications*] ... AVC
Automatic Volume Expander (or Expansion) (SAUS) ... AVE
Automatic Volume Expansion ... AVE
Automatic Volume Regulation (SAUS) ... AVR
Automatic Volume Sensing (SAUS) ... AVS
Automatic Voting Machine ... AVM
Automatic Wage Payments (MCD) ... AWP
Automatic Warning Aid (SAUS) ... AWA
Automatic Warning and Control System ... AWCS
Automatic Warning System (SAUS) ... AWS
Automatic Washing Machine (SAUS) ... AWM
Automatic Water Check (SAUS) ... AUTMWTR CK
Automatic Water Check [*Freight*] ... AUTM WTR CK
Automatic Wave Information Processor (SAUS) ... AWIP
Automatic Wave Information System (SAUS) ... AWIS
Automatic Waveform Digitizing System (MCD) ... AWDS
Automatic Weapon (DNAB) ... AUTOWEAP
Automatic Weapon Data Transmission System (SAUS) ... AWDATS
Automatic Weapons ... AW
Automatic Weapons Control System ... AWCS
Automatic Weapons Effect Signature Simulator (MCD) ... AWESS
Automatic Weapons Effects Signature Simulator (SAUS) ... AWESS
Automatic Weapons Release System (DNAB) ... AWRS
Automatic Weapons (Self-Propelled) [*Military*] ... AWSP
Automatic Weather Broadcast (DA) ... AB
Automatic Weather Broadcast Equipment (FAAC) ... AWBE
Automatic Weather Data Acquisition and Archiving System (SAUS) ... AWDAAS
Automatic Weather Observing/Reporting System (FAAC) ... AWOS
Automatic Weather Reporting Station (PIPO) ... AWRS
Automatic Weather Station ... AWS
Automatic Welding ... AW
Automatic Welding (journ.) (SAUS) ... Automat Weld
Automatic Welding Machinery Association [*Defunct*] (EA) ... AWMA
Automatic Welding System ... AWS
Automatic Wind Determination System (SAUS) ... AUTOWINDCO
Automatic Winder (SAUS) ... AU/W
Automatic Winder (IAA) ... AUW
Automatic Wire Data System (MCD) ... AWDS
Automatic Wire Wrap Machine ... AWWM
Automatic With Overdrive (SAUS) ... AUTO W/OD
Automatic Withdrawal Prohibit [*Nuclear energy*] (NRCH) ... AWP
Automatic Word (SAA) ... AW
Automatic Work Control System [*Military*] (MCD) ... AWCS
Automatic Writing Machine ... AWM
Automatic X-Ray Inspection (MCD) ... AXIS
Automatic X-Ray Radiograph ... AXR
Automatic X-ray Radiograph (SAUS) ... AXR
Automatic Yaw Control ... AYC
Automatic Zero Check (SAUS) ... AZC
Automatic Zero Set [*Military*] ... AZS
Automatical Digital Relay (PDAA) ... ADR
Automatical Pre-Punching (SAUS) ... APP
Automatically Compacted Brushes (SAUS) ... AUPAC Brushes
Automatically Controlled Electrical System [*NASA*] (MCD) ... ACES
Automatically Controlled Transportation [*Airport passenger shuttle*] [*Ford Motor Co.*] ... ACT
Automatically Controlled Turbine Run-Up System [*Navigation*] ... ACTRUS
Automatically Cued Target Detecting System (MCD) ... ACTDS
Automatically Data Equalized MODEM [*Computer science*] (IAA) ... ADEM
Automatically Data-Equalized Modem (SAUS) ... ADEM
Automatically Defined Function (SAUS) ... ADF
Automatically Deployable Emergency Locator Transmitter [*Aviation*] (DA) ... ADELT
Automatically Deployable Emergency Locator Transponder (SAUS) ... ADELT
Automatically Directed Outbound Trunk (SAUS) ... ADOT
Automatically Directed Outgoing Intertoll Trunk [*Bell System*] ... ADOIT
Automatically Directed Outgoing Trunk [*Bell System*] ... ADOT
Automatically Erectable Modular Torus ... AEMT
Automatically Generated Test Analysis and Programs (MCD) ... AGTP
Automatically Operated Inlet Valve ... AOIV
Automatically Prepunched Card (SAUS) ... APC
Automatically Processed Wire List (SAUS) ... APWL
Automatically Programmed Remote Indication Logged (or Logging) (SAUS) ... APRIL
Automatically Programmed Tool [*Computer software*] [*Computer science*] ... APT
Automatically Programmed Tool - Advanced Contouring [*IBM Corp.*] ... APT-AC
Automatically Programmed Tool - Intermediate Contouring [*IBM Corp.*] ... APT-IC
Automatically Programmed Tool Language (SAUS) ... APT Language
Automatically Programmed Tool-Basic Positioning (SAUS) ... APT-BP
Automatically Programmed Tooling (SAUS) ... APT
Automatically Programmed Tool-Integrative Graphics System (SAUS) ... APT-IGS
Automatically Programmed Tools (SAUS) ... APT
Automatically Reconfigurable Modular Multiprocessor [*or Multiprocessing*] **System** [*Computer science*] ... ARMMS
Automatically Repaired Computer (SAUS) ... ARC
Automatically Retrieved Microfilm System ... ARMS
Automatically rotatable Phase Shifter (SAUS) ... APS
Automatically Stabilized Maneuvering Unit [*NASA*] ... ASMU
Automatically Synchronous [*Remote-indicating system*] [*Trade name*] [*Western Electric Co.*] ... AUTOSYN
Automatically-Adjustable Shock-Absorber [*System*] [*Automotive engineering*] ... AAS
Automatically-Adjustable Shock-absorber (SAUS) ... AAS
Automatically-Generated Integrated Circuit (DNAB) ... AGIC
Automatiches Schaltgetriebe ... ASG
Automatic-Landing Flight Experiment [*Space program*] [*Japan*] ... AFLEX
Automatic-Landing Flight Experiment [*Space program*] [*Japan*] ... ALFLEX
Automatic/Manual (MDG) ... A/M
Automatic-Patching Verification (SAUS) ... APV
Automatic-Remote-Meter (SAUS) ... ARMETER
automatics (SAUS) ... autos
Automatics Business and Control United Systems, Inc. (SAUS) ... ABACUS
Automating Calculating Machine (SAUS) ... ACM
Automation (DS) ... A
Automation (MSA) ... AUTOMN
Automation ... AUTOMTN
Automation (AFM) ... AUTON
Automation (SAUS) ... Auton
Automation Action (SAUS) ... Automation
Automation and Control (SAUS) ... A&C
Automation and Control ... A & C
Automation and Remote Control (journ.) (SAUS) ... Automat Remote Contr
Automation and Robotics (SAUS) ... A&R
Automation and Robotics (SSD) ... A & R
Automation and Robotics Panel ... ARP
Automation and Robotics Research Institute [*University of Texas at Arlington*] [*Research center*] (RCD) ... ARRI
Automation Center (SAUO) ... AC
Automation Classification Code (SAUS) ... ACC
Automation Co. of Kentucky [*McDonnell Douglas Corp.*] ... AUT/KY
Automation Co. of Texas [*McDonnell Douglas Corp.*] ... AUT/TEX
Automation Communication Resource Management Plan [*Army*] ... ACRMP
Automation Composition System (MCD) ... ACS
Automation Control Corporation (SAUO) ... ACC
Automation Device (IAA) ... AE
Automation Economic Analysis ... AEA
Automation Engineering Laboratory ... AEL
Automation for Storage and Retrieval of Information ... AFSARI
Automation Foundation ... AF
Automation GMBH [*McDonnell Douglas Corp.*] [*Germany*] ... AUT/GMBH
Automation Industries Incorporated (SAUO) ... AII
Automation Industries Research (SAUO) ... AIRL
Automation Industries Research Laboratory (SAUS) ... AIRL
Automation Institute (MCD) ... AI
Automation Instrument Data Service [*Computer-based industrial information system*] [*Indata Ltd.*] [*British*] ... AIDS
Automation Journal of Japan (SAUS) ... amj
Automation Management Office [*Military*] (AABC) ... AMO
Automation of Bibliography through Computerization [*ABC-Clio Press*] ... ABC
Automation of Data Processing/ Computerization of Information Systems (SAUS) ... ADP/CIS
Automation of Data Processing/Computerization of Information Systems [*Food Stamp Program*] [*Department of Agriculture*] (GFGA) ... ADP/CIS
Automation of Field Observations and Services ... AFOS
Automation of Field Operations and Services [*National Weather Service*] (MSC) ... AFOS
Automation of Interlending by Microcomputer [*British*] (NITA) ... AIM
Automation of Procurement and Accounting Data Entry [*Navy*] (GFGA) ... APADE
Automation of Proofs by Mathematical Induction (SAUO) ... MIND/INDUS
Automation of Wartime Functional Supply Requirements (MCD) ... AWFSR
Automation on Air Traffic Flow Management (DA) ... AUT-ATFM
Automation One Association (SAUO) ... AIA
Automation Planning and Liaison Office (SAUS) ... APLO
Automation Planning and Technology ... APT
Automation Resource Group [*Wellesley, MA*] ... ARG
Automation Resources Management System (SAUS) ... ARMS
Automation Robotics and Machine Intelligence System (PDAA) ... ARAMIS
Automation Security Committee [*Military*] (GFGA) ... ASC
Automation Services - System Improvement - Solution and Tracking (MCD) ... ASSIST
Automation Society (EA) ... AS
Automation Source Data (SAUS) ... SDA
Automation System for Scientific Experiments ... ASSE
Automation Systems Manager (WDAA) ... ASM
Automation Techniques, Inc. ... ATI
Automation Techniques, Incorporated (SAUO) ... ATI
Automation Technology Center [*Vicksburg, MS*] [*Army*] ... ATC
Automation Test Facility (AAEL) ... ATF
Automation Training Center (MCD) ... ATC
Automatische Korpsstamunetz [*Tactical Communications System*] [*Germany*] ... Autoko
Automatische Wetterstation (SAUS) ... AWSt
Automatischer Datenme¤platz (SAUS) ... ADaM
Automatischer Thermodesorber-Gaschromatograph (SAUS) ... ATD-GC
Automatisering Landbouwkundige Dokumentatie-En Informatievespreiding in Nederland [*Automation of Agricultural Documentation and Information in the Netherlands*] [*Centre for Agricultural Publishing and Documentation*] (NITA) ... ALADIN
Automative Student Service Educational Training ... ASSET
Automator Control Language [*Computer science*] ... ACL
Auto-Mechanic (SAUS) ... AM
Automedica Corp. [*An association*] [*Defunct*] (EA) ... AM
Automic Fire Control System [*Army*] ... AFSC
Automicrobic System ... AMS
Automix Keyboards, Inc. ... AKI
Automix Keyboards Incorporated (SAUO) ... AKI
Automized Medical Anamnesis Dialog Assistant [*Computer*] ... AMANDA

Automobil Versuchs- und Untersuchungs Strecke [*Automobile Test Track*] [*Department of Energy*] ... AVUS
Automobile ... A
Automobile ... AU
Automobile ... AUTO
Automobile (ADWA) ... auto
Automobile Accident (CPH) ... AA
Automobile Accident, Broadside (MELL) ... AABS
Automobile Accident, Rear End (MELL) ... AARE
Automobile, Aerospace and Agricultural Implement Workers of America (SAUS) ... AAAIWA
Automobile, Aerospace, and Agricultural Implement Workers of America (SAUO) ... AAAIWA
Automobile and Miscellaneous Sales Transactions Office (SAUO) ... AMSTO
Automobile Association (SAUO) ... AA
Automobile Association [*British*] ... AA
Automobile Association and Motor (SAUO) ... AA&MU
Automobile Association of America (SAUO) ... AA of A
Automobile Association of Bengal (SAUO) ... AAB
Automobile Association of Malysia, Penang (SAUO) ... AAM
Automobile Association of South India (SAUO) ... AASI
Automobile Builders' Combination Designed Especially for Getting Hitler including Japan [*Suggested name for Automotive Council for War Production*] [*World War II*] ... ABCDEFGHIJ
Automobile Cases [*Commerce Clearing House*] [*A publication*] (DLA) ... Auto C
Automobile Cases [*Commerce Clearing House*] [*A publication*] (DLA) ... Auto Cas
Automobile Cases, Second Series [*Commerce Clearing House*] [*A publication*] (DLA) ... Auto Cas 2d
Automobile Club ... AC
Automobile Club of America (SAUO) ... ACA
Automobile Club of France (SAUO) ... ACF
Automobile Club of Great Britain and Ireland (SAUO) ... ACGBI
Automobile Club of Great Britain and Ireland [*Later, Royal Automobile Club*] ... ACGBI
Automobile Club of Italy (BARN) ... ACI
Automobile Club of Philadelphia, Philadelphia, PA [*Library symbol*] [*Library of Congress*] [*Obsolete*] (LCLS) ... PPAuC
Automobile Club of Southern California (GEOI) ... ACSC
Automobile Competition Committee for the United States (SAUO) ... ACCUS
Automobile Competition Committee for the United States FIA [*Federation Internationale de l'Automobile*] (EA) ... ACCUS
Automobile Dealers Association (SAUO) ... AD
Automobile Dealers Association ... ADA
Automobile Dealers Association of Indiana (SRA) ... ADAI
Automobile Dealers Association of North Dakota (SRA) ... ADAND
Automobile Dealers Parts Association ... ADPA
Automobile Defog/Defrost System Model (PDAA) ... ADSYM
Automobile Defog-defrost System Model (SAUS) ... ADSYM
Automobile Drivers Radio Information [*System for turning on car radio automatically, e.g. important messages*] (NITA) ... ARi
Automobile Engineering and Manufacturing [*Commercial firm*] [*British*] ... AEM
Automobile Fuel Efficiency Act [*1980*] ... AFEA
Automobile Importer of America (SAUS) ... AIA
Automobile Importers Compliance Association [*Defunct*] (EA) ... AICA
Automobile Importers of America [*Later, AIAM*] (EA) ... AIA
Automobile Industry Action Group (SAUO) ... AIAG
Automobile Information Data Advertising (SAUS) ... AIDA
Automobile Information Disclosure Act [*1958*] ... AIDA
Automobile Insurance Cases [*Commerce Clearing House*] [*A publication*] (DLA) ... Auto Ins Cas
Automobile Labor Board ... ALB
Automobile Law Reporter [*Commerce Clearing House*] [*A publication*] (DLA) ... Auto L Rep
Automobile Leading and Information (SAUS) ... ALI
Automobile Legal Association [*Defunct*] (EA) ... ALA
Automobile Liability [*Insurance*] ... AL
Automobile License Plate Collectors Association (EA) ... ALPCA
Automobile Magazine (journ.) (SAUS) ... Auto Mag
Automobile Manufacturers' Association [*Later, MVMA*] (EA) ... AMA
Automobile Manufacturers Association (SAUO) ... AMA
Automobile Manufacturers Association, Inc., Detroit (SAUS) ... MiDAMA
Automobile Manufacturers' Association, Inc., Detroit, MI [*Library symbol*] [*Library of Congress*] (LCLS) ... MiDAMA
Automobile Mechanic Training Evaluation Project [*Southern Association of Colleges and Schools*] (EDAC) ... AMTEP
Automobile Mutual Insurance Company of America (SAUO) ... AMICA
Automobile Objets d'Art Club (EA) ... AODC
Automobile Owners Action Council [*Defunct*] (EA) ... AOAC
Automobile Parts [*Freight*] ... AUTO PTS
Automobile Parts (SAUS) ... Auto Pts
Automobile Physical Damage [*Insurance*] ... APD
Automobile Protection Association [*Canada*] ... APA
Automobile Protection Corp. [*NASDAQ symbol*] (NQ) ... APCO
Automobile Protection Corp. [*Associated Press*] (SAG) ... AutProt
Automobile Protection-APCO [*NASDAQ symbol*] (TTSB) ... APCO
Automobile Racing Club (SAUO) ... ARC
Automobile Racing Club of America ... ARCA
Automobile Road Information [*Traffic management*] ... ARI
Automobile Safe Driving Center (SAUO) ... ASDC
Automobile Seat Cover Association of America (EA) ... ASCAA
Automobile Shredder Residue ... ASR
Automobile Traffic Density (SAUS) ... ATD
Automobile Transporters Tariff Bureau, Inc. (SAUO) ... ATB
Automobile Transporters Tariff Bureau, Inc., Southfield MI [*STAC*] ... ATB
Automobile Utility Trailer Rental Association (EA) ... AUTRA
automobiles (SAUS) ... autos
Automobili Turismo Sport [*Auto manufacturing company*] [*Italy*] ... ATS
Automobilvertriebs Aktiengesellschaft [*Austria*] [*ICAO designator*] (FAAC) ... MBA
Automobil-Werke Eisenach [*Automobile manufacturer*] [*Germany*] ... AWE
Automotive (MUGU) ... AUTMV
Automotive (MSA) ... AUTOM
Automotive ... AUTOMTV
Automotive (AABC) ... AUTOMV
Automotive Accessories Manufacturers of America (MHDB) ... AAMA
Automotive Advertisers Council [*Chicago, IL*] (EA) ... AAC
Automotive Affiliated Representatives (EA) ... AAR
Automotive Affliated Rcpresentatives (SAUS) ... AAR
Automotive Aftermarket News [*A publication*] ... AAN
Automotive Aftermarket Professional [*AWDA University*] ... AAP
Automotive Air Conditioning Association [*Later, IMACA*] (EA) ... AACA
Automotive and Construction Equipment Overhaul and Repair Plant [*Navy*] ... ACEORP
Automotive and Construction Equipment Parts Depot [*Navy*] ... ACEPD
Automotive Battery Charger Manufacturers Council [*Defunct*] (EA) ... ABCMC
Automotive Billing Module [*GSA*] (TAG) ... AUTOBILL
Automotive Body Parts Association (NTPA) ... ABPA
Automotive Booster Clubs International (EA) ... ABC
Automotive Booster Clubs International (EA) ... ABCI
Automotive Bridge Launching Equipment (SAUS) ... ABLE
Automotive Chemical Manufacturers Council (EA) ... ACMC
Automotive Climate Control ... ACC
Automotive Committee for Air Defense [*World War II*] ... ACAD
Automotive Communications Council (NTPA) ... ACC
Automotive Competitive Assessment Data Bank [*Ward's Research*] [*Database*] ... COMPASS
Automotive Component Group [*Automotive engineering*] ... ACG
Automotive Composites Consortium ... ACC
Automotive Composities Consortium [*General Motors Corp., Ford Motor Co., and Chrysler Corp.*] ... ACC
Automotive Consortium on Recycling and Disposal [*Industry research group*] ... ACORD
Automotive Consumer Action Program (EA) ... AUTOCAP
Automotive Cooling Systems Institute (EA) ... ACSI
Automotive Crash Injury Research ... ACIR
Automotive Development Group [*LTV Steel Corp.*] ... ADG
Automotive Diesel Fuel ... ADF
Automotive Diesel Oil (ADA) ... ADO
Automotive Dismantlers and Recyclers Association (EA) ... ADRA
Automotive Distillate Oil (ADA) ... ADO
Automotive Electric Association [*ASIA*] [*Absorbed by*] (EA) ... AEA
Automotive Electric Association (SAUO) ... AEA
Automotive Electronics Conference and Exposition (SAUO) ... AECE
Automotive Emissions and Fuel Economy Office [*Division of automaker certifying compliance with government exhaust emission and fuel economy standards*] ... AEFEO
Automotive Energy Efficiency Program [*Department of Transportation*] ... AEEP
Automotive Engine Rebuilders Association (EA) ... AERA
Automotive Engine Rebuilders Association. Service Bulletin [*A publication*] (EAAP) ... SB
Automotive Engine Rebuilders Association. Service Bulletin (journ.) (SAUS) ... AERA SB
Automotive Engine Rebuilders Association. Technical Bulletin [*A publication*] (EAAP) ... TB
Automotive Engine Rebuilders Association. Technical Bulletin (journ.) (SAUS) ... AERA TB
Automotive Engineering (journ.) (SAUS) ... Automot Eng
Automotive Exhaust Research Institute [*Defunct*] (EA) ... AERI
Automotive Exhaust Systems Manufacturers Council (EA) ... AESMC
Automotive Exhibitors' Association of South Australia ... AEASA
Automotive Filter Manufacturers Council [*Later, FMC*] (EA) ... AFMC
Automotive Filter Manufacturers Council (SAUS) ... AFMC
Automotive Fine Arts Society ... AFAS
Automotive Fleet and Leasing Association (EA) ... AFLA
Automotive Gas Turbine (ACAE) ... AGT
Automotive Hall of Fame ... AHOF
Automotive Industrial Motor ... AIM
Automotive Industries [*A publication*] ... AI
Automotive Industries Association of Canada ... AIA
Automotive Industries Association of Canada ... AIAC
Automotive Industry Action Group (EA) ... AIAG
Automotive Industry Data [*British*] ... AID
Automotive Industry Matters [*A publication*] (ADA) ... AIM
Automotive Information Council (EA) ... AIC
Automotive Information Management System [*Computer software*] [*Automotive engineering*] ... AIMS
Automotive Information Network Service ... AINS
Automotive Information Test (AABC) ... AIT
Automotive Layshaft Transmission ... ALT
Automotive Legislative Council of America (EA) ... ALCA
Automotive Lift Institute (EA) ... ALI
Automotive List Classification and Profile Production (CIST) ... ALCAPP
Automotive Machine & Parts Association ... AMPA
Automotive Maintenance and Repair Association ... AMRA
Automotive Manufacturers Association (SAUO) ... AMA
Automotive Manufacturers EDP [*Electronic Data Processing*] **Council** (EA) ... AMEDPC
Automotive Market Research Council (SAUO) ... AMCR
Automotive Market Research Council (EA) ... AMRC
Automotive Mechanical and Electrical [*Test*] ... AME
Automotive Mechanics Modular Integrated Training System (SAUO) ... AMMITS

Automotive, Metal, and Engineering Union .... AMEU
Automotive Mutual Insurance Company (SAUO) .... AMIC
Automotive Network Exchange (SAUS) .... ANX
Automotive Occupant Protection Association (EA) .... AOPA
Automotive Occupant Restraints Council (EA) .... AORC
Automotive Oil Change Association (NTPA) .... AOCA
Automotive Organization Team (EA) .... AOT
Automotive Original Equipment Manufacturers .... AOEM
Automotive Parts and Accessories Association (EA) .... APAA
Automotive Parts Association of the Carolinas (SRA) .... APAC
Automotive Parts Manufacturers' Association [Association des Fabricants de
   Pieces d'Automobile] (AC) .... APMA
Automotive Parts Rebuilders Association (EA) .... APRA
Automotive Payment Module [GSA] (TAG) .... AUTOPAY
Automotive Performance Execution and Layout .... APEAL
Automotive Pigeon Loft .... APL
Automotive Planners Handbook (SAUS) .... APH
Automotive Presidents Council (EA) .... APC
Automotive Press Association .... APA
Automotive Products [Commercial firm] [British] .... AP
Automotive Products Emissions Committee (EA) .... APEC
Automotive Products Export Council [Defunct] (EA) .... APEC
Automotive Products Trade Act of 1965 .... APTA
Automotive Professional Training (SAUS) .... APT
Automotive Public Relations Council (EA) .... APRC
Automotive Recyclers Association [Salvage yards] .... ARA
Automotive Recyclers of Indiana (SRA) .... ARI
Automotive Recycling Industry of Nebraska (SRA) .... ARIN
Automotive Refrigeration Products Institute (EA) .... ARPI
Automotive Repair Management Systems [3M Co.] .... ARMS
Automotive Research and Marketing Services .... ARMS
Automotive Restoration Market Organization .... ARMO
Automotive Retailers Association [Canada] .... ARA
Automotive Safety Foundation (EA) .... ASF
Automotive Sales Council (EA) .... ASC
Automotive Satellite Television Network [Automotive engineering] .... ASTN
Automotive Sensor Instrumentation System (ACAE) .... ASIS
Automotive Sensor Instrumentation System Van [Automotive
   engineering] .... ASIS
Automotive Service Association (EA) .... ASA
Automotive Service Association of Georgia (SRA) .... ASAG
Automotive Service Councils [Later, ASA] (EA) .... ASC
Automotive Service Education Program [General Motors] (EDAC) ...... ASEP
Automotive Service Excellence .... ASE
Automotive Service Industry Association (EA) .... ASIA
Automotive Service Reports [A publication] (EAAP) .... ASR
Automotive Services Marketing Association [Canada] .... ASMA
Automotive Specialty Warehouse .... ASW
Automotive Study Unit [American Topical Association] (EA) ... ASU
Automotive Tank Purchase Description (SAUS) .... ATPD
Automotive Technicians Association International (EA) .... ATA
Automotive Technologies Corp. (SAUO) .... AHA
Automotive Technology .... AMT
Automotive Test Rig [Military] (RDA) .... ATR
Automotive Trade Association Executives (EA) .... ATAE
Automotive Trade Association Managers [Later, ATAE] ...... ATAM
Automotive Trades Association Inc. (AC) .... ATA
Automotive Training Managers Council (EA) .... ATMC
Automotive Transportation Center [Purdue University] [Research center]
   (RCD) .... ATC
Automotive Vehicle Manufacturers Association (SAUO) ..... AVMA
Automotive Warehouse Distributors Association (EA) .... AWDA
Automotive Wholesalers Association Executives (EA) .... AWAE
Automotive Wholesalers Association of Alabama and Georgia (SRA) ..... AWAAG
Automotive Wholesalers Association of Tennessee (SRA) .... AWAT
Automotive Wholesalers of Arizona (SRA) .... AWOA
Automotive Wholesalers of Illinois (SRA) .... AWOI
Automotive Wholesalers of New England (SRA) .... AWANE
Automotive Wholesalers of Oklahoma (SRA) .... AWO
Automotive Wholesalers of Texas (SRA) .... AWOT
Automotive Youth Employment Services .... AYES
Automotors Salta SACYF [Argentina] [ICAO designator] (FAAC) ...... LES
Automovil Club Argentino (GEOI) .... ACA
Automovile Journalists Association of Canada [Association des Journalistes
   Automobile du Canada] (AC) .... AJAC
Automtic Synthesis Program (SAUS) .... ASP
Automtic Variable Perforating (SAUS) .... AVP
Automtic Volume Control (SAUS) .... avc
AutoNation, Inc. [NYSE symbol] (SG) .... AN
Autonetics (KSC) .... AN
Autonetics Base-Line Equipment .... ABLE
Autonetics Business & Control United Systems, Inc. .... ABACUS
Autonetics Business and Control United Systems, Inc. (SAUO) ...... ABACUS
Autonetics General Information Learning Equipment .... AGILE
Autonetics Generalized Reset .... AGR
Autonetics ICBM Systems Division (SAUS) .... AISD
Autonetics Kalman Optimum Reset (SAUS) .... ANKOR
Autonetics Kalman Utilization of Reference for Optimal Navigation
   (MCD) .... AKURON
Autonetics Modular Airborne RADAR System .... AMARS
Autonetics Modular Airborne Radar System (SAUS) .... AMARS
Autonetics Strategic Systems Division (SAUS) .... ASSD
Autonome Transfer Unit [Computer science] (DIT) .... ATU
Autonomes Marine System (SAUS) .... AMS
Autonomic Blocking Agent (LDT) .... ABA

Autonomic Dysreflexia [Neurology] (DAVI) .... AD
Autonomic Hyperreflexia [Medicine] .... AH
Autonomic Hyperreflexia [Medicine] (MEDA) .... AHR
Autonomic Lability Score [In ion detection] .... ALS
Autonomic Nervous System [Medicine] .... ANS
Autonomic Nervous System Disorder [Medicine] (MELL) .... ANSD
Autonomic Nervous System Dysfunction [Medicine] (MELL) ... ANSD
Autonomic Neuropathy [Medicine] (MELL) .... AN
Autonomic Perception Questionnaire [Psychology] (EDAC) ... APQ
Autonomous .... AUT
Autonomous (SAUS) .... Auton
Autonomous Aerial Vehicle (SAUS) .... AAV
Autonomous Air Vehicle [Drone-formerly RPV] [Military] (DOMA) ..... AAV
Autonomous Air Vehicle Avionics Suite/Intelligence Munition
   (SAUS) .... AAVAS/IM
Autonomous Anarchist Groups [Spanish] (PD) .... GAS
Autonomous Area .... AA
Autonomous Benthic Explorer [Oceanography] .... ABE
Autonomous Control Subsystem (SAUS) .... ACS
Autonomous Data Transfer .... ADT
Autonomous Domain (VERA) .... AD
Autonomous Energy-Efficiency Index (SAUS) .... AEEI
Autonomous Expendable CTD profiler (SAUS) .... AXCTD
Autonomous Fire and Forget [Military] .... AFAF
Autonomous Free-Flight Dispenser System [Air Force] ...... AFDS
Autonomous Functional Unit (SAUS) .... AFU
Autonomous Guidance for Conventional Weapons [Air Force] .... AGCW
Autonomous Guided Bomb (ACAE) .... AGB
Autonomous Guided Weapon (DOMA) .... AGW
Autonomous Helicopter System [Military] (LAIN) .... AHS
Autonomous Homing Munitions (SAUS) .... AHM
Autonomous Infantry Mortar [Military] (INF) .... AIM
Autonomous Infrared Sensor (ACAE) .... AIRS
Autonomous Intelligent Cruise Control [Automotive engineering] ..... AICC
Autonomous Lagrangian Circulation Explorer [Oceanography] .... ALACE
Autonomous Lagrangian Circulation Explorer (SAUS) .... ALACE
Autonomous Land Vehicle [Military] (RDA) .... ALV
Autonomous Land Vehicle in a Neural Network [Military] .... ALVINN
Autonomous Learner Index .... ALI
Autonomous Line Scanning Unit (MCD) .... ALSU
Autonomous Listening Station (SAUS) .... ALS
Autonomous Listening Stations [Instrumentation] .... ALS
Autonomous Lock-On After Launch (MCD) .... ALOAL
Autonomous Machine Environmental Surveillance System (SAUS) ..... AMESS
Autonomous Maintenance Unit (ACAE) .... AMU
Autonomous Marine Power Source [Navy] .... AMPS
Autonomous Missile Site RADAR (AABC) .... AMSR
Autonomous Multiplexer Channel .... AMC
Autonomous Navigation System .... ANS
Autonomous Navigation System Concept (SAUS) .... ANCS
Autonomous Navigation System Concept (MCD) .... ANSC
Autonomous Navigation Technology (MCD) .... ANT
Autonomous Oblast [Former USSR] .... AO
Autonomous Onboard Computing Complex (ACAE) .... ABKK
Autonomous Payload Control System (SAUS) .... APCS
Autonomous Payload Controller (SAUS) .... APC
Autonomous Precision Approach and Landing System [Lockheed-Martin's
   radical landing-guidance system] .... APALS
Autonomous Precision-Guided Munition [NATO] .... APGM
Autonomous Processing Element (SAUS) .... APE
Autonomous Radio Frequency Target Identification Classification
   (ACAE) .... ARFTIC
Autonomous Remotely Controlled Submersible [Autonomous underwater
   vehicle] .... ARCS
Autonomous Replication Core-Consensus Sequence [Genetics] ..... ACS
Autonomous Replication Sequence [Genetics] .... ARS
Autonomous Republic .... AR
Autonomous Scout Rotorcraft Testbed [Army] .... ASRT
Autonomous Sequential Machine (SAUS) .... ASM
Autonomous Service, Standardisation Directorate and Quality
   Accreditation (SAUS) .... SENORCA
Autonomous Soviet Socialist Republic .... ASSR
Autonomous Space Processor for Orbital Debris (SAUS) .... ASPOD
Autonomous Spacecraft Maintenance (MCD) .... ASM
Autonomous Stand-Off Missile (SAUS) .... ASOM
Autonomous Strike Platform (ACAE) .... ASP
Autonomous Switch Unit [Telecommunications] (NITA) ...... ASU
Autonomous Synthetic Aperture Radar Guidance (ACAE) ... ASARG
Autonomous System [Computer science] (DDC) .... AS
Autonomous System Border Router (SAUS) .... ASBR
Autonomous System Boundary Router (SAUS) .... ASBR
Autonomous System Number .... ASN
Autonomous Tactical All-Weather Strike (MCD) .... ATAWS
Autonomous Tech [NASDAQ symbol] (TTSB) .... ATCI
Autonomous Technologies Corp. [NASDAQ symbol] (SAG) ... ATCI
Autonomous Technologies Corp. [Associated Press] (SAG) ... AutonoT
Autonomous Temperature Line Acquisition System [Moorings] [Marine
   science] (OSRA) .... ATLAS
Autonomous Terminal Homing [Air Force] .... ATH
Autonomous Terminal Homing Program (MCD) .... ATHP
Autonomous Thermal Homing Program (ACAE) .... ATHP
Autonomous Thyroid Nodule (SAUS) .... ATN
Autonomous Transfer Unit (SAUS) .... ATU
Autonomous Undersea (or Underwater) Vehicle (SAUS) ..... AUV
Autonomous Underwater Vehicle [Navy] .... AUV

Autonomous Universal Seeker Study (ACAE)	AUSS
Autonomous Unmanned Reconnaissance Aircraft (SAUS)	AURA
Autonomously Functioning Thyroid Nodule [Endocrinology]	AFTN
Autonomously Functioning Thyroid Nodule [Endocrinology]	ATN
Autonomously Replicating Sequence [Genetics]	ARS
Autonomy (SAUS)	Auton
Auto-Oxidation Inhibitor (BARN)	AI
Autophagic Vacuole [Botany]	AV
Auto-Photovoltaic Measurement (SAUS)	APV-Measurement
Autopilot and Flight Director (SAUS)	APFD
Autopilot Capsule	A/PC
Autopilot Control (AAG)	A/P CTL
Auto-Pilot Controller (SAUS)	APC
Autopilot Controller (SAUS)	APC
Autopilot Disengage Switch (MCD)	ADS
Autopilot Flight Director	APFD
Autopilot Flight Director System (GAVI)	AFDS
Autopilot Ground Control Unit (AAG)	AGCU
Autopilot Ground Control Unit	APGCU
Autopilot Mode Selector	AMS
Autopilot Monitor (AAG)	A/P MON
Autopilot Monitor and Control Unit	A/P MCU
Autopilot Positioning Indicator	A/P POI
Autopilot Rate Control	ARC
Autopilot Surface Servo	ASS
Autopilot Test Monitor (AAG)	A/P TSTMN
Autopilot Test Monitor (SAUS)	A/PTSTMN
Autopilot Test Programmer (AAG)	A/P TSTPG
Autopilot Unit (ACAE)	APU
Autopilot Zero	APO
Autopiloted Vehicle	APV
Autoplot Controller (IEEE)	APC
Auto-Power Spectral Densities (SAUS)	APSDs
AutoPrep 5000 Users Group (EA)	APUG
Auto-Preparation 5000 Users Group (SAUO)	APUG
Autoprogramming Compiler (SAUS)	Autocompiler
Autoprompter (SAUS)	Autogrom
Auto-Protocol Converter (SAUS)	APC
Autopsy [Also, AUT] [Medicine]	AU
Autopsy [Also, AU] [Medicine]	AUT
Autopsy (SAUS)	Autop
Autoquote [Computer science] (TEL)	AQ
Autoradiographic	AR
Autoradiographic Immunoassay (MCD)	ARIA
Autoradiography [Medicine] (DAVI)	AR
Autoradiography	ARG
Autorefraction (SAUS)	AR
Auto-Refresh Direct Memory Access [Computer science] (PDAA)	ARDMA
Auto-Refrigerated Cascade (SAUS)	ARC
Autoregressive [Mathematical bioscience]	AR
Autoregressive Conditional Heteroscedastic [Electronics] (PCM)	ARCH
Autoregressive Moving Average [Statistics]	ARMA
Auto-Regressive Random Field (PDAA)	ARF
Autoregressive-Integrated-Moving-Average [Statistics]	ARIMA
Auto-Regulated Inspiratory Support [Medicine] (DMAA)	ARIS
Auto-Resonant Accelerator [For atomic particles]	ARA
Auto-Restricted Zone [Environmental Protection Agency] (GFGA)	ARZ
Autoroute (DD)	aut
Autosampler	AS
Autosomal Dominant [Genetics]	AD
Autosomal Dominant Disease [Medicine] (MELL)	ADD
Autosomal Dominant Disorder [Medicine] (MELL)	ADD
autosomal dominant familial aniridia (SAUS)	AN1
Autosomal Dominant Non-Syndromic Hearing Loss	ADNSHL
Autosomal Dominant Polycystic Kidney Disease [Medicine]	ADPKD
Autosomal Dominant Retinitis Pigmentosa [Ophthalmology]	ADRP
Autosomal Dominant Vitreo-Retinochoroidopathy [Medicine] (DMAA)	ADVIRC
Autosomal Dominant-Progressive External Ophthalmoplegia	AD-PEO
Autosomal Recessive [Genetics]	AR
Autosomal Recessive Disease [Medicine] (MELL)	ARD
Autosomal Recessive Disorder [Medicine] (MELL)	ARD
Autosomal Recessive Distal Muscular Dystrophy [Medicine]	ARDMD
Autosomal Recessive Juvenile Parkinsonism [Medicine]	AR-JP
Autosomal Recessive Polycystic Disease [Medicine] (DMAA)	ARPD
Autosomal Recessive Polycystic Kidney Disease [Medicine]	ARPKD
Autosomal-Dominant Compelling Helioophthalmic Outburst	ACHOO
Autosomal-dominant Compelling Helio-Ophthalmic Outburst (SAUS)	ACHOO
Autosome [Genetics]	A
AutoSpa Corp. (SAUO)	LUBE
Autostart Job Entry (SAUS)	AJE
Autostore (SAUS)	AS
Autothrottle [Aerospace]	A/T
Auto-Throttle Actuator (MCD)	ATA
Auto-Throttle Actuator Assembly (MCD)	ATAA
Autothrust System (GAVI)	ATHR
Autotote Corp. [Associated Press] (SAG)	Autotote
Autotote Corp. [NASDAQ symbol] (NQ)	TOTE
Autotote Corp. Cl'A' [AMEX symbol] (TTSB)	TTE
Auto-Trace Steam Analysis Program [Computer software]	ASAP
Autotrack Detector Equipment (ACAE)	ADE
Autotrack Interface Processor (ACAE)	AIP
Autotrack Vulcan Air Defense System	AVADS
Autotransformer	AUTOTR
Autotransformer Starter (SAUS)	Autostarter
Auto-trol Technology [NASDAQ symbol] (TTSB)	ATTC

Auto-Trol Technology Corp. [NASDAQ symbol] (NQ)	ATTC
Autotumorolytic Factor [Oncology]	ATF
Autotuned [NAVAID, Navigational Aid] (GAVI)	A
Autovend Technology Corp. [Vancouver Stock Exchange symbol]	AVT
Auto-Voltage Regulator (SAUS)	AVR
AUTOVON (MCD)	AV
AUTOVON Centralized Alarm System	ACAS
Autoweb.com, Inc. [NASDAQ symbol] (SG)	AWEB
Autozone, Inc. [Associated Press] (SAG)	AutoZone
AutoZone Inc. [NYSE symbol] (TTSB)	AZO
Autralasian Quaternary Association (QUAC)	AQUA
Autrex, Inc. [Toronto Stock Exchange symbol]	AUT
Autry Family Association	AFA
Autumn	Au
Autumn	AUT
Autumn (WDAA)	aut
Autumn Circulation Experiment [Denmark, Great Britain, Norway, West Germany] [1987-88] [Oceanography]	ACE
Autumnal Equinox	AE
Autumn-Burned [Ecology]	A
Autun/Bellevue [France] [ICAO location identifier] (ICLI)	LFQF
Aux Bons Soins De [Care Of, c/o] [Correspondence] [French]	ABS
Aux Soins De [Care Of, c/o] [French]	A/S
Aux Soins De [Care Of, c/o] [French]	A/S DE
Auxaire-Bretagne [ICAO designator] (AD)	BS
Auxerre/Moneteau [France] [ICAO location identifier] (ICLI)	LFLA
Auxilary Data System [Computer science] (VERA)	ADS
Auxiliaries (SAUS)	AUXS
Auxiliaries Design Assistance Programme (SAUS)	ADAP
Auxiliaries Flotilla (SAUO)	AUXFLOT
Auxiliaries of Our Lady of the Cenacle (EA)	AOLC
Auxiliaries of the Blessed Sacrament (TOCD)	ABS
Auxiliary (DNAB)	A
Auxiliary (AFM)	AUX
Auxiliary (WDMC)	aux
Auxiliary	AUXIL
Auxiliary (SAUS)	AUXY
Auxiliary Acceleration Pump [Automotive engineering]	AAP
Auxiliary Accumulator (SAUS)	AA
Auxiliary Active Digital Display (SAUS)	A2D
Auxiliary Active Digital Display [Sonar] (DNAB)	AADD
Auxiliary Active Digital Display [Sonar] (DNAB)	A^{2D}
Auxiliary Aiming Mark [Target] (IAA)	AAM
Auxiliary Air Control [Automotive engineering]	AAC
Auxiliary Air Force [Later, R Aux AF] [British]	AAF
Auxiliary Air Force (SAUO)	AFA
Auxiliary Air Force Base	AAFB
Auxiliary Air Force Base Unit (SAUO)	AAFBU
Auxiliary Air Force General List [British military] (DMA)	AAFGL
Auxiliary Air Force Reserve [British]	AAFR
Auxiliary Air Force Reserve (SAUO)	AAFR
Auxiliary Air Force Reserve of Officers (SAUO)	AAFRO
Auxiliary Air Unit (SAUO)	AAU
Auxiliary Air Units [Naval Reserve]	AAU
Auxiliary Airborne Command Post (MCD)	AUXCP
Auxiliary Airborne Power Plant	AAPP
Auxiliary Airborne Power Plant (SAUS)	AAPP
Auxiliary Airborne Power Unit (SAUS)	AAPU
Auxiliary Aircraft Carrier [Navy symbol]	ACV
Auxiliary Aircraft Landing Training Ship (SAUS)	AVT
Auxiliary Aircraft Training Ship	AVT
Auxiliary Aircraft Transport [Navy symbol] [Obsolete]	AVT
Auxiliary Aircraft Warning Service	AAWS
Auxiliary Algorithm (SAUS)	AA
Auxiliary Ambulance Service (DAS)	AAS
Auxiliary Ambulance Service (SAUO)	AAS
Auxiliary Amplifier (AAG)	XA
Auxiliary and Fuel Handling Building [Nuclear energy] (NUCP)	AFHB
Auxiliary and Power Conversion Systems Branch (SAUO)	APCSB
Auxiliary and RADWASTE Area Ventilation System [Nuclear energy] (NRCH)	ARAVS
Auxiliary Apple Unix (SAUS)	AUX
Auxiliary Area Emergency Gas Treatment System [Nuclear energy] (NRCH)	AAEGTS
Auxiliary Area Environmental Control System [Nuclear energy] (NRCH)	AAECS
Auxiliary Array Antenna [Army]	AAA
Auxiliary Array Guard Band [Military]	AAGB
Auxiliary Array Signal Band [Military]	AASB
Auxiliary Artillery Corps [British military] (DMA)	AAC
Auxiliary Assembly [JETDS nomenclature]	AA
Auxiliary Attitude Control System [Aviation] (MCD)	AACS
Auxiliary Aviation Weather Facility (PIPO)	AAWF
Auxiliary Balance Line Evaluation [Nuclear energy] (NUCP)	ABLE
Auxiliary Ballast Tank	ABT
Auxiliary Barracks Ship (Self-Propelled) (DNAB)	APB
Auxiliary Battery Acquisition RADAR (MCD)	ABAR
Auxiliary Battery Acquisition Radar (SAUS)	ABAR
Auxiliary Beam Positioning (ACAE)	ABP
Auxiliary Boiler [of a ship]	AXB
Auxiliary Boiler Survey [of a ship] (DS)	AXBS
Auxiliary Box (SAUS)	AUXBOX
Auxiliary Building Filter System [Nuclear energy] (NRCH)	ABFS
Auxiliary Building Gas Treatment System [Nuclear energy] (NRCH)	ABGTS
Auxiliary Building Isolation [Nuclear energy] (NRCH)	ABI
Auxiliary Building Special Ventilation System [Nuclear energy] (NRCH)	ABSVS

Auxiliary Building Sump [*Nuclear energy*] (IEEE) .... ABS
Auxiliary Building Sump Tank [*Nuclear energy*] (NRCH) .... ABST
Auxiliary Building Ventilation [*Nuclear energy*] (NRCH) .... ABV
Auxiliary Business Service Organization (SAUO) .... ABSO
Auxiliary Carry Flag (VERA) .... AF
Auxiliary Checkpoint .... ACP
Auxiliary Coastal Minesweepers [*Navy symbol*] .... AMC
Auxiliary Coastguard [*British*] .... ACG
Auxiliary Code Storage [*Computer memory*] (NITA) .... ACS
Auxiliary Combat Information Center .... ACIC
Auxiliary Command .... AC
Auxiliary Command Post (SAA) .... ACP
Auxiliary Command Post (SAUO) .... AUXCP
Auxiliary Communications .... AUX COMMO
Auxiliary Communications, Navigation & Identification Panel (SAUS) .... ACNIP
Auxiliary Component Cooling Water System [*Nuclear energy*] (NRCH) ..... ACCWS
Auxiliary Computer Input Multiplexer .... ACIM
Auxiliary Computer Power Unit .... ACPU
Auxiliary Computer Room [*Apollo*] [*NASA*] .... ACR
Auxiliary Conditioning Unit .... ACU
Auxiliary Console (SAA) .... AC
Auxiliary Contractor Logistic Support [*Military*] .... ACLS
Auxiliary Control Element (SAUS) .... ACE
Auxiliary Control Panel [*Aerospace*] (AAG) .... ACP
Auxiliary Control Process (SAUS) .... ACP
Auxiliary Control Propulsion System (SAUS) .... ACPS
Auxiliary Control Station (SAUS) .... ACS
Auxiliary Controller Bus (SAUS) .... ACB
Auxiliary Conversion Equipment .... ACE
Auxiliary Cooling Loop (SAUS) .... ACL
Auxiliary Cooling System [*Nuclear energy*] (NRCH) .... ACS
Auxiliary Core Memory [*Computer science*] (MCD) .... ACM
Auxiliary Core Storage [*Computer science*] (BUR) .... ACS
Auxiliary Core Store (SAUS) .... ACS
Auxiliary Crane Ship [*Navy symbol*] .... TACS
Auxiliary Crew Compartment (MCD) .... ACC
Auxiliary Current Transformer .... AuCT
Auxiliary Data Acquisition Unit [*Computer science*] (MHDI) .... ADAU
Auxiliary Data Annotation Set [*or System*] .... ADAS
Auxiliary Data Processing Equipment .... ADPE
Auxiliary Data Record (ACAE) .... ADR
Auxiliary Data Transfer Unit (SAUS) .... ADTU
Auxiliary Data Translator Unit .... ADTU
Auxiliary Deception Generator (MCD) .... ADG
Auxiliary Deep Submergence Support Ship [*Navy symbol*] (NVT) .... AGDS
Auxiliary Detonating Fuze (SAUS) .... ADF
Auxiliary Detonation Fuze (NG) .... ADF
Auxiliary Display Equipment Group (KSC) .... ADEG
Auxiliary Display Request Keyboard .... ADRK
Auxiliary Display Unit .... ADU
Auxiliary Display-Remote View (ACAE) .... ADRV
Auxiliary Drum (CET) .... AXD
Auxiliary Emission Control Device [*Automotive engineering*] .... AECD
Auxiliary Encoder (or Encoding) System (SAUS) .... AES
Auxiliary Encoder System .... AES
Auxiliary Engineering Signal Processor .... AESP
Auxiliary Equation [*Mathematics*] (OA) .... AE
Auxiliary Equipment (KSC) .... AE
Auxiliary Equipment Building [*Nuclear energy*] (NRCH) .... AEB
Auxiliary Essential Raw Cooling Water [*Nuclear energy*] (NRCH) .... AERCW
Auxiliary Feed [*Nuclear energy*] (NRCH) .... AF
Auxiliary Feed Pump Turbine (IEEE) .... AFPT
Auxiliary Feedwater [*Nuclear energy*] (NRCH) .... AF
Auxiliary Feedwater [*Nuclear energy*] (NRCH) .... AFW
Auxiliary Feedwater Actuating System [*Nuclear energy*] (NRCH) .... AFAS
Auxiliary Feedwater Actuating System [*Nuclear energy*] (NRCH) .... AFWAS
Auxiliary Feedwater Control [*Nuclear energy*] (NRCH) .... AFWC
Auxiliary Feedwater Storage Tank [*Nuclear energy*] (IEEE) .... AFST
Auxiliary Feedwater System [*Nuclear energy*] (NRCH) .... AFS
Auxiliary Feedwater System [*Nuclear energy*] (NRCH) .... AFWS
Auxiliary Ferry Service Unit .... AFSU
Auxiliary Field (MUGU) .... AF
Auxiliary Fighter Director Ship [*Navy*] .... AFDS
Auxiliary Fire Service [*British*] .... AFS
Auxiliary Fire Service (SAUO) .... AFS
Auxiliary Fire Station (SAUS) .... AUX FS
Auxiliary Fire Tube Boiler [*of a ship*] (DS) .... AXFTB
Auxiliary Fire Tube Boiler Survey [*of a ship*] (DS) .... AXFBS
Auxiliary Fire Tube Boiler Survey [*of a ship*] (DS) .... AXFTBS
Auxiliary Flight Control System (SAUS) .... AFCS
Auxiliary Flight Reference System .... AFRS
Auxiliary Flight Service Station [*Aviation*] (FAAC) .... XFSS
Auxiliary Floating Dry Dock [*Navy symbol*] .... AFD
Auxiliary Floating Dry Dock (Big) [*Non-self-propelled*] [*Navy symbol*] .... AFDB
Auxiliary Floating Dry Dock (Concrete) [*Non-self-propelled*] [*Navy symbol*] .... AFDC
Auxiliary Floating Dry Dock (Little) [*Non-self-propelled*] [*Navy symbol*] .... AFDL
Auxiliary Floating Dry Dock Little (SAUS) .... AFDL
Auxiliary Floating Dry Dock (Little, Concrete) [*Non-self-propelled*] [*Navy symbol*] .... AFDL(C)
Auxiliary Floating Dry Dock (Medium) [*Non-self-propelled*] [*Navy symbol*] .... AFDM
Auxiliary Force, India [*British military*] (DMA) .... AFI
Auxiliary Force, India (SAUO) .... AuxF
Auxiliary Force Medical Corps [*British military*] (DMA) .... AFMC
Auxiliary Force Veterinary Corps [*British military*] (DMA) .... AFVC

Auxiliary Frame (SAUS) .... AUXF
Auxiliary Fresh Water (DNAB) .... AFW
Auxiliary Fuel Oil (System) [*Nuclear energy*] (NRCH) .... AFO(S)
Auxiliary Function (SAUS) .... AUXFUN
Auxiliary Function Bit (SAUS) .... AFB
Auxiliary Functional Unit [*Data link*] (NG) .... AFU
Auxiliary General Electronics Research Ship [*Navy*] .... AGERS
Auxiliary General for Environmental Research [*Ship*] [*Military*] (LAIN) .... AGER
Auxiliary General Missile .... AGM
Auxiliary General Oceanographic Research Ship [*Navy*] (MSC) .... AGOR
Auxiliary General Oceanographic Research Vessel (SAUS) .... AGOR Vessel
Auxiliary General Survey [*Navy*] (MSC) .... AGS
Auxiliary Generating Plant [*Aviation*] (AIA) .... AGP
Auxiliary Geographical Ship .... AGS
Auxiliary Ground Control Station (SAUS) .... AUX GCS
Auxiliary Ground Control Station [*NASA*] (KSC) .... AUXGCS
Auxiliary Ground Equipment .... AGE
Auxiliary Handling Machine [*Nuclear energy*] (NRCH) .... AHM
Auxiliary Hydraulic Power Supply .... AHPS
Auxiliary Inerting Gas Subsystem [*Nuclear energy*] (NRCH) .... AIGS
Auxiliary Input/Output Software (SAUS) .... AIOS
Auxiliary Input/Output Statement (SAUS) .... AIOS
Auxiliary Inshore Minesweeper [*NATO*] .... AMI
Auxiliary Intelligence Collection Ship [*Navy*] (CAAL) .... AGI
Auxiliary Interface Adapter (ACAE) .... AIA
Auxiliary Interface Cabinet (IUSS) .... AIC
Auxiliary Interface Unit [*NASA*] .... AIU
Auxiliary Intermediate Heat Exchanger [*Nuclear energy*] (NRCH) ...... AIHX
Auxiliary Junctor (SAUS) .... AJ
Auxiliary Killing Ground [*British and Canadian*] [*World War II*] .... AKG
Auxiliary Landing Field .... ALF
Auxiliary Language Processor (SAUS) .... ALP
Auxiliary Library Service Collections .... ALSC
Auxiliary Library Service Organization .... ALSO
Auxiliary Light [*Navigation signal*] .... Aux
Auxiliary Lighter (SAUS) .... ALS
Auxiliary Lighter Ship (DNAB) .... ALS
Auxiliary Liquid Metal System [*Nuclear energy*] (NRCH) .... ALMS
Auxiliary Loans to Assist Students .... ALAS
Auxiliary Machine Casing Bulkhead (SAUS) .... AMCBH
Auxiliary Machinery (SAUS) .... AUXM
Auxiliary Machinery Room (CAAL) .... AMR
Auxiliary Machinery Space (DNAB) .... AMS
Auxiliary Magnetic Memory (SAUS) .... AMM
Auxiliary Maintenance Engineering Analysis (ACAE) .... AUX-MEA
Auxiliary Marine Power Source [*For submarines*] (DOMA) .... AMPS
Auxiliary Marker [*Telecommunications*] (TEL) .... AM
Auxiliary Measuring Sonde (SAUS) .... AMS
Auxiliary Memory .... AM
Auxiliary Memory Drum .... AMD
Auxiliary Memory Management System (SAUS) .... AMMS
Auxiliary Memory Set (MCD) .... AMS
Auxiliary Memory Unit .... AMU
Auxiliary Memory Unit Controller (ACAE) .... AMU
Auxiliary Mexican Border Veterans (EA) .... AMBV
Auxiliary Military Pioneer Corps [*British*] .... AMPC
Auxiliary Military Pioneer Corps (SAUO) .... AMPC
Auxiliary Mine Layer (SAUS) .... AML
Auxiliary Minelayer [*Navy symbol*] .... ACM
Auxiliary Minelayer .... AML
Auxiliary Minesweeper [*NATO*] .... AM
Auxiliary Minesweeper [*NATO*] .... AMS
Auxiliary Mission Equipment (SAUS) .... AME
Auxiliary Motor Launches (NATG) .... MLA
Auxiliary Motor Minesweeper [*Navy symbol*] .... YMS
Auxiliary Motormine-Sweeper (SAUS) .... AMS
Auxiliary Nuclear Powered Submarine (SAUS) .... SSAN
Auxiliary Ocean Tug [*Navy symbol*] .... ATA
Auxiliary of the Decalogue Society of Lawyers (EA) .... ADSL
Auxiliary Office (COE) .... AO
Auxiliary of/to the American Osteopathic Association (SAUO) .... AAOA
Auxiliary Oil Replenisher [*or Replenishment*] [*Navy*] [*British*] .... AOR
Auxiliary Oil Replenisher (or Replenishment) (SAUS) .... AOR
Auxiliary Oiler (MCD) .... AO
Auxiliary Oiler [*Military Sea Transportation Service*] .... TAO
Auxiliary Operation .... AO
Auxiliary Operational Members [*Coast Guard*] .... AUXOPS
Auxiliary Operator Service System (SAUS) .... AOSS
Auxiliary Oscillator .... AO
Auxiliary Oscillator .... AUXOSC
Auxiliary Output Tester .... AOT
Auxiliary Pastoral Ministry [*Church of England*] .... APM
Auxiliary Patrol [*British military*] (DMA) .... AP
Auxiliary Patrol (SAUS) .... Aux Pat
Auxiliary Patrol Officer (SAUS) .... APO
Auxiliary Payload Power System (MCD) .... APPS
Auxiliary Personnel, Attack [*Navy designation for combat landing craft*] [*World War II*] .... APA
Auxiliary Personnel Attack (SAUS) .... APA
Auxiliary Personnel, Destroyer [*British military*] (DMA) .... APD
Auxiliary Pneumatic (AAG) .... APNEU
Auxiliary Pneumatics Panel .... APP
Auxiliary Point (SAUS) .... AP
Auxiliary Pointing Unit (ACAE) .... APU
Auxiliary Police (LAIN) .... AP

Auxiliary Police Association (SAUO)	APA
Auxiliary Potential Transformer	AuPT
Auxiliary Power (CAAL)	AP
Auxiliary Power Distribution (KSC)	APD
Auxiliary Power Package (MCD)	APP
Auxiliary Power Plant	APP
Auxiliary Power Subsystem (MCD)	APS
Auxiliary Power Supplies (SAUS)	APS
Auxiliary Power Supply	APS
Auxiliary Power Supply Module (CIST)	APSM
Auxiliary Power Supply Unit (MCD)	APSU
Auxiliary Power System (NRCH)	APS
Auxiliary Power [or Propulsion] Unit [Military]	APU
Auxiliary Power Unit (ADWA)	apu
Auxiliary Power Unit Subsystem (MCD)	APUS
Auxiliary Power Unit System Module (MCD)	APUSM
Auxiliary Power Unit Test (MCD)	APUT
Auxiliary Printer (ECII)	AP
Auxiliary Processing Machine (SAUS)	APM
Auxiliary Processing Unit	APU
Auxiliary Program Storage [Computer science] (BUR)	APS
Auxiliary Propelled Anti-Tank [Military] (PDAA)	APAT
Auxiliary Propulsion System [or Subsystem] [Apollo] [NASA]	APS
Auxiliary Propulsion System Aft POP (MCD)	APSAP
Auxiliary Propulsion System Aft Prod (SAUS)	APSAP
Auxiliary Propulsion Unit (SAUS)	APU
Auxiliary Pump-Drive Assembly	APDA
Auxiliary Reactor Area	ARA
Auxiliary Read-Out (SAUS)	ARO
Auxiliary Read-Out Unit [Computer science] (MHDB)	ARU
Auxiliary Recording Circuit	AUXRC
Auxiliary Recording Control [Circuit] [Bell System]	AUXRC
Auxiliary Recovery Aerial (or Antenna) (SAUS)	ARA
Auxiliary Recovery Antenna [NASA] (KSC)	ARA
Auxiliary Register	AUXR
Auxiliary Regulation Excitation Principle [Industrial engines]	AREP
Auxiliary Removable Memory Media/Tape-Transport Cartridge (MCD)	ARMM/TTC
Auxiliary Repair Battle Damage [British military] (DMA)	ARB
Auxiliary Repair Dry Dock [Non-self-propelled] [Navy ship symbol]	ARD
Auxiliary Repair Dry Dock (SAUS)	ARD Dock
Auxiliary Repair Dry Dock, Concrete [Later, AFDL] [Navy symbol] [Obsolete]	ARDC
Auxiliary Report (SAUS)	XREP
Auxiliary Rescue Team Chief [Air Force]	ARTC
Auxiliary Rescue Tug (SAUS)	RTA
Auxiliary Research Submarine (SAUS)	AGSS
Auxiliary Resources Control Office	ARCO
Auxiliary Rocket Engine	ARE
Auxiliary Roll Control	ARC
Auxiliary Routine (IAA)	AR
Auxiliary Seaplane Tender [Ship symbol]	XAV
Auxiliary Segment Table [Electronics] (OA)	AST
Auxiliary Sensor Unit (MCD)	ASU
Auxiliary Service Force, Transition Training Squadron, Pacific	ASFTRNTRARONPAC
Auxiliary Ship Information System [Navy] (CAAL)	ASIS
Auxiliary Society of Lace Workers (SAUO)	ASLW
Auxiliary Software (SAUS)	AS
Auxiliary Spacecraft Power [NASA] (MCD)	ASAP
Auxiliary Spooling Analysis Program (SAUS)	ASAP
Auxiliary Stabilizing Support - "A" Frame	ASF
Auxiliary Stage [NASA] (NASA)	A/S
Auxiliary State Estimator (ACAE)	ASE
Auxiliary Steam [Nuclear energy] (NRCH)	AS
Auxiliary Steam Generator [Nuclear energy] (NRCH)	ASG
Auxiliary Steam (System) [Nuclear energy] (NRCH)	AS(S)
Auxiliary Storage [Computer science]	AS
Auxiliary Storage and Playback [Assembly] [Apollo Telescope Mount] [NASA]	ASAP
Auxiliary Storage and Playback Assembly [Apollo Telescope Mount] [NASA] (KSC)	ASPA
Auxiliary Storage Manager [Computer science]	ASM
Auxiliary Storage Unit [Computer science] (IAA)	ASU
Auxiliary Store Area (SAUS)	ASA
Auxiliary Store Capacity (SAUS)	ASC
Auxiliary Store Carrier (SAUS)	ASC
Auxiliary Store System (SAUS)	ASS
Auxiliary Submarine [Navy symbol]	AGSS
Auxiliary Submarine [Navy symbol]	SSAC
Auxiliary Submarine	SSAG
Auxiliary Submarine Rescue (SAUS)	ASR
Auxiliary Submarine Rescue Ship [Navy symbol]	ASR
Auxiliary Support Reaction System	ASRS
Auxiliary Supporting Feature (IEEE)	ASF
Auxiliary Surface Simulator Platform [Navy] (CAAL)	ASSP
Auxiliary Survey Vessel [Oceanography] (MSC)	ASV
Auxiliary Sustainer Cut-Off (SAUS)	ASCO
Auxiliary Switch [Electricity]	ASW
Auxiliary Switch [Electricity]	AuS
Auxiliary Switch (SAUS)	AuxS
Auxiliary Switch Closed	ASC
Auxiliary Switch [Breaker] Normally Closed [Electricity]	ASC
Auxiliary Switch [Breaker] Normally Open [Electricity]	ASO
Auxiliary Switch Open (SAUS)	ASO

Auxiliary System for Interactive Statistics [Sweden] [Information service or system] (IID)	AXIS
Auxiliary systems (SAUS)	AX
Auxiliary Systems Function Test Stand [NASA] (KSC)	ASFTS
Auxiliary Tank Set (SAUS)	AT Set
Auxiliary Tape Input (SAUS)	ATI
Auxiliary Tape Memory [Spacecraft guidance]	ATM
Auxiliary Territorial Service (SAUO)	AT
Auxiliary Territorial Service (SAUO)	ATS
Auxiliary Territorial Service [Later, WRAC] [British women's service] [World War II]	ATS
Auxiliary Territorial Service Expeditionary Force Institutes (SAUO)	ATSEFI
Auxiliary Territorial Service Expeditionary Force Institutes (SAUS)	ATSEFI
Auxiliary Test Unit	ATU
Auxiliary Timer	AT
Auxiliary Timer Assembly	ATA
Auxiliary to Sons of Union Veterans of the Civil War (EA)	ASUVCW
Auxiliary to the American Dental Association (EA)	AADA
Auxiliary to the American Optometric Association [Later, AFVA] (EA)	AAOA
Auxiliary to the National Dental Association (EA)	ANDA
Auxiliary to the National Medical Association (EA)	ANMA
Auxiliary Tool Production (MCD)	ATP
Auxiliary Track (MUGU)	AUXTRAC
Auxiliary Track Data Storage (SAUS)	ATDS
Auxiliary Training Submarine [Navy symbol]	ATSS
Auxiliary Transport Aviation (SAUS)	ATA
Auxiliary Transport Service (SAUO)	ATS
Auxiliary Tug Salvage (SAUS)	ATS
Auxiliary Tug Service (PDAA)	ATS
Auxiliary Turbopump Assembly	ATPA
Auxiliary Unit	AU
Auxiliary Utility Equipment Area (NRCH)	AUEA
Auxiliary Verb (ADWA)	AUX
Auxiliary Vessel (NOAA)	AV
Auxiliary Vessels [Navy symbol] (MUGU)	AA
Auxiliary Video Switching Matrix	AVSM
Auxiliary Waste Heat Boiler [of a ship] (DS)	AXWHB
Auxiliary Waste Heater Boiler Survey [of a ship] (DS)	AXWHBS
Auxiliary Waste Tube Boiler Survey [of a ship] (DS)	AXWTBS
Auxiliary Water Tube Boiler [of a ship] (DS)	AXWTB
Auxiliary Winding	AW
Auxilium Meum a Deo [My Help Cometh from the Lord] [(Ps., CXXI. 2) Motto of Christian, Margrave of Brandenburg-Baireuth (1581-1655)]	AMAD
Auxilary Control Process [Computer science] (VERA)	ACP
Auxin Response Factor [Biochemistry]	ARF
Auxin-Binding Protein [Biology]	ABP
Auyuittuq National Park, Parks Canada [Parc National Auyuittuq, Parcs Canada] Pangnirtung, Northwest Territories [Library symbol] [National Library of Canada] (NLC)	NWPPCA
AV Panasonic Users Group (SAUO)	AVPUG
AV [Audiovisual] Pansophic Users Group [Defunct] (EA)	AVPUG
Ava, IL [FM radio station call letters]	WXAN
Ava, MO [Location identifier] [FAA] (FAAL)	AOV
Ava, MO [AM radio station call letters]	KKOZ
Ava, MO [FM radio station call letters]	KKOZ-FM
'Avadim (BJA)	'Avad
Avado Brands [NASDAQ symbol] (SG)	AVDO
Avaible Frame Capacity Count (SAUS)	AFCC
Availability (NITA)	AV
Availability (ACAE)	Av
Availability	AVBLTY
Availability	AVLBLTY
Availability Balance File [Military] (AABC)	ABF
Availability Centered Inventory Model (MCD)	ACIM
Availability Centred Inventory Model (SAUS)	ACIM
Availability Check (SAUS)	AC
Availability Code	AC
Availability Computation - Element Transient and Asymptotic Repair Process (PDAA)	AVACOM-ETARP
Availability Control File (SAUS)	ACF
Availability Control Unit (IAA)	ACU
Availability Date [Banking]	AD
Availability Factor [Generating time ratio] (IEEE)	AF
Availability Factor	AVF
Availability Guarantee [Military]	AG
Availability of Logistics Support Elements (MCD)	ALSE
Availability Rate	AR
Availability, Reliability, and Maintainability [Computer performance]	ARM
Availability Status Messages [Travel industry] (TRID)	AVS
Availability, Steady	AS
Availability Store (SAUS)	AS
Availability Table (SAUS)	AT
Available [or Availability] (MCD)	A
Available [or Availability] [Online database field identifier] [Computer science]	AV
Available [or Availability] (KSC)	AVAIL
Available (REAL)	avail
Available [or Availability] (AFM)	AVAL
Available [or Availability]	AVBL
Available (ECII)	AVBLE
Available (ADWA)	AVL
Available (ADWA)	avlbl
Available [or Availability] (MSA)	AVLBL
Available Bit Rate [Computer science] (VERA)	ABR
Available but Not Installed	ABNI
Available Cell Rate (MLOA)	ACR

Available Database Management System ... ADBMS
Available for Local Use (MCD) ... AFLU
Available for Obligations (SAUS) ... AFO
Available for Reassignment ... AVFR
Available for Release (MCD) ... AFR
Available for Sale ... AFS
Available Hours [*Electronics*] (IEEE) ... AH
Available Labor Pool Model (MCD) ... AVPOOL
Available Machine Time ... AMT
Available Manhours (AFM) ... AVMH
Available Memory (SAUS) ... AM
Available Page Queue (SAUS) ... APQ
Available Pay Survey Reports [*Information service or system*] (IID) ... APSR
Available Phosphoric Acid ... APA
Available Potential Energy [*Geophysics*] ... APE
Available Power Efficiency ... APE
Available Power Response ... APR
Available Seat Miles [*Airlines term*] ... ASM
Available Seat-Kilometres [*Air travel*] ... ASK
Available Solar Energy (ADWA) ... ASE
Available Solar Radiation (ADWA) ... ASR
Available Space List [*Computer science*] ... ASL
Available Space List [*Computer science*] (IAA) ... AVSL
Available Store (SAUS) ... AS
Available Supply Rate ... ASR
Available Time ... AT
Available Time (AFM) ... AVT
Available Ton-Kilometres (SAUS) ... ATK
Available Tonne-Kilometer (ADA) ... ATK
Available Vehicle Occupancy [*VDOT*] (TAG) ... AVO
Available Water-Holding Capacity [*Soil science*] ... AWC
Available Water-Holding Capacity [*Soil science*] (OA) ... AWHC
Available-to-Load Date (AABC) ... ALD
Avair, Inc. [*ICAO designator*] (FAAC) ... FVA
Avaj [*Iran*] [*ICAO location identifier*] (ICLI) ... OIHJ
Avalanche Controlled Rectifier (PDAA) ... ACR
Avalanche Diode (KSC) ... AD
Avalanche Diode Oscillator ... ADO
Avalanche Injection Diode ... AID
Avalanche Injection Metal-Oxide Semiconductor ... AMOS
Avalanche Memory Triode (SAUS) ... AMT
Avalanche Mode Photodiode ... AMP
Avalanche Photodiode [*Solid state physics*] ... APD
Avalanche Photodiode Detector ... APD
Avalanche Photon Device (CCCA) ... APD
Avalanche Punch-Through Erase (MCD) ... APTE
Avalanche Resonance Pumped (SAUS) ... ARP
Avalanche Resonance Pumped-Betrieb (SAUS) ... ARP-Betrieb
Avalanche Transit Time ... ATT
Avalanche Transit Time Diode ... ATTD
Avalanche Transit Time Oscillator (IAA) ... ATTO
Avalanche-Included Migration Process (SAUS) ... AIM Process
Avalanche-Induced Migration (MCD) ... AIM
Avalanching Junction Light Output ... AJLO
Avallon [*France*] [*ICAO location identifier*] (ICLI) ... LFGE
Avalon [*Australia*] [*ICAO location identifier*] (ICLI) ... AMAV
Avalon Bay [*Santa Catalina, California*] [*Airport symbol*] (AD) ... AVX
Avalon Bay Communities [*NYSE symbol*] [*Formerly, Bay Apartment Communities*] ... AVB
Avalon, CA [*Location identifier*] [*FAA*] (FAAL) ... AVX
Avalon, CA [*Television station call letters*] (BROA) ... KBJO
Avalon, CA [*AM radio station call letters*] ... KBRT
Avalon, CA [*FM radio station call letters*] ... KISL
Avalon, CA [*FM radio station call letters*] (BROA) ... KLIT-FM
Avalon, CA [*FM radio station call letters*] ... KRCI
Avalon Capital [*NASDAQ symbol*] (TTSB) ... MIST
Avalon Capital, Inc. [*Associated Press*] (SAG) ... AvalonC
Avalon Capital, Inc. [*NASDAQ symbol*] (SAG) ... MIST
Avalon Community Services, Inc. [*Associated Press*] (SAG) ... Avalon
Avalon Community Services, Inc. [*NASDAQ symbol*] (SAG) ... CITY
Avalon Community Svcs [*NASDAQ symbol*] (TTSB) ... CITY
Avalon Hill (SAUS) ... AH
Avalon Holdings'A' [*AMEX symbol*] (SG) ... AWX
Avalon, NJ [*FM radio station call letters*] ... WCZT
Avalon Prop 9% Sr'A'Pfd [*NYSE symbol*] (TTSB) ... AVNPrA
Avalon Properties [*Associated Press*] (SAG) ... Avaln
Avalon Properties [*Associated Press*] (SAG) ... AvalonPr
Avalon Properties [*NYSE symbol*] (SPSG) ... AVN
Avalon Resources, Inc. [*Vancouver Stock Exchange symbol*] ... AGM
Avanavero [*Surinam*] [*ICAO location identifier*] (ICLI) ... SMVO
Avance International, Inc. [*Vancouver Stock Exchange symbol*] ... AVA
Avanced Contract Administrator (SAUS) ... ACA
Avancer [*Fast, as clocks*] [*French*] ... A
Avanguardia Operaia [*Worker's Vanguard*] [*Italy*] [*Political party*] (PPE) ... AO
Avanir Pharmaceuticals 'A' [*AMEX symbol*] (SG) ... AVN
Avant Corp. [*Associated Press*] (SAG) ... Avanti
Avant Corp. [*NASDAQ symbol*] [*Formerly, ArcSys, Inc.*] (SG) ... AVNT
Avant Go, Inc. [*NASDAQ symbol*] ... AVGO
Avant Immunotherapeutics [*Formerly, T Cell Sciences*] [*NASDAQ symbol*] ... AVAN
Avant Jesus-Christ [*Before Christ*] [*French*] ... AV J-C
Avant-Garde (VRA) ... av-gd
Avantgarde de la Revolution Malgache [*Vanguard of the Malagasy Revolution*] [*Political party*] (PPW) ... AREMA
Avant-Garde Francaise d'Amerique [*French Avant-Garde of America*] [*Canada*] ... AGFA
Avanti Air [*Austria*] [*ICAO designator*] (FAAC) ... ATV
Avanti Owners Association International (EA) ... AOAI
Avanti Productions, Inc. [*Vancouver Stock Exchange symbol*] ... AVN
Avaric [*MARC language code*] [*Library of Congress*] (LCCP) ... ava
Avarua/Rarotonga International [*Cook Islands*] [*ICAO location identifier*] (ICLI) ... NCRG
Avascular Necrosis [*Medicine*] (AAMN) ... AN
Avascular Necrosis of Bone [*Medicine*] (DMAA) ... ANB
Avascular Necrosis of Bone [*Medicine*] ... AVNB
Avascular Necrosis of the Femoral Head [*Medicine*] (DMAA) ... AVNFH
Avascular Zone [*Medicine*] (DMAA) ... AVZ
Avastar Jet Charter and Management Services, Inc. [*FAA designator*] (FAAC) ... SJC
Avatar Hldgs [*NASDAQ symbol*] (TTSB) ... AVTR
Avatar Holdings, Inc. [*Associated Press*] (SAG) ... Avatar
Avatar Holdings, Inc. [*NASDAQ symbol*] (NQ) ... AVTR
Avatar Resources Corp. [*Vancouver Stock Exchange symbol*] ... AAV
Avaya, Inc. [*NYSE symbol*] ... AV
AVCAL Change Request (MCD) ... ACR
AVCO Airborne Laser Mapping System (SAUS) ... ALMS
Avco Airway Express, Inc. [*FAA designator*] (FAAC) ... AEX
Avco Corp. (SAUO) ... AV
Avco Data Analysis and Prediction Technique [*for sunspot prediction*] ... ADAPT
AVCO Data Analysis and Prediction Techniques (SAUS) ... ADAPT
Avco Systems Development (MCD) ... AVSD
AVCO Systems Textron (SAUS) ... AST
AVCO-Everett Research Laboratory (SAUS) ... AERL
Avco-Everett Research Laboratory (MCD) ... AERL
Avco-Everett Research Laboratory, Everett, MA [*OCLC symbol*] (OCLC) ... AVC
Avco-Everett Research Laboratory, Everett, MA [*Library symbol*] [*Library of Congress*] (LCLS) ... MEvA
Avcon AG [*Switzerland*] [*ICAO designator*] (FAAC) ... AVX
Avcon, Aviation Consulting Ltd. [*Switzerland*] [*FAA designator*] (FAAC) ... VCN
Avcorp Industries, Inc. [*Toronto Stock Exchange symbol*] ... AVP
Ave Maria ... AM
Ave Maria ... AVM
Avecor Cardiovascular [*NASDAQ symbol*] (TTSB) ... AVEC
Avecor, Inc. [*NASDAQ symbol*] (SAG) ... AVEC
Avecor, Inc. [*Associated Press*] (SAG) ... Avecor
Aveiro [*Portugal*] [*ICAO location identifier*] (ICLI) ... LPAV
AVEMCO Corp. [*NYSE symbol*] (SPSG) ... AVE
AVEMCO Corp. [*Associated Press*] (SAG) ... AVEMCO
Avenal, CA [*Tactical Air Navigation Station*] [*Air Force*] ... AVE
Avenal, CA [*FM radio station call letters*] ... KAAX
Avenger Control Electronics [*Navy*] ... ACE
Avenida [*Avenue*] (EY) ... AVDA
Avenor Inc. [*TS Symbol*] (TTSB) ... AVR
Avensa Aerovias Venezolanas SA [*Venezuela*] [*ICAO designator*] (FAAC) ... AVE
Aventi Cristo [*Before Christ*] [*Italian*] ... AvC
Avenue (WDAA) ... A
Avenue (DD) ... av
Avenue [*Correspondence*] (EY) ... AV
Avenue (GEOI) ... Av
Avenue [*Correspondence*] (AFM) ... AVE
Avenue (TBD) ... Ave
Avenue (VRA) ... ave
Avenue [*Commonly used*] (OPSA) ... AVEN
Avenue [*Commonly used*] (OPSA) ... AVENU
Avenue [*Commonly used*] (OPSA) ... AVENUE
Avenue [*Commonly used*] (OPSA) ... AVN
Avenue [*Commonly used*] (OPSA) ... AVNUE
Avenue Entertainment Grp [*AMEX symbol*] (SG) ... PIX
Avenue of Approach [*Army*] (AABC) ... AA
Avenue Resources, Inc. [*Vancouver Stock Exchange symbol*] ... AVE
Average (DAVI) ... A
Average ... AV
Average (MARI) ... Av
Average (ADWA) ... av
Average ... AVE
Average ... AVER
average (SAUS) ... Aver
Average (AFM) ... AVG
Average (EBF) ... Avg
Average (ABAC) ... avg
Average (ADA) ... AVGE
Average Absolute Control Movement (MCD) ... AACM
Average Absolute Deviation [*Statistics*] ... AAD
Average Absolute Error (MCD) ... AAE
Average Absolute Percentage Error [*Statistics*] ... AAPE
Average Acceleration ... AA
Average Access Time (SAUS) ... AAT
Average Adjuster [*Insurance*] (DS) ... AA
Average Adjustment Factor (MCD) ... AAF
Average Alarm ... AVA
Average All Pig Price [*British*] (NUMA) ... AAPP
Average and Excess Demand (IAA) ... AED
Average Annual Cost [*Business term*] (MHDB) ... AAC
Average Annual Daily Traffic [*FHWA*] (TAG) ... AADT
Average Annual Earnings (SAUS) ... AAE
Average Annual Full-Time Equivalent (SAUS) ... AAFTE
Average Annual Growth Rate (MHDI) ... AAGR
Average Annual Performance Rate ... AAPR
Average Annual Precipitation (PDAA) ... AAP

Average Annual Rainfall (PDAA)	AAR
Average Annual Temperature (PDAA)	AAT
Average Annual weekday Traffic (SAUS)	AADT
Average Aptitude Requirement per Unit Time	AARPUT
Average Audience [Television ratings]	AA
Average Blank Data [Computer science]	AVEBD
Average Body Dose [Radiation technology] (WDAA)	ABD
Average Body Weight (DMAA)	ABW
Average Branching Factor (IAA)	ABF
Average Business Day [Bell System]	ABD
Average Busy Hour [Telecommunications] (TEL)	ABH
Average Busy Season [Telecommunications] (TEL)	ABS
Average Busy Season Busy Hour [Telecommunications] (TEL)	ABSBH
Average Busy Stream [Computer science] (ACRL)	ABS
Average Calculating Operation (SAUS)	ACO
Average Calculating Speed (SAUS)	ACS
Average Calculating Time (SAUS)	ACT
Average Carbonaceous Chondrite [Meteorology]	AVCC
Average Carbonaceous Chondrites (SAUS)	AVCC
Average Circulated [Numismatic term]	AVG
Average Consumer	AC
Average Consumer Extraodinaire .	ACE
Average Correlation Coefficient (PDAA)	ACC
Average Cost	AC
Average Cost [Accounting term]	AVCO
Average Cost per Patient Day [Medicine]	ACPPD
Average Crop Yield [Agriculture] (WDAA)	ACY
Average Cumulative Error (PDAA)	ACE
Average Current-Mantle Adiabat [Geochemistry]	ACMA
Average Customer Wait Time	ACWT
Average Daily Allowance (ADA)	ADA
Average Daily Attendance	ADA
Average Daily Balance	ADB
Average Daily Census	ADC
Average Daily Consumption (MELL)	ADC
Average Daily Dose [Pharmacy] (DAVI)	ADD
Average Daily Gain [of weight] [Cattle]	ADG
Average Daily Member Load	ADML
Average Daily Membership	ADM
Average Daily Patient Load [Medicine]	ADPL
Average Daily Rate [Hotels]	ADR
Average Daily Service Charge [Hospitals]	ADSC
Average Daily Traffic	ADT
Average Daily Traffic (SAUS)	adt
Average Daily Trips (PA)	ADT
Average Data Technique (SAUS)	ADT
Average Day (SAUS)	AVEDAY
Average Decreasing Line	ADL
Average Deferral Percentage	ADP
Average Depth (IAA)	AD
Average Depth (NOAA)	AVDTH
Average Deviation [Statistics]	AD
Average Diameter	AD
Average Diastolic Pressure Avoirdupois [Medicine] (MELL)	AVDP
Average Dose (MELL)	AD
Average Effectiveness Level (IAA)	AEL
Average Efficiency (IAA)	AVEFF
Average Efficiency (SAUS)	AvEff
Average Efficiency Index	AEI
Average Electrode Current	AEC
Average Electroencephalic Response [Medicine] (DB)	AER
Average Emission Factor (CARB)	AEF
Average Error (MCD)	AE
Average Evoked Potential [Neurophysiology]	AEP
Average Evoked Response [Neurophysiology]	AER
Average Evoked Response Technique (DIPS)	AERT
Average Excitation Energy [Physics]	AEE
Average Extent of Burning	AEB
Average Failure Number	AFN
Average Female Mass [Ecology]	FMA
Average Female Weekly Earnings	AFWE
Average Fixed Cost [Economics]	AFC
Average Flying Hours per Sortie [Air Force] (AFIT)	AFHS
Average for Gestational Age [Medicine] (DAVI)	AGA
Average Fractional Overflow (SAUS)	AFO
Average Freight Rate Assessement (SAUS)	AFRA
Average Freight Rate Assessment [Shipping]	AFRA
Average Global Automobile [Emissions to atmosphere]	AGA
Average Goals Against per Period [Hockey]	AGP
Average Gradient	AG
Average Grid Heading (SAA)	AVGH
Average Heading	AVH
Average Hearing Level	AHL
Average Holding Time [Telecommunications] (TEL)	AHT
Average Index Sequential Access Method [Computer science] (MHDI)	AVISAM
Average Indexed Monthly Earnings [Social Security Administration]	AIME
Average Indexed Yearly Earnings (GFGA)	AIYE
Average Injection Rate (SAUS)	AIR
Average Input Pulse Rate	AIPR
Average Instruction Execution Time [Computer parameter]	AIET
Average Instructions per Second [Computer science]	AIP
Average Instructions per Second (SAUS)	AIPS
Average Integral Square Error (PDAA)	AISE
Average Intravascular Pressure [Medicine] (MAE)	AIP
Average Inventory Level	AIL
Average Length (SAUS)	AVL
Average Length of Detection (SAUS)	ALD
Average Length of Stay [of patients in a health care institution]	ALOS
Average Linear Planar Heat Generation Rate [Nuclear energy] (NRCH)	ALPHGR
Average Load Factor	ALF
Average Logistic Time (CIST)	ALT
Average Lymphocyte Output [Medicine] (DB)	ALO
Average Magnitude Difference Function (SAUS)	AMDF
Average Magnitude for Velocity [Military]	AMV
Average Magnitude of Error (SAUS)	AME
Average Male Mass	MMA
Average Male Weekly Earnings	AMWE
Average Man-Hours per Day (DNAB)	AMHD
Average Mean Pressure	AMP
Average Miles Driven Per Day [DOE] (TAG)	AMPD
Average Modulation Transfer Function (VERA)	AMTE
Average Modulation Transfer Function (SAUS)	AMTF
Average Molecular Weight (SAUS)	AMW
Average Month Program [Air Force] (AFIT)	AMP
Average Monthly Consumption (MCD)	AMC
Average Monthly Demand	AMD
Average Monthly Earnings	AME
Average Monthly Limit (EEVL)	AML
Average Monthly Sales (MCD)	AMS
Average Monthly Usage (KSC)	AMU
Average Monthly Wage	AMW
Average Mutual Information (PDAA)	AMI
Average Nearest Neighbour (SAUS)	ANN
Average Net Cost [Insurance]	ANC
Average Number (SAUS)	Av No
Average Octane Number	AON
Average of Normals	AON
Average of Percent Differences (SAUS)	APD
Average on Board (IUSS)	AOB
Average Operating Cost (KSC)	AOC
Average Operation Time	AOT
Average Out [Business term]	AO
Average Outgoing Count Limit (SAUS)	AOCL
Average Outgoing Quality [Quality control]	AOQ
Average Outgoing Quality Laboratory	AOQL
Average Outgoing Quality Level [or Limit] [Quality control]	AOQL
Average Oxidation State [Physical chemistry]	AOS
Average Page Exposure [Advertising] (WDMC)	apx
Average Particle Diameter	APD
Average Particle Volume (SAUS)	APV
Average Payable (SAUS)	AP
Average Peak Noise (MAE)	APN
Average per Pupil Expenditure [Education] (GFGA)	APPE
Average Percent Complete (IUSS)	APC
Average Percentage Damage [Meteorology]	APD
Average Percentage Difference [Mathematics]	APD
Average Picture Level	APL
Average Picture Level (MSA)	AVPL
Average Planar Heat Generation Rate [Nuclear energy] (NRCH)	APLHGR
Average Pore Diameter [Filtration]	APD
Average Potential Model (SAUS)	APM
Average Power (COE)	AP
Average Power Control [Telecommunications] (TEL)	APC
Average Power Dissipation	APD
Average Power Laser	APL
Average Power Laser Experiment (SAUS)	APLE
Average Power Range Monitor [Nuclear energy] (NRCH)	APRM
Average Price	AP
Average Process Time Inverted File [Computer science] (CIST)	APTIF
Average Product [Economics]	AP
Average Product of Labor	AP_L
Average Propensity to Consume [Economics]	APC
Average Propensity to Save [Economics]	APS
Average Quality Level (SAUS)	AQL
Average Quality Limit	AQL
Average Quantity Repaired Monthly	AQRM
Average Quarter Hour (WDMC)	AQH
Average Quarter Hour Rating [Television] [Radio] (WDMC)	AQH
Average Quarter-Hour Rating [Of radio and television programming] (WDMC)	AQR
Average Quarterly Demand	AQD
Average Rating	AR
Average Rectified Forward Current [Electronics] (IAA)	ARFC
Average Rectified Slope [FHWA] (TAG)	ARS
Average Recurrent Interval	ARI
Average Relationship Index	ARI
Average Relative Representation Error (IAA)	ARRE
Average Remaining Lifetime (MAE)	ARL
Average Response Amplitude	ARA
Average Response Amplitude Data	ARAD
Average Response Computer	ARC
Average Response Data	ARD
Average Response Latency [Biochemistry]	ARL
Average Retrieval Time (OA)	ART
Average Revenue	AR
Average Revenue Per Message (SAUS)	ARPM
Average Revenue/Average Physical Product [Economics]	ARAP
Average Revenue/Marginal Physical Product [Economics]	ARMP
Average Roughness (SAUS)	RA

Average Run Length [*Statistics*] ... ARL
Average Run-Time (SAUS) ... ART
Average Sample Number [*Quality control*] ... ASN
Average Sample Run Length [*Statistics*] (PDAA) ... ASRL
Average Sampling Time [*Statistics*] ... AST
Average Season Busy Hour Call Attempts [*Telecommunications*] (TEL) ... ASBHCA
Average Season Busy Hour Call Completions [*Telecommunications*] (TEL) ... ASBHCC
Average Selling Price (SAUS) ... ASP
Average Service Life ... ASL
Average Shifted Histograms (SAUS) ... ASH
Average Sortie Duration (SAUS) ... ASD
Average Sorties per Aircraft Actually Possessed [*Air Force*] (AFIT) ... ASAXP
Average Sorties per Day [*Air Force*] (AFIT) ... ASD
Average Speach Power (SAUS) ... ASP
Average Specific Polymerization Rate (OA) ... ASPR
Average Staffing Level ... ASL
Average Standing Crop ... ASC
Average Straight Time Hourly Earning (SAUS) ... ASTHE
Average Straight Time Hourly Earnings [*Accounting*] ... ASTHE
Average Student Hours [*Education*] (AIE) ... ASH
Average Task Time ... ATT
Average Temperature (NOAA) ... AVTMP
Average Temperature (SAUS) ... AV TMP
Average Temperature (NRCH) ... TAVE
Average Threshold of Pain Reaction (MELL) ... ATPR
Average Time Between Maintenance (SAUS) ... ATBM
Average Time of Burning ... ATB
Average Time to Repair (MCD) ... ATTR
Average T-Matrix Approximation (MCD) ... ATA
Average Total Cost ... ATC
Average Total Diametrical Displacement (IAA) ... ATDD
Average Total Episode Cost [*Medicine*] ... ATEC
Average Total Inspection [*QCR*] ... ATI
Average Total Operating Cost (KSC) ... ATOC
Average Total Time [*Computer science*] (CIST) ... ATT
Average Total Unit Cost ... ATUC
Average Transfer Rate of Information BITS [*Binary Digits*] [*Computer science*] (IEEE) ... ATRIB
Average Turnaround [*Computer science*] ... ATA
Average Unit Cost ... AUC
Average Unit of Council Funding [*Higher Education Funding Council*] (AIE) ... AUCF
Average Unit Procurement Cost [*Military*] (DOMA) ... AUPC
Average Useful Life ... AUL
Average Utilization Factor ... AUF
Average Value (NASA) ... AV
Average Value (SAUS) ... Av Val
Average Variability ... AV
Average Variable Cost [*Of production*] ... AVC
Average Variable Costs ... AVC
Average Vehicle Ridership (PA) ... AVR
Average Visual Evoked Potential [*Neurophysiology*] ... AVEP
Average Voltage (SAUS) ... Eavg
Average Wage ... AW
Average Wait Time (SAUS) ... AWT
Average Weekday Daily Traffic [*TXDOT*] (TAG) ... AWDT
Average Weekly Earnings ... AWE
Average White Back [*Football*] ... AWB
[*The*] **Average White Band** [*Rock music group*] ... AWB
Average Wholesale Price ... AWP
Average Width ... AVW
Average Width (SAUS) ... AV W
Average Word Length (SAUS) ... AWL
Average Word Load (SAUS) ... AWL
Average Work Load ... AWL
Average Work Time ... AWT
Average Working Depth ... AWD
Average Yarding Distance [*Forestry*] ... AYD
Average Yearly Demands ... AYD
Averaged [*Motor Octane Number*] [*Antiknock index*] [*Fuel technology*] ... R & M/2
Averaged Evoked Potential (SAUS) ... AEP
Averaged Magnitude Squared Coherence (MCD) ... AMSC
Averaged Motor Unit Potential (SAUS) ... AMUP
Averaged Probability Ratio Sequential Test (MHDI) ... APRST
Averaged-Coupled Pair Functional [*Quantum chemistry*] ... ACPF
Averaging Enhancement (SAUS) ... AVE
Averbach on Handling Accident Cases [*A publication*] (DLA) ... Averbach Acci Cas
Averett College (SAUO) ... AC
Averette College, Danville, VA [*Library symbol*] [*Library of Congress*] (LCLS) ... ViDA
Avermectin (LDT) ... AVM
Averroes [*Morocco*] [*Seismograph station code, US Geological Survey*] (SEIS) ... AVE
Avert Disruption of Operation ... AVERDISROP
Avert, Inc. [*Associated Press*] (SAG) ... Avert
Avert, Inc. [*NASDAQ symbol*] (SAG) ... AVRT
Avert Inc. Wrrt [*NASDAQ symbol*] (TTSB) ... AVRTW
Averting AIDS & HIV. AIDS Education & Research Trust (SAUO) ... AVERT
Avery [*Printer of U.S. postage stamps*] (BARN) ... AVR
Avery and Hobb's Bankrupt Law [*A publication*] (DLA) ... Av & HBL
Avery and Hobbs' Bankrupt Law of United States [*A publication*] (DLA) ... A & H Bank
Avery Dennison Corp. [*Associated Press*] (SAG) ... AveryD
Avery Dennison Corp. [*NYSE symbol*] (SPSG) ... AVY
Avery Island (SAUS) ... AI
Avery Point [*Connecticut*] [*Seismograph station code, US Geological Survey*] [*Closed*] (SEIS) ... APT
Avery-Mitchell-Yancey Regional Library, Spruce Pine, NC [*Library symbol*] [*Library of Congress*] (LCLS) ... NcSppA
Avery-Morrison Public Library, Newland, NC [*Library symbol*] [*Library of Congress*] (LCLS) ... NcNew
Aves [*Birds*] [*of Aristophanes*] [*Classical studies*] (OCD) ... Av
Avesen SA de CV [*Mexico*] [*ICAO designator*] (FAAC) ... ESE
Avesta [*Language, etc.*] ... Av
Avesta [*MARC language code*] [*Library of Congress*] (LCCP) ... ave
Avesta [*Sweden*] [*ICAO location identifier*] (ICLI) ... ESVA
Avestan (BARN) ... Av
Avestan (ADWA) ... Avest
AVHRR Data Reception and Processing System (SAUS) ... ADAPS
AVHRR Global Area Coverage (SAUS) ... AVHRR GAC
AVHRR Local Area Coverage (SAUS) ... AVHRR LAC
Avia [*Francis Lombardi eC*] [*Italy*] [*ICAO aircraft manufacturer identifier*] (ICAO) ... AD
Avia Airlines [*South Africa*] [*FAA designator*] (FAAC) ... AGW
Avia Airlines [*Ghana*] [*FAA designator*] (FAAC) ... VIL
Avia Express Ltd. [*Hungary*] [*ICAO designator*] (FAAC) ... AEH
Avia Filipines International, Inc. [*Philippines*] [*ICAO designator*] (FAAC) ... FIL
Avia Kargo Sisitem, AS [*Turkey*] [*FAA designator*] (FAAC) ... AVK
Avia Sud [*France*] [*ICAO designator*] (FAAC) ... AVU
Aviacion Colombiana Ltd. [*Colombia*] [*ICAO designator*] (FAAC) ... VCO
Aviacion Comercial de America, SA de DV [*Mexico*] [*FAA designator*] (FAAC) ... VME
Aviacion de Chiapas [*Mexico*] [*ICAO designator*] (FAAC) ... CHP
Aviacion del Noroeste SA de CV [*Mexico*] [*ICAO designator*] (FAAC) ... ANW
Aviacion Ejecutiva del Noroeste SA de CV [*Mexico*] [*ICAO designator*] (FAAC) ... NST
Aviacion Ejecutiva Mexicana SA [*Mexico*] [*ICAO designator*] (FAAC) ... AVM
Aviacion y Comercio SA [*Aviation and Trade Corporation*] [*Airline*] [*Spain*] ... AVIACO
Aviacion y Comercio SA [*Spain*] [*ICAO designator*] (FAAC) ... AYC
Aviacor [*Former USSR*] [*FAA designator*] (FAAC) ... VCR
Aviaeskadra [*Russian term for an air squadron*] ... AS
Aviair Aviation Ltd. [*Canada*] [*ICAO designator*] (FAAC) ... AVF
Avial (Russian Co. Ltd.) [*Former USSR*] [*ICAO designator*] (FAAC) ... RLC
Avialgarve, Taxis Aereos do Algarve Ltd. [*Portugal*] [*ICAO designator*] (FAAC) ... AVG
Aviall, Inc. [*Associated Press*] (SAG) ... Aviall
Aviall, Inc. [*NYSE symbol*] (SPSG) ... AVL
Aviamilano [*Construzioni Aeronautiche SpA*] [*Italy*] [*ICAO aircraft manufacturer identifier*] (ICAO) ... AM
Avian Adeno-Associated Virus (SAUS) ... AAAV
Avian Aircraft Ltd. [*Canada*] [*ICAO aircraft manufacturer identifier*] (ICAO) ... VA
Avian Basal Medium [*Culture media*] ... ABM
Avian Diseases (journ.) (SAUS) ... Avian Dis
Avian Embryo Nutrient Cartridge ... AENC
Avian Encephalomyelitis [*Medicine*] (DB) ... AEM
Avian erythroblastic leukemia viral oncogene (SAUS) ... ERBB2
Avian Erythroblastosis [*Medicine*] (DMAA) ... AEB
Avian Erythroblastosis Virus ... AEV
Avian Herpes Virus [*Medicine*] (DB) ... AHV
Avian Infectious Bronchitis [*Medicine*] (DMAA) ... AIB
Avian Influenza ... AI
Avian Laryngotracheitis [*Medicine*] (DB) ... ALT
Avian Leukemia Virus [*Medicine*] (DB) ... ALV
Avian Leukosis [*Medicine*] (DB) ... AL
Avian Leukosis Complex (MAE) ... ALC
Avian Leukosis Virus ... ALV
Avian Leukosis Virus [*Medicine*] (MELL) ... AVL
Avian Leukosis Virus Keratomileusis [*Medicine*] (MELL) ... ALK
Avian Lymphoblastosis [*Medicine*] (DMAA) ... ALB
Avian Lymphomatosis [*Medicine*] (DB) ... ALB
Avian Myeloblastic Virus Reverse Transcription [*Genetics*] ... AMVRT
Avian Myeloblastitis Virus (SAUS) ... AMV
Avian Myeloblastosis [*Medicine*] (DMAA) ... AMB
Avian Myeloblastosis Virus ... AMV
Avian Nephritis Virus [*Medicine*] (DMAA) ... ANV
Avian Pancreatic Polypeptide ... APP
Avian Philately Unit [*Defunct*] (EA) ... APU
Avian Pneumoencephalitis [*Medicine*] (DB) ... APE
Avian Propagation Center (SAUO) ... APC
Avian Retrovirus ... ARV
Avian Retrovirus ... AVRV
Avian Sarcoma Virus [*Same as RSV*] ... ASV
Avian Sarcoma-Leukosis Virus ... ASLV
Avian Tumor Virus [*Medicine*] (DMAA) ... ATV
Avianca [*ICAO designator*] (AD) ... AV
AVIANCA [*Aerovias Nacionales de Colombia SA*] [*Colombian airline*] ... AVN
Avianca, Aerovias Nacionales de Colombia SA [*ICAO designator*] (FAAC) ... AVA
Aviano [*Italy*] [*ICAO location identifier*] (ICLI) ... LIPA
Aviano [*Italy*] [*ICAO location identifier*] (ICLI) ... LIYW
Avianova SpA [*Italy*] [*ICAO designator*] (FAAC) ... NOV
Aviaobshemash [*Former USSR*] [*FAA designator*] (FAAC) ... OBM
Aviapaslauga [*Lithuania*] [*FAA designator*] (FAAC) ... AVX
Aviapolk [*Russian term for an air regiment*] ... AP
Aviaprima [*Russian Federation*] [*ICAO designator*] (FAAC) ... PRL
Aviaross [*Russian Federation*] [*ICAO designator*] (FAAC) ... RAR
Aviata [*Former USSR*] [*FAA designator*] (FAAC) ... TVL
Aviateca [*ICAO designator*] (AD) ... GU

Aviation [*FCC*] (NTCM)	A
Aviation [*Special duties officer*] [*British*]	AV
Aviation (DLA)	AVI
Aviation (AFM)	AVN
Aviation (ADWA)	avn
Aviation (SAUS)	Avn
Aviation Administrative Communication (DA)	AAC
Aviation Amos [*M et J*], Inc. [*Canada*] [*ICAO designator*] (FAAC)	AMJ
Aviation and Air Defense Division [*US Army Human Engineering Laboratory, Aberdeen Proving Ground, MD*] (RDA)	AADD
Aviation and Astronautics Electronics (SAUS)	Avionics
Aviation and Computer Enthusiasts [*Defunct*] (EA)	ACE
Aviation and Fire Management Centre, Ontario Ministry of Natural Resources, Sault Ste. Marie [*Library symbol*] [*National Library of Canada*] (BIB)	OSTMNA
Aviation and Surface Effects Department [*David W. Taylor Naval Ship Research and Development Center*]	ASED
Aviation and Surface Material Command [*Air Force*]	AVSCOM
Aviation and Troop Command [*Army*]	ATCOM
Aviation and Troop Support Command [*Army*] (RDA)	ATCOM
Aviation Annex [*Air Force*]	AA
Aviation Antisubmarine Warfare Basic Operational Trainer	AAWBOT
Aviation Applied Technology Directorate [*Fort Eustis, VA*] [*Army*] (RDA)	AATD
Aviation Armament Bulletin (MCD)	AAB
Aviation Armament Change (MCD)	AAC
Aviation Armament Laboratory [*Later, Naval Air Development Center*] [*Navy*]	AAL
Aviation Associates, Inc. [*St. Croix*] [*ICAO designator*] (FAAC)	SUA
Aviation Association of Indiana (SRA)	AAI
Aviation ASW [*Antisubmarine Warfare*] Operator [*Navy rating*]	AW
Aviation ASW [*Antisubmarine Warfare*] Operator, First Class [*Navy rating*]	AW1
Aviation ASW [*Antisubmarine Warfare*] Operator, Master Chief [*Navy rating*]	AWCM
Aviation ASW [*Antisubmarine Warfare*] Operator, Second Class [*Navy rating*]	AW2
Aviation ASW [*Antisubmarine Warfare*] Operator, Senior Chief [*Navy rating*]	AWCS
Aviation ASW [*Antisubmarine Warfare*] Operator, Third Class [*Navy rating*]	AW3
Aviation ASW [*Antisubmarine Warfare*] Technician [*Navy rating*]	AX
Aviation ASW [*Antisubmarine Warfare*] Technician, Chief [*Navy rating*]	AXC
Aviation ASW [*Antisubmarine Warfare*] Technician, First Class [*Navy rating*]	AX1
Aviation ASW [*Antisubmarine Warfare*] Technician, Master Chief [*Navy rating*]	AXCM
Aviation ASW [*Antisubmarine Warfare*] Technician, Second Class [*Navy rating*]	AX2
Aviation ASW [*Antisubmarine Warfare*] Technician, Senior Chief [*Navy rating*]	AXCS
Aviation ASW [*Antisubmarine Warfare*] Technician, Third Class [*Navy rating*]	AX3
Aviation Automated Weather-Observation System (SAUS)	AV-AWOS
Aviation Base Responsibility List (AFIT)	ABRL
Aviation Baseship	AVB
Aviation Battalion [*Army*]	AB
Aviation Battalion [*Army*]	AVBAT
Aviation Beauport Ltd. [*British*] [*ICAO designator*] (FAAC)	AVB
Aviation Billet Indicator (DNAB)	ABI
Aviation Bird Unit (SAUS)	ABU
Aviation Boatswain [*Navy rating*]	AB
Aviation Boatswain's Mate [*Navy*] (MUSM)	AB
Aviation Boatswain's Mate [*Navy rating*]	ABM
Aviation Boatswain's Mate, Arresting Gear and Barriers [*Navy rating*]	ABMAG
Aviation Boatswain's Mate, Catapult [*Navy rating*]	ABMCP
Aviation Boatswains Mate, Catapult (SAUS)	ABMCP
Aviation Boatswain's Mate, Chief [*Navy rating*]	ABC
Aviation Boatswain's Mate, First Class [*Navy rating*]	AB1
Aviation Boatswains Mate, First Class (SAUS)	AB1
Aviation Boatswain's Mate, Fuel [*Navy rating*]	ABF
Aviation Boatswain's Mate, Fuel, Airman [*Navy rating*]	ABFAN
Aviation Boatswain's Mate, Fuel, Airman Apprentice [*Navy rating*]	ABFAA
Aviation Boatswain's Mate, Fuel, Second Class [*Navy rating*] (DNAB)	ABF2
Aviation Boatswain's Mate, Fuel, Third Class [*Navy rating*] (DNAB)	ABF3
Aviation Boatswain's Mate, Gasoline System [*Navy rating*]	ABMGA
Aviation Boatswain's Mate, Handler [*Navy rating*]	ABH
Aviation Boatswains Mate, Handler (SAUS)	ABMH
Aviation Boatswain's Mate, Handler, Airman [*Navy rating*]	ABHAN
Aviation Boatswain's Mate, Handler, Airman Apprentice [*Navy rating*]	ABHAA
Aviation Boatswain's Mate, Handler, First Class [*Navy rating*] (DNAB)	ABH1
Aviation Boatswain's Mate, Handler, Second Class [*Navy rating*] (DNAB)	ABH2
Aviation Boatswain's Mate, Handler, Third Class [*Navy rating*] (DNAB)	ABH3
Aviation Boatswain's Mate, Launch and Recovery Equipment [*Navy rating*]	ABE
Aviation Boatswain's Mate, Launch and Recovery Equipment, Airman [*Navy rating*]	ABEAN
Aviation Boatswain's Mate, Launch and Recovery Equipment, Airman Apprentice [*Navy rating*]	ABEAA
Aviation Boatswain's Mate, Plane Handler [*Navy rating*]	ABMPH
Aviation Boatswains Mate, Plane Handler (SAUS)	ABMPH
Aviation Boatswains Mate, Second Class (SAUS)	AB2
Aviation Boatswain's Mate, Second Class [*Navy rating*]	AB2
Aviation Boatswain's Mate, Senior Chief [*Navy rating*]	ABCS
Aviation Boatswain's Mate, Third Class [*Navy rating*]	AB3
Aviation Boatswains Mate, Third Class (SAUS)	AB3
Aviation Cadet [*Air Force*]	AC
Aviation Cadet [*Navy*]	AvC
Aviation Cadet [*Navy*]	AVCAD
Aviation Cadet Alumni Association (EA)	ACAA
Aviation Cadet Qualifying Test [*Military*]	ACQT
Aviation Calibration Equipment (MCD)	AVCAL
Aviation Career Incentive Act [*1974*] (AABC)	ACIA
Aviation Career Incentive Pay [*Air Force*] (AFM)	ACIP
Aviation Carrier Air Turbine fuel (SAUS)	AVCAT
Aviation Carrier Turbine Fuel	AVCAT
Aviation Cases [*Commerce Clearing House*] [*A publication*] (DLA)	Av Cas
Aviation Center [*Army*]	AVNC
Aviation Charter & Management [*British*] [*ICAO designator*] (FAAC)	FTN
Aviation Chief Boatswain's Mate, Arresting Gear and Barriers [*Navy rating*]	ACBMAG
Aviation Chief Boatswain's Mate, Catapult [*Navy rating*]	ACBMCP
Aviation Chief Boatswains Mate, Catapult (SAUS)	ACBMCP
Aviation Chief Boatswains Mate, Gasoline System (SAUS)	ACBMGA
Aviation Chief Boatswain's Mate, Gasoline System [*Navy rating*]	ACBMGA
Aviation Chief Boatswain's Mate, Plane Handler [*Navy rating*]	ACBMPH
Aviation Chief Boatswains Mate, Plane Handler (SAUS)	ACBMPH
Aviation Chief Electricians Mate (SAUS)	ACEM
Aviation Chief Electrician's Mate [*Navy*]	ACEM
Aviation Chief Fire Controlman [*Navy*]	ACFC
Aviation Chief Machinist's Mate [*Navy*]	ACMM
Aviation Chief Machinists Mate (SAUS)	ACMM
Aviation Chief Machinist's Mate, Carburetor Mechanic [*Navy*]	ACMMC
Aviation Chief Machinist's Mate, Flight Engineer [*Navy*]	ACMMF
Aviation Chief Machinist's Mate, Gas Turbine Mechanic [*Navy*]	ACMMT
Aviation Chief Machinists Mate, Gas Turbine Mechanic (SAUS)	ACMMT
Aviation Chief Machinist's Mate, Hydraulic Mechanic [*Navy*]	ACMMH
Aviation Chief Machinist's Mate, Instrument Mechanic [*Navy*]	ACMMI
Aviation Chief Machinist's Mate, Propeller Mechanic [*Navy*]	ACMMP
Aviation Chief Metalsmith [*Navy*]	ACM
Aviation Chief Ordnanceman [*Navy*]	ACOM
Aviation Chief Ordnanceman, Turret Mechanic [*Navy*]	ACOMT
Aviation Chief Radio Technician [*Navy*]	ACRT
Aviation Chief Radioman [*Navy*]	ACRM
Aviation Circular Letter	ACL
Aviation Classification Repair Activity Depot [*Army*] (RDA)	AVCRAD
Aviation Classification Repair Activity Depots (SAUS)	AVCRAD
Aviation Classification Test	ACT
Aviation Clothing and Survival Equipment Bulletin (MCD)	ACSEB
Aviation Co. Meridian [*Former USSR*] [*FAA designator*] (FAAC)	MMM
Aviation Co. Mostransgas [*Former USSR*] [*FAA designator*] (FAAC)	MTG
Aviation Combat Development Agency [*CDC*]	ACDA
Aviation Combat Element [*Marine Corps*] (DOMA)	ACE
Aviation Combat Training System [*Military*]	ACTS
Aviation Combined Arms Tactical Trainer (SAUS)	AVCAT
Aviation Combined Arms Tactical Trainer [*Army*]	AVCATT
Aviation Combined Arms Team Trainer	ACATT
Aviation Combined Arms Team Trainer (SAUS)	AVCATT
Aviation Command (SAUS)	AVCOM
Aviation Command Screening Board (DNAB)	ACSB
Aviation Commission Date (DNAB)	ACD
Aviation Company [*Military*] (VNW)	AVN
Aviation Consolidated Allowance List [*Military*] (NVT)	AVCAL
Aviation Consortium for Education & Training (SAUS)	ACET
Aviation Construction Engineers [*Military*]	ACE
Aviation Consumer Action Process (SAUS)	ACAP
Aviation Consumer Action Project (EA)	ACAP
Aviation Continuation Pay [*Navy*] (DOMA)	ACP
Aviation Control Center	ACC
Aviation Coordinated Allowance List (SAUS)	AVCAL
Aviation Corporation (SAUO)	Avco
Aviation Crash Injury Research (MUGU)	ACIR
Aviation Credit Corps	ACC
Aviation Crime Prevention Institute (EA)	ACPI
Aviation Cruiser (MCD)	CH
Aviation Daily	AD
Aviation Data Analysis Center (MCD)	AVDAC
Aviation Data and Analysis System [*BTS*] (TAG)	ADA
Aviation Data Service, Inc. [*Information service or system*] (IID)	ADS
Aviation Delay (SAUS)	AD
Aviation Depot Group (AAG)	ADG
Aviation Depot Level Repairables (MCD)	AVDLRS
Aviation Depot Squadron [*Air Force*]	ADS
Aviation Depot Squadron [*Air Force*]	AVDS
Aviation Design Research [*Navy*]	ADR
Aviation Detachment [*Military*] (VNW)	AD
Aviation Development Advisory Committee (SAUO)	ADAC
Aviation Development Advisory Committee (SAUS)	ADAC
Aviation Development Board	ADB
Aviation Development Co. Nigeria Ltd. [*ICAO designator*] (FAAC)	ADK
Aviation Development Council (EA)	ADC
Aviation Development Tactics and Evaluation Department [*Military*]	ADTE
Aviation Development Test Activity [*Test and Evaluation Command*] [*Army*] (RDA)	ADTA
Aviation Development Test Activity [*Test and Evaluation Command*] [*Army*] (RDA)	AVNDTA
Aviation Development Test Facility (MCD)	ADTF
Aviation Digital Data Service (SAUS)	ADDS
Aviation Distributors and Manufacturers Association (EA)	ADMA
Aviation Distributors and Manufacturers Association (SAUS)	ADMA
Aviation Distributors, Inc. [*NASDAQ symbol*] (SAG)	ADIN
Aviation Distributors, Inc. [*Associated Press*] (SAG)	AviDist

Aviation Division [*Forecast Systems Laboratory*] (USDC) .... AD
Aviation Division [*Marine science*] (OSRA) .... AD
Aviation Electric, Limited [*Canada*] (ACAE) .... AEL
Aviation Electric Limited (SAUO) .... AEL
Aviation Electric Ltd. (SAUS) .... AEL
Aviation Electric Ltd., Montreal, PQ, Canada [*Library symbol*] [*Library of Congress*] (LCLS) .... CaQMAE
Aviation Electric Ltd., Montreal, Quebec [*Library symbol*] [*National Library of Canada*] (NLC) .... QMAE
Aviation Electrical & Radio Co. Ltd. (SAUO) .... AERCO
Aviation Electrician's Mate [*Navy rating*] .... AE
Aviation Electrician's Mate [*Navy rating*] .... AEM
Aviation Electrician's Mate, Chief [*Navy rating*] .... AEC
Aviation Electrician's Mate, First Class [*Navy rating*] AE1
Aviation Electrician's Mate, Master Chief [*Navy rating*] .... AECM
Aviation Electrician's Mate, Second Class [*Navy rating*] AE2
Aviation Electrician's Mate, Senior Chief [*Navy rating*] .... AECS
Aviation Electrician's Mate, Third Class [*Navy rating*] AE3
Aviation Electronic Combat [*Army*] (RDA) .... AEC
Aviation Electronic Equipment Information Exchange System (MCD) .... AVEXS
Aviation Electronic Technician's Mate [*Navy*] .... AETM
Aviation Electronic Technicians Mate (SAUS) .... AETM
Aviation Electronic Technicians Mate, Combat Aircrewman (SAUS) .... AETAC
Aviation Electronic Technician's Mate, Combat Aircrewman [*Navy*] .... AETAC
Aviation Electronic Technicians Mate, Combat Aircrewman (SAUS) .... AETCA
Aviation Electronics .... AVIONICS
Aviation Electronics Technician [*Navy rating*] .... AT
Aviation Electronics Technician Airborne CIC [*Combat Information Center*] **Equipment** .... ATW
Aviation Electronics Technician, Chief [*Navy rating*] .... ATC
Aviation Electronics Technician, First Class [*Navy rating*] AT1
Aviation Electronics Technician, Master Chief [*Navy rating*] .... ATCM
Aviation Electronics Technician, Second Class [*Navy rating*] AT2
Aviation Electronics Technician, Senior Chief [*Navy rating*] .... ATCS
Aviation Electronics Technician, Third Class [*Navy rating*] AT3
Aviation Electronicsman [*Military*] .... AL
Aviation Engineer (IAA) .... AE
Aviation Engineer Battalion [*Marine Corps*] .... AVNENGRBN
Aviation Engineer Command (SAUS) .... AEC
Aviation Engineer Force .... AEF
Aviation Engineering (SAUS) .... AE
Aviation Engineering & Maintenance (SAUS) .... AEM
Aviation Engineering and Maintenance Co. Ltd. (SAUO) .... AEM
Aviation Engineering Corp. (MCD) .... AVIEN
Aviation Engineering Corporation, Inc. (SAUO) .... AVIEN
Aviation Engineering Flight Activity [*Formerly, ASTA*] [*Edwards Air Force Base, CA*] [*Army*] .... AEFA
Aviation Enterprises [*Denmark*] [*ICAO designator*] (FAAC) .... AVP
Aviation Evaluation Group (SAUO) .... AEG
Aviation Facilities Energy Association [*Defunct*] (EA) .... AFEA
Aviation Facilities Service [*of FAA*] .... AFS
Aviation Financial Services, Inc. .... AFSI
Aviation Financial Services, Incorporated (SAUO) .... AFSI
Aviation Fire Control Technician [*Navy rating*] .... AQ
Aviation Fire Control Technician, Bomb Direction [*Navy rating*] .... AQB
Aviation Fire Control Technician, Chief [*Navy rating*] .... AQC
Aviation Fire Control Technician, Fire Control [*Navy rating*] .... AQF
Aviation Fire Control Technician, First Class [*Navy rating*] AQ1
Aviation Fire Control Technician, First Class (SAUS) .... AQI
Aviation Fire Control Technician, Master Chief [*Navy rating*] .... AQCM
Aviation Fire Control Technician, Second Class [*Navy rating*] AQ2
Aviation Fire Control Technician, Senior Chief [*Navy rating*] .... AQCS
Aviation Fire Control Technician, Third Class [*Navy rating*] AQ3
Aviation Fire Controlman [*Navy*] .... AFC
Aviation Fleet Maintenance (NVT) .... AFM
Aviation Fluids Service Inc. (SAUO) .... AFS
Aviation Foot Lockers [*Army*] (RDA) .... AFL
Aviation Force Structure for the Army (MCD) .... AFSA
Aviation Force Structure of the Army (SAUO) .... AFSA
Aviation Forecast Verification Program [*Marine science*] (OSRA) .... AFVP
Aviation Forum [*British*] .... AF
Aviation Fuel (MSA) .... AVFUEL
Aviation Fuel (SAUS) .... AVFuel
Aviation Fuel [*Gasoline/Kerosene*] [*NATO*] .... AVTAG
Aviation Fuel and Ammunition Park (SAUO) .... AFAP
Aviation Fuel Depot (SAUO) .... AFD
Aviation Fuel, High-Flash Point [*NATO*] .... AVCAT
Aviation Fuels Logistical Area Summary [*Air Force*] (AFIT) .... AFLAS
Aviation Fuels, Lubricants, and Associated Products [*NATO*] (NATG) .... F & L
Aviation Fuels Management System (SAUO) .... FUELS
Aviation Gas Turbine (KSC) .... AGT
Aviation Gas Turbine fuel (SAUS) .... AVTUR
Aviation Gasoline [*Navy*] .... AGAS
Aviation Gasoline .... AVGAS
Aviation Gasoline (ADWA) .... avgas
Aviation General Policy (SAUS) .... AGP
Aviation Gridded Forecast System [*Marine science*] (OSRA) .... AGFS
Aviation Ground Equipment (AAGC) .... AGE
Aviation Ground Power Unit (MCD) .... AGPU
Aviation Ground Support Equipment (SAUS) .... AGSE
Aviation Ground Unit [*Naval Reserve*] .... AGU
Aviation Group, Inc. (SAUO) .... LIFT
Aviation Guided Flight (MUGU) .... AGF
Aviation Gunnery Officers School .... AGOS
Aviation High School (SAUO) .... AHS
Aviation High-Flash Turbine Fuel (SAUS) .... AVCAT
Aviation Historical Society (EA) .... AHS
Aviation Historical Society of Australia. Journal (journ.) (SAUS) .... J Aviat Hist S Aust
Aviation Historical Society of New Zealand (SAUO) .... AHSNZ
Aviation Horsepower (SAUS) .... AHP
Aviation Human Research Unit [*Army*] .... AHRU
Aviation Impact Variable (USDC) .... AIV
Aviation Indoctrination Program [*Military*] (DNAB) .... AIP
Aviation Industries of China (ECON) .... AVIC
Aviation Industry Advisory Council (ADA) .... AVIAC
Aviation Industry Association (SAUO) .... AIA
Aviation Information Services Ltd. (IID) .... AISL
Aviation Infrastructure Roundtable (ACAE) .... AIR
Aviation Instrument Laboratory [*Navy*] .... AIL
Aviation Insurance Association (NTPA) .... AIA
Aviation Insurance Officers Association (DA) .... AIOA
Aviation Insurance Rating Bureau [*Defunct*] (EA) .... AIRB
Aviation Intensive Management Items (AABC) .... AIMI
Aviation Intermediate Maintenance [*Army*] (MCD) .... AVIM
Aviation Investigator (LAIN) .... AI
Aviation Item Reports .... AIR
Aviation Kamchatka-California Organization for Reconstruction and Development (ECON) .... AKCORD
Aviation Laboratories [*Army*] .... AVLABS
Aviation Laboratories (SAUS) .... Av Labs
Aviation LASER Device .... AVLD
Aviation Law Reporter [*Commerce Clearing House*] [*A publication*] (DLA) .... Av L Rep
Aviation Leadership Program (SAUS) .... ALP
Aviation Legere de l'Armee de Terre [*France*] [*ICAO designator*] (FAAC) .... LAT
Aviation Liaison Officer [*Army*] .... AVLNO
Aviation Life Support Equipment (AABC) .... ALSE
Aviation Life Support Systems (MCD) .... ALSS
Aviation Logistic Platform (SAUS) .... ALP
Aviation Logistic Support Ship (SAUS) .... TAVB
Aviation Logistics and Operations Center [*Military*] (DOMA) .... ALOC
Aviation Logistics Officer Course [*Army*] (INF) .... AVLOC
Aviation Lubricant (MUGU) .... AVLUB
Aviation Machinist Mate Jet, Chief [*Navy rating*] .... ADJC
Aviation Machinist Mate Jet, Master Chief [*Navy rating*] .... ADJM
Aviation Machinist Mate Jet, Senior Chief [*Navy rating*] .... ADJS
Aviation Machinist's Mate [*Navy rating*] .... AD
Aviation Machinist's Mate [*Navy rating*] .... AMM
Aviation Machinist's Mate, Carburetor Mechanic [*Navy rating*] .... AMMC
Aviation Machinist's Mate, Combat Aircrewman [*Navy rating*] .... AMMAC
Aviation Machinists Mate First Class (SAUS) AMM1c
Aviation Machinists Mate, Flight Engineer (SAUS) .... AMMF
Aviation Machinist's Mate, Flight Engineer [*Navy rating*] .... AMMF
Aviation Machinist's Mate, Hydraulic Mechanic [*Navy rating*] .... AMMH
Aviation Machinists Mate, Hydraulic Mechanic (SAUS) .... AMMH
Aviation Machinists Mate, Instrument Mechanic (SAUS) .... AMMI
Aviation Machinist's Mate, Instrument Mechanic [*Navy rating*] .... AMMI
Aviation Machinist's Mate, Jet Engine Mechanic [*Navy rating*] .... ADJ
Aviation Machinist's Mate, Jet Engine Mechanic, First Class [*Navy rating*] (DNAB) ADJ1
Aviation Machinist's Mate, Jet Engine Mechanic, Second Class [*Navy rating*] (DNAB) ADJ2
Aviation Machinist's Mate, Jet Engine Mechanic, Third Class [*Navy rating*] (DNAB) ADJ3
Aviation Machinist's Mate, Propeller Mechanic [*Navy rating*] .... AMMP
Aviation Machinist's Mate, Reciprocating Engine Mechanic [*Navy rating*] .... ADR
Aviation Machinist's Mate, Reciprocating Engine Mechanic, Chief [*Navy rating*] .... ADRC
Aviation Machinist's Mate, Reciprocating Engine Mechanic, First Class [*Navy rating*] ADR1
Aviation Machinists Mate, Reciprocating Engine Mechanic, First Class (SAUS) ADR1
Aviation Machinist's Mate, Reciprocating Engine Mechanic, Master Chief [*Navy rating*] .... ADRCM
Aviation Machinist's Mate, Reciprocating Engine Mechanic, Second Class [*Navy rating*] ADR2
Aviation Machinist's Mate, Reciprocating Engine Mechanic, Senior Chief [*Navy rating*] .... ADRCS
Aviation Machinist's Mate, Reciprocating Engine Mechanic, Third Class [*Navy rating*] ADR3
Aviation Machinists Mate Second Class (SAUS) AMM2c
Aviation Machinists Mate Third Class (SAUS) AMM3c
Aviation Machinist's Mate, Turret Mechanic [*Navy rating*] .... AMMT
Aviation Maintenance Administrationman [*Navy rating*] .... AZ
Aviation Maintenance Administrationman, Chief [*Navy rating*] .... AZC
Aviation Maintenance Administrationman, First Class [*Navy rating*] AZ1
Aviation Maintenance Administrationman, Master Chief [*Navy rating*] .... AZCM
Aviation Maintenance Administrationman, Second Class [*Navy rating*] AZ2
Aviation Maintenance Administrationman, Senior Chief [*Navy rating*] .... AZCS
Aviation Maintenance Administrationman, Third Class [*Navy rating*] AZ3
Aviation Maintenance and Logistics Evaluation (MCD) .... AMLE
Aviation Maintenance Costs .... AMC
Aviation Maintenance Foundation (SAUO) .... AMFI
Aviation Maintenance Foundation, Inc. (EA) .... AMFI
Aviation Maintenance Officer [*Military*] (NVT) .... AMO
Aviation Maintenance Technician [*Military*] (DNAB) .... AVMAINTECH
Aviation Management Corp. [*ICAO designator*] (FAAC) .... AAM
Aviation Management Information System (GEOI) .... AMIS
Aviation Marine-Outillage .... AMO

Aviation Marketing Services (SAUO)	AMS
Aviation Material Change (SAA)	AMC
Aviation Material Combat Ready In-Country (MCD)	AMCRIC
Aviation Material Laboratory (SAUO)	AML
Aviation Material Management Program (SAUO)	AMMP
Aviation Material Office [Military] (AFIT)	AMO
Aviation Material Office, Atlantic [Military] (DNAB)	AVNMATOLANT
Aviation Material Office, Reserve [Military] (DNAB)	AVNMATORES
Aviation Materiel Command [St. Louis, MO] [Army]	AVCOM
Aviation Materiel Laboratories [Army]	AML
Aviation Materiel Management Center (AABC)	AMMC
Aviation Materiel Management Improvement Program [Military] (NG)	AMMIP
Aviation Mechanic, Hydraulics (SAUS)	AMH
Aviation Medical	AVM
Aviation Medical Acceleration Laboratory (MCD)	AMAL
Aviation Medical Examiner	AME
Aviation Medical Examiners (SAUO)	AME
Aviation Medical Officer [Military] (AABC)	AMO
Aviation Medical (or Medicine) Society of Australia and New Zealand (SAUO)	AMSANZ
Aviation Medical Reports	AMR
Aviation Medicine [Medical officer designation] [British]	A/M
Aviation Medicine (SAUO)	AM
Aviation Medicine [Military] (AABC)	AVNMED
Aviation Medicine Technician [Navy]	AVT
Aviation Metalsmith	AM
Aviation Metalsmith Second Class (SAUS)	AM2c
Aviation Metalsmith Third Class (SAUS)	AM3c
Aviation Meteorological Facsimile [National Weather Service]	AMFAX
Aviation Mission Planning System (SAUS)	AMPS
Aviation Model Verification Program (SAUS)	AMVP
Aviation Modernization Plan (SAUS)	AMP
Aviation Modernization Program (SAUS)	AMP
Aviation Network	Avnet
Aviation Network (IAA)	AVNET
Aviation News Features	ANF
Aviation News (journ.) (SAUS)	AVN
Aviation Observation (NOAA)	AVIOB
Aviation Officer [MTMC] (TAG)	AO
Aviation Officer Advanced Course (SAUS)	AVOAC
Aviation Officer Cadet (SAUO)	AOC
Aviation Officer Candidate [Navy]	AOC
Aviation Officer Candidate Airman [Navy] (DNAB)	AOCAN
Aviation Officer Candidate School [Navy]	AOCS
Aviation Officer Continuation Pay [Navy]	AOCP
Aviation Officer of the Day [MTMC] (TAG)	AOD
Aviation Officers' Quarters	AOQ
Aviation Officers Quarters (SAUS)	AOQ
Aviation Officers Training Corps	AOTC
Aviation Oil [Military]	A OIL
Aviation Oil [Military]	AVOIL
Aviation Operating Detachment (CINC)	AOD
Aviation Operational Research Branch (SAUO)	AORB
Aviation Operations Technician (DNAB)	AVOPTECH
Aviation Ordnance Man Second Class (SAUS)	AOM2c
Aviation Ordnance Man Third Class (SAUS)	AOM3c
Aviation Ordnance Officer	AOO
Aviation Ordnance Safety Supervisor (COE)	AOSS
Aviation Ordnance Technician (DNAB)	AVORDTECH
Aviation Ordnance Test Station (SAUS)	AOTS
Aviation Ordnanceman [Navy rating]	AO
Aviation Ordnanceman [Navy rating] [Obsolete]	AOM
Aviation Ordnanceman, Airman Apprentice, Striker [Navy rating]	AOAA
Aviation Ordnanceman, Airman, Striker [Navy rating]	AOAN
Aviation Ordnanceman, Bombsight Mechanic [Navy rating] [Obsolete]	AOMB
Aviation Ordnanceman, Bombsight Mechanic (SAUS)	AOMB
Aviation Ordnanceman, Chief [Navy rating]	AOC
Aviation Ordnanceman, Combat Aircrewman [Navy rating] [Obsolete]	AOMAC
Aviation Ordnanceman, Combat Aircrewman, Air Bomber [Navy rating] [Obsolete]	AOACB
Aviation Ordnanceman, First Class [Navy rating]	AO1
Aviation Ordnanceman, Master Chief [Navy rating]	AOCM
Aviation Ordnanceman, Second Class [Navy rating]	AO2
Aviation Ordnanceman, Senior Chief [Navy rating]	AOCS
Aviation Ordnanceman, Third Class [Navy rating]	AO3
Aviation Ordnanceman, Turret Mechanic [Navy rating]	AOMT
Aviation Pay [Navy]	AVIA
Aviation Pay (Crewmember) [Navy]	AVN(CM)
Aviation Pay (Non-Crewmember) [Navy]	AVN(NCM)
Aviation Performance Assessment in a Chemical Environment (PDAA)	APACHE
Aviation Personnel and Survival Equipment Team [Navy] (NG)	APSET
Aviation Personnel Planning Data [Navy] (NG)	APPD
Aviation Petroleum Coordinating Committee, Latin America (SAUO)	APCCLA
Aviation Petroleum Coordinating Committee, Latin American	APCCLA
Aviation Petroleum Coordinating Committee, Latin American Air Pollution Control District (SAUS)	APCCLAAPCD
Aviation Petroleum, Oil & Lubricants (SAUS)	AVPOL
Aviation Petroleum Products Allocation Committee	APPAC
Aviation Petroleum Products Allocation Committee, London	APPAC-L
Aviation Pilot [Navy]	AP
Aviation Pilot, Airship [Navy]	APLA
Aviation Pilot Second Class (SAUS)	AP2c
Aviation Pilot Third Class (SAUS)	AP3c
Aviation Pilots Airship (SAUS)	APLA

Aviation POL [Petroleum, Oil, and Lubrication] Handling Equipment (NATG)	PHE
Aviation Procurement Authorization [Army]	APA
Aviation Procurement, Navy (MCD)	APN
Aviation Professionals International [New Orleans]	API
Aviation Psychology Laboratory [Ohio State University] [Research center] (RCD)	APL
Aviation Publication (MCD)	AVP
Aviation Qualification Test	AQT
Aviation Quebec Labrador Ltd. [Canada] [ICAO designator] (FAAC)	QLA
Aviation Radio and RADAR Countermeasures Technician [Navy]	RCM
Aviation Radio Technician	ART
Aviation Radioman [Navy]	ARM
Aviation Radioman, Combat Aircrewman [Navy]	ARMAC
Aviation Radioman First Class (SAUS)	ARM 1c
Aviation Radioman Second Class (SAUS)	ARM 2c
Aviation Radioman Third Class (SAUS)	ARM 3c
Aviation Radionavigation (SAUS)	AR
Aviation Radionavigation, Land [FCC] (IEEE)	AR
Aviation Readiness Evaluation (NVT)	ARE
Aviation Regulatory Advisory Committee [FAA] (TAG)	ARAC
Aviation Repair and Overhaul Unit	AROU
Aviation Repair Supply Depot	ARSD
Aviation Reports (SAUS)	US Aviation
Aviation Requirements for the Combat Structure of the Army (AABC)	ARCSA
Aviation Research and Development Command (SAUO)	AVRADCOM
Aviation Research and Development Service [FAA]	ARDS
Aviation Research and Technology Activity [Moffett Field, CA] [Army] (RDA)	ARTA
Aviation Research Development and Engineering Center [Army] (RDA)	AVRDEC
Aviation Research Laboratory [University of Illinois] (MCD)	ARL
Aviation Reserve Officers Candidate Program	AVROC
Aviation Resources Management and Control System	ARMACS
Aviation Route Forecast (MCD)	ARF
Aviation Route Weather Report (SAUO)	METAR
Aviation Routine Weather Report [ICAO] (FAAC)	METAR
Aviation Rulemaking Advisory Committee (GAVI)	ARAC
Aviation Safety Analysis System [FAA] (GFGA)	ASAS
Aviation Safety and Health Association (EA)	ASHA
Aviation Safety District Office	ASDO
Aviation Safety Engineering and Research (KSC)	AVSER
Aviation Safety Institute (EA)	ASI
Aviation Safety Office [or Officer] [Military] (MCD)	ASO
Aviation Safety Program [FAA] (SAUO)	ASP
Aviation Safety Programs, Transport Canada [Programme de la Securite Aerienne, Transports Canada], Vancouver, British Columbia [Library symbol] [National Library of Canada] (NLC)	BVATAS
Aviation Safety Regulation	ASR
Aviation Safety Reporting System (MCD)	ASRS
Aviation Sales [NYSE symbol] (SG)	AVS
Aviation Sales Co. [Associated Press] (SAG)	Aviation
Aviation Sales Co. [NYSE symbol] (SAG)	AVS
Aviation Satellite (DNAB)	AVSAT
Aviation School [Army]	AVNS
Aviation School (SAUS)	Avn Sch
Aviation School of Medicine	ASM
Aviation Section Signal Corps (SAUO)	ASSC
Aviation Section, Signal Reserve Corps (SAUO)	ASSRC
Aviation Section Signal Reserve Corps	ASSRC
Aviation Security Association of America - International [Defunct] (EA)	ASAA-I
Aviation Security Command [Philippines]	AVSECOM
Aviation Security Improvement Act [FAA] (TAG)	ASIA
Aviation Security Panel [ICAO] (DA)	AVSEC
Aviation Security System (SAUS)	ASS
Aviation Selected Reserve Programs Branch [BUPERS]	ASRPB
Aviation Selected Special Weather Report (SAUS)	SPECI
Aviation Service Code (AFM)	ASC
Aviation Service Date (AFM)	ASD
Aviation Service Entry Data (AABC)	ASED
Aviation Services [ICAO designator] (AD)	ML
Aviation Services, Inc. [ICAO designator] (FAAC)	AVQ
Aviation Services Incorporated (SAUO)	ASI
Aviation Services International (SAUS)	ASI
Aviation Services Ltd. [Guam] [ICAO designator] (FAAC)	FRE
Aviation Seychelles Ltd. [ICAO designator] (FAAC)	AVS
Aviation Ships Planning Document (MCD)	ASPD
Aviation Signal Light Gun [Military] (PDAA)	ASLG
Aviation Simulations International (SAUO)	ASI
Aviation, Space & Environmental Medicine (SAUS)	AS&EM
Aviation Space and Environmental Medicine (SAUS)	Aviat Space Environ Med
Aviation Spares Ltd (SAUS)	ASL
Aviation Standards [FAA] (TAG)	AVS
Aviation Standards National Field Office [ICAO designator] (FAAC)	FLC
Aviation Status Indicator (DNAB)	ASI
Aviation Storekeeper [Navy rating]	AK
Aviation Storekeeper, Chief [Navy rating]	AKC
Aviation Storekeeper, First Class [Navy rating]	AK1
Aviation Storekeeper, Master Chief [Navy rating]	AKCM
Aviation Storekeeper, Second Class [Navy rating]	AK2
Aviation Storekeeper, Senior Chief [Navy rating]	AKCS
Aviation Storekeeper, Third Class [Navy rating]	AK3
Aviation Structural Mechanic [Navy rating]	AM
Aviation Structural Mechanic (SAUS)	AMS

Aviation Structural Mechanic, Chief [*Navy rating*] .... AMC
Aviation Structural Mechanic, First Class [*Navy rating*] AM1
Aviation Structural Mechanic, Hydraulic Mechanic [*Navy rating*] .... AMH
Aviation Structural Mechanic, Hydraulics, Airman [*Navy rating*] .... AMHAN
Aviation Structural Mechanic, Hydraulics, Airman Apprentice [*Navy rating*] .... AMHAA
Aviation Structural Mechanic, Hydraulics, Chief [*Navy rating*] (DNAB) .... AMHC
Aviation Structural Mechanic, Hydraulics, First Class [*Navy rating*] (DNAB) AMH1
Aviation Structural Mechanic, Hydraulics, Second Class [*Navy rating*] (DNAB) AMH2
Aviation Structural Mechanic, Hydraulics, Third Class [*Navy rating*] (DNAB) AMH3
Aviation Structural Mechanic, Master Chief [*Navy rating*] .... AMCM
Aviation Structural Mechanic, Safety Equipment [*Navy rating*] .... AME
Aviation Structural Mechanic, Safety Equipment, Airman [*Navy rating*] .... AMEAN
Aviation Structural Mechanic, Safety Equipment, Airman Apprentice [*Navy rating*] .... AMEAA
Aviation Structural Mechanic, Safety Equipment, First Class [*Navy rating*] (DNAB) AME1
Aviation Structural Mechanic, Safety Equipment, Second Class [*Navy rating*] (DNAB) AME2
Aviation Structural Mechanic, Safety Equipment, Third Class [*Navy rating*] (DNAB) AME3
Aviation Structural Mechanic, Second Class [*Navy rating*] AM2
Aviation Structural Mechanic, Senior Chief [*Navy rating*] .... AMCS
Aviation Structural Mechanic, Structures [*Navy rating*] .... AMS
Aviation Structural Mechanic, Structures, Airman [*Navy rating*] .... AMSAN
Aviation Structural Mechanic, Structures, Airman Apprentice [*Navy rating*] .... AMSAA
Aviation Structural Mechanic, Structures, First Class [*Navy rating*] (DNAB) AMS1
Aviation Structural Mechanic, Structures, Second Class [*Navy rating*] (DNAB) AMS2
Aviation Structural Mechanic, Structures, Third Class [*Navy rating*] (DNAB) AMS3
Aviation Structural Mechanic, Third Class [*Navy rating*] AM3
Aviation Supplies & Academics .... ASA
Aviation Supply Annex .... ASA
Aviation Supply Control Center (NVT) .... ASCC
Aviation Supply Depot .... ASD
Aviation Supply Depot - Naval Supply Center (MCD) .... ASD-NSC
Aviation Supply Office [*Philadelphia, PA*] [*Navy*] .... ASO
Aviation Supply Office Philadelphia [*Navy*] .... ASOP
Aviation Supply Office/Inventory Control Point .... ASO/ICP
Aviation Supply Officer (DOMA) .... ASO
Aviation Supply Ship [*Navy symbol*] .... AVS
Aviation Support Command [*Military*] (DOMA) .... AVSCOM
Aviation Support, Electrical [*Navy rating*] .... ASE
Aviation Support Equipment (CAAL) .... ASE
Aviation Support Equipment Technician [*Navy rating*] .... AS
Aviation Support Equipment Technician, Chief [*Navy rating*] .... ASC
Aviation Support Equipment Technician, Electrical, Airman Apprentice [*Navy rating*] (DNAB) .... ASEAA
Aviation Support Equipment Technician, Electrical, Second Class [*Navy rating*] (DNAB) ASE2
Aviation Support Equipment Technician, Electrical, Third Class [*Navy rating*] (DNAB) ASE3
Aviation Support Equipment Technician, First Class [*Navy rating*] AS1
Aviation Support Equipment Technician, Hydraulics and Structures, Airman [*Navy rating*] (DNAB) .... ASHAN
Aviation Support Equipment Technician, Hydraulics and Structures, Airman Apprentice [*Navy rating*] (DNAB) .... ASHAA
Aviation Support Equipment Technician, Hydraulics and Structures, Second Class [*Navy rating*] (DNAB) ASH2
Aviation Support Equipment Technician, Hydraulics and Structures, Third Class [*Navy rating*] (DNAB) ASH3
Aviation Support Equipment Technician, Master Chief [*Navy rating*] .... ASCM
Aviation Support Equipment Technician, Mechanical, Airman [*Navy rating*] (DNAB) .... ASMAN
Aviation Support Equipment Technician, Mechanical, Airman Apprentice [*Navy rating*] (DNAB) .... ASMAA
Aviation Support Equipment Technician, Mechanical, Second Class [*Navy rating*] (DNAB) ASM2
Aviation Support Equipment Technician, Mechanical, Third Class [*Navy rating*] (DNAB) ASM3
Aviation Support Equipment Technician, Second Class [*Navy rating*] AS2
Aviation Support Equipment Technician, Senior Chief [*Navy rating*] .... ASCS
Aviation Support Equipment Technician, Third Class [*Navy rating*] AS3
Aviation Support, Hydraulic [*Navy rating*] .... ASH
Aviation Support Material and Equipment (MCD) .... ASME
Aviation Support, Mechanical [*Navy rating*] .... ASM
Aviation Support Ship (SAUS) .... ASS
Aviation Support Technology International Inc. (SAUO) .... ASTI
Aviation Surface Material Command (MCD) .... ASMC
Aviation Survivalman [*Coast Guard*] (MUSM) .... ASM
Aviation System Capacity Plan [*FAA*] (TAG) .... ASCP
Aviation Systems Command [*Army*] (RDA) .... ASC
Aviation Systems Command (SAUO) .... AV
Aviation Systems Command [*St. Louis, MO*] [*Army*] .... AVSCOM
Aviation Systems Command [*Army*] (MCD) .... AVSYCOM
Aviation Systems Laboratory (MCD) .... ASL
Aviation Systems Program Review (MCD) .... ASPR
Aviation Systems Test Activity [*Later, AEFA*] (MCD) .... ASTA
Aviation Tactical Coordinator [*Navy*] (NVT) .... ATACCO
Aviation Tactical Data System .... ATDS
Aviation Technical Test Center [*Army*] (RDA) .... ATTC
Aviation Technical Training Center .... ATTC
Aviation Technical Training Division [*Military*] (DNAB) .... ATTD
Aviation Technician Education Council (EA) .... ATEC
Aviation Technician, Navigation .... ATN
Aviation Technician, RADAR .... ATR
Aviation Test Bed (SAUS) .... AVTB
Aviation Test Office [*Edwards Air Force Base, CA*] [*Army*] .... ATO
Aviation Traders Engineering Ltd. [*British*] .... ATEL
Aviation Traders Limited (SAUO) .... ATL
Aviation Training Aids .... ATA
Aviation Training Aids Branch [*Military*] (DNAB) .... ATAB
Aviation Training Association (COBU) .... ATA
Aviation Training Center .... ATC
Aviation Training Devices (Provisional) [*Army*] (RDA) .... AVD
Aviation Training Jacket (DNAB) .... ATJ
Aviation Training Record .... ATR
Aviation Training Ship (SAUS) .... ATS
Aviation Training Support System [*Navy*] (GFGA) .... ATSS
Aviation Transport Services [*Italy*] [*ICAO designator*] (FAAC) .... ATS
Aviation Turbine (SAUS) .... AVTUR
Aviation Turbine Fuel .... ATF
Aviation Turbine Fuel (ADA) .... AVTUR
Aviation Turbine Fuel (PIAV) .... avtur
Aviation Turbine Gasoline (SAUS) .... ATG
Aviation Turbine Kerosene (SAUS) .... Avtur
Aviation Turbine Kerosine (IAA) .... ATK
Aviation Unit [*Marine Corps*] .... AVNU
Aviation Unit Maintenance [*Army*] (MCD) .... AVUM
Aviation VHF [*Very High Frequency*] **Packet Communications** [*Computer science*] (TNIG) .... AVPAC
Aviation Warfare Specialist (DNAB) .... AWS
Aviation Warrant Officer Career Course [*Army*] .... WOCAR
Aviation Weapons Movement Control System (MCD) .... AWMCS
Aviation Weather and Notice to Airmen System (SAUS) .... AWANAS
Aviation Weather and Notice to Airmen System (MCD) .... AWANS
Aviation Weather Center .... AWC
Aviation Weather Development Laboratory [*FAA*] (TAG) .... AWDL
Aviation Weather Development Program (SAUS) .... AWDP
Aviation Weather Facility .... AWF
Aviation Weather Forecasting Task Force (SAUS) .... AWFTF
Aviation Weather Network (SAUS) .... AWN
Aviation Weather Processor [*ICAO designator*] (FAAC) .... AWP
Aviation Weather Products Generator [*FAA*] (TAG) .... AWPG
Aviation Weather Program (SAUS) .... AWP
Aviation Weather Reporting Station .... AWRS
Aviation Weather Service [*of National Weather Service*] .... AWS
Aviation Week & Space Technology (CCCA) .... AWST
Aviation Week and Space Technology (journ.) (SAUS) .... Aviat Week Space Technol
Aviation Wide-Angle Visual System (MCD) .... AWAVS
Aviation Wide-cut Turbine Fuel (SAUS) .... AVTAG
Aviation Writers Association (SAUO) .... AWA
Aviation-Automatic/Weather Observing System Developmental Model (T) (MCD) .... AV-AWOS-T
Aviation-Electromagnetic Efects Policy Board [*Military*] .... A-EMEPB
Aviation/Space Writers Association (SAUO) .... A/S WA
Aviation/Space Writers Association (EA) .... AWA
Aviaton [*Ukraine*] [*FAA designator*] (FAAC) .... UAN
Aviator (AABC) .... AVR
Aviator Readiness Level (MCD) .... ARL
Aviator SA [*Greece*] [*ICAO designator*] (FAAC) .... AVW
Aviator Training Research Simulator (ACAE) .... ATRS
Aviator's Breathing Oxygen [*Air Force*] .... ABO
Aviators Breathing Oxygen (SAUS) .... ABO
Aviators Certificate (SAUS) .... Av Cert
Aviators Night Vision Imaging System (SAUS) .... ANVIS
Aviator's Night Vision Imaging System/Heads-up Display [*Military*] .... ANVIS/HUD
Aviator's Oxygen Helmet (NG) .... AOH
Aviators Oxygen Helmet (SAUS) .... AOH
Aviators Protective Helmet (SAUS) .... APH
Aviator's Protective Helmet (NG) .... APH
Aviatrans [*Former USSR*] [*ICAO designator*] (FAAC) .... VAS
Aviatsiia Dalnego Deistviia [*Long-Range Aviation*] [*Strategic bombing force of USSR*] .... ADD
Aviatsionnaya Diviziya [*Air Division*] [*Former USSR*] .... AD
Aviatsiya Voenno Morskogo Flota [*Aviation - Naval Fleet*] [*Former USSR*] .... AVMF
AVIC Group International, Inc. [*AMEX symbol*] (SAG) .... AV
AVIC Group International, Inc. [*Associated Press*] (SAG) .... AVIC Gp
Avicaya [*Bolivia*] [*ICAO location identifier*] (ICLI) .... SLAV
Avicultural Advancement Council of Canada (AC) .... AACC
Avicultural Federation of Australia .... AFA
Avicultural Magazine (SAUS) .... Avic Mag
[*The*] **Avicultural Society** [*British*] .... AS
Avicultural Society (SAUO) .... AS
Avicultural Society of America (EA) .... ASA
Avicultural Society of America (EA) .... ASOA
Avid Technology [*NASDAQ symbol*] (TTSB) .... AVID
Avid Technology, Inc. [*NASDAQ symbol*] (SAG) .... AVID
Avid Technology, Inc. [*Associated Press*] (SAG) .... AvidTch
Avidin-Biotin Complex [*Immunochemistry*] .... ABC
Avies [*Estonia*] [*FAA designator*] (FAAC) .... AIA
Avigen Inc. [*NASDAQ symbol*] (TTSB) .... AVGN
Avigen, Inc. [*Associated Press*] (SAG) .... Avigen

Avignon [France] [Airport symbol] (OAG)	AVN
Avignon/Caumont [France] [ICAO location identifier] (ICLI)	LFMV
Avignon-Pujaut [France] [ICAO location identifier] (ICLI)	LFNT
Avijet SA de CV [Mexico] [ICAO designator] (FAAC)	IJE
Avila College, Kansas City (SAUS)	MoKAr
Avila College, Kansas City, MO [OCLC symbol] (OCLC)	HOO
Avila College, Kansas City, MO [Library symbol] [Library of Congress] (LCLS)	MoKAv
Aviles/Asturias [Spain] [ICAO location identifier] (ICLI)	LEAS
Avilond, TAC [Ukraine] [FAA designator] (FAAC)	LON
Avimo Singapore Ltd. (SAUO)	AVS
Avinda Video, Inc. [Toronto Stock Exchange symbol]	AVV
Avino Mines & Resources Ltd. [Vancouver Stock Exchange symbol]	AVO
Aviogenex [Yugoslavia] [ICAO designator] (FAAC)	AGX
Avioimpex [Yugloslavia] [ICAO designator] (FAAC)	AXX
Avion a Grande Vitesse [French high-speed train]	AGV
Avion Myeloblastosis Virus (SAUS)	AMV
Avion Taxi Canada, Inc. [ICAO designator] (FAAC)	ADQ
Aviona [ICAO designator] (AD)	RD
Avionair, Inc. [Canada] [ICAO designator] (FAAC)	ANU
Aviones Are, SA de CV [Mexico] [FAA designator] (FAAC)	NRE
Aviones de Renta de Quintana Roo, SA de CV [Mexico] [FAA designator] (FAAC)	AQT
Aviones de Sonora SA [Mexico] [ICAO designator] (FAAC)	ADS
Aviones Ejecutivos, JFA [Mexico] [FAA designator] (FAAC)	JFA
Aviones Unidos SA de CV [Mexico] [ICAO designator] (FAAC)	AUN
Aviones y Servicios del Golfo SA de CV [Mexico] [ICAO designator] (FAAC)	ADG
Avionic	AVNC
Avionic Control Unit (SAUS)	ACU
Avionic Flight Control System	AFCS
Avionic Instrument (MCD)	AI
Avionic Instruments Inc. (SAUO)	AI2
Avionic Integrated Maintenance Department (SAUO)	AIMD
Avionic Integration Support Facility (MCD)	AISF
Avionic Intermediate Shop (SAUS)	AIS
Avionic Ltd. [Greece] [FAA designator] (FAAC)	VIO
Avionic Observation of Intruder Danger Systems [Army]	AVOIDS
Avionic Requirements (SAUS)	AR
Avionic Subsystem Requirement Document (MCD)	ASRD
Avionic System Integration Plan (MCD)	ASIP
Avionic System Simulation (SAUS)	AVSIM
Avionic Systems Demonstrator Rig (PDAA)	ASDR
Avionic Test Set (MCD)	ATS
Avionics (NASA)	AV
Avionics Advanced Development Task (ACAE)	AADT
Avionics and Electrical System Advanced Trainer (ACAE)	AESAT
Avionics Automatic Transmission Line	AATE
Avionics Automatic Transmission Line (SAUS)	AATL
Avionics Bay (MCD)	AB
Avionics Bay (MCD)	AVBAY
Avionics Bay (SAUS)	AV BAY
Avionics Bay Cooling System	ABCS
Avionics Bulletin (MCD)	AVB
Avionics Bus Interface (SAUS)	ABI
Avionics Change (MCD)	AVC
Avionics Communications and Information Processing (SAUS)	ACIP
Avionics Components and Subsystems (SAUS)	AVCS
Avionics Computer Control (SAUS)	ACC
Avionics, Control, and Information Systems (MCD)	ACIS
Avionics, Control and Information Systems (SAUS)	ACIS
Avionics Cooling Loop (MCD)	ACL
Avionics Cooling System (SAUS)	ACS
Avionics Cooling Unit [Aerospace] (NASA)	ACU
Avionics Cooling Unit Operator (MCD)	ACUO
Avionics Corrosion Prevention Control (ACAE)	ACPC
Avionics Data Utilization System (SAUS)	ADUS
Avionics Decision Notice (MCD)	ADN
Avionics Depot Test Station (MCD)	ADTS
Avionics Depot Test System (ACAE)	ADTS
Avionics Development and Integration Facility (MCD)	ADIF
Avionics Development Facility (SAUS)	ADP
Avionics Development Laboratory [Rockwell International-Space Division] [NASA] (NASA)	ADL
Avionics Display Unit (SAUS)	ADU
Avionics Electrical Distribution (MCD)	AED
Avionics Engineering Development and Integration Facility (ACAE)	AEDIF
Avionics Engineering Division [Air Force]	AVED
Avionics Equipment Design Review	AEDR
Avionics Expert System (MCD)	AES
Avionics Fault Tree Analyzer (MCD)	AFTA
Avionics Improvement Program (SAUS)	AIP
Avionics Integrated Fuzing (ACAE)	AIF
Avionics Integrated Maintenance Expert System (MCD)	AIMES
Avionics Integrated Support (SAUS)	AIS
Avionics Integrated Support Networks (PDAA)	AVISNET
Avionics Integration	AI
Avionics Integration Bench (MCD)	AIB
Avionics Integration Laboratories [NASA] (NASA)	AIL
Avionics Integration Laboratory (SAUS)	AIL
Avionics Integration Plan [NASA] (NASA)	AIP
Avionics Integration Research (SSD)	AIR
Avionics Integration Support Technology (ACAE)	AIST
Avionics Integrity Master Plan (SAUS)	AIMP
Avionics Integrity Program (ACAE)	AIP
Avionics Integrity Program (ACAE)	AVIP
Avionics Interface Unit (MCD)	AIU
Avionics Interim Contractor Support (ACAE)	AICS
Avionics Intermediate Maintenance Depot (SAUS)	AIMD
Avionics Intermediate Shop (MCD)	AIS
Avionics Intermediate Shop Mobile Facility Support (DWSG)	AISMF
Avionics Intermediate Supporter Station (SAUO)	AIS
Avionics Laboratory [Air Force]	AL
Avionics Laboratory Predictive Operations and Support (MCD)	ALPOS
Avionics Laboratory Technical Information Handling Profile	ALTIHP
Avionics Logistics Effects (ACAE)	ALE
Avionics Maintenance (ACAE)	AM
Avionics Maintenance Conference (EA)	AMC
Avionics Maintenance Modifier (ACAE)	AMM
Avionics Maintenance Shop	AMS
Avionics Maintenance Squadron [Air Force/Navy] (MCD)	AMS
Avionics Maintenance Squadron [Air Force] (AFM)	AMSq
Avionics Maintenance Trainer [Military] (IUSS)	AMT
Avionics Maintenance Training System (SAUS)	AMTS
Avionics Management System (SAUS)	AMS
Avionics Master Plan (ACAE)	AMP
Avionics Modernization Program [Air Force] (DOMA)	AMP
Avionics Module Repair Improvement Program [Navy]	AMRIP
Avionics Module Unit	AMU
Avionics Multiple Bus (ACAE)	AMUX
Avionics Multiplex	AMUX
Avionics Multiplexing (ACAE)	AMUX
Avionics Operating Instruction (MCD)	AOI
Avionics Operating Time (MCD)	AOT
Avionics Overall Test (NASA)	AOT
Avionics Planning Activity (ACAE)	APA
Avionics Planning Baseline (ACAE)	APB
Avionics Processing System	APS
Avionics Reconfiguration Technology (ACAE)	ART
Avionics Repairable Assemblies (AFIT)	ARA
Avionics Requirements (MCD)	AR
Avionics Research Aircraft (MCD)	ARA
Avionics Research and Development Activity [Fort Monmouth, NJ] [Army] (GRD)	AVRADA
Avionics Sensor Adaptive Planner (ACAE)	ASAP
Avionics Shop Maintenance	ASM
Avionics Situation Awareness Trainer (SAUS)	ASAT
Avionics Software Integration Facilities (SAUS)	ASIF
Avionics Software Support Cost Model (MCD)	ASSCM
Avionics Specialist Incorporated (SAUO)	ASI
Avionics Specification (ACAE)	AS
Avionics Standard Communications Bus (DA)	ASCB
Avionics Status Panel (MCD)	ASP
Avionics Subsystem for Strategic Bombers	ASSB
Avionics Subsystem Group [NASA] (NASA)	ASG
Avionics Subsystem Interface Unit (MCD)	ASSIU
Avionics Subsystems Interface Contractor [Air Force]	ASIC
Avionics System Integration and Acquisition (MCD)	ASIA
Avionics System Project Officer	ASPO
Avionics System Review (NASA)	ASR
Avionics System Test Equipment Comparator (MCD)	ASTEC
Avionics System Test Specification	ASTS
Avionics Systems Engineering Division [Johnson Space Center] [NASA] (NASA)	ASED
Avionics Systems Trainers (SAUS)	AST
Avionics Technical Note	ATN
Avionics Test Article (NASA)	ATA
Avionics Test Station (MCD)	ATS
Avionics Unit Maintenance (MCD)	AVUM
Avionics Update Programme (SAUS)	AUP
Avionics Upgrade Programme (SAUS)	AUP
Avionics Verification Laboratory (MCD)	AVL
Avionics Verification Status Room [NASA] (NASA)	AVSR
Avionics Visual System (ACAE)	AVS
Avionics/Electronics Integrity Program (ACAE)	AVIP
Avions Mudry & Cie. [France] [ICAO aircraft manufacturer identifier] (ICAO)	CE
Avions Mudry & Cie. [France], Lockheed Aircraft Corp. [ICAO aircraft manufacturer identifier] (ICAO)	CP
Avion-Station-Relais de Transmissions Exceptionelles (SAUS)	ASTARTE
Avior [ICAO designator] (AD)	XP
Avior Pty Ltd. [Australia] [ICAO designator] (FAAC)	AVR
Aviorrenta SA [Mexico] [ICAO designator] (FAAC)	AVI
Aviron [NASDAQ symbol] (SAG)	AVIR
Aviron [Associated Press] (SAG)	Aviron
Avirulence	AVR
Avis de Reception [Return Receipt] [French]	AR
Avis International Secretary Club (SAUO)	AVISC
Avis Licensee Association (EA)	ALA
Avis, PA [FM radio station call letters]	WQBR
Avis Rent a Car	ARAC
Avis Rent A Car [NYSE symbol] (SG)	AVI
Avisco [ICAO designator] (AD)	AO
Aviser SA [Spain] [ICAO designator] (FAAC)	AVH
Avista, Corp. [NYSE symbol] (SG)	AVA
Avistar (Cyprus) Ltd. [ICAO designator] (FAAC)	KJA
Avitar, Inc. [NASDAQ symbol] (SAG)	AVIT
Avitar, Inc. [Associated Press] (SAG)	Avitar
Avitar, Inc. [AMEX symbol] (SG)	AVI
Avitar Inc. Wrrt [NASDAQ symbol] (TTSB)	AVITW
Avitat [British] [ICAO designator] (FAAC)	ESO

Avitour Airlines (SAUS) ... EB
Aviva Petroleum Dep [*AMEX symbol*] (TTSB) ... AVV
Aviva Petroleum, Inc. [*Associated Press*] (SAG) ... AvivaPet
Aviva Petroleum, Inc. [*AMEX symbol*] (SAG) ... AVV
Aviva Resources, Inc. [*Vancouver Stock Exchange symbol*] ... AVS
AVKO Educational Research Foundation (EA) ... AVKOERF
Avnet, Inc. [*Associated Press*] (SAG) ... Avnet
Avnet, Inc. [*NYSE symbol*] (SPSG) ... AVT
Avno [*Denmark*] [*ICAO location identifier*] (ICLI) ... EKAV
Avoca Journal-Herald, Avoca, IA [*Library symbol*] [*Library of Congress*] (LCLS) ... IaAvJH
Avoca Public Library, Avoca, IA [*Library symbol*] [*Library of Congress*] (LCLS) ... IaAv
Avocado (SAUS) ... Avo
Avocado Growers' Association of Western Australia ... AGAWA
Avocado Growers Bargaining Council [*Defunct*] (EA) ... AGBC
Avocado Growers Council [*Later, AGBC*] (EA) ... AGC
Avocado Growers Council (SAUO) ... AGC
Avocado-Sunblotch Viroid ... ASBV
Avocado-Sunblotch Viroid [*Plant pathology*] ... ASBVd
Avocat General [*District Attorney*] [*French*] (ILCA) ... Av Gen
Avocet Ventures, Inc. [*Vancouver Stock Exchange symbol*] ... AVZ
'Avodah Zarah (BJA) ... 'AvZar
Avogadro Constant [*Symbol*] [*IUPAC*] ... L
Avogadro Number [*Number of molecules in one gram-molecular weight of a substance*] ... N
Avogadro's Number [*Chemistry*] (DAVI) ... Na
Avoid Verbal Instructions [*DoD*] (MCD) ... AVI
Avoid Verbal Orders [*Military*] ... AVO
Avoidable Delay ... AD
Avoidable Mortality from Cancer in Black Populations Survey [*Department of Health and Human Services*] (GFGA) ... AMCBPS
Avoidable Shock (SAUS) ... AS
Avoidance of Adverse Effect [*Environmental science*] (COE) ... AOAE
Avoir [*Credit*] [*French*] ... AV
Avoirdupois (SAUS) ... A/d
Avoirdupois ... AV
Avoirdupois [*Unit of measurement*] (KSC) ... AVDP
Avoirdupois (NTIO) ... avdp
Avoirdupois [*Unit of measurement*] ... AVDPS
Avoirdupois ... AVOIR
Avoirdupois (SAUS) ... Avoir
Avoirdupois (ADA) ... AVP
Avoirdupois Ounce ... advp oz
Avoirdupois Weight (SAUS) ... Av Wt
Avon [*Australia*] [*Seismograph station code, US Geological Survey*] (SEIS) ... AVO
Avon, CO [*FM radio station call letters*] ... KZYR
Avon, CO [*Location identifier*] [*FAA*] (FAAL) ... VON
Avon Elementary School, Avon, MN [*Library symbol*] [*Library of Congress*] (LCLS) ... MnAvoE
Avon Junior/Senior High School Library, Avon, NY [*OCLC symbol*] (OCLC) ... RVP
Avon, NY [*FM radio station call letters*] (RBYB) ... WHRR
Avon, NY [*FM radio station call letters*] (BROA) ... WQRV-FM
Avon, NY [*FM radio station call letters*] (RBYB) ... WRQV-FM
Avon, NY [*AM radio station call letters*] ... WYSL
Avon Park, FL [*Location identifier*] [*FAA*] (FAAL) ... AGR
Avon Park, FL [*Location identifier*] [*FAA*] (FAAL) ... AVO
Avon Park, FL [*AM radio station call letters*] ... WAVP
Avon Park, FL [*FM radio station call letters*] ... WWOJ
Avon Products [*NYSE symbol*] (TTSB) ... AVP
Avon Products, Inc. [*Associated Press*] (SAG) ... Avon
Avon Products, Inc. [*NYSE symbol*] (SPSG) ... AVP
Avon Products, Inc., Suffern, NY [*Library symbol*] [*Library of Congress*] (LCLS) ... NSufA
Avondale Financial [*NASDAQ symbol*] (TTSB) ... AVND
Avondale Financial Corp. [*NASDAQ symbol*] (SAG) ... AVND
Avondale Financial Corp. [*Associated Press*] (SAG) ... AvondF
Avondale Industries [*NASDAQ symbol*] (TTSB) ... AVDL
Avondale Industries, Inc. [*NASDAQ symbol*] (NQ) ... AVDL
Avondale Industries, Inc. [*Associated Press*] (SAG) ... Avndle
Avondale Public Library, Avondale, AZ [*Library symbol*] [*Library of Congress*] (LCLS) ... AzAv
Avondale Resources, Inc. [*Vancouver Stock Exchange symbol*] ... AVD
Avonics Management System ... AMS
Avonmore Branch, Stormont, Dundas, and Glengarry County Public Library, Ontario [*Library symbol*] [*National Library of Canada*] (BIB) ... OAVSDG
Avord [*France*] [*ICAO location identifier*] (ICLI) ... LFOA
Avoyelles Parish Library, Marksville, LA [*Library symbol*] [*Library of Congress*] (LCLS) ... LMarA
Avranches/Le Val Saint-Pere [*France*] [*ICAO location identifier*] (ICLI) ... LFRW
Avril Sur Loire [*France*] [*Seismograph station code, US Geological Survey*] (SEIS) ... AVF
Avro International Aerospace [*British*] [*FAA designator*] (FAAC) ... WFD
A.V.Roe & Co. Ltd. (SAUO) ... AVRO
AVSCOM [*Aviation Systems Command*] **Integrated Microfilm Systems** [*Army*] ... AIMS
AVTEAM, Inc. [*NASDAQ symbol*] (SAG) ... AVTM
Avtomat Kalashnikov [*Submachine Gun*] [*Commonwealth of Independent States*] ... AK
Avtomobilei Zavod Lenin Komsomol [*Lenin Collective Automobile Works*] [*Former USSR*] ... AZLK
Avu Avu [*Solomon Islands*] [*Airport symbol*] (OAG) ... AVU
Avulsion (SAUS) ... AV
Avulsion Fracture [*Medicine*] (MELL) ... AF
AVVI [*Altimeter Vertical Velocity Indicator*] **RADAR Altitude** (GFGA) ... ARA
Avvocato [*Solicitor*] [*Italian*] (EY) ... AVV
AVX Corp. [*NYSE symbol*] (SAG) ... AVX
AVX Corp. [*Associated Press*] (SAG) ... AVX Cp
AW Computer Systems [*Associated Press*] (SAG) ... AW
AW Computer Systems, Inc. [*NASDAQ symbol*] (NQ) ... AWCS
AW Computer Systems'A' [*NASDAQ symbol*] (TTSB) ... AWCSA
Awadhi [*MARC language code*] [*Library of Congress*] (LCCP) ... awa
Await ... AWT
Awaiting Action Deck Court Material (SAUS) ... AADCM
Awaiting Action Deck Court-Martial ... AADCM
Awaiting Action General Court-Martial ... AAGCM
Awaiting Action [*of*] **Higher Authority** [*Army*] ... AAHA
Awaiting Action of Higher Authority (SAUS) ... AAHA
Awaiting Action Summary Court Martial (SAUS) ... AASCM
Awaiting Action Summary Court-Martial ... AASCM
Awaiting Additional Funds (AAGC) ... AAF
Awaiting Aircraft Availability ... AAA
Awaiting Bad Conduct Discharge [*Military*] ... ABCD
Awaiting Berth [*Military*] (DNAB) ... AWBER
Awaiting Combat Assignment (MUGU) ... ACA
Awaiting Connection [*Telecommunications*] (TEL) ... AC
Awaiting Contract Record Disposition Notice (AAGC) ... ACRDN
Awaiting Delivery (MCD) ... A/D
Awaiting Delivery of Data (AAGC) ... ADD
Awaiting Discharge [*Military*] (DNAB) ... AWDISCH
Awaiting Disciplinary Action This Command [*Army*] ... AWDISCOM
Awaiting Disconnection [*Telecommunications*] (TEL) ... AD
Awaiting Final Invoice (AAGC) ... AFI
Awaiting Forward Release [*Telecommunications*] (TEL) ... AFR
Awaiting Incoming Continuity [*Telecommunications*] (TEL) ... AIC
Awaiting Incoming Message [*Telecommunications*] (TEL) ... AIM
Awaiting Installation (ACAE) ... AWI
Awaiting Instruction [*Military*] (DNAB) ... AI
Awaiting Laboratory Input ... ALI
Awaiting Maintenance ... AM
Awaiting Maintenance (AFM) ... AWM
Awaiting Number Received [*Telecommunications*] (TEL) ... ANR
Awaiting Office Hours ... AOH
Awaiting Orders [*Military*] (DNAB) ... AWORD
Awaiting Outgoing Continuity [*Telecommunications*] (TEL) ... AOC
Awaiting Overhaul (NG) ... AOH
Awaiting Parts ... AP
Awaiting Parts (AFM) ... AWP
Awaiting Patent and Royalty Clearance (AAGC) ... APRC
Awaiting Plant Clearance (AAGC) ... APC
Awaiting Price Redetermination (AAGC) ... APR
Awaiting Receipt of Application (MELL) ... ARA
Awaiting Removal of Excess Funds (AAGC) ... AREF
Awaiting Reply [*Telecommunications*] (TEL) ... AR
Awaiting Report of Survey (AAGC) ... ARS
Awaiting Results of Trial [*Military*] ... ARTL
Awaiting Sentence [*of court-martial*] ... AWS
Awaiting Transportation (AFM) ... AT
Awaiting Trial ... ATL
Awaiting Trial [*by court-martial*] ... AWT
Awaiting Weather [*Military*] (DNAB) ... AWEA
Awake, Alert, and Oriented (HGAA) ... AAO
Awake and Aware [*Neurology*] (DAVI) ... A & A
Awake and Oriented Times Four [*Neurology and psychiatry*] (DAVI) ... A & OX4
Awake and Oriented Times Three [*Neurology and psychiatry*] (DAVI) ... A & OX3
Awake and Oriented to Person, Place, and Time [*Neurology and psychiatry*] (DAVI) ... A & OX3
Awake and Oriented to Person, Place, Time, and Date [*Neurology and psychiatry*] (DAVI) ... A & OX4
Awake and Oriented to Time, Place, and Person [*Neurology*] (DAVI) ... AAOX3
Awake Indication (SAUS) ... AWI
Awake-Alert-Oriented (ADWA) ... A-A-O
Awami Action Committee [*India*] [*Political party*] (PPW) ... AAC
Awami League [*Bangladesh*] [*Political party*] (FEA) ... AL
Awami League (SAUO) ... AL
Awami National Party [*Pakistan*] [*Political party*] (FEA) ... ANP
Awana Clubs International (EAIO) ... ACI
Awana Youth Association (EA) ... AYA
Award (AABC) ... AWD
Award ... AWRD
Award Central Control Unit [*NASA*] (NASA) ... ACCU
Award Fee ... AF
Award Fee Determination Official (COE) ... AFDO
Award Fee Determination Plan (AAGC) ... AFDP
Award Fee Determining Official (AAGC) ... AFDO
Award Fee Evaluation Board [*NASA*] (NASA) ... AFEB
Award Fee Evaluation Committee [*NASA*] (NASA) ... AFEC
Award Fee Review Board ... AFRB
Award for Effective Advertising (SAUS) ... Effie
Award Hunters Club (SAUO) ... AHC
Award Of Contract (SAUS) ... AOC
Award of Merit [*Royal Horticultural Society*] [*British*] ... AM
Award of Merit [*Boy Scouts of America*] ... AOM
Award of Merit for Group Achievement [*Military*] (DNAB) ... AMGA
Award Processing [*Social Security Administration*] (OICC) ... AP
Award Resources [*Vancouver Stock Exchange symbol*] ... ADR
Award Scheme for Science, Industry and School-Teaching [*Science Research Council*] (PDAA) ... ASSIST
Award Software International, Inc. [*NASDAQ symbol*] (SAG) ... AWRD

Award Software International, Inc. [*Associated Press*] (SAG) ...... AwrdSft	Axial Power Shaping Rods Assembly [*Nuclear energy*] (NRCH) .... APSRA
Award to Honor Excellent Newspaper Advertising (DGA) ...... ATHENA	Axial Pressure Angle [*Gears*] .... APA
Awardee [*Database terminology*] (NITA) .... AW	Axial Ratio (SAUS) .... AR
Awards Almanac [*A publication*] .... AA	Axial Rotating Filtration .... ARF
Awards and Obligations (GFGA) .... AO	Axial Seamount Hydrothermal Emissions Study [*Marine science*]
Awards and Recognition Association (NTPA) .... ARA	(OSRA) .... ASHES
Awards Committee (SAUS) .... ACOM	Axial Shape Index (NRCH) .... ASI
Awards for Cablecasting Excellence .... ACE	Axial Summit Caldera [*Volcanology*] .... ASC
Awards for Publication Excellence .... APEX	Axial Thrust Misalignment .... ATM
Awards for Trivial Animal Research (WDAA) .... AFTAR	Axial Turbo Machine .... ATM
Awards, Honors, and Prizes [*A publication*] .... AHP	Axial Vapor Deposition [*Coating technology*] .... AVD
Aware, Inc. [*Associated Press*] (SAG) .... Aware	Axial Vapor-Phase Oxidation Process [*Optical fibre technology*] (EECA) ...... AVPO
Aware, Inc. [*NASDAQ symbol*] (SAG) .... AWRE	Axial Vector Dominance Model (SAUS) .... ACDM
AWARE International (SAUO) .... AWARE	Axial Vector Dominance Model .... AVDM
Awareness (KSC) .... AWRN	Axial Velocity Ratio .... AVR
Awareness and Preparedness for Emergencies at Local Level (HEAS) ...... APELL	Axial Width .... AW
Awareness Center [*Defunct*] (EA) .... AC	Axially Magnetized Plasma .... AMP
Awareness Research Foundation (EA) .... ARF	Axially Scattering Spectrometer Probe (MCD) .... ASSP
Awareness Vision Imagination Responsibility Action .... AVIRA	Axially Symmetric Nozzle .... ASN
Awarness and Preparedness for Industrial Accident at Local Level	Axidistocervical (SAUS) .... ADC
(SAUS) .... APELL	Axidistogingival (SAUS) .... ADG
Awaruwaunawa [*Guyana*] [*ICAO location identifier*] (ICLI) .... SYAW	Axilla (DAVI) .... ax
Awash [*Ethiopia*] [*ICAO location identifier*] (ICLI) .... HAAW	Axilla, Shoulder, Elbow [*Bandage*] .... ASE
Awash [*Ethiopia*] [*ICAO location identifier*] (ICLI) .... HALA	Axillary [*Medicine*] .... AX
Awash National Park (SAUS) .... ANP	Axillary Crutches [*Medicine*] (MELL) .... AC
Awassa Agricultural Research Station (SAUO) .... AARS	Axillary Dissection [*Medicine*] (DMAA) .... AXD
Away from Home .... AFH	Axillary Fossa [*Medicine*] (MELL) .... AF
Away from Keyboard [*Computer hacker terminology*] (NHD) .... AFK	Axillary Lymph Node Carcinoma [*Medicine*] (MELL) .... ALNC
Away From Keyboard (SAUS) .... AFK	Axillary Lymph Node Dissection [*Medicine*] (MELL) .... ALND
Away from Reactor [*Storage facilities*] .... AFR	Axillary Nodal Irradiation [*Medicine*] (MELL) .... ANI
Away from Reactor Storage [*Nuclear energy*] (NUCP) .... AFRS	Axillary Node [*Medicine*] (MELL) .... AN
Away without Authorization .... AWA	Axillary Node Dissection [*Medicine*] (MELL) .... AND
Aweil [*Sudan*] [*ICAO location identifier*] (ICLI) .... HSAW	Axim [*Ghana*] [*ICAO location identifier*] (ICLI) .... DGTX
Awesome Resources Ltd. [*Vancouver Stock Exchange symbol*] .... AWE	Axinite (SAUS) .... Ax
AWIPS Forecast Preparation System (SAUS) .... AER	Axiobuccal [*Dentistry*] (MAE) .... AB
AWIPS [*Advanced Weather Interactive Processing System*] **Forecast**	Axiobuccocervical [*Dentistry*] .... ABC
Preparation System [*Marine science*] (OSRA) .... AFPS	Axiobuccogingival [*Dentistry*] .... ABG
AWIPS Forecast Preparation System (SAUS) .... AFPS	Axiobuccolingual [*Dentistry*] .... ABL
AWIPS Program Office (SAUS) .... APO	Axio-Buco-Cervical (SAUS) .... ABC
AWIPS [*Advanced Weather Interactive Processing System*] **Program Office**	Axiocervical [*Dentistry*] .... AC
[*Marine science*] (OSRA) .... APO	Axiocisal (SAUS) .... AI
A-Wire (SAUS) .... AW	Axiodistal [*Dentistry*] .... AD
AWIS Meteorological Applications (SAUS) .... AMA	Axiodistocervical [*Dentistry*] .... ADC
Awkward (ADWA) .... awk	Axiodistoclusal (SAUS) .... Adnok
Awkward Expression or Construction [*Used in correcting manuscripts,*	Axiodistogingival [*Dentistry*] .... ADG
etc.] .... AWK	Axiodistoincisal [*Dentistry*] .... ADI
Awning (MSA) .... AWN	Axiodistoinclusal (SAUS) .... ADI
Awning Deck [*of a ship*] (DS) .... Adk	Axiodisto-Occlusal [*Dentistry*] .... ADO
Awning Deck [*of a ship*] (DS) .... AWD	Axiogingival [*Dentistry*] .... AG
Awood Air Ltd. [*Canada*] [*ICAO designator*] (FAAC) .... AWO	Axiogist (SAUS) .... Axio
AWOS Data Acquisition System [*FAA*] (TAG) .... ADAS	Axioincisal [*Dentistry*] .... AI
AWOS/ASOS Data Acquisition System (SAUS) .... ADAS	Axiolabial [*Dentistry*] .... ALa
AWS Ammunition Magazine (MCD) .... AAM	Axiolabial (SAUS) .... ALA
AXA ADS [*NYSE symbol*] (SAG) .... AXA	Axiolabiogingival (SAUS) .... ALAG
Axa Midi Assurances [*Commercial firm*] [*France*] .... AMA	Axiolabiogingival [*Dentistry*] .... ALaG
Axactic Polypropylene .... APP	Axiolabiolingual [*Dentistry*] .... ALaL
AXAF Imaging Optical/UV Monitor (SAUS) .... AXIOM	Axiolabiolingual (SAUS) .... Alal
Axcess, Inc. [*NASDAQ symbol*] [*Formerly, Lasertechnics, Inc.*] .... AXSI	Axiolingual [*Dentistry*] .... AL
Axel Heiberg Island [*Canada*] .... AHI	Axiolinguocervical [*Dentistry*] .... ALC
Axel L. Wenner Automatic Computer (RALS) .... ALWAC	Axiolinguoclusal (SAUS) .... ALO
Axel Lennard Wenner Gren (SAUS) .... Alweg	Axiolinguogingival [*Dentistry*] .... ALG
Axel Rent SA [*Mexico*] [*ICAO designator*] (FAAC) .... AXR	Axiolinguo-Occlusal [*Dentistry*] .... ALO
Axel-Wennergren Automatic Computer (SAUS) .... ALWAC	axiologically (SAUS) .... axio
AXENT Technologies [*NASDAQ symbol*] (TTSB) .... AXNT	Axiology (SAUS) .... Axio
Axent Technologies, Inc. [*Associated Press*] (SAG) .... AxentT	Axiom .... AX
Axent Technologies, Inc. [*NASDAQ symbol*] (SAG) .... AXNT	Axiom (ADWA) .... ax
Axes (SAUS) .... AX	Axiom (SAUS) .... Axio
Axial .... A	Axiom Information Resources .... AIR
Axial (DAVI) .... ax	Axiom International Development Corp. [*Formerly, Axiom Explorations, Inc.*]
Axial Centrifugal (AAG) .... AC	[*Vancouver Stock Exchange symbol*] .... AXX
Axial Flow (AAG) .... AF	Axiom of Choice [*Logic*] .... AC
Axial Flow .... AXFL	Axiomatic Language (SAUS) .... AXM Language
Axial Flow Compressor .... AFC	Axiomatic Requirements Engineering (MCD) .... ARE
Axial Flow Reactor [*Chemical engineering*] .... AFR	Axiomesial [*Dentistry*] .... AM
Axial Flow Wheel .... AFW	Axiomesiocervical [*Dentistry*] .... AMC
Axial Flux Density (IEEE) .... AFD	Axiomesiodistal [*Dentistry*] .... AMD
Axial Flux Difference [*Nuclear energy*] (NRCH) .... AFD	Axiomesiogingival [*Dentistry*] .... AMG
Axial Flux Difference Alarm (IEEE) .... AFDA	Axiomesioincisal [*Dentistry*] .... AMI
Axial Flux Offset (IEEE) .... AFO	Axiomesio-Occlusal [*Dentistry*] .... AMO
Axial Folding Bridge (SAUS) .... AFB	Axio-Occlusal [*Dentistry*] .... AO
Axial Gear Differential (OA) .... AGD	Axioocclusal (SAUS) .... AO
Axial Gear Differential/Constant-Speed Drive (DNAB) .... AGD/CSD	Axiopulpal [*Dentistry*] .... AP
Axial Gradient (MAE) .... ax grad	Axis (ABBR) .... A
Axial Gradient (SAUS) .... Ax Grad	Axis (AAG) .... AX
Axial Magma Chamber [*Geology*] .... AMC	Axis (DIPS) .... Ax
Axial Next-Nearest-Neighbor Interactions [*Crystallography*] .... ANNNI	Axis (SAUS) .... ax
Axial Pitch (IEEE) .... AXP	Axis [*of a cylindrical lens*] [*Ophthalmology*] (DAVI) x
Axial Pneumatic Pilot Assisted Relief Valve (SAUS) ...... APPA Relief Valve	Axis Controlled Carrier (SAUS) .... ACC
Axial Power Distribution monitoring system (SAUS) .... APDCS	Axis Controller .... AXCON
Axial Power Distribution Monitoring Systems [*Nuclear energy*] (NRCH) .... APDMS	Axis Crossing Interval Meter [*SONAR*] .... ACIM
Axial Power Imbalance Limit (IEEE) .... APIL	Axis Deviation (MAE) .... AD
Axial Power Indicator [*Environmental science*] (COE) .... API	Axis of Orientation [*Imaginary vertical line at the left of a block of text*] [*Also,*
Axial Power Monitor [*Environmental science*] (COE) .... APM	*mental margin*] (WDMC) .... A/O
Axial Power Shape (SAUS) .... APS	Axis [*or Axes*] of Signal Communication [*Army*] .... AXSIGCOMM
Axial Power Shaping Rods [*Nuclear energy*] (NRCH) .... APSR	Axis Select (IAA) .... AS

Axis-Crossing Interval Meter (SAUS) ... ACIM
Axisymmetric Blunt Body ... ABB
Axisymmetric Duct Aeroacoustic Modeling (MCD) ... ADAM
Axisymmetric Duct Aeroacoustic Modelling (SAUS) ... ADAM
Axisymmetric Jet Stretcher ... AJS
Axisymmetric Spiral [*Astronomy*] ... ASS
Axisymmetric Vectoring Exhaust Nozzle (SAUS) ... AVEN
Axisymmetrical and Planar Structural Analysis (SAUS) ... APS
Axisymmetrical and Planar Structural Analysis (MCD) ... APSA
Axisymmetrical Conical Flow ... ACF
Axisymmetrical Flow Field ... AFF
Axle Detector ... AD
Axle Flange Gasket [*Automotive engineering*] ... AF
Axle Fluid (SAUS) ... AF
Axle Housing Cover Gasket [*Automotive engineering*] ... AX
Axle Nut (DICI) ... AN
Axle-Load Survey Recorder (SAUS) ... ALSER
Axminster [*England*] ... AXMIN
Axogen Ltd. [*AMEX symbol*] (SAG) ... AXG
Axogen Ltd. [*Associated Press*] (SAG) ... Axogen
Axon Cylinder Membrane ... ACM
Axonal Arborization [*Medicine*] (DMAA) ... AA
Axonal Neuropathy [*Medicine*] (MELL) ... AN
Axonal Terminal (DB) ... AT
Axonometric (VRA) ... axon
Axsys Technologies, Inc. [*Associated Press*] (SAG) ... AxsysTch
Axsys Technologies, Inc. [*NASDAQ symbol*] (SAG) ... AXYS
Axum [*Ethiopia*] [*Airport symbol*] (OAG) ... AXU
Axum [*Ethiopia*] [*ICAO location identifier*] (ICLI) ... HAAX
AxW Next-Nearest-Neighbor Interactions (SAUS) ... ANNNI
AxyS Pharmaceuticals [*NASDAQ symbol*] (SG) ... AXPH
Ayacucho [*Peru*] [*Airport symbol*] (OAG) ... AYP
Ayacucho/Coronel FAP Alfredo Mendivil Duarte [*Peru*] [*ICAO location identifier*] (ICLI) ... SPHO
Ayagualo [*El Salvador*] [*Seismograph station code, US Geological Survey*] [*Closed*] (SEIS) ... AYA
Ayckbourn's Chancery Forms [*A publication*] (DLA) ... Ayck Ch F
Ayckbourn's Chancery Practice [*A publication*] (DLA) ... Ayck Ch Pr
Ayckbourn's Jurisdiction of the Supreme Court of Judicature [*A publication*] (DLA) ... Ayck Jur
Aydin [*Turkey*] [*Airport symbol*] (AD) ... ADN
Aydin [*Turkey*] [*ICAO location identifier*] (ICLI) ... LTBD
Aydin Corp. [*NYSE symbol*] (SPSG) ... AYD
Aydin Corp. [*Associated Press*] (SAG) ... Aydin
Ayeet Aviation & Tourism [*Israel*] [*FAA designator*] (FAAC) ... AYT
Ayenquera [*Peru*] [*Seismograph station code, US Geological Survey*] (SEIS) ... AYE
Ayer, Ft. Devens, MA [*Location identifier*] [*FAA*] (FAAL) ... DKO
Ayer Information Center [*Information service or system*] (IID) ... AIC
Ayer Public Library, Delavan, IL [*Library symbol*] [*Library of Congress*] (LCLS) ... IDelav
Ayer Public Library, Delavan, IL [*OCLC symbol*] (OCLC) ... ISG
Ayerok Petroleum [*Vancouver Stock Exchange symbol*] ... AYK
Ayers Rock [*Australia*] [*Airport symbol*] (OAG) ... AYQ
Ayers Rock Mount of a National Park (SAUS) ... AR/MONP
Ayers Rock National Park (SAUS) ... Ayers
Ayerst Laboratories [*Research code symbol*] ... AY
Ayerst, McKenna & Harrison, Inc. Montreal, Quebec [*Library symbol*] [*National Library of Canada*] (NLC) ... QMAY
Ayerst, McKenna & Harrison Ltd., Montreal, PQ, Canada [*Library symbol*] [*Library of Congress*] (LCLS) ... CaQMAy
Ayerst Science Laboratory, Rouses Point, NY [*Library symbol*] [*Library of Congress*] (LCLS) ... NRpA
Ayian Leukosis [*Medicine*] (DMAA) ... AL
Aylesbeare [*England*] ... AYLB
Aylesbury [*England*] ... AYLB
Aylesbury/Thame [*British*] [*ICAO location identifier*] (ICLI) ... EGTA
Ayliffe's Calendar of Ancient Charters [*1774*] [*A publication*] (DLA) ... Ayl Char
Ayliffe's Introduction to the Calendar of Ancient Charters [*A publication*] (DLA) ... Ayl Int
Ayliffe's Pandect of the Roman Civil Law [*A publication*] (DLA) ... Ayl Pan
Ayliffe's Pandect of the Roman Civil Law [*A publication*] (DLA) ... Ayl Pand
Ayliffe's Pandects [*A publication*] (DLA) ... Ayliffe
Ayliffe's Parergon Juris Canonici Anglicani [*A publication*] (DLA) ... Ayliffe
Ayliffe's Parergon Juris Canonici Anglicani [*A publication*] (DLA) ... Ayl Par
Aylmer District Museum, Aylmer, ON, Canada [*Library symbol*] [*Library of Congress*] (LCLS) ... CaOAYM
Aylmer District Museum, Ontario [*Library symbol*] [*National Library of Canada*] (BIB) ... OAYM
Aylmer Heritage Association (AC) ... AHA
Ay-Luri [*Bolivia*] [*ICAO location identifier*] (ICLI) ... SLAX
Aymara [*MARC language code*] [*Library of Congress*] (LCCP) ... aym
Aymo Cravetta [*Deceased, 1569*] [*Authority cited in pre-1607 legal work*] (DSA) ... Aym
Ayn Rand Institute (EA) ... ARI
Ayn Rand Memorial Library Association [*Defunct*] (EA) ... ARMLA
Ayolas [*Paraguay*] [*ICAO location identifier*] (ICLI) ... SGAY
Ayr and Wigton's Registration Cases [*Scotland*] [*A publication*] (DLA) ... Ayr & Wig
Ayr Research Station [*Queensland, Australia*] ... ARS
Ayres Space Test [*Psychology*] ... AST
Ayr's Registration Cases [*Scotland*] [*A publication*] (DLA) ... Ayr
Ayrshire [*County in Scotland*] (WGA) ... AYR
Ayrshire (SAUS) ... Ayr
Ayrshire [*County in Scotland*] ... AYRS
Ayrshire Archaeological and Natural History Society (SAUO) ... AANHS
Ayrshire Artillery Volunteers [*British military*] (DMA) ... AAV
Ayrshire Breeders' Association (EA) ... ABA
Ayrshire Breeders Association (SAUO) ... ABA
Ayrshire Breeders Association of Canada (AC) ... ABAC
Ayrshire Cattle Society of Australia ... ACSA
Ayrshire Imperial Yeomanry [*British military*] (DMA) ... AIY
Ayrshire Yeomanry [*British military*] (DMA) ... AY
Ayrshire Yeomanry (SAUO) ... AYR
Ayrshire Yeomanry (SAUO) ... AYR YEO
Ayrton's Land Transfer Act [*A publication*] (DLA) ... Ayr Land Tr
A-Z Investigative Services of New York City (SAUO) ... A-Z
Aza [*As substituent on nucleoside*] [*Biochemistry*] ... z
Azacitidine [*Pharmacology*] (DAVI) ... 5-AC
Azacycloheptane Diphosphonate [*Organic chemistry*] ... AHDP
Azacytidine [*or Azacitidine*] [*Also, AZA, Aza-C*] [*Antineoplastic drug*] ... AC
Azacytidine [*or Azacitidine*] [*Also, AC, Aza-C*] [*Antineoplastic drug*] ... AZA
Azacytidine [*or Azacitidine*] [*Also, AC, AZA*] [*Antineoplastic drug*] ... Aza-C
Azad Hind Fauj [*Indian National Army*] ... AHF
Azad Kashmir Muslim Conference [*Pakistan*] [*Political party*] (FEA) ... AKMC
Azad Shahr [*Iran*] [*ICAO location identifier*] (ICLI) ... OINP
Azaguanine (MAE) ... azg
Azahypoxanthine [*Biochemistry*] ... AHX
Azalavia-Azerbaijan Hava Yollari [*ICAO designator*] (FAAC) ... AHY
Azalea Society of America (EA) ... ASA
Azamat [*Kazakhstan*] [*ICAO designator*] (FAAC) ... AZB
Aza(methyl)pregnanedione [*Biochemistry*] ... AMPD
Azania Liberation Front [*South Africa*] ... ALF
Azanian Co-Ordinating Committee [*South Africa*] [*Political party*] (EY) ... AZACCO
Azanian People's Organization [*South Africa*] (PPW) ... AZAPO
Azar Shahr [*Iran*] [*ICAO location identifier*] (ICLI) ... OITW
Azathioprine [*Also, AZA, AZT*] [*Immunosuppressive drug*] ... AZ
Azathioprine [*Also, AZ, AZT*] [*Immunosuppressive drug*] ... AZA
Azathioprine [*Also, AZ, AZA*] [*Immunosuppressive drug*] ... AZT
Azauracil [*Antineoplastic drug*] (DAVI) ... AZU
Azauridine (MAE) ... AU
Azauridine [*Antineoplastic drug*] (DAVI) ... AZUR
Azco Mining [*AMEX symbol*] (TTSB) ... AZC
Azco Mining, Inc. [*AMEX symbol*] (SAG) ... AZC
Azco Mining, Inc. [*Associated Press*] (SAG) ... Azco
Azerbaidzhan (SAUS) ... Azb
Azerbaidzhan (SAUS) ... Azer
Azerbaijan [*Internet country code*] ... AZ
Azerbaijan (ADWA) ... AZE
Azerbaijan Democratic Party [*Iran*] [*Political party*] ... ADP
Azerbaijan Soviet Socialist Republic [*MARC country of publication code*] [*Library of Congress*] (LCCP) ... ajr
Azerbaijan Soviet Socialist Republic (SAUO) ... ASSR
Azerbaijan Soviet Socialist Republic [*MARC geographic area code*] [*Library of Congress*] (LCCP) ... e-ur-aj
Azerbaijani [*MARC language code*] [*Library of Congress*] (LCCP) ... aze
Azerbaijani (BARN) ... Azerb
Azerbaijanian (SAUS) ... Azb
Azerbaydzhani Soviet Socialist Republic ... AzerSSR
Azia Keizai Kenkyujo [*Institute for Developing Economies*]**, Tokyo, Japan** [*Library symbol*] [*Library of Congress*] (LCLS) ... JTA
Azide Dextrose Agar (SAUS) ... ADA
Azide Dextrose-broth (SAUS) ... AD
Azido Dideoxythymidine (SAUS) ... AZT
Azidodeoxythymidine [*Biochemistry*] ... AZT
Azidodideoxyadenosine [*Antiviral*] ... AZA
Azidodideoxyguanosine [*Antiviral*] ... AZG
Azidodideoxyuridine [*Antiviral*] ... AZDDU
Azidodideoxyuridine [*Antiviral*] ... AZDU
Azido(ethyl)dideoxyuridine [*Antiviral*] ... AZEU
Azidonitrophenyl Phosphate [*Also, ACN*] [*Organic chemistry*] ... ANPP
Azidophenyl Norisocarbacyclin [*Organic chemistry*] ... APNIC
Azidophenylglyoxal [*Organic chemistry*] ... APG
(Azidophenylthio)phthalimide [*Organic chemistry*] ... APTP
Azidothymidine [*Later, ZDV*] [*Antiviral*] ... AZI
Azidothymidine [*Antiviral agent*] [*Medicine*] (TAD) ... AZT
Azidothymidine-Triphosphate [*Biochemistry*] ... AZT-TP
Azilda Branch, Rayside-Balfour Public Library, Ontario [*Library symbol*] [*National Library of Canada*] (NLC) ... OARB
Azimut SA [*Spain*] [*ICAO designator*] (FAAC) ... AZT
Azimuth (IAA) ... A
Azimuth (AFM) ... AZ
Azimuth (SAUS) ... Azi
Azimuth (SAUS) ... Azm
Azimuth ... AZM
Azimuth Alignment System [*Aerospace*] (AAG) ... AAS
Azimuth and Elevation (IAA) ... AAE
Azimuth and Elevation ... A & E
Azimuth and Elevation (SAUS) ... A&E
Azimuth and Elevation (SAUS) ... Az/EL
Azimuth and Elevation (MSA) ... AZEL
Azimuth and Range ... AZRAN
Azimuth and Range (SAUS) ... AZ/RAN
Azimuth and Range (MSA) ... AZRNG
Azimuth and Speed Indicator (SAUS) ... ASI
Azimuth Angle (ARMP) ... AZA
Azimuth Angle ... Z
Azimuth Angle Increment ... AAI
Azimuth Angle Measuring Unit (SAUS) ... AAM Unit
Azimuth, Bias, Level Equalization (SAUS) ... ABLE
Azimuth Change Pulse ... ACP

Azimuth Comparator	AC
Azimuth Control Amplifier	ACA
Azimuth Control System	ACS
Azimuth Control Torquer	ACT
Azimuth Determining System [*Army Space Technology and Research Office*] (RDA)	ADS
Azimuth Drive (GFGA)	AD
Azimuth Drive Assembly (MCD)	ADA
Azimuth Drive Local Control	ADLC
Azimuth, Elevation, and Range Overtake (SAA)	AERO
Azimuth Elevation Range (KSC)	AER
Azimuth Error Indicator	AEI
Azimuth Error Test Feature	AETF
Azimuth Error Test Fixture (MCD)	AETF
Azimuth Follow-Up Amplifier	AFA
Azimuth Follow-up Amplifier (SAUS)	AFA
Azimuth Follow-Up System	AFS
Azimuth Gimbal Assembly (MCD)	AGA
Azimuth Guidance Nose in Stands (MCD)	AGNIS
Azimuth Indicator	AI
Azimuth Laying Set (AABC)	ALS
Azimuth Mark Pulse Amplifier	AMPA
Azimuth Only	AZON
Azimuth Orientation System [*Military*]	AOS
Azimuth Orientation Unit [*Military*] (AABC)	AOU
Azimuth per Gyrocompass (SAUS)	Znpgc
Azimuth Position & Elevation System (SAUS)	APES
Azimuth, Predicted (SAUS)	AP
Azimuth Pulse Generator	APG
Azimuth Quantized Gated Video [*Air Force*]	AQGV
Azimuth Range and Timing Group (KSC)	ARTG
Azimuth Reference Pulse (SAUS)	ARP
Azimuth Reference System (MCD)	ARS
Azimuth Relative Pulse (SAUS)	ARP
Azimuth Reset Pulse	ARP
Azimuth Ridge (SAUS)	AR
Azimuth Scan Limit (ACAE)	ASL
Azimuth Servo Assembly	ASA
Azimuth, Speed, Altitude	AZUSA
Azimuth Speed Indicator	ASI
Azimuth Steering Line (MCD)	ASL
Azimuth Target Intelligence & Acquisition System (SAUS)	ATLAS
Azimuth Torque Amplifier (SAUS)	ATA
Azimuth Torquer Amplifier	ATA
Azimuth Versus Amplitude	AVA
azimuthal (SAUS)	a
Azimuthal Quantum Number	AQN
Azimuthal Quantum Number [*or Orbital Angular Momentum Quantum Number*] [*Symbol*]	l
Azimuthal Quantum Number [*or Orbital Angular Momentum Quantum Number*] - Total [*Symbol*]	L
Azimuthal Speed Indicator (SAUS)	ASI
Azimuthal Torque Amplifier (SAUS)	ATA
Azimuthally Varying Field	AVF
Azimuthally Varying Field Accelerator (SAUS)	AVF Accelerator
Azimuth-Elevation (IDOE)	AZ-EL
Azimuth/Range (RDA)	A/R
Azimuth/Range (SAUS)	AR
Azimuth-Stabilized Plan Position Indicator (DEN)	ASPPI
Azione Dynamico-Specifico [*Dynamic-Specific Action*] [*Italian*] [*Medicine*]	ADS
Aziridinyl Benzoquinone [*Organic chemistry*]	AZQ
Azna [*Iran*] [*ICAO location identifier*] (ICLI)	OICA
Azo Group [*Chemical group with two nitrogen atoms*] (MEDA)	N:N
Azobenzene Derivative [*Organic chemistry*]	ABD
Azobenzenearsonate [*Also, ARS*] [*Organic chemistry*]	ABA

Azobenzenearsonate [*Also, ABA*] [*Organic chemistry*]	ARS
Azobisformamide [*Organic chemistry*]	ABFA
Azobisisobutyronitrile (DB)	ABIBN
Azobisisobutyronitrile [*Organic chemistry*]	AIBN
Azobisisobutyronitrile (SAUS)	AZBN
Azodicarbonamide (OA)	ADA
Azoisobutyronitrile (SAUS)	AIBN
Azoospermia Factor [*Genetics*]	AZF
Azora Minerals [*Vancouver Stock Exchange symbol*]	AZM
Azores (VRA)	Azo
Azores (SAUS)	Azr
Azores Air Transport Station (SAUO)	AATS
Azores Air Transport System (SAUS)	AATS
Azores Fixed Acoustic Range [*NATO*]	AFAR
Azores Hot Spot [*Geology*]	AHS
Azores Islands	AZ
Azores Islands (SAUS)	Azores
Azores Islands [*MARC geographic area code*] [*Library of Congress*] (LCCP)	Inaz-
Azores Time (SAUS)	AT
Azote [*Nitrogen*] [*French*]	AZ
Azoxymethane (DB)	AOM
Azoxymethane [*A carcinogen*]	AZM
Aztar Corp. [*NYSE symbol*] (SPSG)	AZR
Aztar Corp. [*Associated Press*] (SAG)	Aztar
Aztec Manufacturing Co. [*NASDAQ symbol*] (NQ)	AZTC
Aztec Manufacturing Co. [*Associated Press*] (SAG)	AztcM
Aztec Mfg Co. [*NASDAQ symbol*] (TTSB)	AZTC
Aztec Mfg Co. [*NYSE symbol*] (SG)	AZZ
Aztec, NM [*AM radio station call letters*]	KCQL
Aztec, NM [*FM radio station call letters*]	KWYK
Aztec Oil & Gas Co. (SAUO)	AOG
Aztec Ruins National Monument (SAUS)	Arnm
Aztec Ruins National Monument (SAUS)	Azru
Aztec Ruins National Monument	AZRU
Aztec Ruins National Monument (SAUS)	Aztec Ruins
Azul [*Race of maize*]	AZU
Azul [*Argentina*] [*ICAO location identifier*] (ICLI)	SAZA
Azuni's Maritime Law [*A publication*] (DLA)	Az Mar Law
Azuni's Maritime Law [*A publication*] (DLA)	Azuni Mar Law
Azure (ABBR)	A
Azure [*Heraldry*] [*Philately*]	AZ
Azure (ADWA)	az
Azure Laid [*Paper*] (DGA)	AL
Azure Laid (ADA)	AZLD
Azure Resources [*Vancouver Stock Exchange symbol*]	AZR
Azure Wove [*Paper*] (DGA)	AW
Azure Wove (ADA)	AZWO
Azure Wove (SAUS)	Az Wo
Azurin (SAUS)	AZN
Azurin	AZU
Azurix Corp. [*NYSE symbol*] (SG)	AZX
Azurophil-Derived Bactericidal Factor	ADBF
Azurophilic Granule (DB)	AG
Azusa College (SAUO)	AC
Azusa Ground Station	AZGS
Azusa Pacific College, Azusa, CA [*OCLC symbol*] (OCLC)	CAP
Azusa Pacific College, Azusa, CA [*Library symbol*] [*Library of Congress*] (LCLS)	CAzPC
Azusa Pacific University (GAGS)	Azusa Pac U
Azusa Public Library, Azusa, CA [*Library symbol*] [*Library of Congress*] (LCLS)	CAz
Azusa Transponder	AZT
Azusa Transponder Coherent	AZTC
Azyme (SAUS)	Azy
Azza Transport Co. Ltd. [*Sudan*] [*FAA designator*] (FAAC)	AZZ

B
By Meaning

B Adress Register (SAUS) .... BAR
B & B Productions [New Jersey] [Record label] .... B & B
B and Better [Lumber] .... BB
B and Better Lumber (SAUS) .... BB Lumber
B & H Maritime Carriers Ltd. [Associated Press] (SAG) .... B & H Mr
B & H Ocean Carriers Ltd. [Associated Press] (SAG) ..... B & HO
B & H Ocean Carriers Ltd. [AMEX symbol] (CTT) .... BHO
B Battery (SAUS) .... B Btry
B Cell Lymphoma [Medicine] (MELL) .... BCL
"B" Corp. [Toronto Stock Exchange symbol] .... XBC
B. F. Goodrich Chemical Co. [of B. F. Goodrich Co.], Development Center
  Library, Avon Lake, OH [Library symbol] [Library of Congress] (LCLS) .... OAvG
B. F. Goodrich Co., Akron, OH [Library symbol] [Library of Congress]
  (LCLS) .... OAkGr
B. F. Goodrich Co., Information Center, Brecksville, OH [OCLC symbol]
  (OCLC) .... OGR
B. F. Goodrich Co., Technical Library, Brecksville, OH [Library symbol]
  [Library of Congress] (LCLS) .... OBrG
B. F. Goodrich Collegiate Inventors Program (SAUS) ...... BFG-CIP
B. F. Goodrich Institute for Personnel Development .... GIPD
B. F. Jones Memorial Library, Aliquippa, PA [OCLC symbol] (OCLC) ..... BFJ
B. F. Jones Memorial Library, Aliquippa, PA [Library symbol] [Library of
  Congress] (LCLS) .... PA
B. J. Thomas Fan Club (EA) .... BJTFC
B M J Financial [NASDAQ symbol] (TTSB) .... BMJF
B Minus (SAUS) B-1
B Negative (SAUS) .... B-
B negative [Blood type] (DAVI) .... BNEG
B Plus (SAUS) .... B+
B Positive (SAUS) .... B +
B Protein Precursor [Medicine] (MELL) .... BPP
B Pulse (SAUS) .... BP
B radio code (SAUS) .... Bravo letter
B Register B Bit (SAUS) .... BRBB
B scanner (SAUS) .... B scan
B. W. Flinn Middle School, Rockford, IL [Library symbol] [Library of
  Congress] (LCLS) .... IRoFM
B-1 Division [Rockwell] (NAKS) .... B-1 DIV
B9 Mixed Tumor (SAUS) .... BMT
Ba [Fiji] [Airport symbol] (OAG) .... BFJ
Ba [Fiji] [ICAO location identifier] (ICLI) .... NFFA
BA Merchant Services, Inc. [Associated Press] (SAG) ..... BA Mrch
BA Merchant Services, Inc. [NYSE symbol] (CTT) .... BPI
BA Resources [Vancouver Stock Exchange symbol] .... BAP
Baader-Meinhof Group [Revolutionary group] [Germany] ... BMG
Baalbek (SAUS) .... Baal
Baan Co. NV [NASDAQ symbol] (SAG) .... BAAN
Baan Co.NV [NASDAQ symbol] (TTSB) .... BAANF
Baastrup Disease [Medicine] (MELL) .... BD
BAB Holdings [NASDAQ symbol] (TTSB) .... BAGL
BAB Holdings, Inc. [Associated Press] (SAG) .... BABHld
BAB Holdings, Inc. [NASDAQ symbol] (SAG) .... BAGL
Baba Bathra [or Bava Batra] (BJA) .... BB
Baba Kama [or Bava Kamma] (BJA) .... BK
Baba Mezi'a [or Bava Mezi'a] (BJA) .... BM
Baba Qama [or Bava Qamma] (BJA) .... BQ
Babahoyo [Ecuador] [ICAO location identifier] (ICLI) ...... SEBA
Babar Islands of Indonesia (SAUS) .... Babars
Babbage Society (SAUO) .... BABS
Babbing [Fishing for eels] .... BAB
Babbitt [Metallurgy] .... BAB
Babbitt [Metallurgy] .... Bb
Babbitt, Inc. (SAUO) .... BAB
Babbitt Metal [Freight] .... BAB MTL
Babbitt, MN [FM radio station call letters] (RBYB) ..... KAOD
Babbitt Public Library, Babbitt, MN [Library symbol] [Library of Congress]
  (LCLS) .... MnBab
Babcock and Wilcox Co. (SAUO) .... B&W
Babcock & Wilcox Co. (SAUO) .... BAW
Babcock & Wilcox Co., Alliance, OH [Library symbol] [Library of Congress]
  (LCLS) .... OAIB
Babcock & Wilcox Co., Lynchburg, VA [Library symbol] [Library of
  Congress] (LCLS) .... ViLBW
Babcock & Wilcox Hanford Co. (ABAC) .... BWHC
Babcock and Wilcox Nuclear Environmental Services (GAAI) ... B&W-NES

Babcock & Wilcox Standard Safety Analysis Report [Nuclear energy]
  (NRCH) .... BSSAR
Babcock & Wilcox Test Reactor .... BAWTR
Babcock & Wilcox Test Reactor .... BWTR
Babcock Easy Terminal Access System (MCD) .... BETA
Babcock English Electric Nuclear Ltd. (SAUO) .... BEEN
Babcock International, Inc. (EFIS) .... BII
Babcock Test of Mental Efficiency [Psychology] .... BTME
Babcock Woodall-Duckham Ltd. [British] (IRUK) .... BWD
Babe Ruth Baseball (EA) .... BRB
Babe Ruth Baseball/Softball [An association] (EA) .... BRB
Babe Ruth Birthplace Foundation (EA) .... BRBF
Babe Ruth League (EA) .... BRL
Babel Language Editing and Checking (PDAA) .... BLEACH
Babenhausen [Germany] [ICAO location identifier] (ICLI) .... EDEF
Babesiasis Card-agglutination Test (SAUS) .... BCT
Babilonia [Costa Rica] [ICAO location identifier] (ICLI) ..... MRBB
Babine Mountains (SAUS) .... Babines
Babinet Absorption Rule .... BAR
Babinet Jamin Compensator .... BJC
Babinet-Soleil Compensator (SAUS) .... BSC
Babington's Law of Auctions [A publication] (DLA) ...... Bab Auc
Babington's Law of Set-Off [A publication] (DLA) ...... Bab Set-Off
Babinski [Reflex] [Medicine] .... BAB
Babinski-Nageotte [Syndrome] [Medicine] (DB) .... BN
Babinski's Sign [Medicine] (MELL) .... BS
Babo [Indonesia] [Airport symbol] (OAG) .... BXB
Babo [Indonesia] [ICAO location identifier] (ICLI) .... WASO
Babolsar [Iran] [ICAO location identifier] (ICLI) .... OINB
Baboon Endogenous Virus .... BaEV
Baboon Endogenous Virus .... BEV
Baboon Kidney (DMAA) .... BabK
Babson College (GAGS) .... Babson C
Babson College, Babson Park, MA [OCLC symbol] (OCLC) .... BAB
Babson College, Babson Park, MA [Library symbol] [Library of Congress]
  (LCLS) .... MBBI
Babson Institute (SAUO) .... BI
Babson Institute of Business Administration [Massachusetts] .... BIBA
Babson's Reports, Inc. (IIA) .... BRI
Baby Advanced Technology (VERA) .... BAT
Baby Bond [Investment term] .... BB
Baby Boomers in Debt [Lifestyle Classification] .... Biddies
Baby Born Dead [Medicine] .... BBD
Baby Brother Tender Love [Doll manufactured by Mattel, Inc.] ...... BBTL
Baby Hamster Kidney .... BHK
Baby Incendiary Bomb .... B/B
Baby Incendiary Bomb .... BIB
Baby Life Support System (DI) .... BLISS
Baby Mouse Kidney Cells .... BMK
Baby "N" Connector (IEEE) .... BNC
Baby Neill Concelman [Electronics] (MED) .... BNC
Baby or Doll [Freight] .... BB DL
Baby Rat Kidney [Immunology] .... BRK
Baby Superstore [NASDAQ symbol] (TTSB) .... BSST
Baby Superstore, Inc. [Associated Press] (SAG) ...... BabySst
Baby Superstore, Inc. [NASDAQ symbol] (SAG) .... BSST
Baby with Reflux [Medicine] (MELL) .... BWR
Babylon (SAUS) .... Bab
Babylon, NY [Location identifier] [FAA] (FAAL) .... BBN
Babylon, NY [FM radio station call letters] .... WBAB
Babylon, NY [AM radio station call letters] .... WGLI
Babylon, NY [AM radio station call letters] .... WNYG
Babylon, NY [AM radio station call letters] (RBYB) .... WZZU-AM
Babylon Public Library, Babylon, NY [Library symbol] [Library of Congress]
  (LCLS) .... NBab
Babylonia (BJA) .... Bab
Babylonia [or Babylonian] .... BABYL
[The] Babylonian Genesis [A publication] (BJA) .... BG
Babylonian Historical Texts Relating to the Capture and Downfall of
  Babylon [A publication] (BJA) .... BHT
Babylonian Inscriptions in the Collection of James B. Nies (BJA) ..... BIN
Babylonian Legal and Business Documents [A publication] (BJA) .... BLBD
Babylonian Records in the Library of J. Pierpont Morgan (BJA) ..... BRM
Babylonian Seleucid Era (BJA) .... SelBab
Babylonian Talmud (BJA) .... Bab
Babylonian Talmud (BJA) .... BT

Babylonian Vocalization (BJA) ... BV
Babylonien und Assyrien [*A publication*] (BJA) ... BuA
Babylonische Briefe aus der Zeit der Hammurapi Dynastie [*A publication*] (BJA) ... BB
Babylonische Busspsalmen [*A publication*] (BJA) ... BB
Babylonische Rechtsurkunden aus der Regierungszeit Artaxerxes I und Darius II [*A publication*] (BJA) ... BRU
Babylonische Texte [*A publication*] (BJA) ... BT
Babysitting Association of South Australia ... BASA
Babystar, Inc. [*Associated Press*] (SAG) ... Babyst
Babystar, Inc. [*Associated Press*] (SAG) ... Babystr
Babystar, Inc. [*NASDAQ symbol*] (SAG) ... DATA
BAC Aircraft Ltd. [*British*] [*ICAO designator*] (FAAC) ... RPX
BAC Leasing Ltd. [*British*] [*FAA designator*] (FAAC) ... BAC
Baca County Public Library, Springfield, CO [*Library symbol*] [*Library of Congress*] (LCLS) ... CoSp
Bacau [*Romania*] [*Seismograph station code, US Geological Survey*] (SEIS) ... BAC
Bacau [*Romania*] [*Airport symbol*] (OAG) ... BCM
Bacau [*Romania*] [*ICAO location identifier*] (ICLI) ... LRBC
Baccalaureat des Sciences Politiques [*French*] (CPGU) ... BScPol
Baccalaureat des Sciences, Relations Industrielles [*French*] (CPGU) ... BSRI
Baccalaureat en Administration [*French*] [*Bachelor of Administration Studies*] (CPGU) ... BAdmin
Baccalaureat en Administration des Affaires [*Canada*] (DD) ... BAA
Baccalaureat en Agriculture [*French*] (CPGU) ... BAg
Baccalaureat en Analyse [*French*] (CPGU) ... BAAn
Baccalaureat en Architecture [*French*] (CPGU) ... BAr(ch)
Baccalaureat en Education [*French*] [*Bachelor of Education*] (CPGU) ... BEd
Baccalaureat en Genie [*French*] [*Bachelor of Engineering*] (CPGU) ... BE(ng)
Baccalaureat en Ingenerie [*Canada*] (DD) ... Bing
Baccalaureat en Loisirs [*Canada*] (DD) ... BL
Baccalaureat en Musique [*French*] [*Bachelor of Music*] (CPGU) ... BMus
Baccalaureat en Sciences Administratives [*Canada*] (DD) ... BAS
Baccalaureat en Sciences Administratives [*Canada*] (DD) ... BSA
Baccalaureat en Sciences Sociales [*French*] [*Bachelor of Social Science*] (CPGU) ... BScSoc
Baccalaureat Specialise en Commerce [*French*] (CPGU) ... BComm
Baccalaureate ... B
Baccalaureate ... BACC
Baccalaureate Exam [*France*] ... BAC
Baccalaureus ... BAC
Baccalaureus Artium [*Bachelor of Arts*] [*Latin*] ... BA
Baccalaureus Chirurgiae [*Bachelor of Surgery*] ... BC
Baccalaureus Chirurgiae [*Bachelor of Surgery*] ... B Ch
Baccalaureus Chirurgiae [*Bachelor of Surgery*] ... B Chir
Baccalaureus Chirurgiae Dentium [*Bachelor of Dental Surgery*] ... B Ch D
Baccalaureus in Arte Ingeniaria [*Bachelor of Engineering*] (EY) ... BAI
Baccalaureus Juris [*Bachelor of Law*] (DLA) ... B Jur
Baccalaureus Legum [*Bachelor of Laws*] ... BLL
Baccalaureus Literarum [*Bachelor of Literature*] [*Latin*] ... LB
Baccalaureus Medicinae, Chirurgiae Magister [*Bachelor of Medicine, Master of Surgery*] ... MBCM
Baccalaureus Procurationis (DLA) ... B Proc
Baccalaureus Scientiae [*Bachelor of Science*] [*Latin*] ... B Sc
Baccalaureus Scientiae Didacticae [*Bachelor of Didactic Science*] ... BSD
Baccalaureus Utriusque Juris [*Bachelor of Both Laws; i.e., Canon and Civil Laws*] ... BUJ
Baccaulaureat Specialisee en Administration Publique [*French*] (ASC) ... BAdmPub
Bacchae [*of Euripides*] [*Classical studies*] (OCD) ... Bacch
Bacchides [*of Plautus*] [*Classical studies*] (OCD) ... Bacch
Bacchylides [*Fifth century BC*] [*Classical studies*] (OCD) ... Bacchyl
Bac-Giang [*Vietnam*] [*Seismograph station code, US Geological Survey*] (SEIS) ... BGV
Bach, Beethoven and Brahms (SAUS) ... BBB
Bach Choir [*Record label*] ... BC
Bach Jahrbuch [*A publication*] ... B-J
Bach Society of Queensland [*Australia*] ... BSQ
Bach Werke-Verzeichnis [*Music*] ... BWV
Bachad Organization of North America (EA) ... BONA
Bache Group Company (SAUO) ... BAC
Bachelier des Arts [*Bachelor of Arts*] [*French*] ... B des A
Bachelier des Lettres [*Bachelor of Letters*] [*French*] ... B des L
Bachelier des Sciences [*Bachelor of Science*] [*French*] ... B des S
Bachelier en Arts Visuels [*Bachelor of Visual Arts*] [*French*] ... BAV
Bachelier en Droit [*Bachelor of Laws*] [*French*] ... B en Dr
Bachelier en Droit Canonique [*Bachelor of Canon Law*] [*French*] ... BDC
Bachelier en Medicine Veterinaire [*Bachelor of Veterinary Medicine*] [*French*] (ASC) ... BMV
Bachelier en Sciences Administratives [*Bachelor in Administrative Sciences*] [*French*] ... BSA
Bachelier en Service Social [*Bachelor of Social Work*] [*French*] ... BSerSoc
Bachelier es Arts [*Bachelor of Arts*] [*French*] (ASC) ... BesA
Bachelier es Science [*Bachelor of Science*] [*French*] (ASC) ... BesSc
Bachelier es Science Appliquee [*Bachelor of Applied Science*] [*French*] (ASC) ... BesScApp
Bachelier es Sciences [*Bachelor of Science*] [*French*] (ROG) ... B es SC
Bachelier es Sciences Appliquees [*Bachelor of Applied Science*] [*French*] ... BScA
Bachelor ... B
Bachelor (GEAB) ... ba
Bachelor (GEAB) ... bach
Bachelor ... BACH
Bachelor ... BACHR
Bachelor ... BCHLR
Bachelor Airmen's Quarters [*Air Force*] ... BAQ
Bachelor Churgerie (SAUS) ... BCH
Bachelor Degrees for Soldiers [*Program*] ... BDFS
Bachelor Enlisted Quarters ... BEQ
Bachelor in Arts in Library Science (SAUS) ... BALS
Bachelor in Dental Science [*British*] ... BDentSc
Bachelor in Fine Arts (SAUS) ... BFA
Bachelor in Interior Architecture ... BIntArch
Bachelor in Interior Design ... BIntDesign
Bachelor in Landscape Architecture ... BLandArch
Bachelor in Law (DD) ... BL
Bachelor in Library Science (ADA) ... BLibSc
Bachelor in Psychology (SAUS) ... BPs
Bachelor in Surgery (DD) ... BCh
Bachelor in Surgery (DD) ... BChir
Bachelor in Technology (SAUS) ... BTech
Bachelor in Telecommunications Engineering (SAUS) ... BTelE
Bachelor Lake Gold Mines, Inc. [*Toronto Stock Exchange symbol*] ... BLG
Bachelor Noncommissioned Officers' Quarters [*Air Force*] (AFM) ... BNCOQ
Bachelor of Accountancy ... B Acc
Bachelor of Accounting [*Canada*] (ASC) ... BAcc
Bachelor of Accounts ... B Ac
Bachelor of Accounts (SAUS) ... BAc
Bachelor of Accounts ... B Acc's
Bachelor of Actuarial Sciences (DD) ... BActSci
Bachelor of Acupuncture [*British*] (DBQ) ... BAc
Bachelor of Administration ... B Adm
Bachelor of Administration ... BAdmin
Bachelor of Administrative Engineering ... B Adm Eng
Bachelor of Advertising Arts and Design ... B of Adv Art & Des
Bachelor of Aeronautical Administration ... B of AA
Bachelor of Aeronautical and Astronautical Engineering (WGA) ... BAAE
Bachelor of Aeronautical Engineering ... BAE
Bachelor of Aeronautical Engineering [*Canada*] (ASC) ... BAeE
Bachelor of Aeronautical Engineering ... B Ae Eng
Bachelor of Aeronautical Engineering ... B Aero E
Bachelor of Aeronautical Engineering ... B of AE
Bachelor of Aeronautical Science ... B Ae S
Bachelor of Aeronautical Science ... B Ae Sc
Bachelor of Aeronautics ... B Ae
Bachelor of Agricultural Economics (IIA) ... BAE
Bachelor of Agricultural Economics (ADA) ... BAgEc
Bachelor of Agricultural Economics (WDAA) ... B AG ECO
Bachelor of Agricultural Economics (NADA) ... BAgoEco
Bachelor of Agricultural Economics (SAUS) ... BAgrEco
Bachelor of Agricultural Economics ... BAgrEcon
Bachelor of Agricultural Engineering ... BAE
Bachelor of Agricultural Engineering ... B Ag E
Bachelor of Agricultural Engineering ... B Agr E
Bachelor of Agricultural Engineering ... B Eng A
Bachelor of Agricultural Research and Economics ... BAgResEcon
Bachelor of Agricultural Science ... B Agr S
Bachelor of Agricultural Science ... B Agr Sc
Bachelor of Agricultural Science (ADA) ... BAgSc
Bachelor of Agricultural Science (BARN) ... BAgSci
Bachelor of Agricultural Science ... BAS
Bachelor of Agricultural Science ... BA Sc
Bachelor of Agricultural Science (NADA) ... BSA
Bachelor of Agriculture ... BA
Bachelor of Agriculture ... B Ag
Bachelor of Agriculture ... B Agr
Bachelor of Agriculture ... BAgri
Bachelor of Agriculture [*British*] ... BAgric
Bachelor of Air Conditioning Engineering ... BACE
Bachelor of Air Conditioning Engineering ... BAC Eng
Bachelor of Animal Science ... BAnimSc
Bachelor of Applied Arts ... B/A
Bachelor of Applied Arts ... BAA
Bachelor of Applied Arts (NADA) ... BAppArts
Bachelor of Applied Chemistry ... BA Chem
Bachelor of Applied Economics (ADA) ... BAppEc
Bachelor of Applied Mathematics ... BAM
Bachelor of Applied Music ... BMusA
Bachelor of Applied Science ... B Applied Sc
Bachelor of Applied Science (ADA) ... BAppSc
Bachelor of Applied Science (WDAA) ... B APP SCI
Bachelor of Applied Science [*Canada*] (ASC) ... BAS
Bachelor of Applied Science ... BA Sc
Bachelor of Applied Science (ADA) ... BScApp
Bachelor of Applied Science - Built Environment ... BAppSc-BltEnvir
Bachelor of Applied Science - Computing ... BAppSc-Comptg
Bachelor of Applied Science - Construction Management ... BAppSc-ConstMgmt
Bachelor of Applied Science - Electronic Systems and Computing ... BAppSc-ElectSysComptg
Bachelor of Applied Science - Information ... BAppScInfo
Bachelor of Applied Science - Optometry ... BAppSc-Optom
Bachelor of Applied Science - Quantity Surveying ... BAppSc-QuantSurv
Bachelor of Applied Science - Surveying ... BAppSc-Surv
Bachelor of Applied Science (Nursing) (ADA) ... BAppSci(Nsg)
Bachelor of Applied Science (Optometry) ... BAppSci(Optom)
Bachelor of Applied Science (Social Ecology) ... BAppSci(SocEcol)
Bachelor of Architectural Design ... B Arch Des
Bachelor of Architectural Engineering ... BAE
Bachelor of Architectural Engineering ... B Arc E
Bachelor of Architectural Engineering (NADA) ... BArchE
Bachelor of Architectural Engineering ... B Arch Eng

Bachelor of Architectural Engineering	B Ar E
Bachelor of Architectural History	BArchHist
Bachelor of Architectural Science	BAS
Bachelor of Architectural Studies	BArchSt
Bachelor of Architectural Studies	BArchStudies
Bachelor of Architectural Technology	BArchTech
Bachelor of Architecture	B Ar
Bachelor of Architecture	B Arch
Bachelor of Architecture (NADA)	BArch
Bachelor of Architecture and Town Planning (ADA)	BArch & TP
Bachelor of Architecture and Town Planning (SAUS)	B Arch&TP
Bachelor of Architecture in Architectural Engineering	B Arch (ArchE)
Bachelor of Architecture in Architecture	B Arch (Arch)
Bachelor of Architecture in City Planning	B Arch in City Pl
Bachelor of Art and Architecture (ADA)	BAA
Bachelor of Art Education	BAE
Bachelor of Art Education	BA Ed
Bachelor of Art Education	BArtEd
Bachelor of Art of Oratory	BAO
Bachelor of Art Theory	BArtTh
Bachelor of Arts (AEE)	AB
Bachelor of Arts	BA
Bachelor of Arts - Classical	BA Class
Bachelor of Arts - Non-Classical	BA Non-Class
Bachelor of Arts and Science (SAUS)	BASc
Bachelor of Arts and Sciences	B Ar Sc
Bachelor of Arts and Sciences	BAS
Bachelor of Arts (Asian Studies)	BA(AsianStudies)
Bachelor of Arts (Economics)	BA (Econ)
Bachelor of Arts (Education)	BA(Educ)
Bachelor of Arts in Arts and Science (SAUS)	BA in A&Sci
Bachelor of Arts in Arts and Sciences	BA in A & Sci
Bachelor of Arts in Bible	AB (Bible)
Bachelor of Arts in Business Administration (SAUS)	BABA
Bachelor of Arts in Business Administration	BA in BA
Bachelor of Arts in Business and Economics	BA in B & E
Bachelor of Arts in Business and Economics (SAUS)	BA in B&E
Bachelor of Arts in Ceramic Art	BA in Cer A
Bachelor of Arts in Chemical Engineering	AB in Ch E
Bachelor of Arts in Chemistry (WDAA)	BA CHEM
Bachelor of Arts in Chemistry (SAUS)	BA Chem
Bachelor of Arts in Civil Engineering	AB in CE
Bachelor of Arts in Economics (SAUS)	BAEcon
Bachelor of Arts in Economics and Business (SAUS)	BA in E&B
Bachelor of Arts in Economics and Business	BA in E & B
Bachelor of Arts in Education	AB Ed
Bachelor of Arts in Education	BAE
Bachelor of Arts in Education	BA Ed
Bachelor of Arts in Electrical Engineering	AB in EE
Bachelor of Arts in Elementary Education (WGA)	BAEE
Bachelor of Arts in Elementary Education	BA in E Ed
Bachelor of Arts in Elementary Education (SAUS)	BA in E ed
Bachelor of Arts in General Studies [British] (DBQ)	BA(GenStud)
Bachelor of Arts in General Studies	BAGS
Bachelor of Arts in Home Economics	AB in H Ec
Bachelor of Arts in Human Relations	BAH Re
Bachelor of Arts in Information Systems	BAIS
Bachelor of Arts in Journalism	AB in J
Bachelor of Arts in Journalism	BA in J
Bachelor of Arts in Journalism	BAJ
Bachelor of Arts in Journalism (BARN)	B A Jour
Bachelor of Arts in Law	BA(Law)
Bachelor of Arts in Library Science	ABLS
Bachelor of Arts in Mathematics (SAUS)	ABMath
Bachelor of Arts in Mechanical Engineering	AB in ME
Bachelor of Arts in Mechanical Engineering	ABME
Bachelor of Arts in Music	BAM
Bachelor of Arts in Music Education	BA in M Ed
Bachelor of Arts in Music Education (BARN)	BAMusEd
Bachelor of Arts in Nursing (WDAA)	BA NURS
Bachelor of Arts in Nursing (SAUS)	BA Nurs
Bachelor of Arts in Obstetrics (SAUO)	BAO
Bachelor of Arts in Oratory (SAUS)	BAO
Bachelor of Arts in Pedagogy (DD)	BAPed
Bachelor of Arts in Physical Education (NADA)	BAPE
Bachelor of Arts in Practical Christian Training	BAPCT
Bachelor of Arts in Recreation and Physical Education (CPGU)	BAP
Bachelor of Arts in Religious Education	BA in Rel Ed
Bachelor of Arts in Sacred Music (BJA)	BASM
Bachelor of Arts in Secondary Education	AB in Sec Ed
Bachelor of Arts in Secretarial Studies (ADA)	BASecStud
Bachelor of Arts in Social Science (WDAA)	BASS
Bachelor of Arts in Social Studies (SAUS)	BASS
Bachelor of Arts in Speech	BA in Sp
Bachelor of Arts in Speech	BAS
Bachelor of Arts in Teaching	BAT
Bachelor of Arts in Theology	AB in TH
Bachelor of Arts in Theology	BA Theo
Bachelor of Arts in Theology (BARN)	B A Theol
Bachelor of Arts in Theology (SAUS)	BA Theol
Bachelor of Arts in Town Planning (SAUS)	BATP
Bachelor of Arts in Visual Communication	BAVisCom
Bachelor of Arts (Information Management)	BA(InfoMan)
Bachelor of Arts (journ.) (SAUS)	Bach of Arts
Bachelor of Arts (Leisure Studies)	BA(LeisureStud)
Bachelor of Arts (Library Science)	BA(LibSc)
Bachelor of Arts, Master of Science	BASM
Bachelor of Arts (Music)	BA (Mus)
Bachelor of Arts of Architecture (SAUS)	BAA
Bachelor of Arts (Open University) [British] (DI)	BA(OU)
Bachelor of Arts (Special) (CPGU)	BASp
Bachelor of Arts (Visual Arts)	BA(VA)
Bachelor of Arts with Religious Major	AB (Rel)
Bachelor of Arts/Bachelor of Laws (ADA)	BA/LLB
Bachelor of Arts/Bachelor of Management Combines (DD)	BA/BMgmt
Bachelor of Arts/Bachelor of Science Combined (DD)	BA/BS
Bachelor of Asian Studies	BAsianStudies
Bachelor of Association Science	B As S
Bachelor of Association Science	B As Sc
Bachelor of Automobile Engineering	B Au E
Bachelor of Automobile Engineering	B Au Eng
Bachelor of Ayurvedic Medicine	BAM
Bachelor of Ayurvedic Medicine and Surgery (SAUS)	BAMS
Bachelor of Bacteriology	BB
Bachelor of Bacteriology	B Bac
Bachelor of Beauty Culture	BBC
Bachelor of Behavioral Sciences	BBehavSci
Bachelor of Behavioural Science	BBSc
Bachelor of Biblical Arts (SAUS)	B Bib Art
Bachelor of Biblical Arts	B Bib Arts
Bachelor of Biological Chemistry	B Bi Ch
Bachelor of Biological Chemistry	B Bi Chem
Bachelor of Biological Engineering	B Bi E
Bachelor of Biological Engineering	B Bi Eng
Bachelor of Biological Physics	B Bi Phy
Bachelor of Biological Sciences	B Bi S
Bachelor of Biological Sciences	B Bi Sc
Bachelor of Biomedical Sciences	BBiomed
Bachelor of Building (ADA)	BBldg
Bachelor of Building (ADA)	BBuild
Bachelor of Building	BBuilding
Bachelor of Building Construction	BBC
Bachelor of Building Construction	B of BC
Bachelor of Building Science	BBldgSc
Bachelor of Building Science (ADA)	BBldSc
Bachelor of Business	BB
Bachelor of Business (ADA)	BBus
Bachelor of Business - Accountancy	BBus-Accy
Bachelor of Business - Communication	BBus-Comn
Bachelor of Business - Computing	BBus-Comptg
Bachelor of Business - Health Administration	BBusHA
Bachelor of Business - Health Administration	BBus-HealthAdmin
Bachelor of Business - Management	BBus-Mgt
Bachelor of Business - Public Administration	BBus-PubAdmin
Bachelor of Business Administration	BBA
Bachelor of Business Administration	BB Ad
Bachelor of Business Administration	BB Adm
Bachelor of Business Administration (CPGU)	BBAd(min)
Bachelor of Business Administration (ADA)	BBusAd
Bachelor of Business Administration	BBusAdmin
Bachelor of Business Education	BB Ed
Bachelor of Business Management	BBM
Bachelor of Business Management	BBusMgmt
Bachelor of Business Science	BBS
Bachelor of Business Science	BB Sc
Bachelor of Business Studies	BBS
Bachelor of Canon Law	B Can L
Bachelor of Canon Law	BCL
Bachelor of Canon Law (SAUS)	JCB
Bachelor of Cement Engineering	B Ce Eng
Bachelor of Ceramic Engineering	B Cer E
Bachelor of Ceramic Engineering	B Cer Eng
Bachelor of Chemical Engineering	BCE
Bachelor of Chemical Engineering	B Ch E
Bachelor of Chemical Engineering	B Chem E
Bachelor of Chemical Engineering (DD)	BChemEng
Bachelor of Chemical Engineering	B Ch Eng
Bachelor of Chemical Engineering (ADA)	BEChem
Bachelor of Chemical Science	BCS
Bachelor of Chemistry	BC
Bachelor of Chemistry	B Ch
Bachelor of Chemistry	B Chem
Bachelor of Chemistry	Ch B
Bachelor of Christian Education	BCE
Bachelor of Christian Education	B Chr Ed
Bachelor of Christian Science	BSC
Bachelor of Christian Science	CSB
Bachelor of Christian Training	BCT
Bachelor of Chromatic (SAUS)	B Chrom
Bachelor of Chromatics	BChrom
Bachelor of Church Music	BCM
Bachelor of City Forestry	BCF
Bachelor of City Planning	BCP
Bachelor of Civil Engineering [Canada] (ASC)	BCE
Bachelor of Civil Law	BCL
Bachelor of Civil Law	CLB
Bachelor of Civil Law (SAUS)	JCB
Bachelor of Classic (SAUS)	BC
Bachelor of Classics	BC
Bachelor of College Studies	BCS

Bachelor of Combined Studies [*British*] (DBQ) .... BCombStuds
Bachelor of Combined Studies [*British*] (DI) .... BComStuds
Bachelor of Commerce .... BC
Bachelor of Commerce .... B Com
Bachelor of Commerce (SAUO) .... BCom
Bachelor of Commerce .... B Comm
Bachelor of Commerce (Accounting) .... BCom(Acc)
Bachelor of Commerce and Administration (BARN) .... BCA
Bachelor of Commerce-Bachelor of Laws .... BCom-LLB
Bachelor of Commercial Administration .... B Com Adm
Bachelor of Commercial Arts .... BCA
Bachelor of Commercial Education .... BC Ed
Bachelor of Commercial Law .... BCL
Bachelor of Commercial Science .... BCommSc
Bachelor of Commercial Science .... BComSc
Bachelor of Commercial Science .... BCS
Bachelor of Commercial Science .... BC Sc
Bachelor of Commercial Science .... BScCom
Bachelor of Commercial Science (DD) .... BScComm
Bachelor of Commercial Service .... BC Se
Bachelor of Community Welfare .... BCW
Bachelor of Community Work .... BCW
Bachelor of Computer and Mathematical Sciences .... BCM
Bachelor of Computer Management (DD) .... BCM
Bachelor of Computer Science .... BCompSc
Bachelor of Computer Science .... BCS
Bachelor of Computer Science and Engineering .... BCompScEng
Bachelor of Computer Systems Engineering .... BComSysEng
Bachelor of Computing .... BComp
Bachelor of Construction Economics .... BConstrucEc
Bachelor of Creative Arts .... BA(Creative)
Bachelor of Creative Arts .... BCA
Bachelor of Creative Arts .... BCreativeArts
Bachelor of Criminal Science (NADA) .... BCS
Bachelor of Criminology .... B Cr
Bachelor of Dental Science [*British*] (BABM) .... BDentSci
Bachelor of Dental Science (SAUS) .... BDent Sci
Bachelor of Dental Science .... BD Sc
Bachelor of Dental Sciences (SAUS) .... BDSc
Bachelor of Dental Surgery (SAUS) .... BDS
Bachelor of Dental Surgery .... BDS
Bachelor of Dentistry .... BDentistry
Bachelor of Design .... B Des
Bachelor of Design [*Canada*] (ASC) .... BDes
Bachelor of Design .... BDesign
Bachelor of Design in Art Education .... B Des A Ed
Bachelor of Didactics .... BDi
Bachelor of Didactics (SAUS) .... B Di
Bachelor of Didactics .... B Did
Bachelor of Diesel Engineering .... B Di E
Bachelor of Diesel Engineering .... B Di Eng
Bachelor of Diplomacy .... B Dipl
Bachelor of Divine Literature .... BDL
Bachelor of Divinity .... BD
Bachelor of Divinity (CPGU) .... BD(iv)
Bachelor of Divinity .... DB
Bachelor of Divinity and Master of Hebrew Literature (BJA) .... BDMHL
Bachelor of Divinity in Education .... BD in E
Bachelor of Domestic Arts .... ADB
Bachelor of Domestic Arts .... BDA
Bachelor of Dramatic Art .... BDA
Bachelor of Dramatic Art .... B Dr Art
Bachelor of Dramatic Arts (SAUS) .... BDA
Bachelor of Economics .... B Ec
Bachelor of Economics (SAUO) .... BEC
Bachelor of Economics .... BEcon
Bachelor of Economics in Industrial Administration (SAUS) .... BEconIA
Bachelor of Economics in Public Administration (SAUS) .... BEconPA
Bachelor of Economics (Social Sciences) .... BEc(SocSc)
Bachelor of Economics/Bachelor of Laws (ADA) .... BEc/LLB
Bachelor of Education .... BE
Bachelor of Education .... B Ed
Bachelor of Education [*British*] (DET) .... BEd
Bachelor of Education (SAUO) .... BED
Bachelor of Education .... Ed B
Bachelor of Education (SAUS) .... EdB
Bachelor of Education (SAUO) .... EDB
Bachelor of Education in Nursing (SAUS) .... BEdN
Bachelor of Education in Physical Education (SAUS) .... B Ed in Phys Ed
Bachelor of Education in Physical Education (SAUS) .... BEdPE
Bachelor of Education (Industrial Arts) .... BEd(IndArts)
Bachelor of Education (Preliminary Studies) .... BEd(Prelim)
Bachelor of Education (Technical and Further Education) .... BEd(TAFE)
Bachelor of Education (Technological and Applied Studies) .... BEd(TAS)
Bachelor of Educational Science (ADA) .... BEdSc
Bachelor of Educational Studies (ADA) .... BEdSt
Bachelor of Educational Studies .... BEdStud
Bachelor of Electrical Engineering .... BEE
Bachelor of Electrical Engineering .... BEngE
Bachelor of Electrical Engineering, Communication Option .... B of EE (Com Opt)
Bachelor of Electrical Engineering, Power Option .... B of EE (Power Opt)
Bachelor of Electro-Chemical Engineering .... BECE
Bachelor of Electronics and Telecommunication Engineering (SAUS) .... BElec&Tel Eng

Bachelor of Electronics and Telecomunications Engineering (NADA) .... BElec&TelEng
Bachelor of Elementary Didactics (SAUS) .... BED
Bachelor of Elements .... B Ele
Bachelor of Elocution .... BE
Bachelor of Elocution .... B El
Bachelor of Engineering .... BE
Bachelor of Engineering .... BEn
Bachelor of Engineering .... B Eng
Bachelor of Engineering (WGA) .... B Engr
Bachelor of Engineering - Civil .... BEng-Civil
Bachelor of Engineering - Electrical .... BEng-Elec
Bachelor of Engineering - Electrical .... BEng-Elect
Bachelor of Engineering - Mechanical .... BEng-Mech
Bachelor of Engineering (Agriculture) .... BE(Ag)
Bachelor of Engineering Construction .... BEC
Bachelor of Engineering in Agriculture (SAUS) .... B Eng A
Bachelor of Engineering in Mechanical Engineering .... BE-ME
Bachelor of Engineering of Mines .... BEM
Bachelor of Engineering Physics (SAUS) .... B Eng Physics
Bachelor of Engineering Physics .... BEP
Bachelor of Engineering Physics .... BE Phy
Bachelor of Engineering Physics .... B of EP
Bachelor of Engineering Science (DD) .... BE
Bachelor of Engineering Science (WGA) .... B Eng S
Bachelor of Engineering Science (ADA) .... BEngSc
Bachelor of Engineering Science (NADA) .... BEngSci
Bachelor of Engineering Science .... BESc
Bachelor of Engineering Sciences .... BES
Bachelor of Engineering (Technology) .... B Eng (Tech)
Bachelor of Engineering Technology (SAUS) .... B Eng Tech
Bachelor of Engineering Technology .... BET
Bachelor of Engineering/Bachelor of Business .... BEng/BBus
Bachelor of English .... BE
Bachelor of English .... B En
Bachelor of English Divinity .... BED
Bachelor of English Literature .... BEL
Bachelor of English Literature .... ELB
Bachelor of Entomology .... B Ent
Bachelor of Environmental Design Studies [*Canada*] (ASC) .... BEDS
Bachelor of Environmental Science .... BEnvSc
Bachelor of Environmental Science .... BEnvSci
Bachelor of Environmental Studies .... BES
Bachelor of Expression .... BE
Bachelor of Expression .... B Ex
Bachelor of Family Life .... BFL
Bachelor of Film and Television .... BFTV
Bachelor of Finance .... BF
Bachelor of Finance .... BFin
Bachelor of Financial Administration .... BFA
Bachelor of Financial Administration (ADA) .... BFinAdmin
Bachelor of Fine Arts .... BFA
Bachelor of Fine Arts in Dramatic Art .... BFA in DA
Bachelor of Fine Arts in Education .... BFA in Ed
Bachelor of Fine Arts in Landscape Architecture .... BFALA
Bachelor of Fine Arts in Music .... BFA in Mus
Bachelor of Fine Arts in Painting and Sculpture .... BFA in PS
Bachelor of Fine Arts in Speech .... BFA in Sp
Bachelor of Fisheries Science .... BFSc
Bachelor of Foreign Service .... BFS
Bachelor of Foreign Trade .... BFT
Bachelor of Forest Engineering .... BFE
Bachelor of Forest Engineering .... BF Eng
Bachelor of Forestry .... BF
Bachelor of Forestry (ADA) .... B For
Bachelor of Forestry Science (ADA) .... BForSc
Bachelor of Forestry Science (NADA) .... BForSci
Bachelor of General Education .... B Gen Ed
Bachelor of General Laws (DLA) .... BGL
Bachelor of General Laws (SAUS) .... BGL
Bachelor of General Studies .... BGS
Bachelor of Geological Engineering .... BGE
Bachelor of Geological Engineering .... B Ge E
Bachelor of Geological Engineering .... B Ge Eng
Bachelor of Graphic Design .... BGD
Bachelor of Hamburgerology [*McDonald's Corp. Hamburger University*] .... BH
Bachelor of Health Science .... BHlthSc
Bachelor of Health Science .... BHS
Bachelor of Health Science .... BHSc
Bachelor of Health Science .... BHthSc
Bachelor of Hebrew .... BH
Bachelor of Hebrew Letters .... BHL
Bachelor of Hebrew Literature .... BHL
Bachelor of Home Economics (NADA) .... BHE
Bachelor of Home Economics .... BH Ec
Bachelor of Home Science .... BHS
Bachelor of Horticultural Science .... BHortSc
Bachelor of Horticultural Science .... BHortSci
Bachelor of Horticulture .... B Hor
Bachelor of Horticulture .... BHort
Bachelor of Hospital Administration .... BHA
Bachelor of Hospital Administration .... BH Adm
Bachelor of Hospitality .... BHospitality
Bachelor of Household Economics .... BHE
Bachelor of Household Economics (SAUS) .... BHEc

Bachelor of Household Economy	B Ho Ec
Bachelor of Household Science	B Ho Sc
Bachelor of Household Science	BHSc
Bachelor of Household Science (NADA)	BHSci
Bachelor of Human Biology	BHB
Bachelor of Human Movement	BHUMMVT
Bachelor of Human Movement Studies	BHMS
Bachelor of Humane Letter (SAUO)	LHB
Bachelor of Humane Letters	BHL
Bachelor of Humane Letters [or Bachelor of Literature or Bachelor of the More Humane Letters]	LHB
Bachelor of Humanics	BH
Bachelor of Humanities	B Hu
Bachelor of Hygiene	B Hy
Bachelor of Hygiene	B HYG
Bachelor of Hygiene (SAUS)	BHyg
Bachelor of Indian Medicine (NADA)	BIM
Bachelor of Industrial Administration (WGA)	BIA
Bachelor of Industrial Arts	BIA
Bachelor of Industrial Design	BID
Bachelor of Industrial Design	BIndDes
Bachelor of Industrial Education	B Ind Ed
Bachelor of Industrial Engineering	BIE
Bachelor of Industrial Engineering	BI Eng
Bachelor of Industrial Engineering	B Ind E
Bachelor of Industrial Management	BIM
Bachelor of Industrial Management	B Ind Mgt
Bachelor of Industrial Management	B of IM
Bachelor of Industrial Relations (CPGU)	BIndR
Bachelor of Industrial Relations (DD)	BIR
Bachelor of Industrial Technology	BIndTech
Bachelor of Industrial Technology	BIT
Bachelor of Industry	B Ind
Bachelor of Informatics	BIn
Bachelor of Information Science	BInfoSc
Bachelor of Information Systems	BInfoSys
Bachelor of Information Technology and Communication	BInfoTech
Bachelor of Interdisciplinary Studies	BIS
Bachelor of Interior Architectural Engineering	BI Arch E
Bachelor of Interior Architectural Engineering	BI Arch Eng
Bachelor of Interior Architecture	BI Arch
Bachelor of Interior Design	B of ID
Bachelor of International Law	B Int L
Bachelor of Irrigation Engineering	B Ir E
Bachelor of Irrigation Engineering	B Ir Eng
Bachelor of Jewish Education (BJA)	BJE
Bachelor of Jewish Education	BJ Ed
Bachelor of Jewish Literature (BJA)	BJL
Bachelor of Jewish Pedagogy	BJP
Bachelor of Journalism	BJ
Bachelor of Journalism (CPGU)	BJ(our)
Bachelor of Judicial Science	JSB
Bachelor of Juridical and Social Sciences (DLA)	B Jur & Soc S
Bachelor of Jurisprudence	BJ
Bachelor of Jurisprudence	BJuris
Bachelor of Land Information	BLandInfo
Bachelor of Land Management (NADA)	BLM
Bachelor of Land Resource Science	BLandResSc
Bachelor of Landscape Architecture	BLA
Bachelor of Landscape Architecture	BL Arch
Bachelor of Landscape Design [British] (DBQ)	BLD
Bachelor of Landscape Design	BL Des
Bachelor of Landscape Engineering	BL Eng
Bachelor of Landscape Management	BLM
Bachelor of Languages [British] (DBQ)	BA(Lan)
Bachelor of Latin Letters	B La L
Bachelor of Latin Letters	BLL
Bachelor of Law Administration	BLAdmin
Bachelor of Law and Administration	BLA
Bachelor of Laws	BL
Bachelor of Laws (CPGU)	BLL
Bachelor of Laws (SAUS)	JB
Bachelor of Laws (DD)	LLB
Bachelor of Legal Studies (ADA)	BLegS
Bachelor of Legal Studies	BLegSt
Bachelor of Leisure Studies	BLeisureStud
Bachelor of Letters	BL
Bachelor of Letters	B Lit
Bachelor of Letters	B Litt
Bachelor of Letters (ODBW)	BLitt
Bachelor of Letters in Journalism	BLJ
Bachelor of Letters or Literature (SAUO)	LittB
Bachelor of Liberal Arts	BLA
Bachelor of Liberal Arts (SAUS)	BLA
Bachelor of Liberal Studies	BLibSt
Bachelor of Liberal Studies	BLibStudies
Bachelor of Liberal Studies	BLS
Bachelor of Librarianship (SAUS)	BLib
Bachelor of Library and Information Studies	BLS
Bachelor of Library Economics	BLE
Bachelor of Library Economics	BL Ec
Bachelor of Library Science (ADA)	BLib
Bachelor of Library Science (NADA)	BLibS
Bachelor of Library Science (NADA)	BLibSci
Bachelor of Library Science	BLS

Bachelor of Library Science	BL Sc
Bachelor of Library Service (NADA)	BLS
Bachelor of Life Science	LSB
Bachelor of Linguistics, University of Manchester [British] (DBQ)	BLing
Bachelor of Literary Interpretation	BLI
Bachelor of Literature	BL
Bachelor of Literature	B Lit
Bachelor of Literature (SAUO)	BLit
Bachelor of Literature	B Litt
Bachelor of Literature	B Lt
Bachelor of Literature (SAUO)	LHB
Bachelor of Literature (SAUS)	Lit B
Bachelor of Literature	Lt B
Bachelor of Literature and Communication	BLittComm
Bachelor of Management (DD)	BMgmt
Bachelor of Management Arts (DD)	BMA
Bachelor of Management Engineering	B Mgt E
Bachelor of Management Engineering (NADA)	BMgtEng
Bachelor of Manufacturing Management	BMfgMgt
Bachelor of Manufacturing Technology	BManufTech
Bachelor of Marine Engineering	B Ma E
Bachelor of Marine Engineering	B Ma Eng
Bachelor of Marine Engineering	B Mar E
Bachelor of Marine Engineering (NADA)	BMarEng
Bachelor of Marine Science	BMS
Bachelor of Marine Science (SAUS)	BMS
Bachelor of Mathematics	BM
Bachelor of Mathematics	BMath
Bachelor of Mathematics (SAUS)	BMath
Bachelor of Mathematics	BMaths
Bachelor of Mechanic Arts	AMB
Bachelor of Mechanical Engineering	BME
Bachelor of Mechanical Engineering	B Mech E
Bachelor of Mechanical Engineering	BM Eng
Bachelor of Mechanical Engineering (Aeronautical Option)	BME (Aero Option)
Bachelor of Mechanical Engineering, Manufacture, and Management [British] (DBQ)	BEng and Man
Bachelor of Mechanical Science	BMS
Bachelor of Mechanical Science	BM Sc
Bachelor of Mechanical Sciences	B Ms Sc
Bachelor of Mechanics	B Mech
Bachelor of Medical Biology	B Med Biol
Bachelor of Medical Biology (SAUS)	BMedBiol
Bachelor of Medical Engineering (SAUO)	BME
Bachelor of Medical Laboratory Science	BMedLabSc
Bachelor of Medical Science	BMS
Bachelor of Medical Science, University of Dundee [British] (DBQ)	BMSc
Bachelor of Medical Sciences	B Med Sc
Bachelor of Medical Sciences	B Med Sci
Bachelor of Medical Technology	BMT
Bachelor of Medicine	BM
Bachelor of Medicine	B Med
Bachelor of Medicine [Other than from Oxford]	MB
Bachelor of Medicine and Bachelor of Science [British] (ROG)	MBBSC
Bachelor of Medicine and Bachelor of Surgery	BMBS
Bachelor of Medicine, Bachelor of Surgery	BMBCh
Bachelor of Medicine, Master of Surgery	MBMS
Bachelor of Metallurgical Engineering	B Metal E
Bachelor of Metallurgical Engineering	B Met E
Bachelor of Metallurgical Engineering	B Met Eng
Bachelor of Metallurgy	B Met
Bachelor of Metaphysics (SAUO)	MeB
Bachelor of Metaphysics	Me B
Bachelor of Microbiology	B Mic
Bachelor of Mining and Metallurgy	BMM
Bachelor of Mining Engineering	BEM
Bachelor of Mining Engineering	BME
Bachelor of Mining Engineering	B Mi E
Bachelor of Mining Engineering	B Mi Eng
Bachelor of Mining Engineering	BMinE
Bachelor of Mining Engineering	BMiningE
Bachelor of Ministry	BMin
Bachelor of Modern Languages	BML
Bachelor of Municipal Administration	BMA
Bachelor of Music (BARN)	BAC MUS
Bachelor of Music	BM
Bachelor of Music	B Mu
Bachelor of Music (ODBW)	B Mus
Bachelor of Music (SAUO)	BMus
Bachelor of Music (WDAA)	MB
Bachelor of Music Education	BME
Bachelor of Music Education	BM Ed
Bachelor of Music Education	B Mus E
Bachelor of Music Education	BMusEd
Bachelor of Music Education	Mus Ed B
Bachelor of Music in Education (SAUS)	B Mus Ed
Bachelor of Music in Public School Music	B Mus (PSM)
Bachelor of Music in School Music (SAUS)	BMSM
Bachelor of Music (Performance)	BMusPerf
Bachelor of Music Teaching	BMusT
Bachelor of Natural Resources (ADA)	BNatRes
Bachelor of Natural Science (BARN)	BNS
Bachelor of Naval Architecture	BN Arch
Bachelor of Naval Engineering	BNE
Bachelor of Naval Engineering	BN Eng

Bachelor of Naval Science	BNS
Bachelor of Navigation	B Na
Bachelor of Navigation (NADA)	BNav
Bachelor of Nursing	BN
Bachelor of Nursing	BNursing
Bachelor of Nursing Education	BN Ed
Bachelor of Nursing, Nursing Studies, University of Southampton [British] (DBQ)	BN Nursing Studies
Bachelor of Nursing Science	BNS
Bachelor of Nursing Science	BN Sc
Bachelor of Nursing, University of Manchester [British] (DBQ)	BNurs
Bachelor of Nutrition and Dietetics	BND
Bachelor of Obstetrics (SAUS)	BAO
Bachelor of Occupational Therapy (ADA)	BOccThy
Bachelor of Occupational Therapy	BOT
Bachelor of Optometry	B Opt
Bachelor of Optometry (ADA)	BOptom
Bachelor of Optometry	BOptometry
Bachelor of Oral English	BOE
Bachelor of Oratory	BO
Bachelor of Oratory	B Or
Bachelor of Oratory Science (SAUS)	B Or Sc
Bachelor of Oriental Languages (SAUS)	BOL
Bachelor of Oriental Learning (SAUS)	BOL
Bachelor of Oriental Studies	B Orient
Bachelor of Orientation (SAUS)	BOr
Bachelor of Osteopathy	BO
Bachelor of Paediatrics (ADA)	BPaed
Bachelor of Painting	BP
Bachelor of Painting	B Pa
Bachelor of Patent Law	BPL
Bachelor of Pedagogy	BP
Bachelor of Pedagogy	BPaed
Bachelor of Pedagogy [or Pedagogics]	B Pd
Bachelor of Pedagogy	B Pe
Bachelor of Pedagogy [or Pedagogics]	B Ped
Bachelor of Pedagogy	B Py
Bachelor of Pedagogy	Pd B
Bachelor of Pedagogy (ROG)	PE B
Bachelor of Pedagogy	Ped B
Bachelor of Pedagogy	Pg B
Bachelor of Pedagogy (SAUS)	PyB
Bachelor of Pedagogy	Py B
Bachelor of Pediatrics	Pe B
Bachelor of Pediatrics (WDAA)	PED B
Bachelor of Performing Arts	BPerfArts
Bachelor of Petroleum Engineering (WGA)	BPE
Bachelor of Petroleum Engineering	B Pe E
Bachelor of Petroleum Engineering	B Pe Eng
Bachelor of Petroleum Engineering	B Pet E
Bachelor of Pharmaceutical Chemistry	B Ph C
Bachelor of Pharmaceutical Chemistry (SAUS)	BPhC
Bachelor of Pharmacy	BP
Bachelor of Pharmacy (DD)	BPh
Bachelor of Pharmacy	B Pharm
Bachelor of Pharmacy [Academic degree] (WDAA)	BPharm
Bachelor of Pharmacy (CPGU)	BPhm
Bachelor of Pharmacy	Ph B
Bachelor of Pharmacy	Phm B
Bachelor of Philosophy	BP
Bachelor of Philosophy	B Ph
Bachelor of Philosophy	B Phil
Bachelor of Philosophy [Academic degree] (WDAA)	BPhil
Bachelor of Philosophy (WDAA)	PB
Bachelor of Philosophy (DAVI)	PhB
Bachelor of Philosophy (Education), University of Birmingham [British] (DBQ)	BPhil(Ed)
Bachelor of Philosophy in Architecture	Ph B in Arch
Bachelor of Philosophy in Commerce	Ph B in Com
Bachelor of Philosophy in Education	Ph B in Ed
Bachelor of Philosophy in Journalism (NADA)	PhBJ
Bachelor of Philosophy in Journalism (SAUS)	Ph BJ
Bachelor of Philosophy in Speech (SAUS)	Ph B Sp
Bachelor of Philosophy in Speech (NADA)	PhBSp
Bachelor of Photography	B Pho
Bachelor of Physic	BM
Bachelor of Physical and Health Education	BPHE
Bachelor of Physical Biology	BPB
Bachelor of Physical Culture	Ph B
Bachelor of Physical Education	BPE
Bachelor of Physical Education	BP Ed
Bachelor of Physical Education (CPGU)	BP(h)E(d)
Bachelor of Physical Education	BPhysEd
Bachelor of Physical Health Education	BPhysHlthEd
Bachelor of Physical Science	B Ph S
Bachelor of Physical Therapy (WDAA)	B PHYS THY
Bachelor of Physical Therapy (SAUS)	BPhysThy
Bachelor of Physical Therapy	BPT
Bachelor of Physics	B Phy
Bachelor of Physics (NADA)	BPhys
Bachelor of Physiotherapy (ADA)	BPhty
Bachelor of Physiotherapy	BPhysio
Bachelor of Physiotherapy (NADA)	BPT
Bachelor of Planning and Design	BPD
Bachelor of Planning, University of Manchester [British]	BPI

Bachelor of Political Science	B Pol Sc
Bachelor of Practical Theology	P Th B
Bachelor of Professional Arts	BPA
Bachelor of Professional Studies	BPS
Bachelor of Psychic Sciences	B Ps Sc
Bachelor of Psychology	B Ps
Bachelor of Psychology	BPsy
Bachelor of Psychology	BPsych
Bachelor of Psychotherapy	B Ps Th
Bachelor of Public Administration	BPA
Bachelor of Public Administration	BP Adm
Bachelor of Public Administration	BPubAdmin
Bachelor of Public Health	BPH
Bachelor of Public Health Education	BPH Ed
Bachelor of Public Health Engineering	BPHE
Bachelor of Public Health Engineering	BPH Eng
Bachelor of Public Health Nursing	BPHN
Bachelor of Public Policy	BPubPol
Bachelor of Public School Art	BPSA
Bachelor of Public School Music	BPSM
Bachelor of Radio and Television Engineering	BRTE
Bachelor of Radio and Television Engineering	BRT Eng
Bachelor of Radio Engineering	B Ra E
Bachelor of Radio Engineering	B Ra Eng
Bachelor of Recreation Education (DD)	BRE
Bachelor of Refrigeration Engineering	B Re E
Bachelor of Refrigeration Engineering	B Re Eng
Bachelor of Regional and Town Planning (ADA)	BRTP
Bachelor of Religion	B Re
Bachelor of Religious Education	BRE
Bachelor of Religious Education	BR Ed
Bachelor of Religious Sciences	BRSc
Bachelor of Religious Studies	BRS
Bachelor of Rural Engineering	B Ru E
Bachelor of Rural Engineering	B Ru Eng
Bachelor of Rural Science (ADA)	BRurSc
Bachelor of Rural Science (NADA)	BRuSci
Bachelor of Rural Science Education	BRurScEd
Bachelor of Sacred Literature	BSL
Bachelor of Sacred Music	BSM
Bachelor of Sacred Music	BS Mu
Bachelor of Sacred Music	BS Mus
Bachelor of Sacred Music	SMB
Bachelor of Sacred Sciences	B Sa Sc
Bachelor of Sacred Theology	BST
Bachelor of Sacred Theology (NADA)	STB
Bachelor of Sanitary Engineering	BSE
Bachelor of Sanitary Engineering	BS Eng
Bachelor of Sanitary Science	BSS
Bachelor of Sanitary Science	BS Sc
Bachelor of School Music	B Sch Mus
Bachelor of School Music	BSM
Bachelor of School Music	BS Mus
Bachelor of School Music	Sch Mus B
Bachelor of Science	BS
Bachelor of Science (SAUO)	BSC
Bachelor of Science [Academic degree] (AIE)	BSc
Bachelor of Science	SB
Bachelor of Science	Sc B
Bachelor of Science and English Literature	BSEL
Bachelor of Science (Animal Husbandry) (ADA)	BSc(AH)
Bachelor of Science (Architecture)	BSc(Arch)
Bachelor of Science (Chemical Engineering) (ADA)	BSc(ChemEng)
Bachelor of Science (Civil Engineering)	BSCE
Bachelor of Science Degree in Computer Science	BSCS
Bachelor of Science (Dentistry)	BSc (Dent)
Bachelor of Science (Design Studies)	BSc(DesStud)
Bachelor of Science (Domestic Science)	B Sc (Dom Sc)
Bachelor of Science (Education)	BSc(Educ)
Bachelor of Science Education (NADA)	BSE
Bachelor of Science, Engineering (DD)	BScE
Bachelor of Science (Engineering) (EY)	BSc(Eng)
Bachelor of Science (Engineering)	BSc(Engg)
Bachelor of Science (Engineering)	BSc(Engin)
Bachelor of Science Engineering (SAUS)	BSE
Bachelor of Science (Estate Management)	B Sc (Est Man)
Bachelor of Science (Forestry)	BSc(Forestry)
Bachelor of Science (General Science) (ADA)	BSc(GenSc)
Bachelor of Science (Home Science)	BSc(HomeSc)
Bachelor of Science (Home Science)	BSc(HomeSci)
Bachelor of Science in Accounting	BS (Acc)
Bachelor of Science in Accounting (WDAA)	B SC ACC
Bachelor of Science in Accounting	BS in Acc
Bachelor of Science in Administration (CPGU)	BScAdmin
Bachelor of Science in Administrative Engineering	BS in AE
Bachelor of Science in Advertising	BS Adv
Bachelor of Science in Aeronautical Administration	BS in Aero Adm
Bachelor of Science in Aeronautical Education (SAUS)	BS Aero E
Bachelor of Science in Aeronautical Engineering	BSAE
Bachelor of Science in Aeronautical Engineering	BS Ae E
Bachelor of Science in Aeronautical Engineering	BS (Aero E)
Bachelor of Science in Aeronautical Engineering	BS in AE
Bachelor of Science in Aeronautical Engineering	BS in Ae E
Bachelor of Science in Aeronautical Engineering	BS in Aero E
Bachelor of Science in Aeronautical Engineering - Electronics Major	BSAE-E

Bachelor of Science in Agricultural Administration	BSA Adm
Bachelor of Science in Agricultural Administration	BS in AM
Bachelor of Science in Agricultural Administration (SAUS)	BS in AN
Bachelor of Science in Agricultural Biology (NADA)	BScAgrBio
Bachelor of Science in Agricultural Economics (SAUS)	BScAEco
Bachelor of Science in Agricultural Economics (NADA)	BScAgrEco
Bachelor of Science in Agricultural Education	BS in AD
Bachelor of Science in Agricultural Education	BS in Agr Ed
Bachelor of Science in Agricultural Engineering (WGA)	BSAE
Bachelor of Science in Agricultural Engineering	BS Ag E
Bachelor of Science in Agricultural Engineering (NADA)	BScAgrEng
Bachelor of Science in Agricultural Engineering	BSc(AgricEng)
Bachelor of Science in Agricultural Engineering	B Sc in Agr Engr
Bachelor of Science in Agricultural Engineering	BS in Ag E
Bachelor of Science in Agricultural Engineering	BS in Agr E
Bachelor of Science in Agricultural Engineering	BS in Agr Eng
Bachelor of Science in Agricultural Engineering	BS in AN
Bachelor of Science in Agriculture (DD)	BAS
Bachelor of Science in Agriculture	BSA
Bachelor of Science in Agriculture	BS Ag
Bachelor of Science in Agriculture	BS Agr
Bachelor of Science in Agriculture	BScA
Bachelor of Science in Agriculture	BScAg
Bachelor of Science in Agriculture	B Sc Ag
Bachelor of Science in Agriculture	BScAgri
Bachelor of Science in Agriculture	BScAgric
Bachelor of Science in Agriculture	BS in Ag
Bachelor of Science in Agriculture and Animal Husbandry (NADA)	BScAg&AH
Bachelor of Science in Agriculture and Chemistry	BS in Agr & Chem
Bachelor of Science in Agriculture and Education	BS in Ag & Ed
Bachelor of Science in Agriculture and Education (SAUS)	BS in Ag&Ed
Bachelor of Science in Agriculture in Dairy Manufacturing	BS in Ag (DM)
Bachelor of Science in Air Transportation	BSAT
Bachelor of Science in Aircraft Maintenance Engineering	BSAME
Bachelor of Science in Applied Arts (WGA)	BSAA
Bachelor of Science in Applied Mathematics	BS (A Math)
Bachelor of Science in Applied Mathematics (SAUS)	BS A Math
Bachelor of Science in Applied Mathematics	BS in Math
Bachelor of Science in Applied Mathematics	Sc BAM
Bachelor of Science in Architectural Engineering	BSAE
Bachelor of Science in Architectural Engineering	BS Arch E
Bachelor of Science in Architectural Engineering (NADA)	BSArchEng
Bachelor of Science in Architectural Engineering	BS in AE
Bachelor of Science in Architecture (NADA)	BSArch
Bachelor of Science in Architecture (NADA)	BScArch
Bachelor of Science in Architecture	BS in Arch
Bachelor of Science in Architecture in Architectural Engineering	BS Arch (Arch E)
Bachelor of Science in Architecture in Architecture	BS Arch (Arch)
Bachelor of Science in Art Education	BS Art Ed
Bachelor of Science in Bacteriology	B Sc in Bact
Bachelor of Science in Basic Medical Science	BS in Med S
Bachelor of Science in Basic Medical Sciences	BS in BMS
Bachelor of Science in Biology	BS Biol
Bachelor of Science in Biomedical Engineering	BS in Biomed Eng
Bachelor of Science in Business	BSB
Bachelor of Science in Business	BS Bus
Bachelor of Science in Business	BS in Bus
Bachelor of Science in Business - Medical Records	BS (Bus-MR)
Bachelor of Science in Business Administration	BSBA
Bachelor of Science in Business Administration	BSB Ad
Bachelor of Science in Business Administration	BS Bus Ad
Bachelor of Science in Business Administration (NADA)	BScBA
Bachelor of Science in Business Administration	BS in BA
Bachelor of Science in Business Administration	BS in B Ad
Bachelor of Science in Business Administration	BS in Bus Ad
Bachelor of Science in Business and Public Administration (SAUS)	BS Bus and Public Adm
Bachelor of Science in Business Education	BSB Ed
Bachelor of Science in Business Education	BSBusEd
Bachelor of Science in Business Education	BS in B Ed
Bachelor of Science in Business Education	BS in Bus Ed
Bachelor of Science in Business-Medical Records (SAUS)	BS Bus-MR
Bachelor of Science in Cartography	BS in Cart
Bachelor of Science in Ceramic Engineering	BS (Cer E)
Bachelor of Science in Ceramic Engineering	BS Cr E
Bachelor of Science in Ceramic Engineering	BS in Cer E
Bachelor of Science in Ceramic Technology	BS in Cer Tech
Bachelor of Science in Ceramics	BS in Cer
Bachelor of Science in Chemical Engineering (NADA)	BScChemE
Bachelor of Science in Chemical Engineering	BS Ch E
Bachelor of Science in Chemical Engineering	BS Chem E
Bachelor of Science in Chemical Engineering	BS Ch Eng
Bachelor of Science in Chemical Engineering	BS in CE
Bachelor of Science in Chemical Engineering	BS in Ch E
Bachelor of Science in Chemical Engineering	BS in Chem E
Bachelor of Science in Chemical Engineering	BS in Ch Eng
Bachelor of Science in Chemical Engineering	BS in Chm E
Bachelor of Science in Chemical Engineering	BS in CN
Bachelor of Science in Chemical Technology	BS in Chem Tech
Bachelor of Science in Chemistry	BSCh
Bachelor of Science in Chemistry (NADA)	BSChm
Bachelor of Science in Chemistry	BS in C
Bachelor of Science in Chemistry	BS in Ch
Bachelor of Science in Chemistry	BS in Chm
Bachelor of Science in Chemistry	Sc BC
Bachelor of Science in Christian Education - Music	BS in CE - Music
Bachelor of Science in Christian Education-Music (SAUS)	BS in CE-Music
Bachelor of Science in Civil Engineering (NADA)	BScCE
Bachelor of Science in Civil Engineering	B Sc in CE
Bachelor of Science in Civil Engineering	BS in CE
Bachelor of Science in Civil Engineering	SBCE
Bachelor of Science in Commerce	BSC
Bachelor of Science in Commerce	BS in C
Bachelor of Science in Commerce	BS in Com
Bachelor of Science in Commerce	BS in Comm
Bachelor of Science in Commerce and Business	BS in Com & Bus
Bachelor of Science in Commerce and Business (SAUS)	BS in Com&Bus
Bachelor of Science in Commerce and Economics (SAUS)	BS C and E
Bachelor of Science in Commerce and Economics (SAUS)	BS in C&Ec
Bachelor of Science in Commerce and Economics	BS in C & Ec
Bachelor of Science in Commercial and Business Administration	BS in C & BA
Bachelor of Science in Commercial and Business Administration (SAUS)	BS in C&BA
Bachelor of Science in Commercial Education	BS in Com Ed
Bachelor of Science in Communications	BS Com
Bachelor of Science in Community Recreation	BS in Comm Rec
Bachelor of Science in Computer Science	BSCompSci
Bachelor of Science in Criminal Justice	BSCJ
Bachelor of Science in Dental Hygiene (NADA)	BSDH
Bachelor of Science in Dental Hygiene	BSD Hyg
Bachelor of Science in Dental Hygiene	BS in DH
Bachelor of Science in Dentistry (ADA)	BSD
Bachelor of Science in Dentistry (NADA)	BSDent
Bachelor of Science in Dentistry	BS in Dent
Bachelor of Science in Design	BSD
Bachelor of Science in Design	BS Des
Bachelor of Science in Design in Decorative Design	BS Des (Dec Des)
Bachelor of Science in Dianoetics	B Sc (Dn)
Bachelor of Science in Didactics (SAUS)	BSD
Bachelor of Science in Domestic Science (SAUS)	BScDomSc
Bachelor of Science in Economics (CPGU)	BScEc
Bachelor of Science in Economics	B Sc Econ
Bachelor of Science in Economics	BS Ec
Bachelor of Science in Economics (WGA)	BS Econ
Bachelor of Science in Economics	BS in Ec
Bachelor of Science in Economics and Business Administration (SAUS)	BS Ec and Bus Adm
Bachelor of Science in Education	BScEd
Bachelor of Science in Education	BSE
Bachelor of Science in Education	BS Ed
Bachelor of Science in Education	BS in E
Bachelor of Science in Education	BS in Ed
Bachelor of Science in Education, Music Supervision (SAUS)	BS Ed Music Super
Bachelor of Science in Education-Physical Education (SAUS)	BS Ed-Phys Ed
Bachelor of Science in Electrical and Mechanical Engineering	BSEE-ME
Bachelor of Science in Electrical Engineering	B Sc in EE
Bachelor of Science in Electrical Engineering	BSEE
Bachelor of Science in Electrical Engineering	BS in EE
Bachelor of Science in Electrical Engineering	SBEE
Bachelor of Science in Electronic Engineering	BS El E
Bachelor of Science in Electronic Engineering	BS in Elect Eng
Bachelor of Science in Elementary Education (ADA)	BScElEd
Bachelor of Science in Elementary Education	BSEE
Bachelor of Science in Elementary Education	BS El Ed
Bachelor of Science in Elementary Education	BS Elem
Bachelor of Science in Elementary Education	BS in Elem Ed
Bachelor of Science in Engineering (DD)	BE
Bachelor of Science in Engineering	BES
Bachelor of Science in Engineering (DD)	BSc(Eng)
Bachelor of Science in Engineering	BSE
Bachelor of Science in Engineering (NADA)	BSEng
Bachelor of Science in Engineering	BS in E
Bachelor of Science in Engineering	BS in Eng
Bachelor of Science in Engineering	Sc BE
Bachelor of Science in Engineering Administration	BS Engr Ad
Bachelor of Science in Engineering and Civil Engineering	BSE (CE)
Bachelor of Science in Engineering and Economics	BSE & E
Bachelor of Science in Engineering and Economics (SAUS)	BSE&E
Bachelor of Science in Engineering in Aeronautical Engineering	BSE (Ae E)
Bachelor of Science in Engineering in Chemical Engineering	BSE (Ch E)
Bachelor of Science in Engineering in Electrical Engineering	BSE (EE)
Bachelor of Science in Engineering in Engineering Mechanics	BSE (EM)
Bachelor of Science in Engineering in Geodesy and Surveying	BSE (Geod & Surv)
Bachelor of Science in Engineering in Industrial Engineering	BSE (Ind E)
Bachelor of Science in Engineering in Materials Engineering	BSE (Mat E)
Bachelor of Science in Engineering in Mechanical and Industrial Engineering	BSE (M & Ind E)
Bachelor of Science in Engineering in Mechanical Engineering	BSE (ME)
Bachelor of Science in Engineering in Metallurgical Engineering	BSE (Met E)
Bachelor of Science in Engineering in Naval Architecture and Marine Engineering	BSE (Nav Arch & Mar E)
Bachelor of Science in Engineering Mathematics	BS in E Math
Bachelor of Science in Engineering Mechanics	BS in Mech
Bachelor of Science in Engineering of Mines	BSEM
Bachelor of Science in Engineering of Mines	BS in EM
Bachelor of Science in Engineering Physics	BS Engr Phys

Bachelor of Science in Engineering Physics .... BSEP
Bachelor of Science in Engineering Physics .... BSE Phys
Bachelor of Science in Engineering Physics .... BS in EP
Bachelor of Science in Engineering Physics .... BS in E Phys
Bachelor of Science in Engineering Science .... BS Engr Sci
Bachelor of Science in Engineering Sciences .... BS Eng Sci
Bachelor of Science in Engineering Sciences .... BSES
Bachelor of Science in Engineering Sciences .... BSE Sc
Bachelor of Science in Engineering Sciences .... BS in ES
Bachelor of Science in Engineering Technology (IEEE) .... BSET
Bachelor of Science in Finance .... BS (Fin)
Bachelor of Science in Finance .... BS in Fin
Bachelor of Science in Fisheries Management .... BSF Mgt
Bachelor of Science in Foreign Service .... BSFS
Bachelor of Science in Foreign Service .... BS in FS
Bachelor of Science in Forest Management .... BSFM
Bachelor of Science in Forestry [*Canada*] (ASC) .... BScF
Bachelor of Science in Forestry .... B Sc For
Bachelor of Science in Forestry .... BSF
Bachelor of Science in Forestry .... BS For
Bachelor of Science in Forestry .... BS Fsty
Bachelor of Science in Forestry .... BS in For
Bachelor of Science in Forestry .... BS in Fy
Bachelor of Science in Forestry Engineering [*Canada*] (ASC) .... BScFE
Bachelor of Science in Fuel Technology .... BSFT
Bachelor of Science in Game Management .... BSG Mgt
Bachelor of Science in General Business .... BS in Gen Bus
Bachelor of Science in General Education .... BS Gen Ed
Bachelor of Science in General Engineering .... BSGE
Bachelor of Science in General Engineering .... BS in GE
Bachelor of Science in General Engineering .... BS in Gen Eng
Bachelor of Science in General Home Economics (SAUS) .... BS Gen Home Econ
Bachelor of Science in General Nursing (NADA) .... BSGenNur
Bachelor of Science in General Nursing .... BS in Gen Nurs
Bachelor of Science in General Science .... BS in Gen Sci
Bachelor of Science in General Science and Mathematics .... BS in GSM
Bachelor of Science in General Studies .... BS in Gen Std
Bachelor of Science in General Studies .... BS in GS
Bachelor of Science in Geodesy and Surveying .... BS in Geod & Surv
Bachelor of Science in Geodesy and Surveying (SAUS) .... BS in Geod&Surv
Bachelor of Science in Geography .... BS (Geog)
Bachelor of Science in Geography .... BS Ggr
Bachelor of Science in Geological Engineering (NADA) .... BCGeolEng
Bachelor of Science in Geological Engineering .... BS Geol E
Bachelor of Science in Geological Engineering .... BS Gl E
Bachelor of Science in Geological Engineering .... BS in Ge E
Bachelor of Science in Geological Engineering .... BS in Geol E
Bachelor of Science in Geology .... BS (Geol)
Bachelor of Science in Geology .... BS Gl
Bachelor of Science in Geology and Physics .... BSGP
Bachelor of Science in Geophysical Engineering .... BS in Gph E
Bachelor of Science in Geophysics .... BS Gph
Bachelor of Science in Group Work Administration (SAUO) .... BS Group Work Admin
Bachelor of Science in Group Work Education (SAUS) .... BS Group Work Ed
Bachelor of Science in Group Work Education .... BS in GWE
Bachelor of Science in Health (CPGU) .... BSH
Bachelor of Science in Health and Physical Education (SAUS) .... BS Health and Phy Ed
Bachelor of Science in Health and Physical Education (SAUS) .... BS in H&PE
Bachelor of Science in Health and Physical Education .... BS in H & PE
Bachelor of Science in Health and Physical Education .... BS in HPE
Bachelor of Science in Health Education .... BSHE
Bachelor of Science in Health Education (NADA) .... BSHEd
Bachelor of Science in Health Education .... BS in H Ed
Bachelor of Science in Hebrew Education (BJA) .... BSHE
Bachelor of Science in Home Economics .... BSc(HEc)
Bachelor of Science in Home Economics .... B Sc in HE
Bachelor of Science in Home Economics .... BSHE
Bachelor of Science in Home Economics .... BS H Ec
Bachelor of Science in Home Economics (NADA) .... BSHEco
Bachelor of Science in Home Economics (SAUS) .... BS Home Econ
Bachelor of Science in Home Economics .... BS in HE
Bachelor of Science in Home Economics .... BS in H Ec
Bachelor of Science in Home Economics .... BS in H Econ
Bachelor of Science in Home Economics Education .... BS in HD
Bachelor of Science in Home Economics Education (SAUS) .... BS in Home Econ Ed
Bachelor of Science in Home Science .... BSc(HomeScience)
Bachelor of Science in Horticulture .... BSc(Hort)
Bachelor of Science in Hospital Administration .... BSHA
Bachelor of Science in Hotel and Restaurant Administration .... BS in H & RA
Bachelor of Science in Hotel and Restaurant Administration (SAUS) .... BS in H&RA
Bachelor of Science in Hygiene (SAUS) .... BS Hyg
Bachelor of Science in Industrial Art (NADA) .... BSIndArt
Bachelor of Science in Industrial Art .... BS in Ind Art
Bachelor of Science in Industrial Arts .... BS in IA
Bachelor of Science in Industrial Chemistry (NADA) .... BSIndChem
Bachelor of Science in Industrial Chemistry .... BS in Ind Ch
Bachelor of Science in Industrial Education .... BSIE
Bachelor of Science in Industrial Education .... BSIndEd
Bachelor of Science in Industrial Education .... BS in Ind Ed
Bachelor of Science in Industrial Engineering .... BSIE
Bachelor of Science in Industrial Engineering .... BS Ind Eng
Bachelor of Science in Industrial Engineering .... BS in IE
Bachelor of Science in Industrial Engineering .... BS in Ind E
Bachelor of Science in Industrial Engineering and Management .... BS in IE & M
Bachelor of Science in Industrial Engineering and Management (SAUS) .... BS in IE&M
Bachelor of Science in Industrial Management .... BSIM
Bachelor of Science in Industrial Management .... BS Ind Mgt
Bachelor of Science in Industrial Management .... BS in IM
Bachelor of Science in Industrial Relations .... BSIR
Bachelor of Science in Industrial Technology .... BSIndTech
Bachelor of Science in Industrial Technology .... BSIT
Bachelor of Science in Jewish Education (BJA) .... BSJE
Bachelor of Science in Journalism .... BS in J
Bachelor of Science in Journalism .... BSJ
Bachelor of Science in Journalism .... BS Jr
Bachelor of Science in Judaic Studies (BJA) .... BSJS
Bachelor of Science in Labor Relations .... BS Lab Rel
Bachelor of Science in Laboratory Technology .... BS in LT
Bachelor of Science in Land Planning .... BS in LP
Bachelor of Science in Land Surveying (ADA) .... BScSur
Bachelor of Science in Landscape Architecture .... BSLA
Bachelor of Science in Landscape Architecture .... BSL Arch
Bachelor of Science in Landscape Management .... BSLM
Bachelor of Science in Languages .... BSL
Bachelor of Science in Latin .... BS in Lat
Bachelor of Science in Law .... BSL
Bachelor of Science in Letters and Science .... BS in L & S
Bachelor of Science in Letters and Science (SAUS) .... BS in L&S
Bachelor of Science in Liberal Arts (SAUS) .... BS Lib Arts
Bachelor of Science in Liberal Arts and Medicine (SAUS) .... BSLA and Med
Bachelor of Science in Library Science .... BSLS
Bachelor of Science in Library Service .... BS in LS
Bachelor of Science in Light Building Industry (SAUS) .... BS Light Bldg Industry
Bachelor of Science in Linguistics .... BSL
Bachelor of Science in Management Engineering .... BS in Mgt Engr
Bachelor of Science in Management Science .... BS in Mgt Sc
Bachelor of Science in Management Science (NADA) .... BSMgtSci
Bachelor of Science in Marine Engineering (NADA) .... BSMarEng
Bachelor of Science in Mathematical Statistics .... BS in Math Stat
Bachelor of Science in Mathematics and Chemistry .... BSMC
Bachelor of Science in Mechanical Arts .... BS in MA
Bachelor of Science in Mechanical Engineering .... B Sc in ME
Bachelor of Science in Mechanical Engineering .... BS in ME
Bachelor of Science in Mechanical Engineering .... BS in Mech Eng
Bachelor of Science in Mechanical Engineering .... BS in M Engr
Bachelor of Science in Mechanical Engineering .... BSME
Bachelor of Science in Mechanical Industries .... BS in Mech Ind
Bachelor of Science in Mechanics .... BS in Mech
Bachelor of Science in Medical Laboratory Science (ADA) .... BSc(MLS)
Bachelor of Science in Medical Record Library Science .... BS in MRL
Bachelor of Science in Medical Record Library Science (SAUS) .... BS in MRL Sc
Bachelor of Science in Medical Records .... BS in Med Rec
Bachelor of Science in Medical Records (NADA) .... BSMedRec
Bachelor of Science in Medical Records Librarianship (NADA) .... BSMedRecLib
Bachelor of Science in Medical Records Librarianship .... BS in Med Rec Lib
Bachelor of Science in Medical Science (SAUS) .... BS Med Sc
Bachelor of Science in Medical Secretarial Science .... BS in Med Sc
Bachelor of Science in Medical Technology .... B Sc in Med Tech
Bachelor of Science in Medical Technology .... BS in Md
Bachelor of Science in Medical Technology (SAUS) .... BS in MdT
Bachelor of Science in Medical Technology .... BS in Med Tech
Bachelor of Science in Medical Technology .... BS in MT
Bachelor of Science in Medical Technology .... BS Med T
Bachelor of Science in Medical Technology .... BS Med Tech
Bachelor of Science in Medical Technology .... BSMT
Bachelor of Science in Medicine .... B Sc in Med
Bachelor of Science in Medicine .... BS in Med
Bachelor of Science in Medicine .... BSM
Bachelor of Science in Medicine (NADA) .... BSMed
Bachelor of Science in Metallurgical Engineering .... BS in Met E
Bachelor of Science in Metallurgical Engineering .... BS in Met Engin
Bachelor of Science in Metallurgical Engineering .... BS Met E
Bachelor of Science in Metallurgical Engineering .... BS Met Eng
Bachelor of Science in Metallurgical Engineering .... BS Mt E
Bachelor of Science in Metallurgy .... B Sc Met
Bachelor of Science in Metallurgy .... BS in Met
Bachelor of Science in Metallurgy (NADA) .... BSMet
Bachelor of Science in Meteorology .... BS in Met
Bachelor of Science in Meteorology .... BS Met
Bachelor of Science in Military Science .... BS in MS
Bachelor of Science in Mineralogy .... BS Min
Bachelor of Science in Mining (ADA) .... BScMin
Bachelor of Science in Mining .... BS in Min
Bachelor of Science in Mining (NADA) .... BSMIN
Bachelor of Science in Mining Engineering (DAS) .... BScME
Bachelor of Science in Mining Engineering .... BS in Min E
Bachelor of Science in Mining Engineering .... BS in Min Eng
Bachelor of Science in Mining Engineering .... BSME
Bachelor of Science in Mining Engineering .... BS Mg E
Bachelor of Science in Mining Engineering .... BS Min E
Bachelor of Science in Mining Engineering (NADA) .... BSMinEng
Bachelor of Science in Mining Engineering .... BS Mng E
Bachelor of Science in Music .... BSM
Bachelor of Science in Music .... BS Mus
Bachelor of Science in Music Education .... BS in M Educ

Bachelor of Science in Music Education	BS in Mu Ed
Bachelor of Science in Music Education	BSME
Bachelor of Science in Music Education	BSM Ed
Bachelor of Science in Music Education	BS Mus Ed
Bachelor of Science in Musical Education	BS in Mus Ed
Bachelor of Science in Natural History	BS in Nat Hist
Bachelor of Science in Natural History (NADA)	BSNatHist
Bachelor of Science in Natural Science	BS in NS
Bachelor of Science in Natural Science	BS in N Sc
Bachelor of Science in Natural-Gas Engineering	BS in Nat G Engin
Bachelor of Science in Nautical Industrial Technology (NADA)	BSNIT
Bachelor of Science in Nursing	B Sc in Nurs
Bachelor of Science in Nursing	BScN
Bachelor of Science in Nursing (NADA)	BScNurs
Bachelor of Science in Nursing	BS in N
Bachelor of Science in Nursing	BS in Nr
Bachelor of Science in Nursing	BS in Nurs
Bachelor of Science in Nursing	BSN
Bachelor of Science in Nursing	BS Nurs
Bachelor of Science in Nursing Administration	BSNA
Bachelor of Science in Nursing Education	BS in NE
Bachelor of Science in Nursing Education	BS in N Ed
Bachelor of Science in Nursing Education	BS in Nurs Ed
Bachelor of Science in Nursing Education	BSNE
Bachelor of Science in Nursing Education	BSN Ed
Bachelor of Science in Nursing Education	BS Nurs Ed
Bachelor of Science in Occupational Therapy	B Sc in Occ Ther
Bachelor of Science in Occupational Therapy	BS in Occ Ther
Bachelor of Science in Occupational Therapy	BS in OT
Bachelor of Science in Occupational Therapy (NADA)	BSOccTher
Bachelor of Science in Occupational Therapy	BSOT
Bachelor of Science in Oceanography	BS in Ocean
Bachelor of Science in Optics	BS in Opt
Bachelor of Science in Optometry	B Sc in Opt
Bachelor of Science in Optometry	BS in opt
Bachelor of Science in Optometry	BS (Opt)
Bachelor of Science in Ornamental Horticulture	BS in OH
Bachelor of Science in Ornamental Horticulture	BS Orn Hort
Bachelor of Science in Orthoptics	BS in Ortho
Bachelor of Science in Personnel and Industrial Relations	BS (Per & Ind Rel)
Bachelor of Science in Personnel and Public Relations (NADA)	BSPer&PubRel
Bachelor of Science in Personnel and Public Relations (SAUS)	BS Per&Pub Rel
Bachelor of Science in Petroleum	BS in Pet
Bachelor of Science in Petroleum (NADA)	BSPet
Bachelor of Science in Petroleum Engineering	BS in PE
Bachelor of Science in Petroleum Engineering	BS in Pet Engin
Bachelor of Science in Petroleum Engineering	BS in Petr E
Bachelor of Science in Petroleum Engineering (NADA)	BSPetEng
Bachelor of Science in Pharmacy	B Sc in Phar
Bachelor of Science in Pharmacy (DAS)	BScP
Bachelor of Science in Pharmacy	BSc(Pharm)
Bachelor of Science in Pharmacy (CPGU)	BS(c)P(hm)
Bachelor of Science in Pharmacy	BS in Ph
Bachelor of Science in Pharmacy	BS in Phar
Bachelor of Science in Pharmacy	BSP
Bachelor of Science in Pharmacy	BS Ph
Bachelor of Science in Pharmacy	BS Phar
Bachelor of Science in Pharmacy	BSPharm
Bachelor of Science in Physical and Occupational Therapy	BSc (P & OT)
Bachelor of Science in Physical and Occupational Therapy	BS in Th
Bachelor of Science in Physical Education	BSc(PE)
Bachelor of Science in Physical Education (ADA)	BSc(PEd)
Bachelor of Science in Physical Education	BS in PE
Bachelor of Science in Physical Education	BS in P Ed
Bachelor of Science in Physical Education	BS in Phy Ed
Bachelor of Science in Physical Education	BS in Phys Ed
Bachelor of Science in Physical Education	BSPE
Bachelor of Science in Physical Education (NADA)	BSPhysEd
Bachelor of Science in Physical Education (NADA)	BSPhysEdu
Bachelor of Science in Physical Therapy	B Sc in Phys Ther
Bachelor of Science in Physical Therapy	BS in Phys Th
Bachelor of Science in Physical Therapy	BS in Phys Ther
Bachelor of Science in Physical Therapy	BS in PT
Bachelor of Science in Physical Therapy	BS Ph Th
Bachelor of Science in Physical Therapy (NADA)	BSPhysTher
Bachelor of Science in Physical Therapy	BSPT
Bachelor of Science in Physics	B Sc in Phys
Bachelor of Science in Physics	BS Phys
Bachelor of Science in Physics	Sc BP
Bachelor of Science in Practical Arts	BS in PA
Bachelor of Science in Practical Arts	BS in Prac Arts
Bachelor of Science in Practical Arts and Letters	BS in PAL
Bachelor of Science in Professional Geology	BS in Pr Ge
Bachelor of Science in Professional Meteorology	BS in Pr Met
Bachelor of Science in Public Administration	BS in PA
Bachelor of Science in Public Administration	BSPA
Bachelor of Science in Public Health	BSPH
Bachelor of Science in Public Health and Preventative Medicine	BS in PHPM
Bachelor of Science in Public Health Nursing	BS in PHN
Bachelor of Science in Public Health Nursing	BSPHN
Bachelor of Science in Public School Music	BS in PSM
Bachelor of Science in Pure Science	BS
Bachelor of Science in Quantity Surveying (ADA)	BSc(QS)
Bachelor of Science in Radiologic Technology (ADA)	BScRT
Bachelor of Science in Radiologic Technology (SAUS)	BSCRT
Bachelor of Science in Radiological Technology	BS in RT
Bachelor of Science in Radiological Technology	BSRT
Bachelor of Science in Railway and Mechanical Engineering	BS in Ry ME
Bachelor of Science in Railway and Mechanical Engineering (SAUS)	BS Ry ME
Bachelor of Science in Range Animal Husbandry	BS in RAH
Bachelor of Science in Recreation	BS in Rec
Bachelor of Science in Recreation	BSR
Bachelor of Science in Recreation	BS Rec
Bachelor of Science in Recreation Leadership	BS in Rec Lead
Bachelor of Science in Rehabilitation (NADA)	BSR
Bachelor of Science in Religious Education (BJA)	BSinRE
Bachelor of Science in Restaurant Management	B Sc in Rest Mgt
Bachelor of Science in Retailing	BS Ret
Bachelor of Science in Sanitary Engineering	BS in San E
Bachelor of Science in Sanitary Engineering	BSSanE
Bachelor of Science in Sanitary Engineering (SAUS)	SBSA
Bachelor of Science in Sanitary Engineering	SBSanE
Bachelor of Science in Sanitary Science	BS in San Sci
Bachelor of Science in School Library Science (SAUS)	BS School LS
Bachelor of Science in School Music (SAUS)	BS School Mus
Bachelor of Science in School Supervision (SAUS)	BS School Supv
Bachelor of Science in Science	BSS
Bachelor of Science in Science Engineering	BS Sc E
Bachelor of Science in Science Engineering (NADA)	BSScEng
Bachelor of Science in Secondary Education	BS in Sec Ed
Bachelor of Science in Secondary Education	BSSE
Bachelor of Science in Secondary Education	BS Sec
Bachelor of Science in Secondary Education	BS Sec Ed
Bachelor of Science in Secretarial Administration	BSSA
Bachelor of Science in Secretarial Administration	BS (Sec Adm)
Bachelor of Science in Secretarial Science	BS in Sec Sc
Bachelor of Science in Secretarial Science	BS in Sec Sci
Bachelor of Science in Secretarial Science (NADA)	BSSecSci
Bachelor of Science in Secretarial Science	BSS Sci
Bachelor of Science in Secretarial Studies (ADA)	BScSS
Bachelor of Science in Secretarial Studies	BSSS
Bachelor of Science in Social Administration	B Sc in Soc Adm
Bachelor of Science in Social Science	BS in SS
Bachelor of Science in Social Science	BS in S Sc
Bachelor of Science in Social Science	BSSS
Bachelor of Science in Social Science (NADA)	BSSSc
Bachelor of Science in Social Service	BS in Soc Serv
Bachelor of Science in Social Service (NADA)	BSSocServ
Bachelor of Science in Social Service (SAUS)	BS Soc Serv
Bachelor of Science in Social Studies	BS in Soc St
Bachelor of Science in Social Studies (NADA)	BSSocSt
Bachelor of Science in Social Work	BS (Soc Wk)
Bachelor of Science in Sociology (SAUS)	BS Soc
Bachelor of Science in Special Fields	BS in Spec Flds
Bachelor of Science in Speech	BS Sp
Bachelor of Science in Statistics	BS in Stat
Bachelor of Science in Structural Engineering	BS in Struc E
Bachelor of Science in Structural Engineering (NADA)	BSStrucEng
Bachelor of Science in Structural Engineering (SAUS)	BS Struc Eng
Bachelor of Science in Surveying (SAUS)	BScSur
Bachelor of Science in Teaching (ADA)	B Sc Tchg
Bachelor of Science in Teaching	BST
Bachelor of Science in Technology	BSTech
Bachelor of Science in Textile Engineering (ADA)	BSc(TE)
Bachelor of Science in Textile Engineering	BS in TE
Bachelor of Science in Textiles	BA in Text
Bachelor of Science in Textiles (ADA)	BSc(Text)
Bachelor of Science in Textiles (NADA)	BSText
Bachelor of Science in the Social Sciences, University of Southampton [British]	BSc(Social Sciences)
Bachelor of Science in Trade and Industrial Engineering	BST & IE
Bachelor of Science in Trade and Industrial Engineering (SAUS)	BST&IE
Bachelor of Science in Transportation	BS Trans
Bachelor of Science in Veterinary Science (NADA)	BScVetSc
Bachelor of Science in Veterinary Science (SAUS)	B Sc Vet Sc
Bachelor of Science in Vocational Agriculture	BS in Voc Ag
Bachelor of Science in Vocational Education	BS in Voc Ed
Bachelor of Science in Vocational Education (NADA)	BSVocEd
Bachelor of Science in Zoological Sciences	BS in ZS
Bachelor of Science (Industrial Arts)	BSc(IndArts)
Bachelor of Science (Mechanical Engineering)	BSc(MechEng)
Bachelor of Science (Medical)	BSc(Med)
Bachelor of Science (Medical Science)	B Sc (Med Sci)
Bachelor of Science (Nursing)	BSc(Nursing)
Bachelor of Science (Nutrition)	BSc(Nutr)
Bachelor of Science (Occupational Therapy)	BSc(OT)
Bachelor of Science (Oenology)	BSc(Oen)
Bachelor of Science (Physical Therapy)	BSc(PT)
Bachelor of Science (Rural Science)	BSc(RS)
Bachelor of Science (Social Science), University of Edinburgh [British]	BSc(Social Science)
Bachelor of Science (Social Sciences)	BSc(SocSc)
Bachelor of Science (Sociology)	B Sc (Soc)
Bachelor of Science (Surgery)	BSc(Surg)
Bachelor of Science (Technology)	B Sc (Tech)
Bachelor of Science (Town and Regional Planning), University of Dundee [British] (DBQ)	BSc(Town & Regional Planning)
Bachelor of Science, United States Military Academy (SAUS)	BSUSMA

Bachelor of Science, United States Naval Academy (SAUS)	BSUSNA
Bachelor of Science (Veterinary)	BSc(Vet)
Bachelor of Science with Aeronautical Engineering Electives	BS (Ae Elec)
Bachelor of Science with Chemical Engineering Electives	BS (Ch E Elect)
Bachelor of Science with Mechanical Engineering Electives	BS (ME Elect)
Bachelor of Scientific Agriculture	BSA
Bachelor of Scientific Didactics	BS Di
Bachelor of Scientology	B Scn
Bachelor of Secretarial Arts	B Se A
Bachelor of Secretarial Science	B Sec Sc
Bachelor of Secretarial Science	BSS
Bachelor of Secretarial Studies	B Se St
Bachelor of Sience in Mechanical Engineering (SAUS)	BS Mech E
Bachelor of Social Administration	BSocAdmin
Bachelor of Social Science	BScSoc
Bachelor of Social Science (NADA)	BSocSci
Bachelor of Social Science	B So Sc
Bachelor of Social Science	BSS
Bachelor of Social Science	BS Sc
Bachelor of Social Sciences	BSocSc
Bachelor of Social Service	B So Se
Bachelor of Social Studies (ADA)	BSocSt
Bachelor of Social Studies (SAUS)	B Soc St
Bachelor of Social Studies (ADA)	BSocStud
Bachelor of Social Work	BSocW
Bachelor of Social Work	BSocWk
Bachelor of Social Work	B So W
Bachelor of Social Work	BSW
Bachelor of Sociology	B So
Bachelor of Sociology (SAUS)	BSo
Bachelor of Special Education	BSpecEd
Bachelor of Special Education	BSpEd
Bachelor of Special Studies	BSS
Bachelor of Speech	B Sp
Bachelor of Speech Therapy	BSpeechTherapy
Bachelor of Speech Therapy (ADA)	BSpThy
Bachelor of Statistics	B St
Bachelor of Structural Engineering	B St E
Bachelor of Structural Engineering	B St Eng
Bachelor of Suddha Ayurvedic Medicine (SAUS)	BSAM
Bachelor of Surgery (SAUO)	BCH
Bachelor of Surgery	BS
Bachelor of Surgery	B Sur
Bachelor of Surgery (DD)	ChB
Bachelor of Surgery (SAUO)	CHB
Bachelor of Surveying	BSúrv
Bachelor of Surveying Science	BSurvSc
Bachelor of Systematic Theology	B Sy Th
Bachelor of Teaching	BT
Bachelor of Teaching	BTeach
Bachelor of Technical Science	B Sc Tech
Bachelor of Technical Science (SAUO)	BScTech
Bachelor of Technical Science	BTechSc
Bachelor of Technological Science	BTS
Bachelor of Technology	BT
Bachelor of Technology	B Tech
Bachelor of Technology [Canada] (ASC)	BTech
Bachelor of Technology Education	BTechEd
Bachelor of Technology in Information Systems	BTechInfSys
Bachelor of Telecommunication Engineering (SAUS)	BE Te-Com
Bachelor of Telecommunication Engineering (SAUS)	B Tel E
Bachelor of Telecommunications Engineering (ADA)	BTelE
Bachelor of Textile Chemistry	B of TC
Bachelor of Textile Chemistry	BTC
Bachelor of Textile Chemistry	BT Ch
Bachelor of Textile Design	BT Des
Bachelor of Textile Dyeing	BTD
Bachelor of Textile Engineering	B of TE
Bachelor of Textile Engineering	BTE
Bachelor of Textile Engineering	BT Eng
Bachelor of Textile Management	B of TM
Bachelor of Textile Technology	BTT
Bachelor of Textiles	BText
Bachelor of the Art of Obstetrics	BAO
Bachelor of the Elements	BE
Bachelor of the More Humane Letters (SAUO)	LHB
Bachelor of the Science of Law	B Sc L
Bachelor of the Science of Oratory	B Or Sc
Bachelor of the Science of Oratory	B Sc O
Bachelor of the Science of Oratory	BSO
Bachelor of the Science of Theology	STB
Bachelor of Theatre	BT
Bachelor of Theology	BT
Bachelor of Theology	B Th
Bachelor of Theology (CPGU)	BTh(eo)
Bachelor of Theology	BTheol
Bachelor of Theology (SAUS)	Th B
Bachelor of Town and Country Planning (SAUS)	BTCP
Bachelor of Town and Regional Planning (ADA)	BT & RP
Bachelor of Town and Regional Planning (ADA)	BTRP
Bachelor of Town Planning	BTP
Bachelor of Unani Medicine and Surgery	BUMS
Bachelor of Urban and Regional Planning	BUrbRegPlan
Bachelor of Urban and Regional Planning	BURP
Bachelor of Urban Planning	B Urb Pl
Bachelor of Urban Studies	BUS
Bachelor of Veterinary Medicine	B Vet Med
Bachelor of Veterinary Medicine	BVM
Bachelor of Veterinary Medicine	Vet MB
Bachelor of Veterinary Medicine and Science [Academic degree] (DMAA)	BVMS
Bachelor of Veterinary Medicine and Surgery	BVM & S
Bachelor of Veterinary Medicine and Surgery	BVMS
Bachelor of Veterinary Science (ADA)	BVetSc
Bachelor of Veterinary Science (NADA)	BVetSci
Bachelor of Veterinary Science	BVS
Bachelor of Veterinary Science	BV Sc
Bachelor of Veterinary Science and Animal Husbandry	BVSc & AH
Bachelor of Veterinary Science and Animal Husbandry (SAUS)	B V Sc&AH
Bachelor of Veterinary Surgery (NADA)	BVetSur
Bachelor of Veterinary Surgery	BVS
Bachelor of Visual Arts	BVA
Bachelor of Vocational Adjustment (SAUS)	BVA
Bachelor of Vocational Agriculture	BVA
Bachelor of Vocational Arts	BVocArts
Bachelor of Vocational Education	BVE
Bachelor of Vocational Education	BVocEd
Bachelor of Welding Engineering	BWE
Bachelor of Zoological Science	BZ Sc
Bachelor Officers' Quarters [Military] (MUSM)	BOQ
Bachelor or Chirurgie (CMD)	BChir
Bachelor Sergeant Quarters [Air Force]	BSQ
Bachelor Staff Quarters [Military] (DNAB)	BSQ
Bachelors' and Spinsters' Dance (ADA)	B & S
Bachelor's Degree (Honours) [British]	Bh
Bachelors Degree in Electronics Technology (SAUS)	BET
Bachelor's Degree (Pass) [British]	Bp
Bache's Pennsylvania Justice's Manual [A publication] (DLA)	Bache Pa Just
Bachman Information Systems [NASDAQ symbol] (SPSG)	BACH
Bachman Information Systems, Inc. [Associated Press] (SAG)	BachInf
Bachmanns Bundle (SAUS)	BB
Bachman-Turner Overdrive [Rock music group]	BTO
Bach's Reports [19-21 Montana] [A publication] (DLA)	Bach
Bacillary Angiomatosis [Medicine]	BA
Bacillary Angiomatosis-Bacillary Peliosis	BAP
Bacillary Dysentery [Medicine] (MELL)	BD
Bacillary Emulsion [Tuberculin] [Medicine] (MAE)	BE
Bacillary Peliosis [Medicine] (MELL)	BP
Bacillary White Diarrhea [Veterinary medicine]	BWD
Bacille Acido-Resistant [Acid-Fast Bacillus] [Medicine]	BAR
Bacillen Emulsion [Clinical chemistry] (AAMN)	BE
bacilli (SAUS)	bac
Bacillus [Bacteriology]	B
Bacillus [or Bacilli] [Bacteriology] (WDAA)	BAC
Bacillus (DB)	Bac
Bacillus Abortus (DB)	BA
Bacillus Anthracis (MELL)	BA
Bacillus Calmette-Guerin [TB vaccine] (GPO)	BCG
Bacillus Emulsion [Medicine] (DAVI)	TBN
Bacillus globigii [Biological warfare with bacteria]	BG
Bacillus Pumilis [Bacteriology]	BP
Bacillus Subtilis (DB)	BS
Bacillus Thuringiensis [Pesticide] (EDCT)	BT
Bacillus Thuringiensis Israelensis [Bacteriology]	BTI
Bacitracin Methylene Disalicylate [Animal antibiotic]	BMD
Bacitracin, Polymyxin B, Neomycin Sulfate [Medicine] (DMAA)	BPN
Bacitracin V [Antibacterial compound]	BV
Bacitracin V and X [Antibacterial compound]	BVX
Bacitracin X [Antibacterial compound]	BX
Back	B
Back	BCK
Back [Dance terminology]	BK
Back Again to Hoover [Slogan during 1974 economic downturn]	BATH
Back, Arm, Neck, Scalp [Medicine]	BANS
Back Artwork (SAUS)	BAW
Back Association of Canada	BAC
Back at Keyboard [Online dialog]	BAK
Back Bay National Refuge (SAUS)	BBNR
Back Bay Restaurant Group, Inc. [Associated Press] (SAG)	BackBay
Back Bay Restaurant Group, Inc. [NASDAQ symbol] (SAG)	PAPA
Back Bearing (SAUS)	BB
Back Bias Detector (SAUS)	BBD
Back Bone Ring (VERA)	BBR
Back Care (SAUS)	BC
Back Connected (SAUS)	BC
Back Contact (SAUS)	B-contact
Back Country Adventurer (SAUS)	BCA
Back Country Comfort Seeker (SAUS)	BCC
Back Country Huts (SAUS)	BCH
Back Course (FAAC)	BC
Back Course Marker (FAAC)	BCM
Back Cover [Publishing] (WDMC)	BC
Back Cover [Publishing] (WDAA)	bc
Back Cross (WDAA)	BC
Back Dividends	BD
Back Door Trot [i.e., a call of nature] [Obsolete slang]	BDT
Back Electromotive Force (DEN)	BEMF
Back Emergency Speed (DNAB)	BEM
Back End (MSA)	BE
Back Face (SAA)	BF

Back Fat [Animal husbandry]	BF
Back Feed (SAUS)	BF
Back Focal	BF
Back Focal Distance (MSA)	BFD
Back Focal Length [Optics]	BFL
Back Focal Plane (ACAE)	BFP
Back Folded [Freight]	BF
Back Full Speed (DNAB)	BF
Back Gear [Technical drawings]	BG
Back in the Day (SAUS)	BITD
Back Judge [Football]	BJ
Back Lay Welding (NUCP)	BLW
Back Loading Point [Military] [British]	BLP
Back Marker [Aviation]	BM
Back of Board (MSA)	B of B
Back of Book	BOB
Back of Book (SAUS)	B of B
Back of the Envelope (SAUS)	BOTE
Back of the Envelope Calculation (SAUS)	BOTEC
Back Office Crunch [Business term]	BOC
Back on Topic [Computer hacker terminology]	BOT
Back Order	BO
Back Order (WDAA)	bo
Back Order and Selection	BOS
Back Order Release (DNAB)	BO REL
Back Orifice (SAUS)	BO
Back Outlet Eccentric (SAUS)	Boe
Back Pain [Medicine] (MELL)	BP
Back Pain Association [British] [Research center] (EAIO)	BPA
Back Pain Classification Scale [Medicine] (DMAA)	BPCS
Back Panels (SAUS)	BPs
Back Plane (MCD)	BP
Back Plaster [Technical drawings]	BP
Back Porch Effect	BPE
Back Pressure	BP
Back Pressure Regulator	BPR
Back Pressure Transducer [Automotive engineering]	BPT
Back Pressure Valve (COE)	BPV
Back Projection (DEN)	BP
Back Receive Data (SAUS)	BRD
Back Reflection (DNAB)	BR
Back Request to Send (SAUS)	BRTS
Back Scatter Factor [Medicine] (MAE)	BSF
Back Shelf	BKSLF
Back Shunt Keying	BSK
Back Space Control (SAUS)	BSC
Back Space File (SAUS)	BSF
Back Space Mechanism (SAUS)	BSM
Back Space Pawl (SAUS)	BSP
Back Space Record [Computer science] (CIST)	BSR
Back Space Statement (SAUS)	BSS
Back Spacing Control (SAUS)	BSC
Back Spacing Key (SAUS)	BSK
Back Spacing Time (SAUS)	BST
Back Spread [Investment term]	BS
Back Stage Left [A stage direction]	BSL
Back Stage Right [A stage direction]	BSR
Back Stamp (SAUS)	B/S
Back Street Boys (SAUS)	BSB
Back Surface Field [Photovoltaic energy systems]	BSF
Back Surface Field Reflector (SAUS)	BSFR
Back Surface Reflectance [Photovoltaic energy systems]	BSR
Back Surface Reflection (SAUS)	BSR
Back Tape Reader	BTR
Back Taxiing [Aviation] (FAAC)	BT
Back Telling (SAA)	B-TELL
Back Telling (SAUS)	B-Tell
Back to Back [Technical drawings]	B to B
Back to Bed (MELL)	BTB
Back To Keyboard (SAUS)	BTK
Back to School (WDAA)	BTS
Back to the Bible Broadcast (NTCM)	BBB
Back to the City [An association] [Defunct] (EA)	BC
Back to the Future Fan Club	BTTFFC
Back to the Future, the Fan Club (EA)	BTTFTFC
Back to Work (SAUS)	BTW
Back, Training [Parachute]	BT
Back Trajectory (ARMP)	BT
Back Transient Diode Logic (SAUS)	BTDL
Back Transmit Data (SAUS)	BTD
Back Up [Automotive engineering]	B/UP
Back View (MSA)	BV
Back Widow Spider Toxin [Medicine] (DMAA)	BWST
Back Yard Burgers [NASDAQ symbol] (TTSB)	BYBI
Back Yard Burgers, Inc. [Associated Press] (SAG)	BackYrd
Back Yard Burgers, Inc. [NASDAQ symbol] (SAG)	BYBI
Backache [Medicine]	BA
Backache (SAUS)	B/A
Back-Action Evasion [Physics]	BAE
Backamo [Sweden] [ICAO location identifier] (ICLI)	ESGA
Backarc Basin (SAUS)	BABI
Back-Arc-Basin Basalt [Geology]	BABB
Backboard [Telecommunications] (TEL)	BB
Backbone Concentrator Node [Routing device] [Telecommunications] (PCM)	BCN
Backbone Interface (SAUS)	BI
Backbone Message Transfer Agent (SAUS)	BMTA
Backbone Network Service (SAUS)	BNS
Backbone Ring (SAUS)	BBR
Backbone Service Area (SAUS)	BSA
Backbord [Portside] [German military]	BB
Back-Connected [Technical drawings]	BC
Back-Cross generation (SAUS)	BC generation
Backdoor Financing [Public debt transactions] [Investment term]	BF
Backed With [Used by record companies and trade papers to indicate music on the alternative side of a disk]	b/w
Back-End of Line (AAEL)	BEOL
Back-End Processor [Computer] (TSSD)	BEP
Back-end Storage Network [Computer science] (EECA)	BSN
Back-End-Chip (VERA)	BEC
Backend-image Database Management Network (SAUS)	BDMN
Backer Petroleum Corp. [Vancouver Stock Exchange symbol]	BCM
Backer Resources [Vancouver Stock Exchange symbol]	BAK
Backer Spielvogel Bates Worldwide [Commercial firm] [British] (ECON)	BSBW
Backface (SAUS)	BF
Backfile Conversion Project [European Patent Office]	BACON
Backfire Suppressor Valve [Automotive engineering]	BSV
Back-Gate Metal-Oxide Semiconductor (IAA)	BMOS
Back-Gate Metal-Oxide Semiconductor Field-Effect Transistor (IAA)	BMOSFET
Back-Geared (SAUS)	BGR
Background	BCGD
Background [Low-priority processing] [Computer science]	BG
Background (WDMC)	bg
Background (NTCM)	BKG
Background	BKGD
Background (ADWA)	bkgd
Background (VRA)	bkgr
Background [Low-priority processing] [Computer science]	BKGRD
Background Air Pollution Monitoring (QUAC)	BAPMON
Background Air Pollution Monitoring Network (GNE)	BAPMoN
Background Analysis Center (SAUO)	BAC
Background Atmospheric Pollution Monitoring (SAUS)	BAPMoN
Background Color (SAUS)	BGCOLOR
Background Compiler COBOL [Common Business-Oriented Language] (IAA)	BGCOB
Background Diabetic Retinopathy [Endocrinology and ophthalmology] (DAVI)	BDR
Background Display Dataset (SAUS)	BDD
Background Document (EEVL)	BD
Background Elimination Technique (MCD)	BET
Background Emission Index [Automotive engineering]	BGEI
Background Equivalent Activity	BEA
Background Equivalent Concentration [Computer science]	BEC
Background File Transfer Protocol (SAUS)	BFTP
Background Heat Flux	BHF
Background Hold (SAUS)	BHOLD
Background Illumination Intensity	BII
Background Information (MCD)	BI
Background Information Document [Environmental Protection Agency]	BID
Background Investigation	BI
Background Limited Infrared Photoconductive (ACAE)	BLIP
Background Limited Infrared Photodetector (SAUS)	BLIP
Background Limited Performance (ACAE)	BLIP
Background Listening [Music]	BL
Background Luminance Monitor [Aviation] (DA)	BLM
Background Mapping Sensor	BMS
Background Measurement Satellite (NASA)	BMS
Background Measurements Program (MCD)	BMP
Background Menu (SAUS)	BGM
Background Music (WDAA)	BGM
Background Natural Organic Matter [Environmental chemistry]	BNOM
Background Natural Sound	BGNS
Background Noise [Medicine] (MELL)	BGN
Background Noise Level (SAUS)	BLN
Background Noise Level (CAAL)	BNL
Background Noise Level (CAAL)	LN
Background Noise Power	BNP
Background Noise Suppression Amplifier (DICI)	BNSA
Background Operating System (IEEE)	BOS
Background Paper	BP
Background Perfume	BGP
Background Processing (SAUS)	BP
Background Radiation (SAA)	BR
Background Storage and Control Unit	BSCU
Background/Foreground	B/F
Background-Limited Infrared Photoconductor (IAA)	BIP
Background-Limited Infrared Photography	BLIP
Background-Limited Performance (SAUS)	BLIP
Backhaul Check (TRID)	BHC
Backhoe	BCKHOE
Backhoe Trench [Archaeology]	BHT
Backhoe Trench [Archaeology]	T
Backing [Publishing] (WDMC)	back
Backing (FAAC)	BCKG
Backing Storage (SAUS)	BS
Backing Store Unit (SAUS)	BSU
Backjumping (SAUS)	BJ
Backlash (MSA)	BL
Backlash Allowance (MSA)	BA
Backlight Burtek Trainer	BBT

Backlight Compensation [*Photography*] ... BLC
Backlit (SAUS) ... BL
Backloading Point (SAUS) ... BLP
Backlog of Essential Maintenance and Repair (AFM) ... BEMAR
Backlog of Maintenance and Repair (MCD) ... BMAR
Backmarking with Backjumping (SAUS) ... BMJ
Backmixing [*Chemical engineering*] ... BM
Back-Off Sub (SAUS) ... BOS
Back-Off System ... BOS
Backorder Problem Working Group [*DoD*] ... BOPWG
Backpack ... BP
Backpack Palsy [*Medicine*] (MELL) ... BPP
Backpack Survival Kit (MCD) ... BSK
Backpackers Club [*Reading, Berkshire, England*] (EAIO) ... BC
Backplane Integrated Test System (SAUS) ... BITS
Backplane Interconnect (SAUS) ... BI
Backplane Transceiver Logic (AEBE) ... BTL
Back-Pressure Control ... BPC
Back-Propagation Net (VERA) ... BPN
Backscatler / Absorption Chamber (PDAA) ... BACH
Backscatter Absorption Gas Imaging (SAUS) ... BAGI
Backscatter Electron ... BSE
Backscatter Imaging Tomography [*Factory automation*] (BTTJ) ... BIT
Backscatter Kikuchi Diffraction (SAUS) ... BKD
Backscatter Ultraviolet [*Spectrometry*] (MCD) ... BUV
Backscatter Ultraviolet Spectrometer ... BUS
Backscatter Ultraviolet Spectrometer ... BUVS
Backscattered Electron (MCD) ... BE
Back-Scattered Electron [*Microscopic imaging*] ... BSE
Back-Scattered Electron Imaging (DB) ... BEI
Backscattered Electron Microscopy ... BSEM
Backscattered LASER Energy Digitizing Equipment (MCD) ... BLEDE
Back-scattered Scanning Electron Microscopy (SAUS) ... BSEM
Backscattering Spectroscopy [*Surface analysis*] ... BS
Backsight (DNAB) ... BS
Backspace (SAUS) ... BKSP
Backspace Block (SAUS) ... BSB
Backspace Character [*Keyboard*] [*Computer science*] (BUR) ... BKSP
Backspace Character [*Keyboard*] [*Computer science*] ... BS
Backspace Contact ... BSC
Backspace File (BUR) ... BSF
Backspace or End of Message (SAUS) ... BS or EOM
Backspace Pawl (SAUS) ... BP
Backspace Recorder ... BSR
Backspace Register (SAUS) ... BSR
Backstage [*Theater*] (WDMC) ... back
Backstage (ADA) ... BS
Backstairs [*Gossip*] ... BS
Backstamp ... BKST
Backstrip [*Book-binding*] (WDMC) ... back
Backstrip (WGA) ... BKS
Backtell (IAA) ... BTL
Backtell Lateraltell Output (SAA) ... BLO
Backup (KSC) ... BKUP
Backup (KSC) ... BU
Backup (SAUS) ... XLK
Backup Acquisition System ... BACS
Backup Aerospace Vehicle [*or Aircraft*] ... BA
Backup Aerospace Vehicle [*or Aircraft*] **Authorization** ... BAA
Backup Aerospace Vehicle [*or Aircraft*] **Inventory** ... BAI
Backup Air Data Sensor Assembly (MCD) ... BADSA
Backup Aircraft Authorization (ACAE) ... BAA
Backup Aircraft Inventory (ACAE) ... BAI
Backup Alert Force ... BAF
Backup Attitude Reference System ... BARS
Backup Auxiliary Transformer [*Nuclear energy*] (GFGA) ... BAT
Backup Avionics Subsystem Software (MCD) ... BASS
Backup Avionics System Software (SAUS) ... BASS
Backup Block (MCD) ... BUB
Backup Bus Controller [*Computer science*] ... BBC
Backup Computational Facility (CCCA) ... BCF
Backup Computer (CET) ... BUC
Back-Up Computer System (SAUS) ... BUCS
Backup Control & Audio Unit (SAUS) ... BCAU
Backup Control Electronics (MCD) ... BCE
Backup Control System ... BCS
Backup Control System (MCD) ... BUCS
Back-Up Control System (SAUS) ... BUCS
Backup Controller (MCD) ... BUC
Backup Courier Time Server (SAUS) ... BCTS
Back-Up Decoder (ACAE) ... BUD
Backup Digital Computer ... BDC
Backup Digital Computer ... BUDC
Backup Digital System ... BUDS
Backup Domain Controller (SAUS) ... BDC
Backup Drive Amplifier (MCD) ... BDA
Backup Emergency Communications ... BUEC
Backup Facility [*Nuclear war games*] ... BUF
Backup File [*Computer science*] ... BAK
Backup File (CDE) ... BAK file
Backup Flight Computer (SAUS) ... BFC
Backup Flight Control (MCD) ... BFC
Backup Flight Control System (NAKS) ... BCFS
Backup Flight Control System [*NASA*] (NASA) ... BFCS
Backup Flight Control System (MCD) ... BUFCS
Backup Flight System (MCD) ... BFS
Backup Force ... BF
Backup Gimbal Servo ... BGS
Backup Guidance System [*NASA*] ... BGS
Backup Guidance System [*NASA*] ... BUGS
Backup Interceptor Control [*System*] [*Air Force*] ... BUIC
Backup Interceptor Control System [*Air Force*] ... BUICS
Backup Maintenance Activity (MCD) ... BMA
Backup North-South Stationkeeping (ACAE) ... BNS
Backup Operating System (NASA) ... BOS
Backup Optical Storage System [*Aquidneck Data Corp.*] (NITA) ... BOSS
Backup Optical Unit (NASA) ... BUOU
Backup Plate ... BUP
Backup Plate, Perforated ... BUPP
Back-Up Processor (SAUS) ... BUP
Back-Up Quantity ... BQ
Backup Rate [*Ventilator*] [*Medicine*] (DAVI) ... BUR
Backup Rate of Pitch ... BURP
Backup Rate of Roll ... BURR
Backup Rate of Yaw ... BURY
Backup Register (SAUS) ... BUR
Backup Scram System [*Nuclear energy*] (NRCH) ... BUSS
Back-Up Store (SAUS) ... BUS
Backup Study Sheets [*Military*] ... BUSS
Backup System Services [*NASA*] (NASA) ... BSS
Backup System Test Console ... BUSTC
Back-Up Unit (ACAE) ... B/U
Backus Naur [*or Normal*] **Form** [*ALGOL*] [*Computer science*] (BUR) ... BNF
Backus Normal [*or Naur*] **Form** [*ALGOL*] [*Computer science*] ... BNO
Backus on Sheriffs [*A publication*] (DLA) ... Back Sher
Backus School, Backus, MN [*Library symbol*] [*Library of Congress*] (LCLS) ... MnBacS
Backus-Naur Form (SAUS) ... BN Form
Backward (WDAA) ... BKD
Backward (KSC) ... BKWD
Backward [*Telecommunications*] (TEL) ... BWD
Backward Chaining [*Psychology*] ... BC
Backward Diode ... BD
Backward Edge [*Skating*] ... B
Backward Error Correction (SAUS) ... BEC
Backward Indicator [*Telecommunications*] (TEL) ... BI
Backward Indicator BIT [*Binary Digit*] [*Telecommunications*] (TEL) ... BIB
Backward Internal Rotation [*Orthopedics*] (DAVI) ... BIR
Backward Interworking Telephony Event [*Telecommunications*] (TEL) ... BITE
Backward Limit Photocell ... BLPC
Backward Linkage [*Computer science*] (CIST) ... BLINK
Backward Optimistic-oriented Concurrency Control (SAUS) ... BOCC
Backward Sequence Number [*Telecommunications*] (TEL) ... BSN
Backward Sequence Number Received (SAUS) ... BSNR
Backward Set-up Message (SAUS) ... BSM
Backward Signaling [*Telecommunications*] (TEL) ... BS
Backward Society Education (SAUO) ... BASE
Backward Space File (SAUS) ... BSF
Backward Traveling Wave ... BTW
Backward Volume Wave [*Telecommunications*] (TEL) ... BVW
Backward Wave [*Telecommunications*] (IAA) ... BW
Backward Wave Amplifier ... BWA
Backward Wave Converter (CET) ... BWC
Backward Wave Magnetron (MSA) ... BWM
Backward Wave Oscillator ... BWO
Backward Wave Oscillator Synchronizer ... BWOS
Backward Wave Oscillator Tube ... BWOT
Backward Wave Parametric Amplifier (SAUS) ... BWPA
Backward Wave Power Amplifier ... BWPA
Backward Wave Sweep Oscillator ... BWSO
Backward Wave Tube [*Physics*] ... BWT
Backwardation [*Commodity futures trading*] (ROG) ... BACK
backwardation (SAUS) ... back
Backwardation [*Commodity futures trading*] ... BK
Backward-Compatible (SAUS) ... BC
Backward-Explicit Congestion Notification [*Computer science*] ... BECN
Backwards Differentiation Formula (MHDI) ... BDF
Backwards Differentiation Formulas (SAUS) ... BDF
Backwater Valve (SAUS) ... BWV
Back-Water Valve ... BWV
BackWeb Technologies [*NASDAQ symbol*] (SG) ... BWEB
Backyard Boat Builders [*USCG*] (TAG) ... BYBB
BACM Industries Ltd. [*Formerly, British-American Construction & Materials Ltd.*] ... BACM
Baco [*Ethiopia*] [*ICAO location identifier*] (ICLI) ... HABC
Bacolod [*Philippines*] [*Airport symbol*] (OAG) ... BCD
Bacolod, Negros Occidental [*Philippines*] [*ICAO location identifier*] (ICLI) ... RPVB
Bacon and Meat Manufacturers' Association [*British*] ... BMMA
Bacon & Woodrow [*British*] ... B&W
Bacon. Arguments in Law [*A publication*] (DLA) ... Bacon
Bacon Curers Federation (SAUO) ... BCF
Bacon Families Association [*Defunct*] (EA) ... BFA
Bacon Joint Industrial Committee (SAUO) ... BJIC
Bacon, Lettuce, and Tomato Sandwich ... BLT
Bacon Memorial Public Library, Wyandotte, MI [*Library symbol*] [*Library of Congress*] (LCLS) ... MiWy
Bacon on Benefit Societies and Life Insurance [*A publication*] (DLA) ... Bac Ben Soc
Bacon on Benefit Societies and Life Insurance [*A publication*] (DLA) ... Bac Ins
Bacon on Government [*A publication*] (DLA) ... Bac Gov

Bacon on Government [*A publication*] (DLA) ... Bacon
Bacon on Leases and Terms of Years [*A publication*] (DLA) ... Bac Lease
Bacon on Leases and Terms of Years [*A publication*] (DLA) ... Bacon
Bacone College (SAUO) ... BC
Bacon's Abridgment [*1736-1832*] [*A publication*] (DLA) ... Bac Ab
Bacon's Abridgment [*1736-1832*] [*A publication*] (DLA) ... Bac Abr
Bacon's Abridgment [*1736-1832*] [*A publication*] (DLA) ... Bacon
Bacon's Case of Treason [*1641*] [*A publication*] (DLA) ... Bac Ca
Bacon's Chancery Cases [*England*] [*A publication*] (DLA) ... Bac Chanc
Bacon's Complete Arbitrator [*A publication*] (DLA) ... Bac Comp Arb
Bacon's Complete Arbitrator [*A publication*] (DLA) ... Bacon
Bacon's Decisions (Ritchie) [*England*] [*A publication*] (DLA) ... Bac Dec
Bacon's Decisions (Ritchie) [*England*] [*A publication*] (DLA) ... Bac Rep
Bacon's Elements of the Common Law [*A publication*] (DLA) ... Bac El
Bacon's Elements of the Common Law [*A publication*] (DLA) ... Bacon
Bacon's Essay on Uses [*A publication*] (DLA) ... Bacon
Bacon's Essay on Uses [*A publication*] (DLA) ... Bac Uses
Bacon's Georgia Digest [*A publication*] (DLA) ... Bac Dig
Bacon's Liber Regis [*A publication*] (DLA) ... Bacon
Bacon's Liber Regis, vel Thesaurus Rerum Ecclesiasticarum [*A publication*] (DLA) ... Bac Lib Reg
Bacon's Liber Regis, vel Thesaurus Rerum Ecclesiasticarum [*A publication*] (DLA) ... Bac TE
Bacou USA [*NASDAQ symbol*] (TTSB) ... BACU
Bacou USA [*NYSE symbol*] ... BAU
Bactenology (SAUS) ... BAC
Bacteria (DAVI) ... BAC
Bacteria (WDAA) ... bact
Bacteria Free Stool virus (SAUS) ... BFS
Bacteria Survival Ratio (SAUS) ... BSR
Bacteria-Derived Nuclei (SAUS) ... BDN
Bacterial (SAUS) ... Bac
Bacterial (ADWA) ... bact
Bacterial Adherent Colonies ... BAC
Bacterial Adhesion to Hydrocarbons ... BATH
Bacterial Agglutination (MAE) ... BA
Bacterial Alkaline Phosphatase [*or Bacterial Alkaline Phosphomonoesterase*] [*An enzyme*] ... BAP
Bacterial Antigen Assay [*Medicine*] (MELL) ... BAA
Bacterial Antigen Complex [*Immunochemistry*] ... BAC
Bacterial Artificial Chromosome [*Genetics*] ... BAC
Bacterial Automated Identification Technique ... BAIT
Bacterial Carbon Demand [*Marine biology*] ... BCD
Bacterial Disk Infection [*Medicine*] (MELL) ... BDI
Bacterial Endocarditis [*Medicine*] ... BE
Bacterial Endocarditis ... BEC
Bacterial Flora [*Medicine*] (MELL) ... BF
Bacterial Ice Nucleation Diagnosis [*DNA Plant Technology Corp. test*] ... BIND
Bacterial Identification ... BID
Bacterial Intravenous Protein (MAE) ... BIP
Bacterial Kidney Disease [*Ichthyology*] ... BKD
Bacterial Meningitis [*Medicine*] (MELL) ... BM
Bacterial Mutagenicity Test (DB) ... BMT
Bacterial Organic Carbon [*Water chemistry*] ... BOC
Bacterial Phosphatidylethanolamine [*Physiological chemistry*] ... BPE
Bacterial Polysaccharide Immune Globulin [*Medicine*] (MELL) ... BPIG
Bacterial Quantity Unit (EEVL) ... BQU
Bacterial Releasing Agent [*Microbiology*] ... BRA
Bacterial Secondary Production [*Water chemistry*] ... BSP
Bacterial Sulfate Reduction ... BSR
Bacterial Vaginosis [*Medicine*] ... BV
Bactericidal Concentration (MAE) ... BC
Bactericidal/Permeability Increasing [*Protein*] [*Immunology*] ... BPI
Bacteriochlorophyll [*Biochemistry*] ... BChl
Bacteriochlorophyll-B [*Biochemistry*] ... BC-B
Bacteriologic Index [*Clinical microbiology*] ... BI
Bacteriological ... BAC
Bacteriological (WDAA) ... bacteriol
Bacteriological Analytical Manual [*A publication*] ... BAM
Bacteriological Index (SAUS) ... BI
Bacteriological Laboratory (SAUO) ... Balby
Bacteriological (or Biological) & Chemical weapons (SAUS) ... B&C
Bacteriological (or Biological) & Toxic Weapons Convention (SAUS) ... BWC
Bacteriological Oxygen Demand [*Water pollution*] ... BOD
Bacteriological Reviews (SAUS) ... BR
Bacteriological Reviews (journ.) (SAUS) ... Bacteriol Rev
Bacteriological Warfare ... BW
Bacteriological Warfare, Defence [*British*] [*World War II*] ... BW(D)
Bacteriological Warfare, Operational Panel [*British*] [*World War II*] ... BW(O)
Bacteriological Warfare, Policy Panel [*British*] [*World War II*] ... BW(P)
Bacteriological Warhead ... BW
Bacteriological Weapons (SAUS) ... BW
Bacteriology [*Biochemistry*] (DAVI) ... bact
Bacteriology ... BACTER
Bacteriology (BEE) ... Bacteriol
Bacteriology (ADWA) ... bacteriol
Bacteriology ... BACTLGY
Bacteriology Laboratory (DAVI) ... Bacti Lab
Bacteriopheophytin [*Biochemistry*] ... Bphe
Bacteriopheophytin [*Biochemistry*] ... BPheo
Bacteriopheophytin-B [*Biochemistry*] ... BP-B
Bacteriorhodopsin [*Biochemistry*] ... bR
Bacteriostatic Water for Injection [*Medicine*] ... BWFI
Bacterium [*Bacteria*] [*Latin*] ... BACT
Bacterium (SAUS) ... Bact
Bacteriuria [*Medicine*] (MELL) ... BU
Bacteroids Bile Esculin [*Agar*] [*Microbiology*] ... BBE
Bactine Bag (SAUS) ... Bac Bag
Bactometer Data Management System ... BDMS
Bactrian (VRA) ... Bactr
Bactrian Camel (SAUS) ... Bactrian
Baculovirus Expression Vector [*Biochemistry*] ... BEV
Bacus/B'Gosh Families [*An association*] [*Defunct*] (EA) ... BBF
bad (SAUS) ... bd
Bad and Doubtful Debt (DCTA) ... B & D
Bad Attitude (SAUS) ... BA
Bad Axe, MI [*Location identifier*] [*FAA*] (FAAL) ... BAX
Bad Axe, MI [*Television station call letters*] (BROA) ... WDCP
Bad Axe, MI [*AM radio station call letters*] ... WLEW
Bad Axe, MI [*FM radio station call letters*] ... WLEW-FM
Bad Axe, MI [*Television station call letters*] ... WUCX-TV
Bad Axe Public Library, Bad Axe, MI [*Library symbol*] [*Library of Congress*] (LCLS) ... MiBa
Bad Black Brother ... BBB
Bad Bramstedt [*Germany*] [*ICAO location identifier*] (ICLI) ... EDHX
Bad Breath ... BB
Bad Cannstatt Hospital [*Germany*] [*ICAO location identifier*] (ICLI) ... EDOG
Bad Character ... BC
Bad Check [*Banking*] ... BC
Bad Conduct [*British military*] (DMA) ... BC
Bad Conduct Discharge [*Military*] ... BCD
Bad Conduct Discharge (SAUS) ... BC Dis
Bad Conduct Discharge, General Court-Martial, after Confinement in Prison [*Navy*] ... BDGC
Bad Conduct Discharge, General Court-Martial, after Violation of Probation [*Navy*] ... BDGP
Bad Conduct Discharge, General Court-Martial, Immediate [*Navy*] ... BDGI
Bad Conduct Discharge, Sentence of Summary Court-Martial, Immediate [*Navy*] ... BDSI
Bad Conduct Discharge, Summary Court-Martial, after Violation of Probation [*Navy*] ... BDSP
Bad Data Lister ... BDL
Bad Delivery [*Investment term*] ... BD
Bad Demographic Risk [*Television*] ... BDR
Bad Duerkheim [*Germany*] [*ICAO location identifier*] (ICLI) ... EDRF
Bad Flag (SAUS) ... BF
Bad Frame Indicator (SAUS) ... BFI
Bad Gandersheim [*Germany*] [*ICAO location identifier*] (ICLI) ... EDVA
Bad Hersfeld [*Germany*] [*ICAO location identifier*] (ICLI) ... EDOZ
Bad Kissingen [*Germany*] [*ICAO location identifier*] (ICLI) ... EDEG
Bad Kissingen [*Germany*] [*ICAO location identifier*] (ICLI) ... EDFK
Bad Kreuznach [*Germany*] [*ICAO location identifier*] (ICLI) ... EDEH
Bad Order [*i.e., requiring repair*] ... BO
Bad Parity (SAUS) ... BP
Bad Ragaz [*Switzerland*] [*ICAO location identifier*] (ICLI) ... LSZC
Bad Ragaz [*Switzerland*] [*ICAO location identifier*] (ICLI) ... LSZE
Bad Register (SAUS) ... BR
Bad Reichenhall [*Federal Republic of Germany*] [*Seismograph station code, US Geological Survey*] (SEIS) ... BHG
Bad Tolz [*Germany*] [*ICAO location identifier*] (ICLI) ... EDOV
Bad Weather Watch (SAUO) ... BWW
Bada [*Indonesia*] [*ICAO location identifier*] (ICLI) ... WAMQ
Badajoz [*Spain*] [*Airport symbol*] (OAG) ... BJZ
Badajoz/Talavera La Real [*Spain*] [*ICAO location identifier*] (ICLI) ... LEBZ
Badan Koordiansis Survey Dan Pemetaan Nasianal (SAUS) ... BAKOSURTANAL
Badan Pembinaan dan Penerapan Teknologi [*Indonesia*] (GEOI) ... BPPT
Badana [*Saudi Arabia*] [*Airport symbol*] [*Obsolete*] (OAG) ... BDN
Badbury [*England*] ... BADB
Bade [*Indonesia*] [*Airport symbol*] (OAG) ... BXD
Bade [*Indonesia*] [*ICAO location identifier*] (ICLI) ... WAKE
Baden Community Services (SAUO) ... BCS
Baden Explorations [*Vancouver Stock Exchange symbol*] ... BEX
Baden Hills Golf Club (SAUO) ... BHGC
Baden Intermediate Hockey League (SAUO) ... BIHL
Baden-Baden [*Germany*] [*ICAO location identifier*] (ICLI) ... EDTB
Badfinger Fan Club (EA) ... BFC
Badge Card Reader (MHDI) ... BCR
Badge Collectors Circle [*British*] [*An association*] (DBA) ... BCC
Badge Office Security Sytem (SAUS) ... BOSS
Badge Readout (SAUS) ... BRO
Badger Army Ammunition Plant (AABC) ... BAAP
Badger Meter, Inc. [*Associated Press*] (SAG) ... BadgrM
Badger Meter, Inc. [*AMEX symbol*] (SPSG) ... BMI
Badger Mountain [*Washington*] [*Seismograph station code, US Geological Survey*] (SEIS) ... BDG
Badger Paper Mills [*NASDAQ symbol*] (TTSB) ... BPMI
Badger Paper Mills, Inc. [*Associated Press*] (SAG) ... BadgrP
Badger Paper Mills, Inc. [*NASDAQ symbol*] (NQ) ... BPMI
Badger School, Badger, MN [*Library symbol*] [*Library of Congress*] (LCLS) ... MnBadS
Badger State Car Wash Association [*Wisconsin*] (SRA) ... BSCWA
Badger Union High School District, Lake Geneva, WI [*Library symbol*] [*Library of Congress*] (LCLS) ... WLagB
Badgery's Creek Airport [*Australia*] ... BCA
Badgingarra Research Station (SAUO) ... BRS
Badio Technical Commission for Marines (SAUS) ... RTCM
Badische Anilin und Soda-Fabrik [*Automotive industry supplier*] ... BASF
Badlands National Monument [*South Dakota*] ... BADL
Badlands National Monument (SAUS) ... BNM
Badlands Natural History Society (SAUO) ... BNHA

Badminton Association of England (EAIO) .... BAE
Badminton Association of England (SAUO) .... BA of E
Badminton Association of England (DBA) .... BA of E
Badminton Association of Western Australia .... BAWA
Badminton Library [*A publication*] .... BL
Badminton Union of Ireland (EAIO) .... BUI
Bado Lite [*Zaire*] [*Airport symbol*] (OAG) .... BDT
Badocol Chemicals Pty, Ltd., Melbourne (SAUO) .... Badocol
Baehr-Schiffrin [*Disease*] [*Medicine*] (DB) .... BS
Baende [*Volumes*] [*German*] .... BDE
Baerman Aircraft Corporation (SAUO) .... BAC
Bafata [*Guinea-Bissau*] [*ICAO location identifier*] (ICLI) .... GGBF
Baffle [*Regulating device*] (KSC) .... BAF
Baffle/Liner Interface Seal [*Nuclear energy*] (NRCH) .... BLIS
Bafgh [*Iran*] [*ICAO location identifier*] (ICLI) .... OIYB
Bafia [*Cameroon*] [*ICAO location identifier*] (ICLI) .... FKAF
Bafoulabe [*Mali*] [*ICAO location identifier*] (ICLI) .... GABF
Bafour, Blanchard, and Raymond [*Computer typesetting*] (DGA) .... BBR
Bafoussam [*Cameroon*] [*Airport symbol*] (OAG) .... BFX
Bafoussam [*Cameroon*] [*ICAO location identifier*] (ICLI) .... FKKU
Baft [*Iran*] [*ICAO location identifier*] (ICLI) .... OIKF
Bag [*Shipping*] .... B
Bag .... BG
Bag All Garbage .... BAG
Bag Cell Peptide [*Biochemistry*] .... BCP
Bag in Box [*Packaging*] .... BIB
Bag of Waters [*Medicine*] .... BOW
Bagabag, Neuva Viscaya [*Philippines*] [*ICAO location identifier*] (ICLI) .... RPUZ
Bagala [*Ship's rigging*] (ROG) .... BLA
Bagarottus dei Corradi da Bologna [*Flourished, 1200-42*] [*Authority cited in pre-1607 legal work*] (DSA) .... B
Bagarottus dei Corradi da Bologna [*Flourished, 1200-42*] [*Authority cited in pre-1607 legal work*] (DSA) .... Ba
Bagarottus dei Corradi da Bologna [*Flourished, 1200-42*] [*Authority cited in pre-1607 legal work*] (DSA) .... Bag
Bagatelle .... BGTTL
Bagdad, AZ [*FM radio station call letters*] (RBYB) .... KAKP
Bagdad, AZ [*FM radio station call letters*] (BROA) .... KBJU-FM
Bagdogra [*India*] [*Airport symbol*] (OAG) .... IXB
Bage [*Brazil*] [*Airport symbol*] (OAG) .... BGX
Bagehot. English Constitution [*8th ed.*] [*1904*] [*A publication*] (DLA) .... Bag Eng Const
Bagehot. English Constitution [*8th ed.*] [*1904*] [*A publication*] (DLA) .... Bag Engl Const
Baggage (AFM) .... BAG
Baggage and Mail car (SAUS) .... BM car
Baggage Express Messenger (SAUS) .... BEM
Baggage for Air Cargo .... CARBAGAIR
Baggage Improvement Program [*IATA*] (DS) .... BIP
Baggage, Mail and Dormitory car (SAUS) .... BMD car
Baggage, Mail and Express car (SAUS) .... BME car
Bagged White Cell Study [*Cytology*] (DAVI) .... BWCS
Baggett, Texas Foreclosure-Law and Practice (SAUS) .... TF
Baghdad (SAUS) .... Bag
Baghdad [*Iraq*] [*Airport symbol*] (OAG) .... BGW
Baghdad Local Time (SAUS) .... BLT
Baghdad Pact (CINC) .... BP
Baghdad Time (SAUS) .... BT
Baghdad/Muthenna [*Iraq*] [*ICAO location identifier*] (ICLI) .... ORBW
Baghdad/Rasheed [*Iraq*] [*ICAO location identifier*] (ICLI) .... ORBR
Baghdad-Saddam [*Iraq*] [*Airport symbol*] (OAG) .... SDA
Baghdad/Saddam International [*Iraq*] [*ICAO location identifier*] (ICLI) .... ORBS
Baghdad/Soica Headquarters [*Iraq*] [*ICAO location identifier*] (ICLI) .... ORBC
Baghdogra [*India*] [*ICAO location identifier*] (ICLI) .... VEBD
Baghlan [*Afghanistan*] [*ICAO location identifier*] (ICLI) .... OABG
Bagley and Harman's Reports [*17-19 California*] [*A publication*] (DLA) .... Bagl & H
Bagley and Harman's Reports [*17-19 California*] [*A publication*] (DLA) .... Bagl & Har
Bagley and Harman's Reports [*17-19 California*] [*A publication*] (DLA) .... Bagl & Har (Cal)
Bagley Elementary School, Bagley, MN [*Library symbol*] [*Library of Congress*] (LCLS) .... MnBagE
Bagley Gazette, Bagley, IA [*Library symbol*] [*Library of Congress*] (LCLS) .... IaBagG
Bagley Public Library, Bagley, IA [*Library symbol*] [*Library of Congress*] (LCLS) .... IaBag
Bagley Public Library, Bagley, MN [*Library symbol*] [*Library of Congress*] (LCLS) .... MnBag
Bagley's Practice at Chambers [*1834*] [*A publication*] (DLA) .... Bag Ch Pr
Bagley's Reports [*16 California*] [*A publication*] (DLA) .... Bagl
Bagley's Reports [*16-19 California*] [*A publication*] (DLA) .... Bagl (Cal)
Baglung [*Nepal*] [*Airport symbol*] (OAG) .... BGL
Baglung [*Nepal*] [*ICAO location identifier*] (ICLI) .... VNBL
Bagneres De Bigorre [*France*] [*Seismograph station code, US Geological Survey*] (SEIS) .... BDB
Bagneres De Luchon [*France*] [*ICAO location identifier*] (ICLI) .... LFCB
Bagnole-De-L'Orne [*France*] [*ICAO location identifier*] (ICLI) .... LFAO
Bagong Alyansang Makabayan [*Philippines*] [*Political party*] (EY) .... Bayan
Bagotville Canadian Forces Base, PQ [*ICAO location identifier*] (ICLI) .... CYBG
Bagra [*Pakistan*] [*Seismograph station code, US Geological Survey*] (SEIS) .... BGP
Bags .... BGS
Bags (SAUS) .... B/s
Bags, Barrels, or Boxes [*Freight*] .... BBB
Bagua [*Peru*] [*ICAO location identifier*] (ICLI) .... SPGU
Baguio [*Philippines*] [*Seismograph station code, US Geological Survey*] (SEIS) .... BAG
Baguio, Benguet [*Philippines*] [*ICAO location identifier*] (ICLI) .... RPUB
Bag-Valve Mask (SAUS) .... BVM
Baha Resources Ltd. [*Vancouver Stock Exchange symbol*] .... BAH
Bahaa Esperanto-Ligo (EA) .... BEL
Baha'i Community [*Australia*] .... BC
Baha'i Faith .... BF
Baha'i International Community .... BIC
Baha'i National Spiritual Assembly [*Australia*] .... BNSA
Bahama Inseln (SAUS) .... Bah
Bahama Islands (WDAA) .... BA I
Bahama Islands (BARN) .... Ba Is
Bahama Islands (SAUO) .... BI
Bahama Islands Ministry of Tourism (SAUO) .... BIMT
Bahama Resources Ltd. [*Vancouver Stock Exchange symbol*] .... BHA
Bahama Route [*Aviation*] (FAAC) .... BR
Bahamas [*IYRU nationality code*] (IYR) .... BA
Bahamas (ROG) .... BAH
Bahamas (VRA) .... Baha
Bahamas [*MARC country of publication code*] [*Library of Congress*] (LCCP) .... bf
Bahamas [*ANSI three-letter standard code*] (CNC) .... BHS
Bahamas [*ANSI two-letter standard code*] (CNC) .... BS
Bahamas [*Aircraft nationality and registration mark*] (FAAC) C6
Bahamas [*MARC geographic area code*] [*Library of Congress*] (LCCP) .... nwbf-
Bahamas Air [*ICAO designator*] (AD) .... UP
Bahamas Airways, Ltd. (SAUO) .... BAL
Bahamas Billfish Championship .... BBC
Bahamas Broadcasting and Television Commission (SAUO) .... BB&TC
Bahamas Environment, Science and Technology Commission (SAUO) .... BEST
Bahamas Federation of Labor (SAUO) .... BFL
Bahamas International Trust Company (SAUO) .... BITC
Bahamas Lands and Surveys Department (GEOI) .... BLS
Bahamas Law Reports [*A publication*] (DLA) .... Bah LR
Bahamas Law Reports [*A publication*] (DLA) .... BLR
Bahamas National Park (SAUS) .... BNP
Bahamas Oil Refining Co. (SAUO) .... Borco
Bahamas Red Cross Society (EAIO) .... BRCS
Bahamas Telecommunications Corp. [*Telecommunications service*] (TSSD) .... BATELCO
Bahamasair Holdings Ltd. [*Bahamas*] [*ICAO designator*] (FAAC) .... BHS
Bahamian Democratic Party [*Political party*] (PPW) .... BDP
Bahar Dar [*Ethiopia*] [*Airport symbol*] (OAG) .... BJR
Bahar Dar [*Ethiopia*] [*ICAO location identifier*] (ICLI) .... HABD
Bahau [*Malaysia*] [*ICAO location identifier*] (ICLI) .... WMAA
Bahawalnagar [*Pakistan*] [*ICAO location identifier*] (ICLI) .... OPBR
Bahawalpur [*Pakistan*] [*Airport symbol*] (AD) .... BWP
Bahawalpur [*Pakistan*] [*ICAO location identifier*] (ICLI) .... OPBW
Bahc, Loicz, Pages (SAUS) .... BLOP
BAHC Scientific Steering Committee (SAUS) .... BAHC-SSC
Bahia (SAUS) .... Bah
Bahia Blanca [*Argentina*] [*Airport symbol*] (OAG) .... BHI
Bahia Blanca/Comdte. Espora [*Argentina*] [*ICAO location identifier*] (ICLI) .... SAZB
Bahia De Caraquez [*Ecuador*] [*ICAO location identifier*] (ICLI) .... SEBC
Bahia De Los Angeles [*Mexico*] [*Seismograph station code, US Geological Survey*] (SEIS) .... LAX
Bahia Oral Language Test (EDAC) .... BOLT
Bahia Solano [*Colombia*] [*Airport symbol*] (OAG) .... BSC
Bahia Solano/Jose Celestino Mutis [*Colombia*] [*ICAO location identifier*] (ICLI) .... SKBS
Bahn Post Amt [*Railway Post Office*] [*German*] .... BPA
Bahrain [*Aircraft nationality and registration mark*] (FAAC) A9C
Bahrain (SAUO) .... A 9 C
Bahrain [*MARC geographic area code*] [*Library of Congress*] .... a-ba-
Bahrain [*MARC country of publication code*] [*Library of Congress*] (LCCP) .... ba
Bahrain .... BAHR
Bahrain (VRA) .... Bahr
Bahrain [*IYRU nationality code*] [*ANSI two-letter standard code*] (CNC) .... BH
Bahrain (SAUS) .... BH
Bahrain [*ANSI three-letter standard code*] (CNC) .... BHR
Bahrain (MILB) .... Brn
Bahrain (SAUO) .... BRN
Bahrain [*Bahrain*] [*ICAO location identifier*] (ICLI) .... OBBB
Bahrain Amiri Air Force (SAUS) .... BAAF
Bahrain Development Bank (EY) .... BDB
Bahrain Dinar [*Monetary unit*] (BJA) .... BD
Bahrain Inter-Bank Offered Rate [*Finance*] .... BIBOR
Bahrain Islands [*Airport symbol*] (OAG) .... BAH
Bahrain Middle East Bank .... BMB
Bahrain Monetary Agency (IMH) .... BMA
Bahrain Petroleum Company (SAUO) .... BAPCO
Bahrain Petroleum Company (SAUO) .... BPC
Bahrain Telecommunications Co. .... BATELCO
Bahrain Tourism Co. (EY) .... BTC
Bahraini Saudi Bank (EY) .... BSB
Bahrain/International [*Bahrain*] [*ICAO location identifier*] (ICLI) .... OBBI
Bahrein Islands (SAUO) .... Bhrn
Bahrein Islands (SAUO) .... BRN
Bahrein Ship Repairing and Engineering Company (SAUO) .... BASREC
Baht [*Monetary unit*] [*Thailand*] .... B
Baht [*Monetary unit*] [*Thailand*] .... BHT
Baia Mare [*Romania*] [*Airport symbol*] (OAG) .... BAY
Baia Mare/Tauti Magherusi [*Romania*] [*ICAO location identifier*] (ICLI) .... LRBM
Baibara [*Papua New Guinea*] [*Airport symbol*] (OAG) .... BAP
Baidoa [*Somalia*] [*ICAO location identifier*] (ICLI) .... HCMB
Baie Comeau [*Canada*] [*Airport symbol*] (OAG) .... YBC
Baie Comeau, PQ [*FM radio station call letters*] .... CBMI

Baie Comeau, PQ [*AM radio station call letters*] ... CHLC
Baie Comeau, PQ [*FM radio station call letters*] (RBYB) ... CHLC-FM
Baie Comeau, PQ [*ICAO location identifier*] (ICLI) ... CYBC
Baie Comeau, Quebec [*FM radio station call letters*] (BROA) ... CBMI-FM
Baie Johan Beetz [*Canada*] [*Airport symbol*] (OAG) ... YBJ
Baie Verte, NF [*Television station call letters*] ... CBNAT-1
Baie Verte, NF [*AM radio station call letters*] ... CKIM
Baie Verte Public Library, Baie Verte, NF, Canada [*Library symbol*] [*Library of Congress*] (LCLS) ... CaNfBV
Baie Verte Public Library, Newfoundland [*Library symbol*] [*National Library of Canada*] (NLC) ... NFBV
Baie-Trinite, PQ [*Television station call letters*] ... CIVF
Baika Women's College [*EDUCATSS*] [*UTLAS symbol*] ... BAI
Baikal [*Russian Federation*] [*ICAO designator*] (FAAC) ... BKL
Baikal Commodity Exchange [*Russian Federation*] (EY) ... BCE
Baikal Drilling Project (SAUS) ... BDP
Baikal International Centre for Ecological Research (SAUO) ... BICER
Baikal-Amur Mainline [*USSR railroad in Siberia*] ... BAM
Baikal-Amur-Magistral (SAUS) ... BAM
Baikonur [*Satellite launch complex*] [*Former USSR*] ... BAI
Bail Bond (DLA) ... BB
Bail Court [*Legal term*] (DLA) ... BC
Bail Court Cases [*A publication*] ... Bail CC
Bail Court Cases [*Legal*] [*British*] ... BCC
Bail Court Cases (Lowndes and Maxwell) [*England*] [*A publication*] (DLA) ... BCR
Bail Court Cases (Lowndes and Maxwell) [*England*] [*A publication*] (DLA) ... BC Rep
Bail Court Reports [*Legal*] [*British*] ... BCR
Bail Court Reports (Saunders and Cole) [*England*] [*A publication*] (DLA) ... Bail Ct R
Bail Court Reports (Saunders and Cole) [*England*] [*A publication*] (DLA) ... BCC
Bail Court Reports (Saunders and Cole) [*England*] [*A publication*] (DLA) ... BCR
Bail Court Reports (Saunders and Cole) [*England*] [*A publication*] (DLA) ... BC Rep
Bail Out ... BO
Bailadores [*Venezuela*] [*Seismograph station code, US Geological Survey*] (SEIS) ... BLV
Baildon's Select Cases in Chancery [*Selden Society Publication, Vol. 10*] [*A publication*] (DLA) ... Baild
Bailed Aircraft Repairables (MCD) ... BAR
Bailett Weighting Function ... BWF
Bailey Bridge (SAUS) ... BB
Bailey Corp. [*NASDAQ symbol*] (CTT) ... BAIB
Bailey Corp. [*Associated Press*] (SAG) ... Bailey
Bailey Elementary School, Pasadena, TX [*Library symbol*] [*Library of Congress*] (LCLS) ... TxPBE
Bailey, G. R., Escanaba MI [*STAC*] ... BGR
Bailey Oil Content Monitor [*Ship ballast discharge*] ... BOCM
Bailey-Borwein-Plouffe (SAUS) ... BBP
Bailey's Chancery Reports [*South Carolina*] [*A publication*] (DLA) ... Bailey Ch
Bailey's Equity Reports [*South Carolina*] [*A publication*] (DLA) ... Bai Eq
Bailey's Equity Reports [*South Carolina*] [*A publication*] (DLA) ... Bail Eq
Bailey's Equity Reports [*South Carolina*] [*A publication*] (DLA) ... Bail Eq (SC)
Bailey's Equity Reports [*South Carolina*] [*A publication*] (DLA) ... Bailey
Bailey's Equity Reports, South Carolina Court of Appeals [*A publication*] (DLA) ... Bailey Eq
Bailey's Law of Master's Liability for Injuries to Servant [*A publication*] (DLA) ... Bailey Mast Liab
Bailey's Law Reports [*South Carolina*] [*A publication*] (DLA) ... Bai
Bailey's Law Reports [*South Carolina*] [*A publication*] (DLA) ... Bail
Bailey's Law Reports [*South Carolina*] [*A publication*] (DLA) ... Bailey
Bailey's Law Reports [*South Carolina*] [*A publication*] (DLA) ... Bail L
Bailey's Law Reports [*South Carolina*] [*A publication*] (DLA) ... Bail L (SC)
Bailey's North Carolina Digest [*A publication*] (DLA) ... Bail Dig
Bailie [*British*] (ROG) ... B
Bailiff Grand Cross ... BGC
Bailiff Grand Cross of [*the Order of*] **Saint John of Jerusalem** [*British*] (ADA) ... GCStJ
Bailing ... BLG
Bailleau-Armenonville [*France*] [*ICAO location identifier*] (ICLI) ... LFFL
Bailliere's Medical Transparencies [*A publication*] (DAVI) ... BMT
Baillie's Digest of Mohammedan Law [*A publication*] (DLA) ... Baill Dig
Baillie's Mohammedan Law of Inheritance [*A publication*] (DLA) ... Baill Inher
Bailly Generating Station [*Nuclear energy*] (NRCH) ... BGS
Bailment [*Legal term*] (DLA) ... Bailm
Bailment (AAGC) ... BLMT
Bailment Flight Test Program ... BFTP
Bailment Test Program (SAUS) ... BTP
Baimuru [*Papua New Guinea*] [*Airport symbol*] (OAG) ... VMU
Bainbridge, GA [*Location identifier*] [*FAA*] (FAAL) ... BGE
Bainbridge, GA [*AM radio station call letters*] ... WMGR
Bainbridge, GA [*FM radio station call letters*] ... WMGR-FM
Bainbridge, GA [*Television station call letters*] ... WTLH
Bainbridge Junior College, Bainbridge, GA [*Library symbol*] [*Library of Congress*] (LCLS) ... GBaB
Bainbridge Naval Training Center (SAUO) ... BNTC
Bainbridge, OH [*FM radio station call letters*] ... WKHR
Bainbridge on Mines and Minerals [*A publication*] (DLA) ... Bainb M & M
Bainbridge on Mines and Minerals [*A publication*] (DLA) ... Bainb Mines
Baird Atomic (SAUO) ... BA
Baird-Associates, Inc. (MCD) ... BAI
Bairnco Corp. [*Associated Press*] (SAG) ... Bairnco
Bairnco Corp. [*NYSE symbol*] (SPSG) ... BZ
Bairnsdale [*Australia*] [*Airport symbol*] [*Obsolete*] (OAG) ... BSJ
Baitadi [*Nepal*] [*Airport symbol*] (OAG) ... BIT
Baitadi [*Nepal*] [*ICAO location identifier*] (ICLI) ... VNBT
Baiting Hollow Free Library, Calverton, NY [*Library symbol*] [*Library of Congress*] (LCLS) ... NCalv
Baiyer River [*New Guinea*] [*Airport symbol*] (AD) ... BYV
Baja California [*Mexico*] ... BC
Baja California - Territorio Norte ... BCTN
Baja California - Territorio Sur ... BCTS
Bajawa [*Indonesia*] [*Airport symbol*] (OAG) ... BJW
Bajawa/Padhameleda [*Indonesia*] [*ICAO location identifier*] (ICLI) ... WRKB
Baje/Cmt. Gustavo Kraemer [*Brazil*] [*ICAO location identifier*] (ICLI) ... SBBG
Bajhang [*Nepal*] [*Airport symbol*] (OAG) ... BJH
Bajhang [*Nepal*] [*ICAO location identifier*] (ICLI) ... VNBG
Bajocian [*Geology*] ... B
Bajura [*Nepal*] [*ICAO location identifier*] (ICLI) ... VNBR
Bakalalan [*Malaysia*] [*Airport symbol*] (OAG) ... BKM
Bake House (WDAA) ... Bk H
Baked ... BKD
Bakel [*Senegal*] [*Seismograph station code, US Geological Survey*] (SEIS) ... BKL
Bakel [*Senegal*] [*Airport symbol*] (OAG) ... BXE
Bakel [*Senegal*] [*ICAO location identifier*] (ICLI) ... GOTB
Bakelalan [*Malaysia*] [*ICAO location identifier*] (ICLI) ... WBGQ
Bakelite Xylonite Limited (SAUO) ... BXL
Baken (SAUS) ... Bkn
Bakeout (SAUS) ... BO
Baker [*Phonetic alphabet*] [*World War II*] (DSUE) ... B
Baker [*Diocesan abbreviation*] [*Oregon*] (TOCD) ... BAK
Baker ... BKR
Baker Analyzed Reagent [*Chemistry*] ... BAR
Baker and Taylor Automated Buying [*A teleordering system*] (NITA) ... BATAB
Baker & Taylor Co. ... B & T
Baker & Taylor Co. [*ACCORD*] [*UTLAS symbol*] ... BTE
Baker & Taylor Electronic Book Ordering Service [*Baker & Taylor Companies*] [*Trademark*] ... BaTaSYSTEMS
Baker and Taylor's Automated Buying System [*Teleordering system*] [*Baker & Taylor Companies*] [*Information service or system*] (IID) ... BATAB
Baker Aviation, Inc. [*ICAO designator*] (FAAC) ... BAJ
Baker, Botts, Shepherd & Coates, Houston, TX [*Library symbol*] [*Library of Congress*] (LCLS) ... TxHBB
Baker, CA [*FM radio station call letters*] ... KBXY
Baker, CA [*FM radio station call letters*] ... KIXF
Baker City, OR [*AM radio station call letters*] ... KBKR
Baker City, OR [*FM radio station call letters*] ... KCMB
Baker City, OR [*FM radio station call letters*] ... KKBC
Baker [*Michael*] **Corp.** [*Associated Press*] (SAG) ... Baker
Baker [*Michael*] **Corp.** [*AMEX symbol*] (SPSG) ... BKR
Baker County Public Library, Baker, OR [*Library symbol*] [*Library of Congress*] (LCLS) ... OrBak
Baker Elementary School, Great Neck, NY [*Library symbol*] [*Library of Congress*] (LCLS) ... NGrnBE
Baker, Fentress & Co. [*Associated Press*] (SAG) ... BakrF
Baker, Fentress & Co. [*NYSE symbol*] (CTT) ... BKF
Baker First Class (SAUS) ... BKR1c
Baker, FL [*FM radio station call letters*] ... WTJT
Baker Gold Ltd. [*Vancouver Stock Exchange symbol*] ... BKG
Baker High School, Baker, MT [*Library symbol*] [*Library of Congress*] (LCLS) ... MtBaHS
Baker Hughes, Inc. [*Associated Press*] (SAG) ... BakrHu
Baker Hughes, Inc. [*NYSE symbol*] (SPSG) ... BHI
Baker Hughes Video (SAUS) ... BHV
Baker [*J.*], **Inc.** [*Associated Press*] (SAG) ... BakerJ
Baker [*J.*], **Inc.** [*NASDAQ symbol*] (NQ) ... JBAK
Baker Industries, Inc. (SAUO) ... BAK
Baker Island Army Air Field [*Baker Island*] [*ICAO location identifier*] (ICLI) ... PBAR
Baker, LA [*FM radio station call letters*] ... WBBU
Baker Lake [*Northwest Territories*] [*Seismograph station code, US Geological Survey*] (SEIS) ... BLC
Baker Lake [*Canada*] [*Airport symbol*] (OAG) ... YBK
Baker Lake, NT [*FM radio station call letters*] ... CKQN
Baker Lake, NT [*ICAO location identifier*] (ICLI) ... CYBK
Baker, Michael [*AMEX symbol*] (SG) ... BKR
Baker, MT [*Location identifier*] [*FAA*] (FAAL) ... BKU
Baker, MT [*AM radio station call letters*] ... KFLN
Baker, MT [*FM radio station call letters*] (BROA) ... KJJM-FM
Baker Oil Tools, Inc. (SAUO) ... BKO
Baker on the Law Relating to Burials [*A publication*] (DLA) ... Bak Bur
Baker, OR [*Location identifier*] [*FAA*] (FAAL) ... BKE
Baker River Audiovisual Center [*Library network*] ... BRAVC
Baker School of Navigation (SAUO) ... BSN
Baker Street Irregulars (EA) ... BSI
Baker Street Irregulars (SAUS) ... TBSI
Baker University (SAUO) ... BU
Baker University, Baldwin City, KS [*Library symbol*] [*Library of Congress*] (LCLS) ... KBB
Baker University, Baldwin City, KS [*OCLC symbol*] (OCLC) ... KKB
Bakers' and Allied Traders' Golfing Society [*British*] (BI) ... BATS
Bakers and Pastrycooks' Association of Tasmania [*Australia*] ... BPAT
Baker's Antifol, Cyclophosphamide, Adriamycin, and Cisplatin [*Antineoplastic drug regimen*] (DAVI) ... T-CAP
Baker's Cyst [*Medicine*] (MELL) ... BC
Bakers' Food and Allied Workers' Union [*British*] (DCTA) ... BFAWU
Baker's Health Laws [*A publication*] (DLA) ... Bak Health L
Baker's Law of Highways [*A publication*] (DLA) ... Bak Highw
Baker's Law of Quarantine [*A publication*] (DLA) ... Baker Quar
Baker's New York Corporation Laws [*A publication*] (DLA) ... Bak Corp
Bakers' Union [*British*] (DI) ... BU

Baker-Schmidt Telescope (PDAA) ... BST
Baker-Schulberg Community Mental Health Ideology Scale [*Psychology*] ... CMHI
Bakersfield [*California*] [*Airport symbol*] (OAG) ... BFL
Bakersfield, CA [*TACAN station*] (NASA) ... BFL
Bakersfield, CA [*AM radio station call letters*] ... KAFY
Bakersfield, CA [*Television station call letters*] ... KBAK
Bakersfield, CA [*AM radio station call letters*] ... KBID
Bakersfield, CA [*AM radio station call letters*] ... KCWR
Bakersfield, CA [*AM radio station call letters*] ... KERN
Bakersfield, CA [*FM radio station call letters*] ... KERN-FM
Bakersfield, CA [*Television station call letters*] ... KERO
Bakersfield, CA [*FM radio station call letters*] (RBYB) ... KFRB-FM
Bakersfield, CA [*AM radio station call letters*] ... KGEO
Bakersfield, CA [*Television station call letters*] ... KGET
Bakersfield, CA [*FM radio station call letters*] ... KGFM
Bakersfield, CA [*AM radio station call letters*] ... KHIS
Bakersfield, CA [*FM radio station call letters*] ... KHIS-FM
Bakersfield, CA [*FM radio station call letters*] (BROA) ... KISV-FM
Bakersfield, CA [*FM radio station call letters*] ... KIWI
Bakersfield, CA [*FM radio station call letters*] ... KKBB
Bakersfield, CA [*AM radio station call letters*] ... KNZR
Bakersfield, CA [*FM radio station call letters*] ... KPRX
Bakersfield, CA [*FM radio station call letters*] (BROA) ... KSMJ-FM
Bakersfield, CA [*FM radio station call letters*] ... KTIE
Bakersfield, CA [*FM radio station call letters*] ... KTQX
Bakersfield, CA [*Television station call letters*] (BROA) ... KUVI
Bakersfield, CA [*FM radio station call letters*] ... KUZZ
Bakersfield, CA [*Television station call letters*] ... KUZZ-TV
Bakersfield, CA [*AM radio station call letters*] ... KWAC
Bakersfield, CA [*AM radio station call letters*] (RBYB) ... KXEM
Bakersfield, CA [*AM radio station call letters*] ... KZPM
Bakersfield College (SAUO) ... BC
Bakersfield Individualized Process (EDAC) ... BIP
Bakersfield/Meadows Field [*California*] [*ICAO location identifier*] (ICLI) ... KBFL
Bakertalc, Inc. [*Toronto Stock Exchange symbol*] ... BKT
Bakery ... BAK
bakery (SAUS) ... bak
Bakery (AABC) ... BKRY
Bakery and Allied Trades Association Ltd. [*British*] (BI) ... BATA
Bakery and Confectionery Workers' International Union of America [*Later, BCTWIU*] (EA) ... BCWIU of A
Bakery, Confectionary, Tobacco Workers, and Grain Millers International Union ... BCTGM
Bakery, Confectionery and Tobacco Workers International (SAUO) ... BCTWI
Bakery, Confectionery, and Tobacco Workers' International Union (EA) ... BCTWIU
Bakery Employees and Salesmen's Federation of Australia ... BESFA
Bakery Equipment Manufacturers Association (EA) ... BEMA
Bakery Industry Employees' Association of New South Wales [*Australia*] ... BIEANSW
Bakery Students Association of Scotland (BI) ... BSAS
Bakhon Phanom/Mukdahan [*Thailand*] [*ICAO location identifier*] (ICLI) ... VTUB
Bakhtar Afghan Airlines [*ICAO designator*] (AD) ... BJ
Bakhtaran [*Iran*] [*ICAO location identifier*] (ICLI) ... OICC
Bakhtaran [*Iran*] [*ICAO location identifier*] (ICLI) ... OICT
Bakhuys [*Surinam*] [*ICAO location identifier*] (ICLI) ... SMBG
Baking ... BKG
Baking Industry and Teamster Labor Conference (EA) ... BITLC
Baking Industry Association of New South Wales [*Australia*] ... BIANSW
Baking Industry Sanitation Standards Committee (EA) ... BISSC
Baking Powder (WDAA) ... B/P
Baking Powder (SAUS) ... BP
Baking Sands Tactical Underwater Range [*Oahu, HI*] ... BASTUR
Baking Trade Union of South Australia ... BTUSA
Baking Trades Employees' Union of New South Wales [*Australia*] ... BTEUNSW
Bakkafjordur [*Iceland*] [*Airport symbol*] (OAG) ... BJD
Bakken Library of Electricity in Life, Minneapolis, MN [*Library symbol*] [*Library of Congress*] (LCLS) ... MnMBL
Bako National Park (SAUS) ... BNP
Bakosurtanal Image Analysis System (SAUS) ... BIAS
Bakra Resources Ltd. [*Vancouver Stock Exchange symbol*] ... BKQ
Baksan Neutrino Observatory (SAUS) ... Baksan
Bakshi Ka Talab [*India*] [*ICAO location identifier*] (ICLI) ... VIBL
Baku [*Former USSR*] [*Seismograph station code, US Geological Survey*] (SEIS) ... BAK
Baku (SAUS) ... Bak
Bakuai [*China*] [*ICAO location identifier*] (ICLI) ... RCUK
Bakuriani [*Former USSR*] [*Seismograph station code, US Geological Survey*] (SEIS) ... BKR
Balair AG [*Switzerland*] [*ICAO designator*] (FAAC) ... BBB
Balalae [*Solomon Islands*] [*Airport symbol*] (OAG) ... BAS
Balalae, Shortland Islands [*Solomon Islands*] [*ICAO location identifier*] (ICLI) ... AGGE
Balalaika and Domra Association of America (EA) ... BDAA
Balance [*Accounting*] (AFM) ... BAL
Balance [*Medicine*] (DAVI) ... bal
Balance [*Bookkeeping*] (ODBW) ... bal
Balance [*Accounting*] (ROG) ... BALCE
Balance (EBF) ... Balce
Balance (WGA) ... BLC
Balance (SAUS) ... blc
Balance (ADA) ... BLCE
Balance Agriculture with Industry (SAUO) ... BAWI
Balance Calibration Machine ... BCM
Balance Card (SAUS) ... BC
Balance Column (SAUS) ... BC
Balance Contrast Enhancement Technique (SAUS) ... BCET
Balance Control (SAUS) ... BC
Balance Counter (SAUS) ... BC
Balance de Radiaciãn de Superficie (SAUS) ... SRB
Balance Fixture (MCD) ... BAF
Balance Forward Master ... BFM
Balance, Gate, Station (SAUS) ... BGS
Balance General Mobilization Reserve Acquisition Objective [*DoD*] ... BGMRAO
Balance Location ... BALOC
Balance Magnetometric Zero (NOAA) ... BMZ
Balance Mobilization Reserve Materiel Objective [*Army*] (AABC) ... BMRMO
Balance of Commitments ... BCOM
Balance of Material (MCD) ... BM
Balance of Need Campaign [*Red Cross fund-raising*] ... BON
Balance of Payments [*Accounting*] ... BALPA
Balance of Payments [*International trade*] ... B-of-P
Balance of Payments [*International trade*] ... BOP
Balance of Payments [*International trade*] ... BP
Balance of Payments Act [*International trade*] (AABC) ... BOPA
Balance of Payments Program (AAGC) ... BALPRO
Balance of Payments Programmed [*International trade*] (AABC) ... BOPP
Balance of Payments Report [*A publication*] (DLA) ... Bal Pay't Rep
Balance of Plant [*Nuclear energy*] (NRCH) ... BOP
Balance of Plant Standard Safety Analysis Report [*Nuclear energy*] (NRCH) ... BOPSSAR
Balance of Power (IEEE) ... BOP
Balance of Space to Space Control Agencies ... BALSPACON
Balance of State [*Department of Labor*] ... BOS
Balance of Time (SAUS) ... BOT
Balance of Trade [*International trade*] ... B-of-T
Balance of Trade [*International trade*] ... BOT
Balance Reading Device (SAUS) ... BRD
Balance Resources Ltd. [*Vancouver Stock Exchange symbol*] ... BLD
Balance Return Loss [*Telecommunications*] (TEL) ... BRL
Balance Selection (SAUS) ... BS
Balance Sheet [*Accounting*] ... BS
Balance Test (SAUS) ... Bal T
Balance to Follow (WDAA) ... BTF
Balance Totalizing Mechanism (SAUS) ... BTM
Balance Transferred (SAUS) ... B/TF
Balance Voltage (SAUS) ... BAL V
Balanced ... B
Balanced (SAUS) ... BAL
Balanced Asynchronous (ACRL) ... BA
Balanced Asynchronous Class (SAUS) ... BAC
Balanced Biological Communities [*Environmental science*] (COE) ... BBC
Balanced Budget ... BB
Balanced Budget Amendment ... BBA
Balanced Budget and Emergency Deficit Control Reaffirmation Act [*1987*] ... BBEDCRA
Balanced Capacitor Read Only Storage (SAUS) ... BCROS
Balanced Care [*AMEX symbol*] (SG) ... BAL
Balanced Colorimeter Chamber (MCD) ... BCC
Balanced Crystal Mixer (IAA) ... BCM
Balanced Current [*Electronics*] (IAA) ... BC
Balanced Diet Certificates [*Economics simulation game*] ... BALDICER
Balanced Digital Transmission Device [*Army*] ... BDTD
Balanced, Effective, State-related and Training-oriented Program (SAUS) ... BEST Program
Balanced Electrolyte Solution [*Physiology*] ... BES
Balanced Emitter Transistor (SAUS) ... BET
Balanced Emotional Empathy Scale [*Test*] (TMMY) ... BEES
Balanced Expansion Technique (MCD) ... BET
Balanced Extravehicular Training Aircraft [*NASA*] ... BETA
Balanced File Organization Scheme (MHDI) ... BFS
Balanced Force Requirements Analysis (MCD) ... BALFRAN
Balanced Force Requirements Analysis Model (CCCA) ... BALFRAM
Balanced Forearm Orthosis [*Medicine*] ... BFO
Balanced Fund [*Investment term*] ... B
Balanced Half-Sample Replication [*Statistics*] ... BHSR
Balanced in Plane (IEEE) ... BIP
Balanced Income & Growth Fund Trust Units [*Toronto Stock Exchange symbol*] ... BIF
Balanced Incomplete Block [*Statistical design*] ... BIB
Balanced Incomplete Block Design [*Mathematics*] ... BIBD
Balanced Incomplete Repeated Measures Design ... BIRMD
Balanced Indigenous Population ... BIP
Balanced Inductor Logical Element ... BILE
Balanced Input Converter (SAUS) ... BALINVERTER
Balanced Job Execution on Remote Network (SAUS) ... BJOERN
Balanced Line Driver (MSA) ... BLD
Balanced Line Logical Element ... BLLE
Balanced Line System ... BLS
Balanced Magnetic Amplifier ... BMA
Balanced Magnetic Switch (SAUS) ... BMS
Balanced Nuclear Economy Code (IAA) ... BANEC
Balanced Nutrient Solution ... BNS
Balanced Parametric Amplifier ... BPA
Balanced Pressure Joint ... BPJ
Balanced Pressure Plane Swivel Joint ... BPPSJ
Balanced Pressure Swivel Joint ... BPSJ
Balanced Processing Monitor [*Mitsubishi*] (NITA) ... BPM
Balanced Property Management (ADA) ... BPM

Balanced Property Trust (ADA) ... BPT
Balanced Repeated Replication [*Statistics*] ... BRR
Balanced Resource Allocation Information for Logical Lucid Evaluation (PDAA) ... BRAILLE
Balanced Salt Solution [*Cell incubation medium*] ... BSS
Balanced Swivel Joint ... BSJ
Balanced Tape Drive ... BTD
Balanced Technology Initiative [*DoD*] (RDA) ... BTI
Balanced Technology Institute (AAGC) ... BTI
Balanced Ternary (SAUS) ... BT
Balanced, Total [*Business term*] ... BT
Balanced Traction (MELL) ... BT
Balanced Transformer (IAA) ... BTL
Balanced Transformer-Less (SAUS) ... BTL
Balanced Unbalanced (SAUS) ... BALUN
Balanced Valve Regulator ... BVR
Balanced Voltage ... BV
Balanced-Deficit Diet ... BDD
Balanced-Emitter Technology (IAA) ... BET
Balanced-Emitter Transistor (SAUS) ... BET
Balanced-Pressure System (SAUS) ... BPS
Balanced-to-Unbalanced Line Transformer [*Telecommunications*] (TEL) ... BALUN
Balanced-Tree [*Technique for organizing indexes*] (CDE) ... B-tree
Balanced-Unbalanced [*Adapter*] (VERA) ... BALUN
Balance-of-System [*Power plant efficiency*] ... BOS
Balance-to-Unbalance Network [*Telecommunications*] ... BALUN
Balancing ... BALNCNG
Balancing Machine (SAUS) ... BM
Balancing Network (SAUS) ... BAL NET
Balancing Network (IAA) ... BALNET
Balancing Network ... BN
Balancing Rheostat ... BALRHEO
Balancing Rheostat (SAUS) ... bal rheo
Balancing Set (IEEE) ... BALS
Balancing the Budget on the Backs of the Elderly [*Political charge*] ... B^3E
Balancing the Budget on the Backs of the Poor [*Political charge*] ... B^3P
Balancing Transformer (IAA) ... BALTR
Balancing Transformer (SAUS) ... BAL TR
Balancing Unit (SAUS) ... balun
Balancing Unit [*Radio*] ... BALUN
Balanitis Xerotica Obliterans (DMAA) ... BXO
Balantidium [*Biochemistry*] (DAVI) ... B
Balao Chico [*Ecuador*] [*ICAO location identifier*] (ICLI) ... SEBH
Balasingham's Notes of Cases [*Ceylon*] [*A publication*] (DLA) ... Balas NC
Balasingham's Notes of Cases [*Ceylon*] [*A publication*] (ILCA) ... Bal Notes
Balasingham's Reports [*Ceylon*] [*A publication*] (DLA) ... Bal
Balasingham's Reports of Cases [*Ceylon*] [*A publication*] (ILCA) ... Balasingham Rep
Balasingham's Reports of Cases [*1904-09*] [*Ceylon*] [*A publication*] (DLA) ... Balas RC
Balasingham's Reports of Cases [*Ceylon*] [*A publication*] (ILCA) ... Bal Rep
Balasingham's Supreme Court Reports [*Ceylon*] [*A publication*] (DLA) ... Balas
Balaton Public Library, Balaton, MN [*Library symbol*] [*Library of Congress*] (LCLS) ... MnBa
Balaton Public Schools, Balaton, MN [*Library symbol*] [*Library of Congress*] (LCLS) ... MnBaPS
Balboa [*Monetary unit*] [*Panama*] ... B
Balboa (SAUS) ... Balb
Balboa (SAUS) ... Boa
Balboa, Canal Zone [*Location identifier*] [*FAA*] (FAAL) ... ZLB
Balboa Heights [*Canal Zone*] [*Seismograph station code, US Geological Survey*] (SEIS) ... BHP
Balboa High School (SAUO) ... BHS
Balboa/Albrook [*Panama*] [*ICAO location identifier*] (ICLI) ... MPLB
Balch Institute [*Philadelphia, PA*] ... BI
Balch Institute Library, Philadelphia, PA [*OCLC symbol*] (OCLC) ... BAI
Balch Institute, Philadelphia, PA [*Library symbol*] [*Library of Congress*] (LCLS) ... PPBI
Balch Springs, TX [*AM radio station call letters*] ... KSKY
Balchem Corp. [*Associated Press*] (SAG) ... Balchem
Balchem Corp. [*AMEX symbol*] (SAG) ... BCP
Balco Industries [*Toronto Stock Exchange symbol*] [*Vancouver Stock Exchange symbol*] ... BFP
Balcones Research Center (SAUO) ... BRC
balconette (SAUS) ... balc
Balcony (NTIO) ... bal
Balcony (WDAA) ... BAL
Balcony [*Classified advertising*] (ADA) ... BALC
Balcony (ADWA) ... balc
Balcony [*Travel industry*] (TRID) ... BLCY
Balcor Resources Corp. [*Vancouver Stock Exchange symbol*] ... BAL
Bald Eagle [*District of Columbia*] [*Seismograph station code, US Geological Survey*] [*Closed*] (SEIS) ... BED
Bald Eagle Protection Act [*1940*] ... BEPA
Bald Eagle Total Value ... BETV
Bald Headed Men of America (SAUO) ... BHMA
Bald Knob, AR [*AM radio station call letters*] ... KAPZ
Bald Knob, AR [*FM radio station call letters*] ... KKSY
Bald with Bridgework, Bifocals, Baywindow, and Bunions [*A humorous unofficial Selective Service Class*] ... 5B
Baldachino (VRA) ... baldc
Baldasseroni on Maritime Law [*A publication*] (DLA) ... Bald
Baldasseroni on Maritime Law [*A publication*] (DLA) ... Bald CC
Baldeva Ram Dave. Privy Council Judgment [*India*] [*A publication*] (DLA) ... Baldev PC
Baldeva Ram Dave. Privy Council Judgment [*India*] [*A publication*] (DLA) ... Bal RD
Baldor Electric [*NYSE symbol*] (TTSB) ... BEZ
Baldor Electric Co. [*Associated Press*] (SAG) ... Baldor
Baldus & Cole, Statistical Proof of Discrimination (SAUS) ... SPD
Baldus Bartolinus Novellus [*Deceased, 1490*] [*Authority cited in pre-1607 legal work*] (DSA) ... Bald Novell
Baldus Bartolinus Novellus [*Deceased, 1490*] [*Authority cited in pre-1607 legal work*] (DSA) ... Bal Novel
Baldus (Commentator on the Code) [*A publication*] (DLA) ... Bald
Baldus (Commentator on the Code) [*A publication*] (DLA) ... Bald CC
Baldus de Ubaldis [*Deceased, 1400*] [*Authority cited in pre-1607 legal work*] (DSA) ... B
Baldus de Ubaldis [*Deceased, 1400*] [*Authority cited in pre-1607 legal work*] (DSA) ... Bal
Baldwin & Lyons Cl'A' [*NASDAQ symbol*] (TTSB) ... BWINA
Baldwin & Lyons Cl'B' [*NASDAQ symbol*] (TTSB) ... BWINB
Baldwin & Lyons, Inc. [*Associated Press*] (SAG) ... BaldLy
Baldwin & Lyons, Inc. [*Associated Press*] (SAG) ... BaldLyB
Baldwin & Lyons, Inc. [*Associated Press*] (SAG) ... BaldwLy
Baldwin & Lyons, Inc. [*NASDAQ symbol*] (NQ) ... BWIN
Baldwin. Appendix to 11 Peters [*A publication*] (DLA) ... Bald App 11 Pet
Baldwin City, KS [*FM radio station call letters*] ... KNBU
Baldwin, FL [*FM radio station call letters*] ... WXQL
Baldwin. Law of Bankruptcy [*11th ed.*] [*1915*] [*A publication*] (DLA) ... Bald Bank
Baldwin Locomotive Works, Eddystone, PA [*Library symbol*] [*Library of Congress*] [*Obsolete*] (LCLS) ... PEddyB
Baldwin on Bankruptcy [*A publication*] (DLA) ... Baldwin
Baldwin Piano [*NASDAQ symbol*] (SAG) ... BPAO
Baldwin Piano & Organ [*NASDAQ symbol*] (TTSB) ... BPAO
Baldwin Piano & Organ Co. [*Associated Press*] (SAG) ... BaldPia
Baldwin Piano & Organ Co. (EFIS) ... BPO
Baldwin Public Library, Baldwin (SAUS) ... NBald
Baldwin Public Library, Baldwin, NY [*Library symbol*] [*Library of Congress*] (LCLS) ... NBald
Baldwin Public Library, Birmingham, MI [*Library symbol*] [*Library of Congress*] (LCLS) ... MiBir
Baldwin Senior High School, Baldwin, NY [*Library symbol*] [*Library of Congress*] (LCLS) ... NBaldSH
Baldwin Technology Corp. [*Associated Press*] (SAG) ... Baldw
Baldwin Technology Corp. [*AMEX symbol*] (SPSG) ... BLD
Baldwin Technology'A' [*AMEX symbol*] (TTSB) ... BLD
Baldwin Wallace College (SAUS) ... BWD
Baldwin-Lima-Hamilton Co., Inc. (SAUO) ... BLH
Baldwin's Connecticut Digest [*A publication*] (DLA) ... Bald Conn Dig
Baldwin's Connecticut Digest [*A publication*] (DLA) ... Baldw Dig
Baldwin's Kentucky Revised Statutes, Annotated [*A publication*] (DLA) ... KY Rev Stat Ann
Baldwin's Patent, Copyright, Trade-Mark Cases [*A publication*] (DLA) ... Bald Pat Cas
Baldwin's Patent, Copyright, Trade-Mark Cases [*A publication*] (DLA) ... Bald Pat Etc Cas
Baldwin's United States Circuit Court Reports [*A publication*] (DLA) ... Bald
Baldwin's United States Circuit Court Reports [*A publication*] (DLA) ... Bald CC
Baldwin's United States Circuit Court Reports [*A publication*] (DLA) ... Bald Cir C
Baldwin's United States Circuit Court Reports [*A publication*] (DLA) ... Bald Rep
Baldwin's United States Circuit Court Reports [*A publication*] (DLA) ... Baldw
Baldwin's United States Circuit Court Reports [*A publication*] (DLA) ... Baldwin's CC US Rep
Baldwin's United States Circuit Court Reports [*A publication*] (DLA) ... Baldwin's Rep
Baldwin's View of the United States Constitution with Opinions [*A publication*] (DLA) ... Bald Const
Baldwin's View of the United States Constitution with Opinions [*A publication*] (DLA) ... Bald Op
Baldwinsville, NY [*FM radio station call letters*] ... WBXL
Baldwinsville, NY [*AM radio station call letters*] ... WFBL
Baldwinsville, NY [*FM radio station call letters*] ... WSEN
Baldwin-Wallace College [*Berea, OH*] ... BWC
Baldwin-Wallace College, Berea, OH [*Library symbol*] [*Library of Congress*] (LCLS) ... OBerB
Baldwin-Wallace College, Berea, OH [*OCLC symbol*] (OCLC) ... OXB
Baldwyn, MS [*FM radio station call letters*] ... WESE
Baldy Mountain, MB [*Television station call letters*] ... CBWST
Bale [*Shipping*] ... B
Bale ... BE
Bale ... BL
Bale (ADWA) ... bl
Bale [*Switzerland*] [*ICAO location identifier*] (ICLI) ... LSZM
Bale Feet, Cubic (SAUS) ... bfc
Bale Mountains National Park (SAUS) ... BMNP
Baleares (SAUS) ... Bal
Balearic Islands ... BAL IS
Balearic Islands ... Bal Isls
Balearic Islands (SAUS) ... Bals
Balearic Islands ... BI
Balearic Islands (SAUO) ... BI
Baled ... Bld
Bale/Grain (SAUS) ... b/g
Bale/Mulhouse [*France/Switzerland*] [*ICAO location identifier*] (ICLI) ... LFSB
Balen/Keiheuvel [*Belgium*] [*ICAO location identifier*] (ICLI) ... EBKH
Baler, Aurora Sub-Province [*Philippines*] [*ICAO location identifier*] (ICLI) ... RPUR
Bales (MARI) ... Bls
Bales (SAUS) ... B/s
Bales of Cotton [*Shipping*] ... B/C

Bales or Rolls [Freight] .... B or R
Balescu-Lenard-Quernsey Equation (SAUS) .... BLQ Equation
Balfour Declaration [1917] [For protection of the Jewish settlement of Palestine] (BJA) .... BD
Balfour's Practice Laws of Scotland [A publication] (DLA) .... Balf
Balfour's Practice Laws of Scotland [A publication] (DLA) .... Balf Pr
Bali [Papua New Guinea] [Airport symbol] (OAG) .... BAJ
Bali [Cameroon] [Airport symbol] (OAG) .... BLC
Bali [Cameroon] [ICAO location identifier] (ICLI) .... FKKG
Bali [Indonesia] [ICAO location identifier] (ICLI) .... WRRZ
Bali International Air Service [Indonesia] [ICAO designator] (FAAC) .... BLN
Bali International/Ngurah Rai [Indonesia] [ICAO location identifier] (ICLI) .... WRRR
Balikesir [Turkey] [Airport symbol] (AD) .... BZI
Balikesir [Turkey] [ICAO location identifier] (ICLI) .... LTBF
Balikpapan [Indonesia] [Airport symbol] (OAG) .... BPN
Balikpapan/Sepinggan [Indonesia] [ICAO location identifier] (ICLI) .... WRLL
Balimo [Papua New Guinea] [Airport symbol] (OAG) .... OPU
Balkan [ICAO designator] (AD) .... LZ
Balkan Endemic Nephropathy [Medicine] (MELL) .... BEN
Balkan Environment Research and Development Institute (SAUS) .... BERDI
Balkan grippe or nine-mile fever (SAUS) .... Q fever
Balkan Intelligence Centre [British] [World War II] .... BIC
Balkan Supply Center [Navy] .... BSC
Balkan Turks of America [Later, BTAA] (EA) .... BTA
Balkan Turks of America Association (EA) .... BTAA
Balkan-Bulgarian Airlines [ICAO designator] (FAAC) .... LAZ
Balkan-ji-Bari International [Children's Own Garden International - COGI] (EAIO) .... BjBI
Balks [Baseball] .... BK
Ball .... B
Ball .... BA
Ball Aerospace Systems Division (NAKS) .... BASD
Ball and Beatty's Irish Chancery Reports [1807-14] [A publication] (ILCA) .... Ba & B
Ball and Beatty's Irish Chancery Reports [1807-14] [A publication] (DLA) .... Ba & Be
Ball and Beatty's Irish Chancery Reports [1807-14] [A publication] (DLA) .... Ball & B
Ball and Beatty's Irish Chancery Reports [1807-14] [A publication] (DLA) .... Ball & Beatty
Ball and Beatty's Irish Chancery Reports [1807-14] [A publication] (DLA) .... Ball & B (Ir)
Ball and Beatty's Irish Chancery Reports [1807-14] [A publication] (DLA) .... B & B
Ball and Chain [Slang for a wife] .... B & C
Ball and Flange (SAUS) .... B&F
Ball and Lever (SAUS) .... B&L
Ball and Roller Bearing Manufacturers Association (SAUO) .... BRBMA
Ball and Socket Joint .... BSJ
Ball and Socket Upper Bearing .... BSUB
Ball and Tube [Photography] .... B & T
Ball Bearing [Technical drawings] .... BB
Ball Bearing .... BBRG
Ball Bearing Joint .... BBJ
Ball Bearing Swivel Joint .... BBSJ
Ball Bearing Torque .... BBT
Ball Bearings (SAUS) .... BBs
Ball Brothers Research Corp., Boulder, CO [Library symbol] [Library of Congress] (LCLS) .... CoBBRC
Ball Brothers Research Corporation (SAUO) .... BBRC
Ball Change [Dance terminology] .... BC
Ball Check Valve .... BCV
Ball Corp. [Associated Press] (SAG) .... Ball
Ball Corp. [NYSE symbol] (SPSG) .... BLL
Ball Grid Array (AAEL) .... BFA
Ball Grid Array (VERA) .... BGA
Ball Joint [Automotive engineering] .... B/JNT
Ball Joint Actuator .... BJA
Ball Joint Fitting .... BJF
Ball, LA [FM radio station call letters] (BROA) .... KHFX-FM
Ball, LA [AM radio station call letters] .... KWDF
Ball Lightning .... BL
Ball Limiting Memory (SAUS) .... BLM
Ball Lock Pin .... BLP
Ball Manufacturers Engineers Committee (EA) .... BMEC
Ball on Back (DAVI) .... BOB
Ball On Cylinder Lubricity Evaluator [Fuels and lubricants testing] .... BOCLE
Ball on National Banks [A publication] (DLA) .... Ball Banks
Ball on National Banks [A publication] (DLA) .... BB
Ball On Three Disk .... BOTD
Ball Reduction Drive .... BRD
Ball Space Systems Division (SAUS) .... BSSD
Ball Spin Frequency [Machinery] .... BSF
Ball Spinning Friction .... BSF
Ball State Teachers College [Later, Ball State University] [Indiana] .... BSTC
Ball State University .... Ball St U
Ball State University, Muncie, IN [OCLC symbol] (OCLC) .... IBS
Ball State University, Muncie, IN [Library symbol] [Library of Congress] (LCLS) .... InMuB
Ball Stop (SAUS) .... BSP
Ball Tooth Gear .... BTG
Ball Tooth Gear Joint .... BTGJ
Ball Tooth Joint .... BTJ
[The] Ballad Book [A publication] .... BaBo
Ballantine Laboratories, Inc. (SAUO) .... BL

Ballantine. Statute of Limitations [1810] [A publication] (DLA) .... Ball Lim
Ballantine/Del Rey/Fawcett/Ivy [Publishing group] .... B/DR/F/I
Ballantyne of Omaha, Inc. [Associated Press] (SAG) .... Ballntyn
Ballantyne of Omaha, Inc. [AMEX symbol] (SAG) .... BTN
Ballarat Music Lovers' Club [Australia] .... BMLC
Ballarat Tramway Preservation Society [Australia] .... BTPS
Ballard Community Hospital Library, Seattle, WA [Library symbol] [Library of Congress] (LCLS) .... WaSBH
Ballard Medical Products [Associated Press] (SAG) .... Ballard
Ballard Medical Products [NYSE symbol] (SPSG) .... BMP
Ballard Power Systems [NASDAQ symbol] (SG) .... BLDP
Ballard Power Systems [NASDAQ symbol] (TTSB) .... BLDPF
Ballard Power Systems, Inc. [Associated Press] (SAG) .... Ballard
Ballard Power Systems, Inc. [NASDAQ symbol] (SAG) .... BLDP
Ballard Research, Inc., North Vancouver, BC, Canada [Library symbol] [Library of Congress] (LCLS) .... CaBNvBR
Ballard Research, Inc., North Vancouver, British Columbia [Library symbol] [National Library of Canada] (NLC) .... BNVBR
Ballard's Somerton Court Rolls [Oxford Archaeological Society, No. 50] [England] [A publication] (DLA) .... Ball
Ballast (IAA) .... B
Ballast (KSC) .... BALL
Ballast (MSA) .... BLST
Ballast Aerating Retrieval Boom (MCD) .... BARB
Ballast Control Panel .... BCP
Ballast Flood Valve .... BFV
Ballast Lamp .... BALL LP
Ballast Lumen Factor (PDAA) .... BLF
Ballast Rack (MCD) .... BR
Ballast, Sand and Allied Trades Association (SAUO) .... BSATA
Ballast Tank Meter .... BTM
Ballast Tube (IAA) .... BALLT
Ballast Tube Resistor .... BTR
Ballast Undercutter-Cleaner (SAUS) .... BUC
Ballastable Earthmoving Sectionalized Tractor [Formerly, UET] [Army] .... BEST
Ballastable Tractor .... BALTRAC
Ballatar Explorations [Vancouver Stock Exchange symbol] .... BLE
Ball-Burton-Hill-Hatch Plan [Senate resolution calling for international cooperation during wartime, named after four senators who introduced plan] B2H2
Balled [Freight] .... BLD
Balled and Burlapped [Plant industry] .... B & B
Ballen Booksellers International, Inc. [UTLAS symbol] .... BII
Ballentine's Law Dictionary [A publication] (DLA) .... Ballentine
Ballentine's Self Pronouncing Law Dictionary [A publication] (DLA) .... Ballentine's Law Dict
Baller .... BLLR
Ballerup (SAUS) .... Ball
Ballet America Concert Dancers .... BACD
Ballet Contemporani de Barcelona .... BCB
Ballet Intensive from Moscow .... BIM
Ballet Theatre Foundation (EA) .... BTF
Ballet Theatre of Queensland [Australia] .... BTQ
Ballets de San Juan [Puerto Rico] .... BST
Ballett der Deutschen Opera [Berlin] .... BDO
Balletto di Toscana [Florence, Italy] .... BDT
Ballina [Australia] [Airport symbol] .... BNK
Ballinger Publishing Co. .... B
Ballinger, TX [FM radio station call letters] (RBYB) .... KCSE-FM
Ballinger, TX [AM radio station call letters] .... KRUN
Ballinger, TX [FM radio station call letters] .... KRUN-FM
Ballinger's Annotated Codes and Statutes [Washington] [A publication] (DLA) .... Bal Ann Codes
Ballinger's Annotated Codes and Statutes [Washington] [A publication] (DLA) .... Ballinger's Ann Codes & St
Balliol College [Oxford, England] (BARN) .... Ball
Balliol College (SAUO) .... BC
Balliol College, Oxford (SAUO) .... Ball
Ballismus (SAUS) .... Ball
Ballistic .... B
Ballistic [or Ballistics] (MSA) .... BAL
Ballistic (AFM) .... BALL
Ballistic Advanced Missile (MCD) .... BAM
Ballistic Aerial Target System .... BATS
Ballistic Aimpoint [Military] (CAAL) .... BAP
Ballistic Analysis Research System .... BARS
Ballistic and LASER Eye Protection Spectacles [Army] (INF) .... BLEPS
Ballistic & Laser Protection Spectacles (SAUS) .... BLPS
Ballistic and LASER Protective Spectacles [Military] (RDA) .... BLPS
Ballistic Anti-ballistic Missile Boost Intercept (SAUS) .... BAMBI
Ballistic Armor Subsystem [Military] (DOMA) .... BASS
Ballistic Attack Game .... BAG
Ballistic Camera .... BC
Ballistic Camera Control (KSC) .... BCC
Ballistic Coefficient .... BC
Ballistic Compressor Computer Code .... BCCC
Ballistic Computation Technology (SAUS) .... BCT
Ballistic Computer System (SAUS) .... BCS
Ballistic Computer Systems (AAGC) .... BCS
Ballistic Computer/Weapon Controller (SAUS) .... BC/WC
Ballistic Correction of the Moment .... BCM
Ballistic Correction to Normal .... BCN
Ballistic Damage Tolerance (MCD) .... BDT
Ballistic Data Acquisition System (MCD) .... BALDAS
Ballistic Defense Missile .... BDM

Ballistic Density ... BALDNY
Ballistic Electron Emission Microscopy ... BEEM
Ballistic Electron Emission Spectroscopy ... BEEM
Ballistic Electron Emmission Spectroscopy (AAEL) ... BEEM
Ballistic Environmental Characteristics and Measurement Program [*Army*] (AABC) ... BECAMP
Ballistic Evaluation Motor (MCD) ... BEM
Ballistic Evaluation Static Test (MCD) ... BEST
Ballistic Flight Test Missile (MCD) ... BFTM
Ballistic Height Correction ... BHC
Ballistic Hull and Turret Vehicle (MCD) ... BH & T
Ballistic Identification (SAUS) ... BALID
Ballistic Intercept Missile (SAUS) ... BIM
Ballistic LASER Holographic System (MCD) ... BLHS
Ballistic LASER Protection System [*Army*] (INF) ... BLEPS
Ballistic Loran Assist Device (SAUS) ... BALLAD
Ballistic Missile (MUGU) ... BALMI
Ballistic Missile (AFM) ... BM
Ballistic Missile Acquisition RADAR ... BMAR
Ballistic Missile Analyst Technician (SAUS) ... BMAT
Ballistic Missile Analyst Technician-Specialist ... BMAT/S
Ballistic Missile Bombardment [*or Boost*] **Interceptor** [*Military*] ... BAMBI
Ballistic Missile Bombardment Interceptor (SAUS) ... BAMBI
Ballistic Missile Boost Intercept (SAUS) ... BAMBI
Ballistic Missile Branch ... BMB
Ballistic Missile Burning Intercept (SAUS) ... BAMBI
Ballistic Missile Center [*Air Materiel Command*] [*Obsolete*] ... BMC
Ballistic Missile Center, Air Materiel Command [*Obsolete*] ... BMC/AMC
Ballistic Missile Checker (SAUS) ... BMC
Ballistic Missile Checkout Equipment Technician-Specialist ... BMCET/S
Ballistic Missile Construction Office ... BMCO
Ballistic Missile Cost Study (SAUS) ... BMCS
Ballistic Missile Defense ... BMD
Ballistic Missile Defense - Nuclear Effects and Threat Committee (AABC) ... BMD-NEAT
Ballistic Missile Defense Advanced Technology Center (AABC) ... BMDATC
Ballistic Missile Defense Center (MCD) ... BMDC
Ballistic Missile Defense Command ... BMDC
Ballistic Missile Defense Command Post (AABC) ... BMDCP
Ballistic Missile Defense Committee ... BMDC
Ballistic Missile Defense Communications Agency (SAUS) ... BMDCA
Ballistic Missile Defense Emergency Action Report (AABC) ... BMDEAR
Ballistic Missile Defense Engagement Simulator ... BMDES
Ballistic Missile Defense Integrated Training Plan (AABC) ... BMDITP
Ballistic Missile Defense Master Plan (AABC) ... BMDMP
Ballistic Missile Defense Materials Program Office (MCD) ... BMDMPO
Ballistic Missile Defense Missile Battalion (AABC) ... BMDMB
Ballistic Missile Defense Operations [*or Organization*] [*or Office*] (AABC) ... BMDO
Ballistic Missile Defense Operations Activity (AABC) ... BMDOA
Ballistic Missile Defense Operations Center (ACAE) ... BMDOC
Ballistic Missile Defense Organization ... BMDO
Ballistic Missile Defense Organization (AAGC) ... BUDO
Ballistic Missile Defense Program Manager (AABC) ... BMDPM
Ballistic Missile Defense Program Office (AABC) ... BMDPO
Ballistic Missile Defense Surveillance Battalion (AABC) ... BMDSB
Ballistic Missile Defense System ... BMDS
Ballistic Missile Defense Systems Command [*Huntsville, AL*] ... BMD
Ballistic Missile Defense Systems Command (ACAE) ... BMDSC
Ballistic Missile Defense Systems Command (AABC) ... BMDSCOM
Ballistic Missile Defense Systems Technology Program (SAUO) ... BMDSTP
Ballistic Missile Defense Test and Evaluation Center (ACAE) ... BMDTEC
Ballistic Missile Defense-Nuclear Effects and Threat Committee (SAUS) ... BMD-NEAT Committee
Ballistic Missile Division [*Ballistic Research Laboratory*] ... BMD
Ballistic Missile Division - Field Office [*Ballistic Research Laboratory*] (SAA) ... BMD-FO
Ballistic Missile Division Field Office (SAUO) ... BMDFO
Ballistic Missile Early Warning [*System*] ... BMEW
Ballistic Missile Early Warning System ... BMEWS
Ballistic Missile Inertial Guidance Technician (IAA) ... BMIGT
Ballistic Missile Inertial Guidance Technician-Mechanic ... BMIGT/M
Ballistic Missile Interceptor ... BMI
Ballistic Missile Launch Equipment Technician-Repairman ... BMLET/R
Ballistic Missile Logistics Office ... BMLO
Ballistic Missile Manager ... BMM
Ballistic Missile Office [*Norton Air Force Base, CA*] [*United States Air Force Systems Command*] (GRD) ... BMO
Ballistic Missile Operational Training Readiness ... BMOTR
Ballistic Missile Organization (SAUS) ... BMO
Ballistic Missile Orientation Course ... BMOC
Ballistic Missile Radiation Analysis Center ... BAMIRAC
Ballistic Missile Reentry System ... BMRS
Ballistic Missile Reentry System (AABC) ... BMRSYS
Ballistic Missile Ship [*Navy*] ... BMS
Ballistic Missile Specification (IAA) ... BMS
Ballistic Missile Submarine [*Navy symbol*] ... SSB
Ballistic Missile Surface Force ... BMSF
Ballistic Missile System Branch (SAUO) ... BMSB
Ballistic Missile Systems Command [*Army*] (RDA) ... BMSC
Ballistic Missile Target System (MCD) ... BMTS
Ballistic Missile Technology (ADWA) ... BMT
Ballistic Missile Terminal Defense ... BMTD
Ballistic Missile Test System (IEEE) ... BMTS
Ballistic Missile Test Vessel ... BMTV
Ballistic Missile Threat (ACAE) ... BMT
Ballistic Missile Weapon System (SAUS) ... BMWS
Ballistic Missile with Self Contained Guidance (SAUO) ... LANCE
Ballistic Missiles Committee (SAUO) ... BMC
Ballistic Missiles European Task Organization [*Military*] ... BMETO
Ballistic Missiles Management Group (SAUO) ... BMMG
Ballistic Missiles Weapon System ... BMWS
Ballistic Missle Defense Control Center (ACAE) ... BMDCC
Ballistic Number (MCD) ... BN
Ballistic Offense Suppressive System [*Military*] ... BOSS
Ballistic Offensive Suppression System (SAUS) ... BOSS
Ballistic Particle Manufacturing [*Desktop manufacturing*] ... BPM
Ballistic Processor [*Military*] (CAAL) ... BP
Ballistic Protected Shelter (MCD) ... BPS
Ballistic Range for Aircraft Survivability Studies (DNAB) ... BRASS
Ballistic Recording System ... BRS
Ballistic Recoverable Booster (MCD) ... BRB
Ballistic Recovery of Orbiting Man (KSC) ... BROOM
Ballistic Reentry Body ... BRB
Ballistic Reentry Vehicle ... BRV
Ballistic Research Laboratories (SAUO) ... BLR
Ballistic Research Laboratories Electronic Scientific Computer ... BRLESC
Ballistic Research Laboratory [*Aberdeen Proving Ground, MD*] [*Army*] ... BRL
Ballistic Rocket Air Suppression ... BRAS
Ballistic Shell ... BS
Ballistic Sight Technology Improving Night/(Day) Gunnery [*Project*] [*Military*] ... BSTING
Ballistic Simulated Round (MCD) ... BSR
Ballistic Systems Division [*Norton Air Force Base, CA*] ... BSD
Ballistic Systems Education Division [*Air University*] [*Air Force*] ... BSED
Ballistic Systems Zeus [*Aerospace*] ... BSZ
Ballistic Test and Evaluation Systems (KSC) ... BATES
Ballistic Test Evaluation and Sealing (SAUS) ... BATES
Ballistic Test Facility [*Air Research and Development Command*] (AAG) ... BTF
Ballistic Test Site Terminal (MCD) ... BTST
Ballistic Test Submodule (RDA) ... BTSM
Ballistic Track Assignor (AAG) ... BTA
Ballistic Trajectory (DNAB) ... BT
Ballistic Trajectory calculators allowing for Meteorological conditions (SAUS) ... BALMET
Ballistic Wind ... BALLWIN
Ballistic Wind ... BALWND
Ballistic Wind Plotter ... BWP
Ballistically Launched Aerodynamic Missile ... BLAM
Ballistic/Laser Armour Protective Posture (SAUS) ... BLAPP
Ballistic/Laser Eyeware Protective System (SAUS) ... BLEPS
Ballistics Computer Unit ... BCU
Ballistics Dispensing System (MCD) ... BDS
Ballistics Force Integrator and Analyzer System (MCD) ... BFIAS
Ballistics Identification (SAUS) ... BALID
Ballistocardiogram [*Medicine*] ... BCG
Ball-Jointed [*Body*] [*Doll collecting*] ... bj
Ball-Lock Separation Bolt ... BLSB
Ballon De Servance [*France*] [*Seismograph station code, US Geological Survey*] (SEIS) ... BSF
Balloon (AFM) ... BLN
Balloon Altitude Mosaic Measurements (MCD) ... BAMM
Balloon and Nike Scaled High Explosive Experiment (KSC) ... BANSHEE
Balloon and Parachute (SAUS) ... BALLUTE
Balloon Angioplasty [*Medicine*] (MELL) ... BA
Balloon Aortic Valvuloplasty [*Medicine*] (MELL) ... BAV
Balloon Aortic Valvuloplasty [*Cardiology*] (DAVI) ... BAVP
Balloon Astronomy ... BALAST
Balloon Atmospheric Propagation Experiment [*NASA*] ... BAPE
Balloon Atrial Septostomy [*Cardiology*] (DMAA) ... BAS
Balloon Barrage ... BB
Balloon Barrage Group (SAUO) ... BBG
Balloon Barrage Training Center [*Army*] ... BBTC
Balloon Catheter [*Medicine*] (MELL) ... BC
Balloon Catheter Angioplasty ... BCA
Balloon Command (DAS) ... BC
Balloon Command (SAUO) ... BC
Balloon Corps (SAUO) ... BC
Balloon Destroyer [*British*] ... BD
Balloon Dilation Angioplasty [*Cardiology*] (DMAA) ... BDA
Balloon Electronics Package (SAUS) ... BEP
Balloon Federation of America (EA) ... BFA
Balloon Infrared Astronomy Platform ... BIRAP
Balloon Interrogation Package ... BIP
Balloon Launch Drop Test Vehicle (SAUS) ... BLDTV
Balloon Launching Station ... BLS
Balloon Microwave Limb Sounder (SAUS) ... BMLS
Balloon Observations of Millimetric Extragalactic Radiation and Geophysics (SAUS) ... BOOMERANG
Balloon Parachute ... BALLUTE
Balloon Parachute (SAUS) ... BALUTE
Balloon Platoon of America [*Later, HBC*] (EA) ... BPA
Balloon Post Collectors Club (EA) ... BPCC
Balloon Radio System ... BRS
Balloon Squadron (SAUO) ... BS
Balloon Supported Rocket ... BSR
Balloon Telecom Manager (SAUS) ... BTM
Balloon Temperature and Humidity [*Sonde*] [*Meteorology*] ... BALTHUM
Balloon Training Unit (SAUO) ... BTU
Balloon Training Unit (SAUS) ... BTU
Balloon Transport System ... BTS

Balloon Valvuloplasty [*Medicine*] (MELL) .... BVP
Balloon-Assisted Takeoff [*Air Force*] .... BATO
Balloon-Borne Astronomical Studies (MCD) .... BBAS
Balloon-Borne Filter .... BBF
Balloon-Borne Filter Radiometer .... BBFR
Balloon-Borne LASER In-Situ Sensor [*Spectrometer*] .... BLISS
Balloon-Borne Microwave Limb Sounder [*Atmospheric research*] .... BMLS
Balloon-Borne Nephelometer .... BBN
Balloon-Borne Particle Counter (SAUS) .... DUSTSONDE
Balloon-Borne Polar Nephelometer .... BBPN
Balloon-Borne Polar Nephelometer .... BPN
Balloon-Borne Radio .... BBR
Balloon-Borne Radio System .... BBRS
Balloon-Borne Solar Pointer .... BBSP
Balloon-Borne Sounding System (ARMP) .... BBSS
Balloon-Borne Ultraviolet Stellar Spectrometer .... BUSS
Balloon-Launched Decelerator Test [*Air Force*] .... BLDT
Balloon-Tipped Catheter [*Medicine*] (MELL) .... BTC
Ball-Pass Frequency, Inner Race [*Machinery*] .... BPF(I)
Ball-Pass Frequency, Outer Race [*Machinery*] .... BPF(O)
Ballroom .... BLLRM
Ballroom Dancers Federation [*British*] (DBA) .... BDF
Ball's Digest of the Common Law [*A publication*] (DLA) .... Ball Dig
Ball's Index to Irish Statutes [*A publication*] (DLA) .... Ball Ind
Ball's Popular Conveyancer [*A publication*] (DLA) .... Ball Conv
Ball's Student Guide to the Bar [*A publication*] (DLA) .... Ball St Guide
Ballston Spa, NY [*FM radio station call letters*] (RBYB) .... WXCR-FM
Ballston Spa, NY [*FM radio station call letters*] .... WZRQ
Ballstop (MSA) .... BSP
Ball-Strut-Tie-Rod Assembly (SAUS) .... BSTRA
Ball-Valve Assembly (SAUS) .... BVA
Ballwin, MO [*FM radio station call letters*] .... KYMC
Bally Entertainment Corp. [*Formerly, Bally Manufacturing*] [*Associated Press*] (SAG) .... BallyEnt
Bally Entertainment Corp. [*Formerly, Bally Manufacturing*] [*NYSE symbol*] (SAG) .... BLY
Bally Entertain't8.00%'PRIDES' [*NYSE symbol*] (TTSB) .... BLYPrP
Bally Gaming International [*NASDAQ symbol*] (SPSG) .... BGII
Bally Gaming International Corp. [*Associated Press*] (SAG) .... BalyGm
Bally Gaming Intl. [*NASDAQ symbol*] (TTSB) .... BGII
Bally Manufacturing Comp. (SAUO) .... BLY
Bally Total Fitness Holding [*NYSE symbol*] (SG) .... BFT
Bally Total Fitness Holding Corp. [*Associated Press*] (SAG) .... BallyTot
Bally Total Fitness Holding Corp. [*NASDAQ symbol*] (SAG) .... BFIT
Ballykelly [*British*] [*ICAO location identifier*] (ICLI) .... EGQB
Bally's Grand [*NASDAQ symbol*] (TTSB) .... BGLV
Ballys Grand, Inc. [*Associated Press*] (SAG) .... Ballys
Ballys Grand, Inc. [*Associated Press*] (SAG) .... BallysGr
Ballys Grand, Inc. [*NASDAQ symbol*] (SAG) .... BGLV
Ballys Grand Wrrt [*NASDAQ symbol*] (TTSB) .... BGLVW
Balmaceda [*Chile*] [*Airport symbol*] (OAG) .... BBA
Balmaceda/Balmaceda [*Chile*] [*ICAO location identifier*] (ICLI) .... SCBA
Balmertown Public Library, Ontario [*Library symbol*] [*National Library of Canada*] (NLC) .... OBAL
Balmoral Shoe [*Orthosis*] .... Bal
Balneum [*Bath*] [*Medicine*] .... B
Balneum [*Bath*] [*Medicine*] (ROG) .... BALN
Balneum Arenae [*Sand Bath*] [*Medicine*] .... BA
Balneum Arenae [*Sand Bath*] [*Medicine*] .... BAL ARENAE
Balneum Calidum [*Warm Bath*] [*Medicine*] (ROG) .... BALN CAL
Balneum Mariae [*Salt-Water Bath*] [*Medicine*] .... BAL MAR
Balneum Marinum [*Sea-Water Bath*] [*Medicine*] .... BM
Balneum Vaporis [*Vapor Bath*] [*Medicine*] .... BAL VAP
Balneum Vaporis [*Vapor Bath*] [*Medicine*] .... BV
Balopticon [*An opaque projector*] (WDMC) .... balop
Balopticon (IEEE) .... BALOP
Balopticon (SAUS) .... Balop
Balsa Wood (VRA) .... bal wd
Balsam Lake, WI [*FM radio station call letters*] (RBYB) .... WWLC-FM
Balsam Resources, Inc. [*Vancouver Stock Exchange symbol*] .... BSM
Balsam School, Bovey, MN [*Library symbol*] [*Library of Congress*] (LCLS) .... MnBovS
Balsamic [*Mild, Healing*] [*Medicine*] (ROG) .... BAL
Balsamum [*Balsam*] [*Pharmacy*] .... BALS
Balsas [*Brazil*] [*Airport symbol*] (AD) .... BSS
Baltek Corp. [*Associated Press*] (SAG) .... Baltek
Baltek Corp. [*NASDAQ symbol*] (NQ) .... BTEK
Balthazar Scales of Adaptive Behavior [*Psychology*] .... BSAB
Baltia Air Lines, Inc. [*ICAO designator*] (FAAC) .... BTL
Baltic (ADWA) .... Balt
Baltic [*MARC language code*] [*Library of Congress*] (LCCP) .... bat
Baltic (SAUS) .... Bltc
Baltic Airlines Ltd. [*ICAO designator*] (FAAC) .... HOT
Baltic Air-Sea Ice Study (SAUS) .... BASIS
Baltic American Freedom League (EA) .... BAFL
Baltic and Bothnian Echoes from the Lithosphere [*Collaborative seismic project*] [*Britain, Denmark, Finland, Germany, and Sweden*] .... BABEL
Baltic and International Maritime Conference (SAUO) .... BIMC
Baltic and International Maritime Conference [*or Council*] [*Copenhagen, Denmark*] (EAIO) .... BIMCO
Baltic and International Maritime Conference Uniform Time Charter Party for Offshore Service Vessels (SAUS) .... Supplytime
Baltic and International Maritime Council (SAUO) .... BIMCO
Baltic and North Sea Radiotelephone Conference (SAUO) .... BNRC
Baltic and North Sea Telecommunication Meeting (SAUO) .... BNTM
Baltic Appeal to the United Nations (SAUO) .... BATUN
Baltic Approaches (SAUS) .... Baltap
Baltic Aviation, Inc. [*ICAO designator*] (FAAC) .... BLT
Baltic Bankers Ltd. [*Finland*] .... BBL
Baltic BATHY-TESAC Pilot Project (SAUS) .... BALTEPP
Baltic Conference Ready Berth Clause 1938 (SAUS) .... Readyberth
Baltic Conference Stoppage of Suez Canal Traffic Clause 1956 (SAUS) .... Suezstop
Baltic Conference Waiting for Berth Clause 1962 (SAUS) .... Waitberth
Baltic Council of Victoria [*Australia*] .... BCV
Baltic Dry Index (SAUO) .... BDI
Baltic Experiment for ERS-1 (SAUS) .... BEERS
Baltic Floating University (SAUO) .... BFU
Baltic Freight Index [*of spot market rates*] [*Shipping*] (DS) .... BFI
Baltic Futures Exchange [*British*] (NUMA) .... BFE
Baltic International Airlines [*Latvia*] [*ICAO designator*] (FAAC) .... BIA
Baltic International Freight Futures Exchange [*London, England*] .... BIFFEX
Baltic International USA, Inc. [*Associated Press*] (SAG) .... Baltic
Baltic International USA, Inc. [*Associated Press*] (SAG) .... BalticInt
Baltic International USA, Inc. [*NASDAQ symbol*] (SAG) .... BISA
Baltic Intl USA Wrrt [*NASDAQ symbol*] (TTSB) .... BISAW
Baltic Marine Cooperation (SAUO) .... BMC
Baltic Marine Environment Protection Commission - Helsinki Commission (EAIO) .... HELCOM
Baltic Mercantile and Shipping Exchange (SAUO) .... BMSE
Baltic Monitoring Programme (SAUS) .... BMP
Baltic Open Sea Experiment (GNE) .... BOSEX
Baltic Operations 1982 (SAUO) .... BALTOPS 82
Baltic Operations multi-national exercise (SAUS) .... BALTOPS
Baltic Panamax Index (SAUO) .... BPI
Baltic Pulp and Paper (SAUS) .... BALTPULP
Baltic Research Foundation [*Australia*] (EAIO) .... BRF
Baltic Sea (SAUS) .... BSEA
Baltic Sea Experiment (QUAC) .... BALTEX
Baltic Sea Hydrographic Commission (SAUO) .... BSHC
Baltic Sea Protected Area (SAUS) .... BSPA
Baltic sea region on-Line Environmental information Resources for Internet Access (SAUS) .... BALLERINA
Baltic Sea Salmon Standing Committee (SAUO) .... BSSC
Baltic Sea Seismic Programme (SAUS) .... BABEL
Baltic Sea System Study (SAUS) .... BASYS
Baltic Sea Vertical Mixing and Advection Experiment (SAUS) .... BAVAMEX
Baltic States [*MARC geographic area code*] [*Library of Congress*] (LCCP) .... eb---
Baltic States Freedom Council (SAUO) .... BSFC
Baltic Steamship Co. (MHDB) .... BSC
Baltic Student Federation .... BSF
Baltic Women's Council (EA) .... BWC
Baltic Wood (SAUS) .... Baltwood
Baltic World Conference (SAUO) .... BWC
Baltic World Council [*Defunct*] (EA) .... BWC
Baltimore [*Diocesan abbreviation*] [*Maryland*] (TOCD) .... BAL
Baltimore [*Maryland*] .... BALT
Baltimore [*Maryland*] .... BALTO
Baltimore [*Maryland*] [*Name derived from Baltimore-Washington International Airport*] [*Airport symbol*] .... BWI
Baltimore Aircoil International (SAUO) .... BAC
Baltimore & Annapolis Railroad Co. (IIA) .... B & A
[*The*] **Baltimore & Annapolis Railroad Co.** [*AAR code*] .... BLA
Baltimore and Annapolis Railroad Co. (SAUO) .... BLA
Baltimore & Eastern Railroad Co. [*Absorbed into Consolidated Rail Corp.*] [*AAR code*] .... BE
Baltimore and Ohio (ADWA) .... B&O
Baltimore & Ohio - Chesapeake & Ohio (SAUO) .... B&O-C&O
[*The*] **Baltimore & Ohio Chicago Terminal Railroad Co.** .... B & OCT
[*The*] **Baltimore & Ohio Chicago Terminal Railroad Co.** [*AAR code*] .... BOCT
Baltimore & Ohio Railroad (SAUO) .... B&ORR
[*The*] **Baltimore & Ohio Railroad Co.** [*Chessie System, Inc.*] .... B & O
[*The*] **Baltimore & Ohio Railroad Co.** [*Chessie System, Inc.*] .... B & O RR
Baltimore & Ohio Railroad Co. (SAUO) .... BO
[*The*] **Baltimore & Ohio Railroad Co., Employees' Library, Baltimore, MD** [*Library symbol*] [*Library of Congress*] [*Obsolete*] (LCLS) .... MdBBO
Baltimore & Ohio Railroad Historical Society (EA) .... B & ORHS
Baltimore Bar Library, Baltimore, MD [*Library symbol*] [*Library of Congress*] (LCLS) .... MdBB
Baltimore Biological Laboratory .... BBL
Baltimore City Court House, Baltimore, MD [*Library symbol*] [*Library of Congress*] (LCLS) .... MdBCH
Baltimore City Hospitals, Doctors' Library, Baltimore, MD [*Library symbol*] [*Library of Congress*] (LCLS) .... MdBH
Baltimore City Reports [*A publication*] (DLA) .... Balt C Rep
Baltimore City Reports [*A publication*] (DLA) .... BR
Baltimore College of Commerce [*Maryland*] .... BCC
Baltimore Colts [*National Football League*] [*1950, 1953-83*] (NFLA) .... Bal
Baltimore Conference, Inc., United Methodist Historical Society, Baltimore, MD [*Library symbol*] [*Library of Congress*] (LCLS) .... MdBBC
Baltimore County Public Library, Towson, MD [*Library symbol*] [*Library of Congress*] (LCLS) .... MdBCP
Baltimore Gas and Electric (SAUS) .... BG&E
Baltimore Gas & Electric Co. [*Associated Press*] (SAG) .... BaltGE
Baltimore Gas & Electric Co. [*NYSE symbol*] (SPSG) .... BGE
Baltimore Gas & Electric Co. [*Associated Press*] (SAG) .... BltGE
Baltimore Hebrew College (BJA) .... BHC
Baltimore Hebrew College, Baltimore, MD [*Library symbol*] [*Library of Congress*] (LCLS) .... MdBHC

Baltimore Huntington's Disease Project [*Johns Hopkins University*] [*Research center*] (RCD) .... BHDP
Baltimore Junior College [*Maryland*] .... BJC
Baltimore Law Transcript [*A publication*] (DLA) .... Balt LT
Baltimore Law Transcript [*A publication*] (DLA) .... Balt L Tr
Baltimore Law Transcript [*A publication*] (DLA) .... BLT
Baltimore Longitudinal Study of Aging [*Department of Health and Human Services*] (GFGA) .... BLSA
Baltimore, Maryland, and Ohio .... BM & O
Baltimore, MD [*Location identifier*] [*FAA*] (FAAL) .... FND
Baltimore, MD [*Location identifier*] [*FAA*] (FAAL) .... IUB
Baltimore, MD [*Location identifier*] [*FAA*] (FAAL) .... MDV
Baltimore, MD [*Location identifier*] [*FAA*] (FAAL) .... MTN
Baltimore, MD [*Location identifier*] [*FAA*] (FAAL) .... OEH
Baltimore, MD [*Location identifier*] [*FAA*] (FAAL) .... RUX
Baltimore, MD [*AM radio station call letters*] .... WBAL
Baltimore, MD [*Television station call letters*] (BROA) .... WBAL-DT
Baltimore, MD [*Television station call letters*] .... WBAL-TV
Baltimore, MD [*Television station call letters*] .... WBFF
Baltimore, MD [*AM radio station call letters*] .... WBGR
Baltimore, MD [*FM radio station call letters*] .... WBJC
Baltimore, MD [*AM radio station call letters*] .... WBMD
Baltimore, MD [*FM radio station call letters*] .... WBYQ
Baltimore, MD [*AM radio station call letters*] .... WCAO
Baltimore, MD [*AM radio station call letters*] .... WCBM
Baltimore, MD [*FM radio station call letters*] .... WEAA
Baltimore, MD [*FM radio station call letters*] .... WERQ
Baltimore, MD [*Television station call letters*] .... WHSW
Baltimore, MD [*AM radio station call letters*] .... WITH
Baltimore, MD [*FM radio station call letters*] .... WIYY
Baltimore, MD [*AM radio station call letters*] .... WJFK
Baltimore, MD [*FM radio station call letters*] .... WJHU
Baltimore, MD [*Television station call letters*] .... WJZ
Baltimore, MD [*Television station call letters*] (BROA) .... WJZ-DT
Baltimore, MD [*FM radio station call letters*] .... WLIF
Baltimore, MD [*Television station call letters*] .... WMAR
Baltimore, MD [*Television station call letters*] (BROA) .... WMAR-DT
Baltimore, MD [*Television station call letters*] .... WMPB
Baltimore, MD [*Television station call letters*] .... WNUV
Baltimore, MD [*FM radio station call letters*] .... WOCT
Baltimore, MD [*AM radio station call letters*] .... WOLB
Baltimore, MD [*FM radio station call letters*] .... WPOC
Baltimore, MD [*FM radio station call letters*] .... WRBS
Baltimore, MD [*Television station call letters*] (BROA) .... WUTB
Baltimore, MD [*AM radio station call letters*] .... WWIN
Baltimore, MD [*AM radio station call letters*] .... WWLG
Baltimore, MD [*FM radio station call letters*] .... WWMX
Baltimore, MD [*FM radio station call letters*] .... WXYV
Baltimore Motor Yacht Club (SAUO) .... BMYC
Baltimore Museum of Art (SAUO) .... BMA
Baltimore Museum of Art, Baltimore, MD [*Library symbol*] [*Library of Congress*] (LCLS) .... MdBMA
Baltimore, Ohio & Southwestern Railway .... BO & SW
Baltimore Photo & Blue Print Co., Baltimore, MD [*Library symbol*] [*Library of Congress*] (LCLS) .... BPB
Baltimore Publishers Association (EA) .... BPA
Baltimore Ravens [*National Football League*] [*1996-present*] (NFLA) .... BRv
Baltimore Regional Planning Commission [*Library network*] .... RPC
Baltimore Steam Packet Co. [*AAR code*] .... BSP
Baltimore Symphony Orchestra (SAUO) .... BSO
Baltimore Vegetarians [*Later, VRG*] (EA) .... BV
Baltimore Yacht Club (SAUO) .... BYC
Baltimore/Baltimore-Washington International [*Maryland*] [*ICAO location identifier*] (ICLI) .... KBWI
Baltischer Weltrat [*Baltic World Council*] (EAIO) .... BW
Baluchi [*MARC language code*] [*Library of Congress*] (LCCP) .... bal
Baluchi Students' Organization [*Pakistan*] (PD) .... BSO
Baluchistan (SAUS) .... Baluch
Baluchistan Liberation Front [*Pakistan*] [*Political party*] (PD) .... BLF
Baluchistan, Pakistan (ILCA) .... Bal Pak
Baluhya Political Union (SAUO) .... BPU
Balurghat [*India*] [*ICAO location identifier*] (ICLI) .... VEBG
Balustrade (VRA) .... balstr
Balwin Wallace College (SAUO) .... BWC
Balzac Deflection Door .... BDD
Balzers/FL [*Switzerland*] [*ICAO location identifier*] (ICLI) .... LSXB
Bam [*Iran*] [*ICAO location identifier*] (ICLI) .... OIKM
Bam Bolster Upper (SAUS) .... BBU
Bama Band Fan Club (EA) .... BBFC
Bamaga [*Australia*] [*Airport symbol*] (OAG) .... ABM
Bamako [*Mali*] [*Airport symbol*] (OAG) .... BKO
Bamako [*Mali*] [*ICAO location identifier*] (ICLI) .... GABV
Bamako Initiative Management Unit (SAUO) .... BIMU
Bamako/Senou [*Mali*] [*ICAO location identifier*] (ICLI) .... GABS
Bamar [*Afghanistan*] [*ICAO location identifier*] (ICLI) .... OABR
Bambadinca [*Guinea-Bissau*] [*ICAO location identifier*] (ICLI) .... GGBB
Bambara [*MARC language code*] [*Library of Congress*] (LCCP) .... bam
Bambari [*Central African Republic*] [*ICAO location identifier*] (ICLI) .... FEFM
Bamberg [*Germany*] [*ICAO location identifier*] (ICLI) .... EDEJ
Bamberg, SC [*FM radio station call letters*] .... WWBD
Bamberg Symphony Orchestra (SAUO) .... BSO
Bamberg-Denmark, SC [*AM radio station call letters*] .... WRIT
Bamberger-Marie [*Disease*] [*Medicine*] (DB) .... BM
Bambili-Dingila [*Zaire*] [*ICAO location identifier*] (ICLI) .... FZKB
Bamboo Mosaic Virus [*Plant pathology*] .... BAMV
Bamburi [*Kenya*] [*Airport symbol*] [*Obsolete*] (OAG) .... BMQ
Bamenda [*Cameroon*] [*ICAO location identifier*] (ICLI) .... FKKV
Bamfield Marine Station, Bamfield, British Columbia [*Library symbol*] [*National Library of Canada*] (BIB) .... BBAM
Bamian [*Afghanistan*] [*Airport symbol*] [*Obsolete*] (OAG) .... BIN
Bampoor [*Iran*] [*ICAO location identifier*] (ICLI) .... OIZP
Bampton [*England*] .... BAMP
Bamu [*Papua New Guinea*] [*Airport symbol*] (OAG) .... BMZ
Bamyan [*Afghanistan*] [*ICAO location identifier*] (ICLI) .... OABN
Ban (WGA) .... B
Ban Houei Sai [*Laos*] [*Airport symbol*] (AD) .... OUI
Ban Large Office Buildings (SAUO) .... BLOB
Ban the Soviets Coalition (EA) .... BTSC
Ban Unsafe Schoolbuses Which Regularly Endanger Children [*Student legal action organization*] .... BUSWREC
Banak [*Norway*] [*ICAO location identifier*] (ICLI) .... ENNA
Banana and Fruit Development Corporation (SAUO) .... BFDC
Banana Bunchy Top Virus (SAUS) .... BBTV
Banana Growers Federation (SAUO) .... BGF
Banana Growers' Federation Cooperative [*Australia*] .... BGFC
Banana Industry Committee [*New South Wales, Australia*] .... BIC
Banana Industry Protection Board [*Australia*] .... BIPB
Banana Plug Resistor .... BPR
Banana, Rice Cereal, Apple Sauce, and Tea [*Diet*] (DAVI) .... BRAT
Banana River Repeater Station [*NASA*] (KSC) .... BRRS
Bananas, Rice, Apple Sauce, Tea, and Toast [*Diet*] (DAVI) .... BRATT
Bananas, Rice Cereal, Applesauce, and Toast [*Bland diet*] [*Medicine*] .... BRAT
Bananera [*Guatemala*] [*ICAO location identifier*] (ICLI) .... MGBN
Banankoro/Gbenko [*Guinea*] [*ICAO location identifier*] (ICLI) .... GUGO
Banaras Law Journal [*India*] [*A publication*] (DLA) .... Banaras LJ
Banaras Law Journal [*India*] [*A publication*] (DLA) .... Ban LJ
Banares Hindu University (SAUO) .... Ban
Banat Air Service Ltd. [*Romania*] [*FAA designator*] (FAAC) .... BAT
Banbury [*British depot code*] .... BAN
Banbury. English Exchequer Reports [*145 English Reprint*] [*A publication*] (DLA) .... Banbury (Eng)
Banbury Gold Mines [*Vancouver Stock Exchange symbol*] .... BBG
Banc Cymru [*Bank of Wales*] .... BC
Banc Galicia-Buenos AiresADR [*NASDAQ symbol*] (SG) .... BGALY
Banc One $3.50 Cv Pfd [*NASDAQ symbol*] (TTSB) .... BONEO
Banc One Corp. [*Associated Press*] (SAG) .... BancOne
Banc One Corp. [*Associated Press*] (SAG) .... BcOne
Banc One Corp. [*NASDAQ symbol*] (SAG) .... BONE
Banc Texas Group [*Associated Press*] (SAG) .... BanTex
Banca, Borsa, e Titoli di Credito [*A publication*] (ILCA) .... Banca Borsa Tit Cred
Banca Brignone [*Italy*] .... BB
Banca Commerciale Italiana [*Italy*] .... BCI
Banca del Gottardo [*Gotthard Bank*] [*Switzerland*] .... BG
Banca della Svizzera Italiana [*Swiss-Italian Bank*] [*Switzerland*] .... BSI
Banca Europea degli Investimenti [*European Investment Bank - EIB*] [*Italian*] .... BEI
Banca Internationala de Investitii [*International Investment Bank*] .... BII
Banca Mondiale [*World Bank*] [*Italian*] .... BM
Banca Nazionale del Lavoro [*National Bank of Labor*] [*Italy*] (ECON) .... BNL
Banca Nazionale dell'Agricoltura [*National Bank of Agriculture*] [*Italy*] (ECON) .... BNA
Banca QuadruADS [*NASDAQ symbol*] (TTSB) .... QDRMY
Banca Quadrum SA [*Associated Press*] (SAG) .... BncQuad
Banca Quadrum SA [*NASDAQ symbol*] (SAG) .... QDRM
BanCal Tri-State Corporation (SAUO) .... BNC
BancFirst Corp. [*NASDAQ symbol*] (TTSB) .... BANF
BancFirst Corp. Oklahoma [*NASDAQ symbol*] (SAG) .... BANF
BancFirst Corp. Oklahoma [*Associated Press*] (SAG) .... BncFstOK
Bancfirst Ohio Corp. [*NASDAQ symbol*] (SAG) .... BFOH
Bancfirst Ohio Corp. [*Associated Press*] (SAG) .... BncfstOH
Bancinsurance Corp. [*Associated Press*] (SAG) .... Bancins
Bancinsurance Corp. [*NASDAQ symbol*] (SAG) .... BCIS
Banco Amazonas [*Amazon Bank*] [*Ecuador*] .... BA
Banco BHIF [*Associated Press*] (SAG) .... BcoBHIF
Banco BHIF ADS [*NYSE symbol*] (SG) .... BB
Banco Bilbao Vizcaya (ECON) .... BBV
Banco Bilbao Vizcaya [*NYSE symbol*] (SPSG) .... BVG
Banco Bilbao Vizcaya 9% ADS [*NYSE symbol*] (TTSB) .... BVGPrB
Banco Bilbao Vizcaya ADS [*NYSE symbol*] (TTSB) .... BBV
Banco Bilbao Vizcaya International [*Associated Press*] (SAG) .... BncBil
Banco Bilbao Vizcaya International [*Associated Press*] (SAG) .... BncBl
Banco Bilbao Vizcaya SA [*NYSE symbol*] (CTT) .... BBV
Banco Bilbao Vizcaya SA [*Associated Press*] (SAG) .... BcBilV
Banco Cent Hispanoamer ADS [*NYSE symbol*] (TTSB) .... BCH
Banco Central [*Toronto Stock Exchange symbol*] .... BCY
Banco Central de Nicaragua [*Central Bank of Nicaragua*] .... BCN
Banco Central Hispanoamericano [*NYSE symbol*] (SAG) .... BCH
Banco Central Hispanoamericano SA [*Associated Press*] .... BncCtrl
Banco Centroamericano de Integracion Economica [*Central American Bank for Economic Integration*] [*Spanish*] (BARN) .... BCIE
Banco Comercial de Mocambique .... BCM
Banco Comercial Portugues [*Portuguese Commercial Bank*] (ECON) .... BCP
Banco Comercial Portugues SA [*Associated Press*] (SAG) .... BnCPort
Banco Coml Portugues ADS [*NYSE symbol*] (TTSB) .... BPC
Banco de A. Edwards [*Associated Press*] (SAG) .... BcoAEdw
Banco de A Edwards ADS [*NYSE symbol*] (TTSB) .... AED
Banco de Bilbao [*Spain*] .... BB
Banco de Bilbao [*Italian*] .... BB
Banco de Cabo Verde [*Bank of Cape Verde*] (EY) .... BCV
Banco de Credito Nacional SA [*Private bank*] [*Brazil*] (EY) .... BCN

Banco de Desenvolvimento de Minas Gerais SA [*Brazil*] (EY) .... BDMG
Banco de Desenvolvimento do Estado de Sao Paulo SA [*Brazil*] (EY) .... BADESP
Banco de Galicia y Buenos Aires [*NASDAQ symbol*] (SAG) .... BGAL
Banco de Galicia y Buenos Aires [*Commercial firm*] [*Associated Press*] (SAG) .... BncGalic
Banco de Galicia-Buenos Aires [*NASDAQ symbol*] (TTSB) .... BGALY
Banco de la Nacion [*National Bank*] [*Peru*] .... BN
Banco de la Nacion Argentina [*National Bank of Argentina*] .... BNA
Banco de Latinoamerica, SA [*Panama*] (EY) .... BANCOLAT
Banco de Mexico [*ICAO designator*] (FAAC) .... BMX
Banco de Santander SA [*NYSE symbol*] (SPSG) .... STD
Banco de Santander Sociedad Anonima de Credito [*Associated Press*]..... BnSant
Banco De Santiago [*Associated Press*] (SAG) .... BcoSanti
Banco De Santiago [*NYSE symbol*] (SAG) .... SAN
Banco di Napoli [*Italy*] .... BDN
Banco di Sicilia [*Italy*] .... BdS
Banco do Estado do Rio de Janiero SA [*Brazil*] (EY) .... BANERJ
Banco Espanol de Credito [*Spain*] (ECON) .... BANESTO
Banco Europeo de Inversion [*European Investment Bank - EIB*] [*Spanish*] ...... BEI
Banco Europeu para a America Latina [*Bank*] [*Portuguese*] (EY) .... BEAL
Banco Fonsecas & Burnay [*Fonsecas & Burnay Bank*] [*Portugal*] .... BFB
Banco Frances del Rio ADS [*NYSE symbol*] (TTSB) .... BFR
Banco Frances del Rio La Plata [*NYSE symbol*] (SAG) .... BFR
Banco Frances del Rio La Plata [*Associated Press*] (SAG) .... BncoFrn
Banco Ganadero [*Associated Press*] (SAG) .... BGanadro
Banco Ganadero [*Associated Press*] (SAG) .... BGandro
Banco Ganadero [*Associated Press*] (SAG) .... BGndo
Banco Ganadero ADS [*NYSE symbol*] (TTSB) .... BGA
Banco Ganadero 'C'Pref ADS [*NYSE symbol*] (TTSB) .... BGAPr
Banco Hipotecario de la Construccion SA [*The Dominican Republic*] (EY) .... BANHICO
Banco Holandes Unido [*Dutch Union Bank*] [*Ecuador*] .... BHU
Banco Indl Colombiano Pref ADS [*NYSE symbol*] (TTSB) .... CIB
Banco Industrial Columbiano SA [*Associated Press*] (SAG) .... BcoIndl
Banco Industrial Columbiano SA [*NYSE symbol*] (SAG) .... CIB
Banco Industrial del Mediterraneo [*Industrial Bank of the Mediterranean*] [*Spain*] .... BIM
Banco Inmobilario [*Nicaragua*] (EY) .... BIN
Banco Interamericano de Desarrollo [*Inter-American Development Bank*] [*Spanish*] .... BID
Banco Internacional [*International Bank*] [*Ecuador*] .... BI
Banco Internacional de Reconstruccion y Fomento [*International Bank for Reconstruction and Development; also known as World Bank*] [*Spanish*]..... BIRF
Banco Latinamericano de Exportaciones [*Associated Press*] (SAG) .... BcLatn
Banco Latinoamericano de Export 'E' [*NYSE symbol*] (SPSG) .... BLX
Banco Mundial [*World Bank*] [*Spanish*] .... BM
Banco Nacional de Angola [*National Bank of Angola*] .... BNA
Banco Nacional de Comercio Exterior (SAUO) .... BANCOMEXT
Banco Nacional de Desarrollo [*National Development Bank*] [*Argentina*] .... BND
Banco Nacional de Mexico [*National Bank of Mexico*] .... Banamex
Banco Nacional de Obras y Servicios Publicos [*Mexico*] (GEOI) .... Banobras
Banco Nacional de Trabajadores [*Paraguay*] (EY) .... BNT
Banco Nacional do Desenvolvimento Economico [*National Economic Development Bank*] [*Brazil*] .... BNDE
Banco OHiggins [*Associated Press*] (SAG) .... BcOHig
Banco OHiggins [*NYSE symbol*] (SAG) .... OHG
Banco O'Higgins ADS [*NYSE symbol*] (TTSB) .... OHG
Banco Osorno y La Union [*Associated Press*] (SAG) .... BcOsorno
Banco Osorno y La UnionADS [*NYSE symbol*] (TTSB) .... BOU
Banco Panamericano [*Panama*] (EY) .... PANABANK
Banco Popular de Desenvolvimento .... BPD
Banco Portugues do Atlantico [*Portuguese Bank of the Atlantic*] (ECON) .... BPA
Banco Portugues do Investimento [*Portuguese Investment Bank*] .... BPI
Banco Regis [*or Reginae*] [*The King's (or Queen's) Bench*] [*Latin*] .... BR
Banco Resources Ltd. [*Vancouver Stock Exchange symbol*] .... BAR
Banco Rio De La Plata ADS [*NYSE symbol*] (SG) .... BRS
Banco Santander ADS [*NYSE symbol*] (TTSB) .... STD
Banco Santander Cent Hispano ADS [*NYSE symbol*] (SG) .... STD
Banco Santander Central Hispano [*Spain*] .... BSCH
Banco Santander Chile [*Associated Press*] (SAG) .... BcSantCh
Banco Santander Chile [*NYSE symbol*] (SAG) .... BSB
Banco Santander-Chile ADS [*NYSE symbol*] [*Formerly, Banco Osorno y La Union ADS*] (SG) .... BSB
Banco Santander-Puerto Rico [*NYSE symbol*] (SG) .... SBP
Banco Santiago ADS [*NYSE symbol*] [*Formerly, Banco de Santiago ADS*] (SG) .... SAN
Banco Wiese ADS [*NYSE symbol*] (TTSB) .... BWP
Banco Wiese Limitado [*Associated Press*] (SAG) .... BcoWiese
Banco Wiese Limitado [*NYSE symbol*] (SAG) .... BWP
BancoBilbaoVizcaya8.00%ADS [*NYSE symbol*] (TTSB) .... BVGPrC
BancoBilbaoVizcaya9.75% ADS [*NYSE symbol*] (TTSB) .... BVGPr
Bancode A Edwards [*NYSE symbol*] (SAG) .... AED
Bancode A Edwards [*Associated Press*] (SAG) .... BcoAEd
BancOklahoma (EFIS) .... BOK
Bancom Development Corporation (SAUO) .... Bancom
Bancorp Connecticut [*NASDAQ symbol*] (TTSB) .... BKCT
Bancorp Connecticut, Inc. [*NASDAQ symbol*] (SAG) .... BKCT
Bancorp Connecticut, Inc. [*Associated Press*] (SAG) .... Bncp CT
Bancorp Hawaii, Inc. [*Associated Press*] (SAG) .... BcpHaw
Bancorp Hawaii, Inc. [*Associated Press*] (SAG) .... BcpHw
Bancorp Hawaii, Inc. [*NYSE symbol*] (SPSG) .... BOH
Bancorp South, Inc. [*Associated Press*] (SAG) .... BcpSou
Bancorp South, Inc. [*NASDAQ symbol*] (SAG) .... BOMS
BancorpSouth [*NYSE symbol*] (SG) .... BXS
Bancroft, Avery & McAlister, San Francisco, CA [*Library symbol*] [*Library of Congress*] (LCLS) .... CSFBA
Bancroft Convertible Fund, Inc. [*Associated Press*] (SAG) .... BanFd
Bancroft Convertible Fund, Inc. [*AMEX symbol*] (SPSG) .... BCV
Bancroft Library of the University of California (SAUS) .... BLUCB
Bancroft Library of the University of California at Berkeley (SAUO) .... BLUCB
Bancroft, ON [*Television station call letters*] CIII-2
Bancroft, ON [*AM radio station call letters*] .... CJNH
Bancroft Public Library, Bancroft, ON, Canada [*Library symbol*] [*Library of Congress*] (LCLS) .... CaOBan
Bancroft Public Library, Ontario [*Library symbol*] [*National Library of Canada*] (NLC) .... OBAN
Bancroft Public Library, Salem, NY [*Library symbol*] [*Library of Congress*] (LCLS) .... NSa
Bancroft Register, Bancroft, IA [*Library symbol*] [*Library of Congress*] (LCLS) .... IaBanR
Bancshare Portfolio Corp. [*Toronto Stock Exchange symbol*] .... XBP
Banctec, Inc. [*Associated Press*] (SAG) .... Banctec
BancTec, Inc. [*NASDAQ symbol*] (NQ) .... BTEC
BancTec,Inc. [*NYSE symbol*] (TTSB) .... BTC
Banctexas Group, Inc. [*NYSE symbol*] (SPSG) .... BTX
Bancus [*Common Bench*] [*Legal*] [*British*] (ROG) .... B
Bancus Superior [*King's Bench*] [*British*] [*Legal term*] (ROG) .... BANC SUP
Bancus Superior [*King's Bench*] [*British*] [*Legal term*] (DLA) .... BS
BancWest Corp. [*Formerly, First Hamilton*] [*NYSE symbol*] .... BWE
Band .... B
Band [*Volume*] [*German*] .... BD
Band (KSC) .... BND
Band (SAUS) .... Bnd
Band Amplitude Product .... BAP
Band and Orchestra [*Musical slang*] .... B & O
[*The*] **Band Appreciation Society** (EAIO) .... TBAS
Band Approximation Method (MCD) .... BAM
Band Archive Management Service (IAA) .... BAMS
Band Association of New South Wales (SAUO) .... BANSW
Band Block (SAUS) .... BB
Band Colour Sergeant [*British military*] (DMA) .... Bd/CSgt
Band Corporal .... BC
Band Corporal [*British military*] (DMA) .... Bd/Cpl
Band Display .... BNDDIS
Band Edge (AAEL) .... BE
Band Edge Energy .... BEE
Band Elimination .... BE
Band Elimination Filter .... BEF
Band Filter Cut-Off (SAUS) .... BFCO
Band Filter Set .... BFS
Band Gap (AAEL) .... BG
Band Gap Engineering (AAEL) .... BGE
Band Gap Reduction (SAUS) .... BGR
Band Ignitor Tube .... BIT
Band Interleaved by Line (TELE) .... BIL
Band Interleaved by Pixel (ADWA) .... BIP
band keratopathy (SAUS) .... band
Band Keratopathy [*Medicine*] (MELL) .... BK
Band Limiting Filter [*Electronics*] (OA) .... BLF
Band of Hope [*British*] .... B of H
Band of Hope [*British*] (DAS) .... BOH
Band of Hope Union (SAUO) .... B of H
Band of the Royal Military College (SAUO) .... BRMC
Band Pass Filter (SAUS) .... BPF
Band Predictive Code Modulation (SAUS) .... BPCM
Band Pressure Level .... BPL
Band Rate (SAUS) .... BR
Band Reject (IAA) .... BR
Band Saw (SAUS) .... BS
Band Sequential (GEOI) .... BSQ
Band Sergeant [*British military*] (DMA) .... Bd/Sgt
Band Setting (IAA) .... BS
Band Splitting Effect (SAUS) .... BSE
Band System (IAA) .... BS
Band Training and Advisory Services Branch [*Canada, Indian and Inuit Affairs Program*] [*Canada*] .... BTAS
Banda [*Indonesia*] [*ICAO location identifier*] (ICLI) .... WAPC
Banda Aceh [*Indonesia*] [*Airport symbol*] (OAG) .... BTJ
Banda Aceh/Blangbintang [*Indonesia*] [*ICAO location identifier*] (ICLI) .... WITT
Banda Aceh/Maimun Saleh [*Indonesia*] [*ICAO location identifier*] (ICLI) .... WIAB
Banda Atjeh [*Indonesia*] [*Airport symbol*] (AD) .... BTJ
Bandag, Inc. [*Associated Press*] [*Associated Press*] (SAG) .... Bandag
Bandag, Inc. [*Associated Press*] (SAG) .... Bandg
Bandag, Inc. [*NYSE symbol*] (SPSG) .... BDG
Bandag Inc.'A' [*NYSE symbol*] (TTSB) .... BDG A
Bandage (SAUS) .... BAN
Bandanaira [*Indonesia*] [*Airport symbol*] (OAG) .... NDA
Bandar Abbas [*Iran*] [*Airport symbol*] (OAG) .... BND
Bandar Abbas [*Iran*] [*ICAO location identifier*] (ICLI) .... OIKB
Bandar Anzali [*Iran*] [*ICAO location identifier*] (ICLI) .... OIGP
Bandar Deylam [*Iran*] [*ICAO location identifier*] (ICLI) .... OIBD
Bandar Khamir [*Iran*] [*ICAO location identifier*] (ICLI) .... OIKI
Bandar Lampung [*Indonesia*] [*Airport symbol*] (OAG) .... TKG
Bandar Lengeh [*Iran*] [*Airport symbol*] (OAG) .... BDH
Bandar Lengeh [*Iran*] [*ICAO location identifier*] (ICLI) .... OIBL
Bandar Mahshahr [*Iran*] [*ICAO location identifier*] (ICLI) .... OIAM
Bandar Seri Begawan [*Brunei*] [*Airport symbol*] (OAG) .... BWN
Bandar Torkaman [*Iran*] [*ICAO location identifier*] (ICLI) .... OINY
Bandaranaike Centre for International Studies (SAUO) .... BCIS

Bandblock (IAA) ... BB
Band-by-Band (SAUS) ... BB
Bande Dessinee [*Comic strip*] [*French*] ... BD
Banded Iron Formation [*Geology*] ... BIF
Banded Signaling (VERA) ... BS
Banded Two Sides and One End [*Lumber*] (DAC) ... B2S1E
Band-Edge Coupling (SAUS) ... BE COUP
Bandeirante [*Airplane code*] ... Emb
Bandelier National Monument (SAUS) ... BNM
Bandelier National Movement (SAUO) ... BAND
Bandera, TX [*FM radio station call letters*] ... KEEP
B&H Maritime Carriers [*AMEX symbol*] (TTSB) ... BHM
B&H Ocean Carriers [*AMEX symbol*] (TTSB) ... BHO
Bandiagara [*Mali*] [*ICAO location identifier*] (ICLI) ... GABD
Bandinus Familiatus de Pisa [*Deceased, 1218*] [*Authority cited in pre-1607 legal work*] (DSA) ... Ba
Bandinus Familiatus de Pisa [*Deceased, 1218*] [*Authority cited in pre-1607 legal work*] (DSA) ... Ban
Bandinus Familiatus de Pisa [*Deceased, 1218*] [*Authority cited in pre-1607 legal work*] (DSA) ... Band
Bandipur Wildlife Sanctuary (SAUS) ... BWS
Bandirma [*Turkey*] [*ICAO location identifier*] (ICLI) ... LTBG
Bandkamalkhan [*Afghanistan*] [*ICAO location identifier*] (ICLI) ... OABK
Band-Limited Hiss [*NASA*] ... BLH
Band-Limited Signal ... BLS
Band-Limiting Filter (SAUS) ... BLF
Bandmaster [*Military*] [*British*] (ROG) ... BANDMR
Bandmaster [*Military*] [*British*] (ROG) ... BANDR
Bandmaster (SAUS) ... Bdmr
Bandmaster [*Military*] [*British*] (ROG) ... BDR
Bandmaster (ROG) ... BM
Bandmaster ... BMSTR
Bandmaster [*Military*] [*British*] (DMA) ... Bndr
Bandmaster of the Bandsmen's College of Music (WDAA) ... BBCM
Bando McGlocklin Adj Rt'A'Pfd [*NASDAQ symbol*] (TTSB) ... BMCCP
Bando McGlocklin Capital [*NASDAQ symbol*] (TTSB) ... BMCC
Bando McGlocklin Capital Corp. [*Associated Press*] (SAG) ... Bando
Bando McGlocklin Capital Corp. [*Associated Press*] (SAG) ... BandoM
Bando McGlocklin Capital Corp. [*NASDAQ symbol*] (NQ) ... BMCC
Bandolier ... BAND
Bandolier (MSA) ... BDLR
Bandon, OR [*FM radio station call letters*] (RBYB) ... KBDN
Bandon Public Library, Bandon, OR [*Library symbol*] [*Library of Congress*] (LCLS) ... OrBan
B&P Instrumentation Ltd. (SAUO) ... BPI
Bandpass (IDOE) ... bp
Bandpass ... BP
Bandpass Amplifier (SAUS) ... BPA
Bandpass Crystal ... BPC
Bandpass Crystal Filter ... BCF
Bandpass Crystal Filter ... BPCF
Bandpass Detector (SAUS) ... BPD
Bandpass Filter ... BF
Bandpass Filter ... BPF
Bandpass Limiter (IAA) ... BPL
Band-Pass Limiter (SAUS) ... BPL
Bandpass Network ... BPN
Bandpass Transformer ... BPT
Bandrejection Filter (IAA) ... BRF
Bands (Civilian and Military) [*Public-performance tariff class*] [*British*] ... B
Bands of America (EA) ... BA
Bandsman [*Military*] [*British*] ... BDSM
Bandsman (SAUS) ... Bdsm
Bandsman [*Military*] [*British*] ... BDSMN
Bands-of-Performance (MCD) ... BOP
Bandstop [*Electronics*] (IAA) ... BS
Band-Stop (SAUS) ... BS
Bandstop Filter (PDAA) ... BSF
Bandstop Filter (MSA) ... BSFL
Band-To-Band Tunneling (SAUS) ... BTBT
Bandundu [*Zaire*] [*Airport symbol*] (OAG) ... FDU
Bandundu [*Zaire*] [*ICAO location identifier*] (ICLI) ... FZBO
Bandung [*Indonesia*] [*Airport symbol*] (OAG) ... BDO
Bandung [*Indonesia*] [*Seismograph station code, US Geological Survey*] [*Closed*] (SEIS) ... BND
Bandung Institute of Technology, Indonesia (SAUS) ... ITB
Bandung Technical Institute (SAUS) ... BTI
Bandung/Husein Sastranegara [*Indonesia*] [*ICAO location identifier*] (ICLI) ... WIIB
B&V Waste Science and Technology Corp. (EFIS) ... BVWST
Bandwidth [*Frequency range*] ... B
Bandwidth [*Frequency range*] ... BW
Bandwidth (IDOE) ... bw
Bandwidth Allocation Control Protocol [*Telecommunications*] (ACRL) ... BACP
Bandwidth Allocation Control Protocol (SAUS) ... BAPC
Bandwidth Allocation Protocol [*Telecommunications*] (ACRL) ... BAP
Bandwidth Balancing Mechanism (VERA) ... BWBM
Bandwidth Broker (SAUS) ... BB
Bandwidth Compression (ROAS) ... BWC
Bandwidth Compression Technique ... BCT
Bandwidth Conservation Society (SAUO) ... BCS
Bandwidth Demand Assignment (CCCA) ... BDA
Bandwidth Efficient Zero Suppression (ADWA) ... BEZS
Bandwidth Expansion (SAUS) ... BWE
Bandwidth Management Services (SAUS) ... BMS
Bandwidth on Demand (SAUS) ... BOD
Bandwidth on Demand (PCM) ... BOND
Bandwidth on Demand Interoperability Working Group [*Telecommunications*] (ACRL) ... BONDING
Bandwidth Radio (MCD) ... BWR
Bandwidth Ratio ... BWR
Bandwidth Ratio [*Telecommunications*] (NITA) ... BWT
Bandwidth Reduction and Intelligence Target Tracking (MCD) ... BRITT
Bandwidth Shape Factor ... BSF
Bandwidth Test Set (ROAS) ... BWTS
Bandwidth Time (CCCA) ... BT
Bane Houei Say [*Laos*] [*ICAO location identifier*] (ICLI) ... VLHS
Baneh [*Iran*] [*ICAO location identifier*] (ICLI) ... OICB
Banff [*Alberta*] [*Seismograph station code, US Geological Survey*] [*Closed*] (SEIS) ... BAN
Banff, AB [*ICAO location identifier*] (ICLI) ... CYBA
Banff Centre Library, Alberta [*Library symbol*] [*National Library of Canada*] (NLC) ... ABSFA
Banff Library, Alberta [*Library symbol*] [*National Library of Canada*] (NLC) ... AB
Banff Library, Banff, AB, Canada [*Library symbol*] [*Library of Congress*] (LCLS) ... CaAB
Banff Municipal Library, Improvement District No. 9, Banff, AB, Canada [*Library symbol*] [*Library of Congress*] (LCLS) ... CaABIDM
Banff National Park (SAUS) ... BNP
Banff Park Natural History Museum (SAUO) ... BPNHM
Banff School of Fine Arts, Banff, AB, Canada [*Library symbol*] [*Library of Congress*] (LCLS) ... CaABSFA
Banfora [*Burkina Faso*] [*ICAO location identifier*] (ICLI) ... DHOB
Bang for the Buck ... BFB
Bang on a Can Festival ... BOAC
Banga [*Zaire*] [*ICAO location identifier*] (ICLI) ... FZCI
Bangala Law Reporter [*India*] [*A publication*] (DLA) ... Bang LR
Bangalore [*India*] [*Airport symbol*] (OAG) ... BLR
Bangalore [*India*] [*ICAO location identifier*] (ICLI) ... VOBG
Bangalore Torpedo banir bombing and navigation inertial (SAUS) ... Bang Torp
Bangalore Volunteer Rifles [*British military*] (DMA) ... BVR
Bangamba [*Congo*] [*ICAO location identifier*] (ICLI) ... FCPB
Bangassou [*Central African Republic*] [*ICAO location identifier*] (ICLI) ... FEFG
Bang-Bang Erection System [*Electronics*] (IAA) ... BBES
Bang-Bang-Bang Surfaces (PDAA) ... BBBS
Bangkok (SAUS) ... Bank
Bangkok (SAUS) ... Bgk
Bangkok [*Thailand*] (WDAA) ... BGK
Bangkok [*Thailand*] [*Airport symbol*] (OAG) ... BKK
Bangkok [*Thailand*] [*ICAO location identifier*] (ICLI) ... VTBA
Bangkok [*Thailand*] [*ICAO location identifier*] (ICLI) ... VTBB
Bangkok Airways [*Thailand*] [*ICAO designator*] (FAAC) ... BKP
Bangkok Bank [*Thailand*] ... BB
Bangkok Bank Limited (SAUO) ... BBL
Bangkok Bank of Commerce ... BBC
Bangkok Interbank-Offered Rate (SAUS) ... BIBOR
Bangkok Metropolitan Administration (SAUO) ... BMA
Bangkok/International [*Thailand*] [*ICAO location identifier*] (ICLI) ... VTBD
Bangladash ... BANGLA
Bangladesh [*MARC geographic area code*] [*Library of Congress*] ... a-bg-
Bangladesh (ILCA) ... Bang
Bangladesh [*ANSI two-letter standard code*] (CNC) ... BD
Bangladesh [*MARC country of publication code*] [*Library of Congress*] (LCCP) ... bg
Bangladesh [*ANSI three-letter standard code*] (CNC) ... BGD
Bangladesh (MILB) ... Bng
Bangladesh (WDAA) ... BNGL
Bangladesh [*Aircraft nationality and registration mark*] (FAAC) ... S2
Bangladesh Agricultural Union (SAUO) ... BAU
Bangladesh Biman [*ICAO designator*] (FAAC) ... BBC
Bangladesh Biman [*ICAO designator*] (AD) ... BG
Bangladesh Council of Scientific and Industrial Research (SAUO) ... BSCIR
Bangladesh Cultural Association (EA) ... BCA
Bangladesh House Building Finance Corp. (EY) ... BHBFC
Bangladesh Institute of Development Economics (SAUO) ... BIDE
Bangladesh International Action Group (SAUO) ... BIAG
Bangladesh Krishi Bank (EY) ... BKB
Bangladesh Library Association (SAUO) ... BLA
Bangladesh Medical Association of North America (EA) ... BMA
Bangladesh Medical Research Council Bulletin (SAUO) ... Bangladesh Med Res Counc Bull
Bangladesh National Awami Party [*Political party*] (PPW) ... NAP
Bangladesh National Party [*Bangladesh Jatiyabadi Dal*] (PPW) ... BNP
Bangladesh National Scientific and Technical Documentation Centre [*Information service or system*] (IID) ... BANSDOC
Bangladesh Navy (SAUS) ... BN
Bangladesh News Agency ... BNA
Bangladesh Open University (SAUO) ... BOU
Bangladesh Population and Health Consortium/NGO Project ... BPHC
Bangladesh Power Development Board ... BPDB
Bangladesh Press International ... BPI
Bangladesh Railway (SAUS) ... BR
Bangladesh Rural Advancement Committee [*Development program*] ... BRAC
Bangladesh Samabaya Bank Ltd. (EY) ... BSBL
Bangladesh Samajtantrik Dal [*Bangladesh Socialist Party*] (PPW) ... BSD
Bangladesh Sanwad Sanstha [*News agency*] ... BSS
Bangladesh Shilpa Bank [*Industrial Development Bank*] (EY) ... BSB
Bangladesh Technical Education Board (SAUO) ... BTED
Bangladesh University of Engineering and Technology (SAUO) ... BUET
Bangladesh Water Development Board (SAUO) ... BWDB
Bangladesh-Australia Society of South Australia ... BASSA

Bangledesh [*E. Pakistan*] (VRA) ... Bangl
Bangles Fan Club [*Later, Bangles n' Mash International*] [*Defunct*] (EA) ... BFC
Bangles n' Mash International [*Defunct*] (EA) ... BMI
Bango Whiplash [*Military*] ... BW
Bangong-Nujiang Suture [*Paleogeography*] ... BNS
Bangor [*City in Wales*] (ROG) ... BAN
Bangor [*Maine*] [*Airport symbol*] (OAG) ... BGR
Bangor (SAUS) ... Bng
Bangor Air Defense Sector (SAA) ... BAADS
Bangor and Aroostook (SAUO) ... BA
Bangor & Aroostook (SAUS) ... B&A
Bangor & Aroostook Railroad Co. (IIA) ... B & A
Bangor & Aroostook Railroad Co. ... B & AR
Bangor & Aroostook Railroad Co. [*AAR code*] ... BAR
Bangor Historical Society, Bangor, ME [*Library symbol*] [*Library of Congress*] (LCLS) ... MeBaHi
Bangor Hydro Electric Co. [*NYSE symbol*] (SPSG) ... BGR
Bangor Hydro-Electric Co. [*Associated Press*] (SAG) ... BangH
Bangor International Airport ... BIA
Bangor, ME [*Location identifier*] [*FAA*] (FAAL) ... JVH
Bangor, ME [*AM radio station call letters*] ... WABI
Bangor, ME [*Television station call letters*] ... WABI-TV
Bangor, ME [*FM radio station call letters*] ... WEZQ
Bangor, ME [*FM radio station call letters*] ... WHCF
Bangor, ME [*FM radio station call letters*] ... WHSN
Bangor, ME [*Television station call letters*] ... WLBZ
Bangor, ME [*FM radio station call letters*] ... WMEH
Bangor, ME [*Television station call letters*] ... WVII
Bangor, ME [*FM radio station call letters*] (RBYB) ... WWBX
Bangor, ME [*AM radio station call letters*] ... WZON
Bangor Mental Health Institute, Bangor, ME [*OCLC symbol*] (OCLC) ... MEB
Bangor [*Wales*] **Orange Position Estimating Equipment for Pastures** [*Electronic beeper to be attached to sheep*] ... BO PEEP
Bangor Public Library, Bangor, ME [*OCLC symbol*] (OCLC) ... BYN
Bangor Public Library, Bangor, ME [*Library symbol*] [*Library of Congress*] (LCLS) ... MeBa
Bangor Punta Corporation (SAUO) ... BNK
Bangor Theological Seminary, Bangor, ME [*Library symbol*] [*Library of Congress*] (LCLS) ... MeBaT
Bangor University College (SAUO) ... BUC
Bangor, Wicklow, McClure, and Monteagle Union Public Library, Maynooth, Ontario [*Library symbol*] [*National Library of Canada*] (BIB) ... OMBW
Bangor/International [*Maine*] [*ICAO location identifier*] (ICLI) ... KBGR
Bangsa Moro National Liberation Front [*Philippines*] [*Political party*] (FEA) ... BMNLF
Bangui [*Central African Republic*] [*Airport symbol*] (OAG) ... BGF
Bangui [*Central African Republic*] [*Seismograph station code, US Geological Survey*] (SEIS) ... BNG
Bangui [*Central African Republic*] [*ICAO location identifier*] (ICLI) ... FEFV
Bangui/M'Poko [*Central African Republic*] [*ICAO location identifier*] (ICLI) ... FEFF
Bangula [*Malawi*] [*ICAO location identifier*] (ICLI) ... FWBG
Bani [*Monetary unit*] [*Romania*] ... B
Banihal [*India*] [*ICAO location identifier*] (ICLI) ... VIBH
Banished (ROG) ... BAN
Banister Continental Ltd. [*Toronto Stock Exchange symbol*] ... BAC
Banister Foundation [*Formerly, Banister, Inc.*] [*AMEX symbol*] (SPSG) ... BAN
Banister, Foundation [*Associated Press*] (SAG) ... Banstr
Banja Luka [*Yugoslavia*] [*Seismograph station code, US Geological Survey*] (SEIS) ... BLY
Banja Luka [*Former Yugoslavia*] [*ICAO location identifier*] (ICLI) ... LYBK
Banjarbaru Research Institute for Food Crops (SAUO) ... BARIF
Banjarmasin [*Indonesia*] [*Airport symbol*] (OAG) ... BDJ
Banjarmasin Sector [*Indonesia*] [*ICAO location identifier*] (ICLI) ... WRBZ
Banjarmasin/Syamsuddin Noor [*Indonesia*] [*ICAO location identifier*] (ICLI) ... WRBB
Banjo ... bjo
Banjo ... BJO
Banjul [*Gambia*] [*Airport symbol*] (OAG) ... BJL
Banjul [*Gambia*] [*ICAO location identifier*] (ICLI) ... GBYD
Bank ... B
Bank (EBF) ... Bk
Bank ... BK
Bank (ROG) ... BNK
Bank Acceptance ... BA
Bank Account Debits Tax (ADA) ... BAD
Bank Account Debits Tax (ADA) ... BADT
Bank Administration [*Bank Administration Institute*] [*A publication*] ... BA
Bank Administration Institute (EA) ... BAI
Bank America Corp. (SAUO) ... BAM
Bank Americard Authorization System Exchange (SAUS) ... BASE
Bank Analysis System [*Robinson-Humphrey Co.*] [*Defunct*] [*Information service or system*] (CRD) ... BANKANAL
Bank and Office Interiors (SAUO) ... B&OI
Bank and Trust ... B & T
Bank and Turn Indicator [*Aviation*] ... BTI
Bank Angle [*Aviation*] (PIPO) ... B/A
Bank Angle (SAUS) ... BA
Bank Atlantic Bancorp, Inc. [*NASDAQ symbol*] (SAG) ... BANCA
Bank Atlantic Bancorp, Inc. [*Associated Press*] (SAG) ... BkAtlB
Bank Automated Service Information System (BUR) ... BASIS
Bank Book ... BB
Bank Book ... BK
Bank Bumiputra Malaysia Berhad (FEA) ... BBMB
Bank Burglary ... BB
Bank Buying Rate (TRID) ... BBR
Bank Cable (IAA) ... BKCA
Bank Cable (SAUS) ... bk ca
Bank Capital Markets Association [*Washington, DC*] (EA) ... BCMA
Bank Cash Ratio (ADA) ... BCR
Bank Cash Reserve (ADA) ... BCR
Bank Clearing [*Business term*] (ADA) ... BC
Bank [*Joseph A.*] **Clothiers, Inc.** [*NASDAQ symbol*] (SAG) ... JOSB
Bank [*Joseph A.*] **Clothiers, Inc.** [*Associated Press*] (SAG) ... JosBank
Bank Control System (SAUS) ... BCS
Bank Corp. of Georgia [*NASDAQ symbol*] (SAG) ... BCGA
Bank Corp. of Georgia [*Associated Press*] (SAG) ... BkCpGa
Bank Credit Transfer (DI) ... BCT
Bank Descriptor Index [*Computer science*] ... BDI
Bank Descriptor Registers [*Computer science*] ... BDR
Bank Descriptor Word [*Computer science*] ... BDW
Bank Dividend (IIA) ... BD
Bank Draft ... BD
Bank Draft (DS) ... B/DFT
Bank Draft Number (TEL) ... BDN
Bank Economic and Social Database [*World Bank*] [*United Nations*] (DUND) ... BESD
Bank Education Service [*British*] (BI) ... BES
Bank Error ... BE
Bank Export Services Act [*1982*] ... BESA
Bank for Cooperatives ... BC
Bank for Foreign Trade of the USSR ... BFT
Bank for International Settlements [*Basel, Switzerland*] (AF) ... BIS
Bank for International Settlements, Quarterly [*Database*] [*I. P. Sharp Associates*] [*Information service or system*] (CRD) ... BISQ
Bank for International Settlements, Semi-Annual [*Database*] [*I. P. Sharp Associates*] [*Information service or system*] (CRD) ... BISS
Bank fuer Gemeinwirtschaft [*Germany*] ... BfG
Bank fuer Internationalen Zahlungsausgleich [*Bank for International Settlements*] [*German*] ... BIZ
Bank fuer Kredit und Aussenhandel AG [*Bank for Credit and Export Trade*] [*German*] ... BKA
Bank Giro Credit [*British*] (DCTA) ... BGC
Bank Guaranteed (EBF) ... BG
Bank Handlowy Spălka Akcyjna (SAUS) ... BHSA
Bank Holding Company ... BHC
Bank Holding Company Act [*of 1956*] (TDOB) ... BHCA
Bank Holiday ... BH
Bank Identification Number ... BIN
Bank Identifier Code (TBD) ... BIC
Bank in Liechtenstein ... BIL
Bank Information Center (SAUO) ... BIC
Bank Information System Network ... BISNET
Bank Instrument Contract (EBF) ... BIC
Bank Insurance Fund ... BIF
Bank Investment Contract ... BIC
Bank Larceny ... BL
Bank Management Information System ... BMIS
Bank Markazi Iran. Bulletin [*A publication*] ... BMIB
Bank Marketing Association [*Chicago, IL*] (EA) ... BMA
Bank Marketing Association, Chicago, IL [*Library symbol*] [*Library of Congress*] (LCLS) ... ICBM
Bank Marketing Association, Chicago, IL [*OCLC symbol*] (OCLC) ... IDZ
Bank Mees & Hope NV ... BMH
Bank Melli Iran ... BMI
Bank Note (SAUS) ... BN
Bank Number (SAUS) ... BNKNO
Bank of Africa [*Mali*] (EY) ... BOA
Bank of Alberta [*Toronto Stock Exchange symbol*] ... BNT
Bank of Alexandria (SAUO) ... BOA
Bank of America ... BA
Bank of America [*NYSE symbol*] (SG) ... BAC
Bank of America (SAUO) ... BOA
Bank of America ... B of A
Bank of America Australia ... BAA
Bank of America, National Trust and Savings Association (SAUO) ... BA
Bank of America, National Trust and Savings Association (SAUO) ... BofA
Bank of American International (SAUO) ... BAI
Bank of American National Trust and Savings Association (MHDW) ... BANTSA
Bank of Boston [*NYS*] (TTSB) ... BKB
Bank of Boston 7.875%DepPfd [*NYSE symbol*] (TTSB) ... BKBPrF
Bank of Boston 8.60% Dep Pfd [*NYSE symbol*] (TTSB) ... BKBPrE
Bank of Boston Adj Rt A Pfd [*NYSE symbol*] (TTSB) ... BKBPrA
Bank of Boston Adj Rt B Ptd [*NYSE symbol*] (TTSB) ... BKBPrB
Bank of Boston Adj Rt C Pfd [*NYSE symbol*] (TTSB) ... BKBPrC
Bank of Boston Corp. [*NYSE symbol*] (SPSG) ... BKB
Bank of Boston Corp. [*Associated Press*] (SAG) ... BkBost
Bank of British Columbia [*Toronto Stock Exchange symbol*] [*Vancouver Stock Exchange symbol*] ... BBC
Bank of California, San Francisco, CA [*Library symbol*] [*Library of Congress*] (LCLS) ... CSfB
Bank of Canada [*Banque du Canada*] ... BC
Bank of Canada, Ottawa, ON, Canada [*Library symbol*] [*Library of Congress*] (LCLS) ... CaOOB
Bank of Canada [*Banque du Canada*] **Ottawa, Ontario** [*Library symbol*] [*National Library of Canada*] (NLC) ... OOB
Bank of Canada Weekly Financial Statistics [*I. P. Sharp Associates*] [*Information service or system*] (CRD) ... WBANK
Bank of China Trust and Consultancy Co. ... BOCTC
Bank of Commerce (California) [*Associated Press*] (SAG) ... BCmCA

Bank of Commerce (California) [*NASDAQ symbol*] (SAG) .... BCOM
Bank of Commerce, Technical Information Facility, Toronto, ON, Canada
  [*Library symbol*] [*Library of Congress*] (LCLS) .... CaOTBCO
Bank of Communications [*China*] .... BOC
Bank of Communications [*China*] .... BoCom
Bank of Credit and Commerce Australia .... BCCA
Bank of Credit & Commerce International [*Facetious Translation: Bank of
  Crooks and Criminals International*] (ECON) .... BCCI
Bank of Credit and Commerce International (SAUO) .... BCCI
Bank of Credit and Commerce Niger (EY) .... BCCN
Bank of England (SAUO) .... BE
Bank of England (SAUO) .... BOE
Bank of England (SAUO) .... B of E
Bank of England .... B of E
Bank of England Staff Organisation .... BESO
Bank of England Statistical Summary (SAUS) .... BESS
Bank of Ghana .... B of G
Bank of Granite [*Associated Press*] (SAG) .... BkGranit
Bank of Granite [*NASDAQ symbol*] (SAG) .... GRAN
Bank of Hawaii (SAUO) .... BoH
Bank of Ireland Asset Management .... BIAM
Bank of Ireland Governor & Co ADS [*NYSE symbol*] (SG) .... IRE
Bank of Japan (SAUS) .... B of J
Bank of Japan (ODBW) .... BoJ
Bank of Kuwait & the Middle East (ECON) .... BKME
Bank of London and South America (SAUO) .... BL & SA
Bank of London & South America, Ltd. (SAUO) .... BOLSA
Bank of Los Angeles [*Associated Press*] (SAG) .... BankLA
Bank of Los Angeles [*NASDAQ symbol*] (SAG) .... BKLA
Bank of Los Angeles [*Associated Press*] (SAG) .... BnkLA
Bank of Maldives Ltd. (FEA) .... BML
Bank of Melbourne [*Australia*] .... BOM
Bank of Mitsubishi Ltd. [*Associated Press*] (SAG) .... BkTokyo
Bank of Mitsubishi Ltd. [*NYSE symbol*] (SAG) .... MBK
Bank of Montreal [*Associated Press*] (SAG) .... BkMont
Bank of Montreal [*Toronto Stock Exchange symbol*] [*Vancouver Stock
  Exchange symbol*] .... BMO
Bank of Montreal (SAUS) .... B of M
Bank of Montreal, Canadian Imperial Bank of Commerce, Bank of Nova
  Scotia, and Toronto-Dominion Bank .... MINT
Bank of Montreal, Montreal, PQ, Canada [*Library symbol*] [*Library of
  Congress*] (LCLS) .... CaQMBMo
Bank of Montreal [*Banque de Montreal*], Quebec [*Library symbol*] [*National
  Library of Canada*] (NLC) .... QMBMO
Bank of Montreal, Technical Information Centre, Willowdale, ON, Canada
  [*Library symbol*] [*Library of Congress*] (LCLS) .... CaOTBM
Bank of Nashville [*Associated Press*] (SAG) .... BkNash
Bank of Nashville [*Associated Press*] (SAG) .... BkNsh
[*The*] Bank of Nashville [*NASDAQ symbol*] (NQ) .... TBON
Bank of Nauru .... BON
Bank of New Hampshire Corp. [*NASDAQ symbol*] (NQ) .... BNHC
Bank of New Hampshire Corp. [*Associated Press*] (SAG) .... BnkNH
Bank of New Orleans (SAUO) .... BNO
Bank of New South Wales. Circular [*A publication*] .... Bank NSW Circular
Bank of New York [*Associated Press*] (SAG) .... Bank NY
Bank of New York .... BONY
Bank of New York Co., Inc. [*NYSE symbol*] (SPSG) .... BK
Bank of New York Co., Inc. [*Associated Press*] (SAG) .... BkNY
Bank of Nova Scotia [*Toronto Stock Exchange symbol*] [*Vancouver Stock
  Exchange symbol*] .... BNS
Bank of Nova Scotia (SAUS) .... Scotiabank
Bank of Nova Scotia, Toronto, ON, Canada [*Library symbol*] [*Library of
  Congress*] (LCLS) .... CaOTNS
Bank of Nova Scotia [*Banque de Nouvelle-Ecosse*], Toronto, Ontario [*Library
  symbol*] [*National Library of Canada*] (NLC) .... OTNS
Bank of Queensland Ltd. .... BOQ
Bank of Queensland Ltd. [*Australia*] .... BQL
Bank of San Diego (SAUO) .... BSD
Bank of Santa Clara [*Associated Press*] (SAG) .... BkSClara
Bank of Santa Clara [*NASDAQ symbol*] (SAG) .... BNSC
Bank of Scotland .... BOS
Bank of Singapore .... BOS
Bank of Small Industries and Commerce [*Bangladesh*] (EY) .... BASIC
[*The*] Bank of South Carolina [*NASDAQ symbol*] (NQ) .... BKSC
Bank of South Carolina (The) Charleston [*Associated Press*] (SAG) .... BankSC
Bank of Southington [*Associated Press*] (SAG) .... BkSthg
Bank of Southington [*AMEX symbol*] (TTSB) .... BSO
Bank of Southington (SAUS) .... TBOS
Bank of Spain .... BOS
Bank of Thailand (IMH) .... BOT
Bank of the Commonwealth (SAUO) .... BOC
Bank of the Philippine Islands (SAUO) .... BPI
Bank of the United States .... BUS
Bank of Tokyo .... BOT
Bank of Tokyo Australia Ltd. .... BOTA
Bank of Tokyo-MitsubishiADS [*NYSE symbol*] (TTSB) .... MBK
Bank of Tonga .... BT
Bank of Uganda .... BoU
Bank of Valletta [*Malta*] .... BV
Bank of Western Samoa .... BWS
Bank of Yorba Linda [*NASDAQ symbol*] (SAG) .... BOYL
Bank of Yorba Linda [*Associated Press*] (SAG) .... BYrbLin
Bank Officers Union (SAUO) .... BOU
Bank Official Loan Act [*1933*] .... BOLA
Bank One Corp. [*NYSE symbol*] (SG) .... ONE

Bank Pass Book (ROG) .... BPB
Bank Personnel Selection Inventory [*Test*] .... BPSI
Bank Plus Corp. [*Associated Press*] (SAG) .... BnkPlus
Bank Plus Corp. [*NASDAQ symbol*] [*Formerly, Fidelity Federal Bank*] (SG) .... BPLS
Bank Post Bill [*Business term*] .... BPB
Bank Proof Machine (SAUS) .... BPM
Bank Public Relations and Marketing Association [*Later, BMA*] .... BPRMA
Bank Rate [*Banking*] .... BR
Bank Robbery .... BR
Bank Secrecy Act (TDOB) .... BSA
Bank Settlement Plan (ADA) .... BSP
Bank Sorter-Reader (SAUS) .... BSR
Bank South Corp. [*NASDAQ symbol*] (NQ) .... BKSO
Bank South Corp. [*Associated Press*] (SAG) .... BkSouth
Bank Standing Order (DI) .... BSO
Bank Stationers Association [*Later, FSA*] (EA) .... BSA
Bank Street College (SAUO) .... BSC
Bank Street College of Education (GAGS) .... Bank St C
Bank Street College of Education, New York, NY [*Library symbol*] [*Library of
  Congress*] (LCLS) .... NNBSC
Bank Street Writer [*A computer program manufactured by Bank Street and
  Intentional Educations, Inc.*] .... BSW
Bank Subsidiaries/Other or Nonbank Subsidiaries/Parent
  Company/Consolidated (EBF) .... BOPEC
Bank Teller Job Trial [*Test*] [*Vocational Research Institute*] (TES) .... BTJT
Bank Teller Terminal (SAUS) .... BTT
Bank to Turn [*Aviation*] (MCD) .... BTT
Bank United 'A' [*NYSE symbol*] (SG) .... BNKU
Bank United Corp. [*NASDAQ symbol*] (SAG) .... BNKU
Bank United Corp. [*Associated Press*] (SAG) .... BnkUntd
Bank United of Texas FSB [*NYSE symbol*] (SPSG) .... BKU
Bank United of Texas FSB [*Associated Press*] (SAG) .... BKUtd
Bank Utd Texas 9.60% 'B' Pfd [*NYSE symbol*] (TTSB) .... BKUPrB
Bank Utd Texas FSB Pfd [*NYSE symbol*] (TTSB) .... BKUPrA
Bank West Financial [*NASDAQ symbol*] (TTSB) .... BWFC
Bank West Financial Corp. [*Associated Press*] (SAG) .... Bk West
Bank West Financial Corp. [*NASDAQ symbol*] (SAG) .... BWFC
Bank Wire Transfer of Funds .... BWTF
Bankair [*ICAO designator*] (AD) .... JA
Bankair, Inc. [*ICAO designator*] (FAAC) .... BKA
BankAmer 7.875% cm Ser'M'Pfd [*NYSE symbol*] (TTSB) .... BACPrM
BankAmer 8.16% cm Ser'L'Pfd [*NYSE symbol*] (TTSB) .... BACPrL
BankAmer 8.375% cm Ser'K'Pfd [*NYSE symbol*] (TTSB) .... BACPrK
BankAmer 8.50% cm Ser'N'Pfd [*NYSE symbol*] (TTSB) .... BACPrN
BankAmer 9% cm Ser'H'Pfd [*NYSE symbol*] (TTSB) .... BACPrH
BankAmer Adj cm A Pfd [*NYSE symbol*] (TTSB) .... BACPrA
BankAmer Adj cm B Pfd [*NYSE symbol*] (TTSB) .... BACPrB
BankAmerica Corp. [*Formerly, Security Pacific Corp.*] [*NYSE symbol*]
  (SPSG) .... BAC
BankAmerica Corp. [*Associated Press*] (SAG) .... BankAm
BankAmerica Corp. [*Associated Press*] (SAG) .... BkA
BankAmerica Corp. [*Associated Press*] (SAG) .... BkAm
BankAmericard [*Later, Visa*] [*Credit card*] .... BA
BankAmericard [*Later, Visa*] [*Credit card*] .... BAC
BankAmericard Service Exchange .... BASE
Bank-Americard Service Exchange (SAUO) .... BASE
BankAtlantic, a Federal Savings Bank [*Associated Press*] (SAG) .... BankAtl
BankAtlantic Bancorp 'A' [*NYSE symbol*] (SG) .... BBX
BankAtlantic Bancorp, Inc. [*NASDAQ symbol*] (SAG) .... BANC
BankAtlantic Bancorp, Inc. [*Associated Press*] (SAG) .... BnkAtla
BankAtlantic Bancorp'A' [*NASDAQ symbol*] (TTSB) .... BANCA
BankAtlantic Bancorp'B' [*NASDAQ symbol*] (TTSB) .... BANC
BankAtlantic Financial (EFIS) .... BFC
BankBoston Corp. [*NYSE symbol*] (SG) .... BKB
Bankcard .... BC
Bankcard (TBD) .... Bkcd
Bankcard Holders of America (EA) .... BHA
Bankcard Services Association (NTPA) .... BSA
BankcAtlantic Bancorp, Inc. [*NASDAQ symbol*] (SAG) .... BANC
Banked Breast Milk [*Neonatology*] (DAVI) .... BBM
Banked Position Withdrawal Sequence (IEEE) .... BPWS
Bankeno Resources Ltd. [*Toronto Stock Exchange symbol*] .... BKE
Banker (TBD) .... Bnkr
Banker .... BNKR
Bankers' [*Rate*] [*Value of the English pound*] .... BK
Bankers Acceptance (SAUS) .... BA
Bankers Association for Foreign Trade [*Washington, DC*] (EA) .... BAFT
Bankers Automated Clearing Service (SAUS) .... BAC
Bankers' Automated Clearing Services [*British*] (DCTA) .... BACS
Bankers' Blanket Bond [*Investment term*] .... BBB
Bankers Clearing House [*California*] (SRA) .... BCH
Bankers Committee (EA) .... BC
Bankers Committee for Tax Equality [*of the National Tax Equality
  Association*] (EA) .... BCTE
Bankers Committee to Eliminate Favoritism to Credit Unions (EA) .... BCEFCU
Bankers Corp. [*Associated Press*] (SAG) .... Bankrs Cp
Bankers Corp. [*NASDAQ symbol*] (SAG) .... BKCO
Bankers First Corp. [*NASDAQ symbol*] (NQ) .... BNKF
Bankers First Corp. [*Associated Press*] (SAG) .... BnkFst
Bankers Institute of New Zealand (SAUO) .... BINZ
Banker's Law Journal [*A publication*] (DLA) .... Banker's LJ
Bankers Life Co. (EFIS) .... BLC
Bankers Life Holding Corp. [*Associated Press*] (SAG) .... BkrsLH
Bankers Life Holding Corp. [*NYSE symbol*] (SPSG) .... BLH
Banker's Note [*Associated Press*] (SAG) .... BnkrN

Banker's Note [*AMEX symbol*] (SAG) .... TBN
Banker's Note [*ECM Symbol*] (TTSB) .... TBN.EC
Banker's Note, Inc. (EFIS) .... BKNT
Banker's Order .... BO
Bankers Tr N.Y. 7.625%Dep Pfd [*AMEX symbol*] (TTSB) .... BPR
Bankers Tr N.Y. Adj Dep'Q'Pfd [*NYSE symbol*] (TTSB) .... BTPrQ
Bankers Tr N.Y. Adj Dep'R'Pfd [*NYSE symbol*] (TTSB) .... BTPrR
Bankers Tr N.Y.7.50% Dep Pfd [*AMEX symbol*] (TTSB) .... BPB
Bankers Tr N.Y.7.75% Dep'S'Pfd [*NYSE symbol*] (TTSB) .... BTPrS
Bankers Tr N.Y.8.55% Sr'l'Pfd [*NYSE symbol*] (TTSB) .... BTPrl
Bankers Tr6% Cap Sec [*AMEX symbol*] (TTSB) .... BTB
Bankers Tr6.125%CapSec [*AMEX symbol*] (TTSB) .... BND
Bankers Trust Co. (MHDW) .... BTC
Bankers Trust Information Service [*Database producer*] .... BTIS
Bankers Trust International, Inc. (SAUO) .... BTI
Bankers Trust New York Corp. [*Associated Press*] (SAG) .... BankTr
Bankers Trust New York Corp. [*AMEX symbol*] (SPSG) .... BND
Bankers Trust New York Corp. [*Associated Press*] (SAG) .... BnkT
Bankers Trust New York Corp. [*AMEX symbol*] (SAG) .... BPB
Bankers Trust New York Corp. [*AMEX symbol*] (SAG) .... BPR
Bankers Trust New York Corp. [*NYSE symbol*] (SPSG) .... BT
Bankers Trust New York Corp. [*AMEX symbol*] (SPSG) .... BTB
Bankers Trust New York Corp. [*NYSE symbol*] (SAG) .... BTU
Bankfull (QUAC) .... bkf
bankfull (SAUS) .... bkf
Bank/Fund Conferences Office [*World Bank, IMF*] .... BFCO
Bankgesellschaft Berlin [*Germany*] (ECON) .... BGB
Bankim Barotra [*Commerce Bank*] [*Malagasy*] (AF) .... BB
Banking .... BKG
Banking (WDAA) .... Bkg
Banking (WDAA) .... bkg
Banking (ADA) .... BNKG
Banking (TBD) .... Bnkg
Banking .... BNKNG
Banking and Currency (SAUO) .... B&C
Banking and Currency Committee [*US Senate*] .... B & C
Banking and Securities Industry Committee [*Inactive*] .... BASIC
Banking Cases [*A publication*] (DLA) .... Bank Cas
Banking Center (SAUS) .... TBCX
Banking Clause (SAUS) .... Bank Cl
Banking Code [*A publication*] (DLA) .... Bank C
Banking Communication Standard (VERA) .... BCS
Banking Communication System (IAA) .... BCS
Banking Federation of the European Economic Community [*Belgium*] (EAIO) .... BFEC
Banking Federation of the European Economic Community [*Belgium*] (EAIO) .... BFEEC
Banking, Finance, and Urban Affairs (DLA) .... BFUA
Banking, Housing, and Urban Affairs (DLA) .... BHUA
Banking Information Processing System [*Computer science*] (BUR) .... BIPS
Banking Information Service [*British*] .... BIS
Banking, Insurance, and Finance Union [*British*] (DBA) .... BIFU
Banking Law Bulletin [*Australia*] [*A publication*] .... BLB
Banking Law Institute (EA) .... BLI
Banking Literature Index [*A publication*] .... BLI
Banking On-Line Package System (BUR) .... BOPS
Banking Profession Political Action Committee [*Acronym now used as official name of organization*] (EA) .... BANKPAC
Banking Research and Economic Analysis [*Unit*] [*Department of the Treasury*] (GRD) .... BR & EA
Banking Systems Information Exchange .... BSIE
Banking Users' Group [*British*] .... BAKUP
Bankit Resource Corp. [*Vancouver Stock Exchange symbol*] .... BKR
Banknorth Group [*NASDAQ symbol*] (TTSB) .... BKNG
Banknorth Group, Inc. [*NASDAQ symbol*] (NQ) .... BKNG
Banknorth Group, Inc. [*Associated Press*] (SAG) .... Bknth
Banknote .... BN
Banknote Corp of America [*Printer of U.S. postage stamps*] (BARN) .... BCA
Bank-Parameter-Datei (SAUS) .... BPD
Bankroll [*Slang*] .... BR
Bankrupt (WDAA) .... Bkpt
Bankrupt (WDAA) .... bkpt
Bankrupt (ROG) .... BKPT
Bankrupt .... BKRPT
Bankrupt (ROG) .... BKRUPT
Bankrupt [*or Bankruptcy*] (DCTA) .... BRUPT
Bankrupt Court Reporter [*New York*] [*A publication*] (DLA) .... Bank Ct Rep
Bankrupt Register [*A publication*] (DLA) .... B Reg
Bankruptcy [*Legal term*] (DLA) .... Bank
Bankruptcy .... BANKCY
Bankruptcy [*Legal term*] (DLA) .... Bankr
Bankruptcy [*Legal term*] (DLA) .... Bcy
Bankruptcy .... BKCY
Bankruptcy (ODBW) .... bkcy
Bankruptcy [*Legal shorthand*] (LWAP) .... BKPTCY
Bankruptcy (ADA) .... BKRPCY
Bankruptcy .... BKRPTCY
Bankruptcy .... BKTCY
Bankruptcy .... BKY
Bankruptcy Act [*Legal term*] (DLA) .... Bankr Act
Bankruptcy and Insolvency (SAUS) .... B&I
Bankruptcy and Insolvency Cases [*Legal*] [*British*] .... B & I
Bankruptcy and Insolvency Reports [*1853-55*] [*England*] [*A publication*] (DLA) .... B & I

Bankruptcy and Insolvency Reports [*1853-55*] [*England*] [*A publication*] (DLA) .... Bank & Ins
Bankruptcy and Insolvency Reports [*1853-55*] [*England*] [*A publication*] (DLA) .... Bank & Insol Rep
Bankruptcy and Insolvency Reports [*1853-55*] [*England*] [*A publication*] (DLA) .... Bank & Ins R
Bankruptcy and Insolvency Reports [*1853-55*] [*England*] [*A publication*] (DLA) .... Bank Insol Rep
Bankruptcy and Insolvency Reports [*1853-55*] [*England*] [*A publication*] (DLA) .... Bankr Ins R
Bankruptcy Annulment Order [*Legal term*] (DLA) .... BAO
Bankruptcy Bar Bulletin [*A publication*] (DLA) .... Bankr B Bull
Bankruptcy Cases [*A publication*] (DLA) .... BC
Bankruptcy Court [*Legal term*] (DLA) .... Bank
Bankruptcy Court [*Legal term*] (DAS) .... BC
Bankruptcy Court (SAUO) .... BC
Bankruptcy Court Decisions [*A publication*] (DLA) .... Bankr Ct Dec
Bankruptcy Fee (ADA) .... BF
Bankruptcy File [*Canada Systems Group*] [*Ottawa, ON*] [*Information service or system*] (IID) .... BKRP
Bankruptcy Forms [*A publication*] (DLA) .... Bankr Form
Bankruptcy Gazette [*A publication*] (DLA) .... Bank Gaz
Bankruptcy Law Reports [*CCH*] [*A publication*] (AAGC) .... Bankr L Rep
Bankruptcy Official Receivers' Information System .... BORIS
Bankruptcy Reform Act [*1978*] .... BRA
Bankruptcy Register [*A publication*] (DLA) .... Bank Reg
Bankruptcy Register [*A publication*] (DLA) .... BR
Bankruptcy Reporter [*West*] [*A publication*] (AAGC) .... BR
Bankruptcy Reports [*A publication*] (DLA) .... BR
Banks & Barns [*Commercial firm*] [*British*] .... B & B
Banks Automated Clearing Services (SAUS) .... BACS
Banks Automated Clearing System [*British*] (NITA) .... BACS
Banks Community Library, Banks, OR [*Library symbol*] [*Library of Congress*] (LCLS) .... OrBa
Banks Multi-Access in Real Time (SAUS) .... BANKMART
Banks, OR [*FM radio station call letters*] (BROA) .... KBBT-FM
Banks, OR [*FM radio station call letters*] .... KDBX
Banks' Reports [*1-5 Kansas*] [*A publication*] (DLA) .... Banks
Bank-Share Owners Advisory League [*Inactive*] .... BSOAL
Bankson Language Screening Test [*Child development test*] .... BLST
Bankson Language Screening Test-2 (TES) BLT-2
Bank-Switching [*Computer technology*] .... BS
Bankter's Institutes of Scottish Law [*A publication*] (DLA) .... Bank I
Bankter's Institutes of Scottish Law [*A publication*] (DLA) .... Bank Inst
Bankter's Institutes of Scottish Law [*A publication*] (DLA) .... Bankt I
BankUnited Financial Corp. [*NASDAQ symbol*] (NQ) .... BKUN
BankUnited Financial Corp. [*Associated Press*] (SAG) .... BkUtF
BankUnited Financial Corp. [*Associated Press*] (SAG) .... BnkUt
BankUnited Financial Corp. [*Associated Press*] (SAG) .... BnkUtd
BankUnited Financial'A' [*NASDAQ symbol*] (TTSB) .... BKUNA
BankUnited Finl 8% Cv Pfd [*NASDAQ symbol*] (TTSB) .... BKUNP
BankUnited Finl 9% Perp Pfd [*NASDAQ symbol*] (TTSB) .... BKUNO
Banner [*Record label*] .... Ban
Banner Aerospace [*Associated Press*] (SAG) .... BanrAer
Banner Aerospace [*NYSE symbol*] (SPSG) .... BAR
Banner Blade Length [*Botany*] .... BBLL
Banner Claw Length [*Botany*] .... BCLL
Banner Elk, NC [*Location identifier*] [*FAA*] (FAAL) .... BAR
Banner Elk, NC [*FM radio station call letters*] .... WZJS
Banner Entertainment [*Vancouver Stock Exchange symbol*] .... BNN
Banner Reflex [*Botany*] .... BREX
Banning and Arden's Patent Cases [*United States*] [*A publication*] (DLA) .... Ban & A
Banning and Arden's Patent Cases [*United States*] [*A publication*] (DLA) .... Bann & A
Banning and Arden's Patent Cases [*United States*] [*A publication*] (DLA) .... Bann & A Pat Cas
Banning and Arden's Patent Cases [*United States*] [*A publication*] (DLA) .... Bann & Ard
Banning and Arden's Patent Reports [*United States*] [*A publication*] (DLA) .... B & A
Banning, CA [*Location identifier*] [*FAA*] (FAAL) .... BNG
Banning, CA [*AM radio station call letters*] .... KMET
Banning. Limitations of Actions [*3rd ed.*] [*1906*] [*A publication*] (DLA) .... Bann Lim
Banning Union Public Library, Banning, CA [*Library symbol*] [*Library of Congress*] (LCLS) .... CBan
Bannister Research & Consulting .... BRC
Bannister's Disease [*Medicine*] (MELL) .... BD
Bannister's Edition of Orlando Bridgman's English Common Pleas Reports [*A publication*] (DLA) .... Bann Br
Bannister's Reports, English Common Pleas [*A publication*] (DLA) .... Bann
Bannock Regional Medical Center, Medical Library [*Library symbol*] [*Library of Congress*] (LCLS) .... IdPBH
Bannon, E. J., Buffalo NY [*STAC*] .... BEJ
Bannu [*Pakistan*] [*Airport symbol*] (OAG) .... BNP
Bannu [*Pakistan*] [*ICAO location identifier*] (ICLI) .... OPBN
BanPonce 8.35%.Mthly Inc. Pfd [*NASDAQ symbol*] (TTSB) .... BPOPP
BanPonce Corp. [*Associated Press*] (SAG) .... BanPn
BanPonce Corp. [*Associated Press*] (SAG) .... BanPonc
BanPonce Corp. [*NASDAQ symbol*] (NQ) .... BPOP
Banque Africaine de Developpement [*African Development Bank*] [*Use ADB*] (AF) .... BAD
Banque al-Baraka Mauritanienne Islamique (EY) .... BAMIS
Banque Arabe de Developpement Economique en Afrique [*Arab Bank for Economic Development in Africa*] .... BADEA

Banque Arabe et Internationale d'Investissement [*France*] .... BAII

Banque Arabe-Libyenne-Burkinabe pour le Commerce et le Developpement (EY) .... BALIB

Banque Bruxelles Lambert [*Belgium*] (ECON) .... BBL

Banque Canadienne Nationale .... BCN

Banque Centrale de Compensation (SAUS) .... BCC

Banque Centrale de la Republique de Guinee [*Central Bank of the Republic of Guinea*] (AF) .... BCRG

Banque Centrale de Syrie [*Central Bank of Syria*] (BJA) .... BCS

Banque Centrale de Tunisie [*Central Bank of Tunisia*] (AF) .... BCT

Banque Centrale des Etats de l'Afrique de l'Ouest [*Central Bank of the West African States*] [*Dakar, Senegal*] (AF) .... BCEAO

Banque Centrale des Etats de l'Afrique Equatoriale et de Cameroun [*Central Bank of the States of Equatorial Africa and Cameroon*] (AF) .... BCEAEC

Banque Centrale du Congo Belge et du Ruanda-Urundi [*Central Bank of the Belgian Congo and Rwanda-Urandi*] .... BCCBRU

Banque Commerciale du Burundi (EY) .... BANCOBU

Banque Commerciale du Rwanda [*Commercial Bank of Rwanda*] (AF) .... BCR

Banque Commerciale du Senegal (EY) .... BCS

Banque d'Afrique Occidentale [*Bank of French West Africa*] .... BAO

Banque Dahomeenne de Developpement [*Dahomean Development Bank*] .... BDD

Banque de Credit Agricole et de Developpement [*Central African Republic*] (EY) .... BCAD

Banque de Developpement de la Republique du Niger [*Development Bank of the Republic of Niger*] (AF) .... BDRN

Banque de Developpement de l'Afrique de l'Est [*East African Development Bank - EADB*] (EAIO) .... BDAE

Banque de Developpement des Etats du Grand Lac [*Development Bank of the Great Lakes States*] (EAIO) .... BDEGL

Banque de Developpement du Tchad [*Development Bank of Chad*] (AF) .... BDT

Banque de Developpement Local [*Algeria*] (EY) .... BDL

Banque de Developpment des Etats de l'Afrique Centrale [*Central African States Development Bank*] .... BDEAC

Banque de Donnees a acces direct de l'Universite du Quebec [*Database of the holdings of the University of Quebec*] [*Canada*] (NITA) .... BADADUQ

Banque de Donnees Internationales de Biometrie Humaine et d'Ergonomie [*International Database of Human Biometrics and Ergonomics*] [*Universite Rene Descartes*] [*France*] [*Information service or system*] (CRD) .... ERGODATA

Banque de Donnees Locales [*Local Area Data Bank*] [*National Institute of Statistics and Economic Studies*] [*Information service or system*] (IID) .... BDL

Banque de Donnees Macroeconomiques [*Macroeconomic Data Bank*] [*National Institute of Statistics and Economic Studies*] [*Information service or system*] .... BDM

Banque de Donnees Socio-Economiques des Pays Mediterraneens [*Socioeconomic Data Bank on the Mediterranean Countries*] [*International Center for Advanced Mediterranean Agronomic Studies*] [*Information service or system*] (IID) .... MEDISTAT

Banque de Donnees Urbaines de Paris et de la Region d'Ile-De-France [*Urban Data Bank of Paris and the Paris Region*] [*Paris Office of Urbanization*] [*France*] [*Information service or system*] (IID) .... BDU

Banque de France [*Bank of France*] .... BF

Banque de l'Union Europeenne [*European Union Bank*] [*France*] .... BUE

Banque de Madagascar et des Comores [*Bank of Madagascar and of the Comoro Islands*] (AF) .... BMC

Banque de Nouvelle - Caledonie (EY) .... BNC

Banque de Terminologie de Quebec [*Terminology Bank of Quebec*] [*French Language Board*] [*Information service or system*] .... TERMINOQ

Banque de Terminologie du Quebec [*Terminology Bank of Quebec*] [*French Language Board*] [*Information service or system*] (IID) .... BTQ

Banque des Connaissances et des Techniques [*Knowledge and Technique Bank*] [*National Agency for the Promotion of Research*] [*Information service or system*] (IID) .... BCT

Banque des Estats de l'Afrique Centrale (EBF) .... BCEA

Banque des Etats de l'Afrique Centrale [*Bank of Central African States*] (AF) .... BEAC

Banque des Reglements Internationaux [*Bank for International Settlements*] .... BRI

Banque d'Expansion Industrielle [*Industrial Development Bank*] [*Canada*] .... BEI

Banque d'Information Automatisee sur les Medicaments Principes Actifs [*Databank on active ingredients of drugs*] [*French*] (NITA) .... BIAM PA

Banque d'Information Industrielle [*Industrial Information Data Base*] [*Industrial Research Center of Quebec*] [*Information service or system*] (IID) .... BII

Banque d'Information Industrielle de Pont-A-Mousson et du CTIF [*Centre Technique des Industries de la Fonderie*] [*French*] [*Information service or system*] (CRD) .... BIIPAM-CTIF

Banque d'Information Robert Debre [*Centre International de l'Enfance*] [*Database*] .... BIRD

Banque d'Information sur les Recherches [*INSERM Research Information Bank*] [*National Institute for Health and Medical Research*] [*Information service or system*] (IID) .... BIR

Banque d'Informations Automatisees sur les Medicaments [*Data Bank for Medicaments*] [*Information service or system*] (IID) .... BIAM

Banque d'Informations Politiques et d'Actualite [*Political and Current Events Information Bank*] [*Database*] [*Telesystems - Questel*] [*Information service or system*] (IID) .... BIPA

Banque du Congo Belge [*Bank of the Belgian Congo*] .... BCB

Banque Europeenne de Credit [*Belgium*] .... BEC

Banque Europeenne d'Investissement [*European Investment Bank - EIB*] [*French*] .... BEI

Banque Europeenne pour l'Amerique Latine [*Bank*] [*French*] (EY) .... BEAL

Banque Exterieure d'Algerie [*Algerian Foreign Bank*] (AF) .... BEA

Banque Federale de Developpement [*Federal Business Development Bank - FBDB*] [*Canada*] .... BFD

Banque Francaise Commerciale Ocean Indian [*Reunion*] (EY) .... BFCOI

Banque Francaise du Commerce Exterieur [*French state-owned bank*] .... BFCE

Banque Francaise pour le Commerce [*French Commercial Bank*] (AF) .... BFC

Banque Franco-Arabe d'Investissements Internationaux .... FRAB

Banque Gabonaise de Developpement [*Gabonese Development Bank*] (AF) .... BGD

Banque Guineenne du Commerce Exterieur [*Guinean Bank of Foreign Commerce*] (AF) .... BGCE

Banque Interamericaine de Developpement [*Inter-American Development Bank*] [*French*] .... BID

Banque International de Placement .... BIP

Banque Internationale a Luxembourg SA (ECON) .... BIL

Banque Internationale des Comores (EY) .... BIC

Banque Internationale du Burkina [*Burkina Faso*] (EY) .... BIB

Banque Internationale pour la Reconstruction et le Developpement [*International Bank for Reconstruction and Development; also known as the World Bank*] [*French*] .... BIRD

Banque Internationale pour l'Afrique en Guinee (EY) .... BIAG

Banque Internationale pour l'Afrique Occidentale [*International Bank for West Africa*] [*France*] (AF) .... BIAO

Banque Internationale pour l'Afrique Occidentale - Cote d'Ivoire (EY) .... BIAO-CI

Banque Ivoirienne de Developpement Industriel [*Ivorian Bank for Industrial Development*] (AF) .... BIDI

Banque Malgache de l'Ocean Indien [*Indian Ocean Malagasy Bank*] [*Madagascar*] (EY) .... BMOI

Banque Malgache d'Escompte et de Credit [*Malagasy Discount and Credit Bank*] (AF) .... BAMES

Banque Malienne de Credits et de Depots [*Malian Credit and Deposits Bank*] (AF) .... BMCD

Banque Marocaine pour le Commerce Exterieur [*Moroccan Foreign Trade Bank*] (AF) .... BMCE

Banque Mauritanienne de Developpement [*Mauritanian Development Bank*] (AF) .... BMD

Banque Nationale Agricole [*National Agricultural Bank*] [*Tunisia*] (AF) .... BNA

Banque Nationale de Belgique [*National Bank of Belgium*] .... BNB

Banque Nationale de Credit Rural [*Gabon*] (EY) .... BNCR

Banque Nationale de Devellopement du Burkina (EY) .... BNDB

Banque Nationale de Developpement de la Haute-Volta [*National Development Bank of Upper Volta*] (AF) .... BNDHV

Banque Nationale de Developpement du Congo [*National Development Bank of the Congo*] (AF) .... BNDC

Banque Nationale de Developpement Economique [*National Economic Development Bank*] [*France*] (AF) .... BNDE

Banque Nationale de Mauritanie (EY) .... BNM

Banque Nationale de Paris [*National Bank of Paris*] [*France*] .... BNP

Banque Nationale du Canada, Centre de Documentation, Montreal, PQ, Canada [*Library symbol*] [*Library of Congress*] (LCLS) .... CaQMBAN

Banque Nationale du Congo [*National Bank of the Congo*] .... BNC

Banque Nationale Malgache de Developpement [*Malagasy National Development Bank*] (AF) .... BNM

Banque Nationale pour le Commerce et l'Industrie [*National Bank for Commerce and Industry*] [*Togo*] [*French*] .... BNCI

Banque Nationale pour le Developpement Agricole [*National Agricultural Development Bank*] [*Ivory Coast*] (AF) .... BNDA

Banque Nationale pour le Developpement Economique [*National Bank for Economic Development*] [*Morocco*] (IMH) .... BNDE

Banque Ouest Africaine de Developpement [*West African Development Bank - WADB*] (EAIO) .... BOAD

Banque pour le Financement du Commerce et des Investissements du Burkina (EY) .... BFCIB

Banque pour l'Expansion Industrielle [*Industrial Development Bank*] [*France*] (EY) .... BANEXI

Banque Senegalo-Koweitienne [*Senegal-Kuwait Bank*] .... BSK

Banque Senegalo-Tunisienne (EY) .... BST

Banque Tchadienne de Credit et de Depots [*Chad*] (EY) .... BTCD

Banquet Event Order [*Food service industry*] .... BEO

Banqueting/Catered Functions [*Public-performance tariff class*] [*British*] .... BF

Banta Corp. [*Associated Press*] (SAG) .... Banta

Banta Corp. [*NYSE symbol*] (SG) .... BN

Banta Corp. [*NASDAQ symbol*] (NQ) .... BNTA

Bantam (ABBR) .... BTM

Bantam (SAUO) .... ISBN 0-553

Bantam Books (SAUS) .... Bantam

Bantam, Doubleday, Dell Publishing Group .... BDD

Bantam Inertial Reference (SAUS) .... BANIR

Bantam Reconnaissance-Command [*Jeep prototype*] .... BRC

Bantamweight (ABBR) .... BTMWT

Banting Research Centre Library, Department of National Health and Welfare [*Bibliotheque du Centre de Recherches Banting, Ministere de la Sante Nationale et du Bien-Etre Social*] **Ottawa, Ontario** [*Library symbol*] [*National Library of Canada*] (NLC) .... OONHBR

Banting-Best Physiology Library, University of Toronto, Ontario [*Library symbol*] [*National Library of Canada*] (NLC) .... OTUBP

Bantock Society (EA) .... BS

Bantu (SAUS) .... Ban

Bantu Administration and Development (SAUO) .... BAD

Banyan Hotel Inv Fund [*AMEX symbol*] (TTSB) .... VHT

Banyan Hotel Investment Fund (SAG) .... BanyHI

Banyan Hotel Investment Fund (SAUS) .... VHI

Banyan Hotel Investment Fund [*Formerly, VMS Hotel Investment Fund*] [*AMEX symbol*] (SPSG) .... VHT

Banyan Mortgage Inv Fund [*NYSE symbol*] (TTSB) .... VMG

Banyan Mortgage Investment Fund [*Associated Press*] (SAG) .... BanyMF

Banyan Mortgage Investment Fund [*Formerly, VMS Mortgate Investment Fund*] [*NYSE symbol*] (SPSG) .... VMG

Banyan Short Term Inc. Trust (SAUS) .... VST

Banyan Short Term Income Trust [*Associated Press*] (SAG) ..... BanynSh
Banyan Short Term Income Trust [*Formerly, VMS Short Term Income Trust*] [*AMEX symbol*] (SPSG) ..... VST
Banyan Strategic Land Fd II [*NASDAQ symbol*] (TTSB) ..... VSLF
Banyan Strategic Land Fund [*Associated Press*] (SAG) ..... BanySL
Banyan Strategic Land Fund [*NASDAQ symbol*] (SAG) ..... VSLF
Banyan Strategic Land Fund II [*Associated Press*] (SAG) BanySL2
Banyan Strategic Land Fund II [*NASDAQ symbol*] (SAG) ..... VSLF
Banyan Strategic Realty Tr [*NASDAQ symbol*] (TTSB) ..... VLANS
Banyan Strategic Realty Trust [*Associated Press*] (SAG) ..... BanyRT
Banyan Strategic Realty Trust [*NASDAQ symbol*] (SAG) ..... VLAN
Banyan Systems [*NASDAQ symbol*] (TTSB) ..... BNYN
Banyan Systems, Inc. [*Associated Press*] (SAG) ..... BanynSy
Banyan Systems, Inc. [*NASDAQ symbol*] (SAG) ..... BNYN
Banyan VINES Control Protocol (SAUS) ..... BVCP
Banyo [*Cameroon*] [*ICAO location identifier*] (ICLI) ..... FKAB
Banyumas/Wirasaba [*Indonesia*] [*ICAO location identifier*] (ICLI) ..... WIAP
BANZ [*British-Australian-New Zealand*] [*Papua New Guinea*] [*Airport symbol*] [*Obsolete*] (OAG) ..... BNZ
Banza-Lute [*Zaire*] [*ICAO location identifier*] (ICLI) ..... FZCL
Baombardement (SAUS) ..... BBT
Baoshan [*China*] [*Airport symbol*] (OAG) ..... BSD
Baotou [*China*] [*Airport symbol*] (OAG) ..... BAV
Baotou [*China*] [*ICAO location identifier*] (ICLI) ..... ZBOW
BAPTA [*Bearing and Power Transfer Assembly*] **Accelerometer and Conditioner** [*Aerospace*] ..... BAC
Baptism (GEAB) ..... bap
Baptism (SAUS) ..... BAP
Baptist ..... B
Baptist ..... BAP
Baptist (NTIO) ..... Bap
Baptist (WDAA) ..... Bapt
Baptist (VRA) ..... bapt
Baptist ..... BAPT
Baptist (SAUS) ..... Bapt
Baptist Association of Hospital Chaplains (EA) ..... BAHC
Baptist Bible College, Denver, CO [*Library symbol*] [*Library of Congress*] (LCLS) ..... CoDBB
Baptist Bible College of Pennsylvania, Clarks Summit, PA [*Library symbol*] [*Library of Congress*] (LCLS) ..... PCsB
Baptist Bible College, Springfield, MO [*Library symbol*] [*Library of Congress*] (LCLS) ..... MoSpBB
Baptist Bible Fellowship International (EA) ..... BBFI
Baptist College at Charleston, Charleston, SC [*OCLC symbol*] (OCLC) ..... SBC
Baptist College at Charleston, Charleston, SC [*Library symbol*] [*Library of Congress*] (LCLS) ..... ScCB
Baptist Community Service [*Australia*] ..... BCS
Baptist Convention of Ontario & Quebec (AC) ..... BCOQ
Baptist Counselling Service [*Australia*] ..... BCS
Baptist General Conference of Canada (AC) ..... BGC
Baptist Historical Society (SAUO) ..... BHS
[*The*] **Baptist Historical Society** [*British*] ..... BHS
Baptist Historical Society of New South Wales [*Australia*] ..... BHSNSW
Baptist Holiday Fellowship, Ltd. (SAUO) ..... BHF
Baptist Hospital Association (EA) ..... BHA
Baptist Hospital, Medical Library, Nashville, TN [*Library symbol*] [*Library of Congress*] (LCLS) ..... TNBH
Baptist Hospital of Miami, Health Sciences Library, Miami, FL [*Library symbol*] [*Library of Congress*] (LCLS) ..... FMBH
Baptist Independent Church [*Also, BIC*] ..... BI
Baptist Independent Church [*Also, BI*] ..... BIC
Baptist Information Retrieval System [*Southern Baptist Convention*] [*Nashville, TN*] [*Library network*] [*Defunct*] ..... BIRS
Baptist Joint Committee on Public Affairs (EA) ..... BJCPA
Baptist Life Association [*Buffalo, NY*] (EA) ..... BLA
Baptist Medical Center (Montclair), Medical Library, Birmingham, AL [*Library symbol*] [*Library of Congress*] (LCLS) ..... ABBM-M
Baptist Medical Center (Princeton), Medical Library, Birmingham, AL [*Library symbol*] [*Library of Congress*] (LCLS) ..... ABBM-P
Baptist Medical Center, School of Nursing, Birmingham, AL [*Library symbol*] [*Library of Congress*] (LCLS) ..... ABBM
Baptist Memorial Hospital, Kansas City, MO [*Library symbol*] [*Library of Congress*] (LCLS) ..... MoKBH
Baptist Memorial Hospital, Memphis, TN [*Library symbol*] [*Library of Congress*] (LCLS) ..... TMBH
Baptist Memorial Hospital, School of Nursing, Memphis, TN [*Library symbol*] [*Library of Congress*] (LCLS) ..... TMBH-N
Baptist Mid-Missions (EA) ..... BMM
Baptist Mission of North America [*Defunct*] (EA) ..... BMNA
Baptist Mission Society ..... BMS
Baptist Missionary (SAUO) ..... BMS
Baptist Missionary Association Theological Seminary, Jacksonville, TX [*Library symbol*] [*Library of Congress*] (LCLS) ..... TxJaB
Baptist Peace Fellowship (EA) ..... BPF
Baptist Peace Fellowship of North America (EAIO) ..... BPFNA
Baptist Public Relations Association (EA) ..... BPRA
Baptist Revival Fellowship [*British*] ..... BRF
Baptist Student Union (IIA) ..... BSU
Baptist Students Concerned [*Defunct*] (EA) ..... BSC
Baptist Students Federation (SAUO) ..... BSF
Baptist Telecommunications Network [*Nashville, TN*] [*Cable-television system*] ..... BTN
Baptist Union ..... BU
Baptist Union Corporation Limited (SAUO) ..... BUCL
Baptist Union of Australia ..... BUA
Baptist Union of Great Britain and Ireland (SAUO) ..... BU
Baptist Union of Western Canada (ROAS) ..... BUWC
Baptist Women in Ministry/Folio (EA) ..... BWIM/FOLIO
Baptist Women's Missionary Auxilliary [*British*] (BI) ..... BWMA
Baptist Women's Union of the South West Pacific [*Australia*] ..... BWUSWP
Baptist World Aid (EA) ..... BWA
Baptist World Aid (EA) ..... BWAid
Baptist World Alliance (EA) ..... BWA
Baptist World Relief [*Later, Baptist World Aid*] (EA) ..... BWARF
Baptist Young People's Union ..... BYPU
Baptists for Life (EA) ..... BFL
Baptized ..... BA
Baptized ..... BAP
Baptized ..... BAPT
Baptized (ADWA) ..... bapt
Baptized ..... BP
Baptized (SAUS) ..... Bp
Baptized (GEAB) ..... bpt
Bar (ABAC) ..... b
Bar ..... B
Bar [*Freight*] ..... BA
Bar ..... BR
Bar Address Register [*Computer science*] (NITA) ..... BAR
Bar and Legal World [*England*] [*A publication*] (DLA) ..... Bar & Leg W
Bar Association Bulletin, Los Angeles [*A publication*] (DLA) ..... BA Bull LA
Bar Association for Commerce, Finance, and Industry [*British*] (DBA) ..... BACA
Bar Association for Commerce, Finance and Industry (SAUO) ..... BACFI
Bar Association for Human Rights of Greater New York (EA) ..... BAHRGNY
Bar Association of Metropolitan St. Louis. Bankruptcy Reporter [*A publication*] (DLA) ..... BAMSL
Bar Association of Queensland [*Australia*] ..... BAQ
Bar Association of the District of Columbia (SRA) ..... BADC
Bar Association of the District of Columbia, Washington, DC [*Library symbol*] [*Library of Congress*] (LCLS) ..... DBA
Bar Bulletin [*A publication*] (DLA) ..... B Bull
Bar Bulletin, New York County Lawyers' [*A publication*] (DLA) ..... Bar Bull (NY County La)
Bar Chair (SAUS) ..... BC
Bar Chart Report (MCD) ..... BCR
Bar Code Information System (GEOI) ..... BARCIS
Bar Coded Label (NITA) ..... BCL
Bar. Das Internationale Privat-und-Strafrecht [*A publication*] (DLA) ..... Bar Int Pr R
Bar Double-X (SAUS) ..... BDX
Bar Draft (SAUS) ..... BD
Bar Draft [*Depth of water over a bar*] ..... BD
Bar Draught (SAUS) ..... BD
Bar Examination Annual [*1893-94*] [*A publication*] (DLA) ..... Bar Ex Ann
Bar Examination Guide [*1895-99*] [*A publication*] (DLA) ..... Bar Ex Guide
Bar Examination Journal [*A publication*] (DLA) ..... Bar Ex J
Bar Examination Journal [*A publication*] (DLA) ..... Bar Ex Jour
Bar Examination Journal [*A publication*] (DLA) ..... B Exam J
Bar (Handle) Control [*Early automobiles*] (ROG) ..... BC
Bar Harbor [*Maine*] [*Airport symbol*] (OAG) ..... BHB
Bar Harbor Airlines [*ICAO designator*] (FAAC) ..... AJC
Bar Harbor Airlines [*ICAO designator*] (AD) ..... QO
Bar Harbor Bankshares [*AMEX symbol*] (SG) ..... BHB
Bar Harbor, ME [*FM radio station call letters*] ..... WLKE
Bar Harbor, ME [*FM radio station call letters*] ..... WMDI
Bar Joist [*Building construction*] (OA) ..... BJ
Bar Journal [*A publication*] ..... BJ
Bar Keel [*Shipping*] (DS) ..... BK
Bar Leader [*A publication*] (DLA) ..... B Leader
Bar Library Association of Kansas City, Kansas City, MO [*Library symbol*] [*Library of Congress*] (LCLS) ..... MoKB
Bar Line Printer (SAUS) ..... BLP
Bar Mitzvah (BJA) ..... BM
Bar Reports [*1865-71*] [*A publication*] (DLA) ..... Bar Rep
Bar Reports in All Courts [*England*] [*A publication*] (DLA) ..... Bar
Bar Reports in All Courts [*England*] [*A publication*] (DLA) ..... Bar Re
Bar Resources Ltd. [*Vancouver Stock Exchange symbol*] ..... BSL
Bar to Bar (ACAE) ..... BB
Baraboo, WI [*FM radio station call letters*] ..... WOLX
Baraboo, WI [*AM radio station call letters*] ..... WRPQ
Barack Inventory Accounting (SAUS) ..... BIA
Baracoa [*Cuba*] [*Airport symbol*] (OAG) ..... BCA
Baracoa Playa/Habana [*Cuba*] [*ICAO location identifier*] (ICLI) ..... MUPB
Baracoa/Oriente [*Cuba*] [*ICAO location identifier*] (ICLI) ..... MUBA
Baraga, MI [*FM radio station call letters*] (BROA) ..... WBUM-FM
Barahona [*Dominican Republic*] [*Airport symbol*] (OAG) ..... BRX
Barahona [*Dominican Republic*] [*ICAO location identifier*] (ICLI) ..... MDBH
Barair SA [*Spain*] [*ICAO designator*] (FAAC) ..... BAI
Barakoma [*Solomon Islands*] [*Airport symbol*] (OAG) ..... VEV
Baramita [*Guyana*] [*Airport symbol*] (OAG) ..... BMJ
Baramita [*Guyana*] [*ICAO location identifier*] (ICLI) ..... SYBR
Barandium Resources [*Vancouver Stock Exchange symbol*] ..... BRM
Baranof, AK [*Location identifier*] [*FAA*] (FAAL) ..... BNF
Baranof Island Housing Authority (SAUO) ..... BIHA
Barany's Caloric Test [*Medicine*] (MELL) ..... BCT
Barat [*Yemen*] [*ICAO location identifier*] (ICLI) ..... OYBT
Barat College of the Sacred Heart [*Later, Barat College*] [*Lake Forest, IL*] ..... BCSH
Barat College of the Sacred Heart, Lake Forest, IL [*OCLC symbol*] (OCLC) ..... ICB
Barat College of the Sacred Heart, Lake Forest, IL [*Library symbol*] [*Library of Congress*] (LCLS) ..... ILfB
Barbacena [*Brazil*] [*ICAO location identifier*] (ICLI) ..... SBBQ
Barbadensis [*Pharmacy*] (ROG) ..... BB

Barbadensis [Pharmacy] (ROG)	Bbds
Barbados [Aircraft nationality and registration mark] (FAAC)	8P
Barbados (ROG)	BARB
Barbados (VRA)	Barb
Barbados [ANSI two-letter standard code] (CNC)	BB
Barbados [MARC country of publication code] [Library of Congress] (LCCP)	bb
Barbados (SAUS)	Bbados
Barbados [Seismograph station code, US Geological Survey] (SEIS)	BDS
Barbados (ADWA)	Bds
Barbados [Airport symbol] (OAG)	BGI
Barbados [Seismograph station code, US Geological Survey] [Closed] (SEIS)	BRB
Barbados [ANSI three-letter standard code] (CNC)	BRB
Barbados (SAUS)	Brbds
Barbados [IYRU nationality code] (IYR)	KBA
Barbados [MARC geographic area code] [Library of Congress] (LCCP)	nwbb-
Barbados Board of Tourism (EA)	BBT
Barbados Environmental Association (EAIO)	BEA
Barbados Industrial Development Corporation (SAUO)	Barbados IDC
Barbados Labor Party	BLP
Barbados Law Reports [A publication] (DLA)	Barb LR
Barbados Law Reports [A publication] (DLA)	BLR
Barbados National Party (SAUO)	BNP
Barbados National Standards Institution (SAUO)	BNSI
Barbados Oceanographic and Meteorological Analysis Program (SAUS)	BOMAP
Barbados Oceanographic and Meteorological Analysis Project	BOMAP
Barbados Oceanographic and Meteorological Experiment [National Oceanic and Atmospheric Administration]	BOMEX
Barbados Tourist Board (SAUO)	BTB
Barbara Bain International	BBI
Barbara Bush Foundation for Family Literacy (EA)	BBFFL
Barbara Eden International Fan Club (EA)	BEIFC
Barbara Eden's Official Fan Club (EA)	BEOFC
barbarian (SAUS)	barb
Barbarossa Day (SAUS)	B Day
Barbary Ape (SAUS)	Barb
Barbary Horse (SAUS)	Barb
Barbecon, Inc. [Toronto Stock Exchange symbol]	BEC
Barbecue (ADA)	BBQ
Barbecue Briquet Institute [Later, BIA]	BBI
Barbecue Industry Association (EA)	BIA
Barbed Tape Obstacle (SAUS)	BTO
Barber [Charles E.] [Designer's mark, when appearing on US coins]	B
Barber	BARB
Barber, Albert P., Kenosha WI [STAC]	BAA
Barber Coin Collector Society (EA)	BCCS
Barber Colman Co., Technical Library, Loves Park, IL [Library symbol] [Library of Congress] (LCLS)	ILpB
Barber Hairstyling for Men and Women [Associated Press] (SAG)	BarHair
Barber Hairstyling for Men and Women [NASDAQ symbol] (SAG)	BBHF
Barber Middle East Line (SAUO)	BMEL
Barber Oil Corp. (SAUO)	BBO
Barber on Insurance [A publication] (DLA)	Barb Ins
Barber Pole (KSC)	BP
Barber Steamship Lines (MHDW)	BSL
Barber Suggestibility Scale [Psychology]	BBS
Barber West African Line (SAUO)	BWAL
Barber's Digest [New York] [A publication] (DLA)	Barb App Dig
Barber's Digest of Kentucky [A publication] (DLA)	Barb Dig
Barber's Gold Law [South Africa] [A publication] (DLA)	B
Barber's Gold Law [South Africa] [A publication] (DLA)	Barb
Barber's Gold Law [South Africa] [A publication] (DLA)	Barber
Barbers, Hairdressers, and Cosmetologists International Union of America (SAUO)	BHCIUS
Barbers, Hairdressers, Cosmetologists (SAUO)	BHC
Barbers Point Naval Air Station, Oahu Island [Hawaii] [ICAO location identifier] (ICLI)	PHNA
Barber's Reports [14-42 Arkansas] [A publication] (DLA)	Bar
Barber's Reports [14-42 Arkansas] [A publication] (DLA)	Barb
Barber's Reports [14-42 Arkansas] [A publication] (DLA)	Barb Ark
Barber's Reports [14-42 Arkansas] [A publication] (DLA)	Barbe
Barber's Reports [14-42 Arkansas] [A publication] (DLA)	Barber
Barber-Scotia College [Concord, NC]	BSC
Barber-Scotia College, Concord, NC [OCLC symbol] (OCLC)	NCB
Barber-Scotia College, Concord, NC [Library symbol] [Library of Congress] (LCLS)	NcCoB
Barberton [South Africa] [ICAO location identifier] (ICLI)	FABN
Barberton Public Library, Barberton, OH [Library symbol] [Library of Congress] (LCLS)	OBarb
Barbette [Military]	BARB
Barbeyrac's Edition of Grotius on War and Peace [A publication] (DLA)	Barb Gro
Barbeyrac's Edition of Puffendorf's Law of Nature and Nations [A publication] (DLA)	Barb Puf
Barbil [India] [ICAO location identifier] (ICLI)	VEBL
Barbital Poisoning [Medicine] (MELL)	BP
Barbital-Dependent [Medicine] (DMAA)	BD
Barbiturate [Pharmacology]	barb
Barbiturate (SAUS)	Barb
Barbiturate Dependence [Medicine] (DMAA)	BD
Barbiturate Screen [Biochemistry] (DAVI)	BARB
Barbour and Carroll's Kentucky Statutes [A publication] (DLA)	Barb & C KY St
Barbour Elementary School, Rockford, IL [Library symbol] [Library of Congress] (LCLS)	IRoBaE
Barbour on Parties in Law and Equity [A publication] (DLA)	Barb Par
Barbour on the Law of Set-Off [A publication] (DLA)	Barb Set-Off
Barbour's Abstracts of Chancellor's Decisions [New York] [A publication] (DLA)	Barb Abs
Barbour's Chancery Practice [New York] [A publication] (DLA)	Barb Ch Pr
Barbour's Chancery Reports [New York] [A publication] (DLA)	Barb Ch
Barbour's Chancery Reports [New York] [A publication] (DLA)	Barb Chancery Rep
Barbour's Chancery Reports [New York] [A publication] (DLA)	Barb Ch (NY)
Barbour's Chancery Reports [New York] [A publication] (DLA)	Barb Ch Rep
Barbour's Chancery Reports [New York] [A publication] (DLA)	Barbour's Ch R
Barbour's Chancery Reports [New York] [A publication] (DLA)	B Ch
Barbour's Criminal Law [A publication] (DLA)	Barb Cr L
Barbour's Criminal Law [A publication] (DLA)	Barb Cr Law
Barbour's Criminal Pleadings [A publication] (DLA)	Barb Cr P
Barbour's Criminal Practice [A publication] (DLA)	Barb Cr P
Barbour's New York Reports [A publication] (DLA)	B
Barbour's Supreme Court Reports [New York] [A publication] (DLA)	Barb
Barbour's Supreme Court Reports [New York] [A publication] (DLA)	Barb (NY) SCR
Barbour's Supreme Court Reports [New York] [A publication] (DLA)	Barbour
Barbour's Supreme Court Reports [New York] [A publication] (DLA)	Barbour (NY)
Barbour's Supreme Court Reports [New York] [A publication] (DLA)	Barbour's Sup Court Rep
Barbour's Supreme Court Reports [New York] [A publication] (DLA)	Barb R
Barbour's Supreme Court Reports [New York] [A publication] (DLA)	Barb SC
Barbour's Supreme Court Reports [New York] [A publication] (DLA)	Barb SCR
Barbour's Supreme Court Reports [New York] [A publication] (DLA)	Barb Sup Ct
Barbour's Supreme Court Reports [New York] [A publication] (DLA)	Barb Sup Ct Reports
Barbour's Supreme Court Reports [New York] [A publication] (DLA)	Bar SC Rep
Barbourville, KY [AM radio station call letters]	WYWY
Barbourville, KY [FM radio station call letters]	WYWY-FM
Barbuda [West Indies] [Airport symbol] (OAG)	BBQ
Barbuda [MARC geographic area code] [Library of Congress] (LCCP)	nwbc-
Barbuda People's Movement [Antigua] [Political party] (PD)	BPM
Barca [Ship's rigging] (ROG)	BCA
Barcaldine [Australia] [Airport symbol] (OAG)	BCI
Barcan Communications, Inc. [Vancouver Stock Exchange symbol]	BNC
Barcelona [Spain] [Airport symbol] (OAG)	BCN
Barcelona [Venezuela] [Airport symbol] (OAG)	BLA
Barcelona [Spain] [ICAO location identifier] (ICLI)	LEBL
Barcelona [Spain] [ICAO location identifier] (ICLI)	LECB
Barcelona Convention Secretariat	BCS
Barcelona Olympic Organizing Committee [Spain] (EAIO)	BOOC
Barcelona, Oslo, Budapest, Copenhagen, Amsterdam, Tampere, Sheffield, Szombathely, and Stuttgart [Library school collaboration] (TELE)	BOBCATSSS
Barcelona, Spain - Pisa, Italy [Submarine cable] [Telecommunications]	BAPI
Barcelona/Gral. Jose Antonio Anzoategui Internacional Anzoategui [Venezuela] [ICAO location identifier] (ICLI)	SVBC
Barceloneta, PR [AM radio station call letters]	WBQN
Barcelonnette/Saint-Pons [France] [ICAO location identifier] (ICLI)	LFMR
Barch, John R., New York NY [STAC]	BJR
Barcklay Flying Service [ICAO designator] (FAAC)	ACH
Barclay Classroom Assessment System [Student personality test]	BCAS
Barclay Early Childhood Skill Assessment Center (EDAC)	BECSAS
Barclays Australia Investment Services Consensus Earnings Profile	BARCEP
Barclays Australia Ltd. (SAUO)	BAL
Barclays Bank [Associated Press] (SAG)	BarB
Barclays Bank (SAUO)	BB
Barclays Bank [NYSE symbol] (SPSG)	BCB
Barclays Bank Australia	BBA
Barclays Bk C1/C2Unit ADS [NYSE symbol] (TTSB)	BCBPrC
Barclays Bk D1/D2Unit ADS [NYSE symbol] (TTSB)	BCBPrD
Barclays Bk E1/E2 UnitADS [NYSE symbol] (TTSB)	BCBPr
Barclays de Zoete Wedd [Banking]	BZT
Barclays de Zoete Wedd [Investment firm] [British]	BZW
Barclay's Development Fund [Barclay's Bank] [British]	BDF
Barclay's Digest of the Law of Scotland [A publication] (DLA)	Barc Dig Law Sc
Barclay's Digest of the Law of Scotland [A publication] (DLA)	Bar Dig
Barclays Global Investors [British]	BGI
Barclays Group Staff Union [British] (WDAA)	BGSU
Barclays Home Mortgage Rate [British] (DCTA)	BHMR
Barclay's Law of Highways [A publication] (DLA)	Barc High
Barclays Ltd. [Associated Press] (SAG)	Barclay
Barclays Ltd. [NYSE symbol] (SPSG)	BCS
Barclays Merchant Bank [British]	BMB
Barclay's Missouri Digest [A publication] (DLA)	Barc Dig
Barclay's Missouri Digest [A publication] (DLA)	Barc Mo Dig
Barclays Overseas Development Corporation (SAUO)	BODC
Barclays PLC [Associated Press] (SAG)	Barclay
Barclays plc ADS [NYSE symbol] (TTSB)	BCS
Barco Rotary Joint	BRJ
Barcode Decal (SAUS)	BCD
Barcode Information System (SAUS)	BARCIS
Bar-Code Reader/Sorter [Marketing] (PDAA)	BCRS
Barcoded Lightweight Interview Package (SAUS)	BLIP
BARCODE/DECAL Systems (SAUS)	BARCDECAL
Bard College (SAUO)	BC
Bard College, Annandale-On-Hudson, NY [Library symbol] [Library of Congress] (LCLS)	NAnB
Bard College, Annandale-On-Hudson, NY [OCLC symbol] (OCLC)	VVP

Bard [*C.R.*]**, Inc.** [*Associated Press*] (SAG) ... Bard
Bard [*C. R.*]**, Inc.** [*NYSE symbol*] (SPSG) ... BCR
Bard Silver & Gold [*Vancouver Stock Exchange symbol*] ... BDS
Bardai-Zougra [*Chad*] [*ICAO location identifier*] (ICLI) ... FTTZ
Bardeen-Cooper-Schrieffer Theory [*Theoretical physics*] ... BCS
Bardeen-Cooper-Schrieffer Theory (SAUS) ... BCS-Theory
Bardenas Reales [*Spain*] [*ICAO location identifier*] (ICLI) ... LEBR
Bardera [*Somalia*] [*ICAO location identifier*] (ICLI) ... HCMD
Bardet-Beidl Syndrome [*Medicine*] ... BBS
Bardine Oils Ltd. [*Vancouver Stock Exchange symbol*] ... BAO
Barding Sands Underwater Test Range (SAUS) ... BARSTUR
Bard-Pic [*Syndrome*] [*Medicine*] (DB) ... BP
Bardsey Bird and Field Observatory, Ispley, near Redditch, Worcestershire (SAUO) ... BBFO
Bardsey Observatory Report (journ.) (SAUS) ... RBOBDY
Bardstown, KY [*Location identifier*] [*FAA*] (FAAL) ... BRY
Bardstown, KY [*AM radio station call letters*] ... WBRT
Bardstown, KY [*FM radio station call letters*] ... WOKH
Bardufoss [*Norway*] [*Airport symbol*] (OAG) ... BDU
Bardufoss [*Norway*] [*ICAO location identifier*] (ICLI) ... ENDU
Bare and Acid Resisting Paint (SAUS) ... B&ARP
Bare and Painted (SAUS) ... B and P
Bare and Painted (BARN) ... b & p
Bare Base [*Air Force*] (AFM) ... BB
Bare Base Set [*Air Force*] ... BBS
Bare Base Support Package (MCD) ... BBSP
Bare Beryllium Copper Wire ... BBCW
Bare Brass Wire ... BBW
Bare Copper ... BC
Bare Copper Wire ... BCW
Bare Copper-Clad Wire ... BCCW
Bare Equipment Modernization Officer [*Military*] (DNAB) ... BEMO
Bare Essentials of Surface Transfer ... BEST
Bare Eyed Cockatoo [*Bird*] ... BE2
Bare Gold Plated Wire (SAUS) ... BGPW
Bare Lymphocytes Syndrome [*Medicine*] ... BLS
Bare Metal Arc Welding ... BMAW
Bare Molybdenum Wire ... BMW
Bare Nickel Chrome Wire ... BNCW
Bare of Armatures (SAUS) ... BOA
Bare Phosphor Bronze Wire ... BPBW
Bare Platinum Wire ... BPW
Bare Reactor Experiment at Nevada ... BREN
Bare Refractory, Double Containment [*Boiler*] [*NASA*] ... BRDC
Bare Sight Tunnel (SAUS) ... BST
Bare Silver-Plated Wire ... BSPW
Bare Stainless-Steel Wire ... BSSW
Bare Steel Wire ... BSW
Bare Tungsten Wire ... BTW
Bare Wire and Telephone System Development Schedule (SAUS) ... BWTSDS
Bare Zirconium Wire ... BZW
Bareback Riding [*Rodeo term*] ... BB
Bareboat (RIMS) ... Bb
Bareboat Charter (DNAB) ... BBC
Bareboat Charter (DNAB) ... BC
Barefoot, Inc. [*NASDAQ symbol*] (SPSG) ... BARE
Barefoot, Inc. [*Associated Press*] (SAG) ... Barefoot
Bareilly [*India*] [*ICAO location identifier*] (ICLI) ... VIBY
Barely Noticeable Difference [*Medicine*] (MELL) ... BND
Barents Sea (SAUS) ... Barents
Barents Sea Impact Study (SAUS) ... BASIS
Barexor Minerals, Inc. [*Vancouver Stock Exchange symbol*] ... BXR
Barfield Corp. (SAUO) ... BIC
Bargain (ADA) ... BARG
Bargain (SAUS) ... Barg
Bargain (ROG) ... BARGN
Bargain ... BRGN
Bargain Purchase Option (ADWA) ... BPO
Bargaining Unit (GFGA) ... BU
Bargaining Unit Member [*of a faculty union*] ... BUM
Barge ... B
Barge ... BG
Barge (ROG) ... BGE
Barge Aboard Catamaran ... BACAT
Barge, Amphibious, Resupply, Cargo ... BARC
Barge, Amphibious, Resupply Craft [*Navy*] (VNW) ... BARC
Barge and Canal Development Association [*British*] ... BCDA
Barge Builders Trade Union [*British*] ... BBTU
Barge Cargo (AAG) ... BC
Barge Cargo Ship ... TALS
Barge Carrying Vessel ... BCV
Barge, Knockdown (MSA) ... BK
Barge Off Loading Facility ... BOLF
Barge, Refrigerated, Large (SAUS) ... BRL
Barge, Training (MSA) ... BT
Barge Transportation Appraisal Program [*Military*] (MCD) ... BARTAP
Bargeldloser Zahlungsverkehr (SAUS) ... BZV
Barge-Mounted Methanol Plant [*Chemical industry*] ... BMMP
Barge-Mounted Production and Storage System (DS) ... BPSS
Barges on Board [*Shipping*] ... BOB
Bargmann Bowen and Kemp, Inc. [*Telecommunications service*] (TSSD) ... BBK
Bargraph Display Unit (SAUS) ... BDU
Barham's Student's Guide to the Preliminary Examinations [*A publication*] (DLA) ... Barh Pre Ex
Bari [*Italy*] [*Seismograph station code, US Geological Survey*] [*Closed*] (SEIS) ... BAI
Bari [*Italy*] [*Airport symbol*] (OAG) ... BRI
Baric Computing Services (SAUO) ... BARIC
Bar-Ilan Centre for Strategic Studies (SAUS) ... BCSS
Bar-Ilan University (SAUO) ... B-I U
Bar-Ilan University (BJA) ... BIU
Barile-Yaguchi-Eveland [*Growth medium*] [*Microbiology*] ... BYE
Barinas [*Venezuela*] [*Airport symbol*] (OAG) ... BNS
Barinas, Barinas [*Venezuela*] [*ICAO location identifier*] (ICLI) ... SVBI
Baring Brothers Hambrecht & Quist Ltd. (SAUO) ... BBHQ
Baring Unit Trust Management Service [*Finance*] [*British*] ... BUTM
Bario [*Malaysia*] [*Airport symbol*] (OAG) ... BBN
Bario [*Malaysia*] [*ICAO location identifier*] (ICLI) ... WBGZ
Bari/Palese Macchie [*Italy*] [*ICAO location identifier*] (ICLI) ... LIBD
Barisal [*Bangladesh*] [*Airport symbol*] (AD) ... BZL
Barisan Mountains (SAUS) ... Barisans
Barisan Nasional [*Malaysia*] [*Political party*] (EY) ... BN
Barisan Nasional Penbebasan Pattani [*Thailand*] [*Political party*] ... BNPP
Barisan Revolusi Nasional [*Thailand*] [*Political party*] ... BRN
Barite (SAUS) ... Ba
Baritone [*Music*] ... B
Baritone [*Music*] ... BAR
Baritone [*Music*] (ADA) ... barit
Baritone Saxophone ... barsx
Barium [*Chemical element*] ... Ba
Barium Boron Oxide [*Inorganic chemistry*] ... BBO
Barium Chloranilate [*Organic chemistry*] ... BCA
Barium Cloud Experiment [*NASA*] ... BCE
Barium Contrast Enema [*Medicine*] (CPH) ... BCE
Barium Crown ... BC
Barium Enema [*Medicine*] (DMAA) ... Ba
Barium Enema [*Medicine*] ... BaE
Barium Enema [*Medicine*] (MEDA) ... BaEn
Barium Enema [*Medicine*] (BABM) ... Ba enem
Barium Enema [*Medicine*] ... BE
Barium Ferrite Magnet ... BFM
Barium Ion Cloud [*NASA*] ... BIC
Barium Meal [*Medicine*] ... BaM
Barium Meal Test (SAUS) ... BMT
Barium Metaborate (SAUS) ... BMB
Barium Oxide ... BaO
Barium Oxide Ferrite ... BOF
Barium Sodium Niobate [*Crystal*] ... BSN
Barium Strontium Calcium Copper Oxide (SAUS) ... BSCCO
Barium Strontium Titanate (AAEL) ... BST
Barium Sulfate (SAUS) ... Barite
Barium-Magnesia-Alumina-Silicate [*Inorganic chemistry*] ... BMAS
Bark (WGA) ... BAR
Bark [*or Barque*] (ROG) ... BK
Bark (VRA) ... brk
Bark Dieback [*Plant pathology*] ... BD
Bark Forager [*Ornithology*] ... BF
Bark Necrosis Virus (SAUS) ... BNV
Bark Split Virus (SAUS) ... BSV
Bark Thickness [*Botany*] ... BARKTH
Barkcloth (VRA) ... brkcth
Barken International, Inc. [*ICAO designator*] (FAAC) ... BKJ
Barkentine (SAUS) ... Bkn
Barker & Dobson [*British*] ... B & D
Barker Code Processing ... BCP
Barker Free Library, Barker, NY [*Library symbol*] [*Library of Congress*] (LCLS) ... NBar
Barker, Storey, Matthews (WDAA) ... BSM
Barker-Henderson [*Theory*] [*Chemical physics*] ... BH
Barkerville Historic Park, British Columbia [*Library symbol*] [*National Library of Canada*] (NLC) ... BBHP
Barkhausen-Kurz Oscillator ... BKO
Barkhausen-Kurz Oscillator ... BO
Barkhor Resources, Inc. [*Vancouver Stock Exchange symbol*] ... BHO
Barking [*Borough in England*] ... BARK
Barking Sands, Kauai Island [*Hawaii*] [*ICAO location identifier*] (ICLI) ... PHBK
Barking Sands Tactical Underwater Range [*Naval Oceanographic Office*] ... BARSTUR
Barking Sands Underwater Range Expansion [*Naval Oceanographic Office*] (MCD) ... BSURE
Barkley Dam [*TVA*] ... BD
Barksdale, LA [*Location identifier*] [*FAA*] (FAAL) ... BYU
Barkston Ashe and Skyrac Volunteers [*British military*] (DMA) ... B & SV
Barkston Heath [*British*] [*ICAO location identifier*] (ICLI) ... EGYE
Barkston-Heath FTU [*British*] [*Military*] [*FAA designator*] (FAAC) ... BHH
Bar-Le-Duc [*France*] [*ICAO location identifier*] (ICLI) ... LFEU
Barley (SAUS) ... Bly
Barley Alkaline Protease Inhibitor [*Medicine*] (DMAA) ... BAPI
Barley and Malt Institute [*Defunct*] (EA) ... BMI
Barley Canyon [*New Mexico*] [*Seismograph station code, US Geological Survey*] (SEIS) ... BRC
Barley Leaf Piece Agar [*Microbiology*] ... BLPA
Barley Marketing Board of New South Wales [*Australia*] ... BMBNSW
Barley Research Committee for Queensland [*Australia*] ... BRCQ
Barley Research Committee for South Australia ... BRCSA
Barley Research Committee for Western Australia ... BRCWA
Barley Research Committee, New South Wales [*Australia*] ... BRCNSW
Barley Research Council [*Australia*] ... BRC
Barley Stripe Mosaic Virus ... BSMV

Barley Yellow Dwarf [*Plant pathology*] .... BYD
Barley Yellow Dwarf Virus .... BYDV
Barley Yellow Mosaic Virus [*Plant pathology*] .... BAYMV
Barley Yellow Striate Mosaic Virus [*Plant pathology*] .... BYSMV
Barleycorn [*Unit of weight*] [*Obsolete*] [*British*] (ROG) .... BAR
Barleycorn [*Unit of weight*] [*Obsolete*] [*British*] (ROG) .... BC
Barling, AR [*FM radio station call letters*] .... KOLX
Barlow. Justice of Peace [*1745*] [*A publication*] (DLA) .... Barl Just
Barlow Sanatorium, Elks Tuberculosis Library, Los Angeles, CA [*Library symbol*] [*Library of Congress*] (LCLS) .... CLE
Barlow's Disease [*Medicine*] (MELL) .... BD
Barn [*Area of nuclear cross-section*] .... b
Barn .... BN
Barn (WDAA) .... Bn
Barn Cleaner, Cattle Feeder and Silo Unloader Association (SAUO) .... BCCFSUA
Barn Equipment Association [*Later, FEA*] (EA) .... BEA
Barnabites [*Also, CRSP*] [*Roman Catholic men's religious order*] .... Barn
Barnard [*Star second closest to the sun*] (BARN) .... Barn
Barnard College (SAUO) .... BC
Barnard College, Columbia University, New York, NY [*Library symbol*] [*Library of Congress*] (LCLS) .... NNBa
Barnardiston's English Chancery Cases [*1740-41*] [*A publication*] (DLA) .... Barnardiston CC
Barnardiston's English Chancery Reports [*A publication*] (DLA) .... Bar Ch
Barnardiston's English Chancery Reports [*A publication*] (DLA) .... Bar Chy
Barnardiston's English Chancery Reports [*1740-41*] [*A publication*] (DLA) .... Barnard Ch
Barnardiston's English Chancery Reports [*1740-41*] [*A publication*] (DLA) .... Barnard Ch (Eng)
Barnardiston's English Chancery Reports [*1740-41*] [*A publication*] (DLA) .... Barnard Ch Rep
Barnardiston's English Chancery Reports [*1740-41*] [*A publication*] (DLA) .... Barn C
Barnardiston's English Chancery Reports [*1740-41*] [*A publication*] (DLA) .... Barn Ch
Barnardiston's English King's Bench Reports [*A publication*] (DLA) .... Bar
Barnardiston's English King's Bench Reports [*A publication*] (DLA) .... Barn
Barnardiston's English King's Bench Reports [*A publication*] (DLA) .... Barnard
Barnardiston's English King's Bench Reports [*A publication*] (DLA).... Barnard KB
Barnardiston's English King's Bench Reports [*A publication*] (DLA) .... Barn KB
Barnardiston's Tempore Hardwicke Reports, Chancery [*1740-41*] [*England*] [*A publication*] (DLA) .... Barnard
Barnaul [*Former USSR*] [*ICAO location identifier*] (ICLI) .... UNBB
Barncade-Penetrating Cartridge (SAUS) .... B-P Cartridge
Barner Ready Light System (SAUS) .... BRL Sys
Barnes and Noble (SAUO) .... ISBN 0-88029
Barnes & Noble, Inc. (SAUO) .... B&N
Barnes & Noble, Inc. [*Associated Press*] (SAG) .... BarNbl
Barnes & Noble, Inc. [*NYSE symbol*] (SPSG) .... BKS
Barnes Engineering Company (SAUO) .... BEC
Barnes' English Common Pleas Reports [*A publication*] (DLA) .... Barn
Barnes' Equity Practice [*A publication*] (DLA) .... Barn Eq Pr
Barnes' Exposition of the Law Respecting Sheriff [*1816*] [*A publication*] (DLA) .... Barn Sh
Barnes Group [*NYSE symbol*] (TTSB) .... B
Barnes Group, Inc. [*NYSE symbol*] (SPSG) .... B
Barnes Group, Inc. [*Associated Press*] (SAG) .... BarnGp
Barnes, Hickam, Pantzer & Boyd, Indianapolis, IN [*OCLC symbol*] (OCLC).... IHB
Barnes, Hickam, Pantzer & Boyd, Law Library, Indianapolis, IN [*Library symbol*] [*Library of Congress*] (LCLS) .... InIBHP
Barnes' Notes of Cases of Practice in Common Pleas [*94 English Reprint*] [*A publication*] (DLA) .... Bar N
Barnes' Notes of Cases of Practice in Common Pleas [*94 English Reprint*] [*A publication*] (DLA) .... Barnes
Barnes' Notes of Cases of Practice in Common Pleas [*94 English Reprint*] [*A publication*] (DLA) .... Barnes NC
Barnes' Notes of Cases of Practice in Common Pleas [*94 English Reprint*] [*A publication*] (DLA) .... Barnes Notes
Barnes' Notes of Cases of Practice in Common Pleas [*94 English Reprint*] [*A publication*] (DLA) .... Barnes Notes (Eng)
Barnes' Notes of Cases of Practice in Common Pleas [*94 English Reprint*] [*A publication*] (DLA) .... Barn No
Barnes' Notes on the New Testament [*A publication*] .... BNNT
barnesandnoble.com, Inc.'A' [*NASDAQ symbol*] (SG) .... BNBN
Barnesboro, PA [*AM radio station call letters*] .... WNCC
Barnes-Hind Pharmaceutical (DAVI) .... B-H
Barnes-Hind/Hydrocurve [*Commercial firm*] (DAVI) .... BH
Barnes's Federal Code [*A publication*] (DLA) .... Barnes's Fed Code
Barnesville, GA [*AM radio station call letters*] .... WBAF
Barnesville High School, Barnesville, MN [*Library symbol*] [*Library of Congress*] (LCLS) .... MnBarH
Barnesville, OH [*FM radio station call letters*] .... WBNV
Barnesville Public Library, Barnesville, MN [*Library symbol*] [*Library of Congress*] (LCLS) .... MnBar
Barnesville Public Library, Barnesville, OH [*Library symbol*] [*Library of Congress*] (LCLS) .... OBarn
Barnet's English Central Criminal Courts Reports [*27-92*] [*A publication*] (DLA) .... Barnet
Barnett Banks, Inc. [*Associated Press*] (SAG) .... Barnett
Barnett Banks, Inc. [*Associated Press*] (SAG) .... Barnt
Barnett Banks, Inc. [*NYSE symbol*] (SPSG) .... BBI
Barnett, Inc. [*Associated Press*] (SAG) .... Barnett
Barnett Inc. [*NASDAQ symbol*] (TTSB) .... BNTT
Barnett Mortage Trust (SAUO) .... BMT
Barnewall and Adolphus' English King's Bench Reports [*109-110 English Reprint*] [*1830-34*] [*A publication*] (DLA) .... B & A
Barnewall and Adolphus' English King's Bench Reports [*109-110 English Reprint*] [*1830-34*] [*A publication*] (DLA) .... B & Ad
Barnewall and Adolphus' English King's Bench Reports [*109-110 English Reprint*] [*1830-34*] [*A publication*] (DLA) .... Bar & Ad
Barnewall and Adolphus' English King's Bench Reports [*109-110 English Reprint*] [*1830-34*] [*A publication*] (DLA) .... Barn & A
Barnewall and Adolphus' English King's Bench Reports [*109-110 English Reprint*] [*A publication*] (DLA) .... Barn & Ad
Barnewall and Adolphus' English King's Bench Reports [*109-110 English Reprint*] [*A publication*] (DLA) .... Barn & Ad (Eng)
Barnewall and Adolphus' English King's Bench Reports [*109-110 English Reprint*] [*1830-34*] [*A publication*] (DLA) .... Barn & Adol
Barnewall and Alderson's English King's Bench Reports [*1817-22*] [*A publication*] (DLA) .... B & A
Barnewall and Alderson's English King's Bench Reports [*A publication*] (DLA) .... B & Ald
Barnewall and Alderson's English King's Bench Reports [*A publication*] (DLA) .... Bar & Al
Barnewall and Alderson's English King's Bench Reports [*A publication*] (DLA) .... Barn & A
Barnewall and Alderson's English King's Bench Reports [*A publication*] (DLA) .... Barn & Ald
Barnewall and Alderson's English King's Bench Reports [*A publication*] (DLA) .... Barn & Ald (Eng)
Barnewall and Alderson's English King's Bench Reports [*1st part*] [*A publication*] (DLA) .... Selw & Barn
Barnewall & Aldersons K.B. Reports, 1st part (SAUS) .... Selw&Barn
Barnewall and Cresswell's English King's Bench Reports [*107-109 English Reprint*] [*A publication*] (DLA) .... B & C
Barnewall and Cresswell's English King's Bench Reports [*A publication*] (DLA) .... Bar & Cr
Barnewall and Cresswell's English King's Bench Reports [*107-109 English Reprint*] [*A publication*] (DLA) .... Barn & C
Barnewall and Cresswell's English King's Bench Reports [*107-109 English Reprint*] [*A publication*] (DLA) .... Barn & C (Eng)
Barnewall and Cresswell's English King's Bench Reports [*107-109 English Reprint*] [*A publication*] (DLA) .... Barn & Cr
Barnewall and Cresswell's English King's Bench Reports [*107-109 English Reprint*] [*A publication*] (DLA) .... Barn & Cress
Barney Children's Medical Center, Dayton, OH [*Library symbol*] [*Library of Congress*] (LCLS) .... ODaMC
Barnfield and Stiness' Reports [*20 Rhode Island*] [*A publication*] (DLA) .... Barnf & S
Barnfield's Reports [*19-20 Rhode Island*] [*A publication*] (DLA) .... Barn
Barnhart Dictionary of Etymology [*A publication*] .... BDE
barns (SAUS) .... b
Barns Olson Aeroleasing Ltd. [*British*] [*ICAO designator*] (FAAC) .... CLN
Barnstable Law Library, Barnstable, MA [*Library symbol*] [*Library of Congress*] (LCLS) .... MBarL
Barnstable, MA [*FM radio station call letters*] .... WQRC
Barnstaple [*Municipal borough in England*] .... BARNST
Barnstaple's Printed Minutes and Proceedings [*A publication*] (DLA) .... Barn Pr M
Barnum Elementary School, Barnum, MN [*Library symbol*] [*Library of Congress*] (LCLS) .... MnBmE
Barnum High School, Barnum, MN [*Library symbol*] [*Library of Congress*] (LCLS) .... MnBmH
Barnum Woods Elementary School, East Meadow, NY [*Library symbol*] [*Library of Congress*] (LCLS) .... NEmBWE
Barnwall's Digest of the Year Books [*A publication*] (DLA) .... Barnw Dig
Barnwell Fuel Receiving and Storage Station (SAUO) .... BFRSS
Barnwell Industries, Inc. [*Associated Press*] (SAG) .... Barnwl
Barnwell Industries, Inc. [*Toronto Stock Exchange symbol*] .... BNW
Barnwell Industries, Inc. [*AMEX symbol*] (SPSG) .... BRN
Barnwell Municipal Library, Alberta [*Library symbol*] [*National Library of Canada*] (NLC) .... ABARM
Barnwell Nuclear Fuel Plant (NRCH) .... BNFP
Barnwell Plutonium Product Facility (SAUO) .... BPPF
Barnwell, SC [*Commercial waste site*] (GAAI) .... BARN
Barnwell, SC [*Location identifier*] [*FAA*] (FAAL) .... BNL
Barnwell, SC [*AM radio station call letters*] .... WBAW
Barnwell, SC [*FM radio station call letters*] .... WBAW-FM
Baroclinic (SAUS) .... BACLIN
Baroclinic Prognosis [*NWS*] (FAAC) .... BACLIN
Baroclinic Waves [*Astronomy*] .... BW
Baroda Law Reports [*India*] [*A publication*] (DLA) .... Baroda LR
Baroda/Vadodara [*India*] [*ICAO location identifier*] (ICLI) .... VABO
Barograph Display Unit .... BDU
Baromedical Nurses Association (EA) .... BNA
Barometer [*or Barometric*] .... BAR
Barometer (NTIO) .... bar
Barometer (SAUS) .... Bar
Barometer (AABC) .... BARO
Barometer (FAAC) .... BRM
Barometric [*Medicine*] (DAVI) .... B
barometric (SAUS) .... bar
Barometric (WGA) .... BRMC
Barometric Absolute Pressure [*Automotive engineering*] .... BAP
Barometric Altimeter (MCD) .... BA
Barometric Altimeter (SAUS) .... B/A
Barometric Altitude (MCD) .... BALT
Barometric Altitude (GAVI) .... HBARO
Barometric Altitude Control .... BAC
Barometric Altitude Indicator (NASA) .... BAI

Barometric Altitude Reference Unit .... BARU
Barometric and Manifold Absolute Pressure [*Automotive engineering*] .... BMAP
Barometric Pressure .... BP
Barometric Pressure [*Medicine*] (STED) .... PB
Barometric Pressure Correction [*Symbol*] .... B
Barometric Read Solenoid [*Automotive engineering*] .... BRS
Barometric Switch (SAUS) .... BAROSWITCH
Baron .... B
Baron (ROG) .... BA
Baron .... BN
Baron (ROG) .... BON
Baron (ROG) .... BR
Baron Aviation Services, Inc. [*ICAO designator*] (FAAC) .... BVN
Baron of Exchequer [*British*] (ROG) .... BE
Baron on Chattel Mortgages [*A publication*] (DLA) .... Baron Ch Mort
Baron Users Group [*National Shorthand Reporters Association*] .... BUG
Baroness (ROG) .... BNSS
Baroness (ROG) .... BSS
Baroness Publications Ltd., Inc. [*Publisher*] .... B
Baronet [*British*] .... BART
Baronet (WDAA) .... Bart
Baronet (WDAA) .... Bt
Baronet (EY) .... BT
Baronet of British Kingdom [*Initials used by Arthur Orton in his diary*]
    (ROG) .... B of BK
Baronial Order of Magna Charta (EA) .... BOMC
Baronne [*Baroness*] [*French*] (BARN) .... Bonnet
Barons Oil Ltd. [*Toronto Stock Exchange symbol*] .... BN
Barony of Urie Court Records [*1604-1747*] [*Scotland*] [*A publication*]
    (DLA) .... Baron
Baroque (SAUS) .... Bar
Baroque (VRA) .... Barq
Baroque All Style High [*Acronym is title of silk screen by sculptor Eduardo
    Paolozzi*] .... BASH
Baroque Resources Ltd. [*Vancouver Stock Exchange symbol*] .... BRQ
Barora [*Solomon Islands*] [*Airport symbol*] (OAG) .... RRI
Baroreceptor Reflex [*Medicine*] (MELL) .... BRR
Barossa Valley Vintage Festival Association [*Australia*] .... BVVFA
Barossa Winemakers' Association [*Australia*] .... BWA
Barostat (KSC) .... BARO
Baroswitch .... BS
Barotropic Electromagnetic and Pressure Experiment [*North Pacific, 1986-
    87*] [*Marine science*] (OSRA) .... BEMPEX
Barotropic Prognosis (FAAC) .... BATROP
Barotropic Vorticity Equation (SAUS) .... BVE
Bar-Pattern Response [*Computer science*] (IAA) .... BPR
Barque [*Bark, Boat*] [*French*] (ROG) .... BAR
Barque .... BK
Barque [*Bark, Boat*] [*French*] .... BQ
Barque [*Bark, Boat*] [*French*] .... BQUE
Barquentine [*Ship*] .... BKN
Barquisimeto [*Venezuela*] [*Airport symbol*] (OAG) .... BRM
Barquisimeto/Internacional, Lara [*Venezuela*] [*ICAO location identifier*]
    (ICLI) .... SVBM
Barr and Stroud Dentrometer User (SAUS) .... BASDU
Barr Laboratories, Inc. [*Associated Press*] (SAG) .... BarrLb
Barr Laboratories, Inc. [*AMEX symbol*] (SPSG) .... BRL
Barra [*Brazil*] [*Airport symbol*] (OAG) .... BQQ
Barra [*Hebrides Islands*] [*Airport symbol*] (OAG) .... BRR
Barra [*British*] [*ICAO location identifier*] (ICLI) .... EGPR
Barra Colorado [*Costa Rica*] [*Airport symbol*] (OAG) .... BCL
Barra De Parismina [*Costa Rica*] [*ICAO location identifier*] (ICLI) .... MRBP
Barra De Tortuguero [*Costa Rica*] [*ICAO location identifier*] (ICLI) .... MRBT
Barra Del Colorado [*Costa Rica*] [*ICAO location identifier*] (ICLI) .... MRBC
Barra Do Garcas [*Brazil*] [*ICAO location identifier*] (ICLI) .... SBBW
Barra Do Garcas/Xingu [*Brazil*] [*ICAO location identifier*] (ICLI) .... SBXG
Barra, Inc. [*Associated Press*] (SAG) .... Barra
BARRA, Inc. [*NASDAQ symbol*] (SPSG) .... BARZ
Barra Side Processor (SAUS) .... BSP
Barraca [*Peru*] [*ICAO location identifier*] (ICLI) .... SPCA
Barrack Department [*British military*] (DMA) .... BD
Barrack Officers Quarters (SAUS) .... BOQ
Barrack Store Accountant (SAUS) .... BSA
Barrack Warden [*British military*] (DMA) .... BW
Barracks .... BAKS
Barracks [*Military*] (MUSM) .... BK
Barracks [*Military*] (WDAA) .... Bks
Barracks (ADWA) .... bks
Barracks (AABC) .... BKS
Barracks and Quarters [*Army*] .... B & Q
Barracks and Quarters .... B&Q
Barracks Craft [*Non-self-propelled*] [*Navy symbol*] .... APL
Barracks Master-at-Arms .... BMAA
Barracks Officer (SAUS) .... BO
Barracks Petty Officer (DNAB) .... BPO
Barracks Regulations (SAUS) .... BR
Barrackville, WV [*FM radio station call letters*] .... WMMN
Barrackville, WV [*FM radio station call letters*] (RBYB) .... WVUC
Barracuda Resources Ltd. [*Vancouver Stock Exchange symbol*] .... BCZ
Barradall. Manuscript Reports [*Virginia*] [*A publication*] (DLA) .... Barr M
Barradall. Manuscript Reports [*Virginia*] [*A publication*] (DLA) .... Barr MSS
Barrage (SAUS) .... Bar
Barrage Balloon (SAUS) .... BAR BLN
Barrage Balloon .... BRGBLN
Barrage Balloon [*Navy symbol*] .... ZK

Barrage Balloon Battalion (SAUO) .... Bar Bln Bn
Barrage Fire (SAUS) .... BF
Barrage Jammers [*RADAR*] .... BJ
Barrage Jamming (SAUS) .... BJ
Barrage Mansour Eddahbi [*Morocco*] [*Seismograph station code, US
    Geological Survey*] (SEIS) .... BME
Barrage Rocket (NATG) .... BR
Barrancabermeja [*Colombia*] [*Airport symbol*] (OAG) .... EJA
Barrancabermeja/Yariguis [*Colombia*] [*ICAO location identifier*] (ICLI) .... SKEJ
Barranquilla [*Colombia*] [*Airport symbol*] (OAG) .... BAQ
Barranquilla [*Colombia*] [*ICAO location identifier*] (ICLI) .... SKEC
Barranquilla/Ernesto Cortissoz [*Colombia*] [*ICAO location identifier*]
    (ICLI) .... SKBQ
Barranquitas, PR [*AM radio station call letters*] .... WOLA
Barraquer-Kreimeich-Swinger procedure (SAUS) .... BKS
Barratry [*FBI standardized term*] .... BARR
Barre & Chelsea Railroad (IIA) .... B & C
Barre and Chelsea Railroad Co. (SAUO) .... BC
Barre Granite Association (EA) .... BGA
Barre, VT [*FM radio station call letters*] (RBYB) .... WCMD-FM
Barre, VT [*FM radio station call letters*] .... WORK
Barre, VT [*AM radio station call letters*] .... WSNO
Barreau de Montreal, Bibliotheque des Avocats, Montreal, PQ, Canada
    [*Library symbol*] [*Library of Congress*] (LCLS) .... CaQMAv
Barred .... BRRD
Barred Trunk [*Telecommunications*] (NITA) .... BT
Barre-Guillain [*Syndrome*] [*Medicine*] (DB) .... BG
Barreiras [*Brazil*] [*Airport symbol*] (OAG) .... BRA
Barrel [*Shipping*] .... B
Barrel [*Shipping*] .... BAR
Barrel (SAUS) .... Bar
Barrel (AFM) .... BBL
Barrel (EDCT) .... bbl
Barrel [*Automotive term*] .... Bbl
Barrel (MCD) .... BL
Barrel (ADWA) .... brl
Barrel .... BRL
Barrel Bulk [*Shipping*] (ROG) .... BB
Barrel Cactus Virus [*Plant pathology*] .... BACV
Barrel Cactus Virus .... BCV
Barrel Coating .... BC
Barrel Futurities of America (EA) .... BFA
Barrel Racing [*Rodeo term*] .... GB
Barrel Roll (CINC) .... BR
Barrel Roller (SAUS) .... Brl Roll
Barrel Stave Projector. Acoustic projector (SAUS) .... BSP
Barrel Switch (IAA) .... BSW
Barrel Vault (VRA) .... bar vlt
Barre-Lieou [*Syndrome*] [*Medicine*] (DB) .... BL
Barrel-Launched Adaptive Munitions .... BLAM
Barrels (SAUS) .... Bars
Barrels [*or Boxes*] [*Freight*] .... BB
Barrels (SAUS) .... Bbl
Barrels [*Shipping*] .... BBLS
Barrels (ROG) .... BLL
Barrels [*Shipping*] .... BLS
Barrels, Boxes, or Crates [*Freight*] .... BBC
Barrels of New Oil (MHDB) .... BNO
Barrels of Oil and Water (SAUS) .... BO&W
Barrels of Oil Equivalent .... BOE
Barrels of Oil Equivalent per Day .... BOED
Barrels of Oil per Calendar Day (SAUS) .... BOCD
Barrels of Oil per Day (WGA) .... BOPD
Barrels of Total Fluid (SAUS) .... BTF
Barrels or Bags [*Freight*] .... B BGS
Barrels per Calendar Day (IAA) .... BCD
Barrels per Calendar Day .... BPCD
Barrels per Calender Day (EDCT) .... bpcd
Barrels per Day (IMH) .... bbl/d
Barrels per Day (SAUS) .... BBLS/DAY
Barrels per Day .... BD
Barrels per Day .... BPD
Barrels per Day (ADWA) .... bpd
Barrels per Day Oil Equivalent .... B/DOE
Barrels per Hour .... BPH
Barrels per Minute .... BPM
Barrels per Month (IAA) .... BM
Barrels per Month (IAA) .... BPM
Barrels per Stream Day (EDCT) .... bpsd
Barrels per Stream Day [*Also, BSD*] .... BPSD
Barrels per Stream Day [*Also, BPSD*] .... BSD
Barrel-Tile Roof [*Technical drawings*] .... BTR
Barremian-Aptian [*Paleontology*] .... BA
Barre-Montpelier, VT [*Location identifier*] [*FAA*] (FAAL) .... VKN
Barren Foundation [*Defunct*] (EA) .... BF
Barren Grounds Nature Reserve (SAUS) .... BGNR
Barretos [*Brazil*] [*ICAO location identifier*] (ICLI) .... SBBT
Barrett [*California*] [*Seismograph station code, US Geological Survey*]
    (SEIS) .... BAR
Barrett Business Services [*Associated Press*] (SAG) .... BarrettB
Barrett Business Services, Inc. [*NASDAQ symbol*] (SAG) .... BBSI
Barrett Business Svcs [*NASDAQ symbol*] (TTSB) .... BBST
Barrett Memorial Library, Petersburg, IN [*Library symbol*] [*Library of
    Congress*] (LCLS) .... InPet

Barrett Memorial Library, Williams Bay, WI [*Library symbol*] [*Library of Congress*] (LCLS) ... WWil
Barrett Resources [*Associated Press*] (SAG) ... BaretRs
Barrett Resources [*NYSE symbol*] (TTSB) ... BRR
Barrett Soft Mount. Rifle mount (SAUS) ... BSM
Barrette [*Hawaii*] [*Seismograph station code, US Geological Survey*] [*Closed*] (SEIS) ... BAH
Barrett-Lennard Relationship Inventory (EDAC) ... BLRI
Barrett's Esophagus [*Medicine*] ... BE
[*The*] **Barretts of Wimpole Street** [*A play by Rudolf Besier*] ... BOWS
Barrhead Public Library, Alberta [*Library symbol*] [*National Library of Canada*] (NLC) ... ABARR
Barriada ... BDA
Barrick Gold [*NYSE symbol*] (TTSB) ... ABX
Barrick Gold Corp. [*NYSE symbol*] (SAG) ... ABX
Barrick Gold Corp. [*Associated Press*] (SAG) ... BarrickG
Barrick Resources Corp. [*Toronto Stock Exchange symbol*] ... BRC
Barrick-Cullaton Gold Trust Units [*Toronto Stock Exchange symbol*] ... BC
Barrie & Jenkins [*Publisher's imprint*] ... B & J
Barrie, ON [*FM radio station call letters*] ... CFJB
Barrie, ON [*FM radio station call letters*] ... CHAY
Barrie, ON [*FM radio station call letters*] (RBYB) ... CIQB
Barrie, ON [*Television station call letters*] ... CKVR
Barrie Public Library, Barrie, ON, Canada [*Library symbol*] [*Library of Congress*] (LCLS) ... CaOBa
Barrie Public Library, Ontario [*Library symbol*] [*National Library of Canada*] (NLC) ... OBA
Barriefield Branch, Frontenac County Library, Ontario [*Library symbol*] [*National Library of Canada*] (BIB) ... OBFC
Barrier (NVT) ... BAR
Barrier (MSA) ... BARR
Barrier and Countersurveillance Division [*Army*] (RDA) ... B & CD
Barrier Arresting (SAUS) ... BAK
Barrier Arresting Kit (PDAA) ... BAK
Barrier Coat (MSA) ... BC
Barrier Combat Air Patrol [*Navy*] ... BARCAP
Barrier Development Program Plan (ABAC) ... BDPP
Barrier Doctrine [*Military*] (NVT) ... BARDOC
Barrier Film Rectifier ... BFR
Barrier Filter [*Medicine*] ... BF
Barrier Forces, Atlantic (SAUO) ... BARLANT
Barrier Forces, Pacific (SAUO) ... BARPAC
Barrier, Grease Proof (MSA) ... BGP
Barrier Injected Transit Time (CCCA) ... BARRITT
Barrier Injection Transit Time [*Physics*] ... BARITT
Barrier Isolation Unit [*Medicine*] (DB) ... BIU
Barrier Layer Cell ... BLC
Barrier Layer Rectifier ... BLR
Barrier, Moisture Vapor Proof (MSA) ... BMVP
Barrier Operations [*Military*] (NVT) ... BAROPS
Barrier Paper Manufacturers Association [*Defunct*] (EA) ... BPMA
Barrier Preparation (MCD) ... BP
Barrier Pressure [*Medicine*] ... BRP
Barrier Ready Light System (MSA) ... BRLS
Barrier Ready Light System (IAA) ... BRLSYS
Barrier Reef Resources [*Vancouver Stock Exchange symbol*] ... BAF
Barrier Tech [*Vancouver Stock Exchange symbol*] ... BAE
Barrier Technical Advisory Board (ABAC) ... BTAB
Barrier Terminal Strip ... BTS
Barrier Up Indicator System (MSA) ... BUIS
Barrier Up Indicator System ... BUISYS
Barrier, Waterproof (MSA) ... BWP
Barriered Landscape Water Renovation System (SAUS) ... BLWRS
Barrier-Equivalent Velocity [*Automotive safety*] ... BEV
Barrigada, GU [*FM radio station call letters*] (RBYB) ... KHMG
Barrincorp Industries, Inc. [*Toronto Stock Exchange symbol*] ... BCP
Barring ... BRRG
Barring of All Incoming Calls (CGWS) ... BAIC
Barring of All Outgoing Calls (CGWS) ... BAOC
Barringer Reflectance Spectrometer (SAUS) ... REFSPEC
Barringer Research Ltd., Rexdale, ON, Canada [*Library symbol*] [*Library of Congress*] (LCLS) ... CaOTBR
Barringer Research Ltd., Rexdale, Ontario [*Library symbol*] [*National Library of Canada*] (NLC) ... OTBR
Barringer Resources [*Associated Press*] (SAG) ... BarrngTch
Barringer Resources, Inc. [*NASDAQ symbol*] (NQ) ... BARR
Barringer Resources, Inc. [*Associated Press*] (SAG) ... BarTc
Barringer Resources, Inc. [*Associated Press*] (SAG) ... BarTch
Barringer Technologies Inc. [*NASDAQ symbol*] (TTSB) ... BARR
Barrington Area Library District, Barrington, IL [*Library symbol*] [*Library of Congress*] (LCLS) ... IBa
Barrington Bancorp [*NASDAQ symbol*] (TTSB) ... BABC
Barrington Bancorp, Inc. [*NASDAQ symbol*] (SAG) ... BABC
Barrington Bancorp, Inc. [*Associated Press*] (SAG) ... Barrngtn
Barrington College (SAUO) ... BC
Barrington College, Barrington, RI [*Library symbol*] [*Library of Congress*] (LCLS) ... RBaB
Barrington Historical Society (SAUS) ... NjBarHi
Barrington Historical Society, Barrington, NJ [*Library symbol*] [*Library of Congress*] (LCLS) ... NjBarHi
Barrington Petroleum Ltd. [*Formerly, Barrington Properties Ltd.*] [*Toronto Stock Exchange symbol*] ... BPL
Barrington Properties Ltd. [*Toronto Stock Exchange symbol*] [*Vancouver Stock Exchange symbol*] ... BGP
Barrington Public Library (SAUS) ... RB
Barrington Public Library, Barrington, RI [*Library symbol*] [*Library of Congress*] (LCLS) ... RBa
Barrington's Magna Charta [*A publication*] (DLA) ... Bar Mag
Barrington's Observations upon the Statutes from Magna Charta to 21 James [*A publication*] (DLA) ... Bar Ob Stat
Barrington's Observations upon the Statutes from Magna Charta to 21 James [*A publication*] (DLA) ... Barr Ob
Barrington's Observations upon the Statutes from Magna Charta to 21 James I [*A publication*] (DLA) ... Bar Anc Stat
Barrington's Observations upon the Statutes from Magna Charta to 21 James I [*A publication*] (DLA) ... Bar Obs St
Barrington's Observations upon the Statutes from Magna Charta to 21 James I [*A publication*] (DLA) ... Barring Obs St
Barrington's Observations upon the Statutes from Magna Charta to 21 James I [*A publication*] (DLA) ... Barring St
Barrington's Observations upon the Statutes from Magna Charta to 21 James I [*A publication*] (DLA) ... Barr Obs St
Barrington's Observations upon the Statutes from Magna Charta to 21 James I [*A publication*] (DLA) ... Barr St
Barrio Florida [*Puerto Rico*] [*Seismograph station code, US Geological Survey*] (SEIS) ... PWP
Barrister (ADA) ... bar
Barrister ... BARR
Barrister ... BRRSTR
Barrister (ABBR) ... BRSTR
Barrister Information Systems Corp. [*Associated Press*] (SAG) ... Baristr
Barrister Information Systems Corp. [*AMEX symbol*] (SPSG) ... BIS
Barrister-at-Law ... BL
Barristers and Solicitors Admission Board of New South Wales [*Australia*] ... BSABNSW
Barristers and Solicitors' Admission Board of the Australian Capital Territory ... BSABACT
Barro Colorado Island [*Canal Zone*] [*Site of Smithsonian Tropical Research Institute*] ... BCI
Barro Misery Index [*Economics*] ... BMI
Barroll. Chancery Practice [*Maryland*] [*A publication*] (DLA) ... Barr Ch Pr
Barron and Arnold's English Election Cases [*1843-46*] [*A publication*] (DLA) ... B & A
Barron and Arnold's English Election Cases [*1843-46*] [*A publication*] (DLA) ... B & Arn
Barron and Arnold's English Election Cases [*1843-46*] [*A publication*] (DLA) ... Bar & Arn
Barron and Arnold's English Election Cases [*1843-46*] [*A publication*] (DLA) ... Barr & Arn
Barron and Austin's English Election Cases [*1842*] [*A publication*] (DLA) ... B & A
Barron and Austin's English Election Cases [*1842*] [*A publication*] (DLA) ... B & Aust
Barron and Austin's English Election Cases [*1842*] [*A publication*] (DLA) ... B & Aust Cases (Eng)
Barron and Austin's English Election Cases [*1842*] [*A publication*] (DLA) ... Bar & Au
Barron and Austin's English Election Cases [*1842*] [*A publication*] (DLA) ... Bar & Aust
Barron and Austin's English Election Cases [*1842*] [*A publication*] (DLA) ... Barr & Aus
Barron and Holtzoff's Federal Practice and Procedure [*A publication*] (DLA) ... Barron & H Fed Pr & Proc
Barron, WI [*FM radio station call letters*] (BROA) ... WBFE-FM
Barron's Mirror of Parliament [*A publication*] (DLA) ... Barron Mir
Barron-Welsh Art Scale [*Psychology*] ... BWAS
Barros & Associates Ltd. [*Information service or system*] (IID) ... B & A
Barrow [*Alaska*] [*Airport symbol*] (OAG) ... BRW
Barrow [*Alaska*] [*Seismograph station code, US Geological Survey*] [*Closed*] (SEIS) ... BRW
Barrow [*Alaska*] [*ICAO location identifier*] (ICLI) ... PABR
Barrow, AK [*Location identifier*] [*FAA*] (FAAL) ... IEY
Barrow, AK [*AM radio station call letters*] ... KBRW
Barrow, AK [*FM radio station call letters*] (RBYB) ... KBRW-FM
Barrow, AK [*Location identifier*] [*FAA*] (FAAL) ... NMT
Barrow and District Association of Engineers (SAUO) ... BDAE
Barrow Environmental Observatory (SAUS) ... BEO
Barrow High School, Barrow, AK [*Library symbol*] [*Library of Congress*] (LCLS) ... AkBarH
Barrow Observatory (SAUO) ... BRW
Barrow Technical Services (SAUS) ... BTS
Barrows' Reports [*18 Rhode Island*] [*A publication*] (DLA) ... Bar
Barrows' Reports [*18 Rhode Island*] [*A publication*] (DLA) ... Barr
Barrows' Reports [*18 Rhode Island*] [*A publication*] (DLA) ... Barrows
Barrows' Reports [*18 Rhode Island*] [*A publication*] (DLA) ... Barrows (RI)
Barrow/Walney Island [*British*] [*ICAO location identifier*] (ICLI) ... EGNL
Barr's Body (MELL) ... BB
Barr's Reports [*1-10 Pennsylvania*] [*A publication*] (DLA) ... Barr
Barr's Reports [*1-10 Pennsylvania*] [*A publication*] (DLA) ... Barr (PA)
Barry [*Cardiff*] [*Welsh depot code*] ... BRY
Barry All the Time (EA) ... BATT
Barry Bostwick Fan Club (EA) ... BBFC
Barry College (SAUO) ... BC
Barry College, Miami Shores, FL [*Library symbol*] [*Library of Congress*] (LCLS) ... FMsB
Barry College, North Miami, FL [*OCLC symbol*] (OCLC) ... FBC
Barry College, North Miami, FL [*Library symbol*] [*Library of Congress*] (LCLS) ... FNmB
Barry [*R.G.*] **Corp.** [*Associated Press*] (SAG) ... BarryR
Barry Gibb Record (EA) ... BGR

Barry Melton Band [*Pop music group*] ... BMB
Barry Morse Fan Club (EA) ... BMFC
Barry on Building Societies [*A publication*] (DLA) ... Barry Build Soc
Barry on Forms and Precedents in Conveyancing [*A publication*] (DLA) ... Barry Forms Conv
Barry on Tenures [*A publication*] (DLA) ... Barr Ten
Barry on Tenures [*A publication*] (DLA) ... Barry Ten
Barry. Practice of Conveyancing [*1865*] [*A publication*] (DLA) ... Barry Conv
Barry Railway [*Wales*] ... BR
Barry Railway Co. (SAUO) ... BR
Barry (R.G.) [*NYSE symbol*] (TTSB) ... RGB
Barry (R.G.) Corp. [*NYSE symbol*] (SAG) ... RGB
Barry. Statutory Jurisdiction of Chancery [*1861*] [*A publication*] (DLA) ... Barry Ch Jur
Barry. Statutory Jurisdiction of Chancery [*1861*] [*A publication*] (DLA) ... Barry Ch Pr
Barry University (GAGS) ... Barry U
Barry's Babes [*Later, BGR*] (EA) ... BB
Barry's Bay Public Library, Ontario [*Library symbol*] [*National Library of Canada*] (NLC) ... OBB
Barrys Jewelers [*Associated Press*] (SAG) ... BarryJwl
Barry's Jewelers [*NASDAQ symbol*] (TTSB) ... BARY
Barry's Jewelers, Inc. [*NASDAQ symbol*] (NQ) ... BARY
Barry's Jewelers, Inc. [*Associated Press*] (SAG) ... BaryJ
Barry's Jewelers, Inc. [*Associated Press*] (SAG) ... BaryJw
Barry's Jewelers Wrrt [*NASDAQ symbol*] (TTSB) ... BARYW
Barryton Public Library, Barryton, MI [*Library symbol*] [*Library of Congress*] (LCLS) ... MiBar
Barsalogho [*Burkina Faso*] [*ICAO location identifier*] (ICLI) ... DHCB
Barsand Resources, Inc. [*Vancouver Stock Exchange symbol*] ... BSD
Barstow, CA [*Location identifier*] [*FAA*] (FAAL) ... BYS
Barstow, CA [*FM radio station call letters*] ... KDUC
Barstow, CA [*Television station call letters*] ... KHIZ
Barstow, CA [*AM radio station call letters*] ... KIQQ
Barstow, CA [*AM radio station call letters*] ... KSZL
Barstow, CA [*FM radio station call letters*] ... KXXZ
Barstow School, Kansas City, MO [*Library symbol*] [*Library of Congress*] (LCLS) ... MoKBa
Bar-Sur-Seine [*France*] [*ICAO location identifier*] (ICLI) ... LFFR
Bart Resources Ltd. [*Vancouver Stock Exchange symbol*] ... BK
Bartender (ABBR) ... BRTNDR
Barter (ABBR) ... BRTR
Barter Clubs (EA) ... BC
Barter Island [*Alaska*] [*Seismograph station code, US Geological Survey*] (SEIS) ... BI1
Barter Island [*Alaska*] [*Seismograph station code, US Geological Survey*] (SEIS) ... BI2
Barter Island [*Alaska*] [*Seismograph station code, US Geological Survey*] (SEIS) ... BI3
Barter Island [*Alaska*] [*Seismograph station code, US Geological Survey*] (SEIS) ... BI4
Barter Island [*Alaska*] [*Airport symbol*] (OAG) ... BTI
Barter Island [*Alaska*] [*ICAO location identifier*] (ICLI) ... PABA
Barter Worldwide, Inc. [*Information service or system*] (IID) ... BWW
Barth [*Germany*] [*ICAO location identifier*] (ICLI) ... ETBH
Bartholin and Skene [*Glands*] [*Medicine*] ... B & S
Bartholin Gland Carcinoma [*Medicine*] (MELL) ... BGC
Bartholin's Skene's, and Urethral [*Glands*] [*Gynecology*] (DAVI) ... BSU
Bartholin's, Urethral, and Skene's Glands and External Genitalia [*Gynecology*] (DAVI) ... BUSEG
Bartholin's, Urethral, Skene's [*Glands*] [*Medicine*] ... BUS
Bartholomaeus [*Authority cited in pre-1607 legal work*] (DSA) ... Barto
Bartholomaeus Archamonus [*Authority cited in pre-1607 legal work*] (DSA) ... Bar Ar
Bartholomaeus Archamonus [*Authority cited in pre-1607 legal work*] (DSA) ... Bar Archa
Bartholomaeus Belenzinus de Modena [*Deceased, 1478*] [*Authority cited in pre-1607 legal work*] (DSA) ... Barth Belenz
Bartholomaeus Belenzinus de Modena [*Deceased, 1478*] [*Authority cited in pre-1607 legal work*] (DSA) ... Bartho Belenz
Bartholomaeus Belenzinus (Mutinensis) [*Deceased, 1478*] [*Authority cited in pre-1607 legal work*] (DSA) ... Bartho Mutinen
Bartholomaeus Brixiensis [*Deceased circa 1258*] [*Authority cited in pre-1607 legal work*] (DSA) ... B
Bartholomaeus Brixiensis [*Deceased circa 1258*] [*Authority cited in pre-1607 legal work*] (DSA) ... Bar
Bartholomaeus Brixiensis [*Deceased circa 1258*] [*Authority cited in pre-1607 legal work*] (DSA) ... Bar Brix
Bartholomaeus Brixiensis [*Deceased circa 1258*] [*Authority cited in pre-1607 legal work*] (DSA) ... Bar Brixi
Bartholomaeus Brixiensis [*Deceased circa 1258*] [*Authority cited in pre-1607 legal work*] (DSA) ... Bar Brixien
Bartholomaeus Brixiensis [*Deceased circa 1258*] [*Authority cited in pre-1607 legal work*] (DSA) ... Bart Bri
Bartholomaeus Brixiensis [*Deceased circa 1258*] [*Authority cited in pre-1607 legal work*] (DSA) ... Barth
Bartholomaeus Brixiensis [*Deceased circa 1258*] [*Authority cited in pre-1607 legal work*] (DSA) ... Barth Brix
Bartholomaeus Brixiensis [*Deceased circa 1258*] [*Authority cited in pre-1607 legal work*] (DSA) ... B Bri
Bartholomaeus Brixiensis [*Deceased circa 1258*] [*Authority cited in pre-1607 legal work*] (DSA) ... B Brix
Bartholomaeus Brixiensis [*Deceased circa 1258*] [*Authority cited in pre-1607 legal work*] (DSA) ... B Bx
Bartholomaeus Brixiensis [*Deceased circa 1258*] [*Authority cited in pre-1607 legal work*] (DSA) ... Bthol
Bartholomaeus Camerarius [*Deceased, 1564*] [*Authority cited in pre-1607 legal work*] (DSA) ... Bartol Camer
Bartholomaeus Cepolla [*Deceased, 1477*] [*Authority cited in pre-1607 legal work*] (DSA) ... Bart Cepol
Bartholomaeus de Capua [*Deceased, 1328*] [*Authority cited in pre-1607 legal work*] (DSA) ... B
Bartholomaeus de Capua [*Deceased, 1328*] [*Authority cited in pre-1607 legal work*] (DSA) ... Ba de Ca
Bartholomaeus de Capua [*Deceased, 1328*] [*Authority cited in pre-1607 legal work*] (DSA) ... Bar de C
Bartholomaeus de Capua [*Deceased, 1328*] [*Authority cited in pre-1607 legal work*] (DSA) ... Bar de Ca
Bartholomaeus de Capua [*Deceased, 1328*] [*Authority cited in pre-1607 legal work*] (DSA) ... Bar de Cap
Bartholomaeus de Capua [*Deceased, 1328*] [*Authority cited in pre-1607 legal work*] (DSA) ... Bart de Cap
Bartholomaeus de Capua [*Deceased, 1328*] [*Authority cited in pre-1607 legal work*] (DSA) ... B de C
Bartholomaeus de Capua [*Deceased, 1328*] [*Authority cited in pre-1607 legal work*] (DSA) ... B de Ca
Bartholomaeus de Exeter [*Flourished, 12th century*] [*Authority cited in pre-1607 legal work*] (DSA) ... Barthol
Bartholomaeus de Saliceto [*Deceased, 1411*] [*Authority cited in pre-1607 legal work*] (DSA) ... Bar
Bartholomaeus de Saliceto [*Deceased, 1411*] [*Authority cited in pre-1607 legal work*] (DSA) ... Bar de Sa
Bartholomaeus de Saliceto [*Deceased, 1411*] [*Authority cited in pre-1607 legal work*] (DSA) ... Bar de Sal
Bartholomaeus de Saliceto [*Deceased, 1411*] [*Authority cited in pre-1607 legal work*] (DSA) ... Bar de Sali
Bartholomaeus de Saliceto [*Deceased, 1411*] [*Authority cited in pre-1607 legal work*] (DSA) ... Bartho de Sali
Bartholomaeus de Saliceto [*Deceased, 1411*] [*Authority cited in pre-1607 legal work*] (DSA) ... B de Sa
Bartholomaeus Socinus [*Deceased, 1507*] [*Authority cited in pre-1607 legal work*] (DSA) ... Bart Socin
Bartholoman's Reports, Yorkshire Lent Assize [*March 9, 1911*] [*England*] [*A publication*] (DLA) ... Bartholoman
Bartholomew County Historical Society, Columbus, IN [*Library symbol*] [*Library of Congress*] (LCLS) ... InColuHi
Bartholomew County Library, Columbus, IN [*OCLC symbol*] (OCLC) ... INB
Bartholomew County Library, Columbus, IN [*Library symbol*] [*Library of Congress*] (LCLS) ... InColo
Bartholomew County Library, Columbus, IN [*Library symbol*] [*Library of Congress*] (LCLS) ... InColu
Bartholomew Sales & Distribution Services [*British*] ... BSDS
Barth's Aviation [*France*] [*ICAO designator*] (FAAC) ... BTH
Bartica [*Guyana*] [*Airport symbol*] (OAG) ... GFO
Bartica [*Guyana*] [*ICAO location identifier*] (ICLI) ... SYBT
Bartle Bogle Hegarty [*Commercial firm*] [*British*] ... BBH
Bartlesville [*Oklahoma*] [*Airport symbol*] (AD) ... BVO
Bartlesville Energy Research Center [*Department of Energy*] ... BERC
Bartlesville Energy Technology Center [*Later, NIPER*] [*Department of Energy*] [*Bartlesville, OK*] [*Information service or system*] (GRD) ... BETC
Bartlesville, OK [*Location identifier*] [*FAA*] (FAAL) ... BVO
Bartlesville, OK [*Television station call letters*] ... KDOR
Bartlesville, OK [*AM radio station call letters*] ... KWON
Bartlesville, OK [*FM radio station call letters*] ... KYFM
Bartlesville Project Office [*Bartlesville, OK*] [*Department of Energy*] (GRD) ... BPO
Bartlesville Public Library, Bartlesville, OK [*Library symbol*] [*Library of Congress*] (LCLS) ... OkB
Bartlet & Richardes, Windsor, Ontario [*Library symbol*] [*National Library of Canada*] (BIB) ... OWBR
Bartlett Cove, AK [*Location identifier*] [*FAA*] (FAAL) ... BQV
Bartlett Nuclear Inc. (SAUO) ... BNI
Bartlett, TN [*AM radio station call letters*] (RBYB) ... WGSF
Bartlett, TN [*FM radio station call letters*] (RBYB) ... WMFS
Bartlett's Congressional Election Cases [*A publication*] (DLA) ... Bart Cong Election Cases
Bartlett's Congressional Election Cases [*A publication*] (DLA) ... Bart El Cas
Bartlett's Congressional Election Cases [*A publication*] (DLA) ... Bart Elec Cas
Bartlett's Index of the Laws of Rhode Island [*A publication*] (DLA) ... Bart Ind
Bartlett's Law of Mining [*1850*] [*A publication*] (DLA) ... Bart Mines
Bartley Herbarium, Ohio University [*Athens, OH*] ... BHO
Bartoc Archives Z-symbol Rhythm Extraction (SAUS) ... BARZREX
Bartok Archives Z-Symbol Rhythm Extraction [*Computer science*] ... BARZREX
Bartok Recording Studio [*Record label*] ... BRS
Bartolus de Sassoferrato [*Deceased, 1357*] [*Authority cited in pre-1607 legal work*] (DSA) ... B
Bartolus de Sassoferrato [*Deceased, 1357*] [*Authority cited in pre-1607 legal work*] (DSA) ... Bar
Bartolus de Sassoferrato [*Deceased, 1357*] [*Authority cited in pre-1607 legal work*] (DSA) ... Bart
Bartolus de Sassoferrato [*Deceased, 1357*] [*Authority cited in pre-1607 legal work*] (DSA) ... Barto
Bartolus de Sassoferrato [*Deceased, 1357*] [*Authority cited in pre-1607 legal work*] (DSA) ... Bto
Barton & Guestier (SAUO) ... B&G
Barton & Guestier [*Wine*] ... B & G
Barton County Community College, Great Bend, KS [*Library symbol*] [*Library of Congress*] (LCLS) ... KGbB
Barton Regis [*England*] ... BART REG
Bartone [*Record label*] ... Bne

Bartoni International Gallery (SAUO) ... BIG
Bartonian Metaphysical Society, Ottawa, ON, Canada [Library symbol]
  [Library of Congress] (LCLS) ... CaOOBM
Bartonian Metaphysical Society, Ottawa, Ontario [Library symbol] [National
  Library of Canada] (NLC) ... OOBM
Barton's Law Practice [A publication] (DLA) ... Bart L Pr
Barton's Maxims in Conveyancing [A publication] (DLA) ... Bart Max
Barton's Modern Precedents in Conveyancing [A publication]
  (DLA) ... Bar Prec Conv
Barton's Modern Precedents in Conveyancing [3rd ed.] [1826]
  [A publication] (DLA) ... Bart Prec Conv
Barton's Science of Conveyancing [2nd ed.] [1810-22] [A publication]
  (DLA) ... Bart Conv
Barton's Suit in Equity [A publication] (DLA) ... Bar Eq
Barton's Suit in Equity [A publication] (DLA) ... Bart Eq
Bartonville, IL [FM radio statio call letters] (RBYB) ... WIXO-FM
Bartow, FL [Location identifier] [FAA] (FAAL) ... BOW
Bartow, FL [AM radio station call letters] ... WBAR
Bartow, FL [AM radio station call letters] ... WWBF
Bartow Public Library, Bartow, FL [Library symbol] [Library of Congress]
  (LCLS) ... FB
Bartram Trail Regional Library, Washington, GA [Library symbol] [Library of
  Congress] (LCLS) ... GWasB
Baruch [Book of the Bible] (BJA) ... Ba
Baruch [Book of the Bible] ... Bar
Baruch College (SAUS) ... BC
Baruch College, New York, NY [OCLC symbol] (OCLC) ... VVB
Baruch Retrieval of Automated Information for Negotiations [City University
  of New York] [Information service or system] (IID) ... BRAIN
Barwick Community Library, Barwick, ON, Canada [Library symbol] [Library
  of Congress] (LCLS) ... CaOBC
Barwick Community Library, Ontario [Library symbol] [National Library of
  Canada] (BIB) ... OBC
Barycentric Dynamical Time (SAUS) ... TDB
Barye (SAUS) ... Ba
Barymin Explorations Ltd. [Toronto Stock Exchange symbol] ... BYX
Baryon Scale (WDAA) ... B
Baryon Symmetric Big Band (PDAA) ... BSBB
Baryonic Dark Matter [Galactic science] ... BDM
Baryon-Isobar Rest System ... BARS
Baryta Light Fling (MSA) ... BLF
Barytex Resources Corp. [Vancouver Stock Exchange symbol] ... BTX
Barzona Breeders Association of America (EA) ... BBAA
BAS Airlines [ICAO designator] (AD) ... GS
Bas Relief (VRA) ... barlf
BASA [British Australian Studies Association] Magazine [A publication] ... BASA Mag
Basaba Enterprises, Inc. [Vancouver Stock Exchange symbol] ... BSE
Basair AB [Sweden] [ICAO designator] (FAAC) ... BSR
Basal (ADWA) ... bas
Basal (SAUS) ... Bas
Basal Acid Output [Medicine] ... BAO
Basal Acid Output to Maximal Acid Output [Ratio] [Medicine]
  (AAMN) ... BAO-MAO
Basal Area [Cross-sectional area of three at breast height] (WPI) ... BA
Basal Area Increment [Forestry] ... BAI
Basal Body Temperature [Medicine] ... BBT
Basal Cell Atypia [Medicine] (DAVI) ... BCA
Basal Cell Carcinoma [Medicine] ... BCC
Basal Cell Carcinoma [Medicine] (DAVI) ... BCCA
Basal Cell Dysplasia [Medicine] (DAVI) ... BCD
Basal Cell Epithelioma [Obsolete] [Medicine] ... BCE
Basal Cell Hyperplasia [Medicine] ... BCH
Basal Cell Nevus [Medicine] (MELL) ... BCN
Basal Cell Nevus Syndrome [Medicine] (DMAA) ... BCNS
Basal Cell Vigilance (DAVI) ... BCV
Basal Cerebral Vigilance [Sleep] ... BCV
Basal Energy Expenditure [Nutrition] (DMAA) ... BEE
Basal Energy Requirement [Nutrition] ... BER
Basal Fold ... BF
Basal Forebrain Area (SAUS) ... BFA
Basal Ganglion [Medicine] (DMAA) ... BG
Basal Gastric Acid Output [Medicine] (MELL) ... BAO
Basal Granule ... BGR
Basal Groove ... BG
Basal Heart Rate [Medicine] ... BHR
Basal Insulin Level [Medicine] (DMAA) ... BIL
Basal Lamina [Neuroanatomy] ... BL
Basal Layer of Endometrium [Medicine] (MELL) ... BLE
Basal Leaf Area [Botany] ... BAREA
Basal Level Element [Genetics] ... BLE
Basal Level Enhancer [Genetics] ... BLE
Basal Medium [Microbiology] ... BM
Basal Medium, Eagle's [Diploid cell cultures] (MAE) ... BME
Basal Metabolic Rate (CPH) ... BMET
Basal Metabolic Rate [Medicine] ... BMR
Basal Metabolism [Medicine] ... BM
Basal Metabolism Rate (NTIO) ... BMR
Basal Metabolism Reading (SAUS) ... BMR
Basal Optic Root (DB) ... BOR
Basal Pepsin Output [Medicine] (DMAA) ... BPO
Basal Period ... BP
Basal Retinal Neuron [Neurology] ... BRN
Basal [or Baseline] Skin Resistance [Medicine] ... BSR
Basal Starch Cycloheximide Antibiotic Agar [Microbiology] ... BSCAA
Basal Temperature Charting [Medicine] (MELL) ... BTC

Basal Transcription Apparatus [Biochemistry] ... BTA
Basal Web ... BW
Basal-Ganglion Calcification [Neurology] (DAVI) ... BGC
Basalt (VRA) ... bst
Basalt, CO [FM radio station call letters] (RBYB) ... KNFO
Basalt Public Library, Basalt, CO [Library symbol] [Library of Congress]
  (LCLS) ... CoBa
Basalt Very High Alumina Basalt (SAUS) ... VHA
Basalt Waste Isolation Project [Department of Energy] ... BWIP
Basalt Waste Isolation Project Office (SAUO) ... BWIPO
Basaltic Achondrite Best Initial (DICI) ... BABI
Basaltic Achondrite Parent [Planetary body] (OAG) ... BAP
Basaltic Termite Barrier (SAUS) ... BTB
Basaltic Volcanism Study Project [Planetary science] ... BVSP
Basankusu [Zaire] [Airport symbol] (OAG) ... BSU
Basankusu [Zaire] [ICAO location identifier] (ICLI) ... FZEN
Basco [Philippines] [Airport symbol] (OAG) ... BSO
Basco, Batanes Island [Philippines] [ICAO location identifier] (ICLI) ... RPUO
Base ... B
Base (DCTA) ... BAS
Base (IAA) ... BS
Base (SAUS) ... Bs
Base Accountable Supply Officer [Air Force] ... BASO
Base Accounting and Finance Office [Air Force] (AFM) ... BAFO
Base Activation ... BA
Base Activation Central Control Committee ... BACCC
Base Activation Change Order ... BACO
Base Activation Instruction ... BAI
Base Activation Notice ... BAN
Base Activation Statistical Control ... BASC
Base Activation Test Equipment ... BATE
Base Adder Register (SAUS) ... BAR
Base Address and Transfer [Military] ... BAT
Base Address Register [Computer science] (BUR) ... BAR
Base Adressing (SAUS) ... BA
Base Air Defense Ground Environment [Air Force] ... BADGE
Base Air Defense Ground Environment System (SAUS) ... BADGES
Base Air Depot (SAUO) ... BAD
Base Air Depot Area [Air Force] ... BADA
Base Air Post Depot (SAUO) ... BAPD
Base Air Traffic Control (SAUS) ... BATC
Base Aircraft Maintenance and Engineering Organization [Canadian
  Navy] ... BAMEO
Base Allowance List (MUGU) ... BAL
Base Ammunition and Petroleum Depot (SAUO) ... BAPD
Base Ammunition Depot (NATG) ... BAD
Base Ammunition Depot (SAUO) ... BAmD
Base Ammunition Depot (SAUS) ... B Am D
Base and Increment (SAUS) ... B&I
Base and Increment [Technical drawings] ... B & I
Base and Installation Security System [Military] ... BISS
Base Area Commandant ... BAC
Base Area Defense Ground Environment (SAUS) ... BADGE
Base Area Refueling Equipment ... BARE
Base Assembly ... BA
Base Assembly and Test Equipment (SAA) ... BATE
Base Assembly Parts List (IAA) ... BAPL
Base Augmentation Support Set (MCD) ... BASS
Base Authorization List ... BAL
Base Automated Budget System (ACAE) ... BABS
Base Automated Mobility System (MCD) ... BAMS
Base Automotive Maintenance ... BAM
Base Auxiliary Power (KSC) ... BAP
Base Band (SAUS) ... BB
Base Bleed (SAUS) ... BB
Base Bleed Unit (SAUS) ... BBU
Base Budget Automation System (ACAE) ... BBAS
Base Burn (SAUS) ... BB
Base Burning (MCD) ... BB
Base Burning/Lateral Injection Propulsion (MCD) ... BBLIP
Base Camp (SAUO) ... C
Base Capacitance (IDOE) ... C_B
Base Case Coordinating Instructions (DOMA) ... BCCI
Base Catalyzed Destruction (ABAC) ... BCD
Base Central Technical Facility (SAUO) ... BCTF
Base Central Test Facility (SAUO) ... BCTF
Base Checkout Equipment (SAUS) ... BCE
Base Circle Diameter (IAA) ... BCD
Base Civil Engineer [Military] (AFM) ... BCE
Base Civil Engineer Real Property Office (SAA) ... BCERPO
Base Civil Engineering Course [Air Force] ... BCECRS
Base Civil Engineering School [Air Force] ... BCESCH
Base Closing Economic Injury [Loan] ... BCEI
Base Closure Action (MCD) ... BCA
Base Closure and Realignment Act [Military] ... BCRA
Base Closure and Realignment Commission [DoD] ... BCARS
Base Cluster Operations Center [Environmental science] (COE) ... BCOC
Base Cluster Operations Centers (SAUO) ... BCOC
Base Coat/Clear Coat [Automotive body and refinishing] ... BC/CC
Base Collector ... BC
Base Command (SAUO) ... Ba Com
Base Command ... BC
Base Command Payment Office (SAUO) ... BCPO
Base Communications Center (SAUO) ... BCC
Base Communications Center Strategy Working Group (SAUO) ... BCCSWG

Base Communications Plan [*United States Army Communications Command*] (MCD) .... BASCOP
Base Communications Processor (CCCA) .... BCP
Base Communications-computer Center (SAUS) .... BCC
Base Composite Price Index (MCD) .... BI
Base Condemnation Percent (NASA) .... BCP
Base Connection [*Engineering*] (IAA) .... BC
Base Connection (SAUS) .... bc
Base Consolidation Control Office (AFM) .... BCCO
Base Consolidation Control Officer (SAUS) .... BCCO
Base Construction Depot Detachment [*Navy*] .... BCDD
Base Construction Liaison Unit (SAA) .... BCLU
Base Contracting Automated System [*Computer science*] .... BCAS
Base Contracting Office (SAUO) .... BCO
Base Contracting Officer [*Military*] .... BCO
Base Correlation Matrix [*Air Force*] (DOMA) .... BCM
Base Count (IAA) .... BC
Base Course Wear Rate [*Tire testing*] .... BCWR
Base Current Branch (SAUS) .... BCB
Base Damage Report (SAUS) .... BASEDAM
Base Data Processing Installation .... BDPI
Base Data System (AFM) .... BDS
Base de Datos Geomagneticos [*Instituto Geografico Nacional*] [*Database*] .... BASEMAG
Base de Documentos en Politica Criminal [*Criminal Law Documents Data Base*] [*United Nations Latin American Institute for Crime Prevention and Treatment of Offenders*] (IID) .... DPOC
Base de Donnees des Obligations Francaises [*DAFSA*] [*Database*] .... BDO
Base Defence Zone (SAUS) .... BDZ
Base Defense Force [*Military*] (NVT) .... BDF
Base Defense Measure (ACAE) .... BDM
Base Defense Operations Center (SAUO) .... BDOC
Base Deficit .... BD
Base Deflection Right (SAUS) .... BDR
Base Depot (SAUO) .... BD
Base Depot (SAUO) .... B dep
Base Depot and General Hospital (SAUO) .... BDGH
Base Depot and General Hospital (SAUS) .... BDGH
Base Depot of Medical Stores (SAUO) .... BDMS
Base Depot Stockage Model (SAUS) .... BDSM
Base Depot Veterinary Stores (SAUS) .... BDVS
Base des Forces Canadiennes [*Canadian Forces Base - CFB*] .... BFC
Base Design Section [*Military*] (IAA) .... BDS
Base Design Section - Operational Facility Installation [*Military*] (IAA) ..... BDSOFI
Base Design Section - Support Facility Installation [*Military*] (IAA) .... BDSSFI
Base Design Section-Support Facilities Installations (SAUS) .... BDS-SFI
Base Detonating .... BD
Base Detonating Fuse .... BDF
Base Detonating Fuze (MCD) .... BDEF
Base Detonating, Self-Destroying .... BDSD
Base Development Board [*Military*] (AABC) .... BDB
Base Development Feasibility Study [*Navy*] .... BDFS
Base Development Plan (AABC) .... BDP
Base Development Report .... BASEDEV
Base Development Survey (MCD) .... BDS
Base Diameter .... BD
Base Diameter .... BDIA
Base Diameter [*Manufacturing term*] .... Db
Base Diffusion Isolation .... BDI
Base Diffusion Process (SAUS) .... BDP
Base d'Information Robert Debre [*Robert Debre Information Base*] [*International Children's Center*] [*Information service or system*] (IID) .... BIRD
Base Distribution System [*Air Force*] (AFM) .... BDS
Base Divider Strip (AAG) .... BDS
Base Down (SAUS) .... BD
Base Drag Reduction (SAUS) .... BDR
Base Ejection .... BE
Base Electronics System Engineering Plan (NG) .... BESEP
Base Electronics Systems Engineering Plan (SAUO) .... BESEP
Base Engineer Automated Management System (SAUS) .... BEAMS
Base Engineer Depot (SAUO) .... BED
Base Engineer Emergency Force [*Air Force*] (AFM) .... BEEF
Base Engineer Store Depot (SAUO) .... BESD
Base Engineering Automated Management System (AFM) .... BEAMS
Base Engineering Course (SAUS) .... BEC
Base Equation (SAUS) .... BE
Base Equipment Container .... BEC
Base Equipment Management Office [*Air Force*] (AFM) .... BEMO
Base Equipment Unit (SAUO) .... BEU
Base Equipment Unit (SAUS) .... BEU
Base Examination Course (SAUS) .... BEC
Base Excess [*Medicine*] .... BE
Base Excess [*Biochemistry*] (DAVI) .... Bex
Base Excess [*Medicine*] .... BXS
Base Exchange .... BX
Base Extension Course .... BEC
Base Facilities for SACLANT [*NATO*] (NATG) .... BFS
Base Field Effect Register [*Electronics*] (OA) .... BFER
Base Field-Effect Resistor (SAUS) .... BFER
Base File .... BF
Base Flight Management Data System (AFM) .... BFMDS
Base Flood Elevation (DEMM) .... BFE
Base Flood Elevation (SAUS) .... BSE
Base for Information and Communication in Europe (SAUS) .... BICE
Base for Uniform Language Definition [*Computer science*] (IEEE) .... BUILD

Base Force .... BASEFOR
Base Formula (SAUS) .... BF
Base Frequency (ADA) .... BF
Base Fuel Supply Officer (SAUS) .... BFSO
Base Fuels Management Officer [*Air Force*] (AFM) .... BFMO
Base Fuels Supply Officer [*Air Force*] (AFM) .... BFSO
Base Funded (AFM) .... BF
Base Fuse (or Fuze) (SAUS) .... BF
Base Fuze Hole Plug .... BFHP
Base Heat Shield .... BHS
Base Helix Angle [*NASA*] .... BHA
Base Hospital [*Military*] .... BH
Base Identifier (SAUS) .... BI
Base Ignition .... BI
Base In (SAUS) .... BI
Base Indexed (SAUS) .... BX
Base Individual Mobilization Augmentee Administrator (SAUS) .... BIMAA
Base Industrial Relations Office [*or Officer*] [*Military*] .... BIRO
Base Infantry .... BI
Base Information Data Distribution System (SAUS) .... BIDDS
Base Information Digital Distribution System (ACAE) .... BIDDS
Base Information System Management Center (SAUO) .... BISMC
Base Information Transfer Center [*Military*] .... BITC
Base Information Transfer System [*Navy*] (GFGA) .... BITS
Base Injection (IAA) .... BI
Base Inspection Questionnaire [*Air Force*] .... BIQ
Base Installation - Minuteman [*Military*] (IAA) .... BIMM
Base Installation Action Requirements .... BIAR
Base Installation Department (SAA) .... BID
Base Installation Minuteman (SAUS) .... BI-MM
Base Installation Officer .... BIO
Base Installation Test Equipment [*Military*] (IAA) .... BITE
Base Intelligence Officer (SAUS) .... B Intel O
Base Interface Surveillance Unit (IAA) .... BISU
Base Interrupt Address Register (IAA) .... BIAR
Base Intrusion Detection System (MCD) .... BIDS
Base Intrusion Surveillance System (MCD) .... BISS
Base Island Transistor (SAUS) .... BIT
Base Isolation Level (IAA) .... BIL
Base Junction Transistor (SAUS) .... BJT
Base Level Accounting & Reporting System (SAUS) .... BLARS
Base Level Commercial Equipment [*DoD*] .... BCE
Base Level Data Automation Program (SAUS) .... PHASE IV
Base Level Inquiry System .... BLIS
Base Level Maintenance Cost System (AFIT) .... BLMCS
Base Level Military Personnel System (SAUS) .... BLMPS
Base Level Military Personnel System (ACAE) .... BLMS
Base Level of Treatment (DICI) .... BLT
Base Level Operations .... BLO
Base Level Personnel System [*Air Force*] (GFGA) .... BLPS
Base Level Self-Sufficiency [*Air Force*] .... BLSS
Base Level System Modernization (SAUS) .... BLSM
Base Liaison Officer (SAUS) .... BLO
Base Line Configuration Identification (SAA) .... BCI
Base Loaded Aerial (SAUS) .... BLA
Base Loaded Antenna .... BLA
Base Loading System (DNAB) .... BLS
Base Locator Linkage (MHDI) .... BLL
Base Logistical Command (SAUS) .... BALOC
Base Logistical Command .... BALOG
Base Machine (SAUS) .... BM
Base Mail Distribution Scheme [*Air Force*] (AFM) .... BMDS
Base Maintenance [*Air Force*] (AFM) .... BM
Base Maintenance and Operations Model .... BMOM
Base Maintenance and Repair .... BMAR
Base Maintenance Building (MCD) .... BMB
Base Maintenance Division [*Navy*] .... BMD
Base Maintenance Operation (MCD) .... BMO
Base Maintenance Removal Interval [*Air Force*] (AFIT) .... BMRI
Base Management Engineering Data System .... BMEDS
Base Manager Data System .... BMDS
Base Manager's Notice .... BMN
Base Manpower Data System [*Air Force*] (OAG) .... BMDS
Base Marambio [*Argentina*] [*ICAO location identifier*] (ICLI) .... SAWB
Base Marshalling Yard (SAUO) .... BMY
Base Mechanical Transport Depot (SAUO) .... BMTD
Base Medical Equipment Depot (SAUO) .... BMED
Base Medical Supply Office [*or Officer*] [*Air Force*] (AFM) .... BMSO
Base Metal Catalyst [*Automotive engineering*] .... BMC
Base Metal Sulfides (SAUS) .... BMS
Base Military Training (ACAE) .... BMT
Base Mount Valve .... BMV
Base Network Control Center .... BNCC
Base, Neutral, and Acid (EEVL) .... BNA
Base Neutralizing Capacity [*Chemistry*] .... BNC
Base Notation (SAUS) .... BN
Base Number (SAUS) .... BN
Base of Air Operations .... BAO
Base of Bank (WDAA) .... BB
Base of Dorsal Left (SAUS) .... BDL
Base of Dorsal Lip .... BDL
Base of Lateral Lip .... BLL
Base of Natural Logarithms [*Mathematics*] (DAVI) .... e
Base of Overcast [*Meteorology*] .... BOVC
Base of Preference Program [*for reenlisting airmen*] .... BOP

Base of Prism Down [Medicine] (DMAA)	BD
Base of prism In (SAUS)	BI
Base of Stack Register (SAUS)	BOSR
Base of Terminal Service [for airmen]	BTS
Base of Tongue [Anatomy and otorhinolaryngology] (DAVI)	BOT
Base Officers Quarters (SAUS)	BOQ
Base on Balls (SAUS)	bb
Base Only Density (DGA)	BOD
Base Operacional de Tropas Paraquedistas [Paratroopers Operational Base] [Air Force] [Portugal]	BOTP
Base Operating Centre (SAUS)	BOC
Base Operating Information System [Formerly, COCOAS]	BASOPS
Base Operating Information System (Supply Management System)	BASOPS (SMS)
Base Operating Service [Contract] [DoD]	BOS
Base Operating Supplies	BOS
Base Operating Supply System	BOSS
Base Operating Support (AFM)	BOS
Base Operating System (ACAE)	BASOPS
Base Operating System (SAUS)	BOS
Base Operation Manager	BOM
Base Operations	BAOPS
Base Operations	BASEOPS
Base Operations [Army]	BASOPS
Base Operations Contract (SSD)	BOC
Base Operations Division [NASA] (KSC)	BOD
Base Operations Maintenance Simulator (MHDI)	BOMS
Base Operations Office	BASOPS
Base Operations Officer (SAUS)	BOO
Base Order	BO
Base Ordnance Depot	BOD
Base Ordnance Officer (SAUS)	BOO
Base Ordnance Workshop [British and Canadian]	BOW
Base Organization and Maintenance Processor (IEEE)	BOMP
Base Page (ACAE)	BP
Base Pairs [Genetics] (DOG)	bp
Base Pairs in DNA [Genetics]	BP
Base Patrol Center (or Centre) (SAUS)	BPC
Base Pay [Military]	BP
Base Pay Office (SAUO)	BPO
Base Percussion	BP
Base Perimeter Security System	BPSS
Base Period Density	BPD
Base Personnel Office (SAUO)	BPO
Base Personnel Staff Officer [Air Force] [British]	BPSO
Base Petrol Installation (SAUO)	BPI
Base Pioneer [Cell neuron]	BP
Base Pitch (MSA)	BP
Base Planning Board [Military] (DNAB)	BPB
Base Point	BP
Base Point	BPT
Base Point Configuration (AAG)	BPC
Base Point Defense Launching System (DNAB)	BPDLS
Base Pointer [Computer science]	BP
Base Position [Phylogenetic analysis]	BP
Base Post Office	BPO
Base Postal Section [Air Force] (AFM)	BPS
Base Precision Measurement Equipment Laboratories (AFM)	BPMEL
Base Procured (AFM)	BP
Base Procured/Central Procured (AFM)	BP/CP
Base Procurement Office [Air Force] (AFM)	BPO
Base Procurement Service Stores [Air Force] (AFM)	BPSS
Base Production Unit [Army] (AABC)	BPU
Base Productivity Factor (MCD)	BPF
Base Program Preparation Facility [Computer science] (MHDI)	BPPF
Base Protein	BP
Base Quartermaster [Marine Corps]	BQM
Base Quota	BQ
Base Rate Area [Telecommunications] (TEL)	BRA
Base Rate Boundary [Telecommunications] (TEL)	BRB
Base Realignment Aid Closure [Military]	BRAC
Base Realignment and Closure [DoD] (RDA)	BRAC
Base Realignment Contract (COE)	BRAC
Base Recirculation Insulation (IAA)	BRI
Base Reclamation [of critical materials] (AAG)	BR
Base Record (SAUS)	BR
Base Records Unit (SAA)	BRU
Base Recovery After Attack (ACAE)	BRAA
Base Recovery After Attack (MCD)	BRAAT
Base Recovery After Attack Team (SAUO)	BRAAT
Base Recovery After Attack Training (SAUS)	BRAAT
Base Recovery After Attack Transport (ACAE)	BRAAT
Base Recovery Course [Military] (NVT)	BRC
Base Register [Computer science] (IAA)	BAR
Base Register (CMD)	BR
Base Register [Computer science]	BX
Base Register Contents (SAUS)	BRC
Base Register Designator	BRD
Base Remount Depot [British military] (DMA)	BRD
Base Repair Cycle (MCD)	BRC
Base Repair Cycle Time (ACAE)	BRCT
Base Requirements Overseas (CINC)	BRO
Base Residence Course	BRC
Base Resistance (IDOE)	R_B
Base Resistance Transistor	BRT
Base [or Basic] Retirement Date [Air Force]	BRD
Base Salvage (AAG)	BS
Base Salvage Officer (MCD)	BSO
Base Section [Military]	BASEC
Base Section [Military]	BS
Base Security Council [Air Force] (AFM)	BSC
Base Selection Unit (SAUS)	BSU
Base Service Battalion [Marine Corps]	BSERBN
Base Service Store [Air Force] (AFIT)	BSS
Base Service Unit [Navy]	BASESERVUNIT
Base Service Unit [Navy]	BSU
Base Sheet Resistance	RBB
Base Shell	BS
Base Shield (IAA)	BS
Base Shop Test Facility [Military]	BSTF
Base Shop Test Station [Military]	BSTS
Base Shop Tester	BST
Base Signal Officer [Military] (IAA)	BSO
Base Site Control (SAUS)	BSC
Base Skirt	BS
Base Spares Allowance List (MCD)	BSAL
Base Spares Group	BSG
Base Spatial Unit (GEOI)	BSU
Base Station (SAUS)	BS
Base Station [ITU designation] (CET)	FB
Base Station Control Function (VERA)	BCF
Base Station Controller (VERA)	BSC
Base Station Identification Code (VERA)	BSIC
Base Station System [Telecommunications] (ITD)	BSS
Base Station System Management Application Part (VERA)	BSSMAP
Base station Video Imaging Terminal (SAUS)	B-VIT
Base Statistical Control (AAG)	BSC
Base Stop Tester (SAUS)	BST
Base Supplies and Transport Depot (SAUS)	BSTD
Base Supply (KSC)	BS
Base Supply Airfield (SAUS)	B Sup Airfd
Base Supply Airfield [British and Canadian]	B Sup Airfld
Base Supply and Transport Depot (SAUO)	BSTD
Base Supply Depot	BSD
Base Supply Management Office [Air Force] (AFM)	BSMO
Base Supply Office (SAUO)	BSO
Base Supply Officer [Navy]	BSO
Base Supply System (ACAE)	BSS
Base Support Area [Military]	BSA
Base Support Equipment [Military]	BSE
Base Support Group [Air Force]	BSGP
Base Support Group (SAUO)	BSGp
Base Support Group System [Air Force]	BSGS
Base Table Image (SAUS)	BTI
Base Target (MCD)	BT
Base Telecommunications Modernization (SAUS)	SCOPE DIAL
Base Ten Sys CI'A' [NASDAQ symbol] (TTSB)	BASEA
Base Ten Sys CI'B' [NASDAQ symbol] (TTSB)	BASEB
Base Ten Systems [Associated Press] (SAG)	BsTn
Base Ten Systems, Inc. [NASDAQ symbol] (NQ)	BASE
Base Topo (GEOI)	BT
Base Training Unit (SAUO)	BTU
Base Transceiver Station	BTS
Base Transceiver Systems (AAEL)	BTS
Base Transfusion Unit (SAUS)	BTU
Base Transit Depot (SAUO)	BTD
Base Unit	BU
Base Value (IDOE)	V
Base Vehicle Depot (SAUO)	BVD
Base Vehicle Reporting Officer	BVRO
Base Video Handler (SAUS)	BVH
Base Voltage (IDOE)	V_B
Base Weather Station (MCD)	BWS
Base Wire and Telephone System [Air Force] (MCD)	BWTS
Base Wire and Telephone System Development Schedule [Air Force]	BWTSDS
Base Wire Communications Program [Air Force]	BWCP
Base Wire Communications System [Air Force] (CET)	BWCS
Base Work Order (AAG)	BWO
Base Workshop [British and Canadian] [Military]	B Wksp
Base Workshop Facility (SAUO)	BWF
Base Year (DOMA)	BY
Base Year Dollars (MCD)	BYS
Baseball	BB
Baseball (ABBR)	BSBL
Baseball	BSBLL
Baseball Assistance Team (NDBD)	BAT
Baseball Association of Great Britain (SAUO)	BAGB
Baseball Canada [Also, Canadian Federation of Amateur Baseball] (AC)	CFAB
Baseball Club (SAUO)	BBC
Baseball Club	BBC
Baseball Elbow [Medicine] (MELL)	BBE
Baseball Elbow [Medicine] (MELL)	BE
Baseball Finger [Medicine] (MELL)	BBF
Baseball Foot [Medicine] (MELL)	BBF
Baseball Hall of Fame Committee on Baseball Veterans (EA)	BHFCBV
Baseball Hall of Shame [Defunct] (EA)	BHS
Baseball Umpires Council of Australia	BUCA
Baseball Writers Association (SAUO)	BWA
Baseball Writers Association of America (EA)	BWAA
Baseband (AAG)	BB

Baseband (MUGU) .... BSB
Baseband Adaptive Transversal Equalizer (SAUS) .... BATE
Baseband Amplifier (SAUS) .... BBA
Baseband Assembly Unit .... BAU
Baseband Breadboard .... BBB
Baseband Control & Traffic Exchange System (SAUS) .... BCTE
Baseband Distribution Unit .... BDU
Baseband Intrinsic Noise Ratio (SAUS) .... BINR
Baseband Level Control (MCD) .... BLC
Baseband Matrix (SAUS) .... BMX
Baseband Modulator-Demodulator (IAA) .... BMD
Baseband National Television Standards Committee (SAUS) .... B-NTSC
Baseband Processor .... BBP
Baseband Radar Bag Initiator (SAUS) .... BARBI
Baseband RADAR Sensor Technology (PDAA) .... BARS
Baseband Separation Unit (MCD) .... BSU
Baseband Unit (SAUS) .... BBU
Baseboard (ABBR) .... BSBD
Baseboard Hot Water [*Heating system*] [*Classified advertising*] .... BBHW
Base-Catalysed Dechlorination .... BCD
Base-Catalyzed Decomposition Process .... BCDP
Base-Catalyzed Destination [*Environmental science*] .... BCD
Base-Coupled Logic [*Computer science*] (PDAA) .... BCL
Based (ABBR) .... BSD
Based Store (SAUS) .... BS
Base-Diffusion Isolation Technique (SAUS) .... BDI Technique
Base-Diffusion Isolation Technology (SAUS) .... BDI Technology
Basedow type (SAUS) .... B-type
Base-Down (Prism) [*Ophthalmology*] .... BD
Base-Emitter (DNAB) .... BE
Base-Emitter Self-aligned Technology (SAUS) .... BEST
Base-Excision Repair [*Genetics*] .... BER
Basegram [*Navy*] .... BGM
Base-Height Ratio .... B/H
Base-In (Prism) [*Ophthalmology*] .... BI
Basel [*Bale*] [*Switzerland*] [*Seismograph station code, US Geological Survey*] .... BAS
Basel (SAUS) .... Bas
Basel Club (EAIO) .... BC
Baseless (ABBR) .... BSLS
Base-Level Self-Sufficiency Spare [*Air Force*] (DOMA) .... BLSSS
Baseline (SAUS) .... BAS
Baseline (ACAE) .... B/l
Baseline .... BL
Baseline Accounting and Reporting System (NASA) .... BARS
Baseline Air Pollution Monitoring Network (SAUS) .... BAPMon
Baseline Air Pollution Station (AUEG) .... BAPS
Baseline Allocation Requirements Document (ACAE) .... BARD
Baseline Armor Reliability Test [*Army*] (MCD) .... BART
Baseline Automated Test System (SAUS) .... BATS
Baseline Calibration Equipment .... BLCE
Baseline Change Control Board (SAUS) .... BCCB
Baseline Change Request (ARMP) .... BCR
Baseline Comparison System [*Army*] .... BCS
Baseline Configuration .... BLC
Baseline Configuration Description (ACAE) .... BCD
Baseline Configuration Document (SSD) .... BCD
Baseline Correlation Matrix [*Air Force*] (AAGC) .... BCM
Baseline Cost Estimate (AABC) .... BCE
Baseline Data Collection Facility (MCD) .... BDCF
Baseline Definition Document (NASA) .... BDD
Baseline Demonstration Laser (SAUS) .... BDL
Baseline Design Data Book (MCD) .... BDDB
Baseline Document Change Request (MCD) .... BDCR
Baseline Documentation (MCD) .... BLD
Baseline Electronic Warfare System (MCD) .... BLEWS
Baseline Flight Vehicle Mission Time Line .... BFVMTL
Baseline Information System (SAUS) .... BLIS
Baseline Information Tracking System (ABAC) .... BITS
Baseline Intelligence Summary Supplement (MCD) .... BIS
Baseline Iteration Zero (SAUS) .... BLITZ
Baseline Jamming Assets (SAUS) .... BJA
Baseline Monitoring Report [*Environmental Protection Agency*] (GFGA) .... BMR
Baseline Operational Evaluation (ACAE) .... BOE
Baseline Operations Plan (MCD) .... BOP
Baseline Program Document (NASA) .... BPD
Baseline Program Documentation (SAUS) .... BPD
Baseline Radar Bag Initiator (SAUS) .... BARBI
Baseline Reduction Intelligent Target Tracker (ACAE) .... BRITT
Baseline Reference Flight Plan (KSC) .... BRFP
Baseline Reference Mission (MCD) .... BRM
Baseline Restorer (IEEE) .... BLR
Baseline Schedule Plan (MCD) .... BSP
Baseline Standardized Subsystem (ACAE) .... BLSS
Baseline Surface Radiation Network [*World Meteorological Organization*] (USDC) .... BSRN
Baseline Test Facilities (ACAE) .... BTF
Baseline Upper Air Network (SAUS) .... BUAN
Baseline Waste Management Strategy (NUCP) .... BWMS
Baselined Software Library (MCD) .... BSL
Basel/Mulhouse [*Switzerland*] [*Airport symbol*] (OAG) .... BSL
Base-machine Microinstruction Cycle (SAUS) .... BMC
Base-machine Microroutine Execution (SAUS) .... BMX
Base-machine Microroutine Length (SAUS) .... BML
Base-machine Microroutine Overhead (SAUS) .... BMO
Basement .... BSMNT
Basement (REAL) .... bsmt
Basement [*Classifed advertising*] .... BSMT
Basement Membrane [*Medicine*] .... BM
Basement Membrane Associated Protein [*Biochemistry*] (DB) .... BMAP
Basement Membrane Matrix [*Biochemistry*] .... BMM
Basement Membrane Zones [*Anatomy*] .... BMZ
Base-message Switching Center (SAUS) .... BSC
Base-Neutralized Acid (SAUS) .... BNA
Basenji Club of America (EA) .... BCA
Basenji Club of America (EA) .... BCOA
Basenpaare (SAUS) .... bp
Baseops International, Inc. [*ICAO designator*] (FAAC) .... XBO
Base-Out (Prism) [*Ophthalmology*] .... BO
Baseplate [*Technical drawings*] .... BAPE
Baseplate [*Technical drawings*] .... BP
Baseplate [*Technical drawings*] .... BPL
Base-Region Width (IDOE) .... W_B
Bases and Stations Information System [*Navy*] (GFGA) .... BASIS
Bases Integrated Electronics Package (ACAE) .... BIEP
Bases on Balls [*Baseball*] .... BB
Base-Station Control (WDAA) .... BSC
Base-Stored Image Sensor .... BASIS
Base-Up (Prism) [*Ophthalmology*] .... BU
Base-Voltage Supply (IDOE) .... V_{BB}
BASF AG ADS [*NYSE symbol*] .... BF
BASF Chemicals Limited (SAUO) .... BCL
Bashaw Public Library, Alberta [*Library symbol*] [*National Library of Canada*] (NLC) .... ABASH
Bashful (ABBR) .... BSHFL
Bashfully (ABBR) .... BSHFLY
Bashfulness (ABBR) .... BSHFLNS
Bashkir [*MARC language code*] [*Library of Congress*] (LCCP) .... bak
Bashkir Soviet Socialist Republic .... BashSSR
Bashkirian Airlines [*Former USSR*] [*International*] (FAAC) .... BTC
Bashkirian Autonomous Soviet Socialist Republic (SAUO) .... BASSR
Basic (SAUS) .... BA
Basic [*Rate*] [*Value of the English pound*] .... BAS
Basic (MUGU) .... BSC
Basic Access Interface (SAUS) .... BAI
Basic Access Method [*Computer science*] .... BAM
Basic Achievement Skills Individual Screener [*Educational test*] .... BASIS
Basic Acoustic Warfare System (MCD) .... BAWS
Basic Acrylic Monomer Manufacturers Association (EA) .... BAMM
Basic Active Service Date (AABC) .... BASD
Basic Activity Subset [*Telecommunications*] (OSI) .... BAS
Basic Adaptive Hardware .... BAH
Basic Additional Teleprocessing Support [*Computer science*] (BUR) .... BATS
Basic Additional Teleprocessing System (SAUS) .... BATS
Basic Address Register (SAUS) .... BAR
Basic Administration and Management .... BAAM
Basic Advance Training .... Bas Adv Tra
Basic Advanced Integrated Navigation System .... BAINS
Basic Agreement .... BA
Basic Air Defense Ground Environment (ACAE) .... BADGE
Basic Air Navigation School [*Military*] (OA) .... BANS
Basic Air Speed (SAUS) .... BAS
Basic Air Temperature .... BAT
Basic Aircraft Checkout Equipment (SAUS) .... BACE
Basic Airman (SAUS) .... BA
Basic Airman [*Air Force*] E1
Basic Airspeed [*Aviation*] .... BAS
Basic Algebraic Symbolic Interpretive Compiler (IEEE) .... BASIC
Basic Allowance for Housing [*Army*] .... BAH
Basic Allowance for Quarters [*Military*] .... BAQ
Basic Allowance for Quarters for Adopted Child [*Military*] .... BAQ(AC)
Basic Allowance for Quarters for Father [*Military*] .... BAQ(F)
Basic Allowance for Quarters for Husband [*Military*] .... BAQ(H)
Basic Allowance for Quarters for Legitimate Children [*Military*] .... BAQ(LC)
Basic Allowance for Quarters for Mother [*Military*] .... BAQ(M)
Basic Allowance for Quarters for Stepchildren [*Military*] .... BAQ(SC)
Basic Allowance for Quarters for Wife [*Military*] .... BAQ(W)
Basic Allowance for Quarters Pending Disability Retirement [*Military*] .... BAQ(DIS RET)
Basic Allowance for Subsistence [*Military*] .... BAS
Basic Alteration Class Drawing [*Navy*] (CAAL) .... BACD
Basic American Medical (EFIS) .... BAMI
Basic Analysis and Mapping Program (SAUS) .... BANMP
Basic and Applied Myology [*A publication*] .... BAM
Basic and Logically Applied Norms-Civil Engineering (SAUS) .... BALANCE
Basic and Long-term Research .... BLR
Basic and Traditional Food Association [*Inactive*] (EA) .... BTFA
Basic Angle System .... BAS
Basic Application Run Time [*Computer science*] (VERA) .... BART
Basic Application Runtime (SAUS) .... BART
Basic Applications Programmer Training (SAUS) .... BAPT
Basic Appraisal System for Incoming Components .... BASIC
Basic Approved Jury Instructions (HGAA) .... BAJI
Basic Area of Interest [*Army*] (ADDR) .... BAI
Basic Arithmetic Order (SAUS) .... BAO
Basic Armed Forces Communication Plan .... BAFCOM
Basic Armed Forces Communication Plan (SAUO) .... BAFCom
Basic Armor Reliability Test (MCD) .... BART
Basic Armor Training (MCD) .... BAT
Basic Army Administrative Course .... BAAC

Basic Army Regulations (SAUS) ... BAR
Basic Army Strategic Estimate [*A document*] ... BASE
Basic Artillery Force Simulation Model (MCD) ... BAFSM
Basic Artillery Observer Subsystem (SAUS) ... BAOS
Basic Assembler [*Computer science*] (IAA) ... BA
Basic Assembler Program [*Computer science*] ... BAP
Basic Assembly Language [*Programming language*] [*Sperry UNIVAC*] [*Computer science*] ... BAL
Basic Assembly Unit (WDAA) ... BAU
Basic Assessment System for Children ... BASC
Basic Assurance Test (SAUS) ... BAT
Basic Attack Helicopter Team [*Army*] (RDA) ... BAHT
Basic Attack Option (MCD) ... BAO
Basic Attention Handling (SAUS) ... BAH
Basic Authorization ... BA
Basic Automatic Checkout Equipment ... BACE
Basic Automatic Stored Instruction Computer (BUR) ... BASIC
Basic Automation Systems Elements ... BASE
Basic Aviation Sub-System Integration Concept (PDAA) ... BASIC
Basic Aviation Trainer (SAUS) ... BAT
Basic Avionics Procedure Trainer [*British military*] (DMA) ... BAPT
Basic Bank Skills Battery [*Test*] [*London House, Inc.*] (TES) ... BBSB
Basic Bibliographic Citation (SAUS) ... BBC
Basic Bload Graphics (SAUS) ... BLD
Basic Block (SAUS) ... BB
Basic Border Agreement (SAUS) ... BBA
Basic Boxed Base ... BBB
Basic Brazeau Medium [*Culture media*] ... BBM
Basic Building Code ... BBC
Basic Business Language [*Computer science*] (IEEE) ... BBL
Basic Business-Oriented Language (SAUS) ... BASBOL
Basic Cadet Training (SAUS) ... BCT
Basic Calcium Phosphate [*Biochemistry*] (DAVI) ... BCP
Basic Calculating Operation (SAUS) ... BCO
Basic Call Process (VERA) ... BCP
Basic Call Processing System [*Telecommunications*] (NITA) ... BCPS
Basic Call Sate Modell (SAUS) ... BCSM
Basic Carbonate White Lead [*Paint technology*] ... BCWL
Basic Cardiac Life Support [*System*] [*Medicine*] ... BCLS
Basic Carriage Service [*Telecommunications*] ... BCS
Basic Cell Hyperplasia [*Medicine*] (DB) ... BCH
Basic Channel Adapter (SAUS) ... BCA
Basic Code (SAUS) ... BC
Basic Combat Maneuver (MCD) ... BCM
Basic Combat Training [*Later, BT*] [*Army*] ... BCT
Basic Combined Programming Language ... BCPL
Basic Combined Subset [*Telecommunications*] (OSI) ... BCS
Basic Command Interpreter [*Computer science*] (CIST) ... BCI
Basic Command Language (SAUS) ... BCL
Basic Commercial Pilot's License (PIAV) ... BCPL
Basic Communication Access Method [*Computer science*] (IAA) ... BCAM
Basic Communications Support (SAUS) ... BCS
Basic Comparison Element (MHDI) ... BCE
Basic Component (SAUS) ... BC
Basic Computer System (SAUS) ... BCS
Basic Computer Unit ... BCU
Basic Concepts Inventory [*Psychology*] ... BCI
Basic Configuration ... BSC
Basic Consolidated Requirements Document (NASA) ... BCRD
Basic Contour Line ... BCL
Basic Contract Specification ... BCS
Basic Control [*Mode*] [*Computer science*] ... BC
Basic Control Frequency ... BCF
Basic Control Memory (SAUS) ... BCM
Basic Control Mode (SAUS) ... BC Mode
Basic Control Monitor (BUR) ... BCM
Basic Control System [*For satellites*] (MDG) ... BCS
Basic Controller (SAUS) ... BC
Basic Conversational Verb Set (SAUS) ... BCVS
Basic Copy [*Genetics*] ... BC
Basic Cost Information (AFIT) ... BCI
Basic Counter Unit (SAUS) ... BCU
Basic Court System (PDAA) ... BCS
Basic Cryptanalysis Course ... BCC
Basic Cycle Length [*Medicine*] (DAVI) ... BCL
Basic Daily Food Allowance (AABC) ... BDFA
Basic Damage Control Exercise (SAUO) ... BDCE
Basic Data (SAUS) ... BD
Basic Data Access Method [*Computer science*] (EECA) ... BDAM
BASIC Data Acquisition (SAUS) ... BASEDAC
Basic Data Base Environment [*Computer science*] (MHDI) ... BDBE
Basic Data Management (SAUS) ... BDM
Basic Data Records (SAUS) ... BDR
Basic Data Service (SAUS) ... BDS
Basic Data Set Project [*National Science Foundation*] ... BDSP
Basic Data Transmission Routine (IAA) ... BDTR
Basic Dead Load [*Construction*] (DICI) ... BDL
Basic Decision Height [*Aviation*] (DA) ... BCH
Basic Democrats [*Pakistan*] ... BD
Basic Design Engineering (MCD) ... BDE
Basic Design Language (SAUS) ... BDL
Basic Device Unit [*Computer science*] (IBMDP) ... BDU
Basic Direct Access Method [*IBM Corp.*] [*Computer science*] (BUR) ... BDAM
Basic Direct Shipping Instructions ... BDSI
Basic Disk Access Method (MCD) ... BDAM
Basic Disk Filing System (SAUS) ... BDFS
Basic Disk Operating (or Operation) System (SAUS) ... BDOS
Basic Display File (SAUS) ... BDF
Basic Display Unit [*Computer science*] ... BDU
Basic Dungeons & Dragons (SAUS) ... BD&D
Basic Earthquake Education (SAUS) ... BEE
Basic ECM Environment Simulator (SAUS) ... BEES
Basic Economic Education (SAUS) ... BEE
Basic Economics Test [*Educational test*] ... BET
Basic Editor Monitor [*Computer science*] (MHDI) ... BEM
Basic Education Act [*1977*] ... BEA
Basic Education Assistance Material Service [*National Multimedia Center for Adult Basic Education*] (IID) ... BEAMS
Basic Education Centre (SAUO) ... BEC
Basic Education Development System (OICC) ... BEDS
Basic Education Program (EDAC) ... BEP
Basic Education Resource Centre (SAUO) ... BERC
Basic Educational Opportunity Grants [*Office of Education*] ... BEOG
Basic Educational Skills Test ... BEST
Basic Educational Skills through Technology Project [*U.S. Department of Education*] (EDAC) ... BEST
Basic Electric Arc (PDAA) ... BEA
Basic Electrical Rhythm [*Neurophysiology*] ... BER
Basic Electricity and Electronics ... BE & E
Basic Electricity and Electronics Individualized Learning System [*Military*] (DNAB) ... BE/E INLS
Basic Electricity and Electronics School [*Military*] (DNAB) ... BEES
Basic Electronics Maintenance Trainer ... BEMT
Basic Element of Performance [*Medicine*] (DMAA) ... BEP
Basic Encoding Rule [*Telecommunications*] (OSI) ... BER
Basic Encoding Unit ... BEU
Basic Encyclopedia [*Army*] (AABC) ... BE
Basic Encyclopedic Redundancy Media (IEEE) ... BERM
Basic Energy Foods (SAUS) ... BEF
Basic Energy Sciences Committee [*Department of Energy*] [*Washington, DC*] (EGAO) ... BESAC
Basic Energy Sciences Program [*Department of Energy*] [*Washington, DC*] ... BES
Basic Energy Sciences Program [*Department of Energy*] [*Washington, DC*] ... BESP
Basic Engineering (DNAB) ... BENG
Basic Engineering Casualty Control Exercise [*Military*] (NVT) ... BECCE
Basic Engineering Damage Control Exercise [*Military*] (NVT) ... BEDCE
Basic Engineering Development ... BED
Basic Engineering Product Assumption ... BEPA
Basic English ... BE
Basic English for Testing Applications (PDAA) ... BETA
Basic English in the Native Language ... BENL
Basic English Skills Test ... BEST
Basic Enlisted Service Date (AABC) ... BESD
Basic Enlisted Submarine School [*Navy*] (DOMA) ... BESS
Basic Entry Pay Date ... BEPD
Basic Equation (SAUS) ... BE
Basic Equipment List (MCD) ... BEL
Basic Error Control System ... BECS
Basic Essential Skills Testing ... BEST
Basic Essential Skills Training (SAUO) ... BEST
Basic Exchange Rate Planning Model [*Telecommunications*] (TEL) ... BERPM
Basic Exchange Telecommunications Radio Service (CIST) ... BETRS
Basic Exchange Telephone Radio [*Telecommunications*] (TNIG) ... BETR
Basic Exchange Telephone Radio Systems [*Telecommunications*] (OTD) ... BETRS
Basic Executive Scheduler and Timekeeper (PDAA) ... BEST
Basic Executive System [*Honeywell, Inc.*] ... BES
Basic Exercises ... BX
Basic Experimental Automatic Syntactic Translator [*Bunker Ramo Corp.*] (NITA) ... BEAST
Basic Experimental Language [*Computer science*] (IAA) ... BASEX
Basic Experimental Language (SAUS) ... BASEX Language
Basic Extended Acronym Human Users Guide (SAUS) ... BEAR HUG
Basic Extension to Alpha [*Alaska long period array*] ... BETA
Basic External Function (SAUS) ... BEF
Basic Extraction Sludge Treatment ... BEST
Basic Facility Requirements List [*Navy*] ... BFRL
Basic Fetoprotein (DB) ... BFP
Basic Fibroblast Growth Factor [*Biochemistry*] ... BFGF
Basic Field Descriptor (SAUS) ... BFD
Basic Field Manual [*Military*] ... BFM
Basic Fighter Maneuver [*Air Force*] (MCD) ... BFM
Basic Fighter Manoeuvres (SAUS) ... BFM
Basic Fighter Transition [*Air Force*] (DOMA) ... BFT
Basic File Access System ... BFAS
Basic File Channel (SAUS) ... BFC
BASIC [*Bank Automated Service Information System*] **File Directory** (HGAA) ... BFD
BASIC [*Bank Automated Service Information System*] **File System** [*Computer science*] (HGAA) ... BFS
Basic Filter Power Handling Capacity (IAA) ... BFPHC
Basic Fitness Test [*British military*] (DMA) ... BFT
Basic Fitness Training (SAUS) ... BFT
Basic Flight Data Acquisition System (SAUS) ... BFDAS
Basic Flight Maneuvering [*Navy*] (DOMA) ... BFM
Basic Floppy Disk ... BFD
Basic Fluid Power Research Program (IAA) ... BFPR
Basic Flying School (SAUO) ... BFS
Basic Format (SAUS) ... BF
Basic Gastrin [*Medicine*] (DMAA) ... BG

Basic Graphic Access Method (IAA) .... BGAM
Basic Graphic System (SAUS) .... BGS
Basic Ground Instructor [*Aviation*] (PIPO) .... BGI
Basic Group (SAUO) .... BG
Basic Group Formation (SAUO) .... BGF
Basic Group Translator (SAUO) .... BGT
Basic Hardware (SAUS) .... BH
Basic Health Management .... BHM
Basic Health Profile .... BHP
Basic Health Unit (DB) .... BHU
Basic Helix-Loop-Helix [*Genetics*] .... BHLH
Basic Helix-Loop-Helix .... bHLH
Basic Heterostructure (IAA) .... BH
Basic High Layer Functions (SAUS) .... BHLF
Basic Hole System .... BHS
Basic Human Factor Technology (SSD) .... BHFT
Basic Human Needs .... BHN
Basic Hydrological Network Assessment Project (SAUS) .... BNAP
Basic Hytran Simulation Language [*Computer science*] (PDAA) .... BHSL
Basic Identification Number (EECA) .... BIN
Basic Identity Data Element (COE) .... BIDE
Basic Ideology Research Unit (SAUO) .... BIRU
Basic Image Classification and Enhancement Package (SAUS) .... BICEP
Basic Imagery File (MCD) .... BIF
Basic Imagery Interpretation Brief (MCD) .... BIIB
Basic Imagery Interpretation Report (MCD) .... BIIR
Basic Impulse Insulation Level [*Electronics*] .... BIL
Basic Impulse Level (ACAE) .... BIL
Basic Impulse Level Tests (ACAE) .... BILT
Basic in Flow (NRCH) .... BIF
Basic Incidence Rate [*Medicine*] .... BIR
Basic Income Unit (WDAA) .... BIU
Basic Incorporated (SAUO) .... BAI
Basic Index (NITA) .... BI
Basic Indexed Sequential Access Method [*IBM Corp.*] [*Computer science*] .... BISAM
Basic Indexing and Retrieval System [*Computer science*] (DIT) .... BIRS
Basic Indexing Sequential Access Method (SAUS) .... BISAM
Basic Indissoluble Information (SAUS) .... bit
Basic Industrial Control Engineering Programming System (IAA) .... BICEPS
Basic Industrial Materials [*Program*] [*Navy*] .... BIM
Basic Industries Group (SAUO) .... BIG
Basic Industry Research Laboratory .... BIRL
Basic Infantry .... BI
Basic Infantry Training (SAUS) .... BIT
Basic Information Package .... BIP
Basic Information Retrieval System (NITA) .... BIRS
Basic Information Unit (BUR) .... BIU
Basic Initial Entry Test (MCD) .... BIET
Basic Initial Entry Training (MCD) .... BIET
Basic Input Power (SAUS) .... BIP
BASIC Input/Output Supervisor (SAUS) .... BIOS
Basic Input-Output Support Program Package (IAA) .... BIO
Basic Input/Output System [*Computer science*] (WDMC) .... bio
Basic Input-Output System [*IBM Corp.*] .... BIOS
Basic Inspection (HEAS) .... BAS
Basic Institutional Development Program [*Under Title III of the Higher Education Act*] .... BIDP
Basic Instruments and Selected Documents of the GATT (AAGC) .... BISD
Basic Insulation Level (SAUS) .... BIL
Basic Integrated Aircraft Command and Control [*Navy*] .... BIACC
Basic Interchange System (SAUS) .... BIS
Basic Interconnection Test (SAUS) .... BIT
Basic Interpersonal Communicative Skills (EDAC) .... BICS
BASIC Interpreter Package [*Computer science*] .... BIP
Basic Intrinsic Noise Ratio (CET) .... BINR
Basic Inventory of Natural Language [*Test*] .... BINL
Basic Investigation of Remotely Detectable Deposits of Oil and Gas.... BIRDDOG
Basic Iron Aluminum Silicate [*Du Pont trademark*] .... BIASILL
Basic Issue Item Code (ACAE) .... BIIC
Basic Issue Item List (SAUS) .... BIIL
Basic Issue Items [*Army*] (AABC) .... BII
Basic Issue Items List [*Army*] (AABC) .... BIIL
Basic Issue List Items [*Army*] .... BILI
Basic Jet Navigation (DNAB) .... BJN
Basic Journal Abstracts [*A publication*] .... BJA
Basic Jumbo Group (SAUS) .... BJG
Basic Jumbogroup (SAUO) .... BJG
Basic Knowledge and Skills [*Training*] [*Military*] .... BK & S
Basic Land and Property Unit (GEOI) .... BLPU
Basic Landsat Image Processing (SAUS) .... BLIP
Basic Language (SAUS) .... BAS
Basic Language Concepts Test [*Child development test*] .... BLCT
Basic Language for the Implementation of System Software [*Computer science*] .... BLISS
Basic Language Machine [*Computer*] (BUR) .... BLM
BASIC [*Beginner's All-Purpose Symbolic Instruction Code*] **Language Translator** [*Computer science*] (MCD) .... BLT
Basic Launch Plan [*NASA*] (KSC) .... BLP
Basic Learning Institute .... BLI
Basic Letter (SAUS) .... BL
Basic Level Automation of Data through Electronics .... BLADE
Basic Liberation of Smokers and Sympathizers of Marijuana .... BLOSSOM
Basic Library Inquiry Subsystem [*Computer science*] .... BLISS
Basic Life Support [*System*] .... BLS

Basic Linear Algebra for Distributed Environments (VERA) .... BLADE
Basic Linear Algebra Subprograms (SAUS) .... BLAS
Basic Linear Algebra Subroutines (SAUS) .... BLAS
Basic Link Unit [*Computer science*] (BUR) .... BLU
Basic Linkage (SAUS) .... BL
Basic List-oriented Information Structures System (SAUS) .... BLISS
Basic Literal Automatic Coding .... BALITAC
Basic Load [*Ammunition*] (AABC) .... BL
Basic Load Storage Area [*Military*] .... BLSA
Basic Local Alignment Search Tool [*Computer program*] .... BLAST
Basic Logic Unit (IEEE) .... BLU
Basic Logistics Plan (SAUS) .... BLP
Basic Low Layer Functions (SAUS) .... BLLF
Basic Machine Cycle (IAA) .... BMC
Basic Machine Language (SAUS) .... BML
Basic Magnesium, Inc., Las Vegas, NV [*Library symbol*] [*Library of Congress*] [*Obsolete*] (LCLS) .... NvLBM
Basic Main Frame (NATG) .... BMF
Basic Maintenance Allowance .... BMA
Basic Management Information System (SAUS) .... BMIS
Basic Manufacturing Division .... BMD
Basic Mapping Support (SAUS) .... BMP
Basic Mapping Support [*Computer science*] .... BMS
Basic Marksmanship Training Range (SAUS) .... BMTR
Basic Mass Empty (SAUS) .... BME
Basic Material Laboratory (SAUO) .... BML
Basic Measurement Unit (SAUS) .... BMU
Basic Medical Insurance Plan [*UN Food and Agriculture Organization*] .... BMIP
Basic Medium Edition (SAUS) .... BME
Basic Memory Access Controller [*Memory management unit*] [*Computer science*] .... BMAC
Basic Message Switching Center [*Computer science*] .... BSC
Basic Metabolic Rate [*Biochemistry*] (DAVI) .... BMR
Basic Metabolic Unit [*Medicine*] (DMAA) .... BMU
Basic Metabolism Rate and Electrocardiogram [*Medicine*] .... BMR & ECG
Basic Metals and Minerals Processing Industry Council [*Australia*] .... BMMPIC
Basic Metals Industry Council [*Australia*] .... BMIC
Basic Meteorological Services (FAAC) .... BMS
Basic Military Compensation (MCD) .... BMC
Basic Military Journalist [*Department of Defense Information School course*] (DNAB) .... BMJ
Basic Military Requirement .... BMR
Basic Military Training .... BMT
Basic Military Training Group (SAUO) .... BMTG
Basic Military Training School .... BMTS
Basic Military Training School, United States Air Force .... BMTS USAF
Basic Military Training Squadron [*Air Force*] .... BMTS
Basic Minimum Descent Height [*Aviation*] (DA) .... BMDH
Basic Minute Value (PDAA) .... BMV
Basic Missile Checker (NATG) .... BMC
Basic Mission, Design Number, and Series [*Aircraft*] (AFM) .... BMDNS
Basic Mission Design Number and Series (SAUS) .... BMDNS
Basic Mission Qualified [*NASA*] .... BMQ
Basic Mobile Facility (MCD) .... BMF
Basic Modular Memory (SAUS) .... BMM
Basic Monthly Maintenance Charge (NITA) .... BMMC
Basic Morse Mission Trainer [*Military*] .... BMMT
Basic Motion Time (SAUS) .... BMT
Basic Motion-Time Study .... BMT
Basic Motor Ability Test [*Education*] .... BMAT
Basic Multicellular Unit [*Medicine*] (DMAA) .... BMU
Basic Multiline Controller [*Computer science*] (MHDI) .... BMLC
Basic Multi-Minutes (PDAA) .... BMM
Basic Multi-Role Avionics (PDAA) .... BMRA
Basic National Security Police (MCD) .... BNSP
Basic Naval Aviation Officers School (DNAB) .... BANAVAVNOFFSCOL
Basic Naval Aviation Officers School (DNAB) .... BNAO
Basic Naval Establishment Plan .... BNEP
Basic Navigation Battery (SAUS) .... BNB
Basic Net Radio Interface Device (MCD) .... BNRID
Basic Network (IAA) .... BASNET
Basic Network (SAUS) .... Bas Net
Basic Networking Utilities .... BNU
Basic Noncommissioned Officer Course [*Army*] (INF) .... BNCOC
Basic Noncommissioned Officer Course [*Army*] .... BNOC
Basic Notch Unit .... BNU
Basic Object Adapter [*Computer science*] (VERA) .... BOA
Basic Oblate Spheroid .... BOS
Basic Occupational Language Training .... BOLT
Basic Occupational Literacy Test .... BOLT
Basic Occupational Preparation .... BOP
Basic Officer Military Orientation Program (SAUS) .... BOMOP
Basic Officers Training Battalion [*Army*] (INF) .... BOTB
Basic Online Memory (SAUS) .... BOM
Basic Open Hearth (SAUS) .... BOH
Basic Operating Agreement (SAUS) .... BOA
Basic Operating Companies (SAUO) .... BOC
Basic Operating Consumer-Oriented Language [*Computer science*] .... BOCOL
Basic Operating Memory (SAUS) .... BOM
Basic Operating Monitor .... BOM
Basic Operating Program [*Computer science*] (NITA) .... BOP
Basic Operating Programming Aid [*Computer science*] (CIST) .... BOPA
Basic Operating System [*IBM Corp.*] [*Computer science*] .... BOS
Basic Operating System [*Computer science*] (NITA) .... BOSS
Basic Operating System Software [*Toshiba Corp.*] [*Japan*] .... BOSS

Basic Operating Weight (SAUS) .... BOW
Basic Operation Memory [*Computer science*] (IAA) .... BOM
Basic Operation Plan [*Army*] .... BOP
Basic Operational Capability (SSD) .... BOC
Basic Operational Data .... BOD
Basic Operational Kinetic Kill Vehicle [*Military*] (ACAE) .... BOKKV
Basic Operational Requirements and Planning Criteria Group [*ICAO*] (DA) .... BORG
Basic Operational Sea Training (SAUS) .... BOST
Basic Operational Training Unit (Fixed Wing) .... BOTU(FW)
Basic Operational Training Unit (Rotary Wing) .... BOTU(RW)
Basic Operator Console (SAUS) .... BOC
Basic Order Agreement .... BOA
Basic Ordering Agreement .... BOA
Basic Ordering Unit .... BOU
Basic Organization of Associated Labour (SAUO) .... BOAL
Basic Organizing/Optimizing Training Schedules (MCD) .... BOOTS
Basic Output Report (SAUS) .... BOR
Basic Overall Polarity (IAA) .... BOP
Basic Oxygen Demand (SARE) .... BOD
Basic Oxygen Furnace [*Steelmaking*] .... BOF
Basic Oxygen Process [*Steelmaking*] .... BOP
Basic Oxygen Process Furnace [*Steelmaking*] (EG) .... BOPF
Basic Oxygen Steel [*Steelmaking*] .... BOS
Basic Package Computer (SAUS) .... BASICPAC
Basic Packet Switched System (SAUS) .... BPSS
Basic Packet Switching Service (SAUS) .... BPSS
Basic Pancreatic Trypsin Inhibitor (DB) .... BPTI
BASIC Paper Tape System (SAUS) .... BASIC/PTS
Basic Parameter Input Tape [*Computer science*] (IAA) .... BPIT
Basic Partitioned Access Method [*IBM Corp.*] [*Computer science*] .... BPAM
Basic Partitioned Data Access Method (SAUS) .... BPDA Method
Basic Partitioned File Access Method (SAUS) .... BPFA Method
Basic Parts List .... BPL
Basic Parts Records Summary (SAUS) .... BPRS
Basic Pay .... BP
Basic Pay Entry Date .... BPED
Basic Peripheral Channel .... BPC
Basic Petroleum International Ltd. [*Associated Press*] (SAG) .... BasPetr
Basic Petroleum International Ltd. [*NASDAQ symbol*] (NQ) .... BPIL
Basic Petroleum Intl. [*NASDAQ symbol*] (TTSB) .... BPILF
Basic Phrase Marker (SAUS) .... BPM
Basic Physical Fitness Test (MCD) .... BPFT
Basic Planning Data and Assumption (SAUS) .... BPD&A
Basic Planning Document [*Military*] (AABC) .... BPD
Basic Planning Memorandum (NATG) .... BASPM
Basic Point Defense [*Military*] (NVT) .... BPD
Basic Point Defense Missile System (MCD) .... BPDMS
Basic Point Defense Ship Missile System (ACAE) .... BPDSMS
Basic Point Defense Surface Missile System (NVT) .... BPDSMS
Basic Point Defense System (MCD) .... BPDS
Basic Pole Unit .... BPU
Basic Polyvalent Trypsin Inhibitor (DB) .... BPTI
Basic Postflight (MCD) .... BPO
Basic Pressure Altitude .... BPA
Basic Principles Training Simulator (SAUS) .... BPTS
Basic Process (ECII) .... BP
Basic Processed Radar Training (SAUS) .... BPRT
Basic Processing Unit (CET) .... BPU
BASIC [*Beginner's All-Purpose Symbolic Instruction Code*] **Processor and Computer** .... BASICPAC
Basic Processor and Computer (SAUS) .... BASICPAC
Basic Production Scheduling System (IAA) .... BPSS
Basic Products Corp. (SAUO) .... BPD
BASIC [*Beginner's All-Purpose Symbolic Instruction Code*] **Program File** [*Computer science*] .... BAS
Basic Programming Extensions (SAUS) .... BPE
Basic Programming for Computers (SAUS) .... BPC
Basic Programming Knowledge Test (MCD) .... BPKT
Basic Programming Support [*IBM Corp.*] (BUR) .... BPS
Basic Programming System .... BPS
Basic Proline-Rich Protein (DMAA) .... PRB
Basic Protein [*Immunology*] .... BP
Basic Psychological Study (MCD) .... BPS
Basic Purchase Agreement (MCD) .... BPA
Basic Qualification (SAUS) .... BQ
Basic Qualification Course (DNAB) .... BQC
Basic Query Language [*Computer science*] (BUR) .... BQL
Basic Query System (SAUS) .... BQS
Basic Radiation Effects Reactor .... BRER
Basic Rapid Alarm Security System (SAUS) .... BRASS
Basic Rate Access .... BRA
Basic rate Interface (SAUS) .... BAI
Basic Rate Interface [*Telecommunications*] (PCM) .... BRI
Basic Rate Interface Transmission Equipment [*Telecommunications*] (ACRL) .... BRITE
Basic Rate Service .... BRS
Basic Read Data Flow (SAUS) .... BRDF
Basic Read Only Storage (SAUS) .... BROS
Basic Reading Inventory (EDAC) .... BRI
Basic Real Constant (SAUS) .... BRC
Basic Real-Time Monitor [*Computer science*] (CIST) .... BRTM
Basic Recommended Reading (ADA) .... BRR
Basic Reconfigurable Interactive Editing Facility [*Computer science*] (VERA) .... BRIEF
Basic Record Audit (SAUS) .... BRA
Basic Record Tape (SAUS) .... BRT
Basic Reference Book (ACAE) .... BRB
Basic Reference Coordinate System (MCD) .... BRCS
Basic Reference Lottery Ticket (PDAA) .... BRLT
Basic Reference Model .... BRM
Basic Regular Expression (SAUS) .... BRE
Basic Remote Module (SAUS) .... BRM
Basic Requirements (SAUS) .... BR
Basic Research .... BAS-R
Basic Research .... BR
Basic Research and Human Resources (ADWA) .... BRHR
Basic Research in Adaptive Intelligence [*EEC*] .... BRAIN
Basic Research in Industrial Technology for Europe .... BRITE
Basic Research, Inc. (EA) .... BRINC
Basic Research Vehicle [*Automotive engineering*] .... BRV
Basic Resolution Unit [*Computer science*] .... BRU
Basic Rest-Activity Cycle [*Medicine*] (DMAA) .... BRAC
Basic Retirement Date (SAUS) .... BRD
Basic Rifle Maintenance .... BRM
Basic Rifle Marksmanship [*Program of instruction*] [*Army*] (INF) .... BRM
Basic RNAV (SAUS) .... BRNAV
Basic Routine (SAUS) .... BR
Basic Safety Standards Directive (HEAS) .... BSS
Basic Salt Solution (MELL) .... BSS
Basic Save Graphics (SAUS) .... BSV
Basic Saville System (ACAE) .... BASS
Basic Schedule of Quantified Items (MHDI) .... BSQI
#The Basic School [*Marine Corps*] (DOMA) .... TBS
Basic School Skills Inventory [*Education*] .... BSSI
Basic School Skills Inventory - Diagnostic .... BSSI-D
Basic School Skills Inventory - Screen .... BSSI-S
Basic Sediment [*Petroleum*] .... BS
Basic Sediment and Water [*in crude oil*] .... BS & W
Basic Sediment And Water (SAUS) .... BS&W
Basic Selection Unit [*Computer science*] (IAA) .... BSU
Basic Semantic Element [*Computer science*] (DIT) .... BASE
Basic Sequential Access Method [*IBM Corp.*] [*Computer science*] .... BSAM
Basic Service Arrangement (ACRL) .... BSA
Basic Service Element [*Computer science*] (TNIG) .... BSE
Basic Service Set (SAUS) .... BSS
Basic Service Tier [*Telecommunications*] (OTD) .... BST
Basic Services Terminal .... BST
Basic Serving Arrangements (SAUS) .... BSA
Basic Shaft System .... BSS
Basic Shelter Facility (ACAE) .... BSF
Basic Shipping Instructions (NASA) .... BSI
Basic Sine In (TRID) .... BSI
Basic Sine Out (TRID) .... BSO
Basic Size [*Printing*] (WDMC) .... BS
Basic Skill Film (SAUS) .... BSF
Basic Skills Assessment Program [*Academic achievement and aptitude test*] .... BSAP
Basic Skills Education Program [*Army*] .... BSEP
Basic Skills Learning System (EDAC) .... BSLS
Basic Skills Trainer [*Army*] (INF) .... BST
Basic Sounding Unit [*Telecommunications*] (TEL) .... BSU
Basic Spline (DOM) .... B-spline
Basic Standard Definition (SAUS) .... BSD
Basic Standardization Agreement [*Military*] .... BSA
Basic Statement (SAUS) .... BS
Basic Status Register [*IBM*] (CIST) .... BSTAT
Basic Stock Allowance [*Military*] .... BSA
Basic Stock Allowance List [*Military*] (NVT) .... BSAL
Basic Storage Module (MCD) .... BSM
Basic Storage Unit [*Computer science*] (IAA) .... BST
Basic Striping Unit (SAUS) .... BSU
Basic Stripping Method (DICI) .... BSM
Basic Structural Design Gross Weight (MCD) .... BSDG
Basic Structural Unit .... BSU
Basic Subsystem Module .... BSM
Basic Super Mastergroup (SAUO) .... BSMG
Basic Super Mastergroup Signal (SAUO) .... BSMG Signal
Basic Support for Cooperative Work (SAUS) .... BSCW
Basic Support for Institutionalized Child Support (SAUO) .... BASIC
Basic Support for Institutionalizing Child Survival (SAUO) .... BASICS
Basic Surface Radiation Network (SAUS) .... BSRN
Basic Sustainment Materiel [*Army*] .... BSM
Basic Switching Impulse Insulation Level (IAA) .... BSIL
Basic Switching-Surge Level (IAA) .... BSL
Basic Symbol (SAUS) .... BS
Basic Synchronized Subset [*Telecommunications*] (OSI) .... BSS
Basic Synchronous Communication [*Computer science*] (IAA) .... BSC
Basic Synoptic Network of World Weather Watch (SAUS) .... BSN
Basic System (IEEE) .... BASYS
Basic System Memory [*Computer science*] (BUR) .... BSM
Basic System Reference Frequency (ACRL) .... BSRF
Basic System Release (MCD) .... BSR
Basic Systems, Inc., Huntington, WV [*Library symbol*] [*Library of Congress*] (LCLS) .... WvHuB
Basic Systems Language (SAUS) .... BSL
Basic Tables of Commissioning Allowances [*Navy*] .... BTCA
Basic Takeoff Gross Weight [*Aviation*] (MCD) .... BTOGW
Basic Tape Access Method [*Computer science*] .... BTAM
Basic Tape System (SAUS) .... BTS

Basic Technical Course [*Military*] .... BTC
Basic Technique [*Parapsychology*] .... BT
Basic Telecommunication (MCD) .... BTMA
Basic Telecommunications Access Method [*IBM Corp.*] [*Computer science*] .... BTAM
Basic Teleprocessing Access Method .... BTAM
Basic Terminal Access Method [*Computer science*] .... BTAM
Basic Terminal Unit (SAUS) .... BTU
Basic Terminal/Network Support (SAUS) .... BTNS
Basic Test Battery [*Navy*] .... BTB
Basic Thermometer Input Tape (SAUS) .... BPIT
Basic Timesharing, Inc. [*Later,*] (NITA) .... BTI
Basic Time-Sharing System (BUR) .... BTSS
Basic Trading Area (ACRL) .... BTA
[*Rand McNally*] **Basic Trading Areas** .... BTA
Basic Traffic Control Center (IAA) .... BTCC
Basic Trainer [*Air Force*] .... BT
Basic Training [*Military*] (NVT) .... BASICTNG
Basic Training [*Military*] .... BT
Basic Training Center [*Military*] .... BTC
Basic Training for Skill Development (SAUS) .... BTSD
Basic Training Group (SAUO) .... BTG
Basic Training School .... BTS
Basic Training Target (SAUS) .... BTT
Basic Training Unit (SAUS) .... BTU
Basic Transcription Factor [*Genetics*] .... BTF
Basic Transient Diode Logic [*Computer science*] (BUR) .... BTDL
Basic Transmission Header [*Computer science*] (IBMDP) .... BTH
Basic Transmission Unit [*Computer science*] .... BTU
Basic Transmission Unit per Square Foot per Minute (IAA) .... BTUSQFTMIN
Basic Transport Mechanism (SAUS) .... BTM
Basic Transportation Vehicle .... BTV
Basic Trauma Life Support [*Medicine*] (DMAA) .... BTLS
Basic Travel Allowance .... BTA
Basic Typing (SAUS) .... BT
Basic Underwater Demolition Team [*Marine Corps*] .... BUD
Basic Underwater Demolition/SEAL [*Sea, Air, and Land Capability*] **Training Department** [*Navy*] .... BUD/S
Basic Unformatted Real System (SAUS) .... BURS
Basic Unit Test Equipment (ACAE) .... BUTE
Basic Unit Training .... BUT
Basic Update Generator (MHDB) .... BUG
Basic Update Matrix Program .... BUMP
Basic User Unit (MCD) .... BUU
Basic Utility Routine (SAUS) .... BUR
Basic Utility System (SAUS) .... BUS
Basic Vehicle (SAUS) .... BV
Basic Vulcan Air Defense System (SAUS) .... BVADS
Basic War Plan [*Navy*] .... BWP
Basic Weapons (SAUS) .... BW
Basic Weather Network (SAUS) .... BWN
Basic Weight (SAUS) .... BAS WT
Basic Weight Calculator (SAUS) .... BWC
Basic Weight Controller .... BWC
Basic Work Data (MHDB) .... BWD
Basic Zinc Arsenate (SAUS) .... Adamite
BASIC-52 Computer/Controller BCC-52
Basically (ABBR) .... BSCY
Basically Qualified (SAUS) .... BQ
BASIC-Extended (SAUS) .... BASIC-X
Basic-Extension (IAA) .... BASEX
Basic/Four Corporation (SAUO) .... BFC
Basics of Adult Teaching (OICC) .... BOAT
Basics of Language [*Method*] .... BOL
Basics of Supervisory Skills .... BOSS
Basil (SAUS) .... Bas
Basilar Artery [*Anatomy*] .... BA
Basilar Membrane [*Ear anatomy*] .... BM
Basilar Papilla [*Anatomy*] .... BP
Basile, LA [*FM radio station call letters*] (BROA) .... KQIS-FM
Basile, LA [*FM radio station call letters*] .... KSIG
Basilian Fathers (TOCD) .... csb
Basilian Fathers (TOCD) .... CSB
Basilian Salvatorian Fathers [*Roman Catholic religious order*] .... BS
Basilian Salvatorian Fathers (TOCD) .... BSO
Basilic Vein [*Anatomy*] (AAMN) .... BV
Basilica (SAUS) .... Bas
Basilica (VRA) .... basl
Basilicata (SAUS) .... Bas
Basin [*of a river*] [*Geology*] .... B
Basin [*Board on Geographic Names*] .... BSN
Basin Exploration [*NASDAQ symbol*] (SAG) .... BSNX
Basin Exploration, Inc. [*Associated Press*] (SAG) .... BasExpl
Basin Petroleum Resources Ltd. [*Vancouver Stock Exchange symbol*] .... BSN
Basin Planning Report. New York State Water Resources Commission. Series ENB (journ.) (SAUS) .... NWRBBE
Basin Rainfall Monitoring System (SAUS) .... BRMS
Basin Sustainability Business Plan (SAUS) .... BSBP
Basin Sustainability Business Plan Working Group (SAUO) .... BSBPWG
Basing (ABBR) .... BSG
Basing Point Pricing System (SAUS) .... BPPS
Basing Test & System Support (SAUS) .... BT&SS
Basin-wide Extended Climate Study (SAUS) .... BECS
Basioccipital [*Anatomy*] .... BO
Basion [*Craniometric point*] .... BA
Basis Advance Training (SAUS) .... Bas Adv Tra
Basis Computer Center (IAA) .... BCC
Basis Contour Line (SAUS) .... BCL
Basis Counter Line (SAUS) .... BCL
Basis Energy Reduction Technology (SAUS) .... BERT
BASIS History (SAUS) .... BASIS-H
Basis of Allocation .... BOA
Basis of Estimate (AAGC) .... BOE
Basis of Issue [*Army*] .... BOI
Basis of Issue Monitoring and Recording System [*Army*] (AABC) .... BOIMARS
Basis of Issue Plan [*Army*] .... BOIP
Basis of Issue Plan - Complete [*Army*] .... BOIP-C
Basis of Issue Plan - Tentative [*Army*] .... BOIP-T
Basis of Issue Plan II [*Army*] (AABC) .... BOIP II
Basis of Issue System [*Army*] .... BOIS
Basis of Standard System (IAA) .... BOSS
Basis Point [*Finance*] (ODBW) .... BP
BASIS Political science, public administration, urban studies and international (SAUS) .... BASIS-P
Basis Quote [*Investment term*] .... BQ
Basis Set Extension [*Physical chemistry*] .... BSE
Basis Set Superposition Error [*Physical chemistry*] .... BSSE
Basiscreme (SAUS) .... BSC
Basisian Salvatorian Fathers (TOCD) .... bso
Basisphenoid [*Anatomy*] .... BS
Bask [*Iran*] [*ICAO location identifier*] (ICLI) .... OIZR
Basked (ABBR) .... BSKD
Basket .... Bas
Basket .... bast
Basket .... bkt
Basket .... BKT
Basket (ADWA) .... bsk
Basket .... BSK
Basket (KSC) .... BSKT
Basket (VRA) .... bskt
Basket Ball Association (SAUO) .... BBA
Basket Case (SAUS) .... BC
Basket Loading Pool [*Nuclear energy*] (NRCH) .... BLP
Basket Range Stone .... RS
Basket, Skip, and Hamper Makers Association [*A union*] [*British*] .... BSHMA
Basketball (ADA) .... BB
Basketball .... bskb
Basketball (ABBR) .... BSKBL
Basketball .... BSKTBLL
Basketball Australia [*An association*] .... BA
Basketball Club (SAUO) .... BC
Basketball Federation of the United States of America [*Defunct*] .... BFUSA
Basketball Northern Territory [*Australia*] [*An association*] .... BNT
Basketball Referees Association of New Zealand (SAUO) .... BRANZ
Basketball Saskatchewan Inc. [*Formerly, Saskatchewan Basketball*] (AC) .... BSI
Basketball-Related Income .... BRI
Basketry (ABBR) .... BSKTY
Baskets or Hampers [*Freight*] .... BH
Basking (ABBR) .... BSKG
Basking in Reflected Glory (DIPS) .... BIRG
Basle Nomina Anatomica [*Basel Anatomical Nomenclature*] [*Medicine*] .... BNA
Basler Airlines, Inc. [*Air carrier designation symbol*] .... BASX
Basler Flight Service, Inc. [*ICAO designator*] (FAAC) .... BFC
Basolateral [*Anatomy*] .... BL
Basongo [*Zaire*] [*ICAO location identifier*] (ICLI) .... FZVR
Basophil [*Hematology*] .... B
Basophil [*Hematology*] .... Bas
Basophil [*Hematology*] (DHSM) .... BASO
Basophil Chemotactic Factor [*Hematology*] .... BCF
Basophil-Associated Mononuclear (DB) .... BAM
Basophile (SAUS) .... Baso
Basophilic Degeneration [*Hematology*] .... BD
Basophilic Stippling [*Biochemistry*] (DAVI) .... STIP
Basophils (SAUS) .... BS
Basotho Congress Party [*Lesotho*] [*Political party*] (PPW) .... BCP
Basotho Democratic Alliance [*Lesotho*] [*Political party*] (EY) .... BDA
Basotho National Party [*Lesotho*] [*Political party*] (PPW) .... BNP
Basotho Unity Party [*South Africa*] [*Political party*] (PPW) .... BUP
Basque [*MARC language code*] [*Library of Congress*] (LCCP) .... bag
Basque (ABBR) .... BSQ
Basque (SAUS) .... Bsq
Basque Educational Organization (EA) .... BEO
Basque Left - Left for Socialism (PPW) .... EE-IS
Basra [*Iraq*] [*Airport symbol*] (AD) .... BSR
Basrah/Magal [*Iraq*] [*ICAO location identifier*] (ICLI) .... ORMM
Basrah/Shaibah [*Iraq*] [*ICAO location identifier*] (ICLI) .... ORMS
Bass (IDOE) .... b
Bass [*or Basso*] [*Music*] .... B
Bass [*or Basso*] [*Music*] .... Bs
Bass ADS [*NYSE symbol*] (SPSG) .... BAS
Bass Anglers Sportsman Society (EA) .... BASS
Bass Baritone [*Music*] .... BBAR
Bass Clarinet .... BC
Bass Clarinet .... bcl
Bass Clarinet [*Music*] .... BCLAR
Bass Equalizer System (SAUS) .... BES
Bass Guitar .... bgtr
Bass Klarinette [*Bass Clarinet*] [*Music*] .... B Kl
Bass PLC [*NYSE symbol*] (SAG) .... BAS
Bass Public Ltd. [*Associated Press*] (SAG) .... Bass

Bass Research Foundation (EA) .... BRF
Bass Strait (SAUS) .... Bas
Bass Transistor (IDOE) .... b
Bass Trombone .... btbn
Bassano Del Grappa [Italy] [ICAO location identifier] (ICLI) ...... LIPJ
Bassano Public Library, Alberta [Library symbol] [National Library of Canada] (NLC) .... ABAS
Bassari [Togo] [ICAO location identifier] (ICLI) .... DXBS
Basse Pression [Low Pressure] [French] .... BP
Basse Tension [Low Tension] [French] .... BT
Bassein [Myanmar] [Airport symbol] (OAG) .... BSX
Bassein [Myanmar] [ICAO location identifier] (ICLI) ...... VBBS
Bassel, Sullivan & Leake, Toronto, Ontario [Library symbol] [National Library of Canada] (NLC) .... OTBSL
Bassen-Kornzweig [Syndrome] [Medicine] (DB) .... BK
Basses-Alpes [Lower Alps] [French] (BARN) .... B Alp
Basset Horn .... bthn
Basset Hound Club of America (EA) .... BHCA
Basse-Terre [Guadeloupe] [Airport symbol] (OAG) ...... BBR
Basse-Terre (SAUS) .... TFFB
Basse-Terre/Baillif [French Antilles] [ICAO location identifier] (ICLI) .... TFFB
Basseterre/Golden Rock [St. Kitts Island] [ICAO location identifier] (ICLI) ...... TKPK
Bassett Furniture [Associated Press] (SAG) .... BassettF
Bassett Furniture [NASDAQ symbol] (TTSB) .... BSET
Bassett Furniture Industries, Inc. [NASDAQ symbol] (NQ) ...... BSET
Bassett, NE [FM radio station call letters] .... KMNE
Bassett, NE [Television station call letters] .... KMNE-TV
Bassett, NE [Location identifier] [FAA] (FAAL) .... RBE
Bassett, VA [AM radio station call letters] .... WCBX
Bassett's Illinois Criminal Pleading and Practice [A publication] (DLA) ...... Bass Crim Pl
Basso [Music] .... BAS
Basso Continuo [Continued Bass] [Music] (ROG) ... BAS CON
Basso Continuo [Continued Bass] [Music] .... BASS CON
Basso Continuo [Continued Bass] [Music] .... BASS CONT
Basso Continuo [Continued Bass] [Music] .... BC
Basso Continuo [Continued Bass] [Music] (ROG) C
Bassoon [Music] (ROG) .... B
Bassoon [Music] .... BN
Bassoon .... bn
Bassoon [Music] .... Bsn
Bassposaune [Bass Trombone] [Music] .... BP
Basswood (VRA) .... baswd
Bastak [Iran] [ICAO location identifier] (ICLI) .... OIBH
Bastard [Slang] (DSUE) .... B
Bastard [Slang] (DSUE) .... BAS
Bastard (DLA) .... BAST
Bastard [Size or material] .... BSTD
Bastard (ABBR) .... BSTRD
Bastard Amber [Stage-lighting filter] (WDMC) .... BA
Bastardize (ABBR) .... BSTRDZ
Bastardized (ABBR) .... BSTRDZD
Bastardizing (ABBR) .... BSTRDZG
Bastardly (ABBR) .... BSTRDY
Bastardy [FBI standardized term] .... BAST
Baste (ABBR) .... BST
Basted (ABBR) .... BSTD
Bastia [Corsica] [Airport symbol] (OAG) .... BIA
Bastia/Poretta, Corse [France] [ICAO location identifier] (ICLI) ...... LFKB
Basting (ABBR) .... BSTG
Bastogne (SAUS) .... Bas
Bastrop (SAUS) .... Bas
Bastrop, LA [Location identifier] [FAA] (FAAL) .... BQP
Bastrop, LA [FM radio station call letters] (BROA) ... KAXV-FM
Bastrop, LA [FM radio station call letters] (RBYB) ... KLMB-FM
Bastrop, LA [FM radio station call letters] .... KRVV
Bastrop, LA [AM radio station call letters] .... KTRY
Bastrop, LA [FM radio station call letters] .... KTRY-FM
Bastrop, TX [FM radio station call letters] .... KGSR
Bastrop, TX [FM radio station call letters] (BROA) .. KYCM-FM
Basuto (SAUS) .... Bas
Basutoland (BARN) .... Bas
Basutoland .... BL
Basutoland Factory Estate Development Company, Lesotho (SAUO) ...... BAFED
Basutoland Police Force (SAUO) .... BPolF
Bat .... B
Bat Conservation International (EA) .... BCI
Bat Conservation Society of Canada (AC) .... BCSC
Bat Conservation Trust [British] (EAIO) .... BCT
Bat Groups of Britain (EAIO) .... BGB
BAT Industries Ltd. [Associated Press] (SAG) .... BAT
BAT Industries Ltd. [AMEX symbol] (SPSG) .... BTI
Bat National Action Plan (SAUS) .... BATNAP
Bata [Spanish Guinea] [Airport symbol] (AD) .... BSG
Bata [Equatorial Guinea] [ICAO location identifier] (ICLI) ...... FGBT
Bata Shoe Museum Foundation (AC) .... BSMF
Bataan [Costa Rica] [ICAO location identifier] (ICLI) ...... MRBN
Bataan Export-Processing Zone (SAUO) .... BEPZ
Bataan Ocean Petroleum Depot (CINC) .... BOPD
Batabano [Cuba] [ICAO location identifier] (ICLI) ..... MUBO
Bataillon de Commandement et d'Appui [Headquarters and Support Battalion] [Algeria] (AF) ...... BCA
Batallon Vasco Espanol [Spanish Basque Battalion] (PD) ...... BVE
Batam/Hang Nadim [Indonesia] [ICAO location identifier] (ICLI) ...... WIKB
Batavia (SAUS) .... Bat

Batavia [Indonesia] [Later, TNG] [Geomagnetic observatory code] ...... BTV
Batavia Area Office (SAUO) .... BA
Batavia Area Office [Energy Research and Development Administration] ...... BAO
Batavia Beacon, Batavia, IA [Library symbol] [Library of Congress] (LCLS) ...... IaBatB
Batavia, NY [Location identifier] [FAA] (FAAL) .... GVQ
Batavia, NY [TV station call letters] (RBYB) .... WAQF-TV
Batavia, NY [AM radio station call letters] .... WBTA
Batavia, NY [FM radio station call letters] .... WGCC-FM
Batavia, OH [FM radio station call letters] .... WOBO
Batboy (NDBD) .... BB
Batch [Computer science] .... B
Batch [Computer science] (CDE) .... BAT
Batch 2 Trafalgar-Class submarine (SAUS) B2TC
Batch Assembly (SAUS) .... BA
Batch Automated Balancing System [Computer science] (MHDI) ...... BABS
Batch Bulk Processing (SAUS) .... BBP
Batch Change Supplement (SAUS) .... BCS
Batch Command Language [Computer science] .... BCL
Batch Data Class [Telecommunications] .... BDC
Batch Data Transmission System .... BDTS
Batch Disk Operating System .... BDOS
Batch Distribution Coefficient (SAUS) .... KD
Batch Execution System [Computer science] [Engineering] ...... BES
Batch Executive (IAA) .... BATEX
Batch Fabrication .... BF
Batch Fabrication Technique .... BFT
Batch File [Computer science] .... BAT
Batch File [Computer science] .... BAT File
Batch File Transfer Protocol (SAUS) .... BFTP
Batch Freeform Input [Computer science] (MHDI) .... BFI
Batch Input (NITA) .... BI
Batch Job Foreground [Computer science] .... BJF
Batch Job Format (SAUS) .... BJF
Batch Message Processing (SAUS) .... BMP
Batch Message Processing Program [Computer science] (ITCA) ...... BMP
Batch Mixer .... BMXR
Batch News Receive Via UUCP (SAUS) .... BNRCVUUCP
Batch Number (SAUS) .... BCHNR
Batch Numbering (SAUS) .... BN
Batch Operating Software System .... BOSS
Batch Operating System [Computer science] .... BOS
Batch Processing (SAUS) .... BAT
Batch Processing .... BP
Batch Processing Monitor [Xerox Corp.] [Computer science] (MCD) ...... BPM
Batch Processing Multilanguage Operating System [Computer science] (IAA) ...... BAMOS
Batch Processing Operating System (IAA) .... BPOS
Batch Processing System .... BPS
Batch Query Language [Programming language] .... BQL
Batch Reactor [Chemical engineering] .... BR
Batch Simple Message Transfer Protocol (SAUS) .... BSMTP
Batch Spool Monitor (SAUS) .... BSM
Batch, Stirred-Tank Reactor (PDAA) .... BSTR
Batch Terminal Controller [Computer science] (IAA) ... BTC
Batch Terminal Simulator [Computer science] .... BTS
Batch Time-Sharing Monitor [Xerox Corp.] [Computer science] (MCD) ...... BTM
Batch Transfer Program .... BTP
Batch Weighing Kit .... BWK
Batch Weighing System .... BWS
Batched (ABBR) .... BTCHD
Batched Compilation (SAUS) .... BC
Batchelder's Law of Massachusetts Manufacturing Corporations [A publication] (DLA) ...... Batch Mfg Cor
Batchewana Indian Band, Sault Ste. Marie, Ontario [Library symbol] [National Library of Canada] (NLC) ...... OSTMB
Batching (ABBR) .... BTCHG
Batean [Ship's rigging] (ROG) .... BAT
Bateau Torpilleur [Torpedo Boat] [French] .... BT
Bateaux Resources, Inc. [Vancouver Stock Exchange symbol] ...... BTU
Batelle Development Corporation (ABAC) .... BDC
Batelle Project Management Division (ABAC) .... BPMD
Bateman. General Laws of Excise [2nd ed.] [1840] [A publication] (DLA) ...... Bate Exc
Bateman. Law of Auctions [11th ed.] [1953] [A publication] (DLA) ...... Bate Auct
Bateman on Agency [A publication] (DLA) .... Bate Ag
Bateman's Commercial Law [A publication] (DLA) ... Bate Com L
Bateman's United States Constitutional Law [A publication] (DLA) ...... Bate Const
Bater Surname Organization (EA) .... BSO
Bateria Artifical Chromosome [Genetics] .... BAC
Bateria de Examenes de Aptitud General [General Aptitude Test Battery] [Spanish] ...... BEAG
Bateria General de Preubas de Aptitud [General Aptitude Test Battery] [Spanish] ...... BGPA
Bateria Woodcock-Munoz: Pruebas de Habilidad Cognitiva-Revisada [Test] (TMMY) ...... Bateria-RCOG
Bates' Annotated Revised Statutes [Ohio] [A publication] (DLA) ...... Bates' Ann St
Bates College (SAUO) .... BC
Bates College, Lewiston, ME [OCLC symbol] (OCLC) ... BTS
Bates College, Lewiston, ME [Library symbol] [Library of Congress] (LCLS) ...... MeLB
Bates' Delaware Chancery Reports [A publication] (DLA) ...... Bates
Bates' Delaware Chancery Reports [A publication] (DLA) ...... Bates Ch
Bates' Digest [Ohio] [A publication] (DLA) .... Bates' Dig
Bates Large Acceptance Spectrometer Toroid ...... BLAST

Bates' Law of Partnership [*A publication*] (DLA) .... Bates Part
Bates Manufacturing Co., Inc. (SAUO) .... BAT
Batesburg, SC [*AM radio station call letters*] .... WBLR
Batesburg, SC [*FM radio station call letters*] .... WKWQ
Batesville [*Arkansas*] [*Airport symbol*] (OAG) .... BVX
Batesville, AR [*Location identifier*] [*FAA*] (FAAL) .... BVX
Batesville, AR [*Location identifier*] [*FAA*] (FAAL) .... INY
Batesville, AR [*AM radio station call letters*] .... KAAB
Batesville, AR [*AM radio station call letters*] .... KBTA
Batesville, AR [*FM radio station call letters*] (BROA) .... KBTA-FM
Batesville, AR [*FM radio station call letters*] .... KZLE
Batesville, AR [*Location identifier*] [*FAA*] (FAAL) .... LYY
Batesville Herald Tribune, Batesville, IN [*Library symbol*] [*Library of Congress*] (LCLS) .... InBaHT
Batesville, IN [*Location identifier*] [*FAA*] (FAAL) .... HLB
Batesville, IN [*FM radio station call letters*] .... WRBI
Batesville, MS [*FM radio station call letters*] .... WBLE
Batesville, MS [*AM radio station call letters*] .... WJBI
Bath .... B
Bath (WGA) .... BA
Bath (ADA) .... BTH
Bath and Basin [*Classified advertising*] (ADA) .... B & B
Bath & Body Works .... BBW
Bath & Hammondsport Railroad Co. [*AAR code*] .... BH
Bath and West and Southern Counties Society (SAUO) .... BWSCS
Bath Blanket [*Medicine*] (MEDA) .... BB
Bath Branch, Lennox and Addington County Public Library, Ontario [*Library symbol*] [*National Library of Canada*] (NLC) .... OBLAC
Bath Industries, Inc. (SAUO) .... BIW
Bath Information and Data Services [*Computer science*] [*British*] (TNIG) .... BIDS
Bath Institute of Medical Engineering [*University of Bath*] [*British*] (IRUK) .... BIME
Bath Iron Works [*Maine*] (DOMA) .... BIW
Bath Iron Works Corp. (SAUO) .... BIW
Bath, Laxative, Enema, Shampoo, and Shower [*Medicine*] (AAMN) .... BLESS
Bath, ME [*FM radio station call letters*] (RBYB) .... WBC
Bath, ME [*FM radio station call letters*] (RBYB) .... WBCI-FM
Bath, ME [*AM radio station call letters*] .... WJTO
Bath, NY [*AM radio station call letters*] .... WABH
Bath, NY [*FM radio station call letters*] .... WCIK
Bath, NY [*FM radio station call letters*] .... WVIN
Bath Road [*Bristol*] [*British depot code*] .... BL
Bath Royal Literary and Scientific Institution (SAUO) .... BRLSI
Bath Unit [*British and Canadian*] [*Military*] .... BU
Bath University Comparative Catalogue Study (SAUO) .... BUCCS
Bath University Computing Services [*British*] (AIE) .... BUCS
Bath University ISI Data Service (SAUS) .... BIDS
Bathometer (SAUS) .... Batho
Bathophenanthroline [*Organic chemistry*] .... BP
Bathophenanthroline [*Analytical chemistry*] .... BPT
Bathophenanthroline Disulphonate [*Organic chemistry*] .... BPDS
Bathroom [*Classified advertising*] .... BA
Bathroom (ADWA) .... ba
Bathroom (VRA) .... bathrm
Bathroom [*Classified advertising*] (ADA) .... BATHRM
Bathroom .... BR
Bathroom (ADA) .... BTH
Bathroom (REAL) .... bth
Bathroom [*Classified advertising*] (ADA) .... BTHRM
Bathroom Privileges [*Medicine*] .... BP
Bathroom Privileges [*Medicine*] .... BRP
Bathtub (ABBR) .... BT
Bathurst [*Australia*] [*Airport symbol*] (OAG) .... BHS
Bathurst [*Gambia*] [*Airport symbol*] (AD) .... BTH
Bathurst College, Bathurst, NB, Canada [*Library symbol*] [*Library of Congress*] (LCLS) .... CaNBBB
Bathurst Island [*Australia*] [*Airport symbol*] (OAG) .... BRT
Bathurst, NB [*AM radio station call letters*] .... CKBC
Bathurst, NB [*FM radio station call letters*] .... CKLE
Bathurst Paper Ltd. [*Toronto Stock Exchange symbol*] .... BAT
Bathyconductograph .... BC
Bathymeter (SAUS) .... Bathy
Bathymetric Estimator Search Technique (SAUS) .... BEST
Bathymetric Navigation Equipment .... BNE
Bathymetric Navigation Planning Chart (GEOI) .... BNPC
Bathymetric Navigation System (SAUS) .... BNS
Bathymetric Plotting Sheets (SAUS) .... BPS
Bathymetric Swath [*Survey System*] [*National Ocean Survey*] (PDAA) .... BS
Bathymetric Swath Survey System [*National Ocean Survey*] (MSC) .... BSSS
Bathyscaphe (SAUS) .... Bathy
Bathyscaphe Oceanographic Program .... BOP
Bathysphere (SAUS) .... Bathy
Bathythermal Data (MCD) .... BTD
Bathythermal Traces .... BT
Bathythermograph [*Oceanography*] (MSC) .... BATHY
Bathythermograph [*Oceanography*] .... BT
Bathythermograph (SAUS) .... BY
Bathythermograph Report (SAUS) .... BATHY
Bathythermographic Data Collection and Processing Facility [*Oceanography*] .... BTDCPF
Bathythermographic Data Processing and Analysis Facility [*Oceanography*] .... BTDPAF
Batibus Club International (SAUO) .... BCI
Batie [*Burkina Faso*] [*ICAO location identifier*] (ICLI) .... DHCE
Batik (ABBR) .... BTK
Batik (VRA) .... btk
Batka Party (SAUO) .... BP
Batman [*Turkey*] [*ICAO location identifier*] (ICLI) .... LTCJ
Batman and Robin .... B&R
Batman Forever .... BF
Batman Returns .... BR
Batman, the Animated Series .... BAS
Batman the Animated Series [*Television program*] .... BTAS
Batna [*Algeria*] [*ICAO location identifier*] (ICLI) .... DABT
Baton (WDAA) .... BTN
Baton Broadcasting, Inc. [*Toronto Stock Exchange symbol*] .... BNB
Baton Rouge [*Diocesan abbreviation*] [*Louisiana*] (TOCD) .... BR
Baton Rouge [*Louisiana*] [*Airport symbol*] (OAG) .... BTR
Baton Rouge, LA [*Location identifier*] [*FAA*] (FAAL) .... CLZ
Baton Rouge, LA [*AM radio station call letters*] .... KBRH
Baton Rouge, LA [*FM radio station call letters*] .... KLSU
Baton Rouge, LA [*Television station call letters*] .... WAFB
Baton Rouge, LA [*FM radio station call letters*] .... WBRH
Baton Rouge, LA [*Television station call letters*] .... WBRZ
Baton Rouge, LA [*FM radio station call letters*] (BROA) .... WDGL-FM
Baton Rouge, LA [*FM radio station call letters*] .... WFMF
Baton Rouge, LA [*FM radio station call letters*] .... WGGZ
Baton Rouge, LA [*Television station call letters*] .... WGMB
Baton Rouge, LA [*AM radio station call letters*] .... WIBR
Baton Rouge, LA [*AM radio station call letters*] .... WJBO
Baton Rouge, LA [*FM radio station call letters*] .... WJFM
Baton Rouge, LA [*Television station call letters*] .... WLPB
Baton Rouge, LA [*FM radio station call letters*] (RBYB) .... WLSS-FM
Baton Rouge, LA [*AM radio station call letters*] .... WNDC
Baton Rouge, LA [*FM radio station call letters*] .... WRKF
Baton Rouge, LA [*FM radio station call letters*] .... WTGE
Baton Rouge, LA [*Television station call letters*] .... WVLA
Baton Rouge, LA [*FM radio station call letters*] (BROA) .... WXCT-FM
Baton Rouge, LA [*AM radio station call letters*] .... WXOK
Baton Rouge, LA [*AM radio station call letters*] .... WYNK
Baton Rouge, LA [*FM radio station call letters*] .... WYNK-FM
Baton Rouge Public Library (SAUO) .... BRPL
Baton Rouge/Ryan Field [*Louisiana*] [*ICAO location identifier*] (ICLI) .... KBTR
Batouri [*Cameroon*] [*ICAO location identifier*] (ICLI) .... FKKI
Batouri [*Cameroon*] [*Airport symbol*] (OAG) .... OUR
Batrachomyomachia (SAUS) .... Batr
Batrachotoxin [*Biochemistry*] .... BTX
Batrachotoxinin A [*Toxicology*] (LDT) .... BTX-A
Bats Both Right-Handed and Left-Handed [*Baseball*] .... BB
Bats Left-Handed [*Baseball*] .... BL
Bats Right-Handed [*Baseball*] .... BR
Batse Coordinates Distribution Network .... BACODINE
Batsfjord [*Norway*] [*Airport symbol*] (OAG) .... BJF
Batsfjord [*Norway*] [*ICAO location identifier*] (ICLI) .... ENBS
Batsman (ADA) .... B
Battaillon des Jeunes Ruraux [*Rural Youth Battalion*] [*Zaire*] .... BJR
Battalion .... BAT
Battalion (ADWA) .... bat
battalion (SAUO) .... bat
Battalion (ROG) .... BATN
Battalion .... BATT
Battalion (SAUO) .... Batt
Battalion (ADWA) .... batt
Battalion (ADA) .... BATTN
Battalion (AFM) .... BN
Battalion (WDAA) .... Bn
Battalion (MILB) .... bn
Battalion (SAUO) .... Bon
Battalion (ABBR) .... BTLN
Battalion .... BTN
Battalion Administration Officer (MCD) .... BAO
Battalion Aid Station [*Army*] .... BAS
Battalion Analyzer and Tactical Trainer for Local Engagements (MCD) .... BATTLE
Battalion and Below Command and Control [*Army*] B2C2
Battalion Antitank Recoilless Rifle .... BAT
Battalion Anti-Tank rifle (SAUS) .... BAT rifle
Battalion Artillery Group (MCD) .... BAG
Battalion Automated Personnel System .... BAPERS
Battalion Battle Simulation [*Army*] .... BBS
Battalion Beachhead [*Army*] .... BBH
Battalion Casualty Station (SAUS) .... BCS
Battalion Close Support Weapon System (MCD) .... BCSWS
Battalion Combat Team .... BCT
Battalion Combat Train (SAUO) .... BCT
Battalion Command and Coordination [*Military*] .... BCAC
Battalion Command Centre (SAUO) .... BCC
Battalion Command Inspection [*Army*] (INF) .... BCI
Battalion Command Post (DNAB) .... BN-CP
Battalion Command Post (SAUS) .... Bn CP
Battalion Command Post (SAUO) .... Bn DP
Battalion Commander (MCD) .... BC
Battalion Commander (SAUS) .... Bn Comdr
Battalion Control Group [*Army*] .... BCG
Battalion Equipment Evaluation Program [*DoD*] .... BEEP
Battalion Etranger de Parachutistes [*Foreign Battalion of Parachutists*] [*French Foreign Legion*] .... BEP
Battalion Executive (SAUS) .... Bn Ex
Battalion Expeditionary Force (CINC) .... BEF
Battalion Field Exercise [*Military*] (NVT) .... BNFEX
Battalion Field Training Days (MCD) .... BFTD

Battalion Fire Distribution Center (AABC) .... BFDC
Battalion Ground Surveillance Section [Army] (AABC) .... BGSS
Battalion Group (SAUO) .... Bn Gp
Battalion Headquarters [British military] (DMA) .... BHQ
Battalion Headquarters [Marine Corps] .... BNHQ
Battalion Headquarters (SAUO) .... BnHQ
Battalion Headquarters (SAUS) .... Bn Hqu
Battalion Infantry (CINC) .... BI
Battalion Information Group (SAUO) .... BIG
Battalion Information Unit (SAUO) .... BIU
Battalion Input/Output Device (MCD) .... BIOD
Battalion Landing Exercise [Military] (NVT) .... BLTLEX
Battalion Landing Team [Marine Corps] (DOMA) .... BLT
Battalion Landing Team Landing Exercise [Military] (NVT) .... BTLEX
Battalion Level Training Model [DoD] .... BLTM
Battalion Loading Officer (SAUS) .... BLO
Battalion Logistical Operations Center [Military] (INF) .... BLOC
Battalion Maintenance Equipment [Military] .... BME
Battalion Maintenance Officer [Army] (INF) .... BMO
Battalion Maintenance Sergeant [Military] (INF) .... BMS
Battalion Maintenance Technician [Military] (INF) .... BMT
Battalion Medical Officer (SAUS) .... Bn MO
Battalion Mortar and Davy Crockett Platoon [Army] (AABC) .... BMDCP
Battalion Mortar System [Army] .... BMS
Battalion Motor Officer [Military] (INF) .... BMO
Battalion Officer-of-the-Watch (DNAB) .... BOOW
Battalion Operated Surveillance System [Army] (INF) .... BOSS
Battalion Operations Center (AABC) .... BOC
Battalion Orderly Corporal [British and Canadian] .... BOC
Battalion Orderly Room [British] .... BOR
Battalion Orderly Sergeant [British and Canadian] .... BOS
Battalion Orders [British military] (DMA) .... BO
Battalion Reserve Line (SAUS) .... BRL
Battalion Routine Orders (SAUS) .... Bn RO
Battalion Sergeant-Major (SAUS) .... BSM
Battalion Shore Fire Control Party .... BNSFCP
Battalion Shore Fire Control Party (SAUO) .... BnSFCP
Battalion Signal Officer (INF) .... BSO
Battalion Standing Order (SAUS) .... BSO
Battalion Supply and Maintenance Equipment [Military] .... BSME
Battalion Supply Point (SAUS) .... Bn Sup P
Battalion Supply Point [Army] (INF) .... BSP
Battalion Tactical Initialization [Military] .... BATI
Battalion Tactical Operations Center [Army] .... BN TOC
Battalion Tactical Operations Center [Military] .... BTOC
Battalion Targeting System (DOMA) .... BTS
Battalion Task Force (MCD) .... BNTF
Battalion Task Force (SAUO) .... BTF
Battalion Terminal (SAUS) .... BT
Battalion Training Management System [Army] (INF) .... BTMS
Battalion Training Model [Military] .... BTM
Battalion Transport Officer [British military] (DMA) .... BTO
Battalion/Brigade Signal Officer Course [Military] (INF) .... BBSOC
Battambang [Cambodia] [ICAO location identifier] (ICLI) .... VDBG
Batted In [Short form for RBI, Runs Batted In] [Baseball] .... BI
Battella Developmental Inventory [Psychology] (DHP) .... BDI
Battelle - Defense Information Analysis Center [Battelle Memorial Institute] .... BDIAC
Battelle - Defense Information Center [Battelle Memorial Institute] (MCD) ..... BDIC
Battelle Automated Search Information System [Database management system] [Battelle Memorial Institute] [Information service or system] .... BASIS
Battelle Columbus Laboratories Decommissioning Project [Department of Energy] (GAAI) .... BCLDP
Battelle Columbus Laboratories (or Laboratory) (SAUS) .... BCL
Battelle Defense Document Center [Battelle Memorial Institute] (SAA) .... BDDC
Battelle Energy Information Center (SAUS) .... BEIC
Battelle Europe (ABAC) .... BE
Battelle Human Affairs Research Center [Seattle, WA] .... BHARC
Battelle Human Affairs Research Center, Seattle, WA [Library symbol] [Library of Congress] (LCLS) .... WaSBa
Battelle Institute Learning Automation [Battelle Memorial Institute] (IEEE) .... BILA
Battelle Interactive Resources Management System (SAUS) .... BIRMS
Battelle Marine Sciences Laboratory (SAUS) .... BMSL
Battelle Memorial Institute (EA) .... BMI
Battelle Memorial Institute, Columbus, OH [OCLC symbol] (OCLC) .... BKM
Battelle Memorial Institute, Pacific Northwest Laboratory, Richland, WA [Library symbol] [Library of Congress] (LCLS) .... WaRiB
Battelle Monte Carlo [Computer science] .... BMC
Battelle New England Marine Research Laboratory [Battelle Memorial Institute] [Research center] (RCD) .... BNEMRL
Battelle Northwest (SAUS) .... BNW
Battelle Northwest Laboratories .... BNL
Battelle Northwest Laboratories (KSC) .... BNWL
Battelle North-West Laboratory .... BNWL
Battelle Pacific Northwest Laboratories [Nuclear energy] (NRCH) .... BPNL
Battelle Portland Operations (ABAC) .... BPO
Battelle Research Reactor .... BRR
Battelle Seattle Research Center (ABAC) .... BSRC
Battelle Seminars and Studies Program (SAUS) .... BSSP
Battelle Seminars and Study Program (SAUO) .... BSSP
Battelle Washington Office (ABAC) .... BWO
Battelle-Columbus Laboratories, Columbus, OH [Library symbol] [Library of Congress] (LCLS) .... OCoB
Battelle-Defender Information Analysis Center (SAUO) .... BDIAC

Battelle-Northwest Hospital, Life Science Library, Richland, WA [Library symbol] [Library of Congress] (LCLS) .... WaRiBN
Battelle's Educational Computer User's Network [Battelle Memorial Institute] [Information service or system] (IID) .... BECUN
Battelles Internal Telephone System (SAUS) .... IBX
Battelles Office Automation Research and Development (SAUS) .... BOARD
Batten (SAUS) .... Batt
Batten (KSC) .... BATT
Batten, Barton, Durstine & Osborn [Advertising agency] .... BBD & O
Batten, Barton, Durstine, and Osborn [An advertising agency] [New York, NY] (WDMC) .... BBDO
Batten on the Stannaries Act [A publication] (DLA) .... Bat Stan
Batten. Specific Performance on Contracts [1849] [A publication] (DLA) .... Bat Sp Perf
Batten-Mayou [Syndrome] [Medicine] (DB) .... BM
Battens (SAUS) .... Bttns
Batten's Disease [Medicine] .... BD
Batten's Disease Gene (HGEN) .... BDG
Batten's Disease Support and Research Association (EA) .... BDSRA
Batten-Spielmyer-Vogt [Syndrome] [Medicine] (AAMN) .... BSV
Batten-Steinert [Syndrome] [Medicine] (DB) .... BS
Batten-Turner Muscular Dystrophy [Syndrome] [Medicine] .... BTMD
Batter .... BAT
Batter (SAUS) .... Bat
Battered Child (CPH) .... BC
Battered Child Syndrome .... BCS
Battered Woman (MELL) .... BW
Battered Woman [or Wife] Syndrome [Medicine] [Defunct] .... BWS
Batterers Anonymous (EA) .... BA
Batterie Experimental (SAUS) .... BATEX
Batteries (SAUS) .... Batt
Batteries Batteries, Inc. [NASDAQ symbol] (SAG) .... BATS
Batteries Batteries, Inc. [Associated Press] (SAG) .... Batter
Batteries Batteries, Inc. [Associated Press] (SAG) .... Batteries
Batteries Batteries Wrrt [NASDAQ symbol] (TTSB) .... BATSW
Batteries Not Included (SAUS) .... BNI
Batters Faced by Pitcher [Baseball] .... BFP
Battery .... B
Battery (IAA) .... BA
Battery (AAG) .... BAT
Battery .... BATRY
Battery (SAUS) .... Batry
Battery [FBI standardized term] .... BATT
Battery (SAUO) .... Batt
Battery .... BATTY
Battery [Military] (WDAA) .... btry
Battery (AFM) .... BTRY
Battery (ADWA) .... btty
Battery (SAUO) .... Btty
Battery .... BTY
Battery (WDAA) .... Bty
Battery (MILB) .... bty
Battery Acid (EDCT) .... BAA
Battery Acquisition Radar (SAUS) .... BAR
Battery Adjust (AABC) .... BA
Battery Aiming Point (SAUS) .... BAP
Battery and Earth Loop (SAUS) .... BEL
Battery Backup [Computer science] (CIST) .... BBU
Battery Backup Random Access Memory [Computer science] (CIST) .... BBRAM
Battery Block (SAUS) .... BB
Battery Booster Cable .... BBC
Battery Capability .... BC
Battery Captain (SAUS) .... BK
Battery Cell Voltage Monitor (ACAE) .... BCVM
Battery Charge and Reconditioning Unit (ACAE) .... BCRU
Battery Charge Controller (ACAE) .... BCC
Battery Charge Regulator .... BCR
Battery Charger [Military] (MSA) .... BAT CHG
Battery Charger [Military] .... BC
Battery Chargers (SAUS) .... BCs
Battery Charging (SAUS) .... Bat Chg
Battery Command Centre (SAUO) .... BCC
Battery Command Post [Army] .... BCP
Battery Command Post [Army] .... BTRY CP
Battery Commander [Army] .... BC
Battery Commander Assistant (SAUS) .... BCA
Battery Commanders Station (SAUS) .... BCS
Battery Computer System (MCD) .... BCS
Battery Computer Unit (SAUS) .... BCU
Battery Condition Indicator (MCD) .... BCI
Battery Control (SAUS) .... BC
Battery Control and Monitor [Army] .... BCM
Battery Control Area [Army] .... BCA
Battery Control Building [Army] .... BCB
Battery Control Center (ACAE) .... BCC
Battery Control Central [Army] .... BCC
Battery Control Data Processor [Army] .... BCDP
Battery Control Officer [Army] (AABC) .... BCO
Battery Control Post [Army] .... BCP
Battery Control RADAR [Army] .... BCR
Battery Control System [Army] .... BCS
Battery Control Trailer (NATG) .... BCT
Battery Control Van (NATG) .... BCV
Battery Coolant Unit (SAUS) .... BCU
Battery Council International (EA) .... BCI

Battery Cutoff [Telecommunications] (IAA) .... BATCO
Battery Cutoff [Telecommunications] (TEL) .... BCO
Battery Data Link [Air Force] .... BDL
Battery Data Link System [Air Force] .... BDLS
Battery Discharge Controller (ACAE) .... BDC
Battery Discharge Regulator (ADWA) .... BDR
Battery Display Unit [Army] .... BDU
Battery Disposal Technology (EFIS) .... BDT
Battery Echelon Operating Control (AFM) .... BEOC
Battery Electronic Pack (SAUS) .... BEP
Battery Energy Storage System (DWSG) .... BESS
Battery Energy Storage Test .... BEST
Battery Exhaust Emergency Recirculation (DNAB) .... BEER
Battery Fire Support Vehicle (SAUS) .... BFSV
Battery Firing Device (MCD) .... BFD
Battery Fuse (IAA) .... BATFU
Battery Fuse (SAUS) .... BAT FU
Battery Fuse Panel (IAA) .... BFP
Battery Guidance Command Group .... BGCG
Battery Headquarters (SAUO) .... BHQ
Battery Holder (SAUS) .... BAT HOLD
Battery Information Index [Battelle Memorial Institute] (IID) .... BII
Battery Integration and RADAR Display Equipment [Air defense system] .... BIRDIE
Battery Integration Routing Display Equipment (MCD) .... BIRDIE
Battery Interconnecting Cables (NATG) .... BIC
Battery Interface Unit (MCD) .... BIU
Battery Inverter (AAG) .... BI
Battery Inverter Accessory Power Supply .... BIAPS
Battery Inverter Accessory Power Supply (SAUS) .... BI-APS
Battery Inverter Instrument Power Supply (IAA) .... BIIPS
Battery Leader (SAUS) .... BL
Battery Left (SAUS) .... BL
Battery Level Computer (MCD) .... BLC
Battery Maintenance Group [Military] .... BMG
Battery Observation Post (SAUS) .... BOP
Battery of Leukocyte Tests [Clinical medicine] .... BLT
Battery Operated (IAA) .... BATTOPER
Battery Operated (SAUS) .... BATT OPER
Battery Operated Device .... BOD
Battery Operations Center [Air Force] .... BOC
Battery Operations Centre Vehicle (SAUS) .... BOCV
Battery, Overvoltage Protection, Ringing, Supervision, Coding, Hybrids, Testing [Seven basic functions performed by line circuits] [Telecommunications] .... BORSCHT
Battery, Overvoltage, Ring, Supervision, Hybrid Test (CIST) .... BORSHT
Battery Package .... BP
Battery Park City [New York City] .... BPC
Battery Plotting Room .... BPR
Battery Power Feed, Overvoltage Protection, Ringing, Supervision (SAUS) .... BORSCHT
Battery Protection and Reconditioning Circuit (MCD) .... BPRC
Battery Protection Unit (ACAE) .... BPU
Battery Quartermaster-Sergeant [British] .... BQMS
Battery Random Access Memory [External storage system] [Computer science] .... BATRAM
Battery Reconditioning Unit (ADWA) .... BRU
Battery Repair and Test Facility (SAUO) .... BRTF
Battery Replacement Unit (MCD) .... BRU
Battery Right (SAUS) .... BR
Battery Sergeant-Major .... BSM
Battery Shop Maintenance [NASA] (KSC) .... BSM
Battery Signal Conditioning Unit (ACAE) .... BSCU
Battery Simulator .... BS
Battery Status Indicator (NATG) .... BSI
Battery Supply (IAA) .... BATSUP
Battery Supply (SAUS) .... BAT SUP
Battery Target [British and Canadian] [Military] .... BT
Battery Tech, Inc. [Associated Press] (SAG) .... BatTech
Battery Tech, Inc. [NASDAQ symbol] (SAG) .... BTIO
Battery Technologies [NASDAQ symbol] (TTSB) .... BTIOF
Battery Terminal Equipment .... BTE
Battery Test Set .... BTS
Battery Timing Equipment (AAG) .... BTE
Battery Timing Group .... BTG
Battery Training Corps [British] .... BTC
Battery Training Corps (SAUO) .... BTC
Battery Training Exercise (SAUO) .... BTE
Battery Vehicle Society [British] .... BVS
Battery Voltage (SAUS) .... BATT VOLT
Battery Voltage [Automotive engineering] .... VBAT
Battery-Powered (ADA) .... BP
Battery-Powered Electrically Heated Catalyst [Automotive exhaust emissions] .... BPEHC
Battery-Powered Recorder .... BPR
Battery-Voltage Limit System .... BVLS
Batticaloa [Ceylon] [Airport symbol] (AD) .... BTC
Batticaloa [Sri Lanka] [ICAO location identifier] (ICLI) .... VCCB
Batting Average [Baseball] .... BA
Batting Practice [Baseball] .... BP
Battle .... B
Battle (AABC) .... BAT
Battle (WGA) .... BATT
Battle (ABBR) .... BTL
Battle Area Clearance (SAUS) .... BAC

Battle Area Control Unit [Military] .... BACU
Battle Area Surveillance and Integrated Communications System [Marine Corps] .... BASIC
Battle Area Surveillance and Integrated Communications System [Marine Corps] (IEEE) .... BASICS
Battle Area Surveillance and Integrated Communications System Processor and Computer [Marine Corps] .... BASICPAC
Battle Area Surveillance Intelligence Communications System (ACAE) .... BASICS
Battle Area Tactical Scenario (SAUS) .... BATS
Battle Area Tactical Simulation (SAUS) .... BATS
Battle Bridge Tier [Shipping] (ROG) .... BBTR
Battle Casualities (SAUS) .... BC
Battle Casualty (MAE) .... BC
Battle Casualty Replacement (SAUS) .... BCR
Battle Casualty Vietnam .... BCV
Battle Code (SAUS) .... BATCO
Battle Command Battle Laboratory [Army] .... BCBL
Battle Command Training Program [Army] .... BCTP
Battle Commander (SAUS) .... BC
Battle Commanders Training Facility (SAUO) .... BCTF
Battle Coordination Element [Army] (MCD) .... BCE
Battle Coordination Team (SAUO) .... BCT
Battle Correlator Display .... BCD
Battle Creek [Michigan] [Airport symbol] (OAG) .... BTL
Battle Creek College (SAUS) .... MiBaC
Battle Creek College, Battle Creek, MI [Library symbol] [Library of Congress] [Obsolete] (LCLS) .... MiBatC
Battle Creek, MI [AM radio station call letters] .... WBCK
Battle Creek, MI [FM radio station call letters] .... WBXX
Battle Creek, MI [AM radio station call letters] .... WELL
Battle Creek, MI [Television station call letters] .... WJUE
Battle Creek, MI [FM radio station call letters] .... WKFR
Battle Creek, MI [AM radio station call letters] .... WOLY
Battle Creek, MI [Television station call letters] .... WOTV
Battle Creek, MI [AM radio station call letters] (BROA) .... WRCC
Battle Creek, MI [AM radio station call letters] (RBYB) .... WWKN-AM
Battle Creek, MI [Television station call letters] (BROA) .... WZPX
Battle Creek Public School, Battle Creek, MI [Library symbol] [Library of Congress] (LCLS) .... MiBat
Battle Creek Times, Battle Creek, IA [Library symbol] [Library of Congress] (LCLS) .... IaBcT
Battle Cruiser [Navy] .... BC
Battle Cruiser [Navy symbol] .... CB
Battle Cruiser [Navy] CC
Battle Cruiser Flag [Navy] [British] .... BC
Battle Cruiser Fleet (SAUS) .... BCF
Battle Cruiser Flotilla (SAUO) .... BCF
Battle Cruiser Force [British military] (DMA) .... BCF
Battle Cruiser Squadron [Navy] .... BCS
Battle Cruiser Squadron (SAUO) .... BCS
Battle Damage and Assessment Review [Military] .... BDAR
Battle Damage Assessment .... BDA
Battle Damage Assessment and Reporting Team .... BDART
Battle Damage Assessment System (ACAE) .... BDAS
Battle Damage Assessment Team [Navy] (DOMA) .... BDAT
Battle Damage Information Script (SAA) .... BDIS
Battle Damage Repair [Army] (RDA) .... BDR
Battle Damage Repair Ship [Navy symbol] .... ARB
Battle Damage Umpire (SAA) .... BDU
Battle Director (SAUO) .... BD
Battle Doctrine (SAUS) .... BD
Battle Dress [Military] .... BD
Battle Dress Overgarment [Military] (INF) .... BDO
Battle Dress Uniform [Military] .... BDU
Battle Dressing Station [Military] (NVT) .... BDS
Battle Energy Corp. [Vancouver Stock Exchange symbol] .... BTE
Battle Fatigue (INF) .... BF
Battle Field Tactical Trainer .... BFTT
Battle Fleet (SAUO) .... BF
Battle Force .... BATFOR
Battle Force (ACAE) .... BF
Battle Force Combatant [Navy] .... BFC
Battle Force Inport Training [Navy] (DOMA) .... BFIT
Battle Force In-port Training (SAUS) .... BFIT
Battle Force Tactical Training (SAUS) .... BFTT
Battle Ground, IN [FM radio station call letters] (RBYB) .... WASK-FM
Battle Group .... BG
Battle Group Anti-Air Warfare Coordinator [No longer used] [Navy] (DOMA) .... BGAAWC
Battle Group Commander (MCD) .... BG/CDR
Battle Group Commanders Team Training (DOMA) .... BGCTT
Battle Group Exercise [Navy] (DOMA) .... BGE
Battle Group Interactive Gaming System (ACAE) .... BGIGS
Battle Group Landing Team .... BGLT
Battle Group Operational Readiness System (DOMA) .... BGORS
Battle Group Passive Horizon Extension System [Reconnaissance] .... BGPHES
Battle Group Passive Horizon Extension System - Surface Terminal [Reconnaissance] (DWSG) .... BGPHES-ST
Battle Group Tactical Training [Navy] (DOMA) .... BGTT
Battle Harbour, NF [ICAO location identifier] (ICLI) .... CWBF
Battle Honours Committee (SAUO) .... BHC
Battle Information Management Laboratory (SAUO) .... BIML
Battle Injury or Wound .... BIW
Battle Inoculation Test [Military] (WDAA) .... BIT

Battle Lake Public School, Battle Lake, MN [*Library symbol*] [*Library of Congress*] (LCLS) .... MnBatS
Battle Management [*Military*] (SDI) .... BM
Battle Management Algorithm (ACAE) .... BMA
Battle Management Command Control & Communications (SAUS) BMC3
Battle Management Information System (SAUS) .... BMIS
Battle Management Laboratory (ACAE) .... BML
Battle Management Node .... BMN
Battle Management Processing and Display (SAUS) .... BMPAD
Battle Management System (ACAE) .... BMS
Battle Management Test Bed (ACAE) .... BMTB
Battle Management Training Facility (SAUS) .... BMTF
Battle Management/Command, Control, Communications (MCD) BM/C3
Battle Management/Command, Control, Communications, and Intelligence [*Military*] .... BM/C³I
Battle Manning (DNAB) .... BM
Battle Mountain [*Nevada*] [*Airport symbol*] [*Obsolete*] (OAG) .... BAM
Battle Mountain [*Nevada*] [*Seismograph station code, US Geological Survey*] (SEIS) .... BMN
Battle Mountain Gold Co. [*Associated Press*] (SAG) .... BatlMt
Battle Mountain Gold Co. [*Toronto Stock Exchange symbol*] [*NYSE symbol*] .... BMG
Battle Mtn Gold $3.25 Cv Pfd [*NYSE symbol*] (TTSB) .... BMGPr
Battle of Atlantic [*World War II*] .... BA
Battle of Britain Memorial Flight (SAUS) .... BBMF
Battle of Britain Memorial Flight (WDAA) .... BOBMF
Battle Planning Simulation (ACAE) .... BPS
Battle Point Astronomical Association .... BPAA
Battle Position (AABC) .... BP
Battle Practice Target [*Obsolete*] [*Navy*] [*British*] .... BPT
Battle Readiness and Competition Instructions (NVT) .... BATREADCOM
Battle Readiness and Competition Instructions (NVT) .... BATREADCOMP
Battle Reconnaissance (MCD) .... BATRECON
Battle Reconnaissance (SAUS) .... B RCN
Battle Ship (SAUS) .... BS
Battle Short (ACAE) .... BS
Battle Short Relay .... BSR
Battle Simulation Center (MCD) .... BSC
Battle Simulation Officer (SAA) .... BSO
Battle Simulation Team (SAUO) .... BST
Battle Staff Coordinator (SAUO) .... BSC
Battle Staff Director (SAUO) .... BSD
Battle Staff Exercise [*Air Force*] (MUSM) .... BSX
Battle Staff Noncommissioned Officer Course [*Army*] (INF) .... BSNCOC
Battle Staff Operations Officer (ACAE) .... BSOO
Battle Staff Support Center [*Air Force*] .... BSSC
Battle Staff Team .... BST
Battle Staff Training Facility [*Marine Corps*] .... BSTF
Battle Star .... BS
Battle Surveillance Airship System (ACAE) .... BSAS
Battle Watch Captain (MCD) .... BWC
Battle Wound Injury (CINC) .... BWI
Battlecars (SAUS) .... BC
Battled (ABBR) .... BTLD
Battlefield (ABBR) .... BTLFLD
Battlefield Air Interdiction (MCD) .... BAI
Battlefield Airborne Illumination System (CINC) .... BAIS
Battlefield Area Evaluation (ACAE) .... BAE
Battlefield Area Interdiction (ACAE) .... BAI
Battlefield Area Reconnaissance System [*RADAR*] [*Army*] .... BARCS
Battlefield Area Surveillance System (MCD) .... BASS
Battlefield Artillery Target Engagement System (MCD) .... BATES
Battlefield Automated System Engineering Support [*Army*] .... BASES
Battlefield Automated Tactical Support System (MCD) .... BATSS
Battlefield Automation Appraisal (MCD) .... BAA
Battlefield Automation Interoperability System Engineering Management Plan [*Army*] .... BAISEMP
Battlefield Automation Management (MCD) .... BAM
Battlefield Automation Management Program (SAUO) .... BAMP
Battlefield Awareness and Data Dissemination [*Army*] .... BADD
Battlefield Circulation Control [*Military*] (MUSM) .... BCC
Battlefield Combat Identification [*Army*] (RDA) .... BCID
Battlefield Combat Identification System [*Army*] (RDA) .... BCIS
Battlefield Command Terminal (SAUS) .... BCT
Battlefield Command Trainer (SAUS) .... BCT
Battlefield Commanders' Aid [*Army*] .... BCA
Battlefield Communications Review .... BCR
Battlefield Computer System .... BCS
Battlefield Control Element (SAUS) .... BCE
Battlefield Damage Assessment and Repair [*Technical manual*] [*Army*] (RDA) .... BDAR
Battlefield Data System .... BDS
Battlefield Day (RDA) .... BFD
Battlefield Development Plan (RDA) .... BDP
Battlefield Distributed (or Distribution) Simulation-Development (SAUS) .... BDS-D
Battlefield Distributed Simulation - Developmental Program [*Army*] (RDA) .... BDS-D
Battlefield Distribution Simulation (SAUS) .... BDS
Battlefield Electromagnetic Environment Office [*Fort Huachuca, AZ*] [*United States Electronic Proving Ground*] (GRD) .... BEEO
Battlefield Electronic Communications System (DWSG) .... BECS
Battlefield Environment (MCD) .... BE
Battlefield Environment Directorate (SAUO) .... BED
Battlefield Environment LASER Designator [*MIRADCOM*] (MCD) .... BELD

Battlefield Environment LASER Designator/Weapon System Simulation [*MIRADCOM*] (RDA) .... BELDWSS
Battlefield Environmental Effects Software [*Army*] .... BEES
Battlefield Estimate .... BFE
Battlefield Exercise (DNAB) .... BFE
Battlefield Exploitation and Target Acquisition (MCD) .... BETA
Battlefield Exploitation and Target Acquisition System (ACAE) .... BETAS
Battlefield Functional Area [*Army*] .... BFA
Battlefield Functional Area Control System (SAUS) .... BFACS
Battlefield Functional Mission Area (SAUS) .... BFMA
Battlefield Functional System (MCD) .... BFS
Battlefield Functional System Concept (MCD) .... BFSC
Battlefield Guided Weapon (MCD) .... BGW
Battlefield Identification Friend or Foe (MCD) .... BIFF
Battlefield Identification Management System (SAUS) .... BIMS
Battlefield Identification System Study [*NATO*] (NATG) .... BISS
Battlefield Illumination (AABC) .... BI
Battlefield Illumination Airborne System (AFM) .... BIAS
Battlefield Illumination Integrated Night Vision Devices (MCD) .... BIINVD
Battlefield Illumination L System (MCD) .... BTL ILUM-L
Battlefield Illumination System .... BIS
Battlefield Information and Control Center (SAUO) .... BICC
Battlefield Information Center [*Army*] .... BIC
Battlefield Information Collection and Exploitation System .... BICES
Battlefield Information Communications Center (MCD) .... BICC
Battlefield Information Control Center [*Army*] (AABC) .... BICC
Battlefield Information Control System (SAUS) .... BICS
Battlefield Information Distribution System (MCD) .... BIDS
Battlefield Information System [*Army*] (RDA) .... BIS
Battlefield Information Targeting System (ACAE) .... BITS
Battlefield Information Transmission System [*Army*] .... BITS
Battlefield Inoculation Remote Initiation System (SAUS) .... BIRIS
Battlefield Integrated Information Center (MCD) .... BIIC
Battlefield Integration (SAUS) .... BI
Battlefield Integration Coordination Center .... BICC
Battlefield Integration Management System [*Army*] .... BIMS
Battlefield Intelligence Coordinator [*Army*] (DOMA) .... BIC
Battlefield Interdiction (MCD) .... BFI
Battlefield Interdiction (MCD) .... BI
Battlefield Laser Acquisition Sensor Test (SAUS) .... BLAST
Battlefield Laser Implication Program (ACAE) .... BLIP
Battlefield Location and Information System [*Army*] (RDA) .... BLAIS
Battlefield Management System [*Military*] (INF) .... BMS
Battlefield Meteorological System (SAUS) .... BMETS
Battlefield Mission Management System (SAUS) .... BMMS
Battlefield Mobility / Target Acquistion [*Military*] .... BM/TA
Battlefield Nuclear Warfare [*Army*] .... BNW
Battlefield Operating System [*Military*] (RDA) .... BOS
Battlefield Operations Laser Designator (SAUS) .... BOLD
Battlefield Operations Systems (SAUS) .... BOS
Battlefield Optical Munition (SAUS) .... BOM
Battlefield Optimized Artillery Rocket (SAUS) .... BOAR
Battlefield Period (MCD) .... BFP
Battlefield Plan Development (MCD) .... BPD
Battlefield Recovery & Evacuation (SAUS) .... BRE
Battlefield Related Electronic Warfare Simulator (MCD) .... BREWS
Battlefield Related Evaluation of Countermeasure Hardware [*Model*] (MCD) .... BREACH
Battlefield Sensor Simulator (SAUS) .... BSS
Battlefield Situation Display [*DoD*] .... BSD
Battlefield Surveillance (SAUS) .... BFS
Battlefield Surveillance (MCD) .... BS
Battlefield Surveillance Airship System (PDAA) .... BSAS
Battlefield Surveillance and Target Acquisition RADAR (MCD) .... BSTAR
Battlefield Surveillance Devices (MCD) .... BSD
Battlefield Surveillance [*RADAR*] Electronics (MCD) .... BASE
Battlefield Surveillance RADAR (MCD) .... BSR
Battlefield Surveillance/Moving Target Acquisition Plan (MCD) .... BS/MTAR
Battlefield System Architecture (MCD) .... BSA
Battlefield System Integration Center (MCD) .... BSICEN
Battlefield System International (SAUS) .... BSI
Battlefield Systems Integration (MCD) .... BSI
Battlefield Systems Project Management .... BSPM
Battlefield Visualization Graphics (AABC) .... BVG
Battlefield Weapons System .... BWS
Battlefield Weapons System Laboratory .... BWSL
Battlefield Weather Observation & Forecast System (SAUS) .... BWOFS
Battleford Union Hospital Memorial Library, North Battleford, Saskatchewan (SAUS) .... SNBH
Battleford Union Hospital Memorial Library, North Battleford, Saskatchewan [*Library symbol*] [*National Library of Canada*] (BIB) .... SNBH
Battlefords Early Childhood Intervention Home-Based Program Inc. (AC) .... BECIP
Battlegroup Passive Horizon System (ACAE) .... BPHS
Battlement (WDAA) .... BATT
Battlement (ABBR) .... BTLMT
Battle's Digest [*North Carolina*] [*A publication*] (DLA) .... Bat Dig
Battles Nomenclature Committee (SAUO) .... BNC
Battle's Revised Statutes of North Carolina [*1873*] [*A publication*] (DLA) .... Bat Rev St
Battle's Revised Statutes of North Carolina [*1873*] [*A publication*] (DLA) .... Bat Stat
Battle's Revised Statutes of North Carolina [*1873*] [*A publication*] (DLA) .... Battle's Revisal
Battle's Sign [*Medicine*] (MELL) .... BS

Battleship (MUGU) .... BAT
Battleship .... BATSHIP
Battleship [*Navy symbol*] .... BB
Battleship .... BS
Battleship (ABBR) .... BTLSP
Battleship Aircraft Carrier (SAUS) .... BAC
Battleship Battle Group [*Usually BBG*] [*Navy*] (DOMA) .... BBBG
Battleship Battle Group [*Sometimes the more awkward BBBG*] [*Navy*] (DOMA) .... BBG
Battleship Division .... BATDIV
Battleship Firing (SAA) .... BF
Battleship Flag [*Navy*] [*British*] .... BS
Battleship Observation Squadron [*Navy symbol*] .... VO
Battleship Squadron .... BATRON
Battleship Squadron .... BS
Battleship Surface Action Group (SAUO) .... BBSAG
Battleships and Cruisers, Atlantic Fleet .... BATCRULANT
Battleships and Cruisers, Pacific Fleet .... BATCRUPAC
Battleships, Atlantic Fleet .... BATLANT
Battleships, Atlantic Fleet .... BATSHIPSLANT
Battleships, Battle Force, Pacific Fleet .... BATSHIPSBATFORPAC
Battleships, Pacific Fleet .... BATPAC
Battleships, Pacific Fleet .... BATSHIPSPAC
Battlesight Zero (MCD) .... BSZ
Battle-Unit Short-Range Antitank Weapon System (NATG) .... BUSRAT
Battling (ABBR) .... BTLG
Batts' Annotated Revised Civil Statutes [*Texas*] [*A publication*] (DLA) .... Batts' Ann St
Batts' Annotated Revised Civil Statutes [*Texas*] [*A publication*] (DLA) .... Batts' Rev St
Batty's Irish King's Bench Reports [*A publication*] (DLA) .... Batt
Batty's Irish King's Bench Reports [*A publication*] (DLA) .... Batty (Ir)
Batu Besar [*Indonesia*] [*Airport symbol*] (OAG) .... BTH
Batu Licin [*Indonesia*] [*ICAO location identifier*] (ICLI) .... WRBC
Batu Pahat [*Malaysia*] [*ICAO location identifier*] (ICLI) .... WMAB
Batu Putih/Talisayam [*Indonesia*] [*ICAO location identifier*] (ICLI) .... WRLD
Batumi [*Former USSR*] [*Airport symbol*] (OAG) .... BUS
Bau [*Zaire*] [*ICAO location identifier*] (ICLI) .... FZFF
Bau Bau [*Indonesia*] [*Airport symbol*] (OAG) .... BUW
Bau Bau/Betoambari [*Indonesia*] [*ICAO location identifier*] (ICLI) .... WAAB
Baucau [*East Timor*] [*ICAO location identifier*] (ICLI) .... WPEC
Baud [*Unit of data transmission speed*] (MCD) .... B
Baud [*Unit of data transmission speed*] (CET) .... Bd
Baud (ABAC) .... bd
Baud Programming System [*Computer science*] (IAA) .... BPS
Baud Rate [*Data transmission speed*] [*Computer science*] .... BDRT
Baud Rate Generator [*Computer science*] .... BRG
Baudeloeque's Diameter [*External conjugate diameter of pelvis*] [*Obstetrics*] (DAVI) .... DB
Baudette [*Minnesota*] [*ICAO location identifier*] (ICLI) .... KBDE
Baudette, MN [*Location identifier*] [*FAA*] (FAAL) .... BDE
Baudette Public Library, Baudette, MN [*Library symbol*] [*Library of Congress*] (LCLS) .... MnBau
Baudot (IAA) .... BAUD
Baudot Code .... BAUD
Baudot Code (SAUS) .... BAUD Code
Baudot Code (IAA) .... BD
Baudot-Verdan Differential Analyzer [*Electronics*] (IAA) .... BV
baud-per-second (SAUS) .... bps
Bauer Hospital-Saint Mary Medical Center, Long Beach, CA [*Library symbol*] [*Library of Congress*] (LCLS) .... CLobB
Bauer Publishing & Printing Ltd., Rahway, NJ [*Library symbol*] [*Library of Congress*] (LCLS) .... NjRahB
Bauforschungsprojekte [*Building Research Projects*] [*Fraunhofer Society*] [*Information service or system*] (IID) .... BAUFO
Baughan, E. F., Baltimore MD [*STAC*] .... BEF
Baulk (WDAA) .... B
Baume [*Scale*] [*Measurement*] (GPO) .... B
Baume .... BA
Baume [*Hydrometer scale or specific gravity*] [*Organic chemistry*] (DAVI) .... Be
Baume & Mercier .... BM
Baumholder [*Germany*] [*ICAO location identifier*] (ICLI) .... EDEK
Bauobjektdokumentation [*Buildings Documentation*] [*Fraunhofer Society*] [*Germany*] [*Information service or system*] (IID) .... BODO
Baures [*Bolivia*] [*ICAO location identifier*] (ICLI) .... SLBU
Bauru [*Brazil*] [*Airport symbol*] (OAG) .... BAU
Bauru [*Brazil*] [*ICAO location identifier*] (ICLI) .... SBBU
Bausch & Lomb, Inc. (EFIS) .... B&L
Bausch & Lomb, Inc. [*Associated Press*] (SAG) .... BauschL
Bausch & Lomb, Inc. (EFIS) .... BL
Bausch & Lomb, Inc. [*NYSE symbol*] (SAG) .... BOL
Bausch & Lomb, Inc., Library, Rochester, NY [*OCLC symbol*] (OCLC) .... VQB
Bausch & Lomb, Inc., Rochester, NY [*Library symbol*] [*Library of Congress*] (LCLS) .... NRBL
Bausch & Lomb, Inc., SOFLENS Division, Technical Information Center, Rochester, NY [*Library symbol*] [*Library of Congress*] (LCLS) .... NRBL-S
Bausch & Lomb Optical Co. (SAUO) .... B&L
Bauxite Alumina Study Company Limited (SAUO) .... BASCOL
Bauxite & Northern Railway Co. [*Later, BXN*] [*AAR code*] .... BN
Bauxite & Northern Railway Co. [*AAR code*] .... BXN
Bavanat [*Iran*] [*ICAO location identifier*] (ICLI) .... OISB
Bavaria (SAUS) .... Bav
Bavaria [*State in West Germany*] (ROG) .... BAV
Bavarian (SAUS) .... Bav
Bavarian Amateur Radio Translator on Balloon (SAUS) .... Bartob
Bavarian Border Police [*Germany*] .... BBP
Bavarian Dance Group of North America (EA) .... BDGNA
Bavarian Lion Industries Ltd. [*Vancouver Stock Exchange symbol*] .... BAV
Bavarian Truck Company (SAUO) .... BTC
Bavli [*or Babylonian Talmud*] (BJA) .... b
Baw Faw Mountain [*Washington*] [*Seismograph station code, US Geological Survey*] (SEIS) .... BFW
Bawdsey [*British*] [*ICAO location identifier*] (ICLI) .... EGVB
Bawlf Municipal Library, Alberta [*Library symbol*] [*National Library of Canada*] (NLC) .... ABAM
Baxley, GA [*FM radio station call letters*] .... WBYZ
Baxley, GA [*Television station call letters*] (BROA) .... WGSA
Baxley, GA [*Television station call letters*] .... WUBI
Baxley, GA [*AM radio station call letters*] .... WUFE
Baxter Elementary School, Baxter, MN [*Library symbol*] [*Library of Congress*] (LCLS) .... MnBaxE
Baxter International [*NYSE symbol*] (SPSG) .... BAX
Baxter International, Inc. [*Associated Press*] (SAG) .... Baxter
Baxter Laboratories, Inc. [*of Baxter Travenol Laboratories, Inc.*] [*Research code symbol*] .... BAX
Baxter, MN [*AM radio station call letters*] .... WWWI
Baxter New Era, Baxter, IA [*Library symbol*] [*Library of Congress*] (LCLS) .... IaBaxNE
Baxter on Judicature Acts and Rules [*A publication*] (DLA) .... Bax Jud Acts
Baxter Springs, KS [*FM radio station call letters*] .... KMOQ
Baxter Technologies Corp. [*Toronto Stock Exchange symbol*] .... BTC
Baxter, TN [*FM radio station call letters*] .... WBXE
Baxter Women's Club, Baxter, IA [*Library symbol*] [*Library of Congress*] (LCLS) .... IaBaxWC
Baxter's Reports [*60-68 Tennessee*] [*A publication*] (DLA) .... Bax
Baxter's Reports [*60-68 Tennessee*] [*A publication*] (DLA) .... Baxt
Baxter's Reports [*60-68 Tennessee*] [*A publication*] (DLA) .... Baxter
Baxter's Reports [*60-68 Tennessee*] [*A publication*] (DLA) .... Baxt (Tenn)
Bay [*Maps and charts*] .... B
Bay [*Thoroughbred racing*] .... B
Bay (ADA) .... BY
Bay Air Aviation [*New Zealand*] [*ICAO designator*] (FAAC) .... BAY
Bay Air Cargo, SA [*Brazil*] [*FAA designator*] (FAAC) .... BAO
Bay Ann Resources, Inc. [*Vancouver Stock Exchange symbol*] .... BYA
Bay Apartment Communities [*Associated Press*] (SAG) .... BayApt
Bay Apartment Communities [*NYSE symbol*] (SAG) .... BYA
Bay Area Air Pollution Control District (SAUS) .... BAAPCD
Bay Area Air Quality Management District (SAUO) .... BAAQMD
Bay Area Army Terminal Center, San Francisco (SAUO) .... BAATC
Bay Area Automated Mapping Association (GEOI) .... BAAMA
Bay Area Cryonics Society [*Later, American Cryonics Society*] (EA) .... BACS
Bay Area Digital GeoResource (GEOI) .... BADGER
Bay Area Functional Performance Evaluation [*Personality research*] [*Psychology*] .... BAFPE
Bay Area Gigabit Network [*Computer science*] (TNIG) .... BAGNet
Bay Area GNU Enthusiasts League (SAUO) .... BAGEL
Bay Area Library and Information System [*Library network*] .... BALIS
Bay Area Library and Information System [*Library network*] .... EBC
Bay Area Library and Information System, Hayward, CA [*OCLC symbol*] (OCLC) .... BAS
Bay Area Library and Information System, Hayward, CA [*Library symbol*] [*Library of Congress*] (LCLS) .... CHB
Bay Area Multimedia Technology Alliance .... BAMTA
Bay Area Physicians for Human Rights (EA) .... BAPHR
Bay Area Pollution Control District (SAUS) .... BAAPCD
Bay Area Quality Management District (SAUO) .... BAAQMD
Bay Area Rapid Transit [*San Francisco area, California*] .... BART
Bay Area Rapid Transit District (SAUO) .... BARTD
Bay Area Rapid Transit District (SAUS) .... BAR TD
Bay Area Rapid Transit System (SAUS) .... BART System
Bay Area Reference Center [*San Francisco Public Library*] [*San Francisco, CA*] [*Library network*] .... BARC
Bay Area Regional Database (SAUS) .... BARD
Bay Area Regional Research Network [*Acquired from Stanford University by Bolt Beranek and Newman*] [*Internet service*] [*Also, an information service or system*] .... BARRnet
Bay Area Religious Channel [*Cable TV programming service*] .... BARC
Bay Area Research Collective (SAUO) .... BARC
Bay Area Research Wireless Access Network (VERA) .... BARWAN
Bay Area Seismic Imaging Experiment [*Geology*] .... BASIX
Bay Area Shared Information Consortium (SAUS) .... BASIC
Bay Area Spatial Information System [*Geogroup Corp.*] [*Information service or system*] (IID) .... BASIS
Bay Area Transportation Study Commission (SAUO) .... BATSC
Bay Cabinet Unit .... BCU
Bay City Junior College [*Michigan*] .... BCJC
Bay City, MI [*FM radio station call letters*] .... WCHW
Bay City, MI [*FM radio station call letters*] .... WHNN
Bay City, MI [*FM radio station call letters*] .... WIOG
Bay City, MI [*AM radio station call letters*] .... WMAX
Bay City, MI [*Television station call letters*] .... WNEM
Bay City, MI [*FM radio station call letters*] .... WTRK
Bay City, MI [*FM radio station call letters*] .... WUCX
Bay City, MI [*AM radio station call letters*] .... WXOX
Bay City Public Library, Bay City, MI [*Library symbol*] [*Library of Congress*] (LCLS) .... MiBay
Bay City, TX [*Location identifier*] [*FAA*] (FAAL) .... BYY
Bay City, TX [*AM radio station call letters*] (RBYB) .... KFCC
Bay City, TX [*FM radio station call letters*] .... KMKS
Bay City, TX [*FM radio station call letters*] .... KXGJ

Bay City-Midland-Saginaw [*Michigan*] [*Airport symbol*] (AD) .... MBS
Bay Conservation and Development Commission (GEOI) .... BCDC
Bay County Library System, Auburn Branch Library, Auburn, MI [*Library symbol*] [*Library of Congress*] (LCLS) .... MiBayS-A
Bay County Library System, Bay City, MI [*Library symbol*] [*Library of Congress*] (LCLS) .... MiBayS
Bay County Library System, Broadway Branch Library, Bay City, MI [*Library symbol*] [*Library of Congress*] (LCLS) .... MiBayS-B
Bay County Library System, Linwood Branch Library, Linwood, MI [*Library symbol*] [*Library of Congress*] (LCLS) .... MiBayS-L
Bay County Library System, Pinconning Branch Library, Pinconning, MI [*Library symbol*] [*Library of Congress*] (LCLS) .... MiBayS-P
Bay County Library System, Sage Branch Library (SAUS) .... MiBay-S
Bay County Library System, Sage Branch Library, Bay City, MI [*Library symbol*] [*Library of Congress*] (LCLS) .... MiBayS-S
Bay County Public Library, Panama City, FL [*Library symbol*] [*Library of Congress*] (LCLS) .... FPc
Bay de Noc Community College (SAUO) .... BNCC
Bay De Noc Community College, Escanaba, MI [*Library symbol*] [*Library of Congress*] (LCLS) .... MiEscB
Bay Gelding [*Horse*] .... BG
Bay Horse (BARN) .... b h
Bay Meadows Operating Co. [*Associated Press*] (SAG) .... BayMea
Bay Meadows Operating Co. [*AMEX symbol*] (SPSG) .... CJ
Bay Meadows Oper(Unit) [*AMEX symbol*] (TTSB) .... CJ
Bay Medical Center, Bay City, MI [*Library symbol*] [*Library of Congress*] (LCLS) .... MiBayM
Bay Microfilm, Incorporated, Palo Alto, CA [*Library symbol*] [*Library of Congress*] (LCLS) .... BMI
Bay Mills Ltd. [*Toronto Stock Exchange symbol*] .... BAY
Bay Minette, AL [*FM radio station call letters*] .... WAVH
Bay Minette, AL [*AM radio station call letters*] .... WBCA
Bay Minette, AL [*FM radio station call letters*] .... WNSP
Bay Networks, Inc. [*NYSE symbol*] (SAG) .... BAY
Bay Networks, Inc. [*Associated Press*] (SAG) .... BayNtwk
Bay Networks, Inc. [*NASDAQ symbol*] (SAG) .... BNET
Bay of Bengal (SAUS) .... BoB
Bay of Biscay (SAUS) .... B Bisc
Bay of Biscay Subarea [*NATO*] .... BISCLANT
Bay of Fundy (SAUS) .... Fundy
Bay of Islands Complex [*Newfoundland*] [*Geology*] .... BOI
Bay of Pigs Veterans Association (EA) .... BPVA
Bay Path Junior College [*Longmeadow, MA*] .... BPJC
Bay Resources [*Vancouver Stock Exchange symbol*] .... BAU
Bay Ridge Bancorp [*Associated Press*] (SAG) .... BayRidge
Bay Ridge Bancorp [*NASDAQ symbol*] (SAG) .... BRBC
Bay Ridge High School (SAUO) .... BRHS
Bay Roberts Public Library, Bay Roberts, NF, Canada [*Library symbol*] [*Library of Congress*] (LCLS) .... CaNfBR
Bay Roberts Public Library, Newfoundland [*Library symbol*] [*National Library of Canada*] (NLC) .... NFBR
Bay Shore, NY [*FM radio station call letters*] .... WBZO
Bay Shore Senior High School, Bay Shore, NY [*Library symbol*] [*Library of Congress*] (LCLS) .... NBysSH
Bay Shore-Brightwaters Public Library, Brightwaters, NY [*Library symbol*] [*Library of Congress*] (LCLS) .... NBri
Bay Springs, MS [*AM radio station call letters*] .... WIZK
Bay Springs, MS [*FM radio station call letters*] .... WIZK-FM
Bay Springs, MS [*FM radio station call letters*] (BROA) .... WKZW-FM
Bay St. George Community College [*UTLAS symbol*] .... BSG
Bay St. George Community College, Stephenville, Newfoundland [*Library symbol*] [*National Library of Canada*] (NLC) .... NFSBS
Bay St. Louis, MS [*AM radio station call letters*] .... WBSL
Bay State Bancorp [*AMEX symbol*] (SG) .... BYS
Bay State Gas [*NYSE symbol*] (SAG) .... BGC
Bay State Gas Co. [*Associated Press*] (SAG) .... BaySGs
Bay State Teachers College (SAUO) .... BSTC
Bay Valley Conference (PSS) .... BVC
Bay View Capital [*NYSE symbol*] (SG) .... BVC
Bay View Capital [*NASDAQ symbol*] (TTSB) .... BVFS
Bay View Capital Corp. [*Associated Press*] (SAG) .... BayVw
Bay View Capital Corp. [*NASDAQ symbol*] (NQ) .... BVFS
Bay View Elementary School, Duluth, MN [*Library symbol*] [*Library of Congress*] (LCLS) .... MnDuBVE
Bay Window Villa .... BV
Bayamo [*Cuba*] [*Airport symbol*] (OAG) .... BYM
Bayamo [*Cuba*] [*ICAO location identifier*] (ICLI) .... MUBY
Bayamon Central University , Bayamon, Puerto Rico (SAUS) .... PrBayC
Bayamon Central University, Bayamon, PR [*OCLC symbol*] (OCLC) .... BCU
Bayamon Central University (Universidad Central de Bayamon), Bayamon, Puerto Rico [*Library symbol*] [*Library of Congress*] (LCLS) .... PrBayC
Bayamon, PR [*FM radio station call letters*] (RBYB) .... WCOM
Bayamon, PR [*Television station call letters*] .... WDWL
Bayamon, PR [*AM radio station call letters*] .... WLUZ
Bayamon, PR [*AM radio station call letters*] .... WRSJ
Bayamon, PR [*FM radio station call letters*] .... WXYX
Bayandai [*Former USSR*] [*Seismograph station code, US Geological Survey*] [*Closed*] (SEIS) .... BAY
Bayard News, Bayard, IA [*Library symbol*] [*Library of Congress*] (LCLS) .... IaBayN
Bayard, NM [*AM radio station call letters*] .... KNFT
Bayard, NM [*FM radio station call letters*] .... KNFT-FM
Bayard on Evidence [*A publication*] (DLA) .... Bay Ev
Bayard on the Constitution of the United States [*A publication*] (DLA) .... Bay Cons
Bayard Public Library, Bayard, IA [*Library symbol*] [*Library of Congress*] (LCLS) .... IaBay
Bayard Taylor Memorial Library, Kennett Square, PA [*Library symbol*] [*Library of Congress*] (LCLS) .... PKs
Bayard-Alpert gauge (SAUS) .... BA-gauge
Bay-Area Random Access Information Network [*Defunct*] (TSSD) .... BRAIN
Baybanks, Inc. [*Associated Press*] (SAG) .... BayBks
BayBanks, Inc. [*NASDAQ symbol*] (NQ) .... BBNK
Bayboro, NC [*FM radio station call letters*] (BROA) .... WBHU-FM
Bayboro, NC [*FM radio station call letters*] .... WKZF
Baycorp Holdings [*AMEX symbol*] (SG) .... MWH
Bayer Foreign Investments Ltd. (SAUO) .... Bayforin
Bayerische Flugzeug Werke [*Bavarian Airplane Works*] [*German*] .... BFW
Bayerische Koenigpartei [*Bavarian Royalist Party*] [*Pre-World War II*] .... BKP
Bayerische Motoren Werke [*Bavarian Motor Works*] [*German automobile manufacturer; initialism used as name of its cars and motorcycles*] .... BMW
Bayerische Motoren Werke [*Bavarian Motor Works*] **North America** .... BMWNA
Bayerische Rundfunk [*Radio network*] [*West Germany*] .... BR
Bayerische Staatspartei [*Bavarian State Party*] [*Germany*] (PPW) .... BSP
Bayerische Vereinsbank [*Union Bank of Bavaria*] [*Munich, West Germany*] .... BV
Bayerische Volkspartei [*Bavarian People's Party*] [*Germany*] [*Political party*] (PPE) .... BVP
Bayerisches Landwirtschaftliches Informationssystem [*Bavarian Agricultural Information System*] [*Databank*] [*Germany*] (IID) .... BALIS
Bayernpartei [*Bavarian Party*] [*Germany*] [*Political party*] (PPE) .... BP
Bayes Empirical-Distribution Function (SAUS) .... BEF
Bayes Fixed Sample-Size Procedure [*Statistics*] .... BFP
Bayes Information Criterion .... BIC
Bayes Operating Characteristic .... BOC
Bayes Sequential Procedure [*Statistics*] .... BSP
Bayesian Analysis Modified by Inspection [*Computer science*] .... BAMBI
Bayesian Decision-Support System (SAUS) .... BDSS
Bayesian Information Criteria (IDAI) .... BIC
Bayesian Network [*Graphical Model*] (IDAI) .... BN
Bayesian Network Interchange Format (IDAI) .... BNIF
Bayesian Reliability Demonstration Test [*Computer science*] .... BRDT
Bayesian Zero-Failure [*Computer science*] (MCD) .... BAZE
Bayfield Laboratory, Ocean Science and Surveys, Fisheries and Oceans Canada [*Laboratoire Bayfield, Science et Leves Oceaniques, Peches et Oceans Canada*] **Burlington, Ontario** [*Library symbol*] [*National Library of Canada*] (NLC) .... OBUFBL
Bayfield Public Library, Bayfield, CO [*Library symbol*] [*Library of Congress*] (LCLS) .... CoBay
Baykit [*Former USSR*] [*ICAO location identifier*] (ICLI) .... UNKW
Bayley Infant Neurodevelopmental Screener [*Test*] (TMMY) .... BINS
Bayley on Bills [*A publication*] (DLA) .... Bayl B
Bayley on Bills [*A publication*] (DLA) .... BB
Bayley on Bills and Notes [*A publication*] (DLA) .... Bay Bills
Bayley on Fines and Recoveries [*A publication*] (DLA) .... Bayl F & R
Bayley Scales of Infant Development .... BSID
Bayley's Commentaries on the Laws of England [*A publication*] (DLA) .... Bayl Ch Pr
Bayley's Questions and Answers for Students [*A publication*] (DLA) .... Bayl Q & A
Baylies' Digested Index of English and American Reports [*A publication*] (DLA) .... Bay Dig Ind
Baylies on Domestic Servants [*A publication*] (DLA) .... Bay Dom Serv
Baylis Elementary School, Syosset, NY [*Library symbol*] [*Library of Congress*] (LCLS) .... NSyoBaE
Baylis Public Library, Sault Ste. Marie, MI [*Library symbol*] [*Library of Congress*] (LCLS) .... MiSsB
Baylles on Sureties and Guarantors [*A publication*] (DLA) .... Baylles Sur
Baylor College of Dentistry, Dallas, TX [*OCLC symbol*] (OCLC) .... IBD
Baylor College of Medicine (HGEN) .... BCM
Baylor Computing Center [*Baylor College of Medicine*] [*Research center*] (RCD) .... BCC
Baylor Rapid Autologous Transfusion [*System*] [*Medicine*] (DMAA) .... BRAT
Baylor University (GAGS) .... Baylor U
Baylor University (SAUO) .... BaylUniv
Baylor University (SAUO) .... BU
Baylor University (SAUO) .... BUniv
Baylor University, Armstrong Browning Library, Waco, TX [*Library symbol*] [*Library of Congress*] (LCLS) .... TxWB-B
Baylor University in Dallas, Dallas, TX [*Library symbol*] [*Library of Congress*] (LCLS) .... TxDaBU
Baylor University, Law School Library, Waco (SAUS) .... TxWBL
Baylor University, Law School Library, Waco, TX [*Library symbol*] [*Library of Congress*] (LCLS) .... TxWB-L
Baylor University, Museum Collection, Waco (SAUS) .... TxWBMus
Baylor University, Museum Collection, Waco, TX [*Library symbol*] [*Library of Congress*] (LCLS) .... TxWB-Mus
Baylor University School of Nursing, Dallas, TX [*Library symbol*] [*Library of Congress*] (LCLS) .... TxWB-N
Baylor University, Waco, TX [*OCLC symbol*] (OCLC) .... IYU
Baylor University, Waco, TX [*Library symbol*] [*Library of Congress*] (LCLS) .... TxWB
Bayly Moore. English Common Pleas Reports [*A publication*] (DLA) .... B Moore
Bayonet (MSA) .... BAY
Bayonet (SAUS) .... Bay
Bayonet Automobile Cap (SAUS) .... BA Cap
Bayonet Base [*Lens mount*] (NTCM) .... BB
Bayonet Base Socket (SAUS) .... BB Socket
Bayonet Candelabra .... BAYC
Bayonet Candelabra Double Contact .... BAYCANDDC
Bayonet Candelabra Single Contact .... BAYCANDSC
Bayonet Candelabra Single Contact (SAUS) .... BAY CAND SC

Bayonet Cap ..... BC
Bayonet Catch (SAUS) ..... BC
Bayonet Coaxial Connector [*Telecommunications*] (ECII) ..... BNC
Bayonet Fiber Optic Connector (SAUS) ..... BFOC
Bayonet Fighting ..... BF
Bayonet Naval Connector [*Electronics*] (NTCM) ..... BNC
Bayonet Neil Councilman [*Telecommunications*] (ACRL) ..... BNC
Bayonet Nipple Connector (SAUS) ..... BNC
Bayonet Nut Connection (SAUS) ..... BNC
Bayonet Nut Connector Socket (SAUS) ..... BNC SKT
Bayonet Nut Connector Straight Adapter (SAUS) ..... BNC STR ADAPT
Bayonet Nut Connector Tee Adapter (SAUS) ..... BNC T ADAPT
Bayonet Nut Coupling [*Telecommunications*] (EECA) ..... BNC
Bayonet Pin (SAUS) ..... BP
Bayonet Skirted ..... BAYSK
Bayonet Workers' Trade Society [*A union*] [*British*] ..... BWTS
Bayonette Connector, for Coaxial Cable [*Electronics*] (NITA) ..... BNC
Bayonne Free Public Library, Bayonne, NJ [*Library symbol*] [*Library of Congress*] (LCLS) ..... NjBa
Bayoo [*Commonly used*] (OPSA) ..... BAYOO
Bayou [*Maps and charts*] ..... B
Bayou ..... BYU
Bayou Preservation Society (SAUO) ..... BPS
Bayou Steel Corp. of La Place [*Associated Press*] (SAG) ..... Bayou
Bayou Steel Corp. of La Place [*AMEX symbol*] (SPSG) ..... BYX
Bayou Steel'A' [*AMEX symbol*] (TTSB) ..... BYX
Bayou Vista, LA [*AM radio station call letters*] ..... KDLP
Bayou Vista, LA [*FM radio station call letters*] ..... KQKI
Bayport Restaurant Group [*NASDAQ symbol*] (TTSB) ..... PORT
Bayport Restaurant Group, Inc. [*Associated Press*] (SAG) ..... Bayport
Bayport Restaurant Group, Inc. [*NASDAQ symbol*] (SAG) ..... PORT
Bayport-Blue Point Public Library, Blue Point, NY [*Library symbol*] [*Library of Congress*] (LCLS) ..... NBp
Bayport-Blue Point Public Library, Blue Point, NY [*Library symbol*] [*Library of Congress*] (LCLS) ..... NBpP
Bayrak Radio & TV Corp. [*Turkish Cyprus*] (EY) ..... BRTK
Bayrak Radyo-Televisyon [*Bayrak Radio-Television*] ..... BRT
Bayram-Ali [*Former USSR*] [*Seismograph station code, US Geological Survey*] [*Closed*] (SEIS) ..... BAT
Bayreuth [*Germany*] [*Airport symbol*] (OAG) ..... BYU
Bayreuth [*Germany*] [*ICAO location identifier*] (ICLI) ..... EDEL
Bayreuth [*Germany*] [*ICAO location identifier*] (ICLI) ..... EDQD
Bayridge Development [*Vancouver Stock Exchange symbol*] ..... BYD
Bayrock Utility Securities, Inc. (SAUO) ..... BAY
Bay's Reports [*1-3, 5-8 Missouri*] [*A publication*] (DLA) ..... Bay
Bay's South Carolina Reports [*1783-1804*] [*A publication*] (DLA) ..... Bay
Bayshore Independent, Matawan, NJ [*Library symbol*] [*Library of Congress*] (LCLS) ..... NjMatB
Bayside, CA [*FM radio station call letters*] ..... KZPN
Bayside Electronics, Inc. (SAUO) ..... BEI
Bayside, VA [*AM radio station call letters*] (BROA) ..... WBVA
Bayside Yacht Club (SAUO) ..... BYC
Baytoun, TX [*Television station call letters*] ..... KVVV
Baytown, TX [*Location identifier*] [*FAA*] (FAAL) ..... HPY
Baytown, TX [*AM radio station call letters*] ..... KWWJ
Bayu Indonesia Air PT [*ICAO designator*] (FAAC) ..... BYU
Bayuk Cigars, Inc. (SAUO) ..... BYK
Bayview Avenue Elementary School, Freeport, NY [*Library symbol*] [*Library of Congress*] (LCLS) ..... NFreeBE
Bayview Community Hospital, Mastic Beach, NY [*Library symbol*] [*Library of Congress*] (LCLS) ..... NMbCH
Bayville Elementary School, Bayville, NY [*Library symbol*] [*Library of Congress*] (LCLS) ..... NBayvE
Bayville Free Library (SAUS) ..... NBayr
Bayville Free Library, Bayville, NY [*Library symbol*] [*Library of Congress*] (LCLS) ..... NBayv
Bayville Intermediate School, Bayville, NY [*Library symbol*] [*Library of Congress*] (LCLS) ..... NBayvI
Bayville Intermediate School, Locust Valley, NY [*Library symbol*] [*Library of Congress*] (LCLS) ..... NLvBI
Bayville Primary School, Bayville, NY [*Library symbol*] [*Library of Congress*] (LCLS) ..... NBayvP
Baywest Capital [*Vancouver Stock Exchange symbol*] ..... BAW
Baz Resources Ltd. [*Vancouver Stock Exchange symbol*] ..... BZR
Bazaar ..... BZR
Bazianus [*Deceased, 1197*] [*Authority cited in pre-1607 legal work*] (DSA) ..... B
Bazianus [*Deceased, 1197*] [*Authority cited in pre-1607 legal work*] (DSA) ..... Bas
Bazianus [*Deceased, 1197*] [*Authority cited in pre-1607 legal work*] (DSA) ..... Baz
Bazianus [*Deceased, 1197*] [*Authority cited in pre-1607 legal work*] (DSA) ..... Baza
Bazianus [*Deceased, 1197*] [*Authority cited in pre-1607 legal work*] (DSA) ..... Bazan
Bazianus de Baldone de Vaude [*Flourished, 13th century*] [*Authority cited in pre-1607 legal work*] (DSA) ..... Baz
Bazil [*Red sheep*] [*Bookbinding*] (ROG) ..... BAZ
Bazillenemulsion [*Bacillary emulsion*] [*Immunology*] ..... BE
Bazman [*Iran*] [*ICAO location identifier*] (ICLI) ..... OIZN
BB&T Corp. [*NYSE symbol*] (SG) ..... BBT
BBC Realty Investors [*Toronto Stock Exchange symbol*] [*Vancouver Stock Exchange symbol*] ..... BBT
BBN Combined Programming Language (SAUS) ..... BCPL
BBN Corp. [*NYSE symbol*] (SAG) ..... BBN
BC [*British Columbia*] **Bancorp** [*Toronto Stock Exchange symbol*] [*Vancouver Stock Exchange symbol*] ..... BBC
BC Biotechnology Alliance (AC) ..... BCBA
BC Central Credit Union, Vancouver, BC, Canada [*Library symbol*] [*Library of Congress*] (LCLS) ..... CaBVaCCU
BC Council for the Family (AC) ..... BCCF
BC [*British Columbia*] **Court House Library Society, Vancouver, British Columbia,** [*Library symbol*] [*National Library of Canada*] (NLC) ..... BVAL
BC Deaf Sports Federation (AC) ..... BCDSF
BC Environmental Network (AC) ..... BCEN
BC Gas [*TS Symbol*] (TTSB) ..... BCG
BC Gymnastics Association (AC) ..... BCGA
B.C. Health Information Management Professionals Society (SAUO) ..... BCHIMPS
BC Lung Association (AC) ..... BCLA
BC Multicultural Education Society (AC) ..... BCMES
B.C. Native Women's Society, Kamloops, BC, Canada [*Library symbol*] [*Library of Congress*] (LCLS) ..... CaBKNW
BC Parents in Crisis Society (AC) ..... BCPIC
BC [*British Columbia*] **Rail Ltd.** [*Toronto Stock Exchange symbol*] [*Vancouver Stock Exchange symbol*] ..... BCL
BC Salmon Farmers Association (AC) ..... BCSFA
BC Shellfish Growers Association (AC) ..... BCSGA
BC Snowmobile Federation (AC) ..... BCSF
BC [*British Columbia*] **Sugar Refinery Ltd.** [*Toronto Stock Exchange symbol*] ..... BCS
BC Therapeutic Riding Association (AC) ..... BCTRA
BCA Charter [*British*] [*ICAO designator*] (FAAC) ..... BRC
BCA Credit Information [*Later, Broadcast Credit Association*] (EA) ..... BCA
BCAM International, Inc. [*Associated Press*] (SAG) ..... BCAM
BCAM International, Inc. [*Associated Press*] (SAG) ..... BCAM Int
BCAM Intl Wrrt'B' [*NASDAQ symbol*] (TTSB) ..... BCAML
BCAM Intl Wrrt'E' [*NASDAQ symbol*] (TTSB) ..... BCAMZ
BCB Financial Services Corp. [*NASDAQ symbol*] (SAG) ..... BCBF
BCB Financial Services Corp. [*Associated Press*] (SAG) ..... BCB Fin
BCB Financial Svcs [*NASDAQ symbol*] (TTSB) ..... BCBF
BCC Library, CANMET, Energy, Mines, and Resources Canada [*Bibliotheque du CBC, CANMET, Energie, Mines, et Ressources Canada*], **Nepean, Ontario** [*Library symbol*] [*National Library of Canada*] (NLC) ..... ONEMRCM
BCE, Inc. [*Formerly, Bell Canada Enterprises*] [*Toronto Stock Exchange symbol*] ..... B
BCE, Inc. [*Formerly, Bell Canada Enterprises*] [*NYSE symbol*] (SPSG) ..... BCE
BCE Mobile Communic [*NYSE symbol*] (SG) ..... BCX
BCE Mobile Communications, Inc. [*Associated Press*] (SAG) ..... BCE MC
BCE Mobile Communications, Inc. [*Toronto Stock Exchange symbol*] ..... BCX
BCE Place Finance Corp. [*Toronto Stock Exchange symbol*] [*Vancouver Stock Exchange symbol*] ..... BDF
BCED Capital Investment Corp. [*Toronto Stock Exchange symbol*] [*Vancouver Stock Exchange symbol*] ..... BDP
B-Cell Activating Factor [*Immunology*] ..... BAF
B-Cell Acute Lymphoblastic Leukemia [*Medicine*] ..... B-ALL
B-Cell Antigen Receptor [*Immunology*] ..... BCR
B-Cell Chronic Lymphocytic Leukemia [*Medicine*] ..... B-CLL
B-Cell Differentiation Factor [*Immunology*] ..... BCDF
B-Cell Growth Factor [*Biochemistry*] ..... BCGF
B-Cell Growth Factor (SAUS) ..... B-cgf
B-Cell Line [*Cytology*] ..... BCL
B-Cell Maturation Factor [*Immunology*] ..... BMF
B-Cell Precursor [*Biochemistry*] ..... BCP
B-Cell Prolymphocytic Leukemia ..... B-PLL
B-Cell Stimulatory Factor [*Biochemistry*] ..... BSF
B-Cell-Lymphadenopathy Associated Virus ..... B-LAV
Bchelor of Science in Group Work Education (SAUO) ..... BS Group Work Ed
BCNU [*Carmustine*] **and Triazinate** [*Antineoplastic drug*] (DAVI) ..... BT
BCNU [*Carmustine*], **ara-C, Cyclophosphamide, Thioguanine** [*Antineoplastic drug regimen*] ..... BACT
BCNU [*Carmustine*], **Cyclophosphamide, Oncovin , Prednisone** [*Vincristine*] [*Antineoplastic drug regimen*] ..... BCOP
BCNU [*Carmustine*], **Cyclophosphamide, Prednisone** [*Antineoplastic drug regimen*] ..... BCP
BCNU [*Carmustine*], **Cyclophosphamide, Vinblastine, Procarbazine, Prednisone** [*Antineoplastic drug regimen*] ..... BCVPP
BCNU [*Carmustine*], **Cyclophosphamide, Vincristine, Prednisone** [*Antineoplastic drug regimen*] ..... BCVP
BCNU [*Carmustine*], **Hydroxyurea, Dacarbazine** [*Antineoplastic drug regimen*] ..... BHD
BCNU [*Carmustine*], **Hydroxyurea, Dacarbazine, Vincristine** [*Antineoplastic drug regimen*] ..... BHDV
BCNU [*Carmustine*], **Methotrexate, Procarbazine** [*Antineoplastic drug regimen*] ..... BMP
BCNU [*Carmustine*], **Prednisone** [*Antineoplastic drug regimen*] ..... BP
BCNU [*Carmustine*], **Vinblastine, Cyclophosphamide, Procarbazine, Prednisone** [*Antineoplastic drug regimen*] ..... BVCPP
BCNU [*Carmustine*], **Vinblastine, Procarbazine, and Prednisone** [*Antineoplastic drug regimen*] (DAVI) ..... BCUPP
BCNU [*Carmustine*], **Vincristine, Adriamycin, Prednisone** [*Antineoplastic drug regimen*] ..... BVAP
BCNU [*Carmustine*], **Vincristine, and arbazine** [*DTIC*] [*Antineoplastic drug regimen*] (DAVI) ..... BVD
BCNU [*Carmustine*], **Vincristine, Procarbazine, Prednisone** [*Antineoplastic drug regimen*] ..... BVPP
B-Colony Forming Cells ..... B-CFC
BCP International Bank Ltd. [*Associated Press*] (SAG) ..... BCP Bk
BCP International Bank Ltd. [*NYSE symbol*] (SAG) ..... BPC
BCR [*Bituminous Coal Research*] **National Laboratory** [*Defunct*] (EA) ..... BCRNL
BCS [*Boeing Computer Services*] **Interactive Graphics** ..... BIG
BCT International [*NASDAQ symbol*] (SAG) ..... BCTI
BCT International, Inc. [*Associated Press*] (SAG) ..... BCT Int
BCT.TELUS Communications [*Toronto Stock Exchange symbol*] (SG) ..... BTS
BCU Industries, Inc. [*Toronto Stock Exchange symbol*] ..... BCU

BDM Corp., Albuquerque, NM [*Library symbol*] [*Library of Congress*] (LCLS) ... NmABD
BDM Federal, Inc. (GAAI) ... BDM
BDM International, Inc. (SAUO) ... BDM
BDM International, Inc. [*NASDAQ symbol*] (SAG) ... BDMI
BDM International, Inc. [*Associated Press*] (SAG) ... BDMInt
BDM International, Information Service Center, Kettering, OH [*Library symbol*] [*Library of Congress*] (LCLS) ... OKetBD
BDM Intl. [*NASDAQ symbol*] (TTSB) ... BDM
BDM Service Co. (MCD) ... BDMSC
BE Aerospace, Inc. [*Associated Press*] (SAG) ... BE Aero
BE Aerospace, Inc. [*NASDAQ symbol*] (SPSG) ... BEAV
Be Back in A Minute (SAUS) ... BBIAM
Be Back Later [*Computer hacker terminology*] (NHD) ... BBL
Be Back Later [*Internet language*] [*Computer science*] ... bbl
Be Back Soon [*Online dialog*] ... BBS
Be Ever Alert, Vigilant/Error Removal [*United States Air Force Security System's acronym for the Zero Defects Program*] ... BEAVER
BE Method (SAUS) ... BEM
Be On the Lookout [*Police term*] ... BOL
Be On the Lookout [*Police term*] ... BOLO
Be Right Back [*Internet language*] [*Computer science*] ... brb
Be Right Back [*Computer hacker terminology*] (NHD) ... BRB
Be Seein' You [*Computer science*] (DOM) ... BCNU
Be Seeing You [*Amateur radio shorthand*] (WDAA) ... BCNU
BE Semiconductor Indus [*NASDAQ symbol*] (SG) ... BESI
BE Semiconductor Indus [*NASDAQ symbol*] (TTSB) ... BESIF
Be Specific ... BS
Be Undressed, Ready, My Angel [*Correspondence*] (DSUE) ... BURMA
BEA Conference and Congress Advisory Bureau (SAUO) ... CCAB
BEA Income Fund [*Associated Press*] (SAG) ... BEA Inco
BEA Income Fund [*NYSE symbol*] (SAG) ... FBF
BEA Strategic Income Fd [*NYSE symbol*] (TTSB) ... FBI
BEA Strategic Income Fund [*Associated Press*] (SAG) ... BEA Strat
BEA Strategic Income Fund [*NYSE symbol*] (SAG) ... FBI
BEA Systems [*NASDAQ symbol*] (SG) ... BEAS
Beach (MCD) ... BCH
Beach [*Commonly used*] (OPSA) ... BEACH
Beach (ADA) ... BH
Beach Abort ... BA
Beach Amphibious Resupply Cargo (SAUS) ... BARC
Beach and Coastal Stability Project in the Lesser Antilles (SAUS) ... COSALC-I
Beach Armored Recovery Vehicle ... BARV
Beach Boys Fan Club (EA) ... BBFC
Beach Boys Freaks United (EA) ... BBFU
Beach Boys Stomp Fan Club (EAIO) ... BBSFC
Beach City, OH [*FM radio station call letters*] (BROA) ... WOFN-FM
Beach Club ... BC
Beach, Dewey W., Denver CO [*STAC*] ... BDW
Beach Discharge Lighter ... BDL
Beach Discharge Point (MCD) ... BDP
Beach Erosion Board [*Army*] ... BEB
Beach Front USA [*An association*] (EA) ... BFUSA
Beach Group ... BG
Beach Grove, IN [*AM radio station call letters*] ... WNTS
Beach Interface Unit [*Environmental science*] (COE) ... BIU
Beach Jumper Unit ... BJU
Beach Landing Site [*Military*] (DOMA) ... BLS
Beach Lighterage Control Point [*Environmental science*] (COE) ... BLCP
Beach Maintenance Area [*British and Canadian*] [*World War II*] ... BMA
Beach Master Unit [*Navy*] ... BMU
Beach Modulator Oscillator ... BMO
Beach on Contributory Negligence [*A publication*] (DLA) ... Beach Contrib Neg
Beach on Injunctions [*A publication*] (DLA) ... Beach Inj
Beach on Private Corporations [*A publication*] (DLA) ... Beach Priv Corp
Beach on Public Corporations [*A publication*] (DLA) ... Beach Pub Corp
Beach on the Law of Receivers [*A publication*] (DLA) ... Beach Rec
Beach Ordnance Company (SAUO) ... BOC
Beach Party ... BP
Beach Party Division [*Navy*] (NVT) ... BPD
Beach Party Group [*Navy*] (NVT) ... BPG
Beach Party Guard [*Navy*] (NVT) ... BPG
Beach Party Team [*Navy*] (NVT) ... BPT
Beach Patrol Craft [*British military*] (DMA) ... BPC
Beach Protection Program [*Australia*] ... BPP
Beach Signal Office [*Military*] (IAA) ... BSO
Beach Support Area (CINC) ... BSA
Beach Support Unit [*Military*] (DNAB) ... BSU
Beach Support Vehicle [*Navy*] (CAAL) ... BSV
Beachcomber, Ship Bottom, NJ [*Library symbol*] [*Library of Congress*] (LCLS) ... NjSbB
[*The*] **Beaches Environmental Assessment, Closure, and Health Act 1993** ... BEACH
Beachfront [*Travel industry*] (TRID) ... BCHFT
Beachhead (AFM) ... BHD
Beachhead Air Defense (MCD) ... BHAD
Beaching Cradle (SAUS) ... BHC
Beachmaster ... BM
Beachmaster ... BMR
Beachmaster Company (SAUO) ... BMCO
Beachmasters Net (SAUS) ... BMN
Beach's Commentaries on Modern Equity Jurisprudence [*A publication*] (DLA) ... Beach Mod Eq Jur
Beach's Modern Practice in Equity [*A publication*] (DLA) ... Beach Eq Prac
Beachville Ye Olde Museum, Beachville, ON, Canada [*Library symbol*] [*Library of Congress*] (LCLS) ... CaOBEM
Beachville Ye Olde Museum, Ontario [*Library symbol*] [*National Library of Canada*] (BIB) ... OBEM
Beacon [*Aviation*] ... B
Beacon [*Aviation*] (AFM) ... BCN
Beacon (ADWA) ... bcn
Beacon ... BN
Beacon Aerial Equipment (SAUS) ... BAE
Beacon Aided Radar Bombing (ACAE) ... BARB
Beacon Airborne S-band (SAUS) ... BAS
Beacon Airborne X-Band (IAA) ... BAX
Beacon Aircraft Position (MUGU) ... BAP
Beacon and Auroral Research (SAUS) ... BEAR
Beacon and Wayland News, Winfield, IA [*Library symbol*] [*Library of Congress*] (LCLS) ... IaWinfB
Beacon Antenna Equipment ... BAE
Beacon Available [*Aviation*] (PIPO) ... B
Beacon Buoy (IAA) ... BB
Beacon College [*Defunct*] (EA) ... BC
Beacon Collision Avoidance Program (SAUS) ... BCAP
Beacon Collision Avoidance System [*Aviation*] (DA) ... BACS
Beacon Collision Avoidance System [*Aviation*] ... BCAS
Beacon Control Console (IAA) ... BCC
Beacon Data [*Aviation*] (FAAC) ... BDAT
Beacon Data Generation (SAA) ... BDG
Beacon Drive Assemblies (SAUS) ... BDA
Beacon Experiment and Auroral Research ... BEAR
Beacon Explorer [*Satellite*] [*NASA*] ... BE
Beacon Explorer A [*Satellite*] [*NASA*] ... BE-A
Beacon Explorer B [*Satellite*] [*NASA*] ... BE-B
Beacon Explorer B Satellite (SAUS) ... BE-B Satellite
Beacon Ground S-Band (SAUS) ... BGS
Beacon Identification Method (DNAB) ... BIM
Beacon Instrumented Guided Ordnance (MCD) ... BINGO
Beacon, NY [*AM radio station call letters*] ... WBNR
Beacon Observation Laser Team (SAUS) ... BOLT
Beacon Only Bombing System ... BOBS
Beacon, Pequannock, NJ [*Library symbol*] [*Library of Congress*] (LCLS) ... NjPeqB
Beacon Point ... BP
Beacon Portable Packset ... BPP
Beacon Portable Set (SAUS) ... BPS
Beacon Present Signal (ACAE) ... BPS
Beacon Press [*Publisher*] ... BP
Beacon Processing System ... BPS
Beacon Properties Corp. [*NYSE symbol*] (SAG) ... BCN
Beacon Properties Corp. [*Associated Press*] (SAG) ... BeacnP
Beacon Properties Corp. [*Associated Press*] (SAG) ... BeacnPr
Beacon Ranging Pulse ... BRP
Beacon Receiver (SAUS) ... BR
Beacon Reply Group [*Aviation*] (OA) ... BRG
Beacon Reply Processor (SAUS) ... BRP
Beacon Track Receiver (ACAE) ... BTR
Beacon Tracking Level (KSC) ... BTL
Beacon Tracking System ... BTS
Beacon Transmitter (SAUS) ... BT
Beacon Transmitter (ADWA) ... BTX
Beacon Transmitter (ACAE) ... BXMTR
Beacon Trigger Generator ... BTG
Beacon, Ultra Portable "S" Band [*Navy*] ... BUPS
Beacon, Ultra Portable X Band [*Navy*] (IAA) ... BUPX
Beacon Video Digitizer ... BVD
Beacon Video Processing System ... BVPS
Beacon Video Processor ... BVP
Beacon-Automated Processing System (SAUS) ... BAPS
Beacon-Radio Set ... BRS
Beacons and Blind Landing (IAA) ... BBL
Beacons and Blind Landing (SAUS) ... bbl
Beaconsfield [*Urban district in England*] ... BEAC
Beaconsfield Public Library, Beaconsfield, PQ, Canada [*Library symbol*] [*Library of Congress*] (LCLS) ... CaQBE
Beaconsfield Public Library, Quebec [*Library symbol*] [*National Library of Canada*] (NLC) ... QBE
Bead (IAA) ... BD
Bead and Stone Importers Association (EA) ... BSIA
Bead Butt (SAUS) ... BB
Bead Flush (SAUS) ... BF
Bead Society (EA) ... BS
Bead/Bead (SAUS) ... B/B
Beaded [*or Banded*] **One Side** [*Lumber*] ... B1S
Beaded [*or Banded*] **Two Sides** [*Lumber*] ... B2S
Beading Device [*Tool*] (AAG) ... BDDV
Beading Die ... BDDI
Beads (VRA) ... bea
Beadwork (VRA) ... beawk
Beagle Pup Club [*British*] ... BPC
Beak ... B
Beak Consultants, Mississauga, ON, Canada [*Library symbol*] [*Library of Congress*] (LCLS) ... CaOMBC
Beak Consultants, Mississauga, Ontario [*Library symbol*] [*National Library of Canada*] (NLC) ... OMBC
Beak Line ... BL
Bealanana [*Madagascar*] [*Airport symbol*] (OAG) ... WBE
Beale Cypher Association (EA) ... BCA
Beall Family Association (EA) ... BFA

Beam [*of a ship*] ... B
Beam (KSC) ... BM
Beam (ADWA) ... bm
Beam Accelerator for Novel Super High Energy Electron (SAUS) ... BANSHEE
Beam Accessed Metal Oxide Semiconductor [*Memory technology*] (NITA) ... BEAMOS
Beam Addressed Metal Oxide Semiconductor [*Memory technology*] ... BEAMOS
Beam Alignment System (ACAE) ... BAS
Beam and Plate System (PDAA) ... BAPS
Beam Approach (DEN) ... B/A
Beam Approach Beacon System [*Aviation*] (KSC) ... BABS
Beam Approach Seeker Evaluation System [*Air Force*] (MCD) ... BASES
Beam Approach Training [*Military*] ... BAT
Beam Approach Training Flight [*British military*] (DMA) ... BATF
Beam Calibrator (PDAA) ... BECA
Beam Candle Watt Power (MCD) ... BCWP
Beam Candle Watt Seconds (MCD) ... BCWS
Beam Candlepower ... BCP
Beam Candlepower Seconds ... BCPS
Beam Catcher (SAUS) ... BC
Beam Collimation Error (MUGU) ... BCE
Beam Collimator ... BC
Beam Communication Set (SAUS) ... BCS
Beam Communications Set ... BCS
Beam Control Subsystem (MCD) ... BCS
Beam Control System (ACAE) ... BCS
Beam Correction Factor ... BCF
Beam Coupling (SAUS) ... BC
Beam Coupling Coefficient ... BCC
Beam Coupling Tube (NATG) ... BEACOTRON
Beam Deflection Tube ... BDT
Beam Degrader ... BD
Beam Deviation Factor (SAUS) ... BDF
Beam Electron-Beam Coating (SAUS) ... EBC
Beam Electron-Beam Direct-Write (SAUS) ... EBDW
Beam Entry Buffer (SAUS) ... BEB
Beam Expander (SAUS) ... BE
Beam Experiment Aboard Rocket (MCD) ... BEAR
Beam Extreme (SAUS) ... BExtreme
Beam Forming ... BF
Beam Forming & Switching Network (CCCA) ... BFSN
Beam Heated Cathode (SAUS) ... BHC
Beam Injected Distributed-Emission Magnetron (SAUS) ... BIDEMATRON
Beam Injected Magnetron (SAUS) ... BIMATRON
Beam Landing Correction (SAUS) ... BLC
Beam Lead Sealed Junction [*Electronics*] (IAA) ... BLSJ
Beam Lead Sealed Junction Integrated Circuit Package (AABC) ... BLSJICP
Beam Line Operations and Safety Awareness (SARE) ... BLOSA
Beam Management Terminal ... BMT
Beam Monitor ... BM
Beam of Light Transistor (MSA) ... BOLT
Beam of Light Transmitter ... BOLT
Beam Packing Loss (IAA) ... BPL
Beam Plasma Amplification (MCD) ... BPA
Beam Position Monitor ... BPM
Beam Positioning Drive (OA) ... BPD
Beam Positioning Magnet ... BPM
Beam Power (SAUS) ... BP
Beam Propagation Method (SAUS) ... BPM
Beam Ride (AAG) ... BR
Beam Ride Actuator ... BRA
Beam Ride Error ... BRE
Beam Rider (SAUS) ... BR
Beam Rider Tail Control Fragmentation [*Missile*] (MCD) ... BTF
Beam Riding Platform (ACAE) ... BRP
Beam Shape Loss (IAA) ... BSL
Beam Spacer (DAC) ... BS
Beam Splitter [*Instrumentation*] ... BS
Beam Stabilization Auto-Alignment Subsystem (ACAE) ... BSAS
Beam Steering ... BS
Beam Steering Computer ... BSC
Beam Steering Device ... BSD
Beam Steering Group ... BSG
Beam Steering Processor [*Military*] ... BSP
Beam Steering Programmer Microprocessor [*Military*] ... BSPUP
Beam Steering Shift Register [*Military*] ... BSSR
Beam Steering System ... BSS
Beam Steering Transducer ... BST
Beam Steering Ultrasonic Transducer ... BSUT
Beam Steering Unit (DA) ... BSU
Beam Stop ... BS
Beam Switching Tube (SAUS) ... BST
Beam Tape Packaging [*Computer science*] ... BTP
Beam to Waterline Length ... B/LWL
Beam Tracking Nuclear [*Military*] (CAAL) ... BTN
Beam Transfer Area [*LASER technology*] ... BTA
Beam Transport System ... BTS
Beam Width (CET) ... BW
Beam Zero Indication (MCD) ... BZI
Beam-Alignment Sensor (SAUS) ... BAS
Beam-Driven Thermonuclear (MCD) ... BDTN
Beames' Commitments in Bankruptcy [*A publication*] (DLA) ... Bea Bank
Beames' Costs in Equity [*A publication*] (DLA) ... Bea CE
Beames' Costs in Equity [*A publication*] (DLA) ... Bea Costs
Beames' Costs in Equity [*A publication*] (DLA) ... CE
Beames' Equity Pleading [*A publication*] (DLA) ... Bea Eq Pl
Beames' Glanville [*A publication*] (DLA) ... Beames Glanv
Beames on the Writ of Ne Exeat Regno [*A publication*] (DLA) ... Bea Ne Ex
Beames' Orders in Chancery [*England*] [*A publication*] (DLA) ... Bea Ord
Beames' Pleas in Equity [*A publication*] (DLA) ... Bea Pl Eq
Beam-Foil (PDAA) ... BF
Beam-Foil Spectroscopy ... BFS
Beam-Forming Electrode ... BFE
Beam-Forming Interfact (PDAA) ... BFI
Beam-Forming Network ... BFN
Beam-Forming Plate (SAUS) ... BP
Beam-induced Light Emission (SAUS) ... BLE
Beaminster [*England*] ... BEAM
Beam-Lead Device (IEEE) ... BLD
Beam-Lead Individual Carrier (PDAA) ... BLIC
Beam-Lead Interconnect Packaging (SAUS) ... BLIP
Beam-Rider Tail Control ... BT
Beam-Rider Terrier [*Missile*] (MCD) ... BT
Beam-Riding Tail-Controlled Nuclear Missile ... BTN
Beams and Stringers [*Technical drawings*] ... B & S
Beams and Stringers (SAUS) ... B&S
Beams and Stringers (SAUS) ... B and S
Beamsplitter Control Electronics (SAUS) ... BCE
Beamsteering (MSA) ... BMSTRG
Beamsville District Secondary School, Beamsville, ON, Canada [*Library symbol*] [*Library of Congress*] (LCLS) ... CaOBeD
Beamsville District Secondary School, Ontario [*Library symbol*] [*National Library of Canada*] (NLC) ... OBED
Beam-Switching Tube ... BST
Beam-to-Beam Correlation (NVT) ... BBC
Beamwidth (MSA) ... BMW
Bean Common Mosaic Virus ... BCMV
Bean Curly Dwarf Mosaic Virus [*Plant pathology*] ... BCDMV
Bean Golden Mosaic Virus ... BGMV
Bean Growers Cooperative Association [*Australia*] ... BGCA
Bean Markup Language (SAUS) ... BML
Bean Mild Mosaic Virus [*Plant pathology*] ... BMMV
Bean Pod Mottle Virus [*Plant pathology*] ... BPMV
Bean Rugose Mosaic Virus [*Plant pathology*] ... BRMV
Bean Summer Death Virus [*Plant pathology*] ... BSDV
Bean Yellow Mosaic Virus ... BYMV
Bean Yellow Vein Banding Virus [*Plant pathology*] ... BYVBV
Beance Tubaire Volontaire [*Voluntary opening of eustachian tubes*] [*Deep-sea diving*] [*French*] ... BTV
Beans Development Kit (SAUS) ... BDK
Bear Canyon [*Utah*] [*Seismograph station code, US Geological Survey*] [*Closed*] (SEIS) ... BCU
Bear Canyon School, Alberta [*Library symbol*] [*National Library of Canada*] (BIB) ... ABCS
Bear Creek, AK [*Location identifier*] [*FAA*] (FAAL) ... BCC
Bear Creek Township, MI [*FM radio station call letters*] (BROA) ... WTLI-FM
Bear Gulch [*California*] [*Seismograph station code, US Geological Survey*] (SEIS) ... BGH
Bear Identification Code (SAUS) ... BIC
Bear Island [*Formerly, Bjornoya*] [*Norway*] [*Geomagnetic observatory code*] ... BJN
Bear Lake County District Library, Montpelier, ID [*Library symbol*] [*Library of Congress*] (LCLS) ... IdMonB
Bear Lake County District Paris Branch, Paris, ID [*Library symbol*] [*Library of Congress*] (LCLS) ... IdMonB-P
Bear Lake, MI [*FM radio station call letters*] ... WZTU
Bear Lake Resources Ltd. [*Vancouver Stock Exchange symbol*] ... BLA
Bear Market [*Investment term*] ... BM
Bear Mountain Trailside Museum, Bear Mountain, NY [*Library symbol*] [*Library of Congress*] (LCLS) ... NBmtT
Bear Point Community Library, Bear Canyon, AB, Canada [*Library symbol*] [*Library of Congress*] (LCLS) ... CaABcBC
Bear Point Community Library, Bear Canyon, Alberta [*Library symbol*] [*National Library of Canada*] (NLC) ... ABCBC
Bear River Historical Society, Bear River, NS, Canada [*Library symbol*] [*Library of Congress*] (LCLS) ... CaNSBrH
Bear River Historical Society, Nova Scotia [*Library symbol*] [*National Library of Canada*] (NLC) ... NSBRH
Bear River Migratory Bird Refuge (SAUS) ... BRMBR
Bear River Range [*Idaho*] [*Seismograph station code, US Geological Survey*] (SEIS) ... BEI
Bear Stearns [*Associated Press*] (SAG) ... BS VPt
Bear Stearns 7.60%'C'Dep Pfd [*NYSE symbol*] (TTSB) ... BSCPrC
Bear Stearns 7.88%'B'Dep Pfd [*NYSE symbol*] (TTSB) ... BSCPrB
Bear Stearns Adj Rt Pfd [*NYSE symbol*] (TTSB) ... BSCPrA
Bear Stearns Companies, Inc. [*Associated Press*] (SAG) ... BearS
Bear Stearns Companies, Inc. [*Associated Press*] (SAG) ... BearSt
Bear Stearns Companies, Inc. [*AMEX symbol*] (SAG) ... BJC
Bear Stearns Companies, Inc. [*AMEX symbol*] (SAG) ... BJP
Bear Stearns Companies, Inc. [*NYSE symbol*] (SPSG) ... BSC
Bear Stearns Companies, Inc. [*Associated Press*] (SAG) ... BSCUB
Bear Stearns Companies, Inc. [*Associated Press*] (SAG) ... BSHK
Bear Stearns Companies, Inc. [*Associated Press*] (SAG) ... BSJpn
Bear Stearns Companies, Inc. [*Associated Press*] (SAG) ... BS MRK
Bear Stearns Companies, Inc. [*Associated Press*] (SAG) ... BSNk
Bear Stearns Companies, Inc. [*Associated Press*] (SAG) ... BSYn
Bear Stearns Companies, Inc. [*AMEX symbol*] (SAG) ... BYE
Bear Stearns Companies, Inc. [*AMEX symbol*] (SAG) ... BYN
Bear Stearns Companies, Inc. [*AMEX symbol*] (SAG) ... HXC
Bear Stearns Companies, Inc. [*AMEX symbol*] (SAG) ... HXP
Bear Stearns Companies, Inc. [*AMEX symbol*] (SAG) ... KBB

Bear Stearns Companies, Inc. [AMEX symbol] (SAG) ..... MCP
Bear Stearns Companies, Inc. [AMEX symbol] (SAG) ..... NKB
Bear Stearns Cos.'CUBS''98 [AMEX symbol] (TTSB) ..... KBB
Bear Stearns Fin LLC'EPICS' [NYSE symbol] (TTSB) ..... BSCPrZ
Bear Sterns 5.50%MRK'CHIPS' [AMEX symbol] (TTSB) ..... MCP
Bear Valley [California] [Seismograph station code, US Geological Survey]
  (SEIS) ..... BVL
Bear Valley Observatory [California] [Seismograph station code, US
  Geological Survey] [Closed] (SEIS) ..... BVC
Bearbeiter [Editor] [German] (BARN) ..... Bearb
Bearbeitet [Revised] [German] (BARN) ..... bearb
Bearblock. Treatise upon Tithes [6th ed.] [1832] [A publication]
  (DLA) ..... Bear Tithes
Beard Co. [Associated Press] (SAG) ..... BeardCo
Beard Co. [AMEX symbol] (SPSG) ..... BOC
Beard Oil Co. (EFIS) ..... BOC
Bearded Collie Club of America (EA) ..... BCCA
Bearded Iris Mosaic Virus [Plant pathology] ..... BIMV
Beardlsey-Brown Valley Public Schools, Beardlsey, MN [Library symbol]
  [Library of Congress] (LCLS) ..... MnBeaPS
Beardmore Public Library, Ontario [Library symbol] [National Library of
  Canada] (NLC) ..... OBEAR
Beardmore Resources [Vancouver Stock Exchange symbol] ..... BDR
Beardsley-Browns Valley Public Schools, Browns Valley, MN [Library
  symbol] [Library of Congress] (LCLS) ..... MnBrvPS
Beardstown, IL [AM radio station call letters] ..... WRMS
Beardstown, IL [FM radio station call letters] ..... WRMS-FM
Beardstown Public Library, Beardstown, IL [Library symbol] [Library of
  Congress] (LCLS) ..... IBea
Bearer ..... BRR
Bearer Bond [Investment term] (ADA) ..... BB
Bearer Capability (SAUS) ..... BC
Bearer Channel (SAUS) ..... B-CHANNEL
Bearer Channel [A component of ISDN interfaces] (PCM) ..... B-channel
Bearer Company [British military] (DMA) ..... Br Coy
Bearer Depository Receipt [Investment term] ..... BDR
Bearer Identification Code (SAUS) ..... BIC
Bearer Participation Certificate (EBF) ..... BPC
Bearer Switchover Unit (SAUS) ..... BSU
Bearing [Angle] ..... B
Bearing (SAUS) ..... BEAR
Bearing ..... BG
Bearing (WDAA) ..... BR
Bearing (AFM) ..... BRG
Bearing (ADWA) ..... brg
Bearing ..... BRNG
Bearing Altitude Indicator [Aerospace] ..... BAI
Bearing and Power Transfer Assembly [Aerospace] ..... BAPTA
Bearing and Range Indicator ..... BRI
Bearing Bronze [Metallurgy] ..... BBz
Bearing Capacity Ratio [Materials technology] ..... BCR
Bearing Deviation Indicator [Aerospace] ..... BDI
Bearing, Distance, and Heading ..... BDH
Bearing, Distance, and Heading Indicator ..... BDHI
Bearing Distance Indicator (SAUS) ..... BDI
Bearing Error [Military] (CAAL) ..... BE
Bearing Factor [Mechanical engineering] ..... BF
Bearing Frequency Indicator (NVT) ..... BFI
Bearing Frequency Plot (SAUS) ..... BFP
Bearing Inch (SAUS) ..... BI
Bearing Indicator (MCD) ..... BI
Bearing Indicator and Navigator to Grounded Operator (MCD) ..... BINGO
Bearing Magnetic [Navigation] (IAA) ..... BM
Bearing Materials Tester (SAUS) ..... BMT
Bearing Mounted Clutch ..... BMC
Bearing Pennant [Navy] [British] ..... BG
Bearing per Gyro Compass [Navigation] ..... BPGC
Bearing per Standard Compass [Navigation] ..... BPSC
Bearing per Steering Gyro Compass [Navigation] ..... BPSTGC
Bearing Pile [Technical drawings] (DAC) ..... BP
Bearing Plate [Technical drawings] ..... BPL
Bearing Point (SAUS) ..... BP
Bearing Procurement Specification (MSA) ..... BPS
Bearing Range Indicator (SAUS) ..... BRI
Bearing Ratio (SAUS) ..... BR
Bearing Repeater Unit (IAA) ..... BRU
Bearing Seals and Materials Tester (SAUS) ..... BSMT
Bearing Specialists Association (EA) ..... BSA
Bearing Supplies Ltd. [British] [ICAO designator] (FAAC) ..... PVO
Bearing Technology ..... BT
Bearing Time Recorder ..... BTR
Bearing/Confidence ..... B/CONF
Bearing/Frequency Display (SAUS) ..... BFD
Bearingless Main Rotor (RDA) ..... BMR
Bearing-Only Launch [Navy] (CAAL) ..... BOL
Bearings (SAUS) ..... bs
Bearings, Inc. [Associated Press] (SAG) ..... Bearng
Bearings, Inc. [NYSE symbol] (SPSG) ..... BER
Bearn-Fabre, PQ [Television station call letters] CKRN-3
Bears, Lions, Eagles, Steelers, Vikings, Colts, Dolphins, and Bills
  [Computerized scouting combine for professional football teams; name
  comprises membership teams] ..... BLESTO-VIII
Bearskin Lake [ICAO designator] (AD) ..... JV
Bearskin Lake Air Service Ltd. [Canada] [ICAO designator] (FAAC) ..... BLS
Beasley's New Jersey Chancery Reports [A publication] (DLA) ..... Beas

Beasley's New Jersey Equity Reports [12-13] [A publication] (DLA) ..... Beas
Beasley's New Jersey Equity Reports [A publication] (DLA) ..... Beasl
Beat ..... BT
Beat Frequency Generator (SAUS) ..... BFG
Beat Frequency Oscillator (SAUS) ..... BFO
Beat Frequency Oscillator (SAUS) ..... bfo
Beat Matsushita Whatsoever [Facetious translation of BMW - Bavarian Motor
  Works, Originated by Sony Corp.] (ECON) ..... BMW
Beat Oscillator ..... BO
Beata Maria [The Blessed Virgin] [Latin] ..... BM
Beata Maria Virgo [Blessed Mary the Virgin] [Latin] ..... BMV
Beata Virgo [Blessed Virgin] [Latin] ..... BV
Beata Virgo Maria [Blessed Virgin Mary] [Latin] ..... BVM
Beatae Memoriae [Of Blessed Memory] [Latin] ..... BM
Beaten Favourite [Horse racing] [British] ..... BF
Beaten It to Death (SAUS) ..... BITD
Beaten Zone (SAUS) ..... BZ
Beat-Frequency ..... BF
Beat-Frequency Detection (IAA) ..... BFD
Beat-Frequency Interferometer (PDAA) ..... BFI
Beat-frequency Oscillator Transformer (SAUS) ..... BOT
Beating [FBI standardized term] ..... BTG
Beating Inflation in Local Government Establishment (SAUS) ..... BILGE
Beating the Gun [Investment term] ..... BTG
Beatissime Pater [Most Holy Father] [Latin] ..... BP
Beatitudo Vestra [Your Holiness] [Latin] ..... BV
Beatles Connection [An association] (EA) ..... BC
Beatles Fan Club: Good Day Sunshine (EA) ..... BFCGDS
Beatles Information Center [Sweden] (EAIO) ..... BIC
Beatles Unlimited (EA) ..... BU
Beatrice Foods Co., Chicago, IL [Library symbol] [Library of Congress]
  (LCLS) ..... ICBF
Beatrice Foods Company (SAUO) ..... BRY
Beatrice M. Murphy Foundation (EA) ..... BMMF
Beatrice, NE [Location identifier] [FAA] (FAAL) ..... BIE
Beatrice, NE [Location identifier] [FAA] (FAAL) ..... BJU
Beatrice, NE [FM radio station call letters] ..... KTGL
Beatrice, NE [AM radio station call letters] ..... KWBE
Beatrice Public Library, Beatrice, NE [Library symbol] [Library of Congress]
  (LCLS) ..... NbB
Beatrice Public Library, Beatrice, NE [Library symbol] [Library of Congress]
  (LCLS) ..... NbBea
Beatrix Mine [South Africa] [ICAO location identifier] (ICLI) ..... FABX
Beats per Minute [Medicine] (DMAA) ..... bpm
Beats per Minute [Cardiology] ..... BPM
Beats per Second [Cardiology] ..... BPS
Beatty [Nevada] [Seismograph station code, US Geological Survey] [Closed]
  (SEIS) ..... BEA
Beatty [Nevada] [Seismograph station code, US Geological Survey] [Closed]
  (SEIS) ..... BTY
BEATTY, NV [Commercial waste site] (GAAI) ..... BETY
Beatty, NV [Location identifier] [FAA] (FAAL) ..... BTY
Beatty's Irish Chancery Reports [1814-36] [A publication] (DLA) ..... Beat
Beatty's Irish Chancery Reports [1814-36] [A publication] (DLA) ..... Beatt
Beatty's Irish Chancery Reports [1814-36] [A publication] (DLA) ..... Beatty
Beatty's Irish Chancery Reports [1814-36] [A publication] (DLA) ..... Beatty Ir Ch
Beattyville, KY [FM radio station call letters] ..... WLJC
Beattyville, KY [Television station call letters] ..... WLJC-TV
Beau Canada Exploration Ltd. [Toronto Stock Exchange symbol] ..... BAU
Beau Val Mines [Vancouver Stock Exchange symbol] ..... BVM
Beauard Parish Library, DeRidder (SAUS) ..... LDeB
Beauchamp Exploration, Inc. [Vancouver Stock Exchange symbol] ..... BPE
Beauchemin, Beaton, LaPointe, Inc., Montreal, PQ, Canada [Library symbol]
  [Library of Congress] (LCLS) ..... CaQMBBL
Beauchemin, Beaton, Lapointe, Inc., Montreal, Quebec [Library symbol]
  [National Library of Canada] (NLC) ..... QMBBL
Beauchemin-Beaton-Lapointe Inc. (SAUO) ..... BBL
Beaufield Resources, Inc. [Toronto Stock Exchange symbol] ..... BFD
Beauford Resources Ltd. [Vancouver Stock Exchange symbol] ..... BFR
Beaufort [South Carolina] [Airport symbol] (OAG) ..... BFT
Beaufort and Arctic Storms Experiment (QUAC) ..... BASE
Beaufort & Morehead (SAUO) ..... B&M
Beaufort & Morehead Railroad (SAUO) ..... BEM
Beaufort & Morehead Railroad Co. [AAR code] ..... BMH
Beaufort County Library (SAUS) ..... ScB
Beaufort County Library, Beaufort, SC [Library symbol] [Library of
  Congress] (LCLS) ..... ScB
Beaufort County Technical Institute, Washington, NC [Library symbol]
  [Library of Congress] (LCLS) ..... NcWaB
Beaufort Force (WEAT) ..... Bf
Beaufort, Hyde, Martin Regional Library, Washington, NC [Library symbol]
  [Library of Congress] (LCLS) ..... NcWaBHM
Beaufort Leasing Ltd. [Canada] [FAA designator] (FAAC) ..... QTX
Beaufort, NC [Location identifier] [FAA] (FAAL) ..... MRH
Beaufort, NC [AM radio station call letters] ..... WBTB
Beaufort, SC [Location identifier] [FAA] (FAAL) ..... NBC
Beaufort, SC [Location identifier] [FAA] (FAAL) ..... NGJ
Beaufort, SC [FM radio station call letters] ..... WAGP
Beaufort, SC [AM radio station call letters] ..... WBEU
Beaufort, SC [FM radio station call letters] ..... WJWJ
Beaufort, SC [Television station call letters] ..... WJWJ-TV
Beaufort, SC [AM radio station call letters] ..... WVGB
Beaufort, SC [FM radio station call letters] ..... WYKZ
Beaufort Technical College, Beaufort, SC [Library symbol] [Library of
  Congress] (LCLS) ..... ScBTC

Beaufort West [*South Africa*] [*ICAO location identifier*] (ICLI) .... FABW
Beaufort West/Wes Town [*South Africa*] [*ICAO location identifier*] (ICLI) .... FABY
Beaufort Wind Scale .... BWS
Beaufort/Beaufort Marine Corps Air Station [*South Carolina*] [*ICAO location identifier*] (ICLI) .... KNBC
Beaulieu Vineyard (SAUO) .... BV
Beaume Scale (ADWA) .... Be
Beaumont [*Diocesan abbreviation*] [*Texas*] (TOCD) .... BEA
[*Francis*] **Beaumont and** [*John*]**Fletcher** [*17th century English dramatists*] (BARN) .... Beau & Fl
Beaumont Art Museum, Beaumont, TX [*Library symbol*] [*Library of Congress*] (LCLS) .... TxBeaAM
Beaumont. Bills of Sale [*1855*] [*A publication*] (DLA) .... Beau Bills
Beaumont, CA [*Location identifier*] [*FAA*] (FAAL) .... BUO
Beaumont, CA [*FM radio station call letters*] .... KAEH
Beaumont Enterprise & Journal, Beaumont, TX [*Library symbol*] [*Library of Congress*] (LCLS) .... TxBeaE
Beaumont Library District Library, Beaumont, CA [*Library symbol*] [*Library of Congress*] (LCLS) .... CBea
Beaumont. Life and Fire Insurance [*2nd ed.*] [*1846*] [*A publication*] (DLA) .... Beau Ins
Beaumont Municipal Library, Alberta [*Library symbol*] [*National Library of Canada*] (NLC) .... ABEAM
Beaumont Port-Arthur/Jefferson County [*Texas*] [*ICAO location identifier*] (ICLI) .... KBPT
Beaumont, Sour Lake & Western Railway Co. (SAUO) .... BSL&W
Beaumont, Sour Lake & Western Railway Co. .... BSL & W
Beaumont, TX [*Location identifier*] [*FAA*] (FAAL) .... BMT
Beaumont, TX [*Location identifier*] [*FAA*] (FAAL) .... GDE
Beaumont, TX [*AM radio station call letters*] (RBYB) .... KAYD
Beaumont, TX [*FM radio station call letters*] .... KAYD-FM
Beaumont, TX [*Television station call letters*] .... KBMT
Beaumont, TX [*Television station call letters*] .... KFDM
Beaumont, TX [*Television station call letters*] .... KITU
Beaumont, TX [*AM radio station call letters*] (RBYB) .... KJUS
Beaumont, TX [*AM radio station call letters*] .... KLVI
Beaumont, TX [*FM radio station call letters*] .... KQXY
Beaumont, TX [*AM radio station call letters*] (BROA) .... KRCM
Beaumont, TX [*FM radio station call letters*] (RBYB) .... KTCX-FM
Beaumont, TX [*FM radio station call letters*] .... KTXB
Beaumont, TX [*FM radio station call letters*] .... KVLU
Beaumont, TX [*AM radio station call letters*] (BROA) .... KWBK-AM
Beaumont, TX [*FM radio station call letters*] .... KXTJ
Beaumont, TX [*FM radio station call letters*] .... KYKR
Beaumont, TX [*AM radio station call letters*] .... KZZB
Beaumont/Port Arthur [*Texas*] [*Airport symbol*] (OAG) .... BPT
Beaune/Challanges [*France*] [*ICAO location identifier*] (ICLI) .... LFGF
Beaunit Corp. (SAUO) .... BEM
Beaupre Explorations [*Vancouver Stock Exchange symbol*] .... BPD
Beauregard. Organisation de la Famille [*A publication*] (DLA) .... Beaur Org
Beauregard Parish Library, DeRidder, LA [*Library symbol*] [*Library of Congress*] (LCLS) .... LDeB
Beausoleil Indian Band Library, Christian Island, Ontario [*Library symbol*] [*National Library of Canada*] (BIB) .... OCIB
Beauti Control Cosmetics, Inc. [*Associated Press*] (SAG) .... BeauCtl
Beautician (ABBR) .... BTCN
BeautiControl Cosmetics [*NASDAQ symbol*] (TTSB) .... BUTI
BeautiControl Cosmetics, Inc. [*NASDAQ symbol*] (NQ) .... BUTI
Beautification (ABBR) .... BTFCN
Beautiful [*Classified advertising*] .... BEAUT
Beautiful (SAUS) .... Beaut
Beautiful (ABBR) .... BTFL
Beautiful Books [*A publication*] .... BB
Beautiful British Columbia (SAUS) .... BBC
Beautiful Music (NTCM) .... BM
Beautiful Music Friends (EA) .... BMF
Beautiful Music/Easy Listening [*Radio station format*] (WDMC) .... B/EZ
Beautiful Old House .... BOH
Beautiful People [*Slang for the wealthy, world-traveling, partying set*] .... BP
Beautiful Poems on Jesus [*A publication*] .... BePJ
Beautiful Wife (IIA) .... BW
Beautifully (REAL) .... beaut
beautifully (SAUS) .... beaut
Beautifully (ABBR) .... BTFLY
Beautifulness (ABBR) .... BTFLNS
Beautify (ABBR) .... BTFY
Beautifying (ABBR) .... BTFYG
Beauty .... BTY
Beauty and Barber Supply Institute (EA) .... BBSI
Beauty and the Beast International [*An association*] [*Defunct*] (EA) .... BBI
Beauty Counselors International, Inc. [*Toronto Stock Exchange symbol*] .... BCN
Beauty, Divinity, Wisdom, Power, Honor, Glory, Strength [*Freemasonry*] (ROG) .... BDWPHGS
Beauty [*or Bottom*] **(Quark)** [*Atomic physics*] .... b
Beauty Quotient (SAUS) .... BQ
Beauty Without Cruelty, Incorporated (SAUO) .... BWCI
Beauty Without Cruelty International (SAUO) .... BWC
Beauty Without Cruelty Society [*Australia*] .... BWCS
Beauty without Cruelty USA (EA) .... BWC
Beauvais [*France*] [*Airport symbol*] (AD) .... BVA
Beauvais/Tille [*France*] [*ICAO location identifier*] (ICLI) .... LFOB
Beauval Public Library, Beauval, SK, Canada [*Library symbol*] [*Library of Congress*] (LCLS) .... CaSBe
Beauval Public Library, Saskatchewan [*Library symbol*] [*National Library of Canada*] (NLC) .... SB
Beauvechain [*Belgium*] [*ICAO location identifier*] (ICLI) .... EBBE
Beauvoir, the Jefferson Davis Shrine, Biloxi, MS [*Library symbol*] [*Library of Congress*] (LCLS) .... MsBB
Beaux Arts Gallery (SAUO) .... BAG
Beaux-Arts Institute of Design (SAUO) .... BAID
Beavan and Walford's Railway and Canal Cases [*England*] [*A publication*] (DLA) .... Beav & W
Beavan and Walford's Railway and Canal Cases [*England*] [*A publication*] (DLA) .... Beav & Wal
Beavan and Walford's Railway and Canal Cases [*England*] [*A publication*] (DLA) .... Beav & Wal Ry Cas
Beavan and Walford's Railway and Canal Cases [*England*] [*A publication*] (DLA) .... Beav & W Ry Cas
Beavan. Railway and Canal Cases [*England*] [*A publication*] (DLA) .... Beav R & C
Beavan's English Rolls Court Reports [*A publication*] (DLA) .... B
Beavan's English Rolls Court Reports [*A publication*] (DLA) .... Beav
Beavan's English Rolls Court Reports [*A publication*] (DLA) .... Beavan Ch
Beavan's English Rolls Court Reports [*A publication*] (DLA) .... Beav (Eng)
Beavan's Ordines Cancellariae [*A publication*] (DLA) .... Beav OC
Beaver [*On lead tokens used as payment in the Canadian fur trade during the 1700's*] .... B
Beaver [*Record label*] [*Canada*] .... Bea
Beaver [*A publication*] (BRI) .... Beav
Beaver .... BVR
Beaver [*Alaska*] [*Airport symbol*] (OAG) .... WBQ
Beaver, AK [*Location identifier*] [*FAA*] (FAAL) .... WBQ
Beaver Army Terminal [*Oregon*] .... BEART
Beaver College (SAUO) .... BC
Beaver College, Glenside, PA [*OCLC symbol*] (OCLC) .... BEA
Beaver College, Glenside, PA [*Library symbol*] [*Library of Congress*] (LCLS) .... PGIB
Beaver County Court House, Beaver, PA [*Library symbol*] [*Library of Congress*] (LCLS) .... PBeC
Beaver Dam, KY [*FM radio station call letters*] (BROA) .... WAUE-FM
Beaver Dam, KY [*FM radio station call letters*] (BROA) .... WKLX-FM
Beaver Dam, WI [*AM radio station call letters*] .... WBEV
Beaver Dam, WI [*FM radio station call letters*] .... WXRO
Beaver Defenders (EA) .... BD
Beaver Falls [*Pennsylvania*] [*Airport symbol*] (OAG) .... BFP
Beaver Falls, PA [*Location identifier*] [*FAA*] (FAAL) .... BVI
Beaver Falls, PA [*FM radio station call letters*] (BROA) .... WAMO-FM
Beaver Falls, PA [*AM radio station call letters*] .... WBVP
Beaver Falls, PA [*FM radio station call letters*] .... WGEV
Beaver Falls, PA [*FM radio station call letters*] .... WITX
Beaver Falls, PA [*FM radio station call letters*] (RBYB) .... WXDX
Beaver Island Mormon Colony Library, St. James, Beaver Island, MI [*Library symbol*] [*Library of Congress*] [*Obsolete*] (LCLS) .... MiBeiM
Beaver Lake Branch, Walden Public Library, Ontario [*Library symbol*] [*National Library of Canada*] (NLC) .... OWBL
Beaver, Meade & Englewood [*AAR code*] .... BME
Beaver Memorial Library, Beaver, PA [*Library symbol*] [*Library of Congress*] (LCLS) .... PBe
Beaver Resources, Inc. [*Toronto Stock Exchange symbol*] [*Vancouver Stock Exchange symbol*] .... BGI
Beaver Springs, PA [*FM radio station call letters*] (RBYB) .... WLZS-FM
Beaver Springs, PA [*FM radio station call letters*] .... WWBV
Beaver Valley Power Station (NRCH) .... BVPS
Beaver Valley Public Library, Fruitvale, British Columbia [*Library symbol*] [*National Library of Canada*] (NLC) .... BFBV
Beaverbrook Art Gallery (SAUO) .... BAG
Beaverbrook Branch, Kanata Public Library, Ontario [*Library symbol*] [*National Library of Canada*] (NLC) .... OKAB
Beaverbrook Collection, New Brunswick Archives, Fredericton, New Brunswick [*Library symbol*] [*National Library of Canada*] (NLC) .... NBFB
Beaverbrook Newspapers Ltd., London, United Kingdom [*Library symbol*] [*Library of Congress*] (LCLS) .... UkLB
Beavercreek, OH [*FM radio station call letters*] (RBYB) .... WXEG
Beaverhead Resources [*Vancouver Stock Exchange symbol*] .... BVH
Beaverlodge Elementary School, Alberta [*Library symbol*] [*National Library of Canada*] (BIB) .... ABES
Beaverlodge High School, Alberta [*Library symbol*] [*National Library of Canada*] (BIB) .... ABBS
Beaverton Branch, Brock Township Public Library, Ontario [*Library symbol*] [*National Library of Canada*] (BIB) .... OBEAB
Beaverton City Library, Beaverton, OR [*Library symbol*] [*Library of Congress*] (LCLS) .... OrB
Beaverton, MI [*FM radio station call letters*] .... WMRX
Beaverton, OR [*FM radio station call letters*] .... KKCW
Beaverton-Thorah Eldon Historical Society, Inc., Ontario [*Library symbol*] [*National Library of Canada*] (NLC) .... OBEATE
Beavertown Historical Society, Lincoln Park, NJ [*Library symbol*] [*Library of Congress*] (LCLS) .... NjLpBHi
Beawes' Lex Mercatoria [*England*] [*A publication*] (DLA) .... Beaw
Beawes' Lex Mercatoria [*England*] [*A publication*] (DLA) .... Beawes' Lex Merc
Beawes' Lex Mercatoria [*England*] [*A publication*] (DLA) .... Beaw Lex Mer
Beazer Homes USA [*Associated Press*] (SAG) .... BeazHm
Beazer Homes USA [*Associated Press*] (SAG) .... Beazr
Beazer Homes USA [*Associated Press*] (SAG) .... BeazrHm
Beazer Homes USA [*NYSE symbol*] (SAG) .... BZH
Beazer HomesUSA$2.00CvExPfd [*NYSE symbol*] (TTSB) .... BZHPrA
Bebe Stores [*Stock market symbol*] .... BEBE
BEC Energy [*NYSE symbol*] [*Formerly, Boston Edison*] .... BSE
BEC Group [*NYSE symbol*] [*Formerly, Benson Eyecare*] (SG) .... EYE
BEC Group, Inc. [*Associated Press*] (SAG) .... BEC Gp
BEC Group, Inc. [*NYSE symbol*] (SAG) .... EYE

Became (GEAB) ... bec
Because (SAUS) ... b/c
Because (SAUS) ... bec
Because (ADWA) ... bec
Because (ADA) ... BEC
Because (ADWA) ... BK
Because It's There Network [*Electronic mail system*] (TNIG) ... BITNET
Because It's Time Network [*Interuniversity communications network*] ... BITNET
Beccaria on Crimes and Punishments [*A publication*] (DLA) ... Bec Cr
Beccles [*British*] [*ICAO location identifier*] (ICLI) ... EGSM
Bechar [*Algeria*] [*Airport symbol*] (OAG) ... CBH
Bechard. Histoire du Droit Municipal [*A publication*] (DLA) ... Bech Hist
Bechar/Ouakda [*Algeria*] [*ICAO location identifier*] (ICLI) ... DAOC
Bechar/Ouakda [*Algeria*] [*ICAO location identifier*] (ICLI) ... DAOR
Bechtel Client Letter (IEEE) ... BCL
Bechtel Corporation (SAUO) ... BECH
Bechtel Group Inc. (SAUO) ... BGI
Bechtel Group, Inc., San Francisco, CA [*Library symbol*] [*Library of Congress*] (LCLS) ... CSfBe
Bechtel Group, Inc., Technical Library, Houston, TX [*Library symbol*] [*Library of Congress*] (LCLS) ... TxHBec
Bechtel Hanford Incorporated (ABAC) ... BHI
Bechtel Information Services (IID) ... BIS
Bechtel National, Inc. (GAAI) ... BNI
Bechuana (SAUS) ... Bechu
Bechuanaland (SAUO) ... Bech
Bechuanaland Police (SAUO) ... BechP
Beck Anxiety Inventory [*Test*] (TMMY) ... BAI
Beck Depression Inventory [*Psychology*] ... BDI
Beck Hopelessness Scale [*Test*] (TMMY) ... BHS
Beck Scale for Suicide Ideation [*Test*] (TMMY) ... BSS
Becker [*Blood group*] ... Be
Becker & Hayes, Inc. [*Information service or system*] (IID) ... B & H
Becker County Historical Society, Detroit Lakes, MN [*Library symbol*] [*Library of Congress*] (LCLS) ... MnDlHi
Becker Elementary School, Becker, MN [*Library symbol*] [*Library of Congress*] (LCLS) ... MnBE
Becker High School, Becker, MN [*Library symbol*] [*Library of Congress*] (LCLS) ... MnBH
Becker Junior College, Worcester, MA [*Inactive*] [*OCLC symbol*] (OCLC) ... BQM
Becker Junior College, Worcester, MA [*Library symbol*] [*Library of Congress*] (LCLS) ... MWBe
Becker Milk Co. Ltd. [*Toronto Stock Exchange symbol*] ... BEK
Becker Muscular Dystrophy [*Medicine*] ... BMD
Becker Public Library, Becker Elementary School, Becker, MN [*Library symbol*] [*Library of Congress*] (LCLS) ... MnB
Becker Work Adjustment Profile (TES) ... BWAP
Becker's Muscular Dystrophy [*Medicine*] (DMAA) ... BDM
Becket [*Bracket*] ... BCKT
Beckley [*West Virginia*] [*Airport symbol*] (OAG) ... BKW
Beckley College (SAUO) ... BC
Beckley College, Beckley, WV [*Library symbol*] [*Library of Congress*] (LCLS) ... WvBC
Beckley, WV [*Location identifier*] [*FAA*] (FAAL) ... MQU
Beckley, WV [*FM radio station call letters*] ... WCIR
Beckley, WV [*AM radio station call letters*] ... WIWS
Beckley, WV [*AM radio station call letters*] ... WJLS
Beckley, WV [*FM radio station call letters*] ... WJLS-FM
Beckley, WV [*FM radio station call letters*] ... WVPB
Beckley, WV [*AM radio station call letters*] ... WWNR
Beckley-Raleigh County Library, Beckley, WV [*Library symbol*] [*Library of Congress*] (LCLS) ... WvB
Becklin-Neugebauer [*Astronomy*] ... BN
Beckman Coulter [*NYSE symbol*] [*Formerly, Beckman Instruments*] ... BEC
Beckman Instruments, Inc. [*Associated Press*] (SAG) ... BckIns
Beckman Instruments, Inc. [*NYSE symbol*] (CTT) ... BEC
Beckman Instruments, Inc. (SAUS) ... BII
Beckman Instruments, Inc., Fullerton, CA [*Library symbol*] [*Library of Congress*] (LCLS) ... CFIB
Beckman Instruments, Inc., Technical Library, Palo Alto, CA [*Library symbol*] [*Library of Congress*] (LCLS) ... CPaB
Beckman Translation [*Programming language*] [*Beckman Instruments, Inc.*] ... BECKTRAN
Beck's Colorado Reports [*12-16 Colorado and 1 Colorado Court of Appeals*] [*A publication*] (DLA) ... Beck
Beck's Colorado Reports [*12-16 Colorado and 1 Colorado Court of Appeals*] [*A publication*] (DLA) ... Beck (Colo)
Beck's Depression Index-Short Form [*Psychiatry*] (DAVI) ... BDI SF
Beck's Medical Jurisprudence [*A publication*] (DLA) ... Beck Med Jur
Beckwith-Wiedemann Support Network (EA) ... BWSN
Beckwith-Wiedemann Syndrome [*Medicine*] ... BWS
Beclobrinic Acid [*Biochemistry*] ... BBA
Beclomethasone Dipropionate [*Pharmacology*] ... BDP
Become (DA) ... BC
Become (FAAC) ... BCM
Becoming [*ICAO*] (FAAC) ... BECMG
Becoming One's Own Man [*Psychology*] ... BOOM
Becoming the Gift [*Religious education test*] ... BTG
Becquerel [*Symbol*] [*SI unit of activity of ionizing radiation source*] ... Bq
Becquerel (ABAC) ... bq
Becton, Dickinson & Co. [*Initialism used in titles of a series of technical publications*] ... B-D
Becton, Dickinson & Co. [*NYSE symbol*] (SPSG) ... BDX
Becton, Dickinson & Co. [*Associated Press*] (SAG) ... BectDk
Becton, Dickinson & Co., Paramus, NJ [*OCLC symbol*] (OCLC) ... JBD
Becton, Dickinson & Co. Research Center ... BDRC
Becton, Dickinson & Co., Research Center Library, Research Triangle Park, Durham, NC [*Library symbol*] [*Library of Congress*] (LCLS) ... NcDurBD
Becton, Dickinson & Co., Rutherford, NJ [*Library symbol*] [*Library of Congress*] (LCLS) ... NjRuB
Becton Dickinson Diagnostics [*Commercial firm*] (DAVI) ... BDI
Becton, Dickinson Research Center (SAUO) ... BDRC
Becton-Dickinson [*Spinal needle*] [*Medicine*] (DAVI) ... BD
Bed [*Medicine*] ... b
Bed [*Amateur radio shorthand*] (WDAA) ... BD
Bed and Board (WDAA) ... B & B
Bed and Board (SAUS) ... B&B
Bed and Breakfast [*Tourist accommodations*] ... B & B
Bed and Breakfast (TRID) ... B&B
Bed and Breakfast Inns of North America (SAUO) ... BBINA
Bed and Breakfast League (EA) ... BBL
Bed & Breakfast Reservation Services World-Wide [*An association*] ... B&BRSWW
Bed and Chair [*Rest*] [*Medicine*] ... B & C
Bed and Light Breakfast [*Hotel accomodations*] ... BLB
Bed Bath [*Medicine*] ... BB
Bed Bath & Beyond [*NASDAQ symbol*] (TTSB) ... BBBY
Bed Bath & Beyond, Inc. [*NASDAQ symbol*] (SAG) ... BBBY
Bed Bath & Beyond, Inc. [*Associated Press*] (SAG) ... BedBath
Bed Board [*Medicine*] (MELL) ... BB
Bed, Breakfast, and Bath [*Tourist accommodations*] ... BBB
Bed, Breakfast, and Evening Meal [*Tourist accommodations*] ... BB & EM
Bed Depth Service Time [*Wastewater treatment*] ... BDST
Bed Joint [*Technical drawings*] ... BJT
Bed Nucleus of the Stria Terminalis [*Brain anatomy*] ... BNST
Bed Pan [*Medicine*] (MELL) ... bp
Bed Pan (SAUS) ... BP
Bed Plate (SAUS) ... BP
Bed Rest [*Medicine*] ... BR
Bed Volume (ABAC) ... BV
Beda [*Deceased, 735*] [*Authority cited in pre-1607 legal work*] (DSA) ... B
Beda [*Deceased, 735*] [*Authority cited in pre-1607 legal work*] (DSA) ... Be
Bedanda [*Guinea-Bissau*] [*ICAO location identifier*] (ICLI) ... GGBE
Bedarfsflugunternehmen Dr. L. Polsterer [*Austria*] [*ICAO designator*] (FAAC) ... OPV
Bedarieux-La-Tour-Sur-Orb [*France*] [*ICAO location identifier*] (ICLI) ... LFNX
Bedarride. Droit Commercial [*A publication*] (DLA) ... Bed Dr Comm
Bedbug Rash [*Medicine*] (MELL) ... BDR
Bedded (SAUS) ... BDD
Bedding (MSA) ... BDNG
Bedding ... BEDG
Bedding Plane (SAUS) ... Bdg Pl
Beddingfield High School Library, Wilson, NC [*Library symbol*] [*Library of Congress*] (LCLS) ... NcWilB
Bedell Advertising Selling Improvement Corporation (SAUO) ... BASIC
Bedell's Reports [*163-191 New York*] [*A publication*] (DLA) ... Bedell
Bederation of British Tape Recordists (DBA) ... FBTR
Bedford [*Massachusetts*] [*Airport symbol*] (OAG) ... BED
Bedford [*Borough and county in England*] ... BEDFD
Bedford [*British*] [*ICAO location identifier*] (ICLI) ... EGVW
Bedford Bancshares [*NASDAQ symbol*] (TTSB) ... BFSB
Bedford Bancshares, Inc. [*Associated Press*] (SAG) ... BedfrdBc
Bedford Bancshares, Inc. [*NASDAQ symbol*] (SAG) ... BFSB
Bedford College for Women (SAUO) ... BCW
Bedford Free Library, Bedford, NY [*Library symbol*] [*Library of Congress*] (LCLS) ... NBed
Bedford Free Public Library, Bedford, MA [*Library symbol*] [*Library of Congress*] (LCLS) ... MBd
Bedford Hills Free Library, Bedford Hills, NY [*Library symbol*] [*Library of Congress*] (LCLS) ... NBedh
Bedford, IN [*Location identifier*] [*FAA*] (FAAL) ... BFR
Bedford, IN [*AM radio station call letters*] ... WBIW
Bedford, IN [*FM radio station call letters*] ... WQRK
Bedford Institute of Oceanography (SAUO) ... BIO
Bedford Institute of Oceanography [*Canada*] (MSC) ... BIO
Bedford Institute of Oceanography [*Institut Oceanographique de Bedford*] **Dartmouth, Nova Scotia** [*Library symbol*] [*National Library of Canada*] (NLC) ... NSDB
Bedford, MA [*Location identifier*] [*FAA*] (FAAL) ... BED
Bedford, MA [*Location identifier*] [*FAA*] (FAAL) ... SKR
Bedford, MA [*Location identifier*] [*FAA*] (FAAL) ... ULJ
Bedford, NH [*FM radio station call letters*] ... WAEF
Bedford, NH [*FM radio station call letters*] (RBYB) ... WOXF-FM
Bedford, NH [*FM radio station call letters*] (BROA) ... WQLL-FM
Bedford, NS [*ICAO location identifier*] (ICLI) ... CWHX
Bedford, PA [*AM radio station call letters*] ... WAYC
Bedford, PA [*AM radio station call letters*] ... WBFD
Bedford, PA [*FM radio station call letters*] ... WOOX
Bedford, PA [*FM radio station call letters*] ... WWCW
Bedford Park Public Library District, Bedford Park, IL [*Library symbol*] [*Library of Congress*] (LCLS) ... IBpB
Bedford Prop Investors(New) [*NYSE symbol*] (TTSB) ... BED
Bedford Property Investors [*Associated Press*] (SAG) ... BedfrdP
Bedford Property Investors, Inc. [*NYSE symbol*] (SPSG) ... BED
Bedford Property Investors, Inc. [*Associated Press*] (SAG) ... BedfrdPr
Bedford Public Library, Bedford, IN [*Library symbol*] [*Library of Congress*] (LCLS) ... InB
Bedford Public Library, Bedford, OH [*Library symbol*] [*Library of Congress*] (LCLS) ... OBed
Bedford Rae [*British*] [*ICAO designator*] (FAAC) ... RRS
Bedford Software Ltd. [*Toronto Stock Exchange symbol*] ... BFS

Bedford Systems Users Group (EA) ... BSUG
Bedford Times-Mail, Bedford, IN [*Library symbol*] [*Library of Congress*] (LCLS) ... InBTM
Bedford Times-Press, Bedford, IA [*Library symbol*] [*Library of Congress*] (LCLS) ... IaBedTP
Bedford, VA [*AM radio station call letters*] ... WBLT
Bedford, VA [*FM radio station call letters*] (RBYB) ... WLQE-FM
Bedford/Castle Mill [*British*] [*ICAO location identifier*] (ICLI) ... EGSB
Bedford/Laurence G. Hanscom Field [*Massachusetts*] [*ICAO location identifier*] (ICLI) ... KBED
Bedfordshire [*England*] (BARN) ... Bedford
Bedfordshire [*County in England*] (ODBW) ... Beds
Bedfordshire [*County in England*] ... BEDS
Bedfordshire (SAUS) ... Beds
Bedfordshire and Hertfordshire Regiment (SAUO) ... Bedfs & Herts R
Bedfordshire and Hertfordshire Regiment (SAUO) ... BEDFS HERTS
Bedfordshire Historical Record Society (SAUO) ... BHRS
Bedfordshire Imperial Yeomanry [*British military*] (DMA) ... BIY
Bedfordshire Regiment (SAUO) ... BR
Bedfordshire Yeomanry [*British military*] (DMA) ... BY
Bedliner ... BDLNR
Bedlington Terrier Club of America (EA) ... BTCA
Bedourie [*Australia*] [*Airport symbol*] [*Obsolete*] (OAG) ... BEU
Bedpan (MSA) ... BDPN
Bedpan ... BP
Bedrest (SAUS) ... BR
Bedrock (SAUS) ... BR
Bedrock Resources Ltd. [*Vancouver Stock Exchange symbol*] ... BDK
Bedrohung (SAUS) ... Bedr
Bedroom (ROG) ... B
Bedroom ... BDRM
Bedroom (REAL) ... bdrm
Bedroom (SAUS) ... Bdrm
Bedroom (SAUS) ... Bed
Bedroom (VRA) ... bedrm
Bedroom [*Classified advertising*] (ADA) ... BEDRM
Bedroom (ADWA) ... br
Bedroom [*Classified advertising*] ... BR
Bedroom [*Classified advertising*] (ADA) ... B'RM
Bedroom Farce [*Literary genre*] (WDAA) ... BF
Bedroom Steward [*In the first class aboard an ocean liner*] ... BR
Bedrooms (SAUS) ... Bdrms
Beds and Patients Report (SAUS) ... BAP REPT
Beds and Patients Report ... BAPREPT
Beds Occupied ... BEDOC
Bedside [*Medicine*] ... BS
Bedside Commode (CPH) ... BSC
Bedside Drainage [*Medicine*] (DMAA) ... BSD
Bedside Glucose Monitoring [*Medicine*] (DMAA) ... BGM
Bedside Network of the Veterans Hospital Radio and TV Guild [*Later, VBN*] (EA) ... BNVHRTVG
Bedside X-Ray Examination (MELL) ... BXE
Bedsore (MELL) ... BS
Bedspread Blanket ... BB
Bedstead Alliance [*A union*] [*British*] ... BA
Bedstead Workmens Association [*A union*] [*British*] ... BWA
Bedtime ... BT
Bedtime Insulin, Daytime Sulfonylurea [*Therapy*] [*Pharmacology*] (DAVI) ... BIDS
Bed-Wetting (MELL) ... BW
Bee Biology and Systematics Laboratory [*Department of Agriculture*] [*Research center*] (RCD) ... BBSL
Bee County College, Beeville, TX [*Library symbol*] [*Library of Congress*] (LCLS) ... TxBeeC
Bee County Public Library, Beeville, TX [*Library symbol*] [*Library of Congress*] (LCLS) ... TxBee
Bee Industries Association [*Defunct*] (EA) ... BIA
Bee Industries Association of America (SAUO) ... BIAA
Bee Keepers Association ... BKA
Bee Research Association [*Later, IBRA*] ... BRA
Bee Research Association (SAUS) ... BRA-8
Bee Venom [*Entomology*] ... BV
Beebas [*NASDAQ symbol*] (SAG) ... BEBA
Beeba's Creations, Inc. [*Associated Press*] (SAG) ... Beebas
Beebe, AR [*FM radio station call letters*] ... KPIK
Beebe Ranch [*California*] [*Seismograph station code, US Geological Survey*] (SEIS) ... BBR
Beebee's Analysis of Common Law Practice [*A publication*] (DLA) ... Bee Anal
Beebe's Ohio Citations [*A publication*] (DLA) ... Beebe Cit
Beech (VRA) ... becwd
Beech Aerospace Services Inc. (SAUO) ... BASI
Beech Aircraft Company (SAUO) ... B
Beech Aircraft Corp. (SAUO) ... BCX
Beech Aircraft Corp. [*ICAO aircraft manufacturer identifier*] (ICAO) ... BE
Beech Aircraft Corp. [*ICAO designator*] (FAAC) ... BEC
Beech Aircraft Corporation (SAUO) ... BAC
Beech Bottom Power Company (SAUO) ... BBP
Beech Creek Railroad Co. (SAUO) ... BCH
Beech Mountain, NC [*FM radio station call letters*] ... WECR
Beech Mountain Railroad (MHDB) ... BMRR
Beech Mountain Railroad Co. [*AAR code*] ... BEEM
Beecham Bovril Brands [*Commercial firm*] [*British*] ... BBB
Beecham Laboratories, White Hall, IL [*Library symbol*] [*Library of Congress*] (LCLS) ... IWhhB
Beecham Products-Western Hemisphere Research, Parsippany, NJ [*OCLC symbol*] (OCLC) ... BEE
Beecham Research Laboratories Ltd. [*Great Britain*] [*Research code symbol*] ... BRL
Beechcraft (SAUS) ... BCFT
Beechcraft [*Airplane code*] ... Bec
Beechcraft Kingair [*Airplane code*] ... Bek
Beech-Nut Life Savers, Inc. (SAUO) ... BLS
Beef (ROG) ... BF
Beef Assurance Scheme (SAUS) ... BAS
Beef Cattle Price Index ... BCPI
Beef Cattle Research Center [*Michigan State University*] [*Research center*] (RCD) ... BCRC
Beef Friesian Society (EA) ... BFS
Beef Heart Infusion Broth [*Microbiology*] ... BHIB
Beef Heart Infusion Supplement [*Broth or agar*] [*Growth medium*] (DAVI) ... BHIS
Beef Heart Mitochondria (SAUS) ... BHM
Beef Improvement Association of Australia ... BIAA
Beef Improvement Federation (EA) ... BIF
Beef Industry Council (EA) ... BIC
Beef Island [*British Virgin Islands*] [*Airport symbol*] (AD) ... EIS
Beef Liver Catalase [*An enzyme*] (OA) ... BLC
Beef Promotion and Research Board (EA) ... BPRB
Beef Recording Association [*British*] (BI) ... BRA
BEEF [*Base Engineer Emergency Forces*] **Reporting, Analysis, and Status System** [*Air Force*] (AFM) ... BRASS
Beef Research and Information Act [*1976*] ... BRIA
Beef Serum Albumin [*Medicine*] (MEDA) ... BSA
Beef Shorthorn [*Cattle*] ... BS
Beef Shorthorn Society of Australia ... BSSA
Beef Tapeworm [*Medicine*] (MELL) ... BTW
Beef Thyroid-Stimulating Hormone [*Endocrinology*] (MAE) ... BTSH
Beefmaster Breeders Universal (EA) ... BBU
Beefy-Meaty-Peptide (SAUS) ... BMP
Beehive Office Supervisory System (SAUS) ... BOSS
Beekeeper ... BK
Beekeeper Serum [*Medicine*] (DMAA) ... BKS
Beekman Community Library Reading Center, Poughquag, NY [*Library symbol*] [*Library of Congress*] (LCLS) ... NPoq
Beeler, J. L., Los Angeles CA [*STAC*] ... BJL
Beeler's Reports [*Tennessee*] [*A publication*] (DLA) ... Beeler
Been ... BN
Been Here Since Day One [*Group of Reagan administration staffers*] ... BHSDO
Been There, Done That [*Internet dialog*] ... BTDT
Been to America [*Slang*] [*British*] ... BTA
Beeper Obliterans [*Medicine*] (MELL) ... BO
Beer [*Phonetic alphabet*] [*Pre-World War II*] (DSUE) ... B
Beer Barrel (WDAA) ... BB
Beer, Bum, and Bacca [*Nautical*] [*Slang*] [*British*] (DSUE) ... 3B's
Beer Can Collectors of America (EA) ... BCCA
Beer Drinkers of America (EA) ... BDA
Beer Firkin ... BF
Beer House (ROG) ... BH
Beer Industry League of Louisiana (SRA) ... BILL
Beer Industry of Florida (SRA) ... BIF
Beer Institute (EA) ... BI
Beer Wholesalers Association of New Jersey (SRA) ... BWANJ
Be-'eravon Mugbal (BJA) ... BM
Beersheba [*Israel*] [*Airport symbol*] [*Obsolete*] (OAG) ... BEV
Beersheba/Teyman [*Israel*] [*ICAO location identifier*] (ICLI) ... LLBS
Beery Development Test of Visual-Motor Integration [*Psychiatry*] (DAVI) ... BDTVMI
Bee's Admiralty. An Appendix to Bee's District Court Reports [*A publication*] (DLA) ... Bee Adm
Bee's English Crown Cases Reserved [*A publication*] (DLA) ... Bee CCR
Bee's United States District Court Reports [*A publication*] (DLA) ... Bee
Beeswax (ABBR) ... BSWX
Beet Armyworm Larvae [*Entomology*] ... BAW
Beet Cryptic Virus [*Plant pathology*] ... BCV
Beet Curly Top Virus [*Plant pathology*] ... BCTV
Beet Growers Association (SAUS) ... BGA
Beet Invert Syrup [*Food sweetener*] ... BIS
Beet Leaf Curl Virus [*Plant pathology*] ... BLCV
Beet Medium Invert Syrup [*Food sweetener*] ... BMIS
Beet Mild Yellowing Virus [*Plant pathology*] ... BMYV
Beet Mosaic Virus [*Plant pathology*] ... BTMV
Beet Necrotic Yellow Vein Virus ... BNYVV
Beet Sugar Development Foundation (EA) ... BSDF
Beet Temperate Virus [*Plant pathology*] ... BTEV
Beet Western Yellows Virus ... BWYV
Beet Yellow Stunt Virus [*Plant pathology*] ... BYSV
Beet Yellows Virus ... BYV
Beeton Public Library, Ontario [*Library symbol*] [*National Library of Canada*] (BIB) ... OBEE
Beevers-Ross [*Beta-alumina crystallography*] ... BR
Beeville, TX [*Location identifier*] [*FAA*] (FAAL) ... BEA
Beeville, TX [*AM radio station call letters*] ... KIBL
Beeville, TX [*FM radio station call letters*] ... KTKO
Beeville, TX [*FM radio station call letters*] ... KYTX
Beeville, TX [*Location identifier*] [*FAA*] (FAAL) ... NIR
Beeville, TX [*Location identifier*] [*FAA*] (FAAL) ... NNL
Beeville/Chase Field Naval Air Station [*Texas*] [*ICAO location identifier*] (ICLI) ... KNIR
Befandriana [*Madagascar*] [*Airport symbol*] (OAG) ... WBD
Befandriana Nord [*Madagascar*] [*ICAO location identifier*] (ICLI) ... FMNF
Befindlichkeitsskala (DB) ... BfS
Before ... B

Before [*Slang*] (DAVI) ... B4
Before [*Internet language*] [*Computer science*] ... b4
Before (VRA) ... bef
Before ... BEF
before (SAUS) ... bef
Before ... BEFE
Before (MSA) ... BFR
before (SAUS) ... bfr
Before Birth Control (SAUS) ... BBC
Before Bottom Center [*Valve position*] ... BBC
Before Bottom Dead Center [*Valve position*] ... BBDC
Before Breaking Bulk (RIMS) ... BBB
Before Business Clearance (NASA) ... BBC
Before Calculators ... BC
Before Casinos ... BC
Before Christ ... BC
Before Christian Era ... BCE
Before Cloning [*Cytology*] ... BC
Before Columbus Foundation (EA) ... BCF
Before Commercialism ... BC
Before Competition [*Term associated with the divestiture of AT & T*] ... BC
Before Cook [*Era preceding discovery of Australia by British explorer, James Cook*] (ECON) ... BC
Before Credit Cards [*Slang*] ... BC
Before Croonery [*Musical slang*] ... BC
Before Dark (FAAC) ... BFDK
Before Dead Center [*Valve position*] ... BDC
Before Divestiture [*AT & T*] (IT) ... BD
Before Flight (MCD) ... BF
Before Flight Abort [*NASA*] (MCD) ... BFA
Before Flight Reliability (MCD) ... BFR
Before Full Moon [*Freemasonry*] (ROG) ... BFM
Before Girls [*i.e., before women became part of armed forces*] [*Military*] ... BG
Before Goetz [*A reference to "vigilante" Bernhard Goetz, who shot four youths on a New York subway in 1984 after allegedly being threatened by them*] [*See also AG*] ... BG
Before Image (SAUS) ... BIM
Before Infantry Light and Lethal [*Antitank*] (MCD) ... BILL
Before Initial Release [*Information system*] (MCD) ... BIR
Before Marriage ... BM
Before Meals and At Bedtime [*Pharmacy*] (DAVI) ... AC & HS
Before Mentioned [*Legal*] [*British*] (ROG) ... BEFEMENTD
Before Midnight (ROG) ... BM
Before Morning Twilight (SAA) ... BMT
Before New Moon [*Freemasonry*] (ROG) ... BNM
Before Next Interaction (SAUS) ... BNI
Before Present ... BP
Before Proceeding on Course [*Aviation*] ... BPOC
Before Queues [*Referring to pre-World War II period*] [*Slang*] [*British*] ... BQ
Before Record Signal (SAUS) ... BRR Signal
Before Recorded Time (SAUS) ... BRT
Before Rotary Cutting [*Quilting*] ... BRC
Before Sleep [*Pharmacy*] (DAVI) ... BS
Before Stephen Sondheim [*A reference to simpler, less sophisticated, and more sentimental musicals*] ... BSS
Before the Common Era [*Jewish equivalent of BC*] ... BCE
Before the Crash [*i.e., before the 1929 stock market collapse*] [*Slang*] ... BC
Before the Euro ... BE
Before the Present ... BP
Before the Romantics [*A publication*] ... BeR
Before Top Center [*Valve position*] ... BTC
Before Top Dead Center [*Valve position*] ... BTDC
Before Total (SAUS) ... BT
Before Touching [*Parapsychology*] ... BT
Before Upper Dead Center ... BUDC
Before Video ... BV
Before Your Very Eyes (DGA) ... BVE
Befrienders International [*Later, BISW*] (EAIO) ... BI
Befrienders International Samaritans Worldwide (EA) ... BISW
Begg. Conveyancing Code [*Scotland*] [*A publication*] (DLA) ... Begg Code
Begg. Law Agents [*Scotland*] [*A publication*] (DLA) ... Begg L Ag
Beggign Paroxysmal Positional Vertigo [*Medicine*] ... BPPV
Begin (SAUS) ... BE
Begin (ADWA) ... beg
Begin Block (SAUS) ... BB
Begin Bracket [*Indicator*] [*Computer science*] (IBMDP) ... BB
Begin Chain (SAUS) ... BC
Begin Column (SAUS) ... BC
Begin Of Partition (SAUS) ... BOP
Begin Of Transaction (SAUS) ... BOT
Begin Standard Radar Refuel Orbit (SAUS) ... BSRRO
Begin Standard Refuel Orbit [*Aviation*] (FAAC) ... BSRO
Begin Subroutine (SAUS) ... BEGSR
Begin TAG (SAUS) ... BTAG
Begin Telemetry Cycle ... BTC
Begin Transmission, Break ... BT
Beginn der Bestellung (SAUS) ... BST
Beginn der Blattentfaltung (SAUS) ... BO
Beginn der Gelbreife (SAUS) ... GR
Beginn der Knospenbildung (SAUS) ... KNO
Beginn der Teigreife (SAUS) ... TR
Beginn der Vollreife (SAUS) ... VR
Beginn des Auflaufens (SAUS) ... AU
Beginners Algebraic Symbolic Interpretive Compiler [*Computer science*] (NITA) ... BASIC
Beginners All Purpose Standard Instruction Code (SAUS) ... BASIC
Beginners All purpose Symbolic Instruction Code (SAUS) ... BASIC
Beginners All Symbolic Instruction Code (SAUS) ... BASIC
Beginner's All-Purpose Symbolic Instruction Code [*Programming language invented by T. E. Kurtz and J. G. Kemeny at Dartmouth College in 1963-64*] ... BASIC
Beginner's All-Purpose Symbolic Instruction Code A [*Computer science*] (DDC) ... BASICA
Beginning (VRA) ... beg
Beginning ... BEG
Beginning ... BGNG
Beginning Address (SAUS) ... BA
Beginning and Ending (SAUS) ... B&E
Beginning and Ending (ADA) ... B & E
Beginning Assessment Test of Reading (EDAC) ... BATR
Beginning At A Point (SAUS) ... BAP
Beginning Character (SAUS) ... BC
Beginning Climb [*Aviation*] (FAAC) ... BC
Beginning Descent (SAUS) ... BD
Beginning Descent [*Aviation*] (FAAC) ... BGND
Beginning Education Assessment [*Educational development test*] ... BEA
Beginning Entrepreneurial Support Team ... BEST
Beginning Evening Nautical Twilight ... BENT
Beginning Event (DNAB) ... BE
Beginning Experience (SAUS) ... BE
Beginning File Label (SAUS) ... BFL
Beginning Mark (SAUS) ... BM
Beginning Morning Astronomical Twilight [*Navigation*] (MCD) ... BMAT
Beginning Morning Civil Twilight [*Navigation*] ... BMCT
Beginning Morning Nautical Twilight [*Navigation*] ... BMNT
Beginning Morning Nautical Twilight [*Navigation*] (CINC) ... BMT
Beginning, Negative, Positive, Finish [*ASCII subset*] ... BNPF
Beginning Number (SAUS) ... BEGNR
Beginning of Business ... BOB
Beginning of Cycle (NRCH) ... BOC
Beginning of Equilibrium Cycle [*Nuclear energy*] (NRCH) ... BEC
Beginning of Equilibrium Cycle [*Nuclear energy*] (NRCH) ... BOEC
Beginning of Equilibrium Life (NUCP) ... BOEL
Beginning of Extent (SAUS) ... BOE
Beginning of File (NASA) ... BOF
Beginning of Group (SAUO) ... BOG
Beginning of Information [*Computer science*] (NITA) ... BOI
Beginning of Information Marker [*Computer science*] ... BIM
Beginning of Life ... BOL
Beginning of Magnetic Tape [*Computer science*] (MDG) ... BMT
Beginning of Message (IAA) ... BOM
Beginning of Month [*Accounting*] (NASA) ... BOM
Beginning of Period ... BOP
Beginning of Quarter [*Accounting*] ... BOQ
Beginning of Record (SAUS) ... Beg o Rec
Beginning of Record [*Computer science*] (IAA) ... BOR
Beginning of Record (SAUS) ... OR
Beginning Of Table (SAUS) ... BOT
Beginning of Tape [*Computer science*] ... BOT
Beginning of Tape [*Computer science*] (IAA) ... BT
Beginning of Year [*Accounting*] ... BOY
Beginning of Year Significant Non-Complier [*Environmental Protection Agency*] (ERG) ... BOYSNC
Beginning Of Year violator (SAUS) ... BOY
Beginning Period (AABC) ... BP
Beginning Procedure Turn (FAAC) ... BPT
Beginning Professional Salary ... BPS
Beginning Reel Label (SAUS) ... BRL
Beginning Standard Holding Procedure [*Aviation*] (FAAC) ... BSHP
Beginning Standard Instrument Approach [*Aviation*] (IAA) ... BGSIA
Beginning Standard Range Approach [*Aviation*] (FAAC) ... BSRAP
Beginning Straight-In Approach [*Aviation*] (IAA) ... BGSTA
Beginning Straight-In Approach [*Aviation*] (FAAC) ... BSIAP
Beginning Tape Label [*Computer science*] (BUR) ... BTL
Beginning Teacher Evaluation Study (EDAC) ... BTES
Beginning to Tape Test ... BTT
Begleiter (SAUS) ... Begl
Begleitung [*Accompaniment*] [*Music*] ... BEGL
Behalf (ROG) ... BEHF
Behavior (WGA) ... B
Behavior (AAMN) ... BEH
Behavior Analysis in Ireland (EAIO) ... BAI
Behavior Analyst Certification Board (SAUO) ... BACB
Behavior and Systems Research Laboratory [*Army*] ... BESERL
Behavior and Systems Research Laboratory [*Arlington, VA*] [*Army*] (IEEE) ... BESRL
Behavior Assessment System for Children [*Test*] (TMMY) ... BASC
Behavior Based Safety (SARE) ... BBS
Behavior Cards [*Psychological testing*] ... BC
Behavior Classification Checklist [*Psychology*] ... BCC
Behavior Disorder ... BD
Behavior Engineering Model (EDAC) ... BEM
Behavior Evaluation Scale [*Educational testing*] ... BES
Behavior Evaluation Table [*Psychology*] (DHP) ... BET
Behavior Genetics Association (EA) ... BGA
Behavior Intervention Plan ... BIP
Behavior Management Plan ... BMP
Behavior Management Plan ... BMT
Behavior Modification [*Psychology*] (DAVI) ... AMOD
Behavior Modification [*Psychology*] ... B-MOD

Behavior Monitor System ... BMS
Behavior of Offshore Structures [*Conference*] ... BOSS
Behavior Pattern (ADA) ... BP
Behavior Problem Checklist (EDAC) ... BPC
Behavior Rating Instrument for Autistic and Other Atypical Children [*Child development test*] [*Psychology*] ... BRIAAC
Behavior Rating Profile [*Educational testing*] ... BRP
Behavior Replication by Analog Instruction of the Nervous System [*Electrical stimulation of the brain*] ... BRAINS
Behavior Research Institute (EA) ... BRI
Behavior Science Corporation (SAUO) ... BASICO
Behavior Sciences and the Law [*A publication*] (DLA) ... Behav Sci & L
Behavior Status Inventory [*Personality development test*] [*Psychology*] ... BSI
Behavior Style Questionnaire [*Medicine*] (DMAA) ... BSQ
Behavior Therapy [*Psychology*] ... BT
Behavior Therapy and Research Society (EA) ... BTRS
Behavioral ... BEHAV
Behavioral (AFM) ... BEHVL
Behavioral ... BHVRL
Behavioral Academic Self-Esteem [*Student personality test*] [*Psychology*] ... BASE
Behavioral Activation System ... BAS
Behavioral Alcohol Research Laboratory (DICI) ... BARLAB
Behavioral and Brain Sciences (SAUO) ... BBS
Behavioral and Social Sciences ... BSS
Behavioral and Social Sciences Survey Committee (EA) ... BSSSC
Behavioral Approach Scale [*Psychology*] ... BAS
Behavioral Approach System (DIPS) ... BAS
Behavioral Assertiveness Test for Children ... BAT-C
Behavioral Assessment Grid ... BAG
Behavioral Assessment of Speech Anxiety (EDAC) ... BASA
Behavioral Avoidance Test [*Psychometrics*] ... BAT
Behavioral Books Institute [*Book club*] ... BBI
Behavioral Characteristics Progression [*Scale*] ... BCP
Behavioral Checklist [*Psychology*] ... BCL
Behavioral Differential ... BD
Behavioral Effects of Infectious Diseases [*Army*] ... BEID
Behavioral Emergency Committee [*Medicine*] (HCT) ... BEC
Behavioral Inhibition System ... BIS
Behavioral Intervention [*Medicine*] (MELL) ... BI
Behavioral Inventory ... BI
Behavioral Kinesiology [*Book title*] ... BK
Behavioral Medicine (MELL) ... BM
Behavioral Neurogenetics and Neuroimaging Research Center (ADWA) ... BNNRC
Behavioral Neuropsychology Special Interest Group (EA) ... BNSIG
Behavioral Objective ... BO
Behavioral Observation Scale for Autism [*Medicine*] (DB) ... BOS
Behavioral Pharmacology Society (EA) ... BPS
Behavioral Research Aspects of Safety and Health Working Group [*University of Kentucky*] [*Research center*] (RCD) ... BRASH
Behavioral Research Council (EA) ... BRC
Behavioral Research Laboratories ... BRL
Behavioral Risk Factor (MELL) ... BRF
Behavioral Risk Factor Surveillance System ... BRESS
Behavioral Risk Factor Surveillance System [*Health survey*] ... BRFSS
Behavioral Role-Playing Test (EDAC) ... BRPT
Behavioral Science Programming Language [*Computer science*] ... BSPL
Behavioral Science Research Laboratory (SAUO) ... BESRL
Behavioral Sciences Laboratory [*University of Cincinnati*] [*Information service or system*] (IID) ... BSL
Behavioral Sciences Research Laboratory (SAUO) ... BERSL
Behavioral Skills Training [*Navy*] ... BEST
Behavioral Skills Training Unit [*Navy*] (DNAB) ... BEHSTU
Behavioral Task Analysis (MCD) ... BTA
Behaviorally Anchored Rating Scale ... BARS
Behaviorally Handicapped ... BH
Behaviorally/Emotionally Handicapped ... BEH
Behavior-Based Incentive Compensation [*Human resources*] (WYGK) ... BBIC
Behaviorism [*Psychology*] (DAVI) ... beh
Behaviorists for Social Action (EA) ... BFSA
Behavior-Level Deviation (AAEL) ... BDEV
Behaviour Modification Information Test (AIE) ... BMIT
Behaviour Pattern (SAUS) ... BP
Behaviour Research and Therapy (SAUS) ... BRAT
Behavioural Ecology (SAUS) ... Behav Ecol
Behavioural Ecology and Sociobiology (SAUS) ... Behav Ecol Sociobiol
Behavioural Sciences Research Division (HEAS) ... BSRD
Behaviour-Based Personnel Systems (SAUS) ... BBPS
Behcet Syndrome [*Medicine*] (DMAA) ... BS
Behcet's Disease [*Medicine*] ... BD
Behcet-Touraine [*Syndrome*] [*Medicine*] (DB) ... BT
Beheaded (ROG) ... BEH
Behind (ROG) ... BEHD
Behind (FAAC) ... BHND
Behind Armor Debris [*Army*] (RDA) ... BAD
Behind Armor Effect [*Military*] (MUSM) ... BAE
Behind Completion Date ... BCD
Behind Schedule ... B/S
Behind Tape Reader (MCD) ... BTR
Behind the Ear [*Hearing aid*] [*Audiology*] ... BTE
Behind the Lens (NTCM) ... BTL
Behind the Line [*Air Force*] ... BTL
Behind The Scenes [*Film*] [*Television*] (WDMC) ... BTS
Behind-The-Reader (SAUS) ... BTR
Behnken's Unit [*Of Roentgen-Ray Exposure*] [*Radiology*] (DAVI) ... R
Behshahr [*Iran*] [*ICAO location identifier*] (ICLI) ... OINH
Behsood [*Afghanistan*] [*ICAO location identifier*] (ICLI) ... OABD
Bei [*At, With*] [*German*] ... B
BEI Electronics [*NASDAQ symbol*] (TTSB) ... BEII
BEI Electronics, Inc. [*Associated Press*] (SAG) ... BEI El
BEI Electronics, Inc. [*NASDAQ symbol*] (NQ) ... BEII
BEI Medical Systems [*NASDAQ symbol*] [*Formerly, BEI Electronics*] (SG) ... BMED
BEI Technologies [*NASDAQ symbol*] (SG) ... BEIQ
Beica [*Ethiopia*] [*Airport symbol*] (OAG) ... BEI
Beica [*Ethiopia*] [*ICAO location identifier*] (ICLI) ... HABE
Beida [*Libya*] [*Airport symbol*] (OAG) ... LAQ
Beifolgend [*Herewith*] [*German*] ... BEIF
Beige (WGA) ... BG
Beigebunden [*Bound With*] [*German*] (BARN) ... beigeb
Beigetretene Teile Deutschlands [*Newly Adhered Parts of Germany*] [*Name given to former East German territory after unification*] ... BGTD
Beihan [*People's Democratic Republic of Yemen*] [*ICAO location identifier*] (ICLI) ... ODAB
Beijer Institute Centre for Resource Assessment and Management [*British*] (IRUK) ... BICRAM
Beijing [*China*] [*Airport symbol*] (OAG) ... PEK
Beijing [*China*] [*ICAO location identifier*] (ICLI) ... ZBPE
Beijing Astronomical Observatory [*China*] ... BAO
Beijing City [*China*] [*ICAO location identifier*] (ICLI) ... ZBBB
Beijing Computer Center [*China*] (BUAC) ... GBCC
Beijing Dance Institute [*China*] ... BDI
Beijing Electron-Positron Collider [*High-energy physics*] [*China*] ... BEPC
Beijing Institute of Computer Technology (SAUS) ... BICT
Beijing Institute of Modern Physics [*China*] ... BIMP
Beijing Institute of Technology [*China*] ... BIT
Beijing Polytechnic University [*China*] ... BPU
Beijing Proton Synchrotron [*China*] ... BPS
Beijing Publications Import & Export Corp. ... BPIEC
Beijing Royal Jelly [*Biochemistry*] ... BRJ
Beijing Underground-Network Information System [*China*] (GEOI) ... BUPNIS
Beijing University of Chemical Technology ... BUCT
Beijing Yanhua Petrochem'H' ADS [*NYSE symbol*] (SG) ... BYH
Beijing/Capital [*China*] [*ICAO location identifier*] (ICLI) ... ZBAA
Beilingries [*Germany*] [*ICAO location identifier*] (ICLI) ... EDYG
Beilstein Registry Connection Tables [*Chemistry*] ... BRET
Beilstein Unique Sequence [*Chemistry*] ... BUS
Beilstein Unique Sequence Number [*Chemistry*] ... BUSEN
Beilstein-Institut, Frankfurt/Main, Germany [*Library symbol*] [*Library of Congress*] (LCLS) ... GyFmB
Being (ROG) ... BEG
Being ... BG
Being for Carter before the Convention [*One of the Carter Administration's criteria for appointment of federal judges*] ... BCBC
Beira [*Mozambique*] [*Airport symbol*] (OAG) ... BEW
Beira [*Mozambique*] [*ICAO location identifier*] (ICLI) ... FQBE
Beira [*Mozambique*] [*ICAO location identifier*] (ICLI) ... FQBR
Beirut [*Lebanon*] [*Airport symbol*] (OAG) ... BEY
Beirut [*Lebanon*] [*ICAO location identifier*] (ICLI) ... OLBV
Beirut [*Lebanon*] [*ICAO location identifier*] (ICLI) ... OLDD
Beirut [*Lebanon*] [*ICAO location identifier*] (ICLI) ... OLLL
Beirut/International [*Lebanon*] [*ICAO location identifier*] (ICLI) ... OLBA
Beiseker Municipal Library, Alberta [*Library symbol*] [*National Library of Canada*] (NLC) ... ABEM
Beiseker Municipal Library, Beiseker, AB, Canada [*Library symbol*] [*Library of Congress*] (LCLS) ... CaABeM
Beispiel [*Example*] [*Music*] [*German*] ... BEISP
Beit Bridge [*Zimbabwe*] [*ICAO location identifier*] (ICLI) ... FVBB
Beit Memorial Trust (SAUO) ... BMT
Beit Mikra (BJA) ... BM
Beit Zeiroth Mizrachi (BJA) ... BZM
Beitraeg [*or Beitraege*] [*Contribution, Share*] [*German*] (OCD) ... Beitr
Beitraege zum Altbabylonischen Privatrecht [*A publication*] (BJA) ... BAbPr
Beitraege zum Assyrischen Woerterbuch [*A publication*] (BJA) ... BaWb
Beitraege zur Danziger Statistik [*Danzig*] ... BDS
Beitraege zur Semitischen Sprachwissenschaft [*A publication*] (BJA) ... BSS
Beitraege zur Statistik der Republik Oesterreich [*Austria*] ... BSRO
Beja [*MARC language code*] [*Library of Congress*] (LCCP) ... bej
Beja [*Portugal*] [*ICAO location identifier*] (ICLI) ... LPBE
Beja [*Portugal*] [*ICAO location identifier*] (ICLI) ... LPBJ
Bejaia [*Algeria*] [*Airport symbol*] (OAG) ... BJA
Bejaia/Soummam [*Algeria*] [*ICAO location identifier*] (ICLI) ... DAAE
Beker Industries Corp. (SAUO) ... BKI
Beker Industries Corp. (SAUS) ... QBKI
Bekesy Ascending Descending Gap Evaluation ... BADGE
Bekily [*Madagascar*] [*ICAO location identifier*] (ICLI) ... FMSL
Bekily [*Madagascar*] [*Airport symbol*] (OAG) ... OVA
Bekol/Thomas [*Congo*] [*ICAO location identifier*] (ICLI) ... FCMT
Bel [*Ten decibels*] ... B
Bel Air, MD [*FM radio station call letters*] ... WHFC
Bel Air, MD [*AM radio station call letters*] ... WHRF
Bel and the Dragon [*Old Testament book*] [*Apocrypha*] ... Bel and Dr
Bel Exemplaire [*Typography*] (DGA) ... BEL EX
Bel Fuse, Inc. [*NASDAQ symbol*] (NQ) ... BELF
Bel Fuse, Inc. [*Associated Press*] (SAG) ... BelFuse
Bel Fuse, Inc.'A' [*NASDAQ symbol*] (SG) ... BELFA
Bela [*Pakistan*] [*ICAO location identifier*] (ICLI) ... OPBL
Bela Lugosi Society [*Defunct*] (EA) ... BLS
Bela Lyons Pratt [*Designer's mark, when appearing on US coins*] ... BLP
Bela Vista [*Brazil*] [*Airport symbol*] (AD) ... BVS
Belacker [*France*] [*Seismograph station code, US Geological Survey*] (SEIS) ... BAF

Belady Optimum Replacement [*Algorithm*] [*Computer science*] .... BOR
Belaga [*Malaysia*] [*Airport symbol*] (OAG) .... BLG
Belaga [*Malaysia*] [*ICAO location identifier*] (ICLI) .... WBGC
Belair [*Belarus*] [*ICAO designator*] (FAAC) .... BLI
Bel-Air Ltd. [*Slovakia*] [*FAA designator*] (FAAC) .... BLJ
Belair National Park (SAUS) .... BNP
Bel-Air Resources [*Vancouver Stock Exchange symbol*] .... BLS
Belarus (MILB) .... Bel
Belarus [*Internet country code*] .... BY
Belarus (SAUS) .... by
Belarusian Congress Committee of America .... BCCA
Belarusian-American Association in the United States of America .... BAZA
Belarusky Narodny Front [*Belarussian Popular Front*] [*Political party*] (EY) .... BNF
Belarussian Literary Association [*Canada*] (EAIO) .... BLA
Belastungswert (SAUS) .... BW
Belavia [*Belarus*] [*ICAO designator*] (FAAC) .... BRU
Belbek-5P [*Ukraine*] [*FAA designator*] (FAAC) .... BEK
Belchamp [*England*] .... BELCH
Belco Oil & Gas Corp. [*Associated Press*] (SAG) .... Belco
Belco Oil & Gas Corp. [*NYSE symbol*] (SAG) .... BOG
Belco Petroleum Corp. (SAUO) .... BPC
Belcourt, ND [*FM radio station call letters*] .... KEYA
Belden & Blake Corp. [*NASDAQ symbol*] (TTSB) .... BELD
Belden & Blake Energy Co. [*NASDAQ symbol*] (SAG) .... BELD
Belden & Blake Energy Co. [*Associated Press*] (SAG) .... BeldBlk
Belden Corp. (SAUO) .... BEL
Belden, Inc. [*Associated Press*] (SAG) .... Belden
Belden, Inc. [*NYSE symbol*] (SPSG) .... BWC
Belding Heminway Co., Inc. [*Associated Press*] (SAG) .... BeldHem
Belding Heminway Co., Inc. [*NYSE symbol*] (SPSG) .... BHY
Beleaguered (AABC) .... BEL
Belem [*Brazil*] [*Airport symbol*] (OAG) .... BEL
Belem [*Brazil*] [*ICAO location identifier*] (ICLI) .... SBBL
Belem/Julio Cesar [*Brazil*] [*ICAO location identifier*] (ICLI) .... SBJC
Belem/Val-De-Caes [*Brazil*] [*ICAO location identifier*] (ICLI) .... SBBE
Belen, NM [*AM radio station call letters*] .... KARS
Belen, NM [*FM radio station call letters*] (RBYB) .... KLVO
Belep [*New Caledonia*] [*Airport symbol*] (OAG) .... BMY
Belet Uen [*Somalia*] [*ICAO location identifier*] (ICLI) .... HCMN
Belfast [*City in Northern Ireland*] (ROG) .... BELF
Belfast [*Northern Ireland*] [*Airport symbol*] (OAG) .... BFS
Belfast [*City in Northern Ireland*] .... BLFST
Belfast and County Dow Railway (SAUO) .... BCD
Belfast and County Down Railway (SAUO) .... B&CoD
Belfast & Moosehead Lake (SAUO) .... B&M L
Belfast & Moosehead Lake (SAUS) .... BML
Belfast & Moosehead Lake Railroad Co. [*AAR code*] .... BML
Belfast and North Counties Railway [*British*] (ROG) .... B & NCR
Belfast Association of Engineers [*Northern Ireland*] (BARN) .... BAE
Belfast Banking Co. [*Ireland*] .... BBC
Belfast Chamber of Trade (SAUO) .... BCT
Belfast Citizens Commission (SAUO) .... BCC
Belfast City Library (SAUS) .... BCL
Belfast [*Northern Ireland*] **Harbour** [*Airport symbol*] (OAG) .... BHD
Belfast Harbour [*British*] [*ICAO location identifier*] (ICLI) .... EGAC
Belfast, ME [*Location identifier*] [*FAA*] (FAAL) .... BST
Belfast, ME [*FM radio station call letters*] (BROA) .... WBFB-FM
Belfast, ME [*FM radio station call letters*] .... WWFX
Belfast, Mersey and Manchester [*Steamship*] (MHDB) .... BMM
Belfast Public Library (SAUO) .... BPL
Belfast Public Library, Belfast, NY [*Library symbol*] [*Library of Congress*] (LCLS) .... NBelf
Belfast und Northern Counties Railway (SAUO) .... B&NCR
Belfast Urban Area (SAUO) .... BUA
Belfast/Aldergrove [*British*] [*ICAO location identifier*] (ICLI) .... EGAA
Belfer Graduate School of Science (SAUO) .... BGSC
Belfort [*France*] [*Airport symbol*] (OAG) .... BOR
Belfort Laser Ceilometer (ARMP) .... BLC
Belfort/Chaux [*France*] [*ICAO location identifier*] (ICLI) .... LFGG
Belfort/Fontaine [*France*] [*ICAO location identifier*] (ICLI) .... LFSQ
Belga [*Monetary unit*] [*Belgium*] .... B
Belga Esperantista Federacio (SAUO) .... BEF
Belga Esperanto-Instituto (SAUO) .... BEI
Belgaum [*India*] [*Airport symbol*] (OAG) .... IXG
Belgaum [*India*] [*ICAO location identifier*] (ICLI) .... VABM
Belgavia (Societe de Handling) [*Belgium*] [*ICAO designator*] (FAAC) .... BLG
Belgian (ODBW) .... Bel
Belgian (ADWA) .... Belg
Belgian Academy of Esthetic Dentistry (SAUO) .... BAED
Belgian African Line (SAUO) .... BAL
Belgian Air Force .... BAF
Belgian Air Staff [*NATO*] (NATG) .... BELAIR
Belgian American Chamber of Commerce in the United States (NTPA) .... BACC
Belgian American Educational Foundation (EA) .... BAEF
Belgian and Luxembourg Association of Penal Law (EAIO) .... BLAPL
Belgian Antarctic Expedition [*1897-99,1957-58*] .... BelgAE
Belgian Archives for the Social Sciences [*Information service or system*] (IID) .... BASS
Belgian Army (SAUO) .... BAR
Belgian Army Allied Club (SAUO) .... BELAAC
Belgian Association for Development Cooperation (SAUO) .... BADECO
Belgian Begonia Growers Association [*Defunct*] (EA) .... BBGA
Belgian Chamber of Commerce for Australia .... BCCA
Belgian Chamber of Commerce in the United States (SAUO) .... BCCUS
Belgian Circle in Victoria [*An association*] [*Australia*] .... BCV
Belgian Committee for Electroheat and Electrochemistry (SAUO) .... BCEE
Belgian Congo (SAUS) BC/62FAB
Belgian Congo .... CB
Belgian Co-ordinated Collections of Micro-organisms (SAUS) .... BCCM
Belgian Defence Industries (SAUO) .... BDI
Belgian Defence Industry Group (SAUO) .... BDIG
Belgian Draft Horse Corporation of America (SAUO) .... BDHCA
Belgian Educational Student Travel Service .... BESTS
Belgian Engineers & Constructors S.A. (SAUO) .... BECSA
Belgian Engineers in North America [*Defunct*] (EA) .... BENA
Belgian Flight Centre [*ICAO designator*] (FAAC) .... ABF
Belgian Fourragere [*Military decoration*] .... BEFOURRA
Belgian Fourragere [*Military decoration*] .... BEFourragere
Belgian Fourragere [*Military decoration*] .... BF
Belgian Franc (SAUS) .... BEF
Belgian Franc [*Monetary unit*] .... BFc
Belgian Franc (SAUS) .... BFr
Belgian Fruit Line (SAUO) .... BFL
Belgian Fund for Development Cooperation (SAUO) .... FOSBel
Belgian Futures and Options Exchange [*Stock exchange*] [*Belgium*] (EY) .... BELFOX
Belgian Hand Group (SAUO) .... BHG
Belgian Information and Dissemination Service [*European host database system*] [*Ministry of Economic Affairs*] (IID) .... BELINDIS
Belgian Information System by Telephone (SAUS) .... BISTEL
Belgian Institute for Automatic Control (SAUO) .... BIRA
Belgian Institute for Posts and Telecommunications (SAUO) .... BIPT
Belgian Institute for Space Aeronomy (SAUS) .... BISA
Belgian Institute in London (SAUS) .... BIL
Belgian Institute in London (SAUO) .... BIL
Belgian International Air Carriers [*ICAO designator*] (FAAC) .... BIC
Belgian International Air Services (SAUO) .... BIAS
Belgian Linen Association [*Later, ILPC*] (EA) .... BLA
Belgian Mechanical Fabrication (SAUS) .... BMF
Belgian Military Communications (SAUS) .... BEMILCOM
Belgian Nautical Research Association (SAUO) .... BNRA
Belgian Naval Ship (SAUS) .... BNS
Belgian Naval Staff [*NATO*] (NATG) .... BELNAV
Belgian Nuclear Research Centre (SAUO) .... BNRC
Belgian Online Libraries Directory (SAUO) .... BOLD
Belgian Organisation for Testing Laboratories and Inspection Bodies (SAUS) .... BELTEST
Belgian Organisation for the Certification of Quality Systems, products and personnel (SAUS) .... BELCERT
Belgian package (SAUS) .... BIBLIO
Belgian package for HP 3000 (SAUS) .... BIBOSS
Belgian PC package (SAUS) .... ATBiB
Belgian PC package (SAUS) .... BIDOC
Belgian PC package (SAUS) .... GIBUS
Belgian Reactor .... BR
Belgian Research Network (SAUO) .... Belnet
Belgian Review of International Law [*A publication*] (DLA) .... Belg Rev Int'l L
Belgian Sheepdog Club of America (EA) .... BSCA
Belgian Shipbuilders Corp. (SAUS) .... BSC
Belgian Socialist Party .... BSP
Belgian Society of Medicine and Surgery of the Foot (SAUS) .... SBMCP
Belgian Tank Storage Company (SAUO) .... Beltanco
Belgian Technical Foundry Association (SAUO) .... BTGV
Belgian Telecommunications User Group (ACRL) .... BELTUG
Belgian Tourist Bureau (SAUO) .... BTB
Belgian Tourist Office (EA) .... BTO
Belgian Unidentified Flying Objects Investigation (SAUO) .... BUFOI
Belgian Unix User Group (SAUS) .... BUUG
Belgian UNIX Users Group (SAUO) .... BUUG
Belgian Veterinary Computer Association (GVA) .... BCVA
Belgian-American Association (EAIO) .... ABA
Belgian-Luxembourg American Studies Association [*Belgium*] (EAIO) .... BLASA
Belgic [*Language*] (BARN) .... Bel
Belgique Judiciaire [*A publication*] (ILCA) .... Belg Jud
Belgique Judiciaire [*A publication*] (ILCA) .... ILCA
Belgische Radio en Televisie [*Belgian Radio and Television - Dutch Service*] .... BRT
Belgische Socialistische Partij [*Belgian Socialist Party*] (PPW) .... BSP
Belgische Werkliedenpartij [*Belgian Workers' Party*] [*Later, Belgian Socialist Party*] [*Political party*] (PPE) .... BWP
Belgisch-Luxembourg Wissel Instituut [*Benelux*] .... BLWI
Belgium [*IYRU nationality code*] .... B
Belgium [*ANSI two-letter standard code*] (CNC) .... BE
Belgium [*MARC country of publication code*] [*Library of Congress*] (LCCP) .... be
Belgium (MILB) .... Be
Belgium (ODBW) .... Bel
Belgium [*ANSI three-letter standard code*] (CNC) .... BEL
Belgium .... BELG
Belgium (VRA) .... Belg
Belgium [*MARC geographic area code*] [*Library of Congress*] (LCCP) .... e-be-
Belgium [*International civil aircraft marking*] (ODBW) .... OO
Belgium and Luxembourg (SAUS) .... Belgolux
Belgium Centre for Information Processing (SAUS) .... BCIP
Belgium Netherland Luxembourg Economic Union (SAUO) .... Benelux
Belgium Pharmacopoeia [*A publication*] .... Belg P
Belgium Philatelic Society (EA) .... BPS
Belgium Tourist Reservations (SAUO) .... BTR
Belgium-Luxembourg (SAUS) .... B-L
Belgium-Luxembourg Chamber of Commerce [*Australia*] .... B-LCC
Belgium-Luxembourg Economic Union [*Political party*] (PPE) .... BLEU

Belgrade [*Former Yugoslavia*] [*Airport symbol*] (OAG) .... BEG
Belgrade (SAUS) .... Bel
Belgrade Elementary School, Belgrade, MN [*Library symbol*] [*Library of Congress*] (LCLS) .... MnBgE
Belgrade High School, Media Center, Belgrade, MN [*Library symbol*] [*Library of Congress*] (LCLS) .... MnBgH
Belgrade, MT [*AM radio station call letters*] .... KGVW
Belgrade, MT [*FM radio station call letters*] .... KSCY
Belhaven College (SAUO) .... BC
Belhaven College, Jackson, MS [*Library symbol*] [*Library of Congress*] (LCLS) .... MsJB
Belhaven, NC [*FM radio station call letters*] .... WKJA
Beli, AK [*Location identifier*] [*FAA*] (FAAL) .... BEK
Beliefs about Science and Science Education Scale (EDAC) .... BSSE
Believe [*Amateur radio shorthand*] (WDAA) .... BLV
Believe It or Not .... BION
Believe the Children [*An association*] (EA) .... BTC
Belinfante-Swihart [*Theory*] .... BS
Beling and Vanderstraaten's Ceylon Reports [*A publication*] (DLA) .... B & V
Beling and Vanderstraaten's Ceylon Reports [*A publication*] (DLA) .... Beling & Van
Beling's Ceylon Reports [*A publication*] (DLA) .... Bel
Beling's Ceylon Reports [*A publication*] (DLA) .... Beling
Belize (BARN) .... Bel
Belize [*ANSI three-letter standard code*] (CNC) .... BLZ
Belize [*ANSI two-letter standard code*] (CNC) .... BZ
Belize (MILB) .... Bze
Belize [*International civil aircraft marking*] (ODBW) V3
Belize Action Movement (PD) .... BAM
Belize Airways [*ICAO designator*] (AD) .... ST
Belize Broadcasting Network (EY) .... BBN
Belize City [*Belize*] [*Airport symbol*] (OAG) .... BZE
Belize Defense Forces [*Military*] .... BDF
Belize Institute of Social Research (SAUO) .... BISRA
Belize Institute of Social Research and Action .... BISRA
Belize Popular Party [*Political party*] (EY) .... BPP
Belize Trans Air [*ICAO designator*] (FAAC) .... JGR
Belize Transair [*ICAO designator*] (FAAC) .... BTR
Belize/International [*Belize*] [*ICAO location identifier*] (ICLI) .... MZBZ
Belkin, Inc. [*Toronto Stock Exchange symbol*] .... BKN
Belknap's Probate Law of California [*A publication*] (DLA) .... Bel Prob
Bell (NFPA) .... B
Bell [*Computer science*] (DOM) .... BEL
Bell (IEEE) .... BL
Bell Adjustment Inventory (EDAC) .... BAI
Bell Administrative Network Communication System [*Telecommunications*] (TEL) .... BANCS
Bell Administrative Network Communications System [*Telecommunications*] (ACRL) .... BANCS
Bell Advanced Tilt Rotor (MCD) .... BAT
Bell Aerospace Co. .... BAC
Bell Aerospace Co., New Orleans, LA [*Library symbol*] [*Library of Congress*] (LCLS) .... LNBA
Bell Aerospace Corporation (SAUO) .... BAC
Bell Aerospace Textron .... BAT
Bell Aerospace Textron, Technical Library, Niagara Falls, NY [*Library symbol*] [*Library of Congress*] (LCLS) .... NNiaB
Bell Aerosystems Co. (KSC) .... BA
Bell Aerosystems Co. (SAUO) .... ba
Bell Aerosystems Co., Buffalo, NY [*Library symbol*] [*Library of Congress*] (LCLS) .... NBuBA
Bell Aerosystems Company (SAUS) .... BA
Bell Aircraft Corp. (SAUO) .... Bell
Bell Alarm (IAA) .... BA
Bell Alarm Switch (AAG) .... BASW
Bell and Bell [*Technical drawings*] .... B & B
Bell and Bell (SAUS) .... B&B
Bell and Flange (SAUS) .... B and F
Bell and Flange [*Technical drawings*] .... B & F
Bell and Gossett Company (SAUO) .... BLG
Bell & Howell Co. (EFIS) .... B&H
Bell & Howell Co. .... BH
Bell & Howell Co., Research Laboratories, Pasadena, CA [*Library symbol*] [*Library of Congress*] (LCLS) .... CPBH
Bell & Howell Holdings Co. [*Associated Press*] (SAG) .... BellHwl
Bell & Howell Holdings Co. [*NYSE symbol*] (SAG) .... BHW
Bell & Howell/Mamiya Co. .... BHMC
Bell and Spigot [*Technical drawings*] .... B & S
Bell and Spigot (SAUS) .... B&S
Bell Application Network Control System (SAUS) .... BANCS
Bell Atlantic .... BA
Bell Atlantic Corp. (EFIS) .... BAC
Bell Atlantic Corp. (EFIS) .... BATCO
Bell Atlantic Corp. [*NYSE symbol*] (SPSG) .... BEL
Bell Atlantic Corp. [*Associated Press*] (SAG) .... BellAtl
Bell Atlantic Mobile Systems [*Telecommunications*] .... BAMS
Bell Atlantic Nynex Mobil (SAUS) .... BANM
Bell Atlantic Regional Timesharing (SAUO) .... BARTS
Bell Audit Relate System [*Bell Laboratories*] .... BARS
Bell Audit System [*Bell Laboratories*] .... BAS
Bell Bancorp, Inc. [*NASDAQ symbol*] (SAG) .... BELL
Bell Bancorp, Inc. [*Associated Press*] (SAG) .... BellBcp
Bell Cablemedia [*NASDAQ symbol*] (TTSB) .... BCMPY
Bell Cablemedia Ltd. [*NASDAQ symbol*] (SAG) .... BCMP
Bell Cablemedia Ltd. [*Associated Press*] (SAG) .... BellCabl
Bell. Calcutta Reports [*A publication*] (DLA) .... Bell
Bell Canada [*Toronto Stock Exchange symbol*] .... BC
Bell Canada Data Resource Center, Ottawa, ON, Canada [*Library symbol*] [*Library of Congress*] (LCLS) .... CaOOBDR
Bell Canada Documentation Resource Center, Hull, PQ, Canada [*Library symbol*] [*Library of Congress*] (LCLS) .... CaQHB
Bell Canada Enterprises (SAUS) .... BCE
Bell Canada Enterprises, Inc. [*Toronto Stock Exchange symbol*] [*Vancouver Stock Exchange symbol*] .... B
Bell Canada, Headquarters Economics Library, Hull, PQ, Canada [*Library symbol*] [*Library of Congress*] (LCLS) .... CaQHBE
Bell Canada, Headquarters Engineering Economics Reference Centre, Hull, PQ, Canada [*Library symbol*] [*Library of Congress*] (LCLS) .... CaQHBEER
Bell Canada Headquarters Regulatory Matters-Regulatory Information Bank, Hull, PQ, Canada [*Library symbol*] [*Library of Congress*] (LCLS) .... CaQHBRM
Bell Canada Headquarters, Regulatory Matters-Regulatory Information Bank, Hull, Quebec [*Library symbol*] [*National Library of Canada*] (NLC) .... QHBRM
Bell Canada Information Resource Centre, Toronto, ON, Canada [*Library symbol*] [*Library of Congress*] (LCLS) .... CaOTBCIR
Bell Canada Information Resource Centre, Toronto, Ontario [*Library symbol*] [*National Library of Canada*] (NLC) .... OTBCIR
Bell Canada International, Inc. [*Ottawa, ON*] [*Telecommunications*] (TSSD) .... BCI
Bell Canada Intl. [*NASDAQ symbol*] (SG) .... BCICF
Bell Canada Market Information Centre, Ottawa, ON, Canada [*Library symbol*] [*Library of Congress*] (LCLS) .... CaOOBMI
Bell Canada Market Information Centre, Ottawa, Ontario [*Library symbol*] [*National Library of Canada*] (NLC) .... OOBMI
Bell Character [*Keyboard*] .... BEL
Bell College of Technology Information Service (SAUS) .... BECTIS
Bell College Technical Information Service, Hamilton [*British*] (NITA) .... BECTIS
Bell College Technology Information System (SAUS) .... BECTIS
Bell Communications Research, Inc. (SAUS) .... BCR
Bell Communications Research, Inc. (TSSD) .... Bellcore
Bell Communications Research, Inc. (SAUO) .... BELLCORE
Bell Companies .... BELCOS
Bell. Competing Titles [*Scotland*] [*A publication*] (DLA) .... BCT
Bell. Competing Titles [*Scotland*] [*A publication*] (DLA) .... Bell CT
Bell Cord [*Technical drawings*] .... BC
Bell Crank [*Automotive engineering*] .... B/CRK
Bell Crank [*Automotive engineering*] .... BELCRK
Bell Data Network [*Telecommunications*] .... BDN
Bell Doesn't Ring [*Telecommunications*] (TEL) .... BDR
Bell. Election Law of Scotland [*A publication*] (DLA) .... Bell Elec
Bell End .... BE
Bell FLICKS [*Programming language*] [*1973*] (CSR) .... BEFLIX
Bell Helicopter Co. (SAUO) .... bh
Bell Helicopter Co., Brantly Helicopter Corp., Brditschka [*Heinrich Brditschka Flugzeugbau*] [*ICAO aircraft manufacturer identifier*] (ICAO) .... HB
Bell Helicopter Co., Fort Worth, TX [*Library symbol*] [*Library of Congress*] (LCLS) .... TxFBH
Bell Helicopter Company (SAUO) .... BHC
Bell Helicopter International (ACAE) .... BHI
Bell Helicopter, Textron Canada [*FAA designator*] (FAAC) .... TXB
Bell Helicopter Textron, Inc. .... BHT
Bell Helicopter Textron-Europe (SAUS) .... BHT-E
Bell Indexing (SAUS) .... BELLDEX
Bell Industries, Inc. [*Associated Press*] (SAG) .... BellInd
Bell Industries, Inc. [*NYSE symbol*] (SPSG) .... BI
Bell Information Flow System (SAUS) .... BIFS
Bell Information Network .... BIN
Bell Integrated Optical Device [*Electronics*] (EECA) .... BIOD
Bell International Corp. (SAUO) .... BLL
Bell Island, AK [*Location identifier*] [*FAA*] (FAAL) .... KBE
Bell Island Public Library, Bell Island, NF, Canada [*Library symbol*] [*Library of Congress*] (LCLS) .... CaNfBI
Bell Island Public Library, Newfoundland [*Library symbol*] [*National Library of Canada*] (NLC) .... NFBI
Bell Jar System .... BJS
Bell Jar System (SAUS) BJS-58
Bell Laboratories Automatic Design System [*Computer program*] .... BLADES
Bell Laboratories Automatic Design System [*Computer program*] .... BLADS
Bell Laboratories Automatic Device .... BLADE
Bell Laboratories Formula Translation Assembly Program (IAA) .... BETAP
Bell Laboratories FORTRAN Assembly Program [*Computer science*] (IEEE) .... BEFAP
Bell Laboratories Interpratative System (SAUS) .... BLIS
Bell Laboratories Interpretive System [*Computer program*] .... BLIS
Bell Laboratories Library Real-Time Loan System .... BELLREL
Bell Laboratories Library Real-time Loan System (SAUS) .... BELLREL System
Bell Laboratories Machine Aided Technical Information Center (SAUS) .... BELLMATIC
Bell Laboratories Machine-Aided Technical Information Center (SAUS) BELLMATIC-1
Bell Laboratories Record (journ.) (SAUS) .... Bell Lab Rec
Bell Laboratories Record (journ.) (SAUS) .... BeLR
Bell Laboratories Record (journ.) (SAUS) .... BLRC
Bell Labs Engineering Scholarship Program (SAUS) .... BLESP
Bell Labs Layered Space-Time .... BLAST
Bell. Lecture on Conveyancing [*Scotland*] [*A publication*] (DLA) .... Bell Convey
Bell Little Electrodata Symbolic System for the Electrodata [*Symbolic assembly program*] .... BLESSED
Bell Log System .... BLS

Bell Memorial Public Library, Mentone, IN [Library symbol] [Library of Congress] (LCLS) .... InMe
Bell Metal (SAUS) .... BM
Bell Microproducts [NASDAQ symbol] (TTSB) .... BELM
Bell Microproducts, Inc. [Associated Press] (SAG) .... BellMic
Bell Microproducts, Inc. [NASDAQ symbol] (SAG) .... BELM
Bell Molybdenum Mines [Vancouver Stock Exchange symbol] .... BLY
Bell Northern Research [Telecommunications] (TEL) .... BNR
Bell Northern Research, Bramalea, ON, Canada [Library symbol] [Library of Congress] (LCLS) .... CaOBramB
Bell Northern Research, Bramalea, Ontario [Library symbol] [National Library of Canada] (NLC) .... OBRAMB
Bell Northern Research, Inc., Learning Resources Center, Morrisville, NC [Library symbol] [Library of Congress] (LCLS) .... NcMorB
Bell Northern Research, Montreal, PQ, Canada [Library symbol] [Library of Congress] (LCLS) .... CaQMBNR
Bell Northern Research, Montreal, Quebec [Library symbol] [National Library of Canada] (NLC) .... QMBNR
Bell Northern Research, Ottawa, ON, Canada [Library symbol] [Library of Congress] (LCLS) .... CaOONorE
Bell Northern Research, Ottawa, Ontario [Library symbol] [National Library of Canada] (NLC) .... OONORE
Bell Northern Software Research, Toronto, ON, Canada [Library symbol] [Library of Congress] (LCLS) .... CaOTBNS
Bell Northern Software Research, Toronto, Ontario [Library symbol] [National Library of Canada] (NLC) .... OTBNS
Bell Number Screening [Telecommunications] (TEL) .... BNS
Bell Object Relations Inventory (SAUS) .... BORI
Bell on Excise [A publication] (DLA) .... Bel Ex
Bell on Expert Testimony [A publication] (DLA) .... Bell Exp Test
Bell on Landlord and Tenant [Bengal] [A publication] (DLA) .... Bell L & T
Bell on Leases [Scotland] [A publication] (DLA) .... Bell Leas
Bell on Leases [A publication] (DLA) .... BL
Bell Operating Co. [Also, BSOC] [Post-divestiture division of American Telephone & Telegraph Co.] .... BOC
Bell Operating Companies (SAUO) .... BOCs
Bell Operating System (SAUS) .... BESYS
Bell Operating System [Telecommunications] (TEL) .... BOS
Bell Owned and Maintained [Telecommunications] (TEL) .... BOAM
Bell Point Of Contact (SAUS) .... BPOC
Bell. Property as Arising from the Relation of Husband and Wife [1849] [A publication] (DLA) .... Bell HW
Bell Propulsion Laboratory (IAA) .... BPL
Bell Rings Faintly [Telecommunications] (TEL) .... BRF
Bell. Sale of Food and Drugs [14th ed.] [1968] [A publication] (DLA) .... Bell S
Bell. Sale of Food and Drugs [14th ed.] [1968] [A publication] (DLA) .... Bell Sale
Bell Shock Force (SAUS) .... BSF
Bell Sports [NASDAQ symbol] (TTSB) .... BSPT
Bell Sports Corp. [Associated Press] (SAG) .... BellSpt
Bell Sports Corp. [NASDAQ symbol] (SAG) .... BSPT
Bell System (SAUS) .... Bell
Bell System Center for Technical Education .... BSCTE
Bell System Common Language [Telecommunications] (TEL) .... BSCL
Bell. System of the Forms of Deeds [Scotland] [A publication] (DLA) .... Bell Deeds
Bell. System of the Forms of Deeds (Styles) [Scotland] [A publication] (DLA) .... Bell Sty
Bell System Operating Co. [Also, BOC] [Post-divestiture division of American Telephone & Telegraph Co.] .... BSOC
Bell System Practices .... BSP
Bell System Reference Frequency Standard (SAUS) .... BCRFS
Bell System Reference Frequency Standard [Telecommunications] (TEL) .... BSRFS
Bell System Reference System (SAUS) .... BSRF
Bell System Repair Specification [Telecommunications] (TEL) .... BSRS
Bell System Technical Journal (journ.) (SAUS) .... Bell Sys Tech
Bell Systems Data Processing (SAUS) .... BSDP
Bell Systems Technical Journal [A publication] (CCCA) .... BSTJ
Bell Tech Group Ltd [NASDAQ symbol] (TTSB) .... BELT
Bell Technology Group Ltd. [Associated Press] (SAG) .... BellTch
Bell Technology Group Ltd. [Associated Press] (SAG) .... BellTech
Bell Technology Group Ltd. [NASDAQ symbol] (SAG) .... BELT
Bell Technology Wrrt [NASDAQ symbol] (TTSB) .... BELTW
Bell Telephone Co. of Canada (IIA) .... BTC
Bell Telephone Co. of Canada, Law Department Library, Montreal, PQ, Canada [Library symbol] [Library of Congress] (LCLS) .... CaQMBL
Bell Telephone Co. of Canada, Montreal, PQ, Canada [Library symbol] [Library of Congress] (LCLS) .... CaQMB
Bell Telephone Laboratories (SAUO) .... Bell
Bell Telephone Laboratories (SAUO) .... BELLTEL
Bell Telephone Laboratories, Inc. [Murray Hill, NJ] .... BTL
Bell Telephone Laboratories, Inc., Holmdel, NJ [OCLC symbol] (OCLC) .... BTL
Bell Telephone Laboratories, Inc., Murray Hill, NJ [Library symbol] [Library of Congress] (LCLS) .... NjMuB
Bell Telephone Laboratories, Inc., Technical Information Library, Holmdel, NJ [Library symbol] [Library of Congress] (LCLS) .... NjHolB
Bell Telephone Laboratories, Inc., Technical Information Library, Whippany, NJ [Library symbol] [Library of Congress] (LCLS) .... NjWhiB
Bell Telephone Manufacturing (SAUS) BTM-13
Bell Telephone Manufacturing Co. [Telecommunications] .... BTM
Bell. Testing of Deeds [Scotland] [A publication] (DLA) .... Bell TD
Bell. Testing of Deeds [Scotland] [A publication] (DLA) .... BTD
Bell Wire .... BW
Bella Bella [Canada] [Airport symbol] (OAG) .... ZEL
Bella Coola [Canada] [Airport symbol] (OAG) .... QBC

Bella Coola Museum, Bella Coola, BC, Canada [Library symbol] [Library of Congress] (LCLS) .... CaBBCM
Bella Coola Museum, British Columbia [Library symbol] [National Library of Canada] (NLC) .... BBCM
Bella Union [Bolivia] [ICAO location identifier] (ICLI) .... SLBN
Bella Vista [Paraguay] [ICAO location identifier] (ICLI) .... SGBV
Bella Vista, AR [FM radio station call letters] .... KBVA
Bellabon Resources [Vancouver Stock Exchange symbol] .... BLJ
Belladonna [Deadly Nightshade (or its medicinal extract)] .... BD
belladonna .... bell
Belladonna (SAUS) .... Bella
Belladonna [Deadly Nightshade (or its medicinal extract)] (ROG) .... BELLAD
Belladonna [Deadly Nightshade (or its medicinal extract)] (ROG) .... BELLADON
belladonna alkaloids (SAUS) .... bell alk
Belladonna & Opium (SAUS) .... B&O
Belladonna and Opium [Toxicology] .... B & O
Belladonna Mottle Virus [Plant pathology] .... BEMV
Belladonna/Opium (DB) .... BO
Bell-Air [ICAO designator] (AD) LL
Bell-Air Executive Air Travel Ltd. [New Zealand] [ICAO designator] (FAAC) .... BEL
Bellaire City Library, Bellaire, TX [Library symbol] [Library of Congress] (LCLS) .... TxBl
Bellaire, MI [Location identifier] [FAA] (FAAL) .... ACB
Bellaire, MI [Location identifier] [FAA] (FAAL) .... CXK
Bellaire, OH [Location identifier] [FAA] (FAAL) .... AIR
Bellaire, OH [AM radio station call letters] .... WOMP
Bellaire, OH [FM radio station call letters] .... WOMP-FM
Bellaire Public Library, Bellaire, MI [Library symbol] [Library of Congress] (LCLS) .... MiBela
Bellaire, TX [AM radio station call letters] (BROA) .... KILE
Bellaire, Zanesville & Cincinnati Railroad [Nickname: Bent, Zigzagged, and Crooked] .... BZ & C
Bellaire, Zanesville and Cincinnati Railroad (SAUO) .... BZ&C
Bellairs Research Institute [Canada] (MSC) .... BRI
Bellamy Brothers Fan Club (EA) .... BBFC
Bellanca Aircraft Corp. [ICAO aircraft manufacturer identifier] (ICAO) .... BL
Bellanca Aircraft Corp., Champion Aircraft Corp. [ICAO aircraft manufacturer identifier] (ICAO) .... CH
Bellanca Contact (EA) .... BC
Bellar & Lichtenberg [Device] .... B & L
Bellarmine College (SAUO) .... BC
Bellarmine College, Louisville, KY [OCLC symbol] (OCLC) .... KBC
Bellarmine College, Louisville, KY [Library symbol] [Library of Congress] (LCLS) .... KyLoB
Bellarmine College, Plattsburgh, NY [Library symbol] [Library of Congress] (LCLS) .... NPlaB
Bellarmine College, Thomas Merton Studies Center (SAUS) .... KyloB-M
Bellarmine College, Thomas Merton Studies Center, Louisville, KY [Library symbol] [Library of Congress] (LCLS) .... KyLoB-M
Bellary [India] [ICAO location identifier] (ICLI) .... VOBI
Bellasis. Bombay Reports [A publication] (DLA) .... Bel
Bellasis. Bombay Reports [A publication] (DLA) .... Bell
Bellasis. Civil Cases [Bombay] [A publication] (DLA) .... Bellas
Bellasis. Civil Cases [Bombay] [A publication] (DLA) .... Bell CC
Bellasis. Criminal Cases [Bombay] [A publication] (DLA) .... Bellas
Bellasis. Criminal Cases [Bombay] [A publication] (DLA) .... Bell CC
Bellavista/Huallaga [Peru] [ICAO location identifier] (ICLI) .... SPBL
Bellco Energy Corp. [Vancouver Stock Exchange symbol] .... BLO
BELLCORE AMA Format (SAUS) .... BAMAF
Belle Chasse, LA [FM radio station call letters] .... KMEZ
Belle Chasse State School, Belle Chasse, LA [Library symbol] [Library of Congress] (LCLS) .... LBcS
Belle Fourche Public Library, Belle Fourche, SD [Library symbol] [Library of Congress] (LCLS) .... SdBf
Belle Fourche, SD [AM radio station call letters] .... KBFS
Belle Fourche, SD [FM radio station call letters] (RBYB) .... KZZI
Belle Glade, FL [FM radio station call letters] .... WBGF
Belle Glade, FL [AM radio station call letters] .... WSWN
Belle Plaine, IA [FM radio station call letters] .... KXPW
Belle Plaine, IA [FM radio station call letters] (BROA) .... KZAT-FM
Belle Plaine, KS [FM radio station call letters] .... KANR
Belle Plaine Union, Belle Plaine, IA [Library symbol] [Library of Congress] (LCLS) .... IaBepU
Belle River Public Library, Ontario [Library symbol] [National Library of Canada] (NLC) .... OBRI
Belle Valley School, Belleville, IL [Library symbol] [Library of Congress] (LCLS) .... IBelVS
Bellechasse [Switzerland] [ICAO location identifier] (ICLI) .... LSTB
Belleek Collectors' International Society (EA) .... BCS
Belleek Collector's Society [Commercial firm] (EA) .... BCS
Bellefontaine, OH [Location identifier] [FAA] (FAAL) .... RUV
Bellefontaine, OH [AM radio station call letters] .... WBLL
Bellefontaine, OH [FM radio station call letters] .... WPKO
Bellefonte, AR [AM radio station call letters] .... KNWA
Bellefonte Central Railroad Co. [AAR code] .... BFC
Bellefonte District Library Center [Library network] .... CPDLC
Bellefonte Nuclear Plant (NRCH) .... BNP
Bellefonte, PA [AM radio station call letters] .... WBLF
Bellefonte, PA [FM radio station call letters] .... WZWW
Bellefonte-Clearfield-Philipsburg [Pennsylvania] [Airport symbol] (AD) .... PSB
Bellegarde, SK [Television station call letters] CBKFT-9
Bellegarde/Vouvray [France] [ICAO location identifier] (ICLI) .... LFHN
Bellerive Foundation (EAIO) .... BF
Bellerophon [of Euripides] [Classical studies] (OCD) .... Beller
Beller's Criminal Cases [Bombay] [A publication] (DLA) .... Bell Cr C

Beller's Criminal Cases [Bombay] [A publication] (DLA) .... Bell Cr Ca
Beller's Criminal Cases [Bombay] [A publication] (DLA) .... Bell Cr Cas
Beller's Delineation of Universal Law [A publication] (DLA) .... Bell UL
Beller's Delineations of Universal Law [A publication] (DLA) .... Bell Del
Bellerville/Scott Air Force Base [Illinois] [ICAO location identifier] (ICLI) .... KBLV
Belles Lettres [A publication] (BRI) .... Belles Let
Belleview, FL [FM radio station call letters] (BROA) .... WWKO-FM
Belleville [Diocesan abbreviation] [Illinois] (TOCD) .... BEL
Belleville & District Chamber of Commerce (AC) .... BCC
Belleville Area College, Belleville, IL [Library symbol] [Library of Congress]
    (LCLS) .... IBelC
Belleville Area College, Belleville, IL [OCLC symbol] (OCLC) .... IDF
Belleville Astronomy Club (SAUO) .... BAC
Belleville Free Public Library, Belleville, NJ [Library symbol] [Library of
    Congress] (LCLS) .... NjBe
Belleville, IL [Location identifier] [FAA] (FAAL) .... BLV
Belleville, IL [Location identifier] [FAA] (FAAL) .... OXK
Belleville, IL [Location identifier] [FAA] (FAAL) .... RCC
Belleville, IL [Location identifier] [FAA] (FAAL) .... SKE
Belleville, IL [AM radio station call letters] .... WIBV
Belleville, KS [FM radio station call letters] .... KREP
Belleville, KS [Location identifier] [FAA] (FAAL) .... RPB
Belleville, ON [FM radio station call letters] .... CIGL
Belleville, ON [AM radio station call letters] .... CJBQ
Belleville, ON [FM radio station call letters] .... CJLX
Belleville, ON [FM radio station call letters] .... CJOJ
Belleville Public Library, Belleville, IL [Library symbol] [Library of Congress]
    (LCLS) .... IBel
Belleville Public Library, Belleville, ON, Canada [Library symbol] [Library of
    Congress] (LCLS) .... CaOBE
Belleville Public Library, Ontario [Library symbol] [National Library of
    Canada] (NLC) .... OBE
Belleville Public Schools District 118, Belleville, IL [Library symbol] [Library
    of Congress] (LCLS) .... IBelSD
Belleville Telegram, Belleville, NJ [Library symbol] [Library of Congress]
    (LCLS) .... NjBeT
Belleville Township High School District 201, Belleville, IL [Library symbol]
    [Library of Congress] (LCLS) .... IBelTSD
Belleville-Villie-Morgon [France] [ICAO location identifier] (ICLI) .... LFHW
Bellevue Community College, Bellevue, WA [Library symbol] [Library of
    Congress] (LCLS) .... WaBB
Bellevue Herald-Leader, Bellevue, IA [Library symbol] [Library of Congress]
    (LCLS) .... IaBevHL
Bellevue Index of Depression .... BID
Bellevue Municipal Library, Alberta [Library symbol] [National Library of
    Canada] (NLC) .... ABELM
Bellevue, NE [AM radio station call letters] (BROA) .... KAZP-AM
Bellevue, NE [AM radio station call letters] .... KOIL
Bellevue, OH [FM radio station call letters] .... WNRR
Bellevue Oil & Minerals [Vancouver Stock Exchange symbol] .... BEU
Bellevue Public Library, Bellevue, IA [Library symbol] [Library of Congress]
    (LCLS) .... IaBev
Bellevue Public Library, Bellevue, ID [Library symbol] [Library of Congress]
    (LCLS) .... IdBe
Bellevue Public Library, Bellevue, NE [OCLC symbol] (OCLC) .... BLL
Bellevue Public Library, Bellevue, NE [Library symbol] [Library of Congress]
    (LCLS) .... NbBe
Bellevue Public Library, Bellevue, NE [Library symbol] [Library of Congress]
    (LCLS) .... NbBeL
Bellevue Public Library, Bellevue, OH [Library symbol] [Library of
    Congress] (LCLS) .... OBv
Bellevue School District, Instructional Materials Center, Bellevue, WA
    [Library symbol] [Library of Congress] (LCLS) .... WaBS
Bellevue Township Library, Bellevue, MI [Library symbol] [Library of
    Congress] (LCLS) .... MiBel
Bellevue Ventures Ltd. [Vancouver Stock Exchange symbol] .... BVL
Bellevue, WA [Location identifier] [FAA] (FAAL) .... BVU
Bellevue, WA [FM radio station call letters] .... KASB
Bellevue, WA [FM radio station call letters] .... KBCS
Bellevue, WA [Television station call letters] .... KBEH
Bellevue, WA [Television station call letters] (RBYB) .... KBGE
Bellevue, WA [AM radio station call letters] .... KBLV
Bellevue, WA [FM radio station call letters] .... KLSY
Bellevue, WA [Television station call letters] (BROA) .... KWPX
Bellewe New York City Hospital (SAUS) .... Belle
Bellewe's Cases Tempore Henry VIII [Brooke's New Cases] [England]
    [A publication] (DLA) .... Pet Br
Bellewe's Cases Tempore Richard II [1378-1400] [A publication]
    (ILCA) .... Bel Cas T R II
Bellewe's Cases Tempore Richard II [1378-1400] [A publication]
    (DLA) .... Bellewe's Ca Temp R II
Bellewe's English King's Bench Reports [A publication] (DLA) .... Bell
Bellewe's English King's Bench Reports [A publication] (DLA) .... Bellewe
Bellewe's English King's Bench Reports [A publication] (DLA) .... Bellewe (Eng)
Bellewe's English King's Bench Reports Tempore Richard II [1378-1400]
    [A publication] (DLA) .... Bel
Bellewe's English King's Bench Reports Tempore Richard II [1378-1400]
    [A publication] (DLA) .... Bell Cas T Rich II
Bellewe's English King's Bench Reports Tempore Richard II [1378-1400]
    [A publication] (DLA) .... Bell Cas T R II
Bellewe's Les Ans du Roy Richard le Second [1378-1400] [A publication]
    (DLA) .... YB Rich II
Belley-Peyrieu [France] [ICAO location identifier] (ICLI) .... LFKY
Bellfield [Australia] [Seismograph station code, US Geological Survey]
    (SEIS) .... BFD

Bellin Memorial Hospital, Green Bay, WI [Library symbol] [Library of
    Congress] (LCLS) .... WGrB
Bell-Independent Relations [Telecommunications] (TEL) .... B-IR
Belling .... BLNG
Bellinger and Cotton's Annotated Codes and Statutes [Oregon]
    [A publication] (DLA) .... Ann Codes & St
Bellinger and Cotton's Annotated Codes and Statutes [Oregon]
    [A publication] (DLA) .... B & C Comp
Bellinger's Reports [4-8 Oregon] [A publication] (DLA) .... Bel
Bellinger's Reports [4-8 Oregon] [A publication] (DLA) .... Bell
Bellinger's Reports [4-8 Oregon] [A publication] (DLA) .... Bellinger
Bellinger's Reports [4-8 Oregon] [A publication] (DLA) .... Bell (Or)
Bellingham [Washington] [Airport symbol] (OAG) .... BLI
Bellingham [Washington] [Seismograph station code, US Geological Survey]
    [Closed] (SEIS) .... BLL
Bellingham Public Library, Bellingham, WA [Library symbol] [Library of
    Congress] (LCLS) .... WaBe
Bellingham Public Schools, Bellingham, MN [Library symbol] [Library of
    Congress] (LCLS) .... MnBelPS
Bellingham, WA [FM radio station call letters] .... KAFE
Bellingham, WA [Television station call letters] .... KBCB
Bellingham, WA [AM radio station call letters] .... KGMI
Bellingham, WA [FM radio station call letters] (RBYB) .... KISM-FM
Bellingham, WA [AM radio station call letters] .... KPUG
Bellingham, WA [FM radio station call letters] .... KUGS
Bellingham, WA [Television station call letters] .... KVOS-TV
Bellingham, WA [FM radio station call letters] .... KZAZ
Bellingham, WA [Location identifier] [FAA] (FAAL) .... LUM
Bellingham-Ferndale, WA [AM radio station call letters] .... KBFW
Bellingham/International [Washington] [ICAO location identifier] (ICLI) .... KBLI
Bellini-Tose System .... BT
Bellini-Tose System .... BTS
Bellini-Tosi system (SAUS) .... BT system
Belli's Modern Trials [A publication] (DLA) .... Belli's Mod Trials
Bellmore Memorial Library, Bellmore, NY [Library symbol] [Library of
    Congress] (LCLS) .... NBellm
Bellmouth [Design engineering] .... BLMTH
Bellofram Rolling Diaphragm .... BRD
Bellona Island [Solomon Islands] [Airport symbol] (OAG) .... BNY
Bellows (MSA) .... BLWS
Bellows Falls, VT [FM radio station call letters] .... WBFL
Bellows Falls, VT [FM radio station call letters] (BROA) .... WZSH-FM
Bellows Tankage Module .... BTM
Bellows Valve .... BV
Bellport Memorial Library, Bellport, NY [Library symbol] [Library of
    Congress] (LCLS) .... NBel
Bellport Senior High School, Brookhaven, NY [Library symbol] [Library of
    Congress] (LCLS) .... NBrooHS
Bell's Appeals to House of Lords from Scotland [A publication]
    (DLA) .... Bell Sc App
Bell's Cases in Parliament: Scotch Appeals [A publication] (DLA) .... Bell PC
Bell's Cases in the Scotch Court of Session [A publication] (DLA) .... Bell
Bell's Cases in the Scotch Court of Session [A publication] (DLA) .... Bell Cas
Bell's Cases in the Scotch Court of Session [A publication] (DLA) .... Bell Sc Cas
Bell's Cases in the Scotch Court of Session [A publication] (DLA) .... Bell Ses Cas
Bell's Commentaries on the Laws of Scotland [A publication] (DLA) .... BC
Bell's Commentaries on the Laws of Scotland [A publication] (DLA) .... Bell Comm
Bell's Decisions, Scotch Court of Session [A publication]
    (DLA) .... Bell Ct of Sess Fol R
Bell's Dictionary and Digest of the Laws of Scotland [A publication]
    (DLA) .... Bell Dict
Bell's Dictionary of Decisions, Scotch Court of Session [A publication]
    (DLA) .... Bell Dict Dec
Bell's Dictionary of Decisions, Scotch Court of Session [A publication]
    (DLA) .... Bell's Dict
Bell's English Crown Cases [A publication] (DLA) .... Bell Cr C
Bell's English Crown Cases [A publication] (DLA) .... Bell Cr Ca
Bell's English Crown Cases [A publication] (DLA) .... Bell Cr Cas
Bell's English Crown Cases Reserved [169 English Reprint] [A publication]
    (DLA) .... Bell
Bell's English Crown Cases Reserved [169 English Reprint] [A publication]
    (DLA) .... Bell CC
Bell's English Crown Cases Reserved [169 English Reprint] [A publication]
    (DLA) .... Bell CC (Eng)
Bell's Folio Reports, Scotch Court of Session [1794-95] [A publication]
    (DLA) .... Bell Fol
Bell's House of Lords Scotch Appeal Cases [1842-50] [A publication]
    (DLA) .... Bell App
Bell's House of Lords Scotch Appeal Cases [1842-50] [A publication]
    (DLA) .... Bell App Bell (SC)
Bell's House of Lords Scotch Appeal Cases [1842-50] [A publication]
    (DLA) .... Bell App Cas
Bell's House of Lords Scotch Appeal Cases [1842-50] [A publication]
    (DLA) .... Bell HL
Bell's House of Lords Scotch Appeal Cases [1842-50] [A publication]
    (DLA) .... Bell HL Sc
Bell's House of Lords Scotch Appeal Cases [1842-50] [A publication]
    (DLA) .... Bell's App
Bell's House of Lords Scotch Appeal Cases [1842-50] [A publication]
    (DLA) .... S Bell
Bells House of Lords Scotch Appeal Cases (journ.) (SAUS) .... S Bell
Bell's Illustrations of Principles [A publication] (DLA) .... Bell Illus
Bell's Law of Arbitration in Scotland [A publication] (DLA) .... Bell Arb
Bell's Law of Awards [A publication] (DLA) .... Bell Aw
Bell's Medico-Legal Journal [A publication] (DLA) .... Bell Med LJ

Bell's Octavo Reports, Scotch Court of Sessions [1790-92] [A publication]
(DLA) .... Bell 8vo
Bell's Octavo Reports, Scotch Court of Sessions [1790-92] [A publication]
(DLA) .... Bell Oct
Bell's Palsy [Medicine] (DMAA) .... BP
Bell's Principles of the Law of Scotland [10 eds.] [1829-99] [A publication]
(DLA) .... Bell Prin
Bell's Putative Marriage Case [Scotland] [A publication] (DLA) .... Bell Put Mar
Bell's Reports, Court of Session [1790-92] [Scotland] [A publication]
(DLA) .... Bell C
Bell's Reports, High Court of Calcutta [India] [A publication] (DLA) .... Bell CHC
Bell's Reports, High Court of Calcutta [India] [A publication] (DLA) .... Bell HC
Bell's Reports, High Court of Calcutta [India] [A publication] (DLA) .... Bell (In)
Bell's Science Series [A publication] .... BSS
Bell's Scotch Appeal Cases [A publication] (DLA) .... Bell
Bell's Scotch Appeal Cases [A publication] (DLA) .... Bell Ap Ca
Bell's Scotch Appeal Cases [A publication] (DLA) .... Bell Sc App Cas
Bell's Scottish Digest [A publication] (DLA) .... Bell Sc Dig
Bell's Scottish Digest [A publication] (DLA) .... Bell Scot Dig
Bell's Supplemented Notes to Hume on Crimes [A publication] (DLA) .... Bell No
Bells, TX [FM radio station call letters] (BROA) .... KMKT-FM
Bellsouth Advertising & Publishing Company (SAUO) .... BAPCO
BellSouth Corp. [Associated Press] (SAG) .... BellSo
BellSouth Corp. [NYSE symbol] (SPSG) .... BLS
Bellsouth Services, Birmingham, AL [Library symbol] [Library of Congress]
(LCLS) .... ABBsS
Bellum Actiacum [of Ausonius] [Classical studies] (OCD) .... B Act
Bellum Africum [of Ausonius] [Classical studies] (OCD) .... B Afr
Bellum Alexandrinum [of Ausonius] [Classical studies] (OCD) .... B Alex
Bellum Catilinae [or De Catilinae Coniuratione] [of Sallust] [Classical studies]
(OCD) .... Cat
Bellum Civile [of Caesar] [Classical studies] (OCD) .... BCiv
Bellum Gallicum [of Caesar] [Classical studies] (OCD) .... BGall
Bellum Iugurthinum [of Sallust] [Classical studies] (OCD) .... Iug
Bellum Judaicum [Josephus] [Classical studies] (BJA) .... BelJud
Bellum Judaicum [Josephus] [Classical studies] (OCD) .... BJ
Bellum Judaicum [Josephus] [Classical studies] (BJA) .... JBJ
Bell-View Airlines Ltd. [Nigeria] [ICAO designator] (FAAC) .... BLV
Bellview, MN [FM radio station call letters] (BROA) .... KBGP-FM
Bellville, TX [AM radio station call letters] .... KFRD
Bellwether Expl Co. [Associated Press] (SAG) .... Bellweth
Bellwether Exploration [NASDAQ symbol] (TTSB) .... BELW
Bellwether Exploration Co. [Associated Press] (SAG) .... Bellweth
Bellwether Exploration Co. [NASDAQ symbol] (NQ) .... BELW
Bellwether Resources [Vancouver Stock Exchange symbol] .... BLW
Bellwether Stock [Investment term] .... BS
Bellwood, PA [FM radio station call letters] .... WALY
Bellwood Public Library, Bellwood, IL [Library symbol] [Library of Congress]
(LCLS) .... IBelw
Belly Button to Medial Malleolus [Measurement] [Anatomy] (DAVI) .... BB to MM
Belmac Corp. [Associated Press] (SAG) .... Belmac
Belmac Corp. [AMEX symbol] (SPSG) .... BLM
Belmar Public Library, Belmar, NJ [Library symbol] [Library of Congress]
(LCLS) .... NjBel
Belmar/Farmingdale, NJ [Location identifier] [FAA] (FAAL) .... BLM
Belmond Independent, Belmond, IA [Library symbol] [Library of Congress]
(LCLS) .... IaBelmI
Belmond Public Library, Belmond, IA [Library symbol] [Library of Congress]
(LCLS) .... IaBelm
Belmont [Australia] [Airport symbol] .... BEO
Belmont Abbey College [North Carolina] .... BAC
Belmont Abbey College, Belmont, NC [Library symbol] [Library of Congress] (LCLS) ... NcBe
Belmont and Methuen Township Public Library, Nephton, Ontario [Library
symbol] [National Library of Canada] (BIB) .... ONBM
Belmont Bancorp [Associated Press] (SAG) .... BelBcp
Belmont Bancorp [NASDAQ symbol] (SAG) .... BLMT
Belmont College (SAUO) .... BC
Belmont College, Nashville, TN [OCLC symbol] (OCLC) .... TBC
Belmont College, Nashville, TN [Library symbol] [Library of Congress]
(LCLS) .... TNBe
Belmont Elementary School, North Babylon, NY [Library symbol] [Library of
Congress] (LCLS) .... NNbBE
Belmont Homes [Associated Press] (SAG) .... BelmH
Belmont Homes [NASDAQ symbol] (SAG) .... BHIX
Belmont Memorial Library, Belmont, MA [Library symbol] [Library of
Congress] (LCLS) .... MBelm
Belmont, NC [AM radio station call letters] .... WCGC
Belmont, NC [Television station call letters] .... WJZY
Belmont, NH [FM radio station call letters] .... WNHI
Belmont Resources [Vancouver Stock Exchange symbol] .... BEO
Belmont Technical Institute, St. Clairsville, OH [Library symbol] [Library of
Congress] (LCLS) .... OStcB
Belmonte [Brazil] [Airport symbol] (OAG) .... BVM
Belmoral Mines Ltd. [Toronto Stock Exchange symbol] .... BME
Belo [Madagascar] [Airport symbol] (OAG) .... BMD
Belo [A.H.] Corp. [Associated Press] (SAG) .... BeloAH
Belo [A. H.] Corp. [NYSE symbol] (SPSG) .... BLC
Belo Horizonte [Brazil] [Airport symbol] (OAG) .... BHZ
Belo Horizonte/Confins [Brazil] [ICAO location identifier] (ICLI) .... SBCF
Belo Horizonte/Pampulha [Brazil] [ICAO location identifier] (ICLI) ...... SBBH
Belo Information Systems Online Network [A. H. Belo Corp.] [Discontinued
service] [Information service or system] (IID) .... BISON
Beloit College (SAUO) .... BC
Beloit College, Beloit, WI [Library symbol] [Library of Congress] (LCLS) ...... WBB

Beloit College Library, Beloit, WI [OCLC symbol] (OCLC) .... WII
Beloit, KS [AM radio station call letters] .... KVSV
Beloit, KS [FM radio station call letters] .... KVSV-FM
Beloit Memorial Hospital, Beloit, WI [Library symbol] [Library of Congress]
(LCLS) .... WBM
Beloit, WI [FM radio station call letters] .... WBCR
Beloit, WI [AM radio station call letters] .... WGEZ
Beloit/Janesville [Wisconsin] [Airport symbol] (OAG) .... JVL
Belo-Luxembourg Chamber of Commerce (DS) .... BLCC
Belorussia (SAUS) .... Bel
Belorussian [MARC language code] [Library of Congress] (LCCP) ...... bel
Belorussian Soviet Socialist Republic [MARC country of publication code]
[Library of Congress] (LCCP) .... bwr
Belorussian Soviet Socialist Republic [MARC geographic area code] [Library
of Congress] (LCCP) .... e-ur-bw
Belorussian Yiddish (BJA) .... BrY
Belo-Sur-Tsiribihina [Madagascar] [ICAO location identifier] (ICLI) ...... FMML
Belousov-Zhabotinskii [Physical chemistry] .... BZ
Belousov-Zhabotinsky reaction (SAUS) .... BZ reaction
Below (SAUS) .... Bel
Below [Technical drawings] .... BEL
Below .... BLO
Below (SAUS) .... Blo
Below (MSA) .... BLW
Below All Clouds [Aviation] .... BAC
Below Bridges [Navigation] .... BB
Below Bridges (SAUS) .... bb
Below Bridges [Transportation] .... BBS
Below Center of Mass [Command report] [Army] (INF) .... BCM
Below Clouds [Aviation code] .... BLO
Below Costal Margin [Medicine] (MELL) .... BCM
Below Datum (SAUS) .... BD
Below Datum (QUAC) .... bd
Below Deck [of a ship] (DS) .... BD
Below Deck Communications System [Navy] (LAIN) .... BDCS
Below Diaphragm [Medicine] (DAVI) .... BD
Below Elbow [Medicine] .... BE
Below Elbow [Orthopedics] (DAVI) .... BELB
Below Ground Level (WDAA) .... BGL
Below Ground Net Primary Productivity (SAUS) .... BNPP
Below Ground Surface .... BGS
Below Knee [Medicine] .... BK
Below Knee Amputation [Medicine] .... BKA
Below Knee Amputation (SAUS) .... BK Amp
Below Knee to Toe [Medicine] (MAE) .... BKTT
Below Knee Walking Cast (MEDA) .... BKWC
Below Knee Walking Plaster [Medicine] (MAE) .... BKWP
Below Layer Range (NVT) .... BLR
Below Left Costal Margin [Medicine] (MELL) .... BLCM
Below Limit of Detection .... BLD
Below Lower Limit (IEEE) .... BLL
Below Market Interest Rate (GFGA) .... BMIR
Below Minimum Standards [TV ratings] .... BMS
Below or Equal (SAUS) .... BE
Below Proof .... BP
Below Regulatory Concern [Nuclear Regulatory Commission classification] .... BRC
Below Rig Floor (SAUS) .... BRF
Below Right Costal Margin [Anatomy] (DAVI) .... BRCM
Below Sea Floor (SAUS) .... BSF
Below Sea Level (SAUS) .... BSL
Below Sea-Level Flying Club (SAUO) .... BSLFC
Below Slab (OA) .... BS
Below Surface (QUAC) .... bs
Below Surface (SAUS) .... BS
Below the Detectable Limit .... BDL
Below the Horizon (ACAE) .... BTH
Below the Line [Budget] .... BTL
Below the Promotion Zone (ACAE) .... BPZ
Below the Treatment Zone (GNE) .... BTZ
Below Threshold Change [Air Force] .... BTC
Below Umbilicus [Medicine] (MELL) .... BU
Below Upper Limit (SAUS) .... BUL
Below Waist [Medicine] .... BW
Below Watch .... BW
Below Water (NG) .... BW
Below-Ground Pool (SAUS) .... BGP
Below/Hook Lifters Section of the Material Handling Institute (EA) ... BHLS
Below-Knee Cast [Medicine] (MELL) .... BKC
Below-Knee Orthosis [Orthopedics] (DAVI) .... BKO
Belozyorsk [Former USSR] [ICAO location identifier] (ICLI) .... ULWB
Belpre, OH [FM radio station call letters] .... WCVV
Belpre, OH [FM radio station call letters] .... WMBP
Belpre, OH [FM radio station call letters] .... WNUS
Belsk [Poland] [Seismograph station code, US Geological Survey] [Closed]
(SEIS) .... BEL
Belt (SAUS) .... BLT
Belt Association (EA) .... BA
Belt Driven Retrofit [Cosworth racing engines] [Automotive engineering] .... BDR
Belt Driven Turbocharged [Cosworth racing engines] [Automotive
engineering] .... BDT
Belt Driven Type A [Cosworth racing engines] [Automotive engineering] .... BDA
[The] Belt Railway Co. of Chicago [AAR code] .... BRC
[The] Belt Railway Co. of Chicago .... BR of C
Belt Railway Company of Chicago (SAUO) .... BRC
Belt Railway Company of Chicago (SAUO) .... BR of C

Belt Weather Kit (MCD) ... BWK
Belt Work Line ... BWL
Beltec Enterprises Ltd. [*Vancouver Stock Exchange symbol*] ... BET
Belted Galloway Society (EA) ... BGS
Belting [*Freight*] ... BLTG
Belton Railroad Co. [*AAR code*] ... BRR
Belton, SC [*FM radio station call letters*] ... WEPC
Belton, SC [*AM radio station call letters*] ... WHPB
Belton, TX [*Television station call letters*] ... KNCT
Belton, TX [*FM radio station call letters*] ... KOOC
Belton, TX [*AM radio station call letters*] ... KTON
Beltrami and Indusi (SAUS) ... B-I
Belt's Edition of Brown's Chancery Reports [*1778-94*] [*A publication*] (DLA) ... Belt Bro
Belt's Edition of Vesey, Senior's, English Chancery Reports [*A publication*] (DLA) ... Belt Ves Sen
Belt's Supplement to Vesey, Senior's, English Chancery Reports [*1746-56*] [*A publication*] (DLA) ... Belt's Supp (Eng)
Belt's Supplement to Vesey, Senior's, English Chancery Reports [*1746-56*] [*A publication*] (DLA) ... Belt Sup
Belt's Supplement to Vesey, Senior's, English Chancery Reports [*1746-56*] [*A publication*] (DLA) ... Belt Supp
Belt's Supplement to Vesey, Senior's, English Chancery Reports [*1746-56*] [*A publication*] (DLA) ... Belt Sup Ves
Beltsville Agricultural Research Center [*Maryland*] [*Department of Agriculture*] ... BARC
Beltsville Human Nutrition Research Center [*Department of Agriculture*] ... BHNRC
Beltsville Space Center [*Later, Goddard Space Flight Center*] [*NASA*] ... BSC
Beluga, AK [*Location identifier*] [*FAA*] (FAAL) ... BLG
Belvedere, SC [*FM radio station call letters*] ... WAFJ
Belves-Saint-Pardoux [*France*] [*ICAO location identifier*] (ICLI) ... LFIB
Belvidere, IL [*FM radio station call letters*] ... WXRX
Belvidere, NJ [*FM radio station call letters*] ... WRNJ
Belvidere, NJ [*FM radio station call letters*] (BROA) ... WWYY-FM
Belview Public School, Bleview, MN [*Library symbol*] [*Library of Congress*] (LCLS) ... MnBevPS
Belvoir Fuels and Lubricants Research Facility [*Southwest Research Institute*] [*San Antonio, TX*] ... BFLRF
Belvoir Research, Development, and Engineering Center [*Fort Belvoir, VA*] [*Army*] (RDA) ... BRDEC
Belzoni, MS [*FM radio station call letters*] (BROA) ... WBYP-FM
Belzoni, MS [*AM radio station call letters*] ... WELZ
Belzoni, MS [*FM radio station call letters*] (BROA) ... WGNG-FM
Belzoni, MS [*FM radio station call letters*] ... WVRD
Bem Sex-Role Inventory [*Research test*] [*Psychology*] ... BSRI
Bema Gold Corp. [*Associated Press*] (SAG) ... BemaGold
Bema Gold Corp. [*AMEX symbol*] (SAG) ... BGO
Bema Gold Ltd. [*Toronto Stock Exchange symbol*] [*Vancouver Stock Exchange symbol*] ... BGO
Bemba [*MARC language code*] [*Library of Congress*] (LCCP) ... bem
Bembridge [*British*] [*ICAO location identifier*] (ICLI) ... EGHJ
Bement Community Unit School District, Bement, IL [*Library symbol*] [*Library of Congress*] (LCLS) ... IBemSD
Bement Public Library, St. Johns (SAUS) ... MiStjo
Bement Public Library, St. Johns, MI [*Library symbol*] [*Library of Congress*] (LCLS) ... MiStjo
Bement Township Library, Bement, IL [*Library symbol*] [*Library of Congress*] (LCLS) ... IBem
Bemichi [*Guyana*] [*Airport symbol*] (OAG) ... BCG
Bemidji [*Minnesota*] [*Airport symbol*] (OAG) ... BJI
Bemidji Aviation Services, Inc. [*ICAO designator*] (FAAC) ... BMJ
Bemidji High School, Bemidji, MN [*Library symbol*] [*Library of Congress*] (LCLS) ... MnBemH
Bemidji, MN [*Television station call letters*] (BROA) ... KAGR
Bemidji, MN [*Television station call letters*] ... KAWE
Bemidji, MN [*FM radio station call letters*] ... KBHP
Bemidji, MN [*FM radio station call letters*] ... KBSB
Bemidji, MN [*AM radio station call letters*] ... KBUN
Bemidji, MN [*FM radio station call letters*] ... KCRB
Bemidji, MN [*AM radio station call letters*] ... KKBJ
Bemidji, MN [*FM radio station call letters*] ... KKBJ-FM
Bemidji, MN [*FM radio station call letters*] (BROA) ... KKZY-FM
Bemidji, MN [*FM radio station call letters*] ... KNBJ
Bemidji, MN [*Location identifier*] [*FAA*] (FAAL) ... MDI
Bemidji Public Library, Bemidji, MN [*Library symbol*] [*Library of Congress*] (LCLS) ... MnBem
Bemidji State College [*Later, Bemidji State University*] [*Minnesota*] ... BSC
Bemidji State College [*Later, Bemidji State University*], **Bemidji, MN** [*Library symbol*] [*Library of Congress*] (LCLS) ... MnBemS
Bemidji State University (GAGS) ... Bemidji St U
Bemidji State University, Bemidji, MN [*OCLC symbol*] (OCLC) ... MNB
Bemis Co., Inc. [*Associated Press*] (SAG) ... Bemis
Bemis Co., Inc. [*NYSE symbol*] (SPSG) ... BMS
Bemis Memorial Library, Robbinsville, NC [*Library symbol*] [*Library of Congress*] (LCLS) ... NcRob
Bemoair [*Czechoslovakia*] [*FAA designator*] (FAAC) ... BMI
Ben (BJA) ... b
Ben & Jerry's Cl'A' [*NASDAQ symbol*] (TTSB) ... BJICA
Ben & Jerry's Homemade, Inc. [*Associated Press*] (SAG) ... BenJerry
Ben & Jerry's Homemade, Inc. [*NASDAQ symbol*] (NQ) ... BJIC
Ben Asia Container Service (SAUO) ... BACS
Ben Chajim (BJA) ... BCh
Ben Franklin Retail Stores, Inc. [*Associated Press*] (SAG) ... BFrankR
Ben Franklin Retail Stores, Inc. [*NASDAQ symbol*] (SAG) ... BFRS
Ben Franklin Society [*Defunct*] (EA) ... BFS
Ben Franklin Technology Center [*Research center*] (RCD) ... BFTC
Ben Gurion [*Israel*] [*ICAO location identifier*] (ICLI) ... LLAD
Ben Hur Life Association [*Crawfordsville, IN*] (EA) ... BHLA
Ben Line Steamers (MHDB) ... BLS
BEN LINE Wm. Thompson & Co. (SAUO) ... BEN LINE
Ben Marcato [*Well Marked*] [*Music*] (ROG) ... BM
Ben May Laboratory for Cancer Research [*University of Chicago*] [*Research center*] (RCD) ... BML
Ben Monroe's Kentucky Reports [*A publication*] (DLA) ... Ben Monroe
Ben Monroe's Kentucky Reports [*A publication*] (DLA) ... BM
Ben Monroe's Kentucky Reports [*A publication*] (DLA) ... B Mon (KY)
Ben Monroe's Kentucky Reports [*A publication*] (DLA) ... B Monr
Ben Monroe's Kentucky Supreme Court Reports [*A publication*] (DLA) ... B Mon
Ben Naphtali (BJA) ... BN
Ben R. Oppenheimer [*California Institute of Technology*] ... BRO
Ben Slimane [*Morocco*] [*ICAO location identifier*] (ICLI) ... GMMB
Benactyzine (SAUS) ... BZ
Bena-Dibele [*Zaire*] [*ICAO location identifier*] (ICLI) ... FZVO
Benair [*Italy*] [*ICAO designator*] (FAAC) ... BEI
Benard Convection Cell ... BCC
Benbecula [*Hebrides Islands*] [*Airport symbol*] (OAG) ... BEB
Benbecula [*British*] [*ICAO location identifier*] (ICLI) ... EGPL
Bence Jones [*As in Bence Jones protein, Bence Jones reaction, etc.*] [*Named for Henry Bence Jones, 19th century London physician*] ... BJ
Bence Jones Protein [*Named for Henry Bence Jones, 19th century London physician*] (MAE) ... BJP
Bence Jones Protein [*Named for Henry Bence Jones, 19th century London physician*] (DAVI) ... B J PR
Bench (SAUS) ... BEN
Bench (MSA) ... BNCH
Bench Check (NASA) ... B/C
Bench Check Serviceable (ACAE) ... BCS
Bench Checkout Equipment ... BCE
Bench Checkout Equipment ... BCOE
Bench Craft, Inc. (SAUS) ... SOFA
Bench Detergency Dispersancy Test (PDAA) ... BDDT
Bench Maintenance [*NASA*] (KSC) ... BM
Bench Maintenance Equipment [*NASA*] (KSC) ... BME
Bench Maintenance Test Set (SAA) ... BMTS
Bench Mark (SAUS) ... BM
Bench Mark Control Point (NASA) ... BCP
Bench Mark Control Point [*Nautical charts*] ... BM
Bench Mark Test Files (MCD) ... BMTF
Bench Model Solar Receiver (MCD) ... BMSR
Bench Order ... BO
Bench Press (SAUS) ... BEN Press
Bench Replaceable Assembly (MCD) ... BRA
Bench Scale Calorimeter ... BSC
Bench Stock [*Air Force*] (AFIT) ... B/S
Bench Stock List (ACAE) ... BSL
Bench Stock Support Unit [*Military*] ... BSSU
Bench Test and Calibration Equipment (ACAE) ... BTCE
Bench Test Console ... BTC
Bench Test Cooler (ACAE) ... BTC
Bench Test Equipment (ACAE) ... BTE
Bench Test Fixture ... BTF
Bench Test Instruction (SAUS) ... BTI
Bench Test Kit (ACAE) ... BTK
Bench Test Specification ... BTS
Bench Welder Control Panel ... BWCP
Benchboard (KSC) ... BNCHBD
Benchers of the Inns of Court (SAUO) ... BIC
Benchmark [*Computer system evaluation*] ... BM
Benchmark Control Point (SAUS) ... BCP
Benchmark Electronics, Inc. [*Associated Press*] (SAG) ... BenchE
Benchmark Electronics, Inc. [*AMEX symbol*] (SAG) ... BHE
Benchmark Interchange Format [*Computer science*] (VERA) ... BIF
Benchmark Interface Format [*Computer science*] (BTTJ) ... BIF
Benchmark Monitor Display (SAUS) ... BMD
Benchmark Monitor Display System [*Sperry UNIVAC*] ... BMD
Benchmark of Concurrent Architectures for their Use in Scientific Engineering (SAUS) ... BECAUSE
Benchmark Plan (SAUS) ... BMP
Benchmark Portability System (PDAA) ... BPS
Benchmark Report Format (SAUS) ... BRF
Benchmark Reporting Format (VERA) ... BRF
Benchmark Soils Project [*University of Hawaii, University of Puerto Rico*] ... BSP
Benchmark Timing Methodology (VERA) ... BTM
BENCHMARQ Microelectronics [*NASDAQ symbol*] (TTSB) ... BMRQ
Bench-Test Fixture (SAUS) ... BTF
Benckiser N.V.'B' [*NYSE symbol*] (SG) ... BNV
Bend [*Commonly used*] (OPSA) ... BEND
Bend ... BND
Bend Down ... BD
Bend Down ... BDN
Bend Line (MSA) ... BL
Bend, OR [*AM radio station call letters*] ... KBND
Bend, OR [*FM radio station call letters*] ... KICE
Bend, OR [*FM radio station call letters*] ... KNLR
Bend, OR [*FM radio station call letters*] ... KOAB
Bend, OR [*Television station call letters*] ... KOAB-TV
Bend, OR [*FM radio station call letters*] ... KQAK
Bend, OR [*Television station call letters*] ... KTVZ
Bend, OR [*FM radio station call letters*] ... KTWS
Bend, OR [*FM radio station call letters*] ... KXIX

Bend, OR [*AM radio station call letters*] ... KXUX
Bend Radius (MCD) ... BR
Bend Radius Template (MCD) ... BRT
Bend Research, Inc., Bend, OR [*Library symbol*] [*Library of Congress*] (LCLS) ... OrBeBR
Bend Senior High School, Bend, OR [*Library symbol*] [*Library of Congress*] (LCLS) ... OrBeHS
Bend Tangency Line (MCD) ... BTL
Bend Up ... BU
Bend Up [*Technical drawings*] ... BUP
Benday [*Type of dye*] (WDMC) ... BD
Benday [*Engraving*] (NTCM) ... DAY
Bend-Down Virginia [*A picked-up stub of a cigarette*] ... BDV
Bender Visual-Motor Gestalt [*Test*] [*Psychology*] (DAVI) ... BVMG
Bender Visual-Motor Gestalt Test [*Education*] ... BVMGT
Bender-Gestalt Test [*Psychology*] ... B-G
Bender-Gestalt Test [*Psychology*] ... BGT
Bendigo Agricultural Show Society [*Australia*] ... BASS
Bendigo & District Environment Council (SAUO) ... BDEC
Bendigo School of Mines (SAUO) ... BSM
Bending (MSA) ... BNG
Bending Allowance [*Engineering*] (IAA) ... BA
Bending Die (SAUS) ... BDDI
Bending Feedback Control ... BFC
Bending Form [*Tool*] (AAG) ... BEFM
Bending Magnet ... BM
Bending Mode Filters ... BMF
Bending Moment [*Aerospace*] ... BM
Bending Moment (SAUS) ... bm
Bending Moment [*Aerospace*] (AAG) ... M
Bendix Antiskid System [*Automotive engineering*] ... BAS
Bendix Atlantic Inflator Co. [*Automotive industry supplier*] ... BAICO
Bendix Aviation (SAUS) ... BDXAV
Bendix Aviation Corp. [*Later, Bendix Corp.*] ... BAC
Bendix Aviation Corp. [*Later, Bendix Corp.*] (MCD) ... BDX
Bendix Aviation Corp. [*Later, Bendix Corp.*], **Pacific Division, North Hollywood, CA** [*Library symbol*] [*Library of Congress*] (LCLS) ... CNhB
Bendix Aviation Corporation (SAUO) ... BDXAV
Bendix Aviation Corporation (SAUO) ... BXC
Bendix Corp., Baltimore, MD [*Library symbol*] [*Library of Congress*] (LCLS) ... MdBBR
Bendix Corp., Electrical Components Division, Engineering Library, Sidney, NY [*Library symbol*] [*Library of Congress*] (LCLS) ... NSidS
Bendix Corp., Engineering Development Center, Bendix Center, Southfield, MI [*Library symbol*] [*Library of Congress*] (LCLS) ... MiSfB
Bendix Corp., Technical Information Center, Kansas City, MO [*Library symbol*] [*Library of Congress*] (LCLS) ... MoKBen
Bendix Corporation (SAUO) ... BX
Bendix Elementary School Annandale, MN [*Library symbol*] [*Library of Congress*] (LCLS) ... MnAdBE
Bendix Engineering Development Center, Southfield, MI [*OCLC symbol*] (OCLC) ... EEB
Bendix Field Engineering Corporation (SAUO) ... BFEC
Bendix Integrated Data System ... BIDS
Bendix Interactive Geographic Information System (SAUS) ... BIGIS
Bendix Missile Systems Division (MCD) ... BMSD
Bendix Optimum Configuration Satellite (IEEE) ... BOCS
Bendix Technical Journal (SAUS) ... Bendix TechJ
Bendix-Westinghouse Automotive Air Brake Co. ... BW
Bendloe's [*or Benloe's*] **English Common Pleas** [*1531-1628*] [*A publication*] (DLA) ... Bendl
Bendloe's [*or Benloe's*] **Reports, English Common Pleas** [*Edition of 1661*] [*A publication*] (DLA) ... Bendloe
Bend-Over Point (PDAA) ... BOP
Bendroflumethiazide [*Organic chemistry*] (MEDA) ... BFM
Bene [*Well*] [*Pharmacy*] ... BEN
Bene Merenti [*To the Well-Deserving*] [*Latin*] ... BM
Bene Merenti [*To the Well-Deserving*] [*Latin*] ... BMT
Bene Merenti Fecit [*He Erected This to the Well-Deserving*] [*Latin*] ... BMF
Bene Quiescat [*May He, or She, Rest Well*] [*Latin*] ... BQ
Bene Vale [*Farewell*] [*Latin*] ... BV
Bene Vixit [*He Lived a Good Life*] [*Latin*] ... BV
Beneath (FAAC) ... BNTH
Benecke on Marine Insurance [*A publication*] (DLA) ... Ben Ins
Benedicite [*Bless You*] [*Latin*] ... Bte
Benedict College (SAUO) ... BC
Benedict College, Columbia (SAUS) ... ScCoB
Benedict College, Columbia, SC [*OCLC symbol*] (OCLC) ... BDC
Benedict College, Columbia, SC [*Library symbol*] [*Library of Congress*] (LCLS) ... ScCoB
Benedictine ... BENED
Benedictine and Brandy ... B & B
Benedictine College, Atchison, KS [*OCLC symbol*] (OCLC) ... KKA
Benedictine College, North Campus, Atchison, KS [*Library symbol*] [*Library of Congress*] (LCLS) ... KAS
Benedictine College, South Campus, Atchison, KS [*Library symbol*] [*Library of Congress*] (LCLS) ... KAM
Benedictine Congregation of Our Lady of Monte (TOCD) ... OSB
Benedictine Heights College [*Oklahoma*] ... BHC
Benedictine High School, Cleveland, OH [*Library symbol*] [*Library of Congress*] (LCLS) ... OCIBHS
Benedictine Hospital, Medical Library, Kingston, NY [*Library symbol*] [*Library of Congress*] (LCLS) ... NKiB
Benedictine Monks (TOCD) ... OSB
Benedictine Monks, Olivetan Benedictines, Sylvestrine Benedictines (TOCD) ... osb
Benedictine Nuns (TOCD) ... OSB
Benedictine Nuns of the Congregation of Solesmes (TOCD) ... OSB
Benedictine Nuns of the Primitive Observance (TOCD) ... OSB
Benedictine Sisters (TOCD) ... OSB
Benedictine Sisters of Liberty (TOCD) ... OSB
Benedictine Sisters of Pontifical Jurisdiction (TOCD) ... OSB
Benedictine Sisters of Sacred Heart (TOCD) ... OSB
Benedictines for Peace (EA) ... BP
Benedictio [*Blessing*] [*Latin*] (ADA) ... BEN
Benediction ... B
Benedict's American Admiralty Practice [*A publication*] (DLA) ... Ben Adm
Benedict's American Admiralty Practice [*A publication*] (DLA) ... Ben Adm Prac
Benedict's New York Civil and Criminal Justice [*A publication*] (DLA) ... Ben Just
Benedict's United States District Court Reports [*A publication*] (DLA) ... Ben
Benedict's United States District Court Reports [*A publication*] (DLA) ... Bene
Benedict's United States District Court Reports [*A publication*] (DLA) ... Bened
Benedict's United States District Court Reports [*A publication*] (DLA) ... Benedict
Benedict's United States District Court Reports [*A publication*] (DLA) ... Bt
Benedictus [*Blessed*] [*Latin*] ... Bs
Benedictus de Isernia [*Flourished, 1221-52*] [*Authority cited in pre-1607 legal work*] (DSA) ... B
Benedictus de Isernia [*Flourished, 1221-52*] [*Authority cited in pre-1607 legal work*] (DSA) ... Be
Benedictus de Isernia [*Flourished, 1221-52*] [*Authority cited in pre-1607 legal work*] (DSA) ... Bene
Benedictus de Isernia [*Flourished, 1221-52*] [*Authority cited in pre-1607 legal work*] (DSA) ... Bn
Benedict-Webb-Rubin [*Equation of state*] ... BWR
Benedict-Webb-Rubin Equation (SAUS) ... BWR-Equation
Benediktinische Monatsschrift [*A publication*] (BJA) ... BenM
Benedum Civic Center Public Library, Bridgeport, WV [*Library symbol*] [*Library of Congress*] (LCLS) ... WvBri
Benefical Standard Mortgage Investors (SAUO) ... BSM
Benefice ... BNFC
Beneficial (ROG) ... BENEFL
Beneficial ... BNFCL
Beneficial Communications [*Computer system*] [*Beneficial Management Corp.*] ... BENCOM
Beneficial Corp. [*Associated Press*] (SAG) ... Benef
Beneficial Corp. [*Wall Street slang name: "Big Nose Louie"*] [*Associated Press*] (SAG) ... BenefCp
Beneficial Corp. (EFIS) ... BFC
Beneficial Corp. [*NYSE symbol*] (SAG) ... BNL
Beneficial Corp.,$4.30 Pfd [*NYSE symbol*] (TTSB) ... BNLPrB
Beneficial Corp.,$4.50 Pfd [*NYSE symbol*] (TTSB) ... BNLPrA
Beneficial Corp.,5% Pfd [*NYSE symbol*] (TTSB) ... BNLPrV
Beneficial Corp.,$5.50 Cv Pfd [*NYSE symbol*] (TTSB) ... BNLPrC
Beneficial Insects Research Laboratory [*Department of Agriculture*] [*Newark, DE*] (GRD) ... BIRL
Beneficial Insurance Group (SAUO) ... BIG
Beneficial Occupancy ... BO
Beneficial Occupancy Date ... BOD
Beneficial Rays of the Sun [*In reference to suntanning, supposedly occuring between 10am and 2pm*] [*See also SROTS*] ... BROTS
Beneficial Suggestion (SAUO) ... BENNY SUGG
Beneficial Suggestion (SAUO) ... BEN SUG
Beneficial Suggestion (MCD) ... BS
Beneficial Suggestions [*Program*] ... BENNY SUGG
Beneficial Suggestions [*Program*] (DNAB) ... BENNY SUGGS
Beneficial Suggestions [*Program*] (DNAB) ... BEN SUG
Beneficial Use Date ... BUD
Beneficial Uses Shipping System (SAUO) ... BUSS
Beneficiary [*Legal shorthand*] (LWAP) ... BEN
Beneficiary ... BENE
Beneficiary (AFM) ... BENEF
Beneficiary (ROG) ... BENEFY
Beneficiary ... BFCY
Beneficiary Data Exchange System [*between state welfare agencies and the Social Security Administration*] ... BENDEX
Beneficiary Developing Country [*Trade status*] ... BDC
Beneficiary Evaluation Survey Service [*LIMRA*] ... BESS
Beneficiary Government Production Program ... BGPP
Beneficiary Identification Records Location Subsystem (MCD) ... BIRLS
Benefit (TBD) ... Bnft
Benefit ... BNFT
Benefit (ADA) ... BT
Benefit and Donation Claims, Selected Decisions of Umpire [*England*] [*A publication*] (DLA) ... OUUISD
Benefit Assessment for System Change (MHDB) ... BASYC
Benefit Cost Analysis [*Accounting*] ... BCA
Benefit Decisions of the British Umpire [*A publication*] (DLA) ... OUUIBD
Benefit Eligibility Interview [*Unemployment insurance*] (OICC) ... BEI
Benefit Performance [*Theater*] [*Slang*] (WDMC) ... ben
Benefit Principles (DLA) ... BP
Benefit Rights Interview [*Unemployment insurance*] ... BRI
Benefit Service Series, Unemployment Insurance [*Department of Labor*] [*A publication*] [*A publication*] (DLA) ... BSSUI
Benefit Service Series, Unemployment Insurance [*Department of Labor*] [*A publication*] ... BSUI
Benefit Systems Testing Section [*Social Security Administration*] ... BSTS
Benefit Trust Fund (SAUS) ... BTF
Benefit Week Number [*Unemployment insurance*] (OICC) ... BWN
Benefit Year Ending [*Unemployment insurance*] ... BYE

Benefit-Cost [*Ratio*] ... B-C
Benefit-Cost Analysis of Federal Programs: Guidelines and Discounts [*OMB Circular*] (AAGC) ... A-94
Benefit-Cost Ratio [*Finance*] ... BCR
Benefit-Cost ratio (SAUS) ... B/C ratio
Benefits (BARN) ... bnfts
Benefits Analysis Program [*Environmental Protection Agency*] (GFGA) ... BAP
Benefits and Use Division [*Environmental Protection Agency*] (GFGA) ... BUD
Benefits Control System [*Insurance*] ... BCS
Benefits Exceed Costs (COE) ... BExC
Benefits Review Board [*Department of Labor*] (OICC) ... BRB
Benefits Review Board Service (Matthew Bender) [*A publication*] (DLA) ... BRBS
Benelli Owner's Club of America (EA) ... BOCA
Benelux Countries [*MARC geographic area code*] [*Library of Congress*] (LCCP) ... el---
Benelux Economic Union (SAUO) ... BEU
BENELUX Economische Union [*Belgium, Netherlands, and Luxembourg Economic Union*] (EAIO) ... BEU
Benelux Falcon Service [*Belgium*] [*ICAO designator*] (FAAC) ... BFS
BENELUX Group on Mortality (EAIO) ... BGM
Benelux Phlebology Society (EA) ... BPS
BENELUX [*Belgium, Netherlands, Luxembourg*] **Subarea Channel** [*NATO*] (NATG) ... BENECHAN
Benelux Trademark Office (SAUO) ... BBM
Benelux-American Motors (SAUO) ... BAM
Benet on Military Law and Courts-Martial [*A publication*] (DLA) ... Benet Ct-M
Benetton Group ADS [*NYSE symbol*] (TTSB) ... BNG
Benetton Group SpA [*Associated Press*] (SAG) ... Beneton
Benetton Group SpA [*NYSE symbol*] (SPSG) ... BNG
Benetton Group S.p.A [*ML, exchange symbol*] (TTSB) ... BTON
Benevento [*Italy*] [*Seismograph station code, US Geological Survey*] [*Closed*] (SEIS) ... BNV
Benevolent (ROG) ... BENEV
benevolent (SAUS) ... benev
Benevolent ... BNVLNT
Benevolent and Loyal Order of Pessimists (EA) ... BLOOP
Benevolent and Protective Order of Elks (EA) ... BPOE
Benevolent Association for Naming All Nonentities After Schools ... BANANAS
Benevolent Order of Nurses under Sedation (SAUO) ... BONUS
Benevolent Orders (DLA) ... Ben Ord
Benevolent Protective Order-Wolves of the World (SAUO) ... BPO-WOW
Benevolent Society of Coachmakers [*British*] ... BSC
Benevolent Society of New South Wales [*Australia*] ... BSNSW
Benevolent Society of St. Patrick ... BSSP
Benevolent Society of St. Patrick (SAUO) ... BSSP
Benevolenti Lectori Salutem [*Greeting to the Well-Wishing Reader*] [*Latin*] ... BLS
Benewah County Library District, St. Maries, ID [*Library symbol*] [*Library of Congress*] (LCLS) ... IdSmB
Bengal ... BENG
Bengal (ADWA) ... Beng
Bengal [*or Bengalese*] (WDAA) ... BG
Bengal and North-Western Railway (SAUO) ... B&N-W Ry
Bengal & North-Western Railway Battalion [*British military*] (DMA) ... B & NW RY BN
Bengal Army Native Hospital Corps [*British military*] (DMA) ... BANHC
Bengal, Bay of [*MARC geographic area code*] [*Library of Congress*] (LCCP) ... ab---
Bengal Cavalry [*British military*] (DMA) ... BC
Bengal Civil Service [*British*] ... BCS
Bengal Civil Service (SAUO) ... BCS
Bengal Civil Service (SAUO) ... BenCS
Bengal Civil Service [*British*] (ROG) ... BEN CS
Bengal Full Bench Rulings [*North-Western Provinces, India*] [*A publication*] (DLA) ... Full BR
Bengal Fusiliers [*British military*] (DMA) ... BF
Bengal Horse Artillery [*British military*] (DMA) ... BHA
Bengal Lancers [*British military*] (DMA) ... BL
Bengal Law Reports [*India*] [*A publication*] (DLA) ... Ben
Bengal Law Reports [*India*] [*A publication*] (DLA) ... Beng
Bengal Law Reports [*India*] [*A publication*] (DLA) ... Beng LR
Bengal Law Reports, Appeal Cases [*India*] [*A publication*] (DLA) ... Beng LR App Cas
Bengal Law Reports, Appeal Cases [*India*] [*A publication*] (DLA) ... BLRAC
Bengal Law Reports, High Courts [*India*] [*A publication*] (DLA) ... BLR
Bengal Law Reports, Privy Council [*India*] [*A publication*] (DLA) ... Beng LRPC
Bengal Law Reports, Privy Council [*India*] [*A publication*] (DLA) ... BLRPC
Bengal Law Reports, Supplement [*India*] [*A publication*] (DLA) ... Beng LR Supp
Bengal Law Reports, Supplemental Volume, Full Bench Rulings [*India*] [*A publication*] (DLA) ... BLR Suppl Vol
Bengal Law Reports, Supplemental Volume, Full Bench Rulings [*India*] [*A publication*] (ILCA) ... BLR Sup Vol
Bengal Light Cavalry [*British military*] (DMA) ... BLC
Bengal Medical Department [*British military*] (DMA) ... BMD
Bengal Nagpur Railway (SAUO) ... BNRy
Bengal Native Infantry (SAUO) ... BengNI
Bengal Native Infantry (SAUO) ... BenNI
Bengal Native Infantry [*Military*] [*British*] (ROG) ... BEN NI
Bengal Native Infantry [*Military*] [*British*] ... BNI
Bengal Native Infantry (SAUO) ... BNI
Bengal North Western Railway (SAUO) ... BNWR
Bengal Nygpur Railway (SAUO) ... BN
Bengal Press Advisory Committee (SAUO) ... BPAC
Bengal Sadr Diwani Adalat Cases [*India*] [*A publication*] (DLA) ... Beng SDA
Bengal Sadr Diwani Adalat Decisions [*A publication*] (DLA) ... Dec SDA
Bengal Staff Corps [*Military*] [*British*] (ROG) ... BEN SC
Bengal Staff Corps (SAUO) ... BenSC
Bengal Staff Corps (SAUO) ... BSC
Bengal Staff Corps [*British*] [*Military*] ... BSC
Bengal Yeomanry Cavalry [*British military*] (DMA) ... BYC
Bengali [*MARC language code*] [*Library of Congress*] (LCCP) ... ben
Bengali [*Language, etc.*] (ROG) ... BENG
Bengal-Nagpore Railway Volunteer Rifles [*British military*] (DMA) ... BNRVR
Benghazi [*Libya*] [*Airport symbol*] (OAG) ... BEN
Benghazi (SAUS) ... Bzi
Benghazi/Benina [*Libya*] [*ICAO location identifier*] (ICLI) ... HLLB
Bengis Aviation (Pty) Ltd. [*South Africa*] [*FAA designator*] (FAAC) ... SPT
Bengkalis/Sungai Pakning [*Indonesia*] [*ICAO location identifier*] (ICLI) ... WIBS
Bengkayang [*Indonesia*] [*ICAO location identifier*] (ICLI) ... WIOB
Bengkulu [*Indonesia*] [*Airport symbol*] (OAG) ... BKS
Bengkulu/Padang Kemiling [*Indonesia*] [*ICAO location identifier*] (ICLI) ... WIPL
Bengston, DeBell, Elkin & Titus Ltd. (GEOI) ... BDET
Benguela [*Angola*] [*Airport symbol*] (OAG) ... BUG
Benguela [*Angola*] [*ICAO location identifier*] (ICLI) ... FNBG
Benguela Current (SAUS) ... Ben Cur
Benguela Environment Fisheries Interaction & Training (SAUS) ... BENEFIT
Benguela Sources and Transports (SAUS) ... BEST
Benguet Consolidated, Inc. (SAUO) ... BE
Benguet Corp. [*Associated Press*] (SAG) ... BengtB
Benguet Corp.Cl'B' [*NYSE symbol*] (SG) ... BE
Ben-Gurion University (BJA) ... BGU
Beni [*Zaire*] [*ICAO location identifier*] (ICLI) ... FZNP
Beni Abbes [*Algeria*] [*Airport symbol*] (AD) ... KBA
Beni Hasan [*Egyptology*] (ROG) ... BH
Beni-Abbes [*Algeria*] [*Seismograph station code, US Geological Survey*] (SEIS) ... BAB
Benicia Free Public Library, Benicia, CA [*Library symbol*] [*Library of Congress*] (LCLS) ... CBen
Benidji Middle School, Bemidji, MN [*Library symbol*] [*Library of Congress*] (LCLS) ... MnBemMS
Benign Acute Nephritis [*Medicine*] (MELL) ... BAN
Benign Asbestos Pleural Effusion (HEAS) ... BAPE
Benign Breast Disease [*Medicine*] (DMAA) ... BBD
Benign Breast Syndrome [*Medicine*] (MELL) ... BBS
Benign Childhood Epilepsy [*Medicine*] (MELL) ... BCE
Benign Cystic Teratoma [*Medicine*] (MELL) ... BCT
Benign Epileptiform Transients of Sleep [*Neurology*] (DAVI) ... BETS
Benign Essential Blepharospasm [*Medicine*] (EA) ... BEB
Benign Essential Blepharospasm Research Foundation (EA) ... BEBRF
Benign Essential Hypertension [*Medicine*] (MELL) ... BEH
Benign Exertional Headache [*Medicine*] (DMAA) ... BEH
Benign Familial Hematuria [*Medicine*] (DMAA) ... BFH
Benign Familial Neonatal Convulsions [*Medicine*] ... BFNC
Benign Febrile Convulsion [*Medicine*] (MAE) ... BFC
Benign Focal Epilepsy of Childhood [*Medicine*] (DMAA) ... BFEC
Benign Hypertrophic Prostate (SAUS) ... BHP
Benign Hypertrophy of Prostate [*Medicine*] (MELL) ... BHP
Benign Intracranial Hypertension [*Medicine*] ... BIH
Benign Intradermal Nevus [*Dermatology*] (DAVI) ... BIN
Benign Intrauterine Growth [*Medicine*] (MELL) ... BIUG
Benign Lichenoid Keratosis [*Medicine*] ... BLK
Benign Lymphocytic Angiitis and Granulomatosis [*Medicine*] ... BLAG
Benign Metastasizing Leiomyomas [*Medicine*] (MELL) ... BML
Benign Monoclonal B-Cell Lymphocytosis [*Medicine*] (DMAA) ... BMBL
Benign Monoclonal Gammopathy [*Immunochemistry*] ... BMG
Benign Monoclonal Hypergammaglobulinemia [*Medicine*] ... BMH
Benign Mucous Membrane Pemphigoid (SAUS) ... BMMP
Benign Mucous Membrane Pemphigus [*Medicine*] (MAE) ... BMMP
Benign Mucous Membrane Pemphigus [*Dermatology*] (DAVI) ... BMPP
Benign Neonatal Convulsions [*Medicine*] (MELL) ... BNC
Benign Neonatal Familial Epilepsy [*Medicine*] (MELL) ... BNFE
Benign Neoplasm [*Medicine*] (MELL) ... BN
Benign Nephrosclerosis [*Medicine*] (MAE) ... BNS
Benign Occipital Epilepsy [*Medicine*] (DMAA) ... BOE
Benign Ovarian Tumor [*Medicine*] (MELL) ... BOT
Benign Paroxysmal Positioning Nystagmus [*Medicine*] (DMAA) ... BPPN
Benign Paroxysmal Positioning Vertigo ... BPPV
Benign Paroxysmal Torticollis [*Medicine*] (DMAA) ... BPT
Benign Paroxysmal Vertigo [*Medicine*] (DMAA) ... BPV
Benign Positional Vertigo [*Neurology*] (DAVI) ... BPV
Benign Proliferative Lesion [*Medicine*] (DMAA) ... BPL
Benign Prostatic Hyperplasia [*Medicine*] (CDI) ... BPH
Benign Prostatic Hypertrophy [*Medicine*] ... BPH
Benign Pseudohypertropic Muscular Dystrophy [*Medicine*] (MELL) ... BPMD
Benign Recurrent Hematuria [*Medicine*] (MELL) ... BRH
Benign Recurrent Intrahepatic Cholestasis [*Medicine*] (DMAA) ... BRIC
Benign Senescent Forgetfulness [*Medicine*] ... BSF
Benign Sexual Headache [*Medicine*] (DMAA) ... BSH
Benign Symmetric Lipomatosis [*Medicine*] ... BSL
Benign Tertian Malaria [*Medicine*] (DMAA) ... BTM
Benign Tumor (MELL) ... BT
Benignus EEG Evoked Potential (SAUS) ... BEEP
Benihana Inc. [*NASDAQ symbol*] (TTSB) ... BNHN
Benihana Inc.'A' [*NASDAQ symbol*] (TTSB) ... BNHNA
Benihana National Corp. [*Associated Press*] (SAG) ... Benhn
Benihana National Corp. [*Associated Press*] (SAG) ... Benihan
Benihana National Corp. [*NASDAQ symbol*] (NQ) ... BNHN
Beni-Mellal [*Morocco*] [*ICAO location identifier*] (ICLI) ... GMMD
Benin [*ANSI three-letter standard code*] (CNC) ... BEN
Benin [*ANSI two-letter standard code*] (CNC) ... BJ
Benin (MILB) ... Bn

Benin [*Nigeria*] [*ICAO location identifier*] (ICLI) .... DNBE
Benin [*Aircraft nationality and registration mark*] (FAAC) .... TY
Benin Air Express [*ICAO designator*] (FAAC) .... BEX
Benin City [*Nigeria*] [*Airport symbol*] (OAG) .... BNI
Benin Internet Society (SAUO) .... BIN
Benishangul People's Liberation Movement [*Ethiopia*] .... BPLM
Benishangul Peoples Liberation Movement (SAUO) .... GBPLM
Benito Juarez [*Argentina*] [*ICAO location identifier*] (ICLI) .... SAZJ
Benjamin and Slidell's Louisiana Digest [*A publication*] (DLA) .... Ben & S Dig
Benjamin Franklin High School (SAUO) .... BFHS
Benjamin Franklin High School Library, Rochester, NY [*OCLC symbol*] (OCLC) .... RVQ
Benjamin Franklin Junior Stamp Club [*Later, BFSC*] (EA) .... BFJSC
Benjamin Franklin Literary and Medical Society (EA) .... BFLMS
Benjamin Franklin Stamp Club (EA) .... BFSC
Benjamin Franklin University [*Washington, DC*] .... BFU
Benjamin Harrison [*US president, 1833-1901*] .... BH
Benjamin Harrison Memorial Home (SAUO) .... BHMH
Benjamin on Sales of Personal Property [*1868-1955*] [*A publication*] (DLA) .... Benj
Benjamin on Sales of Personal Property [*1868-1955*] [*A publication*] (DLA) .... Benj Sa
Benjamin on Sales of Personal Property [*1868-1955*] [*A publication*] (DLA) .... Benj Sales
Benjamin/Cummings Publishing Co. Inc. (SAUO) .... B/C
Benjamin/Cumnings (SAUO) .... ISBN 0-8053
Benjamin's Chalmer's Bills and Notes [*A publication*] (DLA) .... Benj Chalm Bills & N
Benjamin's New York Annotated Cases [*A publication*] (DLA) .... Benj
Benloe and Dalison's English Common Pleas Reports [*A publication*] (DLA) .... B & D
Benloe and Dalison's English Common Pleas Reports [*A publication*] (DLA) .... Ben & D
Benloe and Dalison's English Common Pleas Reports [*A publication*] (DLA) .... Ben & Dal
Benloe and Dalison's English Common Pleas Reports [*A publication*] (DLA) .... Benl
Benloe and Dalison's English Common Pleas Reports [*A publication*] (DLA) .... Benl & D
Benloe and Dalison's English Common Pleas Reports [*A publication*] (DLA) .... Benl & Dal
Benloe and Dalison's English Common Pleas Reports [*A publication*] (DLA) .... Benl & D (Eng)
Benloe and Dalison's English Common Pleas Reports [*A publication*] (DLA) .... Benl Old
Benloe and Dalison's English Common Pleas Reports [*A publication*] (DLA) .... Dal
Benloe at the End of Ashe's Tables [*A publication*] (DLA) .... Benl in Ashe
Benloe in Benloe and Dalison's English Common Pleas Reports [*A publication*] (DLA) .... Old Ben
Benloe in Benloe and Dalison's English Common Pleas Reports [*A publication*] (DLA) .... Old Benloe
Benloe in Keilway's Reports [*A publication*] (DLA) .... Benl in Keil
Benloe's English King's Bench and Common Pleas Reports [*A publication*] (DLA) .... Ben
Benloe's English King's Bench and Common Pleas Reports [*A publication*] (DLA) .... Benl New
Benloe's English King's Bench Reports [*73 English Reprint*] [*1531-1628*] [*A publication*] (DLA) .... Ben in Keil
Benloe's English King's Bench Reports [*73 English Reprint*] [*1531-1628*] [*A publication*] (DLA) .... Benl
Benloe's English King's Bench Reports [*73 English Reprint*] [*1531-1628*] [*A publication*] (DLA) .... Benl (Eng)
Benloe's English King's Bench Reports [*73 English Reprint*] [*1531-1628*] [*A publication*] (DLA) .... Benl KB
Benloe's English King's Bench Reports [*73 English Reprint*] [*1531-1628*] [*A publication*] (DLA) .... Benloe
Bennett and Heard's Leading Criminal Cases [*England*] [*A publication*] (DLA) .... B & H Cr Cas
Bennett and Heard's Leading Criminal Cases [*England*] [*A publication*] (DLA) .... B & H Crim Cas
Bennett and Heard's Leading Criminal Cases [*England*] [*A publication*] (DLA) .... B & H Lead Ca
Bennett and Heard's Leading Criminal Cases [*England*] [*A publication*] (DLA) .... B & H Lead Cas
Bennett and Heard's Leading Criminal Cases [*England*] [*A publication*] (DLA) .... Ben & HLC
Bennett and Heard's Leading Criminal Cases [*England*] [*A publication*] (DLA) .... Benn & H Cr Cas
Bennett and Heard's Leading Criminal Cases [*England*] [*A publication*] (DLA) .... Benn & H Lead Crim Cas
Bennett and Heard's Massachusetts Digest [*A publication*] (DLA) .... B & H Dig
Bennett and Heard's Massachusetts Digest [*A publication*] (DLA) .... Benn & H Dig
Bennett College (SAUO) .... BC
Bennett College, Greensboro, NC [*OCLC symbol*] (OCLC) .... BEN
Bennett College, Greensboro, NC [*Library symbol*] [*Library of Congress*] (LCLS) .... NcGB
Bennett College, Millbrook, NY [*Library symbol*] [*Library of Congress*] (LCLS) .... NMbrB
Bennett County Library, Martin, SD [*Library symbol*] [*Library of Congress*] (LCLS) .... SdMa
Bennett, D. L., Wheeling WV [*STAC*] .... BDL
Bennett Junior College [*New York*] .... BJC
Bennett Mechanical Comprehension Test [*Mechanical ability test*] .... BMCT
Bennett on Receivers [*A publication*] (DLA) .... Benn Rec
Bennett, Richard A., Stockton CA [*STAC*] .... BRA
Bennett's Dakota Cases [*A publication*] (DLA) .... Benn (Dak)
Bennett's Dissertation on Practice of Masters in Chancery [*A publication*] (DLA) .... Benn Pr MC
Bennett's Fire Insurance Cases [*A publication*] (DLA) .... Ben Fl Cas
Bennett's Fire Insurance Cases [*A publication*] (DLA) .... Benn Fl Cas
Bennett's Insurance Cases [*A publication*] (DLA) .... Ben Ins Cas
Bennett's Missouri Cases [*A publication*] (DLA) .... Benn (MO)
Bennett's Reports [*16-21 Missouri*] [*A publication*] (DLA) .... Benn
Bennett's Reports [*1 Dakota*] [*A publication*] (DLA) .... Benn
Bennett's Reports [*1 California*] [*A publication*] (DLA) .... Benn
Bennett's Reports [*1 California*] [*A publication*] (DLA) .... Benn Cal
Bennett's Rights and Liabilities of Farmers [*A publication*] (DLA) .... Benn Farm
Bennett's Transport [*Commercial firm*] [*British*] .... BET
Bennettsville & Cheraw Railroad (IIA) .... B & C
Bennettsville, SC [*Location identifier*] [*FAA*] (FAAL) .... BBP
Bennettsville, SC [*Location identifier*] [*FAA*] (FAAL) .... BES
Bennettsville, SC [*AM radio station call letters*] .... WBSC
Bennington Aviation, Inc. [*ICAO designator*] (FAAC) .... BEN
Bennington Bunch [*An association*] (EA) .... BB
Bennington College (SAUO) .... BC
Bennington College (GAGS) .... Bennington C
Bennington College, Bennington, VT [*OCLC symbol*] (OCLC) .... BNT
Bennington College, Bennington, VT [*Library symbol*] [*Library of Congress*] (LCLS) .... VtBennC
Bennington Free Library, Bennington, VT [*Library symbol*] [*Library of Congress*] (LCLS) .... VtBenn
Bennington Museum, Inc., Bennington, VT [*Library symbol*] [*Library of Congress*] (LCLS) .... VtBennM
Bennington, NE [*FM radio station call letters*] .... KRRK
Bennington, NE [*FM radio station call letters*] (RBYB) .... KTNP-FM
Bennington, VT [*AM radio station call letters*] .... WBTN
Bennington, VT [*FM radio station call letters*] (BROA) .... WBTN-FM
Bennington, VT [*FM radio station call letters*] .... WHGC
Benny Goodman [*Clarinetist*] .... BG
Benny Wilson Fan Club (EA) .... BWFC
Beno [*Zaire*] [*ICAO location identifier*] (ICLI) .... FZBE
Benoctol [*French illicit drug available in Vietnam*] (VNW) .... BT's
Benoist scale (SAUS) .... B
Benrus Corp. (SAUO) .... BEN
Bensbach [*Papua New Guinea*] [*Airport symbol*] (OAG) .... BSP
Bensberg [*Federal Republic of Germany*] [*Seismograph station code, US Geological Survey*] (SEIS) .... BNS
Benson [*British*] [*ICAO location identifier*] (ICLI) .... EGUB
Benson & Hedges (ADA) .... B & H
Benson, AZ [*FM radio station call letters*] .... KAVV
Benson Eyecare Corp. [*Associated Press*] (SAG) .... BenEye
Benson Eyecare Corp. [*NYSE symbol*] (SAG) .... EYE
Benson Financial [*NASDAQ symbol*] (TTSB) .... BFCX
Benson Financial Corp. [*Associated Press*] (SAG) .... BensonF
Benson Financial Corp. [*NASDAQ symbol*] (SAG) .... BFCX
Benson, MN [*Location identifier*] [*FAA*] (FAAL) .... BBB
Benson, MN [*AM radio station call letters*] .... KSCR
Benson, MN [*FM radio station call letters*] .... KSCR-FM
Benson, NC [*AM radio station call letters*] .... WPYB
Benson Needham Univas [*International advertising network*] .... BNU
Benson Public Library, Benson, AZ [*Library symbol*] [*Library of Congress*] (LCLS) .... AzBe
Benson Public Schools, Benson, MN [*Library symbol*] [*Library of Congress*] (LCLS) .... MnBenPS
Bensonhurst Yacht Club (SAUO) .... BYC
Benson's Disease [*Medicine*] (MELL) .... BD
Benson's Relaxation Response [*Psychology*] (DHP) .... BRR
Benson's Remarkable Trials and Notorious Characters [*A publication*] (DLA) .... Rem Tr No Ch
Bensons Remarkable Trials and Notorious Characters (SAUS) .... Rem Tr No Ch
Bensselaerville, NY [*FM radio station call letters*] (RBYB) .... WGKP-FM
Bent .... BNT
Bent (MSA) .... BT
Bent Knee Walker [*Doll collecting*] .... BKW
Bent Knees [*Doll collecting*] .... BK
Bent Logarithmically Periodic Zig-Zags .... BLPZZ
Bent of Tau Beta Pi (journ.) (SAUS) .... BENT
Bent Up Trailing Edge [*Aviation*] (PIPO) .... BUTE
Bent Wire Antenna .... BWA
Benta [*Malaysia*] [*ICAO location identifier*] (ICLI) .... WMAC
Bentall Capital Corp. [*Toronto Stock Exchange symbol*] .... BCC
Bentayan [*Indonesia*] [*ICAO location identifier*] (ICLI) .... WIPY
Bentham on Rationale of Judicial Evidence [*A publication*] (DLA) .... Benth Ev
Bentham on Rationale of Judicial Evidence [*A publication*] (DLA) .... Benth Jud Ev
Bentham's Act of Packing as Applied to Special Juries [*1821*] [*A publication*] (DLA) .... Bent Pack Jur
Bentham's Codification [*A publication*] (DLA) .... Bent Cod
Bentham's Constitutional Code for All Nations [*A publication*] (DLA) .... Bent Const Code
Bentham's Judicial Evidence [*A publication*] (DLA) .... Bent Ev
Bentham's Judicial Evidence [*A publication*] (DLA) .... Benth Jud Ev
Bentham's Judicial Evidence [*A publication*] (DLA) .... Bent Jud Ev
Bentham's Principles of Morals and Legislation [*A publication*] (DLA) .... Bent Mor Leg
Bentham's Rationale of Punishment [*A publication*] (DLA) .... Bent Pun
Bentham's Theory of Legislation [*A publication*] (DLA) .... Bent The Leg
Benthic Acoustic Stress Sensor [*Oceanographic instrument*] .... BASS
Benthic Boundary Layer [*Oceanography*] .... BBL
Benthic Boundary Zone (SAUS) .... BBZ
Benthic Foraminiferal Oxygen Index (SAUS) .... BFOI

Benthic Inflatable Toolstore Enclosure (PDAA) .... BITE
Benthic Layer Interactive Profiling System [*Marine science*] (OSRA) .... BLIPS
Benthic Metabolism Measurement .... BMM
Benthic Mixed Layer [*Nuclear energy*] (NUCP) .... BML
Benthic Nepheloid Layer [*Oceanography*] .... BNL
Benthic Organic Matter (SAUS) .... BOM
Benthos, Inc. [*NASDAQ symbol*] (SG) .... BTHS
Bentley College, Waltham, MA [*OCLC symbol*] (OCLC) .... BET
Bentley College, Waltham, MA [*Library symbol*] [*Library of Congress*] (LCLS) .... MWalBe
Bentley Drivers Club (EA) .... BDC
Bentley Pharmaceutical [*Associated Press*] (SAG) .... BentPh
Bentley Pharmaceuticals [*AMEX symbol*] [*Formerly, Belmac Corp.*] (SG) .... BNT
Bentley Public Library, Alberta [*Library symbol*] [*National Library of Canada*] (NLC) .... ABEN
Bentley Resources Ltd. [*Vancouver Stock Exchange symbol*] .... BYT
Bentley School, New York, NY [*Library symbol*] [*Library of Congress*] (LCLS) .... NNBeS
Bentley Systems, Inc. (VERA) .... BSI
Bentley's Irish Chancery Reports [*A publication*] (DLA) .... Bent
Bentley's Reports [*13-19 Attorneys-General's Opinions*] [*A publication*] (DLA) .... Bentl Atty-Gen
Bent-Mescalero School Library, Mescalero, NM [*Library symbol*] [*Library of Congress*] (LCLS) .... NmMeB
Benton & Bowles [*Advertising agency*] .... B & B
Benton & Bowles (SAUO) .... B&B
Benton, AR [*AM radio station call letters*] .... KEWI
Benton, AR [*FM radio station call letters*] .... KMVK
Benton County Historical Museum, Sauk Rapids, MN [*Library symbol*] [*Library of Congress*] (LCLS) .... MnSrB
Benton County Public Library, Fowler, IN [*Library symbol*] [*Library of Congress*] (LCLS) .... InFo
Benton County Recorder's Office, Fowler, IN [*Library symbol*] [*Library of Congress*] (LCLS) .... InFoCR
Benton, Franklin, Walla Walla County Air Pollution Control Authority (SAUO) .... BFWWCAPCA
Benton Harbor [*Michigan*] [*Airport symbol*] (OAG) .... BEH
Benton Harbor Engineering Works (SAUO) .... BHEW
Benton Harbor, MI [*AM radio station call letters*] .... WHFB
Benton Harbor, MI [*FM radio station call letters*] .... WHFB-FM
Benton Harbor, MI [*FM radio station call letters*] (BROA) .... WYKL-FM
Benton Harbor Public Library, Benton Harbor, MI [*Library symbol*] [*Library of Congress*] (LCLS) .... MiBh
Benton, IL [*Location identifier*] [*FAA*] (FAAL) .... BEE
Benton, IL [*FM radio station call letters*] .... WQRL
Benton, KY [*FM radio station call letters*] (RBYB) .... WAAJ-FM
Benton, KY [*AM radio station call letters*] .... WCBL
Benton, KY [*FM radio station call letters*] .... WCBL-FM
Benton, KY [*FM radio station call letters*] (BROA) .... WTRT-FM
Benton, KY [*FM radio station call letters*] .... WVHM
Benton, LA [*FM radio station call letters*] .... KLKL
Benton Lake National Refuge (SAUS) .... BLNR
Benton Oil & Gas [*NYSE symbol*] (SG) .... BNO
Benton Oil & Gas [*NASDAQ symbol*] (TTSB) .... BNTN
Benton Oil & Gas Co. [*Associated Press*] (SAG) .... BentOG
Benton Oil & Gas Co. [*NASDAQ symbol*] (SAG) .... BNTN
Benton Oil & Gas Co. [*Associated Press*] (SAG) .... BntOG
Benton Oil & Gas Wrrt [*NASDAQ symbol*] (TTSB) .... BNTNW
Benton, PA [*FM radio station call letters*] (BROA) .... WGGI-FM
Benton, PA [*FM radio station call letters*] .... WKXP
Benton Resources Ltd. [*Vancouver Stock Exchange symbol*] .... BRX
Benton, TN [*AM radio station call letters*] .... WBIN
Benton, TN [*FM radio station call letters*] .... WBIN-FM
Benton, TN [*FM radio station call letters*] (BROA) .... WOCE-FM
Benton Township - Potterville District Library, Potterville, MI [*Library symbol*] [*Library of Congress*] (LCLS) .... MiPot
Benton Visual Retention Test [*Psychology*] (DAVI) .... BVRT
Benton Visual Retention Test, Revised [*Psychology*] (DAVI) .... BVRTR
Benton Visual Retention Time [*Psychiatry*] .... BVRT
Bentong [*Malaysia*] [*ICAO location identifier*] (ICLI) .... WMAD
Bentonite Agglutination (OA) .... BA
Bentonite Agglutination Inhibition (OA) .... BAI
Bentonite Flocculation [*Test*] .... BF
Benton's Abridgement of the Debates of Congress [*A publication*] (DLA) .... Bent Abr
Benton/Stearns Special Education Professional Library, St. Cloud, MN [*Library symbol*] [*Library of Congress*] (LCLS) .... MnStclBS
Bentonville, AR [*FM radio station call letters*] (RBYB) .... KFAY
Bentonville-Bella Vista, AR [*AM radio station call letters*] (RBYB) .... KESE
Bent's Old Fort National Historic Site .... BEOL
Bentu [*Sudan*] [*ICAO location identifier*] (ICLI) .... HSBT
Bentwaters [*British*] [*ICAO location identifier*] (ICLI) .... EGVJ
Bentwood (VRA) .... bntwd
Benvenuto Club [*Milan, Italy*] .... BV
Benyzlimidazole [*Organic chemistry*] .... BZI
Benzaldehyde [*Organic chemistry*] .... BAL
Benzaldehyde (SAUS) .... BZGAK
Benzaldehyde (EDCT) .... BzH
Benzalkonium and Heparin (MAE) .... BH
Benzalkonium Chloride [*Organic chemistry*] .... BAC
benzalkonium chloride (SAUS) .... benzalk
Benzamide (DMAA) .... Bam
Benzanthracene [*Also, BzAnth*] [*Organic chemistry*] .... BA
Benzanthracene [*Also, BA*] [*Organic chemistry*] .... BzAnth
Benz-a-pyren (SAUS) .... BaP
benzathine (SAUS) .... benz
Benzathine Penicillin G [*Antibacterial*] .... BPG
Benzbromarone (SAUS) .... BBR
Benzedrine .... B
Benzedrine (SAUS) .... Benz
Benzedrine Bomb (SAUS) .... B-Bomb
Benzedrine stimulants benny benzedrine (SAUS) .... Bennies
Benzen Hexa Chlorid (SAUS) .... BHC
Benzene [*Organic chemistry*] (ADA) .... BZ
Benzene (ABAC) .... Bz
Benzene- 1,3-Disulfohydrazide (SAUS) .... DBSH
Benzene Hexachloride (SAUS) .... BHA
Benzene Hexachloride [*Also, GBH, HCH*] [*Insecticide*] .... BHC
Benzene Study Team (EEVL) .... BST
Benzene Task Group (EEVL) .... BTG
Benzene Tetrachloride (SAUS) .... BTC
Benzene, Toluene, and Xylene .... BTX
Benzenecarboxylic Acid [*Organic chemistry*] .... BCA
Benzenediazonium Chloride [*Organic chemistry*] .... BDC
Benzene-Dioxane-Acetic Acid (SAUS) .... BzDA Acid
Benzene-Methanol-Acetic Acid (SAUS) .... BzMA Acid
Benzene-Soluble Organics [*Pollutant*] .... BSO
Benzene-Soluble Particulate Matter (SAUS) .... BSPM
Benzenesulfonic Acid [*Organic chemistry*] .... BSA
Benzenesulfonohydrazide [*Organic chemistry*] .... BSH
Benzenesulfonyl Histamine (SAUS) .... BSH
Benzenetricarboxylate [*Organic chemistry*] .... BTC
Benzethonium Chloride (SAUS) .... BZT
Benzhydryl [*As substituent on nucleoside*] [*Biochemistry*] .... bh
Benzhydryl [*Biochemistry*] .... Bzh
Benzidine [*Carcinogen*] .... BENZ
Benzidine [*Carcinogen*] .... BZD
Benziger Bruce & Glencoe, Inc. (SAUO) .... BBG
Benzilic Acid Tropine Ester [*Also, BETE, BTE*] [*Pharmacology*] .... BAT
Benzilic Acid Tropine Ester [*Also, BAT, BTE*] [*Pharmacology*] .... BETE
Benzilic Acid Tropine Ester [*Also, BAT, BETE*] [*Pharmacology*] .... BTE
Benzimidazole [*Biochemistry*] .... Bza
Benzimidazolyl [*Biochemistry*] .... Bza
Benzimidazolylphenylmaleimide [*Organic chemistry*] .... BIPM
Benzin (SAUS) .... Be
Benzine (SAUS) .... Bene
Benzine (SAUS) .... Benz
Benzing Retrograde (DAVI) .... BR
Benzoate (MAE) .... B
benzocaine (SAUS) .... benzo
Benzo(c)phenanthrene [*Organic chemistry*] .... BcPh
Benzocyclobutene [*Organic chemistry*] .... BCB
Benzodiazepine (DB) .... BDZ
Benzodiazepine [*Also, BZD*] [*Organic chemistry*] .... BZ
Benzodiazepine (SAUS) .... Bz
Benzodiazepine [*Also, BZ*] [*Organic chemistry*] .... BZD
Benzodiazepine [*Pharmacology*] (DAVI) .... BZDZ
Benzo(e)pyridoindole [*Organic chemistry*] .... BePI
benzoic acid (SAUS) .... ben
Benzoic Acid [*Organic chemistry*] .... BOA
Benzoic Acid (SAUS) .... Bz A
Benzoin (SAUS) .... bnzn
Benzon [*Denmark*] [*Research code symbol*] .... U
Benzonia Public Library, Benzonia, MI [*Library symbol*] [*Library of Congress*] (LCLS) .... MiBen
Benzonitrile [*Organic chemistry*] .... BN
Benzophenone Tetracarboxylic Acid Dianhydride (PDAA) .... BTAD
Benzophenone Tetracarboxylic Dianhydride (DB) .... BDTA
Benzophenonetetracarboxylic Dianhydride [*Organic chemistry*] .... BTDA
Benzophenonetetracarboxylic Diethylester [*Organic chemistry*] .... BTDE
Benzopyrene [*or Benzpyrene*] [*Also, BZ*] [*Carcinogen*] .... BP
Benzopyrene [*or Benzpyrene*] [*Also, BP*] [*Carcinogen*] .... BZ
Benzopyrenedihydrodiolepoxide [*Organic chemistry*] .... BPDE
Benzoquinone Acetic Acid (SAUS) .... BQA
Benzothiophene [*Organic chemistry*] .... BT
Benzothiopyranoindazole [*Organic chemistry*] .... BTPI
Benzotrifuroxan [*Organic chemistry*] .... BTF
Benzoyl [*Organic chemistry*] .... Bz
Benzoyl Arginine Amide (SAUS) .... BAA
Benzoyl Arginine Methyl Ester (SAUS) .... BAME
Benzoyl Leuco Methylene Blue [*Organic chemistry*] .... BLMB
Benzoyl Peroxide [*Also, BPO*] [*Organic chemistry*] .... BP
Benzoyl Peroxide [*Also, BP*] [*Organic chemistry*] .... BPO
Benzoyl Peroxide (SAUS) .... BPO
Benzoylacetone [*Organic chemistry*] .... BZAC
Benzoylarginine Amide [*Biochemistry*] .... BAA
Benzoylarginine Ethyl Ester [*Biochemistry*] .... BAEE
Benzoylarginine Methyl Ester [*Biochemistry*] .... BAME
Benzoylarginine p-Nitroanilide [*Also, BAPNA*] [*Biochemistry*] .... BAPA
Benzoylarginine p-Nitroanilide [*Also, BAPA*] [*Biochemistry*] .... BAPNA
Benzoylargininenaphthylamide .... BANA
Benzoylargininenitroanilide [*Organic chemistry*] .... BANI
Benzoyl-Arginine-p-Nitroanilide (SAUS) .... BAPNA
Benzoylated DEAE [*Diethylaminoethyl*] [*Organic chemistry*] .... BD
Benzoylated-Naphthoylated DEAE [*Diethylaminoethyl*] .... BND
Benzoylated-Naphthoylated (DEAE)[*Diethylaminoethyl*]**-Cellulose** [*Analytical biochemistry*] .... BNC
Benzoylbenzoic Acid [*Organic chemistry*] .... BBA
Benzoyl-DL-Arginine-p-Nitroanilide (SAUS) .... DL-BAPNA
Benzoylecgonine [*Cocaine metabolite*] .... BE

Benzoylecgonine [*Biochemistry*] ... BZE
Benzoyloxime [*Organic chemistry*] ... BO
Benzoyl-para-aminosalicylate [*Pharmacology*] ... BPAS
Benzoyl(Phenylalanyl)Proline [*Biochemistry*] ... BPAP
Benzoylphenylhydroxylamine (NRCH) ... BPHA
Benzoyl(sulfamoyl)(thenyloxy)benzoic Acid [*Biochemistry*] ... BSTBA
Benzoylthiamine Disulfide (SAUS) ... BTDS
Benzoyltrifluoroacetone [*Organic chemistry*] ... BTA
Benzoyltrifluoroacetone [*Organic chemistry*] (NRCH) ... BTFA
Benzoyltyrosine [*Biochemistry*] ... BT
Benzoyltyrosine Ethyl Ester [*Biochemistry*] ... BTEE
Benzoyl-Tyrosyl Para-Aminobenzoic Acid [*Organic chemistry*] ... BT PABA
Benzoyl-Tyrosyl-Para-Aminobenzoic Acid [*Test*] (MEDA) ... Bz-Ty-PABA
Benzquinamide [*Pharmacology*] ... BZQ
Benzyl [*Organic chemistry*] ... Bn
Benzyl [*Organic chemistry*] ... Bzl
Benzyl Alcohol (MELL) ... BA
Benzyl Alcohol (SAUS) ... Bz Alc
Benzyl Analogue of Serotonin [*Medicine*] (DAVI) ... BAS
Benzyl Bromide Beriberi [*Medicine*] (MELL) ... BB
Benzyl Butyl Phthalate [*Organic chemistry*] ... BBP
Benzyl Dimethyl Amine (SAUS) ... BDMA
Benzyladenine [*Biochemistry*] ... BA
Benzyl-Aminophenol [*Organic chemistry*] ... BAP
Benzylaminopurine [*Biochemistry*] ... BAP
Benzylantiserotonin [*Pharmacology*] ... BAS
(Benzyl)benzylidenecyclopentanone [*Organic chemistry*] ... BBCP
Benzylcinchonidinium Chloride [*Organic chemistry*] ... BCDC
Benzylcinchoninium Chloride [*Organic chemistry*] ... BCNC
Benzylcyclopropylamine [*Organic chemistry*] ... BCA
Benzyldimethylamine [*Organic chemistry*] ... BDMA
Benzylfurancarboxylic Acid [*Organic chemistry*] ... BFCA
Benzylfurylmethyl Alcohol [*Organic chemistry*] ... BFA
Benzylideneglucose [*Biochemistry*] ... BG
Benzylidenemalononitrile [*Organic chemistry*] ... BMN
Benzyl-Iso-Thiourea [*Organic chemistry*] ... BITU
Benzyloctyladipat (SAUS) ... BOA
Benzyloctylphthalat (SAUS) ... BOP
Benzyloxymethyl [*Organic chemistry*] ... BOM
Benzyl-Para-Aminophenol (EDCT) ... BAP
Benzylpenicilloyl [*Organic chemistry*] ... BPO
Benzylpenicilloyl Polylysine [*Organic chemistry*] ... BPL
Benzylselenocyanate [*Antineoplastic drug*] ... BSC
Benzylthiomethyl [*Biochemistry*] ... Btm
Benzyl-Thiourea (SAUS) ... BITO
Benzyl-Thiourea (SAUS) ... bitu
Benzyltrichlorosilane [*Organic chemistry*] ... BTCS
Benzyltrimethylammonium Chloride [*Also, TMBAC*] [*Organic chemistry*] ... BTM
Benzyl(vinyl)pyridinium Bromide [*Organic chemistry*] ... BVP
Beobachtung [*Observation*] [*German*] ... BB
Beobachtungsstelle [*Observation post*] [*German military - World War II*] ... BST
Beograd [*Belgrade*] [*Yugoslavia*] [*Seismograph station code, US Geological Survey*] (SEIS) ... BEO
Beograd [*Former Yugoslavia*] [*ICAO location identifier*] (ICLI) ... LYBA
Beograd [*Former Yugoslavia*] [*ICAO location identifier*] (ICLI) ... LYBB
Beograd [*Former Yugoslavia*] [*ICAO location identifier*] (ICLI) ... LYBE
Beograd [*Former Yugoslavia*] [*ICAO location identifier*] (ICLI) ... LYYY
Beongo [*Zaire*] [*ICAO location identifier*] (ICLI) ... FZEO
Bepaling [*Provision in statute or contract*] [*Netherlands*] (ILCA) ... Bep
Bephenium Hydroxynaphthoate (MAE) ... BHN
Beppu [*Japan*] [*Seismograph station code, US Geological Survey*] [*Closed*] (SEIS) ... BEP
Bequeath [*Legal term*] (WDAA) ... BEQ
Bequeath [*Legal term*] (ROG) ... BEQTH
Bequeathed [*Legal term*] ... BEQD
Bequeathed [*Legal term*] ... BEQTHD
Bequest ... BEQT
Berachampa [*India*] [*ICAO location identifier*] (ICLI) ... VEBC
Berakhot [*or Berakot*] (BJA) ... Ber
Berar Law Journal [*India*] [*A publication*] (DLA) ... Berar
Berau [*Indonesia*] [*Airport symbol*] (OAG) ... BEJ
Berber [*MARC language code*] [*Library of Congress*] (LCCP) ... ber
Berbera [*Somalia*] [*Airport symbol*] (OAG) ... BBO
Berbera [*Somalia*] [*ICAO location identifier*] (ICLI) ... HCMI
Berberati [*Central African Republic*] [*ICAO location identifier*] (ICLI) ... FEFT
Berck-Sur-Mer [*France*] [*ICAO location identifier*] (ICLI) ... LFAM
Berclair, TX [*Location identifier*] [*FAA*] (FAAL) ... NGT
Berea College (SAUO) ... BC
Berea College, Berea, KY [*OCLC symbol*] (OCLC) ... KBE
Berea College, Berea, KY [*Library symbol*] [*Library of Congress*] (LCLS) ... KyBB
Berea, KY [*AM radio station call letters*] ... WKXO
Berea, KY [*FM radio station call letters*] ... WKXO-FM
Berea, OH [*FM radio station call letters*] ... WBWC
Berean Bible College, Calgary, AB, Canada [*Library symbol*] [*Library of Congress*] (LCLS) ... CaACBB
Berean Bible Society (EA) ... BBS
Berean Mission, Inc. (EA) ... BMI
Bereave (ABBR) ... BRVE
Bereaved (ABBR) ... BRVED
Bereaved Children's Program [*Later, BC*] (EA) ... BCP
Bereaved Parents' Association (WDAA) ... BPA
Bereavement Center (EA) ... BC
Bereavement Services & Community Education (AC) ... LIFT
Bereina [*Papua New Guinea*] [*Airport symbol*] (OAG) ... BEA
Bereitschaftsstellung [*Line of support*] [*German military - World War II*] ... BST
Berens River [*Canada*] [*Airport symbol*] (OAG) ... YBV
Beresford Public Library, Beresford, SD [*Library symbol*] [*Library of Congress*] (LCLS) ... SdBer
Bereshit Rabba (BJA) ... BerRabb
Berg Analysis and Prediction System (SAUS) ... BAPS
Berg Electronics Corp. [*NYSE symbol*] (SAG) ... BEI
Berg Electronics Corp. [*Associated Press*] (SAG) ... BergElc
Berga [*Sweden*] [*ICAO location identifier*] (ICLI) ... ESQP
Bergamo [*Italy*] [*Airport symbol*] (OAG) ... BGY
Bergamo/Orio Al Serio [*Italy*] [*ICAO location identifier*] (ICLI) ... LIME
Bergdorf Goodman (SAUO) ... B-G
Bergen [*Norway*] [*Seismograph station code, US Geological Survey*] (SEIS) ... BER
Bergen [*Norway*] [*Airport symbol*] (OAG) ... BGO
Bergen [*Norway*] [*ICAO location identifier*] (ICLI) ... ENVV
Bergen Brunswig [*Associated Press*] (SAG) ... BergBr
Bergen Brunswig 'A' [*NYSE symbol*] (TTSB) ... BBC
Bergen Brunswig Corp. [*NYSE symbol*] (SPSG) ... BBC
Bergen Citizen, Edgewater, NJ [*Library symbol*] [*Library of Congress*] (LCLS) ... NjEwB
Bergen Community College, Paramus, NJ [*OCLC symbol*] (OCLC) ... BER
Bergen Community College, Paramus, NJ [*Library symbol*] [*Library of Congress*] (LCLS) ... NjParB
Bergen County Community Library System (SAUS) ... BCCLS
Bergen County Historical Society, North Hackensack, NJ [*Library symbol*] [*Library of Congress*] (LCLS) ... NjNhBHi
Bergen Gazette, Inc., Garfield, NJ [*Library symbol*] [*Library of Congress*] (LCLS) ... NjGaB
Bergen News, Palisades Park, NJ [*Library symbol*] [*Library of Congress*] (LCLS) ... NjPalN
Bergen Reading Center, Bergen, NY [*Library symbol*] [*Library of Congress*] (LCLS) ... NBerR
Bergen Record, Hackensack, NJ [*Library symbol*] [*Library of Congress*] (LCLS) ... NjHackR
Bergenfield Free Public Library, Bergenfield, NJ [*Library symbol*] [*Library of Congress*] (LCLS) ... NjBer
Bergen/Flesland [*Norway*] [*ICAO location identifier*] (ICLI) ... ENBR
Bergen-Hohne [*Germany*] [*ICAO location identifier*] (ICLI) ... EDZB
Bergen-Paterson Pipe Support Corp. (SAUO) ... BP
Berger Hldgs Ltd [*NASDAQ symbol*] (TTSB) ... BGRH
Berger Holdings, Inc. [*Associated Press*] (SAG) ... BergHld
Berger Holdings, Inc. [*NASDAQ symbol*] (SAG) ... BGRH
Berger, Jenson & Nicholson Ltd. (SAUO) ... BJN
Bergerac [*France*] [*Airport symbol*] [*Obsolete*] (OAG) ... EGC
Bergerac/Roumaniere [*France*] [*ICAO location identifier*] (ICLI) ... LFBE
Berger's Disease [*Medicine*] ... BD
Berggiesshubel [*German Democratic Republic*] [*Seismograph station code, US Geological Survey*] (SEIS) ... BRG
Berglynn Resources [*Vancouver Stock Exchange symbol*] ... BGN
Bergneustadt/Auf Dem Dumpel [*Germany*] [*ICAO location identifier*] (ICLI) ... EDKF
Bergstrom and Ridder [*Boating rig*] ... B&R
Bergstrom Capital [*AMEX symbol*] (SPSG) ... BEM
Bergstrom Capital Corp. [*Associated Press*] (SAG) ... BergCa
Berhad [*Public Limited Company*] [*Malaysia*] (FEA) ... BHD
Beriault Branch, Gloucester Public Library, Ontario [*Library symbol*] [*National Library of Canada*] (NLC) ... OGB
Berichte. Verhandlungen der Saechsischen Gesellschaft der Wissenschaften zu Leipzig [*A publication*] (OCD) ... Ber Sachs Ges Wiss
Beriev [*Russian aircraft designation*] (DOMA) ... Be2
Bering [*Komandorsky Islands*] [*Former USSR*] [*Seismograph station code, US Geological Survey*] (SEIS) ... BKI
Bering Air, Inc. [*ICAO designator*] (FAAC) ... BRG
Bering Sea, AK [*Location identifier*] [*FAA*] (FAAL) ... OCV
Bering Sea Expedition [*or Experiment*] ... BESEX
Bering Sea Fisheries-Oceanography Cooperation Investigations [*Marine science*] (OSRA) ... BS FOCI
Bering Sea FOCI [*Fisheries-Oceanography Cooperative Investigations*] (USDC) ... BS FOCI
Bering Sea FOCI (SAUS) ... BS FOCI
Bering Sea Impact Study (SAUS) ... BESIS
Bering Sea Marine Mammal Experiment [*National Oceanic and Atmospheric Administration*] (MSC) ... BESMEX
Bering Sea Patrol [*Navy*] ... BERSEAPAT
Bering Sea Patrol (SAUO) ... BSP
Bering Sea Patrol (SAUS) ... BSP
Bering Slope Current (SAUS) ... BSC
Bering Standard Time (HGAA) ... BST
Bering Strait Time (SAUS) ... BST
Bering Straits Regional Housing Authority (SAUO) ... BSRHA
Beringovsky [*Former USSR*] [*ICAO location identifier*] (ICLI) ... UHMR
Berkeley [*England*] ... BERK
Berkeley [*California*] (BARN) ... Berk
Berkeley Abstract Machine (SAUS) ... BAM
Berkeley Association (EA) ... BA
Berkeley, CA [*Location identifier*] [*FAA*] (FAAL) ... JBK
Berkeley, CA [*FM radio station call letters*] ... KALX
Berkeley, CA [*FM radio station call letters*] (RBYB) ... KBLX
Berkeley, CA [*FM radio station call letters*] ... KPFA
Berkeley, CA [*FM radio station call letters*] ... KPFB
Berkeley, CA [*AM radio station call letters*] ... KVTO
Berkeley County Library, Moncks Corner, SC [*Library symbol*] [*Library of Congress*] (LCLS) ... ScMoc
Berkeley Database Management System (SAUS) ... BDMS
Berkeley Elites Automated Retrieval [*University of California at Berkeley*] [*Information service or system*] (NITA) ... BEAR
Berkeley Enthusiasts Club [*Woking, Surrey, England*] (EAIO) ... BEC

Berkeley Exchange (EA) ..... BE
Berkeley Geochronology Center ..... BGC
Berkeley Historical Society, Berkeley, CA [*Library symbol*] [*Library of Congress*] (LCLS) ..... CBHi
Berkeley Internet Name Domain [*Computer science*] (ITCA) ..... BIND
Berkeley Macintosh Users' Group (IID) ..... BMUG
Berkeley Networking (SAUS) ..... BNET
Berkeley Nuclear Laboratories [*England*] ..... BNL
Berkeley Nucleonics Corporation (SAUO) ..... BNC
Berkeley Packet Filter (SAUS) ..... BPF
Berkeley Particle Data Center ..... BPDC
Berkeley Particle Data Group [*Lawrence Radiation Laboratory*] ..... BPDG
Berkeley Process Flow Language (SAUS) ..... BPFL
Berkeley Public Library, Berkeley, CA [*Library symbol*] [*Library of Congress*] (LCLS) ..... CB
Berkeley Public Library, Berkeley, IL [*Library symbol*] [*Library of Congress*] (LCLS) ..... IBerk
Berkeley Quality Software (SAUS) ..... BQS
Berkeley Reliability Tools (SAUS) ..... BeRT
Berkeley Review (journ.) (SAUS) ..... BeR
Berkeley Roundtable on the International Economy [*University of California*] ..... BRIE
Berkeley Scientific Laboratories (SAUS) ..... BSL
Berkeley Software Design, Inc (SAUS) ..... BSDI
Berkeley Software Distribution [*University of California*] [*Computer science*] (TNIG) ..... BSD
Berkeley Software Distribution UNIX (CDE) ..... BSD UNIX
Berkeley Springs, WV [*AM radio station call letters*] ..... WCST
Berkeley Springs, WV [*FM radio station call letters*] ..... WCST-FM
Berkeley Springs, WV [*FM radio station call letters*] (RBYB) ..... WDHC-FM
Berkeley Standard Distribution [*Computer science*] (BYTE) ..... BSD
Berkeley Stress Analysis Finite Elements (SAUS) ..... BERSAFE
Berkeley System Distribution (SAUO) ..... BSD
Berkeley Version (BJA) ..... BV
Berkeley-Byerly [*California*] [*Seismograph station code, US Geological Survey*] (SEIS) ..... BKS
Berkeley-Haviland [*California*] [*Seismograph station code, US Geological Survey*] (SEIS) ..... BRK
Berkeley-Illinois-Maryland Array ..... BIMA
Berkeley-Illinois-Maryland Association [*Consortium for astronomical study*] ..... BIMA
Berkeley-Oakland Service System [*Library network*] ..... BOSS
Berkeley/San Diego License (SAUO) ..... BSDL
Berkelium [*Chemical element*] ..... Bk
Berkely [*W.R.*] **Corp.** [*Associated Press*] (SAG) ..... Berkly
Berkley [*W.R.*] **Corp.** [*Associated Press*] (SAG) ..... Berkley
Berkley [*W. R.*] **Corp.** [*NASDAQ symbol*] (NQ) ..... BKLY
Berkley Heights Public Library, Berkley Heights, NJ [*Library symbol*] [*Library of Congress*] (LCLS) ..... NjBh
Berkley Resources, Inc. [*Vancouver Stock Exchange symbol*] ..... BKS
Berkley, W.R. [*NASDAQ symbol*] (SG) ..... BKLY
Berkley(W.R.)7.375% Dep'A'Pfd [*NASDAQ symbol*] (TTSB) ..... BKLYZ
Berko Rotary Joint (SAUS) ..... BRJ
Berks Community Television [*Reading, PA*] [*Telecommunications*] (TSSD) ..... BCTV
Berkshire [*County in England*] ..... BERKS
Berkshire [*County in England*] (ODBW) ..... Berks
Berkshire (SAUS) ..... Berks
Berkshire (FAAC) ..... BRKSHR
Berkshire and Westminster Dragoons [*British military*] (DMA) ..... B & W Dgns
Berkshire Archaeological Society (SAUO) ..... BAS
Berkshire Archaeological Society (SAUS) ..... BAS
Berkshire Athenaeum, Pittsfield, MA [*Library symbol*] [*Library of Congress*] (LCLS) ..... MPB
Berkshire Athenium (SAUS) ..... BA
Berkshire Christian College, Lenox, MA [*Library symbol*] [*Library of Congress*] (LCLS) ..... MLenB
Berkshire Community College [*Pittsfield, MA*] ..... BCC
Berkshire Community College, Pittsfield, MA [*Library symbol*] [*Library of Congress*] (LCLS) ..... MPBC
Berkshire Gas Co. [*Associated Press*] (SAG) ..... BerkGs
Berkshire Gas Co. [*NASDAQ symbol*] (NQ) ..... BGAS
Berkshire Hathaway [*Associated Press*] (SAG) ..... BerkH
Berkshire Hathaway, Inc. [*Associated Press*] (SAG) ..... BerkHa
Berkshire Hathaway, Inc. [*NYSE symbol*] (CTT) ..... BRK
Berkshire Hills Bancorp [*AMEX symbol*] ..... BHL
Berkshire Law Library Association, Pittsfield, MA [*Library symbol*] [*Library of Congress*] (LCLS) ..... MPBL
Berkshire Realty Co., Inc. [*Associated Press*] (SAG) ..... BerkR
Berkshire Realty Company, Inc. [*Associated Press*] (SAG) ..... BerkRty
Berkshire Realty, Inc. [*NYSE symbol*] (SPSG) ..... BRI
Berkshire Yeomanry Cavalry [*British military*] (DMA) ..... BYC
Berle Resources Ltd. [*Vancouver Stock Exchange symbol*] ..... BRL
Berlevag [*Norway*] [*Airport symbol*] (OAG) ..... BVG
Berlevag [*Norway*] [*ICAO location identifier*] (ICLI) ..... ENBV
Berlin [*Germany*] [*Airport symbol*] (OAG) ..... BER
Berlin (ROG) ..... BERL
Berlin [*New Hampshire*] [*Seismograph station code, US Geological Survey*] (SEIS) ..... BNH
Berlin [*West Germany*] [*Seismograph station code, US Geological Survey*] (SEIS) ..... BRN
Berlin [*Germany*] [*ICAO location identifier*] (ICLI) ..... EDBA
Berlin [*Germany*] [*Airport symbol*] (OAG) ..... SXF
Berlin [*Germany*] [*Airport symbol*] (OAG) ..... TXL
Berlin - Free University [*West Germany*] [*Seismograph station code, US Geological Survey*] (SEIS) ..... BRL
Berlin Air Safety Center ..... BASC
Berlin Air Traffic Central Center (SAUO) ..... BARTCC
Berlin Airlift Device [*Military decoration*] ..... BAD
Berlin Airlift Device [*Military decoration*] (AABC) ..... BerADev
Berlin Airlift Device [*Military decoration*] ..... BERDEV
Berlin Airways Control Approach (SAUO) ..... BACA
Berlin ATM LAN Interconnection (SAUS) ..... BALI
Berlin Border Guard [*East Germany*] ..... BBG
Berlin Brigade ..... BB
Berlin Brigade ..... BBDE
Berlin Command [*Allied German Occupation Forces*] ..... BC
Berlin Commission British [*Post-World War II*] ..... BERCOMB
Berlin Conference of Catholic Christians in European Countries (SAUO) ..... BC
Berlin Contingency [*NATO*] (NATG) ..... BERCON
Berlin Continuing Engineering Education Program (SAUS) ..... BECEEP
Berlin Control Zone [*Allied German Occupation Forces*] ..... BCZ
Berlin, CT [*FM radio station call letters*] ..... WERB
Berlin Declaration (SAUS) ..... BD
Berlin District [*Allied German Occupation Forces*] ..... BD
Berlin Document Center [*Allied German Occupation Forces*] ..... BDC
Berlin Documentary (or Documents) Center (SAUS) ..... BDC
Berlin Electron Storage Ring for Synchrotron Radiation ..... BESSY
Berlin European [*ICAO designator*] (FAAC) ..... ECJ
Berlin European [*ICAO designator*] (AD) ..... WZ
Berlin Fan Club [*Defunct*] (EA) ..... BFC
Berlin Kommandatura ..... BK
Berlin Kommandatura Commandents' Letter ..... BKC/L
Berlin, MD [*FM radio station call letters*] ..... WOCQ
Berlin Military Post (SAUO) ..... BMP
Berlin Mills [*AAR code*] ..... BMS
Berlin, NH [*Location identifier*] [*FAA*] (FAAL) ..... BML
Berlin, NH [*Location identifier*] [*FAA*] (FAAL) ..... HXK
Berlin, NH [*AM radio station call letters*] ..... WMOU
Berlin, NH [*FM radio station call letters*] (RBYB) ..... WPKQ-FM
Berlin, NH [*FM radio station call letters*] ..... WZPK
Berlin, NJ [*FM radio station call letters*] ..... WNJS
Berlin Overseas News Service (SAUO) ..... BONS
Berlin Papyri [*A publication*] (OCD) ..... PBerol
Berlin Philharmonic Orchestra ..... BPO
Berlin Public Library, Berlin, WI [*Library symbol*] [*Library of Congress*] (LCLS) ..... WBer
Berlin Quadripartite Document ..... BQD
Berlin Regional Test Bed (VERA) ..... BRTB
Berlin Regional Testbed (SAUS) ..... BRTB
Berlin Research Area Information Network (VERA) ..... BRAIN
Berlin Sector [*Allied German Occupation Forces*] ..... BS
Berlin State Opera Orchestra ..... BSOO
Berlin Task Force ..... BTF
Berlin U.S.A. [*ICAO designator*] (AD) ..... ZF
Berlin, VT [*AM radio station call letters*] (BROA) ..... NEW AM
Berlin, WI [*FM radio station call letters*] (BROA) ..... WBJZ-FM
Berlin, WI [*AM radio station call letters*] ..... WISS
Berlin, WI [*FM radio station call letters*] ..... WISS-FM
[*The*] **Berline, Berlin-Brandenburgisches Luftfahrtunternehmen GmbH** [*Germany*] [*ICAO designator*] (FAAC) ..... TBL
Berliner Beitraege zur Keilschriftforschung [*A publication*] (BJA) ..... BBK
Berliner, Cohen & Biogini, Law Library, San Jose, CA [*Library symbol*] [*Library of Congress*] (LCLS) ..... CSjB
Berliner, Coher & Biogini, Law Library, San Jose, CA [*Library symbol*] [*Library of Congress*] (LCLS) ..... CSjBC
Berliner Griechische Urkunden [*A publication*] (OCD) ..... BGU
Berliner Handels- & Frankfurter Bank [*Berlin & Frankfurt Bank*] ..... BHF
Berliner Klassikertexte [*A publication*] (OCD) ..... BKT
Berliner Konferenz Europaischer Katholiken [*Berlin Conference of European Catholics*] [*Germany*] (EAIO) ..... BK
Berliner Philologische Wochenschrift [*A publication*] (OCD) ..... B Phil Woch
Berliner Sector (SAUS) ..... BS
Berliner Verkehrs-Gesellschaft [*Later, Berliner Verkehrs-Betriebe*] [*Berlin Transport*] [*West Berlin*] ..... BVG
Berliner Zionistische Vereinigung [*A publication*] (BJA) ..... BZV
Berlinetta Boxer [*Ferrari sports car*] ..... BB
Berlin/Gatow [*Germany*] [*ICAO location identifier*] (ICLI) ..... EDBG
Berlin/Schonefeld [*Germany*] [*ICAO location identifier*] (ICLI) ..... ETBN
Berlin/Schonefeld [*Germany*] [*ICAO location identifier*] (ICLI) ..... ETBS
Berlin/Tegel [*Germany*] [*ICAO location identifier*] (ICLI) ..... EDBT
Berlin/Tempelhof [*Germany*] [*ICAO location identifier*] (ICLI) ..... EDBB
Berlitz International [*Associated Press*] (SAG) ..... Berlitz
Berlitz International [*NYSE symbol*] (SPSG) ..... BTZ
Berlitz School (SAUO) ..... BS
Berman Leasing Co. (SAUO) ..... BMA
Bermejo [*Bolivia*] [*ICAO location identifier*] (ICLI) ..... SLBJ
Bermuda [*Airport symbol*] (OAG) ..... BDA
Bermuda (SAUO) ..... BER
Bermuda (DLA) ..... BERM
Bermuda (SAUS) ..... Berm
Bermuda [*ANSI two-letter standard code*] (CNC) ..... BM
Bermuda [*MARC country of publication code*] [*Library of Congress*] (LCCP) ..... bm
Bermuda [*ANSI three-letter standard code*] (CNC) ..... BMU
Bermuda [*IYRU nationality code*] (IYR) ..... KB
Bermuda [*MARC geographic area code*] [*Library of Congress*] (LCCP) ..... lnbm-
Bermuda - Navy [*Bermuda*] [*Seismograph station code, US Geological Survey*] [*Closed*] (SEIS) ..... BEN
Bermuda Atlantic Time Series [*Oceanographic Station*] ..... BATS

Bermuda Atlantic Time-series Station (SAUS) ..... BATS
Bermuda Atlantic Time-series Study (SAUS) ..... BATS
Bermuda Base Command [*World War II*] ..... BBC
Bermuda Benevolent Association ..... BBA
Bermuda Biological Station (SAUO) ..... BBS
Bermuda Biological Station for Research, Inc. (SAUO) ..... BBSR
Bermuda Botanical Gardens (SAUO) ..... BBG
Bermuda Broadcasting Company Limited (SAUO) ..... BBCL
Bermuda Container Line (SAUO) ..... BCL
Bermuda Dunes, CA [*Location identifier*] [*FAA*] (FAAL) ..... UDD
Bermuda Football Association (SAUO) ..... BFA
Bermuda Island (NASA) ..... BDA
Bermuda Islands (BARN) ..... Ber Is
Bermuda Islands (SAUS) ..... Berm
Bermuda Islands (SAUO) ..... BI
Bermuda Islands ..... BI
Bermuda Law Reports [*A publication*] (DLA) ..... BLR
Bermuda Library, Hamilton, Bermudas [*Library symbol*] [*Library of Congress*] (LCLS) ..... BmuHB
Bermuda Militia (SAUO) ..... BM
Bermuda Militia Artillery (SAUO) ..... BMA
Bermuda Naval Air Station [*Bermuda*] [*ICAO location identifier*] (ICLI) ..... TXKF
Bermuda Plan [*Travel accomodations*] ..... BP
Bermuda Radio and Television Company (SAUO) ..... BR & TC
Bermuda Radio and Television Company (SAUS) ..... BR&TC
Bermuda Range Safety Officer [*NASA*] (KSC) ..... BRSO
Bermuda Resources Ltd. [*Vancouver Stock Exchange symbol*] ..... BDA
Bermuda Star Lines, Inc. (MHDW) ..... BSL
Bermuda Stock Exchange Ltd. ..... BSX
Bermuda Tracking Station [*NASA*] (KSC) ..... BDA
Bermuda Trade Development Board (SAUO) ..... BTDB
Bermuda Triangle (SAUS) ..... Ber Tri
Bermuda Volunteer Rifle Corps (SAUO) ..... BVRC
Bermuda-Columbia [*Bermuda*] [*Seismograph station code, US Geological Survey*] (SEIS) ..... BEC
Bermuda-Kindley Field (SAUO) ..... BDA
Bermudas commercial internet (SAUS) ..... LYNX
Bermuda-Schwortz Industries, Inc. [*Vancouver Stock Exchange symbol*] ..... BWT
Bern. Office Federal de l'Air [*Switzerland*] [*ICAO location identifier*] (ICLI) ..... LSSO
Bern Radio [*Switzerland*] [*ICAO location identifier*] (ICLI) ..... LSSB
Bern Resources Ltd. [*Vancouver Stock Exchange symbol*] ..... BER
Bernadia [*Italy*] [*Seismograph station code, US Geological Survey*] (SEIS) ..... BERI
Bernard Berenson [*American art critic, 1865-1959*] ..... BB
Bernard Geis Associates [*Publisher*] [*Obsolete*] ..... BGA
Bernard Haldane [*Commercial firm*] [*Associated Press*] (SAG) ..... BerHald
Bernard Haldane [*NASDAQ symbol*] (SAG) ..... BHAL
Bernard Haldane Assoc Inc. [*NASDAQ symbol*] (TTSB) ..... BHAL
Bernard Herrmann Society (EA) ..... BHS
Bernard Johnson, Inc., Houston, TX [*Library symbol*] [*Library of Congress*] (LCLS) ..... TxHBJ
Bernard M. Baruch College of the City University of New York (GAGS) ..... Baruch C (CUNY)
Bernard M. Baruch College of the City University of New York, New York, NY [*Library symbol*] [*Library of Congress*] (LCLS) ..... NNBBC
Bernard Shaw Society (EA) ..... BSS
Bernard van Risenburgh [*Label stamped on works by the master ebeniste*] ..... BVRB
Bernard-Henri Levy [*French writer and philosopher*] ..... BHL
Bernard-Horner [*Syndrome*] [*Medicine*] (DB) ..... BH
Bernardine Sisters of the Third Order of St. Francis (TOCD) ..... OSF
Bernardo De Irigoyen [*Argentina*] [*ICAO location identifier*] (ICLI) ..... SATI
Bernard's Church Cases [*Ireland*] [*A publication*] (DLA) ..... Bern
Bernard's Church Cases [*Ireland*] [*A publication*] (DLA) ..... Bern Ch Cas
Bernards Township Library, Inc., Basking Ridge, NJ [*Library symbol*] [*Library of Congress*] (LCLS) ..... NjBas
Bernard-Soulier Syndrome [*Hematology*] ..... BSS
Bernardsville Library Association, Bernardsville, NJ [*Library symbol*] [*Library of Congress*] (LCLS) ..... NjBern
Bernardsville News, Bernardsville, NJ [*Library symbol*] [*Library of Congress*] (LCLS) ..... NBernN
Bernardsville News, Bernardsville, NJ [*Library symbol*] [*Library of Congress*] (LCLS) ..... NjBernN
Bernardus Compostellanus [*Authority cited in pre-1607 legal work*] (DSA) ..... B Compos
Bernardus Compostellanus [*Authority cited in pre-1607 legal work*] (DSA) ..... Ber Compos
Bernardus Compostellanus, Junior [*Deceased, 1267*] [*Authority cited in pre-1607 legal work*] (DSA) ..... B
Bernardus Compostellanus, Senior [*Flourished, 1198-1216*] [*Authority cited in pre-1607 legal work*] (DSA) ..... B
Bernardus Compostellanus, Senior [*Flourished, 1198-1216*] [*Authority cited in pre-1607 legal work*] (DSA) ..... Ber
Bernardus de Bottone de Parma [*Deceased, 1266*] [*Authority cited in pre-1607 legal work*] (DSA) ..... B
Bernardus de Bottone de Parma [*Deceased, 1266*] [*Authority cited in pre-1607 legal work*] (DSA) ..... Ber
Bernardus de Bottone de Parma [*Deceased, 1266*] [*Authority cited in pre-1607 legal work*] (DSA) ..... Bern
Bernardus de Bottone de Parma [*Deceased, 1266*] [*Authority cited in pre-1607 legal work*] (DSA) ..... Bernar
Bernardus de Pavia [*Deceased, 1213*] [*Authority cited in pre-1607 legal work*] (DSA) ..... B
Bernardus Maynardi [*Authority cited in pre-1607 legal work*] (DSA) ..... Ber May
Bernardus Maynardi [*Authority cited in pre-1607 legal work*] (DSA) ..... B May
Bernardus Papiensis [*Deceased, 1213*] [*Authority cited in pre-1607 legal work*] (DSA) ..... B Pa
Bernardus Saporis [*Flourished, 1327-36*] [*Authority cited in pre-1607 legal work*] (DSA) ..... B Sapo
Bernardus Saporis [*Flourished, 1327-36*] [*Authority cited in pre-1607 legal work*] (DSA) ..... B Sapor
Bernay/Saint-Martin [*France*] [*ICAO location identifier*] (ICLI) ..... LFPD
Bern/Belp [*Switzerland*] [*ICAO location identifier*] (ICLI) ..... LSZB
Berne [*Switzerland*] [*Airport symbol*] (OAG) ..... BRN
Berne, IN [*FM radio station call letters*] ..... WZBD
Berne Public Library, Berne, IN [*Library symbol*] [*Library of Congress*] (LCLS) ..... InBer
Berne Public Library, Berne, IN [*OCLC symbol*] (OCLC) ..... XBB
Bernedict-Webb-Rubin Equation (SAUS) ..... BWR-Equation
Berneimer's Basal Medium (DB) ..... BBM
Berner High School, Massapequa, NY [*Library symbol*] [*Library of Congress*] (LCLS) ..... NMassBH
Berner Oberland-Bahnen [*Bernese Overland Railways*] ..... BOB
Berne/Radio Suisse SA [*Switzerland*] [*ICAO location identifier*] (ICLI) ..... LSSR
Bernese Mountain Dog Club of America (EA) ..... BMDCA
Bernhard, Eisenbraun and Associates (GEOI) ..... BEA
Bernheim's Syndrome [*Medicine*] (MELL) ..... BS
Bernice P Bishop Museum (SAUO) ..... BISH
Bernice P Bishop Museum (SAUO) ..... BISHOP
Bernice P. Bishop Museum (SAUO) ..... BPBM
Bernice Pauahi Bishop Museum, Honolulu, HI [*Library symbol*] [*Library of Congress*] (LCLS) ..... HHB
Bernie [*Missouri*] [*Seismograph station code, US Geological Survey*] [*Closed*] (SEIS) ..... BRM
Bernoulli Disk ..... BD
Bernoulli Number [*Mathematics*] ..... B
Bernoulli Society for Mathematical Statistics and Probability [*Voorburg, Netherlands*] (EA) ..... BSMSP
Bernstein & Associates [*Computer science*] ..... B&A
Bernstein, Lee, Yang, Primakoff [*Physicists*] ..... BLYP
Beroroha [*Madagascar*] [*Airport symbol*] (OAG) ..... WBO
Beroroha/Antsoa [*Madagascar*] [*ICAO location identifier*] (ICLI) ..... FMSB
Berre-La-Fare [*France*] [*ICAO location identifier*] (ICLI) ..... LFNR
Berridale [*Airport symbol*] ..... BRE
Berrien Springs, MI [*FM radio station call letters*] ..... WAUS
Berry (ABBR) ..... BRY
Berry Aviation, Inc. [*ICAO designator*] (FAAC) ..... AHS
Berry College (SAUO) ..... BC
Berry College (GAGS) ..... Berry C
Berry College (SAUS) ..... GMtbC
Berry College, Mount Berry, GA [*OCLC symbol*] (OCLC) ..... GBC
Berry College, Mount Berry, GA [*Library symbol*] [*Library of Congress*] (LCLS) ..... GMtbC
Berry, Fruit, or Vegetable [*Freight*] ..... BERRY F V
Berry Hill Elementary School, Syosset, NY [*Library symbol*] [*Library of Congress*] (LCLS) ..... NSyoBE
Berry Hill, TN [*AM radio station call letters*] ..... WVOL
Berry Petroleum Co. [*Associated Press*] (SAG) ..... BerryP
Berry Petroleum Co. Class A [*NYSE symbol*] (SPSG) ..... BRY
Berry Pseudorotation ..... BPR
Berry, R. H., San Leandro CA [*STAC*] ..... BRH
Berrying (ABBR) ..... BRYG
Berryman [*Missouri*] [*Seismograph station code, US Geological Survey*] [*Closed*] (SEIS) ..... BRR
Berry's Reports [*1-28 Missouri Appeals*] [*A publication*] (DLA) ..... Berry
Berryville, AR [*AM radio station call letters*] ..... KTHS
Berryville, AR [*FM radio station call letters*] ..... KTHS-FM
Berryville, VA [*FM radio station call letters*] ..... WAPP
Bersatu Rakyat Jelata Sabah [*Sabah People's Union*] [*Malaysia*] [*Political party*] (PPW) ..... BERJAYA
Berserk (ABBR) ..... BSRK
Bert Leston Taylor [*American columnist, 1866-1921*] [*Initials used as pseudonym*] ..... BLT
Bertan High Voltage (SAUS) ..... BA
Bertelsmann Electronic Edition (SAUS) ..... BEE
Bertelsmann Electronic Publishing (SAUS) ..... BEP
Bertelsmann Music Group [*Record company*] (ECON) ..... BMG
Bertelsmann Printing & Manufacturing Corp. ..... BPMC
Berth (MSA) ..... BTH
Berth Terms [*Shipping*] ..... BT
Bertha Hill [*Idaho*] [*Seismograph station code, US Geological Survey*] [*Closed*] (SEIS) ..... BHI
Bertha-Hweitt School, Bertha, MN [*Library symbol*] [*Library of Congress*] (LCLS) ..... MnBeB
Berthing ..... BERTH
Berthing Latch Interface Mechanism (SSD) ..... BLIM
Berthoud Public Library, Berthoud, CO [*Library symbol*] [*Library of Congress*] (LCLS) ..... CoBer
Bertolotti-Garcin [*Syndrome*] [*Medicine*] (DB) ..... BG
Berton's New Brunswick Reports [*A publication*] (DLA) ..... Ber
Berton's New Brunswick Reports [*A publication*] (DLA) ..... Bert
Berton's New Brunswick Reports [*A publication*] (DLA) ..... NBR Ber
Bertoua [*Cameroon*] [*Airport symbol*] (OAG) ..... BTA
Bertoua [*Cameroon*] [*ICAO location identifier*] (ICLI) ..... FKKO
Bertrand Chaffee Hospital, Springville, NY [*Library symbol*] [*Library of Congress*] (LCLS) ..... NSprvCH
Bertrand Russell Peace Foundation (EA) ..... BRPF
Bertrand Russell Society (EA) ..... BRS
Bertrandus [*Authority cited in pre-1607 legal work*] (DSA) ..... Bert
Bertrandus [*Authority cited in pre-1607 legal work*] (DSA) ..... Bertran

Bertrandus [*Authority cited in pre-1607 legal work*] (DSA) .... Btran
Bertrandus de Montefaventino [*Deceased, 1342*] [*Authority cited in pre-1607 legal work*] (DSA) .... B
Bertrandus de Montefaventino [*Deceased, 1342*] [*Authority cited in pre-1607 legal work*] (DSA) .... B de Monfa
Bertrandus de Montefaventino [*Deceased, 1342*] [*Authority cited in pre-1607 legal work*] (DSA) .... Bertr
Bertrix [*Belgium*] [*ICAO location identifier*] (ICLI) .... EBBX
Bertucci's, Inc. [*NASDAQ symbol*] (SPSS) .... BERT
Bertuccis, Inc. [*Associated Press*] (SAG) .... Bertuci
Beru [*Kiribati*] [*Airport symbol*] (OAG) .... BEZ
Beru [*Kiribati*] [*ICAO location identifier*] (ICLI) .... NGBR
Berufsgenossenschaft der chemischen Industrie (SAUS) .... BG-Chemie
Berufungsgericht [*Court of Appeal*] [*German*] (ILCA) .... BG
Berul Associates Ltd. [*Information service or system*] (IID) .... BAL
Berwick [*Former county in Scotland*] (WGA) .... BERW
Berwick, LA [*FM radio station call letters*] .... KBZE
Berwick, PA [*FM radio station call letters*] .... WKAB
Berwick, PA [*AM radio station call letters*] .... WSQV
Berwickshire [*County in England*] .... Berwicks
Berwyn Public Library, Berwyn, IL [*Library symbol*] [*Library of Congress*] (LCLS) .... IBer
Berwyn School, Alberta [*Library symbol*] [*National Library of Canada*] (BIB) .... ABWS
Berwyn WI Municipal Library, Alberta [*Library symbol*] [*National Library of Canada*] (NLC) .... ABWM
Berwyn W.I. Municipal Library, Berwyn, AB, Canada [*Library symbol*] [*Library of Congress*] (LCLS) .... CaABerWM
Beryl (SAUS) .... be
Beryl [*Jewelry*] (ROG) .... BERL
Beryllium [*Chemical element*] .... Be
Beryllium Aluminate (SAUS) .... Chrysoberyl
Beryllium Aluminum Silicate (SAUS) .... Beryl
Beryllium Atomization and Thermal Spray Facility (SAUS) .... BATSF
Beryllium Oxide .... BeO
Beryllium Oxide (IDOE) .... beO
Beryllium Oxide Microwave Integrated Circuit (SAUS) .... BOMIC
Beryllium Oxide Reactor Experiment [*Formerly, EBOR*] [*Nuclear energy*] .... BORE
Beryllium Oxide Washer .... BOW
Beryllium Physics Reactor (NRCH) .... BPR
Beryllium Thrust Chamber .... BTC
Besah (BJA) .... Bes
Besalampy [*Madagascar*] [*Airport symbol*] (OAG) .... BPY
Besalampy [*Madagascar*] [*ICAO location identifier*] (ICLI) .... FMNQ
Besancon [*France*] [*Seismograph station code, US Geological Survey*] (SEIS) .... BES
Besancon-La-Veze [*France*] [*ICAO location identifier*] (ICLI) .... LFQM
Besancon/Thise [*France*] [*ICAO location identifier*] (ICLI) .... LFSA
Beschwerdenliste (DB) .... BL
Beseech (ABBR) .... BSCH
Beseech (ABBR) .... BSECH
Beseeched (ABBR) .... BSCHD
Beseeched (ABBR) .... BSECHD
Beseeching (ABBR) .... BSCHG
Besicorp Group [*Associated Press*] (SAG) .... Besicp
Besicorp Group [*AMEX symbol*] (SAG) .... BGI
Besicorp Group [*ECM Symbol*] (TTSB) .... BGIEC
Beside (ABBR) .... BSD
Beside (ABBR) .... BSID
Besiege (ABBR) .... BSEG
Besiege (ABBR) .... BSG
Besieged (ABBR) .... BSEGD
Besieged (ABBR) .... BSGD
Besieging (ABBR) .... BSEGG
Besieging (ABBR) .... BSGG
Besloten Vennootschap [*Private or Closed Limited Company*] [*Dutch*] .... BV
Besmear (ABBR) .... BSMER
Besmear (ABBR) .... BSMR
Besmeared (ABBR) .... BSMRD
Besmearing (ABBR) .... BSMRG
Besmirch (ABBR) .... BSMRCH
Besnier-Boeck [*Disease*] [*Medicine*] (DB) .... BB
Besonders [*Particularly*] [*German*] .... BSD
Bess Kaiser Foundation Hospital, Medical Library, Portland, OR [*Library symbol*] [*Library of Congress*] (LCLS) .... OrPBK
Bess Kaiser Foundation Hospital, Medical Library, Portland, OR [*Library symbol*] [*Library of Congress*] (LCLS) .... OrPK
Bess Tilson Sprinkle Memorial Library, Weaverville, NC [*Library symbol*] [*Library of Congress*] (LCLS) .... NcWea
Bessel Function [*Mathematics*] (IAA) .... BES
Bessel Function Model (MCD) .... BFM
Besseler. Musik des Mittelalters und der Renaissance [*A publication*] .... BeMMR
Bessemer [*Metallurgy*] .... BESS
Bessemer Acid Steel (SAUS) .... BAS
Bessemer, AL [*Location identifier*] [*FAA*] (FAAL) .... BEQ
Bessemer, AL [*AM radio station call letters*] .... WSMQ
Bessemer and Lake Erie Railroad Co. (SAUO) .... B&LE
Bessemer & Lake Erie Railroad Co. .... B & LE
Bessemer & Lake Erie Railroad Co. [*AAR code*] .... BLE
Bessemer Public Library, Bessemer, MI [*Library symbol*] [*Library of Congress*] (LCLS) .... MiBes
Bessemer Steel (SAUS) .... BS
Bessey-Lowry Unit [*Medicine*] (MAE) .... BL
Bessey-Lowry Unit (MAE) .... BLU
Bessey-Lowry-Brock Unit [*Medicine*] (MAE) .... BLB

Bessie Smith Society (EA) .... BSS
Besson [*Frank S.*] Memorial Award [*American Defense Preparedness Association*] (RDA) .... BMA
Besson's New Jersey Precedents [*A publication*] (DLA) .... Bess Prec
Best [*Moody's bond rating*] [*Investment term*] .... Aaa
Best (IAA) .... B
Best (ROG) .... BST
Best Adaptive Path [*NASA*] .... BAP
Best Alignment True Heading (SAUS) .... BATH
Best Alternative Equally Effective Data System .... BAEDS
Best Amplitude (DB) .... BA
Best & Company, Inc. (SAUO) .... BST
Best and Final Offer [*DoD*] (MCD) .... BAFO
Best and Final Offer .... B/F
Best and Revised Final Offer [*DoD*] .... BARFO
Best and Smith's English Queen's Bench Reports [*A publication*] (DLA) .... B & S
Best and Smith's English Queen's Bench Reports [*A publication*] (DLA) .... Best & S
Best and Smith's English Queen's Bench Reports [*A publication*] (DLA) .... Best & S (Eng)
Best and Smith's English Queen's Bench Reports [*A publication*] (DLA) .... Best & Sm
Best Asymptotically Normal [*Estimates*] [*Econometrics*] .... BAN
Best Available (WDMC) .... ba
Best Available (WDMC) .... BA
Best Available and Safest Technology .... BAST
Best Available Control Measures [*Environmental science*] (COE) .... BACM
Best Available Control Technology [*Environmental Protection Agency*] .... BACT
Best Available Controls [*Environmental science*] (COE) .... BAC
Best Available Demonstrated Control Technology [*Environmental Protection Agency*] .... BADCT
Best Available Demonstrated Technology [*Environmental Protection Agency*] (FFDE) .... BADT
Best Available Retrofit Facility [*Environmental Protection Agency*] (GFGA) .... BARF
Best Available Retrofit Technology [*Environmental Protection Agency*] .... BART
Best Available Scientific Information [*Environmental science*] (COE) .... BASI
Best Available Shelter Survey [*of fallout shelters*] [*Civil Defense*] .... BASS
Best Available Technology .... BAT
Best Available Technology Economically Achievable [*Wastewater treatment*] .... BATEA
Best Available Technology Not Entailing Excessive Costs [*British*] .... BATNEEC
Best Available Treatment (MCD) .... BAT
Best Available Treatment Economically Achievable (SAUS) .... BATEA
Best Available True Heading (MCD) .... BATH
Best Average Definition Over the Picture Area (SAA) .... BADOPA
Best Berlin Broadcast [*Radio program broadcast from Berlin by Robert H. Best, former South Carolina journalist*] [*World War II*] .... BBB
Best Best (SAUS) .... BB
Best Black [*Pencil leads*] (ROG) .... BB
Best British Briar (SAUS) .... BBB
Best Buddies International [*An association*] (EA) .... BBI
Best Building Economic Solutions Together [*Committee redesigning the defunct Charleston Navy Base and Shipyard*] (ECON) .... BEST
Best Buy [*NYSE symbol*] (SG) .... BBY
Best Buy Cap 6.50%'MIPS' [*NYSE symbol*] (TTSB) .... BBYPrM
Best Buy Capital LP [*NYSE symbol*] (SAG) .... BBY
Best Buy Capital Ltd. [*Associated Press*] (SAG) .... BestB
Best Buy Co. [*Associated Press*] (SAG) .... BestBuy
Best Candidate Committee (EA) .... BCC
Best Commercial Flight Line Test Set (MCD) .... BCFLS
Best Control Technology [*Environmental Protection Agency*] (ERG) .... BCT
Best Controlled Similar Source Emission [*Environmental Protection Agency*] .... BCSSE
Best Conventional Pollutant Control Technology (EPAT) .... BCPCT
Best Conventional Pollutant Control Technology (GNE) .... BCT
Best Conventional Pollutant Technology [*Environmental science*] (COE) .... BCPT
Best Conventional Technology [*Environmental Protection Agency*] .... BCT
Best Copy Available .... BCA
Best Corrected Visual Acuity [*Ophthalmology*] .... BVA
Best Critical Region (IAA) .... BCR
Best Cruise Altitude .... BCA
Best Cruise Mach Number [*Aviation*] .... BCM
Best Current Practice (SAUS) .... BCP
Best Current Practices Documents [*Computer science*] (IGQR) .... BCP documents
Best Dark Virginia [*Tobacco*] [*British*] (ROG) .... BDV
Best Delay [*Audiometry*] .... BD
Best Demonstrated Achievable Technology [*Environmental science*] (EPAT) .... BDAT
Best Demonstrated Available Technology .... BDAT
Best Demonstrated Control Technology [*Environmental science*] (EPAT) .... BDCT
Best Demonstrated Technology (GFGA) .... BDT
Best Depth Range [*Military*] (NVT) .... BDR
Best Developed Alternate [*Environmental Protection Agency*] .... BDAT
Best Dressed List .... BDL
Best Educational Systems for Teaching .... BEST
Best Efficiency Point (KSC) .... BEP
BEST [*Beneficial Employees Security Trust*] Employers Association (EA) .... BEA
Best Engineering Judgement [*Environmental Protection Agency*] (FFDE) .... BEJ
Best Enhanced Advanced Technology (VERA) .... BEAT
Best Estimate (SAUS) .... BE
Best Estimate Constrained .... BEC
Best Estimate Model (NRCH) .... BE
Best Estimate of Orbital Parameters .... BEOP
Best Estimate of Track (ACAE) .... BET
Best Estimate of Trajectory [*Apollo*] [*NASA*] .... BET

Best Estimate Unconstrained ... BEU
Best Estimated Quantity (AAGC) ... BEQ
Best Ever Bottled [*Wines and spirits*] ... BEB
Best Evidence Rule [*Legal shorthand*] (LWAP) ... BER
Best Excitatory Frequency [*Neurophysiology*] ... BEF
Best Execution Analysis Tabulation [*Computer science*] ... BEAT
Best Expert Judgment [*Environmental Protection Agency*] (ERG) ... BEJ
Best Fit Algorithm [*Mathematics*] (IAA) ... BF
Best Fit Algorithm (SAUS) ... BF Algorithm
Best Fit Sphere (MCD) ... BFS
Best Fixed-Sample Procedure [*Statistics*] ... BFSP
Best Foods Inc. (SAUO) ... BF
Best Foods, Inc. (SAUO) ... BFX
Best Friend [*Initialism used by author E. B. White to describe his wife*] ... BF
Best Game [*Billiards*] (BARN) ... BG
Best Grade [*Business term*] (EBF) ... A1
Best Holiday Trav-L-Park Association (EA) ... BHTPA
Best Ice Cream You Ever Ate ... BICYEA
Best in Class (SAUS) ... BIC
Best in Group ... BIG
Best in Match ... BIM
Best in Show [*Dog show term*] ... BIS
Best Index Slope Extraction (SAUS) ... BISE
Best Inhibitory Frequency [*Neurophysiology*] ... BIF
BEST Instruments [*Test*] (TMMY) ... BEST
Best Linear Unbiased Estimator [*Statistics*] ... BLUE
Best Linear Unbiased Prediction [*Genetics*] ... BLUP
Best Loiter Mach Number [*Aviation*] ... BLM
Best Loiter Mach Number (SAUS) ... BLM Number
[*The*] **Best Love Story Poems** [*A publication*] ... BeLS
Best Loved Poems of the American People [*A publication*] ... BLPA
Best Loved Religious Poems [*A publication*] ... BLRP
Best Management Practice [*Environmental Protection Agency*] ... BMP
Best Management Practices Evaluation Program (WPI) ... BMPEP
Best Management Program (PA) ... BMP
Best Manufacturing Practices (ACAE) ... BMP
Best Noise Figure (IAA) ... BNF
Best Null Detector and Flip Flop (SAUS) ... BNDAFF
Best of a Bad Situation ... BBS
Best of a Kind (BARN) ... A
Best of Both Worlds (ADWA) ... BOBW
Best of Both Worlds [*Apple Computer's Macintosh Due System's nickname*] [*Pronounced as a proper name: Bob W.*] ... Bob W
Best of Breed ... BB
Best of Breed ... BOB
Best of the U.S. (SAUS) ... BOTUS
Best of Variety (WDAA) ... BOV
Best of Winners [*Dog show term*] ... BW
Best Offer [*Classified advertising*] ... BO
Best Offer (SAUS) ... Boffer
Best on Best (MCD) ... BOB
Best on Evidence [*A publication*] (DLA) ... Best Ev
Best on Presumptions of Law and Fact [*A publication*] (DLA) ... Best Pres
Best on Presumptions of Law and Fact [*A publication*] (DLA) ... Best Presumptions
Best on the Right to Begin and Reply [*A publication*] (DLA) ... Best Beg & Rep
Best on Trial by Jury [*A publication*] (DLA) ... Best Jur Tr
Best Operating Procedure (SAUS) ... BOP
Best Operational Capability ... BOC
Best Opposite Sex (to Best of Breed) [*Dog show term*] ... BOS
Best Output and Color [*Computer science*] (IAA) ... BOC
Best Paint Solid (SAUS) ... BPS
Best Play for Imperfect Player (SAUS) ... BPIP
Best Practicable Control Technology [*Wastewater treatment*] ... BPCT
Best Practicable Control Technology (SAUS) ... BPT
Best Practicable Control Technology Currently Available (MCD) ... BPCTCA
Best Practicable Control Technology Currently Available (EEVL) ... BPT
Best Practicable Control Technology Currently Available [*Clean Water Act*] (ERG) ... BPTCA
Best Practicable Environmental Option (ECON) ... BPEO
Best Practicable Means ... BPM
Best Practicable Technology [*Environmental Protection Agency*] ... BPT
Best Practicable Treatment (GNE) ... BPT
Best Practicable Waste Treatment Technology (EG) ... BPWTT
Best Practical Control Method [*Wastewater treatment*] (DICI) ... BPCM
Best Practical Means [*Business term*] (DCTA) ... BPM
Best Practical Wastewater Treatment Technology (EEVL) ... BPWTT
Best Practice Technology (SAUS) ... BPT
Best Preliminary Estimate (AFM) ... BPE
Best Products Co. (SAUO) ... BES
Best Products Co., Inc. [*NASDAQ symbol*] (SAG) ... BEST
Best Products Company, Inc. [*Associated Press*] (SAG) ... BestPd
Best Professional Judgment [*Environmental Protection Agency*] ... BPJ
Best Qualified ... BQ
Best Range of Aging Verified Oscillator (MUGU) ... BRAVO
Best Regards [*Amateur radio shorthand*] (WDAA) ... 73s
Best Replacement Factor (CAAL) ... BRF
Best Resources, Inc. [*Vancouver Stock Exchange symbol*] ... BST
Best Speed Rating [*of a horse*] ... BSR
Best Straight Line [*Mathematics*] ... BSL
Best Support Concept Approach ... BSCA
Best Technical Approach [*Military*] (AABC) ... BTA
Best Technology Generally Available [*Environmental Protection Agency*] ... BTGA
Best Time of the Day [*Automotive racing*] ... BTD
Best Times Available [*Television*] ... BTA
Best Value Selection (AAGC) ... BVS
Best Vision Antenna Services [*Australia*] (CIST) ... BVA
Best Western International, Inc. (EFIS) ... B-W
Best Western Motels [*Motel chain*] ... BWM
Bestand Juedischer Gemeinden in Staatsarchiv Hamburg [*A publication*] (BJA) ... BJG
Best-Estimated Evaluation Trajectory [*NASA*] (KSC) ... BEET
Best-Fit Central Y-Plane ... BFCY-P
Best-Fit Optic Z-Plane ... BFOZ-P
Bestfoods [*NYSE symbol*] (SG) ... BFO
Bestial (ABBR) ... BSTL
Bestiality (ABBR) ... BSTLT
Bestially (ABBR) ... BSTLY
Bestow (ABBR) ... BSTO
Bestow (ABBR) ... BSTW
Bestowable (ABBR) ... BSTWB
Bestowal (ABBR) ... BSTWL
Bestowed (ABBR) ... BSTWD
Bestowing (ABBR) ... BSTWG
Bestowment (ABBR) ... BSTWT
Best's Disease [*Medicine*] (MELL) ... BD
Best's Law Dictionary [*A publication*] (DLA) ... Best Law Dic
Bestwall Gypsum Co. (SAUO) ... BWG
Bestway Inc. [*NASDAQ symbol*] (TTSB) ... BSTW
Bet 'Eked Sefarim (BJA) ... BES
BET Holdings [*NYSE symbol*] (SPSG) ... BTV
Bet Holdings, Inc. [*Associated Press*] (SAG) ... BetHld
BET Holdings'A' [*NYSE symbol*] (TTSB) ... BTV
Bet Ltd. ADS [*NYSE symbol*] [*Toronto Stock Exchange symbol*] (SPSG) ... BEP
Bet Midrash le Torah (BJA) ... BMT
Bet Nahrain (EA) ... BN
BET PLC [*Associated Press*] (SAG) ... BET Plc
BET Public Ltd ADS [*NYSE symbol*] (TTSB) ... BEP
Bet Ya'akov Lekhu ve-Nelkhah (BJA) ... BILU
Beta ... B
Beta Absorption Gauge ... BAG
Beta Activity [*Measure of radioactivity*] ... BA
Beta Alpha Psi (EA) ... BAP
Beta Alternating Transmission System (MCD) ... BATS
Beta Analytic (SAUS) ... Beta-
Beta Anneal (PDAA) ... BA
Beta, Atla, and Themis [*Regions on planet Venus*] ... BAT
Beta Barium Borate (SAUS) ... BBO
Beta Beta Beta [*An association*] (NTPA) ... TriBeta
Beta, Beta-Dicyano-O-Chlorostyrene [*Organic chemistry*] (DAVI) ... CS
Beta Disintegration Energy ... BDE
Beta Environmental Fine Structure [*Physics*] ... BEFS
Beta Gamma Sigma ... BGS
Beta Human Chorionic Gonadotropin [*Endocrinology*] (DAVI) ... B-HCG
Beta Kappa Chi (EA) ... BKX
Beta Lambda (SAUS) ... BL
Beta Lighted Infantry Telescope System (SAUS) ... BLITS
Beta Methyl Umbelliferone (SAUS) ... BMU
Beta Solar Array Drive (SSD) ... BSAD
Beta Spectrometer ... BS
Beta Thickness Gauge (DEN) ... BTG
Beta-1-C [*Also called complement C_3*] [*Biochemistry*] (DAVI) ... B-1-C
Beta-2-Mikroglobulin (SAUS) ... B2MG
Beta-Adrenergic Agonist [*Medicine*] (MELL) ... BAA
Beta-Alumina Solid Electrolyte ... BASE
Beta-Aminopropionitrile [*Organic chemistry*] ... BAPN
Beta-Amyloid Precursor Protein ... BAPP
Beta-Androgenic Receptor Kinase [*An enzyme*] ... B-ARK
Beta-Anyloid Protein Bi-Anyloid Protein ... BAP
Beta-Binomial Distribution (SAUS) ... BBD
Beta-Blocker [*Pharmacology*] (DAVI) ... BB
Beta-Blocker Heart Attack Trial [*Cardiology*] ... BHAT
Beta-Carotene [*Biochemistry*] ... BC
Beta-Cedrene ... BCDR
Beta-Cyclodextrin [*Organic chemistry*] ... BCD
Beta-Endorphin [*Biochemistry*] ... B-END
Beta-Galactosidase (DB) ... BG
Betagalactoside ... BGal
Beta-Gamma ... BG
Beta-Glucuronidase [*Organic chemistry*] (DAVI) ... GRS
Beta-Glycerophosphatase (MAE) ... BGP
Beta-Hemolytic Streptococcus [*Medicine*] ... BHS
Betahemolytic Streptococcus (SAUS) ... BHS
Beta-Hydroxy Acid [*Organic chemistry*] ... BHA
Beta-Hydroxybutyrate [*Medicine*] (MELL) ... BHB
Beta-Hydroxybutyric Acid (MAE) ... BHBA
Beta-Hydroxybutyric Acid Dehydrogenase (DB) ... BHBAD
Beta-Hydroxyethylhydrazine [*Plant growth compound*] ... BOH
(Beta-Hydroxyethyl)theophylline [*Biochemistry*] ... BHET
(Beta-Hydroxypropyl)theophylline [*Biochemistry*] ... BHPT
Beta-Hydroxysteroid Dehydrogenase [*An enzyme*] ... BHD
Beta-Hydroxytheophylline [*Medicine*] (DMAA) ... BHT
Betail Research Foundation (SAUS) ... RRF
Beta-Ionone [*Biochemistry*] ... BI
Beta-Lactamase Inhibitory Protein [*Biochemistry*] ... BLIP
Beta-Lactoglobulin [*Biochemistry*] ... BLG
Betalactoglobulin (SAUS) ... BLG
Beta-Lipoprotein [*Biochemistry*] (DB) ... BLP
Betamax [*First home VCR (Video Cassette Recorder) format*] (CDE) ... Beta
Beta-Mercaptoethanol [*Organic chemistry*] ... BME
Betamethasone (DB) ... BM

Betamethasone Acetate [*Medicine*] (DMAA) .... BA
Betamethasone Valerate [*Glucocorticoid*] .... BV
Beta-Methylamino-alanine [*An amino acid*] .... BMAA
Beta-Methylheptadecanoic Acid [*Organic chemistry*] .... BMHDA
Beta-Naphthoflavone [*Organic chemistry*] .... BNF
Beta-Naphthoflavone (SAUS) .... BNT
Beta-Naphthol [*Organic chemistry*] .... BN
Beta-Naphthoxyacetic Acid [*Plant growth compound*] .... BNOA
Beta-Naphthylamine [*Organic chemistry*] .... BNA
Beta-Nitropropionic Acid [*Organic chemistry*] .... BNPA
Beta-Oxalylamino-alanine [*An amino acid*] .... BOAA
Beta-Oxybutyric Acid [*Organic chemistry*] (MAE) .... BOBA
Beta-Oxynaphthoic Acid [*Also, BONA*] [*Organic chemistry*] .... BON
Beta-Oxynaphthoic Acid [*Also, BON*] [*Organic chemistry*] .... BONA
Beta-Propriolactone [*Organic chemistry*] .... BPL
Betar Brith Trumpeldor (EA) .... BBT
Betare-Oya [*Cameroon*] [*ICAO location identifier*] (ICLI) .... FKAO
Beta-Resorcylic Acid [*Organic chemistry*] .... BRA
Beta-S-Fetoprotein (SAUS) .... BSF
Beta-Site Amyloid Precursor Protein-Cleaving Enzyme .... BACE
Beta-Streptococcus Group A [*Bacteriology*] (DAVI) .... BSGA
Beta-Thromboglobulin [*Hematology*] .... BTG
Betera [*Spain*] [*ICAO location identifier*] (ICLI) .... LEBT
Beth Din of America (EA) .... BDA
Beth Israel (BJA) .... BI
Beth Israel Ambulatory Center (DAVI) .... BIAC
Beth Israel Hospital (SAUO) .... BIH
Beth Israel Hospital, Medical Library, Denver, CO [*Library symbol*] [*Library of Congress*] (LCLS) .... CoDBI-M
Beth Israel Medical Center, New York, NY [*Library symbol*] [*Library of Congress*] (LCLS) .... NNBI
Beth Israel Medical Center, New York, NY [*OCLC symbol*] (OCLC) VVI
Beth Simchat Torah (BJA) .... BST
Bethalto Community Unit 8, Bethalto, IL [*Library symbol*] [*Library of Congress*] (LCLS) .... IBethCU
Bethalto, IL [*FM radio station call letters*] .... WFUN
Bethalto Public Library, Bethalto, IL [*Library symbol*] [*Library of Congress*] (LCLS) .... IBeth
Bethania Mennonite Personal Care Home, Winnipeg, Manitoba [*Library symbol*] [*National Library of Canada*] (NLC) .... MWBM
Bethania Mennonite Personal Care Home, Winnipeg, MB, Canada [*Library symbol*] [*Library of Congress*] (LCLS) .... CaMWBM
Bethany and Northern Baptist Theological Seminaries Library, Oak Brook, IL [*OCLC symbol*] (OCLC) .... IDI
Bethany and Northern Baptist Theological Seminaries Library, Oak Brook, IL [*Library symbol*] [*Library of Congress*] (LCLS) .... IObT
Bethany Beach, DE [*FM radio station call letters*] (BROA) .... WJYN-FM
Bethany Beach, DE [*FM radio station call letters*] .... WOSC
Bethany Beach, DE [*FM radio station call letters*] (RBYB) .... WZSK
Bethany College (SAUO) .... BC
Bethany College, Bethany, WV [*OCLC symbol*] (OCLC) .... WVB
Bethany College, Bethany, WV [*Library symbol*] [*Library of Congress*] (LCLS) .... WvBeC
Bethany College, Lindsborg, KS [*OCLC symbol*] (OCLC) .... KFB
Bethany College, Lindsborg, KS [*Library symbol*] [*Library of Congress*] (LCLS) .... KLindB
Bethany Fellowship Missions (EA) .... BFM
Bethany Lutheran College, Mankato, MN [*OCLC symbol*] (OCLC) .... MBE
Bethany Lutheran College, Mankato, MN [*Library symbol*] [*Library of Congress*] (LCLS) .... MnManBC
Bethany Lutheran Theological Seminary, Mankato, MN [*OCLC symbol*] (OCLC) .... MBS
Bethany Lutheran Theological Seminary, Mankato, MN [*Library symbol*] [*Library of Congress*] (LCLS) .... MnManBS
Bethany Medical Center, Kansas City, KS [*Library symbol*] [*Library of Congress*] (LCLS) .... KKcBM
Bethany, MO [*AM radio station call letters*] .... KAAN
Bethany, MO [*FM radio station call letters*] .... KAAN-FM
Bethany, MO [*AM radio station call letters*] (BROA) .... KIRK-AM
Bethany Nazarene College [*Oklahoma*] .... BNC
Bethany Nazarene College, Bethany, OK [*OCLC symbol*] (OCLC) .... OKA
Bethany Nazarene College, Bethany, OK [*Library symbol*] [*Library of Congress*] (LCLS) .... OkBetC
Bethany, OK [*FM radio station call letters*] .... KNTL
Bethany, WV [*FM radio station call letters*] .... WVBC
Bethel [*Alaska*] [*Seismograph station code, US Geological Survey*] [*Closed*] (SEIS) .... BET
Bethel [*Alaska*] [*ICAO location identifier*] (ICLI) .... PABE
Bethel, AK [*Location identifier*] [*FAA*] (FAAL) .... JBT
Bethel, AK [*FM radio station call letters*] .... KYKD
Bethel, AK [*AM radio station call letters*] .... KYUK
Bethel, AK [*Television station call letters*] .... KYUK-TV
Bethel, AK [*Location identifier*] [*FAA*] (FAAL) .... OSE
Bethel Bancorp [*Associated Press*] (SAG) .... BethlBc
Bethel Bancorp [*NASDAQ symbol*] (NQ) .... BTHL
Bethel College (SAUO) .... BC
Bethel College, Learning Resources Center, St. Paul, MN [*OCLC symbol*] (OCLC) .... MNK
Bethel College, McKenzie, TN [*Library symbol*] [*Library of Congress*] (LCLS) .... TMckB
Bethel College, Mishawaka, IN [*Library symbol*] [*Library of Congress*] (LCLS) .... InMisB
Bethel College, North Newton, KS [*Library symbol*] [*Library of Congress*] (LCLS) .... KNnB
Bethel College, St. Paul, MN [*Library symbol*] [*Library of Congress*] (LCLS) .... MnSB
Bethel Hospital, Winkler, Manitoba [*Library symbol*] [*National Library of Canada*] (NLC) .... MWBH
Bethel Hospital, Winkler, MB, Canada [*Library symbol*] [*Library of Congress*] (LCLS) .... CaMWinBH
Bethe-Salpeter Equation [*Physics*] (OA) .... BS
Bethe-Salpeter Equation [*Physics*] .... BSE
Bethesda Base Hospital, Information Resource Center, Cincinnati, OH [*Library symbol*] [*Library of Congress*] (LCLS) .... OCBH
Bethesda Hospital, Medical Library, Denver, CO [*Library symbol*] [*Library of Congress*] (LCLS) .... CoDBH-M
Bethesda Lutheran Hospital, St. Paul, MN [*Library symbol*] [*Library of Congress*] (LCLS) .... MnSBH
Bethesda, MD [*FM radio station call letters*] .... WARW
Bethesda, MD [*FM radio station call letters*] .... WMMJ
Bethesda, MD [*AM radio station call letters*] .... WTEM
Bethesda Military Librarians Group [*Library network*] .... NMCLA
Bethesda National Christian Resource Center (EA) .... BNCRC
Bethesda Research Laboratories [*Life Technologies, Inc.*] [*Gaithersburg, MD*] .... BRL
Bethesda System (MELL) .... BS
Bethlehem [*South Africa*] [*ICAO location identifier*] (ICLI) .... FABM
Bethlehem Corp. [*AMEX symbol*] (SPSG) .... BET
Bethlehem Corp. [*Associated Press*] (SAG) .... BethCp
Bethlehem Natural Science Association (SAUO) .... BNSA
Bethlehem, PA [*Television station call letters*] .... WBPH
Bethlehem, PA [*AM radio station call letters*] .... WGPA
Bethlehem, PA [*FM radio station call letters*] .... WLVR
Bethlehem, PA [*FM radio station call letters*] .... WZZO
Bethlehem Public Library, Bethlehem, PA [*Library symbol*] [*Library of Congress*] (LCLS) .... PB
Bethlehem Public Library, Bethlehem, PA [*OCLC symbol*] (OCLC) .... PBL
Bethlehem Resources Corp. [*Toronto Stock Exchange symbol*] [*Vancouver Stock Exchange symbol*] .... BTH
Bethlehem Steel (SAUS) .... Beth Steel
Bethlehem Steel $5 cm Cv Pfd [*NYSE symbol*] (TTSB) .... BSPr
Bethlehem Steel Co. (SAUO) .... BSCO
Bethlehem Steel Corp. (SAUO) .... Bethlehem
Bethlehem Steel Corp. (SAUO) .... Beth Steel
Bethlehem Steel Corp. [*Associated Press*] (SAG) .... BethStl
Bethlehem Steel Corp. [*Wall Street slang name: "Bessie"*] [*NYSE symbol*] (SPSG) .... BS
Bethlehem Steel Corp. [*Wall Street slang name: "Bessie"*] [*Associated Press*] (SAG) .... BthS
Bethlehem Steel Corp. [*Wall Street slang name: "Bessie"*] [*Associated Press*] (SAG) .... BthSt
Bethlehem Steel Corp., Charles H. Herty, Jr., Memorial Library, Bethlehem, PA [*Library symbol*] [*Library of Congress*] (LCLS) .... PBS
Bethlehem Steel Corp., Charles M. Schwab Memorial Library, Bethlehem, PA [*Library symbol*] [*Library of Congress*] (LCLS) .... PBSteel
Bethlehem Steel Corporation (SAUS) .... Bethlehem
Bethlehem Steel Corporation (SAUO) .... BSC
Bethlehem Steel Corporation (SAUO) .... BStC
Bethlehem Steel$2.50cmCv Pfd [*NYSE symbol*] (TTSB) .... BSPrB
Bethlehem Transportation Company (SAUO) .... BTC
Bethlehem Transportation Corp. [*Steamship*] (MHDW) .... BTC
Bethlehem, WV [*FM radio station call letters*] .... WHLX
Bethlehem, WV [*FM radio station call letters*] (RBYB) .... WRIR-FM
Bethlehem, WV [*FM radio station call letters*] (BROA) .... WZNW-FM
Bethlemita, Daughters of the Sacred Heart of Jesus (TOCD) .... Bethl
Bethnal Green Museum (SAUO) .... BGM
Bethnal Green Museum (SAUS) .... BGM
Bethpage, NY [*Location identifier*] [*FAA*] (FAAL) .... BPA
Bethpage Public Library, Bethpage, NY [*Library symbol*] [*Library of Congress*] (LCLS) .... NBet
Bethpage Senior High School, Bethpage, NY [*Library symbol*] [*Library of Congress*] (LCLS) .... NBethSH
Bethpage Senior High School, Bethpage, NY [*Library symbol*] [*Library of Congress*] (LCLS) .... NBetSH
Bethune-Cookman College [*Daytona Beach, FL*] .... BCC
Bethune-Cookman College, Daytona Beach, FL [*OCLC symbol*] (OCLC) .... DBB
Bethune-Cookman College, Daytona Beach, FL [*Library symbol*] [*Library of Congress*] (LCLS) .... FDbBC
Betioky [*Madagascar*] [*Airport symbol*] (OAG) .... BKU
Betioky [*Madagascar*] [*ICAO location identifier*] (ICLI) .... FMSV
Bet-Nahrain Democratic Party [*Political party*] (BJA) .... BNDP
Betoken (ABBR) .... BTKN
Betonite Flocculation Test (SAUS) .... BFT
Betonvereniging van Suidelike Africa [*Concrete Society of South Africa*] (EAIO) .... BSA
Betoota [*Queensland*] [*Airport symbol*] (AD) .... BTX
Betou [*Congo*] [*ICAO location identifier*] (ICLI) .... FCOT
Betreffend [*Referring To*] [*German*] .... BETR
Betriebsberufsschule [*Factory Training School*] [*Germany*] .... BBS
Betriebsforschungsinstitut [*Institute for Industrial Research*] [*German Iron and Steel Engineers Association*] [*Dusseldorf*] [*Information service or system*] (IID) .... BFI
Betriebsgewerkschaftsleitung [*Factory Union Headquarters*] [*Germany*] .... BGL
Betriebsrategesetz [*Law on Works Councils*] [*German*] (ILCA) .... BetrRG
Betriebsverfassungsgesetz [*Law on the Representation of Workers and Works Councils*] [*German*] (ILCA) .... BetrVG
Betriebswirtschaftliches Literatursuchsystem [*Business Literature Search System*] [*Society for Business Information*] [*Information service or system*] (IID) .... BLISS

Betroka [*Madagascar*] [*ICAO location identifier*] (ICLI) .... FMSE
Betrust Investments [*Vancouver Stock Exchange symbol*] .... BTR
Bets Settlement Investment Engine (SAUS) .... BETSIE
Betschuana Protectorate (SAUO) .... BP
Betsie Valley District Library, Thompsonville, MI [*Library symbol*] [*Library of Congress*] (LCLS) .... MiTho
Betsy Ross High School (SAUO) .... BRHS
Betsy-Tacy Society (EA) .... BTS
Bettendorf, IA [*FM radio station call letters*] (RBYB) .... KORB
Bettendorf News, Bettendorf, IA [*Library symbol*] [*Library of Congress*] (LCLS) .... IaBetN
Better .... BETR
better (SAUS) .... betr
Better .... btr
Better (BARN) .... BTR
Better [*Wood industry*] (WPI) .... Btr
Better Access to Manuscripts and Browsing of Images (TELE) .... BAMBI
Better Assessment Science Integrating Point and Nonpoint Systems (GEOI) .... BASINS
Better Boys Foundation (EA) .... BBF
Better Business Bureau .... BBB
[*A*] Better Chance (EA) .... ABC
Better Cities Program (SAUS) .... BCP
Better Education thru Simplified Spelling (EA) .... BEtSS
Better Education thru Spelling Improvement (SAUO) .... BEtSI
Better Electronic Service Technicians .... BEST
Better Fabrics Test Bureau .... BFTB
Better Farming (journ.) (SAUS) .... Better F
Better Government Association (EA) .... BGA
Better Hearing and Speech Month .... BH & SM
Better Hearing Australia [*An association*] (EAIO) .... BHA
Better Hearing Institute (EA) .... BHI
Better Heating-Cooling Council [*Later, HI*] (EA) .... BHC
Better Heating-Cooling Council (SAUO) .... BHCC
Better Highways Information Foundation [*Later, ARTBA*] .... BHIF
Better Home Heat Council of New Hampshire (SRA) .... BHHCNH
Better Homes and Gardens (SAUO) .... B H&G
Better Homes and Gardens [*Information service or system*] [*A publication*] (IID) .... BH & G
Better Homes and Gardens (journ.) (SAUS) .... BH&G
Better Humanity League [*Commercial firm*] .... BHL
Better Image Software with Help On-Line for Programs (SAUS) .... BISHOP
Better Independent Grocers (SAUO) .... BIG
Better Kitchens Institute (EA) .... BKI
Better Known As (SAUS) .... BKA
Better Lawn and Turf Institute (EA) .... BLTI
Better Light Better Sight Bureau [*Defunct*] (EA) .... BLBSB
Better Occupational Awareness Training (SAUS) .... BOAT
Better on Lips than on Paper [*Put at the end of a letter with kisses*] [*British*] .... BOLTOP
Better Opportunities for Single Soldiers [*Army*] .... BOSS
Better Packaging Advisory Council (EA) .... BPAC
Better Postcard Collectors' Club [*Later, D of A*] (EA) .... BPCC
Better Resources Ltd. [*Vancouver Stock Exchange symbol*] .... BRZ
Better Roads and Transportation Council (EA) .... BR & TC
Better Sleep Council [*National Association of Bedding Manufacturers*] (EA) .... BSC
Better Sound Reproduction (IAA) .... BSR
Better Speech Institute of America (SAUO) .... BSIA
Better than Average .... BTA
Better than Expected [*Politics*] .... BTE
Better Than Nothing (SAUS) .... BTN
Better Than Open Look (SAUS) .... BTOL
Better Vision Institute (EA) .... BVI
Better World Society [*Defunct*] (EA) .... BWS
Better World Society International (SAUO) .... BWS
Better World Zine (SAUS) .... BWZ
Bettering Oregon's Opportunity for Saving Talent [*Educational project*] (EA) .... BOOST
Betting Office Licensees Association [*British*] (DBA) .... BOLA
Bettis Atomic Power Laboratory (SAUO) .... BL
Bettis Corp. [*NASDAQ symbol*] (SAG) .... BETT
Bettis Corp. [*Associated Press*] (SAG) .... Bettis
Bettits Atomic Power Laboratory (SAUO) .... BAPL
Bettles [*Alaska*] [*Airport symbol*] (OAG) .... BTT
Bettles [*Alaska*] [*ICAO location identifier*] (ICLI) .... PABT
Bettles, AK [*Location identifier*] [*FAA*] (FAAL) .... EAV
[*The*] Bettmann Archive [*A publication*] .... TBA
Betts' Admiralty Practice [*A publication*] (DLA) .... Betts' Adm Pr
Betts Open Shop System (SAUS) .... BOSS
Betty Ford Clinic (SAUS) .... BFC
Betty Lake, AK [*Location identifier*] [*FAA*] (FAAL) .... BDY
Betty White Fan Club (EA) .... BWFC
Between (VRA) .... bet
Between (KSC) .... BET
between (SAUS) .... bet
Between (ROG) .... BETN
Between (ROG) .... BETW
Between (ADWA) .... betw
Between .... Betw
Between .... BTN
Between .... BTW
Between (AABC) .... BTWN
Between and Brunauer-Emmett-Teller (SAUS) .... BET
Between Centers [*Technical drawings*] .... BC
Between Centers (or Centres) (SAUS) .... BC

Between Chain (SAUS) .... BETC
Between Comfort and Discomfort .... BCD
Between Commands Testing [*Computer science*] .... BCT
Between Great Trochanters [*Orthopedics*] (DAVI) .... BiT
Between Ischial Spines [*Pelvic measurement*] [*Gynecology*] .... BISp
Between Ischial Spines .... BISP
Between Ischial Tuberosities [*Gynecology*] (BABM) .... Bi Isch
Between Ischial Tuberosities [*Medicine*] (MEDA) .... Bi Isch
Between Job Monitor [*Computer science*] .... BJM
Between Layers [*ICAO*] (FAAC) .... BTL
Between Perpendiculars [*Technical drawings*] .... BP
Between Two Outfielders [*Baseball*] [*Also, a lifestyle classification*] .... Tweener
Betz Laboratories [*NYSE symbol*] (SPSG) .... BTL
Betz Laboratories, Inc. [*Associated Press*] (SAG) .... BetzLb
Betz Laboratories, Inc. (EFIS) .... BL
Betz Laboratories, Inc., Trevose, PA [*Library symbol*] [*Library of Congress*] (LCLS) .... PTrB
BetzDearborn, Inc. [*Associated Press*] (SAG) .... BetzDearb
BetzDearborn, Inc. [*NYSE symbol*] (SAG) .... BTL
Betzdorf/Kirchen [*Germany*] [*ICAO location identifier*] (ICLI) .... EDKI
Beulah, MI [*FM radio station call letters*] (RBYB) .... WBVE-FM
Beulah, ND [*FM radio station call letters*] (BROA) .... KAVG-FM
Beulah, ND [*AM radio station call letters*] .... KHOL
Beulah Public Library, Beulah, MI [*Library symbol*] [*Library of Congress*] (LCLS) .... MiBeu
Beurmann-Gougerot [*Disease*] [*Medicine*] (DB) .... BG
Beurre, Oeufs, Fromages [*Butter, Eggs, Cheese*] [*French*] .... BOF
Bev Tyme 10% Cv'C' Pfd [*NASDAQ symbol*] (TTSB) .... BEVTP
Beva [*A prefix meaning multiplied by one billion; same as "giga"*] .... B
Bevatron .... BEV
Bevatron/Super-HILAC [*Combination of accelerators*] .... BEVALAC
Bevel .... BEV
Bevel (VRA) .... bev
Bevel Gear .... BG
Bevel Gear (SAUS) .... BG
Beveled [*Technical drawings*] .... BVL
Beveled Edge (SAUS) .... BE
Beveled on Four Edges [*Lumber*] (DAC) B4E
Beveled on Three Edges [*Lumber*] (DAC) B3E
Beveled Plate Glass (DAC) .... BPG
Beveled Wood Siding [*Technical drawings*] .... BWS
Bevelled Deckle Edges [*Cards*] (DGA) .... BDE
Bevelled Edges [*Printing*] (DGA) .... BE
Beven and Siebel's Reports [*Ceylon*] [*A publication*] (DLA) .... B & S
Beven and Siebel's Reports [*Ceylon*] [*A publication*] (DLA) .... Bev & Sieb
Beven on Negligence in Law [*1889-1928*] [*A publication*] (DLA) .... Beven
Beven's Ceylon Reports [*A publication*] (DLA) .... Be (Ceylon)
Beven's Ceylon Reports [*A publication*] (ILCA) .... Bev Ceylon
Beven's Ceylon Reports [*A publication*] (DLA) .... Beven
Beverage .... BEV
Beverage (DMAA) .... bev
Beverage (KSC) .... BV
Beverage (MSA) .... BVGE
Beverage Canners International Corp. .... BCI
Beverage Container Control Coalition [*Later, WCFR*] (EA) B3C
Beverage Container Recycling and Litter Reduction Act (SAUS) .... BCRLRA
Beverage Industry Recycling Program (SAUS) .... BIRP
Beverage Machinery Manufacturers Association (EA) .... BMMA
Beverage Management, Inc. (EFIS) .... BMI
Beverage Manufacturers' Agents Association (EA) .... BMAA
Beverage Network [*An association*] (EA) .... BN
Beveren Rabbit Club [*Defunct*] (EA) .... BRC
Beverley [*Jamaica*] [*Seismograph station code, US Geological Survey*] [*Closed*] (SEIS) .... BEV
Beverley Yacht Club (SAUO) .... BYC
Beverly Bancorporation, Inc. [*NASDAQ symbol*] (SAG) .... BEVB
Beverly Bancorporation, Inc. [*Associated Press*] (SAG) .... BevBanc
Beverly Development, Inc. [*Toronto Stock Exchange symbol*] .... BVD
Beverly Enterprises [*NYSE symbol*] (SPSG) .... BEV
Beverly Enterprises [*Associated Press*] (SAG) .... Bevrly
Beverly Farms Public Library, Beverly, MA [*Library symbol*] [*Library of Congress*] (LCLS) .... MBev-F
Beverly Foundation (EA) .... BF
Beverly Hills (IIA) .... BH
Beverly Hills 90210 [*Television program title*] 90210
Beverly Hills Bar Association. Journal [*A publication*] (DLA) .... Bev Hills BAJ
Beverly Hills, CA [*AM radio station call letters*] (BROA) .... KGIL-AM
Beverly Hills, CA [*AM radio station call letters*] (RBYB) .... KNNS
Beverly Hills, FL [*FM radio station call letters*] .... WXOF
Beverly Hills Intermediate School, Houston, TX [*Library symbol*] [*Library of Congress*] (LCLS) .... TxHBhI
Beverly Hills Public Library, Beverly Hills, CA [*OCLC symbol*] (OCLC) .... BHP
Beverly Hills Public Library, Beverly Hills, CA [*Library symbol*] [*Library of Congress*] (LCLS) .... CBev
Beverly Hills Racquets Club [*Book title*] .... BHRC
Beverly Historical Society, Beverly, MA [*Library symbol*] [*Library of Congress*] (LCLS) .... MBevHi
Beverly, MA [*Location identifier*] [*FAA*] (FAAL) .... BVY
Beverly, MA [*Location identifier*] [*FAA*] (FAAL) .... TOF
Beverly, MA [*AM radio station call letters*] .... WNSH
Beverly Public Library, Beverly, MA [*Library symbol*] [*Library of Congress*] (LCLS) .... MBev
Beverly Springs [*Australia*] [*Airport symbol*] [*Obsolete*] (OAG) .... BVZ
Beverly Times, Beverly, MA [*Library symbol*] [*Library of Congress*] (LCLS) .... MBevT

Bevier and Southern [Railroad] (MHDB) .... B & S
Bevier & Southern Railroad Co. [AAR code] .... BVS
Bevil on Homicide [A publication] (DLA) .... Bev Hom
Bevill's Patent Cases [England] [A publication] (DLA) .... Bev Pat
Bevin and Mill's Reports [Ceylon] [A publication] (DLA) .... Bev & M
Bevin on Employer's Liability for Negligence of Servants [A publication]
    (DLA) .... Bev Emp L
Bevitron Orbit Code .... BOC
Bev-Tyme, Inc. [Associated Press] (SAG) .... BevT
Bev-Tyme, Inc. [NASDAQ symbol] (SAG) .... BEVT
Bev-Tyme Inc. [NASDAQ symbol] (TTSB) .... BEVTC
Bev-Tyme, Inc. [Associated Press] (SAG) .... BevTym
Bev-Tyme Inc.Wrrt'C' [NASDAQ symbol] (TTSB) .... BEVTZ
Bewani [Papua New Guinea] [Airport symbol] (OAG) .... BWP
Bewley and Naish on Common Law Procedure [A publication]
    (DLA) .... Bew & N Pr
Bewusstein [Consciousness] [Psychology] .... BW
Bex [Switzerland] [ICAO location identifier] (ICLI) .... LSTX
Bexar County Medical Library Association, San Antonio, TX [Library
    symbol] [Library of Congress] (LCLS) .... TxSaBM
Bexhill Museum [British] .... BEX
Bexley Public Library, Columbus, OH [Library symbol] [Library of Congress]
    (LCLS) .... OCoBex
Bexley-Maudsley Automated Psychological Screening [Test] .... BMAPS
Beyelorussian Liberation Front (SAUO) .... BLF
Beyer Elementary School, Rockford, IL [Library symbol] [Library of
    Congress] (LCLS) .... IRoBeE
Beyla [Guinea] [ICAO location identifier] (ICLI) .... GUBL
Beynes/Thiverval [France] [ICAO location identifier] (ICLI) .... LFPF
Beynhurst [England] .... BEYN
Beyond (FAAC) .... BYD
Beyond Baroque Foundation (EA) .... BBF
Beyond Capability of Maintenance (SAUS) .... BCM
Beyond Capacity of Intermediate Maintenance [Army] (MCD) .... BCIM
Beyond Capacity of Maintenance (MCD) .... BCM
Beyond Economic Repair (SAUS) .... BER
Beyond Economical Repair (MCD) .... BER
Beyond Line of Sight (MCD) .... BLOS
Beyond Local Repair [Weaponry] [British] .... BLR
Beyond the Horizon (MCD) .... BTH
Beyond Very High Speed Integration (CIST) .... BHSI
Beyond Visual Range (MCD) .... BVR
Beyond Visual Range Air-to-Air Missile (MCD) .... BVRAAM
Beyond Visual Range Missile (MCD) .... BVRM
Beyond War Foundation (EA) .... BWF
Beyond.com Corp. [NASDAQ symbol] (SG) .... BYND
Beyond-the-Horizon Communication (SAUS) .... Troposcatter
Bezafibrate Coronary Atherosclerosis Intervention Trial .... BECAIT
Bezah (BJA) .... Bez
Bezanson School, Alberta [Library symbol] [National Library of Canada]
    (BIB) .... ABEZS
Bezene, Toluene, Ethylbenzene, and Xylene [Organic mixture] .... BTEX
Beziehungsweise [Respectively] [German] .... BEZW
Beziehungsweise [Respectively] [German] .... BZW
Beziers [France] [Airport symbol] (OAG) .... BZR
Beziers/Vias [France] [ICAO location identifier] (ICLI) .... LFMU
Bezirksgericht [District Court] [German] (DLA) .... Bez G
Bezirksgericht [District Court] [German] (DLA) .... Bez Ger
Bezold-Type Reflex [Medicine] (MAE) .... BTR
Bezpartyjny Blok Wspolpracy z Rzadem [Non-Party Bloc of Cooperation with
    the Government] [Poland] [Political party] (PPE) .... BBWR
Bezueglich [Concerning] [German] .... BEZ
Bezueglich [In Regard To, With Reference To] [German] .... BZGL
Bezugsdicke der i-ten Farbglasschicht (SAUS) .... DOi
BF Enterprises [NASDAQ symbol] (TTSB) .... BFEN
BF Enterprises, Inc. [NASDAQ symbol] (NQ) .... BFEN
BF Enterprises, Inc. [Associated Press] (SAG) .... BF Ent
B.F. Goodrich Co. (SAUO) .... BFG
B.F. Goodrich Co. (SAUO) .... GR
BF Goodrich Co. Economic and Business Facts and Forecasts (journ.)
    (SAUS) .... Goodrich
BF Realty Holdings Ltd. [Toronto Stock Exchange symbol] (SPSG) .... BFR
BFC Construction [AMEX symbol] [Formerly, Banister Foundation] (SG) .... BNC
BFS Bancorp, Inc. [Associated Press] (SAG) .... BFS NY
BFS Bankorp, Inc. [NASDAQ symbol] (TTSB) .... BFSI
BFS Bankorp, Inc. [NASDAQ symbol] (NQ) .... BFSI
BFS [Berliner Spezial Flug], Luftahrtunternehmen GmbH [Germany] [ICAO
    designator] (FAAC) .... SBY
BFX Hospitality Group [AMEX symbol] (SG) .... BFX
BG Attendant Call Transfer (SAUS) .... XFR
BG plc ADS [NYSE symbol] (SG) .... BRG
B-Glycerophosphase (SAUS) .... BGP
BGM Diversified Energy, Inc. [Vancouver Stock Exchange symbol] .... BGD
BGR Precious Metals, Inc. [Toronto Stock Exchange symbol] .... BPT
BGS Systems [NASDAQ symbol] (TTSB) .... BGSS
BGS Systems, Inc. [Associated Press] (SAG) .... BGS
BGS Systems, Inc. [NASDAQ symbol] (NQ) .... BGSS
BHA Group [NASDAQ symbol] (SG) .... BHAG
BHA Group, Inc. [Associated Press] (SAG) .... BHA
BHA Group, Inc. [NASDAQ symbol] (NQ) .... BHAG
BHA Group'A' [NASDAQ symbol] (TTSB) .... BHAG
Bhaba Atomic Research Centre (SAUS) .... BARC
Bhaba Atomic Research Committee (SAUS) .... BARC
Bhabba Atomic Research Centre [India] .... BARC
Bhadrapur [Nepal] [Airport symbol] (OAG) .... BDP

Bhagtanwala [Pakistan] [ICAO location identifier] (ICLI) .... OPBG
Bhairawa [Nepal] [Airport symbol] (OAG) .... BWA
Bhairawa [Nepal] [ICAO location identifier] (ICLI) .... VNBW
Bhakra [India] [Seismograph station code, US Geological Survey] (SEIS) .... BHK
Bhaktapur District Hospital (SAUS) .... BHAKHOS
Bhamo [Myanmar] [Airport symbol] (OAG) .... BMO
Bhamo [Myanmar] [ICAO location identifier] (ICLI) .... VBBM
Bharat Aluminium Corporation (SAUO) .... BALCO
Bharat Dynamics Ltd. (SAUO) .... BDL
Bharat Heavy Electricals Ltd. [India] .... BHEL
Bharat Heavy Plates & Vessels (SAUO) .... BHPV
Bharatiya Agro-Industries Foundation (SAUO) .... BAIF
Bharatiya Janata Party [Indian People's Party] [Political party] .... BJ
Bharatiya Janata Party [Indian People's Party] [Political party] (PPW) .... BJP
Bharatiya Lok Dal [India] [Political party] (PPW) .... BLD
Bharatpur [Nepal] [Airport symbol] [Obsolete] (OAG) .... BHR
Bharatpur [Nepal] [ICAO location identifier] (ICLI) .... VNBP
Bhatinda [India] [ICAO location identifier] (ICLI) .... VIBT
Bhatnagar-Gross-Krook [Equation] .... BGK
Bhatnagar-Gross-Krook equation (SAUS) .... BGK-equation
Bhaunagar [India] [ICAO location identifier] (ICLI) .... VABV
Bhavnagar [India] [Airport symbol] (OAG) .... BHU
BHC Communications [Associated Press] (SAG) .... BHC
BHC Communications, Inc. [AMEX symbol] (SPSG) .... BHC
BHC Communications'A' [AMEX symbol] (TTSB) .... BHC
BHC Financial [NASDAQ symbol] (TTSB) .... BHCF
BHC Financial, Inc. [NASDAQ symbol] (SAG) .... BHCF
BHC Financial, Inc. [Associated Press] (SAG) .... BHC Fncl
BHI Corp. [Associated Press] (SAG) .... BHI Cp
BHI Corp. [NASDAQ symbol] (SAG) .... BHIK
BHI Corp. [NASDAQ symbol] (TTSB) .... BHIKF
Bhiwani [India] [ICAO location identifier] (ICLI) .... VIBW
Bhoja Airlines [Pakistan] [ICAO designator] (FAAC) .... BHO
Bhojpur [Nepal] [Airport symbol] (OAG) .... BHP
Bhojpur [Nepal] [ICAO location identifier] (ICLI) .... VNBJ
Bhojpuri [MARC language code] [Library of Congress] (LCCP) .... bho
Bhopal [India] [Airport symbol] (OAG) .... BHO
Bhopal [India] [ICAO location identifier] (ICLI) .... VABP
B-horizon (SAUS) .... B&hor
BHP [Broken Hill Proprietary Ltd.] Journal [A publication] .... BHP JI
Bhubaneswar [India] [Airport symbol] (OAG) .... BBI
Bhubaneswar [India] [ICAO location identifier] (ICLI) .... VEBS
Bhuj [India] [Airport symbol] (OAG) .... BHJ
Bhuj [India] [ICAO location identifier] (ICLI) .... VABJ
Bhumibol Dam [Thailand] [Seismograph station code, US Geological Survey]
    (SEIS) .... BDT
Bhutan [Aircraft nationality and registration mark] (FAAC) A5
Bhutan [MARC geographic area code] [Library of Congress] .... a-bt-
Bhutan .... Bhu
Bhutan (SAUS) .... Bhu
Bhutan .... BHUT
Bhutan [ANSI two-letter standard code] (CNC) .... BT
Bhutan [MARC country of publication code] [Library of Congress] (LCCP) .... bt
Bhutan [ANSI three-letter standard code] (CNC) .... BTN
Bhutan Broadcasting Service (EY) .... BBS
Bhutan People's Party [Political party] .... BPP
Bhutan Philatelic Society (EA) .... BPS
Bhutan Tourism Corp. (EY) .... BTC
BI, Inc. [NASDAQ symbol] (NQ) .... BIAC
BI, Inc. [Associated Press] (SAG) .... BI Inc
Bi Post (SAUS) .... BPT
Biacore International AB [NASDAQ symbol] (SAG) .... BCOR
Biacore International AB [Associated Press] (SAG) .... Biacore
Biafra [MARC geographic area code] [Library of Congress] (LCCP) .... f-by-
Biafra Relief Services Foundation (EA) .... BRSF
Biafran Air Force (SAUO) .... BAF
Biak [Indonesia] [Airport symbol] (OAG) .... BIK
Biak [Indonesia] [ICAO location identifier] (ICLI) .... WABZ
Biak/Frans Kaisiepo [Indonesia] [ICAO location identifier] (ICLI) .... WABB
Biak/Manuhua [Indonesia] [ICAO location identifier] (ICLI) .... WABU
Bialla [Papua New Guinea] [Airport symbol] (OAG) .... BAA
Biamperometric [Electromagnetics] .... Biamp
Biarritz [France] [Airport symbol] (OAG) .... BIQ
Biarritz-Bayonne/Anglet [France] [ICAO location identifier] (ICLI) .... LFBZ
Biaru [Papua New Guinea] [Airport symbol] (OAG) .... BRP
Bias [Telecommunications] .... B
Bias Contrast (AAEL) .... BC
Bias Discrete Spot (SAUS) .... BDS
Bias, Equalization, Sensitivity of the Tape (SAUS) .... BEST
Bias Oscillator Frequency .... BOF
Bias Power and Temperature Step Stress (PDAA) .... BPATSS
Bias Telegraph Distortion .... BTD
Bias Temperature .... BT
Biased Antiworld Paw Entry [Testing of left and right laterality in mice] .... BAWPE
Biased Optimal Steering Selector (PDAA) .... BOSS
Biased Predictive Proportional Guidance .... BPPG
Biased Proportional Guidance .... BPG
Biased Random Walk [Mathematics] .... BRW
Biased World Paw Entry [Testing of left and right laterality in mice] .... BWPE
Biax Element Memory (SAUS) .... BEM
Biax Element Store (SAUS) .... BES
Biax Memory Core (SAUS) .... BMC
Biax Memory Element (SAUS) .... BME
Biaxial (IAA) .... BIAX
Biaxial Shock Test Machine [CERL] [Army] (RDA) .... BSTM

Biaxially-Oriented Nylon film (SAUS) ... BON
Biaxially-Oriented Polypropylene [*Plastics technology*] ... BOPP
Biaxially-Oriented Polypropylene film (SAUS) ... BOPP
BIB Received (SAUS) ... BIBR
BIB to be Transmitted (SAUS) ... BIBT
Bibanga [*Zaire*] [*ICAO location identifier*] (ICLI) ... FZWB
Bibas in Christo [*May You Live in Christ*] [*Latin*] ... BIC
Bibbia e Oriente [*A publication*] (BJA) ... BO
Bibbia e Oriente [*A publication*] (BJA) ... BOr
Bibbia e Oriente Fossano, Cuneo (BJA) ... BibO
Bibbia e Oriente Fossano, Cuneo (BJA) ... BieOr
Bibb's Kentucky Reports [*4-7 Kentucky*] [*1808-17*] [*A publication*] (DLA) ... Bibb
Bibb's Kentucky Reports [*4-7 Kentucky*] [*1808-17*] [*A publication*] (DLA) ... Bibb (KY)
Bibe [*Drink*] [*Pharmacy*] ... BIB
Bibel und Liturgie [*A publication*] (BJA) ... BL
Bibelforskaren (BJA) ... BF
Bibel-Lexikon [*A publication*] (BJA) ... BL
Biberach Aerodrome Riss [*Germany*] [*ICAO location identifier*] (ICLI) ... EDMB
Bibi Besch Fan Club (EA) ... BBFC
Bible ... B
Bible (WDMC) ... b
Bible ... BB
Bible (NTIO) ... Bib
Bible ... BIB
[*The*] **Bible - An American Translation (1935)** [*A publication*] (BJA) ... AT
Bible and Medical Missionary Fellowship [*Later, BMMFI/USA*] (EA) ... BMMF
Bible Atlas [*Hurblut*] [*A publication*] (BJA) ... HBA
Bible Christian Union (EA) ... BCU
Bible Churchmen's Missionary Society [*Church of England*] ... BCMS
Bible Club Movement (EA) ... BCM
Bible de Jerusalem [*A publication*] (BJA) ... BJer
Bible Dictionary [*A publication*] (BJA) ... BD
Bible du Centenaire [*A publication*] (BJA) ... BCent
Bible et Terre Sainte [*A publication*] (BJA) ... BTS
Bible Grove, IL [*Location identifier*] [*FAA*] (FAAL) ... BIB
Bible Holiness Movement (EA) ... BHM
[*The*] **Bible in Current Catholic Thought** [*A publication*] ... BCCT
Bible Institute of Los Angeles ... BILA
Bible Key Words [*London, 1949-1965*] [*A publication*] (BJA) ... BKW
Bible Lands' Missions Aid Society [*British*] (BI) ... BLMAS
Bible League (EA) ... BL
Bible Literature International (EA) ... BLI
Bible Meditation League [*Later, BLI*] (EA) ... BML
Bible Memory Association, International (EA) ... BMA
Bible Protestant Missions (EA) ... BPM
Bible Reading Fellowship [*British*] ... BRF
Bible Research Library (SAUO) ... BRL
Bible Research Systems [*Information service or system*] (IID) ... BRS
Bible Sabbath Association (EA) ... BSA
Bible Seminary in New York ... BSNY
Bible Speaks Today (WDAA) ... BST
Bible Study League of America [*Defunct*] (EA) ... BSLA
Bible Translation Society (SAUO) ... BTS
Bible Version [*As opposed to the Prayer Book version of the Psalms*] ... BV
Bibles for the World (EA) ... BFW
Bibles for the World (EA) ... BW
Bible-Science Association (EA) ... BSA
Bibletone [*Record label*] ... Bib
Biblia Hebraica (BJA) ... BH
Biblia Hebraica (R. Kittel) [*A publication*] (BJA) ... BHK
Biblia Hebraica Stuttgartensia [*A publication*] (BJA) ... BHS
Biblia Rabbinica [*A publication*] (BJA) ... BR
Biblia Revuo [*A publication*] (BJA) ... BRe
Biblial Research Institute, Inc., Buffalo, NY [*Library symbol*] [*Library of Congress*] (LCLS) ... NBuBR
Biblica [*A publication*] (BJA) ... Bb
Biblica et Orientalia. Sacra Scriptura Antiquitatibus Orientalibus Illustrata [*Rome*] [*A publication*] (BJA) ... BietOr
Biblical (ROG) ... B
Biblical (ROG) ... BIB
Biblical (WDAA) ... Bib
Biblical (ADWA) ... bib
Biblical (ADWA) ... bibl
Biblical (WDAA) ... Bibl
Biblical ... BIBL
Biblical Aramaic (BJA) ... BA
Biblical Archaeologist Reader [*A publication*] (BJA) ... BAR
Biblical Colloquium [*Defunct*] (EA) ... BC
Biblical Creation Society [*British*] ... BCS
Biblical Essays [*A publication*] (BJA) ... BE
Biblical Evangelism (EA) ... BE
Biblical Fine Arts Association (EA) ... BFAA
Biblical Hebrew (BJA) ... BH
Biblical History and Literature (BJA) ... BHL
Biblical Institute for Social Change (EA) ... BISC
Biblical Numismatic Society [*Defunct*] (EA) ... BNS
Biblical Research [*A publication*] (BJA) ... BRe
Biblical Research in Palestine (SAUO) ... BRP
Biblical Review (journ.) (SAUS) ... BibR
Biblical School of Theology, Hatfield, PA [*Library symbol*] [*Library of Congress*] (LCLS) ... PHatfB
Biblical Seminary in New York, New York, NY [*Library symbol*] [*Library of Congress*] (LCLS) ... NNBS
Biblical Theologians (EA) ... BT
Biblical Theology Bulletin [*A publication*] (BRI) ... BTB
Biblical Topics Study Unit [*American Topical Association*] (EA) ... BTSU
Biblical Witness Fellowship (EA) ... BWF
Biblical World (journ.) (SAUS) ... BibWorld
Biblio Service Data Bank (SAUS) ... BSBD
Biblioclasm (SAUS) ... Biblioc
Biblioclast (SAUS) ... Biblioc
Bibliogenesis (SAUS) ... Biblin
Bibliognost (SAUS) ... Biblin
Bibliogony (SAUS) ... Biblin
Bibliografia di Informatica e Diritto [*Bibliography of Legal/Rights Information*] [*CSC-Corte Suprema di Cassazione*] [*Italy*] (NITA) ... BID
Bibliografia Espanola [*Ministerio de Cultura*] [*Spain*] [*Information service or system*] (CRD) ... BIBL
Bibliografia Espanola de Ciencias de la Informacion [*Database*] [*Universidad Complutense de Madrid*] [*Spanish*] [*Information service or system*] (CRD) ... BECI
Bibliografia Extranjera Depositada en la Biblioteca Nacional [*Ministerio de Cultura*] [*Spain*] [*Information service or system*] (CRD) ... BNBE
Bibliografia General Espanola e Hispanoamericana [*A bibliographic publication*] [*Spain*] ... BEH
Bibliografia (Nazionale Italiano) (NITA) ... BIBLIO
Bibliograph (SAUS) ... Biblio
Bibliographee (SAUS) ... Bibliog
Bibliographer (AL) ... Bibl
Bibliographer (ADWA) ... bibliog
Bibliographia Huntiana [*Computer-based bibliography*] ... BH
Bibliographic (AL) ... Bibl
Bibliographic Access and Control System [*Washington University*] [*Information service or system*] (IID) ... BACS
Bibliographic Access System (EDAC) ... BAS
Bibliographic and Grouping System [*A software program for iconography*] (NITA) ... BAG
Bibliographic and Information Technology Department (SAUS) ... BITD
Bibliographic and Library Information Search Service [*Louisiana State University*] ... BLISS
Bibliographic and Library Instruction for Secondary Schools ... BLISS
Bibliographic Author or Subject Interactive Search (SAUS) ... BA-SIS
Bibliographic Author or Subject Interactive Search-History (SAUS) ... BA-SIS-H
Bibliographic Author or Subject Interactive Search-Political science (SAUS) ... BA-SIS-P
Bibliographic Author or Subject Interactive Search-Sociology (SAUS) ... BA-SIS-S
Bibliographic Automation of Large Library Operations on a Time Sharing System (SAUS) ... BALLOTS System
Bibliographic Automation of Large Library Operations using Time Sharing (SAUS) ... BALLOTS
Bibliographic Center for Research, Denver (SAUS) ... TPS
Bibliographic Center for Research, Denver, CO [*OCLC symbol*] (OCLC) ... TPS
Bibliographic Center for Research, Denver, CO [*OCLC symbol*] (OCLC) ... TPT
Bibliographic Centre, Ontario Ministry of Government Services, Toronto, Ontario [*Library symbol*] [*National Library of Canada*] (NLC) ... OTGSB
Bibliographic Classification [*System of library classification devised by Henry Evelyn Bliss*] ... BC
Bibliographic Computer System (SAUS) ... BIBLICOS
Bibliographic Control System (ADA) ... BCS
Bibliographic Cooperative Program [*American Library Association*] ... BIBCO
Bibliographic Data (SAUS) ... BD
Bibliographic Data (ADA) ... BIBDATA
Bibliographic Data Entry System [*Computer science*] (PDAA) ... BIBDES
Bibliographic Data Exchange System (SAUS) ... BDES
Bibliographic Data Processing Program [*For keyword indexing*] [*Information retrieval software*] ... BIDAP
Bibliographic Database ... BDB
Bibliographic Database Search Service [*University of Wyoming Libraries*] (OLDSS) ... BDS
Bibliographic Index of Library Documents [*Helsinki School of Economics*] [*Database*] ... BILD
Bibliographic Information on Southeast Asia [*University of Sydney Library*] [*Database*] [*Information service or system*] (IID) ... BISA
Bibliographic Information Publication System (SAUS) ... BIPS
Bibliographic Information Retrieval and Dissemination (SAUS) ... BIRD
Bibliographic Information Retrieval Online Service (SAUS) ... BIROS
Bibliographic Information Service for Vocational Training [*ILO*] [*United Nations*] (DUND) ... BISVOT
Bibliographic Information System (SAUS) ... BIS
Bibliographic Instruction [*Library science*] ... BI
Bibliographic Instruction Section [*Association of College and Research Libraries*] ... BIS
Bibliographic Network [*OCLC retrieval system*] [*Computer science*] ... BIBNET
Bibliographic On-Line Display [*Document storage and retrieval system*] [*Computer science*] ... BOLD
Bibliographic Online Library Display [*Scientific Documentation Centre*] [*British*] (NITA) ... BOLD
Bibliographic On-Line Organized Knowledge [*Computer science*] (KSC) ... BOOK
Bibliographic Pattern Discovery Algorithm (PDAA) ... BPDA
Bibliographic Reference (SAUS) ... RF
Bibliographic Reference Service [*Library science*] (TELE) ... BRS
Bibliographic Retrieval Services, Inc. [*Database host system*] [*Scotia, NY*] ... BRS
Bibliographic Retrieval System (SAUS) ... BRS
Bibliographic Search Services [*University of Minnesota*] (OLDSS) ... BSS
Bibliographic Service Development Program [*Council on Library Resources*] (NITA) ... BSDP
Bibliographic Services Division [*The British Library*] (NITA) ... BSD
Bibliographic Systems Center [*Case Western Reserve University*] (IID) ... BSC

Bibliographical (AL) ... Bibl
Bibliographical Center for Research, Rocky Mountain Region [*Library network*] ... BCR
Bibliographical Center for Research, Rocky Mountain Region, Denver, CO [*Library symbol*] [*Library of Congress*] (LCLS) ... CoDB
Bibliographical Footnotes ... bibl-f
Bibliographical Imprint or Note (SAUS) ... Biblin
Bibliographical Note (DSUE) ... BIBLIO
Bibliographical Services Section [*of a library*] ... BSS
Bibliographical Society [*British*] (DIT) ... BS
Bibliographical Society (SAUO) ... BS
Bibliographical Society of America (SAUS) ... Bib Soc Am
Bibliographical Society of America (EA) ... BSA
Bibliographical Society of America Papers [*A publication*] (BRI) ... BSA-P
Bibliographical Society of Canada (SAUO) ... Bib Soc Can
Bibliographical Society of Canada (DGA) ... BSC
Bibliographical Society of the University of Virginia (EA) ... BSUV
Bibliographical Society Publications (journ.) (SAUS) ... BSP
Bibliographie Linguistischer Literatur [*Bibliography of Linguistic Literature*] [*Stadt- und Universitatbibliothek Frankfurt*] [*Information service or system*] [*Information service or system*] (CRD) ... BLL
Bibliographie Topographique des Principales Cites Grecques de l'Italie Meridionale et de la Sicile dans l'Antiquite [*A publication*] (OCD) ... Bibl Topogr
Bibliographie zur Offentlichen Unternehmung und Verwaltung [*Bibliography of Public Management and Administration*] [*NOMOS Datapool*] [*Information service or system*] ... BOWI
Bibliographies (SAUS) ... Bibs
Bibliography (ROG) ... BIB
Bibliography ... BIBL
Bibliography (AL) ... Bibl
Bibliography (WDAA) ... bibl
Bibliography (WDAA) ... bibliog
Bibliography ... BIBLIOG
Bibliography (ADWA) ... bibliogr
Bibliography (GEAB) ... bl
Bibliography and Index of Geology ... BiblGeo
Bibliography Master Index [*A database*] [*Gale Research*] (NITA) ... BMI
Bibliography of Agriculture [*Oryx Press*] [*Phoenix, AZ*] [*A publication*] ... B of A
Bibliography of American Literature [*A publication*] ... BAL
Bibliography of Australian Medicine and Health Services [*A publication*] ... BIBAM
Bibliography of Bioethics [*A publication*] ... BOB
Bibliography of Dutch language and literature studies (SAUS) ... BNTL
Bibliography of Jewish Communities in Europe [*Catalog at General Archives for the History of the Jewish People, Jerusalem*] [*A publication*] (BJA) ... BJCE
Bibliography of Medical Reviews (SAUS) ... BMR
Bibliography of Medical Translations [*A publication*] ... BMT
Bibliography of Newfoundland, Memorial University [*UTLAS symbol*] ... BON
Bibliography of Old Norse-Icelandic Studies [*A publication*] ... BONIS
Bibliography of Research Studies in Education, 1926-1940 [*A publication*] ... BRSE
Bibliography of Soil Science [*A publication*] ... BSS
Bibliography of Soil Science (journ.) (SAUS) ... BSS
Bibliography of the Computer in Environmental Design [*A publication*] ... BCED
Bibliography on Cable Television [*A publication*] (TSSD) ... BCTV
Bibliography on Cold Regions Science and Technology [*A publication*] ... BCRST
Bibliography on Incineration of Refuse and Waste [*Air Pollution Control Association*] [*A publication*] ... BIR
Bibliography Section, Alberta Public Affairs Bureau, Edmonton, Alberta [*Library symbol*] [*National Library of Canada*] (NLC) ... AEPA
bibliolater (SAUS) ... bibliol
bibliolatrous (SAUS) ... bibliol
bibliolatry (SAUS) ... bibliol
bibliological (SAUS) ... bibliol
bibliologist (SAUS) ... bibliol
bibliology (SAUS) ... bibliol
bibliomancy (SAUS) ... bibliom
bibliomane (SAUS) ... bibliom
bibliomania (SAUS) ... bibliom
bibliomaniac (SAUS) ... bibliom
bibliomanist (SAUS) ... bibliom
bibliopegic (SAUS) ... bibliop
bibliopegist (SAUS) ... bibliop
bibliopegy (SAUS) ... bibliop
bibliophagist (SAUS) ... bibliop
bibliophile (SAUS) ... bibliop
bibliophilia (SAUS) ... bibliop
bibliophobe (SAUS) ... bibliop
bibliophobia (SAUS) ... bibliop
bibliopole (SAUS) ... bibliop
bibliopsychology (SAUS) ... bibliopsy
bibliotec- (SAUS) ... bibl
Biblioteca Apostolica Vaticana, Vatican City, Vatican City [*Library symbol*] [*Library of Congress*] (LCLS) ... VatBA
Biblioteca Benjamin Franklin (SAUO) ... BBF
Biblioteca Benjamin Franklin, Guadalajara, Mexico [*Library symbol*] [*Library of Congress*] (LCLS) ... MxGuBF
Biblioteca Benjamin Franklin, Mexico City, Mexico [*Library symbol*] [*Library of Congress*] (LCLS) ... MxMBF
Biblioteca Berenson, Florence, Italy [*Library symbol*] [*Library of Congress*] (LCLS) ... ItFB
Biblioteca Centrala de Stat a R.S. Romania [*Central State Library of Romania*], **Bucharest, Romania** [*Library symbol*] [*Library of Congress*] (LCLS) ... RoBBC
Biblioteca Comunale "Angelillo", Servizio Prestito, Bari, Italy [*Library symbol*] [*Library of Congress*] (LCLS) ... ItBa
Biblioteca Comunale di Barletta, Barletta, Italy [*Library symbol*] [*Library of Congress*] (LCLS) ... ItBar
Biblioteca Marucelliana di Firenze, Servizio Prestito, Florence, Italy [*Library symbol*] [*Library of Congress*] (LCLS) ... ItFBM
Biblioteca Nacional, Buenos Aires, Argentina [*Library symbol*] [*Library of Congress*] (LCLS) ... Aa
Biblioteca Nacional, Caracas, Venezuela [*Library symbol*] [*Library of Congress*] (LCLS) ... Ve
Biblioteca Nacional de Agricultura [*National Library of Agriculture*] [*Brazil*] [*Information service or system*] (IID) ... BINAGRI
Biblioteca Nacional de Chile, Santiago, Chile [*Library symbol*] [*Library of Congress*] (LCLS) ... Chl
Biblioteca Nacional de Mexico, Mexico City, Mexico [*Library symbol*] [*Library of Congress*] (LCLS) ... MxMBN
Biblioteca Nacional, Madrid, Spain [*Library symbol*] [*Library of Congress*] (LCLS) ... Sp
Biblioteca Nacional, Rio De Janeiro, Brazil [*Library symbol*] [*Library of Congress*] (LCLS) ... Br
Biblioteca Nazional Universitaria di Torino, Servizio Prestito, Turin, Italy [*Library symbol*] [*Library of Congress*] (LCLS) ... ItTU
Biblioteca Nazionale Centrale, Florence [*Italy*] ... BNCF
Biblioteca Nazionale Centrale, Rome, Italy [*Library symbol*] [*Library of Congress*] (LCLS) ... It
Biblioteca Publica, Palma De Mallorca, Spain [*Library symbol*] [*Library of Congress*] (LCLS) ... SpPm
Biblioteca Statale di Cremona, Cremona, Italy [*Library symbol*] [*Library of Congress*] (LCLS) ... ItCr
Biblio-Tech Ltd., Three Fathom Harbor, Nova Scotia [*Library symbol*] [*National Library of Canada*] (NLC) ... NSTB
Biblio-Techniques Library and Information System [*Washington Library Network*] (NITA) ... BLIS
Bibliotechno-Bibliograficheskaya Klassifikatsiya [*Library Bibliographical Classification*] [*Russian Federation*] (NITA) ... BBK
Biblioteka Golowna Politechniki Warszawsjiej (Warsaw Technical University Central Library), Warsaw, Poland [*Library symbol*] [*Library of Congress*] (LCLS) ... PoWP
Biblioteka Narodowa [*National Library*], **Warsaw, Poland** [*Library symbol*] [*Library of Congress*] (LCLS) ... PoWBN
Bibliotekernes Oplysningskontor, Centre de Pret International, Kobenhavn, Denmark [*Library symbol*] [*Library of Congress*] (LCLS) ... DnKBO
Bibliotekstjanst AB [*Library Service Ltd.*] [*Sweden*] [*Information service or system*] (IID) ... BTJ
bibliothec- (SAUS) ... bibl
Bibliotheca [*of Apollodorus*] [*Classical studies*] (OCD) ... Bibl
Bibliotheca [*of Photius*] [*Classical studies*] (OCD) ... Bibl
Bibliotheca [*Library*] [*Latin*] ... BIBL
Bibliotheca Hagiographica Graeca [*A publication*] (ODCC) ... BHG
Bibliotheca Hagiographica Latina Antiquae et Mediae Aetatis [*A publication*] (ODCC) ... BHL
Bibliotheca Hagiographica Orientalis [*A publication*] (ODCC) ... BHO
Bibliotheca Judaica [*A publication*] (BJA) ... BJ
Bibliotheca Orientalis [*A publication*] (BJA) ... BiblOr
Bibliotheca Parsoniana, New Orleans, LA [*Library symbol*] [*Library of Congress*] [*Obsolete*] (LCLS) ... LNP
bibliothecal (SAUS) ... bibliothec
Bibliothekarisch-Analytisches System zur Informations Speicherung-Erschleissung [*Library analytical system for information storage/retrieval*] [*Federal Republic of Germany*] (NITA) ... BASIS-E
Bibliotheks Ausleihverwaltungsystem [*Library circulation system*] [*Federal Republic of Germany*] (NITA) ... BIAS
Bibliotheks Automatisierung-System [*Online Cataloguing System*] [*Federal Republic of Germany*] (NITA) ... BAS
Bibliotheks- und Informationssystem [*Library and Information System*] [*German*] ... BIS
Bibliothek-Verbund-System [*Library Network System*] [*Siemens AG*] [*Information service or system*] (IID) ... BVS
Bibliotheque (VRA) ... bibl
Bibliotheque Adelard-Berger, St.-Jean-Sur-Richelieu, Quebec [*Library symbol*] [*National Library of Canada*] (BIB) ... QSTJA
Bibliotheque Administrative du Quebec [*UTLAS symbol*] ... BAQ
Bibliotheque Administrative, (Edifice H), Ministere des Communications du Quebec, Quebec [*Library symbol*] [*National Library of Canada*] (NLC) ... QQMCH
Bibliotheque Administrative, Ministere des Affaires Inter-Gouvernementales du Quebec, Quebec, Quebec [*Library symbol*] [*Obsolete*] [*National Library of Canada*] (NLC) ... QQAI
Bibliotheque Americaine de Nantes, Universite de Nantes Chemin du Tertre, Nantes, France [*Library symbol*] [*Library of Congress*] (LCLS) ... FrNALP
Bibliotheque Americaine, Universite de Grenoble III, Domaine Universitaire, Grenoble, France [*Library symbol*] [*Library of Congress*] (LCLS) ... FrGrALP
Bibliotheque Americaine, Universite de Nancy II, Nancy, France [*Library symbol*] [*Library of Congress*] (LCLS) ... FrNanALP
Bibliotheque Americaine, Universite de Toulouse-Le Mirail, Toulouse, France [*Library symbol*] [*Library of Congress*] (LCLS) ... FrTIALP
Bibliotheque Americaine, Universite Paul-Valery, Montpellier, France [*Library symbol*] [*Library of Congress*] (LCLS) ... FrMpALP
Bibliotheque Battelle, Centre de Recherche, Geneve, Switzerland [*Library symbol*] [*Library of Congress*] (LCLS) ... SzGB
Bibliotheque Calvet, Avignon, France [*Library symbol*] [*Library of Congress*] (LCLS) ... FrAv
Bibliotheque Cantonal et Universitaire de Lausanne, Lausanne, Switzerland [*Library symbol*] [*Library of Congress*] (LCLS) ... SzLaCU

Bibliotheque Centrale de Pret d'Abitibi-Temiscamingue, Rouyn-Noranda, Quebec [*Library symbol*] [*National Library of Canada*] (NLC) .... QRBC

Bibliotheque Centrale de Pret de la Cote-Nord, Sept-Iles, Quebec [*Library symbol*] [*National Library of Canada*] (NLC) .... QSIBCP

Bibliotheque Centrale de Pret de la Mauricie, Trois-Rivieres, PQ, Canada [*Library symbol*] [*Library of Congress*] (LCLS) .... CaQTBC

Bibliotheque Centrale de Pret de la Mauricie, Trois-Rivieres, Quebec [*Library symbol*] [*National Library of Canada*] (NLC) .... QTBC

Bibliotheque Centrale de Pret de l'Estrie, Sherbrooke, Quebec [*Library symbol*] [*National Library of Canada*] (BIB) .... QSHERB

Bibliotheque Centrale de Pret d'Outaouais, Hull, Quebec [*Library symbol*] [*National Library of Canada*] (BIB) .... QHBC

Bibliotheque de Documentation des Archives, Ville de Montreal, Quebec [*Library symbol*] [*National Library of Canada*] (NLC) .... QMCIH

Bibliotheque de Droit, Universite de Moncton, New Brunswick [*Library symbol*] [*National Library of Canada*] (NLC) .... NBMOUD

Bibliotheque de Droit, Universite de Sherbrooke, Quebec [*Library symbol*] [*National Library of Canada*] (NLC) .... QSHERUD

Bibliotheque de la Faune, Ministere du Loisir, de la Chasse et de la Peche, Montreal, Quebec [*Library symbol*] [*National Library of Canada*] (NLC) .... QMLCPF

Bibliotheque de la Faune, Ministere du Loisir, de la Chasse, et de la Peche, Orsainville, Quebec [*Library symbol*] [*National Library of Canada*] (NLC) .... QOLCPF

Bibliotheque de la Legislature de la Province de Quebec, Quebec, PQ, Canada [*Library symbol*] [*Library of Congress*] (LCLS) .... CaQQL

Bibliotheque de la Sante, Centre Hospitalier Restigouche, Campbellton, New Brunswick [*Library symbol*] [*National Library of Canada*] (BIB) ...... NBCHR

Bibliotheque de la Ville de Montreal, Montreal, PQ, Canada [*Library symbol*] [*Library of Congress*] (LCLS) .... CaQMBM

Bibliotheque de la Ville de Montreal, Quebec [*Library symbol*] [*National Library of Canada*] (NLC) .... QMBM

Bibliotheque de l'Ambassade de France, Ottawa, ON, Canada [*Library symbol*] [*Library of Congress*] (LCLS) .... CaOOAF

Bibliotheque de l'Ambassade de France, Ottawa, Ontario [*Library symbol*] [*National Library of Canada*] (BIB) .... OOAF

Bibliotheque de l'Arsenal, Paris, France [*Library symbol*] [*Library of Congress*] (LCLS) .... FrPBA

Bibliotheque de l'Assemblee Nationale, Quebec, Quebec [*Library symbol*] [*National Library of Canada*] (NLC) .... QQL

Bibliotheque de l'Institut d'Etudes Medievales, Universite de Montreal, Quebec [*Library symbol*] [*National Library of Canada*] (NLC) .... QMUE

Bibliotheque de Quebec, Quebec [*Library symbol*] [*National Library of Canada*] (NLC) .... QQ

Bibliotheque de Theologie, les Facultes de la Compagnie de Jesus, Montreal, Quebec [*Library symbol*] [*National Library of Canada*] (NLC) .... QMFCJ

Bibliotheque Dentinger [*Dentinger Library*] Falher, Alberta [*Library symbol*] [*National Library of Canada*] (NLC) .... AFD

Bibliotheque des Archives de la Province de Quebec, Quebec, PQ, Canada [*Library symbol*] [*Library of Congress*] (LCLS) .... CaQQA

Bibliotheque des Avocats, Barreau de Montreal, Quebec [*Library symbol*] [*National Library of Canada*] (NLC) .... QMAV

Bibliotheque des Ecoles Francaises d'Athenes et de Rome [*A publication*] (OCD) .... Bibl Ec Franc

Bibliotheque des Freres des Ecoles Chretiennes, Quebec [*Library symbol*] [*National Library of Canada*] (NLC) .... QQBL

Bibliotheque des Instituteurs, Montreal, PQ, Canada [*Library symbol*] [*Library of Congress*] (LCLS) .... CaQMBI

Bibliotheque des Nations Unies, Geneve, Switzerland [*Library symbol*] [*Library of Congress*] (LCLS) .... SzGBNU

Bibliotheque des Sciences de la Sante, Universite de Sherbrooke, Quebec [*Library symbol*] [*National Library of Canada*] (NLC) .... QSHERC

Bibliotheque des Sciences, Universite de Sherbrooke, Quebec [*Library symbol*] [*National Library of Canada*] (NLC) .... QSHERUS

Bibliotheque des Sciences, Universite du Quebec, Montreal [*Library symbol*] [*National Library of Canada*] (BIB) .... QMUQS

Bibliotheque des Services Diocesains, Archeveche de Quebec, Quebec [*Library symbol*] [*National Library of Canada*] (BIB) .... QQAQ

Bibliotheque des Services Infirmiers, Hopital Notre-Dame, Montreal, Quebec [*Library symbol*] [*National Library of Canada*] (NLC) .... QMHNDI

Bibliotheque Deschatelets, Peres Oblats, Ottawa, ON, Canada [*Library symbol*] [*Library of Congress*] (LCLS) .... CaOOSJ

Bibliotheque d'Ingenierie, BG Checo International Ltee., Montreal, Quebec [*Library symbol*] [*National Library of Canada*] (NLC) .... QMBGC

Bibliotheque du Grand Seminaire, Sherbrooke, Quebec [*Library symbol*] [*National Library of Canada*] (NLC) .... QSHERG

Bibliotheque du Monastere des Augustines, Quebec, PQ, Canada [*Library symbol*] [*Library of Congress*] (LCLS) .... CaQQMAB

Bibliotheque du Monastere des Augustines, Quebec, Quebec [*Library symbol*] [*National Library of Canada*] (NLC) .... QQMAB

Bibliotheque du Parlement [*Library of Parliament*] [*Canada*] .... BP

Bibliotheque Felix-Leclerc, Val-Belair, Quebec [*Library symbol*] [*National Library of Canada*] (NLC) .... QVBFL

Bibliotheque Franciscaine, Quebec, PQ, Canada [*Library symbol*] [*Library of Congress*] (LCLS) .... CaQQF

Bibliotheque Franciscaine, Quebec, Quebec [*Library symbol*] [*National Library of Canada*] (NLC) .... QQF

Bibliotheque Gabrielle-Roy, Quebec, PQ, Canada [*Library symbol*] [*Library of Congress*] (LCLS) .... CaQQGR

Bibliotheque Gabrielle-Roy, Quebec, Quebec [*Library symbol*] [*National Library of Canada*] (BIB) .... QQGR

Bibliotheque Gaspesienne, Cap-Chat, PQ, Canada [*Library symbol*] [*Library of Congress*] (LCLS) .... CaQCC

Bibliotheque Gaspesienne, Cap-Chat, Quebec [*Library symbol*] [*National Library of Canada*] (NLC) .... QCC

Bibliotheque Generale et Archives, Rabat, Morocco [*Library symbol*] [*Library of Congress*] (LCLS) .... MorR

Bibliotheque Generale, Universite de Sherbrooke, Quebec [*Library symbol*] [*National Library of Canada*] (NLC) .... QSHERU

Bibliotheque Intermunicipale de Pierrefonds et Dollard-des-Ormeaux, Pierrefonds,PQ, Canada [*Library symbol*] [*Library of Congress*] (LCLS) .... CaQPfD

Bibliotheque Intermunicipale de Pierrefonds et Dollard-Des-Ormeaux, Pierrefonds,Quebec [*Library symbol*] [*National Library of Canada*] (NLC) .... QPD

Bibliotheque Lasallienne, Quebec, PQ, Canada [*Library symbol*] [*Library of Congress*] (LCLS) .... CaQQBL

Bibliotheque Medicale, Hopital Charles Lemoyne, Greenfield Park, Quebec [*Library symbol*] [*National Library of Canada*] (NLC) .... QMHCL

Bibliotheque Medicale, Hopital du Haut-Richelieu, St.-Jean-Sur-Richelieu, Quebec [*Library symbol*] [*National Library of Canada*] (BIB) .... QSTJH

Bibliotheque Medicale, Hopital General La Salle, Quebec [*Library symbol*] [*National Library of Canada*] (NLC) .... QLSHG

Bibliotheque Medicale, Hopital Regional Chaleur [*Medical Library, Chaleur Regional Hospital*] Bathurst, New Brunswick [*Library symbol*] [*National Library of Canada*] (NLC) .... NBBC

Bibliotheque Medicale, Hotel-Dieu de Roberval, Quebec [*Library symbol*] [*National Library of Canada*] (NLC) .... QRHD

Bibliotheque Medicale, Hotel-Dieu Saint-Joseph-De-Tracadie, New Brunswick [*Library symbol*] [*National Library of Canada*] (BIB) .... NBTH

Bibliotheque Municipale, Alma, Quebec [*Library symbol*] [*National Library of Canada*] (NLC) .... QA

Bibliotheque Municipale, Arthabaska, PQ, Canada [*Library symbol*] [*Library of Congress*] (LCLS) .... CaQArM

Bibliotheque Municipale, Arthabaska, Quebec [*Library symbol*] [*National Library of Canada*] (NLC) .... QARM

Bibliotheque Municipale, Asbestos, PQ, Canada [*Library symbol*] [*Library of Congress*] (LCLS) .... CaQAsB

Bibliotheque Municipale, Asbestos, Quebec [*Library symbol*] [*National Library of Canada*] (NLC) .... QASB

Bibliotheque Municipale, Aylmer, Quebec [*Library symbol*] [*National Library of Canada*] (NLC) .... QAY

Bibliotheque Municipale, Beauport, Quebec [*Library symbol*] [*National Library of Canada*] (BIB) .... QBEAU

Bibliotheque Municipale, Becancour, PQ, Canada [*Library symbol*] [*Library of Congress*] (LCLS) .... CaQBEC

Bibliotheque Municipale, Becancour, Quebec [*Library symbol*] [*National Library of Canada*] (NLC) .... QBEC

Bibliotheque Municipale, Boucherville, PQ, Canada [*Library symbol*] [*Library of Congress*] (LCLS) .... CaQBO

Bibliotheque Municipale, Boucherville, Quebec [*Library symbol*] [*National Library of Canada*] (NLC) .... QBO

Bibliotheque Municipale, Brossard, Quebec [*Library symbol*] [*National Library of Canada*] (BIB) .... QB

Bibliotheque Municipale, Buckingham, Quebec [*Library symbol*] [*National Library of Canada*] (NLC) .... QBU

Bibliotheque Municipale, Candiac, Quebec [*Library symbol*] [*National Library of Canada*] (BIB) .... QCA

Bibliotheque Municipale, Cap-De-La Madeleine, PQ, Canada [*Library symbol*] [*Library of Congress*] (LCLS) .... CaQCmM

Bibliotheque Municipale, Cap-De-La-Madeleine, Quebec [*Library symbol*] [*National Library of Canada*] (NLC) .... QCMM

Bibliotheque Municipale, Cap-Rouge, Quebec [*Library symbol*] [*National Library of Canada*] (BIB) .... QCRM

Bibliotheque Municipale, Charlesbourg, Quebec [*Library symbol*] [*National Library of Canada*] (BIB) .... QQBMC

Bibliotheque Municipale, Chateauguay, Quebec [*Library symbol*] [*National Library of Canada*] (BIB) .... QCM

Bibliotheque Municipale, Coaticook, PQ, Canada [*Library symbol*] [*Library of Congress*] (LCLS) .... CaQCB

Bibliotheque Municipale, Coaticook, Quebec [*Library symbol*] [*National Library of Canada*] (NLC) .... QCB

Bibliotheque Municipale, Cowansville, Quebec [*Library symbol*] [*National Library of Canada*] (BIB) .... QC

Bibliotheque Municipale de la Ville de Montreal-Est, Quebec [*Library symbol*] [*National Library of Canada*] (BIB) .... QMEM

Bibliotheque Municipale de Lachine, Quebec [*Library symbol*] [*National Library of Canada*] (NLC) .... QLM

Bibliotheque Municipale de Lyon, Lyon, France [*Library symbol*] [*Library of Congress*] (LCLS) .... FrLy

Bibliotheque Municipale de Saint Raphael de l'Ile Bizard, Saint Raphael de l'IleBizard, PQ, Canada [*Library symbol*] [*Library of Congress*] (LCLS) .... CaQStR

Bibliotheque Municipale de Saint-Laurent [*UTLAS symbol*] .... STL

Bibliotheque Municipale de Saint-Raphael-De-L'Ile-Bizard, Quebec [*Library symbol*] [*National Library of Canada*] (NLC) .... QSTR

Bibliotheque Municipale de Sherbrooke, Sherbrooke, PQ, Canada [*Library symbol*] [*Library of Congress*] (LCLS) .... CaQSherN

Bibliotheque Municipale, Dorval, Quebec [*Library symbol*] [*National Library of Canada*] (BIB) .... QD

Bibliotheque Municipale, Drummondville, PQ, Canada [*Library symbol*] [*Library of Congress*] (LCLS) .... CaQDM

Bibliotheque Municipale, Gatineau, Quebec [*Library symbol*] [*National Library of Canada*] (NLC) .... QG

Bibliotheque Municipale, Granby, PQ, Canada [*Library symbol*] [*Library of Congress*] (LCLS) .... CaQGM

Bibliotheque Municipale, Granby, Quebec [*Library symbol*] [*National Library of Canada*] (NLC) .... QGM

Bibliotheque Municipale, Grand'Mere, PQ, Canada [*Library symbol*] [*Library of Congress*] (LCLS) ... CaQGmM
Bibliotheque Municipale, Grand'Mere, Quebec [*Library symbol*] [*National Library of Canada*] (NLC) ... QGMM
Bibliotheque Municipale, Hull, PQ, Canada [*Library symbol*] [*Library of Congress*] (LCLS) ... CaQH
Bibliotheque Municipale, Hull, Quebec [*Library symbol*] [*National Library of Canada*] (NLC) ... QH
Bibliotheque Municipale, Jonquiere, Quebec [*Library symbol*] [*National Library of Canada*] (BIB) ... QJ
Bibliotheque Municipale, La Salle, PQ, Canada [*Library symbol*] [*Library of Congress*] (LCLS) ... CaQLs
Bibliotheque Municipale, La Salle, Quebec [*Library symbol*] [*National Library of Canada*] (NLC) ... QLS
Bibliotheque Municipale, La Tuque, PQ, Canada [*Library symbol*] [*Library of Congress*] (LCLS) ... CaQLt
Bibliotheque Municipale, La Tuque, Quebec [*Library symbol*] [*National Library of Canada*] (NLC) ... QLT
Bibliotheque Municipale, Lachine, PQ, Canada [*Library symbol*] [*Library of Congress*] (LCLS) ... CaQLaM
Bibliotheque Municipale, Laval, PQ, Canada [*Library symbol*] [*Library of Congress*] (LCLS) ... CaQLA
Bibliotheque Municipale, Laval, Quebec [*Library symbol*] [*National Library of Canada*] (NLC) ... QLA
Bibliotheque Municipale, Levis, PQ, Canada [*Library symbol*] [*Library of Congress*] (LCLS) ... CaQLe
Bibliotheque Municipale, Levis, Quebec [*Library symbol*] [*National Library of Canada*] (NLC) ... QLE
Bibliotheque Municipale, Longueuil, PQ, Canada [*Library symbol*] [*Library of Congress*] (LCLS) ... CaQLo
Bibliotheque Municipale, Longueuil, Quebec [*Library symbol*] [*National Library of Canada*] (NLC) ... QLO
Bibliotheque Municipale, Magog, PQ, Canada [*Library symbol*] [*Library of Congress*] (LCLS) ... CaQMgB
Bibliotheque Municipale, Magog, Quebec [*Library symbol*] [*National Library of Canada*] (NLC) ... QMAGB
Bibliotheque Municipale, Mascouche, Quebec [*Library symbol*] [*National Library of Canada*] (BIB) ... QMASC
Bibliotheque Municipale, Mont-Laurier, Quebec [*Library symbol*] [*National Library of Canada*] (BIB) ... QMLM
Bibliotheque Municipale, Montreal-Nord, PQ, Canada [*Library symbol*] [*Library of Congress*] (LCLS) ... CaQMn
Bibliotheque Municipale, Nantes, France [*Library symbol*] [*Library of Congress*] (LCLS) ... FrN
Bibliotheque Municipale, Plessisville, PQ, Canada [*Library symbol*] [*Library of Congress*] (LCLS) ... CaQPIM
Bibliotheque Municipale, Plessisville, Quebec [*Library symbol*] [*National Library of Canada*] (NLC) ... QPLM
Bibliotheque Municipale, Port-Alfred, PQ, Canada [*Library symbol*] [*Library of Congress*] (LCLS) ... CaQPA
Bibliotheque Municipale, Port-Alfred, Quebec [*Library symbol*] [*National Library of Canada*] (NLC) ... QPA
Bibliotheque Municipale, Port-Cartier, Quebec [*Library symbol*] [*National Library of Canada*] (BIB) ... QPCM
Bibliotheque Municipale, Princeville, PQ, Canada [*Library symbol*] [*Library of Congress*] (LCLS) ... CaQPrM
Bibliotheque Municipale, Princeville, Quebec [*Library symbol*] [*National Library of Canada*] (NLC) ... QPRM
Bibliotheque Municipale, Quebec, PQ, Canada [*Library symbol*] [*Library of Congress*] (LCLS) ... CaQQ
Bibliotheque Municipale, Repentigny, PQ, Canada [*Library symbol*] [*Library of Congress*] (LCLS) ... CaQRe
Bibliotheque Municipale, Repentigny, Quebec [*Library symbol*] [*National Library of Canada*] (NLC) ... QRE
Bibliotheque Municipale, Rimouski, Quebec [*Library symbol*] [*National Library of Canada*] (NLC) ... QRM
Bibliotheque Municipale, Riviere-Du-Loup, Quebec [*Library symbol*] [*National Library of Canada*] (BIB) ... QRL
Bibliotheque Municipale, Rock Island, PQ, Canada [*Library symbol*] [*Library of Congress*] (LCLS) ... CaQRIB
Bibliotheque Municipale, Saint-Bruno-De-Montarville, Quebec [*Library symbol*] [*National Library of Canada*] (BIB) ... QSTB
Bibliotheque Municipale, Saint-Jean, PQ, Canada [*Library symbol*] [*Library of Congress*] (LCLS) ... CaQStJB
Bibliotheque Municipale, Saint-Jean, Quebec [*Library symbol*] [*National Library of Canada*] (NLC) ... QSTJB
Bibliotheque Municipale, Saint-Jerome, PQ, Canada [*Library symbol*] [*Library of Congress*] (LCLS) ... CaQStJe
Bibliotheque Municipale, Saint-Jerome, Quebec [*Library symbol*] [*National Library of Canada*] (NLC) ... QSTJE
Bibliotheque Municipale, Saint-Laurent, PQ, Canada [*Library symbol*] [*Library of Congress*] (LCLS) ... CaQStL
Bibliotheque Municipale, Saint-Laurent, Quebec [*Library symbol*] [*National Library of Canada*] (NLC) ... QSTL
Bibliotheque Municipale, Saint-Leonard, PQ, Canada [*Library symbol*] [*Library of Congress*] (LCLS) ... CaQStLe
Bibliotheque Municipale, Saint-Leonard, Quebec [*Library symbol*] [*National Library of Canada*] (NLC) ... QSLE
Bibliotheque Municipale, Sept-Iles, PQ, Canada [*Library symbol*] [*Library of Congress*] (LCLS) ... CaQSi
Bibliotheque Municipale, Sept-Iles, Quebec [*Library symbol*] [*National Library of Canada*] (NLC) ... QSI
Bibliotheque Municipale, Sherbrooke, Quebec [*Library symbol*] [*National Library of Canada*] (NLC) ... QSHERN
Bibliotheque Municipale, Sorel, PQ, Canada [*Library symbol*] [*Library of Congress*] (LCLS) ... CaQSo
Bibliotheque Municipale, Sorel, Quebec [*Library symbol*] [*National Library of Canada*] (NLC) ... QSO
Bibliotheque Municipale, Ste.-Foy, PQ, Canada [*Library symbol*] [*Library of Congress*] (LCLS) ... CaQSF
Bibliotheque Municipale, Ste.-Foy, Quebec [*Library symbol*] [*National Library of Canada*] (NLC) ... QSF
Bibliotheque Municipale, St.-Eustache, Quebec [*Library symbol*] [*National Library of Canada*] (BIB) ... QE
Bibliotheque Municipale, Terrebonne, Quebec [*Library symbol*] [*National Library of Canada*] (NLC) ... QTER
Bibliotheque Municipale, Trois-Rivieres, PQ, Canada [*Library symbol*] [*Library of Congress*] (LCLS) ... CaQT
Bibliotheque Municipale, Trois-Rivieres, Quebec [*Library symbol*] [*National Library of Canada*] (NLC) ... QT
Bibliotheque Municipale, Verdun, Quebec [*Library symbol*] [*National Library of Canada*] (BIB) ... QVE
Bibliotheque Municipale, Victoriaville, PQ, Canada [*Library symbol*] [*Library of Congress*] (LCLS) ... CaQV
Bibliotheque Municipale, Victoriaville, Quebec [*Library symbol*] [*National Library of Canada*] (NLC) ... QV
Bibliotheque Nationale de Luxembourg, Service du Pret, Luxembourg, Luxembourg [*Library symbol*] [*Library of Congress*] (LCLS) ... LuxLBN
Bibliotheque Nationale du Canada [*National Library of Canada - NLC*] ... BNC
Bibliotheque Nationale du Quebec [*UTLAS symbol*] ... BNQ
Bibliotheque Nationale du Quebec, Montreal, PQ, Canada [*Library symbol*] [*Library of Congress*] (LCLS) ... CaQMBN
Bibliotheque Nationale du Quebec, Montreal, Quebec [*Library symbol*] [*National Library of Canada*] (NLC) ... QMBN
Bibliotheque Nationale et Universitaire, Affaires Generales, Strasbourg, France [*Library symbol*] [*Library of Congress*] (LCLS) ... FrSU
Bibliotheque Nationale, Paris, France [*Library symbol*] [*Library of Congress*] (LCLS) ... FrPBN
Bibliotheque Pere Champagne [*Pere Champagne Library*], **Notre-Dame-De-Lourdes, Manitoba** [*Library symbol*] [*National Library of Canada*] (BIB) ... MNDP
Bibliotheque Publique Cambridge-St-Albert, St.-Albert, ON, Canada [*Library symbol*] [*Library of Congress*] (LCLS) ... CaOSTAC
Bibliotheque Publique Cambridge-St.-Albert, St.-Albert, Ontario [*Library symbol*] [*National Library of Canada*] (NLC) ... OSTAC
Bibliotheque Publique de Dubreuilville, Ontario [*Library symbol*] [*National Library of Canada*] (NLC) ... ODUB
Bibliotheque Publique de St.-Isidore, Ontario [*Library symbol*] [*National Library of Canada*] (NLC) ... OSTI
Bibliotheque Publique du Canton d'Alfred [*Alfred Township Public Library*],**Lefaivre, Ontario** [*Library symbol*] [*National Library of Canada*] (BIB) ... OLAL
Bibliotheque Publique Mgr. Paquet, Caraquet, New Brunswick [*Library symbol*] [*National Library of Canada*] (NLC) ... NBCBP
Bibliotheque Regionale du Haut Saint-Jean, Edmundston, NB, Canada [*Library symbol*] [*Library of Congress*] (LCLS) ... CaNBEBR
Bibliotheque Regionale du Haut Saint-Jean, Edmundston, New Brunswick [*Library symbol*] [*National Library of Canada*] (NLC) ... NBEBR
Bibliotheque Royale d'Albert 1er, American Studies Center, Bruxelles, Belgium [*Library symbol*] [*Library of Congress*] (LCLS) ... Be-Am
Bibliotheque Royale d'Albert 1er, Bruxelles, Belgium [*Library symbol*] [*Library of Congress*] (LCLS) ... Be
Bibliotheque Scientifique Nationale [*National Science Library*] [*Canada*] ... BSN
Bibliotheque Scientifique, Universite Laval, Quebec, Quebec [*Library symbol*] [*National Library of Canada*] (NLC) ... QQLAS
Bibliotheques Vertes pour le Monde [*Green Library - GL*] [*Saint Egreve, France*] (EAIO) ... BVM
bibliotherapeutic (SAUS) ... bibliother
bibliotherapist (SAUS) ... bibliother
bibliotherapy (SAUS) ... bibliother
Bibliotherapy Forum [*Association of Specialized and Cooperative Library Agencies*] ... BF
Biblische Untersuchungen [*A publication*] (BJA) ... BU
Biblische Zeit-und Streitfragen (BJA) ... BZStF
Biblischer Kommentar zum Alten Testament [*A publication*] (BJA) ... BK
Biblisches Reallexikon [*A publication*] (BJA) ... BR
Biblisch-Historisches Handwoerterbuch [*A publication*] (BJA) ... BHH
Biblisch-Historisches Handwoerterbuch [*A publication*] (BJA) ... BHHW
Biblisch-Theologisches Handwoerterbuch [*A publication*] (BJA) ... BTHW
Biblitheque et Audiovisuel, Alma, Quebec [*Library symbol*] [*National Library of Canada*] (NLC) ... QABA
Bic Corp. [*NYSE symbol*] (SAG) ... BIC
Bic Corp. [*Associated Press*] (SAG) ... BicCp
Bicarbonate ... BICARB
Bicarbonate (SAUS) ... Bicarb
Bicarbonate [*Pharmacology*] (DAVI) ... HCO_3
Bicaval Venous Cannulation [*Medicine*] (MELL) ... BCVS
Bicaz [*Romania*] [*Seismograph station code, US Geological Survey*] (SEIS) ... BIZ
Bicentenary [*or Bicentennial*] ... BICENT
Bicentennial Council of the Thirteen Original States [*Later, CTOS*] [*Defunct*] (EA) ... BCTOS
Bicentennial Information Network [*American Revolution Bicentennial Administration*] ... BINET
Bicentennial Junior Committees of Correspondence [*American Revolution Bicentennial Administration, US Postal Service, and National Association of Elementary School Principals*] ... BJCC
Bicentennial Park Trust [*Australia*] ... BPT
Bicentennial Youth Debates [*National Endowment for the Humanities program*] ... BYD

Biceps (SAUS) ... Bic
Biceps Brachii [*A muscle*] ... BB
Biceps Femoris [*A muscle*] [*Anatomy*] ... BF
Biceps Femoris Muscle [*Medicine*] (MELL) ... BFM
Biceps Femoris muscles (SAUS) ... BF muscles
Biceps Jerk [*Neurology*] ... BJ
Biceps Muscle of Arm (MELL) ... BMA
Biceps Reflex (MELL) ... BR
Biceps Tendon [*Anatomy*] ... BT
Biceps Tendon Reflex [*Medicine*] (DMAA) ... BTR
Bicer Medical Systems [*Vancouver Stock Exchange symbol*] ... BCJ
Bichloromethylether (SAUS) ... BCME
Bichon Frise Club of America (EA) ... BFCA
Bichromate (VRA) ... BICH
B-ICI Signaling ATM Adaptation Layer (SAUS) ... B-ICI SAAL
Biciklista Esperantista Movado Internacia [*International Movement of Esperantist Bicyclists - IMEB*] (EAIO) ... BEMI
Bicinchoninic Acid [*Organic chemistry*] ... BCA
Bicknell and Hawley's Reports [*10-20 Nevada*] [*A publication*] (DLA) ... Bick
Bicknell and Hawley's Reports [*10-20 Nevada*] [*A publication*] (DLA) ... Bick & H
Bicknell and Hawley's Reports [*10-20 Nevada*] [*A publication*] (DLA) ... Bick & Hawl
Bicknell, IN [*FM radio station call letters*] ... WUZR
Bicknell's Indiana Civil Practice [*A publication*] (DLA) ... Bick Civ Pr
Bicknell's Indiana Criminal Practice [*A publication*] (DLA) ... Bick Cr Pr
Bicknell's Reports [*India*] [*A publication*] (DLA) ... Bick (In)
BiCMOS Bus-Interface Technology (SAUS) ... BCT
Bicoastal Corp. (SAUS) ... SIGP
Bicol Experiment Station (SAUO) ... BEST
Bicol Region Integrated Agricultural Research (SAUO) ... BRIARC
Bicolor ... Bi
Bicolor Guaiac [*Test*] [*Medicine*] ... BCG
Bicolor Guaiac [*Test*] [*Medicine*] ... BG
Bicomponent [*Laboratory tubing*] ... BC
Biconcave (SAUS) ... BICV
Biconditional (SAUS) ... BICHS
Biconditional ... BICOND
Biconvex ... BCVX
Biconvex (SAUS) ... BICX
Bi-County Community Hospital, Warren, MI [*Library symbol*] [*Library of Congress*] (LCLS) ... MiWarBH
Bicuculline [*Organic chemistry*] ... BIC
Bicuculline ... Bicuc
Biculturalism and Bilingualism [*Canada*] ... B & B
Biculturalism and Bilingualism [*Canada*] ... Bl & Bl
Bicuspid [*Dentistry*] ... B
Bicuspid Aortic Valve [*Cardiology*] (DMAA) ... BAV
Bicycle (MSA) ... BCL
Bicycle (ROG) ... BIKE
Bicycle (SAUS) ... Bike
Bicycle (SAUS) ... Cycle
Bicycle Association of Great Britain (EAIO) ... BAGB
Bicycle Australia [*An association*] ... BA
Bicycle Club [*Generic term*] (WGA) ... BC
Bicycle Club (SAUO) ... BC
Bicycle Club of America (EA) ... BCA
Bicycle Ergometer Stress Test (SAUS) ... BEST
Bicycle Exercise Stress Test [*Medicine*] (MELL) ... BEST
Bicycle Federation of America (EA) ... BF of A
Bicycle Federation of America (EA) ... PRO BIKE
Bicycle Helmet Safety Institute (EA) ... BHSI
Bicycle Institute of America [*Defunct*] (EA) ... BIA
Bicycle Institute of NSW (SAUO) ... BINSW
Bicycle Manufacturers Association of America (EA) ... BMA
Bicycle Motocross ... BMX
Bicycle Network (EA) ... BN
Bicycle Polo Association (SAUO) ... BPA
Bicycle Polo Association of Great Britain (SAUO) ... BPAGB
Bicycle Ride Directors Association of America (EA) ... BRDAA
Bicycle Spoke Injury (MELL) ... BSI
Bicycle Stamps Club (EA) ... BSC
Bicycle Study Unit [*American Topical Association*] (EA) ... BSU
Bicycle Touring Club [*British*] ... BTC
Bicycle Touring Club (SAUO) ... BTC
Bicycle Traders' Association of South Australia ... BTASA
Bicycle Transportation Action (EA) ... BTA
Bicycle Wholesale Distributors Association (EA) ... BWDA
Bicycle-Motocross Industrial Guild (EA) ... BIG
Bicycle-Powered Airplane (SAUS) ... Bicyplane
Bicycles on Stamps [*Study unit*] [*American Topical Association*] (EA) ... BOS
Bicycling Parking Foundation (EA) ... BPF
Bicycling Promotion Organization [*Later, BIA*] (EA) ... BPO
Bicyclists Educational and Legal Foundation (EA) ... BELF
Bicycloheptadien (SAUS) ... BCH
Bi-Cylindrical-Conical (SAUS) ... BCC
Bid [*Stock exchange term*] (SPSG) ... B
Bid Analysis and Reporting System (AAGC) ... BARS
Bid and Asked [*Investment term*] ... B & A
Bid and Proposal ... B & P
Bid and Proposal (SAUS) ... B&P
Bid Bond Service Undertaking ... BBSU
Bid in Die [*Twice a Day*] [*Symbol*] [*Pharmacology*] (DAVI) ... ii
Bid Opening Date ... BOD
Bid Price (SG) ... B
Bid Wanted [*Business term*] ... BW
Bida [*Nigeria*] [*ICAO location identifier*] (ICLI) ... DNBI
Bidar [*India*] [*ICAO location identifier*] (ICLI) ... VOBR
Bid-Asked Electronic Quotation System (SAUS) ... BAEQS
Biddeford, ME [*FM radio station call letters*] ... WCYY
Biddeford, ME [*AM radio station call letters*] ... WIDE
Biddeford, ME [*Television station call letters*] ... WMEA
Bidder's Court of Referees Reports [*England*] [*A publication*] (DLA) ... Bid
Bidders Early Alert Message (PDAA) ... BEAM
Bidder's List Control (SAA) ... BILCO
Bidder's Locus Standi Reports [*England*] [*A publication*] (DLA) ... Bid
Bidder's Locus Standi Reports, I [*1820-36*] [*A publication*] (DLA) ... Bidd
Bidders Mailing List (AAGC) ... BML
Bidders Master File Listing [*DoD*] ... BMFL
Bidding Category Codes (ACAE) ... BCFX
Bidding Expense (ACAE) ... BE
Biddle on Insurance [*A publication*] (DLA) ... Bid Ins
Biddle on Retrospective Legislation [*A publication*] (DLA) ... Bid Retr Leg
Biddle on Warranties in Sale of Chattels [*A publication*] (DLA) ... Bid War Sale Chat
Biddle's Table of Statutes [*A publication*] (DLA) ... Bid Tab Stat
BIDDS Management Subsystem (SAUS) ... BMS
Biddy [*Slang*] (DSUE) ... BID
Bide-a-Wee Home Association (EA) ... BAWHA
Bidecimal Code (SAUS) ... BC
Bideford [*Municipal borough in England*] ... BIDEF
Bidens Mottle Virus [*Plant pathology*] ... BIMV
Bi-Directional (SAUS) ... BiDi
Bidirectional (SAUS) ... BiDi
Bidirectional Associative Memory [*Computer science*] ... BAM
Bidirectional Asymmetric Multipoint-to-Multipoint (SAUS) ... BAMM
Bidirectional Asymmetric Point-to-Multipoint (SAUS) ... BAPM
Bidirectional Asymmetric Point-to-Point (SAUS) ... BAPP
Bidirectional Categorical Grammar ... BCG
Bidirectional Category System ... BCS
Bidirectional Computer Interface Program ... BCI
Bi-Directional Converter (NASA) ... BDC
Bidirectional Converter (SAUS) ... BDC
Bidirectional Counter (SAUS) ... BC
Bidirectional Current Monitoring Relay (SAUS) ... BCMR
Bidirectional Diffraction Distribution Function (CIST) ... BDDF
Bidirectional Field-Effect Transistor (SAUS) ... BiFET
Bidirectional Line Switched Ring [*Telecommunications*] (ACRL) ... BLSR
Bi-Directional Line-Switched Rings ... BLSR
Bidirectional Loop Switching (SAUS) ... BDLS
Bidirectional Output Switch Field Effect Transistor [*Electronics*] (NITA) ... BOSFET
Bidirectional Polarization Distribution Function (SAUS) ... BPDF
Bidirectional Reference Array, Internally Derived [*Computer science*] (DIT) ... BRAID
Bidirectional Reflectance (SAUS) ... BDR
Bidirectional Reflectance Distribution Function (SAUS) ... BRFD
Bidirectional Reflectance Factor (SAUS) ... BRF
Bidirectional Reflectance Field Instrument (SAUS) ... BRFI
Bidirectional Reflectance-Distribution Function ... BRDF
Bidirectional Surface-Scattering Distribution Function [*Computer graphics*] ... BSSDF
Bidirectional Symmetric Multipoint-to Multipoint (SAUS) ... BSMM
Bidirectional Symmetric Point-to Multipoint (SAUS) ... BSPM
Bidirectional Symmetric Point-to Point (SAUS) ... BSPP
Bidirectional Test Fixture (MCD) ... BTF
Bidirectional Transceiver Element [*Telecommunications*] ... BTE
Bidirectional Transmittance Distribution Function (CIST) ... BTDF
Bi-Doppler Scoring System (MCD) ... BIDOPS
Bidor [*Malaysia*] [*ICAO location identifier*] (ICLI) ... WMAE
Bi-Drive Recreational All-Terrain Transporter [*Subaru automobile*] ... BRAT
Bids Accepted for the Following Vacancies (FAAC) ... BAFVC
Bids and Acceptances Committee (SAUO) ... BIDAC
Bids per Circuit per Hour [*Telecommunications*] ... BCH
Bids Solicited (FAAC) ... BDSLD
Bids Solicited as Follows ... BSAF
Bidston [*England*] [*Seismograph station code, US Geological Survey*] [*Closed*] (SEIS) ... BID
Bi-Duplexed Redundancy [*Telecommunications*] ... BDR
Bidwell Mansion State Historic Park, Chico, CA [*Library symbol*] [*Library of Congress*] (LCLS) ... CChiBP
Bie [*Angola*] [*Airport symbol*] (OAG) ... SVP
Bielefeld/Windelsbleiche [*Germany*] [*ICAO location identifier*] (ICLI) ... EDLI
Biel/Kappelen [*Switzerland*] [*ICAO location identifier*] (ICLI) ... LSZP
Biel's Microfilm Co., West Seneca, NY [*Library symbol*] [*Library of Congress*] (LCLS) ... BMC
Bielschowsky-Jansky Syndrome [*Medicine*] (DMAA) ... BJ
Biennale of Illustrations Bratislava (SAUO) ... BIB
Biennial ... B
Biennial ... BE
Biennial [*Botany*] ... bien
Biennial ... BIENN
Biennial Flight Review [*Aviation*] (DA) ... BFR
Biennial General Meeting ... BGM
Biennial Infrastructure Review (SAUS) ... BIR
Biennial National Atomic Spectroscopy Symposium ... BNASS
Biennial Report and Official Opinions of the Attorney General of the State of West Virginia [*A publication*] (DLA) ... Biennial Rep & Op W Va Atty's Gen
Biennial Report of the Attorney General of the State of Iowa [*A publication*] (DLA) ... Biennial Rep Iowa Att'y Gen
Biennial Report of the Attorney General of the State of Michigan [*A publication*] (DLA) ... Mich Att'y Gen Biennial Rep

Biennial Report of the Attorney General of the State of South Dakota [*A publication*] (DLA) .... Biennial Rep SD Att'y Gen
Biennial Report of the Attorney General of the State of Vermont [*A publication*] (DLA) .... Biennial Rep VT Att'y Gen
Biennial Report on Carcinogens (SAUO) .... BRC
Biennial Reporting System [*Environmental Protection Agency*] (AEPA) .... BRS
Bienville Parish Library, Arcadia, LA [*Library symbol*] [*Library of Congress*] (LCLS) .... LArB
Bier Block [*Medicine*] (MELL) .... BB
Bier House (WDAA) .... BH
Biet-Dong-Quan [*South Vietnamese Rangers*] (VNW) .... BDQ
Bifascicular Block [*Electrocardiogram*] (CPH) .... BFB
Bifidus Acidophilus Live [*Health-food product*] .... BA
Bi-Field Effect Transistor (SAUS) .... BIFET
Bifurcation (SAUS) .... BIFN
Bifurcation Analysis and Catastrophy Theory Methodology (MCD) .... BACTM
Big .... BG
Big 10 Conference (PSS) BIG10
Big 12 Conference (PSS) BIG12
Big 8 Conference (PSS) BIG8
Big Apple Triathlon Club (EA) .... BATC
Big B, Inc. [*Associated Press*] (SAG) .... Big B
Big B, Inc. [*NASDAQ symbol*] (NQ) .... BIGB
Big Bag Of Pages (SAUS) .... BIBOP
Big Band [*Music*] (WDMC) .... BB
Big Band [*Radio station format*] (WDMC) .... BBnd
Big Band Academy of America (EA) .... BBAA
Big Bands Collectors' Club (EA) .... BBCC
Big Bar Gold Corp. [*Vancouver Stock Exchange symbol*] .... BBK
Big Bear [*California*] [*Seismograph station code, US Geological Survey*] [*Closed*] (SEIS) .... BBC
Big Bear City, CA [*FM radio station call letters*] .... KBHR
Big Bear Lake, CA [*AM radio station call letters*] .... KBBV
Big Bear Lake, CA [*FM radio station call letters*] (RBYB) .... KXSB
Big Bear Solar Observatory [*California Institute of Technology*] [*Research center*] (RCD) .... BBSO
Big Bear Stores Co. (IIA) .... BB
Big Belt Mountains of Montana (SAUS) .... Big Belts
Big Ben Council (SAUO) .... BBC
Big Ben Report [*World War II*] .... BENREP
Big Ben Resources, Inc. [*Vancouver Stock Exchange symbol*] .... BGB
Big Bend [*Idaho*] [*Seismograph station code, US Geological Survey*] (SEIS) .... BBI
Big Bend [*Montana*] [*Seismograph station code, US Geological Survey*] [*Closed*] (SEIS) .... BBM
Big Bend Community College (SAUO) .... BBCC
Big Bend Community College, Moses Lake, WA [*Library symbol*] [*Library of Congress*] (LCLS) .... WaMIB
Big Bend National Park (SAUS) .... BBNP
Big Bend National Park .... BIBE
Big Bend Natural History Association (EA) .... BBNHA
Big Big Gastrin [*Endocrinology*] .... BBG
Big Block [*Series of Chevrolet V-8 engines*] .... BB
Big Board [*The New York Stock Exchange, Inc.*] [*Slang*] .... BB
Big Board (SAUO) .... BB
Big Brand Names [*i.e., well-established writers*] [*Publishing slang*] .... BBN
Big Brother [*From George Orwell's novel, "1984"*] .... BB
Big Brothers League (SAUO) .... BBL
Big Brothers of America [*Later, BB/BSA*] (EA) .... BBA
Big Brothers/Big Sisters of America (EA) .... BB/BSA
Big Capitalization (SAUS) .... Big-Cap
Big City Bagels [*NASDAQ symbol*] (TTSB) .... BIGC
Big City Bagels, Inc. [*Associated Press*] (SAG) .... BgCtyB
Big City Bagels, Inc. [*NASDAQ symbol*] (SAG) .... BIGC
Big City Bagels, Inc. [*Associated Press*] (SAG) .... BigCityB
Big City Bagels Wrrt [*NASDAQ symbol*] (TTSB) .... BIGCW
Big City Radio 'A' [*AMEX symbol*] (SG) .... YFM
Big Close-Up [*A photograph or motion picture sequence taken from a short distance*] .... BCU
Big Creek [*Nevada*] [*Seismograph station code, US Geological Survey*] [*Closed*] (SEIS) .... BGN
Big Creek Baldy [*Montana*] [*Seismograph station code, US Geological Survey*] [*Closed*] (SEIS) .... BCB
Big Creek News, Polk City, IA [*Library symbol*] [*Library of Congress*] (LCLS) .... IaPolcN
Big Deal [*An association*] (EA) .... BD
Big Delta [*Alaska*] [*ICAO location identifier*] (ICLI) .... PABG
Big Dumb Booster (SAUS) .... BDB
Big Dumb Booster Rocket .... BDB
Big Dutch Hollow [*Utah*] [*Seismograph station code, US Geological Survey*] (SEIS) .... BDU
Big East Conference (EA) .... BEC
Big Eight Conference (EA) .... BEC
Big Eight Council on Black Student Government (EA) .... BECBSG
Big Electronic Human-Energized Machine, Only Too Heavy [*High technology*] .... BEHEMOTH
Big Emerging Markets (ACII) .... BEM
Big Entertainment, Inc. [*NASDAQ symbol*] (SAG) .... BIGE
Big Entertainment, Inc. [*Associated Press*] (SAG) .... BigEnt
Big Entertainment'A' [*NASDAQ symbol*] (TTSB) .... BIGE
Big European Bubble Chamber [*Nuclear particle detector*] .... BEBC
Big Evil Grin [*Online dialog*] .... BEG
Big Falls Elementary School, Big Falls, MN [*Library symbol*] [*Library of Congress*] (LCLS) .... MnBfaE
Big Fat Wide Shot [*Photography*] (WDMC) .... BFWS
Big Fatal Disease [*Slang*] (DNAB) .... BFD
Big F-in Spatula 9000 (SAUS) BFS-9000
Big Fine Deal .... BFD
Big Flats, NY [*FM radio station call letters*] .... WGMM
Big Flower Holdings, Inc. [*NYSE symbol*] (SAG) .... BGF
Big Flower Holdings, Inc. [*Associated Press*] (SAG) .... BigFlower
Big Flower Holdings, Inc. [*Associated Press*] (SAG) .... BigFlwr
Big Flower Press Hldgs [*NYSE symbol*] (TTSB) .... BGF
Big Foot Financial Corp. [*NASDAQ symbol*] (SAG) .... BFFC
Big Foot Financial Corp. [*Associated Press*] (SAG) .... BigFoot
Big Friendly Giant [*In the children's bestseller "The BFG" by Roald Dahl*] .... BFG
Big Grin (SAUS) .... BG
Big Hole Battlefield National Monument (SAUS) .... BHBNM
Big Hole National Battlefield .... BIHO
Big Horn County Public Library, Hardin, MT [*Library symbol*] [*Library of Congress*] (LCLS) .... MtHar
Big I Development Ltd. [*Vancouver Stock Exchange symbol*] .... BID
Big, Intrusive Government .... BIG
Big Island Air, Inc. [*ICAO designator*] (FAAC) .... BIG
Big Island Rainforest Action Group (EA) .... BIRAG
Big Lake, AK [*Location identifier*] [*FAA*] (FAAL) .... BGQ
Big Lake Elementary School, Big Lake, MN [*Library symbol*] [*Library of Congress*] (LCLS) .... MnBIE
Big Lake High School, Big Lake, MN [*Library symbol*] [*Library of Congress*] (LCLS) .... MnBIH
Big Lake National Wildlife Refuge (SAUS) .... BLNWR
Big Lake Public Library, Big Lake, MN [*Library symbol*] [*Library of Congress*] (LCLS) .... MnBI
Big Lake, TX [*FM radio station call letters*] (BROA) .... KWTR-FM
Big Lake, TX [*Location identifier*] [*FAA*] (FAAL) .... LUJ
Big Little Book [*of comic strips*] .... BLB
Big Little Book Collector's Club of America (EA) .... BLBCCA
Big Liver and Spleen Disease [*Poultry*] .... BLS
Big Look Improvement Program (SAUO) .... BLIP
Big Lost River [*Idaho*] [*Seismograph station code, US Geological Survey*] [*Closed*] (SEIS) .... LRI
Big M Petroleum, Inc. [*Vancouver Stock Exchange symbol*] .... BIM
Big Machine on Campus [*Computer*] .... BMOC
Big Mahogany Desk .... BMD
Big Man on Campus [*Slang*] .... BMOC
Big Man's Fan Club (EA) .... BMFC
Big Maria Mountains [*California*] [*Seismograph station code, US Geological Survey*] (SEIS) .... BMM
Big Mountain [*Alaska*] [*Seismograph station code, US Geological Survey*] (SEIS) .... BIG
Big Mountain Air Force Station [*Alaska*] [*ICAO location identifier*] (ICLI) .... PABM
Big Name Fan [*of science fiction or fantastic literature*] [*See also LNF*] .... BNF
Big O Tires, Inc. [*NASDAQ symbol*] (NQ) .... BIGO
Big O Tires, Inc. [*Associated Press*] (SAG) .... BigOTir
Big Office Head Office [*Business term*] (PCM) .... BOHO
Big Oil Bail Out [*Reference by Rep. James H. Scheuer (NY) to a particular toxic waste clean-up bill*] .... BOBO
Big Optical Array [*Proposed, 1992*] .... BOA
Big Orange Switch (SAUS) .... BOS
Big Pine, CA [*FM radio station call letters*] (RBYB) .... KRHV
Big Pine Key, FL [*FM radio station call letters*] .... WWUS
Big Piney, WY [*Location identifier*] [*FAA*] (FAAL) .... BPI
Big Plasma Glucagon [*Endocrinology*] .... BPG
Big Rapids Community Library, Big Rapids, MI [*Library symbol*] [*Library of Congress*] (LCLS) .... MiBr
Big Rapids, MI [*AM radio station call letters*] .... WBRN
Big Rapids, MI [*FM radio station call letters*] .... WBRN-FM
Big Rapids, MI [*FM radio station call letters*] .... WYBR
Big Red Bike Ride [*Fundraising event*] [*British*] .... BRBR
Big Red Switch [*Computer science*] (NHD) .... BRS
Big Rock Brewery [*NASDAQ symbol*] (SAG) .... BEER
Big Rock Brewery [*NASDAQ symbol*] (TTSB) .... BEERF
Big Rock Brewery [*Associated Press*] (SAG) .... BigRck
Big Rock Point Nuclear Plant (NRCH) .... BRPNP
Big Safari Detachment four, Ontario, California (SAUS) .... Det 4
Big Sandy, TX [*Location identifier*] [*FAA*] (FAAL) .... ABG
Big Sandy, TX [*FM radio station call letters*] (RBYB) .... KBAU
Big Sister Association (SAUO) .... BSA
Big Sisters Association of Ontario (AC) .... BSAO
Big Six (SAUO) .... BS
Big Sky Airline [*ICAO designator*] (FAAC) .... BSY
Big Sky Airlines [*ICAO designator*] (AD) .... GQ
Big Sky Conference (PSS) .... BSC
Big Sky Hospice, Billings, MT [*Library symbol*] [*Library of Congress*] (LCLS) .... MtBilBH
Big Sky, MT [*FM radio station call letters*] (BROA) .... KBFN-FM
Big Smiling Grin (SAUS) .... BSG
Big Smith Brands [*NASDAQ symbol*] (TTSB) .... BSBI
Big Smith Brands, Inc. [*NASDAQ symbol*] (SAG) .... BSBI
Big Smith Brands, Inc. [*Associated Press*] (SAG) .... BSmith
Big Smith Brands Wrrt [*NASDAQ symbol*] (TTSB) .... BSBIW
Big Spring [*Texas*] [*Airport symbol*] (AD) .... HCA
Big Spring, TX [*Location identifier*] [*FAA*] (FAAL) .... BGS
Big Spring, TX [*FM radio station call letters*] (BROA) .... KBCX-FM
Big Spring, TX [*AM radio station call letters*] .... KBST
Big Spring, TX [*FM radio station call letters*] .... KBST-FM
Big Spring, TX [*FM radio station call letters*] .... KBTS
Big Spring, TX [*AM radio station call letters*] .... KBYG
Big Spring, TX [*Television station call letters*] .... KWAB
Big Spring/Webb Air Force Base [*Texas*] [*ICAO location identifier*] (ICLI) .... KBGS
Big State Conference (PSS) .... BSTC

Big Stone Gap, VA [*FM radio station call letters*] ... WAXM
Big Stone Gap, VA [*AM radio station call letters*] ... WLSD
Big Stone Hutterite Colony School, Graceville, MN [*Library symbol*] [*Library of Congress*] (LCLS) ... MnGraBS
Big Strike Resources [*Vancouver Stock Exchange symbol*] ... BTK
Big Sur, CA [*Location identifier*] [*FAA*] (FAAL) ... BSR
Big System (SAUS) ... BS
Big Ten Conference (EA) ... BTC
Big Thicket Association (EA) ... BTA
Big Thicket Conservation Association (EA) ... BTCA
Big Thicket Coordinating Committee [*Defunct*] (EA) ... BTCC
Big Three Industries Inc. (SAUO) ... BIG
Big Trout Lake [*Canada*] [*Airport symbol*] (OAG) ... YTL
Big Trout Lake, ON [*ICAO location identifier*] (ICLI) ... CYTL
Big Ugly Dish [*Traditional satellite dish antenna*] ... BUD
Big Ugly Fat Fellow [*Nickname for B-52 bomber*] ... BUFF
Big Ugly Fellow [*Slang for B-52 bomber or other large aircraft*] [*Bowdlerized version*] (DOMA) ... BUF
Big West Conference (EA) ... BWC
Big Whale Cay, Berry Island [*Bahamas*] [*ICAO location identifier*] (ICLI) ... MYBW
Big White Set [*Type of lush movie set used in 1930's musical-comedy films*] ... BWS
Big White Ski Village, BC [*FM radio station call letters*] (RBYB) ... CKFR-FM
Big White Ski Village, BC [*FM radio station call letters*] ... CKIQ
Big Woman on Campus [*Slang*] ... BWOC
Bigamy [*or Bigamist*] (WDAA) ... BIG
Bigelow on Equity [*A publication*] (DLA) ... Big Eq
Bigelow on Estoppel [*A publication*] (DLA) ... Bigelow Estop
Bigelow on Estoppel [*A publication*] (DLA) ... Big Est
Bigelow on Frauds [*A publication*] (DLA) ... Big Fr
Bigelow on Torts [*A publication*] (DLA) ... Big Torts
Bigelow's Bench and Bar of New York [*A publication*] (DLA) ... Big B & B
Bigelow's Cases on Bills and Notes [*A publication*] (DLA) ... Big B & N
Bigelow's Cases on Bills and Notes [*A publication*] (DLA) ... Big Cas B & N
Bigelow's Cases, William I to Richard I [*A publication*] (DLA) ... Big Cas
Bigelow's Cases, William I to Richard I [*A publication*] (DLA) ... Cas Wm I
Bigelow's Edition of Jarman on Wills [*A publication*] (DLA) ... Big Jarm Wills
Bigelow's English Procedure [*A publication*] (DLA) ... Big Eng Proc
Bigelow's English Procedure [*A publication*] (DLA) ... Big Proc
Bigelow's Leading Cases on Bills and Notes, Torts, or Wills [*A publication*] (DLA) ... Bigelow Lead Cas
Bigelow's Leading Cases on Bills and Notes, Torts, or Wills [*A publication*] (DLA) ... Big Lead Cas
Bigelow's Leading Cases on Torts [*A publication*] (DLA) ... Big Cas Torts
Bigelow's Life and Accident Insurance Cases [*A publication*] (DLA) ... Big L & A Ins Cas
Bigelow's Life and Accident Insurance Cases [*A publication*] (DLA) ... Big LI Cas
Bigelow's Life and Accident Insurance Reports [*A publication*] (DLA) ... Big L & A Ins Rep
Bigelow's Life and Accident Insurance Reports [*A publication*] (DLA) ... Life and Acc Ins R
Bigelow's Overruled Cases [*United States, England, Ireland*] [*A publication*] (DLA) ... Big Ov Cas
Bigelow's Placita Anglo-Normanica [*A publication*] (DLA) ... Big Plac
Bigelow's Placita Anglo-Normanica [*A publication*] (DLA) ... Plac Ang Nor
Bigelow-Sanford, Inc. (SAUO) ... BGS
Bigfork School, Bigford, MN [*Library symbol*] [*Library of Congress*] (LCLS) ... MnBfoS
Biggers, Whitten, and Whittingham [*Growth medium*] [*Gynecology*] ... BWW
Biggin Executive Aviation Ltd. [*British*] [*ICAO designator*] (FAAC) ... BHE
Biggin Hill [*British*] [*ICAO location identifier*] (ICLI) ... EGKB
Biggleswade [*Urban district in England*] ... BIGGL
Bigg's Criminal Law [*A publication*] (DLA) ... Bigg Cr L
Biggs Free Public Library, Biggs, CA [*Library symbol*] [*Library of Congress*] (LCLS) ... CBi
Biggs Free Public Library, Biggs, CA [*Library symbol*] [*Library of Congress*] (LCLS) ... CBiP
Biggs on Acts Relating to Railways [*A publication*] (DLA) ... Bigg RR Acts
Biggs Wall (SAUS) ... BW
Bighorn Airways, Inc. [*ICAO designator*] (FAAC) ... BHR
Bighorn Canyon National Recreation Area (SAUS) ... BCNRA
Bighorn Canyon National Recreation Area ... BICA
Bighorn Development Corp. [*Vancouver Stock Exchange symbol*] ... BHD
Bight ... B
Bight (SAUS) ... BGHT
Bight (ROG) ... BGT
Bignell's Reports [*India*] [*A publication*] (DLA) ... Big
Bignell's Reports [*India*] [*A publication*] (DLA) ... Bign
Bigstone Minerals [*Vancouver Stock Exchange symbol*] ... BIG
Big-Time Operator [*Slang*] ... BTO
Bihar Agricultural Research Institute (SAUO) ... BARI
Bihar Industrial and Technical Consultancy Organisation (SAUO) ... BITCO
Bihar Law Journal Reports [*India*] [*A publication*] (DLA) ... Bih LJ Rep
Bihar Law Journal Reports [*India*] [*A publication*] (DLA) ... BLJ
Bihar Light Horse [*British military*] (DMA) ... BLH
Bihar Mineral Development Corporation (SAUO) ... BMDC
Bihar Mounted Rifles [*British military*] (DMA) ... BMR
Bihar Reports [*India*] [*A publication*] (DLA) ... Bih Rep
Bihar State Finance Corporation (SAUO) ... BSFC
Biharmonic Equation ... BHE
Bi-Harmonic Equation (SAUS) ... BHE
Bihorium [*During Two Hours*] [*Pharmacy*] ... BIHOR
BII Enterprises, Inc. [*Toronto Stock Exchange symbol*] ... BII
Biin Open System Interface Extension (SAUS) ... BOSIX
Bijar [*Iran*] [*ICAO location identifier*] (ICLI) ... OICE
Bijbels Woordenboek [*A publication*] (BJA) ... BW
Bijou ... BIJ
Bijouterie ... BIJTR
Bikaner [*India*] [*ICAO location identifier*] (ICLI) ... VIBK
Biker Enforcement Team (SAUO) ... BET
Bikers Against Manslaughter (EA) ... BAM
Bikes for Africa (EA) ... BA
Bikes Not Bombs (EA) ... BNB
Bikini Atoll Rehabilitation Committee [*Federal government*] ... BARC
Bikini Photo Drone (SAUS) ... BPD
Bikitaite [*A zeolite*] ... BIK
Bikoro [*Zaire*] [*ICAO location identifier*] (ICLI) ... FZBC
Bilaspur [*India*] [*ICAO location identifier*] (ICLI) ... VABI
Bilateral [*Anatomy*] (DAVI) ... B
Bilateral ... BIL
Bilateral (ADWA) ... bil
bilateral (DMAA) ... bilat
Bilateral ... BILAT
Bilateral (SAUS) ... Bilat
Bilateral (SAUS) ... BI
Bilateral Acoustic Neurofibromatosis [*Medicine*] ... BANF
Bilateral Acute Renal Vein Thrombosis [*Medicine*] (MELL) ... BARVT
Bilateral Agreements ... BLA
Bilateral Arterial Occlusion [*Medicine*] (MELL) ... BAO
Bilateral Assistance Subcommittee of the DCC (SAUO) ... BAS
Bilateral Asymmetrical [*Medicine*] (DMAA) ... BA
Bilateral Breath Sounds [*Medicine*] (DAVI) ... BBS
Bilateral Bundle Branch Block [*Cardiology*] ... BBBB
Bilateral Cartoid Body Resection [*Medicine*] (DMAA) ... BCBR
Bilateral Cleft of Lip and Palate [*Medicine*] (DMAA) ... BCLP
Bilateral Closed User Group (SAUO) ... BCUG
Bilateral Closed User Group with Outgoing Access (CIST) ... BCUGO
Bilateral Cortical Necrosis [*Medicine*] ... BCN
Bilateral Cystogram [*Radiography*] (DAVI) ... BCG
Bilateral Diffuse Uveal Melanocytic Proliferation (SAUS) ... BDUMP
Bilateral Firm (Hand) Grips (MEDA) ... BLFG
Bilateral Hilar Adenopathy [*Medicine*] (MELL) ... BHA
Bilateral Hilar Lymphadenopathy [*Medicine*] (DMAA) ... BHL
Bilateral Hilar Lymphoma syndrome (SAUS) ... BHL syndrome
Bilateral Impedance Rheograph [*Instrumentation*] ... BR
Bilateral, Independent, Periodic, Lateralized Epileptiform Discharge [*Medicine*] (DMAA) ... BIPLED
Bilateral Inguinal Herniae [*Gastroenterology*] (DAVI) ... BIH
Bilateral Intellectual Property Rights Agreement (SAUO) ... BIPRA
Bilateral Internal Mammary Arteries [*Anatomy*] (DAVI) ... BIMA
Bilateral Investment Treaties ... BIT
Bilateral Iterative Network ... BITN
Bilateral Kinaesthetic Differences (SAUS) ... BKD
Bilateral lower Lung fields (SAUS) ... BL
Bilateral Lung Transplantation (ADWA) ... BLT
Bilateral Myringotomy Tubes [*Otorhinolaryngology*] (DAVI) ... BMT
Bilateral Observation (SAUS) ... Bi Obsn
Bilateral Otitis Externa [*Otorhinolaryngology*] (DAVI) ... BOE
Bilateral Otitis Media [*Medicine*] (MAE) ... BOM
Bilateral Pelvic Lymph Node [*Medicine*] (DAVI) ... BPLN
Bilateral Pelvic Lymph Node Dissection [*Medicine*] (DAVI) ... BPLND
Bilateral Private Circuit (SAUS) ... BPC
Bilateral Program Review (SPST) ... BPR
Bilateral Quarantine Agreement ... BQA
Bilateral Renal Agenesis [*Medicine*] (DMAA) ... BRA
Bilateral Sagittal Osteotomy [*Medicine*] (MAE) ... BSO
Bilateral Sagittal Split Osteotomy [*Medicine*] (MELL) ... BSSO
Bilateral Salpingo-Oophorectomy [*Gynecology*] (DAVI) ... BILAT SXO
Bilateral Salpingo-Oophorectomy [*Gynecology*] ... BSO
Bilateral Salpingo-oophorectomy (SAUS) ... BSP
Bilateral Salpingo-Oophorectomy with Hysterectomy [*Medicine*] ... BSOTH
Bilateral School [*British*] ... B
Bilateral Serous Otitis [*Otorhinolaryngology*] (DAVI) ... BSO
Bilateral Serous Otitis Media [*Otorhinolaryngology*] (DAVI) ... BSOM
Bilateral Short-Leg Casts [*Orthopedics*] (DAVI) ... BILAT SLC
Bilateral Sphenoethmoidectomy [*Medicine*] ... BSE
Bilateral Staff (COE) ... BS
Bilateral Stellate Ganglionectomy (SAUS) ... BSTG
Bilateral, Symmetrical, and Equal (MAE) ... BSE
Bilateral Tape Card (SAUS) ... BTC
Bilateral Tubal Anastomosis [*Medicine*] (MELL) ... BTA
Bilateral Tubal Interruption [*Gynecology*] ... BTI
Bilateral Tubal Ligation [*Gynecology*] (DAVI) ... BLT
Bilateral Tubal Ligation [*Gynecology*] ... BTL
Bilateral Upper Dorsal Sympathectomy [*Medicine*] (DMAA) ... BUDS
Bilateral Upper Extremity [*Occupational therapy*] ... BUE
Bilateral Ureteral Obstruction [*Medicine*] (MELL) ... BUO
Bilateral Vas Ligation [*Medicine*] ... BVL
Bilateral/Non-Governmental Organization (ADA) ... BI/NGO
Bilateration Ranging Transponder (MCD) ... BRT
Bilateration Ranging Transponder System (MCD) ... BRTS
Bilayer Lipid Membrane [*Physical chemistry*] ... BLM
Bilbao [*Spain*] [*Airport symbol*] (OAG) ... BIO
Bilbao [*Spain*] [*ICAO location identifier*] (ICLI) ... LEBB
Bilbiligraphic Records Conversion (EDAC) ... BIBCON
Bild Zeitung [*Picture newspaper*] [*German*] ... BZ
Bilderberg Continuum Atmosphere ... BCA
Bildner & Sons Inc. (SAUO) ... JBIL
Bildschirmtext [*Viewdata system*] [*Federal Ministry of Posts and Telecommunications*] [*Germany*] ... BTX

Bildudalur [*Iceland*] [*Airport symbol*] (OAG) ... BIU
Bile [*Blood group*] ... Bi
Bile Acid [*Gastroenterology*] (AAMN) ... BA
Bile Acid Concentration [*Gastroenterology*] ... BAC
Bile Acid Independent Flow [*Medicine*] (DB) ... BAIF
Bile Acid-Dependent Fraction [*Medicine*] ... BADF
Bile Acid-Independent Canalicular Fraction [*Medicine*] ... BAICF
Bile Acid-Independent Fraction [*Medicine*] ... BAIF
Bile Acid-Losing Syndrome [*Medicine*] (DB) ... BALS
Bile Canalicular Membrane ... BCM
Bile Canaliculi [*Anatomy*] ... BC
Bile Driver (DWSG) ... BD
Bile Duct [*Medicine*] ... BD
Bile Duct Atresia [*Medicine*] (MELL) ... BDA
Bile Duct Examination [*Medicine*] ... BDE
Bile Duct Exploration [*Gastroenterology*] (DAVI) ... BDE
Bile Duct Growth Factor [*Biochemistry*] ... BDGF
Bile Duct Obstruction [*Medicine*] ... BDO
Bile Esculin [*Medicine*] ... BE
Bile Flow [*Physiology*] ... BF
Bile Flow Rate [*Physiology*] ... BFR
Bile Salt Independent Fraction [*Medicine*] (DMAA) ... BSIF
Bile Salt Metabolism (DB) ... BSM
Bile Salts [*Biochemistry*] ... BS
Bile Salts/Phospholipid [*Ratio*] ... BS/PL
Bilene [*Mozambique*] [*ICAO location identifier*] (ICLI) ... FQBI
Bile-Salt Limited Lipase [*An enzyme*] ... BSL
Bilevel (MCD) ... BL
Bilevel Positive Airway Pressure [*Medicine*] (DMAA) ... BIPAP
Bilevel Pulse (MCD) ... BLP
Bilevel Quality Assurance Program [*NASA*] (KSC) ... BQAP
Bilevel Response Unit ... BRU
Bilevel Stimulus Unit ... BSU
Bilge Keel (SAUS) ... BilK
Bilge Keel (SAUS) ... BK
Biliary Atresia [*Medicine*] (DMAA) ... BA
Biliary Atresia & Liver Transplant Network (SAUO) ... BALT
Biliary Colic [*Medicine*] (DMAA) ... BC
Biliary Obstruction [*Medicine*] (MELL) ... BO
Biliary Protein Fraction ... BPF
Biliary Tract Disease [*Medicine*] (DMAA) ... BTD
Biliary Tract Infection [*Medicine*] (MELL) ... BTI
Biliary Tract Pain [*Medicine*] (MELL) ... BTP
Bilin-Binding Protein [*Biochemistry*] ... BBP
Bilinear Target Factor Analysis [*Mathematics*] ... BTFA
Bilingual [*Texts*] (BJA) ... bil
Bilingual Community Educator ... BCE
Bilingual Counsellor ... BC
Bilingual Education (EDAC) ... BE
Bilingual Education (SAUS) ... BE
Bilingual Education Bibliographic Abstracts [*National Clearinghouse for Bilingual Education*] [*Rosslyn, VA*] [*Database*] ... BEBA
Bilingual Education Multifunctional Resource Center (SAUO) ... BEMRC
Bilingual Education Telecommunications Network [*National Clearinghouse for Bilingual Education*] [*Wheaton, MD*] (TSSD) ... BETNET
Bilingual Evaluation Technical Assistance Project (EDAC) ... BETA
Bilingual Foundation of the Arts (EA) ... BFA
Bilingual Information Instructor ... BII
Bilingual Information Officer ... BIO
Bilingual Obstetric Liaison Officer ... BOLO
Bilingual Recording Club of Canada (SAUO) ... BRC
Bilingual Syntax Measure [*English and Spanish test*] ... BSM
Bilingualism & Biculturalism (SAUS) ... BIBI
Bilinugal Education Act of 1968 (EDAC) ... BEA
Bilirubin [*Biochemistry*] (AAMN) ... BIL
Bilirubin [*Clinical chemistry*] ... bili
Bilirubin [*Gastroenterology and neonatology*] (DAVI) ... BILIR
Bilirubin [*Gastroenterology and neonatology*] (DAVI) ... bilirub
Bilirubin [*Biochemistry*] ... BR
Bilirubin Clearance [*Gastroenterology*] (DAVI) ... C_{BR}
Bilirubin Diglucuronide [*Biochemistry*] ... BDG
Bilirubin, Direct and Indirect [*Clinical chemistry*] (CPH) ... Bili D/I
Bilirubin Monoglucuronide [*Biochemistry*] ... BMG
Bilirubin of Unknown Origin [*Gastroenterology*] (DAVI) ... BUO
Bilirubin Oxidase [*An enzyme*] ... BOX
Bilirubin Oxidase (DB) ... BRO
Bilirubin Production [*Biochemistry*] (MAE) ... BRP
Bilirubin Production Rate (DB) ... BPR
Bilirubin, Total [*Clinical chemistry*] (CPH) ... Bili T
Bill Blass [*Couturier*] ... BB
Bill Book [*Shipping*] ... BB
Bill Farrar Fan Club (EA) ... BFFC
Bill Feed Device (SAUS) ... BFD
Bill Feed Printer (SAUS) ... BFP
Bill Glass Evangelistic Association (EA) ... BGEA
Bill Glass Ministries (EA) ... BGM
Bill in Care Of [*Telecommunications*] (TEL) ... BCO
Bill Lodged [*British*] (ADA) ... BL
Bill Number Screening (SAUS) ... BNS
Bill of Entry [*Shipping*] ... B/E
Bill of Exchange [*Accounting*] ... BE
Bill of Health ... BH
Bill of Lading ... BIL
Bill of Lading [*Shipping*] (NOAA) ... BILDG
Bill of Lading [*Shipping*] ... BL
Bill of Lading [*Shipping*] ... BLADING
Bill of Lading [*Shipping*] ... BoL
Bill of Lading Attached (EBF) ... B/L Atchd
Bill of Lading, Clean (SAUS) ... B of L cl
Bill of Lading, Through (SAUS) ... B of L t
Bill of Lading Ton (MARI) ... B/L Ton
Bill of Loading (SAUS) ... BL
Bill of Material (ACAE) ... B/M
Bill of Material Processor (IAA) ... BIMAP
Bill of Material Processor ... BOMP
Bill of Material Status (MCD) ... BOMS
Bill of Material System (MCD) ... BMS
Bill of Materials [*Manufacturing*] (MUGU) ... BM
Bill of Materials (DNAB) ... BMAT
Bill of Materials [*Digital Dynamics Ltd.*] [*Software package*] ... BOM
Bill of Materials [*Manufacturing*] (ODBW) ... bom
Bill of Materials Processor (SAUS) ... BMP
Bill of Parcels ... BP
Bill of Rights ... BR
Bill of Rights Foundation (EA) ... BORF
Bill of Rights Journal [*A publication*] (DLA) ... Bill of Rights J
Bill of Rights Journal [*A publication*] (DLA) ... Bill Rts J
Bill of Rights Journal [*A publication*] (DLA) ... BRJ
Bill of Rights of Virginia [*A publication*] (DLA) ... BRV
Bill of Rights Review [*A publication*] (DLA) ... Bill Rights Rev
Bill of Sale ... BS
Bill of Sale (ADWA) ... b/s
Bill of Sight [*Customs*] ... BS
Bill of Sight [*Customs*] ... B/ST
Bill of Sight (ODBW) ... B/St
Bill of Store ... BS
Bill of Work (NASA) ... BOW
Bill Processor System (SAUS) ... BPS
Bill Tomorrow [*Business term*] ... BT
Billable Time Authorization (SAUS) ... BTA
Billable Time Report (SAUS) ... BTR
Billards Worldcup Association (SAUO) ... BWA
Billboard (VRA) ... bilbd
Billboard Information Network [*Billboard Publications, Inc.*] [*Information service or system*] (IID) ... BIN
Billboard Publications, Inc. ... BPI
Billed At [*Commerce*] ... B/A
Billed at (SAUS) ... B/a
Billed but Not Received (AFIT) ... BNR
Billed Number Screening ... BNS
Billed Office Account Code [*Army*] (AFIT) ... BOAC
Billerica Historical Society, Billerica, MA [*Library symbol*] [*Library of Congress*] (LCLS) ... MBilHi
Billericay [*England*] ... BILL
Billet [*Bill*] [*French*] [*Business term*] (ROG) ... BET
Billet (AABC) ... BIL
Billet (MSA) ... BL
Billet a Payer [*Bill Payable*] [*French*] [*Business term*] ... BAP
Billet a Recevoir [*Bill Receivable*] [*French*] [*Business term*] ... BAR
Billet Master [*Military*] [*British*] (ROG) ... BM
Billet Occupational Code [*Military*] (CAAL) ... BOC
Billet Selection Program [*Military*] (DNAB) ... BSP
Billet Sequence Code ... BSC
Billet Specialty Training (SAUS) ... BST
Billet Split Lens ... BSL
Billet Steel (MSA) ... BLSTL
Billeting ... BLLTNG
Billeting (SAUS) ... Bltg
Billeting and Accommodations Advisory [*Military communications*] ... BAA
Billeting and Acommodations Advisory (SAUS) ... BAA
Billeting and Inventory (SAUS) ... B&I
Billeting and Inventory [*Military*] ... B & I
Billeting Distribution List (SAUS) ... BDL
Billhead (SAUS) ... Bhd
Billiard [*Freight*] ... BILLD
Billiard and Bowling Institue of America (SAUO) ... BBIA
Billiard Congress of America (EA) ... BCA
Billiard Players Association of America ... BPA
Billiards ... BILL
Billiards and Snooker Association of Western Australia ... BSAWA
Billiards and Snooker Control Council [*An association*] (EAIO) ... BSCC
Billiards Association (SAUO) ... BA
Billiards Association [*British*] (BI) ... BA
Billiards Association Control Council (SAUO) ... BACC
Billiards Association Control Council and Billiards for the Services Fund (SAUO) ... BACCBSF
Billiards Club (SAUO) ... BC
Billiards Trade Association (SAUO) ... BTA
Billiards Trade Association [*British*] (BI) ... BTA
Billie Jo Spears Fan Club (EA) ... BJSFC
Billikin Resources, Inc. [*Vancouver Stock Exchange symbol*] ... BIL
Billing ... BLLKNG
Billing, Accounts Receivable, Sales Analysis (IBMDP) ... BARSA
Billing Adjustment Code (ACAE) ... BAC
Billing Advice Code ... BAC
Billing and Accounting Computer (SAUS) ... BAC
Billing and Instruction Book ... B & IB
Billing and Order Support System (SAUS) ... BOSS
Billing and Ordering Forum [*Exchange Carriers Standards Association*] [*Telecommunications*] ... BOF

Billing and Prince's Law and Practice of Patents [*A publication*] (DLA) ... Bill & Pr Pat
Billing Cease Date (TEL) ... BC
Billing Concepts [*NASDAQ symbol*] (SG) ... BILL
Billing Data Transmitter (SAUS) ... BDT
Billing Day (DCTA) ... BD
Billing Group [*Telecommunications*] (TEL) ... BG
Billing Information Concepts [*NASDAQ symbol*] (SAG) ... BILL
Billing Information Concepts [*Associated Press*] (SAG) ... Bill Info
Billing Instructions [*Telecommunications*] (TEL) ... BI
Billing, Inventory Control, Accounts Receivable, Sales Analysis (IBMDP) ... BICARSA
Billing. Law of Awards and Arbitration [*1845*] [*A publication*] (DLA) ... Bil Aw
Billing. Law Relating to Pews [*1845*] [*A publication*] (DLA) ... Bil Pews
Billing Log Number (ACAE) ... BLN
Billing Machine (SAUS) ... BM
Billing Memo Charge [*Business term*] ... BMC
Billing Name and Address ... BNA
Billing Telephone Number [*Telecommunications*] (TEL) ... BTN
Billing Validation Application ... BVA
Billing Validation Center (ROAS) ... BVC
Billing-Collecting-Remitting [*Accounting*] (TEL) ... BCR
Billings [*Montana*] [*Airport symbol*] (OAG) ... BIL
Billings Area Office (SAUO) ... BI
Billings Clinic, Billings, MT [*Library symbol*] [*Library of Congress*] (LCLS) ... MtBilC
Billings Family Life Center [*Australia*] ... BFLC
Billings Mental Health Center, Billings, MT [*Library symbol*] [*Library of Congress*] (LCLS) ... MtBilMH
Billings, MT [*FM radio station call letters*] (RBYB) ... KBBB-FM
Billings, MT [*FM radio station call letters*] (BROA) ... KBEX-FM
Billings, MT [*FM radio station call letters*] (RBYB) ... KBKO
Billings, MT [*AM radio station call letters*] ... KBLG
Billings, MT [*AM radio station call letters*] (BROA) ... KBUL
Billings, MT [*FM radio station call letters*] (BROA) ... KCMT-FM
Billings, MT [*FM radio station call letters*] ... KCTR-FM
Billings, MT [*AM radio station call letters*] (RBYB) ... KDWG
Billings, MT [*FM radio station call letters*] ... KEMC
Billings, MT [*AM radio station call letters*] ... KGHL
Billings, MT [*FM radio station call letters*] ... KIDX
Billings, MT [*FM radio station call letters*] ... KKBR
Billings, MT [*AM radio station call letters*] ... KMAY
Billings, MT [*AM radio station call letters*] (BROA) ... KMZK-AM
Billings, MT [*FM radio station call letters*] ... KRKX
Billings, MT [*Television station call letters*] ... KSVI
Billings, MT [*Television station call letters*] ... KTVQ
Billings, MT [*Television station call letters*] ... KULR
Billings, MT [*AM radio station call letters*] ... KURL
Billings, MT [*FM radio station call letters*] ... KYYA
Billings, MT [*Location identifier*] [*FAA*] (FAAL) ... LKO
Billings Ovulation Method Association of the United States (EA) ... BOM
Billings Public Library, Billings, MT [*Library symbol*] [*Library of Congress*] (LCLS) ... MtBil
Billings Public Schools, Billings, MT [*Library symbol*] [*Library of Congress*] (LCLS) ... MtBils
Billings Township Public Library, Kagawong, Ontario [*Library symbol*] [*National Library of Canada*] (NLC) ... OKBT
Billion (MCD) ... B
Billion ... BIL
Billion (SAUS) ... Bil
Billion (EECA) ... BILLI
Billion ... BN
Billion (SAUS) ... Bn
Billion Barrels [*Shipping*] ... BB
Billion Barrels (SAUS) ... Bbbl
Billion Barrels of Oil ... BBO
Billion Channel Extra Terrestrial Array (SAUS) ... BETA
Billion Channel Extraterrestrial Assay [*Search for intelligent life*] ... BETA
Billion Conductor Feet [*Telecommunications*] (TEL) ... BCF
Billion Cubic Feet ... BCF
Billion Cubic Feet (ADWA) ... bcf
Billion Cubic Meters ... BCM
Billion Electron Volts ... BeV
Billion Electron Volts (AEBE) ... BEV
Billion Electron Volts (SAUS) ... GeV
Billion Floating-Point Operations per Second [*Computer science*] ... BFLOPS
Billion Gallons (EPA) ... BG
Billion Gallons per Day ... BGD
Billion Instructions [*Power measurement*] [*Computer science*] (IAA) ... BIN
Billion Instructions per Second [*Computing power measurement*] [*Computer science*] ... BIPS
Billion Liters per Day ... BLD
Billion Operations Per Second (SAUS) ... BOPS
Billion Passenger Kilo Metre (SAUS) ... BPKM
Billion Years (SAUS) ... BY
Billion Years (EES) ... by
Billion Years ... BY
Billion Years ... BYR
Billionaire Boys Club (EA) ... BBC
Billions (SAUS) ... Bils
Billions of Actions Per Second (SAUS) ... GAPS
Billions of Barrels of Oil Equivalent (MCD) ... BBOE
Billions of Cubic Feet per Day [*of gas*] ... BCFD
Billions of Floating Point Instructions Per Second (SAUS) ... GFLOPS
Billions of Instructions per Second (SAUS) ... GIPS
Billions of Operations per Second (DOMA) ... BOPS
Billionth (SAUS) ... Billi
Billionth (IDOE) ... nano-
Billot. Traite de l'Extradition [*A publication*] (DLA) ... Billot Extrad
Bills (ROG) ... B
Bills and Notes [*Legal term*] (DLA) ... B & N
Bills and Notes ... BN
Bills Discounted ... BD
Bills of Exchange Act [*1882*] [*British*] ... BEA
Bills of Lading (WDAA) ... BsL
Bills of Lading (SAUS) ... Bs/L
Bills of Lading Act ... BLA
Bills Payable [*Business term*] ... BP
Bills Payable [*Business term*] ... BSP
Bills Receivable [*Business term*] ... BR
Bills Receivable [*Business term*] (ODBW) ... b rec
Bills Receivable (SAUS) ... BRec
Bills Recoverable [*Business term*] (ADA) ... BREC
Billund [*Denmark*] [*Airport symbol*] (OAG) ... BLL
Billund [*Denmark*] [*ICAO location identifier*] (ICLI) ... EKBI
Billy Barty Foundation (EA) ... BBF
Billy Barty Foundation for Little People (EA) ... BBFLP
Billy Blanton Fan Club (EA) ... BBFC
Billy Blanton Fan Club International (EA) ... BBFCI
Billy Cate Fan Club (EA) ... BCFC
Billy "Crash" Craddock Fan Club (EA) ... BCCFC
Billy Graham Evangelistic Association (EA) ... BGEA
Billy Troy Fan Club [*Defunct*] (EA) ... BTFC
Bilma [*Niger*] [*ICAO location identifier*] (ICLI) ... DRRI
Biloela [*Australia*] [*Airport symbol*] ... THG
Biloxi [*Diocesan abbreviation*] [*Mississippi*] (TOCD) ... BLX
Biloxi, MS [*Location identifier*] [*FAA*] (FAAL) ... BIX
Biloxi, MS [*Location identifier*] [*FAA*] (FAAL) ... EKE
Biloxi, MS [*Location identifier*] [*FAA*] (FAAL) ... OLQ
Biloxi, MS [*Television station call letters*] ... WLOX
Biloxi, MS [*FM radio station call letters*] ... WMAH
Biloxi, MS [*Television station call letters*] ... WMAH-TV
Biloxi, MS [*FM radio station call letters*] ... WMJY
Biloxi, MS [*AM radio station call letters*] ... WVMI
Biloxi, MS [*AM radio station call letters*] ... WXBD
Biloxi Public Library, Biloxi, MS [*Library symbol*] [*Library of Congress*] (LCLS) ... MsB
Biloxi/Keesler Air Force Base [*Mississippi*] [*ICAO location identifier*] (ICLI) ... KBIX
Bilspedition Transport & Logistics (SAUS) ... BTL
Biltine [*Chad*] [*ICAO location identifier*] (ICLI) ... FTTE
Biltmore Forest, NC [*FM radio station call letters*] ... WZLS
Biltmore Forest, NC [*FM radio station call letters*] (BROA) ... WZRQ-FM
Biltrite Nightingale, Inc. [*Toronto Stock Exchange symbol*] ... BLT
Bima [*Indonesia*] [*Airport symbol*] (OAG) ... BMU
Bima/Palibelo [*Indonesia*] [*ICAO location identifier*] (ICLI) ... WRRB
Bimbereke [*Benin*] [*ICAO location identifier*] (ICLI) ... DBBR
Bimetal Heat Sensor [*Automotive engineering*] ... BHS
Bimetal Steel-Aluminum (OA) ... BSA
Bimetal Turbine Wheel ... BTW
Bimetal Vacuum Switching Valve [*Automotive engineering*] ... BVSV
Bimetallic ... BMTLC
Bimetallic (SAUS) ... Bmtlc
Bimini [*Bahamas*] [*Airport symbol*] (OAG) ... BIM
Bimini-North [*Bahamas*] [*Airport symbol*] (OAG) ... NSB
B-Iminodiproprionitrile (SAUS) ... IDPN
Bimodal Filter (PDAA) ... BMF
Bi-modal Transit Vehicle (SAUS) ... BTV
Bimodular [*Journalism*] (WDMC) ... bimo
Bimolecular Lipid Membrane ... BLM
Bimolecular Lipid Membranes (SAUS) ... BLMs
Bimolecular Liquid Membrane [*Biochemistry*] (DAVI) ... BLM
Bi-Monthly ... b
Bimonthly ... BI-M
bi-monthly (SAUS) ... bi-m
Bimonthly ... BM
Bi-Monthly Law Review. University of Detroit [*A publication*] (DLA) ... Bi-Mo L Rev
Bimonthly Progress Report ... BMPR
Bimonthly Progress Report ... BPR
Bi-monthly Research Notes (SAUS) ... Bi-mon Res Notes
Bimotor (SAUS) ... Bimot
Bin Card (SAUS) ... BC
Bin Data Cell (SAUS) ... BDC
Binary (BUR) ... B
Binary (SAUS) ... Base 2
Binary (AFM) ... BIN
Binary (SAUS) ... Bnry
Binary 8 Zero Suppression [*Computer science*] (VERA) ... B8ZS
Binary 8-Zero Substitution (SAUS) ... B8ZS
Binary Adaptation Kit [*Computer science*] (PCM) ... BAK
Binary Add [*Computer science*] ... BA
Binary Addition (SAUS) ... BA
Binary Alloy Solidification Experiment (SAUS) ... BASE
Binary and Zero Substitution (SAUS) ... B&ZS
Binary Angular Measurement [*Military*] (CAAL) ... BAM
Binary Asymmetric Channel ... BAC
Binary Asymmetric Dependent Channel ... BADC
Binary Asymmetric Independent Channel ... BAIC
Binary Automatic Computer [*Eckert-Maudely Computer Corp.*] ... BINAC
Binary Automatic Data Annotation System ... BADAS
Binary Base (SAUS) ... BB

Binary BIT [*Binary Digit*] Mapped [*Computer science*]	BBM
Binary Block Coding (SAUS)	BBC
Binary Block Encoding (SAUS)	BBE
Binary Boolean Operation (SAUS)	BBO
Binary Card (SAUS)	BC
Binary Cell (SAUS)	BC
Binary Cell (SAUS)	Bin Cl
Binary Channel (SAUS)	BC
Binary Character (SAUS)	BC
Binary Chemical Warhead (SAUS)	BCW
Binary Choice Model (SAUS)	BCM
Binary Code	BC
Binary Code (SAUS)	BINCODE
Binary Code Box	BCB
Binary Code Conversion (SAUS)	BCC
Binary Code Memory (SAUS)	BCM
Binary Code Procedural Language [*Computer science*]	BCPL
Binary Code Word (SAUS)	BCW
Binary Code Word Length (SAUS)	BCWL
Binary Coded Character (SAUS)	BCC
Binary Coded Data (SAUS)	BCD
Binary Coded Decimal (NITA)	BCD
Binary Coded Decimal Code (SAUS)	BCD Code
Binary Coded Decimal Digit (IAA)	BCDD
Binary Coded Decimal Interchange Code (SAUS)	BEKBC DIC
Binary Coded Decimal Notation (SAUS)	BCD Notation
Binary Coded Decimal Number (SAUS)	BCD Number
Binary Coded Decimal System (SAUS)	BCD System
Binary Coded Decimal System (SAUS)	Bin Cde Dec S
Binary Coded Decimal Translation (SAUS)	BCD Translation
Binary Coded Decimal/Quarternary (SAUS)	BCD/Q
Binary Coded Digit (SAUS)	BCD
Binary Coded Frequency Shift Keying (SAUS)	BCFSK
Binary Coded Matrix [*Telecommunications*] (TEL)	BCM
Binary Coded Notation (SAUS)	BCN
Binary Coded Number (SAUS)	BCN
Binary Coded Number System (SAUS)	BCN System
Binary Coded Range Time Signal (SAUS)	BCRTS
Binary Coded Tape (SAUS)	BCT
Binary Coding (SAUS)	BC
Binary Colloidal Alloy Tests (SAUS)	BCAT
Binary Command (SAUS)	BC
Binary Communications Protocol (VERA)	BCP
Binary Communications: Synchronous [*Computer science*] (NITA)	BCS
Binary Compatibility Layer [*Computer science*] (PCM)	BCL
Binary Compatibility Specification [*Computer science*] (PCM)	BCS
Binary Compatibility Standard (SAUS)	BCS
Binary Computer-Generated Hologram (SAUS)	BCGH
Binary Constitution Information Service (MCD)	BCIS
Binary Control Protocol (VERA)	BCP
Binary Conversion (SAUS)	BC
Binary Conversion Matrix (SAUS)	BCM
Binary Convolution Code (SAUS)	BCC
Binary Convolutional Self-Orthogonal Code [*Computer science*] (PDAA)	BCSOC
Binary Counting Unit (IEEE)	BCU
Binary Cycle High-Temperature Gas-Cooled Reactor [*Nuclear energy*] (NUCP)	BI-HTGR
Binary Data Word (SAUS)	BDW
Binary Decimal Converter (SAUS)	BDC
Binary Decimal Counter [*Computer science*]	BDC
Binary Decision Diagram (RALS)	BDD
Binary Deck-to-Tape [*Computer science*]	BDT
Binary Decode Scaler [*Computer science*]	BDS
Binary Decoder [*Computer science*]	BD
Binary Delta Modulation	BDM
Binary Differential Counter (SAUS)	BDC
Binary Differential Phase-Shift Keying [*Telecommunications*] (TEL)	BDPSK
Binary Digit [*Computer science*] (MCD)	BD
Binary Digit (IAA)	BIGIT
Binary Digit (SAUS)	Bigit
Binary Digit (SAUS)	Bin Dig
Binary Digit (SAUS)	Binit
Binary Digit [*Computer science*]	BIT
Binary Digit (IDOE)	bit
Binary Digit Adder (SAUS)	BDA
Binary Digit Eight	byte
Binary Digit System (SAUS)	BDS
Binary Digital Data [*Computer science*]	BDD
Binary Digital Multiplier [*Computer science*]	BDM
Binary Digits (SAUS)	BITS
Binary Digits per Second [*Computer science*] (HGAA)	BIT/SEC
Binary Discrete (MCD)	BD
Binary Discrete Input (SAUS)	BDI
Binary Discriminant Analysis [*Statistics*]	BDA
Binary Display (SAUS)	BD
Binary Distribution Format (SAUS)	BDF
Binary Divide	BD
Binary Divide (MSA)	BDV
Binary Dump Routine	BDR
Binary Editor And Viewer	BEAV
Binary Electromagnetic Signal Signature	BESS
Binary Electronics Sequence Computer (BARN)	BESC
Binary Element String (SAUS)	BYTE
Binary Elementary Unit (SAUS)	BEU
Binary Encoded Quaternary (MCD)	BEQ
Binary Encoded Ternary (MCD)	BET
Binary Encounter Approximation [*Nuclear physics*]	BEA
Binary Entity-Relationship Model [*Computer science*] (HGAA)	BERM
Binary Envelope Locked Loop (MCD)	BELL
Binary Error Erasure Channel (IEEE)	BEEC
Binary Error Exchange Rate (SAUS)	BEER
Binary Exponential Backoff [*Telecommunications*] (OSI)	BEB
Binary Fault Analysis Program [*Computer science*] (MHDB)	BFAP
Binary Fault Isolation Chart [*Computer science*] (MHDB)	BFIC
Binary File Descriptor [*Unix*] (VERA)	BFD
Binary File Descriptors [*Computer science*] (IGQR)	BFD
Binary File Format (SAUS)	BFF
Binary File Transfer (CDE)	BFT
Binary Floating Point Digital Differential Analyzer (SAUS)	BFPDDA
Binary Floating Point Resistor [*Computer science*] (MHDB)	BFPR
Binary Fourier Representation (PDAA)	BIFORE
Binary Frequency Generator (IEEE)	BFG
Binary Frequency Shift Keying (CCCA)	BFSK
Binary Function (SAUS)	BF
Binary Group Code (SAUO)	BGC
Binary Hexadecimal (SAUS)	BINHEX
Binary Homing Device	BHD
Binary Image Processor [*Computer science*]	BIP
Binary Independence Retrieval (SAUS)	BIR
Binary Information (SAUS)	BI
Binary Information Exchange	BIX
Binary Information File [*Computer science*]	BIF
Binary Information Signal (SAUS)	BIS
Binary Information Transfer System (IAA)	BITS
Binary information with a Residue Check Digest (SAUS)	BRCD
Binary Input - Binary Output Machine (IAA)	BIBOM
Binary Input Signal (SAUS)	BIS
Binary Input-Binary Output Moore Machine (SAUS)	BIBOMM
Binary Input-Output Fuzzy Adaptive Memory (IDAI)	BIOFAM
Binary Intensity Mask (AAEL)	BIM
Binary Interchange File Format (CDE)	BIFF
Binary Intersystem Transmission Standard	BITS
Binary Item (SAUS)	BI
Binary Large Object [*Computer science*]	BLOB
Binary Light Beam Deflector	BLBD
Binary Light Switch (SAUS)	BLS
Binary Line Generalization (GEOI)	BLG
Binary Load Dump [*Computer science*] (MHDI)	BLD
Binary Load Generation (SAUS)	BILGE
Binary Load/Dump (SAUS)	BLD
Binary Logarithmic Arbitration Method (SAUS)	BLAM
Binary Logic Element [*Computer science*] (BUR)	BLE
Binary Logical Association	BLA
Binary Magnetic Core	BMC
Binary Memory Cell (SAUS)	BMC
Binary Memory Element (SAUS)	BME
Binary Metal and Metalloid Constitution Data Center [*Illinois Institute of Technology*]	BMMCDC
Binary Mobile Phase [*Chromatography*]	BMP
Binary Multiplication (SAUS)	BM
Binary Multiply	BM
Binary Munitions	BIN MUN
Binary Non-Consecutive Ones (CCCA)	BNO
Binary Northrop Automatic Computer [*Computer science*] (HGAA)	BINAC
Binary Notation (SAUS)	BN
Binary Number [*Computer science*]	BN
Binary Number System (SAUS)	Bin No Sys
Binary Number System [*Computer science*]	BNS
Binary Object Storage System (AAEL)	BOSS
Binary One-Address Computer (SAUS)	B1AC
Binary One-Address System (SAUS)	B1AS
Binary Operation (SAUS)	BO
Binary Order of Magnitude [*Computer science*]	BOM
Binary Output	BO
Binary Output Program	BOP
Binary Oxide Film [*Memory*]	BOF
Binary Packing Problem (SAUS)	BPP
Binary Pattern Detector	BIPAD
Binary Pattern Laser Extraction (SAUS)	BIPLEX
Binary Pattern Logic Extraction (SAUS)	BIPLEX
Binary Phase Code (ACAE)	BPC
Binary Phase Shifting Key [*Computer science*] (ACRL)	BPSK
Binary Phase-Only Filter [*Optics*]	BPOF
Binary Phase-Shift Keying [*Computer science*] (IEEE)	BPSK
Binary Place (SAUS)	BP
Binary Point (SAUS)	Bin Pt
Binary Point (SAUS)	BP
Binary Program Loader	BPL
Binary Program Space [*Computer science*]	BPS
Binary Punch (SAUS)	BP
Binary Punched Card (SAUS)	BPC
Binary Rate Divider	BRD
Binary Rate Multiplier (IAA)	BRM
Binary Read [*Computer science*] (HGAA)	BRD
Binary Reflected Gray Code	BRGC
Binary Relationship Model [*Computer science*] (NITA)	BRM
Binary Relocatable Loader (SAUS)	BRL
Binary Ring Sequence	BRS
Binary Run Tape [*Computer science*] (BUR)	BRT
Binary Scale (AAG)	BS

Binary Search (SAUS) ... BS
Binary Search Tree (IAA) ... BST
Binary Sequential Access Method (SAUS) ... BSAM
Binary Shift Register (SAUS) ... BSR
Binary Shift/Substract Euclidean Algorithm (SAUS) ... BSSE Algorithm
Binary Signal (SAUS) ... BS
Binary Space Partition [*Computer science*] (PCM) ... BSP
Binary Space Partitioning (SAUS) ... BSP
Binary Store Circuit (SAUS) ... BSC
Binary Store Element (SAUS) ... BSE
Binary Subtract ... BS
Binary Switching Algebra (SAUS) ... BSA
Binary Symbol (SAUS) ... BS
Binary Symmetric Channel [*Computer science*] ... BSC
Binary Symmetric Dependent Channel [*Computer science*] ... BSDC
Binary Symmetric Erasure Channel (CCCA) ... BSEC
Binary Symmetric Independent Channel [*Computer science*] ... BSIC
Binary Synchronous (SAUS) ... BISYNC
Binary Synchronous [*Telecommunications*] (NITA) ... BSC
Binary Synchronous (SAUS) ... BSY
Binary Synchronous Adapter (SAUS) ... BSA
Binary Synchronous Coded [*Computer science*] (VERA) ... BSC
Binary Synchronous Communication (SAUS) ... BISYNC
Binary Synchronous Communication [*IBM Corp.*] [*Computer science*] ... BSC
Binary Synchronous Communication (SAUS) ... BSCom
Binary Synchronous Communication Process (SAUS) ... BSC Process
Binary Synchronous Communication System (MHDB) ... BSCS
Binary Synchronous Communications (SAUS) ... BCS
Binary Synchronous Communications [*Protocol*] [*IBM Co.*] (ACRL) ... BSC
Binary Synchronous Communications Adapter [*Computer science*] ... BSCA
Binary Synchronous Communications Controller [*Computer science*] (MHDI) ... BSCC
Binary Synchronous Communications Macro ... BSCM
Binary Synchronous Communications Module [*Computer science*] (VERA) ... BSCM
Binary Synchronous Communications protocol [*IBM Co.*] (ACRL) ... BISYNC
Binary Synchronous Communications/Start-Stop ... BSC/SS
Binary Synchronous Computer (SAUS) ... BISYNC
Binary Synchronous Control ... BSC
Binary Synchronous Transmission [*or Communication*] [*Computer science*] ... BISYNC
Binary Synchronous Transmission (SAUS) ... BST
Binary System (SAUS) ... BS
Binary Table [*Computer science*] (IGQR) ... byte
Binary Term [*Computer science*] ... byte
Binary Time Code (MCD) ... BTC
Binary to ASCII (SAUS) ... BTOA
Binary to Decimal [*Computer science*] ... B/D
Binary to Decimal (SAUS) ... BIDEC
Binary to Decimal [*Computer science*] (BUR) ... BTD
Binary to Hexadecimal (SAUS) ... B2X
Binary to Hexadecimal (SAUS) ... B-H
Binary to Hexadecimal (BUR) ... BH
Binary to Octal [*Computer science*] (BUR) ... BO
Binary to Octal (SAUS) ... B-O
Binary to Seven Segment [*Computer science*] ... BINSS
Binary to Text Encoding [*Computer science*] ... UUEncode
Binary Translation (SAUS) ... BT
Binary Transversal Filter (IAA) ... BTF
Binary Trigger (SAUS) ... Bin Tr
Binary Trigger (SAUS) ... BT
Binary Twos Complement (SAUS) ... BTC
Binary Universal for Representation [*Computer science*] ... BUFR
Binary Utility System (SAUS) ... BUS
Binary Value (SAUS) ... BV
Binary Voltage Weigher ... BVW
Binary Workstation [*Computer science*] ... BW
Binary-Analog Conversion [*Computer science*] (DIT) ... BAC
Binary-Coded Decimal Counter ... BCDC
Binary-Coded Decimal Interchange Code (IEEE) ... BCDIC
Binary-Coded Decimal Interchange Code ... BDIC
Binary-Coded Decimal Nonadjacent Form [*Computer science*] (MHDI) ... BCDNAF
Binary-Coded Decimal/Binary (DEN) ... BCD/B
Binary-Coded Hexadecimal (MCD) ... BCH
Binary-Coded Hollerith ... BCH
Binary-Coded Information ... BCI
Binary-Coded Octal [*Computer science*] ... BCO
Binary-Coded Range Time (MUGU) ... BCRT
Binary-Element Error Ratio (IAA) ... BEER
Binary-Erasure Channel (IAA) ... BEC
Binary-File Transfer - Non-Standard Facilities Frame [*Microsoft Corp.*] (PCM) ... BFT-NSF
Binary-Floating-Decimal [*Computer science*] ... BFD
Binary-to-Decimal Conversion (SAUS) ... BDC
Binary-to-Decimal Converter (SAUS) ... BDC
Binary-to-Decimal Converter [*Computer science*] ... BIDEC
Binary-to-Decimal Counter (SAUS) ... BDC
Binary-to-Decimal Decoder [*Computer science*] ... BDD
Binary-to-Decimal Transmitter [*Computer science*] (NOAA) ... BDT
Binary-to-Digital Decoder (SAUS) ... BDD
Binasal Pharyngeal Airway [*Anatomy*] (MAE) ... BNPA
Binational Agricultural Research and Development Foundation (SAUO) ... BARD
Binational Agricultural Research and Development Fund [*US-Israeli*] [*Research center*] (IRC) ... BARD
Binational Industrial Research and Development Foundation (SAUO) ... BIRD
Binational Science Foundation [*U.S.-Israel*] [*Research center*] ... BSF
Binaural Alternate Loudness Balance Test (MAE) ... BALB
Binaural Analysis System [*Noise testing*] [*Automotive engineering*] ... BAS
Binaural Hearing Impairment ... BHI
Binaural Intensity Effect ... BIE
Binaural Masking Level Difference (PDAA) ... BMLD
Binaural Phase Effect ... BPE
Binbrook [*British*] [*ICAO location identifier*] (ICLI) ... EGXB
Binder (MSA) ... BDR
Binder [*MARC relator code*] [*Library of Congress*] (LCCP) ... bnd
Binder ... BNDR
Binder (VRA) ... bndr
Binder ... BR
Binder Aviatik, Scheibe-Bruns, Schleicher-Bruns [*Germany*] [*ICAO aircraft manufacturer identifier*] (ICAO) ... BS
Binder Control Subsystem ... BINCOS
Binder Twine Association (SAUO) ... BTA
Binders' Guild (EA) ... BG
Bindery ... BDRY
Binding (ADWA) ... bdg
Binding (MSA) ... BDG
Binding ... BDNG
Binding (ROG) ... BIND
Binding (SAUS) ... Bind
Binding Capacity ... BC
Binding Chain [*Toxin*] ... B
Binding Designer [*MARC relator code*] [*Library of Congress*] (LCCP) ... bdd
Binding Edge (ADA) ... BE
Binding Energy ... BE
Binding Energy per Atom (IAA) ... BEPA
Binding Energy per Particle (IAA) ... BEPP
Binding Head ... BDGH
Binding Head (IAA) ... BDH
Binding Head (SAUS) ... Bind H
Binding Head Steel (IAA) ... BHS
Binding Industries of America (EA) ... BIA
Binding Margin [*Bookbinding*] (ADA) ... BM
Binding Post (KSC) ... BP
Binding Post Chamber [*Telecommunications*] (TEL) ... BPC
Binding Protein [*Biochemistry*] ... BP
Binding Unit (IEEE) ... BU
Binding/No Date [*Publishing*] (DGA) ... B/ND
Bindings [*Publishing*] ... BDS
Bindja [*Zaire*] [*ICAO location identifier*] (ICLI) ... FZBQ
Bindley Western Industries [*NYSE symbol*] (SAG) ... BDY
Bindley Western Industries [*Associated Press*] (SAG) ... Bindly
Bindley Western Industries, Inc. (EFIS) ... BW
Bindura [*Zimbabwe*] [*ICAO location identifier*] (ICLI) ... FVBD
Binet-Simon [*Test*] [*Psychology*] (DAVI) ... BS
Bing Crosby Historical Society (EA) ... BCHS
Bing Crosby Productions ... BCP
Binge Eating [*Medicine*] (MELL) ... BE
Binge Eating Disorder ... BED
Binge-and-Purge Syndrome [*Medicine*] (MELL) ... BPS
Bingham and Colvin on Rents [*A publication*] (DLA) ... Bing & Colv Rents
Bingham body (SAUS) ... B-body
Bingham. Infancy and Coveture [*1826*] [*A publication*] (DLA) ... Bing Inf
Bingham. Judgments and Executions [*1815*] [*A publication*] (DLA) ... Bing Ex
Bingham. Judgments and Executions [*1815*] [*A publication*] (DLA) ... Bing Judg
Bingham. Landlord and Tenant [*1820*] [*A publication*] (DLA) ... Bing L & T
Bingham Memorial Hospital, Medical Library, Blackfoot, ID [*Library symbol*] [*Library of Congress*] (LCLS) ... IdBfBH
Bingham. New Cases, English Common Pleas [*131-133 English Reprint*] [*A publication*] (DLA) ... Bing NC
Bingham. New Cases, English Common Pleas [*131-133 English Reprint*] [*A publication*] (DLA) ... Bing N Cas
Bingham. New Cases, English Common Pleas [*131-133 English Reprint*] [*A publication*] (DLA) ... Bing NC (Eng)
Bingham. New Cases, English Common Pleas [*A publication*] (DLA) ... BNC
Bingham Oceanographic Collection ... BOC
Bingham Oceanographic Laboratory (NOAA) ... BOL
Bingham on the Law of Real Property [*A publication*] (DLA) ... Bing RP
Bingham on the Laws of Descent [*A publication*] (DLA) ... Bing Des
Bingham Township Library, Suttons Bay, MI [*Library symbol*] [*Library of Congress*] (LCLS) ... MiSb
Bingham's Actions and Defences in Real Property [*A publication*] (DLA) ... Bing Act & Def
Bingham's English Common Pleas Reports [*130-131 English Reprint*] [*A publication*] (DLA) ... Bing
Bingham's English Common Pleas Reports [*130-131 English Reprint*] [*A publication*] (DLA) ... Bing (Eng)
Bingham's Executory Contracts, Etc. [*A publication*] (DLA) ... Bing Ex Cont
Binghamton [*New York*] [*Airport symbol*] (OAG) ... BGM
Binghamton [*New York*] [*Seismograph station code, US Geological Survey*] (SEIS) ... BNY
Binghamton, NY [*Location identifier*] [*FAA*] (FAAL) ... AAJ
Binghamton, NY [*Location identifier*] [*FAA*] (FAAL) ... IMZ
Binghamton, NY [*FM radio station call letters*] ... WAAL
Binghamton, NY [*Television station call letters*] ... WBNG
Binghamton, NY [*FM radio station call letters*] ... WHRW
Binghamton, NY [*FM radio station call letters*] ... WHWK
Binghamton, NY [*Television station call letters*] ... WICZ
Binghamton, NY [*AM radio station call letters*] ... WINR
Binghamton, NY [*Television station call letters*] (BROA) ... WIVT
Binghamton, NY [*FM radio station call letters*] ... WJIK

Binghamton, NY [*AM radio station call letters*] ... WKOP
Binghamton, NY [*Television station call letters*] ... WMGC
Binghamton, NY [*AM radio station call letters*] ... WNBF
Binghamton, NY [*FM radio station call letters*] ... WSKG
Binghamton, NY [*Television station call letters*] ... WSKG-TV
Binghamton, NY [*FM radio station call letters*] ... WSQX
Binghamton Public Library (SAUS) ... BPL
Binghamton Public Library, Binghamton, NY [*Library symbol*] [*Library of Congress*] (LCLS) ... NBi
Bingo ... BNG
Bingo Clubs and Halls [*Public-performance tariff class*] [*British*] ... BO
Bingold's Myorenal [*Syndrome*] [*Medicine*] (DB) ... BM
Bing's Friends and Collectors Society (EA) ... BFCS
Bin-Hexed File (SAUS) ... HQX
Biniguni [*Papua New Guinea*] [*Airport symbol*] (OAG) ... XBN
Binks Manufacturing Co. [*AMEX symbol*] (SPSG) ... BIN
Binks Manufacturing Co. [*Associated Press*] (SAG) ... BinkMf
Binks Mfg. [*AMEX symbol*] (TTSB) ... BIN
Binmore's Index-Digest of Michigan Reports [*A publication*] (DLA) ... Bin Dig
Binmore's Index-Digest of Michigan Reports [*A publication*] (DLA) ... Binm Ind
Binnacle (MSA) ... BNCL
Binney's Pennsylvania Reports [*1799-1814*] [*A publication*] (DLA) ... Bin
Binney's Pennsylvania Reports [*1799-1814*] [*A publication*] (DLA) ... Binn (PA)
Binney's Pennsylvania Supreme Court Reports [*1799-1814*] [*A publication*] (DLA) ... Binn
Binns' Pennsylvania Justice [*A publication*] (DLA) ... Binn Jus
Binns' Pennsylvania Justice [*A publication*] (DLA) ... Binns' Just
Binocular (MSA) ... BNCLR
Binocular Deprivation [*Optics*] ... BD
Binocular Earth Sensor (MCD) ... BES
Binocular Omni-Orientation (or Oriented) Monitor (SAUS) ... BOOM
Binocular Single Vision [*Ophthalmology*] ... BSV
Binocular Visual Efficiency ... BVE
Binoculars [*Slang*] [*British*] (DSUE) ... BINOCS
Binoculars (VNW) ... BINO(S)
Binolar Disorder [*Medicine*] (MELL) ... BD
Binomial Expansion [*Mathematics*] ... BINOMEXP
Binomial Probability Distributions (MCD) ... BINDIS
Binomial Proportion Test (MCD) ... BITEST
Bin-Tainer [*Shipping*] (DCTA) ... B
Binter Canarais [*Spain*] [*ICAO designator*] (FAAC) ... IBB
Binter-Mediterraneo [*Spain*] [*ICAO designator*] (FAAC) ... BIM
Bintulu [*Malaysia*] [*Airport symbol*] (OAG) ... BTU
Bintulu [*Malaysia*] [*ICAO location identifier*] (ICLI) ... WBGB
Bintuni [*Indonesia*] [*Airport symbol*] (OAG) ... NTI
Binural Intensity Effect (SAUS) ... BIE
Binza [*Leopoldville*] [*Zaire*] [*Seismograph station code, US Geological Survey*] (SEIS) ... BIN
Bio Imaging Technol Wrrt'G' [*NASDAQ symbol*] (TTSB) ... BITIW
Bio Imaging Technologies Inc. [*NASDAQ symbol*] (TTSB) ... BITI
Bio Response (SAUS) ... BIORESP
Bio Technica Intl. [*NASDAQ symbol*] (TTSB) ... BIOT
Bio Technology Gen Wrrt'A' [*NASDAQ symbol*] (TTSB) ... BTGCL
Bio Telemetry System (SAUS) ... BTS
Bioaccumulation Factor [*Nuclear energy*] (NRCH) ... BAF
Bio-Activated Mineral Iotion (SAUS) ... BAM
Bioactive ... B
bioactive (SAUS) ... bioact
Bioactive Aortic Substance [*Biochemistry*] ... BAS
bioactivity (SAUS) ... bioact
Bioaerosol Flux (SAUS) ... BioFlux
Bioanalytical Systems ... BAS
Bio-Aqua Systems 'A' [*AMEX symbol*] (SG) ... SEA
Bioartificial Liver ... BAL
Bioassay Program ... BP
Bioassay Reagent ... BR
Bioassay Studies (SAUS) ... BIOSTU
Bioassay Tank [*Spacecraft*] [*NASA*] ... BAT
Bioastronautic Orbital (or Orbiting) Space System (SAUS) ... BOSS
Bioastronautic Orbiting Space System (SAUO) ... BOSS
Bioastronautics Laboratory Research Tool (IEEE) ... BIOALRT
Bioastronautics Operational Support Unit (MCD) ... BOSU
Bioastronautics Orbital Space Program [*Air Force*] ... BOSP
Bio-Automated Roving Target [*Gun-like toy*] ... BART
Bioavailability/Bioequivalence [*Drug evaluation*] ... BA/BE
Bioavailable Testosterone Concentration [*Medicine*] (MELL) ... BTC
Biobreeding/Worcester [*Rat variety*] ... BB/W
BioChem Pharma [*NASDAQ symbol*] (SG) ... BCHE
BioChem Pharma [*NASDAQ symbol*] (TTSB) ... BCHXF
Biochem Pharma, Inc. [*NASDAQ symbol*] (SAG) ... BCHX
Biochem Pharma, Inc. [*Associated Press*] (SAG) ... BioPhar
Biochemical [*or Biochemistry*] ... BIOCHEM
biochemical (SAUS) ... biochem
Biochemical and Biophysical Research Communications (journ.) (SAUS) ... Biochem Biophys Res Commun
Biochemical Detector (SAUS) ... BCD
Biochemical Genetics (journ.) (SAUS) ... Biochem Genet
Biochemical Journal (SAUS) ... Biochem J
Biochemical Journal (SAUS) ... Biochem Jour
Biochemical Journal (SAUO) ... BJ
Biochemical Medicine (journ.) (SAUS) ... Biochem Med
Biochemical Modeling [*Computer science*] ... BIOMOD
Biochemical Oxygen Demand ... BOD
Biochemical Oxygen Demand as Measured in the Standard 5-Day Test (EEVL) ... BOD5
Biochemical Oxygen Demand Over Five Days [*Biological*] (GNE) ... BOD5
Biochemical Pathways of Artificial Radionuclides (SAUS) ... RADPATH
Biochemical Pharmacology [*A publication*] (MEC) ... Biochem Pharmacol
Biochemical Pharmacology (journ.) (SAUS) ... Biochem Pharmacol
Biochemical Process Industry ... BPI
Biochemical Profile (DAVI) ... BCP
Biochemical Research Foundation (SAUO) ... BIRF
Biochemical Research Foundation, Franklin Institute, Newark, DE [*Closed*] [*Library symbol*] [*Library of Congress*] (LCLS) ... PPF-B
Biochemical Research Foundation of the Franklin Insitute (SAUO) ... BRFFI
Biochemical Research Foundation of the Franklin Institute (SAUS) ... BRFFI
Biochemical Society [*London, England*] (EAIO) ... BS
Biochemical Society of London (SAUO) ... BSL
Biochemical Society Symposia (SAUO) ... Biochem Soc Symp
Biochemical Society Transactions (SAUO) ... Biochem Soc Trans
Biochemical Systems Theory ... BST
Biochemical Test Monitor ... BTM
Biochemische Zeitschrift [*A publication*] (MEC) ... Biochem Z
biochemist (SAUS) ... biochem
Biochemistry ... BIOCHEM
Biochemistry (DD) ... Biochem
Biochemistry And Molecular Biology International (SAUO) ... BAMBI
Biochimica et Biophysica Acta [*A publication*] (MEC) ... Biochim Biophysic Acta
Biochronometry (SAUS) ... Biochron
biocidal (SAUS) ... biocid
Biocidal Products Directive [*European Union*] ... BPD
biocide (SAUS) ... biocid
Biocide Injection System (MCD) ... BIS
Biocircuits Corp. [*NASDAQ symbol*] (SAG) ... BIOC
Biocircuits Corp. [*Associated Press*] (SAG) ... Biocirc
Bioclimatic Prediction and Modelling System (SAUS) ... BIOCLIM
Biocompatible Dialysis [*Medicine*] (MELL) ... BCDM
Biocompatible Orthopedic Polymer [*Medicine*] ... BOP
Biocomputer Statistics (SAUS) ... BCS
Bioconcentration Factor [*of chemicals by living organisms*] ... BCF
Bioconcentration Potential (ADWA) ... BCP
Biocontamination (SAUS) ... Biocon
Biocontrol Science and Technology [*A publication*] ... BST
Biocontrol Technology, Inc. [*NASDAQ symbol*] (NQ) ... BICO
Biocontrol Technology, Inc. [*Associated Press*] (SAG) ... Bioctrl
Bio-Conversion (SAUS) ... BC
Biocraft Laboratories, Inc. [*NYSE symbol*] (SPSG) ... BCL
Biocraft Laboratories, Inc. [*Associated Press*] (SAG) ... Biocft
Biocryst Pharmaceuticals, Inc. [*NASDAQ symbol*] (SAG) ... BCRX
Biocryst Pharmaceuticals, Inc. [*Associated Press*] (SAG) ... Biocryst
BioCryst Pharm'l [*NASDAQ symbol*] (TTSB) ... BCRX
Biocular and Indirect View Display (ACAE) ... BIVD
Biocular Display Drivers Viewer (SAUS) ... BDDV
Biocular Sensor and Symbology (ACAE) ... BOSS
biocybernetics (SAUS) ... biocyb
biodegradability (SAUS) ... biodeg
Bio-Degradable Plastics, Inc. ... BPI
Biodegradable Volatile Solids [*Analytical chemistry*] ... BVS
biodegradation (SAUS) ... biodeg
Biodegradation, Hydrolysis and Photolysis ... BHP
Biodegradation of Environmental Chemicals Modeled with Aquatic, Relative-Rate Coefficients (AUEG) ... BENCHMARC
Biodegrade [*or Biodegradable*] (WDAA) ... BIODEG
biodegrade (SAUS) ... biodeg
biodegraders (SAUS) ... biodeg
biodegrading (SAUS) ... biodeg
Bio-Dental Technologies [*NASDAQ symbol*] (TTSB) ... BDTC
BioDental Technologies Corp. [*NASDAQ symbol*] (SAG) ... BDTC
BioDental Technologies Corp. [*Associated Press*] (SAG) ... BioDent
biodestructible (SAUS) ... biodes
biodeterioration (SAUS) ... biodet
Biodeterioration Information Centre [*British*] ... BIC
Biodeterioration Society (SAUS) ... TBS
Biodiversity Action Network (SAUO) ... BIONET
Biodiversity Action Plan (SAUS) ... BAP
Biodiversity Analysis for Africa (SAUS) ... BAA
Biodiversity and Biological Collections Web Server (SAUS) ... BBCWS
Biodiversity and Conservation (SAUS) ... Biodivers Conserv
Biodiversity and Ecosystems Network (SAUO) ... BENE
Biodiversity and Fluxes in Glacial Arctic Fjords (SAUS) ... BIODAFF
Biodiversity Conservation Information System (SAUO) ... BCIS
Biodiversity Conservation Network (SAUO) ... BCN
Biodiversity Conservation Network (SAUO) ... BCNet
Biodiversity Data Bank (SAUO) ... BDB
Biodiversity Data Management (SAUS) ... BDM
Biodiversity Information Management System (SAUO) ... BIMS
Biodiversity Information Network (SAUO) ... BIN
Biodiversity Information Network 21 (SAUO) ... BIN 21
Biodiversity Information System (SAUS) ... BIS
Biodiversity Institute [*Center established to inventory wildlife*] (PS) ... INBio
Biodiversity Letters (SAUS) ... Biodivers Lett
Biodiversity Mapping for Protection and Sustainable Use of Natural Resources (GEOI) ... BIOMAPS
Biodiversity Policy Coordination Division (SAUO) ... BPCD
Biodiversity Recovery Unit (SAUS) ... BRU
Biodiversity Unit (SAUS) ... BDU
Bio-Dynamic Agricultural Association [*British*] ... BDAA
Bio-Dynamic Farm and Gardening Association (SAUO) ... BDFGA
Bio-Dynamic Farming and Gardening Association (EA) ... BDFGA
Biodynamic Farming and Gardening Association [*Australia*] ... BFGA

Bio-Dynamics Association Australia (SAUO) .... BDAA
Bio-Dynamics, Inc., BMC Library, Indianapolis, IN [Library symbol] [Library of Congress] (LCLS) .... InlBio
Biodynamics International [NASDAQ symbol] (SAG) .... BDYN
Biodynamics International [Associated Press] (SAG) .... BiodyInt
Biodynamics Intl. [NASDAQ symbol] (TTSB) .... BDYN
Bio-Dyne Corp. [Associated Press] (SAG) .... Bio-Dyn
Bio-Dyne Corp. [NASDAQ symbol] (SPSG) .... BODY
Bioelectric Impedance Analysis (DIPS) .... BIA
Bioelectrical Repair and Growth Society (EA) .... BRAGS
Bioelectrochemical Society (EA) .... BES
Bioelectrochemistry .... BEC
Bio-Electro-Chemistry (SAUS) .... BEC
Bioelectrogenesis (SAUS) .... Bioelectrog
Bio-Electro-Magnetics Institute (EA) .... BEMI
Bioelectromagnetics Society (EA) .... BEMS
Bioelectromagnetics Special Interest Group (EA) .... BEM SIG
Bioelectronics (SAUS) .... Bioelectron
Bio-Energy Council [Defunct] (EA) .... BEC
Bioengineering .... BIOENG
Bioengineering and Research to Aid the Handicapped Program [Washington, DC] [National Science Foundation] (GRD) .... BRAH
Bioenvironmental .... BIOENVMT
Bioenvironmental Engineering Services (SAUO) .... BES
Bio-Environmental Health Center (SAUO) .... BEHC
Bioenvironmentalist (SAUS) .... Bioenv
Bioethic Citation Maintenance System (DMAA) .... BCMS
Bioethics Online [Database] .... BIOETHICSLINE
Bio-Event (SAUS) .... BIE
Bio-Feed Industries Ltd. [Vancouver Stock Exchange symbol] .... BOF
Biofeedback [Medicine] (MELL) .... BF
Biofeedback .... BFB
Biofeedback and Self Regulation (SAUS) .... Biofeedback Self Regul
Bio-Feedback Research Society [Later, BSA] (EA) .... BFRS
Biofeedback Research Society [Later, BSA] (EA) .... BRS
Biofeedback Society of America [Later, AAPB] (EA) .... BSA
Biofeedback Systems Ltd. (SAUS) .... BSL
Bio-Feedback Training (SAUS) .... BFT
Biofeedback Training [Physiology] .... BFT
Bioferm Corp., Research Library, Wasco, CA [Library symbol] [Library of Congress] (LCLS) .... CWasB
Biofield Corp. [Associated Press] (SAG) .... Biofield
Biofield Corp. [NASDAQ symbol] (SAG) .... BZET
Biofilm Electrode .... BFE
Biogas Transfer in Estuaries (SAUS) .... BIOGEST
Biogen, Inc. [NASDAQ symbol] (NQ) .... BGEN
Biogen, Inc. [Associated Press] (SAG) .... Biogen
Biogenic (SAUS) .... BIG
Biogenic Amines [Medicine] (MELL) .... BGA
Biogenic Carbon [Chemistry] .... BC
Biogenic Institutes of America [Later, AHMI] (EA) .... BIA
Biogenic Silica [In water sediments] .... BSI
Bio-Geochemical Cycle (SAUS) .... BGC
Biogeochemical Cycle (SAUS) .... BGC
Biogeochemical Ocean Flux Study [Oceanography] .... BOFS
biogeographer (SAUS) .... biogeog
Bio-geographic Information System (SAUS) .... BIS
biogeography (SAUS) .... biogeog
Biogeography (ADA) .... BIOGEOG
biogeology (SAUS) .... biogeo
Biografias [Database] [Ministerio de Cultura] [Spanish] [Information service or system] (CRD) .... BIOG
Biographer (ROG) .... BIOG
biographer (SAUS) .... biog
Biographical Dictionaries and Related Works [A publication] .... BD
Biographical Dictionaries and Related Works. Supplement [A publication] .... BDS
Biographical Dictionaries Master Index [A publication] .... BDMI
Biographical Dictionary of Australian Librarians [A publication] .... BDAL
Biographical Dictionary of Federal Judiciary [A publication] .... BDFJ
Biographical Index of South Australians [A publication] (APTA) .... BISA
Biographical Information Blank .... BIB
Biographical Inventory Creativity .... BIC
Biographical Inventory for Medicine .... BIM
Biographical Inventory for Students [Psychology] .... BIS
Biographical Memoirs of the National Academy of Science [A publication] (MEC) .... Biog Mem Nat Acad Sci
Biographical Memoirs of the Royal Society [A publication] (MEC) .... Biog Memoirs Roy Soc
Biographically (SAUS) .... Biog
Biographics (AABC) .... BIO
Biography (WDMC) .... bio
Biography (WDAA) .... biog
Biography .... BIOG
Biography (AL) .... Biog
Biography Almanac [Later, Almanac of Famous People] [A publication] .... BA
Biography: An Interdisciplinary Quarterly [A publication] (BRI) .... Biography
Biography and Genealogy Master Index [A publication] .... BGMI
Biography Index .... Biol
Biography Master Index [Gale Research, Inc.] [Information service or system] [A publication] (IID) .... BMI
Bio-Imaging Technologies [NASDAQ symbol] (SAG) .... BITI
Bio-Imaging Technologies, Inc. [Associated Press] (SAG) .... BioIm
Bio-Imaging Technologies, Inc. [Associated Press] (SAG) .... BioImag
Bioimmunoassay [Medicine] (MELL) .... BIA
Bioimpedance Venous Analysis [Biochemistry] (DAVI) .... BVA

Bioindustry Association [Great Britain] .... BIA
BioInformatics Molecular Analysis Section .... BIMAS
Bio-Informatics Molecular Analysis Section (SAUO) .... BIMAS
bioinstrumentation (SAUS) .... bioinstru
Bioinstrumentation Advisory Council [Defunct] .... BIAC
Bioinstrumentation Harness Assembly .... BHA
Bio-Integral Resource Center (EA) .... BIRC
Bioisolator Suit System [NASA] (MCD) .... BISS
Bio-Isolator Suit System (SAUS) .... BISS
Bioject Medical Systems Ltd. [Vancouver Stock Exchange symbol] .... BJM
Bioject Medical Technologies [NASDAQ symbol] (NQ) .... BJCT
Bioject Medical Technologies, Inc. [Associated Press] (SAG) .... Bioject
Bioject Medl Technologies [NASDAQ symbol] (TTSB) .... BJCT
Biola College, La Mirada, CA [OCLC symbol] (OCLC) .... CBC
Biola Library, La Mirada, CA [Library symbol] [Library of Congress] (LCLS) .... CLamB
BIOLASE Technology [NASDAQ symbol] (TTSB) .... BLTI
BioLase Technology, Inc. [Associated Press] (SAG) .... BioLase
BioLase Technology, Inc. [NASDAQ symbol] (SAG) .... BLTI
Biologic False Positive Reaction (DB) .... BFPR
Biologic False Reactor (SAUS) .... BFR
Biologic False-Positive Reactor (MAE) .... BFR
Biologic License Application .... BLA
Biologic Response (DB) .... BR
Biologic Rhythms (MELL) .... BR
Biologic Safety Level .... BSL
Bio-Logic Systems [NASDAQ symbol] (TTSB) .... BLSC
Bio-Logic Systems Corp. [Associated Press] (SAG) .... BioLogic
Bio-Logic Systems Corp. [NASDAQ symbol] (NQ) .... BLSC
Biological (ROG) .... BIOL
Biological (AL) .... Biol
Biological Abstract on Tape (SAUS) .... BAT
Biological Abstracts .... BioAb
Biological Abstracts (journ.) (SAUS) .... BA
Biological Abstracts (journ.) (SAUS) .... Biol Abstr
Biological Abstracts on Tape [Biosciences Information Service] [Information service or system] .... BAT
Biological Abstracts Previews (SAUS) .... BAP
Biological Abstracts' Subjects in Context [A publication] .... BASIC
Biological Abstracts/Reports, Reviews, Meetings (SAUO) .... BA/RRM
Biological Activated Carbon [Water treatment] .... BAC
Biological Activity .... BA
Biological Aerosol Detection [Army] (MCD) .... BAD
Biological Aerosol Test Facility [Army] .... BATF
Biological Agent Casualty Assessment System (MCD) .... BACAS
Biological Agent Decontamination Simulant (MCD) .... BADS
Biological Agent Simulant (MCD) .... BAS
Biological Agricultural Reactor of the Netherlands .... BARN
Biological Analysis Detection Instrumentation and Control .... BADIC
Biological and Agricultural Index .... BioAg
Biological and Agricultural Sciences Information Service [University of Minnesota, St. Paul] [Information service or system] (IID) .... BASIS
Biological and Chemical .... BC
Biological and Chemical Research Institute (SAUO) .... BCRI
Biological and Chemical Warfare (NATG) .... BC
Biological and Chemical Warfare .... BCW
Biological and Chemical Warfare Division [DoD] .... BCWD
Biological & Chemical Weapon Disposal (SAUS) .... BCWD
Biological and Climatic Effects Research .... BACER
Biological and Climatological Effects Research [Environmental science] (COE) .... BACER
Biological and Conservation Data (SAUS) .... BCD
Biological and Electronic (NITA) .... BIONIC
Biological and Environmental Reference Materials .... BERM
Biological and Environmental Research (HGEN) .... BER
Biological and Environmental Research Program [Department of Energy] .... BER
Biological and Social Sciences (SAUO) .... BSS
Biological and Toxin Weapons Convention .... BTWC
Biological Anthropological Section (EA) .... BAS
Biological Anthropological Section (SAUO) .... BIO
Biological Antiseptic Tampon (IIA) .... BAT
Biological Aspects of the Hydrological Cycle (SAUS) .... BAHC
Biological Assessment Laboratory .... BAL
Biological Attack Report (journ.) (SAUS) .... BIOREP
Biological, Behavioral, and Social Sciences [Directorate] .... BBS
Biological Bulletin (SAUS) .... Biol Bull
Biological Chemicals of Concern [Environmental science] .... BCC
Biological Chemistry Hoppe-Seyler (SAUS) .... Biol Chem Hoppe Seyler
Biological Component of the Air Pollution Studies (SAUS) .... BCAPS
Biological Computer Laboratory (SAUO) .... BCL
Biological Conservation (SAUS) .... BC
Biological Conservation (SAUS) .... Biol Conserv
Biological Control Acts (SAUO) .... BCA
Biological Control Agent [Agriculture] .... BCA
Biological Control of Insects Research Laboratory [Department of Agriculture] (GRD) .... BCIRL
Biological Control Products (SAUS) .... BCP
Biological Cosmic Ray Experiment (MCD) .... BIOCORE
Biological Damage Indicator .... BDI
Biological Data Management System (SAUS) .... BIOLOGS
Biological Data System [Environmental Protection Agency] (AEPA) .... BIOS
Biological Defense .... BD
Biological Defense [Military] .... BIODEF
Biological Defense [Military] (AABC) .... BIOLDEF
Biological Defense Research Laboratory .... BDRL

Biological Defense Research Program [*DoD*] .... BDRP
Biological Defense System .... BDS
Biological Detection and Alarm Training Simulant (MCD) .... BDATS
Biological Detection System .... BDS
Biological Diversity Advisory Committee [*Australia*] .... BDAC
Biological Diversity Advisory Committee (SAUO) .... BIDAC
Biological Effect Monitoring [*Toxicology*] .... BEM
Biological Effects [*of Nonionizing*] **Electromagnetic Radiation** (MCD) .... BEER
Biological Effects of Atomic Radiation .... BEAR
Biological Effects of Ionizing Radiation .... BEIR
Biological Effects Program [*IDOE project*] [*Terminated, 1978*] (MSC) .... BEP
Biological Electronics (IEEE) .... BIONICS
Biological Energy Research [*Department of Energy*] .... BER
Biological Engineering (SAUS) .... BE
Biological Engineering (SAUS) .... Bioeng
Biological Engineering Society [*British*] .... BES
Biological Engineering Society (SAUO) .... BES
Biological Environment Monitor (SAUS) .... BEM
Biological Experiment Scientific Satellite (SAUS) .... BESS
Biological Exposure Index .... BEI
Biological Exposure Indices [*Medicine*] (MELL) .... BEI
Biological Exposure Limits (HEAS) .... BELS
Biological False Positive [*Clinical chemistry*] .... BFP
Biological Farmers of Australia .... BFA
Biological Half Life (SAUS) .... BHL
Biological Hazard Potential [*Atomic energy*] .... BHP
Biological Imaging and Observational Mission to Earth (SAUS) .... BIOME
Biological Indicator [*Microbiology*] .... BI
Biological Indicator Evaluator Resistometer (DB) .... BIER
Biological Indicator Unit [*Food testing*] .... BIU
Biological Information Service (SAUO) .... BIS
Biological Information-Processing Organization [*Later, SIGBIO*] .... BIO
Biological Institute of Tropical America (EA) .... BIOTA
Biological Integrated Detection System [*Army*] .... BIDS
Biological Inventory .... BI
Biological Investigation of Marine Antarctic Systems and Stocks Program [*Texas A & M University*] [*Research center*] (RCD) .... BIOMASS
Biological Investigation of Space [*NASA*] .... BIOS
Biological Investigations of Terrestrial Antarctic Systems (SAUS) .... BIOTAS
Biological Isolation Garment [*NASA*] .... BIG
Biological Isolator Suit System (MCD) .... BISS
Biological Journal of the Linnean Society (SAUO) .... Biol J Linn Soc
Biological Laboratories (SAUO) .... BioLab
Biological Laboratory [*Army*] (MCD) .... BL
Biological Laboratory, Brunswick, Georgia [*US Bureau of Commercial Fisheries; later, National Marine Fisheries Service*] .... BLBG
Biological Limit Value [*Toxicology*] (LDT) .... BLV
Biological Mass source of ethanol and methanol from crops and trees (SAUS) .... bio-mass
Biological Material Oxidizer (SAUS) .... BMO
Biological Medical (SAUS) .... BIOMED
Biological Medicine .... BIOMED
Biological Modelling (SAUS) .... BIOMOD
Biological Monitoring and Abatement Program (SAUS) .... BMAP
Biological Nitrogen Fixation [*Agriculture*] .... BNF
Biological Nuclear Solvent [*Physiology*] .... BNS
Biological Oceanography (SAUS) .... Biol Oceanogr
Biological Operations [*Military*] (GFGA) .... BIOLOPS
Biological Orbiting Satellite (MCD) .... BIOS
Biological Orbiting Space Station (IAA) .... BOSS
Biological Origin .... BO
Biological Oxygen Demand .... BOD
Biological Oxygen Demand of Five Days (LDT) BOD5
Biological Pack (SAUS) .... BIOPACK
Biological Packs (DNAB) .... BIOPAC
Biological Packs (NG) .... BIOPACK
Biological Parent [*Medicine*] (MELL) .... BP
Biological Pesticides Data [*Environmental Protection Agency*] (AEPA) .... BPD
Biological Photographers Association (SAUO) .... BPA
Biological Photographic Association (EA) .... BPA
Biological Processing (SSD) .... BP
Biological Production Module (SSD) .... BPM
Biological Radio Communications .... BRC
Biological Reagent [*Peptide grade*] .... bR
Biological Receptors - Atrial Natriuretic Factor .... B-ANF
Biological Recording in Scotland Committee (SAUS) .... BRISC
Biological Records Centre [*Institute of Terrestrial Ecology*] [*Information service or system*] (IID) .... BRC
Biological Records Centre (SAUO) .... BRC
Biological Reference Materials .... BRM
Biological Report (AABC) .... BIOLREPT
Biological Report .... BIOREP
Biological Research (AABC) .... BIOLRSCH
Biological Research (NVT) .... BR
Biological Research Center [*Philippines*] .... BRC
Biological Research Institute (SAUO) .... BRI
Biological Research Institute of America (SAUO) .... BRIA
Biological Research Laboratories [*Syracuse University*] [*Research center*] (RCD) .... BRL
Biological Research Module [*NASA*] (NASA) .... BIO
Biological Research Module [*NASA*] (NASA) .... BRM
Biological Research Resources .... BRR
Biological Resource Division .... BRD
Biological Resources Development (SAUS) .... BIORED
Biological Resources Development Team (SAUO) .... BIORED
Biological Response Modifier Technology [*Biotechnology*] .... BRM
Biological Response Modifiers Program [*National Cancer Institute*] .... BRMP
Biological Review (journ.) (SAUS) .... Biol Rev
Biological Reviews of the Cambridge Philosophical Society (SAUO) .... Biol Rev Camb Philos Soc
Biological Safety Cabinet [*Pharmaceutical processing*] .... BSC
Biological Safety Officer [*National Institutes of Health*] .... BSO
Biological Satellite .... BIOS
Biological Satellite (KSC) .... BIOSAT
Biological Sciences Center (ADWA) .... BSC
Biological Sciences Communication Project [*American Institute of Biological Sciences*] .... BSCP
Biological Sciences Curriculum Study [*Colorado College*] [*Research center*] [*National Science Foundation*] .... BSCS
Biological Sciences Division [*Office of Naval Research*] (DNAB) .... BSD
Biological Sciences Research Center [*University of North Carolina at Chapel Hill*] [*Research center*] (RCD) .... BSRC
Biological Sequence/Structure Computational Facility (HGEN) .... BS/SCF
Biological Serial Record Center (SAUO) .... BSRC
Biological Services Program (SAUO) .... BSP
Biological, Social, Machine [*Combination*] .... BIOSOMA
Biological Society (SAUO) .... BS
Biological Society of Washington (SAUO) .... BSW
Biological Space Experiments (MCD) .... BIOSPEX
Biological Species Concept [*Theory of E. Mayr-1942*] .... BSC
Biological Stain Commission (EA) .... BSC
Biological Standards Control Laboratory [*Medical Research Council*] (PDAA) .... BSCL
Biological Station, Fisheries and Oceans Canada [*Station de Biologie, Peches et Oceans Canada*] **St. Andrews, New Brunswick** [*Library symbol*] [*National Library of Canada*] (NLC) .... NBAB
Biological Synoptic Ocean Prediction (CARB) .... BIOSYNOP
Biological Technical Assistance Group (SAUO) .... BTAG
Biological Therapies in Dentistry (SAUS) .... BTD
Biological Threshold Limit Value (PDAA) .... BTLV
Biological Tolerance Value (HEAS) .... BAT
Biological Trace Element Research (SAUS) .... Biol Trace Elem Res
Biological Transformations (SAUS) .... BIOTRANS
Biological Treatment Facility [*Environmental science*] (COE) .... BTF
Biological Urge (SAUS) .... BU
Biological Value .... BV
Biological Variation .... BV
Biological War Laboratory (SAUS) .... BWL
Biological Warfare .... BIOWAR
Biological Warfare .... BW
Biological Warfare Defense .... BWD
Biological Warfare Laboratory .... BWL
Biological Warfare Rapid Warning System [*Army*] .... BWRWS
Biological Warfare Research Center (SAUO) .... BWRC
Biological Warfare Research Establishment (SAUO) .... BWRE
Biological Warfare Weapons (SAUS) .... BWWs
Biological Warfare/Chemical Warfare (NG) .... BW/CW
Biological Weapons [*Military*] (AABC) .... BIOLWPN
Biological Weapons [*Military*] .... BW
Biological Weapons Command (DOMA) .... BWC
Biological Weapons Convention .... BWC
Biological Weapons System [*Military*] (AABC) .... BIOLWPNSYS
Biological Weapons System [*Military*] .... BWS
Biological-Chemical .... BIO-CHEM
Biological/Chemical Attack Report .... BIOREP/CHEMREP
Biological/Chemical Detector (DOMA) .... BCD
Biological-Instrumentation (SAUS) .... BIO-INSTR
Biologically Active Substance [*Biochemistry*] (DB) .... BAS
biologically clean (SAUS) .... bioclean
Biologically Equivalent [*Medicine*] (MELL) .... BE
Biologically Important Trace Species (SAUS) .... BITS
Biologically Induced Mineralization [*Microbial metabolism*] .... BIM
Biologically Liberated Organo-Beasties [*Environmental science*] (COE) .... BLOB
Biologist .... BIOGST
Biologist (ADWA) .... biol
Biologist (SAUS) .... Biol
Biologist's Toolbox .... BT
Biologix (BC) Ltd. [*Vancouver Stock Exchange symbol*] .... BGX
Biology [*Secondary school course*] [*British*] .... B
Biology (DSUE) .... BI
Biology [*or Biological*] (KSC) .... BIO
Biology (DD) .... Bio
Biology (NTIO) .... bio
Biology (WDAA) .... biol
Biology (AL) .... Biol
Biology Abstracts and Zoological Records (SAUS) .... BIOSIS
Biology and Electronics (SAUS) .... Bionics
Biology and Fertility of Soils (SAUS) .... Biol Fertil Soils
Biology Branch Herbarium, Biological and Chemical Research Institute (SAUS) .... DAR
Biology, Chemistry, Physics (DD) .... BCP
Biology Classroom Activity Checklist (EDAC) .... BCAC
Biology Electronics (SAUS) .... BIONICS
Biology, Electronics, Aesthetics, Mechanics [*Robotics competition*] .... BEAM
Biology Information Retrieval System [*Marine science*] (MSC) .... BIRS
Biology of Reproduction (SAUS) .... BOR
Biology Unit [*American Topical Association*] (EA) .... BU
Bioluminescence .... BL
Bioluminescence Immunoassay .... BIA
Biomagnetic Tech [*NASDAQ symbol*] (TTSB) .... BTIX

Biomagnetic Technology [*Commercial firm*] [*Associated Press*] (SAG) .... Biomag
Biomagnetic Technology [*NASDAQ symbol*] (SAG) .... BTIX
Biomagnification Factor [*Toxicology*] (LDT) .... BMF
Biomass [*Biology*] .... B
Biomass and Biofuels Association (COBU) .... BABA
Biomass Burned (CARB) .... BB
Biomass Burning Experiment (SAUS) .... BIBEX
Biomass Energy and Alcohol Fuels Act of 1980 .... BEAFA
Biomass Energy Coordinating Committee [*Department of Energy*] .... BECC
Biomass Energy Research Association (EA) .... BERA
Biomass Energy Systems Program [*Department of Energy*] .... BES
Biomass Integrated Gasifier Steaminjected Gas Turbine (SAUS) .... BIGSTIG
Biomass Production Chamber (ADWA) .... BPC
Biomass Protein .... BMP
Biomass quantity burned in Fields (SAUS) .... BF
Biomass Research Center [*University of Arkansas*] .... BRC
Biomass Users Network (SAUS) .... BUN
Biomaterials Profiling Center [*University of Utah*] [*Research center*] (RCD) .... BPC
biomathematician (SAUS) .... biomath
biomathematics (SAUS) .... biomath
Bio-Mathematics (journ.) (SAUS) .... RBIMBZ
Biomatrix .... BM
Biomatrix, Inc. [*Associated Press*] (SAG) .... Biomatr
Biomatrix, Inc. [*NYSE symbol*] (SG) .... BXM
Biomechanical Combined Oxidation [*Water treatment*] .... BMCO
Biomechanically Faithful Side Impact Dummy [*Automotive engineering*].... BIOSID
Biomechanics Corp. of America [*NASDAQ symbol*] (SAG) .... BCAM
Bio-Mechanics Laboratory (SAUO) .... BML
Biomechanics Laboratory (SAUS) .... BML
Biomedical .... BIOMDCL
biomedical (SAUS) .... biomed
Biomedical .... BMD
Biomedical and Environmental Assessment Group (SAUO) .... BEAG
Biomedical & Environmental Science Laboratory (SAUO) .... BE
Biomedical Application Team (SAUO) .... BAT
Biomedical Application Teams [*NASA*] .... BAT
Biomedical Applications (journ.) (SAUS) .... JCBADL
Biomedical Applications of Computers (SAUS) .... BAC
Biomedical Belt [*NASA*] .... BMB
Biomedical Chromatography [*A publication*] .... BMC
Biomedical Communications Inventory [*National Library of Medicine*] .... BCI
Biomedical Communications Network [*Proposed*] [*National Library of Medicine*] .... BCN
Biomedical Computer .... BMC
Biomedical Computing Council of California Universities (SAUO) .... BCCCU
Biomedical Computing Society [*Later, SIGBIO*] (BUR) .... BCS
Biomedical Computing Technology Information Center [*Oak Ridge National Laboratory*] [*Department of Energy*] (IID) .... BCTIC
Biomedical Data Analysis and Display System [*NASA*] .... BMDADS
Bio-Medical Data Package .... BMDP
Biomedical Data Processing (CIST) .... BMDP
Biomedical Display Unit (KSC) .... BDU
Biomedical Electronics (MCD) .... BME
Biomedical Engineering (DD) .... BiomedEng
Biomedical Engineering (SAUO) .... BMT
Biomedical Engineering and Instrumentation Branch [*National Institutes of Health*] .... BEIB
Biomedical Engineering and Instrumentation Program [*Medicine*] (MELL).... BEIP
Biomedical Engineering and the Research to AID Persons with Disabilities (SAUO) .... BME/RAPD
Biomedical Engineering Current Awareness Notification [*Database, publication*] [*Brunel University*] [*Information service or system*] (CRD) ..... BECAN
Bio-Medical Engineering (journ.) (SAUS) .... Bio-Med Eng
Biomedical Engineering (journ.) (SAUS) .... Biomed Eng
Bio-Medical Engineering (journ.) (SAUS) .... BME
Biomedical Engineering Program [*Carnegie-Mellon University*] [*Research center*] (RCD) .... BME
Biomedical Engineering Research Corporation (SAUO) .... BERC
Bio-Medical Engineering Society (SAUO) .... BMES
Biomedical Engineering Society (EA) .... BMES
Biomedical Engineering Unit [*McGill University*] [*Canada*] [*Research center*] (RCD) .... BMEU
Biomedical Equipment Technology .... BMET
Biomedical Experiment Scientific [*or Support*] **Satellite** [*NASA*] (NASA) .... BESS
Biomedical Experiment Support Satellite (SAUS) .... BESS
Biomedical Informatics Today (ACII) .... BMIT
Biomedical Information Processing Organization (SAUO) .... BIO
Biomedical Information Service [*University of Minnesota, Minneapolis*] [*Information service or system*] (IID) .... BIS
Biomedical Instrumentation Advisory Service [*Clinical Research Centre*] [*British*] (NITA) .... BIAS
Biomedical Instrumentation Consultant .... BIC
Bio-medical Instrumentation Development Unit (SAUO) .... BIDU
Biomedical Interdisciplinary Curriculum Project [*National Science Foundation*] .... BICP
Biomedical Laboratory, Aberdeen Proving Grounds, MD [*OCLC symbol*] (OCLC) .... ADF
Biomedical Library Acquisitions Bulletin (SAUO) .... BLAB
Biomedical Marketing Association (EA) .... BMA
Bio-medical Materials and Engineering (SAUS) .... Biomed Mater Eng
Biomedical Measurement and Control Panel (ACII) .... BCMP
Biomedical Measurement and Control Panel (SAUS) .... BMCP
Biomedical Monitoring System .... BMS
Biomedical Office [*Kennedy Space Center Directorate*] (NAKS) .... MD
Biomedical Optics Society (SAUO) .... BiOS
Biomedical Primate Research Centre [*The Netherlands*] .... BPRC
Biomedical Recovery Capsule (MUGU) .... BRC
Biomedical Research and Development Laboratory [*Army*] (RDA) .... BRDL
Biomedical Research Defense Fund [*Defunct*] (EA) .... BRDF
Biomedical Research Development Grants .... BRDG
Biomedical Research Education Trust (GVA) .... BRET
Biomedical Research in Progress (ECII) .... BRIP
Biomedical Research Institute [*American Foundation for Biological Research*] [*Research center*] (RCD) .... BRI
Biomedical Research Support Advisory Committee [*National Institutes of Health*] (EGAO) .... BRSAC
Biomedical Research Support Grants .... BRSG
Biomedical Research Support Program [*Bethesda, MD*] [*National Institutes of Health*] (GRD) .... BRS
Biomedical Research Technology Program [*Bethesda, MD*] [*National Institutes of Health*] (GRD) .... BRTP
Biomedical Sciences Corps [*Air Force*] (AFM) .... BSC
Biomedical Sciences Instrumentation Symposium (SAUO) .... BSIS
Biomedical Sciences Program (DMAA) .... BMSP
Biomedical Sciences Support Grant (SAUO) .... BSSG
Biomedical Signal Conditioner .... BSC
Biomedical Studies Section [*Oak Ridge National Laboratory*] (IID) .... BMS
Biomedical Technology Transfer Team .... BATEAM
Biomedical Urine Sampling System (KSC) .... BUSS
Biomedical Waste .... BMW
Biomedical Waste Incinerator [*or Incineration*] .... BMWI
biomedicine (SAUS) .... biomed
Biomedicine and Health Program .... BMHP
Bio-Mega, Inc., Montreal, Quebec [*Library symbol*] [*National Library of Canada*] (NLC) .... QMBIM
Biomerica, Inc. [*Associated Press*] (SAG) .... Biomer
Biomerica, Inc. [*Associated Press*] (SAG) .... Biomerica
Biomerica, Inc. [*NASDAQ symbol*] (NQ) .... BMRA
Biomet, Inc. [*Associated Press*] (SAG) .... Biomet
Biomet, Inc. [*NASDAQ symbol*] (NQ) .... BMET
Biomet Incorporated (SAUO) .... BMET
Biomet Tech, Inc. [*Vancouver Stock Exchange symbol*] .... BTS
Biometric Computer Service, Inc. .... BCSI
Biometric Society .... BS
Biometric Society, Eastern North American Region (SAUO) .... ENAR
Biometric Society, Western North American Region (EA) .... WNAR
Biometrics Laboratory Information Processing System (DB) .... BLIPS
Biometrics Research Laboratory (DAVI) .... BRL
Biometrie Humaine (journ.) (SAUS) .... SBHRAL
Biometry .... BIOMET
Biometry and Epidemiology Program [*Department of Health and Human Services*] (GFGA) .... BEPP
Biometry and Risk Assessment Program (GNE) .... BRAP
Biomimetic Affinity Chromatography .... BMC
Biomira, Inc. [*NASDAQ symbol*] (SAG) .... BIOM
Biomira Inc. [*NASDAQ symbol*] (TTSB) .... BIOMF
Biomira, Inc. [*Associated Press*] (SAG) .... Biomira
Biomira, Inc. [*Toronto Stock Exchange symbol*] .... BRA
Biomolecular Engineering Program [*EC*] (ECED) .... BEP
Biomolecular Engineering Research Institute [*Formerly, PERI*] [*Japan*] .... BERI
Biomune Systems [*NASDAQ symbol*] (TTSB) .... BIME
Biomune Systems, Inc. [*NASDAQ symbol*] (SAG) .... BIME
Biomune Systems, Inc. [*Associated Press*] (SAG) .... Biomne
Bionaire, Inc. [*Toronto Stock Exchange symbol*] .... ION
Bionet Intelligent Gateway (VERA) .... BIG
Bionetics Research Institute [*Rockville, MD*] .... BRI
Bionetics Research Laboratory (SAUO) .... BRL
Bionet-International (SAUS) .... BI
Bionet-International (SAUS) .... BioNET-INT
Bionics Adaptive Network .... BAN
Bionomic .... BIONMC
Bionomics, Environment, Plasmodium, Treatment, Immunity [*Malaria epidemiology*] (AAMN) .... BEPTI
Bionomics, Environment, Plasmodium, Treatment, Immunity (SAUS) .... BEPTL
Bionucleonics .... BIONUCL
Biopack [*NASA*] (KSC) .... BP
Biopack Subsystem [*NASA*] (KSC) .... BPSS
Biopedagocical Research Organization on Intensive Learning Environment Reactions (SAUO) .... BROILER
Biopedagogical Research Organization on Intensive Learning Environment Reactions (SAUS) .... BROILER
BioPharmaceutical Technology Center Institute (SAUS) .... BTCI
Biopharmaceutical Technology Center Institute (SAUO) .... BTCI
Biopharmaceutics Classification System [*Drug evaluation*] .... BCS
Biopharmaceutics Coordinating Committee [*Drug evaluation*] .... BCC
Biopharmaceutics Research Branch [*Washington, DC*] [*Department of Health and Human Services*] (GRD) .... BRB
biophysical (SAUS) .... biophys
Biophysical Journal (SAUS) .... Biophys J
Biophysical Profile [*Medicine*] (MELL) .... BPP
Biophysical Society .... BP
Biophysical Society (EA) .... BPS
Biophysical Society (MCD) .... BS
Biophysical Society of Canada [*La Societe de Biophysique du Canada*] (AC) .... BSC
Biophysicist (SAUS) .... Biophys
Biophysics (ADA) .... BIO
Biophysics (DAVI) .... Biophys
Bio-Plexus, Inc. [*Associated Press*] (SAG) .... BioPlex
Bio-Plexus, Inc. [*NASDAQ symbol*] (SAG) .... BPLX

Biopolymer Crosslinking System (DB) ... BCS
Biopool International, Inc. [*Associated Press*] (SAG) ... Biopool
Biopool International, Inc. [*NASDAQ symbol*] (NQ) ... BIPL
Biopool Intl. [*NASDAQ symbol*] (TTSB) ... BIPL
BioProcess Engineering Society International (EA) ... BESI
Bioprocessing Aid ... BPA
Bioprocessing Research Facility [*Oak Ridge, TN*] [*Oak Ridge National Laboratory*] [*Department of Energy*] (GRD) ... BRF
Bioprocessing Technology [*Technical Insights, Inc.*] [*Information service or system*] (CRD) ... BT
Bio-Products Laboratory [*Central Blood Laboratories Authority*] [*British*] (IRC) ... BPL
Biopropellant Valve (SAUS) ... BPV
Biopsy [*Medicine*] ... B
biopsy (SAUS) ... bi
biopsy (SAUS) ... biop
biopsy (SAUS) ... bx
Biopsy [*Medicine*] ... BX
Biopsy and Curettage [*Medicine*] (MELL) ... B & C
Bio-Psychology Doctor (SAUS) ... BPD
Bioquant ... BQ
Biorack (SAUS) ... BR
Bio-Rad Laboratories, Inc. [*AMEX symbol*] (SPSG) ... BIO
Bio-Rad Laboratories, Inc. [*Associated Press*] (SAG) ... BioR
Bio-Rad Labs Cl'A' [*AMEX symbol*] (TTSB) ... BIO.A
Bio-Rad Labs Cl'B' [*AMEX symbol*] (TTSB) ... BIO.B
Bioradioimmunoassay ... BRIA
Bioradiotelemetric System ... BRTS
Bio-Reference Laboratories, Inc. [*Associated Press*] (SAG) ... BioRef
Bio-Reference Laboratories, Inc. [*Associated Press*] (SAG) ... BioRf
Bio-Reference Laboratories, Inc. [*NASDAQ symbol*] (NQ) ... BRLI
Bio-Reference Labs [*NASDAQ symbol*] (TTSB) ... BRLI
Bio-Reference Labs Wrrt'A' [*NASDAQ symbol*] (TTSB) ... BRLIW
Bio-Reference Labs Wrrt'B' [*NASDAQ symbol*] (TTSB) ... BRLIZ
Bioregional Project (EA) ... BP
Bioremediation Action Committee [*Environmental science*] (EPAT) ... BAC
Bioren and Duane's United States Laws [*A publication*] (DLA) ... Bior & D Laws
BioResearch, Inc., Farmingdale, NY [*Library symbol*] [*Library of Congress*] (LCLS) ... NFarB
Bio-Research Laboratories Ltd., Pointe-Claire, PQ, Canada [*Library symbol*] [*Library of Congress*] (LCLS) ... CaQMBR
Bio-Research Laboratories Ltd., Pointe-Claire, Quebec [*Library symbol*] [*National Library of Canada*] (NLC) ... QMBR
Bio-Research Laboratory, Senneville, Quebec [*Library symbol*] [*National Library of Canada*] (NLC) ... QSBR
BioResearch Titles (DIT) ... BRT
Bioresmethrin [*Biochemistry*] ... BR
Bioresources Research Facility [*University of Arizona*] [*Research center*] (RCD) ... BRF
Biorex, Ste.-Foy, Quebec [*Library symbol*] [*National Library of Canada*] (BIB) ... QSFB
Biorka [*Alaska*] [*Seismograph station code, US Geological Survey*] [*Closed*] (SEIS) ... BIO
BIOS Data Area (SAUS) ... BDA
BIOS [*Basic Input-Output System*] **Parameter Block** [*Computer science*] (PCM) ... BPB
BioSafe International, Inc. [*Associated Press*] (SAG) ... BioSafe
BioSafe International, Inc. [*Associated Press*] (SAG) ... BioSf
BioSafe International, Inc. [*NASDAQ symbol*] (SAG) ... BSFE
BioSafe Intl. [*NASDAQ symbol*] (TTSB) ... BSFE
BioSafe Intl. Wrrt'C' [*NASDAQ symbol*] (TTSB) ... BSFEW
BioSafe Intl. Wrtt'E' [*NASDAQ symbol*] (TTSB) ... BSFEL
Biosafety in Microbiological and Biomedical Laboratories (SAUO) ... BMBL
Biosafety Information Network and Advisory Service (SAUS) ... BINAS
Biosafety Level - Large Scale [*For laboratories utilizing biological agents*] ... BL-LS
Biosafety Level 4 ... BL_4
Biosafety Special Working Group (SAUO) ... BSWG
Biosafety Systems [*NASDAQ symbol*] (SAG) ... BSSI
Biosafety Systems, Inc. [*Associated Press*] (SAG) ... BioSafety
Biosatellite (SAUS) ... Biosat
Bioscience ... Biosci
BioScience [*A publication*] (BRI) ... BioSci
BioScience Information Services (SAUO) ... BSIS
Bioscience Program [*NASA*] ... BP
Bio-Sciences Information Exchange [*Smithsonian Institution*] ... BSIE
Biosciences Information Network for Latin America and the Caribbean (SAUO) ... BINLAC
BioSciences Information Service [*Database producer*] [*Philadelphia, PA*] ... BIOSIS
Biosciences Information Service of Biological Abstracts (SAUS) ... BIOSIS
bioscientific (SAUS) ... biosci
bioscientist (SAUS) ... biosci
Bioscope [*The cinema*] [*Obsolete*] [*British*] (DSUE) ... BIO
Bioscript (SAUS) ... BST
Biosedra [*France*] [*Research code symbol*] ... B
Bioseparation (SAUS) ... BIO
Biosepra, Inc. [*Associated Press*] (SAG) ... Biosepra
BioSepra Inc. [*NASDAQ symbol*] (TTSB) ... BSEP
BioSequence Markup Language (RALS) ... BSML
Bioserve-Instrumentation Technology Associate Materials Dispersion Analysis (SAUO) ... BIMDA
Bioshield Power Assembly [*NASA*] ... BPA
Bioshield Pyrotechnic Control Assembly [*for Mariner Venus-Mercury Project spacecraft*] [*NASA*] ... BPCA
BIOSIS [*BioSciences Information Service*] **Information Transfer Service** ... BITS
BIOSIS/CAS [*BioSciences Information Service/Chemical Abstracts Service*] **Registry Number Concordance** [*American Chemical Society*] [*Information service or system*] (CRD) ... BIOCAS
Biosophical Institute, Inc. [*Defunct*] ... BII
BioSource International [*NASDAQ symbol*] (SAG) ... BIOI
BioSource International [*Associated Press*] (SAG) ... BioSrce
Biospecific Affinity Chromatography ... BAC
Biospecific Interaction Analysis (SAUS) ... BIA
BioSpecifics Technologies, Inc. [*Associated Press*] (SAG) ... BioSpecif
BioSpecifics Technologies, Inc. [*NASDAQ symbol*] (SAG) ... BSTC
biospeliology (SAUS) ... biospel
Biosphere [*Self-contained scientific experimental community*] ... B2
Biosphere Reserve (GNE) ... BR
Biosphere-Atmosphere Chemistry (SAUS) ... BAC
Biosphere-Atmosphere Exchange of Pollutants (SAUS) ... BIATEX
Biosphere-Atmosphere Exchange of Trace Gases (SAUS) ... BIATEX
Biosphere-Atmosphere Interactions in the Tropics (SAUS) ... BAIT
Biosphere-Atmosphere Interactions project (SAUS) ... BAI
Biosphere-Atmosphere Stable Isotope Network (SAUS) ... BASIN
Biosphere-Atmosphere Transfer, Ecological Research and in situ Studies in Amazonia (SAUS) ... BATERISTA
Biosphere-Atmosphere Transfer Scheme [*Meteorology*] ... BATS
Biosphere-Atmosphere Transfer Scheme Version 1e (SAUS) ... BATS1E
Biospheric Aspects of the Hydrological Cycle [*Marine science*] (OSRA) ... BAHC
Biospheric Controls on Trace Gas Fluxes in Northern Wetlands (SAUO) ... CONGAS
Biospheric Model Validation Study (SAUS) ... BIOMOVS
Biospherical Instruments, Inc. (SAUO) ... BSI
Biospherics [*NASDAQ symbol*] (TTSB) ... BINC
Biospherics, Inc. [*NASDAQ symbol*] (NQ) ... BINC
Biospherics, Inc. [*Associated Press*] (SAG) ... Biosph
Biospherics Research on Emissions from Wetlands (SAUS) ... BREW
Biossay of Luteinizing Hormone (DMAA) ... bioLH
Biostack (SAUS) ... BSK
Biostatistics ... BIOSTAT
Biostructures Participating Research Team [*Biostructures Institute*] (RCD) ... BPRT
Biosynthetic Antibody Binding Site [*Biochemistry*] ... BABS
Biosynthetic Human Insulin [*Medicine*] ... BHI
Biosys [*Associated Press*] (SAG) ... Biosys
Biosys, Inc. [*NASDAQ symbol*] (NQ) ... BIOS
Biosys Medical [*NASDAQ symbol*] (TTSB) ... BIOP
Biosystematic Code [*Databank terminology*] (NITA) ... BC
Biosystematic Code [*Online database field identifier*] ... BS
Biosystematics Research Institute [*Canada*] (ARC) ... BRI
Biot [*Also, aA*] [*Unit of electric current*] ... Bi
Biotech Electronics Ltd. [*Toronto Stock Exchange symbol*] ... ION
Biotech Knowledge Sources (SAUS) ... BKS
Biotechnic Research and Development (SAUS) ... BRAD
Biotechnica Canada, Calgary, AB, Canada [*Library symbol*] [*Library of Congress*] (LCLS) ... CaACBC
Biotechnica Canada, Calgary, Alberta [*Library symbol*] [*National Library of Canada*] (BIB) ... ACBC
Biotechnica International, Inc. ... BII
Biotechnica International, Inc. ... BIT
Biotechnica International, Inc. ... BTI
Biotechnical Research Project [*EC*] (ECED) ... BIOREP
Biotechnical Research Technology [*NIH*] ... BRT
Biotechnics International, Inc. [*NASDAQ symbol*] (NQ) ... BIOT
Biotechnics International, Inc. [*Associated Press*] (SAG) ... BioTInt
Biotechnology ... BIOTEC
Biotechnology ... BIOTECH
Biotechnology (ADWA) ... biotech
Biotechnology ... BT
Biotechnology Advisory Committee [*Environmental Protection Agency*] (GFGA) ... BAC
Biotechnology and Applied Biochemistry (SAUO) ... BAB
Biotechnology and Biological Sciences Research Council [*British*] ... bbscrc
Biotechnology and Biological Sciences Research Council [*British*] ... BBSRC
Biotechnology and Human Research ... BHR
Biotechnology and Human Research Office (SAUO) ... B & HRO
Biotechnology Branch, CISTI , Montreal, Quebec [*Canada Institute for Scienctific and Technical Information*] [*Annexe de Biotechnologie, ICIST*] [*Library symbol*] [*National Library of Canada*] (BIB) ... QMNB
Biotechnology Citation Index (SAUO) ... BCI
Biotechnology Equipment Suppliers [*Deutsche Gesellschaft fuer Chemisches Apparatewesen, Chemische Technik, und Biotechnologie eV*] [*Germany*] (IID) ... BIOQUIP
Bio-Technology Exhibition (TSPED) ... BIOTEX
Biotechnology Facility (SAUS) ... BF
Biotechnology Facility (SSD) ... BTF
Biotechnology Gen Corp. [*Associated Press*] (SAG) ... BioTcG
Biotechnology Gen Corp. [*Associated Press*] (SAG) ... BioTG
Bio-Technology General Corp. [*NASDAQ symbol*] (SP86) ... BTGC
Bio-Technology Genl [*NASDAQ symbol*] (TTSB) ... BTGC
Biotechnology Industry Organization ... BIO
Biotechnology Information Knot for Europe (SAUO) ... BIKE
Biotechnology Information Toolkit Software (SAUS) ... BITS
Biotechnology Investment Opportunities [*Database*] [*High Tech Publishing Co.*] [*Information service or system*] (CRD) ... BIO
Biotechnology Orbital Laboratory (KSC) ... BOL
Bio-Technology Purchasing Management Association [*Defunct*] (EA) ... BPMA
Biotechnology Research Council (WDAA) ... BRC
Biotechnology Research for Innovation, Development, and Growth in Europe [*EC*] (ECED) ... BRIDGE

Biotechnology Research Institute [*Montreal, PQ*] [*Canada*] ... BRI
Biotechnology Science Advisory Committee (SAUO) ... BSAC
Biotechnology Science Coordinating Committee [*An interagency governmental group*] [*Washington, DC*] ... BSCC
Biotechnology Thrust ... BT
Biotechnology Training Program (HGEN) ... BTP
biotelemetric (SAUS) ... biotel
biotelemetry (SAUS) ... biotel
Biotelemetry System ... BTS
Biotic Potential ... BP
BioTime, Inc. [*Associated Press*] (SAG) ... Biotime
Biotime, Inc. [*NASDAQ symbol*] (SAG) ... BTIM
Biotin ... B
Biotin [*Pharmacology*] (DAVI) ... B_7
biotin (SAUS) ... vit H
Biotin Carboxyl Carrier Protein [*Biochemistry*] ... BCCP
Biotin-Avidin-Linked Immunoassay [*Immunochemistry*] ... BALIA
Biotin-Carboxylase (SAUS) ... BC
Biotinoyl (Iodoacetyl) Ethylenediamine [*An enzyme*] ... BIE
Biotin-X Cadaverine [*Biochemical labelling compound*] ... BXC
Biotinyl-para-aminobenzoate [*Biochemistry*] ... BPAB
Biotite (SAUS) ... bi
Biotite Granite Schist [*Geology*] ... BIOT GR SCH
Biotransformation (SAUS) ... Biotrans
BioTransplant, Inc. [*Associated Press*] (SAG) ... BioTrans
BioTransplant, Inc. [*NASDAQ symbol*] (SAG) ... BTRN
Biot-Savart Law [*Physics*] ... BSL
Biovail Corp. International [*Associated Press*] (SAG) ... Biovail
Biovail Corp. International [*AMEX symbol*] (SAG) ... BVF
Biovail Corp. Intl. [*AMEX symbol*] (TTSB) ... BVF
Bio-Vascular, Inc. [*Associated Press*] (SAG) ... BioVasc
Bio-Vascular, Inc. [*NASDAQ symbol*] (NQ) ... BVAS
Biowaste Monitoring System (MCD) ... BMS
BioWhittaker, Inc. [*Associated Press*] (SAG) ... Biowht
BioWhittaker, Inc. [*NYSE symbol*] (SPSG) ... BWI
Biozone (SAUS) ... BIZ
Bipara [*Having borne two children*] [*Gynecology and Obstetrics*] (DAVI) ... Para II
Biparietal Diameter (SAUS) ... BDP
Biparietal Diameter [*Gynecology*] (MAE) ... BIP
Biparietal Diameter [*Obstetrics*] (DAVI) ... BiPD
Biparietal Diameter [*Gynecology*] ... BP
Biparietal Diameter [*Gynecology*] ... BPD
Biparting Door ... BIPD
Biparting Doors (SAUS) ... BIPD
Bipartisan [*Politics*] (WDMC) ... bipart
Bipartite (SAUS) ... BIP
Bipartite and Bizonal Reorganization Committee (SAUO) ... BBRC
Bipartite Board [*Post-World War II, Germany*] ... BIB
Bipartite Board, Berlin (SAUO) ... BIB
Bipartite Civil Aviation Panel [*Post-World War II, Germany*] ... BCAP
Bipartite Civil Aviation Panel Berlin District (SAUO) ... BCAPBD
Bipartite Civil Service Advisors [*Post-World War II, Germany*] ... BICIV
Bipartite Civil Service Group (SAUO) ... BIPCIV
Bipartite Commerce and Industry Group (SAUO) ... BCIG
Bipartite Commerce and Industry Group (SAUO) ... BIPC&I
Bipartite Communications Panel [*Post-World War II, Germany*] ... BICOM
Bipartite Control Group (SAUO) ... BCG
Bipartite Control Office [*Post-World War II, Germany*] ... BICO
Bipartite Decartelization Commission [*Berlin*] [*Post-World War II, Germany*] ... BIDEC
Bipartite Decartelization Sub-Commission [*Minden*] [*Post-World War II, Germany*] ... BIDESC
Bipartite Economic Control Group (SAUO) ... BIGECO
Bipartite Economic Panel [*Post-World War II, Germany*] ... BIECO
Bipartite Economic Panel Railway Supplies Committee [*Post-World War II, Germany*] ... BIECO/RAIL
Bipartite Economics Control Group [*Post-World War II, Germany*] ... BECG
Bipartite Finance Group (SAUO) ... BIPFIN
Bipartite Finance Panel [*Post-World War II, Germany*] ... BIFIN
Bipartite Food, Agriculture and Forestry Group (SAUS) ... BIPFA
Bipartite Food and Agriculture Panel [*Post-World War II, Germany*] ... BIF & A
Bipartite Food and Agriculture Panel (SAUO) ... BIF&A
Bipartite Legislation Review Board (SAUO) ... BLRB
Bipartite Matching Code (SAUS) ... BIPM
Bipartite News Office [*Post-World War II, Germany*] ... BNO
Bipartite (or Bizonal) Economic Council (SAUO) ... BEC
Bipartite Secretariat [*Post-World War II, Germany*] ... BISEC
Bipartite Transport Control Group [*Post-World War II, Germany*] ... BTCG
Bipartite Transportation Group (SAUO) ... BIPTPT
Bipartite Vetting Party (SAUO) ... BVP
Bi-Petro Resources [*Vancouver Stock Exchange symbol*] ... BIP
Bi-Phase Mark (MHDI) ... BIO-M
Bi-Phase Modulation (IAA) ... BPM
Bi-Phase Shift Keyed (or Keying) (SAUS) ... BPSK
Bi-phase Space (SAUS) ... Bi-Phase-S
Bi-Phase-Level (SAUS) ... Bi-Phase-L
Bi-Phase-Mark (SAUS) ... Bi-Phase-M
Biphasic Positive Airway Pressure (SAUS) ... BIPAP
Biphenyl [*Medicine*] (MELL) ... BP
Biphenyl Dianhydride [*Organic chemistry*] ... BPDA
Biphenyl Work Group (EA) ... BWG
Biphenylamine [*Organic chemistry*] ... BPA
(Biphenylyl)phenyloxazole [*Organic chemistry*] ... BPO
Biphetamine (SAUS) ... Biphet
Bipiperidyl Mustard [*Pharmacology*] ... BPM
Biplabi Bangla Congress [*India*] [*Political party*] (PPW) ... BBC
Biplane ... B
Biplane Experimental [*Aircraft*] [*World War I*] ... BE
Biplane Ultra-Light Research Device (PDAA) ... BURD
Bipod Heavy Barrel [*Weaponry*] [*Military*] (INF) ... BHB
Bipolar [*Medicine*] (MELL) ... BP
Bipolar Active-plastic Cell (SAUS) ... BAC
Bipolar Affective Disorder [*Psychology*] (DAVI) ... BAD
Bipolar Affective Disorder [*Genetics*] ... BPAD
Bipolar Cell [*Biochemistry*] ... BC
Bipolar Cell [*In the retina*] ... Bi
Bipolar Coagulation Probe (SAUS) ... BICAP
Bipolar Complementary Metal Oxide Semiconductor [*Electronics*] (BARN) ... BICMOS
Bipolar Complementary Metal-Oxide Semiconductor (IAA) ... BCMOS
Bipolar Field Effect Transistor (IAA) ... BIFET
Bipolar Illness [*Psychiatry*] (CPH) ... BPI
Bipolar Insulated Gate Field-Effect Transistor [*Bell Laboratories*] ... BIGFET
Bipolar Insulated-Gate Field-Effect Transistor (SAUS) ... BIG-FET
Bipolar Integrated Circuit [*Electronics*] (EECA) ... BIC
Bipolar Integrated Technology Inc (SAUS) ... BIT
Bipolar Inversion Channel Field Effect Transistor (MCD) ... BICFET
Bipolar Junction Transistor [*Electronics*] ... BJT
Bipolar Junction Transistor (SAUS) ... BjT
Bipolar Line Unit [*Electronics*] (IAA) ... BLU
Bipolar Magnetic Region (OA) ... BMR
Bipolar Manic-Depressive Disorder [*Medicine*] (MELL) ... BMDD
Bipolar Memory Technology (SAUS) ... BMT
Bipolar Metal-Oxide Semiconductor (IEEE) ... BiMOS
Bipolar Operational Amplifier ... BOA
Bipolar Operational Power ... BOP
Bipolar Operational Power Supplies (SAUS) ... BOPs
Bipolar Power Supply (DWSG) ... BPS
Bipolar PROM (SAUS) ... BPROM
Bipolar Prosthesis [*Medicine*] (MELL) ... BP
Bipolar Psychological Inventory [*Personality development test*] [*Psychology*] ... BPI
Bipolar Read Only Memory [*Computer science*] (MHDI) ... BROM
Bipolar Read-Only Memories (SAUS) ... BROMs
Bipolar Return to Zero [*Electronics*] (ACRL) ... BPRZ
Bipolar Transistor (SAUS) ... BPT
Bipolar Twos-Complement Code (SAUS) ... BTC Code
Bipolar Violation (SAUS) ... BPV
Bipolar with Eight-Zero Substitution [*Coding*] [*Telecommunications*] ... B8ZS
Bipolar with N Zeros Substitution [*Electronics*] (NITA) ... BNZS
Bipolar with Six Zero Substituting (SAUS) ... B6ZS
Bipolar-CMOS-DMOS (MCD) ... BCDMOS
Bipolar-Mode Static Induction Transistor (MCD) ... BSIT
Bipost [*Lamp base*] (NTCM) ... Bp
Bipost ... BPT
Bipropellant (KSC) ... BIP
Bipropellant (SAUS) ... BIPROP
Bipropellant Valve (MCD) ... BPV
Bi-purpose Triple Coil (SAUS) ... BTC
Bipyridine [*Also, BPY*] [*Organic chemistry*] ... BIPY
Bipyridine [*Also, BIPY*] [*Organic chemistry*] ... BPY
Bipyridinium Chlorochromate [*Organic chemistry*] ... BPCC
Bi-Quinary (SAUS) ... Bi-Quin
Biquinary Code (SAUS) ... BC
Biquinary Coded Decimal Notation (SAUS) ... BCD Notation
Biquinary Coded Decimal Number (SAUS) ... BCD Number
Biquinary Notation (SAUS) ... BN
Biquinary Number (SAUS) ... BN
Biquinary Number Notation (SAUS) ... BNN
Biquinary System (SAUS) ... BS
Bir Moghrein [*Mauritania*] [*ICAO location identifier*] (ICLI) ... GQPT
Birao [*Central African Republic*] [*ICAO location identifier*] (ICLI) ... FEFI
Birao [*Central African Republic*] [*Airport symbol*] (AD) ... IRO
Biratnagar [*Nepal*] [*Airport symbol*] (OAG) ... BIR
Biratnagar [*Nepal*] [*ICAO location identifier*] (ICLI) ... VNVT
Biratnagar CBR Project (SAUS) ... BIRCBR
Birch (VRA) ... bir
Birch Creek [*Alaska*] [*Airport symbol*] (OAG) ... KBC
Birch Elementary School, Massapequa, NY [*Library symbol*] [*Library of Congress*] (LCLS) ... NMassBE
Birch Elementary School, Merrick, NY [*Library symbol*] [*Library of Congress*] (LCLS) ... NMerkBE
Birch Hill [*Alaska*] [*Seismograph station code, US Geological Survey*] [*Closed*] (SEIS) ... BRH
Birch, Raymond Sr., Southampton PA [*STAC*] ... BRS
Birch Tree, MO [*AM radio station call letters*] ... KBMV
Birch Tree, MO [*FM radio station call letters*] ... KBMV-FM
Bircham Newton Training Centre (SAUO) ... BNTC
Birchler & Co. AG (SAUO) ... bico
Birchwood Elementary School, Duluth, MN [*Library symbol*] [*Library of Congress*] (LCLS) ... MnDuBE
Birchwood Elementary School, Huntington Station, NY [*Library symbol*] [*Library of Congress*] (LCLS) ... NHsBE
Bird Aircraft Strike Hazard ... BASH
Bird Airplane Club (EA) ... BAC
Bird and Bat Banding Scheme (SAUS) ... BBBS
Bird Association of California (EA) ... BAC
Bird Avoidance Model (SAUS) ... BAM
Bird Breeder's Lung [*Medicine*] (MELL) ... BBL
Bird Clubs of America (EA) ... BCA

Bird Combat Air Patrol (SAUS) .... BIRDCAP
Bird Control Unit (SAUS) .... BCU
Bird Corp. [*NASDAQ symbol*] (NQ) .... BIRD
Bird Corp. [*Associated Press*] (SAG) .... BirdC
Bird Corp. [*Associated Press*] (SAG) .... BirdCp
Bird Corp. $1.85 Cv Pref [*NASDAQ symbol*] (TTSB) .... BIRDP
Bird Dog Association, International (EA) .... BDAI
Bird Electronic Co. (SAUO) .... BE
Bird Friends Society [*Defunct*] (EA) .... BFS
Bird Impact Resistant Transparency (PDAA) .... BIRT
Bird Investigation, Review, and Deterrent [*NASA*] .... BIRD
Bird Island [*Seychelles Islands*] [*Airport symbol*] (OAG) .... BDI
Bird Island Public Library, Bird Island, MN [*Library symbol*] [*Library of Congress*] (LCLS) .... MnBi
Bird Island-Danube-Renville-Sacred Heart (BDRSH) Public Schools, Renville, MN [*Library symbol*] [*Library of Congress*] (LCLS) .... MnRenBPS
Bird. Laws Respecting Landlords, Tenants, and Lodgers [*11th ed.*] [*1833*] [*A publication*] (DLA) .... Bird L & T
Bird Leasing, Inc. [*ICAO designator*] (FAAC) .... BIR
Bird Lovers Anthology [*A publication*] .... BLA
Bird. New Pocket Conveyancer [*5th ed.*] [*1830*] [*A publication*] (DLA) .... Bird Conv
Bird Observers Club of Australia (SAUO) .... BOC
Bird Protection League of South Australia .... BPLSA
Bird Resistant [*Sorghum variety*] .... BR
Bird. Solution of Precedents of Settlements [*1800*] [*A publication*] (DLA) .... Bird Sol Pr
Bird Strike Committee Europe [*Denmark*] (EAIO) .... BSCE
Bird Study (SAUS) .... Bird Stud
Bird Sweep Completed [*Aviation*] (FAAC) .... BSC
Bird-Fanciers Lung [*Medicine*] .... BFL
Birds and Wildlife .... B&W
Birds Mouth (SAUS) .... BM
Birds of a Feather Session (SAUS) .... BOFS
Birds of Prey Rehabilitation Foundation (EA) .... BPRF
[*The*] **Birds of Western Palearctic** [*Book series*] [*British*] [*A publication*] .... BWP
Birds Protection Act (SAUS) .... BPA
Bird's Supplement to Barton's Conveyancing [*A publication*] (DLA) .... Bird Supp
Birdseye's Statutes [*New York*] [*A publication*] (DLA) .... Birds St
Bird's-Eye-View .... BEV
Birdsville [*Australia*] [*Airport symbol*] (OAG) .... BVI
Birdwood's Printed Judgments [*India*] [*A publication*] (DLA) .... Birdw
Birgenair [*Turkey*] [*ICAO designator*] (FAAC) .... BHY
Birjand [*Iran*] [*ICAO location identifier*] (ICLI) .... OIMB
Birkbeck College Computation Laboratory [*British*] .... BCCL
Birkenhead [*British depot code*] .... BHD
Birkenhead's Judgments, House of Lords [*1919-22*] [*England*] [*A publication*] (DLA) .... Birk J
Birlesmis Milletler Turk Dernegi [*United Nations Association of Turkey*] (EAIO) .... BMTD
Birma (SAUO) .... BUR
Birmingham [*City, county borough, and university in England*] .... BHAM
Birmingham [*Alabama*] [*Airport symbol*] .... BHM
Birmingham [*England*] [*Airport symbol*] (OAG) .... BHX
Birmingham [*Diocesan abbreviation*] [*Alabama*] (TOCD) .... BIR
Birmingham [*City, county borough, and university in England*] .... BIRM
Birmingham [*British*] [*ICAO location identifier*] (ICLI) .... EGBB
Birmingham [*Alabama*] [*ICAO location identifier*] (ICLI) .... KBHM
Birmingham Aerocentre, Ltd. [*British*] [*FAA designator*] (FAAC) .... HOT
Birmingham, AL [*Location identifier*] [*FAA*] (FAAL) .... ROE
Birmingham, AL [*Location identifier*] [*FAA*] (FAAL) .... VUZ
Birmingham, AL [*Television station call letters*] .... WABM
Birmingham, AL [*AM radio station call letters*] .... WAGG
Birmingham, AL [*AM radio station call letters*] .... WAPI
Birmingham, AL [*AM radio station call letters*] .... WATV
Birmingham, AL [*AM radio station call letters*] .... WAYE
Birmingham, AL [*FM radio station call letters*] .... WBFR
Birmingham, AL [*FM radio station call letters*] .... WBHM
Birmingham, AL [*Television station call letters*] .... WBIQ
Birmingham, AL [*Television station call letters*] .... WBMG
Birmingham, AL [*Television station call letters*] .... WBRC
Birmingham, AL [*AM radio station call letters*] (RBYB) .... WDJC-AM
Birmingham, AL [*FM radio station*] (RBYB) .... WDJC-FM
Birmingham, AL [*FM radio station call letters*] .... WENN
Birmingham, AL [*AM radio station call letters*] .... WERC
Birmingham, AL [*AM radio station call letters*] (BROA) .... WEZN
Birmingham, AL [*FM radio station call letters*] .... WGIB
Birmingham, AL [*Television station call letters*] (BROA) .... WIAT
Birmingham, AL [*AM radio station call letters*] .... WJOX
Birmingham, AL [*FM radio station call letters*] .... WJSR
Birmingham, AL [*FM radio station call letters*] .... WLJR
Birmingham, AL [*FM radio station call letters*] .... WMJJ
Birmingham, AL [*AM radio station call letters*] (BROA) .... WMKI
Birmingham, AL [*FM radio station call letters*] .... WMXQ
Birmingham, AL [*FM radio station call letters*] .... WODL
Birmingham, AL [*Television station call letters*] .... WTTO
Birmingham, AL [*FM radio station call letters*] .... WVSU
Birmingham, AL [*Television station call letters*] .... WVTM
Birmingham, AL [*AM radio station call letters*] .... WYDE
Birmingham, AL [*FM radio station call letters*] (BROA) .... WYSF-FM
Birmingham, AL [*FM radio station call letters*] .... WZRR
Birmingham, AL [*AM radio station call letters*] .... WZZK
Birmingham, AL [*FM radio station call letters*] .... WZZK-FM
Birmingham and Fire Counties Architectural Association (SAUO) .... BFCAA
Birmingham and Loughborough Electronic Network Device (SAUS) .... BLEND
Birmingham and Loughborough Electronic Networking Development (SAUS) .... BLEND
Birmingham and Midland Institute (SAUO) .... BMI
Birmingham and Midland Institute School of Music (SAUO) .... BSM
Birmingham and Midland Motor Omnibus Co. (SAUO) .... BMMO
Birmingham & Midland Motor Omnibus Co. Ltd. [*British*] (DCTA) .... BMMD
Birmingham and Midlands Scientific Society (SAUO) .... BMSS
Birmingham & Southeastern (SAUS) .... B&SE
Birmingham & Southeastern R. R. [*AAR code*] .... BSE
Birmingham and Warwickshire Archaeological Society (SAUO) .... BWAS
Birmingham Aviation Ltd. [*British*] [*ICAO designator*] (FAAC) .... ATX
Birmingham Belt R. R. [*AAR code*] .... BB
Birmingham Botanical and Horticultural Society (SAUO) .... BBHS
Birmingham College of Advanced Technology (SAUO) .... BCAT
Birmingham Contemporary Music Group [*British*] .... BCMG
Birmingham Electric Co. (SAUO) .... BME
Birmingham European Airways [*Airline flight code*] (ODBW) .... VB
Birmingham Group Training Association (SAUO) .... BGTA
Birmingham Libraries Cooperative Mechanisation Project [*Later, Library Services Ltd.*] (NITA) .... BLCMP
Birmingham Library and Information Network [*British*] (NITA) .... B-LINK
Birmingham Medical Institute (SAUO) .... BMI
Birmingham Metallurgical Association (SAUO) .... BMetA
Birmingham Metallurgical Society (SAUO) .... BMS
Birmingham, MI [*FM radio station call letters*] .... WCSX
Birmingham Natural History Society (SAUO) .... BNHS
Birmingham Nitro Proof (SAUS) .... BNP
Birmingham Post & Mail Ltd., Birmingham, United Kingdom [*Library symbol*] [*Library of Congress*] (LCLS) .... UkBP
Birmingham Pregnancy Advisory Serivice (SAUO) .... BPAS
Birmingham Procurement District (SAUS) .... BIRMPDIS
Birmingham Productivity Association (SAUO) .... BPA
Birmingham Public and Jefferson County Free Library (SAUO) .... BP&JC FL
Birmingham Public and Jefferson County Free Library, Birmingham, AL [*Library symbol*] [*Library of Congress*] (LCLS) .... AB
Birmingham Public Libraries, Birmingham, United Kingdom [*Library symbol*] [*Library of Congress*] (LCLS) .... UkB
Birmingham Public Library [*Alabama*] .... BPL
Birmingham Reference Library (SAUO) .... BRL
Birmingham Repair [*British military*] (DMA) .... BR
Birmingham Revision [*of BNA*] [*Medicine*] [*British*] .... BR
Birmingham School of Music (SAUO) .... BSM
Birmingham School of Printing (SAUO) .... BSP
Birmingham School of Printing (SAUS) .... BSP
Birmingham Small Arms, Inc. (MCD) .... BSA
Birmingham Solar Oscillations Network .... BISON
Birmingham Sound Reproducers, Ltd. (SAUO) .... BSR
Birmingham Southern College [*Alabama*] .... BSC
Birmingham Southern College, Birmingham, AL [*Library symbol*] [*Library of Congress*] (LCLS) .... ABS
Birmingham Southern Railroad Co. [*AAR code*] .... BS
Birmingham Standard [*Wire gauge*] .... BS
Birmingham Steel Corp. [*NYSE symbol*] (SPSG) .... BIR
Birmingham Steel Corp. [*Associated Press*] (SAG) .... BirStl
Birmingham Steel Corp. (EFIS) .... BSC
Birmingham Symphony Orchestra (SAUO) .... BSO
Birmingham Technology Ltd. at Aston Science Park [*Research center*] [*British*] (IRUK) .... BTL
Birmingham Transport Historical Group (SAUO) .... BTHG
Birmingham University, Birmingham, United Kingdom [*Library symbol*] [*Library of Congress*] (LCLS) .... UkBU
Birmingham University Industrial Liaison for Technology [*Research center*] [*British*] .... BUILT
Birmingham University Railway and Inland Waterway Society (SAUO) .... BURIWS
Birmingham Utilities, Inc. [*NASDAQ symbol*] (SAG) .... BIRM
Birmingham Utilities, Inc. [*Associated Press*] (SAG) .... BirmUtl
Birmingham Utils [*NASDAQ symbol*] (TTSB) .... BIRM
Birmingham Wire Gauge (IDOE) .... BG
Birmingham Wire Gauge .... BWG
Birmingham-Jefferson Library, Birmingham, AL [*OCLC symbol*] (OCLC) .... ABJ
Birnamwood, WI [*FM radio station call letters*] .... WHET
Birrfeld [*Switzerland*] [*ICAO location identifier*] (ICLI) .... LSZF
Birsa Agricultural University (SAUO) .... BAU
Birth .... B
Birth (ADA) .... BTH
Birth Certificate .... BC
Birth Certificate (GEAB) .... bcer
Birth Control .... BC
Birth Control Advisory Bureau [*British*] (BI) .... BCAB
Birth Control Association (SAUO) .... BCA
Birth Control Campaign (SAUS) .... BCC
Birth Control Clinic .... BCC
Birth Control Glasses [*Military*] (MUSM) .... BCG
Birth Control Institute (SAUS) .... BCI
Birth Control Investigation Committee (BABM) .... BCIC
Birth Control Investigation Committee (SAUO) .... BICIC
Birth Control League of America (SAUO) .... BCLA
Birth Control Medication .... BCM
Birth Control Pill [*Medicine*] .... BCP
Birth Control Regimen [*Medicine*] (MELL) .... BCR
Birth Control-Abortion Referral Service (SAUS) .... BC-ARS
Birth Date [*Medicine*] (MELL) .... BD
Birth Date (GEAB) .... bdt
Birth Defect [*Neonatology*] (DAVI) .... BD

Birth Defect and Clinical Genetic Society [*Defunct*] (EA) ... BDCGS
Birth Defects Foundation (SAUO) ... BDF
Birth Defects Information System [*Center for Birth Defects Information Services, Inc.*] [*Information service or system*] (IID) ... BDIS
Birth Defects Monitoring Program (SAUO) ... BDMP
Birth Education, Training, and Acceptance ... BETA
Birth Injury [*Medicine*] (MELL) ... BI
Birth Support Providers, International [*Affiliated with National Association of Childbirth Assistants (NACA)*] (PAZ) ... BSPI
Birth Trauma (MELL) ... BT
Birth Visit (ROG) ... BV
Birth Weight [*Medicine*] ... BW
Birth Weight [*Medicine*] ... BWT
Birthdate (DD) ... b
Birthday (ABBR) ... BRTDY
Birthday (ABBR) ... BRTHDY
Birthday Honours [*Titles conferred on the sovereign's birthday*] [*British*] ... BH
Birthing Room (MELL) ... BR
Birthmark (MELL) ... BM
Birthmark [*Dermatology*] (DAVI) ... BMK
Birthmark (ABBR) ... BRTHMK
Birthmark (ABBR) ... BRTMK
Birthparent & Relative Group Society (AC) ... BRGS
Birthplace (ADWA) ... bp
Birthplace ... BP
Birthplace ... BPL
Birthplace (ADWA) ... bpl
Birthplace (ABBR) ... BRTHPL
Birthplace (ABBR) ... BRTPLC
Birthrate ... BR
Birthright (ABBR) ... BRTHRGT
Birthright (ABBR) ... BRTRT
Births, Deaths, and Marriages ... BDM
Births, Marriage and Deaths (WDAA) ... BMD
Birthstone (ABBR) ... BRTHSTN
Birthstone (ABBR) ... BRTST
Birthweight (NTIO) ... bw
Bis [*Twice*] [*Pharmacy*] ... B
bis Acetylacetonate (SAUS) ... ACA
Bis Horis [*Every Two Hours*] [*Pharmacy*] (ROG) ... BIS HOR
Bis in Die [*Twice a Day*] [*Pharmacy*] ... BD
Bis in Die [*Twice a Day*] [*Pharmacy*] ... BID
Bis in Die [*Twice a Day*] [*Pharmacy*] (ROG) ... BIS in D
Bis in Die Sumendus [*To Be Taken Twice a Day*] [*Pharmacy*] ... BDS
Bis in Noctus [*Twice a Night*] [*Pharmacy*] ... BIN
Bis in Septem Diebus [*Twice a Week*] [*Pharmacy*] ... bi7d
Bis in Septem Dies [*Twice in Seven Days*] [*Pharmacy*] (ROG) ... BIS in 7 D
Bis Terve in Die [*Two or Three Times a Day*] [*Pharmacy*] ... BTID
Bis Tris Propane [*Biological buffer*] ... BTP
bis-4-Decyloxybenziliden-2-chloro-1,4-phenylendiamin (SAUS) ... DOBCP
Bis(acetatomercurimethyl)dioxane [*Organic chemistry*] ... BAMD
Bis(acryloyl)cystamine [*Organic chemistry*] ... BAC
Bis(amidino-benzimidazolyl)methane [*Biochemistry*] ... BABIM
Bis(aminomethyl)cyclohexane [*Organic chemistry*] ... BAC
Bis(aminophenoxy)ethanetetraacetic Acid [*Organic chemistry*] ... BAPTA
Bisaminophenyloxadiazole [*Organic chemistry*] ... BAO
Bis(aminopropyl)piperazine [*Organic chemistry*] ... BAPP
Bisbee [*Arizona*] [*Airport symbol*] (OAG) ... BSQ
Bisbee, AZ [*FM radio station call letters*] (RBYB) ... KRMB-FM
Bisbee, AZ [*FM radio station call letters*] ... KWCD
Bisbee, AZ [*FM radio station call letters*] (RBYB) ... KWRB
Bis-Benzimidazo Benzophenanthroline (SAUS) ... BBB
Bis(benzimidazole) [*Organic chemistry*] ... BBI
Bis-Benzimidazole Perylene (SAUS) ... BBIP
Bis-Benzimidazole perylene (SAUS) ... BBZ
Bis(benzylidene)thiocarbohydrazone [*Organic chemistry*] ... BTH
Bis(biphenyl)oxadiazole [*Organic chemistry*] ... BBOD
Bis(biphenylyl)oxazole [*Organic chemistry*] ... BBO
Bis(bromomethyl)oxetane [*Organic chemistry*] ... BBMO
Bisbutoxybenzylidenebitoluidine [*Organic chemistry*] ... BBBT
Bis(carboxyethyl)carboxyfluorescein [*Organic chemistry*] ... BCECF
Biscarosse/Parentis [*France*] [*ICAO location identifier*] (ICLI) ... LFBS
Biscayan (SAUS) ... Bisc
Biscayan ... BISC
Biscayne Apparel, Inc. [*Formerly, Biscayne Holdings, Inc.*] [*AMEX symbol*] (SPSG) ... BHA
Biscayne Apparel, Inc. [*Associated Press*] (SAG) ... BiscApp
Biscayne Bay, FL [*Location identifier*] [*FAA*] (FAAL) ... BSY
Biscayne Chemical Laboratories, Inc., Miami, FL [*Library symbol*] [*Library of Congress*] (LCLS) ... FMB
Biscayne College, Miami, FL [*OCLC symbol*] (OCLC) ... FBM
Biscayne College, Miami, FL [*Library symbol*] [*Library of Congress*] (LCLS) ... FMBC
Biscayne College, St. Thomas University Law School, Miami, FL [*Library symbol*] [*Library of Congress*] (LCLS) ... FMBC-L
Bis-Chlorethyl-Nitroso-Urea (SAUS) ... BCNU
Bis-Chlormethyl Ether (SAUS) ... BCME
Bis(chloroethyl)nitrosourea [*Carmustine*] [*Also, BiCNU*] [*Antineoplastic drug regimen*] ... BCNU
Bis(chloroethyl)nitrosourea [*Carmustine*] [*Also, BCNU*] [*Antineoplastic drug regimen*] ... BiCNU
Bis(chloroethyl)sulfide [*Biochemistry*] ... BCES
Bis(chloromethyl) Ether [*Organic chemistry*] ... BCME
Bis-Chloromethyl Ether (SAUS) ... BCME
Bis(chloromethyl)oxetane [*Organic chemistry*] ... BCMO
Bis(chlorosulfophenyl)phenanthrolinedicarboxylic Acid [*Organic chemistry*] ... BCPDA
Biscuit ... BSCT
Biscuit (ABBR) ... BSCUT
Biscuit and Cracker Distributors Association (EA) ... BCDA
Biscuit and Cracker Manufacturers' Association (EA) ... B & CMA
Biscuit and Cracker Manufacturers' Association (NTPA) ... BCMA
Biscuit Bakers Institute [*B & CMA*] [*Absorbed by*] (EA) ... BBI
Biscuit, Cake, Chocolate, and Confectionery Alliance (EAIO) ... BCCCA
Bis-diazotized Benzidine [*Hematology*] ... BDB
Bis(dimethylamino) Propane [*Organic chemistry*] ... BDAP
Bis((dimethylaminoethyl)indole)sulfide [*Biochemistry*] ... BDIS
Bis(dimethylsilyl)acetamide [*Organic chemistry*] ... BDSA
Bisector (SAUS) ... bis
Bisegmental Neuron [*Neurology*] ... BSN
Biserial Coefficient of Correlation (DIPS) ... rbis
Bis(ethylenedithiolo)tetrathiafulvalene [*Organic chemistry*] ... BEDT-TTF
Bis(ethylhexyl) Phthalate [*Organic chemistry*] ... BEHP
Bisethylhexyl Phthalate (SAUS) ... BEHP
Bisexual [*Psychiatry and infectious disease*] (DAVI) ... AC-DC
Bisexual (DSUE) ... BI
Bisexual (ADWA) ... Bi
Bisexual (TAD) ... bi
Bisexual (SAUS) ... BISEX
Bisexual Asian Female (ADWA) ... BIAF
Bisexual Asian Male (ADWA) ... BIAM
Bisexual Black Female (ADWA) ... BIBF
Bisexual Black Male (ADWA) ... BIBM
Bisexual Center [*Defunct*] (EA) ... BC
Bisexual Hispanic Female (ADWA) ... BIHF
Bisexual Hispanic Male (ADWA) ... BIHM
Bisexual Jewish Female (ADWA) ... BIJF
Bisexual Jewish Male (ADWA) ... BIJM
Bisexual White Male ... BiWM
bis-Fulvene-6.6-Dithiol (SAUS) ... FDT
Bisha [*Saudi Arabia*] [*Airport symbol*] (OAG) ... BHH
Bisha [*Saudi Arabia*] [*ICAO location identifier*] (ICLI) ... OEBH
Bis(hexamethylene)triamine [*Organic chemistry*] ... BHMT
Bishop [*Chess*] ... B
Bishop [*Ecclesiastical*] ... B
Bishop ... BHP
Bishop [*California*] [*Airport symbol*] (OAG) ... BIH
Bishop (DSUE) ... BISH
Bishop (GEAB) ... bish
Bishop (NTIO) ... Bish
Bishop (SAUS) ... Bish
Bishop (WDAA) ... bp
Bishop ... BP
Bishop (WA) ... Bp
Bishop ... BSHP
Bishop and Martyr [*Church calendars*] ... BM
Bishop Baraga Assiocation (SAUO) ... BBA
Bishop, CA [*Location identifier*] [*FAA*] (FAAL) ... CDT
Bishop, CA [*AM radio station call letters*] ... KBOV
Bishop, CA [*FM radio station call letters*] ... KIBS
Bishop College (SAUO) ... BC
Bishop College, Dallas, TX [*Inactive*] [*OCLC symbol*] (OCLC) ... BIS
Bishop College, Dallas, TX [*Library symbol*] [*Library of Congress*] (LCLS) ... TxDaBC
Bishop. First Book of the Law [*A publication*] (DLA) ... Bish First Bk
Bishop Kearney High School Library, Rochester, NY [*OCLC symbol*] (OCLC) ... RVR
Bishop Method of Clothing Construction Council (EA) ... BMCCC
Bishop Museum (SAUS) ... Bish Mus
Bishop Museum Press (SAUS) ... Bishop
Bishop of Carlisle [*British*] ... CARIOL
Bishop of Chichester [*British*] ... CICESTR
Bishop of Durham [*British*] ... DUNELM
Bishop of Salisbury [*British*] ... SARUM
Bishop on Contracts [*A publication*] (DLA) ... Bish Con
Bishop on Contracts [*A publication*] (DLA) ... Bish Cont
Bishop on Criminal Law [*A publication*] (DLA) ... Bish Cr Law
Bishop on Criminal Procedure [*A publication*] (DLA) ... Bich Crim Proc
Bishop on Criminal Procedure [*A publication*] (DLA) ... Bish Cr Proc
Bishop on Insolvent Debtors [*A publication*] (DLA) ... Bish Ins
Bishop on Marriage and Divorce [*A publication*] (DLA) ... Bish Mar & Div
Bishop on Marriage, Divorce, and Separation [*A publication*] (DLA) ... Bish Mar Div & Sep
Bishop on Married Women [*A publication*] (DLA) ... Bish Mar Wom
Bishop on Non-Contract Law, Rights, and Torts [*A publication*] (DLA) ... Bish Non-Cont Law
Bishop on Statutory Crimes [*A publication*] (DLA) ... Bish Stat Cr
Bishop on Statutory Crimes [*A publication*] (DLA) ... Bish St Crimes
Bishop on Written Law [*A publication*] (DLA) ... Bish Wr L
Bishop Resources Development Ltd. [*Vancouver Stock Exchange symbol*] ... BIS
Bishop Routhier School, High Prairie, Alberta [*Library symbol*] [*National Library of Canada*] (BIB) ... AHPBS
Bishop State Junior College, Mobile, AL [*Library symbol*] [*Library of Congress*] (LCLS) ... AMobB
Bishop Suffragan ... BS
Bishop Suffrogan [*or Suffrogan Bishop*] (BARN) ... Bp Suff
Bishop, TX [*FM radio station call letters*] ... KFLZ
Bishopric ... BHPRIC
Bishops (ADA) ... BB
Bishops' Advisory Group on Urban Priority Areas (WDAA) ... BAGUPA

Bishops' Committee for Ecumenical and Interreligious Affairs (EA) ... BCEIA
Bishops' Committee for Education [*Australia*] ... BCE
Bishops' Committee for Industrial Affairs [*Australia*] ... BCIA
Bishops' Committee for the Spanish Speaking [*Later, SHA*] ... BCSS
Bishops' Committee on Priestly Formation (EA) ... BCPF
Bishops' Committee on the Liturgy (EA) ... BCL
Bishop's Committee on Vocations (EA) ... BCV
Bishops Court [*British*] [*ICAO location identifier*] (ICLI) ... EGOC
Bishop's Digest [*Montana*] [*A publication*] (DLA) ... Bishop Dig
Bishop's Edition of Burrill on Assignments [*A publication*] (DLA) ... Bish Burr
Bishops Falls Public Library, Bishops Falls, NF, Canada [*Library symbol*] [*Library of Congress*] (LCLS) ... CaNfBF
Bishops Falls Public Library, Newfoundland [*Library symbol*] [*National Library of Canada*] (NLC) ... NFBF
Bishop's Law of Nolle Prosequi [*A publication*] (DLA) ... Bish Noll Pros
Bishop's New Criminal Law [*A publication*] (DLA) ... Bish New Cr Law
Bishop's New Criminal Procedure [*A publication*] (DLA) ... Bish New Cr Proc
Bishop's Transcript [*British*] (ROG) ... BT
Bishop's Trial [*A publication*] (DLA) ... B Tr
Bishop's University, Department of Geography, Lennoxville, PQ, Canada [*Library symbol*] [*Library of Congress*] (LCLS) ... CaQLBG
Bishop's University, Lennoxville, PQ, Canada [*Library symbol*] [*Library of Congress*] (LCLS) ... CaQLB
Bishop's University, Lennoxville, Quebec [*Library symbol*] [*National Library of Canada*] (NLC) ... QLB
Bishop's University Library [*UTLAS symbol*] ... BHP
Bishopville, SC [*AM radio station call letters*] ... WAGS
Bishopville, SC [*FM radio station call letters*] ... WKHT
Bis(hydroxybenzyl)ethylenediaminediacetic Acid [*Organic chemistry*] ... HBED
Bishydroxycoumarin (SAUS) ... BHC
Bis(hydroxycyclohexyl)nitrosourea [*Antineoplastic drug*] ... BHCNU
Bis(hydroxyethyl)aminoethanesulfonic Acid [*A buffer*] [*Organic chemistry*] ... BES
Bis(hydroxyethyl)dimerate [*Organic chemistry*] ... BHED
Bis(hydroxyethyl)glycine [*A buffer*] [*Organic chemistry*] ... BICINE
Bis(hydroxyethyl)piperazine [*Organic chemistry*] ... BHEP
Bis(hydroxyethyl)terephthalate [*Organic chemistry*] ... BHET
Bis(hydroxymethyl)ferrocene [*Organic chemistry*] ... BHMF
Bis(hydroxymethyl)furan [*Organic chemistry*] ... BHMF
Bis(hydroxymethyl)peroxide [*Organic chemistry*] ... BHMP
Bis(hydroxyphenyl)trichloroethane [*Organic chemistry*] ... HPTE
Biskra [*Algeria*] [*Airport symbol*] (OAG) ... BSK
Biskra [*Algeria*] [*ICAO location identifier*] (ICLI) ... DAUB
Bislig [*Philippines*] [*Airport symbol*] (OAG) ... BPH
Bislig, Surigao Del Sur [*Philippines*] [*ICAO location identifier*] (ICLI) ... RPWZ
Bismaleimide Triazine (AAEL) ... BT
Bis(maleimido)hexane [*Organic chemistry*] ... BMH
Bismarck [*North Dakota*] [*Airport symbol*] (OAG) ... BIS
Bismarck Archipelago (SAUS) ... Bis Arch
Bismarck Hospital, School of Nursing Library, Bismarck, ND [*Library symbol*] [*Library of Congress*] (LCLS) ... NdBH
Bismarck Junior College [*North Dakota*] ... BJC
Bismarck Junior College, Bismarck, ND [*Library symbol*] [*Library of Congress*] (LCLS) ... NdBC
Bismarck, ND [*Location identifier*] [*FAA*] (FAAL) ... BZX
Bismarck, ND [*FM radio station call letters*] (RBYB) ... KACL-FM
Bismarck, ND [*Television station call letters*] ... KBME
Bismarck, ND [*Television station call letters*] (BROA) ... KBME-DT
Bismarck, ND [*AM radio station call letters*] ... KBMR
Bismarck, ND [*Television station call letters*] ... KBMY
Bismarck, ND [*FM radio station call letters*] ... KBYZ
Bismarck, ND [*FM radio station call letters*] ... KCND
Bismarck, ND [*AM radio station call letters*] ... KFYR
Bismarck, ND [*Television station call letters*] ... KFYR-TV
Bismarck, ND [*FM radio station call letters*] ... KKCT
Bismarck, ND [*Television station call letters*] (BROA) ... KNDX
Bismarck, ND [*FM radio station call letters*] ... KQDY
Bismarck, ND [*FM radio station call letters*] ... KSSS
Bismarck, ND [*Television station call letters*] ... KXMB
Bismarck, ND [*AM radio station call letters*] (RBYB) ... KXMR
Bismarck, ND [*FM radio station call letters*] ... KYYY
Bismarck [*Veterans Memorial*] **Public Library, Bismarck, ND** [*Library symbol*] [*Library of Congress*] (LCLS) ... NdBV
Bismarck-Henning Community Unit School District, Bismarck, IL [*Library symbol*] [*Library of Congress*] (LCLS) ... IBisSD
Bismarck-Mandan, ND [*AM radio station call letters*] ... KLXX
Bismark District Office (SAUO) ... BIS
Bis(methyloxybenzylidene)bitoluidine [*Organic chemistry*] ... BMBT
Bis(methylstyryl)benzene [*Organic chemistry*] ... BMSB
Bismorpholinecarbamylsulfenamide [*Organic chemistry*] ... BCMS
Bismuth [*Chemical element*] ... Bi
Bismuth [*Chemical element*] (ROG) ... BIS
bismuth (SAUS) ... bis
Bismuth Formic Iodide (SAUS) ... BFI
Bismuth Germanate [*Inorganic chemistry*] ... BGO
Bismuth, Germanium, and Oxygen [*Inorganic chemistry*] ... BGO
Bismuth Glycine Glucose Yeast [*Medicine*] (DMAA) ... BIGGY
Bismuth Institute [*Brussels, Belgium*] (EAIO) ... BI
Bismuth Iodoform and Paraffin Paste [*Medicine*] ... BIPP
Bismuth Iodoform Paraffin [*Medicine*] ... BIP
Bismuth Iodoform Petrolatum Paste [*Biochemistry*] (DAVI) ... BIPP
Bismuth Silicon Oxide [*LASER Crystal*] (NITA) ... BSO
Bismuth, Strontium, Calcium, Copper, Oxide [*Inorganic chemistry*] ... BSCCO
bismuth subcarbonate (SAUS) ... bis subcarb
bismuth subgallate (SAUS) ... bis subgall
bismuth subnitrate (SAUS) ... bis subnit
bismuth subsalicylate (SAUS) ... bis subsal
Bismuth Subsalicylate [*Antidiarrhea agent*] ... BS
Bismuth Subsalicylate (MELL) ... BSS
Bismuth Sulfite [*Agar*] [*Bacteriology*] ... BS
Bismuthinite (SAUS) ... bs
Bismuth-Sulfite Agar [*Medicine*] (MAE) ... BSA
Bismuth-Tin crystal growth (SAUS) ... BiSn
Bismuthum (SAUS) ... Bi
Bis(nitrophenyl)ethyl [*Organic radical*] ... BNPE
Bis(nitrophenyl)ethyloxycarbonyl [*Organic radical*] ... BNPEOC
Bison (ABBR) ... BSN
Bison Petroleum & Minerals [*Vancouver Stock Exchange symbol*] ... BSP
Bispham's Principles of Equity [*A publication*] (DLA) ... Bisp Eq
Bispham's Principles of Equity [*A publication*] (DLA) ... Bisph Eq
Bisphenol A (EDCT) ... BPA
Bisphenol A-Glycidyl Methacrylate [*Organic chemistry*] ... BIS-GMA
Bisphosphoglycerate [*Biochemistry*] ... BPG
Bisphosphonomethylglycine (DB) ... BPMG
Bispinous [*or Interspinous*] [*Gynecology*] ... bisp
Bispinous [*or Interspinous*] **Diameter** [*Orthopedics*] (DAVI) ... Bisp
Bispinous Diameter [*Pelvic measurement*] (CPH) ... Bisp Diam
Bis(pyridiniumtrimethylene) [*Dichloride*] [*Biochemistry*] ... BPT
Bissau [*Portuguese Guinea*] [*Airport symbol*] (OAG) ... BXO
Bissau/Oswaldo Vieira International [*Guinea-Bissau*] [*ICAO location identifier*] (ICLI) ... GGOV
Bissell's Minnesota Statutes [*A publication*] (DLA) ... Biss Stat
Bissell's United States Circuit Court Reports [*A publication*] (DLA) ... Bis
Bissell's United States Circuit Court Reports [*A publication*] (DLA) ... Biss
Bissell's United States Circuit Court Reports, Seventh Circuit [*A publication*] (DLA) ... Bissell
Bissell's United States Circuit Court Reports, Seventh Circuit [*A publication*] (DLA) ... Biss (US)
Bisset's Partnership and Joint Stock Companies [*1847*] [*A publication*] (DLA) ... Biss Part
Bissett and Smith's Digest [*South Africa*] [*A publication*] (DLA) ... Biss & Sm
Bissett on Estates for Life [*A publication*] (DLA) ... Biss Est
Bissett on Estates for Life [*A publication*] (DLA) ... Bissett Est
Bissextile Year [*Leap Year*] (ROG) ... BIS
Bissora [*Guinea-Bissau*] [*ICAO location identifier*] (ICLI) ... GGBI
Bissync Data Link Control (LAIN) ... BDLC
Bista Bancorp [*Associated Press*] (SAG) ... VistaBcP
Bistable (NRCH) ... B/S
Bistable Diode Laser (SAUS) ... BDL
Bistable Laser Diode (SAUS) ... BILD
Bistable Laser Diode (SAUS) ... BSLD
Bistable Light Emitting Diode (SAUS) ... BILED
Bistable Magnetic (SAUS) ... BIMAG
Bi-stable Magnetic Core (SAUS) ... BIMAC
Bistable Magnetic Core [*Computer science*] ... BIMAC
Bistable Magnetic Core [*Computer science*] ... BIMAG
Bistable Magnetic Core (SAUS) ... BIMAG Core
Bistable Multivibrator [*Electronics*] (IAA) ... BM
Bistable Multivibrator ... BMV
Bistable Multivibrator ... BSM
Bi-Stable Multivibrator (SAUS) ... BSM
Bistable Multivibrator (MUGU) ... BSMV
Bistable Optical Device ... BOD
Bistable Optical Differential Amplifier (MCD) ... BODA
Bistable Optically Controlled Semiconductor Switch (IAA) ... BOSS
Bistable Thermal Donors (AAEL) ... BTD
Bistable Trigger (SAUS) ... BT
Bistaple ... BSTL
Bi-State Academic Libraries [*Library network*] ... BI-SAL
Bi-State Conference (PSS) ... BISC
Bi-State East Conference (PSS) ... BISEC
Bi-State West Conference (PSS) ... BISWC
Bistatic Array (SAUS) ... BISAR
Bistatic Auroral Radar System (SAUS) ... BARS
Bistatic Coherent RADAR Display (MCD) ... BICORD
Bistatic doppler radar receiver Network (SAUS) ... BINET
Bi-Static Fleet Defense (ACAE) ... BFD
Bistatic Identification, Friend or Foe (MCD) ... BIFF
Bistatic Parasitic Radar (SAUS) ... BIPAR
Bistatic RADAR (LAIN) ... B/R
Bistatic RADAR Identification of Hostile Target ... BRIHT
Bistatic RADAR Intelligence Generation and Analysis System (NVT) ... BRIGAND
Bistatic RADAR System (MCD) ... BRASS
Bistatic Receiver and Display System (SAUS) ... BIRADS
Bistatic Reflected Energy Target (MCD) ... BRET
Bistatic SONAR (CAAL) ... BSS
Bistatic Spaceborne Radar (SAUS) ... BSR
Bistatic Synthetic Aperture Harmonic RADAR (MCD) ... BISAHR
Bistatic Thinned Array RADAR (MCD) ... BISTAR
Bis(tert-butylbenzoxazolyl)thiophene [*Organic chemistry*] ... BBOT
Bistre [*Yellowish Brown*] (ROG) ... BIS
Bistre (VRA) ... bist
Bis(tribromophenoxy)ethane [*Flame retardant*] [*Organic chemistry*] ... BTBPE
bis(Trichlorophenyl) Oxalate [*Organic chemistry*] ... TCPO
Bistrifluoroacetamide [*Organic chemistry*] ... BTFA
Bis(trimethylsilyl)acetamide [*Organic chemistry*] ... BSA
Bistrimethylsilylacetamide (SAUS) ... BSA
Bis(trimethylsilyl)acetylene [*Organic chemistry*] ... BTMSA
Bis(trimethylsilyl)carbamate [*Organic chemistry*] ... BSC
Bis(trimethylsilyl)formamide [*Organic chemistry*] ... BSF
Bis(trimethylsilyl)trifluoroacetamide [*Organic chemistry*] ... BSTFA

Bis(trimethylsilyl)urea [*Organic chemistry*] ..... BSU
Bis(tri-n-butyltin) Oxide [*Wood preservative*] (WPI) ..... TBTO
Bis(trinitroethyl)carbonate [*An explosive*] ..... BTNEC
Bis(trinitroethyl)nitramine [*An explosive*] ..... BTNEN
Bistro ..... BSTR
Bistrymethyllacetamide (SAUS) ..... BSA
Bisymmetric Spiral [*Astronomy*] ..... BSS
Bisync [*Protocol*] (PCM) ..... BSC
Bisynchronous (NITA) ..... BISYNC
Bisynchronous Communications Adapter (CIST) ..... BCA
Bisynchronous Communications Module (SAUS) ..... BSCM
Bisynchronous Communications Processor (NITA) ..... BCP
Bisynchronous Frame Level [*Telecommunications*] (NITA) ..... BSCFL
Bisynchronous Oriented Communications System (SAUS) ..... BOCS
Bisynchronous Packet Assembler/ Disassembler (SAUS) ..... BPAD
Bisynchronous Synchronous Communication (SAUS) ..... BSC
BISYS Group [*NASDAQ symbol*] (TTSB) ..... BSYS
BISYS Group, Inc. [*Associated Press*] (SAG) ..... BISYS
BISYS Group, Inc. [*NASDAQ symbol*] (SAG) ..... BSYS
BIT [*Binary Digit*] [*Data transmission speed*] [*Computer science*] (DIT) ..... B
Bit (SAUS) ..... BT
Bit Access Test System (SAUS) ..... BATS
Bit Address (SAUS) ..... BA
Bit Anomaly Detector (SAUS) ..... BAD
BIT [*Binary Digit*] **Attention Deficit Disorder** [*Computer science*] ..... BADD
Bit Block Transfer [*Computer science*] ..... bitBLT
BIT [*Binary Digit*] **Buffer Unit** [*Computer science*] (CET) ..... BBU
Bit Capacity (SAUS) ..... BC
Bit Chain (SAUS) ..... BC
Bit Check (SAUS) ..... BC
Bit Code (SAUS) ..... BC
Bit Combination (SAUS) ..... BC
Bit Configuration (SAUS) ..... BC
BIT [*Binary Digit*] **Control** ..... BC
BIT [*Binary Digit*] **Control Block** [*Computer science*] (IBMDP) ..... BCB
BIT [*Binary Digit*] **Control Panel** [*Computer science*] (MCD) ..... BCP
BIT [*Binary Digit*] **Count Appendage** [*Computer science*] (MHDI) ..... BCA
BIT [*Binary Digit*] **Count Integrity** [*Telecommunications*] (TEL) ..... BCI
BIT [*Binary Digit*] **Density** [*Computer science*] ..... BD
BIT [*Binary Digit*] **Effectiveness Report** (CAAL) ..... BER
Bit Efficient Storage Technique (SAUS) ..... BEST
Bit Error Comparator (ACAE) ..... BEC
Bit Error Correction Rate (SAUS) ..... BECR
BIT [*Binary Digit*] **Error Probability** [*Computer science*] (KSC) ..... BEP
Bit Error Rate (SAUS) ..... BDC
BIT [*Binary Digit*] **Error Rate** [*Computer science*] ..... BER
BIT [*Binary Digit*] **Error Rate Monitor** ..... BERM
BIT [*Binary Digit*] **Error Rate Test** [*Computer science*] ..... BERT
Bit Error Rate Test System (SAUS) ..... BERTS
Bit Error Ratio (COE) ..... BER
Bit Evaluation Report (ACAE) ..... BER
Bit Group (SAUO) ..... BG
BIT [*Binary Digit*] **Image Memory** [*Computer science*] ..... BIM
Bit Independence Criterion (SAUS) ..... BIC
Bit Interleaved Parity [*Electronics*] (ACRL) ..... BIP
Bit Interleaved Parity Violation (VERA) ..... BIPV
BIT [*Binary Digit*] **Light Inspection** (DNAB) ..... BLIN
Bit Location (SAUS) ..... BL
BIT [*Binary Digit*] **Manipulate Load** ..... BML
BIT [*Binary Digit*] **Manipulate Store** ..... BMS
BIT [*Binary Digit*] **Map** [*Computer science*] (PCM) ..... BMP
Bit Map Controller (ACAE) ..... BMC
BIT [*Binary Digit*] **Map Font** [*Computer science*] (PCM) ..... BMF
BIT [*Binary Digit*] **Mark Sequencing** [*Computer science*] (IAA) ..... BMS
BIT [*Binary Digit*] **Matched Filter** ..... BMF
[*A*] **Bit of Money and a Cat** [*Lifestyle classification*] ..... Abomac
Bit Operation Unit (SAUS) ..... BOU
Bit Organized Memory (SAUS) ..... BOM
Bit Organized Store (SAUS) ..... BOS
Bit Oriented Line Discipline (SAUS) ..... BOLD
Bit Oxide (SAUS) ..... BO
Bit Pair (SAUS) ..... BP
BIT [*Binary Digit*] **per Circuit per Hour** [*Computer science*] (IAA) ..... BCH
Bit Position (SAUS) ..... BP
Bit Processor (NITA) ..... BP
BIT [*Binary Digit*] **Rate** [*Data transmission speed*] [*Computer science*] (MCD) ..... BR
BIT [*Binary Digit*] **Rate Low** [*Computer science*] (IAA) ..... BRL
Bit Rate Multiplier (SAUS) ..... BRM
Bit Resolution (SAUS) ..... BR
BIT [*Binary Digit*] **Reversion Circuit** [*Computer science*] (MHDI) ..... BRC
BIT [*Binary Digit*] **Scan** [*Computer science*] (BUR) ..... BSCN
BIT [*Binary Digit*] **Scan Command** [*Computer science*] ..... BSC
Bit Scan Forward (SAUS) ..... BSF
Bit Scan Reverse (SAUS) ..... BSR
Bit Sequence Independence (SAUS) ..... BSI
BIT [*Binary Digit*] **Serial Link** ..... BSL
Bit Shifting Register (SAUS) ..... BSR
Bit Slippage Rate (SAUS) ..... BSR
BIT [*Binary Digit*] **Slippage Rate** [*Computer science*] ..... BSR
BIT [*Binary Digit*] **Space** [*Computer science*] (IAA) ..... BS
Bit Status Register (SAUS) ..... BSR
BIT [*Binary Digit*] **Storage and Sense** [*Computer science*] (IAA) ..... BSS
BIT [*Binary Digit*] **Storage Density** [*Computer science*] ..... BSD
Bit String Operator (SAUS) ..... BSO
Bit Strip Tape Memory (SAUS) ..... BST Memory
BIT [*Binary Digit*] **Sync** [*Computer science*] ..... BS
BIT [*Binary Digit*] **Sync Acquisition** [*Computer science*] ..... BSA
BIT [*Binary Digit*] **Sync Generator** [*Computer science*] ..... BSG
BIT [*Binary Digit*] **Sync Matched Filter** [*Computer science*] ..... BSMF
BIT [*Binary Digit*] **Synchronizer / Signal Conditioner** (PDAA) ..... BSSC
Bit Systems Engineering (ACAE) ..... BSE
Bit Test (ROAS) ..... BT
BIT [*Binary Digit*] **Test** [*Computer science*] ..... BTST
Bit Test and Complement (ROAS) ..... BTC
Bit Test and Reset [*Telecommunications*] (ROAS) ..... BTR
Bit Test and Set (ROAS) ..... BTS
Bit Test Bus Terminator (SAUS) ..... BT
BIT [*Binary Digit*] **Time Counter** [*Computer science*] ..... BTC
Bit Transmitter Noise Test (ACAE) ..... BXNT
Bit Unit (SAUS) ..... BU
Bit Universal Readout Tester (ACAE) ..... BURT
Bit Word (SAUS) ..... BW
Bit Zone Recording (VERA) ..... BZR
Bitam [*Gabon*] [*Airport symbol*] (OAG) ..... BMM
Bitam [*Gabon*] [*ICAO location identifier*] (ICLI) ..... FOOB
Bit-Block Transfer (ADWA) ..... BitBit
BIT [*Binary Digit*]**-Block Transfer** ..... BITBLT
Bit-Block Transfer (SAUS) ..... BitBLT
Bit-Block Transfers [*Computer science*] ..... blts
BITBLT [*Binary Digit-Block Transfer*] **Processing Unit** ..... BPU
Bitburg [*Germany*] [*ICAO location identifier*] (ICLI) ..... EDAB
BIT [*Binary Digit*]**/Byte Conversion** [*Telecommunications*] (TEL) ..... BB
Bitch ..... B
Bit-Compression Multiplexer [*Telecommunications*] (ITD) ..... BCM
Bite Detector ..... BD
Bitec Development Corp. [*Vancouver Stock Exchange symbol*] ..... BTD
Bitemporal (ROG) ..... BT
bitemporal (SAUS) ..... bt
Bitemporal Hemianopia [*Medicine*] (MELL) ..... BTH
Bite-Wing X-Ray (MELL) ..... BWX
Bithionol [*A Bacteriostatic*] [*Pharmacology*] (DAVI) ..... TBP
Bithionol Sulfoxide [*Pharmacology*] ..... BTS
Bithlo, FL [*AM radio station call letters*] (BROA) ..... WNTF
Bithorax Complex [*Gene cluster in fruit fly*] ..... BX-C
Biting (ABBR) ..... BTG
Biting the Carpet (SAUS) ..... BTC
Bitmap Description Format (SAUS) ..... BDF
Bitmap Description/Display Format [*Computer science*] (VERA) ..... BDE
Bitmap Display Format (SAUS) ..... BDF
Bitmap Distribution Format (SAUS) ..... BDF
BitMap Image [*Computer science*] ..... bmp
BITmap Images ..... BMAP
Bitmap Picture (SAUS) ..... BMP
Bit-Mapped File ..... BMP
Bit-Mapped Graphics [*Computer science*] ..... BMP
BITNET [*Because It's Time Network*] **Development and Operations Center** ..... BITDOC
Bitnet Network Information Center (SAUO) ..... BITNIC
BITNET [*Because It's Time Network*] **Network Support Center** ..... BITNSC
Bitolterol [*Pharmacology*] ..... BTL
Bitonic Merge (SAUS) ..... BM
Bitonic Sort (SAUS) ..... BS
BIT [*Binary Digit*]**-Oriented Message** (RDA) ..... BOM
BIT [*Binary Digit*]**-Oriented Protocol** ..... BOP
BIT [*Binary Digit*]**-Plane Encoding** [*Computer science*] ..... BPE
Bi-Trinitroethylnitramine (EDCT) ..... BTNENA
Bi-Trinitroethylurea (EDCT) ..... BTNEU
Bits (SAUS) ..... BI
Bits and Pieces (ACAE) ..... B/P
Bits per Inch (IDOE) ..... bpi
BITs [*Binary Digits*] **per Inch** [*Data density measurement*] [*Computer science*] ..... BPI
BITs [*Binary Digits*] **per Millimeter** [*Data density measurement*] [*Computer science*] ..... BPMM
BITs [*Binary Digits*] **per Minute** [*Data transmission speed*] [*Computer science*] ..... BPM
Bits per Pixel [*Computer science*] (VERA) ..... BPP
Bits per Record (ACAE) ..... BPR
BITs [*Binary Digits*] **per Sample** (MCD) ..... BISMPL
BITs [*Binary Digits*] **per Sample** (NASA) ..... B/SMPL
BITS [*Binary Digits*] **per second** (NITA) ..... BIT/s
BITs [*Binary Digits*] **per Second** [*Data transmission speed*] [*Computer science*] ..... BPS
Bits Per Second [*Computer science*] (WDMC) ..... bps
BITs [*Binary Digits*] **per Second** [*Data transmission speed*] [*Computer science*] (CET) ..... B/S
BITs [*Binary Digits*] **per Second** [*Data transmission speed*] [*Computer science*] (NASA) ..... B/sec
BITS [*Binary Digit*] **per Second per Hertz** [*Telecommunications*] (NITA) ..... B/S/Hz
bits per second per Hertz (SAUS) ..... b/s/Hz
BITs [*Binary Digits*] **per Square Inch** [*Data density measurement*] [*Computer science*] ..... BPSI
Bits per Word (SAUS) ..... B/W
Bits to Bytes Conversion (SAUS) B2BCONV
Bit-Sliced Microprocessor (SAUS) ..... BSM
Bitstream font [*Bitstream Inc.*] (CDE) ..... BT font
Bitstream, Inc. [*NASDAQ symbol*] (SAG) ..... BITS
Bitstream, Inc. [*Associated Press*] (SAG) ..... Bitstrm
Bitter and Burton [*British*] (DSUE) ..... BB
Bitter Lake National Wildlife Refuge (SAUS) ..... BLNWR

Bitter National Magnet Laboratory ... BNML
Bitter Root Public Library, Hamilton, MT [*Library symbol*] [*Library of Congress*] (LCLS) ... MtHam
Bitterroot Resources Ltd. [*Vancouver Stock Exchange symbol*] ... BTT
Bitterwater Creek [*California*] [*Seismograph station code, US Geological Survey*] (SEIS) ... BTW
Bittleston and Wise. New Magistrates' Cases [*England*] [*A publication*] (DLA) ... Bit & Wise
Bittleston, Wise, and Parnell's Magistrates' Cases [*England*] [*A publication*] (DLA) ... Mag Cas
Bittleston, Wise, and Parnell's Reports [*2, 3 New Practice Cases*] [*England*] [*A publication*] (DLA) ... Bitt W & P
Bittleston's Chamber Cases [*1883-84*] [*A publication*] (DLA) ... Bitt Cha Cas
Bittleston's Chamber Cases [*1883-84*] [*A publication*] (DLA) ... Rep in Cha
Bittlestons Chamber Cases (SAUS) ... Repin Cha
Bittleston's Practice Cases [*A publication*] (ILCA) ... Bitt Prac Cas
Bittleston's Practice Cases under Judicature Acts [*England*] [*A publication*] (DLA) ... Bit Prac Cas
Bittleston's Practice Cases under Judicature Acts [*England*] [*A publication*] (DLA) ... Bitt PC
Bittleston's Practice Cases under Judicature Acts [*England*] [*A publication*] (DLA) ... Bitt Pr Cas
Bittleston's Practice Cases under Judicature Acts [*England*] [*A publication*] (DLA) ... Bitt Pr Case
Bittleston's Reports in Chambers, Queen's Bench Division [*England*] [*A publication*] (DLA) ... Bitt
Bittleston's Reports in Chambers, Queen's Bench Division [*England*] [*A publication*] (DLA) ... Bitt Ch
Bittleston's Reports in Chambers, Queen's Bench Division [*England*] [*A publication*] (DLA) ... Bitt Chamb Rep
Bittleston's Reports in Chambers, Queen's Bench Division [*England*] [*A publication*] (DLA) ... Bitt Ch Cas
Bittleston's Reports in Chambers, Queen's Bench Division [*England*] [*A publication*] (DLA) ... Bitt Rep in Ch
Bituberous [*Anatomy*] (DAVI) ... BT
Bitumen ... BITN
Bitumen Mortar (SAUS) ... BM
Bitumen Product (SAUS) ... BIP
bituminized (SAUS) ... bitumd
Bituminized [*Freight*] ... BITUMD
Bituminous [*Technical drawings*] ... BIT
Bituminous (MSA) ... BITUM
Bituminous Aggregate Mixture (OA) ... BAM
Bituminous and Aggregate Equipment Bureau (EA) ... BAEB
Bituminous Coal Division (SAUO) ... BCD
Bituminous Coal Institute [*Absorbed by NCA*] ... BCI
Bituminous Coal Operators' Association (EA) ... BCOA
Bituminous Coal Research, Inc. (SAUO) ... BCR
Bituminous Concrete Producers Association (SAUO) ... BCPA
Bituminous Equipment Manufacturers Bureau [*Later, BAEB*] (EA) ... BEMB
Bituminous Pipe Institute [*Defunct*] (EA) ... BPI
Bituminous Roads Development Group (SAUO) ... BRDG
Bituminous Surface (SAUS) ... BS
Bituminous Treated Base (DAC) ... BTB
Bituninous Coal Research Institute (SAUO) ... BCRI
Bitwise Designs [*Associated Press*] (SAG) ... Bitwse
Bitwise Designs [*NASDAQ symbol*] (SAG) ... BTWS
Biundulant Meningoencephalitis [*Medicine*] (DB) ... BME
Bi-University Institutional Liaison for Development (SAA) ... BUILD
Biuret Test (MELL) ... BT
Biuret-Reactive Material [*Biochemistry*] (MAE) ... BRM
Bivariant (SAUS) ... BIVAR
Bivariant Function Generator (DEN) ... BIVAR
Bivariate Exponential [*Distribution*] [*Statistics*] ... BVE
Bivariate Exponential distribution (SAUS) ... BVE didtribution
Bivariate Normal Mixture [*Statistics*] ... BVN
Bivariate Normal Probability Density (GEOI) ... BNPD
Bivariate Thematic Mapping ... BVTM
Biventricular Assist Device [*Medicine*] (DMAA) ... BVAD
Biventricular Assistance [*Cardiology*] ... BVA
Biventricular Hypertrophy [*Cardiology*] ... BVH
Bivouac (AABC) ... BIV
bivouac (SAUS) ... biv
Biwako Broadcasting Corporation (SAUO) ... BBC
Biweekly ... BI-W
bi-weekly (SAUS) ... bi-w
Biweekly ... BW
Biweekly Progress Report (SAUS) ... BPR
Biweekly Report (MCD) ... BWR
Bixby Memorial Free Library, Vergennes, VT [*Library symbol*] [*Library of Congress*] (LCLS) ... VtVe
Bixby, OK [*FM radio station call letters*] ... KJMM
Bizant [*Australia*] [*Airport symbol*] [*Obsolete*] (OAG) ... BZP
Bizarre (DAVI) ... BIZ
Bizarre People [*Extension of BP - Beautiful People*] [*Slang*] ... BP
Bizerte/Sidi Ahmed [*Tunisia*] [*ICAO location identifier*] (ICLI) ... DTTB
Bizonal I.G. Farben Dispersal Panel (SAUO) ... Fardip
Bizonal International Control Administration (SAUO) ... BICA
Bizonal Supply Committee (SAUO) ... BSC
BJ Services Co. [*NYSE symbol*] (SPSG) ... BJS
BJ Services Wrrt [*NYSE symbol*] (TTSB) ... BJS.WS
Bjerrum Double Band [*Physics*] ... BDB
Bjorkvik [*Sweden*] [*ICAO location identifier*] (ICLI) ... ESKX
Bjornoya [*Norway*] [*ICAO location identifier*] (ICLI) ... ENBJ
BJ's Wholesale Club [*NYSE symbol*] (SG) ... BJ
Bk of N.Y.8.60% Dep Pfd [*NYSE symbol*] (TTSB) ... BKPrB
BKC Semiconductors [*NASDAQ symbol*] (TTSB) ... BKCS
BKC Semiconductors, Inc. [*NASDAQ symbol*] (SAG) ... BKCS
BKC Semiconductors, Inc. [*Associated Press*] (SAG) ... BKC Sem
BKR International (NTPA) ... BKR
Blach & Veatch (SAUO) ... BV
Black (VRA) ... b
Black [*Buoy*] ... B
Black [*Philately*] ... B
Black [*Pencils*] ... B
Black ... BK
Black (ADWA) ... bk
Black (WDMC) ... bl
Black ... BL
Black ... BLCK
Black (ADWA) ... blk
Black [*Thoroughbred racing*] ... BLK
Black (WDMC) ... K
Black Academy of Arts and Letters [*Defunct*] (EA) ... BAAL
Black Action Committee (SAUO) ... BAC
Black Action Movement ... BAM
Black Activist Militant Society (SAUO) ... BAMS
Black Affairs Center [*Later, BACTOD*] (EA) ... BAC
Black Affairs Center for Training and Organizational Development (EA) ... BACTOD
Black Affairs Council (SAUO) ... BAC
Black Afro Militant Movement (SAUO) ... BAMM
[*The*] **Black Agenda** [*An association*] ... TBA
Black American Baptist Churchmen [*An association*] (EA) ... BABC
Black American Cinema Society (EA) ... BACS
Black American Colleges and Universities [*A publication*] ... BACU
Black American Law Students Association (EA) ... BALSA
Black American Response to the African Community [*An association*] (EA) ... BARAC
Black American Response to the African Crisis (EA) ... BARAC
Black American Travel Association [*Defunct*] ... BATA
Black Americans for Bush [*Defunct*] (EA) ... BAB
Black Americans Information Directory [*A publication*] ... BAID
Black and Coloured Sheep Breeders' Association of New South Wales [*Australia*] ... BCSBANSW
Black & Decker (SAUS) ... B&D
Black & Decker Corp. [*NYSE symbol*] (SPSG) ... BDK
Black & Decker Corp. [*Associated Press*] (SAG) ... BlackD
Black & Decker Mfg Co. (SAUO) ... B&D
Black & Decker Mfg. Co. (SAUO) ... BDK
Black and Multiethnic Christian Education Resources Center (EA) ... BMCERC
Black and Non-White YMCA Staffs [*An association*] [*Defunct*] (EA) ... BANWYS
Black & Veatch Consulting Engineers, Central Library, Kansas City, MO [*Library symbol*] [*Library of Congress*] (LCLS) ... MoKBV
Black and White [*Photography, television, etc.*] ... B
Black and White (IDOE) ... B&W
Black & White (VRA) ... b&w
Black and White [*Photography, television, etc.*] ... B & W
Black and White [*Milk of magnesia and aromatic cascara fluid extract*] [*Pharmacy*] ... B & W
Black and White [*Photography, television, etc.*] (KSC) ... BW
Black and White ... B/W
Black and White [*Photography*] [*Art*] (WDMC) ... b/w
Black and White Film Recorder (SAUS) ... BWFR
Black and White Horizontal Bands [*Navigation markers*] ... BWHB
Black and White Horizontal Stripes (SAUS) ... BWHS
Black and White Imagery (SAUS) ... BW-Imagery
Black and White Photography (SAUS) ... BW-Photography
Black and White Vertical Blinds [*Navigation markers*] (DNAB) ... BWVB
Black and White Vertical Stripes [*Navigation markers*] ... BWVS
Black Art (journ.) (SAUS) ... BIA
Black Audio Network, Inc. (NTCM) ... BAN
Black Awareness in Television (EA) ... BAIT
Black Ball Transport, Inc. [*AAR code*] ... BBT
Black Beetle Virus ... BBV
Black Body Cavity (PDAA) ... BBC
Black Body Radiator ... BBR
Black Bolt and Nut Association [*British*] (DBA) ... BBNA
Black Box Corp. [*NASDAQ symbol*] (SAG) ... BBOX
Black Box Corp. [*Associated Press*] (SAG) ... BlackBx
Black Box Model Description Language (SAUS) ... BOMOL
Black Box Under Glass Variable Angle Controllled Temperature [*Automotive paint durability testing*] ... BBUGVACT
Black Brant (SAUS) ... BB
Black, Brown, Red, Orange, Yellow, Green, Blue, Violet, Grey, White [*Electronic component color codes*] (ROAS) ... BBROYGBVGW
Black Business Alliance (EA) ... BBA
Black Business & Professional Association (AC) ... BBPA
Black Business Women - International [*French*] (EAIO) ... BBWI
Black Butte [*New Mexico*] [*Seismograph station code, US Geological Survey*] [*Closed*] (SEIS) ... BBN
Black Butte [*Montana*] [*Seismograph station code, US Geological Survey*] [*Closed*] (SEIS) ... BLK
Black Cancer [*Medicine*] (MELL) ... BC
Black Cancer Virus (SAUS) ... BCV
Black Canyon, AZ [*AM radio station call letters*] (RBYB) ... KUET
Black Canyon of the Gunnison National Monument (SAUS) ... BCGNM
Black Canyon of the Gunnison National Monument ... BLCA
Black Carbon [*Chemistry*] ... BC
Black Caucus of Health Workers (EA) ... BCHW

Black Caucus of the American Library Association (EA) ... BCALA
Black Child Development Institute [*Later, NBCDI*] (EA) ... BCDI
Black Christian Female (ADWA) ... BCF
Black Christian Male (ADWA) ... BCM
Black Christian Nationalist Church ... BCNC
Black Citizens for a Fair Media (EA) ... BCFM
Black Cliff Mines Ltd. [*Toronto Stock Exchange symbol*] ... BKC
Black Coaches Association (EA) ... BCA
Black Code [*Law passed after the Civil War limiting the rights of Negroes in the South*] ... BC
Black College Educational Network (TSSD) ... BCEN
Black Colt (ROG) ... BC
Black Community Crusade for Children [*Children's Defense Fund (CDF)*] (PAZ) ... BCCC
Black Country Development Corp. [*Department of Environment*] [*British*] ... BCDC
Black Country Society [*British*] ... BCS
Black Crossover Vote [*Political science*] ... BCROS
Black Cultural Association (SAUO) ... BCA
Black Cultural Centre for Nova Scotia, Westphal [*Library symbol*] [*National Library of Canada*] (BIB) ... NSWBC
Black Data Processing Associates (EA) ... BDPA
Black Data Processing Associates (EA) ... DPA
Black Death [*1348-49*] ... BD
Black Development Foundation ... BDF
Black Diamond Municipal Library, Alberta [*Library symbol*] [*National Library of Canada*] (NLC) ... ABDM
Black Diamond Municipal Library, Black Diamond, AB, Canada [*Library symbol*] [*Library of Congress*] (LCLS) ... CaABdM
Black Diamond Resources [*Vancouver Stock Exchange symbol*] ... BLK
Black Diamond Steamship Corp. (MHDW) ... BDSC
Black Economic Development Conference (SAUO) ... BEDC
Black Economic Research Center (EA) ... BERC
Black Educational Resources Center [*Later, BMCERC*] (EA) ... BERC
Black Educational Science Trust (SAUS) ... BEST
Black Educational Services, Inc. ... BESI
Black Efforts for Soul in Television ... BEST
Black Elderly Twin Study [*National Institute on Aging*] ... BETS
Black Elected Official ... BEO
Black Employees of the Library of Congress (EA) ... BELC
Black Employment Program (EPA) ... BEP
Black Enamel Slate (MSA) ... BES
Black Enamelled ... BE
Black English [*Dialect*] ... BE
Black English Vernacular [*Dialect*] ... BEV
Black Enterprise [*A publication*] ... BE
Black Enterprise [*A publication*] (BRI) ... B Ent
Black Entertainment and Sports Lawyers Association (EA) ... BESLA
Black Entertainment Lawyers Association [*Later, BESLA*] (EA) ... BELA
Black Entertainment Television [*Cable-television system*] ... BET
Black Executive Exchange Program [*of The National Urban League*] (EA) ... BEEP
Black Faculty and Staff Association (SAUO) ... BFSA
Black Faculty Association (SAUO) ... BFA
Black Family Research Organization (EA) ... BFRO
Black Female ... BF
Black Female (SAUS) ... B/F
Black, Female Republican ... BFR
Black Filly [*Horse racing*] (ROG) ... BF
Black Film & Video Network (AC) ... BFVN
Black Filmmaker Foundation (EA) ... BFF
Black Filmmakers Hall of Fame, Inc. (EA) ... BFHFI
Black Firsts [*A publication*] ... BF
Black Fox Nuclear Station (NRCH) ... BFNS
Black Fox Station [*Nuclear energy*] (NRCH) ... BFS
Black Gelding [*Horse racing*] (ROG) ... BG
Black Generation (SAUS) ... BG
Black Giant Mines Ltd. [*Vancouver Stock Exchange symbol*] ... BG
Black Gold Cooperative Library System, Ventura, CA [*OCLC symbol*] (OCLC) ... BGC
Black Gold Cooperative Library System, Ventura, CA [*Library symbol*] [*Library of Congress*] (LCLS) ... CVtB
Black Granite Gage (SAUS) ... BGG
Black Granite Gauge ... BGG
Black Hawk [*Military*] (MCD) ... BH
Black Hawk College (SAUO) ... BHC
Black Hawk College, East Campus, Gustav E. Lundberg Learning Center, Kewanee, I L [*OCLC symbol*] (OCLC) ... ISY
Black Hawk College, East Campus, Kewanee, IL [*Library symbol*] [*Library of Congress*] (LCLS) ... IKeB
Black Hawk College, Moline, IL [*Library symbol*] [*Library of Congress*] (LCLS) ... IMolB
Black Hawk County Sun, Evansdale, IA [*Library symbol*] [*Library of Congress*] (LCLS) ... IaEvS
Black Hawk Gaming & Development [*Associated Press*] (SAG) ... BlkHG
Black Hawk Gaming & Development Co. [*Associated Press*] (SAG) ... BlkHwkG
Black Hawk Gaming & Development Co., Inc. [*NASDAQ symbol*] (SAG) ... BHWK
Black Hawk Gaming & Dvlp [*NASDAQ symbol*] (TTSB) ... BHWK
Black Hawk Gaming Wrrt 'A' [*NASDAQ symbol*] (TTSB) ... BHWKW
Black Hawk Gaming Wrrt 'B' [*NASDAQ symbol*] (TTSB) ... BHWKZ
Black Hawk Helicopter (SAUS) ... UH-60
Black Hawk Mining, Inc. [*Toronto Stock Exchange symbol*] ... BHK
Black Hill [*Scotland*] [*Seismograph station code, US Geological Survey*] (SEIS) ... EBH
Black Hill Resources Ltd. [*Vancouver Stock Exchange symbol*] ... BHR
Black Hills (FAAC) ... BLKHLS
Black Hills Army Depot ... BHAD
Black Hills Corp. [*NYSE symbol*] (SPSG) ... BKH
Black Hills Corp. [*Associated Press*] (SAG) ... BlkHlCp
Black Hills State College (GAGS) ... Black Hills St C
Black Hills State College, Spearfish, SD [*OCLC symbol*] (OCLC) ... BHS
Black Hills State College, Spearfish, SD [*Library symbol*] [*Library of Congress*] (LCLS) ... SdSpeT
Black Hills Teachers College [*Later, Black Hills State College*] [*South Dakota*] ... BHTC
Black History Month Resource Book [*A publication*] ... BHMRB
Black Hole ... BH
Black Hole Ocarina (MCD) ... BHO
Black Human Resources Network [*An association*] (EA) ... BHRN
Black Incorporation Time (SAUO) ... BIT
Black Incumbent ... BINC
Black, Indian, Hispanic, and Asian Women in Action [*An association*] (EA) ... BIHA
Black Information [*Banking*] [*British*] ... BI
Black Intelligence Test of Cultural Homogeneity [*Sometimes facetiously translated "Black Intelligence Test to Counter Honkeyism"*] ... BITCH
Black Iron ... BI
Black, James F., Baltimore MD [*STAC*] ... BJF
Black Jumbo [*Diplomatic codes*] [*World War II*] ... BJ
Black Knight [*Missile*] ... BK
Black Label Resources, Inc. [*Vancouver Stock Exchange symbol*] ... BLB
Black Law Student Association (EA) ... BLSA
Black Legal Action for Soul in Television [*Student legal action organization*] ... BLAST
Black Leghorn [*Poultry*] ... BL
Black Letter [*Printing*] ... BKLR
Black Letter (ADWA) ... bklr
Black Letter [*Printing*] ... BL
Black Liberation Army (EA) ... BLA
Black Librarians Caucus (EA) ... BCALA
Black Light ... BL
Black Light (SAUS) ... BLK LT
Black Light Blue [*Source for near ultraviolet radiation*] ... BLB
Black Liquor [*Pulp and paper technology*] ... BL
Black Liquor Oxidation [*For pollution control in paper mills*] ... BLO
Black Liquor Solids [*Pulp and paper technology*] ... BLS
Black Literature Criticism [*A publication*] ... BLC
Black Lung [*Social Security Administration*] (OICC) ... BL
Black Lung Association (EA) ... BLA
Black Lung Benefits [*Social Security Administration*] (DHP) ... BLB
Black Lung Benefits Act [*1972*] ... BLBA
Black Magic Project Ltd. [*British*] [*ICAO designator*] (FAAC) ... BLM
Black Male ... BM
Black Marlin Energy [*Vancouver Stock Exchange symbol*] ... BMY
Black Mental Health Alliance (EA) ... BMHA
Black Mesa & Lake Powell [*AAR code*] ... BLKM
Black Mesa and Lake Powell (SAUS) ... BM&LP
Black Mesa Defense Fund (EA) ... BMDF
Black Methodists for Church Renewal (EA) ... BMCR
Black, Middle-Aged Male (MELL) ... BMM
Black Military History Institute of America (EA) ... BMHIA
Black Mountain [*California*] ... BM
Black Mountain College [*1933-1956*] ... BMC
Black Mountain, NC [*AM radio station call letters*] ... WFGW
Black Mountain, NC [*FM radio station call letters*] ... WMIT
Black Mountain, NC [*AM radio station call letters*] (BROA) ... WTZK
Black Mountain, NC [*AM radio station call letters*] ... WZQR
Black Mountain Public Library, Black Mountain, NC [*Library symbol*] [*Library of Congress*] (LCLS) ... NcBlm
Black Moving Object [*Military*] (MUSM) ... BMO
Black Music Association [*Defunct*] (EA) ... BMA
Black Music Association of Canada (AC) ... BMAC
Black Muslim ... BM
Black Muslims (SAUO) ... BMs
Black Nation of Islam (SAUO) ... BNI
Black Oil Finish Slate (MSA) ... BOFS
Black on Constitutional Law [*A publication*] (DLA) ... Black Const Law
Black on Construction and Interpretation of Laws [*A publication*] (DLA) ... Black Interp Laws
Black on Construction and Interpretation of Laws [*A publication*] (DLA) ... Black St Const
Black on Employer's Liability [*A publication*] (DLA) ... Black Emp Li
Black on Employer's Liability [*A publication*] (DLA) ... Bl Emp L
Black on Judgments [*A publication*] (DLA) ... Black Judg
Black on Judgments [*A publication*] (DLA) ... Black Judgm
Black on Judgments [*A publication*] (DLA) ... Bl Judgm
Black on the Laws Regulating the Manufacture and Sale of Intoxicating Liquors [*A publication*] (DLA) ... Black Intox Liq
Black on Tone [*Printing*] (DGA) ... BOT
Black Ordinary Working People ... BOWP
Black Panel Temperature [*Automotive paint durability testing*] ... BPT
Black Panther Party [*Defunct*] [*Political party*] ... BPP
Black Peak [*Arizona*] [*Seismograph station code, US Geological Survey*] [*Closed*] (SEIS) ... BPK
Black Pearl Resources Ltd. [*Vancouver Stock Exchange symbol*] ... BKP
Black People's Convention [*South Africa*] (PD) ... BPC
Black People's Party [*South Africa*] [*Political party*] (PPW) ... BPP
Black Photo Corp. Ltd. [*Toronto Stock Exchange symbol*] ... BPK
Black Pigmented Bacteria [*Microbiology*] ... BPB
Black Political Women's Caucus ... BPWC
Black Powder ... BP
Black Power (SAUS) ... BP

Black Prisoners' Support Group (WDAA) .... BPSG
Black Professional Female (ADWA) .... BPF
Black Professional Male (ADWA) .... BPM
Black Psychiatrists of America (EA) .... BPA
Black Radical Action Group .... BRAG
Black Rapids [Alaska] [Seismograph station code, US Geological Survey]
   (SEIS) .... BLR
Black Raspberry Latent Virus [Plant pathology] .... BRLV
Black Resources and Information Centre [Canada] .... BRIC
Black Resources Information Coordinating Services [Information service or
   system] (IID) .... BRICS
Black Retail Action Group (NTPA) .... BRAG
Black Revolutionary War Patriots Foundation (EA) .... BRWPF
Black River [Jamaica] [Seismograph station code, US Geological Survey]
   [Closed] (SEIS) .... BRJ
Black River & Western Corp. [AAR code] .... BRW
Black River Falls, WI [Location identifier] [FAA] (FAAL) .... BCK
Black River Falls, WI [AM radio station call letters] .... WWIS
Black River Falls, WI [FM radio station call letters] .... WWIS-FM
Black Rock Coalition (EA) .... BRC
Black Scale (MSA) .... BS
Black Scholar [A publication] (BRI) .... Bl S
Black Sea and Area [MARC geographic area code] [Library of Congress]
   (LCCP) .... mb---
Black Sea Expedition [1969] [Turkey, US] (MSC) .... BSE
Black Sea Fisheries Commission (SAUO) .... BSCF
Black Sea Fisheries Commission (SAUS) .... BSFC
Black September Organization [Israel] .... BSO
Black Sheep Ventures, Inc. [Vancouver Stock Exchange symbol] ..... BSV
Black Silent Majority Committee of the USA (EA) .... BSMC
Black Silk Suture [Medicine] .... BSS
Black, Sivalls & Bryson (SAUO) .... BS&B
Black Squad (SAUO) .... BS
Black Star Line [Steamship] (MHDB) .... BSL
Black Students Psychological Association .... BSPA
Black Students Union .... BSU
Black Stuntmen's Association (EA) .... BSA
Black Swan Gold Mines Ltd. [Vancouver Stock Exchange symbol] ..... BSW
Black, Syvalls & Bryson, Inc., HOMCO Division, Houston, TX [Library
   symbol] [Library of Congress] (LCLS) .... TxHH
Black Tennis and Sports Foundation (EA) .... BTSF
Black Theater Alliance (EA) .... BTA
Black Theater Alliance (SAUO) .... BTA
Black Thunder Petroleum [Vancouver Stock Exchange symbol] .... BTP
Black Tie Bureau (NTPA) .... BTB
Black Top and National Delaine Merino Sheep Association (EA) ..... BLNDMSA
Black Top and National Delaine-Merino Sheep Breeders Association
   (NTPA) .... BTNDMSA
Black Turnout [Political science] .... BTURN
Black Turtle Soup .... BTS
Black Unaccountable Machine (SAUS) .... BUM
Black United Front [South Africa] (PD) .... BUF
Black Urban Professional [Lifestyle classification] .... Buppie
Black Urban Professional (ACAE) .... BUPPIE
Black Varnish Cambric [Insulation] (MSA) .... BVC
Black Veterans for Social Justice (EA) .... BVSJ
Black Veterans, Inc. (EA) .... BV
Black Void Reactor .... BVR
Black Vomit [Medicine] (MELL) .... BV
Black Watch (SAUO) .... BlW
Black Watch [Military unit] [British] .... BW
Black Watch Regiment (SAUO) .... Black Watch
Black Water Fever [Medicine] (MELL) .... BWF
Black Widow Spider Toxin .... BWSTx
Black Widow Spider Venom .... BWSV
Black Women in Church and Society (EA) .... BWCS
Black Women in Publishing (EA) .... BWIP
Black Women Organized for Educational Development (EA) .... BWOED
Black Women's Association (EA) .... BWA
Black Women's Educational Alliance (EA) .... BWEA
Black Women's Educational Policy and Research Network (EA) ...... BWEPRN
Black Women's Health Project [Later, NBWHP] (EA) .... BWHP
Black Women's Network [An association] (EA) .... BWN
Black Women's Roundtable on Voter Participation (EA) .... BWRVP
Black World Foundation (EA) .... BWF
Black Writers [A publication] .... BW
Blackader/Lauterman Library of Architecture and Art, McGill University,
   Montreal, Quebec [Library symbol] [National Library of Canada]
   (NLC) .... QMMB
Blackall [Australia] [Airport symbol] (OAG) .... BKQ
Black-and-White Television Set (SAUS) .... B&W TVs
Blackbeard Island National Wildlife Refuge (SAUS) .... BINWR
Blackberry Gold Resources, Inc. [Vancouver Stock Exchange symbol] .. BLC
Blackboard .... BBD
Blackboard (MSA) .... BKD
Blackbody Limited Line (PDAA) .... BBLL
Black-Bordered [Stationery] .... BB
Blackburn (SAUO) .... BV
Blackburn Aeroplane & Motor Co. Ltd. (SAUO) .... B
Blackburn College (SAUO) .... BC
Blackburn College, Carlinville, IL [OCLC symbol] (OCLC) .... IBN
Blackburn College, Carlinville, IL [Library symbol] [Library of Congress]
   (LCLS) .... ICarlB
Blackburn Electronics, Ltd. (SAUO) .... BE
Blackburn Family Association (EA) .... BFA

Blackburn Hamlet Branch, Gloucester Public Library, Ontario [Library
   symbol] [National Library of Canada] (NLC) .... OGBH
Blackburn on Sales [A publication] (DLA) .... Blackb
Blackburn on Sales [A publication] (DLA) .... Blackb Sales
Blackburn on Sales [A publication] (DLA) .... Black Sal
Blackburn Rivet Head (SAUS) .... BRH
Blackbushe [British] [ICAO location identifier] (ICLI) .... EGLK
Black-Capped Chickadee [Ornithology] .... BC
Blackdome Mining Corp. [Toronto Stock Exchange symbol] [Vancouver Stock
   Exchange symbol] .... BDM
Black-Dot Ringworm [Medicine] (MELL) .... BDRW
Blackduck Elementary School, Blackduck, MN [Library symbol] [Library of
   Congress] (LCLS) .... MnBlaE
Blackduck High School, Blackduck, MN [Library symbol] [Library of
   Congress] (LCLS) .... MnBlaH
Blackduck, MN [FM radio station call letters] .... WBJI
Blackduck Public Library, Blackduck, MN [Library symbol] [Library of
   Congress] (LCLS) .... MnBla
Blacken .... BLKN
Blackening .... BLKNG
Blackerby's Justices' Cases [England] [A publication] (DLA) ..... Black Jus
Blackerby's Justices' Cases [England] [A publication] (DLA) ..... Black Just
Blackerby's Magistrates' Reports [1327-1716] [England] [A publication]
   (DLA) .... Black
Blacker-Wood Library of Zoology and Ornithology, McGill University,
   Montreal, Quebec [Library symbol] [National Library of Canada]
   (NLC) .... QMMBZ
Blackeye Cowpea Mosaic Virus [Plant pathology] .... BlCMV
Blackfalds Public Library, Alberta [Library symbol] [National Library of
   Canada] (NLC) .... ABLA
Blackfan-Diamond [Syndrome] [Medicine] (DB) .... BD
Blackfeet Community College Library, Browning, MT [Library symbol]
   [Library of Congress] (LCLS) .... MtBwB
Blackfoot [MARC language code] [Library of Congress] (LCCP) ..... bla
Blackfoot, ID [AM radio station call letters] (BROA) .... KBLI
Blackfoot, ID [FM radio station call letters] .... KCVI
Blackfoot, ID [AM radio station call letters] (RBYB) .... KECN-AM
Blackfoot, ID [FM radio station call letters] .... KLCE
Blackfoot Public Library, Blackfoot, ID [Library symbol] [Library of
   Congress] (LCLS) .... IdBf
Blackford County Historical Society, Hartford City, IN [Library symbol]
   [Library of Congress] (LCLS) .... InHarBHi
Blackford, VA [Location identifier] [FAA] (FAAL) .... GZG
Blackford's Indiana Reports [1817-47] [A publication] (DLA) ..... Bl
Blackford's Indiana Reports [1817-47] [A publication] (DLA) ..... Black
Blackford's Indiana Reports [1817-47] [A publication] (DLA) ..... Blackf
Blackford's Indiana Reports [1817-47] [A publication] (DLA) ..... Blackf (Ind)
Blackford's Indiana Reports [1817-47] [A publication] (DLA) ..... Blackford's la R
Blackford's Indiana Reports [1817-47] [A publication] (DLA) ..... Black R
Blackfriars Settlement (SAUO) .... BS
Blackgram Mottle Virus [Plant pathology] .... BMOV
Blackham, Dundas, and Osborne's Irish Nisi Prius Reports [1846-48]
   [A publication] (DLA) .... BD & O
Blackham, Dundas, and Osborne's Irish Nisi Prius Reports [1846-48]
   [A publication] (DLA) .... Black D & O
Blackham, Dundas, and Osborne's Irish Nisi Prius Reports [1846-48]
   [A publication] (DLA) .... Bl D & O
Blackham, Dundas, and Osborne's Irish Nisi Prius Reports [1846-48]
   [A publication] (DLA) .... Bl D & Osb
Blackhawk Airways, Inc. [ICAO designator] (FAAC) .... BAK
Blackhawk Standbys [An association] (EA) .... BSI
Blackhawk Technical Institute, Janesville, WI [Library symbol] [Library of
   Congress] (LCLS) .... WJaB
Blackhealth Kindergarten School, Long Beach, NY [Library symbol] [Library
   of Congress] (LCLS) .... NLobBK
Blackheath Conservatoire of Music (SAUO) .... BCM
Blackie's Science Text Books [A publication] .... BSTB
Black-Jewish Information Center [Defunct] (EA) .... BJIC
Blackley Order Reception and Invoicing System (SAUS) .... BORIS
Black-Light Region (SAUS) .... BL-Region
Blackman's Volunteer Army of Liberation [An association] (EA) ... BVAL
Blackmist Resources, Inc. [Vancouver Stock Exchange symbol] ...... BKA
Blackmore [England] .... BLACKM
Blackout .... BO
Blackout Door [Military] .... BOD
Blackout Exit Time .... BOE
Blackout Initiation Time .... BOI
Blackout Preparedness .... BP
Blackout Restrictions [British] [World War II] .... BR
Blackout Restrictions in Industrial Establishments [British] [World War II] .... BIE
Blackout Time (SAUS) .... BOT
Blackout Window [Military] .... BOW
Blackpool [England] [Airport symbol] (OAG) .... BLK
Blackpool [British] [ICAO location identifier] (ICLI) .... EGNH
Blackpool Central Library, Blackpool, United Kingdom [Library symbol]
   [Library of Congress] (LCLS) .... UkBl
Blackpool Gazette & Herald Ltd., Blackpool, United Kingdom [Library
   symbol] [Library of Congress] (LCLS) .... UkBlG
Blackrock 1998 Term Trust [NYSE symbol] (SPSG) .... BBT
Blackrock 1998 Term Trust, Inc. [Associated Press] (SAG) Blk1998
Blackrock 1999 Term Trust [Associated Press] (SAG) Blk1999
Blackrock 1999 Term Trust [NYSE symbol] (SAG) .... BNN
Blackrock 2001 Term Trust [Associated Press] (SAG) Blk2001
Blackrock 2001 Term Trust Inc. [NYSE symbol] (SPSG) .... BLK
Blackrock Advantage Term [NYSE symbol] (TTSB) .... BAT

Blackrock Advantage Term Trust [*NYSE symbol*] (SPSG) ... BAT
Blackrock Advantage Term Trust [*Associated Press*] (SAG) ... BlkAdv
Blackrock Broad Investment Grade 2009 Term Trust [*AMEX symbol*] (SPSG) ... BCT
Blackrock Broad Investment Grade 2009Term Trust [*Associated Press*] (SAG) ... BlkBI09
Blackrock CA Inv Qual Muni [*AMEX symbol*] (TTSB) ... RAA
Blackrock California Insurance Municipal 2008 Trade [*NYSE symbol*] (SPSG) ... BFC
Blackrock California Insured Municipal 2008 Term Trust [*Associated Press*] (SAG) ... BlkCA08
Blackrock California Investment Quality Municipal [*AMEX symbol*] (SPSG) ... RAA
Blackrock California Investment Quality Municipal Trust [*Associated Press*] (SAG) ... BCAIQ
Blackrock FL Inv Qual Muni [*AMEX symbol*] (TTSB) ... RFA
Blackrock Florida Insurance Municipal 2008 Trade [*NYSE symbol*] (SPSG) ... BRF
Blackrock Florida Insured Municipal 2008 Term Trust [*Associated Press*] (SAG) ... BlkFL08
Blackrock Florida Investment Quality Municipal [*AMEX symbol*] (SPSG) ... RFA
Blackrock Florida Investment Quality Municipal Trust [*Associated Press*] (SAG) ... BFLIQ
Blackrock Income Trust [*NYSE symbol*] (SPSG) ... BKT
Blackrock Income Trust [*Associated Press*] (SAG) ... BlkIT
Blackrock Insurance Municipal 2008 Trade [*NYSE symbol*] (SPSG) ... BRM
Blackrock Insurance Municipal Term Trust [*NYSE symbol*] (SPSG) ... BMT
Blackrock Insured Municipal 2008 Term Trust [*Associated Press*] (SAG) ... Blk2008
Blackrock Inv Qual Muni Tr [*NYSE symbol*] (TTSB) ... BKN
Blackrock Inv Qual Term Tr [*NYSE symbol*] (TTSB) ... BQT
Blackrock Investment Quality Municipal Trust [*NYSE symbol*] (SPSG) ... BKN
Blackrock Investment Quality Municipal Trust [*Associated Press*] (SAG) ... BlkIQM
Blackrock Investment Quality Term Trust [*Associated Press*] (SAG) ... BlkIQT
Blackrock Investment Quality Term Trust [*NYSE symbol*] (SPSG) ... BQT
Blackrock Municipal Target Term Trust [*Associated Press*] (SAG) ... BlkMTar
Blackrock Municipal Target Term Trust [*NYSE symbol*] (SPSG) ... BMN
Blackrock New Jersey Investment Quality Municipal [*AMEX symbol*] (SPSG) ... RNJ
Blackrock New Jersey Investment Quality Municipal Trust [*Associated Press*] (SAG) ... BNJIQ
Blackrock New York Insurance Municipal 2008 Trade [*NYSE symbol*] (SPSG) ... BLN
Blackrock New York Insured Municipal 2008 Term Trust [*Associated Press*] (SAG) ... BlkNY08
Blackrock New York Investment Quality Municipal [*AMEX symbol*] (SPSG) ... RNY
Blackrock New York Investment Quality Municipal Trust [*Associated Press*] (SAG) ... BNYIQ
Blackrock NJ Inv Qual Muni [*AMEX symbol*] (TTSB) ... RNJ
Blackrock North American Government, Inc. [*NYSE symbol*] (SPSG) ... BNA
Blackrock North American Government Income Trust [*Associated Press*] (SAG) ... BlkNA
Blackrock NY Inv Qual Muni [*AMEX symbol*] (TTSB) ... RNY
Blackrock Strategic Term Trust [*NYSE symbol*] (SPSG) ... BGT
Blackrock Strategic Term Trust [*Associated Press*] (SAG) ... BlkStr
Blackrock Target Term [*NYSE symbol*] (TTSB) ... BTT
Blackrock Target Term Trust [*Associated Press*] (SAG) ... BlkTT
Blackrock Target Term Trust [*NYSE symbol*] (SAG) ... BTT
Blacks Against Nukes (EA) ... BAN
Black's Constitutional Prohibitions [*A publication*] (DLA) ... Black Const Prohib
Black's Decisions in Shipping Cases [*A publication*] (DLA) ... Black Ship Ca
Blacks in Government (EA) ... BIG
Blacks in Law Enforcement [*An association*] (EA) ... BLE
Blacks in Media Broadcasting Organization ... BIMBO
Black's Law Dictionary [*A publication*] (DLA) ... Black Dict
Black's Law Dictionary [*A publication*] (DLA) ... Black Law Dict
Black's Law Dictionary [*A publication*] (DLA) ... Black LD
Black's Law Dictionary [*A publication*] (DLA) ... Black's Law Dict
Black's Law Dictionary [*A publication*] (DLA) ... Bl Dict
Black's Law Dictionary [*A publication*] (DLA) ... Bl LD
Black's Reports [*30-53 Indiana*] [*A publication*] (DLA) ... Black
Black's United States Supreme Court Reports [*66-67 United States Reports*] [*A publication*] (DLA) ... Bk
Black's United States Supreme Court Reports [*66-67 United States Reports*] [*A publication*] (DLA) ... Bl
Black's United States Supreme Court Reports [*66-67 United States Reports*] [*A publication*] (DLA) ... Black
Black's United States Supreme Court Reports [*66-67 United States Reports*] [*A publication*] (DLA) ... Black R
Black's United States Supreme Court Reports [*66-67 United States Reports*] [*A publication*] (DLA) ... Black Rep
Blacksburg [*Virginia*] [*Seismograph station code, US Geological Survey*] (SEIS) ... BAV
Blacksburg [*Virginia*] [*Seismograph station code, US Geological Survey*] (SEIS) ... BLA
Blacksburg Electronic Village ... BEV
Blacksburg, VA [*Location identifier*] [*FAA*] (FAAL) ... BCB
Blacksburg, VA [*Location identifier*] [*FAA*] (FAAL) ... TEC
Blacksburg, VA [*AM radio station call letters*] ... WFNR
Blacksburg, VA [*AM radio station call letters*] ... WKEX
Blacksburg, VA [*FM radio station call letters*] ... WUVT
Blacksburg, VA [*FM radio station call letters*] (RBYB) ... WVMJ
Blackshear, GA [*AM radio station call letters*] ... WGIA
Blackshear, GA [*FM radio station call letters*] ... WKUB
Blacksmith ... BSMITH
Blackstone Advantage Term (EFIS) ... BAT
Blackstone on Magna Charta [*A publication*] (DLA) ... Black Mag Ch
Blackstone, VA [*Location identifier*] [*FAA*] (FAAL) ... BKT
Blackstone, VA [*FM radio station call letters*] ... WBBC
Blackstone, VA [*AM radio station call letters*] ... WKLV
Blackstone's Analysis of the Laws of England [*A publication*] (DLA) ... Black Anal
Blackstone's Commentaries on the Laws of England [*A publication*] (DLA) ... Bl
Blackstone's Commentaries on the Laws of England [*A publication*] (DLA) ... Black Com
Blackstone's Commentaries on the Laws of England [*A publication*] (DLA) ... Blackstone's Commen
Blackstone's Commentaries on the Laws of England [*A publication*] (DLA) ... Bla Com
Blackstone's Commentaries on the Laws of England [*A publication*] (ILCA) ... Bla Comm
Blackstone's Commentaries on the Laws of England [*A publication*] (DLA) ... Bl Com
Blackstone's Commentaries on the Laws of England [*A publication*] (DLA) ... Bl Comm
Blackstone's Commentaries on the Laws of England [*A publication*] (DLA) ... Com
Blackstone's Commentaries on the Laws of England [*A publication*] (DLA) ... Comm
Blackstone's Commentaries on the Laws of England, Abridged [*A publication*] (DLA) ... Black Abr
Blackstone's Law Tracts [*A publication*] (DLA) ... Black L Tr
Blackstone's Law Tracts [*A publication*] (DLA) ... Bl Law Tracts
Blackstone's Law Tracts [*A publication*] (DLA) ... Bl LT
Blackstrap [*Freight*] ... BLKSTP
Black-Top Delaine Merino Sheep Breeders' Association (EA) ... BTDMSBA
Blacktown Agoraphobia Support Group [*Australia*] ... BASG
Blackville, SC [*FM radio station call letters*] (RBYB) ... WIIZ
Blackwall [*Automotive term*] ... BW
Blackware (VRA) ... bwr
Blackwater [*Australia*] [*Airport symbol*] (OAG) ... BLT
Blackwater National Wildlife Refuge (SAUS) ... BNWL
Blackwater National Wildlife Refuge (SAUS) ... BNWR
Blackwell North America, Inc. [*Information service or system*] (IID) ... B/NA
Blackwell North America, Inc. [*New Jersey*] [*ACCORD*] [*UTLAS symbol*] ... BNA
Blackwell North America, Inc. [*Oregon*] [*ACCORD*] [*UTLAS symbol*] ... BNW
Blackwell, OK [*Location identifier*] [*FAA*] (FAAL) ... BWL
Blackwell, OK [*AM radio station call letters*] ... KOKB
Blackwell Retail Group [*British*] ... BRG
Blackwell Science Ltd. (SAUS) ... BSL
Blackwell's Condensed Illinois Reports [*A publication*] (DLA) ... Black Cond
Blackwell's Condensed Illinois Reports [*A publication*] (DLA) ... Black Cond Rep
Blackwell's Condensed Illinois Reports [*A publication*] (DLA) ... Blackw Cond
Blackwell's Scotch Acts [*A publication*] (DLA) ... Blackw Sc Act
Blackwell's Tax Titles [*A publication*] (ILCA) ... Black Tax Tit
Blackwell's Tax Titles [*A publication*] (DLA) ... Blackw Tax Titles
Blackwell's Tax Titles [*A publication*] (DLA) ... Blackw TT
Blackwell's Tax Titles [*A publication*] (DLA) ... Bl TT
Black-White Infrared [*Film*] ... BWIR
Blackwood Catchment Coordinating Group (SAUO) ... BCCG
Blackwood Community Agriculture Centre (SAUO) ... BCAC
Blackwood Hodge (Canada) Ltd. [*Toronto Stock Exchange symbol*] ... BHG
Blackwood, NJ [*FM radio station call letters*] ... WDBK
Blacky Pictures [*Psychological testing*] ... BP
Blacky Test [*Psychology*] (DAVI) ... BT
Blaco Manufacturing Co. (SAUO) ... BLAE
Blacrock Insured Municipal Term Trust [*Associated Press*] (SAG) ... BlkIMT
Bladder (SAUS) ... Blad
Bladder Neck [*Medicine*] (MELL) ... BN
Bladder Neck Contracture [*Medicine*] (MAE) ... BNC
Bladder Neck Obstruction [*Medicine*] ... BNO
Bladder Neck Resection [*Medicine*] ... BNR
Bladder Neck Retraction [*Urology*] (DAVI) ... BNR
Bladder Observation (SAUS) ... BLOBS
Bladder Obstruction [*Medicine*] ... BLOBS
Bladder Outlet Obstruction [*Urology*] (DAVI) ... BOO
Bladder Training Exercise [*Medicine*] (MELL) ... BTE
Bladder Tremor [*Urology*] (DAVI) ... BT
Bladder Tumor [*Oncology and urology*] (DAVI) ... BLT
Bladder Tumor [*Medicine*] ... BT
Bladder Tumor Assay [*Medicine*] (MELL) ... BTA
Bladder Tumor Recheck [*Urology*] (DAVI) ... BTR
Bladder Urine [*Urology*] (DAVI) ... BLAC
Bladder Washout [*Urology*] ... BW
Blade (MSA) ... BL
Blade Area Ratio ... BAR
Blade Element Theory (SAUS) ... BET
Blade Inspection Method ... BIM
Blade Inspection Method System (MCD) ... BIMS
Blade Integrity Monitor [*Aviation*] (DA) ... BIM
Blade Loading Harmonics [*Helicopter*] ... BLH
Blade Passage Tone [*Aviation*] ... BPT
Blade plus Disk fabricated in one piece (SAUS) ... BLISK
Blade Rate (NVT) ... BR
Blade Slap Factor [*Helicopter*] ... BSF
Blade-Brake Clutch [*on lawn mowers*] ... BBC
Bladed Disc [*Turbine component*] ... BLISK
Bladed Ring [*Turbine component*] ... BLING

Bladen County Public Library, Elizabethtown, NC [*Library symbol*] [*Library of Congress*] (LCLS) .... NcE
Bladen Technical College, Dublin, NC [*Library symbol*] [*Library of Congress*] (LCLS) .... NcDubB
Bladen Technical Institute, Elizabethtown, NC [*Library symbol*] [*Library of Congress*] (LCLS) .... NcEB
Blade-Passing Frequency (PDAA) .... BPF
Bladzijde [*Page*] [*Netherlands*] (ILCA) .... blz
Blaettchenpulver [*Flake powder*] [*German military - World War II*] .... BLP
Blagden Management Training Programme [*British*] (AIE) .... BMTP
Blaine County library, Chinook, MT [*Library symbol*] [*Library of Congress*] (LCLS) .... MtCh
Blaine County Medical Center, Medical Library, Hailey, ID [*Library symbol*] [*Library of Congress*] (LCLS) .... IdHIH
Blaine, WA [*AM radio station call letters*] .... KARI
Blair Bell Research Society [*British*] .... BBRS
Blair Corp. [*AMEX symbol*] (SPSG) .... BL
Blair Corp. [*Associated Press*] (SAG) .... BlairCp
Blair County Law Reports [*Pennsylvania*] [*A publication*] (DLA) .... Blair Co
Blair County Law Reports [*Pennsylvania*] [*A publication*] (DLA) .... Blair Co LR
Blair County Law Reports [*Pennsylvania*] [*A publication*] (DLA) .... Blair Co LR (PA)
Blair House Library Foundation [*Defunct*] (EA) .... BHLF
Blair. Manual for Scotch Justices of the Peace [*A publication*] (DLA) .... Blair
Blair, NE [*FM radio station call letters*] .... KDCV
Blair, NE [*FM radio station call letters*] .... KISP
Blair, NE [*FM radio station call letters*] (RBYB) .... KMRV-FM
Blair Public Library, Blair, NE [*Library symbol*] [*Library of Congress*] (LCLS) .... NbBla
Blairmore, AB [*AM radio station call letters*] .... CJPR
Blairmore Public Library, Alberta [*Library symbol*] [*National Library of Canada*] (NLC) .... ABL
Blairstown, NJ [*FM radio station call letters*] .... WHCY
Blairstown Press, Blairstown, NJ [*Library symbol*] [*Library of Congress*] (LCLS) .... NjBlaiP
Blairsville, PA [*Location identifier*] [*FAA*] (FAAL) .... BSI
Blairsville, PA [*FM radio station call letters*] .... WLCY
Blairsville Public Library, Blairsville, PA [*Library symbol*] [*Library of Congress*] (LCLS) .... PBI
Blairsville Public Library, Blairsville, PA [*Library symbol*] [*Library of Congress*] (LCLS) .... PBIP
BLAISE [*British Library Automated Information Service*] **number** [*Database terminology*] (NITA) .... BL
Blake and Hedges' Reports [*2-3 Montana*] [*A publication*] (DLA) .... Blake & H
Blake and Hedges' Reports [*2-3 Montana*] [*A publication*] (DLA) .... Bl & H
Blake, Cassels & Graydon, Law Library, Toronto, ON, Canada [*Library symbol*] [*Library of Congress*] (LCLS) .... CaOTBCG
Blake, Cassels & Graydon, Toronto, Ontario [*Library symbol*] [*National Library of Canada*] (NLC) .... OTBCG
Blake. Chancery Practice [*A publication*] (DLA) .... Bl Chy Pr
Blake Resources Ltd. [*Toronto Stock Exchange symbol*] .... BLE
Blakely, GA [*AM radio station call letters*] .... WBBK
Blakely, GA [*FM radio station call letters*] .... WBBK-FM
Blakely Island [*Washington*] [*Airport symbol*] (OAG) .... BYW
Blake's Reports [*1-3 Montana*] [*A publication*] (DLA) .... Blake
Blakesburg Public Library, Blakesburg, IA [*Library symbol*] [*Library of Congress*] (LCLS) .... IaBlak
Blalock-Taussig [*Cardiology*] .... BT
Blanc Sablon [*Canada*] [*Airport symbol*] (OAG) .... YBX
Blanca Flor [*Bolivia*] [*ICAO location identifier*] (ICLI) .... SLBF
Blanch [*E.W.*] **Holdings, Inc.** [*Associated Press*] (SAG) .... Blanch
Blanch [*E.W.*] **Holdings, Inc.** [*NYSE symbol*] (SPSG) .... EWB
Blanchard and Weeks' Leading Cases on Mines [*A publication*] (DLA) .... Blan & W Lead Cas
Blanchard and Weeks' Leading Cases on Mines [*A publication*] (DLA) .... Blanc & WLC
Blanchard and Weeks' Leading Cases on Mines [*A publication*] (DLA) .... Bl & W Mines
Blanchard Community Library, Santa Paula, CA [*Library symbol*] [*Library of Congress*] (LCLS) .... CStp
Blanchard, LA [*FM radio station call letters*] (BROA) .... KRVQ-FM
Blanchester Public Library, Blanchester, OH [*Library symbol*] [*Library of Congress*] (LCLS) .... OBla
Blanchi-Backlund Transformation [*Engineering*] .... BT
Blandford [*England*] .... BLANDF
Blanding Free Public Library, Rehoboth, MA [*Library symbol*] [*Library of Congress*] (LCLS) .... MReh
Blanding, UT [*Location identifier*] [*FAA*] (FAAL) .... BDG
Blanding, UT [*AM radio station call letters*] .... KUTA
Bland's Chancery Reports [*A publication*] (DLA) .... Bl Chr R
Bland's Maryland Chancery Reports [*A publication*] (DLA) .... Bla Ch
Bland's Maryland Chancery Reports [*A publication*] (DLA) .... Bland
Bland's Maryland Chancery Reports [*A publication*] (DLA) .... Bland Ch (MD)
Bland's Maryland Chancery Reports [*A publication*] (DLA) .... Bland Ch R
Bland's Maryland Chancery Reports [*A publication*] (DLA) .... Bland's Ch
Bland's Maryland Chancery Reports [*A publication*] (DLA) .... Bland's Ch R
Bland's Maryland Chancery Reports [*A publication*] (DLA) .... Bland's Chy Rep
Bland-White-Garland [*Syndrome*] [*Medicine*] (DB) .... BWG
Blaney, Pasternak, Smela, Eagleson & Watson, Toronto, ON, Canada [*Library symbol*] [*Library of Congress*] (LCLS) .... CaOTBP
Blaney, Pasternak, Smela, Eagleson & Watson, Toronto, Ontario [*Library symbol*] [*National Library of Canada*] (NLC) .... OTBP
Blank (BUR) .... B
Blank [*Microtiter plate*] .... BL
Blank (MSA) .... BLK
Blank (HGAA) .... Blnk
Blank Address (SAUS) .... BA
Blank Carbon Copy .... BCC
Blank Card (SAUS) .... BC
Blank Character (SAUS) .... BC
Blank Column Detection Device (SAUS) .... BCD Device
Blank Command (SAUS) .... BC
Blank Corrected Sample Data [*Computer science*] .... BCSD
Blank Die .... BLDI
Blank Display (MHDI) .... BD
Blank Film Door .... BFD
Blank Firing Adaptor [*Army*] (MCD) .... BFA
Blank Firing Attachment (MCD) .... BFA
Blank Flange .... BF
Blank Formatted Disk (SAUS) .... BFD
Blank Instruction (SAUS) .... BI
Blank Line [*Computer science*] .... BL
Blank Punched Card (SAUS) .... BPC
Blank Record (SAUS) .... BR
Blank Recording Disc .... BRD
Blank Space (SAUS) .... BS
Blank Spike .... BS
Blank Spike Duplicate .... BSD
Blank Storage Space (SAUS) .... BSS
Blank Tracer (SAUS) .... BL-T
Blank when Zero .... BZ
Blanke Bevrydingsbeweging [*White Protection Movement*] [*South Africa*] [*Political party*] (EY) .... BBB
Blanked (SAUS) .... BLKD
Blanked Picture Signal .... BPS
Blanked Ventricular Sense [*Medicine*] (DMAA) .... BVS
Blanket (MSA) .... BLKT
Blanket (AAG) .... BLNKT
Blanket (SAUS) .... Blnkt
Blanket Agreement .... BA
Blanket Bath [*Medicine*] .... BB
Blanket Crime Policy [*Insurance*] .... BCP
Blanket Delivery Date [*Military*] (AABC) .... BDD
Blanket Delivery Order (MCD) .... BDO
Blanket Gas (SAA) .... BG
Blanket Open End [*Contract*] [*Business term*] (MCD) .... BOE
Blanket Position Bond [*Insurance*] .... BPB
Blanket Purchase Agreement (KSC) .... BPA
Blanket Purchase Authority .... BPA
Blanket Purchase Award (SAUS) .... BPA
Blanket Purchase Order Agreement (SAUS) .... BPOA
Blanket Purchasing Agreements (SAUO) .... BPA
Blanket Tool Expenditure Control (MCD) .... BTEC
Blanket Tool Order .... BTO
Blanket Travel Order (MCD) .... BTO
Blanket Tritium Recovery [*Subsystem*] (MCD) .... BTR
blanketing Frequency (SAUS) .... Fb
Blanking (DEN) .... BL
Blanking (MSA) .... BLKG
Blanking (SAUS) .... Blkg
Blanking Amplifier (IAA) .... BA
Blanking Circuit (SAUS) .... BC
Blanking Die .... BLKGD
Blanking Input (IEEE) .... BI
Blanking Oscillator (MCD) .... BO
Blanking Press (SAUS) .... BLK Press
Blanking Pulse .... BLKP
Blanking Signal (SAUS) .... BLKS
Blanshard. Statutes of Limitations [*A publication*] (DLA) .... Blan Lim
Blanshard. Statutes of Limitations [*A publication*] (DLA) .... Blansh Lim
Blantyre [*Malawi*] [*Airport symbol*] (OAG) .... BLZ
Blantyre/Chileka [*Malawi*] [*ICAO location identifier*] (ICLI) .... FWCL
Blare Lake, AK [*Location identifier*] [*FAA*] (FAAL) .... TEH
Blaser [*Blower*] [*Wind instrument player*] .... BL
Blashfield. Instructions to Juries [*A publication*] (DLA) .... Blash Juries
Blasinstrumente [*Wind Instruments*] [*Music*] .... Bl
Blasius de Morcono [*Flourished, 14th century*] [*Authority cited in pre-1607 legal work*] (DSA) .... BM
Blasphemy (DLA) .... BLAS
Blast .... BL
Blast Danger Area (NASA) .... BDA
Blast Deflectors Inc. (SAUO) .... BDI
Blast Effect Weapon (SAUS) .... BEW
Blast Environment Wave Simulator (SAUS) .... BEWS
Blast Fragmentation [*Military*] (MUSM) .... BF
Blast Furnace [*Ironmaking*] .... BF
Blast Furnace Cement (SAUS) .... BFC
Blast Furnace Research, Inc. [*Defunct*] (EA) .... BFR
Blast Furnace Slag .... BFS
Blast Furnace Steel Plant (journ.) (SAUS) .... Blast Furn Steel Plant
Blast Gauge (MUGU) .... BG
Blast Propagation (AAG) .... BP
Blast Resistant Artillery Camouflage Screen (MCD) .... BRACS
Blast Response and Collapse of Buildings (MCD) .... BRACOB
Blast Saturation Temperature (PDAA) .... BST
Blast Suppression Device .... BSD
Blast Test .... BT
Blast Test Missile (NG) .... BTM
Blast Test Motor (MCD) .... BTM
Blast Test Vehicle (NG) .... BTV
Blast Wave Yield .... BWY

Blast-Furnace Portland Cement (PDAA)	BPC
Blasthole	BH
Blastic Crisis (DB)	BC
Blast-Induced Distortion (MCD)	BID
Blasting Agent (MCD)	BA
Blasting Gelatine (IAA)	BG
Blasting Powder (SAUS)	Blstg Pwd
Blastocyst (MELL)	B
Blastodermal Cell [Insect embryology]	BC
Blastogenic Factor [Immunochemistry]	BF
Blastomere Analysis before Implantation	BABI
Blastomyces [A fungus] [Biochemistry] (DAVI)	BLASTO
Blastomyces Dermititis (SAUS)	BD
Blatant Self-Promotion	BS
Blatant Self-Promotion (ADWA)	BSP
Blatchford and Howland's Reports [United States] [A publication] (DLA)	Blatchford & H
Blatchford and Howland's United States District Court Reports [A publication] (DLA)	B & H
Blatchford and Howland's United States District Court Reports [A publication] (DLA)	Betts' Dec
Blatchford and Howland's United States District Court Reports [A publication] (DLA)	Bl & H
Blatchford and Howland's United States District Court Reports [A publication] (DLA)	Bl & How
Blatchford and Howland's United States District Court Reports [A publication] (DLA)	Blatch & H
Blatchford and Howland's United States District Court Reports [A publication] (DLA)	Blatchf & H
Blatchford's Prize Cases [United States] [A publication] (DLA)	Blatchf Pr Cas
Blatchford's Prize Cases [United States] [A publication] (DLA)	Blatchf Prize Cas
Blatchford's Prize Cases [United States] [A publication] (DLA)	Bl Pr Cas
Blatchford's Prize Cases [United States] [A publication] (DLA)	Bl Prize
Blatchford's United States Circuit Court Reports [A publication] (DLA)	Bl
Blatchford's United States Circuit Court Reports [A publication] (DLA)	Blat CCR
Blatchford's United States Circuit Court Reports [A publication] (DLA)	Blatch
Blatchford's United States Circuit Court Reports [A publication] (DLA)	Blatchf
Blatchford's United States Circuit Court Reports [A publication] (DLA)	Blatchf CC
Blatchford's United States Circuit Court Reports [A publication] (DLA)	Blatchf CC Rep
Blatchford's United States Circuit Court Reports [A publication] (DLA)	Blatchf (US Circ Ct)
Blatchford's United States Circuit Court Reports [A publication] (DLA)	Blatch (US Cir Ct)
Blatchford's United States Circuit Court Reports [A publication] (DLA)	Bl CC
Blatchford's United States Circuit Court Reports [A publication] (DLA)	Bl CCR
Blatchley Junior High School, Sitka, AK [Library symbol] [Library of Congress] (LCLS)	AkSB
Blatt [Newspaper, Sheet] [German] (BJA)	Bl
Blauvelt Free Library, Blauvelt, NY [Library symbol] [Library of Congress] (LCLS)	NBla
Blaw-Knox Co. (SAUO)	BK
Blaxland's Codex Legum Anglicanum [A publication] (DLA)	Blax Eng Co
Blayney. Life Annuities [1817] [A publication] (DLA)	Blay Ann
Blayney. Life Assurance [1837] [A publication] (DLA)	Bla Life Ass
Blayney. Life Assurance [1837] [A publication] (DLA)	Blay Life Ins
Blaze Software [NASDAQ symbol] (SG)	BLZE
Blazer Horse Association (EA)	BHA
Blazon	BLZN
BLC Financial Svcs [AMEX symbol] (SG)	BCL
BLCMP [Birmingham Libraries Cooperative Mechanisation Project] Online Support Services (NITA)	BOSS
Bleach Filtrate Recycle [Pulp and paper technology]	BFR
Bleach Poisoning [Medicine] (MELL)	BP
Bleach Powder Lime (SAUS)	BPL
Bleachable Absorber Laser Amplifier and Detector (SAUS)	BALAD
Bleach-Accelerator-Releasing Couplers [Photography]	BAR
Bleached [Freight]	BLCHD
Bleached Chemimechanical Pulping Process [Pulp and paper technology]	BCMP
Bleached Chemi-Thermomechanical Pulp	BCTMP
Bleached Eucalypt Kraft	BEK
Bleached Eucalypt Kraft Mill	BEKM
Bleached Kraft Mill Effluent [Pulp and paper processing]	BKME
Bleached Semichemical Pulping Process [Pulp and paper technolgy]	BSCP
Bleach-Fix [Photography]	BLIX
Bleaching [Freight]	BLCHG
Bleaching Treatment [Dentistry]	BT
Bleckley's Reports [34, 35 Georgia] [A publication] (DLA)	Bleck
Bleckley's Reports [34, 35 Georgia] [A publication] (DLA)	Bleckley
Bledisloe [England]	BLED
Bleed (MSA)	BL
Bleed Air Control System (SAUS)	BACS
Bleed Air Precooler	BAP
Bleed Air System	BAS
Bleed Door Actuator	BDA
Bleed Hose Assembly	BHA
Bleed Storage Tank [Nuclear energy] (NRCH)	BST
Bleed Valve (MCD)	BLV
Bleed Valve (MCD)	BV
Bleeder (MSA)	BLDR
Bleeding Frequency [Medicine]	BF
Bleeding [or Bruising] of Undetermined Origin [Medicine]	BUO

Bleeding Time [Hematology] (DAVI)	BLEED
Bleeding Time [Clinical chemistry]	bl x
Bleeding Time [Clinical chemistry]	BT
Bleeding Time Test [Medicine] (MELL)	BTS
Bleid Commissie Remote Sensing (SAUS)	BCRS
Blend	BLEN
Blend (MSA)	BLN
Blend (SAUS)	BLND
Blended Credit Program [Federal government]	BCP
Blended Old Scotch [Whiskey] (ROG)	BOS
Blended Wing Body [Megaplane]	BWB
Blender Control Unit (ECII)	BCU
Blending Octane Number [Petroleum technology]	BON
Blending Octane Value	BOV
Blending Value Octane Number [Petroleum technology]	BVON
Blendkoerper [Frangible-glass smoke grenade] [German military - World War II]	BK
Blenheim [New Zealand] [Airport symbol] (OAG)	BHE
Bleomycin [Also, Bl, Bleo, BLM] [Antineoplastic drug]	B
Bleomycin [Also, B, Bleo, BLM] [Antineoplastic drug]	Bl
Bleomycin [Also, B, Bl, BLM] [Antineoplastic drug]	Bleo
Bleomycin [Sulfate] [Also, B, Bl, Bleo] [Antineoplastic drug]	BLM
Bleomycin, Adriamycin, CCNU [Lomustine], Oncovin [Vincristine] [Antineoplastic drug regimen] (DAVI)	BACO
Bleomycin, Adriamycin, Cyclophosphamide, Oncovin [Vincristine], Dexamethasone [Antineoplastic drug regimen]	BACOD
Bleomycin, Adriamycin, Cyclophosphamide, Oncovin [Vincristine], Prednisone [Antineoplastic drug regimen]	BACOP
Bleomycin, Adriamycin, Cytoxan, Oncovin, Methotrexate with Leucovorin Rescue [Antineoplastic drug] (CDI)	M-BACOS
Bleomycin, Adriamycin, Cytoxan, Tamoxifen [Antineoplastic drug regimen] (DAVI)	BACT
Bleomycin, Adriamycin, Methotrexate, Oncovin [Vincristine], Nitrogen mustard [Antineoplastic drug regimen]	BAMON
Bleomycin, Adriamycin, Prednisone [Antineoplastic drug regimen] (DAVI)	BAP
Bleomycin, Adriamycin, Vinblastine, Imidazole carboxamide [Dacarbazine], Prednisone [Antineoplastic drug regimen]	BAVIP
Bleomycin, CCNU [Lomustine], Adriamycin, and Velban [Antineoplastic drug regimen] (DAVI)	B-CAVe
Bleomycin, CCNU [Lomustine], Adriamycin, Vinblastine [Antineoplastic drug regimen]	BCAVE
Bleomycin, Cyclophosphamide, Dactinomycin [Antineoplastic drug regimen]	BCD
Bleomycin, Cyclophosphamide, Hydroxydaunomycin [Adriamycin], Oncovin , Prednisone [Vincristine] [Antineoplastic drug regimen]	B-CHOP
Bleomycin, Cyclophosphamide, Methotrexate, Fluorouracil [Antineoplastic drug regimen]	BCMF
Bleomycin, Cyclophosphamide, Oncovin [Vincristine], Methotrexate, Fluorouracil [Antineoplastic drug regimen]	BLEO-COMF
Bleomycin, Dacarbazine, Oncovin [Vincristine], Prednisone, Adriamycin [Antineoplastic drug regimen]	B-DOPA
Bleomycin, Dacarbazine [DTIC], Vincristine, Adriamycin, Prednisone [Antineoplastic drug regimen] (DAVI)	BAVIP
Bleomycin, Etoposide, Platinol [Cisplatin] [Antineoplastic drug regimen]	BEP
Bleomycin Hydrochloride (DB)	BLM
Bleomycin Hydrolase [An enzyme]	BH
Bleomycin, Mustargen, Oncovin [Vincristine], Procarbazine, Prednisone [Antineoplastic drug regimen]	B-MOPP
Bleomycin, Nitrogen Mustard, Oncovin [Vincristine], Procarbazine, and Prednisone [Antineoplastic drug regimen] (DAVI)	BLEO-MOPP
Bleomycin, Oncovin [Vincristine], Adriamycin, Prednisone [Antineoplastic drug regimen]	BOAP
Bleomycin, Oncovin [Vincristine], Lomustine, Dacarbazine [Antineoplastic drug regimen]	BOLD
Bleomycin, Oncovin [Vincristine], Natulan , Prednisolone [Procarbazine hydrochloride] [Antineoplastic drug regimen]	BONP
Bleomycin, Oncovin [Vincristine], Prednisone [Antineoplastic drug regimen] (DAVI)	BOP
Bleomycin, Oncovin [Vincristine], Prednisone, Adriamycin, Mustargen , Methotrexate [Nitrogen mustard] [Antineoplastic drug regimen]	BOPAM
Bleomycin Sulfate [Antineoplastic drug] (DAVI)	BLEO
Bleomycin Sulphate [Antineoplastic drug] (DAVI)	BMS
Bleomycin, Vinblastine, Doxorubicin, Streptozocin [Antineoplastic drug regimen]	BVDS
Blepharoconjunctivitis [Medicine] (MELL)	BC
Blepharophimosis, Ptosis, Epicanthus Inversus [Medicine] (DMAA)	BPEI
Blepharophimosis-Ptosis-Epicanthus Inversus Syndrome [Medicine] (DMAA)	BPES
Blepharoplasty [Ophthalmology and plastic surgery] (DAVI)	bleph
Bleriot Experimental [British military] (DMA)	BE
Blessed	B
Blessed (ODCC)	Bl
Blessed	BL
Blessed	BLSSD
Blessed Kateri Tekakwitha League (EA)	BKTL
Blessed Kateri Tekakwitha School, Gloucester, Ontario [Library symbol] [National Library of Canada] (NLC)	OGBKT
Blessed Mary [or Mother] (BARN)	BM
Blessed Mary the Virgin (DAS)	BMV
Blessed Memory (BARN)	BM
Blessed Sacrament	BS
Blessed Sacrament Seminary, Cleveland, OH [Library symbol] [Library of Congress] (LCLS)	OCIBS
Blessed Trinity Society [Defunct]	BTS

Blessed Virgin .... BV
Blessed Virgin Mary .... BVM
Blessed Virgin Missionaries of Carmel (TOCD) .... BVMC
Blesses Religious Institute of Mercenary Missionaries (SAUO) .... BRIMM
Blessings Co. [Associated Press] (SAG) .... Blessings
Blessings Corp. [AMEX symbol] (SPSG) .... BCO
Bletchley [British] [ICAO location identifier] (ICLI) .... EGGE
Bletsoe [England] .... BLET
Blickenaderfer. Law Student's Review [A publication] (DLA) .... Blick Rev
Blida [Algeria] [ICAO location identifier] (ICLI) .... DAAB
Bligh's English House of Lords Reports [A publication] (DLA) .... Bli
Bligh's English House of Lords Reports, New Series [1827-37]
   [A publication] (DLA) .... Bligh NS (Eng)
Bligh's English House of Lords Reports, New Series [1827-37]
   [A publication] (DLA) .... Bli NS
Bligh's English House of Lords Reports, New Series [A publication]
   (DLA) .... Bl NS
Bligh's English House of Lords Reports, Old Series [1819-21]
   [A publication] (DLA) .... Bligh
Bligh's English House of Lords Reports, Old Series [1819-21]
   [A publication] (DLA) .... Bli (OS)
Blimp Squadron [Navy] .... BLIMPRON
Blimp Squadron [Later separated into BLIMPRON and Blimp-HEDRON]
   [Navy] .... ZEDRON
Blimped Noiseless Reflex Camera (NTCM) .... BNC
Blimpie International, Inc. [Associated Press] (SAG) .... Blimpie
Blimpie International, Inc. [NASDAQ symbol] (SAG) .... BMPE
Blimpie Int'l. [AMEX symbol] (SG) .... BLM
Blind .... BLND
Blind & Phisically Handicapped (AL) .... B&PH
Blind Approach [Aviation] .... BA
Blind Approach Beacon System [Aviation] .... BABS
Blind Approach Beam System (SAUS) .... BABS
Blind Approach Instrument System (SAUS) .... BAIS
Blind Approach Landing System [Aviation] .... BALS
Blind Approach System [Aviation] (MCD) .... BAS
Blind Approach Training [Air Force] .... BAT
Blind Blocking [Bookbinding] (DGA) .... BLD BKG
Blind Book Auxiliary (DGA) .... BBA
Blind Bronchial Sampling [Clinical chemistry] .... BBS
Blind Carbon Copy (WDMC) .... bcc
Blind Carbon Copy .... BCC
Blind Child [Social Security Administration] (OICC) .... BC
Blind Children's Fund (EA) .... BCF
Blind Copy (DNAB) .... BC
Blind Copy (NTIO) .... bc
Blind Courtesy Copy (SAUS) .... BCC
Blind Fire Director (NATG) .... BFD
Blind Flange (SAUS) .... BF
Blind Individual [Social Security Administration] (OICC) .... BI
Blind Landing Experimental Unit [Aviation] .... BLEU
Blind Leading the Blind Foundation (SAUO) .... BLB
Blind Learning Aptitude Test [Education] .... BLAT
Blind Loaded (SAUS) .... BL
Blind Loaded and Blind Plugged [Projectile] (MCD) .... BLBP
Blind Loaded and Plugged [Projectile] .... BL & P
Blind Loaded and Plugged (SAUS) .... BLP
Blind Loaded and Traced [Projectile] .... BL & T
Blind Loaded and Traced (SAUS) .... BLT
Blind Loop (MELL) .... BL
Blind Loop Syndrome [Medicine] (DMAA) .... BLS
Blind Manufacturers' Association of Tasmania [Australia] .... BMAT
Blind Matching [Parapsychology] .... BM
Blind Mating Connector (MCD) .... BMC
Blind Mobility Research Unit [University of Nottingham] [British] (IRC) .... BMRU
Blind Navigation .... BN
Blind Operator Interface (SAUS) .... BOI
Blind Outdoor Leisure Development (EA) .... BOLD
Blind Passenger [Travel industry] (TRID) .... BLND
Blind Persons Act (SAUS) .... BPA
Blind Persons Resettlement Officer [Department of Employment] [British] .... BPRO
Blind Persons Technical Officer [British] (AIE) .... BPTO
Blind Post (SAUS) .... BP
Blind Purchase .... BP
Blind River, ON [AM radio station call letters] .... CJNR
Blind River Public Library, Blind River, ON, Canada [Library symbol] [Library of Congress] (LCLS) .... CaOBLR
Blind River Public Library, Ontario [Library symbol] [National Library of Canada] (NLC) .... OBLR
Blind River Refinery, Eldorado Resources Ltd., Ontario [Library symbol] [National Library of Canada] (NLC) .... OBRER
Blind Riveted Joint .... BRJ
Blind School (SAUO) .... BS
Blind Service Association (EA) .... BSA
Blind Soldiers Association of Victoria [Australia] .... BSAV
Blind Sporting Association of New South Wales [Australia] .... BSANSW
Blind Sports [Later, LBSF] (EA) .... BS
Blind Spot [Medicine] (MELL) .... BC
Blind Spot (MELL) .... BS
Blind Spouse [Title XVI] [Social Security Administration] (OICC) .... BS
Blind Test (MELL) .... BT
Blind Tooling [Bookbinding] (DGA) .... BLD TLG
Blind Toss .... BT
Blind Transmission Broadcast [Army] (ADDR) .... BTB
Blind Welfare Society of South Australia .... BWASA

Blind Workers' Union of South Australia .... BWUSA
Blind Workers' Union of Victoria [Australia] .... BWUV
Blinded American Veterans Foundation (EA) .... BAVF
Blinded Soldiers Association (SAUO) .... BSA
Blinded Veterans Association (EA) .... BVA
Blinder (MSA) .... BLD
Blind-Made Products .... BMP
Blindmakers' Association of Australia .... BAA
Blindmakers' Association of New South Wales [Australia] .... BANSW
Blinds [Classified advertising] (ADA) .... BLDS
Blinker Tube .... BKT
Blinkers [Horse racing] .... B
Blinking Light Monitor .... BLM
Blinn College (SAUO) .... BC
Blinn College, Brenham, TX [Library symbol] [Library of Congress] (LCLS) .... TxBreB
Blip Counter System .... BCS
Blip/Frame (CET) .... B/F
Blip-Frame Ratio (MSA) .... BFR
Blip/Scan (MUGU) .... B/S
Blip-Scan Counter .... BSC
Blip-Scan Counter System .... BSCS
Blip-Scan RADAR (IAA) .... BSP
Blip-Scan Radar (SAUS) .... BSR
Blip-Scan Ratio .... BSR
Bliss and Laughlin Industries, Inc. (SAUO) .... BLI
Bliss & Laughlin Industries, Inc. [NASDAQ symbol] (CTT) .... BLIS
Bliss & Laughlin Industries, Inc. [Associated Press] (SAG) .... BlisLau
Bliss Classification .... BC
Bliss Classification Association [London, England] .... BCA
Bliss College (SAUO) .... BC
Bliss Memorial Public Library, Bloomville, OH [Library symbol] [Library of Congress] (LCLS) .... OBlv
Bliss' New York Code [A publication] (DLA) .... Bliss NY Co
Bliss' New York Code, Annotated [A publication] (DLA) .... Bliss NY Code
Bliss on Code Pleading [A publication] (DLA) .... Bliss Co Pl
Bliss on Life Insurance [A publication] (DLA) .... Bliss Ins
Blissymbolics Communication Resource Centre [British] (CB) .... BCRC
Blister Chemical Agent (SAUS) .... H
Blister Fluid [Medicine] (MELL) .... BF
Blister Gas [US Chemical Corps symbol] CX
Blister Pack .... BP
Blit [Computer science] (NHD) .... BLT
Blitter Objects [Amiga computer hardware] .... BOB's
blizzard (SAUS) .... bliz
Blizzard [NWS] (FAAC) .... BLZD
Blizzard Resources, Inc. [Vancouver Stock Exchange symbol] .... BZD
Blizzard Warning [Telecommunications] (OTD) .... BZW
blizzardly (SAUS) .... bliz
blizzardous (SAUS) .... bliz
Bloated Clay Aggregate [Engineering] .... BCA
Bloating and Diarrhea [Medicine] (MELL) .... B & D
Bloc Africain de Guinee [African Bloc of Guinea] .... BAG
Bloc Democratique Gabonais [Gabonese Democratic Bloc] [Later, PDG] .... BDG
Bloc Democratique Senegalais [Senegal] [Political party] (PPW) .... BDS
Bloc des Masses Senegalaises [Bloc of the Senegalese Masses] (AF) .... BMS
Bloc d'Esquerra d'Alliberament Nacional [Left Bloc for National Liberation] [Spain] (PPW) .... BEAN
Bloc Populaire Senegalais [Senegal] (PPW) .... BPS
Bloc pour la Social-Democratie [Benin] [Political party] (EY) .... BSD
Bloc Quebecois [Canada] [Political party] (ECON) .... BQ
Bloch & Co., Cleveland, OH [Library symbol] [Library of Congress] (LCLS) .... BL
Bloch-Sulzberger [Syndrome] [Medicine] (DB) .... BS
Block (WGA) .... BK
Block (WDMC) .... bk
Block .... BL
Block (BUR) .... BLCK
Block [Unit of data] .... BLK
Block (VRA) .... blk
Block (FAAC) .... BLX
Block Acceptance Reporting Mechanism (ADWA) .... BARM
Block Access Method [Computer science] .... BAM
Block Acquisition Sequence (ADWA) .... BAS
Block Adaptive Rate Controlled [Computer science] .... BARC
Block Address Translation [Computer science] (PCM) .... BAT
Block Advisory Committee (SAUO) .... BAC
Block Allocated Transfer Channel (SAUS) .... BATCH
Block Allocating Map (IAA) .... BAM
Block Allocation Map (SAUS) .... BAM
Block Allocator Transfer Channel (SAUS) .... BATCH
Block and List Manipulator [Computer science] (CSR) .... BALM
Block & Quaile (WDAA) .... B&Q
Block Automation System [NYSE trading computer] .... BAS
Block Availability Map (IAA) .... BAM
Block Based Robot (VERA) .... BLOROB
Block Basis (SAUS) .... BB
Block, Betriebs-Lenkungs-Konzentrator (SAUS) .... BLK
Block Boundary Definition Project (SAUS) .... BBDP
Block Boundary Suggestion Project (SAUS) .... BBSP
Block Brazing .... BB
Block Calls Cleared [Telecommunications] (ACRL) .... BCC
Block Character Check (SAUS) .... BCC
Block Check (ACAE) .... BC
Block Check [or Control] Character [Computer science] .... BCC
Block Check Code [Telecommunications] (OSI) .... BCC

Block Check Error [Electronics] (ECII) .... BCER
Block Check Sequence [Computer science] (IAA) .... BCS
Block Coded Decimal (SAUS) .... BCC
Block Coefficient (SAUS) .... b coeff
Block Command (SAUS) .... BC
Block Control Byte (SAUS) .... BCB
Block Control Header [Computer science] (IBMDP) .... BCH
Block Control Sheet [Computer science] .... BCS
Block Control Signal [Telecommunications] (TEL) .... BCS
Block Control Unit [Computer science] (IBMDP) .... BCU
Block Copolymer [Organic chemistry] .... BCP
Block (Copolymerized) [Organic chemistry] .... b
Block Count [Computer science] .... BC
Block Count (SAUS) .... BLKCNT
Block Counter (SAUS) .... BC
Block Data Message (CTAS) .... BDM
Block Data Statement (SAUS) .... BDS
Block Data Transfer (MCD) .... BDT
Block Decoder Assembly [Space Flight Operations Facility, NASA] .... BDA
Block Definition Program (SAUS) .... BDP
Block Delete (IAA) .... BD
Block Demultiplexer [Ground Communications Facility, NASA] .... BDXR
Block Descriptive Word [Computer science] (ITCA) .... BDW
Block Descriptor Word (SAUS) .... BDW
Block Design [Psychometrics] .... BD
Block Diagram (IAA) .... BD
Block Diagram (SAUS) .... BLODI
Block Diagram - Graphics (PDAA) .... BLODI-G
Block Diagram Compiler .... BLODI
Block Diagram Compiler [Engineering program] (IAA) .... BLODIC
Block Diagram Compiler B (IEEE) .... BLODIB
Block Diagram Compiler, B (SAUS) .... BLODICB
Block Diagram Graphics (SAUS) .... BLODIG
Block Downconverter [Satellite communications] .... BD
Block Downconverter [Satellite communications] .... BDC
Block Drug Co. [Associated Press] (SAG) .... BlckD
Block Drug Co., Inc. [NASDAQ symbol] (NQ) .... BLOC
Block Drug'A'non-vtg [NASDAQ symbol] (TTSB) .... BLOCA
Block End (SAUS) .... BE
Block Ended by Symbol [Computer science] (VERA) .... BES
Block Equivalence Tape (SAUS) .... BET
Block Error (SAUS) .... BLER
Block Error Detector (MCD) .... BED
Block Error Rate [Computer science] (MHDI) .... BKER
Block Error Rate (VERA) .... BLER
Block Error Rate Test [Telecommunications] .... BLERT
Block Error Rates (SAUS) .... BKERs
Block Error Ratio Test (SAUS) .... BLERT
Block Error Status (IAA) .... BES
Block Factor (SAUS) .... BF
Block Floating Point Quantizizer (MCD) .... BFPQ
Block Floating Point Quantization (or Quantizer) (SAUS) .... BFPQ
Block Format Recording .... BFR
Block Gap (SAUS) .... BG
Block Gaussian Elimination (SAUS) .... BGE
Block Grant Authority .... BGA
Block Grant/Enumeration District (COE) .... BG/ED
Block Group [Bureau of the Census] (GFGA) .... BG
Block Handler [Computer science] .... BH
Block Handler Routine [Computer science] (BUR) .... BHR
Block Handler Set Association (SAUO) .... BHSASSC
Block Handling Macro (SAUS) .... BH Macro
Block Handling Routine (SAUS) .... BHR
Block Hardware Code (SAUS) .... BHC
Block Head (SAUS) .... BH
Block Header Record [Computer science] .... BHR
Block Improved Abrams [Battle tank] [Army] .... BIA
Block Improvement Program [for M1A1 tank] [Army] .... BIP
Block in Posteroinferior Division of Left Branch [Medicine] (DMAA) .... BIDLB
Block in the Anterosuperior Division of the Left Branch [Cardiology] (DAVI) .... BSDLB
Block [H. & R.], Inc. [Associated Press] (SAG) .... BlckHR
Block [H. & R.], Inc. [NYSE symbol] (SPSG) .... HRB
Block Input Length [Computer science] (BUR) .... BIL
Block Input/Output Input (SAUS) .... BIOI
Block Input-Output Output [Computer science] (MHDI) .... BIOO
Block Instruction (SAUS) .... BI
Block Interaction Diagram (SAUS) .... BID
Block Island [Rhode Island] [Airport symbol] (OAG) .... BID
Block Island - Fisher Island Range [Navy] (GFGA) .... BIFI
Block Island, RI [Location identifier] [FAA] (FAAL) .... SEY
Block Island, RI [FM radio station call letters] .... WBLQ
Block Island, RI [FM radio station call letters] (BROA) .... WERI-FM
Block Island, RI [Television station call letters] .... WOST
Block Island, RI [Television station call letters] (BROA) .... WPXQ
Block Island, RI [FM radio station call letters] .... WVBI
Block Keyboard (SAUS) .... BK
Block Label [Computer science] (IAA) .... BL
Block Length .... BL
Block Length Error [Computer science] (IAA) .... BLE
Block Load Request [Military] .... BLR
Block Loading (SAUS) .... BL
Block Logic Computer .... BLOGIC
Block Marker Track (SAUS) .... BMT
Block Mode Terminal Interface [Computer science] .... BMTI

Block Multiplex Channel (SAUS) .... BLMUX Channel
Block Multiplexer (SAUS) .... BLMPX
Block Multiplexer [Ground Communications Facility, NASA] .... BMXR
Block Multiplexer Channel (MHDI) .... BLMPX
Block Multiplexer Channel (IAA) .... BLMUX
Block Multiplexer Channel .... BMC
Block Multiplexer Channel (SAUS) .... BMUX Channel
Block Name (SAUS) .... BN
Block Numbering Area [Bureau of the Census] (GFGA) .... BNA
Block of Assignment Statements (SAUS) .... BAS
Block of Four [Philately] B4
Block of Information (SAUS) .... B of I
Block of Instructions (SAUS) .... B of I
Block on Tithes [A publication] (DLA) .... Bl Ti
Block Operation (SAUS) .... BO
Block Order (SAUS) .... BO
Block Order Exposure System [Business term] .... BLOX
Block out of Balance [Computer science] .... BOOB
Block Output Length (SAUS) .... BOL
Block Packaging (SAUS) .... BP
Block Packaging Flag .... BPKFL
Block Parity [Error checking method] [Telecommunications] (TEL) .... BP
Block Point Plan Scheduling Procedure (SAA) .... BPPSP
Block Print (VRA) .... blkpr
Block Priority Control (SAUS) .... BPC
Block Proof List [Computer science] .... BPL
Block Proof Record [Computer science] .... BPR
Block Protection Unit (SAUS) .... BPU
Block Punch (SAUS) .... BP
Block Reading (SAUS) .... BR
Block Received Signal [Telecommunications] (TEL) .... BRS
Block Reception (SAUS) .... BR
Block Register (SAUS) .... BR
Block Replacement .... BR
Block Representation Code (SAUS) .... BRC
Block Rule (SAUS) .... BLKR
Block Sale [Investment term] .... BS
Block Scheme (SAUS) .... BS
Block Selection (SAUS) .... BS
Block Sequence Number (CCCA) .... BSN
Block Size (SAUS) .... BS
Block Sort (SAUS) .... BS
Block Specification (MCD) .... BS
Block Started by Symbol [Computer science] (VERA) .... BSS
Block Storage (SAUS) .... BS
Block Storage Segment (SAUS) .... BSS
Block Store Zero [Computer science] (IAA) .... BSZ
Block Structured Assembly Language [Computer science] (NITA) .... BSAL
Block Tag (SAUS) .... BT
Block Tape Recorder .... BTR
Block Template .... BT
Block Terminal [Telecommunications] (NITA) .... BT
Block Terminating Character [Computer science] (IAA) .... BTC
Block Transfer [Computer science] .... BLT
Block Transfer Complete (SAUS) .... BTC
Block Transfer Control (SAUS) .... BTC
Block Transfer Controller [Computer science] .... BTC
Block Transfer Order (SAUS) .... BTO
Block Transfer Unit [Computer science] (IAA) .... BTU
Block Translation Lookaside Buffer [Computer science] (PCM) .... BTLB
Block Truncation Coding (SAUS) .... BTC
Block Type (SAUS) .... BTYPE
Block Type Manipulation Facility .... BTMF
Block Unit Numbers (MCD) .... BUNS
Block-Acknowledged Counter (SAUS) .... BAC
Block-Acknowledged Sequence Number (SAUS) .... BASN
Blockade (AABC) .... BLOC
Blockade Intelligence Department [Ministry of Economic Warfare] [British] [World War II] .... BID
Blockade Operations [Military] (NVT) .... BLOKOPS
Blockage .... BLOC
Block-a-Matic, Block-a-Gram, and Block-a-Text (SAA) .... BAMAGAT
Blockate State Block (SAUS) .... BSB
Block-Completed Counter (SAUS) .... BCC
Block-Completed Sequence Number (SAUS) .... BCSN
Block-Connected Graph [Mathematics] [Used in GPRS] .... BCG
Block-Cutpoint-Tree [Mathematics] [Used in ASAMS] .... BCT
Blocked .... BLKD
Blocked (SAUS) .... Blkd
Blocked Asynchronous Transmission [Message protocol] [Computer science] (PCM) .... BLAST
Blocked Calls Cleared [Telecommunications] .... BCC
Blocked Calls Delayed [Telecommunications] .... BCD
Blocked Calls Held [Telecommunications] .... BCH
Blocked Calls Released [Telecommunications] .... BCR
Blocked Data Format (MCD) .... BDF
Blocked Impurity Band .... BIB
Blocked Precedence Announcement (DNAB) .... BPA
Blocked Random Access Method (MCD) .... BRAM
Blocker Deflector [Aviation] (OA) .... BD
Blockhaus Equipment Switching Test (SAUS) .... BEST
Blockheizkraftwerk (SAUS) .... BHKW
Blockhouse (SAUS) .... B/H
Blockhouse [NASA] (KSC) .... BH
Blockhouse [NASA] (AAG) .... BKHS

Blockhouse Battery Charger [*NASA*] ... BBC
Blockhouse Computer [*NASA*] (KSC) ... BHC
Blockhouse Equipment Switching Test (SAA) ... BEST
Blockhouse Monitor Console (SAUS) ... BMC
Blockhouse Operation [*NASA*] ... BO
Block-In (MCD) ... BI
Blocking (MSA) ... BLKG
Blocking (SAUS) ... Blkg
Blocking (SAUS) ... Blo
Blocking [*Telecommunications*] (TEL) ... BLO
Blocking Acknowledgement Signal [*Telecommunications*] (NITA) ... BLA
Blocking Acknowledgement Signal (SAUS) ... BLA Signal
Blocking Acknowledgment [*Telecommunications*] (TEL) ... BLA
Blocking Antibody [*Immunology*] (MAE) ... BA
Blocking Back [*Football*] ... BB
Blocking, Bracing, and Tie-Down [*Military*] (DOMA) ... BB & T
Blocking, Bracing, Packing, Crating, and Tiedown Materials [*Military*] (INF) ... BBPCT
Blocking Device [*Nuclear energy*] (OA) ... BD
Blocking Factor ... BF
Blocking Factor (CMD) ... BKF
Blocking Factor [*Computer science*] (IAA) ... BLF
Blocking Order (SAUS) ... BO
Blocking Oscillator ... BO
Blocking Signal (SAUS) ... BLKS
Blocking Signal [*Telecommunications*] (NITA) ... BLO
Blocking Signal (SAUS) ... BLO Signal
Blocking-signal Reception (SAUS) ... BLR
Blocking-signal Sending (SAUS) ... BLS
Blocking-Tube Oscillator ... BTO
Block-Iterative Projection (RALS) ... BIP
Block-level Intercensal Geographic Changes and Transactions (SAUS) ... BIGCAT
Block-Multiplexer Input/Output (SAUS) ... XIOP
Block-Multiplexor channel (SAUS) ... BMPX
Block-Oriented Compiler ... BLOC
Block-Oriented Computer ... BOC
Block-Oriented Network Simulator [*Computer science*] ... BONES
Block-Oriented Random-Access Memory [*Computer science*] ... BORAM
Block-Oriented Systems Simulator [*Computer software*] ... BOSS
Blockout ... BO
Block-print Position (SAUS) ... BPOS
Blocks [*Freight*] ... BLKS
Blocks Per Inch (SAUS) ... BPI
Blockseminar (SAUS) ... Bs
Block-Surface-Distance (SAUS) ... BSD
Block-Switching Digital Network ... BSDN
Block-Write Mode [*Computer graphics*] (BYTE) ... BWM
Blodgett Memorial Library, Fishkill, NY [*Library symbol*] [*Library of Congress*] (LCLS) ... NFisk
Bloedel-Donovan Railroad (IIA) ... BD
Bloembergen-Purcell-Pound theory (SAUS) ... BPP-theory
Bloemfontein (SAUS) ... Bfn
Bloemfontein [*South Africa*] [*Airport symbol*] (OAG) ... BFN
Bloemfontein [*South Africa*] [*Seismograph station code, US Geological Survey*] (SEIS) ... BLF
Bloemfontein [*South Africa*] (ROG) ... BLOEMF
Bloemfontein/J. B. M. Hertzog [*South Africa*] [*ICAO location identifier*] (ICLI) ... FABL
Bloemfontein/New Tempe [*South Africa*] [*ICAO location identifier*] (ICLI) ... FATP
Blois/Le Breuil [*France*] [*ICAO location identifier*] (ICLI) ... LFOQ
Blomatrix, Inc. [*NASDAQ symbol*] (SPSG) ... BIOX
Blomkest Elementary School, Blomkest, MN [*Library symbol*] [*Library of Congress*] (LCLS) ... MnBkES
Blond (WGA) ... BLD
Blond (ADWA) ... Blnd
Blonde d'Aquitaine Breeders Society [*British*] (DBA) ... BDABS
Blonde D'Aquitaine Society of Australia and New Zealand ... BDSANZ
Blonder Tongue Laboratories, Inc. [*AMEX symbol*] (SAG) ... BDR
Blonder Tongue Laboratories, Inc. [*Associated Press*] (SAG) ... BlondT
Blonduos [*Iceland*] [*ICAO location identifier*] (ICLI) ... BIBL
Blonduos [*Iceland*] [*Airport symbol*] (OAG) ... BLO
Blood (AAMN) ... B
Blood ... BL
Blood [*Philately*] ... bld
Blood Agar [*Growth medium*] ... BA
Blood Agar Base [*Growth medium*] ... BAB
Blood Agar Plate [*Microbiology*] ... BAP
Blood Alcohol (WGA) ... BA
Blood Alcohol Concentration [*or Content*] [*Sobriety test*] ... BAC
Blood Alcohol Level [*Medicine*] ... BAL
Blood and Bone (ADA) ... b & b
Blood and Guts [*Code name used to refer to Oliver North, National Security Council aide during Reagan administration*] ... BG
Blood and Lymphatic System [*Medicine*] ... BLS
Blood and Marrow Transplant Newsletter (SAUS) ... BMT Newsletter
Blood Bank ... BB
Blood Bank (DAVI) ... Bld Bk
Blood Bank Information and Manage-ment Control System (SAUS) ... BIMACS
Blood Bank Technologist (DAVI) ... BBT
Blood Banking [*Medical specialty*] (DHSM) ... BLB
Blood Brain Barrier [*Neurology*] ... BBB
Blood Buffer (SAUS) ... BB
Blood Buffer Base [*Biochemistry*] (DAVI) ... BB
Blood Cadmium Level ... BCd
Blood Cancer Foundation [*Defunct*] (EA) ... BCF
Blood Cell Separator [*Medicine*] ... BCS
Blood Cells, Molecules and Diseases (SAUS) ... BCMD
Blood Cells, Molecules and Diseases (SAUS) ... Blood Cells Mol Dis
Blood Chemistry (DAVI) ... Bld Chem
Blood Color Analyzer [*Medicine*] ... BCA
Blood Culture [*Medicine*] ... BC
Blood Culture [*Medicine*] (DMAA) ... BIC
Blood Culture [*Medicine*] (AAMN) ... BL CULT
Blood Derived Serum ... BDS
Blood Donor [*Medicine*] (MELL) ... BD
Blood Donor Center (COE) ... BDC
Blood Erythrocytes Particle Counter [*Medicine*] ... BEpc
Blood Ethanol Concentration [*Medicine*] ... BEC
Blood Ethanol Level [*Medicine*] (DMAA) ... BEL
Blood Ethyl Alcohol [*Biochemistry*] (DB) ... BEC
Blood Extracellular Fluid [*Medicine*] (DB) ... BECF
Blood Fasting Sugar [*Medicine*] (DMAA) ... BFS
Blood Flow [*Medicine*] ... BF
Blood Flow Energy [*Medicine*] (DMAA) ... BFE
Blood Flow Monitoring [*Medicine*] (MELL) ... BFM
Blood Flow Rate [*Medicine*] ... BFR
Blood Gas [*US Chemical Corps symbol*] ... AC
Blood Gas Analyzer [*Physiology*] ... BGA
Blood Gas Level [*Medicine*] (MELL) ... BGL
Blood Glucose [*Biochemistry*] (DB) ... BG
Blood Glucose [*Medicine*] (MAE) ... BGlu
Blood Glucose Level [*Medicine*] (MELL) ... BGL
Blood Glucose Reagent Strip [*Endocrinology*] (DAVI) ... BGRS
Blood Granulocyte-Specific Activity [*Hematology*] (MAE) ... BGSA
Blood Group (ADA) ... BG
Blood Group Class ... BGC
Blood Group Substances [*Hematology*] ... BGS
Blood Group-Degrading [*Medicine*] (MAE) ... BGD
Blood Incubation Infectivity Test (SAUS) ... BIIT
Blood Information Service (NITA) ... BIS
Blood Information Service [*Information service or system*] (IID) ... BLDIS
Blood Isotope Clearance [*Medicine*] (DMAA) ... BIC
Blood Lead ... BL
Blood Lead Laboratory Reference System (ADWA) ... BLLRS
Blood Lead Level [*Medicine*] ... BLL
Blood Levels of Enzymes [*Medicine*] (MELL) ... BLE
Blood Loss [*Medicine*] (AAMN) ... BL
Blood Lymphocytes Particle Counter [*Instrumentation*] [*Medicine*] ... Blpc
Blood Monitoring [*Medicine*] ... BM
Blood, Ova, Parasites (SAUS) ... BOP
Blood Oxygen Capacity [*Medicine*] (DMAA) ... BOC
Blood Oxygen Saturation [*On blood gas determinations*] [*Medicine*] (DAVI) ... $B\text{-}O_2S$
Blood Oxygenation Level-Dependent [*Physiology*] ... BOLD
Blood Partial Pressure of Carbon Dioxide [*On blood gas determinations*] (DAVI) ... $B\text{-}PCO_2$
Blood Partial Pressure of Oxygen [*On blood gas determinations*] (DAVI) ... $B\text{-}PO_2$
Blood Plasma Measuring System [*Medicine*] ... BPMS
Blood Precautions [*Isolation*] [*Medicine*] ... B/P
Blood Pressure [*Medicine*] (DMAA) ... BIP
Blood Pressure [*Medicine*] (MAE) ... bl pr
Blood Pressure (SAUS) ... BL PR
Blood Pressure ... BP
Blood Pressure (NTIO) ... bp
Blood Pressure and Pulse (SAUS) ... BPP
Blood Pressure Assembly (KSC) ... BPA
Blood Pressure Cuff [*Cardiology*] (DAVI) ... BCP
Blood Pressure Cuff (SAUS) ... BPC
Blood Pressure Decreased [*Medicine*] (MAE) ... BPD
Blood Pressure Gauge [*Medicine*] ... BPG
Blood Pressure Increased [*Medicine*] (MAE) ... BPI
Blood Pressure, Pulse, Respiration, and Temperature [*On examination*] [*Medicine*] (DAVI) ... BPPRT
Blood Pressure Recorder [*Medicine*] ... BPR
Blood Pressure, Systolic ... BPsys
Blood Products Depot (COE) ... BPD
Blood Program [*Red Cross*] ... BP
Blood Program Directives [*Red Cross*] ... BPD
Blood Program Office (DNAB) ... BPO
Blood Report (COE) ... BLDREP
Blood Research Foundation (EA) ... BRF
Blood Rheology Equipment (SAUS) ... BRE
Blood Rheology Experiment (SAUS) ... BRE
Blood Rheology Experiment Study (SAUS) ... BRES
Blood Sedimentation Rate [*Medicine*] ... BSR
Blood Serological Test [*Medicine*] ... BST
Blood Sugar [*Medicine*] ... Bl S
Blood Sugar [*Medicine*] ... BS
Blood Sugar Level [*Clinical chemistry*] ... BSL
Blood Supply Unit [*Military*] [*British*] ... BSU
Blood, Sweat, and Tears [*Rock music group*] ... BS & T
Blood Test (MELL) ... BT
Blood Transfusion [*Hematology*] (DAVI) ... BT
Blood Transfusion Association (EA) ... BTA
Blood Transfusion Association (SAUO) ... BTA
Blood Transfusion Betterment Association (SAUO) ... BTBA
Blood Transfusion Centre [*British*] ... BTC
Blood Transfusion Reactions (SAUS) ... BTR
Blood Transfusion Recipient [*Medicine*] (DB) ... BTR

Blood Transfusion Service [*Medicine*] .... BTS
Blood Transfusion Society (SAUO) .... BTS
Blood Transshipment Center (COE) .... BTC
Blood Triacylglycerol [*Hematology*] .... BTG
Blood Type [*Medicine*] .... Bl T
Blood Type (SAUS) .... BLT
Blood Type [*Medicine*] (DB) .... BT
Blood Urea [*Medicine*] (MELL) .... BU
Blood Urea Nitrogen [*Medicine*] .... BUN
Blood Uric Acid [*Clinical chemistry*] (CPH) .... BUA
Blood Vessel [*Medicine*] .... BV
Blood Vessel Invasion [*Medicine*] (MAE) .... BVI
Blood Vessel of Branchial Filament .... BVBRF
Blood Vessel of Palp (SAUS) .... BVP
Blood Vessel of Palp .... BVPP
Blood Vessel of Pinnule .... BVP
Blood Vessel Prosthesis [*Medicine*] .... BVP
Blood Viscosity [*Medicine*] (DMAA) .... BIV
Blood Volume [*Medicine*] .... BV
Blood Volume (DAVI) .... Q
Blood Volume Expander [*Medicine*] (MELL) .... BVE
Blood Volume Pulse (ADWA) .... BVP
Blood Volume Quantity per Unit of Time [*Cardiology*] (DAVI) .... QT
Blood Wassermann [*Medicine*] .... BW
Blood-Activated Recalcification [*Medicine*] (DMAA) .... BART
Blood-Air Barrier [*Medicine*] (MELL) .... BAB
Blood-Alcohol Test (SAUS) .... B-A Test
Blood-Aqueous Barrier [*Medicine*] (MELL) .... BAB
Bloodborne Pathogen (SARE) .... BBP
Blood-Brain Barrier (EDCT) .... BB
Blood-Clot Lysis Time [*Medicine*] .... BLT
Blood-Fasting [*Glucose tolerance test*] [*Endocrinology*] (DAVI) .... BL-FST
Blood-Forming Organ [*Medicine*] (DB) .... BFO
Blood/Gas [*Clinical chemistry*] .... B/G
Bloodgood's Disease [*Medicine*] (MELL) .... BD
Blood-Oxygen Release Rate [*Medicine*] (DB) .... BORR
Blood-Products Laboratory [*British*] .... BPL
Blood-Retinal Barrier [*Ophthalmology*] (DAVI) .... BRB
Blood-Stage Variant Antigen Type [*Immunology*] .... BVAT
Bloodstock and Racehorse Industries Confederation (SAUO) .... BRIC
Bloodstone (VRA) .... bldst
Blood-Testis Barrier [*Medicine*] (MELL) .... BTB
Blood-Thymus Barrier [*Medicine*] (MELL) .... BTB
Bloody [*Slang*] [*British*] (DSUE) .... B
Bloody Bastard [*British slang*] .... BB
Bloody Fool [*British slang*] .... BF
Bloody Hell [*British slang*] .... BH
Bloody Nuisance [*British slang*] .... BN
Bloody Public Nuisance [*British slang*] .... BPN
Bloody Young Fool [*Officer under the age of 30*] [*British*] (DSUE) .... BYF
Bloom [*or Blossom*] (ROG) .... BL
Bloom Analogies Test [*Intelligence test*] .... BAT
Bloom Elementary School, Rockford, IL [*Library symbol*] [*Library of Congress*] (LCLS) .... IRoBIE
Bloom Syndrome [*Medicine*] (DMAA) .... BLS
Bloom Syndrome [*Medicine*] .... BS
Bloom Township Community College (SAUO) .... BTCC
Bloomberg Business News (SAUS) .... BBN
Bloomer Learning Test [*Intelligence test*] .... BLT
Bloomer, WI [*FM radio station call letters*] .... WQRB
Bloomfield (BEE) .... Blmfld
Bloomfield College (SAUO) .... BC
Bloomfield College, Bloomfield, NJ [*OCLC symbol*] (OCLC) .... BLO
Bloomfield College, Bloomfield, NJ [*Library symbol*] [*Library of Congress*] (LCLS) .... NjBlC
Bloomfield, CT [*AM radio station call letters*] (BROA) .... WDZK
Bloomfield, CT [*AM radio station call letters*] .... WRDM
Bloomfield Democrat, Bloomfield, IA [*Library symbol*] [*Library of Congress*] (LCLS) .... IaBlD
Bloomfield Evening World and News, Bloomfield, IN [*Library symbol*] [*Library of Congress*] (LCLS) .... InBlWN
Bloomfield Hills, MI [*FM radio station call letters*] .... WBFH
Bloomfield, IA [*Location identifier*] [*FAA*] (FAAL) .... BEX
Bloomfield, IA [*FM radio station call letters*] .... KXOF
Bloomfield, IN [*FM radio station call letters*] .... WBHQ
Bloomfield, NM [*FM radio station call letters*] .... KKFG
Bloomfield Public Library, Bloomfield, IA [*Library symbol*] [*Library of Congress*] (LCLS) .... IaBl
Bloomfield Public Library, Bloomfield, IN [*Library symbol*] [*Library of Congress*] (LCLS) .... InBl
Bloomfield Public Library, Bloomfield, NJ [*Library symbol*] [*Library of Congress*] (LCLS) .... NjBl
Bloomfield-Hallowell Union Library, Bloomfield, Ontario [*Library symbol*] [*National Library of Canada*] (BIB) .... OBLH
Bloomfield's Manumission (or Negro) Cases [*New Jersey*] [*A publication*] (DLA) .... Blm Neg
Bloomfield's Manumission (or Negro) Cases [*New Jersey*] [*A publication*] (DLA) .... Bloom Man
Bloomfield's Manumission (or Negro) Cases [*New Jersey*] [*A publication*] (DLA) .... Bloom Man Neg Cas
Bloomfield's Manumission (or Negro) Cases [*New Jersey*] [*A publication*] (DLA) .... Manum Cas
Bloomfield's Manumission (or Negro) Cases [*New Jersey*] [*A publication*] (DLA) .... Manum Cases
Bloomfield's Manumission (or Negro) Cases [*New Jersey*] [*A publication*] (DLA) .... Neg Cas
Bloomfield's Manumission (or Negro) Cases [*New Jersey*] [*A publication*] (DLA) .... Negro Cas
Blooming Gate (IAA) .... BLG
Blooming Prairie, MN [*FM radio station call letters*] (RBYB) .... KOWZ-FM
Bloomington [*Indiana*] [*Seismograph station code, US Geological Survey*] (SEIS) .... BLO
Bloomington [*Indiana*] [*Airport symbol*] (OAG) .... BMG
Bloomington [*Illinois*] [*Airport symbol*] (OAG) .... BMI
Bloomington (BEE) .... Bton
Bloomington Academic Computer Services [*Indiana University*] [*Research center*] (RCD) .... BACS
Bloomington Area Arts Councilay Area Rapid Transit (SAUO) .... BAAC
Bloomington Herald-Telephone, Bloomington, IN [*Library symbol*] [*Library of Congress*] (LCLS) .... InBloHT
Bloomington, IL [*FM radio station call letters*] .... WBNQ
Bloomington, IL [*FM radio station call letters*] .... WESN
Bloomington, IL [*AM radio station call letters*] .... WJBC
Bloomington, IL [*Television station call letters*] .... WYZZ
Bloomington, IN [*FM radio station call letters*] .... WBWB
Bloomington, IN [*Television station call letters*] .... WCLJ
Bloomington, IN [*FM radio station call letters*] .... WFHB
Bloomington, IN [*FM radio station call letters*] .... WFIU
Bloomington, IN [*AM radio station call letters*] .... WGCL
Bloomington, IN [*Television station call letters*] .... WIIB
Bloomington, IN [*Television station call letters*] .... WTIU
Bloomington, IN [*FM radio station call letters*] .... WTTS
Bloomington, IN [*Television station call letters*] .... WTTV
Bloomington Public Schools, Bloomington, MN [*Library symbol*] [*Library of Congress*] (LCLS) .... MnBloPS
Bloomington, TX [*FM radio station call letters*] .... KLUB
Bloomsburg, PA [*FM radio station call letters*] .... WBUQ
Bloomsburg, PA [*AM radio station call letters*] .... WCNR
Bloomsburg, PA [*FM radio station call letters*] .... WHLM
Bloomsburg, PA [*AM radio station call letters*] .... WJMW
Bloomsburg State College (SAUO) .... BSC
Bloomsburg State College, Bloomsburg, PA [*OCLC symbol*] (OCLC) .... PBB
Bloomsburg State College, Bloomsburg, PA [*Library symbol*] [*Library of Congress*] (LCLS) .... PBbS
Bloomsburg University (SAUO) .... BU
Bloomsburg University of Pennsylvania (GAGS) .... Bloomsburg U
Bloomsbury Review [*A publication*] (BRI) .... Bloom Rev
Bloomsday Club (EA) .... BC
Bloorview Children's Hospital, Health Sciences Library, Willowdale, ON, Canada [*Library symbol*] [*Library of Congress*] (LCLS) .... CaOWBC
Bloque .... BL
Bloque Antiguerrillero del Oriente [*Eastern Anti-Guerrilla Bloc*] [*El Salvador*] (PD) .... BAGO
Bloque de la Vanguardia Revolucionaria [*Bolivia*] [*Political party*] (PPW) .... BVR
Bloque Nacional Popular de Galicia - Partido Socialista Gallego [*Popular National Bloc of Galicia - Galician Socialist Party*] [*Political party*] (PPW) .... BNPG-PSG
Bloque Nacionalista Galego [*Galician Nationalist Block*] [*Spain*] [*Political party*] (EY) .... BNG
Bloque Popular Revolucionario [*Popular Revolutionary Bloc*] [*El Salvador*] (PD) .... BPR
Blotting Paper Manufacturers' Association (DGA) .... BPMA
Blount. Fragmenta Antiquitatis [*A publication*] (DLA) .... Blount Frag Ant
Blount, Inc. (SAUO) .... BLT
Blount, Inc., Montgomery, AL [*Library symbol*] [*Library of Congress*] (LCLS) .... AMB
Blount International [*Associated Press*] (SAG) .... Blount
Blount International [*NYSE symbol*] (SAG) .... BLT
Blount Intl Cl'A' [*NYSE symbol*] (TTSB) .... BLT.A
Blount Intl Cv'B' [*NYSE symbol*] (TTSB) .... BLT.B
Blount Memorial Hospital, Medical Library, Maryville, TN [*Library symbol*] [*Library of Congress*] (LCLS) .... TMaryB
Blount on Tenures [*A publication*] (DLA) .... Blount Ten
Blount's Impeachment Trial [*A publication*] (DLA) .... Blount Tr
Blount's Law Dictionary [*A publication*] (DLA) .... Bl
Blount's Law Dictionary [*A publication*] (DLA) .... Bl D
Blount's Law Dictionary [*A publication*] (DLA) .... Bl LD
Blount's Law Dictionary [*A publication*] (DLA) .... Blount
Blount's Law Dictionary [*A publication*] (DLA) .... Blount LD
Blountstown, FL [*FM radio station call letters*] .... WPHK
Blountstown, FL [*AM radio station call letters*] .... WYBT
Blountville, TN [*AM radio station call letters*] .... WGOC
Blouse Full of Goodies (SAUS) .... BFOG
Blow Back (SAUS) .... BB
Blow Bottle [*Medicine*] (DAVI) .... BB
Blow in Door .... BID
Blow in Place .... BIP
Blow Me Down School/Public Library, Lark Harbour, Newfoundland [*Library symbol*] [*National Library of Canada*] (NLC) .... NFLHB
Blow Me Down School/Public Library, Lark Harbour, NF, Canada [*Library symbol*] [*Library of Congress*] (LCLS) .... CaNfLHB
Blow Molding [*Bottle manufacturing*] .... BM
Blow Molding System .... BMS
Blow Valve .... BV
Blowback .... BB
Blowdown [*Nuclear energy*] (NRCH) .... BD
Blowdown (NASA) .... BLDN
Blowdown [*Chemical engineering*] .... BLWDN
Blowdown Heat Transfer [*Nuclear energy*] .... BDHT

Blowdown Heat Transfer [*Nuclear energy*] (OA) ... BHT
Blowdown Suppression Tank [*Nuclear energy*] (NRCH) ... BST
Blow-Down Valve [*Railroad term*] ... BDV
Blowdown/Emergency Core Cooling [*Nuclear energy*] (NRCH) ... BD/ECC
Blower (IAA) ... B
Blower ... BL
Blower (KSC) ... BLO
Blower (NVT) ... BLR
Blower (KSC) ... BLWR
Blower Access Cover ... BAC
Blower Ramp Sensor [*Automotive air conditioning*] ... BRS
Blower Wheel Housing ... BWH
Blowing [*ICAO*] (FAAC) ... BL
Blowing (SAUS) ... BLWG
Blowing Dust (BARN) ... BD
Blowing Dust [*ICAO*] (FAAC) ... BLDU
Blowing Rock, NC [*AM radio station call letters*] ... WVIO
Blowing Rock, NC [*AM radio station call letters*] (RBYB) ... WXIT-AM
Blowing Sand [*ICAO*] (FAAC) ... BLSA
Blowing Sand [*Meteorology*] (DNAB) ... BS
Blowing Snow [*Meteorology*] (DA) ... BLSN
Blowing Snow [*Meteorology*] (BARN) ... BS
Blowing Spray [*ICAO*] (FAAC) ... BY
Blowline ... BL
Blown Head Gasket [*Automotive term*] ... BHG
Blown in Place (SAUS) ... BIP
Blown Save [*Baseball term*] (NDBD) ... BS
Blowoff ... BO
Blowout ... BLWT
Blowout (IAA) ... BO
Blowout Coil ... BOC
Blow-Out Emergency Team [*British government*] ... BET
Blowout Pipe System ... BPS
Blowout Preventer [*or Prevention*] ... BOP
Blows Per Minute (SAUS) ... BPM
Blowtorch ... BLWT
BLs General Catalogue of Printed Books (SAUS) ... GCPB
BLS Ltd Client Server Library Management System (SAUS) ... TALIS
Blue [*Philately*] ... B
Blue (KSC) ... BL
Blue (VRA) ... bl
Blue (ADWA) ... Blu
Blue (KSC) ... BLU
Blue ... Bu
Blue Affirmative Flag [*Navy*] [*British*] ... BF
Blue Airlines [*Zaire*] [*ICAO designator*] (FAAC) ... BUL
Blue Albion Cattle Society (SAUO) ... BACS
Blue Albion Cattle Society (SAUS) ... BACS
Blue Anchor, Inc. [*Formerly, CFE*] [*Later, BAI*] [*An association*] ... BA
Blue Anchor, Inc. [*An association*] (EA) ... BAI
Blue and Gold Macaw [*Bird*] ... B&G
[*The*] **Blue and the Gray** [*A publication*] ... BIG
Blue Army of Our Lady of Fatima [*Later, World Apostolate of Fatima - WAF*] (EA) ... BALF
Blue Ballistic Missile (ACAE) ... BBM
Blue Bell [*Pennsylvania*] [*Airport symbol*] (OAG) ... BBX
Blue Bell Inc. (SAUO) ... BBL
Blue Bird Corp. (SAUO) ... BB
Blue Blazes Irregulars (EA) ... BBI
Blue Bloaters [*Emphysema*] [*Slang*] [*Medicine*] (MAE) ... BB
Blue Bomber [*Valium tablet*] [*Slang*] ... BB
Blue Book [*Directory of proprietaries*] ... BB
Blue Card (EA) ... BC
Blue Chip [*Investment term*] ... BC
Blue Chip Computerware [*NASDAQ symbol*] (TTSB) ... BCHPE
Blue Chip Computerware, Inc. [*NASDAQ symbol*] (SAG) ... BCHP
Blue Chip Computerware, Inc. [*Associated Press*] (SAG) ... BlChip
Blue Chip Fund [*Associated Press*] (SAG) ... BlueChp
Blue Chip Service (SAUO) ... BCS
Blue Chip Value Fund [*NYSE symbol*] (SPSG) ... BLU
Blue Circle Industries [*British*] ... BCI
Blue Compact Dwarf [*Galaxy*] ... BCD
Blue Compact Galaxy [*Astronomy*] ... BCG
Blue Cone Pigment ... BCP
Blue Crescent [*Later, BCI*] [*An association*] (EAIO) ... BC
Blue Crescent International (EAIO) ... BCI
Blue Cross [*Health insurance plan*] ... BC
Blue Cross and Blue Shield [*Insurance plan*] (DAVI) ... BX BS
Blue Cross and Blue Shield Association [*Chicago, IL*] (EA) ... BCBSA
Blue Cross & Blue Shield of Colorado, Denver, CO [*Library symbol*] [*Library of Congress*] (LCLS) ... CoDBCS
Blue Cross & Blue Shield of North Carolina, Durham, NC [*Library symbol*] [*Library of Congress*] (LCLS) ... NcDurBC
Blue Cross and Blue Shield of Tennessee, Chattanooga, TN [*Library symbol*] [*Library of Congress*] (LCLS) ... TCBCS
Blue Cross Association [*Later, BCBSA*] (EA) ... BCA
Blue Cross Association, Chicago, IL [*Library symbol*] [*Library of Congress*] (LCLS) ... ICBC
Blue Cross Interim Payment [*Insurance*] ... BIP
Blue Cross Plan [*Health insurance*] ... BCP
Blue Cross/Blue Shield [*Health insurance plan*] ... BC/BS
Blue Cross/Blue Shield of Oregon, Portland, OR [*Library symbol*] [*Library of Congress*] (LCLS) ... OrPBC
Blue Crown Conure [*Bird*] ... BC
Blue Danube Network (SAUO) ... BDN
Blue Data Base (ACAE) ... BDB
Blue Diamond Energy [*Vancouver Stock Exchange symbol*] ... BED
Blue Diamond Growers [*An association*] (EA) ... BDG
Blue Diaper Syndrome [*Medicine*] (DMAA) ... BD
Blue Dolphin Energy [*NASDAQ symbol*] (TTSB) ... BDCO
Blue Dolphin Energy Co. [*NASDAQ symbol*] (SAG) ... BDCO
Blue Dolphin Energy Co. [*Associated Press*] (SAG) ... BluDolp
Blue Earth, MN [*AM radio station call letters*] ... KBEW
Blue Earth, MN [*FM radio station call letters*] ... KBEW-FM
Blue Earth, MN [*FM radio station call letters*] ... KJLY
Blue Earth, MN [*Location identifier*] [*FAA*] (FAAL) ... SBU
Blue East (SAUO) ... BE
Blue Emerald Resources [*Vancouver Stock Exchange symbol*] ... BER
Blue Enhanced Silicon Photodiode (SAUS) ... BESP
Blue Etch-Anodize (or Anodizing) (SAUS) ... BEA
Blue Flag (SAUS) ... BF
Blue Flame Gas Association [*Nebraska*] (SRA) ... BFGA
Blue Fluorescent Protein [*Biochemistry*] ... BFP
Blue Force (SAUO) ... BF
Blue Force (DOMA) ... BLUFOR
Blue Force Data Link [*Military*] (CAAL) ... BFDL
Blue Force Tracking [*Military*] ... BFT
Blue Fronted Amazon [*Bird*] ... BFA
Blue Funnel Line (SAUO) ... BFL
Blue Gold Resources [*Vancouver Stock Exchange symbol*] ... BLQ
Blue Grass Depot Activity (SAUS) ... BGDA
Blue Hill, ME [*FM radio station call letters*] ... WERU
Blue Hill Meteorological Observatory [*Harvard University*] (MCD) ... BHMO
Blue Hills Community School, Buffalo Head Prairie, Alberta [*Library symbol*] [*National Library of Canada*] (BIB) ... ABHPBS
Blue Hills Power Plant [*Nuclear energy*] (NRCH) ... BH
Blue Hills Station [*Nuclear energy*] (NRCH) ... BHS
Blue Horizon Travel Club [*ICAO designator*] (FAAC) ... BLH
Blue Horizontal Branch ... BHB
Blue Indicating Lamp (SAUS) ... BIL
Blue Indicator Light ... BIL
Blue Island Public Library, Blue Island, IL [*Library symbol*] [*Library of Congress*] (LCLS) ... IBi
Blue Knights International Law Enforcement Motorcycle Club (EA) ... BK
Blue Laid [*Paper*] (DGA) ... BL
Blue Light Radiation (HEAS) ... BLR
Blue Line (MCD) ... BL
Blue Line (SAUS) ... B/L
Blue Line Copy ... BLC
Blue Line Print ... BLP
Blue Line Requisition ... BL REQ
Blue Military Damage Assessment ... BMDA
Blue Minute Men (SAUO) ... BMM
Blue Mountain [*Alaska*] [*Seismograph station code, US Geological Survey*] (SEIS) ... BLM
Blue Mountain College [*Mississippi*] ... BMC
Blue Mountain College, Blue Mountain, MS [*Library symbol*] [*Library of Congress*] (LCLS) ... MsBm
Blue Mountain Community College (SAUO) ... BMCC
Blue Mountain Community College, Pendleton, OR [*Library symbol*] [*Library of Congress*] (LCLS) ... OrPeB
Blue Mountain Lake [*New York*] [*Seismograph station code, US Geological Survey*] [*Closed*] (SEIS) ... BML
Blue Mountain Lake, NY [*FM radio station call letters*] ... WXLH
Blue Mountain Seismological Observatory ... BMSO
Blue Mountains Array [*Oregon*] [*Seismograph station code, US Geological Survey*] [*Closed*] (SEIS) ... BMO
Blue Mountains Expeditions (SAUO) ... BME
Blue Mountains National Park (SAUS) ... BMNP
Blue Mountains Tourism Authority [*Australia*] ... BMTA
Blue Nevus [*Medicine*] (MELL) ... BN
Blue Nile Bank Ltd. [*Sudan*] ... BNB
Blue Nose Minnow [*Ichthyology*] ... Bn
Blue Oyster Cult [*Rock music group*] ... BOC
Blue Pennant [*Navy*] [*British*] ... BL
Blue Print Files (NRCH) ... BPF
Blue Return [*Round trip fare*] [*British*] ... B
Blue Ribbon Coalition [*An association*] (EA) ... BRC
Blue Ribbon Defense Panel ... BRDP
Blue Ridge, GA [*FM radio station call letters*] ... WPPL
Blue Ridge National Parkway (SAUS) ... BRNP
Blue Ridge Parkway [*National Park Service designation*] ... BLRI
Blue Ridge Railroad (IIA) ... BR
Blue Ridge Regional Library, Martinsville, VA [*Library symbol*] [*Library of Congress*] (LCLS) ... ViMv
Blue Ridge Resources Ltd. [*Vancouver Stock Exchange symbol*] ... BRG
Blue Ridge Technical Institute, Hendersonville, NC [*Library symbol*] [*Library of Congress*] (LCLS) ... NcHvH
Blue Ridge Township Public Library, Mansfield, IL [*Library symbol*] [*Library of Congress*] (LCLS) ... IMan
Blue Ridge, TX [*Location identifier*] [*FAA*] (FAAL) ... BUJ
Blue Rubber Bleb Nevus Syndrome [*Medicine*] (DMAA) ... BRBNS
Blue Screen of Death (SAUS) ... BSOD
Blue Sea Line (SAUO) ... BSL
Blue Second Hydrogen Line in the Solar Spectrum (BARN) ... F
Blue Shade [*Paper*] ... BS
Blue Shield [*Health insurance plan*] ... BS
Blue Shield Association [*Later, BCBSA*] (EA) ... BSA
Blue Shield Medical Care Plans [*Later, BSA*] [*An association*] ... BSMCP
Blue Sky (ROG) ... B

Blue Sky Carrier Co. Ltd. [*Poland*] [*ICAO designator*] (FAAC) ... BSC
Blue Sky Law Reporter [*Commerce Clearing House*] [*A publication*] (DLA) ... Blue Sky L Rep
Blue Sky Laws ... BSL
Blue Springs, MO [*AM radio station call letters*] ... KBEQ
Blue Springs, MO [*AM radio station call letters*] (RBYB) ... KOWW-AM
Blue Square Israel Ltd. [*Associated Press*] (SAG) ... BlueSq
Blue Square Israel Ltd. [*NYSE symbol*] (SAG) ... BSI
Blue Square-Israel ADS [*NYSE symbol*] (SG) ... BSI
Blue Star Line (SAUO) ... BSL
Blue Star Mothers of America (EA) ... BSM
Blue Star Port Lines (SAUO) ... BSPL
Blue Star Ship Management (SAUO) ... BSSM
Blue Star Ship Management Limited (SAUO) ... BSSML
Blue Steel [*Guns*] ... BS
Blue Stellar Object [*Astronomy*] ... BSO
Blue Stern Light (SAUS) ... B ST LT
Blue Straggler [*Star*] [*Astronomy*] ... BS
Blue Streak [*Military*] (SAA) ... BS
Blue Streak Request [*Military*] ... BSR
Blue Supergiant [*Astronomy*] ... BSG
Blue Tetrazolium [*A dye*] ... BT
Blue Toe Syndrome [*Medicine*] (MELL) ... BTS
Blue Tongue Virus [*Medicine*] (DMAA) ... BTV
Blue Tool Steel (MSA) ... BTS
Blue Vein Circle (SAUO) ... BVC
Blue Water Bridge Authority ... BWBA
Blue West (SAUO) ... BW
Blue West, Greenland (SAUO) ... BWG
Blue Willow Collectors Society (EA) ... BWCS
Blue Wove [*Paper*] (DGA) ... BW
Blueberry Leaf Mottle Virus ... BBLMV
Blueberry Mottle Virus ... BBMV
Blueberry Red Ringspot Virus [*Plant pathology*] ... BRRV
Blueberry Shoestring Virus ... BBSSV
Blueberry Shoestring Virus [*Plant pathology*] ... BSSV
Bluebird [*Division of Victor*] [*Record label*] ... BB
Blue-Black ... BB
Blue-Brick University (SAUO) ... BBU
Blue-Collar Ethnic Catholic [*Political demography*] ... BCEC
Blue-Collar Guy [*Lifestyle classification*] ... BCG
Blue-Diaper Syndrome [*Medicine*] (MELL) ... BDS
Bluefeld College (SAUS) ... BC
Bluefield [*West Virginia*] [*Airport symbol*] (OAG) ... BLF
Bluefield College (SAUO) ... BC
Bluefield College, Bluefield, VA [*Library symbol*] [*Library of Congress*] (LCLS) ... ViBluC
Bluefield Public Library, Bluefield, WV [*Library symbol*] [*Library of Congress*] (LCLS) ... WvBl
Bluefield State College [*West Virginia*] ... BSC
Bluefield State College, Bluefield, WV [*Library symbol*] [*Library of Congress*] (LCLS) ... WvBlS
Bluefield, VA [*FM radio station call letters*] ... WBDY
Bluefield, VA [*FM radio station call letters*] (BROA) ... WHKX-FM
Bluefield, VA [*AM radio station call letters*] ... WHYS
Bluefield, WV [*FM radio station call letters*] ... WHAJ
Bluefield, WV [*AM radio station call letters*] ... WHIS
Bluefield, WV [*AM radio station call letters*] (BROA) ... WKEZ-AM
Bluefield, WV [*AM radio station call letters*] ... WKOY
Bluefield, WV [*Television station call letters*] ... WLFB
Bluefield, WV [*FM radio station call letters*] ... WPIB
Bluefield, WV [*Television station call letters*] ... WVVA
Bluefields [*Nicaragua*] [*ICAO location identifier*] (ICLI) ... MNBL
Bluegill [*Ichthyology*] ... BG
Bluegrass (WGA) ... BG
Bluegrass Army Depot ... BGAD
Bluegrass Depot Activity [*Army*] (AABC) ... BGDA
Bluegrass Petroleum, Inc. [*Vancouver Stock Exchange symbol*] ... BGS
Blue-Green Algae [*Water purification*] ... BGA
Blue-Green Algal Virus (OA) ... BGAV
Bluegreen Corp. [*Associated Press*] (SAG) ... Bluegreen
Bluegreen Corp. [*NYSE symbol*] [*Formerly, Patten Corp.*] (SG) ... BXG
Bluejacket's Manual [*Navy*] ... BJM
Blue-Laid [*Paper*] ... BLD
Blue-Line Drawing ... BLD
Blueport Associated Container Transporation (SAUO) ... BP-ACT
Blueprint ... BLUPRNT
Blueprint ... BP
Blueprint Analysis Report (MCD) ... BAR
Blueprint Reading ... BLPRT
Blueprints and Plans (MCD) ... B & P
Blues Foundation (EA) ... BF
Blues Heaven Foundation (EA) ... BHF
Bluesky Oil & Gas [*Toronto Stock Exchange symbol*] [*Vancouver Stock Exchange symbol*] ... BKY
Bluestone [*Inferior gin or whiskey*] [*Slang*] (ADA) ... BL/ST
Bluestone (ABBR) ... BS
Bluetick Breeders of America (EA) ... BBA
Blue-Tongue [*Medicine*] (DMAA) ... BT
Bluetooth (SAUS) ... BT
Bluett's Advocate's Note Book, Isle Of Man [*1720-1846*] [*A publication*] (DLA) ... Blu
Bluett's Isle Of Man Cases [*A publication*] (DLA) ... Bluett
Blue-Visual [*Color index*] ... B-V
Blue-Whale-Unit [*Whaling industry*] ... BWU
Blue/White Pottery Club (EA) ... BWPC
Blue-Winged Olive [*Insect*] ... BWO
Bluff [*Commonly used*] (OPSA) ... BLF
Bluff [*Commonly used*] (OPSA) ... BLUF
Bluff [*Commonly used*] (OPSA) ... BLUFF
Bluff Creek Industries R. R. [*AAR code*] ... BCI
Bluffs [*Postal Service standard*] (OPSA) ... BLFS
Bluffs [*Commonly used*] (OPSA) ... BLUFFS
Bluffton College (SAUO) ... BC
Bluffton College, Bluffton, OH [*OCLC symbol*] (OCLC) ... BLC
Bluffton College, Bluffton, OH [*Library symbol*] [*Library of Congress*] (LCLS) ... OBIC
Bluffton College, Mennonite Historical Library, Bluffton, OH [*Library symbol*] [*Library of Congress*] (LCLS) ... OBIC-M
Bluffton, IN [*FM radio station call letters*] ... WNUY
Bluffton, SC [*FM radio station call letters*] ... WLOW
Bluffton, SC [*FM radio station call letters*] (BROA) ... WWVV-FM
Bluffton-Wells County Public Library, Bluffton, IN [*Library symbol*] [*Library of Congress*] (LCLS) ... InBlu
Bluffton-Wells County Public Library, Bluffton, IN [*OCLC symbol*] (OCLC) ... IWM
Bluie East [*US air bases in Greenland*] [*World War II*] ... BE
Bluie West [*US air bases in Greenland*] [*World War II*] ... BW
Bluish Green ... BG
Blume [*Germany*] [*ICAO aircraft manufacturer identifier*] (ICAO) ... BM
Blumenstiel on Bankruptcy [*A publication*] (DLA) ... Blum B'k'cy
Blunt Cardiac Rupture [*Medicine*] (MELL) ... BCR
Blunt Conical Model ... BCM
Blunt Conical Reentry Vehicle ... BCRV
Blunt End First (SAUS) ... BEF
Blunt End Forward (KSC) ... BEF
Blunt Head Trauma (SAUS) ... BHT
Blunt Injury [*Medicine*] (MELL) ... BI
Blunt Leading Edge ... BLE
Blunt Trailing Edge ... BTE
Blunted Delta Wing ... BDW
Blunted Wedge ... BW
Blur Diameter [*Optics*] ... B/D
Blutkorpersenkung [*Blood Sedimentation Rate*] [*German*] [*Medicine*] ... BKS
Blydenburgh. Law of Usury [*1844*] [*A publication*] (DLA) ... Bly Us
B-Lymphoblastoid Cell Line [*Biochemistry*] ... BLCL
B-Lymphocyte Chemoattractant ... BLC
Blyn Mountain [*Washington*] [*Seismograph station code, US Geological Survey*] (SEIS) ... BLN
Blyth Holdings [*NASDAQ symbol*] (TTSB) ... BLYH
Blyth Holdings, Inc. [*NASDAQ symbol*] (NQ) ... BLYH
Blyth Holdings, Inc. [*Associated Press*] (SAG) ... Blyth
Blyth Industries, Inc. [*Associated Press*] (SAG) ... BlythInd
Blyth Industries, Inc. [*NYSE symbol*] (SAG) ... BTH
Blythe [*California*] [*Airport symbol*] (OAG) ... BLH
Blythe Air Base (SAUO) ... BAB
Blythe, CA [*FM radio station call letters*] ... KJMB
Blythe, CA [*Location identifier*] [*FAA*] (FAAL) ... RPY
Blytheville Air Force Base [*Arkansas*] [*ICAO location identifier*] (ICLI) ... KBYH
Blytheville, AR [*Location identifier*] [*FAA*] (FAAL) ... BYH
Blytheville, AR [*Location identifier*] [*FAA*] (FAAL) ... GOJ
Blytheville, AR [*Location identifier*] [*FAA*] (FAAL) ... HKA
Blytheville, AR [*FM radio station call letters*] ... KHLS
Blytheville, AR [*AM radio station call letters*] ... KLCN
Blythwood, SC [*AM radio station call letters*] ... WBAJ
BlyvoorGold Mng ADR [*NASDAQ symbol*] (TTSB) ... BLYVY
Blyvooruitzicht Gold [*NASDAQ symbol*] (SAG) ... BLYD
Blyvooruitzicht Gold Mining Co. Ltd. [*NASDAQ symbol*] (NQ) ... BLYV
Blyvooruitzicht Gold Mining Co. Ltd. [*Associated Press*] (SAG) ... Blyvoor
BMA [*British Medical Association*] **Press Cuttings Database** [*Information service or system*] (IID) ... BMAP
BMB Compuscience Canada Ltd. [*Toronto Stock Exchange symbol*] ... BMB
BMC Industries, Inc. [*NYSE symbol*] (SPSG) ... BMC
BMC International Corp. (SAUO) ... LITE
BMC Software, Inc. [*NASDAQ symbol*] (NQ) ... BMCS
BMC Softwear [*Associated Press*] (SAG) ... BMC Soft
BMC Softwear, Inc. [*Associated Press*] (SAG) ... BMC Sf
BMC West [*NASDAQ symbol*] (SPSG) ... BMCW
BMC West Corp. [*Associated Press*] (SAG) ... BMC Wst
BMEWS [*Ballistic Missile Early Warning System*] **Operational Simulation System** (IAA) ... BOSS
BMEWS [*Ballistic Missile Early Warning System*] **Performance Test Outline** ... BPTO
BMEWS [*Ballistic Missile Early Warning System*] **Raid Input Generator** (IAA) ... BRIG
BMEWS [*Ballistic Missile Early Warning System*] **Rearward Communications System** (AFM) ... BRCS
BMEWS [*Ballistic Missile Early Warning System*] **Specification** (AFM) ... BSP
BMEWS [*Ballistic Missile Early Warning System*] **System Program Office** (AFM) ... BSPO
BMEWS [*Ballistic Missile Early Warning System*] **Test Procedure** (AFM) ... BTP
BMEWS [*Ballistic Missile Early Warning System*] **Test Report** (AFM) ... BTR
BMI Finance, Regina, Saskatchewan [*Library symbol*] [*National Library of Canada*] (NLC) ... SRBMI
BMI Finance, Regina, SK, Canada [*Library symbol*] [*Library of Congress*] (LCLS) ... CaSRBMI
BMJ Financial Corp. [*Associated Press*] (SAG) ... BMJ
BMJ Financial Corp. [*NASDAQ symbol*] (NQ) ... BMJF
BMMF [*Bible and Medical Missionary Fellowship*] **International** [*Later, IUSA*] (EA) ... BMMFI

BMMF [*Bible and Medical Missionary Fellowship*] **International/USA** [*Later, IUSA*] (EA) ..... BMMFI/USA
BMO II Financial Corp. [*Toronto Stock Exchange symbol*] ..... BMF
BMO II Financial Pr [*Toronto Stock Exchange symbol*] ..... BMFPRA
BMO NT Financial Corp. [*Toronto Stock Exchange symbol*] ..... BMN
B-Mode Receiving Station [*Telecommunications*] (TEL) ..... BRS
BMP Technologies Ltd. [*Vancouver Stock Exchange symbol*] ..... BMP
BMT [*British Maritime Technology Ltd.*] **Abstracts Online** [*Wallsend, Tyne, and Wear, England*] [*Information service or system*] (IID) ..... BOATS
BMW [*Bavarian Motor Works*] **Automobile Club of America** (EA) ..... BMW-ACA
BMW [*Bavarian Motor Works*] **Car Club of America** (EA) ..... BMWCCA
BMW [*Bavarian Motor Works*] **Car Club of Canada** (EAIO) ..... BMW-CCC
BMW Mororcycle Owners of America (SAUO) ..... BMWMOA
BMW [*Bavarian Motor Works*] **Riders Association** (EA) ..... BMWRA
BMW Riders Association (EA) ..... BMW RA
BMW [*Bavarian Motor Works*] **Rolls-Royce AeroEngines** [*Commercial firm*] (ECON) ..... BRRA
BMW [*Bavarian Motor Works*] **Vintage Club of America** (EA) ..... BMWVCA
B'nai Birth Canada [*Also, Children of the Convenant*] (AC) ..... BBC
B'nai B'rith [*Later, BBI*] (EA) ..... BB
B'nai B'rith Bulletin [*A publication*] (ADA) ..... BBB
B'nai B'rith Hillel Foundations (EA) ..... BBHF
B'nai B'rith International (EA) ..... BBI
B'nai B'rith International Commission on Adult Jewish Education [*Later, BBICCJE*] (EA) ..... BBICAJE
B'nai B'rith International Senior Citizens Housing Committee (EA) ..... BBISCHC
B'nai B'rith Senior Citizens Housing Committee (EA) ..... BBSCHC
B'nai B'rith Vocational Service [*Later, B'nai B'rith Career and Counseling Services*] (EA) ..... BBVS
B'nai B'rith Women (EA) ..... BBW
B'nai B'rith Youth Organization (EA) ..... BBYO
Bnai Israel (BJA) ..... BI
Bnai Zion (EA) ..... BZ
BNB database (SAUS) ..... BNBMARC
BNCCORP, Inc. [*Associated Press*] (SAG) ..... BNC
BNCCORP, Inc. [*NASDAQ symbol*] (SAG) ..... BNCC
B-negative (SAUS) B-1
Bnei Akiva of North America (EA) ..... BA of NA
Bnei Akiva of the United States and Canada [*An association*] (EA) ..... BA
BNF Metals Technology Centre (SAUO) ..... BNF
BNH Bancshares [*NASDAQ symbol*] (TTSB) ..... BNHB
BNH Bancshares, Inc. [*Associated Press*] (SAG) ..... BNH
BNH Bancshares, Inc. [*NASDAQ symbol*] (NQ) ..... BNHB
Bnos Agudath Israel (EA) ..... BAI
Bo [*Sierra Leone*] [*Airport symbol*] [*Obsolete*] (OAG) ..... KBS
Boa Vista [*Brazil*] [*Airport symbol*] (OAG) ..... BVB
Boa Vista [*Cape Verde Islands*] [*Airport symbol*] (OAG) ..... BVC
Boa Vista/Internacional [*Brazil*] [*ICAO location identifier*] (ICLI) ..... SBBV
Boaco [*Nicaragua*] [*Seismograph station code, US Geological Survey*] (SEIS) ..... BOA
Boalsburg, PA [*FM radio station call letters*] (BROA) ..... WBUS-FM
Boalsburg, PA [*FM radio station call letters*] ..... WVCV
Boang [*Papua New Guinea*] [*Airport symbol*] (OAG) ..... BOV
Board ..... B
Board (TBD) ..... Bd
Board ..... BD
Board (VRA) ..... bd
Board (ADWA) ..... brd
Board ..... BRD
Board and Care [*Medicine*] (DAVI) ..... B & C
Board and Care [*Medicine*] (DAVI) ..... Bd & C
Board Arbiter (SAUS) ..... BARB
Board Certified [*Physician*] (BARN) ..... BC
Board Certified Associate Behavior Analyst (SAUO) ..... BCABA
Board Certified Behavior Analyst (SAUO) ..... BCBA
Board Command Data Sort (SAUS) ..... BCDS
Board Discrete Wire Equivalent List (SAUS) ..... BDWEL
Board Eligible (MEDA) ..... BE
Board Examined [*of a physician*] (BARN) ..... BE
Board, Family, and Associates [*Company stockholders*] ..... BFA
Board Feet (SAUS) ..... BdFt
Board Foot (ABAC) ..... bd ft
Board Foot Meter (SAUS) ..... FT BM
Board for Aviation Accident Research [*Army*] ..... BAAR
Board for Certification of Genealogists (EA) ..... BCG
Board for Certified Consulting Meteorologists (COE) ..... BCCM
Board for Coordination of Civil Aviation [*NATO*] ..... BOCCA
Board for Correction of Military Records ..... BCMR
Board for Correction of Naval Records ..... BCNR
Board for Engineers' Registration (ACII) ..... BER
Board for Fundamental Education (EA) ..... BFE
Board for International Broadcasting [*Independent government agency*] ..... BIB
Board for International Broadcasting (SAUS) ..... BIP
Board for International Food and Agricultural Development [*Agency for International Development*] [*Washington, DC*] ..... BIFAD
Board for International Food and Agricultural Development and Economic Cooperation (SAUO) ..... BIFADEC
Board for Judicial Administration Rules (SAUO) ..... BJAR
Board for Mission and Unity [*Church of England*] ..... BMU
Board Gardner Denver Data (SAUS) ..... BGDD
Board Information Terminal [*Automotive electronic displays*] ..... BIT
Board Level Computer (MHDI) ..... BLC
Board Measure [*Lumber*] ..... BM
Board Measurement Feet ..... BMF
Board of Action on Letter of Intent Conversion [*Navy*] ..... BALIC
Board of Action on Redetermination [*Navy*] ..... BOAR
Board of Adjustment (PA) ..... BOA
Board of Agriculture (SAUO) ..... BA
Board of Agriculture and Fisheries (SAUO) ..... BAF
Board of Air (SAUO) ..... BA
Board of Airline Representatives (SAUO) ..... BARA
Board of Airline Representatives in the United Kingdom ..... BARUK
Board of Airline Representatives Switzerland (SAUO) ..... BAR
Board of Airlines Representatives in Germany (SAUO) ..... BARIG
Board of Anthropological Research (SAUO) ..... BAR
Board of Appeals (PA) ..... BOA
Board of Appeals and Review [*Later, ARB*] [*Civil Service Commission*] (AFM) ..... BAR
Board of Architects of New South Wales [*Australia*] ..... BANSW
Board of Architects of Queensland [*Australia*] ..... BAQ
Board of Architectural Education [*British*] (BI) ..... BAE
Board of Architectural Examiners (SAUS) ..... BAE
Board of Assistance Appeals [*Environmental Protection Agency*] (GFGA) ..... BAA
Board of Auditors for Infrastructure Accounts (SAUO) ..... BAI
Board of Australian Journals of Scientific Research ..... BAJSR
Board of Aviation Accident Research (SAUS) ..... BAAR
Board of Behavioral Science Examiners (SAUS) ..... BBSE
Board of Brethren Homes and Older Adult Ministries [*Later, BHOAM*] (EA) ..... BBHOAM
Board of Broadcast Governors [*Later, Canadian Radio-Television Commission*] ..... BBG
Board of Broadcasting, European Office ..... BOB/EUR
Board of Broadcasting Governors (SAUO) ..... BBG
Board of Certifed Product Safety Management (SAUS) ..... BCPSM
Board of Certification for Emergency Nursing (SAUO) ..... BCEN
Board of Certification in Anesthesiology (EA) ..... BCA
Board of Certification in Emergency Medicine (SAUO) ..... BCEM
Board of Certification in Pedorthics (EA) ..... BCP
Board of Certification in Professional Ergonomics (SAUS) ..... BCPE
Board of Certification in Surgery (EA) ..... BCS
Board of Certified Hazard Control Management (EA) ..... BCHCM
Board of Certified Healthcare Safety Management (SAUO) ..... BCHSM
Board of Certified Safety Professionals (EA) ..... BCSP
Board of Chief Inspectors (HEAS) ..... BCI
Board of Coast and Geodetic Survey [*Philippines*] (GEOI) ..... BCGS
Board of Contract Appeals (SAUO) ..... BC
Board of Contract Appeals [*Energy Research and Development Administration*] ..... BCA
Board of Contract Appeals Bar Association (AAGC) ..... BCABA
Board of Contract Appeals Bid Protest Decisions 1985-96 [*A publication*] (AAGC) ..... BPD
Board of Contract Appeals Decisions [*CCH*] [*A publication*] (AAGC) ..... BCA
Board of Contract Appeals Decisions [*Commerce Clearing House*] [*A publication*] (DLA) ..... Bd Cont App Dec
Board of Contract Appeals Judges Association (AAGC) ..... BCAJA
Board of Contract Appeals Lawyers Association [*Formerly ASCTLA*] (AAGC) ..... BCALA
Board of Control (SAUO) ..... BC
Board of Control [*British*] (ROG) ..... BC
Board of Cooperative Educational Services - Monroe I, Fairport, NY [*Library symbol*] [*Library of Congress*] (LCLS) ..... NFaiB
Board of Cooperative Educational Services (BOCES), Spencerport, NY [*Library symbol*] [*Library of Congress*] (LCLS) ..... NSpeB
Board of Cooperative Educational Services, Nassau Education Resource Center, Westbury, NY [*Library symbol*] [*Library of Congress*] (LCLS) ..... NWeBE
Board of Cooperative Educational Services, Regional Resource Center, Mexico, NY [*Library symbol*] [*Library of Congress*] (LCLS) ..... NMxB
Board of Cooperative Services (SAUO) ..... BOCS
Board of County Commissioners (PA) ..... BoCC
Board of Crime Control (SAUO) ..... BCC
Board of Customs (SAUO) ..... B/C
Board of Customs (SAUO) ..... BOC
Board of Customs [*British*] (DAS) ..... BOC
Board of Customs (SAUO) ..... B of C
Board of Customs and Excise (SAUO) ..... BCE
Board of Customs and Excise [*British*] ..... BCE
Board of Customs and Excise [*British*] (ODBW) ..... BOCE
Board of Decorations and Medals (SAUO) ..... BD D&M
Board of Decorations and Medals [*Navy*] ..... BD D & M
Board of Dental Examiners (SAUS) ..... BDE
Board of Deputies of British Jews ..... BDBJ
Board of Directors (NATG) ..... BOD
Board of Directors (SAUO) ..... BoD
Board of Directors (SAUS) ..... BofD
Board of Directors NATO Maintenance Supply Service System (NATG) ..... BDNMSSS
Board of Economic Operations (SAUO) ..... BEO
Board of Economic Warfare [*World War II*] ..... BEW
Board of Editors in the Life Sciences (SAUO) ..... BELS
Board of Education (SAUO) ..... BdEd
Board of Education (SAUO) ..... BE
Board of Education ..... BE
Board of Education ..... BEd
Board of Education (SAUO) ..... BOE
Board of Education (AIE) ..... BOE
Board of Education (SAUO) ..... B of E
Board of Education ..... B of E
Board of Education, Cleveland, OH [*Library symbol*] [*Library of Congress*] (LCLS) ..... OCIBE
Board of Education for the Borough of East York [*UTLAS symbol*] ..... EYS

Board of Education for the City of Etobicoke [*UTLAS symbol*] ...... ETS
Board of Education for the City of York Library [*UTLAS symbol*] .... CYS
Board of Education for the City of York, Schools, Toronto, ON, Canada
[*Library symbol*] [*Library of Congress*] (LCLS) .... CaOTYBES
Board of Education Inspectors (SAUO) .... BEI
Board of Education. Juvenile Organisations Committee (SAUO) .... BEJOC
Board of Education of the Methodist Church-Student Loan Fund
(SAUO) .... BEMCSLF
Board of Educational Development [*University of California, Berkeley*] .... BED
Board of Engineering Cooperation (SAUO) .... BEC
Board of Engineers for Rivers and Harbors [*Army*] .... BERH
Board of Engineers for Rivers and Harbors Resident Scholar Program [*Fort
Belvoir, VA*] [*Army*] .... BERH-RSP
Board of Environmental Studies and Toxicology [*NRC*] .... BEST
Board of Ethnic Affairs [*Queensland, Australia*] .... BEA
Board of Examiners for Steam Engine Drivers and Boiler Attendants
[*Victoria, Australia*] .... BOESEDBA
Board of Examiners for the Foreign Service [*Department of State*] .... BEX
Board of Examiners in Watchmakin (SAUS) .... Watch
Board of Examiners of Engineers and Overseers of Works to Local
Authorities [*Australia*] .... BOEEOWLA
Board of Examiners (Scaffolding) [*Victoria, Australia*] .... BOE(S)
Board of Examiners Sex Therapy and Counselling Ontario (CMD) .... BESTCO
Board of Examiners (Welders of Boilers and Pressure Vessels) [*Victoria,
Australia*] .... BOE(WBPV)
Board of Exchequer (SAUO) .... BE
Board of Faculty of Dental Surgery [*British*] .... BFDS
Board of Fellows (SAUS) .... BOF
Board of Fire Commissioners, New South Wales [*Australia*] .... BFCNSW
Board of Fire Underwriters of the Pacific [*Later, ISO*] .... BFUP
Board of Foreign Scholarships [*Department of State*] [*Washington, DC*] .... BFS
Board of Foreign Trade (SAUO) .... BOFT
Board of General Purposes [*Freemasonry*] .... B of GP
Board of Geographic Names .... BGN
Board of Governors .... BG
Board of Governors [*Federal Reserve System*] .... BOG
Board of Governors (SAUO) .... BoG
Board of Governors, Federal Reserve System .... BGFRS
Board of Governors, Federal Reserve System, Washington, DC [*Library
symbol*] [*Library of Congress*] (LCLS) .... DFR
Board of Governors of the California Community Colleges (SAUO) .... BGCCC
Board of Green Cloth (ROG) .... BGC
Board of Greenkeeping Research (SAUO) .... BGR
Board of Guardians [*British*] (ROG) .... BG
Board of Health [*Medicine*] (MELL) .... BH
Board of Health .... B of H
Board of Health (SAUO) .... B of H
Board of Health (DAVI) .... BOH
Board of Higher Education (SAUS) .... B of HE
Board of Home Missions of the National Association of Free Will
Baptists (EA) .... BHMNAFWB
Board of Hospitals and Homes of the Methodist Church (SAUO) .... BHHMC
Board of Immigration Appeals [*Department of Justice*] .... BIA
Board of Immigration Appeals (SAUO) .... BoIA
Board of Incorporated Engineers and Technicians [*British*] (EAIO) .... BIET
Board of Industrial Insurance Appeals (SAUO) .... BIIA
Board of Inland Revenue (SAUO) .... BIR
Board of Inland Revenue [*British*] .... BIR
Board of Inquiry (Army) Rules [*British military*] (DMA) .... BI(A)R
Board of Inspection and Survey [*Navy*] .... BIS
Board of Inspection and Survey [*Navy*] .... B/S
Board of Inspection and Survey (SAUO) .... I&S
Board of Inspection and Survey [*Navy*] .... INSURV
Board of Inspection and Survey, Instructions [*Navy*] .... INSURVINST
Board of Inspection and Survey, Preliminary Evaluation [*Navy*] .... BISPE
Board of Intermediate and Secondary Education (SAUO) .... BISEC
Board of Internal Revenue (SAUO) .... BIR
Board of International Ministries (EA) .... BIM
Board of Investigation and Research -Transportation (SAUO) .... BIRT
Board of Investigations (SAUS) .... BofI
Board of Investments [*Generic term*] .... BOI
Board of Lawyers (SAUO) .... B of L
Board of Life Insurance Medicine (CMD) .... BLIM
Board of Medical Examiners (SAUO) .... BOME
Board of Medical Quality Assurance (DAVI) .... BMQA
Board of Medicine (SAUO) .... BOM
Board of National Estimates [*Terminated*] [*CIA*] .... BNE
Board of National Ministries (EA) .... BNM
Board of Navy Commissioners [*1815-1842*] .... BNC
Board of Nephrology Examiners for Nursing and Technology .... BONENT
Board of Nurse Examiners .... BNE
Board of Nursing (SAUO) .... BON
Board of Nursing Studies [*Queensland, Australia*] .... BNS
Board of Optical Registration [*South Australia and Tasmania*] .... BOR
Board of Optometrical Registration [*New South Wales, Australia*] ..... BOR
Board of Ordnance .... BO
Board of Osteopathic Examiners (SAUO) .... BOE
Board of Parish Education, Lutheran Church in America (EA) .... BPE-LCA
Board of Parole [*Abolished, 1976, functions transferred to United States Parole
Commission*] [*Department of Justice*] .... BP
Board of Patent Interferences [*of Patent Office*] .... BPI
Board of Pharmacy (SAUO) .... BOP
Board of Pharmacy (SAUS) .... B o P
Board of Physician Quality Assurance (MELL) .... BPOA
Board of Podiatric Medicine (SAUS) .... B o PM

Board of Prison Terms (SAUO) .... BPT
Board of Professional Engineers of Queensland [*Australia*] .... BPEQ
Board of Public Utilities (SAUO) .... BPU
Board of Public Works .... BPW
Board of Rabbis .... BR
Board of Realty Information Systems [*Professional Guidance Systems, Inc.*]
[*Information service or system*] (IID) .... BORIS
Board of Regents (DEMM) .... BOR
Board of Registered Nursing .... BRN
Board of Registration for Professional Engineers and Land Surveyors
(SAUS) .... BORPELS
Board of Registration for Professional Engineers and Land Surveyors
[*California*] (GEOI) .... BORPELS
Board of Registration of Medical Auxiliaries [*British*] .... BRMA
Board of Registration of Medical Auxiliaries (SAUO) .... BRMA
Board of Revenue (SAUO) .... BR
Board of Review (SAUO) .... B of R
Board of Review [*Army*] .... BOR
Board of Review [*Army*] .... BR
Board of Review and Judicial Council of the Army (DLA) .... BR-JC (Army)
Board of Review, Discharges and Dismissals (SAUO) .... CBD
Board of Schools of Medical Technology [*Later, NAACLS*] (EA) .... BSMT
Board of Scientific Affairs .... BSA
Board of Scientific and Industrial Research (SAUO) .... BSIR
Board of Secondary Studies .... BSS
Board of Standards Review [*American National Standards Institute*] ..... BSR
Board of State Harbor Commissioners (SAUO) .... BSHC
Board of Supply, Executive (SAUO) .... BOSEG
Board of Supply, Executive Yuan [*Responsible for removing surplus US war
material to China from Guam*] .... BOSEY
Board of Tax Appeals (SAUO) .... BTA
Board of Tax Appeals (SAUO) .... BTA
Board of Tax Appeals (SAUS) .... T A
Board of Tax Appeals Decisions (Commerce Clearing House)
[*A publication*] (DLA) .... BTACCH
Board of Tax Appeals Decisions (Prentice-Hall, Inc.) [*A publication*]
(DLA) .... BTAPH
Board of Tax Appeals Memorandum Decisions (Prentice-Hall, Inc.)
[*A publication*] (DLA) .... BTAM (P-H)
Board of Teacher Education (SAUO) .... BTE
Board of Teacher Registration .... BTR
Board of Technical Assistance (SAUO) .... BTA
Board of the Academy of Professional Reporters .... BAPR
Board of the Air Council (SAUO) .... BAC
Board of the Army Council (SAUO) .... BAC
Board of the Army Council .... BAC
Board of Theological Studies (SAUO) .... BTS
Board of Thoracic Surgery [*Later, American Board of Thoracic Surgery*]
(EA) .... BTS
Board of Trade [*Shipping*] .... B of T
Board of Trade [*Shipping*] .... BOT
Board of Trade [*Shipping*] .... BT
Board of Trade Advisory Committee (SAUO) .... BOTAC
Board of Trade Journal [*A publication*] (DLA) .... BOT Jo
Board of Trade Journal (SAUS) .... BTJ
Board of Trade of Kansas City [*Missouri*] .... B of TKC
Board of Trade of Kansas City, MO (EA) .... KCBT
Board of Trade of the City of Chicago .... B of TCC
Board of Trade of the Wholesale Seafood Merchants (EA) .... BTWSM
Board of Trade Patent Office (SAUO) .... BTPO
Board of Trade Supply Organisation (SAUO) .... BTSO
Board of Trade Survey and Emigration Staff (SAUO) .... BTSES
Board of Trade Unit [*British and Canadian*] [*Military*] .... BOTU
Board of Trade Unit [*British*] .... BTU
Board of Transport [*NATO*] (NATG) .... BOT
Board of Transport Commissioners (SAUO) .... BTC
Board of Transport Economics (SAUO) .... BTE
Board of Transportation Commissioners of Canada (SAUO) .... BTCC
Board of Transportation Commissioners of Canada (SAUO) .... BTC of C
Board of Treasury (SAUO) .... BT
Board of Trustees (EBF) .... BOT
Board of Trustees (SAUS) .... BT
Board of Trustees for Rehabilitation Affairs (SAUO) .... BOTRA
Board of Trustees of the National Police Fund (SAUO) .... BTNPF
Board of Underwriters (SAUO) .... BU
Board of Underwriters of New York (EA) .... BUNY
Board of U.S. Civil Service Examiners (SAUO) .... BCSE
Board of Veterans Appeals [*Veterans Administration*] .... BVA
Board of Veterinary Surgeons of New South Wales [*Australia*] ...... BVSNSW
Board of Visitors (DOMA) .... BOV
Board of Vocational Education and Training [*New South Wales,
Australia*] .... BVET
Board of War Communications [*World War II*] .... BWC
Board of Works [*British*] .... BW
Board of Works (SAUS) .... BW
Board of Zoning Adjustment .... BZA
Board on Agricultural (or Agriculture) and Renewable Resources
(SAUO) .... BARR
Board on Agriculture and Natural Resources (SAUO) .... BA
Board on Approved Reporter Training [*National Shorthand Reporters
Association*] .... BART
Board on Army Science and Technology [*National Research Council,
Academies of Science and Engineering, and Institute of Medicine*] ..... BAST
Board on Atmospheric Science and Climate (SAUO) .... BASC

Board on Atmospheric Science and Climate, National Research Council (SAUS) .... BASC
Board on Geographic Names [Defense Mapping Agency] [Washington, DC] .... BGN
Board on Geographical Names (SAUO) .... BGN
Board on Medicine [of the National Academy of Sciences] [Later, IOM] (EA) .... BOM
Board on Minerals and Energy Resources (SAUS) .... BMER
[The] Board on Natural Disasters [National Research Council] .... BOND
Board on Ocean Science Affairs [National Academy of Science] (MSC) .... BOSA
Board on Personnel Administration (AEBS) .... BPA
Board on Radioactive Waste Management (EA) .... BRWM
Board on Science and Technology for International Development [National Academy of Sciences] .... BOSTID
Board Policy Letter (SAUS) .... BPL
Board President .... B/P
Board Room (VRA) .... bdrm
Board Secretary .... BS
Board Test Language (PDAA) .... BTL
Board Tracking System (ROAS) .... BTS
Board Under Test (SAUS) .... BUT
Board-Certified Diplomate (SAUS) .... BCD
Board/Detached [Bookselling] (DGA) .... BD/DET
Board-Foot (MUGU) .... BD-FT
Board-Foot (SAUS) .... Bd ft
Board-Foot (SAUS) .... BF
Boarding [Schools or pupils] .... B
Boarding (SAUS) .... BDG
Boarding .... BRDNG
Boarding Officer in Charge (SAUO) .... BOIC
Boarding Pass Reserve [Travel industry] (TRID) .... BPR
Boarding School Allowance [Government scholarship] [British] .... BSA
Boarding Schools Association (AIE) .... BSA
Boardman Arm Regional Flux Experiment (SAUS) .... BARFEX
Boardman Atmospheric Radiation Flux Experiment (SAUS) .... BARFEX
Boardman Public Library, Boardman, OR [Library symbol] [Library of Congress] (LCLS) .... OrBo
Board-of-Trade-Ohm (SAUS) .... BOT-Ohm
Board-of-Trade-Unit (SAUS) .... BOT-Unit
Boards (SAUS) .... Bds
Boards [Publishing] (WDAA) .... bds
Boards .... BDS
Board's Minute [Custom house] [British] (ROG) .... BM
Boards of Cooperative Educational Services .... BOCES
Board's Order [British] (ROG) .... BO
Board-to-Trade Unit (SAUS) .... BTU
Boardwalk Casino [Associated Press] (SAG) .... BoardC
Boardwalk Casino [Associated Press] (SAG) .... BoardCas
Boardwalk Casino [NASDAQ symbol] (SAG) .... BWLK
Boardwalk Casino Wrrt [NASDAQ symbol] (TTSB) .... BWLKW
Boat .... B
Boat (AABC) .... BT
Boat (ADWA) .... bt
Boat (SAUS) .... Bt
Boat Allowance List [Navy] (CAAL) .... BAL
Boat and Aircraft (CAAL) .... B & A
Boat and Engine Repair Shop [Coast Guard] .... B & ERS
Boat and Engine Repair Shop (SAUO) .... B&ERS
Boat & Motor Dealer [A publication] .... B & MD
Boat Club .... BC
Boat Engineering Department (SAUO) .... BED
Boat Foreman (DNAB) .... BF
Boat Group Commander [Navy] (NVT) .... BGC
Boat Harbor .... BHBR
Boat Hotel (SAUS) .... Botel
Boat Information Book [Navy] (CAAL) .... BIB
Boat Inlet/High-Capacity [Analytical combustion system] .... BIHC
Boat Landing Team .... BLT
Boat Lanes .... BL
Boat Launching and Recovery Device (PDAA) .... BLARD
Boat Manufacturers Association [Later, NMMA] (EA) .... BMA
Boat Manufacturers' Association of Australia .... BMAA
Boat Operating and Repair Unit [Navy] .... BORU
Boat Operating Unit [Navy] .... BOU
Boat Owners Association (SAUO) .... BOA
Boat Owners Association of the United States .... BOATS
Boat Owners Association of the United States (EA) .... BOAT/US
Boat Owners Council of America [Defunct] .... BOCA
Boat Repair Unit [Navy] .... BRU
Boat Support Unit (SAUO) .... BOATSUPPU
Boat Support Unit (CINC) .... BSU
Boat Trailer Manufacturers Association [Later, TMA] (EA) .... BTMA
Boat Unit (SAUO) .... BOATU
Boat Wave .... BTW
Boating Accident Data Base [Database] [Coast Guard] .... BADB
Boating Accident Reports System [Coast Guard] [Information service or system] (IID) .... BARS
Boating Anti-Pollution Council (EA) .... BAC
Boating Industry Association [Later, NMMA] .... BIA
Boating Industry Association of New South Wales [Australia] .... BIANSW
Boating Industry Association of Queensland [Australia] .... BIAQ
Boating Industry Association of South Australia .... BIASA
Boating Industry Association of Western Australia .... BIAWA
Boating Safety Circular [USCG] (TAG) .... BSC
Boating Safety Detachment [Coast Guard] .... BOSDET

Boating Service Officer .... BSO
Boating Trades Association of Texas (SRA) .... BTAT
Boating While Intoxicated (BARN) .... BWI
Boating Writers International (EA) .... BWI
Boatinus de Mantua [Deceased, 1300] [Authority cited in pre-1607 legal work] (DSA) .... Boa
Boatinus de Mantua [Deceased, 1300] [Authority cited in pre-1607 legal work] (DSA) .... Boat
Boatmen's Bankshares, Inc. [NASDAQ symbol] (NQ) .... BOAT
Boatmen's Bankshares, Inc. [Associated Press] (SAG) .... BoatBnc
Boatowners Unlimited [An association] (EA) .... BU
Boatswain .... B
Boatswain (SAUS) .... Boats
Boatswain (SAUS) .... Bosn
Boatswain (KSC) .... BOSN
Boatswain .... BOSUN
Boatswain (AABC) .... BTSWN
Boatswain, Antisubmarine Service (SAUS) .... BA/S
Boatswain Lieutenant (SAUS) .... BL
Boatswain Sub-Lieutenant (SAUS) .... BSL
Boatswain's Mate [Navy rating] .... BM
Boatswain's Mate, Chief [Navy rating] .... BMC
Boatswain's Mate, Construction Battalion, Boatswain [Navy rating] .... BMCBB
Boatswain's Mate, Construction Battalion, Stevedore [Navy rating] .... BMCBS
Boatswain's Mate, First Class [Navy rating] BM1
Boatswain's Mate, Master Chief [Navy rating] .... BMCM
Boatswain's Mate, Second Class [Navy rating] BM2
Boatswain's Mate, Senior Chief [Navy rating] .... BMCS
Boatswains Mate, Ship Repair, Canvasman (SAUS) .... BMSRC
Boatswain's Mate, Ship Repair, Canvasman [Navy rating] .... BMSRS
Boatswain's Mate, Ship Repair, Crane Operator [Navy rating] .... BMSRC
Boatswain's Mate, Ship Repair, Rigger [Navy rating] .... BMSRR
Boatswain's Mate, Third Class [Navy rating] BM3
Boatswain's Mate-of-the-Watch (DNAB) .... BMOW
Boat-Tail [Bullet] (DICI) .... BT
Boatyard [British Waterways Board sign] .... B
Boavista, Boavista Island [Cape Verde] [ICAO location identifier] (ICLI) .... GVBA
Boaz, AL [AM radio station call letters] .... WBSA
Bob Crane Memorial Fan Club (EA) .... BCMFC
Bob Dylan Fan Club (EA) .... BDFC
Bob Dylan Newsletter [An association] (EA) .... BDN
Bob Evans Farms [NASDAQ symbol] (TTSB) .... BOBE
Bob Evans Farms, Inc. [NASDAQ symbol] (NQ) .... BOBE
Bob Evans Farms, Inc. [Associated Press] (SAG) .... BobEvn
Bob Everhart Fan Club (EA) .... BEFC
Bob Hastings Fan Club [Inactive] (EA) .... BHFC
Bob Homan Fan Club (EA) .... BHFC
Bob Hope Theatre [British] .... BHT
Bob Jones University (SAUO) .... BJI
Bob Jones University [South Carolina] .... BJU
Bob Jones University, Greenville, SC [Library symbol] [Library of Congress] (LCLS) .... ScGBJ
Bob Oscar Plenty [Character in "Dick Tracy" comic strip] .... BO
Bob Rumball Centre for the Deaf (AC) .... BRCD
Bob Webe, Inc. (SAUO) .... BWI
Bobbie Brooks [NASDAQ symbol] (TTSB) .... BBKS
Bobbie Brooks, Inc. [NASDAQ symbol] (NQ) .... BBKS
Bobbie Brooks, Inc. [Associated Press] (SAG) .... BobBrk
Bobbin (KSC) .... BOB
Bobbin Coil Winder .... BCW
Bobbin Core (SAUS) .... BC
Bobby Bare Fan Club (EA) .... BBFC
Bobby Blue Fan Club [Defunct] (EA) .... BBFC
Bobby "C" Fan Club [Defunct] (EA) .... BCFC
Bobby Darin Fan Club (EA) .... BDFC
Bobby Fuller Four-Ever International Fan Club (SAUO) .... BEFFEIFC
Bobby Fuller Four-Ever International Fan Club [Defunct] (EA) .... BFFEIFC
Bobby Goldsboro Fan Club (EA) .... BGFC
Bobby Vinton Booster Club (EA) .... BVBC
Bobby Vinton International Fan Club (EA) .... BVIFC
Bobcaygeon Branch, Victoria County Public Library, Ontario [Library symbol] [National Library of Canada] (BIB) .... OBV
Bobete [Lesotho] [ICAO location identifier] (ICLI) .... FXBB
Bobo Dioulass [Volta] [Airport symbol] (AD) .... BOY
Bobo-Dioulasso [Burkina Faso] [Airport symbol] (OAG) .... BOY
Bobo-Dioulasso [Burkina Faso] [ICAO location identifier] (ICLI) .... DHOO
bo-bo-type locomotive (SAUS) .... bo-bo
Bobov in Israel [An association] (EA) .... BI
Bobs International [An association] (EAIO) .... BI
Bobsleigh Club (SAUO) .... BC
BOC Group [Associated Press] (SAG) .... BOC ADS
BOC Group [NYSE symbol] (SAG) .... BOX
BOC Group ADS [NYSE symbol] (SG) .... BOX
Boca Chapare [Bolivia] [ICAO location identifier] (ICLI) .... SLBC
Boca Do Acre [Brazil] [ICAO location identifier] (ICLI) .... SBBA
Boca Naranjo [Costa Rica] [ICAO location identifier] (ICLI) .... MRBO
Boca Raton [Florida] [ICAO location identifier] (ICLI) .... KBCT
Boca Raton, FL [Location identifier] [FAA] (FAAL) .... BCT
Boca Raton, FL [FM radio station call letters] .... WKIS
Boca Raton, FL [Television station call letters] .... WPPB
Boca Raton, FL [AM radio station call letters] .... WSBR
Boca Raton Public Library, Boca Raton, FL [Library symbol] [Library of Congress] (LCLS) .... FBo
Boca Research [NASDAQ symbol] (TTSB) .... BOCI
Boca Research, Inc. [Associated Press] (SAG) .... BocaRs

Boca Research, Inc. [NASDAQ symbol] (SAG) .... BOCI
Bocanda [Ivory Coast] [ICAO location identifier] (ICLI) .... DIBC
Bocas Del Toro [Panama] [Airport symbol] (OAG) .... BOC
Bocas Del Toro [Panama] [ICAO location identifier] (ICLI) .... MPBO
Boccaccio [Italian author, 1313-1375] (ROG) .... BOCC
Bocce Federation of Australia .... BFA
BOCES [Boards of Cooperative Educational Services] Geneseo Migrant
  Center (EA) .... BGMC
BOCES [Boards of Cooperative Educational Services], Monroe 1, Penfield, NY
  [OCLC symbol] (OCLC) .... VBL
BOCES [Boards of Cooperative Educational Services], Monroe 2, Orleans,
  Spencerport, NY [OCLC symbol] (OCLC) .... VBM
Boch & Limoges [Vancouver Stock Exchange symbol] .... BLL
Bochum [Federal Republic of Germany] [Seismograph station code, US
  Geological Survey] (SEIS) .... BOC
Bochum - University [Federal Republic of Germany] [Seismograph station
  code, US Geological Survey] (SEIS) .... BUG
Bock Diagram Compiler, B (SAUS) .... BLODICB
Bockus International Society of Gastroenterology (EA) .... BISG
Bodansky Unit [Clinical chemistry] .... BD
Bodansky Unit [Clinical chemistry] .... BOD
Bodansky unit (SAUS) .... BOD unit
Bodansky Unit [Also, BD, BOD] [Clinical chemistry] (AAMN) .... BU
Bodaybo [Former USSR] [Seismograph station code, US Geological Survey]
  (SEIS) .... BOD
Bodaybo [Former USSR] [ICAO location identifier] (ICLI) .... UIKB
Boddam and Greenwoods Notanda Digest (SAUS) .... Not Dig
Boddam and Greenwood's Notanda Digest [A publication] (DLA) .... Not Dig
Boddie-Noell Properties, Inc. [AMEX symbol] (SPSG) .... BNP
Boddie-Noell Properties, Inc. [Associated Press] (SAG) .... Boddie
Bode & Babbage Users Group (SAUO) .... BBUG
Bodega Marine Laboratory [University of California] [Research center]
  (RCD) .... BML
Bodegas Rurales Conasupo (SAUO) .... BORUCONSA
Boden [Sweden] [ICAO location identifier] (ICLI) .... ESPG
Bodenstein Number .... Bo
Bodhisattva (VRA) .... bodh
Bodily Injury [Insurance] .... BI
Bodily Injury and Property Damage [Insurance] .... BI/PD
Bodinumu [Papua New Guinea] [Airport symbol] (OAG) .... BNM
Bodleian Library (DAS) .... BL
Bodleian Library (SAUO) .... BL
Bodleian Library (SAUO) .... Bod
Bodleian Library [British] (DGA) .... BOD
Bodleian Library (SAUO) .... Bodl
Bodleian Library [Oxford University] [British] (BARN) .... Bodl
Bodleian Library (DGA) .... BODL LIB
Bodmin [Municipal borough in England] .... BODM
Bodmin [British] [ICAO location identifier] (ICLI) .... EGLA
Bodo [Norway] [Airport symbol] (OAG) .... BOO
Bodo [Norway] [ICAO location identifier] (ICLI) .... ENBD
Bodo [Norway] [ICAO location identifier] (ICLI) .... ENBO
Bodo Oceanic [Norway] [ICAO location identifier] (ICLI) .... ENOB
Bodon [Former USSR] [Seismograph station code, US Geological Survey]
  (SEIS) .... BDN
Bodoni [Printing] (DGA) .... BOD
Body .... B
Body .... BDY
Body (SAUS) .... Bdy
Body (SAUS) .... Bod
Body [Slang] (DSUE) .... BOD
Body Acceleration Synchronous with the Heartbeat [Cardiology] .... BASH
Body and Assembly Operation [Ford Motor Co.] .... B & AO
Body and Assembly Operations .... BAO
Body Armor System Individual Countermine Armor [Army] (INF) .... BASIC
Body Armour Set, Individual Countermine (SAUS) .... BASIC
Body Awareness Resource Network .... BARN
Body Axis Coordinate System (MCD) .... BACS
Body Belts [Medicine] (DAVI) .... B/B
Body Bound Bolts (MSA) .... BBB
Body Burden [of radiation] .... BB
Body Cell Mass .... BCM
Body Centered Cubic (ABAC) .... bcc
Body Computer Module [General Motors' computer system] .... BCM
Body Control Module [Automotive engineering] .... BCM
Body Count [Military] (CINC) .... BC
Body Current (ACAE) .... BC
Body Dysmorphic Disorder [Medicine] .... BDD
Body Electronics Area Network .... BEAN
Body Engineering Office .... BEO
Body Engineering Product Engineering .... BEPE
Body Engineering Product Engineering Office .... BEPEO
Body Fat [Medicine] (MELL) .... BF
Body Flap (NASA) .... BDYFLP
Body Flap (SAUS) .... BF
Body Flap Control (MCD) .... BFC
Body Fluid [Medicine] (MELL) .... BF
Body Guard [Special Air Service] [British] .... BG
Body Heat Content .... BHC
Body Hematocrit-Venous Hematocrit Ratio (MAE) .... BH/VH
Body in White [Automotive manufacturing] .... BIW
Body Length (SAUS) .... BL
Body Lice (MELL) .... BL
Body Line [Typography] (WDMC) .... BL
Body Mass [Medicine] .... BM

Body Mass Index [Medicine] .... BMI
Body Mass Measurements Device (KSC) .... BMMD
Body Mind Centering (SAUS) .... BMC
Body Mounted (MCD) .... BM
Body Odor [Slang] .... BO
Body or Roof [Freight] .... BDY or RF
Body Part [Anatomy] (DAVI) .... BP
Body Point (MCD) .... BPT
Body Restraint System .... BRS
Body Rot of Papaya [Plant pathology] .... BR
Body Sensor Assembly [Military] .... BSA
Body Shell .... BS
Body Side Molding .... BSM
Body Station (MCD) .... BS
Body Support Cradle .... BSC
Body Surface Area .... BSA
Body Surface Burned [Medicine] .... BSB
Body Surface Potential Mapping [Dermatology] (DAVI) .... BSPM
Body Temperature [Medicine] .... BT
Body Temperature [Medicine] .... Tb
Body Temperature and Pressure [Medicine] (WDAA) .... BTP
Body Temperature Charting [Medicine] (MELL) .... BTC
Body Temperature Measuring System .... BTMS
Body Temperature, [Ambient] Pressure, Dry [Medicine] .... BTPD
Body Temperature, [Ambient] Pressure, Saturated [with water] [Medicine] .... BTPS
Body Water [Medicine] .... BW
Body Wave Magnitude (COE) .... Mb
Body Weight .... BW
Body Weight (EEVL) .... bw
Body Weight Change [Medicine] (DB) .... BWC
Body Whorl .... BW
Body Wing (KSC) .... BW
Body-Bound Bolts (SAUS) .... BB/B
Body/Caudal Fin [Ichthyology] .... BCF
Body-Centered [Crystallography] .... BC
Body-Centered Cubic [Also, BCCUB] [Crystallography] .... BCC
Body-Centered Cubic [Also, BCC] [Crystallography] .... BCCUB
Body-Centered Cubic System [Crystallography] (IAA) .... BCCS
Body-Centered Tetragonal [Crystallography] .... BCT
Bodycolor (VRA) .... bdyco
Body-Cooling Garment [NASA] (MCD) .... BCG
Body-Fitted Coordinates [Computer science] .... BFC
Body-Mounted Accelerometer .... BMA
Body-Mounted Attitude Gyro (KSC) .... BMAG
Body-Mounted [Altitude] Gyroscope (SAA) .... BMG
Body-Mounted Radiator (SSD) .... BMR
Body-on-Chassis [Technical drawings] .... BOC
Body-over-Frame [Automotive engineering] .... BOF
Boeck Sarcoid (MELL) .... BS
Boehm Test of Basic Concepts [Psychology] .... BTBC
Boehm Test of Basic Concepts-Revised (TES) .... BOEHM-R
Boehringer Ingelheim Pharmaceuticals, Inc. [Commercial firm] (DAVI) .... BI
Boehringer Mannheim [Test] [Medicine] (DB) .... BM
Boehringer Mannheim Biochemicals .... BMB
Boehringer Mannheim Corp. [Chemical industry supplier] .... BMC
Boehringer Mannheim Corp., Indianapolis, IN [OCLC symbol] (OCLC) .... IBL
Boehringer Mannheim GmbH, Mannheim, Germany [Library symbol] [Library
  of Congress] (LCLS) .... GyMB
Boeing Aerospace Company (SAUO) .... BAC
Boeing Aerospace [or Aircraft] Corp. (MCD) .... BAC
Boeing Air Transport .... BAT
Boeing Airborne Instrumentation Equipment (SAA) .... BAI
Boeing Aircraft Co. (SAUO) .... B
Boeing Aircraft Company (SAUO) .... BAC
Boeing Aircraft Corporation (SAUO) .... BAC
Boeing Aircraft of Canada, Ltd. (SAUO) .... B
Boeing Airplane (SAUS) .... BA
Boeing Airplane Company (SAUO) .... BAC
Boeing Airplane Company Algebraic Interpreter Coding System
  (SAUO) .... BACAICS
Boeing Airplane Company Algebraic Interpretive Computing (SAUO) ..... BACAIC
Boeing Airplane Company Algebraic Interpretive Computing system
  (SAUO) .... BACAIC system
Boeing Airplane Company Design (SAUO) .... BACD
Boeing Applied Computing Service (SAA) .... BACS
Boeing Associated Products (MCD) .... BAP
Boeing Atlantic Test Center (KSC) .... BATC
Boeing Business Jet (SAUS) .... BBJ
Boeing Canada Dash-8 [Airplane code] Dh8
[The] Boeing Co. [ICAO aircraft manufacturer identifier] (ICAO) .... B
[The] Boeing Co. [NYSE symbol] (SPSG) .... BA
Boeing Co. (SAUO) .... BA
Boeing Co. (EFIS) .... BCS
[The] Boeing Co. [Associated Press] (SAG) .... Boeing
[The] Boeing Co., Aerospace Division, Technical Library, Kent, WA [Library
  symbol] [Library of Congress] (LCLS) .... WaSBo-A
[The] Boeing Co., Commercial Airplane Group, Technical Libraries,
  Seattle,WA [Library symbol] [Library of Congress] (LCLS) .... WaSBo
Boeing Co., Technical Libraries, Bellevue, WA [Library symbol] [Library of
  Congress] (LCLS) .... WaSBo-B
Boeing Co., Technical Libraries, Kent, WA [Library symbol] [Library of
  Congress] (LCLS) .... WaSBo-K
Boeing Co., Wichita Division Library (SAUO) .... KWiB
[The] Boeing Co., Wichita Division Library, Wichita, KS [Library symbol]
  [Library of Congress] (LCLS) .... KWiB

Boeing Commercial Airplanes (HLLA) ... BCA
Boeing Commericial Airplane Group [*ICAO designator*] (FAAC) ... BOE
Boeing Computer Services Co. [*Information service or system*] (IID) ... BCS
Boeing Computer Services Richland, Inc. (ABAC) ... BCSR
Boeing Contract Change Proposal (SAUS) ... BCCP
Boeing Data Entry System [*Boeing Computer Services*] (NITA) ... BDES
Boeing Dehavilland Canada [*ICAO designator*] (FAAC) ... DHC
Boeing Development Center (SAUS) ... BDC
Boeing Electronic Analog Computer (SAUS) ... BEAC
Boeing Engineering Analog Computer (IEEE) ... BEAC
Boeing Engineering & Construction (EFIS) ... BEC
Boeing Engineering & Construction Company (SAUO) ... BECC
Boeing Engineering Co. (MCD) ... BEC
Boeing Engineering Thermal Analyzer (MCD) ... BETA
Boeing Extractive Sludge Treatment (SAUS) ... BEST
Boeing Field Test Unit [*NASA*] (IAA) ... BFTU
Boeing Flight Test Center [*NASA*] (IAA) ... BFTC
Boeing Ground Support (KSC) ... BGS
Boeing Gulf Test Section (SAA) ... BGTS
Boeing Industrial Technology Group (ACAE) ... BITG
Boeing Infrared Missile Attack Simulation (MCD) ... BIRMAS
Boeing Intelligent Terminal System [*Boeing Computer Services Co.*] [*Information service or system*] (IID) ... BITS
Boeing Interactive Graphics System (SAUS) ... BIGS
Boeing Interface Surveillance Unit (KSC) ... BISU
Boeing long-Range surface-to-air Missile bearing nuclear warhead (SAUS) ... Bomarc
Boeing Materials Specification ... BMS
Boeing Military Airplane Co. ... BMAC
Boeing Military Airplane Development Organization ... BMADO
Boeing Network Architecture [*Telecommunications*] (TSSD) ... BNA
Boeing of Canada Ltd., Arnprior, ON, Canada [*Library symbol*] [*Library of Congress*] (LCLS) ... CaOArBC
Boeing of Canada Ltd., Arnprior, Ontario [*Library symbol*] [*National Library of Canada*] (BIB) ... OARBC
Boeing on Dock ... BOD
Boeing Operational Supervisory System ... BOSS
Boeing Plastic Analysis Capability for Engines [*Computer science*] [*NASA*] ... BOPACE
Boeing Radiation Effect Laboratory ... BREL
Boeing Robotic Air Vehicles ... BRAVE
Boeing Scientific Research Laboratories ... BSRL
Boeing Services International, Inc. (MCD) ... BSI
Boeing Shaped Scan Correlator (MCD) ... BOSSCO
Boeing Small Research Module [*NASA*] ... BSRM
Boeing Systems Coordinator (MUGU) ... BSC
Boeing Test Support [*NASA*] (KSC) ... BTS
Boeing Vega, Douglas (SAUO) ... BVD
Boeing Wind Tunnel ... BWT
Boeing-Michigan Aeronautical Research Center ... BOMARC
Boeing-Vertol Division [*The Boeing Co.*] [*ICAO aircraft manufacturer identifier*] (ICAO) ... BV
Boeing-Vertol Division [*The Boeing Co.*] [*ICAO aircraft manufacturer identifier*] (ICAO) ... HV
Boeken van het Oude Testament [*Roermond/Maaseik*] [*A publication*] (BJA) ... BoekOT
Boende [*Zaire*] [*Airport symbol*] (OAG) ... BNB
Boende [*Zaire*] [*ICAO location identifier*] (ICLI) ... FZGN
Boere Weerstandsbeweging [*South Africa*] [*Political party*] (EY) ... BWB
Boeren Partij [*Farmers' Party*] [*Netherlands*] [*Political party*] (PPE) ... BP
Boerne, TX [*AM radio station call letters*] ... KBRN
Boevaya Mashina Pekhota [*Infantry Fighting Vehicle*] [*Russian*] ... BMP
Bofors, Infantry, Light & Lethal (SAUS) ... BILL
Bofors Optimized Smart Shell (SAUS) ... BOSS
Bofors Optronic Fire Control Instrument (MILB) ... BOFI
Bofors Spent Acid Concentration [*Chemical industry*] ... BOSAC
Bogalusa, LA [*Location identifier*] [*FAA*] (FAAL) ... BXA
Bogalusa, LA [*Location identifier*] [*FAA*] (FAAL) ... VNL
Bogalusa, LA [*AM radio station call letters*] ... WBOX
Bogalusa, LA [*AM radio station call letters*] ... WIKC
Bogande [*Burkina Faso*] [*ICAO location identifier*] (ICLI) ... DHEB
Bogande [*Burkina Faso*] [*Airport symbol*] (OAG) ... XBG
Bogart-Brociner Associates [*Information service or system*] (IID) ... BBA
Bogazici Hava Tasimacilik AS [*Turkey*] [*ICAO designator*] (FAAC) ... BHT
Bogdaen-Buday [*Disease*] [*Medicine*] (DB) ... BB
Bogdanovka [*Former USSR*] [*Seismograph station code, US Geological Survey*] [*Closed*] (SEIS) ... BGD
Bogen [*Bow*] [*Music*] ... Bg
Bogen Communic Intl Unit [*AMEX symbol*] (TTSB) ... BGN.E
Bogen Communic Intl Wrrt [*AMEX symbol*] (TTSB) ... BGN.WS
Bogen Communications International [*AMEX symbol*] (SAG) ... BGN
Bogen Communications International [*Associated Press*] (SAG) ... Bogen
Bogen Communications International [*Associated Press*] (SAG) ... BogenC
Bogert on Trusts and Trustees [*A publication*] (DLA) ... Bogert Trusts
Boggs and Lewis (GEOI) ... B&L
Boghazkoi-Sammlung des Berliner Museum (BJA) ... Bo
Boghazkoi-Studien [*Leipzig, 1916-1924*] [*A publication*] (BJA) ... BoSt
Boghazkoy [*Museum of the Ancient Orient, Istanbul*] (BJA) ... Bo
Bogie Fan Club [*Canada*] (EAIO) ... BFC
Bogle & Gates, Law Library, Seattle, WA [*Library symbol*] [*Library of Congress*] (LCLS) ... WaSBG
Bognor Regis [*British*] [*ICAO location identifier*] (ICLI) ... EGKC
Bogoliubov-Born-Green-Kirkwood-Yvon [*Plasma kinetic theory hierarchy*] ... BBGKY
Bogong [*Victoria*] [*Australia*] [*Seismograph station code, US Geological Survey*] [*Closed*] (SEIS) ... BOV
Bogor Agriculture Institute, Indonesia (SAUS) ... IPB
Bogor Research Institute for Food Crops (SAUO) ... BORIF
Bogoslovni Vestnik [*Ljubljana*] [*A publication*] (BJA) ... BogVest
Bogoslovska Smotra [*Zagreb*] [*A publication*] (BJA) ... BogSmot
Bogota [*Colombia*] [*Seismograph station code, US Geological Survey*] (SEIS) ... BOCO
Bogota [*Colombia*] [*Seismograph station code, US Geological Survey*] (SEIS) ... BOG
Bogota [*Colombia*] [*ICAO location identifier*] (ICLI) ... SKED
Bogota Public Library, Bogota, NJ [*Library symbol*] [*Library of Congress*] (LCLS) ... NjBo
Bogota/Eldorado [*Colombia*] [*ICAO location identifier*] (ICLI) ... SKBO
Bogue [*Mauritania*] [*ICAO location identifier*] (ICLI) ... GQNE
Bogus Check [*Banking*] ... BC
Bohack Corp. (SAUO) ... BHK
Bohairic Version of the Bible (BJA) ... Boh
Boheme, Butterfly, and Barber of Seville [*Frequently performed operas*] ... 3B's
Bohemia ... BOH
Bohemia Ragtime Society (EA) ... BRS
Bohemian [*Language, etc.*] (ROG) ... BOH
Bohemian [*Language, etc.*] (ROG) ... BOHEM
Bohemian Club (EA) ... BC
Bohemian Club, San Francisco, CA [*Library symbol*] [*Library of Congress*] (LCLS) ... CSfBo
Bohemian Free Thinking School Society (EA) ... BFTSS
Bohemian-Hungarian [*Slang*] ... BOHUNK
Bohemium [*Chemical element*] (MAE) ... Bo
Bohmer [*Germany*] [*ICAO location identifier*] (ICLI) ... EDIJ
Bohmian Quantum Mechanics I [*Physics*] ... BQMI
Bohn Aluminum and Brass Corp. (SAUO) ... BHL
Bohn's Artist's Library [*A publication*] ... BAL
Bohn's Philosophical Library [*A publication*] ... BPL
Bohn's Standard Library [*A publication*] ... BSL
Bohr and Mottleson Model [*of nuclear structure*] ... BMM
Bohr Frequency Condition ... BFC
Bohr Magneton [*Atomic physics*] ... BM
Bohrium [*Chemistry*] (MEC) ... Bh
Bohrium [*Chemical element*] ... BH
Bohr-Kramers-Slater [*Quantum theory*] ... BKS
Bohr-Kramers-Slater theory (SAUS) ... BKS theory
Bohr-Sommerfeld Atom ... BSA
Bohr-Wheeler Theory ... BWT
Bohun. Ecclesiastical Jurisdiction [*A publication*] (DLA) ... Boh Eccl Jur
Bohun. English Lawyer [*A publication*] (DLA) ... Boh Eng L
Bohun. Practising Attorney [*A publication*] (DLA) ... Boh Att
Bohun. Privilegia Londini [*A publication*] (DLA) ... Boh Priv Lond
Bohun. Titles [*A publication*] (DLA) ... Boh Ti
Bohun's Cursus Cancellariae (ILCA) ... Boh Curs Can
Bohun's Cursus Cancellariae [*A publication*] (DLA) ... Bohun Curs Canc
Bohun's Declarations and Pleadings [*A publication*] (DLA) ... Boh Dec
Bohun's Election Cases [*England*] [*A publication*] (DLA) ... Bohun
Bohun's Institutio Legalis (ILCA) ... Boh Inst Leg
Bohun's Institutio Legalis [*A publication*] (DLA) ... Bohun Inst Leg
BOI [*Board of Investments*] **Unit for Industrial Linkage Development** (ECON) ... BUILD
Boil (MELL) ... B
Boil Resistant (SAUS) ... BR
Boiled Grits (SAUS) ... Grits
Boiled [*Linseed*] **Oil** ... BO
Boiler ... B
Boiler (AAG) ... BLR
Boiler (DNAB) ... BOI
Boiler and Industrial Furnace [*Environmental Protection Agency*] ... BIF
Boiler and Machinery ... B & M
Boiler and Pressure Vessel [*Nuclear energy*] (NRCH) ... B + PV
Boiler and Pressure Vessel Code (ABAC) ... BPVC
Boiler and Pressure Vessel Committee [*Nuclear Regulatory Commission*] (GFGA) ... BPVC
Boiler and Pressure Vessel Manufacturers' Association of Australia ... BPVMAA
Boiler and Radiator Manufacturers Association (SAUO) ... BARMA
Boiler Availability Committee (SAUO) ... BAC
Boiler Blower Control (DNAB) ... BBC
Boiler Casing Bulkhead (SAUS) ... BCBH
Boiler Design and Performance ... BODEPE
Boiler Efficiency Improvement Program (SAUO) ... BEIP
Boiler Feed [*Technical drawings*] ... BF
Boiler Feed Compound Tank [*Technical drawings*] ... BFCT
Boiler Feed Pump [*Technical drawings*] ... BFP
Boiler Feed Pump Turbine (SAUS) ... BEPT
Boiler Feed Water [*Technical drawings*] ... BFW
Boiler Feedwater (SAUS) ... BFW
Boiler Horsepower ... BHP
Boiler Horsepower (IAA) ... BOHP
Boiler House [*Technical drawings*] ... BH
Boiler House (WDAA) ... Bo H
Boiler Information Data System [*Southwest Research Institute*] ... BIDS
Boiler Inspection and Insurance ... BI & I
Boiler Manufacturer (DS) ... BO
Boiler Oil (SAUS) ... BO
Boiler Plate ... BP
Boiler Pressure ... BOPRESS
Boiler Pressure ... BP
Boiler Quality (SAUS) ... BQ

Boiler Room ... BR
Boiler Space (SAUS) ... BS
Boiler Stop Valve (SAUS) ... BSV
Boiler Survey ... BS
Boiler System Efficiency (SAUS) ... BSE
Boiler Technician of the Watch (SAUO) ... BTOW
Boiler Turbine Generator (IAA) ... BTG
Boiler Water ... BOWR
Boiler Water/Feedwater Test and Treatment Training (DNAB) ... BW/FWT & TT
Boilermaker [*Navy*] ... B
Boilermaker [*Military*] [*British*] ... BM
Boilermaker (MSA) ... BMKR
Boilermaker [*Navy rating*] ... BR
Boilermaker, Chief [*Navy rating*] ... BRC
Boilermaker First Class (SAUS) ... B1c
Boilermaker, First Class [*Navy rating*] ... BR1
Boilermaker, Master Chief [*Navy rating*] ... BRCM
Boilermaker Second Class (SAUS) ... B2c
Boilermaker, Second Class [*Navy rating*] ... BR2
Boilermaker, Senior Chief [*Navy rating*] ... BRCS
Boilermaker, Ship Repair [*Navy rating*] ... BSR
Boilermaker, Third Class [*Navy rating*] ... BR3
Boilermaker/Welder ... BMW
Boilerman [*Navy rating*] ... BT
Boilerman, Chief [*Navy rating*] ... BTC
Boilerman, First Class [*Navy rating*] ... BT1
Boilerman, Master Chief [*Navy rating*] ... BTCM
Boilerman, Second Class [*Navy rating*] ... BT2
Boilerman, Senior Chief [*Navy rating*] ... BTCS
Boilerman, Third Class [*Navy rating*] ... BT3
Boilerplate (SAUS) ... Blrp
Boilerplates Aerodynamic Test Vehicle (MCD) ... BATV
Boilerwater/Feedwater Test and Treatment ... BFWTT
Boiling ... BOG
Boiling (SAUS) ... Bog
Boiling (SAUS) ... Boil
Boiling Experimental Reactor (SAUS) ... BER
Boiling Heavy Water Reactor ... BHWR
Boiling Light Water [*Nuclear energy*] ... BLW
Boiling Light Water Cooled Plutonium Burner [*Nuclear energy*] (NUCP) ... BLW (PB)
Boiling Liquid Expanding Vapor Explosion [*Chemical engineering*] ... BLEVE
Boiling Nuclear Superheat Critical Experiment (NRCH) ... BONUS-CX
Boiling Nuclear Superheat Reactor ... BONUS
Boiling Point ... BP
Boiling Point (WDAA) ... bp
Boiling Point ... BPT
Boiling Point Elevation ... BPE
Boiling Point Margin [*Engineering*] ... BPM
Boiling Point Number [*Chemical engineering*] ... BPN
Boiling Point Rise ... BPR
Boiling Range ... BR
Boiling Reactor Experiments [*Nuclear energy*] ... BORAX
Boiling Springs, NC [*FM radio station call letters*] ... WGWG
Boiling Transition [*Nuclear energy*] (NRCH) ... BT
Boiling Water Proof (SAUS) ... BWP
Boiling Water Reactor ... BWR
Boiling Water Reactor Experiment (SAUS) ... BORAX
Boiling Water Reactor Owners Group [*Nuclear energy*] (NRCH) ... BWROG
Boiling Water Reactor; Type 6 of GE (SAUS) ... BWR/6
Boiling Water Resistant (SAUS) ... BWR
Boilling/Alleroid (SAUS) ... B/A
Boil-Off ... B-O
Boil-Off Gas [*Petroleum product transportation*] ... BOG
Boils At ... B
BOIP [*Basis of Issue Plan*] **Feeder Data** [*DoD*] ... BOIPFD
BOIP [*Basis of Issue Plan*] **Retrieval Program** [*DoD*] ... BPPRM
Boise [*Diocesan abbreviation*] [*Idaho*] (TOCD) ... B
Boise [*Idaho*] [*Airport symbol*] (OAG) ... BOI
Boise [*Idaho*] [*Seismograph station code, US Geological Survey*] (SEIS) ... BSE
Boise Basin District Library, Idaho City, ID [*Library symbol*] [*Library of Congress*] (LCLS) ... IdIc
Boise Bible College, Boise, ID [*Library symbol*] [*Library of Congress*] (LCLS) ... IdBBC
Boise Cascade [*NYSE symbol*] (SAG) ... BCC
Boise Cascade 7.48% Dep Pfd [*NYSE symbol*] (TTSB) ... BCCPrG
Boise Cascade 9.40% Dep Pfd [*NYSE symbol*] (TTSB) ... BCCPrF
Boise Cascade Corp. [*Associated Press*] (SAG) ... BoisC
Boise Cascade Corp. [*Associated Press*] (SAG) ... BoiseC
Boise Cascade Corp. Library, Boise, ID [*Library symbol*] [*Library of Congress*] (LCLS) ... IdBBC
Boise Cascade Corp., Research Library, International Falls, MN [*Library symbol*] [*Library of Congress*] (LCLS) ... MnIfBC
Boise Cascade Corporation (SAUO) ... BBC
Boise Cascade Office Products [*NYSE symbol*] (SAG) ... BCP
Boise Cascade Office Products [*Associated Press*] (SAG) ... BoisCOff
Boise Cascade Office Products [*NYSE symbol*] (TTSB) ... BOP
Boise City, OK [*Location identifier*] [*FAA*] (FAAL) ... BCY
Boise Creek Resources [*Vancouver Stock Exchange symbol*] ... BOS
Boise, ID [*Television station call letters*] ... KAID
Boise, ID [*Television station call letters*] ... KBCI
Boise, ID [*AM radio station call letters*] ... KBOI
Boise, ID [*AM radio station call letters*] ... KBSU
Boise, ID [*FM radio station call letters*] ... KBSU-FM
Boise, ID [*FM radio station call letters*] (BROA) ... KBSX-FM
Boise, ID [*AM radio station call letters*] ... KGEM
Boise, ID [*AM radio station call letters*] ... KIDO
Boise, ID [*FM radio station call letters*] ... KIZN
Boise, ID [*FM radio station call letters*] ... KJOT
Boise, ID [*AM radio station call letters*] ... KKIC
Boise, ID [*FM radio station call letters*] ... KLTB
Boise, ID [*FM radio station call letters*] ... KQFC
Boise, ID [*AM radio station call letters*] ... KSPD
Boise, ID [*Television station call letters*] ... KTVB
Boise Interagency Fire Center (SAUO) ... BIFC
Boise Interagency Fire Center, Boise, ID [*OCLC symbol*] (OCLC) ... UDF
Boise Junior College [*Idaho*] ... BJC
Boise Peace Quilt Project (EA) ... BPQP
Boise Public Library, Boise, ID [*Library symbol*] [*Library of Congress*] (LCLS) ... IdB
Boise Senior High School, Boise, ID [*Library symbol*] [*Library of Congress*] (LCLS) ... IdBSH
Boise State College, Boise, ID [*Library symbol*] [*Library of Congress*] (LCLS) ... IdBB
Boise State University (GAGS) ... Boise St U
Boise/Boise Air Terminal [*Idaho*] [*ICAO location identifier*] (ICLI) ... KBOI
Boise-Griffin Steamship Company (SAUO) ... BGSC
Boissevain and Morton Regional Library, Boissevain, Manitoba [*Library symbol*] [*National Library of Canada*] (NLC) ... MBOM
Boissevain and Morton Regional Library, Boissevain, MB, Canada [*Library symbol*] [*Library of Congress*] (LCLS) ... CaMBoM
Boissevain Health Centre, Manitoba [*Library symbol*] [*National Library of Canada*] (NLC) ... MBHC
Boissevain, MB [*AM radio station call letters*] ... CJRB
Boisterous (ABBR) ... BSTRU
Boisterous (ABBR) ... BSTRUS
Boisterously (ABBR) ... BSTRUSY
Boisterousness (ABBR) ... BSTRUSNS
Boite Postale [*Post Office Box*] [*French*] ... BP
Boite-a-Musique, Paris [*Record label*] [*France*] ... BaM
Bojnord [*Iran*] [*ICAO location identifier*] (ICLI) ... OIMN
BOK Financial [*NASDAQ symbol*] (TTSB) ... BOKF
BOK Financial Corp. [*Associated Press*] (SAG) ... BOK
BOK Financial Corp. [*NASDAQ symbol*] (SAG) ... BOKF
Bokada [*Zaire*] [*ICAO location identifier*] (ICLI) ... FZFG
Bokaro [*India*] [*Seismograph station code, US Geological Survey*] (SEIS) ... BOK
Bokaro [*India*] [*ICAO location identifier*] (ICLI) ... VEBK
Bokaro Steel Limited (SAUO) ... BSL
Boke/Baralande [*Guinea*] [*ICAO location identifier*] (ICLI) ... GUOK
Bokenge [*Zaire*] [*ICAO location identifier*] (ICLI) ... FZGD
Bokepyin [*Myanmar*] [*ICAO location identifier*] (ICLI) ... VBBP
Bokhara (VRA) ... Bokh
Boko [*Zaire*] [*ICAO location identifier*] (ICLI) ... FZCO
Bokondini [*Indonesia*] [*ICAO location identifier*] (ICLI) ... WAJB
Bokoro [*Chad*] [*ICAO location identifier*] (ICLI) ... FTTK
Bokote/Basengele [*Zaire*] [*ICAO location identifier*] (ICLI) ... FZBW
Bokoudini [*Indonesia*] [*Airport symbol*] (OAG) ... BUI
Boku [*Papua New Guinea*] [*Airport symbol*] [*Obsolete*] (OAG) ... BOQ
Bokungu [*Zaire*] [*ICAO location identifier*] (ICLI) ... FZGF
Bol [*Chad*] [*ICAO location identifier*] (ICLI) ... FTTL
Bol [*Chad*] [*Airport symbol*] (AD) ... OTC
Bola De Oro [*Ecuador*] [*ICAO location identifier*] (ICLI) ... SEBD
Bolama [*Guinea-Bissau*] [*ICAO location identifier*] (ICLI) ... GGBO
Bold (ADA) ... BD
Bold (ADA) ... BLD
Bold and the Beautiful [*Television program title*] ... B&B
Bold Face [*Printing term*] ... BF
Bold Face Capitals [*Printing term*] ... BFC
Bolder Tech [*NASDAQ symbol*] (TTSB) ... BOLD
Boldface [*Typography*] (WDMC) ... bf
Boldface (ADWA) ... bld
Bold-Type Headings ... BTH
Bole [*Ghana*] [*ICAO location identifier*] (ICLI) ... DGLB
Bolero Resources, Inc. [*Vancouver Stock Exchange symbol*] ... BOR
Boletim de Bibliografia Portuguesa [*A bibliographic publication*] [*Portugal*] ... BBP
Boletim. Ministerio de Justica [*Portugal*] [*A publication*] (DLA) ... Bol Min Justica
Boletus Virus [*Plant pathology*] ... BOV
Boliche [*Ecuador*] [*ICAO location identifier*] (ICLI) ... SEBI
Boliden Salt (SAUS) ... BIS
Bolingbroke, GA [*FM radio station call letters*] (RBYB) ... WDBS-FM
Bolinger Road [*California*] [*Seismograph station code, US Geological Survey*] (SEIS) ... BGC
Bolito [*Race of maize*] ... BOL
Bolivar [*Monetary unit*] [*Venezuela*] ... B
Bolivar [*Argentina*] [*ICAO location identifier*] (ICLI) ... SAZI
Bolivar County Library, Cleveland, MS [*Library symbol*] [*Library of Congress*] (LCLS) ... MsCle
Bolivar Free Library, Bolivar, NY [*Library symbol*] [*Library of Congress*] (LCLS) ... NBo
Bolivar Free Library, Bolivar, NY [*Library symbol*] [*Library of Congress*] (LCLS) ... NBoL
Bolivar, MO [*AM radio station call letters*] ... KYOO
Bolivar, TN [*Location identifier*] [*FAA*] (FAAL) ... BAV
Bolivar, TN [*AM radio station call letters*] ... WBOL
Bolivar, TN [*FM radio station call letters*] ... WMOD
Bolivar, TN [*FM radio station call letters*] ... WOJG
Bolivarian Society of the United States (EA) ... BSUS
Bolivia [*MARC country of publication code*] [*Library of Congress*] (LCCP) ... bo
Bolivia [*ANSI two-letter standard code*] (CNC) ... BO
Bolivia (SAUS) ... Bo

Bolivia [*ANSI three-letter standard code*] (CNC) ... BOL
Bolivia (VRA) ... Bol
Bolivia (SAUO) ... Bol
Bolivia [*MARC geographic area code*] [*Library of Congress*] (LCCP) ... s-bo-
Bolivia Inland Mission (SAUO) ... BIM
Bolivia Railway Company (SAUO) ... BRC
Bolivian (ADWA) ... Bol
Bolivian Air-Shower Joint Experiment ... BASJE
Bolivian Hemorrhagic Fever [*Medicine*] (DMAA) ... BHF
Boliviano [*Monetary unit*] [*Bolivia*] ... B
Boll Weevil Research Laboratory [*Department of Agriculture*] [*Mississippi State, MS*] [*Research center*] ... BWRL
Boll Weevil Research Unit [*Mississippi State, MS*] [*Agricultural Research Service*] [*Department of Agriculture*] (GRD) ... BWRU
Bollard [*Shipping*] [*British*] ... Bol
Bollard Pull [*Shipping*] [*British*] ... BP
Bollettino. Commissione Archeologica Comunale in Roma [*A publication*] (OCD) ... Boll Com Arch
Bollettino di Archeologia Cristiana [*A publication*] (BJA) ... BAC
Bollettino di Filologia Classica [*A publication*] (OCD) ... Boll Fil Class
Bollettino di Legislazione Comparata [*A publication*] (ILCA) ... BLC
Bollettino. Istituto di Diritto Romano [*A publication*] (OCD) ... Boll Ist Dir Rom
Bolling Air Force Base (ACAE) ... BAFB
Bolling Family Association (EA) ... BFA
Bologna [*Italy*] [*Airport symbol*] (OAG) ... BLQ
Bologna [*Italy*] [*Seismograph station code, US Geological Survey*] (SEIS) ... BOL
Bologna/Borgo Panigale [*Italy*] [*ICAO location identifier*] (ICLI) ... LIPE
Bolometric Correction ... BC
Bolometric Voltage and Current [*Voltage measurement*] [*National Institute of Standards and Technology*] ... BOLOVAC
Bolsa de Valores do Sao Paulo [*Sao Paulo Stock Exchange*] [*Brazil*] ... BOVESPA
Bolsade Mercadorias and Futuros Exchange (NUMA) ... BM&F
Bolshoi Alt-Azimuth Telescope [*Former USSR*] ... BAT
Bolshoi Ballet Academy [*Former USSR*] ... BA
Bolshoi Ballet Academy [*Moscow*] ... BBA
Bolster (KSC) ... BOLS
Bolt (MSA) ... BLT
Bolt ... BO
Bolt (ABBR) ... BT
Bolt Action [*British military*] (DMA) ... BA
Bolt and Bond Assembly ... BBA
Bolt and Nut ... BN
Bolt, Beranck, & Newman, Inc. (SAUO) ... BB&N
Bolt, Beranek & Newman, Inc. [*NYSE symbol*] (SPSG) ... BBN
Bolt, Beranek & Newman, Inc. [*Associated Press*] (SAG) ... BoltBer
Bolt Circle [*Technical drawings*] ... BC
Bolt Extrusion Thrust Termination (MCD) ... BETT
Bolt Extrusion Thrust Termination System (SAUS) ... BETTS
Bolt Installation and Removal Tool ... BIRT
Bolt Lock (SAUS) ... BL
Bolt Motor Actuator (SPST) ... BMA
Bolt, Nut, and Rivet Makers Association of Scotland [*A union*] ... BNRMAS
Bolt Out of the Blue [*Surprise nuclear attack*] ... BOOB
Bolt Removal Tool ... BRT
Bolt Technology [*AMEX symbol*] (SG) ... BTJ
Bolt Technology Corp. [*Associated Press*] (SAG) ... BoltTch
Bolt Technology Corp. [*AMEX symbol*] (SAG) ... BTJ
bolt with T-shaped square head (SAUS) ... T-bolt
Bolted Bonnet (SAUS) ... BLT BT
Bolted Manhole Cover Plate [*Shipfitting*] ... BM
Bolted on Base (SAUS) ... bo/bs
Bolted Plate [*Technical drawings*] ... BP
Bolted Repair [*Composite structures*] (MCD) ... BREPAIR
Bolted Separable Connector ... BSC
Bolted-on-Base ... BO/BS
Bolton [*Craniometric point*] ... BO
Bolton Environmental Sensing System (NOAA) ... BESS
Bolton Evening News, Bolton, United Kingdom [*Library symbol*] [*Library of Congress*] (LCLS) ... UkBoN
Bolton Institute for a Sustainable Future (EA) ... BISF
Bolt-On Intelligence [*Proposed use for the biochip*] ... BOI
Bolton Point [*Medicine*] (DMAA) ... B
Bolton Point [*Medicine*] (DMAA) ... BP
Bolton Tooth Ratio Analysis [*Medicine*] (MELL) ... BTRA
Bolton, VT [*FM radio station call letters*] (RBYB) ... WCMK
Bolton-Hunter [*Reagent*] (DB) ... BH
Bolton-Hunter Reagent-Labeled Eledoisin [*Analytical biochemistry*] ... BHE
Bolton-Hunter Reagent-Labeled Substance K [*Analytical biochemistry*] ... BHSK
Bolton-Hunter Reagent-Labeled Substance P (DB) ... BHSP
Boltzmann Constant [*Symbol*] [*IUPAC*] ... k
Boltzmann Constant [*Statistical mechanics*] ... S
Boltzmann Equation (SAUS) ... BE
Boltzmann Function [*Physics*] (BARN) ... H
Boltzmann Transport Equation [*Physics*] ... BTE
Bolus (MELL) ... B
Bolus (ADWA) ... bol
Bolus [*Large Pill*] [*Pharmacy*] ... BOL
Bolusan Volcano National Park (SAUS) ... BVNP
Bolworra [*Australia*] [*Airport symbol*] [*Obsolete*] (OAG) ... BCK
Bolzano [*Italy*] [*Seismograph station code, US Geological Survey*] (SEIS) ... BLZ
Bolzano [*Italy*] [*Airport symbol*] (AD) ... BZO
Bolzano [*Italy*] [*ICAO location identifier*] (ICLI) ... LIPB
Bom Jesus Da Lapa [*Brazil*] [*Airport symbol*] (OAG) ... LAZ
Bom Jesus Da Lapa [*Brazil*] [*ICAO location identifier*] (ICLI) ... SBLP
Boma [*Zaire*] [*ICAO location identifier*] (ICLI) ... FZAJ
Bomai [*Papua New Guinea*] [*Airport symbol*] (OAG) ... BMH
BOMARC B Program (SAUS) ... BOB
BOMARC [*Boeing-Michigan Aeronautical Research Center*] **Interceptor** ... BIN
BOMARC [*Boeing-Michigan Aeronautical Research Center*] **Prelaunch Output** (IAA) ... BPO
BOMARC [*Boeing-Michigan Aeronautical Research Center*] **SAGE Compatibility** [*Semiautomatic Ground Environment*] (IAA) ... BOSCO
BOMARC [*Boeing-Michigan Aeronautical Research Center*] **Squadron Simulator** ... BSS
BOMARC [*Boeing-Michigan Aeronautical Research Center*] **Unintegrated Guidance** (IAA) ... BUG
BOMARC [*Boeing-Michigan Aeronautical Research Center*] **Universal SAGE** [*Semiautomatic Ground Environment*] (IAA) ... BUS
Bomb (NG) ... B
Bomb (MUGU) ... BB
Bomb (DNAB) ... BOM
Bomb Aimer (SAUS) ... BA
Bomb Alarm System [*Air Force*] ... BAS
Bomb and Mine Disposal (SAUO) ... B&MD
Bomb and Mine Disposal Officer [*British military*] (DMA) ... BMDO
Bomb Assembly Spares (NG) ... BAS
Bomb Bay [*of an aircraft*] ... BB
Bomb Bay Ring Out (SAA) ... BBRO
Bomb Damage Assessment ... BDA
Bomb Damage Repair ... BDR
Bomb Damage Survey ... BDS
Bomb Data Center [*International Association of Chiefs of Police*] ... BDC
Bomb Director High Speed Aircraft (SAUS) ... BDHSA
Bomb Director Set [*or System*] [*Army*] ... BDS
Bomb Director System (SAUS) ... BDS
Bomb Disposal ... BD
Bomb Disposal Company (SAUO) ... BDC
Bomb Disposal Squad (ADWA) ... BDS
Bomb Disposal Unit (SAUO) ... BDU
Bomb, Dummy Unit (AFM) ... BDU
Bomb Fall Line [*Military*] (NVT) ... BFL
Bomb Group (SAUS) ... BG
Bomb Impact Line (ACAE) ... BIL
Bomb LASER Directed (MCD) ... BOLD
Bomb LASER Tracking (MCD) ... BOLT
Bomb Line (DNAB) ... BL
Bomb Line Unit (MCD) ... BLU
Bomb, Live Unit (AFM) ... BLU
Bomb Maintenance Spares ... BMS
Bomb Mine (MCD) ... BOMINE
Bomb Navigation Guidance System ... BNGS
Bomb Nose Fuze ... BNF
Bomb or Missile Optics (MCD) ... BOMO
Bomb Orbital Strategic System ... BOSS
Bomb Orbital Strategic System - Weapon Development Glide Entry ... BOSS-WEDGE
Bomb Pulsed Release Generator (DWSG) ... BPRG
Bomb Rack Unit ... BRU
Bomb Rack/Rocket Launcher (NG) ... BR/RL
Bomb, Radio, Longitudinal, Generator-Powered ... BRLG
Bomb, Radio, Transverse, Generator-Powered (IAA) ... BRTG
Bomb Release Angle Computer (MCD) ... BRAC
Bomb Release Distance [*Army*] (AABC) ... BRD
Bomb Release Line ... BRL
Bomb Release Safety Lock (SAUS) ... BRSL
Bomb Release Unit (SAUS) ... BRU
Bomb Run Insert (SAA) ... BRI
Bomb Safety Officer [*Navy*] ... BSO
Bomb Savety Officer (SAUS) ... BSO
Bomb Search Team (COE) ... BST
Bomb Service ... BS
Bomb Service Truck (MUGU) ... BSTRK
Bomb Service Truck (SAUS) ... BS Trk
Bomb Sight ... BS
Bomb Store (SAUO) ... BS
Bomb Tail Fuse ... BTF
Bomb Targets Information Committee [*Air Ministry*] [*British*] [*World War II*] ... BTIC
Bomb Testing Device ... BTD
Bomb Thermal Battery (DNAB) ... BTB
Bomb to Warhead Conversion Components (SAUS) ... B/WCA
Bomb-Aimer [*British military*] (DMA) ... B/A
Bombardier ... B
Bombardier ... BDR
Bombardier (AFM) ... BMBDR
Bombardier ... BMDR
Bombardier ... BOM
Bombardier [*British*] (ROG) ... BOMB
Bombardier ... BOMBDR
Bombardier [*British*] (ADA) ... BR
Bombardier Data Indicator (SAUS) ... BDI
Bombardier, Inc. [*Toronto Stock Exchange symbol*] ... BBD
Bombardier Inc.Cl'B' [*TS Symbol*] (TTSB) ... BBD.B
Bombardier-Gunner (SAUS) ... Bdr-Gnr
Bombardier-Navigator (MUGU) ... BN
Bombardier/Navigator (DOMA) ... BOMB/NAV
Bombardiers, Inc. (EA) ... BI
Bombardiers Information File (SAUS) ... BIF
Bombardment (SAUS) ... Bbt
Bombardment (KSC) ... BBT

Bombardment	BOMB
Bombardment Control Unit	BCU
Bombardment Enhanced Etch Rate (IAA)	BEE
Bombardment Enhanced Etch Rate	BEER
Bombardment Excited Amplification in a Semiconductor (SAUS)	BEAR
Bombardment Group (SAUO)	Bm Gr
Bombardment (Heavy) Wing [Air Force]	BHW
Bombardment Liaison Officer [Navy]	BLO
Bombardment (Medium) Wing [Air Force]	BMW
Bombardment Rocket (KSC)	BOMROC
Bombardment Squadron [Air Force]	BMBSq
Bombardment Squadron [Air Force]	BMS
Bombardment Squadron (SAUO)	Bombron
Bombardment Squadron (SAUO)	Bomron
Bombardment Squadron (ACAE)	BS
Bombardment Wing [Air Force]	BW
Bombardment Wing Light (SAUS)	Bmb Wg L
Bombardment Wing Medium (SAUS)	Bmb Wg M
Bombardment-Induced Conductivity	BIC
Bombardment-Induced Light Emission [Physics]	BLE
Bombardon [Musical instrument]	BOMB
Bombay [India] [Seismograph station code, US Geological Survey] (SEIS)	BOM
Bombay [India] [Later, ABG] [Geomagnetic observatory code]	BOM
Bombay [India] [ICAO location identifier] (ICLI)	VABB
Bombay [India] [ICAO location identifier] (ICLI)	VABF
Bombay Art Society (SAUO)	BAS
Bombay, Baroda and Central India Railway (SAUO)	BB&CI
Bombay, Baroda and Central India Railway (SAUO)	BB&CIRly
Bombay, Baroda, and Central India Railway	BB & CIRly
Bombay Bicycle Club (SAUO)	BBC
Bombay Cavalry [British military] (DMA)	BC
Bombay Civil Service (SAUO)	BobCS
Bombay Civil Service (SAUO)	BoCS
Bombay Civil Service (SAUO)	BomCS
Bombay Co. [Associated Press] (SAG)	Bombay
Bombay Company [NYSE symbol] (TTSB)	BBA
Bombay Electric Supply and Transport Undertaking (SAUO)	BEST
Bombay High Court Criminal Rulings [India] [A publication] (DLA)	Bomb Cr Rul
Bombay High Court Printed Judgments [1869-1900] [India] [A publication] (DLA)	BHCPJ
Bombay High Court Printed Judgments [1869-1900] [India] [A publication] (DLA)	PJ
Bombay High Court Reports [1862-75] [India] [A publication] (DLA)	BHC
Bombay High Court Reports [1862-75] [India] [A publication] (DLA)	BHCR
Bombay High Court Reports [1862-75] [India] [A publication] (DLA)	Bom
Bombay High Court Reports [1862-75] [India] [A publication] (DLA)	Bomb HC
Bombay High Court Reports [1862-75] [India] [A publication] (DLA)	Bomb H Ct
Bombay High Court Reports [1862-75] [India] [A publication] (DLA)	Bomb Hg Ct
Bombay High Court Reports [1862-75] [India] [A publication] (DLA)	Bom HCR
Bombay Hook National Wildlife Refuge (SAUS)	BHNWR
Bombay Hook National Wildlife Refuge (SAUS)	Bombay Hook
Bombay Horse Artillery [British military] (DMA)	BHA
Bombay Law Journal [India] [A publication] (DLA)	Bombay LJ
Bombay Law Journal [India] [A publication] (DLA)	Bom LJ
Bombay Law Reporter [India] [A publication] (DLA)	BLR
Bombay Law Reporter [India] [A publication] (DLA)	Bomb LR
Bombay Law Reporter [India] [A publication] (DLA)	Bom LR
Bombay Law Reporter [India] [A publication] (DLA)	Bom LRJ
Bombay Law Reports [India] [A publication] (DLA)	Bom L Rep
Bombay Library Association (SAUO)	BLA
Bombay Light Cavalry [British military] (DMA)	BLC
Bombay Native Infantry (SAUO)	BomNI
Bombay Natural History Society (SAUO)	BNHS
Bombay Port Trust Employees' Union [India]	BPTEU
Bombay Reports, Appellate Juris [India] [A publication] (DLA)	Bom AC
Bombay Reports, Crown Cases [India] [A publication] (DLA)	Bomb Cr Cas
Bombay Reports, Crown Cases [India] [A publication] (ILCA)	Bom Cr Cas
Bombay Reports, Oudh Cases [India] [A publication] (DLA)	Bom OC
Bombay Sadr Diwani Adalat Reports [A publication] (DLA)	Bellasis
Bombay Select Cases, Sadr Diwani Adalat [India] [A publication] (DLA)	Bomb Sel Cas
Bombay Staff Corps [British military] (DMA)	Bomb SC
Bombay Staff Corps (SAUO)	BombSC
Bombay Staff Corps (SAUO)	BomSC
Bombay Staff Corps (SAUO)	BoSC
Bombay Stock Exchange [India]	BSE
Bombay Symphony Orchestra (SAUO)	BSO
Bombay University Library (SAUO)	BUL
Bombay Unreported Criminal Cases [1862-98] [India] [A publication] (DLA)	Bom Unrep Cr C
Bombay Unreported Criminal Cases [1862-98] [India] [A publication] (DLA)	Unrep Cr C
Bombay/Juhu [India] [ICAO location identifier] (ICLI)	VAJJ
Bomb-Disposal Service [Military] (WDAA)	BDS
Bomb-Disposal Unit	BDU
Bombenzielapparat [Bomb sight] [German military - World War II]	BZA
Bombenzielgeraet [Bomb sight] [German military - World War II]	BZG
Bomber [Russian aircraft symbol]	AR
Bomber [Designation for US military aircraft]	B
Bomber [Russian aircraft symbol]	BB
Bomber (MILB)	bbr
Bomber [Military]	BMB
Bomber [Air Force] (AFM)	BMBR
Bomber (AABC)	BMR
Bomber (SAUS)	Bomb

Bomber [Russian aircraft symbol]	B-SCH
Bomber [Russian aircraft symbol]	DB
Bomber [Russian aircraft symbol]	IL
Bomber [Russian aircraft symbol]	SB-RK
Bomber [Russian aircraft symbol]	ZKB
Bomber Activity Weekly Brief (MCD)	BAWB
Bomber Air Relay System - Extension (MCD)	BARS-X
Bomber Air Relay System - Fly Along (MCD)	BARS-F
Bomber Airborne Instrumentation System (SAUS)	BAIS
Bomber Aviation (SAUS)	BA
Bomber Command	BC
Bomber Command (SAUO)	BC
Bomber Command [British military] (DMA)	B Cmd
Bomber Command [Army]	BOMCOM
Bomber Command (SAUO)	Bom Com
Bomber Command Headquarters [British military] (DMA)	BCH
Bomber Command Intelligence Report	BCIR
Bomber Command Intelligence Summary	BCIS
Bomber Command Liaison Officer (NATG)	BCLO
Bomber Command Operational Order	BCOO
Bomber Command Operations Center (SAUO)	BCOC
Bomber Command Tactical Planning Committee	BCTPC
Bomber Control Team [Air Force] (DOMA)	BCT
Bomber Defence Training Flight [British military] (DMA)	BDTF
Bomber Defense Missile [Air Force]	BDM
Bomber Development Establishment (SAUO)	BDE
Bomber Development Establishment (SAUS)	BDE
Bomber Exercise (SAUS)	BOMEX
Bomber Field	B
Bomber Fighter Training System (MCD)	BFTS
Bomber (Intruder) [British military] (DMA)	B(I)
Bomber Operations [Air Ministry] [British] [World War II]	BOPS
Bomber Penetration Evaluation (SAUS)	BPE
Bomber Reconnaissance (SAUS)	BR
Bomber Reconnaissance Aircraft	BR
Bomber Recovery Team [Air Force] (DOMA)	BRT
Bomber Replenishment Area [Military]	BRA
Bomber Squadron (SAUO)	BSq
Bomber Support	BS
Bomber Support Development Unit	BSDU
Bomber Transport [Air Force]	BT
Bomber-Fighter (ACAE)	BF
Bomber-Fighter Squadron (SAUO)	BFS
Bomber-Fighter Squadron [Navy symbol]	VBF
Bomber/Fighter Training System (SAUS)	BFTS
Bomber-Recorder System (SAUS)	BRS
Bomber-Trooper (SAUS)	B-T
Bombes Anti-Personnel (SAUS)	BAP
Bombesin [Biochemistry]	BB
Bombesin [Biochemistry]	BBS
Bombesin [Biochemistry]	Bn
Bombesin-Like Immunoreactivity [Medicine] (MELL)	BLI
Bombesin-Like Peptide [Biochemistry]	BLP
Bombesin-Releasing Immunoreactivity	BRI
Bombing [JETDS nomenclature]	B
Bombing (AABC)	BOM
Bombing Analysis Unit [Supreme Headquarters, Allied Expeditionary Force] [World War II]	BAU
Bombing and Gunnery Flight [British military] (DMA)	B & GF
Bombing and Gunnery Range	BGR
Bombing and Gunnery School [British] (DMA)	BAGS
Bombing & Gunnery School (SAUS)	B&GS
Bombing and Gunnery School [British]	BGS
Bombing and Navigation Inertial Reference	BANIR
Bombing and Reconnaissance Navigation	BARN
Bombing Computer Set	BCS
Bombing Development Unit	BDU
Bombing Encyclopedia (CINC)	BE
Bombing Exercise [Military] (NVT)	BOMBEX
Bombing Landplane	BLP
Bombing over the Horizon	BOTH
Bombing Plane [Navy symbol]	VB
Bombing Post (SAUS)	BP
Bombing RADAR Navigation Equipment	BRANE
Bombing Report [Military]	BOMREP
Bombing Report (NATG)	BOMREPT
Bombing Restriction Area [British military] (DMA)	BRA
Bombing Squadron (SAUO)	Bomron
Bombing Squadron	BOMRON
Bombing Table (SAUS)	BT
Bombing through Overcast [By means of RADAR equipment]	BTO
Bombing, Torpedo Plane [Navy symbol]	VBT
Bombing-Fighting Aircraft [Navy symbol]	VBF
Bombing/Navigation (NG)	B/N
Bombing/Navigation (DOMA)	BOMB/NAV
Bombing-Navigation System (AFM)	BNS
Bomblets Cargo Round (SAUS)	BCR
Bombsight (AABC)	BOMST
Bombsight (SAUS)	BS
Bomb-to-Warhead Conversion (MCD)	B/WC
Bomb-to-Warhead Conversion Components (CINC)	BWCC
Bombyx mori Nuclear Polyhedrosis Virus	BmNPV
BOMEX [Barbados Oceanographic and Meteorological Experiment] Analysis Program (NOAA)	BOMAP
Bomoen [Norway] [ICAO location identifier] (ICLI)	ENBM

Bon Accord Airways [British] [ICAO designator] (FAAC) .... BON
Bon Accord, NB [Television station call letters] (RBYB) CBAT-1
Bon Accord, NB [TV station call letters] (RBYB) .... CBAT-TV
Bon Accord Public Library, Alberta [Library symbol] [National Library of
   Canada] (NLC) .... ABOA
Bon Accord Public Library, Bon Accord, AB, Canada [Library symbol]
   [Library of Congress] (LCLS) .... CaABoa
Bon Chic, Bon Genre [Good Style, Good Family] [Initialism used to denote
   French Yuppies] [Lifestyle classification] .... BCBG
Bon pour Francs [Value in Francs] [French] .... BPF
Bon Secours Medical Library, Baltimore, MD [Library symbol] [Library of
   Congress] (LCLS) .... MdBBS
Bona Fide [In Good Faith] [Latin] .... BF
Bona Fide Occupational Qualification .... BFOQ
Bona Fide Purchaser [Legal term] (DLA) .... BFP
Bona Fide Purchaser for Value [of a security, or other negotiable instrument]
   [Legal term] .... BFPV
Bonae Feminae [To the Good Woman] [Latin] .... BF
Bonae Memoriae [Of Happy Memory] [Latin] .... BM
Bonae Memoriae [of Happy Memory] [Reference to a deceased person]
   [Latin] (BARN) .... Bon Mem
Bonaguida de Aretio [Flourished, 1251-58] [Authority cited in pre-1607 legal
   work] (DSA) .... Bo
Bonaguida de Aretio [Flourished, 1251-58] [Authority cited in pre-1607 legal
   work] (DSA) .... Bona
Bonaguida de Aretio [Flourished, 1251-58] [Authority cited in pre-1607 legal
   work] (DSA) .... Bonag
Bonair Aviation Ltd. [Canada] [ICAO designator] (FAAC) .... BNR
Bonaire [Netherland Antilles] [Airport symbol] (OAG) .... BON
Bonaire Government Tourist Office (EA) .... BGTO
Bonanza [Nicaragua] [ICAO location identifier] (ICLI) .... MNBZ
Bonanza Air Lines, Inc. (SAUO) .... BAL
Bonanza Air Lines, Inc. (SAUO) .... BL
Bonanza Airlines (MHDB) .... BAL
Bonanza Oil & Gas Ltd. [Toronto Stock Exchange symbol] .... BZO
Bonanza, OR [FM radio station call letters] (RBYB) .... KAQX-FM
Bonanza Resources Ltd. [Toronto Stock Exchange symbol] .... BNZ
Bonaparte Record-Republican, Bonaparte, IA [Library symbol] [Library of
   Congress] (LCLS) .... IaBonR
Bonaparte Record-Republican, Bonaparte, IA [Library symbol] [Library of
   Congress] (LCLS) .... IaBonRR
Bonar, Inc. [Toronto Stock Exchange symbol] .... BON
Bonaventure [Canada] [Airport symbol] (OAG) .... YVB
Bonavista Bay, NF [AM radio station call letters] .... CBGY
Bonavista Bay, NF [FM radio station call letters] .... CJOZ
Bonavista, NF [Television station call letters] .... CJWB
Bonavista, NF [ICAO location identifier] (ICLI) .... CWVA
Bonavista Public Library, Bonavista, NF, Canada [Library symbol] [Library of
   Congress] (LCLS) .... CaNfBo
Bonavista Public Library, Newfoundland [Library symbol] [National Library of
   Canada] (NLC) .... NFBO
Bonaza School, Alberta [Library symbol] [National Library of Canada]
   (BIB) .... ABOS
Bond [Investment term] .... B
Bond (EBF) .... Bd
Bond [Investment term] .... BD
Bond (WDAA) .... bd
Bond (ROG) .... BND
Bond Adjustment [Finance] .... AB
Bond Air Services Ltd. [Uganda] [ICAO designator] (FAAC) .... BOD
Bond and Allotment (DNAB) .... B & A
Bond and Burglary .... B & BU
Bond and Etchback (SAUS) .... BESOI
Bond and Preferred [Business term] .... BP
Bond and Share Society [British] (DBA) .... BASS
Bond and Share Society (EA) .... BSS
Bond Anticipation Note [Banking] .... BAN
Bond Buyer Index (EBF) .... BBI
Bond Centered (AAEL) .... BC
Bond Club of New York [New York, NY] (EA) .... BCNY
Bond Corpen Holdings Ltd. (SAUO) .... BCH
Bond County Community Unit, School District 2, De Land, IL [Library
   symbol] [Library of Congress] (LCLS) .... IDelanSD
Bond Dissociation Energy [Chemistry] .... BDE
Bond Enabling Annual Retirement Savings (DFIT) .... BEARS
Bond Equivalent (TDOB) .... BE
Bond Equivalent Yield [Business term] (EMRF) .... BEY
Bond Fund [Finance] .... BF
Bond Helicopters Ltd. [British] [ICAO designator] (FAAC) .... BND
Bond Index to the Determination of Inorganic Crystal Structures [McMaster
   University, Canada] (SAUO) .... BIDICS
Bond Industries, Inc. (SAUO) .... BND
Bond International Gold, Inc. [Toronto Stock Exchange symbol] .... BG
Bond Investors Guaranty Insurance .... BIGI
Bond Law Review [A publication] .... Bond LR
Bond Market Association .... BMA
Bond Maturity [Investment term] .... BM
Bond Molecular Orbitals .... BMO
Bond Negative Resistor .... BNR
Bond Number [Chemistry] .... BN
Bond Number .... Bo
Bond Public Library, Wenona, IL [Library symbol] [Library of Congress]
   (LCLS) .... IWen
Bond Rating (SAUS) .... AA
Bond Rating [Investment term] .... BR

Bond Strength Model of Active Sites .... BSMAS
Bond Test Device (MCD) .... BTD
Bond Trade Analysis Program [IBM Corp.] .... BTAP
Bond Valence Sum [Physical chemistry] .... BVS
Bondage and Discipline [or Domination] .... B & D
Bondage/Domination (WGA) .... B/D
Bonded .... B
Bonded (MSA) .... BND
Bonded and Etchback Silicon on Insulator (AAEL) .... BESOI
Bonded Atom Model (SAUS) .... BAM
Bonded Double Cotton [Wire insulation] (KSC) .... BDC
Bonded Double Paper [Wire insulation] (KSC) .... BDP
Bonded Double Silk [Wire insulation] .... BDS
Bonded Film Lubrication (SAUS) .... BFL
Bonded Goods [International trade] .... B/G
Bonded Laminates Profiled Part [British] .... BLP
Bonded Motors, Inc. [NASDAQ symbol] (SAG) .... BMTR
Bonded Motors, Inc. [Associated Press] (SAG) .... BondMot
Bonded Part [Wire insulation] (IAA) .... BP
Bonded Particle Rolling (SAUS) .... BPR
Bonded Phase Chromatography .... BPC
Bonded Single Cotton [Wire insulation] (MSA) .... BC
Bonded Single Paper [Wire insulation] (IAA) .... BP
Bonded Single Silk [Wire insulation] (MSA) .... BS
Bonded Spoon Type (DNAB) .... BST
Bonded Warehouse .... BW
Bonded Warehouse (SAUO) .... BW
Bonded Wine Cellar .... BWC
Bonded Winery .... BW
Bondell Industries, Inc. [Vancouver Stock Exchange symbol] .... BLI
Bond-Energy Bond-Order [Chemical kinetics] .... BEBO
Bond-Equivalent Effective Margin .... BEEM
Bonderize .... BNDZ
Bondi-Metzner-Sachs [Physics] .... BMS
Bonding .... BNDG
Bonding .... BO
Bonding (SAUS) .... BOND
Bonding Jig (MCD) .... BJ
Bonding Molecular Orbital (SAUS) .... BMO
Bonding Tool (AAG) .... BNTO
Bondo [Zaire] [ICAO location identifier] (ICLI) .... FZKP
Bondoukou [Ivory Coast] [Airport symbol] (OAG) .... BDK
Bondoukou/Soko [Ivory Coast] [ICAO location identifier] (ICLI) .... DIBU
Bonds (SAUS) .... Bds
Bond's United States Circuit Reports [A publication] (DLA) .... Bond
Bondsman .... BNDSMN
Bondsman (GEAB) .... bndsmn
Bone Age [Medicine] .... BA
Bone and Joint [Medicine] .... B & J
Bone and Joint (SAUS) .... B&J
Bone and Joint [Medicine] .... BJ
Bone Apposition Rate [Physiology] .... BAR
Bone Bank [Medicine] (MELL) .... BB
Bone Care International, Inc. [NASDAQ symbol] (SAG) .... BCII
Bone Care International, Inc. [Associated Press] (SAG) .... BoneCre
Bone Care Intl. [NASDAQ symbol] (TTSB) .... BCII
Bone Cement [Medicine] (MELL) .... BC
Bone Conduction [Medicine] .... BC
Bone Connection (SAUS) .... BC
Bone Densitometry [Medicine] (MELL) .... BD
Bone Density Loss [Medicine] (MELL) .... BDL
Bone Dry .... BD
Bone Dry-Weight Basis (IAA) .... BDWB
Bone Dysplasia [Medicine] (MELL) .... BD
Bone Formation .... BF
Bone Formation Rate [Medicine] .... BFR
Bone Fragment [Orthopedics] (DAVI) .... BF
Bone Graft [Orthopedics] .... BG
Bone Greater Than Air [Conduction] .... B + A
Bone Haft and Scale Cutters Society [A union] [British] .... BHSCS
Bone Injury [Medicine] .... BI
Bone Marker [Aviation] .... BM
Bone Marrow .... BM
Bone Marrow Arrest [Medicine] (DB) .... BMA
Bone Marrow Aspirate [Hematology] (DAVI) .... BMA
Bone Marrow Biopsy [Medicine] (MELL) .... BMB
Bone Marrow Cell [Cytology] .... BMC
Bone Marrow Depression [Hematology] (AAMN) .... BMD
Bone Marrow Edema Syndrome [Medicine] .... BMES
Bone Marrow Embolism [Medicine] (MELL) .... BME
Bone Marrow Examination [Medicine] (MELL) .... BME
Bone Marrow Failure [Medicine] (DMAA) .... BMF
Bone Marrow Granulocyte Reserve [Physiology] .... BMGR
Bone Marrow Lymphocytosis [Medicine] (DMAA) .... BML
Bone Marrow Necrosis [Medicine] (DB) .... BMN
Bone Marrow Plasmacytosis [Oncology] .... BMPC
Bone Marrow Pressure [Orthopedics and radiology] (DAVI) .... BMP
Bone Marrow Prostatic Acid Phosphatase .... BMPAP
Bone Marrow Stem Cell [Hematology] .... BMSC
Bone Marrow Transplant [Medicine] .... BMT
Bone Marrow Transplant Unit [Hematology] (DAVI) .... BMTU
Bone Marrow Transplantation (SAUS) .... Bone Marrow Transplant
Bone Mass (MELL) .... BM
Bone Mineral Content [Medicine] .... BMC
Bone Mineral Content/Width [Medicine] .... BMC/W

Bone Mineral Densitometry [*Medicine*] .... BMD
Bone Mineral Density [*Medicine*] .... BMD
Bone Morphogenetic Protein .... BMP
Bone Paste [*Medicine*] (MELL) .... BP
Bone Phosphate of Lime .... BPL
Bone. Precedents in Conveyancing [*1838-40*] [*A publication*] (DLA) .... Bone Prec
Bone Resorption .... BR
Bone Scan [*Medicine*] (MELL) .... BS
Bone Spur (MELL) .... BS
Bone-Derived Growth Factor [*Genetics*] .... BDGF
Bone-Dried Ton .... BDT
Bone-Marrow Derived [*Hematology*] .... B
Bone-Marrow Leucocyte [*Physiology*] .... BML
Bone-Marrow Transfer (SAUS) .... BMT
Bone-Marrow-Derived Cell (ADWA) .... B cell
Bone-Marrow-Derived Cultured Mast Cell .... BMCMC
Bone-Marrow-Derived Lymphocyte [*Hematology*] .... BL
Bone-Marrow-Derived Macrophage [*Biochemistry*] .... BMM
Bone-Marrow-Derived Mast Cells [*Cytology*] .... BMMC
Bone-Marrow-Derived Suppressor Factor [*Immunology*] .... BDSF
Bone-Patellar Tendon-Tubercle Bone [*Graft*] .... BTB
Bone-Resorbing Factor [*Medicine*] (DMAA) .... BRF
Bones, Joints, and Examination [*Medicine*] (DAVI) .... BJE
Bones, Joints, Extremities (SAUS) .... BJE
Bones, Joints, Muscles [*Medicine*] .... BJM
Bones, Muscles, Joints [*Medicine*] (DMAA) .... BMJ
Bonesteel Public Library, Bonesteel, SD [*Library symbol*] [*Library of Congress*] (LCLS) .... SdBo
Bonfield Public Library, Bonfield, ON, Canada [*Library symbol*] [*Library of Congress*] (LCLS) .... CaOBONF
Bonfield Public Library, Ontario [*Library symbol*] [*National Library of Canada*] (NLC) .... OBONF
Bongao/Sanga-Sanga, Sulu [*Philippines*] [*ICAO location identifier*] (ICLI) .... RPWN
Bongimba [*Zaire*] [*ICAO location identifier*] (ICLI) .... FZBB
Bongor [*Chad*] [*ICAO location identifier*] (ICLI) .... FTTB
Bonham, TX [*AM radio station call letters*] .... KFYN
Bonham, TX [*FM radio station call letters*] .... KFYZ
Bonhoffer-Van der Pol Equation (SAUS) .... BVP Equation
Bonhomie & Hattiesburg Southern R. R. [*AAR code*] .... BHS
Bonifati [*Italy*] [*ICAO location identifier*] (ICLI) .... LIBW
Bonifay, FL [*FM radio station call letters*] .... WTBB
Bonifay, FL [*FM radio station call letters*] (BROA) .... WYYX-FM
Bonifay Sand [*A soil type*] .... BS
Bonifide Notice of Intent to Manufacture or Import (EEVL) .... BF
Bonin Islands (SAUS) .... Bon I
Bonita Springs, FL [*FM radio station call letters*] .... WRXK
Bonn [*Germany*] [*Airport symbol*] (OAG) .... BNJ
Bonn (Bad Godesberg-Plittersdorf) [*Germany*] [*ICAO location identifier*] (ICLI) .... EDOJ
Bonn, Frankfurt Am Main [*Germany*] [*ICAO location identifier*] (ICLI) .... EDDA
Bonn Institute for Economic and Social Research (SAUO) .... IWG Bonn
Bonn Scale for the Assesment of Basic Symptoms (SAUS) .... BSABS
Bonne Bay, NF [*Television station call letters*] CBYT-3
Bonne Terre, MO [*FM radio station call letters*] .... KDBB
Bonner Durchmusterung [*Star chart*] .... BD
Bonner General Hospital, Medical Library, Sandpoint, ID [*Library symbol*] [*Library of Congress*] (LCLS) .... IdSanH
Bonner Jahrbuecher [*A publication*] (OCD) .... Bonner Jahrb
Bonner-Bibel (BJA) .... BB
Bonners Ferry, ID [*AM radio station call letters*] .... KBFI
Bonners Ferry, ID [*FM radio station call letters*] .... KRBF
Bonnet (MSA) .... BNT
Bonnet Valve .... BV
Bonnetti's Italian Dictionary [*A publication*] (DLA) .... Bonnetti Ital Dict
Bonneville County District Library, Idaho Falls, ID [*Library symbol*] [*Library of Congress*] (LCLS) .... IdIfC
Bonneville Power Acquisition Guide [*A publication*] (AAGC) .... BAG
Bonneville Power Administration [*Department of Energy*] [*Portland, OR*] .... BPA
Bonneville Power Administration - Low Columbia Area (SAUO) .... BPA-LC
Bonneville Power Administration - Puget Sound Area (SAUO) .... BPA-PS
Bonneville Power Administration - Snake River Office (SAUO) .... BPA-SR
Bonneville Power Administration - Upper Columbia Area (SAUO) .... BPA-UC
Bonneville Power Administration Acquisition [*A publication*] (AAGC) .... BAR
Bonneville Power Administration, Portland, OR [*Library symbol*] [*Library of Congress*] (LCLS) .... OrPB
Bonneville Power Administration Selective Dissemination of Information [*Department of the Interior*] .... BPA-SDI
Bonneville Power Administrator (SAUO) .... BPA
Bonneville Regional Advisory Council [*Terminated, 1978*] [*Department of Energy*] (EGAO) .... BRAC
Bonneville, UT [*Location identifier*] [*FAA*] (FAAL) .... BVL
Bonney on Insurance [*A publication*] (DLA) .... Bon Ins
Bonney on Insurance [*A publication*] (DLA) .... Bonn Ins
Bonney-Fessenden Sociograph [*Psychology*] .... BFS
Bonney's Railway Carriers [*A publication*] (DLA) .... Bonn Car
Bonney's Railway Carriers [*A publication*] (DLA) .... Bon RR Car
Bonn/Hangelar [*Germany*] [*ICAO location identifier*] (ICLI) .... EDKB
Bonnie Hartle Fan Club (EA) .... BHFC
Bonnie Lou Bishop Fan Club (EA) .... BLBFC
Bonnie Lou Bishop International Fan Club (EA) .... BLBIFC
Bonnyville, AB [*Television station call letters*] CBXFT-1
Bonnyville Municipal Library, Alberta [*Library symbol*] [*National Library of Canada*] (NLC) .... ABM
Bonos de Indemnizacián Bancaria (SAUO) .... BIB
Bonos de Renovacián Urbana (SAUO) .... BORES
Bonray Drilling [*NASDAQ symbol*] (TTSB) .... BNRY
Bonray Drilling Corp. [*Associated Press*] (SAG) .... Bonray
Bons Vivants [*An association*] (EA) .... BV
Bonsai .... Bon
Bonsai and Orchid Association (EAIO) .... BOA
Bonsai Clubs International (EA) .... BCI
Bonsai Society of Australia .... BSA
Bonsai Society of Western Australia .... BSWA
Bonso Electronics [*Associated Press*] (SAG) .... Bonso
Bonso Electronics International, Inc. [*NASDAQ symbol*] (NQ) .... BNSO
Bonso Electronics International, Inc. [*NASDAQ symbol*] (SAG) .... BNSW
Bonso Electronics Intl. [*NASDAQ symbol*] (TTSB) .... BNSOF
Bonso Electrs Intl. Wrrt [*NASDAQ symbol*] (TTSB) .... BNSWF
Bontang [*Indonesia*] [*ICAO location identifier*] (ICLI) .... WRLC
Bontebok National Park (SAUS) .... BNP
Bonthe [*Sierre Leone*] [*Airport symbol*] (OAG) .... BTE
Bonthe [*Sierra Leone*] [*ICAO location identifier*] (ICLI) .... GFBN
Bontika [*Zaire*] [*ICAO location identifier*] (ICLI) .... FZBF
Bon-Ton Stores [*NASDAQ symbol*] (TTSB) .... BONT
Bon-Ton Stores, Inc. [*Associated Press*] (SAG) .... BonTon
Bonum Factum [*A Good or Proper Act, Deed, or Decree*] [*Latin*] [*Legal term*] (DLA) .... BF
Bonum Publicum [*The Public Good*] [*Latin*] .... BP
Bonus (ADA) .... BNS
Bonus Aviation [*British*] [*FAA designator*] (FAAC) .... BPT
Bonus Delivery [*Shares*] .... Bnd
Bonus Expeditionary Force .... BEF
Bonus, Extension, and Reenlistment [*Army*] (INF) .... BEAR
Bonus Petroleum Corp. [*Vancouver Stock Exchange symbol*] .... BOU
Bonus Points .... BP
Bonus Vacation Days [*United Auto Workers*] .... BVD
Bony Intraorbital Distance [*Medicine*] (DMAA) .... BIOD
Boob and Bourgeoisie [*H. L. Mencken's portmanteau for the American middle class*] .... BOOBOISIE
BOOG [*British Osborne Owners Group*] **Information Exchange** (NITA) .... BOOGIE
Boogie Down Productions [*Rap recording group*] .... BDP
Book .... B
Book (WDMC) .... b
Book (WDMC) .... bk
Book (AL) .... Bk
Book (AAG) .... BK
Book (SAUS) .... Bk
Book 6 of the WOT series Lord of Chaos (SAUS) .... LoC
Book About Me [*Psychological testing*] .... BAM
Book Acquisition and Bibliographic Service [*National Book Centre*] [*Canada*] .... BABS
Book Action for Nuclear Disarmament [*British*] .... BAND
Book and Periodical Circulation (DGA) .... BPC
Book & Periodical Council (AC) .... BPC
Book and Periodical Development Council (SAUO) .... BPDC
Book Arts Guild (EA) .... BAG
Book Association of Ireland (SAUO) .... BAI
Book Association of Ireland (BARN) .... BAI
Book Auction Records [*A publication*] [*British*] .... BAR
Book Club Associates [*British*] .... BCA
Book Club Edition (ADWA) .... BCE
Book Club of California, San Francisco, CA [*Library symbol*] [*Library of Congress*] (LCLS) .... CSfBk
Book Collector [*A publication*] (BRI) .... BC
Book Collector (journ.) (SAUS) .... BCol
Book Collectors' Society of Australia .... BCSA
Book Communications System [*Information service*] .... BCS
Book Components Manufacturers Association (NTPA) .... BCMA
Book Designer [*MARC relator code*] [*Library of Congress*] (LCCP) .... bkd
Book Development Council [*British*] .... BDC
Book Edge Guilders' Trade Society (DGA) .... BEGTS
Book Exchange (SAUS) .... bk ex
Book Form Drawing (SAUS) .... BFD
[*The*] **Book Guild Ltd.** [*British*] (ECON) .... BG
[*The*] **Book House** [*ACCORD*] [*UTLAS symbol*] .... BKH
Book House Training Centre [*British*] .... BHTC
Book Indexing .... BINDEX
Book Indexing with Context and Entry Points from Text [*Indexing method*] [*Computer science*] (DIT) .... BICEPT
Book Industry Communication [*British*] [*An association*] .... BIC
Book Industry Study Group (EA) .... BISG
Book Industry Systems Advisory Committee [*Book Industry Study Group*] [*New York, NY*] .... BISAC
Book, Insurance, Tax-Fixed Asset Control System (SAUS) .... BIT-FACS
Book Inventory Building and Library Oriented System (EDAC) .... BIBLIOS
Book Inventory Building Library Information Oriented System [*Orange County Public Library, California*] (NITA) .... BIBLIOS
Book Item Contribution Identifier (SAUS) .... BICI
Book Layout and Design [*Publishing*] (WDAA) .... Blad
Book League Monthly (journ.) (SAUS) .... BLM
Book Manufacturers Institute (EA) .... BMI
Book Marketing Council [*British*] .... BMC
Book Marketing Opportunities Database [*Ad-Lib Publications*] [*Information service or system*] (CRD) .... BMO
[*The*] **Book of a Thousand Poems** [*A publication*] .... BoTP
Book of Alternative Services [*Ecclesiastical*] .... BAS
[*The*] **Book of American Negro Poetry** [*A publication*] .... BANP
[*The*] **Book of American Poetry** [*A publication*] .... BAP
[*A*] **Book of American Verse** [*A publication*] .... BAV
[*The*] **Book of Canadian Poetry** [*A publication*] .... BoCaPo

[*A*] **Book of Children's Literature** [*A publication*] ... BoChLi
Book of Classic English Poetry [*A publication*] ... BCEP
Book of Common Prayer [*Episcopalian*] ... BCP
[*A*] **Book of Danish Ballads** [*A publication*] ... BoDaBa
Book of English Literature [*A publication*] ... BEL
Book of Enos (SAUS) ... Enos
Book of Esther (SAUS) ... Esthr
[*The*] **Book of Friendship** [*A publication*] ... BoFr
Book of Helaman (SAUS) ... He
Book of Heroic Verse [*A publication*] ... BHV
[*A*] **Book of Historical Poems** [*A publication*] ... BoHrPo
[*The*] **Book of Humorous Verse** [*A publication*] ... BoHV
Book of Jacob (SAUS) ... Jac
Book of Jarom (SAUS) ... JaG
[*The*] **Book of Joshua in Greek** [*A publication*] (BJA) ... BJG
Book of Jubilees [*Apocalyptic book*] ... BK JUB
Book of Judgments [*England*] [*A publication*] (DLA) ... Book of Judg
Book of Judgments, by Townshend [*A publication*] (DLA) ... Bk Judg
Book of Living Poems [*A publication*] ... BLP
[*The*] **Book of Living Verse** [*A publication*] ... BLV
[*The*] **Book of Living Verse** [*A publication*] ... BOLiVe
[*A*] **Book of Lullabies** [*A publication*] ... BoL
[*The*] **Book of Modern English Poetry** [*A publication*] ... BMEP
Book of Moroni (AD) ... Moro
Book of Mosiah (AD) ... Mos
[*The*] **Book of Nonsense** [*A publication*] ... BoN
Book of Omni (AD) ... Om
Book of Omni (SAUS) ... Om
[*A*] **Book of Personal Poems** [*A publication*] ... BPP
Book of Reference ... BR
Book of Romans (SAUS) ... Rom
[*A*] **Book of Russian Verse** [*A publication*] ... BoR
[*A*] **Book of Scottish Verse** [*A publication*] ... BSV
Book of Semiconductor Equipment and Materials International Standards (AAEL) ... BOSS
[*A*] **Book of South African Verse** [*A publication*] ... BoSA
Book of the Season Scheme [*British*] ... BOSS
Book of the Winter [*A publication*] ... BoW
[*A*] **Book of Treasured Poems** [*A publication*] ... BTP
Book Order ... BO
Book Order and Record Document (PDAA) ... BORD
Book Order and Selection [*Computer science*] ... BOS
Book Order System [*Computer science*] (NITA) ... BOS
Book Ordering, Registering and Inventory System (PDAA) ... BORIS
Book Packagers Association [*British*] (DBA) ... BPA
Book Paper Manufacturers' Association (DGA) ... BPMA
Book Physical Inventory Difference (SAUS) ... BPID
Book Plot Inconsistencies Project (SAUS) ... BPIP
Book Prices Current [*1887-1956*] [*A publication*] [*British*] ... BPC
Book Production Industry (journ.) (SAUS) ... BPI
Book Profit [*Investment term*] ... BP
Book Promoters' Association of Canada (AC) ... BPAC
Book Promotion Society [*Canada*] ... BPS
Book Publisher's Association (NTCM) ... BPA
Book Publishers' Association of Canada ... BPAC
Book Publishers Association of Southern California (SAUO) ... BPASC
Book Publishers Bureau, Incorporated (SAUO) ... BPBI
Book Publisher's Directory [*Later, PD*] [*A publication*] ... BPD
Book Publishers Representatives' Association [*British*] (BI) ... BPRA
Book Publishing ... BP
Book Publishing Development Program [*Canada*] ... BPDP
Book Publishing Record (DIT) ... BPR
Book Rack (MSA) ... BR
Book Records [*Record label*] ... Book
Book Registration Number ... BRN
Book Report [*A publication*] (BRI) ... B Rpt
Book Review ... BR
Book Review Editors File [*University Press of New England*] [*Information service or system*] (IID) ... BREF
Book Review Index ... BoRvI
Book Review Index [*Gale Research, Inc.*] [*Detroit, MI*] [*Information service or system*] [*A publication*] ... BRI
Book Review Index Annual Cumulation [*A publication*] ... BRI-Cum
Book Review Index Master Cumulations [*A publication*] ... BRI-MC
Book Review Index: Periodical Reviews, 1976-1984 [*A publication*] ... BRI-PR
Book Review Index: Reference Books, 1965-1984 [*A publication*] ... BRI-RB
Book Reviews (journ.) (SAUS) ... Book R
Book Services International [*ACCORD*] [*UTLAS symbol*] ... BSI
Book Shelf [*Technical drawings*] (DAC) ... BK SH
Book Stacks Unlimited [*Networked bookseller*] ... BSU
Book Technology Group (SAUO) ... BTG
Book Trade Association of South Africa (SAUO) ... BTASA
Book Trade Benevolent Society [*British*] ... BTBS
Book Trade Electronic Communications Committee [*Library science*] (TELE) ... BTECC
Book Trade Employers' Federation (DGA) ... BTEF
Book Trade Systems Network [*Publishers' Association*] [*British*] ... BTSN
Book Value [*Business term*] ... BV
Book Week Headquarters (SAUO) ... BWH
Book World [*A publication*] (BRI) ... BW
bookable (SAUS) ... bkble
Bookbinder (SAUS) ... Bkbndr
Bookbinder (ADWA) ... bkbndr
Bookbinder (DGA) ... BKBNDR
Bookbinders' Charitable Society (DGA) ... BCS
Bookbindery (DGA) ... BDY
Bookbinding (DGA) ... BKBNDG
bookbinding (SAUS) ... bkbndg
Bookbinding ... BKBNDNG
Bookbinding (ROG) ... BOOKB
Bookbinding and Allied Trades Management Association (DGA) ... BATMA
Bookbinding Cloth (DGA) ... BDG CL
Bookbird [*A publication*] (BRI) ... Bkbird
Bookcase (MSA) ... BC
Bookcase [*s*] [*Freight*] ... BK
Bookcliff Junior High School, Grand Junction, CO [*Library symbol*] [*Library of Congress*] (LCLS) ... CoGjBoJ
Book-Collectors Quarterly (journ.) (SAUS) ... BCQ
Booker Aircraft Museum [*Wycombe Air Park, Booker, Buckinghamshire, England*] ... BAM
Booker Gold Explorations [*Vancouver Stock Exchange symbol*] ... BGE
Booker T. Washington Foundation (EA) ... BTWF
Booker T. Washington High School (SAUO) ... BTWHS
Booker T. Washington National Monument ... BOWA
Bookform Drawing (MSA) ... BFD
Bookham Technology plc ADS [*NASDAQ symbol*] (SG) ... BKHM
Booking (WDAA) ... BKG
Booking Agents Association of Great Britain Ltd. (BI) ... BAA
Booking and Sampling for Indirect Standards [*British*] ... BASIS
Booking Data (SAUS) ... BD
Booking Note (RIMS) ... B/N
Booking Office [*British*] (ROG) ... BO
Booking Register (SAUS) ... BR
Booking Search Control (SAUS) ... BSC
Booking Store (SAUS) ... BS
Bookjacket Designer [*MARC relator code*] [*Library of Congress*] (LCCP) ... bjd
Book-Keeper (ADA) ... BK
Bookkeeper (TBD) ... Bkpr
Bookkeeper (ADWA) ... bkpr
Bookkeeper ... BKPR
Bookkeeper (SAUS) ... Bkpr
Bookkeeping (ADWA) ... bkg
Bookkeeping ... BKG
Bookkeeping (MUGU) ... BKPG
Bookkeeping (TBD) ... Bkpg
Bookkeeping (ADWA) ... bkpg
Bookkeeping (ROG) ... BOOKK
Bookkeeping Address Register (SAUS) ... BAR
Bookkeeping Machine (SAUS) ... BM
Bookkeeping Machine Keyboard (SAUS) ... BMK
Booklet (AFM) ... BKLT
Booklet Category Test [*Brain dysfunction test*] ... BCT
Booklet Pane [*Philately*] ... BP
Booklet Pane Society [*Defunct*] (EA) ... BPS
Book-Library-Management [*System*] ... BLM
Bookline Alert: Missing Books and Manuscripts [*Information service or system*] [*A publication*] ... BAMBAM
Booklist [*A publication*] (BRI) ... BL
Bookmakers' Licensing Board [*South Australia*] ... BLB
Bookmakers' Protection Association Ltd. (BI) ... BPA
Bookmakers' Revision Committee [*New South Wales, Australia*] ... BRC
Bookman's Price Index [*A reference publication listing rare books and their list prices*] ... BPI
Bookmark Exploring Dabbler (SAUS) ... BED
bookmobile (SAUS) ... bkble
Bookmobile (AL) ... Bkmob
Book-of-the-Month Club (WDMC) ... BOM
Book-of-the-Month Club, Inc. (SAUO) ... BOK
Book-of-the-Month Club, Inc. ... BOMC
Book-on-Payment [*Travel industry*] ... BOP
Book-Physical Inventory Difference [*AEC*] ... B-PID
Bookplate (WGA) ... BKP
Bookplate (SAUS) ... Bkp
Bookplate [*Bibliography*] ... B/PL
Bookplate Designer [*MARC relator code*] [*Library of Congress*] (LCCP) ... bpd
Bookplate Society [*London, England*] (EAIO) ... BS
Bookplates [*A publication*] ... BP
Books (WDAA) ... BB
Books (ADWA) ... bb
Books (AL) ... Bks
Books (DLA) ... bks
Books A Million, Inc. [*NASDAQ symbol*] (SAG) ... BAMM
Books A Million, Inc. [*Associated Press*] (SAG) ... BookMill
Books Abroad (journ.) (SAUS) ... BA
Books & Culture [*A publication*] (BRI) ... Bks & Cult
Books and Open-File Report Section (GEOI) ... BOFRS
Books by Mail ... BBM
Books for Bible Students [*A publication*] ... BBS
Books for College Libraries [*A publication of ALA*] ... BCL
Books for College Libraries [*UTLAS symbol*] ... BCLT
Books for Equal Education [*An association*] [*Defunct*] ... BEE
Books for Keeps [*A publication*] (BRI) ... Bks Keeps
Books for Libraries [*Program*] ... BFL
Books for Libraries (SAUS) ... Bks for Libs
Books for Libraries Micropublications, Freeport, NY [*Library symbol*] [*Library of Congress*] (LCLS) ... BFL
Books for Professionals/Miller Accounting Publications [*Harcourt, Brace, Jovanovich, Inc.*] ... BFP/MAP
Books for the Heart [*A publication*] ... BH
Books for the People Fund (EA) ... BPF

Books for Your Children [*A publication*] (BRI) ..... BFYC
Books in Canada [*A publication*] (BRI) ..... BIC
Books in English (AIE) ..... BIE
Books in Print [*Bibliographic database*] [*R. R. Bowker Co.*] [*A publication*] ..... BIP
Books in Series [*A publication*] ..... BIS
Books Magazine [*A publication*] (BRI) ..... Books
Books of Regiam Majestatem [*Scotland*] [*A publication*] (DLA) ..... Reg Maj
Books of Regiam Majestatem (SAUS) ..... Reg Maj
Books of Sederunt [*A publication*] (DLA) ..... Books S
Books of Sederunt [*A publication*] (DLA) ..... Books Sed
Books on Egypt and Chaldea [*A publication*] ..... BEC
Books on Tape ..... BOT
Bookseller ..... BKSLLR
Bookseller [*MARC relator code*] [*Library of Congress*] (LCCP) ..... bsl
Booksellers Association of Great Britain and Ireland (EAIO) ..... BA
Booksellers Association of Great Britain and Ireland (SAUO) ..... BAGBI
Booksellers Association of Philadelphia (SAUO) ..... BAP
Booksellers' Association Service House [*British*] ..... BASH
Booksellers Clearing House [*Commercial firm*] [*British*] ..... BCH
Booksellers of Great Britain ..... BGB
Booksellers of Great Britain and Ireland (DGA) ..... BGD
Booksellers Order Distribution [*British*] ..... BOD
Bookseller's Order Service [*For-profit subsidiary of American Booksellers Association*] [*Defunct*] ..... BOS
Booksellers' Provident Institution [*British*] (DGA) ..... BPI
Booksellers' Provident Institution and Retreat [*British*] (DGA) ..... BPIR
Bookselling (ROG) ..... BOOKS
Bookshelf (SAUS) ..... Bk Sh
Bookshelf ..... BKSHLF
Books-on-File (SAUS) ..... B-o-F
Books-on-Japan-in-English [*A publication*] ..... BJE
Bookstore ..... BKSTR
Booktech.com, Inc. [*AMEX symbol*] (SG) ..... BTC
Booktrade EDI Standards (SAUS) ..... BEDIS
Bookwatch [*A publication*] (BRI) ..... BWatch
Boolarra Virus ..... BOV
Boole & Babbage [*NASDAQ symbol*] (TTSB) ..... BOOL
Boole & Babbage Company (SAUO) ..... BB
Boole & Babbage, Inc. [*NASDAQ symbol*] (NQ) ..... BOOL
Boole & Babbage, Inc. [*Associated Press*] (SAG) ..... BooleB
Boolean [*Mathematics*] ..... B
Boolean [*Mathematics*] ..... BOOL
Boolean Addition (SAUS) ..... BA
Boolean Algebra [*Mathematics*] ..... BA
Boolean Approach for Bivalent Optimization [*Computer science*] (PDAA) ..... BABO
Boolean Array Identifier [*Mathematics*] ..... BAID
Boolean Assignment Statement [*Mathematics*] ..... BAS
Boolean Calculation (SAUS) ..... BC
Boolean Coding (SAUS) ..... BC
Boolean Complementation (SAUS) ..... BC
Boolean Dependency (SAUS) ..... BD
Boolean Differential Calculus (SAUS) ..... BDC
Boolean Encoding (SAUS) ..... BE
Boolean Expression (SAUS) ..... BE
Boolean Factor (SAUS) ..... BF
Boolean Format (SAUS) ..... BF
Boolean Function (SAUS) ..... BF
Boolean Function Designator [*Mathematics*] ..... BFD
Boolean Function Identifier [*Mathematics*] ..... BFID
Boolean Logic (SAUS) ..... BL
Boolean Logic And State Transfer (EECA) ..... BLAST
Boolean Normal Form [*Mathematics*] ..... BNF
Boolean Operation (SAUS) ..... BO
Boolean Operator (SAUS) ..... BO
Boolean Part (SAUS) ..... BP
Boolean Simple Variable [*Mathematics*] ..... BSV
Boolean Term (SAUS) ..... BT
Boolean Time Sequence [*Mathematics*] ..... BTS
Boolean Variable (SAUS) ..... BV
Boom (DS) ..... BM
Boom Antenna (IAA) ..... BMANT
Boom Antenna (SAUS) ..... BM ANT
Boom Control Unit (MCD) ..... BCU
Boom Controller (MCD) ..... BC
Boom Defence [*Navy*] [*British*] ..... BD
Boom Defence (SAUO) ..... BD
Boom Defence Department (SAUO) ..... BDD
Boom Defence Depot [*Navy*] [*British*] ..... BDD
Boom Defence Depot (SAUO) ..... BDP
Boom Defence Officer (SAUS) ..... BDO
Boom Defence Service (SAUO) ..... BDS
Boom Defence Vessel [*Navy*] [*British*] ..... BDV
Boom Defense and Marine Salvage Depot (SAUO) ..... BMSD
Boom Defense Officer ..... BDO
Boom Operator Part Task Trainer (MCD) ..... BOPTT
Boom Operator Part Task Training Simulator ..... BOPTTS
Boom Operator Trainer ..... BOT
Boom Patrol Boat [*British Marines' Special Forces*] [*World War II*] ..... BPB
Boom Time Remaining (NASA) ..... BTR
Boom Vessel (SAUS) ..... bv
Boomerang ..... BO
boomerang (SAUS) ..... boom
Boomerang Association of Australia ..... BAA
Boomerangs Disabled Association [*Australia*] ..... BDA
Boomsail [*Ship's rigging*] (ROG) ..... BMSL
Boomtown, Inc. [*NASDAQ symbol*] (SAG) ..... BMTN
Boomtown, Inc. [*Associated Press*] (SAG) ..... Boomtwn
Boone and Crockett Club (EA) ..... BCC
Boone County Courthouse, Boone, IA [*Library symbol*] [*Library of Congress*] (LCLS) ..... IaBoCoC
Boone County Recorder's Office, Lebanon, IN [*Library symbol*] [*Library of Congress*] (LCLS) ..... InLebCR
Boone, IA [*Location identifier*] [*FAA*] (FAAL) ..... BNW
Boone, IA [*AM radio station call letters*] ..... KFGQ
Boone, IA [*FM radio station call letters*] ..... KFGQ-FM
Boone, IA [*FM radio station call letters*] (RBYB) ..... KRKQ-FM
Boone, IA [*FM radio station call letters*] ..... KRUU
Boone, IA [*AM radio station call letters*] ..... KWBG
Boone Junior College [*Iowa*] ..... BJC
Boone, NC [*FM radio station call letters*] ..... WASU
Boone, NC [*AM radio station call letters*] ..... WATA
Boone News-Republican, Boone, IA [*Library symbol*] [*Library of Congress*] (LCLS) ..... IaBoNR
Boone on Corporations [*A publication*] (DLA) ..... Boone Corp
Booneville, AR [*FM radio station call letters*] ..... KEZU
Booneville, MS [*AM radio station call letters*] ..... WBIP
Booneville, MS [*FM radio station call letters*] ..... WBIP-FM
Booneville, MS [*FM radio station call letters*] ..... WMAE
Booneville, MS [*Television station call letters*] ..... WMAE-TV
Boonton Radio Corporation (SAUO) ..... BRC
Boonville, IN [*AM radio station call letters*] ..... WBNL
Boonville, IN [*FM radio station call letters*] ..... WBNL-FM
Boonville, MO [*FM radio station call letters*] (BROA) ..... KBHO-FM
Boonville, MO [*FM radio station call letters*] ..... KCLR
Boonville, MO [*FM radio station call letters*] (BROA) ..... KCLR-FM
Boonville, MO [*AM radio station call letters*] ..... KWRT
Boonville, MO [*Location identifier*] [*FAA*] (FAAL) ..... VER
Boonville, NY [*AM radio station call letters*] ..... WBRV
Boonville, NY [*FM radio station call letters*] ..... WBRV-FM
Boonville Standard, Boonville, IN [*Library symbol*] [*Library of Congress*] (LCLS) ..... InBooS
Boonville Warrick County Public Library, Boonville, IN [*Library symbol*] [*Library of Congress*] (LCLS) ..... InBoo
Booraem's Reports [*6-8 California*] [*A publication*] (DLA) ..... Boor
Booraem's Reports [*6-8 California*] [*A publication*] (DLA) ..... Booraem
Boosey & Hawkes [*Record label*] [*Great Britain, USA*] (ADA) ..... B & H
Boosey & Hawkes [*Record label*] [*Great Britain, USA*] ..... BH
Boost (ACAE) ..... B
Boost Alcohol Consciousness Concerning the Health of University Students [*In association name BACCHUS of the US*] (EA) ..... BACCHUS
Boost Control piston (SAUS) ..... BC-piston
Boost Discrimination and Track System ..... BDTS
Boost Glide Reentry Vehicle [*Air Force*] ..... BGRV
Boost Glide Vehicle (ACAE) ..... BGV
Boost, Insertion, and Abort [*Aerospace*] ..... BIA
Boost Measurement and Analysis Program (MCD) ..... BMAP
Boost Phase (ACAE) ..... BP
Boost Phase Intercept (AABC) ..... BPHI
Boost Phase Intercept ..... BPI
Boost Phase Leakage (ACAE) ..... BPL
Boost Phase Track System ..... BPTS
Boost Phase Vehicle (ACAE) ..... BPV
Boost Protective Cover [*Apollo*] [*NASA*] ..... BPC
Boost Pump (MCD) ..... BP
Boost Pump Start (MCD) ..... BPS
Boost Regulator (ACAE) ..... B-R
Boost Rocket (SAUS) ..... BST RKT
Boost Stage Discharge Pressure (MCD) ..... BSDP
Boost Surveillance and Tracking System [*Satellite*] [*Military*] ..... BSTS
Boost Vehicle (ACAE) ..... BV
Boostan [*Iran*] [*ICAO location identifier*] (ICLI) ..... OIAB
Boost-Controlled Decelerating Device ..... BCDD
Boosted Anti-Radar Bomb (SAUS) ..... BARB
Boosted Kinetic Energy Penetrator [*Proposed submunition*] ..... BKEP
Booster ..... B
Booster (SAUS) ..... Boost
Booster (MUGU) ..... BST
Booster [*Military*] (AFM) ..... BSTR
booster 1 (SAUS) ..... b 1
booster 1 pitch (SAUS) ..... b 1 p
booster 1 yaw (SAUS) ..... b 1 y
booster 2 (SAUS) ..... b 2
booster 2 pitch (SAUS) ..... b 2 p
booster 2 yaw (SAUS) ..... b 2 y
Booster and Sustainer (SAUS) ..... B&S
Booster and Sustainer ..... B & S
Booster Assembly Building [*NASA*] ..... BAB
Booster Assembly Contractor [*NASA*] (NASA) ..... BAC
Booster Battery ..... BB
Booster Brake [*Automotive engineering*] ..... B/BRK
Booster Burn Time (ACAE) ..... BBT
Booster Burn-Out (IAA) ..... BBO
Booster Change Assembly (MCD) ..... BCA
Booster Cutoff Backup ..... BCOB
Booster Cut-Off Backup (SAUS) ..... BCOB
Booster Development ..... BD
Booster Distribution Amplifier (SAUS) ..... BDA
Booster Dynamic Condition at Abort (SAA) ..... BDCAA
Booster Engine [*Rocketry*] ..... BE
Booster Engine Cutoff [*Rocketry*] ..... BCO

Booster Engine Cutoff [*Rocketry*] ..... BECO
Booster Exhaust Stream ..... BES
Booster Exhaust Study Test [*NASA*] (NASA) ..... BEST
Booster Flight-Acceptance Composite Test [*NASA*] ..... B-FACT
Booster Fuel Jacket ..... BFJ
Booster Gas Generator ..... BGG
Booster Inertial Guidance System [*Aerospace*] ..... BIGS
Booster Insertion and Abort (SAUS) ..... BIA
Booster Interstage Assembly [*Aerospace*] ..... BIA
Booster Jettison ..... BOJ
Booster Lift-Off Mass [*NASA*] (KSC) ..... BLOM
Booster Lift-Off Weight [*NASA*] (KSC) ..... BLOW
Booster Orbiter (MCD) ..... B/O
Booster Press, Howell, NJ [*Library symbol*] [*Library of Congress*] (LCLS) ..... NjHowB
Booster Pump [*Liquid gas carriers*] ..... b
Booster Release Actuator (MCD) ..... BRA
Booster Requirements Document ..... BRD
Booster Separation Motors [*NASA*] (NASA) ..... BSM
Booster Situation Indicator ..... BSI
Booster Solid Rocket Motor [*NASA*] (NASA) ..... BSRM
Booster Stage Discharge Pressure (SAUS) ..... BSDP
Booster Systems Engineer [*NASA*] (KSC) ..... BSE
Booster Technology Simulator (SAUS) ..... BTS
Booster Test Department [*NASA*] (KSC) ..... BST
Booster Trowelable Ablator (SAUS) ..... BTA
Booster Umbilical Assembly ..... BUA
Booster Union Assembly (SAUO) ..... BUA
Booster Vacuum Pump ..... BVP
Booster Vacuum Pump System ..... BVPS
Booster/Adaptor (ACAE) ..... B/A
Booster-Regulator [*NASA*] ..... BR
Boost/Post Boost (ACAE) ..... B/PB
Boot and Floor Polish Trade Board (SAUO) ..... BFPTB
Boot and Shoe Manufacturers' Association and Leather Trades Protection Society [*British*] (BI) ..... BASMA
Boot and Shoe Repair Trade Board (SAUO) ..... BSRTB
Boot and Shoe Travelers Association of New York (EA) ..... BSTANY
Boot and Shoe Workers Union (SAUO) ..... BSW
Boot and Shoe Workers' Union [*Later, UFCWIA*] (IIA) ..... BSWU
Boot Hill (SAUS) ..... BH
Boot or Shoes, or Boot or Shoe Findings [*Freight*] ..... BS BSF
Boot Parameters Protocol [*Computer science*] (ITCA) ..... BOOTP
Boot Read Only Memory [*Computer science*] (DDC) ..... Boot ROM
Boot Top Fracture [*Medicine*] (MELL) ..... BTF
Boot Trade Association, Ltd. (SAUO) ..... BTA
Boote. Action at Law [*A publication*] (ILCA) ..... Boote Act
Boote. Chancery Practice [*A publication*] (DLA) ..... Boote Ch Pr
Bootes [*Constellation*] ..... Boo
Bootes [*Constellation*] ..... Boot
Boote's Suit at Law [*A publication*] (DLA) ..... Boote
Boote's Suit at Law [*A publication*] (DLA) ..... Boote SL
Booth American Shipping Corporation (SAUO) ..... BASC
Booth. Indictable Offences [*A publication*] (DLA) ..... Booth In Of
Booth Library On-Line Circulation [*Data processing system*] [*Eastern Illinois University*] [*Charleston, IL*] ..... BLOC
Booth Memorial Hospital, Flushing, NY [*Library symbol*] [*Library of Congress*] (LCLS) ..... NFB
Booth on Real Actions [*A publication*] (DLA) ..... Boo R Act
Booth on Real Actions [*A publication*] (DLA) ..... Booth R Act
Booth on Real Actions [*A publication*] (DLA) ..... Booth Real Act
Booth on Real Actions [*A publication*] (DLA) ..... BR Act
Booth Steamship Company (SAUO) ..... BSC
Boothbay Harbor, ME [*FM radio station call letters*] ..... WCME
Boothbay Harbor Yacht Club (SAUO) ..... BHYC
Boothby, Lovelace, Bulbulian [*Of Mayo Clinic*] **Unit** (DAVI) ..... BLB
Bootheville, LA [*Location identifier*] [*FAA*] (FAAL) ..... BVE
Booth-Henry-Gorin [*Equations for calculation of net charge and valence of molecule*] ..... BHG
Booth-Henry-Gorin equation (SAUS) ..... BHG equation
Booth's Law of Wills [*A publication*] (DLA) ..... Booth Wills
Boots Combat High (SAUS) ..... BCH
Boots Contract Manufacturing ..... BCM
Boots Pure Drug Co. [*Great Britain*] [*Research code symbol*] ..... RD
Boots Pure Drug Company (SAUO) ..... BPD
Boots&Coots Intl. Well Control [*AMEX symbol*] (SG) ..... WEL
Bootstap Confidence Level [*Mathematics*] ..... BCL
Bootstrap [*Computer science*] ..... BOOT
Bootstrap [*Computer science*] (HGAA) ..... BTSP
Bootstrap (MSA) ..... BTST
Bootstrap Combined Programming Language [*Computer science*] (CSR) ..... BCPL
Bootstrap Commissioning Program [*Air Force*] ..... BCP
Bootstrap Gyro (SAUS) ..... BSG
Bootstrap Gyroscope (IAA) ..... BSG
Bootstrap Memory (SAUS) ..... BM
Bootstrap Protocol [*Telecommunications*] (ACRL) ..... BOOTP
Bootstrap Routine (SAUS) ..... BR
Bootstrap Technique (SAUS) ..... BT
Booue [*Gabon*] [*Airport symbol*] (OAG) ..... BGB
Booue [*Gabon*] [*ICAO location identifier*] (ICLI) ..... FOGB
Booz, Allen and Hamilton Computer Utilization System (SAUS) ..... BACUS
Booz, Allen & Hamilton, Inc., Chicago, IL [*Library symbol*] [*Library of Congress*] (LCLS) ..... ICBAH
Booz-Allen Applied Research, Inc. ..... BAARINC
Booz-Allen-Hamilton (SAUS) ..... BAH
Boozing Urban-Rural Parasites [*Lifestyle classification*] ..... BURPIES
Bop Air (Pty) Ltd. [*South Africa*] [*ICAO designator*] (FAAC) ..... BOP
B-Operator (SAUS) ..... BO
Bophuthatswana Democratic Party [*Political party*] (PPW) ..... BDP
Bophuthatswana National Party (SAUO) ..... BNP
Bor [*Sudan*] [*ICAO location identifier*] (ICLI) ..... HSBR
Bora Bora/Motu-Mute [*French Polynesia*] [*ICAO location identifier*] (ICLI) ..... NTTB
Borabicyclononane [*Organic chemistry*] ..... BBN
Bora-Bora [*Society Islands*] [*Airport symbol*] (AD) ..... BOB
Boral Ltd ADS [*NASDAQ symbol*] (TTSB) ..... BORAY
Borane Methyl Sulfide [*Organic chemistry*] ..... BMS
Boras-Viared [*Sweden*] [*ICAO location identifier*] (ICLI) ..... ESGX
Borate and Aluminum (IIA) ..... BORAL
Borate Oxide (SAUS) ..... SBX
Borated Water Storage Tank [*Environmental science*] (COE) ..... BWST
Borax and Carbon (IIA) ..... BORON
Boray Ltd. [*NASDAQ symbol*] (SAG) ..... BORA
Boray Ltd. [*Associated Press*] (SAG) ..... Boral
Borazjan [*Iran*] [*ICAO location identifier*] (ICLI) ..... OIBN
Borcan Resources [*Vancouver Stock Exchange symbol*] ..... BOA
Bord Gais Eirecann [*Irish Gas Board*] (EY) ..... BGE
Bord Telecom Eireann [*Nationalized industry*] [*Ireland*] (EY) ..... BTE
Bordaire Ltd. [*Canada*] [*ICAO designator*] (FAAC) ..... BOF
Bordano [*Italy*] [*Seismograph station code, US Geological Survey*] (SEIS) ..... BORI
Bordeaux (ADWA) ..... Bdx
Bordeaux [*France*] [*Airport symbol*] (OAG) ..... BOD
Bordeaux [*France*] [*ICAO location identifier*] (ICLI) ..... LFBB
Bordeaux [*France*] [*ICAO location identifier*] (ICLI) ..... LFXJ
Bordeaux Agents Association [*British*] (BI) ..... BAA
Bordeaux or Rouen [*Shipping*] (ROG) ..... B/R
Bordeaux to Hamburg (SAUS) ..... B-H
Bordeaux-Hamburg Inclusive [*Shipping*] ..... B/H
Bordeaux/Hamburg Limits (MARI) ..... B/H
Bordeaux/Merignac [*France*] [*ICAO location identifier*] (ICLI) ..... LFBD
Bordeaux/Saucats [*France*] [*ICAO location identifier*] (ICLI) ..... LFCS
Bordeaux/Souge [*France*] [*ICAO location identifier*] (ICLI) ..... LFDO
Bordeaux-Yvrac [*France*] [*ICAO location identifier*] (ICLI) ..... LFDY
Borden Chemical & Plastics Ltd. [*NYSE symbol*] (SAG) ..... BCU
Borden Chemical, Westhill, ON, Canada [*Library symbol*] [*Library of Congress*] (LCLS) ..... CaOWesBC
Borden Chemical, Westhill, Ontario [*Library symbol*] [*National Library of Canada*] (NLC) ..... OWESBC
Borden Chemicals & Plastics Ltd. [*Associated Press*] (SAG) ..... BordCh
Borden, Inc. (SAUO) ..... BN
Borden, Inc. [*Wall Street slang name: "Moo Moo"*] [*Associated Press*] (SAG) ..... Borden
Borden Museum, Borden, IN [*Library symbol*] [*Library of Congress*] [*Obsolete*] (LCLS) ..... InBoM
Bordentown Historical Society, Bordentown, NJ [*Library symbol*] [*Library of Congress*] (LCLS) ..... NjBorHi
Border (FAAC) ..... BDR
Border Airways [*South Africa*] [*ICAO designator*] (FAAC) ..... BDA
Border Boundary Police [*Thailand*] (CINC) ..... BBP
Border Cargo Selectivity [*USTTA*] (TAG) ..... BCS
Border Collie Club of Queensland [*Australia*] ..... BCCQ
Border Command (SAUO) ..... BC
Border Detection Method [*Radiology*] (DAVI) ..... BDM
Border Ecology Project [*Staff consists of Americans and Mexicans concerned with environmental issues*] (CROSS) ..... BEP
Border Environment Cooperation Commission (SAUO) ..... BECC
Border Environment Infrastructure Fund ..... BEIF
Border Gateway Protocol [*Computer science*] (PCM) ..... BGP
Border Industrial Program (SAUS) ..... BIP
Border Information & Solutions Network (SAUS) ..... BISN
Border Inspection Post (SAUS) ..... BIP
Border Intermediate System ..... BIS
Border Leicester [*Sheep*] ..... BL
Border Leicester Sheepbreeders' Association [*Australia*] ..... BLSA
Border Leicester Sheepbreeders' Association of New South Wales [*Australia*] ..... BLSANSW
Border Line ..... BL
Border Mounted Rifles [*British military*] (DMA) ..... BMR
Border Operations Detachment (SAUO) ..... BOD
Border Patrol ..... BOPAT
Border Patrol ..... BP
Border Patrol Academy ..... BPA
Border Patrol Section Headquarters (SAUO) ..... BPSH
Border Patrol Sector Headquarters ..... BPSH
Border Patrol Station (SAUO) ..... BPS
Border Regiment (SAUO) ..... BORDER
Border Regiment [*British*] ..... BR
Border Rivers Agreement (SAUO) ..... BRA
Border Security Police [*NATO*] (NATG) ..... BSP
Border Surveillance [*Military*] ..... BS
Border Terrier Club of America (EA) ..... BTCA
Border Trade Alliance [*Mexico/US relations*] (CROSS) ..... BTA
Border Union Agricultural Society [*British*] ..... BUAS
Bordereau [*Statement*] [*French*] [*Business term*] ..... BORD
Border-Fault System [*Geology*] ..... BFS
Borderland Sciences Research Foundation (EA) ..... BSRF
Borderline (SAUS) ..... B
Borderline [*Biochemistry*] (DAVI) ..... BOD
Borderline [*Biochemistry*] (DAVI) ..... BORD
Borderline ..... BRD
Borderline Between Comfort and Discomfort glare (SAUS) ..... BCD

Borderline Dull [Medicine] .... BD
Borderline Glucose Tolerance Test [Medicine] (MAE) .... BGTT
Borderline Hypertension (SAUS) .... BLH
Borderline Hypertensive [Medicine] (MELL) .... BH
Borderline Left-Axis Deviation [Cardiology] .... BLAD
Borderline Lepromatous [Medicine] .... BL
Borderline Personality Disorder [Psychology] .... BPD
Borderline Pumping Temperature [Automotive engineering] .... BPT
Borderline Tuberculoid [Medicine] .... BT
Borders Group, Inc. [NYSE symbol] (SAG) .... BGP
Borders Group, Inc. [Associated Press] (SAG) .... Borders
Bordetella [Biochemistry] (DAVI) .... B
Bordetella Pertussis Vaccine .... BPV
Bordet-Gengou [Bacillus] [Microbiology] .... BG
Bordier & Compagnie [Bank] [Switzerland] .... B & Cie
Bordj El Amri [Tunisia] [ICAO location identifier] (ICLI) .... DTTI
Bordj Mokhtar [Algeria] [ICAO location identifier] (ICLI) .... DATM
Bordj Omar Driss [Algeria] [ICAO location identifier] (ICLI) .... DAAW
Bordmechaniker [Flight engineer] [German military - World War II] .... BM
Bore (SAUS) .... BRE
Bore [Freight] .... BRE
Bore and Stroke .... B&S
Bore Autonomic Tester .... BAT
Bore Erosion Gauge Reading .... BEGR
Bore Hole Capsule (SAUS) .... BHC
Bore Hole Seismometer (SAUS) .... BHS
Bore Sight (SAUS) .... BRSIT
Bore Sight Restricted (SAUS) .... BSR
Bore Sight Tracker (SAUS) .... BST
Boreal Asiatic (SAUS) .... BA
Boreal Ecosystem-Atmosphere Study (USDC) .... BOREAS
Boreal Forest Transect Case Study (SAUS) .... BFTCS
Boreal Institute for Northern Studies, University of Alberta, Edmonton, Alberta [Library symbol] [National Library of Canada] (NLC) .... AEUB
Boreal Institute of Northern Studies (SAUS) .... BINS
Boreal Northern Titles [Database] [Boreal Institute for Northern Studies] [Information service or system] (CRD) .... BNT
Borealis Technology Corp. [Associated Press] (SAG) .... Borealis
Borealis Technology Corp. [NASDAQ symbol] (SAG) .... BRLS
Bored Insitu Piles [Camutek] [Software package] (NCC) .... BPILE
Borehole .... BH
Borehole Capsule .... BHC
Borehole Compensated [Sonic log] .... BHC
Borehole Gravity Meter (SAUS) .... BHGM
Borehole Research Group (SAUO) .... BRG
Borehole Seismometer .... BHS
Borehole Televiewer [Drilling technology] .... BHTV
Borehole Water (SAUS) .... BW
Borescope (MSA) .... BS
Boresight (MSA) .... BRSIT
Boresight (KSC) .... BS
Boresight .... BST
Boresight Adjustment System (PDAA) .... BAS
Boresight Axis .... BSA
Boresight Camera .... BC
Boresight Camera (MUGU) .... BSC
Boresight Collimator Test Set (DWSG) .... BSCTS
Boresight Datum Line [Military] .... BSDL
Boresight Error .... BSE
Boresight Error Slope .... BSES
Boresight Fixture (MCD) .... BSF
Boresight Launch (ACAE) .... BRSL
Boresight Range on Target (ACAE) .... BROT
Boresight Reference Line (DNAB) .... BRL
Boresight Reticle Unit (MCD) .... BRU
Boresight Tower (MUGU) .... BST
Borg & Beck [Automotive industry supplier] .... BB
Borg Warner Security Corp. [NYSE symbol] (SAG) .... BOR
Borgarfjordur [Iceland] [Airport symbol] (OAG) .... BGJ
Borge Prien Prove [Danish intelligence test] .... BPP
Borger, TX [Location identifier] [FAA] (FAAL) .... BGD
Borger, TX [FM radio station call letters] (BROA) .... KASV-FM
Borger, TX [FM radio station call letters] (BROA) .... KAVO-FM
Borger, TX [FM radio station call letters] .... KQFX
Borger, TX [AM radio station call letters] .... KQTY
Borgess Hospital, Medical Library, Kalamazoo, MI [Library symbol] [Library of Congress] (LCLS) .... MiKB
Borglanda [Sweden] [ICAO location identifier] (ICLI) .... ESMB
Borginus Cavalcanus [Flourished, 16th century] [Authority cited in pre-1607 legal work] (DSA) .... Borgnin Cavalcan
Borgward Owners' Club (EA) .... BOC
Borg-Warner Automotive [Associated Press] (SAG) .... BorgWAu
Borg-Warner Automotive, Inc. [NYSE symbol] (SPSG) .... BWA
Borg-Warner Chemicals Inc. (SAUO) .... BWC
Borg-Warner Corp. [NYSE symbol] (SPSG) .... BOR
Borg-Warner Corp. .... BW
Borg-Warner Corp., B-J Electronics Division, Santa Ana, CA [Library symbol] [Library of Congress] (LCLS) .... CStaB-E
Borg-Warner Corp., Borg-Warner Chemicals Technical Center, Washington, WV [Library symbol] [Library of Congress] (LCLS) .... WvWaB
Borg-Warner Corp., Des Plaines, IL [OCLC symbol] (OCLC) .... IBW
Borg-Warner Corp., Ingersoll Research Center, Des Plaines, IL [Library symbol] [Library of Congress] (LCLS) .... IDesB
Borg-Warner Corp., York Division, York, PA [Library symbol] [Library of Congress] (LCLS) .... PYB

Borg-Warner Security [NYSE symbol] (TTSB) .... BOR
Borg-Warner Security Corp. [Associated Press] (SAG) .... BorWSc
Boric Acid [Inorganic chemistry] .... BA
Boric Acid [Pharmacology] (DAVI) .... H_3BO_3
Boric Acid Concentrator (NRCH) .... BAC
Boric Acid Injection Tank (IEEE) .... BIT
Boric Acid Mix Tank [Nuclear energy] (NRCH) .... BAMT
Boric Acid Solution (SAUS) .... BAS
Boric Acid Storage Tank (IEEE) .... BAST
Boric Acid Tank [Nuclear energy] (NRCH) .... BAT
Boric Acid Transfer [Nuclear energy] (NRCH) .... BAT
Boric Acid Transfer Pump (IEEE) .... BATP
Boric Oxide (AAEL) B203
Boric-Acid, Tar-oil and Bentonite (SAUS) .... BTB
Boring (SAUS) .... BOR
Boring Bar .... BOBR
Boring But Important Information [Journalism] (WDMC) .... BBI
Boring Fixture (MCD) .... BF
Boring Fixture (AAG) .... BOFX
Boring Institute (EA) .... BI
Boring Old Fart [Slang] (DSUE) .... BOF
Boring Party (EA) .... BP
Boris Becker Fan Club (EA) .... BBFC
Boris Becker of Leimen [Acronym also refers to pretzel produced by German bakers in recognition of this tennis player] .... BOBELE
Borjeson-Forssman-Lehmann Syndrome [Medicine] (DMAA) .... BFLS
Borkenberge [Germany] [ICAO location identifier] (ICLI) .... EDLB
Borkin Industries Corp. [Vancouver Stock Exchange symbol] .... BNI
Borkum [Germany] [Airport symbol] (OAG) .... BMK
Borkum [Germany] [ICAO location identifier] (ICLI) .... EDWR
Borland Database (SAUS) .... BDA
Borland Database Engine [Borland International, Inc.] [Computer science] .... BDE
Borland Enhanced Support and Training (VERA) .... BEST
Borland Graphics Interface [Borland International] (BYTE) .... BGI
Borland International Data Structures (SAUS) .... BIDS
Borland International, Inc. [NASDAQ symbol] (SAG) .... BORL
Borland International, Inc. [Associated Press] (SAG) .... BorInd
Borland Object Component Architecture [Borland International, Inc.] (PCM) .... BOCA
Borland Pascal 7 [Borland International, Inc.] [Computer programming] (PCM) BP7
Borland Pro Quattro (SAUS) .... BORPQU
Borland Quattro (SAUS) .... BORQU
Borland Windows Custom Controls (SAUS) .... BWCC
Borlands Graphics Interface (SAUS) .... BGI
Borlange [Sweden] [Airport symbol] (OAG) .... BLE
Borlange [Sweden] [ICAO location identifier] (ICLI) .... ESSD
Born (WDMC) .... b
Born .... B
Born (ADA) .... BN
Born (SAUS) .... Bn
Born .... BO
Born Again Pagans (EA) .... BAP
Born before Arrival [of mother at hospital] [Medicine] .... BBA
Born Fool (DAS) .... BF
Born in Colony [British] (ADA) .... BC
Born in Japan .... BIJ
Born on Arrival [of mother at hospital] [Medicine] .... BOA
Born Out of Asepsis [Neonatology and obstetrics] (DAVI) .... BOA
Born out of Wedlock (SAUS) .... BOW
Born Young [An association] (EA) .... BY
Borna Disease [Medicine] (PDAA) .... BD
Borna Disease Virus [Veterinary medicine] .... BDV
Born-Again Christian .... BAC
Borne Again Shell (SAUS) .... BASH
Borneo .... Bor
Borneo Island [MARC geographic area code] [Library of Congress] .... a-bn-
Born-Haber Cycle [Physics] .... BHC
Bornier Programmable (IAA) .... BP
Born-Infeld Theory [Physics] .... BIT
Born-Mayer Equation [Physics] .... BME
Born-Oppenheimer Method [Physical chemistry] .... BO
Born-Oppenheimer Method [Physical chemistry] .... BOM
Bornu Youth Movement (SAUO) .... BYM
Bornu Youth Movement - Action Group Alliance [Nigeria] .... BYM-AG
Boro Phosphosilicate (AAEL) .... BPSG
Borobudur (VRA) .... Boro
Borocarbon .... BC
Borocarbon Resistor (CET) .... BCR
Borok [Former USSR] [Geomagnetic observatory code] .... BOX
Boromo [Burkina Faso] [ICAO location identifier] (ICLI) .... DHCO
Boron [Chemical element] .... B
Boron [Symbol is B] [Chemical element] (ROG) .... BOR
Boron and Arsenic (SAUS) .... BORSENIC
Boron Based Fuel (SAUS) .... BBF
Boron Deoxidized Copper (SAUS) .... B-D cu
Boron Electron Center (SAUS) .... BEC
Boron Experiment .... BOREXINO
Boron Fiber (or Fibre) Reinforced Plastics (SAUS) .... BFRP
Boron Fluoride-Ethyl Ether [Organic chemistry] .... BFEE
Boron Injection Tank [Nuclear energy] (NRCH) .... BIT
Boron LePore & Assoc [NASDAQ symbol] (SG) .... BLPG
Boron Management System [Nuclear energy] (NRCH) .... BMS
Boron Measurement (System) [Nuclear energy] (NRCH) .... BM(S)
Boron Metal Fiber .... BMF

Boron Metals Plant (SAA) .... BMP
Boron Neutron Capture Therapy .... BNCT
Boron Nitride [*Inorganic fiber*] .... BN
Boron Nitride Fiber [*Inorganic fiber*] .... BNF
Boron Nitride Image Guide (PDAA) .... BNIG
Boron Plastic .... BP
Boron Potassium Nitrate .... $BKNO_3$
Boron Pyrolytic Graphite .... BPG
Boron Recycle System [*Nuclear energy*] (NRCH) .... BRS
Boron Reinforced Structure (SAUS) .... BRS
Boron Storage Tank [*Nuclear energy*] (NRCH) .... BST
Boron Thermal Regeneration System [*Nuclear energy*] (NRCH) .... BTRS
Boron-Aluminum .... BORAL
Boronated Phenylalanine (SAUS) .... BPA
Boronated Protoporphyrin [*Organic chemistry*] .... BOPP
Boronophenylalanine [*Organic chemistry*] .... BPA
Boron-Oxygen Hole Centre (PDAA) .... BOHC
Boro-Phospho-Silicate Glass (SAUS) .... BPSG
Borophosphosilicate glass from a TEOS & Ocirc (SAUS) .... BPTEOS
Borosilicate Crown (MSA) .... BSC
Boro-Silicate Glass (PDAA) .... BSG
Borosilicate Glass (SAUS) .... BSG
Borough (ROG) .... BGH
Borough .... BO
Borough .... BOR
Borough (ADWA) .... Bor
Borough (BEE) .... Boro
Borough (ROG) .... BORO
Borough Constituency .... BC
Borough Constituency (WDAA) .... Boro Const
Borough Council (SAUO) .... BC
Borough Council .... BC
Borough Education Officer (SAUS) .... BEO
Borough Engineer (SAUS) .... BE
Borough Fiscal [*British*] (ROG) .... BF
Borough of Manhattan Community College, New York, NY [*Library symbol*] [*Library of Congress*] (LCLS) .... NNBMC
Borough of Manhattan Community College, New York, NY [*OCLC symbol*] (OCLC) .... XMC
Borough President (ADWA) .... Beep
Borough President (ADWA) .... BP
Boroujen [*Iran*] [*ICAO location identifier*] (ICLI) .... OIFB
Boroujerd [*Iran*] [*ICAO location identifier*] (ICLI) .... OICJ
Borradaile's Civil Cases, Bombay [*1800-24*] [*India*] [*A publication*] (DLA) .... Borr
Borrego Springs [*California*] [*Airport symbol*] (OAG) .... BXS
Borrelia [*Biochemistry*] (DAVI) .... B
Borroloola [*Airport symbol*] .... BOX
Borromeo Seminary of Ohio, Wickliffe, OH [*Library symbol*] [*Library of Congress*] (LCLS) .... OWicB
Borror Corp. [*NASDAQ symbol*] (SAG) .... BORR
Borror Corp. [*Associated Press*] (SAG) .... Borror
Burroughs Hospital Information Processing System (SAUS) .... BHIPS
Borrowed [*Banking*] (TBD) .... Brw
Borrowed Light (DAC) .... Bit
Borrowed Light (KSC) .... BLT
Borrowed Military Manpower .... BMM
Borrower's Option for Notes and Underwritten Standby [*Finance*] .... BONUS
Borrowings [*Banking*] .... BOR
Borrows, S. A., Detroit, MI [*STAC*] .... BSA
Borthwick. Modes of Prosecuting for Libel [*1830*] [*A publication*] (DLA) .... Borth
Borzhomi [*Former USSR*] [*Seismograph station code, US Geological Survey*] [*Closed*] (SEIS) .... BOR
Borzoi Club of America (EA) .... BCOA
B.O.S. Better Online Sol Wrrt [*NASDAQ symbol*] (TTSB) .... BOSWF
B.O.S. Better Online Solutions [*NASDAQ symbol*] (TTSB) .... BOSCF
BOS Better Online Solutions Ltd. [*NASDAQ symbol*] (SAG) .... BOSC
BOS Better Online Solutions Ltd. [*Associated Press*] (SAG) .... BOSLtd
BOS Better Online Solutions Ltd. [*NASDAQ symbol*] (SAG) .... BOSW
BO-S-AIRE Corp. [*Air carrier designation symbol*] .... BOSX
Bosal International Management NV [*Belgium*] [*ICAO designator*] (FAAC) .... BOS
Bosanquet and Darby's Limitations [*A publication*] (DLA) .... Bos & D Lim
Bosanquet and Puller's English Common Pleas, Exchequer, and House of Lords Rep orts [*1796-1804*] [*A publication*] (DLA) .... B & P
Bosanquet and Puller's English Common Pleas Reports [*126, 127 English Reprint*] [*A publication*] (DLA) .... Bos & P
Bosanquet and Puller's English Common Pleas Reports [*126, 127 English Reprint*] [*A publication*] (DLA) .... Bos & P (Eng)
Bosanquet and Puller's English Common Pleas Reports [*126, 127 English Reprint*] [*A publication*] (DLA) .... Bos & Pu
Bosanquet and Puller's English Common Pleas Reports [*126, 127 English Reprint*] [*A publication*] (DLA) .... Bos & Pul
Bosanquet and Puller's New Reports, English Common Pleas [*1804-07*] [*A publication*] (DLA) .... B & PNR
Bosanquet and Puller's New Reports, English Common Pleas [*1804-07*] [*A publication*] (DLA) .... Bos & PNR
Bosanquet and Puller's New Reports, English Common Pleas [*1804-07*] [*A publication*] (DLA) .... Bos & PNR (Eng)
Bosanquet and Puller's New Reports, English Common Pleas [*1804-07*] [*A publication*] (DLA) .... Bos & Pul NR
Bosanquet and Puller's New Reports, English Common Pleas [*1804-07*] [*A publication*] (ILCA) .... Bos N R
Bosanquet and Puller's New Reports, English Common Pleas [*1804-07*] [*A publication*] (DLA) .... BPNR
Bosanquet and Pullers New Reports, English Common Pleas (SAUS) .... New Rep
Bosanquet and Puller's New Reports, English Common Pleas [*1804-07*] [*A publication*] (DLA) .... New Rep
Bosanquet and Puller's New Reports, English Common Pleas [*1804-07*] [*A publication*] (DLA) .... NR
Bosanquet's Rules of Pleading [*A publication*] (DLA) .... Bos Pl
Bosaso [*Somalia*] [*Airport symbol*] (OAG) .... BSA
Bosaso [*Somalia*] [*ICAO location identifier*] (ICLI) .... HCMF
Boscawen on Convictions [*A publication*] (DLA) .... Bosc Con
Boscombe Down [*British*] [*ICAO location identifier*] (ICLI) .... EGDM
Boscombe Down MOD/PE [*British*] [*ICAO designator*] (FAAC) .... BDN
Bose, Chandhuri and Hocquenghem Code (SAUS) .... BCH Code
Bose-Chaudhuri-Hocquenghem [*Cyclic codes*] [*Telecommunications*] (MCD) .... BCH
Bose-Einstein [*Statistics*] (IAA) .... BE
Bose-Einstein Condensate .... BEC
Bose-Einstein Condensation [*Cryogenius*] [*Physics*] .... BEC
Bose-Einstein Statistics .... BES
Bosler Free Library, Carlisle, PA [*Library symbol*] [*Library of Congress*] (LCLS) .... PCarl
Bosnaair [*Yugoslavia*] [*ICAO designator*] (FAAC) .... BAA
Bosnia and Herzegovina [*Internet country code*] .... BA
Bosnia-Herzegovina (MILB) .... BiH
Bosnian Canadian Relief Association (AC) .... BCRA
Bosnian Serb Air Force (SAUS) .... BSAF
Bosobe-Boshwe [*Zaire*] [*ICAO location identifier*] (ICLI) .... FZBK
Bosondjo [*Zaire*] [*ICAO location identifier*] (ICLI) .... FZGB
Bosphorus Hava Yollari Turizm Ve Ticaret AS [*Turkey*] [*ICAO designator*] (FAAC) .... BSP
Bosque Alegre [*Argentina*] [*Seismograph station code, US Geological Survey*] [*Closed*] (SEIS) .... BOS
Bosque Apache National Wildlife Refuge (SAUS) .... BANWR
Bosque Farms, NM [*FM radio station call letters*] (RBYB) .... KEXT
Boss Operations Support Center (SAUO) .... BOSS
Bossangoa [*Central African Republic*] [*Airport symbol*] (AD) .... BSN
Bossangoa [*Central African Republic*] [*ICAO location identifier*] (ICLI) .... FEFS
Bossembele [*Central African Republic*] [*ICAO location identifier*] (ICLI) .... FEFL
Bossier Parish Library, Benton, LA [*Library symbol*] [*Library of Congress*] (LCLS) .... LBeB
Bost [*Afghanistan*] [*ICAO location identifier*] (ICLI) .... OABT
Boston [*Diocesan abbreviation*] [*Massachusetts*] (TOCD) .... BO
Boston [*Massachusetts*] [*Airport symbol*] .... BOS
Boston [*Massachusetts*] .... BOST
Boston [*Massachusetts*] [*ICAO location identifier*] (ICLI) .... KRBN
Boston Acoustics [*NASDAQ symbol*] (TTSB) .... BOSA
Boston Acoustics, Inc. [*NASDAQ symbol*] (NQ) .... BOSA
Boston Acoustics, Inc. [*Associated Press*] (SAG) .... BostAc
Boston Adult Literacy Fund (SAUO) .... BALF
Boston Air Defense Sector (SAUO) .... BOADS
Boston & Albany Railroad [*AAR code*] .... BA
Boston & Albany Railroad .... B & A
Boston & Albany Railroad .... B & ARR
Boston and Albany Railroad (SAUO) .... B&ARR
Boston & Fitchburg Railroad .... B & F
Boston & Maine Corp. .... B & M
Boston & Maine Corp. [*AAR code*] .... BM
Boston & Maine Railroad [*Later, Boston & Maine Corp.*] .... B & MRR
Boston and Maine Railroad (SAUO) .... BMR
Boston & Maine Transportation Railroad (SAUO) .... BMT
Boston Area Faculty Group on Public Issues (SAUO) .... BAFGOPI
Boston Area Nexrad Demonstration (SAUS) .... BAND
Boston Area Semiconductor Education [*Council*] (AAEL) .... BASE
Boston Assesment of Severe Aphasia [*Medicine*] (DMAA) .... BASA
Boston Athenaeum, Boston, MA [*OCLC symbol*] (OCLC) .... BAT
Boston Athenaeum, Boston, MA [*Library symbol*] [*Library of Congress*] (LCLS) .... MBAt
Boston Bancolp (SAUS) .... SBOS
Boston Bancorp. [*Associated Press*] (SAG) .... BostBc
Boston Bancorp [*Formerly, South Boston Savings Bank*] [*NASDAQ symbol*] (NQ) .... SBOS
Boston Bar Association, Boston, MA [*Library symbol*] [*Library of Congress*] (LCLS) .... MBBA
Boston Bar, BC [*FM radio station call letters*] CKGO-1
Boston Beer Co. [*Associated Press*] (SAG) .... BostBeer
Boston Beer Co. [*Associated Press*] (SAG) .... BstBeer
Boston Beer Co. [*NYSE symbol*] (SAG) .... SAM
Boston Beer 'A' [*NYSE symbol*] (TTSB) .... SAM
Boston Biomedica, Inc. [*NASDAQ symbol*] (SAG) .... BBII
Boston Biomedica, Inc. [*Associated Press*] (SAG) .... BostnBio
Boston Biomedical Library Consortium [*Library network*] .... BBLC
Boston Biomedical Research Institute [*Research center*] (RCD) .... BBRI
Boston Braves [*National Football League*] [*1932*] (NFLA) .... BBr
Boston Bruins Hockey Fan Club (EA) .... BBFC
Boston Bruins Hockey Fan Club (EA) .... BBHFC
Boston Celtics L.P. [*NYSE symbol*] (TTSB) .... BOS
Boston Celtics Ltd. [*Associated Press*] (SAG) .... BCelts
Boston Chicken, Inc. [*NASDAQ symbol*] (SAG) .... BOST
Boston Chicken, Inc. [*Associated Press*] (SAG) .... BostChk
Boston Collaborative Drug Surveillance Program (SAUO) .... BCDSP
Boston College [*Chestnut Hill, MA*] .... BC
Boston College (GAGS) .... Boston C
Boston College Centre for International Higher Education (SAUO) .... BCCIHE
Boston College, Chestnut Hill, MA [*OCLC symbol*] (OCLC) .... BXM
Boston College, Chestnut Hill, MA [*Library symbol*] [*Library of Congress*] (LCLS) .... MChB

Boston College Industrial and Commercial Law Review [*A publication*] (AAGC) .... BC Indus & Com L Rev
Boston College. Law Review [*A publication*] (DLA) .... Boston College L Rev
Boston College Law School, Newton, MA [*OCLC symbol*] (OCLC) .... BXL
Boston College Mathematics Institute [*Boston College*] [*Research center*] (RCD) .... BCMI
Boston College. Third World Law Journal [*A publication*] (DLA) .... BC Third World LJ
Boston College, Weston Observatory, Weston, MA [*Library symbol*] [*Library of Congress*] (LCLS) .... MChB-WO
Boston Communications Group, Inc. [*NASDAQ symbol*] (SAG) .... BCGI
Boston Communications Group, Inc. [*Associated Press*] (SAG) .... BostnCm
Boston Computer Exchange .... BCE
Boston Computer Exchange (CDE) .... BOCOEX
Boston Computer Society (EA) .... BCS
Boston Conservatory of Music .... BCM
Boston Consulting Group (ECON) .... BCG
Boston Consulting Group, Chicago, IL [*Library symbol*] [*Library of Congress*] (LCLS) .... ICBCG
Boston Development Center (SAUS) .... BDC
Boston Diagnostic Aphasia Examination .... BDAE
Boston Diagnostic Inventory of Basic Skills [*Speech and language therapy*] (DAVI) .... BDIBS
Boston Edison (SAUO) .... Bos Ed
Boston Edison 7.75% Dep Ptd [*NYSE symbol*] (TTSB) .... BSEPrB
Boston Edison 8.25% Dep Pfd [*NYSE symbol*] (TTSB) .... BSEPrA
Boston Edison Co. [*Associated Press*] (SAG) .... BosE
Boston Edison Co. [*Associated Press*] (SAG) .... BostEd
Boston Edison Co. [*NYSE symbol*] (SPSG) .... BSE
Boston Elevated Railway (SAUS) .... BE Railway
Boston Exchange Automated Communication Order-Routing Network (DFIT) .... BEACON
Boston, GA [*FM radio station call letters*] .... WTUF
Boston Grain and Flour Exchange (EA) .... BGFE
Boston Group (SAUO) .... BOSGRP
Boston Harbor Software, Inc. (GEOI) .... BHS
Boston Hebrew College (BJA) .... BHC
Boston Hospital for Women (SAUO) .... BHW
Boston Industrial Mission (SAUO) .... BIM
Boston International Choreography Competition .... BICC
Boston Irish .... BI
Boston Law Reporter [*A publication*] (DLA) .... Bost Law Rep
Boston Law Reporter [*A publication*] (DLA) .... Bost LR
Boston Life Sciences [*NASDAQ symbol*] (TTSB) .... BLSI
Boston Life Sciences, Inc. [*NASDAQ symbol*] (SAG) .... BLSI
Boston Life Sciences, Inc. [*Associated Press*] (SAG) .... BostLfSci
Boston Life Sciences Wrrt [*NASDAQ symbol*] (TTSB) .... BLSIW
Boston, MA [*Location identifier*] [*FAA*] (FAAL) .... DGU
Boston, MA [*Location identifier*] [*FAA*] (FAAL) .... LIP
Boston, MA [*Location identifier*] [*FAA*] (FAAL) .... LQN
Boston, MA [*Location identifier*] [*FAA*] (FAAL) .... MDC
Boston, MA [*Location identifier*] [*FAA*] (FAAL) .... NIK
Boston, MA [*Location identifier*] [*FAA*] (FAAL) .... NMF
Boston, MA [*Television station call letters*] .... WABU
Boston, MA [*FM radio station call letters*] .... WBCN
Boston, MA [*FM radio station call letters*] .... WBCS
Boston, MA [*FM radio station call letters*] .... WBMX
Boston, MA [*AM radio station call letters*] .... WBNW
Boston, MA [*FM radio station call letters*] .... WBUR
Boston, MA [*AM radio station call letters*] .... WBZ
Boston, MA [*Television station call letters*] (BROA) .... WBZ-DT
Boston, MA [*Television station call letters*] .... WBZ-TV
Boston, MA [*Television station call letters*] .... WCVB
Boston, MA [*Television station call letters*] (BROA) .... WCVB-DT
Boston, MA [*AM radio station call letters*] .... WEEI
Boston, MA [*FM radio station call letters*] .... WERS
Boston, MA [*AM radio station call letters*] .... WEZE
Boston, MA [*Television station call letters*] .... WFXT
Boston, MA [*Television station call letters*] (BROA) .... WFXT-DT
Boston, MA [*FM radio station call letters*] .... WGBH
Boston, MA [*Television station call letters*] (BROA) .... WGBH-DT
Boston, MA [*Television station call letters*] .... WGBH-TV
Boston, MA [*Television station call letters*] .... WGBX
Boston, MA [*Television station call letters*] (BROA) .... WGBX-DT
Boston, MA [*Television station call letters*] .... WHDH
Boston, MA [*Television station call letters*] (BROA) .... WHDH-DT
Boston, MA [*AM radio station call letters*] .... WILD
Boston, MA [*FM radio station call letters*] .... WJMN
Boston, MA [*AM radio station call letters*] .... WMEX
Boston, MA [*FM radio station call letters*] .... WMJX
Boston, MA [*AM radio station call letters*] (BROA) .... WNFT
Boston, MA [*AM radio station call letters*] (RBYB) .... WNRB
Boston, MA [*FM radio station call letters*] .... WODS
Boston, MA [*AM radio station call letters*] (BROA) .... WPZE-AM
Boston, MA [*FM radio station call letters*] .... WRBB
Boston, MA [*AM radio station call letters*] .... WRKO
Boston, MA [*AM radio station call letters*] .... WROL
Boston, MA [*Television station call letters*] .... WSBK
Boston, MA [*FM radio station call letters*] (BROA) .... WSJZ-FM
Boston, MA [*FM radio station call letters*] .... WUMB
Boston, MA [*FM radio station call letters*] .... WZLX
Boston, MA [*Location identifier*] [*FAA*] (FAAL) .... ZBW
Boston Metropolitan Transit Authority (SAUO) .... BMTA
Boston Museum of Fine Arts .... BMFA
Boston Museum of Science (SAUO) .... BMS
Boston Museum of Science, Boston, MA [*Library symbol*] [*Library of Congress*] (LCLS) .... MBN
Boston Naming Test [*Analysis of lexical processing disorders*] .... BNT
Boston, Nashua [*New Hampshire*] [*ICAO location identifier*] (ICLI) .... KZBW
Boston National Historic Sites Commission [*Government agency, discontinued, 1960*] .... BNHSC
Boston Naval Shipyard .... BNS
Boston Naval Shipyard .... BNSY
Boston Naval Shipyard (SAUO) .... BSNAVSHIPYD
Boston Navy Yard [*Later, Boston Naval Shipyard*] .... BNYD
Boston Neighborhood Hockey League (SAUO) .... BNHL
Boston, New York, Washington [*Proposed name for possible "super-city" formed by growth and mergers of other cities*] .... BOSNYWASH
Boston Opera Group (SAUO) .... BOG
Boston Ordnance District [*Military*] (AAG) .... BOD
Boston Patriots [*National Football League*] [*1960-70*] (NFLA) .... Bos
Boston Police Court. Reports [*A publication*] (DLA) .... Bos Pol Rep
Boston Police Court. Reports [*A publication*] (DLA) .... Bost Pol Rep
Boston Pops Orchestra (SAUO) .... BosPops
Boston Pops Orchestra (SAUO) .... BPO
Boston Private Bancorp [*Associated Press*] (SAG) .... BostPrv
Boston Private Bancorp [*NASDAQ symbol*] (SAG) .... BPBC
Boston Procurement District (SAUS) .... BOSTPDIS
Boston Programming Center (SAUS) .... BPC
Boston Properties [*NYSE symbol*] (SG) .... BXP
Boston Public Latin School (SAUS) .... BPLS
Boston Public Library (SAUO) .... BPL
Boston Public Library and Eastern Massachusetts Regional Public Library System, Boston, MA [*Library symbol*] [*Library of Congress*] (LCLS) .... MB
Boston Public Library Quarterly (journ.) (SAUS) .... BPLQ
Boston Quartermaster Depot (SAUO) .... BQD
Boston Records [*Record label*] .... Bo
Boston Red Sox [*Baseball team*] .... BOSOX
Boston Red Sox (SAUO) .... Bosox
Boston Redevelopment Authority .... BRA
Boston Redskins [*National Football League*] [*1933-36*] (NFLA) .... BRd
Boston Research Data Center (SAUS) .... BRDC
Boston Restaurant Assoc [*NASDAQ symbol*] (TTSB) .... BRAI
Boston Restaurant Assoc Wrrt [*NASDAQ symbol*] (TTSB) .... BRAIW
Boston Restaurant Associates [*Associated Press*] (SAG) .... BostRest
Boston Restaurant Associates [*Associated Press*] (SAG) .... BostRs
Boston Restaurant Associates [*NASDAQ symbol*] (SAG) .... BRAI
Boston Review [*A publication*] (BRI) .... Boston R
Boston School of Occupational Therapy [*Tufts University*] .... BSOT
Boston Scientific [*NYSE symbol*] (TTSB) .... BSX
Boston Scientific Corp. [*Associated Press*] (SAG) .... BostSc
Boston Scientific Corp. [*NYSE symbol*] (SPSG) .... BSX
Boston Shipping Association (EA) .... BSA
Boston Sickle Cell Center [*Boston City Hospital*] [*Research center*] (RCD) .... BSCC
Boston Society of Architects (SAUO) .... BSA
Boston Society of Civil Engineers (SAUO) .... BSCE
Boston Society of Natural History (SAUO) .... BSNH
Boston Society of Natural History, Proceedings (journ.) (SAUS) .... Boston Soc of Nat Hist Proc
Boston Society of Psychiatry and Neurology (SAUO) .... BSPN
Boston Software Works (SAUS) .... BSW
Boston Star Trek Association (EA) .... BSTA
Boston State College, Boston, MA [*Library symbol*] [*Library of Congress*] (LCLS) .... MBSC
Boston State College Library, Boston, MA [*OCLC symbol*] (OCLC) .... BST
Boston Stock Exchange .... B
Boston Stock Exchange [*Massachusetts*] .... BSE
Boston Survey Consultants (GEOI) .... BSC
Boston Symphony Orchestra .... BSO
Boston Tea Party II [*An association*] (EA) .... BTPII
Boston Tea Party II (SAUO) .... BTP II
Boston Technical Publishers (SAUS) .... Boston Tech
Boston Technology [*Associated Press*] (SAG) .... BostTech
Boston Technology [*NYSE symbol*] (SAG) .... BSN
Boston Technology [*NASDAQ symbol*] (SAG) .... BSTN
Boston Technology, Inc. [*Associated Press*] (SAG) .... BostTc
Boston Terminal Co. [*AAR code*] .... BTCO
Boston Terrier Club of America (EA) .... BTCA
Boston Test for Examining Aphasia [*Speech and language therapy*] (DAVI) .... BTEA
Boston Theological Institute (EA) .... BTI
Boston Theological Institute, Cambridge, MA [*OCLC symbol*] (OCLC) .... BTI
Boston Theological Institute, Learning Development Program, Boston, MA [*Library symbol*] [*Library of Congress*] (LCLS) .... MBTI
Boston Theological Institute Library [*Library network*] .... BTI
Boston to Washington [*Proposed name for possible "super-city" formed by growth and mergers between these two*] .... BOSWASH
Boston Transportation Authority (BARN) .... BTA
Boston University (GAGS) .... Boston U
Boston University [*Massachusetts*] .... BU
Boston University (SAUO) .... BU
Boston University, Boston, MA [*OCLC symbol*] (OCLC) .... BOS
Boston University, Boston, MA [*Library symbol*] [*Library of Congress*] (LCLS) .... MBU
Boston University. International Law Journal [*A publication*] (DLA) .... BU Int'l LJ
Boston University Marine Program [*Boston University*] [*Research center*] .... BUMP
Boston University Press (SAUO) .... BUP
Boston University, School of Education, Boston, MA [*Library symbol*] [*Library of Congress*] (LCLS) .... MBU-E
Boston University School of Law (DLA) .... BUSL

Boston University, School of Law, Boston, MA [Library symbol] [Library of Congress] (LCLS) .... MBU-L
Boston University School of Medicine (SAUO) .... BUSM
Boston University, School of Medicine, Boston, MA [OCLC symbol] (OCLC) .... MBU
Boston University, School of Medicine, Boston, MA [Library symbol] [Library of Congress] (LCLS) .... MBU-M
Boston University, School of Theology, Boston, MA [OCLC symbol] (OCLC) .... BZM
Boston University, School of Theology, Boston, MA [Library symbol] [Library of Congress] (LCLS) .... MBU-T
Boston University Studies in English (journ.) (SAUS) .... BUSE
Boston Women's Book Collective [An association] (EA) .... BWBC
Boston Women's Health Book Collective .... BWHBC
Boston Wool Trade Association (EA) .... BWTA
Boston Yacht Club (SAUO) .... BYC
Boston Yanks [National Football League] [1944-48] (NFLA) .... BYk
Bostonfed Bancorp, Inc. [AMEX symbol] (SAG) .... BFD
Bostonfed Bancorp, Inc. [Associated Press] (SAG) .... Bostnfd
Bostonian Society (EA) .... BS
Bostonian Society, Boston, MA [Library symbol] [Library of Congress] (LCLS) .... MBBS
Boston/Logan International [Massachusetts] [ICAO location identifier] (ICLI) .... KBOS
Boston-to-Washington Corridor .... BOWASH
Bostwick, GA [FM radio station call letters] .... WMOQ
Boswell Enterprise, Boswell, IN [Library symbol] [Library of Congress] (LCLS) .... InBosE
Boswell, GA [FM radio station call letters] (RBYB) .... WTHA-FM
Boswell's Reports, Scotch Court of Sessions [A publication] (DLA) .... Bosw
Bosworth's New York Superior Court Reports [A publication] (DLA) .... Bos
Bosworth's New York Superior Court Reports [A publication] (DLA) .... Bosw
Botanic (SAUS) .... Bot
Botanic Garden .... BG
Botanic Gardens Conservation Secretariat (SAUO) .... BGCS
Botanic Gardens Consortium (SAUO) .... BGC
Botanic Gardens of Adelaide and State Herbarium [Australia] .... BGASH
Botanical (ADWA) .... bot
Botanical (SAUS) .... Bot
Botanical .... BOTAN
Botanical Gardens Conservation Secretariat (GNE) .... BGCS
Botanical Gazette (SAUS) .... Bot Gaz
Botanical Journal of the Linnean Society (SAUO) .... Bot J Linn Soc
Botanical Magazine Tokyo (SAUS) .... Bot Mag Tokyo
Botanical Origin .... BO
Botanical Research and Herbarium Management System (SAUO) .... BRAHMS
Botanical Research Centre (SAUS) .... PPB
Botanical Review (SAUS) .... Bot Rev
Botanical Society (SAUO) .... BS
Botanical Society and Exchange Club of British Isles (SAUO) .... BSECBI
Botanical Society, London .... BSL
Botanical Society of America (EA) .... BSA
Botanical Society of Edinburgh (SAUO) .... BSE
Botanical Society of Japan (SAUO) .... BSJ
Botanical Society of Lund (SAUO) .... LBF
Botanical Society of Pennsylvania (SAUO) .... BSP
Botanical Society of the British Isles .... BSBI
Botanical Society of Western Pennsylvania (SAUO) .... BSWP
botanically (SAUS) .... botan
Botanico-Periodicum-Huntianum [Book title] .... B-P-H
Botany [or Botanist] .... BOT
Botany (BEE) .... Bot
Botany (WDAA) .... bot
Botany Bay National Park [Australia] .... BBNP
Botany Bay Regional Planning and Development Committee [Australia] .... BBRPDC
Botany School of Edinburgh (SAUO) .... BSE
Botany School of Edinburgh (SAUS) .... BSE
Botany-Genetics Library, McGill University, Montreal, Quebec [Library symbol] [National Library of Canada] (BIB) .... QMMBG
Bote aus Zion (BJA) .... BoZ
Boteka [Zaire] [ICAO location identifier] (ICLI) .... FZGT
Botetourt-Rockbridge Regional Library, Lexington, VA [Library symbol] [Library of Congress] (LCLS) ViLx
Both (DAVI) .... B
both (SAUS) .... bb
Both Bones [With reference to fractures] [Medicine] .... BB
Both Dates Included (or Inclusive) (SAUS) .... BDI
Both Dates Inclusive [Business term] .... BDI
Both Days Included (or Inclusive) (SAUS) .... BDI
Both Ends (RIMS) .... BE
Both Ends .... BENDS
Both Ends, All Time Saved [Shipping] .... BEATS
Both Eyes [Pharmacy] .... O²
Both Eyes (SAUS) .... Oy
Both Faces [Technical drawings] .... BF
Both Hands [Psychometrics] .... BH
Both Inclusive (RIMS) .... BI
Both Lower Extremities [Medicine] .... BLE
Both Lower Extremities [Neurology and orthopedics] (DAVI) .... BLE's
Both Lower Quadrants [Medicine] (MELL) .... BLQ
Both of This Parish .... BOTP
Both Sideband .... BSB
Both Sides [Technical drawings] .... BS
Both Upper Extremities [Medicine] (DMAA) .... BUE

Both Upper Extremities [Neurology and orthopedics] (DAVI) .... BUE's
Both Upper Quadrants [Medicine] (MELL) .... BUQ
Both Way Trunk .... BWT
Both Ways [Technical drawings] .... BW
Bother (ABBR) .... BTHR
Bothered (ABBR) .... BTHRD
Bothered about Dungeons & Dragons [Video game] .... BADD
Bothering (ABBR) .... BTHRG
Bothersome (ABBR) .... BTHRSM
Bothnia Experiment in Preparation for ERS-1 (SAUS) .... BEPERS
Both-to-Blame [Shipping] .... B/B
Bothway (SAUS) .... B/W
Botopasie [Surinam] [Airport symbol] (OAG) .... BTO
Botopasie [Surinam] [ICAO location identifier] (ICLI) .... SMBO
Botswana [Aircraft nationality and registration mark] (FAAC) A2
Botswana (SAUO) .... A 2
Botswana [Spaceflight Tracking and Data Network] [NASA] .... BOT
Botswana (SAUS) .... Bot
Botswana .... BOTS
Botswana (VRA) .... Botsw
Botswana [MARC country of publication code] [Library of Congress] (LCCP) .... bs
Botswana (MILB) .... Btwa
Botswana [ANSI two-letter standard code] (CNC) .... BW
Botswana [ANSI three-letter standard code] (CNC) .... BWA
Botswana [MARC geographic area code] [Library of Congress] (LCCP) .... f-bs-
Botswana [IYRU nationality code] (IYR) .... RB
Botswana Democratic Party [Political party] (PPW) .... BDP
Botswana Independence Party [Political party] (PPW) .... BIP
Botswana, Lesotho, Swaziland .... BLS
Botswana Liberal Party [Political party] (PPW) .... BLP
Botswana Ministry Agriculture (GEOI) .... BMA
Botswana National Airways .... BNA
Botswana National Front [Political party] (PPW) .... BNF
Botswana National Productivity Centre .... BNPC
Botswana Notes and Records [A publication] .... BNR
Botswana People's Party [Political party] (PPW) .... BPP
Botswana Progressive Union .... BPU
Botswana Protectorate Federal Party .... BPFP
Botswana Renewable Energy Technology Project [Ministry of Mineral Resources and Water Affairs in cooperation with United States Agency for International Development] [Research center] .... BRET
Bottega (VRA) .... btga
Bottineau, ND [FM radio station call letters] .... KBTO
Bottle .... BOT
Bottle (MCD) .... BT
Bottle .... BTL
Bottle (ADWA) .... btl
Bottle Cleaning/Charging Station .... BC/CS
Bottle Drainage .... BD
Bottle-Baby Meal [Airline notation] .... BBML
Bottled .... BOTLD
Bottled (ABBR) .... BTLD
Bottled in Bond [Wines and spirits] .... B/B
Bottled in Bond [Wines and spirits] .... BIB
Bottler .... BTTLR
Bottles (SAUS) .... Bots
Bottles per Minute (WGA) .... BPM
Bottling (ABBR) .... BTLG
Bottom .... B
Bottom .... BO
Bottom (VRA) .... bot
Bottom [Commonly used] (OPSA) .... BOT
Bottom (SAUS) .... Bot
Bottom [Commonly used] (OPSA) .... BOTTM
Bottom [Commonly used] (OPSA) .... BOTTOM
Bottom .... BTM
Bottom Ash (SAUS) .... BA
Bottom Bounce [SONAR propogation mode] [Navy] (NG) .... BB
Bottom Bounce/Omnidirectional Transmission [Navy] .... BB/ODT
Bottom Bounce/Track [Navy] .... BB/T
Bottom Center [Valve position] .... BC
Bottom Chord .... BC
Bottom Contour [Navy] [British] .... BC
Bottom Current (COE) .... BC
Bottom Dead Center [Engineering] .... BDC
Bottom Dead Center (WDAA) .... bdc
Bottom Dead Point .... BDP
Bottom Down (OA) .... BD
Bottom Dropped Out [Investment term] .... BDO
Bottom End Fitting (COE) .... BEF
Bottom Environmental Sensing System .... BESS
Bottom Face [Technical drawings] .... BF
Bottom Finding Pinger .... BFP
Bottom Fitting Insert (COE) .... BFI
Bottom Grille (OA) .... BG
Bottom Hole Assembly [Well drilling technology] .... BHA
Bottom Hole Circulating Temperature [Oil well borehole] .... BHCT
Bottom Hole Pressure [Oil well borehole] .... BHP
Bottom Hole Shut-In Pressure [Oil well borehole] .... BHSIP
Bottom Hole Static Temperature [Oil well borehole] .... BHST
Bottom Hole Temperature [Oil well borehole] .... BHT
Bottom Hole (Treating) Pressure [Oil well borehole] .... BH(T)P
Bottom Input/Output Unit (SAUS) .... BIO Unit
Bottom Layer [Technical drawings] .... BL
Bottom Lead Left (MSA) .... BTLL

Bottom Lead Right (MSA) .... BTLR
Bottom Left Side (MCD) .... BLS
Bottom Level .... BL
Bottom Lug Connection (SAUS) .... BLC
Bottom Ocean Monitor [*Marine science*] (MSC) .... BOM
Bottom of Active Fuel [*Nuclear energy*] (GFGA) .... BAF
Bottom of Conduit (NRCH) .... BOC
Bottom of Edge .... BOE
Bottom of Heart (SAUS) .... BOH
Bottom of Hole [*Geology*] .... BOH
Bottom of Lung (SAUS) .... BOL
Bottom of Range (AAEL) .... BOR
Bottom Of Stack (SAUS) .... BOS
Bottom of Stack-Register (SAUS) .... BOSR
Bottom Plane (MSA) .... BP
Bottom Pressure Fluctuation .... BPF
Bottom Pressure Recorder [*Marine science*] (OSRA) .... BPR
Bottom Pumparound [*Drilling technology*] .... BPA
Bottom Reflection [*Navy*] (NVT) .... BR
Bottom Reflection Active SONAR System .... BRASS
Bottom Refraction Acoustic Telemetry System (MCD) .... BRATS
Bottom Register (OA) .... BR
Bottom Right Side (MCD) .... BRS
Bottom Sediment [*Maps and charts*] .... BS
Bottom Sediment and Water [*in crude oil*] .... BSW
Bottom Settlings [*of crude oil in storage*] .... BS
Bottom Simulating Reflector [*Oceanography*] .... BSR
Bottom SONAR Marker .... BSM
Bottom Time (SAUS) .... BT
Bottom Topography Survey System [*Naval Oceanographic Office*] .... BOTOSS
Bottom Up .... BU
Bottom Value .... BOTVAL
Bottom Water Temperature [*Oceanography*] .... BWT
Bottom Withdrawal [*Tube*] .... BW
Bottomed (ABBR) .... BTMD
Bottomhung (SAUS) .... BH
Bottoming (MSA) .... BOTMG
Bottoming (ABBR) .... BTMG
Bottomless (ABBR) .... BTMLS
Bottom-Loading Transfer Cask [*Nuclear energy*] (NRCH) .... BLTC
Bottom-Mounted Impact Locations System [*Missile technology*] .... BMILS
Bottom-Mounted Instrumentation System (MCD) .... BOMIS
Bottom-Oriented Shrimp Harvester .... BOSH
Bottoms Recycle (ABAC) .... BR
Bottom-Up Greedy .... BUG
Bottom-Up Modular Programming .... BUMP
Bottom-Up Review .... BUR
Bott's Poor Law Cases [*1560-1833*] [*England*] [*A publication*] (DLA) .... Bott PL Cas
Bott's Poor Law Cases [*1560-1833*] [*England*] [*A publication*] (DLA) .... Bott's PL
Bott's Poor Law Cases [*1560-1833*] [*England*] [*A publication*] (DLA) .... BPL
Bott's Poor Law Cases [*1560-1833*] [*England*] [*A publication*] (DLA) .... BPL Cas
Bott's Poor Law Cases [*1560-1833*] [*England*] [*A publication*] (DLA) .... BPL Cases
Bott's Poor Law Settlement Cases [*A publication*] (DLA) .... Bott
Bott's Poor Law Settlement Cases [*A publication*] (DLA) .... Bott Poor Law Cas
Bott's Poor Law Settlement Cases [*A publication*] (DLA) .... Bott Set Cas
Bott's Poor Laws [*A publication*] (DLA) .... Bott PL
Bott's Poor Laws, by Const [*1560-1833*] [*A publication*] (DLA) .... Const
Bott's Poor Laws, by Court [*A publication*] (DLA) .... Court
Bottu [*France*] [*Research code symbol*] .... BO
Botulinal Toxin (ACAE) .... BTX
Botulinium Toxin (SAUS) .... BOTOX
Botulinum Neurotoxin .... BoNT
Botulinum Toxin .... BOT
Botulinum Toxin Therapy [*Medicine*] (MELL) .... BTT
Botulism [*Medicine*] (ABBR) .... BTLM
Botulism Toxoid Pentavalent [*Biochemistry*] (DAVI) .... ABCDE
Botwood Public Library, Botwood, NF, Canada [*Library symbol*] [*Library of Congress*] (LCLS) .... CaNfBot
Botwood Public Library, Newfoundland [*Library symbol*] [*National Library of Canada*] (NLC) .... NFBOT
Bou Saada [*Algeria*] [*ICAO location identifier*] (ICLI) .... DAAD
Bou Sfer [*Algeria*] [*ICAO location identifier*] (ICLI) .... DAOE
Bouake [*Ivory Coast*] [*Airport symbol*] (OAG) .... BYK
Bouake [*Ivory Coast*] [*ICAO location identifier*] (ICLI) .... DIBK
Bouar [*Central African Republic*] [*Airport symbol*] (AD) .... BOP
Bouar [*Central African Republic*] [*ICAO location identifier*] (ICLI) .... FEFO
Boublik, Alder, Chen, Kreglewski Equation [*Physical chemistry*] .... BACK
Bouchard's Node [*Medicine*] (MELL) .... BN
Boucher's Instituts au Droit Maritime [*A publication*] (DLA) .... Bouch Ins Dr Mar
Boufarik [*Algeria*] [*ICAO location identifier*] (ICLI) .... DAAK
Bouffees Delirantes [*An acute delusional disorder*] (DIPS) .... BD
Bougainville Air Service (SAUS) .... JX
Bougainville Copper Ltd. [*Australia*] .... BCL
Bougainville Copper Mine (SAUS) .... BCM
Bougainville Mining Limited (SAUO) .... BML
Bougainville Revolutionary Army [*Papua New Guinea*] [*Political party*] (EY) .... BRA
Bougair [*ICAO designator*] (AD) .... JX
Bought (WGA) .... BGHT
Bought (ROG) .... BGT
Bought (ADWA) .... bgt
Bought .... BO
Bought .... BOT
Bought .... BT
Bought (WDAA) .... Bt
Bought Book [*Tea trade*] (ROG) .... BB
Bought Ledger and Expenditure Analysis Package (PDAA) .... BLEAP
Bought Off (MCD) .... BO
Bougouni [*Mali*] [*ICAO location identifier*] (ICLI) .... GABG
Bouguer Corrected Free-Air Gradient [*Geophysics*] .... BCFAG
Bouillion-Yeast extract (SAUS) .... BY extract
Bouillon Filtre [*Bouillon Filtrate*] .... BF
Boulangerie, Confiserie, Tabac [*Bakery, Confectionary, and Tobacco*] [*Canadian Union*] .... BCT
Boulay-Paty. Droit Commun [*A publication*] (DLA) .... Boul P Dr Com
Boulder [*Wyoming*] [*Seismograph station code, US Geological Survey*] (SEIS) .... BDW
Boulder [*Maps and charts*] .... Bld
Boulder (WDAA) .... Bo
Boulder [*Colorado*] [*Seismograph station code, US Geological Survey*] [*Closed*] (SEIS) BO1
Boulder [*Colorado*] [*Seismograph station code, US Geological Survey*] [*Closed*] (SEIS) .... BOU
Boulder [*Colorado*] [*Airport symbol*] (OAG) .... WBU
Boulder Aeronomy Group (SAUO) .... BAG
Boulder Atmospheric Observatory [*Army*] (OSRA) .... BAO
Boulder City [*Nevada*] [*Seismograph station code, US Geological Survey*] [*Closed*] (SEIS) .... BCN
Boulder City Library, Boulder City, NV [*Library symbol*] [*Library of Congress*] (LCLS) .... NvBc
Boulder City, NV [*Location identifier*] [*FAA*] (FAAL) .... BLD
Boulder City, NV [*FM radio station call letters*] (RBYB) .... KQOL
Boulder City, NV [*FM radio station call letters*] (BROA) .... KSTJ-FM
Boulder, CO [*AM radio station call letters*] .... KBCO
Boulder, CO [*FM radio station call letters*] .... KBCO-FM
Boulder, CO [*AM radio station call letters*] (RBYB) .... KBVI
Boulder, CO [*FM radio station call letters*] .... KGNU
Boulder, CO [*FM radio station call letters*] .... KRKS
Boulder, CO [*Television station call letters*] .... KTVJ
Boulder, CO [*AM radio station call letters*] (BROA) .... KVCU
Boulder Dam [*Arizona*] [*Seismograph station code, US Geological Survey*] [*Closed*] (SEIS) .... BDA
Boulder Emergency Management Center (SAUS) .... BEMC
Boulder Junction, WI [*Location identifier*] [*FAA*] (FAAL) .... BDJ
Boulder Laboratory Macrosystem [*National Institute of Standards and Technology*] .... BOUMAC
Boulder Mountain Resources [*Vancouver Stock Exchange symbol*] .... BMR
Boulder Optimized Field Engineering Estimating Procedure (SAUS) .... BOFEEP
Boulder Public Library, Boulder, CO [*Library symbol*] [*Library of Congress*] (LCLS) .... CoB
Boulder Remote Data Collection and Control System (SAUS) .... BOULD
Boulder Science Resource Network (SAUS) .... BSRN
Boulder Upslope Cloud Observation Experiment (SAUS) .... BUCOE
Boulder Valley School, Boulder, CO [*Library symbol*] [*Library of Congress*] (LCLS) .... CoBVS
Boulder Valley School District, Boulder, CO [*OCLC symbol*] (OCLC) .... BOA
Boulders [*Quality of the bottom*] [*Maps and charts*] .... Blds
Bouldin's Reports [*119 Alabama*] [*A publication*] (DLA) .... Bould
Boulevard (WDAA) .... B
Boulevard (EY) .... BD
Boulevard (GEOI) .... Bl
Boulevard (EY) .... BLD
Boulevard (TBD) .... Blvd
Boulevard [*Postal Service standard*] (OPSA) .... BLVD
Boulevard (VRA) .... blvd
Boulevard (SAUS) .... Blvd
Boulevard (DD) .... boul
Boulevard (NTIO) .... Boul
Boulevard .... BOUL
Boulevard [*Commonly used*] (OPSA) .... BOULEVARD
Boulevard [*Commonly used*] (OPSA) .... BOULV
Boulevard (WDAA) .... BVD
Boulia [*Australia*] [*Airport symbol*] (OAG) .... BQL
Boulmer [*British*] [*ICAO location identifier*] (ICLI) .... EGQM
Boulnois' Reports [*Bengal*] [*A publication*] (DLA) .... Bouln
Boulnois' Reports [*Bengal*] [*A publication*] (DLA) .... Boulnois
Boulsa [*Burkina Faso*] [*ICAO location identifier*] (ICLI) .... DHEA
Boulton & Watt (WDAA) .... B&W
Bouna [*Ivory Coast*] [*Airport symbol*] (OAG) .... BQO
Bouna/Tehini [*Ivory Coast*] [*ICAO location identifier*] (ICLI) .... DIBN
Bouncing-Ball Generator .... BBG
Bound (ADA) .... B
Bound .... BD
Bound (WDMC) .... bd
bound (SAUS) .... bd
Bound (SAUS) .... Bnd
Bound (ADWA) .... bnd
Bound Brook Chronicle, Bound Brook, NJ [*Library symbol*] [*Library of Congress*] (LCLS) .... NjBbC
Bound Brook Memorial Library, Bound Brook, NJ [*Library symbol*] [*Library of Congress*] (LCLS) .... NjBb
Bound Exciton [*Electronics*] (AAEL) .... BE
Bound Hepatitis Antibody [*Medicine*] (DMAA) .... BHA
Bound in Boards .... BDS
Bound in Boards [*Book production*] (WDMC) .... bds
Bound, Ordered, Organized Knowledge (SAUS) .... BOOK
Bound Plasma Tryptophan (PDAA) .... BPT
Bound Seam (DNAB) .... BS
Bound Serum Iron [*Serology*] .... BSI
Bound to Stay Bound Books, Inc. .... BTSB

Bound With (ROG) ... BW
Boundary (WGA) ... BD
Boundary (AABC) ... BDRY
Boundary (ADWA) ... bdry
Boundary (ADWA) ... bdy
Boundary (WDAA) ... Bdy
Boundary (KSC) ... BDY
Boundary (AFM) ... BNDRY
Boundary (DNAB) ... BNDY
Boundary (SAUS) ... Bound
Boundary Address Block (SAUS) ... BAB
Boundary, AK [*Location identifier*] [*FAA*] (FAAL) ... BYA
Boundary Alignment (SAUS) ... BA
Boundary and Annexation Survey [*Bureau of the Census*] (GFGA) ... BAS
Boundary and Interior Layer (MCD) ... BAIL
Boundary Commission for England (WDAA) ... BCE
Boundary Condition (SAUS) ... BC
Boundary County Library District, Bonners Ferry, ID [*Library symbol*] [*Library of Congress*] (LCLS) ... IdBnf
Boundary Element (AAEL) ... BE
Boundary Element Analysis System [*Computational Mechanics Ltd.*] [*Software package*] (NCC) ... BEASY
Boundary Element Method (SAUS) ... BEM
Boundary Element Tape [*Computational Mechanics Ltd.*] [*Software package*] (NCC) ... BET
Boundary Estimate Message [*Aviation code*] ... EST
Boundary Facility (ARMP) ... BF
Boundary Function (SAUS) ... BF
Boundary Integral Equation (MCD) ... BIE
Boundary Intermediate System [*Computer science*] (TNIG) ... BIS
Boundary Layer (SAUS) ... BDL
Boundary Layer ... BL
Boundary Layer Acoustic Monitor (MCD) ... BLAM
Boundary Layer Aerodynamic Technology [*Auto racing*] ... BLAT
Boundary Layer Control ... BLC
Boundary Layer Control Outlet [*Mitsubishi*] [*Aerodynamics*] [*Automotive engineering*] ... BLCO
Boundary Layer Control System [*Fluid mechanics*] (IAA) ... BLCS
Boundary Layer Coolant (SAUS) ... BLC
Boundary Layer Experiment (ARMP) ... BLX
Boundary Layer Flow ... BLF
Boundary Layer Induction Stack Suppressor (CAAL) ... BLISS
Boundary Layer Instrument Package (SAUS) ... BLIP
Boundary Layer Instrumentation Package [*Meteorology*] ... BLIP
Boundary Layer Instrumentation System [*Meteorology*] ... BLIS
Boundary Layer Integral Matrix Procedure (KSC) ... BLIMP
Boundary Layer LIDAR System (MCD) ... BLLS
Boundary Layer Model (MCD) ... BLM
Boundary Layer Profile [*Meteorology*] ... BLP
Boundary Layer Profiler (SAUS) ... BLP
Boundary Layer Profiler System (SAUS) ... BLPS
Boundary Layer Radar (SAUS) ... BLR
Boundary Layer Sensing Group (SAUO) ... BLSG
Boundary Layer Separation ... BLS
Boundary Layer Thrust Vector Control (MCD) ... BLTVC
Boundary Layer Zone ... BLZ
Boundary Light (IAA) ... BOL
Boundary Light (SAUS) ... Bo L
Boundary Lights [*Aviation*] (DA) ... BO
Boundary Line (SAUS) ... BL
Boundary Mark (WDAA) ... Bdy M
Boundary Marker (MCD) ... BM
Boundary marker (SAUS) ... BP
Boundary Monument [*Control point*] [*Nautical charts*] ... Bdy Mon
Boundary Museum, Grand Forks, BC, Canada [*Library symbol*] [*Library of Congress*] (LCLS) ... CaBGFBM
Boundary Museum, Grand Forks, British Columbia [*Library symbol*] [*National Library of Canada*] (NLC) ... BGFBM
Boundary Node (SAUS) ... BN
Boundary Phase Plasticity (PDAA) ... BPP
Boundary Plasma Sheet ... BPS
Boundary Plate (WDAA) ... BP
Boundary Post (WDAA) ... BP
Boundary Profile (SAUS) ... BP
Boundary Representation [*Computer science*] (VERA) ... BR
Boundary Router [*Computer science*] (TNIG) ... BR
Boundary Scan Description Language (SAUS) ... BSDL
Boundary Scan Descriptor Language [*Computer science*] ... BSDI
Boundary Scan Register (CIST) ... BSR
Boundary Stimulus [*To light*] ... BS
Boundary Stone (WDAA) ... BS
Boundary Trap ... BT
Boundary Value (SAUS) ... BV
Boundary Value Analysis [*Computer program test*] ... BVA
Boundary Value Problem ... BVP
Boundary Waters Canoe Area [*Minnesota*] ... BWCA
Boundary Waters Treaty of 1909 (COE) ... BTW
Boundary-Layer Sub-Programme Data Centre [*GARP Atlantic Tropical Experiment*] (MSC) ... BSDC
Boundary-Scan Test [*John Fluke Manufacturing Co., Inc.*] ... BST
Boundary-Spanning Activity (PDAA) ... BSA
Bounded (SAUS) ... Bded
Bounded and Described as Follows (SAUS) ... B&DAF
Bounded Carry Inspection Adder (PDAA) ... BCIA
Bounded Cellular Space (PDAA) ... BCS
Bounded Double Silk (SAUS) ... BDS
Bounded Error Navigation System (MCD) ... BENS
Bounded Right Context (MHDI) ... BRC
Bounded-Input Bounded-Output [*Computer science*] (MHDB) ... BIBO
Bound/Free [*Ratio*] [*Biochemistry*] ... B/F
Boundiali [*Ivory Coast*] [*Airport symbol*] (OAG) ... BXI
Boundiali [*Ivory Coast*] [*ICAO location identifier*] (ICLI) ... DIBI
Boundji [*Congo*] [*Airport symbol*] (OAG) ... BOE
Boundji [*Congo*] [*ICAO location identifier*] (ICLI) ... FCOB
Boundless Corp. [*AMEX symbol*] (SG) ... BND
Bountiful Peak [*Utah*] [*Seismograph station code, US Geological Survey*] [*Closed*] (SEIS) ... BPU
Bountiful, UT [*Location identifier*] [*FAA*] (FAAL) ... BTF
Bountiful, UT [*FM radio station call letters*] (RBYB) ... KURR-FM
Bountiful, UT [*FM radio station call letters*] ... KUTQ
Bounty Information Service (EA) ... BIS
Bounty Land Warrant (SAUS) ... BLWt
Bouraq Indonesia Airlines (FEA) ... BIA
Bouraq Indonesia Airlines [*ICAO designator*] (AD) ... BO
Bouraq Indonesia Airlines PT [*ICAO designator*] (FAAC) ... BOU
Bourbon and Soda (ADWA) ... B and S
Bourbon Public Library, Bourbon, IN [*Library symbol*] [*Library of Congress*] (LCLS) ... InBou
Bourdeaux Resources Ltd. [*Vancouver Stock Exchange symbol*] ... BDX
Bourdin on the Land Tax [*A publication*] (DLA) ... Bourd LT
Bourdon Tube Element ... BTE
Bourem [*Mali*] [*ICAO location identifier*] (ICLI) ... GABR
Bourgas [*Bulgaria*] [*Airport symbol*] (OAG) ... BOJ
Bourg/Ceyreziat [*France*] [*ICAO location identifier*] (ICLI) ... LFHS
Bourgeois [*Typography*] (DGA) ... BOURG
Bourges [*France*] [*ICAO location identifier*] (ICLI) ... LFLD
Bourget College (SAUO) ... BC
Bourjois, Inc. (SAUO) ... BOJ
Bourke [*Australia*] [*Airport symbol*] (OAG) ... BRK
Bourke on the Indian Law of Limitations [*A publication*] (DLA) ... Bourke Lim
Bourke's Parliamentary Precedents [*1842-56*] [*England*] [*A publication*] (DLA) ... Bourke PP
Bourke's Reports, Calcutta High Court [*India*] [*A publication*] (DLA) ... Bourke
Bourn (Cambs) [*British*] [*ICAO location identifier*] (ICLI) ... EGSN
Bourne & Hollingsworth (WDAA) ... B&H
Bourne-Again Shell [*Unix*] (VERA) ... BASH
Bournemouth [*England*] [*Airport symbol*] (OAG) ... BOH
Bournemouth International Centre (SAUO) ... bic
Bournemouth Symphony Orchestra (WDAA) ... BSO
Bournemouth/Hurn [*British*] [*ICAO location identifier*] (ICLI) ... EGHH
Bourns Assist [*Medicine*] (DAVI) ... BA
Bourns, Inc. (SAUO) ... BOU
Boussinesq Viscosity Model (MCD) ... BVM
Bousso [*Chad*] [*ICAO location identifier*] (ICLI) ... FTTS
Bousso [*Chad*] [*Airport symbol*] (AD) ... OUT
Boutilimit [*Mauritania*] [*ICAO location identifier*] (ICLI) ... GQNB
Boutilimit [*Mauritania*] [*Airport symbol*] (AD) ... OTL
Boutique ... BTQ
Boutwell's Manual of the United States Tax System [*A publication*] (DLA) ... Bout Man
Bouvet Island [*ANSI two-letter standard code*] (CNC) ... BV
Bouvet Island [*MARC country of publication code*] [*Library of Congress*] (LCCP) ... bv
Bouvet Island [*ANSI three-letter standard code*] (CNC) ... BVT
Bouvet Island [*MARC geographic area code*] [*Library of Congress*] (LCCP) ... lsbv-
Bouvier's Institutes of American Law [*A publication*] (DLA) ... Bou Inst
Bouvier's Institutes of American Law [*A publication*] (DLA) ... Bouv Inst
Bouvier's Law Dictionary [*A publication*] (DLA) ... Bou Dic
Bouvier's Law Dictionary [*A publication*] (DLA) ... Bouv
Bouvier's Law Dictionary [*A publication*] (DLA) ... Bouvier
Bouvier's Law Dictionary [*A publication*] (DLA) ... Bouv Law Dict
Bouvier's Law Dictionary [*A publication*] (DLA) ... Bouv L Dict
Bouwcentrum International Education (SAUO) ... BIE
Bouygues Offshore ADS [*NYSE symbol*] (SG) ... BWG
Bouygues Offshore SA [*Associated Press*] (SAG) ... Bouygs
Bouygues Offshore SA [*NYSE symbol*] (SAG) ... BWG
Bovey Public Library, Bovey, MN [*Library symbol*] [*Library of Congress*] (LCLS) ... MnBov
Bovie-Assisted Uvulopalatoplasty (DMAA) ... BAUP
Bovill's Patent Cases [*A publication*] (DLA) ... Bov Pat Ca
Bovine Albumin [*Physiology*] (MAE) ... BA
Bovine Albumin in Phosphate Buffer [*Medicine*] (DMAA) ... BAP
Bovine Albumin Phosphate Saline [*Physiology*] ... BAPS
Bovine Alimentary Papilloma Virus [*Medicine*] (DMAA) ... BAPV
Bovine Aortic Endothelium ... BAE
Bovine Artery Endothelial Cell [*Cytology*] ... BAEC
Bovine Beta-Lactoglobulin [*Biochemistry*] ... BBLG
Bovine Capillary Endothelial [*Cytology*] ... BCE
Bovine Carbonic Anhydrase [*An enzyme*] ... BCA
Bovine Chymotrypsin (DMAA) ... BCtr
Bovine Chymotrypsinogen (DB) ... BCtg
Bovine Coronavirus [*Biochemistry*] ... BCV
Bovine Cutaneous Papilloma Virus [*Medicine*] (DMAA) ... BCPV
Bovine Derived Growth Factor [*Biochemistry*] ... BDGF
Bovine Embroyonic Spleen Cells [*Medicine*] (DMAA) ... BESP
Bovine Embryo Skeletal Muscle ... BESM
Bovine Embryonic Kidney Cells [*Medicine*] (DMAA) ... BEK
Bovine Embryonic Lung [*Medicine*] (DMAA) ... BEL
Bovine Enteritis [*Medicine*] (MAE) ... BE
Bovine Enterovirus ... BEV

Bovine Feces Virus [*Veterinary medicine*] (DAVI) .... BFV
Bovine Follicle-Stimulating Hormone [*Biochemistry*] .... BFSH
Bovine Follicular Fluid .... BFF
Bovine Gamma Globulin [*Immunology*] .... BGG
Bovine Growth Hormone [*Endocrinology*] .... BGH
Bovine Hemoglobin [*Biochemistry*] (DB) .... BHb
Bovine Herpesvirus .... BHV
Bovine Immunodeficiency Virus .... BIV
Bovine Immunodeficiency-Like Virus [*Immunology*] (DAVI) .... BIV
Bovine Lactoferrin (DB) .... BLF
Bovine Leukemia Virus .... BLV
Bovine Lumpy Skin Disease [*Medicine*] (DMAA) .... BLSD
Bovine Lung Lipids [*Biochemistry*] .... BLL
Bovine Milk Lysozyme [*Biochemistry*] (OA) .... BML
Bovine Mucosal Disease [*Medicine*] (DB) .... BMD
Bovine Neutrophil Beta-Defensin [*Biochemistry*] .... BNBD
Bovine Pancreatic Enzyme (DB) .... BPE
Bovine Pancreatic Polypeptide .... BPP
Bovine Pancreatic Trypsin Inhibitor [*Biochemistry*] .... BPTI
Bovine Papillomavirus [*Veterinary medicine*] .... BPV
Bovine Papillomavirus Vaccine [*Veterinary medicine*] .... BPV
Bovine Papular Stomatitis (DB) .... BPS
Bovine Paragenital Papilloma Virus [*Medicine*] (DMAA) .... BPPV
Bovine Parathyroid Hormone [*Endocrinology*] .... bPTH
Bovine Pituitary Extract .... BPE
Bovine Plasma Albumin .... BPA
Bovine Protein Kinase C [*An enzyme*] .... bPKC
Bovine Pulmonary Artery Endothelium Cell [*Cell line*] .... BPEC
Bovine Red Blood Cell [*Hematology*] (MAE) .... BRBC
Bovine Research Center at Cornell [*Cornell University*] [*Research center*] (RCD) .... BRCC
Bovine Rhodopsin [*Physiology*] .... bRHOD
Bovine Seminal Vesical Microsomal (DB) .... BSVM
Bovine Serum Albumin [*Immunology*] .... BSA
Bovine Serum Amine Oxidase [*An enzyme*] .... BSAO
Bovine Somatotropin [*Endocrinology*] .... BST
Bovine Spinal Cord Protein [*Medicine*] (DMAA) .... BSCP
Bovine Spongiform Encephalopathy [*Veterinary medicine*] .... BSE
Bovine Substance K .... bSK
Bovine Testicle (SAUS) .... BT
Bovine Thymus Extract (DB) .... BTE
Bovine Thyroid-Stimulating Hormone [*Endocrinology*] .... BTSH
Bovine Thyrotropin [*Endocrinology*] (DAVI) .... BTSH
Bovine Trophoblast Protein [*Biochemistry*] .... BTP
Bovine Trypsin (DB) .... BTr
Bovine Trypsinogen (DB) .... BTg
Bovine Vaginitis Virus [*Veterinary medicine*] (MAE) .... BVV
Bovine Viral Diarrhea .... BVD
Bovine Viral Diarrhea Virus .... BVDV
bovinologist (SAUS) .... bovinol
bovinology (SAUS) .... bovinol
Bow and Stern Thruster [*of a ship*] (DS) .... BS
Bow Buoyancy .... BBYCY
Bow Designation Light (IAA) .... BDLT
Bow Designation Light (SAUS) .... bd lt
Bow Diving .... BDVG
Bow Door .... BDO
Bow Island Public Library, Alberta [*Library symbol*] [*National Library of Canada*] (NLC) .... ABI
Bow Island Public Library, Bow Island, AB, Canada [*Library symbol*] [*Library of Congress*] (LCLS) .... CaABi
Bow Light .... BWLT
Bow Light (SAUS) .... BW LT
Bow Plane .... BPLA
Bow Shock [*Astrophysics*] .... BS
Bow Thruster [*of a ship*] (DS) .... BT
Bow Tie Manufacturers Association (EA) .... BTMA
Bow Valley Naturalists (AC) .... BVN
Bow Valley Resource Services Ltd. [*Toronto Stock Exchange symbol*] .... BOW
Bowater Faculty of Business [*Deakin University*] [*Australia*] .... BFB
Bowater, Inc. [*NYSE symbol*] (SPSG) .... BOW
Bowater, Inc. [*Associated Press*] (SAG) .... Bowat
Bowater, Inc. [*Associated Press*] (SAG) .... Bowatr
Bowater Inc. Dep'B'7%'PRIDES' [*NYSE symbol*] (TTSB) .... BOWPrB
Bowater Inc.'C'8.40% Dep Pfd [*NYSE symbol*] (TTSB) .... BOWPrC
Bowater Paper Corp. Ltd. (SAUO) .... B
Bowater Tutt Industries Pty Ltd. (SAUS) .... Tutts
Bowden Pioneer Museum, Alberta [*Library symbol*] [*National Library of Canada*] (BIB) .... ABOM
Bowden Public Library, Alberta [*Library symbol*] [*National Library of Canada*] (NLC) .... ABOW
Bowdock [*Navy symbol*] .... YBD
Bowdoin College (SAUO) .... BC
Bowdoin College, Brunswick, ME [*OCLC symbol*] (OCLC) .... BBH
Bowdoin College, Brunswick, ME [*Library symbol*] [*Library of Congress*] (LCLS) .... MeB
Bowdoin National Wildlife Refuge (SAUS) .... BNWL
Bowdoin National Wildlife Refuge (SAUS) .... BNWR
Bowdon College, Bowdon, GA [*Library symbol*] [*Library of Congress*] [*Obsolete*] (LCLS) .... GBowdC
Bowdon, GA [*FM radio station call letters*] (BROA) .... WYAI-FM
Bowdon Railway & Transportation (IIA) .... BR & T
Bowdon Railway Co. [*AAR code*] .... BODN
Bowel [*Medicine*] .... BO
Bowel Care of Choice [*Medicine*] (DMAA) .... BCOC

Bowel Impaction [*Gastroenterology*] (DAVI) .... BI
Bowel Incontinence [*Medicine*] (MELL) .... BI
Bowel Injection [*Medicine*] .... BI
Bowel Injury [*Medicine*] (MELL) .... BI
Bowel Movement [*Medicine*] .... BM
Bowel Obstruction [*Medicine*] .... BO
Bowel or Bladder [*Medicine*] (DAVI) .... BB
Bowel Signs Active (SAUS) .... BSA
Bowel Sound Active (SAUS) .... BSA
Bowel Sounds [*Medicine*] .... BS
Bowel Sounds Audible [*Medicine*] (MELL) .... BSA
Bowel Sounds Normal [*Medicine*] .... BSN
Bowel Sounds Normal and Active [*Medicine*] (AAMN) .... BSNA
Bowel Sounds Regular [*Medicine*] (MELL) .... BSR
Bowels [*Medicine*] (BARN) .... B
Bowels Not Open [*Medicine*] .... BNO
Bowels Opened [*Medicine*] .... BO
Bowels Opened Regularly [*Medicine*] (MAE) .... BOR
Bowen [*Australia*] [*Airport symbol*] [*Obsolete*] (OAG) .... ZBO
Bowen Island, BC [*Television station call letters*] (RBYB) CHAN-2
Bowen Island Public Library, British Columbia [*Library symbol*] [*National Library of Canada*] (BIB) .... BBI
Bowen Ratio Energy Balance System (SAUS) .... BREBS
Bowen-McLaughlin-York (SAUO) .... BMY
Bowenoid Papulosis [*Medicine*] (MELL) .... BP
Bowen's Carcinoma In Situ [*Medicine*] (MELL) .... BCIS
Bowen's Political Economy [*A publication*] (DLA) .... Bowen Pol Econ
Bowes Lyon Resources Ltd. [*Vancouver Stock Exchange symbol*] .... BWY
Bowhunters of America (EA) .... BWC
Bowhunters Who Care (EA) .... BWC
Bowie State College, Bowie, MD [*Library symbol*] [*Library of Congress*] (LCLS) .... MdBo
Bowie State College Library, Bowie, MD [*OCLC symbol*] (OCLC) .... BCM
Bowie State University (GAGS) .... Bowie St U
Bowie, TX [*Location identifier*] [*FAA*] (FAAL) .... GMZ
Bowie, TX [*AM radio station call letters*] .... KRJT
Bowie, TX [*FM radio station call letters*] .... KRJT-FM
Bowing of Tibia [*Medicine*] (MELL) .... BOT
Bowker Annual (journ.) (SAUS) .... BA
Bowker Out of Print Books [*Source file*] [*UTLAS symbol*] .... BWK
Bowker's International Serials Database [*R. R. Bowker Co.*] [*Information service or system*] (IID) .... BISD
Bowker's Publisher Authority Database [*R. R. Bowker Co.*] [*Information service or system*] (CRD) .... BPAD
Bowl America CI'A' [*AMEX symbol*] (SG) .... BWLA
Bowl America, Inc. [*Associated Press*] (SAG) .... BowlA
Bowl America, Inc. [*AMEX symbol*] (SPSG) .... BWL
Bowl Championship Series [*Football*] .... BCS
Bowl Vent [*Automotive engineering*] .... BV
Bowled [*Cricket*] .... B
Bowled (WA) .... b
Bowled Out .... B
Bowler and Bowers' United States Comptroller's Decisions [*2, 3*] [*A publication*] (DLA) .... B & B
Bowler and Bowers' United States Comptroller's Decisions [*2, 3*] [*A publication*] (DLA) .... Bow
Bowler's London Session Records [*1605-85*] [*A publication*] (DLA) .... Bow
Bowler's Thumb [*Medicine*] (MELL) .... BT
Bowles Engineering Corp. .... BEC
Bowles Engineering Corporation (SAUO) .... BEC
Bowles on Libel [*A publication*] (DLA) .... Bowl Lib
Bowlin Outdoor Advertising & Travel Ctr., Inc. [*NASDAQ symbol*] (SAG) .... BWLN
Bowlin Outdoor Advertising & Travel Ctr., Inc. [*Associated Press*] (SAG) .... BwlOtdr
Bowlin Outdoor Adv/Travel [*AMEX symbol*] (SG) .... BWN
Bowling .... BOWL
Bowling Apparel Manufacturers of America (EA) .... BAM
Bowling Centers Association of Florida (SRA) .... BCAF
Bowling Centers Association of Michigan (SRA) .... BCAM
Bowling Club (SAUO) .... BC
Bowling Club [*Generic term*] (WGA) .... BC
Bowling Green (SAUS) .... BG
Bowling Green [*Ohio*] [*Seismograph station code, US Geological Survey*] (SEIS) .... BGO
Bowling Green [*Kentucky*] [*Airport symbol*] (AD) .... BWG
Bowling Green College of Commerce (SAUO) .... BGCC
Bowling Green Elementary School, East Meadow, NY [*Library symbol*] [*Library of Congress*] (LCLS) .... NEmBGE
Bowling Green Elementary School, Westbury, NY [*Library symbol*] [*Library of Congress*] (LCLS) .... NWeBGE
Bowling Green Junior High School, Bowling Green, OH [*Library symbol*] [*Library of Congress*] (LCLS) .... OBgJH
Bowling Green, KY [*Location identifier*] [*FAA*] (FAAL) .... BWG
Bowling Green, KY [*AM radio station call letters*] .... WBGN
Bowling Green, KY [*Television station call letters*] .... WBKO
Bowling Green, KY [*FM radio station call letters*] .... WBVR
Bowling Green, KY [*FM radio station call letters*] .... WCVK
Bowling Green, KY [*FM radio station call letters*] .... WDNS
Bowling Green, KY [*AM radio station call letters*] .... WKCT
Bowling Green, KY [*Television station call letters*] .... WKGB
Bowling Green, KY [*Television station call letters*] .... WKNT
Bowling Green, KY [*FM radio station call letters*] .... WKYU
Bowling Green, KY [*Television station call letters*] .... WKYU-TV
Bowling Green, KY [*AM radio station call letters*] .... WLBJ

Bowling Green, KY [*FM radio station call letters*] ..... WWHR
Bowling Green, MO [*AM radio station call letters*] ..... KPCR
Bowling Green, MO [*FM radio station call letters*] ..... KPCR-FM
Bowling Green, OH [*FM radio station call letters*] ..... WBGU
Bowling Green, OH [*Television station call letters*] ..... WBGU-TV
Bowling Green, OH [*AM radio station call letters*] ..... WJYM
Bowling Green, OH [*FM radio station call letters*] ..... WRQN
Bowling Green Senior High School, Bowling Green, OH [*Library symbol*] [*Library of Congress*] (LCLS) ..... OBgSH
Bowling Green State University [*Ohio*] ..... BGSU
Bowling Green State University (GAGS) ..... Bowl Gr St U
Bowling Green State University, Bowling Green, OH [*OCLC symbol*] (OCLC) ..... BGU
Bowling Green State University, Bowling Green, OH [*Library symbol*] [*Library of Congress*] (LCLS) ..... OBgU
Bowling Green State University, Center for Archival Collections, Bowling Green, OH [*Library symbol*] [*Library of Congress*] (LCLS) ..... OBgU-C
Bowling Green, VA [*Location identifier*] [*FAA*] (FAAL) ..... APH
Bowling Green, VA [*FM radio station call letters*] (BROA) ..... WWUZ-FM
Bowling League of Ireland (EAIO) ..... BLI
Bowling Proprietors' Association of America (EA) ..... BPAA
Bowling Proprietors' Association of America - Duckpin Activities Department [*Defunct*] (EA) ..... BPAA-DAD
Bowling Writers Association of America (EA) ..... BWAA
Bowls Club (SAUO) ..... BC
Bowman [*South Carolina*] [*Seismograph station code, US Geological Survey*] (SEIS) ..... BOW
Bowman Aviation, Inc. [*ICAO designator*] (FAAC) ..... BMN
Bowman Gray School of Medicine (SAUO) ..... BGSM
Bowman Gray School of Medicine, Winston-Salem, NC [*OCLC symbol*] (OCLC) ..... NBG
Bowman, ND [*Location identifier*] [*FAA*] (FAAL) ..... BOD
Bowman, ND [*AM radio station call letters*] ..... KPOK
Bowman, SC [*FM radio station call letters*] ..... WACJ
Bowman, SC [*FM radio station call letters*] (BROA) ..... WSPX-FM
Bowman-Birk Soybean Inhibitor [*Medicine*] (DMAA) ..... BBI
Bowman-Birk Trypsin Inhibitor (DB) ..... BBI
Bowman's Capsule (MAE) ..... BC
Bowmanville Museum, Ontario [*Library symbol*] [*National Library of Canada*] (BIB) ..... OBOM
Bowmar Canada Ltd., Ottawa, ON, Canada [*Library symbol*] [*Library of Congress*] (LCLS) ..... CaOOBC
Bowmar Canada Ltd., Ottawa, Ontario [*Library symbol*] [*National Library of Canada*] (NLC) ..... OOBC
Bowmar Instr $3.00 Cv Pfd [*AMEX symbol*] (TTSB) ..... BOMPr
Bowmar Instrument Corp. [*AMEX symbol*] (SPSG) ..... BOM
Bowmar Instrument Corp. [*Associated Press*] (SAG) ..... Bowmr
Bowne & Co. [*NYSE symbol*] (SG) ..... BNE
Bowne & Co., Inc. [*AMEX symbol*] (SPSG) ..... BNE
Bowne & Co., Inc. [*Associated Press*] (SAG) ..... Bowne
Bowne Information Systems (NITA) ..... BIS
Bowns Practice (or Precedents) in Chancery (journ.) (SAUS) ..... Prax
Bowstead on Agency [*1896-1951*] [*A publication*] (DLA) ..... Bowstead
Bowstring ..... BWSTRN
Bowstring Sign (MELL) ..... BSS
Bowstring Test (MELL) ..... BST
Bowtex Energy (Canada) Corp. [*Toronto Stock Exchange symbol*] ..... BXE
Bowyer. Commentaries on the Constitutional Law of England [*2nd ed.*] [*1846*] [*A publication*] (DLA) ..... Bow Cons Law
Bowyer. Commentaries on Universal Public Law [*1854*] [*A publication*] (DLA) ..... Bow Com
Bowyer. Commentaries on Universal Public Law [*1854*] [*A publication*] (DLA) ..... Bow Pub Law
Bowyer. Introduction to the Study and Use of the Civil Law [*1874*] [*A publication*] (DLA) ..... Bow Int
Bowyer's Modern Civil Law [*A publication*] (DLA) ..... Bow Civ Law
Bowyer's Modern Civil Law [*A publication*] (DLA) ..... Bowyer Mod Civil Law
Box ..... BX
Box (VRA) ..... bx
Box Bark Strips [*Construction*] (BARN) ..... BBS
Box Container [*Shipping*] (DS) ..... bx
Box Core [*Marine geology*] ..... BC
Box Culvert Association [*British*] (DBA) ..... BCA
Box Diffusion [*Oceanography*] ..... BD
Box Energy 'B' [*NASDAQ symbol*] (TTSB) ..... BOXXB
Box Energy Corp. [*Associated Press*] (SAG) ..... BoxEn
Box Energy Corp. [*NASDAQ symbol*] (SAG) ..... BOXX
Box Energy'A' [*NASDAQ symbol*] (TTSB) ..... BOXXA
Box Express Messenger (SAUS) ..... BXM
Box External Data ..... BED
Box Fin ..... BXF
Box Hill Systems [*NYSE symbol*] (SG) ..... BXH
Box Keel (SAUS) ..... BxK
Box Manufacturers Association of Greater New York [*Defunct*] (EA) ..... BMAGNY
Box of Bits (SAUS) ..... BOB
Box Office [*Theatrical slang*] ..... BO
Box Office Management International [*An association*] (EA) ..... BOMI
Box Project (EA) ..... BP
Box Van [*Shipping*] (DCTA) ..... B
Boxboard (DGA) ..... BXBD
Boxboard Research and Development Association (EA) ..... BRDA
Boxcar Detector (MSA) ..... BXDT
Boxcar Doppler Filter (PDAA) ..... BDF
Boxed (SAUS) ..... Box
Boxed (SAUS) ..... Bxd
Boxed ..... BXD
Boxed (ADWA) ..... bxd
Boxed Edit [*Control*] [*Computer science*] (PCM) ..... BEDIT
Boxed or Tanked ..... BX/TK
Boxer's Elbow [*Medicine*] (MELL) ..... BE
Boxes (SAUS) ..... Bxs
Boxes, Barrels, or Packages [*Freight*] ..... BBP
Boxes or Crates [*Freight*] ..... BC
Boxes Per Day (SAUS) ..... BPD
Boxford, MA [*FM radio station call letters*] ..... WBMT
Boxing Authority of New South Wales [*Australia*] ..... BANSW
Boxing Club (SAUO) ..... BC
Boxing Writers Association ..... BWA
Box-Office Computer System ..... BOCS
Box-Office Reservation and Information Service ..... BORIS
Boxwood (VRA) ..... bxwd
Boy Clerks Association [*A union*] [*British*] ..... BCA
Boy Entrant [*British military*] (DMA) ..... B/E
Boy Savior Youth Movement [*Defunct*] (EA) ..... BSYM
Boy Scout Movement (SAUO) ..... BSM
Boy Scouts (SAUO) ..... BS
Boy Scouts ..... BS
Boy Scouts (SAUO) ..... BSc
Boy Scouts in Western Europe (SAUO) ..... BSWE
Boy Scouts International Bureau ..... BSIB
Boy Scouts of America (EA) ..... BSA
Boy Scouts of America Alumni Family [*Defunct*] (EA) ..... BSAAF
Boy Scouts of the Philippines (SAUO) ..... BSP
Boy Scouts World Bureau [*Later, WSB*] ..... BSWB
Boyan Action Module (SAUS) ..... BAM
Boyan Script (SAUS) ..... BSC
Boyce and Hart Fan Club (EA) ..... BHFC
Boyce, LA [*FM radio station call letters*] ..... KBCE
Boyce Thompson Institute [*Cornell University*] ..... BTI
Boyce Thompson Institute for Plant Research (SAUO) ..... BTI
Boyce Thompson Institute for Plant Research (SAUS) ..... BTIPR
Boyce Thompson Institute for Plant Research, Yonkers, NY [*Library symbol*] [*Library of Congress*] (LCLS) ..... NYBT
Boyce-Codd Normal Form (RALS) ..... BCNF
Boyce's Delaware Supreme Court Reports [*1909-19*] [*A publication*] (DLA) ..... Boyce
Boyce's Practice in the United States Courts [*A publication*] (DLA) ..... Boyce US Pr
Boyce-Thompson Institute for Plant Research (SAUO) ..... BTIPR
Boycott [*Legal shorthand*] (LWAP) ..... BOY
Boycott Burger King Coalition [*Defunct*] (EA) ..... BBKC
Boycott McDonald's Coalition (EA) ..... BMC
Boyd Bros.Transport'n [*NASDAQ symbol*] (TTSB) ..... BOYD
Boyd Brothers Transportation, Inc. [*NASDAQ symbol*] (SAG) ..... BOYD
Boyd Brothers Transportation, Inc. [*Associated Press*] (SAG) ..... BoydBros
Boyd Gaming [*NYSE symbol*] (SPSG) ..... BYD
Boyd Gaming Corp. [*Associated Press*] (SAG) ..... BoydGm
Boyd. Justice of the Peace [*A publication*] (DLA) ..... Boyd Jus
Boyd. Merchant Shipping Laws [*1876*] [*A publication*] (DLA) ..... Boyd Sh
Boyd's Admiralty Law [*Ireland*] [*A publication*] (DLA) ..... Boyd Adm
Boyds Collection [*NYSE symbol*] (SG) ..... FOR
Boyds Wheels [*NASDAQ symbol*] (TTSB) ..... BYDS
Boyds Wheels, Inc. [*NASDAQ symbol*] (SAG) ..... BYDS
Boyds Wheels, Inc. [*Associated Press*] (SAG) ..... BydWhls
Boyd-Stearns [*Syndrome*] [*Medicine*] (DB) ..... BS
Boyertown, PA [*FM radio station call letters*] ..... WBYN
Boyfriend [*Slang*] ..... BF
Boykin Lodging Co. [*NYSE symbol*] (SAG) ..... BOY
Boykin Lodging Co. [*Associated Press*] (SAG) ..... BoykinL
Boyle. Charities [*1837*] [*A publication*] (DLA) ..... Boy Char
Boyle. Charities [*1837*] [*A publication*] (DLA) ..... Boyle Char
Boyle Public Library, Alberta [*Library symbol*] [*National Library of Canada*] (NLC) ..... ABO
Boyle Public Library, Boyle, AB, Canada [*Library symbol*] [*Library of Congress*] (LCLS) ..... CaABoy
Boyle-Conway Solution [*Neurophysiology*] ..... BC
Boyle's Precis of an Action at Common Law [*A publication*] (DLA) ..... Boyle Act
Boyne City, MI [*FM radio station call letters*] ..... WBCM
Boyne City Public Library (SAUS) ..... MiBoy
Boyne City Public Library, Boyne City, MI [*Library symbol*] [*Library of Congress*] (LCLS) ..... MiBoy
Boyne City Railroad Co. [*AAR code*] ..... BCRR
Boyne Falls, MI [*Location identifier*] [*FAA*] (FAAL) ..... BFA
Boyne Falls Public Library (SAUS) ..... MiBoyf
Boyne Falls Public Library, Boyne Falls, MI [*Library symbol*] [*Library of Congress*] (LCLS) ..... MiBoyf
Boyne Regional Library, Carman, Manitoba [*Library symbol*] [*National Library of Canada*] (NLC) ..... MCB
Boyne Regional Library, Carman, MB, Canada [*Library symbol*] [*Library of Congress*] (LCLS) ..... CaMCB
Boynton Beach, FL [*AM radio station call letters*] (RBYB) ..... WJNA-AM
Boynton Beach, FL [*FM radio station call letters*] ..... WRMB
Boynton Beach, FL [*AM radio station call letters*] ..... WYFX
Boys and Girls Aid Society (SAUO) ..... BGAS
Boys' and Girls' Brigades of America (EA) ..... BGBA
Boys and Girls International Floor Hockey (EA) ..... BGIFH
Boys and Young Men's Apparel Manufacturers Association [*Defunct*] (EA) ..... BAMA
[*The*] **Boy's Book of Verse** [*A publication*] ..... BBV
Boys' Brigade [*British*] ..... BB
Boys Club Professional Association [*Later, ABGCP*] (EA) ..... BCPA

Boys' Club, St. John's, Newfoundland [Library symbol] [National Library of Canada] (NLC) .... NFSBC
Boy's Club, St. John's, NF, Canada [Library symbol] [Library of Congress] (LCLS) .... CaNfSBC
Boys' Clubs of America (EA) .... BCA
Boys High School (SAUS) .... BHS
Boys Hope (EA) .... BH
Boy's Life Brigade .... BLB
Boys of Woodcraft Sportsmen's Clubs [Later, Woodmen Rangers and Rangerettes] (EA) .... BWSC
Boys on Coroners [A publication] (DLA) .... Boys Cor
[The] Boy's Own Paper [Late nineteenth- and early twentieth-century periodical] [British] .... BOP
Boys School [British] .... B
Boys Technical School [British military] (DMA) .... BTS
Boys Town Center for the Study of Youth Development, Omaha, NE [OCLC symbol] (OCLC) .... BTC
Boys Town Center for the Study of Youth Development, Omaha, NE [Library symbol] [Library of Congress] (LCLS) .... NbOB
Boys Town Jerusalem Foundation of America (EA) .... BTJFA
Boys Town Jerusalem Foundation of America (EA) .... BTJFOA
Boys' Towns of Italy (EA) .... BTI
Boysen Reservoir, WY [Location identifier] [FAA] (FAAL) .... BOY
Boyuibe [Bolivia] [ICAO location identifier] (ICLI) .... SLBY
Bozell, Jacobs, Kenyon & Eckhardt [Advertising agency] [New York, NY] .... BJK & E
Bozeman [Montana] [Seismograph station code, US Geological Survey] [Closed] (SEIS) .... BOZ
Bozeman [Montana] [Seismograph station code, US Geological Survey] [Closed] (SEIS) .... BZE
Bozeman [Montana] [Seismograph station code, US Geological Survey] [Closed] (SEIS) .... BZM
Bozeman [Montana] [Airport symbol] (OAG) .... BZN
Bozeman, MT [Location identifier] [FAA] (FAAL) .... AMD
Bozeman, MT [FM radio station call letters] .... KATH
Bozeman, MT [FM radio station call letters] .... KBMC
Bozeman, MT [AM radio station call letters] .... KBOZ
Bozeman, MT [Television station call letters] .... KCTZ
Bozeman, MT [FM radio station call letters] .... KGLT
Bozeman, MT [AM radio station call letters] .... KMMS
Bozeman, MT [FM radio station call letters] .... KMMS-FM
Bozeman, MT [AM radio station call letters] .... KOBB
Bozeman, MT [Television station call letters] .... KUSM
Bozeman, MT [AM radio station call letters] .... KZLO
Bozeman, MT [FM radio station call letters] (BROA) .... KZLO-FM
Bozeman Pubic Library, Bozeman, MT [Library symbol] [Library of Congress] (LCLS) .... MtB
Bozoum [Central African Republic] [ICAO location identifier] (ICLI) .... FEGZ
Bozzel & Jacobs Corp., Information Center, Chicago, IL [Library symbol] [Library of Congress] (LCLS) .... ICBo
Bozzetto (VRA) .... boz
BP Amoco ADS [NYSE symbol] (SG) .... BPA
BP Canada, Inc. [Toronto Stock Exchange symbol] [Vancouver Stock Exchange symbol] .... BPC
BP Exploration Canada Ltd., Calgary, AB, Canada [Library symbol] [Library of Congress] (LCLS) .... CaACBPE
BP Exploration Canada Ltd., Calgary, Alberta [Library symbol] [National Library of Canada] (NLC) .... ACBPE
BP Exploration Information Resource Center, Anchorage, AK [Library symbol] [Library of Congress] (LCLS) .... AkABP
BP Flight Operations Ltd. [British] [ICAO designator] (FAAC) .... BPO
BP Prudhoe Bay Royalty [NYSE symbol] (SPSG) .... BPT
BP Prudhoe Bay Royalty Trust [Associated Press] (SAG) .... BP Pru
BPA International (NTPA) .... BPA
BPC Hydroconsult (SAUS) .... BPCHYDRO
BPI Packaging Tech [NASDAQ symbol] (TTSB) .... BPIE
BPI Packaging Technologies, Inc. [Associated Press] (SAG) .... BPI
BPI Packaging Technologies, Inc. [NASDAQ symbol] (SAG) .... BPIE
BPI Packaging Technologies, Inc. [Associated Press] (SAG) .... BPI Pkg
BPI Pkg Tech 8.50%'A'Pfd [NASDAQ symbol] (TTSB) .... BPIEP
BPI Pkg Technologies Wrrt'B' [NASDAQ symbol] (TTSB) .... BPIEZ
BPI Resources Ltd. [Vancouver Stock Exchange symbol] .... BPY
B-positive (SAUS) .... B+
B-Propriolactone (SAUS) .... BPL
Braathens Helicopter AS [Norway] [ICAO designator] (FAAC) .... BRH
Braathens SAFE Airtransport [ICAO designator] (AD) .... BU
Braathens South American and Far East Airtransport (SAUS) .... SAFE
Braathens South American & Far East Airtransport AS [Norway] [ICAO designator] (FAAC) .... BRA
Brabazon Aircraft [British] (DSUE) .... BRAB
Brabrook. Industrial and Provident Societies [1869] [A publication] (DLA) .... Bra Ind Soc
Brabrook's Law of Trade Unions [A publication] (DLA) .... Bra Tr Un
BRAC [Base Realignment and Closure] Cleanup Plan [Military] (BCP) .... BCP
BRAC [Base Realignment and Closure] Cleanup Team [Military] (BCP) .... BCT
BRAC [Base Realignment and Closure] Environmental Coordinator [Military] (BCP) .... BEC
Bracciera [Ship's rigging] (ROG) .... BRA
Bracco Industria Chimica [Italy] [Research code symbol] .... H
Brace [Medicine] .... B
Brace (MSA) .... BRC
Brace Bit Makers Society [A union] [British] .... BBMS
Brace Resources Ltd. [Vancouver Stock Exchange symbol] .... BCE
Bracebridge, ON [FM radio station call letters] .... CFBG

Bracebridge Public Library, Bracebridge, ON, Canada [Library symbol] [Library of Congress] (LCLS) .... CaOBrac
Bracebridge Public Library, Ontario [Library symbol] [National Library of Canada] (NLC) .... OBRAC
Braced .... BRCD
Braced and Racked [Freight] .... BR
Braced Post (WDAA) .... Br P
Brachial (MELL) .... B
Brachial [Medicine] (DMAA) .... Brach
Brachial Arterial Pressure [Medicine] (MAE) .... Pba
Brachial Artery [Pressure] [Cardiology] (DAVI) .... BA
Brachial Artery [Anatomy] .... BRA
Brachial Artery Output [Medicine] (DB) .... BAO
Brachial Artery Pressure [Medicine] .... BAP
Brachial Neuritis [Medicine] (MAE) .... BN
Brachial Plexus [Medicine] (MELL) .... BP
Brachial Plexus Neuropathy [Medicine] (DMAA) .... BPN
Brachial Plexus Palsy [Medicine] (MELL) .... BPP
Brachial Plexus Paralysis [Medicine] (MELL) .... BPP
Brachio [To the Arm] [Pharmacy] .... BRACH
Brachiocephalic Artery [Cardiology] (DAVI) .... BCA
Brachiocephalic Trunk [Medicine] (MELL) .... BCT
Brachioradialis Jerk [Neurology and orthopedics] (DAVI) .... BRJ
Brachioradialis Reflex [Medicine] (MELL) .... BRR
Brachium [Neurology] .... BC
Brachium Conjunctivum [Neuroanatomy] .... BC
Brachmann-De Lange Syndrome [Medicine] (DMAA) .... BDLS
Brachycardia [Cardiology] .... BC
brachycephalics (SAUS) .... bracbycephs
Bracing (DAC) .... Brcg
Bracken Basic Concept Scale (TES) .... BBCS
Bracken Basic Concept Scale - Diagnostic Scale [Educational development test] .... BBCS-DIAG
Bracken Basic Concept Scale-Screening Test (TES) .... BBCS-SCREENING
Bracken Library, Queen's University, Kingston, Ontario [Library symbol] [National Library of Canada] (NLC) .... OKQH
Brackendale, BC [Television station call letters] (RBYB) CHAN-5
Brackenridge Field Laboratory [University of Texas at Austin] [Research center] (RCD) .... BFL
Brackenridge on the Law of Trusts [A publication] (DLA) .... Brack Tr
Brackenridge's Miscellanies [A publication] (DLA) .... Brack Misc
Bracket .... BKT
Bracket (KSC) .... BRKT
Bracket and Linkage Assembly .... BLA
Bracket Plate (SAUS) .... Bkt Pl
Bracket State Manager (SAUS) .... BSM
Brackish Water Arrival Draft (RIMS) .... BWAD
Brackishwater Aquaculture Information System (SAUS) .... BRAIS
Bracknell [British] [ICAO location identifier] (ICLI) .... EGRR
Bracknell Resources Ltd. [Toronto Stock Exchange symbol] .... BRK
Bracton. De Legibus Angliae [A publication] (DLA) .... Bra
Bracton. De Legibus et Consuetudinibus Angliae [England] [A publication] (DLA) .... Brac
Bracton. De Legibus et Consuetudinibus Angliae [England] [A publication] (DLA) .... Bract
Bracton. De Legibus et Consuetudinibus Angliae [England] [A publication] (DLA) .... Bracton
Bracton's Note Book, King's Bench [1217-40] [A publication] (DLA) .... Brac
Bracton's Note Book, King's Bench [1217-40] [A publication] (DLA) .... Br NB
Bracton's Note Book Tempore Henry III [A publication] (DLA) .... BNB
Brada-Svejda [Tumor] [Medicine] .... BS
Bradbury International Equity [Vancouver Stock Exchange symbol] .... BBE
Bradbury Wilkinson (DGA) .... BW
Bradbury's Pleading and Practice Reports [New York] [A publication] (DLA) .... Bradb
Bradby on Distresses [A publication] (DLA) .... Brad Dis
Braddock, Dunn, and McDonald (SAUO) .... BDM
Braddock Heights, MD [FM radio station call letters] (RBYB) .... WWVZ-FM
Braddock, PA [AM radio station call letters] .... WCXJ
Braddock, PA [FM radio station call letters] .... WRRK
Bradenton, FL [FM radio station call letters] .... WDUV
Bradenton, FL [Television station call letters] .... WFCT
Bradenton, FL [FM radio station call letters] .... WJIS
Bradenton, FL [AM radio station call letters] (RBYB) .... WWPR
Bradenton, FL [Television station call letters] (BROA) .... WXPX
Bradfield [England] .... BRADF
Bradford [Pennsylvania] [Airport symbol] (OAG) .... BFD
Bradford [England] [Airport symbol] (AD) .... BRF
Bradford Action on Teacher Shortages (AIE) .... BATS
Bradford College [Formerly, BJC] [Massachusetts] .... BC
Bradford Community Learning and Education Resource (AIE) .... BE CLEAR
Bradford County Public Library, Starke, FL [Library symbol] [Library of Congress] (LCLS) .... FStaB
Bradford Durfee College of Technology (SAUO) .... BDCT
Bradford Dyers Association, Ltd. (SAUO) .... BDA
Bradford Engineering Society (SAUO) .... BES
Bradford, IL [Location identifier] [FAA] (FAAL) .... BDF
Bradford Institute of Technology (SAUO) .... BIT
Bradford Junior College [Later, BC] [Massachusetts] .... BJC
Bradford Junior College [Later, BC], Bradford, MA [Library symbol] [Library of Congress] (LCLS) .... MBradJ
Bradford, PA [FM radio station call letters] .... WBRR
Bradford, PA [AM radio station call letters] .... WESB
Bradford Public Library, Bradford, IL [Library symbol] [Library of Congress] (LCLS) .... IBra

Bradford Public Library, Bradford, IL [*OCLC symbol*] (OCLC) ... IQX
Bradford Public Library, Bradford, ON, Canada [*Library symbol*] [*Library of Congress*] (LCLS) ... CaOBr
Bradford Public Library, Ontario [*Library symbol*] [*National Library of Canada*] (NLC) ... OBR
Bradford Science Technology and Commercial Services [*Information service or system*] (NITA) ... BRASTACS
Bradford Small Livestock Society (SAUO) ... BSLS
Bradford University Research Ltd. [*British*] (IRUK) ... BURL
Bradford University Software Services Ltd. [*British*] (IRUK) ... BUSS
Bradford's Iowa Supreme Court Reports [*1839-41*] [*A publication*] (DLA) ... Bradford
Bradford's New York Surrogate's Court Reports [*A publication*] (DLA) ... Brad
Bradford's New York Surrogate's Court Reports [*A publication*] (DLA) ... Bradf
Bradford's New York Surrogate's Court Reports [*A publication*] (DLA) ... Bradford's R
Bradford's New York Surrogate's Court Reports [*A publication*] (DLA) ... Bradford's Sur R
Bradford's New York Surrogate's Court Reports [*A publication*] (DLA) ... Bradf Rep
Bradford's New York Surrogate's Court Reports [*A publication*] (DLA) ... Bradf Sur
Bradford's New York Surrogate's Court Reports [*A publication*] (DLA) ... Bradf Sur R
Bradford's New York Surrogate's Court Reports [*A publication*] (DLA) ... Brad R
Bradford's New York Surrogate's Court Reports [*A publication*] (DLA) ... Brad Sur
Bradford's Proceedings in the Court of Star Chamber [*Somerset Record Society Publications, Vol. 27*] [*A publication*] (DLA) ... Bradf
Bradford's Reports [*1838-41*] [*Iowa*] [*A publication*] (DLA) ... Brad
Bradford's Reports [*1838-41*] [*Iowa*] [*A publication*] (DLA) ... Bradf
Bradford's Somerset Star Chamber [*A publication*] (DLA) ... Brad
Bradlees, Inc. [*NYSE symbol*] (SPSG) ... BLE
Bradlees, Inc. [*Associated Press*] (SAG) ... Bradlee
Bradley Aberration Method ... BAM
Bradley Air (Charter) Services Ltd. [*Canada*] [*ICAO designator*] (FAAC) ... BAR
Bradley Commander [*Army*] (INF) ... BC
Bradley Commander Proficiency Course [*Army*] (INF) ... BCPC
Bradley Commander/Gunner Certification Test [*Army*] (INF) ... BCGC
Bradley Crew Evaluator [*Army*] (INF) ... BCE
Bradley Desktop Trainer [*Military*] ... BDT
Bradley Fighting Vehicle [*Army*] ... BFV
Bradley Fighting Vehicle Armament [*Army*] (RDA) ... BFVA
Bradley Fighting Vehicle System [*Army*] ... BFVS
Bradley Fighting Vehicle Systems [*Army*] (RDA) ... BFVS
Bradley Fighting Vehicle Systems Command and Control Vehicle [*Army*] (RDA) ... BFVS-C2V
Bradley Fire Support Team Vehicle [*Army*] ... BFISTV
Bradley Fire Support Vehicle [*Army*] (INF) ... BFSV
Bradley Gunnery and Missile Target System [*Army*] (INF) ... BGMTS
Bradley Gunnery Skills Test [*Army*] (INF) ... BGST
Bradley Infantry Fighting Vehicle [*Army*] (INF) ... BIFV
Bradley International Airport [*FAA*] (TAG) ... BDL
Bradley Leader Course [*Army*] ... BLC
Bradley Memorial Hospital, Cleveland (SAUS) ... TC1eB
Bradley Memorial Hospital, Cleveland, TN [*Library symbol*] [*Library of Congress*] (LCLS) ... TCleB
Bradley Pharm Wrrt 'B' [*NASDAQ symbol*] (TTSB) ... BPRXZ
Bradley Pharm Wrrt 'D' [*NASDAQ symbol*] (TTSB) ... BPRXL
Bradley Pharm Wrrt'A' [*NASDAQ symbol*] (TTSB) ... BPRXW
Bradley Pharmaceuticals, Inc. [*NASDAQ symbol*] (SAG) ... BPRX
Bradley Pharmaceuticals, Inc. [*Associated Press*] (SAG) ... BradP
Bradley Pharmaceuticals, Inc. [*Associated Press*] (SAG) ... BradPhm
Bradley Pharmaceuticals, Inc. [*Associated Press*] (SAG) ... BrdP
Bradley Pharmaceuticals'A' [*NASDAQ symbol*] (TTSB) ... BPRXA
Bradley Polytechnic Institute (SAUO) ... BPI
Bradley Real Estate [*Formerly, Bradley Real Estate Trust*] [*Associated Press*] (SAG) ... BradRE
Bradley Real Estate [*Formerly, Bradley Real Estate Trust*] [*NYSE symbol*] (SAG) ... BTR
Bradley Stinger Fighting Vehicle (SAUS) ... BSFV
Bradley Subcaliber Device [*Army training device*] (INF) ... BSCD
Bradley Table [*Army*] (INF) ... BT
Bradley University (GAGS) ... Bradley U
Bradley University (SAUO) ... BU
Bradley University, Peoria, IL [*OCLC symbol*] (OCLC) ... IBA
Bradley University, Peoria, IL [*Library symbol*] [*Library of Congress*] (LCLS) ... IPB
Bradley, Voorhees, & Day [*A brand name underwear*] ... BVD
Bradley's Point Book [*A publication*] (DLA) ... Bradl PB
Bradley's Rhode Island Reports [*A publication*] (DLA) ... Bradl
Bradley's Rhode Island Reports [*A publication*] (DLA) ... Bradl (RI)
BRADLEY-STINGER Fighting Vehicle-Enhanced [*Army*] ... BSFV-E
Bradner Resources Ltd. [*Vancouver Stock Exchange symbol*] ... BRD
Bradshaw Field, Hawaii Island [*Hawaii*] [*ICAO location identifier*] (ICLI) ... PHSF
Bradsue Resources [*Vancouver Stock Exchange symbol*] ... BDU
Braduskill Intercept Concept ... BIC
Bradwell's Illinois Appellate Reports [*A publication*] (DLA) ... App Ct Rep
Bradwell's Illinois Appellate Reports [*A publication*] (DLA) ... Brad
Bradwell's Illinois Appellate Reports [*A publication*] (DLA) ... Bradw
Bradwells Illinois Appellate Reports (journ.) (SAUS) ... APP Ct Rep
Brady [*W. T.*] **Co.** [*Associated Press*] (SAG) ... BradyW
Brady [*W.H.*] **Co.** [*NASDAQ symbol*] (NQ) ... BRCO
Brady Corp.'A' [*NYSE symbol*] (SG) ... BRC
Brady, TX [*Location identifier*] [*FAA*] (FAAL) ... BBD
Brady, TX [*FM radio station call letters*] ... KIXV
Brady, TX [*AM radio station call letters*] ... KNEL
Brady, TX [*FM radio station call letters*] (RBYB) ... KNEL-FM
Brady, W.T. Co. Class A [*Associated Press*] (SAG) ... BrdyW
Bradycardia [*Cardiology*] (DAVI) ... brady
Bradycardia after Arteriovenous Fistula Occlusion [*Cardiology*] (DMAA) ... BAVFO
Bradykinin [*Biochemistry*] ... BK
Bradykinin Antagonist [*Medicine*] ... BKA
Bradykinin-Potentiating Factor [*Biochemistry*] [*Medicine*] (DMAA) ... BPF
Bradykinin-Potentiating Peptide (DB) ... BPP
Brady's English History [*1648*] [*A publication*] (DLA) ... Bra
Brady's Historical Treatise on Cities [*A publication*] (DLA) ... Bra Cit
Brady's History of the Succession of the Crown of England [*A publication*] (DLA) ... Brad
Brady's Index, Arkansas Reports [*A publication*] (DLA) ... Brady Ind
Brady's Treatise upon Cities and Boroughs [*A publication*] (DLA) ... Brady's Tr
Bradytachy Syndrome (DB) ... BTS
Brady(W.H.)'A'non-vtg [*NASDAQ symbol*] (TTSB) ... BRCOA
Braga [*Portugal*] [*ICAO location identifier*] (ICLI) ... LPBR
Braganca [*Portugal*] [*Airport symbol*] (OAG) ... BGC
Braganca [*Portugal*] [*ICAO location identifier*] (ICLI) ... LPBG
Bragg Cell Receiver (MCD) ... BCR
Bragg Crystal Spectrometer ... BCS
Bragg Crystal Spectrometer/ High Energy Transmission Grating Spectrometer (SAUS) ... BCSS/HETGS
Braham Middle School, Braham, MN [*Library symbol*] [*Library of Congress*] (LCLS) ... MnBhM
Brahma Resources, Inc. [*Vancouver Stock Exchange symbol*] ... BMA
Braid (IAA) ... B
Braid (KSC) ... BRD
Braid-Berheim-Charcot Dissociation (SAUS) ... BBC Dissociation
Braided (SAUS) ... B/D
Braided Memory (SAUS) ... BM
Braided Rug Manufacturers Association [*Defunct*] (EA) ... BRMA
Braided Store (SAUS) ... BS
Braided Trimming Manufacturers Association [*Later, EFMCNTA*] (EA) ... BTMA
Braided Tube Bundle ... BTB
Braided Wire (SAUS) ... bw
Braided Wire Armor (AAG) ... BW
Braidwood Station [*Nuclear energy*] (NRCH) ... BS
Braille and Talking Book Library (ADA) ... B & TBL
Braille and Talking Book Library (SAUO) ... BTBL
Braille Authority of North America (EA) ... BANA
Braille Authority of United Kingdom (SAUO) ... BAUK
Braille Institute (EA) ... BI
Braille Institute Library (SAUO) ... BIL
Braille Institute of America [*Later, BI*] (EA) ... BIA
Braille Institute of America, Los Angeles, CA [*Library symbol*] [*Library of Congress*] (LCLS) ... CLBraille
Braille Printing Terminal (SAUS) ... BPT
Braille Revival League (EA) ... BRL
Braille Technical Press [*Defunct*] (EA) ... BTP
Braille Time-Sharing System ... BTSS
Brailsford-Morquio [*Syndrome*] [*Medicine*] (DB) ... BM
Brain [*Neurology*] (DAVI) ... BRA
Brain ... BRN
Brain, Behavior and Evolution (SAUS) ... Brain Behav Evol
Brain Computer Interface (SAUS) ... BCI
Brain Damage [*Medicine*] (MELL) ... BD
Brain Dead [*Medicine*] (DAVI) ... BD
Brain Derived Growth Factor [*Biochemistry*] ... BDGF
Brain Edema [*Medicine*] (DMAA) ... BE
Brain Electric Activity Monitoring [*Medicine*] (MELL) ... BEAM
Brain Electrical Activity Mapping ... BEAM
Brain Encephalitogen [*Medicine*] (DB) ... BE
Brain Evoked Potential [*Neurophysiology*] ... BEP
Brain Function Diagnostic Unit [*Medicine*] (DB) ... BFDU
Brain Hemorrhage [*Medicine*] (MELL) ... BH
Brain Hormone [*Endocrinology*] ... BH
Brain Information Service (EA) ... BIS
Brain Injured (EDAC) ... BI
Brain Injury [*Medicine*] (MELL) ... BI
Brain Injury and Rehabilitation Trust (WDAA) ... BIRT
Brain Injury Association (SAUO) ... BIA
Brain Injury Association [*Formerly, National Head Injury Foundation*] (EA) ... NHIF
Brain Injury Association of Alberta (SAUO) ... BIAA
Brain Injury Association of California (SAUO) ... BIAC
Brain Injury Association of Florida (SAUO) ... BIAF
Brain Injury Association of Kentucky (SAUO) ... BIAK
Brain Injury Association of Michigan (SAUO) ... BIAMI
Brain Injury Association of Nipissing (SAUO) ... BIAN
Brain Injury Association of North Carolina (SAUO) ... BIANC
Brain Injury Association of Oklahoma (SAUO) ... BIA-OK
Brain Injury Association of Oregon (SAUO) ... BIAO
Brain Injury Association of Tennessee (SAUO) ... BIAT
Brain Injury Association of Virginia (SAUO) ... BIAV
Brain Injury Association of Washington State (SAUO) ... BIAWA
Brain Injury Association of Wisconsin (SAUO) ... BIAW
Brain Injury Society (SAUO) ... BIS
Brain Mapping Technique ... BRAMATEC
Brain Missile Wound [*Medicine*] ... BMW
Brain Natriuretic Peptide [*Biochemistry*] ... BNP
Brain Neurotransmitter [*Medicine*] (DB) ... BNT
Brain Protein Solvent [*Biochemistry*] ... BPS
Brain Research Association [*British*] ... BRA
Brain Research Foundation (EA) ... BRF
Brain Research Institute [*UCLA*] [*Research center*] ... BRI

Brain Response Interface ... BRI
Brain Retraction Pressure [*Neurophysiology*] ... BRP
Brain Simulation Reward (SAUS) ... BSR
Brain State in a Box (SAUS) ... BSB
Brain Stem Auditory Evoked Response [*Neurology and otorhinolaryngology*] (DAVI) ... BSAER
Brain Stem Evoked Potential [*Neurology*] (DAVI) ... BEP
Brain Stem Evoked Potential [*Neurophysiology*] (DMAA) ... BSEP
Brain Stem Evoked Response Audiometry [*Neurology and otorhinolaryngology*] (DAVI) ... BERA
Brain Stem Reticular Formation (SAUS) ... BSRF
Brain Stimulation Reinforcement [*Electrophysiology*] ... BSR
Brain Stimulation Reinforcement [*Neurology*] (DAVI) ... BSS
Brain Tumor [*Medicine*] ... BT
Brain Tumor Research Center [*University of California, San Francisco*] [*Research center*] (RCD) ... BTRC
Brain Tumor Study Group [*National Cancer Institute*] ... BTSG
Brain Uptake Index [*Physiology*] ... BUI
Brain Water ... BW
Brain-Age Quotient [*Medicine*] (DMAA) ... BAQ
Brainard's Legal Precedents in Land and Mining Cases [*United States*] [*A publication*] (DLA) ... BLP L & M Cas
Brainard's Legal Precedents in Land and Mining Cases [*United States*] [*A publication*] (DLA) ... Brain LP
Brain-Associated Small Cell Lung Cancer Antigen [*Medicine*] (DB) ... BASCA
Brain-Derived Neurotrophic Factor [*Neurochemistry*] ... BDNF
Brain-Enriched Hyaluronan Binding [*Neurochemistry*] ... BEHAB
Brainerd [*Minnesota*] [*Airport symbol*] (OAG) ... BRD
Brainerd Community College, Brainerd, MN [*Library symbol*] [*Library of Congress*] (LCLS) ... MnBrC
Brainerd High School, Brainerd, MN [*Library symbol*] [*Library of Congress*] (LCLS) ... MnBrHS
Brainerd International [*Associated Press*] (SAG) ... Brainerd
Brainerd International, Inc. [*NASDAQ symbol*] (NQ) ... BIRI
Brainerd Junior College (SAUO) ... BJC
Brainerd, MN [*Location identifier*] [*FAA*] (FAAL) ... EEE
Brainerd, MN [*Television station call letters*] ... KAWB
Brainerd, MN [*FM radio station call letters*] ... KBPR
Brainerd, MN [*FM radio station call letters*] (RBYB) ... KFGI-FM
Brainerd, MN [*AM radio station call letters*] ... KLIZ
Brainerd, MN [*FM radio station call letters*] ... KLIZ-FM
Brainerd, MN [*AM radio station call letters*] ... KVBR
Brainerd, MN [*FM radio station call letters*] ... KVBR-FM
Brainerd, MN [*FM radio station call letters*] ... WJJY
Brainerd Public Library, Brainerd, MN [*Library symbol*] [*Library of Congress*] (LCLS) ... MnBr
Brain-Heart Infusion [*Growth medium*] ... BHI
Brain-Heart Infusion Agar [*Growth medium*] (OA) ... BHIA
Brain-Heart Infusion Blood Agar [*Growth medium*] ... BHIBA
Brain-Heart Infusion Supplemented [*Broth or agar*] [*Growth medium*] ... BHIS
Brain-Heart Infusion [*Broth*] **with Acetone** [*Growth medium*] ... BHI-Ac
Brain-Reactive Antibody [*Medicine*] (MELL) ... BRA
Brains on Board [*Robot*] [*Androbot, Inc.*] ... BOB
Brainstem Audiometry [*Medicine*] (MELL) ... BSA
Brainstem Auditory Evoked Potential [*Neurophysiology*] ... BAEP
Brainstem Auditory Evoked Response [*Neurophysiology*] ... BAER
Brainstem Encephalitis [*Medicine*] (MELL) ... BSE
Brainstem Injury [*Medicine*] (MELL) ... BSI
Brainstem Transmission Time [*Neurophysiology*] ... BTT
Brainstem-Evoked Response [*Neurophysiology*] ... BSER
Brainstorm (ABBR) ... BRSTRM
Brainstorming (ABBR) ... BRSTRMG
Braintree [*Urban district in England*] ... BRAINT
Braintree Savings Bank [*Associated Press*] (SAG) ... Brantre
[*The*] **Braintree Savings Bank** [*NASDAQ symbol*] (NQ) ... BTSB
Brainware (SAUS) ... Bw
Braithwaite. Oaths in Chancery [*2nd ed.*] [*1864*] [*A publication*] (DLA) ... Braith Oaths
Braithwaite. Oaths in the Supreme Court [*4th ed.*] [*1881*] [*A publication*] (DLA) ... Braith Oaths
Braithwaite. Record and Writ Practice of the Court of Chancery [*1858*] [*A publication*] (DLA) ... Braith Pr
Braithwaite. Times of Procedure in Chancery [*1864*] [*A publication*] (DLA) ... Braith Chy
Braithwaite's Register [*A publication*] (DLA) ... Br Reg
Braj [*MARC language code*] [*Library of Congress*] (LCCP) ... bra
Brake (KSC) ... BK
Brake (SAUS) ... Bk
Brake [*Automotive engineering*] ... BRK
Brake Die ... BKDI
Brake Die (MCD) ... BRD
Brake Electromagnet ... BM
Brake Force Coefficient (SAUS) ... BFC
Brake Force Distributor [*Automotive engineering*] ... BFD
Brake Headquarters USA, Inc. [*NASDAQ symbol*] (SAG) ... BHQU
Brake Headquarters USA, Inc. [*Associated Press*] (SAG) ... BrkeHd
Brake Horsepower ... B
Brake Horsepower (IAA) ... BH
Brake Horsepower (WDAA) ... bhp
Brake Horsepower (EEVL) ... BHP
Brake Horsepower-Hour (AAG) ... BHP-HR
Brake Light Switch [*Automotive engineering*] ... BLS
Brake Manufacturers Council (NTPA) ... BMC
Brake Mean Effective Pressure ... BMEP
Brake Mean Power ... BMP
Brake Mean Pressure (SAUS) ... bmp
Brake On/Off Sensor [*Automotive engineering*] ... BOO
Brake Rating Horsepower [*Automotive engineering*] ... BRHP
Brake Relay ... BR
Brake Release Gross Weight ... BRGW
Brake Release Weight (SAUS) ... BRW
Brake Skid Control [*or Controller*] (NASA) ... B/SC
Brake Skid Controller (SAUS) ... BSC
Brake Specific Carbon Monoxide [*Automotive engineering*] ... BSCO
Brake Specific Carbon Oxide (SAUS) ... BSCO
Brake Specific Fuel Consumption ... BSFC
Brake Specific Hydrocarbons [*Automotive engineering*] ... BSHC
Brake Specific Nitric Oxide (SAUS) ... e BSNO
Brake Specific Oxides of Nitrogen [*Exhaust emissions*] [*Automotive engineering*] ... BSNO
Brake Specific Oxides of Nitrogen [*Automotive engineering*] ... BSNOX
Brake System Parts Manufacturers Council (EA) ... BSPMC
Brake Temperature Monitoring System (MCD) ... BTMS
Brake Thermal Efficiency [*Automotive engineering*] ... BTE
Brake Thermal Efficiency ... BThE
Brake Thermal Efficiency (SAUS) ... BTHEFF
Brakeband (MSA) ... BRKBD
Braked Retarded Parachute (SAUS) ... BRP
Braked Servomotor ... BSM
Brakeman (SAUS) ... brkmm
Brakes (SAUS) ... Bks
Brakes on Pedal Cycle Regulations (SAUS) ... BPCR
Brakes Release Point (ADA) ... BRP
Brake-Transmission Shift Interlock [*Automotive engineering*] ... BTSI
Braking [*Aviation*] (FAAC) ... BRKG
Braking Action (SAUS) ... BA
Braking Action Extremely Poor (SAUS) ... BRAXP
Braking Action Fair [*Aviation*] (FAAC) ... BRAF
Braking Action Good [*Aviation*] (FAAC) ... BRAG
Braking Action Nil [*Aviation*] (FAAC) ... BRAN
Braking Action Poor [*Aviation*] (FAAC) ... BRAP
Braking Force Coefficient (PDAA) ... BFC
Brakpan [*South Africa*] [*ICAO location identifier*] (ICLI) ... FABB
Bralorne Pioneer Museum, Bralorne, BC, Canada [*Library symbol*] [*Library of Congress*] (LCLS) ... CaBBPM
Bralorne Pioneer Museum, British Columbia [*Library symbol*] [*National Library of Canada*] (NLC) ... BBPM
Bralorne Resources Ltd. [*Toronto Stock Exchange symbol*] ... BR
Bram Stoker Club [*Ireland*] (EAIO) ... BSC
Bram Stoker Memorial Association (EA) ... BSMA
Bram Stoker Society (EA) ... BSS
Bramalea Ltd. [*Toronto Stock Exchange symbol*] ... BCD
Bramalea Properties, Inc. [*Toronto Stock Exchange symbol*] ... BPR
Brame's Reports [*66-72 Mississippi*] [*A publication*] (DLA) ... Brame
Brampton [*British*] [*ICAO location identifier*] (ICLI) ... EGYB
Brampton Brick Ltd. [*Toronto Stock Exchange symbol*] ... BBL
Brampton Campus, Sheridan College, Brampton, Ontario [*Library symbol*] [*National Library of Canada*] (BIB) ... OBRASC
Brampton Island [*Australia*] [*Airport symbol*] (OAG) ... BMP
Brampton, ON [*FM radio station call letters*] ... CFNY
Brampton, ON [*AM radio station call letters*] ... CIAO
Brampton Public Library, Brampton, ON, Canada [*Library symbol*] [*Library of Congress*] (LCLS) ... CaOBra
Brampton Public Library, Ontario [*Library symbol*] [*National Library of Canada*] (NLC) ... OBRA
Bran and Multiple Vitamins and Minerals, B-Complex Vitamins, and Yogurt [*A nutritional plan*] ... BAMBY
Branch (IAA) ... B
Branch (ADA) ... BCH
Branch [*Banking*] (TBD) ... Br
Branch (WDAA) ... br
Branch [*Postal Service standard*] (OPSA) ... BR
Branch [*Commonly used*] (OPSA) ... BRANCH
Branch (ADA) ... BRCH
Branch [*Commonly used*] (OPSA) ... BRNCH
Branch Accounting System (SAUS) ... BAS
Branch Address (SAUS) ... BA
Branch Address ... BRA
Branch Always [*Computer science*] ... BRA
Branch and Bound [*Algorithm*] ... BAB
Branch and Bound (SAUS) ... B&B
Branch and Bound Technique (SAUS) ... BB Technique
Branch and Class (DNAB) ... BR & CL
Branch and Condition (SAUS) ... BC
Branch and Condition Status (SAUS) ... BCS
Branch and Count Register (SAUS) ... BCR
Branch and Flow [*Diagram*] ... B & F
Branch and Link (CDE) ... BAL
Branch and Link (IAA) ... BRL
Branch and Mobile Libraries Group (SAUO) ... BMLG
Branch and Store Instruction [*Computer science*] (MDG) ... BSI
Branch Arm Piping [*Nuclear energy*] (NRCH) ... BAP
Branch Arm Piping Enclosure [*Nuclear energy*] (NRCH) ... BAPE
Branch Arm Piping Shielding [*Nuclear energy*] (NRCH) ... BAPS
Branch Assignment (SAUS) ... BA
Branch Assistance Team [*Military*] (AABC) ... BAT
Branch Aviation Supply Office [*Navy*] ... BRASO
Branch Back and Link (SAUS) ... BBL
Branch Back and Load [*Computer science*] ... BBL
Branch Banking and Trust Co. (EFIS) ... BBT

Branch Bill	BB
Branch Circuit Protection Device	BCPD
Branch City [*Databank terminology*] (NITA)	BC
Branch Code (SAUS)	BRCDE
Branch Command Execution (SAUS)	BCE
Branch Conditional (IAA)	BC
Branch Conditional	BRC
Branch Conditionally [*Computer science*]	BCC
Branch Control Unit (SAUS)	BCU
Branch County Library, Coldwater, MI [*Library symbol*] [*Library of Congress*] (LCLS)	MiCwB
Branch Cultural Affairs Officer [*United States Information Service*]	BCAO
Branch Exchange [*Telecommunications*]	BX
Branch Field Post Office (SAUO)	BFPO
Branch Head	BH
Branch Highway (SAUS)	BH
Branch History Table [*Computer science*]	BHT
Branch Hydrographic Office [*Navy*]	BHO
Branch Hydrographic Office (SAUO)	BRANCHHYDRO
Branch Hydrographic Office [*Navy*]	BRANCHYDRO
Branch if Carry Set	BCS
Branch if Greater or Equal (SAUS)	BGE
Branch if Greater Than (SAUS)	BGT
Branch if Higher (SAUS)	BHI
Branch if Higher or Same (SAUS)	BHIS
Branch if Less or Equal (SAUS)	BLE
Branch if Less Than [*Computer science*] (NHD)	BLT
Branch if Lower Or Same (SAUS)	BLOS
Branch If Multiplexer	BIM
Branch if Not Equal (SAUS)	BNE
Branch if Plus (SAUS)	BPL
Branch Immaterial	BI
Branch Immaterial Officer Candidate Course	BIOCC
Branch Information Processing System [*Computer science*]	BIPS
Branch Instruction (SAUS)	BI
Branch Instruction Execution (SAUS)	BIE
Branch Intelligence Officer [*Military*] [*British*]	BIO
Branch Liaison Team [*US Army Chemical School*] [*Fort McClellan, AL*] (RDA)	BLT
Branch Library, Manitoba Veterinarian Services, Winnipeg, Manitoba [*Library symbol*] [*National Library of Canada*] (NLC)	MWVS
Branch Line Society [*British*]	BLS
Branch Loss Factor (SAUS)	BLF
Branch Manager (MCD)	BM
Branch Manager (SAUS)	BRMGB
Branch Material [*Military*] (AABC)	BM
Branch Memorandum	BM
Branch Navy Commissary Store (DNAB)	BRNAVCOMMSTO
Branch No Group [*Computer science*] (MDG)	BNG
Branch of Fall Zero	BFZ
Branch of Full Minus (SAA)	BFM
Branch of Minus (SAUS)	BMI
Branch Office	BO
branch office (SAUO)	bo
Branch Office, Boston [*Office of Naval Research*] (DNAB)	BOB
Branch Office, Chicago [*Office of Naval Research*] (DNAB)	BOC
Branch Office Information System (SAUS)	BOIS
Branch Office Library Inventory Control (SAUS)	BOLIC
Branch Office London [*ONR*]	BOL
Branch Office Manager (EBF)	BOM
Branch Office, Military Intelligence Division [*Army*]	BOMID
Branch Office, Office of Naval Research	ONR BR
Branch Office, Pasadena [*Office of Naval Research*] (DNAB)	BOP
Branch Office Pasadena (SAUO)	BOP
Branch Officer Candidate Course [*DoD*]	BOCC
Branch Officer, Inspector of Naval Material (DNAB)	BRINSMAT
Branch Officer Roster [*Army*]	BOR
Branch on Condition (SAUS)	BC
Branch on Count (IAA)	BCT
Branch on Left Minus (SAA)	BLM
Branch on Load Card (SAUS)	Br LC
Branch on Minus	BM
Branch on Minus (SAUS)	Br Mn
Branch on Nonzero	BN
Branch on Non-Zero (SAUS)	Br NZ
Branch on Overflow (SAUS)	Br OF
Branch on Right Minus (SAA)	BRM
Branch on Zero (SAUS)	Br Z
Branch Operating Instruction [*Air Force*]	BOI
Branch Operating Instruction [*Air Force*] (AFM)	BROI
Branch Output Interrupt [*Computer science*] (MDG)	BOI
Branch Overflow (SAUS)	BROV
Branch Point Sequence [*Genetics*]	BPS
Branch Prediction Unit [*Computer science*] (PCM)	BPU
Branch Processing Unit [*Computer science*]	BPO
Branch Processing Unit [*Computer science*] (VERA)	BPU
Branch Public Affairs Officer [*United States Information Service*]	BPAO
Branch Public Relations Office	BPRO
Branch Pulmonary Dysplasia [*Medicine*] (DB)	BPD
Branch Report	BR
Branch Retinal Artery Occlusion [*Ophthalmology*] (DAVI)	BRAO
Branch Retinal Vein Occlusion [*Ophthalmology*] (DAVI)	BrRvo
Branch Retinal Vein Occlusion [*Ophthalmology*] (CPH)	BRVO
Branch Routine (SAUS)	BR
Branch Stack	BS

Branch State [*Database terminology*] (NITA)	BS
Branch System General License [*Information technology*]	BSGL
Branch Target Buffer [*Computer science*] (PCM)	BTB
Branch Technical Position [*Nuclear energy*] (NRCH)	BTP
Branch Terminal System (SAUS)	BTS
Branch to Subroutine [*Computer science*]	BSR
Branch Training Team [*Army*]	BTT
Branch Transportation Movement Office (SAUO)	BTMO
Branch Transportation Office [*or Officer*] [*Army*]	BTO
Branch Transportation Officer (SAUS)	BTO
Branch Unconditionally	BRU
Branch Unit [*Computer science*] (PCM)	BU
Branch Vein Occlusion [*Medicine*] (DMAA)	BVO
Branch Vein Occlusion Study (SAUS)	BVOS
Branch Warehouse Association (EA)	BWA
Branch Workload Index (SAUS)	BWI
Branch Zip Code [*Database Terminology*] (NITA)	BZ
Branch-Bound Mixed Integer Programming [*Computer science*]	BBMIP
Branche Africaine du Mouvement International des Etudiants Catholiques [*African International Movement of Catholic Students - AIMCS*] (EAIO)	MIEC
Branched Alkylbenzene [*Organic chemistry*]	BAB
Branched Amino Acid (DMAA)	BAA
Branched DNA (SAUS)	bDNA
Branched Ribonucleic Acid [*Genetics*]	bRNA
Branched-Chain Amino Acid [*Biochemistry*]	BAA
Branched-Chain Amino Acid [*Biochemistry*]	BCAA
Branched-Chain Ketoacid [*Biochemistry*]	BCKA
Branched-Chain Ketoacid Dehydrogenase [*Biochemistry*]	BCKD
Branched-Chain Oxoacid Dehydrogenase [*An enzyme*]	BCODH
Branchial Filament	BRF
Branching Filter [*Telecommunications*] (TEL)	BF
Branching Instruction	BI
Branching Process with Markovian Environments (SAUS)	BPME
Branching Process with Random Environments (SAUS)	BPRE
Branching Random Walk with Absorbing Barriers (SAUS)	BRWAB
Branching Ratio (SAUS)	BR
Branching Temporal Logic (RALS)	BTL
Branchioganglionic Neuron [*Neurology*]	BGN
Branchio-Oto-Ureteral [*Syndrome*] [*Medicine*] (DMAA)	BOU
Branch-office Average Maintenance Hours (SAUS)	BAM hrs
Branch's Maxims [*A publication*] (DLA)	Branch Max
Branch's Principia Legis et Equitatis [*Maxims*] [*A publication*] (DLA)	Branch Pr
Branch's Principia Legis et Equitatis [*Maxims*] [*A publication*] (DLA)	Branch Princ
Branch's Reports [*1 Florida*] [*A publication*] (DLA)	Branch
Branch-Target Address Cache [*Computer science*]	BTAC
Branchville, SC [*FM radio station call letters*]	WGFG
Brand Asbestos Control Co., Inc. (EFIS)	BASCO
Brand Development [*Marketing*] (DOAD)	BD
Brand Development Index (WDMC)	BDI
Brand Examination Services & Testing Co. (EFIS)	BESTCO
Brand Name Contract (AABC)	BNC
Brand Name Resale (AABC)	BNR
Brand Names Foundation (EA)	BNF
Brand Potential Index [*Marketing*] (DOAD)	BPI
Brand Rating Index Corp.	BRI
Branded Furniture Society [*British*] (BI)	BFS
Branded Knitting-Wool Association Ltd. [*British*] (BI)	BKWA
Brandeis Memorial Foundation (SAUO)	BMF
Brandeis School, Lawrence, NY [*Library symbol*] [*Library of Congress*] (LCLS)	NLawBS
Brandeis University (GAGS)	Brandeis U
Brandeis University [*Waltham, MA*] (BJA)	BU
Brandeis University, Waltham, MA [*OCLC symbol*] (OCLC)	MBB
Brandeis University, Waltham, MA [*Library symbol*] [*Library of Congress*] (LCLS)	MWalB
Brandeis-Bardin Institute (SAUO)	BBI
Brandenburg, KY [*AM radio station call letters*]	WMMG
Brandenburg, KY [*FM radio station call letters*]	WMMG-FM
Brandenburg's Bankruptcy Digest [*A publication*] (DLA)	Brandenburg Bankr
Brandenburg's Bankruptcy Digest [*A publication*] (DLA)	Brandenburg Dig
Brandenburg's Reports [*21 Opinions Attorneys-General*] [*A publication*] (DLA)	Brand
Brande's Dictionary of Science, Etc. [*A publication*] (DLA)	Brande
Brandevor Enterprises Ltd. [*Toronto Stock Exchange symbol*] [*Vancouver Stock Exchange symbol*]	BVE
Brandl, H. R., Chicago IL [*STAC*]	BHR
Brandon [*Canada*] [*Airport symbol*] (OAG)	YBR
Brandon Call Fan Club (EA)	BCFC
Brandon College (SAUO)	BC
Brandon Films, Inc.	BF
Brandon, FL [*AM radio station call letters*]	WBDN
Brandon Free Public Library, Brandon, VT [*Library symbol*] [*Library of Congress*] (LCLS)	VtBran
Brandon General Hospital, School of Nursing, Brandon, MB, Canada [*Library symbol*] [*Library of Congress*] (LCLS)	CaMBGH
Brandon, MB [*Television station call letters*]	CBWFT-10
Brandon, MB [*AM radio station call letters*]	CKLQ
Brandon, MB [*AM radio station call letters*]	CKX
Brandon, MB [*FM radio station call letters*]	CKX-FM
Brandon, MB [*Television station call letters*]	CKX-TV
Brandon, MB [*Television station call letters*]	CKYB
Brandon, MB [*ICAO location identifier*] (ICLI)	CYBR
Brandon Mental Health Centre, Brandon, MB, Canada [*Library symbol*] [*Library of Congress*] (LCLS)	CaMBMH

Brandon Mental Health Centre, Manitoba [*Library symbol*] [*National Library of Canada*] (NLC) .... MBMH
Brandon, MS [*FM radio station call letters*] .... WRJH
Brandon, MS [*AM radio station call letters*] .... WRKN
Brandon on Foreign Attachment [*A publication*] (DLA) .... Brand F Attachm
Brandon on Foreign Attachment [*A publication*] (ILCA) .... Brand For Att
Brandon on Foreign Attachment [*A publication*] (DLA) .... Brand For Attachm
Brandon. Practice of the Mayor's Court [*1864*] [*A publication*] (DLA) .... Brand May Ct
Brandon Public School, Brandon, MN [*Library symbol*] [*Library of Congress*] (LCLS) .... MnBraS
Brandon Systems [*AMEX symbol*] (SPSG) .... BRA
Brandon Systems Corp. [*Associated Press*] (SAG) .... Brandn
Brandon University, Archives, Brandon, MB, Canada [*Library symbol*] [*Library of Congress*] (LCLS) .... CaMBCA
Brandon University, Brandon, MB, Canada [*Library symbol*] [*Library of Congress*] (LCLS) .... CaMBC
Brandon University, Department of Geography, Brandon, MB, Canada [*Library symbol*] [*Library of Congress*] (LCLS) .... CaMBCG
Brandon University Library [*UTLAS symbol*] .... BUL
Brandon University, Manitoba [*Library symbol*] [*National Library of Canada*] (NLC) .... MBC
Brandon, VT [*FM radio station call letters*] .... WADT
Brandon, VT [*FM radio station call letters*] (BROA) .... WEXP-FM
Brands and Their Companies [*Formerly, TND*] [*A publication*] .... BTC
Brandt Aero Engine Modular Management Aid (SAUS) .... BAEMMA
Brandt on Suretyship and Guaranty [*A publication*] (DLA) .... Brandt Sur
Brandvlei [*South Africa*] [*ICAO location identifier*] (ICLI) .... FABV
Brandy and Benedictine (CDAI) .... B & B
Brandy and Dry Ginger (ADA) .... b & d
Brandy and Soda .... B and S
Brandy Resources [*Vancouver Stock Exchange symbol*] .... BYU
Brandywine College of Widener University, Wilmington, DE [*OCLC symbol*] (OCLC) .... DLB
Brandywine College, Wilmington, DE [*Library symbol*] [*Library of Congress*] (LCLS) .... DeWB
Brandywine Realty Trust [*Formerly, Linpro Specified Properties*] [*AMEX symbol*] (SPSG) .... BDN
Brandywine Realty Trust [*Associated Press*] (SAG) .... Brandyw
Braner Resources [*Vancouver Stock Exchange symbol*] .... BRJ
Branford Savings Bank [*Associated Press*] (SAG) .... BranfdSv
Branford Savings Bank [*NASDAQ symbol*] (NQ) .... BSBC
Branford Savings Bank(CT) [*NASDAQ symbol*] (TTSB) .... BSBC
Branford Steam Railroad [*AAR code*] .... BRFD
Brani Naval Base (SAUS) .... BNB
Braniff Airways, Inc. [*of Braniff International Corp.*] .... BA
Braniff Airways, Inc. [*of Braniff International Corp.*] [*ICAO designator*] (OAG) .... BN
Braniff International Airways (IIA) .... BI
Braniff International Airways (SAUO) .... BN
Braniff International Corp. [*ICAO designator*] .... BNF
Braniff International Council [*Club for frequent flyers*] (EA) .... BIC
Brann-Brawn Family History Association (EA) .... B/BFHA
Brans-Dicke-Jordan [*Scalar-tensor theory*] .... BDJ
Branson, MO [*FM radio station call letters*] .... KLFC
Branson, MO [*AM radio station call letters*] .... KOMC
Branson, MO [*FM radio station call letters*] (RBYB) .... KOZO-FM
Branson, MO [*FM radio station call letters*] .... KRZK
Branson, MO [*Location identifier*] [*FAA*] (FAAL) .... PLK
Branson's Digest [*Bombay*] [*A publication*] (DLA) .... Brans Dig
Brant County Antique Arms Collectors Association (SAUO) .... BCAAC
Brant County Historical Museum, Brantford, ON, Canada [*Library symbol*] [*Library of Congress*] (LCLS) .... CaOBrtBM
Brant County Historical Museum, Brantford, Ontario [*Library symbol*] [*National Library of Canada*] (NLC) .... OBBM
Brantford, ON [*AM radio station call letters*] .... CKPC
Brantford, ON [*FM radio station call letters*] .... CKPC-FM
Brantford Public Library, Brantford, ON, Canada [*Library symbol*] [*Library of Congress*] (LCLS) .... CaOBrt
Brantford Public Library, Ontario [*Library symbol*] [*National Library of Canada*] (NLC) .... OBRT
Brantley, AL [*FM radio station call letters*] (BROA) .... WAOQ-FM
Brantley, AL [*AM radio station call letters*] (BROA) .... WAUL-AM
Brantley Capital Corp. [*NASDAQ symbol*] (SAG) .... BBDC
Brantley Capital Corp. [*Associated Press*] (SAG) .... BrantCp
Brantly's Reports [*80-90 Maryland*] [*A publication*] (DLA) .... Brant
Brantly's Reports [*80-90 Maryland*] [*A publication*] (DLA) .... Brantly
Bras D'Or Mines [*Vancouver Stock Exchange symbol*] .... BRM
Brasair Transportes Aereos [*Brazil*] [*FAA designator*] (FAAC) .... BSI
Brascade Resources, Inc. [*Toronto Stock Exchange symbol*] .... BCA
Brascan Ltd. [*Toronto Stock Exchange symbol*] .... BL
Brascan Ltd. [*AMEX symbol*] (SPSG) .... BRS
Brascan Ltd. [*Associated Press*] (SAG) .... Brscn
Brascon Resources Ltd., Calgary, AB, Canada [*Library symbol*] [*Library of Congress*] (LCLS) .... CaACB
Brascon Resources Ltd., Calgary, Alberta [*Library symbol*] [*National Library of Canada*] (NLC) .... ACB
Brasenose College (SAUO) .... BC
Brasenose College [*Oxford*] .... BNC
Brasenose College (SAUO) .... Bras
Brasenose College (SAUS) .... Bras
Brashear-Hastings Prism .... BHP
Brasil [*Portuguese spelling*] **and Canada** [*In company name "Brascan Ltd."*] .... BRASCAN
Brasil Gold Resources [*Vancouver Stock Exchange symbol*] .... BGZ
Brasil-Central Linhas Areas Regional SA [*Brazil*] [*ICAO designator*] (FAAC) .... BLC
Brasileia [*Brazil*] [*Airport symbol*] (AD) .... BZY
Brasil/Europe Brasil Freight Conference (SAUO) .... BEB
Brasilia [*Brazil*] [*Seismograph station code, US Geological Survey*] (SEIS) .... BAE
Brasilia [*Brazil*] [*Seismograph station code, US Geological Survey*] (SEIS) .... BDF
Brasilia [*Brazil*] [*Airport symbol*] (OAG) .... BSB
Brasilia [*Airplane code*] Em2
Brasilia [*Brazil*] [*ICAO location identifier*] (ICLI) .... SBBS
Brasilia Array [*Brazil*] [*Seismograph station code, US Geological Survey*] (SEIS) .... BAO
Brasilia/Gama [*Brazil*] [*ICAO location identifier*] (ICLI) .... SBGA
Brasilia/Internacional [*Brazil*] [*ICAO location identifier*] (ICLI) .... SBBR
Brass (WGA) .... B
Brass .... BR
Brass .... br
Brass (KSC) .... BRS
Brass (VRA) .... bs
Brass and Bronze Ingot Institute (EA) .... BBII
Brass, Bronze, or Copper [*Freight*] .... BRBZC
Brass Disc (SAUS) .... BD
Brass Divider Strip [*Technical drawings*] .... BDS
Brass Dressers Trade Society [*A union*] [*British*] .... BDTS
Brass Eagle [*Stock market symbol*] .... XTRM
Brass Forging Association (SAUO) .... BFA
Brass Jacket (SAUS) .... bj
Brass Mounted (SAUS) .... bm
Brass or Bronze [*Top*] [*Freight*] .... B or B
Brass or Iron [*Freight*] .... B or I
Brass Plug (SAUS) .... BP
Brass Pounders League [*Unit of American Radio Relay League*] .... BPL
Brass Ring Resources [*Vancouver Stock Exchange symbol*] .... BSG
Brass Ring Society (EA) .... BRS
Brass River (WDAA) .... BR
Brass Washer (SAUS) .... BW
Brassboard Active Optical Fuze (ACAE) .... BAOF
Brassboard Configuration Model (MCD) .... BCM
Brassboard Fault Tolerant Spaceborne Computer (MCD) .... BFTSC
Brassboard Optical Seeker (ACAE) .... BOS
Brasschaat [*Belgium*] [*ICAO location identifier*] (ICLI) .... EBBT
Brasserie .... BRSSR
Brassey's Naval Record [*Brassey's Defence Publishers Ltd.*] [*No longer maintained*] [*Information service or system*] (IID) .... BNR
Brassie Golf Corp. [*Associated Press*] (SAG) .... BrassieG
Brassie Golf Corp. [*NASDAQ symbol*] (SAG) .... PUTT
Brassiere (DSUE) .... BRA
Brassiere (ADWA) .... bra
Brassiere (DSUE) .... BRAS
Brassiere (ABBR) .... BRSSIR
Brassiere Cup Size (SAUS) .... AA
Brassiness (ABBR) .... BRSNS
Brassy (ABBR) .... BRSSY
Brassy (ABBR) .... BRSY
Braswell, J. V., Dallas TX [*STAC*] .... BJV
Bratford & Bingley Building Society (SAUO) .... BBBS
Bratislava [*Czechoslovakia*] [*Seismograph station code, US Geological Survey*] [*Closed*] (SEIS) .... BRA
Bratislava [*Former Czechoslovakia*] [*Airport symbol*] (OAG) .... BTS
Bratislava [*Former Czechoslovakia*] [*ICAO location identifier*] (ICLI) .... LKBB
Bratislava [*Czechoslovakia*] [*Seismograph station code, US Geological Survey*] (SEIS) .... ZST
Bratislava/Ivanka [*Former Czechoslovakia*] [*ICAO location identifier*] (ICLI) .... LKIB
Bratschen [*Viola*] .... BR
Bratsk [*Former USSR*] [*Airport symbol*] (OAG) .... BTK
Bratsk [*Former USSR*] [*ICAO location identifier*] (ICLI) .... UIBB
Brattforsheden [*Sweden*] [*ICAO location identifier*] (ICLI) .... ESSM
Brattleboro, Vermont-Keene, New Hampshire [*Airport symbol*] (AD) .... EEN
Brattleboro, VT [*AM radio station call letters*] .... WKVT
Brattleboro, VT [*FM radio station call letters*] .... WKVT-FM
Brattleboro, VT [*AM radio station call letters*] .... WTSA
Brattleboro, VT [*FM radio station call letters*] .... WTSA-FM
Bratwurst (ADWA) .... brat
Braun Center for Holocaust Studies (EA) .... BCHS
Braun Tool & Instrument Company, Inc. (SAUO) .... BTI
Brauner, Emmett, and Teller Equation [*Chemistry*] (EDCT) .... BET
Braun's Fashions [*NASDAQ symbol*] (TTSB) .... BFCI
Brauns Fashions Corp. [*NASDAQ symbol*] (SAG) .... BFCI
Braun's Fashions Corp. [*Associated Press*] (SAG) .... Brauns
Braunschweig [*Germany*] [*ICAO location identifier*] (ICLI) .... EDVB
Braunschweig [*Germany*] [*ICAO location identifier*] (ICLI) .... EDVE
Braunton [*England*] .... BRAUN
Braunton Burrows National Nature Reserve (SAUS) .... BBNNR
Bravado (ABBR) .... BRVDO
Bravais-Miller Indices [*Physics*] .... BMI
Brave (ABBR) .... BRV
Braved (ABBR) .... BRVD
Bravely (ABBR) .... BRVY
Braveness (ABBR) .... BRVNS
Braverman-Chevigny Auditory Projective Test [*Psychology*] .... BCAPT
Bravery Medal (ADA) .... BM
Braving (ABBR) .... BRVG
Bravo [*International phonetic alphabet*] (DSUE) .... B
Bravo Resources [*Vancouver Stock Exchange symbol*] .... BVO
Bravo Zone (SAA) .... BRZN
Bravo Zulu [*Signal for "job well done"*] [*Navy*] (DOMA) .... BZ

Brawdy [*British*] [*ICAO location identifier*] (ICLI) .... EGDA
Brawled (ABBR) .... BRWLD
Brawley, CA [*Location identifier*] [*FAA*] (FAAL) .... BWC
Brawley, CA [*AM radio station call letters*] (BROA) .... KKSC
Brawley, CA [*AM radio station call letters*] .... KROP
Brawley, CA [*FM radio station call letters*] .... KSIQ
Brawley, CA [*FM radio station call letters*] .... KWST
Brawley Public Library, Brawley, CA [*Library symbol*] [*Library of Congress*] (LCLS) .... CBr
Brawling (ABBR) .... BRWLG
Bray Elementary School, Biwabik, MN [*Library symbol*] [*Library of Congress*] (LCLS) .... MnBiwE
Brayton Heat Exchanger Unit .... BHXU
Brayton Isotope Power System .... BIPS
Brayton Rotating Unit .... BRU
Brayton Turboelectric Engine .... BTE
Brayton Turboelectric Engine .... BTEE
Brayton's Reports [*Vermont*] [*A publication*] (DLA) .... Bray
Brayton's Reports [*Vermont*] [*A publication*] (DLA) .... Bray R
Brayton's Reports [*Vermont*] [*A publication*] (ILCA) .... Brayt
Brayton's Reports [*Vermont*] [*A publication*] (DLA) .... Brayton's Rep
Brayton's Reports [*Vermont*] [*A publication*] (DLA) .... Brayton (VT)
Brayton's Reports [*Vermont*] [*A publication*] (DLA) .... Brayt Rep
Braze .... BRZ
Brazed (VRA) .... braz
Brazed (ABBR) .... BRZD
Brazed Brass Tube Association (SAUO) .... BBTA
Brazed Joint-Face Fed (DNAB) .... BF
Brazed Joint-Preinserted Ring (DNAB) .... BP
Brazen (ABBR) .... BRZN
Brazened (ABBR) .... BRZND
Brazening (ABBR) .... BRZNG
Brazier (MSA) .... BRAZ
Brazier (ABBR) .... BRZIR
Brazier Head .... BRAZH
Brazil [*IYRU nationality code*] [*MARC country of publication code*] [*Library of Congress*] (LCCP) .... bl
Brazil [*ANSI two-letter standard code*] (CNC) .... BR
Brazil (MILB) .... Br
Brazil [*ANSI three-letter standard code*] (CNC) .... BRA
Brazil .... BRAZ
Brazil (VRA) .... Braz
Brazil (SAUO) .... BZ
Brazil (SAUS) .... Bz
Brazil [*International civil aircraft marking*] (ODBW) .... PP
Brazil [*International civil aircraft marking*] (ODBW) .... PT
Brazil [*MARC geographic area code*] [*Library of Congress*] (LCCP) .... s-bl-
Brazil Current (SAUS) .... Bra Cur
Brazil Democratic Movement [*Political party*] .... BDM
Brazil Energy Program (SAUO) .... BEP
Brazil Fast Food [*NASDAQ symbol*] (TTSB) .... BOBS
Brazil Fast Food Corp. [*NASDAQ symbol*] (SAG) .... BOBS
Brazil Fast Food Corp. [*Associated Press*] (SAG) .... Brazil
Brazil Fast Food Corp. [*Associated Press*] (SAG) .... BrazlFst
Brazil Fast Food Wrrt'A' [*NASDAQ symbol*] (TTSB) .... BOBSW
Brazil Fast Food Wrrt'B' [*NASDAQ symbol*] (TTSB) .... BOBSZ
Brazil Fund [*NYSE symbol*] (TTSB) .... BZF
Brazil Fund, Inc. [*Associated Press*] (SAG) .... Brazil
Brazil Fund, Inc. [*NYSE symbol*] (SPSG) .... BZF
Brazil, IN [*AM radio station call letters*] .... WSDM
Brazil, IN [*FM radio station call letters*] .... WSDM-FM
Brazil Labor Information and Resource Center (EA) .... BLI
Brazil Nut Advertising Fund [*Defunct*] (EA) .... BNAF
Brazil Nut Association .... BNA
Brazil Philatelic Association (EA) .... BPA
Brazil Public Library, Brazil, IN [*Library symbol*] [*Library of Congress*] (LCLS) .... InBra
Brazil Standard Time (SAUS) .... BST
Brazil Times, Brazil, IN [*Library symbol*] [*Library of Congress*] (LCLS) .... InBraT
Brazil Tourism Office (EA) .... BTO
Brazila Esperanto-Ligo (SAUO) .... BEL
Brazil-Canary Islands cable (SAUS) .... BRANCAN cable
Brazilian (ADWA) .... Braz
Brazilian (SAUS) .... Bz
Brazilian Agricultural Workers Union (SAUS) .... ULTAB
Brazilian Air Force (SAUO) .... BAF
Brazilian Air Force [*ICAO designator*] (FAAC) .... BRS
Brazilian American Society (SAUS) .... BAS
Brazilian American Survey [*A publication*] .... BAS
Brazilian Angel [*Record label*] .... BrzA
Brazilian Antarcic Program (SAUS) .... PROANTAR
Brazilian Army Aviation [*FAA designator*] (FAAC) .... EXB
Brazilian Association of Information Systems and Office Equipment (SAUO) .... APRIMESC
Brazilian Center of New York (EA) .... BCNY
Brazilian Coffee Institute (EA) .... BCI
Brazilian Columbia [*Record label*] .... BrzC
Brazilian Commission for Space Activities (SAUS) .... COBAE
Brazilian Commission of Space Activities (SAUS) .... COBAE
Brazilian Continental [*Record label*] .... BrzCont
Brazilian Elite [*Record label*] .... BrzEli
Brazilian Energy Regulatory Agency (SAUO) .... ANEEL
Brazilian Environmental Agency (SAUO) .... IBAMA
Brazilian Equity Fund [*Associated Press*] (SAG) .... BrazilEF
Brazilian Equity Fund [*NYSE symbol*] (SPSG) .... BZL
Brazilian Expeditionary Force .... BEF
Brazilian Fund for Biodiversity (SAUO) .... FUNBIO
Brazilian Government Trade Bureau (EA) .... BGTB
Brazilian Infantry Division [*World War II*] .... BID
Brazilian Institute for Space Research (SAUS) .... INPE
Brazilian Institute of Environment and Renewable Natural Resources (SAUO) .... IBMARNR
Brazilian International Airlines .... BIA
Brazilian Journal of Genetics (journ.) (SAUS) RBGED3
Brazilian Marine Geology Programme (SAUS) .... PBGM
Brazilian MGM [*Record label*] .... BrzMGM
Brazilian National Development Bank .... BNDES
Brazilian Navy .... BN
Brazilian News Briefs [*A publication*] (EAAP) .... BNB
Brazilian Oceanographic Data Centre (SAUS) .... BNDO
Brazilian Odeon [*Record label*] .... BrzOd
Brazilian Portuguese (ADWA) .... BrazPg
Brazilian Purpuric Fever [*Medicine*] .... BPF
Brazilian Remote Sensing Experiment (SAUS) .... BRESEX
Brazilian Society for Cartography, Geodesy, Photogrammetry and Remote Sensing (SAUS) .... SBC
Brazilian Space Agency (SAUS) .... INPE
Brazilian Studies Association .... BRASA
Brazilian Thorium Sludge .... BTS
Brazilian Thyroid Sludge (SAUS) .... BTS
Brazilian Tourism Foundation (EA) .... BTF
Brazilian Travel Agency (SAUO) .... BTA
Brazilian Victor [*Record label*] .... BrzV
Brazilian-American Chamber of Commerce (EA) .... BACC
Brazilian-American Cultural Institute (EA) .... BACI
Brazils Irrigation Ministry (SAUS) .... SENIR
Brazils satellite (SAUS) .... Brasilsat
Brazil-US Business Council (EA) .... BUSBC
Brazing .... B
Brazing (SAUS) .... BRAZ
Brazing (KSC) .... BRZG
Brazing Accessory [*Tool*] (AAG) .... BZAC
Brazing Fixture .... BZFX
Brazoria County Library, Angleton, TX [*Library symbol*] [*Library of Congress*] (LCLS) .... TxAng
Brazoria, TX [*Location identifier*] [*FAA*] (FAAL) .... BZT
Brazos Petroleum [*Vancouver Stock Exchange symbol*] .... BRS
Brazos Santiago, TX [*Location identifier*] [*FAA*] (FAAL) .... PIL
Brazosport College, Lake Jackson, TX [*Library symbol*] [*Library of Congress*] (LCLS) .... TxLjB
Brazosport Junior College, Freeport, TX [*Library symbol*] [*Library of Congress*] (LCLS) .... TxFrB
Brazz Axle Pulley (SAUS) .... BAZ
Brazzaville [*People's Republic of the Congo*] [*Airport symbol*] (OAG) .... BZV
Brazzaville [*Congo*] [*ICAO location identifier*] (ICLI) .... FCBV
Brazzaville [*Congo*] [*ICAO location identifier*] (ICLI) .... FCCC
Brazzaville/Maya Maya [*Congo*] [*ICAO location identifier*] (ICLI) .... FCBB
BRC Holdings [*NASDAQ symbol*] [*Formerly, Business Records Cp. Holdings*] (SG) .... BRCP
BRC Holdings, Inc. [*Associated Press*] (SAG) .... BRC Hld
BRC Holdings, Inc. [*NASDAQ symbol*] (SAG) .... BRCP
BRE Properties Cl A [*NYSE symbol*] (SPSG) .... BRE
BRE Properties, Inc. [*Associated Press*] (SAG) .... BRE
Breach [*Legal shorthand*] (LWAP) .... BR
Breach of Community Service Order [*Legal term*] (WDAA) .... BOSCO
Breach of Conditional Discharge Order [*Legal term*] (WDAA) .... BOCDO
Breach of Contract [*Legal term*] .... BOC
Breach of Peace [*FBI standardized term*] .... B of P
Breach of Peace .... BOP
Breach of Probation Order [*Legal term*] (WDAA) .... BOPO
Breach of Promise [*Legal term*] .... B of P
Breach of Promise [*Legal term*] (DLA) .... BRECH PROM
Breach of Suspended Sentence of Imprisonment [*Legal term*] (WDAA) .... BOSS
Breach of Warranty [*Insurance*] (AIA) .... BOW
Breacher's Explosive Access Selectable Tool .... BEAST
Breaching (MSA) .... BRHG
Bread [*Dietetics*] .... Brd
Bread and Puppet Theater [*Vermont*] .... B and P
Bread and Roses (EA) .... B & R
Bread and Water .... B & W
[*The*] **Bread Board System** [*eSoft, Inc.*] [*Computer science*] (PCM) .... TBBS
Bread Bulk (SAUS) .... bb
Bread, Butter, and Marmalade [*Slang*] .... BBM
Bread Equivalent [*Medicine*] (DMAA) .... BE
Bread Exchange [*Dietetics*] .... Brd Ex
Bread for the World (EA) .... BFW
Bread Industry Authority [*Queensland, Australia*] .... BIA
Bread Industry Employees and Salespersons' Association of New South Wales [*Australia*] .... BIESANSW
Bread Loaf Writers Conference (EA) .... BLWC
Bread Manufacturers' Association of New South Wales [*Australia*] .... BMANSW
Bread Manufacturers' Association of South Australia .... BMASA
Bread Manufacturers' Association of Tasmania [*Australia*] .... BMAV
Bread Manufacturers' Association of Western Australia .... BMAWA
Bread Manufacturers' Industrial Association of Australia .... BMIAA
Bread Manufacturers of New South Wales [*Australia*] .... BMNSW
Bread Manufacturers of Queensland Union of Employers [*Australia*] .... BMQUE
Bread Research Institute of Australia .... BRIA
Bread Unit (SAUS) .... BU
Bread Wrapping and Sealing Machine (SAUS) .... BW&SM

Breadalbane Fencibles [*British military*] (DMA)	BF
Breadboard [*NASA*] (KSC)	BB
Breadboard, Brassboard (ACAE)	B/B
Breadboard Float Zone Experiment System (SAUS)	BFZES
Bread-Board Kit (SAUS)	BBK
Breadboard Kit [*NASA*]	BBK
Breadboard of an Electrochemical Air Revitalization System [*NASA*]	BEARS
Breadboard Terminal Landing System [*NASA*] (KSC)	BTLS
Breadboard Verification Equipment [*NASA*]	BVE
Breadboard Visual Reference System [*NASA*]	BVRS
Breadth (ADWA)	b
Breadth	B
Breadth (SAUS)	Bdth
Breadth (RIMS)	Br
Breadth (SAUS)	Brdt
Breadth	BRDTH
Breadth First Search (SAUS)	BFS
Breadth-Length	BL
Breadth-Mouled (SAUS)	BM
Break [*Electronics*]	B
Break (IDOE)	BK
Break (KSC)	BRK
Break Bulk [*Shipping*]	BB
Break Bulk Point [*Transportation*]	BBP
Break Cloud Procedure [*Aviation*] (PIAV)	BCP
Break Control Command Transducers (NASA)	BCCT
Break Corner (SAUS)	brk cor
Break Engage (CAAL)	BK ENG
Break, Enter, and Steal (ADA)	BE & S
Break Even Analysis [*Accounting*]	BEA
Break Even Points (SAUS)	BEPs
Break Field (SAUS)	BF
Break in Overcast [*Meteorology*]	BINOVC
Break Into Other Computers (SAUS)	BIOC
Break Jaw (MSA)	BJ
Break Jaw (SAUS)	BS
Break Line [*Printing*] (DGA)	BK L
Break Load (RIMS)	Brld
Break of Entry (NASA)	BOE
Break of Inspection	BOI
Break of Integrity (NASA)	BOI
Break Over Diode [*Electronics*] (EECA)	BOD
Break Point (SAUS)	BP
Break Point (SAUS)	BRK PT
Break Pressure Tank (PDAA)	BPT
Break Pulse Generator (CET)	BPG
Break Relay (SAUS)	BR
Break Request [*Computer science*] (MDG)	BR
Break Request Signal [*Computer science*]	BRS
Break Transmission (NVT)	BT
Breakage (WGA)	BKG
Breakage (SAUS)	bkg
Breakage-Fusion-Bridge (SAUS)	BFB
Breakaway Piston Head (SAUS)	BPH
Break-Away Torque [*Automotive engineering*]	BAT
Break-Before-Make	BBM
Breakdown (MSA)	BKDN
Breakdown [*Electronics*]	BR
Breakdown Acid (SAUS)	BDA
Breakdown Control Number (MCD)	BCN
Breakdown Diode [*Electronics*]	BKDNDIO
Breakdown Energy of Metal (SAUS)	BEM
Breakdown Lorry (WDAA)	BL
Breakdown Maintenance	BM
Breakdown of Recoverable Items (MCD)	BRI
Breakdown Pressure (SAUS)	BdP
Breakdown Pulse Noise (KSC)	BPN
Breakdown Truck [*British*]	BT
Breakdown Voltage [*Telecommunications*] (TEL)	BDV
Breakdown Voltage	BV
Breaker (KSC)	BKR
Breaker	BRKR
Breaker Block	BB
Breaker End (MSA)	BE
Breaker Failure (IAA)	BF
Breakerless Electronic Ignition (DICI)	BEI
Breakerless Ignition System [*Automotive engineering*]	BIS
Breakers [*Freight*]	BRKS
Break-Even Load Factor (IIA)	BELF
Break-Even Point [*Accounting*]	B/E
Breakfast (CDAI)	B
Breakfast [*Classified advertising*] (ADA)	B'FAST
Breakfast (DAVI)	bkf
Breakfast	bkfst
Breakfast	bkft
Breakfast	BRKF
Breakfast (ADWA)	brkfst
Breakfast (CPH)	brkt
Breakfast and Lunch [*Refers to a late morning or early afternoon meal*]	BRUNCH
Breakfast Fed (MAE)	BF
Breakfast Plan [*Travel industry*] (TRID)	BP
Breakfast Time [*Early morning television program*] [*BBC*]	BT
Break-In (IDOE)	BK
Break-In [*Telecommunications*] (TEL)	BKI
Break-In Cycle (SAA)	BI

Break-In Keying (IAA)	BK
Break-in Keying (SAUS)	BK
Break-In Relay	BIR
Breaking [*FBI standardized term*]	B
Breaking	BRKG
Breaking Action (DNAB)	B/A
Breaking Action (SAUS)	BA
Breaking & Entering [*Legal term*] (WDAA)	B&E
Breaking and Entering and Auto Theft [*Police crime computer*]	BEAT
Breaking and Entering in Nighttime and Petty Larceny	B & ENT & PL
Breaking Capacity (IAA)	BC
Breaking Strain [*Of fishing lines or casts*]	BS
Breaking Strength (MAE)	BS
Breaking Up (ADA)	B/U
Break-Lock ECM [*Electronic Countermeasures*] Training [*Navy*] (ANA)	BKLKTNG
Break-Loose Torque [*Automotive engineering*]	BLT
Break-Off Altitude [*Aviation*] (AFM)	BOA
Breakoff Height (SAUS)	BOH
Break-off Portion (SAUS)	BOP
Breakout (NASA)	B/O
Breakout Box [*Computer service industry*] (MCD)	BO
Breakout Box [*Computer service industry*]	BOB
Break-out Box (SAUS)	BoB
Breakout Procurement Center Representative (AAGC)	BPCR
Breakover [*Electronics*]	BO
Breakpoint [*Telecommunications*] (TEL)	BP
Breakpoint	BPT
Breakpoint Address Register (IAA)	BPA
Breakpoint Cluster Region [*Genetics*]	BCR
Breakpoint Instruction (SAUS)	BI
Break-Point Instruction	BPI
Breakpoint Symbol (SAUS)	BS
Breaks Above	BA
Breaks Below	BB
Breaks in Higher Overcast [*NWS*] (FAAC)	BRKHIC
Breakthrough	BT
Breakthrough Bleeding [*Medicine*]	BB
Breakthrough Bleeding [*Medicine*]	BTB
Breakthrough Curves (SAUS)	BTCs
Breakthrough for Youth [*An association*] (EA)	BTF
Breakthrough Foundation (EA)	BF
Breakthrough Foundation (EA)	BTF
Breakup (SAUS)	BU
Break-Up Missile (MCD)	BUM
Break-Up System (SAUS)	BUS
Breakup Time [*Ophthalmology*]	BUT
Breakwater	BKW
Breakwater (SAUS)	Bkw
Breakwater (WDAA)	BRKWTR
Breakwater Fort (SAUS)	BWF
Breakwater Resources Ltd. [*Toronto Stock Exchange symbol*] [*Vancouver Stock Exchange symbol*]	BWR
Brealy Library, Sir Sandford Fleming College, Peterborough, Ont ario [*Library symbol*] [*National Library of Canada*] (NLC)	OPETSF
Bream Fishermen Association	BFA
Breast (ABBR)	BRST
Breast Biopsy [*Medicine*]	BB
Breast Biopsy [*Medicine*]	B Bx
Breast Biopsy [*Gynecology*] (DAVI)	br bx
Breast Biopsy/Frozen Section (SAUS)	BB/FS
Breast Cancer Advisory Center (EA)	BCAC
Breast Cancer Antigen [*Medicine*] (DB)	BCA
Breast Cancer Awareness Month (journ.) (SAUS)	BCAM
Breast Cancer Detection Center [*University of Michigan*] [*Research center*] (RCD)	BCDC
Breast Cancer Detection Demonstration Project [*NCI/ACS cosponsored project*]	BCDDP
Breast Cancer, Ductal [*Medicine*] (DMAA)	BRCD
Breast Cancer Estrogen-Inducible [*Medicine*] (DMAA)	BCEI
Breast Cancer Fund (SAUO)	BCF
Breast Cancer Information Clearinghouse	BCIC
Breast Cancer Information Service (SAUO)	BCIS
Breast Cancer Prevention Trial (SAUO)	BCPT
Breast Cancer Screening Indicator	BCSI
Breast Cancer Society of Canada (SAUO)	BCSC
Breast Cancer susceptibility gene (SAUS)	BRCA1
Breast Cancer Task Force [*National Cancer Institute*]	BCTF
Breast Care and Mastectomy Association (DBA)	BCMA
Breast Examination (DAVI)	BE
Breast Examination Bras, Inc.	BEBI
Breast Examination through Simultaneous Temperature Evaluation	BEST
Breast Examination Training (ACAE)	BET
Breast Exposure National Trends [*Study*] [*FDA*]	BENT
Breast Fed [*Medicine*]	BF
Breast Feeding	BF
Breast Height (SAUS)	BH
Breast Implant [*Medicine*] (MELL)	BI
Breast Milk [*Neonatology and obstetrics*] (DAVI)	BM
Breast Milk [*Neonatology and obstetrics*] (DAVI)	BrM
Breast Milk Jaundice [*Medicine*] (MELL)	BMJ
Breast Needle Location [*Radiology*] (DAVI)	BNL
Breast Self Exam [*Gynecology*] (DAVI)	BSE
Breast Self-Examination [*for cancer*] [*Medicine*]	BSE
Breast Stimulation Test (SAUS)	BST
Breast Tumor [*Medicine*]	BT

Breast Tumor Frozen Section [*Medicine*] (DMAA) .... BTFS
Breastbone (ABBR) .... BRSTBN
Breast-Conserving Therapy (ADWA) .... BCY
Breast-Cyst Fluid Protein [*Immunochemistry*] .... BCFP
Breast-Feeding Mother (WDAA) .... BFM
Breastplate (ABBR) .... BRSTPLT
Breaststroker's Knee [*Medicine*] (MELL) .... BSK
Breat and Water (SAUS) .... B&W
Breath [*Medicine*] .... BR
Breath [*or Breathe*] (ABBR) .... BRTH
Breath Alcohol Concentration .... BAC
Breath Alcohol Ignition Interlock Device [*Automotive safety*] .... BAIID
Breath Hydrogen Test .... BHT
Breath Length (SAUS) .... BL
Breath Odor [*Medicine*] (MELL) .... BO
Breath Rate per Minute (MCD) .... BRPM
Breath sound (SAUS) .... BR sound
Breath Sounds [*Medicine*] .... BrS
Breath Sounds [*Medicine*] .... BS
Breath Test .... BT
Breath Test [*For determining whether or not an auto driver is legally drunk*] [*British*] .... B (Test)
Breath Units .... BU
Breathable Barrier Film [*Organic chemistry*] .... BBF
Breath-Alcohol Concentration [*Sobriety test*] .... BrAC
Breathe (MSA) .... BRTH
Breathe (ABBR) .... BRTHE
Breathe on Recirculation Ignition System (PDAA) .... BORIS
Breathed (ABBR) .... BRTHD
Breather (MSA) .... BRTHR
Breather Hose/Mouthpiece (MCD) .... BH/MP
Breathers for the Reduction of Atmospheric Hazards to the Environment [*Student legal action organization*] .... BREATHE
Breathers United to Stop Standing Time of Passenger-Buses [*Student legal action organization*] .... BUS STOP
Breath-Hold Diving .... BH
Breath-Hold Time .... BHT
Breathing (ABBR) .... BRTHG
Breathing Air (MCD) .... BA
Breathing Air (NASA) .... BAIR
Breathing Air System (ACAE) .... BAS
Breathing Apparatus .... BA
Breathing Apparatus Entry Control Officer (WDAA) .... BAECO
Breathing Apparatus Search and Rescue (SAUS) .... BASAR
Breathing Apparatus Self-Contained Compressed Air Search and Rescue (PDAA) .... BASAR
Breathing Apparatus Tender (WDAA) .... BAT
Breathing Frequency [*Medicine*] (DAVI) .... f
Breathing Metabolic Simulator [*IBM Corp.*] .... BMS
Breathing Rate (MELL) .... BR
Breathing Reserve (ADA) .... BR
Breathng Apparatus Control Van (WDAA) .... BACV
Breaths per Minute .... BPM
Breaths per Second .... BPS
Breathtaking (ABBR) .... BRTHTKG
Breaux Bridge, LA [*FM radio station call letters*] .... KFTE
Brecciated (SAUS) .... Brec
Brecht Society of America [*Defunct*] (EA) .... BSA
Breckenridge, CO [*FM radio station call letters*] .... KSMT
Breckenridge Elementary School, Breckenridge, MN [*Library symbol*] [*Library of Congress*] (LCLS) .... MnBreE
Breckenridge High School, Breckenridge, MN [*Library symbol*] [*Library of Congress*] (LCLS) .... MnBreH
Breckenridge, MN [*AM radio station call letters*] .... KBMW
Breckenridge, MN [*FM radio station call letters*] .... KLTA
Breckenridge Public Library, Breckenridge, MN [*Library symbol*] [*Library of Congress*] (LCLS) .... MnBre
Breckenridge, TX [*Location identifier*] [*FAA*] (FAAL) .... BKD
Breckenridge, TX [*AM radio station call letters*] .... KBIL
Breckenridge, TX [*FM radio station call letters*] (BROA) .... KLXK-FM
Breckenridge, TX [*FM radio station call letters*] .... KROO
Brecknockshire [*Wales*] (BARN) .... Brec
Brecknockshire [*County in Wales*] (ROG) .... BRECK
Brecknockshire [*County in Wales*] (ROG) .... BRECONS
Brecknockshire [*County in Wales*] (ROG) .... BRK
Brecknockshire [*County in Wales*] .... BRKS
Brecknockshire Battalion (SAUO) .... BRECKNOCKS
Brecon [*Welsh depot code*] .... BCN
Brecon and Merthyr Railway [*Wales*] .... BM
Brecon & Merthyr Tydfil Junction Railway Co. (SAUO) .... BMTJR
Breda News, Breda, IA [*Library symbol*] [*Library of Congress*] (LCLS) .... IaBreN
Bredasdorp [*South Africa*] [*ICAO location identifier*] (ICLI) .... FABR
Bredstedt [*Germany*] [*ICAO location identifier*] (ICLI) .... EDZS
Breech [*Obstetrics*] (DAVI) .... Br
Breech Delivery [*Medicine*] (MELL) .... BD
Breech Loading Gun .... BLG
Breech Mechanism [*of a weapon*] .... BM
Breech Presentation [*Medicine*] (MELL) .... BP
Breechloader (SAUS) .... Br L
Breech-Loading [*Weapon*] .... BL
Breech-Loading Rifle .... BLR
Breech-Loading Rifled Guns .... BLRG
Breed Age Average [*Dairy science*] (OA) .... BAA
Breed of Sire .... BOS
Breed Technologies [*NYSE symbol*] (SPSG) .... BDT
Breed Technologies [*Associated Press*] (SAG) .... BredTch
Breeder .... BRDR
Breeder Reactor .... BR
Breeder Reactor Corporation (SAUO) .... BRC
Breeder Reactor Program (SAUS) .... BRP
Breeders and Hatchermen's Association [*Australia*] .... BHA
Breeding .... BRDG
Breeding Bird Census (BARN) .... BBC
Breeding Bird Survey [*Department of the Interior*] .... BBS
Breeding Gain .... BG
Breeding Ratio [*Nuclear energy*] (NRCH) .... BR
Breema Rug Study Society [*Later, CRSS*] (EA) .... BRSS
Breen, CO [*AM radio station call letters*] .... KLLV
Breese Elementary District 12, Breese, IL [*Library symbol*] [*Library of Congress*] (LCLS) .... IBreD
Breese Public Library, Breese, IL [*Library symbol*] [*Library of Congress*] (LCLS) .... IBre
Breese's Illinois Reports [*1 Illinois*] [*A publication*] (DLA) .... Breese
Breese's Illinois Supreme Court Reports [*1 Illinois*] [*1819-31*] [*A publication*] (DLA) .... Breese
Breeze (ABBR) .... BRZ
Breeze Corporation (SAUO) .... BRZ
Breeze Corporations Inc. (SAUO) .... BC
Breeze Electron Ballistic Accelerometer (SAA) .... BEBA
Breezeway (ABBR) .... BRZWY
Breezier (ABBR) .... BRZIR
Breeziest (ABBR) .... BRZST
Breeziness (ABBR) .... BRZNS
Breezing [*Horse racing*] .... B
Breezy (ABBR) .... BRZY
Breezy Point, MN [*FM radio station call letters*] .... KLKS
Brefeldin A [*Antibiotic*] .... BFA
B-Register 8 Bit (SAUS) .... B Reg BB
Bregma [*Medicine*] (MELL) .... B
Breguet Cruise [*SST*] .... BC
Breguet-Dassault [*Societe Anonyme des Ateliers d'Aviation Louis Breguet*] [*France*] [*ICAO aircraft manufacturer identifier*] (ICAO) .... BG
Breidbart Index (SAUS) .... BI
Breiddalsvik [*Iceland*] [*Airport symbol*] (OAG) .... BXV
Breitband WiN (SAUS) .... BWiN
Breitband-ISDN (SAUS) .... B-ISDN
Breiten-/Tiefengrad (SAUS) .... B/T
Breitkopf & Haertel [*Music*] .... B & H
Breitscheid/Dillkreis [*Germany*] [*ICAO location identifier*] (ICLI) .... EDGB
Breit-Wigner Formula .... BWF
Breit-Wigner-Fano [*Spectra interference*] .... BWF
Bremen [*Germany*] [*Airport symbol*] (OAG) .... BRE
Bremen [*Germany*] [*ICAO location identifier*] (ICLI) .... EDDW
Bremen [*Germany*] [*ICAO location identifier*] (ICLI) .... EDWW
Bremen [*Costa Rica*] [*ICAO location identifier*] (ICLI) .... MRBM
Bremen Demokratische Volkspartei [*Bremen Democratic People's Party*] [*Germany*] [*Political party*] (PPE) .... BDV
Bremen Enquirer, Bremen, IN [*Library symbol*] [*Library of Congress*] (LCLS) .... InBreE
Bremen, GA [*AM radio station call letters*] .... WGMI
Bremen, IN [*FM radio station call letters*] (BROA) .... WHPZ-FM
Bremen, IN [*FM radio station call letters*] .... WYEZ
Bremen Maritime Training Centre (SAUS) .... BMTC
Bremen Port of Embarkation [*West Germany*] .... BPE
Bremer Afrika Archiv (SAUO) .... BAA
Bremer County Courthouse, Waverly, IA [*Library symbol*] [*Library of Congress*] (LCLS) .... IaWavCoC
Bremer County Historical Society, Plainsfield, IA [*Library symbol*] [*Library of Congress*] (LCLS) .... IaPlaBHi
Bremer County Historical Society, Waverly, IA [*Library symbol*] [*Library of Congress*] (LCLS) .... IaWavBHi
Bremer County Independent, Waverly, IA [*Library symbol*] [*Library of Congress*] (LCLS) .... IaWavI
Bremerhaven [*Germany*] [*Airport symbol*] (OAG) .... BRV
Bremerhaven [*Germany*] [*ICAO location identifier*] (ICLI) .... EDEO
Bremerhaven Port of Embarkation (SAUO) .... BPOE
Bremerhaven/Am Luneort [*Germany*] [*ICAO location identifier*] (ICLI) .... EDWB
Bremerton Freight Car Ferry [*AAR code*] .... BFCF
Bremerton, WA [*Location identifier*] [*FAA*] (FAAL) .... BER
Bremerton, WA [*Location identifier*] [*FAA*] (FAAL) .... CAN
Bremerton, WA [*AM radio station call letters*] .... KBRO
Bremerton, WA [*FM radio station call letters*] .... KRWM
Bremerton, WA [*Location identifier*] [*FAA*] (FAAL) .... PWT
Bremgarten [*Germany*] [*ICAO location identifier*] (ICLI) .... EDSG
Bremsstrahlung Isochromat Spectroscopy (MCD) .... BIS
Bren Del Win Centennial Library, Deloraine, Manitoba [*Library symbol*] [*National Library of Canada*] (NLC) .... MDB
Bren Del Win Centennial Library, Deloraine, MB, Canada [*Library symbol*] [*Library of Congress*] (LCLS) .... CaMDB
Bren Gun [*or Gunner*] [*British military*] (DMA) .... BG
Bren Gun Carrier [*British military*] (DMA) .... BGC
Brenair Ltd. [*British*] [*ICAO designator*] (FAAC) .... BNX
Brenau College (SAUO) .... BC
Brenau College, Gainsville, GA [*Library symbol*] [*Library of Congress*] (LCLS) .... GGaB
Brencham Air Charter Ltd. [*British*] [*ICAO designator*] (FAAC) .... BRE
Brenco, Inc. [*NASDAQ symbol*] (NQ) .... BREN
Brenco, Inc. [*Associated Press*] (SAG) .... Brenco
Brenda Lee Fan Club (EA) .... BLFC

Brenda Mines Ltd. [Toronto Stock Exchange symbol] [Vancouver Stock Exchange symbol] .... BND
Brendle's, Inc. [NASDAQ symbol] (NQ) .... BRDL
Brendle's, Inc. [Associated Press] (SAG) .... Brendle
Brenham, TX [Location identifier] [FAA] (FAAL) .... BNH
Brenham, TX [FM radio station call letters] .... KTTX
Brenham, TX [FM radio station call letters] .... KULF
Brenham, TX [AM radio station call letters] .... KWHI
Bren-Mar Resources [Vancouver Stock Exchange symbol] .... BML
Brennard-Paige Industries, Inc. (EFIS) .... BPI
Brent Resources Group Ltd. [Vancouver Stock Exchange symbol] .... BTG
Brenton Banks [NASDAQ symbol] (TTSB) .... BRBK
Brenton Banks, Inc. [NASDAQ symbol] (NQ) .... BRBK
Brenton Banks, Inc. [Associated Press] (SAG) .... BrentBk
Brentwood [Urban district in England] .... BRENTW
Brentwood College (SAUO) .... BC
Brentwood, NY [FM radio station call letters] .... WXBA
Brentwood Public Library, Brentwood, MO [Library symbol] [Library of Congress] (LCLS) .... MoBr
Brentwood Public Library, Brentwood, NY [Library symbol] [Library of Congress] (LCLS) .... NBren
Brentwood, TN [AM radio station call letters] (BROA) .... WNSR
Brentwood, TN [AM radio station call letters] .... WYOR
Brenwest Mining [Vancouver Stock Exchange symbol] .... BWM
Brescia College (SAUO) .... BC
Brescia College, London, ON, Canada [Library symbol] [Library of Congress] (LCLS) .... CaOLBR
Brescia College, London, Ontario [Library symbol] [National Library of Canada] (NLC) .... OLBR
Brescia College, Owensboro, KY [Library symbol] [Library of Congress] (LCLS) .... KyOwB
Bresea Resources Ltd. [Vancouver Stock Exchange symbol] .... BSR
Breslau [Wroclaw] [Poland] [Seismograph station code, US Geological Survey] [Closed] (SEIS) .... BRE
Breslauer Philologische Abhandlungen [A publication] (OCD) .... Bresl Phil Abh
Breslich & Foss [British] .... B & F
Brest [France] [Airport symbol] (OAG) .... BES
Brest [France] [ICAO location identifier] (ICLI) .... LFRR
Brest [France] [ICAO location identifier] (ICLI) .... LFRX
Brest Subarea, Channel [NATO] .... BRESTCHAN
Brest/Guipavas [France] [ICAO location identifier] (ICLI) .... LFRB
Bret Hart Fan Club (EA) .... BHFC
Bret "Hit Man" Hart Fan Club (EA) .... BHMHFC
Brethren (ABBR) .... BRTHRN
Brethren Historical Library and Archives, Elgin, IL [Library symbol] [Library of Congress] (LCLS) .... IElgB
Brethren Homes and Older Adult Ministries [An association] (EA) .... BHOAM
Brethren in Christ World Missions (EA) .... BICWM
Brethren of the White Cross [Book written by James De Mille (1873)] .... BOWC
Brethren Peace Fellowship [Inactive] (EA) .... BPF
Brethren Service Commission [Later, World Ministries Commission] (EA) .... BSC
Brethren Volunteer Service (EA) .... BVS
Brethren/Mennonite Council for Lesbian and Gay Concerns (EA) .... BMC
Bretigny-Sur-Orge [France] [ICAO location identifier] (ICLI) .... LFPY
Breton [MARC language code] [Library of Congress] (LCCP) .... bre
Breton [Language, etc.] (ROG) .... BRET
Breton (ADWA) .... Bret
Breton Municipal Library, Alberta [Library symbol] [National Library of Canada] (NLC) .... ABRM
Bretton Woods Committee (EA) .... BWC
Bretton Woods Fund (EA) .... BWF
Brett's Cases in Modern Equity [A publication] (DLA) .... Brett Ca Eq
Brevard College (SAUO) .... BC
Brevard College, Brevard, NC [Library symbol] [Library of Congress] (LCLS) .... NcBreC
Brevard Community College [Florida] (KSC) .... BCC
Brevard Community College, Cocoa, FL [OCLC symbol] (OCLC) .... EBC
Brevard Community College, Cocoa, FL [Library symbol] [Library of Congress] (LCLS) .... FCoaB
Brevard County Library System, Merritt Island, FL [Library symbol] [Library of Congress] (LCLS) .... FMiB
Brevard Engineering College [Florida] (KSC) .... BEC
Brevard Junior College (SAUO) .... BJC
Brevard, NC [AM radio station call letters] .... WGCR
Brevard, NC [AM radio station call letters] .... WRAQ
Brevard, NC [AM radio station call letters] (BROA) .... WSQL-AM
Brevard's Digest of the Public Statute Law, South Carolina [A publication] (DLA) .... Brev Dig
Brevard's South Carolina Reports [1793-1816] [A publication] (DLA) .... Brev
Brevet [Military] .... BREV
Brevet (ADWA) .... brev
Brevet [Military] .... BT
Brevet [Military] .... BVT
brevet (SAUS) .... bvt
Brevet d'Etudes Professionnelles [French] [Professional Studies Diploma] (CPGU) .... BEP
Brevete [Patent] [French] .... BREV
Brevete [Patent] [French] .... BTE
Brevete sans Garantie du Gouvernement [Patent without Government Guarantee] [French] .... BSGDG
Breveted [Military] [British] (ROG) .... BREV
Brevetoxin [Toxicology] (LDT) .... BTX
Brevetoxin-B [Biochemistry] .... BTX-B
Brevia Judicialia [Judicial Writs] [Latin] [Legal term] (DLA) .... Brev Ju
Brevia Selecta [Choice Writs] [Latin] [Legal term] (DLA) .... Brev Sel

Breviary (VRA) .... brev
breviate (SAUS) .... brev
brevier (SAUS) .... brev
Brevier .... BREV
Brevig Mission [Alaska] [Airport symbol] (OAG) .... KTS
Brevity (ABBR) .... BRVT
Brew House (WDAA) .... Br H
Brewarrina [Australia] [Airport symbol] (OAG) .... BWQ
Brewer (SAUS) .... Brew
Brewer (ABBR) .... BRWR
Brewer, ME [FM radio station call letters] .... WKIT
Brewer, ME [AM radio station call letters] .... WNSW
Brewer, ME [FM radio station call letters] .... WQCB
Brewer,C Homes'A' [NASDAQ symbol] (TTSB) .... CBHI
Breweries and Bottleyard Employees' Industrial Union of Workers of Western Australia .... BBEIUWWA
Breweries and Bottleyards Employees' Union [Australia] .... BBEU
Brewers & Licenced Retailers Association (WDAA) .... BLRA
Brewers Association of America (EA) .... BAA
Brewers Association of Canada, [Association des Brasseurs du Canada], Ottawa, Ontario [Library symbol] [National Library of Canada] (NLC) .... OOBA
Brewers' Association of New South Wales [Australia] .... BANSW
Brewers Association of Scotland (SAUS) .... BAS
Brewers Hop Research Institute [Later, USBA] .... BHRI
Brewer's Reports [19-26 Maryland] [A publication] (DLA) .... Brew
Brewer's Reports [19-26 Maryland] [A publication] (DLA) .... Brewer
Brewer's Reports [19-26 Maryland] [A publication] (DLA) .... Brew (MD)
Brewer's Spent Grain .... BSG
Brewer's Spent Grain Bran .... BSGB
Brewers United for Real Potables (SAUS) .... BURP
Brewers Yeast Council [Later, Brewers Yeast and Grains Council] [Defunct] (EA) .... BYC
Brewery (SAUS) .... Brew
Brewery .... BRWRY
Brewing (ROG) .... BREW
brewing (SAUS) .... brew
Brewing .... BRWNG
Brewing & Malting Barley Research Institute [Institut de Recherche-Brassage et Orge de Maltage] (AC) .... BMBRI
Brewing Industries Research Institute [Defunct] (EA) .... BIRI
Brewing Industry Research Foundation [British] .... BIRF
Brewing Research Association (SAUO) .... BRA
Brewing Research Foundation [British] .... BRF
Brewing Research Foundation International (WDAA) .... BRFI
Brewing Trade Review Law Reports [A publication] (DLA) .... BTRLR
Brewing Trade Review Licensing Law Reports [England] [A publication] (DLA) .... BTR
Brewmaster Systems Ltd. [Vancouver Stock Exchange symbol] .... BWE
Brewmeisters Anonymous (EA) .... BA
Brewster [Unit] [Physics] .... B
Brewster Angle Microscopy .... BAM
Brewster Elementary School, Brewster, MN [Library symbol] [Library of Congress] (LCLS) .... MnBrwES
Brewster Ladies Library, Brewster, MA [Library symbol] [Library of Congress] (LCLS) .... MBre
Brewster, NY [AM radio station call letters] .... WPUT
Brewster Public Library, Brewster, NY [Library symbol] [Library of Congress] (LCLS) .... NBre
Brewster Society (EA) .... BS
Brewsterite [A zeolite] .... BRE
Brewster's Pennsylvania Digest [A publication] (DLA) .... Brewst PA Dig
Brewster's Pennsylvania Reports [A publication] (DLA) .... Brews
Brewster's Pennsylvania Reports [A publication] (DLA) .... Brews (PA)
Brewster's Pennsylvania Reports [A publication] (DLA) .... Brewst
Brewster's Pennsylvania Reports [A publication] (DLA) .... Brewster
Brewton, AL [AM radio station call letters] .... WEBJ
Brewton, AL [FM radio station call letters] .... WKNU
Brewton, AL [FM radio station call letters] (BROA) .... WPHG-FM
Brewton-Parker College, Mount Vernon, GA [Library symbol] [Library of Congress] (LCLS) .... GMtvB
Bre-X Minerals Ltd. [Associated Press] (SAG) .... BreXMn
Bre-X Minerals Ltd. [NASDAQ symbol] (SAG) .... BXMN
Bria [Central African Republic] [ICAO location identifier] (ICLI) .... FEFR
Brian, Eric, John, Apthorp & Marion/Millie [Frozen food store] (WDAA) .... BEJAM
Brian Head, UT [FM radio station call letters] .... KREC
Brian Nolan Spradlin International Fan Club Organization (EA) .... BNSIFCO
Briana Resources Ltd. [Vancouver Stock Exchange symbol] .... BIA
Briar Cliff College [Sioux City, IA] .... BCC
Briar Cliff College, Sioux City, IA [Library symbol] [Library of Congress] (LCLS) .... IaScB
Briar Cliff College, Sioux City, IA [OCLC symbol] (OCLC) .... IOB
Briar Pipe Trade Association [British] (DBA) .... BPTA
Briarcliff College (SAUO) .... BC
Briarcliff College, Briarcliff Manor, NY [Library symbol] [Library of Congress] (LCLS) .... NBmB
Briarcliff Manor, NY [FM radio station call letters] .... WRGX
Briarcliff Manor, NY [FM radio station call letters] (BROA) .... WWXY-FM
Briarcliff Manor Public Library, Briarcliff Manor, NY [Library symbol] [Library of Congress] (LCLS) .... NBm
Briard Club of America (EA) .... BCA
Briare/Chatillon [France] [ICAO location identifier] (ICLI) .... LFEI
Bribery [FBI standardized term] .... BRBY
Bribery (DLA) .... BRIB
Bribery and Secret Conventions Prevention League (SAUO) .... BSCPL
Bribery-Labor [FBI undercover investigation] .... BRILAB

Brican Resources [*Vancouver Stock Exchange symbol*] ... BRI
Brice Henderson Fan Club (EA) ... BHFC
Brice. Law Relating to Public Worship [*1875*] [*A publication*] (DLA) ... Bri Pub Wor
Brices Crossroads National Battlefield Site ... BRCR
Brice's Ultra Vires [*A publication*] (DLA) ... Brice Ult V
Brice's Ultra Vires [*A publication*] (DLA) ... Bri Ult V
Brice's Ultra Vires [*A publication*] (ILCA) ... Br Ult V
Brick (WGA) ... B
Brick [*Classified advertising*] (ADA) ... BK
Brick ... BRCK
Brick (VRA) ... bri
Brick [*Classified advertising*] ... BRK
Brick and Tile (ADA) ... BT
Brick Association of North Carolina (SRA) ... BANC
Brick Association of South Carolina (SRA) ... BASC
Brick Brewing Co. Ltd. [*Toronto Stock Exchange symbol*] ... BRB
Brick Construction ... BR
Brick Development Association [*British*] (DBA) ... BDA
Brick Development Research Institute [*Australia*] ... BDRI
Brick Enclosed Elevator (GEOI) ... BE
Brick Institute of America (EA) ... BIA
Brick Institute of California (SRA) ... BRIC
Brick of Bytes [*Computer software*] [*Army High-Performance Computing Research Center*] (RDA) ... BOB
Brick or Stone Built, Slated or Tiled (MARI) ... bsst
Brick Piers (BARN) ... bp
Brick Protected [*Insurance classification*] ... BP
Brick Township, NJ [*FM radio station call letters*] ... WBGD
Brick Unprotected [*Insurance classification*] ... BU
Brick Unprotected (SAUS) ... bu
Brick Veneer (SAUS) ... B/V
Brick Veneered [*Insurance classification*] ... BV
Brickell's Digest [*Alabama*] [*A publication*] (DLA) ... Brick Ala Dig
Brickell's Digest [*Alabama*] [*A publication*] (DLA) ... Brick Dig
Bricklayer (SAUS) ... Brklyr
Bricklayers, Masons, and Plasterers' International of America [*Later, BAC*] ... BMP
Bricklayers, Masons and Plasteres International Union of America (SAUO) ... BM&PIU of A
Bricklayers, Masons and Plasteres International Union of America (SAUO) ... BMPIU
Bricklayers, Masons Independent Union of Canada ... BMIU
Bricklin International (EA) ... BI
Bricklin International Owners Club (EA) ... BIOC
Brickmakers Society [*A union*] [*British*] ... BS
Bricks, Pottery, Glass, Cement [*Department of Employment*] [*British*] ... BPGC
Brickwork ... BWK
Brickwork (SAUS) ... Bwk
Bridal ... BRDL
Bridal and Bridesmaides Apparel Association (SAUO) ... BBAA
Bridal and Bridesmaids Apparel Association (EA) ... BBAA
Bridal Industry Association (EA) ... BIA
Bridewell Hospital (SAUS) ... BH
Bridge [*Shipping*] ... B
Bridge [*Board on Geographic Names*] (KSC) ... BDG
Bridge (ADA) ... BDGE
Bridge [*Interconnects computer networks*] ... BR
Bridge [*Dentistry*] (DAVI) ... BR
Bridge (NTIO) ... br
Bridge (WDAA) ... Br
Bridge (ROG) ... BRD
Bridge (KSC) ... BRDG
Bridge [*or Bridging*] [*Telecommunications*] (TEL) ... BRG
Bridge ... BRI
Bridge [*Commonly used*] (OPSA) ... BRIDGE
Bridge Across the Pond Tom Jones Fan Club (EA) ... BATP
Bridge Adapter Pallet (SAUS) ... BAP
Bridge Amplifier ... BA
Bridge and Building Supply Association [*Defunct*] ... BBSA
Bridge and Structures Information Center [*University of Pittsburgh Department of Civil Engineering*] [*Information service or system*] (IID) ... BASIC
Bridge Board (SAUS) ... BB
Bridge Boat Erection (SAUS) ... BBE
Bridge Bypass (SAUS) ... BP
Bridge Company (SAUO) ... Br Co
Bridge Company (SAUO) ... BrCoy
Bridge Construction Exercise [*Military*] (NVT) ... BRIDGEX
Bridge Control System (IAA) ... BCS
Bridge Cut Off (SAUS) ... BCO
Bridge Cutoff (IEEE) ... BCO
Bridge Deck (SAUS) ... BDk
Bridge Display Console ... BDC
Bridge Display Panel [*Navy*] (CAAL) ... BDP
Bridge Educational Trust Ltd. [*British*] ... BET
Bridge Erection Boat ... BEB
Bridge Excitation ... BRDGSCIT
Bridge Grid Flooring Manufacturers Association (EA) ... BGFMA
Bridge Link (SAUS) ... B Link
Bridge Needs and Investment Process [*FHWA*] (TAG) ... BNIP
Bridge Number (VERA) ... BN
Bridge Platoon (SAUO) ... BrPlat
Bridge Plotting Room [*Navy*] ... BPR
Bridge Port Pair (VERA) ... BPP
Bridge Protocol Data Unit [*Telecommunications*] (ACRL) ... BPDU
Bridge Rating and Analysis Structural System (MCD) ... BRASS
Bridge Receiving Room [*Navy*] ... BRR
Bridge Relay Element [*Electronics*] (ACRL) ... BRE
Bridge Remote Control (SAUS) ... BRC
Bridge Resources Ltd. [*Vancouver Stock Exchange symbol*] ... BGU
Bridge Router Interface (SAUS) ... BRI
Bridge View Bancorp [*Associated Press*] (SAG) ... BrdgVw
Bridge View Bancorp [*AMEX symbol*] (SAG) ... BVB
Bridge Wing (SAUS) ... BRWg
Bridge Wireless Officer [*British military*] (DMA) ... BWO
Bridged Frequency Ringing [*Telecommunications*] (TEL) ... BFR
Bridged Tap Isolator (IEEE) ... BTI
Bridge-Element Delay (IEEE) ... BED
Bridge/Forecastle [*of a ship*] (DS) ... BF
Bridgehampton, NY [*FM radio station call letters*] (BROA) ... WBSQ-FM
Bridgehampton, NY [*FM radio station call letters*] ... WLIE
Bridgehead (MSA) ... BRGHD
Bridgehead (AABC) ... BRH
Bridgelayer [*British military*] (DMA) ... B/L
Bridgeport [*Connecticut*] [*Airport symbol*] (OAG) ... BDR
Bridgeport [*Diocesan abbreviation*] [*Connecticut*] (TOCD) ... BGP
Bridgeport [*Connecticut*] [*Seismograph station code, US Geological Survey*] [*Closed*] (SEIS) ... BPT
Bridgeport, AL [*AM radio station call letters*] ... WBTS
Bridgeport City Normal School, Bridgeport, CT [*Library symbol*] [*Library of Congress*] [*Obsolete*] (LCLS) ... CtBN
Bridgeport, CT [*AM radio station call letters*] ... WCUM
Bridgeport, CT [*AM radio station call letters*] ... WDJZ
Bridgeport, CT [*Television station call letters*] ... WEDW
Bridgeport, CT [*FM radio station call letters*] ... WEZN
Bridgeport, CT [*Television station call letters*] ... WHAI
Bridgeport, CT [*AM radio station call letters*] ... WICC
Bridgeport, CT [*Television station call letters*] (BROA) ... WIPX
Bridgeport, CT [*FM radio station call letters*] ... WPKN
Bridgeport Engineering Institute [*Connecticut*] ... BEI
Bridgeport Machines [*NASDAQ symbol*] (TTSB) ... BPTM
Bridgeport Machines, Inc. [*NASDAQ symbol*] (SAG) ... BPTM
Bridgeport Machines, Inc. [*Associated Press*] (SAG) ... BptMach
Bridgeport, NE [*FM radio station call letters*] (BROA) ... KAWQ-FM
Bridgeport, NY [*FM radio station call letters*] ... WTKW
Bridgeport Philatelic Club (SAUO) ... BPC
Bridgeport Public Library (SAUS) ... BPL
Bridgeport Public Library, Bridgeport, CT [*OCLC symbol*] (OCLC) ... BPT
Bridgeport Public Library, Bridgeport, CT [*Library symbol*] [*Library of Congress*] (LCLS) ... CtB
Bridgeport Public Library, Bridgeport, MI [*Library symbol*] [*Library of Congress*] (LCLS) ... MiBrid
Bridgeport, TX [*Location identifier*] [*FAA*] (FAAL) ... BPR
Bridgeport, TX [*FM radio station call letters*] (BROA) ... KBFR-FM
Bridgeport, TX [*FM radio station call letters*] ... KBOC
Bridgeport, TX [*FM radio station call letters*] ... KBTT
Bridgeport, WV [*FM radio station call letters*] ... WDCI
Bridger Memorial Public Library, Bladenboro, NC [*Library symbol*] [*Library of Congress*] (LCLS) ... NcBl
Bridger Resources, Inc. [*Vancouver Stock Exchange symbol*] ... BDG
Bridge/Router [*Telecommunications*] (ACRL) ... B/R
Bridge/Router Interface Module (VERA) ... BRIM
Bridges (SAUS) ... BRS
Bridges and Gateways (SAUS) ... B&G
Bridges and Tunnels (SAUS) ... B&T
Bridges and Tunnels Crowd [*Derogatory reference to people who reach Manhattan via these routes*] ... B and T
Bridgestreet Accomodations [*AMEX symbol*] (SG) ... BDS
Bridgeton Evening News, Bridgeton, NJ [*Library symbol*] [*Library of Congress*] (LCLS) ... NjBN
Bridgeton Free Public Library, Bridgeton, NJ [*Library symbol*] [*Library of Congress*] (LCLS) ... NjB
Bridgeton, NJ [*FM radio station call letters*] ... WNJB
Bridgeton, NJ [*AM radio station call letters*] ... WSNJ
Bridgeton, NJ [*FM radio station call letters*] ... WSNJ-FM
Bridgetown [*Barbados*] [*ICAO location identifier*] (ICLI) ... TBPO
Bridgetown/Grantley Adams Internacional [*Barbados*] [*ICAO location identifier*] (ICLI) ... TBPB
Bridgettines [*Roman Catholic religious order*] ... BRIDG
Bridge-Tunnel [*Proposed English Channel link between Britain and France*] ... BRUNNEL
Bridgeview Public Library, Bridgeview, IL [*Library symbol*] [*Library of Congress*] (LCLS) ... IBrv
Bridgeville Savings Bank FSB [*Pennsylvania*] [*NASDAQ symbol*] (SAG) ... BREC
Bridgeville Savings Bank FSB [*Pennsylvania*] [*Associated Press*] (SAG) ... BridgvSv
Bridgeville Savings Bank FSB PA [*NASDAQ symbol*] (SAG) ... BRFC
Bridgeville Savings Bk [*NASDAQ symbol*] (TTSB) ... BRFC
Bridgewater College (SAUO) ... BC
Bridgewater College, Bridgewater, VA [*OCLC symbol*] (OCLC) ... VBC
Bridgewater College, Bridgewater, VA [*Library symbol*] [*Library of Congress*] (LCLS) ... ViBrC
Bridgewater, MA [*FM radio station call letters*] ... WBIM
Bridgewater, NJ [*AM radio station call letters*] ... WBRW
Bridgewater, NJ [*AM radio station call letters*] (BROA) ... WSPW-AM
Bridgewater, NS [*AM radio station call letters*] ... CKBW
Bridgewater State College (GAGS) ... Bridgewater St C
Bridgewater State College, Bridgewater, MA [*OCLC symbol*] (OCLC) ... BDR
Bridgewater State College, Bridgewater, MA [*Library symbol*] [*Library of Congress*] (LCLS) ... MBridT
Bridgewater, VA [*Location identifier*] [*FAA*] (FAAL) ... VBW

Bridgewater, VA [FM radio station call letters] .... WAMM
Bridgewell Hospital (SAUO) .... BH
Bridgewest Development [Vancouver Stock Exchange symbol] .... BWD
Bridgewire (NASA) .... BW
Bridgford Foods [NASDAQ symbol] (TTSB) .... BRID
Bridgford Foods Corp. [NASDAQ symbol] (NQ) .... BRID
Bridging [Graphics] .... BDG
Bridging Amplifier (SAUS) .... BA
Bridging and Routing Packet Control Facility [Network Systems Corp.]
  (PCM) .... BCF/PCF
Bridging Control Protocol (VERA) .... BCP
Bridging for the Nineties (SAUO) BR90
Bridging Hepatic Necrosis [Gastroenterology] (DAVI) .... BHN
Bridging Key [on Dial Assistance Switchboard] (CET) .... BR
Bridging Router [Communications] .... brouter
Bridging Truck [British] .... BT
Bridging Vehicle (SAUS) .... BV
Bridgman. Index to Equity Cases [A publication] (DLA) .... Bridg Eq Ind
Bridgman. Legal Bibliography [1801] [A publication] (DLA) .... Bridg Leg Bib
Bridgman, MI [FM radio station call letters] (RBYB) .... WYTZ
Bridgman on Conveyancing [A publication] (DLA) .... Bridg Conv
Bridgman Public Library, Bridgman, MI [Library symbol] [Library of
  Congress] (LCLS) .... MiBridm
Bridgman. Reflections on the Study of the Law [1804] [A publication]
  (DLA) .... Bridg Ref
Bridgman's Digested Index [A publication] (DLA) .... Bridg Dig Ind
Bridgman's Thesaurus Juridicus [A publication] (DLA) .... Bridg Thes
Bridle Arrester (MCD) .... B/A
Bridle Road (WDAA) .... BR
Bridled with Rainbows [A publication] .... BrR
Bridlington [Yorkshire resort town] [England] (DSUE) .... BRID
Bridport [Municipal borough in England] .... BRIDP
Brief .... BF
Brief .... br
Brief .... BRF
Brief Adaptive Psychotherapy [Psychology] .... BAP
Brief and Time [Photography] .... B & T
Brief, Bright, Brotherly [Religion] (DSUE) .... 3B's
Brief Carroll Depression Rating Scale [Psychology] (DMAA) .... BCDRS
Brief Cognitive Rating Scale [Medicine] (DMAA) .... BCRS
Brief Easy Editing Routine (ADA) .... BEER
Brief Entry .... BE
Brief Index of Adaptive Behavior [Educational development test] .... BIAB
Brief Intelligence Summary (NATG) .... BINSUM
Brief Introduction .... BI
Brief Loss of Consciousness (MELL) .... BLOC
Brief Maximal Effort [Orthopedics and physical therapy] (DAVI) .... BME
Brief Neuropsychological Mental Status Examination .... BNMSE
Brief of the Phi Delta Phi [Menasha, Wisconsin] [A publication] (DLA) .... Brief
Brief Psychiatric Rate Scale (DAVI) .... BPRS
Brief Psychiatric Rating Scale .... BPRS
Brief Psychiatric Reacting Scale (DAVI) .... BPRS
Brief Qualification Evaluation Program (SAUS) .... BQEP
Brief Reactive Psychosis (SAUS) .... BRP
Brief Record Cataloging .... BRC
Brief Repetitive Isometric Maximal Exercise (DMAA) .... BRIME
Brief Short-Action Potential (MAE) .... BSAP
Brief, Small, Abundant Potential (MAE) .... BSAP
Brief Stimulus Therapy [Psychology] .... BST
Brief Stop for Ammunition Lift [Military] (NVT) .... BSA
Brief Stop for Cargo Lift [or Delivery] [Military] (NVT) .... BSC
Brief Stop for Embarking or Debarking Personnel [Military] (NVT) .... BSP
Brief Stop for Fuel [Military] (NVT) .... BSF
Brief Symptom Inventory [Personality development test] [Psychology] .... BSI
Brief Systems Test [NASA] (KSC) .... BST
Brief Task Description (AAG) .... BTD
Brief Task Outline (AAG) .... BTO
Brief Test of Head Injury (TMMY) .... BTHI
Brief Vestibular Disorientation Test .... BVDT
Briefcase (SAUS) .... BFC
Briefcase Terminal [Army] (INF) .... BCT
Briefer .... BFR
Briefing (AABC) .... BFG
Briefing (KSC) .... BRFG
Briefing and Liaison Team (SAUO) .... BLT
Briefing Centre, World University Services of Canada [Centre de
  Ressources, Entraide Universitaire Mondiale du Canada], Ottawa, Ontario
  [Library symbol] [National Library of Canada] (NLC) .... OOWU
Briefing Co-ordination Facility (SAUS) .... BCF
Briefing Papers (AAGC) .... BP
[The] Briefing Papers Collection [A publication] (AAGC) .... BPC
Briefing Room [Navy] .... BR
Briefings/Issues/Projects/Programs (DNAB) .... BIPP
Briefly (SAUS) .... BF
Brief-Stimuli Technique (DIPS) .... BST
Brienne-Le-Chateau [France] [ICAO location identifier] (ICLI) .... LFFN
Brierly Investments Limited (SAUO) .... BIL
Brig [Ship] (ROG) .... BG
Brig .... BR
Brig [Shipping] (ROG) .... BRG
Brig [Switzerland] [Seismograph station code, US Geological Survey]
  [Closed] (SEIS) .... BRI
Brigadas Revolucionarias [Revolutionary Brigades] [Portugal] [Political
  party] (PPE) .... BR
Brigade (ADWA) .... bde

Brigade [Military] (MUSM) .... Bde
Brigade (AABC) .... BDE
Brigade .... BDG
Brigade (SAUO) .... BG
Brigade (SAUO) .... Bgde
Brigade .... BGDE
Brigade (WGA) .... BR
Brigade .... BRIG
Brigade (ADWA) .... brig
Brigade Administrative Area [Military] [British] .... BAA
Brigade Aeroportee Renforcee [Reinforced Airborne Brigade] [Zaire] (AF) .... BAR
Brigade Aid Station [Military] .... BAS
Brigade Air Liaison Officer (SAUS) .... BALO
Brigade Air Support Officer [Military] [British] .... BASO
Brigade Air Support Operations Centre [Military] [British] .... BASOC
Brigade Airborne Alert Force [Military] .... BAAF
Brigade Ammunition Column .... BAC
Brigade & Battle Group Trainer (SAUO) .... BBGT
Brigade and Below Command and Control [Military] (RDA) B2C2
Brigade Area (SAUS) .... BA
Brigade Artillery [Army] (INF) .... BRIGARTY
Brigade Artillery Intelligence Officer [Military] [British] .... BAIO
Brigade Battle Simulation [Army] .... BBS
Brigade Combat Team [Army] (INF) .... BCT
Brigade Commander (SAUS) .... Bde Comdr
Brigade Commander (SAUS) .... Bg C
Brigade Data Center [Military] (AABC) .... BDC
Brigade Data Processing System .... BDPS
Brigade Electrical and Mechanical Engineer [Military] [British] .... BEME
Brigade Engineer Group [Marine Corps] (CINC) .... BEG
Brigade Fire Support Officer [Army] .... BDE FSO
Brigade Force Initiative [Army] .... BFI
Brigade Gas Officer (SAUS) .... BGO
Brigade Group (SAUO) .... BGr
Brigade Headquarters [Army] .... BH
Brigade Headquarters [Army] .... BHQ
Brigade Headquarters [Army] .... BRIGHED
Brigade Headquarters .... Brig Hq
Brigade Intelligence Officer (SAUS) .... BIO
Brigade Landing Exercise [Military] (NVT) .... BRIGLEX
Brigade Landing Team [Army] (AABC) .... BDELT
Brigade Logistic Support Group [Marine Corps] (CINC) .... BLSG
Brigade Logistical Control Point (SAUO) .... BLCP
Brigade Maintenance Area [British military] (DMA) .... BMA
Brigade Major [Military] .... Bde Maj
Brigade Major .... BM
Brigade Major (DAS) .... B Maj
Brigade Major (SAUS) .... BrigMaj
Brigade Major, Medium Artillery (SAUS) .... BMMA
Brigade Major of the Queen's Troops [British] (ROG) .... BMQT
Brigade Major, Royal Artillery [British and Canadian] .... BMRA
Brigade Medical Officer (SAUS) .... BMO
Brigade of Guard (SAUO) .... BOG
Brigade of Guards .... BOG
Brigade of Gurkhas [British military] (DMA) .... BG
Brigade Operations Display and After Action Review System [Army]
  (RDA) .... BODAS
Brigade Ordnance Officer [British] .... BOO
Brigade Ordnance Warrant Officer [British] .... BOWO
Brigade Patrol Troop (SAUS) .... BPT
Brigade Platoon (SAUS) .... Br Plat
Brigade Provost Marshal (SAUS) .... Br PM
Brigade Quartermaster [Marine Corps] .... BRQM
Brigade Receiving Room .... BRR
Brigade Remote Computer Center (SAUO) .... BRCC
Brigade Reporting Centre (SAUO) .... BRC
Brigade Resources, Inc. [Vancouver Stock Exchange symbol] .... BGA
Brigade Rouge d'Occitanie [Red Brigade of Occitania] [France] (PD) .... BROC
Brigade Routine Order [British] .... BRO
Brigade Royal Army Service Corps Officer (SAUS) .... BRASCO
Brigade Staff Petty Officer (SAUS) .... BgSf PO
Brigade Supply Officer (SAUS) .... BSO
Brigade Support Area [Military] (AABC) .... BSA
Brigade Tactical Control Party [Army] .... BDE TAC
Brigade Tactical Operations Center .... BTOC
Brigade Training Officer (WDAA) .... BTO
Brigade Training School (SAUS) .... BTS
Brigade Transport Company (SAUO) .... Bde Tpt Coy
Brigade Transport Officer [British] .... BTO
Brigadearzt (SAUS) .... Br
Brigade/Battalion Simulation [Army] (DOMA) .... BBS
Brigade/Corps/Division (SAUS) .... BCD
Brigadehauptverbandplatz (SAUO) .... BrHVPl
Brigades Revolutionnaires Francaises [Revolutionary French Brigades]
  [French] (PD) .... BRF
Brigadier .... BDR
Brigadier (SAUS) .... Bdr
Brigadier [British military] (DMA) .... Br
Brigadier (SAUS) .... Brd
Brigadier (EY) .... BRIG
Brigadier (WDAA) .... Brig
Brigadier and Deputy Director of Royal Engineers (SAUS) .... BDDRE
Brigadier General .... BG
Brigadier General .... BGEN
Brigadier General (SAUO) .... BGen

Brigadier General (SAUO) ... BrGen
Brigadier General ... BRIGEN
Brigadier General (AFM) ... BRIG GEN
Brigadier General (WDAA) ... Brig Gen
Brigadier General [*Air Force, Army, Marine Corps*] ... O7
Brigadier, General Staff [*Army*] [*British*] ... BGS
Brigadier, Royal Artillery [*British*] ... BRA
Brigadier, Royal Artillery (Antiaircraft Artillery) [*British and Canadian*] ... BRA(AA)
Brigadier-General, General Staff (SAUS) ... BGGS
Brigantine [*Ship*] ... BGN
Brigantine [*Ship*] (ROG) ... BN
Brigantine [*Ship*] (ADA) ... B'TINE
Brigantine National Wildlife Refuge (SAUS) ... BNWL
Brigantine National Wildlife Refuge (SAUS) ... BNWR
Brigantine Times, Brigantine, NJ [*Library symbol*] [*Library of Congress*] (LCLS) ... NjBrigT
Brigate Rosse [*Red Brigades*] [*Italy*] (PD) ... BR
Brigdeport Engravers Supply Co. (SAUO) ... BESCO
Brigford Foods Corp. [*Associated Press*] (SAG) ... BrdgF
Briggian Logarithm (SAUS) ... BL
Briggs & Stratton Corp. ... B & S
Briggs & Stratton Corp. [*NYSE symbol*] (SPSG) ... BGG
Briggs & Stratton Corp. [*Associated Press*] (SAG) ... BrigSt
Briggs & Stratton Corp. [*Associated Press*] (SAG) ... BrigStrat
Brigg's General Railway Acts [*A publication*] (DLA) ... Briggs Ry Acts
Briggs Manufacturing Company (SAUO) ... BG
Briggs, OH [*Location identifier*] [*FAA*] (FAAL) ... BSV
Briggs-Lawrence County Public Library, Ironton, OH [*Library symbol*] [*Library of Congress*] (LCLS) ... OIB
Brigham City, UT [*Location identifier*] [*FAA*] (FAAL) ... BMC
Brigham City, UT [*FM radio station call letters*] (RBYB) ... KLZX-FM
Brigham City, UT [*FM radio station call letters*] (BROA) ... KRAR-FM
Brigham City, UT [*AM radio station call letters*] ... KSOS
Brigham City, UT [*FM radio station call letters*] ... KSOS-FM
Brigham City, UT [*AM radio station call letters*] (BROA) ... KXOL
Brigham Integrated Computing System (RALS) ... BICS
Brigham Young Libraries Information Network [*Brigham Young University*] [*Provo, UT*] [*Information service or system*] (IID) ... BYLINE
Brigham Young University [*Utah*] ... BYU
Brigham Young University (SAUS) ... UPB
Brigham Young University, Hawaii Campus, Laie, HI [*OCLC symbol*] (OCLC) ... BYU
Brigham Young University, Hawaii Campus, Laie, HI [*Library symbol*] [*Library of Congress*] (LCLS) ... HLaB
Brigham Young University, J. Reuben Clark Law Library (SAUS) ... UPB-L
Brigham Young University, J. Reuben Clark Law Library, Provo, UT [*Library symbol*] [*Library of Congress*] (LCLS) ... UPB-L
Brigham Young University Press ... BYUP
Brigham Young University, Provo, UT [*Library symbol*] [*Library of Congress*] (LCLS) ... UPB
Brigham Young University, School of Library and Information Science, Provo, UT [*OCLC symbol*] (OCLC) ... UUB
Brigham Young University Science Bulletin, Biological Series (journ.) (SAUS) ... Brigham Young Univ Sci Bull
Bright [*of stars*] (BARN) ... a
Bright (FAAC) ... BRGT
Bright (MSA) ... BRT
Bright (ADWA) ... brt
Bright Alphanumeric Display System (CAAL) ... BRANDS
Bright Alphanumeric Subsystem (SAUS) ... BANS
Bright [*T. G.*] **& Co. Ltd.** [*Toronto Stock Exchange symbol*] ... BRT
Bright Annealed (DAC) ... BA
Bright Belt Warehouse Association (EA) ... BBWA
Bright Cathode-Ray Tube (DEN) ... BCRT
Bright Display Equipment ... BDE
Bright Display Radar Indicator (SAUS) ... BDRI
Bright Field (SAUS) ... BF
Bright Greenish Yellow [*Fluorescence*] [*A fungal metabolite property*] (OA) ... BGY
Bright Greenish Yellow Fluorescence [*A fungal metabolite property*] ... BGYF
Bright. Husband and Wife [*3rd ed.*] [*1849*] [*A publication*] (DLA) ... Bright H & W
Bright Object Detector (SAUS) ... BOD
Bright Object Sensor (MCD) ... BOS
Bright Old Thing [*A member of established society in Washington, DC*] ... BOT
Bright QUASAR Survey [*Astronomy*] ... BQS
Bright RADAR Indicator-Tower Equipment ... BRITE
Bright RADAR Tube Display (AAG) ... BRTD
Bright Red Blood [*Medicine*] ... BRB
Bright Red Blood per Rectum [*Medicine*] ... BRBPR
Bright Source Protection [*Optics*] ... BSP
Bright Two Sides [*Lumber*] (DAC) ... B2S
Bright Up (SAUS) ... BU
Bright Wire Goods Manufacturers Service Bureau [*Defunct*] (EA) ... BWGMSB
Bright Young Thing (DSUE) ... BYT
Brightest Cluster Member (SAUS) ... BCM
Brightly on the Law of Costs in Pennsylvania [*A publication*] (DLA) ... Bright Costs
Brightly's Analytical Digest of the Laws of the United States [*A publication*] (DLA) ... Bright Dig
Brightly's Analytical Digest of the Laws of the United States [*A publication*] (DLA) ... Brightly Dig
Brightly's Analytical Digest of the Laws of the United States [*A publication*] (DLA) ... Bright US Dig
Brightly's Annotated Bankrupt Law [*A publication*] (DLA) ... Bright Bank Law
Brightly's Digest [*New York*] [*A publication*] (DLA) ... Bright Dig
Brightly's Digest [*Pennsylvania*] [*A publication*] (DLA) ... Bright Dig
Brightly's Digest [*New York*] [*A publication*] (DLA) ... Brightly Dig
Brightly's Digest [*Pennsylvania*] [*A publication*] (DLA) ... Brightly Dig
Brightly's Edition of Purdon's Digest of Pennsylvania Laws [*A publication*] (DLA) ... Bright Purd
Brightly's Edition of Purdon's Digest of Pennsylvania Laws [*A publication*] (DLA) ... Bright Pur Dig
Brightly's Edition of Troubat and Haly's Practice [*A publication*] (DLA) ... Bright Tr & H Pr
Brightly's Equitable Jurisdiction [*Pennsylvania*] [*A publication*] (DLA) ... Bright Eq Jur
Brightly's Federal Digest [*A publication*] (DLA) ... Br Fed Dig
Brightly's Federal Digest [*A publication*] (DLA) ... Bright Fed Dig
Brightly's Leading Election Cases [*Pennsylvania*] [*A publication*] (DLA) ... Bright EC
Brightly's Leading Election Cases [*Pennsylvania*] [*A publication*] (DLA) ... Bright Elec Cas
Brightly's Leading Election Cases [*Pennsylvania*] [*A publication*] (DLA) ... Brightly El
Brightly's Leading Election Cases [*Pennsylvania*] [*A publication*] (DLA) ... Brightly El Cas
Brightly's Leading Election Cases [*Pennsylvania*] [*A publication*] (DLA) ... Brightly Elect Cas
Brightly's Leading Election Cases [*Pennsylvania*] [*A publication*] (DLA) ... Brightly Election Cas (PA)
Brightly's Leading Election Cases [*Pennsylvania*] [*A publication*] (DLA) ... Brightly's Elec Cas
Brightly's New York Digest [*A publication*] (DLA) ... Bright NY Dig
Brightly's Pennsylvania Digest [*A publication*] (DLA) ... Bright PA Dig
Brightly's Pennsylvania Nisi Prius Reports [*A publication*] (DLA) ... Bright
Brightly's Pennsylvania Nisi Prius Reports [*A publication*] (DLA) ... Brightly
Brightly's Pennsylvania Nisi Prius Reports [*A publication*] (DLA) ... Brightly NP
Brightly's Pennsylvania Nisi Prius Reports [*A publication*] (DLA) ... Brightly's Rep
Brightly's Pennsylvania Nisi Prius Reports [*A publication*] (DLA) ... Bright NP
Brightly's Pennsylvania Nisi Prius Reports [*A publication*] (DLA) ... Bright (PA)
Brightly's Pennsylvania Nisi Prius Reports [*A publication*] (DLA) ... PA NP
Brightness ... B
Brightness (KSC) ... BRI
Brightness (GAVI) ... BRT
Brightness Acuity Tester (SAUS) ... BAT
Brightness Contrast ... BC
Brightness Contrast Value ... BCV
Brightness Merit ... BM
Brightness Modulation [*Ultrasound scanning*] [*Medicine*] (DAVI) ... B-Mode
Brightness Temperature (ARMP) ... BT
Brightness Temperature Difference (ARMP) ... BTD
Brightness Temperatures (SAUS) ... TB
Brightness Value Unit (GEOI) ... BVU
Brighton [*County borough in England*] ... BRIGH
Brighton [*England*] [*Airport symbol*] (AD) ... BSH
Brighton (ROG) ... BTON
Brighton and Hove Natural History and Philosophical Society (SAUO) ... BHNHPS
Brighton & South Coast Railway [*British*] (ROG) ... BSC
Brighton & South Coast Railway [*British*] (ROG) ... BSCR
Brighton City Library, Brighton, MI [*Library symbol*] [*Library of Congress*] (LCLS) ... MiBrig
Brighton, CO [*AM radio station call letters*] (RBYB) ... KLDC-AM
Brighton, CO [*AM radio station call letters*] ... KLTT
Brighton Community Hospital, Medical Library, Brighton, CO [*Library symbol*] [*Library of Congress*] (LCLS) ... CoBriH-M
Brighton Enterprise-News, Brighton, IA [*Library symbol*] [*Library of Congress*] (LCLS) ... IaBrBEN
Brighton Enterprise-News, Brighton, IA [*Library symbol*] [*Library of Congress*] (LCLS) ... IaBrEN
Brighton High School Library, Rochester, NY [*OCLC symbol*] (OCLC) ... RVS
Brighton MARC [*Machine-Readable Catalogue*] **Project** [*British*] (NITA) ... BRIMARC
Brighton Memorial Library, Brighton, IL [*Library symbol*] [*Library of Congress*] (LCLS) ... IBri
Brighton, NY [*FM radio station call letters*] (RBYB) ... WAQB-FM
Brighton, NY [*FM radio station call letters*] (BROA) ... WZNE-FM
Brighton Public Library, Ontario [*Library symbol*] [*National Library of Canada*] (BIB) ... OBRIG
Brighton Reading and Individualized Skills Continuum (EDAC) ... BRISC
Brighton-Hove-Worthing Joint Airport Committee (SAUO) ... BHWJAC
Brightpoint, Inc. [*Associated Press*] (SAG) ... Brightpt
Brightpoint, Inc. [*NASDAQ symbol*] (SAG) ... CELL
Brightwells Barrow [*England*] ... BRIGHTW BAR
Brigitte Bardot [*French actress*] ... BB
Brigittine Monks (TOCD) ... osss
Brigus Public Library, Brigus, NF, Canada [*Library symbol*] [*Library of Congress*] (LCLS) ... CaNfBri
Brigus Public Library, Newfoundland [*Library symbol*] [*National Library of Canada*] (NLC) ... NFBRI
Brill, C. D., Washington DC [*STAC*] ... BCD
Brillante [*Brilliantly*] [*Music*] ... BRILL
Brilliance (KSC) ... BRIL
Brilliance China Automotive [*NYSE symbol*] (SPSG) ... CBA
Brilliance China Automotive Holding Ltd. [*Associated Press*] (SAG) ... BrillChA
Brilliant [*Philately*] ... bril
Brilliant [*British*] [*Slang*] ... BRILL
Brilliant and Ivory [*Jewelry*] (ROG) ... B & I
Brilliant Anti-Armor Submunition [*Army*] (RDA) ... BAT
Brilliant Anti-Tank System [*Army*] ... BAT
Brilliant Buff Finishing [*Metal finishing*] ... BBF

[A] Brilliant Career	ABC
Brilliant Computer Products Co. (PCM)	BCP
Brilliant Cresyl Blue [Biological stain]	BCB
Brilliant Digital Entertainment, Inc. [AMEX symbol] (SAG)	BDE
Brilliant Digital Entertainment, Inc. [Associated Press] (SAG)	BrillDig
Brilliant Eyes	BE
Brilliant Green [An indicator] [Chemistry]	BG
Brilliant Green Agar (OA)	BGA
Brilliant Green Bile [Microorganism growth medium]	BGB
Brilliant Green Lactose Broth (MAE)	BGLB
Brilliant Green Suphadiazine-Deoxycholate Agar (PDAA)	BGSDA
Brilliant Pebbles	BP
Brilliant Uncirculated [Condition of coins] [Numismatics]	BU
Brillion, WI [FM radio station call letters]	WEZR
Brillouin Scattering (PDAA)	BS
Brillouin Zone [Physics]	BZ
Brillouin-Wentzel-Kramers [Physics]	BWK
Brill-Symmers [Disease] [Medicine] (DB)	BS
Brimm Energy Corp. [NASDAQ symbol] (SAG)	BRIM
Brimm Energy Corp. [NASDAQ symbol] (TTSB)	BRIMF
Brimm Energy Corp. [Associated Press] (SAG)	Brimm
Brimstone R. R. [AAR code]	BRM
Brinco Ltd. [Toronto Stock Exchange symbol]	BRN
Brindise/Casale [Italy] [ICAO location identifier] (ICLI)	LIBR
Brindisi [Italy] [Airport symbol] (OAG)	BDS
Brindisi [Italy] [ICAO location identifier] (ICLI)	LIBB
Brindled (WGA)	BD
Brine Chiller Test Stand (DWSG)	BCTS
Brine Disposal Program [Environmental Data and Information Service] (MSC)	BDP
Brine Shrimp Nauplii [Ichthyology]	BSN
Brinell Hardness (SAUS)	HB
Brinell Hardness Number [Also, BHN, BHNo, HB]	BH
Brinell Hardness Number [Also, BH, BHNo, HB]	BHN
Brinell Hardness Number [Also, BH, BHN, HB]	BHNo
Brinell Hardness Number [Also, BH, BHN, BHNo]	HB
Brinell Hardness Test (AAEL)	BHT
Bring Back Mark Lindsay Campaign (EA)	BBMLC
Bring 'Em Back Alive [AAA Holiday News Service]	BEBA
Bring Forward	BF
Bring Your Own [Liquor] [Party invitation notation]	BYO
Bring Your Own Beef [Phrase popularized during 1973 beef shortage]	BYOB
Bring Your Own Boat	BYOB
Bring Your Own Booze [or Bottle] [Party invitation notation]	BYOB
Bring Your Own Girl (IIA)	BYOG
Bring Your Own Grog [British] (ADA)	BYOG
Bring Your Own Rocket Launcher [Computer hacker terminology]	BYORL
Bring Your Own TV	BYOTV
Bring Your Own Vehicle	BYOV
Bring Your Own Wine (ADA)	BYOW
Bringham Memorial Library, Sharon, WI [Library symbol] [Library of Congress] (LCLS)	WSha
Bring-Up Security Investigation [Military]	BUSI
Brinker International [Formerly, Chili's, Inc.] [Associated Press] (SAG)	Brinker
Brinker International [Formerly, Chili's, Inc.] [NYSE symbol] (SPSG)	EAT
Brinkley, AR [Location identifier] [FAA] (FAAL)	BKZ
Brinkley, AR [AM radio station call letters]	KBRI
Brinkley, AR [FM radio station call letters]	KQMC
Brinkley, AR [FM radio station call letters] (BROA)	KTRQ-FM
Brinster's Medium for Ovum Culture (DB)	BMOC
Brio Industries [NASDAQ symbol] (SAG)	BRIO
Brio Industries [NASDAQ symbol] (TTSB)	BRIOF
Brio Industries [Associated Press] (SAG)	BrioInd
Brioude-Beaumont [France] [ICAO location identifier] (ICLI)	LFHR
Briquet	BQ
Briquette (ADA)	BRIQ
Briquette	BRQTT
Briquettes (VRA)	briq
Brisa International [Toronto Stock Exchange symbol]	BSA
Brisbane [Australia] [ICAO location identifier] (ICLI)	ABBB
Brisbane [Australia] [ICAO location identifier] (ICLI)	ABBN
Brisbane [Australia] [ICAO location identifier] (ICLI)	ABBR
Brisbane [Australia] [ICAO location identifier] (ICLI)	ABBX
Brisbane [Australia] [ICAO location identifier] (ICLI)	ABEF
Brisbane [Australia] [ICAO location identifier] (ICLI)	ABRF
Brisbane [Australia] [Airport symbol] (OAG)	BNE
Brisbane [Australia]	Bris
Brisbane [Australia] [Seismograph station code, US Geological Survey] (SEIS)	BRS
Brisbane Amateur Turf Club (SAUO)	BATC
Brisbane Amateur Winemakers' Club [Australia]	BAWC
Brisbane Basketball	BB
Brisbane Biennial	BB
Brisbane Bushwalkers Club	BBC
Brisbane Forest Park Administration [Australia]	BFPA
Brisbane Funeral Directors' Association [Australia]	BFDA
Brisbane Jazz Club [Australia]	BJC
Brisbane Latvian Club [Australia]	BLC
Brisbane Market Trust [Australia]	BMT
Brisbane Netball Association [Australia]	BNA
Brisbane Night Tennis Association [Australia]	BNTA
Brisbane Overseas Wharfowners' Association [Australia]	BOWA
Brisbane Produce Merchants' Association [Australia]	BPMA
Brisbane Sand and Gravel Producers' Association [Australia]	BSGPA
Brisbane Sporting Car Club [Australia]	BSCC

Brisbane Theosophical Society [Australia]	BTS
Brisbane Tramway Museum Society [Australia]	BTMS
Brisbane Warana Festival [Australia]	BWF
Brisbane Women's Club [Australia]	BWC
Brisbane Women's Hockey Association [Australia]	BWHA
Brisbane/Archerfield [Australia] [ICAO location identifier] (ICLI)	ABAF
Brisbin's Reports [1 Minnesota] [A publication] (DLA)	Brisbin
Brisbin's Reports [1 Minnesota] [A publication] (DLA)	Brisb Minn
Brisk and Equal [Medicine] (DMAA)	B&E
Brisk and Equal (SAUS)	BE
Brisket (ABBR)	BRSKT
Briskly (ABBR)	BRSKY
Bris-Myr Squibb,$2 Cv Pfd [NYSE symbol] (TTSB)	BMYPr
Bristle (ABBR)	BRSL
Bristle Institute of America (SAUS)	BIA
Bristled (ABBR)	BRSLD
Bristling (ABBR)	BRSLG
Bristol [Board/paper]	B
Bristol [France] [Research code symbol]	B
Bristol [City and county borough in England] (ROG)	BRIS
Bristol [England] [Airport symbol] (OAG)	BRS
Bristol [City and county borough in England]	BRSTL
Bristol [British] [ICAO location identifier] (ICLI)	EGRD
Bristol Aero Engines Ltd., Montreal, PQ, Canada [Library symbol] [Library of Congress] (LCLS)	CaQMBAE
Bristol Aero Engines Ltd., Montreal, Quebec [Library symbol] [National Library of Canada] (NLC)	QMBAE
Bristol Aeroplane Co. (MCD)	BAC
Bristol Aeroplane Company (SAUO)	BAC
Bristol Aerospace Ltd. (SAUO)	BAL
Bristol Aerospace Ltd., Winnipeg, Manitoba [Library symbol] [National Library of Canada] (NLC)	MWBA
Bristol and Birmingham Railway (ROG)	B & BR
Bristol & Wessex Aeroplane Club Ltd. [British] [ICAO designator] (FAAC)	FLP
Bristol BAE [British] [ICAO designator] (FAAC)	GEM
Bristol Bay Oceanographic Processes	B-BOP
Bristol Bay School, Media Center, Naknek, AK [Library symbol] [Library of Congress] (LCLS)	AkNakBS
Bristol Centre for the Advancement of Architecture [British] (CB)	BCAA
Bristol Channel [British]	BC
Bristol Channel [British]	B/CH
Bristol City Line [Steamship] (MHDW)	BCL
Bristol Community College, Fall River, MA [OCLC symbol] (OCLC)	BRC
Bristol Community College, Fall River, MA [Library symbol] [Library of Congress] (LCLS)	MFB
Bristol County Law Library, Taunton, MA [Library symbol] [Library of Congress] (LCLS)	MTaB
Bristol, CT [AM radio station call letters]	WPRX
Bristol Evening Post, Bristol, United Kingdom [Library symbol] [Library of Congress] (LCLS)	UkBrP
Bristol Fighter [Aircraft] [World War I]	BF
Bristol Fighter [British aircraft] (DSUE)	BRISFIT
Bristol Flying Centre Ltd. [British] [ICAO designator] (FAAC)	CLF
Bristol Historical and Preservation Society, Bristol, RI [Library symbol] [Library of Congress] (LCLS)	RBrHi
Bristol Hotel [NYSE symbol] (TTSB)	BH
Bristol Hotel & Resorts [NYSE symbol] (SG)	BH
Bristol Hotel Co. [NYSE symbol] (SAG)	BH
Bristol Hotel Co. [Associated Press] (SAG)	BristHtl
Bristol Ice And Snow Cover Algorithm (SAUS)	BRISCA
Bristol Independent School District Library, Bristol, SD [Library symbol] [Library of Congress] (LCLS)	SdBrS
Bristol Industrial Archaeological Society (SAUO)	BIAS
Bristol Interactive System (SAUS)	BIAS
Bristol Laboratories (SAUO)	BL
Bristol Laboratories	BL
Bristol Laboratories [Research code symbol]	BL-H
Bristol Laboratories [Research code symbol]	P
Bristol Laboratories, Library, Syracuse, NY [OCLC symbol] (OCLC)	ZUD
Bristol Laboratories, Syracuse, NY [Library symbol] [Library of Congress] (LCLS)	NSyBL
Bristol Memorial Hospital, Bristol, TN [Library symbol] [Library of Congress] (LCLS)	TBriH
Bristol Myers Squibb [Associated Press] (SAG)	BrMSq
Bristol Myers Squibb [Associated Press] (SAG)	BrMySq
Bristol Owners Club, US Branch (EA)	BOC
Bristol Polytechnic [Bristol, England]	BP
Bristol Record Society (SAUO)	BRS
Bristol, RI [FM radio station call letters]	WQRI
Bristol Royal Blind Asylum (SAUO)	BRBA
Bristol Siddeley Turbomechanical International (SAUO)	BSTI
Bristol Simplified Reheat [Aircraft] (NATG)	BSR
Bristol Social Adjustment Guides [Psychology]	BSAG
Bristol Steam Navigation Co. (MHDB)	BSNC
Bristol Technology Systems, Inc. [Associated Press] (SAG)	BristIT
Bristol Technology Systems, Inc. [NASDAQ symbol] (SAG)	BTEC
Bristol, TN [Location identifier] [FAA] (FAAL)	BON
Bristol, TN [Location identifier] [FAA] (FAAL)	TRI
Bristol, TN [AM radio station call letters]	WBCV
Bristol, TN [FM radio station call letters]	WHCB
Bristol, TN [FM radio station call letters]	WXBQ-FM
Bristol Tolzey Court (SAUO)	BTC
Bristol United Press Ltd., Bristol, United Kingdom [Library symbol] [Library of Congress] (LCLS)	BUP
Bristol University Medical School [England] (WDAA)	BUMS

Bristol University Spelaeological Society (SAUO) ... BUSS
Bristol Urological Institut (SAUO) ... BUI
Bristol, VA [*Television station call letters*] ... WCYB
Bristol, VA [*AM radio station call letters*] ... WOPI
Bristol, VA [*AM radio station call letters*] ... WXBQ
Bristol, VA [*AM radio station call letters*] ... WZAP
Bristol/Filton [*British*] [*ICAO location identifier*] (ICLI) ... EGTG
Bristol/Lulsgate [*British*] [*ICAO location identifier*] (ICLI) ... EGGD
Bristol-Myers Co. ... B-M
Bristol-Myers Co. (SAUO) ... BMY
Bristol-Myers Co. [*Research code symbol*] ... NSC
Bristol-Myers Co. [*Research code symbol*] ... RP
Bristol-Myers Squibb [*NYSE symbol*] (TTSB) ... BMY
Bristol-Myers Squibb Co. [*NYSE symbol*] (SPSG) ... BMY
Bristol-Myers Squibb Co. [*Associated Press*] (SAG) ... BrMSq
Bristol-Myers Squibb Co. [*Associated Press*] (SAG) ... BrMySq
Bristol-Myers Squibb's ... BMS
Bristol/NOAA Interactive Scheme (SAUS) ... BIAS
Bristol-Washington Township Public Library (Bristol Public Library), Bristol, IN [*Library symbol*] [*Library of Congress*] (LCLS) ... InBri
Bristow Helicopters Group Ltd. [*British*] [*ICAO designator*] (FAAC) ... BHL
Bristow Helicopters Group Ltd. (SAUS) ... UH
Bristow Masayu Helicopter PT [*Indonesia*] [*ICAO designator*] (FAAC) ... BMH
Bristow, OK [*FM radio station call letters*] ... KREK
Bristow Public Library, Bristow, OK [*Library symbol*] [*Library of Congress*] (LCLS) ... OkBr
Brit Chalutzim Datiyim (BJA) ... BACHAD
Brit Ivrit Olamit [*World Association for Hebrew Language and Culture*] (EAIO) ... BIO
Brita Esperantista Asocion (SAUO) ... BEA
Britain (SAUO) ... Br
Britain (ROG) ... BR
Britain (WA) ... Br
Britain [*or British*] ... BRIT
Britain (VRA) ... Brit
Britain (SAUO) ... Brit
Britain and Scandinavia (SAUO) ... Brisc
Britain Nepal Medical Trust (SAUS) ... BNMT
Britain-Australia Society (DBA) ... B-AS
Britain-China Friendship Association (BI) ... BCFA
Britains Atomic Factories (SAUS) ... BAF
Britair SA [*France*] [*ICAO designator*] (FAAC) ... BZH
Britannarium [*Of All the Britains*] [*Coin inscription*] (ROG) ... BRITT
Britannia ... BRIT
Britannia (SAUS) ... Brit
Britannia Airways [*Airline flight code*] (ODBW) ... BY
Britannia Airways Ltd. [*British*] [*ICAO designator*] (FAAC) ... BAL
Britannia Building Society [*British*] ... BBS
Britannia Metal (SAUS) ... Brit Met
Britannia Petite Rabbit Fanciers Association [*Defunct*] (EA) ... BPRFA
Britannia Royal Naval College ... BritColl
Britannia Royal Naval College (SAUO) ... BritColl
Britannia Royal Naval College ... BRNC
Britannica ... BRIT
Britannica (SAUS) ... Brit
Britannica Junior Encyclopedia [*A publication*] ... BJE
Britannica Reading Achievement Center ... BRAC
Britcol Resource Development [*Vancouver Stock Exchange symbol*] ... BTO
Brite Voice System, Inc. [*NASDAQ symbol*] (NQ) ... BVSI
Brite Voice Systems [*NASDAQ symbol*] (TTSB) ... BVSI
Brite Voice Systems, Inc. [*Associated Press*] (SAG) ... BriteV
BriteSmile, Inc. [*Formerly, Ion Laser Technology*] [*AMEX symbol*] ... BWT
Brith Abraham (BJA) ... BA
B'rith Christian Union [*Later, FSJ*] (EA) ... BCU
Brith Sholom (EA) ... BS
Britian Israel Public Affairs Centre ... BIPAC
Briticism (BARN) ... Brit
Britisch-American Tobacco Co. Ltd. (SAUO) ... BAT
British ... B
British (ADWA) ... Br
British (BEE) ... Brit
British (DLA) ... BRIT
British (SAUO) ... Brit
British (ROG) ... BRT
British ... BRTSH
British Ability Scales (EDAC) ... BAS
British Abraham Foundation (SAUO) ... BAF
British Abrasive Federation (EAIO) ... BAF
British Absolute Unit ... BAU
British Academy ... BA
British Academy (SAUO) ... BA
British Academy (SAUO) ... BAFTA
British Academy of Experts (DBA) ... BAE
British Academy of Film and Television Arts ... BAFTA
British Academy of Forensic Science (SAUS) ... BAFS
British Academy of Forensic Sciences (SAUO) ... BAFS
British Academy of Songwriters, Composers, and Authors ... BASCA
British Accounting and Finance Association (PDAA) ... BAFA
British Accounting Association (DBA) ... BAA
British Accreditation Council (SAUO) ... BAC
British Acetylene Association (SAUO) ... BAA
British Acetylene Welding Association (SAUO) ... BAW
British Acoustical Society ... BAS
British Action for Children's Television (AIE) ... BAC
British Activity Holiday Association (DBA) ... BAHA
British Actors' Equity Association [*A union*] (DCTA) ... BAEA
British Acupuncture Association and Register (DBA) ... BAA
British Acupuncture Association and Register (EA) ... BAAR
British Additional Teleprocessing Support (SAUS) ... BATS
British Adhesive and Sealants Association ... BASA
British Adhesive Manufacturers Association (SAUO) ... BAMA
British Admiralty (SAUO) ... BA
British Admiralty ... BA
British Admiralty Delegation [*to Washington*] ... BAD
British Admiralty Delegation to Washington (SAUO) ... BAD
British Admiralty Establishment ... BAE
British Admiralty Maintenance and Supply Representative (SAUO) ... BAMBSR
British Admiralty Maintenance and Supply Representative ... BAMSR
British Admiralty Repair Mission ... BARM
British Admiralty Repair Mission (SAUO) ... BARM
British Admiralty Signal Radar Establishment (SAUO) ... BASRE
British Admiralty Signal Radar Establishment (SAUS) ... B/ASRE
British Admiralty Technical Mission (SAUO) ... BATM
British Admiralty Technical Mission [*World War II*] ... BATM
British Adult Publications Association (SAUO) ... BAPA
British Adult Publications Association Ltd. (SAUO) ... BAPAL
British Advertising Association (SAUO) ... BAA
British Advertising Gift Distributors Association (SAUO) ... BAGDA
British Advisory Committee for Aeronautics ... BACA
British Advisory Mission to South Vietnam ... BRIAM
British Aearospaces Reinforced and Microwave Plastics (SAUS) ... RMP
British Aerial Standards Council (SAUO) ... BASC
British Aerial Transport Ltd. ... BAT
British Aerobatic Association (PDAA) ... BAeA
British Aeromedical Practitioners Association (DBA) ... BAMPA
British Aeromedical Practitioners Association (DA) ... BAPA
British Aeronautical Research Committee ... BARC
British Aerophilatelic Federation (DBA) ... BAeF
British Aerosol Manufacturers Association ... BAMA
British Aerospace ... BAE
British Aerospace Air Combat Maneuvering Instrumentation Range (DA) ... BAACMIR
British Aerospace Aircraft Group (SAUO) ... BAAG
British Aerospace Australia ... BAeA
British Aerospace Commercial Aircraft (SAUS) ... BACA
British Aerospace Corporation (SAUO) ... BAC
British Aerospace Dynamics Group (SAUO) ... BADG
British Aerospace Flying College Ltd. [*ICAO designator*] (FAAC) ... AYR
British Aerospace Jetstream 31 [*Airplane code*] ... J31
British Aerospace Ltd. ... BA
British Aerospace Ltd. ... BAe
British Aerospace PLC [*ICAO designator*] (FAAC) ... BAE
British Aerospace PLC (SAUS) ... HQ
British Aerospace Simulation Ltd. (SAUO) ... BAeSL
British Aerospace Staff Association (SAUO) ... BASA
British Aerospace Systems & Equipment Ltd. (SAUO) ... BASE
British Agencies for Adoption (WDAA) ... BAA
British Agencies for Adoption and Fostering (DI) ... BAAF
British Aggregate Construction Materials Industry ... BACMI
British Agricultural and Garden Machinery Association ... BAGMA
British Agricultural and Horticultural Plastics Association (PDAA) ... BAHPA
British Agricultural Export Council ... BAEC
British Agricultural Export Council (SAUO) ... BAEC
British Agricultural History Society ... BAHS
British Agricultural Machinery Manufacturers Export Group (SAUS) ... BAMMEX
British Agricultural Marketing Development Organisation (SAUO) ... BAMDO
British Agricultural Marketing Research Group ... BAMRG
British Agrochemicals Association ... BAA
British Aikido Association (SAUO) ... BAA
British Air Commission [*Washington*] ... BAC
British Air Cushion Vehicle Safety Requirements (PDAA) ... BACVSR
British Air Ferries (SAUS) ... BAF
British Air Ferries [*ICAO designator*] (AD) ... VF
British Air Force ... BAF
British Air Force in South East Asia (SAUO) ... BAFSEA
British Air Force of Occupation (SAUO) ... BAFO
British Air Force of Occupation Command (SAUO) ... BAFOC
British Air Forces in France [*World War II*] ... BAFF
British Air Forces in Greece [*British military*] (DMA) ... BAFG
British Air Intelligence Service (SAUO) ... BAIS
British Air Line Pilots Association (SAUS) ... BALPA
British Air Mail Society (BI) ... BAMS
British Air Ministry ... BAM
British Air Ministry Control Office ... BAMCO
British Air Survey Association (DBA) ... BASA
British Air Transport Association (DA) ... BATA
British Aircraft Constructors (SAUO) ... BAC
British Aircraft Corp. Ltd. [*ICAO aircraft manufacturer identifier*] (ICAO) ... BA
British Aircraft Corp. Ltd. [*ICAO aircraft manufacturer identifier*] (ICAO) ... BR
British Aircraft Corp. Ltd. [*ICAO aircraft manufacturer identifier*] (ICAO) ... PE
British Aircraft Corp. Ltd. [*ICAO aircraft manufacturer identifier*] (ICAO) ... VC
British Aircraft Corporation Commercial Habitat Under the Sea (SAUO) ... BACCHUS
British Aircraft Corporation Ltd. (SAUO) ... BAC
British Aircraft Corporation Staff Association (SAUO) ... BACSA
British Aircraft Corporation USA (SAUO) ... BACUSA
British Aircraft Manufacturing Company, Limited (SAUO) ... BAMCL
British Aircraft Preservation Council ... BAPC
British Aircraft Users Association (SAUO) ... BAUA
British Airline Stewardesses Association (SAUO) ... BASSA

British Airport Construction and Equipment Association (SAUO) ... BACEA
British Airport Rapid Control and Indication Systems (PDAA) ... BARCIS
British Airports Authority ... BAA
British Airports Information Retrieval [*System*] ... BAIR
British Airports International (SAUO) ... BAI
British Airtours Ltd. [*Airline*] ... BA
British Airtours Ltd. [*British*] [*ICAO designator*] (ICDA) ... KT
British Airways [*British*] [*ICAO designator*] (ICDA) ... BA
British Airways [*ICAO designator*] (FAAC) ... BAW
British Airways (SAUO) ... BE
British Airways [*Associated Press*] (SAG) ... BritAir
British Airways ADS [*NYSE symbol*] [*Toronto Stock Exchange symbol*] (SPSG) ... BAB
British Airways Board (AIA) ... BAB
British Airways, Cairo (SAUO) ... BAC
British Airways European Division (SAUO) ... BAED
British Airways Group (SAUO) ... BAG
British Airways Helicopters (SAUO) ... BAH
British Airways, Ltd. (SAUO) ... BAL
British Airways Overseas Division (SAUO) ... BAOD
British Airways Safety Information System (GAVI) ... BASIS
British Airways Shuttle [*ICAO designator*] (FAAC) ... SHT
British Airways Shuttle Services ... BASS
British Airways Staff Information System (SAUS) ... BASIS
British Allergy Society ... BAS
British Alsatian Association (BI) ... BAA
British Aluminium Building Service (BI) ... BABS
British Aluminium Co. (SAUO) ... BA
British Aluminium Co. Ltd. (ODBW) ... BACO
British Aluminium Foil Rollers Association (BI) ... BAFRA
British Aluminum Company (SAUS) ... BACO
British Amateur Athletic Board ... BAAB
British Amateur Baseball Federation ... BABF
British Amateur Dancers Association (SAUO) ... BADA
British Amateur Electronics Club (PDAA) ... BAEC
British Amateur Gymnastics Association ... BAGA
British Amateur Gymnastics Association (SAUO) ... BAGA
British Amateur Karate Association (SAUO) ... AKA
British Amateur Press Association (BI) ... BAPA
British Amateur Radio Teleprinter Group (BI) ... BARTG
British Amateur Rugby League Association (DBA) ... BARLA
British Amateur Scientific Research Association (SAUO) ... BASRA
British Amateur Strand Pulling Association ... BASPA
British Amateur Tape Recording Society ... BATRS
British Amateur Television Club ... BATC
British Amateur Weight Lifters' Association ... BAWLA
British Amateur Wrestling Association (BI) ... BAWA
British America ... BA
British America (BARN) ... BR AM
British America (SAUS) ... Br Am
British American (SAUO) ... BA
British American (SAUO) ... B/A
British American Bank Note, Inc. [*Toronto Stock Exchange symbol*] [*Vancouver Stock Exchange symbol*] ... BAN
British American Books (SAUS) ... British Am Bks
British American Minesweeper [*British military*] (DMA) ... BAMS
British American Oil (SAUO) ... BAO
British American Oil (SAUS) ... BAO
British American Repertory Company ... BARC
British American Scientific Research Association ... BASRA
British American Security Information Center [*Research Orgainzation*] ... BASIC
British American Security Information Council (SAUO) ... BASIC
British American Standard (SAUS) ... BAS
British American Tobacco ADS [*Formerly, BAT Industries Ltd.*] [*AMEX symbol*] ... BTI
British Amputee Sports Association (DBA) ... BASA
British Amsterdam Maritime Agencies (SAUO) ... BAMA
British Amusement Catering Trades Association (DBA) ... BACTA
British Anaerobic and Biomass Association (PDAA) ... BABA
British Anaerobic & Biomass Association Ltd. ... BABA LTD
British Anaesthetic and Respiratory Equipment Manufacturers Association (DBA) ... BAREMA
British Anatomical Society (SAUO) ... BAS
British and Burmese Steam Navigation Company (SAUO) ... B & B SNC
British and Central-European Chamber of Commerce (SAUO) ... BCECC
British and Colonial Prize Cases [*A publication*] (DLA) ... B & C Pr Cas
British and Colonial Prize Cases [*A publication*] (DLA) ... Br & Col
British and Colonial Prize Cases [*A publication*] (DLA) ... Br & Col Pr Cas
British and Colonial Prize Cases [*A publication*] (DLA) ... Brit & Col Pr Cas
British and Colonial Prize Cases [*A publication*] (DLA) ... PC
British and Colonial Prize Cases [*A publication*] (DLA) ... Trehern
British & Commonwealth [*Company*] ... B & C
British & Commonwealth (SAUO) ... B&C
British & Commonwealth Holdings [*Commercial firm*] (ECON) ... B & C
British and Commonwealth Shipping Company (SAUO) ... B&CS
British and European Geranium Society (EAIO) ... BEGS
British and European Osteopathic Association [*Sutton, Surrey, England*] (EAIO) ... BEOA
British and Foreign Bible Society (SAUO) ... B&FBS
British and Foreign Bible Society ... BFBS
British and Foreign Maritime Agencies (SAUO) ... BAFMA
British and Foreign Maritime Agencies (BARN) ... BAFMA
British and Foreign School Society (SAUO) ... BFSS
British and Foreign Schools Society (AIE) ... BFSS
British and Foreign Temperance Society (SAUO) ... BFTS
British and International Addressing Post [*A publication*] ... BIA
British and Irish Association of Law Librarians (DLA) ... BIALL
British and Irish Basketball Federation (SAUO) ... BIBF
British and Irish Basketball Federation (DBA) ... BIBF
British and Irish Committee for Map Information and Cataglogue Systems (GEOI) ... BRICMICS
British and Irish Communist Organization [*Irish*] ... B & ICO
British and Irish Skeptic (EAIO) ... BIS
British & Irish Steam Packet Co. (MHDB) ... B & I SPC
British and Irish Steamship Co. (SAUO) ... B&I
British and Latin American Chamber of Commerce (SAUO) ... BLACC
British and Midlands Scientific Society (SAUO) ... BMSS
British and South African Forum ... BASAF
British and South Asian Trade Association [*British Overseas Trade Board*] (DS) ... BASATA
British Andrology Society (SAUO) ... BAS
British Angular Rate Bombsight ... BARB
British Animated Film Association (SAUO) ... BAFA
British Animation Group (SAUO) ... BAG
British Anodising Association ... BAA
British Antarctic Expedition ... BAE
British Antarctic Expedition [*1898-1900,1907-09,1910-13*] ... BrAE
British Antarctic Survey (QUAC) ... BAR
British Antarctic Survey [*Research center*] (IRC) ... BAS
British Antarctic Survey Medical Unit (SAUO) ... BASMU
British Antarctic Territory ... BAT
British Anti-Common Market Campaign [*An association*] (DBA) ... BACMC
British Anti-Lewisite [*Also, DMP: Dimercapto, propanol*] [*Detoxicant*] ... BAL
British Antiquarian Booksellers Association (SAUS) ... BABA
British Anti-Smoking Education Society ... BASES
British Antitank Bar Mine System (MCD) ... BATBAMS
British Anti-Zionist Organisation - Palestine Solidarity ... BAZO-PS
British Appaloosa Society (DBA) ... BApS
British Approvals Board for Telecommunications ... BABT
British Approvals for Fire Equipment ... BAFE
British Approvals Service for Electric Cables (PDAA) ... BASEC
British Approvals Service for Electrical Equipment in Flammable Atmospheres (SAUO) ... BASEEFA
British Approved Name ... BAN
British Aqueous Fusion Process (MCD) ... BAF
British Arabian Technical Cooperation (PDAA) ... BATC
British Arachnological Society (SAUO) ... BAS
British Archaeological Association ... BAA
British Archaeological Society (SAUS) ... BAS
British Archaeologists and Developers Liaison Group ... BADLG
British Architectural Library [*Royal Institute of British Architects*] [*Information service or system*] (IID) ... BAL
British Architectural Students Association (SAUO) ... BASA
British Archives Council (DIT) ... BAC
British Armed Forces Special Vouchers [*British military*] (DMA) ... BAFSV
British Armed Forces Special Vouchers (SAUS) ... BAFSVS
British Armed Forces Voucher [*Pronounced "baff"*] [*Paper money used on military bases*] (DSUE) ... BAFV
British Army ... BA
British Army (SAUO) ... BA
British Army Aid Group [*China*] [*World War II*] ... BAAG
British Army Equipment Exhibition (MCD) ... BAEE
British Army Forces Overseas ... BAFO
British Army Forces Overseas (SAUO) ... BAFO
British Army Motoring Association (SAUO) ... BAMA
British Army Motoring Association [*British military*] (DMA) ... BAMA
British Army News Service [*British military*] (DMA) ... BANEWS
British Army News Unit (SAUO) ... BANU
British Army of Occupation [*World War II*] ... BAO
British Army of the Rhine [*NATO/NORTHAG*] ... BAOR
British Army Post Office [*British military*] (DMA) ... BAPO
British Army Review [*A publication*] ... BAR
British Army Staff ... BAS
British Army Staff, Washington (MCD) ... BASW
British Army Training & Liaison Staff (SAUS) ... BATLS
British Army Training Liaison Staff, Kenya ... BATLSK
British Army Training Team ... BATT
British Army Training Unit (SAUS) ... BATU
British Army Training Unit, Suffield [*British military*] (DMA) ... BATUS
British Army/Royal Navy Equipment Exhibition (SAUS) ... BARNEE
British Art Medal Society (DBA) ... BAMS
British Art Metal Manufacturers Export Group (SAUO) ... BAMEX
British Article Number Association (SAUO) ... BANA
British Artists [*A publication*] ... BA
British Artists in Glass ... BAG
British Arts Festivals Association (DBA) ... BAFA
British Association for Accident and Emergency Medicine (SAUO) ... BAEM
British Association for American Studies (SAUO) ... BAAS
British Association for American Studies (EA) ... BAAS
British Association for American Studies Bulletin (journ.) (SAUS) ... BAASB
British Association for Applied Linguistics (SAUO) ... BAAL
British Association for Autogenic Training and Therapy (DBA) ... BAFATT
British Association for Behavioural & Cognitive Psychotherapies (SAUO) ... BABCP
British Association for Brazing and Soldering ... BABS
British Association for Canadian Studies ... BACS
British Association for Cancer Research ... BACR
British Association for Cardiac Rehabilitation (SAUO) ... BACR
British Association for Cemeteries in South Asia ... BACSA
British Association for Chemical Specialities ... BACS

British Association for Commercial and Industrial Education (DCTA) .... BACIE
British Association for Commercial and Industrial Education (SAUO) .... BASIE
British Association for Commercial and Technical Education (SAUO) ...... BACTE
British Association for Construction Heads (AIE) .... BACH
British Association for Counselling .... BAC
British Association for Green Crop Driers (SAUO) .... BAGCD
British Association for Immediate Care (WDAA) .... BASIC
British Association for Information and Library Education and Research (TELE) .... BAILER
British Association for Information and Library Education and Research (SAUO) .... BAILER
British Association for International Understanding (SAUO) .... BAIU
British Association for Irish Studies .... BAIS
British Association for Labour Legislation (SAUO) .... BALL
British Association for Language Teaching .... BALT
British Association for Local History .... BALH
British Association for Open Learning .... Baol
British Association for Paediatric Otolaryngology (SAUO) .... BAPO
British Association for Perinatal Paediatrics (PDAA) .... BAPP
British Association for Psychopharmacology .... BAP
British Association for Romanian Studies (EAIO) .... BARS
British Association for Service to the Elderly (DBA) .... BASE
British Association for Shooting and Conservation .... BASC
British Association for Soviet, Slavonic, and East European Studies (DBA) .... BASSEES
British Association for Surgery of the Knee (SAUO) .... BASK
British Association for the Advancement of Science (SAUO) .... BA
British Association for the Advancement of Science (BI) .... BA
British Association for the Advancement of Science .... BAAS
British Association for the Advancement of Science (SAUO) .... BAAS
British Association for the Advancement of Science (SAUO) .... BritAAS
British Association for the Control of Aircraft Noise (SAUO) .... BACAN
British Association for the Retarded .... BAR
British Association for the Study and Prevention of Child Abuse and Neglect (DI) .... BASPCAN
British Association for the Study of Community Dentistry .... BASCD
British Association for Veterinary Ophthalmology (GVA) .... BrAVO
British Association for/of Immediate Care Schemes (SAUO) .... BASICS
British Association for/of Rheumatology and Rehabilitation (SAUO) .... BARR
British Association for/of Social Psychiatry (SAUO) .... BASP
British Association for/of Surgical Oncology (SAUO) .... BASO
British Association in Forensic Medicine (SAUO) .... BAFM
British Association in/of Forensic Medicine (SAUO) .... BAFM
British Association of Academic Phoneticians (DBA) .... BAAP
British Association of Accountants and Auditors (BI) .... BAA
British Association of Accountants and Auditors (SAUO) .... BAAA
British Association of Accountants and Auditors (SAUO) .... BAA&A
British Association of Advisers and Lecturers in Physical Education .... BAALPE
British Association of Advisers and Lecturers in Pysical Education (SAUO) .... BAALPE
British Association of Advisers in Physical Education (SAUO) .... BAALPE
British Association of Aesthetic Plastic Surgeons (EAIO) .... BAAPS
British Association of Airport Equipment Manufacturers and Services (DA) .... BAAEMS
British Association of Art Therapists Ltd. .... BAAT
British Association of Audiological Scientists (SAUO) .... BAAS
British Association of Barbershop Singers (EAIO) .... BABS
British Association of Beauty Therapy and Cosmetology (DBA) .... BABTAC
British Association of Behavioural Psychotherapy (DI) .... BABP
British Association of Bio-Fuel and Oil .... BABFO
British Association of Cancer United Patients .... BACUP
British Association of Canned and Preserved Food Importers and Distributors (DBA) .... BACFID
British Association of Canoe Traders (DBA) .... BACT
British Association of Caving Instructors (SAUO) .... BACI
British Association of Chemists (SAUO) .... BAC
British Association of Chinese Studies (DBA) .... BACS
British Association of CIRP Industrial Sponsors (SAUO) .... BACIS
British Association of Clinical Anatomists .... BACA
British Association of Clothing Machinery Manufacturers (PDAA) .... BACMM
British Association of Colliery Management (DCTA) .... BACM
British Association of Communicators in Business (WDAA) .... BACB
British Association of Community Physicians (DBA) .... BACP
British Association of Concert Agents .... BACA
British Association of Conference Towns .... BACT
British Association of Consultants in Agriculture and Horticulture (BI) .... BACAH
British Association of Consultants in Agriculture and Horticulture (SAUO) .... BACAH
British Association of Consulting Engineers .... BACE
British Association of Corrosion Engineers (SAUO) .... BACE
British Association of Cosmetic Surgeons .... BACS
British Association of Crystal Growth .... BACG
British Association of Dental Nurses (SAUO) .... BADN
British Association of Dermatologists (SAUO) .... BAD
British Association of Dermatologists [*or Dermatology*] (EAIO) .... BAD
British Association of Dermatology and Syphilology (SAUO) .... BADS
British Association of Early Childhood Education (SAUO) .... BAECE
British Association of Educational Supplies (COBU) .... BESA
British Association of Electrolysists .... BAE
British Association of Feed Supplement and Additives Manufacturers (GVA) .... BAFSAM
British Association of Feed Supplement Manufacturers (DBA) .... BAFSM
British Association of Field and Sports Contractors, Ltd. (SAUO) .... BAFSC
British Association of Fishing Tackle Makers (SAUO) .... BAFTM
British Association of Fitted Furniture Installers (DBA) .... BAFFI
British Association of Former United Nations Civil Servants (SAUO) .... BAFUNCS
British Association of Friends of Museums .... BAFM
British Association of Golf Course Architects (DBA) .... BAGCA
British Association of Grain, Seed, Feed and Agricultural Merchants (SAUO) .... BASAM
British Association of Green Crop Driers (DBA) .... BAGCD
British Association of Helicopter Operators (PDAA) .... BAHO
British Association of Homoeopathic Pharmacists .... BAHP
British Association of Homoeopathic Veterinary Surgeons .... BAHVS
British Association of Homoeopathic Veterinary Surgeons (SAUO) .... BHAVS
British Association of Hotel Accountants (DBA) .... BAHA
British Association of Industrial Editors (EAIO) .... BAIE
British Association of Lace and Embroidery Designers and Draughtsmen (SAUO) .... BALEDD
British Association of Landscape Industries .... BALI
British Association of Lecturers in English for Academic Purposes (AIE) .... BALEAP
British Association of Leisure Parks, Piers, and Attractions (DBA) .... BALPPA
British Association of Lithographic Plate Manufacturers (DBA) .... BALPM
British Association of Machine Tool Merchants (SAUS) .... BAMTM
British Association of Managers of Textile Work (SAUO) .... BAMTW
British Association of Manipulative Medicine .... BAMM
British Association of Meat Wholesalers Ltd. (BI) .... BAMW
British Association of Myasthenics (DBA) .... BAM
British Association of National Coaches (SAUO) .... BANC
British Association of Nature Conservationists .... BANC
British Association of Neurologists (DI) .... BAN
British Association of Neuropathologists (SAUO) .... BAN
British Association of Numismatic Societies .... BANS
British Association of Occupational Therapists .... BAOT
British Association of Operating Department Assistants (DBA) .... BAODA
British Association of Oral and Maxillofacial Surgeons (DBA) .... BAOMS
British Association of Oral and Maxillo-Facial Surgeons .... BAOS
British Association of Oral Surgeons (SAUO) .... BAOS
British Association of Organisers and Lecturers in Physical Education (SAUO) .... BAOLPE
British Association of Orthodontists .... BAO
British Association of Otolaryngologists .... BAO
British Association of Otolaryngologists (DBA) .... BAOL
British Association of Overseas Furniture Removers (SAUO) .... BAOFR
British Association of Overseas Furniture Removers (BI) .... BAOFR
British Association of Paediatric Surgeons (SAUO) .... BAPS
British Association of Palestine-Israel Philatelists (BI) .... BAPIP
British Association of Paper Exporters (PDAA) .... BAPEX
British Association of Parascending Clubs (DBA) .... BAPL
British Association of Pediatric Surgeons (SAUS) .... BAPS
British Association of Physical Medicine (SAUO) .... BA Phys Med
British Association of Physical Medicine (BABM) .... BAPhysMed
British Association of Physical Medicine (BI) .... BAPM
British Association of Physical Medicine (SAUO) .... BAPM
British Association of Physical Medicine and Rheumatology (SAUO) .... BAPM&R
British Association of Physical Training (SAUO) .... BAPT
British Association of Picture Libraries and Agencies (DBA) .... BAPLA
British Association of Pig Producers (BI) .... BAPP
British Association of Pig Producers, Bere Regis, Dorset (SAUO) .... BAPP
British Association of Pool Table Operators (DBA) .... BAPTO
British Association of Print & Copyshops (SAUO) .... BAP&C
British Association of Print and Copyshops (COBU) .... BAPC
British Association of Professional Hairdressing Employers (DBA) .... BAPHE
British Association of Psychological Types (COBU) .... BAPT
British Association of Psychotherapists (DBA) .... BAP
British Association of Radiology and Physiotherapy (SAUO) .... BARP
British Association of Rally Doctors (DBA) .... BARD
British Association of Refrigerators (SAUO) .... BAR
British Association of Rehabilitated Psychotherapy (DI) .... BARP
British Association of Remote Sensing Companies (SAUO) .... BARSC
British Association of Removers (DBA) .... BAR
British Association of Residential Settlements (BI) .... BARS
British Association of Resort Tourist Officers (SAUO) .... BARTO
British Association of Retired Persons (DI) .... BARP
British Association of Rose Breeders .... BARB
British Association of Secretaries (SAUO) .... BAS
British Association of Seed Analysts .... BASA
British Association of Settlements (SAUO) .... BAS
British Association of Settlements and Social Action Centres .... BAS
British Association of Settlements and Social Action Centres .... BASSAC
British Association of Sewing Machine Manufacturers (PDAA) .... BASMM
British Association of Ship Suppliers (DBA) .... BASS
British Association of Ski Instructors (SAUO) .... BASI
British Association of Ski Instructors (DI) .... BASI
British Association of Skin Camouflage (DBA) .... BASC
British Association of Social Workers .... BASW
British Association of Sound Collections (DBA) .... BASC
British Association of Sport Medicine .... BASM
British Association of Sports Ground and Landscape Contractors, Ltd. (SAUO) .... BASLC
British Association of State Colleges in English Language Teaching (DBA) .... BASCELT
British Association of State English Language Teaching .... BASELT
British Association of Surgical Oncologists (SAUO) .... BASO
British Association of Symphonic Bands and Wind Ensembles (EAIO) .... BASBWE
British Association of Synthetic Rubber Manufacturers (PDAA) .... BASRM
British Association of Teachers of Conservative Dentistry (SAUO) .... BATCD

British Association of Teachers of Dancing (SAUO) .... BATD
British Association of Teachers of the Deaf (AIE) .... BATD
British Association of Teachers of the Deaf .... BATOD
British Association of the Hard of Hearing .... BAHOH
British Association of Tourism Officers (EAIO) .... BATO
British Association of Trade Computer Label Manufacturers (DBA) .... BATCLM
British Association of Trauma in Sport (DBA) .... BATS
British Association of Traumatology in Sport (DI) .... BATS
British Association of Urological Surgeons .... BAUS
British Association of Viewdata Information Providers .... BAVIP
British Association of Wheelchair Distributors (DBA) .... BAWD
British Association of Women Entrepreneurs (DBA) .... BAWE
British Association of Women Executives (DI) .... BAWE
British Association of Young Scientists (BI) .... BAYS
British Association Ohm (SAUO) .... BA-ohm
British Association Ohm (SAUS) .... BA-Ohm
British Association Screw Thread .... BA
British Association Service for Elderly (SAUO) .... BASE
British Association Sovereign and Military Order of Malta (SAUO) .... BASMOM
British Association Sovereign and Military Order of Malta (BI) .... BASMON
British Association Standard (IAA) .... BAS
British Association thread (SAUO) .... BA thread
British Association Unit (IAA) .... BAU
British Astronomical Association .... BAA
British Athletics Federation (WA) .... BAF
British Atlantic Committee (EAIO) .... BAC
British Atlantic Committee of NATO (SAUO) .... BACNATO
British Atmosphere (SAUS) .... Br atm
British Atmospheric Data Centre .... BADC
British Atomic Committee .... BAC
British Atomic Energy Agency (SAUO) .... Brit AEA
British Atomic Energy Agency (SAUS) .... Brit AEA
British Atomic Energy Authority (SAUO) .... BAEA
British Atomic Energy Authority .... BAEA
British Atomic Energy Corporation (SAUO) .... BAEC
British Atomic Energy Research Establishment (SAUO) .... BAERE
British Atomic Energy Research Establishment .... B/AERE
British Atomic Scientists Association (SAUS) .... BASA
British Audio Dealers Association (DBA) .... BADA
British Australian Settlers Society .... BASS
British Auto Racing Funatics [*An association*] .... BARF
British Automatic Company (SAUO) .... BAC
British Automatic Sprinkler Association (DBA) .... BASA
British Automation Company (SAUO) .... BAC
British Automobile Manufacturers Association (EA) .... BAMA
British Automobile Manufacturers Association in Canada (PDAA) .... BAMAC
British Automobile Racing Club .... BARC
British Aviation Archaeological Council (SAUO) .... BAAC
British Aviation Insurance Company (SAUO) .... BAIC
British Baby Carriage Manufacturers' Association (BI) .... BBCMA
British Backgammon Association (SAUO) .... BBA
British Bacon Curers Federation (SAUO) .... BBCF
British Baking Industries Research Association (PDAA) .... BBIRA
British Ballet Organisation (SAUO) .... BBO
British Ballet Organization (SAUO) .... BBO
British Balloon and Airship Club .... BBAC
British Bank of the Middle East .... BBME
British Bankers Association (SAUO) .... BBA
British Bankers Association Interest Settlement Rate (NUMA) .... BBAISR
British Barrels per Day (SAUS) .... BBls/D
British Baseball Federation (DBA) .... BBF
British Bath Manufacturers' Association Ltd. (BI) .... BBMA
British Bathroom Council (DBA) .... BBC
British Battery Makers Society (SAUO) .... BBMS
British Battery Manufacturers Association (DBA) .... BBMA
British Bedding Plant Association (DBA) .... BBPA
British Bee-Keeping Centre (SAUO) .... BBKC
British Beer-mat Collectors Society (SAUO) .... BBCS
British Beer-Mat Collectors' Society (EA) .... BB-CS
British Bemberg Limited (SAUO) .... BBL
British Berlin Flying Club (SAUO) .... BBFC
British Binders and Finishers Association (DBA) .... BBFA
British Biophysical Society .... BBS
British Biotech plc ADS [*NASDAQ symbol*] (TTSB) .... BBIOY
British Bio-Technologies, Inc. [*NASDAQ symbol*] (SAG) .... BBIO
British Bio-Technology Group [*Associated Press*] (SAG) .... BritBio
British Bio-Technology Ltd. (IRC) .... BBL
British Bird Breeders' Association (BI) .... BBBA
British Blind and Shutter Association (DBA) .... BBSA
British Blood Transfusion Society (SAUO) .... BBTS
British Bloodstock Agency .... BBA
British Bloodstock Association (SAUO) .... BBA
British Blue [*A British sailor*] .... BB
British Board of Agreement [*Department of the Environment*] [*Research center*] (IRUK) .... BBA
British Board of Deputies (SAUO) .... BBD
British Board of Film Censors (SAUO) .... BBFC
British Board of Film Censors (BI) .... BBFC
British Board of Film Classification .... BBFC
British Board of Jewish Deputies (SAUO) .... BBJD
British Board of Quality Control .... BBQC
British Bobsleigh [*or Bobsled*] **Association** (EAIO) .... BBA
British Bobsleigh Association (SAUO) .... BBA
British Bomb Retarding System (SAUS) .... BBRS
British Bombing Research Mission [*World War II*] .... BBRM
British Bombing Survey Units [*World War II*] .... BBSU
British Bone Society .... BBS
British Bonsai Association (DBA) .... BBA
British Book Center (or Centre) (SAUS) .... Brit Book Centr
British Book Export (SAUO) .... BBE
British Books in Print [*Whitaker & Sons, Ltd.*] [*Information service or system*] (IID) .... BBIP
British Boot and Shoe Institute (SAUS) .... BBSI
British Boot and Shoe Institution (SAUO) .... BBSI
British Boot, Shoe and Allied Trades Research Association (BI) .... BBSATRA
British Borneo Civil Affairs Unit [*World War II*] .... BBCAU
British Bottle Collectors Club (SAUO) .... BBCC
British Bottlers Institute (SAUS) .... BBI
British Box and Packaging Association (DBA) .... BB & PA
British Boxing Board of Control (SAUO) .... BBBC
British Branch of the Radiation Laboratory (SAUS) .... BBRL
British Branded Hosiery Group [*An association*] (DBA) .... BBHG
British Brazing Association (SAUO) .... BBA
British Bridge League (SAUO) .... BBL
British Broadcasting Company (SAUO) .... BBC
British Broadcasting Corp. [*State-operated radio and television*] .... BBC
British Broadcasting Corp. Research Department (SAUS) .... BBCRD
British Broadcasting Corp. Scottish Symphony Orchestra .... BBCSSO
British Broadcasting Corporation Research Department (SAUO) .... BBCRD
British Broadcasting Corporation Symphony Orchestra (SAUO) .... BBCSO
British Broadcasting Corporations first television network (SAUS) BBC-1
British Broadcasting Corporations second telev²sion network (SAUS) BBC-2
British Broiler Growers' Association (BI) .... BBGA
British Brush Manufacturers Association (PDAA) .... BBMA
British Brush Manufacturers Research Association (IRUK) .... BBMRA
British Bryn Mawr College (SAUO) .... BMC
British Bryological Society .... BBS
British Buddy Holly Society (EAIO) .... BBHS
British Building and Engineering Appliances .... BB & EA
British Building Manufacturers Association (SAUO) .... BBMA
British Bulgarian Friendship Society (DBA) .... BBFS
British Bureau of Non-Ferrous Metal Statistics (BI) .... BNFMS
British Bureau of Television Advertising .... BBTA
British Burma .... BR BUR
British Burma (ILCA) .... Brit Burm
British Burn Association (DBA) .... BBA
British Business Association [*Singapore*] (DS) .... BBA
British Business Graduates Society (DBA) .... BBGS
British Business Schools Librarians Group (SAUO) .... BBSLG
British Businessmen's Associaton (DBA) .... BBA
British Butterfly Conservation Society .... BBCS
British Button Manufacturers Association (BI) .... BBMA
British Button Manufacturers Association (SAUO) .... BBMA
British Button Society (DBA) .... BBS
British Cable Makers Confederation (DBA) .... BCMC
British Cable Services (NITA) .... BCS
British Cactus and Succulent Society (DBA) .... BCSS
British Calcium Carbonates Federation (DBA) .... BCCF
British Caledonian Airways [*ICAO designator*] (AD) .... BCAL
British Caledonian Airways (DCTA) .... B Cal
British Caledonian Airways Ltd. .... BCA
British Caledonian Airways Ltd. (SAUO) .... BCAL
British Caledonian Airways Ltd. [*ICAO designator*] (OAG) .... BR
British Caledonian Airways Ltd. (SAUO) .... JB
British Calibration Service [*Research center*] (IRC) .... BCS
British Camp Fire Girls (BI) .... BCFG
British Campaign Against Book Piracy .... BCABP
British Canadian Holstein Society (SAUO) .... BCHS
British Canadian Trade Association (BI) .... BCTA
British Candle (SAUS) .... BC
British Canoe Union .... BCU
British Canoe Union International Canoeing Exhibition [*British*] .... BCUICE
British Car Auctions .... BCA
British Car Parks (WDAA) .... BCP
British Car Rental Association (BI) .... BCRA
British Car Wash Association (DBA) .... BCWA
British Caramel Manufacturers Association (DBA) .... BCMA
British Caravanners Club (DBA) .... BCC
British Carbonisation Research Association (SAUO) .... BCRA
British Cardiac Society (DBA) .... BCS
British Cardiovascular Intervention Society (SAUO) .... BCIS
British Cargo Ship .... BAK
British Caribbean Airways Ltd. [*ICAO designator*] (FAAC) .... BCL
British Caribbean Territory .... BCT
British Carpet Classification Scheme (PDAA) .... BCCS
British Carpet Industry Technical Association (SAUO) .... BCITA
British Carpet Technical Centre (CB) .... BCTC
British Carpet Trade Centre (SAUO) .... BCTC
British Cartographic Society .... BCS
British Carton Association (BI) .... BCA
British Casino Association (DBA) .... BCA
British Caspian Trust .... BCT
British Cast Concrete Federation (SAUO) .... BCCF
British Cast Iron Pressure Pipe Association (PDAA) .... BCIPPA
British Cast Iron Research Association .... BCIRA
British Casting Association (SAUO) .... BCA
British Catalogue of Audiovisual Materials [*British Library*] (NITA) .... BCAVM
British Catalogue of Music [*British National Bibliography*] .... BCM
British Cattle Movement Service (GVA) .... BCMS
British Cattle Veterinary Association (DBA) .... BCVA

British Cave Research Association (SAUO) ... BCRA
British Cave Research Association ... BCRA
British Cement Association [*Also, an information service or system*] (IID) ... BCA
British Central Africa [*Pre-World War II*] ... BCA
British Central Africa Protectorate (SAUO) ... BCAP
British Central Office of Information ... BCOI
British Ceramic Confederation (DBA) ... BCC
British Ceramic Gift and Tableware Manufacturers' Association (DBA) ... BCGTMA
British Ceramic Manufacturers Federation (SAUO) ... BCMF
British Ceramic Plant and Machinery Manufacturers Association (PDAA) ... BCPMMA
British Ceramic Research Association (SAUO) ... B CE RA
British Ceramic Research Association (SAUO) ... BCeram RA
British Ceramic Research Association (PDAA) ... BCeramRA
British Ceramic Research Association (PDAA) ... BCRA
British Ceramic Research Institute (SAUS) ... BCRI
British Ceramic Research Ltd. [*Research center*] (IRC) ... CERAM
British Ceramic Society ... BCS
British Ceramic Society (SAUO) ... BCS
British Ceramic Tile Council Ltd. (BI) ... BCTC
British Cervical Spine Society (SAUO) ... BCSS
British Chain Manufacturers Association (DBA) ... BCMA
British Chamber of Commerce (DS) ... BCC
British Chamber of Commerce, Bangkok (DS) ... BCCB
British Chamber of Commerce for Italy ... BCCI
British Chamber of Commerce in Germany (DBA) ... BCCG
British Chamber of Commerce in Japan (DBA) ... BCCJ
British Chamber of Commerce in Turkey (DBA) ... BCCT
British Channel Island Ferries ... BCIE
British Channel Island Ferries ... BCIF
British Charities Association (SAUO) ... BCA
British Charollais Sheep Society (DBA) ... BCSS
British Charter [*ICAO designator*] (FAAC) ... BCR
British Charter [*British*] [*ICAO designator*] (ICDA) ... SE
British Chemical Defence Department (SAUO) ... BCDD
British Chemical Distributors and Traders Association (DBA) ... BCDTA
British Chemical Engineering and Process Technology (journ.) (SAUS) ... Br Chem Eng Process Technol
British Chemical Engineering Contractors Association (PDAA) ... BCECA
British Chemical Industrial (or Industry) Safety Council (SAUO) ... BCISC
British Chemical Industrial Safety Council (SAUS) ... BCISC
British Chemical Plant Manufacturers Association (SAUO) ... BCPMA
British Cheque Collectors Society (DBA) ... BCCS
British Chess Federation (BI) ... BCF
British Chess Magazine ... BCM
British Chicken Association (SAUO) ... BCA
British Chicken Association Ltd. (BI) ... BCA
British Chief Administrator ... BCA
British Chiefs of Staff ... BCOS
British Chiefs of Staff ... BCS
British Children's Theatre Association ... BCTA
British Chilean Chamber of Commerce (DBA) ... BCCC
British Chilean Council (SAUO) ... BCC
British China and Porcelain Artists Association (DBA) ... BCPAA
British Chip Board Manufacturers' Association (BI) ... BCMA
British Chiropody Association (DBA) ... BChA
British Chiropractic Association (SAUO) ... BCA
British Chiropractors' Association ... BCA
British Christian Pen Pal Club (SAUO) ... BCPPC
British Christmas Tree Growers Association (DBA) ... BCTGA
British Circus Ring, Nottingham (SAUO) ... BCR
British Citizens' Band Council (DBA) ... BCBC
British Civil Air Requirements (PIAV) ... BCAR
British Civil Airworthiness Requirements ... BCAR
British Civil Aviation Regulations (MCD) ... BCAR
British Civil Aviation Standing Conference (SAUO) ... BCASC
British Civil Censorship (SAUO) ... BCC
British Civil Service (SAUO) ... BCS
British Civil Uranium Procurement Directorate (NUCP) ... BCUPO
British Classical Association (SAUO) ... BCA
British classical music programs station (SAUS) ... Radio 3
British Clayware Land Drain Industry [*An association*] (DBA) ... BCLDI
British Cleaning Council Exhibition (ITD) ... BCCE
British Clock and Watch Manufacturers Association (PDAA) ... BCWMA
British Clothing Industry Association (DBA) ... BCIA
British Clothing Industry Productivity and Technology Centre (CB) ... BCC
British Coal Corporation (SAUO) ... BCC
British Coal Enterprise ... BCE
British Coal Utilisation Research Association ... BCURA
British Code of Advertising Practice (ODBW) ... BCAP
British Coke Research Association (PDAA) ... BCRA
British Coking Industry Association (SAUO) ... BCIA
British College of Accountancy, Ltd. ... BCA
British College of Acupuncture (DI) ... BCA
British College of Aeronautics ... B/C of A
British College of Aeronautics (SAUO) ... BC of A
British College of Naturopathy and Osteopathy ... BCNO
British College of Obstetricians and Genaecologists (SAUO) ... BCOG
British College of Ophthalmic Opticians (DBQ) ... BCOO
British College of Optometrists (DBA) ... BCO
British College of Physical Education (SAUO) ... BCPE
British College Sports Association (SAUO) ... BCSA
British Colleges Sports Association ... BCSA
British Colliery Owners Research Association (SAUO) ... BCORA
British Colombia Ladies Curling Association (AC) ... BCLCA
British Colombia Water & Wastewater Association (AC) ... BCWWA
British Colonial Airlines, Inc. ... BCA
British Colostomy Association (DBA) ... BCA
British Colour Council ... BCC
British Colour Education Institute (SAUO) ... BCEI
British Colour Makers' Association (DI) ... BCMA
British Columbia [*Canadian province*] [*Postal code*] ... BC
British Columbia [*MARC country of publication code*] [*Library of Congress*] (LCCP) ... bcc
British Columbia (ILCA) ... Br Col
British Columbia (DLA) ... BRIT COL
British Columbia [*MARC geographic area code*] [*Library of Congress*] (LCCP) ... n-cn-bc
British Columbia Agency ... BCCA
British Columbia and Yukon Chamber of Mines, Vancouver, BC, Canada [*Library symbol*] [*Library of Congress*] (LCLS) ... CaBVaBY
British Columbia and Yukon Chamber of Mines, Vancouver, British Columbia [*Library symbol*] [*National Library of Canada*] (NLC) ... BVABY
British Columbia and Yukon Church Aid Society (SAUO) ... BCYCAS
British Columbia Annual Law Lectures [*Canada*] [*A publication*] (DLA) ... BCL Lectures
British Columbia Art Therapy Association (AC) ... BCATA
British Columbia Artificial Insemination Centre (SAUO) ... BCAI
British Columbia Association for Community Living [*Formerly, British Columbians for Mentally Handicapped People*] (AC) ... BCACL
British Columbia Association of Broadcasters (AC) ... BCAB
British Columbia Association of Community Care (AC) ... BCACC
British Columbia Association of Health Care Auxiliaries (AC) ... BCAHA
British Columbia Association of Medical Radiation Technologists (AC) ... BCAMRT
British Columbia Association of Optometrists (AC) ... BCAO
British Columbia Association of People Who Stutter (SAUO) ... BCAPS
British Columbia Association of Podiatrists (AC) ... BCAP
British Columbia Association of Podiatry (SAUO) ... BCAP
British Columbia Association of Social Workers [*Association des Travailleurs Sociaux de la Colombie-Britannique*] (AC) ... BCASW
British Columbia Association of Speech Language Pathologists and Audiologists (SAUO) ... BCASLPA
British Columbia Automobile Association (AC) ... BCAA
British Columbia Barkerville Restoration Advisory Committee, Victoria, BC, Canada [*Library symbol*] [*Library of Congress*] (LCLS) ... CaBViB
British Columbia Barkerville Restoration Advisory Committee, Victoria, British Columbia [*Library symbol*] [*National Library of Canada*] (NLC) ... BVIB
British Columbia Branch Lectures [*A publication*] (DLA) ... BC Branch Lectures
British Columbia Building Envelope Council [*Formerly, Building Envelope Council of British Columbia*] (AC) ... BCBEC
British Columbia Bureau of Economics and Statistics, Business-Finance Library, Victoria, BC, Canada [*Library symbol*] [*Library of Congress*] (LCLS) ... CaBViBE
British Columbia, Canada (ILCA) ... Brit Col (Can)
British Columbia Cancer Foundation ... BCCF
British Columbia Cancer Research Centre ... BCCRC
British Columbia Central Credit Union, Vancouver, British Columbia [*Library symbol*] [*National Library of Canada*] (NLC) ... BVACCU
British Columbia Chapter, American Foundrymen's Society Archives and Museum, Delta, British Columbia [*Library symbol*] [*National Library of Canada*] (NLC) ... BDEAF
British Columbia Coalition of People with Disabilities (AC) ... BCCPD
British Columbia Coast Terminals [*Canada*] ... BCCT
British Columbia Coastal Service (SAUO) ... BCCS
British Columbia College and Institute Library Services Clearinghouse for the Print Impaired (CILS), Vancouver, British Columbia [*Library symbol*] [*National Library of Canada*] (NLC) ... BVACILS
British Columbia College of Teachers (AC) ... BCCT
British Columbia Colleges Athletic Association (AC) ... BCCAA
British Columbia Council of Licensed Practical Nurses (AC) ... BCCLPN
British Columbia Dietitians' & Nutritionists' Association (AC) ... BCDNA
British Columbia Educational Association of Disabled Students (AC) ... BCEADS
British Columbia Electric (SAUS) ... BCE
British Columbia Electric Co., Ltd. (SAUO) ... BCE
British Columbia Energy Commission, Vancouver, BC, Canada [*Library symbol*] [*Library of Congress*] (LCLS) ... CaBVaEC
British Columbia Energy Commission, Vancouver, British Columbia [*Library symbol*] [*National Library of Canada*] (NLC) ... BVAEC
British Columbia Farm Machinery Museum, Fort Langley, BC, Canada [*Library symbol*] [*Library of Congress*] (LCLS) ... CaBFLFMM
British Columbia Farm Machinery Museum, Fort Langley, British Columbia [*Library symbol*] [*National Library of Canada*] (NLC) ... BFLFMM
British Columbia Federation of Agriculture (AC) ... BCFA
British Columbia Federation of Foster Parent Associations (AC) ... BCFFPA
British Columbia Federation of Labour [*Federation du travail de la Colombie-Britannique*] (AC) ... BCFL
British Columbia Ferry & Marine Workers' Union [*Syndicat des Travailleurs Marins et de Bacs de la Colombie-Britannique*] (AC) ... BCFMWU
British Columbia Ferry Corp., Victoria, British Columbia [*Library symbol*] [*National Library of Canada*] (NLC) ... BVIFC
British Columbia Floor Covering Association (AC) ... BCFCA
British Columbia Forest Museum, Duncan, BC, Canada [*Library symbol*] [*Library of Congress*] (LCLS) ... CaBDUFM
British Columbia Forest Museum, Duncan, British Columbia [*Library symbol*] [*National Library of Canada*] (NLC) ... BDUFM
British Columbia Forest Service, Victoria, BC, Canada [*Library symbol*] [*Library of Congress*] (LCLS) ... CaBViFS

British Columbia Forest Service, Victoria, British Columbia [*Library symbol*] [*National Library of Canada*] (NLC) .... BVIFS
British Columbia Forest Service-Canadian Forestry Service (SAUS) .... JRBSDA
British Columbia Forestry Association [*Formerly, Canadian Forestry Association of BC*] (AC) .... BCFA
British Columbia Forestry Society (SAUO) .... BCFS
British Columbia Fruit Growers Association (SAUS) .... BCFGA
British Columbia Government [*Canada*] [*ICAO designator*] (FAAC) .... BCG
British Columbia Health Association (AC) .... BCHA
British Columbia Heritage Conservation, Branch Resource Information Centre, Victoria, BC, Canada [*Library symbol*] [*Library of Congress*] (LCLS) .... CaBViHCR
[*The*] **British Columbia Humanist Association** [*Also, Humanist Association of BC*] [*Formerly, Humanist Association of Greater Vancouver*] (AC) .... BCHA
British Columbia Hydro and Power Authority [*Formerly, British Columbia Electric Co. Ltd.*] [*AAR code*] .... BCE
British Columbia Hydro and Power Authority (SAUO) .... BCHPA
British Columbia Hydro and Power Authority (SAUS) .... BCHPH
British Columbia Hydro and Power Authority, Surrey, BC, Canada [*Library symbol*] [*Library of Congress*] (LCLS) .... CaBSH
British Columbia Hydro and Power Authority, Surrey, British Columbia [*Library symbol*] [*National Library of Canada*] (NLC) .... BSH
British Columbia Hydro and Power Authority [*Formerly, British Columbia Electric C o. Ltd.*], **Vancouver, BC, Canada** [*Library symbol*] [*Library of Congress*] (LCLS) .... CaBVaH
British Columbia Hydro and Power Authority, Vancouver, British Columbia [*Library symbol*] [*National Library of Canada*] (NLC) .... BVAH
British Columbia Hydro Engineering Library, Vancouver, BC, Canada [*Library symbol*] [*Library of Congress*] (LCLS) .... CaBVaHE
British Columbia Hydro Engineering Library, Vancouver, British Columbia [*Library symbol*] [*National Library of Canada*] (NLC) .... BVAHE
British Columbia Institute of Technology [*Canada*] (ASF) .... BCIT
British Columbia Institute of Technology, Burnaby, BC, Canada [*Library symbol*] [*Library of Congress*] (LCLS) .... CaBBIT
British Columbia Institute of Technology, Burnaby, British Columbia [*Library symbol*] [*National Library of Canada*] (NLC) .... BBIT
British Columbia Institute of Technology Library [*UTLAS symbol*] .... BCI
British Columbia Institute of Technology Staff Society [*Societe du Personnel de l'Institut de la Technolgie de la Colombie-Britannique*] (AC) .... BCITSS
British Columbia Insulation Contractors Association (AC) .... BCICA
British Columbia Interior Curling Association (AC) .... BCICA
British Columbia Labour Relations Board Decisions [*Database*] [*Western Legal Publications Ltd.*] [*Information service or system*] (CRD) .... BCLRBD
British Columbia Law Notes [*A publication*] (DLA) .... BCL Notes
British Columbia Law Reports [*Canada*] [*A publication*] (DLA) .... BC
British Columbia Law Reports [*Canada*] [*A publication*] (DLA) .... BCLR
British Columbia Library Association [*Canada*] (AEBS) .... BCLA
British Columbia Library Association (SAUO) .... BCLA
British Columbia Library Network [*Canada*] (NITA) .... BCLN
British Columbia Library, New Westminster, BC, Canada [*Library symbol*] [*Library of Congress*] (LCLS) .... CaBNWB
British Columbia Library Services Branch, Audiobook Service to the Handicapped, Burnaby, BC, Canada [*Library symbol*] [*Library of Congress*] (LCLS) .... CaBBLA
British Columbia Library Trustees Association (AC) .... BCLTA
British Columbia Lumber Manufacturers' Association [*Canada*] (BI) .... BCLMA
British Columbia Medical Association (AC) .... BCMA
British Columbia Medical Library Service, Vancouver, BC, Canada [*Library symbol*] [*Library of Congress*] (LCLS) .... CaBVaM
British Columbia Medical Library Service, Vancouver, British Columbia [*Library symbol*] [*National Library of Canada*] (NLC) .... BVAM
British Columbia Microelectronics, Burnaby, BC, Canada [*Library symbol*] [*Library of Congress*] (LCLS) .... CaBBBCM
British Columbia Microelectronics, Burnaby, British Columbia [*Library symbol*] [*National Library of Canada*] (NLC) .... BBBCM
British Columbia Ministry of Attorney General, CLEU Library, Victoria, BC, Canada [*Library symbol*] [*Library of Congress*] (LCLS) .... CaBViAGC
British Columbia Ministry of Economic Development, Victoria, BC, Canada [*Library symbol*] [*Library of Congress*] (LCLS) .... CaBViED
British Columbia Ministry of Education [*UTLAS symbol*] .... VME
British Columbia Ministry of Education, Victoria, BC, Canada [*Library symbol*] [*Library of Congress*] (LCLS) .... CaBViDE
British Columbia Ministry of Education, Victoria, British Columbia [*Library symbol*] [*National Library of Canada*] (NLC) .... BVIDE
British Columbia Ministry of Energy, Mines and Petroleum Resources, Victoria, British Columbia [*Library symbol*] [*National Library of Canada*] (NLC) .... BVIM
British Columbia Ministry of Environment, Planning and Resource Management Division, Victoria, BC, Canada [*Library symbol*] [*Library of Congress*] (LCLS) .... CaBViEPR
British Columbia Ministry of Environment, Victoria, British Columbia [*Library symbol*] [*National Library of Canada*] (NLC) .... BVILFW
British Columbia Ministry of Forests, Victoria, British Columbia [*Library symbol*] [*National Library of Canada*] (NLC) .... BVIFO
British Columbia Ministry of Health, Health Information, Victoria, BC, Canada [*Library symbol*] [*Library of Congress*] (LCLS) .... CaBViHI
British Columbia Ministry of Health, Health Promotion Programmes, Victoria, BC, Canada [*Library symbol*] [*Library of Congress*] (LCLS) .... CaBViHPP
British Columbia Ministry of Health, Victoria, BC, Canada [*Library symbol*] [*Library of Congress*] (LCLS) .... CaBViHe
British Columbia Ministry of Health, Victoria, British Columbia [*Library symbol*] [*National Library of Canada*] (NLC) .... BVIHE

British Columbia Ministry of Highways and Public Works, Victoria, BC, Canada [*Library symbol*] [*Library of Congress*] (LCLS) .... CaBViH
British Columbia Ministry of Highways and Public Works, Victoria, British Columbia [*Library symbol*] [*National Library of Canada*] (NLC) .... BVIH
British Columbia Ministry of Human Resources, Staff Development Division, Victoria, BC, Canada [*Library symbol*] [*Library of Congress*] (LCLS) .... CaBViHRS
British Columbia Ministry of Human Resources, Vancouver, British Columbia [*Library symbol*] [*National Library of Canada*] (NLC) .... BVIHRS
British Columbia Ministry of Industry and Small Business Development, Victoria, British Columbia [*Library symbol*] [*National Library of Canada*] (NLC) .... BVIED
British Columbia Ministry of Labour, Victoria, BC, Canada [*Library symbol*] [*Library of Congress*] (LCLS) .... CaBViML
British Columbia Ministry of Labour, Victoria, British Columbia [*Library symbol*] [*National Library of Canada*] (NLC) .... BVIML
British Columbia Ministry of Lands, Parks, and Housing, Parks Library, Victoria,BC, Canada [*Library symbol*] [*Library of Congress*] (LCLS) .... CaBViLPHP
British Columbia Ministry of Mines and Petroleum Resources, Victoria, BC, Canada [*Library symbol*] [*Library of Congress*] (LCLS) .... CaBViM
British Columbia Ministry of Recreation and Conservation, Fish and Game Branch, Victoria, BC, Canada [*Library symbol*] [*Library of Congress*] (LCLS) .... CaBViRC
British Columbia Ministry of Social Services and Housing, Vancouver, British Columbia [*Library symbol*] [*National Library of Canada*] (NLC) .... BVIHRS
British Columbia Ministry of the Attorney General, Law Library, Victoria, BC, Canada [*Library symbol*] [*Library of Congress*] (LCLS) .... CaBViAGL
British Columbia Ministry of the Environment, Environmental Protection, Pollution Control Branch, Victoria, BC, Canada [*Library symbol*] [*Library of Congress*] (LCLS) .... CaBViEP
British Columbia Ministry of the Environment, Victoria, BC, Canada [*Library symbol*] [*Library of Congress*] (LCLS) .... CaBViLFW
British Columbia Motion Picture Association (AC) .... BCMPA
British Columbia Museum of Medicine, Vancouver, BC, Canada [*Library symbol*] [*Library of Congress*] (LCLS) .... CaBVaMUM
British Columbia Museum of Medicine, Vancouver, British Columbia [*Library symbol*] [*National Library of Canada*] (NLC) .... BVAMUM
British Columbia Museum of Mining, Britannia Beach, British Columbia [*Library symbol*] [*National Library of Canada*] (NLC) .... BBBM
British Columbia Museum, Vancouver, British Columbia [*Library symbol*] [*National Library of Canada*] (NLC) .... BVABSM
British Columbia Native Women's Society (AC) .... BCNWS
British Columbia Native Women's Society, Kamloops, British Columbia [*Library symbol*] [*National Library of Canada*] (NLC) .... BKNW
British Columbia Neurofibromatosis Foundation (AC) .... BCNF
British Columbia Nurses' Union [*Syndicat des Infirmieres de la Colombie-Britannique*] (AC) .... BCNU
British Columbia Orchard Archives Society, Delta, BC, Canada [*Library symbol*] [*Library of Congress*] (LCLS) .... CaBDEOA
British Columbia Orchard Archives Society, Delta, British Columbia [*Library symbol*] [*National Library of Canada*] (NLC) .... BDEOA
British Columbia Packers Ltd. [*Toronto Stock Exchange symbol*] .... BCK
British Columbia Packers Ltd. [*Vancouver Stock Exchange symbol*] .... BPQ
British Columbia Packers Ltd., Product Assurance and Development, Vancouver, BC,Canada [*Library symbol*] [*Library of Congress*] (LCLS) .... CaBVaPAD
British Columbia Paint Manufacturers' Association (AC) .... BCPMA
British Columbia Paraplegic Association (AC) .... BCPA
British Columbia Parkinson's Disease Association (AC) .... BCPDA
British Columbia Power and Hydro Authority [*Canada*] [*ICAO designator*] (FAAC) .... BCH
British Columbia Printing Industries Association (AC) .... BCPIA
British Columbia Provincial Museum (SAUS) .... BCPM
British Columbia Provincial Museum, Ethnology Division, Victoria, BC, Canada [*Library symbol*] [*Library of Congress*] (LCLS) .... CaBViPME
British Columbia Provincial Museum, Victoria, BC, Canada [*Library symbol*] [*Library of Congress*] (LCLS) .... CaBViPM
British Columbia Provincial Museum, Victoria, British Columbia [*Library symbol*] [*National Library of Canada*] (NLC) .... BVIPM
British Columbia Rail, Corporate Information, Vancouver, BC, Canada [*Library symbol*] [*Library of Congress*] (LCLS) .... CaBVaBCR
British Columbia Railway (SAUS) .... BCR
British Columbia Railway Co. [*AAR code*] .... BCOL
British Columbia Railway Historical Association (AC) .... BCRHA
British Columbia Real Estate Association (AC) .... BCREA
British Columbia Recreation & Parks Association (AC) .... BCRPA
British Columbia Regiment (SAUO) .... BrColRgt
[*The*] **British Columbia Regional Network** [*Computer science*] [*Canada*] (TNIG) .... BCNET
British Columbia Reports [*A publication*] (DLA) .... BCC
British Columbia Reports [*A publication*] (DLA) .... BCR
British Columbia Reports [*A publication*] (DLA) .... BC Rep
British Columbia Research Council (SAUO) .... BCRC
British Columbia Research Council, Vancouver, BC, Canada [*Library symbol*] [*Library of Congress*] (LCLS) .... CaBVaR
British Columbia Research Council, Vancouver, British Columbia [*Library symbol*] [*National Library of Canada*] (NLC) .... BVAR
British Columbia Resources Investment Corp. [*Toronto Stock Exchange symbol*] [*Vancouver Stock Exchange symbol*] .... BCI
British Columbia Revised Statutes [*Canada*] [*A publication*] (DLA) .... BC Rev Stat
British Columbia Securities Commission, Vancouver, British Columbia [*Library symbol*] [*National Library of Canada*] (BIB) .... BVASEC

British Columbia Society of Artists [*1949-68, founded 1908 as BCSFA*] [*Canada*] (NGC) .... BCSA
British Columbia Society of Fine Arts [*1908, BCSA from 1949*] [*Canada*] (NGC) .... BCSFA
British Columbia Society of Landscape Architects (AC) .... BCSLA
British Columbia Society of Occupational Therapists (SAUO) .... BCSOT
British Columbia Spatial Archive and Interchange Format (SAUS) .... BC-SAIL
British Columbia Special Olympics (AC) .... BCSO
British Columbia Sports Hall of Fame and Museum, Vancouver, British Columbia [*Library symbol*] [*National Library of Canada*] (NLC) .... BVABCS
British Columbia Sports Medicine Clinic [*University of British Columbia*] [*Research center*] (RCD) .... BCSMC
British Columbia Statutes [*Canada*] [*A publication*] (DLA) .... BC Stat
British Columbia Steamship Company (SAUO) .... BCSC
British Columbia Surgical Society (AC) .... BCSS
British Columbia Systems Corp., Victoria, British Columbia [*Library symbol*] [*National Library of Canada*] (NLC) .... BVISC
British Columbia Tax Reporter (Commerce Clearing House) [*A publication*] (DLA) .... BC Tax Rep (CCH)
British Columbia Teacher-Librarians' Association (AC) .... BCTLA
British Columbia Teachers' Federation [*Canada*] (AEBS) .... BC
British Columbia Teachers' Federation [*Federation des Enseignants de la Colombie-Britannique*] (AC) .... BCTF
British Columbia Teachers' Federation Resources Centre, Vancouver, BC, Canada [*Library symbol*] [*Library of Congress*] (LCLS) .... CaBVaTF
British Columbia Teachers' Federation Resources Centre, Vancouver, British Columbia [*Library symbol*] [*National Library of Canada*] (NLC) .... BVATF
British Columbia Telephone Co. [*Toronto Stock Exchange symbol*] [*Vancouver Stock Exchange symbol*] .... BCT
British Columbia Telephone Co., Burnaby, BC, Canada [*Library symbol*] [*Library of Congress*] (LCLS) .... CaBBT
British Columbia Telephone Co., Burnaby, British Columbia [*Library symbol*] [*National Library of Canada*] (NLC) .... BVABT
British Columbia Telephone Co., Vancouver, BC, Canada [*Library symbol*] [*Library of Congress*] (LCLS) .... CaBVaBT
British Columbia Telephone Company (SAUO) .... BC Tel
British Columbia Telephone Ltd. [*Canada*] [*ICAO designator*] (FAAC) .... BCT
British Columbia Trade Development Corporation (ABAC) .... BCTDC
British Columbia Trade Union Group [*Canada*] (CROSS) .... TUG
British Columbia Trucking Association (AC) .... BCTA
British Columbia Union Catalogue, Burnaby, BC, Canada [*Library symbol*] [*Library of Congress*] (LCLS) .... CaBBUC
British Columbia Union Catalogue, Burnaby, British Columbia [*Library symbol*] [*National Library of Canada*] (NLC) .... BBUC
British Columbia Veterinary Association (SAUO) .... BCVA
British Columbia Veterinary Medical Association (AC) .... BCVMA
British Columbia Water Polo Association (AC) .... BCWPA
British Columbia Watershed Protection Alliance (AC) .... BCWPA
British Columbian, New Westminster, British Columbia [*Library symbol*] [*National Library of Canada*] (NLC) .... BNWB
British Columbian Resource Investment Corporation (SAUO) .... BRIC
British Columbias Matsqui Institution (SAUS) .... Abbotsford
British Combustion Equipment Manufacturers Association (SAUO) .... BCEMA
British Commanders-in-Chief Mission to the Soviet Forces in Germany (SAUO) .... BRIXMIS
British Commercial Gas Association (SAUO) .... BCGA
British Commercial Monomark (SAUO) .... BCM
British Commercial Neutral Broadcasting Company (SAUO) .... BCNBC
British Commerical Glasshouse Manufacturers Association (DBA) .... BCGMA
British Commissioner [*Salvation Army*] .... BC
British Committee for Map Information and Catalogue Systems (NITA) .... BRICMICS
British Committee for Polish Welfare (SAUO) .... BCPW
British Committee for Standards in Haematology .... BCSH
British Committee on Radiation Units and Measurements (SAUO) .... BCRUM
British Committee on Radiological Units (HEAS) .... BCRU
British Commonwealth [*MARC geographic area code*] [*Library of Congress*] (LCCP) .... b----
British Commonwealth .... BC
British Commonwealth (SAUO) .... BC
British Commonwealth Air Force (SAUO) .... BCAir
British Commonwealth Air Training Plan [*World War II*] .... BCATP
British Commonwealth Alliance (ADA) .... BCA
British Commonwealth and Empire .... BCE
British Commonwealth and Empire (SAUO) .... BCE
British Commonwealth and European Union (SAUO) .... BCEU
British Commonwealth Chamber of Commerce in the United States (SAUO) .... BCCCUS
British Commonwealth Ex-Services League (SAUO) .... BCEL
British Commonwealth Ex-Services League (SAUO) .... BCESL
British Commonwealth Far East Strategic Reserve .... BCFESR
British Commonwealth Forces .... BCF
British Commonwealth Forces (SAUO) .... BCF
British Commonwealth Forces in Korea (SAUO) .... BCFK
British Commonwealth Forces, Korea [*British military*] (DMA) .... BCFK
British Commonwealth Forest Translation Exchange .... BCFTE
British Commonwealth Games Federation (SAUO) .... BCGF
British Commonwealth Geographical Liaison Office (PDAA) .... BCGLO
British Commonwealth International News Agency .... BCINA
British Commonwealth International Newsfilm Agency (SAUO) .... BCINA
British Commonwealth Korean Base [*British military*] (DMA) .... BCKB
British Commonwealth Occupation Force [*Military*] .... BCOF
British Commonwealth Occupation Force (SAUO) .... BCOF
British Commonwealth of Nations (SAUO) .... BCN
British Commonwealth of Nations .... BCN
British Commonwealth of Nations (SAUO) .... BCON
British Commonwealth of Nations Scientific Liaison Offices (SAUO) .... BCSO
British Commonwealth Pacific Airlines Ltd. (ADA) .... BCP
British Commonwealth Pacific Airlines Ltd. .... BCPA
British Commonwealth Producers' Organization .... BCPO
British Commonwealth Scientific Office .... BCSO
British Commonwealth Scientific Office (North America) [*Washington, DC*] .... BCSO(NA)
British Commonwealth Standards Committee (SAUO) .... BCSC
British Commonwealth Sugar Agreement .... BCSA
British Commonwealth Union (ADA) .... BCU
British Commonwealth Union (SAUO) .... BCU
British Commonwealth War Veterans Association (SAUO) .... BCWVA
British Commonwealth Weightlifting Federation (SAUO) .... BCWLF
British Communications Corporation (SAUO) .... BCC
British Communications Corporation Ltd. (SAUO) .... BCC
British Communist Party (SAUO) .... BCP
British Company Law Cases [*A publication*] .... BCC
British Comparative Education Society (AIE) .... BCES
British Compressed Air Society .... BCAS
British Compressed Gases Association (DBA) .... BCGA
British Computer Associated for the Blind (PDAA) .... BCAB
British Computer Association for the Blind (SAUS) .... BCAB
British Computer Society [*London*] .... BCS
British Computer Society, Nursing Specialist Group (SAUO) .... BCS NSG
British Computer Society Schools Committee (AIE) .... BCSSC
British Concrete Federation (SAUO) .... BCF
British Concrete Pumping Association (PDAA) .... BCPA
British Confectioners' Association (BI) .... BCA
British Conference and Exhibition Centres Export Council (DBA) .... BCECEC
British Conference on Automation and Computation .... BCAC
British Constitution Association (SAUO) .... BCA
British Constructional Steelwork Association (PDAA) .... BCSA
British Consular Mail (SAUS) .... BCM
British Consultants Bureau (CB) .... BCB
British Contact Lens Association .... BCLA
British Continental Airways, Ltd. (SAUO) .... BCA
British Continental Trade Press (SAUO) .... BCTP
British Contingent United Nations Forces in Cyprus (SAUO) .... BRITCON UNFICYP
British Contract Furnishing Association (PDAA) .... BCFA
British Control Commission (SAUO) .... BCC
British Control Investigation Committee (SAUO) .... BCIC
British Control Supply Mission [*World War II*] .... BCSM
British Cooking Industry Association (BI) .... BCIA
British Cookware Manufacturers Association (DBA) .... BCMA
British Cooperative Clinical Group (SAUO) .... BCCG
British Co-Operative Clinical Group (BABM) .... BCCG
British Coordinating Committee for Biotechnology .... BCCB
British Copyright Council (ILCA) .... BCC
British Copyright Council (SAUO) .... BCC
British Copyright Protecting (or Protection) Association (SAUO) .... BCPA
British Corinthian Yacht Club (DI) .... BCYC
British Corp. .... BC
British Correspondence Chess Association (BI) .... BCCA
British Corrosion Journal (SAUS) .... Br Corros J
British Cotton Board (SAUO) .... BCB
British Cotton Industry Research Association (SAUO) .... BCIRA
British Cotton Industry Research Association (DI) .... BCIRA
British Cotton Waste Association (SAUO) .... BCWA
British Cotton-Growing Association (SAUO) .... BCGA
British Council (SAUO) .... BC
British Council .... BC
British Council (SAUO) .... BRICOUN
British Council Cultural Scientific Office (SAUO) .... BCCSO
British Council Film Club (SAUO) .... BCFC
British Council for Aid to Refugees .... BCAR
British Council for Rehabilitation of the Disabled (BI) .... BCRD
British Council for the Promotion of International Trade (BI) .... BCPIT
British Council for the Rehabilitation of the Disabled (SAUO) .... BCRD
British Council in Australia .... BCA
British Council Library (SAUO) .... BCL
British Council of Christian Settlements (SAUO) .... BCCS
British Council of Churches .... BCC
British Council of Maintenance Association (SAUO) .... BCMA
British Council of Productivity Association (PDAA) .... BCPA
British Council of Productivity Associations (SAUO) .... BCPA
British Council of Shopping Centres .... BCSC
British Council Undergraduate Fellowship Scheme (AIE) .... BRUFS
British Country Music Association, Otley Yorks (SAUO) .... BCMA
British Crafts Centre (CB) .... BCC
British Crane Hire Corporation (SAUO) .... BCHC
British Crayfish Marketing Association (DBA) .... BCMA
British Crime Survey (ECON) .... BCS
British Crop Dryers, Ltd. (SAUO) .... BCD
British Crop Protection Council .... BCPC
British [*or English*] **Crown Cases** [*A publication*] (DLA) .... Br CC
British [*or English*] **Crown Cases** [*A publication*] (DLA) .... Br Cr Ca
British [*or English*] **Crown Cases** [*A publication*] (DLA) .... Br Cr Cas
British [*or English*] **Crown Cases** [*A publication*] (DLA) .... Brit Cr Cas
British Crown Colony (SAUO) .... BCC
British Crown Colony .... BCC
British Crown Green Bowling Association (DBA) .... BCGBA
British Cryogenics Council (DBA) .... BCC
British Currency (SAUS) .... BC
British Cutlery and Silverware Association (EAIO) .... BCSA

British Cutlery Federation (SAUO) .... BCF
British Cycle Tourist Competition (SAUO) .... BCTC
British Cycling Federation .... BCF
British Cyclo-Cross Association (SAUO) .... BCCA
British Cyclo-Cross Association (DBA) .... BCCA
British Czechoslovak Friendship League (SAUO) .... BCFL
British Dahlia Growers Association (DBA) .... BDGA
British Darts Organization (DBA) .... BDO
British Database on Research for Aids for the Disabled (SAUS) .... BARD
British Deaf and Dumb Association (BI) .... BDDA
British Deaf Association (DI) .... BDA
British Deaf Sports Council (DBA) .... BDSC
British Decartelization Agency (SAUO) .... BRIDAG
British Decorators Association (DBA) .... BDA
British Deep-Drawing Research Group (SAUO) .... BDDRG
British Deer Farmers Association (DBA) .... BDFA
British Deer Producers' Association (DBA) .... BDPS
British Deer Producers Society (SAUO) .... BDPS
British Deer Society .... BDS
British Defence and Aid Fund for Southern Africa (EAIO) .... BDAFSA
British Defence Co-ordinating Committee (SAUO) .... BDCC
British Defence Co-ordinating Committee, Middle East (SAUO) .... BDCC/ME
British Defence Directory [Brassey's Defence Publishers Ltd.] [Information service or system] (IID) .... BDD
British Defence Forces (SAUO) .... BDF
British Defence Liaison Staff (SAUO) .... BDLS
British Defence Manufacturers Association (PDAA) .... BDMA
British Defence Software (SAUO) .... BDS
British Defence Staff .... BDS
British Defence Staff, Washington, DC [Also, BDSWASHDC] (NATG) .... BDSW
British Defence Staff, Washington, DC [Also, BDSW] (NATG) .... BDSWASHDC
British Defense-notice system for protecting state secrets with the cooperation of the press (SAUS) .... D-notice system
British Deming Association (DBA) .... BDA
British Democratic Party [Political party] .... BDP
British Dental Association .... BDA
British Dental Health Foundation (DI) .... BDHF
British Dental Health Organisation (DI) .... BDHO
British Dental Hygienists Association .... BDHA
British Dental Institute (DI) .... BDI
British Dental Journal [A publication] .... BDJ
British Dental Migraine Study Group [An association] (DBA) .... BDMSG
British Dental Students Association (SAUO) .... BDSA
British Dental Trade Association (DBA) .... BDTA
British Department of Health and Social Security (SAUS) .... DHSS
British Department of Transport .... BDOT
British Destroyer Escort .... BDE
British Diabetic Association (IRUK) .... BDA
British Diabetic Association (SAUO) .... BDA
British Diamond Workers Trade Union .... BDWTU
[The] British Dietetic Association .... BDA
British Dietetic Association (SAUO) .... BDA
British Digest of International Law [A publication] .... BDIL
British Digestive Foundation (IRUK) .... BDF
British Direct Mail Advertising Association (DI) .... BDMAA
British Direct Mail Marketing Association (SAUO) .... BDMMA
British Direct Marketing Association (DBA) .... BDMA
British Disinfectant Manufacturers Association (SAUO) .... BDMA
British Display Society (BI) .... BDS
British Disposable Products Association (PDAA) .... BDPA
British Document Exchange .... BDE
British Document Exchange .... BRITDOC
British Dog Breeders' Council (GVA) .... BDBC
British Doll Artists Association (DBA) .... BDA
British Domestic Appliances, Ltd. (SAUO) .... BDA
British Dominions and Colonies (SAUO) .... BD&C
British Dominions Emigration Society (SAUO) .... BDES
British Door Association, Ltd. (SAUO) .... BDA
British Double Summer Time .... BDST
British Drag Racing Association (BI) .... BDRA
British Drama League (DI) .... BDL
British Drilling Association (DBA) .... BDA
British Driving Society (SAUO) .... BDS
British Driving Society (BI) .... BDS
British Drug Houses Ltd. [Research code symbol] .... BDH
British, Dutch, West German Consortium for Processing Uranium (SAUS) .... URANCO
British Dye-Stuff Corporation (SAUO) .... BDSC
British Dyslexia Association .... BDA
British Eagle Airlines (IIA) .... BE
British Earth Sheltering Association (DBA) .... BESA
British East Africa (SAUO) .... BEA
British East Africa .... BEA
British East Africa (SAUO) .... BrEAf
British East Africa Protectorate [British government] .... BEAP
British East African Army Corps .... BEAAC
British Eastern Merchant Shippers' Association (BI) .... BEMSA
British Ecological Society (SAUO) .... BES
British Education and Training Technology Exhibition (ITD) .... BETT
British Education Index (DET) .... BEI
British Education Management and Administration Society (DBA) .... BEMAS
British Educational Administration Society (SAUO) .... BEAS
British Educational Contractors Group (AIE) .... BECG
British Educational Equipment Association (DS) .... BEEA
British Educational Export Council (SAUO) .... BEEC

British Educational Furniture Manufacturers Council (AIE) .... BEFMC
British Educational Research Association .... BERA
British Educational Suppliers Association (AIE) .... BESA
British Effluent and Water Association [Trade association] .... BEWA
British Egg Association (BI) .... BEA
British Egg Information Service (DI) .... BEIS
British Egg Marketing Board (DI) .... BEMB
British Egg Products Association (DI) .... BEPA
British Egyptian Expeditionary Force (SAUO) .... BEEF
British Elastic Rope Sports Association (HEAS) .... BERSA
British Elbow and Shoulder Society (SAUO) .... BESS
British Electric Cable Testing Organisation (MCD) .... BECTO
British Electric Car Racing Association (SAUO) .... BECRA
British Electric Conduit Systems Manufacturers (SAUO) .... BECSM
British Electric Council (SAUO) .... BEC
British Electric Lamp, Ltd. (SAUO) .... BELL
British Electric Resistance Company (SAUS) .... BERCO
British Electric Resistance Company, Ltd. (SAUO) .... BERCO
British Electric Traction (SAUS) .... bet
[The] British Electric Traction Co. Ltd. .... BET
British Electric Tractions Company (SAUO) .... BET
British Electrical and Allied Industries Research Association (MCD) .... BEAIRA
British Electrical and Allied Industries Research Association (SAUO) .... BERA
British Electrical and Allied Manufacturers Association .... BEAMA
British Electrical Approvals Board .... BEAB
British Electrical Conduit Manufacturers .... BECM
British Electrical Development Association, Inc. (SAUO) .... BEDA
British Electrical Power Convention (SAUO) .... BEPC
British Electrical Power Convention (MCD) .... BEPC
British Electrical Systems Association (DBA) .... BESA
British Electricity Approvals Board (SAUS) .... BEAB
British Electricity Authority .... BEA
British Electricity Board (SAUO) .... BEB
British Electricity International Ltd. (SAUO) .... BEI
British Electro-Ceramic Manufacturers' Association (BI) .... BECMA
British Electronic and Applied Research Association (MCD) .... BEARA
British Electronics Week [Trade show] (ITD) .... BEW
British Electrostatic Control Association (EAIO) .... BECA
British Electrostatic Manufacturers Association (DBA) .... BESMA
British Electrotechnical Approvals Board (NITA) .... BEAB
British Electrotechnical Approvals Board for Household Appliances (SAUO) .... BEAB
British Electrotechnical Committee (SAUO) .... BEC
British Electrotechnical Committee (BARN) .... BEL
British Element .... BE
British Element, Trieste Forces (SAUO) .... BETFOR
British Embassador (SAUS) .... BE
British Embassy (SAUO) .... BE
British Embassy (DS) .... B/E
British Embassy (SAUS) .... BRITEMB
British Embassy (SAUO) .... Brit Emby
British Embassy, Washington, DC [Library symbol] [Library of Congress] (LCLS) .... DBE
British Emergency Air Medical Service (DA) .... BEAMS
British Emigrant Families Association (SAUO) .... BEFA
British Empire (SAUO) .... BE
British Empire .... BE
British Empire and Commonwealth .... BE & C
British Empire and Commonwealth Games Council (SAUO) .... BECGC
British Empire and Commonwealth Games Federation .... BECGF
British Empire and Commonwealth Weight-Lifting Council .... BE & CWLC
British Empire Cancer Campaign (SAUO) .... BECC
British Empire Cancer Campaign for Research (SAUO) .... BECCR
British Empire Cancer Council .... BECC
British Empire Exhibition (SAUO) .... BEE
British Empire Forces (SAUO) .... BEF
British Empire Forces .... BEF
British Empire League .... BEL
British Empire League (SAUO) .... BEL
British Empire Leprosy Relief Association .... BELRA
British Empire Medal .... BEM
British Empire Naturalist Association .... BENA
British Empire Radio Transmission Award (SAUS) .... BERTA
British Empire Receiving Station (SAUS) .... BERS
British Empire Series [A publication] .... BES
British Empire Service League .... BESL
British Empire Service League (SAUO) .... BESL
British Empire Service League Auxiliary (SAUO) .... BESL Aux
British Empire Steam Navigation Co. (SAUO) .... BESN
British Empire Steel Corporation (SAUO) .... BEStC
British Empire Union (SAUO) .... BEU
British Empire Union .... BEU
British Employees Federation (SAUO) .... BEF
British Employers' Confederation .... BEC
British Employers Executive (SAUS) .... BEE
British Endodontic Society .... BES
British Endodontic Society (SAUO) .... BES
British Energy (WDAA) .... BE
British Energy Management Systems .... BEMS
British Engineering Service Traders (SAUO) .... BEST
British Engineering Standards Association .... BESA
British Engineers Association .... BEA
British Engineers Club .... BEC
British English (SAUS) .... BE
British English [Language] (WGA) .... BrE

British Enka Artificial Silk Company (SAUO) .... BEASCO
British Entertainment and Dancing Association (DBA) .... BEDA
British Entomological and Natural History Society .... BENHS
British Epigraphy Society (SAUO) .... BES
British Epilepsy Association .... BEA
British Epilepsy Association (SAUO) .... BEpA
British Epilepsy Association (SAUS) .... B EpA
British Equestrian Federation (DBA) .... BEF
British Equestrian Promotions, Ltd. .... BEP
British Equestrian Trade Association (DBA) .... BETA
British Equine Veterinary Association (DBA) .... BEVA
British Equipment Manufacturers Association (SAUO) .... BEMA
British Equipment Trade Association (SAUO) .... BETA
British Esperanto Association, Inc. (BI) .... BEA
British Esperanto Scientific Association (SAUO) .... BESA
British Essence Manufacturers' Association (BI) .... BEMA
British European Airways Computerized Office Network (SAUO) .... BEACON
British European Airways Corp. [*Later, British Airways*] .... BEA
British European Airways Corp. [*Later, British Airways*] .... BEAC
British European Airways Corp. [*later, British Airways*] **Computerized Office Network** .... BEACON
British European Corporation (SAUO) .... BEC
British Examining and Registration Board in Occupational Hygiene .... BERBOH
British Examining Board in Occupational Hygiene (SAUO) .... BEBOH
British Executive Air Services Ltd. (SAUO) .... BEAS
British Executive and General Aircraft Ltd. (SAUO) .... BEAGLE
British Executive Service Overseas [*Overseas Development Administration*] (DS) .... BESO
British Exhibition Contractors Association (EAIO) .... BECA
British Exhibition Venues Association .... BEVA
British Exhibitors' Association (BI) .... BEA
British Expeditionary Force .... BEF
British Experimental Pile Operation [*Nuclear reactor*] (DEN) .... BEPO
British Experimental Pile Zero (SAUS) .... BEPO
British Experimental Rocket (SAUS) .... BER
British Experimental Rotor Program .... BERP
British Experimental Rotor Programme (SAUO) .... BERP
British Expertise in Science and Technology [*Longman Cartermill Ltd.*] [*Scotland*] [*Information service or system*] (IID) .... BEST
British Export Board (PDAA) .... BEB
British Export Houses Association (SAUO) .... BEHA
British Export Trade Advertising Association (SAUO) .... BETAA
British Export Trade Advertising Corporation (SAUO) .... BETAC
British Export Trade Research Organisation .... BETRO
British Exporters Association (DBA) .... BExA
British Exports Marketing Advisory Committee [*Defunct*] .... BEMAC
British Ex-Services Association [*Australia*] .... BESA
British Ex-Services Womens (United Kingdom) Association .... BESW(UK)A
British Fabric Association (DBA) .... BFA
British Facsimile Industry Compatibility Committee (SAUO) .... BFICC
British Facsimile Industry Consultative Committee (NITA) .... BFICC
British Falconers Club (SAUO) .... BFC
British False Memory Society (WDAA) .... BFMS
British Families Education Service .... BFES
British family phonein and pop programs station (SAUS) .... Radio 2
British Fantasy Society (DBA) .... BFS
British Far Eastern Broadcasting Service (SAUO) .... BFEBS
British Farm Mechanization Association (SAUO) .... BFMA
British Farm Produce Council (SAUO) .... BFPC
British Farm Produce Council (BI) .... BFPC
British Fascists [*Political party*] (WDAA) .... BF
British Federation against Venereal Diseases (SAUO) .... BFVD
British Federation of Aesthetics and Cosmetology (BI) .... BFAC
British Federation of Brass Bands (DBA) .... BFBB
British Federation of Business and Professional Women (ODBW) .... BFBPW
British Federation of Business and Professional Women (SAUO) .... BFBPW
British Federation of Care Home Proprietors (DBA) .... BFCHP
British Federation of Commodity Associations (ODBW) .... BFCA
British Federation of Commodity Associations (SAUO) .... BFCA
British Federation of Elastic Web Manufacturers (SAUO) .... BFEWM
British Federation of Film Societies .... BFFS
British Federation of Folk Clubs (SAUO) .... BFFC
British Federation of Hotel, Guest House, and Self-Catering Associations (DBA) .... BFHGH & SC
British Federation of Iron and Steel Stockholders (BI) .... BFISS
British Federation of Master Printers [*A union*] .... BFMP
British Federation of Master Printers (SAUO) .... BFMP
British Federation of Music Festivals (SAUO) .... BFMF
British Federation of Musical Festivals .... BFMF
British Federation of Plumber Merchants (SAUO) .... BFPM
British Federation of Printing Machinery and Supplies .... BFPMS
British Federation of Sand and Land Yacht Clubs .... BFSLYC
British Federation of Social Workers (SAUO) .... BFSW
British Federation of Textile Technicians (DCTA) .... BFTT
British Federation of University Women (SAUO) .... BFLW
British Federation of University Women, Ltd. (SAUO) .... BFUW
British Federation of Wholesale Confectioners (SAUO) .... BFWC
British Federation of Young Choirs (DBA) .... BFYC
British Federation of Young Cooperators (SAUO) .... BFYC
British Fertility Society (SAUO) .... BFS
British Fibreboard Packaging Association (DBA) .... BFPA
British Field Hospital [*British military*] (DMA) .... BFH
British Field Post Office [*World War II*] .... BFPO
British Field [*Wireless*] **Set** [*British military*] (DMA) .... BF Set
British Field Sports Society .... BFSS
British Film Academy (WDAA) .... BFA
British Film and Television Producers' Association .... BFTPA
British Film Authority (SAUO) .... BFA
British Film Designers Guild (DBA) .... BFDG
British Film Fund Agency .... BFFA
British Film Industries (SAUO) .... BFI
British Film Industries (SAUS) .... BFI
British Film Institute .... BFI
British Film Producers Association (SAUO) .... BFPA
British Fine Arts Society (SAUO) .... BFAS
British Fire Protection Systems Association (PDAA) .... BFPSA
British Fire Services Association (PDAA) .... BFSA
British Fireboard Packaging Employers' Association .... BFPEA
British Firework Manufacturers Safety Association (SAUO) .... BFMSA
British First Airborne Division (SAUO) .... BFAD
British First Airborne Division .... BFAD
British First Army .... BFA
British First Army (SAUO) .... BFA
British Fishing and Small Vessel Equipment Association (SAUO) .... BFSVEA
British Fishing Federation (SAUO) .... BFF
British Fishing Port (SAUO) .... BFP
British Flat Roofing Council (DBA) .... BFRC
British Flight Battalion (SAUO) .... BFB
British Flight Battalion .... BFB
British Floorcovering Manufacturers Association (DBA) .... BFMA
British Flour Industry Association (SAUO) .... BFIA
British Flower Industry Association (PDAA) .... BFIA
British Flue and Chimney Manufacturers Association (DBA) .... BFCMA
British Fluid Power Association (EAIO) .... BFPA
British Fluid Power Distributors Association (DBA) .... BFPDA
British Flying Training School (SAUS) .... BFTS
British Food Classification (BARN) .... A
British Food Export Council (DS) .... BFEC
British Food Manufacturers Research Association (SAUS) .... BFMRA
British Food Manufacturing Industries Research Association (ARC) .... BFMIRA
British Food Mission [*World War II*] .... BFM
British Foods Action Group (DI) .... BFAG
British Football Association (SAUO) .... BFA
British Footpaths Association (SAUO) .... BFA
British Footwear Association (WDAA) .... BFA
British Footwear Manufacturers' Federation .... BFMF
British Forces (DMA) .... BF
British Forces (SAUO) .... BF
British Forces Arabian Peninsula (SAUO) .... BFAP
British Forces, Arabian Peninsula [*British military*] (DMA) .... BFAP
British Forces Broadcasting Service [*or Station*] .... BFBS
British Forces Broadcasting Service-Television (SAUS) .... BFBS-TV
British Forces Broadcasting Station (SAUO) .... BFBS
British Forces Broadcasting Unit (IAA) .... BFBU
British Forces, Falkland Islands (SAUS) .... BFFI
British Forces Germany [*NATO*] .... BFG
British Forces, Hong Kong (SAUS) .... BFHK
British Forces in Germany (SAUO) .... BFIG
British Forces in Greece (SAUO) .... BFG
British Forces in Italy (SAUO) .... BFoI
British Forces in Palestine (SAUO) .... BFIP
British Forces Maintenance Area (SAUO) .... BFMA
British Forces Near East (SAUO) .... BFNE
British Forces Network .... BFN
British Forces Post Office .... BFPO
British Forces Posted Overseas (WDAA) .... BFPO
British Forces West Palestine (SAUO) .... BFWP
British Foreign and Colonial Corp. [*Finance*] .... BFCC
British Foreign and State Papers [*A publication*] (DLA) .... BFSP
British Foreign Legion [*British military*] (DMA) .... BFL
British Forging Industry Association (EAIO) .... BFIA
British Foundation for Age Research (IRUK) .... BFAR
British Foundry Association (DBA) .... BFA
British Franchise Association (DBA) .... BFA
British Franchise Association (SAUO) .... BFA
British Francophone Business Group [*An association*] (DBA) .... BFBG
British Free Corps (SAUO) .... BFC
British Free Corps [*Corps formed by Germans among POW's and civil internees*] [*World War II*] .... BFC
British Friction Materials Council (BI) .... BFMC
British Friesian Cattle Society (SAUO) .... BFCS
British Friesian Cattle Society of Great Britain and Ireland .... BFCS
British Frisian (SAUS) .... BF
British Frontier Service (BARN) .... BFS
British Frozen Food Federation (DBA) .... BFFF
British Frozen Foods Federation (SAUO) .... BFFF
British Fruit and Vegetable Canners Association (DBA) .... BF & VCA
British Fuchsia Society (BI) .... BFS
British Fulbright Scholars Association (PDAA) .... BFSA
British Fur Trade Alliance (SAUO) .... BFTA
British Fur Trade Association (DBA) .... BFTA
British Furniture Manufacturers Federated Associations (SAUO) .... BFM
British Gallantry Medal .... BGM
British Gaming Association (BARN) .... BGA
British Gas (ECON) .... BG
British Gas ADS [*NYSE symbol*] (SPSG) .... BRG
British Gas Corp. [*Toronto Stock Exchange symbol*] .... BGS
British Gas Corporation (SAUO) .... BGC
British Gas Corporation Pension Scheme .... BGCPS
British Gas Council (SAUO) .... BCG

British Gas Council (SAUO) ... BGC
British Gas International ... BGI
British Gas Ltd. [*Associated Press*] (SAG) ... BritGas
British Gas Ltd. American Depository Receipts [*Toronto Stock Exchange symbol*] ... BGSR
British Gas Lurgi (SAUS) ... BGL
British Gas Region ... BGR
British Gas Staff Association [*A union*] ... BGSA
British Gas Staff Association (SAUO) ... BGSA
British Gas Staff Pension Scheme ... BGSPS
British Gauge [*Metal industry*] ... BG
British Gear Manufacturers Association (MCD) ... BGMA
British Gelatine and Glue Research Association (DAVI) ... BGGRA
British General Hospital ... BGH
British Geological Survey ... BGS
British Geomorphological Research Group ... BGRG
British Geotechnical Society ... BGS
British Geotechnical Society ... BGTS
British Geriatric Society (SAUS) ... BGS
British Geriatrics Society ... BGS
British Geriatrics Society (SAUO) ... BGS
British Glaciological Society (SAUO) ... BGIS
British Glaciological Society (NOAA) ... BGS
British Gladiolus Society (BI) ... BGS
British Glass Industry Research Association [*Research center*] (IRC) ... BGIRA
British Glass Manufacturers Confederation (DBA) ... BGMC
British Gliding Association (MCD) ... BGA
British Glucose Manufacturers Association (SAUO) ... BGMA
British Glues and Chemicals Ltd. (SAUO) ... BGC
British Go Association (DBA) ... BGA
British Goat Society ... BGS
British Golf Greenkeepers' Association (BI) ... BGGA
British Goose Producers Association (DBA) ... BGPA
British Government (SAUO) ... BG
British Government (SAUO) ... B Govt
British Government (SAUO) ... BritGovt
British Graham Land Expedition [*1934-37*] ... BGLE
British Granite and Whinstone Federation (PDAA) ... BGWF
British Grassland Society ... BGS
British Grassland Society (SAUO) ... BGS
British Grenadiers (SAUO) ... BG
British Grenadiers ... BG
British Greyhound Racing Association (SAUO) ... BGRA
British Greyhound Racing Board (SAUO) ... BGRB
British Greyhound Racing Federation (SAUO) ... BGRF
British Ground Freezing Society (PDAA) ... BGFS
British Growers' Look Ahead International Exhibition (ITD) ... BGLA
British Guayana (SAUO) ... BRG
British Guiana ... BG
British Guiana ... BGU
British Guiana (SAUO) ... BGu
British Guiana (ILCA) ... Brit Gui
British Guiana Airways (SAUO) ... BGA
British Guiana Airways Ltd. [*A national airline*] ... BGAL
British Guiana Base Command (SAUO) ... BGBC
British Guiana Consolidated Goldfields Ltd. (SAUO) ... BGCG
British Guiana Full Court Reports (Official Gazette) [*A publication*] (DLA) ... FC
British Guiana General Jurisdiction (Official Gazette) [*1899-*] [*A publication*] (ILCA) ... GJ
British Guiana Law Reports [*A publication*] (DLA) ... BG
British Guiana Law Reports (Old and New Series) [*A publication*] (DLA) ... BGLR
British Guiana Limited Jurisdiction (Official Gazette) [*1899-1955*] [*A publication*] (DLA) ... LJ
British Guiana Militia Artillery [*British military*] (DMA) ... BGMA
British Guiana Reports of Opinions [*A publication*] (DLA) ... RBG
British Guiana Supreme Court, Appellate Jurisdiction (DLA) ... AJ
British Guiana Volunteer Force [*British military*] (DMA) ... BGVF
British Guild of Flight Operations Officers (DA) ... BritGFO
British Guillain Barre Syndrome Support Group (BUAC) ... GBS
British Guinea Time (SAUS) ... BGT
British Hacksaw and Bandsaw Manufacturers' Association (DBA) ... BHBMA
British Hacksaw Makers Association (SAUO) ... BHMA
British Handball Association (DBA) ... BHA
British Hang Glider Manufacturers Federation (PDAA) ... BHGMF
British Hang Gliding Association ... BHGA
British Hang-Gliding and Paragliding Association (PIAV) ... BHPA
British Hard Metal Association ... BHMA
British Hard Metal Export Association (SAUO) ... BHMEA
British Hardmetal Association (DBA) ... BHA
British Hardware and Housewares Manufacturers Association (DBA) ... BHHMA
British Hardware Federation (DBA) ... BHF
British Hardware Promotion Council Ltd. (BI) ... BHPC
British Harness Racing Club (DBA) ... BHRC
British Hat Guild (DBA) ... BHG
British Hay and Straw Merchants' Association (DBA) ... BHSMA
British Headwear Industries Federation (DBA) ... BHIF
British Health and Safety Society (HEAS) ... BHSS
British Health Care Association (DBA) ... BHCA
British Health Food Trade Association (DBA) ... BHFTA
British Health-Care Export Council (DS) ... BHCEC
British Health-Care Export Council (EAIO) ... BHEC
British Healthcare Internet Association (SAUO) ... BHIA
British Heart Foundation (EAIO) ... BHF
British Heavy Steel Association (BI) ... BHSA
British Helicopter Advisory Board (AIA) ... BHAB
British Hellenic Chamber of Commerce (DBA) ... BHCC
British Herb Trade Association (DBA) ... BHTA
British Herbal Medicine Association ... BHMA
British Herdsmen's Club (BI) ... BHC
British Heritage Institute (Canada) Inc. (AC) ... BHIC
British Heritage Society (EA) ... BHS
British Herpetological Society ... BHS
British Herpetological Society (SAUO) ... BHS
British Herring Trade Association (SAUO) ... BHTA
British High Commissioner ... BHC
British Hip Society (SAUO) ... BHS
British Hire Cruiser Federation (DBA) ... BHCF
British HIV Association (SAUO) ... BHIVA
British Hockey Board (SAUO) ... BHB
British Holiday and Home Parks Association (DBA) ... BH & HPA
British Holiday and Travel Association (SAUO) ... BHTA
British Holiday Fellowship Ltd. (BI) ... BHF
British Holistic Medical Association [*British*] ... BHMA
British Holistic Medical Society ... BHMS
British Holistic Veterinary Medicine Association (GVA) ... BHVMA
British Holstein Society (DBA) ... BHS
British Home and Hospital for Incurables ... BHHI
British Home Defense Measures (SAUS) ... BHDM
British Home Furnishings Bureau (DBA) ... BHFB
British Home Stores (SAUO) ... BHS
British Home Stores [*Retail chain*] ... BHS
British Homeopathic Association ... BHA
British Homoeopathic Association (SAUO) ... BHA
British Homoeopathic Society (SAUO) ... BHS
British Honduras [*MARC country of publication code*] [*Library of Congress*] (LCCP) ... bh
British Honduras ... BH
British Honduras (SAUO) ... BHond
British Honduras (ILCA) ... Brit Hond
British Honduras [*MARC geographic area code*] [*Library of Congress*] (LCCP) ... ncbh-
British Honduras Airways, Ltd. (SAUO) ... BHA
British Honduras Broadcasting Service (SAUO) ... BHBS
British Honduras Defence Force (SAUO) ... BHondDFce
British Honduras Police Force (SAUO) ... BHondPF
British Honduras Volunteer Guard (SAUO) ... BHVG
British Honey Importers and Packers Association (DBA) ... BHIPA
British Horological Institute ... BHI
British Horse Association (SAUO) ... BHA
British Horse Industry Confederation (GVA) ... BHIC
British Horse Society (SAUO) ... BHS
British Horse Society (DI) ... BHS
British Horsepower ... BHP
British Horseracing Board (GVA) ... BHB
British Hospital (SAUS) ... Brit Hosp
British Hospital Doctors Federation (SAUO) ... BHDF
British Hospital Equipment Display Centre (CB) ... BHEDC
British Hospitality Association (WDAA) ... BHA
British Hospitals Association (SAUO) ... BHA
British Hospitals Contributory Schemes Association (PDAA) ... BHCSA
British Hospitals Export Council [*Later, BHCEC*] (DS) ... BHEC
British Hosta and Hemerocallis Society (EAIO) ... BHHS
British Hotel and Public Building Equipment Group (SAUO) ... HOPBEG
British Hotels and Restaurants Association (BI) ... BHRA
British Hotels Association (BARN) ... BHA
British Hotels, Restaurants and Caterers Association (SAUO) ... BHRCA
British House Rabbit Association (GVA) ... BHRA
British Housewives League (SAUO) ... BHL
British Hovercraft ... BH
British Hovercraft Corporation (SAUO) ... BHC
British Humane Association (SAUO) ... BHA
British Humanist Association (SAUO) ... BHA
British Humanist Association ... BHA
British Humanities Index (TELE) ... BHI
British Humanities Research Board (AIE) ... BHRB
British Hydrological Society (SAUO) ... BHS
British Hydromechanical Research Association (SAUO) ... BHRA
British Hydromechanics Research Association (SAUO) ... BHMRA
British Hydromechanics Research Association (SAUO) ... BHRA
British Hypnosis Research [*An association*] (DBA) ... BHRE
British Hypnosis Research Association ... BHRA
British Hypnotherapy Association ... BHA
British Ice Hockey Association (DI) ... BIHA
British Ichthyological Society ... BIS
British Impact Treatment Association (DBA) ... BITA
British Imperial Metal Industries (SAUO) ... BIM
British Imperial System ... BIS
British Import Union (DBA) ... BIU
British Importers' Confederation (DS) ... BIC
British Incoming Tour Operators Association (DBA) ... BITOA
British Independent Air Transport Association, Ltd. (SAUO) ... BIATA
British Independent Airways [*ICAO designator*] (FAAC) ... BXH
British Independent Airways [*ICAO designator*] (AD) ... RX
British Independent Factors Association (DBA) ... BIFA
British Independent Garages Association (DBA) ... BIGA
British Independent Grocers' Association (DBA) ... BIGA
British Independent Plastic Extruders Association (DBA) ... BIPEA
British Independent Steel Producers Association (PDAA) ... BISPA
British Independent Television (SAUO) ... BIT
British India ... BI

British India (SAUO) ... BrI
British India Commonwealth League (SAUO) ... BICL
British India Line (SAUO) ... BIL
British India Line (SAUO) ... BrIL
British India Steam Navigation Co. (IIA) ... BI
British India Steam Navigation Co. ... BISN
British India Steam Navigation Co. (ROG) ... BISNC
British India Steam Navigation Company (SAUO) ... BISNC
British Indian Ocean Territories (or Territory) (SAUS) ... BIOT
British Indian Ocean Territory [*MARC country of publication code*] [*Library of Congress*] (LCCP) ... bi
British Indian Ocean Territory ... BIOT
British Indian Ocean Territory [*MARC geographic area code*] [*Library of Congress*] (LCCP) ... i-bi-
British Indian Ocean Territory [*ANSI two-letter standard code*] (CNC) ... IO
British Indian Ocean Territory [*ANSI three-letter standard code*] (CNC) ... IOT
British Industrial Advertising Association (SAUO) ... BIAA
British Industrial Advertising Association (PDAA) ... BIAA
British Industrial and Scientific Film Association ... BISFA
British Industrial and Scientific International Translations Service (SAUO) ... BISITS
British Industrial Biological Research Association (ARC) ... BIBRA
British Industrial Ceramic Manufacturers Association (DBA) ... BICMA
British Industrial Collaborative Exponential Program ... BICEP
British Industrial Collaborative Exponential Programme (SAUO) ... BICEP
British Industrial Development (SAUS) ... BID
British Industrial Development Office [*Through foreign branches, encourages investments in Britain from abroad*] ... BIDO
British Industrial Fasteners Federation (DBA) ... BIFF
British Industrial Floor Machine Association (SAUO) ... BIFMA
British Industrial Furnace Construction Association (DBA) ... BIFCA
British Industrial Marketing Association (SAUO) ... BIMA
British Industrial Measuring and Control Apparatus Manufacturers Association (SAUS) ... BIMCAM
British Industrial Measuring and Control Apparatus Manufacturers Association (SAUS) ... BIMCAM Association
British Industrial Plastics (ODBW) ... BIP
British Industrial Plastics Ltd. (SAUO) ... BäläP
British Industrial Truck Association ... BITA
British Industries Agencies (SAUO) ... Britagent
British Industries Fair (SAUO) ... BIF
British Industries Fair ... BIF
British Industries Federation ... BIF
British Industries Film Association (SAUO) ... BIFA
British Industries National Council (SAUO) ... BINC
British Industry [*Vancouver Stock Exchange symbol*] ... BI
British Industry Committee on South Africa ... BICSA
British Industry Roads Campaign (SAUO) ... BIRC
British Industry Steel Producers (SAUO) ... BISP
British Informatics Society Ltd. (NITA) ... BISL
British Information Centre (SAUO) ... BIC
British Information Service Library (SAUO) ... BISL
British Information Services ... BIS
British Information Services (SAUS) ... Brit Info
British Information Services, New York, NY [*Library symbol*] [*Library of Congress*] (LCLS) ... NNBLI
British Information Technology Exhibition and Conference on Engineering Software [*Computational Mechanics Institute*] ... BRITEC
British Infrared Manufacturers Organization (PDAA) ... BIRMO
British Institute for Brain Injured Children ... BIBIC
British Institute for Non-Destructive Testing (SAUO) ... BINDT
British Institute for Recordes Sound (SAUO) ... BIRS
British Institute in Paris (SAUO) ... BIP
British Institute in Paris (SAUS) ... BIP
British Institute of Acupuncture (SAUS) ... BIA
British Institute of Acupuncture (SAUO) ... BIA
British Institute of Adult Education (SAUO) ... BIAE
British Institute of Adult Education (SAUS) ... BIAE
British Institute of Agricultural Consultants (DBA) ... BIAC
British Institute of Architectural Technicians (EAIO) ... BIAT
British Institute of Cinematographers (SAUO) ... BIC
British Institute of Cleaning Science (SAUO) ... BICS
[*The*] **British Institute of Cleaning Science** ... BICS
British Institute of Cleaning Science ... BICSC
British Institute of Dealers in Securities [*Defunct*] ... BIDS
British Institute of Electrical Engineers ... BIEE
British Institute of Embalmers ... BIE
British Institute of Energy Economics (DBA) ... BIEE
British Institute of Engineering Technology (DI) ... BIET
British Institute of Engineering Technology (SAUO) ... BIST
British Institute of Engineers (MCD) ... BIE
British Institute of Facilities Management (COBU) ... BIFM
British Institute of Graphologists (DBA) ... BIG
British Institute of Hardwood Flooring Specialists (BI) ... BIHFS
British Institute of Human Rights (DLA) ... BIHR
British Institute of Industrial Art ... BIIA
British Institute of Industrial Art (SAUO) ... BIIA
British Institute of Industrial Therapy ... BIIT
British Institute of Innkeeping ... BII
British Institute of Interior Design (SAUO) ... BIID
British Institute of International and Comparative Law ... BIICL
British Institute of International and Comparative Law (EA) ... BRICLAW
British Institute of Jazz Studies (BI) ... BIJS
British Institute of Kitchen Architecture (DBA) ... BIKA
British Institute of Management ... BIM
British Institute of Management Secretariat for Overseas Countries (PDAA) ... BIMSOC
British Institute of Materials (SAUO) ... BIM
British Institute of Mental Handicap ... BIMH
British Institute of Metals (SAUO) ... BIM
British Institute of Non-Destructive Testing (PDAA) ... BINDT
British Institute of Non-Destructive Testing (EAIO) ... BInst NDT
British Institute of Occupational Hygiene (HEAS) ... BIOH
British Institute of Organ Studies (DBA) ... BIOS
British Institute of Persian Studies (DBA) ... BIPS
British Institute of Philosophy (SAUO) ... BIP
British Institute of Philosophy (SAUS) ... BIP
British Institute of Physics (SAUO) ... BIP
British Institute of Practical Psychology (SAUO) ... BIPP
British Institute of Practical Psychology ... IPP
British Institute of Practical Psychology Ltd. (BI) ... BIPP
British Institute of Professional Photography (AIE) ... BIPP
British Institute of Public Opinion ... BIPO
British Institute of Radio Engineers ... BIRE
British Institute of Radio Engineers (IAA) ... BRITIRE
British Institute of Radiology (SAUO) ... BIR
British Institute of Radiology (DEN) ... BIR
British Institute of Recorded Sound ... BIRS
British Institute of Regulatory Affairs (DBA) ... BIRA
British Institute of Securities Laws (DBA) ... BISL
British Institute of Sewage Purification ... BISP
British Institute of Sports Coaches (DBA) ... BISC
British Institute of Surgical Technologists (SAUO) ... BIST
British Institute of Surgical Technologists ... BIST
British Institute of Traffic Education Research (DBA) ... BITER
British Institute On-Line Information Service (SAUS) ... BRIOLIS
British Institution (ROG) ... BI
British Institution of Radio Engineers (SAUO) ... BIRE
British Institution of Radio Engineers (SAUO) ... BritIRE
British Institution of Training Officers (PDAA) ... BITO
British Institutions Reflection Profiling Syndicate [*Seismic profiling*] ... BIRPS
British Instrument Industries Exhibition (SAUO) ... BIIE
British Insulated Cables ... BIC
British Insulin Manufacturers (SAUO) ... BIM
British Insurance and Finance Union (DI) ... BIFU
British Insurance and Investment Brokers' Association ... BIIBA
British Insurance Association ... BIA
British Insurance Brokers' Association (DLA) ... BIBA
British Insurance Group (SAUO) ... BIG
British Insurance Law Association (SAUO) ... BILA
British Insurance Law Association (DLA) ... BILA
British Insurance Law Association. Bulletin [*A publication*] (DLA) ... BILA Bull
British Insurers' International Committee (MARI) ... BIIC
British Integrated Programmed Suite (SAUS) ... BIPS
British Intelligence Bureau (SAUO) ... BIB
British Intelligence Department (SAUO) ... BID
British Intelligence General Orders Transferred (SAUS) ... BIGOT
British Intelligence Objectives Sub-Committee (SAUO) ... BIOS
British Intelligence Objectives Subcommittee ... BIOS
British Intelligence Service (SAUO) ... BIS
British Interactive Broadcasting ... BIB
British Interactive Multimedia Association (DDC) ... BIMA
British Interactive Video Association [*Information service or system*] (IID) ... BIVA
British Interlibrary Loan Project (SAUS) ... VISCOUNT
British Interlining Manufacturers Association (DBA) ... BIMA
British Internal Combustion Engine Manufacturers Association (SAUO) ... BICEMA
British Internal Combustion Engine Research Association (SAUO) ... BICERA
British Internal Combustion Engine Research Institute (SAUO) ... BJCERJ
British Internal Combustion Engine Research Institute Ltd. [*Research center*] (IRUK) ... BICERI
British International Freight Association (EAIO) ... BIFA
British International Helicopters [*ICAO designator*] (AD) ... UR
British International Helicopters Ltd. [*ICAO designator*] (FAAC) ... BIH
British International Helicopters Ltd. (SAUO) ... BIHL
British International Law Cases [*A publication*] (DLA) ... BILC
British International Law Society (DLA) ... BILS
British International Motorcycle Association (EA) ... BIMA
British International Pictures (SAUO) ... BIP
British International Postcard Exhibition ... BIPEX
British International Studies Association (DBA) ... BISA
British Interplanetary Society (SAUO) ... BIS
British Interplanetary Society ... BIS
British Intitute in Eastern Africa (SAUO) ... BIEA
British Invasion Force (SAUO) ... BIF
British Investment Casting Trade Association ... BICTA
British Investors Database ... BID
British Iris Society (EAIO) ... BIS
British Iris Society (SAUO) ... BIS
British Iron and Steel Consumers' Council ... BRISCC
British Iron and Steel Corporation (SAUO) ... BISC
British Iron and Steel Corporation (SAUO) ... BISCO
British Iron and Steel Federation ... BISF
British Iron and Steel Industry Translation Service ... BISITS
British Iron and Steel Institute (SAUO) ... BISI
British Iron and Steel Institute Translation Service (NITA) ... BISITS
British Iron and Steel Research Associates (SAUS) ... BISRA
British Iron and Steel Research Association (SAUO) ... BIASRA
British Iron and Steel Research Association ... BISRA
British Iron, Steel and Kindred Trades Association (BI) ... BISAKTA

British Iron, Steel and Kindred Trades Association (SAUO) ... BISAKTA
British Ironfounders Association (BI) ... BIA
British Island Airways [*ICAO designator*] (AD) ... IV
British Island Airways Ltd. ... BIA
British Island Airways Ltd. (SAUO) ... KCZZ
British Isles (SAUO) ... BrI
British Isles Bee Breeders Association (DBA) ... BIBBA
British Isles Bowling Council (SAUO) ... BIBC
British Isles Federation of Agricultural Co-operatives (SAUO) ... BIFAC
British Isles Joint TNM Classification Committee (SAUO) ... BIJC
British Israel World Federation (SAUO) ... BIWF
British, Italian, French, United States (SAUS) ... BIFUS
British Jewellers Association (PDAA) ... BJA
British Jewellery and Giftware Federation (DBA) ... BJGF
British Jewish Cockney ... BJC
British Jigsaw Puzzle Library [*An association*] (DBA) ... BJPL
British Joint Communications and Electronics Board (SAUS) ... BJCEB
British Joint Communications Board [*British military*] (DMA) ... BJCB
British Joint Communications Office (NATG) ... BJCO
British Joint Communications-Electronics Board [*Military*] ... BJCEB
British Joint Corrosion Group (SAUO) ... BJCG
British Joint Services ... BJS
British Joint Services Mission [*Later, SUKLO*] ... BJSM
British Joint Services Mission, Washington, D.C. (SAUO) ... BJSM WASHDC
British Joint Staff Mission [*World War II*] ... BJSM
British Journal for the History of Science [*A publication*] ... BJHS
British Journal for the Philosophy of Science [*A publication*] ... BJPS
British Journal of Addiction (SAUO) ... BJA
British Journal of Administrative Law [*A publication*] (DLA) ... BJAL
British Journal of Administrative Law [*A publication*] (DLA) ... Brit J Admin Law
British Journal of Administrative Law [*A publication*] (DLA) ... Brit J Adm L
British Journal of Aesthetics (journ.) (SAUS) ... BJA
British Journal of Anaesthesia (SAUO) ... BJA
British Journal of Cancer [*A publication*] ... BJC
British Journal of Cancer (SAUS) ... Br J Cancer
British Journal of Clinical Pharmacology (SAUO) ... BJCP
British Journal of Criminology [*A publication*] ... BJ Crim
British Journal of Dermatology (SAUS) ... Br J Dermatol
British Journal of Experimental Pathology (SAUS) ... Br J Exp Pathol
British Journal of General Practice (SAUO) ... BJGP
British Journal of Haematology (SAUS) ... Br J Haematol
British Journal of Healthcare Computing and Information Management (SAUO) ... BJHC&IM
British Journal of Industrial Medicine (SAUS) ... Br J Ind Med
British Journal of Industrial Relations [*A publication*] ... BJIR
British Journal of International Law [*A publication*] (DLA) ... Brit J Int'l L
British Journal of Law & Society [*A publication*] ... BJLS
British Journal of Medical Psychology (journ.) (SAUS) ... BJMPs
British Journal of Non-Destructive Testing (SAUS) ... Br J Non-Destr Test
British Journal of Nursing (SAUO) ... BJN
British Journal of Ophthalmology (SAUS) ... BJO
British Journal of Opthalmology (SAUS) ... Br J Opthalmol
British Journal of Pharmacology (SAUO) ... BJP
British Journal of Plastic Surgery (SAUO) ... BJPS
British Journal of Psychiatry (journ.) (SAUS) ... Brit J Psychiat
British Journal of Radiology (SAUO) ... BJR
British Journal of Radiology (SAUS) ... Br J Radiology
British Journal of Sociology. Published quarterly for the London School of Economics and Political Sience. London (SAUS) ... LSE/BJS
British Journal of Urology (SAUO) ... BJU
British Judo Association ... BJA
British Junior Chamber [*An association*] (DBA) ... BJC
British Junior Chambers of Commerce (BI) ... BJCC
British Jute Trade Research Association (PDAA) ... BJTRA
British Karate Association (SAUO) ... BKA
British Karate Board (DI) ... BKB
British Kidney Fund Association (SAUO) ... BKFA
British Kidney Patient Association (DI) ... BKPA
British Kinematograph Society (SAUO) ... BKS
British Kinematograph Sound and Television Society Journal (SAUO) ... BKSTSJ
British Kinematograph, Sound and Television Society Journal (SAUS) ... BKSTSJ
British Kinematography, Sound, and Television Society ... BKSTS
British Kite Flyers Association (SAUO) ... BKFA
British Knights [*Brand name of athletic shoe*] ... BK
British Knitting and Clothing Export Council (DBA) ... BKCEC
British Knitting Export Council (SAUO) ... BKEC
British Kodaly Academy (DBA) ... BKA
British Korfball Association (EAIO) ... BKA
British Laboratory Animals Veterinary Association (DBA) ... BLAVA
British Laboratory Ware Association Ltd. (BI) ... BLWA
British Labour Esperanto Association (SAUO) ... BLEA
British Labour Movement (SAUO) ... BLM
British Labour Party (SAUO) ... BLP
British Lace Trade Joint Committee (SAUO) ... BLTJC
British Lamp Blown Scientific Glassware Manufacturers' Association Ltd. (BI) ... BLSGMA
British Landing Army (SAUO) ... BLA
British Landrace Pig Society (BI) ... BLPS
British Laryngological, Rhinological, and Otological Association (MAE) ... BLROA
British Latin America Volunteers [*British military*] (DMA) ... BLAV
British Launderers Research Association (PDAA) ... BLRA
British Lawn Mower Racing Association (DBA) ... BLMRA
British Lawnmower Manufacturers Federation (SAUO) ... BLMF
British League of Male Chauvinists (EAIO) ... BLMC
British Leather Confederation (IRUK) ... BLC
British Leather Fashion Council (DBA) ... BLFC
British Leather Federation (BI) ... BLF
British Leather Manufacturers (SAUO) ... BLM
British Leather Manufacturers Research Association ... BLMRA
British Leathergoods Manufacturers Association (DBA) ... BLMA
British Legal Association (DLA) ... BLA
British Legal Services Agency (DLA) ... BLSA
British Legion ... BL
British Legion (SAUO) ... BL
British Legion Headquarters ... BLH
British Legion Village ... BLV
British Lending Library Review (journ.) (SAUS) ... BLL Rev
British Leprosy Relief Association (BI) ... BLRA
British Leprosy Relief Association (IRUK) ... LEPRA
British Leyland [*Later, BL Ltd., then Rover Group*] [*Auto manufacturing company*] ... BL
British Leyland Europe and Overseas [*Commercial firm*] ... BLEO
British Leyland Motor (SAUO) ... BLM
British Leyland Motor Corp. [*Auto manufacturing company*] ... BLMC
British Leyland Motor Holdings [*Auto manufacturing company*] ... BLMH
British Leyland Systems Ltd. (NITA) ... BLSL
British Liaison Mission (SAUO) ... BLM
British Liaison Officer ... BLO
British Liaison Officer (SAUS) ... Brit L Off
British Liaison Team (SAUO) ... BLT
British Liberation Army [*Later, British Army of the Rhine*] ... BLA
British Library [*Formerly, The British Museum Reading Room*] ... BL
British Library (SAUO) ... BL
British Library Association (BARN) ... BLA
British Library Automated Information Service [*European host database system*] (IID) ... BLAISE
British Library Bibliographic Services [*London, England*] ... BLBS
[*The*] **British Library Bibliographic Services Division** (NITA) ... BLBSD
British Library Catalog: Humanities and Social Sciences [*Information service or system*] (CRD) ... HSS
British Library Catalogue (TELE) ... BLC
British Library Cataloguing in Publication (TELE) ... BL CIP
British Library Cataloguing In Publication (SAUS) ... BL CIP
British Library Computing and Telecommunications Department (TELE) ... BLCTD
British Library, Development and Systems Office, London, England [*Library symbol*] [*Library of Congress*] (LCLS) ... Uk-D
British Library Document Supply Centre (CB) ... BLDSC
British Library Document Supply Copyright Clearance Centre (SAUO) ... BLDSCCC
British Library Document Supply Service (SAUS) ... BL DSC
British Library General Catalogue of Printed Books [*A publication*] ... BLC
British Library Humanities and Social Sciences (TELE) ... BL H&SS
British Library Information Sciences Service ... BLISS
British Library Information Skills (AIE) ... BLIS
British Library Lending Division ... BLL
British Library Lending Division ... BLLD
British Library Lending Division in Boston Spa (SAUS) ... Boston Spa
British Library, London, England [*OCLC symbol*] (OCLC) ... BRI
British Library, London, United Kingdom [*Library symbol*] [*Library of Congress*] (LCLS) ... Uk
British Library Name Authority File (TELE) ... BL NAF
British Library National Bibliographic Service (TELE) ... BL NBS
British Library National Bibliographic Service (SAUS) ... BL NBS
British Library National Sound Archive (TELE) ... BL NSA
British Library of Political and Economic Science [*London School of Economics*] ... BLPES
British Library of Tape ... BLOT
British Library of Tape Recordings (SAUO) ... BLOT
British Library of Tape Recordings for Hospital Patients (SAUO) ... BLTRHP
British Library of Wildlife Sound ... BLOWS
[*The*] **British Library Reference Division** (NITA) ... BLRD
British Library Regular Readers' Group (WDAA) ... BLRRG
[*The*] **British Library Research and Development Department** (NITA) ... BLR & DD
British Library Research and Development Department (SAUS) ... BL R&DD
British Library Research and Development Division (AIE) ... BLRDD
British Library Research and Innovation Centre (TELE) ... BL RIC
British Library Science Reference and Information Service (TELE) ... BL SRIS
British Lichen Society (EAIO) ... BLS
British Life, Art and History (SAUS) ... BLAH
British Life Assurance Trust ... BLAT
British Lift Association (DBA) ... BLA
British Light Aviation Center (MCD) ... BLAC
British Light Aviation Center (or Centre) (SAUS) ... BLAC
British Light Tackle Club (SAUO) ... BLTC
British Lighting Council [*Defunct*] ... BLC
British Lighting Industry (SAUO) ... BLI
British Limb Reconstruction Society (SAUO) ... BLRS
British Limbless Ex-Service Men's Association ... BLESMA
British Limousin Cattle Society (DBA) ... BLCS
British Linen Bank ... BLB
British Linen Hire Association (PDAA) ... BLHA
British Lion [*Motion picture company*] ... BL
British List Brokers Association (DBA) ... BLBA
British Literary and Artistic Copyright Association ... BLACA
British Logistics (SAUS) ... BRITLOG
British Lubricants Federation (DBA) ... BLF

British Lubricating Oil and Grease Research Organization (SAUO) .... BLOGRO
British Machine Guarding Authority .... BMGA
British Machine Vision Association .... BMVA
British Machinery Pump Manufacturers (SAUS) .... BPMA
British Magical Society (DBA) .... BMS
British Mail Order Corp. (DGA) .... BMOC
British Maize Starch and Glucose Manufacturers Association (BI) .... BMSGMA
British Majorettes' Association (DI) .... BMA
British Malachological Society (SAUO) .... BMS
British Malaya (SAUO) .... BM
British Malaysian Industry and Trade Association (DS) .... BMITA
British Malaysian Society (DBA) .... BMS
British Malleable Tube Fittings Association (BI) .... BMTFA
British Management Data Foundation (SAUO) .... BMDF
British Mandatory Procurement Office, Herford (SAUO) .... BMPO
British Man-Made Fibres Federation (BI) .... BMFF
British Man-Made Fibres Federation .... BMMFF
British Mantle Manufacturers' Association (BI) .... BMMA
British Manufacture and Research .... BMS
British Manufacture & Research Co. (SAUO) .... BMARC
British Manufactured (SAUS) .... BM
British Manufacturers' Association Ltd. (BI) .... BMA
British Manufacturers of Malleable Tube Fittings Export Group .... BRIMAFEX
British Manufacturers of Petroleum Equipment (SAUO) .... BMPE
British Manufacturing and Research Company (SAUO) .... British MARC
British Marine Aircraft (SAUS) .... BMA
British Marine Aquarist Association .... BMAA
British Marine Equipment Association (DBA) .... BMEA
British Marine Equipment Council (DS) .... BMEC
British Marine Industries Federation (EAIO) .... BMIF
British Marine Mutual (RIMS) .... BMM
British Marine RADAR (IAA) .... BMR
British Marine Underwriters Associations (MARI) .... BMUA
British Maritime Intelligence Support System (SAUS) .... BRITMISS
British Maritime Law Association .... BMLA
British Maritime Technology Ltd. [Research center] (IRC) .... BMT
British Market Research Bureau (SAUO) .... BMRB
British Market Research Bureau Ltd. [Information service or system]
   (IID) .... BMRB
British Mass Transit Consultants [Commercial firm] .... BMTC
British Mat and Matting Manufacturers Association (BI) .... BMMMA
British Match Corporation (SAUO) .... BMC
British Matchbox Label and Booklet Society .... BML-BS
British Matchbox Label Society (SAUO) .... BMLS
British Materials Handling Board (HEAS) .... BMHB
British Materials Handling Federation (DBA) .... BMHF
British Mean Time (DAS) .... BMT
British Measurement and Testing Association (ACII) .... BMTA
British Measurement System (SAUS) .... BMS
British Measures Group .... BMG
British Mechanical Engineering Confederation (SAUO) .... BRIMEC
British Mechanical Engineering Federation (DI) .... BMEF
British Medal (DI) .... BM
British Medical [Vancouver Stock Exchange symbol] .... BMD
British Medical Acupuncture Association (PDAA) .... BMAA
British Medical Acupuncture Society .... BMAS
British Medical Association .... BMA
British Medical Battalion (SAUS) .... BRITMEDBATT
British Medical Board (SAUO) .... BMB
British Medical Bulletin (journ.) (SAUS) .... BMB
British Medical Bulletin (journ.) (SAUS) .... Br Med Bull
British Medical Charter [ICAO designator] (FAAC) .... BMD
British Medical Council .... BMC
British Medical Data Systems (NITA) .... BMDS
British Medical Informatics Society (ACII) .... BMIS
British Medical Journal [A publication] .... BMJ
British Medical Journal (journ.) (SAUS) .... Br Med J
British Medical LASER Association .... BMLA
British Medical Pilots Association (SAUO) .... BMPA
British Medical Protection Society (SAUS) .... BMPS
British Medical Representatives Association (BI) .... BMRA
British Medical Research Council .... BMRC
British Medical Research Council (SAUO) .... BMRC
British Medical Society (SAUO) .... BMS
British Medical Students Association (BI) .... BMSA
British Medical Television .... BMTV
British Medical Ultrasound Society (EAIO) .... BMUS
British Medical Union (SAUO) .... BMU
British Mediterranean Airways Ltd. [FAA designator] (FAAC) .... LAJ
British Menswear Guild Ltd. (BI) .... BMG
British Merchant Banking and Securities Houses Association (EAIO) .... BMBA
British Merchant Navy .... BMN
British Merchant Service Guild (SAUO) .... BMSG
British Merchant Shipping Mission .... BMSM
British Metal Castings Council (DBA) .... BMCC
British Metal Corporation Ltd. (SAUO) .... BMC
British Metal Sintering Association (SAUO) .... BMSA
British Metallurgical Plant Constructors Association (DBA) .... BMPCA
British Metalworking Plant Makers Association (SAUO) .... BMPA
British Meteor Society (EAIO) .... BMS
British Meteorological Office (MCD) .... BMO
British Metrication Board .... BMB
British Mexican Society (DBA) .... BMS
British Micro Manufacturer Group .... BMMG
British Microcirculation Society (EAIO) .... BMS

British Microcomputer Manufacturers Group (SAUO) .... BMMG
British Microfilm Export Group (SAUO) .... BMEG
British Micrographic Manufacturers Association (DBA) .... BMMA
British Microlight Aircraft Association (PDAA) .... BMAA
British Micropalaeontological Research Group .... BMRG
British Micropalaeontological Society (QUAC) .... BMS
British Middle East Office .... BMEO
British Midland Airways [ICAO designator] (AD) .... BD
British Midland Airways Ltd. .... BM
British Midland Airways Ltd. [ICAO designator] (FAAC) .... BMA
British Military Administration .... BMA
British Military Administration, British Borneo .... BMA(BB)
British Military Authority .... BMA
British Military Exchange Mission (WDAA) .... BRIXMIS
British Military Government .... BMG
British Military Hospital .... BMH
British Military Hospital (SAUO) .... BRIMILHOSP
British Military Intelligence (SAUO) .... BMI
British Military Mission .... BMM
British Military Mission in Ethiopia (SAUO) .... BMME
British Military Police Office (SAUO) .... BMPO
British Military Port and Shipping Branch (SAUO) .... BMPS
British Military Supply Mission [World War II] .... BMSM
British Military Volunteer Service (SAUO) .... BMVS
British Mining Tools Association (SAUO) .... BMTA
British Ministry of Agriculture, Food and Fisheries (SAUO) .... MAFF
British Ministry of Information (SAUO) .... BMI
British Ministry of Information (DAS) .... BMI
British Ministry of Supply (AAG) .... B/MOS
British Ministry of Supply (SAUO) .... BMOS
British Ministry of Supply .... BMS
British Ministry of Supply Research and Development
   Establishment .... BMSRDE
British Ministry of War Transport [World War II] .... BMWT
British Mission (SAUO) .... BM
British Missionary Society (SAUO) .... BMS
British Modal Speaking Position (SAUS) .... BMSP
British Model Soldier Society .... BMSS
British Modified Starch Manufacturers Association (SAUO) .... BMSMA
British Monomark (SAUS) .... BM
British Morgan Horse Society .... BMHS
British Mosquito Control Institute (SAUO) .... BMCI
British Motels Federation (SAUO) .... BMF
British Moth Boat Association (BI) .... BMBA
British Motor and Sailing Ship Owners Association (SAUO) .... BMSSOA
British Motor Corp. Ltd. .... BMC
British Motor Cycle Racing Club (DBA) .... BEMSEE
British Motor Cycle Racing Club, Ltd. (SAUO) .... BMCRC
British Motor Heritage .... BMH
British Motor Holdings Ltd. (SAUO) .... BMH
British Motor Racing Marshals Club (DBA) .... BMRMC
British Motor Racing Research Trust .... BMRRT
British Motor Ship Owners Association (DBA) .... BMSOA
British Motor Trade Association (BI) .... BMTA
British Mountaineering Council .... BMC
British Movement [Political party] .... BM
British Movement (SAUO) .... BM
British Museum (SAUO) .... BM
British Museum [London] .... BM
British Museum (SAUO) .... BMu
British Museum (SAUO) .... BMus
British Museum (SAUO) .... BritMus
British Museum - Sloan Herbarium [London] .... MB-SL
British Museum Catalogue .... BMC
British Museum Catalogue of Coins of the Roman Empire [A publication]
   (OCD) .... B M Coins Rom Emp
British Museum Department of Manuscripts (SAUO) .... BMDM
British Museum Department of Manuscripts (SAUS) .... BMDM
British Museum Expeditions to Middle Egypt [London] [A publication]
   (BJA) .... BME
British Museum Library [London] .... BML
British Museum of Natural History (SAUO) .... BMNH
British Museum Quarterly (SAUS) .... BMQ
British Museum Reading Room (SAUS) .... BMRR
British Music Hall Society (BI) .... BMHS
British Music Information Centre (CB) .... BMIC
British Music Society .... BMS
British Music Union .... BMU
British Musical Society (SAUO) .... BMS
British Music-Hall Association (WDAA) .... BMHA
British Musicians' Pensions Society (BI) .... BMPS
British Mycological Society .... BMS
British Mycological Society (SAUO) .... BMS
British Narrow Fabrics Association (DBA) .... BNFA
British National Antarctic Expedition [1901-04] .... BrNAE
British National Association for Soviet and East European Studies
   (PDAA) .... BNASEES
British National Association of Perry Makers .... BNAPM
British National Bibliographical Staff Association .... BNBSA
British National Bibliography (WDAA) .... BNB
British National Bibliography Research Fund .... BNBRF
British National Book Centre .... BNBC
British National Cadet Association (SAUO) .... BNCA
British National Carnation Society (SAUO) .... BNCS
British National Carnation Society (BI) .... BNCS

British National Committee (WDAA) .... BNC
British National Committee for Chemistry (SAUO) .... BNCC
British National Committee for Electroheat (PDAA) .... BNCE
British National Committee for General Information Programme (SAUS) .... BNCGIP
British National Committee for Geography (SAUO) .... BNCG
British National Committee for International Engineering Affairs (PDAA) .... BNCIEA
British National Committee for Non-Destructive Testing (SAUO) ...... BNC for NDT
British National Committee for Non-Destructive Testing (ACII) .... BNCNDT
British National Committee for Scientific Radio (SAUO) .... BNCSR
British National Committee for the International Chamber of Commerce (SAUO) .... BNCICC
British National Committee of Materials (SAUO) .... BNC on Mats
British National Committee of the International Chamber of Commerce (DS) .... BNC/ICC
British National Committee of the International Electrotechnical Commission (SAUO) .... BNC-IEC
British National Committee on Antarctic Research .... BNCAR
British National Committee on Data for Science and Technology (DIT) .... BNCDST
British National Committee on Materials .... BNCM
British National Committee on Ocean Engineering .... BNCOE
British National Committee on Ocean Engineering (SAUO) .... ENCOR
British National Committee on Research .... BNCOR
British National Committee on Space Research .... BNCSR
British National Committee on Surface Active Agents .... BNC
British National Committee on Surface Active Agents (BI) .... BNCSAA
British National Committee on Surface Active Agents (SAUO) .... BNCSAA
British National Conference on Databases (NITA) .... BNCOD
British National Connector (SAUS) .... BNC
British National Discography (SAUS) .... BND
British National Engineering Laboratory (SAUO) .... BNEL
British National Export Council .... BNEC
British National Film Catalogue (DIT) .... BNFC
British National Formulary [A publication] .... BNF
British National Fuels Ltd. (SAUO) .... BNFL
British National Health Insurance (SAUO) .... BNHI
British National Health Service .... BNHS
British National Institute for Medical Research (SAUO) .... BNIMR
British National Institute of Oceanography .... BNIO
British National Insurance Board (SAUO) .... BNIB
British National Lymphoma Investigation .... BNLI
British National Oil Corp. [Pronounced "bee-knock"] [Nationalized industry] [British] .... BNOC
British National Opera Company .... BNOC
British National Overseas (SAUS) .... BNO
British National Party (PPW) .... BNP
British National Radio School (SAUO) .... BNRS
British National Radio School (SAUS) .... BNRS
British National Remote Sensing Centre (SAUS) .... BNRSC
British National Research Development Corporation (SAUO) .... BNRDC
British National Socialist Movement (SAUO) .... BNS
British National Socialist Movement (SAUO) .... BNSM
British National Space Centre .... BNSC
British National Space Council (SAUO) .... BNSC
British National Temperance League (SAUO) .... BNTL
British Natural Hygiene Society .... BNHS
British Naturalists' Association (BARN) .... BNA
British Naturopathic and Osteopathic Association .... BNOA
British Nautical Instrument Trade Association (DBA) .... BNITA
British Naval Air Service .... BNAS
British Naval Air Staff .... BNAS
British Naval Attache (NATG) .... BNA
British Naval Connector (CDE) .... BNC
British Naval Equipment Association (PDAA) .... BNEA
British Naval Gunnery Mission [British military] (DMA) .... BNGM
British Naval Gunnery Mission (SAUO) .... BNGM
British Naval Liaison Officer .... BNLO
British Naval Liaison [Office] US Navy [London] .... BNLUS
British Naval Mission (SAUO) .... BNM
British Naval Representative (SAUS) .... BNR
British Naval Staff .... BNS
British Navy (SAUO) .... BN
British Needlecrafts Council (DBA) .... BNC
British Neuropathological Society .... BNS
British Neuroscience Association (SAUO) .... BNA
British New Foundland Development Corporation (SAUO) .... BRINCO
British New Guinea (ADA) .... BNG
British New Town Movement (WDAA) .... BNTM
British New Zealand Trade Council, Inc. (DBA) .... B-NZTC
British Newfoundland Exploration Ltd (SAUO) .... BRINEX
British Newspaper Society (SAUO) .... BNS
British Non-Commissioned Officer [British military] (DMA) .... BNCO
British Noncommissioned Officers (SAUS) .... BNCOS
British Non-Ferrous Abstracts [A database] [British Non-Ferrous Metals Technology Centre] (NITA) .... BNF ABS
British Non-Ferrous Metals Abstracts [BNF Metals Technology Centre] [Information service or system] (CRD) .... BNF
British Non-Ferrous Metals Federation (BI) .... BNFMF
British Non-Ferrous Metals Research Association .... BNFMRA
British Non-Ferrous Metals Research Association .... BNMRA
British Non-Ferrous Metals Technology Centre (EAIO) .... BNFMTC
British Non-Ferrous Metals Technology Centre (SAUS) .... BNFMTC
British Non-Ferrous Smelters Association (SAUS) .... BNFSA

British Nonwovens Manufacturers Association (DBA) .... BNMA
British North Africa Force (SAUO) .... BNAF
British North Africa Force .... BNAF
British North America .... BNA
British North America (SAUO) .... BNA
British North America Philatelic Society (EA) .... BNAPS
British North American Act .... BNAA
British North Atlantic (DS) .... BNA
British North Borneo .... BNB
British North Borneo (SAUO) .... BNB
British Nuclear Associates (SAUO) .... BNA
British Nuclear Ballistic Missile .... BNBM
British Nuclear Cardiology Group (SAUO) .... BNCG
British Nuclear Design and Construction Limited (SAUS) .... BNDC
British Nuclear Energy Committee (SAUS) .... BNEC
British Nuclear Energy Conference (SAUS) .... BNEC
British Nuclear Energy Conference .... BNEC
British Nuclear Energy Society .... BNES
British Nuclear Engineering Society (SAUO) .... BNES
British Nuclear Export Executives [Group to promote export of nuclear power stations of British design] .... BNX
British Nuclear Forum .... BNF
British Nuclear Fuels Ltd. .... BNF
British Nuclear Fuels Ltd. .... BNFL
British Nuclear Laboratories (SAUO) .... BNL
British Nuclear Medicine Society (SAUO) .... BNMS
British Nuclear Society (SAUO) .... BNS
British Nuclear Test Veterans Association (DBA) .... BNTVA
British Nuclear Waste Ltd. (NUCP) .... BNWL
British Numerical Control Society (MCD) .... BNCS
British Numismatic Society .... BNS
British Numismatic Society (SAUO) .... BNS
British Numismatic Trade Association .... BNTA
British Nursery Goods Association (BI) .... BNGA
British Nursery Goods Association (SAUO) .... BNGA
British Nursing Association (BI) .... BNA
British Nursing Index (SAUO) .... BNI
British Nutrition Foundation Ltd. (SAUO) .... BNF
British Nylon Spinners Ltd. (SAUO) .... BNS
British Oat and Barley Millers Association (DBA) .... BOBMA
British Occupational Hygiene Society (EAIO) .... BOHS
British Oceanographic Data Centre [Marine science] (OSRA) .... BODC
British Oceanographic Data Service (SAUO) .... BODC
British Oceanographic Data Service .... BODS
British Office for Training Exchange .... BOTEX
British Office Systems and Stationery Federation (DBA) .... BOSSF
British Office Technology Manufacturers Alliance (NITA) .... BOTMA
British Officer [British military] (DMA) .... BO
British Offshore Equipment Association (DS) .... BOEA
British Offshore Support Vessel Owners Association (SAUO) .... BOSVA
British Offshore Support Vessels Association (DS) .... BOSVA
British Oil (WDAA) .... BritOil
British Oil and Cake Mills .... BOCM
British Oil and Cake Mills Ltd. (SAUO) .... BOCM
British Oil and Gas Firing Equipment Manufacturers Association (SAUO) .... BOGFEMA
British Oil and Mineral .... BOM
British Oil Burner Manufacturers' Association (BI) .... BOBMA
British Oil Development Co. (SAUO) .... BOD
British Oil Equipment Credits Ltd. .... BOEC
British Oil Shipping (SAUO) .... BOS
British Oil Spill Control Association (ASF) .... BOSCA
British Olympic Association .... BOA
British Oncological Association (DBA) .... BOA
British Oncology Association (SAUO) .... BOA
British Oncology Data Managers (DBA) .... BODMA
British Oncology Data Managers Association (SAUO) .... BODMA
British Onion Growers' Association (BI) .... BOGA
British Ophthalmic Anaesthesia Society (SAUO) .... BOAS
British Ophthalmic Lens Manufacturers and Distributors Association (DBA) .... BOLMADA
British Ophthalmic Mass Manufacturers Association (DBA) .... BOMMA
British Optical and Precision Engineers, Ltd. (SAUO) .... BOPE
British Optical Association (SAUO) .... BoA
British Optical Association .... BOA
British Optical Association (Dispenser) (DI) .... BOA(Disp)
British Optical Association, London, United Kingdom [Library symbol] [Library of Congress] (LCLS) .... UkLBOA
British Order of Ancient Free Gardeners .... BOAFG
British Organ Donor Society (PDAA) .... BODY
British Organic Farmers .... BOF
British Organisation of Non-Parents (DBA) .... BON
British Organisation of Non-Parents (DI) .... BON-P
British Orienteering Federation (DBA) .... BOF
British Orienteering Federation (SAUO) .... BOF
British Origami Society .... BOS
British Ornithologists' Club .... BOC
British Ornithologists' Union .... BOU
British Orphans Adoption Society (SAUO) .... BOAS
British Orthodontics Society (SAUO) .... BOS
British Orthopaedic Association .... BOA
British Orthopaedic Foot Surgery Society (SAUO) .... BOFSS
British Orthopaedic Oncology Society (SAUO) .... BOOS
British Orthopaedic Research Society (SAUO) .... BORS
British Orthopaedic Spine Society (SAUO) .... BOSS

British Orthopaedic Sports Trauma Association (SAUO) .... BOSTA
British Orthopedic Association (SAUO) .... BoA
British Orthoptic Society (SAUO) .... BOS
British Orthoptic Society .... BOS
British Osborne Owners Group [*A user group*] (NITA) .... BOOG
British Osteopathic Association .... BOA
British Osteopathic Association (SAUO) .... BoA
British Other Ranks .... BOR
British Overhead Irrigation, Ltd. (SAUO) .... BOIL
British Overseas African Command (SAUO) .... BOAC
British Overseas Aid Group (DS) .... BOAG
British Overseas Air Charter (SAUS) .... BOAC
British Overseas Airways Corp. [*Later, British Airways*] .... BOA
British Overseas Airways Corp. [*Humorously interpreted as "Better on a Camel"*] [*Later, British Airways*] .... BOAC
British Overseas Airways Digital Information Computer for Electronic Automation (SAUS) .... BOADICEA
British Overseas and Commonwealth Banks Association (DBA) .... BOCBA
British Overseas Citizenship .... BOC
British Overseas Fairs Ltd. (SAUO) .... BOF
British Overseas Media Bureau .... BOMB
British Overseas Mining Association (BI) .... BOMA
British Overseas Mining Association (SAUO) .... BOMA
British Overseas Trade Advisory Committee .... BOTAC
British Overseas Trade Board .... BOTB
British Overseas Trade Group for Israel (DS) .... BOTGI
British Oxygen Co. [*Later, BOC Group*] .... BOC
British Oxygen Engineering Ltd. (SAUO) .... BOE
British Oxygen Research and Development (SAUS) .... BORAD
British Oxygen Research and Development Association (SAUO) .... BORAD
British Pacific [*Vancouver Stock Exchange symbol*] .... BSH
British Pacific Financial, Inc. [*Formerly, British Pacific Resources, Inc.*] [*Vancouver Stock Exchange symbol*] .... BTF
British Pacific Fleet (SAUO) .... BPF
British Pacific Fleet [*Obsolete*] .... BPF
British Pacific Fleet Intelligence Liaison Officer .... BPFILO
British Pacific Fleet Liaison Officer .... BPFLO
British Pacific Islands (SAUS) .... BPI
British Pacing & Electrophysiology Group (SAUO) .... BPEG
British Paediatric Association .... BPA
British Paediatric Cardiac Association (SAUO) .... BPCA
British Paediatric Neurology Association (SAUO) .... BPNA
British Pantomime Association .... BPA
British Paper and Board Industry Federation (DGA) .... BPBIF
British Paper and Board Industry Research Association .... BPBIRA
British Paper and Board Makers' Association (DGA) .... BPBMA
British Paper Bag Federation (SAUO) .... BPBF
British Paper Box Federation (SAUO) .... BPBF
British Paper Box Federation (DGA) .... BPBF
British Paper Box Manufacturers' Federation (DGA) .... BPBMF
British Paper Machinery Makers Association (DBA) .... BPMMA
British Paper Stock Merchants Association (SAUO) .... BPS
British Parachute Association .... BPA
British Paraplegic Sports Society (DBA) .... BPSS
British Parking Association .... BPA
British Passport Control Office (SAUO) .... BPCO
British Pasta Products Association (DBA) .... BPPA
British Patent .... BP
British Patent (IAA) .... BRITPAT
British Patent .... BRP
British Patents Abstracts (SAUS) .... BPA
British Pattern Recognition Association (ACII) .... BPRA
British Payroll Managers Association (DBA) .... BPMA
British Peace Assembly .... BPA
British Peace Committee (SAUO) .... BPC
British Pediatric Association (BARN) .... BPA
British Pelagonium and Geranium Society (SAUO) .... BPGS
British Penny [*Derived from Latin "denarius"*] .... d
British Pensioners and Trade Unions Action Association (SAUO) .... BPTUAA
British Percheron Horse Society (BI) .... BPHS
British Performance Guarantee Corporation (SAUO) .... BPGC
British Pest Control Association (EAIO) .... BPCA
British Petrol ADS [*NYSE symbol*] (TTSB) .... BP
British Petroleum Co. [*NYSE symbol*] [*Toronto Stock Exchange symbol*] (SPSG) .... BP
British Petroleum Co. (IIA) .... BPT
British Petroleum Co. Ltd. (SAUO) .... BP
British Petroleum Co. Ltd. [*Associated Press*] (SAG) .... BritPt
British Petroleum Company Ltd. (SAUO) .... BPC
British Petroleum Exploration [*Columbia*] [*FAA designator*] (FAAC) .... BPX
British Petroleum North America .... BPNA
British Petroleum Tanker (SAUO) .... BPT
British Pharmaceutical Code .... BPC
British Pharmaceutical Codex [*A publication in pharmacy*] .... BPC
British Pharmaceutical Society (SAUO) .... BPS
British Pharmaceutical Students' Association (BI) .... BPSA
British Pharmacological Society (SAUO) .... BPHS
British Pharmacological Society (SAUO) .... BPS
British Pharmacological Society .... BPS
British Pharmacopieia Commission (SAUO) .... BPC
British Pharmacopoeia (SAUO) .... BP
British Pharmacopoeia [*A publication in pharmacy*] .... BP
British Pharmacopoeia [*A publication*] (MAE) .... BPh
British Pharmacopoeia (SAUS) .... Brit Pharm
British Pharmacopoeia (DAVI) .... PhB
British Pharmacopoeia (Veterinary) .... BP(Vet)
British Philatelic Association Ltd. (BI) .... BPA
British Philatelic Federation (DBA) .... BPF
British Philatelic Trust (DI) .... BPT
British Phonograph Industry (SAUO) .... BPI
British Phonographic Industry (CIST) .... BPI
British Phosphate Commission (FEA) .... BPC
British Phosphate Commission (SAUS) .... Brit Phos Comm
British Phosphate Commissioners (SAUO) .... BPC
British Photobiology Society (SAUO) .... BPS
British Photobiology Society .... BPS
British Photographic Association (DBA) .... BPA
British Photographic Export Group (DBA) .... BPEG
British Photographic Importers Association (DBA) .... BPIA
British Photographic Manufacturers Association (DGA) .... BPMA
British Phycological Society .... BPS
British Physical Laboratories Ltd. (NUCP) .... BPL
British Pig Association (GVA) .... BPA
British Pilots Association [*A union*] .... BPA
British Pipe Organ Society (DBA) .... BPOS
British Plain Spirits .... BPS
British Plant Growth Regulator Group (EAIO) .... BPGRG
British Plaster Board Industries (SAUO) .... BPBI
British Plastic Federation Ltd. (SAUO) .... BPF
British Plastics Federation .... BPF
British Plastics Windows Group [*An association*] (DBA) .... BPWG
British Ploughing Association (BI) .... BPA
British Plumbing Fittings Manufacturers Association (DBA) .... BPFMA
British Poets of the Nineteenth Century [*A publication*] .... BPN
British Polarographic Research Institute .... BPRI
British Polarological Research Society (DBA) .... BPRS
British Police Mission (SAUO) .... BPM
British Polio Federation (SAUO) .... BPF
British Polio Fellowship [*British*] .... BPF
British Polished Plate (SAUS) .... BPP
British Polled Hereford Society Ltd. (BI) .... BPHS
British Polytechnics Sports Association (DBA) .... BPSA
British Ports Association (DS) .... BPA
British Ports Federation (DBA) .... BPF
British Post Office .... BPO
British Post Office Corporation (SAUO) .... BPOC
British Postal Chess Federation (BI) .... BPCF
British Postal Equipment Engineering Association (SAUO) .... BPEEA
British Poster Advertising Association (DGA) .... BPAA
British Postgraduate Medical Federation .... BPMF
British Postgraduate Medical Federation (SAUS) .... BpMF
British Postmark Society (EA) .... BPS
British Pot Plant Growers Association (SAUS) .... PPGA
British Pottery Managers Association (DBA) .... BPMA
British Poultry Breeders and Hatcheries Association (DBA) .... BPBHA
British Poultry Federation (EAIO) .... BPF
British Poultry Meat Federation (EAIO) .... BPMF
British Poultrymeat Association (SAUO) .... BPA
British Pound [*Monetary unit*] .... BP
British Powder Metal Federation (DBA) .... BPMF
British Power Press Manufacturers Association (MCD) .... BPPMA
British Powerboating Union (SAUO) .... BPU
British Practice in International Law [*A publication*] (DLA) .... Brit Prac Int'l L
British Precast Concrete Federation (EAIO) .... BPCF
British Precision Pilots Association (DA) .... BPPA
British Press Service (SAUO) .... BPS
British Pressure Gauge Manufacturers Association (BI) .... BPGMA
British Printing & Communication Corporations [*Later, MCC*] .... BPCC
British Printing Corp. [*Later, BPCC*] .... BPC
British Printing Industries' Federation (DCTA) .... BPIF
British Printing Ink Manufacturers (DGA) .... BPIM
British Printing Ink Society (DGA) .... BPIS
British Printing Machinery Association (DGA) .... BPMA
British Printing Society (DGA) .... BPS
British Prisoners of War Books and Game Fund (SAUO) .... BPOWBGF
British Pro Golfers Association (SAUO) .... BPGA
British Pro-Chiropractic Association (SAUO) .... BPCA
British Production and Inventory Control Society (DBQ) .... BPICS
British Productivity Council .... BPC
British Professional Association (DBA) .... BPA
British Professional Cycle Racing Association (SAUO) .... BPCRA
British Promotional Merchandise Association (DBA) .... BPMA
British Property Federation (DBA) .... BPF
British Provident Association for Hospitals and Additional Services (SAUO) .... BPAHAS
British Psychoanalytical Society (EAIO) .... BPS
British Psychodrama Association (DBA) .... BPA
British Psychological Society (EAIO) .... BPS
British Psychological Society (SAUO) .... BPsS
British Psychological Society, Medical Section (SAUO) .... BPSMS
British Pteridological Society (DBA) .... BPS
British Public [*Slang*] .... BP
British Public Schools Association of New South Wales [*Australia*] .... BPSANSW
British Public Works Association (EAIO) .... BPWA
British Publishers Guild (SAUO) .... BPG
British Publishers' Traditional Market (WDAA) .... BPTM
British Pump Manufacturers Association (EAIO) .... BPMA
British Puppet and Model Theatre Guild (SAUO) .... BPMTG
British Purchasing Commission .... BPC
British Pyrotechnists' Association (BI) .... BPA

British Quality Association (DBA)	BQA
British Quality Awards Scheme (AIE)	BQAS
British Quality Vegetable Salad Association (DBA)	BQVSA
British Quarrying and Slag Federation (SAUO)	BQSF
British Quarter Horse Association (DBA)	BQHA
British Quartermaster Unit (SAUO)	BQU
British Rabbit Council (BI)	BRC
British Racing and Sport Car Club	BRSCC
British Racing Drivers Association (SAUO)	BRDA
British Racing Drivers Club	BRDC
British Racing Green (ADA)	BRG
British Racing Motors	BRM
British Racing Tobaggan Association (BI)	BRTA
British Racing Toboggan Association (SAUO)	BRTA
British Racketball Association (DBA)	BRA
British Radiation Protection Association (DBA)	BRadPA
British Radiesthesia Association (BI)	BRA
British Radiesthesia Association (SAUO)	BRA
British Radio and Electronic Equipment Manufacturers Association (DS)	BREEMA
British Radio and Electronic Equipment Manufacturers Association [Formerly, British Radio Equipment Manufacturers Association]	BREMA
British Radio Cabinet Makers Association (SAUO)	BRCMA
British Radio Cabinet Manufacturers' Association (IAA)	BRCMA
British Radio Communication (IAA)	BRC
British Radio Corporation (SAUO)	BRC
British Radio Relay League (SAUO)	BRRL
British Radio Valve Manufacturers' Association	BRVMA
British Radiological Protection Association (DEN)	BRPA
British Rail (SAUO)	Britrail
British Rail Engineering	BRE
British Rail Engineering Limited (SAUO)	BREL
British Rail Hovercraft (PDAA)	BRH
British Rail Hovercraft Limited (SAUO)	BRHL
British Rail Interactive Graphical Aid to Production and Design (SAUS)	BRIGATPAD
British Rail Inter-City Service (SAUO)	BRICS
British Rail Privatisation Safety Unit (HEAS)	BRPSU
British Rail Property Board	BRPB
British Rail Travel Centre (SAUO)	BRTC
British Railway (TRID)	BritRail
British Railway Administration (SAUO)	BRA
British Railway Industry Export Group	BRIEX
British Railway Modellers of North America [Canada]	BRMNA
British Railway Modelling Standards Bureau (SAUO)	BRMSB
British Railwaymen's Touring Club (BI)	BRTC
British Railways	BR
British Railways (SAUS)	Br Rys
British Railways Board	BRB
British Railways Female Mobile Gang (SAUO)	BRFMG
British Rainwear Manufacturers Association (SAUO)	BRMF
British Rainwear Manufacturers Federation (BI)	BRMF
British Rate and Data	BRAD
British Raw Materials Mission [World War II]	BRMM
British Rayon Research Association (SAUO)	BRRA
British Ready Mixed Concrete Association (BI)	BRMCA
British Receiving Station (IAA)	BRS
British Reclamation Industries Confederation (SAUO)	BRIC
British Record Centre (SAUO)	BRS
British Record Fish Committee (SAUO)	BRFC
British Record Society	BRS
British Record Society, Ltd. (SAUO)	BRSL
British Recorded Tape Development Committee (SAUO)	BRTDC
British Records Association (SAUO)	BRA
British Records Association	BRA
British Recovery Unit (SAUO)	BRU
British Red Cross (SAUO)	BRS
British Red Cross Association (SAUO)	BRCA
British Red Cross Society (SAUO)	BRCS
British Red Cross Society	BRCS
British Refractories Research Association (SAUO)	BRRA
British Refrigeration and Air Conditioning Association (SAUO)	BRACA
British Refrigeration Association (SAUO)	BRA
British Refrigeration Association (DBA)	BRA
British Regional Television Association (BI)	BRTA
British Regional Television Association (SAUO)	BRTA
British Regular Army (SAUO)	BRA
British Reinforced Concrete (WDAA)	BRC
British Reinforcement Manufacturers Association (DBA)	BRMA
British Relay Wireless (SAUS)	BRW
British Reports, Translations, and Theses [A publication]	BRTT
British Research and Development Corp. (NUCP)	BRDC
British Research Council (SAUO)	BRC
British Research Establishment (SAUO)	BRE
British Research Library (SAUS)	BRL
British Research Station	BRS
British Resident (SAUS)	BR
British Resin Manufacturers Association (DBA)	BResMA
British Resin Manufacturers Association (SAUO)	BRMA
British Resorts Association	BRA
British Retail Consortium (EAIO)	BRC
British Retail Florist's Association (DBA)	BRFA
British Retail Footwear Market	BRFM
British Retinitis Pigmentosa Society	BRPS
British Revision [of BNA] [Medicine]	BR

British Rheumatism and Arthritis Association (BI)	BRA
British Rhine Army (SAUO)	BRA
British Rigid Urethane Foam Manufacturers Association	BRUFMA
British Rivet Association (SAUO)	BRA
British Rivet Export Group (BI)	BREG
British Road Federation Ltd. (BI)	BRF
British Road Research Laboratory	BRRL
British Road Service Federation Ltd. (SAUO)	BRS
British Road Services	BRS
British Road Services Ltd. (SAUS)	BRSL
British Road Tar Association (BI)	BRTA
British Road Tar Association (SAUO)	BRTA
British Robot Association Ltd.	BRA
British Robotics Systems Ltd. (NITA)	BRSL
British Roentgen Society (MAE)	BRS
British Roll Tuners Trade Society [A union] (DCTA)	BRTTS
British Roller Canary Association (BI)	BRCA
British Roller Canary Club (BI)	BRCC
British Romagnola Cattle Society (DBA)	BRCS
British Romanian Friendship Association (DBA)	BRFA
British Ropeway Engineering Co. Ltd. (SAUO)	BRECO
British Routing Liaison Officer [World War II]	BRLO
British Routing Office	BRO
British Royal Commission on Capital Punishment (SAUO)	BRCCP
British Royal Marine Corps (CINC)	BRMC
British Rubber and Resin Adhesive Manufacturers Association (SAUO)	BRAMA
British Rubber and Resin Adhesive Manufacturers' Association (BI)	BRRAMA
British Rubber Development Board (SAUO)	BRDB
British Rubber Manufacturers' Association (EAIO)	BRMA
British Rubber Products Research Association (MCD)	BRPRA
British Rug Manufacturers Association (SAUO)	BRMA
British Ruling Cases [A publication] (DLA)	BRC
British Ruling Cases [A publication] (DLA)	Brit Rul Cas
British Ruling Cases [A publication] (DLA)	Br Rul Cas
British Safety Council	BSC
British Safety Standards (SAUO)	BSS
British Sailors Institute (SAUS)	BSI
British Sailors Society (BI)	BSS
British Salonica Force	BSF
British Samoa (SAUS)	Brit Sam
British Samoyed Club (BI)	BSC
British Sanitary Fireclay Association (BI)	BSFA
British Satellite Beam (BARN)	BSB
British Satellite Broadcasting [Telecommunications]	BSB
British Savings Bond	BSB
British School at Athens (SAUS)	BSA
British School at Rome [Italy]	BSR
British School of Archaeology at Rome (SAUS)	BSAR
British School of Archaeology in Athens (SAUO)	BSA
British School of Archaeology in Egypt (SAUO)	BSAE
British School of Archaeology in Egypt (SAUS)	BSAE
British School of Archaeology in Iraq (SAUS)	BSAI
British School of Archaeology in Iraq (SAUO)	BSAI
British School of Archaeology in Jerusalem	BSA
British School of Archaeology in Jerusalem (SAUO)	BSAJ
British School of Archaeology in Jerusalem (SAUS)	BSAJ
British School of Archaeology in Rome (SAUO)	BSAR
British School of Archaeology in Rome (SAUO)	BSR
British School of Archeology at Athens (BARN)	BSAA
British School of Athens (SAUO)	BSA
British School of Dowsers (SAUO)	BSD
British School of Egyptian Archaeology (SAUO)	BSEA
British School of Egyptian Archaeology	BSEA
British School of Motoring (DI)	BSM
British School of Osteopathy	BSO
British School Technology (NITA)	BST
British Schools and Universities Club of New York (EA)	BSUCNY
British Schools and Universities Foundation (EA)	BSUF
British Schools Exploration Society	BSES
British Schools Exploring Society (SAUO)	BSES
British Schools Judo Association (SAUO)	BSJA
British Science and Technology in Education (AIE)	BSTF
British Science Fiction Association Ltd.	BSFA
British Scientific Instrument Research Association	BSIRA
British Scouts in Western Europe (SAUO)	BSWE
British Scrap Federation (DBA)	BSF
British Seafarers' Joint Council (DS)	BSJC
British Seafarers' Union	BSU
British Seamans Identity Card (SAUS)	BSIC
British Secondary Metals Association (DBA)	BSMA
British Security Coordination [World War II]	BSC
British Security Coordination	BSC
British Security Coordination Office (SAUO)	BSCO
British Security Industry Association, Ltd. (SAUO)	BSIA
British Security Service Organization	BSSO
British Sedimentological Research Group (QUAC)	BSRG
British Seeds Council (DBA)	BSC
British Service Charities Committee	BSCC
British Service Intelligence and Security Administrative Unit (SAUO)	BSI&SAU
British Service League (SAUO)	BSL
British Sewage Plant Manufacturers Association (PDAA)	BSPMA
British Sheep Dairying Association (DBA)	BSDA
British Shell Collectors Club	BSCC
British Shingon Buddhist Association (EAIO)	BSBA

British Ship Adoption Society ... BSAS
British Ship Research Association [*Research center*] (IRC) ... BSRA
British Ship Research Association (SAUO) ... BSRA
British Ship Research Council ... BSRC
British Shipbreakers' Association (BI) ... BSA
British Shipbuilders ... BS
British Shipbuilding Exports (BI) ... BSE
British Shipbuilding Hydrodynamics ... BSH
British Shipbuilding Integrated Production System (PDAA) ... BRITSHIPS
British Shipbuilding Research Association ... BSRA
British Shippers Council (DS) ... BSC
British Shipping Federation (DS) ... BSF
British Shipping Federation Limited (SAUO) ... BSFL
British Shipping Laws [*A publication*] (DLA) ... Brit Ship L
British Shoe Corp. ... BSC
British Shoe Repair Council (DBA) ... BSRC
British Shooting Sports Council (DBA) ... BSSC
British Shops and Stores Association (DBA) ... BSSA
British Short Wave Correspondence Club (SAUO) ... BSWCC
British Short Wave Correspondence Club (SAUS) ... BSWCC
British Show Jumping Association (DI) ... BSJA
British Show Pony Society (DBA) ... BSPS
British Sign Association (DBA) ... BSA
British Sign Language (DI) ... BSL
British Signal Communications Board (SAUO) ... BSCB
British Silbak Premier Mines [*Vancouver Stock Exchange symbol*] ... BSK
British Silk Research Association (SAUO) ... BSRA
British Sitcom (ADWA) ... Britcom
British Size (IAA) ... BS
British Sjogren's Syndrome Association (DBA) ... BSSA
British Skate Makers' Association (BI) ... BSMA
British Skateboard Association (SAUO) ... BSA
British Ski Club for the Disabled (DBA) ... BSCD
British Ski Federation (EAIO) ... BSF
British Ski Instruction Council (SAUO) ... BSIC
British Sky Broadcasting (WDAA) ... BSB
British Sky Broadcasting [*Satellite-television consortium*] (ECON) ... BSkyB
British Sky Broadcasting Ltd. [*Associated Press*] (SAG) ... BritSky
British Sky Broadcasting Ltd. [*NYSE symbol*] (SAG) ... BSY
British Sky Broadcsting Gp ADS [*NYSE symbol*] (TTSB) ... BSY
British Slag Federation [*A union*] ... BSF
British Slot Car Racing Association (DBA) ... BSCRA
British Small Animal Veterinary Association (EAIO) ... BSAVA
British Snail Farmers Association (DBA) ... BSFA
British Snoring & Sleep Apnoea Association (WDAA) ... BSSAA
British Social Attitudes [*Survey*] ... BSA
British Social Biology Council ... BSBC
British Social Hygiene Association ... BSHA
British Social Hygiene Council (SAUO) ... BSHC
British Socialist Party ... BSP
British Societies Institute (BI) ... BSI
British Society for Agricultural Labour Science ... BSALS
British Society for Allergy and Clinical Immunology ... BSACI
British Society for Allergy, Environmental and Nutritional Medicine (SAUO) ... BSAENM
British Society for Antimicrobial Chemotherapy ... BSAC
British Society for Cell Biology ... BSCB
British Society for Cell Biology (SAUO) ... BSCB
British Society for Clinical Cytology ... BSCC
British Society for Dental Research (DBA) ... BSDR
British Society for Dermatopathology (EAIO) ... BSD
British Society for Developmental Biology ... BSDB
British Society for Digestive Endoscopy ... BSDE
British Society for Disability and oral Health (SAUO) ... BSDH
British Society for Eighteenth Century Studies ... BSECS
British Society for Electronic Music ... BSEM
British Society for Experimental and Clinical Hypnosis (DBA) ... BSECH
British Society for Haematology ... BSH
British Society for Haematology (SAUO) ... BSH
British Society for Histocompatibility and Immunogenetics (SAUO) ... BSHI
British Society for Immunology (SAUO) ... BSI
[*The*] **British Society for Immunology** ... BSI
British Society for Information Science (SAUO) ... BSIS
British Society for International Bibliography [*Later, Aslib*] ... BSIB
British Society for International Health Education (AEBS) ... BSIHE
British Society for International Understanding (BI) ... BSIU
British Society for International Understanding (SAUO) ... BSIU
British Society for Medical and Dental Hypnosis (DBA) ... BSMDH
British Society for Music Therapy ... BSMT
British Society for Mycopathology (DBA) ... BSM
British Society for Non-Destructive Testing (MCD) ... BSNDT
British Society for Parasitology (EAIO) ... BSP
[*The*] **British Society for Phenomenology** ... BSP
British Society for Phenomenology (SAUO) ... BSP
British Society for Plant Growth Regulation (EAIO) ... BSPGR
British Society for Plant Pathology ... BSPP
British Society for Research in Agricultural Engineering (BI) ... BSRAE
British Society for Research in Agricultural Engineering (SAUO) ... BSRAE
British Society for Research on Ageing (EAIO) ... BSRA
British Society for Restorative Dentistry (SAUO) ... BSRD
British Society for Rheology (DBA) ... BSR
British Society for Social Responsibility in Science ... BSSRS
British Society for Strain Measurement ... BSSM
British Society for Strain Measurement (SAUO) ... BSSM
British Society for the History of Mathematics (DBA) ... BSHM
British Society for the History of Pharmacy ... BSHP
[*The*] **British Society for the History of Science** ... BSHS
British Society for the Philosophy of Science ... BSPS
British Society for the Propagation of the Gospel among the Jews (SAUO) ... BJS
British Society for the Study of Mental Subnormality ... BSSMS
British Society for the Study of Orthodontics (BI) ... BSSO
British Society for the Study of Orthodontics (SAUO) ... BSSO
British Society for the Study of Prosthetic Dentistry ... BSSPD
British Society for/of Electronic Music (SAUO) ... BSEM
British Society of Aesthetics ... BSA
British Society of Allergy and Environmental Medicine (DBA) ... BSAEM
British Society of Animal Production ... BSAP
British Society of Animal Science (GVA) ... BSAS
British Society of Audiology ... BSA
British Society of Audiology (SAUO) ... BSA
British Society of Audiology ... BSAUD
British Society of Australian Philately ... BSAP
British Society of Cardiovascular Research (SAUO) ... BSCR
British Society of Chartered Accountants (SAUO) ... BSCA
British Society of Cinematographers (DBA) ... BSC
British Society of Clinical Hypnosis (SAUO) ... BSCH
British Society of Commerce (BI) ... BSC
British Society of Dentistry for the Handicapped (DBA) ... BSDH
[*The*] **British Society of Dowsers** ... BSD
British Society of Dowsers (SAUO) ... BSD
British Society of Echocardiography (SAUO) ... BSE
British Society of Flavourists ... BSF
British Society of Franciscan Studies (SAUO) ... BSFS
British Society of Gastroenterology (SAUO) ... BSG
British Society of Gastroenterology ... BSG
British Society of Gerontology (DBA) ... BSG
British Society of Hypnotherapists ... BSH
British Society of Master Glass Painters (BI) ... BSMGP
British Society of Nutritional Medicines ... BSNM
British Society of Oral Medicine (DBA) ... BSOM
British Society of Perfumers (DBA) ... BSP
British Society of Periodontology ... BSP
British Society of Phenomenology (SAUO) ... BSP
British Society of Plant Breeders (DBA) ... BSPB
British Society of Poster Designers (SAUO) ... BPD
British Society of Poster Designers ... BPD
British Society of Psychosomatic Obstetrics and Gynecology and Andrology (DBA) ... BSPOGA
British Society of Restorative Dentistry ... BSRD
British Society of Scientific Glassblowers ... BSSG
British Society of Social and Behavioural Gerontology ... BSSBG
British Society of Soil Science (SAUO) ... BSSB
British Society of Soil Science ... BSSS
British Society of Sports History (DBA) ... BSSH
British Society of Stamp Journalists (BI) ... BSSJ
British Society of Surgery of the Hand (DBA) ... BSSH
British Society of Toxicological Pathologists (DBA) ... BSTP
British Society of Underwater Photographers (DBA) ... BSoUP
British Sociological Associates ... BSOCA
[*The*] **British Sociological Association** ... BSA
British Sociological Association (SAUO) ... BSA
British Soft Drinks Association (DBA) ... BSDA
British Softball Federation (SAUO) ... BSF
British Software Factory (NITA) ... BSF
British Soil Classification System (NUCP) ... BSCS
British Solomon Islands [*MARC country of publication code*] [*Library of Congress*] (LCCP) ... bp
British Solomon Islands ... BSI
British Solomon Islands [*MARC geographic area code*] [*Library of Congress*] (LCCP) ... pobp-
British Solomon Islands Protectorate (ADA) ... BSIP
British Soluble Coffee Manufacturers Association (DBA) ... BSCMA
British Solvent Oils Co. (SAUO) ... BRISOL
British Sound Recording Association (BI) ... BSRA
British [*formerly, Birmingham*] **Sound Reproduction** [*Initialism is now name of company and brand name of its products*] ... BSR
British South Africa ... BSA
British South Africa Brigade (SAUO) ... BSA Bde
British South Africa Co. (ROG) ... BSAC
British South Africa Corps ... BSAC
British South Africa Corps (SAUO) ... BSAC
British South Africa Police (SAUO) ... BSAP
British South Africa Police ... BSAP
British South African Company (SAUO) ... BSAC
British South American Airways Corp. ... BSAA
British South American Airways Corp. [*Later absorbed by BOAC*] ... BSAAC
British South American Airways Corporation (SAUO) ... BSAAC
British Soviet Friendship Society (SAUO) ... BSFS
British Soviet Friendship Society (BI) ... BSFS
British Soviet Society (SAUO) ... BSS
British Space Development Co. ... BSDC
British Spas Federation (DBA) ... BSF
British Special Ship Equipment Association (PDAA) ... BSSEA
British Spectacle Frame Makers Association (DBA) ... BSFMA
British Speedway Promoters Association (BI) ... BSPA
British Speleological Association (BI) ... BSA
British Spinners and Doublers Association (PDAA) ... BSDA
British Sporting Rifle Club (PDAA) ... BSRC
British Sports and Allied Industries Federation (DBA) ... BSAIF

British Sports and Games Association (SAUO) ... BSGA
British Sports Association for the Disabled ... BSAD
British Sports Photographers Association (SAUO) ... BSPA
British Spotted Pony Society (DBA) ... BSpPS
British Stammering Association (SAUO) ... BSA
British Standard (IAA) ... BRSTD
British standard (SAUS) ... Br std
British Standard ... BS
British Standard Beam [*Engineering*] ... BSB
British Standard Black [*Ink*] (DGA) ... BS BLK
British Standard Brass (SAUS) ... BSB
British Standard Channel (IAA) ... BSC
British Standard Code of Practice ... BSCP
British Standard Cycle (IAA) ... BSC
British Standard Data Code (BUR) ... BSDC
British Standard Dimension ... BSD
British Standard Equal Angle (SAUS) ... BSEA
British Standard Fine Thread ... BSF
British Standard Fine thread (SAUS) ... BSF thread
British Standard for Automobile (SAUS) ... BS AU
British Standard Four-Color Blue [*Ink*] (DGA) ... BS4B
British Standard Gauge [*Telecommunications*] (TEL) ... BSG
British Standard Handful [*Slang*] (DSUE) ... BSH
British Standard Interface (SAUS) ... BSI
British Standard: Marine Series (SAUS) ... BS MA
British Standard Number ... BSN
British Standard of Hardness (SAUS) ... BSH
British Standard Pipe, Tapered (SAUS) ... BSPT
British Standard Pipe Thread ... BSP
British Standard Pipe thread (SAUS) ... BSP thread
British Standard Red [*Ink*] (DGA) ... BSR
British Standard Section (SAUS) ... BSS
British Standard Sieve (SAUS) ... BSS
British Standard Size [*Typography*] (DGA) ... BSS
British Standard Specification ... BSS
British Standard Tee (SAUS) ... BST
British Standard Three-Color Blue [*Ink*] (DGA) ... BS3B
British Standard Time (NATG) ... BST
British Standard Unequal Angle (SAUS) ... BSUA
British Standard Whitworth (MCD) ... BSW
British Standard Wire Gauge ... BSWG
British Standard Yellow [*Ink*] (DGA) ... BSY
British Standard-European (SAUS) ... BS-EN
British Standards Association ... BSA
British Standards Institute (WPI) ... BSI
British Standards Institution (ARC) ... BSI
British Standards Institution (DAVI) ... BSID
British Standards Institution Standards Association (SAUO) ... BSISA
British Standards Society (DBA) ... BSS
British Starch Industry Association (DBA) ... BSIA
British Starter Battery Association (SAUO) ... BSBA
British State Air Lines (SAUO) ... BSAL
British station featuring educational and informational programs on cooking, farming and the theater (SAUS) ... Radio 4
British Stationery and Office Equipment Association (BI) ... BSOEA
British Stationery and Office Products Federation (SAUO) ... BSOPF
British Stationery Council (DGA) ... BSC
British Statistics Office ... BSO
British Steam Specialties Ltd. (SAUO) ... BSS
British Steel ADS [*NYSE symbol*] (TTSB) ... BST
British Steel Castings Research Association [*Later, SCRATA*] (EA) ... BSCRA
British Steel Corp. ... BSC
British Steel Corp. (SAUS) ... BSCorp
British Steel Corporation (SAUO) ... BSCorp
British Steel Export Association (BI) ... BSEA
British Steel (journ.) (SAUS) ... SRI
British Steel Ltd. [*Associated Press*] (SAG) ... BritStl
British Steel Ltd. [*NYSE symbol*] (CTT) ... BST
British Steel Wire Industries Association (SAUO) ... BSWIA
British Steelmakers Creep Committee (SAUO) ... BSCC
British Stickmakers Guild (DBA) ... BSG
British Stock Car Association ... BSCA
British Stone Federation (BI) ... BSF
British Structural Bearings Manufacturers Association (DBA) ... BSBMA
British Student Federalists (SAUO) ... BSF
British Student Travel Centre (SAUO) ... BSTC
British Student Tuberculosis Foundation (BI) ... BSTF
British Students Sports Federation (DBA) ... BSSF
British Studies Intelligencer (EA) ... BSI
British Sub-Aqua Club (BI) ... BSAC
British Sub-Aqua Club (SAUO) ... BSAC
British Subject without Citizenship ... BSWC
British Sugar Beet Seed Producers Association (DBA) ... BSBSPA
British Sugar Beet Society (SAUO) ... BSBS
British Sugar Bureau (SAUO) ... BSB
British Sugar Corp. ... BSC
British Sugar Machinery Manufacturers Association (PDAA) ... BSMMA
British Sulphate of Ammonia Federation Ltd. (BI) ... BSAF
British Sulphate of Copper Association (Export) Ltd. (BI) ... BSCA
British Sulphur Corporation (SAUO) ... BSC
British Summer Time ... BST
British Sunbathing Association (SAUO) ... BSA
British Supervisory Element (SAUO) ... BSE
British Supply Board [*Ottawa*] [*World War II*] ... BSB
British Supply Council ... BSC
British Supply Council (SAUO) ... BSC
British Supply Council in North America (SAUO) ... BSCNA
British Supply Mission [*World War II*] ... BSM
British Supply Office ... BSO
British Support Command (SAUS) ... BRSC
British Support Forces (SAUS) ... BSF
British Surface Treatment Suppliers Association (DBA) ... BSTSA
British Surfing Association ... BSA
British Surgical Export Group (DBA) ... BSEG
British Surgical Support Suppliers Association (BI) ... BSSSA
British Surgical Trades Association (BI) ... BSTA
British Survey (SAUS) ... BS
British Suzuki Institute (EAIO) ... BSI
British Synchronous Clock Conference (SAUO) ... BSCC
British Tabulating Machinery Co. ... BTMC
British Tabulating Machines Co. (SAUO) ... BTM
British Tactical Air Force (SAUO) ... BTAF
British Tactical Air Force ... BTAF
British Tanker Company (SAUO) ... BTC
British Tanning Extract Manufacturers' Association (BI) ... BTEMA
British Tanzania Society (SAUO) ... BTS
British Tape Industry Association (SAUO) ... BTIA
British Tar Industry Association (SAUO) ... BTIA
British Tarantula Society (DBA) ... BTS
British Tarpaviors Federation Ltd. (BI) ... BTF
British Tattoo Artists Federation (DBA) ... BTAF
British Tax Review [*A publication*] ... BTR
British Tea Table Co. (ROG) ... BTT
British Technical Council [*of the Motor and Petroleum Industries*] ... BTC
British Technical Council of Motor and Petroleum Industries ... BTCMPI
British Technology Group [*Research center*] ... BTG
British Technology Index (AIE) ... BTI
British Telecom [*or Telecommunications*] [*Common carrier*] ... BT
British Telecom Action for Disabled Customers (NITA) ... BTADC
British Telecom Business Systems (NITA) ... BTBS
British Telecom Enterprises (NITA) ... BTE
British Telecom Enterprises' Value Added Systems and Services (NITA) ... BTE/Vass
British Telecom Global Satellite Services (WDAA) ... BTGSS
British Telecom International (NITA) ... BTI
British Telecom Lempel Ziv (CDE) ... BTLZ
British Telecom Mobile Communications ... BTMC
British Telecom Phonecards [*Prepaid cards for use in noncoin pay telephones*] ... BTP
British Telecom Requirement (SAUO) ... BTR
British Telecom Research Laboratories ... BTRL
British Telecom Unions Committee ... BTUC
British Telecommn ADR [*NYSE symbol*] (TTSB) ... BTY
British Telecommunications (SAUS) ... Brit Telecom
British Telecommunications (SAUS) ... BT
British Telecommunications Ltd. [*Associated Press*] (SAG) ... BritTel
British Telecommunications Ltd. [*NYSE symbol*] [*Toronto Stock Exchange symbol*] (SPSG) ... BTY
British Telecommunications Research Establishment (SAUO) ... BTRE
British Telecommunications Research Ltd. (SAUO) ... BTR
British Telecommunications Systems Ltd. (TEL) ... BTS
British Television Society (SAUO) ... BTS
British Temperance League (SAUO) ... BTL
British Temperance Society (BI) ... BTS
British Temperance Youth (SAUO) ... BTY
British Tenpin Bowling Association, Ltd. ... BTBA
British Tensional Strapping Association (PDAA) ... BTSA
British term for sonar (DOMA) ... ASDIC
British Tertiary Volcanic Province [*Geology*] ... BTVP
British Textile Confederation (DCTA) ... BTC
British Textile Employers' Association (EAIO) ... BTEA
British Textile Machinery Association (DS) ... BTMA
British Textile Society (SAUO) ... BTS
British Textile Technology Group (ECON) ... BTTG
British Theatre Association [*Defunct*] ... BTA
British Theatre Association (SAUO) ... BTA
British Theatre Institute (EA) ... BTI
British Theatre Museum (BI) ... BTM
British Theatre Museum Association (SAUO) ... BTMA
British Thermal Unit ... BTHU
British Thermal Unit ... BTU
British Thermal Unit (MEC) ... Btu
British Thermal Unit (NTIO) ... btu
British Thermal Unit per Cubic Foot (SAUS) ... BTU/cu ft
British Thermal Unit per Cubic Foot (SAUS) ... Btu/ft3
British Thermal Unit per Cubic Foot times Degree Fahrenheit (SAUS) ... Btu/cu ft degF
British Thermal Unit per Cubic Foot times Degree Fahrenheit (SAUS) ... Btu/ft3 degF
British Thermal Unit per Degree Fahrenheit (SAUS) ... Btu/degF
British Thermal Unit per Degree Rankine (SAUS) ... BtuýR
British Thermal Unit per Foot times Hour times Degree Fahrenheit (SAUS) ... Btu/ft h deg F
British Thermal Unit per Hour (SAUS) ... Btu/h
British Thermal Unit per Pound (SAUS) ... Btu/lb
British Thermal Unit per Pound times Degree Fahrenheit (SAUS) ... Btu/lb deg F
British Thermal Unit per Pound times Degree Rankine (SAUS) ... Btu/lb ýR
British Thermal Unit per Second (SAUS) ... Btu/s
British Thermal Unit per Second times Foot times Degree Fahrenheit (SAUS) ... Btu/s ft degF

British Thermal Unit per Second times Square Foot times Degree Fahrenheit (SAUS) .... Btu/s fty degF
British thermal Unit per Second times Square Foot times Degree Fahrenheit (SAUS) .... Btu/s sqft degF
British Thermal Unit per Second times Square Foot times Square Foot times Degree (SAUS) .... Btu/s fty degF
British Thermal Unit per Square Foot times Hour (SAUS) .... Btu/ftyh
British Thermal Unit per Square Foot times Hour (SAUS) .... Btu/sqft h
British Thermal Unit per Square Inch times Second (SAUS) .... Btu/iny S
British Thermal Unit per Square Inch times Second (SAUS) .... Btu/squin s
British Thermal Units per Hour (MCD) .... BTU/h
British Thermal Units per Hour (DNAB) .... BTU/HR
British Thomson-Houston Co. .... BTH
British Thoracic and Tuberculosis Association .... BTTA
British Thoracic Association (SAUO) .... BTA
[The] British Thoracic Society .... BTS
British Throwsters Association (DBA) .... BTA
British Timber Merchants Association (DBA) .... BTMA
British Timber Production Agency (SAUO) .... BTPA
British Time (IAA) .... BRT
British Time (SAUS) .... Br T
British Tin Box Manufacturers Federation (PDAA) .... BTBMF
British Tinnitus Association .... BTA
British Tire & Rubber Co. .... BTR
British Tissues, Ltd. .... BT
British Tobacco Industry .... BTI
British Touch for Health Association .... BTFHA
British Tourist Authority (EA) .... BTA
British Towing Tank Panel (MCD) .... BTTP
British Toxicology Society (DBA) .... BTS
British Toy and Hobby Association (EAIO) .... BTHA
British Toy and Hobby Manufacturers Association (SAUO) .... BTHMA
British Toy Manufacturers Association (SAUO) .... BTMA
British Toymakers' Guild (BI) .... BTG
British Tractor Pullers Association (DBA) .... BTPA
British Trade and Investment Office (EA) .... BTIO
British Trade Association of New Zealand (SAUO) .... BTANZ
British Trade Development Office [Later, BTIO] (EA) .... BTDO
British Trade Journal [A publication] (ROG) .... BTJ
British Trade Mission .... BTM
British Trade Union (SAUO) .... BTU
British Trade Union Congress (SAUO) .... BTUC
British Trades Mission (SAUO) .... BTM
British Trades Union Congress [TUC] .... BKT
British Trampoline Federation (DBA) .... BTF
British Trans-Atlantic Air Mail Service (IAA) .... BRAMS
British Trans-Atlantic Air Mail Service .... BTAMS
British Trans-Atlantic Air Mail Service (SAUO) .... BTAMS
British Transplantation Society .... BTS
British Transport Advertising .... BTA
British Transport and General Workers Union (SAUS) .... TGWU
British Transport Catering Service (SAUO) .... BTCS
British Transport Commission (SAUO) .... BTC
British Transport Commission .... BTC
British Transport Commission Police .... BTCP
British Transport Docks (SAUS) .... BTD
British Transport Docks Board .... BTDB
British Transport Hotels [Commercial firm] .... BTH
British Transport Officers Guild (DBA) .... BTOG
British Transport Police (HEAS) .... BTP
British Transport Staff College (BI) .... BTSC
British Travel and Holidays Association [Later, British Travel Association] .... BTHA
British Travel Association (BI) .... BTA
British Travel Survey (ECON) .... BTS
British Trawler Federation .... BTF
British Trawler Officers Federation [A union] .... BTOF
British Treaty Series [A publication] (DLA) .... Brit TS
British Trials and Rally Drivers Association .... BTRDA
British Triathlon Association (DBA) .... BTA
British Trolleybus Society (DCTA) .... BTS
British Troops, Austria [World War II] .... BTA
British Troops in Berlin (SAUO) .... BTB
British Troops in Egypt (SAUO) .... BTE
British Troops in Egypt [World War II] .... BTE
British Troops in Germany (DMA) .... BTG
British Troops in Greece (SAUO) .... BTG
British Troops in Iraq (DMA) .... BTI
British Troops in Low Countries (SAUO) .... BTLC
British Troops in North Africa [World War II] .... BTNA
British Troops in Northern Ireland (SAUO) .... BTNI
British Troops in Palestine (SAUO) .... BTIP
British Trout Association (DBA) .... BTA
British Truck Racing Association (DBA) .... BTRA
British Trust for Conservation Volunteers .... BTCV
British Trust for Ornithology .... BTO
British Tuberculosis Association (SAUO) .... BTA
British Tugowners Association (BI) .... BTA
British Tunneling Society (SAUO) .... BTS
British Turf Irrigation Association (DBA) .... BTIA
British Turkey Federation Ltd. (BI) .... BTF
British Turkey Federation, Ltd. (SAUO) .... BTF
British Turned-Parts Manufacturers Association (DBA) .... BTMA
British Tutorial Institute .... BTI
British Twinning and Bilingual Association (BI) .... BTBA

British Typewriter Manufacturers Association (PDAA) .... BTMA
British Tyre & Rubber Co. Ltd. (SAUO) .... BTR
British Ulster Dominion Party (SAUO) .... BUDP
British Ultimate Federation (DBA) .... BUF
British Underground Nuclear Test (MCD) .... BUNT
British Unemployment Resource Network (PDAA) .... BURN
British Unidentified Flying Objects Research Association .... BUFORA
British Union Catalogue of Music Periodicals (SAUO) .... BUCOMP
British Union Catalogue of Periodicals [A publication] .... BUCOP
British Union Catalogue of Periodicals-World List of Scientific Periodicals (SAUO) .... BUCOP-WLSP
British Union for the Abolition of Vivisection .... BUAV
British Union of Fascists .... BUF
British Union of Film Organisations (SAUO) .... BUFO
British Union of Grammar School Attenders (SAUO) .... BUGSA
British Union of Great Britain and Ireland (SAUO) .... BU
British Union Oil Company (SAUO) .... BUOC
British Union Temperance Department (SAUO) .... BUTD
British United Air Ferries (SAUO) .... BUAF
British United Airways (SAUO) .... BR
British United Airways .... BUA
British United Channel Islands Airways (SAUS) .... JY
British United Island Airways .... BUIA
British United Press .... BUP
British United Provident Association (DCTA) .... BUPA
British United Shoe Machinery [Commercial firm] .... BUSM
British United Traction Co. .... BUT
British Universities Accommodation Consortium .... BUAC
British Universities Association of Slavists .... BUAS
British Universities Evangelical Christian Union (SAUO) .... BUECU
British Universities Film and Video Council [Information service or system] (IID) .... BUFVC
British Universities Industrial Relations Association .... BUIRA
British Universities North America Club (EA) .... BUNAC
British Universities Society of Arts .... BUSA
British Universities Sports Federation .... BUSF
British Universities Student Travel Association (SAUO) .... BUSTA
British Universities Transatlantic Exchange Committee (AIE) .... BUTEC
British Uralite Ltd. (SAUO) .... BU
British Urban and Regional Information System Association .... BURISA
British Urban Development .... BUD
British Urban Development Services Unit [Department of Environment] (DI) .... BUDSU
British Urethane Foam Contractors Association (DBA) .... BUFCA
British Vacuum Council (DBA) .... BVC
British Valve and Actuators Manufacturers Association (DBA) .... BVAMA
British Valve Manufacturers Association (PDAA) .... BVMA
British Van Heusen Corporation (SAUO) .... BVH
British Vehicle Registration (SAUS) .... BVR
British Vehicle Rental and Leasing Association (DBA) .... BVRLA
British Venture Capital Association (DBA) .... BVCA
British Veterinary Association .... BVA
British Veterinary Camelid Association (GVA) .... BVCA
British Veterinary Code .... BVC
British Veterinary Codex [A publication] .... BVetC
British Veterinary Dental Association (GVA) .... BVDA
British Veterinary Hospitals Association (DBA) .... BVHA
British Veterinary Journal (SAUS) .... Br Vet J
British Veterinary Nursing Association (DBA) .... BVNA
British Veterinary Radiology Association (DBA) .... BVRA
British Veterinary Zoological Society (DBA) .... BVZS
British Vexillological Society .... BVS
British Videogram Association .... BVA
British Videogram Association (NITA) .... BVGA
British Videotext and Teletext (SAUS) .... BVT
British Vigilance Association (BI) .... BVA
British Vigilance Association (SAUO) .... BVA
British Virgin Island [IYRU nationality code] (IYR) .... KV
British Virgin Islands (SAUO) .... BVI
British Virgin Islands .... BVI
British Virgin Islands [ANSI two-letter standard code] (CNC) .... VG
British Virgin Islands [ANSI three-letter standard code] (CNC) .... VGB
British Virgin Islands Hotel and Commerce Association (EAIO) .... BVIHCA
British Visitor's Passport .... BVP
British Voluntary Euthanasia Society (SAUO) .... BVES
British Volunteer Programme (SAUO) .... BVP
British Volunteer Programme .... BVP
British Volunteers, Latin America [British military] (DMA) .... BVLA
British War Cabinet .... BWC
British War Cabinet (SAUO) .... BWC
British War Comforts Fund (SAUO) .... BWCF
British War Medal .... BWM
British War Medal (SAUS) .... BWM
British War Relief (SAUO) .... BWR
British War Relief Association (SAUO) .... BWRA
British War Relief Society (SAUO) .... BWRS
British War Relief Society [in US] .... BWRS
British War Supplies Committee [Combined Production and Resources Board] [World War II] .... BWSC
British War Veterans of America (EA) .... BWVA
British War Victims Fund (SAUO) .... BWVF
British Warm Air Hand Drier Association (DBA) .... BWAHDA
British Warm-Blood Society (DBA) .... BWBS
British Waste Paper Association (PDAA) .... BWPA
British Waste Paper Utilisation Council (BI) .... BWPUC

British Watch and Clockmakers Guild (DBA) ... BWCMG
British Water and Effluent Treatment Plant Association (PDAA) ... BWETPA
British Water Colour Society (BI) ... BWS
British Water Industries Group (DBA) ... BWIG
British Water International ... BWI
British Water Research Association (SAUO) ... BWRA
British Water Ski Federation (SAUO) ... BWSF
British Water Ski Federation ... BWSF
British Watercolour Society (SAUO) ... BWS
British Waterfowl Association (BI) ... BWA
British Waterways [*State-owned company*] ... BW
British Waterways Board ... BWB
British Waterworks Association ... BWA
British Waterworks Association (SAUO) ... BWWA
British Weed Control Conference (SAUS) ... BWCC
British Welded Steel Tube Manufacturers Association (PDAA) ... BWSTMA
British Welding Research Association [*Later, WI*] (MCD) ... BWRA
British West Africa ... BWA
British West India Regiment (SAUO) ... BWIR
British West Indian Airways Ltd. [*ICAO designator*] (OAG) ... BW
British West Indian Airways Ltd. ... BWIA
British West Indies [*Later, WI*] ... BWI
British West Indies Sugar Association (SAUO) ... BWISA
British Wheat Starch Association (DBA) ... BWSA
British Wheel of Yoga [*An association*] (DBA) ... BWOY
British White Cattle Society of Australia ... BWCSA
British Whiting Federation (BI) ... BWF
British Wholesale Traders Association (DBA) ... BWTA
British Wildlife Appeal (EAIO) ... BWA
British Wind Energy Association (IRUK) ... BWEA
British Wind Engineering Association (SAUO) ... BWEA
British Winter Time (IAA) ... BWT
British Wire Gauge (SAUS) ... bwg
British Wire Netting Manufacturers Association (DBA) ... BWNMA
British Wire Rod Rollers' Association (BI) ... BWRRA
British Wireless Marine Service (DEN) ... BWMS
British Wireless Marine Service (SAUO) ... BWMS
British Withdrawal from Northern Ireland Campaign ... BWNIC
British Women Pilots Association (PDAA) ... BWPA
British Women's Temperance Association (BI) ... BWTA
British Wood Chipboard Manufacturers Association (PDAA) ... BWCMA
British Wood Preserving Association ... BWPA
British Wood Pulp Association (DBA) ... BWPA
British Wood Turners' Association ... BWTA
British Woodwork Manufacturers' Association (BI) ... BWMA
British Woodworking Federation (DBA) ... BWF
British Wool Confederation (SAUO) ... BWC
British Wool Federation ... BWF
British Wool Marketing Board ... BWMB
British Working Men's Club ... BWMC
British Work-Measurement Data Foundation (SAUO) ... BWMDF
British Workmen's Institute (BI) ... BWI
British World Airlines Ltd. [*FAA designator*] (FAAC) ... BWL
British Woven Wire Export Association (DBA) ... BWWEA
British Xylonite (SAUS) ... BX
British Yard Motor Minesweepers ... BYMS
British Yearbook of International Law [*A publication*] ... BYBL
British Young Naturalists Association (BI) ... BYNA
British Youth Band Association (SAUO) ... BYBA
British Youth Council (EAIO) ... BYC
British Youth Science (SAUO) ... BYS
British Yugoslav Society (DBA) ... BYS
British Zeolite Association ... BZA
British Zonal Decartellization Office (SAUO) ... BZDO
British Zone (SAUO) ... BZ
British Zone Petroleum Coordinating Authority [*Post-World War II, Germany*] ... BZPCA
British-American Arts Association (EA) ... BAAA
British-American Business Association (EAIO) ... BABA
British-American Chamber of Commerce (EA) ... BACC
British-American Collectors Club (SAUS) ... BACC
British-American Construction and Materials, Ltd. (SAUO) ... BACM
British-American Coordinating Committee [*Turkey*] ... BACC
British-American Educational Foundation (SAUO) ... BAEF
British-American Hospital (SAUO) ... B-A H
British-American Light Opera Exchange ... BALOE
British-American Parliamentary Group (SAUO) ... BAPG
British-American Rhykenological Society [*Defunct*] (EA) ... B-ARS
British-American Scientific International Commercial (SAUO) ... BASIC
British-American Scientific International Commercial English ... BASIC (English)
British-American Tobacco Co. ... BAT
British-American Tobacco Co. ... BATC
British-American Tobacco Company (SAUO) ... BQB
British-American Wrestling Association (DI) ... BAWA
British-Australian Heritage Society ... BAHS
British-Australian Studies Association ... BASA
British-Australian Wool Realization Association (SAUO) ... BAWRA
British-Australian-New Zealand Antarctic Research Expedition [*1929-31*] ... BANZARE
British-Canadian Holstein-Friesian Association (BI) ... BCHFA
British-Canadian Trade Association (SAUO) ... BCTA
British-Caribbean Association (SAUO) ... BCA
British-Caribbean Philatelic Study Group (SAUO) ... BCPSG
British-Central-European Chamber of Commerce (DAS) ... BCECC
British-China Friendship Association (SAUO) ... BCFA
British-Czechoslovak Centre (SAUO) ... BCC
British-German Trade Council e.V. (SAUO) ... BGTC
British-Irish Association (SAUO) ... BIA
British-Irish Intergovernmental Council (SAUO) ... BIIC
British-Irish Interparliamentary Body (SAUO) ... BIIB
British-Israel Chamber of Commerce (DBA) ... B-ICC
British-Israel World Federation ... BI
British-Israel World Federation ... BIWF
British-Italian League (SAUO) ... BIL
British-Kurdish Friendship Society ... BKFS
British-North American Committee (EA) ... BNAC
British-Romanian Association (EAIO) ... ACARDA
British-Scandinavian Economic Committee (SAUS) ... UNISCAN
British-South African Company (SAUO) ... BRISACO
British-Soviet Chamber of Commerce (DS) ... BSCC
British-Swedish Chamber of Commerce (SAUO) ... BSCC
British-Swiss Chamber of Commerce (SAUO) ... BSCC
British-United States Agreement [*Signed May 17, 1943; formalized cooperation between the communications intelligence agencies of Great Britain and the United States*] ... BRUSA
British-United States Amateur Rocket Bureau ... BUSARB
British-United States Convoy Instructions ... BUSCI
British-United States Routing Agreement [*Shipping*] ... BUSRA
Briton ... Brit
Brits [*South Africa*] [*ICAO location identifier*] (ICLI) ... FABS
Britt Airways [*ICAO designator*] (AD) ... RU
Britt Airways, Inc. [*ICAO designator*] (FAAC) ... BTA
Britt Area Community Library, Britt, Ontario [*Library symbol*] [*National Library of Canada*] (NLC) ... OBRIT
Britt News-Tribune, Britt, IA [*Library symbol*] [*Library of Congress*] (LCLS) ... IaBriNT
Brittany Air International [*Airline*] [*France*] ... BRITAIR
Brittany Air International [*ICAO designator*] (AD) ... DB
Brittany Base Section [*World War II*] ... BBS
Brittany Oceanological Center ... BOC
Brittany Revolutionary Front [*France*] ... FLB
Britten Norman (Bembridge) Ltd. [*British*] [*ICAO aircraft manufacturer identifier*] (ICAO) ... BN
Brittle (ABBR) ... BRTL
Brittle Bone Disease [*Medicine*] (MELL) ... BBD
Brittle Bone Society [*British*] ... BBS
Brittle Hair, Impaired Intelligence, Decreased Fertility, and Short Stature [*Syndrome*] [*Medicine*] (MELL) ... BIDS
Brittle Materials Design (MCD) ... BMD
Brittle Matrix Composite [*Materials science*] ... BMC
Brittle-Ductile Transition [*Geology*] ... BDT
Brittle-to-Ductile Transition [*Metallurgy*] ... BDT
Britton & Koontz Capital Corp. [*NASDAQ symbol*] (SAG) ... BKBK
Britton & Koontz Capital Corp. [*Associated Press*] (SAG) ... Brt&Ktz
Britton, SD [*Location identifier*] [*FAA*] (FAAL) ... BTN
Britton's Ancient Pleas of the Crown [*A publication*] (DLA) ... Brit
Britton's Ancient Pleas of the Crown [*A publication*] (DLA) ... Britt
Brive/La Roche [*France*] [*ICAO location identifier*] (ICLI) ... LFBV
Brive-La-Gaillarde [*France*] [*Airport symbol*] (OAG) ... BVE
Brix (SAUS) ... Bx
Brixton College [*London, England*] ... BC
Brize Norton [*British*] [*ICAO location identifier*] (ICLI) ... EGVN
Brize Norton, FTU [*British*] [*FAA designator*] (FAAC) ... BZN
Brno [*Former Czechoslovakia*] [*Airport symbol*] (OAG) ... BRQ
Brno-Enfield [*Machine gun*] ... BREN
BRO Resources Ltd. [*Vancouver Stock Exchange symbol*] ... BRO
Broach (MSA) ... BRCH
Broach (KSC) ... BRO
Broach Adapter ... BHAD
Broach Fixture ... BHFX
Broach Fixture (MCD) ... BRF
Broaching Tool Institute (SAUS) ... BTI
Broad [*Also, BR*] [*Spectral*] ... B
Broad (ADA) ... BD
Broad [*Also, B*] [*Spectral*] ... BR
Broad Absorption Line [*Quasar*] [*Astrophysics*] ... BAL
Broad Agency Announcement [*National automotive center*] (RDA) ... BAA
Broad Anatomy Marine [*See also HAM*] [*Slang term for female marines*] [*Bowdlerized version*] ... BAM
Broad Area Announcement ... BAA
Broad Area Optical Lightning Telescope Sensor (SAUS) ... BOLTS
Broad Area Review ... BAR
Broad Area Surveillance Executive Committee (ACAE) ... BSEC
Broad Audit Guidelines ... BAG
Broad Band Bearer Capability (SAUS) ... BBC
Broad Band Noise (DMAA) ... BBN
Broad Band Waveguide Circulator (SAUS) ... BBWC
Broad Band X Ray Telescope (SAUS) ... BBXRT
Broad Bean Mottle Virus [*Plant pathology*] ... BBMV
Broad Bean Necrosis Virus [*Plant pathology*] ... BBNV
Broad Bean Stain Virus [*Plant pathology*] ... BBSV
Broad Bean True Mosaic Virus [*Plant pathology*] ... BBTMV
Broad Bean Wilt Virus [*Plant pathology*] ... BBWV
Broad Brucher Shoe [*Medicine*] (MELL) ... BBS
Broad Economic Categories (SAUS) ... BEC
Broad Economic Category ... BEC
Broad Emission Line [*Spectra*] ... BEL
Broad Field of View (MCD) ... BFOV
Broad Folio [*Typography*] (DGA) ... BRD FO
Broad Gage (IAA) ... BG

Broad Gauge (SAUS)	BG
Broad Gauge Railway Operation Division (SAUO)	BGROD
Broad Host Range [Biochemistry]	BHR
Broad Ligament of Uterus [Medicine] (MELL)	BLU
Broad Measure (ADA)	BM
Broad National Bancorp [NASDAQ symbol] (NQ)	BNBC
Broad National Bancorp [Associated Press] (SAG)	BroadN
Broad Natl Bancorp [NASDAQ symbol] (TTSB)	BNBC
Broad Ocean Area	BOA
Broad Ocean Area - Missile Impact Locating System [Navy] (NG)	BOA-MILS
Broad Ocean Deployment	BOD
Broad Ocean Development (MCD)	BOD
Broad Ocean Scoring System [Missiles]	BOSS
Broad Pass [Alaska] [Seismograph station code, US Geological Survey] [Closed] (SEIS)	BDP
Broad Street Pneumonia [Center for Disease Control]	BSP
Broad Sweeping Generalization (SAUS)	BSG
Broad System of Ordering (MCD)	BSO
Broad Thumb-Hallux Syndrome [Medicine] (MELL)	BTHS
Broadax Systems, Inc. (PCM)	BSI
Broadband [Communications channel description] (IEEE)	BB
Broadband Acoustic Array Section	BAAS
Broadband Active Analyzer	BAA
Broadband ADSL (SAUS)	BDSL
Broadband Aerial (SAUS)	BBA
Broadband Aerial Kit (SAUS)	BAK
Broadband Analysis SONAR Surveillance (MCD)	BASS
Broadband Antenna	BBA
Broadband Antenna Kit	BAK
Broad-Band Anti-Reflective (SAUS)	BBAR
Broadband Bearer Capability (VERA)	BBC
Broadband Cable System	BCS
Broadband Chaff (SAUS)	BBC
Broadband Class Of Bearer (SAUS)	BCOB
Broadband Coaxial Cable (SAUS)	BBC Cable
Broadband Code Division Multiple Access [Telecommunications] (ACRL)	B-CDMA
Broadband Communication Network (BUR)	BCN
Broadband Communications Bus (SAUS)	BCB
Broadband Conducted (IEEE)	BBC
Broadband Connectionless Bearer Service [Telecommunications] (ACRL)	BCLB
Broadband Connectionless Data Bearer Service (VERA)	BCDBS
Broadband Connection-Oriented Bearer Service [Telecommunications] (ACRL)	BCOB
Broadband Control (SAUS)	BBC
Broadband Distributive Services [Telecommunications]	BD
Broadband Exchange [Western Union communication system]	BEX
Broadband Exchange over Trans-European Links (SAUO)	BETEL
Broadband Frequency	BF
Broadband Hemispherical in Flux Radiometer (CARB)	BBHIR
Broadband Hemispherical Solar Radiometer (CARB)	BBHSR
Broadband High Layer Information (VERA)	BHLI
Broad-Band High-Reflectance (SAUS)	BBHR
Broadband Information System (SAUS)	BIS
Broadband Integrated Glass Fibre Optical Network [Project] [Federal Republic of Germany] (NITA)	BIGFON
Broadband Integrated Services Digital Network [Telecommunications]	BISDN
Broadband Interface Controller [Motorola, Inc.]	BIC
Broadband Interface Module [Computer science] (VERA)	BIM
Broadband Internet Delivery System (SAUS)	BIDS
Broadband Interneuron [Neuroanatomy]	BBI
Broadband Inter-Switching System Interface (VERA)	BISSI
Broadband ISDN (SAUS)	B-ISDN
Broadband ISDN User Part (SAUS)	BISUP
Broadband ISDN [Integrated Services Digital Network] User Part [Telecommunications] (ACRL)	B-ISUP
Broadband Island (SAUS)	BRIS
Broadband Isotropic Real-Time Electric Field Sensor (MCD)	BIRES
Broadband Klystron Amplifier	BKA
Broadband Latching Circulator	BLC
Broadband Latching Switch	BLS
Broadband Local Exchange [Telecommunications] (ACRL)	B-LE
Broadband Local Management Interface (SAUS)	B-LMI
Broadband Low Layer Information (VERA)	BLLI
Broadband Microwave Power Amplifier	BMPA
Broadband Network Operating System	BNOS
Broadband Network Premises (VERA)	BNP
Broadband Network Service [Telecommunications] (ACRL)	BNS
Broadband Network Termination [Telecommunications]	BNT
Broadband Network Termination (SAUS)	B-NT
Broadband Networking Services [Computer science] (IGQR)	BBNS
Broadband Noise Generator (SAUS)	BNG
Broadband Observatory for the Localization of Transients (SAUS)	BOLT
Broadband Optical Network Termination (SAUS)	BONT
Broadband Outdoor Radiometer Calibration (ARMP)	BORCAL
Broadband Packet Exchange [Telecommunications] (ACRL)	BPX
Broadband Passive Optical Network (SAUS)	BPON
Broadband Power Amplifier (SAUS)	BPA
Broadband Radiated (IEEE)	BBR
Broadband Radiation Station (SAUS)	BRS
Broadband Radiometer Station (SAUS)	BSR
Broadband Rectangular-to-Circular Transition [Telecommunications] (IAA)	BRCT
Broadband Remote Line Unit [Telecommunications] (ACRL)	BRLU
Broadband Remote Oculometer (KSC)	BRO
Broadband Service Expert Group	BSEG
Broadband Service Integration Multiplexer [Telecommunications]	BSIM
Broadband Solid State Preamplifier (SAUS)	BSSP
Broadband Solid-State Preamplifier	BSSP
Broadband Subsystem	BRD
Broadband Switching Element [Telecommunications]	BSE
Broadband Switching Network [Telecommunications]	BSN
Broadband Switching System [Telecommunications] (ACRL)	BSS
Broadband Switching Unit [Telecommunications]	BSU
BroadBand Technologies [NASDAQ symbol] (TTSB)	BBTK
BroadBand Technologies, Inc. [NASDAQ symbol] (SAG)	BBTK
BroadBand Technologies, Inc. [Associated Press] (SAG)	BrdbdTc
Broadband Technology (SAUS)	BBT
Broadband Terminal Adapter [Telecommunications] (ACRL)	B-TA
Broadband Terminal Equipment [Telecommunications] (ACRL)	B-TE
Broadband Transport Manager (SAUS)	BTM
Broadband Trunk Module [Telecommunications]	BTM
Broadband Unbalanced Transformer [Telecommunications] (OA)	BUT
Broadband Unified Messaging System (SAUS)	BUMS
Broadband Waveguide Circulator	BBWC
Broadband Waveguide Circulator	BWC
Broadband Wireless Access	BWA
Broadband Wireless Technology (SAUS)	BWT
Broadband X-Band Klystron	BXK
Broadband X-Ray Telescope	BBXRT
Broadband Y-band Klystron (SAUS)	BYK
Broadband-to-Narrowband Interface (SAUS)	BNI
Broad-Based Consumption Tax (ADA)	BBCT
Broad-Based Enhanced Savings Tax	BEST
Broadbed and Furrow System (GNE)	BBF
Broad-Breasted White (SAUS)	BBW
Broadcast [FCC] (NTCM)	B
Broadcast (IDOE)	BC
Broadcast (SAUS)	B/C
Broadcast [Information transmission] (AFM)	BCST
Broadcast	bcst
Broadcast (SAUS)	BDST
Broadcast	BRDCST
Broadcast	BRDSCT
Broadcast (MUGU)	BRST
Broadcast Advertisers Reports [Information service or system] [Defunct]	BAR
Broadcast Advertisers Reports (journ.) (SAUS)	BAR
Broadcast Advertising Bureau, Inc. (SAUO)	BABI
Broadcast Advertising Producers Society of America (NTCM)	BAPSA
Broadcast Amplifier (IAA)	BCAMPL
Broadcast Amplifier (IAA)	Bc Ampl
Broadcast and Group Translators (VERA)	BGT
Broadcast and Television Receivers (MCD)	BTR
Broadcast and Television Receivers (journ.) (SAUS)	BTR
Broadcast Band	BCB
Broadcast Bureau [of FCC]	BB
Broadcast Bureau of Measurement [FCC] (NTCM)	BBM
Broadcast by Cable TV	Cablecast
Broadcast Cable Credit Association (NTPA)	BCCA
Broadcast Cable Financial Management Association (EA)	BCFMA
Broadcast Capital Fund, Inc. (NTCM)	BROADCAP
Broadcast Channel (CGWS)	BCH
Broadcast Communications Ltd. (SAUO)	BCL
Broadcast Communications System	BCS
Broadcast Control	BC
Broadcast Control Authority (NVT)	BCA
Broadcast Control Center	BCC
Broadcast Control Channel (VERA)	BCCH
Broadcast Control Segment (SAUS)	BCS
Broadcast Control Station (SAUO)	BCS
Broadcast Credit Association (EA)	BCA
Broadcast Designers Association (EA)	BDA
Broadcast Education Association (EA)	BEA
Broadcast Educators Association of Canada (AC)	BEAC
Broadcast Electronic Video Recording (IAA)	BEVR
Broadcast Engineering Officer (ADA)	BEO
Broadcast Exchange (IAA)	BEX
Broadcast, Execute This Command [Telecommunications] [Electronics] (ECII)	BETC
Broadcast Executives Society (AC)	BES
Broadcast Fighter Control [Military]	BROFICON
Broadcast Financial Management Association [Later, BCFMA] (EA)	BFM
Broadcast Industry Automation System [Data Communications Corp.] [Information service or system] (IID)	BIAS
Broadcast Information Bureau, Inc.	BIB
Broadcast Institute of North America (NTCM)	BINA
Broadcast Intercept (MCD)	BI
Broadcast Interference [Telecommunications]	BCI
Broadcast Interrupt (CCCA)	B/I
Broadcast Keying Station (NVT)	BKS
Broadcast Listener [Amateur radio]	BCL
Broadcast Listening (IDOE)	BCL
Broadcast Management/Engineering (journ.) (SAUS)	BM/E
Broadcast Master Antenna Control (SAUS)	B-MAC
Broadcast Measurement Bureau (NTCM)	BMB
Broadcast Message Server (VERA)	BMS
Broadcast Music, Inc. (EA)	BMI
Broadcast Music Incorporated (SAUO)	BMIC
Broadcast Net (NATG)	BRN
Broadcast News Ltd. (NTCM)	BNL

Broadcast News Service (NTCM) ... BNS
Broadcast Officer ... BOR
Broadcast Online TV (SAUS) ... BOT
Broadcast Operations Control (SAUS) ... BOC
Broadcast Operator's Certificate of Proficiency ... BOCP
Broadcast Pioneers (EA) ... BP
Broadcast Pioneers Educational Fund, Inc. (NTCM) ... BPEF
Broadcast Pioneer's Library (NTCM) ... BPL
Broadcast Pioneers Library (SAUO) ... BP Lib
Broadcast Production Officer ... BPO
Broadcast Promotion and Marketing Executives (EA) ... BPME
Broadcast Radio Emergency Communication [*Air Force*] ... BRECOM
Broadcast Rating Council [*Later, EMRC*] ... BRC
Broadcast Rating Council (SAUO) ... BRC
Broadcast Recognition Access Method (VERA) ... BRAM
Broadcast Recognition with Alternating Priorities (VERA) ... BRAP
Broadcast Recognizing Access Method (SAUS) ... BRAM
Broadcast Requested (FAAC) ... BCREQ
Broadcast Satellite [*Japan*] ... BS
Broadcast Satellite International, Inc. [*Dallas, TX*] [*Telecommunications service*] (TSSD) ... BSI
Broadcast Satellite Service ... BSS
Broadcast Services for Windows (PCM) ... BSW
Broadcast Short-Message Service (SAUS) ... BSMS
Broadcast Specialist Course [*Department of Defense Information School*] (DNAB) ... BSC
Broadcast Station (FAAC) ... BCSTN
Broadcast Station (PIPO) ... BS
Broadcast Switched Virtual Connections (VERA) ... BSVC
Broadcast Television Systems (SAUS) ... BTS
Broadcast Television Systems Committee Recommendation [*FCC*] (NTCM) ... BTSC
Broadcast Terminal Very-High Frequency Omni-Range (SAUS) ... BTVOR
Broadcast Transmission Systems (MCD) ... BTS
Broadcast Unknown Server [*Telecommunications*] (ACRL) ... BUS
Broadcast Very-High Frequency Omni-Range (SAUS) ... BVOR
Broadcast Warning Message (ROAS) ... BWM
Broadcast Warning TWX (SAUS) ... BWT
Broadcaster ... BCSTR
Broadcaster ... BRDCSTR
Broadcasters (SAUS) ... B Casters
Broadcasters Audience Research Board [*British*] [*Information service or system*] ... BARB
Broadcasters Database [*Houston, TX*] [*Information service or system*] (IID) ... BDB
Broadcasters Digital Cooperative ... BDC
Broadcaster's Foundation, Inc. (NTCM) ... BFI
Broadcasters Nonprofit Satellite Service [*Ford Foundation*] ... BNS
Broadcasters' Promotion Association [*Later, BPME*] (EA) ... BPA
Broadcasting ... B
Broadcasting (MCD) ... BC
Broadcasting ... BCSTG
Broadcasting ... BRDSCTG
Broadcasting Amplitude Modulation ... BAM
Broadcasting and Entertainment Trades Alliance [*A union*] [*British*] (EAIO) ... BETA
Broadcasting and Film Commission [*Later, CC*] (EA) ... BFC
Broadcasting and Film Commission/National Council of the Churches of Christ in the USA (NTCM) ... BFC/NCC
Broadcasting Co. of America (NTCM) ... BCA
Broadcasting Complaints Commission [*British*] ... BCC
Broadcasting Corp. of China ... BCC
Broadcasting Corp. of the Bahamas ... BCB
Broadcasting Corporation of Japan (SAUO) ... BCJ
Broadcasting Corporation of New Zealand (SAUO) ... BCNZ
Broadcasting Council [*Australia*] ... BC
Broadcasting Entertainment & Cinematograph Technicians' Union (WDAA) ... BECTU
Broadcasting Entertainment Cinematograph and Theatre Union [*British*] (EAIO) ... BECTU
Broadcasting for International Understanding (AC) ... BIU
Broadcasting Foundation of America [*Defunct*] (EA) ... BFA
Broadcasting House (WDAA) ... BH
Broadcasting in Australia [*A publication*] ... BIA
Broadcasting Information Office (SAUO) ... BIO
Broadcasting Maintenance District ... BMD
Broadcasting Operations Recording and Information System ... BORIS
Broadcasting Organizations of Non-Aligned Countries [*Belgrade, Yugoslavia*] (EAIO) ... BONC
Broadcasting Press Guild (SAUO) ... BPG
Broadcasting Program [*Association of Independent Colleges and Schools specialization code*] ... BC
Broadcasting Publications, Inc. (SAUS) ... BPI
Broadcasting Reports [*Australia*] [*A publication*] ... BR
Broadcasting Satellite Experimental [*Japan*] (MCD) ... BSE
Broadcasting Satellite Service (SAUS) ... BSS
Broadcasting Service (SAUS) ... BS
Broadcasting Squadron [*Air Force*] ... BRS
Broadcasting Standards Council [*British*] (WDAA) ... BSC
Broadcasting Station [*ITU designation*] (CET) ... BC
Broadcasting Station ... BS
Broadcasting Station, Television [*ITU designation*] ... BT
Broadcasting Support Services (AIE) ... BSS
Broadcasting System of Niigata (SAUO) ... BSN
Broadcasting Television Systems Philips (SAUS) ... BTS
Broadcasting Video Recording (SAUS) ... BVR
Broadcast-Television Recording Engineers [*An association*] (NTCM) ... BTRE
Broadcom Corp.'A' [*NASDAQ symbol*] (SG) ... BRCM
Broadened Opportunities for Officer Selection and Training [*Navy*] (NVT) ... BOOST
Broader System of Ordering (SAUS) ... BSO
Broader Term [*Cross-reference*] [*Indexing*] ... BT
Broad-Flanged Beam ... BFB
Broadland Noise Generator ... BNG
Broadlaw [*Scotland*] [*Seismograph station code, US Geological Survey*] (SEIS) ... EBL
Broad-Line Radio Galaxy [*Astrophysics*] ... BLRG
Broad-Line Region [*Spectra*] ... BLR
Broad-Line System (SAUS) ... BLR
Broadmoor Criminal Lunatic Asylum (SAUO) ... BCLA
Broadside [*Paper*] (DGA) ... BS
Broad-Spectrum Antibiotic [*Medicine*] (MELL) ... BSA
Broadus, MT [*Location identifier*] [*FAA*] (FAAL) ... BDX
Broadus Public Library, Broadus, MT [*Library symbol*] [*Library of Congress*] (LCLS) ... MtBr
Broadview Public Library, Broadview, IL [*Library symbol*] [*Library of Congress*] (LCLS) ... IBrov
Broadview, SK [*ICAO location identifier*] (ICLI) ... CYDR
BroadVision, Inc. [*Associated Press*] (SAG) ... BroadVis
BroadVision, Inc. [*NASDAQ symbol*] (SAG) ... BVSN
Broadway (WDAA) ... B
Broadway [*A street name*] ... BDWY
Broadway [*A street name*] [*British*] ... BDY
Broadway ... BRDWY
Broadway [*A street name*] ... B'WAY
Broadway (NTIO) ... Bway
Broadway (WDAA) ... BY
Broadway & Seymour, Inc. [*Associated Press*] (SAG) ... BdwySey
Broadway & Seymour Inc. [*NASDAQ symbol*] (TTSB) ... BSIS
Broadway Beverages [*Vancouver Stock Exchange symbol*] ... BEV
[*The*] **Broadway Book of English Verse** [*A publication*] ... BrBEV
Broadway Elementary School, Grand Junction, CO [*Library symbol*] [*Library of Congress*] (LCLS) ... CoBjBrE
Broadway Elementary School, Grand Junction, CO [*Library symbol*] [*Library of Congress*] (LCLS) ... CoGjBrE
Broadway Financial [*NASDAQ symbol*] (TTSB) ... BYFC
Broadway Financial Corp. [*Associated Press*] (SAG) ... BrdwyF
Broadway Financial Corp. [*NASDAQ symbol*] (SAG) ... BYFC
Broadway Memorial Institute (SAUO) ... BMI
Broadway Stores [*Associated Press*] (SAG) ... Bdway
Broadway Stores [*Formerly, Carter Hawley, Hale*] [*NYSE symbol*] (SAG) ... BWY
Broadway Stores Wrrt [*NYSE symbol*] (SG) ... BWY WS
Broadway, VA [*FM radio station call letters*] ... WLTK
Broadway-Hale Stores, Inc. (SAUO) ... BHS
Broadway-Timberville, VA [*AM radio station call letters*] ... WBTX
Broadwoodwidger [*England*] ... BROADWOODW
Brobeck, Phleger & Harrison, San Francisco, CA [*Library symbol*] [*Library of Congress*] (LCLS) ... CSfBPH
Broca Index [*Medicine*] ... BI
Brocade (VRA) ... brcd
Brocade Communication Systems [*NASDAQ symbol*] ... BRCD
Brocades-Stheeman [*Netherlands*] [*Research code symbol*] ... BS
Broccoli Necrotic Yellows Virus [*Plant pathology*] ... BNYV
Brochet, MB [*ICAO location identifier*] (ICLI) ... CYBT
Brock Air Services Ltd. [*Canada*] [*ICAO designator*] (FAAC) ... BRD
Brock Control Systems, Inc. [*NASDAQ symbol*] (SAG) ... BROC
Brock Control Systems, Inc. [*Associated Press*] (SAG) ... BrockCS
Brock Exploration Corp. [*AMEX symbol*] (SPSG) ... BKE
Brock Exploration Corp. [*Associated Press*] (SAG) ... BrockCp
Brock Intl Inc. [*NASDAQ symbol*] (TTSB) ... BROC
Brock Township Public Library, Beaverton Branch, Beaverton, ON, Canada [*Library symbol*] [*Library of Congress*] (LCLS) ... CaOBEAB
Brock Township Public Library, Cannington Branch, Cannington, ON, Canada [*Library symbol*] [*Library of Congress*] (LCLS) ... CaOCAB
Brock Township Public Library, Sunderland, ON, Canada [*Library symbol*] [*Library of Congress*] (LCLS) ... CaOSunB
Brock Township Public Library, Sunderland, Ontario [*Library symbol*] [*National Library of Canada*] (NLC) ... OSUNB
Brock University, Department of Geography, Saint Catharines, ON, Canada [*Library symbol*] [*Library of Congress*] (LCLS) ... CaOStCBG
Brock University Library [*UTLAS symbol*] ... BCK
Brock University, Saint Catharines, ON, Canada [*Library symbol*] [*Library of Congress*] (LCLS) ... CaOStCB
Brock University, St. Catharines, Ontario [*Library symbol*] [*National Library of Canada*] (NLC) ... OSTCB
Brockenbrough and Holmes. Virginia Cases [*A publication*] (DLA) ... Brock & H
Brockenbrough and Holmes. Virginia Cases [*A publication*] (DLA) ... Brock & Ho
Brockenbrough and Holmes. Virginia Cases [*A publication*] (DLA) ... Brock & Hol
Brockenbrough and Holmes. Virginia Cases [*A publication*] (DLA) ... Brock & Hol Cas
Brockenbrough. Virginia Cases [*A publication*] (DLA) ... Brock Cas
Brockenbrough's Marshall's Decisions, United States Circuit Court [*A publication*] (DLA) ... Brock
Brockenbrough's Marshall's Decisions, United States Circuit Court [*A publication*] (DLA) ... Brock CC
Brockenbrough's Marshall's Decisions, United States Circuit Court [*A publication*] (DLA) ... Brock Marsh
Brocket Public Library, Alberta [*Library symbol*] [*National Library of Canada*] (NLC) ... ABRO
Brock-Graham [*Syndrome*] [*Medicine*] (DB) ... BG
Brocklebank & Well Lines [*Steamship*] (MHDB) ... B & W

Brockport High School Library, Brockport, NY [*OCLC symbol*] (OCLC) .... RVT
Brockport, NY [*AM radio station call letters*] .... WASB
Brockport, NY [*FM radio station call letters*] .... WASB-FM
Brockport, NY [*FM radio station call letters*] .... WBSU
Brockton, MA [*AM radio station call letters*] .... WBET
Brockton, MA [*FM radio station call letters*] .... WCAV
Brockton, MA [*FM radio station call letters*] (BROA) .... WCAV-FM
Brockton, MA [*AM radio station call letters*] .... WMSX
Brockton Public Library, Brockton, MA [*Library symbol*] [*Library of Congress*] (LCLS) .... MBrock
Brockville [*Canada*] [*Airport symbol*] (OAG) .... XBR
Brockville, ON [*AM radio station call letters*] .... CFJR
Brockville, ON [*FM radio station call letters*] .... CHXL
Brockville Psychiatric Hospital, Library Resources and Informtion Centre, Brockville, ON, Canada [*Library symbol*] [*Library of Congress*] (LCLS) .... CaOBRPH
Brockville Public Library, Brockville, ON, Canada [*Library symbol*] [*Library of Congress*] (LCLS) .... CaOB
Brockville Public Library, Ontario [*Library symbol*] [*National Library of Canada*] (NLC) .... OB
Brockway Glass Co., Inc. (SAUO) .... BRK
Brockway, PA [*AM radio station call letters*] .... WVCQ
Brockway Standard Holdings, Inc. [*Associated Press*] (SAG) .... BrckwSt
Brockway Standard Holdings, Inc. [*NASDAQ symbol*] (SAG) .... BWAY
Brodart Co. [*ACCORD*] [*UTLAS symbol*] .... BRD
Broderbund Software [*NASDAQ symbol*] (TTSB) .... BROD
Broderbund Software, Inc. [*NASDAQ symbol*] (SPSG) .... BROD
Broderbund Software, Inc. [*Associated Press*] (SAG) .... BrodSft
Broderick and Freemantle's Ecclesiastical Cases [*1840-64*] [*A publication*] (DLA) .... Br & F Ecc
Broderick and Freemantle's Ecclesiastical Cases [*1840-64*] [*A publication*] (DLA) .... Br & Fr
Broderick and Freemantle's Ecclesiastical Cases [*1840-64*] [*A publication*] (DLA) .... Bro & F
Broderick and Freemantle's Ecclesiastical Cases [*1840-64*] [*A publication*] (DLA) .... Bro & Fr
Broderick and Freemantle's Ecclesiastical Cases [*1840-64*] [*A publication*] (DLA) .... Brod
Broderick and Freemantle's Ecclesiastical Cases [*1840-64*] [*A publication*] (DLA) .... Brod & F
Broderick and Freemantle's Ecclesiastical Cases [*1840-64*] [*A publication*] (DLA) .... Brod & F Ecc Cas
Broderick and Freemantle's Ecclesiastical Cases [*1840-64*] [*A publication*] (DLA) .... Brod & Fr
Broderick and Freemantle's Ecclesiastical Cases [*1840-64*] [*A publication*] (DLA) .... Brod & Fr Ecc Cas
Broderick and Freemantle's Ecclesiastical Cases [*1840-64*] [*A publication*] (DLA) .... Brod & Frem
Broderick and Freemantle's English Ecclesiastical Reports [*1840-64*] [*A publication*] (DLA) .... B & F
Broderip and Bingham's English Common Pleas Reports [*A publication*] (DLA) .... B & B
Broderip and Bingham's English Common Pleas Reports [*A publication*] (DLA) .... Br & B
Broderip and Bingham's English Common Pleas Reports [*A publication*] (DLA) .... Brod & B
Broderip and Bingham's English Common Pleas Reports [*129 English Reprint*] [*A publication*] (DLA) .... Brod & Bing
Brodhead Memorial Public Library, Brodhead, WI [*Library symbol*] [*Library of Congress*] (LCLS) .... WBro
Brodie Resource Library, Thunder Bay, ON, Canada [*Library symbol*] [*Library of Congress*] (LCLS) .... CaOTBBR
Brodie Resource Library, Thunder Bay, Ontario [*Library symbol*] [*National Library of Canada*] (NLC) .... OTBBR
Brodie's Notes and Supplement to Stair's Institutions [*Scotland*] [*A publication*] (DLA) .... Brod Stair
Brodie's Notes and Supplement to Stair's Institutions [*Scotland*] [*A publication*] (DLA) .... Bro St
Brodie's Notes and Supplement to Stair's Institutions [*Scotland*] [*A publication*] (DLA) .... Bro Stair
Brodix's American and English Patent Cases [*A publication*] (DLA) .... Brodix Am & Eng Pat Cas
Brodix's American and English Patent Cases [*A publication*] (DLA) .... Brodix Am & E Pat Cas
Brodmann's Areas [*Brain anatomy*] .... BA
Brodsky, David, New York NY [*STAC*] .... BDD
Brody Medical Science Building (SAUS) .... MS
Brohm Resources, Inc. [*Toronto Stock Exchange symbol*] [*Vancouver Stock Exchange symbol*] .... BRH
Broiler and Egg Association of Minnesota (SRA) .... BEAM
Broiler Growers Association (SAUO) .... BGA
Brokaw Hospital Medical Center, Normal, IL [*Library symbol*] [*Library of Congress*] (LCLS) .... INBH
Broke [*Rough finish of paper*] .... B
Broken .... B
Broken .... BKN
Broken (WDAA) .... Bn
Broken [*Quality of the bottom*] [*Nautical charts*] .... brk
Broken .... BRKN
Broken and Repaired (SAUS) .... B/R
Broken Arrow, OK [*FM radio station call letters*] .... KNYD
Broken Arrow, OK [*FM radio station call letters*] (RBYB) .... KOAS
Broken as Designed [*Computer hacker terminology*] (NHD) .... BAD
Broken Bow Carnegie Library, Broken Bow, NE [*Library symbol*] [*Library of Congress*] (LCLS) .... NbBro
Broken Bow, NE [*Location identifier*] [*FAA*] (FAAL) .... BBW
Broken Bow, NE [*Location identifier*] [*FAA*] (FAAL) .... CUZ
Broken Bow, NE [*FM radio station call letters*] .... KBBN
Broken Bow, NE [*AM radio station call letters*] .... KCNI
Broken Bow, OK [*FM radio station call letters*] (RBYB) .... KCGX
Broken Bow, OK [*FM radio station call letters*] .... KKBI
Broken Cloud (WEAT) .... BKN
Broken Clouds (SAUS) .... BKN Clouds
Broken Clouds or Better (MUGU) .... BCOB
Broken Clouds or Better [*Meteorology*] (DA) .... BCOP
Broken Corn and Foreign Material [*Quality measure for grain*] .... BCFM
Broken Cubic Meter (DAC) .... BCM
Broken Cubic Yard (DAC) .... BCY
Broken Hill [*Australia*] [*ICAO location identifier*] (ICLI) .... AABH
Broken Hill [*Australia*] [*ICAO location identifier*] (ICLI) .... APBH
Broken Hill [*Kabwe*] [*Zambia*] [*Seismograph station code, US Geological Survey*] (SEIS) .... BHA
Broken Hill [*Australia*] [*Airport symbol*] (OAG) .... BHQ
Broken Hill Associated Smelters Pty. Ltd. (SAUO) .... BHAS
Broken Hill Chamber of Commerce [*Australia*] .... BHCC
Broken Hill Historical Society. Journal and Proceedings (journ.) (SAUS) .... J Proc Boken Hill Hist S
Broken Hill Municipal Library, Broken Hill, NSW, Australia [*Library symbol*] [*Library of Congress*] (LCLS) .... AuBh
Broken Hill Proprietary ADR [*NYSE symbol*] (SPSG) .... BHP
Broken Hill Proprietary Co. Ltd. [*Associated Press*] (SAG) .... BHP
Broken Hill Pty. Co. Ltd. (SAUO) .... BHP
Broken Hill Pty Limited (SAUS) .... BHP
Broken Orange Pekoe [*Tea*] .... BOP
Broken Orange Pekoe Fannings [*Tea*] .... BOPF
Broken Paper (BARN) XXX
Broken Sea [*Navigation*] .... B
Broken Time Payment [*US Olympic Committee*] .... BTP
Broken-Case Price [*Marketing*] (DOAD) .... BCP
Brokenhead River Regional Library, Beausejour, Manitoba [*Library symbol*] [*National Library of Canada*] (NLC) .... MBBR
Brokenhead River Regional Library, Beausejour, MB, Canada [*Library symbol*] [*Library of Congress*] (LCLS) .... CaMBBR
Broker [*London Stock Exchange*] .... B
Broker [*Business term*] .... BKR
Broker [*Banking*] (TBD) .... Brkr
Broker .... BRKR
Broker (WDAA) .... BROK
Broker Management Council (EA) .... BMC
Broker Services, Inc. [*Englewood, CO*] [*Information service or system*] (IID) .... BSI
Brokerage (SAUS) .... Bkge
Brokerage (TBD) .... Brkg
Brokerage .... BRKRGE
Brokerage (ROG) .... BROK
Brokerage (SAUS) .... Brok
Brokerage Accounting Information System (SAA) .... BRAINS
Brokerage Accounting System Elements [*IBM computer program*] .... BASE
Broker-Dealer (DFIT) .... BD
Broker-Dealer-Investment Advisor Directory [*Securities and Exchange Commission*] (GFGA) .... BDA
Broker's Daily Statement .... BDS
Broker's Order [*Finance*] .... BO
Broker's Order (WDAA) .... bo
Bromacetyl Cellulose (SAUS) .... BAC
Bromacetylcellulose [*or Bromoacetycellulose*] [*Organic chemistry*] .... BAC
Bromatology (SAUS) .... Bromat
Bromchloride Fluormethane Fire Extinguisher (SAUS) .... BCF Extinguisher
Bromcresol Green [*An indicator*] [*Chemistry*] .... BCG
Bromcresol Purple [*An indicator*] [*Chemistry*] .... BCP
Brome County Historical Society, Knowlton, PQ, Canada [*Library symbol*] [*Library of Congress*] (LCLS) .... CaQKB
Brome County Historical Society, Knowlton, Quebec [*Library symbol*] [*National Library of Canada*] (NLC) .... QKB
Bromegrass Mosaic Virus .... BMV
bromeliad (SAUS) .... brome
Bromeliad Society (EA) .... BS
Bromeliad Society (EA) .... BSI
Bromeliad Society of New South Wales [*Australia*] .... BSNSW
Bromeliad Society of Victoria [*Australia*] .... BSV
Bromide [*Chemistry*] (ADA) .... BROM
bromide (SAUS) .... brom
bromide + seltzer (SAUS) .... bromo-seltzer
Bromide-Bromate Number (SAUS) .... BB No
bromidic (SAUS) .... brom
bromidrosis (SAUS) .... bromo
Brominated Isobutene-Isoprene (Butyl) Rubber (EDCT) .... BIIR
Brominated Vegetable Oil [*Soft drink additive*] .... BVO
Bromine [*Chemical element*] .... Br
Bromine Efficiency Factor .... BEF
Bromine Monoxide (EOSA) .... BrO
Bromine Number (SAUS) .... Br No
Bromine Pentafluoride [*Corrosive compound*] .... BPF
Bromine-Loading Potential [*Atmospheric science*] .... BLP
Bromine-Methanol (SAUS) .... BM
Bromma Flygskola/Cabair [*Sweden*] [*ICAO designator*] (FAAC) .... CVN
Bromo [*As substituent on nucleoside*] [*Biochemistry*] .... br
Bromoacetaldehyde Diethyl Acetal [*Organic chemistry*] .... BADEA
Bromoacetamidothymidine [*Antineoplastic drug*] .... BAT
Bromoacetone [*War gas*] .... BA
Bromoacetyl [*Organic chemistry*] .... BA

Bromoacetylcholine [*Biochemistry*] ... BAC
Bromoacetyl-DNP-Diamino-L-Butyric Acid [*Biochemistry*] ... BADB
Bromoacetyl-DNP-Ethylenediamine [*Biochemistry*] ... BADE
Bromoacetyl-DNP-L-Lysine [*Biochemistry*] ... BADL
Bromoacetyl-DNP-L-Ornithine [*Biochemistry*] ... BADO
Bromoacetylmono(azobenzenearsonic Acid)-L-tyrosine [*Biochemistry*] ... BAAT
Bromoamiloride [*Biochemistry*] ... Br-A
(Bromobenzoyl)methyladamantylamine [*Biochemistry*] ... BMA
Bromobenzyl Cyanide [*Tear gas*] ... BBC
Bromobenzyl Cyanide (SAUS) ... CA
Bromobenzylnitrile [*Toxic compound*] ... BBN
Bromochloride Fluormethane Fire Extinguisher (SAUS) ... BCF Extinguisher
Bromochloride-Fluoromethane (SAUS) ... BCF
Bromochlorodifluoromethane [*Fire extinguishing agent*] [*Organic chemistry*] (ADA) ... BCF
Bromochlorofluorocarbon [*Organic chemistry*] ... BCFC
bromo-chloro-fluoromethane (SAUS) ... bcf
Bromo(chloro)indolylphosphate [*Organic chemistry*] ... BCIP
Bromochlorophenol Blue [*Organic chemistry*] ... BCPB
Bromocresol Purple Desoxycholate [*Agar*] [*Chemistry*] (DAVI) ... BCP-D
Bromocresyl Purple (SAUS) ... BCP
Bromocriptine [*Pharmacology*] ... Br
Bromocriptine Growth Hormone Test (SAUS) ... BGHT
Bromocriptine-Dopamine Agonist (MELL) ... BDA
Bromodeoxyuridine [*Also, BDUR, BrDU*] [*Biochemistry*] ... BDU
Bromodeoxyuridine [*Also, BDU, BrDU*] [*Biochemistry*] ... BDUR
Bromodeoxyuridine [*Also, BDU, BDUR*] [*Biochemistry*] ... BrDU
Bromodeoxyuridine (SAUS) ... BrdU
Bromodeoxyuridine [*Also, BDU, BDUR*] [*Antineoplastic drug*] (DAVI) ... BrdUrd
Bromodeoxyuridine [*Antineoplastic drug*] (DAVI) ... BUDU
Bromodiphenyl(ethylphenyl)ethylene [*Endocrinology*] ... BDPE
Bromoergocryptine [*Organic chemistry*] ... BEC
Bromoethanesulfonic Acid [*Organic chemistry*] ... BES
Bromofluorocarbon [*Organic chemistry*] ... BFC
Bromoflurobenzene (ABAC) ... BFB
bromoform (SAUS) ... bromo
Bromoform-Triallyl Phosphate [*Flame retardant*] ... BAP
bromohydrosis (SAUS) ... bromidrosis
Bromoil Print (VRA) ... BRPT
Bromoisobutene Isoprene Rubber [*Organic chemistry*] ... BIIR
Bromoisovalerylurea [*Pharmacology*] ... BVU
Bromomercurihydroxypropane [*Clinical chemistry*] ... BMHP
Bromo-Methoxychalcone [*Organic chemistry*] ... BMC
(Bromomethyl)dimethyl Chlorosilane [*Organic chemistry*] ... BMDMCS
Bromo-Naphthyl-Beta-Galactosidase [*An enzyme*] (MAE) ... BNGase
Bromo-Naphthyl-Beta-Galactoside (MAE) ... BNG
Bromoperoxidase [*An enzyme*] ... BPO
Bromophenacyl Bromide [*Organic chemistry*] ... BPB
Bromophenol Blue [*A pH indicator*] [*Organic chemistry*] (DAVI) ... BPB
Bromopyrogallol Red [*An indicator*] [*Chemistry*] ... BPR
Bromosulfophthalein [*Clinical chemistry*] ... BSP
Bromothymol Blue Lactose [*Medicine*] (DMAA) ... BTBL
bromotology (SAUS) ... bromot
Bromotrifluoroethylene [*Organic chemistry*] ... BFE
Bromotrifluoromethane [*Fire extinguishing agent*] [*Organic chemistry*] (ADA) ... BTM
Bromotrifluoromethane [*Fire-extinguishing material*] (NAKS) ... CBrF3
Bromouracial Deoxyriboside (SAUS) ... BUDR
Bromouracil [*Biochemistry*] ... BU
Bromouracildeoxyriboside [*Antineoplastic drug*] ... BUdR
Bromouridine [*One-letter symbol; see BrUrd*] ... B
Bromouridine [*Also, B*] [*A nucleoside*] ... BrUrd
Bromovinyldeoxyuridine [*Biochemistry*] ... BVDU
(Bromovinyl)uracil [*Antiviral compound*] ... BVU
Brompheniramine Maleate [*Antihistamine*] ... BPM
Brompheniramine Maleate Elixir [*Medicine*] (MELL) ... BME
Brompton Park Military Hospital [*British military*] (DMA) ... BPMH
Bromsulphalein Test (MELL) ... BSPT
Bromsulphalein Test (SAUS) ... BSP Test
Bromthymol [*or Bromothymol*] **Blue** [*A dye*] ... BTB
Bronchial ... BRON
Bronchial Allergen Challenge [*Immunology*] ... BAC
Bronchial Artery Embolization [*Cardiology*] (DAVI) ... BAE
Bronchial Asthma [*Medicine*] ... BA
Bronchial Bars (SAUS) ... BB
Bronchial Blood Flow [*Medicine*] (DMAA) ... BBF
Bronchial Carcinoid ... BC
Bronchial Carcinoma [*Medicine*] (DAVI) ... BC
Bronchial Drainage [*Medicine*] (DAVI) ... BD
Bronchial Foreign Body [*Medicine*] (MELL) ... BFB
Bronchial Hyper-Reactivity [*Medicine*] (MELL) ... BH
Bronchial Lavage [*Medicine*] (MELL) ... BL
Bronchial Lymph Node [*Medicine*] (MAE) ... BLN
Bronchial Node [*Medicine*] (MELL) ... BN
Bronchial Provocation Test [*Medicine*] ... BPT
Bronchial Rings (SAUS) ... BR
Bronchial Smooth Muscle Cell [*Medicine*] (DMAA) ... BSMC
Bronchialcarcinom (SAUS) ... BC
Bronchialcarcinom (SAUS) ... BCA
Bronchidesmus (SAUS) ... BD
Bronchiectasis, Eosinophilia, Asthma, Pneumonia [*Medicine*] (DMAA) ... BEAP
Bronchiectatic Cyst [*Pulmonary medicine*] ... BC
Bronchiolitis Obliteransdiffuse Interstitial Pneumonia [*Medicine*] ... BIP
Bronchiolitis Obliterans-Organizing Pneumonia [*Medicine*] (DMAA) ... BOOP
Bronchitis [*Medicine*] ... BR
Bronchitis (SAUS) ... Bronch
Broncho Vascular Markings (SAUS) ... BVM
Bronchoalveolar Carcinoma [*Medicine*] (MELL) ... BAC
Bronchoalveolar Cells [*Medicine*] ... BAC
Bronchoalveolar Lavage [*Medicine*] ... BAL
Bronchoalveolar Lavage Fluid [*Medicine*] ... BALF
Bronchoalveolar Wash Fluids [*Medicine*] ... BAW
Bronchoarterial Bundle [*Medicine*] (MELL) ... BAB
Bronchodilation Following Deep Inspiration [*Medicine*] (DMAA) ... BFDI
Bronchodilator [*Medicine*] ... B
Bronchodilator (DB) ... BD
Bronchodilator Drug [*Medicine*] (MELL) ... BDD
Bronchoenterology (DB) ... BE
Bronchoesophagology [*Medicine*] ... BE
Bronchogenic Carcinoma [*Medicine*] (DMAA) ... BGCA
Bronchogenic Cyst ... BC
Bronchogenic Cyst [*Medicine*] (MELL) ... BGC
Bronchophony [*Medicine*] (DAVI) ... Brhp
Bronchophony (SAUS) ... BRPH
Bronchopleural [*Medicine*] ... BP
Bronchopleural Fistula [*Anatomy*] ... BPF
Bronchopulmonary [*Medicine*] (DAVI) ... BP
Bronchopulmonary Aspergillosis [*Medicine*] (DB) ... BPA
Bronchopulmonary Dysplasia [*Medicine*] ... BPD
Bronchopulmonary Lavage [*Medicine*] (MELL) ... BPL
Bronchopulmonary Lymph Nodes [*Medicine*] (MELL) ... BPLN
Bronchopulmonary Segmental Artery [*Medicine*] (DMAA) ... BPSA
Bronchopulmonary Segmental Drainage [*Medicine*] (DAVI) ... BPSD
Bronchoscopic (SAUS) ... Bronch
Bronchoscopist (SAUS) ... Bronch
Bronchoscopist [*Medicine*] (DAVI) ... bronch
Bronchoscopy [*Medicine*] (DAVI) ... BRO
Bronchoscopy [*Medicine*] ... BRON
Bronchoscopy [*Medicine*] ... BRONCH
Bronchoscopy [*Medicine*] (DAVI) ... broncho
Bronchospasm [*Medicine*] ... BSp
Bronchovascular Marking [*Medicine*] (MAE) ... BVM
Bronchovesicular [*Breath sounds*] [*Medicine*] ... BV
Bronchus (MELL) ... B
Bronchus Associated Lymphoid Tissue ... BALT
Bronchus-Carcinom (SAUS) ... BC
Bronco Petroleum Ltd. [*Vancouver Stock Exchange symbol*] ... BOP
Broneje Transporter [*Soviet Armored Personnel Carrier*] ... BTR
Bronevaya Mashina Destany [*Soviet airborne combat vehicle*] (INF) ... BMD
Bronfman Science Center [*Williams College*] [*Research center*] (RCD) ... BSC
Bronnoysund [*Norway*] [*Airport symbol*] (OAG) ... BNN
Bronnoysund/Bronnoy [*Norway*] [*ICAO location identifier*] (ICLI) ... ENBN
Bronson, KS [*FM radio station call letters*] (BROA) ... KBJQ-FM
Bronson, MI [*FM radio station call letters*] ... WCVM
Bronsted Acid [*Biochemistry*] ... BA
Bronsted Base [*Biochemistry*] ... BB
Bronsweg [*Surinam*] [*ICAO location identifier*] (ICLI) ... SMBW
Bronte Society (EA) ... BS
Bronx [*New York*] (BARN) ... Bx
Bronx Community College [*New York*] ... BCC
Bronx Community College Library, Bronx, NY [*OCLC symbol*] (OCLC) ... VWB
Bronx Community College, New York (SAUS) ... NNBC
Bronx Community College, New York, NY [*Library symbol*] [*Library of Congress*] (LCLS) ... NNBC
Bronx High School of Science (SAUO) ... BHSS
Bronx Homicide Task Force (SAUS) ... Bronx HTF
Bronx House of Detention (SAUO) ... BHD
Bronx Irish Catholic (SAUO) ... BIC
Bronx Yacht Club (SAUO) ... BYC
Bronxville Public Library, Bronxville, NY [*Library symbol*] [*Library of Congress*] (LCLS) ... NBron
Bronze ... BR
Bronze (WDAA) ... br
Bronze [*Philately*] ... brnz
Bronze (WGA) ... BRO
Bronze (KSC) ... BRZ
Bronze ... BZ
Bronze (VRA) ... bz
Bronze Age ... BA
Bronze Floors [*On ships*] ... BF
Bronze Medal ... BM
Bronze Service Star [*Military decoration*] (AFM) ... BSS
Bronze Star Medal [*Military decoration*] ... BSM
bronzing (SAUS) ... brnz
Broodband Inter-Carrier Interface [*Telecommunications*] ... BICI
Brooder [*s*] [*Freight*] ... BRD
Brook (WGA) ... BK
Brook (MCD) ... BRK
Brook [*Commonly used*] (OPSA) ... BROOK
Brook College, Chicago, IL [*Library symbol*] [*Library of Congress*] (LCLS) ... ICBCL
Brook Reaction Test [*Medicine*] (DMAA) ... BRT
Brookdale Community College, Lincroft, NJ [*OCLC symbol*] (OCLC) ... BCC
Brookdale Community College, Lincroft, NJ [*Library symbol*] [*Library of Congress*] (LCLS) ... NjLincB
Brooke Army Burn Institute (SAUO) ... BABI
Brooke Army Hospital (SAUO) ... BAH
Brooke Army Medical Center ... BAMC
Brooke General Hospital (SAUO) ... BGH
Brooke General Hospital, Medical Library, Fort Sam Houston, TX [*Library symbol*] [*Library of Congress*] (LCLS) ... TxFshBH

Brooke Group Ltd. [*NYSE symbol*] (SPSG) ... BGL
Brooke Group Ltd. [*Associated Press*] (SAG) ... Brooke
Brooke on the Office of a Notary in England [*A publication*] (DLA) ... Bro Not
Brooke, VA [*Location identifier*] [*FAA*] (FAAL) ... BRV
Brooke's Abridgment [*England*] [*A publication*] (DSA) ... B
Brooke's Abridgment [*England*] [*A publication*] (DSA) ... Br
Brooke's Abridgment [*England*] [*A publication*] (DLA) ... Br Abr
Brooke's Abridgment [*England*] [*A publication*] (DLA) ... Bro Ab
Brooke's Abridgment [*England*] [*A publication*] (DLA) ... Bro Abr
Brooke's Abridgment [*England*] [*A publication*] (DLA) ... Brook Abr
Brooke's Abridgment [*England*] [*A publication*] (DLA) ... Brooke Abr
Brooke's Bibliotheca Legum Angliae [*A publication*] (DLA) ... Brooke Bib Leg
Brooke's Churchwarden's Guide [*A publication*] (DLA) ... Brooke Ch W
Brookes Deflection Potentiometer ... BDP
Brooke's Ecclesiastical Cases [*1850-72*] [*England*] [*A publication*] (DLA) ... Brooke
Brooke's Ecclesiastical Judgments [*A publication*] (DLA) ... Brooke Eccl Judg
Brooke's New Cases (Collected by Bellewe) [*A publication*] (DLA) ... Bell
Brooke's New Cases (Collected by Bellewe) [*A publication*] (DLA) ... Bell Cas T H VIII
Brooke's New Cases (Collected by Bellewe) [*A publication*] (DLA) ... Bellewe T H VIII
Brooke's New Cases, English King's Bench [*1515-58*] [*A publication*] (DLA) ... Bell Cas T Hen VIII
Brooke's New Cases, English King's Bench [*1515-58*] [*A publication*] (DLA) ... Bellewe's Ca Temp Hen VIII
Brooke's New Cases, English King's Bench [*1515-58*] [*A publication*] (DLA) ... BNC
Brooke's New Cases, English King's Bench [*1515-58*] [*A publication*] (DLA) ... Br NC
Brooke's New Cases, English King's Bench [*1515-58*] [*A publication*] (DLA) ... Br N Cas
Brooke's New Cases, English King's Bench [*1515-58*] [*A publication*] (DLA) ... Bro NC
Brooke's New Cases, English King's Bench [*1515-58*] [*A publication*] (DLA) ... Brooke
Brooke's New Cases, English King's Bench [*1515-58*] [*A publication*] (DLA) ... Brooke NC
Brooke's New Cases, English King's Bench [*1515-58*] [*A publication*] (DLA) ... Brooke (Petit)
Brooke's New Cases, English King's Bench [*1515-58*] [*A publication*] (DLA) ... Brook N Cas
Brooke's New Cases, English King's Bench [*1515-58*] [*A publication*] (DLA) ... Lit Brooke
Brooke's New Cases, English King's Bench [*1515-58*] [*A publication*] (DLA) ... Little Brooke
Brooke's New Cases (Petit Brooke) [*1515-58*] [*A publication*] (DLA) ... Pet Br
Brooke's Office and Practice of a Notary [*A publication*] (DLA) ... Br Not
Brooke's Office and Practice of a Notary [*A publication*] (DLA) ... Brooke Not
Brooke's Reading on the Statute of Limitations [*A publication*] (DLA) ... Brooke Lim
Brooke's Reading on the Statute of Limitations [*A publication*] (DLA) ... Bro Read
Brooke's Six Ecclesiastical Judgments [*A publication*] (DLA) ... Bro Ecc
Brooke's Six Ecclesiastical Judgments [*A publication*] (DLA) ... Brooke Eccl
Brooke's Six Ecclesiastical Judgments [*A publication*] (DLA) ... Brooke Six Judg
Brookfield [*Connecticut*] [*Seismograph station code, US Geological Survey*] (SEIS) ... BCT
Brookfield, CT [*AM radio station call letters*] ... WINE
Brookfield, CT [*FM radio station call letters*] ... WRKI
Brookfield Free Public Library, Brookfield, IL [*Library symbol*] [*Library of Congress*] (LCLS) ... IBro
Brookfield, MO [*Location identifier*] [*FAA*] (FAAL) ... BZK
Brookfield, MO [*AM radio station call letters*] ... KZBK
Brookfield, MO [*FM radio station call letters*] ... KZBK-FM
Brookfield Properties [*NYSE symbol*] ... BPO
Brookfield, WI [*FM radio station call letters*] (RBYB) ... WFMI
Brookfield, WI [*FM radio station call letters*] (BROA) ... WPNT-FM
Brookhaven Area Office [*Energy Research and Development Administration*] ... BAO
Brookhaven Area Office (SAUO) ... BK
Brookhaven Beam Research Reactor ... BBRR
Brookhaven Energy System Optimization Model (MCD) ... BESOM
Brookhaven Free Library, Brookhaven, NY [*Library symbol*] [*Library of Congress*] (LCLS) ... NBroo
Brookhaven Graphite Research Reactor ... BGRR
Brookhaven High Flux Reactor (SAUS) ... BHFR
Brookhaven Linac Isotope Producer [*Nuclear energy*] ... BLIP
Brookhaven Medical Reactor ... BMR
Brookhaven Medical Research Center ... BMRC
Brookhaven Medical Research Reactor (NRCH) ... BMRR
Brookhaven Memorial Hospital, Patchogue, NY [*Library symbol*] [*Library of Congress*] (LCLS) ... NPatBH
Brookhaven, MS [*Location identifier*] [*FAA*] (FAAL) ... BVV
Brookhaven, MS [*FM radio station call letters*] ... WBKN
Brookhaven, MS [*AM radio station call letters*] ... WCHJ
Brookhaven National Laboratory (EEVL) ... BHNL
Brookhaven National Laboratory [*Department of Energy*] [*Upton, NY*] ... BNL
Brookhaven National Laboratory, Upton, NY [*OCLC symbol*] (OCLC) ... ZBN
Brookhaven National Library (SAUO) ... BNL
Brookhaven Office [*AEC*] ... BH
Brookhaven Portable Cesium Developmental Irradiator Unit [*Nuclear energy*] ... BPCDI
Brookhaven Portable Cesium Developmental Irradiator unit (SAUS) ... BPCDI unit
Brookhaven Press, Washington, DC [*Library symbol*] [*Library of Congress*] (LCLS) ... BkP
Brookhaven Raster Display (SAUS) ... BRAD
Brookhaven Research Reactor ... BRR
Brookhaven Science Associates [*Nonprofit partnership*] ... BSA
Brookhaven Service Center [*IRS*] ... BSC
Brookhaven Town Hall, Historical Collection, Patchogue, NY [*Library symbol*] [*Library of Congress*] (LCLS) ... NPatB
Brookings [*South Dakota*] [*Airport symbol*] (OAG) ... BKX
Brookings Economics and Statistical Translator [*Computer science*] ... BEAST
Brookings Institute (SAUO) ... BI
Brookings Institution (EA) ... BI
Brookings Institution, Washington, DC [*Library symbol*] [*Library of Congress*] (LCLS) ... DBI
Brookings, OR [*Location identifier*] [*FAA*] (FAAL) ... BOK
Brookings, OR [*AM radio station call letters*] ... KURY
Brookings, OR [*FM radio station call letters*] ... KURY-FM
Brookings Public Library, Brookings, SD [*Library symbol*] [*Library of Congress*] (LCLS) ... SdBro
Brookings, SD [*AM radio station call letters*] ... KBRK
Brookings, SD [*FM radio station call letters*] ... KBRK-FM
Brookings, SD [*FM radio station call letters*] ... KESD
Brookings, SD [*Television station call letters*] ... KESD-TV
Brookings, SD [*FM radio station call letters*] ... KSDJ
Brook-Iroquois Public Library, Brook, IN [*Library symbol*] [*Library of Congress*] (LCLS) ... InBro
Brooklands [*British*] [*ICAO location identifier*] (ICLI) ... EGLB
Brooklands Automobile Racing Club (SAUO) ... BARC
Brookline Bancorp [*NASDAQ symbol*] (SG) ... BRKL
Brookline, MA [*FM radio station call letters*] ... WBOS
Brookline, MA [*AM radio station call letters*] ... WUNR
Brooklyn ... BKLN
Brooklyn [*New York*] (BARN) ... Bklyn
Brooklyn (SAUS) ... Bklyn
Brooklyn [*Diocesan abbreviation*] [*New York*] (TOCD) ... BRK
Brooklyn Academy of Music ... BAM
Brooklyn Army Terminal ... BART
Brooklyn Army Terminal (SAUO) ... BAT
Brooklyn Arts Museum (SAUS) ... BAM
Brooklyn Avenue School, Valley Stream, NY [*Library symbol*] [*Library of Congress*] (LCLS) ... NVsBAE
Brooklyn Bancorp, Inc. [*Associated Press*] (SAG) ... BklynBc
Brooklyn Bancorp, Inc. [*NASDAQ symbol*] (SAG) ... BRKB
Brooklyn Botanic Garden [*Brooklyn, NY*] ... BBG
Brooklyn Botanic Garden, Brooklyn, NY [*Library symbol*] [*Library of Congress*] (LCLS) ... NBG
Brooklyn Bridge (SAUS) ... Bklyn Brdg
Brooklyn, Bronx, and Queens [*New York City slang for nightclub or restaurant that has fallen out of favor with the pacesetters*] ... BBQ
Brooklyn Business Library ... BBL
Brooklyn Center for the Performing Arts at Brooklyn College ... BCBC
Brooklyn Children's Museum, Brooklyn, NY [*Library symbol*] [*Library of Congress*] (LCLS) ... NBCMu
Brooklyn Chronicle, Brooklyn, IA [*Library symbol*] [*Library of Congress*] (LCLS) ... IaBroC
Brooklyn College (SAUO) ... BC
Brooklyn College, Brooklyn, NY [*Library symbol*] [*Library of Congress*] (LCLS) ... NBC
Brooklyn College, Brooklyn, NY [*OCLC symbol*] (OCLC) ... VDB
Brooklyn College of Pharmacy, Brooklyn, NY [*Library symbol*] [*Library of Congress*] (LCLS) ... NBCP
Brooklyn College of the City University of New York (GAGS) ... Brooklyn C (CUNY)
Brooklyn Daily Record [*A publication*] (DLA) ... Brookl Rec
Brooklyn Daily Record [*A publication*] (DLA) ... Brooklyn Daily Rec
Brooklyn Dodgers [*National Football League*] [*1930-43*] (NFLA) ... BkD
Brooklyn Eastern District Terminal [*AAR code*] ... BEDT
Brooklyn Eckfords (SAUS) ... ECK
Brooklyn Entomological Society (SAUO) ... BES
Brooklyn Friends School, New York, NY [*Library symbol*] [*Library of Congress*] (LCLS) ... NBF
Brooklyn Homicide Task Force (SAUO) ... Bklyn HTF
Brooklyn Homicide Task Force (SAUS) ... Brooklyn HTF
Brooklyn, IA [*FM radio station call letters*] ... KSKB
Brooklyn Institute of Arts and Sciences ... BIAS
Brooklyn Law School [*New York, NY*] ... BLS
Brooklyn Law School (GAGS) ... Brooklyn Law
Brooklyn Law School, Brooklyn, NY [*Library symbol*] [*Library of Congress*] (LCLS) ... NBL
Brooklyn Law School, Brooklyn, NY [*OCLC symbol*] (OCLC) ... ZBL
Brooklyn Local Economic Development Corporation (SAUO) ... BLEDCO
Brooklyn, MI [*FM radio station call letters*] ... WKHM
Brooklyn Museum (SAUO) ... Bklyn Mus
Brooklyn Museum (SAUO) ... BM
[*The*] **Brooklyn Museum Aramaic Papyri** [*A publication*] (BJA) ... BMAP
Brooklyn Museum, Brooklyn, NY [*Library symbol*] [*Library of Congress*] (LCLS) ... NBB
Brooklyn Museum, Wilbour Library of Egyptology, Brooklyn, NY [*Library symbol*] [*Library of Congress*] (LCLS) ... NBB-E
Brooklyn, NY [*Location identifier*] [*FAA*] (FAAL) ... NOP
Brooklyn, NY [*FM radio station call letters*] ... WKRB
Brooklyn Opera Company (SAUO) ... BOC
Brooklyn Park, MN [*AM radio station call letters*] ... WLOL
Brooklyn Philharmonica Orchestra (SAUO) ... BPO
Brooklyn Polytechnic Institute (SAUO) ... BPI
Brooklyn Post Office (SAUO) ... BPO
Brooklyn Public Library [*New York, NY*] ... BPL

Brooklyn Public Library, Brooklyn, NY [Library symbol] [Library of Congress] (LCLS) .... NB
Brooklyn Public Library, Brooklyn, NY [Library symbol] [Library of Congress] (LCLS) .... NBPu
Brooklyn, Queens, Long Island [Section of New York Times] .... BQLI
Brooklyn Rapid Transit Co. [A New York City subway line] [Became BMT] .... BRT
Brooklyn Technical High School (SAUO) .... BTHS
Brooklyn Tigers [National Football League] [1944] (NFLA) .... BkT
Brooklyn Union Gas [NYSE symbol] (TTSB) .... BU
Brooklyn Union Gas Co. [Associated Press] (SAG) .... BklyUG
Brooklyn Union Gas Co. [Wall Street slang name: "Bug"] [NYSE symbol] (SPSG) .... BU
Brooklyn Union Gas Co. .... BUG
Brooklyn-Manhattan Transit Corp. [A New York City subway line] .... BMT
Brooklyn-Queens Expressway (SAUS) .... BQE
Brooklyn-Queens-Staten Island Health Sciences Group [Library network] .... BQSI
Brookmere Ventures [Vancouver Stock Exchange symbol] .... BKV
Brookneal, VA [AM radio station call letters] (RBYB) .... WODI-AM
Brookport, IL [Location identifier] [FAA] (FAAL) .... BDD
Brookport, IL [AM radio station call letters] .... WRIK
Brooks [Postal Service standard] (OPSA) .... BRKS
Brooks [Commonly used] (OPSA) .... BROOKS
Brooks, AB [AM radio station call letters] .... CIBQ
Brooks Art Gallery, Memphis, TN [Library symbol] [Library of Congress] (LCLS) .... TMBA
Brooks Automation [NASDAQ symbol] (TTSB) .... BRKS
Brooks Automation, Inc. [NASDAQ symbol] (SAG) .... BRKS
Brooks Automation, Inc. [Associated Press] (SAG) .... BrooksA
Brooks Automation, Inc. [Associated Press] (SAG) .... BrooksAu
Brooks Bird Club (EA) .... BBC
Brooks Brothers [Clothing store] .... B²
Brooks Fiber Properties [NASDAQ symbol] (TTSB) .... BFPT
Brooks Fiber Properties, Inc. [NASDAQ symbol] (SAG) .... BFPT
Brooks Fiber Properties, Inc. [Associated Press] (SAG) .... BrooksF
Brooks Free Library, Harwich, MA [Library symbol] [Library of Congress] (LCLS) .... MHar
Brooks Memorial Hospital Medical Center, Dunkirk, NY [Library symbol] [Library of Congress] (LCLS) .... NDunBH
Brooks Memorial Library, Brattleboro, VT [Library symbol] [Library of Congress] (LCLS) .... VtBrt
Brooks Public Library, Alberta [Library symbol] [National Library of Canada] (NLC) .... ABR
Brooks' Reports [106-119 Michigan] [A publication] (DLA) .... Brooks
Brooks Resources Corp. [Vancouver Stock Exchange symbol] .... BRC
Brookside Elementary School, Baldwin, NY [Library symbol] [Library of Congress] (LCLS) .... NBaldBE
Brookside Junior High School, North Merrick, NY [Library symbol] [Library of Congress] (LCLS) .... NNmBJ
Brookston, IN [FM radio station call letters] .... WEZV
Brookston, IN [FM radio station call letters] (BROA) .... WLFF-FM
Brookstone, Inc. [NASDAQ symbol] (SAG) .... BKST
Brookstone, Inc. [Associated Press] (SAG) .... Brookstn
Brooksville, FL [Location identifier] [FAA] (FAAL) .... BKV
Brooksville, FL [AM radio station call letters] .... WWJB
Brooksville, MS [FM radio station call letters] (RBYB) .... WAJV
Brooktree Corp. [Associated Press] (SAG) .... Brktree
Brooktree Corp. [NASDAQ symbol] (SPSG) .... BTRE
Brooktrout, Inc. [NASDAQ symbol] (SG) .... BRKT
Brooktrout Technologies, Inc. [NASDAQ symbol] (SAG) .... BRKT
Brooktrout Technology [NASDAQ symbol] (TTSB) .... BRKT
Brooktrout Technology, Inc. [Associated Press] (SAG) .... Broktrt
Brookview Elementary School, Rockford, IL [Library symbol] [Library of Congress] (LCLS) .... IRoBrE
Brookville American, Brookville, IN [Library symbol] [Library of Congress] (LCLS) .... InBrkvA
Brookville Democrat, Brookville, IN [Library symbol] [Library of Congress] (LCLS) .... InBrkvD
Brookville, NY [FM radio station call letters] .... WCWP
Brookville, PA [FM radio station call letters] (BROA) .... WBEU-FM
Brookville, PA [FM radio station call letters] .... WMKX
Brookwood, AL [Location identifier] [FAA] (FAAL) .... OKW
Brookwood Reservoir [California] [Seismograph station code, US Geological Survey] (SEIS) .... BKC
Broom and Hadley's Blackstone [A publication] (DLA) .... B & H Black
Broom and Hadley's Commentaries on the Laws of England [A publication] (DLA) .... Br & Had
Broom and Hadley's Commentaries on the Laws of England [A publication] (DLA) .... Broom & H Com
Broom and Hadley's Commentaries on the Laws of England [A publication] (DLA) .... Broom & H Comm
Broom and Whisk Makers (MHDB) .... BWM
Broom Closet .... BCL
Broom. Common Law [9th ed.] [1896] [A publication] (DLA) .... Br Com
Broom. Constitutional Law [3rd ed.] [1885] [A publication] (DLA) .... Br Cons Law
Broom. Constitutional Law [3rd ed.] [1885] [A publication] (DLA) .... Broom Const L
Broom on Parties to Actions [A publication] (DLA) .... Broom Part
Broom. Philosophy of Law [3rd ed.] [1883] [A publication] (DLA) ..... Broom Ph Law
Broom. Philosophy of Law [3rd ed.] [1883] [A publication] (DLA) .... Br Phil Law
Broome [Australia] [ICAO location identifier] (ICLI) .... APBR
Broome [Australia] [Airport symbol] (OAG) .... BME
Broome Regional Aboriginal Medical Service [Australia] .... BRAMS
Broome Technical Community College [New York] .... BTCC
Broome Technical Community College, Binghamton, NY [Library symbol] [Library of Congress] (LCLS) .... NBiBT
Broomfield, CO [Television station call letters] .... KBDI

Broom's Commentaries on the Common Law [A publication] (DLA) .... Bro Com
Broom's Commentaries on the Common Law [A publication] (DLA) ...... Broom CL
Broom's Commentaries on the Common Law [A publication] (DLA) .... Broom Com Law
Broom's Legal Maxims [A publication] (DLA) .... Br Leg Max
Broom's Legal Maxims [A publication] (DLA) .... Br Max
Broom's Legal Maxims [A publication] (DLA) .... Bro Leg Max
Broom's Legal Maxims [A publication] (DLA) .... Bro Max
Broom's Legal Maxims [A publication] (DLA) .... Broom
Broom's Legal Maxims [A publication] (DLA) .... Broom Leg Max
Broom's Legal Maxims [A publication] (DLA) .... Broom Max
Broomstick Cast [Medicine] (MELL) .... BSC
Brooten High School, Brooten, MN [Library symbol] [Library of Congress] (LCLS) .... MnBtH
Broth Filtrate [Microbiology] .... BF
Brothel (ABBR) .... BRTHL
Brother [or Brotherhood] .... B
Brother .... BR
Brother (GEAB) .... br
Brother (NTIO) .... Br
Brother (SAUS) .... Br
Brother (ADWA) .... Bro
Brother .... BRO
Brother (DMAA) .... bro
Brother (ROG) .... BROR
Brother to Brother International (EA) .... BBI
Brotherhood (ILCA) .... Bhd
Brotherhood .... BRTHD
Brotherhood Artists Association (SAUO) .... BAA
Brotherhood Association of Military Airmen .... BAMA
Brotherhood Commission (EA) .... BC
Brotherhood Movement (SAUO) .... BM
Brotherhood of Anglican Churchmen [Canada] .... BAC
Brotherhood of Associated Book Travelers (EA) .... BABT
Brotherhood of Boilermakers, Iron Shipbuilders, Blacksmiths, Forgers and Helpers (SAUO) .... BBF
Brotherhood of Book Travelers [Later, ABT] (EA) .... BBT
Brotherhood of Knights of the Black Pudding Tasters (EA) .... BKBPT
Brotherhood of Locomotive Engineers (NTPA) .... BLE
Brotherhood of Locomotive Engineers .... B of LE
Brotherhood of Locomotive Engineers State Legislative Board, Illinois (SRA) .... BLESLB-IL
Brotherhood of Locomotive Firemen and Enginemen [Later, United Transportation Union] [AFL-CIO] .... BLFE
Brotherhood of Locomotive Firemen and Enginemen [Later, United Transportation Union] [AFL-CIO] .... LFE
Brotherhood of Maintenance of Way Employees (SAUO) .... BMWE
[The] Brotherhood of Man under the Fatherhood of God [Journalistic slang for political platitudes; said to be taken from a speech by Hubert H. Humphrey] .... BOMFOG
Brotherhood of Marine Engineers [Later merged with MEBA] .... BME
Brotherhood of Marine Officers (EA) .... BMO
Brotherhood of Painters, Decorators, and Paperhangers of America [Later, IBPAT] (EA) .... B of PDPH of A
Brotherhood of Painters, Decorators, and Paperhangers of America [Later, IBPAT] .... BPDP
Brotherhood of Railroad Clerks (SAUO) .... BRC
Brotherhood of Railroad Signalmen (SAUO) .... B of Rs
Brotherhood of Railroad Signalmen (EA) .... B of RS
Brotherhood of Railroad Signalmen (SAUO) .... BRRS
Brotherhood of Railroad Signalmen (EA) .... BRS
Brotherhood of Railroad Signalmen of America (SAUO) .... BRSA
Brotherhood of Railroad Trainmen (SAUO) .... B of RT
Brotherhood of Railroad Trainmen [Later, United Transportation Union] (EA) .... BRT
Brotherhood of Railway, Airline and Steamship Clerks, Freight Handlers, Express and Station Employees (SAUO) .... BRAC
Brotherhood of Railway, Airline, and Steamship Clerks, Freight Handlers, Express and Station Employees (SAUO) .... BRASCFHESE
Brotherhood of Railway Airline and Steamship Clerks, Freight Handlers, Express and Station Employees (SAUS) .... Railway Employees Union
Brotherhood of Railway, Airline, and Steamship Clerks; Freight Handlers; Expressand Station Employees .... BRASC
Brotherhood of Railway and Airline Clerks (SAUO) .... BRAC
Brotherhood of Railway and Steamship Clerks, Freight Handlers, Express and Station Employees [Later, BRAC] (EA) .... BRSC
Brotherhood of Railway Carmen of America [Later, BRC of US & C] [AFL-CIO] (EA) .... BRC
Brotherhood of Railway Carmen of America (SAUO) .... BRCA
Brotherhood of Railway Carmen of America (SAUO) .... BRCofA
Brotherhood of Railway Carmen of America [Later, BRC of US & C] [AFL-CIO] (EA) .... BRC of A
Brotherhood of Railway Carmen of Amerika (SAUO) .... BRC
Brotherhood of Railway Carmen of the United States & Canada (SAUO) .... BRC of US&C
Brotherhood of Railway Carmen of the United States and Canada [AFL-CIO] (EA) .... BRC of US & C
Brotherhood of Railway Carmen of the United States and Canada (SAUO) .... BRCUSC
Brotherhood of Saint Andrew (EA) .... BSA
Brotherhood of Saint Andrew (EA) .... BStA
Brotherhood of Shoe and Allied Craftsmen (EA) .... BSAC
Brotherhood of Sleeping Car Porters (SAUO) .... B of SCP
Brotherhood of Sleeping Car Porters (IIA) .... BSCP
Brotherhood of Sleeping Car Porters [Later, BRAC] (EA) .... SCP

Brotherhood of St. Barnabas (SAUO) .... BSB
Brotherhood of St. Francis of Assisi (SAUO) .... BSFA
Brotherhood of St. Paul (SAUO) .... BSP
Brotherhood of the American Lutheran Church (SAUO) ... BALC
Brotherhood of the American Lutheran Church [Later, American Lutheran
 Church Men] (EA) .... BALC
Brotherhood of the Holy Cross [Anglican religious community] ...... BHC
Brotherhood of the Holy Cross (SAUO) .... BHCross
Brotherhood of the Holy Name (SAUO) .... BHN
Brotherhood of the Holy Name of Jesus (SAUO) .... BHN
Brotherhood of the Holy Trinity .... BHT
Brotherhood of the Jungle Cock (EA) .... BJC
Brotherhood of the Knights of the Vine (EA) .... BKV
Brotherhood of Traveling Jewelers (EA) .... BTJ
Brotherhood of Utility Workers of New England (EA) .. BUWNE
Brotherhood of Utility Workers of New England (EA) .. UWNE
Brotherhood Railway Carmen Division/Transportation Communications
 Union (EA) .... BRC/TCU
[A] Brotherhood Towards Education .... ABATE
Brother-in-Law (ADA) .... BIL
Brotherly (ABBR) .... BRY
Brotherly Love, Relief, and Truth [Freemasonry] ..... BLRT
Brothers .... BROS
Brothers (ADWA) .... bros
Brothers (WDAA) .... Bros
Brothers (SAUS) .... Bros
Brothers Air Service (SAUO) .... BASCO
Brothers and Sisters in Christ [An association] (EA) . BASIC
Brother's Brother Foundation (EA) .... BBF
Brothers for Christian Community (SAUO) .... BFCC
Brothers Gourmet Coffees [NASDAQ symbol] (SAG) ...... BEAN
Brothers Gourmet Coffees [Associated Press] (SAG) ... BroGour
Brothers of Charity (TOCD) .... fc
Brothers of Charity (TOCD) .... FC
Brothers of Charity of Spokane [Roman Catholic religious order] ... BCS
Brothers of Christian Instruction (TOCD) .... FIC
Brothers of Christian Instruction (TOCD) .... fIc
Brothers of Christian Instruction of Ploermel (SAUO) . La Mennais Brothers
Brothers of Christian Service (TOCD) .... BCS
Brothers of Mercy (TOCD) .... fmm
Brothers of Mercy (TOCD) .... FMM
Brothers of Our Lady, Mother of Mercy [Netherlands] (EAIO) .. BOLMM
Brothers of Our Lady, Mother of Mercy (TOCD) .... CFMM
Brothers of Our Lady of Mercy [Roman Catholic religious order] ... CFMM
Brothers of Our Lady of Providence (TOCD) .... olc
Brothers of Our Lady of Providence (TOCD) .... OLP
Brothers of Saint Pius X (TOCD) .... cspx
Brothers of St. Francis Xavier (TOCD) .... cfx
Brothers of St. Francis Xavier (TOCD) .... CFX
Brothers of St. Patrick (TOCD) .... fsp
Brothers of St. Patrick (TOCD) .... FSP
Brothers of St. Pius X [Roman Catholic religious order] .. CSPX
Brothers of the Christian Schools (SAUO) .... Christian Brothers
Brothers of the Christian Schools (TOCD) .... fsc
Brothers of the Christian Schools (TOCD) .... FSC
Brothers of the Congregation of Holy Cross (TOCD) ... CSC
Brothers of the Congregation of Our Lady of the Holy Rosary (TOCD) .. fsr
Brothers of the Congregation of Our Lady of the Holy Rosary (TOCD) .. FSR
Brothers of the Good Shepherd [Roman Catholic religious order] ... BGS
Brothers of the Holy Eucharist (TOCD) .... fse
Brothers of the Holy Eucharist (TOCD) .... FSE
Brothers of the Immaculate Heart of Mary (TOCD) ..... ihm
Brothers of the Immaculate Heart of Mary (TOCD) ..... IHM
Brothers of the Poor of St. Francis (TOCD) .... cfmm
Brothers of the Poor of St. Francis (TOCD) .... cfp
Brothers of the Sacred Heart (TOCD) .... sc
Brothers of the Sacred Heart (TOCD) .... SC
Brothers to All Men [An association] .... BAM
Brothers to All Men International (SAUO) .... BAM
Brothers to All Men International (EA) .... BAMI
Brothers United for Future Foreskins (EA) .... BUFF
Brothers-in-Law (ABBR) .... BRSNLW
Brough [British] [ICAO location identifier] (ICLI) .. EGNB
Brough's Law of Elections [A publication] (DLA) ..... Brough Elec
Brought (ADA) .... BROT
Brought .... BRT
Brought Down [Horse racing] .... B
Brought Down [Accounting] .... BD
Brought Forward [Business term] .... BF
Brought Forward (EBF) .... b/f
Brought Forward (SAUS) .... Brd Fwd
Brought Forward (SAUS) .... Bt Fwd
Brought in by Ambulance (WDAA) .... BIBA
Brought in by Police Department [Emergency medicine] (DAVI) . BIBPD
Brought in Dead [Medicine] .... BID
Brought into Service [Telecommunications] (TEL) ..... BIS
Brought on Charge (MCD) .... BOC
Brought Over [Business term] .... B/O
Brought Over (SAUS) .... BO
Brought Over (ROG) .... OB
Brought-in-By (HGAA) .... BIB
Broughton [Canada] [Airport symbol] (OAG) .... YVM
Broughton Hospital, Staff Library, Morganton, NC [Library symbol] [Library
 of Congress] (LCLS) .... NcMoBH
Broughton Island, NT [ICAO location identifier] (ICLI) . CYVM

Broughton's Indian Civil Procedure [A publication] (DLA) .. Bro Civ Proc
Broughton's Indian Civil Procedure [A publication] (DLA) .. Brough Civ Pro
Broulan Resources, Inc. [Toronto Stock Exchange symbol] .. BNR
Broun's Reports, Scotch Justiciary Court [1842-45] [A publication]
 (DLA) .... Bro Just
Broun's Reports, Scotch Justiciary Court [1842-45] [A publication]
 (DLA) .... Broun
Broun's Reports, Scotch Justiciary Court [1842-45] [A publication]
 (DLA) .... Broun Just
Brouwer General Pertubations Differential Correction Program
 (SAUS) .... BGPDC Program
Brouwer General Perturbations Differential Correction Program
 (MCD) .... BGPDC
Brouwer-Lyddane Orbit Generation Routine .... BROWRO
Brow (WDAA) .... BR
Broward Community College, Fort Lauderdale, FL [OCLC symbol]
 (OCLC) .... EDB
Broward Community College, Fort Lauderdale, FL [Library symbol] [Library
 of Congress] (LCLS) .... FFIB
Broward County Libraries Division, Fort Lauderdale, FL [Library symbol]
 [Library of Congress] (LCLS) .... FFIBL
Broward County Libraries Division, Pompano Beach, FL [OCLC symbol]
 (OCLC) .... FBR
Browbeat (ABBR) .... BRWBT
Browbeaten (ABBR) .... BRWBTN
Browbeating (ABBR) .... BRWBTG
Brower Exploration, Inc. [Vancouver Stock Exchange symbol] .. BRE
Browerville, MN [FM radio station call letters] ..... KXDL
Browerville Public School, Browerville, MN [Library symbol] [Library of
 Congress] (LCLS) .... MnBvP
Brown [Thoroughbred racing] .... BR
Brown (ADWA) .... Br
Brown (ADWA) .... Brn
Brown (VRA) .... brn
Brown (KSC) .... BRN
Brown .... BRWN
Brown [Telecommunications] (TEL) .... BWN
brown (SAUS) .... bwn
Brown Adipose Tissue [Physiology] .... BAT
Brown, Agency and Trusts [1868] [A publication] (ILCA) .. Bro Ag
Brown Ale and Mild Bitters [British] (DSUE) .... B and M
Brown Algorithm Simulator and Animator [Framework for software
 construction] [Brown University] (NITA) .... BALSA
Brown & Bigelow (EA) .... B&B
Brown & Bigelow (SAUO) .... BWB
Brown & Brown [NYSE symbol] (SG) .... BRO
Brown and Hemingway's Reports [53-58 Mississippi] [A publication]
 (DLA) .... Bro & H
Brown and Hemingway's Reports [53-58 Mississippi] [A publication]
 (DLA) .... Brown & H
Brown and Hemingway's Reports [53-58 Mississippi] [A publication]
 (DLA) .... Brown & Hemingway
Brown and McCall's Yorkshire Star Chamber [Yorkshire Archaeological
 Society Record, Series 44, 45, 51, 70] [A publication] (DLA) .. Bro & M
Brown and Rader's Reports [137 Missouri] [A publication] (DLA) . Br & R
Brown and Rader's Reports [137 Missouri] [A publication] (DLA) . Brown & R
Brown & Root, Inc., Technical Library, Houston, TX [Library symbol] [Library
 of Congress] (LCLS) .... TxHBR
Brown & Root International (ECON) .... BRI
Brown & Root North Africa (WDAA) .... BARNA
Brown & Root-Northrop .... BRN
Brown and Sharp (SAUS) .... B&S
Brown and Sharpe [Wire gauge] .... B & S
Brown and Sharpe Gauge .... B & SG
Brown & Sharpe Manufacturing Co. [NYSE symbol] (SPSG) . BNS
Brown & Sharpe Manufacturing Co. [Associated Press] (SAG) . BwnSh
Brown & Sharpe Mfg'A' [NYSE symbol] (TTSB) .... BNS
Brown and Sharpe Wire Gauge (SAUS) .... B&SWG
Brown & Williamson Tobacco Corp. .... B & W
Brown & Williamson Tobacco Corp. (SAUO) .... B&W
Brown & Williamson Tobacco Corp., Research Department Library,
 Louisville, KY [Library symbol] [Library of Congress] (LCLS) . KyLoBW
Brown Animal Sanatory Institution (SAUS) .... BASI
Brown Animal Sanitary Institution (SAUS) .... BASI
Brown Association Management Services, Inc. (SAUO) .. BAMSI
Brown Bag Institute (EA) .... BBI
Brown Bag Lunch (SAUS) .... BBL
Brown, Boveri & Co. Ltd. [Switzerland] .... BBC
Brown, Boveri-Krupp Reaktorbau [Germany] .... BB/KR
Brown Brothers Harriman (ECON) .... BBH
Brown City Public Library, Brown City, MI [Library symbol] [Library of
 Congress] (LCLS) .... MiBrc
Brown Co. (SAUO) .... BWN
Brown County Democrat, Nashville, IN [Library symbol] [Library of
 Congress] (LCLS) .... InNasD
Brown County Historical Society, Nashville, IN [Library symbol] [Library of
 Congress] (LCLS) .... InNasBHi
Brown County Hospital, Green Bay, WI [Library symbol] [Library of
 Congress] (LCLS) .... WGrBC
Brown County Library, Green Bay, WI [OCLC symbol] (OCLC) . GZG
Brown County Library, Green Bay, WI [Library symbol] [Library of
 Congress] (LCLS) .... WGr
Brown County Public Library, Nashville, IN [Library symbol] [Library of
 Congress] (LCLS) .... InNas

Brown County Recorder's Office, Nashville, IN [*Library symbol*] [*Library of Congress*] (LCLS) ... InNasCR
Brown, Durbin, and Evans [*Statisticians*] ... BDE
Brown Dwarf [*Astronomy*] ... BD
Brown Engineering Co. (KSC) ... BEC
Brown Engineering Company (SAUO) ... BEC
Brown Engineering Company (SAUO) ... BECO
Brown Female (SAUS) ... B/F
Brown Forman, Inc. [*NYSE symbol*] (SAG) ... BF
Brown Forman, Inc. [*Associated Press*] (SAG) ... BrnF
Brown Forman, Inc. [*Associated Press*] (SAG) ... BrwnFA
Brown Forman, Inc. [*Associated Press*] (SAG) ... BrwnFB
Brown Group, Inc. [*NYSE symbol*] (SPSG) ... BG
Brown Group, Inc. [*Associated Press*] (SAG) ... BrwnGp
Brown Group, Inc. (SAUO) ... BWS
Brown [*Alex*], **Inc.** [*Associated Press*] (SAG) ... AlexBrn
Brown [*Tom*], **Inc.** [*Associated Press*] (SAG) ... BrTom
Brown [*Tom*], **Inc.** [*NASDAQ symbol*] (SAG) ... TMBR
Brown, James H., Atlanta GA [*STAC*] ... BJH
Brown Leaf Area Index (SAUS) ... BLAI
Brown. Limitations as to Real Property [*1869*] [*A publication*] (DLA) ... Bro Lim
Brown. Limitations as to Real Property [*1869*] [*A publication*] (DLA) ... Bro RPL
Brown Line Positive ... BR/L
Brown Lung Association (EA) ... BLA
Brown Male (SAUS) ... BM
Brown Norway [*Rat variety*] ... BN
Brown Oil of Vitriol ... BOV
Brown on Agency and Trust [*A publication*] (DLA) ... Bro Ag
Brown on Fixtures [*A publication*] (DLA) ... Bro Fix
Brown on Forestalling, Regrating, and Monopolizing, with Cases [*A publication*] (DLA) ... Bro For
Brown Picton and Hornby Libraries (SAUS) ... BP&HL
Brown Planthopper [*Entomology*] ... BPH
Brown Public Library, Northfield, VT [*Library symbol*] [*Library of Congress*] (LCLS) ... VtN
Brown Sedge Growth with Brown Sedge [*Ecology*] ... BB
Brown Shoe [*NYSE symbol*] (SG) ... BWS
Brown Shoe Co. Inc. (SAUO) ... BWS
Brown Stem Rot [*Plant pathology*] ... BSR
Brown Stock Washer [*Pulp and paper technology*] ... BSW
Brown Strachan Associates, Vancouver, BC, Canada [*Library symbol*] [*Library of Congress*] (LCLS) ... CaBVaBS
Brown Strachan Associates, Vancouver, British Columbia [*Library symbol*] [*National Library of Canada*] (NLC) ... BVABS
Brown Swiss Cattle Breeders Association of America (SAUO) ... BSCBA
Brown Swiss Cattle Breeders Association of the USA (EA) ... BSCBA
Brown, Tax Strategies for Separation and Divorce (SAUS) ... TSSD
Brown Tin (SAUS) ... B-TiN
Brown. Treatise on Law of Sale [*Scotland*] [*A publication*] (DLA) ... Bro Sal
Brown Tree Snake Control Program (COE) ... BTSCP
Brown Trout Club (EA) ... BTC
Brown University (GAGS) ... Brown U
Brown University (SAUO) ... BrUniv
Brown University (SAUO) ... BU
Brown University [*Rhode Island*] ... BU
Brown University, Annmary Brown Memorial Library, Providence, RI [*Library symbol*] [*Library of Congress*] (LCLS) ... RPAB
Brown University Display for Working Set References ... BUDWSR
Brown University Graphic System ... BUGS
Brown University Interactive Language (SAUO) ... BRUIN Language
Brown University Interpreter [*Computer science*] ... BRUIN
Brown University, John Hay Library of Rare Books annd Special Collections, Providence, RI [*Library symbol*] [*Library of Congress*] (LCLS) ... RPB-JH
Brown University Library (SAUO) ... BUL
Brown University Press (SAUO) ... Brown U Pr
Brown University, Providence, RI [*OCLC symbol*] (OCLC) ... RBN
Brown University, Providence, RI [*Library symbol*] [*Library of Congress*] (LCLS) ... RPB
Brown University, Sciences Library, Providence, RI [*Library symbol*] [*Library of Congress*] (LCLS) ... RPB-S
Brown Wrapping Paper (OA) ... BWP
Brown-Curtis Turbine (SAUS) ... BCT
Browndale Community Library, Browndale, AB, Canada [*Library symbol*] [*Library of Congress*] (LCLS) ... CaABrC
Browne. Actions at Law [*1843*] [*A publication*] (DLA) ... Bro Ac
Browne. Actions at Law [*1843*] [*A publication*] (DLA) ... Bro Act
Browne. Actions at Law [*1843*] [*A publication*] (DLA) ... Browne Act
Browne and Gray's Reports [*A publication*] (DLA) ... Browne & G
Browne and Gray's Reports [*A publication*] (DLA) ... Browne & Gray
Browne and MacNamara. Railway Cases [*A publication*] (DLA) ... B & Macn
Browne and MacNamara's English Railway and Canal Cases [*A publication*] (DLA) ... Browne & MacN
Browne and MacNamara's Railway Cases [*A publication*] (DLA) ... B & M
Browne and MacNamara's Railway Cases [*A publication*] (DLA) ... B & Mac
Browne and MacNamara's Railway Cases [*A publication*] (DLA) ... Bro & M
Browne and MacNamara's Railway Cases [*A publication*] (DLA) ... Bro & Mac
Browne and MacNamara's Railway Cases [*A publication*] (DLA) ... Brown & MacN
Browne and Theobald. Railways [*4th ed.*] [*1911*] [*A publication*] (DLA) ... Browne & Th Railw
Browne, Bortz & Coddington, Inc. [*Denver, CO*] [*Telecommunications*] (TSSD) ... BBC
Browne. Georgia Pleading and Practice and Legal Forms, Annotated [*A publication*] (DLA) ... Brown GA Pl & Pr Anno
Browne. Law of Carriers [*1873*] [*A publication*] (DLA) ... Bro Car
Browne. Law of Rating of Hereditaments [*2nd ed.*] [*1886*] [*A publication*] (DLA) ... Bro Hered
Browne on Carriers [*A publication*] (DLA) ... Browne Car
Browne on the Companies' Acts [*A publication*] (DLA) ... Bro Co Act
Browne on the Statute of Frauds [*A publication*] (DLA) ... Bro Fr
Browne on the Statute of Frauds [*A publication*] (DLA) ... Bro St Fr
Browne on the Statute of Frauds [*A publication*] (DLA) ... Browne Fr
Browne on the Statute of Frauds [*A publication*] (DLA) ... Browne St Frauds
Browne on Trade Markets [*A publication*] (DLA) ... Bro Tr M
Browne on Trade Markets [*A publication*] (DLA) ... Browne Tr M
Browne on Usages and Customs [*A publication*] (DLA) ... Browne Us
Browne. Practice in Divorce and Matrimonial Causes [*11th ed.*] [*1931*] [*A publication*] (DLA) ... Browne Div Pr
Browned-Off Passed-Over (SAA) ... BOPO
Browne's Civil and Admiralty Law [*A publication*] (DLA) ... Bro C & AL
Browne's Civil and Admiralty Law [*A publication*] (DLA) ... Bro Civ Law
Browne's Civil and Admiralty Law [*A publication*] (DLA) ... Browne Civ L
Browne's Civil and Admiralty Law [*A publication*] (DLA) ... Browne Civ Law
Browne's Civil Procedure Reports [*New York*] [*A publication*] (DLA) ... Browne
Browne's Digest of Decisions on Divorce and Alimony [*A publication*] (DLA) ... Bro Dig Div
Browne's Divorce Court Practice [*A publication*] (DLA) ... Bro Div Pr
Browne's Divorce Court Practice [*A publication*] (DLA) ... Browne Div
Browne's Judicial Interpretation of Common Words and Phrases [*A publication*] (DLA) ... Browne Jud Interp
Browne's Law of Usages and Customs [*A publication*] (DLA) ... Bro Us & Cus
Browne's Medical Jurisprudence of Insanity [*A publication*] (DLA) ... Bro Ins
Browne's National Bank Cases [*A publication*] (DLA) ... Bro NB Cas
Browne's National Bank Cases [*A publication*] (DLA) ... Browne Bank Cas
Browne's National Bank Cases [*A publication*] (DLA) ... Browne NBC
Browne's New Abridgment of Cases in Equity [*A publication*] (DLA) ... Bro Abr in Eq
Browne's Parliamentary and Municipal Registration Act [*A publication*] (DLA) ... Bro Reg Act
Browne's Patent Office Practice [*A publication*] (DLA) ... Bro Pat Pr
Browne's Pennsylvania Reports [*1801-14*] [*A publication*] (DLA) ... Bro PA
Browne's Practice of the High Court of Chancery [*A publication*] (DLA) ... Bro Ch Pr
Browne's Probate Practice [*A publication*] (DLA) ... Bro Prob Pr
Browne's Probate Practice [*A publication*] (ILCA) ... Browne Prob
Browne's Probate Practice [*A publication*] (DLA) ... Browne Prob Pr
Browne's Reports [*Sri Lanka*] [*A publication*] (DLA) ... Bro
Browne's Reports [*Pennsylvania*] [*A publication*] (DLA) ... Bro
Browne's Reports [*Pennsylvania*] [*A publication*] (DLA) ... Browne
Browne's Reports [*Sri Lanka*] [*A publication*] (DLA) ... Browne
Browne's Reports [*Massachusetts*] [*A publication*] (DLA) ... Browne
Browne's Reports [*Pennsylvania*] [*A publication*] (DLA) ... Browne (PA)
Browne's Reports [*Pennsylvania*] [*A publication*] (DLA) ... Browne PA R
Browne's Reports [*Pennsylvania*] [*A publication*] (DLA) ... Browne's Rep
Browne's Reports [*Pennsylvania*] [*A publication*] (DLA) ... Brown's (Penn)
Browne's Reports [*Pennsylvania*] [*A publication*] (DLA) ... Brown's Penn Rep
Browne's Reports [*Ceylon*] [*A publication*] (DLA) ... Br R
Browne's Reports [*Pennsylvania*] [*A publication*] (DLA) ... PA Browne R
Browne's Reports (Pennsylvania) [*A publication*] (DLA) ... PA Browne (PA)
Brownfield Public Library, Alberta [*Library symbol*] [*National Library of Canada*] (NLC) ... ABROW
Brownfield, TX [*Location identifier*] [*FAA*] (FAAL) ... BFE
Brownfield, TX [*AM radio station call letters*] ... KKUB
Brownfield, TX [*FM radio station call letters*] ... KLZK
Brown-Firth Research Laboratories (SAUO) ... BF
Brown-Firth Research Laboratories (SAUO) ... BFRL
Brown-Forman Cl'B' [*NYSE symbol*] (TTSB) ... BFB
Brown-Forman Inc. 4% Pfd [*NYSE symbol*] (TTSB) ... BFPr
Brown-Forman Industries (SAUO) ... BFI
Brown-Forman'A' [*NYSE symbol*] (TTSB) ... BFA
Brownian Dynamics Simulation (AAEL) ... BDS
Browning Aircraft Machine Gun ... BAMG
Browning and Lushington on Marriage and Divorce [*A publication*] (DLA) ... Bro & Lush M & D
Browning and Lushington on Marriage and Divorce [*A publication*] (DLA) ... Brown & Lush M & D
Browning and Lushington's English Admiralty Reports [*1863-65*] [*A publication*] (DLA) ... B & L
Browning and Lushington's English Admiralty Reports [*1863-65*] [*A publication*] (DLA) ... Br & L
Browning and Lushington's English Admiralty Reports [*1863-65*] [*A publication*] (DLA) ... Br & Lush
Browning and Lushington's English Admiralty Reports [*1863-65*] [*A publication*] (DLA) ... Bro & L
Browning and Lushington's English Admiralty Reports [*1863-65*] [*A publication*] (DLA) ... Bro & Lush
Browning and Lushington's English Admiralty Reports [*1863-65*] [*A publication*] (DLA) ... Brown & L
Browning and Lushington's English Admiralty Reports [*1863-65*] [*A publication*] (DLA) ... Brown & L (Eng)
Browning and Lushington's English Admiralty Reports [*1863-65*] [*A publication*] (DLA) ... Brown & Lush
Browning Automatic Rifle ... BAR
Browning Ferris [*NYSE symbol*] (SAG) ... BFE
Browning Ferris [*NYSE symbol*] (SAG) ... BFI
Browning Ferris [*Associated Press*] (SAG) ... BrnFAC
Browning Ferris [*Associated Press*] (SAG) ... BrwnFr
Browning Ferris Industry (SAUS) ... BFI
Browning Institute (EA) ... BI
Browning Machine Gun ... BMG

Browning on Marriage and Divorce [*A publication*] (DLA) .... Bro M & D
Browning on Marriage and Divorce [*A publication*] (DLA) .... Brown M & D
Browning-Ferries Industries, Inc. (SAUO) .... BFI
Browning-Ferris 7.25% 'ACES' [*NYSE symbol*] (TTSB) .... BFE
Browning-Ferris Industries, Inc. [*NYSE symbol*] (SPSG) .... BFI
Browning-Ferris Industries, Inc. [*Associated Press*] (SAG) .... BrwnFr
Browning's Divorce Court Practice [*A publication*] (DLA) .... Brown Div Pr
Brownish [*Philately*] .... brnsh
Brownish (SAUS) .... Brnsh
Brownish Pink (SAUS) .... BrPk
Brownish-Black .... BB
Brownlow and Goldesborough's English Common Pleas Reports [*A publication*] (DLA) .... Br & G
Brownlow and Goldesborough's English Common Pleas Reports [*A publication*] (DLA) .... Br & Gold
Brownlow and Goldesborough's English Common Pleas Reports [*A publication*] (DLA) .... Bro & G
Brownlow and Goldesborough's English Common Pleas Reports [*A publication*] (DLA) .... Brown
Brownlow and Goldesborough's English Common Pleas Reports [*A publication*] (DLA) .... Brown & G (Eng)
Brownlow and Goldesborough's English Common Pleas Reports [*A publication*] (DLA) .... Brown & Gold
Brownlow and Goldesborough's English Common Pleas Reports [*A publication*] (DLA) .... Brownl
Brownlow and Goldesborough's English Common Pleas Reports [*A publication*] (DLA) .... Brownl & G
Brownlow and Goldesborough's English Common Pleas Reports [*A publication*] (DLA) .... Brownl & Gold
Brownlow and Goldesborough's Nisi Prius Reports [*1569-1624*] [*England*] [*A publication*] (DLA) .... B & G
Brownlow's Brevia Judicialia, Etc. [*1662*] [*A publication*] (DLA) .... Br Brev Jud
Brownlow's Brevia Judicialia, Etc. [*1662*] [*A publication*] (DLA) .... Br Brev Jud & Ent
Brownlow's Brevia Judicialia, Etc. [*1662*] [*A publication*] (DLA) .... Brow Brev
Brownlow's Brevia Judicialia, Etc. [*1662*] [*A publication*] (DLA) .... Brownl Brev
Brownlow's Entries [*A publication*] (DLA) .... Br Ent
Brownlow's Entries [*A publication*] (DLA) .... Brown Ent
Brownlow's Entries [*A publication*] (DLA) .... Brownl Ent
Brownlow's Latine Redivivus [*or Entries*] [*A publication*] (DLA) .... Bro Ent
Brownlow's Latine Redivivus [*or Entries*] [*A publication*] (DLA) .... Brownl Redv
Brown-Roberts-Wells [*Computerized tomographic stereotaxic guide*] [*Radiology*] (DAVI) .... BRW
Brown's Cases in Parliament [*A publication*] (DLA) .... BPC
Brown's Cases in Parliament [*A publication*] (DLA) .... Bro Parl Cas
Brown's Chancery Cases [*England*] [*A publication*] (DLA) .... BCC
Brown's Chancery Cases [*England*] [*A publication*] (DLA) .... BCR
Brown's Chancery Cases [*England*] [*A publication*] (DLA) .... BC Rep
Brown's Chancery Cases [*England*] [*A publication*] (DLA) .... Br CC
Brown's Chancery Cases [*England*] [*A publication*] (DLA) .... Br PC
Brown's Chancery Cases Tempore Lord Thurlow [*England*] [*A publication*] (DLA) .... Brown Ch
Brown's Chancery Cases Tempore Lord Thurlow [*England*] [*A publication*] (DLA) .... Brown Ch C
Brown's English Chancery Cases [*or Reports*] [*A publication*] (DLA) .... Bro CC
Brown's English Chancery Cases [*or Reports*] [*A publication*] (DLA) .... Brown C
Brown's English Chancery Cases [*or Reports*] [*A publication*] (DLA) .... Brown CC
Brown's English Chancery Reports [*28, 29 English Reprint*] [*A publication*] (DLA) .... Bro
Brown's English Chancery Reports [*28, 29 English Reprint*] [*A publication*] (DLA) .... Bro Ch
Brown's English Chancery Reports [*28, 29 English Reprint*] [*A publication*] (DLA) .... Bro Ch Cas
Brown's English Chancery Reports [*28, 29 English Reprint*] [*A publication*] (DLA) .... Bro Ch R
Brown's English Chancery Reports [*28, 29 English Reprint*] [*A publication*] (DLA) .... Brown
Brown's English Ecclesiastical Reports [*A publication*] (DLA) .... Brown Ecc
Brown's English Nisi Prius Cases [*A publication*] (DLA) .... Bro NP
Brown's English Nisi Prius Cases [*A publication*] (DLA) .... Brown NP Cas
Brown's English Parliamentary Cases [*A publication*] (DLA) .... Bro PC
Brown's English Parliamentary Cases [*A publication*] (DLA) .... Brown
Brown's Entries [*A publication*] (DLA) .... Bro Ent
Brown's Epitome and Analysis of Savigny's Treatise on Obligations in Roman Law [*A publication*] (DLA) .... Brown's Roman Law
Browns Ferry Nuclear Plant (NRCH) .... BFNP
Browns Ferry Nuclear Power Plant (NRCH) .... BFNPP
Brown's Formulae Bene Placitandi [*A publication*] (DLA) .... Bro Form
Brown's Formulae Bene Placitandi [*A publication*] (ILCA) .... Form Pla
Brown's Forum [*A publication*] (DLA) .... Bro For
Brown's House of Lords Cases [*England*] [*A publication*] (DLA) .... Brown Parl
Brown's House of Lords Cases [*England*] [*A publication*] (DLA) .... Brown Parl Cas
Brown's House of Lords Cases [*England*] [*A publication*] (DLA) .... Brown PC
Brown's Law Dictionary [*A publication*] (DLA) .... Bro Law Dic
Brown's Law Dictionary [*A publication*] (DLA) .... Brown
Brown's Law Dictionary [*A publication*] (DLA) .... Brown Dict
Brown's Law Dictionary and Institute [*1874*] [*A publication*] (DLA) .... Brown
Brown's Michigan Nisi Prius Reports [*A publication*] (DLA) .... Bro
Brown's Michigan Nisi Prius Reports [*A publication*] (DLA) .... Bro NP
Brown's Michigan Nisi Prius Reports [*A publication*] (DLA) .... Brown
Brown's Michigan Nisi Prius Reports [*A publication*] (DLA) .... Brown NP
Brown's Michigan Nisi Prius Reports [*A publication*] (DLA) .... Brown NP (Mich)
Brown's Michigan Nisi Prius Reports [*A publication*] (DLA) .... Mich Nisi Prius
Brown's Michigan Nisi Prius Reports [*A publication*] (DLA) .... Mich NP
Brown's Modus Intrandi [*A publication*] (DLA) .... Mod Int
Brown's Parliamentary Cases [*England*] [*A publication*] (DLA) .... Bro
Brown's Parliamentary Reports [*England*] [*A publication*] (DLA) .... BPR
Brown's Parties to Actions [*A publication*] (DLA) .... Br Par
Browns Practice or Precedents in Chance (SAUS) .... Prax
Brown's Practice (Praxis) [*or Precedents*] **in Chancery** [*A publication*] (DLA) .... Bro Prac
Brown's Practice (Praxis) [*or Precedents*] **in Chancery** [*A publication*] (DLA) .... Prax
Brown's Reports [*53-65, 80-136 Missouri*] [*A publication*] (DLA) .... Bro
Brown's Reports [*80-137 Missouri*] [*A publication*] (DLA) .... Brown
Brown's Reports [*4-25 Nebraska*] [*A publication*] (DLA) .... Brown
Brown's Reports [*53-65 Mississippi*] [*A publication*] (DLA) .... Brown
Brown's Scotch Reports [*A publication*] (DLA) .... Brown
Brown's Supplement to Morison's Dictionary of Decisions, Scotch Court of Sessions [*A publication*] (DLA) .... Bro Sup to Mor
Brown's Supplement to Morison's Dictionary of Decisions, Scotch Court of Sessions [*A publication*] (DLA) .... BS
Brown's Supplement to Morison's Dictionary, Scotch Court of Sessions [*A publication*] (DLA) .... Bro Supp
Brown's Supplement to Morison's Dictionary, Scotch Court of Sessions [*A publication*] (DLA) .... Brown Sup
Brown's Supplement to Morison's Dictionary, Scotch Court of Sessions [*A publication*] (DLA) .... Brown Sup Dec
Brown's Supplement to Morison's Dictionary, Scotch Court of Sessions [*A publication*] (DLA) .... Br Sup
Brown's Synopsis of Decisions, Scotch Court of Sessions [*1540-1827*] [*A publication*] (DLA) .... Bro Syn
Brown's Synopsis of Decisions, Scotch Court of Sessions [*1540-1827*] [*A publication*] (DLA) .... Bro Synop
Brown's Synopsis of Decisions, Scotch Court of Sessions [*1540-1827*] [*A publication*] (DLA) .... Brown Syn
Brown's Synopsis of Decisions, Scotch Court of Sessions [*1540-1827*] [*A publication*] (DLA) .... Br Syn
Brown's United States Admiralty Reports [*A publication*] (DLA) .... Bro Adm
Brown's United States Admiralty Reports [*A publication*] (DLA) .... Brown
Brown's United States Admiralty Reports [*A publication*] (DLA) .... Brown Adm
Brown's United States Admiralty Reports (Appendix) [*A publication*] (DLA) .... Brown's Adm App
Brown's United States District Court Reports [*A publication*] (DLA) .... Brown
Brown's United States District Court Reports (Admiralty and Revenue Cases) [*A publication*] (DLA) .... Bro A & R
Brown's United States District Court Reports (Admiralty and Revenue Cases) [*A publication*] (DLA) .... Brown A & R
Brown's Vade Mecum [*A publication*] (DLA) .... Bro VM
Brownsburg Guide, Brownsburg, IN [*Library symbol*] [*Library of Congress*] (LCLS) .... InBrbG
Brownsburg, IN [*FM radio station call letters*] .... WQFE
Brownsburg Public Library, Brownsburg, IN [*Library symbol*] [*Library of Congress*] (LCLS) .... InBrb
Brown-Sequard [*Disease*] [*Medicine*] (DB) .... BS
Brownshall [*England*] .... BROWNS
Brownstone (ADWA) .... brwnstn
Brownstone Revival Committee (EA) .... BRC
Brownstown Banner, Brownstown, IN [*Library symbol*] [*Library of Congress*] (LCLS) .... InBrtB
Brownstown Community School District No. 201, Brownstown, IL [*Library symbol*] [*Library of Congress*] (LCLS) .... IBrowSD
Brownstown Public Library, Brownstown, IN [*Library symbol*] [*Library of Congress*] (LCLS) .... InBrt
Brownsville [*Texas*] [*Airport symbol*] (OAG) .... BRO
Brownsville [*Diocesan abbreviation*] [*Texas*] (TOCD) .... BWN
Brownsville Historical Association, Brownsville, TX [*Library symbol*] [*Library of Congress*] (LCLS) .... TxBHi
Brownsville, OR [*FM radio station call letters*] (RBYB) .... KEHK-FM
Brownsville, OR [*FM radio station call letters*] .... KLRF
Brownsville, PA [*AM radio station call letters*] .... WASP
Brownsville, TN [*AM radio station call letters*] .... WNWS
Brownsville, TN [*FM radio station call letters*] .... WTBG
Brownsville, TX [*FM radio station call letters*] .... KBNR
Brownsville, TX [*AM radio station call letters*] .... KBOR
Brownsville, TX [*FM radio station call letters*] .... KKPS
Brownsville, TX [*FM radio station call letters*] .... KTEX
Brownsville, TX [*Television station call letters*] .... KVEO
Brownsville, TX [*Location identifier*] [*FAA*] (FAAL) .... MIH
Brownsville/International [*Texas*] [*ICAO location identifier*] (ICLI) .... KBRO
Brown-Symmers [*Disease*] [*Medicine*] (DB) .... BS
Brownton Public Schools, Brownton, MN [*Library symbol*] [*Library of Congress*] (LCLS) .... MnBroPS
Browntown Public Library, Browntown, MN [*Library symbol*] [*Library of Congress*] (LCLS) .... MnBro
Brownvale Community Library, Alberta [*Library symbol*] [*National Library of Canada*] (NLC) .... ABC
Brownwood [*Texas*] [*Airport symbol*] (OAG) .... BWD
Brownwood Public Library, Brownwood, TX [*Library symbol*] [*Library of Congress*] (LCLS) .... TxBrd
Brownwood, TX [*FM radio station call letters*] (BROA) .... KBUB-FM
Brownwood, TX [*AM radio station call letters*] .... KBWD
Brownwood, TX [*FM radio station call letters*] (BROA) .... KHPU-FM
Brownwood, TX [*FM radio station call letters*] .... KOXE
Brownwood, TX [*FM radio station call letters*] (BROA) .... KPBE-FM
Brownwood, TX [*FM radio station call letters*] .... KPSM
Brownwood, TX [*AM radio station call letters*] .... KXYL
Brownwood, TX [*FM radio station call letters*] .... KXYL-FM
Brows, Lids, and Lashes [*Anatomy*] (DAVI) .... BLL
Browse (ABBR) .... BRWS

Browsed (ABBR) ... BRWSD
Browsing (ABBR) ... BRWSG
Browsing On-Line with Selective Retrieval ... BROWSER
Broxton, GA [*FM radio station call letters*] ... WULS
Broyden-Fletcher-Goldfarb-Shanno optimization algorithm (SAUS) ... BFGS
Broye-Les-Pesmes [*France*] [*ICAO location identifier*] (ICLI) ... LFYH
BRT Realty Trust [*Associated Press*] (SAG) ... BRT
BRT Realty Trust SBI [*NYSE symbol*] (TTSB) ... BRT
Brtish Medical Protection Society (SAUO) ... BMPS
Bruccoli-Clark Publishers ... BCP
Bruce and Williams. Admiralty Jurisdiction [*A publication*] (DLA) ... Bru & Wil Adm
Bruce Artwick Organization (SAUS) ... BAO
Bruce Boxleitner Fan Club (EA) ... BBFC
Bruce County Museum, Southampton, Ontario [*Library symbol*] [*National Library of Canada*] (BIB) ... OSOM
Bruce County Public Library, Port Elgin, ON, Canada [*Library symbol*] [*Library of Congress*] (LCLS) ... CaOPteB
Bruce County Public Library, Port Elgin, Ontario [*Library symbol*] [*National Library of Canada*] (NLC) ... OPEB
Bruce Maximal Stress Test (DB) ... BMST
Bruce Maximum Stress Test [*Medicine*] (DMAA) ... BMST
Bruce Mines & Plummer Additional Union Public Library, Bruce Mines, ON, Canada [*Library symbol*] [*Library of Congress*] (LCLS) ... CaOBMP
Bruce Mines and Plummer Additional Union Public Library, Bruce Mines, Ontario [*Library symbol*] [*National Library of Canada*] (NLC) ... OBMP
Bruce Peel Special Collections Library, University of Alberta, Edmonton, Alberta [*Library symbol*] [*National Library of Canada*] (NLC) ... AEUS
Bruce, Principia Juris Feudalis [*A publication*] (DLA) ... Bru Princip
Bruce Trail Association (EA) ... BTA
Brucella [*Bacteriology*] ... B
Brucella [*Bacteriology*] (AAMN) ... BR
Brucella (DB) ... Bruc
Brucella Agglutinins [*Bacteriology*] (DAVI) ... BRUCL
Brucella Ring Test [*Dairy science*] (OA) ... BRT
Brucella, Vitamin K Blood Agar [*Bacteriology*] (DAVI) ... BRBA
Brucellosis and Tuberculosis Eradication Campaign (SAUO) ... BTEC
Brucellosis and Tuberculosis Eradication Campaign Committee (SAUO) ... BTECC
Brucellosis Information System [*Department of Agriculture*] (GFGA) ... BIS
Brucellus Abortus [*Bacteriology*] ... BA
Bruce's Military Law [*A publication*] (DLA) ... Bru ML
Bruce's Scotch Court of Session Reports [*1714-15*] [*A publication*] (DLA) ... Br
Bruce's Scotch Court of Session Reports [*1714-15*] [*A publication*] (DLA) ... Bru
Bruce's Scotch Court of Session Reports [*1714-15*] [*A publication*] (DLA) ... Bruce
Bruckner Society of America (EA) ... BSA
Bruder [*Brother*] [*Freemasonry*] [*German*] (ROG) ... B
Bruderheim Municipal Library, Alberta [*Library symbol*] [*National Library of Canada*] (NLC) ... ABRUM
Bruderheim Municipal Library, Bruderheim, AB, Canada [*Library symbol*] [*Library of Congress*] (LCLS) ... CaABruM
Brudzinski, Oppenheim, Chaddock, and Gullaird [*Reflexes and signs*] [*Neurology*] (DAVI) ... BOCG
Bruedern [*Brethren*] [*Freemasonry*] [*German*] ... B'n
Bruggemeyer Memorial Library, Monterey Park Public Library, Monterey Park, CA [*Library symbol*] [*Library of Congress*] (LCLS) ... CMp
Bruggen [*Germany*] [*ICAO location identifier*] (ICLI) ... EDUR
Bruininks-Oseretsky Balance Subtest [*Occupational therapy*] ... BOBS
Bruininks-Oseretsky Test of Motor Proficiency [*Occupational therapy*] ... BOTMP
Bruise (ABBR) ... BRUS
Bruised (ABBR) ... BRUSD
Bruiser (ABBR) ... BRUSR
Bruising (ABBR) ... BRUSG
Bruit [*Medicine*] (MELL) ... B
Brule, WI [*FM radio station call letters*] ... WHSA
Brumado [*Brazil*] [*Airport symbol*] (OAG) ... BMS
Brunauer-Emmett-Teller [*Adsorption equation*] ... BET
Brunauer-Emmett-Teller Equation (SAUS) ... BET Equation
Brunauer-Emmett-Teller Isotherm [*Adsorption isotherm equation*] ... BET Isotherm
Brunauer-Emmett-Teller Method (SAUS) ... BET Method
Bruncor, Inc. [*Toronto Stock Exchange symbol*] ... BRR
Brundidge, AL [*FM radio station call letters*] (BROA) ... WTBF-FM
Bruneau District Library, Bruneau, ID [*Library symbol*] [*Library of Congress*] (LCLS) ... IdBr
Brunei [*MARC geographic area code*] [*Library of Congress*] ... a-bx-
Brunei (BARN) ... B
Brunei [*International vehicle registration*] (ODBW) ... BRU
Brunei (MILB) ... Bru
Brunei ... BRUN
Brunei [*MARC country of publication code*] [*Library of Congress*] (LCCP) ... bx
Brunei Broadcasting Service ... BBS
Brunei Darussalam [*ANSI two-letter standard code*] (CNC) ... BN
Brunei Darussalam [*ANSI three-letter standard code*] (CNC) ... BRN
Brunei Darussalam [*Aircraft nationality and registration mark*] (FAAC) ... V8
Brunei Darussalam National Committee for Pacific Economic Cooperation ... BDCPEC
Brunei, Indonesia, Malaysia, Philippines [*International trade*] ... BIMP
Brunei, Indonesia, Malaysia, Philippines East Asian Growth Area [*International trade*] ... BIMP-EAGA
Brunei National Democratic Party [*Political party*] (FEA) ... BNDP
Brunei National United Party [*Political party*] (EY) ... BNUP
Brunei People's Independence Front [*Political party*] (FEA) ... BPIF
Brunei Shell Petroleum (SAUO) ... BSP
Brunei Town [*Brunei*] [*Airport symbol*] (AD) ... BTN
Brunei/International [*Brunei*] [*ICAO location identifier*] (ICLI) ... WBSB
Brunel Institute for Bioengineering [*Brunel University*] [*Information service or system*] (IID) ... BIB
Brunel Institute of Computational Mathematics [*Research center*] [*British*] (IRUK) ... BICOM
Brunel Institute of Organisation and Social Studies (SAUO) ... BIOSS
Brunel University (SAUO) ... Brun U
Brunel University (SAUO) ... BU
Brunet (ABBR) ... BRUT
Brunett Downs [*Northern Territory, Australia*] [*Airport symbol*] (AD) ... BTD
Brunker's Irish Common Law Digest [*A publication*] (DLA) ... Brunk Ir Dig
Brunner Zigzag Incision [*Medicine*] (MELL) ... BZZI
Brunner's Collected Cases [*United States*] [*A publication*] (DLA) ... Brun Col Cas
Brunner's Collected Cases [*United States*] [*A publication*] (DLA) ... Brunn Col Cas (F)
Brunner's Collected Cases [*United States*] [*A publication*] (DLA) ... Brunn Coll Cas
Brunner's Collected Cases [*United States*] [*A publication*] (DLA) ... Brunner Col Cas
Brunner's Gland Adenoma [*Medicine*] (MELL) ... BGA
Brunner's Selected Cases [*United States*] [*A publication*] (DLA) ... Brunn Sel Cas
Brunner's Selected Cases [*United States*] [*A publication*] (DLA) ... Brun Sel Cas
Brunner's Selected Cases, United States Circuit Courts [*A publication*] (DLA) ... Brunner Sel Cas
Bruno Elementary School, Bruno, MN [*Library symbol*] [*Library of Congress*] (LCLS) ... MnBruE
Bruno's, Inc. [*NASDAQ symbol*] (NQ) ... BRNO
Brunskill's Land Cases [*Ireland*] [*A publication*] (DLA) ... Brunskill
Brunskill's Land Cases [*Ireland*] [*A publication*] (DLA) ... Bruns LC
Brunson Electronic Triangulation System (GEOI) ... BETS
Brunswick [*Record label*] [*Great Britain*] ... B
Brunswick [*Georgia*] [*Airport symbol*] (OAG) ... BQK
Brunswick [*Georgia*] [*Airport symbol*] (AD) ... SSI
Brunswick Corp. [*NYSE symbol*] (SPSG) ... BC
Brunswick Corp. [*Associated Press*] (SAG) ... Brnwk
Brunswick, GA [*Location identifier*] [*FAA*] (FAAL) ... BQK
Brunswick, GA [*Location identifier*] [*FAA*] (FAAL) ... SSI
Brunswick, GA [*FM radio station call letters*] (RBYB) ... WAQC-FM
Brunswick, GA [*FM radio station call letters*] (BROA) ... WAYR-FM
Brunswick, GA [*Television station call letters*] ... WBSG
Brunswick, GA [*AM radio station call letters*] ... WGIG
Brunswick, GA [*AM radio station call letters*] ... WMOG
Brunswick, GA [*AM radio station call letters*] ... WPIQ
Brunswick, GA [*FM radio station call letters*] ... WSEG
Brunswick, GA [*AM radio station call letters*] (BROA) ... WSFN
Brunswick, GA [*FM radio station call letters*] (RBYB) ... WSOL-FM
Brunswick, GA [*FM radio station call letters*] ... WWIO
Brunswick, GA [*FM radio station call letters*] (RBYB) ... WWRD
Brunswick, GA [*FM radio station call letters*] (RBYB) ... WWRR-FM
Brunswick General Hospital, Amityville, NY [*Library symbol*] [*Library of Congress*] (LCLS) ... NAmiGH
Brunswick Junior College, Brunswick, GA [*Library symbol*] [*Library of Congress*] (LCLS) ... GBruJC
Brunswick, MD [*AM radio station call letters*] ... WTRI
Brunswick, ME [*Location identifier*] [*FAA*] (FAAL) ... NBT
Brunswick, ME [*Location identifier*] [*FAA*] (FAAL) ... NHZ
Brunswick, ME [*Location identifier*] [*FAA*] (FAAL) ... NMU
Brunswick, ME [*FM radio station call letters*] ... WBOR
Brunswick, ME [*AM radio station call letters*] ... WCLZ
Brunswick, ME [*FM radio station call letters*] ... WCLZ-FM
Brunswick Mining & Smelting Corp. Ltd. [*Toronto Stock Exchange symbol*] ... BMS
Brunswick Port Authority (SAUO) ... BPA
Brunswick Regiment (SAUO) ... Brunsw
Brunswick Regional Library, Brunswick, GA [*Library symbol*] [*Library of Congress*] (LCLS) ... GBru
Brunswick Steam Electric Plant (NRCH) ... BSEP
Brunswick Technical College, Supply, NC [*Library symbol*] [*Library of Congress*] (LCLS) ... NcSupB
Brunswick/Brunswick Naval Air Station [*Maryland*] [*ICAO location identifier*] (ICLI) ... KNHZ
Brunswick/Glynco Naval Air Station [*Georgia*] [*ICAO location identifier*] (ICLI) ... KNEA
Brunswick-Greensville Regional Library, Lawrenceville, VA [*Library symbol*] [*Library of Congress*] (LCLS) ... ViLaw
Brush (MSA) ... BR
Brush (VRA) ... bru
Brush and Broom Trade Board (SAUO) ... BBTB
Brush Back Yearly (SAUS) ... BBY
Brush Beryllium Company (SAUO) ... BBC
Brush Biopsy [*Medicine*] (MELL) ... BB
Brush Border [*of intestinal epithelial cell*] [*Cell physiology*] ... BB
Brush Border Endopeptidase [*Medicine*] (DMAA) ... BBEP
Brush Border Membrane [*Medicine*] (DMAA) ... BBM
Brush Border Membrane Vesicle (DB) ... BBMV
Brush Border Myosin [*Biology*] ... BBMI
Brush Clean and Withe (SAUS) ... BCW
Brush, CO [*FM radio station call letters*] (BROA) ... KPRB-FM
Brush, CO [*AM radio station call letters*] ... KSIR
Brush, CO [*FM radio station call letters*] ... KSIR-FM
Brush Creek Mining & Development [*Associated Press*] (SAG) ... BrushCrk
Brush Creek Mining & Development Co., Inc. [*NASDAQ symbol*] (NQ) ... BCMD
Brush Electrical Machines Ltd. (SAUO) ... BEM
Brush Front Regularly (SAUS) ... BFR
Brush Holder ... BRH
Brush Holder (IAA) ... BRHLR
Brush Holder (SAUS) ... Br Hlr

Brush Lifting and Short-Circuiting Gear (SAUS) .... BLS-C Gear
Brush Owner's Association [*Defunct*] (EA) .... BOA
Brush Public Library, Brush, CO [*Library symbol*] [*Library of Congress*] (LCLS) .... CoBru
Brush Style [*Computer science*] (PCM) .... BS
Brush Wellman, Inc. [*Associated Press*] (SAG) .... BrshWI
Brush Wellman, Inc. [*NYSE symbol*] (SPSG) .... BW
Brushed .... Brshd
Brushless Motor (SAUS) .... BLM
Brushless Torque Motor .... BTM
Brushmakers of Scotland Protection Association [*A union*] .... BSPA
Brush-Off [*Slang*] .... BRO
Brushware Manufacturers' Association of Australia .... BMAA
Brusly, LA [*FM radio station call letters*] .... KRVE
Brusque (ABBR) .... BRSQ
Brusquely (ABBR) .... BRSQY
Brusqueness (ABBR) .... BRSQNS
Brussels [*Belgium*] [*Airport symbol*] (OAG) .... BRU
Brussels [*Belgium*] [*ICAO location identifier*] (ICLI) .... EBBB
Brussels [*Belgium*] [*ICAO location identifier*] (ICLI) .... EBBS
Brussels [*Belgium*] [*ICAO location identifier*] (ICLI) .... EBBU
Brussels [*Belgium*] [*ICAO location identifier*] (ICLI) .... EBBV
Brussels [*Belgium*] [*ICAO location identifier*] (ICLI) .... EBMI
Brussels [*Belgium*] [*ICAO location identifier*] (ICLI) .... EBUM
Brussels [*Belgium*] [*ICAO location identifier*] (ICLI) .... EBUR
Brussels [*Belgium*] [*ICAO location identifier*] (ICLI) .... EBVA
Brussels [*Belgium*] [*ICAO location identifier*] (ICLI) .... EBWM
Brussels Community High School District 37, Brussels, IL [*Library symbol*] [*Library of Congress*] (LCLS) .... IBrusSD
Brussels Institute for Management of the Environment (SAUO) .... BIM
Brussels Inter-Bank Offered Rate [*Finance*] .... BIBOR
Brussels Nomenclature [*Standard customs nomenclature published by the Customs Cooperation Council*] .... BN
Brussels Research Unit for Environmental, Geochemical and Life Sciences Studies (SAUO) .... BRUEGEL
Brussels Sprouts Marketing Program (EA) .... BSMP
Brussels Tariff Nomenclature (ILCA) .... BNT
Brussels Tariff Nomenclature [*See also CCCN*] [*EEC*] [*Belgium*] .... BTN
Brussels Tariff Nomenclature for the Latin American Free Trade Association (BARN) .... NABLOC
Brussels Treaty Organization (SAUO) .... BRUTO
Brussels Treaty Organization [*Later, Western European Union*] .... BTO
Brussels Treaty Permanent Commission (NATG) .... BTPC
Brussels/Grimbergen [*Belgium*] [*ICAO location identifier*] (ICLI) .... EBGB
Brussels/National [*Belgium*] [*ICAO location identifier*] (ICLI) .... EBBR
Brussels-Richwood Community Consolidated School District 41, Brussels, IL [*Library symbol*] [*Library of Congress*] (LCLS) .... IBrusRSD
Brutal (ABBR) .... BRTL
Brutality (ABBR) .... BRTLT
Brutalize (ABBR) .... BRTLZ
Brutalized (ABBR) .... BRTLZD
Brutalizing (ABBR) .... BRTLZG
Brutally (ABBR) .... BRTLY
Brute (ABBR) .... BRT
Brute Force and Ignorance [*Computer science*] [*Slang*] (WDMC) .... BFI
Brute Force and Massive Ignorance (SAUS) .... BFMI
Brute Force Gyro .... BFG
Brute Force [*Unregulated*] **Supply** (IEEE) .... BFS
Brutish (ABBR) .... BRTSH
Brutish (ABBR) .... BRUTH
Brutishly (ABBR) .... BRTSHY
Brutishness (ABBR) .... BRTSHNS
Bruton's Tyrosine Kinase [*An enzyme*] .... Btk
Bruttoregistertonne [*Gross Registered Ton*] [*German*] .... BRT
Brutus [*of Plutarch*] [*Classical studies*] (OCD) .... Brut
Brutus or De Claris Oratoribus [*of Cicero*] [*Classical studies*] (OCD) .... Brut
Bruxelles [*Belgium*] [*City in Belgium*] (ROG) .... BRUX
Bruyere College (SAUO) .... BC
Bruzual [*Venezuela*] [*Airport symbol*] (AD) .... BRZ
Bruzual, Apure [*Venezuela*] [*ICAO location identifier*] (ICLI) .... SVBZ
BRX Mining & Petroleum [*Vancouver Stock Exchange symbol*] .... BXG
Bryan [*Texas*] [*Airport symbol*] (AD) .... CFD
Bryan Adams Fan Club (EA) .... BAFC
Bryan High Titer (DB) .... BH
Bryan, OH [*Location identifier*] [*FAA*] (FAAL) .... BWB
Bryan, OH [*Location identifier*] [*FAA*] (FAAL) .... BYN
Bryan, OH [*FM radio station call letters*] (RBYB) .... WAOX
Bryan, OH [*FM radio station call letters*] .... WBNO
Bryan, OH [*FM radio station call letters*] (RBYB) .... WGBE-FM
Bryan, OH [*AM radio station call letters*] .... WQCT
Bryan Public Library, Bryan, TX [*Library symbol*] [*Library of Congress*] (LCLS) .... TxBry
Bryan, TX [*Location identifier*] [*FAA*] (FAAL) .... CFD
Bryan, TX [*AM radio station call letters*] .... KAGC
Bryan, TX [*FM radio station call letters*] .... KBMA
Bryan, TX [*Television station call letters*] .... KBTX
Bryan, TX [*FM radio station call letters*] .... KKYS
Bryan, TX [*FM radio station call letters*] .... KORA
Bryan, TX [*AM radio station call letters*] .... KTAM
Bryan, TX [*FM radio station call letters*] (BROA) .... KXBK
Bryan, TX [*Television station call letters*] .... KYLE
Bryan-Bennett Public Library, Salem, IL [*Library symbol*] [*Library of Congress*] (LCLS) .... ISal
Bryan/Coulter Field [*Texas*] [*ICAO location identifier*] (ICLI) .... KCFD
Bryansk [*Former USSR*] [*ICAO location identifier*] (ICLI) .... UUBP
Bryant and Stratton. Commercial Law [*A publication*] (DLA) .... Bry & Str Com L
Bryant College (SAUO) .... BC
Bryant College (GAGS) .... Bryant C
Bryant College, Smithfield, RI [*OCLC symbol*] (OCLC) .... BRB
Bryant College, Smithfield, RI [*Library symbol*] [*Library of Congress*] (LCLS) .... RSmB
Bryant Library, Roslyn, NY [*Library symbol*] [*Library of Congress*] (LCLS) .... NRosl
Bryce Canyon National Park (SAUS) .... BCNP
Bryce Canyon National Park .... BRCA
Bryce Canyon National Park (SAUS) .... Bryce
Bryce Canyon, UT [*Location identifier*] [*FAA*] (FAAL) .... BCE
Bryce. Registration of Trade Marks [*A publication*] (DLA) .... Bryce Tr M
Bryce's Study of the Civil Law [*A publication*] (DLA) .... Bryce Civ L
Bry-Lin Hospital, Buffalo, NY [*Library symbol*] [*Library of Congress*] (LCLS) .... NBuBLH
Brymon Airways [*British*] .... BA
Brymon Airways [*ICAO designator*] (AD) .... BC
Brymon Airways [*British*] .... BR
Brymon European Airway [*British*] [*ICAO designator*] (FAAC) .... BRY
Bryn Mawr (SAUS) .... BM
Bryn Mawr Bank Corp. [*NASDAQ symbol*] (NQ) .... BMTC
Bryn Mawr Bank Corp. [*Associated Press*] (SAG) .... BrynMw
Bryn Mawr College (GAGS) .... Bryn Mawr C
Bryn Mawr College, Bryn Mawr, PA [*OCLC symbol*] (OCLC) .... BMC
Bryn Mawr College, Bryn Mawr, PA [*Library symbol*] [*Library of Congress*] (LCLS) .... PBm
Bryne Library Consulting, Richmond, VA [*Library symbol*] [*Library of Congress*] (LCLS) .... ViRBL
Bryology .... BRY
Bryology (ROG) .... BRYOL
Bryson City, NC [*AM radio station call letters*] .... WBHN
Brystol-Myers Pharmaceuticals R & D, Buffalo, NY [*Library symbol*] [*Library of Congress*] (LCLS) .... NBuBM
BSB Bancorp [*Associated Press*] (SAG) .... BSB Bcp
BSB Bancorp [*NASDAQ symbol*] (TTSB) .... BSBN
BSB Bancorp, Inc. [*NASDAQ symbol*] (NQ) .... BSBN
B-shaped nut (SAUS) .... B-nut
BSL Airlines [*Ukraine*] [*FAA designator*] (FAAC) .... BSL
BSR Conter-Terrorist Driving School (SAUO) .... BSR
BSR Monarch Works Ltd. (SAUO) .... BSR
BT Financial Corp. [*NASDAQ symbol*] (NQ) .... BTFC
BT Financial Corp. [*Associated Press*] (SAG) .... BT Fin
BT Office Products International, Inc. [*NYSE symbol*] (SAG) .... BTF
BT Office Products International, Inc. [*Associated Press*] (SAG) .... BT Off
BT Shipping Ltd. [*NASDAQ symbol*] (NQ) .... BTBT
BT Shipping Ltd. [*Associated Press*] (SAG) .... BT Shp
BT Shipping Ltd ADR [*NASDAQ symbol*] (TTSB) .... BTBTY
BTG Inc. [*NASDAQ symbol*] (TTSB) .... BTGI
BTG, Inc. [*Associated Press*] (SAG) .... BTG Inc
BTI Computer Systems [*Formerly, Basic Timesharing, Inc.*] .... BTI
BTL Corp. [*Formerly, Butler Brothers*] .... BTL
B-Track Initiator (SAA) .... BTI
BTU International [*NASDAQ symbol*] (TTSB) .... BTUI
BTU International, Inc. [*NASDAQ symbol*] (CTT) .... BTUI
BTU International, Inc. [*Associated Press*] (SAG) .... BTU Int
Bua [*Fiji*] [*Airport symbol*] [*Obsolete*] (OAG) .... BVF
Bua [*Fiji*] [*ICAO location identifier*] (ICLI) .... NFNU
Buattifel [*Libya*] [*ICAO location identifier*] (ICLI) .... HLFL
Buayan/General Santos, Cotabato (South) [*Philippines*] [*ICAO location identifier*] (ICLI) .... RPWB
Bubaque [*Guinea-Bissau*] [*ICAO location identifier*] (ICLI) .... GGBU
Bubble (KSC) .... BUB
Bubble Bath Detector (OA) .... BBD
Bubble Behavior Unit (SAUS) .... BBU
Bubble Chamber .... BC
Bubble Chamber Experiment .... BCE
Bubble Column [*Engineering*] .... BC
Bubble Column Slurry Reactor [*Chemical engineering*] .... BCSR
Bubble Curtain [*Pisciculture*] .... BC
Bubble Domain Memory .... BDM
Bubble Droplet Particle Unit (SAUS) .... BDPU
Bubble Electromagnetic Pulse .... BEMP
Bubble Growth (PDAA) .... BUBGRO
Bubble Interfacial Microlayer Sampler [*Oceanography*] (MSC) .... BIM
Bubble Interfacial Microlayer Sampler [*Oceanography*] .... BIMS
Bubble Jet Color .... BJC
Bubble Lattice File [*Computer science*] (HGAA) .... BLF
Bubble Memory [*Data storage device*] [*Computer science*] (BUR) .... BM
Bubble Memory [*Data storage device*] [*Computer science*] (MSA) .... BUBMEM
Bubble Memory Controller [*Computer science*] .... BMC
Bubble Memory Device [*Computer science*] .... BMD
Bubble Oxygenator (SAUS) .... BO
Bubble Position Register [*Computer science*] (IAA) .... BPR
Bubble Pulse (IAA) .... BP
Bubble Pulse Period .... BPP
Bubble String Comparator (SAUS) .... BSC
Bubble-Gum Brigade [*Preteens*] .... BGB
Bubblejet Color (SAUS) .... BJC
Bubbles (SAUS) .... Bubs
Bubble-Up Initiation [*Automotive project management*] .... BI
Bubbling Fluidized Bed Combustion .... BFBC
Bubo [*Medicine*] (MELL) .... B
Bucak [*Turkey*] [*Seismograph station code, US Geological Survey*] (SEIS) .... BCK
Bucaramanga [*Colombia*] [*Seismograph station code, US Geological Survey*] (SEIS) .... BCR

Bucaramanga [*Colombia*] [*Airport symbol*] (OAG) .... BGA
Bucaramanga/Palo Negro Sur [*Colombia*] [*ICAO location identifier*] (ICLI) .... SKBG
Buccal [*Pertaining to the cheek*] .... B
Buccal [*Dentistry*] (DAVI) .... Buc
Buccal Cartilage [*Dentistry*] .... BC
Buccal Cavity (SAUS) .... BC
Buccal Commissure [*Dentistry*] .... BC
Buccal Epithelial Cells .... BEC
Buccal Ganglion [*Dentistry*] .... BUG
Buccal Mass [*Dentistry*] .... BM
Buccal Retractor Nerve (SAUS) .... BRN
Buccal Smear Test [*Medicine*] (MELL) .... BST
Buccal-Lingual Syndrome (SAUS) .... BLS
Buccaneer .... BCCNR
Buccaneer Aircraft [*"Banana Bomber"*] [*British*] (DSUE) .... BUCC
Buccaneer National Class Association (EA) .... BNCA
Buccoaxial [*Dentistry*] .... BA
Buccoaxiocervical [*Dentistry*] .... BAC
Buccoaxiogingival [*Dentistry*] .... BAG
Buccocervical [*Dentistry*] .... BC
Buccodistal [*Dentistry*] .... BD
Buccogingival [*Dentistry*] .... BG
Buccolingual [*Dentistry*] .... BL
Buccolingual Masticatory Syndrome (DIPS) .... BLM
Buccomesial [*Dentistry*] .... BM
Bucco-Occlusal [*Dentistry*] .... BO
Buccopharyngeal Fascia [*Medicine*] (MELL) .... BPF
Buccopulpal [*Dentistry*] .... BP
Buchan [*Australia*] [*Seismograph station code, US Geological Survey*] [*Closed*] (SEIS) .... BUV
Buchan [*British*] [*ICAO location identifier*] (ICLI) .... EGQN
Buchanan [*Liberia*] [*ICAO location identifier*] (ICLI) .... GLBU
Buchanan [*Liberia*] [*ICAO location identifier*] (ICLI) .... GLLB
Buchanan [*Liberia*] [*Airport symbol*] (AD) .... UCN
Buchanan. Cape Colony Court of Appeal Reports [*South Africa*] [*A publication*] (DLA) .... AC
Buchanan. Cape Colony Court of Appeal Reports [*South Africa*] [*A publication*] (DLA) .... App Ca
Buchanan County Courthouse, Independence, IA [*Library symbol*] [*Library of Congress*] (LCLS) .... IaIndpBC
Buchanan County Courthouse, Independence, IA [*Library symbol*] [*Library of Congress*] (LCLS) .... IaIndpCoC
Buchanan Foundation (SAUO) .... BF
Buchanan, MI [*FM radio station call letters*] .... WSMK
Buchanan's Appeal Court Reports, Cape Of Good Hope [*A publication*] (DLA) .... BAC
Buchanan's Appeal Court Reports, Cape Of Good Hope [*A publication*] (DLA) .... Buch AC
Buchanan's Appeal Court Reports, Cape Of Good Hope [*A publication*] (DLA) .... Buch App Cas
Buchanan's Appeal Court Reports, Cape Of Good Hope [*A publication*] (DLA) .... Buch Ct Ap Cape GH
Buchanan's Appeal Court Reports, Cape Of Good Hope [*A publication*] (ILCA) .... Buch Ct App Cape G H
Buchanan's Cape Of Good Hope Reports [*A publication*] (DLA) .... Buch
Buchanan's Cape Of Good Hope Reports [*A publication*] (DLA) .... Buch E Cape GH
Buchanan's Cape Of Good Hope Reports [*A publication*] (DLA) .... Buch Rep
Buchanan's Court of Session [*1800-13*] [*Scotland*] [*A publication*] (DLA) .... Buch
Buchanan's New Jersey Equity Reports [*A publication*] (DLA) .... Buch
Buchanan's New Jersey Equity Reports [*A publication*] (DLA) .... Buchan
Buchanan's New Jersey Equity Reports [*A publication*] (DLA) .... Buch Eq (NJ)
Buchanan's Precedents of Pleading [*A publication*] (DLA) .... Buch Pr Pl
Buchanan's Remarkable Criminal Cases [*Scotland*] [*A publication*] (DLA) .... Buch Cas
Buchanan's Remarkable Criminal Cases [*Scotland*] [*A publication*] (DLA) .... Buch Tr
Buchanan's Reports, Cape Of Good Hope [*A publication*] (DLA) .... Buch J Cape GH
Buchanan's Reports, Court of Session and Justiciary [*Scotland*] [*A publication*] (DLA) .... Buchanan
Buchanan's Reports of the Court of Appeal, Cape [*1880-1910*] [*South Africa*] [*A publication*] (ILCA) .... A
Buchanan's Supreme Court Reports [*Cape Colony*] [*A publication*] (DLA) .... Buch
Buchanan's Supreme Court Reports, Cape Of Good Hope [*1868-79*] [*South Africa*] [*A publication*] (DLA) .... B
Buchanan's Supreme Court Reports, Cape Of Good Hope [*1868-79*] [*South Africa*] [*A publication*] (DLA) .... Buch SC Rep
Buchan's California Lien Laws [*A publication*] (DLA) .... Buch Lien Law
Buchans Public Library, Buchans, NF, Canada [*Library symbol*] [*Library of Congress*] (LCLS) .... CaNfBu
Buchans Public Library, Newfoundland [*Library symbol*] [*National Library of Canada*] (NLC) .... NFBU
Bucharest [*Romania*] [*Seismograph station code, US Geological Survey*] (SEIS) .... BUC
Bucharest [*Romania*] [*Seismograph station code, US Geological Survey*] (SEIS) BUC1
Bucharest [*Romania*] [*Seismograph station code, US Geological Survey*] (SEIS) BUC2
Bucharest (SAUS) .... Buchar
Bucharest [*Romania*] [*Airport symbol*] (OAG) .... BUH
Bucharest [*Romania*] **Banesa Airport** [*Airport symbol*] (OAG) .... BBU
Buchberg [*Switzerland*] [*Seismograph station code, US Geological Survey*] (SEIS) .... BUB
Buchel [*Germany*] [*ICAO location identifier*] (ICLI) .... EDSB
Buchtel, OH [*AM radio station call letters*] .... WAIS
Buciclovir Triphosphate [*Antiviral*] .... BCVTP
Buck Island National Monument (SAUS) .... BINM
Buck Island Reef National Monument .... BUIS
Buck Memory Element (MCD) .... BME
Buck Owens Fan Club [*Defunct*] (EA) .... BOFC
Buck-a-Day (PDAA) .... BAD
Buckbee-Mears Automated Plotting System (SAUS) .... BMAPS
Buckbee-Mears Company (SAUO) .... BMC
Buckbee-Mears Cortland (EFIS) .... BMC
Buck-Boost Transformer .... BBT
Bucket .... BCKT
Bucket .... BKT
Bucket Brigade (SAUS) .... BBD
Bucket Brigade Delay Line (SAUS) .... BBDL
Bucket Brigade Shift Register (SAUS) .... BBSR
Bucket Wheel Excavator (DICI) .... BWE
Bucket-Brigade Device [*Electronics*] .... BBD
Buckeye .... BCKEYE
Buckeye Airways International [*Air carrier designation symbol*] .... BAIX
Buckeye Association of School Administrators [*Ohio*] (SRA) .... BASA
Buckeye, AZ [*Location identifier*] [*FAA*] (FAAL) .... BXK
Buckeye, AZ [*FM radio station call letters*] .... KMJK
Buckeye Cellulose Corp. [*NYSE symbol*] (SAG) .... BKI
Buckeye Cellulose Corp. [*Associated Press*] (SAG) .... BuckCel
Buckeye Cellulose Corp., Technical Division Library, Memphis, TN [*Library symbol*] [*Library of Congress*] (LCLS) .... TMBC
Buckeye Partners Ltd. [*Associated Press*] (SAG) .... Buckeye
Buckeye Pipe Line Company (SAUO) .... BKP
Buckeye Ptnrs L.P. [*NYSE symbol*] (TTSB) .... BPL
Buckeye Public Library, Buckeye, AZ [*Library symbol*] [*Library of Congress*] (LCLS) .... AzBu
Buckeye Technologies [*NYSE symbol*] [*Formerly, Buckeye Cellulose*] (SG) .... BKI
Buckham Memorial Library, Faribault, MN [*Library symbol*] [*Library of Congress*] (LCLS) .... MnF
Buckhannon, WV [*FM radio station call letters*] .... WBTQ
Buckhannon, WV [*AM radio station call letters*] .... WBUC
Buckhannon, WV [*FM radio station call letters*] .... WBUC-FM
Buckhannon, WV [*FM radio station call letters*] .... WVPW
Buckhannon, WV [*FM radio station call letters*] .... WVWC
Buckhead America [*NASDAQ symbol*] (TTSB) .... BUCK
Buckhead America Corp. [*NASDAQ symbol*] (SAG) .... BUCK
Buckhead America Corp. [*Associated Press*] (SAG) .... BuckAm
Buckhorn, California [*Spaceflight Tracking and Data Network*] [*NASA*] .... BUC
Bucking Coil (SAUS) .... BC
Bucking Current Generator .... BCG
Bucking Signal .... BS
Buckingham [*Electrostatic measure*] .... B
Buckingham [*Municipal borough in England*] .... BUCK
Buckingham Corp. (SAUO) .... BHM
Buckingham Palace [*British*] .... BP
Buckingham Palace Press Office [*British*] .... BPPO
Buckinghamshire [*County in England*] .... BUCKS
Buckinghamshire [*County in England*] (ODBW) .... Bucks
Buckinghamshire Regiment (SAUO) .... Bucks
Buckland [*Alaska*] [*Airport symbol*] (OAG) .... BKC
Buckland [*England*] .... BUCK
Buckle (ROG) .... BKLE
Buckle, Inc. [*NYSE symbol*] (SG) .... BKE
Buckle, Inc. [*NASDAQ symbol*] (SAG) .... BKLE
Buckle, Inc. [*Associated Press*] (SAG) .... Buckle
Buckled Zone (SAA) .... BZ
Buckley on the Companies Acts [*1873-1949*] [*A publication*] (DLA) .... Buck Comp Act
Buckley on the Companies Acts [*1873-1949*] [*A publication*] (DLA) .... Buckl
Buckley Public Library, Poteau, OK [*Library symbol*] [*Library of Congress*] (LCLS) .... OkPot
Buckley-Loda Community Unit School District, Buckley, IL [*Library symbol*] [*Library of Congress*] (LCLS) .... IBucSD
Buckling of Shells of Revolution [*Computer program*] [*NASA*] (MCD) .... BOSOR
Buckman Laboratories, Inc., Memphis, TN [*Library symbol*] [*Library of Congress*] (LCLS) .... TMBL
Buckminster Fuller Institute (EA) .... BFI
Bucknall Steamship Lines Ltd. (ROG) .... BSL
Bucknell Automated Retrieval and Display System (SAUS) .... BARDS
Bucknell Computer Services [*Bucknell University*] [*Research center*] (RCD) .... BCS
Bucknell University (SAUO) .... BU
Bucknell University (GAGS) .... Bucknell U
Bucknell University, Lewisburg, PA [*OCLC symbol*] (OCLC) .... PBU
Bucknell University, Lewisburg, PA [*Library symbol*] [*Library of Congress*] (LCLS) .... PLeB
Bucknell University Press (SAUO) .... Bucknell U Pr
Buckner's Decisions [*in Freeman's Mississippi Chancery Reports, 1839-43*] [*A publication*] (DLA) .... Buck Dec
Bucknill. Care of the Insane [*1880*] [*A publication*] (DLA) .... Buck Ins
Bucknill on Lunacy [*A publication*] (DLA) .... Buck Lun
Bucknill's Cooke's Cases of Practice, Common Pleas [*England*] [*A publication*] (DLA) .... Buck Cooke
Buckram (ADA) .... BKM
Buckram [*Fabric*] .... BUCK
Bucks County Community College, Newtown, PA [*OCLC symbol*] (OCLC) .... BUC
Bucks County Community College, Newtown, PA [*Library symbol*] [*Library of Congress*] (LCLS) .... PNtB
Bucks County Free Library, Doylestown, PA [*OCLC symbol*] (OCLC) .... DPB
Bucks County Free Library, Doylestown, PA [*Library symbol*] [*Library of Congress*] (LCLS) .... PDoB

Bucks County Historical Society, Doylestown, PA [Library symbol] [Library of Congress] (LCLS) .... PDoBHi
Bucks County Law Reporter [Pennsylvania] [A publication] (DLA) .... Bucks
Bucks County Law Reporter [Pennsylvania] [A publication] (DLA) .... Bucks Co L Rep
Bucks County Law Reporter [Pennsylvania] [A publication] (DLA) .... Bucks Co LR (PA)
Buck's English Cases in Bankruptcy [1816-20] [A publication] (DLA) .... Buck
Buck's English Cases in Bankruptcy [1816-20] [A publication] (DLA) .... Buck Bankr (Eng)
Buck's English Cases in Bankruptcy [1816-20] [A publication] (DLA) ..... Buck Cas
Buck's Massachusetts Ecclesiastical Law [A publication] (DLA) ...... Buck Eccl Law
Buck's Reports [7-8 Montana] [A publication] (DLA) .... Buck
Buckskin (VRA) .... bcksk
Bucksport, SC [FM radio station call letters] .... WGTR
Bucky [Cassette film in Potter-Bucky Diaphragm] [Radiology] (DAVI) ...... B
BUCS [Backup Control System] Self Test (MCD) .... BUCS/ST
Bucuresti [Romania] [ICAO location identifier] (ICLI) ...... LRBB
Bucuresti/Baneasa [Romania] [ICAO location identifier] (ICLI) ...... LRBS
Bucuresti/Otopeni [Romania] [ICAO location identifier] (ICLI) ...... LROP
Bucyrus Intl. [NASDAQ symbol] (TTSB) ...... BCYR
Bucyrus, OH [AM radio station call letters] ...... WBCO
Bucyrus, OH [FM radio station call letters] ...... WQEL
Bucyrus-Erie Co. [NASDAQ symbol] (SAG) ...... BCYR
Bucyrus-Erie Co. ...... BE
Bucyrus-Erie Co. [Associated Press] (SAG) ...... BucyEr
Bucyrus-Erie Company (SAUO) ...... BY
Bud Collins' Modern Encyclopedia of Tennis [A publication] ...... BCMET
Bud Drop Virus (SAUS) ...... BDV
Bud Duct (SAUS) ...... BD
Bud Radio Inc. (SAUO) ...... BDR
Budakeszi [Hungary] [Later, TYH] [Geomagnetic observatory code] ...... BUZ
Budapest [Hungary] [Seismograph station code, US Geological Survey] (SEIS) ...... BUD
Budapest [Hungary] [Airport symbol] (OAG) ...... BUD
Budapest (SAUS) ...... Buda
Budapest (BARN) ...... Budpst
Budapest [Hungary] [ICAO location identifier] (ICLI) ...... LHAA
Budapest [Hungary] [ICAO location identifier] (ICLI) ...... LHCC
Budapest Interbank Offered Rate (SAUO) ...... BUBOR
Budapest, Oslo, Barcelona, Copenhagen, Amsterdam, Tampere, Sheffield, Stuttgart and Szombathely [Names of cities where participating universities of library conference are located] ...... BOBCATSSS
Budapest Symphony Orchestra (SAUO) ...... BSO
Budapest/Ferihegy [Hungary] [ICAO location identifier] (ICLI) ...... LHBP
Budd Canada, Inc. [Toronto Stock Exchange symbol] ...... BUD
Budd Co., Fort Washington, PA [Library symbol] [Library of Congress] (LCLS) ...... PFwB
Budd Company (SAUO) ...... BF
Budd-Chiari [Syndrome] [Medicine] (DB) ...... BC
Budd-Chiari Syndrome [Medicine] ...... BCS
Buddha Sasaba Council (SAUO) ...... BSC
Buddhism ...... BUDD
Buddhist Center of the United States of America (EA) ...... BCUSA
Buddhist Churches of America Federation of Buddhist Women's Associations (EA) ...... BCAFBWA
Buddhist Council for Refugee Rescue and Resettlement (EA) ...... BCRRR
Buddhist Era ...... BE
Buddhist Foundation of Victoria [Australia] ...... BFV
Buddhist League of Esperantists (SAUO) ...... BLE
Buddhist Peace Fellowship (EA) ...... BPF
Buddhist Publication Society [Multinational association based in Sri Lanka] (EAIO) ...... BPS
[The] Buddhist Society [British] (EAIO) ...... TBS
Buddhist Society of Compassionate Wisdom [Canada] (EAIO) ...... BSCW
Buddhist Society of New South Wales [Australia] ...... BSNSW
Buddhist Society of Queensland [Australia] ...... BSQ
Buddhist Text Translation Society (EA) ...... BTTS
Buddhist Union of Europe (EAIO) ...... BUE
Buddhist Vihara Society (EA) ...... BVS
Buddhists Concerned for Animals [Defunct] (EA) ...... BCA
Budding Uninhibited by Benzimidazole [Cytology] ...... BUB
Buddism (SAUS) ...... BUD
Buddy ...... BDDY
Buddy Clark Fan Club [Defunct] (EA) ...... BCFC
Buddy DeFranco Appreciation Society (EA) ...... BDAS
Buddy Holly and the Crickets Fan Club (EAIO) ...... BHCFC
Buddy Holly Memorial Society (EA) ...... BHMS
Buddy Max Fan Club (EA) ...... BMFC
Buddy Rich Fan Club (EA) ...... BRFC
Buddy Secondary Life Support System [Aerospace] ...... BSLSS
Bude, MS [FM radio station call letters] ...... WMAU
Bude, MS [Television station call letters] ...... WMAU-TV
Budgerigar (ODBW) ...... budgie
Budgerigar Society [British] (DBA) ...... BS
Budgerigar Society (SAUO) ...... BS
Budgerigar Society of Australia ...... BSA
Budget (DLA) ...... B
Budget (MILB) ...... bdgt
Budget (SAUS) ...... Bdgt
Budget ...... BGT
Budget (ODBW) ...... bud
Budget (AFM) ...... BUD
Budget, Accounting, and Finance (AFM) ...... BA & F
Budget, Accounting and Finance (SAUS) ...... BA&F

Budget Accounting Information System [IBM Corp.] ...... BACIS
Budget Activity [Navy] ...... BA
Budget Activity Account [Army] (AABC) ...... BAA
Budget Adjustment Request ...... BAR
Budget Advisory Board (SAA) ...... BAB
Budget Advisory Committee [Army] ...... BAC
Budget Allocation Notice (MCD) ...... BAN
Budget Allocation Sheets (MCD) ...... BAS
Budget Allocation Summary (MCD) ...... BAS
Budget Analysis and Review Committee [American Library Association] ..... BARC
Budget Analysis Reporting System (MCD) ...... BARS
Budget and Accounting Officer [Military] ...... BAO
Budget and Finance Division [NATO] (NATG) ...... BUDFIN
Budget and Financial Management (SAUS) ...... BFM
Budget and Forecast Calendarization [Accounting] ...... BFC
Budget and Manpower Guidance [Military] (AABC) ...... BMG
Budget and Planning Office (SAUS) ...... BP
Budget and Plans (SAUS) ...... BUDPLAN
Budget and Program Resources Review [Army] ...... BAPRR
Budget and Reporting (NRCH) ...... B & R
Budget and Reporting Code (COE) ...... B&RC
Budget and Resource Management Division (SAUO) ...... BRMD
Budget at Complete (SAUS) ...... BAC
Budget at Completion (MCD) ...... BAC
Budget at Completion Variance (MCD) ...... BACV
Budget Authority [Office of Management and Budget] ...... BA
Budget Authorization [Air Force] (AFM) ...... BA
Budget Authorization Account Number [Air Force] (AFM) ...... BAAN
Budget Authorization and Updating Form (MCD) ...... BAUF
Budget Center (MCD) ...... BC
Budget Change Document [Accounting] (SSD) ...... BCD
Budget Change Notice (ACAE) ...... BCN
Budget Change Proposal [Accounting] ...... BCP
Budget Change Request [Accounting] (MCD) ...... BCR
Budget Classification Code (NVT) ...... BCC
Budget Code [Air Force] (AFIT) ...... BC
Budget Committee (SAUO) ...... BC
Budget Committee (SAUO) ...... BCOM
Budget Division [Environmental Protection Agency] (GFGA) ...... BD
Budget Divison (SAUS) ...... BUD
Budget Enactment Instruction ...... BEI
Budget Enforcement Act [1990] ...... BEA
Budget Enhancement Act (AAGC) ...... BEA
Budget Estimate Guidance [Military] ...... BEG
Budget Estimate Review (ACAE) ...... BER
Budget Estimate Submission [DoD] ...... BES
Budget Estimates Presentation Instructions (AFM) ...... BEPI
Budget Execution [Army] (AABC) ...... BEXEC
Budget Execution Appropriation Maintenance System [Military] ...... BEAMS
Budget Execution Code ...... BEC
Budget Execution Plan [Army] ...... BEP
Budget Execution Review [Army] (AABC) ...... BER
Budget Executives Institute [Later, PEI] (EA) ...... BEI
Budget Expenditure Plan (ACAE) ...... BEP
Budget Fiscal Year ...... BFY
Budget Formulation [Army] (AABC) ...... BFORM
Budget Formulation and Appropriation Model (MCD) ...... BFAM
Budget Formulation Directive [Military] (AABC) ...... BFD
Budget Formulation Office, Office of the Director of the Army Budget ...... BFOODAB
Budget Furniture Forum [Later, ROFF] (EA) ...... BFF
Budget Group 'A' [NYSE symbol] (SG) ...... BD
Budget Increment Package [DoD] ...... BIP
Budget Industries, Inc. (SAUO) ...... BGT
Budget Information for the States [Office of Management and Budget] (GFGA) ...... BIS
Budget Information Form (OICC) ...... BIF
Budget Line Item Number (MCD) ...... BLIN
Budget Management Information System (SAUS) ...... BMIS
Budget Management System ...... BMS
Budget Obligation [or Overlay] (NRCH) ...... B/O
Budget Obligations (EEVL) ...... BO
Budget Office [Army] ...... BUD
Budget Office, War Department [World War II] ...... BOWD
Budget Planning and Review Committee (SAUO) ...... BPRC
Budget Planning and Systems Group (SAUO) ...... BPSG
Budget Planning Document (SAUS) ...... BPD
Budget, Plans and Information (SAUS) ...... BPI
Budget Policy Statement (SAUS) ...... BPS
Budget Preparation System Master File [Office of Management and Budget] (GFGA) ...... BPS
Budget Program [DoD] (GFGA) ...... BP
Budget Program Activity Code ...... BPAC
Budget Program Activity Code Material Program Code (MCD) ...... BPAC/MPC
Budget Program Estimate (MCD) ...... BPE
Budget Program Sequence Number (ACAE) ...... BPSN
Budget Project [Navy] (CAAL) ...... BP
Budget Project Account [Military] (AABC) ...... BPA
Budget Project Number [Navy] (NG) ...... BPN
Budget Project Officer [Navy] (DNAB) ...... BPO
Budget Project Symbol Number (AFM) ...... BPSN
Budget Related Papers ...... BRP
Budget Review Board (ACAE) ...... BRB
Budget Review Committee (ACAE) ...... BRC
Budget Review Group (IAA) ...... BRG

Budget Surplus Report (SAUS) .... BSR
Budget System .... BUSY
Budget Tracking System .... BTS
Budget Workload Analysis Report [*Navy*] (NG) .... BWAR
Budget Workload Indicators .... BWI
Budget Year (AFM) .... BY
Budgetaire, Comptable, et Financier [*Budget, Accounting, and Finance - BA & F*] .... BCF
Budgetary (TBD) .... Bdgty
Budgetary and Planning (NAKS) .... B&P
Budgetary and Planning Quotations (MCD) .... BPQ
Budgetary and Scheduling Information System (MCD) .... BASIS
Budgetary Control (DCTA) .... BC
Budgetary Cost Information [*Accounting*] .... BCI
Budgetary Policy .... BP
Budget/Cost Account Plan (MCD) .... BCAP
Budgeted Actual Cost .... BAC
Budgeted Cost (ADA) .... BC
Budgeted Cost at Completion (AAGC) .... BAC
Budgeted Cost for Work Performed .... BCWP
Budgeted Cost for/of Work Scheduled (SAUS) .... BCWS
Budgeted Cost of Work (ACAE) .... BCW
Budget-Funded Agency .... BFA
Budget/Housing Policy Committee (SAUO) .... BHP
Budgeting and Reporting (ABAC) .... B&R
Budhana Ligo Esperantista [*Buddhist League of Esperantists - BLE*] [*Germany*] (EAIO) .... BLE
Budingen [*Germany*] [*ICAO location identifier*] (ICLI) .... EDEP
Budkov [*Czechoslovakia*] [*Geomagnetic observatory code*] .... BDV
Budleigh [*England*] .... BUDL
Budoia [*Papua New Guinea*] [*Seismograph station code, US Geological Survey*] (SEIS) .... BDO
Budweiser (ADWA) .... Bud
Bueckeburg [*Germany*] [*ICAO location identifier*] (ICLI) .... EDCB
Buecker Flugzeugbau GmbH & Hagglund-Soner [*Germany*] [*ICAO aircraft manufacturer identifier*] (ICAO) .... BC
Buehlerhoehe [*Federal Republic of Germany*] [*Seismograph station code, US Geological Survey*] (SEIS) .... BUH
Buena Hora [*Bolivia*] [*ICAO location identifier*] (ICLI) .... SLBH
Buena Park, CA [*FM radio station call letters*] .... KBPK
Buena Park Library District Library, Buena Park, CA [*Library symbol*] [*Library of Congress*] (LCLS) .... CBp
Buena Vista [*Guatemala*] [*Seismograph station code, US Geological Survey*] (SEIS) .... BVA
Buena Vista [*Bolivia*] [*ICAO location identifier*] (ICLI) .... SLBW
Buena Vista, CO [*FM radio station call letters*] (BROA) .... KBVC-FM
Buena Vista, CO [*AM radio station call letters*] .... KDMN
Buena Vista College [*Storm Lake, IA*] .... BVC
Buena Vista College, Storm Lake, IA [*Library symbol*] [*Library of Congress*] (LCLS) .... IaSlB
Buena Vista College, Storm Lake, IA [*OCLC symbol*] (OCLC) .... IOE
Buena Vista Public Library, Buena Vista, CO [*Library symbol*] [*Library of Congress*] (LCLS) .... CoBue
Buena Vista, VA [*FM radio station call letters*] .... WREL
Buenaventura [*Colombia*] [*Airport symbol*] (AD) .... BUN
Buenaventura [*Colombia*] [*ICAO location identifier*] (ICLI) .... SKBU
Buenavista, Agusan [*Philippines*] [*ICAO location identifier*] (ICLI) .... RPWV
Buenes Aires Musical (journ.) (SAUS) .... BAM
Buenos Aires [*Argentina*] .... BA
Buenos Aires [*Argentina*] [*Seismograph station code, US Geological Survey*] (SEIS) .... BAA
Buenos Aires [*Argentina*] [*Airport symbol*] (OAG) .... BUE
Buenos Aires [*Costa Rica*] [*ICAO location identifier*] (ICLI) .... MRBA
Buenos Aires [*Argentina*] [*ICAO location identifier*] (ICLI) .... SABA
Buenos Aires (Edificio Condor) [*Argentina*] [*ICAO location identifier*] (ICLI) .... SABC
Buenos Aires Embotell'a ADS [*NYSE symbol*] (TTSB) .... BAE
Buenos Aires Embotelladora [*Commercial firm*] [*Associated Press*] (SAG) .... BAEmb
Buenos Aires [*Argentina*] **Ezeiza** [*Airport symbol*] (OAG) .... EZE
Buenos Aires [*Argentina*] **Jorge Newbery Airport** [*Airport symbol*] (OAG) .... AEP
Buenos Aires (Servicio Meteorologico Nacional) [*Argentina*] [*ICAO location identifier*] (ICLI) .... SABM
Buenos Aires/Aeroparque, Jorge Newbery [*Argentina*] [*ICAO location identifier*] (ICLI) .... SABE
Buenos Aires/Don Torcuato [*Argentina*] [*ICAO location identifier*] (ICLI) .... SADD
Buenos Aires [*Argentina*]**/Ezeiza** [*Argentina*] [*ICAO location identifier*] (ICLI) .... SAEZ
Buerger-Gruetz [*Syndrome*] [*Medicine*] (DB) .... BG
Buergerinitiative Parlament [*Citizens' Parliamentary Initiative*] [*Austria*] [*Political party*] (EY) .... BIP
Buergerinitiativen [*Citizens' action groups*] [*Germany*] .... BI's
Buergerpartei [*Citizens' Party*] [*Germany*] [*Political party*] (PPE) .... BP
Buergerpartei [*Citizens' Party*] [*Germany*] [*Political party*] (PPW) .... BPa
Buestenhalter [*Brassiere*] [*German slang*] .... BH
Bufete Industrial [*Associated Press*] (SAG) .... Bufete
Bufete Industrial SA [*NYSE symbol*] (SPSG) .... GBI
Buff and Polishing Wheel Manufacturers Association [*Defunct*] .... BPWMA
Buff Polish [*Optics*] .... BP
Buffalo (WDAA) .... BFO
Buffalo [*Rat variety*] .... BUF
Buffalo [*New York*] [*Seismograph station code, US Geological Survey*] [*Closed*] (SEIS) .... BUF
Buffalo [*New York*] [*Airport symbol*] .... BUF
Buffalo .... BUFF
Buffalo - Larkin [*New York*] [*Seismograph station code, US Geological Survey*] [*Closed*] (SEIS) .... BFF
Buffalo Airways [*ICAO designator*] (FAAC) .... BVA
Buffalo Airways Ltd. [*Canada*] [*ICAO designator*] (FAAC) .... BFL
Buffalo Americanist Digest (SAUS) .... BAD
Buffalo Americanist Group (SAUO) .... BAG
Buffalo and Erie County Historical Society, Buffalo, NY [*Library symbol*] [*Library of Congress*] (LCLS) .... NBuHi
Buffalo and Erie County Public Library, Buffalo, NY [*Library symbol*] [*Library of Congress*] (LCLS) .... NBu
Buffalo and Erie County Public Library, Buffalo, NY [*Library symbol*] [*Library of Congress*] (LCLS) .... NBuBE
Buffalo and Erie County Public Library, Buffalo, NY [*OCLC symbol*] (OCLC) .... VHB
Buffalo Bill Historical Center (EA) .... BBHC
Buffalo Bill Museum, Cody, WY [*Library symbol*] [*Library of Congress*] (LCLS) .... WyCoB
Buffalo Bills [*National Football League*] [*1960-present*] (NFLA) .... Buf
Buffalo Center Tribune, Buffalo Center, IA [*Library symbol*] [*Library of Congress*] (LCLS) .... IaBucCT
Buffalo City School District, Buffalo, NY [*Library symbol*] [*Library of Congress*] (LCLS) .... NBuSD
Buffalo Color Corp., Buffalo, NY [*Library symbol*] [*Library of Congress*] (LCLS) .... NBuCo
Buffalo Columbus Hospital, Buffalo, NY [*Library symbol*] [*Library of Congress*] (LCLS) .... NBuCoH
Buffalo Creek & Gauley Railroad (SAUO) .... BCG
Buffalo Creek Railroad Co. (SAUO) .... BCK
Buffalo Environmental Law Journal (SAUS) .... BELJ
Buffalo Express Airlines, Inc. [*ICAO designator*] (FAAC) .... BRX
Buffalo Forge Company (SAUO) .... BFC
Buffalo Gap, VA [*FM radio station call letters*] (RBYB) .... WZXI
Buffalo General Hospital (SAUS) .... BGH
Buffalo General Hospital, Buffalo, NY [*Library symbol*] [*Library of Congress*] (LCLS) .... NBuGH
Buffalo General Hospital, School of Nursing, Buffalo, NY [*Library symbol*] [*Library of Congress*] (LCLS) .... NBuGH-N
Buffalo Head Prairie School, Alberta [*Library symbol*] [*National Library of Canada*] (BIB) .... ABHPS
Buffalo Intermediate School, Buffalo, MN [*Library symbol*] [*Library of Congress*] (LCLS) .... MnBfI
Buffalo Junior High School, Buffalo, MN [*Library symbol*] [*Library of Congress*] (LCLS) .... MnBfJ
Buffalo, KY [*AM radio station call letters*] .... WXAM
Buffalo Lake National Wildlife Refuge (SAUS) .... BLNWR
Buffalo Memorial Hospital, Medical Library, Buffalo, MN [*Library symbol*] [*Library of Congress*] (LCLS) .... MnBfH
Buffalo, MN [*AM radio station call letters*] .... KRWC
Buffalo, MO [*FM radio station call letters*] .... KBFL
Buffalo Municipal Housing Authority (SAUO) .... BMHA
Buffalo Museum of Science (SAUO) .... BMS
Buffalo Narrows [*Canada*] [*Airport symbol*] [*Obsolete*] (OAG) .... YVT
Buffalo Narrows Public Library, Buffalo Narrows, SK, Canada [*Library symbol*] [*Library of Congress*] (LCLS) .... CaSBuN
Buffalo Narrows Public Library, Saskatchewan [*Library symbol*] [*National Library of Canada*] (NLC) .... SBN
Buffalo Narrows, SK [*ICAO location identifier*] (ICLI) .... CYVT
Buffalo Niagara Electric Corporation (SAUO) .... BNE
Buffalo, NY [*Location identifier*] [*FAA*] (FAAL) .... GBI
Buffalo, NY [*AM radio station call letters*] .... WBEN
Buffalo, NY [*FM radio station call letters*] .... WBFO
Buffalo, NY [*FM radio station call letters*] .... WBNY
Buffalo, NY [*FM radio station call letters*] .... WDCX
Buffalo, NY [*FM radio station call letters*] (RBYB) .... WEDG
Buffalo, NY [*FM radio station call letters*] .... WFBF
Buffalo, NY [*AM radio station call letters*] .... WGR
Buffalo, NY [*FM radio station call letters*] .... WGRF
Buffalo, NY [*Television station call letters*] .... WGRZ
Buffalo, NY [*AM radio station call letters*] .... WHTT
Buffalo, NY [*FM radio station call letters*] .... WHTT-FM
Buffalo, NY [*Television station call letters*] .... WIVB
Buffalo, NY [*FM radio station call letters*] .... WJYE
Buffalo, NY [*Television station call letters*] .... WKBW
Buffalo, NY [*FM radio station call letters*] (BROA) .... WLCE-FM
Buffalo, NY [*FM radio station call letters*] .... WMJQ
Buffalo, NY [*AM radio station call letters*] .... WNED
Buffalo, NY [*FM radio station call letters*] .... WNED-FM
Buffalo, NY [*Television station call letters*] .... WNED-TV
Buffalo, NY [*Television station call letters*] .... WNEQ
Buffalo, NY [*Television station call letters*] .... WNYB
Buffalo, NY [*TV station call letters*] (RBYB) .... WNYO-TV
Buffalo, NY [*FM radio station call letters*] (RBYB) .... WSJZ-FM
Buffalo, NY [*Television station call letters*] .... WUTV
Buffalo, NY [*AM radio station call letters*] .... WWKB
Buffalo, NY [*AM radio station call letters*] .... WWWS
Buffalo, NY [*FM radio station call letters*] .... WYRK
Buffalo, OK [*Location identifier*] [*FAA*] (FAAL) .... BFK
Buffalo Organization for Social and Technological Innovation (EA) .... BOSTI
Buffalo Organization for Social and Technological Innovation, Inc. (BOSTI), Buffalo, NY [*Library symbol*] [*Library of Congress*] (LCLS) .... NBuBO
Buffalo Orphan Prototype [*Medicine*] (MAE) .... BOP
Buffalo Primary Library, Buffalo, MN [*Library symbol*] [*Library of Congress*] (LCLS) .... MnBfP
Buffalo Psychiatric Center, Buffalo, NY [*Library symbol*] [*Library of Congress*] (LCLS) .... NBuPC

Buffalo Public Library (SAUO) ... BPL
Buffalo Public Library, Buffalo, MN [*Library symbol*] [*Library of Congress*] (LCLS) ... MnBf
Buffalo Range [*Zimbabwe*] [*Airport symbol*] (OAG) ... BFO
Buffalo Rat Liver [*Cytology*] ... BRL
Buffalo Resources [*Vancouver Stock Exchange symbol*] ... BUF
Buffalo Ridge Baptist Academy, Lake Benton, MN [*Library symbol*] [*Library of Congress*] (LCLS) ... MnLbBa
Buffalo, Rochester and Pittsburg Railroad (SAUO) ... BR&PR
Buffalo, Rochester & Pittsburg Railway [*Terminated*] ... BR & PRY
Buffalo, Rochester & Pittsburgh Railroad ... BR & P
Buffalo Sabres Booster Club (EA) ... BSBC
Buffalo, SD [*Location identifier*] [*FAA*] (FAAL) ... BUA
Buffalo Senior High School, Buffalo, MN [*Library symbol*] [*Library of Congress*] (LCLS) ... MnBfS
Buffalo Society of Natural History (SAUO) ... BSNH
Buffalo Society of Natural Sciences (SAUO) ... BSNS
Buffalo Society of Natural Sciences, Buffalo Museum of Science, Buffalo, NY [*Library symbol*] [*Library of Congress*] (LCLS) ... NBuB
Buffalo, Union-Carolina Railroad (IIA) ... BUC
Buffalo, WY [*Location identifier*] [*FAA*] (FAAL) ... BYG
Buffalo, WY [*AM radio station call letters*] ... KBBS
Buffalo, WY [*FM radio station call letters*] (BROA) ... KBUW-FM
Buffalo, WY [*FM radio station call letters*] ... KLGT
Buffalo Yacht Club (SAUO) ... BYC
Buffalo-area Engineering Awareness for Minorities, Inc. (SAUS) ... BEAM
Buffalo/Greater Buffalo International [*New York*] [*ICAO location identifier*] (ICLI) ... KBUF
Buffelsfontein Gold Mines Ltd. [*NASDAQ symbol*] (SAG) ... BLGM
Buffelsfontein Gold Mines Ltd. [*Associated Press*] (SAG) ... Buff ADR
Buffelsfontein Gold Mining Co. [*Associated Press*] (SAG) ... Buffels
Buffelsfontein Gold Mining Co. Ltd. [*NASDAQ symbol*] (NQ) ... BFEL
Buffer [*Computer science*] (TEL) ... B
Buffer [*Computer science*] (MSA) ... BFR
Buffer [*Computer science*] ... BUF
Buffer (NASA) ... BUFF
Buffer A Register (SAUS) ... BA Reg
Buffer Access Card [*Computer science*] (NASA) ... BAC
Buffer Address Array [*Computer science*] (IAA) ... BAA
Buffer Address Counter (SAUS) ... BAC
Buffer Address Register [*Computer science*] ... BAR
Buffer Alignment Information (SAUS) ... BAI
Buffer Allocation Size (SAUS) ... BASize
Buffer Amplification (SAUS) ... BA
Buffer Amplifier (SAUS) ... BA
Buffer Amplifier [*Computer science*] ... BA
Buffer B Register (SAUS) ... BB Reg
Buffer Base (MAE) ... BB
Buffer Boundary Alignment (SAUS) ... BFALN
Buffer Cell (IAA) ... BC
Buffer Control Junction Switch [*Computer science*] ... BCJS
Buffer Control Register (NITA) ... BCR
Buffer Control Unit [*Computer science*] (CET) ... BCU
Buffer Control Word [*Computer science*] ... BCW
Buffer Cycle (IAA) ... BC
Buffer Exchange Column (DB) ... BEC
Buffer Fat (SAUS) ... BF
Buffer Free (SAUS) ... BF
Buffer Index [*Computer science*] ... BI
Buffer Input-Output Memory [*Computer science*] ... BIOM
Buffer Input/Output Processor [*Computer science*] (NITA) ... BIOP
Buffer Interface Unit [*Computer science*] (NASA) ... BIU
Buffer Interlace Controller (SAUS) ... BIC
Buffer Load Point (SAUS) ... BLP
Buffer Location Counter (SAUS) ... BLC
Buffer Location-counter Limit (SAUS) ... BLIM
Buffer Map [*Computer science*] (NASA) ... BMAP
Buffer Mark [*Computer science*] (IAA) ... BM
Buffer Memory ... BM
Buffer Module [*Computer science*] ... BM
Buffer Multiplexer (SAUS) ... BM
Buffer Punch Card (SAUS) ... BPC
Buffer Punch Service (SAUS) ... BPS
Buffer Punch Transfer (SAUS) ... BPT
Buffer Read Card (SAUS) ... BRC
Buffer Read Service (SAUS) ... BRS
Buffer Read Transfer (SAUS) ... BRT
Buffer Register [*Computer science*] ... BR
Buffer Register Under Computer Edict [*Computer science*] (PDAA) ... BRUCE
Buffer Register Under Computer Edit (CIST) ... BRUCE
Buffer Stock Financing Facility [*International Monetary Fund*] ... BSFF
Buffer Store Block (SAUS) ... BSB
Buffer Store Circuit (SAUS) ... BSC
Buffer Store Device (SAUS) ... BSD
Buffer Survey (SAUS) ... bs
Buffer Word Counter [*Computer science*] ... BWC
Buffer Zone [*Environmental science*] (COE) ... BZ
Buffered [*Medicine*] ... BF
Buffered (SAUS) ... Bfrd
Buffered Access Method (SAUS) ... BAM
Buffered Azide Glucose Glycerol [*Broth*] [*Microbiology*] ... BAGG
Buffered Block Channel (MCD) ... BBC
Buffered Communications Adapter [*Computer science*] (IAA) ... BCA
Buffered Computer (SAUS) ... BC
Buffered Data and Control Bus ... BDCB
Buffered Data Transmission Simulator ... BDTS
Buffered Deoxycholate Glucose [*Broth*] [*Microbiology*] ... BDG
Buffered Direct Injection (IAA) ... BDI
Buffered Distilled Water [*Chemistry*] ... BDW
Buffered Emitter Follower ... BEF
Buffered Fast Printer (SAUS) ... BFP
Buffered FET [*Field Effect Transistor*] **Logic** [*Integrated circuitry*] ... BFL
Buffered Field Effect Transistor Logic (SAUS) ... BFET Logic
Buffered Filtered Seawater ... BFSW
Buffered Flip-Flop [*Computer science*] ... BFF
Buffered Hydro Fluoric [*Acid*] (AAEL) ... BHF
Buffered Input/Output (SAUS) ... BI/O
Buffered Input/Output [*Computer science*] (NITA) ... BIO
Buffered Line Selector (SAUS) ... BLS
Buffered Magnetic Tape Transfer [*Computer science*] (NITA) ... BMTT
Buffered Magnetic Tape Transport [*Computer science*] (OA) ... BMTT
Buffered Oxide Etchant (AAEL) ... BOE
Buffered Printing ... BP
Buffered Pyrophosphatase Activity [*Chemistry*] ... BPA
Buffered Remote Interactive Search Console (PDAA) ... BRISC
Buffered Ringer's Solution [*Medicine*] ... BFR
Buffered Ringer's Solution [*Medicine*] (CPH) ... BFR Sol
Buffered Ringers Solution (SAUS) ... BFR Sol
Buffered Saline (MELL) ... BS
Buffered Saline Solution (AAMN) ... BSS
Buffered Salt Solution (SAUS) ... BSS
Buffered Sampler Reader (SAUS) ... BSR
Buffered Selector Channel ... BSELCH
Buffered Send/Receive ... BSR
Buffered Start (SAUS) ... BFRST
Buffered Terminal Multiplexer [*Computer science*] (IAA) ... BTM
Buffered Transmission Control Unit (SAUS) ... BTCU
Buffered-Saline/Glucose [*Clinical chemistry*] ... BSG
Buffer/Formatter (SAUS) ... B/F
Buffering in Progress ... BIP
Buffer/Multiplexer [*Computer science*] (CET) ... B/M
Buffers, Number of (SAUS) ... BUFNOM
Buffet and Bull [*Slang for a political dinner*] ... B & B
Buffet Breakfast [*Travel industry*] (TRID) ... BB
Buffets, Inc. [*NASDAQ symbol*] (NQ) ... BOCB
Buffets, Inc. [*Associated Press*] (SAG) ... Buffets
Buffing (MSA) ... BFG
Buffoons of America (EA) ... BA
Buffs (SAUO) ... Bu
Buffton Corp. [*AMEX symbol*] (SPSG) ... BFX
Buffton Corp. [*Associated Press*] (SAG) ... Buffton
Buford, GA [*FM radio station call letters*] ... WLKQ
Buford, GA [*AM radio station call letters*] ... WXEM
Buford's Boosters Fan Club (EA) ... BBFC
Bug (DSUE) ... B
Bug Eyed Monster (SAUS) ... BEM
Bug Off [*Slang*] ... BO
Bugaboo Creek Steak House [*Associated Press*] (SAG) ... BugCreek
Bugaboo Creek Steak House [*NASDAQ symbol*] (SAG) ... RARE
Bugatti [*Automobile*] ... BUG
Bugger All [*Slang*] [*British*] (DSUE) ... BA
Buginarium [*Nasal Bougie*] [*Pharmacy*] ... BUGINAR
Buglemaster [*Navy*] ... BGM
Buglemaster ... BGMSTR
Buglemaster First Class (SAUS) ... Bgmstr 1c
Buglemaster Second Class (SAUS) ... Bgmstr 2c
Bugler [*British military*] (DMA) ... B
Bugler ... BGLR
Bugler ... BR
Bugler [*Navy*] ... BUG
Bugs Per Line (SAUS) ... BPL
Buhasa [*United Arab Emirates*] [*ICAO location identifier*] (ICLI) ... OMAB
Buhl Foundation (SAUO) ... BF
Buhl, MN [*FM radio station call letters*] (RBYB) ... WIRN-FM
Buhl Public Library, Buhl, ID [*Library symbol*] [*Library of Congress*] (LCLS) ... IdBuh
Buhl Public Library, Buhl, MN [*Library symbol*] [*Library of Congress*] (LCLS) ... MnBul
Buia [*Italy*] [*Seismograph station code, US Geological Survey*] (SEIS) ... BUI
BUIC [*Backup Interceptor Control*] **NOPAD Control Center** ... BNCC
Buick Club of America (EA) ... BCA
Buick Collector's Club of America [*Defunct*] ... BCCA
Buick Compact Club [*Defunct*] (EA) ... BCC
Buick Compact Club of America [*Later, BCC*] (EA) ... BCCA
Buick Grand National (SAUS) ... GN
Buick GS [*Gran Sport*] **Club of America** (EA) ... BGSCA
Buick Motor Division [*General Motors Corp.*] ... BMD
Buick-Oldsmobile-Cadillac Group [*General Motors Corp.*] ... BOC
Buick-Oldsmobile-Pontiac [*General Motors Corp.*] ... BOP
Buie's Creek, NC [*FM radio station call letters*] ... WCCE
Build (DNAB) ... BLD
Build (SAUS) ... bld
Build Absolutely Nothing Anywhere Near Anybody (ADWA) ... Banana
Build Absolutely Nothing Anywhere Near Anything [*Facetious successor to NIMBY*] ... BANANA
Build Ada Main Program [*Computer science*] ... BAMP
Build and Blood Pressure Study [*Society of Actuaries*] ... BBPS
Build Definition Language (SAUS) ... BDL
Build Matrix (SAUS) ... BMX
Build, Operate, Transfer [*Business term*] ... BOT

Build Options, Renew Norms, Free Roles through Educational Equity [*National project to help students choose appropriate future careers*] ..... BORN FREE
Build Out Capacitor [*Telecommunications*] (TEL) ..... BOC
Build Out Lattice [*Telecommunications*] (TEL) ..... BOL
Build, Own, Operate [*Property development*] ..... BOO
Build, Own, Operate, Transfer [*Property development*] ..... BOOT
Build, Own, Transfer [*Property development*] ..... BOT
Builder ..... BLDR
Builder (VRA) ..... bldr
Builder [*Navy rating*] ..... BU
Builder, Concrete [*Navy rating*] ..... BUR
Builder, Constructionman (DNAB) ..... BUCN
Builder, First Class [*Navy rating*] BU1
Builder, Heavy [*Navy rating*] ..... BUH
Builder, Light [*Navy rating*] ..... BUL
Builder, Second Class [*Navy rating*] BU2
Builder, Third Class [*Navy rating*] BU3
Builder's and Sponsor's Profit and Risk Allowance [*Department of Housing and Urban Development*] (GFGA) ..... BSPRA
Builders Association of Minnesota (SRA) ..... BAM
Builders Association of Missouri (SRA) ..... BAM
Builders' Benevolent Institution [*British*] (BI) ..... BBI
Builders' Exchange Association of Texas (SRA) ..... BX
Builders Exchange of Detroit and Michigan (EA) ..... BEDM
Builders Hardware Manufacturers Association, Inc. (AAGC) ..... BHMA
Builders Hardware Manufacturers Association of Canada [*Association Canadienne des Fabricants de Quincaillerie de Batiment*] (AC) ..... BHMAC
Builders of Greater Britain [*A publication*] ..... BGB
Builders Old Measurement ..... BOM
Builders' Registration Board of Western Australia [*Australia*] ..... BRBWA
Builder's Risk [*Insurance*] ..... BR
Builders Supply Association of West Virginia (SRA) ..... BSA-WV
Builders Transport [*NASDAQ symbol*] (TTSB) ..... TRUK
Builders Transport, Inc. [*Associated Press*] (SAG) ..... BuildT
Builders Transport, Inc. [*NASDAQ symbol*] (NQ) ..... TRUK
Builder's Trials [*Shipbuilding*] ..... BT
Builders Warehouse Assn [*NASDAQ symbol*] (TTSB) ..... BWAI
Builders Warehouse Association, Inc. [*Associated Press*] (SAG) ..... BldrWr
Builders Warehouse Association, Inc. [*NASDAQ symbol*] (SAG) ..... BWAI
Buildex, Inc. (SAUO) ..... BLX
Building (ADA) ..... B
Building (ADA) ..... BDG
Building (NATG) ..... BLD
Building (AFM) ..... BLDG
Building (ASC) ..... Bldg
Building (DD) ..... bldg
Building ..... BLG
Building (ROG) ..... BUILD
Building Access Card [*Issued to Senate staff members to ensure security in the Capitol*] ..... BAC
Building Advisor [*Red Cross Disaster Services*] ..... BA
Building Advisory Committee ..... BAC
Building Advisory Service [*British*] (BI) ..... BAS
Building Aid System (SAUS) ..... BASYS
Building and Civil Engineer [*British*] ..... B & CE
Building and Civil Engineering Industries Uniformity Agreement (SAUS) ..... BCEIUA
Building and Construction Contracts [*A publication*] (DLA) ..... Bldg Contr
Building and Construction Council, New South Wales [*Australia*] ..... BCCNSW
Building and Construction Industry Council [*Australia*] ..... BCIC
Building and Construction Industry Long Service Leave Board [*Australia*] ..... BCILSB
Building and Construction Law [*Australia*] [*A publication*] ..... BCL
Building and Construction Trades Council - North Dakota (SRA) ..... BCTC-ND
Building and Construction Trades Council of Delaware (SRA) ..... BCTCD
Building and Construction Trades Department [*AFL-CIO*] ..... BCTD
Building and Contents [*Insurance*] ..... B & C
Building and Engineering [*British*] ..... B & E
Building and Engineering Journal [*A publication*] ..... Building & Eng J
Building and Facilities (SAUO) ..... B & F
Building and Facilities (SAUS) ..... B&F
Building and Loan ..... B & L
Building and Loan (TBD) ..... Bldg & Ln
Building and Loan Association (DLA) ..... B & L
Building and Loan Association (SAUO) ..... B&L
Building and Loan Association (EBF) ..... B&L Assn
Building and Monument Workers Association of Scotland [*A union*] ..... BMWAS
Building and Repair [*Red Cross Disaster Services*] ..... B and R
Building and Repair (SAUS) ..... B&R
Building and Safety Engineering ..... BSE
Building and Service Industry ..... B & SI
Building and Social Housing Foundation [*British*] ..... BSHF
Building and Town-Planning Technical Staff (SAUO) ..... BTPTS
Building and Town-Planning Technical Staff (SAUS) ..... BTPTS
Building Apprenticeship and Training Council (SAUO) ..... BATC
Building Better Boards for Community Organizations Project [*American Association of Community and Junior Colleges*] (EDAC) ..... BBB
Building Better Cities (SAUS) ..... BBC
Building Block (KSC) ..... BB
Building Block Concept [*Army-ROAD concept*] ..... BBC
Building Block Monochromator ..... BBM
Building Block Oriented Language [*Computer science*] (PDAA) ..... BBOL
Building Block Principle ..... BBP
Building Block Signal Processor [*Computer science*] (MHDI) ..... BBSP
Building Block System ..... BBS
Building Center (or Centre) (SAUS) ..... BC
Building Center Trust (PDAA) ..... BCT
Building Centre Trust (SAUO) ..... BCT
Building Code (DAC) ..... BC
Building Conservation Trust [*An association*] (DBA) ..... BCT
Building Construction Forum (SAUO) ..... BCF
Building Construction Materials and Equipment [*A publication*] (ADA) ..... BCME
Building Contractors Association of New Jersey (SRA) ..... BCANJ
Building Control Accreditation Authority [*Victoria, Australia*] ..... BCAA
Building Control Qualifications Board [*Victoria, Australia*] ..... BCQB
Building Control Technical Advisory Council [*Victoria, Australia*] ..... BCTAC
Building Cost Information Service [*Royal Institute of Chartered Surveyors*] [*Information service or system*] (IID) ..... BCIS
Building Data Council (SAUO) ..... BDC
Building Density (SAA) ..... BD
Building Description Language ..... BDL
Building, Design and Management (SAUS) ..... BDM
Building Design Association of South Australia ..... BDASA
Building Design Partnership (SAUS) ..... BDP
Building Design System [*Applied Research of Cambridge Ltd.*] [*Software package*] (NCC) ..... BDS
Building Disputes Tribunal [*Australia*] ..... BDT
Building Distribution Frame [*Telecommunications*] (NITA) ..... BDF
Building Division Council (SAUO) ..... BDC
Building Economic Alternatives [*Co-Op America*] [*A publication*] ..... BEA
Building Economics Research Unit (SAUO) ..... BERU
Building Emergency Plan [*Environmental science*] (COE) ..... BEP
Building Emergency Plan [*Environmental science*] (COE) ..... BEPLAN
Building Emergency Program Administrator [*Environmental science*] (COE) ..... BEPA
Building Emergency Support Team [*Environmental science*] (COE) ..... BEST
Building Employers' Confederation [*A union*] [*British*] ..... BEC
Building Energy Estimating Programme (SAUO) ..... BEEP
Building Energy Management Systems (SAUS) ..... BEMS
Building Energy Performance Analysis Club (SAUO) ..... BEPAC
Building Energy Performance Standards ..... BEPS
Building Energy Standards Program (ABAC) ..... BESP
Building Energy Systems Analysis Project [*Public Works Canada*] ..... BESA
Building Energy Utilization Laboratory [*Iowa State University*] [*Research center*] (RCD) ..... BEUL
Building Engineer (HGAA) ..... BIDGE
Building Engineer ..... Bldg E
Building Envelope Council of Ottawa Region (AC) ..... BECOR
Building Environmental Performance Assessment Criteria (SAUS) ..... BEPAC
Building Equipment Accessories and Materials [*Program*] [*Canada*] ..... BEAM
Building Equipment, Accessories and Materials Programme (SAUO) ..... BEAM
Building Exhibition (SAUO) ..... BE
Building Fire Safety Committee [*South Australia*] ..... BFSC
Building for Environmental and Economic Sustainability (SAUS) ..... BEES
Building Illness Syndrome (SAUS) ..... BIS
Building In Reliability (SAUS) ..... BIR
Building Industries Federation, South Africa (SAUO) ..... BIFEDSA
Building Industries National Council (SAUO) ..... BINC
Building Industry Advisory Council [*Australia*] ..... BIAC
Building Industry Association (ECON) ..... BI
Building Industry Association (SRA) ..... BIA
Building Industry Association of Hawaii (SRA) ..... BIA-HI
Building Industry Association of Washington (SRA) ..... BIAW
Building Industry Consulting Service [*Telecommunications*] (TEL) ..... BICS
Building Industry Consulting Service International [*Tampa, FL*] [*Telecommunications service*] ..... BICSI
Building Industry Consulting Services (SAUS) ..... BICS
Building Industry Development Services ..... BIDS
Building Industry Distributors (SAUO) ..... BID
Building Industry Employers of New York State (SRA) ..... BIENYS
Building Industry Libraries Group (SAUO) ..... BILG
Building Industry Subcontractors Association (SAUO) ..... BISCA
Building Industry Technicians Training Council (SAUO) ..... BITTC
Building Industry Training Board (SAUO) ..... BITB
Building Information Centre [*Cauldon College of Further and Higher Education*] [*British*] (CB) ..... BIC
Building Integrated Timing Supply (ACRL) ..... BITS
Building Item Name Directory [*A publication*] ..... BIND
Building Liaison Officer (ADA) ..... BLO
Building Line [*Technical drawings*] ..... BL
Building Loads Analysis and System Thermodynamics [*Computer program*] ..... BLAST
Building Maintenance Employers Association [*Later, SEA*] (EA) ..... BMEA
Building Maintenance Information Ltd. (DBA) ..... BMI
Building Management Authority of Western Australia ..... BMAWA
Building Management System (ACII) ..... BMS
Building Material Dealers Association (NTPA) ..... BMDA
Building Material Exhibition Association (SAUO) ..... BMEA
Building Material Exhibitors Association [*Defunct*] (EA) ..... BMEA
Building Material Loan (SAUO) ..... BML
Building Material Series [*National Institute of Standards and Technology*] ..... BMS
Building Materials and Equipment Southeast Asia (SAUO) ..... BM&ESA
Building Materials and Structures (SAA) ..... BMS
Building Materials Distribution Group (EFIS) ..... BMDG
Building Materials Export Group [*British*] (DS) ..... BMEG
Building Materials Export Group (SAUO) ..... BMEG
Building Materials Holdings [*NASDAQ symbol*] [*Formerly, BMC West*] (SG) ..... BMHC
Building Materials Producers (SAUS) ..... BMP

Building Materials Research Laboratories (SAUO) ... BMRL
Building Merchants' Federation [*British*] ... BMF
Building Monitoring System (ADA) ... BMS
Building Officials and Code Administrators International (EA) ... BOCA
Building Officials Conference of America, Inc. ... BOCA
Building Omission Area (GEOI) ... BOA
Building One Services [*Formerly, Consolidated Capital*] [*NASDAQ symbol*] ... BOSS
Building Operation (HEAS) ... BO
Building Optimization Program [*Computer science*] ... BOP
Building Out Section ... BOS
Building Owners and Managers Association International (EA) ... BOMA
Building Owners and Managers Association International ... BOMAI
Building Owners and Managers' Association of Australia ... BOMAA
Building Owners and Managers Institute International (NTPA) ... BOMI
Building Owners Federation of Mutual Fire Insurance Companies (SAUO) ... BOF
Building Permit (PA) ... BP
Building Permits Survey (SAUS) ... BPS
Building Power Low Voltage Relay [*Environmental science*] (COE) ... BLVR
Building Products Executives Conference ... BPEC
Building Products Institute (SAUO) ... BPI
Building Products Ltd., Montreal, PQ, Canada [*Library symbol*] [*Library of Congress*] (LCLS) ... CaQMBP
Building Products Ltd., Montreal, Quebec [*Library symbol*] [*National Library of Canada*] (NLC) ... QMBP
Building Products Register [*American Institute of Architects*] ... BPR
Building Registration Board of Queensland [*Australia*] ... BRBQ
Building Regulation Review Task Force ... BRRTF
Building Regulations Advisory Committee [*British*] ... BRAC
Building Related Illness ... BRI
Building Renovating Association ... BRA
Building Research Advisory Board [*Later, ABBE*] [*National Academy of Sciences*] ... BRAB
Building Research Advisory Service [*Building Research Establishment*] [*Department of Industry*] [*British*] (DS) ... BRAS
Building Research Board (EA) ... BRB
Building Research Division (SAUO) ... BRD
Building Research Energy Conservation Support Unit [*British*] ... BRECSU
Building Research Energy Conservation Support Unit (AIE) ... BRESCU
Building Research Establishment [*Research center*] [*British*] (IRC) ... BRE
Building Research Institute [*Later, BRAB, ABBE*] (EA) ... BRI
Building Research Laboratory [*Ohio State University*] [*Research center*] (RCD) ... BRL
Building Research Station [*British*] ... BRS
Building Research Station News [*A publication*] ... BRS
Building Restriction Line [*FAA*] (TAG) ... BRL
Building Risk (SAUS) ... B/R
Building Science (journ.) (SAUS) ... BS
Building Science Series [*National Institute of Standards and Technology*] ... BSS
Building Securities Company (SAUO) ... BSC
Building Seismic Safety Council (SAUO) ... BSSC
Building Service Contractors Association International (EA) ... BSCA
Building Service Contractors Association International (EAIO) ... BSCAI
Building Service Employees' International Union [*Later, SEIU*] (EA) ... BSE
Building Service League [*Later, SEA*] (EA) ... BSL
Building Services Authority [*Queensland, Australia*] ... BSA
Building Services Calculations [*Amazon Computers*] [*Software package*] (NCC) ... BSC
Building Services Engineering Society (SAUO) ... BSES
Building Services Estimating [*Tipdata Ltd.*] [*Software package*] (NCC) ... BSE
Building Services Programs [*Amazon Computers*] [*Software package*] (NCC) ... BSP
Building Services Research and Information Association [*Information service or system*] (IID) ... BSRIA
Building Societies Act [*British*] ... BSA
Building Societies Association [*British*] ... BSA
Building Societies' Commission [*British*] ... BSC
Building Societies Database [*British*] ... BSD
Building Societies Institute (SAUO) ... BSI
Building Societies' Investment Trust (WDAA) ... BSIT
Building Societies Members Association [*British*] (DBA) ... BSMA
Building Societies Ombudsman Scheme [*British*] ... BSOS
Building Society (ODBW) ... BS
Building Society (SAUO) ... BS
Building Space Requirement (DAC) ... BSR
Building Specification Group (SAUO) ... BSG
Building Stone Institute (EA) ... BSI
Building Supply Institute of Technology [*Canada*] ... BSIT
Building Systems Councils of the National Association of Home Builders (NTPA) ... BSC/NAHB
Building Systems Design (journ.) (SAUS) ... BSD
Building Systems Division [*Washington, DC*] [*Department of Energy*] (GRD) ... BSD
Building Systems Industry Forum (NTPA) ... BSIF
Building Systems Institute (EA) ... BSI
Building Technology Division (SAUO) ... BTD
Building Thermal Envelope Systems and Materials ... BTESM
Building Time Delay Relay [*Environmental science*] (COE) ... BTDR
Building Trade Joint Council (SAUO) ... BTJC
Building Trades Council (SAUO) ... BTC
Building Trades Employers Association (SRA) ... BTEA
Building Trades Exhibition (SAUO) ... BTE
Building Trades Group (SAUO) ... BTG
Building Use Studies [*Research firm*] [*British*] ... BUS
Building Utility Design System (MHDI) ... BUDS
Building Ventilation (SAUS) ... BV
Building Wake Factor [*Nuclear energy*] (NRCH) ... BWF
Building Waterproofers Association [*Defunct*] (EA) ... BWA
Building Woodwork [*Freight*] ... BLDG WDWRK
Building Workers' Industrial Union [*British*] ... BWIU
Building Workers' Industrial Union of Australia ... BWIUA
Building-Energy Management System ... BEMS
Buildings (SAUS) ... BLDGS
Buildings and Community Systems (EG) ... BCS
Buildings and Equipment Section [*Library Administration and Management Association*] ... BES
Buildings and Utilities (ABAC) ... B&U
Buildings, Antennas, Spans, and Earth Formations [*Fixed-object parachuting*] ... BASE
Buildings at Risk Trust [*British*] (WDAA) ... BART
Buildings Control Officer ... BUCO
Buildings Energy Technology Transfer Program [*Canada*] ... BETT
Buildings for College and University Libraries Committee [*Library Administration and Management Association*] [*American Library Association*] ... BCUL
build-operate-transfer (SAUS) ... b-o-t
Build-Out Circuits (SAUS) ... BOC
Build-Out Components (SAUS) ... BOC
Build-to-Order [*Compaq Computer Corp.*] [*Computer science*] ... BTO
Build-to-Order Software Selector ... BOSS
Buildup (FAAC) ... BLDUP
Buildup (KSC) ... BU
Buildup Control Office (SAUO) ... BUCO
Build-Up Control Organization [*Established to supervise flow of personnel and equipment to the Continent, immediately following Normandy invasion*] [*British*] [*World War II*] ... BUCO
Build-Up Parts List (SAUS) ... B/UPL
Built (DAC) ... Bit
Built ... BLT
Built (BARN) ... blt
Built (ROG) ... BT
Built for British [*As suffix to plane designation*] ... B
Built on Mask [*Microlithography*] ... BOM
Built Up Area [*Army*] ... BUA
Built-Down [*Military*] (INF) ... BD
Built-In [*Classified advertising*] (ADA) ... B/I
Built-In ... BLTIN
Built-In (SAUS) ... BLT-IN
Built-in Assembler (SAUS) ... BASM
Built-in Ballistic Computer (SAUS) ... BBC
Built-In Bit Error Rate [*Computer science*] ... BER
Built-In Breathing System ... BIBS
Built-In Cleaning Systems Institute [*Defunct*] (EA) ... BCSI
Built-In Diagnostic Equipment [*Analytical chemistry*] ... BIDE
Built-in Electronic System Test (ACAE) ... BEST
Built-In Hold [*of countdown*] [*NASA*] (KSC) ... BIH
Built-In Light Beacon ... BILB
Built-In Logic (ACAE) ... BIL
Built-in Logic Block Observation (or Observer) (SAUS) ... BILBO
Built-In Logic Block Observer [*Computer science*] (MHDB) ... BILBO
Built-In Orderly Organized Knowledge [*Learning device*] ... BOOK
Built-In Self-Test ... BIST
Built-In Test [*or Testing*] [*Computer science*] ... BIT
Built-In Test Equipment ... BITE
Built-In Test System [*Military*] (CAAL) ... BITS
Built-In Test/Built-In Test Equipment [*Military*] (RDA) ... BIT/BITE
Built-In Test/Fault Isolation (SAUS) ... BIT/FI
Built-In Unit (SSD) ... BIU
Built-In Variance (MCD) ... BIV
Built-in-Place Component [*Electronics*] ... BIPCO
Built-up Addressing (SAUS) ... BUA
Built-Up Cast Iron Propeller [*of a ship*] (DS) ... BCP
Built-Up Cast Steel Propeller [*of a ship*] (DS) ... BCSP
Built-Up Edge (MCD) ... BUE
Built-Up Low-Cost Advanced Titanium Structures (MCD) ... BLATS
Built-Up Roofing ... BUR
Buin [*Papua New Guinea*] [*Airport symbol*] (OAG) ... UBI
Buired Capacitance (SAUS) ... BC
Buisiness Information Network (SAUS) ... BIN
Buisson Ardent [*The Burning Bush*] [*Freemasonry*] ... BA
Bujumbura [*Burundi*] [*Airport symbol*] (OAG) ... BJM
Bujumbura [*Burundi*] [*ICAO location identifier*] (ICLI) ... HBBA
Buka Island [*Papua New Guinea*] [*Airport symbol*] (OAG) ... BUA
Bukavu [*Zaire*] [*Airport symbol*] (OAG) ... BKY
Bukavu/Kavumu [*Zaire*] [*ICAO location identifier*] (ICLI) ... FZMA
Bukhara [*Former USSR*] [*Airport symbol*] (OAG) ... BHK
Bukoba [*Tanzania*] [*Airport symbol*] (OAG) ... BKZ
Bukoba [*Tanzania*] [*ICAO location identifier*] (ICLI) ... HTBU
Bul Bul Academy of Fine Arts [*Dacca, Pakistan*] ... BAFA
Bula [*Indonesia*] [*ICAO location identifier*] (ICLI) ... WAPB
Bulan, Sorsogon [*Philippines*] [*ICAO location identifier*] (ICLI) ... RPUU
Bulape [*Zaire*] [*ICAO location identifier*] (ICLI) ... FZUL
Bulawayo [*Zimbabwe*] [*Seismograph station code, US Geological Survey*] (SEIS) ... BUL
Bulawayo [*Zimbabwe*] [*Airport symbol*] (OAG) ... BUQ
Bulawayo/Bulawayo [*Zimbabwe*] [*ICAO location identifier*] (ICLI) ... FVBU
Bulawayo/Induna [*Zimbabwe*] [*ICAO location identifier*] (ICLI) ... FVIN
Bulb ... B
Bulb and Time [*Photography*] ... B & T

Bulb Angle [Shipfitting] .... BA
Bulb Distributors' Association [British] (DBA) .... BDA
Bulbocavernosus [Muscle group] .... BC
Bulbocavernosus Activity [Physiology] .... BCA
Bulbocavernosus Reflex [Medicine] (DAVI) .... BCR
Bulbus Chordae [Cardiology] (DAVI) .... BC
Bulchi [Ethiopia] [ICAO location identifier] (ICLI) .... HABU
Bulford/Salisbury Plain [British] [ICAO location identifier] (ICLI) .... EGDS
Bulgaria [ANSI two-letter standard code] (CNC) .... BG
Bulgaria (MILB) .... Bg
Bulgaria [ANSI three-letter standard code] (CNC) .... BGR
Bulgaria [MARC country of publication] [Library of Congress] (LCCP) .... bu
Bulgaria [IYRU nationality code] .... BU
Bulgaria (WDAA) .... BUL
Bulgaria (VRA) .... BULG
Bulgaria (VRA) .... Bulg
Bulgaria [MARC geographic area code] [Library of Congress] (LCCP) .... e-bu
Bulgaria [License plate code assigned to foreign diplomats in the US] .... QM
Bulgarian (SAUS) .... Blg
Bulgarian [MARC language code] [Library of Congress] (LCCP) .... bul
Bulgarian (ADWA) .... Bulg
Bulgarian Accreditation Service (SAUS) .... BAS
Bulgarian Agrarian Party [Political party] .... BAP
Bulgarian Agrarian People's Party [Political party] (PPW) .... BAPP
Bulgarian Agrarian People's Union - Nikola Petkov [Political party] .... BAPU-NP
Bulgarian Agrarian People's Union-United [Political party] (EY) .... BAPU
Bulgarian Agrarian Union [Political party] .... BAU
Bulgarian Air Cargo [ICAO designator] (FAAC) .... BCA
Bulgarian Astronautical Society (SAUO) .... BAS
Bulgarian Atomic Energy Commission (SAUO) .... BCAE
Bulgarian Communist Party [Bulgarska Komunisticheska Partiia] [Political party] (PPW) .... BCP
Bulgarian Flying Cargo [FAA designator] (FAAC) .... BFB
Bulgarian Liberal Party [Political party] .... BLP
Bulgarian Lucky Flight [ICAO designator] (FAAC) .... BLF
Bulgarian National Committee (EA) .... BNC
Bulgarian National Front (EA) .... BNF
Bulgarian Socialist Labor Federation [Defunct] (EA) .... BSLF
Bulgarian Socialist Party [Political party] (EY) .... BSP
Bulgarian Telegraph Agency [News agency] .... BTA
Bulgarian Turkish Association of Australia .... BTAA
Bulgarian-United States Trade and Economic Council (NTPA) .... BUSTEC
Bulgarska Komunisticheska Partiia [Bulgarian Communist Party] [Political party] (PPE) .... BKP
Bulgarska Rabotnicheska Partiia [Bulgarian Workers Party] [Political party] (PPE) .... BRP
Bulgarska Socialdemokraticheska Partiia [Bulgarian Social Democratic Party] [Political party] (PPE) .... BSDP
Bulgarska Telegrafna Agentsiya [Bulgarian News Agency] .... BTA
Bulgarski Naroden Zemedelski Suiuz [Bulgarian National Agrarian Union] (PPE) .... BNZS
Bulgarski Zemedelski Naroden Soyuz [Bulgarian Agrarian People's Union-United] [Political party] (EY) .... BZNS
Bulgarus de Bulgarinis [Deceased, 1166] [Authority cited in pre-1607 legal work] (DSA) .... B
Bulgarus de Bulgarinis [Deceased, 1166] [Authority cited in pre-1607 legal work] (DSA) .... Bu
Bulgarus de Bulgarinis [Deceased, 1166] [Authority cited in pre-1607 legal work] (DSA) .... Bul
Bulgarus de Bulgarinis [Deceased, 1166] [Authority cited in pre-1607 legal work] (DSA) .... Bulg
Bulgemaster (SAUS) .... BGM
Bulimba [Australia] [Airport symbol] [Obsolete] (OAG) .... BIP
Bulimia [Medicine] (MELL) .... B
Bulimia Anorexia Self Help (SAUS) .... basb
Bulimia Anorexia Self-Help. Inc. (SAUO) .... BASH
Bulimia Cognitive Distortions Scale [Psychology] (DMAA) .... BCDS
Bulimia Nervosa [Medicine] .... BN
Bulimia Test [Personality development test] [Psychology] .... BULIT
Bulimic Investigatory Test [Psychology] (DMAA) .... BITE
Bulk .... BLK
Bulk (SAUS) .... blk
Bulk [Substrate] [Electron device] (MSA) .... BU
Bulk Acoustic Wave [Physics] .... BAW
Bulk Airmail .... BAM
Bulk Biomass Model [Pisciculture] .... BBM
Bulk Breaking Point (SAUS) .... BBP
Bulk Burning (IEEE) .... BB
Bulk Cargo (SAUS) .... BC
Bulk Cargoes Advisory Group (SAUO) .... BCAG
Bulk Carrier (SAUS) .... Blk C
Bulk Carrier [Shipping] (DS) .... BLK CAR
Bulk Carrier of 26,000 Deadweight Tons [Shipping] (DS) .... B 26
Bulk Carrier of 30,000 Deadweight Tons [Shipping] (DS) .... B 30
Bulk Carriers Conference, Arlington VA [STAC] .... BLK
Bulk Cement (SAUS) .... BC
Bulk Chaff Dispenser (SAUS) .... BCD
Bulk Containers [Shipping] (DCTA) .... BK
Bulk Continuous Filament [Textile science] .... BCF
Bulk Copy Program [Computer science] (PCM) .... BCP
Bulk Core (MHDI) .... BC
Bulk Current Injection [Electronics] .... BCI
Bulk Data Network (ACAE) .... BDN
Bulk Data Processing (IAA) .... BDP
Bulk Data Switching .... BDS

Bulk Data Transfer Subsystem [Telecommunications] (TEL) .... BDTS
Bulk Density (IAA) .... BD
Bulk Direct Mail Service (ADA) .... BDMS
Bulk Easy Access Readout (SAUS) .... BEAR
Bulk Electronic Clearance System .... BECS
Bulk Encryption (CCCA) .... BE
Bulk Encryption Unit (SAUS) .... BEU
Bulk Erase Head (SAUS) .... BEH
Bulk Filtering Acquisition and Tracking System (MCD) .... BATS
Bulk Freight Containers [Shipping] (DCTA) .... BU
Bulk Fuel System (COE) .... BFS
Bulk Fuel Tank Assembly (MCD) .... BFTA
Bulk Function Transfer (PDAA) .... BFT
Bulk Grains Queensland [An association] [Australia] .... BGQ
Bulk Head .... BH
Bulk in Barrels [Freight] .... BLK B
Bulk Information Processing (SAUS) .... BIP
Bulk Inland Petroleum, Oil, and Lubrication Transport (NATG) .... BIPOLT
Bulk Input/Output (SAUS) .... BULKIO
Bulk Ion Temperature (AAEL) .... BIT
Bulk Issue (ADA) .... BI
Bulk Issue Store (SAUO) .... BIS
Bulk Items List .... BIL
Bulk Mail .... BM
Bulk Mail Center [Postal Service] .... BMC
Bulk Material Length (NRCH) .... BML
Bulk Media Conversion .... BMC
Bulk Memory (ACAE) .... BM
Bulk Memory Address Register (ACAE) .... BMAR
Bulk Memory Controller (ACAE) .... BMC
Bulk Metal Insulator Semiconductor Structure (SAUS) .... BMIS Structure
Bulk Microdefects (SAUS) .... BMD
Bulk Modulus of Elasticity [Symbol] (DEN) .... k
Bulk Molding Compound .... BMC
Bulk Molding Compound [Plastics technology] .... BMMC
Bulk Negative Conductance [Electronics] (IAA) .... BNC
Bulk Negative Differential Conductivity [Electronics] (IAA) .... BNDC
Bulk Oil Temperature (PDAA) .... BOT
Bulk Optically-controlled Semiconductor Switch (SAUS) .... BOSS
Bulk Packaging and Containerization Institute [Later, CII] (EA) .... BPCI
Bulk Packed on Pallets [Paper] (DGA) .... BPOP
Bulk Packed on Pallets [Paper] (DGA) .... BPP
Bulk Petrol Co. [British and Canadian] [Military] .... BPC
Bulk Petrol Storage Center (SAUS) .... BPSC
Bulk Petrol Storage Section (SAUO) .... BPSS
Bulk Petrol Supply Depot (SAUO) .... BPSD
Bulk Petrol Transport (SAUS) .... BPT
Bulk Petroleum Facilities and Systems .... BPFS
Bulk Petroleum Management System .... BPMS
Bulk Petroleum Products .... BPP
Bulk Pharmaceutical Chemical [Manufacturing] .... BPC
Bulk Polymerization Process [Plastics technology] .... BPP
Bulk Presorted Mail (ADA) .... BPSM
Bulk Processing System (SAUS) .... BPS
Bulk Rate Business Mail .... BBM
Bulk Resistance (IAA) .... BR
Bulk Semiconductor Limiter .... BSL
Bulk Shielding Facility [ORNL] .... BSF
Bulk Shielding Reactor .... BSR
Bulk Silicate Earth [Biology] .... BSE
Bulk Storage Device (IEEE) .... BSD
Bulk Storage System .... BSS
Bulk Store Memory Device (MCD) .... BSMD
Bulk Supply Depot (SAUO) .... BSD
Bulk Supply Tariff (MHDB) .... BST
Bulk Synchronous Parallel (RALS) .... BSP
Bulk Synchronous Parallelism (SAUS) .... BSP
Bulk Tainers [Shipping] (DS) .... Bk
Bulk Tape Degausser .... BTD
Bulk Tape Eraser .... BTE
Bulk Transfer Facility .... BTF
Bulk Transfer Hose .... BTH
Bulk Transmission of Data (SAUS) .... BTD
Bulk Verification Services [British] .... BVS
Bulk Volume (ROAS) .... BV
Bulk Water (CARB) .... BW
Bulk Water System [Environmental science] (COE) .... BWS
Bulk Wet Density .... BWD
Bulk-Channel Charge-Coupled Device [Electronics] (TEL) .... BCCD
Bulk-Cohesion-Dipolarity-Elasticity [Factor analysis of physical property data of liquid compounds] .... BCDE
Bulk/Common Items List (MCD) .... BCIL
Bulked Continous Fibre (SAUS) .... BCF
Bulked Continuous Fiber [or Filament] [Textile] .... BCF
Bulker (SAUS) .... Blkr
Bulkhead (AAG) .... BHD
Bulkhead (ADWA) .... bhd
Bulkhead .... Bkhd
Bulkhead (SAUS) .... BKHD
Bulkhead (MUGU) .... BLKD
Bulkhead (KSC) .... BLKHD
Bulkhead Connector .... BC
Bulkhead Jack .... BHJ
Bulkhead Jack .... BJ
Bulkhead Receptable (SAUS) .... BHR

Bulkhead Receptacle ... BR
Bulk-Oil-Roll-on Carrier (SAUS) ... BO-Ro Carrier
Bulky Mechanical [*Paper*] (DGA) ... BM
Bulky Mechanical Newsprint (DGA) ... BMN
Bull & Bear Group, Inc. [*NASDAQ symbol*] (NQ) ... BNBG
Bull & Bear Group, Inc. [*Associated Press*] (SAG) ... BullBear
Bull & Bear Group'A' [*NASDAQ symbol*] (TTSB) ... BNBGA
Bull & Bear Municipal Income Fund, Inc. [*AMEX symbol*] (SAG) ... BBM
Bull & Bear US Government Securities Fund [*AMEX symbol*] (SAG) ... BBG
Bull Baffles Brains [*Bowdlerized version*] (DSUE) ... 3B's
Bull Elephants (EA) ... BE
Bull General Electric ... BGE
Bull HN [*Honeywell and NEC*] **Information Systems Inc.** [*Billerica, MA*] (CDE) ... Bull HN
Bull, Icl, Siemens, Olivetti und Nixdorf (SAUS) ... BISON
Bull Lines (SAUO) ... B
Bull Nose ... BN
Bull Riders Only [*An association*] ... BRO
Bull Riding [*Rodeo term*] ... BR
Bull Run [*NASDAQ symbol*] (SG) ... BULL
Bull Run Corp. [*NASDAQ symbol*] (NQ) ... BULL
Bull Run Corp. [*Associated Press*] (SAG) ... Bull Run
Bull Session [*Slang for a random conversation*] ... BS
Bull Steamship Lines (SAUO) ... BSL
Bull Terrier Club of America (EA) ... BTCA
Bullard and Curry's Louisiana Digest [*A publication*] (DLA) ... Bull & C Dig
Bullard and Curry's Louisiana Digest [*A publication*] (DLA) ... Bull & Cur Dig
Bullard Company (SAUO) ... BLD
Bullard-Sanford Public Library, Vassar, MI [*Library symbol*] [*Library of Congress*] (LCLS) ... MiVa
Bulldog Clamp [*Medicine*] (MELL) ... BDC
Bulldog Club of America (EA) ... BCA
Bulldozer (SAUS) ... Bdoz
Bulldozer [*Freight*] ... BDOZER
Bulldozer (MSA) ... BDZR
Bulldozing ... BLLDZG
Bulleid Pacific Preservation Society [*British*] (BI) ... BPPS
Bullen and Leake's Pleadings on Actions in King's Bench Decisions [*A publication*] (DLA) ... Bull & L
Bullen and Leake's Precedents of Pleading [*A publication*] (ILCA) ... B & L
Bullen and Leake's Precedents of Pleading [*A publication*] (DLA) ... B & L Pr
Bullen and Leake's Precedents of Pleading [*A publication*] (DLA) ... Bull & L Pr
Buller and Bund's Manual of Bankruptcy [*A publication*] (DLA) ... Bull & B Bank
Buller's Law of Distress for Rent [*A publication*] (DLA) ... Bull Dis
Buller's Law of Nisi Prius [*England*] [*A publication*] (DLA) ... BNP
Buller's Law of Nisi Prius [*England*] [*A publication*] (DLA) ... Buller NP
Buller's Law of Nisi Prius [*England*] [*A publication*] (DLA) ... Bull NP
Buller's Law of Nisi Prius [*England*] [*A publication*] (DLA) ... Bull NP (Eng)
Bullet ... BLLT
Bullet Dispersion Indicator ... BDI
Bullet Drop Compensator (DICI) ... BDC
Bullet Group, Inc. [*Formerly, Bullet Energy Ltd.*] [*Vancouver Stock Exchange symbol*] ... BUL
Bullet Hit Indicator (MCD) ... BHI
Bullet Path [*Ballistics*] ... BP
Bullet Shot Trauma [*Medicine*] (MELL) ... BST
Bullet Sports International, Inc. [*Associated Press*] (SAG) ... BulletSp
Bullet Sports International, Inc. [*NASDAQ symbol*] (SAG) ... PARR
Bullet Through (SAUS) ... B-T
Bullet Trap Universal (SAUS) ... BTU
Bullet Wound (MELL) ... BW
Bulletin ... B
Bulletin ... BLLTN
Bulletin (WGA) ... BU
Bulletin (AFM) ... BUL
Bulletin (ADWA) ... bul
Bulletin ... BULL
Bulletin [*News*] [*Advertising*] (WDMC) ... bull
Bulletin (AL) ... Bull
Bulletin (NTCM) ... BUN
Bulletin. American Academy of Psychiatry and the Law [*A publication*] (DLA) ... Bull Am Acad Psych & L
Bulletin. American Patent Law Association [*A publication*] (DLA) ... APLA Bull
Bulletin. Anglo-Soviet Law Association [*A publication*] (DLA) ... Bull Anglo-Sov LA
Bulletin Articles Information Subsystem [*Computer science*] ... BAIS
Bulletin. Association of the Bar of the City of New York [*A publication*] (DLA) ... New York City BA Bul
Bulletin. Association of the Bar of the City of New York [*A publication*] (DLA) ... NYCBA Bull
Bulletin. Australian Society of Legal Philosophy [*A publication*] ... BASLP
Bulletin Baud Service (SAUO) ... BBS
Bulletin Board [*Computer online message system*] ... BB
Bulletin Board [*Technical drawings*] ... BBD
Bulletin Board for Libraries [*British*] ... BUBL
Bulletin Board Note Manager [*Prodigy offline reader*] ... BBNM
Bulletin Board Service ... BBS
Bulletin Board Software (SAUS) ... BBS
Bulletin Board Systems [*Personal computer message network system*] ... BBS
Bulletin. Committee on Criminal Courts' Law and Procedure. Association of the B ar. City of New York [*A publication*] (DLA) ... CCC Bull
Bulletin. Comparative Law Bureau [*A publication*] (DLA) ... Bulletin Comp L
Bulletin. Department of Agriculture (journ.) (SAUS) ... Tas Dep Agric Bull
Bulletin d'Epigraphie Semitique [*A publication*] (BJA) ... BES
Bulletin des Arrets de la Chambre Criminelle de la Cour de Cassation [*A publication*] (ILCA) ... Bull Crim
Bulletin des Assurances [*A publication*] (ILCA) ... BA
Bulletin des Leo Baeck Instituts (SAUS) ... LBIB
Bulletin. Faculty of Education. Utsunomiya University (journ.) (SAUS) ... UFEBB
Bulletin Far Seas Fisheries Research Laboratory (SAUS) ... Bull Far Seas Fish Res Lab
Bulletin Forestry Commission (SAUS) ... Bull For Comm
Bulletin Francais. Societe Internationale de Musique [*A publication*] ... BSIM
Bulletin. Freshwater Fisheries Research Laboratory (journ.) (SAUS) ... TSKHAY
Bulletin Geological Society of America (SAUO) ... Bull Geol Soc Am
Bulletin Geological Survey of Canada (SAUS) ... Bull Geol Surv Can
Bulletin. Geological Survey of South Australia [*A publication*] ... Bull Geol Survey Sth Aust
Bulletin. Industrial Law Society [*A publication*] (DLA) ... Indust L Soc Bull
Bulletin. Institut Intermediaire International [*A publication*] (DLA) ... Bull III
Bulletin. International Association of Law Libraries [*A publication*] (DLA) ... IALL Bull
Bulletin. International Bar Association [*A publication*] (DLA) ... Bull IBA
Bulletin. International Commission of Jurists [*A publication*] (DLA) ... Bull ICJ
Bulletin International des Sciences Sociales [*A publication*] (DLA) ... Bull Int Sc Soc
Bulletin. International Law Association [*1936-38*] [*A publication*] (DLA) ... Int'l L Ass'n Bull
Bulletin. International Seismological Centre [*A publication*] ... BISC
Bulletin. John Rylands Library [*A publication*] (OCD) ... Bull Rylands Libr
Bulletin. Judge Advocate General of the Army [*United States*] [*A publication*] (DLA) ... Bull JAG
Bulletin. Korean Fisheries Society (journ.) (SAUS) ... HSHKA
Bulletin. Kyoto Educational University. Series B. Mathematics and Natural Science (journ.) (SAUS) ... KBSEA
Bulletin. Kyushu Institute of Technology (journ.) (SAUS) ... KKDKA
Bulletin Legislatif Dalloz [*A publication*] (ILCA) ... BLD
Bulletin. National Tax Association [*A publication*] (DLA) ... Bull Nat Tax Assoc
Bulletin. National Tax Association [*A publication*] (DLA) ... Bull NTA
Bulletin of Animal Behaviour (SAUS) ... Bull Anim Behav
Bulletin of Aquatic Biology (SAUS) ... Bull Aquat Biol
Bulletin of Canadian Welfare Law [*A publication*] (DLA) ... Bull Can Welfare Law
Bulletin of Comparative Labour Relations [*A publication*] (DLA) ... Bull Comp Lab Rel
Bulletin of Czechoslovak Law [*A publication*] (DLA) ... Bull Czech L
Bulletin of Environmental Contamination and Toxicology (SAUS) ... Bull Environ Contam Toxicol
Bulletin of Experimental Biology and Medicine [*A publication*] ... BEBIM
Bulletin of Experimental Biology and Medicine (SAUS) ... Bull Exp Biol Med
Bulletin of Freshwater Fisheries Research Laboratory (SAUS) ... Bull Freshwater Fish Res Lab
Bulletin of Indonesian Economic Studies (SAUS) ... Bull Indones Econ Stud
Bulletin of Law, Science, and Technology [*A publication*] (DLA) ... Bull L Science & Tech
Bulletin of Legal Developments [*A publication*] (DLA) ... Bull Legal Devel
Bulletin of Legal Developments [*A publication*] (DLA) ... Bull Leg Dev
Bulletin of Marine Science (SAUS) ... Bull Mar Sci
Bulletin of Mathematical Biophysics (SAUS) ... Bull Math Biophys
Bulletin of Medieval Canon Law [*A publication*] (DLA) ... Bull Mediev Canon L
Bulletin of Paleomalacology (journ.) (SAUS) ... BPM
Bulletin of Prosthesis Research (SAUS) ... BPR
Bulletin of the Academy of Sciences (journ.) (SAUS) ... Bull Acad Sci
Bulletin of the Academy of Sciences of the USSR, Geologic Series (SAUS) ... Bull Acad Sci USSR Geol S
Bulletin of the Academy of Sciences of the USSR. Physical Sciences (SAUS) ... Bull Acad Sci USSR Phys S
Bulletin of the American Academy of Psychiatry and the Law (SAUS) ... Bull Am Acad Psychiatry Law
Bulletin of the American Astronomical Society (SAUO) ... BAAS
Bulletin of the American Astronomical Society (SAUO) ... Bull Arn Astron Soc
Bulletin of the American Astronomical Society (journ.) (SAUS) ... Bull Arn Astron Soc
Bulletin of the American Mathematical Society (SAUO) ... Bull Amer Math Soc
Bulletin of the American Meteorological Society [*A publication*] (ARMP) ... BAMS
Bulletin of the American Meteorological Society (SAUO) ... Bull Amer Meteorol Soc
Bulletin of the American Physical Society (SAUO) ... Bull Am Phys Soc
Bulletin of the American Physical Society (journ.) (SAUS) ... Bull Am Phys Soc
Bulletin of the American Schools of Oriental Research (SAUS) ... BASOR
Bulletin of the American Society for Information Science (SAUO) ... BASIS
Bulletin of the Astronomical Institutes of the Netherlands (journ.) (SAUS) ... BAN
Bulletin of the Astronomical Institutes of the Netherlands (journ.) (SAUS) ... Bull Astron Inst Neth
Bulletin of the Atomic Scientists [*A publication*] (BRI) ... BAS
Bulletin of the Atomic Scientists (journ.) (SAUS) ... Bull At Sci
Bulletin of the Australian Mathematical Society [*A publication*] ... BAMS
Bulletin of the Australian Mathematical Society (SAUO) ... Bull Aust Math Soc
Bulletin of the Biogeographical Society of Japan (SAUO) ... Bull Biogeogr Soc Jpn
Bulletin of the British Mycological Society (SAUO) ... Bull Br Mycol Soc
Bulletin of the California Agricultural Experiment Station (SAUS) ... Bull Calif Agric Exp Stn
Bulletin of the Chemical Society, Belgrade (SAUS) ... Bull Chem Soc Belgr
Bulletin of the Chemical Society Belgrade (SAUO) ... Bull Chem Soc Belgr
Bulletin of the Chemical Society of Belgium [*A publication*] (MEC) ... Bull Soc Chem Belg
Bulletin of the Chemical Society of Japan (SAUO) ... Bull Chem Soc Jp
Bulletin of the Chemical Society of Japan (journ.) (SAUS) ... Bull Chem Soc Jp
Bulletin of the Faculty of Arts, Cairo (journ.) (SAUS) ... BFAC
Bulletin of the Fisheries Research Board of Canada (SAUS) ... Bull Fish Res Board Can
Bulletin of the Friends Historical Association (journ.) (SAUS) ... BFHA

Bulletin of the Geisinger Medical Center (SAUS) .... Bull Geisinger Med Cent
Bulletin of the Geological Society of Finland (SAUO) .... Bull Geol Soc Finl
Bulletin of the Georgia Academy of Science (SAUS) .... Bull Ga Acad Sci
Bulletin of the Historical Society of Montgomery County (journ.) (SAUS) .... BHSMCo
Bulletin of the Imperial institute. London (SAUS) .... Imperial institute bulletins
Bulletin of the Indian Society of Soil Science (SAUO) .... Bull Indian Soc Soil Sci
Bulletin of the Institute of History and Philology (journ.) (SAUS) .... BIHP
Bulletin of the Institute of Maritime and Tropical Medicine in Gdynia (SAUS) .... Bull Inst Marit Trop Med Gdynia
Bulletin of the Institute of Mathematics and Its Applications [*A publication*] .... BIMA
Bulletin of the International Association of Scientific Hydrology (SAUO) .... Bull Int Assoc Sci Hydrol
Bulletin of the International Committee of Historical Sciences (journ.) (SAUS) .... BICHS
Bulletin of the International Committee on Urgent Anthropological and Ethnological Research. Vienna (SAUS) .... ICUAER/B
Bulletin of the International Social Security Association. Geneva (SAUO) .... ISSA/B
Bulletin of the Japan Society of Mechanical Engineers (SAUO) .... Bull Jap Soc Mech Engrs
Bulletin of the John Rylands Library. Manchester (journ.) (SAUS) .... BJRLM
Bulletin of the John Rylands Library. Manchester (journ.) (SAUS) .... JRL/B
Bulletin of the Judge Advocate General of the Army [*Now LAAWS BBS*] (AAGC) .... Bull JAGA
Bulletin of the Kanagawa Dental College (SAUO) .... BKDC
Bulletin of the Leo Baeck Instituts (SAUO) .... LBIB
Bulletin of the Los Angeles Neurological Society (SAUO) .... Bull Los Angeles Neurol Soc
Bulletin of the Medical Library Association [*A publication*] .... BMLA
Bulletin of the Medical Library Association (journ.) (SAUS) .... Bull Med Libr Ass
Bulletin of the Menninger Clinic (SAUS) .... Bull Menninger Clin
Bulletin of the Metals Museum [*A publication*] [*Sendai, Japan*] .... BMM
Bulletin of the National Research Council [*A publication*] (BARN) .... BNRC
Bulletin of the New York Academy of Medicine (SAUS) .... Bull NY Acad Med
Bulletin of the New York Herpetological Society (SAUO) .... HERP
Bulletin of the New York Zoological Society (SAUO) .... Bull NYZS
Bulletin of the New York Zoological Society (journ.) (SAUS) .... Bull NYZS
Bulletin of the Parenteral Drug Association (SAUO) .... Bull Parenter Drug Assoc
Bulletin of the Philosophical Society of Washington [*A publication*] (BARN) .... BPSW
Bulletin o.f the Seismological Society of America (SAUO) .... Bull Seismol Soc Am
Bulletin of the Seismological Society of America (SAUO) .... Bull Seismol Soc Amer
Bulletin of the Seismological Society of America (journ.) (SAUS) .... Bull Seismol Soc Am
Bulletin of the Southern California Academy of Sciences (SAUS) .... Bull South Calif Acad Sci
Bulletin of the Torrey Botanical Club (SAUS) .... Bull Torrey Bot Club
Bulletin of the Wildlife Society (SAUO) .... Bull Wildl Soc
Bulletin of the World Health Organization (SAUS) .... Bull Wld Hlth Org
Bulletin of the World Health Organization (SAUS) .... Bull World Health Organ
Bulletin of Tokyo Medical and Dental University (SAUO) .... Bull Tokyo Med Dent Univ
Bulletin Officiel des Annonces des Marches Publics [*Direction des Journaux Officiels*] [*Database*] .... BOAMP
Bulletin on the Rheumatic Diseases (SAUS) .... Bull Rheum Dis
Bulletin. Quebec Society of Criminology [*A publication*] (DLA) .... Bull Que Soc Crim
Bulletin. Societe "Union Musicologique" [*A publication*] .... BUM
Bulletin. Sydney Division. Institution of Engineers of Australia [*A publication*] .... Bull Syd Div Instn Eng Aust
Bulletin. Taichung District Agricultural Improvement Station (journ.) (SAUS) .... TCNPEX
Bulletin. Tokyo Gakugei University (journ.) (SAUS) .... TGUBA
Bulletin. United States Trademark Association Series [*A publication*] (DLA) .... Trademark Bull
Bulletin. United States Trademark Association Series (journ.) (SAUS) .... Trademark Bull
Bulletin Usuel des Lois et Arretes [*A publication*] (ILCA) .... Bull Us
Bulletin. Utah Engineering Experiment Station (journ.) (SAUS) .... UEEBA
Bulletin with Newsweek [*A publication*] (APTA) .... B/N
Bulletin/Hospital for Joint Diseases (SAUS) .... Bull Hosp Jt Dis
Bulletin-Press, Sioux Rapids, IA [*Library symbol*] [*Library of Congress*] (LCLS) .... IaSrBP
Bulletins (SAUS) .... Bulls
Bulletins and Orders (NUCP) .... B and O
Bulletins and Orders Task Force [*Nuclear Regulatory Commission*] (NRCH) .... B & OTF
Bulletins (journ.) (SAUS) .... RB
Bulletins of Ordnance Information .... BOI
Bulletproof [*Army*] (AABC) .... BPRF
Bulletproof (SAUS) .... Bull Prf
Bullets At Target Range (SAUS) .... BATR
Bullet-Trap Rifle Grenade [*Army*] (INF) .... BTRG
Bullfighting [*Rodeo term*] .... BF
Bullhead City, AZ [*AM radio station call letters*] .... KBAS
Bullhead City, AZ [*AM radio station call letters*] .... KFLG
Bullhead City, AZ [*FM radio station call letters*] .... KFLG-FM
Bullhead City [*Arizona*]**/Laughlin** [*Nevada*] [*Airport symbol*] (OAG) .... BHC
Bulliat [*Let It Boil*] [*Pharmacy*] .... BULL
Bullientis [*Boiling*] [*Pharmacy*] (ROG) .... BULLIENT
Bulling the Market [*Investment term*] .... BTM
Bullingbroke's Ecclesiastical Law [*A publication*] (DLA) .... Bull Eccl
Bullion (ROG) .... BLLN
Bullion (ROG) .... BLN
Bullion Range Exploration [*Vancouver Stock Exchange symbol*] .... BIN
Bullnose (SAUS) .... BN
Bullnose Morris Club (EA) .... BMC
Bullock Ridge Splitting [*Agriculture*] .... BL
Bullocks Harbour/Great Harbour Cay, Berry Island [*Bahamas*] [*ICAO location identifier*] (ICLI) .... MYBG
Bullous Ichthyosis [*Dermatology*] .... BI
Bullous Impetigo [*Medicine*] (MELL) .... BI
Bullous Pemphigoid [*Medicine*] .... BP
Bullous Pemphigoid Antigen [*Immunology*] .... BPA
Bullous Pemphigoid Antigen [*Medicine*] (DMAA) .... BPAG
Bullpup All-Weather Guidance System [*Naval Ordnance Systems Command*] .... BAGS
Bullpup Board of Directors (SAUO) .... BBOD
Bull's Eye Nonuniformity (AAEL) .... BENU
Bulls Gap, TN [*FM radio station call letters*] (BROA) .... WBGQ-FM
Bullseye Cancel Collectors Club .... BCCC
Bullseye Class Association (EA) .... BCA
Bullseye Engineering and Technical Services (DNAB) .... BETS
Bulolo [*Papua New Guinea*] [*Airport symbol*] (OAG) .... BUL
Bulonge-Kigogo [*Zaire*] [*ICAO location identifier*] (ICLI) .... FZMK
Bulova Watch Company, Inc. (SAUO) .... BVA
Bulstrode's English King's Bench Reports [*1610-25*] [*A publication*] (DLA) .... Buls
Bulstrode's English King's Bench Reports [*1610-25*] [*A publication*] (DLA) .... Bulst
Bulstrode's English King's Bench Reports [*1610-25*] [*A publication*] (DLA) .... Bulstr
Bulwark .... BWK
Bulwark (SAUS) .... Bwk
Bulwer-Lytton Fiction Contest (SAUS) .... BLFC
Bum Boy [*Slang*] [*British*] (DSUE) .... BB
BUM International, Inc. [*Associated Press*] (SAG) .... BUM Int
BUM International, Inc. [*NASDAQ symbol*] (SAG) .... BUMM
Bumba [*Zaire*] [*Airport symbol*] (OAG) .... BMB
Bumba [*Zaire*] [*ICAO location identifier*] (ICLI) .... FZFU
Bum-Fodder [*Toilet paper*] [*Slang*] [*British*] (DSUE) .... BUMF
Bumiputra Malaysia Finance Ltd. (SAUO) .... BMFL
Bump. Federal Procedure [*A publication*] (DLA) .... Bump Fed Pr
Bump on Bankruptcy [*A publication*] (DLA) .... Bump B'k'cy
Bump on Composition in Bankruptcy [*A publication*] (DLA) .... Bump Comp
Bump on Fraudulent Conveyances [*A publication*] (DLA) .... Bump Fraud Conv
Bump on Fraudulent Conveyances [*A publication*] (DLA) .... Bump Fr Conv
Bump Protection Hat .... BPH
Bump, Squeak, and Rattle [*Automotive characterization*] .... BSR
Bump Storage (SAUS) .... BS
Bump. United States Stamp Laws [*A publication*] (DLA) .... Bump St L
Bumped [*Bookselling*] (DGA) .... BMP
Bumped Tape Automated Bonding [*Electronics*] (AAEL) .... BTAB
Bumped Tape Carrier Bonding (SAUS) .... BTCB
Bumper [*Automotive engineering*] .... BMPR
Bumper Fracture [*Medicine*] (MELL) .... BF
Bumper Impulse Detector .... BID
Bumper Lift Jack .... BLJ
Bumper Limiter/Protective Plates (MCD) .... BL/PP
Bumper Recycling Association of North America (EA) .... BRANA
Bumper to Back of Cab [*Automotive engineering*] .... BBC
Bumper to Bumper .... BTB
Bump's Internal Revenue Laws [*A publication*] (DLA) .... Bump Int Rev
Bump's Internal Revenue Laws [*A publication*] (DLA) .... Bump's Int Rev Law
Bump's Law of Patents, Trade-Marks, Etc. [*A publication*] (DLA) .... Bump Pat
Bump's Notes on Constitutional Decisions [*A publication*] (DLA) .... Bump Const Dec
Bump's Notes on Constitutional Decisions [*A publication*] (DLA) .... Bump NC
Bumpstead [*England*] .... BUMP
Bumthills Aviation Ltd. (SAUO) .... JG
Bunbury [*Australia*] [*Airport symbol*] (OAG) .... BUY
Bunbury. English Exchequer Reports [*145 English Reprint*] [*A publication*] (DLA) .... Bunb
Bunbury Institute of Advanced Education [*Australia*] .... BIAE
Bunch (WGA) .... BCH
Bunch (DNAB) .... BH
Bunch Block (SAUS) .... BB
Bunch Of Dumb Terminals (SAUS) .... BODT
[*A*] **Bunch of Guys Seated around a Table Method** [*Facetious description of a decision-making process*] .... BOGSAT
[*A*] **Bunch of Guys Sitting around a Table Method** [*Facetious description of a decision-making process*] .... BOGSAAT
[*A*] **Bunch of Jewish Kids** [*Slang*] (BJA) .... ABOJK
Bunched .... bchd
Bunching (MSA) .... BCHG
Bunching Block (MSA) .... BB
Bund der Amateurtheater (SAUO) .... BdA
Bund deutscher Amateurtheater e.V. (SAUO) .... BdA
Bundaberg [*Australia*] [*ICAO location identifier*] (ICLI) .... ABBU
Bundaberg [*Australia*] [*Airport symbol*] (OAG) .... BDB
Bund-Communist Party [*Political party*] (BJA) .... BCP
Bundelkund Legion [*British military*] (DMA) .... BL
Bundesamt fuer Militarflugplatze [*Switzerland*] [*ICAO designator*] (FAAC) .... BAMF
Bundesamt fuer Verfassungsschutz [*Federal Office for the Protection of the Constitution*] [*West German counterintelligence agency*] .... BfV
Bundesamt fur Militarflugplatze [*Switzerland*] [*ICAO designator*] (FAAC) .... SUI
Bundesamt fur Statistik [*Federal Statistical Office*] [*Information service or system*] (IID) .... BFS

Bundesanstalt fuer Materialforschung und -Pruefung [*Federal Institute for Materials Research and Testing*] [*Database producer*] [*Germany*] [*Information retrieval*] (IID) .... BAM

Bundesanstalt fuer Materialprufung Unter den Eichen [*International Association for Structural Mechanics in Reactor Technology*] (EAIO) .... BAM

Bundesanwalt [*Public Prosecutor or Attorney General*] [*German*] (ILCA) .... BA

Bundesanwaltschaft [*The Office of Public Prosecutor*] [*German*] (ILCA) .... BA

Bundesanzeiger Verlagsgesellschaft, mbH, Koln, Germany [*Library symbol*] [*Library of Congress*] (LCLS) .... GyKoB

Bundesarbeitsgericht [*Federal Supreme Labour Court*] [*German*] (DLA) .... BAG

Bundesarbeitsgericht [*Federal Labor Court*] [*German*] (ILCA) .... BArbG

Bundesaufsichtsamt fur das Kreditwesen [*Federal Supervisory Office for Credit*] [*Germany*] .... BAK

Bundesfinanzhof [*Federal Supreme Fiscal Court*] [*German*] (DLA) .... BFH

Bundesforschungsanstalt fuer Fischerei [*Database producer*] [*Germany*] .... BFF

Bundesgericht [*Federal Supreme Court*] [*German*] (DLA) .... BG

Bundesgerichtshof [*Federal Supreme Court*] [*German*] (DLA) .... BGH

Bundesgesetz [*Federal Act or Statute*] [*German*] (ILCA) .... BdG

Bundesgesetz [*Federal Act or Statute*] [*German*] (ILCA) .... BdGes

Bundesgesetz [*Federal Act or Statute*] [*German*] (ILCA) .... BG

Bundesgesundheitsamt [*Database producer*] .... BGA

Bundesgrenzschutz [*West Germany*] [*Military*] (NATG) .... BGS

Bundesinstitut fuer Sportwissenschaft [*Federal Institute for Sports Science*] [*Germany*] (IID) .... BISp

Bundeskanzler [*Federal Chancellor*] [*German*] (ILCA) .... BK

Bundeskanzleramt [*Federal Chancery*] [*German*] (ILCA) .... BK

Bundeskartellamt [*Federal Cartel Office*] [*German*] (ILCA) .... BKA

Bundeskriminalamt [*Federal Criminal Police Bureau*] [*Germany*] .... BKA

Bundesminister der Justiz [*Federal Minister of Justice*] [*German*] (ILCA) .... BMJ

Bundesministerium fuer Forschung und Technologie [*Ministry for Research and Technology*] [*Information service or system*] [*Germany*] (IID) .... BMFT

Bundesnachrichtendienst [*Federal Intelligence Service*] [*Germany*] .... BND

Bundesrat (SAUO) .... BRt

Bundesrepublik Deutschland [*Federal Republic of Germany*] .... BRD

Bundesrueckerstattungsgesetz [*A publication*] (BJA) .... BRuG

Bundessozialgericht [*Federal Court of Social Security*] [*German*] (ILCA) .... BSG

Bundessozialgericht [*Federal Supreme Social Security Court*] [*German*] (DLA) .... B Soz G

Bundesstelle fuer Aussenhandelsinformation [*Federal Office of Foreign Trade Information*] [*German Ministry of Economics*] (IID) .... BfAi

Bundesverband der Deutschen Industrie [*Federation of German Industries*] .... BDI

Bundesvereinigung Deutscher Apothekerverbande [*German Pharmaceutical Association Research Institute*] [*Information service or system*] (IID) .... ABDA

Bundesverfassungsgericht [*Federal Constitutional Court*] [*German*] (DLA) .... B Verf G

Bundesverwaltungsgericht [*Federal Supreme Administrative Court*] [*German*] (DLA) .... B Verw G

Bundi [*Papua New Guinea*] [*Airport symbol*] (OAG) .... BNT

Bundle (MCD) .... BD

Bundle (WDMC) .... bd

Bundle (ADWA) .... bdl

Bundle .... BDL

Bundle .... BDLE

Bundle (ADWA) .... bdle

Bundle .... BNDL

Bundle Adjustment for SPOT Imagery of CSRSC at Central University (SAUO) .... BASICC

Bundle Assembly (SAA) .... BA

Bundle Branch Block [*Cardiology*] .... BBB

Bundle Controlled Expansion .... BCEX

Bundle Drawing Process [*Metal fiber technology*] .... BDP

Bundle of His [*Cardiology*] (DAVI) .... BH

Bundle-Branch [*Cardiology*] (DAVI) .... BB

Bundle-Branch Heart Block [*Cardiology*] (DAVI) .... BBHB

Bundled Bark Strips (SAUS) .... Bdl bk s

Bundle-Forming Pili [*Microbiology*] .... BFP

Bundles (SAUS) .... Bdles

Bundles .... BDLS

Bundles for Britain (SAUO) .... BFB

Bungalow (REAL) .... bnglw

Bungalow .... BU

Bungalow [*Classified advertising*] (ADA) .... BUNG

Bungarotoxin [*Also, BTX, BuTx*] [*Biochemistry*] .... BGT

Bungarotoxin [*Also, BGT, BuTx*] [*Biochemistry*] .... BTX

Bungarotoxin [*Also, BGT, BTX*] [*Biochemistry*] .... BuTx

Bung-Hole [*i.e., cheese*] [*British slang*] .... BH

bungling bureaucrat (SAUS) .... bb

Bungo Tebo/Pasir Mayang [*Indonesia*] [*ICAO location identifier*] (ICLI) .... WIPI

Bungoma [*Kenya*] [*ICAO location identifier*] (ICLI) .... HKBU

Bunia [*Zaire*] [*Airport symbol*] (AD) .... BUX

Bunia [*Zaire*] [*ICAO location identifier*] (ICLI) .... FZKA

Bunia-Ruampara [*Zaire*] [*Geomagnetic observatory code*] .... B

Bunion (MELL) .... B

Bunion [*Orthopedics and podiatry*] (DAVI) .... BUN

Bunker Adjustment Charge .... BAC

Bunker Adjustment Factor [*Business term*] .... BAF

Bunker Defeat Munition [*Army*] (INF) .... BDM

Bunker Fuel Oil (DS) .... BFO

Bunker Hill Income Securities, Inc. (SAUO) .... BHL

Bunker Hill Mining [*Vancouver Stock Exchange symbol*] .... BNH

Bunker Hill Public Library, Bunker Hill, IL [*Library symbol*] [*Library of Congress*] (LCLS) .... IBun

Bunker on Board (RIMS) .... BOB

Bunker Surcharge (SAUS) .... BS

Bunkered Target Munition (ACAE) .... BTM

Bunker-Ramo Corp. (SAUO) .... BR

Bunker-Ramo Corporation (SAUO) .... BRC

Bunkers Remaining on Board (RIMS) .... BROB

Bunkie, LA [*FM radio station call letters*] .... KEZP

Bunkum [*Nonsense*] [*Slang*] (DSUE) .... BUNK

Bunnie Mills Fan Club (EA) .... BMFC

Bunnies and Burrows (SAUS) .... BB

Bunno Bedele [*Ethiopia*] [*ICAO location identifier*] (ICLI) .... HABB

Bunnythorpe [*New Zealand*] [*Seismograph station code, US Geological Survey*] [*Closed*] (SEIS) .... BUN

Buno-Bonnevaux [*France*] [*ICAO location identifier*] (ICLI) .... LFFB

Bunt [*Baseball term*] (NDBD) .... B

Bunt [*Baseball*] (BARN) .... b

Buntok/Sanggau [*Indonesia*] [*ICAO location identifier*] (ICLI) .... WRBU

Bunyon. Domestic Law [*1875*] [*A publication*] (DLA) .... Buny Dom L

Bunyon. Fire Insurance [*7th ed.*] [*1923*] [*A publication*] (DLA) .... Buny Fire Ins

Bunyon. Life Insurance [*5th ed.*] [*1914*] [*A publication*] (DLA) .... Buny Life Ins

Bunyon on Life Assurance [*A publication*] (DLA) .... Buny Life Ass

Bunzl Flexpack Ltd. [*British*] .... BFL

Bunzl PLC ADS [*NYSE symbol*] (SG) .... BNL

Buoni del Tesoro Poliennali [*Italy*] (ECON) .... BTP

Buonmethuot/Chung Duc [*Viet Nam*] [*ICAO location identifier*] (ICLI) .... VVBM

Buoy (SAUS) .... Bu

Buoy (SAUS) .... By

Buoy Boat .... BU

Buoy Boat, Stern Loading .... BUSL

Buoy Integrated Antenna Submarine [*or System*] (MCD) .... BIAS

Buoy Messenger .... BMSS

Buoy Power Supply .... BPS

Buoy Tender [*Coast Guard symbol*] (DNAB) .... WYTM

Buoy Underwater Sound Signal (NG) .... BUSS

Buoyancy .... B

Buoyancy Actuated Launch and Retrieval Elevator (SAUS) .... BALARE

Buoyancy Compensator Device .... BCD

Buoyancy Compensators .... BC

Buoyancy Control Device (SAUS) .... BCD

Buoyancy Induced Dispersion (GFGA) .... BID

Buoyancy Transport Vehicle (MCD) .... BTV

Buoyant (MSA) .... BYNT

Buoyant Ballistic Inertial Missile (MCD) .... BBIM

Buoyant Cable Antenna (SAUS) .... BCA

Buoyant Capsule (MCD) .... BC

Buoyant Line and Point Source Model [*Environmental Protection Agency*] (GFGA) .... BLP

Buoyant Venus Station [*NASA*] .... BVS

bupivacaine hydrochloride (SAUS) .... bupiv

Buprenorphine [*Analgesic*] .... BUP

Bur Oak Library System [*Library network*] .... BOLS

Bura [*Kenya*] [*ICAO location identifier*] (ICLI) .... HKBR

Buraimi [*Oman*] [*ICAO location identifier*] (ICLI) .... OOBR

Burao [*Somalia*] [*Airport symbol*] (OAG) .... BUO

Burao [*Somalia*] [*ICAO location identifier*] (ICLI) .... HCMV

Buras, LA [*FM radio station call letters*] (RBYB) .... KMRL

Burbank [*California*] [*Airport symbol*] .... BUR

Burbank, CA [*AM radio station call letters*] .... KRCK

Burbank Public Library, Burbank, CA [*Library symbol*] [*Library of Congress*] (LCLS) .... CBb

Burbank/Hollywood-Burbank [*California*] [*ICAO location identifier*] (ICLI) .... KBUR

Burchardus Wormatiensis [*Deceased, 1025*] [*Authority cited in pre-1607 legal work*] (DSA) .... B

Burda-MarketingInfoSystem [*Burda GmbH, Marketing Service Department*] [*Information service or system*] (IID) .... MADIS

Burdekin Agricultural College [*Australia*] .... BAC

Burdekin River Irrigation Area Advisory Committee [*Queensland, Australia*] .... BRIAAC

Burdekin River Irrigation Area Technical Advisory Committee [*Queensland, Australia*] .... BRIATAC

Burden Center .... BC

Burden of Going Forward [*Legal shorthand*] (LWAP) .... BOGF

Burden of Proof [*Legal shorthand*] (LWAP) .... BOP

Burden Rate Adjustment (MCD) .... BRA

Burdett College (SAUO) .... BC

Burdett Resources Ltd. [*Vancouver Stock Exchange symbol*] .... BDT

Burdick [*Suction*] [*Surgery*] (DAVI) .... BURD

Burdick Suction [*Medicine*] (BABM) .... Burd

Burdick's Law of Crime [*A publication*] (DLA) .... Burdick Crime

Burdick's Principles of Roman Law [*A publication*] (DLA) .... Burdick Roman Law

Burdock Yellows Virus [*Plant pathology*] .... BUYV

Bureau (AABC) .... BU

Bureau (ADWA) .... bu

Bureau (SAUO) .... Bu

Bureau .... BUR

Bureau (WDMC) .... bur

Bureau (AL) .... Bur

Bureau Arabe de Presse et de Publications [*Paris*] (BJA) .... BAPP

Bureau Canadien de l'Education Internationale [*Canadian Bureau for International Education - CBIE*] .... BCEI

Bureau Central de Compensation [*Central Bureau of Compensation - CBC*] (EAIO) .... BCC

Bureau Central des Renseignements et d'Action [*French Resistance organization*] .... BCRA

Bureau Central Recreation Fund (SAUO) .... BCRF

Bureau Chief (DEMM) .... BC

Bureau Control Activity Number ... BCAN
Bureau Control Number ... BCN
Bureau Control Number (ACAE) ... BUCON
Bureau County Historical Society, Princeton, IL [*Library symbol*] [*Library of Congress*] (LCLS) ... IPriHi
Bureau d'Amenagement du Nouvel Aeroport International de Montreal [*New Montreal International Airport Project Office - NMIAPO*] [*Canada*] ... BANAIM
Bureau de la Baie James et du Nord Quebecois, Ste.-Foy, PQ, Canada [*Library symbol*] [*Library of Congress*] (LCLS) ... CaQQBJNQ
Bureau de la Baie James et du Nord Quebecois, Ste.-Foy, Quebec [*Library symbol*] [*National Library of Canada*] (NLC) ... QQBJNQ
Bureau de la Cooperation et du Developpement International [*Office for International Cooperation & Development*] (AC) ... BCDI
Bureau de la Science et de la Technologie, Quebec, PQ, Canada [*Library symbol*] [*Library of Congress*] (LCLS) ... CaQQBST
Bureau de la Statistique du Quebec, Quebec, PQ, Canada [*Library symbol*] [*Library of Congress*] (LCLS) ... CaQQBS
Bureau de la Statistique du Quebec, Quebec, Quebec [*Library symbol*] [*National Library of Canada*] (NLC) ... QQBS
Bureau de l'Assistance Technique [*Technical Assistance Bureau*] ... BAT
Bureau de Liaison de l'Information Religieuse dans l'Ocean Indien [*Indian Ocean Religious Information Liaison Office*] (AF) ... BLIROI
Bureau de Liaison des Industries du Caoutchouc de la CEE [*Rubber Industries Liaison Bureau of the EEC*] [*Belgium*] ... BLIC
Bureau de Liaison des Syndicats Europeens (CEE) des Produits Aromatiques [*Liaison Bureau of the European and EEC Unions of Aromatic Products*] (EAIO) ... BLA
Bureau de Recherche et de Consultation en Education [*Bureau of Research and Consultation in Education*] [*Canada*] ... BRCE
Bureau de Recherches Geologiques et Minieres [*Bureau of Geological and MiningResearch*] [*Burkina Faso*] [*Information service or system*] (IID) ... BRGM
Bureau de Traduction, Gouvernement du Nouveau-Brunswick [*Translation Bureau, Governement of New Brunswick*] **Fredericton, New Brunswick** [*Library symbol*] [*National Library of Canada*] (NLC) ... NBFT
Bureau d'Education Ibero-Americain ... BEIA
Bureau des Jeux Olympiques d'Hiver de 1988, Gouvernement du Canada [*Office of the 1988 Winter Olympic Games, Government of Canada*] ... BJOH
Bureau des Plans de Vol Repetitifs [*FAA designator*] (FAAC) ... ZBZ
Bureau d'Etudes Industrielles et de Cooperation, Institut Francais du Petrole [*Office of Industrial Studies and Cooperation, French Institute of Petroleum*] [*Canada*] ... BEICIP
Bureau d'Information et de Presse [*Circulated Allied propaganda in France and informed Allies of resistance activities*] [*World War II*] ... BIP
Bureau d'Informations et de Previsions Economiques [*Office of Economic Information and Forecasting*] [*Information service or system*] (IID) ... BIPE
Bureau d'Interventions Cliniques et Communautaires [*Office of Clinical and Communal Operations*] [*Canada*] ... BICC
Bureau d'Investissement en Afrique [*Office of Investments in Africa*] [*France*] (AF) ... BIA
Bureau du Coordonnateur, Reforme de la Reglementation [*Office of the Coordinator, Regulatory Reform*] [*Canada*] ... BCRR
Bureau du Verificateur General du Canada [*Office of the Auditor-General of Canada*] ... BVG
Bureau Electr Pubg Wrrt [*NASDAQ symbol*] (TTSB) ... BEPIW
Bureau Electronics Equipment Model [*Navy*] (MCD) ... BEEM
Bureau Equipment List (MCD) ... BEL
Bureau Europeen de Controle et d'Etudes Generales ... BECEG
Bureau Europeen de Coordination des Organisations Internationales de Jeunesse [*European Coordination Bureau for International Youth Organizations - ECB*] (EAIO) ... BEC
Bureau Europeen de la Jeunesse et de l'Enfance ... BEJE
Bureau Europeen de l'Education Populaire [*European Bureau of Adult Education - EBAE*] (EAIO) ... BEEP
Bureau Europeen des Unions de Consommateurs [*European Bureau of Consumers' Unions*] (EAIO) ... BEUC
Bureau Federal d'Examen des Evaluations Environnementales [*Federal Environmental Assessment Review Office*] [*Canada*] ... BFEEE
Bureau for Adult Thalidomide Victims [*West Germany*] ... BATV
Bureau for Africa and Europe [*AID*] ... BAE
Bureau for Africa, Office of the Sahel & Francophone W. African Affair (SAUO) ... AFR/SWA
Bureau for Careers in Jewish Service [*Defunct*] (EA) ... BCJS
Bureau for Education Technology and Administration (SAUO) ... BETA
[*The*] **Bureau for Excellence in Durham Region** (AC) ... BEDR
Bureau for Far East (SAUO) ... BFE
Bureau for Latin America [*Agency for International Development*] ... BLA
Bureau for Near East and South Asia (SAUO) ... BNESA
Bureau for Overseas Medical Service [*British*] (CB) ... BOMS
Bureau for Policy and Program Support [*United Nations*] (ECON) ... BPPS
Bureau for Private Enterprise ... PRE
Bureau for Reference and Loan Services [*Library network*] ... R & L
Bureau for the Advancement of Independent Retailing (EA) ... BAIR
Bureau Hydrographique International [*International Hydrographic Organization*] (EAIO) ... BHI
Bureau Inlichtingen [*Netherlands Information Office*] [*World War II*] ... BI
Bureau, Institute, and Division [*National Institutes of Health*] ... BID
Bureau Interafricain de Developpement et de Cooperation [*Inter-African Development and Cooperation Office*] (AF) ... BIDC
Bureau Interafricain des Sols et de l'Economie Rurale [*Inter-African Bureau of Soils and Rural Economy*] ... BIS
Bureau Interafricain des Sols et de l'Economie Rurale [*Inter-African Soils and Rural Economy Office*] (AF) ... BISER
Bureau Interforces de Codification (SAUS) ... BLC
Bureau International Afghanistan (EA) ... BIA
Bureau International Catholique de l'Enfance [*International Catholic Child Bureau - ICCB*] [*Geneva, Switzerland*] (EA) ... BICE
Bureau International d'Anthropologie Differentielle [*International Bureau of Differential Anthropology*] ... BIAD
Bureau International d'Audiophonologie [*International Office for Audiophonology - IOA*] [*Brussels, Belgium*] (EA) ... BIAP
Bureau International de Documentation des Chemins de Fer [*International Office of Railway Documentation*] ... BDC
Bureau International de la Chaussure et du Cuir ... BIC
Bureau International de la Recuperation [*International Bureau of Recuperation*] [*Brussels, Belgium*] (EA) ... BIR
Bureau International de l'Edition Mecanique ... BIEM
Bureau International de l'Heure [*International Time Bureau*] (EAIO) ... BIH
Bureau International de Recherche sur les Implications Sociales du Progres Technique ... BIRISPT
Bureau International d'Education [*International Bureau of Education - IBE*] (EAIO) ... BIE
Bureau International des Containers [*International Container Bureau*] [*Paris, France*] (EAIO) ... BIC
Bureau International des Expositions [*International Bureau of Exhibitions*] (EAIO) ... BIE
Bureau International des Poids et Mesures [*International Bureau of Weights and Measures*] [*Sevres, France*] (EA) ... BIPM
Bureau International des Producteurs d'Assurances et de Reassurances [*International Association of Insurance and Reinsurance Intermediaries - IAIRI*] [*Paris, France*] (EAIO) ... BIPAR
Bureau International des Universites ... BIU
Bureau International d'Information des Chambres de Commerce ... BIICC
Bureau International du Beton Manufacture [*International Bureau for Precast Concrete*] (EAIO) ... BIBM
Bureau International du Cinema [*International Cinematograph Bureau*] ... BIC
Bureau International du Film des Chemins de Fer [*International Railway Film Bureau*] ... BFC
Bureau International du Scoutisme ... BIS
Bureau International du Tourisme Social [*International Bureau of Social Tourism - IBST*] (EAIO) ... BITS
Bureau International du Travail [*International Labour Office*] [*French*] ... BIT
Bureau International Permanent de Chimie Analytique pour les Matieres Destinees a l'Alimentation de l'Homme et des Animaux [*Permanent International Bureau of Analytical Chemistry of Human and Animal Food*] ... BIPCA
Bureau International pour la Standardisation de la Rayonne et des Fibres Synthetiques [*International Bureau for the Standardisation of Manmade Fibres*] (EAIO) ... BISFA
Bureau International pour le Tourisme et les Echanges de la Jeunesse [*International Bureau for Youth Tourism and Exchanges*] (EAIO) ... BITEJ
Bureau International Technique de l'ABS [*Acronitrile-Butadiene-Styrene*] [*of the European Council of Chemical Manufacturers' Federations*] (EAIO) ... BITL
Bureau International Technique des Gelatines (EAIO) ... BITG
Bureau International Technique des "Inorganic Feed Phosphates" [*Inorganic Feed Phosphates International Technical Bureau - IFPITB*] (EAIO) ... BITIFP
Bureau International Technique des Polyesters (EAIO) ... BITP
Bureau International Technique des Polyesters Insatures [*of the European Council of Chemical Manufacturers' Federations*] (EAIO) ... BITPI
Bureau International Technique du Methanol [*European Council of Chemical Manufacturers' Federations*] [*Belgium*] (EAIO) ... BITM
Bureau International Technique du Spathfluor (SAUO) ... BIT Spathfluor
Bureau Issues Association (EA) ... BIA
Bureau Local d'Intervention Traitant du Sida (AC) ... BLITS
Bureau Marcel van Dijk, SA [*Information service or system*] (IID) ... BMvD
Bureau Militaire de Standardisation [*Military Agency for Standardization*] [*NATO*] ... BMS
Bureau Mineral Resources [*Austalia*] (GEOI) ... BMR
Bureau National de l'Information Scientifique et Technique [*National Scientific and Technical Information Bureau*] [*France*] [*Information service or system*] (IID) ... BNIST
Bureau National des Donnees Oceaniques [*National Bureau for Ocean Data*] [*European host database system*] [*France*] [*Information service or system*] (IID) ... BNDO
Bureau Number [*Database terminology*] (NITA) ... BN
Bureau Number [*Aircraft identification*] [*Obsolete*] [*Navy*] ... BUNO
Bureau of Accounts [*Department of the Treasury*] ... BA
Bureau of Accreditation and School Improvement Studies [*University of Michigan*] [*Research center*] (RCD) ... BASIS
Bureau of Administrative Management and Budget [*United Nations Development Program*] ... BAMB
Bureau of Adult and Vocational Education (SAUO) ... BAVE
Bureau of Adult, Vocational and Technical Education (SAUS) ... BAVTE
Bureau of Advertising (SAUO) ... BA
Bureau of Advertising (SAUO) ... BoA
Bureau of Advertising [*American Newspaper Publishers Association*] (NTCM) ... B of A
Bureau of Aeronautics (SAUO) ... Aer
Bureau of Aeronautics [*Later, Naval Air Systems Command*] ... B/A
Bureau of Aeronautics [*Later, Naval Air Systems Command*] ... BAR
Bureau of Aeronautics [*Later, Naval Air Systems Command*] [*Obsolete*] ... BUAER
Bureau of Aeronautics (SAUS) ... BuAer
Bureau of Aeronautics, Department of the Navy (SAUO) ... A
Bureau of Aeronautics General Representative [*Obsolete*] [*Navy*] ... BAGR
Bureau of Aeronautics General Representative, Eastern District [*Obsolete*] [*Navy*] ... BAGRED
Bureau of Aeronautics General Representative, Western District [*Obsolete*] [*Navy*] ... BAGRWD
Bureau of Aeronautics Industrial Reserve [*Obsolete*] [*Navy*] ... BAIR

Bureau of Aeronautics Maintenance Repair Officer [*Obsolete*] [*Navy*] ..... BAMRO
Bureau of Aeronautics Maintenance Representative [*Obsolete*] [*Navy*] ...... BAMR
Bureau of Aeronautics Maintenance Resident Representative Office [*Obsolete*] [*Navy*] ..... BAMRRO
Bureau of Aeronautics Material Officer [*Obsolete*] [*Navy*] ..... BAMO
Bureau of Aeronautics Representative (SAUO) ..... BAMR
Bureau of Aeronautics Representative [*Obsolete*] [*Navy*] ..... BAR
Bureau of Aeronautics Reserve Training Unit (SAUO) ..... BARTU
Bureau of Aeronautics Resident Representative [*Obsolete*] [*Navy*] ..... BARR
Bureau of Aeronautics Shipment Order [*Obsolete*] [*Navy*] ..... BASO
Bureau of Aeronautics Shipping Order (SAUO) ..... BASO
Bureau of Aeronautics Training Unit [*Obsolete*] [*Navy*] ..... BARTU
Bureau of African Affairs [*Department of State*] ..... BAA
Bureau of Agricultural and Industrial Chemistry [*Department of Agriculture*] ..... BAIC
Bureau of Agricultural Chemistry and Engineering (SAUS) ..... BACE
Bureau of Agricultural Chemistry and Engineering (SAUO) ..... BCE
Bureau of Agricultural Economics [*Functions dispersed, 1953*] [*Department of Agriculture*] ..... BAE
Bureau of Agricultural Economics (SAUO) ..... BOAE
Bureau of Agricultural Engineering (SAUO) ..... BAEng
Bureau of Air Commerce [*Later, Civil Aeronautics Authority*] ..... BAC
Bureau of Air Commerce Type Certificate (SAUS) ..... ACRC
Bureau of Air Commerce Type Certificate ..... ACTC
Bureau of Air Commerce Type Certificate (SAUO) ..... ACTC
Bureau of Air Pollution Sciences ..... BAPS
Bureau of Air Quality Control (COE) ..... BAQC
Bureau of Air Traffic Management ..... BATM
Bureau of Aircraft Production (SAUO) ..... BAP
Bureau of Alcohol, Tobacco, and Firearms [*Department of the Treasury*] ..... ATF
Bureau of Alcohol, Tobacco, and Firearms [*Department of the Treasury*] ..... BATF
Bureau of Alcohol, Tobacco, and Firearms Laboratory, Washington, DC [*OCLC symbol*] (OCLC) ..... ATF
Bureau of American Ethnology [*of the Smithsonian Institution*] ..... BAE
Bureau of Analyzed Samples [*British*] ..... BAS
Bureau of Animal Industry [*Department of Agriculture*] ..... BAI
Bureau of Animal Industry (SAUO) ..... BAInd
Bureau of Animal Welfare [*Victoria, Australia*] ..... BAW
Bureau of Applied Social Research [*Columbia University*] (IID) ..... BASR
Bureau of Apprenticeship (SAUO) ..... BA
Bureau of Apprenticeship and Training [*Department of Labor*] ..... BAT
Bureau of Audio-Visual Aids (SAUO) ..... BAVA
Bureau of Audio-Visual Education (SAUO) ..... BAVE
Bureau of Audio-Visual Educational (SAUS) ..... BAVE
Bureau of Automotive Regulation ..... BAR
Bureau of Automotive Repair (SAUO) ..... BAR
Bureau of Aviation Medicine (KSC) ..... BAM
Bureau of Aviation Safety (SAUO) ..... BAS
Bureau of Bilingual Publications (SAUO) ..... BBP
Bureau of Biological and Physical Sciences (SAUO) ..... BBPS
Bureau of Biological Research [*Rutgers University*] [*Research center*] (RCD) ..... BBR
Bureau of Biologics [*Also, BOB*] [*FDA*] ..... BB
Bureau of Biologics [*Also, BB*] [*FDA*] ..... BOB
Bureau of Broadcast Measurement [*Canada*] (NTCM) ..... BBM
Bureau of Business and Economic Research [*Old Dominion University*] [*Norfolk, VA*] [*Research center*] (RCD) ..... BBER
Bureau of Business Research [*University of Texas, Austin*] [*Information service or system*] (IID) ..... BBR
Bureau of Catholic Indian Missions (EA) ..... BCIM
Bureau of Charities and Corrections (SAUO) ..... BCCA
Bureau of Child Welfare (SAUO) ..... BCW
Bureau of Child Welfare (BARN) ..... BCW
Bureau of Commercial Fisheries (SAUO) ..... BCF
Bureau of Commercial Fisheries [*Later, National Marine Fisheries Service*] (MCD) ..... BOCF
Bureau of Commercial Research (SAUO) ..... BCR
Bureau of Commerical Fisheries [*Now National Marine Fisheries Service*] (USDC) ..... BSF
Bureau of Community Corrections (OICC) ..... BCC
Bureau of Community Environmental Management [*Terminated, 1973*] [*HEW*] ..... BCEM
Bureau of Community Facilities (SAUO) ..... BCF
Bureau of Community Health Services [*Health Services Administration*] ..... BCHS
Bureau of Community Health Services (SAUO) ..... BoCHS
Bureau of Competitive Assessment and Business Policy [*Department of Commerce*] ..... BCABP
Bureau of Compliance Planning and Support [*Department of Emergency Management*] (DEMM) ..... BCPS
Bureau of Conference Planning and General Service (SAUO) ..... CPG
Bureau of Construction and Repair [*Until 1940*] [*Navy*] ..... BUC & R
Bureau of Construction and Repair [*Until 1940*] [*Navy*] ..... BUCON
Bureau of Construction and Repair [*Until 1940*] [*Navy*] ..... C & R
Bureau of Construction and Repair (SAUO) ..... C&R
Bureau of Consular Affairs (SAUO) ..... BCA
Bureau of Consular Affairs-Department of State (SAUO) ..... BCA/DoS
Bureau of Consultation [*Federal Trade Commission*] ..... BC
Bureau of Consumer Affairs (SAUO) ..... BCA
Bureau of Contract Information [*Defunct*] (EA) ..... BCI
Bureau of Co-ordination of Arabization (SAUO) ..... BCA
Bureau of Correction (SAUO) ..... BoC
Bureau of Correctional Institutions (SAUO) ..... BCI
Bureau of Cosmotherapy (SAUO) ..... BC
Bureau of Crime Statistics and Research [*New South Wales, Australia*] ..... BCSR
Bureau of Criminal Identification (SAUO) ..... BCI
Bureau of Criminal Investigation (SAUO) ..... BCI
Bureau of Criminal Investigation (BARN) ..... BCI
Bureau of Criminal Statistics (BARN) ..... BCS
Bureau of Current Affairs (SAUO) ..... BCA
Bureau of Customs [*Later, US Customs Service*] [*Department of the Treasury*] ..... BC
Bureau of Customs [*Later, US Customs Service*] [*Department of the Treasury*] ..... BOC
Bureau of Dairy Industry [*Department of Agriculture*] [*Functions transferred to ARS, 1953*] ..... BDI
Bureau of Dangerous Drugs [*Canada*] ..... BDD
Bureau of Data Management and Strategy [*Department of Health and Human Services*] (GFGA) ..... BDMS
Bureau of Data Processing and Accounts [*Social Security Administration*] ..... BDPA
Bureau of Disability Insurance [*Social Security Administration*] ..... BDI
Bureau of Disease Prevention and Environment Control (SAUO) ..... BDPEC
Bureau of Disease Prevention and Environmental Control ..... BDPEC
Bureau of Documents; Dr. Pepper Company (SAUO) ..... DOC
Bureau of Domestic Business Development [*Department of Commerce*] ..... BDBD
Bureau of Domestic Commerce [*Formerly, Business and Defense Services Administration and Office of Field Services*] [*Department of Commerce*] [*Terminated, 1977, functions transferred to Domestic and International Business Administration*] ..... BDC
Bureau of Drug Abuse Control [*Absorbed by Bureau of Narcotics and Dangerous Drugs of Department of Justice*] ..... BDAC
Bureau of Drugs [*Later, Center for Drugs and Biologics*] [*FDA*] ..... BD
Bureau of Drugs (SAUO) ..... BoD
Bureau of East Asian and Pacific Affairs [*Formerly, Bureau of Far Eastern Affairs*] [*Department of State*] ..... BEAPA
Bureau of East-West Trade [*Department of Commerce*] ..... BEWT
Bureau of Economic Advisors (COE) ..... BEA
Bureau of Economic Affairs [*Later, Bureau of Economic and Business Affairs*] [*Department of State*] ..... BEA
Bureau of Economic Affairs (SAUO) ..... Bur Eco Aff
Bureau of Economic Analysis [*Department of Commerce*] [*Washington, DC*] (IID) ..... BEA
Bureau of Economic and Business Affairs [*Formerly, Bureau of Economic Affairs*] [*Department of State*] ..... BEBA
Bureau of Economic and Business Affairs (SAUO) ..... EB
Bureau of Economic and Business Research [*University of Delaware*] [*Research center*] (RCD) ..... BEBR
Bureau of Economic and Business Research [*University of Florida*] [*Gainesville*] [*Information service or system*] (IID) ..... BEBR
Bureau of Economic Geology [*Texas*] (GEOI) ..... BEG
Bureau of Economic Regulation [*of CAB*] ..... BER
Bureau of Economic Research and Development [*Virginia State University*] [*Research center*] (RCD) ..... BERD
Bureau of Economics [*Federal Trade Commission*] ..... BE
Bureau of Education for Fair Trade ..... BEFT
Bureau of Education for the Handicapped [*Office of Education*] [*Later, SEP*] ..... BEH
Bureau of Educational and Cultural Affairs [*Later Known as USIA, then as ICA or USICA, then again as USIA*] ..... BECA
Bureau of Educational and Cultural Affairs (SAUO) ..... ECA
Bureau of Educational Evaluation [*Research center*] (RCD) ..... BEE
Bureau of Educational Personnel Development [*HEW*] ..... BEPD
Bureau of Educational Research and Evaluation [*Mississippi State University*] [*Research center*] (RCD) ..... BERE
Bureau of Educational Research and Service [*Memphis State University*] [*Research center*] (RCD) ..... BERS
Bureau of Educational Research and Service [*University of Tennessee at Knoxville*] [*Research center*] (RCD) ..... BERS
Bureau of Elec Pub [*NASDAQ symbol*] (TTSB) ..... BEPI
Bureau of Electronic and Appliance Repair (SAUS) ..... BEAR
Bureau of Electronic Publishing, Inc. [*NASDAQ symbol*] (SAG) ..... BEPI
Bureau of Electronic Publishing, Inc. [*Associated Press*] (SAG) ..... BurEl
Bureau of Electronic Publishing, Inc. [*Associated Press*] (SAG) ..... BurElP
Bureau of Electronic Repair Dealer Registration (SAUO) ..... BERDR
Bureau of Elementary and Secondary Education [*Office of Education*] ..... BESE
Bureau of Employees' Compensation [*Later, OWCP*] [*Department of Labor*] ..... BEC
Bureau of Employment Security [*Later, US Employment Service*] [*Department of Labor*] ..... BES
Bureau of Enforcement ..... BOE
Bureau of Engineer Surveyors (SAUO) ..... BES
Bureau of Engineering [*Obsolete*] [*Navy*] ..... BUENG
Bureau of Engraving and Printing [*Department of the Treasury*] ..... BEP
Bureau of Entomology and Plant Quarantine [*Department of Agriculture*] [*Functions transferred to ARS, 1953*] ..... BEPQ
Bureau of Entomology and Plant Quarantine (SAUO) ..... B of E
Bureau of Environmental Statistics (SAUS) ..... BES
Bureau of Equipment and Recruiting [*Abolished, 1914*] [*Navy*] ..... BER
Bureau of European Affairs [*Department of State*] ..... BEA
Bureau of European Affairs (SAUO) ..... Bur Eur Aff
Bureau of European Affairs (SAUO) ..... EUR
Bureau of European Designers Associations (EA) ..... BEDA
Bureau of Evaluative Studies and Testing [*Indiana University*] [*Research center*] (RCD) ..... BEST
Bureau of Executive Manpower [*Civil Service Commission*] ..... BEM
Bureau of Explosives [*Later, HMS (BOE)*] ..... BE
Bureau of Explosives [*A publication*] (EAAP) ..... BOE
Bureau of Explosives (SAUO) ..... BUEXPL
Bureau of Export Administration [*Department of Commerce*] ..... BXA
Bureau of Export Development [*Department of Commerce*] ..... BED

Bureau of Facilities and Material (AAGC) ... BFM
Bureau of Family Services [*of SSA*] ... BFS
Bureau of Far Eastern Affairs [*Department of State*] ... BFEA
Bureau of Federal Credit Unions [*Later, NCUA*] [*Social Security Administration*] ... BFCU
Bureau of Federal Supply (AAGC) ... BFS
Bureau of Field Operations (SAUO) ... BFO
Bureau of Finance and Administration [*US Postal Service*] (MCD) ... BFA
Bureau of Financial Assistance (SAUO) ... BFA
Bureau of Fisheries and Aquatic Resources [*Phillippines*] [*Marine science*] (OSRA) ... BFAR
Bureau of Flight Standards (KSC) ... BFS
Bureau of Flora and Fauna [*Australia*] ... BFF
Bureau of Foods Irradiated Foods Committee [*Food and Drug Administration*] ... BFIFC
Bureau of Foods, Pesticides, and Product Safety [*FDA*] ... BFPPS
Bureau of Foreign and Domestic Commerce [*Functions later dispersed*] [*Department of Commerce*] ... BFDC
Bureau of Foreign Commerce [*Abolished, 1961*] [*Department of Commerce*] ... BFC
Bureau of Forensic Ballistics (SAUS) ... BFB
Bureau of Freelance Photographers [*British*] (CB) ... BFP
Bureau of Government Financial Operations [*Department of Treasury*] ... BGFO
Bureau of Governmental Research [*University of California*] [*Research Center*] (AEBS) ... BGR
Bureau of Governmental Research and Service [*University of Oregon*] [*Research center*] (RCD) ... BGRS
Bureau of Health Care Delivery and Assistance [*Department of Health and Human Services*] ... BHCDA
Bureau of Health Insurance [*Social Security Administration*] ... BHI
Bureau of Health Insurance, Social Security Administration (SAUO) ... BHISSA
Bureau of Health Manpower (SAUO) ... BHM
Bureau of Health Manpower (SAUO) ... BoHM
Bureau of Health Manpower Education [*National Institutes of Health*] ... BHME
Bureau of Health Planning and Resource Development (SAUO) ... BHPRD
Bureau of Health Planning and Resources Development (SAUO) ... BoHP&RD
Bureau of Health Professions [*Department of Health and Human Services*] (DAVI) ... BHPr
Bureau of Health Professions Education and Manpower Training [*HEW*] ... BEMT
Bureau of Health Protection Services. State of Nevada. (SAUO) ... BHPS
Bureau of Health Resources Development (SAUO) ... BHRD
Bureau of Health Services [*Public Health Service*] ... BHS
Bureau of Hearings and Appeals [*Social Security Administration*] ... BHA
Bureau of Higher Education [*Later, Bureau of Higher and Continuing Education*] [*Office of Education*] ... BHE
Bureau of Highway Traffic (SAUO) ... BHT
Bureau of Home Economics (SAUO) ... BHE
Bureau of Human Nutrition and Home Economics [*Department of Agriculture*] [*Functions transferred to ARS, 1953*] ... BHNHE
Bureau of Hygiene and Tropical Diseases [*Database producer*] ... BHTD
Bureau of Hygiene and Tropical Diseases (SAUO) ... BHTD
Bureau of Identification (SAUO) ... BId
Bureau of Immigration Research Advisory Committee [*Australia*] ... BIRAC
Bureau of Independent Publishers and Distributors (EA) ... BIPAD
Bureau of Indian Affairs [*Department of the Interior*] ... BIA
Bureau of Indian Affairs [*Better known as BIA*] [*Department of the Interior*] (MCD) ... BOIA
Bureau of Indian Affairs Procurement Regulation [*A publication*] (AAGC) ... BIAPR
Bureau of Industrial Costs and Prices [*India*] (ECON) ... BICP
Bureau of Industrial Economics [*Department of Commerce*] ... BIE
Bureau of Industry Economics (SAUO) ... BEI
Bureau of Industry Economics (SAUO) ... BIE
Bureau of Industry Research (SAUO) ... BIR
Bureau of Information and Research on Student Health (SAUO) ... BIRSH
Bureau of Information for Science and Technology (SAUS) ... BIST
Bureau of Information on Nickel (SAUO) ... BIN
Bureau of Information Science Research (SAUS) ... BISR
Bureau of Inspection and Survey ... BIS
Bureau of Institutional Development [*Office of Education*] ... BID
Bureau of Insular Affairs [*Originally, part of War Department; functions transferred to Department of Interior, 1939*] ... BIA
Bureau of Intelligence and Research [*Department of State*] ... BIR
Bureau of Intelligence and Research [*Department of State*] ... INR
Bureau of Inter-American Affairs (SAUO) ... BIA
Bureau of Inter-American Affairs [*Department of State*] ... BIAA
Bureau of Intergovernmental Personnel Programs ... BIPP
Bureau of Inter-Industrial Statistics and Multiple Regression Analysis (MCD) ... BISMRA
Bureau of Internal Affairs ... BIA
Bureau of Internal Revenue [*Department of the Treasury*] [*Later, Internal Revenue Service*] ... BIR
Bureau of International Affairs (MCD) ... BIA
Bureau of International Affairs (SAUO) ... Bur Intl Aff
Bureau of International Broadcasting (SAUO) ... BIB
Bureau of International Business Operations [*Department of Commerce*] [*Abolished, 1963*] ... BIBO
Bureau of International Commerce [*Department of Commerce*] [*Functions transferred to Domestic and International Business Administration*] ... BIC
Bureau of International Commerce-Commercial Intelligence Division (SAUO) ... BIC-CID
Bureau of International Economic Policy and Research [*Department of Commerce*] ... BIEPR
Bureau of International Expositions (SAUO) ... BEI
Bureau of International Expositions (SAUS) ... BIE
Bureau of International Labor Affairs [*Department of Labor*] ... BILA
Bureau of International Labor Affairs [*Department of Labor*] ... ILAB
Bureau of International Language Coordination (SAUO) ... BILC
Bureau of International Organization Affairs [*Department of State*] ... BIOA
Bureau of International Programs [*Department of Commerce*] ... BIP
Bureau of International Scientific and Technological Affairs [*Department of State*] ... BISTA
Bureau of International Whaling Statistics (SAUO) ... BIWS
Bureau of International Whaling Statistics (BARN) ... BIWS
Bureau of Investigation [*Federal Trade Commission*] ... BI
Bureau of Jewish Education ... BJE
Bureau of Justice Assistance ... BJA
Bureau of Justice Statistics [*Department of Justice*] [*Also, an information service or system*] (IID) ... BJS
Bureau of Justice Statistics (SAUO) ... BJS
Bureau of Juvenile Correction (SAUO) ... BJC
Bureau of Labor - Management Relations and Cooperative Programs [*Department of Labor*] ... BLMRCP
Bureau of Labor Standards [*Absorbed by OSHA*] [*Department of Labor*] [*Washington, DC*] ... BLS
Bureau of Labor Statistics [*Department of Labor*] [*Washington, DC*] ... BLS
Bureau of Labor Statistics. Bulletin [*A publication*] (DLA) ... BLS Bull
Bureau of Labor-Management Reports (SAUS) ... BLMR
Bureau of Land Management [*Department of the Interior*] ... BLM
Bureau of Land Management [*Department of the Interior*] (MCD) ... BOLM
Bureau of Land Management, Billings, MT [*Library symbol*] [*Library of Congress*] (LCLS) ... MtBilB
Bureau of Land Management, Billings, MT [*OCLC symbol*] (OCLC) ... UBD
Bureau of Land Management, Boise District Office, Boise, ID [*OCLC symbol*] (OCLC) ... UDL
Bureau of Land Management, Boise, ID [*Library symbol*] [*Library of Congress*] (LCLS) ... IdBLM-B
Bureau of Land Management, Denver, Denver, CO [*OCLC symbol*] (OCLC) ... UDD
Bureau of Land Management, Library, New Orleans, New Orleans, LA [*OCLC symbol*] (OCLC) ... UDQ
Bureau of Laundry and Dry Cleaning Standards (EA) ... BLDCS
Bureau of Libraries and Educational Technology [*Later, BLLR*] [*HEW*] ... BLET
Bureau of Libraries and Learning Resources [*Formerly, BLET*] [*HEW*] ... BLLR
Bureau of Library and Learning Resources and Community Services (SAUO) ... BLLRCS
Bureau of Litigation [*Federal Trade Commission*] ... BL
Bureau of Management Consulting, Department of Supply and Services [*Bureau des Conseillers en Gestion, Ministere des Approvisionnements et Services*] **Ottawa, Ontario** [*Library symbol*] [*National Library of Canada*] (NLC) ... OOBMC
Bureau of Manpower Utilization [*World War II*] ... BMU
Bureau of Marketing and Modification (SAUO) ... BMM
Bureau of Medical Devices [*Food and Drug Administration*] ... BMD
Bureau of Medical Devices (SAUO) ... BoMD
Bureau of Medical Devices and Diagnostic Products [*FDA*] ... BMDDP
Bureau of Medical Services [*Public Health Service*] ... BMS
Bureau of Medical Services (SAUO) ... BoMS
Bureau of Medical Statistics (SAUO) ... BMS
Bureau of Medicine [*of FDA*] ... BM
Bureau of Medicine and Supply Integrated Allowance List ... BM & SIAL
Bureau of Medicine and Surgery [*Later, Naval Medical Command*] [*Navy*] ... BMS
Bureau of Medicine and Surgery (SAUO) ... BUM&S
Bureau of Medicine and Surgery [*Navy*] ... BUM & S
Bureau of Medicine and Surgery (SAUS) ... Bu M&S
Bureau of Medicine and Surgery (SAUS) ... BuMed
Bureau of Medicine and Surgery [*Obsolete*] [*Navy*] ... BUMED
Bureau of Medicine and Surgery [*Navy*] ... M & S
Bureau of Medicine and Surgery Hospital Corps Publication [*Later, NAVMED*] [*Navy*] ... NMSHC
Bureau of Medicine and Surgery Instructions [*Navy*] ... BUMEDINST
Bureau of Medicine and Surgery Publications [*Navy*] ... NM & S
Bureau of Medicine and Surgery Publications (SAUS) ... NM&S
Bureau of Meteorology (SAUO) ... BM
Bureau of Meteorology (SAUO) ... BoM
Bureau of Meteorology ... BOM
Bureau of Meteorology and Oceanographic Services (SAUS) ... METOC
Bureau of Meteorology Research Center [*Marine science*] (OSRA) ... BMRC
Bureau of Meteorology Training Centre ... BMTC
Bureau of Military Application of Scientific Research (NATG) ... BMASR
Bureau of Mines [*Department of the Interior*] ... BM
Bureau of Mines [*Department of the Interior*] ... B of M
Bureau of Mines (SAUO) ... B of M
Bureau of Mines [*Department of the Interior*] ... BOM
Bureau of Mines [*Department of the Interior*] ... BuM
Bureau of Mines [*Department of the Interior*] ... BUMINES
Bureau of Mines and Geosciences [*Philippines*] (GEOI) ... BMG
Bureau of Mines Chamber (SAUS) ... BOM Chamber
Bureau of Mines. Information Circular [*Department of the Interior*] [*A publication*] ... BMIC
Bureau of Mines, Pittsburg (MCD) ... BMP
Bureau of Mines Technical Paper ... BMTP
Bureau of Mines. Technology News (journ.) (SAUS) ... TNBMD
Bureau of Motor Carrier Safety [*Department of Transportation*] ... BMCS
Bureau of Motor Carriers [*ICC*] ... BMC
Bureau of Motor Vehicles (SAUO) ... BMV
Bureau of Municipal Research [*Canada*] (IRC) ... BMR
Bureau of Narcotics [*Department of the Treasury*] [*Absorbed by BNDD of Department of Justice*] ... BN

Bureau of Narcotics and Dangerous Drugs [*Formerly, Bureau of Narcotics and Bureau of Drug Abuse Control; later, Drug Enforcement Administration*] [*Department of Justice*] ... BNDD
Bureau of National Affairs (EA) ... BNA
Bureau of National Capital Airports [*of FAA*] ... BNCA
Bureau of Natural Gas [*of FPC*] ... BNG
Bureau of Naval Personnel [*Also, BUPERS, NAVPERS*] ... BNP
Bureau of Naval Personnel [*Also, BNP, NAVPERS*] ... BUPERS
Bureau of Naval Personnel [*Also, BNP, BUPERS*] ... NAVPERS
Bureau of Naval Personnel - Personnel Research Division ... NAVPERS-PRD
Bureau of Naval Personnel Circular Letters ... BNPCL
Bureau of Naval Personnel Controlled Instructor Billets ... BUPERSCONINSTRBIL
Bureau of Naval Personnel Instruction ... NAVPERSINST
Bureau of Naval Personnel Manual ... BNPM
Bureau of Naval Ships [*Obsolete*] (MCD) ... BNS
Bureau of Naval Weapons [*Obsolete*] ... BNW
Bureau of Naval Weapons (SAUO) ... BUWEP
Bureau of Naval Weapons [*Obsolete*] ... BUWEPS
Bureau of Naval Weapons [*Obsolete*] ... NAVWEPS
Bureau of Naval Weapons Branch Representative [*Obsolete*] (MCD) ... BWBR
Bureau of Naval Weapons Fleet Readiness [*Obsolete*] (MCD) ... BUWEPS FR
Bureau of Naval Weapons, Fleet Readiness (SAUS) ... BUWEPS FR
Bureau of Naval Weapons Fleet Readiness Representative [*Obsolete*] (MCD) ... BUWEPSFLEREADREP
Bureau of Naval Weapons Fleet Readiness Representative [*Obsolete*] (MUGU) ... BUWEPSFLTREADREP
Bureau of Naval Weapons Fleet Readiness Representative [*Obsolete*] (MCD) ... BWFRR
Bureau of Naval Weapons Fleet Readiness Representative, Atlantic [*Obsolete*] (MCD) ... BUWEPSFLEREADREPLANT
Bureau of Naval Weapons Fleet Readiness Representative, Atlantic [*Obsolete*] (MUGU) ... BWFRRLANT
Bureau of Naval Weapons Fleet Readiness Representative, Central [*Obsolete*] (MCD) ... BUWEPSFLEREADREPCEN
Bureau of Naval Weapons Fleet Readiness Representative, Central [*Obsolete*] (MUGU) ... BWFRRCEN
Bureau of Naval Weapons Fleet Readiness Representative, Pacific [*Obsolete*] (MCD) ... BUWEPSFLEREADREPPAC
Bureau of Naval Weapons Fleet Readiness Representative, Pacific [*Obsolete*] (MUGU) ... BWFRRPAC
Bureau of Naval Weapons Instruction [*Obsolete*] (MCD) ... BUWEPSINST
Bureau of Naval Weapons Notice [*Obsolete*] ... BUWEPSNOTE
Bureau of Naval Weapons Representative [*Obsolete*] (MCD) ... BUWEPSREP
Bureau of Naval Weapons Representative [*Obsolete*] ... BWR
Bureau of Naval Weapons Representatives (AAGC) ... BUWEPSREPS
Bureau of Naval Weapons Resident Representative [*Obsolete*] ... BUWEPSRESREP
Bureau of Naval Weapons Resident Representative [*Obsolete*] (MUGU) ... BWRR
Bureau of Naval Weapons Support Representative, Naval Air Training Command [*Obsolete*] (MUGU) ... BWSRT
Bureau of Naval Weapons Technical Liaison Office [*Obsolete*] (MUGU) ... BUWEPSTLO
Bureau of Naval Weapons Technical Representative [*Obsolete*] (MUGU) ... BUWEPSTECHREP
Bureau of Navigation [*Later, Bureau of Naval Personnel*] [*Navy*] ... BUNAV
Bureau of Navy Yards and Docks [*Later, NFEC*] ... BNYD
Bureau of Near Eastern and South Asian Affairs [*Department of State*] ... BNESAA
Bureau of Occupational and Adult Education [*Office of Education*] ... BOAE
Bureau of Oceans and International Enviromental and Scientific Affairs/ Scientific and Technological Affairs [*Department of State*] (MSC) ... OES/SCI
Bureau of Oceans and International Environmental and Scientific Affairs (SAUO) ... BOIESA
Bureau of Oceans and International Environmental and Scientific Affairs [*Department of State*] ... OES
Bureau of Oceans and International Environmental and Scientific Affairs/ Ocean and Fishery Affairs (SAUS) ... OFS/OFA
Bureau of Oceans and International Environmental and Scientific Affairs/ Environmental and Population Affairs [*Department of State*] (MSC) ... OES/ENP
Bureau of Oceans and International Environmental and Scientific Affairs/ Ocean and Fishery Affairs [*Department of State*] (MSC) ... OES/OFA
Bureau of Oceans, Fisheries, and Scientific Affairs [*Department of State*] ... BOFSA
Bureau of Old-Age and Survivors Insurance [*Social Security Administration*] ... BOASI
Bureau of Operating Rights [*ICC*] ... BOR
Bureau of Operations and Programming [*United Nations Development Program*] ... BOP
Bureau of Ordnance [*Functions transferred to Bureau of Naval Weapons, 1960, and later to Naval Ordnance Systems Command*] [*Navy*] ... BO
Bureau of Ordnance [*Functions transferred to Bureau of Naval Weapons, 1960, and later to Naval Ordnance Systems Command*] [*Navy*] ... BUORD
Bureau of Ordnance and Hydrography [*Obsolete*] [*Navy*] ... BOH
Bureau of Ordnance Design Unit [*Obsolete*] [*Navy*] ... BODU
Bureau of Ordnance Fleet Test Equipment [*Obsolete*] [*Navy*] ... B of TE
Bureau of Ordnance Instructions [*Later, NAVORDINST*] ... BUORDINST
Bureau of Ordnance Publication [*Later, NAVORD*] [*Navy*] ... NORD
Bureau of Ordnance Shipment Order [*Obsolete*] [*Navy*] ... BOSO
Bureau of Ordnance Technical Liaison Officer (SAUS) ... BOTLO
Bureau of Organized Crime and Criminal Intelligence (SAUO) ... BOCCI
Bureau of Outdoor Recreation [*Terminated, 1978, functions transferred to Heritage Conservation and Recreation Service*] [*Department of the Interior*] (MCD) ... BOOR
Bureau of Outdoor Recreation [*Terminated, 1978, functions transferred to Heritage Conservation and Recreation Service*] [*Department of the Interior*] ... BOR
Bureau of Pension Advocates [*Canada*] ... BPA
Bureau of Planning and Entitlement Grants ... BPEG
Bureau of Plant Industry [*Later, BPISAE*] [*Department of Agriculture*] ... BPI
Bureau of Plant Industry, Soils, and Agricultural Engineering [*Formerly, BPI*] [*Functions transferred to ARS, 1953*] [*Department of Agriculture*] ... BPISAE
Bureau of Politico-Military Affairs-Department of State (SAUO) ... BPMA/DoS
Bureau of Postsecondary Education [*Later, Bureau of Higher and Continuing Education*] [*Office of Education*] ... BPE
Bureau of Power [*of FPC*] ... BP
Bureau of Preparedness and Response [*Department of Emergency Management*] (DEMM) ... BPR
Bureau of Primary Health Care ... BPHC
Bureau of Printing (GEOI) ... BOP
Bureau of Prison Terms (SAUO) ... BPT
Bureau of Prisons (SAUO) ... BOP
Bureau of Prisons [*Department of Justice*] ... BP
Bureau of Prisons Acquisition Regulation [*A publications*] (AAGC) ... BPAR
Bureau of Product Safety [*FDA*] ... BPS
Bureau of Professional Education of the American Osteopathic Association (EA) ... BPEAOA
Bureau of Provisions and Clothing [*See also BSA*] [*Navy*] ... BPC
Bureau of Public Administration [*University of Tennessee at Knoxville*] [*Research center*] (RCD) ... BPA
Bureau of Public Affairs (SAUO) ... BuPubAff
Bureau of Public Affairs (SAUO) ... Bur Pub Aff
Bureau of Public Affairs-Department of State (SAUO) ... BPA/DoS
Bureau of Public Assistance [*Later, BFS*] [*Social Security Administration*] ... BPA
Bureau of Public Inquiries ... BPI
Bureau of Public Relations [*War Department*] [*World War II*] ... BPR
Bureau of Public Roads [*Department of Transportation*] ... BPR
Bureau of Public Roads Transport Highway Mobilization [*Federal emergency order*] ... BPR-THM
Bureau of Public Transport Highway Mobilization (SAUS) ... BPRTHM
Bureau of Quality Assurance [*HEW*] ... BQA
Bureau of Quality Control [*Department of Health and Human Services*] (GFGA) ... BQC
Bureau of Radiation and Medical Devices [*Canada*] ... BRMD
Bureau of Radiation Protection (NRCH) ... BRP
Bureau of Radiological Health [*FDA*] ... BRH
Bureau of Radiological Health / Division of Electronics Products [*FDA*] (PDAA) ... BRH/DEP
Bureau of Radiological Health / Division of Environmental Radiation [*FDA*] (PDAA) ... BRH/DER
Bureau of Radiological Health / Division of Medical Radiation Exposure [*FDA*] (PDAA) ... BRH/DMRE
Bureau of Radiological Health / Northeastern Radiological Health Laboratory [*FDA*] (PDAA) ... BRH/NERHL
Bureau of Radiological Health / Office of Regional Operations [*FDA*] (PDAA) ... BRH/ORO
Bureau of Radiological Health / Southeastern Radiological Health Laboratory [*FDA*] (PDAA) ... BRH/SERHL
Bureau of Radiological Health / Southwestern Radiological Health Laboratory [*FDA*] (PDAA) ... BRH/SWRHL
Bureau of Radiological Health, Rockville, MD [*OCLC symbol*] (OCLC) ... BRH
Bureau of Railroad Safety [*Department of Transportation*] ... BRS
Bureau of Railway Economics [*Later, AAR*] ... BRE
Bureau of Raw Materials for American Vegetable Oils and Fats Industries (EA) ... BORM
Bureau of Readjustment Education (SAUO) ... BRE
Bureau of Reclamation [*Later, WPRS*] [*Department of the Interior*] (MCD) ... BOR
Bureau of Reclamation [*Later, WPRS*] [*Department of the Interior*] ... BR
Bureau of Reclamation [*Later, WPRS*] [*Department of the Interior*] ... BUREC
Bureau of Reclamation (SAUO) ... BuREC
Bureau of Recovery and Mitigation [*Department of Emergency Management*] (DEMM) ... BRM
Bureau of Recruiting and Examining [*Civil Service Commission*] ... BRE
Bureau of Rehabilitation (SAUO) ... BRI
Bureau of Relations with Member States (SAUO) ... BMS
Bureau of Research and Community Services [*Duquesne University*] [*Research center*] (RCD) ... BORACS
Bureau of Research and Development (KSC) ... BRAD
Bureau of Research and Development Center [*FAA*] (AAG) ... BRDC
Bureau of Research and Engineering [*US Postal Service*] ... BRE
Bureau of Research Information Control System (SAUS) ... BRICS
Bureau of Resource Assessment and Land Use Planning ... BRALUP
Bureau of Resource Sciences (SAUO) ... BRS
Bureau of Resources and Trade Assistance [*Department of Commerce*] ... BRTA
Bureau of Retirement and Insurance [*Civil Service Commission*] ... BRI
Bureau of Retirement Survivors Insurance [*Social Security Administration*] ... BRSI
Bureau of Safety and Supply Radio Services ... BSSRS
Bureau of Safety Regulations (SAA) ... BSR
Bureau of Salesmen's National Associations (EA) ... BSNA
Bureau of School Systems [*Office of Education*] ... BSS
Bureau of Security and Consular Affairs (SAUO) ... BSCA
Bureau of Ships [*Later, Naval Sea Systems Command*] ... BS
Bureau of Ships [*Later, Naval Sea Systems Command*] ... BUSHIPS
Bureau of Ships Analog Computer [*Obsolete*] [*Navy*] ... BUSAC
Bureau of Ships Journal [*Obsolete*] [*Navy*] ... BSJ
Bureau of Ships Publications [*Obsolete*] [*Navy*] ... NBS
Bureau of Social Hygiene (SAUO) ... BSH
Bureau of Social Sciences Research, Inc. (MCD) ... BSSR

Bureau of Soils and Water Management [*Department of Agriculture*] .... BSWM
Bureau of Solid Waste Management [*Environmental Protection Agency*] ..... BSWM
Bureau of Sport Fisheries and Wildlife [*Superseded by US Fish and Wildlife Service*] [*Department of the Interior*] (MCD) .... BOSFW
Bureau of Sport Fisheries and Wildlife (SAUS) .... BSF&W
Bureau of Sport Fisheries and Wildlife [*Superseded by US Fish and Wildlife Service*] [*Department of the Interior*] .... BSFW
Bureau of Sport Fisheries and Wildlife, Eastern Fish Disease Laboratory, Kearneysville, WV [*Library symbol*] [*Library of Congress*] (LCLS) .... WvKeFW
Bureau of Standards .... B of S
Bureau of Standards (SAUO) .... B of S
Bureau of Standards (SAUO) .... BS
Bureau of Standards .... BS
Bureau of Standards .... BUSTDS
Bureau of State Security [*Later, Department of National Security*] [*South Africa*] .... BOSS
Bureau of State Services [*of Public Health Service*] .... BSS
Bureau of Statistics (SAUO) .... BS
Bureau of Statistics [*Japan*] (GEOI) .... BS
Bureau of Statistics, Alberta Treasury, Edmonton, Alberta [*Library symbol*] [*National Library of Canada*] (NLC) .... AETBS
Bureau of Steam Engineering [*Navy*] .... BSE
Bureau of Strata Mechanics (SAUO) .... BSM
Bureau of Student Support [*Office of Education*] .... BSS
Bureau of Supplies and Accounts [*Later, NSUPSC*] [*Navy*] .... BSA
Bureau of Supplies and Accounts [*Later, NSUPSC*] [*Navy*] .... BUSANDA
Bureau of Supplies and Accounts [*Later, NSUPSC*] [*Navy*] .... NAVSANDA
Bureau of Supplies and Accounts (SAUS) .... S&A
Bureau of Supplies and Accounts [*Later, NSUPSC*] [*Navy*] .... S & A
Bureau of Supplies and Accounts Shipment Order [*Obsolete*] [*Navy*] .... SANDASO
Bureau of Technical Assistance Operations [*UN*] .... BTAO
Bureau of Technical Information (SAA) .... BTI
Bureau of the Budget [*Later, OMB*] .... BB
Bureau of the Budget [*Later, OMB*] .... BOB
Bureau of the Budget [*Later, OMB*] .... BuB
Bureau of the Budget [*Later, OMB*] .... BUBUD
Bureau of the Budget Approval [*Obsolete*] .... BBA
Bureau of the Budget in Exile Unrequited Marching and Chowder Society (EA) .... BBEUMCS
Bureau of the Budget in Exile Unrequited Marching and Chowder Society .... BOBEUMACS
Bureau of the Census [*Department of Commerce*] (MCD) .... BC
Bureau of the Census (GEOI) .... BOC
Bureau of the Census (SAUS) .... BUCEN
Bureau of the Census (SAUO) .... BURCEN
Bureau of the Census, Field Division Library, Washington, DC [*OCLC symbol*] (OCLC) .... CBW
Bureau of the Census of the U.S. Department of Commerce (SAUO) .... Census
Bureau of the Census, Washington, DC [*OCLC symbol*] (OCLC) .... CBU
Bureau of the Comptroller (SAUO) .... BOC
Bureau of the Mint [*Department of the Treasury*] .... BM
Bureau of the Mint, Treasury Division (SAUO) .... BMTD
Bureau of the Public Debt [*Department of the Treasury*] .... BPD
Bureau of Trade Regulation [*Department of Commerce*] .... BTR
Bureau of Transients (SAUO) .... BOT
Bureau of Transport and Communications Economics [*Austria*] [*Also, an information service or system*] (IID) .... BTCE
Bureau of Transport Economics and Statistics [*ICC*] .... BTE & S
Bureau of Transport Economics and Statistics (SAUO) .... BTE&S
Bureau of Transportation and International Services [*US Postal Service*] (MCD) .... BTIS
Bureau of Transportation Statistics [*BTS*] [*OFR*] (TAG) .... BTS
Bureau of Unemployment Compensation (SAUS) .... UCB
Bureau of University Travel [*Defunct*] .... BUT
Bureau of Veterans Reemployment Rights [*Department of Labor*] .... BVRR
Bureau of Veterinary Medicine [*FDA*] .... BVM
Bureau of Vital Statistics (AFM) .... BVS
Bureau of Vocational Rehabilitation (OICC) .... BVR
Bureau of War Information (SAUO) .... BWI
Bureau of War Risk Litigation .... BWRL
Bureau of Water Carriers .... BWC
Bureau of Weapons [*Navy*] .... BUWEAPS
Bureau of Weapons (SAUO) .... BuWeps
Bureau of Weapons Instruction (ACAE) .... BUWEPINST
Bureau of Work Programs (SAUO) .... BWP
Bureau of Work-Training Programs [*Terminated, 1969*] [*Department of Labor*] .... BWTP
Bureau of Yards and Docks [*Later, NFEC*] [*Washington, DC*] [*Navy*] ...... BUDOCKS
Bureau of Yards and Docks [*Later, NFEC*] [*Navy*] .... BUY & D
Bureau of Yards and Docks (SAUO) .... Bu Y&D
Bureau of Yards and Docks [*Later, NFEC*] [*Navy*] (KSC) .... BUYARD
Bureau of Yards and Docks [*Later, NFEC*] [*Navy*] .... BUYDSDOCKS
Bureau of Yards and Docks [*Later, NFEC*] [*Navy*] (MCD) .... BYD
Bureau of Yards and Docks [*Later, NFEC*] [*Navy*] .... Y & D
Bureau of Yards and Docks Publications [*Obsolete*] [*Navy*] .... NAVDOCKS
Bureau of Yards and Docks Publications [*Obsolete*] [*Navy*] .... NAVDOCSP
Bureau on Agriculture and Renewable Resources .... BARR
Bureau on Jewish Employment Problems (EA) .... BJEP
Bureau Permanent Interafricain de la Tse-Tse et de la Trypanosomiase .... BPITT
Bureau Permanent International des Constructeurs d'Automobiles [*International Permanent Bureau of Motor Manufacturers*] (EAIO) .... BPICA
Bureau Permanent International des Constructeurs de Motocycles [*Permanent International Bureau of Motorcycle Manufacturers*] (EAIO) ..... BPICM
Bureau Planned Procurement Guide [*Navy*] .... BPPG
Bureau Politique National [*National Political Bureau*] (AF) .... BPN
Bureau Regional d'Action Sida (AC) .... BRAS
Bureau Regional de l'UNESCO pour la Science et la Technologie en Afrique [*UNESCO Regional Office for Science and Technology in Africa - UNESCO-ROSTA*] [*Nairobi, Kenya*] (EAIO) .... BRUSTA
Bureau Regional de Science et de Technologie pour l'Europe et l'Amerique du Nord [*Regional Office for Science and Technology for Europe and North America*] (EAIO) .... SC/ROSTENA
Bureau Socialiste International [*Brussels*] .... BSI
Bureau Township Consolidated School District 250, Princeton, IL [*Library symbol*] [*Library of Congress*] (LCLS) .... IPriBSD
Bureau [*of Naval Personnel*] **Unit Identification Code** .... BUIC
Bureau +van Dijk, SA (IID) .... BvD
Bureau Veritas [*International register for the classification of shipping and aircraft*] .... BV
Bureau Veritas Quality International Ltd. (SAUO) .... BVQI
Bureau Veritas SA [*France*] [*ICAO designator*] (ICDA) .... XD
Bureau Veritas SA [*France*] [*ICAO designator*] (FAAC) .... XDA
Bureau voor de Industriele Eigendom, Bibliotheek Octrooiraad, The Hague, Netherlands [*Library symbol*] [*Library of Congress*] (LCLS) .... NeHB
Bureau Voucher [*Army*] (AABC) .... BV
Bureau Weather Control .... BWC
Bureaucratic Syndrome [*In book title "B.S.: The Bureaucratic Syndrome"*] .... BS
Bureau-General Committee (SAUO) .... BUR
Bureaux Internationaux Reunis pour la Protection de la Propriete Intellectuelle [*United International Bureau for the Protection of Intellectual Property*] [*Later, WIPO*] .... BIRPI
Bureta [*Fiji*] [*Airport symbol*] (OAG) .... LEV
Bureta [*Fiji*] [*ICAO location identifier*] (ICLI) .... NFNB
Burford Public Library, Ontario [*Library symbol*] [*National Library of Canada*] (BIB) .... OBUR
Burford's Reports [*6-18 Oklahoma*] [*A publication*] (DLA) .... Burf
Burg .... BG
Burg [*Commonly used*] (OPSA) .... BURG
Burg Eltz [*Federal Republic of Germany*] [*Seismograph station code, US Geological Survey*] (SEIS) .... BGG
Burg Feuerstein [*Germany*] [*ICAO location identifier*] (ICLI) .... EDQE
Burgan Bank [*Kuwait*] .... BB
Burgas [*Bulgaria*] [*Airport symbol*] (AD) .... BOJ
Burgas [*Bulgaria*] [*ICAO location identifier*] (ICLI) .... LBBG
Burgaw, NC [*FM radio station call letters*] .... WKXB
Burgaw, NC [*AM radio station call letters*] .... WVBS
Burge on Appellate Jurisdiction [*1841*] [*A publication*] (DLA) .... Burge App
Burge on Colonial and Foreign Law [*A publication*] (DLA) .... Burg Col & For Law
Burge on Colonial and Foreign Law [*A publication*] (DLA) .... Burge Col Law
Burge on Maritime International Law [*A publication*] (DLA) .... Burge Mar Int L
Burge on Suretyship [*A publication*] (DLA) .... Burge Sur
Burge on the Conflict of Laws [*A publication*] (DLA) .... Burge Confl Law
Burgeo Public Library, Newfoundland [*Library symbol*] [*National Library of Canada*] (NLC) .... NFBUR
Burger .... BGR
Burger King Corp. .... BK
Burgerlijk Wetboek [*Civil Code*] [*Netherlands*] (DLA) .... B
Burgerlijk Wetboek [*Civil Code*] [*Netherlands*] (ILCA) .... BW
Burgersdorp [*South Africa*] [*ICAO location identifier*] (ICLI) .... FABD
Burgess .... BURG
Burgess' Reports [*16-49 Ohio*] [*A publication*] (DLA) .... Burgen
Burgess' Reports [*16-49 Ohio*] [*A publication*] (DLA) .... Burgess
Burgess-Manning Co., Dallas, TX [*Library symbol*] [*Library of Congress*] (LCLS) .... TxDaBM
Burgh Constituency (WDAA) .... BC
Burgh Constituency (WDAA) .... Burgh Const
Burgher (ROG) .... BURG
Burglar Alarm .... BA
Burglary .... BU
Burglary .... Burg
Burglary (DLA) .... BURGL
Burglary Larceny Division (SAUO) .... BLD
Burgomaster .... BM
Burgomaster (ROG) .... BURG
Burgos [*Spain*] [*ICAO location identifier*] (ICLI) .... LEBG
Burgs [*Postal Service standard*] (OPSA) .... BGS
Burgs [*Commonly used*] (OPSA) .... BURGS
Burgundy (ADWA) .... Bdy
Burgwyn's Digest Maryland Reports [*A publication*] (DLA) .... Burg Dig
Burgwyn's Digest Maryland Reports [*A publication*] (DLA) .... Burgw MD Dig
Burial Ground [*Environmental science*] (COE) .... BG
Burial Ground (WDAA) .... Burial Gd
Burial Officer (SAUS) .... BO
Buriat Autonomous Soviet Socialist Republic (SAUO) .... BASSR
Buried (ROG) .... B
Buried (ROG) .... BD
Buried (GEAB) .... bd
Buried (ROG) .... BU
Buried .... BUR
Buried Block (WDAA) .... BB
Buried Bumper Syndrome [*Medicine*] (MELL) .... BBS
Buried Capacitance [*Electronics*] (AAEL) .... BC
Buried Coarctate Mesa [*LASER diode technology*] (NITA) .... BCM
Buried Distribution Wire [*Telecommunications*] (TEL) .... BDW
Buried Heterostructure (IAA) .... BH
Buried History: Quarterly Journal of the Australian Institute of Archaeology [*A publication*] (APTA) .... BH
Buried Implanted Layer for Lateral Isolation (SAUS) .... BILLI
Buried Injector Logic (IAA) .... BIL

Buried Isolation Capacitor (SAUS) .... BICyMOS
Buried Line Intrusion Sensor [*Military*] (LAIN) .... BLIS
Buried Logic Macrocell (SAUS) .... BLMC
Buried Mine Detector (SAUS) .... BMD
Buried Mushroom Structure (SAUS) .... BMS
Buried Optical Guide (SAUS) .... BOG
Buried Oxide (AAEL) .... BOX
Buried Ridge Structure (SAUS) .... BRS
Buried Tape (SAUS) .... BT
Buried Tape Armor [*Telecommunications*] (TEL) .... BT
Buried Trench Weapons System (MCD) .... BTWS
Buried Waste Integrated Demonstration (ABAC) .... BWID
Buried Wire [*Telecommunications*] (TEL) .... BW
Buried-BIT [*Binary Digit*] **Line** [*Computer science*] (IAA) .... BBL
Buried-Oxide Metal-Oxide Semiconductor (IAA) .... BOMOS
Burien-Seattle, WA [*AM radio station call letters*] .... KGNW
Burin Public Library, Burin, NF, Canada [*Library symbol*] [*Library of Congress*] (LCLS) .... CaNfBuri
Burin Public Library, Newfoundland [*Library symbol*] [*National Library of Canada*] (NLC) .... NFBURI
Burkburnett, TX [*FM radio station call letters*] .... KYYI
Burke. Copyright [*1842*] [*A publication*] (DLA) .... Burke Cop
Burke. Criminal Law [*2nd ed.*] [*1845*] [*A publication*] (DLA) .... Burke Cr L
Burke. International Copyright [*1852*] [*A publication*] (DLA) .... Burke Int Cop
Burke Mills, Inc. [*NASDAQ symbol*] (NQ) .... BMLS
Burke Mills, Inc. [*Associated Press*] (SAG) .... Burke
Burke on the Law of Public Schools [*A publication*] (DLA) .... Burke Pub Sch
Burke Public Library, Burke, SD [*Library symbol*] [*Library of Congress*] (LCLS) .... SdBu
Burke's Celebrated Trials [*A publication*] (DLA) .... Burke Cel Tr
Burke's Celebrated Trials [*A publication*] (DLA) .... Burke Tr
Burke's Celebrated Trials [*A publication*] (DLA) .... Cel Tr
Burkesville, KY [*AM radio station call letters*] .... WKYR
Burkesville, KY [*FM radio station call letters*] .... WKYR-FM
Burketown [*Australia*] [*Airport symbol*] (OAG) .... BUC
Burkina Faso [*ANSI two-letter standard code*] (CNC) .... BF
Burkina Faso [*ANSI three-letter standard code*] (CNC) .... BFA
Burkina Faso (SAUS) .... Burk Fas
Burkitt's Lymphoma [*Medicine*] .... BL
Burkitt's Lymphoma Receptor [*Immunology*] .... BLR
Burks' Behavior Rating Scale [*Psychology*] (DAVI) .... BBRS
Burks Falls, Armour & Ryerson Union Library, Burks Falls, ON, Canada [*Library symbol*] [*Library of Congress*] (LCLS) .... CaOBfAR
Burks Falls, Armour, and Ryerson Union Library, Burks Falls, Ontario [*Library symbol*] [*National Library of Canada*] (NLC) .... OBFAR
Burks' Reports [*91-98 Virginia*] [*A publication*] (DLA) .... Burks
Burl (VRA) .... br
Burlamaqui's Natural and Political Law [*A publication*] (DLA) .... Burlamaqui
Burlamaqui's Natural and Political Law [*A publication*] (DLA) .... Burl Nat
Burlamaqui's Natural and Political Law [*A publication*] (DLA) .... Burl Natural & Pol Law
Burlap .... BRLP
Burlap (ADWA) .... brlp
Burlap (VRA) .... bur
Burlap and Jute Association (EA) .... BJA
Burleigh-Anstruther and Chandos Union Public Library, Apsley, Ontario [*Library symbol*] [*National Library of Canada*] (BIB) .... OABA
Burlesque (ROG) .... BURL
Burlesque Historical Society (EA) .... BHS
Burley and Dark Leaf Tobacco Association (NTPA) .... BDLTA
Burley and Dark Leaf Tobacco Export Association (EA) .... BDLTEA
Burley Auction Warehouse Association (EA) .... BAWA
Burley, ID [*Location identifier*] [*FAA*] (FAAL) .... BYI
Burley, ID [*AM radio station call letters*] .... KBAR
Burley, ID [*FM radio station call letters*] (BROA) .... KBSY-FM
Burley, ID [*FM radio station call letters*] .... KZDX
Burley Leaf Tobacco Dealers Association (EA) .... BLTDA
Burley Public Library, Burley, ID [*Library symbol*] [*Library of Congress*] (LCLS) .... IdBur
Burley Stabilization Corp. (EA) .... BSC
Burley Tobacco Growers Cooperative Association (EA) .... BTGCA
Burley-Rupert [*Idaho*] [*Airport symbol*] (AD) .... BYI
Burlingame Public Library, Burlingame, CA [*Library symbol*] [*Library of Congress*] (LCLS) .... CBu
Burlingame Research Center (MCD) .... BRC
Burlington [*Iowa*] [*Airport symbol*] (OAG) .... BRL
Burlington [*Vermont*] [*Airport symbol*] (OAG) .... BTV
Burlington [*Vermont*] [*Seismograph station code, US Geological Survey*] [*Closed*] (SEIS) .... BUR
Burlington Air Express [*ICAO designator*] (AD) .... BAX
Burlington Area Office [*Energy Research and Development Administration*] .... BAO
Burlington Association for Nuclear Disarmament (AC) .... BAND
Burlington Atmospheric Density Model Evaluation Program [*IBM Corp.*] .... BADMEP
Burlington Autosport Club (AC) .... BAC
Burlington, Cedar Rapids & Minnesota Railroad .... BCR & M
Burlington, Cedar Rapids & Northern Railway .... BCR & N
Burlington, CO [*AM radio station call letters*] .... KNAB
Burlington, CO [*FM radio station call letters*] .... KNAB-FM
Burlington, CO [*FM radio station call letters*] (BROA) .... KRGD-FM
Burlington Coat Factory [*NYSE symbol*] (TTSB) .... BCF
Burlington Coat Factory Warehouse Corp. [*NYSE symbol*] (SPSG) .... BCF
Burlington Coat Factory Warehouse Corp. [*Associated Press*] (SAG) .... BurlCoat
Burlington Community College (SAUS) .... BCC
Burlington Community College (SAUO) .... BCCA
Burlington County Area Reference Library, Mount Holly, NJ [*Library symbol*] [*Library of Congress*] (LCLS) .... NjMhB
Burlington County Clerk, Mount Holly, NJ [*Library symbol*] [*Library of Congress*] (LCLS) .... NjMhCoC
Burlington County College, Pemberton, NJ [*Library symbol*] [*Library of Congress*] (LCLS) .... NjPeB
Burlington County Herald, Mount Holly, NJ [*Library symbol*] [*Library of Congress*] (LCLS) .... NjMhH
Burlington County Historical Society, Burlington, NJ [*Library symbol*] [*Library of Congress*] (LCLS) .... NjBuHi
Burlington County Lyceum [*Mount Holly Public Library*], **Mount Holly, NJ** [*Library symbol*] [*Library of Congress*] (LCLS) .... NjMhL
Burlington County Prison Museum, Mount Holly, NJ [*Library symbol*] [*Library of Congress*] (LCLS) .... NjMhPM
Burlington County Times, Willingboro, NJ [*Library symbol*] [*Library of Congress*] (LCLS) .... NjWiT
Burlington Fine Arts Club (SAUO) .... BFAC
Burlington Free Public Library, Burlington, IA [*Library symbol*] [*Library of Congress*] (LCLS) .... IaB
Burlington, Great Northern and Northern Pacific railroads (SAUS) .... Northerns
Burlington House (SAUS) .... BH
Burlington House (SAUO) .... BH
Burlington, IA [*AM radio station call letters*] .... KBUR
Burlington, IA [*AM radio station call letters*] .... KCPS
Burlington, IA [*FM radio station call letters*] .... KDMG
Burlington, IA [*FM radio station call letters*] .... KGRS
Burlington, IA [*Television station call letters*] .... KJMH
Burlington, IA [*FM radio station call letters*] .... KKMI
Burlington Industries (EFIS) .... BI
Burlington Industries, Inc. [*NYSE symbol*] (SPSG) .... BUR
Burlington Industries, Inc. [*Formerly, Burlington Industries Equity*] [*Associated Press*] (SAG) .... BurlInds
Burlington Industries, Inc., Information Services Library, Greensboro (SAUS) .... NcGBur
Burlington Industries, Inc., Information Services Library, Greensboro, NC [*Library symbol*] [*Library of Congress*] (LCLS) .... NcGBI
Burlington Industries, Inc., Information Services Library, Greensboro, NC [*Library symbol*] [*Library of Congress*] (LCLS) .... NcGBur
Burlington, KS [*FM radio station call letters*] .... KSNP
Burlington Liars Club (EA) .... BLC
Burlington Magazine [*A publication*] (BRI) .... BM
Burlington, NC [*Location identifier*] [*FAA*] (FAAL) .... BUY
Burlington, NC [*Television station call letters*] .... WAAP
Burlington, NC [*AM radio station call letters*] .... WBBB
Burlington, NC [*Television station call letters*] (BROA) .... WGPX
Burlington, NC [*FM radio station call letters*] (BROA) .... WKXU-FM
Burlington, NC [*FM radio station call letters*] .... WPCM
Burlington, NJ [*Television station call letters*] .... WGTW
Burlington Northern, Inc. [*AAR code*] .... BN
Burlington Northern, Inc. [*NYSE symbol*] (SPSG) .... BNI
Burlington Northern, Inc. (EFIS) .... BNL
Burlington Northern (Manitoba) Limited [*AAR code*] .... BNML
Burlington Northern Santa Fe [*NYSE symbol*] (TTSB) .... BNI
Burlington Northern Santa Fe Corp. [*Associated Press*] (SAG) .... BNSF
Burlington Northern Santa Fe Corp. [*Associated Press*] (SAG) .... BurlNSF
Burlington, ON [*FM radio station call letters*] .... CING
Burlington Public Library [*UTLAS symbol*] .... BUR
Burlington Public Library, Burlington, CO [*Library symbol*] [*Library of Congress*] (LCLS) .... CoBur
Burlington Public Library, Burlington, ON, Canada [*Library symbol*] [*Library of Congress*] (LCLS) .... CaOBU
Burlington Public Library, Burlington, WI [*Library symbol*] [*Library of Congress*] (LCLS) .... WBur
Burlington Public Library, Ontario [*Library symbol*] [*National Library of Canada*] (NLC) .... OBU
Burlington Randomized Controlled Trial [*Criterion for medical evaluation*] .... BRCT
Burlington Res CoalSeamGasRty [*NYSE symbol*] (TTSB) .... BRU
Burlington Resources Coal Seam Gas Royalty Trust [*NYSE symbol*] (SAG) .... BRU
Burlington Resources Coal Seam Gas Royalty Trust [*Associated Press*] (SAG) .... BurlRsCl
Burlington Resources, Inc. [*NYSE symbol*] (SPSG) .... BR
Burlington Resources, Inc. [*Associated Press*] (SAG) .... BrlRsc
Burlington Township Library, Burlington, MI [*Library symbol*] [*Library of Congress*] (LCLS) .... MiBurl
Burlington, VT [*Television station call letters*] .... WCAX
Burlington, VT [*Television station call letters*] .... WETK
Burlington, VT [*FM radio station call letters*] .... WEZF
Burlington, VT [*Television station call letters*] (RBYB) .... WFFF-TV
Burlington, VT [*AM radio station call letters*] .... WJOY
Burlington, VT [*AM radio station call letters*] .... WKDR
Burlington, VT [*FM radio station call letters*] .... WOKO
Burlington, VT [*FM radio station call letters*] .... WRUV
Burlington, VT [*AM radio station call letters*] .... WVMT
Burlington, VT [*Television station call letters*] .... WVNY
Burlington, VT [*FM radio station call letters*] .... WVPS
Burlington, WA [*Location identifier*] [*FAA*] (FAAL) .... BTA
Burlington, WI [*Location identifier*] [*FAA*] (FAAL) .... BUU
Burlington, WI [*FM radio station call letters*] .... WBSD
Burlington-Graham, NC [*AM radio station call letters*] .... WBAG
Burlington-Graham, NC [*FM radio station call letters*] (RBYB) .... WRSN-FM
Burlington-Graham, NC [*FM radio station call letters*] .... WZZU
Burlington/International [*Vermont*] [*ICAO location identifier*] (ICLI) .... KBTV
Burlington-Rock Island Railroad Co. .... B-RI
Burm (SAUS) .... Bm

Burma [*MARC geographic area code*] [*Library of Congress*] (LCCP) ... a-br-
Burma [*IYRU nationality code*] [*MARC country of publication code*] [*Library of Congress*] (LCCP) ... br
Burma [*ANSI two-letter standard code*] (CNC) ... BU
Burma [*ANSI three-letter standard code*] (CNC) ... BUR
Burma (ADWA) ... Bur
Burma (WDAA) ... BURM
Burma [*International civil aircraft marking*] (ODBW) ... XY
Burma Air Force (SAUS) ... BAF
Burma Airways Corp. [*Rangoon*] (EY) ... BAC
Burma Airways Corp. [*Myanmar*] [*ICAO designator*] (ICDA) ... UB
Burma Auxiliary Force (SAUO) ... BAF
Burma Communist Party (SAUO) ... BCP
Burma Communist Party [*"White Flag" party*] [*Political party*] (PD) ... BCP
Burma Defence Council (SAUO) ... BDC
Burma Defense Army [*Later, BNA*] [*World War II*] ... BDA
Burma Economic Development Corporation (SAUO) ... BEDC
Burma Forces (SAUO) ... BF
Burma Frontier Force (SAUO) ... BFF
Burma Frontier Force [*British military*] (DMA) ... BFF
Burma Gallantry Medal (WDAA) ... BGM
Burma Independence Army [*Fighting on the side of the Japanese*] [*World War II*] ... BIA
Burma Law Institute. Journal [*A publication*] (DLA) ... BLIJ
Burma Law Institute. Journal [*A publication*] (DLA) ... Burma Law Inst J
Burma Law Institute. Journal [*A publication*] (DLA) ... Burma L Inst J
Burma Law Journal [*A publication*] (DLA) ... BLJ
Burma Law Journal [*A publication*] (DLA) ... Bur LJ
Burma Law Journal [*A publication*] (DLA) ... Burm LJ
Burma Law Reports [*A publication*] (DLA) ... Bur LR
Burma Law Reports [*A publication*] (DLA) ... Burma LR
Burma Law Reports [*A publication*] (DLA) ... Burm LR
Burma Law Times [*A publication*] (DLA) ... BLT
Burma Law Times [*A publication*] (DLA) ... Bur LT
Burma Law Times [*A publication*] (DLA) ... Burm LT
Burma Military Police [*British military*] (DMA) ... BMP
Burma National Army [*Formerly, BDA*] ... BNA
Burma National Army (SAUO) ... BNA
Burma Office (SAUO) ... BO
Burma Oil Company (SAUO) ... BOC
Burma (or Burmese) Air Force (SAUO) ... BAF
Burma Press Syndicate, Ltd. (SAUO) ... BPS
Burma Regular Forces (SAUO) ... BRF
Burma Socialist Programme Party [*Political party*] (PPW) ... BSPP
Burma Star Association (WDAA) ... BSA
Burma Star Association (SAUO) ... BSA
Burma State Railways (SAUO) ... BR
Burma Territorial Force (SAUO) ... BTF
Burma Trade Union Congress ... BTUC
Burma Translation Society (SAUO) ... BTS
Burma-America Buddhist Association (EA) ... BABA
Burmac Energy Corp. [*Vancouver Stock Exchange symbol*] ... BUS
Burmah Castrol Ltd. [*NASDAQ symbol*] (SAG) ... BURM
Burmah Castrol Ltd. [*Associated Press*] (SAG) ... BurmhC
Burmah Castrol plc ADR [*NASDAQ symbol*] (TTSB) ... BURMY
Burmah Industrial Products Limited (SAUO) ... BIPL
Burman Aviation (Charter) Ltd. [*British*] [*FAA designator*] (FAAC) ... BMM
Burmese [*MARC language code*] [*Library of Congress*] (LCCP) ... bur
Burmese (SAUS) ... Bur
Burmese (ADWA) ... Burm
Burmese Air Force ... BAF
Burmese Army (CINC) ... BA
Burmese Navy (CINC) ... BN
Burmese Socialist Programme Party (SAUO) ... BSPP
Burn Care Unit [*Medicine*] (MELL) ... BCU
Burn Depth Indicator [*A video camera*] [*Medicine*] (DAVI) ... BDI
Burn In (AAEL) ... BI
Burn Index [*Medicine*] ... BI
Burn Intensive Care Unit [*Medicine*] (MELL) ... BICU
Burn on Stock Jobbing [*A publication*] (DLA) ... Burn St Job
Burn Out Velocity (SAUS) ... VBO
Burn Rate ... BR
Burn Scar Contracture [*Medicine*] (MELL) ... BSC
Burn Stress Pseudodiabetes [*Medicine*] (MELL) ... BSPD
Burn Time [*NASA*] ... BT
Burn Time Remaining (MCD) ... BTR
Burn to Depletion [*NASA*] (KSC) ... BTD
Burn Unit [*Medicine*] ... BU
Burn Wound (MELL) ... BW
Burnable Poison Rod [*Nuclear energy*] (NRCH) ... BPR
Burnable Poison Rod Assembly [*Nuclear energy*] (NRCH) ... BPRA
Burnable Poison Water Reactor (IEEE) ... BPWR
Burnaby Art Gallery, British Columbia [*Library symbol*] [*National Library of Canada*] (NLC) ... BBA
Burnaby Art Gallery, Burnaby, BC, Canada [*Library symbol*] [*Library of Congress*] (LCLS) ... CaBBA
[*The*] **Burnaby Association for the Mentally Handicapped** ... BAMH
Burnaby Public Library, British Columbia [*Library symbol*] [*National Library of Canada*] (NLC) ... BB
Burnaby Public Library, Burnaby, BC, Canada [*Library symbol*] [*Library of Congress*] (LCLS) ... CaBB
Burnaby Public Library, Kingsway Branch, Kingsway, BC, Canada [*Library symbol*] [*Library of Congress*] (LCLS) ... CaBBK
Burnaby Village Museum, British Columbia [*Library symbol*] [*National Library of Canada*] (NLC) ... BBVM
Burn-Bash-Bury [*Australian trash disposal policy in Vietnam*] (VNW) ... B-B-B
Burndale Resources Ltd. [*Vancouver Stock Exchange symbol*] ... BDL
Burn-Dressing Change [*Medicine*] ... BDC
Burndy Corp., Technical Library, Norwalk, CT [*Library symbol*] [*Library of Congress*] (LCLS) ... CtNowaB
Burndy Corporation (SAUO) ... BDC
Burndy Engineering Co., Inc. (SAUO) ... BE
Burned [*Ecology*] ... B
Burned Area [*Ecology*] ... BA
Burned in Time Codes ... BITC
Burned, Shaded [*Ecology*] ... BS
Burner (MSA) ... BNR
Burner ... BRNR
Burners Out of Service [*Combustion emission control*] ... BOOS
Burnet. Criminal Law of Scotland [*A publication*] (DLA) ... Burn Cr L
Burnet, Duckworth & Palmer, Calgary, Alberta [*Library symbol*] [*National Library of Canada*] (BIB) ... ACBDP
Burnet. Manuscript Decisions, Scotch Court of Session [*A publication*] (DLA) ... Burnet
Burnet, TX [*Location identifier*] [*FAA*] (FAAL) ... BMQ
Burnet, TX [*FM radio station call letters*] ... KBLK
Burnet, TX [*AM radio station call letters*] ... KHLB
Burnet, TX [*FM radio station call letters*] ... KHLB-FM
Burnett and Rolfe Ltd. (SAUO) ... BR
Burnett Elementary School, Houston, TX [*Library symbol*] [*Library of Congress*] (LCLS) ... TxHBE
Burnettown, SC [*AM radio station call letters*] (RBYB) ... WKRU-AM
Burnettown, SC [*AM radio station call letters*] ... WVAA
Burnett's Reports [*20-22 Oregon*] [*A publication*] (DLA) ... Burnett
Burnett's Wisconsin Reports [*A publication*] (DLA) ... Burn
Burnett's Wisconsin Reports [*A publication*] (DLA) ... Burnett
Burnett's Wisconsin Reports [*A publication*] (DLA) ... Burnett's Rep
Burnett's Wisconsin Reports [*A publication*] (DLA) ... Burnett (Wis)
Burnett's Wisconsin Supreme Court Reports [*1841-43*] [*A publication*] (DLA) ... Bur
Burney, CA [*Location identifier*] [*FAA*] (FAAL) ... BNY
Burney, CA [*FM radio station call letters*] ... KARZ
Burney, CA [*AM radio station call letters*] ... KAVA
Burney, CA [*FM radio station call letters*] ... KIBC
Burney, CA [*AM radio station call letters*] (BROA) ... KMCA-AM
Burney, CA [*FM radio station call letters*] ... KNCA
Burney, CA [*FM radio station call letters*] (BROA) ... KRRX-FM
Burnham [*England*] ... BURN
Burnham City Hospital, Champaign, IL [*Library symbol*] [*Library of Congress*] (LCLS) ... IChamBH
Burnham Committee (SAUO) ... BC
Burnham Fund Cl.A [*Mutual fund ticker symbol*] (SG) ... BURHX
Burnham, J. B., Chicago IL [*STAC*] ... BJB
Burnham, PA [*FM radio station call letters*] ... WVNW
Burnham Pacific Properties [*NYSE symbol*] (SPSG) ... BPP
Burnham Pacific Properties [*Associated Press*] (SAG) ... BurnPP
Burnie High School [*Tasmania*] [*Seismograph station code, US Geological Survey*] (SEIS) ... BNE
Burnie-Wynward [*Tasmania*] [*Airport symbol*] (AD) ... WNY
Burn-In Screening ... BIS
Burn-In/Aging Tester ... BIAT
Burning ... BRNG
Burning ... BRNNG
Burning Anomaly Rate Factor (MCD) ... BARF
Burning Bush [*Freemasonry*] ... BB
Burning Bush Museum, Pictou, Nova Scotia [*Library symbol*] [*National Library of Canada*] (BIB) ... NSPBB
Burning Bush Museum, Pictou, NS, Canada [*Library symbol*] [*Library of Congress*] (LCLS) ... CaNSPBB
Burning Feet Syndrome [*Medicine*] (DMAA) ... BF
Burning of Urination [*Medicine*] (MELL) ... BOU
Burning Rate Extraction Technique (MCD) ... BRET
Burning Surface Area of Propellant [*Symbol*] [*Aerospace*] ... A
Burning Tongue Syndrome [*Medicine*] (MELL) ... BTS
Burnish (KSC) ... BNH
Burnish (MSA) ... BNSH
Burnished (VRA) ... burn
Burnisher (MSA) ... BRNSHR
Burnishing Tool ... BITO
Burnley Engineering Products Ltd. (SAUO) ... BEP
Burnout (KSC) ... BO
Burn-Out (SAUS) ... BO
Burnout Missile Configuration [*Military*] ... BMC
Burnout Proof ... BOP
Burnout Risk [*Environmental science*] (COE) ... BOR
Burnout Safety Factor (SAA) ... BOSF
Burnout Velocity ... BOV
Burns & Laird Line [*Steamship*] (MHDW) ... B & L
Burns and McDonnell Engineering Co., Kansas City, MO [*Library symbol*] [*Library of Congress*] (LCLS) ... MoKBM
Burns & Roe Inc. (SAUO) ... B&R
Burns & Roe, Inc., Branch Library, Hempstead, NY [*Library symbol*] [*Library of Congress*] (LCLS) ... NHemB
Burns & Roe, Inc., Oradell, NJ [*Library symbol*] [*Library of Congress*] (LCLS) ... NjOrdB
Burns and Schreiber Comedy Hour [*Television program*] [*Obsolete*] ... BS
Burns' Annotated Statutes [*Indiana*] [*A publication*] (DLA) ... Burns' Ann St
Burns' Annotated Statutes [*Indiana*] [*A publication*] (DLA) ... Burns' Rev St
Burn's Attorney's Practice [*A publication*] (DLA) ... Burn Att Pr
Burns. Conveyancing Practice [*Scotland*] [*A publication*] (DLA) ... Burns Pract

Burn's Ecclesiastical Law [*A publication*] (DLA) ..... B Ecc L
Burn's Ecclesiastical Law [*A publication*] (DLA) ..... Burn Eccl
Burn's Ecclesiastical Law [*A publication*] (DLA) ..... Burn Ecc Law
Burn's Ecclesiastical Law [*A publication*] (DLA) ..... Burn's Ecc Law
Burns Elementary School, Hicksville, NY [*Library symbol*] [*Library of Congress*] (LCLS) ..... NHickBE
Burns Federation [*Scotland*] (EAIO) ..... BA
Burns Federation (SAUO) ..... BF
Burns' Indiana Administrative Rules and Regulations [*A publication*] (DLA) ..... Ind Admin R
Burns' Indiana Statutes, Annotated Code Edition [*A publication*] (DLA) ..... Ind Code Ann
Burns Intl. Services [*NYSE symbol*] (SG) ..... BOR
Burn's Justice of the Peace [*England*] [*A publication*] (DLA) ..... B Just
Burn's Justice of the Peace [*England*] [*A publication*] (DLA) ..... Burn JP
Burn's Justice of the Peace [*England*] [*A publication*] (DLA) ..... Burn's JP (Eng)
Burns Lake, BC [*AM radio station call letters*] ..... CFLD
Burns Lake Public Library, British Columbia [*Library symbol*] [*National Library of Canada*] (NLC) ..... BBUL
Burn's Law Dictionary [*A publication*] (DLA) ..... Burn Dict
Burn's Law Dictionary [*A publication*] (DLA) ..... Burn Law Dict
Burn's Marine Insurance [*A publication*] (DLA) ..... Burn Mar Ins
Burns, OR [*Location identifier*] [*FAA*] (FAAL) ..... BNO
Burns, OR [*Location identifier*] [*FAA*] (FAAL) ..... ILR
Burns, OR [*FM radio station call letters*] (RBYB) ..... KQHC-FM
Burns, OR [*AM radio station call letters*] ..... KZZR
Burns, Philip, & Co. [*Steamship*] (MHDW) ..... BP & CO
Burns Society of the City of New York (EA) ..... BSCNY
Burns United Support Group (EA) ..... BUSG
Burns, WY [*FM radio station call letters*] ..... KMUS
Burnside, KY [*FM radio station call letters*] ..... WJDJ
Burnside, KY [*AM radio station call letters*] ..... WKEQ
Burnside, KY [*FM radio station call letters*] (BROA) ..... WWZB-FM
Burnside-Ott Aviation Training Center [*Florida*] ..... BATC
Burnsville, NC [*AM radio station call letters*] ..... WKYK
Burnt (ROG) ..... BNT
Burnt [*Philately*] ..... brnt
Burnt (ROG) ..... BT
Burnt Beyond Recognition (SAUS) ..... BBR
Burnt Beyond Repair (SAUS) ..... BBR
Burnt Island Gold Ltd. (NPL) [*Vancouver Stock Exchange symbol*] ..... BUR
Burnt Out But Opulent ..... BOBO
Burnthills [*ICAO designator*] (AD) ..... KB
Burnthrough (NVT) ..... BT
Burnup ..... BU
Burnup Fraction [*of fuel in plasma*] (MCD) ..... BF
Burr Junior High School, Commack, NY [*Library symbol*] [*Library of Congress*] (LCLS) ..... NCoBJ
Burr Oak Township Library, Burr Oak, MI [*Library symbol*] [*Library of Congress*] (LCLS) ..... MiBar
Burr Oak Township Library, Burr Oak, MI [*Library symbol*] [*Library of Congress*] (LCLS) ..... MiBur
Burrard Inlet Environmental Action Program (AC) ..... BIEAP
Burr-Brown Corp. [*NASDAQ symbol*] (NQ) ..... BBRC
Burr-Brown Corp. [*Associated Press*] (SAG) ..... BurrBr
Burrell-Lawrence-Kennedy [*Vacuum milking device*] ..... BLK
Burrell's Admiralty Cases [*1584-1839*] [*A publication*] (DLA) ..... Burr Adm
Burrell's Reports, Admiralty, Edited by Marsden [*167 English Reprint*] [*A publication*] (DLA) ..... Burrell
Burrell's Reports, Admiralty, Edited by Marsden [*167 English Reprint*] [*A publication*] (DLA) ..... Burrell (Eng)
Burrill on Assignments [*A publication*] (DLA) ..... Burr Ass
Burrill on Assignments [*A publication*] (DLA) ..... Burrill Assignm
Burrill on Circumstantial Evidence [*A publication*] (DLA) ..... Bur Circ Ev
Burrill on Circumstantial Evidence [*A publication*] (DLA) ..... Burr Circ Ev
Burrill on Circumstantial Evidence [*A publication*] (DLA) ..... Burrill Circ Ev
Burrill on Voluntary Assignments [*A publication*] (DLA) ..... Bur Ass
Burrill on Voluntary Assignments [*A publication*] (DLA) ..... Burrill Ass
Burrill's Forms [*A publication*] (DLA) ..... Bur Forms
Burrill's Forms [*A publication*] (DLA) ..... Burr Forms
Burrill's Law Dictionary [*A publication*] (DLA) ..... Bur Law Dic
Burrill's Law Dictionary [*A publication*] (DLA) ..... Burr Dict
Burrill's Law Dictionary [*A publication*] (DLA) ..... Burrill
Burrill's Law Dictionary [*A publication*] (DLA) ..... Burr Law Dict
Burrill's New York Practice [*A publication*] (DLA) ..... Bur Pr
Burrill's New York Practice [*A publication*] (DLA) ..... Burr Pr
Burrill's Practice [*A publication*] (DLA) ..... Burrill Pr
Burring Cutter ..... BUCU
Burro Club [*Democratic political organization*] [*Defunct*] (EA) ..... BC
Burro Red Blood Cells ..... BRBC
Burroughs Advanced Statistical Inquiry System [*Computer science*] (BUR) ..... BASIS
Burroughs and Gresson's Irish Equity Pleader [*A publication*] (DLA) ..... Bur & Gres Eq Pl
Burroughs and Gresson's Irish Equity Pleader [*A publication*] (DLA) ..... Burr & Gr Eq Pl
Burroughs and Sperry Information Systems [*Suggested name for the corporation formed by the Burroughs/Sperry merger*] ..... BASIS
Burroughs Applied Statistical Inquiry System (SAUS) ..... BASIS
Burroughs Bibliophiles (EA) ..... BB
Burroughs Common Language [*Computer science*] (BUR) ..... BCL
Burroughs Computer Output to Microfilm (IEEE) ..... BCOM
Burroughs Corp. (AAG) ..... BRC
Burroughs Corp., Western Region Central Technical Library, Pasadena, CA [*Library symbol*] [*Library of Congress*] (LCLS) ..... CPB-E
Burroughs Corporation (SAUO) ..... BC
Burroughs Corporation (SAUO) ..... BGH
Burroughs Current Mode Logic ..... BCML
Burroughs Data Link Control [*Computer science*] (BUR) ..... BDLC
Burroughs Data Management System (SAUS) ..... BDMS
Burroughs Direct Interface (SAUS) ..... BDI
Burroughs Distribution Scheduling System [*Computer science*] (BUR) ..... BURDS
Burroughs Electrographic Printer-plotter for Ordnance Computing (SAUS) ..... BEPOC
Burroughs Electronic Accounting Machine (BUR) ..... BEAM
Burrough's History of the Chancery [*A publication*] (DLA) ..... Bur Chy
Burroughs' History of the Chancery [*A publication*] (DLA) ..... Burr Ch
Burroughs Hospital Accounting System (SAUS) ..... BHAS
Burroughs Hospital Administration System (SAUS) ..... BHAS
Burroughs Hospital Administrative System [*Computer science*] (BUR) ..... BHAS
Burroughs Hospital Information System (SAUS) ..... BHIS
Burroughs Input and Display System (SAUS) ..... BIDS
Burroughs Input and Display Terminal (IAA) ..... BIDS
Burroughs Input and Display Terminal (SAUS) ..... BIDT
Burroughs Inventory Control System [*Computer science*] (BUR) ..... BICS
Burroughs Inventory Planning Analysis and Simulation System [*Computer science*] (BUR) ..... BIPASS
Burroughs Line Printer Adapter (SAUS) ..... BLPA
Burroughs Management System (SAUS) ..... BMS
Burroughs Modular Terminal (SAUS) ..... BMT
Burroughs Network Architecture (SAUS) ..... BNA
Burroughs on Public Securities [*A publication*] (DLA) ..... Burr Pub Sec
Burroughs on Taxation [*A publication*] (DLA) ..... Burr Tax
Burroughs on Taxation [*A publication*] (DLA) ..... Bur Tax
Burroughs Operational System Simulator (SAUS) ..... BOSS
Burroughs Optical Lens Docking System (MCD) ..... BOLDS
Burroughs Poll/Select (SAUS) ..... BPS
Burroughs Programming Language (IAA) ..... BPL
Burroughs Remote Job Entry (SAUS) ..... BRJE
Burroughs Scientific Processor [*Computer science*] (BUR) ..... BSP
Burroughs, UNIVAC, NCR, Control Data, Honeywell [*IBM competitors in computer manufacture*] ..... BUNCH
Burroughs Wellcome & Co. ..... BW
Burroughs Wellcome & Co., Greenville, NC [*Library symbol*] [*Library of Congress*] (LCLS) ..... NcDurW-Gv
Burroughs Wellcome & Co., Kirkland, Quebec [*Library symbol*] [*National Library of Canada*] (NLC) ..... QKBW
Burroughs Wellcome & Co., Research Triangle Park, NC [*OCLC symbol*] (OCLC) ..... NRT
Burroughs Wellcome Fund ..... BWF
Burroughs Wellcome, Inc., Kirkland Lake, ON, Canada [*Library symbol*] [*Library of Congress*] (LCLS) ..... CaQKIBW
Burroughs Wellcome Research Institute [*Great Britain*] [*Research code symbol*] ..... BW
Burrow. English King's Bench Reports [*A publication*] (DLA) ..... Bur
Burrow. English King's Bench Reports Tempore Lord Mansfield [*97, 98 English Reprint*] [*A publication*] (DLA) ..... Burr
Burrow. English King's Bench Reports Tempore Lord Mansfield [*97, 98 English Reprint*] [*A publication*] (DLA) ..... Burr (Eng)
Burrow-Fill Structure (SAUS) ..... BFS
Burrow's English Settlement Cases [*A publication*] (DLA) ..... Burrow Sett Cas
Burrow's English Settlement Cases [*A publication*] (DLA) ..... Burr SC
Burrow's English Settlement Cases [*A publication*] (DLA) ..... Burr S Cas
Burrow's English Settlement Cases [*A publication*] (DLA) ..... Burr S Cases
Burrow's English Settlement Cases [*A publication*] (DLA) ..... Burr Sett Cas
Burrow's English Settlement Cases [*A publication*] (DLA) ..... Burr Sett Cas (Eng)
Burrow's English Settlement Cases [*A publication*] (DLA) ..... Bur SC
Burrow's English Settlement Cases [*A publication*] (DLA) ..... Sett Cas
Burrow's Reports, English King's Bench [*A publication*] (DLA) ..... Burrow
Burrow's Reports Tempore Mansfield [*England*] [*A publication*] (DLA) ..... BM
Burrow's Reports Tempore Mansfield [*England*] [*A publication*] (DLA) ..... B Monr
Burrow's Reports Tempore Mansfield [*England*] [*A publication*] (DLA) ..... Bur M
Burrow's Reports Tempore Mansfield [*England*] [*A publication*] (DLA) ..... Burr TM
Burrows Trail Arts Council (AC) ..... BTAC
Burr's Lane Junior High School, Dix Hills, NY [*Library symbol*] [*Library of Congress*] (LCLS) ..... NDxhBJ
Burr's Trial, Reported by Robertson [*A publication*] (DLA) ..... Burr Tr
Burr's Trial, Reported by Robertson [*A publication*] (DLA) ..... Burr Tr Rob
Burry Port [*Welsh depot code*] ..... BP
Burry Port & Gwendraeth Valley Railway [*Wales*] ..... BPGV
Bursa [*Turkey*] [*Airport symbol*] [*Obsolete*] (OAG) ..... BTZ
Bursa [*Turkey*] [*ICAO location identifier*] (ICLI) ..... LTBE
Bursa Airlines, Inc. [*Turkey*] [*ICAO designator*] (ICDA) ..... FB
Bursa Cells [*Of thymus or lymph nodes*] ..... B
Bursa Copulatrix (SAUS) ..... bc
Bursa Equivalent Lymphocyte (MAE) ..... B-L
Bursa Hava Yollari [*ICAO designator*] (AD) ..... WL
Bursal Dependent [*Cells*] [*Immunology*] ..... BD
Bursal Lymphomas [*Oncology*] ..... BLYM
Bursar (ABBR) ..... BRSR
Bursar ..... BURS
Bursary (ABBR) ..... BRSRY
Bur-Sin (BJA) ..... BS
Bursitis [*Medicine*] ..... B
Bursitis (ABBR) ..... BRSTS
Burst ..... BRST
Burst (IAA) ..... BST
Burst and All Sky Imaging Survey (SAUS) ..... BASIS
Burst and Synchronous BIT [*Binary Digit*] **Generator** [*Computer science*] (IAA) ..... BSBG

Burst and Transient Source Experiment [*Gamma Ray Observatory satellite data collection*] ... BATSE
Burst Arcsecond Imaging and Spectroscopy (SAUS) ... BASIS
Burst Can Detector (SAUS) ... BCD
Burst Cartridge Detection ... BCD
Burst Cladding Detection System [*Nuclear energy*] (NUCP) ... BCD
Burst Communications Systems (MCD) ... BCS
Burst Delay Timer (MCD) ... BDT
Burst EDO [*Extended Data Out*] [*Computer science*] ... BEDO
Burst Error Correction [*Encoder/decoder*] (MCD) ... BEC
Burst Error Detection and Correlation ... BEDAC
Burst Forming Units (SAUS) ... BFU
Burst Height Compensator [*Military*] (CAAL) ... BHC
Burst Limit Switch (MCD) ... BLS
Burst Measuring System ... BMS
Burst Mode Protocol (SAUS) ... BMP
Burst Multiplexer Channel [*Telecommunications*] ... BMC
Burst of Rapid Atrial Pacing [*Medicine*] (DB) ... BRAP
Burst of Ventricular Pacing [*Medicine*] (DMAA) ... BVP
Burst Out Laughing [*Internet dialog*] ... BOL
Burst Position Locator ... BPL
Burst Slug Detection ... BSD
Burst Static RAM (SAUS) ... BS-RAM
Burst Synchronous SRAM (SAUS) ... BSSRAM
Burst Time Indicator (MCD) ... BTI
Burst Time Plan (LAIN) ... BTP
Burst Tolerance [*Telecommunications*] (ACRL) ... BT
Burst Transmission Group ... BTG
Burst Trapping (MHDI) ... BT
Burst Waveform ... BWF
Burster ... BRSTR
Burst-Error Channel (IAA) ... BEC
Burst-Error Processor (SAUS) ... BEP
Burster-Trimmer-Stacker [*Printing*] (DGA) ... BTS
Burst-Forming Unit ... BFU
Burst-Forming Unit erythroid [*Hematology*] ... BFUe
Burst-Height Indicator ... BHI
Bursting (ABBR) ... BRSTG
Bursting Charge [*Military*] ... BC
Bursting Pacemaker Potential [*Electrophysiology*] ... BPP
Bursting Strength (SAUS) ... BTST STR
Bursting with Laughter [*Internet dialog*] ... BWL
Burst-mode Multiplexer Channel (SAUS) ... BMC
Burst-on-Target (MCD) ... BOT
Burst-Promoting Activity [*Cytology*] ... BPA
Burst-Promoting Factor [*Endocrinology; hematology*] ... BPF
Bursts with Memory [*Physics*] ... BWM
Burst-Time Bias (SAUS) ... BTB
Bursty Errored Seconds [*Computer science*] (VERA) ... BES
Burt Reynolds Fan Club (EA) ... BRFC
Burton and Bitter [*Drink served in British public houses*] ... BB
Burton. Cases and Opinions [*A publication*] (DLA) ... Cas Op
Burton. Manual of the Laws of Scotland [*A publication*] (DLA) ... Burt Man
Burton on Bankruptcy [*A publication*] (DLA) ... Burt Bank
Burton on Real Property [*A publication*] (DLA) ... Burt Real Prop
Burton on Real Property [*A publication*] (DLA) ... Burt RP
Burton Public Library, Burton, OH [*OCLC symbol*] (OCLC) ... BVP
Burton Public Library, Burton, OH [*Library symbol*] [*Library of Congress*] (LCLS) ... OBur
Burton-Cabrera-Frank [*Theory in crystallography*] ... BCF
Burton-on-Trent Natural History and Archaeological Society (SAUO) ... BNHAS
Burton-On-Trent Public Library, Burton-On-Trent, United Kingdom [*Library symbol*] [*Library of Congress*] (LCLS) ... UkBot
Burton's Collection of Cases and Opinions [*England*] [*A publication*] (DLA) ... Burt Cas
Burton's Parliamentary Diary [*A publication*] (DLA) ... Burt Parl
Burton's Scotch Trials [*A publication*] (DLA) ... Burt Sc Tr
Burtonwood [*British*] [*ICAO location identifier*] (ICLI) ... EGOB
Burundi [*Aircraft nationality and registration mark*] (FAAC) ... 9U
Burundi [*MARC country of publication code*] [*Library of Congress*] (LCCP) ... bd
Burundi [*ANSI three-letter standard code*] (CNC) ... BDI
Burundi [*ANSI two-letter standard code*] (CNC) ... BI
Burundi (MILB) ... Bu
Burundi (VRA) ... Buru
Burundi [*MARC geographic area code*] [*Library of Congress*] (LCCP) ... f-bd-
Burundi Air Force (SAUO) ... BAF
Burwash, YT [*ICAO location identifier*] (ICLI) ... CYDB
Burwell, NE [*Location identifier*] [*FAA*] (FAAL) ... BUB
Bury Cooper Whitehead Ltd. [*British*] (IRUK) ... BCW
Burying (ABBR) ... BRYG
Bus [*Computer science*] ... B
Bus Access Module ... BAM
Bus Acknowledgement [*Computer science*] (TEL) ... BUSAK
Bus Adapter (SAUS) ... LBA
Bus Adaptor Control (SAUS) ... BAC
Bus Analog Module (ACAE) ... BAM
Bus and Coach Association of New South Wales ... BCANSW
Bus and Coach Council [*British*] ... BCC
Bus and Lining Module (SAUS) ... BLM
Bus Arbitration Module [*Motorola, Inc.*] ... BAM
Bus Association of New York State (SRA) ... BANY
Bus Automation [*Computer science*] (ODBW) ... BA
Bus Available [*Computer science*] ... BA
Bus Block Transfer ... BBLT
Bus Compatible (IAA) ... BC

Bus Configuration Table (MCD) ... BCT
Bus Control (SAUS) ... BUC
Bus Control Card [*Electronics*] (ACRL) ... BCC
Bus Control Electronics (MCD) ... BCE
Bus Control Element (MCD) ... BCE
Bus Control Interface Unit (MCD) ... BCIU
Bus Control Unit (KSC) ... BCU
Bus Controller (MCD) ... BC
Bus Coupler [*Computer science*] (MCD) ... BC
Bus Data Register (SAUS) ... BDR
Bus Data Unit (SAUS) ... BDU
Bus Device Request [*Computer science*] (VERA) ... BDR
Bus Differential [*Electronics*] (IAA) ... BDF
Bus Direction [*Computer science*] (TEL) ... BDIR
Bus Driver [*Electronics*] (IAA) ... BD
Bus Duct [*Electronics*] (IAA) ... BD
Bus Electronic Scanning Indicator (SAUS) ... BESI
Bus Enable [*Computer science*] (MHDI) ... BEN
Bus Enable (SAUS) ... BUSEN
Bus Error Cycle (SAUS) ... Bus Err Cy
Bus Exchange Logic (SAUS) ... BEL
Bus for Data Output (IAA) ... BDO
Bus Fraction (SAUS) ... BF
Bus Grant (IAA) ... BG
Bus History Association (EA) ... BHA
Bus History Association (SAUO) ... BHA
Bus Interconnect (SAUS) ... BI
Bus Interface [*Computer science*] ... B/I
Bus Interface Adapter (SSD) ... BIA
Bus Interface Adaptor (SAUS) ... BIA
Bus Interface Board (VERA) ... BIB
Bus Interface Chip [*Computer science*] (VERA) ... BIC
Bus Interface Circuit [*Computer science*] (MDG) ... BIC
Bus Interface Controller [*Computer science*] (NITA) ... BIC
Bus Interface Module ... BIM
Bus Interface Node (SAUS) ... BIN
Bus Interface Register (SAUS) ... BIR
Bus Interface Unit [*Computer science*] ... BIU
Bus Interrupter Module [*Motorola, Inc.*] ... BIM
Bus Ion Mass Spectrometer [*Space science instrumentation*] ... BIMS
Bus Link (IAA) ... BL
Bus Load (SAUS) ... BL
Bus Master Interface Controller [*Computer science*] (PCM) ... BMIC
Bus Monitor Unit (MCD) ... BMU
Bus Multiplexer ... BM
Bus Multiplexer (ACAE) ... BMUX
Bus Neutral Mass Spectrometer [*Space science instrumentation*] ... BNMS
Bus Operation Valid (SAUS) ... BOV
Bus Oriented Asynchronous Receiver Transmitter (SAUS) ... BOART
Bus Out (SAUS) ... BOUT
Bus Out Check (SAUS) ... BOC
Bus Out Register [*Computer science*] ... BOR
Bus Proprietors' Association, Victoria [*Australia*] ... BPAV
Bus Propulsion System (ACAE) ... BPS
Bus Request [*Computer science*] (IAA) ... BR
Bus Request [*Computer science*] (TEL) ... BUSRQ
Bus Select Relay (SAUS) ... BSR
Bus Selector [*Computer science*] ... BSLR
Bus Service Management System [*FTA*] (TAG) ... BSMS
Bus Services Licensing Authority (SAUO) ... BSLA
Bus, Standard Marine (SAUS) ... BSM
Bus Subsystem Interface Unit (SAUS) ... BSIU
Bus System Control (SAUS) ... BSC
Bus System Inferface unit (SAUS) ... BSIN
Bus Terminal Unit (MCD) ... BTU
Bus Terminator [*Computer science*] (VERA) ... BT
Bus Tie [*Technical drawings*] ... BT
Bus Tie Breaker ... BTB
Bus Tie Contractor (MCD) ... BTC
Bus Tie Relay (MCD) ... BTS
Bus Transceiver Logic (SAUS) ... BTL
Bus Transfer (AAG) ... BTR
Bus Unit [*Computer science*] ... BU
Bus Unit Scan Station (SAUS) ... BUSS
Bus Voltage Limiter (ACAE) ... BVL
Bus Workers' Protection Society [*A union*] [*British*] ... BWPS
Busala [*Zaire*] [*ICAO location identifier*] (ICLI) ... FZCR
Busan [*South Korea*] [*ICAO location identifier*] (ICLI) ... RKPP
Bus-Bar (SAUS) ... BB
Bus-Bar Layout Drawing [*Computer science*] (TEL) ... BB
Busbars (SAUS) ... BBs
Busbee's Criminal Digest [*North Carolina*] [*A publication*] (DLA) ... Busb Cr Dig
Busbee's North Carolina Equity Reports [*A publication*] (DLA) ... Busbee Eq (NC)
Busbee's North Carolina Equity Reports [*A publication*] (DLA) ... Busb Eq
Busbee's North Carolina Equity Reports [*A publication*] (DLA) ... Bus Eq
Busbee's North Carolina Law Reports [*A publication*] (DLA) ... BNC
Busbee's North Carolina Law Reports [*A publication*] (DLA) ... Busb
Busbee's North Carolina Law Reports [*A publication*] (DLA) ... Busb L
Busboy (ABBR) ... BSBY
Busch Grand National [*Auto racing*] ... BGN
Buschke Memory Test [*Psychology*] (DAVI) ... BMT
Bus-Earth Tracking Station Link [*NASA*] ... BEL
Buses and Trucks ... BAT
Buses International Association (EA) ... BIA
Buses Worldwide [*British*] [*An association*] (DBA) ... BWW

Bush, Boake Allen, Inc. [*NYSE symbol*] (SAG) .... BOA
Bush Boake Allen, Inc. [*Associated Press*] (SAG) .... Bush BA
Bush Church Aid Society [*Australia*] .... BCA
Bush Church Aid Society of Australia .... BCASA
Bush Fire Board of Western Australia .... BFBWA
Bush Fire Council of the Northern Territory [*Australia*] .... BFCNT
Bush Fires Board [*Western Australia*] .... BFB
Bush House (WDAA) .... BH
Bush Indus Cl'A' [*NYSE symbol*] (TTSB) .... BSH
Bush Industries [*NYSE symbol*] (SAG) .... BSH
Bush Industries [*Associated Press*] (SAG) .... BushInd
Bush Pilots Airways [*ICAO designator*] (AD) .... QN
Bush Pilots Airways Ltd. [*Australia*] (ADA) .... BPA
Bush Pilots Association (SAUO) .... BPA
Bush Terminal Buildings (SAUO) .... BHB
Bush Terminal R. R. [*AAR code*] .... BUSH
Bush Terminal Railroad (SAUO) .... BUSH
Bush Transfer (SAUS) .... BTR
Bush Universal, Inc. (SAUO) .... BSH
Bushby. Parliamentary Elections [*5th ed.*] [*1880*] [*A publication*] (DLA) .... Bush Elec
Bushed (ABBR) .... BSHD
Bushehr [*Iran*] [*Airport symbol*] (OAG) .... BUZ
Bushehr [*Iran*] [*ICAO location identifier*] (ICLI) .... OIBT
Bushehr/Bushehr [*Iran*] [*ICAO location identifier*] (ICLI) .... OIBB
Bushel (SAUS) .... Bsh
Bushel (ROG) .... BSH
Bushel (ADWA) .... bsh
Bushel (ABBR) .... BSHL
Bushel .... BU
Bushel .... bu
Bushel (SAUS) .... Bu
Bushel .... BUS
Bushel .... BUSH
Bushels (SAUS) .... Bu/S
Bushfires Council of the Northern Territory [*Australia*] .... BCNT
Bushier (ABBR) .... BSHR
Bushiest (ABBR) .... BSHST
Bushiness (ABBR) .... BSHNS
Bushing (SAUS) .... Bn
Bushing (SAUS) .... Bshg
Bushing (MSA) .... BSHG
Bushing (MSA) .... BUSH
Bushing Current Transformer (KSC) .... BCT
Bushing Potential Device (MSA) .... BPD
Bushire [*Iran*] [*Airport symbol*] (AD) .... BUZ
Bushmaster Aircraft Corp. [*ICAO aircraft manufacturer identifier*] (ICAO) .... BU
Bushnell, FL [*AM radio station call letters*] .... WKFL
Bushnell, IL [*FM radio station call letters*] .... WLMD
Bush's Digest of Florida Laws [*A publication*] (DLA) .... Bush Dig
Bush's Kentucky Reports [*64-77 Kentucky*] [*A publication*] (DLA) .... Bush
Bush's Kentucky Reports [*64-77 Kentucky*] [*A publication*] (DLA) .... Bush (KY)
Bushveldt Carabineers [*British military*] (DMA) .... BVC
Bushwaster Armored Turret (MCD) .... BAT
Bushwhack (ABBR) .... BSHWHK
Bushwhacker (ABBR) .... BSHWHKR
Bushwick High School (SAUO) .... BHS
Busia [*Kenya*] [*ICAO location identifier*] (ICLI) .... HKBA
Busily (ABBR) .... BSLY
Businees Environment Risk Information (SAUO) .... Beri
Business [*As in show biz*] (WDMC) .... biz
Business [*Slang*] (DSUE) .... BIZ
Business (ABBR) .... BSNS
Business (AFM) .... BUS
Business (DD) .... bus
Business (AL) .... Bus
Business (SAUS) .... Bus
Business (BARN) .... Busn
Business Account Number File [*IRS*] .... BANF
Business Accounting System (CIST) .... BAS
Business Accounting Systems (SAUS) .... BAS
Business Acronyms [*A publication*] .... BA
Business Administration (SAUS) .... BAD
Business Administration [*A publication*] .... Bus Admin
Business Administration, Management, and/or Marketing Programs [*Association of Independent Colleges and Schools specialization code*] .... BS
Business Administration Manager (ABAC) .... BAM
Business Advisory and Planning Council (SAUO) .... BAPC
Business Advisory Committee on Procurement [*DoD*] .... BACP
Business Advisory Council [*Later, Business Council*] .... BAC
Business Air AG [*Switzerland*] [*ICAO designator*] (FAAC) .... BUR
Business Air Ltd. [*British*] [*ICAO designator*] (FAAC) .... GNT
Business Air Service Ltd. [*Airline*] [*Canada*] .... BAS
Business Air Services (Toronto) Ltd. [*Canada*] [*ICAO designator*] (FAAC) .... BAM
Business Air Taxi [*Switzerland*] [*ICAO designator*] (FAAC) .... BUT
Business Air Transport Service .... BATS
Business Aircraft Users' Association [*British*] .... BAUA
Business Alert to Nuclear War (EA) .... BANW
Business Alliance for Commerce in Hemp (SAUS) .... BACH
Business Alliance on Government Competition [*Defunct*] (EA) .... BAGC
Business Analysis Model (SAUS) .... BAM
Business Analyst Skills Evaluation [*Test*] .... BUSAN
Business and Commerce [*A publication*] (DLA) .... Bus & Com
Business and Commercial Management Group (SAUO) .... BACM
Business and Consumer Affairs (WDAA) .... BACA
Business and Defense Services Administration [*Later, BDC*] [*Department of Commerce*] .... BDSA
Business and Economic Research Center [*Middle Tennessee State University*] [*Research center*] (RCD) .... BERC
Business and Engineering Enriched Formula Translator (SAUS) .... BEEF Translator
Business and Engineering Enriched FORTRAN [*Programming language*] [*Sperry UNIVAC*] .... BEEF
Business and Farm [*IRS*] .... B & F
Business and Finance (journ.) (SAUS) .... Irish Bus
Business and Financial Manager [*Military*] (DOMA) .... BFM
Business and Financial Services (SAUS) .... BFS
Business and Government Services (ACRL) .... BGS
Business and Industrial Coordinating Council (SAUO) .... BICC
Business and Industrial Development Corporation [*Generic term for a for-profit investment company*] .... BIDCO
Business and Industrial Development Institute [*Saginaw Valley State College*] [*Database search service*] (OLDSS) .... BIDI
Business and Industry Advisory Committee [*NATO*] (NATG) .... BIAC
Business and Industry Association of New Hampshire (SRA) .... BIA
Business and Industry Data Center (SAUS) .... BIDC
Business and Industry Management Abstracts [*A publication*] .... BIMA
Business and Industry Nongovernment Organization .... BINGO
Business and Institutional Furniture Manufacturers Association (EA) .... BIFMA
Business and Investments Centre [*British*] .... BIC
Business and Law [*A publication*] (DLA) .... Bus & L
Business and Law Review [*Corporate Agents, Inc.*] [*Information service or system*] (CRD) .... BLR
Business & Legal Reports, Inc. .... BLR
Business and Loan (SAUS) .... B&L
Business and Management Practices .... BAMP
Business and Professional Code (SAUS) .... BPC
Business and Professional Software [*Software publisher*] .... BPS
Business and Professional Women (ADWA) .... BPW
Business and Professional Women's Club [*Australia*] .... BPWC
Business and Professional Women's Club of Perth [*Australia*] .... BPWCP
Business and Professional Women's Foundation .... BPW
Business and Professional Women's Foundation (EA) .... BPWF
Business and Professions [*A publication*] (DLA) .... Bus & Prof
Business and Professions Code (DLA) .... Bus & Prof C
Business and Residence Centrex Services [*Telecommunications*] (ACRL) .... BRCS
Business and Society [*A publication*] (BRI) .... Bus Soc
Business and Technician Education Council [*British*] .... BTEC
Business and Technician Education Council (ACII) .... BTECH
Business and Technology Alliance (SAUS) .... B&TA
Business and Technology Center [*Control Data Corp.*] [*British*] .... BTC
Business and Technology Education Council National Certificate (AIE) .... BTECNC
Business Application Language .... BAL
Business Application Performance Corp. (VERA) .... BAPCO
Business Application Programmer's Interface [*Computer science*] (VERA) .... BAPI
Business Application Programming Interface (SAUS) .... BAPI
Business Applications Performance Corp. (CDE) .... BAPC
Business Applications Performance Corp. .... BAPCo
Business Applications Programming Guide (MCD) .... BAPG
Business Applications written in BASIC (SAUS) .... BA/BASIC
Business Archives Council [*British*] .... BAC
Business Archives Council (SAUO) .... BAC
Business Area Analysis (SAUO) .... BAA
Business as Usual .... BAU
business as usual (SAUS) .... bau
Business Assessment Study and Evaluation (PDAA) .... BASE
Business Association of Latin American Studies (EA) .... BALAS
Business Automation (SAUS) .... BA
Business Automation Specification Reports (SAUS) .... BASR
Business Automobile Policy [*Insurance*] .... BAP
Business Aviation AS [*Denmark*] [*ICAO designator*] (FAAC) .... BUA
Business Batch System (SAUS) .... BBS
Business Book Review [*A publication*] (BRI) .... Bus Bk R
Business Calculating Machine (SAUS) .... BCM
Business Card Collectors International (EA) .... BCCI
Business Card Museum [*An association*] (EA) .... BCM
Business Census .... BC
Business Center Map (SAUS) .... BCM
Business Class [*Also, J*] [*Airline fare code*] C
Business Class [*Also, C*] [*Airline fare code*] .... J
Business Clearance Memorandum (AAGC) .... BCM
Business Clearance Reviewing Authority (AAGC) .... BCRA
Business Coalition for Fair Competition (EA) .... BCFC
Business Committee for the Arts (EA) .... BCA
Business Communications Co., Inc. [*Norwalk, CT*] [*Information service or system*] [*Telecommunications*] (TSSD) .... BCC
Business Communications Sciences, Inc. (SAUO) .... BCS
Business Communications Service [*British Telecommunications International*] [*London*] (TSSD) .... BCS
Business Communications Systems [*Telecommunications*] (TEL) .... BCS
Business Competitive Intelligence .... BCI
Business Comptuer Systems Ltd. [*Later, Business Computer Systems PLC*] [*British*] (NITA) .... BCL
Business Computer (IAA) .... BC
Business Computer Center (SAUS) .... BCC
Business Computer Network, Inc. [*San Antonio, TX*] [*Telecommunications*] (TSSD) .... BCN

Business Computer System (SAUS)	BCS
Business Computer Users Association (SAUO)	BCUA
Business Computer-Aided Manufacturing (AAEL)	BCAD
Business Computers Ltd. [British] (NITA)	BCL
Business Computers Users Association (MHDB)	BCUA
Business Control System	BCS
Business Cooperation Center [EC] (ECED)	BCC
Business Cooperation Centre (SAUO)	BBC
Business Cooperation Centre (SAUO)	BCC
Business Cooperation Network (SAUO)	BC-NET
Business Co-Operation Network (WDAA)	BCNET
Business Cooperation Network (SAUS)	BC-Net
Business Corp. Law [A publication]	BCL
Business Corporation Board	BCB
Business Council (EA)	BC
Business Council for Effective Literacy [Defunct] (EA)	BCEL
Business Council for Fair Trade (AC)	BCFT
Business Council for Improved Transport Policies (EA)	BCITP
Business Council for International Understanding (EA)	BCIU
Business Council for the United Nations (EA)	BCUN
Business Council on National Issues [Canadian research and lobbying organization] (CROSS)	BCNI
Business Council on the Reduction of Paperwork (EA)	BCORP
Business Customer Services [Telecommunications] (TEL)	BCS
Business Cycle Developments [Bureau of the Census] [A publication]	BCD
Business Cycle Indicators (SAUO)	BCI
Business Data Processing	BDP
Business Data Processing Operation	BDPO
Business Dateline Database [Information service or system] (IT)	BDD
Business Defense Services Administration (SAUO)	BDS
Business Definition Language [Computer science] (IAA)	BDL
Business Definition System (MHDI)	BDS
Business Development Consultants International, Ltd. [British]	BDC
Business Development Exercise (WDAA)	BDE
Business Development Group	BDG
Business Development Report [Department of Commerce] (GFGA)	BDR
Business Development Report System [Department of Commerce] [Database]	BDRS
Business Development Specialist (DOMA)	BDS
Business Directory International (ACII)	BDI
Business Directory of Registered Plumbers [A publication]	BDRP
Business Division [Census] (OICC)	BUS
Business EDP [Electronic Data Processing] Systems Technique [NCR Corp.] (IEEE)	BEST
Business Education	BE
Business Education Administrators Association (SAUO)	BEAA
Business Education Connection (OICC)	BEC
Business Education Council	BEC
Business Education Council General Award (AIE)	BGen
Business Education Research Associates (SAUO)	BERA
Business Education Research Foundation (EA)	BERF
Business Education Research of America [Hato Rey, PR] (EA)	BERA
Business Educational Council/Technical Education Council (SAUO)	BEC/TEC
Business Efficiency Exhibition (SAUO)	BEE
Business Efficiency Exhibition [British] (DIT)	BEE
Business Efficiency Exhibition [Business Equipment Association of South Africa]	BEXA
Business Efficiency Unit (HEAS)	BEU
Business Electronic System Technique (SAUS)	BEST
Business Electronics Computer [Used in training]	BEC
Business Emergency Plan	BEP
Business Energy Investment Tax Credit [IRS]	BEITC
Business, Engineering, Appropriate Technology, and Skilled Trades [Peace Corps program]	BEAST
Business Engineering Workbench (VERA)	BEW
Business English Test [Vocational guidance test]	BET
Business Enterprise Center [Australia]	BEC
Business Environment Risk Information [Information service or system] (IID)	BERI
Business Equipment	BE
Business Equipment and Information Technology Association [British]	BEITA
Business Equipment Digest [British] [A publication] (NITA)	BED
Business Equipment Manufacturers Association [Later, CBEMA]	BEMA
Business Equipment Software Techniques [Computer science]	BEST
Business Equipment Trade Association [London, England]	BETA
Business Espionage Controls and Countermeasures Association (EA)	BECCA
Business European Airways Ltd. [British] [FAA designator] (FAAC)	MIN
Business Executive System for Time-sharing (SAUS)	BEST
Business Executives for National Security (EA)	BENS
Business Executives for National Security Education Fund (EA)	BENS/ED
Business Executives Move for New National Priorities [An association] (EA)	BEM
Business Executives Move for Peace [An association] (VNW)	BEM
Business Executives Move for Vietnam Peace (SAUO)	BEM
Business Expansion Scheme [British]	BES
Business Expenditure Research and Development	BERD
Business Experience Training (BARN)	BET
Business Express [ICAO designator] (FAAC)	GAA
Business Express [ICAO designator] (AD)	HQ
Business Express Delivery Ltd. [Canada] [ICAO designator] (FAAC)	EXP
Business Facilitation Center (SAUO)	BFC
Business File System (SAUS)	BFS
Business Firms Master Index [A publication]	BFMI
Business Flight Service [Denmark] [ICAO designator] (FAAC)	BSF
Business Flights Ltd. [Canada] [ICAO designator] (FAAC)	BFA
Business for Social Responsibility	BSR
Business Forecasting (MCD)	BIZFORC
Business Form Institute (SAUO)	BFI
Business Forms Institute [Defunct]	BFI
Business Forms Management Association (EA)	BFMA
Business Funding Scheme	BFS
Business Geographics Conference (GEOI)	BGC
Business Graduates Association (SAUO)	BGA
Business Grant Services [Information service or system]	BGS
Business Group for Latin America [Later, COA]	BGLA
Business Group Services (SAUO)	BGS
Business Health Assessment Program	BHAP
Business Historical Society (SAUO)	BHS
Business History Conference (EA)	BHC
Business History Foundation [Defunct] (EA)	BHF
Business History Review [A publication] (BRI)	BHR
Business Hours	BH
Business Identity Council of America (NTPA)	BICA
Business Improvement Area	BIA
Business Improvement Bulletin (WDAA)	BIB
Business Improvement District (PA)	BID
Business Improvement Services (AIE)	BIS
Business in the Community [British]	BIC
Business in the Environment (SAUS)	BiE
Business Industry Community College Coalition (EDAC)	BICCC
Business Information Analysis and Integration Technique [Computer science]	BIAT
Business Information Center (WDAA)	BIC
Business Information Centre, Bank of Montreal, Toronto, Ontario [Library symbol] [National Library of Canada] (BIB)	OTBMBI
Business Information Centre/SVP [Information service or system] (IID)	BIC/SVP
Business Information Communications (SAUS)	BISCOM
Business Information Desk Reference [A publication]	BIDR
Business Information Exchange Network [Databank] [Canada]	BIEN
Business Information Group [Information service or system] (IID)	BIG
Business Information Management System (SAUS)	BIMS
Business Information Network [Billboard Publications, Inc.] [New York, NY] [Telecommunications] (TEL)	BIN
Business Information Processing	BIP
Business Information Service [Financial Times Business Information Ltd.] [British] [Information service or system] (IID)	BIS
Business Information Services [Control Data Corp.] [Information service or system] (IID)	BIS
Business Information Systems [Bell System]	BIS
Business Information Systems Analysis and Design [Bell System] (DIT)	BISAD
Business Information Systems Communications [Bell System]	BISCOM
Business Information Systems Customer Service [Bell System]	BISCUS
Business Information Systems Customer Service/Facilities Assignment and Control System [Bell System] (MCD)	BISCUS/FACS
Business Information Systems Management [Mountain View, CA] [Telecommunications service] (TSSD)	BISM
Business Information Systems Modeling and Planning System [Bell System]	BISMAPS
Business Information Systems Programs [Bell System]	BISP
Business Information Systems Specialist Group (SAUO)	BISSG
Business Information Systems-Communications System (SAUS)	BISCOM System
Business Information System/Trunks and Special Services [Telecommunications] (TEL)	BISTSS
Business Information Technology	BIT
Business Information Terminal [Computer science] (HGAA)	BIT
Business Information Wire [Database] [The Canadian Press] [Information service or system] (CRD)	BIW
Business Input/Output Rerun [UNIVAC compiling system] [Computer science]	BIOR
Business Institute (SAUS)	TBI
Business Instruction Set [Computer science] (IAA)	BIS
Business Insurance Trust (DLA)	BIT
Business Intelligence	BI
Business Intelligence Center [SRI International] [Information service or system] (IID)	B-I-C
Business Intelligence Program Research Catalog [SRI International] [Information service or system] (IID)	B-I-P
Business Intelligence Services Ltd. [British]	BIS
Business Intelligence Warehouse (SAUS)	BIW
Business International Corp.	BI
Business International Country Assessment Service [Business International Corp.] [Defunct] [Information service or system] (CRD)	BI/CAS
Business International Non-Governmental Organization (MHDB)	BINGO
Business Interruption [Insurance]	BI
Business Interruption Insurance	BII
Business Inventory Management System (HGAA)	BIM
Business Investment Game	BIG
Business Jets [ICAO designator] (AD)	BQ
Business Law Journal (DLA)	Business LJ
Business Law Journal (DLA)	Bus LJ
Business Law Reports (DLA)	Bus L Rep
Business Law Review [A publication]	BLR
Business Lawyer [A publication]	Bus Law
Business Lead Identification System [Timeplace, Inc.] [Database]	BLIS
Business Leader Group [Washington, DC] (EA)	BLG
Business Leadership Forum (EA)	BLF
Business Library Review [A publication] (BRI)	BusLR

Business Library, Saskatchewan Department of Tourism and Small Business, Regina,Saskatchewan [Library symbol] [National Library of Canada] (NLC) .... SRTSB
Business Library, Saskatchewan Department of Tourism and Small Business, Regina (SAUS) .... SRTSB
Business Licence [British] (ADA) .... BL
Business License Information Service .... BLIS
Business Listing Service (SAUS) .... BLS
Business Logistics Game (SAUS) .... BULOGA
Business Machine .... BM
Business Machine Computer .... BISMAC
Business Machine Computer (MHDI) .... BIZMAC
Business Machine Operator (SAUS) .... BMO
Business Machines Group [Burroughs Corp.] .... BMG
Business Mail Foundation [Later, DMMA] (EA) .... BMF
Business Management (DD) .... BusMgmt
Business Management Control System [Computer science] (IAA) .... BMCS
Business Management Control System Research Project (IAA) .... BMCSRP
Business Management Division (SAUO) .... BMD
Business Management Game .... BMG
Business Management Information System (SAUS) .... BMIS
Business Management Layer (SAUS) .... BML
Business Management System (BUR) .... BMS
Business Management System Team [Air Force] (MCD) .... BMST
Business Manager (MCD) .... BM
Business Manager (WDAA) .... BUS MGR
Business Manager (SAUS) .... Bus Mgr
Business Marketing Association (NTPA) .... BMA
Business Master File [OMB] .... BMF
Business Men's Assurance Co. of America (EFIS) .... BMA
Business Men's League of the United States (EA) .... BMLUS
Business Microcomputer (SAUO) .... BMC
Business Modeling Language (MCD) .... BML
Business Name and Address File [IRS] .... BNAF
Business Name and Address Key Index File [IRS] .... BKIF
Business News Netwowrk .... BNN
Business News Publishing (SAUS) .... BNP
Business Object Documents (VERA) .... BOD
Business Object Model (SAUS) .... BOM
Business Object Notation (SAUS) .... BON
Business Objects ADS [NASDAQ symbol] (SG) .... BOBJ
Business Objects ADS [NASDAQ symbol] (TTSB) .... BOBJY
Business Objects SA [NASDAQ symbol] (SAG) .... BOBJ
Business Objects SA [Associated Press] (SAG) .... BusinObj
Business Objects SA [Associated Press] (SAG) .... BusnObj
Business Office Force Administration Data System [Bell System] .... BOFADS
Business Office Must [Copy that must be printed] [Publishing] .... BOM
Business Office Supervisor [Telecommunications] (TEL) .... BOS
Business Open Shop Scheduling (ACAE) .... BOSS
Business Operations (SAUS) .... BUS
Business Operations Research (SAUO) .... BOR
Business Operations Support Services [British] [FAA designator] (FAAC) .... GEN
Business Opportunities Sourcing System [Information service or system] [Canada] .... BOSS
Business Opportunity and Management Advisory Service (SAUO) .... BOMAS
Business Opportunity Bank [Institute for New Enterprise Development] .... BOB
Business Organization Climate Index (MHDB) .... BOCI
Business Organizations, Agencies, and Publications Directory [Formerly, BOAD] [A publication] .... BOAPD
Business Organizations and Agencies Directory [Later, BOAPD] [A publication] .... BOAD
Business Organizer Scheduling System .... BOSS
Business Partnership for Peace (EA) .... BPP
Business Passenger's Extra Option [Proposed] [Travel industry] .... BPEX
Business People, Inc. [Minneapolis, MN] [Telecommunications service] (TSSD) .... BPI
Business Periodicals Circulation Services [Harcourt Brace Jovanovich] .... BPCS
Business Periodicals Directory [A publication] .... BPD
Business Periodicals Index .... BPI
Business Periodicals Ondisc [UMI/Data Courier] [Information service or system] (CRD) .... BPO
Business Plan System .... BPS
Business Planning Board [Later, BTPB] (EA) .... BPB
Business Planning Language [Computer science] (MHDI) .... BPL
Business Planning Unit (SAUS) .... BPU
Business Press Association (SAUO) .... BPA
Business Press International (DGA) .... BPI
Business Process Analysis .... BPA
Business Process Improvement (AAGC) .... BPI
Business Process Readiness [GSA] (AAGC) .... BPR
Business Process Reengineering .... BPR
Business Products Credit Association (NTPA) .... BPCA
Business Products Industry Association (NTPA) .... BPIA
Business Products Standards Association (NITA) .... BPSA
Business Professionals of America .... BPA
Business Professionals of America .... BPOA
Business Programming Language (SAUS) .... BPL
Business Publications Audit (ACAE) .... BPA
Business Publications Audit (DGA) .... BPC
Business Publications Audit of Circulation, Inc. (SAUO) .... BPA
Business Publications Index and Abstracts [A publication] .... BPIA
Business Publishers, Inc. [Silver Spring, MD] [Information service or system] (IID) .... BPI
Business Radio Service .... BRS
Business Rankings Annual [A publication] .... BRA

Business Record, Des Moines, IA [Library symbol] [Library of Congress] (LCLS) .... IaDmBR
Business Records Holding Corp. [NASDAQ symbol] (SPSG) .... BRCP
Business Records Holding Corp. [Associated Press] (SAG) .... BusnRc
Business Records Manufacturers Association [Later, ABPM] (EA) .... BRMA
Business Recovery Plan (SAUS) .... BRP
Business Recovery Service (ACRL) .... BRS
Business Reference and Services Section [American Library Association] .... BRASS
Business Regulation (DLA) .... Bus Reg
Business Regulation Law Report [A publication] (DLA) .... Bus Reg L Rep
Business Regulation Review Unit (SAUS) .... BRRU
Business Reply Card [Advertising] .... BRC
Business Reply Envelope [Advertising] .... BRE
Business Reply Mail [Advertising] .... BRM
Business Reply Mail Accounting System [US Postal Service] .... BRMAS
Business Reply Post [British] (ADA) .... BRP
Business Research Corp. [Boston, MA] [Information service or system] (IID) .... BRC
Business Research Institute (SAUO) .... BRI
Business Research Management Center [Wright-Patterson Air Force Base, OH] .... BRMC
Business Residence Account Tracking system (SAUS) .... BRAT
Business Residence Custom Service .... BRCS
Business Resource Group [NASDAQ symbol] (SAG) .... BRGP
Business Resource Group [Associated Press] (SAG) .... BusnRs
Business Risk and Value of Operation in Space [NASA] (NASA) .... BRAVO
Business Risks International, Inc. [Database producer] (IID) .... BRI
Business Round Table (SAUO) .... BRT
Business Round Table Report (SAUS) .... BRT Report
Business Roundtable (EA) .... BR
Business Roundtable .... BRT
Business Sample Revision (SAUS) .... BSR
Business School .... B (School)
Business Science Experts [NOMOS Datapool] [Germany] [Information service or system] (CRD) .... WEX
Business Sensitive (ABAC) .... BS
Business Service Center .... BSC
Business Service Centers (ADWA) .... BSCs
Business Service Unit [Telecommunications] (TEL) .... BSU
Business Services and Defense Administration [Department of Commerce] (BARN) .... BSDA
Business Services Branch (HEAS) .... BSB
Business Services Division (HEAS) .... BSD
Business Services Manager (SAUO) .... BSM
Business Services on the Net .... BSN
Business Software Alliance [Formerly, Business Software Association] (EA) .... BSA
Business Software Database [Information Sources, Inc.] [Information service or system] (CRD) .... BSD
Business Start-Up Scheme [British] .... BSS
Business Statistics Office [Department of Trade and Industry] [Information service or system] (IID) .... BSO
Business Strategy Group [of ABT Associates, Inc.] [Cambridge, MA] [Telecommunications service] (TSSD) .... BSG
Business Strategy Panel [Military] .... BSP
Business Studies (DD) .... BusStudies
Business System (SAUS) .... BS
Business System Marketing Division (SAUO) .... BSMD
Business System Planning .... BSP
Business Systems and Security Marketing Association (EA) .... BSSMA
Business Systems Association (NTPA) .... BSA
Business Systems Services (MCD) .... BSS
Business Systems Technology, Inc. .... BST
Business Taxpayer Information File [IRS] .... BTIF
Business Technology Association [Kansas City, MO] [An association] (CDE) .... BTA
Business Technology Research, Inc. [Telecommunications service] (TSSD) .... BTR
Business Telecommunications Corp. [Chicago, IL] (TSSD) .... BTC
Business Telecommunications Equipment [Canada] .... BTE
Business Telecommunications Services (ADA) .... BTS
Business Telephony on Passive Optical Network [Telecommunications] (ROAS) .... BTPON
Business Television (WDMC) .... BTV
Business Terminal Equipment [Telecommunications] (TEL) .... BTE
Business The Real-Time Operating System Nucleus [Computer science] (NITA) .... B TRON
Business Training College .... BTC
Business Transfer Tax [Proposed] [Canada] .... BTT
Business Translation Language (SAUS) .... BTL
Business Travel Accident [Insurance] .... BTA
Business Travel Department (TRID) .... BTD
Business Traveler Hotel Guide [National Association of Business Travel Agents] [A publication] .... BTHG
Business Traveler Magazine [National Association of Business Travel Agents] [A publication] .... BT
Business Trend Analysts, Inc. [Commack, NY] [Information service or system] (IID) .... BTA
Business Turnover Tax (IMH) .... BTT
Business Understanding & Crafts Knowledge School (SAUO) .... BUCKS
Business Unit (ROAS) .... BU
Business User Group [Computer science] .... BUG
Business Vehicle Survey .... BVS

Business Venture Profiles [*TECHSTART International, Inc.*] [*Information service or system*] (CRD) .... BVP
Business Visa (SAUS) B-1
Business Visit [*Program*] [*United States Travel Service*] .... BUSIVISIT
Business Visitors Memorandum [*British Overseas Trade Board*] (DS) .... BVM
Business Volunteers for the Arts (NFD) .... BVA
Business Week [*A publication*] (BRI) .... Bus W
Business Week [*A publication*] (AAGC) .... Bus Wk
Business Week [*A publication*] .... BW
Business Who's Who of Australia [*Database*] [*R.G. Riddell Pty. Ltd.*] .... BUWA
Business Wire (ROAS) .... BW
[*The*] **Business World** [*A publication*] .... TBW
Business/Accounts Reporting Operating Network [*Computer science*] (PDAA) .... BARON
Businesses Offering Goods (SAUS) .... STORE
Business-Higher Education Forum [*Washington, DC*] (EA) .... B-HEF
Business/Higher Education Round Table .... BHERT
Business/Industry Data Center [*Bureau of the Census*] (GFGA) .... BIDC
Business-Industry Political Action Committee (EA) .... BIPAC
Business-Industry-Education [*Days*] [*Usually sponsored by chambers of commerce*] .... BIE
Businesslike (ABBR) .... BSNSLK
Businessman .... bsman
Businessman (ABBR) .... BSNSMN
Businessmen for the Public Interest (SAUO) .... BPI
Business-Oriented Search Service [*Information service or system*] (IID) .... BOSS
Business-Oriented Software System [*Digital Equipment Corp.*] [*Computer science*] (BUR) .... BOSS
Business-Oriented Technology Promotion Programme (SAUS) .... PBTS
Businessowners Policy [*Insurance*] .... BOP
Business/Professional Advertising Association [*New York, NY*] (EA) .... B/PAA
Business-to-Business (SAUS) B2B
Business-to-Business [*Advertising*] (WDMC) .... B-B
Business-to-Business [*Advertising*] (WDMC) .... B-to-B
Businesswoman (ABBR) .... BSNSWMN
Businesswomen (ABBR) .... BSNSWMEN
Busiris [*of Isocrates*] [*Classical studies*] (OCD) .... Bus
Buskin (ABBR) .... BSKN
Buskirk. Indiana Practice [*A publication*] (DLA) .... Busk Pr
Buslink-Interface Module (SAUS) .... BIM
Buss Durkee Hostility Inventory (EDAC) .... BDHI
Busse-Buschke [*Disease*] [*Medicine*] (DB) .... BB
Bust (ADA) .... B
Bust Bodice [*Early name for brassiere*] .... BB
Bustamente Industrial Trade Union (SAUO) .... BITU
Busted Aristocrat [*A cadet officer reduced to the ranks*] [*Military slang*] .... BA
Bus-Termination Array (SAUS) .... BTA
Bustle (ABBR) .... BSTL
Bustled (ABBR) .... BSTLD
Bustling (ABBR) .... BSTLG
Bus-to-Bus Access Circuit [*Bell System*] .... BBAC
Busulfan [*Also, BUS*] [*Antineoplastic drug*] .... BSF
Busulfan [*Antineoplastic drug*] (CDI) .... BU
Busulfan [*Also, BSF*] [*Antineoplastic drug*] .... BUS
Buswell and Wolcott. Massachusetts Practice [*A publication*] (DLA) .... Busw & Wol Pr
Busy .... BSY
Busy [*Telecommunications*] (TEL) .... BY
Busy Beaver (SAUS) .... BB
Busy Bee of Norway AS [*ICAO designator*] (FAAC) .... BEE
Busy BIT [*Binary Digit*] [*Computer science*] (IAA) .... BB
Busy Flash [*Telecommunications*] (NITA) .... BFL
Busy Hour (IAA) .... BH
Busy Hour Call [*Telecommunications*] (TEL) .... BHC
Busy Hour Call Attempts [*Telecommunications*] .... BHCA
Busy Hour Call Completions [*Telecommunications*] (ACRL) .... BHCC
Busy Hour Load [*Telecommunications*] (TEL) .... BHL
Busy Hour Mode (SAUS) .... BHM
Busy Hour Model [*Computer science*] .... BHM
Busy Hour Usage (SAUS) .... BHU
Busy Lamp Field [*Phone console*] [*Bell System*] .... BLF
Busy Line Field (SAUS) .... BLF
Busy Line Verification (SAUS) .... BLV
Busy Season Busy Hour [*Telecommunications*] (ACRL) .... BSBH
Busy Tax Practitioner's Digest [*Australia*] [*A publication*] .... BTPD
Busy Tone [*Telecommunications*] (TEL) .... BT
Busy Tone Multiple-Access [*Telecommunications*] (MHDB) .... BTMA
Busy Tone Trunk [*Telecommunications*] .... BTT
Busy Tone Trunks [*Telecommunications*] (TEL) .... BOTTS
Busy Verification [*Telecommunications*] (TEL) .... BV
Busybody (ABBR) .... BSYBDY
Busying (ABBR) .... BSYG
Busy-Tone Start (SAUS) .... BTST
Busy-to-Start Lead .... BTST
But Less Than .... BLT
But Not .... BN
But Not Exceeding .... BNE
But Not Over .... BNOV
But Now For Something Completely Different (SAUS) .... BNFSCD
But Of Course (SAUS) .... BOC
But Seriously Folks (SAUS) .... BSF
But Seriously Though (SAUS) .... BST
But Then Again (SAUS) .... BTA
But Then Again I could Be Wrong (SAUS) .... BTAICBW
But You Knew That [*Online dialog*] .... BYKT
But You Knew That Already (SAUS) .... BYKTA
Buta [*Zaire*] [*Airport symbol*] (OAG) .... BZU
Buta Zega [*Zaire*] [*ICAO location identifier*] (ICLI) .... FZKJ
butabarbital sodium (SAUS) .... butabarb
Butacaine [*Topical anesthetic*] .... BC
Butadiene (SAUS) .... BD
Butadiene Diepoxide (SAUS) .... BDE
Butadiene Extraction [*Chemical engineering*] .... BTX
Butadiene Rubber .... BR
Butadiene Rubber Based on Neodymium Catalyst (SAUS) .... Nd-BR
Butadiene Rubber Based on Nickel Catalyst (SAUS) .... Ni-BR
Butadiene Rubber Based on Titanium Catalyst (SAUS) .... Ti-BR
Butadiene Styrene rubber (SAUS) .... BS
Butadiene-Styrene Copolymer (EDCT) .... BS
butalbital (SAUS) .... butal
Butane (MSA) .... BUTN
Butane Buzzard Aviation Corp. [*British*] [*ICAO designator*] (FAAC) .... BZZ
Butane Secondary Refrigerant .... BSR
Butane-Butene Fraction .... B-B
Butanediol [*Organic chemistry*] .... BDO
Butanediol Diacetate [*Organic chemistry*] .... BDDA
Butanediol Diglycidyl Ether (SAUS) .... BDCE
Butanediol Diglycidyl Ether [*Organic chemistry*] .... BDGE
Butanediol Succinate [*Organic chemistry*] .... BDS
Butanetetracarboxylic Acid [*Organic chemistry*] .... BTCA
Butanetriol Trinitrate [*An explosive*] .... BTTN
Butanol [*Organic chemistry*] .... BUT
Butanol Insoluble Iodine (SAUS) .... BII
Butanol/Acetic Acid/Water [*Solvent system*] .... BAW
Butanol-Acetic-acid Water (SAUS) .... BAW
Butanol/Ethanol/Water [*Solvent system*] .... BEW
Butanol-Extractable Iodine [*Clinical chemistry*] .... BEI
Butare [*Rwanda*] [*Airport symbol*] (AD) .... BQR
Butare [*Astrida*] [*Rwanda*] [*Seismograph station code, US Geological Survey*] [*Closed*] (SEIS) .... BTR
Butare [*Rwanda*] [*ICAO location identifier*] (ICLI) .... HRYI
Butaritari [*Kiribati*] [*Airport symbol*] (OAG) .... BBG
Butaritari [*Kiribati*] [*ICAO location identifier*] (ICLI) .... NGTU
Butazolidin [*Pharmacology*] (DAVI) .... BTZ
Butazolidin (SAUS) .... Bute
Butcher [*Navy*] .... B
Butcher (ABBR) .... BTCHR
Butcher (MSA) .... BTCR
Butchers Charitable Institution (SAUS) .... BCI
Butchery (ABBR) .... BTCHRY
Bute Resources [*Vancouver Stock Exchange symbol*] .... BTA
Butec International Chemical Corp. [*Formerly, Tay River Petroleum Ltd.*] [*Vancouver Stock Exchange symbol*] .... BIC
Butembo [*Zaire*] [*Seismograph station code, US Geological Survey*] (SEIS) .... BTC
Butembo [*Zaire*] [*ICAO location identifier*] (ICLI) .... FZMB
Buteshire [*County in Scotland*] (BARN) .... Bute
Buteshire Natural History Society (SAUO) .... BNHS
Buthionine Sulfoximine [*Biochemistry*] .... BSO
Buthyl (SAUS) .... Bu
Buthylethylmagnesium [*Organic chemistry*] .... BEM
Butler (ABBR) .... BTLR
Butler Air Transport Ltd. .... BAT
Butler, AL [*Location identifier*] [*FAA*] (FAAL) .... BCZ
Butler, AL [*FM radio station call letters*] (BROA) .... WKZB-FM
Butler, AL [*AM radio station call letters*] .... WPRN
Butler, AL [*FM radio station call letters*] .... WQGL
Butler Area Librarians [*Library network*] .... BAL
Butler Bulletin, Butler, IN [*Library symbol*] [*Library of Congress*] (LCLS) .... InBuB
Butler Carnegie Library, Butler, IN [*Library symbol*] [*Library of Congress*] (LCLS) .... InBu
Butler College (SAUO) .... BC
Butler College, Tyler, TX [*Library symbol*] [*Library of Congress*] (LCLS) .... TxTyB
Butler County Courthouse, Allison, IA [*Library symbol*] [*Library of Congress*] (LCLS) .... IaAlnBCo
Butler County Historical Society, Hamilton, OH [*Library symbol*] [*Library of Congress*] (LCLS) .... OHaBHi
Butler County Legal Journal [*Pennsylvania*] [*A publication*] (DLA) .... Butler
Butler County Tribune-Journal, Allison, IA [*Library symbol*] [*Library of Congress*] (LCLS) .... IaAlnTJ
Butler Health Center, Providence, RI [*Library symbol*] [*Library of Congress*] (LCLS) .... RPBH
Butler High School, Augusta, GA [*Library symbol*] [*Library of Congress*] (LCLS) .... GAuBH
Butler International [*Formerly, North American Ventures, Inc.*] [*NASDAQ symbol*] (SPSG) .... BUTL
Butler International, Inc. [*Associated Press*] (SAG) .... Butler
Butler Manufacturing [*NYSE symbol*] (SAG) .... BBR
Butler Manufacturing [*Associated Press*] (SAG) .... ButlerMfg
Butler Manufacturing Co. [*NASDAQ symbol*] (NQ) .... BTLR
Butler Manufacturing Co. [*Associated Press*] (SAG) .... ButlrMf
Butler Mfg [*NASDAQ symbol*] (TTSB) .... BTLR
Butler, MO [*Location identifier*] [*FAA*] (FAAL) .... BUM
Butler, MO [*AM radio station call letters*] .... KMAM
Butler, MO [*FM radio station call letters*] .... KMOE
Butler Mountain Minerals [*Vancouver Stock Exchange symbol*] .... BMM
Butler National Corp. [*NASDAQ symbol*] (SAG) .... BUKS
Butler National Corp. [*Associated Press*] (SAG) .... ButlrNt
Butler Natl [*NASDAQ symbol*] (TTSB) .... BUKS
Butler, PA [*Location identifier*] [*FAA*] (FAAL) .... BTP
Butler, PA [*Location identifier*] [*FAA*] (FAAL) .... GXO

Butler, PA [*AM radio station call letters*] .... WBUT
Butler, PA [*AM radio station call letters*] .... WISR
Butler, PA [*FM radio station call letters*] .... WLER
Butler Public Library, Butler, PA [*Library symbol*] [*Library of Congress*] (LCLS) .... PBut
Butler University (SAUO) .... BU
Butler University (GAGS) .... Butler U
Butler University, College of Pharmacy, Indianapolis, IN [*Library symbol*] [*Library of Congress*] (LCLS) .... InIB-P
Butler University, Indianapolis, IN [*OCLC symbol*] (OCLC) .... IIB
Butler University, Indianapolis, IN [*Library symbol*] [*Library of Congress*] (LCLS) .... InIB
Butler's Horae Juridicae [*A publication*] (DLA) .... Butler Hor Jur
Butler's Lawyer and Client [*A publication*] (DLA) .... But Law & Cl
Butler's Notes to Coke on Littleton [*A publication*] (DLA) .... Butler Co Litt
Butler's Wharf [*Shipping*] [*British*] (ROG) .... BW
Butoxyacetanilide [*Pharmacology*] .... BOA
Butoxycarbonyl [*Also, Boc*] [*Organic chemistry*] .... BOC
Butoxycarbonyl [*or t-BOC*] [*Biochemistry*] .... t-Boc
Butoxycarbonylethyl Polysulfide [*Organic chemistry*] .... BCEPS
Butropium Bromide [*Pharmacology*] .... BHB
Butt Line [*Technical drawings*] .... BL
Butt Plane .... BP
Butt Splice (MCD) .... BUSP
Butt Weld (SAUS) .... BTWLD
Butt Weld (DNAB) .... BW
Butt Welded .... BTWLD
Butt Welded (IAA) .... BW
Butt Welded Filter .... BWF
Butt Welded Joint .... BWJ
Butte [*Montana*] [*Airport symbol*] (OAG) .... BTM
Butte [*Montana*] [*Seismograph station code, US Geological Survey*] (SEIS) .... BUT
Butte, Anaconda & Pacific Railway Co. [*AAR code*] .... BAP
Butte Aviation, Inc. [*FAA designator*] (FAAC) .... PPS
Butte County Historical Society, Oroville, CA [*Library symbol*] [*Library of Congress*] (LCLS) .... COroBHi
Butte County Library, Oroville, CA [*Library symbol*] [*Library of Congress*] (LCLS) .... COroB
Butte Free Public Library, Butte, MT [*Library symbol*] [*Library of Congress*] (LCLS) .... MtBu
Butte, MT [*Location identifier*] [*FAA*] (FAAL) .... BEY
Butte, MT [*Location identifier*] [*FAA*] (FAAL) .... CPN
Butte, MT [*FM radio station call letters*] .... KAAR
Butte, MT [*FM radio station call letters*] (RBYB) .... KAPC-FM
Butte, MT [*AM radio station call letters*] .... KBOW
Butte, MT [*FM radio station call letters*] (BROA) .... KMBR-FM
Butte, MT [*FM radio station call letters*] .... KMSM
Butte, MT [*FM radio station call letters*] .... KOPR
Butte, MT [*FM radio station call letters*] .... KQUY
Butte, MT [*Television station call letters*] .... KTVM
Butte, MT [*Television station call letters*] .... KWYB
Butte, MT [*Television station call letters*] .... KXLF
Butte, MT [*AM radio station call letters*] .... KXTL
Butte Projects Office (SAUO) .... BU
Butter [*Phonetic alphabet*] [*Royal Navy*] [*World War I*] (DSUE) .... B
Butter (AAMN) .... BUT
Butter .... BUTR
Butter and Cheese Association Limited (SAUO) .... BACAL
Butter and Cheese Association Ltd. (SAUO) .... BACAL
Butter Fat (MAE) .... BF
Butter Information Council [*British*] .... BIC
Butter, Lard, and Salt Provisions .... BL & SP
Butter Marketing Board [*Queensland, Australia*] .... BMB
Butterfly .... Bfly
Butterfly (MSA) .... BTFL
Butterfly [*Stroke*] [*Swimming*] .... BUFLY
Butterfly and Moth Stamp Society (EA) .... BMSS
Butterfly Lovers International (EA) .... BLI
Butterfly Rash [*Medicine*] (MELL) .... BR
Butterfly Spread [*Investment term*] .... BS
Butterfly Valve (SAUS) .... BTFLY VLV
Butterfly Valve (DAC) .... BV
Buttermilk [*Freight*] .... BTRMLK
Butterwick Research Laboratories (SAUO) .... BRL
Butterworth [*Malaysia*] [*ICAO location identifier*] (ICLI) .... WMKB
Butterworth Group (SAUO) .... BG
Butterworth Industrial Laws Service (SAUS) .... BILS
Butterworth's Co. Law Bulletin [*Australia*] [*A publication*] .... BCLB
Butterworths Company Law Cases [*A publication*] .... BCLC
Butterworth's Current Law [*A publication*] (DLA) .... B Current L
Butterworths Journal of International Banking & Financial Law [*A publication*] .... BJIB & FL
Butterworths Medico-Legal Reports [*A publication*] .... BMLR
Butterworths Proprietory Ltd., Chatswood, NSW, Australia [*Library symbol*] [*Library of Congress*] (LCLS) .... AuBut
Butterworth's Rating Appeals [*1913-31*] [*England*] [*A publication*] (DLA) .... BRA
Butterworth's Rating Appeals [*1913-31*] [*England*] [*A publication*] (DLA) .... Butt RA
Butterworth's Rating Appeals [*1913-31*] [*England*] [*A publication*] (DLA) .... Butt Rat App
Butterworth's South African Law Review [*A publication*] (DLA) .... Butterworth's SA Law Review
Butterworth's South African Law Review [*A publication*] (DLA) .... Butterworth's South Afr L Rev
Butterworth's South African Law Review [*A publication*] (DLA) .... Butt SA Law Rev
Butterworths Tax Guide [*A publication*] .... BTG
Butterworth's Weekly Tax Bulletin [*Australia*] [*A publication*] .... BWT Bull
Butterworth's Workmen's Compensation Cases [*A publication*] (DLA) .... Butt WCC
Butterworth's Workmen's Compensation Cases [*A publication*] (DLA) .... Butt Work Comp Cas
Butterworth's Workmen's Compensation Cases [*A publication*] (DLA) .... BWCC
Butterworth's Workmen's Compensation Cases [*A publication*] (DLA) .... BWCC (Eng)
Buttes Watch Co. .... BWC
Buttock [*Shipfitting*] .... BTK
Buttock [*Slang*] (DSUE) .... BUTT
Buttock Line [*Engineering*] .... BL
Button (AAG) .... BTN
Button (ADWA) .... btn
Button .... BUT
Button .... BUTN
Button at Right Bottom [*Telephone touch-tone dial*] .... BARB
Button Cell Battery .... BCB
Button Head .... BTNHD
Button Head (SAUS) .... BTN HD
Button Manufacturing Trade Board (SAUO) .... BMTB
Button Switch .... BS
Buttonhole Deformity [*Medicine*] (MELL) .... BHD
Buttons and Bows [*Magazine in Judith Krantz's novel "I'll Take Manhattan"*] .... B & B
Buttres Double Seal (SAUS) .... BDS
Buttress (VRA) .... butr
Buttress (WDAA) .... BUTT
Buttrey Food & Drug Stores [*NASDAQ symbol*] (TTSB) .... BTRY
Buttrey Food & Drug Stores Co. [*NASDAQ symbol*] (SAG) .... BTRY
Buttrey Food & Drug Stores Co. [*Associated Press*] (SAG) .... Butrey
Butts Army Airfield [*Fort Carson, CO*] .... BAAF
Butts' Edition of Shower's English King's Bench Reports [*A publication*] (DLA) .... Butts Sh
Butts Master [*British and Canadian*] [*World War II*] .... BM
Butt-Treated Cedar (IAA) .... BTC
Butt-Treated Douglas-Fir, Larch and Cedar (SAUS) .... BTDF-L-C
Butt-Treated Lodgepole Pine (IAA) .... BTLP
Buttwil [*Switzerland*] [*ICAO location identifier*] (ICLI) .... LSZU
Butuan [*Philippines*] [*Seismograph station code, US Geological Survey*] [*Closed*] (SEIS) .... BTN
Butuan [*Philippines*] [*Airport symbol*] (OAG) .... BXU
Butuan, Agusan [*Philippines*] [*ICAO location identifier*] (ICLI) .... RPWE
Butut [*Monetary unit*] [*Gambia*] .... B
Butwal Plywood Factory (SAUS) .... BPF
Butwal Power Company Private Ltd. (SAUO) .... BPCPL
Butyl [*Organic chemistry*] .... Bu
Butyl Acrylate [*Organic chemistry*] .... BA
Butyl Alcohol (ACAE) .... BUTANOL
Butyl Benzyl Phthalate [*Organic chemistry*] .... BBP
Butyl Carbitol Piperonylate [*Organic chemistry*] .... BCP
Butyl (Chlorophenyl)carbamate [*Organic chemistry*] .... BCPC
Butyl Diglyme (SAUS) .... BDGL
Butyl Di-Iodohydroxybenzoate [*Organic chemistry*] (DAVI) .... DIB
Butyl Ethyl Ketene [*Organic chemistry*] .... BEK
Butyl Glycidyl Ether [*Organic chemistry*] .... BGE
Butyl Hydroperoxide [*Organic chemistry*] .... BHP
Butyl Isocyanate [*Organic chemistry*] .... BIC
Butyl Mesityl Oxide Oxalate (SAUS) .... BMOO
Butyl Methacrylate [*Organic chemistry*] .... BMA
Butyl Phenyl Ether [*Organic chemistry*] .... BPE
Butyl Phthalyl Butyl Glycolate [*Organic chemistry*] .... BPBG
Butyl Ricinoleate (EDCT) .... BR
Butyl Rubber (EDCT) .... BR
butyl rubber (SAUS) .... PIBI
Butyl Vinyl Ether [*Organic chemistry*] .... BVE
Butylacetanilide [*Organic chemistry*] .... BAA
Butylacetyl Ricinoleate (SAUS) .... BAR
Butyl-Alpha-Methyl-Benzylphenol (SAUS) .... BAMBP
Butylated Hydroxyanisole [*Antioxidant*] .... BHA
Butylated Hydroxyanisole [*Antioxidant*] (WGA) .... BTA
Butylated Hydroxytoluene [*Also, DBPC*] [*Antioxidant*] .... BHT
Butylated Hydroxytolulene [*Antioxidant*] (BABM) .... BTH
Butylated Hydroxytoluol (SAUS) .... BHT
Butylazo(hydroxy)(methyl)hexane [*Organic chemistry*] .... BHMH
Butylcarbamic Acid, Methyl Ester (SAUS) .... BCME
Butyldiethanolamine [*Organic chemistry*] .... BDEA
Butylene Dimethacrylate [*Organic chemistry*] .... BDMA
Butylene Glycol [*Organic chemistry*] .... BG
Butylene Glycol Dinitrate [*Organic chemistry*] .... BGDN
Butyl-ethyl-propanediol [*Organic chemistry*] .... BEPD
Butyl(hydroxybutyl)nitrosamine [*Organic chemistry*] .... BHBN
Butylisonitrile (DMAA) .... BIN
Butyl(methoxy)azobenzene [*Organic chemistry*] .... BMAB
Butylnitrosobenzene [*Organic chemistry*] .... BNB
Butyl(octyl)magnesium [*Organic chemistry*] .... BOM
Butylpyridinium Chloride [*Organic chemistry*] .... BPC
Butyrolactone [*Organic chemistry*] .... BLO
Butyrum [*Butter*] [*Pharmacy*] (ROG) .... BUT
Butyrylcholinesterase [*An enzyme*] .... BuChE
Butzbach (Schloss) [*Germany*] [*ICAO location identifier*] (ICLI) .... EDIO
Butzweilerhof [*Germany*] [*ICAO location identifier*] (ICLI) .... EDCU
BUWEPS [*Bureau of Naval Weapons, now obsolete*] **Evaluation** .... BWE
Buxom Belle, International (SAUO) .... BBI
Buxom Belles, International (EA) .... BBI
Buxton's Reports [*123-129 North Carolina*] [*A publication*] (DLA) .... Buxton

Buxton's Reports [*123-129 North Carolina*] [*A publication*] (DLA) .... Buxton (NC)
Buy a Car [*Slogan during automobile sales slump of 1974-75*] .... BAC
Buy American Act (AAGC) .... BAA
Buy Back [*Investment term*] .... BB
Buy Here - Pay Here [*Used car sales*] .... BHPH
Buy One, Get One Free (WDAA) .... BOGOF
Buy Order [*Investment term*] .... BO
Buy Our Spares Smart [*Program*] (AAGC) .... BOSS
Buy per Drawing (SAA) .... BPD
Buy per Manufacturing Specification (SAA) .... BPMS
Buy Support Objective (AFIT) .... BSO
Buy United States Here [*Program to procure US-made supplies from overseas subsidiaries of US firms*] (AFM) .... BUSH
Buy-Build-Operate (AAGC) .... BBO
Buydown (TDOB) .... BD
Buydown Mortgage [*Business term*] (EMRF) .... BD
Buyer .... B
Buyer .... BUYR
Buyer Attitudes and Sales Experiences [*LIMRA*] .... BASE
Buyer Designated Equipment (MCD) .... BDE
Buyer Furnished Equipment (MCD) .... BFE
Buyer Has Seven Days to Take Up [*Securities brokerage*] [*Investment term*] B7D
Buyer has Seven Days to Take Up [*Investment term*] (MHDW) .... BSD
Buyer (or Buying) (SAUS) .... BUY
Buyer Protection Plan [*Sales*] .... BPP
Buyers .... BYRS
Buyer's Fashion Outlet [*Retailing*] .... BFO
Buyers Health Care Action Group [*Minnesota*] .... BHCAG
Buyers Information Advisory (SAUS) .... BIA
Buyers' Market [*Investment term*] .... BM
Buyer's Option [*Business term*] .... BO
Buyer's Option to Double (ROG) .... BOD
Buyers Screening Guide .... BSG
Buying [*Rate*] [*Value of the English pound*] .... BG
Buying Activity [*Air Force*] (AFM) .... BUYAC
Buying on Margin [*Investment term*] .... BOM
Buying Power Index .... BPI
Buying, Receiving, and Accounts Payable Integrated Data (MCD) .... BRAID
Buy-It-Yourself .... BIY
Buy-Off .... B-O
Buy-Off Date .... BOD
Buys Ballot Law .... BBL
Buzz Attenuation Device (CAAL) .... BAD
Buzz Word Quotient [*Computer science*] (NHD) .... BWQ
Buzzcocks Fan Club/Harmony in My Head (EA) .... PSFC/HIMH
Buzzer (IEEE) .... BU
Buzzer (MSA) .... BUZ
Buzzer [*Electronics*] (IAA) .... BZ
Buzzer (FAAC) .... BZR
Buzzing (SAUS) .... BZ
Buzzworm's Earth Journal [*A publication*] .... Buzz E J
BVBA Lucorp [*Belgium*] [*FAA designator*] (FAAC) .... LIM
Bvbalia, MS [*FM radio station call letters*] (RBYB) .... WYLT-FM
BVD Co. [*Initials stand for Bradley, Voorhies, and Day, organizers of the company*] .... BVD
BVL [*Bowlers' Victory Legion*] **Fund** (EA) .... BVL
BVR Technologies Ltd. [*Associated Press*] (SAG) .... BVR
BVR Technologies Ltd. [*NASDAQ symbol*] (SAG) .... BVRT
BVR Technologies Ltd [*NASDAQ symbol*] (TTSB) .... BVRTF
BW Air Services Ltd. [*British*] [*ICAO designator*] (FAAC) .... BWO
BWAY Corp. [*NASDAQ symbol*] [*Formerly, Brockway Standard Holding*] (SG) .... BWAY
BWAY Corp. [*NYSE symbol*] (SAG) .... BY
BWIA International [*ICAO designator*] (AD) .... BW
BWIP Holding, Inc. [*Associated Press*] (SAG) .... BWIP
BWIP, Inc. [*NYSE symbol*] (SAG) .... BWF
BW/IP Inc. [*NASDAQ symbol*] (TTSB) .... BWIP
By (ROG) .... B
By [*As in 9 x 12*] X
By Any Chance (SAUS) .... BAC
By Any Means Necessary .... BAMN
By Direction (NVT) .... BYDIR
By Direction of the President .... DP
By Mouth [*Pharmacy*] (DAVI) .... OS
By Other Means (NVT) .... BOM
By Procuration [*In power of attorney*] [*Legal term*] .... BP
by proxy (SAUS) .... pp
By the Way [*Internet language*] [*Computer science*] .... BTW
By The Way [*Internet language*] [*Computer science*] .... btw
By Visual Reference to the Ground (SAUS) .... VSA
By Volume (SAUS) .... BV
By Weight (SAUS) .... BW
Byblian (BJA) .... Byb
Byblos Librairie Bookshop, Beirut, Lebanon [*Library symbol*] [*Library of Congress*] (LCLS) .... ByB
Bycatch Reduction Device [*Fishing technology*] .... BRD
Bydgoszcz [*Poland*] [*Airport symbol*] [*Obsolete*] (OAG) .... BZG
Bye [*Cricket*] .... B
Bye Bye for Now [*Internet dialog*] BB4N
Bye Bye for Now [*Online dialog*] .... BBFN
Bye for Now (ADWA) .... BFN
By-Election [*Politics*] .... b/e
Byelorussia [*Belarus*] (BARN) .... Bye
Byelorussia (SAUO) .... Bye
Byelorussian Congress Committee of America (EA) .... BCCA
Byelorussian Democratic Bloc [*Political party*] .... BDB
Byelorussian Institute of Arts and Science (EA) .... BIAS
Byelorussian Liberation Front [*Defunct*] (EA) .... BLF
Byelorussian Literary Association (EA) .... BLA
Byelorussian Popular Front [*Political party*] .... BPF
Byelorussian Soviet Socialist Republic .... BelSSR
Byelorussian Soviet Socialist Republic .... BSSR
Byelorussian Soviet Socialist Republic [*ISO two-letter standard code*] (CNC) .... BY
Byelorussian Soviet Socialist Republic [*ISO three-letter standard code*] (CNC) .... BYS
Byelorussian Youth Association of America [*Later, BAYO*] (EA) .... BYAA
Byelorussian-American Veterans Association (SAUO) .... BAVA
Byelorussian-American Women Association (EA) .... BAWA
Byelorussian-American Youth Organization (EA) .... BAYO
Byers, Casgrain, Montreal, Quebec [*Library symbol*] [*National Library of Canada*] (BIB) .... QMBC
Byesville, OH [*FM radio station call letters*] .... WILE
BYG Natural Resources, Inc. [*Toronto Stock Exchange symbol*] .... BYG
Byggvaruregistret [*Building Commodity File*] [*Swedish Building Center*] [*Stockholm*] [*Information service or system*] (IID) .... BVR
Byhalia, MS [*FM radio station call letters*] .... WHLE
Byholma [*Sweden*] [*ICAO location identifier*] (ICLI) .... ESFY
Byk-Gulden Lomberg [*Germany*] [*Research code symbol*] C
Byk-Gulden Lomberg [*Germany*] [*Research code symbol*] .... Do
Bylaws of the American Institute of Certified Public Accountants (SAUO) .... ETBYLAW
Byles' Law of Exchange [*A publication*] (DLA) .... Byl Exch
Byles on Bills of Exchange [*A publication*] (DLA) .... Byl Bills
Byles on Bills of Exchange [*A publication*] (DLA) .... Byles
Byles on the Usury Laws [*A publication*] (DLA) .... Byl Us L
By-Line [*Publishing*] .... BL
Byng, OK [*FM radio station call letters*] .... KYKC
Bynkershoek's Law of War [*A publication*] (DLA) .... Byn War
Bypass .... BP
Bypass (KSC) .... BYP
Bypass (ADWA) .... byp
Bypass [*Commonly used*] (OPSA) .... BYPA
Bypass [*Commonly used*] (OPSA) .... BYPAS
Bypass [*Commonly used*] (OPSA) .... BYPASS
Bypass [*Commonly used*] (OPSA) .... BYPS
Bypass Angioplasty Revascularzation [*Medicine*] (MELL) .... BARI
By-Pass Capacitor (SAUS) .... Byp Cap
Bypass Capacitor [*Electronics*] (IAA) .... BYPCAP
Bypass Condenser [*Electronics*] (IAA) .... BYPCOND
By-Pass Condenser (SAUS) .... Byp Cond
Bypass Electronic Emergency Fuel System .... BEEFS
Bypass Flow Module [*Nuclear energy*] (NRCH) .... BPFM
Bypass Graft (DAVI) .... BPH
Bypass Isolation Switch .... BIS
Bypass Isolation Transfer Switch .... BITS
Bypass Label Processing [*Computer science*] .... BLP
Bypass Monochrome Signal .... BMS
Bypass Ratio .... BPR
Bypass Surgery [*Medicine*] (MELL) .... BPS
Bypass Turbojet Engine Noise .... BTJE
Bypass Valve (NRCH) .... BPV
Bypass Valve (MCD) .... BV
Byproduct (SAUS) .... BP
Byram Foundation (SAUO) .... BF
Byrd [*Antarctica*] [*Seismograph station code, US Geological Survey*] [*Closed*] (SEIS) .... BSA
Byrd [*Antarctica*] [*Seismograph station code, US Geological Survey*] [*Closed*] (SEIS) .... BYR
Byrd - Stanford Research Institute [*Antarctica*] [*Seismograph station code, US Geological Survey*] [*Closed*] (SEIS) BY1
Byrd Antarctic Expedition [*1928-30,1933-35*] .... ByrdAE
Byrd Polar Research Center [*Ohio State University*] [*Information service or system*] (IID) .... BPRC
Byrd Station, Antarctica .... BYA
Byrne. Bills of Sale [*2nd ed.*] [*1870*] [*A publication*] (DLA) .... Byrne BS
Byrne on Patents [*A publication*] (DLA) .... Byrne Pat
Byron Bay, NT [*ICAO location identifier*] (ICLI) .... CYUK
Byron, GA [*FM radio station call letters*] .... WPWB
Byron Preiss Multimedia .... BPM
Byron Resources, Inc. [*Vancouver Stock Exchange symbol*] .... BYN
Byron Society (EA) .... BS
Byron Station (NRCH) .... BS
Bystander Dominates Initial Dominant [*Sociology*] .... BDID
Byte [*Usually 8 BITS*] [*Computer science*] .... B
Byte [*Computer science*] (IAA) .... BT
Byte Address Register (SAUS) .... BAR
Byte Channel Transfer Switch (SAUS) .... BCTS
Byte Control Protocol [*Computer science*] .... BCP
Byte Count Register [*Computer science*] (MHDI) .... BCR
Byte Counter (SAUS) .... BC
Byte Cycle (SAUS) .... Byte-Cy
Byte Device (SAUS) .... BD
Byte Field (SAUS) .... BF
BYTE Information Exchange [*Electronic conferencing system provided by McGraw-Hill's Byte magazine*] .... BIX
Byte Input Control [*Computer science*] .... BIC
Byte Machine [*Computer science*] (IAA) .... BM
Byte Mask (SAUS) .... BM

Byte Multiplex (SAUS) .... BM
Byte Multiplex Channel (SAUS) .... BYMUX Channel
Byte Multiplexer Mode [*Computer science*] (IAA) .... BM
Byte Not Zero (SAUS) .... BNZ
Byte Order Mark (SAUS) .... BOM
Byte Oriented Protocol (SAUS) .... BOP
Byte Out [*Computer science*] (CIST) .... BO
Byte Output Control [*Computer science*] .... BOC
Byte Rate (SAUS) .... BR
Byte Result Trigger (SAUS) .... BRT
Byte Stream Protocol [*Telecommunications*] (OSI) .... BSP
Byte Transfer In (SAUS) .... BTI
Byte Transfer Out (SAUS) .... BTO
Byte-Multiplexer Channel .... BYMUX
Bytes per Inch [*Computer science*] .... BPI
Bytes per Line [*Computer science*] (VERA) .... BPL

Bytes per Second [*Computer science*] (BUR) .... BPS
Bytes per Second (AEBE) .... Bps
Bytes per Second (ADWA) .... bps
Bythewood. Precedents in Conveyancing [*4th ed.*] [*1884-90*] [*A publication*]
(DLA) .... Byth Conv
Bythewood. Precedents in Conveyancing [*4th ed.*] [*1884-90*] [*A publication*]
(DLA) .... Byth Prec
Bythotrephes Cederstroemi [*Zoology*] .... BC
Bytom [*Poland*] [*Seismograph station code, US Geological Survey*] (SEIS) .... BYT
Byzantine .... BYZ
Byzantine (VRA) .... Byz
Byzantine (SAUS) .... Byz
Byzantine .... Byzan
Byzantinische Zeitschrift [*A publication*] (OCD) .... Byz Zeitschr
Byzantinische Zeitschrift [*A publication*] (ODCC) .... BZ
Byzantinisch-Neugriechische Jahrbucher [*A publication*]
(OCD) .... Byz und Neugr Jahrb

C
By Meaning

C (100) Call Seconds [*Telecommunications*] (NITA) ... CCS
C 3-Receptor Lymphocytes (SAUS) ... CRL
C. A Pippy Jr. Medical Library, Grace General Hospital, St. John's, Newfoundland [*Library symbol*] [*National Library of Canada*] (NLC) ... NFSGGH
C & D Technologies [*NYSE symbol*] [*Formerly, Charter Power Systems*] (SG) ... CHP
C & M Aviation, Inc. [*ICAO designator*] (FAAC) ... TIP
C & W [*Cable & Wireless North America, Inc.*] **Network Services** [*Dallas, TX*] [*Telecommunications*] (TSSD) ... CWNS
C. Berger & Co., Wheaton, IL [*Library symbol*] [*Library of Congress*] (LCLS) ... IWB
C Brewer Homes [*NASDAQ symbol*] (SAG) ... CBHI
C Brewer Homes [*Associated Press*] (SAG) ... CBrewer
C Company (SAUO) ... C Coy
C Compiler (SAUS) ... CC
C. F. Braun & Co., Alhambra, CA [*Library symbol*] [*Library of Congress*] (LCLS) ... CAlhB
C++ File (SAUS) ... CPP
C. G. Jung Foundation for Analytical Psychology (SAUS) ... C G Jung Foun
C G Jung Foundation for Analytical Psychology (SAUO) ... C G Jung Foun
C. H. Boehringer Sohn, Ingelheim [*Germany*] [*Research code symbol*] ... Ad
C. H. Boehringer Sohn, Ingelheim [*Germany*] [*Research code symbol*] ... FH
C. H. Boehringer Sohn, Ingelheim [*Germany*] [*Research code symbol*] ... Ko
C. H. Boehringer Sohn, Ingelheim [*Germany*] [*Research code symbol*] ... KSD
C. H. Boehringer Sohn, Ingelheim [*Germany*] [*Research code symbol*] ... KSW
C. H. Boehringer Sohn, Ingelheim [*Germany*] [*Research code symbol*] ... Me
C. H. Boehringer Sohn, Ingelheim [*Germany*] [*Research code symbol*] ... St
C. H. Boehringer Sohn, Ingelheim [*Germany*] [*Research code symbol*] ... Th
C Hardware Specific Module (SAUS) ... CHSM
C. Howard Marcy State Hospital, Pittsburgh, PA [*OCLC symbol*] (OCLC) ... PHY
C. Hurst & Co. [*Publisher*] [*British*] ... CH
C L & P Capital Ltd. [*NYSE symbol*] (SAG) ... CPM
C Library (SAUS) ... CLIB
C Memo Distribution Facility (SAUS) ... CMDF
"C" Message Weighting [*Telecommunications*] (TEL) ... CMSG
C negative (SAUS) ... C-
C or C++ Compiler (SAUS) ... CC
C positive (SAUS) ... C+
C Programming Language (SAUS) ... C
C Pulse (SAUS) ... CP
C Rated (SAUS) ... CTD
C Register (SAUS) ... CR
C. S. Draper Laboratory, Inc. Cambridge, MA [*OCLC symbol*] (OCLC) ... CSD
C. S. [*Charles Sanders*] **Peirce Society** (EA) ... CSPS
C Scanner (SAUS) ... C SCAN
C Shell (SAUS) ... CSH
C source code (SAUS) ... C
C Specific Media Support (SAUS) ... CSMS
C. Stroemgren, Sorel, Quebec [*Library symbol*] [*National Library of Canada*] (NLC) ... QSOCS
C to A Gate (SAUS) ... C-A
C Topology Specific Module (SAUS) ... CTSM
C. W. - Tariff Agency, Inc., Lansing MI [*STAC*] ... CWA
C. W. Post Campus of Long Island University (GAGS) ... C W Post (LIU)
C2 Functional Analysis & Consolidation Review Panel (SAUO) ... C2 FACRP
C2 Integrated Resources Information System (SAUO) ... CIRIS
C2 Manpower & Personnel Contingency Support System (SAUO) ... C2 MPPCS
C3S Planning Programming and Budgeting System (SAUO) ... C3SPPBS
C3S Readiness Information System (SAUO) ... C3RIS
C4 Systems Master Plan (SAUO) ... C4SMP
C4I for the Warrior (SAUS) ... C4IFTW
C-14 dates by the Isotope laboratory of Groningen University (SAUS) ... GrN
C-14 dates produced by Kyoto Sangyo University (SAUS) ... KSU
ca [*About*] [*Latin*] (EES) ... Circa
CA: A Cancer Journal for Clinicians (SAUS) ... CA Cancer J Clin
CAA Calibration Flight [*British*] [*ICAO designator*] (FAAC) ... CLB
CAA Flight Examiners [*British*] [*ICAO designator*] (FAAC) ... EXM
CAA Flying Unit [*British*] [*ICAO designator*] (FAAC) ... CFU
CAA Flying Unit [*British*] [*ICAO designator*] (ICDA) ... MC
CAA Training Standards [*British*] [*ICAO designator*] (FAAC) ... SDS
CAAA Air Martinique [*France*] [*ICAO designator*] (FAAC) ... MTQ
Caaf Ho Nandi [*Fiji*] [*ICAO location identifier*] (ICLI) ... NFHO
Caara Ventures, Inc. [*Vancouver Stock Exchange symbol*] ... CVZ
Cab Alongside Engine [*Automotive engineering*] ... CAE
Cab Behind Engine [*Automotive engineering*] ... CBE
CAB International (SAUO) ... CABI
CAB [*Commonwealth Agricultural Bureaux*] **International Bureau of Animal Breeding and Genetics** (EAIO) ... CBABG
CAB International Insitute of Biological Control (SAUO) ... CIBC
CAB International Institute of Entomology (SAUO) ... CIE
CAB [*Commonwealth Agricultural Bureaux*] **International Institute of Entomology** [*British*] (IRUK) ... CIE
CAB International Institute of Parasitology (SAUO) ... CIP
CAB [*Commonwealth Agricultural Bureaux*] **International Mycological Institute** [*British*] (IRUK) ... CMI
Cab Over Engine [*Type of truck*] ... COE
Cab Over [*Engine*] **Heavy, High** [*Mobility Multipurpose Wheeled*] **Vehicle** [*Army*] ... COHHV
Cab Research Bureau [*Later, ITA*] (EA) ... CRB
Cab Research Bureau (SAUO) ... CRB
Cab to Axle [*GSA*] (TAG) ... CA
Cab Trade Council [*A union*] [*British*] ... CTC
Cab Tyre Sheathed Cable (SAUS) ... CTS Cable
Cab Tyred Sheathed (PDAA) ... CTS
Cababe and Ellis' Queen's Bench Reports [*1882-85*] [*England*] [*A publication*] (DLA) ... Cab & E
Cababe and Ellis' Queen's Bench Reports [*1882-85*] [*England*] [*A publication*] (DLA) ... Cab & El
Cababe and Ellis' Queen's Bench Reports [*1882-85*] [*England*] [*A publication*] (DLA) ... Cab & El (Eng)
Cababe and Ellis' Queen's Bench Reports [*1882-85*] [*England*] [*A publication*] (DLA) ... Cab & Ell
Cababe and Ellis' Queen's Bench Reports [*1882-85*] [*England*] [*A publication*] (DLA) ... C & E
Cababe. Interpleader and Attachment of Debts [*1900*] [*A publication*] (ILCA) ... Cab Int
cabagin (SAUS) ... vit U
Cabalistic (ROG) ... CAB
Caballero [*Cavalier*] [*Spanish*] (DSUE) ... CAB
Caballococha [*Peru*] [*ICAO location identifier*] (ICLI) ... SPBC
Cabana ... cba
Cabanatuan, Nueva Ecija [*Philippines*] [*ICAO location identifier*] (ICLI) ... RPUC
Cabano, PQ [*FM radio station call letters*] ... CFVD-1
Cabano, PQ [*AM radio station call letters*] ... CJAF
Cabaret ... CBRT
Cabaret, Hotel, Restaurant and Retailers Association [*Alaska*] (SRA) ... CHARR
Cabarien [*Cuba*] [*Airport symbol*] (AD) ... CBN
Cabarrus County Health Department, Concord, NC [*Library symbol*] [*Library of Congress*] (LCLS) ... NcCoCH
Cabarrus County Library, Concord, NC [*Library symbol*] [*Library of Congress*] (LCLS) ... NcCoC
Cabbage Looper [*Entomology*] ... CL
Cabbage Patch Kids ... CPK
Cabel & Wireless Limited (SAUO) ... CWL
Cabell-Huntington Public Library [*Western Counties Regional Library*], **Huntington, WV** [*Library symbol*] [*Library of Congress*] (LCLS) ... WvHu
CABI [*Commonwealth Agricultural Bureaux International*] **Institute of Biological Control** [*Research center*] [*British*] (IRC) ... CIBC
CABI [*Commonwealth Agricultural Bureaux International*] **Institute of Parasitology** [*Research center*] [*British*] (IRC) ... CIP
Cabin (MSA) ... CAB
Cabin (SAUS) ... Cab
Cabin ... CBN
Cabin Address System [*Aviation*] (AIA) ... CAS
Cabin Air Manifold Pressure [*Aviation*] ... CAMP
Cabin Air Temperature [*Aviation*] (NG) ... CAT
Cabin Air Temperature Valve [*Aviation*] ... CATV
Cabin Atmosphere Monitoring System [*NASA*] ... CAMS
Cabin Baggage [*Travel industry*] (TRID) ... CBBG
Cabin Bleed Valve [*Aviation*] (MCD) ... CBV
Cabin Communications System [*Aviation*] ... CCS
Cabin Discrepancy Report [*Report for airline log*] ... CDR
Cabin Display Unit [*Aviation*] ... CDU
Cabin Equipment Interface [*Aviation*] ... CEI
Cabin Gas Analysis Unit [*Aviation*] (NASA) ... CGAU
Cabin Heat Exchanger [*Aviation*] (MCD) ... CHX
Cabin Humidity Control Subsystem [*Aviation*] (NASA) ... CHCS
Cabin Management System (ACAE) ... CMS
Cabin Pressure Control System [*Aviation*] ... CPCS
Cabin Pressure Controller [*Aviation*] (MCD) ... CPC
Cabin Pressure Relief Valve [*Aviation*] (KSC) ... CPRV
Cabin Public Address (SAUS) ... CPA

Cabin Service/Management System [*Aviation*] .... CSMS
Cabin Telecommunications Unit [*Telecommunications*] (PCM) ...... CTU
Cabin/Cockpit Temperature Control Systems [*Aviation*] .... CTCS
Cabinda [*Angola*] [*Airport symbol*] (OAG) .... CAB
Cabinda [*Angola*] [*ICAO location identifier*] (ICLI) .... FNCA
Cabinet [*Technical drawings*] (NFPA) C
Cabinet (KSC) .... CAB
Cabinet .... CABNT
Cabinet .... CABT
Cabinet .... CBNT
Cabinet (WGA) .... CBT
Cabinet Card (VRA) .... CABN
Cabinet Casemakers' Union [*British*] .... CCU
Cabinet Committee for Economic Policy [*Later, CEP*] .... CCEP
Cabinet Committee on Economic and Regional Development
  [*Canada*] .... CCERD
Cabinet Committee on International Narcotics Control [*Terminated,
  1977*] .... CCINC
Cabinet Council on Commerce and Trade [*Reagan administration*] .... CCCT
Cabinet Council on Economic Affairs [*Reagan administration*] .... CCEA
Cabinet Council on Management and Administration [*Executive Office of the
  President*] (GFGA) .... CCMA
Cabinet Economic Committee (SAUO) .... ECO
Cabinet File (CDE) .... CAB file
Cabinet for Families and Children (SAUO) .... CFC
Cabinet for Health Services (SAUO) .... CHS
Cabinet Government Administration Subcommittee on State Wages
  (SAUS) .... WAG
Cabinet Lawyer, by John Wade [*England*] [*A publication*] (DLA) .... Cab Lawy
Cabinet Legislation Committee (SAUO) .... LEG
Cabinet Makers' Society [*A union*] [*British*] .... CMS
Cabinet Office [*New South Wales*] [*Australia*] .... CO
Cabinet Office Briefing Room [*British*] .... COBRA
Cabinet Office Deregulation Unit (HEAS) .... CORU
Cabinet Office Economic Advisory Council (SAUO) .... COEAC
Cabinet Offices Cypher Office [*British*] [*World War II*] .... COCO
Cabinet Pressurization System .... CPS
Cabinet Strategy Sub-committee on Appointments and Honours (SAUO) ..... APH
Cabinet Strategy Subcommittee on Expenditure Control and Government
  Administration (SAUO) .... EXG
Cabinet Strategy Subcommittee on Intelligence and Security (SAUS) .... CIS
Cabinet Sub Committee on Labour Relations (SAUO) .... CSCLR
Cabinet Task Force on Oil Import Control (SAUO) .... CTFOIC
Cabinet War Room .... CWR
Cabinetmaker .... CABMKR
Cabinetmaker (SAUS) .... Cabtmkr
Cabinetmakers' Association of Western Australia .... CMAWA
Cabinetwork (SAUS) .... Cabwk
Cable C
Cable (MSA) .... CA
Cable .... CABL
Cable (AAG) .... CBL
Cable Access Cover .... CAC
Cable Access Point [*Telecommunications*] (TSSD) .... CAP
Cable Activity System [*Telecommunications*] (TEL) .... CAS
Cable Aerial Television (SAUS) .... CATV
Cable & Co. Worldwide, Inc. [*Associated Press*] (SAG) .... CableCo
Cable & Co. Worldwide, Inc. [*Associated Press*] (SAG) .... CbleCo
Cable & Co. Worldwide, Inc. [*NASDAQ symbol*] (SAG) .... CCWW
Cable and Satellite Television (NITA) .... CAST
Cable and Satellite Television Authority (SAUO) .... CSTA
Cable and Telegraph Operators' Association [*A union*] [*British*] .... CTOA
Cable and Wireless (SAUS) .... C&W
Cable and Wireless (SAUS) .... CAW
Cable & Wireless AD [*NYSE symbol*] (TTSB) .... CWP
Cable & Wireless ADS [*NYSE symbol*] (SG) .... CWP
Cable & Wireless HKT ADR [*NYSE symbol*] (SG) .... HKT
Cable & Wireless Ltd. [*Associated Press*] (SAG) .... CablWire
Cable & Wireless Ltd. (SAUS) .... C&W
Cable and Wireless Ltd. [*Telecommunications*] (TEL) .... C & W
Cable & Wireless Ltd. (SAUO) .... C&W
Cable and Wireless Ltd. [*Telecommunications*] (IAA) .... CAW
Cable and Wireless, Ltd. (SAUS) .... CWL
Cable & Wireless Ltd. ADS [*NYSE symbol*] (SPSG) .... CWP
Cable Antenna Television (IAA) .... CATV
Cable Arts Foundation, Inc. (NTCM) .... CAF
Cable Assembly .... CA
Cable Assembly Case (ACAE) .... CAC
Cable Assembly Set (KSC) .... CAS
Cable Audit System (SAUS) .... CAS
Cable Authority [*British*] .... CA
Cable Avoiding Tool (PDAA) .... CAT
Cable Budget (SAUS) .... CB
Cable Car Beverage [*NASDAQ symbol*] (TTSB) .... DRNK
Cable Car Beverage Corp. [*Associated Press*] (SAG) .... CblCar
Cable Car Beverage Corp. [*NASDAQ symbol*] (NQ) .... DRNK
Cable Communications Association (WDAA) .... CCA
Cable Communications for Information Transfer (SAUS) .... CCIT
Cable Communications Resource Center (EA) .... CRC
Cable Connector (IAA) CC
Cable Connector Panel .... CCP
Cable Data Tape (SAUS) .... CDT
Cable Delay Line .... CDL
Cable Design Technologies [*Associated Press*] (SAG) .... CblDsgn
Cable Design Technologies [*NYSE symbol*] (SG) .... CDT

Cable Design Technologies [*NASDAQ symbol*] (SAG) .... CDTC
Cable Distribution Frame (NASA) .... CDF
Cable Distribution Head .... CDH
Cable Distribution Head (SAUS) .... cdh
Cable Distribution Unit [*Aerospace*] (AAG) .... CDU
Cable Duct (MSA) .... CD
Cable Electric Products, Inc. (SAUO) .... CBL
Cable End Sealing Kit .... CESK
Cable Entrance Facility (SAUS) .... CEF
Cable Equalizer (SAUS) .... CE
Cable Firing [*or Fuzing*] (NG) .... CF
Cable FM [*Radio*] (NTCM) .... CAFM
Cable, Functional .... CF
Cable Gallery (SAUS) .... C Gal
Cable Health Network [*Cable-television system*] [*Viacom International, Inc.*] ..... CHN
Cable History Tape .... CHT
Cable Households Using Television [*Cable television ratings*] (NTCM) .... CHUT
Cable Hut (SAUS) .... CH
Cable in the Classroom [*An association*] (ECON) CIC
Cable Integrity Group (NASA) .... CIG
Cable Interconnection Diagram (KSC) .... CID
Cable Interface Tape (SAUS) .... CIT
Cable Interface Unit (DGA) .... CIU
Cable Jacket Zipper .... CJZ
Cable Jointing [*Section of the British Royal Navy*] .... J
Cable Launch Control System (SAA) .... CLCS
Cable Laying Ship .... CLS
Cable Link [*Telecommunications*] (OA) CL
Cable Maintenance Center [*Telecommunications*] (TEL) .... CMC
Cable Makers' Association [*British*] (BI) .... CMA
Cable Management Software .... CMS
Cable Marking System .... CMS
Cable Microcell Integrator (SAUS) .... CMI
Cable Microcell Integrator/Headend Interface Converter (SAUS) .... CMI/HIC
Cable Modem Termination System .... CMTS
Cable Monitoring and Rating System (MHDI) .... CMARS
Cable Multiplexer [*Electronics*] (IAA) .... CMX
Cable Network Engineering Program [*Bell System*] .... CNEP
Cable Network Joint Committee .... CNJC
Cable Network Joint Committee (SAUO) .... CNJC
Cable News Financial Network (ADWA) .... CNFN
Cable News Network [*Facetious translation: Chicken Noodle Network*] [*Cable-
  television system*] .... CNN
Cable On-Line Data Exchange [*Nielson Media Research*] [*Information service
  or system*] .... CODE
Cable Operated Zero Impedence Decoupler (MCD) .... COZID
Cable Orderwire Unit (MCD) .... COU
Cable Pair (SAUS) .... Ca Pr
Cable Pair Identification [*Telecommunications*] (TEL) .... CPI
Cable Party (SAUO) .... CP
Cable Patch Panel (SAUS) .... CPP
Cable Pressure Monitoring System [*Bell System*] .... CPMS
Cable Pressurization Equipment .... CPE
Cable Program Providers Group [*British*] (DBA) .... CPPG
Cable Programming Resource Directory [*A publication*] (TSSD) .... CPRD
Cable Programming Service Tier [*Telecommunications*] (OTD) .... CPST
Cable Programming Services (SAUS) .... CPS
Cable Rack (KSC) .... CR
Cable Reed .... CBLRD
Cable Reinforcement Set (MCD) .... CRS
Cable Relay Service [*or Station*] [*Television transmission*] .... CARS
Cable Repair Administrative System (VERA) .... CRAS
Cable Repair Force Management Plan (SAUS) .... CRFMP
Cable Repairing Ship [*Navy symbol*] .... ARC
Cable Retransmission Facility (SAUS) .... CRF
Cable Routing Rotation (MCD) .... CRN
Cable Running Sheets .... CRS
Cable Satellite Public Affairs Network [*Cable-television system*] .... C-SPAN
Cable Satellite Public Affairs Network (SAUO) .... CSPAN
Cable Select (SAUS) .... CSEL
Cable Ship [*Followed by name of cable-laying ship*] .... CS
Cable Splicing Kit .... CSK
Cable Spreading Room [*Nuclear energy*] (NRCH) .... CSR
Cable Subscription Television .... CSTV
Cable Supply & Consulting Co. Pte Ltd. (SAUO) .... CSC
Cable System Terminal Device [*Telecommunications*] (OTD) .... CSTD
Cable Systems International .... CSI
Cable Tank (SAUS) .... CT
Cable Telecommunication and Video (SAUS) .... CATV
Cable Telecommunications and Video (CIST) .... CATV
Cable Telecommunications Association (NTPA) .... CATA
Cable Telemetry System .... CTS
Cable Television (SAUS) .... Cablevision
Cable Television [*Later, CTV*] .... CATV
Cable Television [*Formerly, CATV*] .... CTV
Cable Television Administration and Marketing Society (EA) .... CTAM
Cable Television Association [*British*] (NITA) .... CTA
Cable Television Bureau (SAUS) .... CTB
Cable Television Cable Makers Association [*British*] (NITA) .... CATVCMA
Cable Television Construction Ltd. [*British*] (NITA) .... CTVC
Cable Television Information Center [*Defunct*] (EA) .... CTIC
Cable Television Library Network (SAUS) .... CATLIB Network
Cable Television Outreach Project (SAUS) .... CATVO Project
Cable Television Relay (NTCM) .... CAR
Cable Television Technical Advisory Committee [*FCC*] (NTCM) .... CTAC

Cable Terminal Section [*Telecommunications*] (TEL) ... CTS
Cable Termination Equipment (CET) ... CTE
Cable Termination Network ... CTN
Cable, Test ... CT
Cable Test Set (MCD) ... CTS
Cable Testing Meter ... CTM
Cable Transfer (EBF) ... CT
Cable Transfer Machine [*Nuclear energy*] (NRCH) ... CTM
Cable Tray (KSC) ... C/T
Cable Tray (SAUS) ... CT
Cable Tray Institute (NTPA) ... CTI
Cable Trays Vertical Chase [*Nuclear energy*] (NRCH) ... CTVC
Cable Trouble Ticket [*Telecommunications*] (TEL) ... CTT
Cable Trunk Ticket Number (SAUS) ... CTTN
Cable Tuning Section (SAUS) ... CTS
Cable Turning Section [*Telecommunications*] (TEL) ... CTS
Cable Turning System [*Telecommunications*] (NITA) ... CTS
Cable TV (SAUS) ... CATV
Cable Twist ... CT
Cable Twist Angle ... CTA
Cable Twister Orthosis [*Medicine*] (MELL) ... CTO
Cable Untwist ... CU
Cable Value Network [*Television*] ... CVN
Cable Vault Ground Bar (SAUS) ... CVGB
cablecaster (SAUS) ... cablecast
cablecasting (SAUS) ... cablecast
Cable-Controlled Underwater Research Vehicle ... CURV
Cable-Controlled Unmanned Recovery Vehicle (MCD) ... CURV
cablegram language (SAUS) ... cablese
Cable-Harness Analyzer ... CHA
Cableman (IAA) ... CBLMN
CableMaxx Holdings, Inc. [*Associated Press*] (SAG) ... Cablmax
Cablemaxx, Inc. [*NASDAQ symbol*] (SAG) ... CMAX
Cable-Measuring Device (SAUS) ... CMD
Cable-operated Unmanned Recovery Vehicle (SAUS) ... CURV
Cables [*Business term*] ... CAB
Cables and Wireless (SAUS) ... CAW
Cables and Wireless Company (SAUO) ... CAW
Cableshare, Inc. [*Toronto Stock Exchange symbol*] ... CSH
Cable/Show Cause [*FCC*] (NTCM) ... CSC
Cable/Special Relief [*FCC*] (NTCM) ... CSR
Cable/Special Temporary Authority [*FCC*] (NTCM) ... CSTA
Cable-Suspended Pumping Station (SAUS) ... CSPS
Cabletel Communications [*AMEX symbol*] (TTSB) ... TTV
Cabletel Communications Corp. [*Associated Press*] (SAG) ... Cabeltel
Cabletel Communications Corp. [*Associated Press*] (SAG) ... Cabletel
Cabletel Communications Corp. [*AMEX symbol*] (SAG) ... TTV
Cabletelevision Advertising Bureau [*New York, NY*] (EA) ... CAB
Cabletelevision Advertising Bureau, Inc. ... CAB
Cabletron Systems [*NYSE symbol*] (TTSB) ... CS
Cabletron Systems, Inc. [*Associated Press*] (SAG) ... Cabltrn
Cabletron Systems, Inc. [*NYSE symbol*] (SPSG) ... CS
Cablevision Sys'A' [*AMEX symbol*] (TTSB) ... CVC
CableVision Systems Corp. [*Associated Press*] (SAG) ... Cablvsn
Cablevision Systems Corp. [*AMEX symbol*] (SPSG) ... CVC
CablevisionSys 8.50% Dep Cv Ex Pfd [*AMEX symbol*] (TTSB) ... CVCPr
Cablewave Systems Inc., North Haven (SAUO) ... CSI
Cabline ... CBL
Cabling Data ... CD
Cabling Diagram ... CAD
Cabling Interface Drawing (MCD) ... CID
Cabo Frio [*Costa Rica*] [*Seismograph station code, US Geological Survey*] (SEIS) ... AR7
Cabo Frio Foundation (SAUO) ... CFF
Cabo Rojo [*Dominican Republic*] [*ICAO location identifier*] (ICLI) ... MDCR
Cabo Rojo, PR [*AM radio station call letters*] ... WEKO
Cabo Rojo, PR [*FM radio station call letters*] ... WMIO
Cabo Velas [*Costa Rica*] [*ICAO location identifier*] (ICLI) ... MRCV
Cabochon (VRA) ... cabo
Cabool, MO [*FM radio station call letters*] ... KOZX
Cabool, MO [*Location identifier*] [*FAA*] (FAAL) ... TVB
Caboose [*Freight*] ... CBSE
Caborca [*Mexico*] [*Seismograph station code, US Geological Survey*] (SEIS) ... CBS
Cabot, AR [*AM radio station call letters*] ... KBBL
Cabot, AR [*FM radio station call letters*] ... KBBL-FM
Cabot, AR [*FM radio station call letters*] (RBYB) ... KKRN-FM
Cabot Archives, Neil's Harbour, Nova Scotia [*Library symbol*] [*National Library of Canada*] (NLC) ... NSNHC
Cabot Archives, Neil's Harbour, NS, Canada [*Library symbol*] [*Library of Congress*] (LCLS) ... CaNSNhC
Cabot, Canot & Forbes Land Trust (SAUO) ... CFT
Cabot Corp. [*Associated Press*] (SAG) ... Cabot
Cabot Corp. [*NYSE symbol*] (SPSG) ... CBT
Cabot Corp., Stellite Division, Kokomo, IN [*Library symbol*] [*Library of Congress*] (LCLS) ... InKoC
Cabot Corp., Stellite Division, Kokomo, IN [*OCLC symbol*] (OCLC) ... ISD
Cabot Corp., Technical Information Center, Billerica, MA [*Library symbol*] [*Library of Congress*] (LCLS) ... MBilC
Cabot Industrial Tr [*NYSE symbol*] (SG) ... CTR
Cabot Institute of Applied Arts and Technology, St. John's, Newfoundland [*Library symbol*] [*National Library of Canada*] (NLC) ... NFSCT
Cabot Microelectronics [*NASDAQ symbol*] (SG) ... CCMP
Cabot Oil & Gas [*Associated Press*] (SAG) ... CbtOG
Cabot Oil & Gas [*NYSE symbol*] (SPSG) ... COG
Cabot Oil & Gas'A' [*NYSE symbol*] (TTSB) ... COG
Cab-Over Cargo Truck (SAUS) ... COCT
Cabramurra [*Australia*] [*Seismograph station code, US Geological Survey*] [*Closed*] (SEIS) ... CAB
Cabre Corp. [*NASDAQ symbol*] (SAG) ... CABR
Cabre Corp. [*Associated Press*] (SAG) ... Cabre
Cabre Exploration Ltd. [*Toronto Stock Exchange symbol*] ... CBE
Cabrillo College, Aptos, CA [*Library symbol*] [*Library of Congress*] (LCLS) ... CApC
Cabrillo National Monument ... CABR
Cabrillo National Monument (SAUS) ... CNM
Cabrini College, Library, Radnor, PA [*OCLC symbol*] (OCLC) ... PAB
Cabriolet (ROG) ... CAB
Cab-to-Rear Axle [*Automotive engineering*] ... CA
Cabtyre Sheathing (SAUS) ... CTS
Cacaine (SAUS) ... C
CA-Cancer Journal for Clinicians (journ.) (SAUS) ... CA-Cancer J Clin
Cacao Necrosis Virus [*Plant pathology*] ... CNV
Cacao Producers Alliance (SAUO) ... CPA
Cacao Swollen Shoot Virus [*Plant pathology*] ... CSSV
Cacao Yellow Mosaic Virus [*Plant pathology*] ... CYMV
Cacchi-Ricci [*Disease*] [*Medicine*] (DB) ... CR
Caceres [*Brazil*] [*Airport symbol*] (OAG) ... CCX
Cache Array Routing Protocol [*Computer science*] ... CARP
Cache Bay Public Library, Ontario [*Library symbol*] [*National Library of Canada*] (NLC) ... OCB
Cache Bus Interface [*Computer science*] (BYTE) ... CBI
Cache Coherent Non-Uniform Memory Access [*Computer science*] ... ccNUMA
Cache Control Register (CIST) ... CACR
Cache Control Unit (VERA) ... CCU
Cache County Public Library, Logan, UT [*Library symbol*] [*Library of Congress*] (LCLS) ... ULC
Cache Decision Unit (SAUS) ... CDU
Cache d'Or Resources [*Vancouver Stock Exchange symbol*] ... CCI
Cache DRAM [*Dynamic Random Access Memory*] (CDE) ... CDRAM
Cache Enable [*Computer science*] (PCM) ... CE
Cache Host Intercommunication Unit (SAUS) ... CHIU
Cache Host Memory Access Unit (SAUS) ... CHMAU
Cache, Inc. [*NASDAQ symbol*] (NQ) ... CACH
Cache, Inc. [*Associated Press*] (SAG) ... Cache
Cache Memory Management Unit [*Computer science*] (BYTE) ... CMMU
Cache On A Stick (SAUS) ... COAST
Cache Only Memory Architecture (SAUS) ... COMA
Cache Random Access Memory (SAUS) ... CRAM
Cache Store Unit (SAUS) ... CSU
Cache Valley Historical Society, Logan, UT [*Library symbol*] [*Library of Congress*] (LCLS) ... ULCHi
Cache-Coherent Non Uniform Memory Access (SAUS) ... CCNUMA
Cache/Disk System [*A storage device*] [*Computer science*] (NITA) ... C/DS
Cache/Memory Management Unit (BYTE) ... CAMMU
Cachimbo [*Brazil*] [*ICAO location identifier*] (ICLI) ... SBCC
Caching File System (SAUS) ... CFS
Cachipo, Monagas [*Venezuela*] [*ICAO location identifier*] (ICLI) ... SVCI
Cachoeira do Sul [*Brazil*] [*Airport symbol*] (AD) ... CCQ
Cachucha Ranch [*New Mexico*] [*Seismograph station code, US Geological Survey*] [*Closed*] (SEIS) ... CCN
CACI, Incorporated-Federal (SAUO) ... CACI
CACI Int'l [*NASDAQ symbol*] (TTSB) ... CACI
Cacia International [*Associated Press*] (SAG) ... CACI
Cacia International, Inc. [*NASDAQ symbol*] (NQ) ... CACI
Cacine [*Guinea-Bissau*] [*ICAO location identifier*] (ICLI) ... GGCC
Cacolo [*Angola*] [*ICAO location identifier*] (ICLI) ... FNCC
Cacquot Kite Balloon ... CKB
Cactoblastis [*South American moth brought to Australia to destroy the prickly pear*] (DSUE) ... CACTO
Cactus [*Horticulture*] ... C
Cactus and Succulent Society of America (EA) ... CSSA
Cactus and Succulent Society of America, Inc. (SAUO) ... CSSA
Cactus and Succulent Society of the Australian Capital Territory ... CSSACT
Cactus Virus 2 [*Plant pathology*] ... CV2
Cactus Virus X [*Plant pathology*] ... CVX
Cactus West Explorations Ltd. [*Vancouver Stock Exchange symbol*] ... CWE
Cacwhuacintle [*Race of maize*] ... CAC
CAD [*Computer-Aided Design*] **for VLSI** [*Very Large Scale Integrati on*] **System** [*Electronics*] (NITA) ... CVS
CAD Framework Initiative, Inc. (SAUO) ... CFI
CAD [*Computer-Aided-Design*] **Programming Language** (PCM) ... CPL
Cadarache [*France*] [*Seismograph station code, US Geological Survey*] (SEIS) ... CDR
Cadastral and Land-Use Mapping Information System (PDAA) ... CLUMIS
Cadaver [*Medicine*] ... Cad
Cadaver (SAUS) ... CAD
Cadaver [*Medicine*] (ROG) ... CADAV
Cadaver (SAUS) ... CDV
Cadaver Disposal Center (SAUS) ... CDC
Cadaver Donor [*Medicine*] ... CD
Cadaveric Donor Renal Transplantation [*Medicine*] ... CDRTx
Cadbury [*England*] ... CADB
Cadbury Schwep LP 8.625%'QUIPS' [*NYSE symbol*] (TTSB) ... CSDPrA
Cadbury Schweppes ADS [*NYSE symbol*] (TTSB) ... CSG
Cadbury Schweppes Delaware LP [*Associated Press*] (SAG) ... CadScD
Cadbury Schweppes Delaware LP [*NYSE symbol*] (SAG) ... CSD
Cadbury Schweppes Ltd. [*NASDAQ symbol*] ... CADB
Cadbury Schweppes PLC (MHDW) ... CADBY
Cadbury Schwepps Ltd. [*Associated Press*] (SAG) ... CadbyS
Cadbury Schwepps PLC [*NYSE symbol*] (SAG) ... CSG
Cadburys Dairy Milk (SAUO) ... CDM

CAD/CAM Association of Finland (SAUO) ... CCY
CAD/CAM [*Computer-Aided Design/Computer-Aided Manufacturing*] **Systems** ... CCS
CAD/CAM [*Computer-Aided Design/Computer-Aided Manufacturing*] **Systems** (MCD) ... CCSYS
Caddev Industry, Inc. [*Vancouver Stock Exchange symbol*] ... CJH
Caddo [*MARC language code*] [*Library of Congress*] (LCCP) ... cad
Caddo Mills, TX [*Location identifier*] [*FAA*] (FAAL) ... MII
Caddo Parish Library, Shreveport, LA [*Library symbol*] [*Library of Congress*] (LCLS) ... LShCa
Cade Industries [*NASDAQ symbol*] (TTSB) ... CADE
Cade Industries, Inc. [*NASDAQ symbol*] (NQ) ... CADE
Cade Industries, Inc. [*Associated Press*] (SAG) ... CadeIn
Cadec Systems, Inc. (SAUO) ... KDCK
Cadeguomycin Deazaguanosine [*Antineoplastic drug*] ... CDM
Cadena Azul de Radiodifusion [*Radio network*] [*Spain*] ... CAR
Cadena Garcia Valseca [*Press agency*] [*Mexico*] ... CGV
Cadena Radial Ecuatoriana (EY) ... CRE
Cadence (SAUS) ... CAD
Cadence Design Systems [*NYSE symbol*] (SPSG) ... CDN
Cadence Design Systems, Inc. [*Associated Press*] (SAG) ... Cadence
Cadence Design Systems, Inc. (MHDW) ... CDNC
Cadence Haute Acces Aletoire (SAUS) ... CHACAL
Cadence Industries Corp. (SAUO) ... CDE
Cadenza [*Cadence*] [*Music*] ... CAD
Cadet [*British military*] (DMA) ... C
Cadet ... CAD
Cadet (SAUS) ... Cad
Cadet (SAUS) ... Cdt
Cadet [*British military*] (DMA) ... Cdt
Cadet Administrative Management Information System [*Air Force*] (GFGA) ... CAMIS
Cadet Battalion [*British military*] (DMA) ... CB
Cadet Candidate (SAUS) ... CC
Cadet Captain ... CC
Cadet Corps [*British military*] (DMA) ... CC
Cadet Corps (SAUO) ... CC
Cadet Forces Medal [*British military*] (DMA) ... CFM
Cadet Midshipman (SAUS) ... Cdt Mid
Cadet Practice Squadron ... CADETRON
Cadet Training Team (SAUO) ... CTT
Cadet Troop Leader Training (MCD) ... CTLT
Cadet Troop Leadership Program (SAUO) ... CTLP
Cadets for the Aid of Families of Prisoners of War (SAUO) ... CAFPOW
Cadets Norfolk Artillery [*British military*] (DMA) ... CNA
Cadger (ROG) ... CAD
Cadillac & Lake City Railway Co. [*AAR code*] ... CLK
Cadillac Convertible Owners of America (EA) ... CCOA
Cadillac Fairview [*NYSE symbol*] (SG) ... CDF
Cadillac Fairview Corp. Ltd. [*Toronto Stock Exchange symbol*] [*Vancouver Stock Exchange symbol*] ... CFV
Cadillac, MI [*Location identifier*] [*FAA*] (FAAL) ... CAD
Cadillac, MI [*AM radio station call letters*] ... WATT
Cadillac, MI [*FM radio station call letters*] ... WCKC
Cadillac, MI [*Television station call letters*] ... WCMV
Cadillac, MI [*Television station call letters*] ... WGKI
Cadillac, MI [*AM radio station call letters*] ... WKJF
Cadillac, MI [*FM radio station call letters*] ... WKJF-FM
Cadillac, MI [*FM radio station call letters*] ... WLXV
Cadillac, MI [*FM radio station call letters*] ... WOLW
Cadillac, MI [*Television station call letters*] ... WWTV
Cadillac Motor Car Division [*General Motors Corp.*] ... CMCD
Cadillac Public School, Cadillac, MI [*Library symbol*] [*Library of Congress*] (LCLS) ... MiCadCS
Cadillac-Larder Lake [*Geology*] ... CLDZ
Cadillac-LaSalle Club (EA) ... CLC
Cadillac-Wexford Public Library, Cadillac, MI [*Library symbol*] [*Library of Congress*] (LCLS) ... MiCad
Cadium Sulfide (SAUS) ... CDS
Cadiz, KY [*AM radio station call letters*] ... WKDZ
Cadiz, KY [*FM radio station call letters*] ... WKDZ-FM
Cadiz Land [*NASDAQ symbol*] (TTSB) ... CLCI
Cadiz Land Co., Inc. [*Associated Press*] (SAG) ... Cadiz
Cadiz Land Co., Inc. [*NASDAQ symbol*] (SAG) ... CLCI
Cadiz, OH [*Location identifier*] [*FAA*] (FAAL) ... CFX
Cadiz, OH [*FM radio station call letters*] ... WCDK
Cadiz Public Library, Cadiz, OH [*Library symbol*] [*Library of Congress*] (LCLS) ... OCad
Cadiz Railroad Co. [*AAR code*] ... CAD
Cadkey Object Developer [*Computer science*] ... COD
Cadmium [*Chemical symbol is Cd*] (KSC) ... CAD
Cadmium [*Chemical element*] ... Cd
Cadmium Arsenide (MED) ... CaAs
Cadmium Association [*British*] (EAIO) ... CA
Cadmium Binding Protein ... CdBP
Cadmium Bronze ... CB
Cadmium Bronze Connector ... CBC
Cadmium Council (EA) ... CC
Cadmium Manganese Telluride (SAUS) ... CdMnTe
Cadmium Mercury Telluride (SAUS) ... CdHgTe
Cadmium Mercury Telluride [*Solid state chemistry*] ... CMT
Cadmium Oxide (SAUS) ... CdO
Cadmium Oxide - Ethylenediamine [*Cellulose solvent*] ... CADOXEN
Cadmium Pigments Association (EAIO) ... CPA
Cadmium Plate [*Technical drawings*] ... CDPL
Cadmium Plate (SAUS) ... Cd Pl
Cadmium Red Line ... CRL
Cadmium Sulfide [*Inorganic chemistry*] (WGA) ... CdS
Cadmium Telluride (SAUS) ... CdTe
Cadmium Zinc Telluride (AAEL) ... CZT
Cadmium-Mercury-Telluride Detector (SAUS) ... CMT Detector
Cadmium-Probe (SAUS) ... Cd-Probe
Cadmium-Sulfide Cell ... CSC
Cadmus Communications Corp. [*NASDAQ symbol*] (NQ) ... CDMS
Cadmus Communicatons Corp. [*Associated Press*] (SAG) ... Cadmus
Cadmus Group, Inc. (GAAI) ... CADMUS
CADO [*Computer Access Device Output*] **Actions-Terminal** (IAA) ... CAT
Cadotte Lake School, Alberta [*Library symbol*] [*National Library of Canada*] (BIB) ... ACALS
Cadre ... CDR
Cadre Weather Team (MCD) ... CWT
Cadus Pharmaceutical Corp. [*Associated Press*] (SAG) ... CadusPh
Cadus Pharmaceutical Corp. [*NASDAQ symbol*] (SAG) ... KDUS
Cadwalader's Cases, United States District Court, Eastern District of Pennsylva nia [*A publication*] (DLA) ... Cadwalader
Cadwalader's Digest of Attorney-General's Opinions [*A publication*] (DLA) ... Cadw Dig
Cady Mountains [*California*] [*Seismograph station code, US Geological Survey*] [*Closed*] (SEIS) ... CAD
CAE Electronics Ltd., Montreal, Quebec [*Library symbol*] [*National Library of Canada*] (NLC) ... QMCAE
CAE, Inc. [*Toronto Stock Exchange symbol*] (SG) ... CAE
CAE Industries Ltd. [*Toronto Stock Exchange symbol*] ... CAE
Caecum ... C
Caecum Ligation and Puncture [*Medicine*] ... CLP
Caeharris [*Cardiff*] [*Welsh depot code*] ... CH
Caelebs [*Unmarried*] [*Latin*] (ROG) ... CAEL
Caelum [*Constellation*] ... Cae
Caelum [*Constellation*] ... Cael
Caen [*France*] [*Airport symbol*] (OAG) ... CFR
Caen/Carpiquet [*France*] [*ICAO location identifier*] (ICLI) ... LFRK
Caenorhabditis [*Nematode*] **Genetics Center** ... CGC
Caenorhabditis Genetics Center (SAUO) ... CGC
Caequot Kite Balloon (SAUS) ... CKB
Caere Corp. [*NASDAQ symbol*] (NQ) ... CAER
Caere Corp. [*Associated Press*] (SAG) ... Caere
Caerlaverock National Nature Reserve (SAUS) ... CNNR
Caernarvonshire [*Wales*] (BARN) ... Caern
Caernarvonshire [*County in Wales*] ... Caerns
Caernarvonshire Historical Society (SAUO) ... CHS
Caerulcus [*Blue*] [*Pharmacy*] (ROG) ... CAERL
Caeruleus [*Dark Blue, Dark Green*] [*Pharmacy*] (DAVI) ... caerul
Caesar [*of Plutarch*] [*Classical studies*] (OCD) ... Caes
Caesar (SAUS) ... Caes
Caesar Contardus [*Deceased, 1585*] [*Authority cited in pre-1607 legal work*] (DSA) ... Caes Contar
Caesar Resources Ltd. [*Vancouver Stock Exchange symbol*] ... CER
Caesarean [*or Cesarean*] [*Section*] [*Obstetrics*] (DAVI) ... C
Caesarean [*or Cesarean*] **Birth** [*Obstetrics*] (DAVI) ... CB
Caesarean Delivered [*Medicine*] ... CD
Caesarean Section [*Medicine*] ... CS
Caesarean [*or Cesarean*] **Section** [*Obstetrics*] (DAVI) ... C Sect
Caesarean Section (NTIO) ... C section
Caesarean Section [*Medicine*] ... C (Section)
Caesarean Support Network [*British*] (DBA) ... CSN
Caesarean-Originated, Barrier-Sustained [*Rodent breeding*] ... COBS
Caesarian Delivery (SAUS) ... CD
Caesars World, Inc. (SAUO) ... CAW
Caesium Beam Frequency Standard (IAA) ... CBFS
Caeteris Paribus [*Other Things Being Equal*] [*Latin*] (ROG) ... CAET PAR
Cafe-au-Lait Macules (DMAA) ... CALM
Cafeteria (BARN) ... caf
Cafeteria ... CAFTRA
Cafeteria Benefits [*Health insurance*] (GHCT) ... CB
Caffeic Acid [*Organic chemistry*] ... CA
Caffeine ... CAF
Caffeine, Alcohol, Pepper, and Aspirin [*As in CAPA-free diet*] [*Medicine*] (DAVI) ... CAPA
Caffeine, Alcohol, Pepper, Peppermint, and Alcohol [*As in CAPPA-free diet*] (DAVI) ... CAPPA
Caffeine, Alcohol, Pepper, Spicy Foods [*Nutrition*] ... CAPS
Caffeine Halothane Challenge Test [*Clinical chemistry*] ... CHCT
Caffeine Sodium Benzoate [*Chemistry*] (DAVI) ... CSB
Cagayan De Oro [*Philippines*] [*Airport symbol*] (OAG) ... CGY
Cagayan De Oro, Misamis Oriental [*Philippines*] [*ICAO location identifier*] (ICLI) ... RPWL
Cagayan Integrated Agricultural Development Project (SAUO) ... CIADP
Cage (MSA) ... CG
Cage Container (DCTA) ... C
Cage Inventory Record [*Shipping*] (DS) ... CIR
Cage Test Language (SAUS) ... CTL
CAGE [*Computerized Aerospace Ground Equipment*] **Test Language** [*Computer science*] (KSC) ... CTL
Caging Amplifier Assembly ... CAA
Caging Retainer and Boresight [*Air Force*] ... CRAB
Cagle's, Inc. [*Associated Press*] (SAG) ... Cagle
Cagle's, Inc. [*AMEX symbol*] (SPSG) ... CGL
Cagle's Inc.'A' [*AMEX symbol*] (SG) ... CGLA
Cagliari [*Italy*] [*Airport symbol*] (OAG) ... CAG
Cagliari/Elmas [*Italy*] [*ICAO location identifier*] (ICLI) ... LIEE

Cagney and Lacey [*Television series*] ... C & L
Caguas [*Puerto Rico*] [*Seismograph station code, US Geological Survey*] (SEIS) ... CAG
Caguas [*Diocesan abbreviation*] [*Puerto Rico*] (TOCD) ... CGS
Caguas, PR [*Television station call letters*] ... WLII
Caguas, PR [*AM radio station call letters*] ... WNEL
Caguas, PR [*Television station call letters*] ... WUJA
Caguas, PR [*AM radio station call letters*] ... WVJP
Caguas, PR [*FM radio station call letters*] ... WVJP-FM
Cahiers de Droit Compare [*A publication*] (ILCA) ... CDC
Cahiers de Droit Familial [*A publication*] (ILCA) ... CDF
Cahiers de Droit Fiscal International [*A publication*] (DLA) ... Cahier Dr Fiscal
Cahiers. Faculte de Droit et des Sciences Economiques de Nancy [*A publication*] (DLA) ... Cah de la Fac de Droit Nancy
Cahill's Illinois Statutes [*A publication*] (DLA) ... Cahill's Ill St
Cahners Advertising Research Reports [*A publication*] ... CARR
Cahners Books International, Inc. [*Later, CBI Publishing Co., Inc.*] ... CBI
Cahners Exposition Group [*Telecommunications service*] (TSSD) ... CEG
Cahokia Community Unit School District 187, Cahokia, IL [*Library symbol*] [*Library of Congress*] (LCLS) ... ICahSD
Cahokia Public Library, Cahokia, IL [*Library symbol*] [*Library of Congress*] (LCLS) ... ICah
Cahors/Lalbenque [*France*] [*ICAO location identifier*] (ICLI) ... LFCC
CAI [*Compagnia Aeronautica Italiana SpA*] [*Italy*] [*ICAO designator*] (FAAC) ... KVY
CAI Wireless Systems [*NASDAQ symbol*] (TTSB) ... CAWS
CAI Wireless Systems, Inc. [*Associated Press*] (SAG) ... CAI Wre
CAI Wireless Systems, Inc. [*NASDAQ symbol*] (SAG) ... CAWS
Caibarien [*Cuba*] [*ICAO location identifier*] (ICLI) ... MUCB
Caicara [*Venezuela*] [*Airport symbol*] (OAG) ... CXA
Caicara de Orinoco [*Venezuela*] [*Airport symbol*] (AD) ... CXA
Caicara De Orinoco, Bolivar [*Venezuela*] [*ICAO location identifier*] (ICLI) ... SVCD
Caile Ferate Romane [*Romanian Railways Board*] [*Department of Railways*] ... CFR
Caines and Leigh. Crown Cases [*England*] [*A publication*] (DLA) ... C & LCC
Caines' Cases [*New York*] [*A publication*] (DLA) ... Cai Ca
Caines' Cases [*New York*] [*A publication*] (DLA) ... Cains C
Caines' Lex Mercatoria Americana [*A publication*] (DLA) ... Cai Lex Mer
Caines' New York Cases in Error [*A publication*] (DLA) ... Cai
Caines' New York Cases in Error [*A publication*] (DLA) ... Cai Cas
Caines' New York Cases in Error [*A publication*] (DLA) ... Cai Cas Err
Caines' New York Cases in Error [*A publication*] (DLA) ... Cain
Caines' New York Cases in Error [*A publication*] (DLA) ... Cain Cas in Error
Caines' New York Cases in Error [*A publication*] (DLA) ... Cain CE
Caines' New York Cases in Error [*A publication*] (DLA) ... Cain E
Caines' New York Cases in Error [*A publication*] (DLA) ... Caines
Caines' New York Cases in Error [*A publication*] (DLA) ... Caines Ca in E
Caines' New York Cases in Error [*A publication*] (DLA) ... Caines' Ca in Er
Caines' New York Cases in Error [*A publication*] (DLA) ... Caines Cas
Caines' New York Cases in Error [*A publication*] (DLA) ... Caines' Cas in Er
Caines' New York Cases in Error [*A publication*] (DLA) ... Caines (NY)
Caines' New York Cases in Error [*A publication*] (DLA) ... Cai R
Caines' New York Cases in Error [*A publication*] (DLA) ... Cas Err
Caines' New York Cases in Error [*A publication*] (DLA) ... CCE
Caines' New York Cases in Error [*A publication*] (DLA) ... NY Cas Err
Caines' New York Cases in Error [*A publication*] (DLA) ... NY Cas in Error
Caines' Practical (New York) Forms [*A publication*] (DLA) ... Cai Forms
Caines' Practice [*A publication*] (DLA) ... Cai Pr
Caines' Reports [*New York*] [*A publication*] (DLA) ... Caine R
Caines' Reports [*New York*] [*A publication*] (DLA) ... Caines' R
Caines' Reports [*New York*] [*A publication*] (DLA) ... Caines Rep
Caines' Reports [*New York*] [*A publication*] (DLA) ... Cains R
Caines' Reports [*New York*] [*A publication*] (DLA) ... Cai (NY)
Caines' Reports, New York Supreme Court [*A publication*] (DLA) ... Cai
Caines' Reports, New York Supreme Court [*A publication*] (DLA) ... Cai Cas
Caines' Reports, New York Supreme Court [*A publication*] (DLA) ... Cain
Caines' Reports, New York Supreme Court [*A publication*] (DLA) ... Caines
Caines' Reports, New York Supreme Court [*A publication*] (DLA) ... Caines Cas
Caines' Reports, New York Supreme Court [*A publication*] (DLA) ... Caines (NY)
Caines' Reports, New York Supreme Court [*A publication*] (DLA) ... Cai R
Caines' Term Reports [*New York*] [*A publication*] (DLA) ... NYT Rep
Caines' Term Reports [*New York*] [*A publication*] (DLA) ... TR
Caines' Term Reports [*New York*] [*A publication*] (DLA) ... TR (NY)
Caines' Term Reports, New York Supreme Court [*A publication*] (DLA) ... Cai
Caines' Term Reports, New York Supreme Court [*A publication*] (DLA) ... Cai Cas
Caines' Term Reports, New York Supreme Court [*A publication*] (DLA) ... Cain
Caines' Term Reports, New York Supreme Court [*A publication*] (DLA) ... Caines
Caines' Term Reports, New York Supreme Court [*A publication*] (DLA) ... Caines Cas
Caines' Term Reports, New York Supreme Court [*A publication*] (DLA) ... Caines (NY)
Caines' Term Reports, New York Supreme Court [*A publication*] (DLA) ... Caines Term Rep (NY)
Caines' Term Reports, New York Supreme Court [*A publication*] (DLA) ... Cai R
Caines' Term Reports, New York Supreme Court [*A publication*] (DLA) ... Cai TR
Cain-Levine Social Competency Scale [*Psychology*] ... C-L
Cain-Levine Social Competency Scale [*Psychology*] ... CLSCS
CAINS [*Carrier/Aircraft Inertial Navigation System*] **Covert Data Link** (MCD) ... CCDL
CAINS Readiness & Overhaul Warranty for the Navy (SAUS) ... CROWN
C-Air [*Former USSR*] [*FAA designator*] (FAAC) ... CEE
Cairensis Gnosticus [*Nag Hammadi Codices*] (BJA) ... CG
Cairine Wilson Secondary School, Gloucester, Ontario [*Library symbol*] [*National Library of Canada*] (BIB) ... OGCW
Cairn Energy USA [*NASDAQ symbol*] (TTSB) ... CEUS
Cairn Energy USA, Inc. [*Associated Press*] (SAG) ... Cairn
Cairn Energy USA, Inc. [*NASDAQ symbol*] (SAG) ... CEUS
Cairn Terrier Club of America (EA) ... CTCA
Cairngorm [*Type of quartz*] (ROG) ... CGM
Cairngorm Summit Automatic Weather Station (SAUO) ... CSAWS
Cairngorms National Nature Reserve (SAUS) ... CNNR
Cairns [*Australia*] [*ICAO location identifier*] (ICLI) ... ABCS
Cairns [*Australia*] [*Airport symbol*] (OAG) ... CNS
Cairns Agricultural, Pastoral, and Mining Association [*Australia*] ... CAPMA
Cairns and District Historic Vehicle Club [*Australia*] ... CHHVC
Cairns and Far North Environment Council (SAUO) ... CFNEC
Cairns. Decisions in the Albert Arbitration (Reilly) [*1871-75*] [*England*] [*A publication*] (DLA) ... Cairns Dec
Cairo [*Egypt*] [*Airport symbol*] (OAG) ... CAI
Cairo [*Egypt*] [*ICAO location identifier*] (ICLI) ... HECC
Cairo Air Transport Co. [*Egypt*] [*ICAO designator*] (FAAC) ... CCE
Cairo Demographic Centre (SAUO) ... CDC
Cairo Documents of the Damascus Covenanters [*A publication*] (BJA) ... CDC
Cairo, GA [*Location identifier*] [*FAA*] (FAAL) ... CYR
Cairo, GA [*AM radio station call letters*] ... WGRA
Cairo, GA [*FM radio station call letters*] ... WSLE
Cairo Geniza (BJA) ... CG
Cairo, IL [*Location identifier*] [*FAA*] (FAAL) ... CIR
Cairo, IL [*AM radio station call letters*] ... WKRO
Cairo Institute of Technology (SAUS) ... CIT
Cairo Institute of Technology, Heluan (SAUO) ... CIT
Cairo International Airport (SAUO) ... CIA
Cairo Local Time (SAUS) ... CLT
Cairo Public Library, Cairo, IL [*Library symbol*] [*Library of Congress*] (LCLS) ... ICa
Cairo Public Library, Cairo, IL [*Library symbol*] [*Library of Congress*] (LCLS) ... ICaL
Cairo Studies in English (journ.) (SAUS) ... CaiSe
Cairo Studies in English (journ.) (SAUS) ... CSE
Cairo University Rowing Club (SAUO) ... CURC
Cairo/International [*Egypt*] [*ICAO location identifier*] (ICLI) ... HECA
CAIS Internet [*NASDAQ symbol*] ... CAIS
Caisse Centrale des Banques Populaires (SAUO) ... CCBP
Caisse Commune d'Epargne et d'Investissement [*Finance institutions*] [*Cameroon*] (EY) ... CCEI
Caisse de Depot de Placement du Quebec, Montreal, PQ, Canada [*Library symbol*] [*Library of Congress*] (LCLS) ... CaQMCDP
Caisse de Depot et Placement du Quebec, Montreal, Quebec [*Library symbol*] [*National Library of Canada*] (NLC) ... QMCDP
Caisse Generale d'Epargne et de Retraite [*State-owned bank*] [*Belgium*] (EY) ... CGER
Caisse Nationale de Credit Agricole du Burkina (EY) ... CNCAB
Caisse Postal [*Post Office Box*] [*French*] (ASC) ... CP
Caisse Primaire d'Assurance Maladie [*French*] (DLA) ... CPAM
Caithness [*County in Scotland*] (ROG) ... CAI
Caithness County [*Scotland*] (BARN) ... caith
Caithness Paperweight Collectors Society [*Perth, Scotland*] (EAIO) ... CPCS
Caitlin Raymond International Registry (ADWA) ... CRIR
Caius (ROG) ... C
Caius College [*Cambridge University*] (ROG) ... CC
Caius College (SAUO) ... CC
Cajabamba/Pampa Grande [*Peru*] [*ICAO location identifier*] (ICLI) ... SPJB
Cajal Club (EA) ... CC
Cajamarca [*Peru*] [*Airport symbol*] (OAG) ... CJA
Cajamarca/Mayor General FAP Armando Revoredo Iglesias [*Peru*] [*ICAO location identifier*] (ICLI) ... SPJR
Cajazeiras [*Brazil*] [*Airport symbol*] (AD) ... CJZ
Cajun Nike [*US Navy missile*] ... CAN
Cake (SAUS) ... CAK
Cake ... CK
Cake and Biscuit Alliance [*British*] ... CBA
Cal Aviation SA [*Greece*] [*ICAO designator*] (FAAC) ... CLV
Cal Denver Resources [*Vancouver Stock Exchange symbol*] ... CEV
Cal Dynamics Corp. [*Vancouver Stock Exchange symbol*] ... CYE
Cal Fed Bancorp. [*NYSE symbol*] [*Formerly, California Federal Bank*] (SG) ... CAL
Cal Fed Bk 7.75% CvPfd'A' [*NYSE symbol*] (TTSB) ... CALPr
Cal Graphite Corp. [*Vancouver Stock Exchange symbol*] ... CGP
Cal Owner's Association [*Defunct*] (EA) ... COA
Cal Sierra [*ICAO designator*] (AD) ... QS
Calabar [*Nigeria*] [*Airport symbol*] (OAG) ... CBQ
Calabar [*Nigeria*] [*ICAO location identifier*] (ICLI) ... DNCA
Calabar Emancipation Party (SAUO) ... CEP
Calabozo [*Venezuela*] [*Airport symbol*] (OAG) ... CLZ
Calabozo, Guarico [*Venezuela*] [*ICAO location identifier*] (ICLI) ... SVCL
Calais [*France*] [*Airport symbol*] (AD) ... CQF
Calais, ME [*FM radio station call letters*] ... WMED
Calais, ME [*Television station call letters*] ... WMED-TV
Calais, ME [*AM radio station call letters*] ... WQDY
Calais, ME [*FM radio station call letters*] ... WQDY-FM
Calais Resources Ltd. [*Toronto Stock Exchange symbol*] ... CLJ
Calais/Dunkerque [*France*] [*ICAO location identifier*] (ICLI) ... LFAC
Calama [*Chile*] [*Seismograph station code, US Geological Survey*] (SEIS) ... CAC
Calama [*Chile*] [*Airport symbol*] (OAG) ... CJC
Calama/El Loa [*Chile*] [*ICAO location identifier*] (ICLI) ... SCCF
Calamba Sugar Estate Inc. (SAUO) ... CEE
Calamocha [*Spain*] [*ICAO location identifier*] (ICLI) ... LECH
Calamus Length ... CL
Calamus Length Index ... CLI
Calando [*Dying Away*] [*Music*] ... Cal
Calapan, Oriental Mindoro [*Philippines*] [*ICAO location identifier*] (ICLI) ... RPUK
Calaveras County Free Library, San Andreas, CA [*Library symbol*] [*Library of Congress*] (LCLS) ... CSadC

Calaveras County Museum & Archives Library, San Andreas, CA [Library symbol] [Library of Congress] (LCLS) .... CSadM
Calaveras Reservoir [California] [Seismograph station code, US Geological Survey] (SEIS) .... CVR
Calavo Growers of California (EA) .... CGC
Calbayog [Philippines] [Airport symbol] (OAG) .... CYP
Calbayog, Western Samar [Philippines] [ICAO location identifier] (ICLI) .... RPVC
Calc-Alkaline (SAUS) .... CAL
Calcaneal Spur (MELL) .... CS
Calcaneal Tendon Reflex [Medicine] (MELL) .... CTR
Calcaneus Fracture (MELL) .... CF
Calcareous [Quality of the bottom] [Nautical charts] .... Ca
Calcarine Fissure (MELL) .... CF
Calcarine Sulcus [Medicine] (DMAA) .... CAS
Calcasieu Parish Public Library, Lake Charles, LA [Library symbol] [Library of Congress] (LCLS) LLcC
Calced Carmelites (TOCD) .... OCarm
Calcein Blue Acetoxymethyl Ester [Organic chemistry] .... CBAM
Calciferol (SAUS) .... vit D2
Calciferol and Lumisterol (SAUS) .... vit D1
Calcific Aortic Stenosis [Medicine] (DMAA) .... CAS
Calcification Rate (STED) .... CR
Calcified Alluvium [Archeology] .... Cala
Calcified Aortic Valve Stenosis [Medicine] (MELL) .... CAVS
Calcified Bone Mineral Density .... CBMD
Calcified Pea Gravel [Archeology] .... cpg
Calcified Tissue Research (journ.) (SAUS) .... Calcif Tissue Res
Calcifying Epithelial Odontogenic Tumor [Medicine] (DMAA) .... CEOT
Calcifying Odontogenic Cyst [Medicine] (MELL) .... COC
Calcined Gross Fission Product .... CGFP
Calcined Waste Packaging Cell [Nuclear energy] (NRCH) .... CWPC
Calcineurin [Biochemistry] .... CaN
Calcineurin [Biochemistry] .... CN
calciniert (SAUS) .... calc
Calcinosis, Committee on Reactor Safety Technology (SAUS) .... CREST
Calcinosis Cutis, Raynaud's Phenomenon, Sclerodactyly, and Telangiectasia [A medical syndrome] .... CRST
Calcinosis, Raynaud's Phenomenon, Esophageal Dysfunction, Sclerodactyly, and Telangiectasia [A medical syndrome] .... CREST
Calcinosis, Raynaud's Phenomenon, Esophageal Dysmotility [or Dysfunction],Sclerodactyly, and Telangiectasia [Syndrome] [Rheumatology] (DAVI) .... CREST
Calcite (SAUS) .... Alabaster
Calcite (SAUS) CC
Calcite [CIPW classification] [Geology] cc
Calcite Compensation Depth [Oceanography] .... CCD
Calcitonin [Also, TCA, TCT] [Endocrinology] .... CT
Calcitonin (STED) .... CTN
Calcitonin Cleavage Product (DB) .... CCP
Calcitonin Gene Related Peptide Receptor [Medicine] (DMAA) .... CGRPR
Calcitonin Gene-Related Peptide [Endocrinology] .... CGRP
Calcitonin Receptor [Endocrinology] .... CTR
Calcitonin-Receptor-Like Receptor [Endocrinology] .... CRLR
Calcium [Chemical element] .... Ca
Calcium [Symbol is Ca] [Chemical element] (ROG) .... CAL
Calcium [Test] [Dentistry] (DAVI) .... CAL
calcium (SAUS) .... cal
calcium acetate (SAUS) .... cal ace
Calcium Activated Neutral Protease [An enzyme] .... CANP
Calcium Alginate [Swab] [Medicine] (DAVI) .... CALGI
Calcium Aluminate Cement (PDAA) .... CAC
Calcium Aluminum Inclusion (SAUS) .... CAI
Calcium and Magnesium Free Plus Ethylenediaminetetraacetic Acid (STED) .... CMFE
Calcium- and Magnesium-Free .... CMF
Calcium- and Magnesium-Free Synthetic Seawater .... CMFSW
Calcium Antagonist (DB) .... CA
Calcium Binding Protein [Biochemistry] .... CaBP
Calcium Bone Index [Medicine] (DAVI) .... CaBI
Calcium Carbonate [Pharmacology] (DAVI) .... CACB
Calcium Carbonate [Pharmacology] (DAVI) .... CaCO$_3$
calcium carbonate (SAUS) .... cal carb
Calcium Carbonate (SAUS) .... Chalk
Calcium Carbonate coust (SAUS) .... Caliche
Calcium Carbonate Deposition Test [Organic chemistry] (DICI) .... CCDT
Calcium Channel Antagonist (MELL) .... CCA
Calcium Channel Blocker [Medicine] (CPH) .... CCB
Calcium Chloride [Pharmacology] (DAVI) .... CaCl$_2$
Calcium Chloride Association (SAUO) .... CCA
Calcium Chloride Hexahydrate .... CCH
Calcium Chloride Institute [Defunct] (EA) CCI
calcium citrate (SAUS) .... cal citr
Calcium Compensation Depth (QUAC) .... CCD
Calcium Cyanamide Citrated [or Citrated Calcium Carbimide] [Pharmacology] CCC
Calcium Cyclamate [Sweetener] CC
Calcium Diethylene-Triamine-Pentaacetic Acid (PDAA) .... CDTPA
Calcium Disodium Ethylene Diamine Tetra-Acetate (SAUS) .... CA EDTA
Calcium Disodium Ethylenediaminetetraacetate [Chelating agent] .... CaEDTA
Calcium Entry Blocking [Agent] [Physiology] .... CEB
Calcium Excretion [Medicine] (DMAA) .... CaE
Calcium, Ferrous, Magnesium, Aluminum, Silicon [Oxide system in geology] .... CFMAS
calcium gluconate (SAUS) .... cal gluc
Calcium Glycerophosphate (DB) .... CaGP

calcium glycerophosphate (SAUS) .... cal glyceroph
Calcium Hydroxide [Inorganic chemistry] (OA) .... CH
Calcium in the Solar Spectrum [Astronomy] (BARN) .... K
Calcium Influx Factor [Neurobiology] .... CIF
Calcium Information Center (SAUS) CIC
Calcium Intake Score [Medicine] .... CS
Calcium Ion Concentration (MELL) CIC
Calcium, Ionized [Organic chemistry] (DAVI) .... CA ION
Calcium Lanthanum Silicate Oxyapatite (IEEE) .... CaLaSOAP
Calcium, Lime, Rust Remover [Cleaning product] .... CLR
Calcium Magnesium Acetate .... CMA
Calcium, Magnesium, Aluminum, Silicon [Oxide system in geology] .... CMAS
Calcium Methanearsonate [Herbicide] .... CMA
Calcium Nutrient Agar [Medicine] (DMAA) .... CNA
Calcium Oxalate [Organic chemistry] (AAMN) .... CA OX
Calcium Oxalate (MELL) .... CO
Calcium Oxalate [Organic chemistry] .... COX
Calcium Oxalate Dihydrate Urinary Calculi [Medicine] (MELL) .... CODUC
Calcium Oxalate Stone [Medicine] (MELL) .... COS
Calcium Oxide (LDT) .... calx
Calcium Oxide [Organic chemistry] (DAVI) .... CaO
calcium phosphate (SAUS) .... cal phos
Calcium Phosphate [Organic chemistry] (DAVI) .... CAPC
Calcium Pyrophosphate [Organic chemistry] (DAVI) .... CAPR
Calcium Pyrophosphate Deposition [Medicine] (MELL) .... CPD
Calcium Pyrophosphate Deposition [Medicine] .... CPPD
Calcium Pyrophosphate Deposition Disease [Rheumatology] (DAVI) .... CPDD
Calcium Pyrophosphate Deposition Disease (ADWA) .... CPPD
Calcium Pyrophosphate Dihydrate [Inorganic chemistry] .... CaPDi
Calcium Pyrophosphate Dihydrate [Inorganic chemistry] .... CPPD
Calcium Release Channel [Neurobiology] .... CRC
Calcium Silicate Brick (SAUS) .... CSB
Calcium Silicate Hydrate [Inorganic chemistry] .... CSH
Calcium Sodium Sulfate (SAUS) .... Glauberite
Calcium Store Disease [Medicine] (MELL) .... CSD
Calcium Sulfate (SAUS) .... Gypsum
Calcium Sulfate (SAUS) .... Stucco
Calcium Test (SAUS) .... Ca Test
Calcium Tolerance Test [Medicine] (DMAA) .... CATT
Calcium Urine Spot [Test] [Biochemistry] (DAVI) .... CA-SP
Calcium-Activated Factor [Meat science] .... CAF
Calcium-Activated Sarcoplasmic Factor [A proteolytic enzyme] .... CASF
Calcium-Aluminum-Rich Inclusion [Meteorite composition] .... CAI
Calcium-Ammonium Nitrate [Fertilizer] .... CAN
Calcium-Based Minerals [Inorganic chemistry] .... CBM
Calcium-Binding Modulator Protein .... CMP
Calcium-Binding Para-Albumin [Biochemistry] .... CPA
Calcium-Binding Protein [Biochemistry] (DB) .... CBP
Calcium-Boron-Aluminum [Glasses] .... CABAL
Calcium-Calmodulin-Dependent Protein Kinase II .... CaMKII
Calcium-Chlorid (SAUS) CaCl2
Calcium-Dependent Adenosine Triphophatase (PDAA) .... Ca-ATPase
Calcium-Dependent Cell Adhesion System (DB) .... CADS
Calcium-Dependent Protease Small Subunit [Medicine] (DMAA) .... CDPS
Calcium-Dependent Protein Kinase [An enzyme] .... CDPK
Calcium-Dependent Regulator (SAUS) .... CDR
Calcium-Free Salt .... CFS
Calcium-Induced Calcium Release [Biochemistry] .... CICR
Calcium-Magnesium Silicate (OA) .... CMS
Calcium-Reduced Skim Milk .... CRSM
Calcium-Reduced Skim Milk Powder (OA) .... CRSMP
Calcium-to-Phosphorus [Molar ratio] (DAVI) .... Ca/P
Calcium-Vanadium-Bismuth (SAUS) .... CVB
Calcofluor White [A cotton whitener] .... CFW
Calcraft [Hangman] [Slang] [British] (DSUE) .... CAL
Calcrete [Geology] .... cAL
Calculate (ADWA) .... calc
Calculate [or Calculated] .... CALC
Calculate Polynomial for Row Values (SAUS) .... CPRV
Calculated (ADA) .... CALCD
Calculated Access Method (PDAA) .... CAM
Calculated Air Speed (MSA) .... CAS
Calculated Altitude .... CALALT
Calculated Area under the Curve [Statistics] .... CAUC
Calculated Average Life (AAG) .... CAL
Calculated Cetane Index [Fuel technology] CCI
Calculated Colloidal Osmotic Pressure [Clinical chemistry] .... cCOP
Calculated Date of Confinement [Obstetrics] (DAVI) .... CDC
Calculated D-spacing (SAUS) .... DCALC
Calculated Error Probable .... CEP
Calculated Estimated Time of Departure [Aviation] (DA) .... CETD
Calculated Estimated Time of Overflight [Aviation] (DA) .... CETO
Calculated Landing Time [FAA] (TAG) .... CLT
Calculated Mean Organism (STED) .... CMO
Calculated Particulate Organic Carbon [Oceanography] .... CPOC
Calculated Protein Efficiency Ration [Nutrition] .... C-PER
Calculated Structure Factor (SAUS) .... Fcalc
Calculated Time of Arrival (DA) .... CTA
Calculated Weight C
Calculated Weight Report .... CWR
Calculated Zenith Distance .... CZD
Calculating Capacity (SAUS) CC
Calculating Device (SAUS) .... CD
Calculating Function (SAUS) .... CF
Calculating Machine (SAUS) .... CM

Calculating Memory (SAUS) ... CM
Calculating Register (SAUS) ... CR
Calculating Speed (SAUS) ... CS
Calculating Store (SAUS) ... CS
Calculating, Tabulating, Recording Company (SAUS) ... CTRCO
Calculating Time (SAUS) ... CT
Calculation (IAA) ... CALCN
Calculation Diagram (SAUS) ... CD
Calculation Experiment (SAUS) ... CE
Calculation Fixed Point (SAUS) ... CFP
Calculation Link Processing System [Military] (CAAL) ... CLIPS
Calculation of Drilling Coordinates (MCD) ... CADRIC
Calculation of Indirect Resources and Conversion to Unit Staff [Computer science] ... CIRCUS
Calculation of Inertia (IAA) ... CAIN
Calculation of Miss Distance Between Objects [Naval Research Laboratory] (PS) ... COMBO
Calculation Statement (SAUS) ... CS
Calculation/Experiment (NRCH) ... C/E
Calculations of Patient and Hospitals Education Resources (SAUS) ... CIPHER
Calculations of Reactor Accident Consequences (NRCH) ... CRAC
Calculator (WDAA) ... CALC
Calculator (SAUS) ... Calr
Calculator (MDG) ... CC
Calculator Collectors Club [British] (DBA) ... CCC
Calculator Help in Processing Signals (SAUS) ... CHIPS
Calculator on Substrate (IAA) ... COS
Calculator Printing (IAA) ... CP
Calculator-Aided Design (SAUS) ... CAD
Calculator-Aware Number [Project] (AIE) ... CAN
Calculator-Oriented Processor (MHDB) ... COP
Calculus (MAE) ... C
Calculus (NTIO) ... calc
Calculus (WDAA) ... CALC
Calculus (SAUS) ... Calc
Calculus of Communicating Systems (RALS) ... CCS
Calculus of Variation [NASA] ... COV
Calculus Rate Problem Solver (PDAA) ... CARPS
Calculus Removal (MAE) ... CR
Calculus Surface Index (STED) ... CSI
Calcutta [India] [Seismograph station code, US Geological Survey] (SEIS) ... CAL
Calcutta [India] (ROG) ... CALC
Calcutta [India] [Airport symbol] (OAG) ... CCU
Calcutta [India] [ICAO location identifier] (ICLI) ... VECC
Calcutta [India] [ICAO location identifier] (ICLI) ... VECF
Calcutta (Behala) [India] [ICAO location identifier] (ICLI) ... VEBA
Calcutta Computers [Software manufacturing company] [India] (ECON) ... CC
Calcutta Electric Supply Corporation (SAUO) ... CESC
Calcutta Law Journal [A publication] (DLA) ... Calc LJ
Calcutta Law Journal [A publication] (DLA) ... Calcutta LJ
Calcutta Law Journal [A publication] (DLA) ... CLJ
Calcutta Law Journal Reports [A publication] (DLA) ... Cal LJ
Calcutta Law Reporter [A publication] (DLA) ... Cal LR
Calcutta Law Reporter [A publication] (DLA) ... CLR
Calcutta Legal Adviser [India] [A publication] (DLA) ... Cal Leg Adv
Calcutta Legal Observer [A publication] (DLA) ... Cal Leg Obs
Calcutta Light Horse [British military] (DMA) ... CLH
Calcutta Mathematical Society (SAUO) ... CMS
Calcutta Metropolitan Development Organization (SAUO) ... CMDO
Calcutta Port Shramik Union [India] ... CPSU
Calcutta Reports of Cases in Appeal [A publication] (DLA) ... Sevestre
Calcutta Sadr Diwani Adalat Reports [India] [A publication] (DLA) ... Cal SDA
Calcutta Series, Indian Law Reports [A publication] (DLA) ... Calc Ser
Calcutta Series, Indian Law Reports [A publication] (DLA) ... Cal Ser
Calcutta Statistical Association (SAUO) ... CSA
Calcutta Stock Exchange (SAUS) ... CSE
Calcutta University (SAUO) ... Calc Univ
Calcutta Volunteer Guards [British military] (DMA) ... VCG
Calcutta Volunteer Lancers [British military] (DMA) ... CVL
Calcutta Weekly Notes [A publication] (DLA) ... Calcutta WN
Calcutta Weekly Notes [A publication] (DLA) ... Calc WN
Calcutta Weekly Notes [A publication] (DLA) ... Cal WN
Calcutta Weekly Notes [A publication] (DLA) ... CWN
Calcutta Weekly Notes [A publication] (DLA) ... WN
Calcutta Weekly Notes [A publication] (DLA) ... WN (Calc)
Calcutta Weekly Reporter [A publication] (DLA) ... Cal WR
Calcyclin [Medicine] (DMAA) ... CACY
Caldarium (VRA) ... caldm
Caldecott's English Settlement Cases [1776-85] [A publication] (DLA) ... Cal
Caldecott's Magistrates' and Settlement Cases [1776-85] [England] [A publication] (DLA) ... Cald
Caldecott's Magistrates' and Settlement Cases [1776-85] [England] [A publication] (DLA) ... Cald (Eng)
Caldecott's Magistrates' and Settlement Cases [1776-85] [England] [A publication] (DLA) ... Cald JP
Caldecott's Magistrates' and Settlement Cases [1776-85] [England] [A publication] (DLA) ... Cald Mag Cas
Caldecott's Magistrates' and Settlement Cases [1776-85] [England] [A publication] (DLA) ... Cald M Cas
Caldecott's Magistrates' and Settlement Cases [1776-85] [England] [A publication] (DLA) ... Cald SC
Caldecott's Magistrates' and Settlement Cases [1776-85] [England] [A publication] (DLA) ... Cald Set Cas
Caldecott's Magistrates' and Settlement Cases [1776-85] [England] [A publication] (DLA) ... Cald Sett Cas
Caldeira-Leggett Model [Physics] ... CLM
Caldera [Chile] [Seismograph station code, US Geological Survey] [Closed] (SEIS) ... CLD
Caldera Mines Ltd. [Vancouver Stock Exchange symbol] ... CMM
Caldera Network Desktop [Linux] (VERA) ... CND
Caldera Open Linux (SAUS) ... COL
Caldera Systems [NASDAQ symbol] (SG) ... CALD
Caldera Systems Curriculum Developers (SAUS) ... CSCD
Calderdale Information Service [Library cooperative] [British] (NITA) ... CALDIS
Calderon [Spanish dramatist, 1600-1682] (ROG) ... CALD
Caldor Corp. [Associated Press] (SAG) ... Caldor
Caldor Corp. [NYSE symbol] (SPSG) ... CLD
Caldwell. Arbitration [2nd ed.] [1825] [A publication] (DLA) ... Cald Arb
Caldwell College, Caldwell, NJ [Library symbol] [Library of Congress] (LCLS) ... NjCalC
Caldwell College for Women [New Jersey] ... CCW
Caldwell College for Women, Caldwell, NJ [OCLC symbol] (OCLC) ... CAL
Caldwell Community College and Technical Institute, Lenoir, NC [Library symbol] [Library of Congress] (LCLS) ... NcLeCT
Caldwell Computer Corporation (SAUO) ... CCC
Caldwell County Public Library, Lenoir, NC [Library symbol] [Library of Congress] (LCLS) ... NcLeC
Caldwell Free Public Library, Caldwell, NJ [Library symbol] [Library of Congress] (LCLS) ... NjCal
Caldwell, ID [FM radio station call letters] (RBYB) ... KARO
Caldwell, ID [AM radio station call letters] ... KBGN
Caldwell, ID [FM radio station call letters] ... KBXL
Caldwell, ID [AM radio station call letters] ... KCID
Caldwell, ID [FM radio station call letters] ... KCID-FM
Caldwell, ID [Television station call letters] ... KHDT
Caldwell, ID [TV station call letters] (RBYB) ... KNIN-TV
Caldwell, ID [FM radio station call letters] ... KTSY
Caldwell, NJ [Location identifier] [FAA] (FAAL) ... CDW
Caldwell, OH [FM radio station call letters] ... WWKC
Caldwell Parish Library, Columbia, LA [Library symbol] [Library of Congress] (LCLS) ... LColC
Caldwell Progress, Caldwell, NJ [Library symbol] [Library of Congress] (LCLS) ... NjCalP
Caldwell Public Library, Caldwell, ID [Library symbol] [Library of Congress] (LCLS) ... IdCa
Caldwell Public Library, Caldwell, OH [Library symbol] [Library of Congress] (LCLS) ... OCal
Caldwell Township Public Library, Verner, Ontario [Library symbol] [National Library of Canada] (NLC) ... OVCT
Caldwell-Luc Operation [Medicine] (MELL) ... CLO
Caldwell's Reports [25-36 West Virginia] [A publication] (DLA) ... Cald
Caledon Information & Community Services [Formerly, Bolton Contact Centre] [Formerly, Caledon Information Centre] (AC) ... CICS
Caledon Public Libraries, Bolton, ON, Canada [Library symbol] [Library of Congress] (LCLS) ... CaOBolC
Caledon Public Libraries, Bolton, Ontario [Library symbol] [National Library of Canada] (NLC) ... OBOLC
Caledonia [Scotland] (ROG) ... CAL
Caledonia [Scotland] ... CALED
Caledonia [Panama] [Airport symbol] (OAG) ... CDE
Caledonia [Costa Rica] [ICAO location identifier] (ICLI) ... MRCD
Caledonia MacBrayne [Commercial firm] [British] ... CALMAC
Caledonia Mining [Associated Press] (SAG) ... Caledon
Caledonia Mining [NASDAQ symbol] (SAG) ... CALV
Caledonia Mining [NASDAQ symbol] (TTSB) ... CALVF
Caledonia Mining Corporation (SAUO) ... CMC
Caledonia, MN [Location identifier] [FAA] (FAAL) ... CHU
Caledonia, MN [FM radio station call letters] (BROA) ... KHTW-FM
Caledonia, MN [FM radio station call letters] (BROA) ... KSFF-FM
Caledonia, MN [FM radio station call letters] ... KSOF
Caledonia, NS [Television station call letters] ... CJCH-6
Caledonia Resources Ltd. [Vancouver Stock Exchange symbol] ... CLN
Caledonia-Mumford Junior/Senior High School Library, Caledonia, NY [OCLC symbol] (OCLC) ... RVU
Caledonian [Railway] [Scotland] (ROG) ... C
Caledonian Airways Ltd. [British] [ICAO designator] (FAAC) ... CKT
Caledonian Canal (SAUS) ... Caled Can
Caledonian Railway (SAUO) ... CR
Caledonian Railway [Scotland] ... CR
Caledonian Railway Co. (SAUO) ... Caled
Caledonian Railway Co. (SAUO) ... Caley
Caledonian Railway Co. (SAUO) ... CalRy
Caledonian Society [Australia] ... CS
Caledonian Steam Packet Company (SAUO) ... CSPCo
Calefactus [Made Warm] [Pharmacy] (ROG) ... CALEFACT
Calefiat [Warm It] [Pharmacy] ... CALEF
Calendae [Calends] [The First Day of the Month] [Latin] ... C
Calendae [Calends] [The First Day of the Month] [Latin] (ROG) ... CAL
Calendar ... CAL
Calendar (VRA) ... cal
Calendar Day (AFM) ... CD
Calendar Line (SAUS) ... CL
Calendar Marketing Agreement ... CMA
Calendar Marketing Association (EA) ... CMA
Calendar of Charter Rolls [British] ... CChR
Calendar of Close Rolls [British] ... CCR
Calendar of Coroners Rolls of the City of London [A publication] (DLA) ... Sharpe
Calendar of Coroners Rolls of the City of London (journ.) (SAUS) ... Sharge
Calendar of Liberate Rolls [British] ... CLR
Calendar of Literary Facts [A publication] ... CLF

Calendar of Papal Letters (WDAA) ... CPL
Calendar of Patent Rolls [*British*] ... CPR
Calendar of Proceedings in Chancery Tempore Elizabeth [*1827-32*] [*A publication*] (DLA) ... Cal Ch
Calendar of Proceedings in Chancery Tempore Elizabeth [*1827-32*] [*A publication*] (DLA) ... Cal P Ch
Calendar of State Papers [*British*] (ROG) ... CSP
Calendar Process [*Telecommunications*] (TEL) ... CP
Calendar Reform Foundation [*Defunct*] (EA) ... CRF
Calendar Reform Political Action Group [*Defunct*] (EA) ... CRPAG
Calendar Time ... CT
Calendar Variations Analysis ... CVA
Calendar Year (TEL) ... CY
Calendar Year to Date (ABAC) ... CYTD
Calendaring and Scheduling API (SAUS) ... CSA
Calendarium Rotulorum Patentium [*Calendar of the Patent Rolls*] [*Latin*] ... CAL ROT PAT
Calendarium Rotulorum Patentum [*Calendar of the Patent Rolls*] [*Latin*] ... CRP
Calendars of the Proceedings in Chancery, Record Commission [*A publication*] (DLA) ... Cal
Calender (SAUS) ... Calen
Calendered Paper (BARN) ... Cal
Calendrier Republicain [*Republican Calendar*] [*French*] ... CR
CalEnergy Co. [*NYSE symbol*] [*Formerly, California Energy*] (SG) ... CE
Calenergy Co., Inc. [*Associated Press*] (SAG) ... Calenergy
Calera, AL [*AM radio station call letters*] ... WBYE
Caleta Josefina [*Chile*] [*Airport symbol*] (AD) ... WCJ
Calexico, CA [*Location identifier*] [*FAA*] (FAAL) ... CXL
Calexico, CA [*AM radio station call letters*] ... KICO
Calexico, CA [*FM radio station call letters*] ... KQVO
Calexico, CA [*FM radio station call letters*] ... KUBO
Calexico Public Library, Calexico, CA [*Library symbol*] [*Library of Congress*] (LCLS) ... CCal
Calexico/International [*California*] [*ICAO location identifier*] (ICLI) ... KCXL
Calf (SAUS) ... Cf
Calf [*Calfskin*] [*Bookbinding*] (WDMC) ... cf
Calf ... CF
Calf Blood Flow (DB) ... CF
Calf Certifying Officer [*Ministry of Agriculture, Fisheries, and Food*] [*British*] ... CCO
Calf Embryonic Heart Cell (DB) ... CEHC
Calf Intestinal Phosphatase [*An enzyme*] ... CIP
Calf Kidney (DB) ... CK
Calf Lung Surfactant Extract [*Medicine*] (DMAA) ... CLSE
Calf Processing Aid Scheme (SAUS) ... CPAS
Calf Pulmonary Artery Endthelial [*Cell line*] ... CPAE
Calf Roping [*Rodeo term*] ... CR
Calf Serum [*Biochemistry*] (DAVI) ... CS
Calf Testis (DB) ... CT
Calf Thymus Extract [*Medicine*] (DMAA) ... CTE
Calf Venous Volume (DB) ... CVR
calfbinding (SAUS) ... cf
Calfskin [*Book cover material*] (NTCM) ... CALF
Calfskin (ADWA) ... cf
Calgary [*Canada*] (ROG) ... CALG
Calgary [*Canada*] [*Airport symbol*] (OAG) ... YYC
Calgary, AB [*AM radio station call letters*] ... CBR
Calgary, AB [*FM radio station call letters*] ... CBR-FM
Calgary, AB [*Television station call letters*] ... CBRT
Calgary, AB [*AM radio station call letters*] ... CFAC
Calgary, AB [*Television station call letters*] ... CFCN-TV
Calgary, AB [*AM radio station call letters*] ... CFFR
Calgary, AB [*AM radio station call letters*] ... CFXL
Calgary, AB [*FM radio station call letters*] ... CHFM
Calgary, AB [*FM radio station call letters*] (BROA) ... CHKF-FM
Calgary, AB [*AM radio station call letters*] ... CHQR
Calgary, AB [*Television station call letters*] ... CICT
Calgary, AB [*FM radio station call letters*] ... CJAY
Calgary, AB [*FM radio station call letters*] (BROA) ... CJSI-FM
Calgary, AB [*FM radio station call letters*] ... CJSW
Calgary, AB [*FM radio station call letters*] ... CKIK
Calgary, AB [*FM radio station call letters*] (RBYB) ... CKIS-FM
Calgary, AB [*AM radio station call letters*] (RBYB) ... CKMX
Calgary, AB [*FM radio station call letters*] ... CKRY
Calgary, AB [*FM radio station call letters*] ... CKUA-1
Calgary Air Conditioning & Sheet Metal Association (AC) ... CASMA
Calgary, Alberta [*Television station call letters*] (BROA) ... CKAL-TV
Calgary & District Labour Council (AC) ... CDLC
Calgary and Region Education Television (SAUS) ... CARPET
Calgary Board of Education, Acquisition and Technical Services [*UTLAS symbol*] ... CBE
Calgary Board of Education, Professional Library [*UTLAS symbol*] ... CBP
Calgary Board of Education Professional Library, Alberta [*Library symbol*] [*National Library of Canada*] (NLC) ... ACBEP
Calgary Branch Library, Alberta Research Council, Alberta [*Library symbol*] [*National Library of Canada*] (NLC) ... ACRC
Calgary Centre Holdings Ltd. [*Toronto Stock Exchange symbol*] ... CGY
Calgary Construction Association (AC) ... CCA
Calgary Early Music Society (AC) ... CEMS
Calgary Field Naturalists' Society [*Societe des Champs Etat de Nature de Calgary*] [*Formerly, Calgary Bird Club*] (AC) ... CFNS
Calgary General Hospital, Alberta [*Library symbol*] [*National Library of Canada*] (NLC) ... ACGH
Calgary Herald, Alberta [*Library symbol*] [*National Library of Canada*] (NLC) ... ACCH
Calgary Herald, Calgary, AB, Canada [*Library symbol*] [*Library of Congress*] (LCLS) ... CaACCH
Calgary Immigrant Aid Society (AC) ... CIAS
Calgary Library Service Centre, Alberta [*Library symbol*] [*National Library of Canada*] (NLC) ... ACCL
Calgary Library Service Centre, Calgary, AB, Canada [*Library symbol*] [*Library of Congress*] (LCLS) ... CaACCL
Calgary Milk Producers' Association [*Formerly, United Milk & Cream Producers*] (AC) ... CMPA
Calgary Olympic Development Association (SAUO) ... CODA
Calgary Olympic Organizing Committee [*Calgary, AB*] (EAIO) ... COOC
Calgary Photographic Historical Society (AC) ... CPHS
Calgary Police Association [*Association de la Police de Calgary*] (AC) ... CPA
Calgary Power Ltd., Calgary, AB, Canada [*Library symbol*] [*Library of Congress*] (LCLS) ... CaACPow
Calgary Public Library [*UTLAS symbol*] ... CPL
Calgary Public Library, Alberta [*Library symbol*] [*National Library of Canada*] (NLC) ... AC
Calgary Public Library, Calgary, AB, Canada [*Library symbol*] [*Library of Congress*] (LCLS) ... CaAC
Calgary Public Library Government Documents [*Information service or system*] (IID) ... CALDOC
Calgary Public School Board, Calgary, AB, Canada [*Library symbol*] [*Library of Congress*] (LCLS) ... CaACLS
Calgary Regional Heatlh Authority (SAUO) ... CRHA
Calgary Research Center, Calgary, AB, Canada [*Library symbol*] [*Library of Congress*] (LCLS) ... CaACR
Calgary Research Centre, Alberta [*Library symbol*] [*National Library of Canada*] (NLC) ... ACR
Calgary Research Centre Library, Shell Canada Ltd., Alberta [*Library symbol*] [*National Library of Canada*] (NLC) ... ACSCL
Calgary Round-Up Band Association (AC) ... CRUB
Calgary/International, AB [*ICAO location identifier*] (ICLI) ... CYYC
Calgene, Inc. [*Associated Press*] (SAG) ... Calgene
Calgene, Inc. [*NASDAQ symbol*] (NQ) ... CGNE
Calgon Adsorption Service (SAUS) ... CAS
Calgon Carbon [*NYSE symbol*] (TTSB) ... CCC
Calgon Carbon [*NYSE symbol*] (SAG) ... COC
Calgon Carbon Corp. [*Associated Press*] (SAG) ... Calgon
Calgon Carbon Corp. (MHDW) ... CRBN
Calgon Corp., Pittsburgh, PA [*OCLC symbol*] (OCLC) ... PCA
Calgranulin A (DMAA) ... CAGA
Calgranulin B (DMAA) ... CAGB
Calhoun Community Unit, School District 40, Hardin, IL [*Library symbol*] [*Library of Congress*] (LCLS) ... IHardCSD
Calhoun County Historical Society, Rockwell City, IA [*Library symbol*] [*Library of Congress*] (LCLS) ... IaRcCHi
Calhoun County Public Library, St. Matthews, SC [*Library symbol*] [*Library of Congress*] (LCLS) ... ScStm
Calhoun Falls [*South Carolina*] [*Seismograph station code, US Geological Survey*] (SEIS) ... CHF
Calhoun, GA [*Location identifier*] [*FAA*] (FAAL) ... CZL
Calhoun, GA [*AM radio station call letters*] ... WEBS
Calhoun, GA [*AM radio station call letters*] ... WJTH
Calhoun, TN [*FM radio station call letters*] ... WCLE
Cali [*Colombia*] [*Airport symbol*] (OAG) ... CLO
Cali Realty [*NYSE symbol*] (TTSB) ... CLI
Cali Realty Corp. [*Associated Press*] (SAG) ... CaliRlty
Cali Realty Corp. [*Associated Press*] (SAG) ... CaliRty
Cali Realty Corp. [*NYSE symbol*] (SAG) ... CLI
Cali/Alfonso Bonilla Aragon [*Colombia*] [*ICAO location identifier*] (ICLI) ... SKCL
Caliber (DMAA) ... Cal
Caliber (AFM) ... CAL
Caliber (ADWA) ... cal
Caliber System [*NYSE symbol*] [*Formerly, Roadway Services*] (SG) ... CBB
Caliber Systems, Inc. [*Associated Press*] (SAG) ... Caliber
Caliber Systems, Inc. [*NYSE symbol*] (SAG) ... CBB
Calibrate ... CAB
Calibrate (CET) ... CAL
Calibrate (AAG) ... CALIB
calibrate (SAUS) ... calib
calibrated (SAUS) ... cal
Calibrated Air Speed (SAUS) ... Cal AS
Calibrated Air Speed ... CAS
Calibrated Airborne Measurements Program (MCD) ... CAMP
Calibrated Airborne Multispectral Scanner [*Instrumentation*] ... CAMS
Calibrated Airborne Special Infrared Measurement Systems (PDAA) ... CASIMS
Calibrated Altitude [*Navigation*] ... CA
calibrated altitude (SAUS) ... ca
Calibrated Ancillary System [*NASA*] (SPST) ... CAS
Calibrated Angle of Attack (MCD) ... AOAC
Calibrated Armor Vehicle Simulator (MCD) ... CAVS
Calibrated Data Tape (ACAE) ... CDT
Calibrated Engine Testing ... CET
Calibrated Focal Length (MSA) ... CFL
Calibrated Magnification (MSA) ... CM
Calibrated Optical and Near Infrared Imaging System (MCD) ... CONIRIS
Calibrated Pressure Switch (KSC) ... CALIPS
Calibrated Probability Density Distribution ... CPDD
Calibrated Radiometer for Background Scanning (SAUS) ... CARABAS
Calibrated Sweep Delay ... CSD
Calibrating, Amplitude-Variation, and Level-Correcting Analog-Digital Equipment (DEN) ... CAVALCADE
Calibrating Work Center (AFIT) ... CWC
Calibration (SAUS) ... Cab

Calibration (ADWA) .... cal
Calibration (MSA) .... CAL
Calibration (AABC) .... CALBR
Calibration (AAG) .... CALIBN
Calibration .... CALIBR
Calibration .... CLBR
Calibration (SAUS) .... Clbr
Calibration Advisory Working Group (ACAE) .... CAWG
Calibration and Certification (IAA) .... CAC
Calibration and Certification (SAUS) .... C&C
Calibration and Checkout (IAA) .... CAC
Calibration and Checkout (SAUS) .... C&C
Calibration And Land Applications of ERS-1 SAR Data (SAUS) .... CALA
Calibration and Maintenance (ACAE) .... C&M
Calibration and Measurement Standards System (ACAE) .... CMSS
Calibration and Measurement Summaries [Air Force] (AFIT) .... CMS
Calibration and Repair Center .... CRC
Calibration and Repair Support Center (SAUO) .... CRSC
Calibration and Tracking Visible Sensor (MCD) .... CTVS
Calibration and Validation (SAUS) .... Cal/Val
Calibration Base Line (GEOI) .... CBL
Calibration Blank [Spectroscopy] .... CALBLK
Calibration Check Compound CCC
Calibration Coordinating Group (SAUO) .... CCG
Calibration Count (SAUS) CC
Calibration Curve Data .... CCD
Calibration Cycle (AFIT) CC
Calibration Data (SAUS) .... CD
Calibration Device (KSC) .... CD
Calibration Equipment [Military] .... CAL-E
Calibration Equipment (ACAE) .... CE
Calibration Error (SAUS) .... CE
Calibration Factor .... CF
Calibration Lead Assembly (ACAE) .... CLA
Calibration Magnification (SAUS) .... CM
Calibration Marker .... CM
Calibration Output (SAUS) .... CAL OUT
Calibration Procedure .... CP
Calibration Procedure .... CPC
Calibration Procedure Status Report [Polaris missile] .... CPSR
Calibration Property Action Order (ACAE) .... CPAO
Calibration Recall Information Systems (KSC) .... CRIS
Calibration Recall System [Army] .... CRS
Calibration, Repair, and Return .... CR & R
Calibration Requirements List (NG) .... CARL
Calibration Requirements List (MCD) .... CRL
Calibration Requirements Summaries (SAUS) .... CRS
Calibration Requirements Summary .... CRS
Calibration Rocket [NASA] .... CALROC
Calibration Signal Generator .... CSG
Calibration Sphere (MCD) .... CALSPHERE
Calibration Support Equipment (ACAE) .... CSE
Calibration Team .... CT
Calibration Technician (KSC) .... CT
Calibration Test Box .... CTB
Calibration Test Unit (ACAE) .... CTU
Calibration Validation Unit [Instrumentation] .... CVU
Calibration Verification Sample [Spectroscopy] .... CVS
Calibration Vibration Exciter .... CVE
Calibration/Certification (SAA) .... CAL/CERT
Calibration/Measurement Requirements Summary .... CMRS
Calibration/Validation (EOSA) .... Cal/Val
Calibrator Control Console (ACAE) CCC
Calibrator Output Cathode Follower (SAUS) ...... CAL OUT CF
Calibre-Radius Head [of projectile] [British] .... CRH
Calicivirus [Medicine] (DMAA) .... CaCV
Calico Printers' Association (DGA) .... CPA
Calicut [India] [ICAO location identifier] (ICLI) .... VOCL
Calidus [Warm] [Pharmacy] (ROG) .... CALID
Calidyne Company (SAUO) C
Caliente Resources Ltd. [Vancouver Stock Exchange symbol] ...... CIT
Calif Amplifier [NASDAQ symbol] (TTSB) .... CAMP
Calif Bancshares [NASDAQ symbol] (TTSB) .... CABI
Calif Culinary Academy [NASDAQ symbol] (TTSB) ...... COOK
Calif Fed'l Bk10.625%'B'Pfd [NYSE symbol] (TTSB) ...... CALPrB
Calif Finl Hldg [NASDAQ symbol] (TTSB) .... CFHC
Calif Micro Devices [NASDAQ symbol] (TTSB) .... CAMD
Calif Microwave [NASDAQ symbol] (TTSB) .... CMIC
Calif Pro Sports [NASDAQ symbol] (TTSB) .... CALP
Calif REIT SBI [NYSE symbol] (TTSB) .... CT
Calif Water Svc [NYSE symbol] (TTSB) .... CWT
Calif Water Svc Grp [NYSE symbol] (SG) .... CWT
California [Postal code] .... CA
California .... CAL
California (NTIO) .... Cal
California .... Cali
California (AFM) .... CALIF
California (ODBW) .... Calif
California [MARC country of publication code] [Library of Congress] (LCCP) ...... cau
California [MARC geographic area code] [Library of Congress] (LCCP) ...... n-us-ca
California Academic Libraries Lists of Serials (EDAC) ...... CALLS
California Academy of Family Physicians (SRA) .... CAFP
California Academy of General Dentistry (SRA) .... CAGD
California Academy of Physician Assistants (SRA) ...... CAPA
California Academy of Sciences .... CAS

California Academy of Sciences Geology Type Collection (SAUS) .... CASGTC
California Academy of Sciences, San Francisco, CA [Library symbol] [Library of Congress] (LCLS) .... CSfA
California Academy of Sciences, San Francisco International Acronym (SAUS) .... CAS
California Achievement Test .... CAT
California Administrative Code (SAUS) .... CAC
California Administrative Code [A publication] (DLA) ...... Cal Adm Code
California Administrative Code [A publication] (DLA) ...... Cal Admin Code
California Administrative Register [A publication] (DLA) ...... Cal Admin Reg
California Advance Legislative Service (Deering) [A publication] (DLA) .... Cal Adv Legis Serv
California Advisory Commission on Marine and Coastal Resources (SAUO) .... CMC
California Advisory Council (SAUO) .... CAC
California Advisory Council on Vocational Education (SAUO) ...... CACVE
California Aeronautics Commission (SAUO) .... CAC
California Agricultural Aircraft Association (EA) .... CAAA
California Agricultural Production Consultants Association (SRA) ...... CAPCA
California Agricultural Resources Model (SAUO) .... CARM
California Agricultural Teachers Association (SRA) ...... CATA
California Agriculture Code [A publication] (DLA) .... Cal Agric Code
California Agriculture (journ.) (SAUS) .... Calif Agric
California Air Pollution Control Officers Association (COE) ...... CAPCOA
California Air Resources Board .... CARB
California Alarm Association (SRA) .... CAA
California Alkali Export Association (SAUO) .... CAEA
California Alkali Export Association (SAUO) .... Calkex
California Almond Growers Exchange [Later, BDG] (EA) ...... CAGE
California Ambulance Association (SRA) .... CAA
California Amplifier, Inc. [Associated Press] (SAG) ...... CalAmp
California Amplifier, Inc. [NASDAQ symbol] (NQ) .... CAMP
California Analysis Centers, Inc. [A management consulting company] [Arlington, Virginia] (WDMC) .... CACI
California and Mexico (IIA) .... CALEXICO
California and Texas Telecommunications System (SAUS) ...... CATTS
California Apartment Association (SRA) .... CAA
California Apparel Industries Association [Later, CFC] (EA) ...... CAIA
California Appellate Decisions [A publication] (DLA) ...... Cal App Dec
California Appellate Reports [A publication] (DLA) .... CA
California Appellate Reports [A publication] (DLA) ...... CA A
California Appellate Reports [A publication] (DLA) ...... Cal App
California Appellate Reports, Second Series [A publication] (DLA) ...... CA 2d
California Appellate Reports, Second Series [A publication] (DLA) ...... CA A 2d
California Appellate Reports, Second Series [A publication] (DLA) ...... Cal App 2d
California Appellate Reports, Second Series, Supplement [A publication] (DLA) .... CA 2d Supp
California Appellate Reports, Second Series, Supplement [A publication] (DLA) .... Cal App 2d Supp
California Appellate Reports, Supplement [A publication] (DLA) ...... Cal App Supp
California Appellate Reports, Supplement [A publication] (DLA) ...... CA Supp
California Appellate Reports, Third Series [A publication] (DLA) ...... CA 3d
California Appellate Reports, Third Series [A publication] (DLA) ...... CA A 3d
California Appellate Reports, Third Series [A publication] (DLA) ...... Cal App 3d
California Appellate Reports, Third Series, Supplement [A publication] (DLA) .... CA 3S
California Appellate Reports, Third Series, Supplement [A publication] (DLA) .... Cal App 3d Supp
California Applicants Attorney Association (SRA) .... CAAA
California Apricot Advisory Board (EA) .... CAAB
California Aqueduct Control System .... CACS
California Arabian Standard Oil Co. .... CASOC
California Arabian Standard Oil Company (SAUO) ...... CASOC
California, Arizona, Florida, and Texas .... CAFT
California Artichoke Advisory Board (EA) .... CAAB
California Arts Commission (SAUO) .... CAC
California Arts Council (SAUO) .... CAC
California Asparagus Advisory Board [Defunct] (EA) ...... CAAB
California Asparagus Growers Association (SAUO) ...... CAGA
California Associated Truckers (SRA) .... CAT
California Association for Adult Day Services (SRA) ...... CAADS
California Association for Bilingual Education (SRA) ...... CABE
California Association for Childhood Education (SAUO) ...... CACE
California Association for Counseling and Development (SRA) ...... CACD
California Association for Health, Physical Education, Recreation, and Dance (SRA) .... CAHPERD
California Association for Health Services at Home (SRA) ...... CAHSAH
California Association for Local Economic Development (SRA) ...... CALED
California Association for Medical Laboratory Technology (SRA) ...... CAMLT
California Association for Research in Astronomy (SAUO) ...... CARA
California Association of Acupuncture and Oriental Medicine (SRA) ...... CAAOM
California Association of Alcoholic Recovery Homes (SRA) ...... CAARH
California Association of Catholic Hospitals (SRA) ...... CACH
California Association of Children's Homes (SRA) ...... CCH
California Association of Collectors (SRA) .... CAC
California Association of College Stores (SRA) .... CACS
California Association of Community Managers (SRA) ...... CACM
California Association of County Data Processors (SAUO) ...... CACDP
California Association of Criminalists (SAUO) .... CAC
California Association of Employers (SRA) .... CAE
California Association of Flower Growers and Shippers (SRA) ...... CAFG&S
California Association of Health Facilities (SRA) .... CAHF
California Association of Hearing Instrument Specialists (SRA) ...... CAHIS
California Association of Highway Patrolmen (SRA) ...... CAHP
California Association of Homes and Services for the Aging (SRA) ...... CAHSA

California Association of Independent Business (SRA) .... CAIB
California Association of Independent Insurance Adjusters (SRA) .... CAIIA
California Association of Licensed Investigators (SRA) .... CALI
California Association of Life Underwriters (SRA) .... CALU
California Association of Local Agency Formation Commissions (SRA) .... CALAFCO
California Association of Long Distance Telephone Companies (SRA) .... CALTEL
California Association of Marriage and Family Therapists (SRA) .... CAMFT
California Association of Medical Products Suppliers (SRA) .... CAMPS
California Association of Mortgage Brokers (SRA) .... CAMB
California Association of Nonprofits (SRA) .... CAN
California Association of Nurse Anesthetists (SRA) .... CANA
California Association of Nurserymen (SRA) .... CAN
California Association of Nurses in Substance Abuse (SAUO) .... CANSA
California Association of Ophthalmology (SRA) .... CAO
California Association of Parking Controllers (EA) .... CAPC
California Association of Pet Professionals (EA) .... CAPP
California Association of Photocopiers and Process Servers (SRA) .... CAPPS
California Association of Physically Handicapped (SAUO) .... CAPH
California Association of Polygraph Examiners (SAUO) .... CAPE
California Association of Port Authorities (SRA) .... CAPA
California Association of Postsecondary Educators of the Disabled (SAUO) .... CAPED
California Association of Public Cemeteries (SRA) .... CAPC
California Association of Public Hospitals (SRA) .... CAPH
California Association of Reactors (SAUO) .... CAR
California Association of Reactors Mortgage Assistance Corporation (SAUO) .... Carrie Mac
California Association of Realtors (SRA) .... CAR
California Association of Reclamation Entities of Water (SAUO) .... AQUACARE
California Association of Resourse Conservation Districts (SRA) .... CARCD
California Association of Sanitation Agencies (SRA) .... CASA
California Association of School Psychologists (SRA) .... CASP
California Association of Student Councils (BARN) .... CASC
California Association of Teachers of English to Speakers of Other Languages (EDAC) .... CATESOL
California Association of Temporary and Staffing Services (SRA) .... CATSS
California Association of the Deaf (SAUO) .... CAD
California Association of Thrift and Loan Companies (SRA) .... CATLC
California Association of Tiger-Owners (EA) .... CAT
California Association of Vocational Educators (SAUO) .... CAVE
California Association of Wheat Growers (SRA) .... CAWG
California Association of Window Manufacturers (SRA) .... CAWM
California Association of Winegrape Growers (EA) .... CAWG
California Astronautics and Space Agency (ACAE) .... CASA
California Attorneys for Criminal Justice (SAUO) .... CACJ
California Autobody Association (SRA) .... CAA
California Automobile Assigned Risk Plan .... CAARP
California Automotive Wholesalers' Association (SRA) .... CAWA
California Aviation Business Association (SRA) .... CABA
California Aviation Education Association .... CAEA
California Avocado Advisory Board [*Later, CAC*] .... CAAB
California Avocado Commission (EA) .... CAC
California Avocado Society (EA) .... CAS
California Bancshares, Inc. [*NASDAQ symbol*] (SAG) .... CABI
California Bancshares, Inc. [*Associated Press*] (SAG) .... CalBnc
California Bankers Association (SRA) .... CBA
California Baptist Theological Seminary .... CBTS
California Basic Education Skills Test (ROAS) .... CBEST
California Bearing Ratio [*Aviation*] .... CBR
California Beer and Beverage Distributors (SRA) .... CBBD
California Beet Growers Association (SRA) .... CBGA
California Beverage Merchants (SRA) .... CBM
California Biotechnology, Inc.[*Later, Scios, Inc.*] .... CAL-BIO
California Board of Medical Quality Assurance (SAUS) .... CBMQA
California Botanical Club (SAUO) .... CBC
California Brandy Advisory Board [*Defunct*] (EA) .... CBAB
California Breast Cancer Organizations (SAUO) .... CABCO
California Brief Life History Inventory [*Personality development test*] [*Psychology*] .... CBLHI
California Broadcasters Association (SRA) .... CBA
California Building Industry Association (SRA) .... CBIA
California Building Material Dealers Association (SRA) .... CBMDA
California Business Education Association (SRA) .... CBEA
California Business Properties Association (SRA) .... CBPA
California Cable Television Association (SRA) .... CCTA
California Cactus Growers Association (EA) .... CCGA
California Canning Peach Association (EA) .... CCPA
California Carvers Guild (EA) .... CCG
California Cast Metals Association (SRA) .... CCMA
California Cattlemen's Association (SRA) .... CCA
California Celery Research Advisory Board (SRA) .... CCRAB
California Center for Community Development (SAUS) .... CCCD
California Central Airlines .... CCA
California Certified Organic Farmers .... CCOF
California Chamber of Commerce (SRA) CCC
California Chicano News Media Association (SRA) .... CCNMA
California Children's Hospital Association (SRA) .... CCHA
California Chiropractic Association (SRA) .... CCA
California Christmas Tree Growers (SRA) .... CCTG
California Citrus Mutual (SRA) .... CCM
California Citrus Quality Council (SAUO) .... CCQC
California City, CA [*FM radio station call letters*] (BROA) .... KCEL-FM
California Civil Addict Program .... CAP
California Civil Rights Initiative (ECON) .... CCRI
California Clean Air Act (SARE) .... CCAA
California Clearinghouse for Library Instruction CCLI
California Cling Peach Advisory Board .... CCPAB
California Cling Peach Advisory Board (EA) .... CPAB
California Cling Peach Growers Advisory Board (SRA) .... CCPGAB
California Coalition for Ethical Mental Health Care .... CCEMHC
California Coastal Conference (PSS) .... CALCC
California Code of Regulations [*Also CCR*] [*A publication*] (AAGC) .... Cal Code Regs
California Code of Regulations [*A publication*] (AAGC) .... CCR
California College of Arts and Crafts (GAGS) .... Cal C Arts & Crafts
California College of Arts and Crafts [*Oakland*] .... CCAC
California College of Arts and Crafts, Oakland, CA [*Library symbol*] [*Library of Congress*] (LCLS) .... COC
California College of Arts and Crafts, Oakland, CA [*Library symbol*] [*Library of Congress*] (LCLS) .... COCAC
California College of Chiropody CCC
California College of Medicine (SAUS) .... CCM
California College of Mortuary Science (SAUS) .... CCMS
California Collegiate Athletic Association (PSS) .... CCAA
California Commun Bancshs [*NASDAQ symbol*] (TTSB) .... CCBC
California Community Bancshares Corp. [*Associated Press*] (SAG) .... CalCmB
California Community Bancshares Corp. [*NASDAQ symbol*] (SAG) .... CCBC
California Compensation Cases [*A publication*] (DLA) .... Cal Comp Cases
California Compensation Cases [*A publication*] (DLA) CC
California Comprehensive Ocean Area Plan (SAUO) .... COAP
California Computer Products, Inc. (MCD) .... CALCOMP
California Computer Products, Inc. (SAUO) .... CalComp
California Computer Products, Inc. (SAUS) .... CCP
California Concordia College, Oakland, CA [*Library symbol*] [*Library of Congress*] (LCLS) .... COCC
California Conference of Machinists (SRA) .... CCM
California Conference of Mason Contractor Associations (SRA) .... CCMCA
California Connections [*Information service or system*] (CRD) .... CALCON
California Constitution [*A publication*] (DLA) .... Cal Const
California Contemporary Fashion Guild (SAUO) .... CCFG
California Contract Cities Association (SRA) .... CCCA
California Contract Show [*Western Merchandise Mart*] (TSPED) .... CALICON
California Cooperative Fisheries Investigation (SAUO) .... CALCOFI
California Cooperative Oceanic Fisheries Investigations [*Also, CALCOFI*] (MSC) .... CCOFI
California Cooperative Oceanic Fisheries Investigations (SAUO) .... COFI
California Cooperative Oceanic Fishery Investigations [*Also, CCOFI*] .... CALCOFI
California Cooperative Remote Sensing Project (SAUS) .... CCRSP
California Coordinating Council for Higher Education (SAUO) .... CCHE
California Correctional Peace Officers Association (SRA) .... CCPOA
California Cosmetology Association (SRA) .... CCA
California Council for Geographic Education (SAUO) .... CCGE
California Council for Interior Design Certification (SRA) .... CCIDC
California Council for International Trade (SRA) .... CCIT
California Council of Civil Engineers and Land Surveyors (GEOI) .... CCCELS
California Council of Police and Sheriffs (SRA) .... CAL-COPS
California Council of the American Institute of Architects (SAUO) .... CCAIA
California Court Clerks Association (SRA) .... CCCA
California Court Interpreters and Translators Association (SAUO) .... CCIA
California Credit Union League (SRA) .... CCUL
California Criminal Justice Information System (SAUS) .... CJIS
California Crop Improvement Association (SRA) .... CCIA
California Culinary Academy, Inc. [*Associated Press*] (SAG) .... CalifCul
California Culinary Academy, Inc. [*NASDAQ symbol*] (SAG) .... COOK
California Current (SAUS) .... Calif Cur
California Current System [*Oceanography*] .... CCS
California Dairy Herd Improvement Association (SRA) .... CDHIA
California Data Network [*Claremont McKenna College, Rose Institue of State and Local Government*] [*Information service or system*] (IID) .... CDN
California Data Processors (SAUS) .... Cal Data Procs
California Date Administrative Committee (EA) .... CDAC
California Date Growers Association [*Defunct*] (EA) .... CDGA
California Debris Commission [*Army*] .... CDC
California Debt Advisory Commission (SAUO) .... CALDAC
California Decisions [*A publication*] (DLA) .... Cal Dec
California Defense Counsel (SRA) .... CDC
California Democratic Council (SAUO) .... CDC
California Dental Association (SRA) .... CDA
California Dental Service (SAUS) .... CDS
California Department of Conservation (GEOI) .... CDC
California Department of Fish and Game (GEOI) .... CDFG
California Department of Fish and Game Fish Bulletin (SAUS) .... Calif Dep Fish Game Fish Bull
California. Department of Food and Agriculture (SAUO) .... CDFA
California Department of Food. & Agriculture Agricultural Chemicals & Feed Division (SAUO) .... CDFA-AGC
California Department of Forestry (GEOI) .... CDF
California Department of Forestry Firefighters Association (SRA) .... CDFFA
California Department of Insurance .... CDI
California Department of Parks and Recreation, Sacramento Area State Parks, Sacramento, CA [*Library symbol*] [*Library of Congress*] (LCLS) .... CSPR
California Department of Transportation [*BTS*] (TAG) .... CALTRANS
California Department of Transportation (SARE) .... CalTrans
California Department of Transportation (SAUO) .... Caltrans
California Department of Water Resources (GEOI) .... CDWR
California Depopulation Commission [*Defunct*] (EA) .... CALDEPOP
California Desert Conversion Area (SAUO) .... CDCA
California Diagnostic Mathematics Test (TES) .... CDMT
California Diagnostic Reading Test (TES) .... CDRT

California Dietetic Association (SRA) .... CDA
California Digital Computer (SAUS) .... CALDIC
California Digital Library .... CDL
California Disability Insurance (ACAE) .... CDI
California Disaster Office (SAUO) .... CDO
California Distance Table Bureau, San Francisco CA [*STAC*] .... CDB
California Distributors Association (SRA) .... CDA
California District Attorneys Association (SRA) .... CDAA
California Division of Mines (SAUO) .... CDM
California Division of Mines and Geology (GEOI) .... CDMG
California Division of Occupational Safety and Health (SARE) .... Cal-OSHA
California Dried Fig Advisory Board [*Later, CFAB*] .... CDFAB
California Dried Fruit Export Association (EA) .... CDFEA
California Driver Education Association (SAUO) .... CALDEA
California Dry Bean Advisory Board (EA) .... CDBAB
California Dump Truck Owners Association (SRA) .... CDTOA
California Earthquake Authority .... CEA
California Eastern Airways .... CEA
California Eastern Laboratories (ACAE) .... CEL
California Ecology Corpsmen (SAUS) .... CECs
California Economic Development Agency (SAUS) .... CEDA
California Education and Research Federation .... CERF
California Education and Research Federation Network .... CERFNET
California Education Information System (SAUS) .... CEIS
California Educational and Research Federation Network (SAUO) .... CERFNET
California Educational Computing Consortium (EA) .... CECC
California Educational Data Processing Association (SAUO) .... CEDPA
California Egg Marketing and Research Agreement (SAUO) .... CEMRA
California Electric Power (SAUS) .... CAP
California Elementary School, Uniondale, NY [*Library symbol*] [*Library of Congress*] (LCLS) .... NUnCE
California Emergency Nurses Association (SAUO) .... CAL-ENA
California Encephalitis [*Medicine*] .... CE
California Encephalitis Virus [*Medicine*] (MELL) .... CEV
California Encephalitis-Virus (SAUS) .... CEV
California Energy Co. [*Associated Press*] (SAG) .... CalEng
California Energy Commission (ABAC) .... CEC
California Energy Resources Conservation and Development Commission (SAUO) .... CERCDC
California Engineering Foundation (EA) .... CEF
California Environmental Protection Agency (BCP) .... Cal/EPA
California Environmental Protection Program Fund (SAUO) .... CEPPF
California Environmental Quality Act (DOGT) .... CEQA
California Environmental Resources Evaluation System (AUEG) .... CERES
California Escrow Association (SRA) .... CEA
California Exposition (SAUO) .... Cal Expo
California Fashion Creators (EA) .... CFC
California Federal Bank [*NYSE symbol*] (SPSG) .... CAL
California Federal Bank [*Associated Press*] (SAG) .... CalFd
California Federal Bank [*Associated Press*] (SAG) .... CalFdCt
California Federal Bank [*Associated Press*] (SAG) .... CalFedl
California Federal Bank [*Associated Press*] (SAG) .... CalFSecCt
California Federal Bank [*NASDAQ symbol*] (SAG) .... CALG
California Federation of Research Internets (SAUO) .... CFRI
California Fertilizer Association (SRA) .... CFA
California Fig Advisory Board (EA) .... CFAB
California Fig Institute (EA) .... CFI
California Financial Corp. (SAUO) .... CFI
California Financial Holding Co. [*Associated Press*] (SAG) .... CalFncl
California Financial Holding Co. [*NASDAQ symbol*] (NQ) .... CFHC
California Fiscal Information System (SAUS) .... CFIS
California Fish Canners Association [*Later, TRF*] (EA) .... CFCA
California Fisheries Information Network [*Marine science*] (OSRA) .... CALFIN
California Flyers School of Aeronautics .... CFSA
California Folklore Quarterly (journ.) (SAUS) .... CFQ
California Forestry Association (SRA) .... CFA
California Freezers Association [*AFFI*] [*Absorbed by*] (EA) .... CFA
California Fruit Exchange [*Later, BAI*] (EA) .... CFE
California Fruit Growers Exchange (SAUO) .... CFGE
California General Corporation Law [*A publication*] (DLA) .... CA GCL
California Geotechnical Engineers Association (SRA) .... CGEA
California Glass Association (SRA) .... CGA
California Gold Mines Ltd. [*Toronto Stock Exchange symbol*] [*Vancouver Stock Exchange symbol*] .... CFA
California Grain annd Feed Association (SRA) .... CGFA
California Grape and Tree Fruit League (EA) .... CG & TFL
California Grape and Tree Fruit League (SAUO) .... CGTFL
California Grocers Association (SRA) .... CGA
California Groundwater Association (SRA) .... CGA
California Guaranteed Student Loans (EDAC) .... CGSL
California Health Federation (SRA) .... CHF
California Health Information Association (SRA) .... CHIA
California Healthcare Association (SRA) .... CHA
California Highway Patrol [*Acronym used as title of TV series*] .... CHiPS
California Highway Patrol (SAUO) .... CHP
California Historical Society (SAUO) .... Calif Hist
California Historical Society (SAUO) .... CHS
California Historical Society Quarterly (journ.) (SAUS) .... CHSQ
California Historical Society, San Francisco, CA [*Library symbol*] [*Library of Congress*] (LCLS) .... CHi
California Home Brands, Inc. (EFIS) .... CHB
California Horticultural Society (SAUO) .... CHS
California Hotel and Motel Association (SRA) .... CH&MA
California Housing Council (SRA) .... CHC
California Hungarian American Cultural Foundation (EA) .... CHACF
California Iceberg Lettuce Commission (EA) CILC
California Identification System (SAUS) .... Cal-ID
California Independant Bancorp [*Associated Press*] (SAG) .... Califlnd
California Independant Bancorp [*NASDAQ symbol*] (SAG) .... CIBN
California Independent Petroleum Association (SRA) .... CIPA
California Industrial Accident Commission, Compensation Cases [*A publication*] (DLA) .... Cal IACCC
California Industrial Accident Decisions [*A publication*] (DLA) .... Cal IAC Dec
California Industrial Accident Decisions [*A publication*] (DLA) .... Cal Ind Acci Dec
California Information Network [*Library network*] .... CALINET
California Information Practices Act (SAUS) .... CIPA
California Information Systems Implementation Committee (SAUO) .... CISIC
California Institute for Rural Studies (SAUO) .... CIRS
California Institute of Asian Studies [*An evening graduate school*] (EA) .... CIAS
California Institute of Asian Studies, San Francisco, CA [*Library symbol*] [*Library of Congress*] (LCLS) .... CSfCI
California Institute of Biological Research [*La Jolla*] .... CIBR
California Institute of Pan African Studies (SAUO) .... CIPAS
California Institute of Social Welfare .... CISW
California Institute of Technology [*Also, CALT, CALTECH, CIT*] [*Pasadena*] (MCD) .... CALIT
California Institute of Technology [*Also, CALIT, CALTECH, CIT*] [*Pasadena*] .... CALT
California Institute of Technology (SAUO) .... CalTec
California Institute of Technology [*Also, CALIT, CALT, CIT*] [*Pasadena*] .... CALTECH
California Institute of Technology .... Caltech
California Institute of Technology (GAGS) .... Cal Tech
California Institute of Technology [*Also, CALIT, CALT, CALTECH*] .... CIT
California Institute of Technology Concurrent Computation Project (SAUS) .... CCCP
California Institute of Technology/ Guggenheim Aeronautical Laboratory (SAUS) .... CIT/GAL
California Institute of Technology, Guggenheim Aeronautical Laboratory (SAUO) .... CIT GAL
California Institute of Technology, Jet Propulsion Laboratory (SAUO) .... CIT JPL
California Institute of Technology, Pasadena, CA [*Library symbol*] [*Library of Congress*] (LCLS) .... CPT
California Institute of Technology Synchrotron Laboratory (SAUO) .... CTSL
California Institute of Technology/Jet Propulsion Laboratory (SAUS) .... CIT/JPL
California Institute of the Arts [*Valencia, CA*] .... CalArts
California Institute of the Arts [*Valencia*] [*OCLC symbol*] (OCLC) .... CIA
California Institute of the Arts, Valencia, CA [*Library symbol*] [*Library of Congress*] (LCLS) .... CVaIA
[*The*] **California Institute of the Sisters of the Most Holy and Immaculate Heart of the Blessed Virgin Mary** (TOCD) .... IHM
California Institution for Women .... CIW
California Institution for Women at Frontera (SAUS) .... Frontera Girls
California Insurance Guarantee Association .... CIGA
California Integrated Remote Sensing System (GEOI) .... CIRSS
California Irrigation Management Information System (SAUO) .... CIMIS
California Jurisprudence [*A publication*] (DLA) .... Cal Jur
California Jurisprudence, Second Edition [*A publication*] (DLA) .... Cal Jur 2d
California Jury Instructions, Civil [*A publication*] (DLA) .... CAJI
California Jury Instructions, Criminal [*A publication*] (DLA) .... CAJC
California Jury Instructions, Criminal [*A publication*] (DLA) .... Cal JIC
California Kamchatka Companies (ECON) .... CKC
California Kiwifruit Commission (EA) .... CKC
California Labor Federation AFL-CIO Library, San Francisco, CA [*Library symbol*] [*Library of Congress*] (LCLS) .... CSfSFL
California Land Surveyors Association (GEOI) .... CLSA
California Law Enforcement Telecommunications System .... CLETS
California Law Journal [*A publication*] (DLA) .... Cal LJ
California Law Journal [*A publication*] (DLA) .... CLJ
California Law Journal and Literary Review [*A publication*] (DLA) .... CLJ & Lit Rev
California Law Review [*A publication*] .... Cal LR
California League Enlisting Action Now [*Antiobscenity group*] .... CLEAN
California League of Food Processors (SRA) .... CLFP
California League of Middle Schools (SRA) .... CLMS
California Legal Record [*A publication*] (DLA) .... Cal Leg Rec
California Legal Record [*A publication*] (DLA) .... C Leg Rec
California Legislative Service (West) [*A publication*] (DLA) .... Cal Legis Serv
California Library Association (SAUO) .... CLA
California Library Authority for Systems and Services [*Library network*] .... CLASS
California Library Automation Network (SAUS) .... CLAN
California Library Services Act Statewide Data Base [*California Library Services Board*] [*Information service or system*] (IID) .... CLSA-DB
California Library Services Board (SAUS) .... CLSB
California Licensed Foresters Association (SRA) .... CLFA
California Life Goals Evaluation Schedules [*Psychology*] .... CLGES
California Line Source Model [*Environmental Protection Agency*] (GFGA) .... CALINE
California Loans to Assist Students (EDAC) .... CLAS
California Lodging Industry Association (SRA) .... CLIA
California Low Emissions Vehicle (SAUS) .... CalLEV
California Low-Emission Vehicle [*Automotive industry*] .... CALLEV
California Lutheran College, Thousand Oaks, CA [*OCLC symbol*] (OCLC) .... CCT
California Lutheran College, Thousand Oaks, CA [*Library symbol*] [*Library of Congress*] (LCLS) .... CToL
California Lutheran University (GAGS) .... Cal Luth U
California Macadamia Society (EA) .... CMS
California Malacozoological Society (SAUO) .... CMS
California Manpower Management Information System Project (SAUS) .... CMMISP

California Manufacturers Register [*Database Publishing*] [*Information service or system*] (CRD) ... CMR
California Map Society (GEOI) ... CMS
California Marijuana Initiative (SAUO) ... CMI
California Marine Associates (SAUO) ... CALMA
California Marine Mammal Center [*Research center*] (RCD) ... CMMC
California Maritime Academy [*Vallejo*] ... CMA
California Maritime Academy, Vallejo, CA [*Library symbol*] [*Library of Congress*] (LCLS) ... CVM
California Marriage Readiness Evaluation [*Psychology*] ... CMRE
California Mastitis Test [*Medicine*] (DMAA) ... CM
California Mastitis Test ... CMT
California, MD [*FM radio station call letters*] (BROA) ... WKIK-FM
California, MD [*FM radio station call letters*] ... WRFK
California Medical Association (MELL) ... CMA
California Medical Facility (SAUS) ... CMF
California Medical Survey [*Psychology*] ... CMS
California Medicine (journ.) (SAUS) ... Calif Med
California Melon Research Board (EA) ... CMRB
California Mental Health Analysis [*Testing*] ... CMHA
California Micro Devices Corp. [*Associated Press*] (SAG) ... CalMicr
California Micro Devices Corp. [*NASDAQ symbol*] (SAG) ... CAMD
California Microfilm Co., Fresno, CA [*Library symbol*] [*Library of Congress*] (LCLS) ... CmC
California Microwave, Inc. [*Associated Press*] (SAG) ... CalMic
California Microwave, Inc. [*NASDAQ symbol*] (NQ) ... CMIC
California Microwave, Incorporated (SAUO) ... CMI
California Milk Producers (SRA) ... CMP
California Mine and Safety Code (SAUS) ... CMSC
California Mining Journal (SAUO) ... CMJ
California, MO [*FM radio station call letters*] (RBYB) ... KATI
California, MO [*AM radio station call letters*] (RBYB) ... KREL
California Motor Vehicle Pollution Control Board (SAUO) ... CMVPCB
California Motor Vehicles Pollution Board (SAUS) ... CMVPB
California Museum of Science (SAUS) ... CMS
California Museum of Science and Industry (SAUS) ... CMS&I
California Music Educators Association (SAUO) ... CMEA
California Narcotic Addict Evaluation Authority (SAUS) ... CNAEA
California Narcotic Information Network (SAUS) ... CNIN
California Narcotics Officers Association (SRA) ... CNOA
California National Fuchsia Society [*Later, NFS*] ... CNFS
California National Guard (SAUO) ... CNG
California Native Plant Society (SAUO) ... CNPS
California Natural Diversity Data Base [*California State Department of Fish and Game*] [*Information service or system*] (IID) ... CNDDB
California Natural Gas Association ... CNGA
California Network [*US Geological Survey*] ... CALNET
California Newspaper Publishing Association (SAUO) ... CNPA
California Nurses Association (SRA) ... CNA
California Occupational Preference Inventory [*Psychology*] (DAVI) ... COPI
California Occupational Preference Survey ... COPS
California Occupational Safety and Health Administration (SAUO) ... CAL-OSHA
California Olive Association (EA) ... COA
California Olive Industry News ... COIN
California Optometric Association (SRA) ... COA
California Orthopaedic Association (SRA) ... COA
California Outdoor Recreation Resources Plan (SAUO) ... CORRP
California, PA [*FM radio station call letters*] ... WVCS
California Pacific Conference (PSS) ... CPC
California Pacific University (SAUO) ... CPU
California Packing Corporation (SAUO) ... CFF
California Palace of the Legion of Honor [*San Francisco*] ... CPLN
California Palace of the Legion of Honor, San Francisco, CA [*Library symbol*] [*Library of Congress*] (LCLS) ... CSfLH
California Parks and Wildlife Initiative (SAUS) ... CalPAW
California Penal Code [*A publication*] (DLA) ... Cal Penal Code
California Persimmon Growers Association (EA) ... CPGA
California Personality [*or Psychological*] **Inventory** ... CPI
California Physicians Service (SAUS) ... CPS
California Pistachio Association (EA) ... CPA
California Pistachio Commission (EA) ... CPC
California Pizza Kitchen, Inc. ... CPK
California Podiatric Medical Association (SRA) ... CPMA
California Polytechnic College (SAUS) ... CPC
California Polytechnic State University (PDAA) ... CPSU
California Polytechnic State University in San Luis Obispo (SAUO) ... Cal Poly
California Polytechnic State University, Pomona, CA [*OCLC symbol*] (OCLC) ... CPO
California Polytechnic State University, Pomona, CA [*Library symbol*] [*Library of Congress*] (LCLS) ... CPomCP
California Polytechnic State University, San Luis Obispo, CA [*OCLC symbol*] (OCLC) ... CPS
California Polytechnic State University, San Luis Obispo, CA [*Library symbol*] [*Library of Congress*] (LCLS) ... CSluSP
California Porter-Cologne Water Quality Control Act (SAUS) ... CPCWQCA
California Poultry Industry Federation (SRA) ... CPIF
California Practice [*A publication*] (DLA) ... Cal Prac
California Prehospital Research and Education Foundation (SAUO) ... CPREF
California Preschool Scale of Social Competence (EDAC) ... CPSSC
California Primate Research Center [*Research center*] (RCD) ... CPRC
California Pro Sports, Inc. [*NASDAQ symbol*] (SAG) ... CALP
California Pro Sports, Inc. [*Associated Press*] (SAG) ... CalPro
California Pro Sports Wrrt [*NASDAQ symbol*] (TTSB) ... CALPW
California Probation, Parole, and Correctional Association ... CPPCA
California Production Service (SAUS) ... CPS
California Prune Advisory Board [*Later, CPB*] ... CPAB
California Prune and Apricot Growers Association [*Later, Sunsweet Growers*] ... CPAGA
California Prune Board (EA) ... CPB
California Psychological Inventory (SAUS) ... CPI
California Psychological Inventory Test (DIPS) ... CPIT
California Public Administrator, Public Guardian, and Public Conservator Association (SRA) ... CPAPGPCA
California Public Employee Relations Program (EA) ... CPER
California Public Employees Retirement System [*Pension fund*] ... CalPERS
California Public Interest Research Group (SAUO) ... CALPIRG
California Public Records Act (SAUS) ... CPRA
California Public Television Stations (SAUS) ... CPTS
California Public Utilities Commission (SAUO) ... CPUC
California Q-Set [*Psychology*] ... CQS
California Radiological Society (SAUO) ... CRS
California Railroad Commission Digest of Decisions [*A publication*] (DLA) ... Cal RC Dec
California Railroad Commission Digest of Decisions [*A publication*] (DLA) ... Cal RC Dec Dig
California Railroad Commission Digest of Decisions [*A publication*] (DLA) ... CRC
California Raisin Advisory Board (EA) ... CALRAB
California Raisin Advisory Board (EA) ... CRAB
California Rare Fruit Growers (EA) ... CRFG
California Real Estate Investment Trust [*Associated Press*] (SAG) ... CalRE
California Real Estate Investment Trust SBI [*NYSE symbol*] (SPSG) ... CT
California Redwood Association (EA) ... CRA
California Regional Land Use Information System (SAUS) ... CRLUIS
California Regional Primate Research Center (GVA) ... CRPRC
California Regional Water Quality Control Board (BCP) ... CRWQCB
California Regulatory Notice Register [*A publication*] (AAGC) ... Cal Reg Notice Reg
California Relative Value Studies [*Medicine*] (DHSM) ... CRVS
California Remote Sensing Council (GEOI) ... CRSC
California Reporter [*A publication*] (DLA) ... CA R
California Reporter (West) [*A publication*] (DLA) ... Cal Rptr
California Reports [*A publication*] (DLA) ... C
California Reports [*A publication*] (DLA) ... Cal
California Reports [*A publication*] (DLA) ... Calif
California Reports [*A publication*] (DLA) ... Cal Rep
California Reports, Second Series [*A publication*] (DLA) ... Cal 2d
California Reports, Third Series [*A publication*] (DLA) ... Cal 3d
California Research and Education Network [*Computer science*] (TNIG) ... CALREN
California Research Corp., Richmond, CA [*Library symbol*] [*Library of Congress*] (LCLS) ... CRicCR
California Resource Recovery Association (SAUO) ... CRRA
California Resources Agency, Sacramento, CA [*Library symbol*] [*Library of Congress*] (LCLS) ... CSRes
California Rug Study Society (EA) ... CRSS
California Rural Legal Assistance (BARN) ... CRLA
California Rural Legal Assistance, Inc. (SAUO) ... CRLA
California Scholarship Federation (ACAE) ... CSF
California School Boards Association (SRA) ... CSBA
California School Employees Association (SRA) ... CSEA
California School Library Association ... CSLA
California School Nurses Organization (SAUS) ... CSNO
California School of Fine Arts ... CSFA
California School of Professional Psychology ... CSPP
California School of Professional Psychology, Fresno, CA [*Library symbol*] [*Library of Congress*] (LCLS) ... CFSP
California Seismic Safety Commission (SAUS) ... CSSC
California Self-Insurers Association (SRA) ... CSIA
California Separation Science Society (SAUO) ... CaSSS
California Service Station and Automotive Repair Association (SRA) ... CSSARA
California Society for Healthcare Attorneys (SRA) ... CSHA
California Society of Addiction Medicine (SRA) ... CSAM
California Society of Certified Public Accountants (SRA) ... CSCPA
California Society of Enrolled Agents (SRA) ... CSEA
California Society of Pathologists (SRA) ... CSP
California Society of Periodontists (SRA) ... CSP
California Society of Professional Engineers (SRA) ... CSPE
California Society of Radiologic Technologists (SRA) ... CSRT
California Solar Energy Industries Association (SRA) ... CAL-SEIA
California Space Institute (SAUO) ... CalSpace
California Spanish Language Data Base [*Information service or system*] (IID) ... CSLDB
California Spanish Language Data Base, Oakland, CA [*Library symbol*] [*Library of Congress*] (LCLS) ... COCSL
California Special Districts Association (SRA) ... CSDA
California Spray-Chemical Corp. (SAUO) ... Calspray
California State Automobile Association (ACRL) ... CSAA
California State Bank [*Associated Press*] (SAG) ... CalSBk
California State Bank [*NASDAQ symbol*] (NQ) ... CSTB
California State Bar Journal [*A publication*] (DLA) ... Calif SBJ
California State Bar Journal [*A publication*] (DLA) ... Cal SBJ
California State College at Fresno ... CSCF
California State College, Bakersfield, CA [*OCLC symbol*] (OCLC) ... CBA
California State College, Bakersfield, CA [*Library symbol*] [*Library of Congress*] (LCLS) ... CBaS
California State College, California, PA [*OCLC symbol*] (OCLC) ... CSC
California State College, California, PA [*Library symbol*] [*Library of Congress*] (LCLS) ... PCalS

California State College, Dominguez Hills [*Later, California State University, Dominguez Hills*], Dominguez Hills, CA [*Library symbol*] [*Library of Congress*] .... CDhS
California State College, San Bernardino (PDAA) .... CSCSB
California State College, San Bernardino, San Bernardino, CA [*OCLC symbol*] (OCLC) .... CSB
California State College, San Bernardino, San Bernardino, CA [*Library symbol*] [*Library of Congress*] (LCLS) .... CSbC
California State College, Sonoma, Rohnert Park, CA [*Library symbol*] [*Library of Congress*] (LCLS) .... CRpS
California State College, Stanislaus, Turlock, CA [*OCLC symbol*] (OCLC) ..... CTU
California State College, Stanislaus, Turlock, CA [*Library symbol*] [*Library of Congress*] (LCLS) .... CTurS
California State Department of Fish and Game, Marine Technical Information Center, San Pedro, CA [*Library symbol*] [*Library of Congress*] (LCLS) .... C-F
California State Department of Mental Hygiene, Metropolitan State Hospital Professional Staff Library, Norwalk, CA [*Library symbol*] [*Library of Congress*] (LCLS) .... CNwMH
California State, Division of Highways, Bridge Department (SAUO) ..... CA-HY-BD
California State Division of Mines, San Francisco, CA [*Library symbol*] [*Library of Congress*] (LCLS) .... CSfCSM
California State Electronics Association (SAUO) .... CSEA
California State Employee's Association (SRA) .... CSEA
California State Fire Marshall (SARE) .... CSFM
California State Firefighters Association (SRA) .... CSFA
California State [*University*], Hayward [*California*] [*Seismograph station code, US Geological Survey*] (SEIS) .... CSH
California State Horseman's Association (SRA) .... CSHA
California State Influenza Vaccine Program (SAUS) .... CSIVP
California State Law Library, Sacramento, CA [*Library symbol*] [*Library of Congress*] (LCLS) .... C-L
California State Library, Law (SAUS) .... SLAW
California State Library, Sacramento, CA [*Library symbol*] [*Library of Congress*] (LCLS) C
California State Library, Sutro Branch, San Francisco, CA [*Library symbol*] [*Library of Congress*] (LCLS) .... C-S
California State Managers and Supervisors (SRA) .... CSMSA
California State Polytechnic College [*Later, California Polytechnic State University*] .... CSPC
California State Polytechnic University at Pomona (GAGS) .... Cal St Poly U (Pomona)
California State Polytechnic University at San Luis Obispo (GAGS) .... Cal St Poly U (San Luis Obispo)
California State Polytechnic University of Pomona (MCD) .... CSPUP
California State Psychological Association .... CSPA
California State Supervisors (SRA) .... CSS
California State Universities and Colleges (SAUS) .... CSUC
California State University [*Formerly, San Francisco State College*] .... CSU
California State University and Colleges [*System*] .... CSUC
California State University and Colleges, Tape Profile, Long Beach, CA [*OCLC symbol*] (OCLC) .... CAC
California State University at Chico (GAGS) .... Cal St U (Chico)
California State University at Dominguez Hills (GAGS) .... Cal St U (Dominguez Hills)
California State University at Fresno (GAGS) .... Cal St U (Fresno)
California State University at Fullerton (GAGS) .... Cal St U (Fullerton)
California State University at Hayward (GAGS) .... Cal St U (Hayward)
California State University at Humboldt (SAUO) .... CSUH
California State University at Long Beach (GAGS) .... Cal St U (Long Beach)
California State University at Los Angeles (GAGS) .... Cal St U (LA)
California State University at Los Angeles (SAUO) .... CSULA
California State University at Northridge (GAGS) .... Cal St U (Northridge)
California State University at Sacramento (GAGS) .... Cal St U (Sacramento)
California State University at San Bernardino (GAGS) ..... Cal St U (San Bernardino)
California State University at San Bernardino (SAUO) .... CSUSB
California State University at San Diego (SAUO) .... CSUSD
California State University at San Francisco (SAUO) .... CSUSF
California State University at Stanislaus (GAGS) .... Cal St U (Stanislaus)
California State University, Chico .... CSUC
California State University, Chico, Chico, CA [*OCLC symbol*] (OCLC) .... CCH
California State University, Chico, Chico, CA [*Library symbol*] [*Library of Congress*] (LCLS) .... CChiS
California State University, Dominguez Hills, Carson, CA [*OCLC symbol*] (OCLC) .... CDH
California State University, Fresno (PDAA) .... CSUF
California State University, Fresno, Fresno, CA [*Library symbol*] [*Library of Congress*] [*OCLC symbol*] (LCLS) .... CFS
California State University, Fullerton, Fullerton, CA [*OCLC symbol*] (OCLC) .... CFI
California State University, Fullerton, Fullerton, CA [*Library symbol*] [*Library of Congress*] (LCLS) .... CFIS
California State University, Hayward, Hayward, CA [*Library symbol*] [*Library of Congress*] (LCLS) .... CHS
California State University, Hayward, Hayward, CA [*OCLC symbol*] (OCLC) .... CSH
California State University, Long Beach .... CSULB
California State University, Long Beach, Long Beach, CA [*OCLC symbol*] (OCLC) .... CLO
California State University, Long Beach, Long Beach, CA [*Library symbol*] [*Library of Congress*] (LCLS) .... CLobS
California State University, Los Angeles, Los Angeles, CA [*OCLC symbol*] (OCLC) .... CLA
California State University, Los Angeles, Los Angeles, CA [*Library symbol*] [*Library of Congress*] (LCLS) .... CLS

[*The*] California State University Network [*Computer science*] (TNIG) .... CSUnet
California State University Network (SAUO) .... CSUNET
California State University, Northridge .... CSUN
California State University, Northridge, Northridge, CA [*OCLC symbol*] (OCLC) .... CNO
California State University, Northridge, Northridge, CA [*Library symbol*] [*Library of Congress*] (LCLS) .... CNoS
California State University, Sacramento .... CSUS
California State University, Sacramento, Sacramento, CA [*OCLC symbol*] (OCLC) .... CSA
California State University, Sacramento, Sacramento, CA [*Library symbol*] [*Library of Congress*] (LCLS) .... CSS
California State Water Resources Control Board (SAUO) .... CSWRCB
California Strawberry Advisory Board (EA) .... CSAB
California Student Opportunity and Access Program (EDAC) .... CAL-SOAP
California Superior Court, Reports of Cases in Appellate Departments [*A publication*] (DLA) .... Cal Sup
California Superior Court, Reports of Cases in Appellate Departments [*A publication*] (DLA) .... Cal Sup (Cal)
California Supplement [*A publication*] (DLA) .... Cal Sup
California Supreme Court Reports [*A publication*] (DLA) C
California Supreme Court Reports, Second Series [*A publication*] (DLA) C2d
California Supreme Court Reports, Third Series [*A publication*] (DLA) C3d
California Supreme Court, San Francisco, CA [*Library symbol*] [*Library of Congress*] (LCLS) .... C-SC
California Sweet Potato Growers (SRA) .... CSPG
California Table Grape Commission (EA) .... CTGC
California Teachers Association (SAUO) .... CTA
California Teachers Association, Burlingame, CA [*Library symbol*] [*Library of Congress*] (LCLS) .... CBuCTA
California Technical Industries (SAUO) .... CTI
California Technical Institute (SAUS) .... CTI
California Terms [*Grain shipping*] .... CT
California Test Bureau [*McGraw Hill, Inc.*] [*Psychology*] .... CTB
California Test of Basic Skills [*Education*] .... CTBS
California Test of Mental Maturity .... CTMM
California Test of Personality [*Psychology*] .... CTP
California Texas Oil Co. .... CALTEX
California Texas Oil Corp. (SAUO) .... Caltex
California Tomorrow [*An association*] (EA) .... CT
California Total Educational Information System (SAUO) .... CTEIS
California Traffic Safety Foundation [*Defunct*] (EA) .... CTSF
California Travel Industry Association (SRA) .... CALTIA
California Trial Lawyers Association .... CAOC
California Trial Lawyers Journal [*A publication*] (DLA) .... CTLJ
California Trucking Association (SAUO) .... CTA
California Tumor Registry .... CTR
California Turkey (SAUS) .... CT
California Ultra-Low-Emission Vehicle [*Automotive industry*] .... CALULEV
California Undersea Aqueduct Reconnaissance-Oceanography Study [*Department of the Interior*] (GFGA) .... CUARO
California Union List of Periodicals [*Cooperative Library Agency for Systems and Services*] [*Database*] .... CULP
California Union of Safety Employees (SRA) .... CAUSE
California United Terminal (SAUS) .... CUT
California Universities Council on Space Sciences .... CUCOSS
California University Cyclotron .... CALUTRON
California University of Pennsylvania (GAGS) .... Cal U (Pa)
California Unreported Cases [*1855-1910*] [*A publication*] (DLA) .... Cal Unrep
California Unreported Cases [*1855-1910*] [*A publication*] (DLA) .... Cal Unrep Cas
California Unreported Cases [*1855-1910*] [*A publication*] (DLA) .... Cal Urep
California Unreported Cases [*1855-1910*] [*A publication*] (DLA) .... CA U
California Unreported Cases [*1855-1910*] [*A publication*] (DLA) .... CU
California Upwelling Variability Experiment (SAUS) .... CUVE
California Vehicle Act (SAUS) .... CVA
California Venereal Disease Advisory Council (SAUO) .... Cal-VDAC
California Verbal Learning Test (DHP) .... CVLT
California Verbal Learning Test, Children's Version (TMMY) .... CVLT-C
California Veterinary Diagnostic Laboratory System .... CVDLS
California Video Research Project (SAUS) .... CVRP
California Virtual University .... CVU
California Warehouse Association (SRA) .... CWA
California Water Association (SRA) .... CWA
California Water Resources Association (SAUO) .... CWRA
California Water Service (SAUS) .... CWS
California Water Service Co. [*Associated Press*] (SAG) .... CalWtr
California Water Service Co. [*NYSE symbol*] (SAG) .... CWT
California Western Railroad [*AAR code*] .... CWR
California Western School of Law (GAGS) .... Cal West Sch of Law
California Western School of Law Library, San Diego, CA [*OCLC symbol*] (OCLC) .... CWE
California Western School of Law, San Diego, CA [*Library symbol*] [*Library of Congress*] (LCLS) .... CSdCWL
California Western University (SAUO) .... CWU
California Wheelchair Aviators (EA) .... CWA
California Wilderness Survival League (EA) .... CWSL
California Wildlife Federation (SAUO) .... CWF
California Workers' Compensation Institute .... CWCI
California World Trade Center (SAUS) .... CWTC
California Yoga Teachers Association (EA) .... CYTA
California Youth Activities (SAUO) .... CYA
California-Arizona Citrus League (SRA) .... CACL
California-grown Avocado (SAUS) .... CALAVO
California-Hawaii-Orient Airline (SAUS) .... Transocean
Californian (SAUS) .... Calif

Californian Rabbit Specialty Club (EA) .... CRSC
California-Nevada Conference of Operating Engineers (SRA) .... CNCOE
Californians for Justice (SAUS) .... CFJ
California-Pacific Utilities Co. (SAUO) .... CLP
California's Wine Wonderland [*A publication*] (EAAP) .... CWW
Californium [*Chemical element*] .... Cf
Californium-252 Plasma Desorption Mass Spectrometry .... CFPDMS
Califronia Association of Alcoholism and Drug Abuse Counselors (SRA) .... CAADAC
Caligula [*the Poisoner*] [*the Hun*] [*the Emperor*] [*Initials that form the name of the villain in "Captain Marvel" comic strip and indicate the sources of his power*] .... IBAC
Caliop [*France*] [*ICAO designator*] (FAAC) .... IOP
Calipatria, CA [*Location identifier*] [*FAA*] (FAAL) .... CLR
Calipatria, CA [*Television station call letters*] (BROA) .... KAJB
Calipatria, CA [*FM radio station call letters*] .... KSSB
Caliper .... CLPR
Caliper Disk Brake .... CDB
Caliper Logging Tool (SAUS) .... CALI
Calistoga [*California*] [*Seismograph station code, US Geological Survey*] [*Closed*] (SEIS) .... CLS
Calistoga, CA [*FM radio station call letters*] (BROA) .... KGRP-FM
Calistoga Free Public Library, Calistoga, CA [*Library symbol*] [*Library of Congress*] (LCLS) .... CCali
Calix [*Anatomy*] (MAE) .... K
Calix Society (EA) .... CS
Calking (SAUS) .... CLKG
Call (IAA) C
Call Acceptance Delay (SAUS) .... CAD
Call Accounting Reconciliation Process [*Telecommunications*] (TEL) .... CARP
Call Accounting System [*or Subsystem*] [*Telecommunications*] .... CAS
Call Accounting System for Hotels [*Telecommunications*] (IAA) .... CASH
Call Address (SAUS) .... CA
Call Address Code [*Telecommunications*] (ECII) .... CDC
Call Admission Control (SAUS) .... CAC
Call Aircraft Co. .... CAL
Call Assembly Index (SAUS) .... CAI
Call Attempts per Second [*Telecommunications*] (TEL) .... CAPS
Call Back [*Word processing*] .... CB
Call Back Control Protocol [*Computer science*] (VERA) .... CBCP
Call Box Discrimination [*Telecommunications*] (TEL) .... CBD
Call Box Station (MSA) .... CBS
Call Center (SAUO) CC
Call Charge Record (ADA) .... CCR
Call Check [*Telecommunications*] (NITA) CC
Call Command (SAUS) CC
Call Command Exit [*IBM Corp*] (CIST) .... CCE
Call Completion to Busy Subscriber [*Telecommunications*] (CIST) .... CCBS
Call Confirmation (SAUS) CC
Call Connected (SAUS) CC
Call Contract CC
Call Control (CGWS) CC
Call Control Agent Function (VERA) .... CCAF
Call Control Module (CCCA) .... CCM
Call Control Processing [*Telecommunications*] (TEL) .... CCP
Call Control Systems [*San Clemente, CA*] [*Telecommunications*] (TSSD) .... CCS
Call Count Meter [*Telecommunications*] (NITA) .... CCM
Call Data Accumulator (SAUS) .... CDA
Call Data Transmitter (ROAS) .... CDT
Call Deflection [*Telecommunications*] (DOM) .... CD
Call Description Language [*Computer science*] (PDAA) .... CDL
Call Detail Recording [*Telecommunications*] (TEL) .... CDR
Call Detail Recording and Reporting (SAUS) .... CDRR
Call Detector (IAA) .... CD
Call Directing (or Direction) Character (SAUS) .... CDC
Call Directing (or Direction) Code (SAUS) .... CDC
Call Director (SAA) .... CD
Call Director Unit .... CDU
Call Disconnect [*Telecommunications*] (ACRL) .... CD
Call Dispatch (IAA) .... CD
Call Diverter (NITA) .... CADI
Call Division Multiple Access (SAUS) .... CDMA
Call Failed [*or Failure*] [*Telecommunications*] (TEL) .... CFL
Call Failed (or Failure) (SAUS) .... CFL
Call Failure Detection Equipment [*Telecommunications*] (NITA) .... CFDE
Call Failure Indication (SAUS) .... CFI
Call Failure Indication, Engaged Tone (SAUS) .... CFIET
Call Failure Indication, No Tone (SAUS) .... CFINT
Call Failure Signal (SAUS) .... CFL Signal
Call Finder [*Telecommunications*] .... CF
Call for Action [*An association*] (NTCM) .... CFA
Call for Action, Inc. (EA) .... CFAI
Call for Discussion [*Internet dialogue*] (VERA) .... CFD
Call For Papers (SAUS) .... CFP
Call For Proposals (SAUS) .... CFP
Call for Service (SAUS) .... CFS
Call for Vote [*Computer hacker terminology*] .... CFV
Call Forward Busy .... CFB
Call Forward Directive [*World War II*] .... CFD
Call Forwarding Busy [*Telecommunications*] (DOM) .... CFB
Call Forwarding No Reply [*Telecommunications*] (DOM) .... CFNR
Call Forwarding Unconditional [*Telecommunications*] (DOM) .... CFU
Call Handler for Advanced Telephone Services [*Telecommunications*] (NITA) .... CHATS
Call Hold [*Telecommunications*] (DOM) .... HOLD
Call Hold and Trace [*Telecommunications*] (TEL) .... CHT
Call Holding Time [*Telecommunications*] (TEL) .... CHT
Call Identification Line [*Telecommunications*] (NITA) CIL
Call Identity Index (SAUS) CII
Call Indicator [*Computer science*] CI
Call Information Logging [*Telecommunications*] (NITA) CIL
Call Information Logging Equipment [*Computer science*] (PDAA) .... CILE
Call Information Protocol (SAUS) .... CIP
Call Instruction (SAUS) CI
Call Interception (SAUS) .... CINT
Call Intrusion (SAUS) CI
Call Key [*Telecommunications*] .... CK
Call Level Interface [*Computer science*] CLI
Call Library (SAUS) CL
Call Loan [*Banking*] CL
Call Macro-Instruction (SAUS) .... CMI
Call Management Center (SAUO) .... CMC
Call Management Language [*Telecommunications*] (ACRL) .... CAMEL
Call Management System [*Accounting package*] (CDE) .... CMS
Call Me God (SAUS) .... CMG
Call Modification Complete (SAUS) .... CMC
Call Modification Request (SAUS) .... CMR
Call Money [*Investment term*] .... CM
Call Monitor (NOAA) .... CALM
Call Net Enterprises [*Associated Press*] (SAG) .... CallNet
Call Net Enterprises [*NASDAQ symbol*] (SAG) .... CNEB
Call Number [*Online database field identifier*] .... CN
Call Number Identification (IAA) .... CNI
Call of Business .... COB
Call of Cathulhu (SAUS) .... COC
Call of More [*Stock exchange term*] [*British*] (ROG) .... C/M
Call Offer (SAUO) .... CO
Call on Carry (SAUS) CC
Call on Minus (SAUS) .... CM
Call on No Carry (SAUS) .... CNC
Call on No Zero (SAUS) .... CNZ
Call on Parity Odd (SAUS) .... CPO
Call on Positive (SAUS) .... CP
Call on Zero (SAUS) .... CZ
Call Option [*Investment term*] .... CO
Call Originate Status [*Telecommunications*] (HGAA) .... COS
Call Out (ACAE) .... C/O
Call Out (ACAE) .... CO
Call Paid [*Telecommunications*] (ADA) .... CP
Call Parity Even (SAUS) .... CPE
Call Path Service Architecture (SAUS) .... CSA
Call Process [*Telecommunications*] (NITA) .... CP
Call Processing Subsystem (SAUS) .... CPS
Call Processing/Voice Messaging (BTTJ) .... CP/VM
Call Processor [*Computer science*] .... CP
Call Progress Indicator [*Telecommunications*] (TEL) .... CPI
Call Progress Signal (SAUS) .... CPS
Call Progress Signal (SAUS) .... CP Signal
Call Protocol Message [*Telecommunications*] (TEL) .... CPM
Call Quickly Distress [*International telegrapher's signal for an emergency*] (WDMC) .... CQD
Call Reference (SAUS) .... CaRe
Call Reference Value [*Telecommunications*] (ACRL) .... CRV
Call Request [*Telecommunications*] .... CR
Call Request [*Telecommunications*] (TEL) .... CRQ
Call Request with Identification (SAUS) .... CRI
Call Routine Display Panel (IAA) .... CDP
Call Sign (PIAV) .... c/s
Call Sign [*or Signal*] [*Radio*] .... CS
Call Signs and/or Address Group Remain Same (MUGU) .... CADSAME
Call Statement (SAUS) .... CS
Call Store [*Telecommunications*] (TEL) .... CS
Call Subscriber ID (SAUS) .... CSID
Call Supervision Message (SAUS) .... CSM
Call Supervision Module [*Telecommunications*] (TEL) .... CSM
Call System (SAUS) .... CS
Call Time Adjustor [*Military communications*] .... CTA
Call Time Value (SAUS) .... CT Value
Call to Australia [*Political party*] .... CTA
Call to Australia - Democratic Labor Party Coalition [*Political party*] .... CTA-DLP
Call To Quarter [*Wire-service jargon for correction*] (WDMC) .... cq
Call to Quarters [*General call preceding transmission of radio signals*] .... CQ
Call to Stations (SAUS) .... CTS
Call Transfer (SAUS) .... CT
Call Transfer (SAUS) .... XFR
Call Transfer all Calls Attendant (SAUS) .... XAA
Call Transfer all Calls Internal (SAUS) .... XAI
Call Transfer all Calls, No restrictions (SAUS) .... XAN
Call Transfer all Calls, Outside (SAUS) .... XAO
Call Transfer Incoming only, Internal (SAUS) XII
Call Transfer Incoming only, No Restrictions (SAUS) .... XIN
Call Transfer Incoming only, Outside (SAUS) .... XIO
Call Transfer Outside (SAUS) .... CTO
Call Treatment Flag (SAUS) .... CTF
Call Up [*Unix*] (VERA) .... CU
Call Waiting [*Telephone communication*] .... CW
Call Waiting (SAUS) .... CWT
Call Waiting Indication [*Telecommunications*] (TEL) .... CWI
Call Word (SAUS) .... CW
Calla Lillies (SAUS) .... Callas

Callable Bond [*Investment term*]	CA
Callable Bond [*Investment term*]	CB
Callahan, FL [*AM radio station call letters*]	WELX
Callahan, FL [*FM radio station call letters*] (RBYB)	WPLA
Callahan, FL [*FM radio station call letters*] (RBYB)	WPLA-FM
Callahan Mining Corporation (SAUO)	CMN
Callan's Military Laws of the United States [*A publication*] (DLA)	Call Mil L
Callan's Military Laws of the United States [*A publication*] (DLA)	Cal Mil Laws
Callao Cave National Park	CCNP
Callao Caves [*Philippines*] [*Seismograph station code, US Geological Survey*] (SEIS)	CVP
Callaway Elementary School, Callaway, MN [*Library symbol*] [*Library of Congress*] (LCLS)	MnCalE
Callaway, FL [*FM radio station call letters*]	WDRK
Callaway, FL [*FM radio station call letters*] (BROA)	WMXP-FM
Callaway Golf Co. [*Associated Press*] (SAG)	CallGolf
Callaway Golf Co. [*NYSE symbol*] (SAG)	ELY
Callaway Mills Co. (SAUS)	GLagCM
Callaway Mills Co., Technical Library (SAUO)	GLagCM
Callaway Mills Co., Technical Library, LaGrange, GA [*Library symbol*] [*Library of Congress*] (LCLS)	GLagCM
Callaway Plant (NRCH)	CP
Call-Back Control Protocol (SAUS)	CBCP
Call-Detail Routing [*Telecommunications*] (TSSD)	CDR
Call-Detail-Recording/Station-Message-Detail-Recording [*Telecommunications*]	CDR/SMDR
Calle	CLL
Called	cld
Called [*In stock listings of newspapers*] [*Business term*]	CLD
Called Game [*Baseball*]	Cg
Called Line (ECII)	CLD
Called Line Identification (SAUS)	CLI
Called Line Identity (SAUS)	CLI
Called Number Delivery (SAUS)	CND
Called Number Identification (SAUS)	CNI
Called Output Image	COI
Called Subscriber Answer [*Telecommunications*] (TEL)	CSA
Called Subscriber Busy [*Telecommunications*] (NITA)	CSB
Called Subscriber Held [*Telecommunications*] (TEL)	CSH
Called Subscriber Identification (SAUS)	CSI
Called to See Patient [*Medicine*] (CPH)	CTSP
Called to the Bar [*British*] (ROG)	B
Caller Number Delivery [*Computer science*] (VERA)	CND
Callerlab-International Association of Square Dance Callers (NTPA)	CALLERLAB
Callex Enterprises Ltd. [*Vancouver Stock Exchange symbol*]	CLS
Callex Mineral Exploration [*Vancouver Stock Exchange symbol*]	CXX
Call-for-Fire-Zone [*Army*]	CFFZ
Callier Center for Communication Disorders, Dallas, TX [*Library symbol*] [*Library of Congress*] (LCLS)	TxDaCCD
calligrapher (SAUS)	callig
Calligrapher [*MARC relator code*] [*Library of Congress*] (LCCP)	cll
Calligrapher	CLLGRPHR
calligraphic (SAUS)	callig
Calligraphy (VRA)	calig
calligraphy (SAUS)	callig
Calligraphy Society of Victoria [*Australia*]	CSV
Callimachus [*Third century BC*] [*Classical studies*] (OCD)	Callim
Call-In Time [*Military communications*]	CIT
Calling (ROG)	CALLG
Calling (DEN)	CLG
Calling (SAUS)	CNG
Calling All Stations [*Amateur radio shorthand*] (WDAA)	CQ
Calling card Authorization Center (SAUS)	CAC
Calling Card Service [*Bell System*]	CCS
Calling Card Validation (ROAS)	CCV
Calling Device [*Telecommunications*]	CD
Calling for Bunkers only (SAUS)	CFBO
Calling for Orders [*Shipping*]	CFO
Calling Instruction (SAUS)	CI
Calling Lake School, Alberta [*Library symbol*] [*National Library of Canada*] (BIB)	ACALLS
Calling Line (SAUS)	CL
Calling Line (ECII)	CLG
Calling Line Directory Number	CLDN
Calling Line Identification [*or Identity*] [*Telecommunications*] (TEL)	CLI
Calling Line Identification [*Telecommunications*] (ACRL)	CLID
Calling Line Identification Presentation [*Telecommunications*] (DOM)	CLIP
Calling Line Identification Restriction [*Telecommunications*] (DOM)	CLIR
Calling Name Identification Presentation (SAUS)	CNIP
Calling Name Identification Restriction (SAUS)	CNIR
Calling Number Display [*Telecommunications*]	CND
Calling Party Answer (SAUO)	CPA
Calling Party Cannot Hear [*Telecommunications*] (TEL)	CPCH
Calling Party Forced Release [*Telecommunications*] (TEL)	CPFR
Calling Party Number [*Telecommunications*]	CPN
Calling Party Pays (CGWS)	CPP
Calling Party's Category [*Telecommunications*] (TEL)	CPC
Calling Processing Subsystem [*Telecommunications*] (TEL)	CPS
Calling Station Identifier (SAUS)	CSID
Calling Tone [*Computer science*]	CNG
Calling Tone (SAUS)	CNG Tone
Calling-Line Matrix (SAUS)	CLM
Calling-Line-Identity (SAUS)	CLI
Calling-line-Identity-Request Signal (SAUS)	CIR Signal
Calling-Line-identity-Unavailable Signal (SAUS)	CLU Signal
Calling-On [*Railroad signal arm*] [*British*]	C
Calling-Party Clear Signal (SAUO)	CCL Signal
Callington [*England*]	CALL
Callington Haven Pty Ltd. (SAUO)	CALHAVEN
Callis on Sewers [*A publication*] (DLA)	Callis
Callis on Sewers [*A publication*] (DLA)	Callis Sew
Callis on Sewers [*A publication*] (DLA)	Call Sew
Callis on Sewers [*A publication*] (DLA)	Cal Sew
Callisburg, TX [*FM radio station call letters*] (BROA)	KPFC-FM
Callisthenic Association of South Australia	CASA
Callisthenics Victoria [*Australia*]	CV
Callistratus [*Flourished, 3rd century*] [*Authority cited in pre-1607 legal work*] (DSA)	Calis
Callitrichid Hepatitis Virus	CHV
Callitype (VRA)	calit
Callman on Unfair Competition and Trade Marks [*A publication*] (DLA)	Callman Unfair Comp
Call-Net Enterprises 'B' [*NASDAQ symbol*] (TTSB)	CNEBF
Callon Petroleum [*NASDAQ symbol*] (TTSB)	CLNP
Callon Petroleum [*NYSE symbol*] (SG)	CPE
Callon Petroleum Co. [*Associated Press*] (SAG)	CallonP
Callon Petroleum Co. [*NASDAQ symbol*] (SAG)	CLNP
Callon Petroleum Cv Exch 'A' Pfd [*NASDAQ symbol*] (TTSB)	CLNPP
Callose Platelets [*Botany*]	CP
Calloway's Nursery [*NASDAQ symbol*] (SPSG)	CLWY
Calloways Nursery, inc. [*Associated Press*] (SAG)	Caloway
CallPath Services Architecture (CDE)	CSA
Call/Return Element (SAUS)	CRE
Calls for Service Signal [*Telecommunications*] (TEL)	CFS
Calls for Service Signal (SAUS)	CFS Signal
Calls per Day (IAA)	CD
Calls per Day [*Telecommunications*] (IAA)	CPD
Calls per Minute [*Telecommunications*] (IAA)	CPM
Calls per Second [*Telecommunications*] (TEL)	CS
Calls Underwritten by Swanbrook [*Investment term*] (DFIT)	CUBS
Call's Virginia Reports [*5-10 Virginia*] [*1797-1825*] [*A publication*] (DLA)	Call
Call's Virginia Reports [*5-10 Virginia*] [*1797-1825*] [*A publication*] (DLA)	Call (VA)
Calls Waiting (SAUS)	CW
Callus [*Medicine*] (DAVI)	CAL
Call-Us, Inc.	CU
Call-Waiting Identification [*Telecommunications service*]	CWID
Calm [*i.e., no wind*]	C
Calm Air [*Canada*] [*ICAO designator*] (FAAC)	CAV
Calm Air International [*ICAO designator*] (AD)	MO
Calm Inversion Pollution (SAUS)	CIP
Calm Sea (ACAE)	CS
Calm Water Line	CWL
Calm Water Ramp [*Environmental science*] (COE)	CWR
Calmar Public Library, Alberta [*Library symbol*] [*National Library of Canada*] (NLC)	ACALM
CalMat Co. [*Associated Press*] (SAG)	Calmat
CalMat Co. [*NYSE symbol*] (SPSG)	CZM
Calmato [*More Calm*] [*Music*]	CALM
Calmodulin [*Also, CaM*] [*Biochemistry*]	CalM
Calmodulin [*Also, CalM*] [*Biochemistry*]	CaM
Calmodulin Binding Protein [*Biochemistry*]	CaM-BP
Calmodulin-Dependent Protein Kinase [*An enzyme*]	CAM-PK
Calnetics Corp. [*NASDAQ symbol*] (NQ)	CALN
Calnetics Corp. [*Associated Press*] (SAG)	Calnetcs
Calnexin (DMAA)	CANX
Calnexin	Cnx
Calnor Resources Ltd. [*Vancouver Stock Exchange symbol*]	CUU
Calomel [*Pharmacy*] (ROG)	CAL
Calomel, Rhubarb, Colocynth [*Medicine*]	CRC
Calopezzati [*Italy*] [*ICAO location identifier*] (ICLI)	LICM
Caloric Heat Unit	CHU
Caloric Power (SAUS)	CP
Caloric Restriction	CR
Caloric Value (SAUS)	CV
Calorie	C
Calorie [*Small Calorie*] [*Dietetics*] (DAVI)	c
Calorie (MSA)	CAL
Calorie (NTIO)	Cal
Calorie (IDOE)	cal
Calorie Control Council (EA)	CCC
Calorie Restricted (STED)	CR
calories (SAUS)	cal
Calories Don't Count [*Title of a 1961 book by Dr. Herman Taller; initialism referred to the diet and diet capsules promoted by the book*]	CDC
Calories from Fat	CFF
Calorific Power (IAA)	CP
Calorific Power (SAUS)	CP
Calorific Recovery Anaerobic Process [*Inc*]	CRAP
Calorific Value [*of a fuel*]	CV
Calorimetry Conference (EA)	CC
Calotype (VRA)	CALOT
Caloundra [*Australia*] [*Airport symbol*] (OAG)	CUD
Calpetro Resources, Inc. [*Vancouver Stock Exchange symbol*]	COZ
Calpine Corp. [*Associated Press*] (SAG)	Calpine
Calpine Corp. [*NYSE symbol*] (SAG)	CPN
Calpine Resources, Inc. [*Vancouver Stock Exchange symbol*]	CLP
Calprop Corp. [*Associated Press*] (SAG)	Calprop
Calprop Corp. [*AMEX symbol*] (SPSG)	CPP

Calpurnius Siculus [*First century AD*] [*Classical studies*] (OCD) ... Calp
Calreticulin ... Crt
CALS [*Customs Acts Legislation Service*] **Information Bulletin** [*Australia*] [*A publication*] ... CIB
CALS Management Information Office (SAUO) ... CALS MIO
Calsequestrin (DMAA) ... CASQ
Calspan Corp. [*Formerly, Cornell Aeronautical Laboratory*] ... CAL
Calspan Corporation (SAUO) ... CAL
Calspan On-Line Information Service [*Calspan Corp.*] [*Information service or system*] (IID) ... COINS
Calspan-UB Research Foundation (SAUO) ... CUBRC
Caltech Concurrent Computer Project (SAUS) ... CCCP
Caltech Data Ltd. [*Vancouver Stock Exchange symbol*] ... KAL
Caltech Intermediate Form (SAUS) ... CIF
Cal-Tech Intermediate Format (SAUS) ... CIF
Caltech Millimeter Array (SAUS) ... MMA
Caltech Political Military Exercise [*International relations simulation game*]... PME
Caltech Population Program [*Agency for International Development*] (IID) ... CPP
Caltex Oil Refining Ltd. (SAUS) ... CORIL
Caltex Pacific Indonesia ... CPI
Calthrop on Copyholds [*A publication*] (DLA) ... Calth Copyh
Calthrop's City of London Cases, King's Bench [*England*] [*A publication*] (DLA) ... Calth
Calthrop's City of London Cases, King's Bench [*England*] [*A publication*] (DLA) ... Calth (Eng)
Calthrop's City of London Cases, King's Bench [*England*] [*A publication*] (DLA) ... Calthr
Calthrop's English King's Bench Reports [*80 English Reprint*] [*A publication*] (DLA) ... Cal
Calthrop's English King's Bench Reports [*80 English Reprint*] [*A publication*] (DLA) ... Cal Rep
Calthrop's English King's Bench Reports [*80 English Reprint*] [*A publication*] (DLA) ... Calth
Calthrop's English King's Bench Reports [*80 English Reprint*] [*A publication*] (DLA) ... Calth (Eng)
Calthrop's English King's Bench Reports [*80 English Reprint*] [*A publication*] (DLA) ... Calthr
Calton, Inc. [*Associated Press*] (SAG) ... Calton
Calton, Inc. [*AMEX symbol*] (SPSG) ... CN
Calument City Public Library, Calumet City, IL [*Library symbol*] [*Library of Congress*] (LCLS) ... ICcP
Calumet & Hecla, Inc. (SAUO) ... CAH
Calumet Bancorp [*NASDAQ symbol*] (SAG) ... CBCI
Calumet Bancorp, Inc. [*Associated Press*] (SAG) ... Calumet
Calumet City Public Library, Calumet City, IL [*Library symbol*] [*Library of Congress*] (LCLS) ... ICc
Calumet College, Whiting, IN [*OCLC symbol*] (OCLC) ... ICC
Calumet College, Whiting, IN [*Library symbol*] [*Library of Congress*] (LCLS) ... InWhC
Calumet, MI [*TV station call letters*] (RBYB) ... WBKP-TV
Calumet Public Library, Calumet, MN [*Library symbol*] [*Library of Congress*] (LCLS) ... MnCm
Calumet Public-School Library, Calumet, MI [*Library symbol*] [*Library of Congress*] (LCLS) ... MiCal
Calvada Resources [*Vancouver Stock Exchange symbol*] ... CVH
Calvarium and Scalp [*Anatomy*] (DAVI) ... C & S
Calvary Baptist School of Theology, Lansdale, PA [*Library symbol*] [*Library of Congress*] (LCLS) ... PLdaC
Calvary Christian School, Worthington, MN [*Library symbol*] [*Library of Congress*] (LCLS) ... MnWoCCS
Calvert City, KY [*FM radio station call letters*] ... WCCK
Calvert Cliffs Nuclear Power Plant (NRCH) ... CCNPP
Calvert Gas & Oils Ltd. [*Toronto Stock Exchange symbol*] ... CVT
Calvert Social Inv. Equity Ptfl [*Mutual fund ticker symbol*] (SG) ... CSIEX
Calvert Social Inv. Mgd. Growth [*Mutual fund ticker symbol*] (SG) ... CSIFX
Calvert Social Investment Fund (SAUO) ... CSIF
Calvert TF Reserve Ltd. Term Ptfl [*Mutual fund ticker symbol*] (SG) ... CTFLX
Calverton, NY [*Location identifier*] [*FAA*] (FAAL) ... CCC
Calverton, NY [*Location identifier*] [*FAA*] (FAAL) ... CTO
Calverton, NY [*Location identifier*] [*FAA*] (FAAL) ... PIC
Calverton-Roanoke, NY [*FM radio station call letters*] (BROA) ... WXXP-FM
Calvert's Parties to Suits in Equity [*A publication*] (DLA) ... Calv Par
Calvert's Parties to Suits in Equity [*A publication*] (DLA) ... Calv Parties
Calvi [*Corsica*] [*Airport symbol*] (OAG) ... CLY
Calvi [*Corsica*] [*Seismograph station code, US Geological Survey*] (SEIS) ... CVF
Calviac [*France*] [*Seismograph station code, US Geological Survey*] (SEIS) ... CAF
Calvin and Hobbes [*Comic strip*] ... C & H
Calvin College and Seminary, Grand Rapids, MI [*OCLC symbol*] (OCLC) ... EXC
Calvin College and Seminary, Grand Rapids, MI [*Library symbol*] [*Library of Congress*] (LCLS) ... MiGrC
Calvin Coolidge Memorial Foundation (EA) ... CCMF
Calvin Klein [*Fashion designer, 1942-*] ... CK
Calvinia [*South Africa*] [*ICAO location identifier*] (ICLI) ... FACV
Calvinistic Methodist Church of Wales (SAUO) ... CMCW
Calvinistic Methodist General Assembly Temperance Committee (SAUO) ... CMGATC
Calvi/Sainte-Catherine, Corse [*France*] [*ICAO location identifier*] (ICLI) ... LFKC
Calwall Computer Corporation (SAUO) ... CCC
Calwer Bibellexikon (BJA) ... CBL
Calwestern Automated Clearing House Association (MHDB) ... CACHA
Calypso Development Ltd. [*Vancouver Stock Exchange symbol*] ... CYS
Calypte Biomedical Corp. [*NASDAQ symbol*] (SAG) ... CALY
Calypte Biomedical Corp. [*Associated Press*] (SAG) ... Calypte
Calyx [*Botany*] (ROG) ... C
Calyx Hole (SAUS) ... CXH
Calyx Lateral Lobe Length [*Botany*] ... CLLL
Calyx Lateral Lobe Shape [*Botany*] ... CLLS
Calyx Lateral Lobe Width [*Botany*] ... CLLW
Calyx Tube Length [*Botany*] ... CTBL
Cam Action Wheel ... CAW
Cam Air Management Ltd. [*British*] [*ICAO designator*] (FAAC) ... CMR
Cam Box ... CBX
Cam Case ... CMCS
CAM Control Block [*Computer science*] ... CCB
CAM Data Systems [*NASDAQ symbol*] (SAG) ... CADA
CAM Data Systems, Inc. [*Associated Press*] (SAG) ... CAM Dt
Cam Designs [*NASDAQ symbol*] (TTSB) ... CMDA
Cam Designs Co. [*Associated Press*] (SAG) ... CamDs
Cam Designs Co. [*Associated Press*] (SAG) ... CampDsg
Cam Designs Co. [*NASDAQ symbol*] (SAG) ... CMDA
Cam Designs Wrrt [*NASDAQ symbol*] (TTSB) ... CMDAW
Cam Follower ... CMFLR
CAM [*Central American Mission*] **International** (EA) ... CAM
CAM International (SAUO) ... CAM
Cam Limit Switch ... CLS
Cam Plate Readout ... CPR
Cam Pocket ... CMPKT
Cam Ranh Bay [*Vietnam*] ... CRB
Cam Roller ... CMRLR
Cam Timing Contact ... CTC
Cam Wedge Clamp ... CWC
Cam Wedge Power Clamp ... CWPC
CAMA [*Centralized Automatic Message Accounting*] **Operator Position Exercise** (PDAA) ... COPE
Camabatela [*Angola*] [*ICAO location identifier*] (ICLI) ... FNCM
CAMAC Industry Applications Group (SAUO) ... CIAG
CAMAC [*Computer-Aided Measurement and Control*] **Input-Output Processor** [*Computer*] ... CIOP
Camaguey [*Cuba*] [*Airport symbol*] (OAG) ... CMW
Camaguey/Ignacio Agramonte [*Cuba*] [*ICAO location identifier*] (ICLI) ... MUCM
Camair [*Division of Cameron Iron Works, Inc.*] [*ICAO aircraft manufacturer identifier*] (ICAO) ... CM
Camaldolese Benedictine Sisters (TOCD) ... OSBCam
Camaldolese Hermits (TOCD) ... osbcam
Camaldolese Hermits (TOCD) ... OSBCam
Camaldolese Hermits of the Congregation of Monte Corona (TOCD) ... ercam
Camaldolese Hermits of the Congregation of Monte Corona (TOCD) ... ErCam
Camana [*Peru*] [*ICAO location identifier*] (ICLI) ... SPAM
Camanachd Association (EA) ... CA
Cam-and-Claw [*Pulldown mechanism in a camera or projector*] ... CAM
Camara Brasileira do Livro [*Brazilian Chamber of Publishing*] (EAIO) ... CBL
Camargo Township Library, Villa Grove, IL [*Library symbol*] [*Library of Congress*] (LCLS) ... IVg
Camargue Air Transport [*France*] [*ICAO designator*] (FAAC) ... CMG
Camarillo, CA [*FM radio station call letters*] ... KMRO
Camarillo, CA [*FM radio station call letters*] (RBYB) ... KOCP
Camarillo State Hospital, Camarillo, CA [*Library symbol*] [*Library of Congress*] (LCLS) ... CCamarH
Camaro Owners of America [*Defunct*] (EA) ... COA
Camas County District Library, Fairfield, ID [*Library symbol*] [*Library of Congress*] (LCLS) ... IdFa
Camas National Wildlife Refuge (SAUS) ... CNWR
Camas Prairie [*Railroad*] (MHDW) ... CAP
Camas Prairie Railroad Co. (IIA) ... CAP
Camas Prairie Railroad Co. [*AAR code*] ... CSP
Camas Public Library, Camas, WA [*Library symbol*] [*Library of Congress*] (LCLS) ... WaCa
Camas Resources Ltd. [*Vancouver Stock Exchange symbol*] ... KMS
Camas, WA [*FM radio station call letters*] (RBYB) ... KNRK
Camaxilo [*Angola*] [*ICAO location identifier*] (ICLI) ... FNCX
Cambendazole (SAUS) ... CBZ
Camber (SAUS) ... Cam
Camber [*Aerospace engineering*] ... CAM
Camberley Land Air Wargame System (SAUS) ... CLAWS
Cambex Corp. [*Associated Press*] (SAG) ... Cambex
Cambex Corp. [*NASDAQ symbol*] ... CBEX
Cambior, Inc. [*Associated Press*] (SAG) ... Camb
Cambior, Inc. [*Associated Press*] (SAG) ... Cambior
Cambior, Inc. [*AMEX symbol*] (SAG) ... CBJ
Cambistry [*Finance*] ... CAMB
Cambium (SAUS) ... Ca
Cambodia [*Democratic Kampuchea*] [*MARC geographic area code*] [*Library of Congress*] (LCCP) ... a-cb-
Cambodia (SAUO) ... CA
Cambodia (SAUO) ... Cam
Cambodia (MILB) ... Cam
Cambodia (VRA) ... Camb
Cambodia (WDAA) ... CAMB
Cambodia [*Democratic Kampuchea*] [*MARC country of publication code*] [*Library of Congress*] (LCCP) ... cb
Cambodia [*ANSI two-letter standard code*] (CNC) ... KH
Cambodia [*ANSI three-letter standard code*] (CNC) ... KHM
Cambodia Crisis Center [*Defunct*] (EA) ... CCC
Cambodia Environmental Management Process ... CEMP
Cambodia-IRRI [*International Rice Research Institute*]**-Australia Project** ... CIAP
Cambodian [*MARC language code*] [*Library of Congress*] (LCCP) ... cam
Cambodian Advisory Council of Australia ... CACA
Cambodian Appeal [*Defunct*] (EA) ... CA
Cambodian Association of Victoria [*Australia*] ... CAV
Cambodian Buddhist Association of Victoria [*Australia*] ... CBAV

Cambodian Buddhist Society (EA) .... CBS
Cambodian Community Welfare Centre [*Australia*] .... CCWC
Cambodian Crisis Committee (EA) CCC
Cambodian Development Council (SAUO) .... CDC
Cambodian Investment Board (ECON) .... CIB
Cambodian People's Party [*Political party*] (ECON) .... CPP
Cambodian Women's Association of New South Wales [*Australia*] .... CWANSW
Cambodian-IRRI-Australian Project (SAUO) .... CIAP
Camborne [*Urban district in England*] .... CAMB
Camborne School of Metalliferous Mining [*British*] .... CSMM
Camborne School of Mines [*British*] (IRUK) .... CSM
Cambourne Resources [*Vancouver Stock Exchange symbol*] .... KAV
Cambrai/Epinoy [*France*] [*ICAO location identifier*] (ICLI) .... LFQI
Cambrai/Niergnies [*France*] [*ICAO location identifier*] (ICLI) .... LFYG
Cambrex Corp. [*Associated Press*] (SAG) .... Cambrx
Cambrex Corp. [*AMEX symbol*] (SPSG) .... CBM
Cambria & Indiana Railroad (SAUO) .... C&IRR
Cambria & Indiana Railroad Co. [*AAR code*] CI
Cambria, CA [*FM radio station call letters*] .... KOTR
Cambria County Legal Journal [*Pennsylvania*] [*A publication*] (DLA) .... Cambria
Cambria County Legal Journal [*Pennsylvania*] [*A publication*] (DLA) .... Cambria Co LJ
Cambria County Legal Journal [*Pennsylvania*] [*A publication*] (DLA) .... Cambria Co (PA)
Cambria County Library System, Johnstown, PA [*OCLC symbol*] (OCLC) .... JOC
Cambria County Library System, Johnstown, PA [*Library symbol*] [*Library of Congress*] (LCLS) .... PJo
Cambria County Reports [*Pennsylvania*] [*A publication*] (DLA) .... Camb Co LJ
Cambria Resources Ltd. [*Vancouver Stock Exchange symbol*] .... KMR
Cambrian (SAUS) .... Camb
Cambrian [*Period, era, or system*] [*Geology*] .... CAMB
Cambrian Airways (SAUO) .... CS
Cambrian Airways Ltd. .... CAS
Cambrian Archaeological Association (SAUO) .... CAA
Cambrian College, Sudbury, ON, Canada [*Library symbol*] [*Library of Congress*] (LCLS) .... CaOSUC
Cambrian College, Sudbury, Ontario [*Library symbol*] [*National Library of Canada*] (NLC) .... OSUC
Cambrian Railway [*British*] .... CAM R
Cambrian Railway [*British*] (ROG) .... CR
Cambrian Railway (SAUO) .... CR
Cambrian Railways (SAUO) .... CamR
Cambrian Society of Victoria [*Australia*] .... CSV
Cambridge [*Municipal borough in England*] C
Cambridge (ADWA) .... Cam
Cambridge [*Massachusetts*] [*Seismograph station code, US Geological Survey*] [*Closed*] (SEIS) .... CAM
Cambridge [*Municipal borough in England*] .... CAM
Cambridge [*Municipal borough in England*] .... CAMB
Cambridge [*Record label*] .... Camb
Cambridge [*England*] [*Airport symbol*] [*Obsolete*] (OAG) .... CBG
Cambridge [*British*] [*ICAO location identifier*] (ICLI) .... EGSC
Cambridge Accelerator Project (SAUS) .... CAP
Cambridge Acoustical Associates, Inc. (MCD) .... CAA
Cambridge Algebraic System [*Programming language*] [*1975*] (CSR) .... CAMAL
Cambridge Analog Simulator for Predicting Atomic Reactions [*British*] (DIT) .... CASPAR
Cambridge Ancient History [*1st edition, 1923-39*] [*A publication*] (OCD) .... CAH
Cambridge Ancient History [*2nd edition*] [*A publication*] (OCD) .... CAH^2
Cambridge and County High School Old Boys Society (SAUO) .... CCHSOBS
Cambridge and Isle of Ely Naturalist Trust (SAUS) .... CIENT
Cambridge and Oxford (SAUS) .... Camford
Cambridge Antibody Technology .... CaT
Cambridge Antiquarian Society (SAUO) .... CambAntS
Cambridge Antiquarian Society (SAUO) .... CAS
Cambridge Arctic Shelf Programme (SAUO) .... CASP
Cambridge Atmospheric Density Numerical Integration Programme (SAUO) .... CADNIP
Cambridge Automatic Digital Computer (IEEE) .... CADC
Cambridge Bay [*Canada*] [*Geomagnetic observatory code*] .... CBB
Cambridge Bay [*Canada*] [*Airport symbol*] (OAG) .... YCB
Cambridge Bay, NT [*ICAO location identifier*] (ICLI) .... CYCB
Cambridge Bible [*A publication*] (BJA) .... CambB
[*The*] **Cambridge Bible Commentary: New English Bible** [*A publication*] (BJA) .... CBC
Cambridge Bible Commentary: New English Bible [*A publication*] (BJA) .... CNEB
Cambridge Bible for Schools and Colleges [*A publication*] (BJA) .... CaB
Cambridge Bible for Schools and Colleges [*A publication*] (BJA) .... CBSC
Cambridge Bibliographical Society (SAUO) .... CBS
[*The*] **Cambridge Bibliography of English Literature** [*A publication*] .... CBEL
Cambridge Bicycle Club [*British*] .... CBC
Cambridge Biological Series [*A publication*] .... CBS
Cambridge BioScience Corp. .... CBS
[*The*] **Cambridge Book of Poetry for Children** [*A publication*] .... CBPC
Cambridge Buddhist Association (EA) .... CBA
Cambridge City Public Library, Cambridge City, IN [*Library symbol*] [*Library of Congress*] (LCLS) .... InCc
Cambridge Communication Corp. (MCD) CCC
Cambridge Community College, Cambridge, MN [*Library symbol*] [*Library of Congress*] (LCLS) .... MnCaCC
Cambridge Computer Associates (SAUS) .... CAA
Cambridge Conference on School Mathematics [*National Science Foundation*] .... CCSM
Cambridge Consultants Ltd.[*Arthur D. Little Ltd.*] [*Research center*] [*British*] (IRUK) CCL
Cambridge Crystallographic Data Centre [*University of Cambridge*] [*Information service or system*] (IID) .... CCDC
Cambridge Crystallographic Data File [*Database*] .... CCDF
Cambridge Crystallographic Data Files (SAUS) .... CCDF
Cambridge Crystallographic Database [*England*] .... CCD
Cambridge Crystallography Subroutine Library [*Database*] .... CCSL
Cambridge Cybernetic Society (VERA) .... CCS
Cambridge Display Technology [*British*] .... CDT
Cambridge District Library, Cambridge, ID [*Library symbol*] [*Library of Congress*] (LCLS) .... IdCm
Cambridge Econometrics [*British*] .... CE
Cambridge Economic Policy Group [*British*] .... CEPG
Cambridge Education Consultants Ltd. [*British*] .... CEC
Cambridge Electron Accelerator .... CEA
Cambridge Electron Accelerator Laboratories [*Massachusetts Institute of Technology*] .... CEAL
Cambridge Electronic Industries [*British*] .... CEI
Cambridge Electronic Research Laboratory (KSC) .... CERL
Cambridge Elementary School, Media Center, Cambridge, MN [*Library symbol*] [*Library of Congress*] (LCLS) .... MnCaES
Cambridge Energy Research Group [*University of Cambridge*] [*British*] (IRUK) .... CERG
Cambridge English Classics [*A publication*] .... CEC
Cambridge Evening News [*A publication*] (WDAA) .... CEN
Cambridge Examination in English for Language Teachers .... CEELT
Cambridge, Fitzwilliam Museum (SAUO) .... CaFM
Cambridge Geographical Series [*A publication*] .... CGS
Cambridge Geological Data System (SAUS) .... CGDS
Cambridge Graphic Systems [*Computer science*] (HGAA) .... CGS
[*The*] **Cambridge Greek Testament** [*A publication*] (BJA) .... CGT
Cambridge Greek Testament Commentary [*A publication*] (BJA) .... CGTC
Cambridge Greek Testament for Schools and Colleges [*A publication*] (BJA) .... CGTSC
Cambridge Healthtech Institute [*England*] (HGEN) .... CHI
Cambridge Heart, Inc. [*Associated Press*] (SAG) .... CambHrt
Cambridge Heart, Inc. [*NASDAQ symbol*] (SAG) .... CAMH
Cambridge High School, Media Center, Cambridge, MN [*Library symbol*] [*Library of Congress*] (LCLS) .... MnCaHS
Cambridge Higher Local Examination [*British*] (ROG) .... CHL
Cambridge Historical Series [*A publication*] .... CHS
Cambridge History of English Literature .... CHEL
Cambridge Instrument Co. PLC (MHDW) .... CAMBY
Cambridge Interactive System (SAUS) .... CIS
Cambridge Inter-Collegiate Christian Union (SAUO) .... CICCU
Cambridge International Dictionary of English [*A publication*] .... CIDE
Cambridge International Reference on Current Affairs Ltd. .... CIRCA
Cambridge Junior College [*Massachusetts*] .... CJC
Cambridge Language Research Unit .... CLRU
Cambridge Language Research Unit (SAUO) .... CLRU
Cambridge Law Journal [*A publication*] .... CLJ
Cambridge Library (SAUS) CL
Cambridge Life Sciences [*British*] .... CLS
Cambridge, MA [*FM radio station call letters*] .... WHRB
Cambridge, MA [*AM radio station call letters*] .... WJIB
Cambridge, MA [*Television station call letters*] .... WLVI
Cambridge, MA [*FM radio station call letters*] .... WMBR
Cambridge Manuals of Science and Literature [*A publication*] .... CMSL
Cambridge Mathematical Series [*A publication*] .... CMS
Cambridge, MD [*Location identifier*] [*FAA*] (FAAL) .... CGE
Cambridge, MD [*AM radio station call letters*] .... WCEM
Cambridge, MD [*FM radio station call letters*] .... WCEM-FM
Cambridge, MD [*FM radio station call letters*] .... WFBR
Cambridge Medieval History (SAUS) .... CMH
Cambridge Memorial Hospital, Health Sciences Library, Cambridge, MN [*Library symbol*] [*Library of Congress*] (LCLS) .... MnCaH
Cambridge Memorial Hospital, Ontario [*Library symbol*] [*National Library of Canada*] (BIB) .... OCCMH
Cambridge Memories, Inc. .... CMI
Cambridge Memories, Incorporated (SAUO) .... CMI
Cambridge Middle School, Media Center, Cambridge, MN [*Library symbol*] [*Library of Congress*] (LCLS) .... MnCaM
Cambridge Military Hospital (SAUS) .... CMH
Cambridge Military Library, Halifax, Nova Scotia [*Library symbol*] [*National Library of Canada*] (NLC) .... NSHC
Cambridge Military Library, Halifax, NS, Canada [*Library symbol*] [*Library of Congress*] (LCLS) .... CaNSHC
Cambridge Military Library, Halifax, NS, Canada [*Library symbol*] [*Library of Congress*] (LCLS) .... DaNSHC
Cambridge, MN [*Location identifier*] [*FAA*] (FAAL) .... CBG
Cambridge, MN [*FM radio station call letters*] (BROA) .... KZNT-FM
Cambridge, MN [*FM radio station call letters*] .... WREV
Cambridge Modern History [*A publication*] (ROG) .... CMH
Cambridge Monitor System .... CMS
Cambridge Monitoring System [*IBM Computer Program*] (NAKS) CMS-2
Cambridge Natural Science Manuals [*A publication*] .... CNSM
Cambridge, NE [*Location identifier*] [*FAA*] (FAAL) .... CSB
Cambridge NeuroScience [*NASDAQ symbol*] (TTSB) .... CNSI
Cambridge NeuroScience, Inc. [*Associated Press*] (SAG) .... CambNe
Cambridge NeuroScience, Inc. [*NASDAQ symbol*] (SAG) .... CNSI
Cambridge, NY [*Location identifier*] [*FAA*] (FAAL) .... CAM
Cambridge Observation Error Analysis (SAUS) .... COBERA
Cambridge Observatory (SAUS) .... Camb Obs
Cambridge Observatory (SAUO) .... CambObs
Cambridge, OH [*Location identifier*] [*FAA*] (FAAL) .... CDI
Cambridge, OH [*FM radio station call letters*] .... WCMJ

Cambridge, OH [*AM radio station call letters*] ..... WILE
Cambridge, OH [*FM radio station call letters*] ..... WOUC
Cambridge, OH [*Television station call letters*] ..... WOUC-TV
Cambridge, ON [*AM radio station call letters*] ..... CIAM
Cambridge, ON [*FM radio station call letters*] (BROA) ..... CIZN-FM
Cambridge Optical Aperture Synthesis Telescope ..... COAST
Cambridge Optical Aperture Synthesis Telescope ..... Coast
Cambridge, Oxford and Southern School Examinations Council (SAUO) ..... COSSEC
Cambridge, Oxford & Southern Secondary Examinations Council [*British*] (AIE) ..... COSSEC
Cambridge Philological Society (SAUO) ..... CPS
Cambridge Philological Society, Cambridge, England, Proceedings (SAUS) ..... Proceed of the Canmbridge Philol Soc
Cambridge Philosophical Society (SAUO) ..... CPhS
Cambridge Philosophical Society (SAUO) ..... CPS
Cambridge Physical Series [*A publication*] ..... CPS
Cambridge Public Library, Cambridge, MA [*Library symbol*] [*Library of Congress*] (LCLS) ..... MC
Cambridge Public Library, Cambridge, ON, Canada [*Library symbol*] [*Library of Congress*] (LCLS) ..... CaOGal
Cambridge Public Library, Ontario [*Library symbol*] [*National Library of Canada*] (NLC) ..... OGAL
Cambridge Pulsar (IIA) ..... CP
Cambridge Quarterly of Healthcare Ethics (SAUO) ..... CQ
Cambridge Radio Observatory Committee ..... CAMROC
Cambridge Reports, Inc. [*Database producer*] (IID) ..... CRI
Cambridge Research Biochemicals [*British*] ..... CRB
Cambridge Research Center [*Air Force*] ..... CRC
Cambridge Research Institute, Inc., Cambridge, MA [*Library symbol*] [*Library of Congress*] (LCLS) ..... MCRI
Cambridge Research Instrumentation ..... CRI
Cambridge Research Laboratories (SAUO) ..... CRL
Cambridge Research Laboratory ..... CRL
Cambridge Scientific Abstracts [*Information service or system*] (IID) ..... CSA
Cambridge Scientific Instruments (SAUO) ..... CSI
Cambridge Series for Schools and Training Colleges [*A publication*] ..... CSSTC
Cambridge Seventh Day Adventist Library, Cambridge, MN [*Library symbol*] [*Library of Congress*] (LCLS) ..... MnCaSD
Cambridge Shopping Centres Ltd. [*Toronto Stock Exchange symbol*] ..... CBG
Cambridge Society for Industrial Archaeology (SAUO) ..... CSIA
Cambridge Soundworks, Inc. [*Associated Press*] (SAG) ..... CambSnd
Cambridge Soundworks, Inc. [*NASDAQ symbol*] (SAG) ..... HIFI
Cambridge Springs, PA [*FM radio station call letters*] (BROA) ..... WAQM-FM
Cambridge State Hospital, Staff Library, Cambridge, MN [*Library symbol*] [*Library of Congress*] (LCLS) ..... MnCaSH
Cambridge Structural Database [*Genetics*] ..... CSD
Cambridge Studies in Medieval Life and Thought (journ.) (SAUS) ..... CSMLT
Cambridge Technology, Inc. ..... CTI
Cambridge Technology Partners [*Associated Press*] (SAG) ..... CambTch
Cambridge Technology Partners [*NASDAQ symbol*] (SAG) ..... CATP
Cambridge Technology Partners [*Associated Press*] (SAG) ..... CmbTch
Cambridge Technology Ptnrs [*NASDAQ symbol*] (TTSB) ..... CATP
Cambridge Teritorial Regiment (SAUO) ..... CTR
Cambridge Training and Development [*British*] (AIE) ..... CTAD
Cambridge University [*England*] ..... CAMB
Cambridge University (SAUO) ..... CU
Cambridge University [*England*] ..... CU
Cambridge University Agricultural Society (SAUO) ..... CUAS
Cambridge University Air Squadron [*British*] (DI) ..... CUAS
Cambridge University Association Football Club (SAUO) ..... CUAFC
Cambridge University Athletic Club (SAUO) ..... CUAC
Cambridge University Boat Club (SAUO) ..... CUBC
Cambridge University Boxing Club (SAUO) ..... CUBC
Cambridge University, Cambridge, United Kingdom [*Library symbol*] [*Library of Congress*] (LCLS) ..... UkCU
Cambridge University Conservative Association (ECON) ..... CUCA
Cambridge University Cricket Club (SAUO) ..... CUCC
Cambridge University Cruising Club (SAUO) ..... CUCC
Cambridge University Department of Education [*British*] (AIE) ..... CUDE
Cambridge University Dramatic Society (SAUO) ..... CUDS
Cambridge University Engineering Department, Cambridge (SAUO) ..... CUED
Cambridge University Football Club (SAUO) ..... CUFC
Cambridge University Golf Club (SAUO) ..... CUGC
Cambridge University Hockey Club (SAUO) ..... CUHC
Cambridge University Lacrosse Club (SAUO) ..... CULC
Cambridge University Lawn Tennis Club (SAUO) ..... CULTC
Cambridge University Library (SAUO) ..... CUL
Cambridge University Library [*British*] (DLA) ..... CUL
Cambridge University Marlowe Dramatic Society (SAUO) ..... CUMDS
Cambridge University Mathematical Laboratory (SAUO) ..... CUML
Cambridge University Mission (SAUO) ..... CUM
Cambridge University Mission ..... CUM
Cambridge University Mummers (SAUO) ..... CUM
Cambridge University Musical Society (SAUO) ..... CUMS
Cambridge University Officer Training Corps [*British military*] (DMA) ..... CUOTC
Cambridge University Opera Group (SAUO) ..... CUOG
Cambridge University Prayer Union, Cambridge (SAUO) ..... CUPU
Cambridge University Press (SAUO) ..... Cambridge UP
Cambridge University Press ..... CUP
Cambridge University Press (SAUO) ..... ISBN 0-521
Cambridge University Press Limited Editions ..... CUPLE
Cambridge University Rifle Association (SAUO) ..... CURA
Cambridge University Rifle Club (SAUO) ..... CURC
Cambridge University Rifles [*British military*] (DMA) ..... CUR
Cambridge University Rugby Union Football Club (SAUO) ..... CURUFC
Cambridge University Training Corps, Territorial Army (SAUO) ..... CUTC
Cambridgeshire [*County in England*] ..... CAMBS
Cambridgeshire [*County in England*] (ODBW) ..... Cambs
Cambridgeshire College of Arts and Technology [*British*] (AIE) ..... CCAT
Cambridgeshire Low Temperature Research Station (SAUO) ..... CLTRS
Cambridgeshire Low Temperature Research Station (SAUS) ..... CLTRS
Cambridgeshire Regiment (SAUO) ..... Ca
Cambridgeshire Regiment (SAUO) ..... Camb
Cambridgeshire Regiment (SAUO) ..... CambR
Cambridgeshire Rifle Volunteer Corps [*British military*] (DMA) ..... CRVC
Cambyses (BJA) ..... Camb
Camco Financial [*NASDAQ symbol*] (TTSB) ..... CAFI
Camco Financial Corp. [*NASDAQ symbol*] (SAG) ..... CAFI
Camco Financial Corp. [*Associated Press*] (SAG) ..... CamcoFn
Camco, Inc. [*Toronto Stock Exchange symbol*] ..... COC
Camco International [*NYSE symbol*] (SPSG) ..... CAM
Camco International [*Associated Press*] (SAG) ..... Camco
Camden [*Australia*] [*ICAO location identifier*] (ICLI) ..... ASCN
Camden [*Division of Victor*] [*Record label*] ..... Cam
Camden [*Diocesan abbreviation*] [*New Jersey*] (TOCD) ..... CAM
Camden [*Arkansas*] [*Airport symbol*] (OAG) ..... CDH
Camden, AL [*Location identifier*] [*FAA*] (FAAL) ..... IWE
Camden, AL [*AM radio station call letters*] ..... WCOX
Camden, AL [*FM radio station call letters*] ..... WYVC
Camden, AR [*AM radio station call letters*] ..... KAMD
Camden, AR [*FM radio station call letters*] (RBYB) ..... KAMD-FM
Camden, AR [*FM radio station call letters*] ..... KCAC
Camden, AR [*FM radio station call letters*] ..... KCXY
Camden, AR [*FM radio station call letters*] (RBYB) ..... KMGC
Camden, AR [*AM radio station call letters*] (BROA) ..... KNHD-AM
Camden, AR [*AM radio station call letters*] ..... KOSG
Camden Council for International Cooperation [*British*] CCIC
Camden County College, Blackwood, NJ [*Library symbol*] [*Library of Congress*] (LCLS) ..... NjBlaC
Camden County College, Voorhees, NJ [*OCLC symbol*] (OCLC) ..... NCK
Camden County Historical Society, Camden, NJ [*Library symbol*] [*Library of Congress*] (LCLS) ..... NjCaHi
Camden County Library, Voorhees (SAUS) ..... NCI
Camden County Library, Voorhees, NJ [*OCLC symbol*] (OCLC) ..... NCL
Camden County Times, Collingswood, NJ [*Library symbol*] [*Library of Congress*] (LCLS) ..... NjCoT
Camden County Times, Westmont, NJ [*Library symbol*] [*Library of Congress*] (LCLS) ..... NjWemT
Camden East Branch, Lennox and Addington County Library, Ontario [*Library symbol*] [*National Library of Canada*] (NLC) ..... OCELAC
Camden Free Public Library, Camden, NJ [*Library symbol*] [*Library of Congress*] (LCLS) ..... NjCa
Camden High School (SAUS) ..... Cam High
Camden Library [*A publication*] ..... CLA
Camden Marine Terminals (SAUS) ..... CMT
Camden, ME [*FM radio station call letters*] ..... WQSS
Camden National [*AMEX symbol*] (SG) ..... CAC
Camden News, Camden, NJ [*Library symbol*] [*Library of Congress*] (LCLS) ..... NjCaN
Camden, NJ [*FM radio station call letters*] ..... WKDN
Camden, NJ [*Television station call letters*] ..... WNJS
Camden, NJ [*AM radio station call letters*] ..... WSSJ
Camden, NJ [*AM radio station call letters*] ..... WTMR
Camden Property Trust [*Associated Press*] (SAG) ..... CamdnP
Camden Property Trust [*NYSE symbol*] (SPSG) ..... CPT
Camden, SC [*Location identifier*] [*FAA*] (FAAL) ..... CDN
Camden, SC [*AM radio station call letters*] (RBYB) ..... WAME
Camden, SC [*AM radio station call letters*] ..... WCAM
Camden, SC [*FM radio station call letters*] ..... WPUB
Camden Society (SAUO) ..... CamdS
Camden, TN [*AM radio station call letters*] ..... WFWL
Camden, TN [*FM radio station call letters*] ..... WRJB
Camden Township Library, Camden, MI [*Library symbol*] [*Library of Congress*] (LCLS) ..... MiCam
Camden-Gloucester Newspapers, Blackwood, NJ [*Library symbol*] [*Library of Congress*] (LCLS) ..... NjBlaCG
Camden-Jackson Township Public Library, Camden, IN [*Library symbol*] [*Library of Congress*] (LCLS) ..... InCam
Camden's Britannia [*A publication*] (DLA) ..... Cam Brit
Camden's Britannia [*A publication*] (DLA) ..... Camd Brit
Camden's Britannia [*A publication*] (DLA) ..... Camden
Camdenton, MO [*FM radio station call letters*] ..... KCVO
Came Free (ADA) ..... CF
Cameco Corp. [*Associated Press*] (SAG) ..... Cameco
Cameco Corp. [*NYSE symbol*] (TTSB) ..... CCJ
Cameco Corp. 1st Installment [*NYSE symbol*] (TTSB) ..... CCJPP
Cameco Research Center, Ottawa, Ontario [*Library symbol*] [*National Library of Canada*] (NLC) ..... OOEN
Camegie Group [*NASDAQ symbol*] (TTSB) ..... CGIX
Camel Corps (SAUO) CC
CAMEL [*Critical Aeronautical Material and Equipment List*] **Gate Field Effe ct Transistors** (MCD) ..... CAMFET
Camel Oil & Gas Ltd. [*Toronto Stock Exchange symbol*] ..... CEG
Camelford [*Rural district in England*] ..... CAMELF
Camelopardalis [*Constellation*] ..... Cam
Camelopardalis [*Constellation*] ..... Caml
Camelot Corp. [*Associated Press*] (SAG) ..... Camelot
Camelot Corp. [*NASDAQ symbol*] (NQ) ..... CAML
Camembe [*Angola*] [*ICAO location identifier*] (ICLI) ..... FNCB

Cameo (VRA) ... cmo
Cameo Curtains (EFIS) ... CC
Camer Frequency (SAUS) ... cf
Camera (VRA) ... cam
Camera (KSC) ... CAM
Camera (MSA) ... CAMR
Camera (ABBR) ... CMRA
Camera and Recorder ... Camcorder
Camera Club (SAUO) ... CC
Camera Concealment and Deception (DWSG) ... CCD
Camera Control System (KSC) ... CCS
Camera Control Unit ... CCU
Camera Copy [*or Camera-Ready Copy*] ... CC
Camera de Comercio Mexico-Estados Unidos [*United States-Mexico Chamber of Commerce*] (EAIO) ... CCMEU
Camera Ducata [*Duchy Chamber*] [*Latin*] [*Legal term*] (DLA) ... Cam Duc
Camera Electronic Unit (MCD) ... CEU
Camera Enterprises, Inc. (SAUS) ... UCAM
Camera Europea degli Arbitri Stragiudiziali e dei Periti Esperti Consulenti Tecnici [*European Chamber of Extra-Judicial Adjudicators and Expert Technical Advisors*] (EAIO) ... CEASPECT
Camera Gun ... CG
Camera Industries of West Germany [*Defunct*] ... CIWG
Camera Line-Up Equipment (SAUS) ... CLUE
Camera Model System (MCD) ... CMS
Camera Obscura (VRA) ... cam obs
Camera Optics Manufacturing Corporation (SAUO) ... COC
Camera Override Control System [*NASA*] (KSC) ... COCS
Camera Processor Viewer (NITA) ... CPV
Camera Quality (MUGU) ... CQ
Camera Ready [*Publishing*] (WDMC) ... CR
Camera Rehearsal ... CR
Camera Repairman [*Navy rating*] ... CR
Camera Satellite (SAUS) ... Camsat
Camera Scaccari [*Exchequer Chamber*] [*Latin*] [*Legal term*] (DLA) ... CAM SCAC
Camera Scaccarii [*Exchequer Chamber*] [*Latin*] [*Legal term*] (DLA) ... Cam Scacc
Camera Site [*NASA*] (KSC) ... CS
Camera Station (SAUS) ... CAMSTA
Camera Stellate [*Star Chamber*] [*Latin*] [*Legal term*] (DLA) ... Cam Stell
Camera System (ACAE) ... CS
Camera Talkback (SAUS) ... CTB
Camera Thermique (SAUS) ... CT
Camera, Timing, and Control (NASA) ... CTC
Camera Timing Indicator ... CTI
Camera-Ready Art [*Publishing*] ... CRA
Camera-Ready Copy [*Publishing*] ... CRC
Camera-Ready Mechanical ... CRM
Camera-Synchron (SAUS) ... CASY
Cameri [*Italy*] [*ICAO location identifier*] (ICLI) ... LIMN
Camerino [*Italy*] [*Seismograph station code, US Geological Survey*] [*Closed*] (SEIS) ... CMR
Cameron and Norwood's North Carolina Conference Reports [*A publication*] (DLA) ... Cam & N
Cameron and Norwood's North Carolina Conference Reports [*1800-04*] [*A publication*] (DLA) ... Cam & Nor
Cameron and Norwood's North Carolina Conference Reports [*A publication*] (DLA) ... C & N
Cameron and Norwood's North Carolina Conference Reports [*A publication*] (DLA) ... CN Conf
Cameron Ashley [*Associated Press*] (SAG) ... CamrnAsh
Cameron Ashley Bldg Prod [*NASDAQ symbol*] (TTSB) ... CABP
Cameron Ashley Building Products [*NYSE symbol*] ... CAB
Cameron Ashley Building Products, Inc. [*NASDAQ symbol*] (SAG) ... CABP
Cameron College, Medical Library Resource Center, Lawton, OK [*Library symbol*] [*Library of Congress*] (LCLS) ... OkLC-M
Cameron Financial [*NASDAQ symbol*] (TTSB) ... CMRN
Cameron Financial Corp. [*Associated Press*] (SAG) ... CamrnF
Cameron Financial Corp. [*NASDAQ symbol*] (SAG) ... CMRN
Cameron. Intestate Succession in Scotland [*A publication*] (DLA) ... Cam Int Suc
Cameron Iron Works, Inc., Houston (SAUS) ... TxHCI
Cameron Iron Works, Inc., Houston, TX [*Library symbol*] [*Library of Congress*] (LCLS) ... TxHCI
Cameron, MO [*AM radio station call letters*] ... KMRN
Cameron, MO [*FM radio station call letters*] ... KNOZ
Cameron on Joint Stock Companies [*Scotland*] [*A publication*] (DLA) ... Cam JS Comp
Cameron Parish Library (SAUS) ... LCC
Cameron Parish Library, Cameron, LA [*Library symbol*] [*Library of Congress*] (LCLS) ... LCaC
Cameron. Reports, Upper Canada Queen's Bench [*A publication*] (DLA) ... Cam
Cameron State Agricultural College [*Oklahoma*] ... CSAC
Cameron Station [*Virginia*] [*Army*] (AABC) ... CAMSTA
Cameron, TX [*FM radio station call letters*] ... KHLR
Cameron, TX [*FM radio station call letters*] ... KJKS
Cameron, TX [*AM radio station call letters*] ... KMIL
Cameron University, Lawton, OK [*OCLC symbol*] (OCLC) ... OKC
Cameron University, Lawton, OK [*Library symbol*] [*Library of Congress*] (LCLS) ... OkLC
Cameron-Brown Investment Group (SAUO) ... CB
Cameron's Legal Opinions [*Toronto*] [*A publication*] (DLA) ... Cam Op
Cameron's Practice [*Canada*] [*A publication*] (DLA) ... Cameron Pr
Cameron's Practice [*Canada*] [*A publication*] (DLA) ... Cameron Pr (Can)
Cameron's Privy Council Decisions [*1832-1929*] [*Canada*] [*A publication*] (DLA) ... CAM
Camerons Supreme Court (SAUS) ... SCC
Cameron's Supreme Court Cases [*Canada*] [*A publication*] (DLA) ... CAM
Cameron's Supreme Court Cases [*Canada*] [*A publication*] (DLA) ... Cam Cas
Cameron's Supreme Court Cases [*Canada*] [*A publication*] (DLA) ... Cameron
Cameron's Supreme Court Cases [*Canada*] [*A publication*] (DLA) ... Cameron (Can)
Cameron's Supreme Court Cases [*Canada*] [*A publication*] (DLA) ... Cameron Cas (Can)
Cameron's Supreme Court Cases [*Canada*] [*A publication*] (DLA) ... Cameron SC
Cameron's Supreme Court Cases [*Canada*] [*A publication*] (DLA) ... Cam SC
Cameron's Supreme Court Cases [*Canada*] [*A publication*] (DLA) ... SCC
Cameron's Supreme Court Practice [*Canada*] [*A publication*] (DLA) ... Cam Prac
Cameroon (WDAA) ... CAM
Cameroon ... Camer
Cameroon [*ANSI two-letter standard code*] (CNC) ... CM
Cameroon [*MARC country of publication code*] [*Library of Congress*] (LCCP) ... cm
Cameroon [*ANSI three-letter standard code*] (CNC) ... CMR
Cameroon (MILB) ... Crn
Cameroon [*MARC geographic area code*] [*Library of Congress*] (LCCP) ... f-cm-
Cameroon [*Aircraft nationality and registration mark*] (FAAC) ... TJ
Cameroon Airlines [*ICAO designator*] (AD) ... UY
Cameroon Airlines [*ICAO designator*] (FAAC) ... UYC
Cameroon Motor Industries (SAUO) ... CAMI
Cameroon National Society (SAUS) ... SNC
Cameroon National Union [*Political party*] ... CNU
Cameroon People's National Congress ... CPNC
Cameroon Protestant College ... CPC
Cameroon Tribune [*A publication*] ... CT
Cameroon United Congress [*Political party*] ... CUC
Cameroons Development Corporation (SAUO) ... CAMDEV
Cameroons Expeditionary Force (SAUO) ... CEF
Cameroons National Federation (SAUO) ... CNF
Cameroun (SAUO) ... Cam
Camfrey Resources Ltd. [*Vancouver Stock Exchange symbol*] ... CFB
Camiare [*Bolivia*] [*ICAO location identifier*] (ICLI) ... SLCM
Camilla, GA [*Location identifier*] [*FAA*] (FAAL) ... CXU
Camilla, GA [*FM radio station call letters*] ... WQVE
Camillian Fathers and Brothers (TOCD) ... oscam
Camillus [*of Plutarch*] [*Classical studies*] (OCD) ... Cam
Camillus Plautius [*Flourished, 1533-66*] [*Authority cited in pre-1607 legal work*] (DSA) ... Camil Plaut
Camillus Salernus [*Flourished, 16th century*] [*Authority cited in pre-1607 legal work*] (DSA) ... Cam Sal
Camillus Salernus [*Flourished, 16th century*] [*Authority cited in pre-1607 legal work*] (DSA) ... Cam Salern
Camillus Salernus [*Flourished, 16th century*] [*Authority cited in pre-1607 legal work*] (DSA) ... CS
Camindex Mines Ltd. [*Toronto Stock Exchange symbol*] ... CXM
Caminhos de Ferro Portugueses [*Railway*] [*Portugal*] (EY) ... CP
Caminito ... CMT
Camino ... CAM
Camino Energy Corp. [*Vancouver Stock Exchange symbol*] ... CIY
Camino, Placerville & Lake Tahoe Railroad Co. [*AAR code*] ... CPLT
Camino Resources Ltd. [*Vancouver Stock Exchange symbol*] ... CWM
Caminus Corp. [*NASDAQ symbol*] (SG) ... CAMZ
Camiri [*Bolivia*] [*Airport symbol*] (OAG) ... CAM
Camiri [*Bolivia*] [*ICAO location identifier*] (ICLI) ... SLCA
Camisole (DSUE) ... CAM
Camisole (DSUE) ... CAMI
Camlock Fastener Co. (SAUO) ... CLC
Cammed-Gear Speed Variator ... CSV
Cammel Laird & Co, Ltd. (SAUO) ... CL
Cammooweal [*Queensland*] [*Airport symbol*] (AD) ... CML
Cam-Net Communic Ntwk [*NASDAQ symbol*] (TTSB) ... CWKTF
Cam-Net Communications Network, Inc. [*Vancouver Stock Exchange symbol*] ... CWK
Cam-Net Communications Network, Inc. [*NASDAQ symbol*] (NQ) ... CWKT
Cam-Net Communicatoins Network [*Associated Press*] (SAG) ... CamNt
Camoens [*Portuguese poet, 1524-1579*] (ROG) ... CAM
Cam-Operated Plunger ... COP
Camosun College Library [*UTLAS symbol*] ... CAM
Camosun College, Victoria, BC, Canada [*Library symbol*] [*Library of Congress*] (LCLS) ... CaBViC
Camosun College, Victoria, British Columbia [*Library symbol*] [*National Library of Canada*] (NLC) ... BVIC
Camouflage (ADWA) ... cam
Camouflage (AFM) ... CAM
Camouflage ... CAMO
Camouflage (MSA) ... CAMOF
Camouflage Company (SAUO) ... Cam Co
Camouflage, Concealment, and Deception (MCD) ... CCD
Camouflage Critical [*Designation*] [*Army*] (RDA) ... CC
Camouflage Detection [*Often, in regard to a special photographic film, as, "CD film"*] [*Military*] ... CD
Camouflage Effectiveness Assessment Office [*Army*] (RDA) ... CEAO
Camouflage Mobile Field Kitchen [*Military*] (MCD) ... CMFK
Camouflage Officer [*British*] ... CO
Camouflage Signature Measurement [*Army*] (RDA) ... CSM
Camouflage Squadron (SAUO) ... CAMSQN
Camouflage Support System (SAUS) ... CASS
Camouflage Technology Center [*Battelle Columbus Division, OH*] ... CAMTEC
Camouflage Unit [*Military*] ... CU
Camouflage Unit (SAUO) ... CU
Camouflage-Sensitive [*Designation*] [*Army*] (RDA) ... CS
CAMP [*Commonly used*] (OPSA) ... CAMP
Camp (ABBR) ... CMP
Camp ... CP

Camp Atterbury, IN [Location identifier] [FAA] (FAAL) .... XAY
Camp Avenue Elementary School, North Merrick, NY [Library symbol]
[Library of Congress] (LCLS) .... NNmCE
Camp Beverly Hills [California clothing store] .... CBH
Camp Borden Station Hospital (SAUO) .... CBSH
Camp Century [Greenland] [Seismograph station] CC
Camp Century [Greenland] [Seismograph station code, US Geological Survey]
[Closed] (SEIS) .... CCG
Camp Chair CC
Camp Coles Signal Laboratory [Army] (MCD) .... CCSL
Camp Commandant CC
Camp Commander (SAUO) CC
Camp De Bitche [France] [ICAO location identifier] (ICLI) .... LFXG
Camp De Canjuers [France] [ICAO location identifier] (ICLI) .... LFHK
Camp De Caylus [France] [ICAO location identifier] (ICLI) .... LFXT
Camp De Coetquidan [France] [ICAO location identifier] (ICLI) .... LFXQ
Camp De La Courtine [France] [ICAO location identifier] (ICLI) .... LFXS
Camp De Mourmelon [France] [ICAO location identifier] (ICLI) .... LFXE
Camp De Sissonne [France] [ICAO location identifier] (ICLI) .... LFXP
Camp De Suippes [France] [ICAO location identifier] (ICLI) .... LFXK
Camp Douglas (SAUS) .... VOK
Camp Douglas, WI [Location identifier] [FAA] (FAAL) .... VOK
Camp Du Larzac [France] [ICAO location identifier] (ICLI) .... LFXW
Camp Du Valdahon [France] [ICAO location identifier] (ICLI) .... LFXH
Camp Elliot [California] [Seismograph station code, US Geological Survey]
(SEIS) .... CPE
Camp Evans Signal Laboratory [Army] .... CESL
Camp Fire Boys and Girls (EA) .... CFBG
Camp Fire Club of America (EA) .... CFCA
Camp Fire Conservation Fund (EA) .... CFCF
Camp Fire Girls [Later, CFBG] (EA) .... CFG
Camp Fire, Inc. (AEE) .... CFI
Camp Gagetown Canadian Forces Base, NB [ICAO location identifier]
(ICLI) .... CYCX
Camp Hill Hospital, Halifax, Nova Scotia [Library symbol] [National Library of
Canada] (NLC) .... NSHCH
Camp Hill Hospital, Halifax, NS, Canada [Library symbol] [Library of
Congress] (LCLS) .... CaNSHCH
Camp Horsemanship Association (EA) .... CHA
Camp Hospital (SAUO) .... CH
Camp Lejeune [North Carolina] [Marine Corps] .... CAMLEJ
Camp Lejeune, NC [AM radio station call letters] (RBYB) .... WCTJ-AM
Camp Lejeune, NC [AM radio station call letters] .... WWOF
Camp Lejeune Railroad Co. [AAR code] .... CPLJ
Camp Manufacturing Co., Franklin, VA [Library symbol] [Library of
Congress] (LCLS) .... ViFraC
Camp Military Police [British military] (DMA) .... CMP
Camp New Amsterdam [Netherlands] .... CNA
Camp Newspaper Service .... CNS
Camp of Israel [Freemasonry] (ROG) .... COI
Camp Okavango [Botswana] [ICAO location identifier] (ICLI) .... FBCO
Camp Parks, CA [Location identifier] [FAA] (FAAL) .... PNY
Camp Parks Communication Annex [California] (MCD) .... CPCA
Camp Pendleton [California] [Marine Corps] .... CAMPEN
Camp Pendleton [California] [Seismograph station code, US Geological
Survey] (SEIS) .... CPT
Camp Pohakuloa, HI [Location identifier] [FAA] (FAAL) .... BSF
Camp Quartermasters Store [British military] (DMA) .... CQMS
Camp Reception Station [A kind of field hospital] [British] .... CRS
Camp Ripley/Little Falls, MN [Location identifier] [FAA] (FAAL) .... MTK
Camp Rising Sun (SAUO) .... CRS
Camp Sentinel RADAR [Military] (RDA) .... CRS
Camp Springs, MD [Location identifier] [FAA] (FAAL) .... ADW
Camp Springs, MD [Location identifier] [FAA] (FAAL) .... MXK
Camp Springs, MD [Location identifier] [FAA] (FAAL) .... NSF
Camp Springs, MD [Location identifier] [FAA] (FAAL) .... RWS
Camp Springs/Andrews Air Force Base [Maryland] [ICAO location identifier]
(ICLI) .... KADW
Camp Strike Force [Military] (VNW) .... CSF
Camp Williams [Utah] [Seismograph station code, US Geological Survey]
(SEIS) .... CWU
Camp Wood, TX [FM radio station call letters] (BROA) .... KAYG-FM
Campagne Elementary School, Bethpage, NY [Library symbol] [Library of
Congress] (LCLS) .... NBetCaE
Campaign (SAUS) .... Camp
Campaign .... CMPGN
Campaign Against Arms Trade [British] (EAIO) .... CAAT
Campaign Against Book Piracy [British] (NITA) .... CABP
Campaign Against Censorship [British] (DBA) .... CAC
Campaign Against Council Corruption [British] (DBA) .... CAMACC
Campaign Against Drinking & Driving (WDAA) .... CADD
Campaign Against Foreign Control in New Zealand (SAUO) .... CAFCINZ
Campaign Against Health Fraud [British] (DBA) .... CAHF
Campaign Against Investment in South Africa [Defunct] (EA) .... CAISA
Campaign Against Lead in Petrol [British] .... CALIP
Campaign Against Lorry Menace [British] .... CALM
Campaign Against Marijuana Planting .... CAMP
Campaign Against Moral Persecution (SAUO) .... CAMP
Campaign Against Nuclear War (EA) .... CANW
Campaign Against Pollution .... CAP
Campaign Against Pornography [British] .... CAP
Campaign Against Psychiatric Abuses, Haverhill, Suffolk (SAUO) .... CAPA
Campaign Against Racial Discrimination [British] .... CARD
Campaign Against Racism and Fascism [British] (DI) .... CARF
Campaign Against Racism in the Media [British] (DI) .... CRAM

Campaign Against Secret Records on Schoolchildren (AIE) .... CASROS
Campaign Against US Military Bases in the Philippines (EA) .... CAB
Campaign Against Utility Service Exploration (SAUO) .... CAUSE
Campaign Brief [A publication] .... CB
Campaign Communications Institute [Telemarketing] (WDMC) CCI
Campaign for a British Referendum (ECON) .... CBR
Campaign for a Devolved Parliament (SAUO) .... CDV
Campaign for Action on Navigation and Locks [British] (DI) .... CANAL
Campaign for All Employees to Reduce Errors (SAA) .... CARE
Campaign for Better Broadcasting (SAUO) .... CBB
Campaign for Comprehensive Education [British] (DI) .... CCE
Campaign for Democracy in Ulster (SAUO) .... CDU
Campaign for Democratic Rights in Northern Ireland (SAUO) .... CDRNI
Campaign for Democratic Socialism [British] .... CDS
Campaign for Economic Democracy .... CED
Campaign for Equal Citizenship (SAUO) .... CEC
Campaign for Freedom from Tobacco (WDAA) .... CFT
Campaign for Homosexual Equality [British] (DBA) .... CHE
Campaign for Human Development (EA) .... CHD
Campaign for Independent Financial Advice [British] (ECON) .... CAMIFA
Campaign for Independent Financial Advice [British] .... CIFA
Campaign for Integrated Observations of Solar Flares (SAUO) .... CINOF
Campaign for Justice in Divorce [British] (DI) .... CJD
Campaign for Labour Party Democracy [British] .... CLPD
Campaign for Labour Representation in Northern Ireland (SAUO) .... CLRNI
Campaign for Labour Victory (SAUO) CLV
Campaign for Lead-Free Air [British] .... CLEAR
Campaign for Nuclear Disarmament .... CND
Campaign for Peace and Democracy/East and West (EA) .... CPD/EW
Campaign for Pesticide Reform [Environmental Protection Agency]
(GFGA) .... CPR
Campaign for Political Rights [Defunct] (EA) .... CPR
Campaign for Press and Broadcasting Freedom [British] (DI) .... CPBF
Campaign for Prosperity (EA) .... CP
Campaign for Real Ale (WDAA) .... Camra
Campaign for Real Ale .... CAMRA
Campaign for Real Ale Ltd. (SAUO) .... CRA
Campaign for Real Ice Cream [British] (DI) .... CAFRIC
Campaign for Social Justice in Northern Ireland (SAUO) .... CSJ
Campaign for Space Political Action Committee [Defunct] (EA) .... CSPAC
Campaign for State-Supported Alternative Schools (AIE) .... CSSAS
Campaign for Surplus Rosaries [Defunct] (EA) .... CSR
Campaign for the Abolition of NATO (SAUO) .... CANTO
Campaign for the Advancement of State Education (SAUO) .... CASE
Campaign for the Advancement of State Education [British] .... CASE
Campaign for the Creation of the National Youth Advisor (EA) .... CCNYA
Campaign for the Defence of the Turkish Peace Movement [British] .... CDTPM
Campaign for the Feminine Woman (SAUO) .... CFW
Campaign for the Homeless and Rootless [British] (DI) .... CHAR
Campaign for the Mentally Handicapped [British] .... CMH
Campaign for the Protection of Hunted Animals (GVA) .... CPHA
Campaign for the Protection of Rural Wales [See also YDCW] (EAIO) .... CPRW
Campaign for the Restoration of the National Anthem (SAUO) .... CRNA
Campaign for the Restoration of the National Anthem and Flag [British]
(DBA) .... CRNAF
Campaign for the Revitalisation of Ale (SAUO) .... CAMRA
Campaign for UN Reform (EA) .... CUNR
Campaign for World Government (EA) .... CWG
Campaign Fund for Republican Women [Defunct] (EA) .... CFRW
Campaign on Use and Restriction of Barbiturates [British] (DI) .... CURB
Campaign Poster Award [British] .... CPA
Campaign to Impede Sex Stereotyping in the Young [British] (DI) .... CISSY
Campaign to Oppose Bank Loans to South Africa [Defunct] (EA) .... COBLSA
Campaign to Re-Elect Mrs. [Margaret] Thatcher [British] [Obsolete] .... CREET
Campaign to Remove US Bases from the Philippines [Later, CAB]
(EA) .... CRUSBP
Campaign to Save Native Forests, Western Australia .... CSNFWA
Campaign to Save the People of Palestine (EA) .... CSPP
Campaign to Stop Government Spying [Later, CPR] (EA) .... CSGS
Campaigns Against Rising Prices (SAUO) .... CARP
Campana de Solidaridad con Nicaragua [Nicaragua Solidarity Campaign]
(EAIO) .... CSN
Campanian (SAUS) .... Camp
Campanian .... CAMP
Campanile (VRA) .... cmpnl
Campanology (ADWA) .... campanol
Campbell Army Airfield [Fort Campbell, Kentucky] .... CAAF
Campbell College, Buies Creek, NC [Library symbol] [Library of Congress]
(LCLS) .... NcBuC
Campbell Colpitts Bridge [Electronics] .... CCB
Campbell Contacts in America (EA) .... CCA
Campbell County Public Library, Gilete, WY [Library symbol] [Library of
Congress] (LCLS) .... WyG
Campbell Foundation, Memphis, TN [Library symbol] [Library of Congress]
(LCLS) .... TMCF
Campbell, Godfrey & Lewtas, Toronto, ON, Canada [Library symbol] [Library
of Congress] (LCLS) .... CaOTCGL
Campbell, Godfrey & Lewtas, Toronto, Ontario [Library symbol] [National
Library of Canada] (NLC) .... OTCGL
Campbell Interest and Skill Survey [Test] (TMMY) .... CISS
Campbell Island [New Zealand] [Seismograph station code, US Geological
Survey] (SEIS) .... CBZ
Campbell Island [New Zealand] [ICAO location identifier] (ICLI) .... NZCA
Campbell. Mercantile Law [3rd ed.] [1904] [A publication] (DLA) .... Camp Merc L
Campbell, MO [FM radio station call letters] (BROA) .... KFEB-FM

Campbell. Negligence [*2nd ed.*] [*1878*] [*A publication*] (DLA) .... Camp Neg
Campbell, OH [*AM radio station call letters*] .... WASN
Campbell on Citation and Diligence [*A publication*] (DLA) .... Camp Cit
Campbell on Executors and Administrators in Pennsylvania [*A publication*] (DLA) .... Camp Ex
Campbell Red Lake Mines, Ltd. (SAUO) .... CRK
Campbell Reproductions Ltd., Ottawa, ON, Canada [*Library symbol*] [*Library of Congress*] (LCLS) .... CamR
Campbell Resources [*NYSE symbol*] (TTSB) .... CCH
Campbell Resources, Inc. [*Formerly, Campbell Chibougamau Mines Ltd.*] [*NYSE symbol*] [*Toronto Stock Exchange symbol*] (SPSG) .... CCH
Campbell Resources, Inc. [*Formerly, Campbell Chibougamau Mines Ltd.*] [*Associated Press*] (SAG) .... CmpR
Campbell River [*Canada*] [*Airport symbol*] (OAG) .... YBL
Campbell River, BC [*AM radio station call letters*] .... CFWB
Campbell River, BC [*Television station call letters*] CHEK-5
Campbell River, BC [*ICAO location identifier*] (ICLI) .... CYBL
Campbell River Museum and Archives, British Columbia [*Library symbol*] [*National Library of Canada*] (NLC) .... BCRM
Campbell. Sale of Goods and Commercial Agency [*2nd ed.*] [*1891*] [*A publication*] (DLA) .... Camp Sale
Campbell Soup Co. [*Associated Press*] (SAG) .... CampSp
Campbell Soup Co. [*NYSE symbol*] (SPSG) .... CPB
Campbell Soup Co. Ltd. [*Toronto Stock Exchange symbol*] .... CSC
Campbell University (GAGS) .... Campbell U
Campbell University, Law Library, Buies Creek, NC [*Library symbol*] [*Library of Congress*] (LCLS) .... NcBuC-L
Campbell-Ewald Co. [*Advertising agency*] .... C-E
Campbellford Branch, Northumberland County Public Library, Ontario [*Library symbol*] [*National Library of Canada*] (NLC) .... OCA
Campbellford Public Library, Campbellford, ON, Canada [*Library symbol*] [*Library of Congress*] (LCLS) .... CaOCam
Campbell-Johnston Associates [*Commercial firm*] [*British*] .... CJA
Campbell-Johnston Executice Secretaries Ltd. (SAUO) .... CJES
Campbell-Johnston Recruitment Advertising Ltd. (SAUO) .... CJRA
Campbell-Larsen Potentiometer .... CLP
Campbellpore [*Pakistan*] [*Airport symbol*] (AD) .... CWP
Campbellpur [*Pakistan*] [*Seismograph station code, US Geological Survey*] (SEIS) .... CBP
Campbell's Compendium of Roman Law [*A publication*] (DLA) .... Camp
Campbell's Compendium of Roman Law [*A publication*] (DLA) .... Campb
Campbell's Compendium of Roman Law [*A publication*] (DLA) .... Campbell
Campbell's Compendium of Roman Law [*A publication*] (DLA) .... Camp Rom L
Campbell's Compendium of Roman Law [*A publication*] (DLA) .... Camp Rom L Comp
Campbell's Creek R. R. [*AAR code*] .... CCK
Campbell's English Nisi Prius Cases [*A publication*] (DLA) .... CNPC
Campbell's English Nisi Prius Reports [*A publication*] (DLA) .... Camp
Campbell's English Nisi Prius Reports [*A publication*] (DLA) .... Campb
Campbell's English Nisi Prius Reports [*A publication*] (DLA) .... Campbell
Campbell's English Nisi Prius Reports [*A publication*] (DLA) .... Campb (Eng)
Campbell's English Nisi Prius Reports [*A publication*] (DLA) .... Camp NP
Campbell's Legal Gazette Reports [*Pennsylvania*] [*A publication*] (DLA) .... Camp
Campbell's Legal Gazette Reports [*Pennsylvania*] [*A publication*] (DLA) .... Campb
Campbell's Legal Gazette Reports [*Pennsylvania*] [*A publication*] (DLA) .... Campbell
Campbell's Legal Gazette Reports [*Pennsylvania*] [*A publication*] (DLA) .... Campb (PA)
Campbell's Legal Gazette Reports [*Pennsylvania*] [*A publication*] (DLA) .... Camp LG
Campbell's Legal Gazette Reports [*Pennsylvania*] [*A publication*] (DLA) .... Leg Gaz R
Campbell's Legal Gazette Reports [*Pennsylvania*] [*A publication*] (ILCA) .... Leg Gaz Re
Campbell's Legal Gazette Reports [*Pennsylvania*] [*A publication*] (DLA) .... Leg Gaz Rep
Campbell's Lives of the Chief Justices [*A publication*] (DLA) .... Campbell
Campbell's Lives of the Chief Justices [*A publication*] (DLA) .... Camp Ch Jus
Campbell's Lives of the Lord Chancellors [*A publication*] (DLA) .... Campbell
Campbell's Lives of the Lord Chancellors [*A publication*] (DLA) .... Camp Ld Ch
Campbell's Lives of the Lord Chancellors [*A publication*] (DLA) .... Camp Lives Ld Ch
Campbell's Reports [*27-58 Nebraska*] [*A publication*] (DLA) .... Camp
Campbell's Reports [*27-58 Nebraska*] [*A publication*] (DLA) .... Campb
Campbell's Reports [*27-58 Nebraska*] [*A publication*] (DLA) .... Campbell
Campbell's Reports of Taney's United States Circuit Court Decisions [*A publication*] (DLA) .... Camp
Campbell's Reports of Taney's United States Circuit Court Decisions [*A publication*] (DLA) .... Campb
Campbell's Reports of Taney's United States Circuit Court Decisions [*A publication*] (DLA) .... Campb Dec
Campbell's Reports of Taney's United States Circuit Court Decisions [*A publication*] (DLA) .... Campbell
Campbell's Reports of Taney's United States Circuit Court Decisions [*A publication*] (DLA) .... Camp Dec
Campbell's Ruling Cases [*England*] [*A publication*] (DLA) .... Rul Cas
Campbells Ruling Cases (SAUS) .... Rul Cas
Campbellsville College, Campbellsville, KY [*Library symbol*] [*Library of Congress*] (LCLS) .... KyCambC
Campbellsville, KY [*Location identifier*] [*FAA*] (FAAL) .... AAS
Campbellsville, KY [*FM radio station call letters*] (RBYB) .... WAPD-FM
Campbellsville, KY [*FM radio station call letters*] .... WCKQ
Campbellsville, KY [*Television station call letters*] .... WGRB
Campbellsville, KY [*AM radio station call letters*] .... WTCO
Campbell-Tintah Elementary School, Campbell, MN [*Library symbol*] [*Library of Congress*] (LCLS) .... MnCamE
Campbell-Tintah High School, Campbell, MN [*Library symbol*] [*Library of Congress*] (LCLS) .... MnCamH
Campbellton Centennial Public Library, Campbellton, NB, Canada [*Library symbol*] [*Library of Congress*] (LCLS) .... CaNBCa
Campbellton Centennial Public Library, New Brunswick [*Library symbol*] [*National Library of Canada*] (NLC) .... NBCA
Campbellton, NB [*Television station call letters*] CBAT-4
Campbellton, NB [*Television station call letters*] .... CKCD
Campbellton, NB [*AM radio station call letters*] .... CKNB
Campbeltown [*Scotland*] [*Airport symbol*] (OAG) .... CAL
Campden [*England*] .... CAMP
Campden Food Preservation Research Association [*British*] (DBA) .... CFPRA
Campeau Corp. [*Toronto Stock Exchange symbol*] .... CMP
Campeche [*Mexico*] (BARN) .... Camp
Campeche [*Mexico*] [*Airport symbol*] (OAG) .... CPE
Campeche [*Mexico*] [*ICAO location identifier*] (ICLI) .... MMCP
Camper .... CMPR
Camper Alert Team [*for missile sites*] [*Air Force*] .... CAT
CAMPER Alert Team (SAUO) .... CAT
Campers and Caravanners' Association of New South Wales [*Australia*] .... CCANSW
Campership Outdoor Program of Education [*Federal antipoverty program*] .... COPE
Campground .... CMPGRND
Camphor (SAUS) .... Cam
camphor (SAUS) .... camp
Camphora [*Camphor*] [*Pharmacy*] (ROG) .... CAMPH
Camphorsulfonic Acid [*Organic chemistry*] .... CSA
Campina Grande [*Brazil*] [*Airport symbol*] (OAG) .... CPV
Campina Grande/Joao Suassuna [*Brazil*] [*ICAO location identifier*] (ICLI) .... SBKG
Campinas [*Brazil*] [*Airport symbol*] (OAG) .... CPQ
Camping .... CMPNG
Camping and Outdoor Leisure Association [*British*] (DBA) .... COLA
Camping Club of Great Britain (SAUO) .... CCGB
Camping Club of Great Britain and Northern Ireland (SAUO) .... CCGBI
Camping Club Youth [*British*] .... CCY
Camping Council of Great Britain and Ireland, Ltd. .... CCGBI
Camping Products Division [*of Industrial Fabrics Association International*] (EA) .... CPD
Camping Trade Association of Great Britain (SAUO) .... CTA
Camping Trade Association of Great Britain Ltd. (BI) .... CTA
Camping Trailer Manufacturers Association [*Later, RVIA*] .... CTMA
Camping Women (EA) .... CW
Campionati Sciistici della Truppe Alpini [*Alpini Ski Championships*] [*Italian*] .... CaSTA
Campo Alegre [*Brazil*] [*Airport symbol*] (OAG) .... CMP
Campo, CA [*Location identifier*] [*FAA*] (FAAL) .... CZZ
Campo De Francia/Enrique A. Jimenez [*Panama*] [*ICAO location identifier*] (ICLI) .... MPCF
Campo de Provas da Marambaia (SAUS) .... CprM
Campo Electr Appliances/Comp [*NASDAQ symbol*] (TTSB) .... CMPO
Campo Electronics, Appliances & Computers, Inc. [*Associated Press*] (SAG) .... CampoEl
Campo Electronics, Appliances & Computers, Inc. [*NASDAQ symbol*] (SAG) .... CMPO
Campo Grande [*Brazil*] [*Airport symbol*] (OAG) .... CGR
Campo Grande [*Brazil*] [*ICAO location identifier*] (ICLI) .... SBCD
Campo Grande/Internacional [*Brazil*] [*ICAO location identifier*] (ICLI) .... SBCG
Campobasso [*Italy*] [*ICAO location identifier*] (ICLI) .... LIBS
Campobello Public Library, Campobello, NB, Canada [*Library symbol*] [*Library of Congress*] (LCLS) .... CaNBCAM
Campobello Public Library, New Brunswick [*Library symbol*] [*National Library of Canada*] (BIB) .... NBCAM
Campomelic Dysplasia [*Medicine*] .... CD
Camp-On [*Telecommunications*] (TEL) .... CMP
Campos [*Brazil*] [*Airport symbol*] (OAG) .... CAW
Campos/Bartolomeu Lisandro [*Brazil*] [*ICAO location identifier*] (ICLI) .... SBCP
Campos/Plataforma PNA-1 [*Brazil*] [*ICAO location identifier*] (ICLI) .... SBGP
Campos/Plataforma SS-17 [*Brazil*] [*ICAO location identifier*] (ICLI) .... SBEN
Camp's Reports [*1 North Dakota*] [*A publication*] (DLA) .... Camp
Campsite .... CMPST
Campton, KY [*FM radio station call letters*] (BROA) .... WCBJ-FM
Campton, NH [*FM radio station call letters*] .... WVFM
Camptothecin [*Antineoplastic drug*] (CDI) .... CPT
Camptothecin Sodium [*Biochemistry*] (AAMN) .... CS
Campulung [*Romania*] [*Seismograph station code, US Geological Survey*] (SEIS) .... CMP
Campus .... CAM
Campus (ABBR) .... CMPS
Campus 1, Champlain Regional College, St.-Lambert, Quebec [*Library symbol*] [*National Library of Canada*] (NLC) .... QSLCR
Campus Action Network [*Defunct*] (EA) .... CAN
Campus Americans for Democratic Action [*Defunct*] (EA) .... CADA
Campus Antenna Television System (SAUS) .... KATS
Campus Area Network (SAUO) .... CAN
Campus Chemical Instrument Center [*Ohio State University*] [*Research center*] (RCD) CCIC
Campus Computer Communication Association (VERA) .... CCCA
Campus Computing Network (SAUS) .... CCN
Campus Conference Network [*Services by Satellite, Inc.*] [*Washington, DC*] [*Telecommunications*] (TSSD) .... CCN
Campus Crusade for Christ International (EA) CCC
Campus Crusade for Christ International (EA) CCCI

Campus Custom Publishing (ADWA) .... CCP
Campus Gateway (SAUS) .... CGW
Campus Improvement Council CIC
Campus Instructional Television System (SAUS) .... KITS
Campus Liaison Officer [Military] (DNAB) .... CLO
Campus Ministries of America (EA) .... CMA
Campus Ministry Women (EA) .... CMW
Campus Notre-Dame de Foy, Cap-Rouge, PQ, Canada [Library symbol]
    [Library of Congress] (LCLS) .... CaQCRCN
Campus Notre-Dame-De-Foy, Cap-Rouge, Quebec [Library symbol] [National
    Library of Canada] (NLC) .... QCRCN
Campus Outreach Opportunity League (EA) .... COOL
Campus Safety Association [of the National Safety Council] (EA) .... CSA
Campus Safety Association of the National Safety Council (EA) ..... CSANSC
Campus Safety, Health, and Environmental Management Association
    (SARE) .... CSHEMA
Campus Studies Institute (EA) .... CSI
Campus Wide Information Service (SAUO) .... CWIS
Campus-Based Information System [National Science Foundation] ..... CBIS
Campus-Free College .... CFC
Campus-Wide Information Server .... CWIS
Campus-Wide Information Systems [Internet] .... CWIS
Campylobacteriosis [Medicine] (MELL) .... CB
Campylobacter-Like Organism (PDAA) .... CLO
Camreco, Inc. [Toronto Stock Exchange symbol] .... CMR
Camrose, AB [AM radio station call letters] .... CFCW
Camrose International Institute [L'Institut International de Camrose] [Formerly,
    Camrose One World Institute] (AC) CII
Camrose International Institute (SAUS) .... COWI
Camrose Lutheran College, Alberta [Library symbol] [National Library of
    Canada] (NLC) .... ACAL
Camrose Lutheran College, Camrose, AB, Canada [Library symbol] [Library
    of Congress] (LCLS) .... CaACAL
Camrose Public Library, Alberta [Library symbol] [National Library of
    Canada] (NLC) .... ACA
Camshaft [Automotive engineering] .... CAM
Camshaft (MSA) .... CMSHFT
Camshaft Profile Switching [Automotive engine design] .... CPS
Camurati-Engelmann [Syndrome] [Medicine] (DB) .... CE
Camuy, PR [AM radio station call letters] .... WCHQ
Camuy, PR [FM radio station call letters] .... WCHQ-FM
Camuy, PR [FM radio station call letters] (BROA) .... WDIN-FM
Can [Buoy] [Maps and charts] C
Can .... CN
Can Am Gold Resources [Vancouver Stock Exchange symbol] ..... CAZ
CAN [Controller Area Network] Application Layer (ACII) .... CAL
Can Buoy (SAUS) .... C Buoy
CAN Calibration Protocol (SAUS) .... CCP
Can Do It [Temporary-help agency] .... CDI
Can Go Over (WDMC) .... cgo
Can Go Over [Newspapers] .... CGO
CAN in Automation (SAUS) .... CIA
CAN Manufacturers Institute (SAUS) .... CMI
Can Manufacturers Institute (EA) .... CMI
Can Not Process (SAUS) .... CANTPR
Can We Meet [Online dialog] .... CWM
Can You Come and See Me .... UCM
Canaan, VT [FM radio station call letters] .... WXMX
Canaanite (BJA) .... Can
Canaanite Myths and Legends [A publication] (BJA) .... CML
Cana/Bohicon [Benin] [ICAO location identifier] (ICLI) .... DBBC
Canacord Resources, Inc. [Toronto Stock Exchange symbol] ...... CQD
Canada C
Canada [ANSI two-letter standard code] (CNC) .... CA
Canada (MILB) .... Ca
Canada (ODBW) .... Can
Canada [ANSI three-letter standard code] (CNC) .... CAN
Canada (SAUO) .... Cana
Canada (WGA) .... CANAD
Canada .... CDA
Canada (SAUO) .... CDN
Canada (SAUO) .... CF
Canada [MARC country of publication code] [Library of Congress] (LCCP) ..... cn
Canada (SAUS) .... CND
Canada [IYRU nationality code] (IYR) .... KC
Canada [MARC geographic area code] [Library of Congress] (LCCP) ..... n-cn-
Canada - Transport Canada [Canada] [ICAO designator] (ICDA) ..... GO
Canada - United Kingdom - United States (SAUO) .... CanUKUS
Canada Academy & Association of Chinese Acupuncture/Medicine
    (AC) .... CACA
Canada Agricultural Plant Research Institute (SAUS) .... CAPRI
Canada Air Defence Command (SAUS) .... CADC
Canada & Gulf Terminal Railway (MHDB) .... C & GTR
[The] Canada & Gulf Terminal Railway Co. [AAR code] .... CGT
Canada Arctic Gas Study Ltd., Toronto, ON, Canada [Library symbol]
    [Library of Congress] (LCLS) .... CaOTCAG
Canada Arctic Gas Study Ltd., Toronto, Ontario [Library symbol] [National
    Library of Canada] (NLC) .... OTCAG
Canada Art Council [Conseil des Arts du Canada] .... CAC
Canada Art Council, Ottawa, ON, Canada [Library symbol] [Library of
    Congress] (LCLS) .... CaOOCAC
Canada Asia Working Group .... CAWG
Canada Assistance Plan .... CAP
Canada, Australia and New Zealand .... CANZ
Canada, Australia and New Zealand Group (SAUO) .... CANZ

Canada Awards for Business Excellence .... ACAE
Canada Basin Deep Water [Oceanography] .... CBDW
Canada Bottle Water Federation [Federation Canadienne des Eaux
    Embouteillees] (AC) .... CBWF
Canada Brush, Broom & Mop Manufacturers Association [Association
    Candienne des Fabricants de Brosses, Balais et Vadrouilles] (AC) ..... CBBMMA
Canada Business Opportunity Centre [1986] .... CBOC
Canada Cement Co. Ltd., Montreal, PQ, Canada [Library symbol] [Library of
    Congress] (LCLS) .... CaQMCC
Canada Cement Co., Montreal, Quebec [Library symbol] [National Library of
    Canada] (NLC) .... QMCC
Canada Cement Lafarge Ltd. [Toronto Stock Exchange symbol] ..... CCT
Canada Cement Lafarge Ltd., Belleville, ON, Canada [Library symbol]
    [Library of Congress] (LCLS) .... CaOBCCL
Canada Cement Lafarge Ltd., Belleville, Ontario [Library symbol] [National
    Library of Canada] (NLC) .... OBCCL
Canada Centre for Geomatics (SAUS) .... CCG
Canada Centre for Inland Waters .... CCIW
Canada Centre for Inland Waters [Centre Canadien des Eaux Interieures],
    Burlington, Ontario [Library symbol] [National Library of Canada]
    (NLC) .... OBUC
Canada Centre for Mapping (GEOI) .... CCM
Canada Centre for Mineral and Energy Technology [Department of Energy,
    Mines, and Resources] [Ottawa, ON] .... CANMET
Canada Centre for Remote Sensing, Energy, Mines and Resources Canada
    [Centre Canadien de Teledetection, Energie, Mines et Ressources Canada]
    Ottawa, Ontario [Library symbol] [National Library of Canada] (NLC) ..... OOCCR
Canada Centre for Remote Sensing Library [UTLAS symbol] ..... EMC
Canada Centre for Space Science [National Research Council of Canada]
    [Research center] (RCD) .... CCSS
Canada Club of Victoria [Australia] CCV
Canada Coast Guard College, Sydney, NS, Canada [Library symbol] [Library
    of Congress] (LCLS) .... CaNSSCG
Canada College Library, Redwood City, CA [OCLC symbol] (OCLC) ..... CCG
Canada Committee on Agricultural Engineering .... CCAE
Canada Committee on Ecological (Biophysical) Land Classification G2
    [See also CCCET] .... CCELC
Canada Committee on Plant Gene Resources .... CCPGR
Canada Committee on Socio-Economic Services [See also CCSSE] ..... CCSES
Canada Communicable Disease Report (SAUS) .... CCDR
Canada Community Services Projects .... CCSP
Canada Council (EAIO) CC
Canada Council [Conseil des Arts du Canada] Ottawa, Ontario [Library
    symbol] [National Library of Canada] (NLC) .... OOCAC
Canada Criminal Acts, Taschereau's Edition [A publication] (DLA) ..... Can Cr Acts
Canada Criminal Cases, Annotated [A publication] (DLA) .... Can CC
Canada Department of Agriculture, Animal Diseases Research Institute
    (West), Lethbridge, AB, Canada [Library symbol] [Library of Congress]
    (LCLS) .... CaALADR
Canada Department of Agriculture, Canadian Farm Management Data
    System, Guelph, ON, Canada [Library symbol] [Library of Congress]
    (LCLS) .... CaOGCF
Canada Department of Agriculture, Canadian Grain Commission,
    Winnipeg, MB, Canada [Library symbol] [Library of Congress]
    (LCLS) .... CaMWGR
Canada Department of Agriculture, Economics Branch, Regina, SK,
    Canada [Library symbol] [Library of Congress] (LCLS) ..... CaSRAgE
Canada Department of Agriculture, Entomological Society of British
    Columbia Library, Vancouver, BC, Canada [Library symbol] [Library of
    Congress] (LCLS) .... CaBVaAg
Canada Department of Agriculture, Experimental Farm, La Pocatiere, PQ,
    Canada [Library symbol] [Library of Congress] (LCLS) ..... CaQPAg
Canada Department of Agriculture, Experimental Farm, L'Assomption, PQ,
    Canada [Library symbol] [Library of Congress] (LCLS) ..... CaQAsAg
Canada Department of Agriculture, Lethbridge, AB, Canada [Library symbol]
    [Library of Congress] (LCLS) .... CaALAg
Canada Department of Agriculture, Ottawa, ON, Canada [Library symbol]
    [Library of Congress] (LCLS) .... CaOOAg
Canada Department of Agriculture, Research Institute, Belleville, ON,
    Canada [Library symbol] [Library of Congress] [Obsolete] (LCLS) ..... CaOBP
Canada Department of Agriculture, Research Institute, London, ON,
    Canada [Library symbol] [Library of Congress] (LCLS) ..... CaOLAg
Canada Department of Agriculture, Research Station, Agassiz, BC, Canada
    [Library symbol] [Library of Congress] (LCLS) .... CaBAgAg
Canada Department of Agriculture, Research Station, Beaverlodge, AB,
    Canada [Library symbol] [Library of Congress] (LCLS) ..... CaABeAg
Canada Department of Agriculture, Research Station, Brandon, MB,
    Canada [Library symbol] [Library of Congress] (LCLS) ..... CaMBAg
Canada Department of Agriculture, Research Station, Charlottetown, PE,
    Canada [Library symbol] [Library of Congress] (LCLS) ..... CaPCAg
Canada Department of Agriculture, Research Station, Delhi, ON, Canada
    [Library symbol] [Library of Congress] (LCLS) .... CaODeAg
Canada Department of Agriculture, Research Station, Fredericton, NB,
    Canada [Library symbol] [Library of Congress] (LCLS) ..... CaNBFAg
Canada Department of Agriculture, Research Station, Harrow, ON, Canada
    [Library symbol] [Library of Congress] (LCLS) .... CaOHarAg
Canada Department of Agriculture, Research Station, Kamloops, BC,
    Canada [Library symbol] [Library of Congress] (LCLS) ..... CaBKAg
Canada Department of Agriculture, Research Station, Kentville, NS,
    Canada [Library symbol] [Library of Congress] (LCLS) ..... CaNSKR
Canada Department of Agriculture, Research Station, Lacombe, AB,
    Canada [Library symbol] [Library of Congress] (LCLS) ..... CaALaAg
Canada Department of Agriculture, Research Station, Morden, MB, Canada
    [Library symbol] [Library of Congress] (LCLS) .... CaMMoAg

Canada Department of Agriculture, Research Station, Regina, SK, Canada [*Library symbol*] [*Library of Congress*] (LCLS) .... CaSRAgR
Canada Department of Agriculture, Research Station, Saanichton, BC, Canada [*Library symbol*] [*Library of Congress*] (LCLS) .... CaBSAg
Canada Department of Agriculture, Research Station, Saint-Jean, PQ, Canada [*Library symbol*] [*Library of Congress*] (LCLS) .... CaQStJAg
Canada Department of Agriculture, Research Station, Saskatoon, SK, Canada [*Library symbol*] [*Library of Congress*] (LCLS) .... CaSSAgR
Canada Department of Agriculture, Research Station, St. John's, NF, Canada [*Library symbol*] [*Library of Congress*] (LCLS) .... CaNfSAg
Canada Department of Agriculture, Research Station, Ste.-Foy, PQ, Canada [*Library symbol*] [*Library of Congress*] (LCLS) .... CaQSFAg
Canada Department of Agriculture, Research Station, Summerland, BC, Canada [*Library symbol*] [*Library of Congress*] (LCLS) .... CaBSuAg
Canada Department of Agriculture, Research Station, Swift Current, SK, Canada [*Library symbol*] [*Library of Congress*] (LCLS) .... CaSSCAg
Canada Department of Agriculture, Research Station, Vineland Station, ON, Canada [*Library symbol*] [*Library of Congress*] (LCLS) .... CaOVAgR
Canada Department of Agriculture, Research Station, Winnipeg, MB, Canada [*Library symbol*] [*Library of Congress*] (LCLS) .... CaMWAG
Canada Department of Agriculture, Winnipeg, MB, Canada [*Library symbol*] [*Library of Congress*] (LCLS) .... CaMWA
Canada Department of Communications, Central Region Information Resources Center, Winnipeg, MB, Canada [*Library symbol*] [*Library of Congress*] (LCLS) .... CaMWCCIR
Canada Department of Communications, Communications Research Centre, Ottawa, ON,Canada [*Library symbol*] [*Library of Congress*] (LCLS) .... CaOORPL
Canada Department of Communications, Ottawa, ON, Canada [*Library symbol*] [*Library of Congress*] (LCLS) .... CaOOCO
Canada Department of Consumer and Corporate Affairs, Ottawa, ON, Canada [*Library symbol*] [*Library of Congress*] (LCLS) .... CaOOCI
Canada Department of Energy, Mines, and Resources, Canada Centre for Remote Sensing, Ottawa, ON, Canada [*Library symbol*] [*Library of Congress*] (LCLS) .... CaOOCCR
Canada Department of Energy, Mines, and Resources, Earth Physics Branch, Ottawa,ON, Canada [*Library symbol*] [*Library of Congress*] (LCLS) .... CaOOO
Canada Department of Energy, Mines, and Resources, Energy Development Sector, Ottawa, ON, Canada [*Library symbol*] [*Library of Congress*] [*Obsolete*] (LCLS) .... CaOOEME
Canada Department of Energy, Mines, and Resources, Map Library, Ottawa, ON, Canada [*Library symbol*] [*Library of Congress*] (LCLS) .... CaOOSMM
Canada Department of Energy, Mines, and Resources, Physical Metallurgy Division,Ottawa, ON, Canada [*Library symbol*] [*Library of Congress*] (LCLS) .... CaOOMP
Canada Department of Energy, Mines, and Resources, Resources Economic Library, Ottawa, ON, Canada [*Library symbol*] [*Library of Congress*] (LCLS) .... CaOOMR
Canada Department of Energy, Mines, and Resources, Surveys and Mapping Branch, Ottawa, ON, Canada [*Library symbol*] [*Library of Congress*] (LCLS) .... CaOOSM
Canada Department of External Affairs, Legal Branch, Ottawa, ON, Canada [*Library symbol*] [*Library of Congress*] (LCLS) .... CaOOELB
Canada Department of External Affairs, Ottawa, ON, Canada [*Library symbol*] [*Library of Congress*] (LCLS) .... CaOOE
Canada Department of Finance, Ottawa, ON, Canada [*Library symbol*] [*Library of Congress*] (LCLS) .... CaOOF
Canada Department of Fisheries and Ocean, St. John's, NF, Canada [*Library symbol*] [*Library of Congress*] (LCLS) .... CaNfSF
Canada Department of Fisheries and Oceans, Institute of Ocean Studies, Sidney, BC, Canada [*Library symbol*] [*Library of Congress*] (LCLS) .... CaBSIOS
Canada Department of Fisheries and Oceans, St. Johns, NF, Canada [*Library symbol*] [*Library of Congress*] (LCLS) .... CaNfSEC
Canada Department of Fisheries and Oceans, Vancouver, BC, Canada [*Library symbol*] [*Library of Congress*] (LCLS) .... CaBVaFi
Canada Department of Fisheries and the Environment, Fisheries and Marine Service, Quebec, PQ, Canada [*Library symbol*] [*Library of Congress*] (LCLS) .... CaQQPSM
Canada Department of Indian Affairs and Northern Development, Battleford National HistoricPark, Battleford, SK, Canada [*Library symbol*] [*Library of Congress*] (LCLS) .... CaSBIN
Canada Department of Indian Affairs and Northern Development, Inuvik Research Laboratory, Inuvik, NT, Canada [*Library symbol*] [*Library of Congress*] (LCLS) .... CaNWII
Canada Department of Indian Affairs and Northern Development, Ottawa, ON, Canada [*Library symbol*] [*Library of Congress*] (LCLS) .... CaOORD
Canada Department of Indian Affairs and Northern Development, Parks Canada, Atlantic Regional Office, Halifax, NS, Canada [*Library symbol*] [*Library of Congress*] (LCLS) .... CaNSHIAP
Canada Department of Indian Affairs and Northern Development, Parks Canada, Ontario Regional Office, Cornwall, ON, Canada [*Library symbol*] [*Library of Congress*] (LCLS) .... CaOGIAP
Canada Department of Indian Affairs and Northern Development, Parks Canada, Quebec Regional Office, Ste-Foy, Quebec, PQ, Canada [*Library symbol*] [*Library of Congress*] (LCLS) .... CaQQIAP
Canada Department of Indian Affairs and Northern Development, Parks Canada, Western Regional Office, Calgary, AB, Canada [*Library symbol*] [*Library of Congress*] (LCLS) .... CaACIA
Canada Department of Indian Affairs and Northern Development, Point Pelee National Park, Leamington, ON, Canada [*Library symbol*] [*Library of Congress*] (LCLS) .... CaOLeI
Canada Department of Indian and Northern Affairs, Prince Albert, SK, Canada [*Library symbol*] [*Library of Congress*] (LCLS) .... CaSPAIN
Canada Department of Indian and Northern Affairs, Yellowknife, NT, Canada [*Library symbol*] [*Library of Congress*] (LCLS) .... CaNWYIM
Canada Department of Industry, Ottawa, ON, Canada [*Library symbol*] [*Library of Congress*] [*Obsolete*] (LCLS) .... CaOOI
Canada Department of Industry, Trade, and Commerce, Ottawa, ON, Canada [*Library symbol*] [*Library of Congress*] (LCLS) .... CaOOTC
Canada Department of Insurance, Ottawa, ON, Canada [*Library symbol*] [*Library of Congress*] (LCLS) .... CaOOIn
Canada Department of Justice, Edmonton, AB, Canada [*Library symbol*] [*Library of Congress*] (LCLS) .... CaAEJ
Canada Department of Justice [*Ministere de la Justice*] **Edmonton, Alberta** [*Library symbol*] [*National Library of Canada*] (NLC) .... AEJ
Canada Department of Justice [*Ministere de la Justice*] **Halifax, Nova Scotia** [*Library symbol*] [*National Library of Canada*] (NLC) .... NSHJ
Canada Department of Justice, Halifax, NS, Canada [*Library symbol*] [*Library of Congress*] (LCLS) .... CaNSHJ
Canada Department of Justice, Montreal, PQ, Canada [*Library symbol*] [*Library of Congress*] (LCLS) .... CaQMJM
Canada Department of Justice [*Ministere de la Justice*] **Montreal, Quebec** [*Library symbol*] [*National Library of Canada*] (NLC) .... QMJM
Canada Department of Justice, Occupational Analysis Library, Ottawa, ON, Canada [*Library symbol*] [*Library of Congress*] [*Obsolete*] (LCLS) .... CaOOOA
Canada Department of Justice, Ottawa, ON, Canada [*Library symbol*] [*Library of Congress*] (LCLS) .... CaOOJ
Canada Department of Justice, Toronto, ON, Canada [*Library symbol*] [*Library of Congress*] (LCLS) .... CaOTJ
Canada Department of Justice, Vancouver, BC, Canada [*Library symbol*] [*Library of Congress*] (LCLS) .... CaBVaJ
Canada Department of Justice [*Ministere de la Justice*] **Vancouver, British Columbia** [*Library symbol*] [*National Library of Canada*] (NLC) .... BVAJ
Canada Department of Justice [*Ministere de la Justice*] **Winnipeg, Manitoba** [*Library symbol*] [*National Library of Canada*] (NLC) .... MWJ
Canada Department of Justice, Winnipeg, MB, Canada [*Library symbol*] [*Library of Congress*] (LCLS) .... CaMWJ
Canada Department of Labour, Occupational Safety and Health Branch, Ottawa, ON, Canada [*Library symbol*] [*Library of Congress*] (LCLS) .... CaOOLAP
Canada Department of Labour, Ottawa, ON, Canada [*Library symbol*] [*Library of Congress*] (LCLS) .... CaOOL
Canada Department of Manpower and Immigration, Halifax, NS, Canada [*Library symbol*] [*Library of Congress*] [*Obsolete*] (LCLS) .... CaNSHMI
Canada Department of Manpower and Immigration, Prince Albert, SK, Canada [*Library symbol*] [*Library of Congress*] [*Obsolete*] (LCLS) .... CaSPAMI
Canada Department of Manpower and Immigration, Winnipeg, MB, Canada [*Library symbol*] [*Library of Congress*] (LCLS) .... CaMWMI
Canada Department of Mines and Resources, Centre for Inland Waters, Burlington, ON, Canada [*Library symbol*] [*Library of Congress*] (LCLS) .... CaOBUC
Canada Department of National Defence, Canadian Forces Staff School, Toronto, ON, Canada [*Library symbol*] [*Library of Congress*] (LCLS) .... CaOTRCS
Canada Department of National Defence, Defence Research Establishment, Esquimalt, BC, Canada [*Library symbol*] [*Library of Congress*] (LCLS) .... CaBEPN
Canada Department of National Defence, Defence Research Establishment, Ottawa, ON, Canada [*Library symbol*] [*Library of Congress*] (LCLS) .... CaOODRC
Canada Department of National Defence, Defence Research Establishment Suffield, Ralston, AB, Canada [*Library symbol*] [*Library of Congress*] (LCLS) .... CaARS
Canada Department of National Defence, Headquarters Mobile Command, St. Hubert, PQ, Canada [*Library symbol*] [*Library of Congress*] (LCLS) .... CaQStHuM
Canada Department of National Defence, Northern Region Information System, [*NORIS*], **Yellowknife, NT, Canada** [*Library symbol*] [*Library of Congress*] (LCLS) .... CaNWYND
Canada Department of National Defence, Ottawa, ON, Canada [*Library symbol*] [*Library of Congress*] [*Obsolete*] (LCLS) .... CaOOAM
Canada Department of National Defence, Quality Assurance Division, Ottawa, ON, Canada [*Library symbol*] [*Library of Congress*] (LCLS) .... CaOOQA
Canada Department of National Defence, Reference and Recreational Library [*Stadacona*], **Halifax, NS, Canada** [*Library symbol*] [*Library of Congress*] (LCLS) .... CaNSHND
Canada Department of National Defence Research Establishment Atlantic, Dartmouth, NS, Canada [*Library symbol*] [*Library of Congress*] (LCLS) .... CaNSHN
Canada Department of National Health and Welfare, Food and Drug Directorate, Ottawa, ON, Canada [*Library symbol*] [*Library of Congress*] (LCLS) .... CaOOFD
Canada Department of National Health and Welfare, Health Protection Branch, Laboratory Centre for Disease Control, Ottawa, ON, Canada [*Library symbol*] [*Library of Congress*] (LCLS) .... CaOONHL
Canada Department of National Health and Welfare, Health Protection Branch, Montreal, PQ, Canada [*Library symbol*] [*Library of Congress*] (LCLS) .... CaQMNHH
Canada Department of National Health and Welfare, Health Protection Branch, Toronto, ON, Canada [*Library symbol*] [*Library of Congress*] (LCLS) .... CaOTNHH
Canada Department of National Health and Welfare, Health Protection Branch, Vancouver, BC, Canada [*Library symbol*] [*Library of Congress*] (LCLS) .... CaBVaNH
Canada Department of National Revenue, Customs and Excise Division, Ottawa, ON, Canada [*Library symbol*] [*Library of Congress*] (LCLS) .... CaOONR
Canada Department of National Revenue, Taxation Division, Ottawa, ON, Canada [*Library symbol*] [*Library of Congress*] (LCLS) .... CaOONRT
Canada Department of Public Works, Capital Region Library, Ottawa, ON, Canada [*Library symbol*] [*Library of Congress*] (LCLS) .... CaOOPWC

Canada Department of Public Works, Office of the Dominion Fire Commissioner, Ottawa, ON, Canada [*Library symbol*] [*Library of Congress*] [*Obsolete*] (LCLS) ... CaOOPWD
Canada Department of Public Works, Ottawa, ON, Canada [*Library symbol*] [*Library of Congress*] (LCLS) ... CaOOPW
Canada Department of Public Works, Research and Development Laboratories, Ottawa, ON, Canada [*Library symbol*] [*Library of Congress*] (LCLS) ... CaOOPWR
Canada Department of Regional Economic Expansion, Moncton, NB, Canada [*Library symbol*] [*Library of Congress*] (LCLS) ... CaNBMoRE
Canada Department of Regional Economic Expansion, Ottawa, ON, Canada [*Library symbol*] [*Library of Congress*] (LCLS) ... CaOOREx
Canada Department of Regional Economic Expansion, Prairie Farm Rehabilitation Administration, Regina, SK, Canada [*Library symbol*] [*Library of Congress*] (LCLS) ... CaSRREE
Canada Department of Regional Economic Expansion, Reference and Enquiries Unit, Ottawa, ON, Canada [*Library symbol*] [*Library of Congress*] [*Obsolete*] (LCLS) ... CaOORExR
Canada Department of Regional Economic Expansion, St. John's, NF, Canada [*Library symbol*] [*Library of Congress*] (LCLS) ... CaNfSREx
Canada Department of Regional Economic Expansion, Toronto, ON, Canada [*Library symbol*] [*Library of Congress*] (LCLS) ... CaOTREx
Canada Department of Regional Industrial Expansion [*Ministere de l'Expansion Industrielle Regionale*] **Moncton, New Brunswick** [*Library symbol*] [*National Library of Canada*] (NLC) ... NBMORE
Canada Department of Regional Industrial Expansion [*Ministere de l'Expansion Industrielle Regionale*] **Montreal, Quebec** [*Library symbol*] [*National Library of Canada*] (NLC) ... QMREX
Canada Department of Regional Industrial Expansion [*Ministere de l'Expansion Industrielle Regionale*] **Saskatoon, Saskatchewan** [*Library symbol*] [*National Library of Canada*] (NLC) ... SSREX
Canada Department of Regional Industrial Expansion Saskatoon, Saskatchewan (SAUS) ... SSREX
Canada Department of Regional Industrial Expansion [*Ministere de l'Expansion Industrielle Regionale*] **St. John's, Newfoundland** [*Library symbol*] [*National Library of Canada*] (NLC) ... NFSREX
Canada Department of Regional Industrial Expansion [*Ministere de l'Expansion Industrielle Regionale*] **Toronto, Ontario** [*Library symbol*] [*National Library of Canada*] (NLC) ... OTREX
Canada Department of Revenue, Canada Customs and Excise, Scientific and Technical Information Centre, Laboratory and Scientific Services Division, Ottawa, ON, Canada [*Library symbol*] [*Library of Congress*] (LCLS) ... CaOOSTI
Canada Department of Supply and Services, Bureau of Management and Consulting, Ottawa, ON, Canada [*Library symbol*] [*Library of Congress*] (LCLS) ... CaOOBMC
Canada Department of Supply and Services, Compensation Branch, Superannuation Division, Ottawa, ON, Canada [*Library symbol*] [*Library of Congress*] (LCLS) ... CaOODPS
Canada Department of Supply and Services, Ottawa, ON, Canada [*Library symbol*] [*Library of Congress*] (LCLS) ... CaOODP
Canada Department of the Environment, Atmospheric Environment Service, Atlantic Region, Halifax, NS, Canada [*Library symbol*] [*Library of Congress*] (LCLS) ... CaNSHW
Canada Department of the Environment, Atmospheric Environment Service, Toronto, ON, Canada [*Library symbol*] [*Library of Congress*] (LCLS) ... CaOTM
Canada Department of the Environment, Bedford Institute of Oceanography, Dartmouth, NS, Canada [*Library symbol*] [*Library of Congress*] (LCLS) ... CaNSDB
Canada Department of the Environment, Canadian Wildlife Service, Edmonton, AB, Canada [*Library symbol*] [*Library of Congress*] (LCLS) ... CaAEECW
Canada Department of the Environment, Canadian Wildlife Service, Ottawa, ON, Canada [*Library symbol*] [*Library of Congress*] (LCLS) ... CaOOECW
Canada Department of the Environment, Canadian Wildlife Service, Prairie Migratory Bird Research Centre, Saskatoon, SK, Canada [*Library symbol*] [*Library of Congress*] (LCLS) ... CaSSECW
Canada Department of the Environment, Canadian Wildlife Service, Sackville, NB, Canada [*Library symbol*] [*Library of Congress*] (LCLS) ... CaNBSaCW
Canada Department of the Environment, Environmental Protection Service, Vancouver, BC, Canada [*Library symbol*] [*Library of Congress*] (LCLS) ... CaBVaEP
Canada Department of the Environment, Environmental Protection Services, Montreal, PQ, Canada [*Library symbol*] [*Library of Congress*] (LCLS) ... CaQMEE
Canada Department of the Environment, Fisheries and Marine Service, Halifax, NS, Canada [*Library symbol*] [*Library of Congress*] (LCLS) ... CaNSHF
Canada Department of the Environment, Fisheries and Marine Service, Research and Development Directorate Biological Station, St. Andrews, NB, Canada [*Library symbol*] [*Library of Congress*] (LCLS) ... CaNBAB
Canada Department of the Environment, Fisheries and Marine Service, Research andDevelopment Directorate, Pacific Biological Station, Nanaimo, BC, Canada [*Library symbol*] [*Library of Congress*] (LCLS) ... CaBNP
Canada Department of the Environment, Fisheries and Marine Service, Research andDevelopment Directorate, Vancouver Laboratory, Vancouver, BC, Canada [*Library symbol*] [*Library of Congress*] (LCLS) ... CaBVaF
Canada Department of the Environment, Fisheries and Marine Service, Ste.-Anne-De-Bellevue, PQ, Canada [*Library symbol*] [*Library of Congress*] (LCLS) ... CaQMFR
Canada Department of the Environment, Fontaine Branch Library, Ottawa, ON, Canada [*Library symbol*] [*Library of Congress*] (LCLS) ... CaOOEF
Canada Department of the Environment, Forest Fire Research Institute, Ottawa, ON, Canada [*Library symbol*] [*Library of Congress*] (LCLS) ... CaOOFFR
Canada Department of the Environment, Forest Products Laboratory, Ottawa, ON, Canada [*Cl osed*] [*Library symbol*] [*Library of Congress*] (LCLS) ... CaOOFP
Canada Department of the Environment, Forest Products Laboratory, Vancouver, BC,Canada [*Library symbol*] [*Library of Congress*] (LCLS) ... CaBVaFP
Canada Department of the Environment, Forest Research Laboratory, Quebec, PQ, Canada [*Library symbol*] [*Library of Congress*] (LCLS) ... CaQQMF
Canada Department of the Environment, Forest Research Laboratory, Victoria, BC, Canada [*Library symbol*] [*Library of Congress*] (LCLS) ... CaBViF
Canada Department of the Environment, Institute of Ocean Sciences, Victoria, BC,Canada [*Library symbol*] [*Library of Congress*] (LCLS) ... CaBViEM
Canada Department of the Environment, Maritimes Forest Research Centre, Fredericton, NB, Canada [*Library symbol*] [*Library of Congress*] (LCLS) ... CaNBFE
Canada Department of the Environment, Northern Forest Research Centre, Edmonton,AB, Canada [*Library symbol*] [*Library of Congress*] (LCLS) ... CaAEF
Canada Department of the Environment, Ottawa, ON, Canada [*Library symbol*] [*Library of Congress*] (LCLS) ... CaOOFF
Canada Department of the Environment, Pacific Environment Institute, Vancouver, BC, Canada [*Library symbol*] [*Library of Congress*] (LCLS) ... CaBVaPE
Canada Department of the Environment, Petawawa Forest Experiment Station, Chalk River, ON, Canada [*Library symbol*] [*Library of Congress*] (LCLS) ... CaOCkE
Canada Department of the Environment, Quebec Region, Ste.-Foy, Quebec, PQ, Canada [*Library symbol*] [*Library of Congress*] (LCLS) ... CaQQE
Canada Department of the Environment, Research Station, Sault Ste. Marie, ON, Canada [*Library symbol*] [*Library of Congress*] (LCLS) ... CaOStMF
Canada Department of the Environment, Resource and Environmental Law Library, Ottawa, ON, Canada [*Library symbol*] [*Library of Congress*] [*Obsolete*] (LCLS) ... CaOOERE
Canada Department of the Environment, Sea Lamprey Control Centre, Sault Ste. Marie, ON, Canada [*Library symbol*] [*Library of Congress*] (LCLS) ... CaOStMEF
Canada Department of the Secretary of State, Ottawa, ON, Canada [*Library symbol*] [*Library of Congress*] (LCLS) ... CaOOSS
Canada Department of the Secretary of State, Translation Bureau, Montreal, PQ, Canada [*Library symbol*] [*Library of Congress*] (LCLS) ... CaQMBD
Canada Department of the Secretary of State, Translation Bureau, Multilingual Services Division, Ottawa, ON, Canada [*Library symbol*] [*Library of Congress*] [*Obsolete*] (LCLS) ... CaOOSST
Canada Department of the Secretary of State, Translation Bureau, Terminology Centre Library, Ottawa, ON, Canada [*Library symbol*] [*Library of Congress*] (LCLS) ... CaOOSSTT
Canada Department of the Solicitor General, Ottawa, ON, Canada [*Library symbol*] [*Library of Congress*] (LCLS) ... CaOOSG
Canada Department of Veterans Affairs, Ottawa, ON, Canada [*Library symbol*] [*Library of Congress*] (LCLS) ... CaOOV
Canada Deposit Insurance Corp. ... CDIC
Canada Development Corp. [*Toronto Stock Exchange symbol*] [*Vancouver Stock Exchange symbol*] ... CDC
Canada Development Investment Corp. [*Corp. de Developpement des Inve stissements du Canada*] ... CDIC
Canada Dry Corporation (SAUO) ... CD
Canada East ... CE
Canada East Regional Operational Control Center (SAUO) ... CE ROCC
Canada, EC, Japan and United States (SAUS) ... QUADS
Canada Emergency Measures Organization [*Civil defense*] ... CEMO
Canada Employment and Immigration Advisory Council (EDAC) ... CEIAC
Canada Employment and Immigration Commission ... CEIC
Canada Employment and Immigration Department, Ottawa, ON, Canada [*Library symbol*] [*Library of Congress*] (LCLS) ... CaOOMI
Canada Employment and Immigration Department, Quebec Regional Office, Montreal, PQ, Canada [*Library symbol*] [*Library of Congress*] (LCLS) ... CaQMMIQ
Canada Employment and Immigration Department, Toronto, ON, Canada [*Library symbol*] [*Library of Congress*] (LCLS) ... CaOTMIO
Canada Employment and Immigration Department, Vancouver, BC, Canada [*Library symbol*] [*Library of Congress*] (LCLS) ... CaBVaMI
Canada Employment and Immigration Union ... CEIU
Canada Employment Centre ... CEC
Canada Exchequer Court Reports [*1875-1922*] [*A publication*] (DLA) ... Ex CR
Canada [*or Canadian*] **Farm Building Plan Service** ... CFBPS
Canada Farm Labor Pool ... CFLP
Canada Federal Court Reports [*A publication*] (DLA) ... Can FCR
Canada. Fisheries and Marine Service. Resource Development Branch Maritimes Region Technical Report Series Mar-T (journ.) (SAUS) ... TSMRD9
Canada Fortnightly Law Journal [*A publication*] (DLA) ... FLJ
Canada Foundation for Innovation ... CFI
Canada France Ocean Optics Experiment (SAUS) ... CFOX
Canada, France, United Kingdom, United States (SAUO) ... CANFRUKUS
Canada Gazette (Regulations) [*A publication*] (DLA) ... Can Gaz
Canada Geographic Information System [*Canada Land Data Systems Division*] [*Environment Canada*] [*Information service or system*] (IID) ... CGIS
Canada Geological Survey, Vancouver, BC, Canada [*Library symbol*] [*Library of Congress*] (LCLS) ... CaBVaG
Canada Immigration Centre (SAUO) ... Can Imm Cen
Canada in World Affairs [*A publication*] (DLA) ... Can in Wld Aff
Canada Income Plus Fund 1986 Trust Units [*Toronto Stock Exchange symbol*] ... CNFUN

Canada Income Plus Fund 1987 Trust Units [*Toronto Stock Exchange symbol*] ... CUF
Canada Income Plus Fund Trust Units [*Toronto Stock Exchange symbol*] ... CIB
Canada Institute for Scientific and Technical Information [*National Research Council of Canada*] (IID) ... CISTI
Canada Institute for Scientific and Technical Information, Administration Building Library, Ottawa, ON, Canada [*Library symbol*] [*Library of Congress*] (LCLS) ... CaOONAB
Canada Institute for Scientific and Technical Information, Aeronautical and Mechanical Engineering Branch, Ottawa, ON, Canada [*Library symbol*] [*Library of Congress*] (LCLS) ... CaOONAM
Canada Institute for Scientific and Technical Information, Chemistry Library, Ottawa, ON, Canada [*Library symbol*] [*Library of Congress*] (LCLS) ... CaOONC
Canada Institute for Scientific and Technical Information, Division of Building Research, Ottawa, ON, Canada [*Library symbol*] [*Library of Congress*] (LCLS) ... CaOONBR
Canada Institute for Scientific and Technical Information, National Research Council (CISTI) [*Institut Canadien de l'Information Scientifique et Technique, Conseil National de Recherches (ICIST)*] **Ottawa, Ontario** [*Library symbol*] [*National Library of Canada*] (NLC) ... OON
Canada Institute for Scientific and Technical Information, National Research Council, Ottawa, ON, Canada [*Library symbol*] [*Library of Congress*] (LCLS) ... CaOON
Canada Institute for Scientific and Technical Information, Radio and Electrical Engineering Division, Ottawa, ON, Canada [*Library symbol*] [*Library of Congress*] (LCLS) ... CaOONRE
Canada Institute for Scientific and Technical Information, Sussex Library, Ottawa, ON, Canada [*Library symbol*] [*Library of Congress*] (LCLS) ... CaOONS
Canada Institute for Scientific and Technical Information, Uplands Library, Ottawa, ON, Canada [*Library symbol*] [*Library of Congress*] (LCLS) ... CaOONU
Canada Labour Relations Board ... CLRB
Canada Labour Relations Board, Ottawa, ON, Canada [*Library symbol*] [*Library of Congress*] (LCLS) ... CaOOLRB
Canada Labour Relations Board [*Conseil Canadien des Relations de Travail*] **Ottawa, Ontario** [*Library symbol*] [*National Library of Canada*] (NLC) ... OOLRB
Canada Land Data System ... CLDS
Canada Land Inventory ... CLI
Canada Land Surveyor ... CLS
Canada Land Use Monitoring Program (GEOI) ... CLUMP
Canada Lands Surveys Records (SAUO) ... CLSR
Canada Law Journal [*A publication*] (DLA) ... Can LJ
Canada Law Journal [*A publication*] (DLA) ... CLJ
Canada Law Journal, New Series [*A publication*] (DLA) ... Can LJ NS
Canada Law Journal, Old Series [*A publication*] (DLA) ... UCLJ OS
Canada Law Journal, Old Series (journ.) (SAUS) ... UCLJ OS
Canada Law Reform Commission (DLA) ... CLRC
Canada Law Reports [*A publication*] (DLA) ... CLR
Canada Law Reports, Exchequer Court [*A publication*] (DLA) ... Can Ex
Canada Law Reports, Exchequer Court [*A publication*] (DLA) ... Can Exch
Canada Law Reports, Exchequer Court [*A publication*] (DLA) ... Can Ex CR
Canada Law Reports, Exchequer Court [*A publication*] (DLA) ... Can Ex R
Canada Law Reports, Exchequer Court [*A publication*] (DLA) ... ECR
Canada Law Reports, Exchequer Court [*A publication*] (DLA) ... Exch C
Canada Law Reports, Exchequer Court [*A publication*] (DLA) ... Exch Can
Canada Law Reports, Exchequer Court [*A publication*] (DLA) ... Exch CR
Canada Law Reports, Exchequer Court [*A publication*] (DLA) ... Exch Ct (Can)
Canada Law Reports, Exchequer Court [*A publication*] (DLA) ... Ex CR
Canada Law Reports, Exchequer Court and Supreme Court [*A publication*] (DLA) ... Can LR
Canada Law Reports, Exchequer Court and Supreme Court [*A publication*] (DLA) ... CLR (Can)
Canada Law Reports, Federal Court [*A publication*] (DLA) ... FC
Canada Law Reports, Supreme Court [*A publication*] (DLA) ... Can S Ct
Canada Lease Financing Ltd. [*Toronto Stock Exchange symbol*] ... CQF
Canada Legal News [*A publication*] (DLA) ... Can Leg N
Canada Life Financial [*NYSE symbol*] ... CLU
Canada Malting Co. Ltd. [*Toronto Stock Exchange symbol*] ... CMG
Canada Manpower Centre ... CMC
Canada Manpower Industrial Training ... CMIT
Canada Manpower Mobility Program ... CMMP
Canada Manpower Training Program ... CMTP
Canada Map Office (GEOI) ... CMO
Canada Marketing Assistance Program ... CANMAP
Canada Medal ... CM
Canada Ministry of State for Science and Technology, Ottawa, ON, Canada [*Library symbol*] [*Library of Congress*] (LCLS) ... CaOOMSS
Canada Ministry of State for Urban Affairs, Ottawa, ON, Canada [*Library symbol*] [*Library of Congress*] (LCLS) ... CaOOMUA
Canada Ministry of the Solicitor General, Penitentiary, Federal Training Centre,Laval, PQ, Canada [*Library symbol*] [*Library of Congress*] (LCLS) ... CaQLASGPT
Canada Ministry of Transport, Canadian Air Transportation Administration, Ontario Region, Toronto, ON, Canada [*Library symbol*] [*Library of Congress*] (LCLS) ... CaOTTOA
Canada Ministry of Transport, Marine Library, Halifax, NS, Canada [*Library symbol*] [*Library of Congress*] (LCLS) ... CaNSHMT
Canada Ministry of Transport Training Institute, Ottawa, ON, Canada [*Library symbol*] [*Library of Congress*] (LCLS) ... CaOOTI
Canada Ministry of Transport, Transportation Development Agency, Montreal, PQ, Canada [*Library symbol*] [*Library of Congress*] (LCLS) ... CaQMTD
Canada Ministry of Transport, Waterways Development, Montreal, PQ, Canada [*Library symbol*] [*Library of Congress*] (LCLS) ... CaQMTR
Canada Mink Breeders Association [*Association des Eleveurs de Visions du Canada*] (AC) ... CMBA
Canada Mortgage and Housing Corp. [*Government agency*] ... CMHC
Canada Network [*Computer science*] (TNIG) ... CAnet
Canada News-Wire [*Database*] [*Canada News-Wire Service*] [*Information service or system*] (CRD) ... CNW
Canada Northwest Energy Ltd. [*Toronto Stock Exchange symbol*] ... CNW
Canada Oil and Gas Lands Administration ... COGLA
Canada Oil Low Acid [*Variety of rapeseed*] ... CANOLA
Canada Oil Substitution Program ... COSP
Canada Olympic Park [*Calgary, AB*] ... COP
Canada Orient Resources [*Vancouver Stock Exchange symbol*] ... CDO
Canada Packers Ltd., Toronto, Ontario [*Library symbol*] [*National Library of Canada*] (NLC) ... OTCP
Canada Pension Plan ... CPP
Canada Permanent Mortgage Corp. [*Toronto Stock Exchange symbol*] ... CDP
Canada Plan Service ... CPS
Canada Post Corporation Library [*UTLAS symbol*] ... CPC
Canada Post [*Postes Canada*] **Ottawa, Ontario** [*Library symbol*] [*National Library of Canada*] (NLC) ... OOPO
Canada Privy Council Office, Management Information, Ottawa, ON, Canada [*Library symbol*] [*Library of Congress*] (LCLS) ... CaOOPC
Canada Publishing Corp., Agincourt, ON, Canada [*Library symbol*] [*Library of Congress*] (LCLS) ... CaOAgCP
Canada Publishing Corp., Agincourt, Ontario [*Library symbol*] [*National Library of Canada*] (BIB) ... OACP
Canada Railway Cases [*A publication*] (DLA) ... Can Ry Cas
Canada Regional Industrial Expansion , Prince Albert, Saskatchewan (SAUS) ... SPAREX
Canada Regional Industrial Expansion [*Expansion Industrielle Regionale*], **Prince Albert, Saskatchewan** [*Library symbol*] [*National Library of Canada*] (BIB) ... SPAREX
Canada Remote Systems Ltd. [*Information service or system*] (IID) ... CRS
Canada Road [*California*] [*Seismograph station code, US Geological Survey*] (SEIS) ... CDC
Canada Safety Council (AC) ... CSC
Canada Safety Council, Ottawa, ON, Canada [*Library symbol*] [*Library of Congress*] (LCLS) ... CaOOCSC
Canada Safety Council [*Conseil Canadien de la Securite*] **Ottawa, Ontario** [*Library symbol*] [*National Library of Canada*] (NLC) ... OOCSC
Canada Safeway Ltd. [*Toronto Stock Exchange symbol*] ... CNS
Canada Savings Bond [*Investment term*] ... CSB
Canada Shipping Act (SAUS) ... CSA
Canada Soil Information System (SAUS) ... CANSIS
Canada Southern Petroleum Ltd. [*Associated Press*] (SAG) ... CanSoPt
Canada Southern Petroleum Ltd. [*NASDAQ symbol*] (SAG) ... CSPL
Canada Southern Petroleum Ltd. [*Toronto Stock Exchange symbol*] ... CSW
Canada Southern Railway [*Penn Central*] [*AAR code*] ... CASO
Canada Southern Railway Co. (SAUO) ... CNS
Canada South'n Petrol [*NASDAQ symbol*] (TTSB) ... CSPLF
Canada Standard Size [*Of Clothing*] (BARN) ... CSS
Canada Starch Co. ... CASCO
Canada Steamship Lines ... CSL
Canada Steamship Lines [*AAR code*] ... CSSL
Canada Steamship Lines, Montreal (SAUO) ... CSL
Canada Student Loans Program ... CSLP
Canada Studies Foundation [*See also FEC*] ... CSF
Canada Supreme Court (DLA) ... Can SC
Canada Supreme Court (DLA) ... CSC
Canada Supreme Court Reports [*A publication*] (DLA) ... Can SC
Canada Supreme Court Reports [*A publication*] (DLA) ... Can SCR
Canada Supreme Court Reports [*A publication*] (DLA) ... Can SC Rep
Canada Supreme Court Reports [*A publication*] (DLA) ... Can S Ct
Canada Supreme Court Reports [*A publication*] (DLA) ... Can Sup Ct
Canada. Supreme Court Reports (SAUS) ... SCR
Canada Systems Group [*Database producer*] [*Ottawa, ON*] [*Information service or system*] ... CSG
Canada Systems Group, Mississauga, ON, Canada [*Library symbol*] [*Library of Congress*] (LCLS) ... CaOMCSG
Canada Systems Group, Mississauga, Ontario [*Library symbol*] [*National Library of Canada*] (NLC) ... OMCSG
Canada Tax Appeal Board Cases [*A publication*] (DLA) ... Can Tax App Bd
Canada Tax Appeal Board Cases [*A publication*] (DLA) ... Tax ABC
Canada Tax Appeal Board Cases (SAUS) ... Tax ABC
Canada Tax Appeal Board Cases (journ.) (SAUS) ... Tax ABC
Canada Tax Cases [*A publication*] (DLA) ... Can Tax Cas
Canada Tax Cases [*A publication*] (DLA) ... CTC
Canada Tax Cases, Annotated [*A publication*] (DLA) ... Can Tax Cas Ann
Canada Tax Cases, Annotated [*A publication*] (DLA) ... Cas Tax
Canada Taxation Publications [*Database*] (IID) ... CTP
Canada Training Awards Programme (SAUO) ... CTAP
Canada Treaty Series [*A publication*] (DLA) ... Can TS
Canada Trust Income Investments [*Toronto Stock Exchange symbol*] ... CNN
Canada Trustco Mortgage Co. [*Toronto Stock Exchange symbol*] ... CT
Canada Tungsten Mining Corp. Ltd. [*Toronto Stock Exchange symbol*] ... CTM
Canada VM Users Group (EAIO) ... CVMUG
Canada Water [*Canada*] [*A database*] (NITA) ... CWA
Canada West ... CW
Canada West Air Ltd. [*ICAO designator*] (FAAC) ... CWA
Canada West Gold Rush Museum, Surrey, British Columbia [*Library symbol*] [*National Library of Canada*] (NLC) ... BSURCW
Canada West Regional Operational Control Center (SAUO) ... CW ROCC
Canada West Universities Athletic Association [*Association Sportive Universitaire de l'Ouest Canadien*] [*Formerly, Western Canadian Intercollegiate Athletic Union*] (AC) ... CWUAA

Canada Wire & Cable Co. Ltd., Montreal, PQ, Canada [*Library symbol*] [*Library of Congress*] (LCLS) ... CaQMCW
Canada Wire & Cable Co. Ltd., Montreal, Quebec [*Library symbol*] [*National Library of Canada*] (NLC) ... QMCW
Canada Wire & Cable Co. Ltd., Toronto, ON, Canada [*Library symbol*] [*Library of Congress*] (LCLS) ... CaOTCW
Canada Wire & Cable Co. Ltd., Toronto, Ontario [*Library symbol*] [*National Library of Canada*] (NLC) ... OTCW
Canada Wire and Cable Company (SAUO) ... CW
Canada World Youth (AC) ... CWY
Canada Year Book (SAUS) ... CYB
Canada-Arab Business Council (AC) ... CABC
Canada-Australia Trade Agreement ... CANATA
Canada-British Columbia Consultative Board (SAUO) ... CBCC
Canada-California Chamber of Commerce (SRA) ... CCCC
Canada-Caribbean-Central America Policy Alternatives [*An association*] ... CAPA
Canada-Cuba Sports & Fitness Cultural Festivals (AC) ... CCS&FCF
Canada-France Redshift Survey [*Astronomy*] ... CFRS
Canada-France-Hawaii Observatory (SAUS) ... CFHO
Canada-France-Hawaii Telescope [*Mauna Kea, Hawaii*] ... CFHT
Canada-France-Hawaii Telescope Corp. Kamuela, HI [*Library symbol*] [*Library of Congress*] (LCLS) ... HKamCF
Canadain Native Friendship Centre (AC) ... CNFC
Canada-India Reactor ... CIR
Canada-India Reactor (SAUO) ... CIR
Canadair Limited (SAUO) ... Can Ltd
Canadair Limited (SAUO) ... C-L
Canadair Ltd. (SAUO) ... Canadair
Canadair Ltd. [*Canada*] [*ICAO aircraft manufacturer identifier*] (ICAO) ... CL
Canadair Ltd., Engineering Library, Montreal, PQ, Canada [*Library symbol*] [*Library of Congress*] (LCLS) ... CaQMCa
Canadair Ltd., Missiles and Systems Library, Montreal, PQ, Canada [*Library symbol*] [*Library of Congress*] (LCLS) ... CaQMCam
Canadair Regional Jet ... CRJ
Canada-Israel Foundation for Academic Exchanges [*Foundation Canada-Israel pour les Exchanges Universitaires*] (AC) ... CIFAE
Canada-Latin American Resource Centre (AC) ... CLARC
Canada-Ontario Environmental Sustainability Agreement ... COESA
Canada-Ontario Rideau-Trent-Severn Study Committee ... CORTS
Canada-Pakistan Business Council [*Conseil de Commerce Canada Pakistan*] [*Formerly, Canada-Parkistan Trade & Economic Committee*] (AC) ... CPBC
Canada-Russia Business Council (AC) ... CRBC
Canada-Taiwan Business Association (AC) ... CTBA
Canada-Taiwan Friendship Association (AC) ... CTFA
Canada-Transport Canada [*ICAO designator*] (FAAC) ... TGO
Canada-United Kingdom ... CAN-UK
Canada-United Kingdom Chamber of Commerce (DS) ... CUKCC
Canada-United Kingdom Joint Communications-Electronics Committee (SAUO) ... CAN-UK-JCEC
Canada-United Kingdom-Joint Communications Electronics Committees ... CAN-UK JCEC
Canada-United Kingdom-United States [*Agreement*] ... CANUKUS
Canada-United Kingdom-United States Cryptographic Systems General Publications (MCD) ... CCG
Canada-United Kingdom-United States Joint Communications-Electronics Committees ... CANUKUS JCECS
Canada-United States (COE) ... CANUS
Canada-United States (SAUS) ... CAN-US
Canada-United States Environmental Council (EA) ... CUSEC
Canada/United States Region (NATG) ... CUSR
Canada-United States Regional Planning Group [*NATO*] ... CUSRPG
Canada-United States Scientific Advisory Team (SAUO) ... CUSSAT
Canada-US Military Co-operation Community (SAUO) ... MCC
Canadex Resources Ltd. [*Toronto Stock Exchange symbol*] ... CDX
Canadian (ODBW) ... Can
Canadian (ROG) ... CAN
Canadian (ADWA) ... Canad
Canadian ... CANDN
Canadian (DD) ... Cdn
Canadian (NATG) ... CDN
Canadian ... CNDN
Canadian 88 Energy [*AMEX symbol*] (SG) ... EEE
Canadian Abilities Foundation (SAUO) ... CAF
Canadian Abortion Rights Action League ... CARAL
Canadian Abridgment [*A publication*] (DLA) ... Can Abr
Canadian Abridgment [*2nd ed.*] [*A publication*] (DLA) ... Can Abr (2d)
Canadian Academic Accounting Association [*See also ACPC*] ... CAAA
Canadian Academic Aptitude Test (SAUS) ... CAAT
Canadian Academic Centre in Italy ... CACI
Canadian Academic Decathlon Associations (AC) ... CADA
Canadian Academic Research Libraries ... CARL
Canadian Academy of Clinical Biochemistry (SAUO) ... CACB
Canadian Academy of Endodontics (EAIO) ... CAE
Canadian Academy of Engineering (EAIO) ... CAE
Canadian Academy of Facial Plastic & Reconstructive Surgery [*Academie Canadienne de Chirurgie Plastique et Reconstructive Faciale*] [*Formerly, Canadian Institute of Facial Plastic Surgery*] (AC) ... CAFPRS
Canadian Academy of Oral Radiology [*Academie Canadienne de Radiologie Buccale*] (AC) ... CAOR
Canadian Academy of Podiatric Sports Medicine ... CAPSM
Canadian Academy of Recording Arts and Sciences ... CARAS
Canadian Academy of Sport Medicine [*See also CCMS*] ... CASM
Canadian Academy of the History of Pharmacy [*Academie Canadienne d'Histoire de la Pharmacie*] (AC) ... CAHP
Canadian Accredited Insurance Broker (DD) ... CAIB
Canadian Achievement Test [*Canadian Test Centre*] (TES) ... CAT
Canadian Achievement Test in English [*Education*] (AEBS) ... CATE
Canadian Achievement Test in French [*Education*] (AEBS) ... CATF
Canadian Achievement Test in Mathematics [*Education*] (AEBS) ... CATM
Canadian Achievement Test in Technical and Commercial Mathematics [*Education*] (AEBS) ... CATTCM
Canadian Achievement Tests, Second Edition (TMMY) ... CAT/2
Canadian Acoustical Association ... CAA
Canadian Action for Nicaragua (AC) ... CAN
Canadian Active Control System (GEOI) ... CACS
Canadian Active Service Force (SAUO) ... CASF
Canadian Actors' Equity Association [*Canada*] (WWLA) ... CAEA
Canadian Addiction Foundation, Addictions Librarians Special Interest Section ... CAFALSIS
Canadian Administrative Housekeepers Association (AC) ... CAHA
Canadian Adult Congenital Heart Network (SAUO) ... CACHNET
Canadian Advanced Industrial Materials Forum [*Forum Canadien des Materiaux Industriels de Haute Qualite*] (AC) ... CAIMAF
Canadian Advanced Technology Association [*Ottawa, ON*] [*Telecommunications service*] ... CATA
Canadian Advertising Advisory Board ... CAAB
Canadian Advertising and Sales Association ... CASA
Canadian Advertising Foundation ... CAF
Canadian Advertising Rates and Data ... CARD
Canadian Advertising Research Foundation [*Founded 1949*] ... CARF
Canadian Advisory Committee on Programming Languages ... CAC/PL
Canadian Advisory Committee on Remote Sensing (ACAE) ... CACRS
Canadian Advisory Council on the Status of Women (AC) ... CACSW
Canadian Advisory Council on the Status of Women, Documentation Centre, Ottawa, ON, Canada [*Library symbol*] [*Library of Congress*] (LCLS) ... CaOOCACSW
Canadian Aeronautical Institute (IAA) ... CAEI
Canadian Aeronautical Institute (SAUO) ... C Ae I
Canadian Aeronautical Institute ... CAI
Canadian Aeronautics and Space Institute ... CASI
Canadian Aerophilatelic Society (AC) ... CAS
Canadian African Newcomer Aid Centre of Toronto (AC) ... CANACT
Canadian Agency for International Development [*Defunct*] ... CAID
Canadian Aging Research Network [*University of Toronto*] [*Research center*] (RCD) ... CARNET
Canadian Agri-Business Satellite Intelligence Program (SAUS) ... CANASIP
Canadian Agricultural Chemicals Association (SAUO) ... CACA
Canadian Agricultural Chemics Association ... CACA
Canadian Agricultural Economics and Farm Management Society ... CAEFMS
Canadian Agricultural Economics Society ... CAES
Canadian Agricultural Export Corp. ... CANAGREX
Canadian Agricultural Market Development Fund ... CAMDF
Canadian Agricultural Research Council ... CARC
Canadian Agricultural Services Coordinating Committee ... CASCC
Canadian Agricultural Statistics System (SAUS) ... CASS
Canadian Agriculture, Farm and Food Extension Information Network and Exchange (SAUO) ... CAFFEINE
Canadian Agroindustrial Corporation (SAUO) ... CANACOR
Canadian AIDS Society (SAUO) ... CAS
Canadian Air and Precipitation Monitoring Network (EPAT) ... CAPMoN
Canadian Air Cushion Technology Society (AC) ... CACTS
Canadian Air Defence Command (SAUO) ... CADC
Canadian Air Defence Identification Zone ... CADIZ
Canadian Air Defense Command Headquarters (SAUO) ... CanAirDef
Canadian Air Defense Group Headquarters (SAUO) ... CanAirVan
Canadian Air Defense Zone (PIPO) ... CADIZ
Canadian Air Division (MCD) ... CAD
Canadian Air Division (SAUO) ... CANAIRDIV
Canadian Air Division Headquarters (SAUO) ... CanAirDiv
Canadian Air Division Headquarters [*Allied Air Forces in Europe*] ... CANAIRDIV
Canadian Air Force [*1920-1923*] ... CAF
Canadian Air Force - Winnipeg (SAUO) ... CANAIRPEG
Canadian Air Force Defence Command (SAUS) ... CANAIRDEF Command
Canadian Air Force Defense Command (SAUO) ... CANAIRDEF
Canadian Air Force Division (SAUO) ... CANAIRDIV
Canadian Air Force Headquarters (SAUO) ... CANAIRHED
Canadian Air Force Headquarters (SAUS) ... CanAirHed
Canadian Air Force Joint Staff-London (SAUO) ... CANAIRLON
Canadian Air Force Joint Staff-Washington (SAUO) ... CANAIRWASH
Canadian Air Force Material Command (SAUO) ... CANAIRMAT
Canadian Air Force Material Command (SAUS) ... CANAIRMAT Command
Canadian Air Force Tactical Command (SAUO) ... CANAIRTAC
Canadian Air Force Tactical Command (SAUS) ... CANAIRTAC Command
Canadian Air Force Training Command (SAUO) ... CANAIRTRAIN
Canadian Air Force Training Command (SAUS) ... CANAIRTRAIN Command
Canadian Air Force-Newfoundland (SAUO) ... CANAIRNEW
Canadian Air Force-Northwest (SAUO) ... CANAIRNORWEST
Canadian Air Group (MCD) ... CAG
Canadian Air Line Dispatchers' Association [*See also ACRV*] ... CALDA
Canadian Air Line Employees Association (SAUO) ... CALEA
Canadian Air Line Flight Attendants Association ... CALFAA
Canadian Air Lines Employees Association ... CALEA
Canadian Air Mail Collectors Club (EA) ... CAMCC
Canadian Air Mail Collectors Club (EA) ... CAN
Canadian Air Publication ... CAP
Canadian Air Staff Secretariat (SAUO) ... CAS/Sec
Canadian Air Task Group Middle East (SAUO) ... CATGME
Canadian Air Traffic Control Association ... CATCA
Canadian Air Training Command Headquarters ... CANAIRTRAIN
Canadian Air Transport Association (SAUO) ... CATA

Canadian Air Transport Board .... CATB
Canadian Air Transport Command (SAUS) .... CAFATC
Canadian Air Transport Command (MUGU) .... CATC
Canadian Air Transportation Administration .... CATA
Canadian Airborne Regiment (MCD) .... CAR
Canadian Aircraft Insurance Group .... CAIG
Canadian Aircraft Maintenance Engineers Association (SAUO) .... CAMEA
Canadian Aircraft Products, Ltd. (SAUO) .... CAP
Canadian Air-Ground Environment .... CAGE
Canadian Airline Pilots Association .... CALPA
Canadian Airlines [TS Symbol] (TTSB) .... CA
Canadian Airlines International Ltd. [Canadian Pacific Airlines Ltd. and Pacific Western Airlines Ltd.] [Formed by a merger of] .... CAI
Canadian Airlines International Ltd. [Canadian Pacific Airlines Ltd. and Pacific Western Airlines Ltd.] [Formed by a merger of] .... CAIL
Canadian Airlines International Ltd. [ICAO designator] (FAAC) .... CDN
Canadian Airports Council [Conseil des Aeroports du Canada] (AC) .... CAC
Canadian Air/Sea Transportable (SAUO) .... CAST
Canadian Air-Sea Transportable Brigade (SAUS) .... CAST
Canadian Air/Sea Transportable Combat Group .... CAST
Canadian Airspace Reservation Unit [Aviation] (FAAC) .... CARU
Canadian Airways Ltd. .... CAL
Canadian Alarm & Security Association [Association Canadienne de l'Alarme et de la Securite] (AC) .... CANASA
Canadian Alliance Against Software Theft [Alliance Canadienne Contre le vol de Logiciels] (AC) .... ACCVOL
Canadian Alliance Against Software Theft [Alliance Canadienne Contre le vol de Logiciels] (AC) .... CAAST
Canadian Alliance for Research on Schizophrenia (SAUO) .... CAROS
Canadian Alliance in Solidarity with the Native People (EA) .... CASNP
Canadian Alliance of Black Educators [See also ACEN] .... CABE
Canadian Alliance of Community Health Center Associations (SAUO) .... CACHCA
Canadian All-Terrain Vehicle Distributors Council [Conseil Canadien des Distributeurs de Vehicules Tout Terrain] (AC) .... CATV
Canadian Almanac and Directory [A publication] .... CAD
Canadian Altitude Sensing Experiment Package (MCD) .... CASEP
Canadian Amateur Cowboys Association .... CACA
Canadian Amateur Diving Association Inc. [Association Candienne du Plongeon Amateur Inc.] (AC) .... CADA
Canadian Amateur Football Association .... CAFA
Canadian Amateur Hockey Association .... CAHA
Canadian Amateur Musicians (EAIO) .... CAMMAC
Canadian Amateur Radio Federation (PDAA) .... CARF
Canadian Amateur Radio Teletype Group (HGAA) .... CART
Canadian Amateur Speed Skating Association .... CASA
Canadian Amateur Speed Skating Association .... CASSA
Canadian Amateur Sports Federation .... CASF
Canadian Amateur Synchronized Swimming Association .... CASSA
Canadian Amateur Wrestling Association [Association Canadienne de Lutte Amateur] (AC) .... CAWA
Canadian Amenian Business Council Inc. [Conseil Commercial Canadien-Armenien Inc.] (AC) .... CABC
Canadian American Business Association (AC) .... CABA
Canadian Amputee Sports Association [Association Canadienne des Sports Pour Amputes] (AC) .... CASA
Canadian Anaesthetists Society .... CAS
Canadian and Catholic Confederation of Labour CCCL
Canadian and Catholic Confederation of Labour (SAUO) CCCL
Canadian Angus Resources [Vancouver Stock Exchange symbol] .... AGB
Canadian Animal Health Institute [Institut Canadien de la Sante Animale] (AC) .... CAHI
Canadian Animation Producers Association .... CAPA
Canadian Annual Digest [A publication] (DLA) .... CAD
Canadian Anti-Acoustic Torpedo Gear [World War II] .... CAT
Canadian Antique Dealers Association (AC) .... CADA
Canadian Anti-Racism Education & Research Society (AC) .... CAERS
Canadian Anti-Soviet Action Committee (EAIO) .... CASAC
Canadian Apparel Federation [Federation Canadienne du Vetement] (AC) .... CAF
Canadian Apparel Manufacturers Institute (EAIO) .... CAMI
Canadian Appeal Cases [A publication] (DLA) .... Can App Cas
Canadian Appliance Manufacturers Association (AC) .... CAMA
Canadian Applied Mathematics Society (MCD) .... CAMS
Canadian Aquaculture Producers' Council [Conseil Canadien des Aquiculteurs] (AC) .... CAPC
Canadian Arab Federation [Federation Canado-Arabe] (AC) .... CAF
Canadian Arab Friendship Association .... CAFA
Canadian Arab Friendship Society of Toronto (AC) .... CAFS
Canadian Archaeological Association [SA ACA] .... CAA
Canadian Archaeological Radiocarbon Database (QUAC) .... CARD
Canadian Arctic Gas Pipeline (SAUS) .... CAGP
Canadian Arctic Gas Pipeline Ltd. .... CAGPL
Canadian Arctic Gas Study (SAUS) .... CAGS
Canadian Arctic Island .... CAI
Canadian Arctic Petroleum [Vancouver Stock Exchange symbol] .... CAK
Canadian Arctic Resources Committee [Ottawa, ON] [Research center] ...... CARC
Canadian Arctic Resources Committee, Ottawa, ON, Canada [Library symbol] [Library of Congress] (LCLS) .... CaOOCAR
Canadian Arctic Resources Committee, Ottawa, Ontario [Library symbol] [National Library of Canada] (NLC) .... OOCAR
Canadian Armament Research and Development Establishment (SAUO) .... CADRE
Canadian Armament Research and Development Establishment .... CARDE
Canadian Armament Research and Development Establishment, Valcartier (SAUO) .... CARDE
Canadian Armed Forces .... CAF

Canadian Armed Forces [ICAO designator] (FAAC) .... CFC
Canadian Armed Forces Headquarters (SAUO) .... CAFHO
Canadian Armed Forces Headquarters, Ottawa (SAUS) .... CAFHO
Canadian Armed Forces Identification Bureau (SAUO) .... CAFIB
Canadian Armed Forces Institute of Environmental Medicine (PDAA) .... CFIEM
Canadian Armoured Brigade (SAUO) .... CAB
Canadian Armoured Brigade .... CAB
Canadian Armoured Corps .... CAC
Canadian Armoured Corps Training Centre (SAUO) .... CACTC
Canadian Armoured Division (SAUO) .... CAD
Canadian Army (SAUO) .... CA
Canadian Army .... CA
Canadian Army (NATG) .... CANA
Canadian Army (SAUO) .... CDN Army
Canadian Army Active Service Force (SAUO) .... CAASF
Canadian Army Active Service Force .... CAASF
Canadian Army Dental Corps (DMA) .... CADC
Canadian Army Europe (SAUO) .... CAE
Canadian Army Identification Bureau (SAUO) .... CAIB
Canadian Army Language Bureau (SAUO) .... CALB
Canadian Army Liaison Executive .... CALE
Canadian Army Medical Corps .... CAMC
Canadian Army (Militia) .... CA(M)
Canadian Army Occupation Force (SAUO) .... CAOF
Canadian Army Operational Research Establishment .... CAORE
Canadian Army Operational Research Group (DMA) .... CAORG
Canadian Army Operational Research Group (SAUO) .... CAORG
Canadian Army Orders .... CAO
Canadian Army Pay Corps (DMA) .... CAPC
Canadian Army Post Office (DMA) .... CAPO
Canadian Army Post Office (SAUO) .... CAPO
Canadian Army Provost Corps (SAUO) .... CAPC
Canadian Army (Regular) .... CA(R)
Canadian Army Routine Order (SAUS) .... CARO
Canadian Army Service Corps [British military] (DMA) .... CASC
Canadian Army Signals Engineering Establishment (IAA) .... CASEE
Canadian Army Staff College (SAUO) .... CASC
Canadian Army Tank Brigade (SAUO) .... CATB
Canadian Army Tank Regiment (SAUO) .... CATR
Canadian Army Trophy .... CAT
Canadian Army Veterinary Corps (DMA) .... CAVC
Canadian Arrow Mines Ltd. [Toronto Stock Exchange symbol] .... CGR
Canadian Arsenals Limited .... CAL
Canadian Arsenals Ltd. [Arsenaux Canada Ltee.], Le Gardeur, Quebec [Library symbol] [National Library of Canada] (BIB) .... QLAR
Canadian Arsenals Ltd., Le Gardeur, Quebec (SAUS) .... QLAR
Canadian Art Club, Toronto [1907-15] (NGC) .... CAC
Canadian Art Libraries .... CARLIS
Canadian Art Museum Directors Organization .... CAMDO
Canadian Art Therapy Association (SAUO) .... CATA
Canadian Art Therapy Association-Eastern Chapter (AC) .... CATA
Canadian Arthritis and Rheumatism Society .... CARS
Canadian Arthritis and Rheumatism Society (SAUO) .... CARS
Canadian Artillery Reserve Unit (SAUO) .... CARU
Canadian Artists' Representation .... CAR
Canadian Artists' Representation Manitoba [Also, CARFAC Manitoba] (AC) .... CARMAN
Canadian Artists' Representation Ontario [Front des Artistes Canadiens del'Ontario] (AC) .... CARO
Canadian Artists' Representation/Front des Artistes Canadiens .... CARFAC
Canadian Artists Selected by You [Music award alternative to the Canadian Juno Award] [Established 1985] .... CASBY
Canadian Arts Presenters Association [Association Candienne des Organismes Artistiques] (AC) .... CAPACOA
Canadian Asbestos Information Centre, Montreal, PQ, Canada [Library symbol] [Library of Congress] (LCLS) .... CaQMCAI
Canadian Asbestos Information Centre [Centre Canadien d'Information sur l'Amiante] Montreal, Quebec [Library symbol] [National Library of Canada] (NLC) .... QMCAI
Canadian Asian Studies Association [See also ACEA] .... CASA
Canadian Associated Air Balance Council (AC) .... AABC
Canadian Associated Press (SAUO) .... CAP
Canadian Associated School of Karate-Doh .... CASK
Canadian Association Against Sexual Harassment in Higher Education [Association Canadienne Contre le Harcelement Sexuel en Milieu d'Ensignement Superieur] (AC) .... CAASHHE
Canadian Association for Adult Education .... CAAE
Canadian Association for Adult Education, Toronto, ON, Canada [Library symbol] [Library of Congress] (LCLS) .... CaOTCAE
Canadian Association for American Studies (EA) .... CAAS
Canadian Association for Business Economics .... CABE
Canadian Association for Business Forms Management .... CABFM
Canadian Association for Children of Alcoholics (AC) .... CACOA
Canadian Association for Children with Learning Disabilities .... CACLD
Canadian Association for Clinical Microbiology & Infectious Diseases [Association Canadienne de Microbiologie Clinique et des Maladies Contagieuses] (AC) .... CACMID
Canadian Association for Commonwealth Literature and Language Studies [See also ACELLC] .... CACLALS
Canadian Association for Community Education (SAUO) .... CACE
Canadian Association for Community Living .... CACL
Canadian Association for Composite Structures & Materials (AC) .... CACSMA
Canadian Association for Co-Operative Education [Association Canadienne de l'Enseignement Cooperatif] (AC) .... CACE

Canadian Association for Disable Skiing [*Association Canadienne des Sports pour Skieurs Handicapes*] (AC) .... CADS
Canadian Association for Distance Education .... CADE
Canadian Association for Enterostomal Therapy (AC) .... CAET
Canadian Association for Environmental Analytical Laboratories (AC) .... CAEAL
Canadian Association for Free Expression .... CAFE
Canadian Association for Future Studies .... CAFS
Canadian Association for Graduate Studies (AC) .... CAGS
Canadian Association for Health, Physical Education, and Recreation .... CAHPER
Canadian Association for Health, Physical Education, Recreation & Dance [*Association Canadienne pour la Sante, l'Education Physique, les Loisirs et la Danse*] (AC) .... CAHPERD
Canadian Association for Humane Trapping (SAUO) .... CAHT
Canadian Association for Information Science [*Ottawa, ON*] .... CAIS
Canadian Association for Information Science/Association Canadienne des Sciencesde l'Information (IID) .... CAIS/ACSI
Canadian Association for Irish Studies .... CAIS
Canadian Association for Israel Philately .... CAFIP
Canadian Association for Japanese Language Education (AC) .... CAJLE
Canadian Association for Laboratory Animal Science .... CALAS
Canadian Association for Labour Israel (AC) .... CALI
Canadian Association for Latin America (SAUO) .... ACELA
Canadian Association for Latin American and Caribbean Studies (SAUO) .... CALACS
Canadian Association for Music Therapy .... CAMT
Canadian Association for Nursing Law (AC) .... CANL
Canadian Association for Pastoral Education (AC) .... CAPE
Canadian Association for Peace in the Middle East .... CAFPME
Canadian Association for People who Stutter (SAUO) .... CAPS
Canadian Association for Physical Anthropology .... CAPA
Canadian Association for Production and Inventory Control .... CAPIC
Canadian Association for Quality in Health Care [*Association Canadienne pour la Qualite dans les Services de Sante*] (AC) .... CAQHC
Canadian Association for Research in Home Economics [*See also ACREF*] .... CARHE
Canadian Association for Research in Nondestructive Evaluation (AC) .... CARNDE
Canadian Association for Scottish Studies [*See also ACEE*] .... CASS
Canadian Association for South Asian Studies .... CASAS
Canadian Association for Sport Heritage [*Association Canadienne pour l'Heritage Sportif*] (AC) .... CASH
Canadian Association for Studies in Cooperation [*See also ACEC*] .... CASC
Canadian Association for Suicide Prevention [*L'Association Canadienne pour la Prevention du Suicide*] (AC) .... CASP
Canadian Association for Teacher Education (AC) .... CATE
Canadian Association for the Advancement of Netherlandic Studies G2 [*See also ACAEN*] .... CAANS
Canadian Association for the Advancement of Women & Sport & Physical Activity [*Association Canadienne pour l'Avancement des Femmes du Sport et de l'Activite Physique*] (AC) .... CAAWS
Canadian Association for the History of Nursing (AC) .... CAHN
Canadian Association for the Mentally Retarded .... CAMR
Canadian Association for the Practical Study of Law in Education [*Association Canadienne pour une Etude Pratique de la Loi Dan le Systeme Educatif*] (AC) .... CAPSLE
Canadian Association for the Social Studies .... CASS
Canadian Association for the Study of Adult Education [*See also ACEEA*] .... CASAE
Canadian Association for the Study of International Development [*L'Association Canadienne d'Etudes du Developpement International*] (AC) .... CASID
Canadian Association for the Treatment of Offenders .... CATO
Canadian Association for Underwater Sciences (SAUO) .... CAUS
Canadian Association for University Continuing Education .... CAUCE
Canadian Association for Vocational Evaluation & Work Adjustment [*Association Canadienne des Evaluateur de Capacites de Travail*] (AC) .... CAVEWA
Canadian Association for Young Children .... CAYC
Canadian Association in Support of the Native Peoples (SAUO) .... CASNP
Canadian Association in Support of the Native Peoples, Toronto, ON, Canada [*Library symbol*] [*Library of Congress*] (LCLS) .... CaOTCAS
Canadian Association in Support of the Native Peoples, Toronto, Ontario [*Library symbol*] [*National Library of Canada*] (NLC) .... OTCAS
Canadian Association of Actuaries (SAUO) .... CAA
Canadian Association of Administrators of Labour Legislation .... CAALL
Canadian Association of Advertising Agencies (NTCM) .... CAAA
Canadian Association of Aerial Surveyors .... CAAS
Canadian Association of African Studies [*See also ACEA*] .... CAAS
Canadian Association of Amateur Oarsmen .... CAAO
Canadian Association of Anatomists (AC) .... CAA
Canadian Association of Animal Breeders [*Association Canadienne des Eleveus de Betail*] (AC) .... CAAB
Canadian Association of Animal Health Technologists & Technicians (AC) .... CAAHTT
Canadian Association of Applied Linguistics .... CAAL
Canadian Association of Applied Social Research [*See also ACRSA*] .... CAASR
Canadian Association of Applied Spectroscopy (SAUO) .... CAAS
Canadian Association of Artists Managers (AC) .... CAAM
Canadian Association of Basketball Officials .... CABO
Canadian Association of British Manufacturers and Agencies .... CABMA
Canadian Association of Broadcasters .... CAB
Canadian Association of Broadcasters [*Association Canadienne des Radiodiffuseurs*] Ottawa, Ontario [*Library symbol*] [*National Library of Canada*] (NLC) .... OOCAB

Canadian Association of Burn Nurses (AC) .... CABN
Canadian Association of Business Valuators .... CABV
Canadian Association of Captioning Consumers (AC) .... CACC
Canadian Association of Cardiac Rehabilitation (SAUO) .... CACR
Canadian Association of Cardio-Pulmonary Technologists (AC) .... CACPT
Canadian Association of Certified Executive Accountants [*Formerly, Association of Cost & Executive Acconants in Canada*] (AC) .... CACEA
Canadian Association of Certified Planning Tecnicians (AC) .... CACPT
Canadian Association of Chairmen of English Departments (AC) .... CACE
Canadian Association of Chemical Distributors [*Association Canadienne des Distributeurs de Produits Chimiques*] (AC) .... CACD
Canadian Association of Chiefs of Police .... CACP
Canadian Association of Children's Librarians .... CACL
Canadian Association of College and University Libraries .... CACUL
Canadian Association of College and University Libraries (SAUO) .... CALCUL
Canadian Association of College and University Student Services .... CACUSS
Canadian Association of Communications & Allied Workers [*Association Canadienne des Employes de Communications et Travailleurs Connexes*] (AC) .... CACAW
Canadian Association of Consumers (SAUO) .... CAC
Canadian Association of Critical Care Nurses [*Association Canadienne des Infirmieres et Infirmiers de Soins Intensifs*] [*Formerly, National Society of Critical Care Nurses*] (AC) .... CACCN
Canadian Association of Data and Professional Service Organizations [*Information service or system*] (IID) .... CADAPSO
Canadian Association of Data Processing Organizations (IAA) .... CADAPSO
Canadian Association of Data Processing Service Organizations (NITA) .... CADAPSO
Canadian Association of Deans and Directors of Education .... CADDE
Canadian Association of Drilling Engineers (AC) .... CADE
Canadian Association of Education Development Officers .... CAEDO
Canadian Association of Educational Development Officers (NFD) .... CAEDO
Canadian Association of Electroencephalograph Technologists .... CAET
Canadian Association of Elizabeth Fry Societies [*Association Canadienne des Societes Elizabeth Fry*] (AC) .... CAEFS
Canadian Association of Emergency Physicians .... CAEP
Canadian Association of Energy Service Companies (AC) .... CAESCO
Canadian Association of Equipment Dealers (SAUO) .... CAED
Canadian Association of Ethnic (Radio) [*Association Canadienne des Radiodiffuseurs Ethniques*] (AC) .... CAEB
Canadian Association of Exhibitions [*Association des Expositions du Canada*] (AC) .... CAE
Canadian Association of Exposition Managers .... CAEM
Canadian Association of Family Enterprise [*Association Canadienne des Enterprises Familiales*] (AC) .... CAFE
Canadian Association of Fire Chiefs .... CAFC
Canadian Association of Fire Marshals (SAUO) .... CAFM
Canadian Association of Firefighters [*Association Canadienne des Pompiers*] (AC) .... CAFF
Canadian Association of Fish Exporters (AC) .... CAFE
Canadian Association of Food Banks [*Association Canadienne des Banques Alimentaires*] (AC) .... CAFB
Canadian Association of Footwear Importers Inc. (AC) .... CAFI
Canadian Association of Former International Civil Servants [*Association Canadienne des Anciens Fonctionnaires Internationaux*] (AC) .... CAFICS
Canadian Association of Foundations of Education .... CAFE
Canadian Association of Gastroenterology (SAUO) .... CAG
Canadian Association of General Surgeons .... CAGS
Canadian Association of Geographers .... CAG
Canadian Association of Geographers/Association Canadienne des Geographes .... CAG/ACG
Canadian Association of Geophysical Contractors (AC) .... CAGC
Canadian Association of Gift Planners .... CAGP
Canadian Association of Health-Care Auxiliaries [*Associations des Auxiliaires Benevoles des Etablissements de Sante du Canada*] [*Formerly, Canadian Association of Hospital Auxiliaries*] (AC) .... CAHA
Canadian Association of Hispanists [*See also ACH*] .... CAH
Canadian Association of Home Inspectors (AC) .... CAHI
Canadian Association of Housing and Renewal Officials .... CAHRO
Canadian Association of Hungarian Studies [*See also ACEH*] .... CAHS
Canadian Association of Immersion Teachers (AC) .... CAIT
Canadian Association of Independent Living Centres (AC) .... CAILC
Canadian Association of Independent Schools (EAIO) .... CAIS
Canadian Association of Industrial, Mechanical, and Allied Workers .... CAIMAW
Canadian Association of Interventional Cardiology (SAUO) .... CAIC
Canadian Association of Investment Clubs .... CAIC
Canadian Association of Japanese Automovbile Dealers (AC) .... CAJAD
Canadian Association of Journalists [*L'Association Canadienne des Journalistes*] (AC) .... CAJ
Canadian Association of Labour Media .... CALM
Canadian Association of Latin American and Caribbean Studies .... CALACS
Canadian Association of Latin American Studies .... CALAS
Canadian Association of Law Libraries .... CALL
Canadian Association of Law Teachers [*See also ACPD*] .... CALT
Canadian Association of Legal Assistants .... CALA
Canadian Association of Legal Support Staff (AC) .... CALSS
Canadian Association of Library Schools .... CALS
Canadian Association of Logistics Management (EAIO) .... CALM
Canadian Association of Management Consultants .... CAMC
Canadian Association of Manufacturers of Medical Devices .... CAMMD
Canadian Association of Marketing Research Organization [*Association Canadienne des Organisms de Recherche en Marketing*] (AC) .... CAMRO
Canadian Association of Medical Biochemists (AC) .... CAMB
Canadian Association of Medical Microbiologists [*Association Canadienne des Medecins Microbiologistes*] (AC) .... CAMM

Canadian Association of Medical Radiation Technologists (EAIO) .... CAMRT
Canadian Association of Medical Radiation Technologists, Ottawa, Ontario [*Library symbol*] [*National Library of Canada*] (BIB) .... OOCAM
Canadian Association of Medical Record Librarians .... CAMRL
Canadian Association of Medical Students and Interns .... CAMSI
Canadian Association of Members of Public Utility Tribunals (AC) .... CAMPUT
Canadian Association of Message Exchanges, Inc. [*Association Canadienne d'Echange de Messages, Inc.*] (AC) .... CAM-X
Canadian Association of Metal Finishers .... CAMF
Canadian Association of Mining Equipment & Services for Export (AC) .... CAMESE
Canadian Association of Moldmakers [*Formerly, Windsor Association of Moldmakers*] (AC) .... CAMM
Canadian Association of Motion Picture and Electronic Recording Artists .... CAMERA
Canadian Association of Motion Picture Producers .... CAMPP
Canadian Association of Municipal Administrators (AC) .... CAMA
Canadian Association of Music Libraries .... CAML
Canadian Association of Mutual Insurance Companies (AC) .... CAMIC
Canadian Association of Neuroscience Nurses [*Association Canadienne des infirmieres el Infirmiers en Sciences Neurologiques*] (AC) .... CANN
Canadian Association of Nordic Ski Instructors (AC) .... CANSI
Canadian Association of Numismatic Dealers (AC) .... CAND
Canadian Association of Nurse Administrators (AC) .... CANA
Canadian Association of Nurses in AIDS Care (AC) .... CANAC
Canadian Association of Occupational Therapists [*Association Canadienne des Ergotherapeutes*] (AC) .... CAOT
Canadian Association of Occupational Therapy (HGAA) .... CAOP
Canadian Association of Oilwell Drilling Contractors .... CAODC
Canadian Association of Optometrists (SAUO) .... CAO
Canadian Association of Orthodontists [*Association Canadienne des Orthodontists*] (AC) .... CAO
Canadian Association of Paediatric Surgeons (SAUO) .... CAPS
Canadian Association of Palynologists [*Association Canadienne des Palynologues*] (AC) .... CAP
Canadian Association of Pathologists (SAUO) .... CAP
Canadian Association of Pathologists .... CAP
Canadian Association of Pediatric Nurses (AC) .... CAPN
Canadian Association of Pension Supervisory Authorities [*Association Canadienne des Organismes de Controle des Regimes de Retraite*] (AC) .... CAPSA
Canadian Association of Petroleum Producers (IID) .... CAPP
Canadian Association of Pharmacy Students and Interns (SAUO) .... CAPSI
Canadian Association of Pharmacy Technicians (AC) .... CAPT
Canadian Association of Photographers & Illustrators in Communications [*Association Canadienne de Photographes et Illustrateurs de Publicite*] (AC) .... CAPIC
Canadian Association of Physical Medicine and Rehabilitation (EAIO) .... CAPM & R
Canadian Association of Physicians for the Environment (SAUO) .... CAPE
Canadian Association of Physicists (MCD) .... CAP
Canadian Association of Plastic Surgery (HGAA) .... CAPIS
Canadian Association of Poison Control Centres .... CAPCC
Canadian Association of Police Boards (AC) .... CAPB
Canadian Association of Practical Nursing Assistants .... CAPNA
Canadian Association of Prawn Producers [*Association Canadienne des Producteurs de Crevette*] (AC) .... CAPP
Canadian Association of Primary Air Carriers (SAUO) .... CAPAC
Canadian Association of Principals (AC) .... CAP
Canadian Association of Profession Radio Operators [*Association Canadienne des Professionnels de l'Exploitation Radio*] (AC) .... CAPRO
Canadian Association of Professional Conservators .... CAPC
Canadian Association of Professional Dance Organizations (AC) .... CADPO
Canadian Association of Professional Heritage Consultants [*Association Canadienne des Consultants Patrimoine*] (AC) .... CAPHC
Canadian Association of Professors of Education .... CAPE
Canadian Association of Prosthetists and Orthotists .... CAPO
Canadian Association of Provincial and Territorial Archaeologists (QUAC) .... CAPTA
Canadian Association of Psychoanalytic Child Therapists (AC) .... CAPCT
Canadian Association of Public Data Users (GEOI) .... CAPDU
Canadian Association of Public Libraries .... CAPL
Canadian Association of Publishers' Educational Representatives .... CAPER
Canadian Association of Purchasing Agents (HGAA) .... CAPA
Canadian Association of Purchasing Agents (SAUO) .... CAPA
Canadian Association of Quality Assurance Professionals .... CAQAP
Canadian Association of Radiation Oncologists [*Association Canadienne des Radio-Oncologues*] (AC) .... CARO
Canadian Association of Radio and Television Broadcasters .... CARTB
Canadian Association of Radiologists .... CAR
Canadian Association of Radiologists Journal (SAUO) .... CARJ
Canadian Association of Recycling Industries (AC) .... CARI
Canadian Association of Regulated Importers [*Association Canadienne des Importateurs Reglementes*] (AC) .... CARI
Canadian Association of Rehabilitation Personnel .... CARP
Canadian Association of Research Libraries [*Also, ABRC*] .... CARL
Canadian Association of Retail Travel Agents (AC) .... CARTA
Canadian Association of Retired Persons [*Association Canadienne des Individus Retraites*] (AC) .... CARP
Canadian Association of Rhodes Scholars .... CARS
Canadian Association of Rural Studies .... CARS
Canadian Association of SAS Users (AC) .... CASU
Canadian Association of School Administrators (AC) .... CASA
Canadian Association of School Social Workers & Attendance Counsellors (AC) .... CASSWAC
Canadian Association of Schools of Social Work [*See also ACESS*] .... CASSW
Canadian Association of Second Language Teachers (AC) .... CASLT
Canadian Association of Senior Travellers (AC) .... CAST
Canadian Association of Sexual Assault Centres [*Association Canadienne des Centres Contre le Viol*] (AC) .... CASAC
Canadian Association of Slavists [*See also ACS*] .... CAS
Canadian Association of Smelter and Allied Workers .... CASAW
Canadian Association of Social Work Administrators in Health Facilities [*Associations Canadienne des Administrateurs de Services Sociaux en Milieu de Sante*] (AC) .... CASWAHF
Canadian Association of Social Workers [*See also ACTS*] .... CASW
Canadian Association of Special Libraries (EAIO) .... CASL
Canadian Association of Special Libraries and Information Services (HGAA) .... CASLIS
Canadian Association of Specialty Foods [*L'Association Canadienne des Aliments Fins*] [*Formerly, Canadian Specialty Food Association*] (AC) .... CASF
Canadian Association of Speech-Language Pathologists & Audiologists [*Association Canadienne des Orthophonistes et Audiologistes*] (AC) .... CASLPA
Canadian Association of Sports Sciences .... CASS
Canadian Association of Statutory Human Rights Agencies [*Association Canadienne des Organismes Statutaires pour la Protection des Droits de la Personne*] (AC) .... CASHRA
Canadian Association of Teachers of Community Health [*Association Canadienne des Professeurs de Sante Communautaire*] (AC) .... CATCH
Canadian Association of Teachers of Technical Writing .... CATTW
Canadian Association of Textile Colourists and Chemists (HGAA) .... CATCC
Canadian Association of the Deaf (EAIO) .... CAD
Canadian Association of Token Collectors .... CATC
Canadian Association of Toy Libraries and Parent Resource Centers (EAIO) .... CATL
Canadian Association of Toy Libraries and Parent Resource Centers (EAIO) .... TLRC
Canadian Association of University Business Officers .... CAUBO
Canadian Association of University Research Administrators [*See also ACARU*] .... CAURA
Canadian Association of University Schools of Music .... CAUSM
Canadian Association of University Schools of Nursing [*See also ACEUN*] .... CAUSN
Canadian Association of University Schools of Rehabilitation (AC) .... CAUSR
Canadian Association of University Student Personnel Services .... CAUSPS
Canadian Association of University Teachers .... CAUT
Canadian Association of University Teachers of German .... CAUTG
Canadian Association of Veterinary Ophthalmology (GVA) .... CAVO
Canadian Association of Volunteer Bureaux Centres (AC) .... CAVB
Canadian Association of Warehousing & Distribution Services [*Association Canadienne des Entreposeurs et des Distributeurs*] [*Formerly, Canadian Warehousing Association*] (AC) .... CAWDS
Canadian Association of Women Executives & Entrepreneurs [*Association Canadienne des Femmes Cadres et Entrepreneurs*] (AC) .... CAWEE
Canadian Association of Wooden Money Collectors (AC) .... CAWMC
Canadian Association of Youth Orchestras .... CAYO
Canadian Association of Zoological Parks & Aquariums (AC) .... CAZPA
Canadian Association on Charitable Gift Annuities (NFD) .... CACGA
Canadian Association on Gerontology [*Association Canadienne de Gerontologie*] (AC) .... CAG
Canadian Association on Water Pollution Research and Control (EAIO) .... CAWPRC
Canadian Association on Water Quality [*Also, Canadian National Committee of the International Association on Water Quality*] [*Formerly, Canadian Association on Water Pollution Research & Control*] (AC) .... CAWQ
Canadian Astronautical Society .... CAS
Canadian Astronautics, Ottawa, Ontario [*Library symbol*] [*National Library of Canada*] (NLC) .... OOCAA
Canadian Astronomical Society .... CAS
Canadian Astronomical Society (SAUO) .... CASCA
Canadian Atherosclerosis Society [*Societe Canadienne d'Atherosclerose*] (AC) .... CAS
Canadian Athletic Therapists Association .... CATA
Canadian Atlantic Fisheries Scientific Advisory Committee (ASF) .... CAFSAC
Canadian Atlantic Storm Project (SAUS) .... CASP
Canadian Atlantic Storms Program [*Meteorology*] .... CASP
Canadian Atlantic Subarea [*Canadian Navy*] .... CANLANT
Canadian Atomic Energy Commission (SAUO) .... CAEC
Canadian Australian Line .... CASCO
Canadian Authors Association .... CAA
Canadian Auto Workers Union .... CAW
Canadian Automated Air Traffic System .... CAATS
Canadian Automated Buildings Association [*Association Canadienne pour l'Automatisation des Batiments*] (AC) .... CABA
Canadian Automated Pilot Selection System .... CAPSS
Canadian Automatic Merchandising Association (AC) .... CAMA
Canadian Automatic Sprinkler Association (AC) .... CASA
Canadian Automobile Association .... CAA
Canadian Automobile Association, Ottawa, Ontario [*Library symbol*] [*National Library of Canada*] (BIB) .... OOCAAS
Canadian Automobile Dealers Association [*Formerly, Federation of Automobile Dealer Associations of Canada*] (AC) .... CADA
Canadian Automobile Sports Club .... CASC
Canadian Automobile Transaction Office (SAUO) .... CATO
Canadian Automobile Workers Union, Willowdale, Ontario [*Library symbol*] [*National Library of Canada*] (BIB) .... OWCA
Canadian Automotive Electric Association .... CAEA
Canadian Automotive Historians (AC) .... CAH
Canadian Automotive Trade [*A publication*] .... CAT
Canadian Avalanche Association [*Also, Canadian Avalanche Centre*] (AC) .... CAA

Canadian Aviation Electronics ..... CAE
Canadian Aviation Electronics, Montreal, PQ, Canada [*Library symbol*] [*Library of Congress*] (LCLS) ..... CaQMCAE
Canadian Aviation Historical Society (SAUO) ..... CAHS
Canadian Aviation Historical Society (AC) ..... CAHS
Canadian Aviation Safety Board ..... CASB
Canadian Aviation Safety Board [*Bureau Canadien de la Securite Aerienne*] **Ottawa, Ontario** [*Library symbol*] [*National Library of Canada*] (NLC) ..... OOTAS
Canadian Bacterial Diseases Network (AC) ..... CBDN
Canadian Badminton Association ..... CBA
Canadian Badminton Coaches Association ..... CBCA
Canadian Band Association (EAIO) ..... CBA
Canadian Bankers Association ..... CBA
Canadian Bankruptcy Reports, Annotated [*A publication*] (DLA) ..... Can Bankr Ann
Canadian Bankruptcy Reports, Annotated [*A publication*] (DLA) ..... CBR
Canadian Bankruptcy Reports, Annotated, New Series [*A publication*] (DLA) ..... Can Bankr Ann (NS)
Canadian Bankruptcy Reports, Annotated, New Series [*A publication*] (DLA) ..... CBR (NS)
Canadian Baptist Archives, McMaster Divinity College, McMaster University, Hamilton, Ontario [*Library symbol*] [*National Library of Canada*] (NLC) ..... OHMDBA
Canadian Baptist International Ministries (EAIO) ..... CBIM
Canadian Baptist Overseas Mission Board ..... CBOMB
Canadian Bar Association ..... CBA
Canadian Bar Association/ Association du Barreau Canadien (SAUO) ..... CBA/ABC
Canadian Bar Association. Journal [*A publication*] (DLA) ..... Can BAJ
Canadian Bar Association. Proceedings [*A publication*] (DLA) ..... Can BA
Canadian Bar Association. Year Book [*A publication*] (DLA) ..... Can B Ass'n YB
Canadian Bar Insurance Association [*Association d'Assurance du Barreau Canadien*] (AC) ..... CBIA
Canadian Bar Journal [*A publication*] ..... Can BJ
Canadian Bar Review (journ.) (SAUS) ..... CBR
Canadian Barranca Corp. [*Vancouver Stock Exchange symbol*] ..... CBR
Canadian Base Reinforcement Depot (SAUO) ..... CBRD
Canadian Battery Association (AC) ..... CBA
Canadian Beaver Resources [*Vancouver Stock Exchange symbol*] ..... CBV
Canadian Bible College, Regina, Saskatchewan [*Library symbol*] [*National Library of Canada*] (NLC) ..... SRCB
Canadian Bible College, Regina, SK, Canada [*Library symbol*] [*Library of Congress*] (LCLS) ..... CaSRCB
Canadian Biochemical Society (HGAA) ..... CBS
Canadian Biodiversity Information Network (QUAC) ..... CBIN
Canadian Bioethics Society (SAUO) ..... CBS
Canadian Bison Association [*Association Canadienne du Bison*] (AC) ..... CBA
Canadian Board of Marine Underwriters ..... CBMU
Canadian Boating Federation (SAUO) ..... CBF
Canadian Boiler and Machinery Underwriters Association ..... CBMUA
Canadian Boiler Society [*Societe Canadienne de Manufacturiers Chaudieres*] (AC) ..... CBS
Canadian Bond Rating Service (SAUS) ..... CBRS
Canadian Book and Periodical Development Council ..... CBPDC
Canadian Book Exchange Centre (IID) ..... CBEC
Canadian Book Information Centre ..... CBIC
Canadian Book Manufacturing Association ..... CBMA
Canadian Book Marketing Centre [*Formerly, Canadian Book Information Centre*] (AC) ..... CBMC
Canadian Book Publishers' Council ..... CBPC
Canadian Book Review Annual [*A publication*] (BRI) ..... CBRA
Canadian Bookbinders & Book Artist Guild [*Guide Canadienne des Relieurs et des Artisans du Livre*] (AC) ..... CBBAG
Canadian Bookbinders and Book Artists Guild ..... CBBG
Canadian Booksellers Association ..... CBA
Canadian Botanical Association ..... CBA
Canadian Botanical Conservation Network (QUAC) ..... CBCN
Canadian Breast Cancer Foundation (SAUO) ..... CBCF
Canadian Breast Cancer Network (SAUO) ..... CBCN
Canadian Breast Cancer Research Initiative (SAUO) ..... CBCRI
Canadian Breweries, Ltd. (SAUO) ..... CNB
Canadian Bridge Federation ..... CBF
Canadian Brigade (SAUO) ..... CBD
Canadian British Consultants Ltd., Halifax, Nova Scotia [*Library symbol*] [*National Library of Canada*] (NLC) ..... NSHCBC
Canadian British Consultants Ltd., Halifax, NS, Canada [*Library symbol*] [*Library of Congress*] (LCLS) ..... CaNSHCBC
Canadian Broadcast Program Development Fund ..... CBPDF
Canadian Broadcasting Corp. [*Ottawa, ON*] [*Also facetiously translated as Casual Broadcasting Corp. and Communist Broadcasting Corp.*] [*Telecommunications*] ..... CBC
Canadian Broadcasting Corp., Engineering Headquarters Library, Montreal, PQ, Canada [*Library symbol*] [*Library of Congress*] (LCLS) ..... CaQMCBE
Canadian Broadcasting Corp., Montreal, PQ, Canada [*Library symbol*] [*Library of Congress*] (LCLS) ..... CaQMCB
Canadian Broadcasting Corp. [*Societe Radio-Canada*] **Montreal, Quebec** [*Library symbol*] [*National Library of Canada*] (NLC) ..... QMCB
Canadian Broadcasting Corp., Music and Record Library, Halifax, NS, Canada [*Library symbol*] [*Library of Congress*] (LCLS) ..... CaNSHCB
Canadian Broadcasting Corp., Music and Record Library, Winnipeg, MB, Canada [*Library symbol*] [*Library of Congress*] (LCLS) ..... CaMWC
Canadian Broadcasting Corp., Music Library, Montreal, PQ, Canada [*Library symbol*] [*Library of Congress*] (LCLS) ..... CaQMCBM
Canadian Broadcasting Corp., Ottawa, ON, Canada [*Library symbol*] [*Library of Congress*] (LCLS) ..... CaOOAR
Canadian Broadcasting Corp. [*Societe Radio-Canada*] **Ottawa, Ontario** [*Library symbol*] [*National Library of Canada*] (NLC) ..... OOAR
Canadian Broadcasting Corp., Program Archives, Toronto, ON, Canada [*Library symbol*] [*Library of Congress*] (LCLS) ..... CaOTBCP
Canadian Broadcasting Corp., Toronto, ON, Canada [*Library symbol*] [*Library of Congress*] (LCLS) ..... CaOTBC
Canadian Broadcasting Corp. [*Societe Radio-Canada*] **Toronto, Ontario** [*Library symbol*] [*National Library of Canada*] (NLC) ..... OTBC
Canadian Broadcasting Corp., VTR Library, Vancouver, BC, Canada [*Library symbol*] [*Library of Congress*] (LCLS) ..... CaBVaCBV
Canadian Broadcasting League ..... CBL
Canadian Broadcasting Winnipeg [*Canadian Broadcasting Co. record series pref ix*] ..... CBW
Canadian Brotherhood of Railway Employees (SAUO) ..... CBRE
Canadian Brotherhood of Railway Employees and Other Transport Workers ..... CBRE
Canadian Brotherhood of Railway Transport and General Workers ..... CBRT
Canadian Building Abstracts (SAUS) ..... CBAs
Canadian Bureau for International Education [*See also BCEI*] ..... CBIE
Canadian Bureau for the Advancement of Music (AC) ..... BAM
Canadian Bus Association [*Association Canadienne de l'Autobus*] [*Formerly, Canadian Motor Coach Association*] (AC) ..... CBA
Canadian Business Aircraft Association (EAIO) ..... CBAA
Canadian Business and Current Affairs [*Micromedia Ltd.*] [*Information service or system*] (CRD) ..... CBCA
Canadian Business Equipment Manufacturers Association (HGAA) ..... CBEMA
Canadian Business Forms Association (DGA) ..... CBFA
Canadian Business Manufacturers Association (MCD) ..... CBMA
Canadian Business Newspapers Association (SAUO) ..... CBNA
Canadian Business Periodicals Index ..... CBPI
Canadian Business Press ..... CBP
Canadian Business Telecommunications Alliance (AC) ..... CBTA
Canadian Business Travel Association [*Association Canadienne des Charges de Voyages*] (AC) ..... CBTA
Canadian Cable Television Association ..... CCTA
Canadian Camping Association (AC) ..... CCA
Canadian Cancer Society (BARN) ..... CCS
Canadian Canners Ltd., Burlington, ON, Canada [*Library symbol*] [*Library of Congress*] (LCLS) ..... CaOBUCC
Canadian Canners Ltd., Burlington, Ontario [*Library symbol*] [*National Library of Canada*] (NLC) ..... OBUCC
Canadian Canoe Association ..... CCA
Canadian Canoe, Single Person (ADA) C1
Canadian Canoe, Two Person (ADA) C2
Canadian Canon Law Society (AC) ..... CCLS
Canadian Car & Foundry Co. Ltd. (SAUO) ..... CCF
Canadian Car Demurrage Bureau, The, Montreal PQ CDA [*STAC*] ..... CCD
Canadian Carbonization Research Association (AC) ..... CCRA
Canadian Cardiovascular Society (EAIO) ..... CCS
Canadian Career Information Association (AC) ..... CCIA
Canadian Cariboo Resources Ltd. [*Vancouver Stock Exchange symbol*] CCV
Canadian Carpet Institute (EAIO) CCI
Canadian Cartographic Association [*Association Canadienne de Cartographie*] (AC) ..... CCA
Canadian Casualty Assembly Centre (DMA) ..... CCAC
Canadian Cat Association ..... CCA
Canadian Cataloguing in Publication ..... CCIP
Canadian Catholic Conference CCC
Canadian Catholic Historical Association [*See also SCHEC*] ..... CCHA
Canadian Catholic Organization for Development and Peace (SAUO) ..... CCODP
Canadian Catholic School Trustees' Association [*Association Canadienne des Commissaires d'Ecoles Catolique*] (AC) ..... CCSTA
Canadian Cattle Breeders' Association (AC) ..... CCBA
Canadian Cattlemen's Association ..... CCA
Canadian Celanese Ltd., Drummondville, PQ, Canada [*Library symbol*] [*Library of Congress*] (LCLS) ..... CaQDC
Canadian Celiac Association [*Association Canadienne de la Maladie Coeliaque*] [*Also, Celiac Canada*] (AC) ..... CCA
Canadian Center for Occupational Safety and Health (IID) ..... CCOSH
Canadian Centre for Advanced Instrumentation (SAUS) ..... CCAI
Canadian Centre for Architecture ..... CCA
Canadian Centre for Architecture, New York, NY [*Library symbol*] [*Library of Congress*] (LCLS) ..... NNCCA
Canadian Centre for Creative Technology [*Centre Canadien de Technologie Creative*] (AC) ..... CCCT
Canadian Centre for Drug-Free Sport [*Centre Candien Sur le Dopage Sportif*] (AC) ..... CCDS
Canadian Centre for Films on Art, Ottawa, ON, Canada [*Library symbol*] [*Library of Congress*] (LCLS) ..... CaOOCCFA
Canadian Centre for Films on Art [*Centre Canadien du Film sur l'Art*] **Ottawa, Ontario** [*Library symbol*] [*National Library of Canada*] (NLC) ..... OOCCFA
Canadian Centre for Fisheries Innovation [*Centre Canadien d'Innovations des Peches*] [*Formerly, Centre for Fisheries Innovation*] (AC) ..... CCFI
Canadian Centre for Geoscience Data (SAUS) ..... CCGD
Canadian Centre for GIS in Education (SAUS) ..... CCGISE
Canadian Centre for Global Security [*Centre Canadien pour la Securite Mondiale*] [*Formerly, The Arms Control Centre*] (AC) ..... CCGS
Canadian Centre for Information and Documentation on Archives [*National Archives of Canada*] ..... CCIDA
Canadian Centre for Learning Systems [*Research center*] (RCD) ..... CCLS
Canadian Centre for Occupational Health and Safety [*Ministry of Labour*] ..... CCOHS
Canadian Centre for Occupational Health and Safety compact disk (SAUO) ..... CCINFO

Canadian Centre for Occupational Health and Safety, Hamilton, ON, Canada [Library symbol] [Library of Congress] (LCLS) .... CaOHOHS
Canadian Centre for Occupational Health and Safety [Centre Canadien d'Hygieneet de Securite au Travail] Hamilton, Ontario [Library symbol] [National Library of Canada] (NLC) .... OHOHS
Canadian Centre for Philanthropy, Toronto, ON, Canada [Library symbol] [Library of Congress] (LCLS) .... CaOTCCP
Canadian Centre for Philanthropy, Toronto, Ontario [Library symbol] [National Library of Canada] (NLC) .... OTCCP
Canadian Centre for Policy Alternatives (EAIO) .... CCPA
Canadian Centre for Remote Sensing [See also CCT] .... CCRS
Canadian Centre for Swine Improvment Inc. (SAUO) .... CCSI
Canadian Centre for Toxicology [Research center] (RCD) .... CCT
Canadian Centre for Victims of Torture [Formerly, Canadian Centre for Investigation & Prevention of Torture] (AC) .... CCVT
Canadian Centre on Substance Abuse (AC) .... CCSA
Canadian Ceramic Society (AC) .... CCS
Canadian Cerebral Palsy Sports Association [Association Canadienne Sports de Paralysie Cerebrale] (AC) .... CCPSA
Canadian Certified General Accountants' Association .... CCGAA
Canadian Certified Reference Materials Project (PDAA) ..... CCRMP
Canadian Chamber of Commerce (SAUO) CCC
Canadian Chapter of the International Council of Community Churches [Section Canadienne du Conseil International des Eglises Communautaires] (AC) CCICCC
Canadian Charolais Association .... CCA
Canadian Chartered Accountant Uniform (SAUO) .... CAQEX
Canadian chartered Accountant uniform CPA Qualification Examination (SAUS) .... CAQEX
Canadian Chemical Association (HGAA) .... CCA
Canadian Chemical Processing (journ.) (SAUS) .... Can Chem Process
Canadian Chemical Producers Association .... CCPA
Canadian Chicken Marketing Agency [Office Canadien de Commercialisation des Poulets] (AC) .... CCMA
Canadian Chiefs of Staff Committee .... COSC
Canadian Child and Youth Drama Association .... CCYDA
Canadian Child Care Federation [Formerly, Canadian Child Day Care Federation] (AC) .... CCCF
Canadian Children's Literature [A publication] (BRI) .... Can CL
Canadian Children's Multimedia Foundation (AC) .... CCMF
Canadian Children's Opera Chorus (AC) .... CCOC
Canadian Children's Project, Inc. .... CCP
Canadian Chiropractic Association .... CCA
Canadian Chiropractic Examining Board (SAUS) .... CCEB
Canadian Chiropractic Historical Association (SAUO) .... CCHA
Canadian Chiropractic Protective Association (SAUO) ...... CCPA
Canadian Chlorine Chemistry Association (SAUO) CCCC
Canadian Circulation Management Association [Association Canadienne des Chefs de Tirage] (AC) .... CCMA
Canadian Circulations Audit Board [Founded 1937] .... CCAB
Canadian Circumpolar Institute [University of Alberta] (IRC) CCI
Canadian Circumpolar Library (SAUO) CCL
Canadian Civil Liberties Association .... CCLA
Canadian Civil Liberties Union .... CCLU
Canadian Classical association (SAUO) .... FIEC
Canadian Classification and Dictionary of Occupations [A publication] ..... CCDO
Canadian Classification Research Group [International Federation for Documentation] .... CCRG
Canadian Clean Air Act (GNE) .... CCAA
Canadian Clearinghouse for Ongoing Research in Nursing [University of Alberta] (IID) .... CORN
Canadian Climate Center CCC
Canadian Climate Program (QUAC) .... CCP
Canadian Climate Research Network (QUAC) .... CCRN
Canadian Clinical Nurse Specialist Interest Group (AC) ... CCNSIG
Canadian Club [A whiskey] CC
Canadian Club of New York (EA) .... CCNY
Canadian Coalition for Ecology, Ethics & Religion (AC) ... CCEER
Canadian Coalition for High Blood Pressure Prevention & Control [Coalition Canadienne pour la Prevention et le Controle de l'Hypertension Arterielle] (AC) .... CCHBPPC
Canadian Coalition for Nuclear Responsibility .... CCNR
Canadian Coast Guard .... CCG
Canadian Coast Guard [ICAO designator] (FAAC) .... CTG
Canadian Coast Guard College [College de la Garde Cotiere Canadienne] Sydney, Nova Scotia [Library symbol] [National Library of Canada] (NLC) .... NSSCG
Canadian Coast Guard, Quebec, PQ, Canada [Library symbol] [Library of Congress] (LCLS) .... CaQQTCG
Canadian Coast Guard [Garde Cotiere Canadienne] Quebec, Quebec [Library symbol] [National Library of Canada] (NLC) .... QQTCG
Canadian Coast Guard Service .... CCGS
Canadian Coast Guard [Garde Cotiere Canadienne] St. John's, Newfoundland [Library symbol] [Obsolete] [National Library of Canada] (NLC) .... NFSTCG
Canadian Coastal Radar (SAUS) .... CCR
Canadian Coastal Zone Atlantic .... CCZA
Canadian Coastal Zone Pacific .... CCZP
Canadian Cognitive Abilities Test [Academic achievement and aptitude test] .... CCAT
Canadian College of Health Service Executives [College Canadien des Directeurs de Services de Sante] (AC) .... CCHSE
Canadian College of Medical Geneticists [College Canadien de Geneticiens Medicaux] (AC) .... CCMG
Canadian College of Microbiologists (SAUS) .... CCM

Canadian College of Naturopathic Medicine (SAUS) .... CCNM
Canadian College of Organists .... CCO
Canadian College of Physicists in Medicine [College Canadien des Physiciens en Medecine] (AC) .... CCPM
Canadian College of Teachers [See also CCE] .... CCT
Canadian Colleges Athletic Association .... CCAA
Canadian Colonial Airways .... CCA
Canadian Command Active Sonobuoy System (PDAA) ... CANCASS
Canadian Commander, Army, Pacific (CINC) .... CANCOMARPAC
Canadian Commander, Escort Squadron (SAUO) ... CANCOMCORTRON
Canadian Commander, Mine Sweeping Squadron (SAUO) ..... CANCOMINRON
Canadian Commercial Bank .... CCB
Canadian Commercial Bank [Toronto Stock Exchange symbol] ..... CCU
Canadian Commercial Corp. [Government-owned] (RDA) CCC
Canadian Commercial Law Guide (Commerce Clearing House) [A publication] (DLA) .... Can Com L Guide (CCH)
Canadian Commercial Law Reports [1901-05] [A publication] (DLA) .... Can Com Cas
Canadian Commercial Law Reports [1901-05] [A publication] (DLA) .... Can Com LR
Canadian Commercial Law Reports [1901-05] [A publication] (DLA) .... Can Com R
Canadian Commission for UNESCO, Ottawa, Ontario [Library symbol] [National Library of Canada] (BIB) .... OOCCU
Canadian Committee for Industrial Organization .... CCIO
Canadian Committee for the Bibliographic Control of Cartographic Materials (GEOI) .... CCBCCM
Canadian Committee for the International Biological Programme ..... CCIBP
Canadian Committee of Scientists & Scholars [Comite Canadien des Savants et Scientifiques] (AC) .... CCSS
Canadian Committee on Cataloguing [Librarianship] CCC
Canadian Committee on Financing University Research ...... CCFUR
Canadian Committee on History of Geological Sciences (SAUS) ..... CANHIGEO
Canadian Committee on Sugar Analysis (SAUO) .... CCSA
Canadian Committee on the Dynamics and Evolution of the Lithosphere (SAUS) .... CANDEL
[The] Canadian Committee to Protect Journalists (AC) ...... CPJ
Canadian Commonwealth Association .... CCA
Canadian Communicable Disease Center .... CCDC
Canadian Communicable Disease Centre (SAUO) .... CCDC
Canadian Communication Association .... CCA
Canadian Communications and Transportation Commission ..... CCTC
Canadian Communications Foundation .... CCF
Canadian Communications Law Review [A publication] (DLA) .... Can Com L Rev
Canadian Communications Research Information Centre (SAUS) ..... CCRIC
Canadian Communications Satellite (SAUS) .... ANIK
Canadian Communications Technology Satellite (SAUS) ...... CTS
Canadian Communist League (Marxist-Leninist) .... CCL(ML)
Canadian Communist Party [Political party] .... KKP
Canadian Community Law Journal [A publication] (DLA) ...... Can Com LJ
Canadian Community Newspapers Association [Founded 1919] ..... CCNA
Canadian Community of Computer Educators (AC) .... CCCE
Canadian Comparative Literature Association [See also ACLC] ..... CCLA
Canadian Comprehensive Auditing Foundation (HGAA) ...... CCAF
Canadian Computer Complex (NITA) CCC
Canadian Computer Conference (MCD) CCC
Canadian Computer Dealer Association (EAIO) .... CCDA
Canadian Computer Graphics Association (AC) .... CCGA
Canadian Computer Show .... CCS
Canadian Computer-Based Reference Service [National Library of Canada] [Information service or system] (IID) .... CAN/CRS
Canadian Concerned Fathers Action Committee .... CCFAC
Canadian Concrete Masonry Producers' Association (EAIO) ..... CCMPA
Canadian Concrete Pipe Association (AC) .... CCPA
Canadian Condominium Institute-National Chapter (AC) CCI
Canadian Conference of Catholic Bishops .... CCCB
Canadian Conference of the Arts .... CCA
Canadian Conference of Tourism Officials .... CCTO
Canadian Conference on Industrial Computer Systems (SAUS) ..... CCICS
Canadian Congregational Foreign Missionary Society (SAUO) ..... CCFMS
Canadian Congress for Learning Opportunities for Women ..... CCLOW
Canadian Congress of Applied Mechanics (PDAA) .... CANCAM
Canadian Congress of Applied Mechanics (HGAA) .... CCAM
Canadian Congress of Labour CCL
Canadian Congress of Neurological Sciences [Congres Canadien des Sciences Neurologiques] (AC) .... CCNS
Canadian Conservation Institute [See also ICC] [National Museums of Canada] [Research center] (RCD) CCI
Canadian Conservation Institute, National Museums of Canada [Institut Canadien de Conservation, Musees Nationaux du Canada] Ottawa, Ontario [Library symbol] [National Library of Canada] (NLC) ..... OONMCC
Canadian Conservative Centre (EAIO) CCC
Canadian Consortium for Social Research (IID) .... CCSR
Canadian Construction Association .... CCA
Canadian Consulate General Library, New York, NY [Library symbol] [Library of Congress] (LCLS) .... NNCCG
Canadian Consultative Council on Multiculturalism .... CCCM
Canadian Consulting Agrologists Association [L'Assiciation Canadienne des Agronomes-Conseils] (AC) .... CCAA
Canadian Content (SAUS) .... CANCON
Canadian Continental Oil [Vancouver Stock Exchange symbol] ..... CBO
Canadian Control System [For convoys in Canadian Coastal Zone] ..... CANCON
Canadian Controls and Instrumentation (journ.) (SAUS) ..... Can Contr Instrum
Canadian Cooperation Office (SAUS) .... CCO
Canadian Cooperative Applications Satellite (HGAA) .... CAS
Canadian Co-Operative Association (AC) .... CCA

Canadian Cooperative Credit Society .... CCCS
Canadian Co-operative Implements Ltd. (SAUO) CCIL
Canadian Co-Ordinating Council on Deafness .... CCCD
Canadian Coordinating Office for Health Technology Assessment (SAUS) .... CCOHTA
Canadian Copper and Brass Development Association (SAUO) .... CCBA
Canadian Copper and Brass Development Association .... CCBDA
Canadian Copper Refiners Ltd., Montreal, PQ, Canada [*Library symbol*] [*Library of Congress*] (LCLS) .... CaQMCR
Canadian Copper Refiners Ltd., Montreal, Quebec [*Library symbol*] [*National Library of Canada*] (NLC) .... QMCR
Canadian Copyright Institute CCI
Canadian Corporate Management Co. Ltd. [*Toronto Stock Exchange symbol*] .... CCM
Canadian Corporate Names [*Canada Systems Group*] [*Information service or system*] (IID) .... CNAM
Canadian Corporate Newsnet (SAUS) .... CCN
Canadian Corporate Shareholder Services Association [*Association Canadienne des Services aux Actionnaires*] (AC) .... CCSSA
Canadian Corporation for University Space Science (SAUO) .... CCUSS
Canadian Corporations [*Micromedia Ltd.*] [*Canada*] [*Information service or system*] (CRD) .... CanCorp
Canadian Corps Heavy Artillery [*World War I*] .... CCHA
Canadian Correspondence Art Gallery .... CCAG
Canadian Cosmetic, Toiletry & Fragrance Association [*Association Canadienne des Cosmetiques, Produit de Toilette et Parfums*] (AC) .... CCTFA
Canadian Cosmetics Careers Association .... CCCA
Canadian Council Cardiovascular Nurses [*Conseil Canadien des Infirmieres en Nursing Cardiovasculaire*] (AC) .... CCCN
[*The*] **Canadian Council for Accreditation of Pharmacy Programs** [*Le Conseil Canadien de l'Agrement des Programmes de Pharmacie*] (AC) .... CCAPP
Canadian Council for European Affairs [*Conseil Canadien des Affairs Europeenes*] (AC) .... CCEA
Canadian Council for Fisheries Research (ASF) .... CCFFR
Canadian Council for Human Resources in the Environment Industry [*Le Conseil Canadien des Ressources Humaines de l'Industrie de L'Environnement*] (AC) .... CCHREI
Canadian Council for International Business [*Conseil Canadien pour le Commerce International*] [*Also, Canadian Secretariat ICC/BIAC*] (AC) .... CCIB
Canadian Council for International Cooperation CCIC
Canadian Council for Multicultural & Intercultural Education (AC) .... CCMIE
Canadian Council for Non-Destructive Technology (HGAA) .... CCNDT
Canadian Council for Non-Destructive Testing (SAUO) .... CCNDT
Canadian Council for Racial Harmony (AC) .... CCRH
Canadian Council for Reconstruction through UNESCO (SAUO) .... CCRU
Canadian Council for Refugees [*Conseil Canadien pour les Refugies*] [*Formerly, Standing Conference of Organizations Concerned for Refugees*] (AC) .... CCR
Canadian Council for Research in Education .... CCRE
Canadian Council for Research in Education, Ottawa, ON, Canada [*Library symbol*] [*Library of Congress*] [*Obsolete*] (LCLS) .... CaOORE
Canadian Council for Southeast Asian Studies [*Carleton University*] [*Research center*] (RCD) .... CCSEAS
Canadian Council for the Advancement of Education [*Le Conseil Canadien pour l'Avancement de l'Education*] (AC) .... CCAE
Canadian Council for Tobacco Control (SAUO) .... CCTC
Canadian Council for/of International Law (SAUO) CCIL
Canadian Council of Archives [*Conseil Canadien des Archives*] (AC) .... CCA
Canadian Council of Better Business Bureaus [*Conseil Canadian des Bureaux d'Ethique Commerciale*] (AC) .... CCBBB
Canadian Council of Christian Charities (AC) CCCC
[*The*] **Canadian Council of Christians & Jews** [*Conseil Canadien des Chretiens et des Juifs*] (AC) .... CCCJ
Canadian Council of Churches (EAIO) CCC
Canadian Council of Engineering Students .... CCES
Canadian Council of Grocery Distributors [*Conseil Canadien de la Distribution Alimentaire*] (AC) .... CCDA
Canadian Council of Grocery Distributors [*Conseil Canadien de la Distribution Alimentaire*] (AC) .... CCGD
Canadian Council of Independent Laboratories [*Conseil Canadien des Laboratoires Independents*] (AC) CCIL
Canadian Council of Land Surveyors [*See also CCAG*] .... CCLS
Canadian Council of Library Schools [*Conseil Canadien des Ecoles de Bibliotheconomie*] (AC) .... CCLS
Canadian Council of Management Associations (HGAA) .... CCMA
Canadian Council of Motor Transport Administrators [*Conseil Canadien des Administrateurs en Transport Motorise*] (AC) .... CCMTA
Canadian Council of Professional Engineers .... CCPE
Canadian Council of Resource and Environment Ministers .... CCREM
Canadian Council of Resource Ministers, Montreal, PQ, Canada [*Library symbol*] [*Library of Congress*] (LCLS) .... CaQMCCR
Canadian Council of Resource Ministers [*Conseil Canadien des Ministres des Ressources*] **Montreal, Quebec** [*Library symbol*] [*National Library of Canada*] (NLC) .... QMCCR
Canadian Council of Teachers of English .... CCTE
Canadian Council of Teachers of English & Language Arts (AC) .... CCTELA
Canadian Council of Technicians & Technologists [*Conseil Canadien des Techniciens et Technologues*] (AC) .... CCTT
Canadian Council of the Blind .... CCB
Canadian Council of University Biology Chairs (AC) .... CCUBC
Canadian Council on Animal Care .... CCAC
Canadian Council on Children and Youth [*Research center*] (RCD) .... CCCY
Canadian Council on Geographic Education (GEOI) .... CCGE
Canadian Council on Geomatics (SAUO) .... CCOG
Canadian Council on Geomatics Interchange Format (SAUO) .... CCOGIF
Canadian Council on Health Facilities Accreditation .... CCHFA
Canadian Council on Health Services Accreditation (SAUO) .... CCHSA
Canadian Council on Hospital Accreditation (HCT) .... CCHA
Canadian Council on International Law [*Conseil Canadien de Droit International*] (AC) CCII
Canadian Council on International Relations (SAUO) .... CCIR
Canadian Council on Rehabilitation & Work [*Le Conseil Canadien de la Readaptation et du Travail*] (AC) .... CCRT
Canadian Council on Rehabilitation & Work (AC) .... CCRW
Canadian Council on Smoking and Health .... CCSH
Canadian Council on Social Development (SAUO) .... CCDS
Canadian Council on Social Development .... CCSD
Canadian Council on Social Development, Ottawa, ON, Canada [*Library symbol*] [*Library of Congress*] (LCLS) .... CaOOCW
Canadian Council on Social Development [*Conseil Canadien de Developpement Social*] **Ottawa, Ontario** [*Library symbol*] [*National Library of Canada*] (NLC) .... OOCW
Canadian Council on Urban and Regional Research (EA) .... CCURR
Canadian Country Music Association [*Association de la Musique Country Canadienne*] (AC) .... CCMA
Canadian Court Martial Appeal Reports [*1957-*] [*A publication*] (DLA) .... CMAR
Canadian Cowboys Association .... CCA
Canadian Craft & Hobby Association (AC) .... CCHA
Canadian Crafts Council CCC
Canadian Creative Music Collective [*Jazz group*] .... CCMC
Canadian Credit Institute CCI
Canadian Credit Management Association [*Formerly, Creditel of Canada Ltd.*] .... CREDITEL
Canadian Crew Energy [*Vancouver Stock Exchange symbol*] .... KNC
Canadian Criminal Cases [*A publication*] (DLA) .... Can Cr Cas
Canadian Criminal Cases [*Law Book, Inc.*] [*Information service or system*] CCC
Canadian Criminal Cases, Annotated [*A publication*] (DLA) .... Can Crim Cas
Canadian Criminal Cases, Annotated [*A publication*] (DLA) .... Can Crim Cas Ann
Canadian Criminal Cases, New Series [*A publication*] (DLA) .... Can Crim Cas (NS)
Canadian Criminal Justice Association [*Association Canadienne de Justice Penale*] (AC) .... CCJA
Canadian Criminal Reports [*A publication*] (DLA) .... Can Cr R
Canadian Criminology and Corrections Association .... CCCA
Canadian Critical care Society [*Societe Canadienne de Soins Intensifs*] (AC) .... CCCS
Canadian Crossroads International CCI
Canadian Culinary Institute (AC) CCI
Canadian Cultural Society of the Deaf (SAUO) .... CCSD
Canadian Curtiss-Wright Ltd. [*Toronto Stock Exchange symbol*] .... CCW
Canadian Custom Bonded .... CCB
Canadian Cycling Association .... CCA
Canadian Cystic Fibrosis Foundation .... CCF
Canadian Cystic Fibrosis Foundation .... CCFF
Canadian Daily Newspaper Association (SAUO) .... CDNA
Canadian Daily Newspaper Publishers Association .... CDNPA
Canadian Dairy & Food Industries Supply Association [*Association Canadienne des Fournisseurs des Industries Laitierie et de l'Alimentation*] (AC) .... CDFISA
Canadian Dairy Commission .... CDC
Canadian Dairy Commission (SAUO) .... CDR
Canadian Dairy Foods Service Bureau (SAUS) .... CDFSB
Canadian Dance Teachers Association [*Association Canadienne des Professeurs de Danse*] (AC) .... CDTA
Canadian Data Processing Service Organization (SAUS) .... CDAPSO
Canadian Deaf & Hard of Hearing Forum (AC) .... CDHHF
Canadian Deaf Sports Association [*Association des Sports des Sourds du Canada*] (AC) .... CDSA
Canadian Deafblind & Rubella Association [*Association Canadienne de la Surdi-Cecite et de la Rubeole*] (AC) .... CDBRA
Canadian Deafness Research & Training Institute [*Institut Canadien de Recherche et de Formation sur la Surdite*] (AC) .... CDRTI
Canadian Decorating Products Association [*Association Canadienne de l'Industrie de Decoration*] (AC) .... CDPA
Canadian Defence Civil Institute of Environmental Medicine (SAUS) .... DCIEM
Canadian Defence Education Establishment (PDAA) .... CDEE
Canadian Defence Forces (SAUO) .... CDF
Canadian Defence Liaison Staff (Washington) (AFM) .... CDLS(W)
Canadian Defence Research Board (SAUO) .... CDRB
Canadian Defence Research Board Telecommunications Establishment (SAUO) .... CDRBTE
Canadian Defence Research Boards Telecommunications Establishment (SAUS) .... CDRBTE
Canadian Defense Preparedness Association .... CDPA
Canadian Defense Research Board (SAUS) .... CDRB
Canadian Defense Sector (SAUO) .... CDS
Canadian Defense Staff (SAUO) .... CDS
Canadian Defense System (CCCA) .... CDS
Canadian Dental Assistants Association (AC) .... CDAA
Canadian Dental Association .... CDA
Canadian Dental Association, Ottawa, ON, Canada [*Library symbol*] [*Library of Congress*] (LCLS) .... CaOOCDA
Canadian Dental Association, Ottawa, Ontario [*Library symbol*] [*National Library of Canada*] (NLC) .... OOCDA
Canadian Dental Corps (SAUO) .... CDC
Canadian Dental Hygenists' Association [*Association Canadienne des Hygienistes Denteurs*] (AC) .... CDHA
Canadian Dental Hygiene Council (SAUO) .... CDHC
Canadian Dental Laboratory Conference (SAUS) .... CDLC
Canadian Dental Research Foundation (HGAA) .... CDRF

Canadian Department of Agriculture ... CDA
Canadian Department of Defence Production ... CDDP
Canadian Department of Fisheries and Oceans, Marine Fish Division [*Research center*] (RCD) ... MFD
Canadian Department of Forestry (SAUS) ... CDF
Canadian Department of Industry, Trade, and Commerce (DLA) ... Canada Commerce
Canadian Department of National Defence ... CDND
Canadian Department of Supply and Services (MCD) ... CDSS
Canadian Depository for Securities ... CDS
Canadian Dermatology Association (EAIO) ... CDA
Canadian Destroyers Atlantic ... CANDESLANT
Canadian Destroyers Far East ... CANDESFE
Canadian Destroyers Pacific ... CANDESPAC
Canadian Deuterium Reactor (GAAI) ... CANDU
Canadian Deuterium Uranium [*Family of nuclear reactors developed in Canada*] ... CANDU
Canadian Deuterium Uranium Boiling Light-Water [*Nuclear reactor*] ... CANDU BLW
Canadian Development Institute (AC) ... CDI
Canadian Dexter Cattle Association (AC) ... CDCA
Canadian Diabetic Association ... CDA
Canadian Diamond Drilling Association ... CDDA
Canadian Dietetic Association ... CDA
Canadian Digital Elevation Data (GEOI) ... CDED
Canadian Digital Production System (SAUS) ... CA DPS
Canadian Direct Mail/Marketing Association ... CDMMA
Canadian Direct Marketing Association ... CDMA
Canadian Directory of Completed Master's Theses in Nursing [*University of Alberta*] [*Information service or system*] (IID) ... CAMN
Canadian Disability Rights Council (AC) ... CDRC
Canadian Disaggregated Interdepartmental Economic Model ... CANDIDE
Canadian Disarmament Information Service ... CANDIS
Canadian Disc Jockey Association (AC) ... CDJA
Canadian Division Infantry Reinforcement Unit (SAUO) ... CDIRU
Canadian Documentation [*National Research Council*] (NITA) ... CANDOC
Canadian Documentation Centre, Fitness and Sport, Ottawa, ON, Canada [*Library symbol*] [*Library of Congress*] (LCLS) ... CaOOFS
Canadian Dollar [*Monetary unit*] ... CD
Canadian Dollar [*Vancouver Stock Exchange symbol*] ... XCD
Canadian Dollar Investments (Bermuda) Ltd. [*Toronto Stock Exchange symbol*] ... CDI
Canadian Donkey & Mule Association (AC) ... CDMA
[*The*] **Canadian Doukhobor Society** (AC) ... CDS
Canadian Down Syndrome Society ... CDSS
Canadian Dredge & Dock Co., Ltd. (SAUO) ... CND
Canadian Dressage Owners and Riders Association ... CADORA
Canadian Drilling Association [*Also, Canadian Diamond Drilling Association*] (AC) ... CDA
Canadian Drilling Research Association (HGAA) ... CDRA
Canadian Driver and Safety Educators Association ... CDSA
Canadian Drug Identification Codebook (SAUO) ... CDIC
Canadian Drug Manufactures Association (AC) ... CDMA
Canadian Dry Pin (SAUS) ... CDP
Canadian Dun's Market Identifiers [*Dun & Bradstreet Canada Ltd.*] [*Information service or system*] (CRD) ... CDMI
Canadian Eagle Aviation Ltd. [*ICAO designator*] (FAAC) ... HIA
Canadian Earth Energy Association [*Association Canadienne de l'Energie du Sol*] (AC) ... CEEA
Canadian Earth Observation Network (SAUS) ... CEONet
Canadian Earth Resources Evaluation Satellite (SAUS) ... CERES
Canadian Economics Association [*See also ACE*] ... CEA
Canadian Education Association ... CEA
Canadian Education Association, Toronto, ON, Canada [*Library symbol*] [*Library of Congress*] (LCLS) ... CaOTCEA
[*The*] **Canadian Education Association** [*L'Association Canadienne d'Education*] **Toronto, Ontario** [*Library symbol*] [*National Library of Canada*] (NLC) ... OTCEA
Canadian Education Research Information System (SAUO) ... CERIS
Canadian Educational Researchers Association [*See also ACCE*] ... CERA
Canadian Educational Standards Institute (AC) ... CESI
Canadian Efficiency Decoration [*Military*] (DD) ... ED
Canadian Egg Marketing Agency ... CEMA
Canadian Egg Producers Council ... CEPC
Canadian Electrical Association ... CEA
Canadian Electrical Code ... CEC
Canadian Electrical Distributors Association, Inc. ... CEDA
Canadian Electrical Manufacturers Association (SAUO) ... CEMA
Canadian Electronic & Appliance Service Association [*Organisation Canadienne de Service d'Appareils Domestique*] (AC) ... CEASA
Canadian Electronic Document Ordering Service (SAUO) ... CANDOC
Canadian Embassy, Washington, DC [*Library symbol*] [*Library of Congress*] (LCLS) ... DCaE
Canadian Encyclopedic Digest [*A publication*] (DLA) ... CED
Canadian Energy, Mines and Resources (SAUS) ... CEMR
Canadian Energy Pipeline Association (AC) ... CEPA
Canadian Energy Research Institute [*University of Calgary*] [*Research center*] (RCD) ... CERI
Canadian Energy Services Ltd. [*Toronto Stock Exchange symbol*] ... CE
Canadian Engineer Reserve Unit (SAUO) ... CERU
Canadian Engineering Manpower Council ... CEMC
Canadian Engineering Standards Association [*Later, Canadian Standards Association*] ... CESA
Canadian Engineers (DMA) ... CE
Canadian Engineers (SAUO) ... CE
Canadian Entomologist (journ.) (SAUS) ... Can Entomol
Canadian Environment [*Database*] [*WATDOC*] [*Information service or system*] (CRD) ... CENV
Canadian Environment Industry Association [*Association Canadienne des Industries de l'Environnement*] (AC) ... CEIA
Canadian Environmental Assessment Research Council ... CEARC
Canadian Environmental Auditing Association (AC) ... CEAA
Canadian Environmental Certification Approvals Board (SAUS) ... CECAB
Canadian Environmental Defence Fund (AC) ... CEDF
Canadian Environmental Exposition [*Heating, Refrigerating, and Air Conditioning Institute of Canada*] (TSPED) ... CEX
Canadian Environmental Law Association ... CELA
Canadian Environmental Law Association. Newsletter [*A publication*] (DLA) ... CELA Newsletter
Canadian Environmental Law News [*A publication*] (DLA) ... Can Environ LN
Canadian Environmental Law News [*A publication*] (DLA) ... Can Env L News
Canadian Environmental Law News [*A publication*] (DLA) ... C Environ LN
Canadian Environmental Law Reports [*A publication*] (DLA) ... CELR
Canadian Environmental Law Research Foundation (GNE) ... CELRF
Canadian Environmental Network (GNE) ... CEN
Canadian Environmental Protection Act ... CEPA
Canadian Equestrian Federation [*Federation Equestre Canadienne*] (AC) ... CEF
Canadian Equestrian Team ... CET
Canadian Escort Squadron (SAUO) ... CANCOMNEW
Canadian Estate Land Corp. [*Vancouver Stock Exchange symbol*] ... CZY
Canadian Ethnic Studies Association ... CESA
Canadian Evaluation Society [*Societe Canadienne l'Evaluation*] (AC) ... CES
Canadian EWS (SAUS) ... CANEWS
Canadian Executive Service Organization ... CESO
Canadian Expedition to Study the Alpha Ridge [*1983*] ... CESAR
Canadian Expeditionary Forces ... CEF
Canadian Experiments (SAUO) ... CANEX
Canadian Export Association ... CEA
Canadian Export Association, Montreal, PQ, Canada [*Library symbol*] [*Library of Congress*] (LCLS) ... CaQMCEA
Canadian Export Association [*Association Canadienne d'Exportation*] **Montreal, Quebec** [*Library symbol*] [*National Library of Canada*] (NLC) ... QMCEA
Canadian Express Ltd. [*Toronto Stock Exchange symbol*] [*Vancouver Stock Exchange symbol*] ... XE
Canadian Familial Polyposis Registry (DMAA) ... CFPR
Canadian Farm and Industrial Equipment Institute ... CFIEI
Canadian Farm Management Data System, Agriculture Canada [*Systeme Canadien deDonnees sur la Gestion Agricole, Agriculture Canada*] **Guelph, Ontario** [*Library symbol*] [*National Library of Canada*] (NLC) ... OGCF
Canadian Farmworkers Union (AC) ... CFU
Canadian Federal Corporations and Directors [*Canada Systems Group*] [*Information service or system*] (IID) ... CFCD
Canadian Federal Warning Center ... CFWC
Canadian Federation for the Humanities [*See also FCEH*] [*Research center*] (RCD) ... CFH
Canadian Federation of Agriculture ... CFA
Canadian Federation of Biological Societies ... CFBS
Canadian Federation of Business and Professional Women's Clubs [*Established 1930*] ... CFBPWC
Canadian Federation of Chefs & Cooks [*Federation Canadienne des Chefs et Cuisiniers*] (AC) ... CFCC
Canadian Federation of Communications Workers [*See also FCC*] ... CFCW
Canadian Federation of Deans of Management & Administrative Studies [*Federation Canadienne des Doyens de Gestion et d'Administration*] (AC) ... CFDMAS
Canadian Federation of Engineers and Scientists ... CFES
Canadian Federation of Film Societies ... CFFS
Canadian Federation of Friends of Museums (AC) ... CFFM
Canadian Federation of Humane Societies [*Federation des Societes Candiennes d'Assistance aux Animaux*] (AC) ... CFHS
Canadian Federation of Independent Business ... CFIB
Canadian Federation of Independent Business, Willowdale, Ontario [*Library symbol*] [*National Library of Canada*] (BIB) ... OWCF
Canadian Federation of Independent Grocers [*Federation Canadienne des Epiciers Independants*] (AC) ... CFIG
Canadian Federation of Insurance Agents and Brokers ... CFIAB
Canadian Federation of Labour ... CFL
Canadian Federation of Mayors and Municipalities ... CFMM
Canadian Federation of Music Teachers' Associations ... CFMTA
Canadian Federation of Students ... CFS
Canadian Federation of University Women ... CFUW
Canadian Feed Industry Association [*Association Canadienne des Industries de l'Alimentation Animale*] (AC) ... CFIA
Canadian Feed Information Centre (AC) ... CFIC
Canadian Feed the Children (AC) ... CFTC
Canadian Fencing Association ... CFA
Canadian Fencing Federation [*Federation Canadienne d'Escrime*] (AC) ... CFF
Canadian Fertility & Andrology Society [*Societe Canadienne de Fertilite et d'Andrologie*] (AC) ... CFAS
Canadian Fertility Society (SAUO) ... CFS
Canadian Fiber Foods [*Vancouver Stock Exchange symbol*] ... CKF
Canadian Fibreboard Manufacturers' [*Association Canadienne des Manufacturiers d'Isolant de Fibre de Bois*] (AC) ... CFMA
Canadian Field Artillery ... CFA
Canadian Field Hockey Association ... CFHA
Canadian Field Hockey Council ... CFHC
Canadian Field Park Company (SAUO) ... CFPC
Canadian Field-Naturalist (journ.) (SAUS) ... Can Field-Nat
Canadian Fighter (SAUS) ... CF

Canadian Figure Skating Association ..... CFSA
Canadian Film and Television Association ..... CFTA
Canadian Film & Television Production Association [*Association Canadienne de Production de Film et Television*] (AC) ..... CFTPA
Canadian Film and Videotape Certification Office ..... CFVCO
Canadian Film Centre [*Centre Canadien du Film*] [*Formerly, Canadian Centre for Advanced Film Studies*] (AC) ..... CFC
Canadian Film Development Corporation (SAUO) ..... CFDC
Canadian Film Editors Guild ..... CFEG
Canadian Film Group ..... CFG
Canadian Film Institute [*See also ICF*] ..... CFI
Canadian Film Institute, Ottawa, ON, Canada [*Library symbol*] [*Library of Congress*] (LCLS) ..... CaOOCF
Canadian Film Institute [*Institut Canadien du Film*] **Ottawa, Ontario** [*Library symbol*] [*National Library of Canada*] (NLC) ..... OOCF
Canadian Film-Makers Distribution Centre ..... CFDC
Canadian Film-Makers Distribution Centre ..... CFMDC
Canadian Finance & Leasing Association (AC) ..... CFLA
Canadian Financial Database [*The Globe and Mail*] [*Toronto, ON*] [*Information service or system*] (IID) ..... CFD
Canadian Fire Safety Association (AC) ..... CFSA
Canadian Fire Underwriters' Association [*Later, Canadian Underwriters' Association*] ..... CFUA
Canadian Fitness & Lifestyle Research Institute [*Institut Canadien de la Recherche sur la Condition Physique et le Mode de Vie*] (AC) ..... CFLRI
Canadian Flag Officer Atlantic Coast (SAUO) ..... CANFLAGLANG
Canadian Flag Officer Atlantic Coast (SAUO) ..... CanFlagLant
Canadian Flag Officer Pacific Coast (SAUO) ..... CanFlagPac
Canadian Flexible Foam Manufacturers' Association (AC) ..... CFFMA
Canadian Flight Experiment [*NASA*] ..... CANEX
Canadian Fluid Power Association [*Association Canadienne d'Energie Fluide*] (AC) ..... CFPA
Canadian Folk Music Society ..... CFMS
Canadian Food and Allied Workers ..... CFAW
Canadian Food Brokers Association [*Association Canadienne des Courtiers en Alimentation*] (AC) ..... CFBA
Canadian Food for the Hungry (SAUO) ..... CFH
Canadian Food Inspection Agency (GVA) ..... CFIA
Canadian Food Processors Association ..... CFPA
Canadian Food Products Development Center, Portage La Prairie, Manitoba [*Library symbol*] [*National Library of Canada*] (NLC) ..... MPCFP
Canadian Food Products Development Center, Portage La Prairie, MB, Canada [*Library symbol*] [*Library of Congress*] (LCLS) ..... CaMPCFP
Canadian Food Service Executives Association ..... CFSEA
Canadian Food Service Supervisors Association ..... CFSSA
Canadian Food Technologists Association (SAUO) ..... CFTA
Canadian Food Technologists Association (SAUS) ..... CFTA
Canadian Foodgrains Bank Association Inc. [*Association de la Banque Candienne de Grains Inc.*] (AC) ..... CFGB
Canadian Football League ..... CFL
Canadian Football League Players' Association [*Association des Joueurs de la Ligue de Football Canadienne*] (AC) ..... CFLPA
Canadian Force Communications System ..... CFCS
Canadian Forces (AABC) ..... CF
Canadian Forces - Second Career Assistance Network ..... CF-SCAN
Canadian Forces Administrative Order ..... CFAO
Canadian Forces Aerospace and Navigation School, Canadian Forces Base Winnipeg, Westwin, Manitoba [*Library symbol*] [*National Library of Canada*] (NLC) ..... MWCF
Canadian Forces Affiliate Radio System (SAUO) ..... CFARS
Canadian Forces Air Defense Command [*ICAO designator*] (FAAC) ..... CFADC
Canadian Forces Air Navigation School ..... CFANS
Canadian Forces Airborne Sensing Unit (SAUS) ..... CFASU
Canadian Forces Attache ..... CFA
Canadian Forces Auxiliary Vessels [*Military*] ..... CFAV
Canadian Forces Base (NATG) ..... CFB
Canadian Forces Base Barrington, Stone Horse, Nova Scotia [*Library symbol*] [*National Library of Canada*] (NLC) ..... NSSHCF
Canadian Forces Base Barrington, Stone Horse, NS, Canada [*Library symbol*] [*Library of Congress*] (LCLS) ..... CaNSShCF
Canadian Forces Base, Cornwallis, Nova Scotia [*Library symbol*] [*National Library of Canada*] (NLC) ..... NSCCF
Canadian Forces Base, Cornwallis, NS, Canada [*Library symbol*] [*Library of Congress*] (LCLS) ..... CaNSCoCF
Canadian Forces Base, Ensign, Cornwallis, NS, Canada [*Library symbol*] [*Library of Congress*] (LCLS) ..... CaNSCoCFE
Canadian Forces Base, Gagetown, NB, Canada [*Library symbol*] [*Library of Congress*] (LCLS) ..... CaNBGACF
Canadian Forces Base, Gagetown, New Brunswick [*Library symbol*] [*National Library of Canada*] (NLC) ..... NBGACF
Canadian Forces Base, Greenwood, NS, Canada [*Library symbol*] [*Library of Congress*] (LCLS) ..... CaNSGCFA
Canadian Forces Base Halifax, Ships Recreational Library, Halifax, NS, Canada [*Library symbol*] [*Library of Congress*] (LCLS) ..... CaNSHNS
Canadian Forces Base, Ottawa, Ontario [*Library symbol*] [*National Library of Canada*] (BIB) ..... OOCFB
Canadian Forces Base, Royal Canadian Army Museum, Shilo, MB, Canada [*Library symbol*] [*Library of Congress*] (LCLS) ..... CaMShCFAM
Canadian Forces Base St. Jean [*Base des Forces Canadiennes St.-Jean*], **Quebec** [*Library symbol*] [*National Library of Canada*] (NLC) ..... QSTJCF
Canadian Forces Base Winnipeg, Canadian Forces Aerospace and Navigation School, Westwin, MB, Canada [*Library symbol*] [*Library of Congress*] (LCLS) ..... CaMWCF
Canadian Forces College Library [*UTLAS symbol*] ..... CFL
Canadian Forces College, Toronto, ON, Canada [*Library symbol*] [*Library of Congress*] (LCLS) ..... CaOTRC
Canadian Forces College, Toronto, Ontario [*Library symbol*] [*National Library of Canada*] (NLC) ..... OTRC
Canadian Forces Communication Command (NATG) ..... CFCC
Canadian Forces Decoration ..... CD
Canadian Forces Environmental Medicine Establishment (SAUS) ..... CFEME
Canadian Forces Europe (SAUO) ..... CFE
Canadian Forces Exchange [*Military*] ..... CANEX
Canadian Forces Exchange (SAUO) ..... CFXE
Canadian Forces Headquarters [*NATO*] (NATG) ..... CANFORCEHED
Canadian Forces Headquarters [*NATO*] ..... CFHQ
Canadian Forces Hospital ..... CFH
Canadian Forces in Europe (NATG) ..... CFE
Canadian Forces in the Netherlands (SAUO) ..... CFN
Canadian Forces Institute of Aviation Medicine (PDAA) ..... CFIAM
Canadian Forces Low Level Air Defense System [*Military*] ..... CFLLADS
Canadian Forces Maritime Warfare School [*Canadian Navy*] ..... CFMWFS
Canadian Forces Medical Council (CMD) ..... CFMC
Canadian Forces Medical Service (CMD) ..... CFMS
Canadian Forces Personnel Applied Research Unit (SAUO) ..... CFPARU
Canadian Forces Post Office (SAUO) ..... CFPO
Canadian Forces Postal System ..... CFPS
Canadian Forces Project Management Office (HGAA) ..... CFPMO
Canadian Forces Publication ..... CFP
Canadian Forces Recruiting Centre ..... CFRC
Canadian Forces School of Communications and Electronics, Kingston, Ontario [*Library symbol*] [*National Library of Canada*] (BIB) ..... OKC
Canadian Forces School of Military Engineering (SAUS) ..... CFSME
Canadian Forces Special Projects Laboratory (HGAA) ..... CFSPL
Canadian Forces Staff School, Canada Department of National Defence [*College d'Etat-Major des Forces Canadiennes, Ministere de la Defense Nationale*] **Toronto, Ontario** [*Library symbol*] [*National Library of Canada*] (NLC) ..... OTRCS
Canadian Forces Station ..... CFS
Canadian Forces Supplementary Order ..... CFSO
Canadian Forces Supply System (MCD) ..... CFSS
Canadian Forces Supply System Upgrade ..... CFSSU
Canadian Forces Support Establishment (SAUO) ..... CFSE
Canadian Forces Technical Orders (MCD) ..... CFTO
Canadian Forces Technical Services Detachment (SAUS) ..... CFTSD
Canadian Forces Utility Tactical Transport Helicopter programme (SAUS) ..... CFUTTH
Canadian Foremost Ltd. [*Toronto Stock Exchange symbol*] ..... CFT
Canadian Forest Fire Danger Rating System (SAUS) ..... CFFDRS
Canadian Forest Inventory (SAUS) ..... CFI
Canadian Forest Products (SAUO) ..... CFP
Canadian Forest Resource Data System (SAUS) ..... CFRDS
Canadian Forest Service (SAUO) ..... CFS
Canadian Foresters Life Insurance Society (EA) ..... CFLIS
Canadian Forestry Association [*See also AFC*] ..... CFA
Canadian Forestry Association of British Columbia ..... CFABC
Canadian Forestry Corps [*World War I*] ..... CFC
Canadian Forestry Service ..... CFS
Canadian Forestry Service. Pacific Forest Research Centre. (journ.) (SAUS) ..... RBCPDG
Canadian Forum [*A publication*] (BRI) ..... CF
Canadian Foundation Co. Ltd. [*Toronto Stock Exchange symbol*] ..... CDF
Canadian Foundation for AIDS Research [*Fondation Canadienne de Recherche sur le SIDA*] (AC) ..... CanFar
Canadian Foundation for Caribbean Development and Cooperation (SAUO) ..... CFCDC
Canadian Foundation for Drug Policy (SAUO) ..... CFDP
Canadian Foundation for Economic Education [*Fondation d'Education Economique*] (AC) ..... CFEE
Canadian Foundation for the Advancement of Pharmacy (SAUO) ..... CFAP
Canadian Foundation for the Advancement of Pharmacy [*Fondation Canadienne pour l'Avancement de la Pharmacie*] [*Also, Canadian Foundation for Pharmacy*] (AC) ..... CFP
Canadian Foundation for the Study of Infant Deaths [*Fondation Canadienne sur l'Etude de la Mortalite Infantile*] (AC) ..... CFSID
Canadian Foundation for World Development (AC) ..... CFWD
Canadian Foundation on Alcohol and Drug Dependencies ..... CFADD
Canadian Foundation on Compulsive Gambling (AC) ..... CFCG
Canadian Foundry Association [*Association des Fonderies Canadiennes*] (AC) ..... CFA
Canadian Fourteenth Air Training Group Headquarters, Winnipeg ..... CANAIRPEG
Canadian Fraternal Association [*Association Canadienne des Societes Fraternelles*] (AC) ..... CFA
Canadian Free Trade Agreement (ECON) ..... CFTA
Canadian Freezing Drizzle Experiment II (SAUS) ..... CFDE II
Canadian Freight Association (SAUO) ..... CanFA
Canadian Freight Association ..... CFA
Canadian French [*Language*] (BARN) ..... Can Fr
Canadian French (SAUS) ..... Can-Fr
Canadian Friends of Mine (EA) ..... CFM
Canadian Friends Service Committe [*Also, Religious Society of Friends*] (AC) ..... CFSC
Canadian Fusion Fuels Technology Project ..... CFFTP
Canadian Future Study Group (SAUO) ..... CANFUT
Canadian Futurity Oils Ltd. [*Toronto Stock Exchange symbol*] ..... CAF
Canadian Garrison Artillery ..... CGA
Canadian Garrison Regiment (DMA) ..... CGR
Canadian Gas Association ..... CGA
Canadian Gas Processors Association (AC) ..... CGPA

Canadian Gas Research Institute [*Canadian Gas Association*] (IRC) .... CGRI
Canadian Gas Research Institute, Don Mills, ON, Canada [*Library symbol*] [*Library of Congress*] (LCLS) .... CaOTCGR
Canadian Gas Research Institute, Don Mills, Ontario [*Library symbol*] [*National Library of Canada*] (NLC) .... OTCGR
Canadian General Capital [*Associated Press*] (SAG) .... CdnGn
Canadian General Capital [*NYSE symbol*] (SAG) .... CGG
Canadian General Electric (SAUS) .... CGE
Canadian General Electric Co. Ltd. [*Toronto Stock Exchange symbol*] .... CGE
Canadian General Electric Co. Ltd., Peterborough, ON, Canada [*Library symbol*] [*Library of Congress*] (LCLS) .... CaOPeTCG
Canadian General Electric Co. Ltd., Peterborough, Ontario [*Library symbol*] [*National Library of Canada*] (NLC) .... OPETCG
Canadian General Electric Co. Ltd., Toronto, ON, Canada [*Library symbol*] [*Library of Congress*] (LCLS) .... CaOTGE
Canadian General Investments Ltd. [*Toronto Stock Exchange symbol*] .... CGI
Canadian General Standards Board [*Formerly, Canadian Government Specifications Board*] .... CGSB
Canadian Genetic Diseases Network (AC) .... CGDN
Canadian Genl Cp 9.125%'TOPrS' [*NYSE symbol*] (TTSB) .... CGGPrT
Canadian Genome Analysis and Technology (SAUO) .... CGAT
Canadian Genome Analysis and Technology Bioinformatics Support Services (SAUO) .... CGATBSS
Canadian Geographic [*A publication*] (BRI) .... CG
Canadian Geographic Board (SAUS) .... CGB
Canadian Geographic Information System (SAUS) .... CGIS
Canadian Geographic Journal (SAUS) .... Can Georg J
Canadian Geographical Information System (SAUS) .... CGIS
Canadian Geographical Journal (SAUS) .... Canad Geog J
Canadian Geographical Names Data Base (SAUO) .... CGNDB
Canadian Geographical Society (SAUO) .... CGS
Canadian Geographical Society (BARN) .... CGS
Canadian Geologic Survey (SAUS) .... CGS
Canadian Geological Foundation (SAUO) .... CGF
Canadian Geological Survey (SAUO) .... CGS
Canadian Geomorphology Research Group (SAUO) .... CGRG
Canadian Geophysical Union .... CGU
Canadian Geophysics Congress (AC) .... CGC
Canadian Geoscience Council [*Conseil Geoscientifique Canadien*] (AC) .... CGC
Canadian Geoscience Information Centre (GEOI) .... CGIC
Canadian Geospatial Data Infrastructure (GEOI) .... CGDI
Canadian Geotechnical Society .... CGS
Canadian Geriatrics Research Society .... CGRS
Canadian Geriatrics Research Society, Toronto, Ontario [*Library symbol*] [*National Library of Canada*] (NLC) .... OTOGR
Canadian Gerontological Nursing Association (AC) .... CGNA
Canadian Giant Explorations [*Vancouver Stock Exchange symbol*] .... CEG
Canadian Girls in Training (SAUO) .... CGIT
Canadian Give the Gift of Literacy Foundation (AC) .... CGGLF
Canadian Global Change Program (CARB) .... CGCP
Canadian Global Change Program/Arctic Panel (SAUO) .... CGCP/AP
Canadian Goat Society .... CGS
Canadian Gold Resources [*Vancouver Stock Exchange symbol*] .... CGO
Canadian Golf Superintendents Association [*Association Canadienne des Surintendants de Golf*] (AC) .... CGSA
Canadian Good Roads Association .... CGRA
Canadian Government Expositions Centre, Department of Supply and Services [*Centre des Expositions du Gouvernement Canadien, Ministere des Approvisionnements et Services*] **Ottawa, Ontario** [*Library symbol*] [*National Library of Canada*] (NLC) .... OOGE
Canadian Government Office of Tourism .... CGOT
Canadian Government Photo Centre .... CGPC
Canadian Government Purchasing Service (PDAA) .... CGPS
Canadian Government Specifications Board (SAUO) .... CGSB
Canadian Government Supply Services (SAUO) .... CGSS
Canadian Government Travel Bureau, Reference Library, Ottawa, ON, Canada [*Library symbol*] [*Library of Congress*] (LCLS) .... CaOOTB
Canadian Government Wheat Board (SAUO) .... CGWB
Canadian Government Wheat Borad (SAUS) .... CGWB
Canadian Grain Commission (SAUO) .... CGC
Canadian Grain Commission, Agriculture Canada [*Commission Canadienne des Grains, Agriculture Canada*] **Winnipeg, Manitoba** [*Library symbol*] [*National Library of Canada*] (NLC) .... MWGR
Canadian Graphic Arts Association (SAUO) .... CGAA
Canadian Graphite [*Vancouver Stock Exchange symbol*] .... CDT
Canadian Green Bag [*A publication*] (DLA) .... Can Green Bag
Canadian Grenadier Guards (SAUO) .... CGG
Canadian Ground Water Association [*Association Canadienne des Eaux Souterraine*] [*Formerly, Canadian Water Well Contractors Association*] [*Formerly, Canadian Water Well Association*] (AC) .... CGWA
Canadian Group of Painters [*1933-69*] (NGC) .... CGP
Canadian Group Psychotherapy Association (AC) .... CGPA
Canadian Guard Association [*Association Canadienne des Gardiens*] (AC) .... CGA
Canadian Guards (SAUO) .... Cdn Gds
Canadian Guidance and Counselling Association .... CGCA
Canadian Guidance & Counselling Foundation (AC) .... CGCF
Canadian Guide Dogs for the Blind (AC) .... CGDB
Canadian Hail Underwriters Association .... CHUA
Canadian Handball Association [*Federation de Balle au mur du Canada*] (AC) .... CHA
Canadian Hard of Hearing Association .... CHHA
Canadian Hardware & Housewares Manufacturers' Association [*Association Canadienne des Fabricants en Quincaillerie et Article Menagers*] (AC) .... CHHMA
Canadian Hardwood Plywood Association (AC) .... CHPA
Canadian Head Injury Coalition (AC) .... CHIC
Canadian Health Alliance to Stop Therapist Exploitation Now (AC) .... CHASTEN
Canadian Health Association .... CHA
Canadian Health Economics Research Association [*See also ACRES*] .... CHERA
Canadian Health Education Society (SAUO) .... CHES
Canadian Health Education Specialists Society .... CHESS
Canadian Health Food Association .... CHFA
Canadian Health Insurance Association .... CHIA
Canadian Health Libraries Association .... CHLA
Canadian Health Record Association .... CHRA
Canadian Health Services Research Foundation (SAUO) .... CHSRF
Canadian Healthcare Association (SAUS) .... CHA
Canadian Hearing Society (AC) .... CHS
Canadian Heart Health Initiative-Ontario Project (SAUO) .... CHHIOP
Canadian Heat Exchange & Vessel Manufacturers Association (AC) .... CHEVMA
Canadian Helicopters [*ICAO designator*] (FAAC) .... WSR
Canadian Hemochromatosis Society [*Societe Canadienne de l'Hemochromatose*] (AC) .... CHS
Canadian Hemophilia Society [*Societe Canadienne de l'Hemophilie*] (AC) .... CHS
Canadian Heritage Information Network [*National Museums of Canada*] [*Ottawa, ON*] [*Information service or system*] (IID) .... CHIN
Canadian Heritage River System [*NPPAC*] .... CHRS
Canadian High Acceptance Orbit Spectrometer .... CHAOS
Canadian High Altitude Research Missile (SAUS) .... CHARM
Canadian high energy physics project (SAUO) .... KAON
Canadian High Technology Week [*Trade show*] (ITD) .... CHTW
Canadian Highland Cattle Society [*Societe Canadienne des Eleveurs de Bovins Highland*] (AC) .... CHCS
Canadian Historical Association [*See also SHC*] .... CHA
Canadian Historical Production/Injection File [*Petroleum Information Corp.*] [*Information service or system*] (CRD) .... CHST
Canadian Historical Review [*A publication*] (BRI) .... Can Hist R
Canadian Holistic Medicine Association .... CHMA
Canadian Holistic Nurses Association (AC) .... CHNA
Canadian Holocust Remembrance Association (AC) .... CHRA
Canadian Home & School & Parent-Teacher Federation [*Federation Canadienne des Associations Foyer-Ecole et Parents-Maitres*] (AC) .... CHSPTF
Canadian Home Builders' Association .... CHBA
Canadian Home Care Association [*Association Canadienne de Soins et Services a Domicile*] (AC) .... CHCA
Canadian Home Economics Association [*Association Canadienne d'Economie Familiale*] (AC) .... CHEA
Canadian Home Economics Association Foundation [*Fondation de l'Association Canadienne d'Economie Familiale*] (AC) .... CHEAF
Canadian Home Fitness Test [*Medicine*] .... CHFT
Canadian Home Insulation Plan .... CHIP
Canadian Home Renovation Program .... CHRP
Canadian Home Shopping Club .... CHSC
Canadian Home Shopping Network [*Television*] .... CHSN
Canadian Home Shopping Network Ltd. [*Toronto Stock Exchange symbol*] .... CWS
Canadian Horticultural Council [*Conseil Canadien de l'Horticulture*] (AC) .... CHC
Canadian Horticultural Council [*Conseil Canadien de l'Horticulture*], **Ottawa, Ontario** [*Library symbol*] [*National Library of Canada*] (BIB) .... OOCHC
Canadian Hospital Association .... CHA
Canadian Hospital Association [*Association des Hopitaux du Canada*] **Ottawa,Ontario** [*Library symbol*] [*National Library of Canada*] (NLC) .... OOCHA
Canadian Hospital Association, Toronto, ON, Canada [*Library symbol*] [*Library of Congress*] (LCLS) .... CaOTCHA
Canadian Hospital Association [*Association des Hopitaux du Canada*] **Toronto, Ontario** [*Library symbol*] [*National Library of Canada*] (NLC) .... OTCHA
Canadian Hospital Council (SAUO) .... CHC
Canadian Hospital Engineering Society .... CHES
Canadian Hospital (journ.) (SAUS) .... Can Hosp
Canadian Hospitals Injury Reporting and Prevention Program (SAUO) .... CHIRPP
Canadian Hotel Marketing & Sales Executive (AC) .... CHMSE
Canadian Housing & Renewal Association (AC) .... CHRA
Canadian Housing Design Council [*CMHC*] .... CHDC
Canadian Housing Information Centre, Canada Mortgage and Housing Corp. [*Centre Canadien de Documentation sur l'Habitation, Societe Canadienne d'Hypotheques et de Logement*] **Ottawa, Ontario** [*Library symbol*] [*National Library of Canada*] (NLC) .... OOCM
Canadian Hovercraft Industries Association (SAUO) .... CHIA
Canadian Human Rights Commission [*See also CCDP*] .... CHRC
Canadian Human Rights Commission, Ottawa, ON, Canada [*Library symbol*] [*Library of Congress*] (LCLS) .... CaOOCHR
Canadian Human Rights Commission [*Commission Canadienne des Droits de la Personne*] **Ottawa, Ontario** [*Library symbol*] [*National Library of Canada*] (NLC) .... OOCHR
Canadian Human Rights Reporter [*A publication*] (DLA) .... Can Human Rights Rep
Canadian Humanist Publications (AC) .... CHP
Canadian Hunger Foundation [*Fondation Canadienne Contre la Faim*] (AC) .... CHF
Canadian Hunter Exploration Ltd., Calgary, AB, Canada [*Library symbol*] [*Library of Congress*] (LCLS) .... CaACHE
Canadian Hunter Exploration Ltd., Calgary, Alberta [*Library symbol*] [*National Library of Canada*] (NLC) .... ACHE
Canadian Hussars (SAUO) .... Cdn H
Canadian Hydrocarbons Ltd. [*Toronto Stock Exchange symbol*] (SPSG) .... CDH
Canadian Hydrographic Association [*Association Canadienne d'Hydrographie*] (AC) .... CHA
Canadian Hydrographic Service (MCD) .... CHS
Canadian Hydrological Operational Multipurpose Subprogramme [*Environment Canada*] [*Information service or system*] (CRD) .... CHOMS
Canadian Hyperlexia Association .... CHA

Canadian Hypertension Society [*Societe Canadienne d'Hypertension Arterielle*] (AC) .... CHS
Canadian Icelandic Horse Federation (AC) .... CIHF
Canadian Image Processing and Pattern Recognition Society .... CIPPRS
Canadian Immunodeficiencies Patient Organization (SAUO) .... CIPO
Canadian Imperial Bank of Commerce .... CIBC
Canadian Imperial Bank of Commerce [*Toronto Stock Exchange symbol*] [*Vancouver Stock Exchange symbol*] .... CM
Canadian Imperial Bank of Commerce, Toronto, ON, Canada [*Library symbol*] [*Library of Congress*] (LCLS) .... CaOTCIB
Canadian Imperial Bank of Commerce, Toronto, Ontario [*Library symbol*] [*National Library of Canada*] (NLC) .... OTCIB
Canadian Imperial Bk [*TS, exchange symbol*] (TTSB) .... CM
Canadian Imperial Blk Commerce [*NYSE symbol*] (SG) .... BCM
Canadian Imperial Ginseng Products Ltd. [*Associated Press*] (SAG) .... CdnIGin
Canadian Imperial Ginseng Products Ltd. [*NASDAQ symbol*] (SAG) .... IGPF
Canadian Implant Association (EAIO) .... CIA
Canadian Import Tribunal [*QL Systems Ltd.*] [*Information service or system*] (CRD) .... CIT
Canadian Importers Association .... CIA
Canadian Income Plus Fund 1986 Trust Units [*Toronto Stock Exchange symbol*] .... CNF
Canadian Independent Adjusters Conference .... CIAC
Canadian Independent Record Producers Association .... CIRPA
Canadian Independent Record Production Association (AC) .... CIRPA
Canadian Independent Recording Artists in Concert [*Pronounced "kerrack"*] .... CIRAC
Canadian Independent Telephone Association .... CITA
Canadian Index of Computer Literature [*A publication*] CICL
Canadian Indian/Native Studies Association .... CINSA
Canadian Industrial Emergency Response Association (SAUO) .... CIERA
Canadian Industrial Innovation Centre (AC) CIIC
Canadian Industrial Innovation Centre/Waterloo [*University of Waterloo*] [*Research center*] (RCD) .... CIIC/W
Canadian Industrial Minerals Corp. [*Vancouver Stock Exchange symbol*] .... CIJ
Canadian Industrial Preparedness Association (HGAA) .... CIPA
Canadian Industrial Relations Association [*See also ACRI*] .... CIRA
Canadian Industrial Renewal Board [*Montreal, PQ*] .... CIRB
Canadian Industrial Renewal Program .... CIRP
Canadian Industrial Safety Association (PDAA) .... CISA
Canadian Industrial Sweetener Users (AC) .... CISU
Canadian Industrial Traffic League .... CITL
Canadian Industries Ltd. CIL
Canadian Industries Ltd., Central Research Laboratory, McMasterville, PQ, Canada [*Library symbol*] [*Library of Congress*] (LCLS) .... CaQMCILR
Canadian Industries Ltd., Legal Department, Montreal, PQ, Canada [*Library symbol*] [*Library of Congress*] (LCLS) .... CaQMCILL
Canadian Industries Ltd., Montreal, PQ, Canada [*Library symbol*] [*Library of Congress*] (LCLS) .... CaQMCIL
Canadian Industry Program for Energy Conservation .... CIPEC
Canadian Infantry Association [*Association Canadienne de l'Infanterie*] (AC) .... CIA
Canadian Infantry Brigade (DMA) .... CIB
Canadian Infantry Brigade Group [*British military*] (DMA) .... CIBG
Canadian Infantry Corps CIC
Canadian Infantry Division (SAUO) .... CID
Canadian Infantry Holding Unit (SAUO) .... CIHU
Canadian Infantry Holding Unit .... CIHU
Canadian Infectious Disease Society [*Societe Canadienne de Maladies Infectieuses*] (AC) .... CIDS
Canadian Information and Image Management Society [*Information service or system*] (IID) .... CIIMS
Canadian Information Centre for International Credentials (SAUO) CICIC
Canadian Information Industry Association [*Information service or system*] [*Defunct*] (IID) .... CIIA
Canadian Information Processing Society [*Toronto, ON*] .... CIPS
Canadian Information Service (SAUO) .... CIS
Canadian Information Sharing Service .... CISS
Canadian Initiative on Digital Libraries (TELE) .... CIDL
Canadian Injured Workers Alliance [*L'Alliance Canadienne des Victimes d'Accidents et de Maladies du Travail*] (AC) .... CIWA
Canadian Injury Prevention Foundation (AC) .... CIPF
Canadian In-Line & Roller Skating Association (AC) .... CIRSA
Canadian Insolvency Practitioner (DD) .... CIP
Canadian Insolvency Practitioners Association [*Association Canadienne des Professionnels de l'Insolvabilite*] (AC) .... CIPA
Canadian Institue for the Admistration of Justice (AC) .... CIAJ
Canadian Institue of Hypnotism (AC) .... CIH
Canadian Institute for Advanced Research .... CIAR
Canadian Institute for Climate Studies (QUAC) .... CICS
Canadian Institute for Conflict Resolution [*Institute Canadien pour la Resolution des Conflits*] (AC) .... CICR
Canadian Institute for Development Management (AC) .... CIDM
Canadian Institute for Energy Training Inc. [*L'Institut Canadien de Formation de l'Energie*] (AC) .... CIET
Canadian Institute for Environmental Law and Policy .... CIELAP
Canadian Institute for Environmental Law and Policy .... CIELP
Canadian Institute for Health Information (SAUO) .... CIHI
Canadian Institute for Historical Microreproductions [*Source file*] [*UTLAS symbol*] .... CHM
Canadian Institute for Historical Microreproductions .... CIHM
Canadian Institute for Historical Microreproductions, Ottawa, ON, Canada [*Library symbol*] [*Library of Congress*] (LCLS) .... CaOOCIHM

Canadian Institute for Historical Microreproductions [*Institut Canadien de Microreproductions Historiques*] Ottawa, Ontario [*Library symbol*] [*National Library of Canada*] (NLC) .... OOCIHM
Canadian Institute for International Order (SAUO) .... CIIO
Canadian Institute for International Peace and Security [*UTLAS symbol*] ..... CPS
Canadian Institute for International Peace and Security [*Institut Canadien pour la Paix et la Securite Mondiales*] Ottawa, Ontario [*Library symbol*] [*National Library of Canada*] (NLC) .... OOCIIPS
Canadian Institute for Organization Management (AC) .... CIOM
Canadian Institute for Radiation Safety [*Institut Canadien de Radioprotection*] (AC) .... CAIRS
Canadian Institute for Radiation Safety, Ottawa, Ontario [*Library symbol*] [*National Library of Canada*] (NLC) .... OOCIRS
Canadian Institute for Research .... CIR
Canadian Institute for Research in Atmospheric Chemistry [*York University*] .... CIRAC
Canadian Institute for Scientific and Technical Information - CISTI [*UTLAS symbol*] .... CIS
Canadian Institute for Synchrotron Radiation .... CISR
Canadian Institute for Telecommunications Research [*Research center*] (RCD) .... CITR
Canadian Institute for Theatre Technology (AC) .... CITT
Canadian Institute for Theoretical Astrophysics [*University of Toronto*] [*Research center*] (RCD) .... CITA
Canadian Institute of Academic Medicine [*Institut Canadien de Medecine Academique*] (AC) .... CIAM
Canadian Institute of Actuaries .... CIA
Canadian Institute of Adult Education, Montreal, PQ, Canada [*Library symbol*] [*Library of Congress*] (LCLS) .... CaQMICE
Canadian Institute of Adult Education [*Institut Canadien d'Education des Adultes*] Montreal, Quebec [*Library symbol*] [*National Library of Canada*] (NLC) .... QMICE
Canadian Institute of Biotechnology [*Institut Canadien de la Biotechnologie*] (AC) .... CIB
Canadian Institute of Certified Administrative Managers (AC) .... CICAM
Canadian Institute of Chartered Accountants .... CICA
Canadian Institute of Chartered Accountants (SAUO) .... CICA
Canadian Institute of Chartered Business Valuators [*Formerly, Canadian Association of Business Valuators*] (AC) .... CICBV
Canadian Institute of Chemistry (SAUO) CIC
Canadian Institute of Child Health .... CICH
Canadian Institute of Energy (AC) .... CIE
Canadian Institute of Fisheries Technology [*Technical University of Nova Scotia*] [*Research center*] (RCD) .... CIFT
Canadian Institute of Food Technology Journal (SAUS) .... Can Inst Food Technol J
Canadian Institute of Forestry .... CIF
Canadian Institute of Geomatics [*Association Canadienne des Sciences Geomatiques*] (AC) .... CIG
Canadian Institute of Guided Ground Transport (SAUS) .... CICGT
Canadian Institute of Guided Ground Transport [*Queen's University at Kingston*] [*Research center*] (RCD) .... CIGGT
Canadian Institute of Guided Ground Transport, Queens University, Kingston, Ontario (SAUS) .... OKQCI
Canadian Institute of Guided Ground Transport, Queen's University, Kingston, Ontario [*Library symbol*] [*National Library of Canada*] (NLC) .... OKQCI
Canadian Institute of International Affairs (SAUO) .... CIIA
Canadian Institute of International Affairs .... CIIA
Canadian Institute of International Affairs, Toronto, ON, Canada [*Library symbol*] [*Library of Congress*] (LCLS) .... CaOTCIA
Canadian Institute of International Affairs [*Institut Canadien des Affaires Internationales*] Toronto, Ontario [*Library symbol*] [*National Library of Canada*] (NLC) .... OTCIA
Canadian Institute of Management [*Institut Canadien de Gestion*] (AC) .... CIM
Canadian Institute of Marine Engineering, Canada (SAUS) .... CIMarE
Canadian Institute of Marketing [*Institut Canadien du Marketing*] (AC) .... CIM
Canadian Institute of Metalworking [*McMaster University*] [*Research center*] (RCD) .... CIM
Canadian Institute of Mining .... CIM
Canadian Institute of Mining and Metallurgy .... CIMM
Canadian Institute of Mining and Metallurgy, Montreal, PQ, Canada [*Library symbol*] [*Library of Congress*] (LCLS) .... CaQMCIM
Canadian Institute of Mining and Metallurgy Montreal, Quebec (SAUS) .... QMCIM
Canadian Institute of Personalized Education Inc. (AC) .... CIPE
Canadian Institute of Planners (PDAA) .... CIP
Canadian Institute of Plumbing & Heating [*L'Institut Canadien de Plomberie et de Chauffage*] (AC) .... CIPH
Canadian Institute of Public Affairs .... CIPA
Canadian Institute of Public Health Inspectors [*Institut Canadien des Inspecteurs en Hygiene Publique*] (AC) .... CIPHI
Canadian Institute of Resources Law [*University of Calgary*] [*Research center*] (RCD) .... CIRL
Canadian Institute of Science and Technology Ltd. .... CIST
Canadian Institute of Steel Construction .... CISC
Canadian Institute of Strategic Studies (EAIO) .... CISS
Canadian Institute of Surveying .... CIS
Canadian Institute of Surveying and Mapping (EAIO) .... CISM
Canadian Institute of Surveying and Photogrammetry .... CIS & P
Canadian Institute of Surveying and Photogrammetry (SAUO) ...... CIS&P
Canadian Institute of Technology for the Environment (AC) .... CITE
Canadian Institute of Traffic and Transportation .... CITT
Canadian Institute of Travel Counsellors .... CITC
Canadian Institute of Treated Wood .... CITW

Canadian Institute of Ukrainian Studies [*Institut Canadien d'Etudes Ukrainiennes*] (AC) ... CIUS
Canadian Institute on Pollution Control ... CIPC
Canadian Institutes of Health Research ... CIHR
Canadian Insulock [*Vancouver Stock Exchange symbol*] ... CIK
Canadian Insurance Claims Managers Association ... CICMA
Canadian Intelligence Corps (DMA) ... CIC
Canadian Intelligence Corps ... C Int C
Canadian Interagency Forest Fire Centre [*ICAO designator*] (FAAC) ... TKR
Canadian Intercollegiate Athletic Union ... CIAU
Canadian Intercollegiate Sailing Association ... CISA
Canadian Intergovernmental Conference Secretariat ... CICS
Canadian International Development Agency (SAUO) ... ACDI
Canadian International Development Agency [*Formerly, External Aid Office*] ... CIDA
Canadian International Development Agency, Ottawa, ON, Canada [*Library symbol*] [*Library of Congress*] (LCLS) ... CaOOCD
Canadian International Development Agency [*Agence Canadienne de DeveloppementInternational*] **Ottawa, Ontario** [*Library symbol*] [*National Library of Canada*] (NLC) ... OOCD
Canadian International DX Radio Club (AC) ... CIDX
Canadian International Footwear Exposition (ITD) ... CIFE
Canadian International Freight Forwarders Association, Inc. (AC) ... CIFFA
Canadian International Grains Institute ... CIGI
Canadian International Health Education Network (SAUO) ... CIHEN
Canadian International Institute of Applied Negotiation [*L'Institut International Canadien de la Negociation Pratique*] (AC) ... CIIAN
Canadian International Network Association (AC) ... CINA
Canadian International Paper Co. ... CIP
Canadian International Philatelic Exhibition, Toronto (SAUO) ... CAPEX
Canadian International Trade Association (AC) ... CITA
Canadian International Trade Fair (SAUO) ... CITF
Canadian International Trade Tribunal ... CITT
Canadian International Trade Tribunal [*Tribunal Canadien du Commerce Exterieur*], **Ontario** [*Library symbol*] [*National Library of Canada*] (BIB) ... OOCITT
Canadian International Water and Energy Consultants ... Ciwec
Canadian Intravenous Nurses Association (EAIO) ... CINA
Canadian Inventory of Historic Building [*Environment Canada*] [*Information service or system*] (IID) ... CIHB
Canadian Investment Manager (ASC) ... CIM
Canadian Investor Relations Institute [*Institut Canadien de Relations Avec les Investisseurs*] [*Formerly, National Investor Relations Institute Canada*] (AC) ... CIRI
Canadian Iris Society ... CIS
Canadian Italian Business & Professional Association Inc. [*Association des Gens d'Affaires & Professionnels Italo-Canadiens Inc.*] (AC) ... CIBPA
Canadian Italian Business & Professional Association of British Columbia [*Formerly, Italian Canadian Business & Professional Association of British Columbia*] (AC) ... CIBPA
Canadian Italian Business and Professional Men's Association ... CIBPA
Canadian Jesuits International (SAUS) ... CANJES
Canadian Jewellers Institute ... CJI
Canadian Jewish Congress [*Congres Juif Canadien*] (AC) ... CJC
Canadian Jewish Congress Library, Montreal, PQ, Canada [*Library symbol*] [*Library of Congress*] (LCLS) ... CaQMCJ
Canadian Jewish Congress [*Congres Juif Canadien*] **Montreal, Quebec** [*Library symbol*] [*National Library of Canada*] (NLC) ... QMCJ
Canadian Jewish Historical Society [*See also SCHJ*] ... CJHS
Canadian Jobs Strategy [*Employment and Immigration Canada program launched in 1986*] ... CJS
Canadian Joint Staff ... CJS
Canadian Joint Staff (SAUO) ... CJSW
Canadian Jorex Ltd. [*Toronto Stock Exchange symbol*] ... CJX
Canadian Journal of Animal Science (SAUS) ... Can J Anim Sci
Canadian Journal of Biochemistry (SAUS) ... Can J Biochem
Canadian Journal of Botany (SAUS) ... Can J Bot
Canadian Journal of Chemical Engineering (SAUS) ... Can J Chem Eng
Canadian Journal of Chemistry [*A publication*] (MEC) ... Can J Chem
Canadian Journal of Chemistry (journ.) (SAUS) ... Can J Chem
Canadian Journal of Civil Engineering (SAUS) ... CJCE
Canadian Journal of Corrections [*A publication*] (ILCA) ... Can J Correct
Canadian Journal of Criminology [*A publication*] (DLA) ... Can J Criminol
Canadian Journal of Earth Sciences [*A publication*] (QUAC) ... CJES
Canadian Journal of Economics and Political Science (journ.) (SAUS) ... Can J Econ
Canadian Journal of Fisheries and Aquatic Science (SAUS) ... Can J Fish Aquat Sci
Canadian Journal of Forest Research (SAUS) ... Can J Forest Res
Canadian Journal of Genetics and Cytology (SAUS) ... Can J Genet Cytol
Canadian Journal of Industry (SAUS) ... Canad J of Ind
Canadian Journal of Information Science [*A publication*] (NITA) ... CJIS
Canadian Journal of Law and Society/Revue Canadienne de Droit et Societe [*A publication*] ... CJLS/RCDS
Canadian Journal of Linguistics (journ.) (SAUS) ... CJL
Canadian Journal of Medical Technology (SAUS) ... Can J Med Technol
Canadian Journal of Microbiology (SAUS) ... Can J Microbiol
Canadian Journal of Neurological Sciences (SAUS) ... CJNS
Canadian Journal of Nursing Administration (SAUO) ... CJONA
Canadian Journal of Ophthalmology (SAUS) ... Can J Ophthalmol
Canadian Journal of Pharmaceutical Sciences (SAUS) ... Can J Pharm Sci
Canadian Journal of Physics (journ.) (SAUS) ... Can J Phys
Canadian Journal of Physiology and Pharmacology (SAUS) ... Can J Physiol Pharmacol
Canadian Journal of Plant Pathology (SAUS) ... Can J Plant Pathol
Canadian Journal of Plant Science (SAUS) ... Can J Plant Sci
Canadian Journal of Political and Social Theory [*A publication*] ... CJPST
Canadian Journal of Psychology (journ.) (SAUS) ... CJPs
Canadian Journal of Public Health (SAUS) ... Can J Public Health
Canadian Journal of Remote Sensing (SAUS) ... Can J Remote Sens
Canadian Journal of Research (journ.) (SAUS) ... Can J Res
Canadian Journal of Respiratory Therapy (SAUO) ... CJRT
Canadian Journal of Rural Medicine (SAUO) ... CJRM
Canadian Journal of Soil Science (SAUS) ... Can J Soil Sci
Canadian Journal of Surgery (SAUS) ... CJS
Canadian Journal of Zoology (SAUS) ... Can J Zoo
Canadian Journalism Data Base [*University of Western Ontario*] (IID) ... CJD
Canadian Journalism Foundation [*La Fondation pour le Journalisme Canadien*] (AC) ... CJF
Canadian Kennel Club ... CKC
Canadian Kitchen Cabinet Association (AC) ... CKCA
Canadian L and Surface Scheme ... CLASS
Canadian Laboratory for Integrated Spatial Information Research and Engineering [*University of New Brunswick*] [*Research center*] (RCD) ... CanLabINSPIRE
Canadian Laboratory for Integrated Spatial Information Research and Engineering (SAUS) ... CANLAB INSPIRE
Canadian Labour Arbitration Summaries [*Canada Law Book, Inc.*] [*Information service or system*] (CRD) ... CLAS
Canadian Labour Congress ... CLC
Canadian Labour Congress, Ottawa, ON, Canada [*Library symbol*] [*Library of Congress*] (LCLS) ... CaOOCLC
Canadian Labour Congress [*Congres du Travail du Canada*] **Ottawa, Ontario** [*Library symbol*] [*National Library of Canada*] (NLC) ... OOCLC
Canadian Labour Congress/Congres du Travail du Canada [*Political party*] (ASC) ... CLC/CTC
Canadian Labour Defence League ... CLDL
Canadian Labour Force Development Board [*La Commission Canadienne de Mise en Valeur de la Main-d'Oeuvre*] (AC) ... CLFDB
Canadian Labour Law Cases [*A publication*] (DLA) ... CLLC
Canadian Labour Market & Productivity Centre [*Centre Canadien du Marche du Travail et de la Productivite*] (AC) ... CLMPC
Canadian Labour Market and Productivity Centre [*Centre Canadien du Marche du Travail et de la Productivite*], **Ottawa, Ontario** [*Library symbol*] [*National Library of Canada*] (NLC) ... OOCLM
Canadian Labour Party ... CLP
Canadian Labour Relations Board Reports [*A publication*] (DLA) ... Can LRBR
Canadian Labour Union ... CLU
Canadian Labs Supplies Ltd. (EFIS) ... CANLAB
Canadian Lacrosse Association (AC) ... CLA
Canadian Lacrosse Hall of Fame, New Westminster, British Columbia [*Library symbol*] [*National Library of Canada*] (NLC) ... BNWLH
Canadian Ladies Association of Shooting Sports ... CLASS
Canadian Ladies' Golf Association [*Association Canadienne des Golfeuses*] (AC) ... CLGA
Canadian Ladies Lawn Bowling Council ... CLLBC
Canadian Lake & Ocean Salvage Team [*Commercial firm*] ... CLOST
Canadian Land Forces Command and Staff College, Kingston, ON, Canada [*Library symbol*] [*Library of Congress*] (LCLS) ... CaOKF
Canadian Land Forces Europe Exchange System (SAUO) ... CLFEX
Canadian Land Settlers Association (SAUO) ... CLSA
Canadian Latex Allergy Association (SAUO) ... CLAA
Canadian Latvian Business & Professional Association (AC) ... CLBPA
Canadian Law and Society Association [*See also ACDS*] ... CLSA
Canadian Law Information Council [*Information service or system*] (IID) ... CLIC
Canadian Law Review [*A publication*] (DLA) ... Can L Rev
Canadian Law Review and Corporation Legal Journal [*A publication*] (DLA) ... CLR
Canadian Law Times [*A publication*] (DLA) ... Canada LT
Canadian Law Times [*A publication*] (DLA) ... Can LT
Canadian Law Times [*A publication*] (DLA) ... Can L Times
Canadian Law Times [*A publication*] (DLA) ... CLT
Canadian Law Times. Occasional Notes [*A publication*] (DLA) ... Can LT Occ N
Canadian Law Times. Occasional Notes [*A publication*] (DLA) ... CLT Occ N
Canadian Lawn Bowling Council ... CLBC
Canadian Lawyers Insurance Association [*Association d'Assurances des Juristes Canadiens*] (AC) ... CLIA
Canadian League for the Liberation of Ukraine ... CLLU
Canadian League of Composers ... CLC
Canadian Learning Materials Centre ... CLMC
Canadian Legal Advocacy Information and Research Association of the Disabled ... CLAIR
Canadian Legal Information Centre (EAIO) ... CLIC
Canadian Legal Studies [*A publication*] (DLA) ... Can Leg Stud
Canadian Legal Studies [*A publication*] (DLA) ... Can Leg Studies
Canadian Legal Studies [*A publication*] (ILCA) ... Can LS
Canadian Legion (SAUO) ... CL
Canadian Legion Educational Services (SAUO) ... CLES
Canadian Legion War Service (SAUO) ... CLWS
Canadian Lencourt Mines Ltd. [*Toronto Stock Exchange symbol*] ... CLE
Canadian Lesbian and Gay Rights Coalition ... CLGRC
Canadian Liaison Officer (SAUS) ... CFLO
Canadian Library Association [*Also known as ACB and CLA*] ... CANLA
Canadian Library Association [*Also known as ACB and CANLA*] ... CLA
Canadian Library Association, Ottawa, ON, Canada [*Library symbol*] [*Library of Congress*] (LCLS) ... CanLA
Canadian Library Association, Ottawa, ON, Canada [*Library symbol*] [*Library of Congress*] (LCLS) ... CaOOCLA
Canadian Library Association, Ottawa, Ontario [*Library symbol*] [*National Library of Canada*] (BIB) ... OOCLA

Canadian Library Bulletin (journ.) (SAUS) ... Can Lib Bull
Canadian Library Exhibitors' Association ... CLEA
Canadian Library Journal (SAUS) ... Can Libr J
Canadian Library of Family Medicine (SAUO) ... CLFM
Canadian Library Trustees' Association ... CLTA
Canadian Life & Health Insurance Association Inc. [*Association Canadienne des Compagnies d'Assurances de Personnes Inc.*] [*Formerly, Canadian Life Insurance Association*] (AC) ... CLHIA
Canadian Life Insurance Medical Officers Association [*Association Canadienne des Directeurs Medicaux en Assurance-Vie*] (AC) ... CLIMOA
Canadian Lifeboat Institution Inc. (AC) ... CLI
Canadian Light Rail Vehicle ... CLRV
Canadian Light Source ... CLS
Canadian Linguistic Association [*See also ACL*] ... CLA
Canadian Literary Periodical Index [*Information service or system*] (IID) ... CLPI
Canadian Literature [*A publication*] (BRI) ... Can Lit
Canadian Liver Foundation [*Fondation Canadienne du Foie*] (AC) ... CLF
Canadian Livestock Feed Board ... CLFB
Canadian Livestock Feed Board [*Office Canadien des Provendes*] **Montreal, Quebec** [*Library symbol*] [*National Library of Canada*] (NLC) ... QMOCP
Canadian Livestock Records Corporation [*Societe Canadienne d'Enregistrement des Animaux*] (AC) ... CLRC
Canadian Logistics Operation Center (SAUS) ... CLOC
Canadian Long Distance Riding Association (AC) ... CaLDRA
Canadian Long Term Care Assciation [*Association Canadienne de Soins a Long Terme*] (AC) ... CLS
Canadian Longhorn Petroleum [*Vancouver Stock Exchange symbol*] ... CHN
Canadian Low-Level Air Defence System (SAUS) ... CLLADS
Canadian Lumber Size (DAC) ... CLS
Canadian Lumber Standards (WPI) ... CLS
Canadian Lumbermen's Association ... CLA
Canadian Lung Association [*Association Pulmonaire du Canada*] (AC) ... CLA
Canadian Lung Volume Reduction (SAUO) ... CLVR
Canadian Lutheran World Relief (SAUS) ... CLWR
Canadian Machine Gun Corps [*World War I*] ... CMGC
Canadian Machine Tool Distributors' Association (AC) ... CMTDA
Canadian Machine Tool Show (ITD) ... CMTS
Canadian Machine-Readable Cataloguing [*National Library of Canada*] [*Information service or system*] ... CAN/MARC
Canadian Machinery and Metalworking (journ.) (SAUS) ... Can Mach Metalwork
Canadian Magazine Index [*Micromedia Ltd.*] [*Information service or system*] (IID) ... CMI
Canadian Magazine Publishers Association [*Formerly, Canadian Periodical Publisher's Association*] (AC) ... CMPA
Canadian Maine-Anjou Association (AC) ... CMAA
Canadian Major Junior Hockey League ... CMJHL
Canadian Malignant Hyperthermia Association (SAUO) ... MHA
Canadian Management Associates for Global Development (AC) ... CAMDEV
Canadian Managing Editors' Conference ... CMEC
Canadian Man-Computer Communications Society ... CMCS
Canadian Manoir Industries Ltd. [*Toronto Stock Exchange symbol*] ... CMQ
Canadian Manpower Centre (SAUO) ... Can Man Cen
Canadian Manufacturers Association ... CMA
Canadian Manufacturers of Chemical Specialties Association (EAIO) ... CMCS
Canadian Manufacturers of Chemical Specialties Association ... CMCSA
Canadian MARC [*Machine-Readable Cataloging*] [*Source file*] [*UTLAS symbol*] ... CAN
Canadian Marconi [*AMEX symbol*] (TTSB) ... CMW
Canadian Marconi Co. [*Aerospace*] ... CMA
Canadian Marconi Co. [*Associated Press*] (SAG) ... CMarc
Canadian Marconi Co. [*Toronto Stock Exchange symbol*] ... CMC
Canadian Marconi Co. [*AMEX symbol*] [*Toronto Stock Exchange symbol*] (SPSG) ... CMW
Canadian Marconi Co., Kanata, Ontario [*Library symbol*] [*National Library of Canada*] (NLC) ... OKCM
Canadian Marconi Co., Montreal, PQ, Canada [*Library symbol*] [*Library of Congress*] (LCLS) ... CaQMCM
Canadian Marconi Co., Montreal, Quebec [*Library symbol*] [*National Library of Canada*] (NLC) ... QMCM
Canadian Marine Trade Exhibition and Congress [*SHOWBEX*] (TSPED) ... CAMTEC
Canadian Marine Transportation Administration ... CMTA
Canadian Maritime Command ... CANMARCOM
Canadian Maritime Commander, Atlantic (NATG) ... CANCOMARLANT
Canadian Maritime Commission (SAUO) ... CMC
Canadian Maritime Industries Association [*Association Canadienne des Industries Maritimes*] [*Formerly, Canadian Shipbuilding & Ship Repairing Association*] (AC) ... CMIA
Canadian Maritime Rescue Auxiliary (PDAA) ... CMRA
Canadian Maritime Union (BARN) ... CMU
Canadian Masonry Contractors' Association (AC) ... CMCA
Canadian Massage Therapist Alliance [*Alliance Candienne de Massotherapeutes*] (AC) ... CMTA
Canadian Master Athlete Federation (AC) ... CMAF
Canadian Masters Cross-Country Ski Association [*Association Canadienne des Maitres en Ski de Fond*] (AC) ... CMCSA
Canadian Mathematical Congress (SAUO) ... CMC
Canadian Mathematical Society [*Societe Mathematique du Canada*] (AC) ... CMS
Canadian Mathematics Achievement Test [*Education*] (AEBS) ... CMAT
Canadian Meat Council [*Conseil des Viandes du Canada*] [*Formerly, Meat Packers Council of Canada*] (AC) ... CMC
Canadian Meat Importers Committee (AC) ... CMIC
Canadian Mechanized Brigade Group (MCD) ... CMBG
Canadian Media Guild [*La Guilde Canadienne des Medias*] (AC) ... CMG
Canadian Medical Acupuncture Society (SAUO) ... CMAS
Canadian Medical and Biological Engineering Society ... CMBES
Canadian Medical Association ... CMA
Canadian Medical Association Journal (SAUS) ... Can Med Assoc J
Canadian Medical Association Journal [*A publication*] (MELL) ... CMAJ
Canadian Medical Association, Ottawa, ON, Canada [*Library symbol*] [*Library of Congress*] (LCLS) ... CaOOCMA
Canadian Medical Association, Ottawa, Ontario [*Library symbol*] [*National Library of Canada*] (NLC) ... OOCMA
Canadian Medical Discovery Fund ... CMDF
Canadian Medical Malpractice Prevention Association (AC) ... CMMPA
Canadian Medical Protective Association ... CMPA
Canadian Medical Students Association (SAUO) ... CMSA
Canadian Mediterranean Institute [*Research center*] (RCD) ... CMI
Canadian Member, Canadian Joint Staff, Washington, DC ... CANAVUS
Canadian Memorial Chiropractic College ... CMCC
Canadian Memorial Chiropractic College, Toronto, ON, Canada [*Library symbol*] [*Library of Congress*] (LCLS) ... CaOTCMC
Canadian Memorial Chiropractic College, Toronto, Ontario [*Library symbol*] [*National Library of Canada*] (NLC) ... OTCMC
Canadian Mennonite Bible College ... CMBC
Canadian Mennonite Bible College, Winnipeg, Manitoba [*Library symbol*] [*National Library of Canada*] (NLC) ... MWCM
Canadian Mennonite Bible College, Winnipeg, MB, Canada [*Library symbol*] [*Library of Congress*] (LCLS) ... CaMWCM
Canadian Mental Health Association ... CMHA
Canadian Mental Health Association, Toronto, Ontario [*Library symbol*] [*National Library of Canada*] (BIB) ... OTCMHA
Canadian Merchant Fleet (SAUS) ... CMF
Canadian Merchant Navy (SAUO) ... CMN
Canadian Merchant Navy Association Inc. [*Association de la Marine Marchande Canadienne Inc.*] (AC) ... CMNA
Canadian Merchant Service Guild ... CMSG
Canadian Metal Mining Association ... CMMA
Canadian Metallurgical Quarterly (journ.) (SAUS) ... Can Metall Quart
Canadian Meteorological and Oceanographic Society ... CMOS
Canadian Meteorological and Oceanographic Society Consultant (ASC) ... CMOS
Canadian Meteorological Centre [*Marine science*] (MSC) ... CMC
Canadian Meteorological Service (SAUO) ... Can Met Ser
Canadian Metric Association ... CMA
Canadian Microcool Corp. [*Vancouver Stock Exchange symbol*] ... CQO
Canadian Microfilming Co. Ltd. [*Societe Canadienne du Microfilm, Inc.*] **Montreal, Quebec** [*Library symbol*] [*National Library of Canada*] (NLC) ... QMSCM
Canadian Microfilming Co., Montreal, PQ, Canada [*Library symbol*] [*Library of Congress*] (LCLS) ... CanM
Canadian Micrographic Society ... CMS
Canadian Military Electronics Standards Agency (MCD) ... CAMESA
Canadian Military Electronics Standards Agency (SAUO) ... CMESA
Canadian Military Forces (SAUO) ... CMF
Canadian Military Headquarters (SAUO) ... CMHq
Canadian Military Headquarters (DMA) ... CMHQ
Canadian Military Pattern (DMA) ... CMP
Canadian Militia ... CM
Canadian Militia (SAUO) ... CM
Canadian Mine Sweeping Squadron (SAUO) ... CANMINRON
Canadian Mineral Analysts [*Analystes des Mineraux Canadiens*] (AC) ... CMA
Canadian Mineral Occurrence Index [*Department of Energy, Mines, and Resources*] [*Information service or system*] (IID) ... CANMINDEX
Canadian Mineral Processors (HGAA) ... CMP
Canadian Mines Handbook (SAUO) ... CMH
Canadian Mineworkers Union ... CMU
Canadian Minimum Navigation Performance Specification Airspace [*FAA*] (TAG) ... CMNPS
Canadian Mining Journal (journ.) (SAUS) ... Can Min J
Canadian Minister of Transport (SAUO) ... CMT
Canadian Mobile Home Association ... CMHA
Canadian Mockup and Training Facility (SAUS) ... CMTF
Canadian Modern Language Review/La Revue canadienne des langues vivantes (SAUO) ... CMLR/RCLV
Canadian Modern Rhythmic Gymnastics Federation ... CMRGF
Canadian Monthly (journ.) (SAUS) ... Canad Mo
Canadian Morgan Horse Association Inc. [*Association des Chevaux Morgan Canadien Inc.*] (AC) ... CMHA
Canadian Motion Picture Distributors Association ... CMPDA
Canadian Motor Machine Gun [*World War I*] ... CMMG
Canadian Motor Machine Gun Brigade (DMA) ... CMMGB
Canadian Motor Vehicle Arbitration Program ... CAMVAP
Canadian Motor Vehicle Safety Standard ... CMVSS
Canadian Motor Vehicle Tyre Safety Standard (PDAA) ... CMVTSS
Canadian Motorcycle Association [*Association Motocycliste Canadienne*] (AC) ... CMA
Canadian Mounted Rifles ... CMR
Canadian Municipal Journal [*A publication*] (DLA) ... Can Mun J
Canadian Municipal Journal [*A publication*] (DLA) ... CMJ
Canadian Municipal Utilities (SAUS) ... CMU
Canadian Museum Association, Ottawa, ON, Canada [*Library symbol*] [*Library of Congress*] (LCLS) ... CaOOCANM
Canadian Museum Association [*Association des Musees Canadiens*], **Ottawa, Ontario** [*Library symbol*] [*National Library of Canada*] (NLC) ... OOCANM
Canadian Museum of Civilization (QUAC) ... CMC
Canadian Museum of Civilization, National Museums of Canada [*Musee Canadien des Civilisations, Musees Nationaux du Canada*] **Ottawa, Ontario** [*Library symbol*] [*National Library of Canada*] (NLC) ... OONMM
Canadian Museum of Contemporary Photography ... CMCP

Canadian Museum of Flight and Transportation .... CMFT
Canadian Museum of Health and Medicine (SAUO) .... CMHM
Canadian Museum of Nature (QUAC) .... CMN
Canadian Museums Association .... CMA
Canadian Music Centre .... CMC
Canadian Music Council [*Defunct*] (EAIO) .... CMC
Canadian Music Educators' Association .... CMEA
Canadian Music Library Association (SAUO) .... CMLA
Canadian Music Library Association, Toronto, ON, Canada [*Library symbol*] [*Library of Congress*] (LCLS) .... CaOTCMLA
Canadian Music Library Association [*Association Canadienne des Bibliotheques Musicales*] **Toronto, Ontario** [*Library symbol*] [*National Library of Canada*] (NLC) .... OTCMLA
Canadian Music Publishers Association [*See also ACEM*] .... CMPA
Canadian Music Research Council .... CMRC
Canadian Music Therapy Association .... CMTA
Canadian Musical Heritage Society [*Societe pour le Patrimoine Musical Canadien*] (AC) .... CMHS
Canadian Musical Reproduction Rights Agency .... CMRRA
Canadian Mutual Aid Board [*World War II*] .... CMAB
Canadian National (SAUS) .... CN
Canadian National + Canadian Pacific (SAUS) .... Via Rail
Canadian National Asbestos Council [*Formerly, The Canadian Chapter of the National Asbestos Council*] (AC) .... CANNAC
Canadian National Carbide Company (SAUO) .... CNCC
Canadian National Committee - International Peat Society .... CNC-IPS
Canadian National Committee for Earthquake Engineering .... CANCEE
Canadian National Committee for Mental Hygiene (BARN) .... CNCMH
Canadian National Committee for Pacific Economic Cooperation .... CANCPEC
Canadian National Committee for the International Association on the Properties of Steam (PDAA) .... CNC/IAPS
Canadian National Committee for the International Federation of Automatic Control (EAIO) .... CNC-IFAC
Canadian National Committee of the International Committee on Water Pollution Research and Control (EAIO) .... CNC/IAWPRC
Canadian National Committee of the World Energy Conference (SAUO) .... CANWEC
Canadian National Committee, World Energy Conference .... CANWEC
Canadian National Defence Research Department (SAUO) .... CNDRD
Canadian National Energy Forum .... CNEF
Canadian National Exhibition [*Held annually in Toronto*] .... CNE
Canadian National Federation of Independent Unions [*See also FCNSI*] .... CNFIU
Canadian National Federation of Independent Unions/Federation Canadienne Nationale des Syndicats Independants (ASC) .... CNFIU/FCNSI
Canadian National Institute for the Blind .... CNIB
Canadian National Institute for the Blind, National Library Division, Toronto, ON, Canada [*Library symbol*] [*Library of Congress*] (LCLS) .... CaOTBNL
Canadian National Library (SAUO) .... CNL
Canadian National Library (BARN) .... CNL
Canadian National Library Association (SAUO) .... CNLA
Canadian National Packaging Exposition [*Packaging Association of Canada*] (TSPED) .... PAC-EX
Canadian National Power Alcohol Conference .... CANPAC
Canadian National Railway Co. [*Associated Press*] (SAG) .... CdnNRy
Canadian National Railway Co. [*Associated Press*] (SAG) .... CdnRy
Canadian National Railway Co. [*NYSE symbol*] (SAG) .... CNI
Canadian National Railways [*AAR code*] .... CN
Canadian National Railways [*Facetious translation: Certainly No Rush*] .... CNR
Canadian National Railways, Chemical Library, Montreal, PQ, Canada [*Library symbol*] [*Library of Congress*] (LCLS) .... CaQMCNC
Canadian National Railways, Montreal, PQ, Canada [*Library symbol*] [*Library of Congress*] (LCLS) .... CaQMCN
Canadian National Railways [*Chemins de fer Nationaux du Canada*] **Montreal, Quebec** [*Library symbol*] [*National Library of Canada*] (NLC) .... QMCN
Canadian National Railways Pension Trust Fund [*Montreal-based pension fund*] .... CNRPTF
Canadian National Recreation Association .... CNRA
Canadian National Seismograph Network .... CNSN
Canadian National Steamships (MHDW) .... CNS
Canadian National Steamships [*AAR code*] .... CNSS
Canadian National Telecommunications .... CNT
Canadian National Telecommunications [*Canada*] [*ICAO designator*] (ICDA) .... XN
Canadian National Telecommunications [*FAA designator*] (FAAC) .... XNC
Canadian National Telegraphs (SAUS) .... CNT
Canadian National Telephone Co. (NITA) .... CNT
Canadian National Yellow Pages Service .... CANYPS
Canadian National-Canadian Pacific Railway .... CNCP
Canadian National/Canadian Pacific Telecommunications (NITA) .... CN/CPT
Canadian National/Canadian Pacific Telecommunications (SAUO) .... CNCPT
Canadian Native Arts Foundation (AC) .... CNAF
Canadian Native Law Reporter. Native Law Centre. University of Saskatchewan [*A publication*] (DLA) .... Can Native L Rep
Canadian Natl Railway [*NYSE symbol*] (SG) .... CNI
Canadian Natl Railway [*NYSE symbol*] (TTSB) .... CNI PP
Canadian Natural Deuterium Uranium Pressurized Heavy-Water [*Nuclear reactor*] .... CANDU PHW
Canadian Natural Resources [*Toronto Stock Exchange symbol*] (SG) .... CNQ
Canadian Natural Resources Ltd. [*Toronto Stock Exchange symbol*] .... CNQ
Canadian Nature Federation [*Federation Canadienne de la Nature*] [*Formerly, Canadian Audubon Society*] (AC) .... CNF
Canadian Naturopathic Association [*Association Canadienne de Naturopathie*] (AC) .... CNA
Canadian Nautical Research Society [*Societe Canadienne pour la Recherche Nautique*] (AC) .... CNRS
Canadian Naval Air Station .... CANAS
Canadian Naval Board .... CNB
Canadian Naval Commander Newfoundland .... CANCOMNEW
Canadian Naval Electronic Warfare System .... CANEWS
Canadian Naval Gunboat (SAUS) .... CNG
Canadian Naval Joint Staff in United States (SAUO) .... CANAVUS
Canadian Naval Mission Overseas .... CNMO
Canadian Naval Modifications .... CANAVMODS
Canadian Naval Post Office (SAUO) .... CNPO
Canadian Naval Service .... CNS
Canadian Naval Stores (SAUO) .... CANAVSTORES
Canadian Navigation Society (AC) .... CNS
Canadian Navy Auxiliary Vessel (SAUS) .... CNAV
Canadian Navy Joint Staff in Great Britain (SAUO) .... CANABRIT
Canadian Network for Asthma Care (SAUO) .... CNAC
Canadian Network for Environmental Education and Communication (SAUO) .... EECOM
[*The*] **Canadian Network for Environmental Education & Communication** [*Reseau Canadien d'Education et de Communication Relatives a l'Environnement*] (AC) .... EECOM
Canadian Network for Sampling Precipitation .... CANSAP
Canadian Network for Space Research (AC) .... CNSR
Canadian Network for the Advancement of Research, Industry and Education (IID) .... CANARIE
Canadian Network of Toxicology Centres (AC) .... CNTC
Canadian Neurological Society [*Societe Canadienne de Neurologie*] (AC) .... CNS
Canadian News Index [*Micromedia Ltd.*] [*Information service or system*] [*A publication*] .... CNI
Canadian News Service .... CNS
Canadian Newspaper Unit .... CNU
Canadian NORAD Region [*Aviation*] (FAAC) .... CANR
Canadian Northeast Wideband Systems [*Air Force*] (MCD) .... CNEWS
Canadian Northern Express Co. (SAUO) .... CN
Canadian Northern Express Company (SAUO) .... CanNo
Canadian Northern Pacific Railway .... CNP
Canadian Northern Railway .... CNoR
Canadian Northern Railway (ROG) .... CNR
Canadian Northern Railway (SAUO) .... CNRy
Canadian Northstar Corp. [*Toronto Stock Exchange symbol*] .... CNX
Canadian Northwest Atlantic Area .... CNA
Canadian Nuclear Association .... CNA
Canadian Nuclear Society (NUCP) .... CNS
Canadian Numismatic Association [*Association Canadienne de Numismatique*] (AC) .... CNA
Canadian Numismatic Research Society .... CNRS
Canadian Nurse Educators Association (AC) .... CNEA
Canadian Nursery Trades Association (AC) .... CNTA
Canadian Nurses' Association [*See also AIC*] .... CNA
Canadian Nurses' Association, Ottawa, ON, Canada [*Library symbol*] [*Library of Congress*] (LCLS) .... CaOOCN
Canadian Nurses' Association [*Association Canadienne des Infirmieres*] **Ottawa, Ontario** [*Library symbol*] [*National Library of Canada*] (NLC) .... OOCN
Canadian Nurses Foundation [*Fondation des Infirmieres et Infirmiers du Canada*] (AC) .... CNF
Canadian Nurses Protective Society (AC) .... CNPS
Canadian Nurses Respiratory Society (AC) .... CNRS
Canadian Nut Council [*Conseil Canadien des Noix*] (AC) .... CNC
Canadian Obstetric, Gynecologic & Neonatal Nurses (AC) .... COGNN
Canadian Occidental Petrol [*AMEX symbol*] (TTSB) .... CXY
Canadian Occidental Petroleum Ltd. [*Associated Press*] (SAG) .... CdnOc
Canadian Occidental Petroleum Ltd. [*AMEX symbol*] (SPSG) .... CXY
Canadian Occidental Petroleum Ltd., Calgary, Alberta [*Library symbol*] [*National Library of Canada*] (NLC) .... ACCOP
Canadian Occupational Forecasting Program (EDAC) .... COFOR
Canadian Occupational Health Nurses Association [*Formerly, National Association of Occupational Health Nurses*] (AC) .... COHNA
Canadian Occupational Interest Inventory [*Vocational test*] .... COII
Canadian Ocean Data System .... CODS
Canadian Ocean Escort Vessel .... COEV
Canadian Oceanographic Data Centre [*Later, MEDS*] .... CODC
Canadian Oceanographic Identification Center (HGAA) .... COIC
Canadian Office Employees Union [*See also SCEB*] .... COEU
Canadian Office Machine Dealers Association (HGAA) .... COMDA
Canadian Office Products Association .... COPA
Canadian Officers Training Corps .... COTC
Canadian Offshore Oil Spill Research Association (SAUO) .... COOSRA
Canadian Offshore Resources Exposition (ITD) .... CORE
Canadian Oil and Gas Handbook [*A publication*] (DLA) .... Can Oil & Gas
Canadian Oil and Gas Industries (SAUO) .... COGI
Canadian Oldtimers Hockey Association .... COHA
Canadian Olympic Association .... COA
Canadian Olympic Regatta at Kingston .... CORK
Canadian Oncology Society .... COS
Canadian Online Enquiry System [*Pronounced "can-olay"*] [*National Research Council of Canada*] [*Ottawa, ON*] .... CAN/OLE
Canadian On-Line Record Database .... CORD
Canadian Opera Company .... COC
Canadian Operating Statistics [*Database*] [*Statistics Canada*] [*Information service or system*] (CRD) .... COPS
Canadian Operational Research Society .... CORS
Canadian Operations Research Society (SAUO) .... COReS
Canadian Ophthalmological Society (DAVI) .... COS

Canadian Options for Greenhouse Gas Emissions Reduction (QUAC) ... COGGER
Canadian Oral History Association [*See also SCHO*] ... COHA
Canadian Order of Foresters [*Later, CFLIS*] (EA) ... COF
Canadian Organic Growers ... COG
Canadian Organisation for Development through Education (SAUO) ... CODE International
Canadian Organisation for the Promotion of Education Inc. [*Organization Canadienne pour la Promotion de l'Education Inc.*] (AC) ... COPE
Canadian Organization for Advancement of Computers in Health (EAIO) ... COACH
Canadian Organization for Campus Activities ... COCA
Canadian Organization for Development through Education ... CODE
Canadian Organization for the Rights of Prostitutes (AC) ... CORP
Canadian Organization for the Simplification of Trade Procedures ... COSTPRO
Canadian Organization for the Simplification of Trade Procedures (SAUO) ... COSTPRO
Canadian Organization of Medical Physicists (SAUO) ... COMP
Canadian Organization of Public Housing Tenants ... COPHT
Canadian Organization of Small Business Inc. [*Also, The Voice of Business*] (AC) ... COSBI
Canadian Orienteering Federation ... COF
Canadian Ornamental Plant Foundation [*Fondation Canadienne des Plantes Ornementales*] (AC) ... COPF
Canadian Orthopaedic Association (DAVI) ... COA
Canadian Orthopaedic Nurses' Association ... CONA
Canadian Osteopathic Aid Society (AC) ... COAS
Canadian Osteopathic Association (SAUO) ... COA
Canadian Otolaryngological Society (PDAA) ... COS
Canadian Outdoor Measurement Bureau ... COMB
Canadian Outrigger Racing Association (AC) ... CORA
Canadian Overseas Exploration [*Vancouver Stock Exchange symbol*] ... CVC
Canadian Overseas Military Railway Construction Corps [*World War I*] ... CORCC
Canadian Overseas Telecommunications Corp. ... COTC
Canadian Over-the-Counter Automated Trading System ... COATS
Canadian Owners and Pilots Association ... COPA
Canadian Ownership and Control Determination ... COCD
Canadian Pacer Petroleum [*Vancouver Stock Exchange symbol*] ... CDP
Canadian Pacific (SAUS) ... Can Pac
Canadian Pacific (SAUS) ... CP
Canadian Pacific Air Lines (SAUO) ... CP
Canadian Pacific Air Lines (SAUO) ... CP Air
Canadian Pacific Airlines [*ICAO designator*] (AD) ... CP Air
Canadian Pacific Airlines Ltd. [*Facetious translations: Can't Possibly Arrive, Come Push Along*] ... CPA
Canadian Pacific Airlines Ltd. ... CPAir
Canadian Pacific Airlines Ltd. ... CPAL
Canadian Pacific Express and Transport ... CPET
Canadian Pacific Hotels Ltd. (SAUO) ... CP
Canadian Pacific Limited (SAUO) ... CPL
Canadian Pacific Line (SAUO) ... CPL
Canadian Pacific Ltd. [*Associated Press*] (SAG) ... CdnPc
Canadian Pacific Ltd. [*NYSE symbol*] [*Toronto Stock Exchange symbol*] [*Vancouver Stock Exchange symbol*] (SPSG) ... CP
Canadian Pacific Ltd. [*Le Canadien Pacifique*] **Montreal, Quebec** [*Library symbol*] [*National Library of Canada*] (NLC) ... QMCP
Canadian Pacific Oil and Gas (SAUS) ... CPOG
Canadian Pacific, Ord [*NYSE symbol*] (TTSB) ... CP
Canadian Pacific Police Association [*Association des Policiers du Canadien Pacifique*] (AC) ... CPPA
Canadian Pacific Railroad (SAUO) ... CanPac
Canadian Pacific Railroad (SAUS) ... CP
Canadian Pacific Railroad (MHDB) ... CP Rail
Canadian Pacific Railway [*Facetious translations: Can't Pay Rent, Can't Promise Returns*] ... CPR
Canadian Pacific Railway Co. (SAUO) ... CPRy
Canadian Pacific Railway Co., Montreal, PQ, Canada [*Library symbol*] [*Library of Congress*] (LCLS) ... CaQMCP
Canadian Pacific Route (SAUS) ... CPR
Canadian Pacific Steamship Company Ltd. (SAUO) ... CPSCo
Canadian Pacific Steamship Line (SAUS) ... CPSL
Canadian Pacific Steamships (SAUO) ... CPS
Canadian Pacific Steamships (MHDB) ... CP Ships
Canadian Pacific Telegraphs (SAUO) ... CPT
Canadian Paediatric Society (EAIO) ... CPS
Canadian Paint and Wallpaper Dealers' Association ... CPWDA
Canadian Palliative Care Association (AC) ... CPCA
Canadian Paper Box Manufacturers' Association Inc. [*Association Canadienne des Fabricants de Boites en Cartons*] (AC) ... CPBMA
Canadian Paper Money Society ... CPMS
Canadian Paper Trade Association (AC) ... CPTA
Canadian Paperworkers Union ... CPU
Canadian Paralympic Committee [*Comite Paralympique du Canada*] [*Formerly, Canadian Federation of Sport Organizations for the Disabled*] (AC) ... CPC
Canadian Paraplegic Association [*Ontario*] (AC) ... CPA
Canadian Paraplegic Association Nova Scotia (AC) ... CPA-NS
Canadian Parents for French (AC) ... CPF
Canadian Park Service, Environment Canada [*Service Canadien des Parcs, Environnement Canada*], **Canmore, Alberta** [*Library symbol*] [*National Library of Canada*] (BIB) ... ACACP
Canadian Park Service, Environment Canada [*Service Canadien des Parcs, Environnement Canada*], **Cornwall, Ontario** [*Library symbol*] [*National Library of Canada*] (NLC) ... OCN
Canadian Park Service, Environment Canada [*Service Canadien des Parcs, Environnement Canada*], **Quebec, Quebec** [*Library symbol*] [*National Library of Canada*] (NLC) ... QQPCQ
Canadian Parks & Wilderness Society [*Societe pour la Protection des Parcs et des Sites Naturales du Canada*] (AC) ... CPAWS
Canadian Parks Partnership [*Partenaires des Parcs Canadiens*] (AC) ... CPP
Canadian Parks/Recreation Association [*Association Canadienne des Loisirs/Parcs*] (AC) ... CP/RA
Canadian Particleboard Association [*Canada*] (EAIO) ... CPA
Canadian Passenger Transportation Corp. [*Proposed*] ... CPTC
Canadian Patent (IAA) ... CANPAT
Canadian Patent Office. Record [*A publication*] (DLA) ... Can Pat Off Rec
Canadian Patent Report, Second Series [*A publication*] (DLA) ... CPR (2d)
Canadian Patents and Developments Ltd. ... CPDL
Canadian Patrol Frigate [*Military*] ... CPF
Canadian Patrol Frigates Program [*Canadian Navy*] ... CPFP
Canadian Pawnee Oil [*Vancouver Stock Exchange symbol*] ... CPW
Canadian Payload Specialist (SAUS) ... CPS
Canadian Payments Association ... CPA
Canadian Payments Association, Ottawa, Ontario [*Library symbol*] [*National Library of Canada*] (BIB) ... OOCPA
Canadian Payroll Association [*Association Canadienne de la Paie*] (AC) ... CPA
Canadian Peace Alliance [*Alliance Canadienne pour la Paix*] (AC) ... CPA
Canadian Peace Research and Education Association [*See also ACREP*] ... CPREA
Canadian Peace Research Institute ... CPRI
Canadian Peace Research Institute, London, Ontario [*Library symbol*] [*National Library of Canada*] (NLC) ... OLCPR
Canadian Pediatric Kidney Disease Research Centre (SAUO) ... CPKDRC
Canadian PEN Center (EAIO) ... CPENC
Canadian Penitentiary Service (SAUO) ... Can Pen Ser
Canadian Penitentiary Service ... CPS
Canadian Pension Commission (SAUO) ... Can Pen Ser
Canadian Pension Commission ... CPC
Canadian Pension Commission [*Commission Canadienne des Pensions*], **Charlottetown, Prince Edward Island** [*Library symbol*] [*National Library of Canada*] (BIB) ... PCCP
Canadian People's [*Citizens and Residents*] **Defence Committee** ... CPDC
Canadian Performance Distributors ... CPD
Canadian Periodical Index ... CanI
Canadian Periodical Index [*The Globe and Mail*] [*Information service or system*] (CRD) ... CPI
Canadian Periodical Press Association (SAUO) ... CPPA
Canadian Periodical Publishers Association ... CPPA
Canadian Periodical Reference Services, Ottawa, ON, Canada [*Library symbol*] [*Library of Congress*] [*Obsolete*] (LCLS) ... CaOOCAP
Canadian Permanent Army Service Corps (DMA) ... CPASC
Canadian Permanent Committee on Geographical Names ... CPCGN
Canadian Permanent Force (SAUO) ... CPF
Canadian Permanent Signal Corps [*British military*] (DMA) ... CPSC
Canadian Perspectives on International Law and Organization [*A publication*] (DLA) ... Can Persp
Canadian Pest Management Society [*Societe Canadienne de Lutte Contre les Organismes Nuisibles*] [*Formerly, Agricultural Pesticide Society*] (AC) ... CPMS
Canadian Petroleum Association ... CPA
Canadian Petroleum Association, Calgary, AB, Canada [*Library symbol*] [*Library of Congress*] (LCLS) ... CaACCP
Canadian Petroleum Association, Calgary, Alberta [*Library symbol*] [*National Library of Canada*] (NLC) ... ACCP
Canadian Petroleum Association Statistics [*Information service or system*] (CRD) ... CPASTATS
Canadian Petroleum Geology (SAUO) ... CPG
Canadian Petroleum Products Institute [*Institut Canadien des Produits Petroliers*] [*Formerly, Petroleum Association for Conservation of the Canadian Environment*] (AC) ... CPPI
Canadian Petroleum Writers Association (AC) ... CPWA
Canadian Pharmaceutical Association (MCD) ... CPA
Canadian Pharmaceutical Association (EAIO) ... CPhA
Canadian Pharmacists Association (SAUO) ... CPhA
Canadian Philosophical Association ... CPA
Canadian Philosophical Reviews [*A publication*] (BRI) ... CPR
Canadian Photo Video Trade Association [*Formerly, Canadian Photographic Trade Association*] (AC) ... CPVTA
Canadian Physicians for Aid & Relif (AC) ... CPAR
Canadian Physiological Society [*Societe Canadienne de Physiologie*] (AC) ... CPS
Canadian Physiotherapy Association ... CPA
Canadian Physiotherapy Cardio-Respiratory Society (AC) ... CPCRS
Canadian Phytopathological Society Inc. [*Societe Canadienne de Phytopathologie*] (AC) ... CPS
Canadian Picture Pioneers (AC) ... CPP
Canadian Pinzgauer Association (AC) ... CPA
Canadian Plains Research Center [*University of Regina*] [*Information service or system*] (IID) ... CPRC
Canadian Plastics Institute [*Institut Canadien du Plastique*] (AC) ... CPI
Canadian Play Therapy Association (AC) ... CPTA
Canadian Podiatric Sports Medicine Academy ... CPSMA
Canadian Poetry Association [*Also, London Regional Literary Society*] (AC) ... CPA
Canadian Poetry in English [*A publication*] ... CaP
Canadian Polar Commission (SAUO) ... CPC
Canadian Polar Information System (SAUO) ... CPIS
Canadian Police Association ... CPA
Canadian Police College, Royal Canadian Mounted Police, Ottawa, ON, Canada [*Library symbol*] [*Library of Congress*] (LCLS) ... CaOOCPC
Canadian Police Information Centre ... CPIC

Canadian Political Memorabilia Club (AC) .... CPMC
Canadian Political Science Association .... CPSA
Canadian Polystyrene Recycling Association (AC) .... CPRA
Canadian Population Society [*See also SCP*] .... CPS
Canadian Pork Council [*Formerly, Canadian Swine Council*] (AC) .... CPC
Canadian Port & Harbour Association [*Association des Ports et Havres du Canada*] (AC) .... CPHA
Canadian Portland Cement Association [*Association Canadienne du Ciment Portland*] (AC) .... CPCA
Canadian Postal Corps [*Later, RCPC*] .... CPC
Canadian Poster Advertising Association (SAUO) .... CPAA
Canadian Postmasters and Assistants Association .... CPAA
Canadian Postmaster's Association .... CPA
Canadian Post-MD Education Registry [*Systeme Informatise sur les Stagiaires Post-MD en Formation Clinique*] (AC) .... CAPER
Canadian Posture and Seating Centre [*Research center*] (RCD) .... CPSC
Canadian Potash Producers Association .... CPPA
Canadian Potato Chip/Snack Food Association [*Association Canadienne des Fabricants de Chips/Grignotines*] (AC) .... CPC/SFA
Canadian Poultry & Egg Processors Council [*Formerly, Canadian Produce Council*] (AC) .... CPEPC
Canadian Power Squadrons [*Boating*] .... CPS
Canadian Premium Resources Corp. [*Vancouver Stock Exchange symbol*] .... CIP
Canadian Press .... CP
Canadian Press Information Network (IID) .... CPIN
Canadian Press Newstex [*The Canadian Press*] [*Information service or system*] (IID) .... CPN
Canadian Prestressed Concrete Institute [*See also ICBP*] .... CPCI
Canadian Print Marketers Association [*Association Canadienne des Courtiers en Imprimerie*] (AC) .... CPMA
Canadian Print Measurement Bureau (NITA) .... PMB
Canadian Printing Industries Association (EAIO) .... CPIA
Canadian Printing Ink Manufacturers Association (SAUO) .... CPIMA
Canadian Produce Marketing Association [*Association Canadienne de la Distribution de Fruite et Legumes*] [*Formerly, Canadian Fruit Wholesalers Association*] (AC) .... CPMA
Canadian Professional Logistics Institute [*Institut Canadien Professionnel Logistique*] [*Formerly, Professional Logistics Institute of Canada*] (AC) .... CPLI
Canadian Professional Rodeo Association .... CPRA
Canadian Professional Sales Association [*Association Canadienne des Professionnels de la Vente*] [*Formerly, Commercial Travellers Association of Canada*] (AC) .... CPSA
Canadian Professional Soccer League .... CPSL
Canadian Professors for Peace in The Middle East (AC) .... CPPME
Canadian Programming Service [*Service Canadien de Programmation*] (AC) .... CPS
Canadian Prostate Health Council (SAUO) .... CPHC
Canadian Provost Corps (SAUO) .... Cdn Prov Cor
Canadian Psoriasis Foundation [*Fondation Canadienne du Psoriasis*] (AC) .... CPF
Canadian Psychiatric Association .... CPA
Canadian Psychoanalytic Society (SAUO) .... CPS
Canadian Psychological Association (MCD) .... CPA
Canadian Psychological Association - Interest Group on Women and Psychology .... CPA-IGWAP
Canadian Public Administration [*A publication*] (DLA) .... Can Pub Ad
Canadian public data base retrieval system (SAUS) .... VIDEOTEX
Canadian Public Health Association .... CPHA
Canadian Public Personnel Management Association .... CPPMA
Canadian Public Relations Society .... CPRS
Canadian Public Relations Society [*Societe Canadienne des Relations Publiques*], **Ottawa, Ontario** [*Library symbol*] [*National Library of Canada*] (BIB) .... OOCPR
Canadian Pulp and Paper Association [*See also ACPPP*] .... CPPA
Canadian Pulp and Paper Association, Montreal, PQ, Canada [*Library symbol*] [*Library of Congress*] (LCLS) .... CaQMNA
Canadian Pulp and Paper Asssociation [*Association Canadienne des Producteurs dePates et Papiers*] **Montreal, Quebec** [*Library symbol*] [*National Library of Canada*] (NLC) .... QMNA
Canadian Pulp and Paper Industry (journ.) (SAUS) .... CPPI
Canadian Qualified Products Lists (SAUS) .... CQPL
Canadian Quaternary Association .... CANQUA
Canadian Quilters Association (AC) .... CQA
Canadian Racquetball Association .... CRA
Canadian Radiation Protection Association (SAUO) .... CRPA
Canadian Radio and Television Commission (SAUO) .... CRTC
Canadian Radio Broadcasting Commission [*Later, Canadian Broadcasting Corp.*] .... CRBC
Canadian Radio Relay League (PDAA) .... CRRL
Canadian Radio Technical Planning Board (NTCM) .... CRTPB
Canadian Radio Technical Planning Committee (SAUO) .... CRTPC
Canadian Radio-Direction Finder (MCD) .... CRDF
Canadian Radio-Television and Telecommunications Commission [*Conseil de la Radiodiffusion et des Telecommunications Canadiennes*] [*Ottawa, ON*] [*Telecommunications*] .... CRTC
Canadian Radio-Television and Telecommunications Commission, Ottawa, ON, Canada [*Library symbol*] [*Library of Congress*] (LCLS) .... CaOORT
Canadian Radio-Television and Telecommunications Commission [*Conseil de la Radiodiffusion et des Telecommunications Canadiennes*] **Ottawa, Ontario** [*Library symbol*] [*National Library of Canada*] (NLC) .... OORT
Canadian Railroad Historical Association .... CRHA
Canadian Railway and Transport Cases [*A publication*] (DLA) .... Can Ry & T Cas
Canadian Railway and Transport Cases [*A publication*] (DLA) .... CRTC
Canadian Railway Cases [*A publication*] (DLA) .... Can R Cas
Canadian Railway Cases [*A publication*] (DLA) .... CRC
Canadian Railway Commission .... CRC
Canadian Railway Labour Association .... CRLA
Canadian Railway Labour Executives' Association .... CRLEA
Canadian Railway Troops [*World War I*] .... CRT
Canadian Real Estate Association .... CREA
Canadian Recording Industry Association .... CRIA
Canadian Recreational Canoeing Association .... CRCA
Canadian Recreational Vehicle Association (EAIO) .... CRVA
Canadian Red Cross (SAUO) .... CRC
Canadian Red Cross Committee (SAUO) .... CRCC
Canadian Red Cross Committee (HGAA) .... CRCC
Canadian Red Cross Society, Ottawa, ON, Canada [*Library symbol*] [*Library of Congress*] (LCLS) .... CaOOCRC
Canadian Red Cross Society [*Societe Canadienne de la Croix-Rouge*] **Ottawa, Ontario** [*Library symbol*] [*National Library of Canada*] (NLC) .... OOCRC
Canadian Refrigeration & Air Conditioning Contractors Association (AC) .... CRACCA
Canadian Regional Science Association [*See also ACSR*] .... CRSA
Canadian Registered Safety Professional (ASC) .... CRSP
Canadian Registration Board of Occupational Hygienists (SARE) .... CRBOH
Canadian Regulatory Reporter [*Database*] [*Canadian Law Information Council*] [*Information service or system*] (CRD) .... CRR
Canadian Rehabilitation Council for the Disabled .... CRCD
Canadian Reinforcement Group (SAUO) .... CRG
Canadian Reinforcement Unit (SAUO) .... CRU
Canadian Religious Conference .... CRC
Canadian Remote Sensing Society (EAIO) .... CRSS
Canadian Renewable Fuels Association (AC) .... CRFA
Canadian Reports, Appeal Cases [*1828-1913*] [*A publication*] (DLA) .... AC
Canadian Reports, Appeal Cases [*1828-1913*] [*A publication*] (DLA) .... Can App
Canadian Reports, Appeal Cases [*1828-1913*] [*A publication*] (DLA) .... Can RAC
Canadian Reports, Appeal Cases [*1828-1913*] [*A publication*] (DLA) .... Can R App Cas
Canadian Reports, Appeal Cases [*1828-1913*] [*A publication*] (DLA) .... CR
Canadian Reports, Appeal Cases [*1828-1913*] [*A publication*] (DLA) .... CRAC
Canadian Reprography Collective .... CRC
Canadian Research and Development (journ.) (SAUS) .... Can Res Dev
Canadian Research and Education Network [*Computer science*] (TNIG) .... CDNnet
Canadian Research Institute for the Advancement of Women [*Research center*] (RCD) .... CRIAW
Canadian Research Institute for the Advancement of Women, Ottowa, ON, Canada [*Library symbol*] [*Library of Congress*] (LCLS) .... CaOOCRI
Canadian Research Institute for the Avancement of Women [*Institut Canadien deRecherches sur les Femmes*] **Ottawa, Ontario** [*Library symbol*] [*National Library of Canada*] (NLC) .... OOCRI
Canadian Reserve File [*Petroleum Information Corp.*] [*Information service or system*] (CRD) .... CNDN
Canadian Resident Matching Service (SAUO) .... CaRMS
Canadian Residential Appraiser (ASC) .... CRA
Canadian Resort Development [*Formerly, Canadian Resort & Recreational Development Association*] (AC) .... CRDA
Canadian Resources for Enterprise Development Organization (AC) .... CREDO
Canadian Restaurant and Foodservices Association .... CR & FA
Canadian Restaurant & Foodservices Association [*Association Canadienne des Restaurateurs et des Services Alimentaires*] (AC) .... CRFA
Canadian Restaurant Association .... CRA
Canadian Restricted [*Broadcasting term*] .... CR
Canadian Retail Hardware Association (PDAA) .... CRHA
Canadian Retraining Centre (SAUO) .... CRC
Canadian Retransmission Collective (AC) .... CRC
Canadian Retransmission Right Association (AC) .... CRRA
Canadian Rheumatism Association (HGAA) .... CRA
Canadian Rheumatology Association (SAUO) .... CRA
Canadian Rhythmic Sportive Gymnastic Federation [*Federation Canadienne de Gymnastique Rythmique Sportive*] [*Formerly, Canadian Modern Rhythmic Gymnastic Federation*] (AC) .... CRSGF
Canadian Rights and Liberties Federation, Ottawa, ON, Canada [*Library symbol*] [*Library of Congress*] (LCLS) .... CaOOCRLF
Canadian Rights and Liberties Federation, Ottawa, Ontario [*Library symbol*] [*National Library of Canada*] (NLC) .... OOCRLF
Canadian Risk Manager (DD) .... CRM
Canadian Road Network (GEOI) .... CRN
Canadian Rock Art Research Associates .... CRARA
Canadian Rock Mechanics Association [*Association Candienne de Mechanique des Roches*] (AC) .... CARMA
Canadian Rocket Society (SAUO) .... CRS
Canadian Rocket Vehicle (ACAE) .... CRV
Canadian Roofing Contractors' Association .... CRCA
Canadian Rose Society [*Formerly, Rose Society of Ontario*] (AC) .... CRS
Canadian Roxy Petroleum Ltd. [*Toronto Stock Exchange symbol*] .... CNR
Canadian Royal Mint, Ottawa, ON, Canada [*Library symbol*] [*Library of Congress*] (LCLS) .... CaOOCRM
Canadian Royal Mint [*Monnaie Royale Canadienne*] **Ottawa, Ontario** [*Library symbol*] [*National Library of Canada*] (NLC) .... OOCRM
Canadian Rural Medicine Network (SAUO) .... CaRMeN
Canadian Sailfish Corp. [*See also OCPS*] .... CSFC
Canadian Sales Finance Long Form Report .... CANSAF
Canadian Sales Tax Reporter (Commerce Clearing House) [*A publication*] (DLA) .... Can Sales Tax Rep (CCH)
Canadian Sanitation Standards Association .... CSSA
Canadian Sanitation Supply Association [*Association Canadienne des Fournisseurs de Produits Sanitaires*] [*Formerly, Canadian Sanitation Standards Association*] (AC) .... CSSA
Canadian Satellite (SAUS) .... CANSAT
Canadian Satellite Communications, Inc. [*Mississauga, ON*] [*Telecommunications*] (TSSD) .... CANCOM

Canadian Satellite Communications, Inc. [*Toronto Stock Exchange symbol*] .... SAT
Canadian Saturday Night [*A publication*] .... CSN
Canadian Save the Children Fund .... CANSAVE
Canadian Schizophrenia Foundation (EA) .... CSF
Canadian Scholarship Trust Foundation [*Fondation Fiduciaire Canadienne de Bourses d'Etudes*] [*Formerly, CST Foundation*] (AC) .... CST
Canadian School Boards Association [*Association Canadienne des Commissions/Conseils Scolaires*] [*Formerly, Canadian School Trustees' Association*] (AC) .... CSBA
Canadian School Library Association .... CSLA
Canadian School of Artillery (SAUO) .... CS of A
Canadian School of Missions and Ecumenical Institute, Toronto, ON, Canada [*Library symbol*] [*Library of Congress*] (LCLS) .... CaOTCM
Canadian School of Missions and Ecumenical Institute, Toronto, Ontario [*Library symbol*] [*National Library of Canada*] (NLC) .... OTCM
Canadian Science & Technology Historical Association (AC) .... CSTHA
Canadian Science Film Association .... CSFA
Canadian Science Writers' Association [*Association Canadienne des Redacteurs Sceintifiques*] (AC) .... CSWA
Canadian Scientific Liaison Office (HGAA) .... CSLO
Canadian Scientific Ship (BARN) .... CSS
Canadian Scottish Regiment (SAUO) .... CanScotR
Canadian Scottish Regiment (SAUO) .... Cdn Scots
Canadian Seamen's Union .... CSU
Canadian Search and Rescue Association .... CASARA
Canadian Section International Association of Penal Law (EAIO) .... CSIAPL
[*The*] Canadian Securities [*Institut Canadien des Valeurs Mobilieres*] (AC) .... CSI
Canadian Security and Intelligence Service .... CSIS
Canadian Security and Intelligence Service [*UTLAS symbol*] .... SIS
Canadian Seed Growers Association (HGAA) .... CSGA
Canadian Seed Trade Association (AC) .... CSTA
Canadian Selection, Toronto, Ontario [*Library symbol*] [*National Library of Canada*] (NLC) .... OTCSE
Canadian Selective Dissemination of Information (SAUS) .... Can/SDI
Canadian Semiotic Association [*See also ACS*] .... CSA
Canadian Seniors Packaging Advisory Council [*Conseil Consultatif Canadien pour l'Adaptation de l'Emballage aux Besoins des Aines*] (AC) .... CASPAC
Canadian Serials Industry Systems Advisory Committee .... CSISAC
Canadian Service for Overseas Students and Trainees .... CSOST
Canadian Service for the Selective Dissemination of Information [*National Research Council of Canada*] [*Information service or system*] (IID) .... CAN/SDI
Canadian Services Armament Committee (SAUO) .... CSAC
Canadian Services College .... CANSERVCOL
Canadian Services College (SAUO) .... CanServColl
Canadian Sewing & Needlecraft Association [*Association Canadienne des Travaux d'Aiguilles*] [*Formerly, Canadian Home Sewing & Needlecraft Association*] (AC) .... CSNA
Canadian Sheet Steel Building Institute [*Institut Canadien de la tole d'Acier pour le Batiment*] (AC) .... CSSBI
Canadian Shipbuilding and Ship Repairing Association .... CSSRA
Canadian Shipbuilding and Ship-Repairing Association (SAUO) .... CS&SRA
Canadian Shipowners Association (EAIO) .... CSA
Canadian Shipping Act [*1970*] (MSC) .... CSA
Canadian Shooting Sports Foundation [*La Fondation des Sports de Tir*] (AC) .... CSSF
Canadian Shopcraft Union .... CSU
Canadian Siberian Expeditionary Force .... CSEF
Canadian Signals Training Centre (SAUO) .... CSTC
Canadian Silk Mfg. Ltd. (EFIS) .... CASCO
Canadian Ski Association .... CSA
Canadian Ski Instructors' Alliance .... CSIA
Canadian Ski Marathon [*Marathon Canadien de Ski*] (AC) .... CSM
Canadian Ski Patrol System [*Organisation de la Patrouille Canadienne de Ski*] (AC) .... CSPS
Canadian Sleep Society (AC) .... CSS
Canadian Slovak League .... CSL
Canadian Small Arms School (SAUO) .... CSAS
Canadian Snowbird Association (AC) .... CSA
Canadian Soccer Association .... CSA
Canadian Social Science Abstracts [*York University*] [*Canada*] [*A database*] (NITA) .... CSSA
Canadian Social Science Research Council (SAUO) .... CSSRC
Canadian Society for Aesthetic (Cosmetic) Plastic Surgery (EAIO) .... CSACPS
Canadian Society for Aesthetics (AC) .... CSA
Canadian Society for Aesthetics .... CSAC
Canadian Society for Asian Studies .... CSAS
Canadian Society for Brain, Behavior and Cognitive Sciences (SAUO) .... CSBBCS
Canadian Society for Cell Biology (SAUO) .... CSBC
Canadian Society for Cell Biology (SAUO) .... CSCB
Canadian Society for Chemical Engineering (SAUO) .... CS Ch E
Canadian Society for Chemical Engineering .... CSChE
Canadian Society for Chemical Engineers [*Also, CSChe*] .... CSCE
Canadian Society for Chemical Technology (EAIO) .... CSCT
Canadian Society for Chemistry (EAIO) .... CSC
Canadian Society for Civil Engineering .... CSCE
Canadian Society for Clinical Investigation [*Societe Canadienne de Recherches Cliniques*] (AC) .... CSCI
Canadian Society for Clinical Pharmacology [*Societe Canadienne de Pharmacologie Clinique*] (AC) .... CSCP
Canadian Society for Colour in Art, Industry, and Science (EAIO) .... CSC
Canadian Society for Computation Studies of Intelligence (SAUS) .... CSCSI
Canadian Society for Cultural and Intellectual History .... CSCIH
Canadian Society for Education through Art [*1951*] (NGC) .... CSEA

Canadian Society for Eighteenth-Century Studies (AC) .... CSECS
Canadian Society for Electrical and Computer Engineering (EAIO) .... CSECE
Canadian Society for Electrical Engineering (SAUO) .... CSEE
Canadian Society for Electrical Engineers (MCD) .... CSEE
Canadian Society for Engineering in Agriculture, Food, and Biological Systems .... CSAE
Canadian Society for Engineering Management [*Societe Canadienne de Gestion en Ingenierie*] [*Formerly, EIC General Members Society*] (AC) .... CSEM
Canadian Society for Exercise Physiology [*Formerly, Canadian Association of Sport Sciences*] (AC) .... CSEP
Canadian Society for Horticultural Science (AC) .... CSHS
Canadian Society for Industrial Heritage (AC) .... CSIH
Canadian Society for Industrial Security .... CSIS
Canadian Society for International Health [*Societe Canadienne pour la Sante International*] [*Formerly, Canadian Society for Tropical Medicine & International Health*] (AC) .... CSIH
Canadian Society for Italian Studies .... CSIS
Canadian Society for Mechanical Engineering .... CSME
Canadian Society for Medical Laboratory Science (SAUO) .... CSMLS
Canadian Society for Medical Mycology [*Societe Canadienne de Mycologie Medicale*] (AC) .... CSMM
Canadian Society for Mesopotamian Studies [*Societe Canadienne des Etudes Mesopotamiens*] [*Formerly, Society for Mesopotamian Studies*] (AC) .... CSMS
Canadian Society for Musical Traditions (EAIO) .... CSMT
Canadian Society for Musical Traditions [*Societe Canadienne pour les Traditions Musicales*] [*Formerly, Canadian Folk Music Society*] (AC) .... CSTM
Canadian Society for Non-Destructive Testing .... CSNDT
Canadian Society for Pharmaceutical Sciences (SAUO) .... CSPS
Canadian Society for Professional Engineers (AC) .... CSPE
Canadian Society for Psychomotor Learning and Sport Psychology (EDAC) .... CSPLSP
Canadian Society for Renaissance Studies [*See also SCER*] .... CSRS
Canadian Society for the Advancement of Legal Technology [*Association Canadienne pour l'Advancement de l'Informatique Juridique*] (AC) .... CSALT
Canadian Society for the Comparative Study of Civilizations [*See also SCECC*] .... CSCSC
Canadian Society for the History and Philosophy of Mathematics [*See also SCHPM*] .... CSHPM
Canadian Society for the History and Philosophy of Science [*See also SCHPS*] .... CSHPS
Canadian Society for the History of Medicine [*See also SCHM*] .... CSHM
Canadian Society for the History of Rhetoric [*See also SCHR*] .... CSHR
Canadian Society for the Prevention of Cruelty to Animals (BARN) .... CSPCA
Canadian Society for the Prevention of Cruelty to Animals (SAUO) .... CSPCA
Canadian Society for the Prevention of Cruelty to Children .... CSPCC
Canadian Society for the Study of Education [*See also SCEE*] [*University of Ottawa*] [*Research center*] (RCD) .... CSSE
Canadian Society for the Study of Higher Education [*See also SCEES*] .... CSSHE
Canadian Society for the Study of Names [*See also SCEN*] .... CSSN
Canadian Society for the Study of Religion [*See also SCER*] .... CSSR
Canadian Society for Titanic Education & Preservation (AC) .... CANSTEP
Canadian Society for Transfusion Medicine [*Societe Canadienne de Medecine Transfusionnelle*] [*Formerly, Canadian Association of Immunohematologists*] (AC) .... CSTM
Canadian Society of Addiction Medicine (SAUO) .... CSAM
Canadian Society of Aerospace Medicine [*Societe Medicale Aeronautique du Canada*] (AC) .... CSAM
Canadian Society of Agricultural Engineering .... CSAE
Canadian Society of Agronomy .... CSA
Canadian Society of Allergy & Clinical Immunology [*Societe Canadienne d'Allergie et d'Immunologie Clinique*] (AC) .... CSACI
Canadian Society of Animal Science .... CSAS
Canadian Society of Applied Art [*1905, founded 1903 as Society of Arts and Crafts of Canada*] (NGC) .... CSAP
Canadian Society of Association Executives [*Formerly, Institute of Canadian Trade Association Executives*] (AC) .... CSAE
Canadian Society of Biblical Studies [*See also SCEB*] .... CSBS
Canadian Society of Biochemistry and Molecular & Cell Biology (SAUO) .... CSBMCB
Canadian Society of Church History [*See also SCHE*] .... CSCH
Canadian Society of Cinematographers .... CSC
Canadian Society of Clinical Chemists [*Societe Canadienne des Clinico-Chimistes*] (AC) .... CSCC
Canadian Society of Clinical Neurophysiologists [*Societe Canadienne de Neurophsiologistes Cliniques*] (AC) .... CSCN
Canadian Society of Computational Studies of Intelligence (IAA) .... CSCI
Canadian Society of Computational Studies of Intelligence .... CSCSI
Canadian Society of Copyright Consumers [*Societe Canadienne des Consommaters Copyright*] [*Formerly, Musical Protective Society of Canada*] (AC) .... CSCC
Canadian Society of Corporate Secretaries (AC) .... CSCS
Canadian Society of Cytology .... CSC
Canadian Society of Decorative Arts [*Cercle Canadien des Arts Decoratifs*] (AC) .... CSDA
Canadian Society of Diagnostic Medical Sonographers (AC) .... CSDMS
Canadian Society of Environmental Biologists [*La Societe Canadienne des Biologistes de l'Environnement*] (AC) .... CSEB
Canadian Society of Exploration Geophysicists (AC) .... CSEG
Canadian Society of Extension .... CSE
Canadian Society of Forensic Science (AC) .... CSFS
Canadian Society of Forest Engineers (HGAA) .... CSFE
Canadian Society of Fund Raising Executives (NFD) .... CSFRE
Canadian Society of Graphic Art [*1923-76, founded c.1903 as GAC, SGA from 1912*] (NGC) .... CSGA

Canadian Society of Hospital Pharmacists .... CSHP
Canadian Society of Internal Medicine [*Societe Canadienne de Medecine Interne*] (AC) ... CSIM
Canadian Society of Laboratory Technologists (EAIO) .... CSLT
Canadian Society of Landscape Architects .... CSLA
Canadian Society of Landscape Architects and Town Planners (HGAA) ... CSLATP
Canadian Society of Magazine Editors (AC) ...... CSME
Canadian Society of Marine Artists .... CSMA
Canadian Society of Mechanical Engineers (SAUO) ...... CSME
Canadian Society of Microbiologists (EAIO) ...... CSM
Canadian Society of Military Medals and Insignia ...... CSMMI
Canadian Society of New York (EA) ...... CSNY
Canadian Society of Orthopaedic Technologists (EAIO) ...... CSOT
Canadian Society of Otolaryngology - Head and Neck Surgery (EAIO) ...... CSO-HNS
Canadian Society of Painters in Water Color (AC) ...... CSPWC
Canadian Society of Painters in Water Colour [*1925*] (NGC) ...... CSPWC
Canadian Society of Patristic Studies [*See also ACEP*] ...... CSPS
Canadian Society of Petroleum Geologists [*Formerly, Alberta Society of Petroleum Geologists*] (AC) ...... CSPG
Canadian Society of Plant Physiologists (AC) ...... CSPP
Canadian Society of Plastic Surgeons [*Societe Canadienne des Chirurgiens Plasticiens*] (AC) ...... CSPS
Canadian Society of Public Health Dentists [*Association Canadienne des Dentistes en Sante Publique*] (AC) ...... CSPHD
Canadian Society of Radiological Technicians ...... CSRT
Canadian Society of Respiratory Therapists (AC) ...... CSRT
Canadian Society of Rural Extension ...... CSRE
Canadian Society of Safety Engineering ...... CSSE
Canadian Society of Scientific Photography [*Societe Canadienne de la Photographie Scientifique*] (AC) ...... CSSP
Canadian Society of Soil Science [*Societe Canadienne de la Science du Sol*] (AC) ...... CSSS
Canadian Society of Surgical Oncology [*Societe Canadienne d'Oncologie Chirurgicale*] (AC) ...... CSSO
Canadian Society of Technical Agriculturists (SAUO) ...... CSTA
Canadian Society of Telehealth (SAUO) ...... CST
Canadian Society of Wildlife and Fishery Biologists ...... CSWFB
Canadian Socio-Economic Information Management System [*Statistics Canada*] [*Database*] [*Ottawa, ON*] (IID) ...... CANSIM
Canadian Socioeconomic Information Management System (SAUS) ...... CANSIM System
Canadian Sociology and Anthropology Association [*See also ACSA*] ...... CSAA
Canadian Soft Drink Association [*Association Canadeinne de l'Industrie des Boissons Gazeuses*] [*Formerly, Canadian Association of Carbonated Beverages*] ...... CSDA
Canadian Soil Information System [*Land Resource and Research Institute*] [*Ottawa, ON*] [*Information service or system*] (IID) ...... CanSIS
Canadian Soil Science Society (MCD) ...... CSSS
Canadian Solar Industries Association ...... CSIA
Canadian Solar Industries Association Inc. [*Association des Industries Solaires du Canada Inc.*] (AC) ...... CanSIA
Canadian Space Agency ...... CSA
Canadian Space Agency Engineering Support Center (SAUS) ...... CESC
Canadian Space Centre (SAUS) ...... CSC
Canadian Spatial Reference System (GEOI) ...... CSRS
Canadian Speech Association ...... CSA
Canadian Speech Research Environment (SAUO) ...... CSRE
Canadian Spice Association (AC) ...... CSA
Canadian Spinal Research Organization (SAUO) ...... CSRO
Canadian Spooner Resources, Inc. [*Toronto Stock Exchange symbol*] ...... CSF
Canadian Sport & Fitness Administration Centre [*Centre Canadien d'Administration du Sport et de la Condition Physique*] (AC) ...... CSFAC
Canadian Sport Parachuting Association (EA) ...... CSPA
Canadian Sporting Goods Association [*Association Canadienne d'Article Sport*] (AC) ...... CSGA
Canadian Sports & Fitness Marketing Inc. [*Le Marketing Canadien du Sport et de la Condition Physique*] (AC) ...... CSFM
Canadian Sprinkler Risk Pool ...... CSRP
Canadian Stamp Dealers' Association ...... CSDA
Canadian Standard Freeness [*Drainage rate of synthetic pulps*] ...... CSF
Canadian Standard Seismograph (SAUS) ...... CSS
Canadian Standardbred Horse Society (AC) ...... CSHS
Canadian Standardized Test of Fitness ...... CSTF
Canadian Standards [*Standards Council of Canada*] [*Information service or system*] (CRD) ...... CANSTAN
Canadian Standards Agency (AAEL) ...... CSA
Canadian Standards Approval ...... CSA
Canadian Standards Association ...... CSA
Canadian Standards Association Data Processing Standard Designation (SAUS) Z243
Canadian Standards Association, Rexdale, Ontario [*Library symbol*] [*National Library of Canada*] (NLC) ...... OTCSA
Canadian Standards Association Testing Laboratories (or Laboratory) (SAUO) ...... CSATL
Canadian Standards Association Testing Laboratory (SAUS) ...... CSATL
Canadian Standards Association, Toronto, ON, Canada [*Library symbol*] [*Library of Congress*] (LCLS) ...... CaOTCSA
Canadian Statistical Society ...... CSS
Canadian Steam Navigation Company (SAUO) ...... CanSN
Canadian Steel Can Recycling Council (AC) ...... CSCRC
Canadian Steel Construction Council ...... CSCC
Canadian Steel Environmental Association [*Association Environnemental de la Siderurgie Canadienne*] (AC) ...... AESC

Canadian Steel Environmental Association [*Association Environnemental de la Siderurgie Canadienne*] (AC) ...... CSEA
Canadian Steel Industries Construction Council (HGAA) ...... CSICC
Canadian Steel Industry Research Association ...... CSIRA
Canadian Steel Producers Association (AC) ...... CSPA
Canadian Stock Options [*Toronto Stock Exchange*] [*Canada*] [*Information service or system*] (CRD) ...... CDNOPT
Canadian Street Rod Association ...... CSRA
Canadian String Teachers' Association ...... CSTA
Canadian Student Debating Federation ...... CSDF
Canadian Student Pugwash ...... CSP
Canadian Sub-Aqua Club (SAUO) ...... CSAC
Canadian Submarine Acquisition Programme (SAUS) ...... CASAP
Canadian Sugar Beet Producers' Association (AC) ...... CSBPA
Canadian Sugar Factories Ltd. ...... CSF
Canadian Sugar Institute [*Institut Canadien du Sucre*] (AC) ...... CSI
Canadian Superior Oil Ltd., Calgary, AB, Canada [*Library symbol*] [*Library of Congress*] (LCLS) ...... CaACCS
Canadian Swimming Pool Association ...... CANSPA
Canadian Swine Breeders Association (GVA) ...... CSBA
Canadian Switched Network ...... CSN
Canadian Synthetic Aperature Radar Satellite (SAUS) ...... RADARSAT
Canadian Synthetic Aperture Radar Satellite (EOSA) ...... Radarsat
Canadian Syringomyelia Network (SAUO) ...... CSN
Canadian Table Tennis [*Association Canadienne de Tennis de Table*] (AC) ...... CTTA
Canadian Tactical Air Command Headquarters ...... CANAIRTAC
Canadian Tactical Air Command Headquarters (SAUO) ...... CanAirTac
Canadian Talent Library ...... CTL
Canadian Tank Regiment (SAUO) ...... CTR
Canadian Task Force on Preventive Health Care (SAUO) ...... CTFPHC
Canadian Task Force on the Periodic Health Examination ...... CTFPHE
Canadian Tax Cases [*A publication*] (DLA) ...... C Tax C
Canadian Tax Foundation (AC) ...... CTF
Canadian Tax Foundation. Conference Report [*A publication*] (DLA) ...... Can Tax Found
Canadian Tax Foundation. Report of Proceedings of the Tax Conference [*A publication*] (DLA) ...... Can Tax Found Rep Proc Tax Conf
Canadian Tax Foundation, Toronto, ON, Canada [*Library symbol*] [*Library of Congress*] (LCLS) ...... CaOTCT
Canadian Tax Foundation [*Association Canadienne d'Etudes Fiscales*] Toronto, Ontario [*Library symbol*] [*National Library of Canada*] (NLC) ...... OTCT
Canadian Tax Law Journal [*A publication*] (DLA) ...... Can Tax LJ
Canadian Tax Reporter (Commerce Clearing House) [*A publication*] (DLA) ...... Can Tax Rep (CCH)
Canadian Taxpayers Federation (AC) ...... CTF
Canadian Teachers Federation ...... CTF
Canadian Teachers Federation, Ottawa, ON, Canada [*Library symbol*] [*Library of Congress*] (LCLS) ...... CaOOCT
Canadian Teachers Federation, Ottawa, Ontario [*Library symbol*] [*National Library of Canada*] (NLC) ...... OOCT
Canadian Team Handball Federation ...... CTHF
Canadian Technical Asphalt Association (EAIO) ...... CTAA
Canadian Technical Awareness Programme (SAUS) ...... CANTAP
Canadian Technical Awareness Programme (HGAA) ...... CAN/TAP
Canadian Technology Satellite (MCD) ...... CTS
Canadian Telebook Agency [*ACCORD*] [*Source file*] [*UTLAS symbol*] ...... CTA
Canadian Telebook Agency, Toronto, ON, Canada [*Library symbol*] [*Library of Congress*] (LCLS) ...... CaOTCTA
Canadian Telebook Agency, Toronto, Ontario [*Library symbol*] [*National Library of Canada*] (NLC) ...... OTCTA
Canadian Telecommunications Carriers Association ...... CTCA
Canadian Telecommunications Consultants Association (AC) ...... CTCA
Canadian Telecommunications Satellite (SAUS) ...... CTS
Canadian Telecommunications Satellite System (SAUS) ...... Can Telsat
Canadian Telefunken [*Record label*] ...... CanT
Canadian Telephone Employees' Association [*See also ACET*] ...... CTEA
Canadian Television and Radio Commission (CGWS) ...... CTRC
Canadian Television Network ...... CTV
Canadian Television Producers and Directors Association ...... CTPDA
Canadian Test Centre Inc. (AC) ...... CTC
Canadian Test of Basic Skills [*Education*] ...... CTBS
Canadian Test of Cognitive Skills (TMMY) ...... Canadian TCS
Canadian Test of General Information [*Education*] (AEBS) ...... CTGI
Canadian Test Satellite (SAUS) ...... CTS
Canadian Testing Association ...... CTA
Canadian Textbook Publishers' Institute ...... CTPI
Canadian Textile and Chemical Union ...... CTCU
Canadian Textiles Institute (EAIO) ...... CTI
Canadian Textiles Institute [*Institut Canadien des Textiles*], Ottawa, Ontario [*Library symbol*] [*National Library of Canada*] (BIB) ...... OOCTI
Canadian Theatre Critics Association [*Association des Critiques de Theatre du Canada*] (AC) ...... CTCA
Canadian Theological College ...... CTC
Canadian Theological Seminary ...... CTS
Canadian Theological Society [*See also SCT*] ...... CTS
Canadian Therapeutic Riding Association (SAUO) ...... CanTRA
Canadian Thoracic Society [*Societe Canadienne de Thoracologie*] (AC) ...... CTS
Canadian Thoroughbred Horse Society [*Societe Canadienne du Cheval Thoroughbred*] (AC) ...... CTHS
Canadian Tire Corp. Ltd. [*Toronto Stock Exchange symbol*] ...... CTR
Canadian Tire Coupon Collectors Club [*Club de Collectionneurs de Coupons Canadian Tire*] (AC) ...... CTCCC
Canadian Tobacco Manufacturers' Council ...... CTMC

Canadian Tobacco Manufacturers' Council, Montreal, PQ, Canada [*Library symbol*] [*Library of Congress*] (LCLS) .... CaQMCTM
Canadian Tobacco Manufacturers' Council [*Conseil Canadien des Fabricants des Produits du Tabac*] **Montreal, Quebec** [*Library symbol*] [*National Library of Canada*] (NLC) .... QMCTM
Canadian Tooling Manufacturers' Association [*Association Canadienne des Fabricants d'Outillage*] (AC) .... CTMA
Canadian Towed Array SONAR System .... CANTASS
Canadian Toy Testing Council .... CTTC
Canadian Trace Minerals Ltd. [*Vancouver Stock Exchange symbol*] .... CTJ
Canadian Trade and Tariffs Committee .... CTTC
Canadian Trade Index [*Canada Systems Group*] [*Information service or system*] (IID) .... CTIX
Canadian Trade Marks [*Canada Systems Group*] [*Information service or system*] (IID) .... TMRK
Canadian Trades and Labour Congress (SAUO) .... CTLC
Canadian Training Division [*Canadian Navy*] .... CANTRAINDIV
Canadian Training Squadron [*Canadian Navy*] .... CANTRAINRON
Canadian Trakehner Horse Society (AC) .... CTHS
Canadian Transatlantic Telephone Cable [*Between Canada and England*] .... CANTAT
Canadian Transatlantic Telephones (SAUO) .... CANTAT
Canadian Transport Commission (SAUO) .... Can Tran Comm
Canadian Transport Commission .... CTC
Canadian Transport Commission, Air Transport Committee, Ottawa, ON, Canada [*Library symbol*] [*Library of Congress*] [*Obsolete*] (LCLS) .... CaOOAT
Canadian Transport Commission, Ottawa, ON, Canada [*Library symbol*] [*Library of Congress*] (LCLS) .... CaOOTT
Canadian Transport Emergency Center (HEAS) .... CANUTEC
Canadian Transport Tariff Bureau Association .... CTTBA
Canadian Transport Workers Union [*Syndicat Canadien des Travailleurs du Transport*] (AC) .... CTWU
Canadian Transportation Documentation System [*Database*] [*Transport Canada Library and Information Center*] [*Information service or system*] (CRD) .... CTDS
Canadian Transportation Equipment Association .... CTEA
Canadian Transportation Research Forum .... CTRF
Canadian Transportation Research Information Service .... CTRIS
Canadian Transtech Industries [*Vancouver Stock Exchange symbol*] .... CDA
Canadian Troops Training Centre (SAUO) .... CTTC
Canadian Trotting Association .... CTA
Canadian Trucking Association (SAUO) .... CTA
Canadian Trucking Association (AC) .... CTA
Canadian Trusted Computer Product Evaluation Criteria (VERA) .... CTCPEC
Canadian Tuberculosis and Respiratory Disease Association .... CTRDA
Canadian Tuberculosis Association (DAVI) .... CTA
Canadian Tuberculosis Association (SAUO) .... CTA
Canadian Turkey Marketing Agency [*Office Canadien de Commercialisation du Dindon*] (AC) .... CTMA
Canadian Turnaround Management Association [*Association Canadienne de Restructuration d'Entreprises*] (AC) .... CTMA
Canadian, TX [*Location identifier*] [*FAA*] (FAAL) .... HHF
Canadian, TX [*FM radio station call letters*] .... KRBG
Canadian, TX [*FM radio station call letters*] (RBYB) .... KYEG-FM
Canadian UFO Research Network .... CUFORN
Canadian Ukrainian Youth Association .... CYMK
Canadian Underwriters Association .... CUA
Canadian Union Catalogue of Books [*National Library of Canada*] [*Information service or system*] (IID) .... UCB
Canadian Union Catalogue of Library Materials for the Handicapped [*National Library of Canada*] [*Information service or system*] (IID) .... CANUC:H
Canadian Union Catalogue of Serials [*National Library of Canada*] [*Information service or system*] (IID) .... UCS
Canadian Union College .... CUC
Canadian Union College, College Heights, AB, Canada [*Library symbol*] [*Library of Congress*] (LCLS) .... CaAChCU
Canadian Union College, College Heights, Alberta [*Library symbol*] [*National Library of Canada*] (NLC) .... ACHCU
Canadian Union of Base Metal Workers .... CUBMW
Canadian Union of Educational Workers .... CUEW
Canadian Union of Jewish Students .... CUJS
Canadian Union of Operating Engineers and General Workers .... CUOE
Canadian Union of Postal Workers .... CUPW
Canadian Union of Professional and Technical Employees .... CUPTE
Canadian Union of Public Employees .... CUPE
Canadian Union of Students .... CUS
Canadian Union of Transportation Employees .... CUTE
Canadian Unitarian Council .... CUC
Canadian United Minerals [*Vancouver Stock Exchange symbol*] .... CUN
Canadian Unity Information Centre, Ottawa, ON, Canada [*Library symbol*] [*Library of Congress*] (LCLS) .... CaOOCUI
Canadian Unity Information Office [*Centre d'Information sur l'Unite Canadienne*] **Ottawa, Ontario** [*Library symbol*] [*National Library of Canada*] (NLC) .... OOCUI
Canadian Universities' Reciprocal Insurance Exchange .... CURIE
Canadian University & College Conference Officers Association (AC) .... CUCCOA
Canadian University & College Counselling Association [*Association Canadienne de Counselling Universitaire et Collegial*] [*Formerly, University Counselling & Placement Association*] (AC) .... CUCCA
Canadian University Computer Network (SAUO) .... CANUCNET
Canadian University Computer Network (MCD) .... CANUNET
Canadian University Music Society [*See also SMUC*] .... CUMS
Canadian University Press (DGA) .... CUP
Canadian University Service Overseas .... CUSO
Canadian University Service Overseas, Ottawa, ON, Canada [*Library symbol*] [*Library of Congress*] (LCLS) .... CaOOCUS
Canadian University Teachers of Home Economics [*See also PEDUC*] .... CUTHE
Canadian Uranium Research Foundation (SAUO) .... CURF
Canadian Urban Institute [*Institut Urbain du Canada*] (AC) .... CUI
Canadian Urban Transit Association .... CUTA
Canadian Urethane Manufacturers Association (HGAA) .... CUMA
Canadian Urologic Oncology Group (SAUO) .... CUOG
Canadian Urological Association (SAUO) .... CUA
Canadian Urological Surgeons .... CUA
Canadian Utilities Ltd. [*Toronto Stock Exchange symbol*] .... CU
Canadian Utilities Ltd., Edmonton, AB, Canada [*Library symbol*] [*Library of Congress*] (LCLS) .... CaAECU
Canadian Utilities Ltd., Edmonton, Alberta [*Library symbol*] [*National Library of Canada*] (NLC) .... AECU
Canadian Vegans for Animal Rights (AC) .... C-VAR
Canadian Vent Corp. [*Vancouver Stock Exchange symbol*] .... CVB
Canadian version of WWV (SAUS) .... CHU
Canadian Veterinary Journal (SAUS) .... Can Vet J
Canadian Veterinary Medical Association (EAIO) .... CVMA
Canadian Videotext Consultative Committee (SAUS) CVCC
Canadian Vintage Wireless Association [*Defunct*] (EA) .... CVWA
Canadian Vocational Association (AC) .... CVA
Canadian Voice of Women for Peace [*See also VFCP*] .... VOW
Canadian Volunteer Service Medal (SAUS) .... CVSM
Canadian Volunteers in Corrections Training Project .... CaVIC
Canadian War Museum, Ottawa, ON, Canada [*Library symbol*] [*Library of Congress*] (LCLS) .... CaOONMC
Canadian War Museum [*Musee de Guerre du Canada*] **Ottawa, Ontario** [*Library symbol*] [*National Library of Canada*] (NLC) .... OONMC
Canadian War Narrative Section [*World War I*] .... CWNS
Canadian War Office (DMA) .... CWO
Canadian War Records Office (SAUO) .... CRO
Canadian War Records Office [*World War I*] .... CWRO
Canadian War Services (SAUO) .... CWS
Canadian War Supplies Assignment Board [*World War II*] .... CWSAB
Canadian Warplane Heritage, Inc. .... CWH
Canadian Warplane Heritage Museum [*ICAO designator*] (FAAC) .... CWH
Canadian Waste Technology, Inc., Toronto, Ontario [*Library symbol*] [*National Library of Canada*] (NLC) .... OTCWT
Canadian Water & Wastewater Association (AC) .... CWWA
Canadian Water Quality Association [*Association Canadienne pour la Qualite de l'Eau*] (AC) .... CWQA
Canadian Water Resources Association (EAIO) .... CWRA
Canadian Water Resources Program (GEOI) .... CWRA
Canadian Water Ski Association .... CWSA
Canadian Water Supply Energy Loop .... CANWEL
Canadian Weekly Newspapers Association (DGA) .... CWNA
Canadian Weightlifting Federation/Halterophile Canadienne .... CWFHC
Canadian Welder and Fabricator (SAUS) .... Can Welder Fabr
Canadian Welding Development Institute, Toronto, ON, Canada [*Library symbol*] [*Library of Congress*] (LCLS) .... CaOTCWB
Canadian Welding Society (SAUO) .... CWRU
Canadian Welding Society (SAUO) .... CWS
Canadian Welfare (journ.) (SAUS) .... CW
Canadian Well Logging Society .... CWLS
Canadian Western Amateur Bodybuilding Association .... CWABBA
Canadian Western Approaches .... CWA
Canadian Western Bank [*Toronto Stock Exchange symbol*] .... CWB
Canadian Western Natural Gas Co. Ltd. [*Toronto Stock Exchange symbol*] .... CWN
Canadian Westinghouse Corp. (SAUO) .... CWC
Canadian Westinghouse Library, Hamilton, ON, Canada [*Library symbol*] [*Library of Congress*] (LCLS) .... CaOHW
Canadian Wheat Board .... CWB
Canadian Wheat Board Library [*UTLAS symbol*] .... CWB
Canadian Wheat Board [*Commission Canadienne du Ble*] **Winnipeg, Manitoba** [*Library symbol*] [*National Library of Canada*] (NLC) .... MWCWB
Canadian Wheat Board, Winnipeg, MB, Canada [*Library symbol*] [*Library of Congress*] (LCLS) .... CaMWCWB
Canadian Wheelchair Basketball Association (SAUO) .... CWBA
Canadian Wheelchair Sports Association .... CWSA
Canadian Wholesale Drug Association [*Association des Grossistes en Medicaments du Canada*] (AC) .... CWDA
Canadian Wildlife Federation [*Federation Canadienne de la Fuane*] (AC) .... CWF
Canadian Wildlife Service (SAUS) .... CWS
Canadian Wildlife Service (SAUO) .... CWS
Canadian Wildlife Service, Environment Canada [*Service Canadien de la Faune, Environnement Canada*] **Ottawa, Ontario** [*Library symbol*] [*National Library of Canada*] (NLC) .... OOECW
Canadian Wildlife Service, Environment Canada [*Service Canadien de la Faune, Environnement Canada*] **Sackville, New Brunswick** [*Library symbol*] [*National Library of Canada*] (NLC) .... NBSACW
Canadian Wildlife Service, Environment Canada [*Service Canadien de la Faune, Environnement Canada*] **Winnipeg, Manitoba** [*Library symbol*] [*National Library of Canada*] (NLC) .... MWECW
Canadian Wildlife Service, Environment Canada [*Service Canadien de la Faune, Environnement Canada*] **Yellowknife, Northwest Territories** [*Library symbol*] [*National Library of Canada*] (NLC) .... NWYECW
Canadian Wildlife Service, Quebec Region [*Environment Canada*] [*Research center*] .... CWS
Canadian Wind Energy Association Inc. [*Association Canadienne d'Energie Ecolienne*] (AC) .... CANWEA
Canadian Wind Engineering Association .... CWEA
Canadian Window and Door Manufacturers Association .... CWDMA

Canadian Wireless Telecommunications Association (CGWS) .... CWTA
Canadian Women in Radio & Television (AC) .... CWRT
Canadian Women of Note [*Database*] [*York University*] [*Defunct*] [*Information service or system*] (CRD) .... CWON
Canadian Women's Army Corps .... CWAC
Canadian Women's Intercollegiate Athletic Union .... CWIAU
Canadian Women's Press Club [*Later, Media Club of Canada*] .... CWPC
Canadian Women's Sailboat Racing Association .... CWSRA
Canadian Women's Studies Association [*See also ACEF*] .... CWSA
Canadian Wood Council .... CWC
Canadian Wood Council, Ottawa, ON, Canada [*Library symbol*] [*Library of Congress*] (LCLS) .... CaOOCWC
Canadian Wood Council [*Conseil Canadien du Bois*] **Ottawa, Ontario** [*Library symbol*] [*National Library of Canada*] (NLC) .... OOCWC
Canadian Wood Energy Institute .... CWEI
Canadian Wood Pallet and Container Association (EAIO) .... CWPCA
Canadian Wood Preservers Bureau [*Bureau Canadien de la Preservation du Bois*] (AC) .... CWPB
Canadian Wood Products Industries (SAUO) .... CWPI
Canadian Woodmen of the World (EA) .... CWW
Canadian Workplace Automation Research Centre [*Department of Communications*] (IRC) .... CWARC
Canadian Workplace Automation Research Centre, Laval, PQ, Canada [*Library symbol*] [*Library of Congress*] (LCLS) .... CaQLaCW
Canadian Workplace Automation Research Centre Laval, Quebec (SAUS) .... QLACW
Canadian Workplace Automation Research Centre [*Centre Canadien de Recherche sur l'Informatisation du Travail*] **Laval, Quebec** [*Library symbol*] [*National Library of Canada*] (NLC) .... QLACW
Canadian Worldwide Energy Ltd. [*Toronto Stock Exchange symbol*] .... CWW
Canadian Writers and Illustrators of British Columbia [*Canada*] (WWLA) .... CWILLBC
Canadian Yachting Association .... CYA
Canadian Youth Centre (SAUO) .... CYC
Canadian Youth Congress (SAUO) .... CYC
Canadian Youth for Peace .... CYP
Canadian Youth Foundation (AC) .... CYF
Canadian Youth Hostels Association .... CYHA
Canadian Zionist Federation [*La Federation Sioniste Canadienne*] (AC) .... CZF
Canadiana Acquisitions, National Library of Canada [*Acquisitions pour Canadiana, Bibliotheque Nationale du Canada*] **Ottawa, Ontario** [*Library symbol*] [*National Library of Canada*] (NLC) .... OONLC
Canadiana Department, Royal Ontario Museum, Toronto, Ontario [*Library symbol*] [*National Library of Canada*] (NLC) .... OTRMC
Canadiana/Cataloguing Subsystem .... CAN/CAT
Canadian-American Center [*University of Maine at Orono*] [*Research center*] (RCD) .... CAN-AM
Canadian-American Challenge Cup Series [*Auto racing*] .... CAN-AM
Canadian-American Committee (EA) .... CAC
Canadian-American Free Trade Area .... CAFTA
Canadian-American Law Journal [*A publication*] (DLA) .... Cam Am LJ
Canadian-American Merchant Shipping Instructions .... CAMSI
Canadian-American Motor Carriers Association (EA) .... CAMCA
Canadian-American Women's Association, American Section (EA) .... CAWAAS
Canadian/Audio Cassette Tapes (SAUS) .... CAN/ACT
Canadian-Australian Steamship Company (SAUO) .... CASCO
Canadian-Controlled Private Corp. .... CCPC
Canadian-English Achievement Test [*Education*] (AEBS) .... CEAT
Canadian-National/Canadian-Pacific Telecommunications (SAUS) .... CN/CP Telecommunications
Canadians Against Drunk Driving [*Canadiens Contre l'Alcool au Volant*] (AC) .... CADD
Canadians Against PLO Terrorism (SAUO) .... CAPLOT
Canadians Concerned About Violence in Entertainment (AC) .... C-CAVE
Canadians for Accessible Governmetn & Equal Employment Inc. (AC) .... CAGEE
Canadians for Decency (AC) .... CFD
Canadians for Ethical Treatment of Food Animals (AC) .... CETFA
Canadians for Health Research [*Canadiens pour la Recherche Medicale*] (AC) .... CHR
Canadians for Responsible Government (EAIO) .... CFRG
Canadians Jewellers Association (AC) .... CJA
Canadian-Scandinavian Foundation (AC) .... CSF
Canadian-Soviet Friendship Society (SAUO) .... CSFS
Canadian-Tech Industries, Inc. [*Vancouver Stock Exchange symbol*] .... KT
Canadian-United Kingdom-United States Joint Communications-Electronics Committee (SAUO) .... CanUKUS-JCECS
Canadian-United Kingdown-United States Joint Communications-Electronics Committee (SAUS) .... CANUKUSJCEC
Canadian-United States Eastern Power Complex .... CANUSE
Canadian-United States Trade Agreement (SAUO) .... CUSTA
Canadien Association for Nursing Research (SAUO) .... CANR
Canadien Society of Customs Brokers [*Societe Canadienne des Coutiers en Douane*] (AC) .... CSCB
Canadina Institute of Mining, Metallurgy & Petroleum [*Institut Canadien des Mines, de la Metallurgie et du Petrole*] [*Formerly, Canadian Institute of Mining & Metallurgy*] (AC) .... CIM
Canadore College, North Bay, Ontario [*Library symbol*] [*National Library of Canada*] (NLC) .... ONBCC
Canady, J. G., Charlotte NC [*STAC*] .... CJG
Canaima [*Venezuela*] [*Airport symbol*] (OAG) .... CAJ
Canaima, Bolivar [*Venezuela*] [*ICAO location identifier*] (ICLI) .... SVCN
CanAir [*Canada*] [*FAA designator*] (FAAC) .... CWW
Canair Cargo [*Canada*] [*ICAO designator*] (FAAC) .... TDR
Canajoharie, NY [*FM radio station call letters*] .... WCAN
Canajoharie, NY [*FM radio station call letters*] (BROA) .... WCAN-FM
Canakkale [*Turkey*] [*ICAO location identifier*] (ICLI) .... LTBH
Canal (WDAA) C
Canal (NTIO) .... Can
Canal (ROG) .... CAN
Canal [*Board on Geographic Names*] .... CNL
Canal and Lake .... C and L
Canal and Rail [*Transportation*] .... C & R
Canal Commission (SAUO) CC
Canal Defense Light .... CDL
Canal Flats, BC [*Television station call letters*] CBUBT-1
Canal Fulton Public Library, Canal Fulton, OH [*Library symbol*] [*Library of Congress*] (LCLS) .... OCnf
Canal, Lake, and Rail .... CL & R
Canal, River, and Dock Watchmen's Association [*A union*] [*British*] .... CRDWA
Canal Safe Transit System .... CASTS
Canal Society of New York State (EA) .... CSNYS
Canal Transport Marketing Board [*British*] (BI) .... CTMB
Canal Zone [*Postal code*] (AFM) .... CZ
Canal Zone [*MARC country of publication code*] [*Library of Congress*] (LCCP) .... cz
Canal Zone [*MARC geographic area code*] [*Library of Congress*] (LCCP) .... nccz-
Canal Zone [*ANSI three-letter standard code*] [*Obsolete*] (CNC) .... PCZ
Canal Zone [*ANSI two-letter standard code*] [*Obsolete*] (CNC) .... PZ
Canal Zone Biological Area [*A preserve administered by the Smithsonian Institution*] [*Later, Smithsonian Tropical Research Institute*] .... CZBA
Canal Zone Code [*A publication*] (DLA) .... CZC
Canal Zone Code [*A publication*] (DLA) .... CZ Code
Canal Zone Forces (SAUO) .... CZF
Canal Zone Government [*Superseded by Panama Canal Commission*] .... CZG
Canal Zone Junior College .... CZJC
Canal Zone Merit System (MHDB) .... CZMS
Canal Zone Reports, Supreme and District Courts [*A publication*] (DLA) .... CZ Rep
Canal Zone Study Group (EA) .... CZSG
Canal Zone Supreme Court Reports [*A publication*] (DLA) .... Canal Zone Sup Ct
Canalicular Liver Plasma Membrane [*Anatomy*] .... CLPM
Canalization (SAUS) .... Can
Canalize (SAUS) .... Can
Canal-Randolph Corp. (SAUO) .... CRH
Canam Industry Corp. [*Vancouver Stock Exchange symbol*] .... CAR
Canam Manac Group, Inc. [*Toronto Stock Exchange symbol*] .... CAM
Canamax Resources, Inc. [*Toronto Stock Exchange symbol*] .... CMX
Canamera Explorations, Inc. [*Vancouver Stock Exchange symbol*] .... CXT
Canamin Resources [*Vancouver Stock Exchange symbol*] .... CA
Canandaigua Brands Cl A [*NASDAQ symbol*] [*Formerly, Canadaigua Wine Cl A*] (SG) .... CBRNA
Canandaigua, NY [*AM radio station call letters*] .... WCGR
Canandaigua, NY [*FM radio station call letters*] .... WCIY
Canandaigua, NY [*FM radio station call letters*] (BROA) .... WISY-FM
Canandaigua, NY [*FM radio station call letters*] .... WLKA
Canandaigua, NY [*FM radio station call letters*] (RBYB) .... WMHX-FM
Canandaigua, NY [*AM radio station call letters*] (BROA) .... WRSB
Canandaigua Veterans Administration Medical Center Library, Canandaigua, NY [*OCLC symbol*] (OCLC) .... VQC
Canandaigua Wine Cl'A' [*NASDAQ symbol*] (TTSB) .... WINEA
Canandaigua Wine Cl'B' [*NASDAQ symbol*] (TTSB) .... WINEB
Canandaigua Wine Co., Inc. [*Associated Press*] (SAG) .... CWine
Canandaigua Wine Co., Inc. [*NASDAQ symbol*] (SAG) .... WINE
Cananea [*Mexico*] [*Airport symbol*] (AD) .... CNA
Cananea [*Mexico*] [*ICAO location identifier*] (ICLI) .... MMCA
Canarc Resources [*Vancouver Stock Exchange symbol*] .... CCM
Canarchon Holdings Ltd. [*Toronto Stock Exchange symbol*] .... CAH
Canarctic Ventures [*Vancouver Stock Exchange symbol*] .... CTV
Canard Homing Antimaterial Projectile .... CHAMP
Canard Homing Artillery Modular Projectile (SAUS) .... CHAMP
Canard Rotor/Wing (SAUS) .... CRW
CanArgo Energy [*NASDAQ symbol*] [*Formerly, Fountain Oil*] .... GUSHD
Canari Airlines [*Israel*] [*ICAO designator*] (FAAC) .... CRI
Canarias [*Canary Islands*] [*ICAO location identifier*] (ICLI) .... GCCC
Canarias [*Formerly, Tenerife*] [*Spain*] [*Geomagnetic observatory code*] .... TEN
Canaries Current (SAUS) .... Canar Cur
Canarsie, NY [*Location identifier*] [*FAA*] (FAAL) .... CRI
Canary Current System (SAUS) .... CCS
Canary Islands (SAUO) .... CanIs
Canary Islands (KSC) .... CYI
Canary Islands [*MARC geographic area code*] [*Library of Congress*] (LCCP) .... lnca-
Canary Islands Submarine Cable (SAUS) .... TRANSCAN
Canas [*Costa Rica*] [*ICAO location identifier*] (ICLI) .... MRCA
Canasia Industries Corp. [*Vancouver Stock Exchange symbol*] .... CAJ
Canasil Resources, Inc. [*Vancouver Stock Exchange symbol*] .... CLZ
CanAtom Ltd., Montreal, PQ, Canada [*Library symbol*] [*Library of Congress*] (LCLS) .... CaQMCL
CanAtom Ltd., Montreal, Quebec [*Library symbol*] [*National Library of Canada*] (NLC) .... QMCL
Canaustra Gold Explorations [*Vancouver Stock Exchange symbol*] .... CZX
Canavaninosuccinic Acid [*Organic chemistry*] (MAH) .... CSA
Canaveral [*Obsolete*] [*NASA*] (KSC) .... CAN
Canaveral Administration Complex [*NASA*] (SAA) .... CAC
Canaveral Council of Technical Societies .... CCTS
Canaveral District Office [*Obsolete*] [*NASA*] (KSC) .... CANDO
Canaveral Test Report .... CTR
Canaveral-Mila [*Military*] .... CNM
Canavieiras [*Brazil*] [*Airport symbol*] (OAG) .... CNV
Canbec Resources [*Vancouver Stock Exchange symbol*] .... CCS

Canberra [*Australia*] [*ICAO location identifier*] (ICLI) ... ASCA
Canberra [*Australia*] [*ICAO location identifier*] (ICLI) ... ASCB
Canberra [*Australia*] [*ICAO location identifier*] (ICLI) ... ASCO
Canberra [*Australia*] [*ICAO location identifier*] (ICLI) ... ASMO
Canberra [*Australia*] [*Geomagnetic observatory code*] ... CAA
Canberra [*Australia*] [*Seismograph station code, US Geological Survey*] (SEIS) ... CAN
Canberra [*Australia*] [*Airport symbol*] (OAG) ... CBR
Canberra and District Home Care [*Australia*] ... CDHC
Canberra Archaeological Society [*Australia*] ... CAS
Canberra Blind Society [*Australia*] ... CBS
Canberra Bonsai Society [*Australia*] ... CBS
Canberra Botanic Gardens (SAUO) ... CBG
Canberra Bridge Club [*Australia*] ... CBC
Canberra Bushwalkers' Club [*Australia*] ... CBC
Canberra Business Council [*Australia*] ... CBC
Canberra Canoe Club [*Australia*] ... CCC
Canberra Chamber of Commerce [*Australia*] ... CCC
Canberra Children's Choir [*Australia*] ... CCC
Canberra Churches Centre [*Australia*] ... CCC
Canberra Civil Rehabilitation Committee [*Australia*] ... CCRC
Canberra Classical Association [*Australia*] ... CCA
Canberra Consumers Incorporated [*Australia*] ... CC
Canberra Craft Bookbinders' Guild [*Australia*] ... CCBG
Canberra Development Board [*Australia*] ... CDB
Canberra Entertainment Centre [*Australia*] ... CEC
Canberra Ex-Servicewomen's Association [*Australia*] ... CESA
Canberra Historical Journal [*A publication*] ... Canberra Hist J
Canberra Historical Journal [*A publication*] ... Can HJ
Canberra Horticultural Society [*Australia*] ... CHS
Canberra Income Tax Circular Memorandum [*Australia*] [*A publication*] ... CITCM
Canberra Income Tax Circular Memorandum [*A publication*] ... CM
Canberra Institute of Technology [*Australia*] ... CIT
Canberra Institute of the Arts [*Australia*] ... CIA
Canberra Kennel Club [*Australia*] ... CKC
Canberra Laboratories Automation Software System (SAUS) ... CLASS
Canberra Ornithologists Group (SAUO) ... COG
Canberra Philharmonic Society [*Australia*] ... CPS
Canberra Sar Sea Imaging Experiment (SAUS) ... CASSIE
Canberra Skeptics [*Australia*] ... CS
Canberra Times [*A publication*] ... Can T
Canberra Training Flight (SAUS) ... CTF
Canberra University College (SAUO) ... CUC
Canbra Foods Ltd. [*Toronto Stock Exchange symbol*] ... CBF
Canby Community Hospital, Canby, MN [*Library symbol*] [*Library of Congress*] (LCLS) ... MnCanH
Canby High School, Canby, MN [*Library symbol*] [*Library of Congress*] (LCLS) ... MnCanHS
Canby Public Library, Canby, MN [*Library symbol*] [*Library of Congress*] (LCLS) ... MnCan
Canby Public Library, Canby, OR [*Library symbol*] [*Library of Congress*] (LCLS) ... OrCan
Canby Union High School, Canby, OR [*Library symbol*] [*Library of Congress*] (LCLS) ... OrCanHS
Cancapital Corp. [*Toronto Stock Exchange symbol*] ... CJC
Cancel [*Publishing*] (WDMC) ... can
Cancel (AABC) ... CAN
Cancel (EBF) ... Canc
Cancel [*Computer science*] (BARN) ... CNCL
Cancel [*or Cancellation*] (AFM) ... CNL
Cancel (NVT) ... CNX
Cancel [*or Cancelled*] (CINC) ... CX
Cancel (SAUS) ... xxl
Cancel Approved Arrival [*Aviation*] (FAAC) ... CXA
Cancel Approved Departure [*Aviation*] (FAAC) ... CXD
Cancel Back Order ... CBO
Cancel Character [*Keyboard*] [*Computer science*] ... CAN
Cancel Character (SAUS) ... Can
Cancel Connect (SAUS) ... XN
Cancel Controller Area Network (SAUS) ... CAN
Cancel Corridor Assignment (SAUS) ... CCA
Cancel Disconnect (SAUS) ... XD
Cancel First Choice (SAUS) ... XF
Cancel Flight Plan (FAAC) ... CNLFP
Cancel Form Order (CIST) ... CFO
Cancel Former Order (ADWA) ... CFO
Cancel in Transmission (SAUS) ... CANTRAN
Cancel Last Message (SAUS) ... CLM
Cancel Launch in Progress [*Air Force*] ... CLIP
Cancel Line (SAUS) ... CAN
Cancel Long Lead Connect (SAUS) ... XL
Cancel Lot Cycle (AAEL) ... CLC
Cancel Move Request (AAEL) ... CMR
Cancel on Back [*Deltiology*] ... C/B
Cancel on Face [*Deltiology*] ... C/F
Cancel Previous Order (DI) ... CPO
Cancel Request (SAUS) ... CR
Cancel Transmission (SAUS) ... CANTRAN
Cancelable (ABBR) ... CNCLB
Cancelation Clause [*Business term*] ... CC
Cancel/Clarify Message (SSD) ... CCM
Canceled ... C
Canceled (WDMC) ... can
Canceled (NTIO) ... canc
Canceled ... CANC
Canceled (ABBR) ... CNCLD
Canceled Check [*Banking*] ... CC
Canceled or Postponed ... COP
Canceled to Order [*Philately*] ... CTO
Canceled Transmission (CET) ... CANTRAN
Canceler (ABBR) ... CNCLR
Canceling (DCTA) ... CANCL
Canceling ... CANCLG
Canceling (ABBR) ... CNCLG
Canceling Former Order ... CFO
Cancellation (ADWA) ... can
Cancellation ... CANC
Cancellation (EBF) ... Canc
Cancellation (ROG) ... CANCLN
Cancellation (ABBR) ... CNCLAN
Cancellation (ABBR) ... CNCLN
Cancellation Addendum Sales Order (NASA) ... CASO
Cancellation Message (SAUS) ... CNL Message
Cancellation of Amplitude Modulation (MCD) ... CAM
Cancellation of Instruments [*Legal term*] (DLA) ... CANC INSTR
Cancellation Ratio (CCCA) ... CR
Cancellation Recommended [*Travel industry*] (TRID) ... XR
Cancellation Request (SAUS) ... CR
Cancelled (SAUS) ... Cld
Cancelled (BARN) ... CLD
Cancelled ... CXL
Cancelled [*Travel industry*] (TRID) ... XLD
Cancelled (TRID) ... XX
Cancelled Name [*Travel industry*] (TRID) ... XN
Cancelled Segment [*Travel industry*] (TRID) ... XS
Cancelling (IAA) ... CLG
Cancelling (SAUS) ... Clg
Cancelling Former Orders (SAUS) ... CFO
Cancelling of Policy Returns Only [*Insurance*] (MARI) ... CRO
Cancelling Returns Only (SAUS) ... CRO
Cancellous Bone Graft [*Medicine*] (MELL) ... CBG
Cancer ... C
Cancer [*or Carcinoma*] [*Medicine*] ... CA
Cancer [*Medicine*] (MELL) ... Ca
Cancer [*Constellation*] ... CAN
Cancer [*Oncology*] (DAVI) ... Can
Cancer [*Constellation*] ... Canc
Cancer [*Constellation*] ... Cnc
Cancer (ABBR) ... CNCR
Cancer Aftercare and Rehabilitation Society [*British*] (DBA) ... CARE
Cancer Aid Listening Line [*British*] (DI) ... CALL
Cancer and Leukemia, Group B [*Medicine*] ... CALGB
Cancer and Polio Research Fund (SAUO) ... CPRF
Cancer and Sex Hormone (MELL) ... CASH
Cancer and Steroid Hormonal Study (ADWA) ... CSHS
Cancer Antigen (SAUS) ... CA
Cancer Assessment Group (SAUO) ... CAG
Cancer Attitude Survey [*Oncology and psychiatry*] (DAVI) ... CAS
Cancer Biochemistry Biophysics (SAUS) ... Cancer Biochem Biophys
Cancer Biotherapeutics Newsletter [*A publication*] (ADWA) ... CBN
Cancer Breaking Factor [*Antineoplastic drug*] ... CBF
Cancer Bulletin (journ.) (SAUS) ... Cancer Bull
Cancer Care (EA) ... CC
Cancer Care, Inc. (EA) ... CCI
Cancer Care International (SAUS) ... CCI
Cancer Cell Oncogene [*Medicine*] (LDT) ... c-onc
Cancer Checking Lipid [*Oncology*] ... CCL
Cancer Chemotherapy [*Medicine*] (MELL) ... CCT
Cancer Chemotherapy National Committee (SAUO) ... CCNC
Cancer Chemotherapy National Service Center [*National Institutes of Health*] ... CCNSC
Cancer Chemotherapy Reports (journ.) (SAUS) ... Cancer Chemother Rep
Cancer Coagulative Factor (SAUS) ... CCF
Cancer Connection (SAUO) ... CC
Cancer Control Agency of British Columbia (PDAA) ... CCABC
Cancer Control Agency of British Columbia, Vancouver, British Columbia [*Library symbol*] [*National Library of Canada*] (NLC) ... BVACCA
Cancer Control Science Associates Program [*National Cancer Institute*] ... CCSAP
Cancer Control Society (EA) ... CCS
Cancer Council, New South Wales [*Australia*] ... CCNSW
Cancer Cytology Foundation of America [*Later, National Cancer Cytology Center*] ... CCF
Cancer Cytology Foundation of America [*Later, National Cancer Cytology Center*] ... CCFA
Cancer Detection Centre [*British*] ... CDC
Cancer Dose (NUCP) ... CD
Cancer Epidemiology, Biomarkers and Prevention (SAUS) ... Cancer Epidemiol Biomarkers Prev
Cancer Family Syndrome [*Oncology*] (DAVI) ... CFS
Cancer Federation (SAUO) ... CFI
Cancer Federation, Inc. (EA) ... CFI
Cancer Free [*Medicine*] ... CF
Cancer Fund of America ... CFA
Cancer Genetics Studies Consortium ... CGSC
Cancer Genome Anatomy Project [*A Cooperative database*] ... CGAP
Cancer Guidance Institute (EA) ... CGI
Cancer Hazards Ranking and Information System ... CHRIS
Cancer Hopefuls United for Mutual Support [*Defunct*] (EA) ... CHUMS
Cancer Hot Line [*of Cancer Connection*] (EA) ... CH
Cancer Immunology and Immunotherapy (journ.) (SAUS) ... CII

Cancer Immunology, Immunotherapy (SAUS) ... Cancer Immunol Immunother
Cancer Incidence in North America (SAUS) ... CINA
Cancer Information Clearinghouse [*National Cancer Institute*] [*Database*] ... CIC
Cancer Information Dissemination and Analysis Center ... CIDAC
Cancer Information Online [*Database*] [*Computer science*] (CIST) ... CANCERLINE
Cancer Information Service [*HEW*] ... CIS
Cancer Information Service for Developing Countries (SAUS) ... CISDC
Cancer Information System (SAUO) ... CIS
Cancer International Research Cooperative ... CANCIRCO
Cancer Journal for Clinicians (SAUS) ... CA
Cancer Literature [*National Cancer Institute*] [*Information service or system*] ... CANCERLIT
Cancer Multistep Therapy [*Medicine*] (DMAA) ... CMT
Cancer Normalizing Factor [*Medicine*] (DB) ... CNF
Cancer of Prostate [*Oncology and urology*] (DAVI) ... CAP
Cancer of the Cervix [*Medicine*] ... CACX
Cancer of Unknown Primary Site [*Medicine*] (MELL) ... CUPS
Cancer Online (SAUS) ... CANCER LINE
Cancer Pain Treatment (MELL) ... CPT
Cancer Patients' Assistance Society of New South Wales [*Australia*] ... CPASNSW
Cancer Patients, Weight Losing ... CWL
Cancer Patients, Weight Stable ... CWS
Cancer Potential Index ... CPI
Cancer Prevention Benefit Program [*National Cancer Institute*] ... CPBP
Cancer Prevention Fellowship Program [*NCI*] ... CPFP
Cancer Procoagulant [*Medicine*] (MELL) ... CP
Cancer Project (SAUS) ... CANCERPROJ
Cancer Proneness Phenotype [*Medicine*] (DMAA) ... CPP
Cancer Registry Lower Saxony (SAUO) ... CARLOS
Cancer Rehabilitation Evaluation System [*Medicine*] (DMAA) ... CARES
Cancer Relief Macmillan Fund [*British*] (DBA) ... CRMF
Cancer Research [*A publication*] (MEC) ... Cancer Res
Cancer Research Advisory Centre (SAUO) ... CRAC
Cancer Research Campaign [*British*] ... CRC
Cancer Research Campaign Technology [*British*] ... CRCT
Cancer Research Center [*Research center*] (RCD) ... CRC
Cancer Research Emphasis Grants ... CREG
Cancer Research Foundation (SAUO) ... CRF
Cancer Research Foundation of America (ADWA) ... CRFA
Cancer Research Fund (SAUO) ... CRF
Cancer Research Fund of the Damon Runyon-Walter Winchell Foundation (EA) ... CRFDR-WWF
Cancer Research Institute ... CRI
Cancer Research Projects [*National Cancer Intitute*] [*Information service or system*] [*Defunct*] ... CANCERPROJ
Cancer Research Society Inc. [*Societe de Recherche sur le Cancer Inc.*] (AC) ... CRS
Cancer Research Unit [*Flinders University*] [*Australia*] ... CRU
Cancer Risk-Assessment Verification Endeavor ... CRAVE
Cancer Serum Index ... CSI
Cancer Surveillance System [*Medicine*] (STED) ... CSS
Cancer Therapy Evaluation Program [*Bethesda, MD*] [*National Cancer Institute*] [*Department of Health and Human Services*] (GRD) ... CTEP
Cancer Therapy Facility ... CTF
Cancer Therapy Reviews (SAUO) ... CTR
Cancer Treatment Advisory Committee [*HEW*] (EGAO) ... CTAC
Cancer Treatment Hldgs [*ECM symbol*] (TTSB) ... CTHEC
Cancer Treatment Holdings, Inc. [*Associated Press*] (SAG) ... CancTr
Cancer Treatment Holdings, Inc. [*AMEX symbol*] (SAG) ... CTH
Cancer Watch (SAUO) ... CW
Cancer-Asociated Retinopathy syndrome (SAUS) ... CAR
Cancer-Associated Polypeptide Antigen [*Medicine*] (DMAA) ... CAPA
Cancer-Associated Retinopathy [*Medicine*] (MELL) ... CAR
Cancer-Free White Mouse [*Medicine*] (MEDA) ... CFW
Cancer-Free White Mouse [*Medicine*] (MAE) ... CFWM
Cancermondial (SAUO) ... CANM
Cancer-Potency Factor [*Environmental chemistry*] ... CPF
Cancer-Prone Family (MELL) ... CPF
Cancom Industries, Inc. [*Vancouver Stock Exchange symbol*] ... CCX
CANCOM [*Canadian Satellite Communications, Inc.*] **Teleconference Network, Inc.** [*Telecommunications service*] (TSSD) ... CTN
Cancorp Enterprises [*Vancouver Stock Exchange symbol*] ... CEE
Cancrinite (SAUS) ... ca
Cancrinite [*A zeolite*] ... CAN
Cancrizans of the Duration series (SAUS) ... DC
Cancun [*Mexico*] [*Airport symbol*] (OAG) ... CUN
Cancun [*Mexico*] [*ICAO location identifier*] (ICLI) ... MMUN
Cancun Avioturismo SA [*Mexico*] [*ICAO designator*] (FAAC) ... CAU
Candala [*Somalia*] [*ICAO location identifier*] (ICLI) ... HCMC
Candela [*Formerly, Candlepower*] [*See also cd*] (MDG) ... C
Candela [*Formerly, Candlepower*] [*Symbol*] [*SI unit of luminous intensity*] ... cd
Candela (SAUS) ... CD
Candela Color Management System (SAUS) ... CCMS
Candela Corp. [*NASDAQ symbol*] [*Formerly, Candela Laser*] (SG) ... CLZR
Candela Corp. Wrrt [*NASDAQ symbol*] (TTSB) ... CLZRW
Candela Laser Corp. [*Associated Press*] (SAG) ... Candela
Candela Laser Corp. [*Associated Press*] (SAG) ... Candla
Candela Laser Corp. [*NASDAQ symbol*] (NQ) ... CLZR
Candela per Square Centimetre (SAUS) ... Cd/cmy
Candela per Square Foot (SAUS) ... Cd/fty
Candela per Square Foot (SAUS) ... Cd/sq ft
Candela per Square Inch (WDAA) ... CD/IN^2
Candela per Square Inch (SAUS) ... Cd/sq in
Candela per Square Meter (WDAA) ... CD/M^2
Candela per Square Meter (or Metre) (SAUS) ... Cd/my
Candela per Steradian ... CD/SR
Candela Resources Ltd. [*Vancouver Stock Exchange symbol*] ... CDD
Candelabra (SAUS) ... CAND
Candelabra Edison Screw (IAA) ... CES
Candelabra Prefocused ... CPREF
Candelabra Screw (IAA) ... CANDSC
Candelabra Screw (SAUS) ... Cand Sc
Candelas per Square Foot ... CD/FT^2
Candelas per Square Meter (IDOE) ... cd/m^2
Candelas per Square Meter (SAUS) ... Cd/my
Candida [*Genus of fungi*] (AAMN) ... CAN
Candida Albicans (SAUS) ... CA
Candida Albicans Skin Test Antigen [*Immunology*] ... CASTA
Candida Cylindracea [*A yeast*] ... CCL
Candida Metabolic Antigen (STED) ... CMA
Candida Rugosa Lipase [*An enzyme*] ... CRL
Candida Yeast [*Biochemistry*] (DAVI) ... CANDID
Candidal Onychomycosis (STED) ... CO
Candidate (AFM) ... CAND
Candidate Density Function (MCD) ... CDF
Candidate Environmental Impact Statement (MCD) ... CEIS
Candidate Evaluation ... CE
Candidate for Disposal (MCD) ... CFD
candidate gene for X-inactivation center (SAUS) ... XIST
Candidate in Philosophy ... Fil Kand
Candidate Item File ... CIF
Candidate Material ... CM
Candidate of Historical Sciences ... CSc
Candidate of Pharmacy ... Cand Pharm
Candidate of Science ... C Sc
Candidate of Technical Science ... Cand Techn Sci
Candidate of Theology (IIA) ... CT
Candidate of Theology ... C Th
Candidate of Theology (SAUS) ... ThC
Candidate of Theology ... Th C
Candidate Pass Generator [*NASA*] ... CPG
Candidate Repair Parts Redistribution Report ... CRPRR
Candidate Selection [*Army*] ... CS
Candidate/Nominee Protective Division [*US Secret Service*] ... CNPD
Candidates Reply Date Agreement [*Education*] ... CRDA
Candidatus [*Academic degree*] [*Latin*] ... C
Candidatus Juris [*Doctor of Law*] [*Latin*] (WDAA) ... CAND JUR
Candidatus Magisterii [*Academic Degree*] [*Latin*] ... CMG
Candies, Inc. [*NASDAQ symbol*] (SAG) ... CAND
Candies, Inc. [*NASDAQ symbol*] (SG) ... CANDE
Candies, Inc. [*Associated Press*] (SAG) ... Candi
Candies, Inc. [*Associated Press*] (SAG) ... Candies
Candies Inc. Wrrt'B' [*NASDAQ symbol*] (TTSB) ... CANDL
Candies Inc. Wrrt'C' [*NASDAQ symbol*] (TTSB) ... CANDN
Candilejas [*Colombia*] [*Airport symbol*] (OAG) ... CJD
Candle (IDOE) ... c
Candle [*Illumination*] ... C
Candle ... Ca
Candle (SAUS) ... CA
Candle [*Illumination*] ... CD
Candle, AK [*Location identifier*] [*FAA*] (FAAL) ... CDL
Candle Flames in Microgravity (SAUS) ... CFM
Candle Foot (SAUS) ... Cdl-ft
Candle Foot [*Illumination*] (IAA) ... CF
Candle Manufacturers Association [*Later, NCA*] (EA) ... CMA
Candle Power (IDOE) ... cp
Candle Power/Square Foot (KSC) ... CPSF
Candle-Hour [*Illumination*] ... CH
Candle-Hour [*Illumination*] (AAG) ... C-HR
Candlelight ... CNDLLGHT
Candlelighters Childhood Cancer Foundation (EA) ... CCCF
Candlelighters Childhood Cancer Foundation (EA) ... CF
Candlelighters Childhood Cancer Foundation Canada [*Fondation des Eclaireurs pour le Cancer dans l'Enfance Canada*] [*Also, Candlelighters Canada*] (AC) ... CCCFC
Candlepower [*Physics*] ... CP
Candlepower Hour (IAA) ... CPH
Candles per Square Meter [*Optics*] ... c/m^2
Candles per Square Meter (SAUS) ... c/my
Candles per Square Metre (SAUS) ... c/my
Candlewood Hotel Co., Inc. [*NASDAQ symbol*] (SAG) ... CNDL
Candlewood Hotel Co., Inc. [*Associated Press*] (SAG) ... Cndlewd
C&N Electrical Industries Ltd. (SAUO) ... CNEI
Cando Public Library, Cando, ND [*Library symbol*] [*Library of Congress*] (LCLS) ... NdCan
Candol Developments Ltd. [*Toronto Stock Exchange symbol*] ... CJD
Candorado Mines Ltd. [*Vancouver Stock Exchange symbol*] ... COM
Candover Investments [*Finance*] [*British*] ... CI
CANDU Owners Group (AC) ... COG
Candy ... CNDY
Candy Apple [*Bowdlerized version*] ... CA
Candy Brokers Association of America [*Later, NCBSA*] (EA) ... CBA
Candy, Chocolate and Confectionery Institute (EA) ... CCCI
Candy. Mayor's Court Practice [*1879*] [*A publication*] (DLA) ... Candy MC
Cane and Leigh. Crown Cases Reserved [*England*] [*A publication*] (DLA) ... Cane & L
Cane Farming Development Corporation (SAUO) ... CFDC
Cane Invert Syrup [*Food sweetener*] ... CIS
Cane Medium Invert Syrup [*Food sweetener*] ... CMIS

Cane, Wicker, and Perambucot Operatives' Society [*A union*] [*British*] ..... CWPOS
CANEBSCO Subscription Service Ltd. [*ACCORD*] [*UTLAS symbol*] .... EBS
Canebsco Subscription Service Ltd., Toronto, ON, Canada [*Library symbol*] [*Library of Congress*] (LCLS) .... CaOTCSS
CANEBSCO Subscription Service Ltd., Toronto, Ontario [*Library symbol*] [*National Library of Canada*] (NLC) .... OTCSS
Caneco Audio-Publishers, Inc. [*Vancouver Stock Exchange symbol*] .... CPB
Canertech, Inc., Winnipeg, Manitoba [*Library symbol*] [*National Library of Canada*] (NLC) .... MWCI
Canertech, Inc., Winnipeg, MB, Canada [*Library symbol*] [*Library of Congress*] (LCLS) .... CaMWCI
Canes Venatici [*Constellation*] .... CVen
Canes Venatici [*Constellation*] .... CVn
Canet Nordenfelt Gun .... CN
Canever English History Club .... CEHC
Canewdon [*England*] .... CANEW
Can-Ex Resources Ltd. [*Vancouver Stock Exchange symbol*] .... CXZ
Caney, KS [*FM radio station call letters*] .... KEOJ
Cane-Zebiak [*Marine science*] (OSRA) .... CZ
Canfic Resources Ltd. [*Vancouver Stock Exchange symbol*] .... CNM
Canfield Centre for Logistics and Transportation .... CCLT
Canfield Instructional Styles Inventory [*Teacher evaluation test*] .... CIS
Canfield Learning Styles Inventory [*Educational test*] .... CLS
Canfield, Rodeman, Adams, and Preller [*Philadelphia law firm in Spiro Agnew's book, "The Canfield Decision"*] .... CRAP
Canfor Capital Ltd. [*Toronto Stock Exchange symbol*] .... CCP
Canfor Corp. [*Toronto Stock Exchange symbol*] [*Vancouver Stock Exchange symbol*] .... CFP
Canguard Health Technologies, Inc. [*Vancouver Stock Exchange symbol*] ..... CGD
Canhorn Mining Corp. [*Toronto Stock Exchange symbol*] .... CNH
Canifair Aviation, Inc. [*Canada*] [*ICAO designator*] (FAAC) .... CNF
Canine [*Deciduous*] [*Dentistry*] C
Canine [*K9 Corps - Army Dogs*] [*World War II*] K9
Canine Adenovirus [*Veterinary medicine*] .... CAV
Canine Behavior Institute (EA) .... CBI
Canine Companions for Independence (EA) CCI
Canine Control Council [*Australia*] CCC
Canine Coronavirus [*Veterinary science*] (DB) CCV
Canine Defence League (SAUO) .... CDL
Canine Defense Fund (EA) .... CDF
Canine Distemper [*Veterinary medicine*] .... CD
Canine Distemper Encephalitis [*A disease*] .... CDE
Canine Distemper Virus [*Veterinary medicine*] .... CDV
Canine Dose [*Veterinary medicine*] .... CD
Canine Eye Registration Foundation [*Defunct*] (EA) .... CERF
Canine Gastric Dilatation-Volvulus [*Veterinary medicine*] .... CGDV
Canine Good Citizen [*Purebred canine award*] .... CGC
Canine Health Schemes Management Group [*British*] (GVA) .... CHSMG
Canine Herpes Virus [*Veterinary science*] (DB) .... CHV
Canine Home Protection System [*Acronym is title of 1979 movie*] .... CHOMPS
Canine Kidney [*Physiology*] .... CK
Canine Livestock Animals Welfare Service [*Australia*] .... CLAWS
Canine Myasthenia Gravis (STED) .... CMG
Canine Pancreatic Polypeptide (STED) .... CPP
Canine Parovirus .... CPV
Canine Pulmonary Surfactant .... CPSA
Canine Quarterly: a Parody of the World's Most Elegant Magazine for Men [*A publication*] .... CQ
Canine Tuberculosis (SAUS) .... CanTb
Canine X-Linked Muscular Dystrophy .... CXMD
Canis Major [*Constellation*] .... CMa
Canis Major [*Constellation*] .... CMaj
Canis Minor [*Constellation*] .... CMi
Canis Minor [*Constellation*] .... CMin
Canisco Resources [*NASDAQ symbol*] (TTSB) .... CANRQ
Canisius College (GAGS) .... Canisius C
Canisius College, Buffalo, NY [*Library symbol*] [*Library of Congress*] (LCLS) .... NBuCC
Canisius College, Buffalo, NY [*OCLC symbol*] (OCLC) .... VKC
Canister (AAG) .... CAN
Canister (SAUS) .... Can
Canister .... CN
Canister (SAUS) .... CNT
Canister (KSC) .... CSTR
Canister Assembly Launch Test Program (SAUS) .... CALTP
Canister Harpoon Control and Launch System (MCD) .... CHCLS
Canister Purge [*Automotive engineering*] .... CP
Canister Purge Regulator Valve [*Automotive engineering*] .... CPRV
Canister Purge Solenoid [*Automotive engineering*] .... CANP
Canister Return Purge Valve [*Automotive engineering*] .... CRPV
Canister Treatment Cell [*Nuclear energy*] (NUCP) .... CTC
Canister/Interceptor .... C/I
Canister/Launcher [*Strategic Defense Initiative*] .... C/L
Canister/Launcher Electronic Equipment .... CLEE
Canister/Launcher Electronics .... CLE
Canlan Investment Corp. [*Vancouver Stock Exchange symbol*] .... CAI
Can-Mac Exploration Ltd. [*Vancouver Stock Exchange symbol*] .... CXB
CANMARC [*Canadian Machine-Readable Cataloging*] **English Authority File** [*Source file*] [*UTLAS symbol*] .... CAE
CANMARC [*Canadian Machine-Readable Cataloging*] **French Authority File** [*Source file*] [*UTLAS symbol*] .... CAF
Canmax, Inc. [*Associated Press*] (SAG) .... Canmax
Canmax, Inc. [*NASDAQ symbol*] (SAG) .... CNMX
CANMET [*Canada Centre for Mineral and Energy Technology*] **Library** [*Canada Energy, Mines, and Resources*] [*UTLAS symbol*] .... EMM
CANMET [*Canada Centre for Mineral and Energy Technology*] **Library, Energy, Mines, and Resources Canada , Devon, Alberta** [*Bibliotheque CANMET, Energie, Mines, et Ressources Canada*] [*Library symbol*] [*National Library of Canada*] (NLC) .... ADEMRCM
CANMET [*Canada Centre for Mineral and Energy Technology*] **Library, Energy, Mines, and Resources Canada , Ottawa, Ontario** [*Bibliotheque CANMET, Energie, Mines, et Ressources Canada*] [*Library symbol*] [*National Library of Canada*] (NLC) .... OOM
CANMET [*Canada Centre for Mineral and Energy Technology*] **Library, Western Research Laboratory, Energy, Mines, and Resources Canada , Sherwood Park, Alberta** [*Bibliotheque CANMET, Laboratoire de Recherche de l'Ouest, Energie, Mines, et Ressources Canada*] [*Library symbol*] [*National Library of Canada*] (NLC) .... ASPEMRCM
Canmore, AB [*AM radio station call letters*] .... CFHC
Canmore, AB [*FM radio station call letters*] (BROA) .... CJMT-FM
Canmore Municipal Library, Alberta [*Library symbol*] [*National Library of Canada*] (NLC) .... ACAM
Canmore Municipal Library, Canmore, AB, Canada [*Library symbol*] [*Library of Congress*] (LCLS) .... CaACaM
Canna Yellow Mottle Virus [*Plant pathology*] .... CAYMV
Cannabichromene (SAUS) .... CBC
Cannabicyclol (SAUS) .... CBL
Cannabidiol [*Organic chemistry*] .... CBD
Cannabidiolic Acid [*Organic chemistry*] .... CBDA
Cannabinoid (SAUS) .... Canna
Cannabinol (SAUS) .... Canna
Cannabinol [*A component of marijuana*] .... CBN
Cannabis Action Network (EA) .... CAN
Cannan Electric Co., Los Angeles, CA [*Library symbol*] [*Library of Congress*] (LCLS) .... CLCan
Canned (SAUS) .... CD
Canned and Cooked Meat Importers Association (EA) .... CCMIA
Canned Antiair Warfare Exercise (NVT) .... CAAWEX
Canned Chop Suey Foods Industry [*Defunct*] .... CCSFI
Canned Food Information Council (EA) .... CFIC
Canned Food Marketing Committee (EA) .... CFMC
Canned Ration (ADWA) .... C ration
Canned Salmon Institute [*Later, SI*] (EA) .... CSI
Cannelton, IN [*FM radio station call letters*] .... WLME
Cannelton Public Library, Cannelton, IN [*Library symbol*] [*Library of Congress*] (LCLS) .... InCan
Cannery .... CAN
Cannery Board [*Queensland*] [*Australia*] .... CB
Cannes [*France*] [*Airport symbol*] (AD) .... CEQ
Cannes/Mandelieu [*France*] [*ICAO location identifier*] (ICLI) .... LFMD
Cannet Des Maures [*France*] [*Seismograph station code, US Geological Survey*] [*Closed*] (SEIS) .... CMF
Cannibalistic Humanoid Underground Dwellers [*or Contaminated Hazard Underground Disposal*] [*Acronym used as title of movie*] .... CHUD
Cannibalization Point [*Supply and Maintenance*] [*Military*] .... CP
Cannibalize (MCD) .... K-BALL
Canning .... CNNNG
Canning Machinery and Supplies Association [*Later, FPM & SA*] (EA) ...... CMSA
Canning, NS [*Television station call letters*] CJCH-1
Canning Rvier Wetlands Conservation Society [*Australia*] .... CRWCS
Cannington Branch, Brock Township Public Library, Ontario [*Library symbol*] [*National Library of Canada*] (BIB) .... OCAB
Cannon (MILB) .... can
Cannon (WDAA) .... CAN
Cannon [*Freight*] .... CANN
Cannon (SAUS) .... CN
Cannon Artillery Weapon Systems (MCD) .... CAWS
Cannon Beach, OR [*FM radio station call letters*] (RBYB) .... KCBZ
Cannon Express [*AMEX symbol*] (SG) .... AB
Cannon Express [*NASDAQ symbol*] (TTSB) .... CANX
Cannon Express, Inc. [*Associated Press*] (SAG) .... CannEx
Cannon Express, Inc. [*Associated Press*] (SAG) .... CannExp
Cannon Express, Inc. [*NASDAQ symbol*] (NQ) .... CANX
[*The*] **Cannon Group, Inc.** (MHDW) .... CAN
Cannon House Office Building .... CHOB
Cannon Hunters Association of Seattle [*Defunct*] (EA) .... CHAOS
Cannon Launched Laser Beam Riding Projectile (SAUS) .... CLBRP
Cannon Maintenance Trainer .... CMT
Cannon Memorial YMCA Public Library, Kannapolis, NC [*Library symbol*] [*Library of Congress*] (LCLS) .... NcKa
Cannon Minerals Ltd. [*Vancouver Stock Exchange symbol*] .... CN
Cannon Nonlaunched Guided Projectile .... CNLGP
Cannon Platoon (SAUO) .... Cn Plat
Cannon Printing System Language (SAUS) .... CAPSL
Cannon Street Investments [*Finance*] [*British*] .... CSI
Cannon Street Station [*London*] (ROG) C
Cannon-Caliber Electro-Magnetic Launcher (SAUS) .... CCEML
Cannondale Corp. [*NASDAQ symbol*] (SAG) .... BIKE
Cannondale Corp. [*Associated Press*] (SAG) .... Canondle
Cannon-Launched Beam Rider Projectile (MCD) .... CLBRP
Cannon-Launched Guidance Electronics (SAUS) .... CLGE
Cannon-Launched Guided Projectile .... CLGP
Cannon-Launched Precision Guided Munition (MCD) .... CL-PGM
Cannons Regular of the Immaculate Conception (TOCD) .... crlc
Cannonsburg, KY [*AM radio station call letters*] .... WOKT
Cannot [*Amateur radio shorthand*] (WDAA) .... CNT
Cannot Call Out (SAUS) .... CCO
Cannot Comply (NVT) .... CANTCO
Cannot Duplicate (MCD) .... CND
Cannot Find .... CF

Cannot Find (SAUS) ... CNF
Cannot Hear (SAUS) ... CH
Cannot Hear Of [*Bookselling*] ... C/H/O
Cannot Observe (SAUS) ... CNO
Canobie [*Australia*] [*Airport symbol*] [*Obsolete*] (OAG) ... CBY
CanOcean Resources Ltd., New Westminster, BC, Canada [*Library symbol*] [*Library of Congress*] (LCLS) ... CaBNWCR
CanOcean Resources Ltd., New Westminster, British Columbia [*Library symbol*] [*National Library of Canada*] (NLC) ... BNWCR
Canoe ... C
Canoe South Australia ... CSA
Canoe-Camping Club [*British*] (BI) ... CCC
Canoga Park (SAUS) ... CNP
Canoga Park Area Office [*AEC*] (MCD) ... CPAO
Canoga Test Laboratory [*NASA*] (NASA) ... CTL
Canon ... C
Canon ... CAN
Canon (SAUS) ... Can
Canon ... CN
Canon Auto Tuning [*Photography*] (OA) ... CAT
Canon Auto Tuning System (SAUS) ... CATS
Canon Buffer Transmission [*Computer science*] (VERA) ... CBT
Canon City, CO [*AM radio station call letters*] ... KRLN
Canon City, CO [*FM radio station call letters*] ... KRLN-FM
Canon City, CO [*FM radio station call letters*] ... KSTY
Canon City, CO [*FM radio station call letters*] (BROA) ... KTLC-FM
Canon City Public Library, Canon City, CO [*Library symbol*] [*Library of Congress*] (LCLS) ... CoCc
Canon, Inc. [*NASDAQ symbol*] (NQ) ... CANN
Canon, Inc. (MHDW) ... CANNY
Canon, Inc. [*Associated Press*] (SAG) ... Canonl
Canon, Inc. ADR [*NYSE symbol*] ... CAJ
Canon, Inc. ADR [*NASDAQ symbol*] (SG) ... CANNY
Canon Law Society of America (SAUO) ... CLDA
Canon Law Society of America (EA) ... CLS
Canon Law Society of America (EA) ... CLSA
Canon Printer System Language [*Computer application*] (PCM) ... CaPSL
Canon-Caliber Electromagnetic Launcher ... CCEML
Canonesses Regular of St. Augustine [*Roman Catholic women's religious order*] ... CRA
Canonical Analysis Landsat Model of Chlorophyll A and Turbidity (SAUS) ... CALMCAT
Canonical Conjunctive Normal Form (SAUS) ... CCNF
Canonical Correlation (SAUS) ... CC
Canonical Correlation Analysis [*Mathematics*] ... CCA
Canonical Correspondence Analysis [*Statistical analysis*] ... CANOCO
Canonical Correspondence Analysis (QUAC) ... CCA
Canonical Disjunctive Normal Form (SAUS) ... CDNF
Canonical Encoding Rules (SAUS) ... CER
Canonical List of all Known Acronyms (SAUS) ... CLOAKA
Canonical Minimum Scattering Antenna (SAUS) ... CMS Antenna
Canonical Molecular Orbital [*Physical chemistry*] ... CMO
Canonical Name (SAUS) ... CNAME
Canonical Signed Digit Code (SAUS) ... CSD Code
Canonical Unit of Length ... CUL
Canonical Unit of Time ... CUT
Canonical Variates Analysis [*Mathematics*] ... CVA
Canonically (SAUS) ... Can
Canonically Decoupled (SAUS) ... CD
Canonici Regulares Immaculate Conceptionis [*Canons Regular of the Immaculate Conception*] [*Roman Catholic men's religious order*] ... CRIC
Canonici Regulares Lateranenses [*Canons Regular of the Lateran*] ... CRL
Canonici Regulares Ordinis Sanctae Crucis [*Canons Regular of the Order of the Holy Cross*] [*Crosier Fathers*] [*Roman Catholic religious order*] ... OSC
Canonicorum [*England*] ... CAN
Canonry (SAUS) ... Can
Canons Enacted under King Edgar [*A publication*] (DLA) ... Edg C
Canons of Aelfric [*A publication*] (DLA) ... Aelf C
Canons Regular of Premontre (TOCD) ... OPraem
Canons Regular of Premontre, Premonstratensians, Norbetines (TOCD) ... opraem
Canons Regular of Saint Augustine (SAUO) ... CRSA
Canons Regular of the Immaculate Conception (TOCD) ... CRIC
Canons Regular of the Lateran (TOCD) ... crl
Canons Regular of the Lateran (TOCD) ... CRL
Canons Regular of the Order of the Holy Cross, Crosier Fathers (TOCD) ... osc
Canonsburg, PA [*AM radio station call letters*] ... WWCS
Canopus Acquisition Gate [*NASA*] ... CAG
Canopus Probe near Limb of Venus Angle [*NASA*] ... CPV
Canopy (MSA) ... CAN
Canopy Cover [*Ecology*] ... CNPY
Canopy Removal System [*for helicopters*] (RDA) ... CRS
Canopy Smoke Grenade (DWSG) ... CSG
Canossian Daughters of Charity (TOCD) ... FdCC
Canova Public Library, Canova, SD [*Library symbol*] [*Library of Congress*] (LCLS) ... SdCan
Canova Resources Ltd. [*Vancouver Stock Exchange symbol*] ... CVD
Canpax-Air AG [*Switzerland*] [*ICAO designator*] (FAAC) ... CAX
Canreos Minerals [*Vancouver Stock Exchange symbol*] ... CSL
Canron, Inc. [*Toronto Stock Exchange symbol*] ... CL
Cans or Cartons [*Freight*] ... CC
Cansey, Forbes, Fogarty, Gallagher (SAUO) ... CFFG
Canso Historical Society, Canso, NS, Canada [*Library symbol*] [*Library of Congress*] (LCLS) ... CaNSCaH
Canso Historical Society, Nova Scotia [*Library symbol*] [*National Library of Canada*] (NLC) ... NSCH
Canstar Oil Sands Ltd., Calgary, Alberta [*Library symbol*] [*National Library of Canada*] (NLC) ... ACCOS
Canstar Sports, Inc. [*Toronto Stock Exchange symbol*] ... HKY
Canstat Petroleum Corp. [*Vancouver Stock Exchange symbol*] ... CPT
CanSurmount (EA) ... CS
Cant [*or Canting*] [*Heraldry*] ... CA
Can't Add, Doesn't Even Try [*Computer science*] ... CADET
Can't Be Called [*Telecommunications*] (TEL) ... CBC
Can't Be Heard [*Telecommunications*] (TEL) ... CBH
Can't Break Dial Tone [*Telecommunications*] (TEL) ... CBDT
Can't Call - No Dial Tone [*Telecommunications*] (TEL) ... CC-NDT
Can't Hear [*Telecommunications*] (TEL) ... CH
Can't Manage a Rifle [*Formed by reversing the initials of Royal Army Medical Corps*] [*World War I*] [*British*] ... CMAR
Can't Play and No Chance [*Baseball term*] (NDBD) ... cp and nc
Can't Remember Stuff (ADWA) ... CRS
Can't Say Good-By ... CSG
Can't Tell What [*Accounting slang*] ... CTW
Cantab Pharmaceuticals ADS [*NASDAQ symbol*] (TTSB) ... CNTBY
Cantab Pharmaceuticals Ltd. [*Associated Press*] (SAG) ... Cantab
Cantab Pharmaceuticals Ltd. [*NASDAQ symbol*] (SAG) ... CNTB
Cantabile [*Flowing Style*] [*Music*] ... CANT
Cantabile [*Flowing Style*] [*Music*] ... CANTAB
Cantabrigians or Cantabs-Cambridge University undergraduates (SAUS) ... Tabs
Cantabrigiensis [*Of Cambridge University*] [*Latin*] (ROG) ... CANT
Cantabrigiensis [*Of Cambridge University*] [*Latin*] ... CANTAB
Cantabrigiensis [*Academic degree*] (WDAA) ... Cantab
Cantando [*In a Singing Manner*] [*Music*] (ROG) ... CANTO
Cantate Domino [*Sing Unto the Lord*] [*Music*] ... CAND
Cantchungo [*Guinea-Bissau*] [*ICAO location identifier*] (ICLI) ... GGCG
Canted Fuselage Station (MCD) ... CFS
Canteen (SAUS) ... Can
Canteen for Extreme Climate [*Army*] ... CEC
Canteen Man (SAUS) ... CM
Canteen Van (WDAA) ... CaV
Cantel Industries [*NASDAQ symbol*] (TTSB) ... CNTI
Cantel Industries, Inc. [*Associated Press*] (SAG) ... Cantel
Cantel Industries, Inc. [*NASDAQ symbol*] (SAG) ... CNTL
Canter Background Interference Procedure [*For the Bender Gestalt Test*] [*Psychology*] (DAVI) ... CBIP
Canter Background Interference Procedure for Bender Gestalt [*Test*] [*Psychology*] (DAVI) ... CBIPBG
Canterbury [*Record label*] ... Cant
Canterbury [*City in England*] ... CANT
Canterbury (SAUS) ... Cant
Canterbury [*City and county borough in England*] ... CANTERB
Canterbury and York Society [*British*] (WDAA) ... CYS
Canterbury and York Society (SAUO) ... CYS
Canterbury College Industrial Development Department (SAUO) ... CCIDD
Canterbury Corporate Services [*Associated Press*] (SAG) ... Cantbry
Canterbury Corporate Services [*NASDAQ symbol*] (SAG) ... XCEL
Canterbury Corporate Svcs [*NASDAQ symbol*] (TTSB) ... XCEL
Canterbury Educational Services, Inc. (SAUS) ... SKIL
Canterbury Park Holdings [*Associated Press*] (SAG) ... CantbrPk
Canterbury Park Holdings [*Associated Press*] (SAG) ... CantP
Canterbury Park Holdings [*Associated Press*] (SAG) ... CntPk
Canterbury Park Holdings [*NASDAQ symbol*] (SAG) ... TRAK
Canterbury Pk Hldg Corp. [*NASDAQ symbol*] (TTSB) ... TRAK
Canterbury Pk Hldg Wrrt [*NASDAQ symbol*] (TTSB) ... TRAKW
Canterbury Resources, Inc. [*Vancouver Stock Exchange symbol*] ... CYZ
Canterbury Science Teachers Association (SAUO) ... CSTA
Canterbury, Texas Construction Law Manual (SAUS) ... TCLM
Canterbury University College (SAUO) ... CUC
Canterbury Yeomanry Cavalry [*British military*] (DMA) ... CYC
Canterra Energy Ltd. [*Toronto Stock Exchange symbol*] ... CEN
Canterra Energy Ltd., Calgary, Alberta [*Library symbol*] [*National Library of Canada*] (NLC) ... ACCE
Cantetech, Inc., Winnipeg, MB, Canada [*Library symbol*] [*Library of Congress*] (LCLS) ... CaMWCA
Cantharides [*Spanish Fly*] [*Pharmacy*] (ROG) ... CANTHA
Cantharides [*Spanish Fly*] [*Pharmacy*] (ROG) ... CANTHARD
Cantho [*Viet Nam*] [*ICAO location identifier*] (ICLI) ... VVCT
Canthomeatal Line [*Anatomy*] ... CML
Cantiague Elementary School, Jericho, NY [*Library symbol*] [*Library of Congress*] (LCLS) ... NJerCE
Canticle (WDAA) ... cant
Canticle of Canticles [*Old testament book*] [*Douay version*] ... CANT
Canticles [*Song of Solomon*] [*Old Testament book*] ... Cant
Canticles [*Song of Solomon*] [*Old Testament book*] (BJA) ... Ct
Cantilever ... CANT
Cantilever (MSA) ... CANTIL
Cantilever Bridge (SAUS) ... Cant B
Cantilevered Elevated Causeway [*Army*] ... CANTELCAS
Canto (ROG) ... C
Canto [*Melody*] [*Music*] ... CAN
Canto [*Melody*] [*Music*] ... CANT
Canto Primo [*First Soprano*] [*Music*] ... C1O
Canto Primo [*First Soprano*] [*Music*] (ROG) ... CO 1MO
Canto Primo [*First Soprano*] [*Music*] ... CO1O
Canton [*China*] [*Airport symbol*] (AD) ... CAN
Canton [*Republic of China*] [*Seismograph station code, US Geological Survey*] (SEIS) ... CNT
Canton & Carthage Railroad (IIA) ... C & C

Canton and Carthage Railroad Co. (SAUO) .... C&CA
Canton and Enderbury Islands [*MARC country of publication code*] [*Library of Congress*] (LCCP) .... cp
Canton and Enderbury Islands [*ANSI two-letter standard code*] (CNC) .... CT
Canton and Enderbury Islands [*ANSI three-letter standard code*] (CNC) .... CTE
Canton and Enderbury Islands [*MARC geographic area code*] [*Library of Congress*] (LCCP) .... pocp-
Canton Carnegie Public Library, Canton, SD [*Library symbol*] [*Library of Congress*] (LCLS) .... SdCa
Canton Free Library, Canton, NY [*Library symbol*] [*Library of Congress*] (LCLS) .... NCa
Canton Free Library, Canton, NY [*Library symbol*] [*Library of Congress*] (LCLS) .... NCaL
Canton, GA [*AM radio station call letters*] .... WCHK
Canton, GA [*FM radio station call letters*] .... WGST
Canton, IL [*Location identifier*] [*FAA*] (FAAL) .... CTK
Canton, IL [*FM radio station call letters*] (BROA) .... WBDM-FM
Canton, IL [*AM radio station call letters*] .... WBYS
Canton, IL [*FM radio station call letters*] .... WBYS-FM
Canton Island [*Phoenix Islands*] [*Airport symbol*] (AD) .... CIS
Canton Island [*Phoenix Islands*] [*ICAO location identifier*] (ICLI) .... PCIS
Canton Island Range Communications Control Center [*Military*] (MCD) .... CRCCC
Canton, MO [*FM radio station call letters*] (RBYB) .... KRRY
Canton, MS [*AM radio station call letters*] .... WMGO
Canton, MS [*AM radio station call letters*] .... WONG
Canton, NC [*AM radio station call letters*] .... WPTL
Canton, NC [*AM radio station call letters*] .... WWIT
Canton, NJ [*FM radio station call letters*] (BROA) .... WJKS-FM
Canton, NJ [*FM radio station call letters*] .... WNNN
Canton, NY [*AM radio station call letters*] .... WNYS
Canton, NY [*FM radio station call letters*] .... WSLU
Canton, NY [*FM radio station call letters*] .... WVNC
Canton, NY [*FM radio station call letters*] .... WXQZ
Canton, OH [*AM radio station call letters*] .... WCER
Canton, OH [*Television station call letters*] .... WDLI
Canton, OH [*AM radio station call letters*] .... WHBC
Canton, OH [*FM radio station call letters*] .... WHBC-FM
Canton, OH [*FM radio station call letters*] (BROA) .... WHK-FM
Canton, OH [*AM radio station call letters*] .... WINW
Canton, OH [*Television station call letters*] .... WOAC
Canton, OH [*AM radio station call letters*] .... WRCW
Canton, OH [*FM radio station call letters*] .... WRQK
Canton, OH [*FM radio station call letters*] .... WTOF
Canton, PA [*FM radio station call letters*] .... WHGL
Canton Public Library Association, Canton, OH [*Library symbol*] [*Library of Congress*] (LCLS) .... OCan
Canton Public Library, Canton, MS [*Library symbol*] [*Library of Congress*] (LCLS) .... MsCa
Canton Railroad Co. [*AAR code*] .... CTN
Canton, SD [*FM radio station call letters*] (RBYB) .... KIXK
Canton, SD [*FM radio station call letters*] (BROA) .... KYBB-FM
Cantonese .... CANT
Cantonment .... CNTNMNT
Cantonment, FL [*AM radio station call letters*] .... WNVY
Cantonments [*Military*] (ROG) .... CANTON
Cantor .... CANT
Cantor .... CANTR
Cantoris [*Of the Cantor*] [*Music*] .... CAN
Cantors Assembly (EA) .... CA
Cantors Assembly of America [*Later, CA*] (EA) .... CAA
Cantor's Traumatic Medicine and Surgery for the Attorney [*A publication*] (DLA) .... Cantor Med & Surg
Cantrell and Cochrane [*Initials used as brand name of soft drink*] .... C & C
Cantrell Resources [*Vancouver Stock Exchange symbol*] .... CLJ
Cantuaria [*Canterbury*] [*Latin*] .... CANTUAR
Cantuariensis [*of Canterbury*] [*Latin*] (BARN) .... Cantaur
Cantuariensis [*Of Canterbury*] [*Latin*] (ILCA) .... Cantuar
Cantus [*Record label*] [*Sweden*] .... Cus
Cantus Firmus [*Plain Chant*] [*Music*] .... CF
Cantwell's Cases on Tolls and Customers [*Ireland*] [*A publication*] (DLA) .... Cantwell
Canuck Engineering Ltd., Calgary, AB, Canada [*Library symbol*] [*Library of Congress*] (LCLS) .... CaACCEL
Canuck Engineering Ltd., Calgary, Alberta [*Library symbol*] [*National Library of Canada*] (NLC) .... ACCEL
Canuck Resources Corp. [*Vancouver Stock Exchange symbol*] .... CKC
Canuck Resources, Inc. [*Toronto Stock Exchange symbol*] .... CNC
Canus Laboratories Ltd. [*Vancouver Stock Exchange symbol*] .... CZL
Canusa Financial Corp. [*Vancouver Stock Exchange symbol*] .... CZF
Canutama [*Brazil*] [*Airport symbol*] (AD) .... CUJ
Canute [*King of England, Denmark, and Norway, 994-1035*] (ILCA) .... Can
Canvas (VRA) c
Canvas (DAC) .... Can
Canvas .... CANV
Canvas Awning Institute [*Later, American Canvas Institute*] (EA) .... CAI
Canvas Covers [*Shipping*] (DS) CC
Canvas Products Association International (SAUO) .... CPA
Canvas Products Association International [*Later, IFAI*] (EA) .... CPAI
Canvasback Society (EA) .... CS
Canvas-Covered Wire-Rope Handrail [*Aerospace*] (MSA) .... CCWRH
Canvas-Covered Wire-Rope Handrail [*Aerospace*] (AAG) .... CC WR HDR
CanWest Global Commun [*NYSE symbol*] (SG) .... CWG
Canwest Global Communications Corp. [*Associated Press*] (SAG) .... Canwst
Canwest Global Communications Corp. [*NYSE symbol*] (SAG) .... CWG
Canwest Trustco [*Vancouver Stock Exchange symbol*] .... CWX
Canyon [*Commonly used*] (OPSA) .... CANYN
Canyon [*Commonly used*] (OPSA) .... CANYON
Canyon [*Commonly used*] (OPSA) .... CNYN
Canyon .... CYN
Canyon City, OR [*FM radio station call letters*] (RBYB) .... KJDY-FM
Canyon Country, CA [*AM radio station call letters*] .... KBET
Canyon de Chelly National Monument .... CACH
Canyon de Chelly National Monument (SAUS) .... Canyon de Chelly
Canyon Diablo Troilite [*Geophysics*] .... CDT
Canyon Forest Village .... CFV
Canyon Junction [*Wyoming*] [*Seismograph station code, US Geological Survey*] [*Closed*] (SEIS) .... CJW
Canyon Research Group, Inc., Westlake Village, CA [*Library symbol*] [*Library of Congress*] (LCLS) .... CWlvC
Canyon Resources [*Associated Press*] (SAG) .... CanyonRs
Canyon Resources [*AMEX symbol*] (SAG) .... CAU
Canyon Resources [*NASDAQ symbol*] (TTSB) .... CYNR
Canyon Resources Corp. [*Associated Press*] (SAG) .... Cany
Canyon Resources Corp. [*Associated Press*] (SAG) .... CanyRs
Canyon Resources Corp. [*NASDAQ symbol*] (NQ) .... CYNR
Canyon, TX [*FM radio station call letters*] .... KPUR-FM
Canyon, TX [*FM radio station call letters*] .... KWTS
Canyon, TX [*AM radio station call letters*] (RBYB) .... KZRK
Canyon, TX [*FM radio station call letters*] (RBYB) .... KZRK-FM
Canyon View Group Home, East Wenatchee, WA [*Library symbol*] [*Library of Congress*] (LCLS) .... WaEawC
Canyonlands Field Institute [*An association*] (EA) .... CFI
Canyonlands National Park .... CANY
Canyonlands National Park (SAUS) .... Canyonlands
Canyonlands National Park (SAUS) .... CNP
Caobang [*Viet Nam*] [*ICAO location identifier*] (ICLI) .... VVCB
Cap (SAUS) .... CP
Cap and Gown; a Treasury of College Verse [*A publication*] .... CAG
Cap Haitien [*Haiti*] [*Airport symbol*] (OAG) .... CAP
Cap Haitien Internacional [*Haiti*] [*ICAO location identifier*] (ICLI) .... MTCH
CAP PA Gutierrez [*Hernando R.*] **Ordonez** [*Mexico*] [*ICAO designator*] (FAAC) .... ORD
Cap Rlty Inv TaxExFdL P1 [*AMEX symbol*] (TTSB) .... CRA
Cap Rlty Inv TaxExFdLP II [*AMEX symbol*] (TTSB) .... CRB
Cap Rlty Inv TaxExFdLP III [*AMEX symbol*] (TTSB) .... CRL
Cap Screw (SAUS) .... CAP SCR
Cap Screw and Special Threaded Products Bureau [*Defunct*] (EA) .... CSSTPB
Cap Skirring [*Senegal*] [*Airport symbol*] (OAG) .... CSK
Cap Skirring [*Senegal*] [*ICAO location identifier*] (ICLI) .... GOGS
Capabilities and Procedures .... C & P
Capabilities and Procedures Document (ACAE) .... CAP
Capabilities and Requirements Review (SAUS) .... CRR
Capabilities Assessment Center (SAUO) .... CAC
Capabilities Data (SAA) .... CD
Capabilities Demonstration Satellite (SAUS) .... CDS
Capabilities Engineering Data Report System (MCD) .... CEDRS
Capabilities Exercise [*Army*] .... CAPEX
Capabilities Live Fire Exercise [*Military*] .... CALFEX
Capabilities Master Plan (ACAE) .... CMP
Capability (SAUS) .... CAP
Capability (KSC) .... CAPAB
Capability (SAUS) .... CPBL
Capability and Proficiency Evaluation .... CAPE
Capability Assessment System for Expert Systems (ACAE) .... CASES
Capability Categories (RDA) .... CAPCATS
Capability Data Acknowledgement (SAUS) .... CDA
Capability Design Specifications (AABC) .... CDS
Capability Evaluation Plan .... CEP
Capability Evaluation System (SAUS) .... CAPES
Capability Exercise .... CAPEX
Capability for United States Firms Overseas (SAUO) .... CUSFO
Capability Inspection [*Air Force*] (AFM) CI
Capability Maturity Model .... CMM
Capability Objective Package (MCD) .... COP
Capability Password Level [*Telecommunications*] (TEL) .... CPL
Capability Performance .... CP
Capability Performance, Lower (AAEL) .... CPL
Capability Performance, Upper (SAUS) .... CPU
Capability Release (ACAE) .... CR
Capability Set One (SAUS) CS1
Capability Set Two (SAUS) CS2
Capability Support Plan .... CASP
Capability Upkeep Programme (SAUS) .... CUP
Capable [*or Capability*] (AFM) .... CPBL
Capable of underwater missile launchings (SAUS) .... C-class
Capacitance [*Symbol*] [*IUPAC*] C
Capacitance (IDOE) c
Capacitance (IDOE) .... cap
Capacitance (DEN) .... CAP
Capacitance (SAUS) .... Cb base
Capacitance (SAUS) .... Cp
Capacitance Anode/Grid (SAUS) .... cag
Capacitance as a Function of Voltage (IEEE) .... C(V)
Capacitance Decode Box .... CDB
Capacitance Diaphragm Gauge [*Instrumentation*] .... CDG
Capacitance Discharge Vaporization [*Nuclear energy*] (NRCH) .... CDV
Capacitance Electronic Disc (or Disk) (SAUS) .... CED
Capacitance, External (SAUS) .... CE
Capacitance Factor (SAUS) .... CAPF
Capacitance Grid [*Electronics*] (IAA) .... CG

Capacitance Grid Plate [*Electronics*] (IAA) .... CGP
Capacitance Hole Probe .... CHP
Capacitance of Grid (SAUS) .... CG
Capacitance Plate-Cathode (SAUS) .... CPC
Capacitance, Plate-Filament (SAUS) .... CPF
Capacitance Pressure Transmitter Indicator (SAUS) .... CAPTIN
Capacitance Proximity Sensor (PDAA) .... CPS
Capacitance Resistance Capacitance Resistance Filter (SAUS) .... CRCR Filter
Capacitance Voltage Measurements (MCD) .... CVM
Capacitance-to-Voltage [*Electronics*] (AAEL) CV
Capacitance-Voltage Frequency (SAUS) .... CVF
Capacitation (MELL) C
Capacitative Discharge [*Voltage source*] .... CD
Capacitatively Coupled Microwave Plasma Emission Spectroscopy (MEC) .... CMPES
Capacitatively Coupled Plasma Spectroscopy (MEC) .... CMPS
Capacitive Charge Generation (SAUS) .... CCG
Capacitive Deionization (ADWA) .... CDI
Capacitive Discharge Ignition (SAUS) .... CDI
Capacitive Feedback Transimpedance Amplifier (ADWA) .... CTIA
Capacitive Loss Factor (IEEE) .... CLF
Capacitive Position Sensing Transducer (PDAA) .... CPST
Capacitive Pressure Transducer [*Engineering*] (IAA) .... CPT
Capacitive Reactance Xc
Capacitive Reactance (SAUS) XC
Capacitive Read-Only Memory [*Computer science*] (IEEE) .... CROM
Capacitive Threshold Logic (SAUS) .... CTL
Capacitive Voltage Divider .... CVD
Capacitively Coupled Microwave Plasma .... CMP
Capacitor (CET) C
Capacitor (IAA) .... CA
Capacitor (IDOE) .... cap
Capacitor (MSA) .... CAP
Capacitor and Resistor Technology Symposium (CIST) .... CARTS
Capacitor Bank .... CB
Capacitor Coupled Logic [*Electronics*] (NITA) CCL
Capacitor Diode .... CD
Capacitor Diode FET [*Field Effect Transistor*] **Logic** [*Electronics*] (NITA) .... CDFL
Capacitor Diode Gate .... CDG
Capacitor Diode Voltage Multiplier (ACAE) .... CDVM
Capacitor Discharge [*Automotive engineering*] .... CD
Capacitor Discharge Ignition [*Automotive technology*] .... CDI
Capacitor Discharge Unit (SAUS) .... CDU
Capacitor Flashgun [*Photography*] .... CAPFG
Capacitor Input Filter .... CIF
Capacitor Leakage Indicator CLI
Capacitor Qualification Test .... CQT
Capacitor Rate-Integrating Gyroscope .... CRIG
Capacitor Read-Only Storage [*Computer science*] .... CROS
Capacitor Resonance Frequency .... CRF
Capacitor Start (SAUS) .... CAP ST
Capacitor Start and Run (SAUS) .... CAP ST&R
Capacitor Start and Run (IAA) .... CAPSTAR
Capacitor Store (SAUS) .... CS
Capacitor Test Program .... CTP
Capacitor-Diode Logic (MSA) .... CDL
Capacitor-Resistor (IAA) .... CAPRISTOR
Capacitor-Resistor Diode .... CRD
Capacitors (SAUS) .... CAPS
Capacitor-Start [*Motor*] [*Electricity*] .... CAPST
Capacity [*Electricity*] (DAS) C
Capacity [*Medicine*] c
Capacity (EEVL) .... CA
Capacity (WDAA) .... cap
Capacity (AFM) .... CAP
Capacity (EBF) .... Cap
Capacity [*Insurance; Finance; Transportation*] .... CAPY
Capacity (SAUS) .... Capy
Capacity (FAAC) .... CPTY
Capacity (ADA) .... CY
Capacity (AAG) .... K
Capacity Activated Transducer [*Electronics*] (NITA) .... CAT
Capacity Assurance Plan [*Environmental regulation*] .... CAP
Capacity Bale Space (SAUS) .... Tccbl
Capacity Building for Electronic Communications for Africa (SAUO) .... CABECA
Capacity Change (SAUS) CC
Capacity Coupling CC
Capacity Downchange (SAUS) .... CD
Capacity Engineering Support (ACAE) .... CES
Capacity Exceeding Number (SAUS) .... CEN
Capacity Factor (IAA) .... CAPF
Capacity Factor (IAA) .... CF
Capacity Limiting Constituents (GNE) CLC
Capacity Limiting System (SAUS) .... CLS
Capacity Loading and Schedule System .... CLASS
Capacity Loading and Scheduling System (SAUS) .... CLASS
Capacity Office (SAUO) .... CO
Capacity Planning and Operation Sequencing System (SAUO) .... CAPOSS
Capacity Planning and Operations Sequencing System [*IBM Corp.*] .... CAPOSS
Capacity Planning and Operations Sequencing System - Extended [*IBM Corp.*] .... CAPOSS-E
Capacity Planning System (IAA) .... CPS
Capacity Planning Volume .... CPV
Capacity Record (SAUS) .... CR
Capacity Requirements Planning (MCD) .... CRP
Capacity Selector Valve (MCD) .... CSV
Capacity Ships Force .... CAPSHIPFOR
Capacity Upchange (SAUS) .... CU
Capacity Utilization Bottleneck Efficiency System (AAEL) .... CUBES
Capacity Utilization Factor (SAUS) .... CUF
Capco Automotive Products [*Formerly, Clark Automotive Products*] [*NYSE symbol*] (SAG) .... CAB
Capco Automotive Products [*Formerly, Clark Automotive Products*] [*Associated Press*] (SAG) .... CapcoA
Cape [*Maps and charts*] C
Cape .... CA
Cape [*Commonly used*] (OPSA) .... CAPE
Cape .... CPE
Cape and Orange Free State Native Appeal Court, Selected Decisions (SAUS) .... NAC&O
Cape and Orange Free State Native Appeal Court, Selected Decisions [*A publication*] (DLA) .... NAC & O
Cape Ann Historical Association, Gloucester, MA [*Library symbol*] [*Library of Congress*] (LCLS) .... MGIHi
Cape Arago State Park (SAUS) .... CASP
Cape Ballet [*South Africa*] .... CB
Cape Breton (SAUS) .... CB
Cape Breton Development Corp., Sydney, Nova Scotia [*Library symbol*] [*National Library of Canada*] (NLC) .... NSSCBD
Cape Breton Hospital, Sydney, Nova Scotia [*Library symbol*] [*National Library of Canada*] (NLC) .... NSSCBH
Cape Breton Island .... CB
Cape Breton Island (SAUS) .... CBI
Cape Breton Island [*Nova Scotia*] (BARN) .... CBT
Cape Breton Post, Sydney, Nova Scotia [*Library symbol*] [*National Library of Canada*] (NLC) .... NSSCB
Cape Breton Post, Sydney, NS, Canada [*Library symbol*] [*Library of Congress*] (LCLS) .... CaNSSCB
Cape Breton Regional Library, Sydney, Nova Scotia [*Library symbol*] [*National Library of Canada*] (NLC) .... NSSC
Cape Breton Regional Library, Sydney, NS, Canada [*Library symbol*] [*Library of Congress*] (LCLS) .... CaNSSC
Cape Canaveral (ACAE) CC
Cape Canaveral [*Florida*] (KSC) .... CNV
Cape Canaveral Air Force Station (NASA) .... CCAFS
Cape Canaveral Air Station .... CCAS
Cape Canaveral Auxiliary Air Force Base [*Obsolete*] (AAG) .... CCAAFB
Cape Canaveral, FL [*Location identifier*] [*FAA*] (FAAL) .... XMR
Cape Canaveral Forecast Facility [*NASA*] (NASA) .... CCFF
Cape Canaveral Missile Test Annex [*Later, KSC*] .... CCMTA
Cape Canaveral Missile Test Center [*Later, KSC*] .... CCMTC
Cape Canaveral Public Library, Cape Canaveral, FL [*Library symbol*] [*Library of Congress*] (LCLS) .... FCa
Cape Canaveral Reference Atmosphere [*NASA*] (NASA) .... CCRA
Cape Canaveral Test Annex [*Obsolete*] [*Aerospace*] (AAG) .... CCTA
Cape Central Airways, Inc. [*ICAO designator*] (FAAC) .... SEM
Cape Charles, VA [*Location identifier*] [*FAA*] (FAAL) CCV
Cape Charles, VA [*FM radio station call letters*] (BROA) .... WAZP-FM
Cape Charles, VA [*FM radio station call letters*] .... WROX
Cape Chelyuskin [*Former USSR*] [*Geomagnetic observatory code*] .... CCS
Cape Clear Bird Observatory (SAUS) .... CCBO
Cape Cod CC
Cape Cod Bank & Trust [*Associated Press*] (SAG) .... CCBT
Cape Cod Bank & Trust Co. [*NASDAQ symbol*] (NQ) .... CCBT
Cape Cod Central Railroad CCC
Cape Cod Community College [*West Barnstable, MA*] CCCC
Cape Cod Community College, West Barnstable, MA [*Library symbol*] [*Library of Congress*] (LCLS) .... MWebaC
Cape Cod Direction Center [*Air Force*] .... CCDC
Cape Cod Experiment [*Oceanography*] .... CCE
Cape Cod Museum of Natural History, Brewster, MA [*Library symbol*] [*Library of Congress*] (LCLS) .... MBreC
Cape Cod National Seashore [*National Park Service designation*] .... CACO
Cape Cod National Seashore (SAUS) .... CCNS
Cape Cod System [*Air Force*] .... CCS
Cape Colony [*British Empire*] CC
Cape Colony (SAUO) CC
Cape Colony Court of Appeal Reports (journ.) (SAUS) .... App Cas Buchanan
Cape Colony Cyclist Corps [*British military*] (DMA) CCCC
Cape Colony Supreme Court Reports [*A publication*] (DLA) .... SCR
Cape Colony Supreme Court Reports (SAUS) .... SCR
Cape Communications Control [*NASA*] CCC
Cape Coral (SAUS) .... WAKS
Cape Coral, FL [*Television station call letters*] .... WFTX
Cape Coral, FL [*FM radio station call letters*] .... WXKB
Cape Corps [*British military*] (DMA) CC
Cape Croker Public Library, Wiarton, ON, Canada [*Library symbol*] [*Library of Congress*] (LCLS) .... CaOWCC
Cape Croker Public Library, Wiarton, Ontario [*Library symbol*] [*National Library of Canada*] (NLC) .... OWCC
Cape Decision, AK [*Location identifier*] [*FAA*] (FAAL) .... CDE
Cape Dorset [*Canada*] [*Airport symbol*] (OAG) .... YTE
Cape Dorset, NT [*Canada*] [*ICAO location identifier*] (ICLI) .... CYTE
Cape Douglas [*Alaska*] [*Seismograph station code, US Geological Survey*] (SEIS) .... CDA
Cape Dyer, NT [*ICAO location identifier*] (ICLI) .... CYVN
Cape Eleuthera, Eleuthera Island [*Bahamas*] [*ICAO location identifier*] (ICLI) .... MYEC
Cape Fear Railways, Inc. [*AAR code*] .... CF
Cape Fear Railways, Inc. (SAUO) .... CFR

Cape Fear Technical Institute [*Wilmington, NC*] (ASF) .... CFTI
Cape Fear Technical Institute, Wilmington, NC [*Library symbol*] [*Library of Congress*] (LCLS) .... NcWCF
Cape Fear Valley Hospital, Medical Library, Fayetteville, NC [*Library symbol*] [*Library of Congress*] (LCLS) .... NcFayCFH
Cape Floral Kingdom (SAUS) .... CFK
Cape Garrison Artillery [*British military*] (DMA) .... CGA
Cape Giradeau, MO [*AM radio station call letters*] (RBYB) .... KGIR-AM
Cape Girardeau [*Missouri*] [*Airport symbol*] (OAG) .... CGI
Cape Girardeau [*Missouri*] [*Seismograph station code, US Geological Survey*] (SEIS) .... CGM
Cape Girardeau, MO [*AM radio station call letters*] .... KAPE
Cape Girardeau, MO [*Television station call letters*] .... KBSI
Cape Girardeau, MO [*AM radio station call letters*] .... KCGQ
Cape Girardeau, MO [*FM radio station call letters*] .... KEZS
Cape Girardeau, MO [*Television station call letters*] .... KFVS
Cape Girardeau, MO [*FM radio station call letters*] .... KGMO
Cape Girardeau, MO [*FM radio station call letters*] .... KRCU
Cape Girardeau, MO [*AM radio station call letters*] .... KZIM
Cape Girardeau Public Library, Cape Girardeau, MO [*Library symbol*] [*Library of Congress*] (LCLS) .... MoCg
Cape Gloucester [*Papua New Guinea*] [*Airport symbol*] (OAG) .... CGC
Cape Grim (SAUS) .... CGO
Cape Grim Baseline Air (or Atmospheric) Pollution Station (SAUS) .... CGBAPS
Cape Grim Baseline Air Pollution Station (SAUO) .... CGBAPS
Cape Grim Baseline Atmospheric Pollution Station (SAUO) .... CGBAPS
Cape Grim Photochemical Intensive (SAUO) .... GCPI
Cape Hatteras National Seashore [*National Park Service designation*] .... CAHA
Cape Hatteras National Seashore Recreational Area (SAUS) .... CHNSRA
Cape Henry (GAAI) .... HEN
Cape Horn Current (SAUS) .... C Horn Cur
Cape Kennedy [*NASA*] (KSC) .... CK
Cape Kennedy (SAUO) .... CKN
Cape Kennedy Air Force Station .... CKAFS
Cape Kennedy Forecast Facility [*NASA*] (KSC) .... CKFF
Cape Kennedy Missile Test Annex [*NASA*] (KSC) .... CKMTA
Cape Kennedy Missile Test Area (SAUS) .... CKMTA
Cape Kennedy Missile Test Center (SAUO) .... CKMTC
Cape Kennedy Precipitation Experiment [*Marine science*] (OSRA) .... CAPE
Cape Kennedy Range Safety Officer [*NASA*] (KSC) .... CKRSO
Cape Kennedy Reference Atmosphere [*Later, CCRA*] [*NASA*] (NASA) .... CKRA
Cape Kennedy Reference Atmosphere (SAUS) .... CKRA
Cape Kennedy Space Network, Inc. [*NASA*] .... CKSNI
Cape Kennedy Space Network, Incorporated (SAUO) .... CKSNI
Cape Kumukahi, Hawaii (SAUS) .... KUM
Cape Law Journal [*South Africa*] [*A publication*] (DLA) .... Cape Law J
Cape Law Journal [*South Africa*] [*A publication*] (DLA) .... Cape LJ
Cape Law Journal [*South Africa*] [*A publication*] (DLA) .... CLJ
Cape Law Reports [*South Africa*] [*A publication*] (DLA) .... CLR
Cape Lisburne [*Alaska*] [*Airport symbol*] (OAG) .... LUR
Cape Lisburne Air Force Station [*Alaska*] [*ICAO location identifier*] (ICLI) .... PALU
Cape Lookout National Seashore [*National Park Service designation*] .... CALO
Cape Lookout National Seashore (SAUS) .... CLNS
Cape Lookout State Park (SAUS) .... CLSP
Cape May [*New Jersey*] [*Airport symbol*] (OAG) .... WWD
Cape May County Clerk, Cape May Court House, NJ [*Library symbol*] [*Library of Congress*] (LCLS) .... NjCmCoC
Cape May County Gazette, Cape May Court House, NJ [*Library symbol*] [*Library of Congress*] (LCLS) .... NjCmG
Cape May County Library, Cape May Court House, NJ [*Library symbol*] [*Library of Congress*] (LCLS) .... NjCmCo
Cape May County Times and Seven Mile Beach Reporter, Sea Isle City, NJ [*Library symbol*] [*Library of Congress*] (LCLS) .... NjSicTR
Cape May Court House, NJ [*FM radio station call letters*] .... WBNJ
Cape May Court House, NJ [*FM radio station call letters*] (RBYB) .... WNJZ-FM
Cape May, NJ [*Location identifier*] [*FAA*] (FAAL) .... NMK
Cape May, NJ [*FM radio station call letters*] (BROA) .... WJSX-FM
Cape May, NJ [*FM radio station call letters*] .... WSJL
Cape May, NJ [*FM radio station call letters*] (BROA) .... WWCJ-FM
Cape Medical Staff Corps [*British military*] (DMA) .... CMSC
Cape Monze [*Pakistan*] [*ICAO location identifier*] (ICLI) .... OPKA
Cape Mounted Police (SAUO) .... CMP
Cape Mounted Police [*British*] (ROG) .... CMP
Cape Mounted Rifles [*British*] .... CMR
Cape Mounted Rifles (SAUO) .... CMR
Cape Mounted Rifles, Left Wing [*British*] .... CMRLW
Cape Mounted Rifles, Right Wing [*British*] .... CMRRW
Cape Mounted Yeomanry [*British military*] (DMA) .... CMY
Cape Newenham [*Alaska*] [*Airport symbol*] (OAG) .... EHM
Cape Newenham Air Force Station [*Alaska*] [*ICAO location identifier*] (ICLI) .... PAEH
Cape of Good Hope [*South Africa*] [*Seismograph station code, US Geological Survey*] [*Closed*] (SEIS) .... CGH
Cape of Good Hope [*South Africa*] .... C of GH
Cape Of Good Hope Reports [*South Africa*] [*A publication*] (DLA) .... SC
Cape of Good Hope Reports (SAUS) .... SC
Cape Palmas [*Liberia*] [*Airport symbol*] (OAG) .... CPA
Cape Parry, NT [*ICAO location identifier*] (ICLI) .... CZUE
Cape Peninsula Road Safety Association (SAUO) .... CPRSA
Cape Peninsula Welfare Organisation of the Aged (SAUO) .... CPWOA
Cape Peninsular Rifles [*British military*] (DMA) .... CPR
Cape Perth National Park (SAUS) .... CPNP
Cape Province (SAUO) .... CP
Cape Province [*of South Africa*] .... CP
Cape Provincial Division Reports [*South Africa*] [*A publication*] (DLA) C
Cape Provincial Division Reports [*South Africa*] [*A publication*] (DLA) .... Cape P Div
Cape Provincial Division Reports [*South Africa*] [*A publication*] (DLA) .... CPD
Cape Range National Park (SAUS) .... CRNP
Cape Reinga [*New Zealand*] [*Seismograph station code, US Geological Survey*] (SEIS) .... CRZ
Cape Resources, Inc. [*Vancouver Stock Exchange symbol*] .... CKT
CAPE [*Capability and Proficiency Evaluation*] **Review Period** .... CRP
Cape Roberts Project (SAUS) .... CRP
Cape Rodney [*Papua New Guinea*] [*Airport symbol*] (OAG) .... CPN
Cape Romain National Wildlife Refuge (SAUS) .... CRNWR
Cape Romanzof [*Alaska*] [*Seismograph station code, US Geological Survey*] [*Closed*] (SEIS) .... CPR
Cape Romanzof [*Alaska*] [*Airport symbol*] (OAG) .... CZF
Cape Romanzof Air Force Station [*Alaska*] [*ICAO location identifier*] (ICLI) .... PACZ
Cape Romanzof, AK [*Location identifier*] [*FAA*] (FAAL) .... CZF
Cape Sable (SAUS) .... Sable
Cape Sable Historical Society, Barrington, Nova Scotia [*Library symbol*] [*National Library of Canada*] (NLC) .... NSBCSH
Cape Sable Historical Society, Barrington, NS, Canada [*Library symbol*] [*Library of Congress*] (LCLS) .... CaNSBaCSH
Cape San Juan [*Puerto Rico*] [*Seismograph station code, US Geological Survey*] (SEIS) .... CSJ
Cape Sarichef [*Alaska*] [*Seismograph station code, US Geological Survey*] [*Closed*] (SEIS) .... CSA
Cape Sarichef Air Force Station [*Alaska*] [*ICAO location identifier*] (ICLI) .... PACS
Cape Seppings, AK [*Location identifier*] [*FAA*] (FAAL) .... XCS
Cape Shipunski [*Former USSR*] [*Seismograph station code, US Geological Survey*] (SEIS) .... SPN
Cape Shore Public Library, St. Brides, Newfoundland [*Library symbol*] [*National Library of Canada*] (NLC) .... NFSBCS
Cape Shore Public Library, St. Brides, NF, Canada [*Library symbol*] [*Library of Congress*] (LCLS) .... CaNfSbCS
Cape Skagen or The Skaw (SAUS) .... Skag
Cape Skagen or The Skaw (SAUS) .... Skaw
Cape Smyth Air [*ICAO designator*] (FAAC) .... CMY
Cape Spencer, AK [*Location identifier*] [*FAA*] (FAAL) .... CSP
Cape St. George Public Library, Newfoundland [*Library symbol*] [*National Library of Canada*] (NLC) .... NFCSG
Cape St. Jacques [*South Vietnam*] [*Airport symbol*] (AD) .... CSJ
Cape Support Coordinator [*NASA*] (KSC) .... CSC
Cape Times [*A publication*] (DLA) .... CT
Cape Times Common Law Reports [*South Africa*] [*A publication*] (DLA) .... CTCLR
Cape Times Law Reports, Edited by Shiel [*A publication*] (DLA) .... Shiel
Cape Times Supreme Court Reports, Cape Of Good Hope [*South Africa*] [*A publication*] (DLA) .... Cape TR
Cape Times Supreme Court Reports, Cape Of Good Hope [*South Africa*] [*A publication*] (DLA) .... CTR
Cape Town [*South Africa*] (ROG) .... CAPETN
Cape Town [*South Africa*] [*Airport symbol*] (OAG) .... CPT
Cape Town (SAUO) .... CT
Cape Town [*South Africa*] [*Later, HER*] [*Geomagnetic observatory code*] .... CTO
Cape Town [*South Africa*] [*ICAO location identifier*] (ICLI) .... FACT
Cape Town Cavalry [*British military*] (DMA) .... CTC
Cape Town Computer Services and Bureaux Association (SAUO) .... CT/COSBA
Cape Trafalgar (SAUS) .... Trafalgar
Cape Verde [*ANSI three-letter standard code*] (CNC) .... CPV
Cape Verde [*Islands*] [*MARC country of publication code*] [*Library of Congress*] (LCCP) cv
Cape Verde [*ANSI two-letter standard code*] (CNC) CV
Cape Verde [*Aircraft nationality and registration mark*] (FAAC) D4
Cape Verde [*Islands*] [*MARC geographic area code*] [*Library of Congress*] (LCCP) .... lncv-
Cape Verde Computer Communication Project (SAUO) .... CVCCP
Cape Verde Escudo (ODBW) .... CV Esc
Cape Verde Islands .... C Verd Isls
Cape Verde Islands CVI
Cape Verde Islands [*International civil aircraft marking*] (ODBW) D4
Cape Verde Islands (SAUS) .... Verds
Cape Vincent, NY [*FM radio station call letters*] (BROA) .... WBDR-FM
Cape Vincent, NY [*FM radio station call letters*] .... WKGG
Cape Vincent, NY [*FM radio station call letters*] .... WMHI
Cape Vogel [*Papua New Guinea*] [*Airport symbol*] (OAG) CVL
Cape Volunteer Bearer Corps [*British military*] (DMA) .... CVBC
Cape York Peninsula (GEOI) .... CYP
Cape York Peninsula Land Use Strategy (GEOI) .... CYPLUS
Cape York Peninsula Land Use Study (SAUO) .... CYPLUS
Cape York Space Base (SAUO) .... CYSB
Cape York Space Facility (SAUO) .... CYSF
Cape York Space Port (SAUO) .... CYSP
Cape Young, NT [*ICAO location identifier*] (ICLI) .... CYUI
Capel Court (SAUO) CC
Capel-Cure Myers [*Stockbrokers*] [*British*] .... CCM
Capella [*Chapel*] [*Latin*] (BARN) .... capel
Capella Resources Ltd. [*Vancouver Stock Exchange symbol*] .... CAL
Capetown Performing Arts Board .... CAPAB
CAP-Gemini-Sogeti [*Software manufacturer*] .... CGS
CAPI Connection Service (SAUS) .... CCS
Capiantur [*Let Them Be Taken*] [*Pharmacy*] (ROG) .... CAPIANT
Capias ad Respondendum [*That You Take to Answer*] [*A judicial writ*] [*Latin*] [*Legal term*] (ADA) .... CARE
Capias ad Respondendum [*That You Take to Answer*] [*A judicial writ*] [*Latin*] [*Legal term*] (ROG) .... CA RESP

Capias ad Satisfaciendum [*A writ of execution*] [*Latin*] [*Legal term*] (ROG) ... CA SA
Capiat [*Let the Patient Take*] [*Pharmacy*] ... CAP
Capiat [*Let the Patient Take*] [*Pharmacy*] (ROG) ... CAPT
Capiat [*Let the Patient Take*] [*Pharmacy*] (ROG) ... CPT
Capiat Quantum Vult [*Let the Patient Take as Much as He Will*] [*Pharmacy*] ... CAP QUANT VULT
Capiendus [*To Be Taken*] [*Pharmacy*] ... CAPIEND
Capilano College Media Centre [*UTLAS symbol*] ... CAP
Capilano College, Vancouver, BC, Canada [*Library symbol*] [*Library of Congress*] (LCLS) ... CaBVaC
Capilano College, Vancouver, British Columbia [*Library symbol*] [*National Library of Canada*] (NLC) ... BVAC
Capilano Resources, Inc. [*Vancouver Stock Exchange symbol*] ... CUZ
Capillary (AAMN) ... c
Capillary (MSA) ... CPLRY
Capillary Action Shaping Technique (MCD) ... CAST
Capillary Agglutination (SAUS) ... CA
Capillary Agglutination Test [*Medicine*] (DMAA) ... CAT
Capillary Array Electrophoresis [*Analytical biochemistry*] ... CAE
Capillary Basement Membrane [*Medicine*] (MELL) ... CBM
Capillary Basement Membrane (Thickness) [*Medicine*] (DB) ... CBM(T)
Capillary Bed [*Medicine*] (MELL) ... CB
Capillary Blood [*Medicine*] (DAVI) ... C
Capillary Blood Flow [*Medicine*] (MAE) ... CBF
Capillary Blood Gas [*Biochemistry*] (DAVI) ... CBG
Capillary Blood Gases [*Medicine*] (DAVI) ... CPG
Capillary Blood Glucose [*Biochemistry*] (DAVI) ... CBG
Capillary Blood Volume (DAVI) ... Qc
Capillary Column Gas Chromatography ... CCGC
Capillary Column Usage ... CCU
Capillary Diffusion Capacity [*Medicine*] (DMAA) ... CDC
Capillary Drainage [*Medicine*] (MELL) ... CD
Capillary Electrochromatography [*Computer science*] ... CEC
Capillary Electrophoresis [*Physical chemistry*] ... CE
Capillary Electrophoresis System [*In CES I, manufactured by Dionex Corp.*] [*Analytical biochemistry*] ... CES
Capillary Electrophoresis-Single Cell Biosensor [*Analytical biochemistry*] ... CE-SCB
Capillary Filling Time [*Medicine*] (MELL) ... CFT
Capillary Filtration Coefficient (IEEE) ... CFC
Capillary Fragility Test [*Medicine*] (MELL) ... CFT
Capillary Free Zone [*Medicine*] (DMAA) ... CFZ
Capillary Gas Chromatograph ... CGC
Capillary Gel Electrophoresis ... CGE
Capillary Hemorrhage [*Medicine*] (MELL) ... CH
Capillary Isoelectric Focusing ... CIEF
Capillary Isotachophoresis [*Biochemistry*] ... CITP
Capillary Liquid Chromatography (SAUS) ... CLC
Capillary Lumen [*Medicine*] (MELL) ... CL
Capillary Osmotic Pressure [*Physiology*] ... COP
Capillary Packed Column (DB) ... CPC
Capillary Pressure [*Physiology*] ... CP
Capillary Refill Test [*Medicine*] (MELL) ... CRT
Capillary Suction Times ... CST
Capillary Volume [*Clinical chemistry*] (AAMN) ... VC
Capillary Water Barrier (SAUS) ... CWB
Capillary Whole Blood True Sugar [*Medicine*] (AAMN) ... CWBTS
Capillary Zone Electrophoresis [*Physical chemistry*] ... CZE
Capillary Zone Electrophoresis - Mass Spectrometry [*Analytical chemistry*] ... CZE-MS
Capillary-Driven Heat Transfer (SAUS) ... CHT
Capillary-Like Space [*Medicine*] (MELL) ... CLS
Capistrano [*Hazardous test facility*] ... CAPO
Capistrano Test Site ... CTS
Capita [*Chapters*] [*Latin*] ... CC
Capita Preferred Trust [*Associated Press*] (SAG) ... Capita
Capita Preferred Trust [*NYSE symbol*] (SAG) ... TCC
Capital (WDAA) ... cap
Capital (EY) ... CAP
Capital (EBF) ... Cap
Capital ... Capit
Capital [*Accounting; Finance; Economics*] (ROG) ... CAPL
Capital ... CPTAL
Capital [*Factor of production*] ... K
Capital Account [*Finance*] ... CA
Capital Accumulation [*Business term*] ... CA
Capital Acquisition Deduction [*Business term*] ... CAD
Capital Across America ... CXA
Capital Adequacy, Asset Quality, Management, Earnings, Liquidity [*Formula used by the Federal Deposit Insurance Corp. to evaluate banks*] ... CAMEL
Capital Adequacy Directive [*Chicago Board Options Exchange*] (NUMA) ... CAD
Capital Adequacy Directive [*European Union*] (ECON) ... CAD
Capital Adequacy Ratio ... CAR
Capital Air Service, Inc. [*ICAO designator*] (FAAC) ... CPX
Capital Airlines [*ICAO designator*] (AD) ... BZ
Capital Airlines (SAUS) ... CL
Capital Airlines, Inc. ... CA
Capital Airlines, Inc. [*ICAO designator*] (FAAC) ... CAP
Capital Alliance Income Tr [*AMEX symbol*] (SG) ... CAA
Capital American Financial [*NYSE symbol*] (SPSG) ... CAF
Capital American Financial Co. [*Associated Press*] (SAG) ... CapAm
Capital & Counties [*Property development company*] [*British*] ... C & C
Capital & Counties [*Property development company*] [*British*] ... CAPCO
Capital and Lower Case (WDMC) ... c & lc
Capital and Lower Case (WDMC) ... clc
Capital and Lower Case Letters (SAUS) ... C&LC Letters
Capital and Small Capital Letters (SAUS) ... C&SC Letters
Capital and Small Capitals (WDMC) ... c&sc
Capital Appreciation [*Business term*] ... CA
Capital Appreciation Bond (EBF) ... CAB
Capital Appropriation Request (EBF) ... CAR
Capital Area Library Network ... CALNET
Capital Area, Personnel Service Office (Navy) ... CAPSO-N
Capital Area Regional Library, Raymond, MS [*Library symbol*] [*Library of Congress*] (LCLS) ... MsR
Capital Area Support Center [*Military*] ... CASC
Capital Asset ... CA
Capital Asset Management Process (ABAC) ... CAMP
Capital Asset Pricing Model (EBF) ... CHAPS
Capital Assets Review Board ... CARB
Capital Associates [*NASDAQ symbol*] (TTSB) ... CAII
Capital Associates, Inc. [*NASDAQ symbol*] (NQ) ... CAII
Capital Athletic Conference (PSS) ... CATC
Capital Authorization Request ... CAR
Capital Automotive REIT [*NASDAQ symbol*] (SG) ... CARS
Capital Aviation Services Ltd. [*Canada*] [*ICAO designator*] (FAAC) ... VEN
Capital Bancorp [*NASDAQ symbol*] (SPSG) ... CABK
Capital Bancorp $2 Dep'C'Pfd [*NASDAQ symbol*] (TTSB) ... CABKZ
Capital Bancorp (Florida) [*Associated Press*] (SAG) ... CapBFL
Capital Bancorp (Florida) [*NASDAQ symbol*] (SAG) ... CBCP
Capital Bancorp, Inc. [*Associated Press*] (SAG) ... CapAsc
Capital Bancorp, Inc. [*Associated Press*] (SAG) ... CapBn
Capital Bancorp, Inc. [*Associated Press*] (SAG) ... CapBnc
Capital Brands [*NASDAQ symbol*] (TTSB) ... CAASD
Capital Brands, Inc. [*NASDAQ symbol*] (SAG) ... CAAS
Capital Brands, Inc. [*Associated Press*] (SAG) ... CapBrnd
Capital Builder Account [*Merrill Lynch & Co., Inc.*] [*Finance*] ... CBA
Capital Cities Broadcasting Corp. (SAUO) ... CCB
Capital Cities Communications, Inc. ... CCCI
Capital Cities/ABC, Inc. [*Associated Press*] (SAG) ... CapCities
Capital Cities/ABC, Inc. [*NYSE symbol*] (SPSG) ... CCB
Capital City Bank Grp [*NASDAQ symbol*] (SG) ... CCBG
Capital Collegiate Women's Conference (PSS) ... CCWC
Capital Commitment Request (DNAB) ... CCR
Capital Construction Fund [*FHWA*] (TAG) ... CCF
Capital Consumption Adjustment [*or Allowance*] [*Accounting*] ... CCA
Capital Consumption Allowance (SAUO) ... CCA
Capital Corp. of the West [*Associated Press*] (SAG) ... CapWest
Capital Corp. of the West [*NASDAQ symbol*] (SAG) ... CCOW
Capital Cost Allowance [*Accounting*] ... CCA
Capital Development Fund [*United Nations*] ... CDF
Capital District Library Council for Reference and Research Resources [*Latham, NY*] [*Library network*] ... CDLC
Capital District Library Council, Schenectady, NY [*Library symbol*] [*Library of Congress*] (LCLS) ... NScHLC
Capital District Library Council, Troy, NY [*OCLC symbol*] (OCLC) ... VYD
Capital Dynamics [*Vancouver Stock Exchange symbol*] ... CAP
Capital Equipment (AFIT) ... CE
Capital Equipment Corp. [*Burlington, MA*] ... CEC
Capital Expenditure [*Accounting*] ... CE
Capital Expenditure Price Index ... CEPI
Capital Expenditure Proposal ... CEP
Capital Expenditure Request ... CER
Capital Expenditure Review (DHSM) ... CER
Capital Expenditure Threshold (DMAA) ... CET
Capital Factors Holding, Inc. [*NASDAQ symbol*] (SAG) ... CAPF
Capital Factors Holding, Inc. [*Associated Press*] (SAG) ... CapFact
Capital Federal Financial [*NASDAQ symbol*] (SG) ... CFFN
Capital Formation [*Later, NCCD*] (EA) ... CF
Capital Formation Counselors [*Service mark of Capital Formation Counselors, Inc.*] ... CFC
Capital Gain [*Accounting*] ... CG
Capital Gains Tax ... CGT
Capital Goods [*Finance*] ... CAPG
Capital Goods [*Business term*] ... CG
Capital Guaranteed [*Business term*] ... CG
Capital Guaranty Corp. [*Associated Press*] (SAG) ... CapGty
Capital Guaranty Corp. [*NYSE symbol*] (SPSG) ... CGY
Capital Guaranty Insurance ... CGI
Capital Holding Corporation (SAUO) ... CPH
Capital H-shaped beam (SAUS) ... H-beam
Capital Improved Value (ADA) ... CIV
Capital Improvements Plan (PA) ... CIP
Capital Improvements Program ... CIP
Capital Intensive [*Finance*] ... CI
Capital Investment Analysis [*Business term*] ... CIA
Capital Investment Computer Program [*Economics*] ... CICP
Capital Investment Discard ... CID
Capital Investment Generation Normal (SAUS) ... CIGN
Capital Investment Goal Programming ... CIGP
Capital Investment Model [*Navy*] ... CIM
Capital Investment Plan [*FAA*] (TAG) ... CIP
Capital Investment Program ... CIP
Capital Issues Committee [*British*] (BARN) ... CIC
Capital Legal Foundation (EA) ... CLF
Capital Letter [*Typography*] (WDAA) ... CAP
Capital Library Cooperative, Mason, MI [*OCLC symbol*] (OCLC) ... EEJ
Capital Library Wholesale [*ACCORD*] [*UTLAS symbol*] ... CLW

Capital Library Wholesale, Ottawa, Ontario [*Library symbol*] [*National Library of Canada*] (NLC) ... OOCL
Capital Loss [*Accounting*] ... CL
Capital Maintenance and Rental Funds (DNAB) ... CMRF
Capital Maintenance Fund ... CMF
Capital Market Preferred Stock (EBF) ... CMPS
Capital Market Statistics ... CMS
Capital Marketers Assurance Corporation (TDOB) ... CapMAC
Capital Markets Report [*Dow Jones & Co., Inc.*] [*Information service or system*] (CRD) ... CMR
Capital Media Group Ltd. [*Associated Press*] (SAG) ... CapMdia
Capital Media Group Ltd. [*NASDAQ symbol*] (SAG) ... CPMG
Capital Military Assistance Command (AABC) ... CMAC
Capital Military District [*Vietnam*] ... CMD
Capital Military Region ... CMR
Capital Mortgage Investments (SAUO) ... CMU
Capital Needs Analysis [*Finance*] ... CNA
Capital One Financial [*NYSE symbol*] (TTSB) ... COF
Capital One Financial Corp. [*Associated Press*] (SAG) ... CapOne
Capital One Financial Corp. [*NYSE symbol*] (SAG) ... COF
Capital Pacific Holdings [*Associated Press*] (SAG) ... CapPcHl
Capital Pacific Holdings [*AMEX symbol*] (SAG) ... CPH
Capital PC [*Personal Computer*] **User Group** (EA) ... CPCUG
Capital Planning Information Ltd. [*Information service or system*] (IID) ... CPI
Capital Press Club (EA) ... CPC
Capital Properties [*AMEX symbol*] (SG) ... CPI
Capital Property Accounting and Control (MCD) ... CAPPRO
Capital Punishment Project (EA) ... CPP
Capital Re [*NYSE symbol*] (TTSB) ... KRE
Capital Re Corp. [*Associated Press*] (SAG) ... CapRe
Capital Re Corporation1 [*NYSE symbol*] (SAG) ... KRE
Capital Re LLC'MIPS' [*NYSE symbol*] (TTSB) ... KREPrL
Capital Real Estate [*NYSE symbol*] (SPSG) ... KRE
Capital Realty Investment Tax Exempt Fund Ltd. [*AMEX symbol*] (SPSG) ... CRA
Capital Realty Investment Tax Exempt Fund Ltd. [*AMEX symbol*] (SPSG) ... CRB
Capital Realty Investment Tax Exempt Fund Ltd. [*AMEX symbol*] (SPSG) ... CRL
Capital Realty Investors Tax Exempt Fund Ltd. [*Associated Press*] (SAG) ... CapRI2
Capital Realty Investors Tax Exempt Fund Ltd. [*Associated Press*] (SAG) ... CapRI3
Capital Realty Investors Tax Exempt Ltd. [*Associated Press*] (SAG) ... CapRtyl
Capital Recovery Factor ... CRF
Capital Recovery Schedule ... CRS
Capital Region Centre for the Hearing Impaired [*Centre de la Region de la Capitale pour les Personnes a Deficience Auditive*] (AC) ... CRCHI
Capital Region Library, Public Works Canada [*Bibliotheque de la Region de la Capitale, Travaux Publics Canada*] **Ottawa, Ontario** [*Library symbol*] [*National Library of Canada*] (NLC) ... OOPWC
Capital Research Center ... CRC
Capital ROK [*Republic of Korea*] **Infantry Division** ... CRID
Capital Savings Bancorp [*NASDAQ symbol*] (SAG) ... CAPS
Capital Savings Bancorp [*Associated Press*] (SAG) ... CapSvgs
Capital Secure [*Finance*] ... CS
Capital Senior Living [*NYSE symbol*] (SG) ... CSU
Capital Ship [*Bomb*] ... CS
Capital Southwest [*NASDAQ symbol*] (TTSB) ... CSWC
Capital Southwest Corp. [*Associated Press*] (SAG) ... CapSw
Capital Southwest Corp. [*NASDAQ symbol*] (NQ) ... CSWC
Capital Speakers Club (EA) ... CSC
Capital Special Zone [*Saigon, Vietnam*] (VNW) ... CSZ
Capital Stock ... CS
Capital Stock Model [*Congressional Budget Office*] (GFGA) ... CSM
Capital Stock Tax Ruling, Internal Revenue Bureau [*United States*] [*A publication*] (DLA) ... CST
Capital Systems Group (SAUO) ... CSG
Capital Systems Group, Inc. [*Information service or system*] (IID) ... CSG
Capital Trading Aviation Ltd. [*British*] [*ICAO designator*] (FAAC) ... EGL
Capital Transfer Tax [*British*] ... CTT
Capital Trust 'A' [*NYSE symbol*] (SG) ... CT
Capital Type Rehabilitation Facility (MCD) ... CTR
Capital University (GAGS) ... Capital U
Capital University (SAUO) ... CU
Capital University, Columbus, OH [*OCLC symbol*] (OCLC) ... CAU
Capital University, Columbus, OH [*Library symbol*] [*Library of Congress*] (LCLS) ... OCoC
Capital University, Columbus, OH [*Library symbol*] [*Library of Congress*] (LCLS) ... OCoCU
Capital University, Law Library, Columbus, OH [*OCLC symbol*] (OCLC) ... CAV
Capital University, School of Law, Columbus, OH [*Library symbol*] [*Library of Congress*] (LCLS) ... OCoC-L
Capital Utilization Criteria (SAUS) ... CUCRIT
Capital Work Order (NRCH) ... CWO
Capital-Asset Pricing Model ... CAPM
Capital/Asset Quality/Management/Earnings/Liquidity Regulatory Ratings (EBF) ... CAMEL
Capital-D-shaped ring (SAUS) ... D-ring
Capital-G-shaped string (SAUS) ... G-string
Capital-H-shaped bar (SAUS) ... H-bar
Capital-H-shaped hinge (SAUS) ... H-hinge
Capitalisation ... cap
Capital-I-shaped metal beam (SAUS) ... I-beam
Capitalization [*Real estate*] ... CAP
Capitalization (EBF) ... Cap
Capital-J-shaped bolt (SAUS) ... J-bolt
Capitals [*Printing*] ... C
Capitals [*Printing*] ... CAPS
Capitals and Lower Case [*Printing*] ... C & LC
Capitals and Lower Case (SAUS) ... C&LC
Capitals and Small Capitals [*Printing*] ... C & SC
Capitals, Cassette Programming System (SAUS) ... CAPS
Capital-U-shaped bolt (SAUS) ... U-bolt
Capitated Primary Care Network (STED) ... CPCN
Capitation ... CAP
Capitation ... Cap
Capiteq Ltd., Trading as Air North Regional [*Australia*] [*FAA designator*] (FAAC) ... ANO
Capitol ... CAP
Capitol [*Record label*] ... Cap
Capitol ... CPTOL
Capitol [*Record label*] [*Great Britain*] ... DCap
Capitol Air Express [*ICAO designator*] (FAAC) ... CEX
Capitol Air Lines ... CAL
Capitol Air Service [*ICAO designator*] (AD) ... RX
Capitol American Financial Cp. [*NYSE symbol*] (SAG) ... CAF
Capitol American Financial Cp. [*Associated Press*] (SAG) ... CapAm
Capitol American Finl [*NYSE symbol*] (TTSB) ... CAF
Capitol Area Health Consortium Libraries [*Library network*] ... CAHCL
Capitol Area Library Consortium, Inc. [*Library network*] ... CALCO
Capitol Area Motion Pictures Education Organization [*Washington, DC*] ... CAMEO
Capitol Bancorp Ltd. [*Associated Press*] (SAG) ... CaptlBc
Capitol Bancorp Ltd. [*NASDAQ symbol*] (NQ) ... CBCL
Capitol Consortium Network [*of CUMWA*] [*Information service or system*] ... CAPCON
Capitol Consortium Network, Washington, DC [*OCLC symbol*] (OCLC) ... TPU
Capitol Consortium Network, Washington, DC [*OCLC symbol*] (OCLC) ... TPV
Capitol Emergency Response Plan (DEMM) ... CERP
Capitol Federal Financial [*NASDAQ symbol*] ... CFFN
Capitol Hill Burro Club (EA) ... CHBC
Capitol Hill Restoration Society (EA) ... CHRS
Capitol Hill Women's Political Caucus (EA) ... CHWPC
Capitol Historical Society [*Washington, DC*] ... CHS
Capitol Information Association (EA) ... CIA
Capitol International Airways (MCD) ... CAP
Capitol International Airways [*Air carrier designation symbol*] ... CAPX
Capitol International Airways [*ICAO designator*] (AD) ... CL
Capitol Line-Up [*A publication*] (EAAP) ... CLU
Capitol Multimedia [*NASDAQ symbol*] (TTSB) ... CDIM
Capitol MultiMedia, Inc. [*Associated Press*] (SAG) ... CapMl
Capitol MultiMedia, Inc. [*Associated Press*] (SAG) ... CapMult
Capitol MultiMedia, Inc. [*NASDAQ symbol*] (SAG) ... CDIM
Capitol Multimedia Wrrt 'A' [*NASDAQ symbol*] (TTSB) ... CDIMW
Capitol Peak [*Washington*] [*Seismograph station code, US Geological Survey*] (SEIS) ... CPW
Capitol Publications, Inc. [*Information service or system*] (IID) ... CPI
Capitol Publishing Group [*Information service or system*] (IID) ... CPG
Capitol Radio Engineering Institute [*Now known only by initialism*] ... CREI
Capitol Reef National Monument ... CARE
Capitol Reef National Monument (SAUS) ... CRNM
Capitol Region Library Council [*Library network*] ... CRLC
Capitol Services, Inc. [*Database producer*] [*Information service or system*] (IID) ... CSI
Capitol Transamerica [*Associated Press*] (SAG) ... CapTrns
Capitol Transamerica [*NASDAQ symbol*] (TTSB) ... CATA
Capitol Transamerica Corp. [*NASDAQ symbol*] (NQ) ... CATA
Capitol Wireless, Inc. [*Telecommunications service*] (TSSD) ... CAPWIRE
Capitola, CA [*AM radio station call letters*] (RBYB) ... KMBY
Capitol-Cetra [*Record label*] ... CCet
Capitolo [*Chapter*] [*Italian*] (ILCA) ... Cap
Capitular Degrees [*Freemasonry*] (ROG) ... CAP D
Capitular Masonry [*Freemasonry*] (ROG) ... CM
Capitulo [*Chapter*] [*Latin*] (ROG) ... CALO
Capitulum [*Chapter*] [*Latin*] (ROG) ... C
Capitulum [*Chapter*] [*Latin*] ... CAP
CapMAC Holdings [*Associated Press*] (SAG) ... CapMAC
CapMAC Holdings [*NYSE symbol*] (SAG) ... KAP
Capo [*The Beginning*] [*Music*] ... C
Capo Bellavista [*Italy*] [*ICAO location identifier*] (ICLI) ... LIEB
Capo Caccia [*Italy*] [*ICAO location identifier*] (ICLI) ... LIEH
Capo Carbonara [*Italy*] [*ICAO location identifier*] (ICLI) ... LIEC
Capo Frasca [*Italy*] [*ICAO location identifier*] (ICLI) ... LIEF
Capo Mele [*Italy*] [*ICAO location identifier*] (ICLI) ... LIMU
Capo Palinuro [*Italy*] [*ICAO location identifier*] (ICLI) ... LIQK
Capo S. Lorenzo [*Italy*] [*ICAO location identifier*] (ICLI) ... LIEL
Capo Spartivento [*Italy*] [*ICAO location identifier*] (ICLI) ... LICH
Capodimonte [*Italy*] [*Seismograph station code, US Geological Survey*] [*Closed*] (SEIS) ... CAP
Capoverso [*Paragraph*] [*Italian*] (ILCA) ... Capv
Cappadocian (BJA) ... Capp
Capped (MSA) ... CPPD
Capped Argon Bubbling [*Steelmaking*] ... CAB
Capper Military Occupational Specialty [*Army*] (AABC) ... CMOS
CAPPETRO, Inc. (SAUO) ... CAPPETRO
Capreol Public Library, Ontario [*Library symbol*] [*National Library of Canada*] (NLC) ... OCAP
Capreomycin [*An antibiotic*] (MAE) ... CM
Capri [*Italy*] [*Geomagnetic observatory code*] ... CPI
Capri [*Italy*] [*ICAO location identifier*] (ICLI) ... LIQC
Capri [*Italy*] [*Airport symbol*] (AD) ... PRJ
Capri Class Association (EA) ... CCA

Capri Resources Ltd. [*Vancouver Stock Exchange symbol*] ..... CPI
Capricorn (NTIO) ..... CAP
Capricorn Conservation Council [*Australia*] CCC
Capricorn Resources Ltd. [*Vancouver Stock Exchange symbol*] ..... CAX
Capricornia Wildlife Welfare Association [*Australia*] ..... CWWA
Capricornus [*Constellation*] ..... Cap
Capricornus [*Constellation*] ..... Capr
Caprine Arthritis Encephalitis Virus [*Veterinary medicine*] ..... CAEV
Caprine Arthritis-Encephalitis [*Veterinary medicine*] ..... CAE
Caprine Placental Lactogen [*Medicine*] (DMAA) ..... CPL
Caprock Energy Ltd. [*Vancouver Stock Exchange symbol*] ..... CYG
Caps and Small Caps (IIA) ..... C & SC
Capsaicin-Related Drug (MELL) ..... CRD
Capscrew [*Technical drawings*] ..... CAPSCR
Capsid-Targeted Viral Inactivation [*Immunlogy*] ..... CTVI
Capsill Roller Beam (SAUS) ..... CRB
Capstan ..... CPSN
Capstan Tracking Logic (SAUS) ..... CTL
Capstar Hotel Co. [*Associated Press*] (SAG) ..... Capstar
Capstar Hotel Co. [*NYSE symbol*] (SAG) ..... CHO
Capstead Mortgage [*NYSE symbol*] (SPSG) ..... CMO
Capstead Mortgage Corp. [*Associated Press*] (SAG) ..... CapM
Capstead Mortgage Corp. [*Associated Press*] (SAG) ..... Capstd
Capstead Mtge $1.26 cm Cv Pfd [*NYSE symbol*] (TTSB) ..... CMOPrB
Capstead Mtge $1.60cm Cv Pfd [*NYSE symbol*] (TTSB) ..... CMOPrA
Capstone Capital Trust, Inc. [*Associated Press*] (SAG) ..... CapsCT
Capstone Capital Trust, Inc. [*Associated Press*] (SAG) ..... CapstCT
Capstone Capital Trust, Inc. [*NYSE symbol*] (SAG) ..... CCT
Capstone: Govt. Income Fund [*Mutual fund ticker symbol*] (SG) ..... CGVIX
Capstone: Growth Fund [*Mutual fund ticker symbol*] (SG) ..... TRDFX
Capstone: Japan Fund [*Mutual fund ticker symbol*] (SG) ..... CNJFX
Capstone Material Fielding Plan [*Army*] ..... CMFP
Capstone Pharmacy Services, Inc. [*Associated Press*] (SAG) ..... CapsPh
Capstone Pharmacy Services, Inc. [*Associated Press*] (SAG) ..... CapsPhm
Capstone Pharmacy Services, Inc. [*NASDAQ symbol*] (SAG) ..... DOSE
Capstone Pharmacy Svc [*NASDAQ symbol*] (TTSB) ..... DOSE
Capstone Pharmacy Svcs Wrrt [*NASDAQ symbol*] (TTSB) ..... DOSEW
Capstone Turbine [*NASDAQ symbol*] ..... CPST
Capsula [*Capsule*] [*Pharmacy*] ..... CAP
Capsula [*Capsule*] [*Pharmacy*] ..... CAPS
Capsula [*Capsule*] [*Pharmacy*] (DAVI) ..... capsul
Capsula Amylacea [*A Cachet*] [*Pharmacy*] ..... CAPS AMYLAC
Capsula Gelatina [*A Gelatine Capsule*] [*Pharmacy*] ..... CAPS GELAT
Capsula Mollis [*Soft Capsule*] [*Pharmacy*] ..... CAP MOLL
Capsular Antigen [*Immunology*] (MAE) ..... K
Capsular Polysaccharide [*Biochemistry*] ..... CPS
Capsular Polysaccharide Complex [*Biochemistry*] ..... CPC
Capsulated Torpedo (ACAE) ..... CAPTOR
Capsule [*Medicine*] (MELL) ..... CAP
Capsule (NTIO) ..... Caps
Capsule ..... CAPS
Capsule (MSA) ..... CPSL
Capsule Ariane Technologique (ACAE) ..... CAT
Capsule Assembly Machine (MCD) ..... CAM
Capsule Bus (ACAE) ..... CB
Capsule Cartilage Articular Preservation [*Orthopedics*] (DAVI) ..... CCAP
Capsule Communications [*or Communicator*] [*NASA*] ..... CAPCOM
Capsule Communications [*or Communicator*] [*NASA*] CC
Capsule Communications [*or Communicator*] [*NASA*] (IAA) ..... CPCOM
Capsule Communicator (SAUS) CC
Capsule Control [*NASA*] (KSC) ..... CAPCON
Capsule Drive Core [*Aerospace*] ..... CDC
Capsule Elapsed Time [*Aerospace*] ..... CET
Capsule End Cover [*Aerospace*] ..... CEC
Capsule Escape and Survival Applied Research [*Aerospace*] ..... CESAR
Capsule, Extended Release (SAUS) ..... CER
Capsule Integrated Test Equipment [*Aerospace*] ..... CITE
Capsule Internal Programmer [*Aerospace*] ..... CIP
Capsule Launch System (SAUS) ..... CLS
Capsule Mechanical Training Model [*Aerospace*] (MCD) ..... CMTM
Capsule Observation Panel [*Aerospace*] ..... COP
Capsule Positioning Mechanism [*Aerospace*] ..... CPM
Capsule Separation [*Aerospace*] (AAG) ..... CAPSEP
Capsule Systems Advanced Development [*Aerospace*] (MCD) ..... CSAD
Capsule Systems Test [*NASA*] ..... CST
Capsule Technology Group, Inc. [*Toronto Stock Exchange symbol*] ..... TKG
Capsule Technology International Ltd. ..... CTIL
Capsule Test Conductor [*NASA*] (KSC) ..... CTC
Capsule Test Unit [*Aerospace*] ..... CTU
Capsule-Orbiting Bus Link [*NASA*] ..... COL
Capsule/Tablet (NTIO) ..... caplet
Capsule/Tablet [*Medicine*] ..... Caplet
Capsure Holdings [*Associated Press*] (SAG) ..... Capsure
Capsure Holdings [*NYSE symbol*] (SPSG) ..... CSH
Captain [*Worn on captain's uniform*] [*Hockey*] C
Captain ..... CAP
Captain (ROG) ..... CAPN
Captain (AAG) ..... CAPT
Captain (SAUO) ..... Capt
Captain (WDAA) ..... Capt
Captain (NTIO) ..... Cpt
Captain [*Military*] ..... CPT
Captain [*Air Force, Army, Marine Corps*] O3
Captain [*Navy*] O6
Captain, Coastal Forces [*Navy*] [*British*] ..... CCF
Captain, Coastal Forces, Eastern Theater [*Navy*] ..... CCFET
Captain Consolidated Resources [*Vancouver Stock Exchange symbol*] ..... CTC
Captain Cook [*Hawaii*] [*Seismograph station code, US Geological Survey*] (SEIS) ..... CPH
Captain Cook Study Unit [*American Topical Association*] (EA) ..... CCSU
Captain Engineer (SAUS) ..... CE
Captain [*Commanding*] **Escort Forces** [*Navy*] ..... CEF
Captain Fishery Protection (SAUS) ..... CFP
Captain, Fishery Protection Squadron [*NATO*] ..... CFPS
Captain Fleet Maintenance (SAUS) ..... CFM
Captain in Charge (SAUS) ..... CAPIC
Captain James Smith Memorial Foundation (EA) ..... CJSMF
Captain John Curtis Memorial Library, Brunswick, ME [*Library symbol*] [*Library of Congress*] (LCLS) ..... MeBC
Captain (Naval) ..... Capt (N)
Captain, Naval Drafting (SAUS) ..... CND
Captain, Naval Operations Command Systems [*British military*] (DMA) ..... CNOCS
Captain of Gun [*British military*] (DMA) ..... CG
Captain of Horse [*British*] ..... CH
Captain of Royal Marines [*Military*] [*British*] ..... RMC
Captain of Subsistence (SAUO) ..... CS
Captain of the Dockyard [*Obsolete*] [*British*] ..... CD
Captain of the Fleet [*Navy*] [*British*] ..... COF
Captain of the Guard [*Freemasonry*] ..... CG
Captain of the Gun (SAUS) ..... CG
Captain of the Host [*Freemasonry*] (ROG) ..... CH
Captain of the Parish [*British*] (ROG) ..... CP
Captain of the Port (SAUS) ..... C of P
Captain of the Port [*Coast Guard*] ..... COTP
Captain of the Port (SAUS) ..... CP
Captain of the Yeoman of the Guard [*British*] (ROG) ..... CYG
Captain Professional Military Education [*Army*] ..... CPT-PME
Captain, Signal School (SAUS) ..... CSS
Captain, Submarines (SAUS) ..... Capt SM
Captain Superintendent (SAUS) ..... CS
Captain, Surface Weapons Acceptance [*British military*] (DMA) ..... CSWA
Captain Theodore C. Freeman Memorial Library, Houston, TX [*Library symbol*] [*Library of Congress*] (LCLS) ..... TxHF
Captain-General [*British military*] (DMA) ..... Capt-Gen
Captain-General ..... CG
Captain-General and President (ROG) ..... CGP
Captain-General of the Religious and Military Order of the Temple for Scotland [*Freemasonry*] (ROG) ..... CGR & MOT for S
Captain-Instructor [*Navy*] [*British*] CI
Captain's Imperfect Entry [*Shipping*] ..... CIE
Captains Option (SAUS) ..... C/O
Captec Net Lease Realty [*NASDAQ symbol*] (SG) ..... CRRR
Caption (SAUS) ..... Capt
Caption (ADA) ..... CAPT
Caption Code (DNAB) CC
Caption Sheet [*Television*] [*Publishing*] (WDMC) ..... cap sheet
Captioned Media Program ..... CMP
Captital Computer Suites Ltd. (SAUS) ..... CCS
Captive Adjustable Must-Use System (SAUS) ..... Camus
Captive Air Bubble (DB) ..... CAB
Captive Air Spacecraft (MCD) ..... CASC
Captive Airborne Training Missile (DOMA) ..... CATM
Captive Animals Protection Society [*British*] (DI) ..... CAPS
Captive Boresight Harmonization Kit (MCD) ..... CBHK
Captive Carrier Test [*Military*] ..... CCT
Captive European Nations (NATG) ..... CEN
Captive Firing Test Set [*Aerospace*] (AAG) ..... CFTS
Captive Flight (MUGU) ..... C/FLT
Captive Flight Acceptance Test (ACAE) ..... CFAT
Captive Flight Demonstration (ACAE) ..... CFD
Captive Flight Model [*Military*] (CAAL) ..... CFM
Captive Flight Test Missiles (MCD) ..... CFTM
Captive Flight Trainer (SAUS) ..... CFP
Captive Flight Trainer ..... CFT
Captive Flight Unit (ACAE) ..... CFU
Captive Installation Function [*Telecommunications*] (TEL) ..... CIF
Captive Insurance Companies Association (EA) ..... CICA
Captive Line Parts (ACAE) ..... CLP
Captive Management Plan (SAUO) ..... CMP
Captive Nations Committee (EA) ..... CNC
Captive Nations' Council of New South Wales [*Australia*] ..... CNCNSW
Captive Pod Trainer (ACAE) ..... CPT
Captive Power Plant ..... CPP
Captive Reset Ignitor (NASA) ..... CAPRI
Captive Rest Ignitor (SAUS) ..... CAPRI
Captive Simulation (NASA) ..... CAPSIM
Captive Spot Curve Follower (SAUS) ..... CSCF
Captive Test ..... CT
Captive Test Unit (MCD) ..... CTU
Captive Test Vehicle ..... CTV
Captive Trainer ..... CT
Captive Training Missile (ACAE) ..... CTM
Captive Trajectory System [*Air Force*] ..... CTS
Captivi [*of Plautus*] [*Classical studies*] (OCD) ..... Capt
Captopril [*Also, CPT*] [*Antihypertensive drug*] ..... CP
Captopril [*Antihypertensive drug*] ..... CPT
Captopril Prevention Project [*Study*] [*Medicine*] (DMAA) ..... CAPP
Capture ..... CAP
Capture (AABC) ..... CPTR
Capture Orbit Vehicle Assembly Mode ..... COVAM

Capture Range (SAUS) .... CR
Capture the Flag (ADWA) .... CTF
Capture/Compare [Electronics] [Automotive engineering] .... CAPCOM
Captured (GEAB) .... capt
Captured Air Bubble (MCD) .... CAB
Captured Air Bubble Boat [Navy] .... CABB
Captured Air Bubble Over Water Vehicle [Military] (IAA) .... CABOWV
Captured Documents (SAUS) .... CAP DOC
Captured Enemy Documents [Military] (AFM) .... CED
Captured Enemy Documents Organization (NATG) .... CEDO
Captured Enemy Equipment [Military] (AFM) .... CEE
Captured Enemy Equipment Depot (SAUO) .... CEED
Captured Enemy Material (SAUS) .... cem
Captured Enemy Material [Military] .... CEM
Captured Enemy Signal Equipment [Military] (MCD) .... CESE
Captured Gamma Ray .... CGR
Captured in Action [Military] .... CIA
Captured Steam Bubble Nuclear .... CSBN
Capture-Mark-Recapture [Demography] .... CMR
Capuchin Franciscan Friary .... CFF
Capuchin Franciscans of the Renewal (SAUO) .... CFR
[The] Capuchin Friars (TOCD) .... OFMCap
[The] Capuchin Friars, Franciscan Fathers (TOCD) .... ofmcap
Capuchin Poor Clares (TOCD) .... CPC
Capuchin Poor Clares (TOCD) .... OSCCap
Capuchin Sisters (Spain) (TOCD) .... CDP
Capuchin Theological Seminary, Garrison, NY [Library symbol] [Library of Congress] (LCLS) .... NGaC
Capuchin-Franciscans (Province of St. Joseph) (EA) .... CFPSJ
Capulin Mountain National Monument [National Park Service designation] (SAUS) .... CAMO
Capulin Mountain National Monument (SAUS) .... CMNM
Caput [Head] [Latin] C
Caput [Head] [Latin] .... CAP
Caquetania [Colombia] [Airport symbol] (OAG) .... CQT
Caquiaviri [Bolivia] [ICAO location identifier] (ICLI) .... SLHY
Car (SAUS) C
Car Accountant .... CA
Car and Motorcycle Drivers Association Ltd. [British] (BI) .... CAMDA
Car and Truck Renting and Leasing Association (EA) .... CATRALA
Car Area Network (SAUO) .... CAN
Car Assembly .... CA
Car Audio Specialists Association (EA) .... CASA
Car battery (SAUS) .... Lead-acid battery
Car Business Corporation (SAUO) .... CBC
Car Care Council (EA) CCC
Car Carrier (SAUS) .... Car C
Car Craft [A publication] CC
Car Deck .... CD
Car Department Officers Association (EA) .... CDOA
Car Ferry (SAUS) .... CF
Car Float [Non-self-propelled] [Navy symbol] .... YCF
Car Handling Automation for Fail-Safe European Roadway .... CHAUFFEUR
Car Information and Navigation (SAUS) .... CARIN
Car Information and Navigation System [Compact disc technology] .... CARIN
Car Load (SAUS) CL
Car Nicobar [India] [ICAO location identifier] (ICLI) .... VECX
Car of the Year .... COTY
Car of the Year .... COY
Car Park (ADA) .... CP
Car Park (SAUO) .... CP
Car Post (SAUO) .... CP
Car Pricing .... CP
Car Return (ECII) .... CR
Car Service [Railroads] .... CS
Car Service Department .... CSD
Car Service Order .... CSO
Car Service Section [Railroads] .... CSS
Car Signal Processor (SAUS) .... CSP
Car Wars (SAUS) .... CW
Car Wash Owners and Suppliers Association (EA) .... COSA
Cara [Dear One] [Latin] .... K
Cara Loudtop Altitude Radiometer (SAUS) .... CAR
Cara Operations Ltd. [Toronto Stock Exchange symbol] .... CAO
Caracas [Venezuela] [Seismograph station code, US Geological Survey] (SEIS) .... CAR
Caracas [Venezuela] [Airport symbol] (OAG) .... CCS
Caracas Ciudad Distrito Federal [Venezuela] [ICAO location identifier] (ICLI) .... SVCC
Caracas Maiquetia Distrito Federal [Venezuela] [ICAO location identifier] (ICLI) .... SVCA
Caracas/Generelisimo Francisco De Miranda Base Aerea La Carlota, Miranda [Venezuela] [ICAO location identifier] (ICLI) .... SVFM
Caracas/Internacional del Centro Miranda [Venezuela] [ICAO location identifier] (ICLI) .... SVCS
Caracas/Metropolitano Internacional, Miranda [Venezuela] [ICAO location identifier] (ICLI) .... SVMP
Caracas/Simon Bolivar Internacional Maiquetia Distrito Federal [Venezuela] [ICAO location identifier] (ICLI) .... SVMI
Caraco Pharm Labs [NASDAQ symbol] (TTSB) .... CARA
Caraco Pharm Labs Wrrt [NASDAQ symbol] (TTSB) .... CARAW
Caraco Pharmaceutical Labs [NASDAQ symbol] (SAG) .... CARA
Caraco Pharmaceutical Labs [Associated Press] (SAG) .... Caraco
Caraffa Di Catanzaro [Italy] [ICAO location identifier] (ICLI) .... LIBK
Caramoan National Park (SAUS) .... CNP

Caranavi [Bolivia] [ICAO location identifier] (ICLI) .... SLVI
Caransebes/Caransebes [Romania] [ICAO location identifier] (ICLI) .... LRCS
Carapace Length [Pisciculture] CL
Carapace Width .... CW
Caraquet, NB [AM radio station call letters] .... CJVA
Carat [Unit of measure for precious stones or gold] C
Carat [Unit of measure for precious stones or gold] .... CAR
Carat (NTIO) .... Ct
Carat [Unit of measure for precious stones or gold] .... CT
Carat [Unit of measure for precious stones or gold] .... K
Carat Assembled Logical Loader (IAA) .... CALL
Carat, Clarity, Colour and Cut (SAUS) CCCC
Carat, Metric .... CM
Caratage, Color, Clarity, and Shape [Factors in determining the value of a diamond] .... CCCS
Carate [Costa Rica] [ICAO location identifier] (ICLI) .... MRCE
Carats (SAUS) .... CTS
Carauari [Brazil] [Airport symbol] (AD) .... CAF
Carauari [Brazil] [ICAO location identifier] (ICLI) .... SBUI
Caraustar Industries [NASDAQ symbol] (TTSB) .... CSAR
Caraustar Industries, Inc. [Associated Press] (SAG) .... Caraustr
Carauster Industries, Inc. [NASDAQ symbol] (SAG) .... CSAR
Caravan (SAUS) .... Van
Caravan America-China [Defunct] (EA) .... CAC
Caravan and Camping Industry Association of New South Wales [Australia] .... CCIANSW
Caravan and Camping Industry Association of South Australia [Australia] .... CCIASA
Caravan House [An association] (EA) .... CH
Caravan Mission to Village Children (SAUO) .... CMVC
Caravan of East and West (EA) .... CEW
Caravan Sites Act [Town planning] [British] .... CSA
Caravan Trade and Industries Association of Queensland [Australia] .... CTIAQ
Caravans International (SAUO) CI
Caravela [Guinea-Bissau] [ICAO location identifier] (ICLI) .... GGCV
Caravelas [Brazil] [Airport symbol] (AD) .... CRV
Caravelas [Brazil] [ICAO location identifier] (ICLI) .... SBCV
Caraveli [Peru] [Seismograph station code, US Geological Survey] [Closed] (SEIS) .... CRV
Caraveli [Peru] [ICAO location identifier] (ICLI) .... SPVL
Caravelle jet airplane (SAUS) CVL
Caraz [Peru] [ICAO location identifier] (ICLI) .... SPAA
Carbachol [Cholinergic] .... CCh
Carbamazepine [Also, CBZ] [An analgesic] .... CARB
Carbamazepine [Pharmacology] (DAVI) .... CARBAM
Carbamazepine [Also, CARB] [An analgesic] .... CBZ
Carbamazepine-Epoxide [An analgesic] .... CBZ-E
Carbaminohemoglobin [Medicine] (MELL) .... CAH
Carbamoylcyclopropene [Organic chemistry] .... CCP
Carbamoyldihydropyridine [Organic chemistry] .... CDHP
Carbamyl Phosphate [Also, CP] [Organic chemistry] .... CAP
Carbamyl Phosphate [Also, CAP] [Organic chemistry] .... CP
Carbamyl Phosphate Synthetase (PDAA) .... CPSase
Carbamylcholine [Organic chemistry] CC
Carbamylmethyl [Biochemistry] .... Cam
Carbamyl-Phosphate Synthetase [An enzyme] .... CPS
Carbazilquinone [Antineoplastic drug] .... CQ
Carbazopropionyl - Phosphatidyl Ethanolamine [Organic chemistry] .... CPA-PE
Carben Energy, Inc. [Vancouver Stock Exchange symbol] .... CBZ
Carbenicillin [Bactericide] .... CB
Carbenicillin [Bactericide] .... CBC
Carbenicillin [Medicine] (DMAA) .... CBCN
Carberry/North Cypress Library, Carberry, Manitoba [Library symbol] [National Library of Canada] (NLC) .... MCNC
Carbibbean Labour Congress (SAUO) CLC
Carbide .... CARB
Carbide (MSA) .... CBD
Carbide .... cbd
Carbide Diamond Abrasive (IAA) .... CDA
Carbide-Forming Element [Metal treating] .... CFE
Carbide/Graphite Group [NASDAQ symbol] (TTSB) .... CGGI
[The] Carbide/Graphite Group, Inc. [Associated Press] (SAG) .... CarGrpt
[The] Carbide/Graphite Group, Inc. [NASDAQ symbol] (SAG) .... CGGI
Carbimazole [Pharmacology] (DAVI) .... CGI
Carbine (AABC) .... CBN
Carbine (ADWA) .... cbn
Carbinol Reduction Potential [Chemistry] .... CRP
Carbo Ceramics [NASDAQ symbol] (TTSB) .... CRBO
Carbo Ceramics [NYSE symbol] .... CRR
Carbo Ceramics, Inc. [Associated Press] (SAG) .... CarboCe
Carbo Ceramics, Inc. [NASDAQ symbol] (SAG) .... CRBO
Carbobenzoxide (SAUS) .... CB
Carbobenzoxy [Also, CBZ] [Organic chemistry] .... Cb
Carbobenzoxy (DB) .... Cbo
Carbobenzoxy [Also, Cb] [Organic chemistry] .... CBZ
Carbobenzoxy (SAUS) .... Cbz
Carbobenzoxychloride [Organic chemistry] (DAVI) .... CBz
Carbobenzoxy-L-Arginine Amidehydrolase (DB) .... CAAH
Carbodiimide [Organic chemistry] .... CDI
Carbodiimide Residue [As substituent on nucleoside] [Biochemistry] .... cms
Carbohydrate [Dietetics] C
Carbohydrate [Dietetics] .... Car
Carbohydrate [Dietetics] .... CARB
Carbohydrate [Dietetics] .... CARBO
Carbohydrate (ADWA) .... carbo

Carbohydrate (SAUS) ... Carbo
Carbohydrate [*Organic chemistry*] ... CHO
Carbohydrate ... COH
Carbohydrate Addict's Diet ... CAD
Carbohydrate Antigen [*A tumor marker*] (CDI) ... CA
Carbohydrate Antigen 125 [*Immunology*] (DAVI) ... CA 125
Carbohydrate Craver [*Nutrition*] ... CC
Carbohydrate Deficient Glycoprotein Syndrome [*Medicine*] ... CDGS
Carbohydrate Deficient Transferrin (SAUS) ... CDT
Carbohydrate Information online resources guide (SAUS) ... CARBHYD
Carbohydrate Metabolism Index [*Biochemistry*] ... CMI
Carbohydrate Recognition Domain [*Biochemistry*] ... CRD
Carbohydrate Research Institute [*Queen's University at Kingston*] [*Canada*] [*Research center*] (RCD) ... CRI
Carbohydrate Utilization Test [*Medicine*] (MELL) ... CUT
Carbohydrate Vitamin Nitrogen (SAUS) ... CVN
Carbohydrate-Binding Protein [*Biochemistry*] (DB) ... CBP
Carbohydrate-Craving Obesity [*Medicine*] ... CCO
Carbohydrate-Induced Hyperglyceridemia [*Medicine*] ... CIH
Carbol Fuchsine (SAUS) ... CF
Carbolfuchsin [*A dye*] ... CF
Carbolic Methylene Blue [*Clinical chemistry*] ... CMB
Carboline Carboxylic Acid Ester [*Medicine*] (DMAA) ... CCE
Carbon [*Chemical element*] ... C
Carbon ... CARB
Carbon (SAUS) ... Graphite
Carbon 13 Nuclear Magnetic Resonance [*Informations system Karls rube*] (NITA) ... C13-NMR
Carbon 14 (SAUS) ... Carb 14
Carbon Absorber (EEVL) ... CA
Carbon Absorption Bio-oxidation System (PDAA) ... CABOS
Carbon Absorption (or Adsorption) Unit (SAUS) ... CAU
Carbon Absorption Unit (GFGA) ... CAU
Carbon Adsorber Tube (PDAA) ... CAT
Carbon Adsorption/Absorption [*for vapor recovery*] ... CAA
Carbon and Nitrogen Cycling in Forest Ecosystems (SAUS) ... CANIF
Carbon and Quartz/Phenolic ... CQ/P
Carbon Arc Brazing ... CAB
Carbon Arc Cutting [*Welding*] ... CAC
Carbon Arc Welding ... CAW
Carbon Bed (EEVL) ... CB
Carbon Black (AAEL) ... CB
Carbon Black Export (EA) ... CBE
Carbon Black Feedstock ... CBFS
Carbon Black Producers Traffic Committee ... CBPTC
Carbon Bond [*Chemistry*] ... CB
Carbon Bond Mechanism - Version 4 [*Air pollution*] ... CB4
Carbon Circuit Breaker (SAUS) ... CCB
Carbon Compensation Depth ... CCD
Carbon Content of Dead Biomass (SAUS) ... CCDB
Carbon Content of Living Biomass (SAUS) ... CCLB
Carbon Copies (or Copy) (SAUS) ... CC
Carbon Copy (WDAA) ... cc
Carbon Copy for Windows [*Symantec Corp.*] (PCM) ... CCW
Carbon Country Railway Company (SAUO) ... CBC
Carbon County Railway Co. [*AAR code*] ... CBC
Carbon cycle in certain plant species (SAUS) ... C3
Carbon cycle in certain plant species (SAUS) ... C4
Carbon Cycle Model Linkage Project (SAUS) ... CCMLP
Carbon Design Partnership ... CDP
Carbon Dioxide (SAUS) ... CO
Carbon Dioxide (NAKS) ... CO2
Carbon Dioxide Concentrating [*or Concentrator*] **Module** ... CDCM
Carbon Dioxide Economizer ... CDE
Carbon Dioxide Equivalent [*Environmental science*] ... CDE
Carbon Dioxide Exchange Rate [*Plant biochemistry*] ... CER
Carbon Dioxide Information and Analysis Center [*Department of Energy*] [*Information service or system*] (IID) ... CDIAC
Carbon Dioxide Information Center [*Department of Energy*] [*Oak Ridge, TN*] [*Database*] ... CDIC
Carbon Dioxide Intercalibration Experiment (QUAC) ... CARBICE
Carbon Dioxide Laser (SAUS) ... CDL
Carbon Dioxide LASER Beam (MCD) ... CDLB
Carbon Dioxide LASER Rangefinder [*Army*] ... CO2 LRF
Carbon Dioxide LASER Therapy [*Medicine*] (MELL) ... CDLT
Carbon Dioxide Membrane Lung [*Medicine*] (MELL) ... CDML
Carbon Dioxide Observational Platform System [*NASA*] ... CO-OPS
Carbon Dioxide Production [*Medicine*] (DAVI) ... VCO_2
Carbon Dioxide Reduction [*Factor for metabolism*] ... CDR
Carbon Dioxide Reduction Subsystem (NASA) ... CRS
Carbon Dioxide Research Division [*Oak Ridge National Laboratory*] ... CDRD
Carbon Dioxide Research Program (SAUO) ... CDRP
Carbon Dioxide System [*of a ship*] (DS) ... CAR DI SYS
Carbon Dioxide Tension [*in blood gases*] (DAVI) ... PCO_2
Carbon Dioxide Therapy ... CDT
Carbon Electrode Equipment ... CEE
Carbon Emissions Trajectory Assessment (SAUO) ... CETA
Carbon Equilibrium Loop ... CEL
Carbon Equivalent [*Chemical engineering*] ... CE
Carbon Equivalent Value (PDAA) ... CEV
Carbon Exchange between Vegetation, Soil, and the Atmosphere [*Biology*] ... CEVSA
Carbon Fiber ... CF
Carbon Fiber Reinforced (ACAE) ... CFR
Carbon Fiber Reinforced Composite ... CFC
Carbon Fiber Reinforced Plastic ... CFRP
Carbon Fiber Reinforced Thermoplastic [*Plastics technology*] ... CFRTP
Carbon Fiber-Reinforced Glass (PDAA) ... CFRG
Carbon Fiber-Reinforced Glass-Ceramic (PDAA) ... CFRGC
Carbon Fiber-Reinforced Polymer (PDAA) ... CFRP
Carbon Film ... CF
Carbon Filtered ... CF
Carbon Fraction (CARB) ... CF
Carbon Fraction of Above Ground Biomass (CARB) ... CFAGB
Carbon Fraction of Fuel (SAUS) ... CFF
Carbon from Dissolved Carbonates ... CDC
Carbon Furnace ... CF
Carbon Glass (SAUS) ... CG
Carbon Glass Resistance Thermometer (ACAE) ... CGRT
Carbon, Hydrogen, Nitrogen ... CHN
Carbon Hydrogen Nitrogen Analyzer (SAUS) ... CHN Analyzer
Carbon, Hydrogen, Nitrogen, Oxygen, Phosphorus and Sulfur (SAUS) ... C-H-N
Carbon, Hydrogen, Nitrogen, Oxygen, Phosphorus, and Sulfur [*Compounds*] ... CHNOPS
Carbon Hydrogen Oxidant experiment (SAUS) ... CHOX
Carbon, Hydrogen, Oxygen, Nitrogen [*Composition of interstellar dust*] ... CHON
Carbon Magnetic Resonance [*Also, CNMR*] ... CMR
Carbon Micro-Fiber [*Materials science*] ... CMF
Carbon Molecular Sieve [*Adsorption technology*] ... CMS
Carbon Molybdenum Steel (MSA) ... CMOS
Carbon Monofluoride [*Inorganic chemistry*] ... CMF
Carbon Monoxide ... CO
Carbon Monoxide [*Endogenous production*] [*Medicine*] (DAVI) ... V_{co}
Carbon monoxide Carbon trace gas emission (SAUS) ... CO-C
Carbon Monoxide Concentration ... COC
Carbon Monoxide Dehydrogenase [*An enzyme*] ... CODH
Carbon Monoxide Emission Index [*Automotive engineering*] ... COEI
Carbon Monoxide Hemoglobin [*Medicine*] (MELL) ... HbCO
Carbon Monoxide LASER (MED) ... CO laser
Carbon Monoxide Mass [*Automotive engineering*] ... COM
Carbon Monoxide Measuring System ... CMMS
Carbon Monoxide Poisoning (MELL) ... CMP
Carbon Monoxide Pollution Experiment [*NASA/General Electric*] ... COPE
Carbon Monoxide Tension (DAVI) ... P_{co}
Carbon Municipal Library, Alberta [*Library symbol*] [*National Library of Canada*] (NLC) ... ACARM
Carbon Municipal Library, Carbon, AB, Canada [*Library symbol*] [*Library of Congress*] (LCLS) ... CaACarM
Carbon Nitrogen Phosphorus Ratio (EEVL) ... CNP ratio
Carbon Nitrogen Ratio (EEVL) ... CN ratio
Carbon, Oxygen, Nitrogen, Phosphorus, and Sulphur (QUAC) ... CONPS
Carbon, Oxygen, Nitrogen, Phosphorus and Sulphur (SAUS) ... CONPSC
Carbon Oxysulfide (LDT) ... COS
Carbon Paper and Inked Ribbon Association [*Defunct*] (EA) ... CPIRA
Carbon Paper Feed (SAUS) ... CPF
Carbon Paste ... CP
Carbon Paste Electrode [*Electrochemistry*] ... CPE
Carbon Preference Index [*Organic geochemistry*] ... CPI
Carbon Released from Dead biomass (SAUS) ... CRD
Carbon Released from Living Biomass (CARB) ... CRL
Carbon Ribbon Attachment (SAUS) ... CRA
Carbon Rod Atomizer [*Spectroscopy*] ... CRA
Carbon, Rust, and Undesirable Dirt [*Facetious interpretation of what collects on objects left unprotected*] [*Automotive engineering*] ... CRUD
Carbon Shell System ... CSS
Carbon Source Response Element [*Genetics*] ... CSRE
Carbon Star [*Astronomy*] (BARN) ... N
Carbon Stars [*Astronomy*] (BARN) ... R
Carbon Steel ... CS
Carbon Stored (CARB) ... CS
Carbon Tetrachloride (GNE) ... CCL_4
Carbon Tetrachloride [*Also, CTC*] [*Organic chemistry*] ... CT
Carbon Tetrachloride [*Also, CT*] [*Organic chemistry*] ... CTC
Carbon Tetrachloride Intoxication (MELL) ... CTI
Carbon Tetrachloride Poisoning [*Medicine*] (MELL) ... CTCP
Carbon to Nitrogen Ratio ... C/N
Carbon to Oxygen [*Ratio*] ... C/O
Carbon Usage Rate [*Environmental Protection Agency*] ... CUR
Carbon Vacuum Deoxidized ... CVD
Carbon Zinc Battery ... CZB
Carbon-13 Nuclear Magnetic Resonance [*Also, CMR*] ... CNMR
Carbon-13 Nuclear Magnetic Resonance Search System [*Netherlands Information Combine*] [*Database*] ... CNMR
Carbonaceous (SAUS) ... Carb
Carbonaceous Biochemical Oxygen Demand [*Environmental chemistry*] ... CBOD
Carbonaceous Biological Oxygen Demand 5 (COE) ... CBOD-5
Carbonaceous Chondrite ... CC
Carbonaceous Chondrite Fission [*Geophysics*] ... CCF
Carbonaceous Chondrite Fission Xenon [*Geophysics*] ... CCFXe
Carbonaceous Chondrite Reference Standard [*Geophysics*] ... CCRS
Carbonaceous Mass Fraction (QUAC) ... CMF
Carbonacious Species Methods Comparison Study (SAUS) ... CSMCS
Carbonatanhydrase (SAUS) ... CAH
Carbonate (SAUS) ... Carb
Carbonate ... CARB
Carbonate (GNE) ... CO_3
Carbonate (MSA) ... CRBNT
Carbonate Accumulation [*Archeology*] ... ca
Carbonate Alkalinity (SAUS) ... CALK
Carbonate Analysis (SAUS) ... BOMB

Carbonate Compensation Depth [*Oceanography*] .... CCD
Carbonate Compensation Level [*Oceanography*] CCL
Carbonate Crust [*Archeology*] CC
Carbonate Dehydratase [*An enzyme*] (MAE) .... CD
Carbonate Hydroxy Fluorapatite [*Inorganic chemistry*] .... CHFA
Carbonate Nodule [*Archeology*] .... cn
Carbonate of Flake [*Archeology*] .... cf
Carbonate Platform [*Archaeology*] .... CP
Carbonated .... CARB
Carbonated .... CRBNATD
Carbonated Beverage (SAUS) .... Pop
Carbonated Beverage Can Makers Committee [*Division of CBCMA*]
   (EA) .... CBCMC
Carbonated Beverage Container Manufacturers Association [*Later, CMI*]
   (EA) .... CBCMA
Carbonated Beverage Institute (EA) .... CBI
Carbonated Soft Drink (SAUS) .... CSD
Carbon-Bonded Carbon Fiber .... CBCF
Carbon-Carbon (SAUS) .... C-C
Carbon-Carbon Bond (MELL) .... CCB
Carbon-Carbon Data Base [*Battelle Columbus Laboratories*] [*Database*] ...... CCDB
Carbon-Chloroform Extract (PDAA) .... CCE
Carbon-Cobalt-tungsten Alloy (SAUS) .... Carboloy
Carbondale [*Illinois*] [*Airport symbol*] (OAG) .... MDH
Carbondale, CO [*Location identifier*] [*FAA*] (FAAL) .... CQL
Carbondale, CO [*FM radio station call letters*] .... KDNK
Carbondale, IL [*AM radio station call letters*] .... WCIL
Carbondale, IL [*FM radio station call letters*] .... WCIL-FM
Carbondale, IL [*FM radio station call letters*] (RBYB) .... WDBX-FM
Carbondale, IL [*FM radio station call letters*] .... WSIU
Carbondale, IL [*Television station call letters*] .... WSIU-TV
Carbondale Middle School, Carbondale, CO [*Library symbol*] [*Library of Congress*] (LCLS) .... CoCaCM
Carbondale Mining Technology Center [*Department of Energy*] (GRD) .... CMTC
Carbondale, PA [*AM radio station call letters*] .... WCDL
Carbondale, PA [*FM radio station call letters*] (BROA) .... WCTP-FM
Carbondale, PA [*FM radio station call letters*] .... WSGD
Carbondale/Murphysboro, IL [*Location identifier*] [*FAA*] (FAAL) .... MDH
Carbonear General Hospital, Carbonear, NF, Canada [*Library symbol*] [*Library of Congress*] (LCLS) .... CaNfCGH
Carbonear General Hospital, Newfoundland [*Library symbol*] [*National Library of Canada*] (NLC) .... NFCGH
Carbonear, NF [*AM radio station call letters*] .... CHVO
Carbonear Public Library, Carbonear, NF, Canada [*Library symbol*] [*Library of Congress*] (LCLS) .... CaNfC
Carbonear Public Library, Newfoundland [*Library symbol*] [*National Library of Canada*] (NLC) .... NFC
Carbon-Enhanced Vapor Etching (SAUS) .... CEVE
Carbon-Equivalent, Liquid (SAUS) .... CEL
Carbon-Equivalent, Liquidus (OA) .... CEL
Carbon-Equivalent-Difference (PDAA) .... CED
Carboneum (SAUS) C
Carbon-Fibre Electrode .... CFE
Carbon-Film Resistor .... CFR
Carbon-Free Medium [*Cytology*] .... CFM
Carbon-Hydrogen Bond (MELL) .... CHB
Carbonic Anhydrase [*An enzyme*] .... CA
Carbonic Anhydrase II [*Analytical chemistry*] .... CAII
Carbonic Anhydrase Inhibitor [*Medicine*] (MELL) .... CAI
Carbonic Dichloride [*Phosgene*] [*Poison gas*] [*Army symbol*] .... CG
Carboniferous (SAUS) .... Carbonif
Carbon-in-Column [*Gold ore processing*] CIC
Carbon-in-Leach [*Gold ore processing*] CIL
Carbon-in-Pulp [*Gold ore processing*] .... CIP
Carbonite Trachloride (SAUS) .... CTC
Carbonless Copying Paper (IAA) .... CCP
Carbon-Nitrogen-Oxide (SAUS) .... CNO
Carbon-Nitrogen-Oxygen [*Galactic molecular formation cycle*] .... CNO
Carbon-Nitrogen-Sulfur Analyzer (SAUS) .... CNS
Carbon/Phenolic .... C/P
Carbonprint (VRA) .... CBPT
Carbon-Reactive Protein [*Biochemistry*] (DB) .... CRP
Carbonyl Cyanide m-ChloroPhenylhydrazone (SAUS) .... CCCP
Carbonyl Iron Powder (ACAE) .... CIP
Carbonyl Sulphide (PDAA) .... COS
Carbonyl Value [*Food science*] CV
Carbonylcyanide p-Trifluoromethoxyphenylhydrazone (SAUS) .... FCCP
Carbonylcyanide-meta-chlorophenylhydrazone [*Also, CCP*] [*Organic chemistry*] .... CCCP
Carbonylcyanide-meta-chlorophenylhydrazone [*Also, CCCP*] [*Organic chemistry*] .... CCP
Carbonyldiimidazole [*Organic chemistry*] .... CDI
Carboplatin [*Antineoplastic drug*] (CDI) .... CBDCA
Carboplatin, Doxorubicin, Cytoxan [*Antineoplastic drug*] (CDI) .... CDC
Carboquone (DB) .... CQ
Carborondum (VRA) .... carbor
Carborundum Co., Niagara Falls, NY [*Library symbol*] [*Library of Congress*] (LCLS) .... NNiaCa
Carborundum Company (SAUO) .... CBO
Carboxamidomethyl [*Organic chemistry*] .... CAM
(Carboxamidophenyl)dimethyltriazene [*Biochemistry*] .... CADT
Carboxy Nitrose Rubber (SAUS) .... CNR
Carboxy Nitroso Rubber [*Organic chemistry*] .... CNR
Carboxy Terminal Fragment [*Genetics*] .... CTF
Carboxy Terminated Polyisobutylene (SAUS) .... CTPIB

Carboxy Terminus of Propressophysin [*Laboratory*] (DAVI) .... CPP
Carboxyamidoimidazole [*Organic chemistry*] .... CAI
Carboxyarabitol Bisphosphate [*Biochemistry*] .... CABP
(Carboxybenzoyl)quinolinecarboxaldehyde [*Organic chemistry*] .... CBQCA
Carboxyethyl Acrylate (EDCT) .... CEA
Carboxyfluorescein [*Fluorophore*] .... CF
Carboxyfluorescein Diacetate [*Organic chemistry*] .... CFDA
Carboxyhemoglobin (DB) .... COHb
Carboxyhemoglobin [*Biochemistry*] .... COHB
Carboxyhemoglobin [*Biochemistry*] (AAMN) .... COHgB
Carboxyhemoglobin [*Medicine*] (MELL) .... HbCO
Carboxyhemoglobin A [*Biochemistry*] .... COHbA
Carboxyl Group (SAUS) .... COOH
Carboxyl Terminal (DMAA) .... Ct
Carboxyl Terminated Polybutadiene (SAUS) .... CTPB
Carboxylated Nitrile-Butadiene Rubber (SAUS) .... XNBR
Carboxylated Styrene Butadiene Rubber (SAUS) .... XSBR
Carboxylation Efficiency [*Botany*] .... CE
Carboxyl-Ester Lipase (DMAA) .... CEL
Carboxylesterase [*An enzyme*] .... CE
Carboxylic Acid Reductase [*An enzyme*] .... CAR
Carboxyl-Terminal Domain [*Genetics*] .... CTD
Carboxyl-Terminated Butadiene-Acrylonitrile [*Organic chemistry*] .... CTBN
Carboxyl-Terminated Polybutadiene Binder [*Organic chemistry*] .... CTPB
Carboxyl-Terminated Polyester Propellant (MCD) .... CTPE
Carboxymethyl [*Also, Cm, Cme*] [*Biochemistry*] .... CM
Carboxymethyl [*Also, CM, Cm*] [*Biochemistry*] .... Cme
Carboxymethyl Cyclodextrin [*University of Arizona, Tucson*] .... CMCD
Carboxymethyl Hydroxyethyl Cellulose [*Organic chemistry*] .... CMHEC
Carboxymethyl Oxysuccinate (EDCT) .... CMOS
Carboxymethyl Starch [*Organic chemistry*] .... CMS
Carboxymethylated [*Cotton*] (EDCT) .... CM
Carboxymethylcellulose [*Organic chemistry*] .... CMC
[*Sodium*] Carboxymethylcellulose (BARN) .... CMC-CT
Carboxymethylcellulose (DMAA) .... COMC
carboxymethylcellulose sodium (SAUS) .... cmc
Carboxymethylcysteine [*Biochemistry*] .... CMC
Carboxymethyldextran [*Organic chemistry*] .... CMD
Carboxymuconate Lactonizing Enzyme (SAUS) .... CMLE
Carboxymuconolactone Decarboxylase [*An enzyme*] .... CMD
Carboxymyoglobin [*Biochemistry*] .... COMb
Carboxypeptidase A [*An enzyme*] .... CPA
Carboxypeptidase B [*An enzyme*] .... CPB
Carboxypeptidase E [*An enzyme*] .... CPE
Carboxypeptidase Inhibitor [*in potatoes*] .... CPI
Carboxypeptidase Y [*An enzyme*] .... CPY
(Carboxyphenyl)benzoyl-Aminopenicillanic Acid [*Biochemistry*] .... CBAP
Carboxypolymethylene [*Organic chemistry*] .... CARBOPOL
Carboxypyridine Disulfide [*Biochemistry*] .... CPDS
Carboxyribitol Bisphosphate [*Biochemistry*] .... CRBP
Carboy (MCD) .... CB
Carboy .... CBY
Carburetor (MSA) .... CARB
Carburetor .... CARBTR
Carburetor Air Temperature [*Aviation*] .... CAT
Carburetor Bowl Vent [*Automotive engineering*] .... CBV
Carburetor Deceleration Combustion Controlled Valve [*Automotive engineering*] .... CDCCV
Carburize (SAUS) .... CARB
Carburized, Quenched, and Tempered [*Steel heat treatment*] (IIA) .... CQT
Carcano Rifle .... CARC
Carcass Weight [*Animal husbandry*] .... CW
Carcassonne [*France*] [*Airport symbol*] (OAG) .... CCF
Carcassonne/Salvaza [*France*] [*ICAO location identifier*] (ICLI) .... LFMK
Carcino Embryonales Antigen (SAUS) .... KEA
Carcino-Breaking Factor (DB) .... CBF
Carcinoembryonic Antigen [*Immunochemistry*] .... CEA
Carcinoembryonic Antigen-Like [*Protein*] [*Medicine*] (DMAA) .... CEAL
Carcinogen Assessment Group [*Environmental Protection Agency*] .... CAG
Carcinogen Bioassay in Small Rodents .... CBSR
Carcinogen Information Program (EA) .... CIP
Carcinogen Risk Assessment Verification Endeavor (EEVL) .... CRAVE
Carcinogen Risk Assessment Verification Exercise [*Environmental science*] (COE) .... CRAVE
Carcinogen System (SAUS) .... CARS
Carcinogenesis; a Comprehensive Survey (SAUS) .... Carcinog Compr Surv
Carcinogenesis Bioassay Data System [*National Cancer Institute*] (IID) .... CBDS
Carcinogenic Activity Indicator (FFDE) .... CAI
Carcinogenic Assessment Group (SAUO) .... CAG
Carcinogenic Index CI
Carcinogenic Potency Database [*Toxicology*] .... CPOB
Carcinogenic Potency Factor (SAUS) .... CPE
Carcinogenic Potency Factor (FFDE) .... CPF
Carcinoid Syndrome [*Oncology*] (DAVI) .... CS
Carcinoid-Like Syndrome [*Medicine*] (MELL) .... CLS
Carcinom (SAUS) .... Ca
Carcinoma (SAUS) .... CA
Carcinoma (ADWA) .... ca
Carcinoma Cell Line [*Cytology*] CCL
Carcinoma In Situ [*Oncology*] .... CIS
Carcinoma in Situ of Cervix [*Medicine*] (MELL) .... CISC
Carcinoma in Situ of Vagina [*Medicine*] (MELL) .... CISV
Carcinoma of Undetermined Primary [*A cancer condition*] (CDI) .... CUP
Carcinoma-Bearing Animal (AAMN) .... CBA
Carcinomatous Meningitis [*Oncology*] .... CM

Carcinomatous Neuromyopathy [Medicine] (MELL)	CNM
Card [Manuscript descriptions]	C
Card (VRA)	cd
Card (MSA)	CD
Card (SAUS)	Cd
Card [Amateur radio shorthand] (WDAA)	CRD
Card Adapter Register (SAUS)	CAR
Card Agglutination Trypanosomiasis Test [Clinical chemistry]	CATT
Card Alert [Database terminology] (NITA)	CA
Card Alignment (SAUS)	CA
Card and Light Gun Input (SAA)	CLI
Card and Printer Remote Interface	CAPRI
Card Application (SAUS)	CA
Card Assembler (SAUS)	CA
Card Assembly Plant (SAUS)	CAP
Card Assembly Program (SAUS)	CAP
Card Automated Reproduction and Distribution (SAUS)	CARD
Card Automated Reproduction and Distribution System (ECII)	CARD
Card Automatic Code System [IBM Corp.] (IEEE)	CARDCODER
Card Batch (SAUS)	CB
Card Board Description Tape (SAUS)	CBDT
Card Box (SAUS)	CB
Card Buffer Register (SAUS)	CBR
Card Buffer Store (SAUS)	CBS
Card Capacitive (or Capacitor) Read-Only Storage (SAUS)	CCROS
Card Capacitor Read-Only Storage [Computer science] (IEEE)	CCROS
Card Capacity Read Only Storage (SAUS)	CCROS
Card Capacity Store (SAUS)	CCS
Card Channel (SAUS)	CC
Card Channel Ready (SAUS)	CD-CHRDY
Card Clothing Manufacturers Association [Defunct] (EA)	CCMA
Card Code	CC
Card Collating (SAUS)	CC
Card Collator (SAUS)	CC
Card Column	CC
Card Computer Interface [Computer science] (IID)	CCI
Card Controlled Accounting Machine (SAUS)	CCAM
Card Controlled Billing Machine (SAUS)	CCBM
Card Controlled Calculator (SAUS)	CCC
Card Controlled Invoicing Machine (SAUS)	CCIM
Card Controlled Tape Punch (SAUS)	CCTP
Card Cornering Station (SAUS)	CCS
Card Count [Computer science]	CC
Card Count (SAUS)	CDCT
Card Counter (SAUS)	CC
Card Counting Attachment (SAUS)	CCA
Card Counting Sorter (SAUS)	CCS
Card Counting Unit (SAUS)	CCU
Card Deck (IAA)	CD
Card Design Center (SAUS)	CDC
Card Development Design Daily Status (SAUS)	CDDDS
Card Distribution	CD
Card Distribution Service [Library of Congress]	CDS
Card Document Machine (SAUS)	CDM
Card Duplication (SAUS)	CD
Card Edge Low Profile [Computer science] (IGQR)	CELP
Card Ejection (SAUS)	CE
Card Error [Computer science] (IAA)	CE
Card Extract Counter (SAUS)	CEC
Card Face (SAUS)	CF
Card Feed [Computer science] (IAA)	CF
Card Feed Barrier Strip (SAUS)	CFBS
Card Feed Circuit Breaker (SAUS)	CFCB
Card Feed Compare (SAUS)	CFC
Card Feed Device (SAUS)	CFD
Card Feed Hopper (SAUS)	CFH
Card Feed Stop (SAUS)	CFS
Card Feeding Mechanism (SAUS)	CFM
Card Field (SAUS)	CF
Card File (SAUS)	CF
Card Format Identifier (NASA)	CFI
Card Gripper (SAUS)	CG
Card Guide (SAUS)	CG
Card Holder (SAUS)	CH
Card Hopper (SAUS)	CH
Card Identification Code [DoD] (AFIT)	CIC
Card Image Correction [Computer science]	CIMCO
Card Image Manipulator for Large Entities [Computer science] (PDAA)	CIMPLE
Card Image Tape (SAUS)	CIT
Card Index (SAUS)	CI
Card Inductor Read Only (SAUS)	CIRO
Card Inductor Read Only Memory (SAUS)	CIRO Memory
Card Information Space (SAUS)	CIS
Card Information Structure [Computer science]	CIS
Card Input [Computer science] (BUR)	CI
Card Input Editor [Computer science] (SAA)	CIED
Card Input Station (SAUS)	CIS
Card Input-Preliminary Processing (SAA)	CCP
Card Insertion (SAUS)	CI
Card Interpreter (SAUS)	CI
Card Inventory Control	CIC
Card Jam (SAUS)	CJ
Card Jam Detector (SAUS)	CJD
Card Lever (SAUS)	Cd Lev
Card Lever Control (SAUS)	CLC
Card Lifter (SAUS)	CL
Card Line (SAUS)	CL
Card Load (SAUS)	cl
Card Loading Signal (SAUS)	CLS
Card Magazine (SAUS)	CM
Card Maintenance & Data Recorder (SAUS)	CMDR
Card Manufacturing Daily Status (SAUS)	CMDS
Card Matching (SAUS)	CM
Card Memory (SAUS)	CM
Card Module (SAUS)	Cd Mod
Card Module Tester	CMT
Card Network Planning (SAUS)	CNP
Card on A Stick (SAUS)	COAST
Card on Board (SAUS)	COB
Card Operating System (IAA)	COS
Card Or Tape Reader (SAUS)	COT
Card Oriented Computer (SAUS)	COC
Card Oriented Data Processing System (SAUS)	CODPS
Card Oriented Model (SAUS)	COM
Card Oriented System (SAUS)	COS
Card Packet System (AABC)	CARDPAC
Card Packet System (SAUS)	CARDPACS
Card Part Number (SAUS)	CPN
Card Perforator (SAUS)	CP
Card Pick Up (DCTA)	CPU
Card Print Processor [Computer science] (IAA)	CPP
Card Printing (SAUS)	CP
Card Processing (SAUS)	CP
Card Processing System (SAUS)	CPS
Card Programmable Hand-Held Calculator/Computer (MCD)	CPHHC
Card Programmed Calculator [IBM Corp. - late 1940's] [Computer science]	CPC
Card Programmed Computer (IAA)	CPC
Card Programming Support (SAUS)	CPS
Card Programming System [Computer science] (CMD)	CPS
Card Punch [Computer science] (BUR)	CP
Card Punch and Reader [Computer science]	CP/R
Card Punch Interface (SAUS)	CPI
Card Punch Memory (SAUS)	CPM
Card Punch Operation (SAUS)	CPO
Card Punch Store (SAUS)	CPS
Card Punching Printer [Computer output device] [Computer science] (BUR)	CPP
Card Punching Rate (SAUS)	CPR
Card Punching Unit (SAUS)	CPU
Card Random-Access Memory [NCR Corp.] [Computer science]	CRAM
Card Read Error (SAUS)	CRE
Card Read Punch (SAUS)	CRP
Card Reader [Computer science]	CDR
Card Reader (SAUS)	Cd Rdr
Card Reader [Computer science] (NVT)	CR
Card Reader [Computer science]	CRD
Card Reader In Dispenser (SAUS)	CRIND
Card Reader Operation (SAUS)	CRO
Card Reader Unit [Computer science]	CRU
Card Reader/Punch [Computer science]	CRP
Card Reader-Punch interpreter [Computer science] (DNAB)	CRPI
Card Reading (SAUS)	CR
Card Ready [Computer science] (SAA)	CR
Card Recording (SAUS)	CR
Card Registration (SAUS)	CR
Card Release Daily Status (SAUS)	CRDS
Card Reproducer [Computer science] (IAA)	CR
Card Run (SAUS)	CR
Card Security Number [Banking]	CSN
Card Selection (SAUS)	CS
Card Service [Computer science] (PCM)	CS
Card Service/Socket Service [Computer science] (PCM)	CS/SS
Card Setting Machine Tenters' Society [A union] [British] (DCTA)	CSMTS
Card Size (SAUS)	CS
Card Socket [Electronics] (IAA)	CS
Card Sorting (SAUS)	CS
Card Stacker (SAUS)	CS
Card Station [Computer science] (BUR)	CS
Card Stock (VRA)	cdst
Card Store (SAUS)	CS
Card Store Control [Computer science] (IAA)	CSC
Card to Printer (IAA)	CP
Card Type (DNAB)	CT
Card Unit (SAUS)	CU
Card Virtual Machine (SAUS)	CARDVM
CARDA Coordination Center (SAUO)	CCC
Card-and-heald Wire Gauge (SAUS)	CWG
Cardarelli's Sign [Medicine] (MELL)	CS
Card-Automated Reproduction and Distribution System [Library of Congress]	CARDS
Cardboard (MAE)	cb
Cardboard (VRA)	cdbd
Cardboard (ADA)	CDBD
Cardboard City (WDAA)	CC
Cardboard Film Holder Without Intensifying Screens [Radiology] (DAVI)	cb
Cardboard Heroes (SAUS)	CH
Cardboard Illustrative Aid to Computation [Bell Telephone Co.] [Computer science]	CARDIAC
Cardboard Illustrative Aid to Computation [Computer science] (PDAA)	CARIAC
Carded for Record Only	CRO
Carded Packaging Institute (EA)	CPI

Carded Yarn Association [Later, AYSA] (EA)	CYA
Cardfile (SAUS)	CRD
Cardholder (SAUS)	Cd HL
Cardiac	CRDC
Cardiac Accelerator Center [Physiology]	CAC
Cardiac Adjustment Scale [Psychology]	CAS
Cardiac Allograft [Medicine] (MELL)	CA
Cardiac Ambulatory Monitoring Unit [Cardiology] (DAVI)	CAMU
Cardiac and Pulmonary Rehabilitation [Medicine] (STED)	CPR
Cardiac Angiography [Medicine] (MELL)	CA
Cardiac Apnea [Medicine] (MELL)	CA
Cardiac Arrest [Medicine]	CA
Cardiac Arrest and Asystole [Medicine] (MELL)	CA & A
Cardiac Arrest Code [Medicine]	CAC
Cardiac Arrhythmia Suppression Trial [National Heart, Lung, and Blood Institute]	CAST
Cardiac Arrhythmias Research and Education Foundation (SAUO)	CARE
Cardiac Care Registered Nurse (WGA)	CCRN
Cardiac Care Unit [Medicine]	CCU
Cardiac Catheterization [Cardiology] (DAVI)	CC
Cardiac Contusion [Medicine] (MELL)	CC
Cardiac Cycle [Medicine]	CC
Cardiac Defects, Abnormal Facies, Thymic Hypoplasia, Cleft Palate, and Hypocalcemia from Deletions in Chromosome 22 [Medical syndrome]	CATCH-22
Cardiac Disease [Medicine]	CD
Cardiac Dullness [Physiology]	CD
Cardiac Dysrhythmia [Medicine] (MELL)	CD
Cardiac Embolism [Medicine] (MELL)	CE
Cardiac Emergency [Medicine] (MAE)	CE
Cardiac Enlargement [Medicine]	CE
Cardiac Failure [Medicine]	CF
Cardiac Filling Pressure [Cardiology]	CFP
Cardiac Hypertrophy [Medicine] (MELL)	CH
Cardiac Index [Physiology]	CI
Cardiac Inhibition Center [Physiology]	CIC
Cardiac Insufficiency [Medicine] (MAE)	CI
Cardiac Intensive Care Unit [of a hospital] (AAMN)	CICU
Cardiac Inward Rectifier [Biochemistry]	CIR
Cardiac Lipomas [Medicine] (MELL)	CL
Cardiac Magnetic Resonance Imaging [Cardiology]	CMRI
Cardiac Massage (SAUS)	CM
Cardiac Minute Output [Physiology]	CMO
Cardiac Monitor [Medicine] (MAE)	CM
Cardiac Monitoring Unit [Medicine] (STED)	CMU
Cardiac Muscle [Medicine] (MELL)	CM
Cardiac Observation Unit [Cardiology] (DAVI)	COU
Cardiac Output [Cardiology]	CO
Cardiac Output (DAVI)	Q
Cardiac Output [Cardiology] (DAVI)	QT
Cardiac Output by Thermodilution [Cardiology] (DMAA)	COTD
Cardiac Output Estimation [Medicine] (MELL)	COE
Cardiac Output Recorder [Physiology]	COR
Cardiac Pacemaker (MELL)	CPM
Cardiac Pathways Corp. [Associated Press] (SAG)	CardPth
Cardiac Pathways Corp. [NASDAQ symbol] (SAG)	CPWY
Cardiac Performance [Medicine] (DB)	CP
Cardiac Pool [Medicine] (DB)	CP
Cardiac Pulmonary Reserve [Physiology]	CPR
Cardiac Pump Function [Medicine] (MELL)	CPF
Cardiac Purkinje Fiber [Medicine] (MELL)	CPF
Cardiac Reconditioning Center [Rehabilitation] (DAVI)	CRC
Cardiac Rehabilitation (DAVI)	CR
Cardiac Rehabilitation Unit [Cardiology] (DMAA)	CRU
Cardiac Rescue Technician (SAUO)	CRT
Cardiac Research Laboratory (SAUS)	CRL
Cardiac Respiration (SAUS)	CR
Cardiac Resuscitation Team [Medicine]	CRT
Cardiac Risk Index [Medicine] (MELL)	CRI
Cardiac Society of Great Britain and Ireland (DAVI)	CSGBI
Cardiac Stress Test [Medicine] (MAE)	CST
Cardiac Surgery [Medicine] (MAE)	CAS
Cardiac Surgical Intensive Care Unit [Medicine]	CSICU
Cardiac Surveillance Unit (DAVI)	CSU
Cardiac Sympathetic Nerve [Medicine] (DB)	CSN
Cardiac T Rapid Assay [Medicine] (MELL)	CTRA
Cardiac Tamponade (MELL)	CT
Cardiac Thoracic Intensive Care Unit	CTICU
Cardiac Transplantation [Medicine] (STED)	CTx
Cardiac Troponin C [Biochemistry]	CTnC
Cardiac Type	CT
Cardiac Unit [Medicine] (STED)	CU
Cardiac Valve Procedure [Medicine] (STED)	CVP
Cardiac Volume [Medicine] (MELL)	CV
Cardiac Work [Physiology]	CW
Cardiac Work Index [Physiology]	CWI
Cardiac-Recurrent Nerve [Medicine] (PDAA)	CRN
Cardiac/Thoracic Intensive Care Unit [Medicine] (DAVI)	CTIU
Cardiac/Thoracic Unit [Medicine]	CTU
Cardiff [Welsh depot code]	CDF
Cardiff (SAUS)	Cff
Cardiff [Wales] [Airport symbol] (OAG)	CWL
Cardiff [British] [ICAO location identifier] (ICLI)	EGFF
Cardiff City [British] [ICAO location identifier] (ICLI)	EGRG
Cardiff East Docks [Welsh depot code]	CED
Cardiff Railway [Wales]	CAR R
Cardiff Railway (SAUO)	CarR
Cardiff Railway Co. (SAUO)	CR
Cardiff University Industry Centre [British] (IRUK)	CUIC
Cardiff Valleys [Welsh depot code]	CV
Cardiff/Tremorfa [British] [ICAO location identifier] (ICLI)	EGFC
Cardigan (DSUE)	CARDI
Cardigan [City and county in Wales] (ROG)	CDG
Cardigan Welsh Corgi Club of America (EA)	CWCCA
Cardiganshire [County in Wales] (ROG)	CARD
Cardiganshire [County in Wales] (ROG)	CARDIGS
Cardiganshire [County in Wales]	CARDS
Cardinal	CA
Cardinal (WDAA)	Card
Cardinal	CARD
Cardinal	CDL
Cardinal Airlines (MHDB)	CD
Cardinal Bancshares [NASDAQ symbol] (TTSB)	CARD
Cardinal Bancshares, Inc. [NASDAQ symbol] (SAG)	CARD
Cardinal Bancshares, Inc. [Associated Press] (SAG)	CardBnc
Cardinal Club (EA)	CC
Cardinal Health [NYSE symbol] (TTSB)	CAH
Cardinal Health, Inc. [NYSE symbol] (SAG)	CAH
Cardinal Health, Inc. [Associated Press] (SAG)	CardInlH
Cardinal Health, Inc. [Associated Press] (SAG)	CardnHlt
Cardinal Leger & His Endeavours (AC)	CLE
[Le] Cardinal Leger et Ses Oeuvres (AC)	CLO
Cardinal Mindszenty Foundation (EA)	CMF
Cardinal Mineral Corp. Ltd. [Vancouver Stock Exchange symbol]	CDB
Cardinal Mooney High School Library, Rochester, NY [OCLC symbol] (OCLC)	RVV
Cardinal Point (ROG)	CP
Cardinal Point (SAUS)	CP
Cardinal Points Specification (SAUS)	CPS
Cardinal Public Library, Cardinal, ON, Canada [Library symbol] [Library of Congress] (LCLS)	CaOCARD
Cardinal Public Library, Ontario [Library symbol] [National Library of Canada] (BIB)	OCARD
Cardinal Realty Services, Inc. [Associated Press] (SAG)	CardRlt
Cardinal Realty Services, Inc. [Associated Press] (SAG)	CardRlty
Cardinal Realty Services, Inc. [NASDAQ symbol] (SAG)	CRSI
Cardinal Realty Svcs [NASDAQ symbol] (TTSB)	CRSI
Cardinal Stritch College (GAGS)	Card Stritch C
Cardinal Stritch College [Wisconsin]	CSC
Cardinal Stritch College, Milwaukee, WI [Library symbol] [Library of Congress] (LCLS)	WMCSC
Cardinal Virtues [Freemasonry] (ROG)	CV
Cardinalis [Authority cited in pre-1607 legal work] (DSA)	Car
Cardinalis [Authority cited in pre-1607 legal work] (DSA)	Card
Cardinalis [Authority cited in pre-1607 legal work] (DSA)	Cardi
Cardinalis Florentinus [Franciscus Zabarella] [Deceased, 1417] [Authority cited in pre-1607 legal work] (DSA)	Card Flor
Cardinalis Florentinus (Franciscus Zabarella) [Deceased, 1417] [Authority cited in pre-1607 legal work] (DSA)	Card Zabarel
Cardington Atmospheric Boundary Layer Experiment (PDAA)	CABLE
Cardio Pulmonal Reanimation (SAUS)	CPR
Cardio Scatter Histograph (SAUS)	CSHG
cardioacceleration (SAUS)	cardioac
Cardioacceleratory Peptide [Biochemistry]	CAP
cardioactive (SAUS)	cardioac
cardioactivity (SAUS)	cardioac
Cardiodilatin [Biochemistry]	CDD
Cardioesophageal [Junction] [Gastroenterology] (DAVI)	CE
Cardioesophageal Junction [Gastroenterology] (DAVI)	CEJ
cardiogenesis (SAUS)	cardiog
CardioGenesis Corp. [Associated Press] (SAG)	CardGen
CardioGenesis Corp. [NASDAQ symbol] (TTSB)	CGCP
cardiogenetic (SAUS)	cardiog
Cardiogenic Pulmonary Edema [Cardiology] (DAVI)	CPE
Cardiogenic Shock [Cardiology] (DMAA)	CGS
Cardiogenic Shock	CS
Cardiographic	CRDGRPHC
cardiography (SAUS)	cardiog
cardiogreen (SAUS)	cg
Cardio-Green (Dye) [Trademark]	CG
Cardio-Inhibitor Center (SAUS)	CIC
Cardiokymograph (BARN)	CKG
Cardiolipin [Immunochemistry]	CL
Cardiolipin Complement Fixation [Immunochemistry] (DAVI)	CCF
Cardiolipin Microflocculation Test [Medicine] (DMAA)	CMFT
Cardiolipin Natural Lecithin [Immunochemistry] (MAE)	CNL
Cardiolipin Synthetic Lecithin [Biochemistry] (MAE)	CSL
Cardiology (MAE)	card
Cardiology	CARDIO
Cardiology	cardiol
Cardiology	CRDLGY
Cardiology (DAVI)	Ventricular Rhythm
Cardiology Intensive Care Unit (SAUS)	CICU
Cardiology Office Computer (SAUS)	COC
Cardiology Research Center [Russian]	CRC
Cardiology Technologists' Association of British Columbia (AC)	CTABC
Cardiology Transcription Unit [Medicine]	CTU
cardiolysin (SAUS)	cardiol
cardiomegaly (SAUS)	cardiomeg
Cardiometrics, Inc. [Associated Press] (SAG)	Cardiom

Cardiometrics, Inc. [*NASDAQ symbol*] (SAG) ... CFLO
Cardiomyography [*Cardiology*] ... CM
cardiomyopathy (SAUS) ... cardiomyo
Cardiomyopathy [*Medicine*] ... CM
Cardiomyopathy [*Medicine*] (MAE) ... CMP
Cardiomyopathy and Wooly Haircoat [*Syndrome*] [*Medicine*] (DMAA) ... CWH
Cardion Electronics, Woodbury, NY [*Library symbol*] [*Library of Congress*] (LCLS) ... NWbC
Cardiophrenic Angle (STED) ... CPA
cardiopulmonary (SAUS) ... cardiopul
Cardiopulmonary ... CARDPLMNRY
Cardiopulmonary [*Medicine*] (STED) ... C/P
Cardiopulmonary [*Medicine*] ... CP
Cardiopulmonary Arrest [*Medicine*] (CPH) ... CPA
Cardiopulmonary Blood Volume [*Medicine*] (STED) ... CPBV
Cardiopulmonary Bypass [*Medicine*] ... CPB
Cardiopulmonary Bypass [*Medicine*] (MELL) ... CPBP
Cardiopulmonary Bypass Surgery [*Medicine*] (STED) ... CPBS
Cardiopulmonary Cerebral Resuscitation [*Medicine*] (DMAA) ... CPCR
Cardiopulmonary Corp. [*Associated Press*] (SAG) ... Cardpul
Cardiopulmonary Corp. [*NASDAQ symbol*] (SAG) ... CPCP
Cardiopulmonary Disease (MELL) ... CPD
Cardiopulmonary Exercise Testing [*Medicine*] ... CPX
Cardiopulmonary Research Institute (DAVI) ... CAPRI
Cardiopulmonary Resuscitation [*Medicine*] ... CPR
Cardiopulmonary Support [*Medicine*] (MELL) ... CPS
Cardiopulmonary Technologies (SAUS) ... HART
Cardiorenal Failure [*Medicine*] (MELL) ... CRF
cardiorespiratory (SAUS) ... cr
Cardiorespiratory [*Medicine*] ... CR
Cardiorespiratory Failure [*Medicine*] (MELL) ... CRF
Cardiorespirogram [*Medicine*] (DAVI) ... CRG
Cardiotachometer [*Medicine*] ... CTM
Cardiotech International, Inc. [*Associated Press*] (SAG) ... Cardtch
Cardiotech International, Inc. [*AMEX symbol*] (SAG) ... CTE
Cardiotech Intl. [*AMEX symbol*] (SG) ... CTE
Cardiothoracic Intensive Care Unit ... CTICU
Cardiothoracic Ratio [*Medicine*] ... CT
Cardiothoracic Ratio [*Medicine*] ... CTR
Cardiothoracic Research and Education Foundation (EA) ... CREF
Cardiothoracic Systems [*NASDAQ symbol*] (TTSB) ... CTSI
CardioThoracic Systems, Inc. [*Associated Press*] (SAG) ... CardioTh
CardioThoracic Systems, Inc. [*NASDAQ symbol*] (SAG) ... CTSI
Cardiotocography [*Gynecology*] ... CTG
Cardiotonic Steroid [*Medicine*] ... CTS
Cardiotronics Inc. [*NASDAQ symbol*] (TTSB) ... CDIO
Cardiovascular (SAUS) ... Cardiov
Cardiovascular ... CRDVSCLR
Cardiovascular [*Medicine*] ... CV
Cardiovascular Accident [*Medicine*] (DMAA) ... CVA
Cardiovascular Adverse Effects [*Medicine*] (MELL) ... CVAE
Cardiovascular and Interventional Radiology Society of Europe (EA) ... CIRSE
Cardiovascular Computerized Tomography [*Scanner*] [*Cardiology*] (DAVI) ... CVCT
Cardiovascular Conditioning Suit [*Medicine*] ... CVCS
Cardiovascular Credentialing International (EA) ... CCI
Cardiovascular Data Analysis by Machine Processing (AEBS) ... CARDAMAP
Cardiovascular Deconditioning [*Medicine*] (MEDA) ... CD
Cardiovascular Diagnostics [*NASDAQ symbol*] (TTSB) ... CVDI
Cardiovascular Diagnostics, Inc. [*Associated Press*] (SAG) ... CardiDiag
Cardiovascular Diagnostics, Inc. [*NASDAQ symbol*] (SAG) ... CVDI
Cardiovascular Disease [*Medicine*] ... CD
Cardiovascular Disease [*Medicine*] ... CVD
Cardiovascular Disease Study [*British*] ... CVDS
Cardiovascular Dynamics, Inc. [*Associated Press*] (SAG) ... CardiDy
Cardiovascular Dynamics, Inc. [*NASDAQ symbol*] (SAG) ... CCVD
Cardiovascular Failure [*Medicine*] (MELL) ... CVF
Cardiovascular Incident [*Medicine*] (DMAA) ... CVI
Cardiovascular In-Patient Care Unit ... CICU
Cardiovascular Institute [*Boston University*] [*Research center*] (RCD) ... CVI
Cardiovascular Insufficiency [*Medicine*] (DMAA) ... CVI
Cardiovascular Intensive Care Unit (NUJO) ... CVICU
Cardiovascular Monitor [*Medicine*] ... CVM
Cardiovascular Observation Unit (SAUS) ... CVOU
Cardiovascular Operating Room (STED) ... CVOR
Cardiovascular Pressure [*Medicine*] (WDAA) ... CVP
Cardiovascular Pressure Transducer (SAUS) ... CPT
Cardiovascular Pulmonary Laboratory [*Medicine*] (MAE) ... CVPlab
Cardiovascular Recovery Room [*Medicine*] (DMAA) ... CVRR
Cardiovascular Reflex Conditioning [*Medicine*] ... CRC
Cardiovascular Reflex Conditioning System [*Medicine*] ... CRCS
Cardiovascular Renal Disease [*Medicine*] ... CVRD
Cardiovascular Research and Training Center [*University of Alabama in Birmingham*] [*Research center*] (RCD) ... CVRTC
Cardiovascular Research Center (SAUO) ... CRC
Cardiovascular Research Institute [*University of California, San Francisco*] [*Research center*] (RCD) ... CVRI
Cardiovascular Research (journ.) (SAUS) ... Cardiovasc Res
Cardiovascular Respiratory (SAUS) ... CVR
Cardiovascular Respiratory Disease [*Medicine*] ... CVRD
Cardiovascular Respiratory System [*Medicine*] ... CVR
Cardiovascular Status (SAUS) ... CVS
Cardiovascular Studies Unit [*University of Pennsylvania*] [*Research center*] (RCD) ... CVSU
Cardiovascular Surgery [*Medicine*] ... CVS
Cardiovascular Surgery Unit (DAVI) ... CSU
Cardiovascular System [*Medicine*] ... CVS
Cardiovascular Technologist (DAVI) ... CT
Cardiovascular Technologist (HCT) ... CVT
Cardiovascular Thoracic Intensive Care Unit (DAVI) ... CVT-ICU
Cardiovascular Thoracic Post-Intensive Care Unit (DAVI) ... CVTP-ICU
Cardiovascular-Renal [*Medicine*] ... CVR
Cardiovascular-Thoracic Surgery (DAVI) ... CVT S
Cardiovascular/Thoracic Surgery and Cardiology Assembly (ADWA) ... CSCA
cardioversion (SAUS) ... cardiover
Card-Operated Typewriter (SAUS) ... COT
Card-Pitt [*National Football League*] [*1944*] (NFLA) ... CaP
Cards (SAUS) ... CDs
Cards per Day [*Computer science*] (BUR) ... CPD
Cards per Hour [*Computer science*] ... C/H
Cards per Hour (SAUS) ... C/hour
Cards per Hour [*Computer science*] ... CPH
Cards per Minute [*Computer science*] ... CM
Cards per Minute [*Computer science*] (IAA) ... CMIN
Cards per Minute (SAUS) ... C/min
Cards per Minute [*Computer science*] ... CPM
Cards per Second [*Computer science*] ... CPS
Card-Select Number [*Computer science*] (PCM) ... CSN
Cardston Public Library, Alberta [*Library symbol*] [*National Library of Canada*] (NLC) ... ACAR
Cards-to-Tape Converter (SAUS) ... CTC
Card-to-Disk (SAUS) ... C/D
Card-to-Magnetic Tape Conversion System [*Computer science*] (DIT) ... CTS
Card-to-Punch (SAUS) ... CP
Card-to-Tape Activity (SAUS) ... SITCARD
Card-to-Tape Converter (SAUS) ... C/TC
Card-to-Tape Converter [*Computer science*] (IAA) ... CTC
Card-to-Tape Tape [*Computer science*] ... CTT
Care ... K
Care about the Strays (EA) ... CATS
Care Aggregated Module ... CAM
Care and Maintenance [*British military*] (IAA) ... CAM
Care and Maintenance [*British military*] (DMA) ... C & M
Care and Maintenance (SAUS) ... C&M
Care and Maintenance Instruction [*Nuclear energy*] (NRCH) ... CMI
Care and Maintenance Party (SAUO) ... C & M Pty
Care and Maintenance Unit, Royal Artillery (SAUO) ... CAM RA
Care and Preservation [*Army*] (AABC) ... C & P
Care at Home ... CAH
Care Canada, Ottawa, Ontario [*Library symbol*] [*National Library of Canada*] (BIB) ... OOCARE
Care Custody and Control ... CCC
Care for Life [*An association*] (EA) ... CFL
Care for the Kurds (SAUO) ... CFTK
Care for the Mentally Handicapped (SAUO) ... CMH
Care for the Wild [*An association*] [*British*] (EAIO) ... CW
Care Group [*NASDAQ symbol*] (TTSB) ... CARE
[*The*] **Care Group, Inc.** [*NASDAQ symbol*] (NQ) ... CARE
Care Group, Inc. [*Associated Press*] (SAG) ... CareGp
Care How Others Keep the Environment [*An association*] ... CHOKE
Care International (SAUS) ... CARE
CARE International Car Rental System (SAUO) ... CARE
Care Logic Module (NASA) ... CLM
Care Net [*An association*] (EA) ... CN
Care Of [*Correspondence*] ... C/O
Care Of (NTIO) ... c/o
Care Of (WDMC) ... co
Care of County (WDMC) ... C/O
Care of Ship Checkoff List (DNAB) ... CSCL
Care of Supplies in Storage [*Military*] (AABC) ... COSIS
Care of the Body Surface (DIPS) ... COBS
Care of the Next Infant [*Medicine*] (WDAA) ... CONI
Care Point Medical Centres Ltd. [*Vancouver Stock Exchange symbol*] ... CPJ
Care, Understanding, Research, Organization for the Welfare of Drug Addicts (SAUO) ... CURE
Care Unit Program [*Chemical dependency*] (DAVI) ... CUP
Care Vet Pharmacy [*Vancouver Stock Exchange symbol*] ... VET
Care-Cure Coordination [*Medicine*] (DMAA) ... CCC
Career ... CAR
Career Ability Placement Survey [*Vocational guidance test*] ... CAPS
Career Adaptive Behavior Inventory [*Vocational guidance test*] ... CAB
Career Advancement Network (EA) ... CAN
Career Airmen Reenlistment Reservation System [*Air Force*] ... CAREERS
Career Analysis Procedure [*LIMRA*] ... CAP
Career Apparel Institute (EA) ... CAI
Career Area Rotation Model [*Air Force*] ... CAROM
Career Assessment Inventory [*Vocational guidance test*] ... CAI
Career Assistance Counseling [*Air Force*] (AFM) ... CAC
Career Assistance Program [*Department of Labor*] ... CAP
Career Attitudes and Strategies Inventory: An Inventory for Understanding Adult Careers (TMMY) ... CASI
Career Awareness Inventory [*Vocational guidance test*] ... CAI
Career College Association (NTPA) ... CCA
Career Control (AFM) ... CC
Career Counselor [*Military*] (AABC) ... CARCSLR
Career Criminal Apprehension Unit (LAIN) ... CCAU
Career Criminals Program (SAUO) ... CCP
Career Decision Scale (EDAC) ... CDS
Career Descision-Making System [*Test*] [*Harrington and O'Shea*] (TES) ... CDM
Career Development (WYGK) ... CD

Career Development and Outplacement Association (COBU) ...... CDOA
Career Development Center (EA) ...... CDC
Career Development Center, Shaker Heights (SAUS) ...... SKS
Career Development Center, Shaker Heights, OH [OCLC symbol] (OCLC) .... SKS
Career Development Course (AFM) ...... CDC
Career Development Inventory [Psychology] (DHP) ...... CDI
Career Development Organization, Inc (SAUS) ...... CDO
Career Development Program (OICC) ...... CDP
Career Development Review [Australia] ...... CDR
Career Development Scheme ...... CDS
Career Education Association of Victoria [Australia] ...... CEAV
Career Employment Experience [Office of Youth Programs] [Department of Labor] ...... CEE
Career Employment Group [British military] (DMA) ...... CEG
Career Executive Force [Air Force] ...... CEF
Career Exploration Inventory [Test] (TMMY) ...... CEI
Career Exploration Profile [Vocational guidance test] ...... CEP
Career Exploration Series [Vocational guidance test] ...... CES
Career Factor Checklist (EDAC) ...... CFC
Career Horizons [NYSE symbol] (TTSB) ...... CHZ
Career Horizons, Inc. [Associated Press] (SAG) ...... CareerHz
Career Horizons, Inc. [NASDAQ symbol] (SAG) ...... CARH
Career Information and Counseling [Air Force] ...... CIAC
Career Information Center (DNAB) ...... CARINFOCEN
Career Information Center (OICC) CIC
Career Information Delivery System (OICC) ...... CIDS
Career Information Resource Advisory Group [Canada] ...... CIRAG
Career Information Service (SAUS) ...... CIS
Career Information System [National Career Information System] [Eugene, OR] [Information service or system] (IID) ...... CIS
Career Information Unit (OICC) ...... CIU
Career Interest Test [Vocational guidance test] ...... CIT
Career Intern Program (MCD) ...... CIP
Career is Over [Business term] (MHDB) ...... CIO
Career Laboratories Utilizing Experience (OICC) ...... CLUE
Career Limiting Move (MCD) ...... CLM
Career Management and Assignment [Department of State] ...... CMA
Career Management Field [Military] (AABC) ...... CMF
Career Management Individual Files [Military] (INF) ...... CMIF
Career Management Information File [Military] (AABC) ...... CMIF
Career Maturity Inventory [Vocational guidance test] ...... CMI
Career Maturity Inventory-Competence Test [Psychology] (DHP) ...... CMI-CT
Career Maturity Profile (DHP) ...... CMP
Career Minister [Department of State] ...... CM
Career Motivation (AFM) ...... CM
Career Motivation and Achievement Planning Inventory (EDAC) ...... C-MAP
Career Officer Candidate Development Course [Air Force] ...... COCDC
Career Opportunities and Planning for Employment Center [Public library service] ...... COPE
Career Opportunities for Youth (SAA) ...... COY
Career Opportunities Program [Office of Education] (EA) ...... COP
Career Orientation Placement and Evaluation Survey [Vocational guidance test] ...... COPES
Career Orientation Program [LIMRA] ...... COP
Career Orientations Inventory (DHP) ...... COI
Career Oriented Modules to Explore Topics in Science (EDAC) ...... COMETS
Career Placement Registry, Inc. [Database producer] [Information service or system] (IID) ...... CPR
Career Planning and Adult Development Network (EA) ...... CPADN
Career Planning & Placement (SAUS) ...... CPP
Career Planning Board [Navy] (NVT) ...... CPB
Career Planning Program [Vocational guidance test] ...... CPP
Career Preference Questionnaire (DHP) ...... CPQ
Career Program [Army] (RDA) ...... CP
Career Program Manager (MCD) ...... CPM
Career Progression Military Occupational Specialty (MCD) ...... CPMOS
Career Recruiter Force (DNAB) ...... CRF
Career Reenlistment Objectives [Navy] ...... CREO
Career Reserve Status [Air Force] ...... CRS
Career Resource Center (DHP) ...... CRC
Career Resources Information [JA Micropublishing, Inc.] [Information service or system] (IID) ...... CRI
Career Retrieval Search System [Pittsburgh University] (NITA) ...... CARESS
Career Service Status (SAUS) ...... CRS
Career Structure Review [Australia] ...... CSR
Career Technologies Corp. [Database producer] (IID) ...... CTC
Career Trainee (BARN) ...... ct
Career Training Foundation (EA) ...... CTF
Career Transition for Dancers [An association] (EA) ...... CTFD
Career Vitae [Job applications] (DCTA) CV
Career Woman [A publication] ...... Car Wom
Career Women's Forum (EAIO) ...... CWF
Career-Limiting Maneuver (ADWA) ...... CLM
CareerMosaic ...... CM
Career-Oriented Preparation for Employment [Federal antipoverty program] ...... COPE
Careers ...... CARS
Careers Advisory Service Computerized Aid (SAUS) ...... CASCAID
Careers Advisory Service in Industry for Girls (SAUO) ...... CASIG
Careers and Occupational Information Centre (IID) ...... COIC
Careers and Occupational Information Unit (AIE) ...... COIU
Careers and the Disabled [A publication] ...... Car Dis Ab
Careers' Association of New South Wales [Australia] ...... CANSW
Careers Education and Guidance (AIE) ...... CEG
Careers, Education, and Training Advice Centre [British] (CB) ...... CETAC

Careers Guidance Observed (AIE) ...... CARGO
Careers Literature and Information Prescription Service (AIE) ...... CLIPS
Careers Office Management and Public Appraisal System (AIE) ...... COMPAS
Careers on the Move for Engineers of Tomorrow [An association] ...... COMET
Careers Research and Advisory Centre [British] ...... CRAC
Careers Research and Advisory Centre (SAUO) ...... CRAGC
Careers Service Branch [Department of Employment] [British] (AIE) ...... CSB
Careers Services [Navy] [British] ...... CS
Career-Shortening Gesture ...... CSG
Careerware Reference Centre, STM Systems Corp., Ottawa, Ontario [Library symbol] [National Library of Canada] (BIB) ...... OOSTM
Caregiver Stress (MELL) ...... CGS
Careinsite, Inc. [NASDAQ symbol] ...... CARI
Careless and Negligent Driving [Traffic offense charge] ...... CN
CareInsite, Inc. [NASDAQ symbol] (SG) ...... CARL
Caremark International [NYSE symbol] (SPSG) ...... CK
Caremark International, Inc. [Associated Press] (SAG) ...... Caremk
Carematrix Corp. [Associated Press] (SAG) ...... Caremtx
Carematrix Corp. [AMEX symbol] (SAG) ...... CMD
CareMatrix Corp. [NASDAQ symbol] (SAG) ...... CMDC
Carena-Bancorp, Inc. [Toronto Stock Exchange symbol] ...... CDN
Care-Oriented Medical Record [University of Alabama] ...... COMREC
Careside, Inc. [AMEX symbol] (SG) ...... CSA
Caretaker (SAUS) ...... Crtkr
Caretenders Healthcorp. [Associated Press] (SAG) ...... Caretnd
Caretenders Healthcorp. [NASDAQ symbol] (SPSG) ...... CTND
Carey Diversified LLC [NYSE symbol] (SG) ...... CDC
Carey Foster Bridge [Electronics] ...... CFB
Carga Aerea Dominicana [Dominican Republic] [ICAO designator] (FAAC) ...... CDM
Carga Aerea Venezolana Caraven SA [Venezuela] [ICAO designator] (FAAC) ...... CCR
Carga del Caribe SA de CV [Mexico] [FAA designator] (FAAC) ...... CDC
Carges Collect (SAUS) CC
Cargill Branch, Bruce County Public Library, Ontario [Library symbol] [National Library of Canada] (NLC) ...... OCAR
Cargill Information Center, Wayzata, MN [OCLC symbol] (OCLC) ...... CAR
Cargill Instructional Center, Wayzata, MN [Library symbol] [Library of Congress] (LCLS) ...... MnWayC
Cargill Investor Services (SAUO) ...... CiS
Cargill Technical Services, Ltd. [British] [Commercial firm] ...... CTS
Cargo (WGA) C
Cargo (MSA) ...... CAR
Cargo (AABC) ...... CGO
Cargo ...... CRG
Cargo Acceptance and Load Control (ACAE) ...... CALC
Cargo Accounts Settlement System [IATA] (DS) ...... CASS
Cargo Agents Reservation Airwaybill Insurance and Tracking System (DA) ...... CARAT
Cargo Air Lines [Israel] (BJA) ...... CAL
Cargo Air Lines Ltd. (SAUO) ...... CAL
Cargo Aircraft Mine Laying (MCD) ...... CAML
Cargo Aircraft Minelayer (SAUS) ...... CAML
Cargo Airline Evaluation Model (PDAA) ...... CAEM
Cargo Allocation and Load Control [Aviation] ...... CALC
Cargo and Loading Analysis [Shipping] ...... C & LA
Cargo and Loading Analysis (SAUS) ...... C&LA
Cargo and Loading Analysis Table [Environmental science] (COE) ...... C&LAT
Cargo & Passenger Air Services Ltd. [Switzerland] [ICAO designator] (FAAC) ...... CPS
Cargo & Passenger Air Services Ltd. [Switzerland] [ICAO designator] (FAAC) ...... CPZ
Cargo and Rescue Aircraft ...... CARA
Cargo Apparent Good Order [Shipping] ...... CAGO
Cargo Automation Research Team (SAUO) ...... CART
Cargo Bay Module Personnel Provisions [NASA] (KSC) ...... CBMPP
Cargo Bay Stowage Assembly (NASA) ...... CBSA
Cargo Capacity [Shipping] (DCTA) CC
Cargo Category Code (SAUO) CCC
Cargo Center of Gravity (MSA) ...... CCG
Cargo Compartment Trainer (SAUS) ...... CCT
Cargo Container (KSC) ...... CACON
Cargo Container (SAUS) ...... Cargotainer
Cargo Control CC
Cargo Data Interchange System (MCD) ...... CARDIS
Cargo Data Standards Board [IATA] (DS) ...... CDSB
Cargo Deadweight (SAUS) ...... DWTC
Cargo Delivery Receipt [Shipping] ...... CDR
Cargo Delivery System [Shipping] ...... CDS
Cargo Disposition Instructions [Shipping] ...... CDI
Cargo Dor Ltd. [Ghana] [ICAO designator] (FAAC) ...... CDO
Cargo Drop Reel (NVT) ...... CDR
Cargo Facilities and GSE Projects Office (SAUS) ...... CP-FEO
Cargo Glider [Military] ...... CG
Cargo Handling [Environmental science] (COE) ...... CH
Cargo Handling and Port Group [Navy] (NVT) ...... CHAPGRU
Cargo Handling and Storage Facility ...... CHSF
Cargo Handling Battalion [Obsolete] [Army] ...... CHB
Cargo Handling Charge [Shipping] (DS) ...... CHC
Cargo Handling Cooperative Program [MARAD] (TAG) ...... CHCP
Cargo Handling Equipment [Army] ...... CHE
Cargo Handling Rig (RDA) ...... CHR
Cargo Hazardous Servicing Facility (MCD) ...... CHSF
Cargo Helicopter (AABC) ...... CH
Cargo Increment Number (DOMA) ...... CIN
Cargo Information Message Procedures [IATA] (DS) ...... IMP

Cargo Information System [*Aviation*] (DA)	CIS
Cargo Integration Control Center (MCD)	CICC
Cargo Integration Review (MCD)	CIR
Cargo Integration Test Equipment (NASA)	CITE
Cargo Interface Verification Test (MCD)	CIVT
Cargo Investigation Panel [*IATA*] (DS)	CIP
Cargo Landing Adaptability (SAUS)	CLA
Cargo Left Trailer (KSC)	CLT
Cargo Load Transporter (ACAE)	CLT
Cargo Loaded on Vehicles [*MTMC*] (TAG)	VEHCAR
Cargo Lunar Excursion Module	CLEM
Cargo Management (MCD)	CM
Cargo Management (NAKS)	cm
Cargo Module (MCD)	CAM
Cargo Offload and Discharge System [*Environmental science*] (COE)	COLDS
Cargo Oil (DS)	co
Cargo on Deck (SAUS)	COD
Cargo Operations (NAKS)	Co
Cargo Operations [*NASA*] (MCD)	CO
Cargo Orbit Transfer Vehicle (MCD)	COTV
Cargo Outturn Report (AABC)	COR
Cargo Outturn Reporting System	CORS
Cargo Performance Overview System [*BTS*] (TAG)	CAPOS
Cargo Preference Year [*MARAD*] (TAG)	CPY
Cargo Processing Contract (MCD)	CPC
Cargo Processing Facility [*Shipping*] (NASA)	CPF
Cargo Processing Technician (NASA)	CPT
Cargo Program [*or Projects*] Office [*NASA*] (MCD)	CP
Cargo Projects - Program Control Office [*NASA*] (NASA)	CP-PCO
Cargo Projects Office (NAKS)	CP
Cargo Projects Office-Deployable Payloads Projects Office (NAKS)	CP-DPO
Cargo Projects Office-Spacelab Projects Office (NAKS)	CP-SPO
Cargo Propulsion Module [*NASA*] (KSC)	CPM
Cargo Readiness Review (SAUS)	CRR
Cargo Reinsurance Association [*New York, NY*] (EA)	CRA
Cargo Remaining on Board (RIMS)	CROB
Cargo Routing Information File [*Environmental science*] (COE)	CRIF
Cargo Security Advisory Standards [*Department of Transportation*]	CSAS
Cargo Services Conference [*IATA*] (DS)	CSC
Cargo Ship [*of any type*] [*Navy symbol*]	AK
Cargo Ship	CA
Cargo Ship [*Military Sea Transportation Service*] (CINC)	TAK
Cargo Ship and Aircraft Ferry [*Navy symbol*]	AKV
Cargo Ship and Aircraft Ferry [*Military Sea Transportation Service*] (CINC)	TAKV
Cargo Ship, Dock [*Navy symbol*]	AKD
Cargo Ship Dock (SAUS)	CSD
Cargo Ship, Merchant Marine Manned	XAK
Cargo Short Take Off and Landing (ACAE)	CSTOL
Cargo Submarine [*Navy symbol*] [*Obsolete*]	AK(SS)
Cargo Submarine [*Navy symbol*] [*Obsolete*]	ASSA
Cargo Submarine [*Navy symbol*] [*Obsolete*]	SSA
Cargo Systems and Procedures Committee [*IATA*] (DS)	CSPC
Cargo Tank [*Shipping*] (DS)	CT
Cargo Tank Center (DS)	CTC
Cargo Tank Common [*of a ship*] (DS)	CTX
Cargo Tank Wing [*of a ship*] (DS)	CTW
Cargo Technical Evaluation Task Force [*IATA*] (DS)	CTETF
Cargo Three, Inc. [*Panama*] [*FAA designator*] (FAAC)	CTW
Cargo Traffic Analysis (MCD)	CTA
Cargo Traffic Procedures Committee [*IATA*] (DS)	CTPC
Cargo transport aircraft, Experimental (SAUS)	CX
Cargo Transport Unit (SAUS)	CTU
Cargo Transport Units (SAUO)	CTUs
Cargo Trim Valve (SAUS)	CTV
Cargo Variant [*LSD 41 variant*] (DOMA)	CV
Cargo Vessel (SAUS)	C
Cargo War Rating Committee (SAUO)	CWRC
Cargoes of Particular Hazard [*Environmental Protection Agency*]	COPH
Cargojet [*Formerly, Yugoslav Republic*] [*FAA designator*] (FAAC)	CRJ
Cargolux Airline International [*Luxembourg*] [*ICAO designator*] (FAAC)	CLX
Cargoman [*Oman*] [*ICAO designator*] (FAAC)	CGM
Cargo's Proportion of (General) Average [*Shipping*]	CGA
Cargosur [*Spain*] [*ICAO designator*] (FAAC)	OWS
Cargo/Tanker Branch (DNAB)	C/TB
Cargo/Transport [*Designation for all US military aircraft*]	C
Cargo/Transport Aircraft - Experimental	CX
Cargo/Transport Aircraft Experimental - Heavy Logistics System (KSC)	CX-HLS
Cariana International Industries, Inc. [*Vancouver Stock Exchange symbol*]	CIA
Carib [*MARC language code*] [*Library of Congress*]	car
Carib Aviation Ltd. [*Antigua and Barbuda*] [*FAA designator*] (FAAC)	DEL
Carib Express [*Barbados*] [*FAA designator*] (FAAC)	BCB
Caribair [*Airlines*] (OAG)	CB
Caribbean	CAR
Caribbean (AFM)	CARIB
Caribbean	CRBBN
Caribbean Action Lobby (EA)	CAL
Caribbean Action Plan (SAUS)	CAP
Caribbean Advertising Service (SAUO)	CAS
Caribbean Agricultural and Rural Development, Advisory and Training Service (SAUO)	ARDATS
Caribbean Agricultural and Rural Development Advisory and Training Service (SAUO)	CARDATS
Caribbean Agricultural Trading Company (SAUO)	CATCO
Caribbean Air Cargo (SAUO)	CARICARGO
Caribbean Air Cargo [*Barbados*] [*ICAO designator*] (FAAC)	DCC
Caribbean Air Cargo Ltd. [*Barbados*] (EY)	CARICARGO
Caribbean Air Command [*Air Force*]	CAC
Caribbean Air Command [*Air Force*]	CAIRC
Caribbean Air Transport [*ICAO designator*] (AD)	XC
Caribbean Air Transport Co., Inc. [*Netherlands*] [*ICAO designator*] (FAAC)	CLT
Caribbean Airways [*ICAO designator*] (AD)	IQ
Caribbean Airways [*Barbados*] [*ICAO designator*] (FAAC)	IQQ
Caribbean American Intercultural Organization (EA)	CAIO
Caribbean Amphibious Ready Group [*Navy*] (NVT)	CARG
Caribbean Area [*Services to the Armed Forces*] [*Red Cross*]	CA
Caribbean Area [*MARC geographic area code*] [*Library of Congress*] (LCCP)	cc---
Caribbean Area Division of ORIT (SAUO)	CADORIT
Caribbean Area Small Craft Project	CASCP
Caribbean Area Treaty Organization (SAUO)	CATO
Caribbean Association for Rehabilitation Therapists (SAUO)	CART
Caribbean Association for the Rehabilitation of the Disabled [*Defunct*] (EAIO)	CARD
Caribbean Association of Building Societies and Housing Finance Institutions (SAUO)	CABSHFI
Caribbean Association of Media Workers (SAUO)	CAMWORK
Caribbean Association of National Telecommunications Organizations (SAUO)	CANTO
Caribbean Association of Rehabilitation Therapists [*Guyana*] (EAIO)	CART
Caribbean Atlantic Airlines (SAUS)	CAA
Caribbean Atlantic Airlines [*Puerto Rico*]	CARIBAIR
Caribbean Atlantic Airlines [*Puerto Rico*] [*ICAO designator*]	CBA
Caribbean Atlantic Airlines, Inc. (SAUO)	CBA
Caribbean Atlantic Regional Dental Federation (SAUO)	CARDA
Caribbean Australian Association	CAA
Caribbean Aviation Training Institute (SAUO)	CATI
Caribbean Basin Business Information Center (IMH)	CBIC
Caribbean Basin Corrections Association [*Cayman Islands*] (EAIO)	CBCA
Caribbean Basin Economic Recovery Act	CBERA
Caribbean Basin Information Network [*Caribbean/Central American Action*] [*Information service or system*] (IID)	CBIN
Caribbean Basin Information Network (SAUO)	CBIN
Caribbean Basin Initiative (SAUO)	CBI
Caribbean Basin Initiative [*Financial aid package proposed by President Reagan for Central American and Caribbean countries*]	CBI
Caribbean Basin Radar Network, Extended programme (SAUS)	CBRN-E
Caribbean Broadcasting Company (SAUO)	CBC
Caribbean Broadcasting Corp.	CaBC
Caribbean Broadcasting Union	CBU
Caribbean Cane Farmers' Association [*Kingston, Jamaica*] [*Inactive*] (EAIO)	CCFA
Caribbean Central American Action (SAUO)	C/CAA
Caribbean Christian Communications Network (SAUO)	CCCN
Caribbean Church Women (SAUO)	CCW
Caribbean Cigar Co. [*Associated Press*] (SAG)	CaribCig
Caribbean Cigar Co. [*NASDAQ symbol*] (SAG)	CIGR
Caribbean Cigar Co. [*Associated Press*] (SAG)	CribCig
Caribbean Coastal Marine Productivity [*Marine science*] (OSRA)	CARICOMP
Caribbean Coastal Marine Productivity Programme (SAUO)	CARICOMB
Caribbean Command [*Military*]	CARIBCOM
Caribbean Command Air (SAUO)	CARIC
Caribbean Commission [*Later, Caribbean Organization*]	CC
Caribbean Common Market (EBF)	CARICOM
Caribbean Common Market Standards Council [*Georgetown, Guyana*] (EAIO)	CCMSC
Caribbean Community (ADWA)	Caricom
Caribbean Community [*or Common Market*] [*Barbados, Jamaica, Trinidad-Tobago, Guyana, Belize, Dominica, Grenada, St. Kitts-Nevis-Anguilla, St. Lucia, St. Vincent*] [*Guyana*]	CARICOM
Caribbean Community Agricultural Development and Advisory Service (SAUO)	CADAS
Caribbean Community and Common Market (SAUO)	CARIBCOM
Caribbean Community and Common Market (SAUO)	CARICOM
Caribbean Community and Common Market (WA)	Caricom
Caribbean Community and Common Market (SAUO)	CCCM
Caribbean Conference of Churches (EAIO)	CCC
Caribbean Congress of Labor	CCL
Caribbean Conservation Association [*St. Michael, Barbados*]	CCA
Caribbean Conservation Corp. (EA)	CCC
Caribbean Conservation Program (SAUS)	CCP
Caribbean Consumer Council (SAUO)	CCC
Caribbean Consumers Union [*Antigua-Barbuda*] (EAIO)	CCU
Caribbean Council for Science and Technology (SAUO)	CCST
Caribbean Council of Engineering Organizations (SAUO)	CCEO
Caribbean Council of Legal Education (SAUO)	CLE
Caribbean Council of Legal Education (SAUO)	LE
Caribbean Current (SAUS)	Carib Cur
Caribbean Defense Command [*or Commander*]	CDC
Caribbean Democrat Union (SAUO)	CDU
Caribbean Development and Cooperation Committee [*Economic Commission for Latin America*]	CDCC
Caribbean Development and Cooperation Committee (SAUO)	DCC
Caribbean Development Bank	CARIBANK
Caribbean Development Bank (EBF)	CBD
Caribbean Development Bank [*St. Michael, Barbados*]	CDB
Caribbean Division [*Navy*] (DNAB)	CARIBDIV
Caribbean Division Naval Facilities Engineering Command	CARIBNAVFACENGCOM

Caribbean Division Naval Facilities Engineering Command .... DIRCARIBDOCKS
Caribbean Documentation Centre (SAUO) .... CARIB/DOC
Caribbean Economic Community .... CEC
Caribbean Educational Service .... CES
Caribbean Employers Confederation [Trinidad and Tobago] (EAIO) .... CEC
Caribbean Energy Information System [UNESCO] (DUND) .... CEIS
Caribbean Environment Program [Marine science] (OSRA) .... CEP
Caribbean Environment Programme (SAUO) .... CAR
Caribbean Environmental Information Center (SAUO) .... CEIC
Caribbean Environmental Network project (SAUO) .... CEN
Caribbean Epidemiology Center (SAUO) .... CAREC
Caribbean Epidemiology Centre (SAUS) .... WHO-PAHO-CARET
Caribbean Event Alert Switchboard (SAUS) .... CEAS
Caribbean Examinations Council [St. Michael, Barbados] (EAIO) CXC
Caribbean Express, Inc. [ICAO designator] (FAAC) .... TLC
Caribbean Family Planning Affiliation (EAIO) .... CFPA
Caribbean Federation of Aeroclubs (EA) .... CFA
Caribbean Fisheries Training and Development Institute (SAUO) .... CFTDI
Caribbean Fishery Management Council [National Oceanic and Atmospheric
  Administration] (GFGA) .... CFMC
Caribbean Food Corp. [An association] (EAIO) .... CFC
Caribbean Food Corporation, Port-of-Spain (SAUO) .... CFC
Caribbean Food Crops Society [Isabela, Puerto Rico] (EAIO) .... CFCS
Caribbean Free Trade Area (SAUO) .... CARIFTA
Caribbean Free Trade Association .... CARIFTA
Caribbean Free Trade Organization (SAUO) .... CARIFTA
Caribbean Gamefishing Association .... CGA
Caribbean Group for Cooperation in Economic Development
  (SAUO) .... Caribbean Group
Caribbean Group for Cooperation in Economic Development (EA) .... CGED
Caribbean Hotel Association (EA) .... CHA
Caribbean Industrial Research Institute [Trinidad and Tobago] [Research
  center] (IRC) .... CARIRI
Caribbean Industrial Research Institute .... CIRI
Caribbean Industrial Research Institute Technical Information Service
  (SAUO) .... CARIRI-TIS
Caribbean Information Network (SAUS) .... CARINET
Caribbean Information System for Economic and Social Planning [ECLAC]
  [United Nations] (DUND) .... CARISPLAN
Caribbean Institute and Study Center for Latin America (SAUO) .... CISCLA
Caribbean Institute for Meteorology and Hydrology [Caribbean Meteorologic
  al Institute] [Acronym is based on former name,] (EAIO) .... CMI
Caribbean Institute for Resource Management (SAUO) .... CIRM
Caribbean Institute of Mass Communications (SAUO) .... CARIMAC
Caribbean Institute on Mental Retardation and Developmental Disabilities
  (SAUO) .... CIMR
Caribbean Integrated Management and Engineering Consultants
  (SAUO) .... CARIMECO
Caribbean International [ICAO designator] (AD) .... XQ
Caribbean International Airways (SAUO) .... CIA
Caribbean Investment Corporation (SAUO) .... CARINCO
Caribbean Investment Promotion Service (SAUO) .... CIPS
Caribbean Law Journal [A publication] (DLA) .... Caribbean LJ
Caribbean Law Journal [A publication] (DLA) .... Carib LJ
Caribbean Marine Biological Institute (SAUO) .... CARMABI
Caribbean Marine Biological Institute (BARN) .... CMBI
Caribbean Marine Biological Institute (SAUO) .... CMBI
Caribbean Meteorological Institute [Marine science] (OSRA) .... CMI
Caribbean Meteorological Organisation [Formerly, Caribbean Meteorological
  Service] (EA) .... CMO
Caribbean Meteorological Organization [Marine science] (OSRA) .... CMO
Caribbean Metrology Programme (SAUO) .... CMP
Caribbean National Forest (SAUS) .... CNF
Caribbean Natural Resources Institute (EAIO) .... CANARI
Caribbean Network of Educational Innovation for Development [UNESCO]
  [United Nations] (DUND) .... CARNEID
Caribbean Organisation (or Organization) for Rural Development and
  Education (SAUO) .... CORDE
Caribbean Organization [An international governmental body, of which the US
  was a member] [Terminated, 1965] .... CO
Caribbean Organization of Tax Administrators (EAIO) .... COTA
Caribbean Overseas Lines (SAUO) .... CAROL
Caribbean Planning for Adaptation to Global Climate in the Caribbean.... CPACC
Caribbean Plant Protection Commission [Trinidad and Tobago] (EAIO) .... CPPC
Caribbean Press Association (NTCM) .... CPA
Caribbean Primate Research Center [University of Puerto Rico] [Research
  center] (RCD) .... CPRC
Caribbean Project Development Facility (SAUO) .... CDPF
Caribbean Psychiatric Association (SAUO) .... CarPA
Caribbean Public Services Association [Barbados] (EAIO) .... CPSA
Caribbean Publishers Broadcasters Association (SAUO) .... CPBA
Caribbean Ready Group (SAUO) .... CARG
Caribbean Region [USTTA] (TAG) .... CAR
Caribbean Regional Badminton Confederation [Aruba] (EAIO) .... CAREBACO
Caribbean Regional Council for Adult Education [University of the West
  Indies] (EAIO) .... CARAE
Caribbean Regional Council for Adult Education [Barbados] (EAIO) .... CARCAE
Caribbean Regional Organization of Associations for Science Education
  (SAUO) .... CROASE
Caribbean Regional Program (SAUO) .... CRP
Caribbean Research Institute [College of the Virgin Islands] .... CRI
Caribbean Resources Corp. [Vancouver Stock Exchange symbol] .... CBC
Caribbean Rice Improvement Network (SAUO) .... CRIN
Caribbean Rice Research Network (SAUO) .... CRRN
Caribbean Sailing Yachts, Inc. (SAUO) .... CSY

Caribbean Sea and Adjacent Regions (SAUS) .... CSAR
Caribbean Sea Frontier [Navy] .... CARIBSEAFRON
Caribbean Sea Frontier [Navy] .... CSF
Caribbean Sea Project (SAUS) .... CSP
Caribbean Studies Association (EA) .... CSA
Caribbean Studies. University of Puerto Rico. Institute of Caribbean
  Studies (journ.) (SAUS) .... UPR/CS
Caribbean Super Station [Satellite television system] .... CSS
Caribbean Technical Assistance (SAUO) .... CTA
Caribbean Telecommunication Union (SAUO) .... CTU
Caribbean Tourism Association [Later, Caribbean Tourism Organization]
  (EA) .... CTA
Caribbean Tourism Organization (EAIO) .... CTO
Caribbean Tourism Organization, American Branch (EA) .... CTO
Caribbean Tourism Research and Development Centre [Later, Caribbean
  Tourism Organization] (EAIO) .... CTRC
Caribbean Tourist Association (SAUO) .... CTA
Caribbean Travel Association (SAUO) .... CTA
Caribbean Trust Fund (SAUS) .... CTF
Caribbean University Network (SAUO) .... CUNet
Caribbean Writers Series [Heinemann Educational Books Ltd.] [British] .... CWS
Caribbeana Council [Defunct] (EA) CC
Caribbean-Atlantic Airlines, Inc. (SAUO) .... CAAI
Caribbean-Atlantic Airlines, Inc. (SAUO) .... CARIBAIR
Caribbean/Central American Action (EA) .... C/CAA
Caribbean/Latin American Action [An association] (EA) .... C/CAA
Caribbeans to United States North of Hatteras (SAUS) .... CAR/USNH
Caribe Petroleums [Vancouver Stock Exchange symbol] .... CBP
Caribean Air Express (SAUS) .... CAE
Caribean Sea Frontier (SAUS) .... CSF
Caribiner International [NYSE symbol] (TTSB) .... CWC
Caribiner Intl., Inc. [Associated Press] (SAG) .... Caribinr
Caribiner Intl., Inc. [NYSE symbol] (SAG) .... CWC
Caribintair SA [Haiti] [ICAO designator] (FAAC) .... CRT
Caribjet, Inc. [Antigua and Barbuda] [ICAO designator] (FAAC) .... CBJ
Cariboo College, Kamloops, BC, Canada [Library symbol] [Library of
  Congress] (LCLS) .... CaBKCC
Cariboo College, Kamloops, British Columbia [Library symbol] [National
  Library of Canada] (NLC) .... BKCC
Cariboo College Library [UTLAS symbol] .... CAR
Cariboo Lumber Manufacturers' Association (AC) .... CLMA
Cariboo Tourist Association (AC) .... CTA
Cariboo-Chilcotin Archives, Williams Lake, British Columbia [Library
  symbol] [National Library of Canada] (NLC) .... BWLC
Cariboo-Thompson Nicola Library System, Kamloops, BC, Canada [Library
  symbol] [Library of Congress] (LCLS) .... CaBKCT
Cariboo-Thompson Nicola Library System, Kamloops, British Columbia
  [Library symbol] [National Library of Canada] (NLC) .... BKCT
Caribou [Maine] [Seismograph station code, US Geological Survey] (SEIS) ..... CBM
Caribou [Maine] [ICAO location identifier] (ICLI) .... KCAR
Caribou, ME [Location identifier] [FAA] (FAAL) .... CAR
Caribou, ME [FM radio station call letters] .... WCXU
Caribou, ME [AM radio station call letters] .... WFST
Caribou Performance Test .... CPT
Carica [A Fig] [Pharmacology] (ROG) .... CARIC
Caricature [or Caricaturist] .... caric
Caricaturists Society of America (EA) .... CSA
CARICOM Multilateral Clearing Facility (SAUO) .... CMCF
Caries Resistant (STED) .... CR
Caries Susceptible [Medicine] (MELL) .... CS
Carina [Constellation] .... Car
Carina [Constellation] .... Cari
Carina Minerals Resources Ltd. [Vancouver Stock Exchange symbol] .... CIM
Caring for the Earth (SAUO) .... CFE
Caring for the Older Veteran (journ.) (SAUS) .... Old Vetern
Caring for Young Refugees (SAUO) .... CYR
Caring Relationship Inventory [Psychology] .... CRI
Cariolis Absorber (SAUS) .... CA
Carissimus [Dearest] [Latin] .... K
CARITAS Internationalis (SAUO) .... CARITAS
Caritas Internationalis [International Confederation of Catholic Organizations
  for Charitable and Social Action] [Vatican City, Vatican City State] (EAIO) CI
Carl Duisberg Society [Later, CDSI] (EA) .... CDS
Carl Gustav [King of Sweden] .... CG
Carl H. Pforzheimer Library, New York, NY [Library symbol] [Library of
  Congress] (LCLS) .... NNPf
Carl Hanser Verlag [Publisher] .... CHV
Carl Karcher Enterprises .... CKE
Carl Neuberg Society for International Scientific Relations. Transactions of
  the Symposium (journ.) (SAUS) .... Trans Symp Carl Neuberg Soc
Carl Perkins Fan Club [Defunct] (EA) .... CPFC
Carl Perkins Vocational Education Act [1984] (OICC) .... CPVEA
Carl Reiner, Sheldon Leonard, Dick Van Dyke, Danny Thomas [Acronym is
  name of production company of TV series "The Dick Van Dyke
  Show"] .... CALVADA
Carl Sandburg Birthplace Association, Galesburg, IL [Library symbol]
  [Library of Congress] (LCLS) .... IGS
Carl Sandburg College, Galesburg, IL [Library symbol] [Library of Congress]
  (LCLS) .... IGSC
Carl Sandburg College, LRC, Galesburg, IL [OCLC symbol] (OCLC) .... IHR
Carl Schurz Memorial Foundation [Later, NCSA] (EA) .... CSMF
Carl Vinson Nuclear Powered Carrier [DoD] .... CVN
Carla Riggs-Hall International Fan Club (EA) .... CRHIFC
Carlanita Music [Publisher] .... CMC

Carle Foundation Hospital, Urbana, IL [*Library symbol*] [*Library of Congress*] (LCLS) .... IUrCH
Carle Place High School, Carle Place, NY [*Library symbol*] [*Library of Congress*] (LCLS) .... NCpHS
Carleton and Regiment [*British military*] (DMA) .... CYR
Carleton Board of Education, Ottawa, ON, Canada [*Library symbol*] [*Library of Congress*] (LCLS) .... CaOOCBE
Carleton Board of Education, Ottawa, Ontario [*Library symbol*] [*National Library of Canada*] (NLC) .... OOCBE
Carleton Board of Education, Sir Wilfrid Laurier High School Library, Ottawa, ON, Canada [*Library symbol*] [*Library of Congress*] (LCLS).... CaOOWLS
Carleton College, Northfield, MN [*OCLC symbol*] (OCLC) ...... MNN
Carleton College, Northfield, MN [*Library symbol*] [*Library of Congress*] (LCLS) .... MnNC
Carleton Corp. [*Formerly, Apertus Technologies*] [*NASDAQ symbol*] .... CARL
Carleton County Historical Society, Upper Woodstock, New Brunswick [*Library symbol*] [*National Library of Canada*] (NLC) .... NBUWH
Carleton Library System [*Carleton University*] [*Information service or system*] (IID) .... CLS
Carleton Memorial Hospital, Woodstock, New Brunswick [*Library symbol*] [*National Library of Canada*] (BIB) .... NBWH
Carleton, MI [*Location identifier*] [*FAA*] (FAAL) .... CRL
Carleton Place Public Library, Carleton Place, ON, Canada [*Library symbol*] [*Library of Congress*] (LCLS) .... CaOCp
Carleton Place Public Library, Ontario [*Library symbol*] [*National Library of Canada*] (NLC) .... OCP
Carleton, PQ [*Television station call letters*] .... CHAU
Carleton, PQ [*FM radio station call letters*] (RBYB) .... CIEU
Carleton University (SAUO) .... CU
Carleton University Academic Staff Association [*Association du Personnel Enseignant de l'Universite Carleton*] (AC) .... CUASA
Carleton University, Department of Art History, Ottawa, ON, Canada [*Library symbol*] [*Library of Congress*] (LCLS) ...... CaOOCCAH
Carleton University, Geography Department, Ottawa, ON, Canada [*Library symbol*] [*Library of Congress*] (LCLS) .... CaOOCCG
Carleton University Library [*UTLAS symbol*] .... CTN
Carleton University, Ottawa, ON, Canada [*Library symbol*] [*Library of Congress*] (LCLS) .... CaOOCC
Carleton University, Ottawa, Ontario [*Library symbol*] [*National Library of Canada*] (NLC) .... OOCC
Carleton University, Social Sciences Division, Ottawa, ON, Canada [*Library symbol*] [*Library of Congress*] [*Obsolete*] (LCLS) ...... CaOOCCSS
Carleton's New Brunswick Reports [*A publication*] (DLA) .... Carl
Carleton's New Brunswick Reports [*A publication*] (DLA) .... NBR Carl
Carletonville [*South Africa*] [*ICAO location identifier*] (ICLI) ...... FACR
Carlin Resources Corp. [*Vancouver Stock Exchange symbol*] .... CLM
Carline Assignment Model [*General Motors Corp.*] .... CLAM
Carlinville, IL [*FM radio station call letters*] .... WCNL
Carlinville, IL [*FM radio station call letters*] .... WIBI
Carlinville, IL [*FM radio station call letters*] (BROA) .... WOLG-FM
Carlinville, IL [*FM radio station call letters*] (RBYB) .... WTSG-FM
Carlinville Public Library, Carlinville, IL [*Library symbol*] [*Library of Congress*] (LCLS) .... ICarl
Carlisle [*England*] [*Airport symbol*] (OAG) .... CAX
Carlisle [*British*] [*ICAO location identifier*] (ICLI) .... EGNC
Carlisle Citizen, Carlisle, IA [*Library symbol*] [*Library of Congress*] (LCLS) .... IaCarlC
Carlisle Companies [*Associated Press*] (SAG) .... Carlisle
Carlisle Companies [*NYSE symbol*] (SPSG) .... CSL
Carlisle Corp. (SAUO) .... CSL
Carlisle, KY [*FM radio station call letters*] .... WCAK
Carlisle, KY [*FM radio station call letters*] (BROA) .... WVCM-FM
Carlisle, PA [*FM radio station call letters*] .... WDCV
Carlisle, PA [*AM radio station call letters*] .... WHYL
Carlisle, PA [*FM radio station call letters*] .... WHYL-FM
Carlisle, PA [*AM radio station call letters*] .... WIOO
Carlisle Plastics (EFIS) .... CP
Carlisle Plastics Cl'A' [*NYSE symbol*] (TTSB) .... CPA
Carlisle Plastics, Inc. [*Associated Press*] (SAG) .... CarlislP
Carlisle Public Library, Carlisle, IA [*Library symbol*] [*Library of Congress*] (LCLS) .... IaCarl
Carlisle Public Library, Carlisle, IN [*Library symbol*] [*Library of Congress*] (LCLS) .... InCa
Carlisle Public Library, Carlisle, IN [*Library symbol*] [*Library of Congress*] (LCLS) .... InCaL
Carlo Erba [*Italy*] [*Research code symbol*] I
Carlo Erba [*Italy*] [*Research code symbol*] .... K
Carload (WDMC) cl
Carload CL
Carload Lot [*Commerce*] CL
Carloading .... CRLDNG
Carloforte [*Sardinia*] [*Seismograph station code, US Geological Survey*] [*Closed*] (SEIS) .... CRL
Carlos Cervantes del Rio [*Mexico*] [*ICAO designator*] (FAAC) .... CCD
Carlos Elementary School, Carlos, MN [*Library symbol*] [*Library of Congress*] (LCLS) .... MnCarE
Carlotn High School, Carlton, MN [*Library symbol*] [*Library of Congress*] (LCLS) .... MnCtH
Carlow [*County in Ireland*] (ROG) .... CAR
Carlow College, Our Lady of Mercy Academy, Pittsburgh, PA [*Library symbol*] [*Library of Congress*] (LCLS) .... PPiCa-O
Carlow College, Pittsburgh, PA [*OCLC symbol*] (OCLC) .... CRC
Carlow College, Pittsburgh, PA [*Library symbol*] [*Library of Congress*] (LCLS) .... PPiCa
Carlsbad [*California*] [*Airport symbol*] (OAG) .... CLD

Carlsbad [*New Mexico*] [*Seismograph station code, US Geological Survey*] (SEIS) .... CLN
Carlsbad [*New Mexico*] [*Airport symbol*] (OAG) .... CNM
Carlsbad, CA [*Location identifier*] [*FAA*] (FAAL) .... CRQ
Carlsbad, CA [*Location identifier*] [*FAA*] (FAAL) .... EKG
Carlsbad, CA [*FM radio station call letters*] (BROA) .... KMCG-FM
Carlsbad, CA [*FM radio station call letters*] (BROA) .... KMSX-FM
Carlsbad, CA [*FM radio station call letters*] (RBYB) .... KUPR
Carlsbad Caverns National Park .... CACA
Carlsbad Caverns National Park (SAUS) .... CCNP
Carlsbad City Library, Carlsbad, CA [*Library symbol*] [*Library of Congress*] (LCLS) .... CCarl
Carlsbad City Library, Carlsbad, CA [*OCLC symbol*] (OCLC) .... CCP
Carlsbad, NM [*Location identifier*] [*FAA*] (FAAL) .... CNM
Carlsbad, NM [*AM radio station call letters*] .... KAMQ
Carlsbad, NM [*AM radio station call letters*] .... KATK
Carlsbad, NM [*FM radio station call letters*] .... KATK-FM
Carlsbad, NM [*FM radio station call letters*] (BROA) .... KBFV-FM
Carlsbad, NM [*AM radio station call letters*] .... KCCC
Carlsbad, NM [*FM radio station call letters*] .... KCDY
Carlsbad, NM [*Television station call letters*] .... KOCT
Carlsbad, NM [*Television station call letters*] (BROA) .... KUPC
Carlsbad Public Library, Carlsbad, NM [*Library symbol*] [*Library of Congress*] (LCLS) .... NmC
Carlsbad Ventures [*Vancouver Stock Exchange symbol*] .... KVI
Carlsbad/Cavern City Air Terminal [*New Mexico*] [*ICAO location identifier*] (ICLI) .... KCNM
Carlsberg Automated Meridian Circle [*Astronomy*] .... CAMC
Carlson Elementary School, Rockford, IL [*Library symbol*] [*Library of Congress*] (LCLS) .... IRoCaE
Carlson Mines Ltd. [*Vancouver Stock Exchange symbol*] CLX
Carlson Psychological Survey [*Test*] .... CPS
Carlstadt Leather Finishes (SAUO) .... CLF
Carlton and United Breweries [*Australia*] .... CUB
Carlton and United Breweries Ltd. (SAUO) .... CUB
Carlton College (SAUO) .... Car
Carlton Communications [*NYSE symbol*] (SPSG) .... CCM
Carlton Communications Ltd. [*Associated Press*] (SAG) .... CarlCm
Carlton Communications Ltd. [*Associated Press*] (SAG) .... CarltCm
Carlton Communications Ltd. [*NASDAQ symbol*] (SAG) .... CCTV
Carlton Commun'X-CAPS' [*NYSE symbol*] (TTSB) .... CCMPr
Carlton County Historical Society, Cloquet, MN [*Library symbol*] [*Library of Congress*] (LCLS) .... MnClHi
Carlton Public Library, Carlton, MN [*Library symbol*] [*Library of Congress*] (LCLS) .... MnCt
Carlton University (SAUO) .... Car
Carlyle Barton Laboratory (MCD) .... CBL
Carlyle Energy Ltd. [*Toronto Stock Exchange symbol*] .... CYD
Carlyle Golf, Inc. [*NASDAQ symbol*] (SAG) .... CRLG
Carlyle Golf, Inc. [*Associated Press*] (SAG) .... CrlyGl
Carlyle Golf, Inc. [*Associated Press*] (SAG) .... CrlyleGlf
Carlyle Golf Wrrt [*NASDAQ symbol*] (TTSB) .... CRLGW
Carlyle School, Carlyle, IL [*Library symbol*] [*Library of Congress*] (LCLS) .... ICarlyS
Carma Developers Ltd. [*Toronto Stock Exchange symbol*] .... CDV
Carma Ltd. [*Toronto Stock Exchange symbol*] .... CVP
Carmac Resources [*Vancouver Stock Exchange symbol*] .... CMA
Carmanguay Public Library, Alberta [*Library symbol*] [*National Library of Canada*] (NLC) .... ACARMA
Carmanville Public Library, Carmanville, NF, Canada [*Library symbol*] [*Library of Congress*] (LCLS) .... CaNfCa
Carmanville Public Library, Newfoundland [*Library symbol*] [*National Library of Canada*] (NLC) .... NFCA
Carmarthen [*Welsh depot code*] .... CARM
Carmarthenshire [*County in Wales*] .... CARM
Carmarthenshire [*County in Wales*] (ROG) .... CARMARTHS
Carmarthenshire [*County in Wales*] .... CARMS
Carmel, CA [*FM radio station call letters*] (RBYB) .... KBOQ
Carmel, CA [*AM radio station call letters*] .... KRML
Carmel, CA [*FM radio station call letters*] (RBYB) .... KXDC
Carmel Clay Schools, Carmel IN [*Library symbol*] [*Library of Congress*] (LCLS) .... InCarS
Carmel Community [*Roman Catholic women's religious order*] CC
Carmel Container Sys [*AMEX symbol*] (TTSB) .... KML
Carmel Container Systems Ltd. [*Associated Press*] (SAG) .... Carmel
Carmel Container Systems Ltd. [*AMEX symbol*] (SPSG) .... KML
Carmel de Montreal, Montreal, PQ, Canada [*Library symbol*] [*Library of Congress*] (LCLS) .... CaQMACAR
Carmel de Montreal, Quebec [*Library symbol*] [*National Library of Canada*] (NLC) .... QMCAR
Carmel, IN [*FM radio station call letters*] .... WHJE
Carmel News Journal, Carmel, IN [*Library symbol*] [*Library of Congress*] (LCLS) .... InCarNJ
Carmel, NY [*Location identifier*] [*FAA*] (FAAL) .... CMK
Carmel Public Library, Carmel, IN [*Library symbol*] [*Library of Congress*] (LCLS) .... InCar
Carmel Valley, CA [*AM radio station call letters*] .... KIEZ
Carmelita [*Guatemala*] [*ICAO location identifier*] (ICLI) .... MGCR
Carmelita Petroleum [*Vancouver Stock Exchange symbol*] .... CFH
Carmelitae Divini Cordis Jesu [*Carmelite Sisters of the Divine Heart of Jesus*] [*Roman Catholic religious order*] .... DCJ
Carmelitas del Sagrado Corazon (TOCD) .... OCD
Carmelite .... CARM
Carmelite Brothers of the Holy Eucharist [*Roman Catholic religious order*] .... CFSE
Carmelite Community of the Word (TOCD) .... CCW

Carmelite Fathers and Brothers (TOCD) ... ocarm
Carmelite Fathers and Brothers (TOCD) ... OCarm
Carmelite Missionaries [*Rome, Italy*] (EAIO) ... CM
Carmelite Missionaries of St. Theresa [*Roman Catholic women's religious order*] ... CMST
Carmelite Nuns of the Ancient Observance (TOCD) ... OCarm
Carmelite Sisters (Corpus Christi) (TOCD) ... OCarm
Carmelite Sisters for Aged and Infirm (TOCD) ... OCarm
Carmelite Sisters of Charity (TOCD) ... Cach
Carmelite Sisters of Charity, Institute of Vedruna (SAUO) ... CaCh
Carmelite Sisters of St. Teresa (TOCD) ... CSST
Carmelite Sisters of St. Therese of the Infant Jesus [*Roman Catholic religious order*] ... CST
Carmelite Sisters of the Divine Heart of Jesus (TOCD) ... CarmelDCJ
Carmelite Sisters of the Eucharist (TOCD) ... CSE
Carmelite Sisters of the Most Sacred Heart of Los Angeles (TOCD) ... OCD
Carmelite Third Order [*Rome, Italy*] (EAIO) ... CTO
Carmelite Vietnamese of Our Lady of Mt. Carmel (TOCD) ... OCA
Carmelites of Mary Immaculate (TOCD) ... cmi
Carmelites of Mary Immaculate (TOCD) ... CMI
Carmen Arvale [*of Calpurnius Siculus*] [*Classical studies*] (OCD) ... Carm Arv
Carmen de Bello Aegyptiaco sive Actiaco [*of Ausonius*] [*Classical studies*] (OCD) ... B Aegypt
Carmen de Patagones [*Argentina*] [*Airport symbol*] (AD) ... CPG
Carmen Division of the Brotherhood of Railway, Airline and Steamship Clerks, Freight Handlers, Express and Station Employes (EA) ... CD/BRAC
Carmen Saeculare [*of Horace*] [*Classical studies*] (OCD) ... Carm Saec
Carmen Saliare [*of Calpurnius Siculus*] [*Classical studies*] (OCD) ... Carm Sal
Carmi, IL [*Location identifier*] [*FAA*] (FAAL) ... CUL
Carmi, IL [*AM radio station call letters*] ... WROY
Carmi, IL [*FM radio station call letters*] ... WRUL
Carmichael, CA [*AM radio station call letters*] ... KFIA
Carmike Cinemas, Inc. [*Columbus, GA*] [*Associated Press*] (SAG) ... Carmik
Carmike Cinemas Inc. [*NYSE symbol*] (SPSG) ... CKE
Carmike Cinemas'A' [*NYSE symbol*] (TTSB) ... CKE
Carmina [*or Odes*] [*of Sidonius Apollinaris*] [*Classical studies*] (OCD) ... Carm
Carmina Epigraphica [*of Calpurnius Siculus*] [*Classical studies*] (OCD) ... Carm Epigr
Carmina Latina Epigraphica [*A publication*] (OCD) ... Carm Epigr
Carmina Popularia [*of Calpurnius Siculus*] [*Classical studies*] (OCD) ... Carm Pop
Carminative [*Expelling Wind*] [*Pharmacy*] (ROG) ... CAR
Carmine (ROG) ... CAR
Carmody-Wait. Cyclopedia of New York Practice [*A publication*] (DLA) ... Carmody-Wait NY Prac
Carnal Knowledge [*FBI standardized term*] ... CK
Carnal Knowledge of Female Child [*FBI standardized term*] ... CK of FC
Carnarvon [*Australia*] [*ICAO location identifier*] (ICLI) ... APCR
Carnarvon [*Western Australia*] [*Airport symbol*] (AD) ... CVQ
Carnarvon Horticultural Development Council (SAUO) ... CHDC
Carnarvon Township Public Library, Mindemoya, Ontario [*Library symbol*] [*National Library of Canada*] (NLC) ... OMCT
Carnarvon Tracking Station [*NASA*] ... CRO
Carnarvonshire [*County in Wales*] ... CARN
Carnarvonshire [*County in Wales*] (ROG) ... CARNARVS
Carnarvonshire [*County in Wales*] (ROG) ... CARNS
Carnasaw Mountain - Lookout Tower [*Oklahoma*] [*Seismograph station code, US Geological Survey*] (SEIS) ... CRO
Carnation (DSUE) ... CARN
Carnation Company (SAUO) ... CMK
Carnation Cryptic Virus [*Plant pathology*] ... CARCV
Carnation Etched Ring Virus ... CERV
Carnation Instant Breakfast [*Nestle Beverage Co.*] [*Tradename*] (DAVI) ... CIB
Carnation Italian Ringspot Virus [*Plant pathology*] ... CIRSV
Carnation Latent Virus [*Plant pathology*] ... CLV
Carnation Mottle Virus ... CaMoV
Carnation Mottle Virus ... CarMV
Carnation Necrotic Fleck Virus ... CNFV
Carnation Research Laboratories, Van Nuys, CA [*Library symbol*] [*Library of Congress*] (LCLS) ... CVnCR
Carnation Ringspot Virus ... CRSV
Carnation Vein Mottle Virus [*Plant pathology*] ... CVMV
Carnation Yellow Stripe Virus [*Plant pathology*] ... CYSV
Carnegie Alumni Clan (SAUO) ... CAC
Carnegie Bancorp [*Associated Press*] (SAG) ... CarnB
Carnegie Bancorp [*Associated Press*] (SAG) ... CarnegBc
Carnegie Bancorp [*NASDAQ symbol*] (SAG) ... CBNJ
Carnegie Bancorp Wrrt [*NASDAQ symbol*] (TTSB) ... CBNJW
Carnegie Bookmobile Library, Grafton, ND [*Library symbol*] [*Library of Congress*] (LCLS) ... NdGrC
Carnegie Center for Transnational Studies ... CCTS
Carnegie City Library, Little Falls, MN [*Library symbol*] [*Library of Congress*] (LCLS) ... MnLf
Carnegie Commission on Educational Television (SAUO) ... CCET
Carnegie Commission on Higher Education ... CCHE
Carnegie Commission on Science, Technology, and Government (EA) ... CCSTG
Carnegie Commission Reports Information System (SAUS) ... CCRIS
Carnegie Committee for Music and Drama (SAUO) ... CCMD
Carnegie Corp. of New York (EA) ... CCNY
Carnegie Corp. of New York, New York, NY [*Library symbol*] [*Library of Congress*] (LCLS) ... NNCar
Carnegie Corporation (SAUO) ... CC
Carnegie Council of Policy Studies in Higher Education [*Defunct*] (EA) ... CCPSHE
Carnegie Council on Adolescent Development (EA) ... CCAD
Carnegie Council on Ethics and International Affairs (EA) ... CCEIA
Carnegie Dunfermline Trust (SAUO) ... CDT
Carnegie Ellsworth Public Library, Iowa Falls, IA [*Library symbol*] [*Library of Congress*] (LCLS) ... Ialf
Carnegie Endowment for International Peace (EA) ... CEIP
Carnegie Endowment for International Peace, New York, NY [*Library symbol*] [*Library of Congress*] (LCLS) ... NNCE
Carnegie Forum on Education and the Economy (EA) ... CFEE
Carnegie Foundation for the Advancement of Teaching (EA) ... CFAT
Carnegie Free Library (SAUO) ... CFL
Carnegie Free Library, Beaver Falls, PA [*Library symbol*] [*Library of Congress*] (LCLS) ... PBf
Carnegie Free Library, Braddock, PA [*Library symbol*] [*Library of Congress*] (LCLS) ... PBra
Carnegie Free Library of McKeesport, McKeesport, PA [*Library symbol*] [*Library of Congress*] (LCLS) ... PMck
Carnegie Geophysical Laboratory (SAUO) ... CGL
Carnegie Group, Inc. [*Associated Press*] (SAG) ... Carnegie
Carnegie Group, Inc. [*NASDAQ symbol*] (SAG) ... CGIX
Carnegie Hall (SAUO) ... CH
Carnegie Hall (SAUS) ... CH
Carnegie Hall - Jeunesses Musicales [*Defunct*] (EA) ... CH-JM
Carnegie Hero Fund (SAUO) ... CHF
Carnegie Hero Fund Commission (EA) ... CHFC
Carnegie Hero Fund Trust (SAUO) ... CHFT
Carnegie Institute [*New York*] ... CI
Carnegie Institute of Technology (SAUO) ... Carnegie Tech
Carnegie Institute of Technology (SAUS) ... Carn Inst
Carnegie Institute of Technology [*Later, Carnegie-Mellon University*] [*Pennsylvania*] ... CIT
Carnegie Institute of Technology (SAUO) ... CITY
Carnegie Institution of Washington (SAUO) ... Carnegie Inst
Carnegie Institution of Washington (EA) ... CIW
Carnegie Institution of Washington [*District of Columbia*] [*Seismograph station code, US Geological Survey*] [*Closed*] (SEIS) ... DTM
Carnegie Institution of Washington, Department of Terrestrial Magnetism, Washington, DC [*Library symbol*] [*Library of Congress*] (LCLS) ... DCI-T
Carnegie Institution of Washington Geophysical Laboratory (SAUO) ... CIWGL
Carnegie Institution of Washington, Geophysical Laboratory, Washington, DC [*Library symbol*] [*Library of Congress*] (LCLS) ... DCI-G
Carnegie Institution of Washington, Washington, DC [*Library symbol*] [*Library of Congress*] (LCLS) ... DCI
Carnegie Interest Inventory [*Medicine*] (DMAA) ... CII
Carnegie International [*AMEX symbol*] ... CGY
Carnegie Library (SAUO) ... CL
Carnegie Library, Dawson, MN [*Library symbol*] [*Library of Congress*] (LCLS) ... MnDaw
Carnegie Library of Parkersburg and Wood County, Parkersburg, WV [*Library symbol*] [*Library of Congress*] (LCLS) ... WvP
Carnegie Library of Pittsburgh (SAUS) ... CLP
Carnegie Library of Pittsburgh, Allegheny Regional Branch, Monroeville, PA [*Library symbol*] [*Library of Congress*] (LCLS) ... PPi-A
Carnegie Library of Pittsburgh, Pittsburgh, PA [*OCLC symbol*] (OCLC) ... CPL
Carnegie Library of Pittsburgh, Pittsburgh, PA [*Library symbol*] [*Library of Congress*] (LCLS) ... PPi
Carnegie Library, Rockport, MA [*Library symbol*] [*Library of Congress*] (LCLS) ... MRp
Carnegie Library, Rome, GA [*Library symbol*] [*Library of Congress*] (LCLS) ... GR
Carnegie Mellon University (GAGS) ... Carnegie Mellon U
Carnegie Multi-Mini Processor ... CMMP
Carnegie Museum of Natural History [*Pittsburgh, PA*] ... CM
Carnegie Museum of Natural History ... CMNH
Carnegie Museum of Natural History. Special Publication (journ.) (SAUS) ... SPCHDX
Carnegie Observatories (SAUS) ... TCO
Carnegie, PA [*AM radio station call letters*] ... WPLW
Carnegie, PA [*AM radio station call letters*] (BROA) ... WZUM
Carnegie Public Library, Angola, IN [*OCLC symbol*] (OCLC) ... IIA
Carnegie Public Library, Angola, IN [*Library symbol*] [*Library of Congress*] (LCLS) ... InAng
Carnegie Public Library, Bradford, PA [*Library symbol*] [*Library of Congress*] (LCLS) ... PBr
Carnegie Public Library, Browns Valley, MN [*Library symbol*] [*Library of Congress*] (LCLS) ... MnBrv
Carnegie Public Library, Clarksdale, MS [*Library symbol*] [*Library of Congress*] (LCLS) ... MsCld
Carnegie Public Library, Conneaut, OH [*Library symbol*] [*Library of Congress*] (LCLS) ... OConCL
Carnegie Public Library District, Fortville, IN [*Library symbol*] [*Library of Congress*] (LCLS) ... InFtv
Carnegie Public Library, Las Vegas, NM [*OCLC symbol*] (OCLC) ... LVN
Carnegie Public Library of Corning, Corning, CA [*Library symbol*] [*Library of Congress*] (LCLS) ... CCorn
Carnegie Public Library, Union, OR [*Library symbol*] [*Library of Congress*] (LCLS) ... OrUn
Carnegie Public Library, Washington Court House, OH [*Library symbol*] [*Library of Congress*] (LCLS) ... OWas
Carnegie Public Library, Washington, IN [*Library symbol*] [*Library of Congress*] (LCLS) ... InWas
Carnegie Southern Observatory [*Later, Las Campanas Observatory*] ... CARSO
Carnegie Trust for the Universities of Scotland (SAUO) ... CTUS
Carnegie United Kingdom Trust (BARN) ... CUKT
Carnegie-Mellon Action Project (SAUS) ... C-MAP
Carnegie-Mellon Institute of Research (SAUO) ... CMIR
Carnegie-Mellon University [*Pittsburgh, PA*] ... CMU

Carnegie-Mellon University, Hunt Institute for Botanical Documentation, Pittsburgh, PA [*Library symbol*] [*Library of Congress*] (LCLS) .... PPiHB
Carnegie-Mellon University, Mellon Institute, Pittsburgh, PA [*Library symbol*] [*Library of Congress*] (LCLS) .... PPiM
Carnegie-Mellon University, Pittsburgh, PA [*OCLC symbol*] (OCLC) .... PMC
Carnegie-Mellon University, Pittsburgh, PA [*Library symbol*] [*Library of Congress*] (LCLS) .... PPiC
Carnegie-Mellon University-Design Automation (MCD) .... CMU-DA
Carnegie-Stout Free Public Library, Dubuque, IA [*Library symbol*] [*Library of Congress*] (LCLS) .... IaDu
Carnelian (VRA) .... carnl
Carnelian Bay, CA [*FM radio station call letters*] .... KODS
Carnes Creek Explorations [*Vancouver Stock Exchange symbol*] .... CSK
Carney, William L., Bresman IN [*STAC*] .... CWL
Carnian [*Geology*] C
Carnic Alps (SAUS) .... Carnics
Carnicobar [*India*] [*ICAO location identifier*] (ICLI) .... VOCX
Carnitine-Palmitine Transferase (DB) .... CPT
Carnival (WDAA) .... carn
Carnival .... CARN
Carnival (DSUE) .... CARNI
Carnival Air [*ICAO designator*] (FAAC) .... CAA
Carnival Corp. [*Formerly, Carnival Cruise*] [*Associated Press*] (SAG) .... CarnCp
Carnival Corp. [*Associated Press*] (SAG) .... CarnvCp
Carnival Corp. [*NYSE symbol*] (SAG) CCL
Carnival Corp'A' [*NYSE symbol*] (TTSB) CCL
Carnmarth [*England*] .... CARNM
Carnot [*Central African Republic*] [*Airport symbol*] (AD) .... CRF
Carnow, Coninleas & Associates, Ltd., Chicago, IL [*Library symbol*] [*Library of Congress*] (LCLS) .... ICCaC
Caro, MI [*FM radio station call letters*] .... WIDL
Caro, MI [*AM radio station call letters*] .... WKYO
Carol Burnett Fund for Responsible Journalism (EA) .... CBFRJ
Carol Lawrence National Fan Club (EA) .... CLFC
Carol P&L $5 cm Pfd [*AMEX symbol*] (TTSB) .... CPLPr
Carolian Systems International, Inc. [*Toronto Stock Exchange symbol*] .... CSJ
Carolin Mines Ltd. [*Toronto Stock Exchange symbol*] [*Vancouver Stock Exchange symbol*] CLL
Carolina (BEE) .... Car
Carolina [*United States*] [*Obsolete*] (ROG) .... CAR
Carolina [*Brazil*] [*Airport symbol*] (AD) .... CLN
Carolina [*South Africa*] [*ICAO location identifier*] (ICLI) .... FACL
Carolina [*Brazil*] [*ICAO location identifier*] (ICLI) .... SBCI
Carolina Air Transit, Inc. [*ICAO designator*] (FAAC) .... CTX
Carolina Alliance for Fair Employment .... CAFE
Carolina & North Western [*Railroad*] (MHDB) .... C & NW
Carolina & Northwestern Railroad (IIA) .... C & NW
Carolina & Northwestern Railway Co. [*AAR code*] .... CRN
Carolina Asphalt Pavement Association (SRA) .... CAPA
Carolina Association of Professional Insurance Agents (SRA) .... CAPIA
Carolina Beach, NC [*FM radio station call letters*] .... WLGX
Carolina Beach, NC [*AM radio station call letters*] .... WMYT
Carolina Bird Club (ROAS) .... CBC
Carolina Brahman Breeders Association (GVA) .... CBBA
Carolina Brown Lung Association (ROAS) .... CBLA
Carolina, Clinchfield & Ohio [*Railway*] (MHDB) CCL
Carolina, Clinchfield and Ohio Railroad (SAUO) .... Cc&O
Carolina, Clinchfield and Ohio Railroad Co. (SAUO) .... CCO
Carolina Discipliana Library, Wilson, NC [*Library symbol*] [*Library of Congress*] (LCLS) .... NcWilC
Carolina Financial (EFIS) .... CF
Carolina Fincorp., Inc. [*Associated Press*] (SAG) .... CaroFin
Carolina Fincorp., Inc. [*NASDAQ symbol*] (SAG) .... CFNC
Carolina First Corp. [*NASDAQ symbol*] (NQ) .... CAFC
Carolina First Corp. [*Associated Press*] (SAG) .... CaroF
Carolina First Corp. [*Associated Press*] (SAG) .... CaroFst
Carolina First Corp. [*Associated Press*] (SAG) .... CaroFt
Carolina Freight Carriers (SAUO) .... CAO
Carolina Freight Corp. [*NYSE symbol*] (SPSG) .... CAO
Carolina Geological Society (SAUO) .... CGS
Carolina Gold [*Vancouver Stock Exchange symbol*] .... CJE
Carolina Institute for Research on Early Education for the Handicapped (EDAC) .... CIREEH
Carolina Law Journal [*A publication*] (DLA) .... Car LJ
Carolina Law Journal [*A publication*] (DLA) .... Carolina LJ
Carolina Law Repository [*North Carolina*] [*A publication*] (DLA) .... Car Law Repos
Carolina Law Repository [*North Carolina*] [*A publication*] (DLA) .... Car L Rep
Carolina Law Repository [*North Carolina*] [*A publication*] (DLA) .... Carolina L Repos
Carolina Law Repository [*North Carolina*] [*A publication*] (DLA) .... Law Repos
Carolina Law Repository (Reprint) [*North Carolina*] [*A publication*] (DLA).... Car LR
Carolina Law Repository (Reprint) [*North Carolina*] [*A publication*] (DLA) .... Car L Repos
Carolina Law Repository (Reprint) [*North Carolina*] [*A publication*] (DLA) .... L Rep
Carolina Law Repository (Reprint) [*North Carolina*] [*A publication*] (DLA) .... N Car Law Rep
Carolina Library Services, Inc. (IID) .... CLS
Carolina Panthers [*National Football League*] [*1995-present*] (NFLA) .... Car
Carolina Population Center [*University of North Carolina*] [*Research center*] (IID) .... CPC
Carolina Power & Light Co. [*Associated Press*] (SAG) .... CaroP
Carolina Power & Light Co. [*Associated Press*] (SAG) .... CaroPw
Carolina Power & Light Co. [*Associated Press*] (SAG) CarP8.55
Carolina Power & Light Co. [*NYSE symbol*] (SAG) .... CPD
Carolina Power & Light Co. [*NYSE symbol*] (SPSG) .... CPL

Carolina Power & Light Co., Technical Library, Raleigh, NC [*Library symbol*] [*Library of Congress*] (LCLS) .... NcRCPL
Carolina, PR [*FM radio station call letters*] .... WAHQ
Carolina, PR [*Television station call letters*] .... WDZE
Carolina, PR [*AM radio station call letters*] .... WIDA
Carolina, PR [*FM radio station call letters*] .... WIDA-FM
Carolina, PR [*FM radio station call letters*] (BROA) .... WVOZ-FM
Carolina, PR [*Television station call letters*] (BROA) .... WZDE
Carolina Pwr & Lt 8.55%'QUICS' [*NYSE symbol*] (TTSB) .... CPD
Carolina Quarterly [*A publication*] (BRI) .... CQ
Carolina Record of Individual Behavior (EDAC) .... CRIB
Carolina Regina [*Queen Caroline*] [*Latin*] .... CR
Carolina Sandhills National Wildlife Refuge (SAUS) .... CSNWR
Carolina Southern Bank [*Associated Press*] (SAG) .... CaroSth
Carolina Southern Bank [*NASDAQ symbol*] (NQ) .... CSBK
Carolina Southern Railway Co. [*AAR code*] .... CRS
Carolina Southern Railway Co. (IIA) .... CS
Carolina Steel Corp. (EFIS) .... CSC
Carolina Sthrn Bk Spartn SC [*NASDAQ symbol*] (TTSB) .... CSBK
Carolina Western [*AAR code*] .... CARW
Carolinas Air Pollution Control Association (COE) .... CAPCA
Carolinas Association of Chamber of Commerce Executives (SRA) .... CACCE
Carolinas Concrete Masonry Association (SRA) .... CCMA
Carolinas Electrical Contractors Association (SRA) .... CECA
Carolinas Independent Automobile Dealers Association (SRA) .... CIADA
Carolinas Intercollegiate Athletic Conference (PSS) .... CIAC
Carolinas Junior College Conference (PSS) .... CJCC
Carolinas-Virginia Athletic Conference (PSS) .... CVAC
Carolinas-Virginia Nuclear Power Associates, Inc. .... CVNPA
Carolinas-Virginia Tube Reactor .... CVTR
Carolina-Virginia Power Pool (SAUS) .... CARVA Power Pool
Caroline Chisholm School of Nursing [*Monash University*] [*Australia*] .... CCSN
Caroline Chisholm Society [*Australia*] .... CCS
Caroline County Public Library, Denton, MD [*Library symbol*] [*Library of Congress*] (LCLS) .... MdD
Caroline G. Atkinson Elementary School, Freeport, NY [*Library symbol*] [*Library of Congress*] (LCLS) .... NFreeAtE
Caroline Islands [*Diocesan abbreviation*] (TOCD) CI
Caroline Islands [*MARC geographic area code*] [*Library of Congress*] (LCCP) .... poci- TT
Caroline Islands (VRA) .... TT
Caroline Public Library, Alberta [*Library symbol*] [*National Library of Canada*] (NLC) .... ACARO
Carolus [*Charles*] [*Numismatics*] (ROG) .... CAR
Carolus Cordell, Catholicae Academicae Duacenae Alumnus [*Pseudonym used by Charles Cordell*] .... CCCADA
Carolus Molinaeus [*Deceased, 1566*] [*Authority cited in pre-1607 legal work*] (DSA) .... Carol Molin
Carolus Molinaeus [*Deceased, 1566*] [*Authority cited in pre-1607 legal work*] (DSA) .... Caro Molin
Carolus Rex [*King Charles*] [*Latin*] .... CR
Caronport, SK [*FM radio station call letters*] (RBYB) .... CJOS
Carop-Rent a Car NV (SAUO) .... Carop
Carora, Lara [*Venezuela*] [*ICAO location identifier*] (ICLI) .... SVCO
Carotene [*Biochemistry*] (DAVI) .... CAROT
Carotene Vitamin (SAUS) .... vit A
Carotenoid Vesicle (DB) CV
Carotid Artery [*Anatomy*] (DAVI) .... CA
Carotid Artery Occlusion [*Medicine*] .... CAO
Carotid Artery System [*Medicine*] .... CAS
Carotid Artery Territory Stroke [*Medicine*] (MELL) .... CATS
Carotid Audiofrequency Analysis [*Medicine*] (DMAA) .... CAA
Carotid Bodies Resected [*Medicine*] (AAMN) .... CBR
Carotid Cavernous Fistula [*Medicine*] .... CCF
Carotid Cavernous sinus Fistula (SAUS) .... CCF
Carotid Chemoreceptor Activation [*Medicine*] .... CCRA
Carotid Chemoreflex [*Medicine*] (MELL) .... CCR
Carotid Compression Tomography [*Medicine*] .... CCT
Carotid Doppler Ultrasonography [*Medicine*] (MELL) .... CDUS
Carotid Endarterectomy [*Medicine*] .... CE
Carotid Endarterectomy [*Cardiology*] (DAVI) .... CEA
Carotid Phonoangiography [*Medicine*] .... CPA
Carotid Photoangiography [*Cardiology*] (DAVI) .... CPA
Carotid Pressure (SAUS) .... CP
Carotid Pulse (SAUS) .... CAR Pulse
Carotid Pulse [*Medicine*] (MELL) .... CP
Carotid Pulse Tracing [*Cardiology*] (DAVI) .... CPT
Carotid Sheath [*Cardiology*] (DAVI) .... CS
Carotid Sinus [*Cardiology*] (DAVI) .... CS
Carotid Sinus Denervation (DB) .... CSD
Carotid Sinus Hypersensitivity [*Cardiology*] (DAVI) .... CSH
Carotid Sinus Massage [*Cardiology*] .... CSM
Carotid Sinus Nerve (AAMN) .... CSN
Carotid Sinus Nerve Stimulation [*or Stimulator*] [*Cardiology*] (AAMN) .... CSNS
Carotid Sinus Pressure [*Cardiology*] (CPH) .... CSP
Carotid Sinus Stimulation [*Cardiology*] .... CSS
Carotid Sinus Syndrome [*Medicine*] (STED) .... CSS
Carotid Sinus Transmural Pressure [*Cardiology*] .... CSTMP
Carotid Sympathetic Plexus [*Medicine*] (MELL) .... CSP
Carotid Tracing [*Medicine*] .... CT
Carotid-Thyroid Transit Time (DB) .... CTTT
Carotis Pulse Curve [*Medicine*] .... CPC
Carousel Memory (SAUS) .... CM
Carousel Transfer Tube .... CTT

Carp Lake Township Library, White Pine, MI [*Library symbol*] [*Library of Congress*] (LCLS) .... MiWp
Carpal Tunnel [*Medicine*] .... CT
Carpal Tunnel Decompression [*Medicine*] .... CTD
Carpal Tunnel Release [*Medicine*] (DMAA) .... CTR
Carpal Tunnel Syndrome [*Medicine*] .... CTS
Carpal-Tarsal Osteolysis [*Medicine*] (MELL) .... CTO
Carpathian (SAUS) .... Carp
Carpathian Mountains (BARN) .... Carp
Carpatho-Russian Benevolent Association Liberty (EA) .... CRBAL
Carpel [*Botany*] (BARN) .... cpl
Carpel (SAUS) .... CPL
Carpentaria (ROG) .... CARP
Carpentaria Community Services [*Australia*] .... CCS
Carpenter [*Navy*] [*British*] (ROG) .... CAR
Carpenter [*or Carpentry*] .... CARP
Carpenter [*Theater*] [*Slang*] (WDMC) .... carp
Carpenter .... CARPTR
Carpenter (MSA) .... CPNTR
Carpenter (AABC) .... CPTR
Carpenter Lake Resources [*Vancouver Stock Exchange symbol*] .... CTA
Carpenter Research Project (SAUS) .... CARP
Carpenter Steel Co. (SAUO) .... CRS
Carpenter Technology (SAUS) .... CARTECH
Carpenter Technology [*NYSE symbol*] (TTSB) .... CRS
Carpenter Technology Corp. [*Associated Press*] (SAG) .... CarpTech
Carpenter Technology Corp. [*Formerly, Carpenter Steel Co.*] [*Associated Press*] (SAG) .... CarTec
Carpenter Technology Corp. [*Formerly, Carpenter Steel Co.*] [*NYSE symbol*] (SPSG) .... CRS
Carpenters and Joiners of America (MHDB) .... CJA
Carpenters and Joiners Protection Society [*A union*] [*British*] .... CJPS
Carpenters' Co. (EA) CC
Carpenters' Co., Philadelphia, PA [*Library symbol*] [*Library of Congress*] (LCLS) .... PPCC
Carpenter's Mate [*Navy*] .... CM
Carpenter's Mate, Construction Battalion [*Navy*] .... CMCB
Carpenter's Mate, Construction Battalion, Builder [*Navy*] .... CMCBB
Carpenter's Mate, Construction Battalion, Draftsman [*Navy*] .... CMCBD
Carpenter's Mate, Construction Battalion, Excavation Foreman [*Navy*] .... CMCBE
Carpenter's Mate, Ship Repair [*Navy*] .... CMSR
Carpenter's Mate, Ship Repair, Boatbuilder-Wood [*Navy*] .... CMSRB
Carpenter's Mate, Ship Repair, Carpenter [*Navy*] .... CMSRC
Carpenter's Mate, Ship Repair, Caulker-Boat [*Navy*] .... CMSRK
Carpenter's Mate, Ship Repair, Cement Worker-Concrete [*Navy*] .... CMSRN
Carpenter's Mate, Ship Repair, Joiner [*Navy*] .... CMSRJ
Carpenter's Mate, Ship Repair, Shipwright [*Navy*] .... CMSRS
Carpenter's Reports [*52-53 California*] [*A publication*] (DLA) .... Carp
Carpenter's Reports [*52-53 California*] [*A publication*] (DLA) .... Carpenter
Carpentras [*France*] [*ICAO location identifier*] (ICLI) .... LFNH
Carpentry (SAUS) .... Carp
Carpentry .... CARP
Carpentry (ADWA) .... carp
Carpentry .... CRPNTRY
Carpentry and Joinery .... C & J
Carper Family Association (EA) .... CFA
Carpet (MSA) .... CARP
Carpet (VRA) .... cpt
Carpet [*Classified advertising*] (ADA) .... CPT
Carpet [*Classified advertising*] (ADA) .... CRPT
Carpet and Rug Industry Consumer Action Panel [*Defunct*] .... CRICAP
Carpet and Rug Institute (EA) .... CRI
Carpet and Upholstery Cleaning Association [*Australia*] .... CUCA
Carpet Cleaners Institute of the Northwest (SRA) .... CCINW
Carpet Cushion Council (EA) CCC
Carpet Information Network [*Tapistree Group, Inc.*] [*Information service or system*] (IID) .... C-LINE
Carpet Institute of Australia .... CIA
Carpet Manufacturers Marketing Association (EA) .... CMMA
Carpet Research, Engineering, Aestetics, Technological and Education (SAUS) .... CREATE
Carpet Wool Council [*Defunct*] .... CWC
Carpeted (ADWA) .... cptd
Carpeted [*Classified advertising*] .... CRPT
Carpeting (SAUS) .... Carp
Carpeting Mats or Rugs [*Freight*] .... CPTNG MATS RGS
Carpets and Curtains (ADA) .... C & C
Carpets and Drapes (SAUS) .... C&D
Carpinteria, CA [*FM radio station call letters*] .... KSBL
Carpinteria Valley Historical Association, Carpinteria, CA [*Library symbol*] [*Library of Congress*] (LCLS) .... CCarpHi
Carpita Corp. [*Toronto Stock Exchange symbol*] .... CYY
Carpmael's Patent Cases [*1602-1842*] [*England*] [*A publication*] (DLA) .... Carp
Carpmael's Patent Cases [*1602-1842*] [*England*] [*A publication*] (DLA) .... Carp Pat Cas
Carpmael's Patent Cases [*1602-1842*] [*England*] [*A publication*] (DLA) ..... Carp PC
Carpometacarpal [*Anatomy*] .... CMC
Carpometacarpal Articulation [*Medicine*] (MELL) .... CMA
Carpometacarpal Joint [*Medicine*] (DMAA) .... CMCJ
Carpometacarpal Joint [*Anatomy*] (DAVI) .... CMJ
Carpometacarpal Joint Dislocation [*Medicine*] (MELL) .... CMJD
Carpometacarpal Ligament [*Medicine*] (MELL) .... CMCL
Carpool System (SAUS) .... CARPOOL
carport (SAUS) .... c/p
Carport (ADWA) .... crpt

Carpus (MELL) C
Carr America Realty Corp. [*Associated Press*] (SAG) .... CarrAmR
Carr America Realty Corp. [*NYSE symbol*] (SAG) .... CRE
Carr Boyd Minerals Ltd./ Commonwealth Scientific & Industrial Research Organization (SAUO) .... CBML/CSIRO
Carr Boyd Minerals Ltd./Commonwealth Scientific & Industrial Research Organization (SAUS) .... CBML/CSIRO
Carr Gottstein Foods [*Associated Press*] (SAG) .... CarGot
Carr Gottstein Foods [*Associated Press*] (SAG) .... CarrGott
Carr Gottstein Foods [*NYSE symbol*] (SAG) .... CGF
Carr Realty [*Associated Press*] (SAG) .... CarrRlty
Carr Realty Corp. [*NYSE symbol*] (SPSG) .... CRE
Carrabelle, FL [*FM radio station call letters*] (BROA) .... WCAF-FM
Carrabelle, FL [*FM radio station call letters*] (BROA) .... WOCY-FM
Carrageenan Induced Foot Edema [*Medicine*] (DB) .... CFE
Carrageenin Pleural Reaction (DB) .... CPR
CarrAmerica Realty [*NYSE symbol*] [*Formerly, Carr Realty*] (SG) .... CRE
Carran's Summary Cases [*India*] [*A publication*] (DLA) .... Carr Cas
Carrasco [*Montevideo, Uruguay*] [*Airport symbol*] (AD) .... CSO
Carrau's Edition of Summary Cases [*Bengal*] [*A publication*] (DLA) .... Carrau
Carre (DD) .... car
Carrefour Canadien International [*Canadian Crossroads International*] (EAIO) CCI
Carrefour de Solidarite Internationale (SAUO) .... CSI
Carrefour des Agents de Pastorale en Monde Ouvrier [*Crossroads of Pastoral Agents and Workers of the World*] [*Canada*] .... CAPMO
Carrefour des Employees de Secretariat [*Crossroads of Secretariat Employees*] [*Canada*] .... CES
Carrel-Dakin [*Fluid*] .... CD
Carrer Development and Assessment Center for Librarians (EDAC) .... CDACL
Carretera .... CARR
Carr-Gottstein Foods, Inc. [*NYSE symbol*] (SPSG) .... CGF
Carriacou [*Windward Islands*] [*Airport symbol*] (OAG) .... CRU
Carriage (WDAA) C
Carriage (ROG) .... CARR
Carriage .... CGE
Carriage (MSA) .... CRG
Carriage and Insurance Paid to Named Point [*Shipping*] (DS) .... CIP
Carriage and Packing [*Shipping*] (ADA) .... C & P
Carriage and Packing (SAUS) .... C&P
Carriage and Wagon Work [*British railroad term*] .... C and W
Carriage Association of America (EA) .... CAA
Carriage Control CC
Carriage Control Character [*Computer science*] CCC
Carriage Drive Mechanism (SAUS) .... CDM
Carriage Forward [*Finance*] (ODBW) .... carr fwd
Carriage Forward (SAUS) .... Cge Fwd
Carriage Free (SAUS) .... CF
Carriage, Insurance, and Freight .... CIF
Carriage Interlock (SAUS) CI
Carriage of Dangerous Goods by Rail Regulations (HEAS) .... CDG Rail
Carriage of Explosives Regulations .... CER
Carriage of Goods [*by sea*] [*Shipping*] .... C of G
Carriage of Goods by Sea Act [*Shipping*] .... COGSA
Carriage Paid (EBF) .... Carr pd
Carriage Paid (SAUS) .... Carr Pd
Carriage Paid (SAUS) .... Cge Pd
Carriage Paid .... CP
Carriage Paid to (SAUS) .... CPT
Carriage Reference Number (ACAE) .... CRN
Carriage Release Key (SAUS) .... CRK
Carriage Reset (WDMC) .... CR
Carriage Return .... CR
Carriage Return Character (SAUS) .... CRC
Carriage Return Code (SAUS) .... CRC
Carriage Return Contact .... CRC
Carriage Return Key (SAUS) .... CRK
Carriage Return/Line Feed (SAUS) .... CRLF
Carriage Return/Line Feed [*Computer science*] .... CR/LF
Carriage Return/Line Feed (ADWA) .... cr/lf
Carriage Services, Inc. [*Associated Press*] (SAG) .... CarrSrv
Carriage Services, Inc. [*NASDAQ symbol*] (SAG) .... CRSV
Carriage Tape Punch (SAUS) .... CTP
Carriage Tape Simulator [*Computer science*] (IAA) .... CTS
Carriage Tension Tape (SAUS) .... CTT
Carriage-to-Interference (SAUS) .... C/I
Carribean Basin Radar Network [*Military*] (DOMA) .... CBRN
Carrie Palmer Weber Junior High School, Port Washington, NY [*Library symbol*] [*Library of Congress*] (LCLS) .... NPtwWJ
Carried (ADA) .... CARR
Carried Down [*Bookkeeping*] .... CD
Carried Forward (EBF) .... cd forwd
Carried Forward [*Bookkeeping*] (ODBW) .... cd fwd
Carried Forward (SAUS) .... Cd Fwd
Carried Forward [*Bookkeeping*] (ODBW) .... cf
Carried Forward [*Finance*] (DFIT) .... CF
Carried Over [*Accounting*] .... CO
Carrier [*JETDS nomenclature*] C
Carrier (CINC) .... CAR
Carrier [*Telecommunications*] (AFM) .... CARR
Carrier (ADWA) .... carr
Carrier [*Telecommunications*] (CET) CX
Carrier [*Telecommunications*] .... CXR
Carrier Access Billing System [*Telecommunications*] (ACRL) .... CABS
Carrier Access Code (SAUS) .... CAC

Carrier Air Group [*Navy*] ... CAG
Carrier Air Group [*Canadian military*] ... CANCARAIRGRP
Carrier Air Group [*Navy*] ... CARAIRGROUP
Carrier Air Group (SAUO) ... CARAIRGRU
Carrier Air Group ... CARG
Carrier Air Group [*Navy*] (MUGU) ... CVG
Carrier Air Patrol (SAUS) ... CAP
Carrier Air Support Detachment (SAUO) ... CARAIRSUPPDET
Carrier Air Support Detachment (SAUO) ... CASD
Carrier Air Traffic Control ... CATOC
Carrier Air Traffic Control Center [*Navy*] (DOMA) ... CATCC
Carrier Air Traffic Control Center - Direct Altitude Identity Readout [*Navy*] (MCD) ... CATCC-DAIR
Carrier Air Traffic Control Officer [*Navy*] ... CATCO
Carrier Air Traffic Controller (MCD) ... CATC
Carrier Air Wing [*Navy*] ... CAW
Carrier Air Wing Reserve [*Navy*] ... CAWR
Carrier Airborne Early Warning Squadron [*Navy*] ... CARAEWRON
Carrier Airborne Early Warning Squadron (SAUO) ... CarAEWRon
Carrier Airborne Early Warning Squadron [*Navy symbol*] (NVT) ... VAW
Carrier Airborne Early Warning Training Squadron [*Navy*] (DNAB) ... CARAEWTRARON
Carrier Airborne Early Warning Wing [*Navy*] (NVT) ... CAEWW
Carrier Aircraft (MCD) ... CA
Carrier Aircraft Contractor (ACAE) ... CAC
Carrier Aircraft Data Operations Control System (SAUS) ... CADOCS
Carrier Aircraft Deck Operations Control System [*Navy*] (NG) ... CADOCS
Carrier Aircraft Equipment ... CAE
Carrier Aircraft [*or Alignment*] **Inertial Navigation System** (MCD) ... CAINS
Carrier Aircraft Inertial Navigation System (SAUS) ... Cains
Carrier Aircraft Maintenance Support Improvement (DNAB) ... CAMSI
Carrier Aircraft Modification (NASA) ... CAM
Carrier Aircraft Operational Compatibility System [*Navy*] ... CAOCS
Carrier Aircraft Service Detachment [*Marine Corps*] ... CASD
Carrier Aircraft Service Division [*Navy*] ... CASD
Carrier Aircraft Service Division [*Navy*] ... CASDIV
Carrier Aircraft Service Unit [*Navy*] ... CASU
Carrier Aircraft Squadron Effectiveness Evaluation ... CASEE
Carrier Aircraft Support Study [*Navy*] (NG) ... CASS
Carrier All-Weather Flying ... CAWF
Carrier Amplitude/Phase Modulation (SAUS) ... CAP
Carrier and Bit Timing Recovery [*Computer science*] (LAIN) ... CBTR
Carrier and Field Service Unit (NVT) ... CAFSU
Carrier and Sideband (IAA) ... CBS
Carrier and Sideband (DA) ... CSB
Carrier Antisubmarine Air Group [*Navy*] ... COMCARANTISUBAIRGRU
Carrier Antisubmarine Air Group [*Navy*] (NVT) ... CVSG
Carrier Antisubmarine Warfare Air Group (SAUO) ... CARANTISUBAIRGRU
Carrier Antisubmarine Warfare Group [*Navy*] (DNAB) ... CARANTISUBGRU
Carrier Antisubmarine Warfare Group (SAUO) ... CARASWAIRGRU
Carrier Arresting Gear (ACAE) ... CAG
Carrier Balloon System (SAUS) ... CABALS
Carrier Balloon System (MCD) ... CBS
Carrier Balloon/Omegasonde (SAUS) ... CBO
Carrier Balloon/Omegasonde System [*National Center for Atmospheric Research*] ... CBO
Carrier Battle Force (SAUO) ... CVBF
Carrier Battle Group (SAUO) ... CBG
Carrier Battle Group [*Navy*] ... CVBG
Carrier Battle Group (SAUS) ... VCBG
Carrier, Bomb, Light Store (SAUS) ... CBLS
Carrier, Bomb Triple Ejector (SAUS) ... CBTE
Carrier Bombs Light Store [*Military*] (PDAA) ... CBLS
Carrier Color Signal ... CCS
Carrier Common Line [*Telecommunications*] (IT) ... CCL
Carrier Common Line Charge [*Computer science*] (TNIG) ... CCLC
Carrier Container Council (SAUO) ... CCC
Carrier Control Approach Trainer (SAUS) ... CCAT
Carrier Controlled Approach [*Aircraft carrier RADAR landing system*] ... CCA
Carrier Corp. (SAUO) ... CRR
Carrier Corp., Library, Syracuse, NY [*OCLC symbol*] (OCLC) ... ZUE
Carrier Corp., Syracuse, NY [*Library symbol*] [*Library of Congress*] (LCLS) ... NSyC
Carrier Current (SAUS) ... CARR CUR
Carrier Current (IAA) ... CC
Carrier Current Communication (SAUS) ... CCC
Carrier Detector (SAUS) ... CARD
Carrier Detector (BUR) ... CD
Carrier Division [*Navy*] ... CARDIV
Carrier Division (SAUO) ... Cardiv
Carrier Elimination Filter ... CEF
Carrier Evaluation and Reporting System ... CERS
Carrier Failure Alarm [*Telecommunications*] (ITD) ... CFA
Carrier Frequencies (SAUS) ... CFs
Carrier Frequency (SAUS) ... CARR-FREQ
Carrier Frequency [*Radio*] ... CF
Carrier Frequency (IDOE) ... f_c
Carrier Frequency Alarm [*Telecommunications*] (TEL) ... CFA
Carrier Frequency Line Transformer (SAUS) ... CFLT
Carrier Frequency Oscillator (SAUS) ... CFO
Carrier Frequency Pulse ... CFP
Carrier Frequency Shift ... CFS
Carrier Frequency Telephone Repeater [*Telecommunications*] ... CRF
Carrier Gas Fusion [*Chemistry*] ... CGF
Carrier Group Alarm [*Telecommunications*] ... CGA
Carrier Identification Code ... CIC
Carrier Identification Parameter (VERA) ... CIP
Carrier Input (MSA) ... CIN
Carrier Insertion Oscillator [*Telecommunications*] (EECA) ... CIO
Carrier Instrument Landing System [*Navy*] (CAAL) ... CILS
Carrier Landing-Aid Stabilization System [*Navy*] ... CLASS
Carrier Level Controller (SAUS) ... CLC
Carrier Liaison Committee [*An association*] (EA) ... CLC
Carrier Mills, IL [*FM radio station call letters*] ... WBVN
Carrier Noise Level ... CNL
Carrier of Iron (Ferrum) (MAE) ... Cf
Carrier Onboard Delivery [*Naval aviation*] ... COD
Carrier Onboard Spare Aircraft (ACAE) ... COSA
Carrier Overhaul (MCD) ... COH
Carrier Packed (SAUS) ... CP
Carrier Performance Measurement Plan (SAUS) ... CPMP
Carrier Performance Rating (AABC) ... CPR
Carrier Pigeon (SAUS) ... CP
Carrier Platoon (SAUS) ... CARR PLAT
Carrier Power Supply, Transistorized [*Telecommunications*] (TEL) ... CST
Carrier Qualification [*Navy*] (NG) ... CARQUAL
Carrier Qualification [*Navy*] (CAAL) ... CQ
Carrier Qualification Training Unit ... CQTU
Carrier Qualifications (SAUS) ... Car Quals
Carrier Receiver (SAUS) ... CTR
Carrier Removal Rate (PDAA) ... CRR
Carrier Replacement [*Insurance*] ... CR
Carrier Replacement Air Group [*Navy*] ... CRAG
Carrier Replacement Air Wing [*Navy*] ... CRAW
Carrier Return Character [*Computer science*] ... CRC
Carrier Route (WGA) ... CAR-RT
Carrier Route Information System [*Postal Service*] [*United States*] (WDMC) ... CRIS
Carrier Route Sort [*Postal Service*] [*United States*] (WDMC) ... Car-rt-sort
Carrier Route Sort [*Postal Service*] [*United States*] (WDMC) ... CR-RT SORT
Carrier Selection (VERA) ... CS
Carrier Sense Collision Detection (SSD) ... CSCD
Carrier Sense Multiple Access [*Telecommunications service*] (BARN) ... CSM
Carrier Sense Multiple Access [*Telecommunications*] ... CSMA
Carrier Sense Multiple Access with Collision Avoidance [*Networking technique*] ... CSMA/CA
Carrier Sense Multiple Access with Collision Avoidance (SAUS) ... CSMA-CA
Carrier Sense Multiple Access with Collision Detection (SAUS) ... CSMA-CD
Carrier Sense Multiple Access with Collision Detection [*Networking technique*] ... CSMA/CD
Carrier Sense Multiple Access with Collision Prevention [*Telecommunications*] (OSI) ... CSMA/CP
Carrier Sense Multiple Access with Contention Resolution (SAUS) ... CSMA-CR
Carrier Sense Multiple Access/Collision Elimination (SAUS) ... CSMA-CE
Carrier Serving Area [*Telecommunications*] (ACRL) ... CSA
Carrier squadron (SAUO) ... Caron
Carrier Stability ... CS
Carrier State ... CARSTAT
Carrier Striking Force [*Tactical Air Command*] (NATG) ... CARSTRIKFOR
Carrier Striking Force [*Tactical Air Command*] ... CSF
Carrier Striking Group [*NATO*] ... CARSTRIKGRU
Carrier Striking Group One (SAUO) ... CARSTRIKGRUONE
Carrier Striking Group Two (SAUO) ... CARSTRIKGRUTWO
Carrier Suitability ... CARSUIT
Carrier Suitability (DNAB) ... CS
Carrier Supply (MSA) ... CS
Carrier Supply, Transistorized (SAUS) ... CST
Carrier Suppression Filter (IAA) ... CSF
Carrier System for Control Approach of Naval Aircraft ... C-SCAN
Carrier Tactical Control Zone [*Military*] (NVT) ... CTCZ
Carrier Task Force [*Navy*] ... CARTASKFOR
Carrier Telegraph (SAUS) ... CT
Carrier Telegraph Receiver ... CTR
Carrier Telephone Channel ... CT
Carrier Telephone (or Telephony) (SAUS) ... CT
Carrier Terminal Information Services (DNAB) ... CTIS
Carrier Test Switch (IEEE) ... CTS
Carrier Tracking Loop ... CTL
Carrier Transfer Station ... CTS
Carrier Transmission Maintenance System [*Bell System*] ... CTMS
Carrier Transmission Measuring System (SAUS) ... CTMS
Carrier Trials Unit (SAUO) ... CTU
Carrier Vehicle [*Military*] ... CV
Carrier Vessel Battle Group (COE) ... CVBG
Carrier Vessel, Nuclear (COE) ... CVN
Carrier Vessel Reactor ... CVR
Carrier Virtual Circuit [*Telecommunications*] ... CVC
Carrier Wave [*A form of radio transmission in code*] (KSC) ... CRW
Carrier Wave [*A form of radio transmission in code*] ... CW
Carrier Wave Oscillator [*Radio transmission device*] (IAA) ... CWO
Carrier Wave Telegraphy (IAA) ... CWT
Carrier Wave Transmission (IAA) ... CWT
Carrierband MODEM [*Motorola, Inc.*] ... CBM
Carrier-Based ... CB
Carrier-Based Airborne Tactical Control System (SAA) ... CB/ATCS
Carrier-Based Airborne Tactical Data System (MCD) ... CB/ATDS
Carrier-Based Antisubmarine Warfare Module [*Navy*] (CAAL) ... CV-ASWM
Carrier-Based Tactical Support Center [*Navy*] (NVT) ... CVTSC
Carrier-Borne Air Liaison Officer (SAUS) ... CBALO
Carrier-Borne Air Liaison Section [*Navy*] ... CBALS
Carrier-Borne Air Liaison Section [*Navy*] ... CBLS

Carrier-Borne Ground Liaison Officer [*Military*] [*British*] .... CBGLO
Carrier-Bound [*Ferrum Iron*] (DAVI) .... CF-Fe
Carrier/Commando Ship/Airfield (SAUS) .... CARAF
Carrier/Container (SAUS) .... C/C
Carrier-Controlled Approach System .... CCAS
Carrier-Controlled Intercept (DNAB) CCI
Carrier-Free [*Radioisotope*] .... CF
Carrier-Free Radar (LAIN) .... CFR
Carrier-Interference Ratio [*Electronics*] (MED) .... C/I ratio
Carrier/Interference Ratio (SAUS) .... C/I Ratio
Carrierless Amplitude and Phase-Modulation (SAUS) .... CAP
Carrierless Amplitude/Phase Modulation (ACRL) .... CAP
Carrierless AM/PM (SAUS) .... CAP
Carrier-on-board Delivery (SAUO) .... COD
Carrier-on-Deck [*Navy carrier-based aircraft*] .... COD
Carrier-Operated Device, Antinoise [*Radio*] .... CODAN
Carrier-Operated Noise Suppression .... CONS
Carrier-Operated Relay .... COR
Carriers & General Corp. (SAUO) .... CGR
Carriers Haulage [*Shipping*] (DS) .... CH
Carriers, Pacific Fleet [*Navy*] .... CARPAC
Carrier's Risk [*Shipping*] .... CR
Carrier's Tax (DLA) .... CT
Carrier's Tax Ruling [*IR Bulletin*] [*A publication*] (DLA) .... CT
Carrier-Specific T-Helper [*Cell*] [*Medicine*] (DMAA) .... CTh
Carrier-to-Interface ratio (SAUS) .... C/I
Carrier-to-Interference (SAUS) CI
Carrier-to-Interference Ratio [*Computer science*] .... C/I
Carrier-to-Interference Ratio [*Computer science*] .... CIR
Carrier-to-Noise [*Ratio*] .... C/N
Carrier-to-Noise Density .... C/No
Carrier-to-Noise Density, Downlink .... C/No/d
Carrier-to-Noise Density, Intermodulation .... C/No/im
Carrier-to-Noise Density, Total .... C/No/t
Carrier-to-Noise Density, Uplink .... C/No/u
Carrier-to-Noise, Downlink .... C/N/d
Carrier-to-Noise, Intermodulation .... C/N/im
Carrier-to-Noise Ratio [*Telecommunications*] (OSI) .... C/N
Carrier-to-Noise Ratio .... CNR
Carrier-to-Noise Temperature, Downlink .... C/T/d
Carrier-to-Noise Temperature, Intermodulation .... C/T/im
Carrier-to-Noise Temperature, Total .... C/T/t
Carrier-to-Noise Temperature, Uplink .... C/T/u
Carrier-to-Noise, Total .... C/N/t
Carrier-to-Noise, Uplink .... C/N/u
Carries Ampholytes [*Chemistry*] .... CA
Carrigan Industries Ltd. [*Vancouver Stock Exchange symbol*] .... CCG
Carrigan Industries Ltd. [*Vancouver Stock Exchange symbol*] .... CRN
Carrillo [*Costa Rica*] [*ICAO location identifier*] (ICLI) .... MRCR
Carrington and Dewhurst Group Ltd. (SAUO) .... CD
Carrington and Kirwan's English Nisi Prius Reports [*174, 175 English Reprint*] [*A publication*] (DLA) .... C & K
Carrington and Kirwan's English Nisi Prius Reports [*174, 175 English Reprint*] [*A publication*] (DLA) .... Car & K
Carrington and Kirwan's English Nisi Prius Reports [*174, 175 English Reprint*] [*A publication*] (DLA) .... Car & K (Eng)
Carrington and Kirwan's English Nisi Prius Reports [*174, 175 English Reprint*] [*A publication*] (DLA) .... Car & Kir
Carrington and Marshman's English Nisi Prius Reports [*1840-42*] [*A publication*] (DLA) .... C & M
Carrington and Marshman's English Nisi Prius Reports [*1840-42*] [*A publication*] (DLA) .... C & Mar
Carrington and Marshman's English Nisi Prius Reports [*1840-42*] [*A publication*] (DLA) .... C & Marsh
Carrington and Marshman's English Nisi Prius Reports [*1840-42*] [*A publication*] (DLA) .... Car & M
Carrington and Marshman's English Nisi Prius Reports [*1840-42*] [*A publication*] (DLA) .... Car & Mar
Carrington and Marshman's English Nisi Prius Reports [*1840-42*] [*A publication*] (DLA) .... Car & M (Eng)
Carrington and Marshman's English Nisi Prius Reports [*1840-42*] [*A publication*] (DLA) .... Carr & M
Carrington and Payne's English Nisi Prius Reports [*1823-41*] [*A publication*] (DLA) .... C & P
Carrington and Payne's English Nisi Prius Reports [*1823-41*] [*A publication*] (DLA) .... Car & P
Carrington and Payne's English Nisi Prius Reports [*1823-41*] [*A publication*] (DLA) .... Car & P (Eng)
Carrington Cotton Corporation [*Australia*] CCC
Carrington. Criminal Law [*3rd ed.*] [*1828*] [*A publication*] (DLA) .... Car Cr L
Carrington Laboratories [*NASDAQ symbol*] (TTSB) .... CARN
Carrington Laboratories, Inc. (MHDW) .... CARN
Carrington Labs [*Associated Press*] (SAG) .... Caringtn
Carrington Labs [*NASDAQ symbol*] (SAG) .... CARN
Carrington, ND [*FM radio station call letters*] (RBYB) .... KANG-FM
Carrington, ND [*AM radio station call letters*] .... KDAK
Carrizal [*Costa Rica*] [*ICAO location identifier*] (ICLI) .... MRCZ
Carrizo [*California*] [*Seismograph station code, US Geological Survey*] (SEIS) .... CRR
Carrizo Springs, TX [*Location identifier*] [*FAA*] (FAAL) .... CZT
Carrizo Springs, TX [*Location identifier*] [*FAA*] (FAAL) .... DMD
Carrizo Springs, TX [*AM radio station call letters*] .... KBEN
Carrizo Springs, TX [*FM radio station call letters*] .... KCZO
Carroll Air Service, Inc. [*ICAO designator*] (FAAC) .... ULS
Carroll Aircraft Corp. PLC [*British*] [*ICAO designator*] (FAAC) .... FBO
Carroll Center for the Blind (EA) .... CCB
Carroll College, Helena, MT [*Library symbol*] [*Library of Congress*] (LCLS) .... MtHC
Carroll College, Library, Helena, MT [*OCLC symbol*] (OCLC) .... MTC
Carroll College, Waukesha, WI [*OCLC symbol*] (OCLC) .... GZB
Carroll College, Waukesha, WI [*Library symbol*] [*Library of Congress*] (LCLS) .... WWauC
Carroll County Comet, Delphi, IN [*Library symbol*] [*Library of Congress*] (LCLS) .... InDelCC
Carroll County Heritage Center, Berryville, AR [*Library symbol*] [*Library of Congress*] (LCLS) .... ArBerC
Carroll County Historical Museum, Delphi, IN [*Library symbol*] [*Library of Congress*] (LCLS) .... InDelCHi
Carroll County Historical Society Museum, Carroll, IA [*Library symbol*] [*Library of Congress*] (LCLS) .... IaCarCH
Carroll County Historical Society, Westminister, MD [*Library symbol*] [*Library of Congress*] (LCLS) .... MdWemHi
Carroll County Public Library, Westminster, MD [*Library symbol*] [*Library of Congress*] (LCLS) .... MdWem
Carroll County Recorder's Office, Delphi, IN [*Library symbol*] [*Library of Congress*] (LCLS) .... InDelCR
Carroll, IA [*Location identifier*] [*FAA*] (FAAL) .... CIN
Carroll, IA [*AM radio station call letters*] .... KCIM
Carroll, IA [*FM radio station call letters*] .... KKRL
Carroll, McEntee & McGinley [*Commercial firm*] .... CM & M
Carroll Public Library, Carroll, IA [*Library symbol*] [*Library of Congress*] (LCLS) .... IaCar
Carroll Publishing Co. [*Information service or system*] (IID) .... CPC
Carroll Rating Scale (SAUS) .... CRS
Carroll Shelby Experimental [*Automobile model*] .... CSX
Carrollton, AL [*FM radio station call letters*] (RBYB) .... WALN
Carrollton, AL [*AM radio station call letters*] .... WRAG
Carrollton, AL [*FM radio station call letters*] (RBYB) .... WZBQ
Carrollton Bancorp [*Associated Press*] (SAG) .... CarrollB
Carrollton Bancorp [*NASDAQ symbol*] (SAG) .... CRRB
Carrollton Community Unit, District 1, Carrollton, IL [*Library symbol*] [*Library of Congress*] (LCLS) .... ICarrCD
Carrollton, GA [*Location identifier*] [*FAA*] (FAAL) .... CTJ
Carrollton, GA [*Location identifier*] [*FAA*] (FAAL) .... GPQ
Carrollton, GA [*FM radio station call letters*] .... WBTR
Carrollton, GA [*AM radio station call letters*] .... WLBB
Carrollton, GA [*AM radio station call letters*] .... WPPI
Carrollton, GA [*FM radio station call letters*] .... WWGC
Carrollton, GA [*AM radio station call letters*] (BROA) .... WWWE
Carrollton, KY [*FM radio station call letters*] .... WIKI
Carrollton, MI [*FM radio station call letters*] .... WTCF
Carrollton, MO [*AM radio station call letters*] .... KAOL
Carrollton, MO [*FM radio station call letters*] .... KMZU
Carrollton, OH [*Location identifier*] [*FAA*] (FAAL) .... TSO
Carrollton Press, Inc., Washington, DC [*Library symbol*] [*Library of Congress*] (LCLS) .... CarP
Carrollton Public Library, Carrollton, IL [*Library symbol*] [*Library of Congress*] (LCLS) .... ICarr
[*The*] **Carrollton Railroad** [*AAR code*] .... CARR
Carrollton Railroad (SAUO) .... CARR
Carronade .... CAR
Carrot Latent Virus [*Plant pathology*] .... CALV
Carrot Mottle Dwarf Virus .... CMDV
Carrot Mottle Virus [*Plant pathology*] .... CMOTV
Carrot Red Leaf Virus [*Plant pathology*] .... CARLV
Carrot Thin Leaf Virus [*Plant pathology*] .... CTLV
Carrot Yellow Leaf Virus [*Plant pathology*] .... CYLV
Carrots in Oil [*Health food capsules*] [*British*] .... CIO
Carrousel Transfer Tube (SAUS) .... CTT
Carrow and Oliver's English Railway and Canal Cases [*A publication*] (DLA) .... C & OR Cas
Carrow Auditory-Visual Abilities Test .... CAVAT
Carrow Elicited Language Inventory [*Education*] .... CELI
Carrow, Hamerton, and Allen's New Sessions Cases [*1844-51*] [*England*] [*A publication*] (DLA) .... Car H & A
Carrow, Hamerton, and Allen's New Sessions Cases [*1844-51*] [*England*] [*A publication*] (DLA) .... Carr Ham & Al
Carrow, Hamerton, and Allen's New Sessions Cases [*1844-51*] [*England*] [*A publication*] (DLA) .... CH & A
Carrow Test for Auditory Comprehension [*Speech and language pathology*] (DAVI) .... CTAC
Carr-Purcell Spin-Echo .... CPSE
Carr-Purcell-Meiboom-Gill [*Radiologic instrumentation*] .... CPMG
Carr's Disease Virus [*Medicine*] (DB) .... CDV
Carry C
Carry .... CA
Carry .... CY
Carry Back (ADWA) .... c/b
Carry Entry (SAUS) .... C Ent
Carry Exit (SAUS) .... CEX
Carry Flag [*Computer science*] (PCM) .... CF
Carry Flip-Flop [*Computer science*] (IAA) .... CFF
Carry Flip-Flop (SAUS) .... C-Flip-Flop
Carry Forward (SAUS) .... CF
Carry Forward [*Accounting*] (MUGU) .... C/F
Carry, High Speed (SAUS) .... CARHSPD
Carry In (SAUS) CI
Carry Look Ahead (SAUS) .... CLA
Carry Look Ahead Generator (SAUS) .... CLAG
Carry Lookahead (MHDI) .... CLA
Carry Out (SAUS) .... CO

Carry Out Remainder Basic Orders .... CARBASORD
Carry Over (ADWA) .... c/o
Carry Over Funds (SAUS) .... C/O
Carry Propagate Adder [*Computer*] .... CPA
Carry Propagate/Carry Save Adder (SAUS) .... CP/CS Adder
Carry Register (NITA) .... CR
Carry Ripple Adder [*Computer science*] (IAA) .... CRA
Carry, Simultaneous (SAUS) .... CARSIMS
Carrying (SAUS) .... CAR
Carrying (MSA) .... CRYG
Carrying [*Freight*] .... CRYNG
Carrying a Dangerous Weapon [*Police term*] .... CDW
Carrying Capacity (EA) CC
Carrying Capacity [*Genetics*] (DAVI) .... K
Carrying Capacity Network (WPI) .... CCN
Carrying Concealed Deadly Weapon [*Police term*] .... CCDW
Carrying Concealed Weapon [*Police term*] .... CCW
Carrying Nuclear-Strike Cruiser .... CNSC
Carry-On Box .... COB
Carry-On Laboratory [*NASA*] .... COL
Carry-On Oxygen System (MCD) .... COS
Carry-Over Data (SAUS) .... COD
Carryover from Previous Log [*Aviation*] (FAAC) .... CFPL
Carry-Over Register (SAUS) .... COR
Carry-Over Storage (SAUS) .... COS
Carry-Save Adder [*Computer science*] (IAA) .... CSA
Carry-Save Adder Module (SAUS) .... CSAM
Cars (SAUS) .... CRS
Cars & Concepts [*Auto industry supplier*] .... C & C
[*The*] **Cars Fan Club** (EA) .... TCFC
Cars of the Past [*An association*] [*Defunct*] (EA) .... CP
Carshaltown's Court Rolls [*England*] [*A publication*] (DLA) .... Carsh
Carson and Staughton [*Inventors of a teargas*] (BARN) .... CS
Carson City [*Nevada*] [*Mint mark, when appearing on US coins*] [*Obsolete*] CC
Carson City, NV [*FM radio station call letters*] .... KBUL
Carson City, NV [*FM radio station call letters*] (BROA) .... KBUL-FM
Carson City, NV [*FM radio station call letters*] .... KNIS
Carson City, NV [*AM radio station call letters*] .... KPTL
Carson City, NV [*FM radio station call letters*] .... KTHX-FM
Carson City, NV [*FM radio station call letters*] .... KWNZ
Carson City Public Library, Carson City, MI [*Library symbol*] [*Library of Congress*] (LCLS) .... MiCc
Carson Gold Corp. [*Vancouver Stock Exchange symbol*] .... CQG
Carson Hill [*California*] [*Seismograph station code, US Geological Survey*] (SEIS) .... CRH
Carson, Inc. [*Associated Press*] (SAG) .... Carson
Carson, Inc. [*NYSE symbol*] (SAG) CIC
Carson Pirie Scott [*NYSE symbol*] (TTSB) .... CRP
Carson Pirie Scott & Co. [*Associated Press*] (SAG) .... CarsPir
Carson Pirie Scott & Co. [*NYSE symbol*] (SAG) .... CRP
Carson Times, Carson, IA [*Library symbol*] [*Library of Congress*] (LCLS) .... IaCarsT
Carson-Newman College [*Tennessee*] .... CNC
Carson-Newman College, Jefferson City, TN [*OCLC symbol*] (OCLC) .... TCN
Carson-Newman College, Jefferson City, TN [*Library symbol*] [*Library of Congress*] (LCLS) .... TJefC
Carson's Rule Bandwidth .... CRBW
CARSTAB Corp., Research Library, Cincinnati, OH [*Library symbol*] [*Library of Congress*] (LCLS) .... OCC
Carstairs Public Library, Alberta [*Library symbol*] [*National Library of Canada*] (NLC) .... ACARS
Carswell [*Texas*] [*ICAO location identifier*] (ICLI) .... KAWN
Cart Away (SAUS) .... CA
CART Central Facility (SAUS) .... CF
CART Data Environment (SAUS) .... CDE
CART Extended Facilities (SAUS) .... CEF
Cart Raman Lidar (SAUS) .... CARL
Carta [*Music*] .... CAR
Carta [*Music*] .... CART
Cartage [*Shipping*] .... CART
Cartage .... CTG
Cartage [*Shipping*] .... CTGE
Cartage (ADWA) .... ctge
Cartagena [*Colombia*] [*Airport symbol*] (OAG) .... CTG
Cartagena/Rafael Nunez [*Colombia*] [*ICAO location identifier*] (ICLI) .... SKCG
Cartago [*Colombia*] [*Airport symbol*] (OAG) .... CRC
Cartago, CA [*FM radio station call letters*] .... KWTY
Carte Blanche [*Credit card*] .... CB
Carte Blanche [*Freedom of Action*] [*French*] .... CBL
Carte de Visite [*Visiting Card*] [*French*] .... C de V
Carte de Visite [*Visiting Card*] [*French*] .... CDV
Carted Luggage (ROG) CL
Carte-de-Visite (VRA) .... CDVT
Cartel. Review of Monopoly, Developments, and Consumer Protection [*London, England*] [*A publication*] (DLA) .... Cartel
Cartel Suisse des Associations de Jeunesse [*Switzerland*] .... CSAJ
Carter & Burgess, Inc., Fort Worth, TX [*Library symbol*] [*Library of Congress*] (LCLS) .... TxFCB
Carter Family Fan Club (EA) .... CFFC
Carter Hawley Hale Stores, Inc. (SAUO) .... CHH
Carter, Paterson & Co. (SAUO) .... CP
Carter-Atkinson Lurmann Mechanism [*Air pollution*] .... CAL
Cartercar Registry (EA) .... CR
Carteret Bancorp, Inc. (MHDW) .... CBC
Carteret Technical Institute, Morehead City (SAUS) .... NcMcC
Carteret Technical Institute, Morehead City, NC [*Library symbol*] [*Library of Congress*] (LCLS) .... NcMcC
Carter's Adaptation Procesor to Aid Interception (SAA) .... CAPTAIN
Carters Dam [*Georgia*] [*Seismograph station code, US Geological Survey*] (SEIS) .... CDG
Carter's English Common Pleas Reports [*1664-76*] [*A publication*] (DLA) .... Cart
Carters English Common Pleas Reports tempore O. Bridgman (SAUS) .... ReptOBr
Carter's English Common Pleas Reports Tempore Orlando Bridgman [*A publication*] (DLA) .... Carter
Carter's English Common Pleas Reports Tempore Orlando Bridgman [*A publication*] (DLA) .... Rep T O Br
Carter's Reports [*1, 2 Indiana*] [*A publication*] (DLA) .... Cart
Carter's Reports [*1, 2 Indiana*] [*A publication*] (DLA) .... Carter
Cartersville, GA [*AM radio station call letters*] .... WBHF
Cartersville, GA [*FM radio station call letters*] .... WCCV
Cartersville, GA [*AM radio station call letters*] .... WYXC
Carterville, IL [*FM radio station call letters*] .... WXLT
Carter-Wallace [*NYSE symbol*] (TTSB) .... CAR
Carter-Wallace, Inc. [*NYSE symbol*] (SPSG) .... CAR
Carter-Wallace, Inc. [*Associated Press*] (SAG) .... CartWal
Carter-Wallace, Inc. .... C/W
Cartesian Coordinate Grid (NVT) .... CCG
Cartesian Coordinate System (SAUS) .... XY
Cartesian Mapping Function .... CMF
Cartesian to Polar .... C-P
Cartesian-to-Polar Converter (SAA) .... CPC
Carthage (VRA) .... Carth
Carthage .... CARTH
Carthage College, Kenosha, WI [*OCLC symbol*] (OCLC) .... GZC
Carthage College, Kenosha, WI [*Library symbol*] [*Library of Congress*] (LCLS) .... WKenC
Carthage, IL [*AM radio station call letters*] .... WCAZ
Carthage, IL [*FM radio station call letters*] .... WCAZ-FM
Carthage, IL [*FM radio station call letters*] (BROA) .... WNKK-FM
Carthage, IL [*FM radio station call letters*] (RBYB) .... WZBN
Carthage, MO [*AM radio station call letters*] .... KDMO
Carthage, MO [*FM radio station call letters*] .... KMXL
Carthage, MS [*AM radio station call letters*] .... WSSI
Carthage, MS [*FM radio station call letters*] (BROA) .... WSSI-FM
Carthage, NY [*FM radio station call letters*] .... WTOJ
Carthage, NY [*Television station call letters*] .... WWNY
Carthage (or Carthagian) (SAUS) .... Carth
Carthage Public Library, Carthage, IL [*Library symbol*] [*Library of Congress*] (LCLS) .... ICart
Carthage Public Library, Carthage, SD [*Library symbol*] [*Library of Congress*] (LCLS) .... SdCar
Carthage, TN [*AM radio station call letters*] .... WRKM
Carthage, TN [*FM radio station call letters*] .... WUCZ
Carthage, TX [*AM radio station call letters*] .... KGAS
Carthage, TX [*FM radio station call letters*] .... KGAS-FM
Carthage, TX [*FM radio station call letters*] .... KTUX
Carthaginia (ROG) .... CARTH
Carthew's English King's Bench Reports [*1686-1701*] [*A publication*] (DLA) .... Cart
Carthew's English King's Bench Reports [*1686-1701*] [*A publication*] (DLA) .... Carth
Carthew's English King's Bench Reports [*1686-1701*] [*A publication*] (DLA) .... Carth (Eng)
Carthographic Assistant (SAUS) .... CA
Carthusian .... CARTH
Carti [*Panama*] [*Airport symbol*] (OAG) .... CTE
Cartier Ebel Christalor .... CEC
Cartier Public Library, Ontario [*Library symbol*] [*National Library of Canada*] (NLC) .... OCART
Cartier Resources, Inc. [*Toronto Stock Exchange symbol*] .... CTE
Cartier-McNamara-Mannix-Morrison & Knudson (SAUO) .... CMMMK
Cartilage (SAUS) .... CART
Cartilage Hair Dysplasia (MELL) .... CHD
Cartilage Induction Factor [*Biochemistry*] (DAVI) .... CIF
Cartilage Matrix Protein [*Medicine*] (DMAA) .... CRTM
Cartilage Oligomeric Matrix Protein [*Biology*] .... COMP
Cartilage Residue [*Orthopedics*] (DAVI) .... CR
Cartilage-Derived Growth Factor [*Biochemistry*] .... CDGF
Cartilage-Derived Inhibitor [*To vascularization*] [*Biochemistry*] .... CDI
Cartilage-Derived Morphogenic Proteins [*Medicine*] .... CDMP
Cartilage-Hair Hypoplasia [*Medicine*] (MAE) .... CHH
Cartilaginous Layer (SAUS) CL
Carting to Shipside [*Shipping*] .... C to S
Cartmell's Trade Mark Cases [*1876-92*] [*England*] [*A publication*] (DLA) .... Cartm
cartobibliographer (SAUS) .... cartobib
cartobibliography (SAUS) .... cartobib
Cartografica Iberica S.A. (SAUO) .... CIBESA
Cartographer (SAUS) .... Crtog
Cartographer [*or Cartography*] (AFM) .... CRTOG
Cartographer [*Navy rating*] .... CT
Cartographer [*MARC relator code*] [*Library of Congress*] (LCCP) .... ctg
Cartographer Development Program (GEOI) .... CDP
Cartographic (SAUS) .... Crtog
Cartographic Advanced Terminal (ACAE) .... CAT
Cartographic and Architectural Archives Division (SAUS) .... CAAD
Cartographic and Audio-Visual Archives Division (SAUO) .... CAVA
Cartographic and Geodetic Processing Squadron [*Air Force*] (AFM) .... CGPSq
Cartographic Application for Tactical/Strategic Systems (ACAE) .... CATSS
Cartographic Assistant [*Ministry of Agriculture, Fisheries, and Food*] [*British*] .... CA

Cartographic Automatic Mapping *(PDAA)* .... CAM
Cartographic Catalog *(GEOI)* CC
Cartographic Conversion Station *(MCD)* .... CCS
Cartographic Data Processing Modelling and Output System
 (SAUS) .... CARDAPMOS
Cartographic Data Visualizer *(GEOI)* .... CDV
Cartographic Draftsman *(SAUS)* .... Cart Draft
Cartographic Feature File *(GEOI)* .... CFF
Cartographic Geodetic Squadron *[Air Force]* .... CGEOSq
Cartographic Information Society *(SAUO)* .... CIS
Cartographic Information Systems Research Group *[Hull University]*
 [British] *(NITA)* .... CISRG
Cartographic Material Order and Tracking System *(GEOI)* .... CMOTS
Cartographic Materials *[International Federation of Library Associations]* .... CM
Cartographic Operations Management Information System *(GEOI)* .... COMIS
Cartographic Perspectives *[A publication]* *(GEOI)* .... CP
Cartographic Production System *(SAUS)* .... CPS
Cartographic Publishing House *[China]* *(GEOI)* .... CPH
Cartographic Representation of Data *(SAUO)* .... CARD
Cartographic Reproduction and Interactive Graphic Editing System
 (GEOI) .... CRAIGES
Cartographic Research Laboratory *(GEOI)* .... CRI
Cartographic Research Laboratory *(SAUO)* .... CRL
Cartographic Technology Laboratory *(GEOI)* .... CTL
Cartographic Test Standard *[Air Force]* .... CTS
Cartographic Users Advisory Council *[American Library Association]* .... CUAC
Cartographic Workstation *(SAUO)* .... CWRU
Cartographic Workstation *(GEOI)* .... CWS
Cartography *(GEOI)* C
Cartography .... CART
Cartography *(MUGU)* .... CARTOG
Cartography *(SAUS)* .... Crtog
Cartography and Geographic Information Science *[A publication]*
 (GEOI) .... CaGIS
Cartography and Geographic Information Society *(GEOI)* .... CAGIS
Cartography and Geographic Information Systems *[A publication]*
 (GEOI) .... CaGIS
Cartography Special Group *[Association of American Geographers]* *(GEOI)* .... CSG
Cartoid Sinus Nerve Stimulation *[Medicine]* *(DMAA)* .... CSNS
Cartoid Ultrasound *[Neurology]* *(CPH)* .... CUS
Cartometric Operations *(GEOI)* .... CO
Carton C
Carton *[Packaging]* .... CRTN
Carton *(MCD)* .... CT
Carton .... CTN
Carton *(WDMC)* .... ctn
Carton Communic ADS *[NASDAQ symbol]* *(TTSB)* .... CCTVY
Cartoon *(VRA)* .... crtn
Cartoon Archetypical Slogan Theatre, London *(SAUO)* .... CAST
Cartoon Conservation Scales *[Educational test]* .... CCS
CARTOON-European Association of Animation Film *(SAUO)* .... AEFA
Cartoon/Fantasy Organization *[Defunct]* *(EA)* .... C/FO
Cartoonists Club of Great Britain *(SAUO)* .... CC of GB
Cartoonists Guild *(EA)* .... CG
Carto-Philatelists *(EA)* .... CP
Cartophilic Society of Great Britain .... CSGB
Cartotheque, Departement de Geographie, Universite de Montreal, Quebec
 [Library symbol] *[National Library of Canada]* *(NLC)* .... QMUGC
Cartotheque, Departement de Geographie, Universite de Sherbrooke,
 Quebec *[Library symbol]* *[National Library of Canada]* *(NLC)* .... QSHERUGC
Cartotheque, Departement de Geographie, Universite du Quebec, Trois-
 Rivieres, Quebec *[Library symbol]* *[National Library of Canada]*
 (NLC) .... QTUGC
Cartotheque, INRS-Urbanisation, Montreal, Quebec *[Library symbol]*
 [National Library of Canada] *(NLC)* .... QMUQIC
Cartotheque, Institut de Geologie, Universite de Montreal, Quebec *[Library
 symbol]* *[National Library of Canada]* *(NLC)* .... QMUGL
Cartotheque, Universite du Quebec, Chicoutimi, Quebec *[Library symbol]*
 [National Library of Canada] *(NLC)* .... QCUGC
Cartotheque, Universite du Quebec, Montreal, Quebec *[Library symbol]*
 [National Library of Canada] *(NLC)* .... QMUQC
Cartotheque, Universite du Quebec, Rimouski, Quebec *[Library symbol]*
 [National Library of Canada] *(NLC)* .... QRUC
Cartotheque, Universite Laval, Quebec, Quebec *[Library symbol]* *[National
 Library of Canada]* *(NLC)* .... QQLACA
Cartouche *(VRA)* .... crtch
Car-Tours in Europe, Inc. .... CTE
Cartridge *(WDAA)* .... cart
Cartridge .... CART
Cartridge *(MSA)* .... CRTG
Cartridge *(SAUS)* .... CTDG
Cartridge *(AABC)* .... CTG
Cartridge *(ADWA)* .... ctg
Cartridge + Television *(SAUS)* .... Cartrivision
Cartridge Access Controller-to-Update System *[Primary Rate, Inc.]* .... CACTUS
Cartridge Access System *(SAUS)* .... CAS
Cartridge Activated Device *(ACAE)* .... CAD
Cartridge Active Miniature Electro-Magnetic *(SAUS)* .... CAMEL
Cartridge Actuated Devices Inc. *(SAUO)* .... CAD
Cartridge Assembly Test *(NG)* .... CAT
Cartridge Direct Memory Access .... CDMA
Cartridge Disk Unit *[Computer science]* *(MHDI)* .... CDU
Cartridge Illuminating Signs *(SAUS)* .... CI Sign
Cartridge Image *(SAUS)* CI
Cartridge Loader *(SAUS)* CL

Cartridge Magnetic Tape Unit .... CMTU
Cartridge Module Drive *(PDAA)* .... CMD
Cartridge Storage Case .... CSC
Cartridge Tape *(NTCM)* .... CT
Cartridge Tape Subsystem *(SAUS)* .... CTS
Cartridge Tape Transport *[Computer science]* *(VERA)* .... CTT
Cartridge Tape Transport Controller *[Computer science]* *(VERA)* .... CTTC
Cartridge Tape Unit *[Telecommunications]* *(TEL)* .... CTU
Cartridge Television, Incorporated *(SAUO)* .... CTI
Cartridge-Actuated Compaction Press *(PDAA)* .... CACP
Cartridge-Actuated Device *[Military]* *(NVT)* .... CAD
Cartridge-Actuated Device *(SAUS)* .... cad
Cartridge-Actuated Flame System *[Terminated]* *[Military]* *(MCD)* .... CAFS
Cartrivision *(SAUS)* .... CTV
Cart-to-Tape Tape *(SAUS)* .... CTT
Cartuja *[Granada]* *[Spain]* *[Seismograph station code, US Geological Survey]*
 (SEIS) .... CRT
Cartularium Saxonicum *[A publication]* *(ILCA)* .... Cart Sax
Cartwheel Fracture *(MELL)* .... CWF
Cartwright, NF *[ICAO location identifier]* *(ICLI)* .... CYCA
Cartwright Public Library, Newfoundland *[Library symbol]* *[National Library of
 Canada]* *(BIB)* .... NFCW
Cartwright's Cases *[Canada]* *[A publication]* *(DLA)* .... Cart Cas (Can)
Cartwright's Cases *[Canada]* *[A publication]* *(DLA)* .... Cartwr Cas
Cartwright's Cases on the British North America Act *[Canada]*
 [A publication] *(DLA)* .... Cart
Cartwright's Constitutional Cases *[1868-96]* *[Canada]* *[A publication]*
 (DLA) .... Cart BNA
Cartwright's Constitutional Cases *[1868-96]* *[Canada]* *[A publication]*
 (DLA) .... Cartw CC
Carupano *[Venezuela]* *[Airport symbol]* *(OAG)* .... CUP
Carupano/Gral. en Jefe Jose Francisco Bermudez, Sucre *[Venezuela]* *[ICAO
 location identifier]* *(ICLI)* .... SVCP
Carus .... K
Carus Chemical Co., Inc., LaSalle, IL *[Library symbol]* *[Library of Congress]*
 (LCLS) .... ILasC
Caruscan Corp. *[Toronto Stock Exchange symbol]* .... CAR
Caruther's History of a Lawsuit. Cases in Chancery *[A publication]*
 (DLA) .... Car Laws
Caruthersville, MO *[AM radio station call letters]* .... KCRV
Caruthersville, MO *[FM radio station call letters]* .... KLOW
Carved *(VRA)* .... crv
Carver Corp. *[Associated Press]* *(SAG)* .... Carver
Carver Corp. *[NASDAQ symbol]* *(NQ)* .... CAVR
Carver County Library, Chaska, MN *[Library symbol]* *[Library of Congress]*
 (LCLS) .... MnCh
Carver Federal Savings Bank *[Associated Press]* *(SAG)* .... CarverFS
Carver Federal Svgs Bank *[NASDAQ symbol]* *(TTSB)* .... CARV
Carver FSB *[NASDAQ symbol]* *(SAG)* .... CARV
Carver, J. C., Neptune NJ *[STAC]* .... CJC
Carver School of Missions and Social Work *(SAUS)* .... CSMSW
Carver's Treatise on the Law Relating to the Carriage of Goods by Sea
 [1885-1957] *[A publication]* *(DLA)* .... Carv Carr
Carver's Treatise on the Law Relating to the Carriage of Goods by Sea
 [1885-1957] *[A publication]* *(DLA)* .... Carver
Carver/Scott Humane Society *(EA)* .... CSHS
Carwash Operators Association *(EA)* .... COA
Carworth Farm Mice (Webster strain) *[Research]* *(DAVI)* .... CFWM
Carworth Farm Mouse, Webster Strain *[Medicine]* *(DMAA)* .... CFW
Cary Memorial Library, Lexington, MA *[OCLC symbol]* *(OCLC)* .... LEX
Cary Memorial Library, Lexington, MA *[Library symbol]* *[Library of
 Congress]* *(LCLS)* .... MLex
Cary on Juries *[A publication]* *(DLA)* .... Cary Jur
Cary. Partnership *[1827]* *(ILCA)* .... Cary Part
Carya cardiformis *[Butternut hickory tree]* Cc
Carya glabra *[Pignut hickory]* .... Cg
Carya ovata *[Shagbark hickory]* .... Co
Carya pecan *[Pecan tree]* .... Cp
Caryatid *(VRA)* .... crytd
Cary's Commentary on Littleton's Tenures *[A publication]* *(DLA)* .... Cary Lit
Cary's English Chancery Reports *[1537-1604]* *[A publication]* *(DLA)* .... Cary
Carzinophilin *[Antineoplastic drug]* *(DAVI)* .... CZ
CAS Registry Number *(SAUS)* .... CRN
CAS Source Index *(SAUS)* .... CASSI
CASA *[Construcciones Aeronauticas Sociedad Anonima]* *[Spain]* *[ICAO aircraft
 manufacturer identifier]* *(ICAO)* .... HA
Casa Editrice Dott. A. Milani *[Italian publisher]* .... CEDAM
Casa El Salvador *(EA)* .... CES
Casa Grande, AZ *[Location identifier]* *[FAA]* *(FAAL)* .... CGZ
Casa Grande, AZ *[Location identifier]* *[FAA]* *(FAAL)* .... CZG
Casa Grande, AZ *[AM radio station call letters]* .... KFAS
Casa Grande, AZ *[FM radio station call letters]* *(RBYB)* .... KLVA
Casa Grande, AZ *[AM radio station call letters]* .... KWLL
Casa Grande Engineering & Mines *[Vancouver Stock Exchange symbol]* .... CGZ
Casa Grande National Monument *(SAUS)* .... Casa Grande
Casa Grande National Monument *(SAUS)* .... CGNM
Casa Grande Public Library, Casa Grande, AZ *[Library symbol]* *[Library of
 Congress]* *(LCLS)* .... AzCg
Casa Grande Ruins National Monument *[National Park Service
 designation]* .... CAGR
Casa Ole Restaurants, Inc. *[NASDAQ symbol]* *(SAG)* .... CASA
Casa Ole Restaurants, Inc. *[Associated Press]* *(SAG)* .... CasaOle
Casa Ole-Restaurants *[NASDAQ symbol]* *(TTSB)* .... CASA
Casablanca *[Morocco]* *[Airport symbol]* *(OAG)* .... CAS
Casablanca *[Morocco]* *[ICAO location identifier]* *(ICLI)* .... GMMM

Casablanca/ANFA [*Morocco*] [*ICAO location identifier*] (ICLI) .... GMMC
Casablanca-Mohamed V [*Morocco*] [*Airport symbol*] (OAG) .... CMN
Casablanca/Mohamed V [*Morocco*] [*ICAO location identifier*] (ICLI) .... GMMN
Casablanca/Tit-Mellil [*Morocco*] [*ICAO location identifier*] (ICLI) .... GMMT
Casamari [*Italy*] [*Seismograph station code, US Geological Survey*] [*Closed*] (SEIS) .... CAS
Casamicciolo [*Isola D'Ischia*] [*Italy*] [*Seismograph station code, US Geological Survey*] [*Closed*] (SEIS) .... CSM
Casamino Acids [*Biochemistry*] .... CAA
Casanova, VA [*Location identifier*] [*FAA*] (FAAL) .... CSN
Casau Explorations Ltd. [*Vancouver Stock Exchange symbol*] .... CUX
Cascadable Real-time Integrated Signal Processor (SAUS) .... CRISP
Cascade (MSA) .... CAS
Cascade .... CASC
Cascade [*Meteorology*] (FAAC) .... CASCD
Cascade Access Method [*Computer science*] (NITA) .... CAM
Cascade Activity Numbering (PDAA) .... CAN
Cascade Airways [*ICAO designator*] (AD) .... CZ
Cascade Amplifier (DEN) .... CA
Cascade Bancorp [*NASDAQ symbol*] (SAG) .... CACB
Cascade Bancorp [*Associated Press*] (SAG) .... CascBcp
Cascade Charge Coupled Device [*Electronics*] C3D
Cascade College, Portland, OR [*Library symbol*] [*Library of Congress*] (LCLS) .... OrPC
Cascade Communications [*Associated Press*] (SAG) .... CascCm
Cascade Communications [*NASDAQ symbol*] (SAG) .... CSCC
Cascade Conference (PSS) .... CASC
Cascade Corp. [*NYSE symbol*] (SAG) .... CAE
Cascade Corp. [*NASDAQ symbol*] (NQ) .... CASC
Cascade Corp. [*Associated Press*] (SAG) .... Cascde
Cascade Corp. [*Associated Press*] (SAG) .... CascdeCp
Cascade Filtration [*Medicine*] (DMAA) .... CF
Cascade Financial Corp. [*Washington*] [*NASDAQ symbol*] (SAG) .... CASB
Cascade Financial Corp [*Washington*] [*Associated Press*] (SAG) .... CascFin
Cascade Holistic Economic Consultants (EA) .... CHEC
Cascade Impactor Data Reduction System [*Environmental Protection Agency*] (GFGA) .... CIDRS
Cascade Improvement Program [*AEC*] .... CIP
Cascade Inline Scripting (SAUS) .... CIS
Cascade International Inc. (SAUO) .... KOSM
Cascade Junior High School, Bend, OR [*Library symbol*] [*Library of Congress*] (LCLS) .... OrBeCJ
Cascade Locks, OR [*Location identifier*] [*FAA*] (FAAL) .... CZK
Cascade Microfilm Systems, Inc., Portland, OR [*Library symbol*] [*Library of Congress*] (LCLS) .... CmI
Cascade Natural Gas [*NYSE symbol*] (TTSB) .... CGC
Cascade Natural Gas Corp. [*Associated Press*] (SAG) .... CascNG
Cascade Natural Gas Corp. [*NYSE symbol*] (SPSG) .... CGC
Cascade Nozzle [*Aviation*] (OA) .... CN
Cascade Orificial Restrictive Device (MCD) .... CORD
Cascade Pioneer-Advertiser, Cascade, IA [*Library symbol*] [*Library of Congress*] (LCLS) .... IaCasPA
Cascade Public Library, Cascade, ID [*Library symbol*] [*Library of Congress*] (LCLS) .... IdCs
Cascade Research (SAUO) .... cr
Cascade Uprating Program [*AEC*] .... CUP
Cascade Variable Conductance Heat Pipe (PDAA) .... CVCHP
Cascaded Carry Save Adder (SAUS) .... CCSA
Cascade-Failure Analysis (IEEE) .... CFA
Cascades [*NWS*] (FAAC) .... CASDS
Cascades, Inc. [*Toronto Stock Exchange symbol*] .... CAS
Cascades Volcano Observatory [*US Geological Survey*] .... CVO
Cascadia Accretionary Prism Detailed Planning Group (SAUO) .... CAP-DPG
Cascadia Juvenile Diagnostic Center, Tacoma, WA [*Library symbol*] [*Library of Congress*] (LCLS) .... WaTCJ
Cascadia Mines [*Vancouver Stock Exchange symbol*] .... CAC
Cascading Style Sheet Level 1 [*Computer science*] (IGQR) CSS1
Cascading Style Sheets [*Computer science*] .... CSS
Cascading Style Sheets Level 1 .... CSS1
Cascais [*Portugal*] [*ICAO location identifier*] (ICLI) .... LPCS
Cascara [*A cathartic*] [*Pharmacy*] (DAVI) .... casc
Cascavel [*Brazil*] [*Airport symbol*] (OAG) .... CAC
Cascavel [*Brazil*] [*ICAO location identifier*] (ICLI) .... SBCA
Cascode Emitter-Couple Logic (SAUS) .... CECL
Case C
Case [*Legal term*] (ILCA) .... Ca
Case (WDMC) .... cs
Case (STED) .... Cs
Case .... CS
Case Aide [*Red Cross*] .... CA
Case Assignment Control File [*IRS*] .... CACF
Case at Bar [*Legal shorthand*] (LWAP) .... CAB
Case Based Hospital Management and Clinical Evaluation in Europe (SAUO) .... CAMAC
Case Center for Complex Flow Measurements [*Case Western Reserve University*] [*Research center*] (RCD) C3FM
Case Center for Electrochemical Sciences [*Case Western Reserve University*] [*Research center*] (RCD) .... CCES
Case Collectors Club (EA) CCC
Case Copy [*Computer science*] .... CY
Case Corp. [*Formerly, Case Equipment*] [*Associated Press*] (SAG) .... CaseCp
Case Corp. [*Formerly, Case Equipment*] [*NYSE symbol*] (SAG) .... CSE
CASE [*Computer-Aided Software Engineering*] **Data Interchange Format** (CDE) .... CDIF
Case Data System [*Computer science*] (PDAA) .... CDS
Case Development Inspection .... CDI
Case Existological Laboratories Ltd. (SAUS) .... CELL
Case Fatality Rate (SAUS) .... CFR
Case Fatality Ratio [*Medicine*] .... CFR
Case File (SAUS) .... CF
Case Handling Information Processing System [*National Labor Relations Board*] .... CHIPS
Case Harden [*Metal*] [*Technical drawings*] .... CH
Case Hardened Steel (SAUS) .... CHS
Case History [*Medicine*] (MELL) .... CH
Case Informant [*Criminology*] (LAIN) CI
Case Institute of Technology [*Later, Case Western Reserve University*] [*Ohio*] .... CIT
Case Integration Services (SAUS) .... CIS
CASE Integration Services (SAUO) .... CIS
Case Law Report Updating Service (SAUS) .... CLARUS
Case Makers Association [*British*] (DBA) .... CMA
Case Management Control System (SAUS) .... CMCS
Case Management Organization (WYGK) .... CMO
Case Management Society of America (EA) .... CMSA
Case Management System [*Department of Justice*] (GFGA) .... CMS
Case Mix (SAUS) .... CM
Case Mix Grouping .... CMG
Case Monitoring [*Air Force*] (AFIT) .... CM
Case Of (AAG) .... C/O
Case of Need .... CN
Case of the City of Chester on Quo Warranto [*A publication*] (DLA) .... Chest Ca
Case Officer [*Criminology*] (LAIN) .... CO
Case Oil .... C/O
Case Oil (SAUS) .... CO
Case on Appeal (DLA) .... AC
Case Packaging [*Shipping*] (DS) C
Case Postale (DD) .... CP
Case Preparation .... CP
Case Project [*IRS*] .... C/P
Case Project Master File [*IRS*] .... CPMF
Case Record Form [*Medicine*] (DB) .... CRF
Case Report (STED) .... CR
Case Review Section [*Social Security Administration*] (OICC) .... CRS
Case Study and Justification Folder .... CSJF
Case Supervisor [*Red Cross*] [*Services to the Armed Forces; Disaster Services*] .... CS
Case Telescoped Ammunition (SAUS) .... CTA
Case Tool for Knowledge Engineering (IDAI) .... CAKE
Case Western Reserve University (GAGS) .... Case West Res U
Case Western Reserve University [*Cleveland, OH*] .... CWRU
Case Western Reserve University, Cleveland Health Sciences Library, Cleveland, OH [*Library symbol*] [*Library of Congress*] (LCLS) .... OCIW-H
Case Western Reserve University, Cleveland, OH [*OCLC symbol*] (OCLC) .... CWR
Case Western Reserve University, Cleveland, OH [*Library symbol*] [*Library of Congress*] (LCLS) .... OCIW
Case Western Reserve University Law Library, Cleveland, OH [*OCLC symbol*] (OCLC) .... CWL
Case Western Reserve University, Law Library, Cleveland, OH [*Library symbol*] [*Library of Congress*] (LCLS) .... OCIW-L
Case Western Reserve University, School of Applied Social Science, Cleveland, OH [*Library symbol*] [*Library of Congress*] (LCLS) .... OCIW-SS
Case Western Reserve University, School of Library Science, Cleveland, OH [*Library symbol*] [*Library of Congress*] (LCLS) .... OCIW-LS
Case Western Reserve University, Sears Library, Cleveland, OH [*Library symbol*] [*Library of Congress*] (LCLS) .... OCIW-S
Case-Based Reasoning .... CBR
Cased Telescoped [*Type of ammunition*] (DOMA) .... CT
Case-Halstead Library, Carlyle, IL [*Library symbol*] [*Library of Congress*] (LCLS) .... ICarly
Casein (VRA) .... cas
Casein .... CAS
Casein Glue Manufacturers Association [*British*] (BI) .... CGMA
Casein Hydrolyzate [*Cell growth medium*] .... CH
Casein Importers Association (EA) .... CIA
Casein Kinase (DMAA) .... CSNK
Casein Plastic [*Organic chemistry*] .... CS
Casein Unit (STED) .... CU
Casein Yeast Lactate [*Media*] [*Biochemistry*] (DAVI) .... CYL
Caseinomacropeptide [*Biochemistry*] .... CMP
Caseless Ammunition Aerial Gun System (MCD) .... CAAGS
Caseless Ammunition Rifle System (SAUS) .... CARS
Caseless Round Gun Program [*Military*] (MCD) .... CRGP
Casement [*Technical drawings*] .... CSMT
Casement Aviation [*ICAO designator*] (FAAC) .... CMT
Casement Projected Transom [*Technical drawings*] .... CPT
Case-Mix Index [*Medicare*] (DHSM) .... CMI
Case-Oriented Studies Information Retrieval System [*Later, TISCA*] [*Navy*] .... COSIRS
Caseouslike Necrosis Cervical Lymph Node [*Medicine*] (MELL) .... CLN
Caserio .... CA
Cases (SAUS) .... Ca
Cases (SAUS) .... CS
Cases and Cabinets [*JETDS nomenclature*] [*Military*] (CET) .... CY
Cases and Opinions in Law, Equity, and Conveyancing [*A publication*] (DLA) .... Cas Eq
Cases and Resolutions (of Settlements; not Holt's King's Bench Reports) [*England*] [*A publication*] (DLA) .... Cas BR Holt

Cases Argued and Decreed in Chancery, English [*A publication*] (DLA) .... Cas Arg & Dec
Cases at Nisi Prius [*A publication*] (DLA) .... CNP
Cases at the End of Popham's Reports [*A publication*] (DLA) .... Poph (2)
Cases Banco Regis Tempore William III [*12 Modern Reports*] [*A publication*] (DLA) .... Cas BR
Cases in Chancery [*England*] [*A publication*] (DLA) .... Cas Ch
Cases in Chancery [*England*] [*A publication*] (DLA) .... Cas in C
Cases in Chancery [*England*] [*A publication*] (DLA) .... Cas in Ch
Cases in Chancery [*England*] [*A publication*] (DLA) CC
Cases in Chancery [*England*] [*A publication*] (DLA) .... Chan Cas
Cases in Chancery [*England*] [*A publication*] (DLA) .... Ch Ca
Cases in Chancery [*England*] [*A publication*] (DLA) .... Ch Cas
Cases in Chancery [*England*] [*A publication*] (DLA) .... Ch Cas (Eng)
Cases in Chancery Tempore Car. II [*A publication*] (DLA) .... Cas Ch 1 2 3
Cases in Chancery Tempore George II [*England*] [*A publication*] (DLA) .... Temp Geo II
Cases in Chancery Tempore George II. (journ.) (SAUS) .... Temp Geo II
Cases in Chancery Tempore King [*25 English Reprint*] [*1724-33*] [*A publication*] (DLA) .... Ca Temp King
Cases in Chancery Tempore King, King's Bench [*1724-33*] [*England*] [*A publication*] (DLA) .... Ca Temp K
Cases in Chancery Tempore Plunkett [*1834-39*] [*Ireland*] [*A publication*] (DLA) .... Ca T Plunk
Cases in Chancery Tempore Talbot, King's Bench [*1734-38*] [*England*] [*A publication*] (DLA) .... Ca Temp Talb
Cases in Crown Law [*England*] [*A publication*] (DLA) .... Cas CL
Cases in Equity Abridged [*1667-1744*] [*England*] [*A publication*] (DLA) .... Cas Eq Abr
Cases in Equity, Gilbert's Reports [*A publication*] (DLA) .... Cas Eq
Cases in Gold Coast Law [*A publication*] (DLA) .... Danquah
Cases in King's Bench [*7-10 George II Tempore*] [*A publication*] (DLA) .... Ann
Cases in King's Bench [*8 Modern Reports*] [*England*] [*A publication*] (DLA) .... Cas KB
Cases in King's Bench Tempore Hardwicke [*1733-38*] [*England*] [*A publication*] (DLA) .... BRH
Cases in King's Colorado Civil Practice [*A publication*] (DLA) .... King Cas
Cases in Law and Equity [*10 Modern Reports*] [*A publication*] (DLA) .... Cas L Eq
Cases in Law and Equity [*10 Modern Reports*] [*A publication*] (DLA) .... Ca T Mac
Cases in Parliament [*A publication*] (DLA) .... Ca P
Cases in Parliament [*A publication*] (DLA) .... Cas P
Cases in Parliament [*A publication*] (DLA) .... Cas Parl
Cases in Parliament (Shower) [*1694-99*] [*A publication*] (DLA) .... Ca Parl
Cases in the Eastern District's Local Division of the Supreme Court [*1910-46*] [*South Africa*] [*A publication*] (DLA) .... E
Cases in the Griqualand West Local Division of the Supreme Court [*1910-46*] [*South Africa*] [*A publication*] (DLA) .... GLD
Cases in the Griqualand West Local Division of the Supreme Court [*1910-46*] [*South Africa*] [*A publication*] (DLA) .... GW
Cases in the House of Lords [*England*] [*A publication*] (DLA) .... Cas HL
Cases in the Supreme Court, Cape Of Good Hope [*A publication*] (DLA) .... Cas SC (Cape GH)
Cases of Appeal to the House of Lords [*A publication*] (DLA) .... Cas App
Cases of Contested Elections [*A publication*] (DLA) .... CCE
Cases of Contested Elections [*A publication*] (DLA) .... C of CE
Cases of Practice, English Common Pleas [*1702-27*] [*A publication*] (DLA) .... Cas Prac CP
Cases of Practice, English Common Pleas [*1702-27*] [*A publication*] (DLA) .... Cas Pra CP
Cases of Practice, English Common Pleas [*Cooke's Reports*] [*A publication*] (DLA) .... Cas Pr CP
Cases of Practice, English King's Bench [*A publication*] (DLA) .... Cas Pr
Cases of Practice, English King's Bench [*A publication*] (DLA) .... Cas Prac KB
Cases of Practice, English King's Bench [*A publication*] (DLA) .... Cas Pra KB
Cases of Practice, English King's Bench [*A publication*] (DLA) .... Cas Pr KB
Cases of Settlement, King's Bench [*1713-15*] [*England*] [*A publication*] (DLA) .... Cas SM
Cases of Settlements and Removals [*1710-42*] [*England*] [*A publication*] (DLA) .... Ca Sett
Cases of Settlements and Removals [*1710-42*] [*England*] [*A publication*] (DLA) .... Cas Sett
Cases on the Six Circuits [*1841-43*] [*Ireland*] [*A publication*] (DLA) .... Cas Six Cir
Cases on the Six Circuits [*1841-43*] [*Ireland*] [*A publication*] (DLA) .... Six Circ
Cases on the Six Circuits (journ.) (SAUS) .... Six Circ
Cases per Officer [*Term used by crime laboratories*] .... CPO
Cases Taken and Adjudged [*First Edition of Reports in Chancery*] [*England*] [*A publication*] (DLA) .... Cas Tak & Adj
Cases Temporary [*Legal term*] [*British*] .... CAT
Cases Tempore Charles 2 [*A publication*] (DLA) .... Ca T Ch 2
Cases Tempore Charles II [*A publication*] (DLA) .... Cas T Ch II
Cases Tempore Finch, English Chancery [*1673-81*] [*23 English Reprint*] [*A publication*] (DLA) .... Cas Temp F
Cases Tempore Finch, English Chancery [*1673-81*] [*23 English Reprint*] [*A publication*] (DLA) .... Cas T F
Cases Tempore Finch, English Chancery [*1673-81*] [*23 English Reprint*] [*A publication*] (DLA) .... Cas T Finch (Eng)
Cases Tempore Finch, English Chancery [*1673-81*] [*23 English Reprint*] [*A publication*] (DLA) .... Ca Temp F
Cases Tempore Finch, English Chancery [*1673-81*] [*23 English Reprint*] [*A publication*] (DLA) .... Rept T Finch
Cases Tempore George I, English Chancery [*8, 9 Modern Reports*] [*A publication*] (DLA) .... Cas T Geo I
Cases Tempore Hardwicke [*A publication*] (DLA) .... Cas Temp Hardw
Cases Tempore Hardwicke, by Lee [*England*] [*A publication*] (DLA) .... Cas T Hard by Lee
Cases Tempore Hardwicke, by Lee [*England*] [*A publication*] (DLA) .... Hardw
Cases Tempore Hardwicke, by Lee [*England*] [*A publication*] (DLA) .... Hardw (Eng)
Cases Tempore Hardwicke, by Lee and Hardwicke [*A publication*] (DLA) .... Hardw Cas Temp
Cases Tempore Hardwicke, by Ridgeway [*England*] [*A publication*] (DLA) .... Hardw
Cases Tempore Hardwicke, by Ridgeway [*England*] [*A publication*] (DLA) .... Hardw (Eng)
Cases Tempore Hardwicke, English King's Bench [*95 English Reprint*] [*1733-38*] [*A publication*] (DLA) .... Cas Temp H
Cases Tempore Hardwicke, English King's Bench [*95 English Reprint*] [*1733-38*] [*A publication*] (DLA) .... Ca Temp H
Cases Tempore Hardwicke, English King's Bench [*95 English Reprint*] [*1733-38*] [*A publication*] (DLA) .... Ca Temp Hard
Cases Tempore Hardwicke, English King's Bench [*95 English Reprint*] [*1733-38*] [*A publication*] (DLA) .... Ca TH
Cases Tempore Hardwicke, English King's Bench [*95 English Reprint*] [*1733-38*] [*A publication*] (DLA) .... Ca T Hard
Cases Tempore Hardwicke, English King's Bench (Ridgway, Lee, or Annaly) [*1733-38*] [*A publication*] (DLA) .... Cas T H
Cases Tempore Hardwicke, English King's Bench (Ridgway, Lee, or Annaly) [*1733-38*] [*A publication*] (DLA) .... Cas T Hardw
Cases Tempore Hardwicke (W. Kelynge's English King's Bench Reports) [*A publication*] (DLA) .... Cas KBTH
Cases Tempore Hardwicke (W. Kelynge's English King's Bench Reports) [*A publication*] (DLA) .... Cas KBT Hard
Cases Tempore Holt [*11 Modern Reports*] [*88 English Reprint*] [*1702-10*] [*A publication*] (DLA) .... Ca TH
Cases Tempore Holt [*11 Modern Reports*] [*88 English Reprint*] [*1702-10*] [*A publication*] (DLA) .... Ca T Holt
Cases Tempore Holt [*11 Modern Reports*] [*88 English Reprint*] [*1702-10*] [*A publication*] (DLA) .... Ca T QA
Cases Tempore Holt, English King's Bench [*A publication*] (DLA) .... Cas T H
Cases Tempore Holt, English King's Bench [*A publication*] (DLA) .... Cas T Holt
Cases Tempore Holt, English King's Bench [*A publication*] (DLA) .... Ca Temp Holt
Cases Tempore Holt, English King's Bench [*A publication*] (DLA) .... Rept T Holt
Cases Tempore King, Chancery [*A publication*] (DLA) .... Ca TK
Cases Tempore King, Chancery [*A publication*] (DLA) .... Ca T King
Cases Tempore King, Chancery [*A publication*] (DLA) .... CTK
Cases Tempore Lee [*1752-58*] [*A publication*] (DLA) .... Ca T Lee
Cases Tempore Lee (English Ecclesiastical) [*A publication*] (DLA) .... Cas Temp Lee
Cases Tempore Macclesfield [*10 Modern Reports*] [*1710-25*] [*England*] [*A publication*] (DLA) .... Cas T Mac
Cases Tempore Macclesfield [*10 Modern Reports*] [*1710-25*] [*England*] [*A publication*] (DLA) .... Cas T Maccl
Cases Tempore Northington [*Eden's English Chancery Reports*] [*A publication*] (DLA) .... CTN
Cases Tempore Queen Anne [*11 Modern Reports*] [*1702-30*] [*England*] [*A publication*] (DLA) .... Cas T QA
Cases Tempore Queen Anne [*11 Modern Reports*] [*1702-30*] [*England*] [*A publication*] (DLA) .... Cas T Q Anne
Cases Tempore Sugden, Irish Chancery [*A publication*] (DLA) .... Cas T Sugd
Cases Tempore Talbot [*A publication*] (DLA) .... Cas Temp Talb
Cases Tempore Talbot [*A publication*] (DLA) .... Cas T Talb
Cases Tempore Talbot [*A publication*] (DLA) .... Ca Temp Talbot
Cases Tempore Talbot, English Chancery [*1734-38*] [*A publication*] (DLA) .... Cas T Tal
Cases Tempore Talbot, English Chancery [*1734-38*] [*A publication*] (DLA) .... Ca T Talb
Cases Tempore Talbot, English Chancery [*1734-38*] [*A publication*] (DLA) .... C T T
Cases Tempore Talbot, English Chancery [*1734-38*] [*A publication*] (DLA) .... Tal
Cases Tempore Talbot, English Chancery [*1734-38*] [*A publication*] (DLA) .... Talb
Cases Tempore Talbot, English Chancery (Forrester) [*A publication*] (DLA) .... Cas FT
Cases Tempore William 3 [*12 Modern Reports*] [*A publication*] (DLA) .... Ca T Wm 3
Cases Tempore William III [*12 Modern Reports*] [*A publication*] (DLA) .... Cas CR
Cases Tempore William III [*12 Modern Reports*] [*A publication*] (DLA) .... Cas T Wm III
Cases under Sugden's Act [*1838*] [*England*] [*A publication*] (DLA) .... Cooke
Cases with Opinions by Eminent Counsel [*1700-75*] [*A publication*] (DLA) .... Cas w Op
Case-Telescoped Ammunition Gun Technology (SAUS) .... CTA-GT
Case-Western Reserve School of Medicine (SAUS) .... CWRSM
Casework [*or Caseworker*] .... CW
Casework Supervisor [*Red Cross*] .... CWS
Caseworker (PHSD) .... Cwrkr
Casey [*Australia*] [*Geomagnetic observatory code*] .... CSY
Casey Community Unit School District, Casey, IL [*Library symbol*] [*Library of Congress*] (LCLS) .... ICasSD
Casey, IL [*Location identifier*] [*FAA*] (FAAL) .... CZB
Casey, IL [*FM radio station call letters*] .... WCBH
Casey, IL [*AM radio station call letters*] .... WKZI
Casey Jones Railroad Unit [*An association*] (EA) .... CJRRU
Casey Township Library, Casey, IL [*Library symbol*] [*Library of Congress*] (LCLS) .... ICas
Casey's General Stores, Inc. [*Associated Press*] (SAG) .... Caseys
Casey's General Stores, Inc. [*NASDAQ symbol*] (NQ) .... CASY
Casey's Reports [*25-36 Pennsylvania*] [*A publication*] (DLA) .... Cas
Casey's Reports [*25-36 Pennsylvania*] [*A publication*] (DLA) .... Casey
Casey's Reports [*25-36 Pennsylvania*] [*A publication*] (DLA) .... Cas R
Caseyville Public Library, Caseyville, IL [*Library symbol*] [*Library of Congress*] (LCLS) .... ICasv
Cash [*Stock exchange term*] (SPSG) C

Cash (DCTA) .... CSH
Cash Account [*Banking*] .... CA
Cash Advance (DCTA) .... CADV
Cash Against Bill of Lading (EBF) .... Cash B/L
Cash Against Disbursement [*Sales*] (MHDW) .... CAD
Cash Against Documents [*Sales*] .... CAD
Cash Against Documents (EBF) .... Cash Doc
Cash Against Documents [*Sales*] (ADA) .... C/D
Cash Against Policy [*Insurance*] .... CAP
Cash Amer Intl [*NYSE symbol*] (TTSB) .... PWN
Cash America International, Inc. [*Associated Press*] (SAG) .... CashAm
Cash America International, Inc. [*NYSE symbol*] (SPSG) .... PWN
Cash and Carry (IIA) .... C & C
Cash before Delivery .... CBD
Cash Book .... CB
Cash Book (SAUS) .... C/B
Cash by Return Mail [*Business term*] (IAA) .... CBRM
Cash by Return Mail [*Business term*] .... CRM
Cash by Return Steamer [*Business term*] .... CRS
Cash Clothing Allowance .... CCA
Cash Collection Voucher CCV
Cash Commodity [*Business term*] CC
Cash Concentration and Disbursement .... CCD
Cash Credit [*British*] CC
Cash Disbursements Journal [*Accounting*] .... CDJ
Cash Discount [*Sales*] .... CD
Cash Discount (WDMC) .... cd
Cash Discount Amount (SAUS) .... CDSAM
Cash Discount Code (SAUS) .... CDSCD
Cash Dispenser [*Banking*] (BUR) .... CD
Cash Dispensing Machine [*Banking*] .... CDM
Cash Earnings [*Business term*] .... CE
Cash Equivalent Value (SAUS) .... CEV
Cash Flow .... CF
Cash Flow Component .... CFC
Cash Flow Return on Investment .... CFROI
Cash Free America [*An association*] (EA) .... CFA
Cash Fund and Expense Accounting (SAUS) .... CF and EA
Cash in Advance .... CIA
Cash in First (SAUS) .... CIF
Cash in Fist .... CIF
Cash in Lieu of Rations (SAUS) .... CILOR
Cash Index Participation [*Investment term*] (DFIT) .... CIP
Cash Item [*Accounting*] CI
Cash Letter [*Banking*] .... C/L
Cash Letter (SAUS) CL
Cash Management Account [*Merrill Lynch*] .... CMA
Cash Management Institute (EA) .... CMI
Cash Management Practitioners Association [*Later, NCCMA*] (EA) .... CMPA
Cash Management System (IAA) .... CMS
Cash Management Trust (ADA) .... CMT
Cash [*or Collect*] **on Delivery** [*Business term*] .... COD
Cash on Delivery (EBF) .... cod
Cash on Delivery Service .... CDS
Cash On Receipt (WDMC) .... cor
Cash on Receipt .... COR
Cash on Receipt of Merchandise (EBF) .... CRM
Cash Operating Profits after Tax (DICI) .... COPAT
Cash or Deferred Arrangement .... CODA
Cash Order [*Business term*] .... CO
Cash Order (WDMC) .... co
Cash Purchasing Agent (AFM) .... CPA
Cash Receipts Journal [*Accounting*] .... CRJ
Cash Refund Notice (TRID) .... CRN
Cash Register Tape .... CRT
Cash Reserve [*Business term*] .... CR
Cash Rules Everything Around Me (SAUS) .... CREAM
Cash Sale [*Business term*] (ADA) .... C/S
Cash Surrender Value [*Insurance*] .... Csv
Cash Surrender Value of Life Insurance .... CSVLI
Cash Technologies .... CHNG
Cash Technologies [*AMEX symbol*] (SG) .... TQ
Cash Terminals Systems [*Commercial firm*] (NITA) .... CTS
Cash Trade [*Investment term*] .... CT
Cash Transaction Report [*Finance*] .... CTR
Cash Value Life Insurance CVLI
Cash Versus Documents .... CVD
Cash with Order [*Business term*] .... CWO
Cash with Order (EBF) .... cwo
Cashel [*City in Ireland*] (ROG) .... CASH
Cashel Mercy Sisters (TOCD) .... CMS
Cashew Nutshell Liquid .... CNSL
Cash-Flow Accounting .... CFA
Cash-Flow-Method (SAUS) .... CFM
Cashier (ROG) .... CAS
Cashier .... CASH
Cashier (TBD) .... Cash
Cashier .... CASHR
Cashier and Accountant [*British*] (ROG) .... CA
Cashiers' Automatic Processing System (DIT) .... CAPS
Cashier's Check CC
Cashiers Cheque (SAUS) CC
Cashmere (VRA) .... cashm
Cashmere and Camel Hair Manufacturers Institute (NTPA) .... CCHMI
Cashmere, WA [*FM radio station call letters*] .... KZPH
Cash-on-Hand [*Banking*] (MHDW) .... COH
Cash-on-Shipment .... COS
Cash-To-Futures Basis [*Business term*] (EMRF) .... CFB
Cashtown, PA [*AM radio station call letters*] .... WFKJ
Casigua [*Venezuela*] [*Airport symbol*] (AD) .... CUV
Casimir, Jennings, and Appleby Public Library, St. Charles, Ontario [*Library symbol*] [*National Library of Canada*] (NLC) .... OSCCJA
Casina [*of Plautus*] [*Classical studies*] (OCD) .... Cas
Casing (WGA) .... CAS
Casing (KSC) .... CSG
Casing Cooling Tank Level (IEEE) .... CCTL
Casing Operating Pressure (SAUS) .... COP
Casing-Collar Log (SAUS) CCL
Casino [*Australia*] [*Airport symbol*] (OAG) .... CSI
Casino Advisory Committee [*Tasmania*] [*Australia*] .... CAC
Casino America [*NASDAQ symbol*] (TTSB) .... CSNO
Casino America, Inc. [*Associated Press*] (SAG) .... CasinoAm
Casino America, Inc. [*NASDAQ symbol*] (SAG) .... CSNO
Casino and Theme Party Operators Association (NTPA) .... CTPOA
Casino Chips and Gaming Tokens Collectors Club (EA) .... CC & GTCC
Casino Data Systems [*Commercial firm*] [*Associated Press*] (SAG) .... CasinoD
Casino Data Systems [*NASDAQ symbol*] (SAG) .... CSDS
Casino Fund International N.V. (SAUO) .... CFI
Casino Magic [*NASDAQ symbol*] (TTSB) .... CMAG
Casino Magic Corp. [*Associated Press*] (SAG) .... CasMagic
Casino Magic Corp. [*NASDAQ symbol*] (SAG) .... CMAG
Casino Reinvestment Development Authority .... CRDA
Casino Resource [*NASDAQ symbol*] (TTSB) .... CSNR
Casino Resource Corp. [*Associated Press*] (SAG) .... CasnRsc
Casino Resource Corp. [*Associated Press*] (SAG) .... CasRs
Casino Resource Corp. [*NASDAQ symbol*] (SAG) .... CSNR
Casino Resource Wrrt 'A' [*NASDAQ symbol*] (TTSB) .... CSNRW
Casino Silver Mines [*Vancouver Stock Exchange symbol*] .... CSV
Casinos Czechoslovakia (ECON) CC
Casio Jet Printing (SAUS) .... CJP
Casion Career Institute (SAUO) CCI
Casitas Dam [*California*] [*Seismograph station code, US Geological Survey*] (SEIS) .... BCD
Casitas Lake [*California*] [*Seismograph station code, US Geological Survey*] [*Closed*] (SEIS) .... BCL
Cask .... CK
Cask .... CSK
Cask Decontamination Pit [*Nuclear energy*] (NRCH) .... CDP
Cask Decontamination Station [*Nuclear energy*] (NRCH) .... CDS
Cask Loading Station [*Nuclear energy*] (NRCH) .... CLS
Cask Support Structure [*Nuclear energy*] (NRCH) .... CSS
Cask Tilting Fixture [*Nuclear energy*] (NRCH) .... CTF
Cask Transfer Tunnels [*Nuclear energy*] (NRCH) .... CTT
Cask Unloading Cell [*Nuclear energy*] (NRCH) .... CUC
Cask Unloading Pool [*Nuclear energy*] (NRCH) .... CUP
Cask Unloading Warm Shop [*Nuclear energy*] (NRCH) .... CUWS
Casket .... CSKT
Casket and Funeral Supply Association of America (NTPA) .... CFSA
Casket Manufacturers Association of America (EA) .... CMA
Casket Store (SAUS) .... CS
Casket Tape (SAUS) .... CT
Casks (SAUS) .... Cks
Casks .... CSKS
Caslan Public Library, Alberta [*Library symbol*] [*National Library of Canada*] (NLC) .... ACAS
Caslan Public Library, Caslan, AB, Canada [*Library symbol*] [*Library of Congress*] (LCLS) .... CaACas
Caslon Old Face [*Typeface*] (DGA) .... COF
Casma [*Peru*] [*ICAO location identifier*] (ICLI) .... SPSA
Casomorphin [*Biochemistry*] .... CM
Casoni Intradermal Test [*Medicine*] (MELL) .... CIT
Caspair Ltd. [*Kenya*] [*ICAO designator*] (FAAC) .... SAL
Caspase-Activated Deoxyribonuclease [*An enzyme*] .... CAD
Casper [*Wyoming*] [*Airport symbol*] (OAG) .... CPR
Casper Air Service, Inc. [*ICAO designator*] (FAAC) .... CSP
Casper College, Casper, WY [*Library symbol*] [*Library of Congress*] (LCLS) .... WyCaC
Casper Junior College (SAUO) .... CJC
Casper, WY [*Location identifier*] [*FAA*] (FAAL) .... CPR
Casper, WY [*Location identifier*] [*FAA*] (FAAL) .... HAD
Casper, WY [*FM radio station call letters*] (RBYB) .... KASS
Casper, WY [*FM radio station call letters*] .... KCSP
Casper, WY [*Television station call letters*] (BROA) .... KCWY
Casper, WY [*Television station call letters*] .... KFNB
Casper, WY [*Television station call letters*] .... KGWC
Casper, WY [*FM radio station call letters*] (BROA) .... KHOC-FM
Casper, WY [*FM radio station call letters*] (BROA) .... KKRR-FM
Casper, WY [*AM radio station call letters*] (BROA) .... KMCG
Casper, WY [*FM radio station call letters*] .... KMGW
Casper, WY [*FM radio station call letters*] (BROA) .... KMLD-FM
Casper, WY [*FM radio station call letters*] .... KQLT
Casper, WY [*FM radio station call letters*] .... KTRS
Casper, WY [*AM radio station call letters*] .... KTWO
Casper, WY [*Television station call letters*] .... KTWO-TV
Casper, WY [*FM radio station call letters*] (BROA) .... KUWC-FM
Casper, WY [*AM radio station call letters*] .... KVOC
Casper, WY [*FM radio station call letters*] (BROA) .... KWYY-FM
Casper, WY [*FM radio station call letters*] (BROA) .... KYOD-FM
Casper, WY [*Location identifier*] [*FAA*] (FAAL) .... SYD
Casper's Forensic Medicine [*A publication*] (DLA) .... Casp For Med

Caspian International Petroleum Co. ..... CIPCO
Caspian Sea and Area [*MARC geographic area code*] [*Library of Congress*] (LCCP) ..... ak---
Caspian Sea Level (SAUS) ..... CSL
Cass County Court House, Fargo (SAUS) ..... NdFC
Cass County Extension Office, Walker, MN [*Library symbol*] [*Library of Congress*] (LCLS) ..... MnWalC
Cass County Historical Society Museum Library, Logansport, IN [*Library symbol*] [*Library of Congress*] (LCLS) ..... InLogCHi
Cass County Historical Society, Walker, MN [*Library symbol*] [*Library of Congress*] (LCLS) ..... MnWalHi
Cass County Library, Cassopolis, MI [*Library symbol*] [*Library of Congress*] (LCLS) ..... MiCassC
Cass County Public Library, Harrisonville, MO [*Library symbol*] [*Library of Congress*] (LCLS) ..... MoHarC
Cass Lake Community Library, Lake, MN [*Library symbol*] [*Library of Congress*] (LCLS) ..... MnCas
Cass Lake Elementary School, Cass Lake, MN [*Library symbol*] [*Library of Congress*] (LCLS) ..... MnCasE
Cass Lake High School, Cass Lake, MN [*Library symbol*] [*Library of Congress*] (LCLS) ..... MnCasHS
Cassagnes-Begonhes [*France*] [*ICAO location identifier*] (ICLI) ..... LFIG
Cassandra: Radical Feminist Nurses Network (EA) ..... CRFNN
Cassanova Brown Streak Disease [*Plant pathology*] ..... CBSD
Cassatie [*Appeal to High Court of Justice*] [*Netherlands*] (ILCA) ..... Cass
Cassava Common Mosaic Virus [*Plant pathology*] ..... CSCMV
Cassava Information Centre (SAUO) CIC
Cassava Latent Virus [*Plant pathology*] ..... CALV
Cassava Vein Mosaic Virus [*Plant pathology*] ..... CAVMV
Cassegrain Feed System ..... CFS
Cassegrain Reflector Antenna ..... CRA
Cassel Group Level of Aspiration Test [*Psychology*] ..... CGLAT
Cassel. Procedure in the Court of Canada [*A publication*] (DLA) ..... Cas Proc
Cassel. Procedure in the Court of Canada [*A publication*] (DLA) ..... Cass Proc
Cassel Psychotherapy Progress Record [*Psychology*] ..... CPPR
Cassell's Anthology of English Poetry [*A publication*] ..... CaAEP
Cassells' Family Magazine [*A publication*] (ROG) ..... CFM
Cassel's Digest [*Canada*] [*A publication*] (DLA) ..... Cass Dig
Cassel's Practice Cases [*Canada*] [*A publication*] (DLA) ..... Cass Prac
Cassel's Practice Cases [*Canada*] [*A publication*] (DLA) ..... Cass Prac Cas
Cassel's Supreme Court Decisions [*A publication*] (DLA) ..... Cass SC
Cassel's Supreme Court Digest [*Canada*] [*A publication*] (DLA) ..... SC Dig
Cassels Supreme Court Digest (journ.) (SAUS) ..... SC Dig
Cassel's Supreme Court Practice [*2nd ed., by Masters*] [*A publication*] (DLA) ..... Cass Sup C Prac
Cassenne [*France*] [*Research code symbol*] C
Cassenne [*France*] [*Research code symbol*] ..... CS
Cassette (ADWA) ..... cas
Cassette (MSA) ..... CASS
cassette (SAUS) ..... Cass
Cassette ..... CASSTT
Cassette + Receiver (SAUS) ..... Casseiver
Cassette Camera Recorder (BARN) ..... CCR
Cassette Information Services ..... CIS
Cassette Magnetic Tape ..... CMT
Cassette Magnetic Tape Operating System [*Computer science*] (PDAA) ..... CMTOS
Cassette Module (AAEL) ..... CM
Cassette Module Controller (AAEL) ..... CMC
Cassette Operating Executive (MHDI) ..... COPE
Cassette Operating Monitor ..... COM
Cassette Operating System (NITA) ..... COS
Cassette Player ..... CASS
Cassette Programming System [*Digital Equipment Corp.*] ..... CAPS
Cassette Single [*Trademark of IRS Records*] ..... Cassingle
Cassette Tape ..... CT
Cassette Tape / Selectric Typewriter (HGAA) ..... CT/ST
Cassette Tape Controller (IAA) ..... CTC
Cassette Tape Loader ..... CTL
Cassette Tape Operating System (IEEE) ..... CTOS
Cassette Television (SAUS) ..... CTV
Cassette Transport System ..... CTS
Cassette User Tape System ..... CUTS
Cassette-Operated System (MSA) ..... COS
Cassia Petroleum [*Vancouver Stock Exchange symbol*] ..... CAU
Cassiar Mining Corp. [*Toronto Stock Exchange symbol*] ..... CSQ
Cassidy Class (EA) CC
Cassidy Resources Ltd. [*Vancouver Stock Exchange symbol*] ..... CYT
Cassidy's Ltd. [*Toronto Stock Exchange symbol*] ..... CYL
Cassilandia [*Brazil*] [*Airport symbol*] (OAG) ..... CSS
Cassini Plasma Spectrometer (SAUS) ..... CAPS
Cassiodori Variarum [*A publication*] (DLA) ..... Cassiod Var
Cassiodorus [*Sixth century AD*] [*Classical studies*] (OCD) ..... Cassiod
Cassiopeia [*Constellation*] ..... Cas
Cassiopeia [*Constellation*] ..... Cass
Cassiopeia A [*Constellation*] ..... CasA
Cassiopeium [*An early name for the chemical element lutetium*] ..... Cp
Cassite (BJA) ..... Cass
Cassiterite (SAUS) ..... kt
Casson's Local Government Board Decisions [*1902-16*] [*England*] [*A publication*] (DLA) ..... Cass LGB
Cassopolis, MI [*AM radio station call letters*] (RBYB) ..... WGTO
Cassovia Air [*Slovakia*] [*ICAO designator*] (FAAC) CVI
Cassville, MO [*FM radio station call letters*] ..... KRLK
Cast (AAG) C
Cast (VRA) ..... cst
Cast Aluminum Structure ..... CAS
Cast Aluminum Structure Technology ..... CAST
Cast and Sofati Container Line (SAUS) ..... SCL
Cast Arrested Repeating Persons [*Fictitious fishing term*] ..... CARP
Cast Brass ..... CB
Cast Brass ..... CBR
Cast Bronze (IIA) ..... CB
Cast Bronze Bearings Institute [*Later, NFFS*] ..... CBBI
Cast Bronze Institute [*Defunct*] (EA) ..... CBI
Cast Bullet Association (EA) ..... CBA
Cast Carbon Steel ..... CCS
Cast Coated [*Paper*] (DGA) CC
Cast Copper CC
Cast Double Base ..... CDB
Cast Enamel [*Classified advertising*] (ADA) ..... CE
Cast Frame (SAUS) ..... CF
Cast Iron CI
Cast Iron Electrode (SAUS) ..... ECI
Cast Iron Maintenance Optimization System [*for gas distribution mains*] [*A trademark*] ..... CIMOS
Cast Iron Pipe Research Association [*Later, DIPRA*] (EA) ..... CIPRA
Cast Iron Seat Collectors Association (EA) ..... CISCA
Cast Iron Soil Pipe Foundation [*Defunct*] (EA) ..... CISPF
Cast Iron Soil Pipe Institute ..... CISP
Cast Iron Soil Pipe Institute (EA) ..... CISPI
Cast Metal Coalition (SAUS) ..... CMC
Cast Metal Part ..... CMP
Cast Metals Association (EA) ..... NFA
Cast Metals Federation [*Later, NFA*] (EA) ..... CMF
Cast Number [*In urinalysis*] [*Biochemistry*] (DAVI) ..... CASTNO
Cast Off, to X-Ray [*Performed with the cast off*] [*Orthopedics*] (DAVI) ..... COTX
Cast Polypropylene (SAUS) ..... CPP
CAST [*Computerized Automatic System Tester*] **Programming Language** ..... CPL
Cast Removed, Take to X-Ray [*Orthopedics*] (DAVI) ..... CRTX
Cast Steel ..... CS
Cast Stone (AAG) ..... CS
Cast Stone [*Technical drawings*] ..... CST
Cast Stone Industry (SAUO) ..... CSI
Cast Stone Institute (NTPA) ..... CSI
Castable Smoke Mix Grenade (MCD) ..... CSMG
Castalia Foundation [*Defunct*] (EA) ..... CF
Castalia, OH [*FM radio station call letters*] ..... WGGN
Castana, IA [*FM radio station call letters*] (BROA) ..... KMAP-FM
Castanospermine [*Biochemistry*] ..... CST
Castaway [*Fiji*] [*Airport symbol*] (OAG) ..... CST
CasTech Aluminum Group [*NYSE symbol*] (TTSB) ..... CTA
Castech Aluminum Group, Inc. [*Associated Press*] (SAG) ..... Castech
Castech Aluminum Group, Inc. [*NYSE symbol*] (SAG) ..... CTA
Castel Tesino [*Italy*] [*Geomagnetic observatory code*] ..... CTS
Castellate ..... CSTL
Castellatus (SAUS) ..... Cas
Castelle [*NASDAQ symbol*] (TTSB) ..... CSTL
Castello Resources Ltd. [*Vancouver Stock Exchange symbol*] ..... CZH
Castelnaudary/Villeneuve [*France*] [*ICAO location identifier*] (ICLI) ..... LFMW
Castelnau-Magnoac [*France*] [*ICAO location identifier*] (ICLI) ..... LFDQ
Castelsarrasin/Moissac [*France*] [*ICAO location identifier*] (ICLI) ..... LFCX
Caster and Floor Truck Manufacturers Association [*Later, ICM*] ..... CFT
Caster and Floor Truck Manufacturers Associations (SAUO) ..... CFTMA
Caster Association of America (EA) ..... CAA
Casters and Towbar ..... CT
Castilejo-Dalitz-Dyson ..... CDD
Castilho/Urubupunga [*Brazil*] [*ICAO location identifier*] (ICLI) ..... SBUP
Castillejos, Zambales [*Philippines*] [*ICAO location identifier*] (ICLI) ..... RPUJ
Castillo de San Marcos National Monument ..... CASA
Castinet ..... CAST
Casting ..... CAST
Casting (ADWA) ..... csg
Casting (KSC) ..... CSTG
Casting and Solidification Technology (SAUS) ..... CAST
Casting Division ..... CD
Casting Industry Suppliers Association (EA) ..... CISA
Casting Society of America (WDMC) ..... CSA
Casting Up [*Printing*] (DGA) ..... CU
Castings Research Laboratory (SAUO) ..... CRL
Cast-in-Place Concrete [*Technical drawings*] ..... CIPC
Cast-Iron Pipe [*Technical drawings*] ..... CIP
Cast-Iron Soil Pipe (DNAB) ..... CISP
Castle C
Castle (ADWA) ..... cas
Castle (MSA) ..... CAS
Castle ..... CAST
Castle ..... CASTL
Castle AM & Co. [*Associated Press*] (SAG) ..... CastlAM
Castle [*A. M.*] **& Co.** [*AMEX symbol*] (SPSG) ..... CAS
Castle [*A. M.*] **& Co.** [*Associated Press*] (SAG) ..... CastleAM
Castle & Cooke [*Associated Press*] (SAG) ..... CastCk
Castle & Cooke [*NYSE symbol*] (SAG) ..... CCS
Castle & Cooke Inc. [*NYSE symbol*] (TTSB) ..... CCS
Castle & Cooke, Inc. (SAUO) ..... CKE
Castle Aviation, Inc. [*ICAO designator*] (FAAC) ..... CSJ
Castle Clinton National Monument ..... CACL
Castle Convert Fund [*AMEX symbol*] (TTSB) ..... CVF
Castle Convertible Fund, Inc. [*Associated Press*] (SAG) ..... CasFd
Castle Convertible Fund, Inc. [*AMEX symbol*] (SPSG) ..... CVF
Castle Energy Corp. [*Associated Press*] (SAG) ..... CastleEn

Castle Energy Corp. [NASDAQ symbol] (NQ) .... CECX
Castle Hill Museum, Cobham, VA [Library symbol] [Library of Congress]
(LCLS) .... ViCoC
Castle Mountain [California] [Seismograph station code, US Geological
Survey] (SEIS) .... CTM
Castle Nut (SAUS) .... CAS NUT
Castle on Rating [4th ed.] [1903] [A publication] (DLA) .... Cast Rat
Castle Rock [California] [Seismograph station code, US Geological Survey]
(SEIS) .... CRC
Castle Rock [New York] [Seismograph station code, US Geological Survey]
(SEIS) .... CTR
Castle Rock, CO [FM radio station call letters] (RBYB) .... KJMN-FM
Castle Rock, CO [FM radio station call letters] (RBYB) .... KNRX
Castle Rock, CO [Television station call letters] .... KWHD
Castle Rock, WA [FM radio station call letters] .... KAZL
Castle Rock, WA [FM radio station call letters] (RBYB) .... KRQT-FM
Castlecrag Conservation Society [Australia] .... CCS
Castlegar [Canada] [Airport symbol] (OAG) .... YCG
Castlegar and District Public Library, Castlegar, British Columbia [Library
symbol] [National Library of Canada] (NLC) .... BCD
Castlegar, BC [AM radio station call letters] .... CKQR
Castlegar, BC [FM radio station call letters] (BROA) .... CKQR-FM
Castlegar, BC [ICAO location identifier] (ICLI) .... CYCG
Castleman's Disease [Oncology] .... CD
Castlepoint [New Zealand] [Seismograph station code, US Geological
Survey] (SEIS) .... CAZ
Castles Association (EA) .... CA
Castle's Law of Commerce in Time of War [A publication] (DLA) ...... Cast Com
Castleton State College, Castleton, VT [Library symbol] [Library of
Congress] (LCLS) .... VtCasT
Castleton, VT [FM radio station call letters] .... WIUV
Cast-Off X-Ray [Performed with the cast off] [Orthopedics] (DAVI) ...... COX
Castor Oil .... CO
Castor Oil (SAUS) .... CO
Castor Public Library, Alberta [Library symbol] [National Library of Canada]
(NLC) .... ACAST
Castoreum [Castor] [Pharmacy] (ROG) .... CASTOR
Cast-Out-Nines .... CON
Castrate .... CAST
Castres/Mazamet [France] [ICAO location identifier] (ICLI) .... LFCK
Castries/Vigie [St. Lucia] [ICAO location identifier] (ICLI) .... TLPC
Castro [Chile] [Airport symbol] (AD) .... WCA
Castro/Gamboa [Chile] [ICAO location identifier] (ICLI) .... SCST
Castroville, TX [Location identifier] [FAA] (FAAL) .... CVB
Castrovirreyna [Peru] [Seismograph station code, US Geological Survey]
(SEIS) .... CST
Casual .... CAS
Casual .... CSL
Casual Disability Exclusion [Insurance] .... CDEX
Casual Payment .... CASPMT
Casual Payments Book [British] (ADA) .... CPB
Casual-Associative Network [for medical applications] [Computer
science] .... CASNET
Casualties (SAUS) .... CAS
Casualties Reception Center (SAUO) .... Casu RC
Casualties Union (EA) .... CU
Casualty [Insurance] C
Casualty (AFM) .... CAS
Casualty .... CSLTY
Casualty Actuarial Society (EA) .... CAS
Casualty Air Evacuation Unit [RAF] [British] .... CAEU
Casualty Analysis for Determining Weapon System Effectiveness [Army]
(AABC) .... CAWSE
Casualty and Damage Assessment (MCD) .... CDA
Casualty Assessment System [Army] .... CAS
Casualty Assistance Calls and Funeral Honors Support Program [Military]
(DNAB) .... CAC/FHS
Casualty Assistance Calls Officer .... CACO
Casualty Assistance Calls Program (CINC) .... CACP
Casualty Assistance Control Officer [Navy] (DOMA) .... CACO
Casualty Assistance Officer [Army] (ADDR) .... CAO
Casualty Branch [BUPERS] .... CB
Casualty Canceled [Navy] .... CASCAN
Casualty Clearing Officer (SAUS) .... CCO
Casualty Clearing Officer (SAUO) .... CCO
Casualty Clearing Point (SAUS) .... CCP
Casualty Clearing Station [Military] .... CCS
Casualty Collecting Post (SAUO) .... CCP
Casualty Collecting-Post (NATG) .... CCP
Casualty Collection Point [Army] (INF) .... CCP
Casualty Control Panel (CAAL) .... CCP
Casualty Control Station [Military] (DNAB) .... CASCON
Casualty Corrected [Navy] .... CASCOR
Casualty Correction Report .... CASCOR
Casualty Department [British police] .... CD
Casualty Estimation Study [Military] .... CES
Casualty Evacuation (MILB) .... casevac
Casualty Evacuation .... CASEVAC
Casualty Evacuation (SAUS) .... CE
Casualty Evacuation and Control Ship [Navy] (NVT) .... CECS
Casualty Evacuation Officer .... CEO
Casualty Evacuation Train [British] .... CET
Casualty Exercise (SAUO) .... CASEX
Casualty Firing Panel .... CFP
Casualty Information Support System [Military] (DNAB) .... CASINFOSUPPSYS

Casualty Information Support System [Military] (DNAB) .... CISS
Casualty Information System (MCD) .... CIS
Casualty Insurance Logistics Automated (PDAA) .... CILA
Casualty Mode [Military] (CAAL) .... CM
Casualty Officer [Military] (DAVI) .... CO
Casualty Procedure .... CASPRO
Casualty Receiving and Treatment Ship [Environmental science] (COE) ...... CRTS
Casualty Receiving Hospital [British] .... CRH
Casualty Receiving Hospital (SAUO) .... CRH
Casualty Report [Navy] .... CASREP
Casualty Report [Navy] .... CASREPT
Casualty Situation Report .... CASSIT
Casualty Staging Facility [Military] (AFM) .... CSF
Casualty Staging Unit [Military] (AFM) .... CSU
Casualty Summary Report (ACAE) .... CASREP
Casualty Surgeons Association [British] .... CSA
Casualty Surgeons Association (SAUO) .... CSA
Casualty Transport Ship (SAUS) .... CTS
Casualty Underwriting Manual [Insurance] .... CUM
Casualty Vulnerability Number .... CVN
Casualty Weapon Director .... CWD
Casualty Weapon Director Panel .... CWDP
Caswall. Copyholds [3rd ed.] [1841] [A publication] (DLA) .... Casw Cop
Cat Allergen [Immunology] .... CA
Cat Association of the Northern Territory [Australia] .... CANT
Cat Aviation, AG [Switzerland] [ICAO designator] (FAAC) .... CAZ
Cat Cay [Bahamas] [Airport symbol] (OAG) .... CXY
Cat Collectors [Commercial firm] (EA) CC
Cat Dander [Test] [Medicine] (DB) .... CD
Cat Eye Syndrome [Medicine] .... CES
Cat Fanciers' Association (EA) .... CFA
Cat Fanciers' Federation (EA) .... CFF
Cat Fancy [A publication] (BRI) .... Cat Fan
Cat Fund (EA) .... CF
Cat Island [Bahamas] [Airport symbol] (AD) .... CAT
Cat Kargo Hava Tasima, AS [Turkey] [FAA designator] (FAAC) .... KET
Cat Pack ["Women's Wear Daily" slang for jetsetters] .... CP
Cat Protection Society of New South Wales [Australia] .... CPSNSW
Cat Protection Society of Victoria [Australia] .... CPSV
Cat Scratch [Medicine] (AAMN) .... CS
Cat Scratch Disease [Medicine] .... CSD
Cat Scratch Disease Bacillus [Medicine] (DMAA) .... CSDB
Cata SACIFI [Argentina] [ICAO designator] (FAAC) .... CTZ
Catabolism and Anabolism [Medicine] (MELL) .... C & A
Catabolite Activator Protein [Biochemistry, genetics] .... CAP
Catabolite Gene Activator [Medicine] (DMAA) .... CGA
Catabolite Gene Activator Protein [Biochemistry, genetics] .... CAP
Catabolite Modular Factor (DB) .... CMF
Catacamas [Honduras] [ICAO location identifier] (ICLI) .... MHCA
Cataclysmic Binary [Computer science] .... CB
Cataclysmic Variable [Astronomy, physics] CV
Catacomb (VRA) .... ctmb
Catadioptric [Optics] .... CAT
Catadioptric-Herschelian Telescope (PDAA) .... CHT
Catafalque .... CAT
Catahoula Parish Library, Harrisonburg, LA [Library symbol] [Library of
Congress] (LCLS) .... LHarC
Catalan [MARC language code] [Library of Congress] (LCCP) .... cat
Catalan [Language, etc.] .... CAT
Catalan (ADWA) .... Catal
Catalan National Council (SAUO) .... CNC
Catalan Solidarity [Political party] (PPW) .... SC
Catalan version of MARC (SAUS) .... CATMARC
Catalase [Also, CTS] [An enzyme] .... CAT
Catalase [An enzyme] .... CTS
Catalase B (DMAA) .... CATB
Catalepton [of Vergil] [Classical studies] (OCD) .... Catal
Catalina 22 National Sailing Association (EA) .... CTNSA
Catalina 25 National Association (EA) .... CTNA
Catalina Airlines [ICAO designator] (AD) .... KG
Catalina Flying Boats, Inc. [FAA designator] (FAAC) .... CBT
Catalina Island [California] [Airport symbol] (OAG) .... AVX
Catalina Island [California] [Seismograph station code, US Geological
Survey] (SEIS) .... CIS
Catalina Island [California] [Airport symbol] [Obsolete] (OAG) .... TWH
Catalina Island [California] Airport in the Sky [Airport symbol] (OAG) ...... CIB
Catalina Lighting [Associated Press] (SAG) .... Cata ILt
Catalina Lighting [NYSE symbol] (SAG) .... LTG
Catalina Marine Science Center [University of Southern California] [Research
center] .... CMSC
Catalina Marketing [NYSE symbol] (TTSB) .... POS
Catalina Marketing Corp. [Associated Press] (SAG) .... CatMkt
Catalina Marketing Corp. [NYSE symbol] (SPSG) .... POS
Catalog C
Catalog (WDMC) .... cat
Catalog (KSC) .... CAT
Catalog .... CATA
Catalog (ROG) .... CATAL
Catalog (BUR) .... CATLG
Catalog (AL) .... Catlg
Catalog Access System [Project for automated library systems] .... CATS
Catalog Card Corp. of America [Information service or system] (IID) CCC
Catalog Card Corporation of America (NITA) 3C
Catalog Card Format Program (SAUS) .... CCFP
Catalog Data Activity [Army] .... CDA

Catalog Data Agency (MCD) ... CDA
Catalog Events [*Exhibition of US company product catalogs, etc., in foreign markets*] [*Department of Commerce*] ... CE
Catalog for Information Exchange and Message Standards (MCD) ... CIEMS
Catalog Input Transmittal (DNAB) ... CIT
Catalog Interoperability (SAUS) ... CI
Catalog Management Data Notification [*Army*] (AABC) ... CMDN
Catalog Management System (SAUS) ... CMS
Catalog Master Data File ... CMDF
Catalog Number ... CANO
Catalog of American Portraits [*Smithsonian Institution*] [*Washington, DC*] ... CAP
Catalog of Approved Requirement Documents [*Army*] (RDA) ... CARDS
Catalog of Available and Standard Hardware [*NASA*] ... CASH
Catalog of Data Sources (SAUS) ... CDS
Catalog of Environmental Resource Data (GEOI) ... CERD
Catalog of Federal Domestic Assistance [*A publication*] ... CFDA
Catalog of Galactic Planetary Nebulae (SAUS) ... CGPN
Catalog of Material Improvement Cards (MCD) ... CMIC
Catalog of Museum Publications and Media [*A publication*] ... CMPM
Catalog of Navy Training Courses (NVT) ... CANTRAC
Catalog of Programs ... CAPR
Catalog of the New York Public Library ... CATNYP
Catalog of the Public Documents [*A bibliographic publication*] ... CPD
Catalog of Virginia Library Resources (EDAC) ... CAVALIR
Catalog On-Line [*National Library of Medicine*] [*Bibliographic database*] ... CATLINE
Catalog Online Tool [*DoD*] ... COLT
Catalog Performance Optimizer (CIST) ... CPO
Catalog Recovery Area [*Computer science*] ... CRA
Catalog Services Association [*Defunct*] (EA) ... CSA
Catalog Support System [*UTLAS International Canada*] [*Information service or system*] ... CATSS
Catalog Typing Worksheet [*for MT/ST typist*] ... CWS
Catalog Writing (ACAE) ... CW
Cataloged File (SAUS) ... CF
Cataloger (AL) ... Catlgr
Cataloging (AL) ... Catlg
Cataloging (SAUS) ... CATLG
Cataloging and Classification Section [*of ALA*] ... CCS
Cataloging and Classification Section's Descriptive Cataloging Committee [*of ALA*] ... CCS/DCC
Cataloging and Indexing Number [*Later, AGRICOLA*] [*National Agricultural Library*] [*Database*] ... CAIN
Cataloging and Indexing Systems Special Interest Group (SAUO) ... CISSIG
Cataloging and Provisioning System (MCD) ... CPS
Cataloging and Standardization Center [*Air Force*] ... CASC
Cataloging and Standardization Division (SAUO) ... CSD
Cataloging and Standardization Office [*Air Force*] (AFIT) ... CASO
Cataloging Code Revision Committee [*of ALA*] ... CCRC
Cataloging Distribution Service [*Library of Congress*] [*Washington, DC*] ... CDS
Cataloging in Publication [*Pronounced "sip"*] [*Formerly, CIS*] [*Library science*] ... CIP
Cataloging in Source [*Later, CIP*] [*Library science*] ... CIS
Cataloging Management Data [*Army*] ... CMD
Cataloging Management Team [*American Library Association*] ... CMT
Cataloging Responsibility Code ... CRC
Cataloging Services Department, OCLC [*Online Computer Library Center*], **Inc., Columbus, OH** [*OCLC symbol*] (OCLC) ... SER
Cataloging-in-Publication Program (SAUS) ... CIPP
Catalogo Colectivo de Publicaciones Periodicas [*Database*] [*Ministerio de Cultura*] [*Spanish*] [*Information service or system*] (CRD) ... CPUP
Catalogo Italiano Riviste su Calcolatore Elettronico [*Database*] [*Editrice Bibliografica*] [*Italian*] [*Information service or system*] (CRD) ... CIRCE
Catalogue (GEAB) ... catal
Catalogue ... CTLG
Catalogue and Index (journ.) (SAUS) ... Cat Index
Catalogue Collectif des Periodiques [*A bibliographic publication*] ... CCP
Catalogue Computerization Project (SAUS) ... CCP
Catalogue cooperation project (SAUS) ... SAMKAT
Catalogue Data File (SAUS) ... CDF
Catalogue de l'Edition Francaise ... CEF
Catalogue des Textes Hittites [*Paris*] (BJA) ... CTH
Catalogue des Theses de Doctorat [*A bibliographic publication*] [*France*] ... CTD
Catalogue General des Antiquites Egyptiennes du Musee du Caire (BJA) ... CG
Catalogue Interoperability Experiment [*Marine science*] (OSRA) ... CINTEX
Catalogue Interoperability Protocol (SAUS) ... CIP
Catalogue Magazine ... CATAZINE
Catalogue Management Routine (SAUS) ... CMR
Catalogue Management Table (SAUS) ... CMT
Catalogue Multilingual Natural Language Access/Linguistic Server (TELE) ... CANAL/LS
Catalogue Number (SAUS) ... CLGNR
Catalogue of Approved Scientific and Technical Intelligence Tasks (MCD) ... CAST
Catalogue of Minerals at Yale (SAUO) ... CMY
Catalogue of Minerals Specimens (SAUO) ... CMS
Catalogue of Oriental Manuscripts in Danish Collections (BJA) ... COMDC
Catalogue of Printed Music [*A publication*] ... CPM
Catalogue of the Babylonian Section [*University Museum, Philadelphia*] [*Formerly, CBM*] (BJA) ... CBS
Catalogue of the Greek Coins of Palestine [*A publication*] (BJA) ... CGCP
Catalogue of the Greek Papyri in the John Rylands Library at Manchester [*A publication*] (OCD) ... P Ryl
Catalogue of the Greek Papyri in the John Rylands Library at Manchester (journ.) (SAUS) ... P Ryl
Catalogue of the Literary Papyri in the British Museum [*A publication*] (OCD) ... Cat Lit Pap
Catalogue of UK Official Publications (SAUS) ... UKOP
Catalogue Online (SAUS) ... CATLINE
Catalogue Procedure (SAUS) ... Catproc
Catalogued (SAUS) ... cat
Catalogued ... CD
Cataloguer (SAUS) ... CAT
Catalogues on Microfiche (AIE) ... COM
Cataloguing and Classification Quarterly [*A publication*] ... CCQ
Cataloguing in Advance of Publication [*British Library Bibliographic Services Division*] (NITA) ... CAP
Cataloguing Support System (SAUS) ... CATSS
Catalogus Codicum Astrologorum Graecorum [*A publication*] (OCD) ... CCAG
Catalogus Codicum Orientalium [*The Netherlands*] [*A publication*] (BJA) ... CCON
Catalonian [*Language, etc.*] (ROG) ... CAT
Catalysed Signal Amplification [*Analytical biochemistry*] ... CSA
Catalysis Reviews (journ.) (SAUS) ... Catal Rev
Catalyst ... C
Catalyst (WGA) ... CAT
Catalyst (SAUS) ... Cat
Catalyst (MSA) ... CTLST
Catalyst Bed Heater (ADWA) ... CBH
Catalyst International, Inc. [*Associated Press*] (SAG) ... Catalyst
Catalyst International, Inc. [*NASDAQ symbol*] (SAG) ... CLYS
Catalyst Intl. [*NASDAQ symbol*] (TTSB) ... CLYS
Catalyst Oriented Packing [*Chemical engineering*] ... COP
Catalyst Pass Fraction ... CPF
Catalyst Resource on the Work Force and Women [*Catalyst Information Center*] [*Information service or system*] (IID) ... CRWF
Catalyst Resources for Women [*A database*] [*Bibliographic Retrieval Service*] (NITA) ... CRFW
Catalyst Semiconductor [*NASDAQ symbol*] (TTSB) ... CATS
Catalyst Semiconductor, Inc. [*Associated Press*] (SAG) ... CatalSem
Catalyst Semiconductor, Inc. [*NASDAQ symbol*] (SAG) ... CATS
Catalytic [*Automotive engineering*] ... CATA
Catalytic Coal Gasification [*Fuel technology*] ... CCG
Catalytic Coal Liquefaction ... CCL
Catalytic Construction Co. ... CATCO
Catalytic Construction Co. (MCD) ... CCC
Catalytic Construction Co. (KSC) ... CCCO
Catalytic Construction Company (SAUO) ... CATCO
Catalytic Construction Company (SAUO) ... CCC
Catalytic Converter [*Automotive engineering*] ... CC
Catalytic Cracker [*Chemical engineering*] ... CC
Catalytic Cracking Unit [*Chemical engineering*] ... CCU
Catalytic Dehydrogenative Polycondensation [*Organic chemistry*] ... CDHP
Catalytic Dewaxing [*Petroleum refining*] ... CDW
Catalytic Extraction Process [*Engineering*] ... CEP
Catalytic Extraction Processing [*Recycling*] ... CEP
Catalytic Flame Ionization Detector ... CFID
Catalytic Membrane Reactor [*Chemical engineering*] ... CMR
Catalytic Optimum Profit-Sharing ... COPS
Catalytic Oxidation ... CAT-OX
Catalytic Oxidation (SAUS) ... Cat-Ox
Catalytic Reforming (IAA) ... CR
Catalytic Reforming Unit [*Petroleum refining*] ... CRU
Catalytic Research Unit (SSD) ... CRU
Catalytic Rich Gas ... CRG
Catalytic Surface Effects Experiment (SAUS) ... CSE
Catalytic Transfer Hydrogenation ... CTH
Catalytica, Inc. [*Associated Press*] (SAG) ... Catalyt
Catalytica, Inc. [*NASDAQ symbol*] (SAG) ... CTAL
Catalytically Cracked Clarified Oil [*Petroleum technology*] ... CCCO
Catalytic-Dow (KSC) ... C-D
Catalyzed Electrochemical Oxidation (ABAC) ... CEO
Catalyzed Electrolytic Plutonium Oxide Dissolution [*Chemistry*] ... CEPOD
Catamaran (ADA) ... cat
Catamaran (SAUS) ... Cat
Catamaran Mine Disposal System (MCD) ... CATMDV
Catamarca [*Argentina*] [*Airport symbol*] (OAG) ... CTC
Catamarca [*Argentina*] [*ICAO location identifier*] (ICLI) ... SANC
Catamenia [*Menstruation*] (CPH) ... cta
Catamenia (SAUS) ... CTA
Catania [*Italy*] [*Seismograph station code, US Geological Survey*] (SEIS) ... CAT
Catania [*Italy*] [*Airport symbol*] (OAG) ... CTA
Catania/Fontanarossa [*Italy*] [*ICAO location identifier*] (ICLI) ... LICC
Cataphyll [*Botany*] ... Ct
Catapilco [*Chile*] [*Seismograph station code, US Geological Survey*] (SEIS) ... CTP
Cataplasma [*Poultice*] [*Pharmacy*] ... CAT
Cataplasma [*Medicine*] (WDAA) ... cat
Cataplasma [*Poultice*] [*Pharmacy*] (ROG) ... CATAPL
Cataplasma [*Poultice*] [*Pharmacy*] (ROG) ... CATAPLAS
Cataplasma [*Poultice*] [*Pharmacy*] ... CATAPLSM
Cataplus [*of Lucian*] [*Classical studies*] (OCD) ... Catapl
Catapult (NG) ... CAT
Catapult (ADWA) ... cat
Catapult Aircraft Merchantship [*Used by British RAF to catapult Hurricane fighter planes from ships to defend convoys from enemy bombers*] [*World War II*] ... CAM
Catapult and Arresting Gear [*Aviation*] (DNAB) ... CAG
Catapult and Arresting Gear Field Service Unit (SAUO) ... CAFSU
Catapult and Arresting Gear Pool [*Navy*] ... CAP
Catapult Armed Merchant Ship (WDAA) ... CAMS
Catapult Arresting Gear and Landing Aids Maintenance [*Aviation*] (NG) ... CALM

Catapult Arresting-gear and Landing-gear Maintenance (SAUS) ... CALM
Catapult Bulletin (MCD) ... CB
Catapult Data Acquisition System (DNAB) ... CDAS
Catapult Hookup and Launch Surveillance ... CAHALS
Catapult Launched Fuel Air Expendable Round (DWSG) ... CATFAE
Catapult Lighter [*Navy symbol*] ... YVC
Catapult-Assisted Takeoff ... CATO
Catapult-launched Fuel-Air Explosive (SAUS) ... CATFAE
Cataract (MELL) ... CAT
Cataract [*Ophthalmology*] ... Cat
Cataract (ADWA) ... cat
Cataract Extraction (SAUS) ... CE
Cataract Extraction with Intraocular Lens Implant (SAUS) ... CE/IOL
Cataract-Microcephaly-Arthrogryposis-Kyphosis [*Syndrome*] [*Medicine*] (DMAA) ... CAMAK
Catarama [*Ecuador*] [*ICAO location identifier*] (ICLI) ... SECA
Catarman [*Philippines*] [*Airport symbol*] (OAG) ... CRM
Catarman, Northern Samar [*Philippines*] [*ICAO location identifier*] (ICLI) ... RPVF
Catarrhal Colds [*Medicine*] ... C (Colds)
Catastrophe (SAUS) ... CATO
Catastrophe Defense Organization (SAUO) ... CDO
Catastrophe Theory (DB) ... CT
Catastrophic Disaster Response Group (DEMM) ... CDRG
Catastrophic Failure Rate ... CFR
Catastrophic Health (MELL) ... CHIP
Catastrophic Health Expense Protection Plan [*Insurance*] ... CHEPP
Catastrophic Health Insurance (GFGA) ... CHI
Catastrophic Sexual Transmutation Theory [*Plant genetics*] ... CSTT
Catawba Area Mental Health Center, Hickory, NC [*Library symbol*] [*Library of Congress*] (LCLS) ... NcHyCM
Catawba College, Salisbury, NC [*Library symbol*] [*Library of Congress*] (LCLS) ... NcSalC
Catawba County Library, Newton, NC [*Library symbol*] [*Library of Congress*] (LCLS) ... NcNt
Catawba Memorial Hospital, Northwest AHEC Library at Hickory, Hickory, NC [*Library symbol*] [*Library of Congress*] (LCLS) ... NcHyCH
Catawba Nuclear Station (NRCH) ... CNS
Catawba Valley Technical Institute, Hickory, NC [*Library symbol*] [*Library of Congress*] (LCLS) ... NcHyC
Catboat (SAUS) ... Cat
Catboat Association (EA) ... CA
Catch [*Pisciculture*] ... C
Catch a Horse and Ride [*Fictitious railroad initialism used to indicate one of the most reliable modes of rural transportation*] ... CH & R
Catch All Phaults [*Quality control*] ... CAP
Catch Basin [*Technical drawings*] ... CB
Catch Limit Algorithm (SAUS) ... CLA
Catch per Angler [*Pisciculture*] ... CA
Catch per Hour [*Pisciculture*] ... CPH
Catch per Standard Day of Fishing [*Fishery management*] (MSC) ... CPSDF
Catch per Unit Effort [*Pisciculture*] ... C/E
Catch per Unit Effort [*Pisciculture*] (MSC) ... CPUE
Catch per Unit Effort [*Pisciculture*] ... CUE
Catch Phrase ... CP
Catch Society of America [*Defunct*] (EA) ... CSA
Catch You Later (ADWA) ... CUL
Catcher [*Baseball*] ... C
Catcher's Earned Run Average [*Baseball term*] (NDBD) ... CERA
Catchment and Land Protection (SAUO) ... CALP
Catchment Area Management [*Army medical term*] ... CAM
Catchment Areas Protection Board (SAUO) ... CAPB
Catchment Coordinating Committee (SAUO) ... CCC
Catchment Management Advisory Committee [*Australia*] ... CMAC
Catchment Management Committee (SAUO) ... CMC
Catchment Resource Assessment Model (SAUO) ... CRAM
Catch-per-Effort [*Fishing*] ... CPE
Catchword ... CWD
Catchword and Trade Name Index [*A publication*] ... CATNI
Catear Resources Ltd. [*Vancouver Stock Exchange symbol*] ... CAA
Catechism ... C
Catechism (WDAA) ... cat
Catechism ... CAT
Catechol Methyltransferase (DMAA) ... CCMT
Catecholamine [*or Catecholaminergic*] [*Biochemistry*] ... CA
Catecholamine [*Biochemistry*] ... CAT
Catecholamine and Metabolites (DB) ... CAT-MET
Catecholamine Club (EA) ... CC
Catecholamines (DIPS) ... CAs
Catecholamines Radioenzymic Assay Kit [*Clinical chemistry*] [*Acronym is trademark*] ... CAT-A-KIT
Catecholamin-O-Methyltransferase (SAUS) ... COMT
Catechol-O-Methyltransferase [*An enzyme*] ... CCMT
Catechol-O-Methyltransferase [*An enzyme*] (MAE) ... CMT
Catechol-O-Methyltransferase [*An enzyme*] ... COMT
Catechol-O-Methyl-Transferase (SAUS) ... COMT
Categoriae [*of Aristotle*] [*Classical studies*] (OCD) ... Cat
Categorial Abstract Machine Language (SAUS) ... CAML
Categorical Exclusion (EEVL) ... CE
Categorical Exclusion [*Environmental science*] (COE) ... CX
Categorical Grammar ... CG
Categories of Cable and Wire Facilities [*Telecommunications*] (OTD) ... C&WF
Category ... CA
Category (MILB) ... Cat
Category (AFM) ... CAT
Category ... CATEG
Category (FAAC) ... CTGY
Category 3 Unshielded Twisted (SAUS) ... CAT-3
Category 5 Unshielded Twisted Pair (SAUS) ... CAT-5
Category Assignment Responsibility List (MCD) ... CARL
Category B Flying Accident [*British military*] (DMA) ... BFA
Category Code [*Online database field identifier*] ... CC
Category Codes and Nomenclature (MCD) ... CCN
Category Development Index (WDMC) ... CDI
Category E Flying Accident [*British military*] (DMA) ... EFA
Category Level [*Environmental science*] (COE) ... C-Level
Category Stimulus [*To light*] ... CS
Category Switch [*Electronics*] (IAA) ... CATS
Catellus Development Corp. [*Associated Press*] (SAG) ... Catelu
Catellus Development Corp. [*Associated Press*] (SAG) ... Catelus
Catellus Development Corp. [*NYSE symbol*] (SPSG) ... CDX
Catellus Dvlp $3.75'A'Cv Pfd [*NYSE symbol*] (TTSB) ... CDXPrA
Catenarian Arch [*Freemasonry*] (ROG) ... CA
Catenary Anchor Leg Mooring ... CALM
Caterer [*Military*] [*British*] ... CA
Caterer ... CATR
Cateret County Public Library, Beaufort, NC [*Library symbol*] [*Library of Congress*] (LCLS) ... NcBea
Catering ... CARG
Catering Accountant [*British military*] (DMA) ... CA
Catering Equipment Distributors Association [*British*] (DBA) ... CEDA
Catering Equipment Manufacturers' Association [*British*] (BI) ... CEMA
Catering Industry Employee (journ.) (SAUS) ... CIE
Catering Managers Association of Great Britain and Northern Ireland (BI) ... CMA
Catering Officer [*British military*] (DMA) ... CT O
Catering Sub-Lieutenant (SAUS) ... CaSL
Catering Teachers Association [*British*] ... CTA
Catering Wages Act (SAUS) ... CWA
Catering Wages Commission [*British*] (DAS) ... CWC
Catering Wages Councils (SAUO) ... CWC
Caterpillar (SAUS) ... CAT
Caterpillar Club (EA) ... CC
Caterpillar, Inc. [*Wall Street slang name: "Cat"*] [*NYSE symbol*] (SPSG) ... CAT
Caterpillar, Inc. [*Wall Street slang name: "Cat"*] [*Associated Press*] (SAG) ... Caterp
Caterpillar Micro Oxidation Test [*Automotive lubricant*] ... CMOT
Caterpillar Mining Equipment (SAUO) ... CME
Caterpillar Overseas S.A. (SAUO) ... CAT
Caterpillar Tractor (SAUS) ... CAT
Caterpillar Tractor (SAUS) ... Cater Trac
Caterpillar Tractor Co. (SAUO) ... CAT
Caterpillar Tractor Co. [*NYSE symbol; later, CAT*] [*Wall Street slang name: "Cat"*] (SPSG) ... CTR
Caterpillar Tractor Co., Business Library, Peoria, IL [*Library symbol*] [*Library of Congress*] (LCLS) ... IPCT
Caterpillar Tractor Co., Peoria, IL [*OCLC symbol*] (OCLC) ... IDX
Caterpillar Tractor Co., Technical Information Center, Peoria, IL [*Library symbol*] [*Library of Congress*] (LCLS) ... IPCT-T
Caterpillar Tractor Co., Technical Information Center, Peoria, IL [*OCLC symbol*] (OCLC) ... ISH
Caterpillar Tractor Company (SAUO) ... CTR
Caterpillar Truck Engine Owners Club ... CTEOC
Cates' Reports [*109-127 Tennessee*] [*A publication*] (DLA) ... Cates
Catex Compagnie [*France*] [*ICAO designator*] (FAAC) ... TEX
Catfish ... CTFSH
Catfish Farmers of America (EA) ... CFA
Catfish Institute [*An association*] (EA) ... CI
Catfish Pond [*New Jersey*] [*Seismograph station code, US Geological Survey*] [*Closed*] (SEIS) ... CNJ
Catgut Acoustical Society (EA) ... CAS
Catgut Suture [*Medicine*] ... CGS
Catham House (SAUO) ... CH
Cathartic [*Pharmacy*] ... CATH
Cathartic Compound (IIA) ... CC
Cathartica [*Cathartic*] [*Pharmacy*] (ROG) ... CATHART
Cathay Bancorp [*NASDAQ symbol*] (TTSB) ... CATY
Cathay Bancorp, Inc. [*Associated Press*] (SAG) ... CathBcp
Cathay Bancorp, Inc. [*NASDAQ symbol*] (SAG) ... CATY
Cathay Pacific Airways [*ICAO designator*] (AD) ... CX
Cathay Pacific Airways Ltd. [*British*] [*ICAO designator*] (FAAC) ... CPA
Cathays [*Cardiff*] [*Welsh depot code*] ... CYS
Cathcart Art Society (SAUO) ... CAS
Cathedral ... CATH
Cathedral (VRA) ... cath
Cathedral (NTIO) ... Cath
Cathedral (SAUS) ... Cath
Cathedral ... CATHDRL
Cathedral ... CATHL
Cathedral ... CD
Cathedral ... CTHDL
Cathedral Architects Association [*British*] (DBA) ... CAA
Cathedral City, CA [*AM radio station call letters*] ... KWXY
Cathedral City, CA [*FM radio station call letters*] ... KWXY-FM
Cathedral Gold Corp. [*Toronto Stock Exchange symbol*] ... CAT
Cathedral of Saint John the Divine, New York, NY [*Library symbol*] [*Library of Congress*] (LCLS) ... NNSJD
Cathedral Organists' Association (EA) ... COA
Cathedral Peace Institute (EA) ... CPI
Cathedral Priory ... CDPR
Cathedral Series [*A publication*] ... CS
Cathedrals Advisory Committee [*Church of England*] ... CAC

Cathepsin S (DMAA) .... CTSS
Catherine Booth Hospital, Montreal, PQ, Canada [*Library symbol*] [*Library of Congress*] (LCLS) .... CaQMCBH
Catherine Booth Hospital, Montreal, Quebec [*Library symbol*] [*National Library of Canada*] (NLC) .... QMCBH
[*St.*] **Catherine's College** [*Oxford University*] (BARN) .... Cath
Catherines Stores [*NASDAQ symbol*] (TTSB) .... CATH
Catherines Stores Corp. [*NASDAQ symbol*] (SPSG) .... CATH
Catherines Stores Corp. [*Associated Press*] (SAG) .... CathStr
Catheter (SAUS) .... CAT
Catheter [*Medicine*] .... CATH
Catheter (ADWA) .... cath
Catheter Balloon Valvuloplasty [*Medicine*] (CPH) .... CBT
Catheter Specimen of Urine [*Medicine*] .... CSU
Catheter-Induced Infection [*Medicine*] (MELL) CII
Catheter-Induced Spasm [*Medicine*] (DB) .... CIS
Catheterization [*or Catheterize*] [*Cardiology and urology*] (DAVI) .... CATH
Catheterized Bladder [*Urology*] (DAVI) .... CB
Catheter-Related Bloodstream Infection [*Medicine*] (MELL) .... CRBSI
Catheter-Related Infection [*Medicine*] .... CRI
Catheter-Related Sepsis [*Medicine*] (MELL) .... CRS
Cathodal Closing Tetanus (SAUS) .... CCT
Cathodal Closure Clonus [*Medicine*] (DMAA) CCCI
Cathodal Closure Clonus [*Medicine*] .... CC Cl
Cathodal Closure Clonus (SAUS) CCCL
Cathodal Closure Contraction [*Also, CCC*] [*Physiology*] .... CaCC
Cathodal Closure Contraction [*Also, CaCC*] [*Physiology*] CCC
Cathodal Closure Tetanus [*Physiology*] .... CCT
Cathodal Closure Tetanus [*Physiology*] .... CCTE
Cathodal Closure Tetanus [*Medicine*] (DB) .... CCTe
Cathodal Duration [*Medicine*] (DMAA) .... KD
Cathodal Duration Tetanus [*Physiology*] .... CaDTe
Cathodal Opening [*Medicine*] (ROG) .... CO
Cathodal Opening Clonus (SAUS) .... Ca Ocl
Cathodal Opening Clonus [*Physiology*] (MAE) .... COC
Cathodal Opening Clonus [*Physiology*] .... COCL
Cathodal Opening Contraction [*Also, COC*] [*Physiology*] .... CaOC
Cathodal Opening Contraction [*Also, CaOC*] [*Physiology*] .... COC
Cathodal Opening Tetanus [*Physiology*] .... COT
Cathodal Opening Tetanus [*Physiology*] .... COTe
Cathode [*or Cathodal*] [*Radiology*] (DAVI) C
Cathode .... CA
Cathode (DIPS) .... Ca
Cathode (ADWA) .... cath
Cathode (MSA) .... CATH
Cathode [*Electron device*] (MSA) .... K
Cathode [*Electron device*] (AAMN) .... Ka
Cathode Boundary Charge Neutrality (SAUS) .... CBCN
Cathode Current Efficiency [*Electrochemistry*] .... CCE
Cathode Dark Space .... CDS
Cathode Efficiency (SAUS) .... CE
Cathode Electrodeposited Paint [*Environmental science*] .... CEP
Cathode Flicker Effect .... CFE
Cathode Follower (IAA) .... CATHFOL
Cathode Follower (SAUS) .... Cath Fol
Cathode Follower .... CF
Cathode Follower Mixer .... CFM
Cathode Grid (SAUS) .... CG
Cathode Heating Time .... CHT
Cathode Luminescence (SAUS) CL
Cathode of Diode (SAUS) .... CD
Cathode Polarization (SAUS) .... CP
Cathode Potential Stabilized .... CPS
Cathode Pulse Method (SAUS) .... CPM
Cathode Pulse Modulation .... CPM
Cathode Pulsed (SAUS) .... CP
Cathode Ray .... CR
Cathode Ray Memory (SAUS) .... CRM
Cathode Ray Setter (DGA) .... CRS
Cathode Ray Storage Tube (SAUS) .... CRST
Cathode Ray Store (SAUS) .... CRS
Cathode Ray Tube Controller (NITA) .... CRTC
Cathode Ray Tube Operating System (NITA) .... CRTOS
Cathode Ray Tube Oscilloscope (SAUS) .... CRTO
Cathode Ray Tube Transformer (SAUS) .... CRTT
Cathode Reaction .... CR
Cathode Resistance (IDOE) .... R_K
Cathode Resistor (SAUS) .... Cath Res
Cathode Resistor (SAUS) .... Rk
Cathode Voltage (SAUS) .... Ek
Cathode-Grid Capacitance .... CGC
Cathode-Grid Capacitance (SAUS) .... CGK
Cathode-Ray Direction Finder [*RADAR*] .... CRDF
Cathode-Ray Electron Tube .... CRET
Cathode-Ray Furnace .... CRF
Cathode-Ray Lamp .... CRL
Cathode-Ray Oscillator .... CO
Cathode-Ray Oscilloscope [*or Oscillograph*] .... CRO
Cathode-Ray Screen [*Air Force*] .... C-SCOPE
Cathode-Ray Terminal .... CRT
Cathode-Ray Tube .... CRT
Cathode-Ray Tube (IDOE) .... crt
Cathode-Ray Tube Automatic Direction Finding (IEEE) .... CADF
Cathode-Ray Tube Indicators [*JETDS nomenclature*] [*Military*] (CET) .... IP
Cathode-Ray Tube Oscillograph .... CRTO
Cathode-Ray Tube Shield .... CRTS
Cathode-Ray Tube Tester .... CRTT
Cathode-Ray tube/keyboard Printer (SAUS) .... CRP
Cathode-Ray Typesetting .... CRT
Cathodic Arc Plasma Deposition [*Coating technology*] .... CAPD
Cathodic Dichromate (PDAA) .... CDC
Cathodic Protection (SAUS) .... Capac
Cathodic Protection [*Metallurgy*] .... CP
Cathodic Protection by Automatically-Controlled Impressed Current (PDAA) .... CAPAC
Cathodic Protection Equipment .... CPE
Cathodic Protection Index (PDAA) .... CPI
Cathodic Protection Industry Association (EA) .... CPIA
Cathodic Protection Survey Kit .... CPSK
Cathodic Stripping Voltammetry [*Analytical chemistry*] .... CSV
Cathodic Survey Kit .... CSK
Cathodic Voltametry Stripping [*Marine science*] (OSRA) .... CVS
Cathodochromic [*Cathode-ray tube*] CC
Cathodochromic Cathode Ray Tube (PDAA) .... CCRT
Cathodoluminescence [*Geophysics*] CL
Cathodoluminescence Microscope Attachment .... CMA
Cathodoluminescence/Energy Dispersive Spectroscopy .... CL/EDS
Catholic C
Catholic (ADA) .... CAT
Catholic .... CATH
Catholic (WDAA) .... Cath
Catholic .... CATHOL
Catholic Access Network - Deus Lumen Est! (EA) .... CANDLE
Catholic Accountants Guild (EA) .... CAG
Catholic Action .... CA
Catholic Action Council Against Communism And Creeping Socialism (SAUO) .... CACACACS
Catholic Action Group (SAUO) .... CAG
Catholic Actors Guild of America (EA) .... CAG
Catholic Actors Guild of America (EA) .... CAGA
Catholic Aid Association (EA) .... CAA
Catholic Alumni Clubs International (EA) .... CACI
Catholic Anthropological Association [*Defunct*] (EA) .... CAA
Catholic Anthropological Conference .... CAC
Catholic Anti-Discrimination (SAUO) .... CAD
Catholic Apostolate of Radio, Television, and Advertising (NTCM) .... CARTA
Catholic Archdiocese of Detroit, Archives, Detroit, MI [*Library symbol*] [*Library of Congress*] (LCLS) .... MiDAA
Catholic Archdiocese of Melbourne Schools' Provident Fund [*Australia*] .... CAMSPF
Catholic Archdiocese of Seattle, Archives, Seattle, WA [*Library symbol*] [*Library of Congress*] (LCLS) .... WaSAA
Catholic Art Association [*Defunct*] (EA) .... CAA
Catholic Association (SAUO) .... CA
Catholic Association for International Peace [*Defunct*] (EA) .... CAIP
Catholic Association of Foresters (EA) .... CAOF
Catholic Association of Persons with Visual Impairment (EA) .... CAPVI
Catholic Audio-Visual Educators Association (EA) .... CAVE
Catholic Aviation League of Our Lady of Loreto [*Defunct*] (EA) .... CALOLL
Catholic Bible Society of America (EA) .... CBSA
Catholic Biblical Association of America (EA) .... CBA
Catholic Biblical Association of Canada [*Formerly, Canadian Catholic Biblical Association*] (AC) .... CBAC
Catholic Biblical Encyclopedia. New Testament [*A publication*] (BJA) .... CBENT
Catholic Biblical Encyclopedia. Old Testament [*A publication*] (BJA) .... CBEOT
Catholic Big Brothers (EA) .... CBB
Catholic Bishops' Conference of England and Wales (EAIO) .... CBCEW
Catholic Book Publishers [*Later, CBPA*] (EA) .... CBP
Catholic Book Publishers Association (EA) .... CBPA
Catholic Book Week .... CBW
Catholic Broadcasters Association (EA) .... CBA
Catholic Bushwalking Club [*Australia*] .... CBC
Catholic Business Education Association [*Later, NCBEA*] (EA) .... CBEA
Catholic Campus Ministry Association (EA) .... CCMA
Catholic Central High School, London, ON, Canada [*Library symbol*] [*Library of Congress*] (LCLS) .... CaOLC
Catholic Central High School, London, Ontario [*Library symbol*] [*National Library of Canada*] (NLC) .... OLC
Catholic Central Union [*Later, COF*] .... CCU
Catholic Central Union of America (EA) .... CCUA
Catholic Central Union of America, St. Louis, MO [*Library symbol*] [*Library of Congress*] (LCLS) .... MoSV
Catholic Central Youth Union of America (EA) .... CCYUA
Catholic Charismatic Renewal Movement .... CCRM
Catholic Charities USA (EA) .... CCUSA
Catholic Church, Archdiocese of Kingston, Archives, Kingston, ON, Canada [*Library symbol*] [*Library of Congress*] (LCLS) .... CaOKCAA
Catholic Church, Archdiocese of Vancouver, Archives, Vancouver, BC, Canada [*Library symbol*] [*Library of Congress*] (LCLS) .... CaBVaCAA
Catholic Church Development Fund [*Australia*] .... CCDF
Catholic Church Extension Society of the United States of America (EA) .... CCESUSA
Catholic Church Extension Society of the USA (EA) .... CCES
Catholic Civics Club of America (SAUO) CCC
Catholic Civics Club of America (SAUO) .... CCCA
Catholic Civics Clubs of America [*Defunct*] (EA) .... CCCA
Catholic Clergyman CC
Catholic College Admissions and Information Center (EA) .... CCAIC
Catholic College of Oklahoma for Women, Guthrie, OK [*Library symbol*] [*Library of Congress*] [*Obsolete*] (LCLS) .... OkGuC

Catholic Commission on Intellectual and Cultural Affairs (EA) ... CCICA
Catholic Committee for Inter-European Migration (SAUO) ... CCIEM
Catholic Committee for Refugees (EA) ... CCR
Catholic Committee for Relief Abroad (SAUO) ... CCRA
Catholic Committee of Appalachia (EA) ... CCA
Catholic Committee on Scouting [*Later, NCCS*] ... CCS
Catholic Committee on Urban Ministry (EA) ... CCUM
Catholic Communications Foundation (NTCM) ... CCF
Catholic Community Service (SAUS) ... CCS
Catholic Community Services Inc. [*Services Communautaires Catholiques Inc.*] (AC) ... CCS
Catholic Confraternity Version [*1941, 1952*] (BJA) ... CC
Catholic Construction Workers of America (EA) ... CCWA
Catholic Council for International Relations (SAUO) ... CCIR
Catholic Council for Polish Welfare (SAUO) ... CCPW
Catholic Council of Civil Liberties (SAUO) ... CCCL
Catholic Council on Civil Liberties [*Defunct*] (EA) ... CCCL
Catholic Council on Working Life (EA) ... CCWL
Catholic Curate ... CC
Catholic Daughters of the Americas (EA) ... CDA
Catholic Dictionary of Theology (SAUS) ... CDT
Catholic Douay Version [*of the Bible*] [*1609*] (BJA) ... Dy
Catholic Economic Association [*Later, ASE*] (EA) ... CEA
Catholic Education Aboriginal Advisory Committee [*Australia*] ... CEAAC
Catholic Education Office, Melbourne [*Australia*] ... CEOM
Catholic Education Office of Western Australia ... CEOWA
Catholic Educational Exhibitors Association [*Later, NCEE*] ... CEEA
Catholic Encylopedia [*A publication*] (ODCC) ... CE
Catholic Enquiry Centre [*Australia*] ... CEC
Catholic Epistles (BJA) ... CathEp
Catholic Evidence Guild [*Defunct*] (EA) ... CEG
Catholic Evidence Guild (SAUO) ... CEG
Catholic Evidence Guild of New York [*Defunct*] (EA) ... CEGNY
Catholic Faith Inventory [*Boyack, Duggan, and Huesing*] (TES) ... CFI
Catholic Family Life Insurance (EA) ... CFLI
Catholic Family Missionary Alliance [*Later, MEW*] (EA) ... CFMA
Catholic Fine Arts Society (EA) ... CFAS
Catholic Foreign Mission Society of America (EA) ... CFMSA
Catholic Foreign Missionary Society of America (SAUO) ... Maryknoll Fathers
Catholic Fund for Overseas Development [*British*] ... CAFOD
Catholic Fund for Overseas Development (SAUO) ... CFOD
Catholic Golden Age (EA) ... CGA
Catholic Guardian Society (EA) ... CGS
Catholic Guild for All the Blind [*Later, CCB*] (EA) ... CGFAB
Catholic Health Association of Alberta [*Formerly, Catholic Health Care Conference of Alberta*] (AC) ... CHAA
Catholic Health Association of British Columbia (AC) ... CHABC
Catholic Health Association of Canada ... CHAC
Catholic Health Association of Canada [*Association Catholique Canadienne de la Sante*], **Ottawa, Ontario** [*Library symbol*] [*National Library of Canada*] (NLC) ... OOCHAC
Catholic Health Association of Manitoba (AC) ... CHAM
Catholic Health Association of Ontario (AC) ... CHAO
Catholic Health Association of Saskatchewan (AC) ... CHAS
Catholic Health Association of the United States (EA) ... CHA
Catholic Health Association of the United States (EA) ... CHA-US
Catholic Health Association of Wisconsin (SAUO) ... CHA-W
Catholic Health Care Association of New South Wales [*Australia*] ... CHCNSW
Catholic High Schools Athletic Association ... CHSAA
Catholic Higher Institute of Eastern Africa (SAUO) ... CHIEA
Catholic Historical Review [*A publication*] (BRI) ... CHR
Catholic Homiletic Society [*Later, CPC*] (EA) ... CHS
Catholic Hospital Association [*Canada*] ... CHA
Catholic Hospital Association of Canada ... CHAC
Catholic Housing Aid Society [*British*] (DBA) ... CHAS
Catholic Information Services (SAUS) ... CIS
Catholic Information Society [*Defunct*] (EA) ... CIS
Catholic Institute for International Relations [*British*] (EAIO) ... CIIR
Catholic Institute of the Food Industry (EA) ... CIFI
Catholic Institute of the Press [*Later, Catholic Alliance for Communications*] (EA) ... CIP
Catholic Inter-American Cooperation Program [*Defunct*] ... CICOP
Catholic Intercontinental Press ... CIP
Catholic International Education Office [*Belgium*] ... CIEO
Catholic International Federation for Physical and Sports Education [*See also FICEP*] [*Paris, France*] (EAIO) ... CIFPSE
Catholic International Union for Social Service ... CIUSS
Catholic Interracial Council (SAUO) ... CIC
Catholic Interracial Council of Chicago (EA) ... CICC
Catholic Interracial Council of New York (EA) ... CIC
Catholic Interracial Council of New York (EA) ... CICNY
Catholic Irish Attorneys [*Fictional organization*] ... CIA
Catholic Journalist [*A publication*] (EAAP) ... CJ
Catholic Knights Insurance Society (EA) ... CKIS
Catholic Knights of America (EA) ... CKA
Catholic Knights of Saint George (SAUO) ... CKStG
Catholic Knights of St. George (EA) ... CKSG
Catholic Kolping Society of America (EA) ... CKSA
Catholic Ladies Aid Society ... CLAS
Catholic Ladies of Columbia ... CLC
Catholic Lay Mission Corps (EA) ... CLMC
Catholic League for Religious and Civil Rights (EA) ... CLRCR
Catholic League for Religious Assistance to Poland (EA) ... CLRAP
Catholic Library Association (SAUO) ... Cath Lib Assn
Catholic Library Association ... CATLA
Catholic Library Association (EA) ... CLA
Catholic Library World [*A publication*] (BRI) ... CLW
Catholic Library World (journ.) (SAUS) ... Cath Libr Wld
Catholic Life Insurance Union (EA) ... CLIU
Catholic Listener Library [*Later, Maynard Listener Library*] (EA) ... CLL
Catholic Major Markets Newspaper Association (EA) ... CMMNA
Catholic Marriage Advisory Council (SAUO) ... CMAC
Catholic Media Council [*Aachen, Federal Republic of Germany*] (EAIO) ... CaMeCo
Catholic Medical Center of Brooklyn & Queens, Inc., Jamaica, NY [*Library symbol*] [*Library of Congress*] (LCLS) ... NJMI
Catholic Medical Mission Board (EA) ... CMMB
Catholic Messenger, Davenport, IA [*Library symbol*] [*Library of Congress*] (LCLS) ... IaDaCM
Catholic Microfilm Center [*Defunct*] ... CMC
Catholic Microfilm Center, Berkeley, CA [*Library symbol*] [*Library of Congress*] [*Obsolete*] (LCLS) ... CathMC
Catholic Mission (SAUO) ... CM
Catholic Mission Sisters of St. Francis Xavier (TOCD) ... XS
Catholic Missionary Society ... CMS
Catholic Near East Welfare Association (EA) ... CNEWA
Catholic Negro-American Mission Board (EA) ... CNAMB
Catholic One Parent Organization (EA) ... COPO
Catholic Order of Foresters (EA) ... COF
Catholic Order of Foresters (SAUO) ... COF
Catholic Pamphlet Society of the United States (EA) ... CPS
Catholic Peace Fellowship (EA) ... CPF
Catholic Poetry Society of America [*Defunct*] (EA) ... CPSA
Catholic Press Association (EA) ... CPA
Catholic Press Features ... CPF
Catholic Press Office [*British*] ... CPO
Catholic Reaction Force (SAUO) ... CRF
Catholic Record Society (SAUO) ... CRS
Catholic Record Society (EA) ... CRS
Catholic Relief Secretariat [*Eritrea*] ... CRS
Catholic Relief Service (SAUO) ... CRS
Catholic Relief Service - United States Catholic Conference (SAUO) ... CDS-USCC
Catholic Relief Services [*Later, CRS-USCC*] ... CRS
Catholic Relief Services - National Catholic Welfare Conference [*Later, CRS-USCC*] (EA) ... CRS-NCWC
Catholic Relief Services - US Catholic Conference (EA) ... CRS-USCC
Catholic Renascence Society [*Defunct*] (EA) ... CRS
Catholic Russian Center, San Francisco, CA [*Library symbol*] [*Library of Congress*] (LCLS) ... CSfCR
Catholic Scholarships for Negroes [*Defunct*] (EA) ... CSN
Catholic School Commission, Montreal, PQ, Canada [*Library symbol*] [*Library of Congress*] (LCLS) ... CaQMCEC
Catholic School Commission [*Commission des Ecoles Catholiques*] **Montreal, Quebec** [*Library symbol*] [*National Library of Canada*] (NLC) ... QMCEC
Catholic School Press Association [*Defunct*] (EA) ... CSPA
Catholic Schools Office [*Australia*] ... CSO
Catholic Slovak Brotherhood ... CSB
Catholic Social Guild (SAUO) ... CSG
Catholic Social Services (SAUO) ... CSS
Catholic Sokol Printing Co., Passaic, NJ [*Library symbol*] [*Library of Congress*] (LCLS) ... NjPasCS
Catholic Solo Parents [*Australia*] ... CSP
Catholic Star Herald, Camden, NJ [*Library symbol*] [*Library of Congress*] (LCLS) ... NjCaSH
Catholic Students' Mission Crusade [*Defunct*] ... CSMC
Catholic Tape Recorders, International (EA) ... CTRI
Catholic Teachers College [*Rhode Island*] ... CTC
Catholic Teachers Federation [*British*] (DBA) ... CTF
Catholic Telecommunications Network of America [*Staten Island, NY*] (TSSD) ... CTNA
Catholic Television Network [*Cable-television system*] ... CTN
Catholic Theological Society of America (EA) ... CTSA
Catholic Theological Union [*Australia*] ... CTU
Catholic Theological Union, Chicago, IL [*Library symbol*] [*Library of Congress*] (LCLS) ... ICTU
Catholic Theological Union, Chicago, IL [*OCLC symbol*] (OCLC) ... IDJ
Catholic Total Abstinence Union ... CTAU
Catholic Total Abstinence Union (SAUO) ... CTAU
Catholic Total Abstinence Union of America (EA) ... CTAUA
Catholic Traditionalist Movement (EA) ... CTM
Catholic Truth Society [*British*] (BI) ... CTS
Catholic Truth Society (SAUO) ... CTS
Catholic Union of Great Britain (SAUO) ... CUGB
Catholic Union of the Sick in America (SAUO) ... CUSA
Catholic University ... CU
[*The*] **Catholic University of America** (GAGS) ... Catholic U
Catholic University of America [*Washington, DC*] ... CUA
Catholic University of America, Clementine Library, Washington, DC [*Library symbol*] [*Library of Congress*] (LCLS) ... DCU-C
Catholic University of America, Hyvernat Collection, Washington, DC [*Library symbol*] [*Library of Congress*] (LCLS) ... DCU-H
Catholic University of America, Ibero-American Collection, Washington, DC [*Library symbol*] [*Library of Congress*] (LCLS) ... DCU-IA
Catholic University of America Law School (DLA) ... CUALS
Catholic University of America Press (SAUO) ... Cath U Pr
Catholic University of America Press (SAUO) ... CUAP
Catholic University of America, Washington, DC [*OCLC symbol*] (OCLC) ... CUA
Catholic University of America, Washington, DC [*Library symbol*] [*Library of Congress*] (LCLS) ... DCU

Catholic University of American Studies in Roman Languages and Literatures (journ.) (SAUS) ..... CUASRLL
Catholic University of Louvain (SAUO) Lv
Catholic University of Puerto Rico (GAGS) ..... Catholic U of PR
Catholic University of Puerto Rico ..... CUPR
Catholic University of Puerto Rico, Law Library, Ponce, Puerto Rico [*Library symbol*] [*Library of Congress*] (LCLS) ..... PrPCU-L
Catholic University School (SAUO) ..... CUS
Catholic Walking Club of Victoria [*Australia*] ..... CWCV
Catholic War Veterans Auxiliary of the U.S.A. (EA) ..... CWVA
Catholic War Veterans of the USA (EA) ..... CWV
Catholic War Veterans of the USA Auxiliary (EA) ..... CWVUSAA
Catholic War Veterans of the USA Ladies Auxiliary [*Later, CWVUSAA*] (EA) ..... CWVA
Catholic Weekly [*A publication*] ..... Catholic Wkly
Catholic White Anglo-Saxon Protestant ..... CWASP
Catholic Women for the ERA (EA) ..... CWERA
Catholic Women of the Chapel ..... CWOC
Catholic Women's Benevolent Legion (EA) ..... CWBL
Catholic Women's League (BARN) ..... CWL
Catholic Women's League of Australia [*An association*] ..... CWLA
Catholic Women's Seminary Fund [*Defunct*] (EA) ..... CWSF
Catholic Worker Movement (EA) ..... CWM
Catholic Workman (EA) ..... CW
Catholic World [*A publication*] (BRI) ..... Cath W
Catholic Writers Guild of America (EA) ..... CWGA
Catholic Young Men's Society [*Ireland*] (BI) ..... CYMS
Catholic Youth Adoration Society [*Defunct*] (EA) ..... CYA
Catholic Youth Association [*Lithuania*] (EAIO) ..... CYA
Catholic Youth Council [*Belgium*] (EAIO) ..... CYC
Catholic Youth Organization ..... CYO
Catholic Youth Service Council (SAUO) ..... CYSC
Catholicarum Universitatum Federatio [*Federation of Catholic Universities*] ..... CUF
Catholics for a Free Choice (EA) ..... CFFC
Catholics for Christian Political Action [*Defunct*] (EA) ..... CCPA
Catholics for Latin America ..... CFLA
Catholics Speak Out [*Quixote Center*] (EA) ..... CSO
Catholics United for Life (EA) ..... CUL
Catholics United for Spiritual Action (EA) ..... CUSA
Catholics United for the Faith (EA) ..... CUF
Catholics Unites for Racial Equality (SAUO) ..... CURE
Cathotic Annodic Filaments ..... CAF
Cathy Buchanan Fan Club (EA) ..... CBFC
Caticlan, Aklan [*Philippines*] [*ICAO location identifier*] (ICLI) ..... RPVE
Catifornia Chiropractic Association (SAUO) ..... CCA
Catio [*Guinea-Bissau*] [*ICAO location identifier*] (ICLI) ..... GGCT
Cation Selective Membrane (SAUS) ..... CSM
Cation-Exchange Capacity [*Chemical technology*] ..... CEC
Cation-Exchange Chromatography (SAUS) ..... CEC
Cation-Exchange Resin [*Chemical technology*] ..... CER
Cationic Asphalt-Neoprene Emulsion [*Dust control*] ..... CANE
Cationic Flocculant Producers Association [*Defunct*] (EA) ..... CFPA
Cationic Liposome [*Biology*] CL
Cationized Ferritin [*Biochemistry*] ..... CF
Cation-Ratio Dating (SAUS) ..... CR Dating
Cation-Responsive Electrode ..... CRE
Catlettsburg, KY [*FM radio station call letters*] (RBYB) ..... WRVC-FM
Catlin Public Library, Catlin, IL [*Library symbol*] [*Library of Congress*] (LCLS) ..... ICat
Catlow Resources Ltd. [*Vancouver Stock Exchange symbol*] ..... CTW
Catlow/Whitney Family Organization (EA) ..... CWFO
[*The*] **Cato Corp.** [*NASDAQ symbol*] (NQ) ..... CACO
Cato Corp. [*Associated Press*] (SAG) ..... CatoCp
Cato Corp.'A' [*NASDAQ symbol*] (TTSB) ..... CACOA
Cato Institute (EA) CI
Cato Maior [*of Plutarch*] [*Classical studies*] (OCD) ..... Cat Mai
Cato Minor [*of Plutarch*] [*Classical studies*] (OCD) ..... Cat Min
Cato Township Public Library, Lakeview, MI [*Library symbol*] [*Library of Congress*] (LCLS) ..... MiLakv
Catoctin Mountain Park [*National Park Service designation*] ..... CATO
Catoctin Mountain Park (SAUS) ..... CMP
Catonsville Community College, Baltimore, MD [*OCLC symbol*] (OCLC) ..... CAT
Catonsville Community College, Learning Resources Division, Baltimore, MD [*Library symbol*] [*Library of Congress*] (LCLS) ..... MdBCC
Catonsville, MD [*FM radio station call letters*] ..... WQSR
Cats and Dogs [*i.e., low selling items or speculative stock*] [*Slang*] [*Business term*] ..... C & D
Cats in Industry [*British*] (DI) CII
Cats on Stamps Study Unit [*American Topical Association*] (EA) ..... CSSU
Cats Protection League [*British*] (DBA) ..... CPL
C.ATS Software [*NASDAQ symbol*] (TTSB) ..... CATX
CATS Software, Inc. [*Associated Press*] (SAG) ..... CATS
CATS Software, Inc. [*NASDAQ symbol*] (SAG) ..... CATX
Cat-Scratch Bacillus [*Medicine*] (MELL) ..... CSB
Catskill Airways [*ICAO designator*] (AD) ..... KF
Catskill Airways, Inc. [*FAA designator*] (FAAC) ..... MOW
Catskill Financial [*NASDAQ symbol*] (TTSB) ..... CATB
Catskill, NY [*AM radio station call letters*] ..... WCKL
Catskill, NY [*FM radio station call letters*] ..... WCTW
Catskills (FAAC) ..... CTSKLS
Catskills/Sullivan County [*New York*] [*Airport symbol*] [*Obsolete*] (OAG) ..... MSV
Cattaraugus-Allegany School Library System, Olean, NY [*Library symbol*] [*Library of Congress*] (LCLS) ..... NolSL
Cattell Infant Intelligence Scale [*Psychology*] (DAVI) ..... CIIS
Cattermole Memorial Library, Fort Madison, IA [*Library symbol*] [*Library of Congress*] (LCLS) ..... IaFm
Cattle (ROG) C
Cattle ..... CAT
Cattle (SAUS) ..... Cat
Cattle ..... CTL
Cattle ..... CTTL
Cattle + Buffalohybrid (SAUS) ..... Cattalo
Cattle Birth Record Document (SAUS) ..... CBRD
Cattle Containers (DCTA) ..... CT
Cattle Control Document (SAUS) ..... CCD
Cattle Food Trade Association (SAUO) ..... CFTA
Cattle Hide ..... CATLHD
Cattle Identification Document (SAUS) ..... CID
Cattle Industry Compensation Act (SAUO) ..... CICA
Cattle Industry Compensation Fund (SAUO) ..... CICF
Cattle on Feed (GFGA) ..... COF
Cattle Options Pilot Program (SAUO) ..... COPP
Cattle Tracing System (GVA) ..... CTS
Cattlemans, Inc. [*Associated Press*] (SAG) ..... Catleman
Cattlemans, Inc. [*NASDAQ symbol*] (SAG) ..... CTLO
Cattle-Plague (ROG) ..... CP
Cattle-Prod Approach (SAUS) ..... C-P A
Catullus [*First century BC*] [*Classical studies*] (OCD) ..... Catull
Catwalk [*Technical drawings*] (DAC) ..... CATW
Catwalk ..... CTWALK
Cauayan [*Philippines*] [*Airport symbol*] (OAG) ..... CYZ
Cauayan, Isabela [*Philippines*] [*ICAO location identifier*] (ICLI) ..... RPUY
Cauca Valley Corporation (SAUO) CVC
Caucasia [*Colombia*] [*Airport symbol*] (OAG) ..... CAQ
Caucasian C
Caucasian [*MARC language code*] [*Library of Congress*] (LCCP) ..... cau
Caucasian (AFM) ..... CAU
Caucasian (SAUS) ..... Cau
Caucasian (MAE) ..... Cauc
Caucasian (NTIO) ..... cauc
Caucasian Adult (SAUS) ..... CA
Caucasian Adult Female (SAUS) ..... CAF
Caucasian Adult Male (SAUS) ..... CAM
Caucasian Child (SAUS) CC
Caucasian Except as Otherwise Indicated [*Army*] ..... CAUEOI
Caucasian Female ..... CF
Caucasian Male ..... CM
Caucasus [*MARC geographic area code*] [*Library of Congress*] (LCCP) ..... e-urk-
Cauchy Boundary Condition [*Mathematics*] ..... CBC
Cauchy Convergence Test [*Mathematics*] ..... CCT
Cauchy-Riemann Equation [*Mathematics*] ..... CRE
Caucus for a New Political Science (EA) ..... CNPS
Caucus for Producers, Writers, and Directors (EA) ..... CPWD
Caucus for Women in Statistics (SAUO) ..... CWRU
Caucus for Women in Statistics (EA) ..... CWS
Cauda Equina Syndrome [*Medicine*] (MELL) ..... CES
Caudal [*Anatomy*] C
Caudal [*Anatomy*] (DAVI) ..... CAUD
Caudal [*Medicine*] (DMAA) ..... cd
Caudal [*Anatomy*] ..... CD
Caudal Dysplasia Syndrome [*Medicine*] (MELL) ..... CDS
Caudal Magnocellular [*Nuclei*] [*Neuroanatomy*] ..... CM
Caudal Mediastinal Node [*Medicine*] (DMAA) ..... CMN
Caudal Photoreceptor [*Biology*] ..... CPR
Caudal Portion of the Dorsal Accessory Olive (DB) ..... CDAO
Caudality (DIPS) ..... CA
Caudality Scale [*Psychology*] ..... Ca
Caudality Scale [*Psychology*] (DHP) ..... Ca Scale
Caudate Nucleus [*Anatomy*] ..... CN
Caudate Putamen [*Neuroanatomy*] ..... CP
Caudate Putamen (DMAA) ..... CPU
Caudate-Caudate to Outer Table (Ratio) [*Neuroradiology*] ..... CC/OT
Caudate-Putamen Complex [*Anatomy*] ..... CPU
Caudate-Putamen complex (SAUS) ..... CPU complex
Caudill, Rowlett & Scott [*Architectural firm*] ..... CRS
Caudodorsal Cell Hormone [*Zoology*] ..... CDCH
Caudodorsal Cells [*Anatomy*] ..... CDC
Caudodorsal Cells Autotransmitter [*Zoology*] ..... CDCA
Caught [*by*] [*In cricket*] C
Caught ..... CAT
Caught ..... CT
Caught and Bowled [*Cricket*] ..... C & B
Caught Out C
Caught Stealing [*Baseball*] ..... CS
Caulfield Resources Ltd. [*Vancouver Stock Exchange symbol*] CXI
Cauliflower (SAUS) ..... Cauli
Cauliflower (DSUE) ..... CAULI
Cauliflower Mosaic Virus [*Also, CLMV*] ..... CaMV
Cauliflower Mosaic Virus [*Also, CaMV*] ..... CLMV
Cauliflower Mosaic Virus [*Medicine*] (DB) ..... CLMW
Caulked Joint ..... CAJ
Caulked Joint ..... CLKJ
Caulking (MSA) ..... CLKG
Caulking (ADWA) ..... clkg
Caulking Seam (DAC) ..... CS
Cauchy-Riemann Equation (SAUS) ..... CRE
Causa [*Case or Cause*] C
Causa [*Decretum Gratiani*] [*A publication*] (DSA) ..... Ca
CAUSA Institute (EA) CI

Causa Mortis [*On Occasion of Death*] [*Latin*] ... CM
Causal Factors Analysis [*Engineering*] ... CFA
Causal Tree Method [*Engineering*] ... CTM
Causapscal, PQ [*AM radio station call letters*] ... CJBM
Causation ... CAUS
Causative (BJA) ... Caus
Causative (ADWA) ... caus
Cause ... C
Cause Consequence Diagram Method [*Engineering*] ... CCDM
Cause for Concern [*Defunct*] (EA) ... CC
Cause of Action (MHDB) ... CA
Cause of Action [*Legal shorthand*] (LWAP) ... COA
Cause of Death (SAUS) ... CD
Cause of Death [*Medicine*] ... COD
Cause of Failure [*Telecommunications*] (TEL) ... COF
Cause of Failure, Effect, and Correction (SAA) ... COFF
Cause Undetermined [*Medicine*] (MELL) ... CU
Cause Undetermined [*Medicine*] (DAVI) ... CUD
Cause Unknown [*Medicine*] (DAVI) ... CU
Cause-and-Effect Analysis (CARB) ... CEA
Cause-Effect Graph Language [*Computer science*] (IBMDP) ... CEGL
Cause-Effect Logic Diagram [*Engineering*] ... CELD
Cause-Related Marketing [*Finance*] ... CRM
Causes Celebres [*Quebec Provincial Reports*] [*A publication*] (DLA) ... Ca Celeb
Causes Celebres [*Quebec Provincial Reports*] [*A publication*] (DLA) ... CC
Causeway (WDAA) ... C
Causeway [*Commonly used*] (OPSA) ... CAUSEWAY
Causeway [*Commonly used*] (OPSA) ... CAUSWAY
Causeway ... CSWAY
Causeway (TBD) ... Cswy
Causeway (KSC) ... CSWY
Causeway Ferry (COE) ... CF
Causeway Section, Nonpowered [*Navy*] (ANA) ... CSNP
Caustic (SAUS) ... Caust
Caustic Boundary Layer [*Acoustics*] ... CBL
Caustic Scrubber (EEVL) ... CS
Caustic Slurry Waste (ABAC) ... CSW
Cauterization [*Medicine*] (DMAA) ... caut
Cauterize [*or Cauterization*] (CPH) ... CAUT
Caution (AFM) ... CAUT
Caution ... CTN
Caution Advised Until Further Notice [*Aviation*] (FAAC) ... CAUFN
Caution Against Dangerous Exports [*Shipping*] ... CADE
Caution and Advisory Lamp Panel (ACAE) ... CALP
Caution and Warning [*Aerospace*] (KSC) ... C & W
Caution and Warning (NAKS) ... C&W
Caution and Warning (NAKS) ... C/W
Caution and Warning Advisory Panel (MCD) ... CWAP
Caution and Warning Advisory Panel Indicators (MCD) ... CWAPI
Caution and Warning Advisory Signals (MCD) ... CWAS
Caution and Warning Annunciator (MCD) ... CWA
Caution and Warning Electronics (NASA) ... CWE
Caution and Warning Electronics Assembly [*Apollo*] [*NASA*] ... CWEA
Caution and Warning Electronics Unit (MCD) ... CWEU
Caution and Warning Equipment [*NASA*] (KSC) ... CWE
Caution and Warning Limit Module [*NASA*] (NASA) ... CWLM
Caution and Warning Status (MCD) ... CWS
Caution and Warning Status Unit [*NASA*] (NASA) ... CWSU
Caution and Warning System [*NASA*] (KSC) ... C & WS
Caution and Warning System (SAUS) ... CWS
Caution and Warning Unit (MCD) ... CWU
Caution and Warning/Fire Suppression Panel (MCD) ... CWFSP
Cautious Hawk [*Description of President Reagan's position on foreign affairs, used in book "Gambling with History: Reagan in the White House"*] ... CAWK
Cavalier [*Knight title*] ... CAV
Cavalier Homes [*NYSE symbol*] (TTSB) ... CAV
Cavalier Homes [*Associated Press*] (SAG) ... CavalrH
Cavalier Homes Co. [*NYSE symbol*] (SAG) ... CAV
Cavalier Homes Co. [*Associated Press*] (SAG) ... CavallrH
Cavalier King Charles Spaniel Club of America (EA) ... CKCSC
Cavalier, ND [*FM radio station call letters*] (RBYB) ... KAOC
Cavalry [*British military*] (DMA) ... C
Cavalry (WDAA) ... Cav
Cavalry (WDAA) ... cav
Cavalry ... CAV
cavalry (SAUO) ... cav
Cavalry (SAUO) ... CAV
Cavalry (SAUO) ... Cavy
Cavalry ... CLVRY
Cavalry Benefit Association (SAUO) ... CBA
Cavalry Brigade (SAUO) ... CB
Cavalry Brigade ... CB
Cavalry Brigade (Air Attack) [*Army*] ... CB(AA)
Cavalry Corps Headquarters (SAUO) ... CCHQ
Cavalry Depot (SAUO) ... CD
Cavalry Division [*Army*] ... CD
Cavalry Fighting Vehicle ... CFV
Cavalry Mechanized Group (SAUO) ... Cav Mecz Gp
Cavalry Mobile Veterinary Section [*British military*] (DMA) ... CMVS
Cavalry Navigation System (MCD) ... CAVNAVS
Cavalry Replacement Training Center ... CRTC
Cavalry Transport [*Navy ship symbol*] [*Obsolete*] ... APC
Cavan [*County in Ireland*] (ROG) ... CA
Cavan [*County in Ireland*] (ROG) ... CAV
Cavanagh Communities Corp. (SAUO) ... CAA
Cavanagh's Law of Money Securities [*A publication*] (DLA) ... Cav Mon Sec
Cavare-Westphal [*Syndrome*] [*Medicine*] (DB) ... CW
Cavco Indus [*NASDAQ symbol*] (TTSB) ... CVCO
Cavco Industries, Inc. [*Associated Press*] (SAG) ... Cavco
Cavco Industries, Inc. (EFIS) ... CVC
Cavco Industries, Inc. [*NASDAQ symbol*] (NQ) ... CVCO
CAVDA [*Citizens Alliance for Venereal Disease Awareness*]**-Citizens AIDS Project** (EA) ... CAP
Cave (ROG) ... CV
Cave Automatic Virtual Environment [*Virtual reality*] ... CAVE
Cave City, AR [*FM radio station call letters*] ... KZIG
Cave City, KY [*FM radio station call letters*] ... WHHT
Cave City, KY [*FM radio station call letters*] (BROA) ... WPTQ-FM
Cave Creek, AZ [*AM radio station call letters*] ... KCCF
Cave Creek, AZ [*AM radio station call letters*] (BROA) ... KFNX
Cave Creek Public Library, Cave Creek, AZ [*Library symbol*] [*Library of Congress*] (LCLS) ... AzCc
Cave Divers Group of Great Britain (SAUO) ... CDG
Cave Diving Association of Australia (SAUO) ... CDAA
Cave Exploration Group [*Australia*] ... CEG
Cave Junction (SAUS) ... SSB
Cave Junction, OR [*FM radio station call letters*] ... KCNA
Cave Junction, OR [*Location identifier*] [*FAA*] (FAAL) ... SSB
Cave Rescue Organization [*British*] (PDAA) ... CRO
Cave Rescue Organization of Great Britain (SAUO) ... CRO
Cave Research Associates (EA) ... CRA
Cave Research Association (SAUO) ... CRA
Cave Research Foundation (EA) ... CRF
Cave Research Group of Great Britain (BI) ... CRG
Caveat [*Let Him Beware*] [*A judicial writ*] [*Latin*] [*Legal term*] ... CAV
Caveat (ADWA) ... cav
Caveat [*Let Him Beware*] [*A judicial writ*] [*Latin*] [*Legal term*] (ROG) ... CAVT
Caveat Emptor [*Let the Buyer Beware*] [*Latin*] ... CE
Caveat Emptor Consumer Report [*A publication*] (AAGC) ... Caveat Emptor
Cavedale Road [*California*] [*Seismograph station code, US Geological Survey*] (SEIS) ... CRD
Cavei Avir Lemitanim [*Israel*] [*ICAO designator*] (FAAC) ... ICL
Cavender's Debates on Canada [*A publication*] (DLA) ... Cav Deb Can
Cavendish Laboratory (SAUS) ... Cavendish
Cavendish Public Library (G. Galloway), Ontario [*Library symbol*] [*National Library of Canada*] (BIB) ... OGALL
Cavendish's Debates, House of Commons [*A publication*] (DLA) ... Cav Deb
Cavern (ROG) ... C
Cavern (ROG) ... CAV
Cavernous Sinus (SAUS) ... CS
Cavernous Sinus [*Medicine*] (MELL) ... CV
Cavernous Sinus Infiltration [*Medicine*] (STED) ... CSI
Cavernous Sinus Syndrome [*Medicine*] (MELL) ... CSS
Cavernous Sinus Thrombosis [*Medicine*] ... CST
Cavernous Sinus Thrombosis [*Medicine*] ... CVT
Caviation Tendency Ratio (SAUS) ... CTR
Cavinas [*Bolivia*] [*ICAO location identifier*] (ICLI) ... SLCJ
Cavinas [*Bolivia*] [*ICAO location identifier*] (ICLI) ... SLCV
Caviology (SAUS) ... Caviol
Cavitation ... CAV
Cavitation Intensity Meter ... CIM
Cavitation Tendency Ratio ... CTR
Cavitron Ultrasonic Surgical Aspirator [*Medicine*] ... CUSA
Cavity (MSA) ... CAV
Cavity [*Dentistry*] (DAVI) ... cav
Cavity Alternated Phase Shift (MCD) ... CAPS
Cavity Foam Insulation Association (SAUO) ... CFIA
Cavity Nester [*Ornithology*] ... CN
Cavity Rim Cup [*A contraceptive device*] ... CRC
Cavity Ringdown LASER Absorption Spectroscopy ... CRLAS
Cavity Transfer Mixer [*Chemical engineering*] ... CTM
Cavity Tunable Filter (SAUS) ... CTF
Cavity Tuned Oscillator ... CTO
Cavity Turnable Filter ... CTF
Cavity Wall ... CW
Cavity-Backed Radiator (SAUS) ... CBR
Cavity-Ringdown Spectrometer (CARB) ... CRS
Cavum Conchal Cartilage Graft [*Medicine*] (MELL) ... CCCG
Cavum Septum Pellucidum (DAVI) ... CSP
Cavus Foot (MELL) ... CF
Cawcaw Swamp [*South Carolina*] [*Seismograph station code, US Geological Survey*] (SEIS) ... CCS
Cawkell Information & Technology Services, Ltd. [*Telecommunications*] (IID) ... CITECH
Cawker City, KS [*FM radio station call letters*] (BROA) ... KZDY-FM
Cawley's Laws Concerning Jesuits, Etc. [*1680*] [*A publication*] (DLA) ... Cawl
Caxias [*Brazil*] [*Airport symbol*] (AD) ... CXS
Caxias do Sul [*Brazil*] [*Airport symbol*] (AD) ... CXJ
Caxton Convalescent Home (SAUO) ... CCH
Cay Sal [*Bahamas*] [*ICAO location identifier*] (ICLI) ... MYCS
Cayajabo [*Cuba*] [*ICAO location identifier*] (ICLI) ... MUCY
Cayana [*Surinam*] [*ICAO location identifier*] (ICLI) ... SMCA
Cayce, SC [*FM radio station call letters*] ... WHKZ
Cayce, SC [*FM radio station call letters*] (BROA) ... WLTY-FM
Cayce, SC [*AM radio station call letters*] ... WTGH
Cayce, SC [*FM radio station call letters*] ... WYFV
Cayenne [*French Guiana*] [*Airport symbol*] (OAG) ... CAY
Cayenne Software, Inc. [*Associated Press*] (SAG) ... CayenneSf
Cayenne Software, Inc. [*NASDAQ symbol*] (SAG) ... CAYN
Cayenne/Rochambeau [*French Guiana*] [*ICAO location identifier*] (ICLI) ... SOCA

Cayes [*Haiti*] [*ICAO location identifier*] (ICLI) .... MTCA
Cayey [*Puerto Rico*] [*Seismograph station code, US Geological Survey*] (SEIS) .... SJCC
Cayey, PR [*AM radio station call letters*] .... WLEY
Cayley-Klein Parameter [*Mathematics*] .... CKP
Cayman Airways [*ICAO designator*] (AD) .... KX
Cayman Airways [*Airline flight code*] (ODBW) .... KX
Cayman Airways Ltd. [*British*] [*ICAO designator*] (FAAC) .... CAY
Cayman Airways Ltd. (SAUO) .... KX
Cayman Brac [*West Indies*] [*Airport symbol*] (OAG) .... CYB
Cayman Brac/Gerrard Smith [*Cayman Islands*] [*ICAO location identifier*] (ICLI) .... MWCB
Cayman Golf Association (EA) .... CGA
Cayman Islands CI
Cayman Islands [*MARC country of publication code*] [*Library of Congress*] (LCCP) .... cj
Cayman Islands [*ANSI three-letter standard code*] (CNC) .... CYM
Cayman Islands [*ANSI two-letter standard code*] (CNC) .... KY
Cayman Islands [*MARC geographic area code*] [*Library of Congress*] (LCCP) .... nwcj-
Cayman Islands [*International civil aircraft marking*] (ODBW) .... VR-C
Cayman Islands Department of Tourism (EA) .... CIDT
Cayman Water Co. Ltd. [*Associated Press*] (SAG) .... CayWtr
Cayman Water Co. Ltd. [*NASDAQ symbol*] (SAG) .... CWCO
Cayman Water Co. Ltd [*NASDAQ symbol*] (TTSB) .... CWCOF
Cayo Largo Del Sur [*Cuba*] [*ICAO location identifier*] (ICLI) .... MUCL
Cayo Mambi [*Cuba*] [*Airport symbol*] (AD) .... CMV
Cayo Mambi [*Cuba*] [*ICAO location identifier*] (ICLI) .... MUBI
Cay's Abridgment, or the English Statutes [*A publication*] (DLA) .... Cay Abr
Cayuga County Community College, Auburn, NY [*Library symbol*] [*Library of Congress*] (LCLS) .... NAuC
Cayuga County Historical Society, Auburn, NY [*Library symbol*] [*Library of Congress*] (LCLS) .... NAuHi
Cayuga Herald News, Cayuga, IN [*Library symbol*] [*Library of Congress*] (LCLS) .... InCayHN
Cayuga Syndrome [*Reproductive disturbance in fish*] .... CS
Cazador Explorations [*Vancouver Stock Exchange symbol*] .... CAZ
Cazaux [*France*] [*ICAO location identifier*] (ICLI) .... LFBC
Cazenovia College, Cazenovia, NY [*Library symbol*] [*Library of Congress*] (LCLS) .... NCazC
Cazenovia College, Witherill Learning Center, Cazenovia, NY [*OCLC symbol*] (OCLC) .... ZCZ
Cazenovia Junior College (SAUO) .... CJC
Cazenovia, NY [*FM radio station call letters*] .... WITC
Cazombo [*Angola*] [*ICAO location identifier*] (ICLI) .... FNCZ
CB Bancorp [*NASDAQ symbol*] (TTSB) .... CBCO
CB Bancorp, Inc. [*Associated Press*] (SAG) .... CB Bcp
CB Bancorp, Inc. [*NASDAQ symbol*] (SAG) .... CBCO
CB Bancshares [*NASDAQ symbol*] (TTSB) .... CBBI
CB Bancshares, Inc. [*NASDAQ symbol*] (SAG) .... CBBI
CB Bancshares, Inc. [*Associated Press*] (SAG) .... CB Bnc
CB Commercial Real Estate Services Group, Inc. [*NASDAQ symbol*] (SAG) .... CBCG
CB Commercial Real Estate Services Group, Inc. [*Associated Press*] (SAG) .... CB CoRl
CB Exective Helicopters [*British*] [*ICAO designator*] (FAAC) .... CBH
CB Pak, Inc. [*Toronto Stock Exchange symbol*] .... CBK
CB [*Citizens Band*] **Radio Patrol of American Federation of Police** (EA) .... CBRP
CB Richard Ellis Services [*NYSE symbol*] [*Formerly, CB Commercial R.E. Services*] .... CBG
CBA Engineering Ltd., Vancouver, BC, Canada [*Library symbol*] [*Library of Congress*] (LCLS) .... CaBVaCBA
CBA Engineering Ltd., Vancouver, British Columbia [*Library symbol*] [*National Library of Canada*] (NLC) .... BVACBA
C-Band [*3900-6200 MHz*] .... C/B
C-Band [*3900-6200 MHz*] (NASA) .... C-BD
C-Band Checkout System (KSC) .... CBCS
C-Band Communications Transponder .... CCT
C-Band Frequency Converter .... CFC
C-Band Integrated Radar Imaging System (SAUS) .... C-IRIS
C-Band Monopulse Feed .... CMF
C-Band RADAR Transponder .... CRT
C-Band Scatterometer (USDC) .... C-SCAT
C-Band Sensitivity Improvement [*Navy*] (MCD) .... CSI
C-Band Temperature .... CTF
C-Band Tracking RADAR .... CTR
C-Band Transponder [*Radio*] .... CBX
C-Band Transponder Antenna [*Radio*] (CET) .... CBA
C-Battery .... CB
CBI Industries, Inc. [*Formerly, Chicago Bridge & Iron Co.*] [*Associated Press*] (SAG) .... CBI
C-bit Coding Violation (SAUS) CCV
C-bit Errored Seconds (SAUS) .... CES
C-Bit Severely Errored Seconds [*Computer science*] (VERA) .... CSES
CBL & Associates Prop [*NYSE symbol*] (TTSB) .... CBL
CBL & Associates Properties [*NYSE symbol*] (SPSG) .... CBL
CBL & Associates Properties [*Associated Press*] (SAG) .... CBL Asc
CBN University, Virginia Beach, VA [*Library symbol*] [*Library of Congress*] (LCLS) .... ViVbC
CBNU Learning Resources Center, Virginia Beach, VA [*OCLC symbol*] (OCLC) .... VCB
CBO Resources Corp. [*Vancouver Stock Exchange symbol*] .... CBU
CBPO [*Consolidated Base Personnel Office*] **Strength Summary Card** (AFM) .... CSS
CBPO [*Consolidated Base Personnel Office*] **Strength Summary Card** (AFM) .... CSSC
CBS Corp. [*NYSE symbol*] [*Formerly, Westinghouse Electric*] (SG) .... CBS
CBS, Inc. [*Formerly, Columbia Broadcasting System, Inc.*] [*NYSE symbol*] (SPSG) .... CBS
CBT Corp. [*NASDAQ symbol*] (SAG) .... CBTC
CBT Corp. [*Associated Press*] (SAG) .... CBT Cp
CBT Group ADS [*NASDAQ symbol*] (TTSB) .... CBTSY
CBT Group PLC [*Associated Press*] (SAG) .... CBT
CBT Group PLC [*Associated Press*] (SAG) .... CBT Gp
CBT Group PLC [*NASDAQ symbol*] (SAG) .... CBTS
C.C. Enrique Cuahonte Delgado, Marta Amezcua de Cuahonte [*Mexico*] [*FAA designator*] (FAAC) .... CUO
CCA Industries [*NASDAQ symbol*] (TTSB) .... CCAM
CCA Industries, Inc. [*Associated Press*] (SAG) .... CCA
CCA Industries, Inc. [*NASDAQ symbol*] (NQ) .... CCAM
CCAIR, Inc. [*Associated Press*] (SAG) .... CCAIR
CCAIR, Inc. [*NASDAQ symbol*] (NQ) .... CCAR
CCAir, Inc. [*ICAO designator*] (FAAC) .... CDL
CCAMLR Ecosystem Monitoring Programme (SAUS) .... CEMP
CCATS [*Communications, Command, and Telemetry Systems*] **Command Controller** [*NASA*] CCC
CCATS [*Communications, Command, and Telemetry Systems*] **Telemetry Controller** [*NASA*] .... CTC
CCB Financial [*NYSE symbol*] (SAG) .... CCB
CCB Financial [*NASDAQ symbol*] (TTSB) .... CCBF
CCB Financial Co. [*Associated Press*] (SAG) .... CCB Fn
CCB Financial Corp. [*NASDAQ symbol*] (NQ) .... CCBF
CCC Coded Communications [*Vancouver Stock Exchange symbol*] .... CCE
CCC Countermeasures (SAUS) .... CCCCM
CCC Information Services Group, Inc. [*NASDAQ symbol*] (SAG) .... CCCG
CCC Information Services Group, Inc. [*Associated Press*] (SAG) .... CCC Info
CCCO [*Central Committee for Conscientious Objectors*]**/An Agency for Military and Draft Counseling** (EA) .... CCCO
CCD Airborne Experimental Scanner for Applications in Remote Sensing (SAUS) .... CAESAR
CCD [*Charge-Coupled Device*] **Transit Instrument** [*Telescope*] .... CTI
CCF Holding [*NASDAQ symbol*] (TTSB) .... CCFH
CCF Holding Co. [*Associated Press*] (SAG) .... CCF
CCF Holding Co. [*NASDAQ symbol*] (SAG) .... CCFH
CCH FAR Archives [*Historical FARs on CD-ROM*] (AAGC) .... FARchives
CCH, Inc. [*Associated Press*] (SAG) .... CCH
CCH, Inc. [*NASDAQ symbol*] (SAG) .... CCHI
CCH [*Commerce Clearing House*] **Publications Index** (ADA) .... CCHP
CCITT High Intelligent Level Language (SAUS) .... CHILL
CCITT [*Consultative Committee on International Telegraphy and Telephony*] **High-Level Language** [*Telecommunications*] (TEL) .... CHILL
CCITT recommendation X.200 is the basic (SAUS) X200
CCITT standard for 14400 bps modems (SAUS) V32bis
CCITT standard for 9600 bps modems (SAUS) V32
CCL Industries, Inc. [*Toronto Stock Exchange symbol*] .... CCQ
CCl2F2, dichlorodifluoromethane, Freon-12 (SAUS) CFC-12
CCl3F, trichlorofluoromethane, Freon-11 (SAUS) CFC-11
CCMS Application Programs (SAUS) .... CAP
CCMS [*Checkout, Control, and Monitor Subsystem*] **Application Programs** [*NASA*] (NASA) .... CAP
CCNU [*Lomustine*], **Adriamycin, Bleomycin, Streptozotocin** [*Antineoplastic drug regimen*] .... CABS
CCNU [*Lomustine*], **Adriamycin, Vinblastine** [*Antineoplastic drug regimen*] .... CAVe
CCNU [*Lomustine*], **Bleomycin, Vinblastine, Dexamethasone** [*Antineoplastic drug regimen*] .... CBVD
CCNU [*Lomustine*], **Cyclophosphamide, Adriamycin, Vincristine, VP-16** [*Antineoplastic drug regimen*] (DAVI) .... CCAVV
CCNU [*Lomustine*], **Cyclophosphamide, Methotrexate, Adriamycin** [*Antineoplastic drug regimen*] (DAVI) .... CCMA
CCNU [*Lomustine*], **Cyclophosphamide, Oncovin , Bleomycin** [*Vincristine*] [*Antineoplastic drug regimen*] (DAVI) .... CCOB
CCNU [*Lomustine*], **Cyclophosphamide, Vincristine** [*Antineoplastic drug regimen*] (DAVI) CCV
CCNU [*Lomustine*], **Cyclophosphamide, Vincristine, Alternating with Adriamycin, Vincristine** [*Antineoplastic drug regimen*] .... CCV-AV
CCNU [*Lomustine*], **Cyclophosphamide, Vincristine, Bleomycin** [*Antineoplastic drug regimen*] (DAVI) .... CCVB
CCNU [*Lomustine*], **Cyclophosphamide, Vincristine, Procarbazine, Prednisone** [*Antineoplastic drug regimen*] .... CCVPP
CCNU [*Lomustine*], **Etoposide, Prednimustine** [*Antineoplastic drug regimen*] .... CEP
CCNU [*Lomustine*], **Etoposide, Vindesine, Dexamethasone** [*Antineoplastic drug regimen*] .... CEVD
CCNU [*Lomustine*], **Ifosfamide, Adriamycin** [*Antineoplastic drug regimen*] .... CIA
CCNU Lomustine, Oncovin [*Vincristine*], **Prednisone** [*Antineoplastic drug regimen*] (DAVI) .... CCNU-OP
CCNU [*Lomustine*], **Methotrexate, Procarbazine** [*Antineoplastic drug regimen*] (DAVI) .... CMP
CCNU [*Lomustine*], **Oncovin , Methotrexate, Procarbazine** [*Vincristine*] [*Antineoplastic drug regimen*] .... COMP
CCNU [*Lomustine*], **Oncovin , Prednisone, Adriamycin, Cyclophosphamide** [*Vincristine*] [*Antineoplastic drug regimen*] .... COPAC
CCNU [*Lomustine*], **Oncovin , Procarbazine, Prednisone** [*Vincristine*] [*Antineoplastic drug regimen*] .... COPP
CCNU [*Lomustine*], **Procarbazine, Methotrexate** [*Antineoplastic drug regirnen*] .... CPM
CCNU [*Lomustine*], **Vinblastine, Bleomycin** [*Antineoplastic drug regimen*] .... CVB
CCNU [*Lomustine*], **Vinblastine, Prednisone, Procarbazine** [*Antineoplastic drug regimen*] .... CVPP

C-COR Electronics, Inc. [*NASDAQ symbol*] (NQ) .... CCBL
CCOR Electronics, Inc. [*Associated Press*] (SAG) .... C COR
C-COR Electrs [*NASDAQ symbol*] (TTSB) .... CCBL
C-COR.net Corp [*NASDAQ symbol*] (SG) .... CCBL
Ccos (Keeling) Islands Cooperative Society [*Australia*] .... C(K)ICS
CCP AG Cosendali Computer Products (SAUO) .... CCP
CCRS Airborne Operations (SAUS) .... AOPS
CCRS Image Analysis System (SAUS) .... CIAS
CCSC Project Management System (SAUS) .... PAC II
CCSM Investigators Group (SAUO) .... CCSMIG
C-CUBE Microsystems [*Associated Press*] (SAG) .... C-CUBE
C-CUBE Microsystems [*NASDAQ symbol*] (SAG) .... CUBE
CCW System Ltd. [*Vancouver Stock Exchange symbol*] .... CWI
CD [*Compact Disc*] **Data Report** [*Langley Publications*] [*Information service or system*] [*A publication*] (IID) .... CDDR
CD for Video (SAUS) .... CD-V
CD Player (SAUS) .... CDP
CD Radio, Inc. [*Associated Press*] (SAG) .... CDRad
CD Radio, Inc. [*Associated Press*] (SAG) .... CDRadio
CD Radio, Inc. [*NASDAQ symbol*] (SAG) .... CDRD
CD Radio Inc. Wrrt [*NASDAQ symbol*] (TTSB) .... CDRDW
CD Warehouse, Inc. [*NASDAQ symbol*] (SAG) .... CDWI
CD Warehouse, Inc. [*Associated Press*] (SAG) .... CD Wrhs
CDC Division of Reproductive Health (SAUS) .... DRH
CDC National AIDS Clearinghouse (SAUO) .... CDC NAC
CDC National AIDS Clearinghouse (EA) .... NAC
CDC Wide-ranging Online Data for Epidemiologic Research (SAUO) .... CDC WONDER
CDCs Office of Womens Health (SAUS) .... OWH
CDI Corp. [*NYSE symbol*] (SPSG) .... CDI
CDIAC Computing System Network (SAUS) .... CCCN
CDIAC Information System (SAUO) .... CIS
CDIS Software, Inc. [*Vancouver Stock Exchange symbol*] .... CIS
CDK (Cyclin Dependent Kinae) Activating Kinae [*An enzyme*] .... CAK
CDMA Development Organization (SAUO) .... CDG
CDOS [*Customer Data and Operations System*] **Integration and Test Facility** (SSD) .... CITF
CDOS Operations Management Service (SAUS) .... COMS
CDOS Software Support Environment (SAUS) .... CSSE
CDOS Test and Verification (SAUS) .... CTAV
CDR Discrepancy Notice [*NASA*] (MCD) .... CDN
CDR Discrepancy Notice Record .... CDNR
CDR Resources [*Vancouver Stock Exchange symbol*] .... CDR
CD-ROM catalogue (SAUS) .... BOOKBANK
CD-ROM Consistent Interface Committee (SAUO) .... CD-CINC
CD-ROM [*Compact Disk Read-Only Memory*] **Continuous Information Service** [*International Data Group - IDG*] [*Information service or system*] (IID) .... CIS
CD-ROM Data Origination Working Group (SAUO) .... CDOWG
CD-ROM database equivalent of Index Medicus (SAUS) .... MEDLINE
CD-ROM Index Architecture Specification Working Group (SAUO) .... CIAS
CD-ROM Interactive Multimedia (SAUS) .... CD-ROM DVI
CD-ROM of incunabula (SAUS) .... INCIPIT
CD-ROM service from Book Data (SAUS) .... BOOKFIND
CDS Application Support Programs [*NASA*] (NASA) .... CASP
CDS [*Carl Duisberg Society*] **International** (EA) .... CDSI
CDW Computer Centers [*NASDAQ symbol*] (TTSB) .... CDWC
CDW Computer Centers [*Associated Press*] (SAG) .... CDW Cpt
CDW Computer Centers, Inc. [*NASDAQ symbol*] (SAG) .... CDWC
CE Franklin Ltd. [*Associated Press*] (SAG) .... CE Frnk
CE Franklin Ltd [*AMEX symbol*] (TTSB) .... CFK
CE Software Hldgs [*NASDAQ symbol*] (TTSB) .... CESH
CE Software Holdings, Inc. [*NASDAQ symbol*] (SAG) .... CESH
CE Software Holdings, Inc. [*Associated Press*] (SAG) .... CE Soft
Cease and Desist [*Legal shorthand*] (LWAP) .... C & D
Cease and Desist Order [*Legal shorthand*] (LWAP) .... CDO
Cease Firing (SAUS) .... CF
Ceased Breathing [*Medicine*] (DAVI) .... CB
Ceased to Breathe [*Medicine*] .... CTB
CEBAF Large Acceptance Spectrometer (SAUS) .... CLAS
Cebu [*Philippines*] [*Later, DAV*] [*Geomagnetic observatory code*] .... CCP
Cebu [*Philippines*] [*Airport symbol*] (OAG) .... CEB
Cebu (SAUS) .... Ceb
Cebu City [*Philippines*] [*Seismograph station code, US Geological Survey*] (SEIS) .... CCP
Cebu Stevedores Association [*Philippines*] .... CSA
Cebu/Lahug, Cebu [*Philippines*] [*ICAO location identifier*] (ICLI) .... RPMC
Cebu-Visayan (SAUS) .... Ceb-Vis
CEC Entertainment [*NYSE symbol*] [*Formerly, ShowBiz Pizza Time*] .... CEC
CEC International Partners [*Citizen Exchange Corps*] (EA) .... CEC
CEC [*Council for Exceptional Children*] **Pioneers Division** (PAZ) .... CEC-PD
CEC Project on Genesis and Impact of Tsunamis on European Coasts (SAUS) .... GITEC
CEC Resources [*AMX*] (TTSB) .... CGS
CEC Resources Ltd. [*Associated Press*] (SAG) .... CEC
CEC Resources Ltd. [*AMEX symbol*] (SAG) .... CGS
Cecchetti Council of America (EA) .... CCA
Cechoslovakische Statistik [*Czechoslovakia*] .... CS
Cecil Aviation Ltd. [*ICAO designator*] (FAAC) CIL
Cecil Rhodes University (SAUO) .... CRU
Cecilia Lee International Fan Club (EA) .... CLIFC
Cecils Junior College, Asheville, NC [*Library symbol*] [*Library of Congress*] (LCLS) .... NcAC
Ceco Corporation (SAUO) .... CCP
Ceco Environmental [*NASDAQ symbol*] (SAG) .... CECE
Ceco Environmental [*Associated Press*] (SAG) .... CecoEnv
CECOM Flight Test Activity [*Lakehurst, NJ*] [*Later, AERA*] [*Army*] (GRD) .... CFTA
CECOS International, Buffalo, NY [*Library symbol*] [*Library of Congress*] (LCLS) .... NBuCEC
Cedalion Systems, Inc., Information Resources, Charlotte, NC [*Library symbol*] [*Library of Congress*] (LCLS) .... NcCCed
Cedar .... CEDR
Cedar Bluff, VA [*FM radio station call letters*] .... WBBY
Cedar Bluff, VA [*FM radio station call letters*] (BROA) .... WHQX-FM
Cedar Bluff, VA [*AM radio station call letters*] .... WYRV
Cedar Breaks National Monument .... CEBR
Cedar City [*Utah*] [*Seismograph station code, US Geological Survey*] (SEIS) .... CCU
Cedar City [*Utah*] [*Airport symbol*] (OAG) .... CDC
Cedar City, UT [*AM radio station call letters*] .... KBRE
Cedar City, UT [*FM radio station call letters*] .... KBRE-FM
Cedar City, UT [*Television station call letters*] (BROA) .... KCSG
Cedar City, UT [*Television station call letters*] .... KSGI
Cedar City, UT [*FM radio station call letters*] .... KSSD
Cedar City, UT [*AM radio station call letters*] .... KSUB
Cedar City, UT [*FM radio station call letters*] .... KSUU
Cedar County Courthouse, Tipton, IA [*Library symbol*] [*Library of Congress*] (LCLS) .... IaTipCoC
Cedar County Historical Society, Clarence, IA [*Library symbol*] [*Library of Congress*] (LCLS) .... IaClarCHi
Cedar Creek, FL [*FM radio station call letters*] .... WKSG
Cedar Creek Youth Camp, Littlerock, WA [*Library symbol*] [*Library of Congress*] (LCLS) .... WaLrC
Cedar Crest and Muhlenberg Colleges, Allentown, PA [*OCLC symbol*] (OCLC) .... EVI
Cedar Crest College [*Pennsylvania*] CCC
Cedar Crest College, Allentown, PA [*Library symbol*] [*Library of Congress*] (LCLS) .... PAtC
Cedar Fair LP [*NYSE symbol*] (SAG) .... FUN
Cedar Fair Ltd. [*Associated Press*] (SAG) .... CedrFr
Cedar Falls Historical Society, Cedar Falls, IA [*Library symbol*] [*Library of Congress*] (LCLS) .... IaCfHi
Cedar Falls, IA [*AM radio station call letters*] (RBYB) .... KCNZ
Cedar Falls, IA [*AM radio station call letters*] (BROA) .... KDNZ
Cedar Falls, IA [*FM radio station call letters*] .... KHKE
Cedar Falls, IA [*FM radio station call letters*] .... KKCV
Cedar Falls, IA [*FM radio station call letters*] .... KUNI
Cedar Falls Public Library, Cedar Falls, IA [*Library symbol*] [*Library of Congress*] (LCLS) .... IaCf
Cedar Falls Record, Cedar Falls, IA [*Library symbol*] [*Library of Congress*] (LCLS) .... IaCfR
Cedar Group [*NASDAQ symbol*] (TTSB) .... CGMV
Cedar Group, Inc. [*Associated Press*] (SAG) .... CedarGp
Cedar Group, Inc. [*NASDAQ symbol*] (SAG) .... CGMV
Cedar Grove Public Library, Cedar Grove, NJ [*Library symbol*] [*Library of Congress*] (LCLS) .... NjCg
Cedar Hill, MO [*FM radio station call letters*] (BROA) .... KNLH-FM
Cedar Income Fund [*NASDAQ symbol*] (TTSB) .... CEDR
Cedar Income Fund Ltd. [*Associated Press*] (SAG) .... CedarI
Cedar Income Fund Ltd. [*NASDAQ symbol*] (NQ) .... CEDR
Cedar Key, FL [*Location identifier*] [*FAA*] (FAAL) .... CDK
Cedar Key, FL [*FM radio station call letters*] (RBYB) .... WCQQ
Cedar Key, FL [*FM radio station call letters*] (RBYB) .... WRGO-FM
Cedar Mill Community Library, Portland, OR [*Library symbol*] [*Library of Congress*] (LCLS) .... OrPCM
Cedar Mountain School, Morgan, MN [*Library symbol*] [*Library of Congress*] (LCLS) .... MnMnCMS
Cedar Mt. Elementary School, Franklin, MN [*Library symbol*] [*Library of Congress*] (LCLS) .... MnFrnCES
Cedar Rapids & Iowa City [*Railway*] (MHDB) .... CRANDIC
Cedar Rapids & Iowa City Railway Co. [*AAR code*] CIC
Cedar Rapids Area Library Consortium [*Library network*] .... CRALC
Cedar Rapids Gazette, Cedar Rapids, IA [*Library symbol*] [*Library of Congress*] (LCLS) .... IaCrG
Cedar Rapids, IA [*FM radio station call letters*] .... KCCK
Cedar Rapids, IA [*AM radio station call letters*] .... KCRG
Cedar Rapids, IA [*Television station call letters*] .... KCRG-TV
Cedar Rapids, IA [*FM radio station call letters*] (RBYB) .... KDAT
Cedar Rapids, IA [*Television station call letters*] (RBYB) .... KFXA
Cedar Rapids, IA [*Television station call letters*] .... KGAN
Cedar Rapids, IA [*FM radio station call letters*] .... KHAK-FM
Cedar Rapids, IA [*AM radio station call letters*] .... KMRY
Cedar Rapids, IA [*Television station call letters*] (BROA) .... KPXR
Cedar Rapids, IA [*FM radio station call letters*] .... KTOF
Cedar Rapids, IA [*Television station call letters*] .... KTVC
Cedar Rapids, IA [*FM radio station call letters*] (RBYB) .... KXMX
Cedar Rapids, IA [*FM radio station call letters*] (BROA) .... KZIA-FM
Cedar Rapids, IA [*Location identifier*] [*FAA*] (FAAL) .... RRU
Cedar Rapids, IA [*AM radio station call letters*] .... WMT
Cedar Rapids, IA [*FM radio station call letters*] .... WMT-FM
Cedar Rapids Public Library, Cedar Rapids, IA [*Library symbol*] [*Library of Congress*] (LCLS) .... IaCr
Cedar Rapids Public Library, Cedar Rapids, IA [*OCLC symbol*] (OCLC) .... IWR
Cedar Rapids/Iowa City [*Iowa*] [*Airport symbol*] (OAG) .... CID
Cedar Road Elementary School, Commack, NY [*Library symbol*] [*Library of Congress*] (LCLS) .... NCoCE
Cedar Shake and Shingle Bureau (EA) .... CSSB
Cedar Springs [*California*] [*Seismograph station code, US Geological Survey*] [*Closed*] (SEIS) .... CED
Cedar Springs [*California*] [*Seismograph station code, US Geological Survey*] (SEIS) .... CSP
Cedar Springs Library (SAUS) .... CSL

Cedar Valley Times, Vinton, IA [*Library symbol*] [*Library of Congress*] (LCLS) ... IaVinT
Cedar Waxwing [*Ornithology*] ... CW
Cedarbrae Branch, Scarborough Public Library, Ontario [*Library symbol*] [*National Library of Canada*] (NLC) ... OTSPC
Cedaredge Public Library, Cedaredge, CO [*Library symbol*] [*Library of Congress*] (LCLS) ... CoCe
Cedarholm, Bland, Havens, and Townes [*Ether drift experiment*] (MUGU) ... CBHT
Cedarhurst Elementary School, Lawrence, NY [*Library symbol*] [*Library of Congress*] (LCLS) ... NLawChE
Cedars of Lebanon Hospital (MCD) ... CLH
Cedars-Sinai Medical Center [*Los Angeles, CA*] ... CS
Cedars-Sinai Medical Center, Los Angeles, CA [*Library symbol*] [*Library of Congress*] (LCLS) ... CLCLH
Cedartown, GA [*AM radio station call letters*] ... WGAA
Cedartown, GA [*FM radio station call letters*] ... WJCK
Cedarville College, Cedarville, OH [*OCLC symbol*] (OCLC) ... CDC
Cedarville College, Cedarville, OH [*Library symbol*] [*Library of Congress*] (LCLS) ... OCedC
Cedarville, OH [*FM radio station call letters*] ... WCDR
Cedi [*Monetary unit*] [*Ghana*] ... C
Cedrol ... CDRL
Ceduna [*Australia*] [*ICAO location identifier*] (ICLI) ... AACD
Ceduna [*Australia*] [*ICAO location identifier*] (ICLI) ... APCD
Ceduna [*Australia*] [*Airport symbol*] (OAG) ... CED
Ceelen-Gellerstedt [*Syndrome*] [*Medicine*] (DB) ... CG
Ceeta-Kel Air [*France*] [*ICAO designator*] (FAAC) ... CET
Cefazolin [*Antibacterial compound*] ... CEZ
Cefazolin [*An antibiotic*] ... CZ
Cefazolin Sodium (MELL) ... CZS
Cefi Aviation SRL [*Italy*] [*ICAO designator*] (FAAC) ... IFC
Cefmenoxime (DMAA) ... CMX
Cefoperazone (STED) ... CPZ
Cefotaxime [*An antibiotic*] ... CTX
Cefoxitin (DB) ... CFX
Cefoxitin Cyclosterine Fructose Agar [*Medium*] [*Microbiology*] (DAVI) ... CCFA
Cefoxitin Cyclosterine Fructose Agar Medium [*Medicine*] (BABM) ... CCFA
Cefpodoxime (DMAA) ... CPDX
Ceftriaxone (DMAA) ... CTRX
Cefuroxime [*Antibacterial drug*] ... CXM
Cefuzonam [*Antibacterial*] ... CZON
Cega Aviation Ltd. [*British*] [*ICAO designator*] (FAAC) ... CEG
Cega Services [*An association*] (EA) ... CC
CEGEP [*College d'Enseignement General et Professionnel*] **de Hauterive, BaieComeau, Quebec** [*Library symbol*] [*National Library of Canada*] (NLC) ... QHAC
CEGEP [*College d'Enseignement General et Professionnel*] **de La Pocatiere, Quebec** [*Library symbol*] [*National Library of Canada*] (NLC) ... QPCE
Cegep de Levis-Lauzon, Lauzon, PQ, Canada [*Library symbol*] [*Library of Congress*] (LCLS) ... CaQLCLL
CEGEP [*College d'Enseignement General et Professionnel*] **de Levis-Lauzon, Lauzon, Quebec** [*Library symbol*] [*National Library of Canada*] (BIB) ... QLCLL
CEGEP [*College d'Enseignement General et Professionnel*] **de Limoilou, Quebec, PQ, Canada** [*Library symbol*] [*Library of Congress*] (LCLS) ... CaQQCE
CEGEP [*College d'Enseignement General et Professionnel*] **de Limoilou, Quebec, Quebec** [*Library symbol*] [*National Library of Canada*] (NLC) ... QQCE
CEGEP [*College d'Enseignement General et Professionnel*] **de l'Outaouais, Heritage Campus, Hull, PQ, Canada** [*Library symbol*] [*Library of Congress*] (LCLS) ... CaQHCH
CEGEP [*College d'Enseignement General et Professionnel*] **de l'Outaouais, Hull, Quebec** [*Library symbol*] [*National Library of Canada*] (NLC) ... QHC
CEGEP [*College d'Enseignement General et Professionnel*] **de Rimouski, Quebec** [*Library symbol*] [*National Library of Canada*] (NLC) ... QRIC
CEGEP [*College d'Enseignement General et Professionnel*] **de Riviere-Du-Loup, Quebec** [*Library symbol*] [*National Library of Canada*] (BIB) ... QRLC
CEGEP [*College d'Enseignement General et Professionnel*] **de Sept-Iles, Quebec** [*Library symbol*] [*National Library of Canada*] (BIB) ... QSIC
CEGEP [*College d'Enseignement General et Professionnel*] **de Shawinigan, Quebec** [*Library symbol*] [*National Library of Canada*] (NLC) ... QSHC
CEGEP [*College d'Enseignement General et Professionnel*] **de Shawinigan, Shawinigan, PQ, Canada** [*Library symbol*] [*Library of Congress*] (LCLS) ... CaQSHC
CEGEP [*College d'Enseignement General et Professionnel*] **de St.-Jerome, Quebec** [*Library symbol*] [*National Library of Canada*] (BIB) ... QSTJEC
CEGEP [*College d'Enseignement General et Professionnel*] **F. X. Garneau, Sillery, Quebec** [*Library symbol*] [*National Library of Canada*] (NLC) ... QQCFX
CEGEP John Abbott College Library (SAUS) ... JAC
CEGEP [*College d'Enseignement General et Professionnel*] **John Abbott College Library** [*UTLAS symbol*] ... JAC
CEGEP Montmorency, Laval, Quebec (SAUS) ... QLAC
CEGEP [*College d'Enseignement General et Professionnel*] **Montmorency, Laval, Quebec** [*Library symbol*] [*National Library of Canada*] (NLC) ... QLAC
CEGEP [*College d'Enseignement General et Professionnel*] **Montmorency-Chomedy, Laval, PQ, Canada** [*Library symbol*] [*Library of Congress*] (LCLS) ... CaQLAC
CEGEP [*College d'Enseignement General et Professionnel*]**, Trois-Rivieres, Bibliotheque** [*EDUCATSS*] [*UTLAS symbol*] ... EUG
CEGEP [*College d'Enseignement General et Professionnel*]**, Trois-Rivieres, PQ, Canada** [*Library symbol*] [*Library of Congress*] (LCLS) ... CaQTCE
CEGEP [*College d'Enseignement General et Professionnel*]**, Trois-Rivieres, Quebec** [*Library symbol*] [*National Library of Canada*] (NLC) ... QTCE
CEGEP, Trois-Rivieres, Quebec (SAUS) ... QTCE
Ceiba, PR [*AM radio station call letters*] ... WFAB
Ceiling [*Hazard limit*] ... C
Ceiling (VRA) ... ceil
Ceiling [*Aviation*] ... CEIL
ceiling (SAUS) ... ceil
Ceiling (DA) ... CIG
Ceiling (ADWA) ... clg
Ceiling [*Aviation*] (KSC) ... CLG
Ceiling (WPI) ... Clg
Ceiling and Visibility [*Aviation*] (PIAV) ... CAVOK
Ceiling and Visibility Okay (SAUS) ... CAVOK
Ceiling and Visibility Unrestricted [*or Unlimited*] [*Aviation*] (MCD) ... CAVU
Ceiling Grille [*Technical drawings*] (DAC) ... CG
Ceiling Height (OA) ... CH
Ceiling Height [*Technical drawings*] ... CHT
Ceiling Joist ... CJ
Ceiling Level ... CL
Ceiling Limit Value [*Investment term*] (MHDW) ... CLV
Ceiling Luminance Coefficient (SAUS) ... CLC
Ceiling Price Regulation (DLA) ... CPR
Ceiling Register (OA) ... CR
Ceiling Value (SAUS) ... CL
Ceilings and Interior Systems Construction Association (EA) ... CISCA
Ceilings and Interior Systems Contractors Association (SAUO) ... CISCA
CEIP [*Communications-Electronics Implementation Plan*] **Implementation Directive** [*Air Force*] (CET) ... CID
C-E-I-R Inc., Washington (SAUO) ... C-E-I-R
Ceja Corp., Tulsa, OK [*Library symbol*] [*Library of Congress*] (LCLS) ... OkTC
CEL Industry Ltd. [*Vancouver Stock Exchange symbol*] ... CKL
Celadon (VRA) ... cel
Celadon Group [*Associated Press*] (SAG) ... Celadon
Celadon Group [*NASDAQ symbol*] (SAG) ... CLDN
Celanese Canada, Inc. [*Toronto Stock Exchange symbol*] ... CCL
Celanese Canada Ltd., Montreal, PQ, Canada [*Library symbol*] [*Library of Congress*] (LCLS) ... CaQMCE
Celanese Canada Ltd., Montreal, Quebec [*Library symbol*] [*National Library of Canada*] (NLC) ... QMCE
Celanese Corp. (SAUO) ... CZ
Celanese Corp., Clarkwood, TX [*Library symbol*] [*Library of Congress*] (LCLS) ... TxClwC
Celanese Corp., Narrows, VA [*Library symbol*] [*Library of Congress*] (LCLS) ... ViNarC
Celanese Engineering Resins Division [*Celanese Corp.*] ... CER
Celanese Fibers Co., Technical Information Center, Charlotte (SAUS) ... NcCCel
Celanese Fibers Co., Technical Information Center, Charlotte, NC [*Library symbol*] [*Library of Congress*] (LCLS) ... NcCCel
Celaya [*Race of maize*] ... CEL
Celaya [*Mexico*] [*ICAO location identifier*] (ICLI) ... MMCY
Celeban Standard Time (SAUS) ... CST
Celebes (SAUS) ... Cel
celebrate (SAUS) ... celeb
celebrated (SAUS) ... cel
Celebrated ... CEL
Celebrating Success with Technology [*Education*] ... CST
celebration (SAUS) ... celeb
celebrities (SAUS) ... celebs
Celebrity (ADWA) ... celeb
Celebrity ... CLBRTY
Celebrity Engineering [*Vancouver Stock Exchange symbol*] ... CEC
Celebrity Entertainment [*NASDAQ symbol*] (TTSB) ... CLER
Celebrity Entertainment, Inc. [*Associated Press*] (SAG) ... CelebEn
Celebrity Entertainment, Inc. [*NASDAQ symbol*] (SAG) ... CLEB
Celebrity, Inc. [*Associated Press*] (SAG) ... CelebInc
Celebrity, Inc. [*NASDAQ symbol*] (SAG) ... FLWR
Celendin [*Peru*] [*ICAO location identifier*] (ICLI) ... SPLD
Celeritek Inc. [*NASDAQ symbol*] (TTSB) ... CLTK
Celery and Parsley Cross [*Genetics*] ... CxP
Celery Mosaic Virus [*Plant pathology*] ... CEMV
Celescope Optical Package (KSC) ... COP
Celesta [*Music*] ... CEL
Celesta ... cel
Celeste Resources [*Vancouver Stock Exchange symbol*] ... CST
Celestial (AFM) ... CEL
Celestial (FAAC) ... CLST
Celestial Atomic Trajectile ... CAT
Celestial Canopy [*Freemasonry*] ... CC
Celestial Data Processor (SAUS) ... CDP
Celestial Ephemeris Pole (GEOI) ... CEP
Celestial Equator ... CE
Celestial Infra-Red Mapper (SAUS) ... CIRM
Celestial Infrared Mapping [*Air Force*] (MCD) ... CIRM
Celestial Infrared Measurement (ACAE) ... CIRM
Celestial Infrared Measurement System ... CIRMS
Celestial Mapping Program [*Air Force*] (MCD) ... CMP
Celestial Measurements Program (ACAE) ... CMP
Celestial Mechanics ... CM
Celestial Moving Target Indicator ... CMTI
Celestial Navigation (FAAC) ... CELNAV
Celestial Navigation (SAUS) ... Celnav
Celestial Navigation Trainer ... CNT
Celestial North Pole (DNAB) ... CNP
Celestial Relays and Power (ACAE) ... CRP
Celestial Research Corp. (KSC) ... CELESCO
Celestial Seasonings [*NASDAQ symbol*] (TTSB) ... CTEA
Celestial Seasonings, Inc. [*Associated Press*] (SAG) ... Celestial
Celestial Seasonings, Inc. [*NASDAQ symbol*] (SAG) ... CTEA
Celestial Sensor (ACAE) ... CS
Celestial Sensor Assembly (ACAE) ... CSA

Celestial Telescope [*OAO*] ... CELESCOPE
Celestial Telescope [*OAO*] (DNAB) ... CELSCOPE
Celestial Training Device (MCD) ... CTD
Celestica, Inc. [*NYSE symbol*] (SG) ... CLS
Celex Group [*NASDAQ symbol*] (TTSB) ... CLXG
Celex Group, Inc. [*Associated Press*] (SAG) ... Celex
Celex Group, Inc. [*NASDAQ symbol*] (SAG) ... CLXG
Celgene Corp. [*NASDAQ symbol*] (NQ) ... CELG
Celgene Corp. [*Associated Press*] (SAG) ... Celgene
Celiac Axis [*Anatomy*] ... CA
Celiac Disease [*Medicine*] (DB) ... CD
Celiac Disease Foundation (EA) ... CDF
Celiac Plexus [*Medicine*] (MELL) ... CP
Celiac Sprue [*Medicine*] (DAVI) ... CS
Celiac Sprue Association/United States of America (EA) ... CSA/USA
Celiac, Superior Mesenteric Artery [*Anatomy*] ... CSMA
Celiac, Superior Mesenteric Vein [*Anatomy*] ... CSMV
Celiac Syndrome [*Medicine*] (MELL) ... CS
Celibate ... CEL
Celico Resources [*Vancouver Stock Exchange symbol*] ... CEL
Celina, OH [*Location identifier*] [*FAA*] (FAAL) ... CQA
Celina, OH [*AM radio station call letters*] ... WCSM
Celina, OH [*FM radio station call letters*] ... WCSM-FM
Celina, OH [*FM radio station call letters*] ... WKKI
Celina, TN [*FM radio station call letters*] ... WVFB
Celktic Council of Australia ... CCA
Cell ... C
Cell Activated Factor [*Medicine*] (TAD) ... CAF
Cell Address Set (SAUS) ... CAS
Cell Adhesion Factor [*Cytochemistry*] ... CAF
Cell Adhesion Molecule [*Cytology*] ... CAM
Cell Adhesion Regulator [*Genetics*] ... CAR
Cell Adhesive Molecule (SAUS) ... CAM
Cell Affinity Chromatography ... CAC
Cell Analysis System [*Microscopy*] ... CAS
Cell Antiviral Factor [*Immunochemistry*] ... CAF
Cell Arrival (VERA) ... CA
Cell Associating Molecule [*Cytology*] ... CAM
Cell Atmosphere Processing System [*Nuclear energy*] (NRCH) ... CAPS
Cell Attached [*Microbiology*] ... CA
Cell Attachment Protein [*Cytochemistry*] ... CAP
Cell Broadcast Channel (CGWS) ... CBCH
Cell Calcium (SAUS) ... Cell Calcium
Cell Cap [*Botany*] ... CC
Cell Count [*Medicine*] (MELL) ... CC
Cell Cover Arming Unit (MCD) ... CCAU
Cell Crates ... celcrts
Cell Culture [*Cytology*] ... CC
Cell Culture and Nitrogen Fixation Laboratory [*Department of Agriculture*] ... CC & NF
Cell Current Density ... CCD
Cell Cycle Analyzer [*Instrumentation*] ... CCA
Cell Cycle Nonspecific [*Antitumor agent*] ... CCNS
Cell Cycle Specific [*Antitumor agent*] ... CCS
Cell Cycles [*Medicine*] (MELL) ... CC
Cell Data (SAUS) ... CD
Cell Delay Tolerance (VERA) ... CDT
Cell Delay Variation (VERA) ... CDV
Cell Delay Variation Tolerance [*Telecommunications*] (ACRL) ... CDVT
Cell Dendrites (SAUS) ... CD
Cell Description Language (SAUS) ... CDL
Cell Directory Service (VERA) ... CDS
Cell Dissociation (DB) ... CD
Cell Division Cycle [*Cytology*] ... CDC
Cell Division Cycle Kinases [*Genetics*] (DOG) ... cdc kinases
Cell Error Ratio (VERA) ... CER
Cell Evaluation Chip (AAEL) ... CEC
Cell Factor [*Biology*] ... CF
Cell for Monitoring and Analysis of Sea-level (SAUS) ... CMAS
Cell for Voting (ADWA) ... CFV
Cell Free Extract [*Microbiology*] ... CFE
Cell Genesys [*NASDAQ symbol*] (TTSB) ... CEGE
Cell Genesys, Inc. [*NASDAQ symbol*] (SAG) ... CEGE
Cell Genesys, Inc. [*Associated Press*] (SAG) ... CellGens
Cell Growth and Differentiation (SAUS) ... Cell Growth Differ
Cell Growth & Differentiation (SAUS) ... CG&D
Cell Hemoglobin Concentration [*Biochemistry, medicine*] ... CHC
Cell Hemoglobin Concentration Mean [*Biochemistry, medicine*] ... CHCM
Cell Host Computer ... CHC
Cell in Frames (SAUS) ... CIF
Cell Information Field (SAUS) ... CIF
Cell Inhibition (DB) ... CI
Cell Interaction [*Immunology*] ... CI
Cell Kinetics Society (EA) ... CKS
Cell Line [*Cytology*] ... CL
Cell Loss Payload (SAUS) ... CLP
Cell Loss Priority [*Computer science*] ... CLP
Cell Loss Ratio (VERA) ... CLR
Cell Management Language [*Software*] (BYTE) ... CML
Cell Matrix Adhesion Regulator [*Medicine*] (DMAA) ... CMAR
Cell Mediated Immunity (SAUS) ... CMI
Cell Meeting Our Morphologic Criteria (STED) ... CMOMC
Cell Membrane ... CM
Cell Memory (SAUS) ... CM
Cell Misinsertion Rate (VERA) ... CMR
Cell Missequenced Ratio (SAUS) ... CSR
Cell Multiplication Inhibition ... CMI
Cell Pack ... Clpk
Cell Pack [*Horticulture*] ... CP
Cell Processor System (MCD) ... CPS
Cell Rate Margin (SAUS) ... CRM
Cell Recovery System [*Medicine*] (MELL) ... CRS
Cell Relay Function (MLOA) ... CRF
Cell Relay Service (VERA) ... CRS
Cell Research Institute [*University of Texas at Austin*] [*Research center*] (RCD) ... CRI
Cell Scanning System [*Cytology*] (SAA) ... CELESCAN
Cell Separation [*Cytology*] ... Cel Sep
Cell Sequence (SAUS) ... CS
Cell Simulation [*Programming language*] [*1973*] (CSR) ... CELLSIM
Cell Site Controller (SAUS) ... CSC
Cell Space Simulation Language (SAUS) ... CESSL
Cell Station (SAUS) ... CS
Cell Store (SAUS) ... CS
Cell Surface Antigens [*Immunology*] ... CSA
Cell Surface Fibronectin [*Biochemistry*] ... CSFN
Cell Surface Protein [*Also known as LETS protein*] [*Cytochemistry*] ... CSP
Cell Surfacr (STED) ... Cs
Cell Switch Fabric (SAUS) ... CSF
Cell Switch Router (SAUS) ... CSR
Cell Terminal [*Computer science*] (VERA) ... CTERM
Cell Therapy [*Medicine*] (MELL) ... CT
Cell Tolerance Variation (VERA) ... CTV
Cell Transfer Delay (VERA) ... CTD
Cell Transmitter Stations [*Telecommunications*] (OTD) ... CTS
Cell Transport Integral Calculation (PDAA) ... CELTIC
Cell Volume [*Hematology*] ... CV
Cell Volume Profile [*Hematology*] ... CVP
Cell Wall ... CW
Cell Wall Constituent (OA) ... CWC
Cell Wall Defective [*Microbiology*] ... CWD
Cell Wall Material [*Biochemistry*] ... CWM
Cell Wall Skeleton [*Cytology*] ... CWS
Cell Wall-Deficient Bacterial Form [*Microbiology*] (MAE) ... CWDF
Cell Water Removal Mechanism ... CWRM
Cellar (SAUS) ... Cel
Cell-Associated Peplomer (DB) ... CAPP
Cellatron (SAUS) ... C
Cell-Based Architecture (AAEL) ... CBA
Cell-Based Array (AEBE) ... CBA
Cell-Cell Adhesion Molecules [*Genetics*] (DOG) ... CAMs
Cell-Cycle Box [*Genetics*] ... CCB
Cell-Cycle Box Factor [*Genetics*] ... CCBF
Cell-Cycle Element [*Cytology*] ... CCE
Cell-Directed Inhibitor [*Medicine*] (DMAA) ... CDI
Celle [*Germany*] [*ICAO location identifier*] (ICLI) ... EDCL
Celle/Arloh [*Germany*] [*ICAO location identifier*] (ICLI) ... EDVC
Cellegy Pharmaceutical [*NASDAQ symbol*] (TTSB) ... CLGY
Cellegy Pharmaceuticals [*Associated Press*] (SAG) ... Cellegy
Cellegy Pharmaceuticals [*Associated Press*] (SAG) ... CellegyPh
Cellegy Pharmaceuticals [*Associated Press*] (SAG) ... Cellgy
Cellegy Pharmaceuticals [*NASDAQ symbol*] (SAG) ... CLGY
Cellegy Pharmaceuticals Wrrt [*NASDAQ symbol*] (TTSB) ... CLGYW
Cellex Biosciences [*NASDAQ symbol*] (TTSB) ... CLXX
Cellex Biosciences, Inc. [*Associated Press*] (SAG) ... CellexB
Cellex Biosciences, Inc. [*Associated Press*] (SAG) ... Cellx
Cellex Biosciences, Inc. [*Associated Press*] (SAG) ... CllxBio
Cellex Biosciences, Inc. [*NASDAQ symbol*] (SAG) ... CLXX
Cellex Biosciences Wrrt 2000 [*NASDAQ symbol*] (TTSB) ... CLXXZ
Cell/Flare (SAUS) ... C/F
Cell-Free Elicitor Preparation [*Plant pathology*] ... CFEP
Cell-Growth Potentiating Factor (DB) ... CGPF
Cell-Junctional Molecule [*Embryology*] ... CJM
Cell-Loc, Inc. [*Alberta Stock Exchange*] ... CLQ
Cell-Mediated Cytolysis ... CMC
Cell-Mediated Cytotoxicity [*Medicine*] (MELL) ... CMC
Cell-Mediated Immune Response [*Immunology*] (AAMN) ... CMIR
Cell-Mediated Immune Response (SAUS) ... CMI Response
Cell [*or Cellular*]**-Mediated Immunity** [*Immunochemistry*] ... CMI
Cell-Mediated Lympholysis [*Immunology*] ... CML
Cell-Mediated Mutagenesis (DB) ... CMM
Cell-Mediated Toxicity [*Medicine*] (MELL) ... CMT
CellNet Data Systems, Inc. [*Associated Press*] (SAG) ... CellNet
CellNet Data Systems, Inc. [*NASDAQ symbol*] (SAG) ... CNDS
Cellobiohydrolase [*An enzyme*] ... CBH
Cellophane (VRA) ... celph
Cellophane (DGA) ... C/PHANE
Cellophane (AAG) ... K
CellPro, Inc. [*Associated Press*] (SAG) ... CellPro
CellPro, Inc. [*NASDAQ symbol*] (SPSG) ... CPRO
Cells in Frames [*Telecommunications*] (ACRL) ... CIF
Cells per Colony [*Microbiology*] ... CPC
Cellsite on Wheels (ADWA) ... COW
Cellstar Corp. [*Associated Press*] (SAG) ... Cellstar
Cellstar Corp. [*NASDAQ symbol*] (SAG) ... CLST
Cell-Substrate Attachment [*Immunology*] ... CSAT
Celltech Group ADS [*NYSE symbol*] (SG) ... CLL
Celltech Media, Inc. [*NASDAQ symbol*] (SAG) ... CTMI
Celltropin [*Biochemistry*] ... CTP
Cellular (SAUS) ... cel

Cellular (ADWA) ... cell
Cellular ... CELL
Cellular ... CELLUL
Cellular [*Freight*] ... CEUR
Cellular Absorbed Dose Spectrometer ... CADS
Cellular and Molecular Basis of Disease [*Program*] [*National Institutes of Health*] ... CMBD
Cellular and Molecular Biology ... CMB
Cellular and Molecular Life Sciences [*A publication*] [*Formerly Experientia*] ... CMLS
Cellular and Molecular Pharmacology (GNE) ... CMP
Cellular Anti-Fraud (CGWS) ... CAF
Cellular Array Processor [*Computer science*] (NITA) ... CAP
Cellular Automata (SAUS) ... CA
Cellular Automation [*Computer science*] (IAA) ... CA
Cellular Cellulose Acetate [*Organic chemistry*] ... CCA
Cellular Circuit-Switched Data (SAUS) ... CCSD
Cellular Commun Intl [*NASDAQ symbol*] (TTSB) ... CCIL
Cellular Commun P.R. [*NASDAQ symbol*] (TTSB) ... CCPR
Cellular Communications, Inc. [*Associated Press*] (SAG) ... CelCmA
Cellular Communications, Inc. [*NASDAQ symbol*] (NQ) ... COMM
Cellular Communications Industry Association [*Telecommunications*] (EA) ... CCIA
Cellular Communications International, Inc. [*NASDAQ symbol*] (SAG) ... CCIL
Cellular Communications International, Inc. [*Associated Press*] (SAG) ... Cell Intl
Cellular Communications Puerto Rico [*NASDAQ symbol*] (SAG) ... CCPR
Cellular Communications Puerto Rico [*Associated Press*] (SAG) ... CelCmPR
Cellular Concrete Association (EA) ... CCA
Cellular Data Link Control [*Communications protocol*] ... CDLC
Cellular Digital Packet Data [*Computer science*] (PCM) ... CDPD
Cellular Digital Packet Data (SAUS) ... CPDP
Cellular Directions, Inc. [*Telecommunications service*] (TSSD) ... CDI
Cellular Double Bottom (SAUS) ... CDB
Cellular Envelope [*Embryology*] ... CE
Cellular Expansion Factor (SAUS) ... CEF
Cellular General Purpose Computer ... CGPC
Cellular Geographic Serving Area [*Telecommunications*] ... CGSA
Cellular Immunity (DB) ... CI
Cellular Immunity Deficiency Syndrome [*Medicine*] ... CIDS
Cellular, Inc. [*Telecommunications service*] (TSSD) ... CI
Cellular Intercarrier Billing Exchange Record ... CIBER
Cellular Intercarrier Billing Exchange Roamer Record [*A publication*] (TSSD) ... CIBER
Cellular Logic (SAUS) ... CL
Cellular Logic Computer (SAUS) ... CLC
Cellular Logic Image Processor [*Telecommunications*] (TEL) ... CLIP
Cellular Logic Operation [*Telecommunications*] (IAA) ... CLO
Cellular Logic-array Image Processing (or Processor) (SAUS) ... CLIP
Cellular Logic-In Memory [*Telecommunications*] (IAA) ... CLIM
Cellular Management System [*Stratus Computer, Inc.*] ... CMS
Cellular Message Information Block ... CMIB
Cellular Mobile Carrier ... CMC
Cellular Mobile Radio Service (SAUS) ... CMRS
Cellular Mobile Telephone ... CMT
Cellular Mobile Telephone Service ... CMTS
Cellular Natural Killing (PDAA) ... CNK
Cellular Neoprene Rubber ... CNR
Cellular Non-Linear Network ... CNN
Cellular Phone Company (SAUO) ... CPC
Cellular Provider (CGWS) ... CP
Cellular Provider Equipment (CGWS) ... CPE
Cellular Radio ... CR
Cellular Radio Communications Association [*Later, CCIA*] (EA) ... CRCA
Cellular Radio Ltd. [*British*] (NITA) ... CRL
Cellular Radio Switching Office [*Telecommunications*] ... CRSO
Cellular Remote Access Bulletin Board [*Cellular Communications Industry Association*] [*Information service or system*] (IID) ... CRABB
cellular Retinoic Acid Binding Protein (SAUS) ... cRABP
Cellular Retinoic Acid-Binding Protein [*Biochemistry*] ... CRABP
Cellular Retinol-Binding Protein [*Biochemistry*] ... CRBP
Cellular Sales & Marketing [*Creative Communications*] [*Information service or system*] (IID) ... CS & M
Cellular Size Volume ... CSV
Cellular Slime Mold [*Biology*] ... CSM
Cellular Subscriber Station (CGWS) ... CSS
Cellular Surface Area [*Cytology*] ... CSA
Cellular Technical Services [*Associated Press*] (SAG) ... CellrTch
Cellular Technical Services [*NASDAQ symbol*] (SAG) ... CTSC
Cellular Technical Svcs [*NASDAQ symbol*] (TTSB) ... CTSC
Cellular Telecommunications Industry Association (IGQR) ... CTI
Cellular Telecommunications Industry Association (EA) ... CTIA
Cellular Telephone (SAUS) ... Cellphone
Cellular Telephone Industry Association ... CTIA
Cellular Telephone Service (HGAA) ... CTS
Cellular Telephone-2nd Generation (CGWS) ... CT2
Cellular Therapy [*Medicine*] ... CT
Cellular Vehicle (WDAA) ... CV
Cellular Ventures, Inc. [*Atlanta, GA*] [*Telecommunications*] (TSSD) ... CV
Cellular-Automata Machine [*Computer science*] (BARN) ... CAM
CellularCommunications'A' [*NASDAQ symbol*] (TTSB) ... COMMA
CellularVision USA [*NASDAQ symbol*] (TTSB) ... CVUS
CellularVision USA, Inc. [*Associated Press*] (SAG) ... CellVisin
CellularVision USA, Inc. [*NASDAQ symbol*] (SAG) ... CVUS
Cellules Combattantes Communistes [*Communist Combatant Cells*] [*Belgium*] ... CCC
Cellules Communistes Combattantes [*Terrorist organization*] [*Belgium*] (EY) ... CCC
Cellulitic Phlegmasia [*Medicine*] (MELL) ... CP
Celluloid (ADWA) ... cel
Celluloid ... CEL
Celluloid [*Dentistry*] (DAVI) ... Cell
Cellulolytic Enzyme Biodegradability [*Biochemistry*] ... CEB
Cellulose [*Botany*] ... CEL
Cellulose (SAUS) ... Cel
Cellulose Acetate [*Organic chemistry; plastics*] ... CA
Cellulose Acetate Butyrate [*Organic chemistry*] ... CAB
Cellulose Acetate Diethylaminoacetate (OA) ... CADA
Cellulose Acetate Electrophoresis [*Organic chemistry*] (MAE) ... CAE
Cellulose Acetate Membrane (SAUS) ... CAM
Cellulose Acetate Methacrylate ... CAM
Cellulose Acetate Nitrate (EDCT) ... CAN
Cellulose Acetate Phthalate [*Organic chemistry*] (MAE) ... CAP
Cellulose Acetate Propionate [*Organic chemistry*] ... CAP
Cellulose Acetobutyrate (SAUS) ... CAB
Cellulose Carboxymethyl Cellulose (SAUS) ... CM
Cellulose Celcarbon-Equivalent-liquid (SAUS) ... CEL
Cellulose Ester [*Organic chemistry*] ... CE
Cellulose Industry Standards Enforcement Program (EA) ... CISEP
Cellulose Insulation Manufacturers Association (NTPA) ... CIMA
Cellulose Insulation Manufacturers Association of Canada (AC) ... CIMAC
Cellulose Ion Exchanger (SAUS) ... CIE
Cellulose Manufacturers Association (EA) ... CMA
Cellulose Nitrate (SAUS) ... Cel Nitr
Cellulose Nitrate (PDAA) ... CLN
Cellulose Nitrate [*Organic chemistry*] ... CN
Cellulose Nitrate with Hydrophobic Edge [*Membrane filtration*] ... CN(h)
Cellulose Paper ... CP
Cellulose Polyethylene [*Organic chemistry*] ... CPE
Cellulose Propionate (EDCT) ... CP
Cellulose Propionate Plastic [*Organic chemistry*] ... CP
Cellulose Research Institute [*Syracuse University*] ... CRI
Cellulose Sheet (SAUS) ... Cel Sheet
Cellulose Sodium Phosphate [*Organic chemistry*] ... CSP
Cellulose Sponge Institute [*Defunct*] (EA) ... CSI
Cellulose Synthase Activator [*Biochemistry*] ... CSA
Cellulose Triacetate [*Organic chemistry*] ... CTA
Cellulose Trinitrate [*Organic chemistry*] ... CTN
Cellulose-Binding Domain [*Genetics*] ... CBD
Celmar Servicios Aereos SA de CV [*Mexico*] [*ICAO designator*] (FAAC) ... CER
Celotex (VRA) ... celtx
Celotex Corporation (SAUO) ... CLO
Celox Laboratories [*NASDAQ symbol*] (TTSB) ... CELX
Celox Laboratories, Inc. [*Associated Press*] (SAG) ... CeloxLab
Celox Laboratories, Inc. [*NASDAQ symbol*] (SAG) ... CELX
Celo-Zongo [*Zaire*] [*ICAO location identifier*] (ICLI) ... FZAD
Cel-Sci Corp. [*NASDAQ symbol*] (NQ) ... CELI
Cel-Sci Corp. [*Associated Press*] (SAG) ... CelSc
Cel-Sci Corp. [*Associated Press*] (SAG) ... CelSci
Cel-Sci Corp. Wrrt [*NASDAQ symbol*] (TTSB) ... CELIW
Celsea Industries, Inc. (SAUO) ... CHD
Celsion Corp. [*AMEX symbol*] ... CLN
Celsius [*Centigrade*] [*Temperature scale*] ... C
Celsius [*Centigrade*] [*Temperature scale*] ... CEL
Celsius (ROG) ... CELS
Celsius Heat Unit (ADA) ... CHU
Celsius Temperature [*Symbol*] [*IUPAC*] ... t
Celsus, De Medicina [*First century AD*] [*Classical studies*] (OCD) ... Celsus Med
Celtic (ROG) ... C
Celtic ... CEL
Celtic ... CELT
Celtic (SAUS) ... Celt
Celtic Club Melbourne [*Australia*] ... CCM
Celtic Group [*MARC language code*] [*Library of Congress*] [*Obsolete*] (LCCP) ... cel
Celtic Inernational Ltd. [*British*] [*ICAO designator*] (FAAC) ... CIC
Celtic Investment [*NASDAQ symbol*] (TTSB) ... CELT
Celtic Investment, Inc. [*NASDAQ symbol*] (SAG) ... CELT
Celtic Investment, Inc. [*Associated Press*] (SAG) ... CelticInv
Celtic League [*Peel, Isle of Man, England*] (EAIO) ... CL
Celtic League, American Branch (EA) ... CLAB
Celtic Resources Ltd. [*Vancouver Stock Exchange symbol*] ... CLI
Celtium (SAUS) ... Ct
Celtrix Pharmaceuticals [*Associated Press*] (SAG) ... Celtrx
Celtrix Pharmaceuticals [*NASDAQ symbol*] (SAG) ... CTRX
CEM Corp. [*Associated Press*] (SAG) ... CEM
CEM Corp. [*NASDAQ symbol*] (NQ) ... CEMX
Cembalo [*Cymbals*] [*Music*] (ROG) ... CEMB
Cembratriene-diol [*Organic chemistry*] ... CBT
Cement (VRA) ... cem
Cement (KSC) ... CEM
Cement (SAUS) ... Cem
Cement ... CEMT
Cement [*Classified advertising*] (ADA) ... CMT
Cement (SAUS) ... Ct
Cement Admixtures Association (EAIO) ... CAA
Cement Aggregate Mixture (OA) ... CAM
Cement and Concrete Association [*British*] [*Research center*] (IRUK) ... C & CA
Cement and Concrete Association [*British*] [*Research center*] ... CCA
Cement and Concrete Reference Laboratory (SAUO) ... CCRL
Cement Association of Japan (SAUO) ... CAJ

Cement Base [Technical drawings] .... CB
Cement Block [Construction] (GEOI) .... CB
Cement Block construction (SAUS) .... CB
Cement Bond Log (SAUS) .... CBL
Cement Brick (SAUS) .... C BR
Cement Conduit [Telecommunications] (TEL) .... CEM
Cement Employers Association (EA) .... CEA
Cement Finish (DAC) .... Cem Fin
Cement Floor [Technical drawings] (DAC) .... Cem Fl
Cement Floor (SAUS) .... CEMFL
Cement Floor [Technical drawings] .... CF
Cement Gland [Embryology] .... CG
Cement Kiln Dust (EEVL) .... CKD
Cement Kiln Recycling Coalition (EEVL) .... CKRC
Cement, Lime, Gypsum, and Allied Workers Division (EA) .... CLGAWD
Cement Lime Mortar (SAUS) .... CLM
Cement Manufacturers' Association (CARB) .... CMA
Cement Modified Soil (SAUS) .... CMS
Cement Mortar [Technical drawings] (DAC) .... Cem Mort
Cement Mortar (SAUS) .... CM
Cement or Concrete [Freight] .... CMT CONC
Cement Paint (SAUS) .... CEMP
Cement Plaster (SAUS) .... CEMPLAS
Cement Plaster [Technical drawings] (DAC) .... Cem Plas
Cement Plaster (AAG) .... CPL
Cement Render .... CR
Cement Riverine Assault Boat [Navy] (MCD) .... CRAB
Cement Slurry (SAUS) .... CS
Cement Squeeze Simulator [For testing well drilling material] .... CSS
Cement Statistical and Technical Association (SAUO) .... CEMBUREAU
Cement Tile [Classified advertising] (ADA) .... CT
Cement Water Ratio (IAA) .... CW
Cement-Asbestos Board (DAC) .... CAB
Cement-Asbestos Board (DAC) .... Cem Ab
Cementation-in-Pulp (SAUS) .... CIP
Cement-Coated Heavy Epoxy .... CCHEP
Cement-Coated Single Epoxy .... CCSEP
Cement-Coated Triple Epoxy .... CCTEP
Cemented (SAUS) .... CMTD
Cemented Carbide Producers Association (EA) .... CCPA
Cemented Only [Of envelopes] .... CO
Cement-Enamel Junction [Dentistry] .... CEJ
Cementex [Research code symbol] .... N
Cementitious Barrier Coat [Anticorrosive coating] .... CBC
Cementitious Packaged Products Association (SAUO) .... CPPA
Cement-Modified Soil (PDAA) .... CMS
Cement-Plaster Ceiling [Technical drawings] .... CPC
Cement-Sand-Molasses (PDAA) .... CSM
Cement-Treated Aggregate (SAUS) .... CTA
Cement-Treated Base .... CTB
Cemetery (SAUS) .... Cem
Cemetery (GEOI) .... Cem
Cemetery (AABC) .... CEM
Cemetery (GEAB) .... cem
Cemetery (VRA) .... cemet
Cemetery (ROG) .... CEMET
Cemetery (ABBR) .... CMTRY
Cemetery .... CNTRY
Cemetery & Crematorium Association of British Columbia (AC) .... CCABC
Cemetery Consumer Service Council (EA) .... CCSC
Cemetery Net (CCCA) .... CN
Cemetery Supply Association [Later, ICSA] (EA) .... CSA
Cemetries Association (SAUO) .... CA
CEMR [Canada Energy Mines and Resources] Headquarters Library [UTLAS symbol] .... EME
CEN Tripartite Committee (SAUO) .... CENTRI
CEN-Certification Committee (SAUS) CCC
Cenco, Inc. (SAUO) .... CNC
Cendant Corp. [NYSE symbol] [Formerly, CUC International] (SG) .... CD
Ceneast Airlines Ltd. [Kenya] [ICAO designator] (FAAC) .... CEL
CENELEC Certification Agreement (SAUS) .... CCA
CENELEC [Comite Europeen de Normalisation Electrotechnique] Electronic Components Committee (DS) .... CECC
Cener Diode (SAUS) .... ZD
CENFED Financial [NASDAQ symbol] (TTSB) .... CENF
Cenfed Financial Corp. [NASDAQ symbol] (SAG) .... CENF
Cenfed Financial Corp. [Associated Press] (SAG) .... Cenfed
Cenior Services Ltd., Calgary, AB, Canada [Library symbol] [Library of Congress] (LCLS) .... CaACCES
Cenit Bancorp [Associated Press] (SAG) .... CenitBcp
Cenit Bancorp [NASDAQ symbol] (SAG) .... CNIT
Cenlor Services Ltd., Calgary, Alberta [Library symbol] [National Library of Canada] (NLC) .... ACCES
Cenomanian [Paleontology] C
Cenomanian (SAUS) .... Cenom
Cenomanian Turonian Black Shale Horizon [Nuclear energy] (NUCP) .... CTBSH
Cenomanian/Turonian [Geological boundary zone] .... C/T
Cenozoic (NTIO) .... Cen
Cenozoic [Period, era, or system] [Geology] .... CEN
Cenozoic Investigations of the Western Ross Sea (SAUO) .... CIROS
Cenozoic Reef Evolution in Space and Time (SAUS) .... CREST
Central Alberta AIDS Network Society (AC) .... CAANS
Central Nova Tourist Association (AC) .... CNTA
Censo de Archivos [Database] [Ministerio de Cultura] [Spanish] [Information service or system] (CRD) .... CARC

Censo de Bibliotecas [Database] [Ministerio de Cultura] [Spanish] [Information service or system] (CRD) .... CBIB
Censo de Museos de Espana [Database] [Ministerio de Cultura] [Spanish] [Information service or system] (CRD) .... CMUS
Censor (ROG) C
Censor [or Censorship] (AFM) .... CENS
Censor (SAUS) .... Cens
Censor [MARC relator code] [Library of Congress] (LCCP) .... cns
Censorship of Publications Board [Ireland] .... CPB
Censorship Policy Board [World War II] .... CPB
Censorship Records and Information Middle East [Military] .... CRIME
Censorship Subcommittee (SAUO) .... CSC
Census (GEAB) .... cen
Census .... CS
Census 2000 Publicity Office (SAUS) C2PO
Census Access System [Urban Decision Systems, Inc.] [Information service or system] [Defunct] (CRD) .... CENSAC
Census Administrative Manual (SAUS) .... CAM
Census Advisory Committee (SAUS) .... CAC
Census Agglomeration [Canada] .... CA
Census and Data Users Services [Illinois State University] [Information service or system] (IID) .... CADUS
Census and Economic Information Center [Montana State Department of Commerce] [Helena] [Information service or system] (IID) .... CEIC
Census Awareness and Products Program [Bureau of the Census] (GFGA) .... CAPP
Census Awareness and Products Staff [Bureau of the Census] (GFGA) .... CAPS
Census Bureau [Department of Commerce] .... CB
Census Bureau (SAUS) .... CEN
Census Bureau Software Package (GFGA) .... CENSPAC
Census Bureau Welfare and Recreation Association (SAUO) .... CBWRA
Census Collection District (SAUS) .... CCD
Census Community Awareness Program [Bureau of the Census] (GFGA) .... CCAP
Census Community Communications Council [US Census Bureau] C4
Census Control System [Bureau of the Census] (GFGA) .... CCS
Census County Division [Bureau of Census] .... CCD
Census Data [Database] .... CDATA
Census Data System (SAUS) .... CDS
Census Designated Place [Bureau of the Census] (GFGA) .... CDP
Census Electronic Data Dissemination (SAUS) .... CENDATA
Census Electronic Publication System (SAUS) .... CEPS
Census Entry (SAUS) .... CENTRY
Census Feature Class Code (GEOI) .... CFCC
Census Federal Credit Union (SAUO) .... CFCU
Census File Number (SAUS) .... CFN
Census Grievance Committee [Vietnam] .... CGC
Census Information Retrieval and Analysis System (SAUS) .... CIRAS
Census Legislative Information System (SAUS) .... CLIS
Census Library, Statistics Canada [Bibliotheque du Recensement, Statistique Canada] Ottawa, Ontario [Library symbol] [National Library of Canada] (NLC) .... OOSCL
Census Map Library, Statistics Canada [Cartotheque du Recensement, Statistique Canada] Ottawa, Ontario [Library symbol] [National Library of Canada] (NLC) .... OOSCM
Census Method X (SAUS) .... CMX
Census Metropolitan Area [Canada] .... CMA
Census of Australian Plants (SAUO) .... CAP
Census of Australian Vascular Plants .... CAVP
Census of Construction Industries (SAUS) CCI
Census of Graduate Medical Trainees .... CGMT
Census of Housing (SAUS) .... CH
Census of Manufactures and Mineral Industries (SAUS) .... CMMI
Census of Population (SAUS) .... CP
Census of Population and Housing (SAUS) .... CPH
Census Projections [Database] (IT) .... CENPRO
Census Promotion Office [Bureau of the Census] (GFGA) .... CPO
Census Quality Management (SAUS) .... CQM
Census Registration Working Party [US Military Government, Germany] .... CRWP
Census Servomechanism and Tape Handler .... CENSER
Census Statistical Area Committee (GEOI) .... CSAC
Census Statistical Areas Key Person (SAUS) .... CSAKP
Census Tabulation System (SAUS) .... CENTS
Census Tracking (SAUS) .... CENTRACK
Census Tract (GEOI) .... CT
Census Tract Street Index (SAUS) .... CTSI
Census Transportation Planning Package [BTS] (TAG) .... CTPP
Census User Guide .... CUG
Cent [Monetary unit] C
Cent [Monetary unit] .... CT
Cent Call Seconds [Telecommunications] .... CCS
Centacare Australia (SAUO) .... CA
CENTAG Element (SAUO) .... CENEL
CENTAG Engineer Training Exercise (SAUO) .... CETEX
CENTAG Medical Working Party (SAUO) .... CMWP
CENTAG Movement Coordination Center (SAUO) .... CMCC
CENTAG Signal Support Group (SAUO) .... CSSG
Cental [Short hundredweight] [British] (WGA) C
Cental [Short hundredweight] [British] (ROG) .... CENT
Cental [Short hundredweight] [British] (ROG) .... CT
Cental [Short hundredweight] [British] (ROG) .... CTL
Centare [Unit of area in metric system] .... CA
Centaur [Rocket] [NASA] (KSC) .... CEN
Centaur [Rocket] [NASA] (KSC) .... CENT
Centaur (SAUS) .... CNTR
Centaur Integrated Support Structure (MCD) .... CISS

Centaur Operations at the Space Station (SAUS) .... COSS
Centaur Reliability Control Engineering (SAUS) .... CRCE
Centaur Resources Ltd. (SAUO) .... KNI
Centaur Resources Ltd. [Vancouver Stock Exchange symbol] .... KNL
Centaur Standard Shroud [NASA] .... CSS
Centaurus [Constellation] .... Cen
Centaurus [Constellation] .... Cent
Centaurus Distant Supercluster [Astronomy] .... CDS
Centavo [Monetary unit in many Spanish-American countries] C
Centavo (ADWA) .... ctvo
Centavo [Cent] [Monetary unit in many Spanish-American countries] .... CTVO
Cente de Prevention du Suicide (AC) .... CPS
Cente d'Information et de Recherche en Consommation de Charlevoix-Ouest (AC) .... CIRCCO
Cente d'Inspection et de Prevention Automobile de l'Estrie (AC) .... CIPAE
Cente for Research-Action on Race Relations (AC) .... CRARR
Cente Francophone ASSITEJ Canada (AC) .... ASSITEJ Canada
Cente International de Documentation et d'Echanges de la Francophonie (AC) .... CIDES
Cente Patronal de l'Environnement du Quebec (AC) .... CPEQ
CENTECH Corp. (SAUO) .... CENTECH
Centenary [or Centennial] .... Cent
Centenary College for Women, Hackettstown, NJ [Library symbol] [Library of Congress] (LCLS) .... NjHaC
Centenary College of Louisiana [Shreveport] CCL
Centenary College of Louisiana, Magale Library, Shreveport, LA [OCLC symbol] (OCLC) .... CEN
Centenary College of Louisiana, Shreveport, LA [Library symbol] [Library of Congress] (LCLS) .... LShC
Centenary Junior College (SAUO) .... CJC
Centennial (ROG) .... CEN
Centennial .... CENT
Centennial (SAUS) .... centen
Centennial [Spain] [ICAO designator] (FAAC) .... CNA
Centennial Airlines, Inc. [ICAO designator] (FAAC) .... CNL
Centennial Bancorp [NASDAQ symbol] (SAG) .... CEBC
Centennial Bancorp [Associated Press] (SAG) .... CentlBc
Centennial Branch, Nepean Public Library, Ontario [Library symbol] [National Library of Canada] (NLC) .... ONCB
Centennial Cellular 'A' [NASDAQ symbol] (TTSB) .... CYCL
Centennial Cellular Corp. [Associated Press] (SAG) .... CentCel
Centennial Cellular Corp. [NASDAQ symbol] (SAG) .... CYCL
Centennial Centre of Science and Technology .... CCST
Centennial College of Applied Arts and Technology, Scarborough, ON, Canada [Library symbol] [Library of Congress] (LCLS) .... CaOTARC
Centennial College of Applied Arts and Technology, Scarborough, Ontario [Library symbol] [National Library of Canada] (NLC) .... OTARC
Centennial Collegiate Vocational Institute, Guelph, ON, Canada [Library symbol] [Library of Congress] (LCLS) .... CaOGC
Centennial Collegiate Vocational Institute, Guelph, Ontario [Library symbol] [National Library of Canada] (NLC) .... OGC
Centennial Conference (PSS) CC
Centennial Elementary School, Roosevelt, NY [Library symbol] [Library of Congress] (LCLS) .... NRoosCE
Centennial Flight Centre [Canada] [ICAO designator] (FAAC) .... CNS
Centennial Leasing Corp. (EFIS) CLC
Centennial Legion of Historic Military Commands (EA) .... CLHMC
Centennial Minerals [Toronto Stock Exchange symbol] [Vancouver Stock Exchange symbol] .... CTN
Centennial Museum, Vancouver, BC, Canada [Library symbol] [Library of Congress] (LCLS) .... CaBVaCM
Centennial Museum, Vancouver, British Columbia [Library symbol] [National Library of Canada] (NLC) .... BVACM
Centennial Park Trust [Australia] .... CPT
Centennial Secondary School, Welland, ON, Canada [Library symbol] [Library of Congress] (LCLS) .... CaOWeC
Centennial Secondary School, Welland, Ontario [Library symbol] [National Library of Canada] (NLC) .... OWEC
Centennial Secondary School, Windsor, ON, Canada [Library symbol] [Library of Congress] (LCLS) .... CaOWC
Centennial Secondary School, Windsor, Ontario [Library symbol] [National Library of Canada] (NLC) .... OWC
Centennial Technologies [AMEX symbol] (TTSB) .... CTN
Centennial Technologies, Inc. [Associated Press] (SAG) .... CentenT
Centennial Technologies, Inc. [Associated Press] (SAG) .... CentTc
Centennial Technologies, Inc. [AMEX symbol] (SAG) .... CTN
Center [A position in football, lacrosse, basketball] C
Center [or Central] (AFM) .... CEN
Center (SAUS) .... Cen
Center [Commonly used] (OPSA) .... CENT
Center [Commonly used] (OPSA) .... CENTER
Center [Commonly used] (OPSA) .... CENTR
Center [Commonly used] (OPSA) .... CENTRE
Center [Commonly used] (OPSA) .... CNTER
Center (BEE) .... cntr
Center .... CNTR
Center (DS) .... CR
Center (TBD) .... Ctr
Center (WDMC) .... ctr
Center .... CTR
Center Accessory Compartment (MCD) .... CAC
Center Ad Hoc Data Review Team [NASA] (KSC) .... CAHDRT
Center Aiming Disc (NATG) .... CAD
Center Airman Record File [Air Force] .... CARF
Center Aisle Connector Bracket (MCD) .... CACB

Center Apollo Data Manager [NASA] (KSC) .... CADM
Center Apollo Document Description Standards [NASA] (KSC) .... CADDS
Center Apollo Documentation Administration Instructions [NASA] (KSC) .... CADAI
Center Apollo Program Offices [NASA] (KSC) .... CAPO
Center Area Discrete (SAUS) .... CAD
Center Automated Manpower and Project Update System (SAUO) .... CAMPUS
Center Back [Soccer] .... CB
Center Back Stage [A stage direction] .... CBS
Center Bancorp, Inc. [NASDAQ symbol] (SAG) .... CNBC
Center Bancorp, Inc. [Associated Press] (SAG) .... CntBncp
Center Banks [NASDAQ symbol] (SAG) .... CTBK
Center Banks [Associated Press] (SAG) .... CtrBnk
Center Beam One Side [Lumber] (DAC) CB1S
Center Beam Two Sides [Lumber] (DAC) CB2S
Center Bit (SAUS) .... CB
Center Board (SAUS) .... CB
Center City Commuter Connections (SAUO) CCCC
Center City Report [A publication] (EAAP) .... CCR
Center City Transportation Program .... CCTP
Center Conductor (SAUS) CC
Center Console Panel (MCD) .... CCP
Center Council Meeting (SAUO) .... CCM
Center Current Range Element (SAUS) .... CCRE
Center Data Descriptions Catalog (KSC) .... CDDC
Center Director [John F. Kennedy Space Center Directorate] [NASA] (NASA) .... CD
Center Distance (MSA) .... CD
Center Distance (SAUS) .... cd
Center Door (SAUS) .... CD
Center Engine Cutoff [NASA] (KSC) .... CECO
Center Entrance (SAUS) .... CE
Center Exploration Program Scientist [NASA] (ACAE) .... CEPS
Center Field [Baseball term] (NDBD) .... cf
Center Field [or Fielder] [Baseball] .... CF
Center Financial [NASDAQ symbol] (TTSB) .... CFCX
Center Financial Corp. (Connecticut) [Associated Press] (SAG) .... CenterFn
Center Financial Corp. (Connecticut) [NASDAQ symbol] (SAG) .... CFCX
Center Fire .... CF
Center Focus [Binoculars] .... CF
Center for a New Democracy (EA) .... CND
Center for a Voluntary Society [Defunct] (EA) .... CVS
Center for a Woman's Own Name [An association] [Defunct] (EA) .... CWON
Center for Academic & Administrative Computing [George Washington University] [Research center] (RCD) .... CAAC
Center for Academic Ethics (EA) .... CAE
Center for Academic Precocity [Arizona State University] [Research center] (RCD) .... CAP
Center for Accelerator Mass Spectrometry (SAUO) .... CAMS
Center for Accelerator Technology and Applied Sciences [University of Texas at Arlington] [Research center] (RCD) .... CATAS
Center for Accountability to the Public (EA) .... CAP
Center for Acoustic Studies (SAUS) .... CAS
Center for Acoustical Studies (SAUO) .... CAS
Center for Acquisition Education, Training, and Research [Military] (RDA) .... CAETR
Center for Acquisition Management Policy [DSMC] (AAGC) .... CAMP
Center for Action on Endangered Species (EA) .... CAES
Center for Adhesives, Sealants, and Coatings [Case Western Reserve University] [Research center] (RCD) .... CASC
Center for Administrative Justice [Later, NCAJ] (EA) .... CAJ
Center for Advance Engineering Study (SAUO) .... CAES
Center for Advanced Aviation System Development (CTAS) .... CAASD
Center for Advanced Biotechnology and Medicine [Rutgers University] [Research center] (RCD) .... CABM
Center for Advanced Computation [University of Illinois] (GEOI) .... CAAD
Center for Advanced Computation (SAUO) .... CAC
Center for Advanced Decision Support for Water and Environmental Systems [University of Colorado at Boulder] [Research center] (RCD) .... CADSWES
Center for Advanced Digital Applications [New York University School of Continuing Education] .... CADA
Center for Advanced Feminist Studies [University of Minnesota] [Research center] (RCD) .... CAFS
Center for Advanced Food Technology [Rutgers University] .... CAFT
Center for Advanced Heart Research .... CAHR
Center for Advanced International Studies (SAUO) .... CAIS
Center for Advanced Land Management Information Technologies [University of Nebraska-Lincoln] (GEOI) .... CALMIT
Center for Advanced Macrostructures and Devices [Louisiana State University] .... CAMD
Center for Advanced Management Programs [University of Houston at Clear Lake] [Research center] (RCD) .... CAMP
Center for Advanced Manufacturing and Production [Southern Illinois University at Edwardsville] [Research center] (RCD) .... CAMP
Center for Advanced Materials [Pennsylvania State University] [Research center] (RCD) .... CAM
Center for Advanced Materials [Lawrence Berkeley Laboratory] [Berkeley, CA] [Department of Energy] (GRD) .... CAM
Center for Advanced Materials Processing [Clarkson University] [Research center] (RCD) .... CAMP
Center for Advanced Medical Informatics at Stanford (SAUO) .... CAMIS
Center for Advanced Molecular Biology and Immunology (SAUS) .... CAMBI
Center for Advanced Photonic and Electronic Materials (SAUS) .... CAPEM
Center for Advanced Professional Education [Canada] .... CAPE

Center for Advanced Purchasing Studies [*Arizona State University*] [*Research center*] (RCD) .... CAPS
Center for Advanced Rehabilitation Engineering [*University of Texas at Arlington*] [*Research center*] (RCD) .... CARE
Center for Advanced Research in Biotechnology [*Jointly sponsored by the US National Bureau of Standards and the University of Maryland*] .... CARB
Center for Advanced Research in Phenomenology [*Defunct*] (EA) .... CARP
Center for Advanced Research on Language Research .... CARLA
Center for Advanced Studies in International Business .... CASIB
Center for Advanced Studies in Telecommunications [*Ohio State University*] (TSSD) .... CAST
Center for Advanced Study in Education [*City University of New York*] [*Research center*] (RCD) .... CASE
Center for Advanced Study in Organization Science (SAUS) .... CASOS
Center for Advanced Study in the Behavioral Sciences (EA) .... CASBS
Center for Advanced Study in the Behavioral Sciences, Stanford, CA [*Library symbol*] [*Library of Congress*] (LCLS) .... CStC
Center for Advanced Study in Theatre Arts [*City University of New York*] [*Research center*] (RCD) .... CASTA
Center for Advanced Study of International Development [*Michigan State University*] [*Research center*] (RCD) .... CASID
Center for Advanced Technologies [*Focus: HOPE*] .... CAT
Center for Advanced Technology for Large Structural Systems [*Lehigh University*] [*Research center*] (RCD) .... ATLSS
Center for Advanced Technology in Telecommunications [*Polytechnic Institute of New York*] [*Brooklyn*] [*Telecommunications service*] (TSSD) .... CATT
Center for Advanced Telecommunications Systems and Services .... CATTS
Center for Advanced Television Studies [*British*] (NTCM) .... CATS
Center for Advanced Training in Cell and Molecular Biology (HGEN) .... CATCMB
Center for Advanced Training in Cell and Molecular Biology/ Catholic University of America (SAUO) .... CATCMB/CUA
Center for Advanced Training in Cell and Molecular Biology/Catholic University of America (HGEN) .... CATCMB/CUA
Center for Advanced Visual Studies [*Massachusetts Institute of Technology*] [*Research center*] (RCD) .... CAVS
Center for Aerospace Doctrine, Research, and Education [*Air University*] [*Research center*] (RCD) .... CADRE
Center for Aerospace Information (AAGC) .... CASI
Center for Aerospace Technology [*Weber State College*] [*Research center*] (RCD) .... CAST
Center for Affective Disorders [*University of Wisconsin, Madison*] [*Research center*] (RCD) .... CAD
Center for Afro-American and African Studies [*University of Michigan*] [*Research center*] (RCD) .... CAAS
Center for Afro-American Studies [*University of California, Los Angeles*] [*Research center*] (RCD) .... CAAS
Center for Aging Research .... CAR
Center for Agricultural and Rural Development [*Iowa State University*] [*Research center*] (RCD) .... CARD
Center for Agricultural Meteorology and Climatology [*University of Nebraska - Lincoln*] [*Research center*] (RCD) .... CAMAC
Center for Agricultural Molecular Biology [*Rutgers University*] [*Research center*] (RCD) .... AgBioTech
Center for Agricultural Research and Development (SAUO) .... CARD
Center for Agricultural, Resource, and Environmental Systems [*University of Missouri*] (GEOI) .... CARES
Center for AIDS Prevention Studies [*University of California, San Francisco*] [*Research center*] (RCD) .... CAPS
Center for AIDS Research [*National Institutes of Health*] .... CFAR
Center for Air Environment Studies [*Pennsylvania State University*] [*Research center*] (RCD) .... CAES
Center for Air Pollution Impact and Trend Analysis [*Washington University*] [*Research center*] (RCD) .... CAPITA
Center for Alcohol Research [*University of Florida*] [*Research center*] (RCD) .... CAR
Center for Alcohol Studies (EA) .... CAS
Center for Alternative Living Medicine .... CALM
Center for Alternative Mining Development Policy (EA) .... CAMDP
Center for Alternative Sentencing and Employment Services [*Research center*] (RCD) .... CASES
Center for Alternatives to Animal Testing [*At Johns Hopkins*] .... CAAT
Center for American Archeology (EA) .... CAA
Center for American History [*University of Texas, Austin*] [*Research center*] (RCD) .... CAH
Center for Analysis and Prediction of Storms [*University of Oklahoma*] [*Research center*] (RCD) .... CAPS
Center for Analysis of Developing Economies [*University of Pennsylvania*] [*Research center*] (RCD) .... CADE
Center for Analysis of Dynamics of Atmospheric Regions (SAUS) .... CADRE
Center for Analysis of Environmental Change [*Oregon State University*] [*Research center*] (RCD) .... CAEC
Center for Analysis of the Dynamics of Regional Ecosystems (SAUS) .... CADRE
Center for Analytic Research in Economics and the Social Sciences [*University of Pennsylvania*] [*Research center*] (RCD) .... CARESS
Center for Animal Health Monitoring (SAUO) .... CAHM
Center for Animals and Public Policy (GNE) .... CAPP
Center for Anthropology and Science Communications (SAUS) .... CASC
Center for Anthropometric Research Data (IID) .... CARD
Center for Anti-Fratricide Technology [*Army*] (DOMA) .... CAFT
Center for Application of Sciences and Technology .... CAST
Center for Applications of Psychological Type (EA) .... CAPT
Center for Applications of Remote Sensing [*Oklahoma State University*] [*Research center*] (RCD) .... CARS
Center for Applied Isotope Studies [*University of Georgia*] [*Research center*] (RCD) .... CAIS

Center for Applied Linguistics (EA) .... CAL
Center for Applied Linguistics (SAUS) .... Ctr Appl Ling
Center for Applied Linguistics, Arlington (SAUS) .... ViArAL
Center for Applied Linguistics, Arlington, VA [*Library symbol*] [*Library of Congress*] (LCLS) .... ViArAL
Center for Applied Linguistics, Washington, DC [*Library symbol*] [*Library of Congress*] (LCLS) .... DCAL
Center for Applied Mathematics [*University of Georgia*] [*Research center*] (RCD) .... CAM
Center for Applied Microbiology [*University of Texas at Austin*] [*Research center*] (RCD) .... CAM
Center for Applied Parallel Processing [*University of Colorado, Boulder*] [*Research center*] (RCD) .... CAPP
Center for Applied Polymer Research [*Case Western Reserve University*] [*Research center*] (RCD) .... CAPRI
Center for Applied Research in the Apostolate (EA) .... CARA
Center for Applied Research in the Apostolate [*CARA*], African Research andInformation Center, Washington, DC [*Library symbol*] [*Library of Congress*] (LCLS) .... DARI
Center for Applied Research in the Language Arts [*Texas Tech University*] [*Research center*] (RCD) .... CARLA
Center for Applied Social Science [*Boston University*] [*Research center*] (RCD) .... CASS
Center for Applied Special Technology .... CAST
Center for Applied Studies in International Negotiations [*Switzerland*] (EAIO) .... CASIN
Center for Applied Thermodynamic Studies [*University of Idaho*] [*Research center*] (RCD) .... CATS
Center for Aquatic Plant Research and Technology [*Army*] .... CAPRT
Center for Arab-Islamic Studies (EA) .... CAIS
Center for Archaeological Investigations [*Southern Illinois University at Carbondale*] [*Research center*] (RCD) .... CAI
Center for Architectural Research [*Rensselaer Polytechnic Institute*] [*Research center*] (RCD) .... CAR
Center for Architecture (SAUO) .... CFA
Center for Architecture and Urban Planning Research [*University of Wisconsin - Milwaukee*] [*Research center*] (RCD) .... CAUPR
Center for Arms Control and International Security Studies (SAUO) .... CACISS
Center for Army Leadership [*Fort Leavenworth, KS*] (INF) .... CAL
Center for Army Lessons Learned (INF) .... CALL
Center for Arts Information [*Defunct*] (EA) .... CAI
Center for Aseptic Processing and Packaging Studies [*North Carolina State University*] [*Research center*] (RCD) .... CAPPS
Center for Asian and African Studies, Mexico (SAUO) .... CEAA
Center for Assessment and Demographic Studies [*Gallaudet College*] [*Research center*] (RCD) .... CADS
Center for Assessment and Training [*Peace Corps*] .... CAST
Center for Assistive Technology (SAUS) .... CAT
Center for Astrodynamics Research (SAUS) .... CCAR
Center for Astronomical Data [*Academy of Sciences of the USSR*] [*Information service or system*] (IID) .... CAD
Center for Astrophysical Research in Antarctica [*National Science Foundation*] .... CARA
Center for Astrophysics [*Harvard-Smithsonian*] .... CA
Center for Astrophysics .... CfA
Center for Astrophysics [*Harvard-Smithsonian*] .... CFA
Center for Astrophysics (SAUO) .... CFA
Center for Astrophysics and Space Sciences [*University of California, San Diego*] [*Research center*] (RCD) .... CASS
Center for Astrophysics and Space Scientists (SAUS) .... CASS
Center for Athletes' Rights and Education [*Defunct*] (EA) .... CARE
Center for Atmospheric and Remote Sounding Studies (SAUS) .... CARSS
Center for Atmospheric and Space Sciences [*Utah State University*] [*Research center*] (RCD) .... CASS
Center for Atmospheric Theory and Analysis [*Research center*] (RCD) .... CATA
Center for Atomic Radiation Studies (EA) .... CARS
Center for Attitudinal Healing (EA) .... CAH
Center for Audio Video Instruction via Satellite (ACAE) .... CAVISAT
Center for Auditory and Speech Sciences [*Gallaudet University*] [*Research center*] (RCD) .... CASS
Center for Austrian Studies (EA) .... CAS
Center for Auto Safety (EA) .... CAS
Center for Automation and Intelligent Systems Research [*Case Western Reserve University*] [*Research center*] (RCD) .... CAISR
Center for Automation Research [*University of Maryland*] [*Research center*] (RCD) .... CfAR
Center for Automotive Research [*Wayne State University*] [*Research center*] (RCD) .... CAR
Center for Automotive Safety (COE) .... CAS
Center for Autonomous and Man-Controlled Robotic and Sensing Systems [*Research center*] (RCD) .... CAMRSS
Center for Battlefield Technologies (SAUS) .... CBT
Center for Bibliographical Services [*Modern Language Association*] (BARN) .... CBS
Center for Bigfoot Studies [*An association*] (EA) .... CBS
Center for Bilingual Research and Second Language Education [*Later, CLEAR*] (GRD) .... CBSLE
Center for Bioanalytical Research [*University of Kansas*] .... CBAR
Center for Biochemical and Biophysical Studies [*Northern Illinois University*] [*Research center*] (RCD) .... CBBS
Center for Biochemical Engineering Research [*New Mexico State University*] [*Research center*] (RCD) .... CBER
Center for Bioethics (MELL) .... CFB
Center for Biofilm Engineering [*Montana State University*] .... CBE

Center for Biological Macromolecules [*State University of New York at Albany*] [*Research center*] (RCD) .... CBM
Center for Biologics Evaluation and Research [*FDA*] .... CBER
Center for Biomedical and Toxicological Research [*Florida State University*] [*Research center*] (RCD) .... CBTR
Center for Biomedical Design [*University of Utah*] [*Research center*] (RCD) .... CBD
Center for Blood Research [*Research center*] (RCD) .... CBR
Center for Book Arts (EA) .... CBA
Center for Borderline History (EA) .... CBH
Center for Brain Research [*University of Rochester*] [*Research center*] (RCD) .... CBR
Center for Building Technology [*Gaithersburg, MD*] [*National Institute of Standards and Technology*] .... CBT
Center for Built Environment Research [*Morgan State University*] [*Research center*] (RCD) .... CEBER
Center for Business and Economic Development [*Auburn University at Montgomery*] [*Research center*] (RCD) .... CBED
Center for Business and Economic Research [*University of Alabama*] [*University, AL*] [*Information service or system*] (IID) .... CBER
Center for Business & Economics Research [*University of Nevada - Las Vegas*] [*Research center*] (RCD) .... CBER
Center for Business Economics and Urban Studies (SAUO) .... CBEUS
Center for Business Information [*Information service or system*] (IID) .... CBI
Center for Business, Work and Learning (SAUO) .... CBWL
Center for Byzantine Studies (SAUS) .... Ctr Byz
Center for Canadian Historical Horticultural Studies [*Hamilton, ON*] .... CCHHS
Center for Carburization Heat Treatment Studies [*Worchester Polytechnic Institute*] [*Research center*] (RCD) .... CCHTS
Center for Case Management Accountability (SAUS) .... CCMA
Center for Cell Regulation and Enhancement of Biology/Biomaterial Interfaces (SAUO) .... CREBBI
Center for Cereals Research [*Pennsylvania State University*] [*Research center*] (RCD) .... CCR
Center for Certification Preparation and Review (SAUS) .... CCPR
Center for Chemical Process Safety (EA) .... CCPS
Center for Children and Technology [*Bank Street College of Education*] [*Research center*] (RCD) .... CCT
Center for Children with Chronic Illness and Disability (SAUO) C3ID
Center for Children's Books. Bulletin [*A publication*] (BRI) .... CCB-B
Center for Chinese Research Materials (EA) .... CCRM
Center for Chinese Research Materials, Washington, DC [*Library symbol*] [*Library of Congress*] (LCLS) .... DCCRM
Center for Chinese Studies [*University of Michigan*] [*Research center*] (RCD) .... CCS
Center for Chinese Studies (SAUS) .... Ctr Chin Stud
Center for Christian Response to Asian Issues (SAUO) .... CCRAI
Center for Christian Studies (EA) .... CCS
Center for Citizen Initiatives (EA) CCI
Center for Civil Society in Southeastern Europe [*Zagreb, Croatia*] .... CCS
Center for Civil Society International .... CCSI
Center for Clean Air Policy (EA) .... CCAP
Center for Climate System Research [*Marine science*] (OSRA) .... CCSR
Center for Climatic and Environmental Assessment [*National Oceanic and Atmospheric Administration*] (IID) .... CCEA
Center for Climatic Research [*University of Wisconsin - Madison*] [*Research center*] (RCD) .... CCR
Center for Clinical Psychopharmacology Data Documetation (SAUS) .... CCPDD
Center for Clouds, Chemistry and Climate (SAUS) C4
Center for Clouds, Chemistry and Climate (SAUS) CCCC
Center for Clouds, Chemistry and Climate (SAUS) .... CH
Center for Coastal Studies [*University of California, San Diego*] [*Research center*] (RCD) .... CCS
Center for Cognitive Science at UB (SAUS) .... CCS
Center for Cold Regions Engineering, Science, and Technology [*State University of New York at Buffalo*] [*Research center*] (RCD) .... CREST
Center for Command & Control Communication Systems (SAUO) C4S
Center for Command, Control, Communications, and Intelligence [*George Mason University*] [*Research center*] (RCD) C3I
Center for Communication and Information Research (SAUS) .... CCIR
Center for Communication Programs (EA) .... CCP
Center for Communication Studies (SAUS) .... CCS
Center for Communications Management (SAUS) .... CCM
Center for Communications Media [*University of Massachusetts-Boston*] [*Telecommunications service*] (TSSD) .... CCM
Center for Communications Ministry [*Formerly, NSCS*] [*Defunct*] (EA) .... CCM
Center for Communications Research/Institute for Defense Analyses (SAUS) .... CCR/IDA
Center for Communications Sciences (SAUO) .... CENCOMS
Center for Communications Systems [*CADPL*] [*Army*] (RDA) .... CENCOMS
Center for Community and Regional Research [*University of Minnesota, Duluth*] [*Research center*] (RCD) .... CCRR
Center for Community Change (EA) CCC
Center for Community Development [*Humboldt State University*] [*Research center*] (RCD) .... CCD
Center for Community Economic Development .... CCED
Center for Community Education Facility Planning [*Inactive*] (EA) .... CCEFP
Center for Community Justice (EA) .... CCJ
Center for Community Planning [*HEW*] .... CCP
Center for Community Study [*University of Rochester*] [*Research center*] (RCD) .... CCS
Center for Comparative Sociology .... CCS
Center for Compatible Economic Development [*Leesburg, VA*] .... CCED
Center for Compliance Information (EA) CCI

Center for Composite Materials [*University of Delaware*] [*Research center*] (RCD) .... CCM
Center for Computational Seismology [*Berkeley, CA*] [*Lawrence Berkeley Laboratory*] [*Department of Energy*] (GRD) .... CCS
Center for Computer Aided Analysis (SAUS) .... CCAA
Center for Computer Aided Design [*University of Iowa*] [*Research center*] (RCD) .... CCAD
Center for Computer Aids for Industrial Productivity [*Rutgers University*] [*Research center*] (RCD) .... CAIP
Center for Computer and Information Services [*Rutgers University, The State University of New Jersey*] [*Information service or system*] (IID) .... CCIS
Center for Computer Applications in Electromagnetic Education (SAUS) .... CAEME
Center for Computer Integrated Engineering and Manufacturing [*University of Tennessee at Knoxville*] [*Research center*] (RCD) .... CCIEM
Center for Computer Research in Humanities [*University of Colorado*] (CIST) .... CCRH
Center for Computer Research in Music and Acoustics [*Pronounced "karma"*] [*Stanford University*] .... CCRMA
Center for Computer Sciences and Technology [*Later, ICST*] [*National Institute of Standards and Technology*] .... CCST
Center for Computer Systems Design [*Washington University*] [*Research center*] (RCD) .... CCSD
Center for Computer-Assisted Legal Instruction (SAUO) .... CALI
Center for Computer-Assisted Legal Instruction (EA) .... CCALI
Center for Computer-Based Behavioral Studies [*Research center*] (RCD) .... CCBS
Center for Computer/Law (EA) CCL
Center for Computing Graphics (SAUO) .... CCGM
Center for Conflict Resolution (SAUO) .... CCR
Center for Conscious Evolution (EA) .... CCE
Center for Conservation Biology Network .... CCBN
Center for Constitutional Rights (EA) .... CCR
Center for Consumer Affairs, University of Wisconsin-Extension (SAUO) .... CCA-UWEX
Center for Consumer Affairs, University of Wisconsin-Milwaukee (EA) .... CCA-UWM
Center for Consumer Product Safety [*National Institute of Standards and Technology*] .... CCPS
Center for Consumer Product Technology [*National Institute of Standards and Technology*] (GRD) .... CCPT
Center for Contemporary Arab Studies [*Georgetown University*] [*Research center*] (RCD) .... CCAS
Center for Contemporary Jewish Documentation (SAUO) .... CCJD
Center for Contemporary Opera (EA) .... CCO
Center for Continuing Education for Women .... CCEW
Center for Continuing Study of the California Economy [*Information service or system*] (IID) .... CCSCE
Center for Control Science and Dynamical Systems [*University of Minnesota*] [*Research center*] (RCD) .... CSDS
Center for Cooperative and Labour Studies for Latin America, Spain and Portugal (SAUO) .... CECL
Center for Corporate Economics and Strategy [*Defunct*] (EA) .... CCES
Center for Corporate Public Involvement (EA) .... CCPI
Center for Craniofacial Anomalies [*University of Illinois at Chicago*] [*Research center*] (RCD) .... CCFA
Center for Creative Imaging [*Camden, Maine*] [*Computer art training*] CCI
Center for Creative Leadership (EA) CCL
Center for Creative Leadership, Greensboro, NC [*Library symbol*] [*Library of Congress*] (LCLS) .... NcGCL
Center for Cross-Cultural Studies [*University of Alaska, Fairbanks*] [*Research center*] (RCD) .... CXCS
Center for Cuban Studies (EA) .... CCS
Center for Curriculum Design [*Information service or system*] [*Defunct*] (IID) .... CCD
Center for Curriculum Development (SAUO) .... CCD
Center for Cyber Communities Initiative (VERA) CCCI
Center for Cyberetics System Synergism (SAUS) .... CYSYS
Center for Cybernetic Studies [*University of Texas at Austin*] [*Research center*] (RCD) .... CCS
Center for Cybernetic Studies [*University of Texas*] (PDAA) .... CS
Center for Cybernetics Studies (SAUO) .... CCS
Center for Cybernetics Systems Synergism .... CYSYS
Center for Dance Medicine (EA) .... CDM
Center for Data Systems and Analysis [*Montana State University*] [*Research center*] (RCD) .... CDSA
Center for Death Education and Research (EA) .... CDER
Center for Defense Information (EA) .... CDI
Center for Degree Studies (SAUS) .... CDS
Center for Democracy and Technology (EA) .... CDT
Center for Democratic Alternatives [*Defunct*] (EA) .... CDA
Center for Democratic Policy (EA) .... CDP
Center for Democratic Renewal (EA) .... CDR
Center for Demographic and Population Genetics [*University of Texas*] [*Research center*] (RCD) .... CDPG
Center for Demographic Studies [*Census*] (OICC) .... CDS
Center for Demography and Ecology [*University of Wisconsin - Madison*] [*Research center*] (RCD) .... CDE
Center for Design Planning (EA) .... CDP
Center for Development Information and Evaluation (SAUO) .... CDIE
Center for Development Planning, Projections, and Policies [*United Nations*] .... CDPPP
Center for Development Policy [*Later, ICDP*] (EA) .... CDP
Center for Development Research, Koobenhavn, Denmark [*Library symbol*] [*Library of Congress*] (LCLS) .... DnKDR
Center for Development Studies .... CDS

Center for Developmental Change [*University of Kentucky*] [*Research center*] (RCD) .... CDC
Center for Devices and Radiological Health [*FDA*] .... CDRH
Center for Discrete Mathematics and Theoretical Computer Science [*Rutgers University*] [*Research center*] (RCD) .... DIMACS
Center for Disease Control and Prevention (DHSM) .... CDCP
Center for Disease Control, Atlanta, GA [*OCLC symbol*] (OCLC) .... HNC
Center for Disease Control, Family Planning Evaluation Division, Atlanta, GA [*Library symbol*] [*Library of Congress*] (LCLS) .... GACDC-FP
Center for Disease Control, Main Library, Atlanta, GA [*Library symbol*] [*Library of Congress*] (LCLS) .... GACDC
Center for Dispute Settlement (EA) .... CDS
Center for Documentation and Communication Research [*Case Western Reserve University*] .... CDCR
Center for Documentation on Refugees [*United Nations High Commission for Refugees*] [*Switzerland*] [*Information service or system*] (IID) .... CDR
Center for Dredging Studies (SAUO) .... CDS
Center for Drug Education and Information (SAUO) .... CEDRO
Center for Drug Evaluation and Research [*Food and Drug Administration*] .... CDER
Center for Drugs and Biologics [*FDA*] .... CDB
Center for Early Adolescence (EA) .... CEA
Center for Earth and Environmental Sciences (SAUO) .... CEES
Center for Earth and Planetary Studies .... CEPS
Center for Earth Observation (SAUS) .... CEO
Center for Earth Observations and Remote Sensing [*Boulder, CO*] [*Cooperative Institute for Research in Environmental Sciences*] [*National Oceanic and Atmospheric Administration*] (GRD) .... CEORS
Center for Earthquake Research and Information [*Memphis State University*] [*Research center*] (RCD) .... CERI
Center for Econometrics and Decision Sciences [*University of Florida*] [*Research center*] (RCD) .... CEDS
Center for Economic and Management Research [*University of Oklahoma*] [*Norman*] [*Information service or system*] (IID) .... CEMR
Center for Economic Conversion (EA) .... CEC
Center for Economic Development and Business Research [*Wichita State University*] [*Kansas*] [*Information service or system*] (IID) .... CEDBR
Center for Economic Entomology (SAUO) .... CEE
Center for Economic Policy Research (SAUO) .... CEPR
Center for Economic Renewal and Technology Transfer [*Montana State University*] .... CERTT
Center for Economic Research [*University of Texas at Austin*] [*Research center*] (RCD) .... CER
[*The*] **Center for Economic Research and Graduate Education** [*Prague*] (ECON) .... CERGE
Center for Economic Studies [*Washington, DC*] [*Department of Commerce*] (GRD) .... CES
Center for Editions of American Authors [*Later, CSE*] .... CEAA
Center for Education and Drug Abuse Research (SAUO) .... CEDAR
Center for Education and Research in Free Enterprise [*College Station, TX*] (EA) .... CERFE
Center for Education and/in International Management (SAUO) .... CEI
Center for Education Improvement [*U.S. Department of Education*] (EDAC) .... CEI
Center for Education in International Management [*Canada*] .... CEI
Center for Education Initiatives (SAUS) .... CEI
Center for Education Statistics [*Washington, DC*] [*Department of Education*] [*Also, an information service or system*] (IID) .... CES
Center for Educational Change [*University of California, Berkeley*] .... CEC
Center for Educational Development [*University of Illinois at Chicago*] [*Research center*] (RCD) .... CED
Center for Educational Diffusion and Social Application of Satellite Telecommunications (SAUS) .... EDSAT
Center for Educational Experimentation, Development, and Evaluation [*University of Iowa*] [*Research center*] (RCD) .... CEEDE
Center for Educational Policy and Management [*Department of Education*] (GRD) .... CEPM
Center for Educational Policy Studies (EA) .... CEPS
Center for Educational Reform (EA) .... CER
Center for Educational Research and Development [*University of Maryland*] [*Research center*] (RCD) .... CERD
Center for Educational Technology [*Florida State University*] [*Research center*] .... CET
Center for Electromagnetic Materials & Optical Systems (SAUS) .... CEMOS
Center for Electromagnetics (SAUS) .... CEM
Center for Electromechnics [*University of Texas at Austin*] [*Research center*] (RCD) .... CEM
Center for Electron Optics [*Michigan State University*] [*Research center*] (RCD) .... CEO
Center for Electronic and Electro-optic Materials (SAUS) .... CEEM
Center for Electronic System Technology (SAUS) .... CEST
Center for Electronic Warfare/Reconnaissance, Surveillance, and Target Acquisit ion [*Fort Monmouth, NJ*] [*United States Army Communications-Electronics Command*] (GRD) .... EW/RSTA
Center for Electronics Communications Command (SAUO) .... CECOM
Center for Endocrinology, Metabolism, and Nutrition [*Northwestern University*] .... CEMN
Center for Energy and Economic Development [*US Bureau of Mines*] .... CEED
Center for Energy and Environmental Assessment (SAUO) .... CEEA
Center for Energy and Environmental Information [*Department of Energy*] (GRD) .... CEEI
Center for Energy and Environmental Management (COE) .... CEEM
Center for Energy and Environmental Policy Research [*Formerly, Center for Energy Policy and Research*] .... CEEPR
Center for Energy and Environmental Research [*University of Puerto Rico*] .... CEER
Center for Energy and Environmental Studies [*Carnegie-Mellon University*] [*Research center*] (RCD) .... CEES
Center for Energy and Environmental Studies, Princeton University (SAUO) .... CEES
Center for Energy and Mineral Resources [*Texas A & M University*] [*Research center*] .... CEMR
Center for Energy Information [*Defunct*] .... CEI
Center for Energy Policy and Research (EA) .... CEPR
Center for Energy Studies [*Louisiana State University*] [*Information service or system*] (IID) .... CES
Center for Energy Studies [*University of Texas at Austin*] [*Research center*] (RCD) .... CES
Center for Energy Systems [*General Electric Information Services Co.*] (NITA) .... CFES
Center for Engineering (SAUO) .... CFE
Center for Engineering Applications of Radioisotopes [*North Carolina State University*] [*Research center*] (RCD) .... CEAR
Center for Engineering Development and Research [*University of South Florida*] [*Research center*] (RCD) .... CEDAR
Center for Engineering Plants for Resistance Against Pathogens [*University of California*] [*Research center*] (RCD) .... CEPRAP
Center for Engineering Systems Advanced Research [*Oak Ridge National Laboratory*] [*Oak Ridge, TN*] [*Department of Energy*] .... CESAR
Center for Enhancement of the Biology/Biomaterial Interfaces (SAUO) .... CEBBI
Center for Entrepreneurial Development [*Carnegie-Mellon University*] .... CED
Center for Entrepreneurial Development, Advancement, Research, and Support [*University of Texas, El Paso*] [*Research center*] (RCD) .... CEDAR
Center for Entrepreneurial Management [*New York, NY*] (EA) .... CEM
Center for Entrepreneurial Studies [*New York University*] [*Research center*] (RCD) .... CES
Center for Entrepreneurship and Economic Development [*Pan American University*] [*Research center*] (RCD) .... CEED
Center for Environment Commerce and Energy (SAUO) .... CECE
Center for Environmental and Estuarine Studies [*University of Maryland*] [*Research center*] .... CEES
Center for Environmental and Regulatory Systems (AEPA) .... CERIS
Center for Environmental Assessment Services [*National Oceanic and Atmospheric Administration*] [*Information service or system*] (IID) .... CEAS
Center for Environmental Conflict Resolution (COE) .... CECR
Center for Environmental Conflict Resolution (SAUS) .... RESOLVE
Center for Environmental Design Education and Research [*University of Colorado*] [*Research center*] (RCD) .... CEDER
Center for Environmental Education [*Research center*] (EA) .... CEE
Center for Environmental Education (SAUO) .... CFEE
Center for Environmental Health [*Atlanta, GA*] [*Department of Health and Human Services*] (GRD) .... CEH
Center for Environmental Health and Injury Control [*Atlanta, GA*] [*Centers for Disease Control*] [*Department of Health and Human Services*] (GRD) .... CEHIC
Center for Environmental Information, Inc. [*Information service or system*] (IID) .... CEI
Center for Environmental Intern Programs (EA) .... CEIP
Center for Environmental Research Education [*State University of New York College, Buffalo*] [*Research center*] (RCD) .... CERE
Center for Environmental Research Information [*Environmental Protection Agency*] (EPA) .... CERI
Center for Environmental Sciences [*University of Colorado at Denver*] [*Research center*] (RCD) .... CES
Center for Environmental Studies [*Williams College*] [*Research center*] (RCD) .... CES
Center for Environmental Studies [*Arizona State University*] [*Research center*] (RCD) .... CES
Center for Environmental Studies (or Study) (SAUO) .... CES
Center for Environmental Toxicology [*Michigan State University*] [*Research center*] (RCD) .... CET
Center for Epidemiologic Studies (SAUO) .... CES
Center for Epidemiologic Studies - Depression Scale [*Personality development test*] [*Psychology*] .... CES-D
Center for Epidemiology and Animal Health (SAUO) .... CEAH
Center for Equine Health .... CEH
Center for Ethics and Toxic Substances .... CETOS
Center for Evaluative Clinical Sciences .... CECS
Center for Excellence for Space Data and Information Sciences (SAUS) .... CESDIS
Center for Exhibition Industry Research (NTPA) .... CEIR
Center for Experiment Design and Data Analysis [*National Oceanic and Atmospheric Administration*] .... CEDDA
Center for Experimental Studies in Business [*University of Minnesota*] .... CESB
Center for Exploratory and Perceptual Art (SAUS) .... CEPA
Center for Exposure Assessment Modeling [*Athens, GA*] [*Environmental Protection Agency*] (GRD) .... CEAM
Center for Extraterrestrial Engineering & Construction (SAUS) .... CETEC
Center for Extreme ultraviolet Astrophysics (SAUS) .... CEA
Center for Faith Development [*Later, CRFMD*] (EA) .... CFD
Center for Family Business [*Cleveland, OH*] (EA) .... CFB
Center for Family Support (EA) .... CFS
Center for Fast Kinetics Research [*University of Texas at Austin*] [*Research center*] (RCD) .... CFKR
Center for Federal Policy Review (EA) .... CFPR
Center for Fertility and Reproductive Research [*Vanderbilt University*] [*Research center*] (RCD) .... C-FARR
Center for Field Research (EA) .... CFR
Center for Financial Freedom and Accuracy in Financial Reporting (EA) .... CFFAFR

Center for Food Safety and Applied Nutrition [*Washington, DC*] [*Department of Health and Human Services*] (GRD) .... CFSAN
Center for Foreign Journalists (EA) .... CFJ
Center for Foreign Policy Development (EA) .... CFPD
Center for Free Electron Laser Studies (SAUS) .... CFELS
Center for Future Research (SAUS) .... CFR
Center for GIS (SAUS) .... CGIS
Center for Global Adventure (SAUO) .... CGA
Center for Global Education (EA) .... CGE
Center for Global Environmental Studies (CARB) .... CGES
Center for Global Trade Development (SAUO) .... CGTD
Center for Government Service [*Rutgers University*] [*Research center*] (RCD) .... CGS
Center for Governmental Research, Inc. [*Research center*] (RCD) .... CGR
Center for Governmental Research Inc. (EA) .... CGRI
Center for Governmental Research Library, Rochester, NY [*OCLC symbol*] (OCLC) .... VQD
Center for Great Lakes and Aquatic Sciences [*University of Michigan*] .... CGLAS
Center for Great Lakes Studies [*University of Wisconsin - Milwaukee*] [*Research center*] (RCD) .... CGLS
Center for Group Learning .... CGL
Center for Growth Alternatives [*Defunct*] (EA) .... CGA
Center for Hazardous Materials Research (EA) .... CHMR
Center for Health Action (EA) .... CHA
Center for Health Administration Studies [*University of Chicago*] [*Research center*] (RCD) .... CHAS
Center for Health and Advanced Policy Studies [*Boston University*] [*Research center*] (RCD) .... CHAPS
Center for Health and Gender Equity (SAUO) .... CHANGE
Center for Health Applications of Aerospace Related Technologies .... CHAART
Center for Health Care Access [*League for Hard of Hearing*] .... CHCA
Center for Health Care Strategies (SAUO) .... CHCS
Center for Health Dispute Resolution .... CHDR
Center for Health Effects of Environmental Contamination [*University of Iowa*] (GEOI) .... CHEEC
Center for Health Management Research (SAUO) .... CHMR
Center for Health Policy Research [*University of Florida*] [*Research center*] (RCD) .... CHPR
Center for Health Promotion and Education [*Atlanta, GA*] [*Department of Health and Human Services*] (GRD) .... CHPE
Center for Health Promotion and Preventative Medicine [*Army*] (BCP) .... CHPPM
Center for Health Promotion Research and Development [*University of Texas*] [*Research center*] (RCD) .... CHPRD
Center for Health Research [*Wayne State University*] [*Research center*] (RCD) .... CHR
Center for Health Resources Planning Information [*National Institutes of Health*] .... CHRPI
Center for Health Services and Policy Research [*Northwestern University*] [*Research center*] (RCD) .... CHSPR
Center for Health Services Research [*University of Iowa*] [*Research center*] (RCD) .... CHSR
Center for Healthcare Ethics (SAUO) .... CHCE
Center for Healthcare Information Management (SAUO) .... CHIM
Center for Hellenic Studies, Harvard University, Washington, DC [*Library symbol*] [*Library of Congress*] (LCLS) .... DCHS
Center for Help for Anxiety/ Agoraphobia through New Growth Experience (SAUO) .... CHAANGE
Center for High Angular Resolution Astronomy [*Georgia State University*] [*Research center*] .... CHARA
Center for High Angular Resolution Astronomy Array (SAUS) .... CHARA Array
Center for High Performance Computing (SAUO) .... CHPC
Center for History of Chemistry [*Later, NFHC*] (EA) .... CHOC
Center for Holistic Resource Management (EA) .... CHRM
Center for Holocaust Studies (EA) .... CHS
Center for Hospitality Research and Service (EA) .... CHRS
Center for Housing, Building, and Planning [*United Nations*] .... UNCHBP
Center for Human Environments Associates, Inc. [*City University of New York*] [*Research center*] (RCD) .... CHE INC
Center for Human Genome Studies [*Internet resource*] .... CHGS
Center for Human Growth and Develoment [*University of Michigan*] [*Research center*] (RCD) .... CHGD
Center for Human Information Processing [*Research center*] (RCD) .... CHIP
Center for Human Radiobiology .... CHR
Center for Human Reproduction (SAUO) .... CHR
Center for Human Resource Research [*Ohio State University*] [*Research center*] (RCD) .... CHRR
Center for Human Resources [*Rutgers University*] [*Research center*] (RCD) .... CHR
Center for Human Rights and Responsibilities [*British*] .... CHRR
Center for Human Services (EA) .... CHS
Center for Human Toxicology [*University of Utah*] [*Research center*] (RCD) .... CHT
Center for Humane Options in Childbirth Experiences (EA) .... CHOICE
Center for Humanitarian Outreach and Intercultural Exchange (SAUO) .... CHOICE
Center for Hydrogen Embrittlement of Electroplated Fasteners [*Worchester Polytechnic Institute*] [*Research center*] (RCD) .... CHEEF
Center for Image Processing and Integrated Computing [*University of California at Davis*] [*Research center*] (RCD) .... CIPIC
Center for Imaging and Pharmaceutical Research (ADWA) .... CIPR
Center for Imaging Science [*University of Chicago*] [*Research center*] (RCD) .... CIS
Center for Immigrants Rights (EA) .... CIR
Center for Immigration Studies (CROSS) .... CIS
Center for Immunity Enhancement in Domestic Animals [*Iowa State University of Science and Technology*] [*Research center*] (RCD) .... CIEDA
Center for Improving Mountain Living [*Western Carolina University*] [*Research center*] (RCD) .... CIML
Center for Independent Action (EA) .... CFIA
Center for Independent Education [*Later, Cato Institute*] (EA) .... CIE
Center for Independent Living [*Rehabilitation*] (DAVI) CIL
Center for Independent Living Services .... CILS
Center for Indigenous Peoples Nutrition and Environment (SAUO) .... CINE
Center for Individual Rights .... CIR
Center for Indoor Air Research .... CIAR
Center for Industrial and Engineering Technology [*Central Connecticut University*] [*Research center*] (RCD) .... CIET
Center for Industrial Development [*European Economic Community/African, Caribbean, and Pacific States*] (DS) .... CID
Center for Industrial Research and Service .... CIRAS
Center for Industry Cooperation & Trade (SAUS) .... CICAT
Center for Infectious Diseases [*Department of Health and Human Services*] (GRD) .... CID
Center for Informatics Research (SAUS) .... CIR
Center for Information and Documentation (SAUO) .... CID
Center for Information and Immigration Studies [*Mexico*] (CROSS) .... CIEM
Center for Information and Numerical Data Analysis and Synthesis [*West Lafayette, IN*] [*Department of Commerce*] (MCD) .... CINDAS
Center for Information Biology (SAUO) .... CIB
Center for Information, Education and Services (SAUO) .... CIES
Center for Information of America (SAUS) .... CIAO
Center for Information of America (SAUS) .... Ctr Info Am
Center for Information on America [*Defunct*] (EA) .... CIOA
Center for Information on Language and Teaching (SAUS) .... CILT
Center for Information Research [*Research center*] (IID) .... CIR
Center for Information Sciences (KSC) .... CIS
Center for Information Systems Research [*Massachusetts Institute of Technology*] [*Research center*] (RCD) .... CISR
Center for Information Systems Security [*DoD*] (DOMA) .... CISS
Center for Information Technology [*Stanford University*] [*Stanford, CA*] (CSR) .... CIT
Center for Information Technology Integration [*University of Michigan*] [*Research center*] (RCD) .... CITI
Center for Inherited Disease Research [*Genotyping facility, Maryland*] .... CIDER
Center for Inherited Disease Research [*Baltimore*] [*National Institutes of Health and Johns Hopkins University*] .... CIDR
Center for Inherited Disorders of Energy Metabolism (ADWA) .... CIDEM
Center for Innovation Management Studies [*Lehigh University*] [*Information service or system*] (IID) .... CIMS
Center for Innovative Diplomacy [*Defunct*] (EA) .... CID
Center for Innovative Learning Technologies .... CILT
Center for Innovative Technology (SAUO) .... CIT
Center for Inquiry and Discovery [*Washington, DC, museum*] .... CID
Center for Institutional Reform and the Informal Sector [*University of Maryland*] (ECON) .... IRIS
Center for Instructional and Research Computing Activities [*University of Florida*] [*Research center*] (RCD) .... CIRCA
Center for Instructional Communications (SAUS) CIC
Center for Instructional Services [*Purdue University*] [*Research center*] (RCD) .... CIS
Center for Instructional Services and Research [*Memphis State University*] [*Research center*] (RCD) .... CISR
Center for Integral Medicine [*Defunct*] (EA) .... CIM
Center for Integrated Electronics [*Rensselaer Polytechnic Institute*] [*Research center*] (RCD) .... CIE
Center for Integrated Facility Engineering [*Stanford University*] [*Research center*] (RCD) .... CIFE
Center for Integrated Manufacturing Studies [*Rochester Institute of Technology*] [*Research center*] (RCD) .... CIMS
Center for Integrated Systems [*Stanford University*] [*Research center*] (RCD) .... CIS
Center for Integration of Natural Disaster Information (GEOI) .... CINDI
Center for Intelligence Studies (EA) .... CIS
Center for Intelligent Computing Studies [*Washington University*] [*Research center*] (RCD) .... CICS
Center for Intelligent Machines and Robotics [*University of Florida*] [*Research center*] (RCD) .... CIMAR
Center for Intelligent Vision and Information Systems .... CIVIS
Center for Interactive Computer Graphics [*Rensselaer Polytechnic Institute*] [*Research center*] (RCD) .... CICG
Center for Interactive Programs [*University of Wisconsin-Extension*] [*Madison*] [*Information service or system*] [*Telecommunications*] (TSSD) .... CIP
Center for Interactive Technology, Applications, and Research [*University of South Florida*] [*Research center*] (RCD) .... CITAR
Center for Inter-American and Border Studies [*University of Texas, El Paso*] [*Research center*] (RCD) .... CIABS
Center for Inter-American and Border Studies [*University of Texas, El Paso*] [*Research center*] (RCD) .... CIBS
Center for Inter-American Relations (EA) .... CIAR
Center for Inter-American Relations .... CIR
Center for Interdisciplinary Research in Computer-Based Learning [*University of Delaware*] [*Research center*] (RCD) .... CIRCL
Center for Interdisciplinary Research on Immunologic Diseases [*Department of Health and Human Services*] (GRD) .... CIRID
Center for Interdisciplinary Study of Science and Technology [*Northwestern University*] [*Research center*] (RCD) .... CISST
Center for Interest Measurement [*University of Minnesota*] [*Research center*] (RCD) .... CIMR
Center for International Affairs [*Harvard University*] [*Research center*] (RCD) .... CFIA
Center for International and Environmental Research (SAUS) .... CICERO

Center for International and Strategic Affairs [*Research center*] (RCD) .... CISA
Center for International Business Cycle Research [*Columbia University*] [*New York, NY*] [*Research center*] (RCD) .... CIBCR
Center for International Business Studies [*Research center*] (RCD) .... CIBS
Center for International Community Health Studies [*University of Connecticut*] [*Research center*] (RCD) .... CICHS
Center for International Earth Sciences Information Network (ARMP) ...... CIESIN
Center for International Economic Growth [*Defunct*] (EA) .... CIEG
Center for International Economics (AUEG) .... CIE
Center for International Education and Research in Accounting [*University of Illinois, Urbana-Champaign*] [*Research center*] (RCD) .... CIERA
Center for International Environment Information [*Later, WEC*] (EA) .... CIEI
Center for International Environmental Cooperation (SAUO) .... INENCO
Center for International Environmental Law (SAUO) .... CIEL
Center for International Financial Analysis and Research, Inc. [*Princeton, NJ*] [*Information service or system*] (IID) .... CIFAR
Center for International Forestry Research .... CIFOR
Center for International Health Information (ADWA) .... CIHI
Center for International Higher Education Documentation (EDAC) .... CIHED
Center for International Media Research (SAUO) .... CIMR
Center for International Meeting on Biology (HGEN) .... CIMB
Center for International Policy .... CIP
Center for International Private Enterprise [*Washington, DC*] (EA) .... CIPE
Center for International Programs and Studies [*University of Missouri - Rolla*] [*Research center*] (RCD) .... CIPAS
Center for International Relations [*University of California, Los Angeles*] [*Research center*] (RCD) .... CIR
Center for International Research [*Bureau of the Census*] [*Information service or system*] (IID) .... CIR
Center for International Security [*Defunct*] (EA) .... CIS
Center for International Studies, Albany, NY [*Library symbol*] [*Library of Congress*] (LCLS) .... NAICI
Center for International Systems Research .... CISR
Center for International Trade Development [*Oklahoma State University*] [*Research center*] (RCD) .... CITD
Center for International Trade in Forest Products [*University of Washington*] .... CINTRAFOR
Center for Interreligious Affairs .... CIA
Center for International Education (SAUO) .... CIE
Center for Investigative Reporting (EA) .... CIR
Center for Iron and Steel Research (SAUS) .... CISR
Center for Irrigation (SAUO) .... CIT
Center for Irrigation Technology [*California State University, Fresno*] [*Research center*] (RCD) .... CIT
Center for Japanese Studies [*University of Michigan*] [*Research center*] (RCD) .... CJS
Center for Judicial Studies (EA) .... CJS
Center for Labor and Industrial Relations [*New York Institute of Technology*] [*Research center*] (RCD) .... CLIR
Center for Labor Education and Research [*University of Colorado*] .... CLEAR
Center for Labor Education and Research [*University of Hawaii*] [*Research center*] (RCD) .... CLEAR
Center for Labor Education and Research [*University of Alabama at Birmingham*] [*Research center*] (RCD) .... CLEAR
Center for Labor Research and Studies [*Florida International University*] [*Research center*] (RCD) .... CLRS
Center for Lake Erie Area Research [*Ohio State University*] .... CLEAR
Center for Lake Superior Environmental Studies [*University of Wisconsin - Superior*] [*Research center*] (RCD) .... CLSES
Center for Language Education and Research [*Los Angeles, CA*] [*Department of Education*] (GRD) .... CLEAR
Center for Latin American and Caribbean Studies, Michigan (SAUO) .... CLACS
Center for Latin American and Iberian Studies [*Vanderbilt University*] [*Research center*] (RCD) .... CLAIS
Center for Latin American, University of Wisconsin-Milwaukee (SAUS) .... UWCLA
Center for Law and Education (EA) .... CLE
Center for Law and Religious Freedom (EA) .... CLRF
Center for Law & Research International [*Nairobi, Kenya*] .... CLARION
Center for Law and Social Policy (EA) .... CLASP
Center for Law and Social Policy (EPA) .... CLSP
Center for Law in the Public Interest (EA) .... CLIPI
Center for Leadership Development (EA) .... CLD
Center for Leadership in School Reform [*Kentucky*] .... CLSR
Center for Learning and Telecommunications [*American Association for Higher Education*] [*Information service or system*] (IID) .... CLT
Center for Lesbian and Gay Studies (EA) .... CLAGS
Center for Libertarian Studies (EA) .... CLS
Center for Life Cycle Software Engineering [*Communications-Electronics Command*] [*Army*] .... CLCSE
Center for Lifelong Education [*Ball State University*] [*Research center*] (RCD) .... CLLE
Center for Living Democracy (EA) .... CLD
Center for Local Government Technology [*Oklahoma State University*] [*Research center*] (RCD) .... CLGT
Center for Local Tax Research (EA) .... CLTR
Center for Loss in Multiple Birth .... CLIMB
Center for Loss in Multiple Birth (EA) .... CLMB
Center for Low-Intensity Conflict [*Army*] CLIC
Center for Machine Intelligence [*Research center*] (RCD) .... CMI
Center for Magnetic Recording Research [*University of California, San Diego*] [*Research center*] (RCD) .... CMRR
Center for Male Medicine (SAUS) .... CMM
Center for Management Development [*American Management Association*] (EA) .... CMD

Center for Management Effectiveness [*Pacific Palisades, CA*] (EA) .... CME
Center for Management Systems (EA) .... CMS
Center for Management Technology [*Commercial firm*] (EA) .... CMT
Center for Manufacturing Productivity and Technology Transfer [*Rensselaer Polytechnic Institute*] [*Research center*] (RCD) .... CMP
Center for Manufacturing Systems [*New Jersey*] .... CMS
Center for Marine Affairs [*Scripps Institution of Oceanography*] .... CMA
Center for Marine and Environmental Studies (SAUO) .... CMES
Center for Marine Conservation (EA) .... CMC
Center for Marine Exploration (GNE) .... CME
Center for Marine Resources [*National Oceanic and Atmospheric Administration*] .... CMR
Center for Maritime Studies [*Later, MRD*] [*Webb Institute of Naval Architecture*] [*Research center*] (EA) .... CMS
Center for Market and Trade Development [*China*] .... CMTD
Center for Marketing Communications [*Later, Advertising Research Foundation*] (EA) .... CMC
Center for Marxist Research [*Defunct*] (EA) .... CMR
Center for Mass Communication [*Columbia University*] .... CMC
Center for Mass Communications Research and Policy [*University of Denver*] [*Research center*] (RCD) .... CMCRP
Center for Massachusetts Data [*Information service or system*] (IID) .... CMD
Center for Materials Research [*Johns Hopkins University*] [*Research center*] (RCD) .... CMR
Center for Materials Research [*Stanford University*] [*Research center*] (RCD) .... CMR
Center for Materials Science [*Los Alamos, NM*] [*Los Alamos National Laboratory*] [*Department of Energy*] (GRD) .... CMS
Center for Materials Science and Engineering [*MIT*] [*Research center*] (RCD) .... CMSE
Center for Materials Science Electron Microscope Laboratory (SAUS) .... CMSEML
Center for Measurement Science (BARN) .... CMS
Center for Media and Public Affairs (EA) .... CMPA
Center for Media Education .... CME
Center for Medical Consumers and Health Care Information (EA) .... CMC
Center for Medical Consumers and Health Care Information (EA) .... CMCHCI
Center for Medical Devices and Radiologic Health (MELL) .... CMDRH
Center for Medical Manpower Studies [*Northeastern University*] [*Research center*] (RCD) .... CMMS
Center for Medieval and Early Renaissance Studies (EA) .... CEMERS
Center for Medieval and Renaissance Studies (EA) .... CMRS
Center for Mental Health Services (USGC) .... CMHS
Center for Metals Production [*Carnegie Mellon University*] [*Research center*] (RCD) .... CMP
Center for Metric Education [*Western Michigan University*] .... CME
Center for Metrology (SAUS) .... CENAM
Center for Metropolitan Studies [*University of Missouri - Saint Louis*] [*Research center*] (RCD) .... CMS
Center for Microcontamination Control [*Research center*] (RCD) .... CMC
Center for Middle Eastern Studies [*Harvard University*] [*Research center*] (RCD) .... CMES
Center for Middle Eastern Studies [*University of California, Berkeley*] [*Research center*] (RCD) .... CMES
Center for Migration Studies of New York (EA) .... CMS
Center for Mining and Mineral Exploration Research (SAUS) .... CIMMER
Center for Modern Dance Education [*Hackensack, NJ*] .... CMDE
Center for Modern Psychoanalytic Studies (SAUO) .... CMPS
Center for Molecular and Genetic Medicine [*Stanford University*] [*Research center*] .... CMGM
Center for Molecular Medicine [*Germany*] .... CMM
Center for Multinational Studies [*Defunct*] (EA) .... CMS
Center for Music Psychology (SAUS) .... CFM
Center for Narcolepsy Research (SAUO) .... CNR
Center for National Food and Agricultural Policy (SAUO) .... CNFAP
Center for National Policy (EA) .... CNP
Center for National Policy Review [*Defunct*] (EA) .... CNPR
Center for National Security Studies (EA) .... CNSS
Center for Nationalist Studies (EA) .... CNS
Center for Natural Areas (EA) .... CNA
Center for Naval Analyses [*Alexandria, VA*] [*Navy*] .... CNA
Center for Naval Analyses Research Contribution (SAUO) .... CRC
Center for Naval Analysis [*Marine science*] (OSRA) .... CNA
Center for Naval Research (CCCA) .... CNR
Center for Near Eastern and North African Studies [*University of Michigan*] [*Research center*] (RCD) .... CNENAS
Center for Neighborhood Technology (EA) .... CNT
Center for Neo-Hellenic Studies (EA) .... CNHS
Center for Networked Information (SAUO) .... CNI
Center for Networked Information Discovery and Retrieval .... CNIDR
Center for Neural Basis of Cognition (VERA) .... CNBC
Center for Neuroscience [*Rutgers University*] .... CNS
Center for Neuroscience, University of Pittsburgh .... CNUP
Center for New Corporate Priorities [*Defunct*] (EA) .... CNCP
Center for New Creation (EA) .... CNC
Center for New National Security (EA) .... CNNS
Center for New Schools (EA) .... CNS
Center for Night Vision and Electro-Optics [*Fort Belvoir, VA*] [*Army*] (INF) .... CNVEO
Center for Non-Broadcast Television [*Defunct*] (EA) .... CNB-TV
Center for Nonlinear Studies [*Los Alamos, NM*] [*Department of Energy*] (GRD) .... CNLS
Center for Nonprofit Organizations [*Defunct*] (EA) .... CNO
Center for Nonviolent Alternatives [*Defunct*] (EA) .... CNVA
Center for Nonviolent Communication (EA) .... CNC

Center for Nonviolent Studies [*An association*] (EA) ... CNS
Center for Northern Studies [*Research center*] (RCD) ... CNS
Center for Nuclear Research (SAUS) ... CERN
Center for Nuclear Studies [*Memphis State University*] [*Research center*] (RCD) ... CNS
Center for Numerical Analysis [*University of Texas at Austin*] [*Research center*] (RCD) ... CNA
Center for Nursing Education, Spokane, WA [*Library symbol*] [*Library of Congress*] (LCLS) ... WaSpCN
Center for Nursing Research [*Ohio State University*] [*Research center*] (RCD) ... CNR
Center for Nursing Research and Evaluation [*University of Wisconsin - Milwaukee*] [*Research center*] (RCD) ... CNRE
Center for Nutrition Policy and Promotion (SAUO) ... CNPP
Center for Occupational Hazards (EA) ... COH
Center for Occupational Health and Safety [*University of Waterloo*] [*Research center*] (RCD) ... COHS
Center for Occupational Research and Development [*Research center*] (RCD) ... CORD
Center for Occupational Research and Development (SAUO) ... CORD
Center for Ocean Analysis and Prediction [*Monterey, CA*] [*NOAA*] ... COAP
Center for Ocean Atmospheric Modeling (SAUS) ... COAM
Center for Ocean Climate Chemistry [*Canada*] [*Marine science*] (OSRA) ... COCC
Center for Ocean, Land and Atmospheric Interactions (SAUS) ... COLAI
Center for Oceanic Analysis and Prediction [*Monterey, CA*] [*National Oceanic and Atmospheric Administration*] ... COAP
Center for Ocean-Land-Atmosphere Studies [*Marine science*] (OSRA) ... COLA
Center for Oceans Law and Policy (EA) ... COLP
Center for Office Technology (EA) ... COT
Center for Oil Spill, Oil Spill Public Information Center, Anchorage, AK [*Library symbol*] [*Library of Congress*] (LCLS) ... AkAOS
Center for OPEC Studies (SAUO) ... CENTROPEP
Center for Operations Research [*MIT*] (MCD) ... COR
Center for Optics Manufacturing (RDA) ... COM
Center for Optics, Photonics, and LASERS [*Laval University*] [*Research center*] (RCD) ... COPL
Center for Optimum Environments (EA) ... COE
Center for Oral Health Research [*University of Pennsylvania*] [*Research center*] (RCD) ... COHR
Center for Orbit Determination in Europe (SAUO) ... CODE
Center for Organ Recovery and Education [*Medicine*] ... CORE
Center for Organizational and Community Development (EA) ... COCD
Center for Orientation, Diagnosis and Treatment of Sexually Transmitted Diseases (SAUO) ... CODETS
Center for Orthopaedic Research (ADWA) ... COR
Center for Overseas Program Analysis [*Department of State*] ... COPA
Center for Packaging Education (EA) ... CPE
Center for Parallel Computers (SAUS) ... PDC
Center for Parapsychological Research [*Defunct*] (EA) ... CPR
Center for Particle Astrophysics (SAUO) ... CfPA
Center for Particle Theory [*University of Texas at Austin*] [*Research center*] (RCD) ... CPT
Center for Patient Advocacy (MELL) ... CPA
Center for Peace Studies (EA) ... CPS
Center for Peace through Culture (SAUO) ... CPC
Center for Peaceful Change (SAUO) ... CPC
Center for Petroleum Engineering (SAUS) ... CPE
Center for Philosophy and Public Policy [*Later, IPPP*] (EA) ... CPPP
Center for Philosophy, Law, Citizenship (EA) ... CPLC
Center for Philosophy of Science [*University of Pittsburgh*] [*Research center*] (RCD) ... CPS
Center for Plant Conservation (EA) ... CPC
Center for Plutonium Production [*France*] (NRCH) ... CPP
Center for Policy Alternatives (EA) ... CPA
Center for Policy and Law in Education [*University of Miami*] [*Research center*] (RCD) ... CPLE
Center for Policy Process [*Defunct*] ... CPP
Center for Policy Research (EA) ... CPR
Center for Policy Research in Education [*New Brunswick, NJ*] [*Department of Education*] (GRD) ... CPRE
Center for Political Research [*Later, Government Research Corp.*] ... CPR
Center for Popular Economics (EA) ... CPE
Center for Popular Music, Middle Tennessee State University, Murfreesboro, TN [*Library symbol*] [*Library of Congress*] (LCLS) ... TMurS-M
Center for Population Activities (SAUO) ... CEFPA
Center for Population and Family Health [*Columbia University*] [*Research center*] (RCD) ... CPFH
Center for Population Options (EA) ... CPO
Center for Population Options' Media Project (EA) ... CPOMP
Center for Population Research (SAUO) ... CPR
Center for Population Research - National Institute of Child Health and Human Development [*Bethesda, MD*] [*Department of Health and Human Services*] (GRD) ... CPR-NICHD
Center for Population Research and Census [*Portland State University*] [*Oregon*] [*Information service or system*] (IID) ... CPRC
Center for Population Studies (SAUS) ... CPS
Center for Populations Options (SAUS) ... CFPO
Center for Positron Emission Tomography (SAUS) ... CPET
Center for Pre-Columbian Studies (SAUS) ... Ctr Pre-Col
Center for Preservation Research ... CPR
Center for Prevention of Premature Arterial Sclerosis ... CPPA
Center for Prevention Services [*Department of Health and Human Services*] (GFGA) ... CPS
Center for Preventive Medicine (SAUS) ... CPM
Center for Process Analytical Chemistry [*University of Washington*] [*Research center*] (RCD) ... CPAC
Center for Process Studies (EA) ... CPS
Center for Produce Quality ... CPQ
Center for Professional Development [*University of Kentucky*] [*Research center*] (RCD) ... CPD
Center for Professional Development and Training [*University of Texas at Austin*] (RDA) ... CPDT
Center for Professional Well-Being [*Formerly, Center for the Well-Being of Health Professionals*] (EA) ... CWBHP
Center for Propellant and Missile Completion [*France*] ... CAPE
Center for Public Administration and Policy [*Virginia Polytechnic Institute and State University*] [*Research center*] (RCD) ... CPAP
Center for Public Affairs [*Arizona State University*] [*Research center*] (RCD) ... CPA
Center for Public Dialogue (EA) ... CPD
Center for Public Health Studies [*Portland State University*] [*Research center*] (RCD) ... CPHS
Center for Public Integrity ... CPI
Center for Public Justice (EA) ... CPJ
Center for Public Policy, Union Institute (EA) ... CPPUI
Center for Public Representation (EA) ... CPR
Center for Public Resources (EA) ... CPR
Center for Quality Assurance in International Education (SAUO) ... CQAIE
Center for Radiation Research [*National Institute of Standards and Technology*] ... CRR
Center for Radiation-hardened Microelectronics (SAUO) ... CRM
Center for Radiophysics and Space Research [*Cornell University*] [*Research center*] ... CRSR
Center for Rate Controlled Recordings [*Defunct*] (EA) ... CRCR
Center for Reflection on the Second Law (EA) ... CFRSL
Center for Reformation Research (EA) ... CRR
Center for Reformation Research, St. Louis, MO [*Library symbol*] [*Library of Congress*] (LCLS) ... MoSCRR
Center for Rehabilitation Technology [*Georgia Institute of Technology*] [*Research center*] (RCD) ... CRT
Center for Religion, Ethics, and Social Policy [*Cornell University*] [*Research center*] (RCD) ... CRESP
Center for Remote Sensing and Cartography [*University of Utah Research Institute*] [*Research center*] (RCD) ... CRSC
Center for Remote Sensing and Environmental Optics (SAUO) ... CRSEO
Center for Renewable Resources (EA) ... CRR
Center for Reproduction of Endangered Species (SAUS) ... CRES
Center for Reproduction of Endangered Wildlife [*Research center*] (RCD) ... CREW
Center for Reproductive and Sexual Health [*Defunct*] (EA) ... CRASH
Center for Reproductive Law and Policy (EA) ... CRLP
Center for Research and Applications in Image and Signal Processing (SAUO) ... CRAISP
Center for Research and Development in Masonry, Calgary, AB, Canada [*Library symbol*] [*Library of Congress*] (LCLS) ... CaACRDM
Center for Research and Documentation on the European Community [*American University*] [*Research center*] (RCD) ... CERDEC
Center for Research and Documentation on the European Community [*American University*] [*Research center*] ... CRDEC
Center for Research and Education in Optics and Lasers (SAUS) ... CREOL
Center for Research and Education in Sexuality [*San Francisco State University*] [*Research center*] (RCD) ... CERES
Center for Research and Evaluation in Applications of Technology in Education [*Palo Alto, CA*] ... CREATE
Center for Research and Lessons Learned [*Army*] ... CENTRALL
Center for Research & studies on Strategy & Technology (SAUS) ... CREST
Center for Research Animal Resources [*Cornell University*] [*Research center*] (RCD) ... CRAR
Center for Research for Mothers and Children [*National Institutes of Health*] (GRD) ... CRMC
Center for Research in Ambulatory Health Care Administration (EA) ... CRAHCA
Center for Research in College Instruction of Science and Mathematics (EA) ... CRICISAM
Center for Research in Computer Graphics (VERA) ... CRCG
Center for Research in Computing Technology [*Harvard University*] [*Research center*] (RCD) ... CRCT
Center for Research in Electro-Optics and Lasers [*University of Central Florida*] [*Research center*] (RCD) ... CREOL
Center for Research in Engineering Science [*University of Kansas*] ... CRES
Center for Research in Faith and Moral Development (EA) ... CRFMD
Center for Research in Innovative Services for the Communicatively Impaired [*Memphis State University*] [*Research center*] (RCD) ... CRISCI
Center for Research in Integrated Manufacturing [*University of Michigan*] [*Research center*] (RCD) ... CRIM
Center for Research in Management Science [*University of California*] (MCD) ... CRMS
Center for Research in Oral Biology [*University of Washington*] [*Research center*] (RCD) ... CROB
Center for Research in Psychotherapy (SAUO) ... CRP
Center for Research in Scientific Communication [*Johns Hopkins University*] (IID) ... CRSC
Center for Research in Scientific Documentation (SAUS) ... CRSD
Center for Research in Security Prices [*University of Chicago*] [*Chicago, IL*] [*Information service or system*] (IID) ... CRSP
Center for Research in Social Behavior [*University of Missouri - Columbia*] [*Research center*] (RCD) ... CRSB
Center for Research in Social Change [*Emory University, Atlanta, GA*] ... CRSC
Center for Research in Social Systems [*American University*] (MCD) ... CRESS

Center for Research in Social Systems of the American University (IEEE) .... CRESS/AU

Center for Research in Surface Science and Submicron Analysis [*Montana State University*] [*Research center*] (RCD) .... CRISS

Center for Research in System Sciences (SAUS) .... CRISS

Center for Research in the Hospitality Service Industries (EA) .... CRHSI

Center for Research in Water Resources [*University of Texas at Austin*] [*Research center*] (RCD) .... CRWR

Center for Research Initiatives and Strategies for the Communicatively Impaired [*Memphis State University*] [*Research center*] (RCD) .... CRISCI

Center for Research Libraries [*Library network*] (EA) .... CRL

Center for Research Libraries, Chicago, IL [*Inactive*] [*OCLC symbol*] (OCLC) .... CRL

Center for Research Libraries, Chicago, IL [*Library symbol*] [*Library of Congress*] (LCLS) .... ICRL

Center for Research on Economic Development [*University of Michigan*] [*Research center*] (RCD) .... CRED

Center for Research on Educational Accountability and Teacher Evaluation [*Western Michigan University*] [*Research center*] (RCD) .... CREATE

Center for Research on Effective Schooling for Disadvantaged Students [*Johns Hopkins University*] [*Research center*] (RCD) .... CDS

Center for Research on Evaluation, Standards, and Student Testing [*Los Angeles, CA*] [*Department of Education*] (GRD) .... CRESST

Center for Research on Industrial Strategy and Policy [*Illinois Institute of Technology*] [*Research center*] (RCD) .... CRISP

Center for Research on Judgment and Policy [*University of Colorado - Boulder*] [*Research center*] (RCD) .... CRJP

Center for Research on Language and Language Behavior [*University of Michigan*] [*Research center*] (RCD) .... CRLLB

Center for Research on Learning and Teaching [*University of Michigan*] [*Research center*] (RCD) .... CRLT

Center for Research on Multi-Ethnic Education [*University of Oklahoma*] [*Research center*] (RCD) .... CRME

Center for Research on Occupational and Environmental Toxicology [*Oregon Health Sciences University*] [*Research center*] (RCD) .... CROET

Center for Research on Parallel Computation (VERA) .... CRPC

Center for Research on Population and Security (SAUS) .... CRPS

Center for Research on Social Organization [*University of Michigan*] [*Research center*] (RCD) .... CRSO

Center for Research on Utilization of Scientific Knowledge [*University of Michigan*] .... CRUSK

Center for Research on Women [*Stanford University*] (RCD) .... CROW

Center for Research on Women [*Duke University*] [*Research center*] (RCD) .... CROW

Center for Resource Development in Adult Education [*University of Missouri - Kansas City*] [*Research center*] (RCD) .... CRD

Center for Resource Management (SAUO) .... CRM

Center for Resourceful Building Technology (SAUS) .... CRBT

Center for Respect of Life and Environment (GNE) .... CRLE

Center for Responsive Design [*Defunct*] (EA) .... CRD

Center for Responsive Governance (EA) .... CRG

Center for Responsive Politics (EA) .... CRP

Center for Responsive Psychology (EA) .... CRP

Center for Ressearch in System Development (SAUS) .... CRISD

Center for Robotic Systems in Microelectronics [*Research center*] (RCD) .... CRSM

Center for Rural Affairs (EA) .... CRA

Center for Rural Studies [*University of Vermont*] [*Research center*] (RCD) ...... CRS

Center for Russian and East European Jewry [*Later, CREEJ*] (EA) .... CFRJ

Center for Russian and East European Jewry (EA) .... CREEJ

Center for Russian and East European Studies [*University of Michigan*] [*Research center*] (RCD) .... CREES

Center for Russian and East European Studies [*University of Pittsburgh*] [*Research center*] (RCD) .... REES

Center for Safety in the Arts (PAZ) .... CSA

Center for Scholarly Editions [*Formerly, CEAA*] (EA) .... CSE

Center for Science and International Affairs [*Harvard University*] [*Research center*] .... CSIA

Center for Science and Technology for Development (SAUO) .... CSTD

Center for Science in the Public Interest (GNE) .... CSPI

Center for Science in the Public Interest (SAUS) .... Ctr Sci Pub

Center for Science Information (EA) .... CSI

Center for Scientific Anomalies Research [*Ann Arbor, MI*] .... CSAR

Center for Scientific Computing (SAUO) .... CSC

Center for Scientific Information on Vivisection (EA) .... CIVITAS

Center for Scientific Review [*National Institutes of Health*] .... CSR

Center for Seafarers' Rights (EA) .... CSR

Center for Security Policy (EA) .... CSP

Center for Self-Sufficiency (EA) .... CSS

Center for Semiarid Agroforestry (WPI) .... CSA

Center for Separation Science [*University of Arizona*] .... CSS

Center for Short-Lived Phenomena [*Cambridge, MA*] .... CFSLP

Center for Short-Lived Phenomena (EA) .... CSLP

Center for Short-Lived Phenomena, Miami (SAUO) .... CSLP

Center for Sickle Cell Disease (EA) .... CSCD

Center for Signals Warfare [*Warrenton, VA*] [*Army*] (GRD) .... CSW

Center for Slavic and East European Studies [*University of Connecticut*] [*Research center*] (RCD) .... CSEES

Center for Social Analysis [*State University of New York at Binghamton*] [*Research center*] (RCD) .... CSA

Center for Social and Behavior Science Research [*Research center*] (RCD) .... CSBSR

Center for Social Concerns (SAUS) .... CSC

Center for Social Epidemiology (ADWA) .... CSE

[*The*] Center for Social Gerontology (EA) .... TCSG

Center for Social Organization of Schools [*Department of Education*] [*Research center*] (GRD) .... CSOS

Center for Social Organization Studies [*University of Chicago*] [*Research center*] (RCD) .... CSOS

Center for Social Research [*City University of New York*] [*Research center*] (RCD) .... CSR

Center for Social Research [*Stanford University*] [*Research center*] (RCD) ..... CSR

Center for Social Research and Education (EA) .... CSRE

Center for Social Science Research and Documentation for the Arab Region [*UNESCO*] [*Information service or system*] (IID) .... ARCSS

Center for Social Studies Education (EA) .... CSSE

Center for Socialist History (EA) .... CSH

Center for Software Engineering [*Army*] .... CSE

Center for Solid State Electronics [*Arizona State University*] [*Research center*] (RCD) .... CSSER

Center for Solid State Electronics Research (SAUS) .... CSSER

Center for South and Southeast Asian Studies [*University of Michigan*] [*Research center*] (RCD) .... CSSEAS

Center for Southern Folklore (EA) .... CSF

Center for Soviet and East European Studies [*University of Connecticut*] [*Research center*] (RCD) .... CSEES

Center for Soviet-American Dialogue (EA) .... CSAD

Center for Space and Advanced Technology (SAUS) .... CSAT

Center for Space Environmental Health (SAUO) .... CSEH

Center for Space Policy, Inc. [*Cambridge, MA*] [*Telecommunications*] (TSSD) .... CSP

Center for Space Research [*Massachusetts Institute of Technology*] [*Research center*] (RCD) .... CSR

Center for Space Research and Applications [*University of Texas at Austin*] [*Research center*] (RCD) .... CSR

Center for Space Structures and Controls [*University of Colorado at Boulder*] [*Research center*] (RCD) .... CSSC

Center for Spatially Integrated Social Sciences (SAUO) .... CSISS

Center for Sports Sponsorship (EA) .... CSS

Center for Standards .... CFS

Center for State Employment Security Automated Systems .... CSESAS

Center for Statistical Consultation and Research .... CSCAR

Center for Statistics [*Later, CES*] [*Department of Education*] (IID) .... CS

Center for Strategic and International Studies [*Georgetown University*] .... CSIS

Center for Strategy Research, Inc. [*Information service or system*] (IID) .... CSR

Center for Student Testing, Evaluation, and Standards [*Later, CRESST*] [*Department of Education*] (GRD) .... CSTES

Center for Studies and Legislative Assistance (SAUO) .... CEAL

Center for Studies in Criminal Justice (EA) .... CSCJ

Center for Studies in Criminology and Criminal Law [*Later, SCSCCL*] (EA) .... CSCCL

Center for Studies in Demography and Ecology [*University of Washington*] [*Research center*] (RCD) .... CSDE

Center for Studies in Education and Human Development [*Gallaudet College*] [*Research center*] (RCD) .... CSEHD

Center for Studies in Language and Communication [*Gallaudet College*] [*Research center*] (RCD) .... CSLC

Center for Studies in Music Technology [*Yale University*] [*Research center*] (RCD) .... CSMT

Center for Studies of Ethnicity and Race in America [*University of Colorado at Boulder*] [*Research center*] (RCD) .... CSERA

Center for Studies of Mental Health of the Aging [*National Institute of Mental Health*] (GRD) .... CSMHA

Center for Studies of Nonlinear Dynamics [*Research center*] (RCD) .... CSND

Center for Studies of Suicide Prevention [*National Institute of Mental Health*] .... CSSP

Center for Studies, Research and Training in International Understanding and Cooperation (SAUO) .... CERFCI

Center for Study of Federalism [*Temple University*] [*Research center*] (RCD) .... CSF

Center for Study of Higher and Postsecondary Education [*University of Michigan*] [*Research center*] (RCD) .... CSHPE

Center for Study of Multiple Birth (EA) .... CSMB

Center for Study of Responsive Law (EA) .... CSRL

Center for Subatomic Structure of Matter [*Australia*] .... CSSM

Center for Substance Abuse Prevention [*Department of Health and Human Services*] .... CSAP

Center for Substance Abuse Research (SAUO) .... CESAR

Center for Substance Abuse Treatment [*Department of Health and Human Services*] .... CSAT

Center for Subsurface Modeling Support [*Environmental Protection Agency*] (AEPA) .... CSMoS

Center for Supercomputing Research and Development [*University of Illinois*] [*Urbana*] [*Information service or system*] (IID) .... CSRD

Center for Supplying Services by Redemptorists for North America ..... CSSRNA

Center for Surface Coatings Research [*Lehigh University*] .... CSCR

Center for Surrogate Parenting (EA) .... CSP

Center for Survey Methods Research [*Bureau of the Census*] (GFGA) ... CSMR

Center for Survey Research [*University of Massachusetts*] [*Research center*] (RCD) .... CSR

Center for Sustainable Agriculture (EA) .... CSA

Center for Sustainable Transportation (EA) .... CST

Center for System Engineering and Integration (SAUO) .... CENSEI

Center for Systems Engineering and Integration [*Army*] (GRD) .... CENSEI

Center for Systems Interoperability and Integration (SAUO) .... CSII

Center for Tactical Computer Systems [*CADPL*] [*Army*] (MCD) .... CENTACS

Center for Talented Youth [*Johns Hopkins University*] (PAZ) .... CTY

Center for Teaching about China (EA) .... CTAC

Center for Teaching Effectiveness [*University of Texas at Austin*] [*Research center*] (RCD) .... CTE

Center for Teaching International Relations .... CTIR
Center for Technical Services [Air Force] .... CTS
Center for Technological Industrial Development (SAUO) .... CDTI
Center for Technology and Administration [American University] [Research center] (RCD) .... CTA
Center for Technology, Environment, and Development [Clark University] .... CENTED
Center for Telecommunications Management [UCLA] (TSSD) ...... CTM
Center for Telecommunications Research [Columbia University] [New York, NY] [Telecommunications service] (TSSD) .... CTR
Center for Telecommunications Studies [Formerly, Broadcast Research Center] [Ohio University] [Research center] (RCD) .... CTS
Center for Telemedicine Law (SAUO) .... CTL
Center for Telephone Information [Laguna Hills, CA] [Telecommunications] (TSSD) .... CTI
Center for the Administration of Justice (SAUO) .... ADJUST
Center for the Advanced Study of Educational Administration .... CASEA
Center for the Advanced Study of Technology, United States International University (SAUO) .... CAST
Center for the Advancement of Community Based Public Health (SAUO) .... CACCBPH
Center for the Advancement of Electronic Health Records (ADWA) .... CAEHR
Center for the Advancement of Health (SAUO) .... CFAH
Center for the Advancement of Human Co-Operation (EA) .... CAHC
Center for the Advancement of Human Service Practice (EA) .... CAHSP
Center for the American Woman and Politics (EA) .... CAWP
Center for the Analysis of Public Issues [Princeton, NJ] .... CAPI
Center for the Application of Information Technology (SAUO) .... CAIT
Center for the Application of Mathematics (SAUO) .... CAM
Center for the Applied Behavioral Sciences [St. Louis University] [Research center] (RCD) .... CABS
Center for the Assessment and Monitoring of Forest and Environmental Resources [University of California, Berkeley] (GEOI) .... CAMFER
Center for the Biology of Natural Systems [Washington University] .... CBNS
Center for the Book in the Library of Congress (EA) .... CBLC
Center for the Coordination of Foreign Manuscript Copying [Library of Congress] .... CCFMC
Center for the Defense of Free Enterprise [Bellevue, WA] (EA) .... CDFE
Center for the Development of Human Resources in Rural Asia (EAIO) .... CENDHRRA
Center for the Education of Women .... CEW
Center for the Environment and Man, Inc. [Research center] (RCD) .... CEM
Center for the Exploitation of Science and Techology [British] .... CEST
Center for the History of American Needlework (EA) .... CHAN
Center for the Humanities [State University of New York at Albany] [Research center] (RCD) .... CHUM
Center for the Improvement of Reasoning in Early Childhood (EA) .... CIREC
Center for the Improvement of Student Learning .... CISL
Center for the Information Sciences (SAUO) .... CIS
Center for the Integrative Study of Animal Behavior (GVA) .... CISAB
Center for the Ministry of Teaching (EA) .... CMT
Center for the New Leadership (EA) .... CTNL
Center for the Progress of Peoples (EAIO) .... CPP
Center for the Promotion of Electoral Assistance (SAUO) .... CAPEL
Center for the Reproduction of Endangered Species .... CRES
Center for the Rights of Campus Journalists (EA) .... CRCJ
Center for the Rights of the Terminally Ill (EA) .... CRTI
Center for the Scientific Study of Religion (SAUS) .... Ctr Sci Study Rel
Center for the Social Sciences [Columbia University] [Research center] (RCD) .... CSS
Center for the Studies of Narcotic and Drug Abuse (SAUS) .... CSNDA
Center for the Study of African Archaeology (SAUO) .... CSAA
Center for the Study of Aging (EA) .... CSA
Center for the Study of American Business .... CSAB
Center for the Study of Architecture (SAUS) .... CSA
Center for the Study of Beadwork [An association] (EA) .... CSB
Center for the Study of Commercialism (EA) .... CSC
Center for the Study of Data Processing [Washington University] [Research center] (RCD) .... CSDP
Center for the Study of Democratic Institutions [Later, Robert Maynard HutchinsCenter for the Study of Democratic Institutions] (EA) .... CSDI
Center for the Study of Democratic Societies (EA) .... CSDS
Center for the Study of Development and Aging [University of Detroit] [Research center] (RCD) .... CSDA
Center for the Study of Drug Development [Tufts University] [Research center] (RCD) .... CSDD
Center for the Study of Drug Policy [NORML] [Absorbed by] (EA) .... CSDP
Center for the Study of Earth from Space [University of Colorado] [National Oceanic and Atmospheric Administration] [Research center] (GRD) .... CSES
Center for the Study of Economics [Columbia, MD] (EA) .... CSE
Center for the Study of Environmental Endocrine Effects (ADWA) .... CSEEE
Center for the Study of Ethics in the Professions [Illinois Institute of Technology] [Research center] (RCD) .... CSEP
Center for the Study of Evaluation [Department of Education] (GRD) .... CSE
Center for the Study of Evolution and the Origin of Life [University of California at Los Angeles] [Research center] (RCD) .... CSEOL
Center for the Study of Extraterrestrial Intelligence .... CSETI
Center for the Study of Foreign Affairs (EA) .... CSFA
Center for the Study of Futures Markets (SAUO) .... CSFM
Center for the Study of Human Rights (EA) .... CSHR
Center for the Study of Information and Education [Syracuse University] (IID) .... CSIE
Center for the Study of Instruction [of NEA] .... CSI
Center for the Study of Intelligence .... CSI

Center for the Study of Japanese Industry and Management of Technology (SAUO) .... JIMP
Center for the Study of Language and Information [Stanford University] [Research center] (RCD) .... CSLI
Center for the Study of Law and Politics (EA) .... CSLP
Center for the Study of Law and Society [University of California, Berkeley] [Research center] (RCD) .... CSLS
Center for the Study of Learning [Pittsburgh, PA] [Department of Education] (GRD) .... CSL
Center for the Study of Legal Authority and Mental Patient Status (EA) .... LAMP
Center for the Study of Liberal Education for Adults (EA) .... CSLEA
Center for the Study of Market Alternatives (EA) .... CSMA
Center for the Study of Multiple Gestation [Later, CSMB] (EA) .... CSMG
Center for the Study of Nigerian Languages (SAUO) .... CSNL
Center for the Study of Non-Medical Drug Use [Later, CSDP] (EA) .... CSNMDU
Center for the Study of Parent Involvement (EA) .... CSPI
Center for the Study of Parental Acceptance and Rejection [University of Connecticut] [Research center] (RCD) .... CSPAR
Center for the Study of Pharmacy and Therapeutics for the Elderly (EA) .... CSPTE
Center for the Study of Political Graphics [An association] .... CSPG
Center for the Study of Power [Later, SPI] (EA) .... CSP
Center for the Study of Race, Crime, and Social Policy [Cornell University] [Research center] (RCD) .... CSRCSP
Center for the Study of Random Geophysical Phenomena (SAUS) .... CEPRAG
Center for the Study of Reading [Later, RREC] [Department of Education] (GRD) .... CSR
Center for the Study of Responsive Law (GNE) .... CSRL
Center for the Study of Sensory Integrative Dysfunction [American Occupational Therapy Association] .... CSSID
Center for the Study of Social Policy (EA) .... CSSP
Center for the Study of the American Family Farm (EA) .... CSAFF
Center for the Study of the Authority and Mental Patient Status (SAUS) .... LAMP
Center for the Study of the College Fraternity (EA) .... CSCF
Center for the Study of the Evaluation of Instructional Programs .... CSEIP
Center for the Study of the Future (EA) .... CSF
Center for the Study of the Presidency (EA) .... CSP
Center for the Study of Urban Poverty (SAUS) .... CSUB
Center for the Study of Writing [Berkeley, CA] [Department of Education] (GRD) .... CSW
Center for the Survival of Western Democracies (EA) .... CSWD
Center for the Utilization of Federal Technology [National Technical Information Service] [Springfield, VA] .... CUFT
Center for the Well-Being of Health Professionals (EA) .... CWBHP
Center for Theoretical Studies [University of Miami] [Research center] (RCD) .... CTS
Center for Thermal/Fluids Engineering (SAUS) .... CTFE
Center for Third World Organizing (EA) .... CTWO
Center for Tissue Trauma Research and Education (EA) .... CTTRE
Center for Total Access [Army] .... CTA
Center for Toxicology and Environmental Health (SAUO) .... CTEH
Center for Trace Characterization [Texas A & M University] [Research center] (RCD) .... CTC
Center for Trade and Agricultural Policy (SAUO) .... CTAP
Center for Trade & Investment Services (SAUO) .... CTIS
Center for Training, Experimentation, and Research on Education (IID).... CPEIP
Center for Transportation Research [University of Texas at Austin] [Research center] (RCD) .... CTR
Center for Transportation Studies [Morgan State University] [Research center] (RCD) .... CTS
Center for Transportation Training and Research [Texas Southern University] [Research center] (RCD) .... CTTR
Center for Tropical Agriculture [University of Florida] [Research center] (RCD) .... CTA
Center for Tropical and Subtropical Aquaculture [Department of Agriculture] .... CTSA
Center for Tropical and Subtropical Architecture Planning and Construction [University of Florida] [Research center] (RCD) .... TROPARC
Center for Tropical Animal Health [Texas A & M University] [Research center] (RCD) .... CTAH
Center for Turbulence Research (ACAE) .... CTR
Center for UFO [Unidentified Flying Object] Studies [Information service or system] (IID) .... CUFOS
Center for Ulcer Research and Education [University of California, Los Angeles] [Research center] (RCD) .... CURE
Center for UN Reform Education (EA) .... CUNRE
Center for UN Reform Education (EA) .... CURE
Center for UN Studies (EAIO) .... CUNS
Center for Urban Affairs and Community Services [North Carolina State University] [Research center] (RCD) .... CUACS
Center for Urban Analysis (SAUS) .... CUA
Center for Urban and Regional Affairs [University of Minnesota] [Research center] (RCD) .... CURA
Center for Urban and Regional Studies (EA) .... CURS
Center for Urban Black Studies (EA) .... CUBS
Center for Urban Economics Development [University of Illinois at Chicago] [Research center] (RCD) .... CUED
Center for Urban Education [Research center] (RCD) .... CUE
Center for Urban Environmental Studies (EA) .... CUES
Center for Urban Policy [Loyola University of Chicago] [Research center] (RCD) .... CUP
Center for Urban Programs [St. Louis University] [Research center] (RCD) .... CUP
Center for Urban Programs and Research [St. Louis University] [Research center] (RCD) .... CUPR

Center for Urban Studies [*Wayne State University*] [*Research center*]
(RCD) .... CUS
Center for Urban Studies [*University of Chicago*] [*Research center*] (RCD) ..... CUS
Center for US Capital Markets (EA) .... CUSCM
Center for US-USSR Initiatives (EA) .... CUSUSSRI
Center for US-USSR Initiatives (EAIO) .... CUUI
Center for Venture Research (EA) .... CVR
Center for Veterinary Biologics (SAUO) .... CVB
Center for Veterinary Medicine [*Food and Drug Administration*] .... CVM
Center for Vietnamese Studies [*Southern Illinois University at Carbondale*]
[*Research center*] (RCD) .... CVS
Center for Violence and Injury Control (ADWA) CVIC
Center for Visual History (SAUS) .... CVH
Center for Visual Science [*University of Rochester*] [*Research center*]
(RCD) .... CVS
Center for Vocational and Technical Education, Ohio State University,
Columbus, OH [*Inactive*] [*OCLC symbol*] (OCLC) .... CVT
Center for Vocational and Technical Education, Ohio State University,
Columbus, OH [*Library symbol*] [*Library of Congress*] (LCLS) .... OCoV
Center for Vocational, Technical, and Adult Education [*University of
Wisconsin - Stout*] [*Research center*] (RCD) .... CVTAE
Center for War, Peace, and the News Media (EA) .... CWPNM
Center for War, Peace and the News Media (SAUO) .... CWPNM
Center for War/Peace Studies (EA) .... CW/PS
Center for Waste Reduction Technologies (EA) .... CWRT
Center for Water and Environment [*University of Minnesota*] .... CWE
Center for Water Policy [*International Ground Water Modeling Center*] .... CWP
Center for Water Resources Research [*University of Nevada*] .... CWRR
Center for Welding Research [*Ohio State University*] [*Research center*]
(RCD) .... CWR
Center for Wildlife Ecology (SAUO) .... CFE
Center for Wildlife Ecology (SAUO) .... CWE
Center for Women and Sport [*Defunct*] (EA) .... CWS
Center for Women Policy Studies (EA) .... CWPS
Center for Women's Studies and Services (EA) .... CWSS
Center for Wooden Boats (EA) .... CWB
Center for World Christian Interaction (EA) .... CWCI
Center for World Thanksgiving (EA) .... CWT
Center for Youth and Social Development [*India*] (EAIO) .... CYSD
Center for Zoroastrian Research (EA) .... CZR
Center for/of Documentation and Research on Peace and Conflict
(SAUO) .... CDRPC
Center Forward [*Soccer*] .... CF
Center Frequency .... CF
Center Frequency (SAUS) .... C/F
Center Frequency (MSA) .... CTRF
Center Frequency Modulation .... CFM
Center Frequency Stabilization [*Radio*] .... CFS
Center Front (SAUS) .... CF
Center Groove Two Edges [*Lumber*] (DAC) CG2E
Center Half (SAUS) .... CH
Center Halfback [*Soccer*] .... CH
Center Halfback [*Soccer*] .... CHB
Center High-Mounted Stop Lamp [*Pronounced "chimsel"*] [*Automotive
engineering*] .... CHMSL
Center (Hospital and Domiciliary) [*Veterans Administration*] .... C(H & D)
Center Hospital and Domiciliary (SAUS) .... CH&D
Center Housing Rotating Assembly [*Automotive engineering*] .... CHRA
Center Information Network [*Support servicing center*] (SSD) .... CIN
Center International de Vol Libre [*Aguessac, France*] (EAIO) CIVL
Center International des Civilisations Bantu (EAIO) .... CICB
Center Island [*Nuclear energy*] (NRCH) CI
Center Island Vessel [*Nuclear energy*] (NRCH) CIV
Center Landing Gear (MCD) .... CLG
Center Launch and Flight Instrumentation Center [*NASA*] (KSC) ...... CLFIC
Center Left [*Theatrical term*] (WDMC) CL
Center Light [*Aviation*] (DA) .... C/L
Center Line CL
Center Line Average .... CLA
Center Line Bend (MSA) .... CLB
Center Line Block [*Philately*] .... CLB
Center Line Data (GEOI) .... CLD
Center Matched [*Technical drawings*] .... CM
Center Materials Representative [*NASA*] (NASA) .... CMR
Center Moriches Free Public Library, Center Moriches, NY [*Library symbol*]
[*Library of Congress*] (LCLS) .... NCm
Center Moriches, NY [*FM radio station call letters*] (BROA) .... WLVG-FM
Center of Advanced Studies (SAUO) .... CAS
Center of Advanced Technology in Electronic Imaging Systems [*New York
State Science and Technology Foundation*] (RDA) .... CAT-EIS
Center of Buoyancy .... CB
Center of Burst (SAUS) .... CB
Center of Concern (EA) CC
Center of Effort [*Sailing*] .... CE
Center of Electoral Assistance and Promotion (SAUO) .... CEPAL
Center of Excellence for Document Analysis and Recognition (SAUS) .... CEDAR
Center of Experimentation in the Pacific Ocean (BARN) .... CEP
Center of Figure [*Topographical coordinate system*] .... COF
Center of Filtering and Plotting (NATG) .... CFP
Center of Flotation .... CF
Center of Fruiting Period [*Ecology*] .... CFP
Center of Genetic Diversity .... CGD
Center of Gravity .... CG
Center of Gravity .... C of G
Center of Gravity .... COG

Center of Gravity above Keel (MCD) .... KG
Center of Gravity Factor (SAUS) .... CGF
Center of Health Technology (SAUO) .... CHT
Center of Impact CI
Center of Influence [*Military*] .... COI
Center of Innovative Computer Applications (VERA) .... CICA
Center Of Interest (SAUS) .... COI
Center of International Studies [*MIT*] [*Research center*] (MCD) .... CIS
Center of Lateral Resistance (IAA) .... CLR
Center of Lift CL
Center of Macula (SAUS) .... COM
Center of Marine Biology [*University of Maryland*] .... COMB
Center of Marine Biotechnology [*Marine science*] (OSRA) .... COMB
Center of Mass [*Atomic physics*] .... CM
Center of Mass (NAKS) .... cm
Center of Mass .... C of M
Center of Mass [*Coordinate system*] (MCD) .... COM
Center of Mass System (SAUS) .... CMS
Center of Military History (AABC) .... CMH
Center of Momentum (SAUS) .... CM
Center of Naval Warfare Studies (SAUO) .... CNWS
Center of Nuclear Image (DMAA) .... CNI
Center of Pillar .... CPLR
Center of Pressure .... CP
Center of Pressure Back .... CPB
Center of Programmed Instruction (DIT) .... CPI
Center of Radio Astronomy and Astrophysics Mackenzie University
(SAUO) .... CRAAM
Center of Research in Administrative Sciences [*University of Moncton*]
[*Research center*] (RCD) .... CRSA
Center of Resistance .... CR
Center of Rotation .... COR
Center of Science and Industry [*Ohio*] (AEBS) .... COSI
Center of Scientific and Technological Information (SAUS) .... COSTI
Center of Technical Excellence [*Army*] (RDA) .... CTX
Center of the Earth (SAUS) .... O
Center of the New Information Processing Technologies [*Russia*] (DDC) ..... CNIT
center of visual impact (SAUS) cvi
Center on Aging [*University of Maryland*] [*Research center*] (RCD) .... COA
Center on Budget and Policy Priorities (EA) .... CBPP
Center on Destructive Cultism (EA) .... CDC
Center on Human Policy (EA) .... CHP
Center on International Race Relations [*University of Denver*] .... CIRR
Center on Law and Pacifism [*Defunct*] (EA) .... CLP
Center on National Labor Policy (EA) .... CNLP
Center on Religion and Society [*Rockford Institute*] (EA) .... CRS
Center on Social Welfare Policy and Law (EA) .... CSWPL
Center on Technology and Society, Inc. [*Research center*] (RCD) ...... CTS
Center on the Consequences of Nuclear War (EA) .... CCNW
Center on Transnational Corporations [*United Nations*] .... CTC
Center on War and the Child (EA) .... CWC
Center Operations Area .... COA
Center Operations Directorate (MCD) .... COD
Center (or Centre) Drill (SAUS) .... CDRILL
Center (or Centre) for Earth Observation (SAUO) .... CEO
Center (or Centre) for Field Research (SAUO) .... CFR
Center (or Centre) for Futures Research (SAUO) .... CFR
Center (or Centre) for Geographical Information and Analysis (SAUO) .... CGIA
Center (or Centre) for Global Education (SAUO) .... CGE
Center (or Centre) for Operations Research and Econometrics (SAUO) ..... CORE
Center (or Centre) for Southeast Asian Studies (SAUO) .... CSEAS
Center (or Centre) for Technical Geoscience (SAUO) .... CTG
Center (or Centre) of Filtering and Plotting (SAUO) .... CFP
Center Overage Pending Assignment (MCD) .... COPA
Center Pivot Irrigation System .... CPIS
Center po Atomn. i Jadernum Dannym [*Center for Nuclear Structure and
Reaction Data*] [*USSR State Committee on the Utilization of Atomic Energy*]
[*Information service or system*] (IID) .... CAJAD
Center Point, TX [*Location identifier*] [*FAA*] (FAAL) .... CSI
Center pour les Droits de l'Homme [*Center for Human Rights*] [*Switzerland*]
(EAIO) .... CDH
Center Pressure Index .... CPI
Center Program Director [*NASA*] (KSC) .... CPD
Center Program Manager [*NASA*] (KSC) .... CPM
Center Projects Working Group (SAUO) .... CPWG
Center Punch (MSA) .... CP
Center Range Control Station [*NASA*] (KSC) .... CRCS
Center (Regional Office and Hospital) [*Veterans Administration*] .... C(RO & H)
Center (Regional Office and Insurance) [*Veterans Administration*] ...... C(RO & INS)
Center Right [*Theatrical term*] (WDMC) .... CR
Center Science Assessment Team [*NASA*] .... CSAT
Center Section .... CS
Center Special Slotted Container [*Packaging*] .... CSSC
Center Stage [*A stage direction*] .... CS
Center Stage Back [*A stage direction*] .... CSB
Center Stage Front [*A stage direction*] .... CSF
Center Standards Officer [*Job Corps*] .... CSO
Center Street Elementary School, Williston Park, NY [*Library symbol*]
[*Library of Congress*] (LCLS) .... NWpCsE
Center Tank (RIMS) .... ce Ta
Center Tap [*Technical drawings*] .... CT
Center Thickness [*Optics*] .... CT
Center to Center .... C-C
Center to Center [*Technical drawings*] .... C to C
Center to End .... C to E

Center to Face (SAUS) .... C to F
Center to Prevent Handgun Violence (EA) .... CPHV
Center to Protect Workers' Rights (SARE) .... CPWR
Center to Study Human-Animal Relationships and Environments [*University of Minnesota*] [*Research center*] (RCD) .... CENSHARE
Center Tracon Automation System [*FAA*] (PS) .... CTAS
Center Traffic Management Advisor [*FAA*] (TAG) ...... CTMA
Center Trust [*NYSE symbol*] (SG) .... CTA
Center Trust Retail Properties [*Formerly, Alexander Haagen Properties*] [*AMEX symbol*] .... ACH
Center, TX [*Location identifier*] [*FAA*] (FAAL) .... CZJ
Center, TX [*AM radio station call letters*] .... KDET
Center, TX [*FM radio station call letters*] .... KDET-FM
Center Vee One Side [*Lumber*] (DAC) CV1S
Center Vee Two Sides [*Lumber*] (DAC) CV2S
Center Voltage Range Element (SAUS) .... CVRE
Center Weather Advisory [*FAA*] (TAG) .... CWA
Center Weather Service Unit [*FAA*] (TAG) .... CWSU
Center Wireless Station (SAUS) .... CWS
Center Work System [*NASA*] (KSC) .... CWS
Centerboard (MSA) .... CNTBRD
Center-Clipping Echo Suppressor (MCD) .... CCES
Center-Cracked Tension (MCD) .... CCT
Centerfold .... Cent
Centering (SAUS) .... CENT
Centering .... CTRG
Centerior Energy [*NYSE symbol*] (SAG) CX
Centerior Energy Corp. [*Associated Press*] (SAG) .... CentEn
Centerless Ground (DNAB) .... CG
Centerline (WDMC) C
Centerline (FAAC) .... CNTRLN
Centerline Contractors & Engineers (EFIS) .... CC&E
Centerline Light [*Aviation*] (DA) CL
Centerline Lighting Will be Provided [*Aviation*] (DA) .. CLL
Centerline of Occupant [*Automotive engineering*] ...... CLO
Center-Line Plotting (MCD) .... CLPLOT
Centerline Vertical Keel .... CVK
Center-Mounted Thermistor (SAUS) .... CMT
Centerns Kvinnoforbund [*Women's Association of the Centre Party*] [*Sweden*] [*Political party*] (EAIO) .... CKF
Center-of-Gravity Locator .... CGL
Center-of-Inertia System .... CIS
Centerpartiet [*Center Party*] [*Sweden*] [*Political party*] (PPE) .... CP
CenterPoint Prop TrSBI [*NYSE symbol*] (SG) .... CNT
CenterPoint Properties [*AMEX symbol*] (SPSG) .... CNT
Centerpoint Properties Corp. [*Associated Press*] (SAG) .. CentrpPr
Centers [*Commonly used*] (OPSA) .... CENTERS
Centers [*Postal Service standard*] (OPSA) .... CTRS
Centers and Regional Associations (EA) .... CARA
Centers for Disease Control [*Formerly, Communicable Disease Center*] [*Department of Health and Human Services*] [*Atlanta, GA*] .... CDC
Centers for Disease Control and Prevention .... CDC
Centers for Disease Control and Prevention. Epidemiology Program Office (SAUO) .... EPO
Centers for Disease Control/Centers for Disease Control Prevention .... CDC/CDCP
Centers for Education and Research in Therapeutics [*FDA*] .. CERT
Centers for Health, Education, and Social Systems Studies [*Formerly, Center for H ealth and Social Systems Research*] [*Research center*] (RCD) .... CHESS
Centers for Radiological Physics .... CRP
Centers for the Analysis of Science and Technical Information (NITA) ..... CASTI
Centers for the Commercial Development of Space ... CCDS
Centers of Excellence [*Army*] (RDA) .... COE
Centers of Excellence [*Marine science*] (OSRA) .... COEs
Centerville and Center Township Library, Centerville, IN [*Library symbol*] [*Library of Congress*] (LCLS) .... InCe
Centerville Community College [*Iowa*] CCC
Centerville, IA [*AM radio station call letters*] .... KCOG
Centerville, IA [*FM radio station call letters*] .... KMGO
Centerville, IN [*AM radio station call letters*] .... WHON
Centerville, OH [*FM radio station call letters*] .... WCWT
Centerville Public Library, Centerville, MA [*Library symbol*] [*Library of Congress*] (LCLS) .... MCen
Centerville, TN [*Location identifier*] [*FAA*] (FAAL) .... GHM
Centerville, TN [*AM radio station call letters*] .... WNKX
Centerville, TN [*FM radio station call letters*] ..... WNKX-FM
Centerville, UT [*FM radio station call letters*] .... KCPX
Centerville, UT [*AM radio station call letters*] (RBYB) .. KCPX-AM
Centerville, UT [*FM radio station call letters*] .... KUMT
Centesimo [*or Centimo*] [*Monetary unit in many Spanish-American countries*] .... CTMO
Centex Construction Prod [*NYSE symbol*] (TTSB) ...... CXP
Centex Construction Products [*Associated Press*] (SAG) .. CentxCn
Centex Construction Products [*NYSE symbol*] (SAG) ... CXP
Centex Corp. [*Associated Press*] (SAG) .... Centex
Centex Corp. [*NYSE symbol*] (TTSB) .... CTX
Centi [*A prefix meaning divided by 100*] [*SI symbol*] c
centi (SAUS) c
Centibar (ADWA) .... cb
Centibar .... CB
Centibel (SAUS) .... Cb
Centibels [*Telecommunications*] .... Cb
Centified Professional Public Buyer (AAGC) .... CPPB
Centigrade [*Celsius*] [*Temperature scale*] C

Centigrade [*Celsius*] [*Temperature scale*] (KSC) .... CENT
Centigrade [*Celsius*] [*Temperature scale*] (ROG) ..... CENTIG
Centigrade Heat Unit .... CHU
Centigrade Thermal Unit .... CTU
Centigram C
Centigram (NTIO) .... cg
Centigram .... Cg
Centigram .... CGM
Centigram Communications [*NASDAQ symbol*] (SPSG) .. CGRM
Centigram Communications Corp. [*Associated Press*] (SAG) .. Centgrm
Centigrams (ROG) CC
Centigray [*Radiation therapy*] (ADDR) .... CGY
centiGrey (SAUS) .... cGy
centiliter (SAUS) cl
Centiliter (GPO) CL
Centiliter (ADWA) cl
centilitre (SAUS) cl
Centillium Communic. [*NASDAQ symbol*] .... CTLM
Centime [*Monetary unit*] [*France*] C
Centime [*Monetary unit*] [*France*] .... CENT
Centimes [*Monetary unit*] [*France*] (GPO) .... ces
Centimes (EBF) .... Cts
Centimeter C
Centimeter (MAE) .... cent
Centimeter (GPO) .... cm
centimeter (SAUS) .... cm
Centimeter, Gram, Second (SAUS) .... CGS
Centimeter Height-Finder [*RADAR*] .... CMH
Centimeter per Second [*Measurement*] (DAVI) .... cm/s
Centimeter-Candle .... CM C
Centimeter-Gram-Second (IDOE) .... cgs
Centimeter-Gram-Second [*System of units*] (AAG) ..... CGS
Centimeter-Gram-Second Electrostatic (SAUS) .... CGSE
Centimeter-Gram-Second Magnetic (SAUS) .... CGSM
Centimeter-Gram-Second Unit .... CGSU
Centimeter-Gram-Second-Biot (SAUS) .... CGSB
Centimeter-Gram-Second-Biot [*System of units*] .... cm-g-s-Bi
Centimeter-Gram-Second-Electromagnetic .... CGSM
Centimeter-Gram-Second-Electrostatic .... CGSE
Centimeter-Gram-Second-Franklin (SAUS) .... CGSF
Centimeter-Gram-Second-Franklin [*System of units*] .. cm-g-s-Fr
centimeters (SAUS) .... cent
centimeters (SAUS) .... cm
Centimeters of Water [*Cuff pressure*] [*Medicine*] (DAVI) .. CmH_2O
Centimeters of Water Pressure [*Measurement*] (DAVI) .. CWP
Centimeters per Second .... CMPS
Centimeters per Second (DMAA) .... cmps
Centimeters per Second [*Telecommunications*] (TEL) .. CM/SEC
Centimetre (SAUS) .... cm
centimetre cube (SAUS) .... cmc
Centimetre Height (SAUS) .... CMH
Centimetre-Gramme-Second- Electrostatic (SAUS) .. CGSE
Centimetric Early Warning RADAR (IAA) .... CEWR
Centimo (ADWA) .... ctmo
Centimorgan [*Unit of genetic map distance*] .... cM
centimorgan (SAUS) .... cM
Centimorgan [*Unit of genetic map distance*] (MAE) ...... cMo
Centipig (SAUS) .... cp
Centipoise (STED) .... cp
Centipoise (ABAC) .... cP
Centipoise [*Unit of viscosity*] .... CP
Centipoise [*Unit of viscosity*] .... CPS
Centipoise (BARN) .... cpse
Centissime (ROG) C
Centistere [*Metric*] .... CS
Centistoke (BARN) .... ck
Centistoke (STED) .... cS
Centistoke [*Also, cSt*] [*Unit of kinematic viscosity*] .... cs
Centistoke [*Also, cs*] [*Unit of kinematic viscosity*] ...... cSt
Centistokes [*Unit of kinematic viscosity*] .... CKS
Centl Hispano Cap 10.50% Pref [*NYSE symbol*] (TTSB) .. HCLPr
Centl Hispano Intl9.875% 'MIPS' [*NYSE symbol*] (TTSB) .. HPNPr
Centner (SAUS) .... Ctr
Cento [*Composition compiled from other works*] C
CENTO [*Central Treaty Organization*] Institute of Nuclear Science (EY) .... CINS
CENTO [*Central Treaty Organization*] Military Communications System (MCD) .... CMCS
Cento Nuptialis [*of Ausonius*] [*Classical studies*] (OCD) .. Cent Nupt
Centocelle [*Italy*] [*ICAO location identifier*] (ICLI) .... LIRC
Centocor, Inc. [*Associated Press*] (SAG) .... Centocor
Centocor, Inc. [*NASDAQ symbol*] (NQ) .... CNTO
Centra Dana Esperantista Ligo (SAUO) .... CDEL
Centra Oficejo (SAUO) .... CO
Centraide, Montreal, PQ, Canada [*Library symbol*] [*Library of Congress*] (LCLS) .... CaOMCCS
Centraide, Montreal, PQ, Canada [*Library symbol*] [*Library of Congress*] (LCLS) .... CaQMCCS
Centraide, Montreal, Quebec [*Library symbol*] [*National Library of Canada*] (NLC) .... QMCCS
Central C
Central (SSD) .... CE
Central [*Alaska*] [*Airport symbol*] (OAG) .... CEM
Central (BEE) .... cen
Central (AAGC) .... Cent
Central (NTIO) .... cent

Central	CENT
Central (ROG)	CENTR
Central	CNTL
Central (VRA)	cntr
Central (MSA)	CTL
Central	CTRL
Central (AL)	Ctrl
Central [Wisconsin] [Airport symbol] (AD)	WIS
Central Abstracting and Indexing Service [American Petroleum Institute] [Information service or system] (IID)	CAIS
Central Academy of Information Technology (VERA)	CAIT
Central Access Monitor Program (NITA)	CAMP
Central Access Routing [Computer science] (VERA)	CAR
Central Accounting Office [Military] (AFM)	CAO
Central Accounting Officer (SAUS)	CAO
Central Accounts Division (SAUO)	CAD
Central Accounts Records Officer (SAUS)	CARO
Central Action Office [Army]	CAO
Central Acts, India [A publication] (DLA)	India Cen Acts
Central Address Buffer Register (SAUS)	CABR
Central Address Memory [Computer science]	CAM
Central Address Register (SAUS)	CAR
Central Administrative Support Center [Marine science] (OSRA)	CASC
Central Advisory Committee (SAUO)	CAC
Central Advisory Committee [British]	CAC
Central Advisory Council for Education (SAUO)	CACE
Central Advisory Council for Science and Technology [British]	CACST
Central Advisory Council of Training for the Ministry (SAUO)	CACTM
Central Advisory Service (SAUO)	CAS
Central Aero-Hydrodynamical Institute [Former USSR]	CAHI
Central Aerohydrodynamics Institute (SAUS)	TAGSI
Central Aero-Hydrodynamics Institute (SAUS)	TsAGI
Central Aerological Observatory (SAUS)	CAO
Central Aerospace Rescue and Recovery Center [Air Force]	CARRC
Central Africa	CAfr
Central Africa (SAUS)	Cent Afr
Central Africa Building Society (SAUO)	CABS
Central Africa Party (SAUO)	CAP
Central Africa Party [Southern Rhodesia]	CAP
Central Africa Protectorate [British government]	CAP
Central Africa Standard (SAUS)	CAS
Central African Airways Corp.	CAA
Central African Broadcasting Station (SAUO)	CABS
Central African Customs and Economic Union (SAUS)	UDEAC
Central African Customs and Economic Union (EBF)	UNDEAC
Central African Empire [Later, CAR]	CAE
Central African Federation [Disbanded Dec. 31, 1963]	CAF
Central African Federation (SAUO)	C Afr Fed
Central African Franc (SAUS)	CAF
Central African Mineral Recources Development Centre (SAUO)	CAMRDC
Central African Mineral Resources Development Centre [Congo] (EAIO)	CAMRDC
Central African Regiment [British military] (DMA)	CAR
Central African Regional Program for the Environment (SAUO)	CARPE
Central African Republic [ANSI three-letter standard code] (CNC)	CAF
Central African Republic	CAfrRep
Central African Republic (SAUO)	CAR
Central African Republic	CAR
Central African Republic (WDAA)	CEN AFR REP
Central African Republic (VRA)	Cent Afr Rep
Central African Republic [ANSI two-letter standard code] (CNC)	CF
Central African Republic [MARC country of publication code] [Library of Congress] (LCCP)	cx
Central African Republic [MARC geographic area code] [Library of Congress] (LCCP)	f-cx-
Central African Republic [International civil aircraft marking] (ODBW)	TL
Central After Care Association [British]	CACA
Central After-Care Association (SAUO)	CACA
Central Agramonte [Cuba] [ICAO location identifier] (ICLI)	MUAG
Central Aguirre Sugar Company (SAUO)	CEG
Central Air Conditioning [Classified advertising] (CDAI)	C/A
Central Air Conditioning (REAL)	c/a
Central Air Conditioning [Classified advertising]	CAC
Central Air Conditioning [Classified advertising]	CENT
central air conditioning (SAUS)	cent/air
Central Air Conditioning (REAL)	cent/air
Central Air Data Computer	CADC
Central Air Data Computer / Central Computer (PDAA)	CADC/CC
Central Air Data Computer Test Set	CADCTS
Central Air Data Subsystem (SAUS)	CADS
Central Air Data System [Air Force]	CADS
Central Air Defense Force	CADF
Central Air Documents Office [Air Force]	CADO
Central Air Force, Command (SAUS)	CENTAF
Central Air Forces	CENTAF
Central Air Materiel Area, Europe	CAMAE
Central Air Medical Board (SAUO)	CAMB
Central Air Procurement District	CEAPD
Central Air Traffic Control School (SAUO)	CATCS
Central Air Transport	CATR
Central Air Transport Corporation (SAUO)	CATC
Central Airborne Performance Analyzer (MCD)	CAPA
Central Aircraft Dispatch	CAD
Central Aircraft Manufacturing Company (SAUO)	CAMCO
Central Aircrew Medical Review Board [Military] (AFM)	CAMRB

Central Airlines, Inc.	CEN
Central Airlines, Inc.	CN
Central Airlines, Inc. [ICAO designator] (FAAC)	CTL
Central Airlines Ltd. [Nigeria] [ICAO designator] (ICDA)	HU
Central Airways (SAUO)	CA
Central Airways [Medicine] (DMAA)	CAW
Central Airways Corp. (AAG)	CA
Central Airways Corp. [Canada] [ICAO designator] (FAAC)	CEN
Central Alarm Station (IEEE)	CAS
Central Alarm System (NUCP)	CARS
Central Alarm System (NRCH)	CAS
Central Alarm Unit (SAUS)	CAU
Central Alaska Time (VERA)	CAT
Central Allied Tactical Air Command (SAUS)	CATAC
Central Altitude Reservation Facility [or Function]	CARF
Central Altitude Reservation Function [FAA] (TAG)	CARF
Central Amancio Rodriguez [Cuba] [ICAO location identifier] (ICLI)	MUFC
Central America	CA
Central America (SAUO)	CAm
Central America	CENTAM
Central America [MARC geographic area code] [Library of Congress] (LCCP)	nc---
Central America and Panama (IID)	CAP
Central America Health Rights Network (SAUO)	CAHRN
Central America Information Center [An association] (EA)	CAIC
Central America Information Office [Defunct] (EA)	CAMINO
Central America Monetary Union (SAUO)	CAMU
Central America Peace Campaign [Defunct] (EA)	CAPC
Central America Research Institute (EA)	CARIN
Central America Resource Center (EA)	CARC
Central America Resource Center, Austin (SAUO)	CARC
Central America Services (SAUO)	CAS
Central America Task Force (EA)	CATF
Central America Week	CAW
Central American (VRA)	Cent Am
Central American Airways (SAUO)	CAA
Central American Airways [Air carrier designation symbol]	CAAX
Central American and Caribbean Sports Organization (EAIO)	CACSO
Central American and Mexico Coniferous Resources Cooperative (GNE)	CAMCORE
Central American Association of Families of Disappeared Persons [See also ACAFADE] [San Jose, Costa Rica] (EAIO)	CAAFDP
Central American Association of Shipowners (SAUO)	ACAMAR
Central American Bank for Economic Integration	CABEI
Central American Bureau (SAUO)	CAB
Central American Center for Economic and Social Documentation (SAUO)	CEDESC
Central American Clearing House (EBF)	CAGH
Central American Club of New York (EA)	CAC
Central American Commission for Environment and Development (SAUO)	CCAD
Central American Committee for Human Rights [British] (EAIO)	CACHR
Central American Common Market (BARN)	CACM
Central American Common Market	CACOM
Central American Common Market (EBF)	CACUM
Central American Confederation of Workers (EAIO)	CACW
Central American Cooperative Corn Improvement Project (SAUO)	CACIP
Central American Council for Tourism (SAUO)	CCT
Central American Defence Council. Latin America (SAUO)	CONDECA
Central American Defense Council (SAUO)	CADC
Central American Development Coordination Council	CADCC
Central American Development Organization (SAUO)	CADO
Central American Economic Council (SAUO)	CEC
Central American Economics Association	CAEA
Central American Energy Commission (EAIO)	CAEC
Central American Federation (SAUO)	CAF
Central American Free Trade Area	CAFTA
Central American Human Rights Committee [British]	CAHRC
Central American Indian [MARC language code] [Library of Congress] (LCCP)	cai
Central American Institute for Public Administration (SAUO)	CAIPA
Central American Integration Secretariat (SAUO)	CAIS
Central American International [Air carrier designation symbol]	CAIX
Central American Mission (SAUO)	CAM
Central American Monetary Council	CAMC
Central American Monetary Stabilization Fund (SAUO)	CAMSF
Central American Parliament (SAUS)	Parlacen
Central American Protected Areas System (SAUO)	CAPAS
Central American Refugee Center (EA)	CARECEN
Central American Refugee Defense Fund (SAUO)	CARDF
Central American Regional Communications Network (SAUO)	CARCN
Central American republic of El Salvador (VRA)	Salvador
Central American Research Institute for Industrial Technology (SAUS)	ICAITI
Central American Research Institute for Industry (SAUO)	CAIT
Central American Research Station (SAUO)	CARS
Central American Society of Pharmacology [Panama] (EAIO)	CASP
Central American Tropical [In CATHOUSES, a reference to temporary US Army barracks in Honduras, 1984]	CAT
Central America-USA Alliance	CONCAUSA
Central Ammunition Depot (NATG)	CAD
Central Ammunition Management Office (SAUO)	CAMO
Central Ammunition Management Office - Pacific [Army] (MCD)	CAMO-P
Central Ammunition Management Office - Pacific [Army] (AABC)	CAMO-PAC
Central Ammunition Supply Status Point	CASSP
Central Amplifier Station [Telecommunications] (OA)	CAS

Central Analog Data Distributing and Computing System (KSC) ... CADDAC
Central Analysis Center (SAUS) ... CAC
Central and Associated Chambers of Agriculture (SAUS) ... CACA
Central and Associated Chambers of Agriculture (SAUO) ... CACA
Central and East European Education and University Systems (SAUO) ... CEUS
Central and East European Law Institute (SAUO) ... CEELI
Central and East European Publishing Project (SAUO) ... CEEPP
Central and East European Studies Association of Canada [*See also AEECEEC*] ... CEESAC
Central and East European Working Group for the Enhancement of Biodiversity (SAUO) ... CEEWEB
Central and Eastern Europe (SAUO) ... C&EE
Central and Eastern Europe ... CEE
Central and Eastern European Academic and Research Networking Organization (TELE) ... CEENet
Central and Eastern European Copyright User Platform (TELE) ... CECUP
Central and Eastern European Countries (SAUO) ... CEECs
Central and Eastern European Countries EDIFACT Board (SAUO) ... CEECEB
Central and Eastern European Country (ECON) ... CEEC
Central and Eastern Pacific Detailed Planning Group (SAUO) ... CEPDPG
Central and Eastern Pacific Panel (SAUO) ... CEPAC
Central and Local Trades Committees [*Australia*] ... CLTC
Central & So. West [*NYSE symbol*] (TTSB) ... CSR
Central and South African Basic Encyclopedia [*A publication*] ... CSABE
Central & South West Corp. [*Associated Press*] (SAG) ... CenSoWst
Central & South West Corp. [*NYSE symbol*] (SPSG) ... CSR
Central & Southern Holding [*NASDAQ symbol*] (TTSB) ... CSBC
Central & Southern Holding Co. [*NASDAQ symbol*] (NQ) ... CSBC
Central & Southern Holding Co. [*Associated Press*] (SAG) ... CtlSou
Central and Southern Line Islands [*gb (Gilbert Islands) used in records cataloged after October 1978*] [*MARC country of publication code*] [*Library of Congress*] (LCCP) ... ln
Central and Southern Line Islands [*MARC geographic area code*] [*Library of Congress*] (LCCP) ... poln-
Central & Southern Motor Freight Tariff Association, Inc. ... CSMFTA
Central & Southern Motor Freight Tariff Association, Inc., Louisville KY [*STAC*] ... CSA
Central Angle (SAUS) ... CA
Central Annunciator Display Panel (MCD) ... CADP
Central Apollo Data Index [*NASA*] (MCD) ... CADI
Central Apparatus Room (DEN) ... CAR
Central Applications Office [*Ireland*] ... CAO
Central Arbiter (SAUS) ... CARB
Central Arbitration Committee [*British*] (ILCA) ... CAC
Central Arbitration Control Point (BYTE) ... CACP
Central Arbitration Point [*Computer science*] (PCM) ... CAP
Central Archive for Reusable Defense Software (SAUO) ... CARDS
Central Archives for the History of the Jewish People [*Jerusalem*] [*A publication*] (BJA) ... CAHJP
Central Archives of Fiji, Suva, Fiji [*Library symbol*] [*Library of Congress*] (LCLS) ... Fj-Ar
Central Archives of the Jewish People [*Jerusalem*] [*A publication*] (BJA) ... CAJP
Central Arctic Geological Expedition (SAUO) ... CAGE
Central Arctic Herd (SAUO) ... CAH
Central Arctic Management Area (SAUO) ... CAMA
Central Area ... CA
Central Area (SAUS) ... Cen A
Central Area, Military Traffic Management and Terminal Service (AABC) ... CAMTMTS
Central Area Power Coordination (SAUS) ... CAPCO
Central Area Power Coordination Group [*Nuclear Regulatory Commission*] (GFGA) ... CAPCO
Central Area Training Aboriginal Resource Accounting Committee [*Australia*] ... CATARAC
Central Arid Asia (CARB) ... CAA
Central Arid Zone Research Institute (WDAA) ... CAZRI
Central Arid Zones Research Institute (SAUO) ... CAZRI
Central Arizona College, Instructional Materials Center, Coolidge, AZ [*Library symbol*] [*Library of Congress*] (LCLS) ... AzCoC
Central Arizona Project [*Federal water-and-power project, similar to TVA*] ... CAP
Central Arizona Project Association (EA) ... CAPA
Central Arizona Speculative Fiction Society (SAUO) ... CASFS
Central Arkansas Library System ... CALS
Central Arkansas Library System, Little Rock, AR [*OCLC symbol*] (OCLC) ... AKD
Central Army Group (SAUO) ... CAG
Central [*European*] **Army Group** [*NATO*] ... CENTAG
Central Artificial Leather Research Institute (SAUO) ... CALRI
Central Asian Research Centre (SAUO) ... CARC
Central Asian Review (journ.) (SAUS) ... CAsR
Central Asian States (ECON) ... CAS
Central Asian-American Enterprise Fund [*Commercial firm*] [*Republic of Kazakstan*] ... CAAEF
Central Assets Account [*Finance*] ... CAA
Central Associated Engineers, Inc. [*Versailles, KY*] [*Telecommunications service*] (TSSD) ... CAE
Central Association for Mental Warfare (SAUO) ... CAMW
Central Association of Agricultural Valuers [*British*] ... CAAV
Central Association of Experimental Stations (SAUO) ... CAES
Central Association of Irish Schoolmistresses (SAUO) ... CAISM
Central Association of Irish Schoolmistresses (BI) ... CAISM
Central Association of London and Provincial Angling Clubs (SAUO) ... CALPAC
Central Association of Obstetricians and Gynecologists (PDAA) ... CAOG
Central Association of Science and Mathematics Teachers [*Later, SSMA*] ... CASMT
Central Association of the Lime and Limestone Industry of Great Britain (SAUO) ... CALLIGB
Central Association of the Miraculous Medal (EA) ... CAMM
Central Atlantic (SAUS) ... CENTLANT
Central Atlantic Collegiate Conference (PSS) ... CACC
Central Atlantic Regional Ecological Test Site [*Department of the Interior*] ... CARETS
Central Atlantic Regional Ecological Test Site project (SAUO) ... CARETS
Central Atlantic Regional Educational Laboratory ... CAREL
Central Atmosphere Monitoring System [*Military*] (CAAL) ... CAMS
Central Audio Management Unit (SAUS) ... CAMU
Central Auditory Nervous System (DMAA) ... CANS
Central Aural Warning System (MCD) ... CAW
Central Aural Warning System (MCD) ... CAWS
Central Australian Aboriginal Congress Inc. (SAUS) ... CAACI
Central Australian Aboriginal Legal Aid Scheme ... CAALAS
Central Australian Folk Society ... CAFS
Central Australian Motels Association ... CAMA
Central Australian Museum (SAUO) ... CAM
Central Australian Museum, Alice Springs (SAUS) ... CAM
Central Australian Show Society ... CASS
Central Australian Tourism Industry Association ... CATIA
Central Austrian Training in Technologies Salzburg/Linz (SAUS) ... CATT-Salzburg/Linz
Central Autentica Nacionalista [*Nationalist Authentic Central*] [*Guatemala*] [*Political party*] (PPW) ... CAN
Central Automated Inventory and Referral Activity [*Organization for operation of CAIRS*] [*Air Force*] ... CAIRA
Central Automated Inventory and Referral System [*Air Force*] ... CAIRS
Central Automated Personnel Security Transaction or Notification Exchange [*DoD*] ... CAPSTONE
Central Automated Replenishment Technique (IEEE) ... CART
Central Automated Support System (DNAB) ... CASS
Central Automatic Digital Data Encoder [*NASA*] ... CADDE
Central Automatic Message Accounting System (CET) ... CAMAS
Central Automatic Reliability Tester (IEEE) ... CART
Central Aviation, Inc. [*ICAO designator*] (FAAC) ... YOG
Central Avionics Information System (ACAE) ... CAINS
Central Axis Depth Dose [*Medicine*] (MELL) ... CADD
Central Band Filter (ACAE) ... CBF
Central Bank [*Philippines*] (IMH) ... CB
Central Bank for Crops (SAUO) ... CBFC
Central Bank Money ... CBM
Central Bank of China ... CBoC
Central Bank of Malta ... CBM
Central Bank of West African States (SAUO) ... CBWAS
Central Baptist Seminary and Bible College, Toronto, Ontario [*Library symbol*] [*National Library of Canada*] (NLC) ... OTCBS
Central Baptist Theological Seminary, Kansas City, KS [*Library symbol*] [*Library of Congress*] (LCLS) ... KKcB
Central Battery (NATG) ... CB
Central [*Common*] **Battery Alarm Signaling** [*Electronics*] ... CBAS
Central [*Common*] **Battery Apparatus** [*Electronics*] ... CBA
Central Battery Exchange [*Electronics*] (IAA) ... CBE
Central Battery Signaling (NATG) ... CBS
Central Battery Signalling (SAUS) ... cbs
Central Battery Supply (SAUS) ... CBS
Central [*Common*] **Battery Supply** [*Electronics*] ... CBS
Central [*Common*] **Battery Switchboard** [*Electronics*] ... CBS
Central [*Common*] **Battery System** [*Electronics*] ... CBS
Central Battery System (SAUS) ... CBS
Central Battery Telephone [*Telecommunications*] ... CBT
Central Battery Telephone Apparatus [*Telecommunications*] ... CBTA
Central Battery Telephone Set [*Telecommunications*] ... CBTS
Central Battle Manager ... CBM
Central Bible College, Springfield, MO [*Library symbol*] [*Library of Congress*] (LCLS) ... MoSpCB
Central Bible Institute [*Missouri*] ... CBI
Central Bibliographic System [*Library of Congress*] ... CBS
Central Bidder's List ... CBL
Central Black Soil Region, RSFSR [*MARC geographic area code*] [*Library of Congress*] (LCCP) ... e-urc-
Central Blood Laboratories Authority [*British*] ... CBLA
Central Blood Volume [*Medicine*] ... CBV
Central Board ... CB
Central Board for Conscientious Objectors (SAUO) ... CBCO
Central Board of Finance (SAUO) ... CBF
Central Board of Finance of the Church of England (SAUO) ... CBFCE
Central Board of Health [*South Australia*] [*Australia*] ... CBH
Central Bomber Establishment [*British military*] (DMA) ... CBE
Central Borrowing Authorities ... CBA
Central Boykott Office (SAUO) ... CBO
Central Branch, Nepean Public Library, Ontario [*Library symbol*] [*National Library of Canada*] (NLC) ... ON
Central Branch Processing Unit (SAUS) ... CBPU
Central Brasil [*Cuba*] [*ICAO location identifier*] (ICLI) ... MUNU
Central British Columbian Airways (SAUO) ... CBCA
Central British Fund for World Jewish Relief (EAIO) ... CBF
Central Broadcasting Administration [*China*] ... CBA
Central Building Research Institute (SAUO) ... CBRI
Central Bureau, Catholic Central Union of America (EA) ... CBCCUA
Central Bureau for Astronomical Telegrams (EA) ... CBAT
Central Bureau for Education Visits and Exchanges (SAUO) ... CBEVE
Central Bureau for Educational Visits and Exchanges ... CBEVE
Central Bureau for the Jewish Aged (EA) ... CBJA

Central Bureau of Astronomical Telegrams (SAUS) .... CBAT
Central Bureau of Compensation [*See also BCC*] [*Belgium*] (EAIO) .... CBC
Central Bureau of Hospital Information (SAUO) .... CBHI
Central Bureau of Identification (WDAA) .... CBI
Central Bureau of Information (SAUO) .... CBI
Central Bureau of Investigation (SAUO) .... CBI
Central Bureau of Nuclear Measurements (SAUS) .... CBLCBNM
Central Bureau of Nuclear Measurements [*European Atomic Energy Community*] .... CBNM
Central Bureau of Statistics [*Information service or system*] (IID) .... CBS
Central Bureau voor Schimmelcultures (DB) .... CBS
Central Business Area (SAUO) .... CBA
Central Business District .... CBD
Central Buying Compnay (SAUO) .... CBC
Central Calculator Unit (SAUS) .... CCU
Central California Coastal Circulation Study (SAUS) .... CCCCS
Central California Traction Co. [*AAR code*] .... CCT
Central Canada Broadcast Engineers (ROAS) .... CCBE
Central Canada Broadcasting Association .... CCBA
Central Canada Exhibition Association .... CCEA
Central Canada University Geological Conference .... CCUGC
Central Canal [*Anatomy*] CC
Central Capabilities Unit (SAUO) .... CCU
Central Capital Corp. [*Toronto Stock Exchange symbol*] .... CEH
Central Caraibes SA (SAUS) .... VG
Central Cardiac Monitoring System .... CCMS
Central Caribbean Air Ltd. (SAUO) .... JK
Central Carolina Technical Institute, Sanford, NC [*Library symbol*] [*Library of Congress*] (LCLS) .... NcSaC
Central Casualty Section (SAUS) .... CCS
Central Certificate Service [*Stock exchange automation program*] .... CCS
Central Certificate System (SAUS) .... CCS
Central Cervical Spinal Cord Syndrome [*Medicine*] (DMAA) .... CCSCS
Central Chamber of Agriculture (SAUS) .... CCA
Central Chamber of Agriculture (SAUO) .... CCA
Central Chancery of the Orders of Knighthood (SAUO) .... CCOK
Central Charging Panel [*Navy*] .... CCP
Central Chemical & Mechanical Research Institute (SAUS) .... CCMRI
Central Circulating Blood Volume [*Physiology*] .... CCBV
Central Citizens' Defence Committee [*Northern Ireland*] .... CCDC
Central Citroen Club [*Defunct*] (EA) CCC
Central Citrus Council of Western Australia .... CCCWA
Central City, KY [*Location identifier*] [*FAA*] (FAAL) .... CCT
Central City, KY [*AM radio station call letters*] .... WMTA
Central City, KY [*AM radio station call letters*] .... WNES
Central City, KY [*FM radio station call letters*] .... WQXQ
Central City, NE [*FM radio station call letters*] .... KZEN
Central City, PA [*FM radio station call letters*] (BROA) .... WSRA-FM
Central City, PA [*FM radio station call letters*] .... WYSN
Central Civilian Personnel Office [*Military*] .... CCPO
Central Classification Committee [*International Federation for Documentation*] CCC
Central Clearance Facility [*Military*] (GFGA) .... CCF
Central Clock (SAUS) CCL
Central Clock Generator [*Telecommunications*] (ACRL) .... CCG
Central CO2 Laboratory (SAUO) CCL
Central Coast (ADA) CC
Central Coast Counties Development Corporation (SAUO) .... CCCDC
Central Coast Country Music Association .... CCCMA
Central Coast Gruens [*Political party*] [*Australia*] .... CCG
Central Coding Office (SAUO) .... CCO
Central College Collegiate Conference (PSS) CCCC
Central College of Kentucky .... CCK
Central College, Pella, IA [*Library symbol*] [*Library of Congress*] (LCLS) .... IaPeC
Central College, Pella, IA [*OCLC symbol*] (OCLC) .... IOP
Central Collegiate Hockey Association (EA) .... CCHA
Central Collegiate Ski Association (PSS) .... CCSA
Central Collegiate Skiing Conference (PSS) .... CCSC
Central Colorado Regional Library Service System [*Library network*] .... CCLS
Central Command [*Persian Gulf War*] .... CENTCOM
Central Command Air Force (SAUO) .... CENTAF
Central Command and Control System Network (ACAE) .... CCCSN
Central Command Decoder [*Spacecraft assembly*] (MCD) .... CCD
Central Command for Land, Sea and Air Forces (SAUO) .... CCLSAF
Central Command, Land, Sea and Air Forces (SAUS) .... CCLSAF
Central Command Network .... CCN
Central command/Southern command Integrated Data System (SAUS) .... CSIDS
Central Commercial Company (SAUO) .... CECOCO
Central Commission for Navigation of the Rine (SAUO) .... CCR
Central Commission for the Navigation of the Rhine [*France*] (EAIO) .... CCNR
Central Commissioning Detail [*Navy*] .... CCD
Central Committee CC
Central Committee for Community Medicine (SAUS) .... CCCM
Central Committee for Forest Ownership in the EEC (EAIO) .... CCFOE
Central Committee for Hospital Medical Services [*British*] (DAVI) .... CCHMS
Central Committee for the Architectural Advisory Panels [*British*] .... CCAAP
Central Committee of Lithuanian Jurists (EA) .... CCLJ
Central Committee of Scottish Chambers of Commerce (SAUO) .... CCSCC
Central Committee of the Chinese Communist Party (SAUO) .... CC CCP
Central Committee of the Communist Party of the Soviet Union (SAUO) .... CC of CPSU
Central Committee of the Communist Party of Yugoslavia (SAUO) .... CC of CPY
Central Committee of Toy Industries (SAUO) .... CCTI
Central Committee on Communications Facilities .... CCCF
Central Committee on Lumber Standards (SAUS) .... CCLS
Central Committee on Ursigrams (SAUO) .... CCU
Central Commodity Budget Office (SAUO) .... CCBO
Central Communication Unit (SAUO) .... CCU
Central Communications Controller CCC
Central Communications Processor (SAUS) .... CCP
Central Communications Region [*Air Force*] .... CCOMMRGN
Central Communications Region [*Air Force*] (MCD) .... CCR
Central Communications Region (SAUS) .... CENCOMMERGN
Central Communications Region [*Air Force*] (AFM) .... CENCOMMRGN
Central Community Relations Unit (SAUO) .... CCRU
Central Compartment (DB) CC
Central Composite Design [*Statistical design of experiments*] .... CCD
Central Computational Computer CCC
Central Computer CC
Central Computer Accounting .... CCA
Central Computer Accounting Corp. .... CCAC
Central Computer Agency [*Civil Service Department*] [*British*] (NITA) .... CCA
Central Computer and Display Facility [*Air Force*] (CET) .... CC & DF
Central Computer and Sequencer [*NASA*] .... CC & S
Central Computer and Sequencer (SAUS) .... CC and S
Central Computer and Sequencer [*NASA*] (IAA) .... CCAS
Central Computer and Sequencing (SAUS) .... CCAS
Central Computer and Telecommunications Agency [*British*] .... CCTA
Central Computer and Telecommunications Authority (COBU) .... CCTA
Central Computer Center CCC
Central Computer Center (AABC) .... CCMPTC
Central Computer Complex CCC
Central Computer Complex (NAKS) ccc
Central Computer Station .... CCS
Central Computer Support Programming System (SAUS) .... CCSPS
Central Computer Unit .... CCU
Central Computing Facility [*NASA*] .... CCF
Central Computing Facility Backup (ACAE) .... CCFB
Central Computing Site (IAA) .... CCS
Central Computing System [*Computer science*] .... CCS
Central Concentrator (SAUS) CC
Central Conduction Time (MELL) .... CCT
Central Conference of American Rabbis (EA) .... CCAR
Central Configuation Management .... CCM
Central Connecticut State College [*Later, Central Connecticut State University*] [*New Britain*] .... CCSC
Central Connecticut State College, New Britain, CT [*Library symbol*] [*Library of Congress*] (LCLS) .... CtNbT
Central Connecticut State University (GAGS) .... Cent Conn St U
Central Console CC
Central Contact Management Region (SAUS) .... CCMR
Central Contract Management Region [*Air Force*] .... CCMR
Central Contractor Register .... CCR
Central Control (KSC) CC
Central Control Agency (SAUO) .... CCA
Central Control and Display Console .... CCDC
Central Control and Distribution Point (SAUO) .... CCDP
Central Control and Monitoring System [*for managing buildings' heating, ventilation, and security needs*] .... CCMS
Central Control Board (SAUO) .... CCB
Central Control Channel Command (MCD) CC
Central Control Commission (SAUO) CCC
Central Control Complex (SAUS) CCC
Central Control Computer System .... CCCS
Central Control Desk (SAUS) .... CCD
Central Control Evaluation and Warning Team (CINC) .... CCEWT
Central Control Facility [*Military*] (AABC) .... CCF
Central Control Function [*Aviation*] (DA) .... CCF
Central Control Indicator (MCD) CCI
Central Control Module (SAUS) .... CCM
Central Control of Quality (SAUS) .... CCQ
Central Control Point (AAGC) .... CCP
Central Control Position (SAUS) .... CCP
Central Control Room (DEN) .... CCR
Central Control Section (NASA) .... CCS
Central Control Ship [*Navy*] (NVT) .... CCS
Central Control Station (MCD) .... CCS
Central Control System (SAUO) .... CCS
Central Control Terminal (ROAS) .... CCT
Central Control/Analysis (SAUS) .... CCA
Central Coolant Supply Station (MCD) .... CCSS
Central Co-Operative Bank [*NASDAQ symbol*] (NQ) .... CEBK
Central Cooperative Bank [*Associated Press*] (SAG) .... CtrCOp
Central Cooperative Society [*United Arab Republic*] .... CCS
Central Co-Operative Society Council [*Rangoon, Burma*] (EY) .... CCS
Central Co-ordinating Allocation Committee for University Project Research (SAUO) .... CCACU
Central Co-ordinating Board (SAUO) .... CCB
Central Coordinating Staff, Canada (AFM) .... CCS-C
Central Core Disease (MELL) .... CCD
Central Corporate Design .... CCD
Central Council for Agricultural and Horticultural Co-Operation [*British*] .... CCAC
Central Council for Agricultural and Horticultural Cooperation (or Cooperatives) (SAUO) .... CCAHC
Central Council for Agricultural and Horticultural Cooperatives (SAUS) .... CCAHC
Central Council for British Naturism (SAUO) .... CCBN
Central Council for British Naturism (BI) .... CCBN
Central Council for District Nursing (SAUO) .... CCDN
Central Council for Education and Training in Social Work [*British*] .... CCETSW

Central Council for Health Education [*British*] (AEBS) .... CCHE
Central Council for Health Education (SAUO) .... CCHE
Central Council for Recreative Physical Training (SAUO) .... CCRPT
Central Council for Rivers Protection (SAUO) .... CCRP
Central Council for the Care of Cripples (SAUO) CCCC
Central Council for the Disabled (SAUO) .... CCD
Central Council for the Social Welfare of Girls and Women (SAUO) ..... CCSWGW
Central Council for the Welfare of Girls and Women (SAUO) .... CCfWGW
Central Council of Ceylon Trade Unions .... CCCTU
Central Council of Church Bell Ringers [*British*] .... CCCBR
Central Council of Economic Leagues (SAUO) .... CCEL
Central Council of International Touring (SAUO) .... CCIT
Central Council of National Retail Associations (EA) .... CCNRA
Central Council of Physical Recreation [*British*] .... CCPR
Central Counteradaptive Change (AAMN) CCC
Central Criminal Court [*Old Bailey*] [*British*] CCC
Central Criminal Court Cases [*1834-1913*] [*England*] [*A publication*]
(DLA) .... CC Ct Cas
Central Criminal Court Cases, Sessions Papers [*1834-1913*] [*England*]
[*A publication*] (DLA) .... CCC Cas
Central Criminal Court Cases, Sessions Papers [*1834-1913*] [*England*]
[*A publication*] (DLA) .... CCC Sess Pap
Central Criminal Court Cases, Sessions Papers [*1834-1913*] [*England*]
[*A publication*] (DLA) .... Cent Crim C Cas
Central Criminal Court Cases, Sessions Papers [*1834-1913*] [*England*]
[*A publication*] (DLA) .... Centr Cr Ct R
Central Criminal Court Cases, Sessions Papers [*1834-1913*] [*England*]
[*A publication*] (ILCA) .... Sess Pap CC
Central Criminal Court Cases, Sessions Papers [*1834-1913*] [*England*]
[*A publication*] (DLA) .... Sess Pap CCC
Central Criminal Court Reports [*England*] [*A publication*] (DLA) .... Cent Crim CR
Central Criminal Court Reports [*England*] [*A publication*] (ILCA) .... Centr Cr Ct R
Central Criminal Court Session Papers (SAUS) .... Sess Pap CCC
Central Crude Ltd. [*Vancouver Stock Exchange symbol*] CLC
Central Cultural Movement [*China*] .... CCM
Central Cultural Movement (SAUO) .... CCM
Central Customer Manager .... CCM
Central Data Acquisition System .... CDAS
Central Data Analysis Area (KSC) .... CDAA
Central Data and Cataloging Center (AFM) .... CD & CC
Central Data and Cataloging Center (SAUO) .... CD&CC
Central Data & Switching Center (SAUS) .... CD&SC
Central Data and Switching Center [*NASA*] (KSC) .... CD & SC
Central Data Bank, EUROCONTROL [*Belgium*] [*ICAO location identifier*]
(ICLI) .... EBBD
Central Data Bank (or Base) (SAUS) .... CDB
Central Data Base Administrator (SAUO) .... CDBA
Central Data Base Server (DOMA) .... CDBS
Central Data Buffer [*Computer science*] (MCD) .... CDB
Central Data Collection Agency (ACAE) .... CDCA
Central Data Collection Point [*Army*] .... CDCP
Central Data Collection System (AFM) .... CDCS
Central Data Control (SAUS) .... CDC
Central Data Conversion Equipment (CIST) .... CDEC
Central Data Corporation (SAUO) .... CDC
Central Data Display .... CDD
Central Data Distribution Facility [*National Oceanic and Atmospheric
Administration*] .... CDDF
Central Data Distribution Service (SAUS) .... CDDS
Central Data Distribution System (SAUS) .... CDDS
Central Data Facility [*NASA*] (NASA) .... CDF
Central Data Flow Control .... CFC
Central Data Handling Facility (ADWA) .... CDHF
Central Data Management (NRCH) .... CDM
Central Data Processing Center .... CDPC
Central Data Processing Computer .... CDPC
Central Data Processing Facility [*NASA*] .... CDPF
Central Data Processing System (ACAE) .... CDPS
Central Data Processing Unit (SAUS) .... CDPU
Central Data Processor (ACAE) .... CDP
Central Data Recording .... CDR
Central Data Station .... CDS
Central Data System [*or Subsystem*] (MCD) .... CDS
Central Data Terminal (SAUO) .... CDT
Central Database System (DA) .... CDBS
Central Data-Conversion Equipment .... CDCE
Central Datum .... CEN
Central Daylight Saving Time .... CDST
Central Daylight Time .... CDT
Central Decode Unit (SAUS) .... CDU
Central Defence Staff [*British*] .... CDS
Central Demand Data Base (SAUO) .... CDDB
Central Dental Laboratories [*Army*] .... CDL
Central Department (SAUO) .... CD
Central Design Activity (MCD) .... CDA
Central Design and Management Team (SAUO) .... CDMT
Central Design Authority (ACAE) .... CDA
Central Design Group .... CDG
Central Detector .... CD
Central Development Unit .... CDU
Central Developmental Groove [*Medicine*] (DMAA) .... CDG
Central Diabetes Insipidus [*Medicine*] (DB) .... CDI
Central Differential Analyzer Control .... CEDAC
Central Digital Computer .... CDC
Central Digital Interface Unit (SAUS) .... CDIU

Central Digital-tone Sample-generator (SAUS) .... CDS
Central Directed Audit [*Military*] .... CDA
Central Directorate on Environmental Protection [*British*] (DCTA) .... CDEP
Central Disbursing Officer (SAUO) .... CDO
Central Disc [*of flowers*] [*Botany*] .... CD
Central Dispatch Center (SAUS) .... CDC
Central Dispatching Board for Unified Power Systems (SAUO) .... CDB
Central Dispatching Organization of the Interconnected Power System
(SAUO) .... CDO
Central Dispatching Organization of the Interconnected Power Systems
(SAUO) .... CDIPS
Central Display Generator (MCD) .... CDG
Central Display Unit .... CDU
Central Distributing Office (SAUO) .... CDO
Central Distribution Center [*Army*] (DOMA) .... CDC
Central Distribution Frame (CDE) .... CDF
Central Distribution Panel .... CDP
Central Distribution Point .... CDP
Central Distribution Programmer (IAA) .... CDP
Central Distribution System [*Publications*] [*Navy*] .... CDS
Central District .... CD
Central Districts Airlines [*Former USSR*] [*FAA designator*] (FAAC) .... CDS
Central Dockyard Laboratory [*British*] .... CDL
Central Document Control [*Jet Propulsion Laboratory, NASA*] .... CDC
Central Document Exchange (SAUS) .... CDE
Central Drafting Officer [*Navy*] .... CENDRAFT
Central Dredging Association (EA) .... CEDA
Central Drug Research Institute [*India*] [*Research code symbol*] X
Central Drugs and Illegal Immigration Intelligence Unit [*British*] (DI) .... CDIIIU
Central DuPage Hospital, Medical Library, Winfield, IL [*Library symbol*]
[*Library of Congress*] (LCLS) .... IWinfC
Central Dynamic Store (PDAA) .... CDS
Central East Coast .... CEC
Central East Pacific [*Region*] .... CEP
Central Eastern Pacific Routes (PIPO) .... CEPAC
Central Eastern Personnel Organization [*Computerized scouting combine for
professional football teams*] .... CEPO
Central Economic Committee .... CEC
Central Economic Information Service [*British*] .... CEIS
Central Economic Planning Staff (SAUO) .... CEPS
Central Economic Zone .... CEZ
Central Editorial Board for the International Geological/Geophysical
Atlases of the Atlantic and Pacific Oceans, short name: GAPA Central
Editor (SAUS) .... CEB-GAPA
Central Education Library (SAUO) .... CEL
Central Education Network [*Des Plaines, IL*] [*Telecommunications service*]
(TSSD) .... CEN
Central Educational Committee at NTH (SAUS) .... SUK
Central Educational Network (SAUS) .... CEN
Central Electric Railfans' Association (EA) .... CERA
Central Electricity and Water Administration (SAUO) .... CEWA
Central Electricity Authority [*British*] .... CEA
Central Electricity Board [*British*] .... CEB
Central Electricity Board (SAUO) .... CEB
Central Electricity Generating Board [*British*] .... CEGB
Central Electricity Generating Board Digest (SAUS) .... CEGB Digest
Central Electricity Research Laboratories [*British*] .... CERL
Central Electro-Chemical Research Institute (SAUS) .... CECRI
Central Electrochemical Research Institute (SAUO) .... CECRI
Central Electrochemical Research Institute .... CERI
Central Electromagnetic Radiation Laboratory (SAUO) .... CERL
Central Electron Microscopy Laboratory [*University of Georgia*] [*Research
center*] (RCD) .... CEML
Central Electronic Complex (SAUS) .... CEC
Central Electronic Management System .... CEMS
Central Electronics Engineering Research Institute (SAUO) .... CEERI
Central Electronics Limited (SAUO) .... CEL
Central Electronics System (KSC) .... CES
Central Elementary School, Bemidji, MN [*Library symbol*] [*Library of
Congress*] (LCLS) .... MnBemCE
Central Elementary School, Bethpage, NY [*Library symbol*] [*Library of
Congress*] (LCLS) .... NBetCE
Central Elementary School, Lawrence, NY [*Library symbol*] [*Library of
Congress*] (LCLS) .... NLawCE
Central Elementary School, Worthington, MN [*Library symbol*] [*Library of
Congress*] (LCLS) .... MnWoCES
Central Emergency Government Headquarters (MCD) .... CEG
Central Emergency Revolving Fund (SAUO) .... CERF
Central Employment Bureau for Women (SAUO) .... CEBW
Central Employment Search and Retrieval (SAUS) .... CESAR
Central Employment Service (SAUO) .... CES
Central Engine [*Galactic radio source*] .... CE
Central Engine Room Control .... CERC
Central Engineer Park (SAUO) .... CEP
Central Engineering (IIA) .... CE
Central Engineering Establishment (SAUO) .... CEE
Central Engineering Establishment (SAUS) .... CEE
Central Engineering Projects Office [*NATO*] (NATG) .... CEPO
Central England Temperature [*Record since 1659*] .... CET
Central England Winter Temperature (PDAA) .... CEWT
Central Enhancement and Maintenance (CIST) .... CEM
Central Environmental Satellite Computer System (SAUO) .... CEMSCS
Central Environmental Satellite Data System (SAUS) .... CEMSDS
Central Episiotomy [*Obstetrics*] (DAVI) .... CE
Central Episiotomy and Repair [*Obstetrics*] (DAVI) .... CE & R

Central Equatorial Pacific Experiment [*Marine science*] (OSRA) ... CEPEX
Central Equipment Group [*Military*] (CAAL) ... CEG
Central Equipment Management and Inventory Control System (MCD) ... CEMICS
Central ERIC (SAUS) ... ERIC/C
Central Error Module (CAAL) ... CEM
Central Euro Media Enter'A' [*NASDAQ symbol*] (TTSB) ... CETV
Central Europe (NATG) ... CE
Central Europe Airways and Communication Service Region (SAUS) ... CENEUR AACS Reg
Central Europe Computer Measurement Group (SAUO) ... CECMG
Central Europe Frequency Distribution Agency (SAUO) ... CE/FDA
Central Europe Joint Emergency Defense Plan [*NATO*] (NATG) ... CEJEDP
Central Europe Operating Agency [*Versailles, France*] [*NATO*] ... CEOA
Central Europe Pipeline Agency [*Later, CEOA*] [*NATO*] (NATG) ... CEPA
Central Europe Pipeline Office [*NATO*] ... CEPO
Central Europe Pipeline Policy Committee [*NATO*] ... CEPPC
Central Europe Pipeline System [*NATO*] (NATG) ... CEPS
Central Europe Railroad Transport [*NATO*] (NATG) ... CE/RRT
Central Europe Road Transport [*NATO*] (NATG) ... CE/RT
Central Europe Wagon Pool (SAUO) ... CEWP
Central European Air Defense Sector ... CEADS
Central European Airlines [*Czechoslovakia*] [*ICAO designator*] (FAAC) ... CMA
Central European Buffer Zone (SAUO) ... CEBZ
Central European Communication Region [*Air Force*] (MCD) ... CECR
Central European Development Corp. ... CEDC
Central European Encephalitis Virus [*Medicine*] (MAE) ... CEEV
Central European Eq Fd [*NYSE symbol*] (TTSB) ... CEE
Central European Equity Fund [*NYSE symbol*] (SAG) ... CEE
Central European Equity Fund [*Associated Press*] (SAG) ... CentEur
Central European Exchange Program for University Studies (SAUS) ... CEEPUS
Central European Federal Youth Movement ... CEFYM
Central European Federalist (journ.) (SAUS) ... Cent Eur Fed
Central European Federation of Christian Trade Unions (EA) ... CEFCTU
Central European Forces Distribution Agency [*NATO*] (NATG) ... CEFDA
Central European Forests (SAUS) ... Cent Eur For
Central European Free Trade Area (SAUO) ... CEFTA
Central European Frisbee Disc Association (SAUO) ... CEFA
Central European History [*A publication*] (BRI) ... CEH
Central European International Bank Ltd. (SAUO) ... CIB
Central European Line [*Oil pipeline*] ... CEL
Central European Media Enterprises ... CME
Central European Media Enterprises Ltd. [*NASDAQ symbol*] (SAG) ... CETV
Central European Media Enterprises Ltd. [*Associated Press*] (SAG) ... CEurMda
Central European Movements Control System (SAUO) ... CMCS
Central European Pipeline Policy Committee (SAUS) ... CEPPC
Central European Pipeline System (SAUO) ... CEPS
Central European Rehabilitation Association (SAUO) ... CERA
Central European Standard Time (SAUS) ... CEST
Central European Summer Time (SAUO) ... CEST
Central European Tactical Zone (SAUS) ... CETZ
Central European Tick Virus (SAUS) ... CET Virus
Central European Tick-Borne Encephalitis [*Medicine*] (DB) ... CETE
Central European Time (DEN) ... CET
Central European Treaty Organization (MCD) ... CENTO
Central European Union (SAUO) ... CEU
Central European University [*Hungary*] ... CEU
Central Europe/Inland Waterways Transport (SAUO) ... CE/IWT
Central Evidence of Research and Development Report (SAUS) ... CERD REPORT
Central Evidence of Research and Development Reports ... CERD
Central Exchange (SAUS) ... CE
Central Exchange ... CENTREX
Central Exchange ... CX
Central Exchange Area [*Telecommunications*] (NITA) ... CXA
Central Excitatory State (SAUS) ... CES
Central [*Nervous System*] **Excitatory State** ... CES
Central Executive System ... CES
Central Executive Unit (DA) ... CEU
Central Experimental and Proving Establishment [*Canada*] (MCD) ... CEPE
Central Experimental and Proving Establishment (SAUO) ... CEPE
Central Experimental Farm (SAUO) ... CEF
Central External Liaison Department [*Chinese Secret Service*] ... CELD
Central Facilities - National Reactor Test Station (SAA) ... CF-NRTS
Central Facilities Area ... CFA
Central Facility (ARMP) ... CF
Central Facility Maintenance (SAUS) ... CFM
Central Fault Display System (SAUS) ... CFDS
Central Fibrous Body [*Medicine*] (DMAA) ... CFB
Central Fidelity Bank [*Associated Press*] (SAG) ... CFidBk
Central Fidelity Banks [*NASDAQ symbol*] (TTSB) ... CFBS
Central Fidelity Banks, Inc. [*NASDAQ symbol*] (NQ) ... CFBS
Central Field [*Ophthalmology*] (CPH) ... CF
Central Fighter Establishment [*British*] ... CFE
Central Fighter Establishment (SAUO) ... CFE
Central Fighter Weapons Instructor School (NATG) ... CFWIS
Central Fighter Weapons Instructors School (SAUO) ... CFWIS
Central File Document Control ... CFDC
Central Files Repository ... CFR
Central Filing (SAUS) ... CF
Central Film Library [*British*] ... CFL
Central Financial Acceptance Corp. [*Associated Press*] (SAG) ... CenFAcc
Central Financial Acceptance Corp. [*NASDAQ symbol*] (SAG) ... CFAC
Central Financial Management Activities [*Military*] (AABC) ... CFMA
Central Fire Brigades Advisory Council [*British*] ... CFBAC
Central Fire Control [*Military*] ... CFC
Central Firing Unit ... CFU
Central Fisheries Research Station (SAUS) ... CFRS
Central Fisheries Research Station, Pusan (SAUO) ... CFRS
Central Flight Instructor (SAUS) ... CFI
Central Flight Instructor Course [*Military*] ... CFIC
Central Flight Status Selection Board [*Air Force*] ... CFSSB
Central Flood Cell (WDAA) ... CFC
Central Florida Community College, Ocala, FL [*Library symbol*] [*Library of Congress*] (LCLS) ... FOcC
Central Florida Information Research Service, Inc. [*Information service or system*] (IID) ... CFIRS
Central Florida Library Consortium, Sanford, FL [*Library symbol*] [*Library of Congress*] (LCLS) ... FsanLC
Central Florida Regional Library, Ocala, FL [*Library symbol*] [*Library of Congress*] (LCLS) ... FOc
Central Florida Research Park ... CFRP
Central Flow Control Facility (SAUO) ... CF2
Central Flow Control Facility [*or Function*] (MCD) ... CFCF
Central Flow Management Unit of Eurocontrol (SAUO) ... CFMU
Central Flow Weather Service Unit [*FAA*] (TAG) ... CFMWP
Central Flow Weather Service Unit (FAAC) ... CFWSU
Central Flying School [*RAF*] [*British*] [*Australia*] ... CFS
Central Flying Training Command [*AAFCFTC*] ... CFTC
Central Food Preparation Facility [*Military*] (AABC) ... CFPF
Central Food Preparation System [*Military*] (AABC) ... CFPS
Central Food Technology Research Institute [*India*] ... CFTRI
Central Forcasting Station (SAUO) ... CFS
Central Forecast Office (DA) ... CFO
Central Forecasting Office (SAUO) ... CFO
Central Forms Committee [*Defunct*] (EA) ... CFC
Central Fracture Dislocation [*Medicine*] (MELL) ... CFD
Central Freight Association ... CFA
Central Freight Bureau (DS) ... CFB
Central Freight Tariff Bureau ... CFTB
Central Frequency (SAUS) ... Fc
Central Frequency Sounding (SAUS) ... CFS
Central Frequency Synthesizer ... CFS
Central Fuel Injection [*Automotive engineering*] ... CFI
Central Fuel Research Institute, Bihar (SAUO) ... FRI
Central Fund of Canada Ltd. [*AMEX symbol*] [*Toronto Stock Exchange symbol*] ... CEF
Central Fund of Canada Ltd. [*Associated Press*] (SAG) ... CFCda
Central Fund,Cda'A' [*AMEX symbol*] (TTSB) ... CEF
Central Garden & Pet [*NASDAQ symbol*] (TTSB) ... CENT
Central Garden & Pet Co. [*Associated Press*] (SAG) ... CenGardn
Central Garden & Pet Co. [*NASDAQ symbol*] (SAG) ... CENT
Central Gear Box (MCD) ... CGB
Central General Hospital, Plainview, NY [*Library symbol*] [*Library of Congress*] (LCLS) ... NPICH
Central Geographic Data Base (GEOI) ... CGDB
Central Geological Survey (SAUO) ... CGS
Central Georgia Associated Libraries [*Library network*] ... CGAL
Central German Administrative Department [*Economic*] **Committee** [*US Military Government, Germany*] ... CADM
Central Germany Area Exchange (SAUO) ... CENGAX
Central Germany Gee Chain (SAUS) ... CGGC
Central Gland [*of the prostate*] ... CG
Central Glass and Ceramic Research Institute (SAUS) ... CGCRI
Central Gliding School [*British military*] (DMA) ... CGS
Central Government Borrowing Requirement [*British*] ... CGBR
Central Grant Aid [*British*] ... CGA
Central Graphics Processor [*Computer science*] (NITA) ... CGP
Central Gray [*Brain anatomy*] ... CG
Central Gray Matter [*Physiology*] ... CGM
Central Grounding Point (NASA) ... CGP
Central Groundwater Board (SAUO) ... CGB
Central Group of Forces (MCD) ... CGF
Central Guaranty Trustco Ltd. [*Toronto Stock Exchange symbol*] ... CGA
Central Guatemala [*Cuba*] [*ICAO location identifier*] (ICLI) ... MUPS
Central Gunnery School (SAUO) ... CGS
Central Gunnery School [*British military*] (DMA) ... CGS
Central Gyro Reference System ... CGRS
Central Heading System (SAA) ... CHS
Central Headquarters (DCTA) ... CHQ
Central Health Services Council (AIE) ... CHSC
Central Health Services Executive [*British*] (DI) ... CHSE
Central Heating ... CH
Central Heating Plant (KSC) ... CHP
Central Hemorrhagic Necrosis [*Medicine*] (MAE) ... CHN
Central High School, Crookston,MN [*Library symbol*] [*Library of Congress*] (LCLS) ... MnCrCH
Central High School, Duluth, MN [*Library symbol*] [*Library of Congress*] (LCLS) ... MnDuCH
Central High School, Grand Junction, CO [*Library symbol*] [*Library of Congress*] (LCLS) ... CoGjCeH
Central Highway Operations Center (SAUO) ... CHOC
Central Hispano Cap 9.43% Pref [*NYSE symbol*] (TTSB) ... HCLPrB
Central Hispano Capital Ltd. [*Associated Press*] (SAG) ... CHisC
Central Hispano Capital Ltd. [*NYSE symbol*] (SAG) ... HCL
Central Hispano International, Inc. [*Associated Press*] (SAG) ... CHisIn
Central Hispano International, Inc. [*NYSE symbol*] (SAG) ... HPN
Central Hockey League ... CHL
Central Hole in Pintle [*Diesel engineering*] ... CHIP
Central Hospital Supply Service Committee (SAUO) ... CHSSC
Central Housing Advisory Committee (SAUO) ... CHAC

Central Hudson Gas & Electric Corp. [*Associated Press*] (SAG) ... CenHud
Central Hudson Gas & Electric Corp. [*NYSE symbol*] (SPSG) ... CNH
Central Hudson Gas&El [*NYSE symbol*] (TTSB) ... CNH
Central [*Atom*] **Hyperfine Structure** ... CHFS
Central Hyperfine Structure (SAUS) ... CHFS
Central I11 Lt4 1/2% cm Pfd [*NYSE symbol*] (TTSB) ... CERPr
Central Ice Data Exploration (SAUS) ... CIDEX
Central Identification, Friend or Foe [*DoD*] ... CIFF
Central Identification Laboratory [*Hawaii*] [*Army*] ... CIL
Central Identification Laboratory - Hawaii [*Army*] ... CIL-HI
Central Illinois Light Co. [*NYSE symbol*] (SAG) ... CER
Central Illinois Light Co. [*Associated Press*] (SAG) ... CnILt
Central Illinois Light Co., Resource Center, Peoria, IL [*Library symbol*] [*Library of Congress*] (LCLS) ... IPCL
Central Illinois Light Company (SAUO) ... CILCO
Central Illinois Lighting Company (SAUO) ... CILC
Central Illinois Public Service (SAUO) ... CIPS
Central Illinois Public Service Co. (SAUO) ... CIP
Central Illinois Public Service Company (SAUO) ... CIPSCO
Central Illinois Quota Zone (SAUO) ... CIQZ
Central Illinois Rainfall Chemistry Experiment (SAUS) ... CIRCE
Central Imagery Office [*Formerly, NRO; changed in 1992*] [*DoD*] (DOMA) ... CIO
Central Independent Television [*British*] (DI) ... CIT
Central Independiente de Obreros Agricolas y Campesinos [*Member of RMALC*] [*Mexico*] (CROSS) ... CIOAC
Central Index File ... CIF
Central Index File - Europe (NATG) ... CIFE
Central Index of Dose Information (HEAS) ... CIDI
Central Index Unit (SAUS) ... CIU
Central India Horse [*British military*] (DMA) ... CIH
Central Indiana Railroad (IIA) ... CI
Central Indiana Railway Co. [*Absorbed into Consolidated Rail Corp.*] [*AAR code*] ... CIND
Central Industrial Applications Center [*Southeastern Oklahoma State University*] [*Information service or system*] (IID) ... CIAC
Central Inertial Guidance Test Facility [*Air Force*] ... CIGTF
Central Inertial Reference Instrumentation System (MCD) ... CIRIS
Central Infantile Hypotonic Syndrome [*Medicine*] (DMAA) ... CIHS
Central Information Dispatch [*Genesis Electronics Corp.*] [*Folsom, CA*] [*Telecommunications*] (TSSD) ... CINDI
Central Information Exchange [*Community Service Council of Broward County, Inc.*] [*Information service or system*] (IID) ... CIE
Central Information Facility (SAUS) ... CIF
Central Information File ... CIF
Central Information Library and Editorial Section (SAUO) ... CILES
Central Information Office (SAUO) ... CIO
Central Information Processor (MCD) ... CIP
Central Information Reference and Control (DIT) ... CIRC
Central Information Reference and Control On-Line System (MCD) ... CIRCOL
Central Information Retrieval and Cartridge Update System [*Computer science*] (NITA) ... CIRCUS
Central Information Service [*University of London*] (IID) ... CIS
Central Information Service on occupational health and safety (SAUO) ... CIS
Central Information System (SAUS) ... CIS
Central Information Unit (SAUS) ... CIU
Central Inhibition [*Medicine*] (MELL) ... CIN
Central Inhibitory State [*Neurology*] (DAVI) ... CIS
Central Initial Zone [*in inflorescence*] [*Botany*] ... CIZ
Central Inland Fisheries Research Institute (SAUO) ... CIFRI
Central Input System (SAUS) ... CIS
Central Input-Output (SAUS) ... CIO
Central Input-Output Multiplexer [*Computer science*] ... CIO
Central Input-Output Unit [*Computer science*] (CIST) ... CIOU
Central Insecticide Board (SAUS) ... CIB
Central Inspection Institue of Weights and Measures (SAUO) ... CII
Central Inspectorate of Vehicles [*British military*] (DMA) ... CIV
Central Installation Supply [*Air Force*] ... CIS
Central Institute for Art (SAUO) ... CIA
Central Institute for Art and Design (SAUS) ... CIAD
Central Institute for Industrial Research (AAG) ... CIIR
Central Institute for Molecular Biology [*East Berlin*] ... CIMB
Central Institute for Physics of the Earth (SAUO) ... CIPE
Central Institute for Scientific and Technical Information (SAUS) ... CISTI
Central Institute for the Deaf (MCD) ... CID
Central Institute of Agricultural Engineering (SAUO) ... CIAE
Central Institute of Art and Design (SAUO) ... CIAD
Central Institute of Aviation Motors (SAUS) ... CIAM
Central Institute of Education (SAUO) ... CIE
Central Institute of Foreign Affairs Research ... CIFAR
Central Institute of Indian Languages (SAUO) ... CIIL
Central Institution [*Scotland*] (AIE) ... CI
Central Instructor School ... CIS
Central Instrument Warning System [*Aviation*] (DA) ... CIWS
Central Instrumentation Control and Data (MCD) ... CICADA
Central Instrumentation Department [*David W. Taylor Naval Ship Research and Development Center*] [*Bethesda, MD*] ... CID
Central Instrumentation Facility [*NASA*] ... CIF
Central Integrated Checkout System ... CICS
Central Integrated Test Set (SAUS) ... CITS
Central Integrated Test System ... CITS
Central Integrated Test System Multiplex (CIST) ... CITS
Central Integrated Test System Multiplex (PDAA) ... CITS-Mux
Central Integrated Traffic Control (PDAA) ... CITRAC
Central Integration Facility ... CIF
Central Integration Site (NASA) ... CIS
Central Intelligence Agency [*Acronym has been facetiously translated "Casey in Action," a reference to the agency's former director*] ... CIA
Central Intelligence Agency / Counter-Terrorism Center (LAIN) ... CIA/C-TC
Central Intelligence Agency, Atlantic (MCD) ... CIALANT
Central Intelligence Agency, McLean, VA [*Library symbol*] [*Library of Congress*] (LCLS) ... ViMcC
Central Intelligence Agency Retirement and Disability System ... CIARDS
Central Intelligence Board ... CIB
Central Intelligence Group (LAIN) ... CIG
Central Intelligence Organizations [*South Vietnam*] ... CIO
Central Intelligence Report (ACAE) ... CIR
Central Intelligence Retirees Association (EA) ... CIRA
Central Intelligence Retrieval Center (MCD) ... CIRC
Central Intercollegiate Athletic Association (EA) ... CIAA
Central Interface Converter Unit ... CICU
Central Interface Unit (SAUS) ... CIU
Central Interior Logging Association (AC) ... CILA
Central Internet Exchange (SAUS) ... CIX
Central Interpretation Unit [*Military*] ... CIU
Central Interval ... CI
Central Inventory Management (SAUS) ... CIM
Central Inventory of Production Equipment Records [*Army*] ... CIPER
Central Investment Program [*Army*] (MCD) ... CIP
Central Iowa Railway Co. [*AAR code*] ... CIRC
Central Iowa Regional Library [*Library network*] ... CIRL
Central Iowa Regional Library System, Des Moines, IA [*Library symbol*] [*Library of Congress*] (LCLS) ... IaDmCI
Central Iron and Steel Research Institute [*China*] ... CISRI
Central Ironmoulders Association of Scotland [*A union*] ... CIAS
Central Islip Public Library, Central Islip, NY [*Library symbol*] [*Library of Congress*] (LCLS) ... NCi
Central Islip State Hospital, Central Islip, NY [*Library symbol*] [*Library of Congress*] (LCLS) ... NCiSH
Central Isolated Unit Welfare Fund (SAUO) ... CIUWF
Central Issue Facility [*Army*] ... CIF
Central Issuing Facility [*Army*] ... CIF
Central Jersey Financial Corp. [*Associated Press*] (SAG) ... CJerFin
Central Jersey Financial Corp. [*NASDAQ symbol*] (NQ) ... CJFC
Central Jersey Finl [*NASDAQ symbol*] (TTSB) ... CJFC
Central Joint Advisory Committee on Tutoral Classes [*British*] ... CJAC
Central Junior College (SAUO) ... CJC
Central Junior High School, Alexandria, MN [*Library symbol*] [*Library of Congress*] (LCLS) ... MnAleCJ
Central Junior High School, Grand Forks, MN [*Library symbol*] [*Library of Congress*] (LCLS) ... MnEgfJ
Central Juvenile Index ... CJI
Central Kalgoorlie Gold [*Australia*] ... CKG
Central Kansas Library System [*Library network*] ... CKLS
Central Kansas Library System, Book Processing Center, Great Bend, KS [*OCLC symbol*] (OCLC) ... KKV
Central Kansas Library System, Great Bend, KS [*Library symbol*] [*Library of Congress*] (LCLS) ... KGbLS
Central Kansas Medical Center, Great Bend, KS [*Library symbol*] [*Library of Congress*] (LCLS) ... KGbMC
Central La Elec [*NYSE symbol*] (TTSB) ... CNL
Central Labor Relations Commission [*Japan*] ... CLRC
Central Laboratory ... CL
Central Laboratory Equipment Management (MCD) ... CLEM
Central Laboratory for Geodesy (SAUO) ... CLG
Central Laboratory for Parallel Processing [*Bulgaria*] (DDC) ... CLPP
Central Laboratory of the Research Councils (SAUO) ... CLRC
Central Labour Board, Bombay (SAUO) ... CLB
Central Labour College [*Railroad*] [*British*] (ROG) ... CLC
Central Labour Relations Board (SAUO) ... CLRB
Central Lake Township Library, Central Lake, MI [*Library symbol*] [*Library of Congress*] (LCLS) ... MiCenl
Central Land Board (SAUO) ... CLB
Central Land Council (SAUO) ... CLC
Central Landowners Association (SAUO) ... CLA
Central Latinamericana de Trabajadores [*Latin American Central of Workers*] (EA) ... CLAT
Central Law Journal [*A publication*] (DLA) ... Cent Law J
Central Law Journal [*A publication*] (DLA) ... Cent LJ
Central Law Journal [*A publication*] (DLA) ... Central LJ
Central Law Journal [*A publication*] (DLA) ... Centr LJ
Central Law Journal [*A publication*] (DLA) ... CLJ
Central Law Monthly [*A publication*] (DLA) ... Cent L Mo
Central Leather Research Institute [*British*] ... CLRI
Central Legal Office (SAUO) ... CLO
Central Liaison Committee (SAUO) ... CLC
Central Library, Albright & Wilson Americas, Islington, Ontario [*Library symbol*] [*National Library of Canada*] (NLC) ... OIE
Central Library and Documentation (SAUO) ... CLD
Central Library and Documentation Branch [*International Labor Organization*] (IEEE) ... CLD
Central Library and Information Services (SAUS) ... CLIS
Central Library, C-I-L, Inc., North York, Ontario [*Library symbol*] [*National Library of Canada*] (NLC) ... OTCIL
Central Library, Dow Chemical of Canada Ltd., Fort Saskatchewan, Alberta [*Library symbol*] [*National Library of Canada*] (NLC) ... AFSD
Central Library for Students (SAUO) ... CL for S
Central Library Network [*Library network*] ... CLN
Central Library, North York, ON, Canada [*Library symbol*] [*Library of Congress*] (LCLS) ... CaOTCe

Central Library, North York, Ontario [*Library symbol*] [*National Library of Canada*] (NLC) ..... OTCE
Central Library of the University of Baghdad (SAUO) ..... CLUB
Central Library Union Catalog (SAUO) ..... CLUC
Central Licensing Agency (SAUO) ..... CLA
Central Life Interests (SAUS) CLI
Central Light Loss (OA) CLL
Central Limit Order Book [*Singapore*] ..... CLOB
Central Limit Theorem [*Statistics*] ..... CLT
Central Line CL
Central Line Power (ACAE) ..... CLP
Central Liquidity Facility [*National Credit Union Administration*] ..... CLF
Central Listening Ability (SAUS) ..... CLA
Central Load Dispatching Office [*US Military Government, Germany*] ..... CLDO
Central Locking [*Automotive accessory*] CL
Central Logic Bus [*Computer science*] ..... CLB
Central Logic Complex (SAUS) CLC
Central Logic Control [*Computer science*] CLC
Central Logic Rack [*Telecommunications*] (TEL) ..... CLR
Central Logic Unit [*Computer science*] ..... CLU
Central Logistics Command [*Republic of Vietnam Armed Forces*] CLC
Central Logistics Management Center (NASA) ..... CLMC
Central London Land Use System and Employment Register (SAUS) ..... CLUSTER
Central London Productivity Association (SAUO) ..... CLPA
Central London Railway (SAUO) ..... CLR
Central London Underground Railway ..... CLR
Central Louisiana Electric Co. (SAUO) ..... CEL
Central Louisiana Electric Co., Inc. [*Associated Press*] (SAG) ..... CenLAEl
Central Louisiana Electric Co., Inc. [*NYSE symbol*] (SPSG) ..... CNL
Central Louisiana Electric Company (SAUO) ..... CLECO
Central Louisiana State Hospital, Medical Library, Pineville, LA [*Library symbol*] [*Library of Congress*] (LCLS) ..... LPiC
Central Lutheran Theological Seminary, Fremont, NE [*Library symbol*] [*Library of Congress*] (LCLS) ..... NbFC
Central Luzon State University (SAUO) ..... CLSU
Central Machine Gun ..... CMG
Central Machine Tool Institute, Bangalore (SAUO) ..... CMTI
Central Magistrates' Court Committee [*British*] ..... CMCC
Central Magnetic Tape Exchange [*Computer science*] (ADA) ..... CEMTEX
Central Mail Exchange [*British*] (ADA) ..... CME
Central Main Interactive Telecommunications System (EDAC) ..... CMITS
Central Maine Power [*NYSE symbol*] (TTSB) ..... CTP
Central Maine Power Co. [*Associated Press*] (SAG) ..... CeMP
Central Maine Power Co. [*Associated Press*] (SAG) ..... CeMPw
Central Maine Power Co. [*Associated Press*] (SAG) ..... CenM
Central Maine Power Co. [*AMEX symbol*] (SAG) ..... CTP
Central Maine Pwr 7.875% Pfd [*NYSE symbol*] (TTSB) ..... CTPPrA
Central Maine Pwr,3 1/2% Pfd [*AMEX symbol*] (TTSB) ..... CTPPr
Central Maintenance Computer (GAVI) ..... CMC
Central Maintenance Facility (NRCH) ..... CMF
Central Management Army Commissaries (AABC) ..... CMAC
Central Management Information Center (SAUS) ..... CMIC
Central Management Services (SAUO) ..... CMS
Central Management Staff Record (PDAA) ..... CMSR
Central Manufacturing District (SAUO) ..... CMD
Central Mapping Agency [*New South Wales*] (GEOI) ..... CMA
Central Marine Chamber of Commerce [*Defunct*] (EA) ..... CMCC
Central Marine Depot (SAUO) ..... CMD
Central Marine Research and Design Institute (SAUO) ..... CNIIMF
Central Massachusetts Regional Public Library System [*Library network*] ..... CMRLS
Central Master Control (MCD) ..... CMC
Central Material Section [*Medicine*] (DAVI) ..... CMS
Central Material Service (SAUO) ..... CMS
Central Material Supply [*Medicine*] (DAVI) ..... CMS
Central Materiel Service Team [*Military*] ..... CMS
Central Meat Cutting Plant (SAUO) ..... CMCP
Central Meat Processing Facility [*Army*] (AABC) ..... CMPF
Central Mechanical Engineering Research Institute (MCD) ..... CMERI
Central Medical Board (BARN) ..... CMB
Central Medical Emergency Dispatcher (SAUS) ..... CMED
Central Medical Equipment Depot (SAUO) ..... CMED
Central Medical Establishment (SAUO) ..... CME
Central Medical Establishment, Aviation [*Air Force*] ..... CMEA
Central Medical Library Association (SAUO) ..... CMLA
Central Medical War Committee (SAUO) ..... CMWC
Central Mediterranean Area [*NATO*] ..... MEDCENT
Central Mediterranean Force [*Later, AAI*] [*British*] [*World War II*] ..... CMF
Central Mediterranean Forces (SAUO) ..... CMF
Central Memory [*Computer science*] (BUR) ..... CM
Central Memory Access Priority [*Computer science*] ..... CMAP
Central Memory Extension [*Computer science*] ..... CME
Central Merchandising Office (SAUO) ..... CMO
Central Meridian (SAUS) ..... CM
Central Meridian Distance [*NASA*] ..... CMD
Central Meridian Longitude [*Planetary science*] ..... CML
Central Meridian Passage (SAUS) ..... CMP
Central Mesabi Medical Center, Hibbing, MN [*Library symbol*] [*Library of Congress*] (LCLS) ..... MnHibM
Central Mess Party (SAUO) ..... CMP
Central Meteorological Observatory [*Japan*] ..... CMO
Central Methodist College, Fayette, MO [*Library symbol*] [*Library of Congress*] (LCLS) ..... MoFC
Central Methodist Mission (SAUS) ..... CMM
Central Michigan College of Education (SAUO) ..... CMCE
Central Michigan Library System [*Library network*] ..... CMLS
Central Michigan University (GAGS) ..... Cent Mich U
Central Michigan University [*Mount Pleasant*] ..... CMU
Central Michigan University, Mount Pleasant, MI [*OCLC symbol*] (OCLC) ..... EZC
Central Michigan University, Mount Pleasant, MI [*Library symbol*] [*Library of Congress*] (LCLS) ..... MiMtpT
Central Microfilm Service Corp., St. Louis, MO [*Library symbol*] [*Library of Congress*] (LCLS) ..... CeM
Central Midwest Regional Educational Laboratory ..... CEMREL
Central Midwest Regional Educational Laboratory (AEBS) ..... CMREL
Central Midwives Board ..... CMB
Central Military Commission [*China*] ..... CMC
Central Military Establishment (SAUS) ..... CME
Central Milk Distributive Committee [*British*] ..... CMDC
Central Mine Action Training School (SAUO) ..... CMATS
Central Mine Data Systems ..... CMDS
Central Mines Action Office [*United Nations*] (WDAA) ..... CMAO
Central Mining Research Station (SAUO) ..... CMRS
Central Minnesota Christian School, Prinsburg, MN [*Library symbol*] [*Library of Congress*] (LCLS) ..... MnPrbMCS
Central Minnesota Educational Cooperative Service Unit, St. Cloud, MN [*Library symbol*] [*Library of Congress*] (LCLS) ..... MnStclEC
Central Minnesota Educational Research and Development Council, Film Library, St. Cloud, MN [*Library symbol*] [*Library of Congress*] (LCLS) ..... MnStclER
Central Minnesota Seismic Array [*Minnesota*] [*Seismograph station code, US Geological Survey*] (SEIS) CM6
Central Missile Support Base (ACAE) ..... CMSB
Central Mission Control Centre (SAUO) ..... CMCC
Central Mississippi Library Council [*Library network*] ..... INFO PASS
Central Missouri Astronomical Association ..... CMAA
Central Missouri State College [*Later, Central Missouri State University*] ..... CMSC
Central Missouri State University (GAGS) ..... Cent Mo St U
Central Missouri State University ..... CMSU
Central Missouri State University, Warrensburg, MO [*OCLC symbol*] (OCLC) ..... MCW
Central Missouri State University, Warrensburg, MO [*Library symbol*] [*Library of Congress*] (LCLS) ..... MoWarbT
Central Molecular Zone [*Galactic science*] ..... CMZ
Central Monitor and Control System (MCD) ..... CMACS
Central Monitoring and Control (SAUS) ..... CEMAC
Central Monitoring Position (IAA) ..... CMP
Central Monitoring Stations (SAUS) ..... CMS
Central Mortgage and Housing Corp. [*Canada*] (BARN) ..... CMHC
Central Mortgage & Housing Corp., Children's Environments Advisory Service, Ottawa, ON, Canada [*Library symbol*] [*Library of Congress*] (LCLS) ..... CaOOCMC
Central Mortgage & Housing Corp., Ottawa, ON, Canada [*Library symbol*] [*Library of Congress*] (LCLS) ..... CaOOCM
Central Mortgage & Housing Corp., Standards Information Centre, Ottawa, ON, Canada [*Library symbol*] [*Library of Congress*] (LCLS) ..... CaOOCMS
Central Mountain Air Ltd. [*Canada*] [*ICAO designator*] (FAAC) ..... GLR
Central Munitions System (SAUO) ..... CMS
Central Music Library (SAUO) ..... CML
Central Music Library (SAUS) ..... CML
Central Naval Ordnance Management Information System ..... CENO
Central Naval Ordnance Management Information System Office (DNAB) ..... CENOMISO
Central Navigation and Control School (SAUO) ..... CNCS
Central Navigation Computer ..... CNC
Central Navigation School ..... CNS
Central Navigation School (SAUO) ..... CNS
Central Nervous System [*Physiology*] ..... CNS
Central Nervous System (DIPS) ..... cns
Central Nervous System Dysfunction [*Medicine*] (MELL) ..... CNSD
Central Nervous-Tissue Mass (SAUS) ..... CNM
Central Network Management Software [*Computer science*] ..... CNMS
Central Neurogenic Hyperpnea [*Medicine*] (DAVI) ..... CNH
Central Neurogenic Hyperventilation [*Medicine*] ..... CNH
Central Neurogenic Hyperventilation [*Medicine*] ..... CNHV
Central Neuropsychiatric Association (EA) ..... CNA
Central Neutralization Facility (SAUO) ..... CNF
Central Nevada Field Laboratory [*University of Nevada - Reno*] [*Research center*] (RCD) ..... CNFL
Central Nevada Seismic Zone ..... CNSZ
Central New Brunswick Woodmen's Museum, Boiestown, New Brunswick [*Library symbol*] [*National Library of Canada*] (NLC) ..... NBBWM
Central New York Library Resources Council [*Syracuse, NY*] [*Library network*] ..... CENTRO
Central New York Library Resources Council, Syracuse, NY [*OCLC symbol*] (OCLC) ..... SRR
Central New York Railroad Corp. [*AAR code*] ..... CNYK
Central New York Union List of Serials, Syracuse, NY [*OCLC symbol*] (OCLC) ..... ZUA
Central Newfoundland Hospital, Grand Falls, Newfoundland [*Library symbol*] [*National Library of Canada*] (NLC) ..... NFGFH
Central Newfoundland Hospital, Grand Falls, NF, Canada [*Library symbol*] [*Library of Congress*] (LCLS) ..... CaNfGfH
Central News Agency (DGA) ..... CNA
Central News Service (SAUO) ..... CNS
Central Newspapers, Inc. Class A [*NYSE symbol*] (SPSG) ..... ECP
Central Night Vision Training School [*Military*] [*British*] ..... CNVTS
Central, NM [*FM radio station call letters*] (RBYB) ..... KNUW-FM
Central Noel Fernandez [*Cuba*] [*ICAO location identifier*] (ICLI) ..... MUCS

Central Nonprofit Agency (AAGC) ... CNA
Central Normal College, Danville, IN [*Library symbol*] [*Library of Congress*] [*Obsolete*] (LCLS) ... InDanN
Central Norseman Gold Corp. Ltd. [*Australia*] ... CNG
Central North American Water Project (SAUO) ... CeNAWP
Central North Carolina Regional Library, Burlington, NC [*Library symbol*] [*Library of Congress*] (LCLS) ... NcBur
Central North Pacific [*Aviation*] (FAAC) ... CENPAC
Central North Pacific ... CNP
Central North Pacific Ocean ... CNP
Central Northern Airways (SAUO) ... CNA
Central NOTAM [*Notice to Airmen*] **Facility** [*Military*] ... CNF
Central Nova Therapeutic Riding Association (AC) ... CENTRA
Central Nucleus Thermal Deposition (SAUS) ... CNTD
Central Obesity (MELL) ... CO
Central Obesity Index [*Medicine*] (DMAA) ... COI
Central of Georgia Railroad Co. ... CG
Central of Georgia Railroad Co. [*AAR code*] ... CGA
Central of Georgia Railroad Co. ... CGARY
Central of Georgia Railroad Co. ... C of GA
Central of Georgia Railway (SAUO) ... CGARY
Central of Georgia Railway Co. (SAUO) ... CG
Central of Georgia Railway Co. (SAUO) ... GEO
Central Off-Equatorial Pacific Upper Layer Temperature [*Oceanography*] ... CULT
Central Office ... CO
Central Office - Local Area Network ... CO-LAN
Central Office Connection [*Telecommunications*] (TSSD) ... COC
Central Office Data Connecting Facility [*Computer science*] (VERA) ... CODCF
Central Office Equipment [*Bell System*] ... COE
Central Office Equipment Estimation System [*Bell System*] ... COEES
Central Office Executives Association of National Panhellenic Conference (EA) ... COEA/NPC
Central Office Executives Association of the National Panhellenic Conference (NTPA) ... COEANPC
Central Office for Environmental Protection [*Basle, Switzerland*] ... COEP
Central Office for General Defense (SAUS) ... OCD
Central Office for International Railway Transport (SAUO) ... COIRT
Central Office for International Transport of Materials (SAUO) ... CIM
Central Office Ground (SAUS) ... COG
Central Office Line Tester (IAA) ... COLT
Central Office Maintenance and Administration System (SAUS) ... COMAS
Central Office Maintenance Management System [*Telecommunications*] (TEL) ... COMMS
Central Office Maintenance Management System - Preventive Maintenance [*Telecommunications*] (TEL) ... COMMS-PM
Central Office Maintenance Printout Analysis and Suggestion System [*Computer science*] (MHDB) ... COMPASS
Central Office Network Access (SAUO) ... CONTAC
Central Office of Information [*London, England*] ... COI
Central Office of Record [*DoD*] ... COR
Central Office of Scientific, Technical and Economic Information (SAUS) ... COSTEI
Central Office of South Vietnam [*North Vietnamese high command in the South*] ... COSVN
Central Office of Statistics [*Malta*] (GEOI) ... COS
Central Office of the Industrial Tribunal [*Department of Employment*] [*British*] ... COIT
Central Office Signaling Panel [*Telecommunications*] (TEL) ... COSP
Central Office Switch (SAUS) ... COS
Central Office Systems Analyst [*Computer science*] ... COSA
Central Office Terminal [*Telecommunications*] (TEL) ... COT
Central Office to Central Office [*Bell System*] ... CO-CO
Central Office-based Local Area Network [*Telecommunications*] (ACRL) ... COLAN
Central Office-Based Multiplexing (SAUS) ... COBM
Central Officers' Training School ... COTS
Central Officials Training Institute (SAUO) ... COTI
Central Ohio Biomedical Engineering Community Council (SAUO) ... COBECC
Central Ohio Breeding Association (SAUO) ... COBA
Central Ohio Federation of Information Processing Societies (SAUO) ... COFIPS
Central Ohio Fibrositis Association (EA) ... COFA
Central Ohio Information Network (SAUS) ... COIN
Central Ohio Interlibrary Network [*Library network*] ... COIN
Central Oil Identification Laboratory [*Groton, CT*] [*Coast Guard*] (MSC) ... COIL
Central Okanagan Foundation (AC) ... COF
Central on Board Softwear (ADWA) ... COBS
Central Oncology Group (DAVI) ... COG
Central On-Line Data Directory (ACAE) ... CODD
Central Ontario Mopar Owners Association (AC) ... COMOA
Central Ontario Regional Library, Richmond Hill, ON, Canada [*Library symbol*] [*Library of Congress*] (LCLS) ... CaORhCO
Central Ontario Regional Library, Richmond Hill, Ontario [*Library symbol*] [*National Library of Canada*] (NLC) ... ORCO
Central Ontario Regional Library System (SAUS) ... CORLS
Central Opera Service (EA) ... COS
Central Operating Agency (NATG) ... COA
Central Operating Authority (SAUO) ... COA
Central Operations System (PDAA) ... COS
Central Operations/Command Center (SAUO) ... COCC
Central Operator Panel (IAA) ... COP
Central Orchid Society [*British*] (DBA) ... COS
Central Ordering Point (IAA) ... COP
Central Ordnance Depot (SAUO) ... COD
Central Ordnance Supply Depot (SAUO) ... COSD
Central Oregon Community College, Bend, OR [*Library symbol*] [*Library of Congress*] (LCLS) ... OrBeC
Central Oregon Community College, Library, Bend, OR [*OCLC symbol*] (OCLC) ... CEO
Central Oregon District Hospital, Medical Library, Redmond, OR [*Library symbol*] [*Library of Congress*] (LCLS) ... OrRedDH
Central Organization for Jewish Education (EA) ... COJE
Central Organization for Rural Cooperatives (SAUO) ... CORC
Central Organization for Technical Training (SAUO) ... COTT
Central Organization of Liaison for Allocation of Circuit (NATG) ... COLAC
Central Organization of Liaison for Application of Circuit (SAUS) ... COLAC
Central Organization of Trade Unions ... COTU
Central Ouality Service (SAUS) ... SCQ
Central Output (SAUS) ... CENOUT
Central Overseas Recruiting and Rotation Office [*Military*] ... CORRO
Central Pac Minerals NL [*NASDAQ symbol*] (TTSB) ... CPMINY
Central Pacific Air Chemistry Experiment (SAUS) ... CPACE
Central Pacific Area [*Navy*] ... CENPAC
Central Pacific Area [*Hawaiian area*] [*World War II*] ... CPA
Central Pacific Bank, Inc. (EFIS) ... CPB
Central Pacific Base Command [*Navy*] ... CENTPACBACOM
Central Pacific Base Command [*Hawaiian Islands*] [*World War II*] ... CPBC
Central Pacific Combat Air Transport Service ... CENCATS
Central Pacific Combat Area Transport Service (SAUO) ... CENCATS
Central Pacific Communications Instructions ... CENTCOM
Central Pacific Fisheries Research Center [*National Oceanic and Atmospheric Administration*] ... CPFRC
Central Pacific Forces ... CENPACFOR
Central Pacific Hurricane Center [*Honolulu*] [*National Weather Service*] (NOAA) ... CPHC
Central Pacific Minerals [*Associated Press*] (SAG) ... CPcMn
Central Pacific Minerals Ltd. (SAUO) ... CPM
Central Pacific Minerals NL [*NASDAQ symbol*] (NQ) ... CPMN
Central Pacific Search and Rescue Coordinator [*Coast Guard*] (DNAB) ... CENPACSARCOORD
Central Pain Syndrome [*Medicine*] ... CPS
Central Park Zoo (SAUS) ... CPZ
Central Parking [*NYSE symbol*] (SG) ... CPC
Central Parking [*NYSE symbol*] (TTSB) ... PK
Central Parking Corp. [*Associated Press*] (SAG) ... CentPkg
Central Parking Corp. [*NYSE symbol*] (SAG) ... PK
Central Parts Contractor (SAUS) ... CPC
Central Pastry Kitchen [*Army*] (AABC) ... CPK
Central Patch and Test [*Facility*] ... CENPAT
Central Patents Index [*A publication*] ... CPI
Central Path Method [*Computer science*] ... CPM
Central Pattern Generator [*Neurochemistry*] ... CPG
Central Pay Accounts Division [*Navy*] ... CPAD
Central Pay Office (AIE) ... CPO
Central Paying and Transfer Agent [*Business term*] (EMRF) ... CPTA
Central Pennsylvania District Library Center, Bellefonte, PA [*OCLC symbol*] (OCLC) ... PCB
Central Pennsylvania Medical Librarians [*Library network*] ... CPHSLA
Central Pennsylvania Youth Ballet ... CPYB
Central Perfusion Pressure [*Medicine*] ... CPP
Central Personnel Data File [*Office of Personnel Management*] [*Washington, DC*] ... CPDF
Central Personnel Department (SAUO) ... CPD
Central Personnel Directorate [*British*] ... CPD
Central Personnel Security Clearance Facility [*Army*] (MCD) ... CCF
Central Personnel Security Clearance Index [*Nuclear energy*] (NRCH) ... CPSCI
Central Physical Evaluation Board [*Navy*] (NVT) ... CPEB
Central Piedmont Community College, Charlotte, NC [*Library symbol*] [*Library of Congress*] (LCLS) ... NcCCP
Central Plains Experimental Range (GNE) ... CPER
Central Plains Turfgrass Foundation [*Later, KTF*] (EA) ... CPTF
Central Planned Economy (SAUO) ... CPE
Central Planning Center (NASA) ... CPC
Central Planning Office [*NASA*] (KSC) ... CPO
Central Planning Team (NATG) ... CPT
Central Plasma Sheet ... CPS
Central Pocket Whorl [*Fingerprint*] (MELL) ... CPW
Central Point ... CP
Central Point Anti-Virus [*Central Point Software, Inc.*] [*Computer science*] (PCM) ... CPAV
Central Point Management Services (SAUS) ... CPMS
Central Point Recuperator [*Computer program*] (PCM) ... CPR
Central Point Software (SAUS) ... CPS
Central Policy Office (SAUS) ... CPO
Central Policy Review Staff [*British*] ... CPRS
Central Pontine Myelinolysis [*Medicine*] ... CPM
Central Port Call Office [*Army*] (AABC) ... CPCO
Central Post Fund [*Army*] ... CPF
Central Post Office (SAUS) ... CPO
Central Post, South Brunswick, NJ [*Library symbol*] [*Library of Congress*] (LCLS) ... NjSobC
Central Postal Directory [*Army*] (AABC) ... CPD
Central Postal Enquiry Bureau (SAUO) ... CPEB
Central Posterior Curve [*Ophthalmology*] ... CPC
Central Poststroke Pain [*Medicine*] (DMAA) ... CPSP
Central Power and Light (SAUO) ... CPL
Central Power Council (SAUO) ... CPC
Central Power Supply ... CPS
Central Power System ... CPS
Central Powerhouse ... CPH
Central Practitioners of Great Britain (SAUO) ... CPGB
Central Premonitions Registry (EA) ... CPR

Central Press ... CP
Central Price Regulation Committee (SAUO) ... CPRC
Central Primero De Enero [*Cuba*] [*ICAO location identifier*] (ICLI) ... MUVA
Central Problem [*Psychometrics*] ... CP
Central Processing (SAUS) ... CP
Central Processing Area (ADA) ... CPA
Central Processing Communications (SAUS) ... CPCOM
Central Processing Complex (SAUS) ... CPC
Central Processing Console [*NBDS*] ... CPC
Central Processing Element [*Computer science*] ... CPE
Central Processing Element BIT Slice [*Computer science*] (NITA) ... CPEBS
Central Processing Facility (MCD) ... CPF
Central Processing Group (SAUO) ... CPG
Central Processing Modules [*Computer science*] (MCD) ... CPM
Central Processing Point [*Computer science*] ... CPP
Central Processing Subsystem [*Computer science*] ... CPSS
Central Processing System [*Computer science*] ... CPS
Central Processing Unit (SAUS) ... Cen Proc U
Central Processing Unit [*Computer science*] ... CPU
Central Processing Unit Diagnostic Program ... CPUD
Central Processing Unit Identification Number [*Computer science*] ... CPUID
Central Processor [*Computer science*] ... CP
Central Processor (IDOE) ... cp
Central Processor and Controller (ACAE) ... CENPAC
Central Processor Element (SAUS) ... CPE
Central Processor Input Output (ACAE) ... CPIO
Central Processor Memory Address [*Computer science*] ... CPMA
Central Processor Molecules (NITA) ... CPM
Central Processor Subsystem (SAUS) ... CPS
Central Processor Subunit [*Computer science*] ... CPSU
Central Processor Test Console [*Computer science*] ... CPTC
Central Processor Unit (SAUS) ... CPU
Central Procurement [*or Centrally Procured*] (AFM) ... CP
Central Procurement Accounting System [*Air Force*] (GFGA) ... CPAS
Central Procurement Division [*Marine Corps*] ... CPD
Central Procurement Office (AABC) ... CPO
Central Procurement Unit (SAUS) ... CPU
Central Procurement-Nonstock Fund (SAUO) ... CP-NSF
Central Product Classification (SAUS) ... COC
Central Production Unit [*Publishing services*] [*American Library Association*] ... CPU
Central Professional Hockey League ... CPHL
Central Programmer and Evaluator ... CPE
Central Programming Service (SAUS) ... CPS
Central Project Office [*of ARS, Department of Agriculture*] ... CPO
Central Property Control ... CPC
Central Property Control System (MCD) ... CPCS
Central Propulsion System (ACAE) ... CPS
Central Provident Fund [*Singapore*] (ECON) ... CPF
Central Provinces [*Later, Madhya Pradesh, India*] ... CP
Central Provinces (SAUO) ... CP
Central Provinces, India (DLA) ... CP Ind
Central Provinces Law Reports [*India*] [*A publication*] (DLA) ... Cent Prov LR
Central Provinces Law Reports [*India*] [*A publication*] (DLA) ... CPLR
Central Provision Office [*World War II*] ... CPO
Central Psi Research Institute (EA) ... CPRI
Central Psychiatric Hospitals Association (SAUO) ... CPHA
Central Public Health Laboratory [*British*] (IRUK) ... CPHL
Central Public House Trust Association (SAUO) ... CPHTA
Central Public Library (SAUO) ... CPL
Central Public Library (SAUS) ... CPL
Central Puget Sound Growth Planning Hearings Board (SAUO) ... CPSGPHB
Central Pulmonary Vessels Enlargement [*Medicine*] ... CVE
Central Pulse Amplifier (MCD) ... CPA
Central Pulse Amplifier/Symbol Generator (SAUS) ... CPA/SG
Central Pulse Distributor [*Telecommunications*] (TEL) ... CPD
Central Purchasing Authority [*Military*] (NVT) ... CPA
Central Purchasing Organization ... CPO
Central Queensland Articled Law Clerks' Association [*Australia*] ... CQALCA
Central Queensland Consumers Association [*Australia*] ... CQCA
Central Queensland Egg Marketing Board [*Australia*] ... CQEMB
Central Queensland Grain Sorghum Marketing Board [*Australia*] ... CQGSMB
Central Queensland Speleological Society [*Australia*] ... CQSS
Central Queensland University [*Australia*] ... CQU
Central R. R. of Pennsylvania [*AAR code*] ... CRP
Central Radio Bureau (SAUS) ... CRB
Central Radio Bureau (SAUO) ... CRB
Central Radio Office [*Telecommunications*] (TEL) ... CRO
Central Radio Propagation Laboratory [*Later, ITS*] ... CRPL
Central Railroad Co. of New Jersey [*Absorbed into Consolidated Rail Corp.*] [*AAR code*] ... CNJ
Central Railroad Co. of New Jersey [*Absorbed into Consolidated Rail Corp.*] ... CRR of NJ
Central Railroad Company of New Jersey (SAUO) ... CNJ
Central Railroad Company of New Jersey (SAUO) ... CRR
Central Railroad of Pennsylvania (SAUO) ... CRP
Central Railway (SAUO) ... CR
Central Railway [*British*] (ROG) ... CR
Central Rainfed and Upland Rice Research Station (SAUO) ... CRURRS
Central Rappahannock Regional Library, Fredericksburg, VA [*Library symbol*] [*Library of Congress*] (LCLS) ... ViFre
Central Ray (STED) ... CR
Central Ray, Pella, IA [*Library symbol*] [*Library of Congress*] (LCLS) ... IaPeCR
Central Read Control (SAUS) ... CRC
Central Real Estate Office [*Military*] ... CREO
Central Receiver Test Facility [*Department of Energy*] ... CRTF
Central Reconnaissance Establishment [*British military*] (DMA) ... CRE
Central Reconnaissance Establishment (SAUO) ... CRE
Central Record, Medford, NJ [*Library symbol*] [*Library of Congress*] (LCLS) ... NjMedR
Central Record Officer (SAUS) ... CRO
Central Recorder (ACAE) ... C/R
Central Recorder Subsystem [*NASA*] ... CR
Central Recorder Subsystem [*NASA*] ... CRS
Central Records Control Area (SAA) ... CRCA
Central Records Department (SAUO) ... CR Dept
Central Records Depository ... CRD
Central Records Facility, United States Army Intelligence Center ... CRFUSAIC
Central Records Library, Newfoundland Light and Power Co. Ltd., St. John's, Newfoundland [*Library symbol*] [*National Library of Canada*] (NLC) ... NFSLP
Central Records Office ... CRO
Central Records, Ontario Hydro, Toronto, Ontario [*Library symbol*] [*National Library of Canada*] (NLC) ... OTOHCR
Central Recruiting Depot (SAUO) ... CRD
Central Recruiting Depot (SAUS) ... CRD
Central Recruiting Division [*Military*] ... CRD
Central Red-Only Memory (SAUS) ... CROM
Central Reference Library [*British*] (DIT) ... CRL
Central Reference Room Bulletin (SAA) ... CRRB
Central Reference Supply ... CRS
Central Region (GEOI) ... CR
Central Region Air Operations Center (SAUO) ... CRAOC
Central Region Airlift Control Center (SAUO) ... CRALCC
Central Region Airlift Division (SAUO) ... CRALD
Central Region Cultural Authority [*South Australia*] ... CRCA
Central Region Headquarters, Atmospheric Environment Service, Environment Canada[*Quartier-General de la Region Centrale, Service de l'Environnement Atmosphe rique, Environnement Canada*] **Winnipeg, Manitoba** [*Library symbol*] [*National Library of Canada*] (NLC) ... MWEAE
Central Region Information Resources Center, Canada Department of Communications[*Centre de Documentation Region du Centre, Ministere des Communications*] **Winnipeg, Manitoba** [*Library symbol*] [*National Library of Canada*] (NLC) ... MWCCIR
Central Region Initial ACCS Programme (SAUS) ... CRIAP
Central Region Integrated Communications System (SAUO) ... CRICS
Central Region Interface Working Group [*NATO*] (NATG) ... CRIWG
Central Region Libraries, Grand Falls, Newfoundland [*Library symbol*] [*National Library of Canada*] (NLC) ... NFGFC
Central Region Libraries, Grand Falls, NF, Canada [*Library symbol*] [*Library of Congress*] (LCLS) ... CaNfGfC
Central Region, RSFSR [*MARC geographic area code*] [*Library of Congress*] (LCCP) ... e-url-
Central Region SEATO [*Southeast Asia Treaty Organization*] **Field Forces** (CINC) ... CRSFF
Central Regional Automated Funds Transfer System ... CRAFTS
Central Regional Laboratory [*Environmental Protection Agency*] (GFGA) ... CRL
Central Regional Library, Transport Canada [*Bibliotheque Regionale du Centre,Transports Canada*], **Winnipeg, Manitoba** [*Library symbol*] [*National Library of Canada*] (NLC) ... MWTCR
Central Register and Clearing House [*British*] ... CRACH
Central Registration Depository [*Investment term*] ... CRD
Central Registry [*of the Ordnance Survey*] [*British*] ... CR
Central Registry of Charities [*British*] ... CRC
Central Registry of Magazine Subscription Solicitors [*Defunct*] (EA) ... CRMSS
Central Registry of War Criminals and Security Suspects [*World War II*] ... CROWCASS
Central Registry of World Dancers (EA) ... CROWD
Central Regulatory Electronic Stenographic System (NRCH) ... CRESS
Central Religious Advisory Committee [*British*] ... CRAC
Central Religious Advisory Committee (SAUO) ... CRAC
Central Repair Depot (NATG) ... CRD
Central Repair Facility (MCD) ... CRF
Central Repair Service (SAUS) ... CRS
Central Repeater System (MCD) ... CRS
Central Reporter [*A publication*] (DLA) ... Cent
Central Reporter [*A publication*] (DLA) ... Cent Rep
Central Reporter [*Pennsylvania*] [*A publication*] (DLA) ... Cent R (PA)
Central Reporter [*A publication*] (DLA) ... CR
Central Reporting Team (SAUO) ... CRT
Central Requirements Committee ... CRC
Central Research Agency [*Cuc Nghien-Chu Trung-Uong*] [*North Vietnamese intelligence agency*] ... CRA
Central Research and Support Establishment [*Information service or system*] (IID) ... CRSE
Central Research Establishment [*Home Office Forensic Science Service*] [*British*] [*Information service or system*] (IID) ... CRE
Central Research Institute for Animal Science (SAUS) ... PUSLITBANGNAK
Central Research Institute for Food Crops (SAUO) ... CRIFC
Central Research Institute for Food Crops (SAUS) ... PPPTP
Central Research Institute of the Electric Power Industry (SAUO) ... CRIEPI
Central Research Institute of the Electrical Power Industry (SAUS) ... CRIEPI
Central Research Laboratories Inc. (SAUO) ... CRL
Central Research Laboratory (SAUS) ... CRL
Central Research Laboratory of Tashiba ... CRLT
Central Reserve Air Fleet ... CRAF
Central Reserve Life [*NASDAQ symbol*] (SAG) ... CRLC
Central Reserve Life Corp. [*Associated Press*] (SAG) ... CRsLfe
Central Reserve Police (WDAA) ... CRP
Central Resistance Council (SAUO) ... CRC

Central Resource Center (SAUO) .... CRC
Central Resource Centre, Carleton Roman Catholic School Board, Nepean, Ontario [*Library symbol*] [*National Library of Canada*] (NLC) .... ONCRC
Central Resource Centre, Prairie View School Division No. 74, Milestone, Saskatchewan (SAUS) .... SMPVS
Central Resource Centre, Prairie View School Division No. 74, Milestone, Saskatchewan [*Library symbol*] [*National Library of Canada*] (NLC) .... SMPVS
Central Retinal Artery [*Ophthalmology*] .... CRA
Central Retinal Artery Occlusion [*Ophthalmology*] .... CRAO
Central Retinal Vein [*Ophthalmology*] .... CRV
Central Retinal Vein Occlusion [*Ophthalmology*] .... CRVO
Central Retransmission Facility (IAA) .... CRF
Central Rhine Commission [*Post-World War II*] .... CRC
Central Rice Research Institute (GNE) .... CRRI
Central Rivers Search and Rescue Coordinator [*Coast Guard*] (DNAB) .... CENRIVSARCOORD
Central Road Research Institute (SAUO) .... CRRI
Central ROC (SAUS) .... ROCCENT
Central Route Charge Office of Eurocontrol (SAUO) .... CRCO
Central Rural Construction Command [*Military*] (CINC) .... CRCC
Central Savannah River Area (SAUS) .... CSRA
Central Savings Bank (SAUO) .... CSB
Central Schengen Information System (SAUO) .... CSIS
Central School (ADA) .... CS
Central Science Laboratory .... CSL
Central Scientific Agricultural Library (SAUS) .... CSAL
Central Scientific Company (SAUO) .... cenco
Central Scientific Computing Center (SAUS) .... CSCC
Central Scientific Computing Facility (SAUS) .... CSCF
Central Scientific Instruments Organisation (SAUO) .... CSIO
Central Scientific Services DPEE (SAUS) .... CSS/DPEE
Central Scotland Aviation Group (SAUO) .... CSAG
Central Scrap Management Office (SAUO) .... CSMO
Central Sec$2cmCv D Pfd [*AMEX symbol*] (TTSB) .... CETRrD
Central Secondary Item Stratification [*Military*] (AFIT) .... CSIS
Central Securities Corp. [*Associated Press*] (SAG) .... CentSE
Central Securities Corp. [*AMEX symbol*] (SPSG) .... CET
Central Securities Corp. [*Associated Press*] (SAG) .... CnS
Central Security Control [*Military*] (AFM) .... CSC
Central Security Control System (SAUS) .... CSCS
Central Security Force (SAUS) .... CSF
Central Security Service [*National Security Agency*] [*Obsolete*] (AABC) .... CSS
Central Selling Organization [*London diamond exchange*] .... CSO
Central Senior High School, Valley Stream, NY [*Library symbol*] [*Library of Congress*] (LCLS) .... NVsCSH
Central Sephardic Jewish Community of America (EA) .... CSJCA
Central Sericulure Research Station (SAUO) .... CSRS
Central Serous Chorioretinopathy [*or Choroidopathy*] [*Ophthalmology*] .... CSC
Central Serous Retinopathy [*Medicine*] (CPH) .... CSP
Central Serous Retinopathy [*Medicine*] (MELL) .... CSR
Central Service [*Medicine*] (DHSM) .... CS
Central Service Facility (NRCH) .... CSF
Central Service Point [*DoD*] (AFIT) .... CSP
Central Service Works Engineering (COE) .... CSWE
Central Services division (SAUS) .... CS
Central Services Organization .... CSO
Central Services Unit for Careers and Appointments Services (SAUO) .... CSUCAS
Central Services Unit for University Careers and Appointments Services [*British*] .... CSU
Central Servicing Development Establishment (SAUO) .... CSDE
Central Servicing Development Establishment (MCD) .... CSDE
Central Ships Alignment Console [*Navy*] (NG) .... CSAC
Central Sierra Snow Laboratory [*Norden, CA*] .... CSSL
Central Sign Off (AAG) .... CSO
Central Signal Processor .... CSP
Central Signals Establishment [*Military*] [*British*] .... CSE
Central Site .... C/S
Central Site Queueing (SAUS) .... CSQ
Central Skyport, Inc. [*ICAO designator*] (FAAC) .... CSI
Central Sleep Apnea [*Medicine*] (MELL) .... CSA
Central Society for Chemical Research (SAUO) .... CSCR
Central Society for Clinical Research (EA) .... CSCR
Central Software Engineering Facility (ACAE) .... CSEF
Central Soil Salinity Research Institute (SAUO) .... CSRRI
Central Solar Heating Plant with Seasonal Storage [*Pronounced "chips"*] [*Thermal technology*] (PS) .... CSHPSS
Central Source Data File (MCD) .... CSDF
Central South Africa Railway (ROG) .... CSA
Central South Africa Railway (SAUO) .... CSA
Central South Africa Railway (SAUO) .... CSAR
Central Soya Company, Inc. (SAUO) .... CSY
Central Sprinkler [*NASDAQ symbol*] (TTSB) .... CNSP
Central Sprinkler Corp. [*NASDAQ symbol*] (NQ) .... CNSP
Central Sprinkler Corp. [*Associated Press*] (SAG) .... CnSprn
Central Standard Summer Time .... CSST
Central Standard Time .... CST
Central Standards Office (OICC) .... CSO
Central State College [*Ohio, Oklahoma*] .... CSC
Central State Hospital, Waupun, WI [*Library symbol*] [*Library of Congress*] (LCLS) .... WWpC
Central State University [*Wilberforce, OH*] .... CSU
Central State University, Edmond, OK [*Library symbol*] [*Library of Congress*] (LCLS) .... OkEdT
Central State University, Edmond, OK [*OCLC symbol*] (OCLC) .... OKX
Central State University, Wilberforce, OH [*OCLC symbol*] (OCLC) .... CNC
Central State University, Wilberforce, OH [*Library symbol*] [*Library of Congress*] (LCLS) .... OWibfC
Central States [*An association*] (EA) .... CS
Central States Anthropological Society (EA) .... CSAS
Central States College Association [*Defunct*] .... CSCA
Central States Communication Association .... CSCA
Central States Conference on the Teaching of Foreign Languages (SAUO) .... CSC
Central States Conference on the Teaching of Foreign Languages (SAUO) .... CSCTFL
Central States Football League .... CSFL
Central States Gas Corporation (SAUO) .... CSGA
Central States Motor Freight Bureau (SAUO) .... CMB
Central States Motor Freight Bureau .... CSMFB
Central States Motor Freight Bureau, Chicago IL [*STAC*] .... CMB
Central States Pension Fund .... CSPF
Central States Roller Canary Breeders Association (EA) .... CSRCBA
Central States Speech Association (AEBS) .... CSSA
central station (SAUS) .... cent sta
Central Station [*NASA*] .... C/S
Central Station Alarm Association (EA) .... CSAA
Central Station Electrical Protection Association [*Later, CSAA*] (EA) .... CSEPA
Central Statistical Board [*Functions taken over by Bureau of the Budget, 1940*] .... CSB
Central Statistical Board (SAUO) .... CSB
Central Statistical Office [*British*] [*Information service or system*] (IID) .... CSO
Central Statistical Unit [*of VLRL*] .... CSU
Central Statistics Bureau [*British Columbia Ministry of Industry and Small Business Development*] [*Information service or system*] (IID) .... CSB
Central Sterile Supply [*Medicine*] (CPH) .... CSS
Central Sterile Supply Department [*Medicine*] (DAVI) .... CSSD
Central Sterile Supply Unit [*Medicine*] (DMAA) .... CSSU
Central Still-Photo Depository (DNAB) .... CSPD
Central Stock Control Point (SAUS) .... CSCP
Central Storage (SAUS) .... CS
Central Storage Device (SAUS) .... CSD
Central Storage Module (SAUS) .... CSM
Central Structure Storage [*Computer science*] (BYTE) .... CSS
Central Subarea, Atlantic [*NATO*] .... CENTLANT
Central Suffolk Hospital, Riverhead, NY [*Library symbol*] [*Library of Congress*] (LCLS) .... NRvCH
Central Sugar Cane Prices Board [*Queensland*] [*Australia*] .... CSCPB
Central Sunday Closing Association (SAUO) .... CSCA
Central Supplies Agency (NATG) .... CSA
Central Supply (KSC) .... CS
Central Supply Association [*Later, ASA*] (EA) .... CSA
Central Supply Facility (MCD) .... CSF
Central Supply Office (SAUO) .... CSO
Central Supply Room .... CSR
Central Supply Support Activity .... CSSA
Central Support Facility (SAUO) .... CSF
Central Support Services [*National Weather Service*] (USDC) .... CSS
Central Switching Center [*Telecommunications*] (TEL) .... CSC
Central Switching Concept (KSC) .... CSC
Central Switching Facility .... CSF
Central Switching Point (SAUS) .... CSP
Central Switching Unit .... CSU
Central Switching-network Control (SAUS) .... CSC
Central Sydney PHU (SAUO) .... CS PHU
Central System Maintenance Support (NATG) .... CSMS
Central System Management Computer (ACAE) .... CSMC
Central Systems Design Agency .... CSDA
Central Systems Management Segment (ACAE) .... CSMS
Central Tactical Processing program (SAUS) .... CTTP
Central Tactical System [*RAF*] (MCD) .... CTS
Central Tactical Unit [*Drug Enforcement Administration*] .... CENTAC
Central Tactics & Trials Organisation (SAUS) .... CTTO
Central Tactics and Trials Organization (SAUO) .... CTTO
Central Tap [*Electronics*] (ECII) .... CT
Central Target Director [*Military*] (CAAL) .... CTD
Central Target Simulator [*Navy*] (MCD) .... CTS
Central Task Force .... CTF
Central Task Force (SAUO) .... CTF
Central Technical Authority (MCD) .... CTA
Central Technical Catalogue [*Library science*] (TELE) .... CTC
Central Technical Community College, Hastings, NE [*Library symbol*] [*Library of Congress*] (LCLS) .... NbHCC
Central Technical Doctrine Officer (DNAB) .... CTDO
Central Technical Documents Office [*Naval Ordnance Systems Command*] [*Information service or system*] (IID) .... CTDO
Central Technical Institute [*Netherlands*] .... CTI
Central Technical Library, Cominco Ltd., Trail, British Columbia [*Library symbol*] [*National Library of Canada*] (NLC) .... BTC
Central Technical Manual Management Activity [*Navy*] (NVT) .... CTMMA
Central Technical Operations (HLLA) .... CTO
Central Technical Order Control [*or Coordination*] **Unit** (MCD) .... CTOCU
Central Technical Order Coordination Unit .... CTOC
Central Technical Services (SAUS) .... CTS
Central Technical Support Facility [*Military*] .... CTSF
Central Technological Development Fund (SAUS) .... KMUFA
Central Telegraph Exchange [*British*] .... CTE
Central Telegraph Male Superintending Officers' Association [*A union*] [*British*] .... CTMSOA
Central Telegraph Office [*British*] (ROG) .... CTO

Central Telegraph Superintending Officers' Association [*A union*] [*British*] .... CTSOA
Central Telegraph Test Center (SAUS) .... CTTC
Central Telemetry Unit (ACAE) .... CTU
Central Telephone & Electronics (SAUS) .... CTE
Central Telephone and Utilities Corp. (NITA) .... CTU
Central Telephone Co. (EFIS) .... CENTEL
Central Telephone Operator [*British*] (ROG) .... CTO
Central Terminal Computer Controller (SAUS) .... CTCC
Central Terminal Exchange (SAUS) .... CENTREX
Central Terminal of Wilson (DAVI) .... CTW
Central Terminal Signaling Interface [*Telecommunications*] (TEL) ..... CTSI
Central Terminal Station (SAUS) .... CTS
Central Terminal Unit [*Telecommunications*] .... CTU
Central Territory Railroad Tariff Bureau .... CTR
Central Test Center (SAUS) .... CTC
Central Test Control (SAUS) .... CTC
Central Test Facility (SAUS) .... CTF
Central Test Site for Personnel and Training Evaluation Program [*Military*] (DNAB) .... CTSPTEP
Central Test Site for Personnel and Training Evaluation Program Detachment [*Military*] (DNAB) .... CTSPTEPDET
Central Test Technology Coordinating Office [*Army*] (RDA) .... CTTCO
Central Texas College, Killeen, TX [*Library symbol*] [*Library of Congress*] (LCLS) .... TxKiC
Central Texas Library System [*Library network*] .... CTLS
Central Time (GPO) .... CT
Central Time and Frequency Control .... CTFC
Central Timing and Data Distribution System (SAA) .... CT & DDS
Central Timing Equipment .... CTE
Central Timing Signal Generator [*Air Force*] (MCD) .... CTSG
Central Timing System .... CTS
Central Timing Unit (KSC) .... CTU
Central Tire Inflation System [*Automotive engineering*] .... CTIS
Central TMDE [*Test, Measuring, and Diagnostic Equipment*] **Activity** [*Army*] (MCD) .... CTA
Central to Peripheral Ratio [*Anatomy*] .... C/P
Central Tool Room .... CTR
Central Torpedo Office .... CTO
Central Township Junior College (SAUO) .... CTJC
Central Tracing Bureau [*Post-World War II*] .... CTB
Central Tracing Policy Board [*Post-World War II*] .... CTPB
Central Track Store Locator (MCD) .... CTSL
Central Track Stores Index (MCD) .... CTSX
Central Tracking Center (IAA) .... CTC
Central Tractor Farm & Country [*NASDAQ symbol*] (TTSB) ...... CTFC
Central Tractor Farm & Country, Inc. [*NASDAQ symbol*] (SAG) .... CTFC
Central Tractor Farm & Country, Inc. [*Associated Press*] (SAG) .... CtrlTrac
Central Trade Test Board [*British*] .... CTTB
Central Trade Test Board (SAUO) .... CTTB
Central Trades' Union [*British*] .... CTU
Central Traffic Control .... CTC
Central Train Control (IAA) .... CTC
Central Training Academy (SAUO) .... CTA
Central Training Council [*Department of Employment*] [*British*] ... CTC
Central Training Depot (SAUS) .... CTD
Central Training Depot (SAUO) .... CTD
Central Training Facility (MCD) .... CTF
Central Training Institute for Instructors (SAUO) .... CTI
Central Training Program (SAUO) .... CTP
Central Training Section [*Air Force*] (AFM) .... CTS
Central Trans Rental Gp ADS [*NYSE symbol*] (TTSB) .... TPH
Central Transfer Point .... CTP
Central Transformer Corporation (SAUO) .... CTC
Central Translation Evidence .... CTE
Central Transport Authority (ADA) .... CTA
Central Transport Consultative Committee [*British*] .... CTCC
Central Transport Rental (WDAA) .... CTR
Central Transport Rental Group Ltd. [*Formerly, Tiphook Ltd. ADS*] [*Associated Press*] (SAG) .... CnTrnRtl
Central Transport Rental Group Ltd. [*Formerly, Tiphook Ltd. ADS*] [*NYSE symbol*] (SAG) .... TPH
Central Treaty Organization [*Also, CTO*] [*Formerly, Baghdad Pact*] ... CENTO
Central Treaty Organization [*Also, CENTO*] [*Formerly, Baghdad Pact*] ... CTO
Central Treaty Organization Allied Military Publication .... CENTAMP
Central TRON (SAUS) .... CTRON
Central Trunk Terminal .... CTT
Central Trust Co. [*Toronto Stock Exchange symbol*] .... CET
Central Trust of China .... CTC
Central Trypanosomiasis Research Laboratory (SAUO) .... CTRL
Central Tuber Crops Research Institute .... CTCRI
Central Tumor Registry [*Medicine*] (BARN) .... CTR
Central Tyre Inflation (SAUS) .... CTI
Central Union for Child Welfare [*Finland*] (EAIO) .... CUCW
Central Union of Hungarian Cooperative Societies (SAUO) .... MOSZK
Central Unit [*Computer science*] (IAA) .... CU
Central Unit for Scientific Photography [*Royal Aircraft Establishment*] [*British*] .... CUSP
Central Unit on Environmental Pollution [*British*] .... CUEP
Central Unit-Buffer (IAA) .... CUB
Central United States Earthquake Consortium (GEOI) .... CUSEC
Central United States Registry [*Army*] .... CUSR
Central Unit-Memory (MCD) .... CUM
Central Unit-Memory Programmer (MCD) .... CUMP
Central U.S. Earthquake Consortium (SAUS) .... CUSEC

Central Utah Project [*Federal aqueduct-and-reservoir plan*] .... CUP
Central Utility Building (AAEL) .... CUB
Central Vacuum (REAL) .... cent/vac
Central Vacuum (REAL) .... c/v
Central Vacuum Loading System .... CVLS
Central Valley, CA [*FM radio station call letters*] .... KNNN
Central Valley Conference (PSS) CVC
Central Valley Project [*California*] (ECON) .... CVP
Central Valley Trucks CV
Central Valuation Committee (SAUO) CVC
Central Vancouver Island Multicultural Society (AC) .... CVIMS
Central Vehicle Depot (SAUO) .... CVD
Central Vehicle Depot Workshop (SAUO) .... CVDW
Central Vehicle Index [*Record of cars lost or stolen in London*] CVI
Central Vehicle Monitoring [*Automotive engineering*] .... CVM
Central Vein [*or Venous*] [*Anatomy*] CV
Central Vein Occlusion [*Medicine*] (DMAA) .... CVO
Central Venous Catheter [*Medicine*] CVC
Central Venous Catheter [*Medicine*] (DMAA) .... CV cath
Central Venous Infusions [*Medicine*] (MELL) CVI
Central Venous Nutrient (STED) .... CVN
Central Venous Oxygen [*Medicine*] (DB) .... CVO
Central Venous Pressure [*Medicine*] .... CVP
Central Verband der Siebenburger Sachsen of the United States [*Later, Alliance of Transylvanian Saxons*] (EA) .... CVSSUS
Central Vermillion County Schools Cooperative, Danville, IL [*Library symbol*] [*Library of Congress*] (LCLS) .... IDanviCS
Central Vermont Airways (SAUO) .... CVA
Central Vermont Public Service Corp. [*NYSE symbol*] (SPSG) ... CV
Central Vermont Public Service Corp. (SAUO) .... CVPS
Central Vermont Public Service Corp. [*Associated Press*] (SAG) ... CVtPS
Central Vermont Railway, Inc. [*AAR code*] CV
Central Vermont Railway, Inc. .... CVT
Central Vermont Railway, Inc. (SAUO) .... CVt
Central Vermont Railway, Inc. (SAUO) .... CVtRy
Central Veterinary Laboratory [*Research center*] [*British*] (IRC) ... CVL
Central Virginia Bankshares [*Associated Press*] (SAG) .... CtrlVA
Central Virginia Bankshares [*NASDAQ symbol*] (SAG) .... CVBK
Central Virginia Community College, Lynchburg, VA [*Library symbol*] [*Library of Congress*] (LCLS) ViLCV
Central Visual Field [*Optics*] .... CVF
Central Volunteer Bureau of Ottawa-Carleton [*Bureau Central des Benevoles d'Ottawa-Carleton*] **Ottawa, Ontario** [*Library symbol*] [*National Library of Canada*] (BIB) .... OOCVB
Central Volunteer Headquarters [*Military*] [*British*] .... CVHQ
Central VT Pub Svc [*NYSE symbol*] (SG) CV
Central Wages Board (SAUO) .... CWB
Central War Time (SAUS) .... CWT
Central Warning Center (SAUS) .... CWC
Central Warning Site (SAUS) .... CWS
Central Washington Hospital, Health Sciences Library, Wenatchee, WA [*Library symbol*] [*Library of Congress*] (LCLS) ...... WaWeC
Central Washington State College, Ellensburg, WA [*Library symbol*] [*Library of Congress*] (LCLS) .... WaElC
Central Washington University (GAGS) .... Cent Wash U
Central Waste Disposal Facility [*Oak Ridge National Laboratory*] ... CWDF
Central Water Advisory Committee (SAUO) .... CWAC
Central Water and Power Department (SAUS) .... CWPD
Central Water and Power Development (SAUO) .... CWPD
Central Water and Power Research Station, Poona (SAUO) ... CWPRS
Central Waterpower, Irrigation and Navigation Research Station (SAUO) .... CWINRS
Central Waterways, Irrigation and Navigation Commission (SAUO) ...... CWINC
Central Weather Bureau [*Taiwan*] (USDC) .... CWB
Central Weather Processor [*FAA*] (TAG) .... CWP
Central Weather Service Unit [*FAA*] (USDC) .... CWSU
Central Welfare Fund (SAUO) .... CWF
Central Welsh Board (SAUO) .... CWB
Central Welsh Board .... CWB
Central Wesleyan College, Central, SC [*Library symbol*] [*Library of Congress*] (LCLS) .... ScCenW
Central Western Law Society [*Australia*] .... CWLS
Central Western Region .... CWR
Central Wholesalers Association (EA) .... CWA
Central Wind Extraction Unit (SAUS) .... CWEU
Central Winter Time (IAA) .... CWT
Central Wireless Station [*Air Force*] [*British*] .... CWS
Central Wisconsin Colony, Staff Library, Madison, WI [*Library symbol*] [*Library of Congress*] (LCLS) .... WMaC
Central Wisconsin Colony, Staff Library, Madison, WI [*Library symbol*] [*Library of Congress*] (LCLS) .... WMaCW
Central Wyoming Community College, Riverton, WY [*Library symbol*] [*Library of Congress*] (LCLS) .... WyRiC
Central Yiddish (BJA) .... CY
Central Yiddish Culture Organization (EA) .... CYCO
Central YMCA Community College, Chicago, IL [*Library symbol*] [*Library of Congress*] (LCLS) .... ICCYM
Central Youth Employment Executive [*Department of Employment*] [*British*] .... CYEE
Central Zionist Archives (SAUO) .... CZA
Centrala Filmarkivet Ab, Stockholm, Sweden [*Library symbol*] [*Library of Congress*] (LCLS) .... CeF
Central-American General Market (SAUO) .... CAGM
Central-Anzeiger fuer Juedische Litteratur [*A publication*] (BJA) ... CAJL

Centrale Bemiddeling bij Medefinanciering Ontuikkelingsprogramma's [*Netherlands*] ... CEBEMO
Centrale de l'Enseignement du Quebec [*Quebec Teaching Congress*] (AC) ... CEQ
Centrale de l'enseignment du Quebec [*Canada*] [*An association*] (CROSS) ... CEQ
Centrale de Livraison de Valeurs Mobilieres ... CEDEL
Centrale des Bibliotheques, Centre Documentaire, Montreal, PQ, Canada [*Library symbol*] [*Library of Congress*] (LCLS) ... CaQMCD
Centrale des Bibliotheques, Services Documentaires Multimedia, Inc., Montreal, Quebec [*Library symbol*] [*National Library of Canada*] (NLC) ... QMECB
Centrale des Professionnelles et Professionnels de la Sante (AC) ... CPS
Centrale des Syndicats Democratiques [*Congress of Democratic Unions*] ... CSD
Centrale des Syndicats Democratiques/Congress of Democratic Unions [*Political party*] [*Canada*] (ASC) ... CSD/CDU
Centrale Nucleaire Europeenne a Neutrons Rapides SA [*France*] (PDAA) ... NERSA
Centralforbundet for Alkohol- och Narkotikaupplysning [*Swedish Council for Information on Alcohol and Other Drugs*] [*Information service or system*] (IID) ... CAN
Centralia College, Centralia, WA [*Library symbol*] [*Library of Congress*] (LCLS) ... WaCeC
Centralia Correctional Center, Centralia, IL [*Library symbol*] [*Library of Congress*] (LCLS) ... ICenC
Centralia District High School, District 200, Centralia, IL [*Library symbol*] [*Library of Congress*] (LCLS) ... ICenHS
Centralia, IL [*Location identifier*] [*FAA*] (FAAL) ... ENL
Centralia, IL [*AM radio station call letters*] ... WILY
Centralia, IL [*FM radio station call letters*] ... WRXX
Centralia, MO [*FM radio station call letters*] ... KMFC
Centralia Public Library, Centralia, IL [*Library symbol*] [*Library of Congress*] (LCLS) ... ICen
Centralia Township Junior College [*Illinois*] ... CTJC
Centralia, WA [*FM radio station call letters*] ... KCED
Centralia, WA [*Television station call letters*] ... KCKA
Centralia, WA [*FM radio station call letters*] ... KMNT
Centralia-Chehalis, WA [*AM radio station call letters*] ... KELA
Centralia-Chehalis, WA [*AM radio station call letters*] ... KITI
Centralinstitut for Nordisk Asienforskning [*Scandinavian Institute of Asian Studies*] [*Later, NIAS*] (EAIO) ... CINA
Centralis Lateralis [*Neuroanatomy*] ... CL
Centralised Air Warning System (SAUO) ... CAWS
Centralised Aircraft Servicing System (SAUS) ... CASS
Centralised Fault Display Interface Unit (SAUS) ... CFDIU
Centralised Information Service for Complementary Medicine (SAUO) ... CISCOM
Centralised Warning Panel (SAUS) ... CWP
Centralization (SAUS) ... cen
Centralization of Supply Management Operations [*DoD*] ... COSMOS
Centralized Accounting and Billeting [*Military*] (DNAB) ... CAB
Centralized Accounting and Billing (MCD) ... CAB
Centralized Accounting and Polling Software [*Computer science*] (PCM) ... CAPS
Centralized Accounting for Local Management [*Veterans Administration*] ... CALM
Centralized Administrative Systems Control and Design (PDAA) ... CASCADE
Centralized Air Defense System (SAA) ... CADS
Centralized Alarm and Control System [*Telecommunications*] (TEL) ... CACS
Centralized Army Passenger Port Call System (AABC) ... CAPPS
Centralized Army Tracking and Control of Hazardous Material (BCP) ... CATCHMAT
Centralized Asset Visibility and Management Program for Vietnam [*Army*] (RDA) ... CAVAMP-V
Centralized Assignment Procedures [*Military*] (INF) ... CAP
Centralized Assignment Procedures Computer System [*Military*] ... CAP III
Centralized Attendants Service [*Bell System*] ... CAS
Centralized Authorization File (SAUS) ... CAF
Centralized Authorized File [*IRS*] ... CAF
Centralized Automated Loop Reporting System (SAUS) ... CARLS
Centralized Automated Military Pay System ... CAMPS
Centralized Automated Pay System ... CAPS
Centralized Automatic Loop Reporting System [*Telecommunications*] (TEL) ... CALRS
Centralized Automatic Message Accounting [*Bell System*] ... CAMA
Centralized Automatic Message Accounting - Computerized [*Bell System*] (TEL) ... CAMA-C
Centralized Automatic Message Accounting - Operator Number Identification [*Telecommunications*] (TEL) ... CAMA-ONI
Centralized Automatic Recorder and Tester ... CART
Centralized Automatic Recording on Trunks [*Bell System*] ... CAROT
Centralized Automatic Test System [*Navy*] (MCD) ... CATES
Centralized Automatic Test System [*Navy*] (MCD) ... CATS
Centralized Automatic Testing ... CAT
Centralized Automatic Toll Ticketing [*Telecommunications*] (TEL) ... CATT
Centralized Automatic Trouble-Locating and Analysis System [*AT & T*] (TEL) ... CATLAS
Centralized Automotive Reporting System [*DARCOM*] (MCD) ... CARS
Centralized Branch Exchange [*Telecommunications*] (TEL) ... CBE
Centralized Branch Exchange [*Telecommunications*] (NITA) ... CBX
Centralized Cancer Patient Data System ... CCPDS
Centralized COMINT Communications Center [*National Security Agency*] ... CCCC
Centralized Command Selection System (MCD) ... CCSS
Centralized Computing Services ... CCS
Centralized Control (SAUS) ... CENTCON
Centralized Control Facility ... CENTCON
Centralized Correspondence Study [*Alaska*] (EDAC) ... CC/S
Centralized Customer Order Processing (SAUS) ... CCOP
Centralized Data Acquisition (SAUS) ... CDA
Centralized Data Base (RDA) ... CDB
Centralized Data Management System (SAUO) ... CDMS
Centralized Data Processing (IEEE) ... CDP
Centralized Dealer Inventory Control System (MHDB) ... CDICS
Centralized Digital Control System [*Computer science*] (PDAA) ... CDCS
Centralized Digital Telecommunications System [*Telecommunications*] (HGAA) ... CDTS
Centralized Electrification and Traffic Control (MCD) ... CETC
Centralized Electronic Control [*Navy*] ... CEC
Centralized Employment Program ... CEP
Centralized Engine Room Control (SAUS) ... CERC
Centralized Environmental Facility ... CEF
Centralized Excess Personal Property [*Department of Agriculture*] (GFGA) ... CEPO
Centralized Expenditure/Reimbursement Processing System (NVT) ... CERPS
Centralized Fault Display System (HLLA) ... CFDS
Centralized Flow Management Unit (DA) ... CFMU
Centralized Fuels Management System (SAUO) ... CFMS
Centralized IFF (SAUS) ... CIFF
Centralized Information Acquisition (SAUS) ... CIA
Centralized Information Reference and Control ... CIRC
Centralized Information Reference and Control System (SAUS) ... CIRC System
Centralized Input/Output System (DNAB) ... CINOS
Centralized Integrated System Compiler (MCD) ... CISIL
Centralized Integrated Systems for International Logistics ... CISIL
Centralized Integrated Technical Information System (DIT) ... CITIS
Centralized Intercept Bureau [*Bell System*] ... CIB
Centralized Intermediate Logistics Concept (MCD) ... CILC
Centralized Intermediate Logistics System (MCD) ... CILS
Centralized Intermediate Repair Facility ... CIRF
Centralized Knowledge Base (SAUS) ... CKB
Centralized Library Automation Service System (SAUS) ... CLASS
Centralized Library Information Processor [*United States Computer Corp.*] [*Information service or system*] (IID) ... CLIP
Centralized Lighting System [*Automotive engineering*] ... CLS
Centralized Local Area Selective Signaling (VERA) ... CLASS
Centralized Lubrication [*Automotive engineering*] ... CL
Centralized Mail Remittance [*Telecommunications*] (TEL) ... CMR
Centralized Main Remittance (SAUS) ... CMR
Centralized Maintenance and Administration Center ... CMAC
Centralized Maintenance System [*Telecommunications*] ... CMS
Centralized Maintenance Test System (SAUS) ... CMTS
Centralized Materials Section ... CMS
Centralized Message Data System [*Bell System*] ... CMDS
Centralized Message Distribution [*Computer science*] ... CMD
Centralized Munitions Systems [*USARPAC*] (MCD) ... CMS
Centralized Network Reference Service (SAUS) ... CNRS
Centralized Online Processing Environment (SAUS) ... COPE
Centralized Operating System (IAA) ... COS
Centralized or Distributed Integrated Access Control [*Computer science*] ... CODIAC
Centralized Payroll System (ADA) ... CPS
Centralized Personnel Record System [*Telecommunications*] (TEL) ... CPRS
Centralized Receiving Point ... CRP
Centralized Records Business Office [*Telecommunications*] (TEL) ... CRBO
Centralized Referral Activity [*Military*] (AFM) ... CRA
Centralized Referral System [*Military*] (AFM) ... CRS
Centralized Reliability Data Organization [*Nuclear Regulatory Commission*] (GFGA) ... CREDO
Centralized Repair Activity [*Air Force*] (AFIT) ... CRA
Centralized Repair Service Answering Bureau (SAUS) ... CRSAB
Centralized Repair Service Attendants [*Telecommunications*] (TEL) ... CRSA
Centralized Requisitioning Accounting and Billing ... CRAB
Centralized Results System [*Telecommunications*] (TEL) ... CRS
Centralized Scheduling (SAUS) ... CS
Centralized Service Observation [*Telecommunications*] (TEL) ... CSO
Centralized Ships Force Management System ... CSFMS
Centralized Status, Alarm, and Control System [*Bell System*] ... CSACS
Centralized Storm Information System (SAUS) ... CSIS
Centralized Structure Store (SAUS) ... CSS
Centralized Supervisory and Control (BUR) ... CSC
Centralized Support Base [*Military*] ... CSB
Centralized System for Analysis Reporting (SAUS) ... CSAR
Centralized Theater Surveillance Database (MCD) ... CTSDB
Centralized Ticket Investigation [*Telecommunications*] ... CTI
Centralized Title Services (SAUS) ... CTS
Centralized Traffic Control [*TRB*] (TAG) ... CTC
Centralized Traffic Control Selector (SAUS) ... CTC Selector
Centralized Train Central (GAVI) ... CTC
Centralized Training [*Material management subsystem*] (MCD) ... CENTRA
Centralized Transient Accounting System (MCD) ... CTAS
Centralized Translation System [*Communications*] ... CTS
Centralized Warning Indicator (SAUS) ... CWI
Centrally Controlled Interconnection System (ACAE) ... CCIS
Centrally Directed Audit (SAUS) ... CDA
Centrally Directed Audit Program (SAUO) ... CDAP
Centrally Funded (AFM) ... CF
Centrally Funded Second Destination Transportation [*Army*] ... CFSDT
Centrally Funded Short Course Program ... CFSCP
Centrally Planned Asia (CARB) ... CPA
Centrally Planned Economy ... CPE
Centrally Planned Europe (SAUO) ... CPE
Centrally Procured (SAUS) ... CP
Centrally Procured Items (MCD) ... CPI
Centrally Reportable Equipment (AAGC) ... CRE

Centrally-Planned Economies (SAUO) .... CPEs
Centralny Osrodek Informacji Normalizacyjnej i Metrologicznej [*Center for Information on Standardization and Metrology*] [*Poland*] (EAIO) .... COINIM
Centralny Urzad Geodezji i Kartografil [*Poland*] (GEOI) .... CUGiK
Central-Processor-Chip (SAUS) .... CPC
Centralverein-Zeitung [*A publication*] (BJA) .... CVZ
Centration Distance (SAUS) .... CD
Centration Point (SAUS) .... CP
Centre (SAUS) .... Cntr
Centre Academique Canadien en Italie [*Canadian Academic Centre in Italy*] .... CACI
Centre Acadien, Universite Sainte-Anne, Church Point, Nova Scotia [*Library symbol*] [*National Library of Canada*] (BIB) .... NSCSA
Centre Africain de Formation et de Recherche Administratives pour la Developpement [*African Training and Research Center in Administration for Development*] (IID) .... CAFRAD
Centre Africain de Recherche Appliquee et de Formation en Matiere de Developpement Social [*African Center for Applied Research and Training in Social Development - ACARTSD*] (EAIO) .... CAFRADES
Centre Africaine d'Etudes Monetaires [*African Centre for Monetary Studies*] [*Senegal*] (EAIO) .... CAEM
Centre Afro-Americain du Travail [*Afro-American Labor Center*] (AF) .... CAAT
Centre Against Apartheid [*United Nations*] (DUND) .... CAA
Centre Airlines, Inc. [*ICAO designator*] (FAAC) .... DTV
Centre, AL [*AM radio station call letters*] .... WAGC
Centre, AL [*AM radio station call letters*] .... WEIS
Centre, AL [*FM radio station call letters*] .... WRHY
Centre Alliance Students' Association [*Australia*] .... CASA
Centre Antonien, Quebec, PQ, Canada [*Library symbol*] [*Library of Congress*] (LCLS) .... CaQQCA
Centre Board (SAUS) .... CB
Centre Canadien d'Architecture [*Canadian Centre for Architecture*] **Montreal, Quebec** [*Library symbol*] [*National Library of Canada*] (NLC) .... QMCCA
Centre Canadien de Lutte Contre l'Alcoolisme et les Toxicomanies (AC) .... CCLAT
Centre Canadien de Recherche en Politiques de Rechange [*Canadian Centre for Policy Alternatives*] (EAIO) .... CCRPR
Centre Canadien de Teledetection [*Canadian Centre for Remote Sensing - CCRS*] .... CCT
Centre Canadien d'Etudes et de Cooperation Internationale, Montreal, Quebec [*Library symbol*] [*National Library of Canada*] (NLC) .... QMCECI
Centre Canadien d'Etudes et de Cooperation Internationle, Montreal, PQ, Canada [*Library symbol*] [*Library of Congress*] (LCLS) .... CaQMCECI
Centre Canadien d'Hygiene et de Securite au Travail [*Canadian Centre for Occupational Health and Safety - CCOHS*] .... CCHST
Centre Catholique International pour l'UNESCO [*France*] CCIC
Centre College of Kentucky, Danville, KY [*OCLC symbol*] (OCLC) .... KCC
Centre College of Kentucky, Danville, KY [*Library symbol*] [*Library of Congress*] (LCLS) .... KyDC
Centre Commun de Recherche (SAUS) .... CCR
Centre Commun de Recherches Nucleaires [*Joint Nuclear Research Center*] [*EURATOM*] .... CCRN
Centre Commun d'Etudes de Television et de Telecommunications [*Videotex research center*] [*France*] .... CCETT
Centre County Court House, Bellefonte, PA [*Library symbol*] [*Library of Congress*] (LCLS) .... PBelC
Centre County Legal Journal [*Pennsylvania*] [*A publication*] (DLA) .... CCLJ
Centre County Library, Bellefonte, PA [*Library symbol*] [*Library of Congress*] (LCLS) .... PBel
[*Le*] **Centre Culturel Francophone de Vancouver** [*Vancouver French Cultural Centre*] (AC) .... CCFV
Centre Culturel, Verdun, PQ, Canada [*Library symbol*] [*Library of Congress*] (LCLS) .... CaQVeC
Centre d'Accueil Domremy-Montreal, Ste.-Genevieve, Quebec [*Library symbol*] [*National Library of Canada*] (NLC) .... QMCADM
Centre d'Action Europeenne Federaliste [*European Center for Federalist Action*] .... AEF
Centre d'Adaptation de la Main-d'Oeuvre Aerospatiale du Quebec (AC) .... CAMAQ
Centre d'Analyse et de Recherche Documentaires pour l'Afrique Noire .... CARDAN
Centre d'Analyse et de Recherche Operationnelle [*Operational Research and Analysis Establishment*] [*Canadian Department of National Defense*] .... CARO
Centre d'Analyse et de Traitement Automatique de la Bible [*Centre of Analysis and Automatic Treatment of the Bible*] [*Canada*] .... CATAB
Centre d'Animation de Developpement et de Recherche en Education (AC) .... CADRE
Centre d'Animation, de Developpement, et de Recherche en Education, Montreal, PQ, Canada [*Library symbol*] [*Library of Congress*] (LCLS) .... CaQMCAD
Centre d'Animation, de Developpement, et de Recherche en Education, Montreal, Quebec [*Library symbol*] [*National Library of Canada*] (NLC) .... QMCAD
Centre d'Animation des Femmes de Hull (AC) .... CAF
Centre d'Animation Pedagogique, Conseil des Ecoles Separees Catholiques d'Ottawa, Ontario [*Library symbol*] [*National Library of Canada*] (BIB) .... OOCESC
Centre d'Arbitrage Commerical National et International du Quebec [*Quebec National & International Commerical Arbitration Centre*] (AC) .... CACNIQ
Centre de Compilation de Donnees Neutroniques [*Neutron Data Compilation Center*] [*France*] [*Information service or system*] (IID) .... CCDN
Centre de Conditionnement Pre-Natal [*Pre-Natal Conditions Centre*] [*Canada*] .... CCPN
Centre de Controle Mixte [*Joint Control Center*] [*NATO*] (NATG) .... CCM
Centre de Controle Tactique Aerien [*Air Tactical Control Center*] [*NATO*] (NATG) .... CCTA
Centre de Cooperation pour les Recherches Scientifiques Relatives au Tabac [*Cooperation Center for Scientific Research Relative to Tobacco*] [*Paris, France*] (EA) .... CORESTA
Centre de Creation Industrielle [*Center for Industrial Creation*] [*Information service or system*] (IID) CCI
Centre de Danse International [*France*] .... CDI
Centre de Documentation - DGTI [*Direction Generale des Technologies de l'Information*], **Ministere des Communications du Quebec, Ste.-Foy, Quebec** [*Library symbol*] [*National Library of Canada*] (BIB) .... QQCOC
Centre de Documentation, APO Quebec, Montreal, PQ, Canada [*Library symbol*] [*Library of Congress*] (LCLS) .... CaQMAPO
Centre de Documentation, APO Quebec, Montreal, Quebec [*Library symbol*] [*National Library of Canada*] (NLC) .... QMAPO
Centre de Documentation, Assurance-Vie Desjardins, Levis, Quebec [*Library symbol*] [*National Library of Canada*] (NLC) .... QLAVD
Centre de Documentation Astrologique (AC) .... CDA
Centre de Documentation, Banque Nationale du Canada, Montreal, Quebec [*Library symbol*] [*National Library of Canada*] (NLC) .... QMBAN
Centre de Documentation, Bureau de la Protection Civile du Quebec, Ste.-Foy, Quebec [*Library symbol*] [*National Library of Canada*] (BIB) .... QSFPC
Centre de Documentation, Bureau des Economies d'Energie du Quebec, Mont real, Quebec [*Library symbol*] [*National Library of Canada*] (NLC) .... QMBE
Centre de Documentation, Centrale de l'Enseignement du Quebec, Ste.-Foy, Quebec [*Library symbol*] [*National Library of Canada*] (NLC) .... QSTFCE
Centre de Documentation, Centre de Recherche Informatique de Montreal, Quebec [*Library symbol*] [*National Library of Canada*] (BIB) .... QMCRIM
Centre de Documentation, Centre de Services Sociaux de Quebec, Quebec [*Library symbol*] [*National Library of Canada*] (BIB) .... QQCSS
Centre de Documentation, Centre Hospitalier Anna-Laberge, Chateauguay, Quebec [*Library symbol*] [*National Library of Canada*] (BIB) .... QCAL
Centre de Documentation, Centre Hospitalier des Laurentides et Centre d'Accueil et de Readaptation des Hautes-Vallees, L'Annonciation, Quebec [*Library symbol*] [*National Library of Canada*] (BIB) .... QACHL
Centre de Documentation, Centre Hospitalier Fleury, Montreal, PQ, Canada [*Library symbol*] [*Library of Congress*] (LCLS) .... CaQMCHF
Centre de Documentation, Centre Hospitalier Fleury, Montreal, Quebec [*Library symbol*] [*National Library of Canada*] (NLC) .... QMCHF
Centre de Documentation, Centre Hospitalier Pierre Boucher, Longueuil, Quebec [*Library symbol*] [*National Library of Canada*] (NLC) .... QLOPB
Centre de Documentation, Centre Hospitalier Regional de Rimouski, Quebec [*Library symbol*] [*National Library of Canada*] (NLC) .... QRCH
Centre de Documentation, CGI [*Conseillers en Gestion et Informatique*], **I nc., Quebec** [*Library symbol*] [*National Library of Canada*] (NLC) .... QQCGI
Centre de Documentation, Charette, Fortier, Hawey, Touche, Ross, Montreal, Quebec [*Library symbol*] [*National Library of Canada*] (NLC) .... QMCFH
Centre de Documentation, CLSC de Hull, Quebec [*Library symbol*] [*National Library of Canada*] (NLC) .... QHCL
Centre de Documentation, CLSC de l'Aquilon, Baie-Comeau, Quebec [*Library symbol*] [*National Library of Canada*] (BIB) .... QBCCL
Centre de Documentation, Commission d'Acces a l'Information, Quebec, Quebec [*Library symbol*] [*National Library of Canada*] (NLC) .... QQCAI
Centre de Documentation, Commission de la Fonction Publique du Quebec, Quebec, Quebec [*Library symbol*] [*National Library of Canada*] (BIB) .... QQCFP
Centre de Documentation, Commission des Normes du Travail, Quebec [*Library symbol*] [*National Library of Canada*] (NLC) .... QQCDT
Centre de Documentation, Commission Rochon, Ste.-Foy, Quebec [*Library symbol*] [*National Library of Canada*] (BIB) .... QSFCRO
Centre de Documentation, Conseil de la Science et de la Technologie du Quebec, Ste.-Foy, Quebec [*Library symbol*] [*National Library of Canada*] (NLC) .... QQCPS
Centre de Documentation, Conseil de la Science et de la Technologie, Quebec [*Library symbol*] [*National Library of Canada*] (NLC) .... QQST
Centre de Documentation, Conseil des Colleges du Quebec, Quebec, Quebec [*Library symbol*] [*National Library of Canada*] (BIB) .... QQCC
Centre de Documentation, Conseil Superieur de l'Education du Quebec, Ste.-Foy, Quebec [*Library symbol*] [*National Library of Canada*] (BIB) .... QSFCSE
Centre de Documentation de la Direction Generale de l'Energie du Ministere des Richesses Naturelles du Quebec, Quebec, PQ, Canada [*Library symbol*] [*Library of Congress*] [*Obsolete*] (LCLS) .... CaQQRNC
Centre de Documentation de la Mecanique [*Documentation Center for Mechanics*] [*Technical Center for Mechanical Industries*] [*Information service or system*] (IID) .... CDM
Centre de Documentation de la Regie du Logement, Montreal, PQ, Canada [*Library symbol*] [*Library of Congress*] (LCLS) .... CaQMRL
Centre de Documentation de la Regie du Logement, Montreal, PQ, Canada [*Library symbol*] [*Library of Congress*] (LCLS) .... CaQQCRS
Centre de Documentation, Departement de Sante Communautaire, Centre Hospitalier,Universite Laval, Quebec [*Library symbol*] [*National Library of Canada*] (NLC) .... QQLACHC
Centre de Documentation, Departement de Sante Communautaire de Lanaudiere, Joliette, Quebec [*Library symbol*] [*National Library of Canada*] (BIB) .... QJCH
Centre de Documentation, Departement de Sante Communautaire du Haut-Richelieu, St.-Jean, Quebec [*Library symbol*] [*National Library of Canada*] (NLC) .... QSTJSC
Centre de Documentation, Departement de Sante Communautaire, Hopital du Saint-Sacrement, Quebec, Quebec [*Library symbol*] [*National Library of Canada*] (BIB) .... QQHSSC

Centre de Documentation, Directeur General des Elections du Quebec, Ste.-Foy, Quebec [*Library symbol*] [*National Library of Canada*] (BIB) ...... QSFE
Centre de Documentation, Direction de l'Environnement, Hydro-Quebec, Montreal, Quebec [*Library symbol*] [*National Library of Canada*] (NLC) ...... QMHDE
Centre de Documentation, Direction Generale de la Planification, Ministere de laMain-d'Oeuvre et de la Securite du Revenu du Quebec, Quebec [*Library symbol*] [*National Library of Canada*] (BIB) ...... QQMSRP
Centre de Documentation, Direction Generale de l'Enseignement et de la RechercheUniversitaires, Ministere de l'Enseignement Superieur et de la Science du Quebe c, Quebec, Quebec [*Library symbol*] [*National Library of Canada*] (BIB) ...... QQESE
Centre de Documentation, Direction Generale des Medias, Ministere des Communications du Quebec, Quebec, Quebec [*Library symbol*] [*National Library of Canada*] (BIB) ...... QQCOM
Centre de Documentation, Direction Generale des Ressources Informationnelles, Ministere de la Main d'Oeuvre et de la Securite du Revenu du Quebec, Quebec, Quebec [*Library symbol*] [*National Library of Canada*] (NLC) ...... QQMSRD
Centre de Documentation DSC, Hotel-Dieu de Riviere-Du-Loup, Quebec [*Library symbol*] [*National Library of Canada*] (BIB) ...... QRLH
Centre de Documentation du 200, Ministere de l'Agriculture, des Pecheries, et del'Alimentation, Quebec, Quebec [*Library symbol*] [*National Library of Canada*] (NLC) ...... QQAG
Centre de Documentation du Personnel, Hopital de Convalescents Julius Richardson[*Staff Library, Julius Richardson Convalescent Hospital, Inc.*], **Montreal, Quebec** [*Library symbol*] [*National Library of Canada*] (NLC) ...... QMHJR
Centre de Documentation, Ecole Secondaire de Plantagenet [*Documentation Centre, Plantagenet Secondary School*], **Ontario** [*Library symbol*] [*National Library of Canada*] (BIB) ...... OPES
Centre de Documentation en Theatre Quebecois, Trois-Rivieres, PQ, Canada [*Library symbol*] [*Library of Congress*] (LCLS) ...... CaQTUTH
Centre de Documentation en Theatre Quebecois, Trois-Rivieres, Quebec [*Library symbol*] [*National Library of Canada*] (NLC) ...... QTUTH
Centre de Documentation et d'Audio-Visuel, Hopital d'Youville de Sherbrooke, Quebec [*Library symbol*] [*National Library of Canada*] (NLC) ...... QSHERY
Centre de Documentation et d'Information Interuniversitaire en Sciences Sociales[*Interuniversity Documentation and Information Center for the Social Science s*] [*Information service or system*] (IID) ...... CENDIS
Centre de Documentation, Hotel-Dieu d'Arthabaska, Quebec [*Library symbol*] [*National Library of Canada*] (BIB) ...... QAHD
Centre de Documentation, Hydro-Quebec International, Montreal, Quebec [*Library symbol*] [*National Library of Canada*] (BIB) ...... QMHI
Centre de Documentation, INRS [*Institut National de la Recherche Scientifique*]**-Eau, Quebec, Quebec** [*Library symbol*] [*National Library of Canada*] (NLC) ...... QQUIE
Centre de Documentation, INRS [*Institut National de la Recherche Scientifique*]**-Energie, Varennes, Quebec** [*Library symbol*] [*National Library of Canada*] (NLC) ...... QVAI
Centre de Documentation, INRS [*Institut National de la Recherche Scientifique*]**-Georessources, Ste.-Foy, Quebec** [*Library symbol*] [*National Library of Canada*] (NLC) ...... QSFIG
Centre de Documentation, INRS [*Institut National de la Recherche Scientifique*]**-Sante, Montreal, Quebec** [*Library symbol*] [*National Library of Canada*] (NLC) ...... QMUQIS
Centre de Documentation INRS [*Institut National de la Recherche Scientifique*]**-Urbanisation, Montreal, Quebec** [*Library symbol*] [*National Library of Canada*] (NLC) ...... QMUQIU
Centre de Documentation, Institut de Recherche Appliquee sur le Travail, Montreal, Quebec [*Library symbol*] [*National Library of Canada*] (NLC) ...... QMRAD
Centre de Documentation, Institut de Technologie Agro-Alimentaire de La Pocatiere, Quebec [*Library symbol*] [*National Library of Canada*] (NLC) ...... QPES
Centre de Documentation, Institut Raymond-Dewar, Montreal, Quebec [*Library symbol*] [*National Library of Canada*] (NLC) ...... QMISM
Centre de Documentation Internationale des Industries Utilisatrices de Produits Agricoles [*International Documentation Center for Industries Using Agricultural Products*] [*Database producer*] [*Information service or system*] (IID) ...... CDIUPA
Centre de Documentation, La Presse Ltee., Montreal, Quebec [*Library symbol*] [*National Library of Canada*] (NLC) ...... QMLP
Centre de Documentation, Laurentienne Mutuelle d'Assurance, Quebec, Quebec [*Library symbol*] [*National Library of Canada*] (BIB) ...... QQLM
Centre de Documentation, le Verificateur General du Quebec, Quebec, Quebec [*Library symbol*] [*National Library of Canada*] (BIB) ...... QQV
Centre de Documentation, Loto-Quebec, Montreal, Quebec [*Library symbol*] [*National Library of Canada*] (NLC) ...... QMLQ
Centre de Documentation, Ministere de la Main-d'Oeuvre et de la Securite du Revenu du Quebec, Montreal, Quebec [*Library symbol*] [*National Library of Canada*] (NLC) ...... QMMSR
Centre de Documentation, Ministere de l'Agriculture, des Pecheries, et de l'Alimentation, Ste.-Foy, Quebec [*Library symbol*] [*National Library of Canada*] (NLC) ...... QSTFAG
Centre de Documentation, Ministere de l'Education du Quebec, Quebec, Quebec [*Library symbol*] [*National Library of Canada*] (BIB) ...... QQED
Centre de Documentation, Ministere de l'Enseignement Superieur et de la Science du Quebec, Ste.-Foy, Quebec [*Library symbol*] [*National Library of Canada*] (NLC) ...... QQBST
Centre de Documentation, Ministere des Affaires Municipales du Quebec, Quebec, Quebec [*Library symbol*] [*National Library of Canada*] (NLC) ...... QQAM
Centre de Documentation, Ministere des Transports - Rue Dorchester, Quebec [*Library symbol*] [*National Library of Canada*] (NLC) ...... QQTRD
Centre de Documentation, Ministere des Transports du Quebec, Montreal, Quebec [*Library symbol*] [*National Library of Canada*] (NLC) ...... QMTRA
Centre de Documentation, Ministere du Commerce Exterieur et du Developpement Technologique du Quebec, Montreal, Quebec (SAUS) ...... QMCED
Centre de Documentation, Ministere du Travail du Quebec, Montreal, Quebec [*Library symbol*] [*National Library of Canada*] (NLC) ...... QMTMO
Centre de Documentation, Ministere du Travail du Quebec, Quebec [*Library symbol*] [*National Library of Canada*] (BIB) ...... QQTQ
Centre de Documentation, Musee Beaulne, Coaticook, Quebec [*Library symbol*] [*National Library of Canada*] (NLC) ...... QCMB
Centre de Documentation, Musee de la Civilisation, Quebec [*Library symbol*] [*National Library of Canada*] (BIB) ...... QQMUC
Centre de Documentation, Musee Laurier, Arthabaska, Quebec [*Library symbol*] [*National Library of Canada*] (NLC) ...... QAML
Centre de Documentation, Office de Planification et de Developpement du Quebe c, Trois-Rivieres, Quebec [*Library symbol*] [*National Library of Canada*] (NLC) ...... QTOPDQ
Centre de Documentation, Office de Planification et de Developpement du Quebec, Montreal, Quebec [*Library symbol*] [*National Library of Canada*] (BIB) ...... QMOP
Centre de Documentation, Office des Professions du Quebec, Quebec [*Library symbol*] [*National Library of Canada*] (NLC) ...... QQEDOP
Centre de Documentation, Pavillon St.-Joseph, Centre Hospitalier Regional de Beauceville, Quebec [*Library symbol*] [*National Library of Canada*] (BIB) ...... QBCH
Centre de Documentation, Peches Maritimes, Ministere de l'Agriculture, des Pe cheries, et de l'Alimentation du Quebec, Gaspe, Quebec [*Library symbol*] [*National Library of Canada*] (NLC) ...... QGAP
Centre de Documentation pour le Sport [*Sport Information Resource Centre*] [*Coaching Association of Canada*] ...... CDS
Centre de Documentation, Programme de Recherche sur l'Amiante, Universite de Sherbrooke, Quebec [*Library symbol*] [*National Library of Canada*] (NLC) ...... QSHERURA
Centre de Documentation, Projet Archipel de Montreal, Quebec [*Library symbol*] [*National Library of Canada*] (NLC) ...... QMPA
Centre de Documentation, Redaction et Terminologie, Hydro-Quebec, Montreal, Quebec [*Library symbol*] [*National Library of Canada*] (BIB) ...... QMHRT
Centre de Documentation, Regie de la Securite dans les Sports du Quebec, Trois-Rivieres, Quebec [*Library symbol*] [*National Library of Canada*] (NLC) ...... QTRRSS
Centre de Documentation, Roche Associes Ltee., Ste.-Foy, Quebec [*Library symbol*] [*National Library of Canada*] (NLC) ...... QSTFRA
Centre de Documentation Sciences Humaines [*Documentation Center for Human Sciences*] [*France*] [*Information service or system*] (IID) ...... CDSH
Centre de Documentation, Secretariat a la Condition Feminine du Quebec, Quebec, Quebec [*Library symbol*] [*National Library of Canada*] (BIB) ...... QQSCF
Centre de Documentation, Secretariat aux Affaires Autochtones, Quebec [*Library symbol*] [*National Library of Canada*] (BIB) ...... QQSAA
Centre de Documentation, Secteur Affaires Sociales, Association pour la Sante etla Securite du Travail, Montreal, Quebec [*Library symbol*] [*National Library of Canada*] (NLC) ...... QMASSAS
Centre de Documentation, Societe d'Habitation du Quebec, Montreal, Quebec [*Library symbol*] [*National Library of Canada*] (BIB) ...... QMSHQ
Centre de Documentation, Societe d'Habitation du Quebec, Quebec [*Library symbol*] [*National Library of Canada*] (BIB) ...... QQSHQ
Centre de Documentation, SOGIC [*Societe Generale des Industries Culturelles du Quebec*], **Montreal, Quebec** [*Library symbol*] [*National Library of Canada*] (BIB) ...... QMSDI
Centre de Documentation, Syndicat de Professionnels et de Professionnelles du Gouvernement du Quebec, Quebec [*Library symbol*] [*National Library of Canada*] (BIB) ...... QQSP
Centre de Documentation, Verification Generale, Hydro-Quebec, Montreal, Quebec [*Library symbol*] [*National Library of Canada*] (BIB) ...... QMHVG
Centre de Documentation-Energie, Ministere de l'Energie et des Ressources du Quebec, Quebec, Quebec [*Library symbol*] [*National Library of Canada*] (NLC) ...... QQERE
Centre de Documentation-Mines, Ministere de l'Energie et des Ressources du Quebec, Quebec, Quebec [*Library symbol*] [*National Library of Canada*] (NLC) ...... QQERM
Centre de Documentation-Terres et Forets, Ministere de l'Energie et des Ressources du Quebec, Quebec, Quebec [*Library symbol*] [*National Library of Canada*] (NLC) ...... QQERT
Centre de Donnees Stellaires [*Stellar Data Center*] [*France*] [*Information service or system*] (IID) ...... CDS
Centre de Formation et de Recyclage des Enseignants des Droits de l'Homme [*France*] ...... CIFREDH
Centre de Gravite Verticale [*Vertical Center of Gravity*] [*Shipping*] [*French*] ...... CGV
Centre de l'Abitibi-Temiscamingue, Archives Nationales du Quebec, Rouyn-Noranda,Quebec [*Library symbol*] [*National Library of Canada*] (BIB) ...... QRAAT
Centre de Liaison des Industries de Traitement des Algues Marines de la CEE [*Liaison Center of the Industries for the Treatment of Seaweeds in the European Economic Community*] ...... CLITAM
Centre de Liaison des Industries Transformatrices de la CEE [*Liaison Center of the Meat Processing Industries of the EEC*] [*Belgium*] ...... CLITRAVI
Centre de Liaison International des Marchands de Machines Agricoles et Reparateurs [*International Liaison Center for Agricultural Machinery Distributors and Maintenance*] [*Common Market*] ...... CLIMMAR
Centre de Maintenance, VIA Rail, Montreal, Quebec [*Library symbol*] [*National Library of Canada*] (BIB) ...... QMVRM
Centre de Preparation Documentaire a la Traduction [*Center for Translation Documentation*] [*Information service or system*] (IID) ...... CPDT
Centre de Promotion du Logiciel Quebecois (AC) ...... CPLQ

Centre de Protection de l'Enfance et de la Jeunesse de l'Outaouais (AC) .... CPEJO

Centre de Readaptation Constance-Lethbridge [*Constance Lethbridge Rehabilition Centre*] (AC) .... CRCL

Centre de Readaptation le Jeunes de l'Outaouais (AC) .... CRJO

Centre de Recherche, Centre Hospitalier, Universite Laval, Quebec, Quebec [*Library symbol*] [*National Library of Canada*] (BIB) .... QQLACHR

Centre de Recherche de Mathematiques Appliquees [*University of Montreal*] [*Research center*] (RCD) .... CRMA

Centre de Recherche Documentaire [*Documentary Research Center*] [*Information service or system*] (IID) .... CREDOC

Centre de Recherche en Biologie Marine [*Marine Biology Research Center*] [*Research center*] (RCD) .... CRBM

Centre de Recherche en Civilisation Canadienne-Francaise [*Center for Research in French Canadian Civilisation*] .... CRCCF

Centre de Recherche en Civilisation Canadienne-Francaise, Universite d'Ottawa [*Centre for Research on French Canadian Culture, University of Ottawa*], Ontario [*Library symbol*] [*National Library of Canada*] (BIB) ..... OOURC

Centre de Recherche en Developpement Humain [*Centre for Research in Human Development*] [*Concordia University*] [*Canada*] [*Research center*] (RCD) .... CRDH

Centre de Recherche en Droit Public [*Center for Research in Public Law*] [*Canada*] (IRC) .... CRDP

Centre de Recherche en Geomatique (SAUS) .... CRG

Centre de Recherche en Litterature Quebecoise [*Universite Laval, Quebec*] [*Canada*] .... CRELIQ

Centre de Recherche en Sciences Neurologiques [*Center for Research in Neurological Sciences*] [*Canada*] (IRC) .... CRSN

Centre de Recherche et d'Etudes sur les Societes Mediterraneennes [*Center for Research and Studies on Mediterranean Societies*] [*Information service or system*] (IID) .... CRESM

Centre de Recherche et Developpement en Economique (AC) .... CRDE

Centre de Recherche Industrielle du Quebec [*Industrial Research Center of Quebec*] [*Information service or system*] (IID) .... CRIQ

Centre de Recherche Industrielle du Quebec, Montreal, PQ, Canada [*Library symbol*] [*Library of Congress*] (LCLS) .... CaQMCRI

Centre de Recherche Industrielle du Quebec, Montreal, Quebec [*Library symbol*] [*National Library of Canada*] (NLC) .... QMCRI

Centre de Recherche Industrielle du Quebec, Ste.-Foy, Quebec [*Library symbol*] [*National Library of Canada*] (NLC) .... QSFCR

Centre de Recherche Informatique de Montreal [*Canada*] .... CRIM

Centre de Recherche sur la Croissance Humaine [*University of Montreal*] [*Research center*] (RCD) .... CRCH

Centre de Recherche sur l'Amerique Latine et le Tiers-Monde [*France*] .... CETRAL

Centre de Recherche sur l'Enseignement du Francais [*St. Anne University*] [*Canada*] [*Research center*] (RCD) .... CREF

Centre de Recherche sur les Transports [*Center for Transport Research*] [*University of Montreal*] [*Research center*] (RCD) .... CRT

Centre de Recherche, Tourbieres Premier Ltee., Riviere-Du-Loup, Quebec [*Library symbol*] [*National Library of Canada*] (BIB) .... QRLP

Centre de Recherches Biologiques Tropicales [*Algeria*] (GEOI) .... CRBT

Centre de Recherches en Amenagement et en Developpement [*Laval University*] [*Canada*] [*Research center*] (RCD) .... CRAD

Centre de Recherches en Relations Humaines, Montreal, PQ, Canada [*Library symbol*] [*Library of Congress*] (LCLS) .... CaQMRH

Centre de Recherches en Relations Humaines, Montreal, Quebec [*Library symbol*] [*National Library of Canada*] (NLC) .... QMRH

Centre de Recherches et de Documentation des Institutions Chretiennes [*Christian Institutions Research and Documentation Center*] [*France*] [*Information service or system*] (IID) .... CERDIC

Centre de Recherches et Investigations Eridermiques et Sensorielles [*The Epidermal and Sensory Research and Investigation Center*] [*Funded by Chanel*] [*France*] .... CERIES

Centre de Recherches Forestieres des Laurentides [*Laurentian Forest Research Center*] [*Canada*] (ARC) .... CRFL

Centre de Recherches Industrielles en Afrique Centrale .... CRIAC

Centre de Recherches pour le Developpement International [*International Development Research Centre*] [*Canada*] .... CIID

Centre de Recherches Scientifiques et Techniques de l'Industrie des Fabrications Metalliques [*Center for Scientific and Technical Research for the Metal Manufacturing Industry*] [*Information service or system*] (IID) ..... CRIF

Centre de Recherches sur l'Afrique Mediterraneenne .... CRAM

Centre de Recherches sur les Communications [*Sherbrooke University*] [*Canada*] [*Research center*] (RCD) .... CRCS

Centre de Recherches sur l'Opinion Publique [*Research Centre on Public Opinion*] [*Canada*] .... CROP

Centre de Reflexion sur le Monde Non Occidental [*Center for the Study of the Non-Occidental World*] (EA) .... CRM

Centre de Regroupement Africain [*Center for African Regroupment*] [*Congo - Leopoldville*] .... CEREA

Centre de Rencontres et d'Echanges Internationaux du Pacifique [*Center of International Cultural and Linguistic Exchanges in the Pacific*] [*Noumea, New Caledonia*] (EAIO) .... CREIPAC

Centre de Reperage des Debouches du Canada [*Canada Business Opportunity Centre - CBOC*] .... CRDC

Centre de Ressources, Ecole Secondaire Algonquin, North Bay, Ontario [*Library symbol*] [*National Library of Canada*] (NLC) .... ONBA

Centre de Sensibilisation au Developpement International (AC) .... CSDI

Centre de Service Social Ville-Marie [*Ville-Marie Social Service Centre*] Montreal, Quebec [*Library symbol*] [*National Library of Canada*] (NLC) .... QMSVM

Centre de Services Sociaux Richelieu, Longueuil, Quebec [*Library symbol*] [*National Library of Canada*] (NLC) .... QLOCSS

Centre de Services Sociaux, Trois-Rivieres, PQ, Canada [*Library symbol*] [*Library of Congress*] (LCLS) .... CaQTCSS

Centre de Services Sociaux, Trois-Rivieres, Quebec [*Library symbol*] [*National Library of Canada*] (NLC) .... QTCSS

Centre de Toxicologie, Centre Hospitalier, Universite Laval, Quebec, Quebec [*Library symbol*] [*National Library of Canada*] (BIB) .... QQLACHT

Centre de Traitement de l'Information [*Data Processing Center*] [*Ministry of Economic Affairs*] [*Belgium*] [*Information service or system*] (IID) .... CTI

Centre de Transit [*International routing term*] [*Telecommunications*] (NITA) .... CT

Centre de Valorisation du Patrimoine Vivant (AC) .... CVPV

Centre d'Ecologie des Ressources Renouvelables [*France*] (GEOI) .... CERR

Centre d'Ecologie et de Toxicologie de l'Industrie Chimique Europeenne [*European Chemical Industry Ecology and Toxicology Center - ECETOC*] (EAIO) .... CETICE

Centre d'Education et d'Action des Femmes de Montreal (AC) .... CEAF

Centre d'Education Interculturelle et de Comprehension Internationale [*Centre for Intercultural Education & International Understanding*] (AC) ...... CEICI

Centre Democratique [*Democratic Center*] [*Later, Center of Social Democrats*] [*France*] [*Political party*] (PPE) ..... CD

Centre des Auteurs Dramatiques (AC) .... CEAD

Centre des Democrates Sociaux [*Center of Social Democrats*] [*France*] [*Political party*] (PPW) .... CDS

Centre des Dossiers et de Documentation, Direction de Montreal, Ministere des Affaires Culturelles du Quebec [*Library symbol*] [*National Library of Canada*] (BIB) .... QMACM

Centre des Hautes Etudes Administratives sur l'Afrique et l'Asie Modernes [*Center for Advanced Administrative Studies on Modern Africa and Asia*] [*French*] (AF) .... CHEAM

Centre des Hautes Etudes Americaines [*Paris*] .... HEA

Centre des Medias, CEGEP [*College d'Enseignement General et Professionnel*]de Ste.-Foy, Quebec [*Library symbol*] [*National Library of Canada*] (NLC) .... QSFC

Centre des Nations Unies pour les Etablissements Humains [*United Nations Centre for Human Settlements*] [*French*] (DUND) .... CNUEH

Centre des Recherches Historiques, Quebec, PQ, Canada [*Library symbol*] [*Library of Congress*] [*Obsolete*] (LCLS) .... CaQQCRH

Centre des Technologies Textiles (AC) .... CTT

Centre d'Essaies Vehicule Automobile [*Motor Vehicle Test Center*] [*French*] .... CEVA

Centre d'Essais en Vol [*France*] [*ICAO designator*] (FAAC) .... CEV

Centre d'Essais Regional Europeen [*European Regional Test Center*] [*NATO*] (NATG) .... CERE

Centre d'Etude de l'Energie Nucleaire/Studiecentrum voor Kernenergie [*Belgium*] (EY) .... CEN/SCK

Centre d'Etude des Supports Publicitaires [*Center for the Study of Advertising Support*] [*Database producer*] [*Paris, France*] .... CESP

Centre d'Etude du Polymorphisme Humain [*Paris, France*] (ECON) .... CEPH

Centre d'Etude et de Cooperation International [*International Study and Cooperation Centre*] [*Canada*] .... CECI

Centre d'Etudes Anti-Imperialistes [*France*] .... CEDETIM

Centre d'Etudes de l'Asie de l'Est [*University of Montreal*] [*Research center*] (RCD) .... CEAE

Centre d'Etudes des Consequences Generales des Grands Techniques Nouvelles [*Center for the Study of the General Results of New Technologies*] (EA) .... CTN

Centre d'Etudes des Problemes d'Outre-Mer [*Center for the Study of Overseas Problems*] [*France*] (AF) .... CEPOM

Centre d'Etudes des Systemes d'Information des Administrations [*Center for the Study on Information Systems in Government*] [*Information service or system*] (IID) .... CESIA

Centre d'Etudes en Administration Internationale [*Canada*] .... CETAI

Centre d'Etudes en Geographie Tropicale [*Centre of Studies in Tropical Geography*] [*France*] .... CEGET

Centre d'Etudes en Relations Humaines [*Centre of Studies in Human Relations*] [*Canada*] .... CERHU

Centre d'Etudes et de Documentation d'Amerique Latine (AC) .... CEDAL

Centre d'Etudes et de Documentation Europeennes [*Montreal*] .... CEDE

Centre d'Etudes et de Realisations Cartographiques Geographiques [*France*] (GEOI) .... CERCG

Centre d'Etudes et de Recherches de Biologie et d'Oceanographie Medicale .... CERBOM

Centre d'Etudes et de Recherches Documentaires sur l'Afrique Centrale .... CERDAC

Centre d'Etudes et de Recherches sur les Qualifications (AIE) .... CEREQ

Centre d'Etudes et d'Experimentation du Machinisme Agricole Tropical [*Center for the Study and Experimentation of Tropical Agriculture Machinery*] [*International Cooperation Center of Agricultural Research for Development*] [*Information service or system*] [*France*] (IID) .... CEEMAT

Centre d'Etudes Franco-Canadiennes de l'Ouest [*Centre of Studies of French-Canadians of Western Canada*] .... CEFCO

Centre d'Etudes Industrielles [*Center for education in international management*] [*Switzerland*] (DCTA) .... CEI

Centre d'Etudes Internationales de la Propriete Industrielle .... CEIPI

Centre d'Etudes Nord-Americaines, Aix-En-Provence, France [*Library symbol*] [*Library of Congress*] (LCLS) .... FrAipNA

Centre d'Etudes Politiques et Administratives du Quebec [*University of Quebec*] [*Research center*] (RCD) .... CEPAQ

Centre d'Etudes Scientifiques et Techniques d'Aquitaine [*France*] .... CESTA

Centre d'Etudes sur la Langue, les Arts, et les Traditions Populaires des Francophones en Amerique du Nord [*Laval University*] [*Canada*] [*Research center*] (RCD) .... CELAT

Centre d'Etudes Theoriques de la Detection et des Communications .... CETHEDEC

Centre d'Etudis Historics Internacionals [*Center for International Historical Studies*] (EA) .... CEHI

Centre d'Excellence pour le Developpement de la Technologie Telidon [*Telidon Technology Development Center*] [*Polytechnical School of Montreal*] [*Quebec*] [*Information service or system*] (IID) .... CDT
Centre d'Histoire de l'Aeronautique et de l'Espace [*Aeronautics and Space Historical Center - ASHC*] (EAIO) .... CHAE
Centre d'Information de Presse [*Press agency*] [*Belgium*] .... CIP
Centre d'Information des Chemins de Fer Europeens [*Information Center of the European Railways*] .... CICE
Centre d'Information des Nations Unies .... CINU
Centre d'Information Documentaire Come-Saint-Germain, Drummondville, Quebec [*Library symbol*] [*National Library of Canada*] (NLC) .... QDM
Centre d'Information en Temps Reel pour l'Europe [*European Center for Information in Real Time*] [*France*] [*Information service or system*] (IID) .... CITERE
Centre d'Information et de Documentation Atlantique [*Brussels, Belgium*] .... CIDA
Centre d'Information, IST [*Industriel Services Techniques*], **Montreal, Quebec** [*Library symbol*] [*National Library of Canada*] (BIB) .... QMIST
Centre d'Information sur la Sante de l'Enfant, Hopital Sainte-Justine, Montreal,Quebec [*Library symbol*] [*National Library of Canada*] (NLC).... QMSTJ
Centre d'Information Sur les Sciences de la Terre [*Canada*] (GEOI) .... CIST
Centre d'Information Textile Habillement [*Textile and Clothing Information Center*] [*Information service or system*] (IID) .... CITH
Centre d'Informations Catholiques pour la France et l'Etranger CIC
Centre d'Informations Spectroscopiques [*Spectroscopic Information Center*] [*Group for the Advancement of Spectroscopic Methods and Physicochemical Analysis*] [*Information service or system*] (IID) .... CIS
Centre d'Informatique Appliquee au Developpement et a l'Agriculture Tropicale [*Center for Informatics Applied to Development and Tropical Agriculture*] [*Royal Museum of Central Africa*] [*Information service or system*] (IID) .... CIDAT
Centre d'Informatique et Documentation Automatique [*Center for Automated Information and Documentation*] [*France*] [*Information service or system*] (IID) .... CIDA
Centre d'Ingenierie Nordique [*University of Montreal*] [*Research center*] (RCD) .... CINEP
Centre d'Inter-Action Culturelle [*Center for Inter-Cultural Action*] (EAIO) .... CIAC
Centre d'Intervention et de Prevention en Toxicomanie de l'Outaouais (AC) .... CIPTO
Centre d'Intervention et de Recherche pour l'Amelioration des Situations de Travail [*University of Quebec at Rimouski*] [*Research center*] (RCD) .... CIRAST
Centre Documentaire, Centrale des Bibliotheques, Montreal, Quebec [*Library symbol*] [*National Library of Canada*] (NLC) .... QMCD
Centre du Commerce International [*International Trade Center - ITC*] [*Geneva, Switzerland*] [*French*] (EAIO) CCI
Centre Ecologique Albert Schweitzer [*Albert Schweitzer Ecological Centre*] [*Switzerland*] (EAIO) .... CEAS
Centre Economique de Secours Europeens [*European Economic Relief Committee*] [*NATO*] (NATG) .... CESE
Centre Elementary School, East Rockaway, NY [*Library symbol*] [*Library of Congress*] (LCLS) .... NErCE
Centre European de Recherches Nucleaires [*Switzerland*] (USDC) .... CERN
Centre Europeen d'Aviation Agricole .... CEAA
Centre Europeen de Documentation et de Compensation .... CEDEC
Centre Europeen de Formation des Statisticiens Economistes des Pays en Voie de Developpement [*European Center for Training Statisticians and Economists from Developing Countries*] .... CESD
Centre Europeen de Formation et de Recherche en Action Sociale [*European Centre for Social Welfare Training and Research - ECSWTR*] [*United Nations*] (EAIO) .... CEFRAS
Centre Europeen de la Culture [*European Cultural Centre - ECC*] (EAIO) .... CEC
Centre Europeen de l'Entreprise Publique [*European Center of Public Enterprise - ECPE*] (EAIO) .... CEEP
Centre Europeen de Recherche et de Documentation Parlementaires [*European Centre for Parliamentary Research and Documentation - ECPRD*] [*Luxembourg*] (EAIO) .... CERDP
Centre Europeen de Recherches Mauvernay [*France*] [*Research code symbol*] .... CERM
Centre Europeen de Recherches sur l'Investissement (EAIO) .... CERI
Centre Europeen de Traduction [*European Translation Center*] .... CET
Centre Europeen de Traitement de l'Information Scientifique [*EURATOM*] .... CETIS
Centre Europeen des Parents de l'Ecole Publique (AIE) .... CEPEP
Centre Europeen des Silicones [*of the European Council of Chemical Manufacturers' Federations*] (EAIO) .... CES
Centre Europeen d'Etudes de l'Acide Sulfurique [*European Center for Studies of Sulfuric Acid*] (EAIO) .... CEEAS
Centre Europeen d'Etudes de Population [*European Center for Population Studies*] .... CEEP
Centre Europeen du Commerce de Detail [*European Center of the Retail Trade*] [*Common Market*] .... CECODE
Centre Europeen pour la Promotion de la Formation Milieu Agricole et Rural [*European Training and Development Centre for Farming and Rural Life - ETDCFRL*] (EAIO) .... CEPFAR
Centre Europeen pour le Developpement de la Formation Professionnelle [*European Centre for the Development of Vocational Training*] (EAIO) .... CEDEFOP
Centre Europeen pour l'Enseignement Superieur [*European Centre for Higher Education*] (EAIO) .... CEPES
Centre Europeen pour les Loisirs et l'Education [*European Centre for Leisure and Education - ECLE*] (EAIO) .... CLE
Centre Europe-Tiers Monde [*Switzerland*] .... CETIM
Centre for Aboriginal and Islander Studies [*Northern Territory*] [*Australia*].... CAIS
Centre for Addiction and Mental Health (SAUO) .... CAMH
Centre for Administrative Studies (SAUO) .... CAS
Centre for Advanced Land Use Studies (SAUS) .... CALCUS
Centre for Advanced Land Use Studies [*College of Estate Management*] [*British*] (CB) .... CALUS
Centre for Advanced Materials Technology [*Monash University*] [*Australia*] .... CAMT
Centre for Advanced Numerical Computation in Engineering and Science [*Australia*] .... CANCES
Centre for Advanced Spatial Analysis [*University College, London*] (GEOI) .... CASA
Centre for Advanced Study in the Developmental Sciences [*British*] .... CASDS
Centre for Advanced Technology Education [*Ryerson Polytechnical Institute*] [*Canada*] [*Research center*] (RCD) .... CATE
Centre for Advancement in Work & Living (AC) .... CAWL
Centre for Advancement of Counselling [*British*] .... CAC
Centre for African Family Studies [*Kenya*] (EAIO) .... CAFS
Centre for African Settlement Studies and Development (SAUO) .... CASSAD
Centre for African Studies [*International Planned Parenthood Federation*] (ECON) .... CAFS
Centre for Aging Studies [*Flinders University*] [*Australia*] .... CAS
Centre for Agricultural Commerce [*University of New England*] [*Australia*] .... CAC
Centre for Agricultural Publications and Documents, Wageningen, Netherlands [*OCLC symbol*] (OCLC) .... NET
Centre for Agricultural Strategy [*University of Reading*] [*British*] (CB) .... CAS
Centre for Agricultural Strategy (SAUO) .... CAS
Centre for Agriculture and Biosciences (SAUS) .... CAB
Centre for Agriculture and Biosciences International (SAUO) .... CABI
Centre for Agrobiological Research (SAUS) .... CABO
Centre for Alcohol and Road Safety Education [*British*] (AIE) .... CARSE
Centre for Alternative Industrial and Technological Systems [*British*] (CB) .... CAITS
Centre for Alternative Technology [*British*] (CB) .... CAT
Centre for American and Commonwealth Arts and Studies [*British*] (CB) .... AmCAS
Centre for Analysis and Dissemination of Demonstrated Energy Technologies (SAUO) .... CADDET
Centre for Analysis of Science (SAUO) .... CAN
Centre for Analysis of Social Exclusion [*Great Britain*] .... CASE
Centre for Applied Economic Research (SAUO) .... CAER
Centre for Applied Health Research (SAUO) .... CAHR
Centre for Applied Health Studies [*University of Ulster at Coleraine*] [*British*] (CB) .... CAHS
Centre for Applied Language Studies [*Carleton University*] [*Canada*] [*Research center*] (RCD) .... CALS
Centre for Applied Linguistics, University of South Australia .... CALUSA
Centre for Applied Microbiology and Research [*Public Health Laboratory Service*] [*British*] .... CAMR
Centre for Applied Research and Engineering Design [*McMaster University, Hamilton, ON*] .... CARED
Centre for Applied Research Engineering and Design (SAUS) .... CARED
Centre for Applied Research in Education [*University of East Anglia*] [*British*] (CB) .... CARE
Centre for Applied Social Research [*Macquarie University*] [*Australia*] .... CASR
Centre for Applied Studies in Development (SAUO) .... CASD
Centre for Applied Studies in International Negotiations (SAUO) .... CASIN
Centre for Architectural Research and Development Overseas [*University of Newcastle upon Tyne*] [*British*] (CB) .... CARDO
Centre for Arid Zone Studies [*University College of North Wales*] [*British*] (CB) .... CAZS
Centre for Asia-Pacific Initiatives (SAUO) .... CAPI
Centre for Astrophysical Research in Antarctica (ECON) .... CARA
Centre for Atmospheric Science .... CAS
Centre for Australian Languages and Linguistics [*Batchelor College*] .... CALL
Centre for Behavioural Research and Program Evaluation (SAUO) .... CBRPE
Centre for Bibliographic Management [*British*] (TELE) .... CBM
Centre for Brain Injury Rehabilitation and Development [*British*] (CB) .... BIRD
Centre for British Teachers (SAUO) .... CBT
Centre for Business Research [*Manchester Business School*] [*British*] (CB) .... CBR
Centre for Business Systems Analysis [*City University*] [*British*] (CB) .... CBSA
Centre for Canadian Population Studies .... CCPS
Centre for Career Development, Revenue Canada - Taxation [*Centre de Developpement Professionnel, Revenu Canada - Impot*] **Ottawa, Ontario** [*Library symbol*] [*National Library of Canada*] (NLC) .... OONRTC
Centre for Catalogue Research [*University of Bath*] [*British*] (CB) .... CCR
Centre for Cell and Tissue Research [*University of York*] [*Research center*] [*British*] (CB) .... CCTR
Centre for Child Study [*University of Birmingham*] [*British*] (CB) .... CCS
Centre for Chiropractic and Osteopathy [*Macquarie University*] [*Australia*] .... CCO
Centre for Chiropractic and Osteopathy [*Macquarie University*] [*Australia*] .... CPO
Centre for Clinical Epidemiology and Biostasis [*University of Newcastle*] [*Australia*] .... CCEB
Centre for Coastal & Marine Sciences .... CCMS
Centre for Cold Ocean Resources Engineering [*Memorial University of Newfoundland*] [*Research center*] (RCD) .... C-CORE
Centre for Comparative Literature and Cultural Studies [*Monash University*] [*Australia*] .... CCLCS
Centre for Computers in Education and Training [*University of Salford*] [*British*] (CB) .... CCET
Centre for Computing and Automation (SAUO) .... CCA
Centre for Conflict Resolution [*Macquarie University*] [*Australia*] .... CCR
Centre for Conservation Farming [*Charles Sturt University*] [*Australia*] .... CCF
Centre for Conservation Studies (SAUO) .... CECON
Centre for Construction Market Information Ltd. [*British*] (CB) .... CCMT

Centre for Contemporary Cultural Studies [*University of Birmingham*] [*British*] (CB) .... CCCS
Centre for Contemporary Jewish Documentation (SAUS) .... CCJD
Centre for Contemporary Studies [*British*] (CB) .... CCS
Centre for Continuing Education in the Building Industry [*Polytechnic of the South Bank*] [*British*] (CB) .... CCEBI
Centre for Cooperation in Agricultural Research (SAUS) .... SACCAR
Centre for Criminological Research [*University of Alberta*] [*Canada*] (IRC) .... CCR
Centre for Criminology and the Social and Philosophical Study of Law [*University of Edinburgh*] [*British*] (CB) .... CCSPSL
Centre for Curriculum Renewal and Educational Development Overseas .... CREDO
Centre for Deafness Studies and Research [*Griffith University*] [*Research center*] [*Australia*] .... CDSR
Centre for Democracy and Development (SAUO) .... CDD
Centre for Developing-Area Studies [*McGill University*] [*Canada*] (IRC) ... CDAS
Centre for Development and Environment (SAUS) .... CDE
Centre for Development and Industrial Productivity (SAUO) .... CDPI
Centre for Development and Population Activities (SAUS) .... CDPA
Centre for Development and Population Activities (EA) .... CEDPA
Centre for Development of Appropriate Agriculture Engineering Technology (SAUO) .... CDAET
Centre for Development of Instructional Technology .... CENDIT
Centre for Development of International Technology (SAUO) .... CENDIT
Centre for Development Research (SAUO) .... CDR
Centre for Development Studies [*Flinders University*] [*Australia*] .... CDS
Centre for Digestive Diseases (SAUO) .... CDD
Centre for Distance Learning [*University of Central Queensland*] [*Australia*] .... CDL
Centre for Earth Observation Science .... CEOS
Centre for Earth Resource Management Applications (SAUS) .... CERMA
Centre for Earth Resources Research [*Memorial University of Newfoundland*] [*Research center*] (RCD) .... CERR
Centre for East Asian Cultural Studies (SAUO) .... CEACE
Centre for Economic and Environmental Development [*British*] (CB) .... CEED
Centre for Economic and Social Information [*United Nations*] .... CESI
Centre for Economic and Social Studies of the Third World (SAUO) ..... CESSTW
Centre for Economic and Social Studies on the Environment (SAUO) ...... CESSE
Centre for Economic Cooperation (AC) .... CEC
Centre for Economic Development of Australia (SAUO) .... CEDA
Centre for Economic Forecasting [*London Business School*] [*British*] (CB) ..... CEF
Centre for Economic Policy Research [*Australian National University*] [*Economics*] [*Australia*] .... CEPR
Centre for Economic Research and Industrial Planning (SAUO) .... Ecoplan International
Centre for Economic Research on Retirement and Aging (SAUO) .... CERRA
Centre for Ecudation for All (SAUS) .... CEFA
Centre for Editing Early Canadian Texts .... CEECT
Centre for Education and Information on Drugs and Alcohol (SAUO) .... CEIDA
Centre for Educational Development and Administration (SAUS) .... CEDA
Centre for Educational Development and Training [*Manchester Polytechnic*] [*British*] (CB) .... CEDAT
Centre for Educational Development, Appraisal and Research [*University of Warwick*] [*British*] (AIE) .... CEDAR
Centre for Educational Development Overseas .... CEDO
Centre for Educational Research and Innovation (EAIO) .... CERI
Centre for Educational Resourses in the Construction Industry (SAUO) .... CERCI
Centre for Educational Sociology [*University of Edinburgh*] [*British*] (CB) .... CES
Centre for Educational Studies [*King's College, London*] [*British*] (CB) .... CES
Centre for Educational Television Overseas [*British*] .... CETO
Centre for Educational Television Overseas, London (SAUO) .... CETO
Centre for Electrical Power Engineering [*Glasgow*] .... CEPE
Centre for Electronics in Agriculture [*University of New England*] [*Australia*] .... CEA
Centre for Employment Initiatives Ltd. [*British*] (CB) .... CEI
Centre for Endangered Reptiles [*Centre Pour Reptiles Menaces*] [*Formerly, The Reptile Breeding Foundation*] (AC) .... CER
Centre for Energy Studies [*Technical University of Nova Scotia*] [*Research center*] (RCD) .... CES
Centre for English Cultural Tradition and Language [*University of Sheffield*] [*British*] (CB) .... CECTAL
Centre for English Language Teaching [*University of Stirling*] [*British*] (CB) .... CELT
Centre for Environment and Development for/in the Arab Region and Europe (SAUO) .... CEDARE
Centre for Environment and Development in the Arab Region and Europe (SAUS) .... CEDARE
Centre for Environmental Education [*British*] (AIE) .... CCE
Centre for Environmental Health (SAUO) .... CEH
Centre for Environmental Interpretation [*Manchester Polytechnic*] [*British*] (CB) .... CEI
Centre for Environmental Management [*University of Newcastle*] [*Australia*] .... CEM
Centre for Environmental Studies [*British*] .... CES
Centre for Ergonomics and Human Factors [*Australia*] .... CEHF
Centre for European Agricultural Studies [*British*] (ARC) .... CEAS
Centre for European Industrial Studies [*University of Bath*] [*British*] (CB) ..... CEIS
Centre for European Legal Studies [*University of Exeter*] [*British*] (CB) .... CELS
Centre for European Policy Studies (ECON) .... CEPS
Centre for European Security and Cooperation [*Netherlands*] .... CESC
Centre for European Social and Economic Policy (SAUO) .... CESEP
Centre for European Social and Economic Policy (SAUO) .... ESEP
Centre for European Social and Economic Policy (SAUO) .... GESEP
Centre for European Studies [*Monash University*] [*Australia*] ...... CES
Centre for Evidence-Based Dentistry (SAUO) .... CEBD
Centre for Evidence-Based Medicine (SAUO) .... CEBM

Centre for Evidence-Based Mental Health (SAUO) .... CEBMH
Centre for Exploitation of Science and Technology [*British*] (ECON) ...... CEST
Centre for Field Research (SAUS) .... CFR
Centre for Financial Assistance to African Countries (SAUO) .... FINAFRICA
Centre for Fiscal Studies [*University of Bath*] [*British*] (CB) .... CFS
Centre for Foreign Policy Studies [*Dalhousie University*] [*Canada*] (IRC) ...... CFPS
Centre for Frontier Engineering Research [*University of Alberta*] [*Canada*] (IRC) .... C-FER
Centre for Global Atmospheric Modelling .... CGAM
Centre for Habilitation Education and Research [*University of Waterloo*] [*Research center*] (RCD) .... CHER
Centre for Health Economics (SAUO) .... CHE
Centre for Health Economics and Policy Analysis (SAUO) .... CHEPA
Centre for Health Evidence (SAUO) .... CHE
Centre for Health Informatics (SAUO) .... CHI
Centre for Health Informatics & Multiprofessional Education (SAUO) .... CHIME
Centre for Health Information Management Research (SAUO) .... CHIMR
Centre for Health Policy (SAUO) .... CHP
Centre for Health Program Evaluation (SAUO) .... CHPE
Centre for Health Services Management [*Leicester Polytechnic*] [*British*] (CB) .... CHSM
Centre for Higher Education in Latin America and the Caribbean (SAUO) .... CRESALC
Centre for Higher Education Management Policy (SAUO) .... CHEMP
Centre for Higher Education Policy Studies [*British*] (AIE) .... CHEPS
Centre for Higher Education Studies (SAUO) .... CHES
Centre for Housing, Building and Planning (SAUO) .... CHBP
Centre for Human Development [*British*] (CB) .... CHD
Centre for Human Ecology and Health Advancement [*University of Newcastle*] [*Australia*] .... CHEHA
Centre for Human Relations and Community Studies [*Concordia University*] [*Canada*] [*Research center*] (RCD) .... CHRCS
Centre for Human Rights Legal Aid .... CHRLA
Centre for Image Analysis [*Charles Sturt University*] [*Australia*] ...... CIA
Centre for Independent Living in Toronto (AC) .... CILT
Centre for Industrial Consultancy and Liaison (SAUO) CICL
Centre for Industrial Control [*Concordia University*] [*Canada*] [*Research center*] (RCD) CIC
Centre for Industrial Control Science [*University of Newcastle*] [*Australia*] .... CICS
Centre for Industrial Innovation [*British*] (ARC) CII
Centre for Information and Advice on Educational Disadvantage [*British*] .... CED
Centre for Information and Documentation [*EURATOM*] (MCD) .... CID
Centre for Information and Technical Assistance, Institute of Man and Resources, Charlottetown, Prince Edward Island [*Library symbol*] [*National Library of Canada*] (NLC) .... PCIMR
Centre for Information Media and Technology [*British*] (EAIO) .... CIMTECH
Centre for Information of Language Teaching (SAUS) .... CILT
Centre for Information on Language Teaching and Research [*Regent's College*] [*British*] (CB) .... CILT
Centre for Information on Language Training [*British*] .... CILT
Centre for Information on Standardization and Metrology [*Information service or system*] (IID) .... CIS
Centre for Information Services [*Council for Scientific and Industrial Research - CSIR*] [*South Africa*] [*Information service or system*] (IID) ...... CIS
Centre for Information Technology and Communications [*Queensland*] [*Australia*] [*Information service or system*] .... CITC
Centre for Innovation and Chemical Research (SAUO) .... CIRC
Centre for Institutional Studies [*North East London Polytechnic*] [*British*] (CB) .... CIS
Centre for Integrated Rural Development (SAUS) .... CIRD
Centre for Integrated Rural Development for Asia and the Pacific .... CIRDAP
Centre for Interdisciplinary Research and/on Development (SAUO) ...... CIRD
Centre for Interdisciplinary Research in the Liberal Arts (SAUS) ..... CIRLA
Centre for Interdisciplinary Studies in Chemical Physics [*University of Western Ontario*] [*Canada*] (IRC) .... CCP
Centre for Interfirm Comparison [*British*] .... CIFC
Centre for Inter-Firm Comparison (SAUO) .... CIFC
Centre for International and Strategic Studies [*York University*] [*Research center*] (RCD) .... CISS
Centre for International Business Studies (SAUO) .... CETAI
Centre for International Cooperation and Appropriate Technology (SAUO) .... CICAT
Centre for International Development Education and Action (SAUO) ...... IDEA
Centre for International Education [*Netherlands*] (EAIO) .... CEVNO
Centre for International Education and Business (SAUO) .... CIEB
Centre for International Education and Development (SAUO) .... CIED
Centre for International Mobility (SAUO) .... CIMO
Centre for International Projects (SAUO) .... CIP
Centre for International Studies [*Canada*] (CROSS) .... CIS
Centre for Internationalising the Study of English .... CIE
Centre for Inventions and Scientific Information (SAUS) .... CISI
Centre for Japanese Business Language [*Australia*] .... CJBL
Centre for Japanese Economic Studies [*Macquarie University*] [*Australia*] ..... CJES
Centre for Journalism Studies [*British*] (CB) .... CJS
Centre for Land and Biological Resource Research [*Canada*] .... CLBRR
Centre for Language Studies [*University of Newcastle*] [*Australia*] ...... CLS
Centre for Latin American Linguistic Studies [*University of St. Andrews*] [*British*] (CB) .... CLALS
Centre for Learning and Development [*British*] (AIE) .... CLD
Centre for Legumes and/in Mediterranean Agriculture (SAUO) .... CLIMA
Centre for Library and Information Management [*Loughborough University of Technology*] [*British*] [*Information service or system*] (IID) ...... CLAIM
Centre for Literacy and Linguistic Computing [*University of Newcastle*] [*Australia*] CLLC
Centre for Local Economic Strategies Ltd. [*British*] (CB) .... CLES

Centre for Machine Condition Monitoring [*Monash University*] [*Australia*] .... CMCM
Centre for Management in Agriculture/Indian Institute of Management (SAUO) .... CMA/IIM
Centre for Manufacturing Renewal [*University of Warwick*] [*British*] (CB) .... CMR
Centre for Marine Conservation (SAUO) .... CMC
Centre for Maritime Cooperation (SAUO) .... CMC
Centre for Mass Communication Research [*University of Leicester*] [*British*] (CB) .... CMCR
Centre for Mathamatical Analysis (SAUS) .... CMA
Centre for Mathematical Modeling and Computer Simulation (SAUO) .... C-MACCS
Centre for Measurement and Information in Medicine [*City University*] [*British*] (CB) .... CMIM
Centre for Medical (SAUS) .... CMERD
Centre for Medicines Research [*British*] (CB) .... CMR
Centre for Medicines Research International (SAUO) .... CMR
Centre for Medieval Studies [*University of Toronto*] [*Canada*] (IRC) .... CMS
Centre for Mennonite Brethren Studies in Canada, Winnipeg, Manitoba [*Library symbol*] [*National Library of Canada*] (NLC) .... MWCMS
Centre for Metrology and Accreditation (SAUS) .... CMA
Centre for Middle Eastern and Islamic Studies [*University of Durham*] [*British*] (CB) .... CMEIS
Centre for Minerals Engineering (SAUO) .... CME
Centre for Mining and Mineral Exploration Research (SAUS) .... CIMMER
Centre for Mining Technology (SAUO) .... CMT
Centre for Molecular Biology and Medicine [*Monash University*] [*Australia*] .... CMBM
Centre for Molecular Structure and Function [*Australian National University*] .... CMSF
Centre for Monitoring the Indian Economy (ECON) .... CMIE
Centre for Multicultural Education [*University of London Institute of Education*] [*British*] (CB) .... CME
Centre for Multicultural Studies [*Flinders University*] [*Australia*] .... CMS
Centre for Natural Resources, Energy, and Transport [*United Nations*] ..... CNRET
Centre for Networked Access to Scholarly Information (SAUO) .... CNASI
Centre for Neuroscience [*University College, London*] [*British*] (CB) .... CNS
Centre for Nonlinear Studies [*University of Leeds*] [*British*] (CB) .... CNLS
Centre for North-West Regional Studies [*University of Lancaster*] [*British*] (CB) .... CNWRS
Centre for Nuclear Magnetic Resonance [*University of Warwick*] [*British*] (CB) .... NMR
Centre for Nursing and Health Care Practices [*Southern Cross University*] [*Medicine*] [*Australia*] .... CFN&HCP
Centre for Ocean, Land and Atmosphere (SAUO) .... COLA
Centre for Ocean Technology [*Canada*] (IRC) .... COT
Centre for Offshore and Remote Medicine [*Memorial University of Newfoundland*] [*Research center*] (RCD) .... MEDICOR
Centre for Operational Research & Development Analysis (SAUS) .... CORDA
Centre for Our Common Future (SAUO) .... COCF
Centre for Overseas Pest Research [*England*] .... COPR
Centre for Pastoral Work in Europe [*See also CPE*] (EAIO) .... CPWE
Centre for Peace and Conflict Studies (SAUO) .... CPACS
Centre for Personal Construct Psychology [*British*] (CB) .... PCP
Centre for Pest Management [*Simon Fraser University*] [*Canada*] [*Research center*] (RCD) .... CPM
Centre for Petroleum and Mineral Law Studies [*University of Dundee*] [*British*] (CB) .... CPMLS
Centre for Petrology and Lithospheric Studies [*Macquarie University*] [*Australia*] .... CPLS
Centre for Physical Distribution Management (SAUO) .... CPDM
Centre for Plant Conservation (SAUO) .... CPC
Centre for Plant Molecular Biology [*McGill University*] [*Canada*] (IRC) .... CPMB
Centre for Policy in Nursing Research (SAUO) .... CPNR
Centre for Policy on Ageing (EAIO) .... CPA
Centre for Policy Research (SAUO) .... CPR
Centre for Policy Research on Science and Technology (SAUO) .... CPROST
Centre for Policy Studies [*British*] .... CPS
Centre for Policy Studies [*Monash University*] [*Australia*] .... CPS
Centre for Precision Technology [*Australia*] .... CPT
Centre for Protection Against Corrosion (SAUO) .... CPAC
Centre for Protein and Enzyme Technology [*La Trobe University*] [*Australia*] .... CPET
Centre for Public Information on Nuclear Energy (SAUO) .... CNIIAtomInform
Centre for Public Sector Research [*University of Canberra*] [*Australia*] .... CPSR
Centre for Radiation and Nuclear Safety (SAUS) .... STUK
Centre for Regional Economic Analysis [*Australia*] .... CREA
Centre for Rehabilitation of Wildlife .... CROW
Centre for Remote Sensing [*Imperial College of Science and Technology*] [*British*] (CB) .... CRS
Centre for Remote Sensing [*James Cook University*] [*Australia*] .... CRS
Centre for Research & Development in Masonry [*Centre de Recherche et de Developpement en Maconnerie*] **Calgary, Alberta** [*Library symbol*] [*National Library of Canada*] (NLC) .... ACRDM
Centre for Research and Documentation on Oral Traditions and African Languages (SAUO) .... CERDOTOLA
Centre for Research and Education on Gender [*University of London*] [*British*] (AIE) .... CREG
Centre for Research in Comparative Medicine [*Canada*] (IRC) .... CRCM
Centre for Research in Education and Work [*Macquarie University*] [*Australia*] .... CREW
Centre for Research in Ethnic Relations [*University of Warwick*] [*British*] (CB) .... CRER
Centre for Research in Experimental Space Science [*York University*] [*Canada*] [*Research center*] (RCD) .... CRESS

Centre for Research in Finance [*University of New South Wales*] [*Information service or system*] (IID) .... CRIF
Centre for Research in Industrial Democracy and Participation [*University of Glasgow*] [*British*] (CB) .... CRIDP
Centre for Research in Librarianship [*University of Toronto*] [*Research center*] (RCD) .... CRL
Centre for Research in Philosophy and Literature [*University of Warwick*] [*British*] (CB) .... CRPL
Centre for Research into Communist Economies [*Research center*] [*British*] (IRC) .... CRCE
Centre for Research Into Economics and Finance in South Africa [*London School of Economic and Political Science*] (ECON) .... CREFSA
Centre for Research into Information Training (SAUS) .... CRIT
Centre for Research into Public Health and Nursing [*La Trobe University*] [*Australia*] .... CRPHN
Centre for Research into Strategic Information Systems [*University of Bath*] [*British*] .... CRSIS
Centre for Research of/on the Epidemiology of Disasters (SAUO) .... CRED
Centre for Research on Arabic and the Culture of the Arab Countries (SAUO) .... CRACAC
Centre for Research on Atoms and Molecules [*Laval University*] [*Canada*] [*Research center*] (RCD) .... CRAM
Centre for Research on European Women [*Belgium*] (EAIO) .... CREW
Centre for Research on International Institutions (SAUO) .... CRII
Centre for Research on Latin America and the Caribbean [*York University*] [*Canada*] [*Research center*] (RCD) .... CERLAC
Centre for Research on Perception and Cognition [*University of Sussex*] [*British*] (CB) .... CRPC
Centre for Research on User Studies [*University of Sheffield*] [*England*] [*Information service or system*] (IID) .... CRUS
Centre for Resource and Environmental Studies .... CRES
Centre for Resource Studies [*Queen's University at Kingston*] [*Canada*] [*Research center*] (RCD) .... CRS
Centre for Rural Research Management [*University of New England*] [*Australia*] .... CRRM
Centre for Rural Social Research [*Charles Sturt University*] [*Australia*] .... CRSR
Centre for Rural Transport [*St. David's University College*] [*British*] (CB) .... CRT
Centre for Russian and East European Studies [*University of Toronto*] [*Canada*] (IRC) .... CREES
Centre for Russian and East European Studies [*University of Birmingham*] [*British*] (CB) .... CREES
Centre for Sanitary Engineering and Environmental Sciences (SAUO) .... CSEES
Centre for Science and Mathematics Education [*British*] (AIE) .... CSME
Centre for Science & Technology Information (SAUO) .... CESTI
Centre for Scientific and Technical Information (SAUS) .... CSTI
Centre for Scientific and Technological Information [*Council for Scientific and Industrial Research*] [*Pretoria, South Africa*] .... CSTI
Centre for Scientific Research (SAUO) .... CSR
Centre for Social and Economic Research on the Global Environment (SAUO) .... CSERGE
Centre for Social Development and Humanitarian Affairs [*United Nations*] (EAIO) .... CSDHA
Centre for Social Research (SAUO) .... CSR
Centre for Social Science Research and Documentation for the Arab Region (SAUO) .... ARCSS
Centre for Socio-Legal Studies [*British*] (CB) .... CSLS
Centre for Software Engineering Ltd. [*British*] (CB) .... CSE
Centre for Software Reliability [*City University*] [*British*] (IRUK) .... CSR
Centre for South Australian Economic Studies [*Flinders University*] [*Australia*] .... CSAES
Centre for Southeast Asia Studies of Kyoto University (SAUS) .... SEAS
Centre for Southeast Asian Studies [*Monash University*] [*Australia*] .... CSAS
Centre for Southern African Studies [*University of York*] [*British*] (CB) .... CSAS
Centre for Spatial Database Management and Solutions (SAUO) .... CSDMS
Centre for Speech Technology Research [*British*] (CB) .... CSTR
Centre for Studies in Money, Banking, and Finance [*Macquarie University*] [*Australia*] .... CSMBF
Centre for Studies in Science and Mathematical Education [*University of Leeds*] [*British*] (CB) .... CSSME
Centre for Studies in Social Policy (SAUO) .... CSSP
Centre for Studies on Integration in Education [*British*] (CB) .... CSIE
Centre for Study of Education in Developing Countries [*Netherlands*] (EAIO) .... CSEDC
Centre for Study of Insurance Operations (AC) .... CSIO
Centre for Teaching and Learning Services [*McGill University*] [*Canada*] [*Research center*] (RCD) .... CTLS
Centre for Technology and Social Change (EERA) .... TASC
Centre for Telecommunications Development [*ITU*] [*United Nations*] (DUND) .... CTD
Centre for Thai National Standard Specifications (SAUO) .... CTNSS
Centre for the Advancement and Study of the European Currency [*France*] (EAIO) .... CASEC
Centre for the Advancement of Mathematical Education in Technology [*Loughborough University of Technology*] [*Research center*] [*British*] (CB) .... CAMET
Centre for the Analysis of Conflict [*Research center*] [*British*] (IRC) .... CAC
Centre for the Analysis of Social Policy [*University of Bath*] [*British*] (CB) .... CASP
Centre for the Analysis of Technical Change (SAUO) .... CATCH
Centre for the Automation of Weapon & Command Systems (SAUS) .... CAWCS
Centre for the Coordination of Social Science Research and Documentation in Africa South of the Sahara (SAUO) .... CERDAS
Centre for the Economics and Management of Aquatic Resources (SAUS) .... CEMARE

Centre for the Independence of Judges and Lawyers [*See also CIMA*] [*Geneva, Switzerland*] (EAIO) .... CIJL
Centre for the Study of Ancient Documents (SAUS) .... CSAD
Centre for the Study of Arms Control and International Security [*University of Lancaster, Fylde College*] [*British*] (CB) .... CSACIS
Centre for the Study of Communication and Culture [*British*] (CB) .... CSCC
Centre for the Study of Community and Race Relations [*Brunel University*] [*British*] (CB) .... CSCRR
Centre for the Study of Comprehensive Schools [*Wentworth College, University of York*] [*British*] (CB) .... CSCS
Centre for the Study of Conflict (SAUO) .... CSC
Centre for the Study of Developing Societies [*Information service or system*] (IID) .... CSDS
Centre for the Study of Economics and Religion [*Fraser Institute*] [*Canada*] (IRC) .... CSER
Centre for the Study of Education in an International Context (SAUO) .... CEIC
Centre for the Study of Education in Developing Countries (SAUO) .... CESO
Centre for the Study of Human Learning [*Brunel University*] [*British*] (CB) .... CSHL
Centre for the Study of International Economic Relations [*University of Western Ontario*] [*Canada*] (IRC) .... CSIER
Centre for the Study of International Relations (SAUO) .... CSIR
Centre for the Study of Mental Retardation [*Canada*] .... CSMR
Centre for the Study of Public Policy [*University of Strathclyde*] [*British*] (CB) .... CSPP
Centre for the Study of Regulated Industries [*McGill University*] [*Canada*] [*Research center*] (RCD) .... CSRI
Centre for Trade Policy and Law [*Established to promote greater public understanding of trade policies*] [*Canada*] (CROSS) .... CTPL
Centre for Translation Studies (SAUO) .... CTS
Centre for Transport Engineering Practice [*Loughborough University of Technology*] [*British*] (CB) .... CTEP
Centre for Transport Studies (SAUO) .... CTS
Centre for Transportation Studies [*University of British Columbia*] [*Canada*] (IRC) .... CTS
Centre for Tropical Marine Ecology (SAUS) .... ZMT
Centre for Tropical Veterinary Medicine [*Overseas Development Administration*] [*British*] (DS) .... CTVM
Centre for Urban and Community Studies [*University of Toronto*] [*Research center*] (RCD) .... CUCS
Centre for Urban and Regional Development Studies [*University of Newcastle upon Tyne*] [*British*] (CB) .... CURDS
Centre for Visual Arts [*University of New England*] [*Australia*] .... CVA
Centre for Water Policy Research [*University of New England*] [*Australia*] .... CWPR
Centre for Wireless Communications [*Singapore*] (DDC) .... CWC
Centre for Women's Development Studies [*India*] (EAIO) .... CWDS
Centre for Women's Health Studies [*Cumberland College of Health Sciences*] [*Australia*] .... CWHS
Centre for World Development Education [*Regent's College*] [*British*] (CB) .... CWDE
Centre for/of African Family Studies (SAUO) .... CAFS
Centre Francais de la Couleur [*Online service*] .... CFC
Centre Francois Charron, Quebec, Quebec [*Library symbol*] [*National Library of Canada*] (BIB) .... QQCF
Centre Franco-Ontarien de Folklore [*Formerly, Institut de Folklore*] [*Research center*] (RCD) .... CFOF
Centre Franco-Ontarien de Ressources Pedagogiques (AC) .... CFORP
Centre Francophone de Recherche en Informatisation des Organisations (AC) .... CEFRIO
Centre Frequency Modulation (SAUS) .... CFM
Centre Frequency Stabilization (SAUS) .... CFS
Centre Half (SAUS) .... CH
Centre Hospitalier Christ-Roi, Quebec, Quebec [*Library symbol*] [*National Library of Canada*] (BIB) .... QQCR
Centre Hospitalier Cooke, Trois-Rivieres, Quebec [*Library symbol*] [*National Library of Canada*] (NLC) .... QTCHC
Centre Hospitalier de Charlevoix, Baie St. Paul, PQ, Canada [*Library symbol*] [*Library of Congress*] (LCLS) .... CaQBSPH
Centre Hospitalier de Charlevoix, Baie St.-Paul, Quebec [*Library symbol*] [*National Library of Canada*] (BIB) .... QBSPH
Centre Hospitalier de Gatineau, Gatineau, PQ, Canada [*Library symbol*] [*Library of Congress*] (LCLS) .... CaQGatCH
Centre Hospitalier de Gatineau, Quebec [*Library symbol*] [*National Library of Canada*] (NLC) .... QGCH
Centre Hospitalier de Lachine, Montreal, PQ, Canada [*Library symbol*] [*Library of Congress*] (LCLS) .... CaQMCHL
Centre Hospitalier de Lachine, Montreal, Quebec [*Library symbol*] [*National Library of Canada*] (NLC) .... QMCHL
Centre Hospitalier de l'Universite Laval, Quebec, Quebec [*Library symbol*] [*National Library of Canada*] (NLC) .... QQLACH
Centre Hospitalier de Verdun, Montreal, PQ, Canada [*Library symbol*] [*Library of Congress*] (LCLS) .... CaQMHGC
Centre Hospitalier de Verdun, Quebec [*Library symbol*] [*National Library of Canada*] (NLC) .... QMHGC
Centre Hospitalier du Sacre-Coeur, Hull, PQ, Canada [*Library symbol*] [*Library of Congress*] (LCLS) .... CaQHSC
Centre Hospitalier Hotel-Dieu, Sherbrooke, PQ, Canada [*Library symbol*] [*Library of Congress*] (LCLS) .... CaQSherHD
Centre Hospitalier Hotel-Dieu, Sherbrooke, Quebec [*Library symbol*] [*National Library of Canada*] (NLC) .... QSHERHD
Centre Hospitalier Jacques Viger, Montreal, PQ, Canada [*Library symbol*] [*Library of Congress*] (LCLS) .... CaQMHM
Centre Hospitalier Jacques Viger, Montreal, Quebec [*Library symbol*] [*National Library of Canada*] (NLC) .... QMHM
Centre Hospitalier Jeffery Hale, Quebec, Quebec [*Library symbol*] [*National Library of Canada*] (BIB) .... QQCHJH
Centre Hospitalier Le Gardeur, Repentigny, PQ, Canada [*Library symbol*] [*Library of Congress*] (LCLS) .... CaQRECHL
Centre Hospitalier Le Gardeur, Repentigny, Quebec [*Library symbol*] [*National Library of Canada*] (NLC) .... QRECHL
Centre Hospitalier Pierre Boucher, Longueuil, PQ, Canada [*Library symbol*] [*Library of Congress*] (LCLS) .... CaQLoPB
Centre Hospitalier Pierre Janet, Hull, PQ, Canada [*Library symbol*] [*Library of Congress*] (LCLS) .... CaQHPJ
Centre Hospitalier Pierre Janet, Hull, Quebec [*Library symbol*] [*National Library of Canada*] (NLC) .... QHPJ
Centre Hospitalier Regional de La Mauricie, Shawinigan, Quebec [*Library symbol*] [*National Library of Canada*] (NLC) .... QSHCH
Centre Hospitalier Regional de Lanaudiere, Joliette, Quebec [*Library symbol*] [*National Library of Canada*] (NLC) .... QJH
Centre Hospitalier Regional de l'Outaouais, Hull, Quebec [*Library symbol*] [*National Library of Canada*] (NLC) .... QHSC
Centre Hospitalier Robert Giffard, Beauport, Quebec [*Library symbol*] [*National Library of Canada*] (NLC) .... QBRG
Centre Hospitalier Robert Giffard, Quebec, PQ, Canada [*Library symbol*] [*Library of Congress*] (LCLS) .... CaQBRG
Centre Hospitalier Rouyn-Noranda, Noranda, PQ, Canada [*Library symbol*] [*Library of Congress*] (LCLS) .... CaQNCHRN
Centre Hospitalier Rouyn-Noranda, Noranda, Quebec [*Library symbol*] [*National Library of Canada*] (NLC) .... QNCHRN
Centre Hospitalier St.-Augustin, Beauport, Quebec [*Library symbol*] [*National Library of Canada*] (BIB) .... QBSA
Centre Hospitalier St.-Vincent-De-Paul, Sherbrooke, PQ, Canada [*Library symbol*] [*Library of Congress*] (LCLS) .... CaQSherSV
Centre Hospitalier St.-Vincent-De-Paul, Sherbrooke, Quebec [*Library symbol*] [*National Library of Canada*] (NLC) .... QSHERSV
Centre Informatique Geologique [*Geological Information Centre*] [*Canada*] .... CIG
Centre Interafricain pour le Developpement de la Formation Professionnelle [*Inter-African Center for the Development of Professional Training*] [*Abidjan, Ivory Coast*] (EAIO) .... CIADFOR
Centre Interamericain d'Education Rurale .... CIER
Centre Interculturel Monchanin, Montreal, Quebec [*Library symbol*] [*National Library of Canada*] (NLC) .... QMCICM
Centre Intergouvernemental de Documentation sur l'Habitat et l'Environnement [*Intergovernmental Center for Documentation on Dwellings and the Environment*] (PDAA) .... CIDHEC
Centre Internacional Escarre per a les Minories Etniques i Nacionalitats (EAIO) .... CIEMEN
Centre International d'Alcoologie / Toxixomanies [*International Center of Alcohol/Drug Addiction*] (PDAA) .... CIATO
Centre International d'Aviation Agricole [*International Agricultural Aviation Center*] .... CIAA
Centre International de Conferences de Geneve [*International Conference Center of Geneva*] [*Switzerland*] (PDAA) .... CICG
Centre International de Coordination pour la Celebration des Anniversaires .... CICCA
Centre International de Criminologie Comparee [*International Center for Comparative Criminology - ICCC*] [*Montreal, PQ*] (EA) CICC
Centre International de Developpement de l'Aluminium .... CIDA
Centre International de Documentation [*International Center for Documentation*] .... CID
Centre International de Documentation Arachnologique [*International Centre for Arachnological Documentation*] (EAIO) .... CIDA
Centre International de Documentation Concernant les Expressions Plastiques .... CIDEP
Centre International de Documentation de l'Inspection Technique des Vehicules Automobiles .... CIDITVA
Centre International de Documentation Economique et Sociale Africaine [*International Center for African Social and Economic Documentation*] .... CIDESA
Centre International de Documentation et d'Information .... CIDI
Centre International de Documentation Parlementaire [*International Center for Parliamentary Documentation*] (EAIO) .... CIDP
Centre International de Formation Europeenne [*France*] .... CIFE
Centre International de Gerontologie Sociale [*International Center of Social Gerontology - ICSG*] [*Paris, France*] [*Defunct*] .... CIGS
Centre International de Hautes Etudes Agronomiques Mediterraneennes .... CIHEAM
Centre International de la Tapisserie Ancienne et Moderne [*Switzerland*] .... CITAM
Centre International de l'Actualite Fantastique et Magique .... CIAFMA
Centre International de l'Eau et l'Assainissement [*IRC International Water and Sanitation Centre*] (EAIO) .... CIR
Centre International de l'Enfance [*International Children's Centre*] [*Paris, France*] (EAIO) .... CIE
Centre International de Liaison des Ecoles de Cinema et de Television [*International Liaison Centre for Film and Television Schools*] (EAIO) .... CILECT
Centre International de Mathematiques Pures et Appliquees [*International Center for Pure and Applied Mathematics - ICPAM*] [*United Nations*] (EA) .... CIMPA
Centre International de Phenomenologie Clinique (EAIO) .... CIPC
Centre International de Recherche, de Creation, et d'Animation [*France*] .... CIRCA
Centre International de Recherche en Amenagement Linguistique (AC) .... CIRAL
Centre International de Recherches et d'Etudes en Management [*International Centre for Research and Studies in Management*] [*Canada*] .... CIREM
Centre International de Recherches sur l'Anarchisme [*International Research Center on Anarchism*] [*Geneva, Switzerland*] (EAIO) .... CIRA

Centre International de Recherches sur le Bilinguisme [*International Center for Research on Bilingualism*] [*Universite Laval, Quebec*] [*Canada*] .... CIRB

Centre International de Recherches sur le Bilinguisme, Universite Laval, Quebec,Quebec [*Library symbol*] [*National Library of Canada*] (NLC) .... QQLACI

Centre International de Recherches sur les Communautes Cooperatives Rurales [*International Research Center on Rural Cooperative Communities*] .... CIRCOM

Centre International de Solidarite Ouvriere (AC) .... CISO

Centre International d'Enseignement Superieur de Journalisme [*UNESCO*] (NTCM) .... CIESJ

Centre International des Antiparasitaires .... CIA

Centre International des Civilisations Bantu [*International Center for the Bantu Civilizations*] [*Gabon*] [*Research center*] (IRC) .... CICIBA

Centre International des Engrais Chimiques [*International Center of Fertilizers*] .... CIEC

Centre International des Etudes de la Musique Ancienne [*International Center of Studies on Early Music*] .... CIEMA

Centre International des Marees Terrestres [*International Centre for Earth Tides*] (EAIO) .... CIMT

Centre International des Sciences Mecaniques .... CISM

Centre International des Syndicalistes Libres en Exil [*International Center of Free Trade Unionists in Exile*] [*Defunct*] .... CISLE

Centre International d'Etude des Textiles Anciens [*International Center for the Study of Ancient Textiles*] [*France*] (SLS) .... CIETA

Centre International d'Etudes des Textiles Anciens [*International Center for the Study of Ancient Textiles*] [*Lyon, France*] .... CIETA

Centre International d'Etudes du Lindane [*International Research Centre on Lindane - IRCL*] (EAIO) .... CIEL

Centre International d'Etudes et de Recherches en Socio-Economie de la Sante [*International Health Centre of Socioeconomics, Researches and Studies - IHCSERS*] [*Lailly En Val, France*] (EAIO) .... CIERSES

Centre International d'Exploitation des Oceans [*See also ICOD*] [*Canada*] .... CIEO

Centre International d'Information de la Mutualite .... CIIM

Centre International d'Information et de Recherche sur la Formation Professionnelle .... CIRF

Centre International d'Information sur le Gaz Naturel et tous Hydrocarbures Ga zeux [*International Information Center on Natural Gas and Gaseous Hydrocarbons*] [*France*] (PDAA) .... CEDIGAZ

Centre International d'Informations de Securite et d'Hygiene du Travail [*International Occupational Safety and Health Information Center*] [*International Labour Office*] (IID) .... CIS

Centre International du Commerce de Gros [*International Center for Wholesale Trade*] .... CICG

Centre International du Film pour l'Enfance et la Jeunesse [*International Center of Films for Children and Young People*] .... CIFEJ

Centre International Humanae Vitae [*International Centre Humanae Vitae*] [*Paris, France*] (EAIO) .... CIHV

Centre International pour Education Artistique [*International Centre for Art Education*] (EAIO) .... CIEA

Centre International pour la Coordination des Recherches en Agriculture .... CICRA

Centre International pour la Formation et les Echanges Geologiques [*International Center for Training and Exchanges in the Geosciences*] (EAIO) .... CIFEG

Centre International pour la Terminologie des Sciences Sociales [*France*] (EAIO) .... CITSS

Centre International pour le Developpement [*International Center for Development*] [*French*] (AF) .... CID

Centre International pour le Reglement des Differends Relatifs aux Investissements [*International Center for Settlement of Investment Disputes*] .... CIRDI

Centre International pour les Etudes Chimiques [*International Center for Chemical Studies - ICCS*] (EAIO) .... CIEC

Centre International pour l'Etude de la Marionnette Traditionnelle [*International Center for Research on Traditional Marionettes*] .... CIPEMAT

Centre International Provisoire de Calcul .... CIPC

Centre Interuniversitaire d'Etudes Europeennes [*Interuniversity Centre for European Studies*] [*Canada*] .... CIEE

Centre Islamique pour le Developpement du Commerce [*Islamic Center for Development of Trade - ICDT*] [*Casablanca, Morocco*] (EAIO) .... CIDC

Centre Left [*Australian Labor Party*] [*Political party*] CL

Centre Marin, Shippagan, NB, Canada [*Library symbol*] [*Library of Congress*] (LCLS) .... CaNBShCM

Centre Marin, Shippagan, New Brunswick [*Library symbol*] [*National Library of Canada*] (NLC) .... NBSCM

Centre Matched (SAUS) .... CM

Centre Meteorologique de Concentration et de Diffusion, French Air Force [*France*] [*ICAO location identifier*] (ICLI) .... LFYF

Centre Mondial d'Information sur l'Education Bilingue [*World Information Centre for Bilingual Education - WICBE*] (EAIO) .... CMIEB

Centre National de Documentation [*National Documentation Center*] [*Morocco*] [*Information service or system*] (IID) .... CND

Centre National de Documentation Pedagogique [*National Center for Pedagogical Documentation*] [*Ministry of Education*] [*Information service or system*] (IID) .... CNDP

Centre National de Documentation Scientifique et Technique [*National Scientific and Technical Documentation Center*] [*Royal Library of Belgium*] [*Belgium*] [*Information service or system*] (IID) .... CNDST

Centre National de la Recherche Scientifique [*France*] [*Marine science*] (OSRA) .... CNRS

Centre National de la Recherche Scientifique et Technologique [*Burkina Faso*] (GEOI) .... CNRST

Centre National de l'Information Chimique [*National Center for Chemical Information*] [*Information service or system*] (IID) .... CNIC

Centre National de Prevention et de Traitement des Intoxications [*National Poison Control Center*] [*Information service or system*] (IID) .... CNPTI

Centre National de Recherches Geomorphologiques [*Belgium*] (GEOI) .... CNRG

Centre National de Recherches Meteorologiques [*Toulouse, France*] [*Marine science*] (OSRA) .... CNRM

Centre National des Biologistes (SAUO) .... CNB

Centre National des Documents du Personnel [*National Personnel Records Center - NPRC*] .... CNDP

Centre National des Expositions et Concours Agricoles .... CENECA

Centre National des Independants [*National Center of Independents*] [*France*] [*Political party*] (PPE) .... CNI

Centre National des Independants et des Paysans [*National Centre of Independents and Peasants*] (EAIO) .... CNI

Centre National des Independants et des Paysans [*National Center of Independents and Peasants*] [*France*] [*Political party*] (PPW) .... CNIP

Centre National des Republicains Sociaux [*National Center of Social Republicans*] [*France*] [*Political party*] (PPE) .... CNRS

Centre National d'Etudes des Telecommunications [*France*] [*ICAO designator*] (FAAC) .... CNET

Centre National d'Etudes des Telecommunications [*France*] [*ICAO designator*] (FAAC) .... CNT

Centre National d'Etudes et d'Experimentation du Machinisme Agricole .... CNEEMA

Centre National d'Etudes Spatiales [*National Center for Space Studies*] [*France*] .... CNES

Centre National d'Information et de Recherche sur l'Aide Juridique [*National Legal Aid Research Centre*] [*Canada*] .... CNIRA

Centre National d'Informations Toxicologiques Veterinaires (GVA) .... CNITV

Centre National pour l'Exploitation des Oceans [*France*] (GEOI) .... CNEXO

Centre of Administrative Studies (SAUS) .... CAS

Centre of Advanced European Studies and Research [*Germany*] .... CAESAR

Centre of Asian Studies (SAUO) .... CAS

Centre of Balance (SAUS) .... C-B

Centre of Buoyancy (SAUS) .... CB

Centre of Burst (SAUS) .... CB

Centre of Christian Spirituality [*Australia*] .... CCS

Centre of Criminology, University of Toronto, Ontario [*Library symbol*] [*National Library of Canada*] (NLC) .... OTUCR

Centre of Democratic Studies of Latin America (SAUO) .... CEDAL

Centre of European Governmental Studies [*University of Edinburgh*] [*British*] (CB) .... CEGS

Centre of Films for Children and Young People [*British*] (DI) .... CFCYP

Centre of Forensic Sciences, Ontario Solicitor General, Toronto, ON, Canada [*Library symbol*] [*Library of Congress*] (LCLS) .... CaOTCF

Centre of Gravity [*Aviation*] (PIAV) .... c of g

Centre of Gravity (SAUS) .... COG

Centre of Gravity Control Computer (SAUS) .... CGCC

Centre of Gravity Factor [*Yachting*] .... CGF

Centre of Indian Trade Unions .... CITU

Centre of Industrial Microbiological Investigationes (SAUO) .... CIMI

Centre of Information and Documentatioin in Medical Education and Health Care (SAUO) .... CIDEMS

Centre of Information on Research and Engineering (SAUO) .... CNTI

Centre of Information Resource & Technology, Singapore [*Information service or system*] (IID) .... CIRTS

Centre of Lateral Resistance (SAUS) .... CLR

Centre of Latin American Studies [*University of Cambridge*] [*British*] (CB) .... CLAS

Centre of Lift (SAUS) CL

Centre of Management in Agriculture [*British*] (CB) .... CMA

Centre of Marine Geological survey Data (SAUO) .... CMGD

Centre of Mathematical Research (SAUO) .... CRM

Centre of Polish Research [*Institute of Comparative Civilizations*] [*Canada*] (IRC) .... CPR

Centre of Pressure [*Aviation*] (PIAV) .... C of P

Centre of Pressure (SAUS) .... CP

Centre of Research and Statistics on Science (SAUO) .... CISN

Centre of Resistance (SAUS) .... CR

Centre of Right (SAUS) .... CR

Centre of South-East Asian Studies [*University of Hull*] [*British*] (CB) .... SEAS

Centre of Studies and Recherches on Arab Provinces during the Ottoman Period (SAUO) .... CERPAO

Centre of studies and Researches on Arab Provinces during the Ottoman Period (SAUO) .... CERPAO

Centre of Transnational Corporations (SAUO) .... CTC

Centre of West African Studies [*University of Birmingham*] [*British*] (CB) .... CWAS

Centre on Addiction and Substance Abuse [*Columbia University*] .... CASA

Centre on Environment for the Handicapped [*British*] (CB) .... CEH

Centre on Integrated Rural Development for Africa (SAUO) .... CIRD-Africa

Centre on Integrated Rural Development for Africa (SAUO) .... CIRDAFRICA

Centre on Juvenile and Criminal Justice .... CJCJ

Centre on Scientific and Technical Information [*Israel*] (NITA) .... COST

Centre on Transnational Corporations (SAUO) .... CTNC

Centre Party (SAUO) .... CP

Centre point of a polygon (SAUS) .... Centroid

Centre pour Democratie et Progres [*Center for Democracy and Progress*] [*Later, Center of Social Democrats*] [*France*] [*Political party*] (PPE) .... CDP

Centre pour l'Avancement des Associations du Quebec (AC) .... CEPAQ

Centre pour le Developpement Industriel [*Centre for the Development of Industry*] (EAIO) .... CDI

Centre pour l'Independance des Magistrats et des Avocats [*Centre for the Independence of Judges and Lawyers - CIJL*] (EA) .... CIMA

Centre Quebecois de Relations Internationales [*Quebec Center for International Relations*] [*Canada*] (IRC) .... CQRI

Centre Quebecois des Sciences de l'Eau, Universite du Quebec, Quebec, Quebec [*Library symbol*] [*National Library of Canada*] (NLC) .... QQQE

Centre Quebecois du Droit de l'Environnement [Quebec Environmental Law Centre] (AC) .... CQDE
Centre Quebecois du PEN [Poets, Playwrights, Editors, and Novelists] International [Canada] (EAIO) .... CQPEN
Centre Regional Africain de Conception et de Fabrication Techniques [African Regional Centre for Engineering Design and Manufacturing - ARCEDEM] (EAIO) .... CRAFT
Centre Regional Africain de Technologie [African Regional Centre for Technology - ARCT] (EA) .... CRAT
Centre Regional de Documentation Pedagogique, Commission Scolaire de Le Gardeur,Repentigny, Quebec [Library symbol] [National Library of Canada] (BIB) .... QRECS
Centre Regional de Formation aux Techniques des Leves Aeriens [Regional Center for Training in Aerial Surveys - RECTAS] (EAIO) .... CRFTLA
Centre Regional de la Cote-Nord, Archives Nationales du Quebec, Sept-Iles, Quebec [Library symbol] [National Library of Canada] (BIB) .... QSIA
Centre Regional de l'Estrie, Archives Nationales du Quebec, Sherbooke, Quebec [Library symbol] [National Library of Canada] (NLC) .... QSHERAN
Centre Regional de l'Outaouais, Archives Nationales du Quebec, Hull, Quebec [Library symbol] [National Library of Canada] (BIB) .... QHQAR
Centre Regional de Montreal, Archives Nationales du Quebec, Quebec [Library symbol] [National Library of Canada] (NLC) .... QMQAR
Centre Rennais d'Information pour le Developpement et la Liberation des Peuples [France] .... CRIDEV
Centre Section (SAUS) .... CS
Centre Technique de Cooperation Agricole et Rural [Technical Centre for Agricultural and Rural Cooperation] (EAIO) .... CTA
Centre Technique des Industries de la Fonderie [Database producer] .... CTIF
Centre Technique International de l'Embouteillage [International Technical Center of Bottling] .... CETIE
Centre Terry Fox de la Jeunesse Canadienne [Terry Fox Canadian Youth Centre] .... CTFJC
Centre to Centre (SAUS) .... C to C
Centre to Face (SAUS) .... C to F
Centre Universitaire de Shippagan, New Brunswick [Library symbol] [National Library of Canada] (NLC) .... NBSCU
Centre Universitaire de Shippagan, Shippagan, NB, Canada [Library symbol] [Library of Congress] (LCLS) .... CaNBSCU
Centre Universitaire Saint-Louis Maillet, Edmundston, New Brunswick [Library symbol] [National Library of Canada] (NLC) .... NBESLM
Centre Wellington District High School, Fergus, ON, Canada [Library symbol] [Library of Congress] (LCLS) .... CaOFerC
Centre Wellington District High School, Fergus, Ontario [Library symbol] [National Library of Canada] (NLC) .... OFERC
Centreboard Factor [IOR] .... CBF
Centred' Etudes de la Navigation Aerienne [France] (GAVI) .... CENA
Centre-Line [Aviation] (PIAV) .... C/L
Centreline Air Services Ltd. [British] [ICAO designator] (ICDA) .... HG
Centres Biblio-Culturels de Montreal-Nord, Quebec [Library symbol] [National Library of Canada] (NLC) .... QMN
[Les] Centres Jeunesse de Quebec (AC) .... CJQ
Centres of Excellence in Molecular and Interfacial Dynamics [Research center] (RCD) .... CEMAID
Centreville, AL [Location identifier] [FAA] (FAAL) .... CKL
Centreville, AL [AM radio station call letters] .... WBIB
Centreville, MS [FM radio station call letters] (RBYB) .... WPAE-FM
Centreville Public Library, Centreville, NF, Canada [Library symbol] [Library of Congress] (LCLS) .... CaNfCe
Centreville Public Library, Newfoundland [Library symbol] [National Library of Canada] (NLC) .... NFCE
Centreville Township Hospital, East St. Louis, IL [Library symbol] [Library of Congress] (LCLS) .... IEsCTH
Centrex Central Office [Telecommunications] (TEL) .... CTXCO
Centrex Customer [Telecommunications] (TEL) .... CTXCU
Centrex Line-Assignment Service [Telecommunications] (ITD) .... CLAS
Centrex System Number [Bell System] [Telecommunications] (TEL) .... CTX
Centri Elettronici Reteconnessi Valutazione Elaborazione Dati [Central Electronic Network for Data Processing and Analysis] [Information service or system] (IID) .... CERVED
Centriacinar Emphysema [Medicine] (MELL) .... CAE
Centric Jaw Relationship [Dentistry] (DAVI) .... CJR
Centric Occlusion [Dentistry] .... CO
Centric Relation [Dentistry] .... CR
Centric Relation Occlusion [Dentistry] .... CRO
Centrifugal C
Centrifugal (KSC) .... CENT
Centrifugal .... CENTF
Centrifugal (MSA) .... CNTFGL
Centrifugal (AABC) .... CNTRF
Centrifugal [Freight] .... CNTRFUGL
Centrifugal Air Package Compressor (SAUS) .... CAP Compressor
Centrifugal Barrel Finishing [of metal surfaces] .... CBF
Centrifugal Cast Tube (SAUS) .... CCT
Centrifugal Charging Pump (IEEE) .... CCP
Centrifugal Coating CC
Centrifugal Countercurrent Chromatography CCCC
Centrifugal Electrostatic Focusing [Engineering] (IAA) .... CEF
Centrifugal Fast Analyzer [Analytical chemistry] .... CFA
Centrifugal Fault Display System .... CFDS
Centrifugal Fluidized Bed [Chemical engineering] .... CFB
Centrifugal Force .... CF
Centrifugal Liquid Extraction [Chemistry] .... CLE
Centrifugal Lockup Converter [Automotive engineering] CLC
Centrifugal Partition Chromatography .... CPC
Centrifugal Photosedimentation .... CP

Centrifugal Solids Recovery (SAUS) .... Censor
Centrifugal Spray Deposition [Steelmaking] .... CSD
Centrifugal Spraying .... CS
Centrifugal Throwout [Automotive engineering] .... C/T
Centrifugal Turning Moment (SAUS) .... CTLO
Centrifugal Urine Separator Assembly [Aerospace] (MCD) .... CUSA
Centrifugation Extractable Fluid .... CEF
Centrifugation Interaction CI
Centrifugation-Sugar Flotation [Soil testing] .... CSF
Centrifuge Moisture Equivalent .... CME
Centrifuge Plant Demonstration Facility [Department of Energy] .... CPDF
Centrifuged Microaggregate Filter (STED) .... CMAF
Centrilobular Emphysema [Medicine] (MAE) .... CLE
Centriole (MELL) C
Centripetal Force .... CF
Centripetal Rub [Medicine] .... CPR
Centris Group [NYSE symbol] (SG) .... CGE
Centristas de Cataluna [Political party] [Spain] (EY) CC
Centro Academico da Democracia Crista [Academic Center for Christian Democracy] [Portugal] [Political party] (PPE) .... CADC
Centro Agronomico Tropical Investigacion y Ensenanza [Tropical Agricultural Research and Training Center] [Turrialba, Costa Rica] (EAIO) .... CATIE
Centro Anglo-Espanol (EA) .... CAE
Centro Argentino de Informacion Cientifica y Tecnologica [Argentine Center for Scientific and Technological Information] [Information service or system] (IID) .... CAICYT
Centro Calculo Sabadell [Sabadell Computing Center] [Information service or system] (IID) .... CCS
Centro Catolico Portugues [Portuguese Catholic Center] [Political party] (PPE) .... CCP
Centro Coordinador de Proyectos Ecumenicos [Promotes exchanges between Mexico, US, and Canada] (CROSS) .... CECOPE
Centro de Analisis e Investigacion Economica [Participant in the Inter-American Bank Research Network] [Mexico] (CROSS) .... CAIE
Centro de Apoyo para Mujeres Violadas [An association] [Mexico] (EAIO) .... CAMVAC
Centro de Arte y Communicacion [Center of Art and Communication] [Argentina] (EAIO) .... CAYC
Centro de Calculo Electronico Universidad Nacional Autonoma de Mexico [National Autonomous University of Mexico, Data Processing Center] [Mexico] .... CCE
Centro de Comercio Internacional [International Trade Center - ITC] [Spanish] CCI
Centro de Documentacao Cientifica e Tecnica [Scientific and Technical Documentation Center] [Portugal] [Information service or system] (IID) .... CDCT
Centro de Encuentros y Dialogos [Member of RMALC] (CROSS) .... CED
Centro de Epidemiologia Molecular, Network for Epidemiologic Tracking [An international alliance of hospitals that track drug resistance] .... CEM/NET
Centro de Esploro kaj Dokumentado pri la Monda Lingvo-Problemo [Center for Research and Documentation on International Language Problems] (EAIO) .... CED
Centro de Estudios Democraticos de America Latina .... CEDAL
Centro de Estudios Economicos y Sociales del Tercer Mundo [Center for Economic and Social Studies of the Third World] [Canada] .... CEESTEM
Centro de Estudios Estrategicos [Center for Strategic Studies] [Mexico] (CROSS) .... CEE
Centro de Estudios Interplanetarios [Spain] (EAIO) .... CEI
Centro de Estudios Monetarios Latinoamericanos [Center for Latin American Monetary Studies] [Mexico City, Mexico] (EAIO) .... CEMLA
Centro de Estudios para el Cambio del campo en Mexico [A Mexican think tank which works on policies and training for growers] (CROSS) .... CECCAM
Centro de Estudios Puertorriquenos, New York, NY [Library symbol] [Library of Congress] (LCLS) .... NNCEP
Centro de Estudios Puertorriquenos, New York, NY [OCLC symbol] (OCLC) .... VXY
Centro de Estudos Franciscanos e Pastorais para a America Latina .... CEFEPAL
Centro de Hidratacian Infantil John Gordon (SAUS) .... CHIJGM
Centro de Informacao e Documentacao Amilcar Cabral [Portugal] .... CIDAC
Centro de Informacion Cientifica y Humanistica [Center for Scientific and Humanistic Information] [Mexico] [Information service or system] (IID) .... CICH
Centro de Informacion de Medicamentos [Spanish Drug Information Center] [Information service or system] (IID) .... CINIME
Centro de Informacion, Documentacion, y Analisis Latinoamericano .... CIDAL
Centro de Informacion Tecnica [Technical Information Center] [University of Puerto Rico] [Information service or system] (IID) .... CIT
Centro de Informacion y Solidaridad con el Paraguay [Switzerland] .... CISP
Centro de Informacoes Nucleares [Center for Nuclear Information] [Brazil] [Information service or system] (IID) .... CIN
Centro de Informativo y Documentacion [Press agency] [Argentina] .... CID
Centro de Investigacion Laboral y Asesoria Sindical [Member of RMALC] [Mexico] (CROSS) .... CILAS
Centro de Investigacion para el Desarrollo [Mexican government funded political and economic research center] (CROSS) .... CIDAC
Centro de Investigacion y Aplicacion de Sensores Remotos [Bolivia] (GEOI) .... CIACER
Centro de Investigacion y de Estudios Avanzados, Instituto Politecnico Nacional,Mexico City, Mexico [Library symbol] [Library of Congress] (LCLS) .... MxMC
Centro de Investigacion y Docencia Economica [Institute which focuses on Mexica n/US relations] (CROSS) .... CIDE
Centro de Investigaciones en Percepcion Remota (SAUS) .... CIAF
Centro de Investigaciones sobre Estados Unidos de America [Mexico/US relations] [Member of UNAM] (CROSS) .... CISEUA

Centro de las Naciones Unidas para los Asentamientos Humanos [*United Nations Centre for Human Settlements*] [*Spanish*] (DUND) .... CNUAH
Centro de Observacao Astronomica no Algarve .... COAA
Centro de Recursos Naturales [*El Salvador*] (GEOI) .... CENREN
Centro de Utilizacion y Promocion de Productos Forestales [*Forestry project*] [*Honduras*] .... CUPRFOR
Centro Democratico de Macau [*Macao Democratic Center*] (PPW) .... CDM
Centro Democratico y Social [*Democratic and Social Center*] [*Spain*] [*Political party*] (PPE) .... CDS
Centro di Azione e Documentazione sull'America Latina .... CADAL
Centro di Documentazione Umberto Nobile, Museo Storico, Rome, Italy [*Library symbol*] [*Library of Congress*] (LCLS) .... ItRUN
Centro di Riferimento Italiano DIANE [*Italian Reference Center for EURONET DIANE*] [*National Research Council*] [*Information service or system*] (IID) .... CRID
Centro di Studi Nucleari Enrico Fermi [*Nuclear Engineering Institute - Enrico Fermi Nuclear Center*] [*Italy*] (NRCH) .... CESNEF
Centro Economico Italia Africa [*Italian-African Economic Center*] (AF) .... CEIA
Centro Educativo Matriz (SAUO) .... CEM
Centro Filatelico Internazionale .... CFI
Centro Gerontologico Latino [*An association*] (EA) .... CGL
Centro Hispano Catolico [*Catholic Spanish Center*] (EA) .... CHC
Centro Informatico Cientifico de Andalucia [*Group of eight universities in Spain*] .... CICA
Centro Informazione, Studi Ed Esperienze (SAUS) .... CISE
Centro Interamericano de Administracion del Trabajo [*Inter-American Center for Labor Administration*] [*Lima, Peru*] (EAIO) .... CIAT
Centro Interamericano de Administradores Tributarios [*Inter-American Center of Tax Administrators*] (EAIO) .... CIAT
Centro Interamericano de Documentacion e Informacion Agricola [*Inter-American Center for Documentation and Agricultural Information*] [*Inter-American Institute for Cooperation on Agriculture*] [*Information service or system*] (IID) .... CIDIA
Centro Interamericano de Ensenanza de Estadistica .... CIENES
Centro Interamericano de Fotointerpretacion [*Bogota, Colombia*] .... CIAF
Centro Interamericano de Investigacion y Documentacion sobre Formacion Profesional [*Inter-American Centre for Research and Documentation on Vocational Training - IACRDVT*] (EAIO) .... CINTERFOR
Centro Interamericano de Libros Academicos [*Inter-American Scholarly Book Center*] .... CILA
Centro Interamericano de Promocion de Exportaciones [*Inter-American Export Promotion Center*] .... CIPE
Centro Interamericano de Vivienda .... CINVA
Centro Interamericano para el Desarrollo Regional [*Inter-American Center for Regional Development*] [*Venezuela*] (EAIO) .... CINDER
Centro Intercultural de Documentacion [*Center for Intercultural Documentation*] [*Cuernavaca, Mexico*] .... CIDOC
Centro Internacional de Agricultura Tropical [*International Center for Tropical Agriculture*] [*Colombia*] .... CIAT
Centro Internacional de Arreglo de Diferencias Relativas a Inversiones [*International Center for Settlement of Investment Disputes*] .... CIADI
Centro Internacional de Educacion y Desarrollo [*Venezuela*] .... CIED
Centro Internacional de Estudios Superiores de Periodisma para America Latina [*Press agency*] [*Ecuador*] .... CIESPAL
Centro Internacional de Formacion en Ciencias Ambientales para Paises de Habla Espanol [*International Center for the Preparation of Personnel in Environmental Sciences in Spanish-Speaking Countries*] [*Spain*] .... CIFCA
Centro Internacional de Informacion Economica .... CIDIE
Centro Internacional de Informacion sobre Seguridad e Higiene del Trabajo [*International Occupational Safety and Health Information Center*] [*Spain*] .... CIS
Centro Internacional de Investigaciones sobre el Cancer [*International Agency for Research on Cancer*] CIIC
Centro Internacional de la Infancia [*International Children's Center*] CII
Centro Internacional de la Papa [*International Potato Center*] [*ICSU*] (EAIO) .... CIP
Centro Internacional de Mejoramiento de Maiz y Trigo [*International Maize and Wheat Improvement Center*] [*ICSU*] (EAIO) .... CIMMYT
Centro Internazionale di Fisica Teorica [*International Center for Theoretical Physics - ICTP*] (EAIO) .... CIFT
Centro Internazionale di Studi sui Trasporti [*International Center for Transportation Studies - ICTS*] (EAIO) .... CIST
Centro Internazionale di Studi sull'Economia Turistica [*International Center of Studies on the Tourist Economy*] [*University of Venice*] [*Italy*] .... CISET
Centro Internazionale Radio-Medico [*International Radio Medical Center; gives emergency medical advice to ships at sea*] .... CIRM
Centro Italiano di Studi Europei (SAUO) .... CISE
Centro Latinoamericana de Demografia [*Latin American Demographic Center*] [*Economic Commission for Latin America and the Caribbean*] [*Chile*] [*United Nations*] .... CELADE
Centro Latinoamericano de Administracion para el Desarrollo [*Latin American Center for Development Administration*] [*Research center*] [*Venezuela*] (IRC) .... CLAD
Centro Latinoamericano de Ciencias Biologicas [*Latin American Center of Biological Sciences*] [*Research center*] [*Venezuela*] (IRC) .... CLAB
Centro Latinoamericano de Documentacion Economica y Social [*Latin American Center for Economic and Social Documentation*] [*Economic Commission for Latin America and the Caribbean*] [*United Nations*] [*Information service or system*] (IID) .... CLADES
Centro Latinoamericano de Quimica [*Latin American Center for Chemistry*] (PDAA) .... CLAQ
Centro Nacional de Desenvolvimento do Gerenciamento da Informacao [*National Center for Information Management Development*] [*Brazil*] [*Information service or system*] (IID) .... CENADEM
Centro Nacional de Informacao Documental Agricola [*National Center for Agricultural Documentary Information*] [*Ministry of Agriculture*] [*Brazil*] [*Information service or system*] (IID) .... CENAGRI
Centro Nacional de Informacion y Documentacion [*National Center for Information and Documentation*] [*Chile*] [*Information service or system*] .... CENID
Centro Nacional de Informacion y Documentacion [*National Information and Documentation Center*] [*Ministry of Labour*] [*Information service or system*] (IID) .... CNID
Centro Nacional de Informacion y Documentacion en Salud [*National Center for Health Information and Documentation*] [*Mexico*] [*Information service or system*] (IID) .... CENIDS
Centro Nacional de Informaciones [*National Information Center*] [*Supersedes DINA*] [*Chile*] .... CNI
Centro Nacional de Microfilm, Madrid, Spain [*Library symbol*] [*Library of Congress*] (LCLS) .... CnM
Centro Nacional de Reconhecimento e Ordenamento Agrario [*Portugal*] (GEOI) .... CNROA
Centro Nacional de Tecnologia Agropecuaria [*El Salvador*] (GEOI) .... CENTA
Centro Nacionalista [*Nationalist Center*] [*Bolivia*] [*Political party*] (PPW) .... CEN
Centro Nazionale Universitario di Calcalo Electronico [*National University Center for Electronic Calculation*] [*Italy*] (NITA) .... CNUCE
Centro Oftalmolágico de Occidente (SAUS) .... COMCISOR
Centro Panamericano de Estudios e Investigaciones Geograficas [*Pan American Center for Geographical Studies and Research - PACGSR*] (EAIO) .... CEPEIGE
Centro Panamericano de Fiebre Aftosa [*South American Commission for the Control of Foot-and-Mouth Disease*] (EAIO) .... COSALFA
Centro Panamericano de Ingenieria Sanitaria y Ciencias del Ambiente [*Pan American Center for Sanitary Engineering and Environmental Sciences*] [*Peru*] [*Research center*] (IRC) .... CEPIS
Centro para la Independencia de Jueces y Abogados [*Switzerland*] .... CIJA
Centro Regional de Educacion de Adultos y Alfabetizacion Funcional para America Latina [*Regional Center for Adult Education and Functional Literacy for Latin America*] [*Mexico*] (EAIO) .... CREFAL
Centro Regional de Sismologia para America del Sur [*Regional Seismology Center for South America*] [*Peru*] [*Research center*] (IRC) .... CERESIS
Centro Regional de Sismologia para America del Sur [*Regional Center for Seismology for South America - RCSSA*] (EAIO) .... CRSAS
Centro Regional para el Fomento del Libro en America Latina .... CERLAL
Centro Regional para la Educacion Superior en America Latina y el Caribe [*Regional Center for Higher Education in Latin America and the Caribbean-Venezuela*] [*United Nations*] (IID) .... CRESALC
Centro Ricerche Interdisciplinari sul Suicidio [*Interdisciplinary Research Center on Suicide*] [*Italy*] (EAIO) .... CRIS
Centro Studi Politica Economica [*of the Italian Communist Party*] .... CESPE
Centro Studi Terzo Mondo [*Study Center for the Third World*] [*Italy*] (EAIO) .... CSTM
Centro Televisivo Vaticano [*Vatican Television Center*] [*1984*] .... CTV
Centroblastic/Centrocytic [*Biochemistry*] .... CB-CC
centroblastisch (SAUS) .... cb
Centroid Moment Tensor Solutions [*A publication*] .... CMTS
Centroid-Moment Tensor [*Seismology*] .... CMT
Centrolateral [*Nucleus of thalamus*] [*Neuroanatomy*] CL
Centromere Protein (DMAA) .... CENP
Centromeric Indices [*Chromosomes*] CI
Centronics Data Computer Corp. (SAUO) .... CEN
Centrophenoxine (DB) .... CPH
Centrum Medyczne Ksztalcenia Podyplomowego (SAUS) .... CMKP
Centrum Partii [*Center Party*] [*Netherlands*] [*Political party*] (EY) .... CP
Centrum voor de Studie van het Onderwijs in Ontwikkelingslanden [*Centre for Study of Education in Developing Countries*] [*Netherlands*] (EAIO) .... CESO
Centrum voor Informatie Beleid [*Netherlands Center for Information Policy*] [*The Hague*] [*Information service or system*] (IID) .... CIB
Centrum voor Informatie en Documentatie [*Center for Information and Documentation*] [*Netherlands Organization for Applied Scientific Research*] [*Delft*] [*Information service or system*] (IID) .... CID
Centrum voor Landbouwpublikaties en Landbouwdocumentatie [*Center for Agricultural Publishing and Documentation*] [*Ministry of Agriculture and Fisheries*] [*Information service or system*] (IID) .... PUDOC
Centrum voor Postoraal in Europa [*Centre for Pastoral Work in Europe*] (EAIO) .... CPE
Centrum-Demokraterne [*Center Democrats*] [*Denmark*] [*Political party*] (PPE) .... CD
Cents (EBF) c
Cents (EBF) .... Cts
Cents per Available Seat Statute Mile [*Aviation*] .... C/ASSM
Cents per Kilometer (ADA) .... CPK
Cents Per Litre .... cpl
Cents per Share (ODBW) .... CPS
Cents-Off Coupon [*Advertising*] .... C/O
Centum [*Hundred*] C
Centum [*Hundred*] .... CENT
Centum [*Hundred*] .... CT
Centum Call-Seconds [*Telecommunications*] (PCM) .... CCS
Centum Milia [*One Hundred Thousand*] [*Latin*] C
Centum Weight [*Hundredweight*] [*Latin*] (GPO) .... CWT
Centura Banks [*NYSE symbol*] (SPSG) .... CBC
Centura Banks [*Associated Press*] (SAG) .... CentBk
Centura Software Corp. [*Associated Press*] (SAG) .... CenturaSft
Centura Software Corp. [*NASDAQ symbol*] (SAG) .... CNTR
Centuries CC
centuries (SAUS) cc
centuries (SAUS) .... cents
Centurion COLIDAR [*Coherent Light Detecting and Ranging*] **System** .... CCS

Centurion Gold Ltd. [Vancouver Stock Exchange symbol] [Toronto Stock Exchange symbol] ... CEU
Centurion LASER Range-Finder ... CLR
Centurion Mines [NASDAQ symbol] (SAG) ... CTMC
Centurion Mines Corp. [Associated Press] (SAG) ... CntMne
Centurium (SAUS) ... Cn
Centurium (SAUS) ... Ct
Century ... C
Century (VRA) ... c
Century ... CEN
Century ... CENT
Century (GEAB) ... cent
Century (BARN) ... centy
Century Airlines [ICAO designator] (AD) ... QX
Century Aluminum [NASDAQ symbol] (TTSB) ... CENX
Century Aluminum Co. [Associated Press] (SAG) ... CentAl
Century Aluminum Co. [NASDAQ symbol] (SAG) ... CENX
Century Association, New York, NY [Library symbol] [Library of Congress] (LCLS) ... NNCenC
Century Aviation International Ltd. [Canada] [FAA designator] (FAAC) ... HAI
Century Aviation, SA de CV [Mexico] [FAA designator] (FAAC) ... URY
Century BanCorp, Inc. [NASDAQ symbol] (NQ) ... CNBK
Century Bancorp, Inc. [Associated Press] (SAG) ... CntyBc
Century Bancorp(MA) [NASDAQ symbol] (TTSB) ... CNBKA
Century Bible [A publication] ... CB
Century Bible [A publication] (BJA) ... CentB
Century Business Svcs [NASDAQ symbol] (SG) ... CBIZ
Century Casinos [NASDAQ symbol] (TTSB) ... CNTY
Century Casinos, Inc. [Associated Press] (SAG) ... CentC
Century Casinos, Inc. [Associated Press] (SAG) ... CentCas
Century Casinos, Inc. [NASDAQ symbol] (SAG) ... CNTY
Century Casinos Wrrt [NASDAQ symbol] (TTSB) ... CNTYW
Century Communic'ns'A' [NASDAQ symbol] (TTSB) ... CTYA
Century Computer International (SAUS) ... CCI
Century Data Systems Inc. (SAUO) ... CDS
Century Dictionary [A publication] (ROG) ... CD
Century Dictionary [A publication] (DLA) ... Cent Dict
Century Dictionary and Cyclopedia [A publication] (DLA) ... Cent Dict and Cyc
Century Dictionary and Encyclopedia [A publication] (DLA) ... Cent Dict & Ency
Century Edition of the American Digest System (West) [A publication] (DLA) ... CD
Century Edition of the American Digest System (West) [A publication] (DLA) ... Cent Dig
Century Electric (SAUS) ... CEY
Century Electric Company (SAUO) ... CEY
Century Financial Corp. [Associated Press] (SAG) ... CentFin
Century Financial Corp. [NASDAQ symbol] (SAG) ... CYFN
Century, FL [FM radio station call letters] ... WKGT
Century, FL [FM radio station call letters] (RBYB) ... WPFL-FM
Century Hutchinson [Publisher] [British] ... CH
Century Industries Co., Inc. (SAUO) ... CTY
Century Minerals and Mining [Australia] ... CMM
[A] Century of Excavation in Palestine [A publication] (BJA) ... HAI
[A] Century of Humorous Verse [A publication] ... CenHV
[A] Century of Lyrics [A publication] ... CenL
Century Publishing Co. ... CPC
Century Research Center Corp. [Information service or system] (IID) ... CRC
Century Service Bulletin (SAUS) ... CSB
Century Shares Trust-Vance, Sanders & Co. (SAUO) ... CST
Century South Banks [NASDAQ symbol] (TTSB) ... CSBI
Century South Banks, Inc. [NASDAQ symbol] (SAG) ... CSBI
Century South Banks, Inc. [Associated Press] (SAG) ... CtrySo
Century Sports Network ... CSN
Century Stand [Filmmaking] (WDMC) ... C-stand
Century Technologies, Inc. (SAUO) ... CENTECH
Century Tel Enterp [NYSE symbol] (TTSB) ... CTL
Century Tel, Inc. [NYSE symbol] (SG) ... CTL
Century Telecommunications [Associated Press] (SAG) ... CntyCm
Century Telecommunications [NASDAQ symbol] (SAG) ... CTYA
Century Telephone Co. [Associated Press] (SAG) ... CntyTl
Century Telephone Enterprises, Inc. [NYSE symbol] (SPSG) ... CTL
Century Village, Lang, ON, Canada [Library symbol] [Library of Congress] (LCLS) ... CaOLgCV
Century Village, Lang, Ontario [Library symbol] [National Library of Canada] (BIB) ... OLCV
Centus [Constellation] ... Cet
Centus [Constellation] ... Ceti
CEOS International Directory Network (SAUS) ... CEOS-IDN
CEP Reporting Official (SAUO) ... CEPRO
CEPEX Integrated Data System (SAUS) ... CIDS
Cephacetril (SAUS) ... CA
Cephalic (ROG) ... CEPH
Cephalic Artery ... CA
Cephalic Index ... CI
Cephalic Sinus ... CS
Cephalic Vasomotor Response [Medicine] (DMAA) ... CVR
Cephalic-Phase Insulin Release [Medicine] (DMAA) ... CPIR
Cephalin Cholesterol Antigen [Immunochemistry] ... CCA
Cephalin Flocculation [Clinical chemistry] (AAMN) ... CEPH-FLOC
Cephalin-Cholesterol Flocculation [Clinical chemistry] ... CCF
Cephalo Pedal Sinus ... CPS
Cephalo-Facial Deformity [Medicine] (DMAA) ... CFD
Cephalon, Inc. [NASDAQ symbol] (SPSG) ... CEPH
Cephalon, Inc. [Associated Press] (SAG) ... Cephln
Cephalopelvic Disproportion [Gynecology] ... CPD

Cephalopod International Advisory Council (SAUO) ... CIAC
Cephalosporin [Pharmacology] (DAVI) ... CEPH
Cephalosporium gramineum [Plant pathology] ... Cg
Cephalosporium Stripe [of wheat] [Plant pathology] ... Cs
Cephalothin [Medicine] (CPH) ... CF
Cephalotin (SAUS) ... Ct
Cepheus [Constellation] ... Cep
Cepheus [Constellation] ... Ceph
Cepi Corpus [Latin] [Legal term] (DLA) ... CC
Cepi Corpus [I Have Taken the Body] [Latin] [Legal term] (DLA) ... CE C
Cepi Corpus and Bail Bond [Legal term] (DLA) ... CC & BB
Cepi Corpus and Committitur [Legal term] (ILCA) ... CC & C
Cepstrum ... CEP
Cepstrum Method (SAUS) ... CEP Method
Cepu/Ngloram [Indonesia] [ICAO location identifier] (ICLI) ... WRSC
Ceradyne, Inc. [Associated Press] (SAG) ... Cerdyn
Ceradyne, Inc. [NASDAQ symbol] (NQ) ... CRDN
Ceramic (SAUS) ... CC
Ceramic (MSA) ... CER
Ceramic (ROG) ... CERAM
Ceramic ... CRMC
Ceramic Age (journ.) (SAUS) ... Ceram Age
Ceramic and Allied Trade Union [British] (DCTA) ... CATU
Ceramic and Alloy [NASA] ... CERAMAL
Ceramic and Graphite Information Center [Air Force] (MCD) ... C & G
Ceramic and Graphite Information Center (SAUO) ... C&G
Ceramic and Graphite Information Center (SAUO) ... CGIC
Ceramic and Metal (SAUS) ... CERMET
Ceramic Applications for Turbine Engines (ACAE) ... CATE
Ceramic Arts Federation International (EA) ... CAFI
Ceramic Association of New Jersey (SAUO) ... CANJ
Ceramic Association of New York State (SAUO) ... CANYS
Ceramic Audio Tone Transducer (PDAA) ... CATT
Ceramic Awareness Bulletin [Defense Ceramic Information Center] [A publication] ... CAB
Ceramic Ball Grid Array (AAEL) ... CBGA
Ceramic Ball Grid Array (SAUS) ... CGBA
Ceramic Based Microcircuit (SAUS) ... CBM
Ceramic Beam Pentode ... CBP
Ceramic Capacitor (IAA) ... CC
Ceramic Cards (ACAE) ... CC
Ceramic Chip Carrier ... C3
Ceramic Chip Carrier ... CCC
Ceramic Delay Line ... CDL
Ceramic DIP [Dual In-line Package] (CDE) ... CERDIP
Ceramic Disc Capacitor (SAUS) ... CDC
Ceramic Disk Capacitor ... CDC
Ceramic Dual In-Line (SAUS) ... CERDIL
Ceramic Dual In-Line Package (CIST) ... CDIP
Ceramic Dual In-Line Package ... CER-DIP
Ceramic Educational Council (EA) ... CEC
Ceramic Engineer ... Cer E
Ceramic Engineer [Canada] (ASC) ... CerE
Ceramic Engineering Research Laboratory (SAUO) ... CERL
Ceramic Fiber Optics ... CFO
Ceramic Filled Polymer Armor System (SAUS) ... CFPAS
Ceramic Flat Pack (AAEL) ... CFP
Ceramic Foam Insulation ... CFI
Ceramic, Glass and Mineral Products Training Board (SAUO) ... CGMPTB
Ceramic Glazed Structural Facing Units (SAUS) ... CGSFU
Ceramic [or Clear] Glazed Structural Facing Units [Technical drawings] ... CGSFU
Ceramic [or Clear] Glazed Structural Unit Base [Technical drawings] ... CGSUB
Ceramic Glazed Structural Unit Base (SAUS) ... CGSUB
Ceramic Glazed Unit [Technical drawings] ... CGU
Ceramic Gold Coating ... CGC
Ceramic Gravitational Containment Vessel [i.e., cup] [Slang] ... CGCV
Ceramic Hotform Die (MCD) ... CHFD
Ceramic Insulated Wire ... CIW
Ceramic Leaded Chip Carrier (NITA) ... CLCC
Ceramic Leadless Chip Carrier (SAUS) ... CLCC
Ceramic Manufacturers Association (NTPA) ... CerMA
Ceramic Manufacturers' Association of Australia ... CMAA
Ceramic Manufacturers' Association of New South Wales [Australia] ... CMANSW
Ceramic Matrix Composite [Materials science] ... CMC
Ceramic Metal Element [NASA] ... CERMET
Ceramic Metal Fuel [NASA] (IAA) ... CERMET
Ceramic Metal Terminal [NASA] (IAA) ... CERAMETERM
Ceramic Metallic (SAUS) ... CERMET
Ceramic Metallized (SAUS) ... CERMET
Ceramic Mosaic Tile [Technical drawings] ... CMT
Ceramic Non-Oxide (SAUS) ... Ceranox
Ceramic Oceanographic Buoy ... COB
Ceramic Package [NASA] (IAA) ... CERPACK
Ceramic Pin Grid Array [Computer science] (VERA) ... CPGA
Ceramic Planar Tube ... CPT
Ceramic Printed Circuit (IAA) ... CPC
Ceramic Quad Flat Pack (CIST) ... CQFP
Ceramic Quad J-Bend (SAUS) ... CQJB
Ceramic Refraction Coating ... CRC
Ceramic Reusable Surface Insulation (NASA) ... CRSI
Ceramic Silicone Foam [Chemistry] ... CSF
Ceramic Table Case (SAUS) ... CERATAB Case
Ceramic Tile [Technical drawings] ... CT
Ceramic Tile Contractors & Industry Association of British Columbia (AC) ... CTCIA

Ceramic Tile Distributors Association (EA) .... CTDA
Ceramic Tile Institute (SAUS) .... CTI
Ceramic Tile Institute of America (EA) .... CTIOA
Ceramic Tile Marketing Federation [Defunct] (EA) .... CTMF
Ceramic Tube Fabrication .... CTF
Ceramic Vacuum Relay .... CVR
Ceramic-Based Microcircuit .... CBM
Ceramic-Heated Tunnel [Langley Research Center] .... CHT
Ceramics (VRA) .... cer
Ceramics Advanced Manufacturing Development Engineering Center
   [Defunct] (EA) .... CAMDEC
Ceramics and Graphite Branch [Air Force] .... CGB
Ceramics and Graphite Information Center [Air Force] .... CGIC
Ceramics and Industrial Minerals (SAUO) .... CIM
Ceramics Applications in Reciprocating Engines [Research group]
   [British] .... CARE
Ceramics Distributors of America (EA) .... CDA
Ceramics, Glass, and Solid State Science Division [National Institute of
   Standards and Technology] (GRD) .... CGSS
Ceramics Industry Advisory Committee (HEAS) .... CERIAC
Ceramics Industry Training Organisation [British] (AIE) .... CITO
Ceramics Information Analysis Center (IID) .... CIAC
Ceramics International Association [Defunct] (EA) .... CIA
Ceramics Monthly [A publication] (BRI) .... Ceram Mo
Ceramics Process Systems (ACAE) .... CPS
Ceramic-Tile Base [Technical drawings] .... CTB
Ceramic-Tile Floor [Technical drawings] .... CTF
Ceramic-to-Metal Seal .... CERMET
Ceramic-to-Metal Seal .... CTMS
Ceramic-Wafer Printed Circuit .... CPC
Ceramide [Biochemistry] .... Cer
Ceramide Activated Protein Phosphatase [An enzyme] .... CAPP
Ceramide Dihexoside [Biochemistry] .... CDH
Ceramide Monohexoside [Biochemistry] .... CMH
Ceramide Trihexosides [Biochemistry] .... CTH
Ceramide-Activated Protein [Biochemistry] .... CAP
Ceratobasidium Anastomosis Group [Phytopathology] .... CAG
Ceratum [Wax Ointment] [Pharmacy] .... CERAT
CERBCO, Inc. [NASDAQ symbol] (NQ) .... CERB
Cerbco, Inc. [Associated Press] (SAG) .... Cerbco
Cerberus Central Ltd. (SAUS) CCL
Cercarienhullen Reaktion [Medicine] .... CHR
CERCLA [Comprehensive Environmental Response, Compensation, and
   Liability Act] Enforcement Division [Environmental Protection Agency]
   (GFGA) .... CED
CERCLA Enforcement Division (SAUO) .... CED
CERCLA Information System .... CERCLIS
Cerclage Wire (MELL) .... CW
Cercle Culturel Camerounais CCL
Cercle de la Finance Internationale de Montreal (AC) .... CEFIM
Cercle Populaire Europeen [European Popular Circle - EPC] (EAIO) .... CPE
Cercle pour le Renouveau et le Progres [Gabon] [Political party] (EY) .... CRP
Cerdas [Bolivia] [ICAO location identifier] (ICLI) .... SLCS
Cereal Agar .... CER
Cereal Chemistry (journ.) (SAUS) .... Cereal Chem
Cereal Chlorotic Mottle Virus [Plant pathology] .... CECMV
Cereal Cyst Nematode [Medicine] .... CCN
Cereal Institute [Defunct] (EA) CI
Cereal Municipal Library, Alberta [Library symbol] [National Library of
   Canada] (NLC) .... ACERM
Cereal Municipal Library, Cereal, AB, Canada [Library symbol] [Library of
   Congress] (LCLS) .... CaACerM
Cereal Rust Laboratory [Department of Agriculture] (GRD) .... CRL
Cereal Ryegrowers' Association [Australia] .... CRA
Cereal Science Today (journ.) (SAUS) .... Cereal Sci Today
Cereal Tillering Disease Virus [Plant pathology] .... CTDV
Cereals and Baltic Friendly Society (SAUO) .... CBFS
Cerebellar Ataxia [Medicine] (MELL) .... CA
Cerebellar Ataxia (DB) .... CLR
Cerebellar Ataxia and Chorioretinal Degeneration [Medicine] (MELL) .... CA & CD
Cerebellar Cortical Degeneration [Medicine] (MELL) .... CCD
Cerebellar Degeneration [Medicine] (MELL) .... CD
Cerebellar Model Articulation Control [System] [National Institute of
   Standards and Technology] .... CMAC
Cerebellar Purkinje Cell [Medicine] (DMAA) .... CPC
Cerebellar-Pontine Angle (SAUS) .... CPA
Cerebellopontine [Anatomy] (AAMN) .... CP
Cerebellopontine Angle [Syndrome] (DB) .... CA
Cerebellopontine Angle [Brain anatomy] .... CPA
Cerebellum [Medicine] (MELL) C
Cerebellum [Brain anatomy] .... CB
Cerebral Amyloid Angiopathy [Medicine] .... CAA
Cerebral Aneurysm [Medicine] (MELL) .... Ca
Cerebral Aqueduct [Brain anatomy] .... CA
Cerebral Arteriosclerosis [Medicine] (MAE) .... CAS
Cerebral Artery Embolism [Medicine] (MELL) .... CAE
Cerebral Autosomal Dominant Arteriopathy with Subcortical Infarcts and
   Leukoencephalopathy [Medicine] .... CADASIL
Cerebral Blood Flow [Medicine] .... CBF
Cerebral Blood Flow Autoregulation .... CBFA
Cerebral Blood Flow Laboratories [Research center] (RCD) .... CBF Labs
Cerebral Blood Flow Studies [Cardiology] (DAVI) .... CBFS
Cerebral Blood Flow Velocity [Cardiology] (DAVI) .... CBFV
Cerebral Commissure [Brain anatomy] CC
Cerebral Cortex Perfusion Rate [Medicine] (MAE) .... CPR

Cerebral Cortical Degeneration [Medicine] (MELL) .... CCD
Cerebral Edema [Medicine] (CPH) .... CE
Cerebral Edema Syndrome [Medicine] (MELL) .... CES
Cerebral Electrotherapy (DIPS) .... CET
Cerebral Embolism [Medicine] (MELL) .... CE
Cerebral Embolism of Unknown Source [Medicine] (MELL) .... CEUS
Cerebral Fissure [Medicine] (MELL) .... CF
Cerebral Function Monitor (PDAA) .... CFM
Cerebral Ganglion [Medicine] .... CG
Cerebral Gigantism [Medicine] (MELL) .... CG
Cerebral Glucose Oxygen Quotient [Medicine] (MAE) .... CG/OQ
Cerebral Hemisphere [Medicine] (MELL) .... CH
Cerebral Infarction [Medicine] CI
Cerebral Lateral Sulcus [Medicine] (MELL) .... CLS
Cerebral Lipidosis [Medicine] (AAMN) .... CLIP
Cerebral Longitudinal Fissure [Medicine] (MELL) .... CLF
Cerebral Malaria [Medicine] .... CM
Cerebral Mantle (DB) .... CM
Cerebral Metabolic Rate [Medicine] .... CMR
Cerebral Metabolic Rate for Oxygen (SAUS) CMR2
Cerebral Metabolic Rate for Oxygen .... CMRO$_2$
Cerebral Metabolic Rate of Glucose [Also, CMRglc] [Biochemistry] .... CMRG
Cerebral Metabolic Rate of Glucose [Also, CMRG] [Biochemistry] .... CMRglc
Cerebral Metabolic Rate of Lactate [Medicine] (DMAA) .... CMRI
Cerebral Metabolic Rate of Oxygen [Biochemistry] (DAVI) .... CMRO
Cerebral Motor Dysfunction [Medicine] .... CMD
Cerebral Palsy [Medicine] .... CP
Cerebral Palsy - International Sports and Recreation Association
   (SAUO) .... CP-ISRA
Cerebral Palsy Association of Quebec, Inc., Quebec, PQ, Canada [Library
   symbol] [Library of Congress] (LCLS) .... CaQQAPC
Cerebral Palsy Association of Quebec, Inc. [L'Association de Paralysie
   Cerebrale du Quebec, Inc.] Quebec, Quebec [Library symbol] [National
   Library of Canada] (NLC) .... QQAPC
Cerebral Palsy Clinic .... CPC
Cerebral Palsy Coordinating Council (SAUO) .... CPCC
Cerebral Palsy International Sports and Recreation Association [Arnhem,
   Netherlands] (EAIO) .... CPISRA
Cerebral Palsy Ireland (EAIO) .... CPI
Cerebral Palsy Overseas (SAUO) .... CPO
Cerebral Palsy Sports Association of British Columbia (AC) .... CPSA-BC
Cerebral Palsy-International Sports and Recreation Association
   (SAUO) .... CP-ISTRA
Cerebral Peduncle [Brain anatomy] .... CP
Cerebral Percutaneous Transluminal Angioplasty [Medicine] (MELL) .... CPTA
Cerebral Performance Category .... CPC
Cerebral Perfusion Pressure [Medicine] .... CPP
Cerebral Ridge [Medicine] .... CR
Cerebral Subarachnoid Venous Pressure [Medicine] (DMAA) .... CSAVP
Cerebral Thrombosis [Medicine] .... CT
Cerebral Tissue Perfusion Pressure [Medicine] (DMAA) .... CTPP
Cerebral Toxoplasmosis [Medicine] (DB) .... cTOX
Cerebral Transient Ischemic Attack [Medicine] (MELL) .... CTIA
Cerebral Tumor [Medicine] .... CT
Cerebral Vascular Profile Study [Cardiology] (DAVI) .... C-Vasc
Cerebral Venous Sinus Thrombosis [Medicine] .... CVST
Cerebral-Pedal Regulator [Neurobiology] .... CPR
Cerebriform Intradermal Nevus [Medicine] (AAMN) .... CIN
Cerebro-Buccal Commissure [Medicine] .... CBC
Cerebrobuccal Commissure (SAUS) .... CBC
Cerebrobuccal Connectives (SAUS) .... CBC
Cerebrocostomandibular Syndrome [Medicine] (DMAA) .... CCM
Cerebro-Costo-Mandibular Syndrome [Medicine] (MELL) .... CCMS
Cerebrohepatorenal [Medicine] (MELL) .... CHR
Cerebrohepatorenal Syndrome [Medicine] .... CHRS
Cerebro-Oculo-Facial-Skeletal Syndrome [Medicine] (DMAA) .... COFS
Cerebro-Oculo-Facio-Skeletal Syndrome [Medicine] (MELL) .... COFSS
Cerebrooculomuscular Syndrome [Medicine] (DMAA) .... COMS
Cerebro-Pedal Commissure [Medicine] .... CPC
Cerebropontine [Angle] [Neurosurgery] (DAVI) .... CP
Cerebrospinal [Medicine] .... CS
Cerebro-Spinal (SAUS) .... CS
Cerebrospinal Fluid [Medicine] (AAMN) C
Cerebrospinal Fluid [Medicine] .... CSF
Cerebrospinal Fluid Leukocyte Particle Counter [Instrumentation] .... CSFLpc
Cerebrospinal Fluid Pressure [Medicine] (AAMN) .... CSFP
Cerebrospinal Fluid Protein [Biochemistry] (DAVI) .... CFP
Cerebrospinal Fluid-Wassermann Reaction [Medicine] (AAMN) .... CSF-WR
Cerebrospinal Meningitis [Medicine] .... CSM
Cerebrotendinous Xanthomatosis [Medicine] .... CTX
Cerebrovascular [Medicine] (MELL) CV
Cerebrovascular (SAUS) .... CVA
Cerebrovascular Accident [Medicine] .... CVA
Cerebrovascular Amyloid [Medicine] .... CA
Cerebrovascular Amyloid Peptide [Medicine] (DMAA) .... CVAP
Cerebrovascular Disease [Medicine] (DMAA) .... CBVD
Cerebrovascular Disease [Neurology and psychiatry] (DAVI) .... CVD
Cerebrovascular Episode [Medicine] (CPH) .... CVE
Cerebrovascular Incident [Medicine] (MELL) CVI
Cerebrovascular Insufficiency [Medicine] CVI
Cerebrovascular Obstructive Disease (MAE) .... CVOD
Cerebrovascular Profile [Cardiology] (DAVI) .... CVP
Cerebrovascular Resistance [Medicine] .... CVR
Cerebroventricular Hemorrhage [Medicine] (DMAA) .... CVH
Cerebrum [Medicine] (MELL) C

Ceremony ..... CRMNY
Ceremony of Installation [*Freemasonry*] (ROG) ..... C of I
Cerenkov Low Energy Sampling and Timing Experiment (SAUS) ..... CELESTE
Cereolus [*An urethral bougie*] [*Pharmacy*] ..... CEREOL
Ceres [*South Africa*] [*Seismograph station code, US Geological Survey*] (SEIS) ..... CER
Ceres [*Argentina*] [*ICAO location identifier*] (ICLI) ..... SANW
Ceres, CA [*FM radio station call letters*] ..... KBES
Ceres, CA [*TV station call letters*] (RBYB) ..... KBSV-TV
Ceres, CA [*AM radio station call letters*] ..... KLOC
Ceres Group [*NASDAQ symbol*] (SG) ..... CERG
Ceric Ammonium Nitrate [*Inorganic chemistry*] ..... CAN
Ceridian Corp. [*Formerly, Control Data Corp.*] [*NYSE symbol*] (SPSG) ..... CEN
Ceridian Corp. [*Associated Press*] (SAG) ..... Ceridian
Ceridian Corp. [*Associated Press*] (SAG) ..... Ceridn
Ceridian Cp Cv Ex Dep Pfd [*NYSE symbol*] (TTSB) ..... CENPr
Cerion Technologies, Inc. [*NASDAQ symbol*] (SAG) ..... CEON
Cerion Technologies, Inc. [*Associated Press*] (SAG) ..... CerionT
Cerise [*Philately*] ..... cer
Cerium [*Chemical element*] ..... Ce
Cerium Magnesium Nitrate [*Inorganic chemistry*] ..... CMN
Cerknica [*Yugoslavia*] [*Seismograph station code, US Geological Survey*] (SEIS) ..... CEY
CERMET [*Ceramic Metal Element*] **Hybrid Integrated Circuit** ..... CHIC
CERMET [*Ceramic Metal Element*] **Resistor Network** ..... CRN
CERN Accounting System (SAUS) ..... ORIAC
CERN Commercial Purchasing System (SAUS) ..... SIRIAC
CERN Electron Storage and Accumulating Ring (SAUS) ..... CESAR
CERN Hybrid Oscillation Research apparatus (SAUS) ..... CHORUS
CERN [*Conseil Europeen pour la Recherche Nucleaire*] **Linear Collider** [*Particle physics*] CLIC
CERN [*Conseil European pour la Recherche Nucleaire*]**-Dortmund-Heidelberg-Saclay Collaboration** ..... CDHS
Cerner Corp. [*NASDAQ symbol*] (NQ) ..... CERN
Cerner Corp. [*Associated Press*] (SAG) ..... Cerner
Cero Gradient Synchrotron (SAUS) ..... ZGS
Cerous Magnesium Nitrate (SAUS) ..... CMN
Cerplex Group [*Associated Press*] (SAG) ..... Cerplex
Cerplex Group [*NASDAQ symbol*] (SAG) ..... CPLX
Cerprobe Corp. [*Associated Press*] (SAG) ..... Cerprbe
Cerprobe Corp. [*NASDAQ symbol*] (NQ) ..... CRPB
Cerrada ..... CER
Cerre Les Noroy [*France*] [*Seismograph station code, US Geological Survey*] [*Closed*] (SEIS) ..... CNF
Cerritos Junior College, Artesia, CA [*Library symbol*] [*Library of Congress*] (LCLS) ..... CArtC
Cerro Catedral [*Argentina*] [*ICAO location identifier*] (ICLI) ..... SAZK
Cerro Corporation (SAUO) ..... CDP
Cerro De Punta [*Puerto Rico*] [*Seismograph station code, US Geological Survey*] (SEIS) ..... CDP
Cerro Del Durzno [*New Mexico*] [*Seismograph station code, US Geological Survey*] (SEIS) ..... CDN
Cerro La Pandura [*Puerto Rico*] [*Seismograph station code, US Geological Survey*] (SEIS) ..... CPD
Cerro Sombrero [*Chile*] [*Airport symbol*] (AD) ..... SMB
Cerro Tolo Interamerican Observatory (SAUS) ..... CTIO
Cerro-Negro [*Argentina*] [*Seismograph station code, US Geological Survey*] (SEIS) ..... CEN
Cerro-Tololo Inter-American Observatory [*Chile*] [*National Science Foundation*] ..... CTIO
Certain (SAUS) ..... Cert
Certain (ROG) ..... CERTN
Certain Borough [*British*] ..... CB
Certain Data Processing (SAUS) ..... CDP
Certain Information Processing (SAUS) ..... CIP
Certain Lethal Dose (SAUS) ..... CLD
Certain Submarine [*Navy*] (NVT) ..... CERTSUB
Certainly (ADWA) ..... cert
Certainly Affordable Mortgage Loan (EBF) ..... CAML
[*A*] **Certainty** ..... CERT
Certainty Equivalent Coefficient [*Finance*] ..... CE
Certainty Equivalent of Revenues [*Business term*] ..... CEOR
Certainty Factor [*Mathematics*] (BARN) ..... CF
Certifed Dental Technician (SAUS) ..... CDT
Certifed Invoice (SAUS) ..... Cert Inv
Certifed Medical Assistant Administrative and Clinical (SAUS) ..... CMAAC
Certificado de Abono Tributario [*Tax Credit Certificate*] [*Spanish*] ..... CAT
Certificant, Acupuncture Foundation of Canada (CMD) ..... CAFC
Certificant, American Board of Emergency Medicine (CMD) ..... CABEM
Certificant, American Board of Surgery (CMD) ..... CABS
Certificant, Board of Life Insurance Examiners (CMD) ..... CBLIE
Certificant, Canadian Board of Occupational Medicine (DD) ..... CCBOM
Certificant, College of Family Physicians, Emergency Medicine (CMD) ..... CCFP(EM)
Certificant, College of Family Physicians of Canada (CPGU) ..... CCFP(c)
Certificat d'Aptitude Professionelle [*Certificate of Professional Ability*] [*French*] (BARN) ..... CAP
Certificate (GEAB) ..... cer
Certificate (ADWA) ..... cert
Certificate (DD) ..... Cert
Certificate [*or Certification*] (AFM) ..... CERT
Certificate (ROG) ..... CERTC
Certificate ..... CERTIF
Certificate (ADWA) ..... ct
Certificate [*Stock exchange term*] (SPSG) ..... CT
Certificate ..... CTF
Certificate (SAUS) ..... Ctf
Certificate (NTIO) ..... ctf
Certificate as a Qualified Social Worker [*British*] ..... CQSW
Certificate Authority ..... CA
Certificate, College of Family Physicians (CMD) ..... CCFP
Certificate Depository [*New York Stock Exchange*] ..... CEDE
Certificate for Amortizing Revolving Debts [*Salomon Brothers*] [*Accounting*] ..... CARD
Certificate for Automobile Receivables [*Investment term*] (DFIT) ..... CAR
Certificate For Automobile Receivables [*Business term*] (EMRF) ..... CARS
Certificate for Physical Education [*British*] (ROG) ..... CPE
Certificate for Vocational Preparation Tutors (AIE) ..... CVPT
Certificate, Health in the Workplace (CMD) ..... CST
Certificate, Hospital Administration (CMD) ..... CHA
Certificate in Advanced Social Research (PGP) ..... CASR
Certificate in Advanced Standing (GAGS) ..... CAS
Certificate in Advanced Study in Business (GAGS) ..... CAGSB
Certificate in Applied Linguistics (PGP) ..... CAL
Certificate in Architectural Drafting ..... CertArchDraft
Certificate in Art ..... CertArt
Certificate in Art Studies ..... CertArtStud
Certificate in Astrology ..... CertAst
Certificate in Basic Health Sciences (PGP) ..... CBHS
Certificate in Business Administration [*Academic degree*] (AIE) ..... CBA
Certificate in Business Management ..... CertBusMan
Certificate in Business Studies ..... CertBusStud
Certificate in Communication, Advertising, and Marketing (ODBW) ..... Cert CAM
Certificate in Community Development ..... CertComDev
Certificate in Community Health (PGP) ..... CCH
Certificate in Computer Programming [*Designation awarded by Institute for the Certification of Computer Professionals*] ..... CCP
Certificate in Counselling ..... CertCouns
Certificate in Criminal Justice Administration (PGP) ..... CCJA
Certificate in Data Education (BUR) ..... CDE
Certificate in Data Processing [*Designation awarded by Institute for Certification of Computer Professionals*] ..... CDP
Certificate in Dietetics ..... CertDiet
Certificate in Early Childhood Teacher Education ..... CertECTEd
Certificate in Education [*British*] (DBQ) ..... CertEd
Certificate in Education (ODBW) ..... Cert Ed
Certificate in Electrical Engineering ..... CertElecEng
Certificate in Electronic Data Processing Auditing (IAA) ..... CEDPA
Certificate in Electronics and Communication ..... CertElecComm
Certificate in English Language Teaching for Adults ..... CELTA
Certificate in Family Systems Studies ..... CertFSStud
Certificate in Fine Arts ..... CertFA
Certificate in Gerontology (PGP) ..... CG
Certificate in Health Services Management [*Academic degree*] (AIE) ..... CertHSM
Certificate in Higher Education ..... CertHEd
Certificate in History and Philosophy of Science ..... CertHisPhilSc
Certificate in Home Health Nursing (PGP) ..... CHHN
Certificate in Horticulture ..... CertHort
Certificate in Human Resources Management (DD) ..... CHRM
Certificate in Industrial Relations ..... CI Rel
Certificate in International Finance (PGP) ..... CIF
Certificate in Journalism ..... CertJourn
Certificate in Library Science (BARN) ..... Cls
Certificate in Library Science (SAUS) ..... CLS
Certificate in Lieu [*of*] CIL
Certificate in Management ..... CIM
Certificate in Management Accounting [*Institute of Man agement Accounting of the National Association of Accountants*] [*Designation awarded by*] ..... CMA
Certificate in Marketing Management ..... CertMarkMan
Certificate in Marriage and Family Therapy ..... CertMFTh
Certificate in Medical Humanities (PGP) ..... CMH
Certificate in Medical Parasitology (ADA) ..... CMP
Certificate in Ministerial Studies (PGP) ..... CMS
Certificate in Music Studies (PGP) ..... CMS
Certificate in Nonprofit Management (PGP) ..... CNM
Certificate in Pacific Administration ..... CertPacAdm
Certificate in Performance (PGP) ..... CP
Certificate in Planning Information (PGP) ..... CPI
Certificate in Professional Counseling (PGP) ..... CPC
Certificate in Professional Writing and Editing ..... CertProWriEd
Certificate in Psychotherapy ..... CertPsychTh
Certificate in Public Administration ..... CP Adm
Certificate in Public Health [*British*] ..... CPH
Certificate in Public Management (PGP) ..... CPM
Certificate in Public Relations ..... CertPR
Certificate in Public Service Studies (SAUS) ..... CPSS
Certificate in Publications and Communications (PGP) ..... CPC
Certificate in Residential Social Work [*British*] (DI) ..... CRSW
Certificate in Sales Engineering ..... CS En
Certificate in Social Service [*British*] (DBQ) ..... CSS
Certificate in Social Work (ADWA) ..... CSW
Certificate in Spiritual Direction (PGP) ..... CSD
Certificate in Statistics (SAUS) ..... CS
Certificate in Systems Analysis (IAA) ..... CSA
Certificate in Teaching ..... CertTeach
Certificate in Teaching English as a Second Language ..... CertTESL
Certificate in Teaching English to Speakers of Other Languages [*Australia*] ..... CertTesol
Certificate in Textiles ..... CertText

Certificate in the Residential Care of Children and Young People [*British*] (DI) ... CRCCYP
Certificate in the Teaching and Training of Subnormal Children (SAUS) ... CTTSC
Certificate in the Teaching of English as a Foreign Language to Adults ... CTEFLA
Certificate in the Teaching of Handicapped Children (ADA) ... CTHC
Certificate in Tourism ... CertTour
Certificate in Transport Administration ... CertTransAdm
Certificate in Tropical Community Medicine and Health [*British*] (DI) ... CTCM and H
Certificate in University Education ... CertUniEd
Certificate in Urban and Regional Planning (PGP) ... CURP
Certificate in Veterinary Practice Management (GVA) ... CVPM
Certificate Issuing System (ACRL) ... CIS
Certificate, Mental Health Association (CMD) ... CMHA
Certificate of Accrual on Treasury Securities [*Salomon Brothers*] [*Finance*] ... CATS
Certificate of Advanced Educational Specialization (PGP) ... CAES
Certificate of Advanced Graduate Study ... CAGS
Certificate of Advanced Librarianship (PGP) ... CAL
Certificate of Advanced Management Studies (PGP) ... CAMS
Certificate of Advanced Professional Studies (PGP) ... CAPS
Certificate of Advanced Studies (or Study) (SAUS) ... CAS
Certificate of Advanced Study in Public Administration (PGP) ... CASPA
Certificate of Airworthiness ... CA
Certificate of Airworthiness [*Aviation*] (PIAV) ... C of A
Certificate of Amortizing Revolving Debt (EBF) ... CARD
Certificate of Analysis ... C of A
Certificate of Assignment of Quarters [*Navy*] ... C/Q
Certificate of Authenticity (ADWA) ... COA
Certificate of Authority ... COA
Certificate of Bank Deposit ... CBD
Certificate of Beneficial Ownership ... CBO
Certificate of Clearance for Use (SAUS) ... CCU
Certificate of Clinical Competence ... CCC
Certificate of Clinical Competence in Audiology ... CCC-A
Certificate of Clinical Competence in Speech ... CCC-S
Certificate of Competency [*Small Business Administration*] ... COC
Certificate of Competency [*Education*] ... C of C
Certificate of Competent Authority [*Department of Energy*] ... COCA
Certificate of Compliance [*FCC*] (NTCM) ... COC
Certificate of Conformance [*DoD*] ... COC
Certificate of Consignment/Origin [*Shipping*] (DS) ... CC/O
Certificate of Coverage [*Insurance*] ... COC
Certificate of Damage [*Tea trade*] (ROG) ... C/D
Certificate of Delivery ... C/D
Certificate of Deposit [*Banking*] ... CD
Certificate of Deposit [*Banking*] ... CDS
Certificate of Deposit [*Banking*] ... COD
Certificate of Deposit [*Banking*] ... C of D
Certificate of Deposit Rate [*Banking*] ... CD RATE
Certificate of Designer of the Royal College of Art [*British*] (DBQ) ... CertDesRCA
Certificate of Destruction (AFM) ... CD
Certificate of Destruction [*Environmental science*] (COE) ... COD
Certificate of Disability for Discharge [*Military*] ... CDD
Certificate of Disposal (ADA) ... CD
Certificate of Disposal [*Environmental science*] (COE) ... COD
Certificate of Disposition of Classified Documents (AAG) ... CDCD
Certificate of Distribution ... CD
Certificate of Educational Achievement (SAUO) ... CEA
Certificate of Eligibility [*Navy*] ... COE
Certificate of Eligibles (COE) ... CERT
Certificate of Exemption ... C of E
Certificate of Experience [*Aviation*] (PIAV) ... C of E
Certificate of Extended Education [*British*] (DI) ... CEE
Certificate of Flight Readiness [*NASA*] (NASA) ... COFR
Certificate of Flight Worthiness [*NASA*] (KSC) ... COFW
Certificate of Gameness [*Purebred canine award*] ... CG
Certificate of General Education ... CGE
Certificate of Graduate Studies (PGP) ... CGS
Certificate of Health Education [*British*] (DI) ... CertHE
Certificate of Incorporation [*Business law*] ... COI
Certificate of Indebtedness [*Finance*] ... C/I
Certificate of Indebtedness [*Finance*] ... COI
Certificate of Individual Theological Studies (PGP) ... CITS
Certificate of Industrial Health ... CIH
Certificate of Insurance ... CI
Certificate of Insurance (HCT) ... COI
Certificate of Internal Auditing (TDOB) ... CIA
Certificate of Internal Auditing (EBF) ... cia
Certificate of Library and Information Science (PGP) ... CLIS
Certificate of Merit [*National Court Reporters Association*] ... CM
Certificate of Merit ... C of M
Certificate of Need ... C of N
Certificate of Need ... CON
Certificate of Neo-Natal Intensive Care Nursing ... CertNNICU
Certificate of Occupancy [*Business term*] (EMRF) ... CO
Certificate of Office Studies [*Academic degree*] (AIE) ... COS
Certificate of Origin [*Investment term*] (DFIT) ... CO
Certificate of Origin (ADWA) ... C/O
Certificate of Origin and Consignment [*Shipping*] (DS) ... C/OC
Certificate of Origin and Interest (SAUS) ... COI
Certificate of Participation ... COP
Certificate of Posting [*Post Office receipt*] [*British*] ... COP
Certificate of Pre-Vocational Education [*Academic degree*] (AIE) ... CPVE
Certificate of Prior Submission [*Navy*] ... CPS
Certificate of Professional and Vocational Education [*British*] ... CPVE
Certificate of Professional Competence [*British*] (DI) ... CPC
Certificate of Professional Studies (PGP) ... CPS
Certificate of Proficiency [*New Zealand*] (WDAA) ... COP
Certificate of Proficiency [*National Shorthand Reporters Association*] ... CP
Certificate of Proficiency in English [*Cambridge*] [*British*] (AIE) ... CPE
Certificate of Public Convenience (CGWS) ... CPC
Certificate of Public Convenience and Necessity ... CPC & N
Certificate of Qualification (KSC) ... COQ
Certificate of Reasonable Value [*Veterans Administration*] ... CRV
Certificate of Registration (ADA) ... C of R
Certificate of Retirement (MUGU) ... C/R
Certificate of Sanitary Science [*British*] ... CSS
Certificate of Secondary Education [*British*] ... CSE
Certificate of Security Clearance (NATG) ... CSC
Certificate of Service [*Military*] (MCD) ... CS
Certificate of Service (SAUS) ... C/S
Certificate of Sixth Year Studies [*Scotland*] (DBQ) ... CSYS
Certificate of Special Studies (PGP) ... CSS
Certificate of Successful Completion of an Examination (OTD) ... CSCE
Certificate of Tax Deposit [*British*] ... CTD
Certificate of the College of Family Physicians of Canada (DD) ... CCFP
Certificate of the Royal College of Physicians [*British*] ... CRCP
Certificate of the Royal College of Surgeons [*British*] ... CRCS
Certificate of the Royal College of Surgeons [*Canada*] (CPGU) ... CRCS(C)
Certificate of the Sanitary Inspectors Examination Joint Board (SAUS) ... CSIEJB
Certificate of Theological Studies (PGP) ... CTS
Certificate of Title ... CT
Certificate of Transport (WPI) ... COT
Certificate of Value (DS) ... C/V
Certificate of Value and Origin (DS) ... CVO
Certificate of Vocational Preparation (AIE) ... VOC
Certificate of War Necessity [*World War II*] ... CWN
Certificate Receipt Voucher (SAUS) ... CRV
Certificate Revocation List (ACRL) ... CRL
Certificate Signing Unit (ACRL) ... CSU
Certificate, Society of Clinical Chemists (CMD) ... CSCC
Certificate, Tropical Medicine & Hygiene (CMD) ... CTM&H
Certificate Trust Lists ... CTL
Certificated (ADWA) ... certif
Certificated (SAUS) ... Certif
Certificated Associate of the Institute of Bankers [*British*] (DI) ... CertAIB
Certificated Bailiffs Association [*British*] (DBA) ... CBA
Certificated Flight Instructor (SAUS) ... CFI
Certificated Master [*or Mistress*] [*British*] ... CM
Certificated Personnel Information Report (SAUO) ... CPIR
Certificates (SAUS) ... Certs
Certificates [*in bond listings of newspapers*] [*Investment term*] ... CF
Certificates (SG) ... Ctf
Certificates (EBF) ... Ctfs
Certificates for Amortizing Revolving Debts [*Finance*] (DFIT) ... CARDS
Certificates of Automobile Receivables [*Salomon Bros.*] ... CAR's
Certificates of Government Receipt (EBF) ... COUGR
Certificati del Tesoro in Euroscudi [*Italy*] (ECON) ... CTE
Certificati di Credito del Tesoro [*Italy*] (ECON) ... CCT
Certification (EBF) ... Cert
Certification (SAUS) ... CERT
Certification ... CTRFCTN
Certification Analysis Network (NASA) ... CAN
Certification Approval Request (NASA) ... CAR
Certification as Professional Contract Manager (RDA) ... CPCM
Certification Authority (ACRL) ... CA
Certification Authority for Reinforcing Steels (PDAA) ... CARES
Certification Board for Music Therapists (EA) ... CBMT
Certification Body (IAA) ... CB
Certification Committee [*American National Standards Institute*] (IEEE) ... CERTICO
Certification Control Number (MCD) ... CCN
Certification Data (AFIT) ... CD
Certification Division [*Environmental Protection Agency*] (GFGA) ... CD
Certification Evaluation Review ... CER
Certification Examination for Practical and Vocational Nurses (SAUO) ... CEPN
Certification Examination for Practical and Vocational Nurses in Long-Term Care (SAUO) ... CEPN-LTC
Certification for Emergency Nursing ... CEN
Certification for Issue (MCD) ... CFI
Certification Inspection (MCD) ... CI
Certification Management Committee (SAUO) ... CMC
Certification of Air Moving Equipment [*British*] (IRUK) ... CAME
Certification of Completion ... COC
Certification of Compliance (SAUS) ... COC
Certification of Computer Professionals (SAUS) ... CCP
Certification of Electrical Equipment for Mining Advisory Council (HEAS) ... CEEMAC
Certification of Equipment Completion (SAA) ... CEC
Certification of Equivalency [*Air Force*] ... COE
Certification of Flight Readiness [*NASA*] (SPST) ... CoFR
Certification of Fund Availability (EEVL) ... COFA
Certification of Nonavailability [*DoD*] ... C/NA
Certification of Proposal ... COP
Certification of Purchase ... CP
Certification Office [*Trade union regulation*] [*British*] ... CO
Certification Print Routine (SAUS) ... CPR

Certification Questionnaire-Minority/ Women Business Enterprise (SAUS) .... MBE/WBE
Certification Questionnaire-Minority/Women Business Enterprise (SAUO) .... MBE/WBE
Certification Reciprocity Consortium/Alcoholism and Other Drug Abuse [*Later, NCRC/AODA*] (EA) .... CRC/AODA
Certification Requirement (MCD) .... CR
Certification Short Test [*Exhaust emissions testing*] [*Automotive engineering*] .... CST
Certification Status Report (NASA) .... CSR
Certification Test Network [*NASA*] (KSC) .... CTN
Certification Test Requirement [*NASA*] .... CTR
Certification Test Specification [*NASA*] (KSC) .... CTS
Certification Test System (MCD) .... CERTS
Certification Unit .... CU
Certified (AAG) C
Certified .... CERT
Certified (EBF) .... Cert
Certified .... CERTD
Certified (ROG) .... CERTFD
Certified (ADWA) .... ctf
Certified Acupuncturist [*Medicine*] .... CA
Certified Addictions Registered Nurse (NUJO) .... CARN
Certified Administrative Manager [*Administrative Manag ement Society*] [*Designation awarded by*] .... CAM
Certified Administrator (CPGU) .... CAdm
Certified Advertising Agency Practitioner .... CAAP
Certified Aircraft Dispatch, Inc. [*ICAO designator*] (FAAC) .... XAD
Certified Alcoholic and Dependency Counselor (DHP) .... CADC
Certified Alcoholic Counselor (DHP) .... CAC
Certified Alcoholism Counselor .... CAC
Certified Alfalfa Seed Council (EA) .... CASC
Certified American Indian Lineage Specialist .... CAILS
Certified American Lineage Specialist .... CALS
Certified Arbitrator [*Canada*] (DD) .... CArb
Certified Assistant Export Manager [*American Society of International Executives*] [*Designation awarded by*] .... CAEM
Certified Associate Contracts Manager [*Exam*] (AAGC) .... CACM
Certified Associate of the Institute of Bankers [*Canada*] (DD) .... CAIB
Certified Association Executive [*American Society of A ssociation Executives*] [*Designation awarded by*] .... CAE
Certified Athletic Trainer (DAVI) .... ATC
Certified Automotive Repairmen Society (SAUO) .... CARS
Certified Automotive Repairmen's Society [*Defunct*] (EA) .... CARS
Certified Baliffs Association of England and Wales (SAUO) .... CBA
Certified Ballast Manufacturer (SAUS) .... CBM
Certified Ballast Manufacturers Association (EA) .... CBM
Certified Ballast Manufacturers Association .... CBMA
Certified Bank Examiner .... CBE
Certified Banyan Engineer (VERA) .... CBE
Certified Banyan Specialist (VERA) .... CBS
Certified Bath Designer [*Certification from the Societies of the National Kitchen & Bath Association*] .... CBD
Certified Biomedical Equipment Technician (RDA) .... CBET
Certified Breastfeeding Educator (NUJO) .... CBE
Certified Building Code Official [*Canada*] (AAGC) .... CBCO
Certified Building Society Executive [*Canada*] (DD) .... CBSE
Certified Business Appraiser [*Institute of Business Appraisers*] [*Designation awarded by*] .... CBA
Certified Business Solutions .... CBS
Certified by the Association for Healthcare Philanthropy (NFD) .... CAHP
Certified Cardiographic Technician (MELL) .... CCT
Certified Case Manager (NUJO) .... CCM
Certified Cash Manager [*National Corporate Cash Management Association*] [*Designation awarded by*] .... CCM
Certified Cell Line [*ATCC*] CCL
Certified Chamber Executive [*American Chamber of Comme rce Executives*] [*Designation awarded by*] .... CCE
Certified Check [*Banking*] CC
Certified Checkpoint Security Administrator (SAUS) .... CCSA
Certified Checkpoint Security Engineer (SAUS) .... CCSE
Certified Chemical Dependency Professional (DHP) .... CCDP
Certified Chemical Engineer .... CChE
Certified Claims Professional .... CCP
Certified Claims Professional Accreditation Council (EA) .... CCPAC
Certified Clinic Account Manager [*American Guild of Patient Account Manag ement*] [*Designation awarded by*] .... CCAM
Certified Clinical Mental Health Counselor (DHP) .... CCMHC
Certified Clinical Nutritionist [*Medicine*] .... CCN
Certified Club Manager [*Club Managers Association of America*] [*Designation awarded by*] .... CCM
Certified Cold Fur Storage Association (EA) .... CCFSA
Certified Collateral Corp. (IID) CCC
Certified Color Manufacturers Association (EA) .... CCMA
Certified Commercial Investment Member [*Realtors Natio nal Marketing Institute of the National Association of Realtors*] [*Designation awarded by*] .... CCIM
Certified Communication Counselor (SAUS) CCC
Certified Computer Professional (RALS) .... CCP
Certified Computer Programmer (ROAS) .... CCP
Certified Computing Professional (SAUS) .... CCP
Certified Configuration Manager .... CCM
Certified Configuration Specialist .... CCS
Certified Construction Specifier [*Construction Specifications Institute*] [*Automotive engineering*] .... CCS
Certified Consultants International [*Defunct*] (EA) CCI
Certified Consumer Credit Executive [*International Con sumer Credit Association*] [*Designation awarded by*] .... CCCE
Certified Corporate Travel Executive [*National Passenger Traffic Associat ion*] [*Designation awarded by*] .... CCTE
Certified Corrective Therapist .... CCT
Certified Cost Estimator/Analyst (AAGC) .... CCE/A
Certified Court Reporter .... CCR
Certified Credit Bureau Executive [*Society of Certified Consumer Credit E xecutives*] [*Designation awarded by*] .... CCBE
Certified Critical Care Registered Nurse (NUJO) .... CCRN
Certified Data Educator (HGAA) .... CDE
Certified Data Manager .... CDM
Certified Data Plan (SAUS) .... CDP
Certified Data Processing Auditor [*EDP Auditors Foundation*] [*Designation awarded by*] .... CDPA
Certified Data Processor (DD) .... CDP
Certified Data Specialist .... CDS
Certified Decal Manufacturers (EA) .... CDM
Certified Degree of Indian Blood (GEAB) .... CBID
Certified Dental Assistant .... CDA
Certified Dental Laboratory (SAUO) .... CDL
Certified Dental Technician .... CDT
Certified Deposit (ROAS) .... CD
Certified Developmental Disabilities Nurse (NUJO) .... CDDN
Certified Diabetes Educator (MEDA) .... CDE
Certified Diabetes Educator (SAUS) .... CDE
Certified Diploma in Accounting and Finance [*British*] (DBQ) .... CDipAF
Certified Direct Marketing Practitioner [*Direct Marketing Association Ins urance Council*] [*Designation awarded by*] .... CDMP
Certified Disability Management Specialist (NUJO) .... CDMS
Certified Document Imaging Architect (SAUS) .... CDIA
Certified Documentary Specialist [*Designation awarded by American Society of International Executives, Inc.*] .... CDS
Certified Drug and Alcohol Counselor (NUJO) .... CDAC
Certified Drug Counselor (MELL) .... CDC
Certified Electrical Technician (SAUS) .... CET
Certified Electronics Technician (SAUS) .... CET
Certified Emergency Nurse (SAUO) .... CEN
Certified Emission Reduction (SAUS) .... CER
Certified Employee Assistance Professional .... CEAP
Certified Employee Benefit Specialist [*Trademark of the International Foundation of Employee Benefit Plans, Inc.*] .... CEBS
Certified Engineering Geologist [*Environmental science*] .... CEG
Certified Engineering Operations Executive [*American Hotel and Motel Asso ciation*] [*Designation awarded by*] .... CEOE
Certified Engineering Technologist [*Environmental science*] .... CET
Certified Enterostomal Therapy Nurse (NUJO) .... CETN
Certified Environmental Auditor [*Environmental science*] .... CEA
Certified Environmental Professional [*Environmental science*] .... CEP
Certified Environmental Trainer .... CET
Certified Exchangor [*International Exchangors Association*] [*Designation awarded by*] .... CE
Certified Exchangors [*An association*] (EA) .... CE
Certified Exhibit Specialist (WDMC) .... CES
Certified Exposition Manager [*National Association of Exposition Managers , Inc.*] [*Designation awarded by*] .... CEM
Certified Family Life Educator .... CFLE
Certified Family Nurse Practitioner (SAUO) .... CFNP
Certified Fast Shipment (SAUS) .... CFS
Certified Financial Consultant [*Canada*] (DD) .... CHFC
Certified Financial Examiner [*Society of Financial Examiners*] [*Designation awarded by*] .... CFE
Certified Financial Planner [*College of Financial Planning*] [*Designation awarded by*] [*Business term*] .... CFP
Certified Financial Planner (SAUO) .... CFP
Certified First Responder (SAUS) .... CFR
Certified Fitness Appraiser [*Canadian Association of Sports Sciences*] .... CFA
Certified Flight Instructor [*Aviation*] .... CFI
Certified Flight Instructor IFR (SAUO) .... CFII
Certified Flight Instructor, Instrument [*Aviation*] .... CFII
Certified Flight Registered Nurses (SAUO) .... CFRN
Certified Food and Beverage Executive [*Educational Institute of the Ameri can Hotel and Motel Association*] [*Designation awarded by*] .... CFBE
Certified Fragrance Sales Specialist (ADWA) .... CFSS
Certified Fraud Examiner [*Canada*] (DD) .... CFE
Certified From [*or Certified To*] [*Legal term*] (DLA) .... cert
Certified Fund-Raising Executive .... CFRE
Certified Gastroenterological Registered Nurse (NUJO) .... CGRN
Certified Gastrointestinal Clinician (MEDA) .... CGC
Certified Genealogical Instructor .... CGI
Certified Genealogical Lecturer .... CGL
Certified Genealogical Record Searcher .... CGRS
Certified Genealogical Records Specialist (SAUS) .... CGRS
Certified Genealogist .... CG
Certified General Accountant .... CGA
Certified Graduate Remodeler [*National Association of Home Builders*] .... CGR
Certified Graphoanalyst .... CGA
Certified Guitar Player [*Monogram used by Chet Atkins*] .... CGP
Certified Hardware List (MCD) .... CHL
Certified Hazardous Materials Manager [*Environmental science*] .... CHMM
Certified Health Education Specialist (ADWA) .... CHES
Certified Health Education Specialists (SAUO) .... CHES
Certified Health Executive (CMD) .... CHE
Certified Health Physicist (SARE) .... CHP

Certified Health Professional (SARE) ... CHP
Certified Hemodialysis Nurse (MEDA) ... CHN
Certified Hemodialysis Technician (NUJO) ... CHT
Certified Herbalist ... CH
Certified Hospice and Palliative Care Nurse (NUJO) ... CHPN
Certified Hospital Administration Program (SAUS) ... CHAP
Certified Hospital Admission Program (DAVI) ... CHAP
Certified Hospitality Housekeeping Executive [*Educational Institute of th e American Hotel and Motel Association*] [*Designation awarded by*] ... CHHE
Certified Hospitals Administration Program (SAUO) ... CHAP
Certified Hotel Administrator [*Educational Institute of the American Hote l and Motel Association*] [*Designation awarded by*] ... CHA
Certified Human Resources Professional [*Canada*] (DD) ... CHRP
Certified Hypnotherapist [*Medicine*] ... CHt
Certified in Education for Public Relations [*Public Relations Society of America*] [*New York, NY*] (WDMC) ... CEPR
Certified Incentive Travel Executive [*Society of Incentive Travel Executi ves*] [*Designation awarded by*] ... CITE
Certified Industrial Hygienist ... CIH
Certified Industrial Manager ... CIM
Certified Infection Control (MEDA) ... CIC
Certified Information Systems Auditor [*EDP Auditors Foundation*] [*Designation awarded by*] ... CISA
Certified Inhalation Protection (SAUS) ... CIP
Certified Institution for the Mental Defective [*British*] ... CIMD
Certified Insurance Counselor [*Society of Certified Insurance Counselors*] [*Designation awarded by*] ... CIC
Certified Insurance Data Manager ... CIDM
Certified Insurance Rehabilitation Specialist (NUJO) ... CIRS
Certified Internal Auditor [*The Institute of Internal Auditors, Inc.*] [*Designation awarded by*] ... CIA
Certified International Executive [*American Society of International Exec utives*] [*Designation awarded by*] ... CIE
Certified International Executive - Air Forwarding [*Am erican Society of International Executives, Inc.*] [*Designation awarded by*] ... CIE-AF
Certified International Executive - Export Management [*American Society of International Executives, Inc.*] [*Designation awarded by*] ... CIE-EM
Certified International Executive - Forwarding [*Americ an Society of International Executives, Inc.*] [*Designation awarded by*] ... CIE-F
Certified International Executive - Traffic Management [*American Society of International Executives, Inc.*] [*Designation awarded by*] ... CIE-TM
Certified International Traffic Manager [*American Society of Internationa l Executives, Inc.*] [*Designation awarded by*] ... CITM
Certified Investment Management Consultant ... CIMC
Certified Investment Management Specialist ... CIMS
Certified Invoice (SAUS) ... Cert Inv
Certified Kitchen Designer ... CKD
Certified Kosher [*Food labeling*] (IIA) ... CK
Certified Kosher [*Food labeling*] ... K
Certified Lab Program [*Environmental science*] (COE) ... CLP
Certified Laboratory Assistant (WGA) ... CLA
Certified Laundry Manager ... CLM
Certified Legal Assistant ... CLA
Certified Legal Nurse Consultant (NUJO) ... CLNC
Certified Legal Video Specialist ... CLVS
Certified Lenders Program [*Small Business Administration*] ... CLP
Certified Licensed Evaluation Facility ... CLEF
Certified Life Care Planner (NUJO) ... CLCP
Certified Life Underwriter [*Insurance*] ... CLU
Certified Life Underwriters (SAUO) ... CLU
Certified Linux Engineer (SAUS) ... CLE
Certified Linux Expert (SAUS) ... CLE
Certified Linux Wizard (SAUS) ... CLW
Certified Literate Community Program ... CLCP
Certified Livestock Marketing Association [*Later, Livestock Marketing Association*] ... CLMA
Certified Logging Professional (WPI) ... CLP
Certified Lotus Engineer (VERA) ... CLE
Certified Management Accountant (DD) ... CMA
Certified Management Consultant [*Institute of Management Consultants, Inc .*] [*Designation awarded by*] ... CMC
Certified Manager of Reporting Services ... CMRS
Certified Manufacturing Engineer (DD) ... CMgE
Certified Market Technician (DD) ... CMT
Certified Marketing Director [*International Council of Shopping Centers*] [*Designation awarded by*] ... CMD
Certified Master [*British*] ... CM
Certified Master Locksmith ... CML
Certified Material Test Report [*Nuclear energy*] (NRCH) ... CMRT
Certified Medical Assistant ... CMA
Certified Medical Assistant-Administrative (WGA) ... CMA-A
Certified Medical Assistant-Administrative and Clinical (WGA) ... CMA-AC
Certified Medical Assistant-Clinical ... CMA-C
Certified Medical Electroencephalographic Technician (WGA) ... CMET
Certified Medical Practice Executive (ADWA) ... CMPE
Certified Medical Representative (MAE) ... CMR
Certified Medical Representatives Institute (SAUO) ... CMR
Certified Medical Representatives Institute (EA) ... CMRI
Certified Medical Transcriptionist ... CMT
Certified Meeting Professional (TRID) ... CMP
Certified Member, American Society of Traffic and Transportation [*America n Society of Transportation and Logistics*] [*Designation awarded by*] ... CM-ASTT
Certified Member of AHP [*Association of Healthcare Philanthropy*] ... CAHP
Certified Member of the Institute of Wood Science [*British*] (DBQ) ... CMIWSc
Certified Metrication Specialist (DICI) ... CMS
Certified Midwife ... CM
Certified Milk Producers Association of America (EA) ... CMPAA
Certified Mistress (SAUS) ... CM
Certified Mortgage Banker ... CMB
Certified Municipal Manager [*Canada*] (ASC) ... CMM
Certified Navy Twill (DNAB) ... CNT
Certified Nephrology Nurse (NUJO) ... CNN
Certified Net Ware Instructor [*Computer science*] ... CNI
Certified NetWare Administrator (SAUO) ... CNA
Certified NetWare Engineer [*Novell, Inc.*] [*Computer science*] (PCM) ... CNE
Certified Netware Engineers Professional Association (VERA) ... CNEPA
Certified Netware Expert (SAUS) ... CNE
Certified Network Administrator (SAUS) ... CNA
Certified Network Engineer (SAUS) ... CNE
Certified Network Expert (SAUS) ... CNX
Certified Neuroscience Registered Nurse (MEDA) ... CNRN
Certified Niche Specialist (TRID) ... CNS
Certified Normal Accommodation (WDAA) ... CNA
Certified Novell Administrator (SAUS) ... CNA
Certified Novell Engineer (SAUS) ... CNE
Certified Novell Instructor [*Computer science*] (IGQR) ... CNI
Certified Novell Salesperson (SAUS) ... CNS
Certified Nuclear Medicine Technologist (MAE) ... CNMT
Certified Nurse Midwife [*Medicine*] ... CNM
Certified Nurse, Operating Room (MEDA) ... CNOR
Certified Nurse Practitioner (SAUO) ... CNP
Certified Nursery Nurse (SAUO) ... CNN
Certified Nurse's Aide ... CNA
Certified Nurses Assistant (SAUS) ... CNA
Certified Nursing Assistant (SAUO) ... CNA
Certified Nutrition Support Dietitian (NUJO) ... CNSD
Certified Nutrition Support Nurse (MEDA) ... CNSN
Certified Nutritionist [*Medicine*] ... CN
Certified Occupational Health Nurse (NUJO) ... COHN
Certified Occupational Health Nurse Specialist (NUJO) ... COHN-S
Certified Occupational Therapy Assistant ... COTA
Certified Office Administrator ... COA
Certified Official Government Business ... COGB
Certified Operating Room Technician ... CORT
Certified Ophthalmic Assistant (NUJO) ... COA
Certified Ophthalmic Medical Assistant (DAVI) ... COMT
Certified Ophthalmic Medical Technologist (NUJO) ... COMT
Certified Ophthalmic Technician (NUJO) ... COT
Certified Orthotist ... CO
Certified Pain Practitioner (NUJO) ... CPP
Certified Park Operators Program (EA) ... CPOP
Certified Parts List (SAUS) ... CPL
Certified Patient [*British*] ... CP
Certified Patient Account Manager [*American Guild of Patient Account Mana gement*] [*Designation awarded by*] ... CPAM
Certified Pediatric Nurse (SAUO) ... CPN
Certified Pediatric Nurse Practitioner (SAUO) ... CPNP
Certified Pediatric Nurse Practitioner/Associate (MEDA) ... CPNP/A
Certified Pediatric Oncology Nurse (NUJO) ... CPON
Certified Pediatric Worker (BARN) ... CPW
Certified Pedorthist ... CPed
Certified Personnel Consultant [*Designation awarded by National Association of Personnel Consultants*] ... CPC
Certified Personnel Information (SAUO) ... CPI
Certified Post-Anesthesia Nurse (MEDA) ... CPAN
Certified Products List (SAUS) ... CPL
Certified Professional Bureau Executive [*Medical-Dental-Hospital Bureaus of America*] [*Designation awarded by*] ... CPBE
Certified Professional Chemist ... CPC
Certified Professional Contracts Manager [*Exam*] (AAGC) ... CPCM
Certified Professional Ergonomist (SAUS) ... CPE
Certified Professional Geologist ... CPG
Certified Professional in Disability Management [*Insurance*] ... CPDM
Certified Professional in Healthcare Quality (NUJO) ... CPHQ
Certified Professional in Quality Assurance (HCT) ... CPQA
Certified Professional Insurance Agents Society (NTPA) ... CPIA
Certified Professional Insurance Woman [*National Association of Insurance Women*] [*Designation awarded by*] ... CPIW
Certified Professional Insurance Women's Association [*Canada*] (DD) ... CPIW
Certified Professional Logistician (MCD) ... CPL
Certified Professional Purchaser [*Canada*] (DD) ... CPP
Certified Professional Secretary [*Institute for Certifying Secretaries*] [*Designation awarded by*] ... CPS
Certified Professional Soil Scientist [*Environmental science*] ... CPSS
Certified Program Generator (IAA) ... CPG
Certified Project Manager [*Environmental science*] (COE) ... CPM
Certified Project Officer [*Environmental Protection Agency*] (GFGA) ... CPO
Certified Property Exchanger (SAUS) ... CPE
Certified Property Manager [*Institute of Real Estate Management*] [*Designation awarded by*] ... CPM
Certified Prosthetist ... CP
Certified Prosthetist and Orthotist ... CPO
Certified Protection Professional [*American Society for Industrial Securi ty*] [*Designation awarded by*] ... CPP
Certified Psychologist [*Canada*] (DD) ... CPsych
Certified Public Accountant ... CPA
Certified Public Accountant/Personal Financial Specialist ... CPA/PFS
Certified Public Purchasing Officer [*Canadian*] ... CPPO
Certified Public Secretary ... CPS
Certified Public Weigher (SAUS) ... CPW

Certified Pulmonary Function Technician (NUJO) .... CPFT
Certified Purchasing Manager [*National Association of Purchasing Manageme nt, Inc.*] [*Designation awarded by*] .... CPM
Certified Radio Marketing Consultant (NTCM) .... CRMC
Certified Radiologic Technician (SAUS) .... CRT
Certified Raw Milk (MEDA) .... CRM
Certified Real Estate Appraiser [*National Association of Real Estate Appr aisers*] [*Designation awarded by*] ...... CREA
Certified Real Estate Brokerage Manager .... CRB
Certified Real Estate Securities Member [*Real Estate Securities and Syndi cation Institute of the National Association of Realtors*] [*Designation awarded by*] .... CRSM
Certified Real Estate Securities Sponsor [*Real Estate Securities and Synd ication Institute of the National Association of Realtors*] [*Designation awarded by*] .... CRSS
Certified Realtime Reporter .... CRR
Certified Record Librarian .... CRL
Certified Records Manager [*Institute of Certified Records Managers*] [*Designation awarded by*] (MCD) ...... CRM
Certified Reference Librarian (BARN) .... CRL
Certified Reference Materials .... CRM
Certified Registered Nurse Anesthetist .... CRNA
Certified Registered Nurse First Assistant (NUJO) .... CRNFA
Certified Registered Nurse Hospice (NUJO) .... CRNH
Certified Registered Nurse in Ophthalmology (NUJO) ... CRNO
Certified Registered Nurse of Infusion .... CRNI
Certified Registered Nurse Practicner (DAVI) .... CRNP
Certified Registered Nurse Practitioner (SAUO) .... CRNP
Certified Rehabilitation Counselor .... CRC
Certified Rehabilitation Registered Nurse .... CRRN
Certified Reliability Data Sheet (SAUS) .... CRDS
Certified Reliability Data Shell [*Computer science*] (PDAA) .... CRDS
Certified Remodeller .... CR
Certified Reporting Instructor .... CRI
Certified Reporting Limit (ABAC) .... CRL
Certified Rescue Technician (SAUO) .... CRT
Certified Residential Broker [*Realtors National Marketing Institute of th e National Association of Realtors*] [*Designation awarded by*] .... CRB
Certified Residential Specialist [*Realtors National Marketing Institute o f the National Association of Realtors*] [*Designation awarded by*] ... CRS
Certified Residential Specialist (SAUS) .... CRS
Certified Respiratory Therapy Technician (DAVI) ...... CRRT
Certified Respiratory Therapy Technician .... CRTT
Certified Retinal Angiographer .... CRA
Certified Review Appraiser [*Finance*] (EMRF) .... CRA
Certified Rooms Division Executive [*Educational Institute of the American Hotel and Motel Association*] [*Designation awarded by*] .... CRDE
Certified Round Assembly Facility [*Military*] .... CRAF
Certified Safety Professional [*Designation awarded by Board of Certified Safety Professionals*] .... CSP
Certified School Nurse (MEDA) .... CSN
Certified Security and Safety Professional [*Environmental science*] ... CSSP
Certified Sex Counselor (DHP) .... CSC
Certified Sex Therapist (DHP) .... CST
Certified Shopping Center Manager [*International Council of Shopping Cent ers*] [*Designation awarded by*] .... CSM
Certified Shorthand Reporter .... CSR
Certified Social Worker .... CSW
Certified Speaking Professional .... CSP
Certified Specialist in Poison Information .... CSPI
Certified Surgical Assistant (NUJO) .... CSA
Certified Surgical Technician (STED) .... CST
Certified Surgical Technologist (HCT) .... CST
Certified Survey Technician (SAUO) .... CST
Certified Systems Engineer (CDE) .... CSE
Certified Systems Professional (CDE) .... CSP
Certified Tax Specialist (PGP) .... CTS
Certified Teacher (SAUS) .... CT
Certified Technician (ASC) .... CTech
Certified Test Data .... CTD
Certified Test Record (IAA) .... CTR
Certified Test Results (NRCH) .... CTR
Certified Tool List (AAG) .... CTL
Certified Traffic Manager .... CTM
Certified Transactional Analysist (SAUO) .... CTA
Certified Transplant Nurse (NUJO) .... CTN
Certified Travel Counselor [*Institute of Certified Tra vel Agents*] [*Designation awarded by*] .... CTC
Certified Tumor Registrar [*Medicine*] (BARN) .... CTR
Certified Urological Registered Nurse (MEDA) .... CURN
Certified Value Specialist (SAUO) .... CVS
Certified Vendor Information (NRCH) CVI
Certified Wound Care Nurse (NUJO) .... CWCN
Certifiled Parts List (SAUS) .... CPL
Certify (DLA) .... cert
Certify (FAAC) .... CRTFY
Certiorari [*Legal term*] (DLA) .... CERT
Certiorari [*To be certified*] [*A writ from a superior to an inferior court*] [*Latin*] (AAGC) ...... cert
Certiorari Denied [*Legal term*] (DLA) .... cert den
Certiorari Denied by United States Supreme Court [*Legal term*] (DLA) ...... US Cert Den
Certiorari Dismissed [*Legal term*] (DLA) .... cert dis
Certiorari Dismissed by United States Supreme Court [*Legal term*] (DLA) ...... US Cert Dis

Certiorari Granted [*Legal term*] (DLA) .... CERT GR
Certron Corp. [*Associated Press*] (SAG) .... Certron
Certron Corp. [*NASDAQ symbol*] (NQ) .... CRTN
Cerulein [*Biochemistry*] .... CRL
Cerulein and Secretin (Test) [*Clinical chemistry*] .. CS
Ceruloplasmin [*Biochemistry*] (DAVI) .... CERULO
Ceruloplasmin [*Biochemistry*] .... Cp
Cerussite (SAUS) .... ce
Cervia [*Italy*] [*ICAO location identifier*] (ICLI) . LIPC
Cervical [*Medicine*] C
Cervical (SAUS) .... Cerv
Cervical and Thoracic Vertebrae [*Medicine*] (DMAA) .. CTV
Cervical Biopsy [*Medicine*] (MELL) .... CxBx
Cervical Collar [*Medicine*] CC
Cervical Collar (MELL) .... CS
Cervical Compression Overloading Test [*Medicine*] (DMAA) ... CCOT
Cervical Connective [*Neuroanatomy*] CC
Cervical Degenerative Disk Disease [*Medicine*] (MELL) ... CDDD
Cervical dilation (SAUS) .... Cervical dil
Cervical Disk Disease [*Medicine*] (MELL) .... CDD
Cervical Disk Syndrome [*Medicine*] (MELL) .... CDS
Cervical Dysplasia [*Medicine*] (MELL) .... CD
Cervical Internal Cartoid Artery [*Medicine*] (DMAA) . CICA
Cervical Intraepithelial Neoplasia [*Medicine*] (MELL) ... CIEN
Cervical Intraepithelial Neoplasia [*Medicine*] ...... CIN
Cervical Intraepithelial Neoplasia [*Mild*] [*Medicine*] (MELL) ... CIN I
Cervical Intraepithelial Neoplasia [*Moderate*] [*Medicine*] (MELL) ... CIN II
Cervical Laminectomy [*Neurology and orthopedics*] (DAVI) ... C LAM
Cervical Lymph Node [*Anatomy*] .... CLN
Cervical Mediastinal Exploration (AAMN) .... CME
Cervical Motion Tenderness [*Medicine*] (DAVI) .... CMT
Cervical Motion Tenderness [*Gynecology*] (DAVI) ..... CxMT
Cervical Mucous Basal Body Temperature [*Gynecology and obstetrics*] (DAVI) .... CMBBT
Cervical Mucous Solution [*Gynecology*] (DAVI) .... CMS
Cervical Mucus [*Obstetrics*] (DAVI) .... CM
Cervical Mucus Penetration [*Medicine*] (STED) .... CMP
Cervical Orthosis [*Medicine*] .... CO
Cervical Pain Syndrome [*Medicine*] (MELL) .... CPS
Cervical Plexus [*Medicine*] (MELL) .... CP
Cervical Prevertebral Soft Tissue Measurement [*Medicine*] (DMAA) ... CSTM
Cervical Range of Motion [*Medicine*] (DMAA) .... CROM
Cervical Rib Syndrome [*Medicine*] (MELL) .... CRS
Cervical Smear (MELL) .... CS
Cervical Spine [*Neurology and orthopedics*] (DAVI) .. CS
Cervical Spine (SAUS) .... CSP
Cervical Spine (ADWA) .... C-spine
Cervical Spine Hyperextension-Flexion Injury [*Medicine*] (MELL) ... CSHFI
Cervical Spine Injury [*Medicine*] (MELL) .... CSI
Cervical Spine Research Society (SAUO) .... CSRS
Cervical Sponge (MELL) .... CS
Cervical Stimulation [*Neurology and orthopedics*] (DAVI) ... CS
Cervical, Thoracic, and Lumbar [*Medicine*] (STED) ... CTL
Cervical Traction [*Neurology, orthopedics, and physical therapy*] (DAVI) ... CT
Cervical Traction [*Medicine*] (MELL) .... CxTx
Cervical Vertebra [*Medicine*] CV
Cervical-Thoracic (SAUS) .... CT
Cervico [*Vertical*] [*Medicine*] (ROG) CV
Cervicoaxial [*Dentistry*] .... CA
Cervicoaxial [*Dentistry*] (DAVI) .... CO
Cervicobrachial Syndrome [*Medicine*] (MELL) .... CBS
Cervico-Dorsal Syndrome (SAUS) .... CDS
Cervicofacial Actinomycosis [*Medicine*] (MELL) ...... CFA
Cervicolinguoaxial [*Dentistry*] .... CLA
Cervico-Oculo-Acoustic Syndrome [*Medicine*] (MELL) .. COAS
Cervicothoracic Orthosis [*Also, CTO*] [*Medicine*] .. CER
Cervicothoracic Orthosis [*Also, CER*] [*Medicine*] .. CTO
Cervicothoracolumbar Orthosis [*Medicine*] .... CTLO
Cervicothoracolumbosacral Orthosis [*Medicine*] ...... CTLSO
Cervicovaginal Antibody [*Medicine*] (STED) .... CVA
Cervicovaginal Fistula [*Medicine*] (MELL) .... CVF
Cervicovaginal Fluid [*Medicine*] (MELL) .... CVF
Cervicovaginal Hood [*Medicine*] (DMAA) .... CVH
Cervix [*Anatomy*] .... CERV
Cervix [*Gynecology*] (DMAA) .... cerv
Cervix (ADWA) cx
Cervix (DMAA) Cx
Cervix [*Anatomy*] CX
Cervoaxial (SAUS) .... CA
Cervus [*Deer*] (ROG) C
[*The*] Cesarean Connection (EA) .... TCC
Cesarean Prevention Movement (EA) .... CPM
Cesarean Section (ADWA) .... cs
Cesarean Section [*Obstetrics*] (STED) .... CS
Cesarean Section (ADWA) .... C-section
Cesarean-Obtained Barrier-Sustained [*Germ-free animals*] (DB) ... COBS
Cesareans/Support, Education, and Concern [*An association*] (EA) ... C/SEC
Cesium [*Chemical element*] .... Cs
Cesium Atomic Beam Tube (IAA) .... CABT
Cesium Beam Frequency Standard (SAUS) .... CBFS
Cesium Beam Time Standard .... CBTS
Cesium Beam Tube .... CBT
Cesium Bombardment Engine .... CBE
Cesium Chloride .... CsCl
Cesium Chloride Polymerizable [*Analytical chemistry*] ... CCP

Cesium Contact Engine	CCE
Cesium Contact Thruster	CCT
Cesium Demonstration Unit *(ABAC)*	CDU
Cesium Dihydrogen Arsenate	CDA
Cesium Feed System	CFS
Cesium Implant [*Oncology and radiation therapy*] *(DAVI)*	CI
Cesium Iodide	CSI
Cesium Ion Emission	CIE
Cesium Ion Propulsion System	CIPS
Cesium Ion Source	CIS
Cesium Lodide *(SAUS)*	CsL
Cesium Loside *(SAUS)*	Csl
Cesium Time Standard	CTS
Cesium Trifluoroacetate [*Reagent*]	CsTFA
Cesium Vapor Cathode	CVC
Cesium Vapor Feed System	CVFS
Cesium-137	Cs-137
Ceskoslovenska Bioklimaticka Spolecnost [*Czechoslovak Bioklimatological Society*] [*Multinational association*] *(EAIO)*	CSBkS
Ceskoslovenska Socialnedemokraticka Strana Delnicka [*Czechoslovak Social Democratic Workers' Party*] *(PPE)*	CSSD
Ceskoslovenska Socialni Demokracie v Exilu [*Czechoslovak Social Democratic Party*] *(EAIO)*	CSDE
Ceskoslovenska Strana Lidova [*Czechoslovak People's Party*] *(PPE)*	CSL
Ceskoslovenska Strana Socialisticka [*Czechoslovak Socialist Party*] *(PPE)*	CSS
Ceskoslovenska Tiskova Kancelar [*Czechoslovak News Agency*]	CTK
Ceskoslovenske Aerolinie [*Czechoslovakia*] [*ICAO designator*] *(FAAC)*	CSA
Cessford Community Library, Alberta [*Library symbol*] [*National Library of Canada*] *(NLC)*	ACC
Cessford Community Library, Cessford, AB, Canada [*Library symbol*] [*Library of Congress*] *(LCLS)*	CaACeC
Cessna [*Airplane code*]	Cna
Cessna Aircraft Co. [*ICAO aircraft manufacturer identifier*] *(ICAO)*	C
Cessna Aircraft Co.	CAC
Cessna Aircraft Company *(SAUO)*	CEA
Cessna Airmaster Club *(EA)*	CAC
Cessna Owners Organization *(EA)*	COO
Cessna Pilots Association *(EA)*	CPA
Cessnock [*Australia*] [*Airport symbol*] *(OAG)*	CES
Cesspits *(ROG)*	CP
Cesspool *(AAG)*	CP
Cesspool Detergent Chemistry *(SAUS)*	CDC
C'Est-a-Dire [*That Is to Say*] [*French*]	C-A-D
Cestan-Chenais [*Syndrome*] [*Medicine*] *(DB)*	CC
Cestodes *(MELL)*	C
Cestriensis [*Signature of the Bishops of Chester*] *(ROG)*	CESTR
Cestriensis [*Signature of the Bishops of Chester*] *(ROG)*	CESTRIEN
CET Environmental Services [*Associated Press*] *(SAG)*	CET EnvS
CET Environmental Services [*Associated Press*] *(SAG)*	CET ES
CET Environmental Services [*AMEX symbol*] *(SAG)*	ENV
Cetacean and Turtle Assessment Program [*University of Rhode Island*] [*Research center*] *(RCD)*	CETAP
Cetacean Society International *(EA)*	CSI
Cetane [*Organic chemistry*]	Cet
Cetane Index [*Fuel technology*]	CI
Cetane Number [*Fuel technology*]	CN
Cetec Engineering Co., Inc. [*Vancouver Stock Exchange symbol*]	CEK
Cetedoc Index of Latin Forms *(SAUS)*	CILF
Cetera [*Remainder*] [*Latin*] *(EES)*	cet
Ceteris Paribus [*Other Things Being Equal*] [*Latin*]	CET PAR
Cetfa SA [*Spain*] [*ICAO designator*] *(FAAC)*	CTF
cetologist *(SAUS)*	cetol
cetology *(SAUS)*	cetol
Cetra [*Record label*] [*Italy*]	Cet
Cetrimonium Bromide [*Organic chemistry*] *(DAVI)*	CTBA
Cetty Taxi Aereo Nacional, SA de CV [*Mexico*] [*FAA designator*] *(FAAC)*	CCT
Cetus [*Whale constellation*] [*Latin*] *(BARN)*	Cet
Cetyl Pyridinium Bromide *(SAUS)*	CPB
Cetyl Pyridinium Chloride *(SAUS)*	CPC
Cetyl Trimethyl Ammonium Bromide *(SAUS)*	CTAB
Cetyl Trimethylammonium Tosylate [*Organic chemistry*]	CTAT
Cetyldimethylbenzylammonium Chloride [*A surfactant*]	CDAC
Cetyl(dimethyl)ethylammonium Bromide [*A surfactant*]	CDEA
Cetylpyridinium Bromide [*Medicine*] *(DMAA)*	CPB
Cetylpyridinium Chloride [*Organic chemistry*]	CPC
Cetyltrimethylammonium [*Organic chemistry*]	CTA
Cetyltrimethylammonium Bromide [*Also, CTAB, CTBM*] [*Antiseptic*]	CETAB
Cetyltrimethylammonium Bromide [*Also, CETAB, CTBM*] [*Antiseptic*]	CTAB
Cetyltrimethylammonium Bromide [*Also, CETAB, CTAB*] [*Antiseptic*] *(AAMN)*	CTBM
Cetyltrimethylammonium Chloride [*Organic chemistry*]	CTACl
Cetyltrimethylammonium Cyanide [*Organic chemistry*]	CTACN
Cetyltrimethylammonium Toluenesulfonate [*Organic chemistry*]	CETATS
Ceuta Unida [*Political party*] *(EY)*	CEU
Cevacin *(SAUS)*	CC
CevionTechnologies [*NASDAQ symbol*] *(TTSB)*	CEON
Ceylon [*Sri Lanka*] [*MARC geographic area code*] [*Library of Congress*] *(LCCP)*	a-ce-
Ceylon [*Sri Lanka*] [*MARC country of publication code*] [*Library of Congress*] *(LCCP)*	ce
Ceylon	Cey
Ceylon *(SAUO)*	Cey
Ceylon *(VRA)*	Ceyl
Ceylon [*Sri Lanka*]	CL
Ceylon [*Sri Lanka*] *(ROG)*	CY
Ceylon Air Force *(SAUS)*	CAF
Ceylon Air Force *(SAUO)*	CAF
Ceylon and Mauritius Royal Garrison Artillery [*British military*] *(DMA)*	CMRGA
Ceylon Army Service Corps [*British military*] *(DMA)*	CASC
Ceylon Broadcasting Corporation *(SAUO)*	CBC
Ceylon Broadcasting Corporation *(SAUO)*	CeBC
Ceylon Civil Service *(SAUO)*	CCS
Ceylon Civil Service [*Obsolete*]	CCS
Ceylon Corps of Military Police [*British military*] *(DMA)*	CCMP
Ceylon Criminal Appeal Reports [*A publication*] *(DLA)*	Ceyl Cr App R
Ceylon Defence Force *(SAUO)*	CDefF
Ceylon Federation of Labor [*Obsolete*]	CFL
Ceylon Fisheries Corporation *(SAUO)*	CFC
Ceylon Forester *(SAUS)*	Ceylon For
Ceylon Government Railways *(SAUO)*	CGR
Ceylon Institute of Scientific and Industrial Research *(SAUO)*	CISIR
Ceylon Labor Union [*Obsolete*]	CLU
Ceylon Labour Law Journal [*A publication*] *(DLA)*	Cey Lab LJ
Ceylon Law Journal [*A publication*] *(DLA)*	Ceyl LJ
Ceylon Law Journal [*A publication*] *(DLA)*	CLJ
Ceylon Law Recorder [*A publication*] *(DLA)*	Ceyl LR
Ceylon Law Recorder [*A publication*] *(DLA)*	Ceyl L Rec
Ceylon Law Recorder [*A publication*] *(DLA)*	Ceylon Law Rec
Ceylon Law Recorder [*A publication*] *(DLA)*	Law Rec
Ceylon Law Recorder *(SAUS)*	Rec
Ceylon Law Recorder (journ.) *(SAUS)*	Law Rec
Ceylon Law Reports [*A publication*] *(DLA)*	CLR
Ceylon Law Review [*A publication*] *(DLA)*	Ceyl L Rev
Ceylon Law Review and Reports [*A publication*] *(DLA)*	Ceylon LR
Ceylon Law Society. Journal [*A publication*] *(DLA)*	Ceylon L Soc J
Ceylon Law Weekly [*A publication*] *(DLA)*	Ceyl LW
Ceylon Law Weekly [*A publication*] *(ILCA)*	CLW
Ceylon Legal Miscellany [*A publication*] *(DLA)*	Ceyl Leg Misc
Ceylon Lines [*Steamship*] *(MHDW)*	CL
Ceylon Mercantile Union [*Obsolete*]	CMU
Ceylon Military Force *(SAUO)*	CMF
Ceylon National Library Services Board *(SAUO)*	CNLSB
Ceylon National Trade Union Confederation *(SAUO)*	CNTUC
Ceylon Plantation Workers' Union [*Obsolete*]	CPWU
Ceylon Railway Clerical Service Union [*Obsolete*]	CRCSU
Ceylon Rubber Research Staff *(SAUO)*	CRRS
Ceylon Society for Quality Control *(SAUO)*	CSQC
Ceylon Tamil Association [*Victoria*] [*Australia*]	CTA
Ceylon Tourist Board *(EAIO)*	CTB
Ceylon Trade Union Federation [*Sri Lanka*] *(FEA)*	CTUF
Ceylon Weekly Reporter [*A publication*] *(ILCA)*	CWR
Ceylon Workers Congress *(SAUO)*	CWC
Ceylonese Importers and Exporters Association *(SAUO)*	CIEA
Ceylonese Welfare Organisation [*Australia*]	CWO
CF Bancorp [*NASDAQ symbol*] *(SAG)*	CFBC
CF Bancorp [*Associated Press*] *(SAG)*	CF Bcp
CFA Franc *(SAUS)*	XOF
CF&I Steel Corp. *(SAUO)*	CF
CFB Bancorp [*NASDAQ symbol*] *(TTSB)*	CFBN
CFB Bancorp, Inc. [*Associated Press*] *(SAG)*	CFB Bcp
CFB Bancorp, Inc. [*NASDAQ symbol*] *(SAG)*	CFBN
CFC Financial Communications [*An association*] *(EA)*	CFC
CFC International, Inc. [*NASDAQ symbol*] *(SAG)*	CFCI
CFC International, Inc. [*Associated Press*] *(SAG)*	CFCIntl
CFC Intl. [*NASDAQ symbol*] *(TTSB)*	CFCI
CFCF, Inc. [*Toronto Stock Exchange symbol*]	CF
CFI Industries [*NASDAQ symbol*] *(NQ)*	CFIB
CFI Industries [*Associated Press*] *(SAG)*	CFI Ind
CFI ProServices [*NASDAQ symbol*] *(TTSB)*	PROI
CFI Proservices, Inc. [*Associated Press*] *(SAG)*	CFI Pro
CFI Proservices, Inc. [*NASDAQ symbol*] *(SAG)*	PROI
CFM Technologies, Inc. [*Associated Press*] *(SAG)*	CFM T
CFM Technologies, Inc. [*NASDAQ symbol*] *(SAG)*	CFMT
CFP Franc *(SAUS)*	XPF
CFS Bancorp [*NASDAQ symbol*] *(SG)*	CITZ
CFS Group, Inc. [*Toronto Stock Exchange symbol*]	CFZ
CFSB Bancorp [*NASDAQ symbol*] *(TTSB)*	CFSB
CFSB Bancorp, Inc. [*NASDAQ symbol*] *(SAG)*	CFSB
CFU [*Croatian Fraternal Union of America*] **Junior Cultural Federation** *(EA)*	CFUJCF
CFW Communications [*NASDAQ symbol*] *(TTSB)*	CFWC
CFW Communications Co. [*NASDAQ symbol*] *(SAG)*	CFWC
CFW Communications Co. [*Associated Press*] *(SAG)*	CFW Cm
CFX Corp. [*Formerly, Chesire Financial*] [*AMEX symbol*] *(SAG)*	CFX
CFX Corp. [*Formerly, Cheshire Financial*] [*Associated Press*] *(SAG)*	CFX Cp
CGA - Canada Research Foundation *(AC)*	CGARF
CGBAPS Computing System *(SAUO)*	GRIMCO
CGC, Inc. [*Toronto Stock Exchange symbol*]	GYP
CGD Advisory Panel *(SAUS)*	CAP
CGD Computing Advisory Board *(SAUS)*	CCAB
CGI Group [*NYSE symbol*] *(SG)*	GIB
CH Academic DecNet *(SAUS)*	CHADNET
CH Financial Co. [*Vancouver Stock Exchange symbol*]	CFQ
C.H. Reinhard School, Bellmore, NY [*Library symbol*] [*Library of Congress*] *(LCLS)*	NBellmR
C.H. Robinson Worldwide [*NASDAQ symbol*] *(SG)*	CHRW
CH2M Hill Library, Boise, ID [*Library symbol*] [*Library of Congress*] *(LCLS)*	IdBCH
Ch3 Albedo Test *(SAUS)*	C3AT
Chabazite [*A zeolite*]	CHA

Chablis Resources Ltd. [*Vancouver Stock Exchange symbol*] ... CHK
Chabot College, Hayward, CA [*Library symbol*] [*Library of Congress*] (LCLS) ... CHC
Chabot Observatory, Oakland, CA [*Library symbol*] [*Library of Congress*] (LCLS) ... COCh
Chabua [*India*] [*Airport symbol*] (AD) ... CHU
Chacarita [*Argentina*] [*Seismograph station code, US Geological Survey*] [*Closed*] (SEIS) ... CCR
Chacarita [*Costa Rica*] [*ICAO location identifier*] (ICLI) ... MRCH
Chachapoyas [*Peru*] [*ICAO location identifier*] (ICLI) ... SPPY
Chachoengsao/Phanom Sarakhan [*Thailand*] [*ICAO location identifier*] (ICLI) ... VTBF
Chachro [*Pakistan*] [*ICAO location identifier*] (ICLI) ... OPCR
Chaco Canyon National Monument ... CHCA
Chaco Cave National Monument (SAUS) ... CCNM
Chad [*MARC country of publication code*] [*Library of Congress*] (LCCP) ... cd
Chad (MILB) ... Cha
Chad [*MARC geographic area code*] [*Library of Congress*] (LCCP) ... f-cd-
Chad [*ANSI three-letter standard code*] (CNC) ... TCD
Chad [*ANSI two-letter standard code*] (CNC) ... TD
Chad [*International civil aircraft marking*] (ODBW) ... TT
Chad Therapeutics [*AMEX symbol*] (TTSB) ... CTU
Chad Therapeutics, Inc. [*Associated Press*] (SAG) ... ChadThr
Chad Therapeutics, Inc. [*AMEX symbol*] (SAG) ... CTU
Chadashoth Archeologioth [*Israel*] [*A publication*] (BJA) ... ChadArch
Chadbourn, Inc. (SAUO) ... CGI
Chadbourn, NC [*AM radio station call letters*] ... WVOE
Chadbourne & Parke, New York, NY [*Library symbol*] [*Library of Congress*] (LCLS) ... NNCh
Chaddock's Toe Sign [*Medicine*] (MELL) ... CTS
Chadron [*Nebraska*] [*Airport symbol*] (OAG) ... CDR
Chadron, NE [*Location identifier*] [*FAA*] (FAAL) ... HIN
Chadron, NE [*FM radio station call letters*] (RBYB) ... KALG
Chadron, NE [*FM radio station call letters*] ... KCNE
Chadron, NE [*AM radio station call letters*] ... KCSR
Chadron, NE [*FM radio station call letters*] ... KQSK
Chadron Public Library, Chadron, NE [*Library symbol*] [*Library of Congress*] (LCLS) ... NbCh
Chadron State College (GAGS) ... Chadron St C
Chadron State College, Chadron, NE [*Library symbol*] [*Library of Congress*] (LCLS) ... NbChS
Chadron State College, Chadron, NE [*OCLC symbol*] (OCLC) ... NCC
Chadwell, Kayser, Ruggles, McGee & Hasting, Chicago, IL [*Library symbol*] [*Library of Congress*] (LCLS) ... ICCK
Chadwell, Kayser, Ruggles, McGee & Hastings, Chicago, IL [*OCLC symbol*] (OCLC) ... ILQ
Chadwick Trust (SAUO) ... CT
Chadwick-Goldhaber Effect [*Physics*] ... CGE
Chadwyck-Healey Ltd., Bishops Stortford, Herts., United Kingdom [*Library symbol*] [*Library of Congress*] (LCLS) ... ChaH
Chaff Dispensing System [*or Subsystem*] (MCD) ... CDS
Chaff Flare Dispenser (ACAE) ... CFD
Chaff Rocket [*Military*] (NVT) ... CHAFFROC
Chaff/Delivery (SAA) ... C/D
Chaff-dispensing Rocket (SAUS) ... Chaffroc
Chaffee, MO [*FM radio station call letters*] ... KYRX
Chaffey College, Alta Loma, CA [*Library symbol*] [*Library of Congress*] (LCLS) ... CAltaC
Chaff/Flare (MCD) ... C/F
Chaff/Flare Countermeasures Dispenser System (PDAA) ... CMDS
Chafford [*England*] ... CHAF
Chagan-Uzun [*Former USSR*] [*Seismograph station code, US Geological Survey*] (SEIS) ... CUR
Chagos Islands (SAUS) ... IO
Chagrin Falls Public Library, Chagrin Falls, OH [*Library symbol*] [*Library of Congress*] (LCLS) ... OCf
Chah Bahar/Konarak [*Iran*] [*ICAO location identifier*] (ICLI) ... OIZC
Chah-Bahar [*Iran*] [*Airport symbol*] (OAG) ... ZBR
Chai Na Ta Corp. [*NASDAQ symbol*] (SAG) ... CCCF
Chai Na Ta Corp. [*Associated Press*] (SAG) ... ChaiNT
Chaillotine Air Service [*France*] [*ICAO designator*] (FAAC) ... CIS
Chain ... CH
Chain (WDMC) ... ch
Chain [*Measure*] ... CHN
Chain [*Symbol*] [*A part of the immunoglobulin molecular structure*] (DAVI) ... J
Chain Acquisition System (SAUS) ... CAS
Chain Address (SAUS) ... CA
Chain Arrester Gear (MCD) ... CHAG
Chain Belt Company (SAUO) ... CHB
Chain Block Character [*Computer science*] (NITA) ... CBC
Chain Block Controller (SAUS) ... CBC
Chain Break [*Broadcasting*] (WDMC) ... CB
Chain Command Flag (IAA) ... CCF
Chain Component ID (SAUS) ... CCID
Chain Crossing Model [*Semiconductor technology*] (OA) ... CCM
Chain Data (CIST) ... CD
Chain Data Flag (SAUS) ... CDF
Chain Delivery [*Press*] (DGA) ... CD
Chain Drug Marketing Association (NTPA) ... CDMA
Chain Elongation Proteins (SAUS) ... CEP
Chain Field Number (SAUS) ... CFN
Chain Flag (SAUS) ... CF
Chain Grate (MSA) ... CG
Chain Gun (SAUS) ... CG
Chain Handling Automated Overlay System (SAA) ... CHAOS
Chain Home [*Aviation*] ... CH
Chain Home Beamed [*Aviation*] ... CHB
Chain Home Extra Low [*Aviation*] ... CHEL
Chain Home High [*Aviation*] ... CHH
Chain Home Low [*Aviation*] ... CHL
Chain Ignition Hazard ... CIH
Chain Index (ADA) ... CI
Chain Input Pointing [*Computer science*] ... CHIP
Chain Length Distribution (SAUS) ... CLD
Chain Link Fence Manufacturers Institute (EA) ... CLFMI
Chain Makers' and Strikers' Association [*A union*] [*British*] ... CMSA
Chain Makers' Providential Association [*A union*] [*British*] ... CMPA
Chain Memory (SAUS) ... CM
Chain of Command (IAA) ... CC
Chain of Command ... CHACOM
Chain of Custody ... COC
Chain Operator (AAG) ... CO
Chain Overseas [*Aviation*] ... CO
Chain Overseas, Extra Low (SAUS) ... COEL
Chain Overseas Extremely Low [*Aviation*] ... COEL
Chain Overseas Low [*Aviation*] ... COL
Chain Pointer Word (SAUS) ... CPW
Chain Procedure [*Indexing*] (NITA) ... CP
Chain Radar (SAUS) ... CR
Chain RADAR System ... CRS
Chain Saw Manufacturers Association [*Later, PPEMA*] (EA) ... CSMA
Chain Store (SAUS) ... CS
Chain Store Renovation and Maintenance, Materials, Modernization ... CRAMMM
Chain Testers Association of Great Britain (BI) ... CTA
Chain Trade Board (SAUO) ... CTB
Chain Weizmann Institute of Science (SAUS) ... CWIS
Chai-Na-Ta Corp. [*NASDAQ symbol*] (TTSB) ... CCCFF
Chai-Na-Ta Ginsing Products Ltd. [*Associated Press*] (SAG) ... ChaiNaTa
Chai-Na-Ta-Ginseng [*Vancouver Stock Exchange symbol*] ... CJG
Chained Addressing (SAUS) ... CA
Chained Command (SAUS) ... CC
Chained Data (SAUS) ... CD
Chained File Management System [*IBM Corp.*] ... CFMS
Chained Schedule of Reinforcement (DIPS) ... CHAIN
Chained Segment Buffering (SAUS) ... CSB
Chained Sequential Operation ... CSO
Chain-Extended Polyethylene (PDAA) ... CEPE
Chaining (SAUS) ... CHN
Chaining Address (SAUS) ... CA
Chaining Data [*Computer science*] (IAA) ... CD
Chaining Error (SAUS) ... CE
Chaining Field (SAUS) ... CF
Chaining File (SAUS) ... CF
Chaining Instruction (SAUS) ... CI
Chainl Command (SAUO) ... CC
Chains (SAUS) ... CHNS
Chain-Transfer Agent [*Organic chemistry*] ... CTA
Chair ... CH
Chair ... CHR
Chair and Bed Rest [*Medical directive*] (CPH) ... C & B
Chair Frame Manufacturers' Association [*British*] (BI) ... CFMA
Chair of Economic Geology (SAUO) ... CEG
Chair of the Board (DD) ... chr
Chair Shower [*Medical rehabilitation*] (DAVI) ... C-Sh
Chaired ... CHRD
Chairmakers' Protection Society [*A union*] [*British*] ... CPS
Chairman [*or Chairwoman or Chairperson*] ... C
Chairman ... CH
Chairman (EY) ... CHAIR
Chairman ... CHM
Chairman (TBD) ... Chm
Chairman (WDAA) ... chm
Chairman ... CHMAN
Chairman (AFM) ... CHMN
Chairman (CMD) ... Chmn
Chairman (ROG) ... CHN
Chairman (SAUS) ... Chn
Chairman ... CHRM
Chairman ... CHRMN
Chairman, Chief of Staff (SAUS) ... CCOS
Chairman, Communications-Electronics Committee [*NATO*] (NATG) ... CCEC
Chairman, Joint Chiefs of Staff (AFM) ... CJCS
Chairman, Military Committee Memorandum [*NATO*] ... CMCM
Chairman, Naval Job Analysis (SAUS) ... CNJA
Chairman of Defense Committee (NATG) ... CODEF
Chairman of Military Committee (NATG) ... COMIL
Chairman of the Board ... CB
Chairman of the Joint Chiefs of Staff Instruction (SAUO) ... CJCSI
Chairman of the Office of Savings Associations ... COSA
Chairman of Volunteers [*Red Cross*] ... CV
Chairman, Operational Planners Group [*Military*] ... COPG
Chairman, Special Studies Group [*Joint Chiefs of Staff*] ... CSSG
Chairman's Guidance (DOMA) ... CG
Chairman's Memorandum ... CM
Chairman's Net Assesment of Strategic Planning (DOMA) ... CNASP
Chairman's Program Assessment [*Joint Chiefs of Staff*] (DOMA) ... CPA
Chairman's Staff Group [*DoD*] ... CSG
Chairperson (AL) ... Ch
Chairperson (PROS) ... chp
Chairperson (ADWA) ... chpn

Chairperson (BARN) .... Chpr
Chairperson .... CHRPRSN
Chairwoman .... CHRWMN
Chairwoman (PROS) .... chwn
Chaiten [Chile] [Airport symbol] (AD) .... WCH
Chaiten/Chaiten [Chile] [ICAO location identifier] (ICLI) .... SCTN
Chaitya (VRA) .... chya
Chaix Hill [Alaska] [Seismograph station code, US Geological Survey]
  (SEIS) .... CHX
Chaiyaphum [Thailand] [ICAO location identifier] (ICLI) .... VTUC
Chaiyaphum/Phu Khieo [Thailand] [ICAO location identifier] (ICLI) .... VTUG
Chajangni [South Korea] [ICAO location identifier] (ICLI) .... RKSI
Chajnantor Observatory Sub-Millimeter International Collaboration .... COSMIC
Chakcharan [Afghanistan] [Airport symbol] [Obsolete] (OAG) .... CCN
Chakhamenu Zikhronam Livrakhah [A publication] (BJA) .... CHaZaL
Chakhcharan [Afghanistan] [ICAO location identifier] (ICLI) .... OACC
Chakulia [India] [ICAO location identifier] (ICLI) .... VECK
Chala [Peru] [Seismograph station code, US Geological Survey] [Closed]
  (SEIS) .... CLA
Chala [Peru] [ICAO location identifier] (ICLI) .... SPHC
Chalais [France] [ICAO location identifier] (ICLI) .... LFIH
Chalan Kanoa [Diocesan abbreviation] (TOCD) .... CHK
Chalcedon Foundation (EA) .... CF
Chalcedony (VRA) .... chldy
Chalcedony (SAUS) .... CN
Chalcocite (SAUS) .... Chale
Chalcone Isomerase [An enzyme] .... CHI
Chalcone Synthase [An enzyme] .... CHS
Chalcophyrite (SAUS) .... CP
Chaldaeisches Woerterbuch ueber die Targumim [A publication] (BJA) .... CWbT
Chaldea (ROG) .... CH
Chaldea [or Chaldean or Chaldaic] .... CHALD
Chaldean (ADWA) .... Chal
Chaldean (ADWA) .... Chald
Chaldean (SAUS) .... Chald
Chaldron [Unit of measure] [Obsolete] .... CH
Chaldron [Unit of measure] [Obsolete] .... CHAL
Chaldron [Unit of measure] [Obsolete] .... CHD
Chaldron [Unit of measure] [Obsolete] (SAUS) .... Chd
Chaldron [Unit of measure] [Obsolete] (ROG) .... CHL
Chaleur Environment Protection Association (AC) .... CEPA
Chaleur Library Region, Campbellton, NB, Canada [Library symbol] [Library of Congress] (LCLS) .... CaNBCaC
Chaleur Library Region, Campbellton, New Brunswick [Library symbol] [National Library of Canada] (NLC) .... NBCAC
Chalgrove [British] [ICAO location identifier] (ICLI) .... EGLJ
Chalice Mining, Inc. [Vancouver Stock Exchange symbol] .... CLG
Chalk [Quality of the bottom] [Nautical charts] .... Ck
Chalk (VRA) .... ck
Chalk Board [Technical drawings] .... CHBD
Chalk Lime and Allied Industries Research Association (SAUS) .... CLAIRA
Chalk, Lime and Allied Industries Research Association (SAUO) .... CLAIRA
Chalk Quarrying Association (SAUO) .... CQA
Chalk Quarrying Association [British] (BI) .... CQA
Chalk River Bibliographic Data Information System [Atomic Energy of Canada Ltd.] (NITA) .... CHARIBDIS
Chalk River Nuclear Laboratories [Atomic Energy of Canada Ltd.] [Information service or system] [Research center] (IID) .... CRNL
Chalk River Public Library, Ontario [Library symbol] [National Library of Canada] (BIB) .... OCK
Chalk River Unidentified Deposit [Nuclear energy] (GFGA) .... CRUD
Chalk's International Airline [ICAO designator] (AD) .... BK
Chalky [Philately] .... chlk
Chalkyitsik [Alaska] [Airport symbol] (OAG) .... CIK
Challanger International Ltd. [Associated Press] (SAG) .... ChalInt
Challengair [Belgium] [FAA designator] (FAAC) .... CHG
Challeng'Air [France] [FAA designator] (FAAC) .... PWA
Challenge (AABC) .... CHAL
Challenge Air Cargo, Inc. [ICAO designator] (FAAC) .... CWC
Challenge Air Transport, Inc. [ICAO designator] (FAAC) .... OFF
Challenge Authentication Protocol (SAUS) .... CHAP
Challenge Aviation Pty Ltd. [Australia] [ICAO designator] (FAAC) .... CHS
Challenge Certificate [In dog shows] (BARN) CC
Challenge Handshake Authentication Protocol [Telecommunications] (PCM) .... CHAP
Challenge Position [Dancing] .... CH-P
Challenge Test Plan .... CTP
Challenge Virus Strain .... CVS
Challenger Armored Repair and Recovery Vehicle [British] .... CARRV
Challenger Armored Repair and Recovery Vehicle [British] .... CR-ARRV
Challenger Armoured Repair & Recovery Vehicle (SAUS) .... CR ARRV
Challenger Chieftain Armament (SAUS) .... CHARM
Challenger Communications Consultants Ltd. [British] [Telecommunications service] (TSSD) CCC
Challenger Improvement Programme (SAUS) .... CHIP
Challenger International [NASDAQ symbol] (SAG) .... ICOM
Challenger International Ltd. [Formerly, Coastal International Ltd.] [Toronto Stock Exchange symbol] .... CTT
Challenger School, Pasadena, TX [Library symbol] [Library of Congress] (LCLS) .... TxPCS
Challenger Society (SAUO) .... CS
Challenger Society for Marine Science [British] (EAIO) .... CSMS
Challenger Training Tank (SAUS) .... CTT
Challenging Adults to Read Effectively (EDAC) .... CARE
Challis, ID [Location identifier] [FAA] (FAAL) .... LLJ

Challis on Real Property [1885-1911] [A publication] (DLA) .... Challis
Challis Public Library, Challis, ID [Library symbol] [Library of Congress] (LCLS) .... IdCha
Challock [British] [ICAO location identifier] (ICLI) .... EGKE
Chalmers' Colonial Opinions [England] [A publication] (DLA) .... Ch
Chalmers' Colonial Opinions [England] [A publication] (DLA) .... Ch Col Op
Chalmers on Bills of Exchange [1878-1952] [A publication] (DLA) .... Chalmers
Chalmers' Opinions, Constitutional Law [1669-1809] [England] [A publication] (DLA) .... Chal Op
Chalmette National Historical Park .... CHAL
Chalna [Bangladesh] [Airport symbol] (AD) .... CHL
Chalon/Champforgeuil [France] [ICAO location identifier] (ICLI) .... LFLH
Chalone Wine Group [NASDAQ symbol] (NQ) .... CHLN
Chalone Wine Group Ltd. [Associated Press] (SAG) .... Chalone
Chalons/Ecury-Sur-Coole [France] [ICAO location identifier] (ICLI) .... LFQK
Chalons/Vatry [France] [ICAO location identifier] (ICLI) .... LFOK
Chalous [Iran] [ICAO location identifier] (ICLI) .... OINC
Chalqueno [Race of maize] .... CHL
Chalumeau [Reed] [Music] .... CHAL
Chalumeau [Reed] [Music] (ROG) .... CHALM
Chama [New Mexico] [Seismograph station code, US Geological Survey] [Closed] (SEIS) .... CNM
Chama Cha Mapinduzi [Revolutionary Party] [Tanzania] [Political party] (PPW) .... CCM
Chamaeleon [Constellation] .... Cha
Chamaeleon [Constellation] .... Cham
Chamaephyt (SAUS) C
Chamber (ADA) .... CH
Chamber .... Cha
Chamber (MSA) .... CHAMB
Chamber (VRA) .... chbr
Chamber (AAG) .... CHM
Chamber (SAUS) .... Chm
Chamber (MSA) .... CHMBR
Chamber Coolant Valve (NASA) CCV
Chamber Coolant Valve Actuator (MCD) .... CCVA
Chamber Flow-Field Code (MCD) .... CFC
Chamber Music America (EA) .... CMA
Chamber Music Society of Lincoln Center .... CMS/LC
Chamber of Agriculture (SAUO) .... CA
Chamber of Agriculture (SAUS) .... CA
Chamber of Automotive Industries of New South Wales [Australia] .... CAINSW
Chamber of Automotive Industries of Queensland (SAUO) .... CAIQ
Chamber of Coal Traders [British] (DBA) .... CCT
Chamber of Commerce CC
Chamber of Commerce .... COC
Chamber of Commerce (SAUO) .... COC
Chamber of Commerce (SAUO) .... C of C
Chamber of Commerce .... C of C
Chamber of Commerce and Industry of South Australia .... CCISA
Chamber of Commerce and Industry of Western Australia .... CCIWA
Chamber of Commerce Association (SAUO) .... CCA
Chamber of Commerce of the Americas (SAUO) .... CCA
Chamber of Commerce of the Apparel Industry (EA) .... CCAI
Chamber of Commerce of the United States (EA) .... CCUS
Chamber of Commerce of the United States (EA) .... COCUSA
Chamber of Commerce of the United States, Washington, DC [Library symbol] [Library of Congress] (LCLS) .... DCC
Chamber of Deputies (DAS) .... COD
Chamber of Deputies (SAUO) .... COD
Chamber of Destination of Ships .... CDS
Chamber of Fruit and Vegetable Industries (SAUO) .... CFVI
Chamber of Manufacturers (SAUO) .... CM
Chamber of Metallurgical Engineers (SAUS) .... CME
Chamber of Mineral Resources of Nova Scotia (AC) .... CMRNS
Chamber of Mines and Energy (SAUO) .... CME
Chamber of Mines and Energy of Western Australia .... CMEWA
Chamber of Mines and Research Laboratories (SAUS) .... CMRL
Chamber of Mines, Metals, and Extractive Industries [Australia] .... CMMEI
Chamber of Mines of South Africa (SAUO) .... CMSA
Chamber of Mines of Western Australia .... CMWA
Chamber of Princes (SAUO) .... CP
Chamber of Shipping (SAUO) .... Ch of S
Chamber of Shipping (DAS) .... COS
Chamber of Shipping (SAUO) .... CS
Chamber of Shipping of the United Kingdom (SAUO) .... CSUK
Chamber Orchestra of Europe .... COE
Chamber Pressure .... CP
Chamber Pressure .... Pc
Chamber Reports, Upper Canada [A publication] (DLA) .... Chamber
Chamber Reports, Upper Canada [A publication] (DLA) .... Chr Rep
Chamberlain [California] [Seismograph station code, US Geological Survey] (SEIS) .... CBC
Chamberlain (ROG) .... CHAMB
Chamberlain Armor Protection System (SAUS) .... CHAPS
Chamberlain Public Library, Chamberlain, SD [Library symbol] [Library of Congress] (LCLS) .... SdCh
Chamberlin's American Commercial Law [A publication] (DLA) .... Cham Com Law
Chambers .... CHAS
Chambers (ROG) .... CHRS
Chambers and Parsons' Railroad Laws [A publication] (DLA) .... Cham & PRR
Chambers and Pretty. Cases on Finance Act [1909-10] [England] [A publication] (DLA) .... Ch & P
Chambers' Chancery Jurisdiction as to Infants [A publication] (DLA) .... Cham Chy Jur

Chambers' Common Law [*Upper Canada*] [*A publication*] (DLA) .... CL Chamb
Chambers' Common Law [*Upper Canada*] [*A publication*] (DLA) .... CL Chambers
Chambers. Commons and Open Spaces [*1877*] [*A publication*]
(DLA) .... Cham Com
Chambers' Digest of Public Health Cases [*A publication*] (DLA) .... Chamb Dig PHC
Chambers. Estates and Tenures [*A publication*] (DLA) .... Cham Est
Chambers. Landlord and Tenant [*1823*] [*A publication*] (DLA) .... Cha L & T
Chambers. Landlord and Tenant [*1823*] [*A publication*] (DLA) .... Cham L & T
Chambers. Leases [*1819*] [*A publication*] (DLA) .... Cham Leas
Chambers of Commerce and Industry [*ASEAN*] (DS) CCI
Chambers of Commerce of Ireland (EAIO) CCI
Chambers Practice [*A publication*] (DLA) .... Cham Pr
Chambers. Rates and Rating [*2nd ed.*] [*1889*] [*A publication*] (DLA) ...... Cham Rat
Chambers Technical Dictionary (SAUS) .... CTD
Chambers' Upper Canada Reports [*1849-82*] [*A publication*] (DLA) .... Cham
Chambers' Upper Canada Reports [*1849-82*] [*A publication*] (DLA) .... Chamb
Chambers' Upper Canada Reports [*1849-82*] [*A publication*] (DLA) .... Cham Rep
Chambersburg, PA [*Location identifier*] [*FAA*] (FAAL) .... EQB
Chambersburg, PA [*AM radio station call letters*] .... WCBG
Chambersburg, PA [*AM radio station call letters*] .... WCHA
Chambersburg, PA [*FM radio station call letters*] .... WIKZ
Chambers's Encyclopaedia [*A publication*] (ROG) .... Chamb Ency
Chambery [*France*] [*Airport symbol*] (OAG) .... CMF
Chambery/Aix-Les-Bains [*France*] [*ICAO location identifier*] (ICLI) .... LFLB
Chambery/Challes-Les-Eaux [*France*] [*ICAO location identifier*] (ICLI) .... LFLE
Chambon-La-Foret [*France*] [*Seismograph station code, US Geological
Survey*] [*Closed*] (SEIS) .... CLF
Chambre d'Appel [*French*] [*Legal term*] (DLA) .... Ch App
Chambre de Commerce du Sud-Ouest de l'Ile de Montreal (AC) .... CCSOIM
Chambre de Commerce et d'Industrie de Paris [*Paris Chamber of Commerce
and Industry*] [*France*] [*Information service or system*] (IID) .... CCIP
Chambre de Commerce Internationale [*The International Chamber of
Commerce - ICC*] [*Paris, France*] (EAIO) CCI
Chambre de Compensation de l'Afrique de l'Ouest [*West African Clearing
House - WACH*] (EAIO) .... CCAO
Chambre de Compensation des Instruments Financiers de Paris .... CCIFP
Chambre Europeenne pour le Developpement du Commerce, de
l'Industrie, et des Finances [*European Chamber for the Development of
Trade, Industry, and Finances*] [*Brussels, Belgium*] (EAIO) .... CECIF
Chambre Immobiliere de la Haute Yamaska Inc. [*Haute Yamaska Real Estate
Board*] (AC) .... CIHY
Chambre Islamique de Commerce, d'Industrie et d'Echange des
Marchandises [*Islamic Chamber of Commerce, Industry, and Commodity
Exchange - ICCICE*] [*Karachi, Pakistan*] (EAIO) .... CICIEM
Chambre Syndicale des Fabricants de Papiers a Cigarettes et Autres
Papiers Minces (EAIO) .... CSFPCPM
Chameleon Micro Implementation Language [*1978*] [*Computer science*]
(CSR) .... CHAMIL
Chameleon Time Sharing System (SAUS) .... CTSS
Chameleonic Light Altering Simulated System (SAUS) .... CLASS
Chamfer [*Design engineering*] (IAA) .... CH
Chamfer [*Design engineering*] .... CHAM
Chamizal National Memorial .... CHAM
CHAMMP Interagency Organization for Numerical Simulations
(SAUS) .... CHAMMPions
CHAMMP Science Team (SAUO) .... CST
Chamois (SAUS) .... Cham
Chamois [*Philately*] .... cham
Chamois Contagious Ecthyma [*Medicine*] (DMAA) .... CCE
Chamomile [*Pharmacology*] (ROG) .... CHAM
Champ Du Feu [*France*] [*Seismograph station code, US Geological Survey*]
(SEIS) .... CDF
Champagne (ROG) .... CHAM
Champagne d'Argent Federation (EA) .... CDF
Champagne Gift Service [*De Courcy Pere et Fils*] [*British*] .... CGS
Champagne News and Information Bureau (EA) .... CNIB
Champagne Resources Ltd. [*Vancouver Stock Exchange symbol*] .... CPG
Champagne-Mumm Admiral's Cup [*Yacht racing*] .... C-MAC
Champagnole/Crotenay [*France*] [*ICAO location identifier*] (ICLI) .... LFGX
Champaign [*Illinois*] [*Airport symbol*] (OAG) .... CMI
Champaign, IL [*FM radio station call letters*] .... WBGL
Champaign, IL [*Television station call letters*] .... WCIA
Champaign, IL [*AM radio station call letters*] .... WDWS
Champaign, IL [*FM radio station call letters*] .... WEFT
Champaign, IL [*FM radio station call letters*] .... WHMS
Champaign, IL [*Television station call letters*] .... WICD
Champaign, IL [*FM radio station call letters*] .... WIXY
Champaign, IL [*FM radio station call letters*] .... WLRW
Champaign, IL [*FM radio station call letters*] .... WPCD
Champaign Public Library, Champaign, IL [*Library symbol*] [*Library of
Congress*] (LCLS) .... ICham
Champaign Public Library, Champaign, IL [*OCLC symbol*] (OCLC) .... IKG
Champaign Urbana (SAUS) .... CMI
Champaign-Urbana Dining Guide (SAUO) .... CUDG
Champaign/Urbana, IL [*Location identifier*] [*FAA*] (FAAL) .... CMI
Champerty and Maintenance [*A publication*] (DLA) .... Champ
Champion [*Dog show term*] .... CH
Champion (DSUE) .... CHAMP
Champion (ADWA) .... Champ
Champion Aircraft Co. .... CAC
Champion Distributed Processing System (SAUS) .... CDPS
Champion Enterprises [*NYSE symbol*] (TTSB) .... CHB
Champion Enterprises [*Associated Press*] (SAG) .... ChmpE
Champion Enterprises, Inc. [*AMEX symbol*] (SPSG) .... CHB
Champion Enterprises, Inc. [*Associated Press*] (SAG) .... ChpEn

Champion Fleet Owners Association (EA) .... CFOA
Champion Healthcare [*AMEX symbol*] (TTSB) .... CHC
Champion Healthcare Corp. [*AMEX symbol*] (SAG) .... CHC
Champion Healthcare Corp. [*Associated Press*] (SAG) .... ChmpH
Champion Industries [*NASDAQ symbol*] (TTSB) .... CHMP
Champion Industries, Inc. [*NASDAQ symbol*] (SAG) .... CHMP
Champion Industries, Inc. [*Associated Press*] (SAG) .... ChmpIn
Champion International (SAUO) .... CHA
Champion International Corp. [*NYSE symbol*] (SPSG) .... CHA
Champion International Corp. (MHDW) .... CHAP
Champion International Corp. [*Associated Press*] (SAG) .... ChmpIn
Champion Oil & Gas [*Vancouver Stock Exchange symbol*] .... CHP
Champion Papers, Inc. (SAUO) .... CPP
Champion Papers, Inc., Pasadena, TX [*Library symbol*] [*Library of
Congress*] (LCLS) .... TxPC
Champion Parts [*NASDAQ symbol*] (TTSB) .... CREB
Champion Parts Rebuilders, Inc. [*Associated Press*] (SAG) .... ChmpPr
Champion Parts Rebuilders, Inc. [*NASDAQ symbol*] (NQ) .... CREB
Champion Public Library, Alberta [*Library symbol*] [*National Library of
Canada*] (NLC) .... ACHAM
Champion Road Machinery [*NASDAQ symbol*] (TTSB) .... CRMLE
Champion Road Machinery Ltd. [*Associated Press*] (SAG) .... ChpRM
Champion Road Machinery Ltd. [*Associated Press*] (SAG) .... ChRM
Champion Road Machinery Ltd. [*NASDAQ symbol*] (SAG) .... CRML
Champion Spark Plug Co. (SAUO) .... CHM
Champion Tracker .... CT
Champions (SAUS) .... CHA
Champion's Cases, Wine and Beer-Houses Act [*England*] [*A publication*]
(DLA) .... Champ
Championship .... CHP
Championship Association of Mechanics (EA) .... CAM
Championship Auto Racing [*NYSE symbol*] (SG) .... MPH
Championship Auto Racing Teams (EA) .... CART
Championship Auto Racing Teams [*An association*] (EA) .... IndyCar
Championship Drivers Licensing Group [*Automobile racing*] .... CDLG
Champlain College, Burlington, VT [*Library symbol*] [*Library of Congress*]
(LCLS) .... VtBC
Champlain College, Plattsburgh, NY [*Library symbol*] [*Library of Congress*]
[*Obsolete*] (LCLS) .... NPlaC
Champlain Enterprises, Inc. [*ICAO designator*] (FAAC) .... UCA
Champlain, NY [*AM radio station call letters*] .... WCHP
Champlain Regional College, Campus 1, St.-Lambert, PQ, Canada [*Library
symbol*] [*Library of Congress*] (LCLS) .... CaQSICR
Champlain Society (EA) .... CS
Champlain Valley Physicians Hospital, Plattsburgh, NY [*Library symbol*]
[*Library of Congress*] (LCLS) .... NPlaP
Champlain Valley School of Nursing, Plattsburgh, NY [*Library symbol*]
[*Library of Congress*] (LCLS) .... NPlaCN
Champleve (VRA) .... champ
Champlin Oil & Refining Company (SAUO) .... CHI
Champps Entertainment, Inc. [*Associated Press*] (SAG) .... Champps
Champps Entertainment, Inc. [*NASDAQ symbol*] (SAG) .... CHPP
CHAMPUS [*Civilian Health and Medical Program of the Uniformed Services*]
Reform Initiative (GFGA) .... CRI
CHAMPUS [*Civilian Health and Medical of the Uniformed Services*] **Regional
Review System** .... CRRS
Chan Hills Military Police [*British military*] (DMA) .... CHMP
Chanaral [*Chile*] [*Seismograph station code, US Geological Survey*] (SEIS) ..... CAA
Chanaral [*Chile*] [*Airport symbol*] (AD) .... CNR
Chanarin Syndrome [*Medicine*] .... CS
Chance (FAAC) .... CHC
Chance Failure Rate (IAA) .... CFR
Chance on Powers [*1831*] [*Supplement, 1841*] [*A publication*] (DLA) ...... Chanc Pow
[*A*] Chance to Grow (EA) .... ACTG
Chance Vought Aircraft, Inc. [*Obsolete*] .... CVA
Chance-Constrained Programming (PDAA) .... CCP
Chancellor C
Chancellor (ADA) .... CH
Chancellor (DLA) .... Chan
Chancellor .... CHANC
Chancellor (NTIO) .... Chanc
Chancellor .... CHANCLLR
Chancellor .... Chllr
Chancellor Broadcasting "A" [*NASDAQ symbol*] [*Formerly, Chancellor Corp.
"A"*] (SG) .... CBCA
Chancellor Broadcstg'A' [*NASDAQ symbol*] (TTSB) .... CBCA
Chancellor Corp. [*NASDAQ symbol*] (SAG) .... CBCA
Chancellor Corp. [*Associated Press*] (SAG) .... Chncellr
Chancellor Energy Resources, Inc. [*Toronto Stock Exchange symbol*] .... CHC
Chancellor Media Corp. A [*NASDAQ symbol*] [*Formerly, Evergreen Media
Corp. A.*] (SG) .... AMFM
Chancellor of the Chamber of Princes (SAUO) .... CCP
Chancellor of the Duchy of Lancaster [*British*] .... CDL
Chancellor of the Exchequer [*British*] .... CE
Chancellor of the Exchequer (SAUO) .... CE
Chancellor of the Exchequer [*British*] (DLA) .... Chanc Ex
Chancellor's Court [*England*] (DLA) .... Ch
Chancery C
Chancery (SAUO) C
Chancery [*British*] .... CH
Chancery .... CHAN
Chancery (GEAB) .... chan
Chancery (SAUO) .... Chan
Chancery (SAUO) .... Chanc
Chancery (ROG) .... CHANC

Chancery .... CHY
Chancery Appeal Cases [1865-75] [A publication] (DLA) .... LR Ch App
Chancery Appeal Cases, English Law Reports [A publication] (DLA) .... CA
Chancery Appeal Cases, English Law Reports [A publication] (DLA) .... Cha App
Chancery Appeal Cases, English Law Reports [A publication]
    (DLA) .... Ch App Cas
Chancery Appeals (SAUO) .... ChApp
Chancery Cases [2 Notes of King's Bench Cases] [England] [A publication]
    (DLA) .... Keny Ch
Chancery Cases Chronicle [Ontario] [A publication] (DLA) .... CC Chr
Chancery Cases Chronicle [Ontario] [A publication] (DLA) .... CC Chron
Chancery Cases Tempore Talbot [England] [A publication] (DLA) .... Forester
Chancery Chambers [Upper Canada] (DLA) .... Ch Chamb
Chancery Chambers [Upper Canada] (DLA) .... Ch Chamb (Can)
Chancery Chambers Reports, Ontario [A publication] (DLA) .... Chamb Rep
Chancery Chambers Reports, Upper Canada [1857-72] [A publication]
    (DLA) .... Chan Chamb
Chancery Court (DLA) .... Chan Ct
Chancery Court (SAUO) .... ChC
Chancery Court (SAUO) .... ChCt
Chancery Division (SAUO) .... CD
Chancery Division .... CD
Chancery Division (SAUO) .... ChD
Chancery Division (SAUO) .... ChyDiv
Chancery Divisional Court [England] (DLA) .... Ch Div'l Ct
Chancery Practice [A publication] (DLA) .... Ch Pr
Chancery Proceedings [British] (ROG) .... CHAN PROC
Chancery Reports Tempore Car. I to Queen Anne [A publication] (DLA) .... CR
Chancery Sentinel [New York] [A publication] (DLA) .... Chan Sentinel
Chancery Sentinel [New York] [A publication] (DLA) .... Ch Sent
Chancery Sentinel [New York] [A publication] (DLA) .... Ch Sent (NY)
Chancery Sentinel [New York] [A publication] (DLA) .... NY Ch
Chances Accepted [Baseball] .... CA
Chancroid Ulcer Disease [Medicine] (MELL) .... CUD
Chandalar [Alaska] [Airport symbol] (OAG) .... WCR
Chandalar Lake, AK [Location identifier] [FAA] (FAAL) .... CQR
Chandalar Lake, AK [Location identifier] [FAA] (FAAL) .... WCR
Chandeleur Bay [Vancouver Stock Exchange symbol] .... CYJ
Chandigarh [India] [Airport symbol] (OAG) IXC
Chandigarh [India] [ICAO location identifier] (ICLI) .... VICG
Chandler .... CHANL
Chandler and Price Letterpress Printing Press (WDMC) .... C&P press
Chandler, AZ [Location identifier] [FAA] (FAAL) .... AMS
Chandler, AZ [Location identifier] [FAA] (FAAL) .... CHD
Chandler, AZ [Location identifier] [FAA] (FAAL) .... HAN
Chandler, AZ [FM radio station call letters] .... KMLE
Chandler, AZ [Location identifier] [FAA] (FAAL) .... UTE
Chandler Evans Corp. .... CECO
Chandler, IN [FM radio station call letters] .... WNTC
Chandler Insurance Co. Ltd. [NASDAQ symbol] .... CHAN
Chandler Insurance Co. Ltd. [Associated Press] (SAG) .... ChanIn
Chandler Insurance Ltd. (MHDW) .... CHANF
Chandler, OK [Location identifier] [FAA] (FAAL) .... CQB
Chandler Public Library, Chandler, AZ [Library symbol] [Library of
    Congress] (LCLS) .... AzCh
Chandler-Lake Wilson High School, Chandler, MN [Library symbol] [Library
    of Congress] (LCLS) .... MnChaHS
Chandler's American Criminal Trials [A publication] (DLA) ...... Chand Crim Tr
Chandler's American Criminal Trials [A publication] (DLA) ...... Chand Cr T
Chandler's Reports [20, 38-44 New Hampshire] [A publication] (DLA) .... Chand
Chandler's Reports [20, 38-44 New Hampshire] [A publication] (DLA) .... Chandl
Chandler's Reports [20, 38-44 New Hampshire] [A publication]
    (DLA) .... Chand (NH)
Chandler's Wisconsin Reports [1849-52] [A publication] (DLA) .... Chand
Chandler's Wisconsin Reports [1849-52] [A publication] (DLA) .... Chandl
Chandler's Wisconsin Reports [1849-52] [A publication] (DLA) .... Chandler
Chandler's Wisconsin Reports [1849-52] [A publication] (DLA) .... Chandler Wis
Chandler's Wisconsin Reports [1849-52] [A publication] (DLA) .... Chand R
Chandler's Wisconsin Reports [1849-52] [A publication] (DLA) .... Chand (Wis)
Chandler/Williams Air Force Base [Arizona] [ICAO location identifier]
    (ICLI) .... KCHD
Chandpur [Bangladesh] [Airport symbol] (AD) .... CDP
Chandra X-Ray Observatory (SAUS) .... CXO
Chandragarhi [Nepal] [ICAO location identifier] (ICLI) .... VNCG
Chandraprabha Wildlife Sanctuary (SAUS) .... CWS
Chanduy [Ecuador] [ICAO location identifier] (ICLI) .... SEUY
Chane Bedoya [Bolivia] [ICAO location identifier] (ICLI) .... SLHN
Chaney's Digest, Michigan Reports [A publication] (DLA) .... Cha Dig
Chaney's Digest, Michigan Reports [A publication] (DLA) .... Ch Dig
Chaney's Michigan Reports [37-58 Michigan] [A publication] (DLA) .... Chan
Chaney's Michigan Reports [37-58 Michigan] [A publication] (DLA) .... Chaney
Chaney's Michigan Reports [37-58 Michigan] [A publication]
    (DLA) .... Chaney (Mich)
Chang Conjunctiva Cells [Medicine] (DMAA) .... CHANG C
Chang Liver [Cell culture] (DB) .... CH
Chang Liver Cells [Medicine] (DMAA) .... CHANG L
Changalane [Mozambique] [Seismograph station code, US Geological
    Survey] (SEIS) .... CNG
Changan Airlines [China] [FAA designator] (FAAC) .... CGN
Changchu International Symposium on Analytical Chemistry [1990] .... CISAC
Changchun [China] [Airport symbol] (OAG) .... CGQ
Changchun [Republic of China] [Seismograph station code, US Geological
    Survey] (SEIS) .... CNH
Changchun [China] [ICAO location identifier] (ICLI) .... ZYCC
Changchun Institute of Applied Chemistry [China] .... CIAC

Change [Used in combinations only] [Army] (AABC) C
Change (AABC) .... CH
Change (AAG) .... CHG
Change (ADWA) .... chg
Change [Telecommunications] (TEL) .... CHN
Change .... CHNG
Change [A publication] (BRI) .... Cng
Change a Column (SAUS) .... CNGCOL
Change Administration .... CA
Change Administration Conference .... CAC
Change Administration Cover Sheet .... CA/CS
Change Agent Questionnaire [Interpersonal skills and attitudes test] .... CAQ
Change Agent Research (PDAA) .... CAR
Change Analysis Board .... CAB
Change Analysis Commitment (SAA) .... CAC
Change Analysis Group .... CAG
Change Analysis Section .... CAS
Change and Configuration Control (SAUS) CCC
Change and Configuration Control System (SAUS) .... CCCS
Change Approaching (SAUS) .... Orange Light
Change Board (MCD) .... CB
Change Board Analysis Record (SAA) .... CBAR
Change Board Comment Record .... CBCR
Change Board Register .... CBR
Change Board Support System (SAUS) .... CBSS
Change Bulletin .... CB
Change Code (MCD) CC
Change Code Page (SAUS) .... CHCP
Change Column Measure [Typesetting] (WDMC) cc
Change Commitment Record (SAA) .... CCR
Change Configuration Control/Development and Maintenance
    (ACAE) .... CCC/DM
Change Configuration Management (VERA) .... CCM
Change Control (ACAE) CC
Change Control and Reporting System (ACAE) .... CCARS
Change Control Board [Social Security Administration] .... CCB
Change Control Board [NASA] (KSC) .... CHGCB
Change Control Board Directive [NASA] (MCD) .... CCBD
Change Control Board Screening Group (SAUO) .... CCBSG
Change Control Board Summary [NASA] (MCD) .... CCBS
Change Control Center (ACAE) CCC
Change Control Determine (MCD) .... CCD
Change Control Engineer .... CCE
Change Control Form (SAUS) .... CCF
Change Control Sub-Board (DNAB) .... CCSB
Change Control System .... CCS
Change Coordination Form (ACAE) .... CCF
Change Course CC
Change Design Order [Navy] (NG) .... CDO
Change Diagram (SAUS) .... CD
Change Diameter (MCD) .... CD
Change Direction (SAUS) .... CD
Change Directive (AAG) .... CD
Change Directory [Computer science] .... CD
Change Directory [Computer science] .... CHDIR
Change Directory Extended [Computer science] (PCM) .... CDX
Change Display [Utility] .... CHAD
Change Evaluation (NASA) .... CE
Change Evaluation Board [NASA] (SSD) .... CEB
Change Evalution/Analysis [Engineering] .... CE/A
Change Facilitator Stages of Concern Questionnaire [Educational
    test] .... CFSOCQ
Change Film Frame (SAA) .... CFF
Change Finger (SAUS) .... CHFN
Change Flight Plan .... CFP
Change Font [Typesetting] (WDMC) .... cf
Change for Children [An association] (EA) CC
Change for Children Association (AC) .... CFCA
Change for Good [An association] (EA) .... CFG
Change for Good (EA) .... CG
Change Frequency (SAUS) .... CF
Change Full Name (SAUS) .... CHFN
Change Group .... CHGRP
Change Identification Control Number CIC
Change Identification Control Schedule Analysis .... CICSA
Change Identification Control Schedule Summary .... CIC-SS
Change Identification Number (NASA) .... CIN
Change Impact Board (NASA) .... CIB
Change Impact Summary (NASA) .... CIS
Change Implementation Board [NASA] (GFGA) .... CIB
Change in Business Inventories (SAUO) .... CBI
Change in Design .... CID
Change in Drawing Authorization (MCD) .... CIDA
Change in Drawing Notice .... CIDN
Change in Formula .... CF
Change in Procurement Instructions (SAUS) .... CIPI
Change Incorporation Notice [Business law] .... CIN
Change Incorporation Record (SAUO) .... CIR
Change Indicator (SSD) CI
Change Indicator Code (SAA) CIC
Change Indicator Control (SAUS) CIC
Change Initiation Request (KSC) .... CIR
Change Instrumentation Notice .... CIN
Change Islands Public Library, Newfoundland [Library symbol] [National
    Library of Canada] (NLC) .... NFCI

Change Leading [*Typesetting*] (WDMC)	cl
Change Leading [*Typography*] (WDMC)	CL
Change Letter Control (NASA)	CLC
Change List	CL
Change Log (SAUS)	CLog
Change Management Center (ACAE)	CMC
Change Management Programme (HEAS)	CHAMP
Change Management System (SAUS)	CMS
Change Management Term (ACAE)	CMT
Change Management/Tracking [*IBM Corp.*]	CM/T
Change Mode	CHMOD
Change My Operation Order [*Military*]	CHORD
Change My Operation Plan [*Military*] (AABC)	CHOPLN
Change My Operation Schedule [*Military*] (MUGU)	CHSKED
Change Name To [*Travel industry*] (TRID)	CHNT
Change Notice	CN
Change Notice Card (AFIT)	CNC
Change Notice Request (MCD)	CNR
Change of Address [*Postal term*] [*United States*] (WDMC)	C/A
Change of Address [*Direct marketing*] (WDMC)	CHAD
Change of Address	COA
Change of Appointing Office (FAAC)	CAO
Change of Assignment	COA
Change of Command	COC
Change of Contract [*Business law*] (AAG)	COC
Change of Course [*Aviation*]	C/C
Change of Initial Condition (MCD)	CIC
Change of Location of Command (SAUO)	COLOC
Change of Locations of Command (SAUS)	COLOC
Change of Operation Plan (SAUS)	CHOPLN
Change of Operational Control [*Military*]	CHOP
Change of Operational Control of Air Cover [*Military*] (NVT)	CHOPAIR
Change of Operational Control Summary [*Military*] (NVT)	CHOPSUM
Change of Operational Order (SAUS)	CHORD
Change of Personal Particulars (ADA)	COPP
Change of Plaster [*Medicine*]	COP
Change of Quarters (DNAB)	CQ
Change of Rating	C/R
Change of Shift (STED)	cos
Change of Speed (DNAB)	C/S
Change of Status (ACAE)	COS
Change of Status (NASA)	CS
Change of Subscribers (TEL)	COS
Change Operations Directive (MCD)	COD
Change [*of*] Order	CO
Change Order (NAKS)	Co
Change Order (SAUO)	CO
Change Order Account (AFM)	COA
Change Order (Aircraft)	CO(A)
Change Order Board (AAG)	COB
Change Order Conference (AAG)	COC
Change Order (Electronic)	CO(E)
Change Order Modification (KSC)	COM
Change Order Request (DNAB)	COR
Change Order Work Sheet (DNAB)	COWS
Change Over	CHGOV
Change Over (DEN)	CO
Change Over Point [*Aviation*] (PIPO)	COP
Change Owner	CHOWN
Change Package (AAG)	CP
Change Package Engineer (SAUS)	CPE
Change Package Identification	CPI
Change Package Identification Number	CPIN
Change Pages (MCD)	CP
Change Plane (SAUS)	Chg Pl
Change Planning Group (NASA)	CPG
Change Point [*Surveying*]	CP
Change Priority Mask (SAUS)	CHPM
Change Process Authorization (MCD)	CPA
Change Processing Station (AAG)	CPS
Change Proposal (KSC)	CP
Change Proposal Request (ACAE)	CPR
Change Recommendation (AFM)	CR
Change Record (TRID)	CR
Change Record Sheet (MCD)	CRS
Change Release [*Military*]	CR
Change Request	CR
Change Request Control System (ACAE)	CRCS
Change Request Directive (MCD)	CR/DIR
Change Request Disposition (MCD)	CRD
Change Request Forms	CRF
Change Request Management (SAUS)	CRM
Change Request Material (AAG)	CRM
Change Request Reply (SAUS)	CRR
Change Request Review Board (USDC)	CRRB
Change Review Authorization (ACAE)	CRA
Change Review Board [*NASA*] (KSC)	CRB
Change Review Board Directive (SAUS)	CRBD
Change Review Committee [*Military*] (AABC)	CRCOM
Change Review Group [*NASA*] (GFGA)	CRG
Change Review Panel (SAUO)	CRP
Change Routing Indicator (MCD)	CRI
Change Schedule Chart	CSC
Change Seeker Index	CSI
Change Sheet [*Marine Corps*]	CS

Change Status (SAUS)	CS
Change Status (NAKS)	cs
Change Status Page (MCD)	CSP
Change Status Report (MCD)	CSR
Change to Approach Control (FAAC)	CAC
Change to Center Control (SAUS)	CTCC
Change to Data Field (SAUS)	CDF
Change to Initial Release (MCD)	CIR
Change to Lower Grade [*Army*]	CLG
Change to Navy Regulations	CNR
Change to Tower Frequency (SAUS)	CTF
Change Tracker (SAUS)	CT
Change Transfer Device (MCD)	CTD
Change Transfer Photography (SAUS)	CTP
Change Verification Notice	CVN
Change Verification Record	CVR
Change Verification System (SAUS)	CVS
Change Weight Manifest [*Aviation*] (FAAC)	CWM
Change Working Directory (SAUS)	CWD
Changeable (SAUS)	Chgbl
Changeable Message Sign [*Highway engineering*]	CMS
Changeable Type-Plate Style	CT-PS
Change-Back Acknowledgement Signal (SAUS)	CBA Signal
Change-Back Control (SAUS)	CBC
Changed (SAUS)	Chgd
Changed (WGA)	CHGD
Changed Course (SAUS)	CC
Changed Number Interception [*Telecommunications*] (TEL)	CNI
Changed Particle Research Laboratory (SAUS)	CPRL
Changeout (NASA)	C/O
Change-Over (SAUS)	Chgov
Changeover [*Aviation*] (FAAC)	CHOV
Changeover (AAG)	CHOVR
Change-Over (SAUS)	Chovr
Change-Over Acknowledgement Signal (SAUS)	COA Signal
Change-over and Change-back Messages (SAUS)	CHM
Change-Over Control (SAUS)	COC
Change-Over Delay (AEBS)	COD
Change-Over Order Signal (SAUS)	COO Signal
Changeover Point (SAUS)	CHOP
Change-Over Signal (SAUS)	COV Signal
Changeover Switch (NATG)	COS
Changeover Time (SAUS)	CT
Change-Parity Time (SAUS)	CPT
Changes and Specifications	C & S
Changes Being Effected [*Food and Drug Administration*]	CBE
Changes in Global National Security Environment (DOMA)	CGNSE
Changes in Itinerary to Proceed to Additional Places [*Military*]	CIPAP
Changes in Law (MCD)	CIL
Changes Islands Public Library, Changes Islands, NF, Canada [*Library symbol*] [*Library of Congress*] (LCLS)	CaNfCI
Changes per Inch (IAA)	CPI
Change-Transfer-to-Solvent [*Physical chemistry*]	CTTS
Changhe Aircraft Factory (SAUS)	CAF
Changing Men [*A publication*] (BRI)	Cha Men
Changing Over (FAAC)	CHGO
Changing Path of Operation	CPO
Changing Pulse Radar (ACAE)	CPR
Changing Radio Automatic Frequency Transmission	CRAFT
Changing Role of the Secondary Head [*Project*] (AIE)	CROSH
Changing to Approach Control (SAUS)	CAC
Changing to Center Control (SAUS)	CTCC
Changsha [*China*] [*Airport symbol*] (OAG)	CSX
Changsha/Datuopu [*China*] [*ICAO location identifier*] (ICLI)	ZGCS
Changuinola [*Panama*] [*Airport symbol*] (OAG)	CHX
Changuinola/Cap. Manuel Nino [*Panama*] [*ICAO location identifier*] (ICLI)	MPCH
Changzhi [*China*] [*Airport symbol*] (OAG)	CIH
Chania [*Greece*] [*Airport symbol*] (OAG)	CHQ
Channel (WDAA)	C
Channel (NTIO)	Ch
Channel (WDMC)	ch
Channel	CH
Channel [*Computer science*] (AABC)	CHAN
Channel (WDMC)	chan
Channel (ADWA)	Chan
Channel (NASA)	CHL
Channel [*Electrical transmission*] (AFM)	CHNL
Channel	CHNNL
Channel 4 [*Television*] [*British*]	C4
Channel Active (SAUS)	ACT
Channel Adapter [*Computer science*] (IBMDP)	CA
Channel Address [*Military*]	CAD
Channel Address Bus (SAUS)	CAB
Channel Address Field (SAUS)	CAF
Channel Address Register [*Computer science*]	CAR
Channel Address Word [*Computer science*]	CAW
Channel Air Bridge (SAUO)	CAB
Channel Air Ferries (SAUO)	CAF
Channel Allocation and Routing Data (IEEE)	CARD
Channel Allocation Monitor and Controller (SAUS)	CAMAC
Channel Amplitude Class [*Electrical engineering*]	CAC
Channel and Isolation Supervision [*Telecommunications*] (TEL)	CIS
Channel and Technical Control Facility [*In a tape-relay station in the AIRCOMNET*]	CTCF
Channel and Traffic Control Agency (SAUO)	CTC

Channel and Traffic Control Agency [*of AACS*] .... CTCA
Channel and Traffic Control Unit [*Subordinate unit of the Channel and Traffic Control Agency*] .... CTCU
Channel Area Difference (SAUS) .... CAD
Channel Associated Signaling [*Telecommunications*] (ACRL) .... CAS
Channel Available Interruption (SAUS) .... CAI
Channel Aviation Ltd. [*British*] [*ICAO designator*] (FAAC) .... GID
Channel Aviation Ltd. [*British*] [*FAA designator*] (FAAC) .... GJD
Channel Bank (ACRL) .... CB
Channel Base Section [*World War II*] .... CBS
Channel Catfish Virus CCV
Channel Check .... CHCK
Channel Check Handler (SAUS) .... CCH
Channel Code Letter (SAUS) CCL
Channel Code Number (SAUS) .... CCN
Channel Coding (SAUS) CC
Channel Command [*Refers to English Channel*] [*Military*] CC
Channel Command (SAUO) .... CHANCOM
Channel Command [*or Control*] Block [*Computer science*] (IAA) .... CCB
Channel Command Call (SAUS) CCC
Channel Command Control (SAUS) CCC
Channel Command Entry (SAUS) .... CCE
Channel Command [*or Control*] Entry [*Computer science*] (IAA) .... CCE
Channel Command or Control [*Computer science*] (IAA) CCC
Channel Command [*or Control*] Register [*Computer science*] (IAA) .... CCR
Channel Command [*or Control*] Word [*Computer science*] .... CCW
Channel Committee [*NATO*] (NATG) .... CHANCOM
Channel Committee [*NATO*] (NATG) .... CHANCOMTEE
Channel Committee Secretary [*NATO*] (NATG) .... CHANSEC
Channel Control (BUR) .... CHC
Channel Control Block (SAUS) .... CCB
Channel Control Check [*Electronics*] (IAA) CCC
Channel Control Check [*Electronics*] (OA) .... CCK
Channel Control Error (SAUS) .... CCE
Channel Control Field [*Telecommunications*] (ECII) .... CCF
Channel Control Orderwire (CAAL) .... CCOW
Channel Control Processor [*Computer science*] (NITA) .... CCP
Channel Control Reconfiguration [*Computer science*] (MHDI) .... CCR
Channel Control Routine (SAUS) .... CCR
Channel Control System (SAUS) .... CCS
Channel Control Unit (CMD) .... CCU
Channel Control Unit (MCD) .... CHCU
Channel Controller (MCD) CC
Channel Controller (NAKS) cc
Channel Coordinator [*Telecommunications*] (NITA) CC
Channel Counter (ACAE) CC
Channel Data Check .... CDK
Channel Data Error (SAUS) .... CDE
Channel Data Register (SAUS) .... CDR
Channel Definition Format [*Microsoft Corp.*] [*Computer science*] .... CDF
Channel Descriptor Table (SAUS) .... CDT
Channel Designator (SAUO) .... CD
Channel Disable (SAUS) .... CD
Channel Divider/User Assignment Switch (ACAE) .... CD/UAS
Channel Down [*Biochemistry*] (DAVI) .... CD
Channel Effluent Limit [*Environmental science*] (COE) .... CEL
Channel Electron Multiplier (MCD) .... CEM
Channel Electron Multiplier Array (MCD) .... CEMA
Channel Enable (SAUS) .... CE
Channel End (OA) .... CE
Channel End (BUR) .... CHE
Channel Equipment Error (SAUS) .... CEE
Channel Error Register (SAUS) .... CER
Channel Error Routine (SAUS) .... CER
Channel Evaluation and Call (IEEE) .... CHEC
Channel Express (Air Services) Ltd. [*British*] [*ICAO designator*] (FAAC) .... EXS
Channel Extension Unit .... CEU
Channel Failure Record (SAUS) .... CFR
Channel Flow Control .... CFC
Channel Flying [*ICAO designator*] (AD) .... IH
Channel for Orders [*Business term*] .... CFO
Channel Frequency Class [*Electrical engineering*] .... CFC
Channel Handicap System [*Yacht racing*] .... CHS
Channel Identification (CET) .... CID
Channel Inboard Record (SAUS) .... CIR
Channel Indirect Data Addressing (IBMDP) .... CIDA
Channel Instruction (SAUS) CI
Channel Interface .... CHIF
Channel Interface Adapter (SAUS) .... CIA
Channel Interface Base (SAUS) .... CIB
Channel Interface Bus (NITA) .... CIB
Channel Interface Processor [*Telecommunications*] (ACRL) .... CIP
Channel Interface Unit (SAUS) .... CIU
Channel Island Aviation [*ICAO designator*] (FAAC) .... CHN
Channel Island Ferries [*British*] .... CIF
Channel Islands (SAUS) .... Chan Is
Channel Islands CI
Channel Islands (SAUS) .... CIM
Channel Islands Militia (SAUO) .... CIM
Channel Islands National Monument .... CHIS
Channel Islands National Monument (SAUS) .... CINM
Channel Level Control (MCD) CLC
Channel Linearity Measurement Assembly (ACAE) .... CLMA
Channel Load Table (SAUS) .... CLT
Channel Loading (SAUS) CL
Channel Local Address Register (SAUS) .... CLAR

Channel Multiplier Array .... CMA
Channel Navigation Information Service [*British Coast Guard*] (PDAA) .... CNIS
Channel One [*French television station*] TF1
Channel Operation Complete (SAUS) .... COC
Channel Operator (SAUS) .... CHOP
Channel Oscilloscope .... C/O
Channel Piezoresistance Effect (SAUS) .... CPE
Channel Port Index .... CPI
Channel Processor .... CHP
Channel Program Area [*Computer science*] (IAA) .... CPA
Channel Program Block [*Computer science*] .... CPB
Channel Program Commands .... CPC
Channel Quality Measurement (CGWS) .... CQM
Channel Queue Limit (SAUS) .... CQL
Channel Queue Table (CCCA) .... CQT
Channel Reconfiguration Hardware (SAUS) .... CRH
Channel Reference Tone (MCD) .... CRT
Channel Register (ACAE) .... CR
Channel Request-High Priority (MHDB) .... CR-HI
Channel Request-Low Priority (MHDB) .... CR-LO
Channel Request-Medium Priority (MHDB) .... CR-MED
Channel Resources Ltd. [*Vancouver Stock Exchange symbol*] .... CHU
Channel Response Time (IAA) .... CRT
Channel Scheduling Process (SAUS) .... CSP
Channel Search (SAUS) .... CS
Channel Select Register [*Telecommunications*] (NITA) .... CSR
Channel Selection (SAUS) .... CS
Channel Selector (SAUS) .... CHAN SEL
Channel Selector (SAUS) .... CS
Channel Service Register (SAUS) .... CSR
Channel Service Unit [*Telecommunications*] (TEL) .... CSU
Channel Service Unit/Data Service Unit .... CSU/DSU
Channel Shifter (SAUS) .... CHAN SHFTR
Channel Signaling System No. 7 [*Computer science*] (TNIG) CSS7
Channel Spread Function (SAUS) .... CSF
Channel State Feedback (PDAA) .... CSFB
Channel Status .... CS
Channel Status Byte [*Computer science*] (IAA) .... CBS
Channel Status Byte (SAUS) .... CSB
Channel Status Field [*Electronics*] (ECII) .... CSF
Channel Status Indicator (SAUS) .... CSI
Channel Status Indicator [*Computer science*] (MDG) .... CST
Channel Status Register (SAUS) .... CSR
Channel Status Table [*Computer science*] (IAA) .... CST
Channel Status Word [*Computer science*] (BUR) .... CSW
Channel Stopping Diffusion (SAUS) .... CHANSTOP Diffusion
Channel SubSystem (SAUS) .... CSS
Channel Swimming Association [*British*] (EAIO) .... CSA
Channel Switching Unit (SAUS) .... CSU
Channel Synchronizer Unit [*Computer science*] .... CSU
Channel System Address Register (SAUS) .... CSAR
Channel Television [*Channel Islands network*] .... CTV
Channel Terminal Bay .... ChTB
Channel Terminating Unit (CCCA) .... CTU
Channel Terminator (HGAA) .... CT
Channel Testing Unit [*Telecommunications*] (OA) .... CTU
Channel Time Slot (SAUS) .... CTS
Channel to Channel Adapter [*Computer science*] (IBMDP) .... CTCA
Channel to Interference Ratio [*Telecommunications*] (OSI) .... C/I
Channel Traffic Control (IAA) .... CTC
Channel Translating Equipment [*Telecommunications*] (TEL) .... CTE
Channel Transmission and Engineering Activation .... CTEA
Channel Transport Model (EEVL) .... CHNTRN
Channel Tunnel [*Joint British-French project in English Channel*] .... CHUNNEL
[*The*] Channel Tunnel Association [*British*] .... CTA
Channel Tunnel Developments (SAUO) .... CTD
Channel Tunnel Group [*British*] .... CTG
Channel Tunnel Project (SAUS) .... Chunnel Project
Channel Tunnel Safety Authority (HEAS) .... CTSA
Channel Tunnel Study Group (SAUO) .... CTSG
Channel Unit Address (SAUS) .... CUA
Channel Unit Signal Controller (IAA) .... CUSC
Channel Verification Signal Generator .... CVSG
Channel Word (IAA) .... CW
Channel Work Area Expansion [*Computer science*] (ECII) .... CWAE
Channel-Activating Protease [*An enzyme*] .... CAP
Channel-Check Handler [*Japan*] (MCD) .... CCH
Channeled Arizona Information Network (SAUS) .... CHAIN
Channeled-Substrate-Planar [*Materials science*] .... CSP
Channel-Forming Integral Protein [*Biochemistry*] .... CHIP
Channeling and Diffusion in Ion Damage (SAUS) .... CHANDID
Channeling Effect Factor .... CEF
Channell Commercial [*NASDAQ symbol*] (SG) .... CHNL
Channell Commercial Corp. [*Associated Press*] (SAG) .... Channell
Channell Commercial Corp. [*NASDAQ symbol*] (SAG) .... CHNL
Channelled Narrow Stripe [*LASER diode technology*] (NITA) .... CNS
Channel/Port Aux Basques Public Library, Channel/Port Aux Basques, NF, Canada [*Library symbol*] [*Library of Congress*] (LCLS) .... CaNfCP
Channel/Port Aux Basques Public Library, Newfoundland [*Library symbol*] [*National Library of Canada*] (NLC) .... NFCP
Channels of English Literature [*A publication*] .... CEL
Channels Ratio .... CR
Channel-to-Channel (MCD) .... CTC
Channel-to-Channel Adapter [*Computer science*] .... CCA
Channel-to-Channel Adapter (SAUS) .... C-C Adapter

Channel-to-Drain Depletion (SAUS) ... CDD
Chanson [*Song*] [*Music*] ... CHANS
Chant du Monde [*Record label*] [*France*] ... CdM
Chantal Pharmaceutical [*NASDAQ symbol*] (TTSB) ... CHTL
Chantal Pharmaceutical Corp. [*Associated Press*] (SAG) ... Chantal
Chantal Pharmaceutical Corp. [*NASDAQ symbol*] (NQ) ... CHTL
Chanthaburi [*Thailand*] [*ICAO location identifier*] (ICLI) ... VTBC
Chantry Certificates [*British*] (ROG) ... CHANT CERT
Chanute Air Force Base [*Illinois*] (SAA) ... CAFB
Chanute Air Force Base [*Illinois*] (AAG) ... CHAFB
Chanute, KS [*Location identifier*] [*FAA*] (FAAL) ... CNU
Chanute, KS [*AM radio station call letters*] ... KKOY
Chanute, KS [*FM radio station call letters*] ... KKOY-FM
Chanute Technical Training Center [*Air Force*] ... CTTC
Chaos Computer Club (VERA) ... CCC
Cha-Pa [*Vietnam*] [*Geomagnetic observatory code*] ... CPA
Chapacura [*Bolivia*] [*ICAO location identifier*] (ICLI) ... SLCH
Chapais, PQ [*AM radio station call letters*] ... CFED
Chapalote [*Race of maize*] ... CHP
Chaparral [*Colombia*] [*Airport symbol*] (AD) ... CPL
Chaparral Airlines [*ICAO designator*] (FAAC) ... CPL
Chaparral Airlines [*ICAO designator*] (AD) ... FC
Chaparral Resources [*NASDAQ symbol*] (TTSB) ... CHAR
Chaparral Resources, Inc. [*Associated Press*] (SAG) ... Chapral
Chaparral Resources, Inc. [*NASDAQ symbol*] (NQ) ... CHAR
Chaparral Steel Co. [*Associated Press*] (SAG) ... ChpStl
Chaparral Steel Co. [*NYSE symbol*] (SPSG) ... CSM
Chaparral Vulcan [*Army*] ... CV
Chaparral/Forward Area Alert RADAR [*Military*] (RDA) ... CHAP/FAAR
Chapeau, PQ [*Television station call letters*] ... CIVP
Chapeco [*Brazil*] [*ICAO location identifier*] (ICLI) ... SBCH
Chapeco [*Brazil*] [*Airport symbol*] (OAG) ... XAP
Chapel ... C
Chapel ... CHAP
Chapel (SAUS) ... Chap
Chapel ... CPL
Chapel (VRA) ... cpl
Chapel Hill [*North Carolina*] [*Seismograph station code, US Geological Survey*] (SEIS) ... CEH
Chapel Hill [*North Carolina*] [*Seismograph station code, US Geological Survey*] [*Closed*] (SEIS) ... CHC
Chapel Hill, NC [*AM radio station call letters*] ... WCHL
Chapel Hill, NC [*AM radio station call letters*] ... WRTP
Chapel Hill, NC [*FM radio station call letters*] ... WUNC
Chapel Hill, NC [*Television station call letters*] ... WUNC-TV
Chapel Hill, NC [*FM radio station call letters*] ... WXYC
Chapel Hill Public Library, Chapel Hill, NC [*Library symbol*] [*Library of Congress*] (LCLS) ... NcCh
Chapel of Ease [*Church of England*] ... CHE
Chapel Resources, Inc. [*Vancouver Stock Exchange symbol*] ... CPL
Chapelco [*Argentina*] [*Airport symbol*] (OAG) ... CPC
Chapelry [*Geographical division*] [*British*] ... CHAP
Chapin Memorial Library, Myrtle Beach, SC [*Library symbol*] [*Library of Congress*] (LCLS) ... ScMb
Chapin Social Insight Test [*Psychology*] ... CSIT
Chaplain (AFM) ... CH
Chaplain (ADWA) ... Chap
Chaplain ... CHAP
Chaplain ... CHAPL
Chaplain ... CHPLN
Chaplain Area Representative [*Air Force*] ... CHAPAR
Chaplain Corps ... CHC
Chaplain Corps (SAUO) ... ChC
Chaplain Fund Accounting System (SAUO) ... CFAS
Chaplain General [*British*] (DAS) ... CGen
Chaplain of His Holiness ... CHH
Chaplain of the Fleet [*Navy*] [*British*] ... CF
Chaplain of the Fleet [*Navy*] [*British*] ... ChF
Chaplain of the Fleet [*Navy*] [*British*] ... CH of F
Chaplain of the Fleet [*Navy*] [*British*] ... C of F
Chaplain of the Forces (SAUS) ... CF
Chaplain of the Jewish Faith (SAUS) ... CJF
Chaplain of the Order of St. John of Jerusalem ... Chap St J
Chaplain of the Order of St. John of Jerusalem ... Ch St J
Chaplain of the Order of St. John of Jerusalem ... CHSTJJ
Chaplain of the Order of St Lazarus of Jerusalem [*Australia*] ... CHLJ
Chaplain of the Territorial Army [*British*] ... CTA
Chaplain Service Personnel [*Air Force*] ... CSP
Chaplain Territorial Army (SAUO) ... CTA
Chaplain to Foreign Immigrants [*British*] (DI) ... CFI
Chaplain to the Forces [*British*] ... CF
Chaplain to the Forces - Emergency Commission [*British*] ... CF(EC)
Chaplain to the Forces - Reserve of Officers [*British*] ... CF(R of O)
Chaplain to the Forces (Jewish) [*British*] ... CF(J)
Chaplain to the Forces (Territorial Army) [*British*] ... CF(TA)
Chaplain to the Territorial Forces (SAUO) ... CTF
Chaplain to the Territorial Forces [*British*] ... CTF
Chaplaincy Services Advisory Committee (SAUO) ... CSAC
Chaplain-General (SAUO) ... CG
Chaplain-General (SAUO) ... Chap-Gen
Chaplain-General to the Forces [*British*] (ROG) ... CHAP-GEN
Chaplain-in-Chief [*British*] ... CH-in-C
Chaplains' Aid Association [*Later, CAA/SEF*] (EA) ... CAA
Chaplains' Aid Association/Seminary Education Fund (EA) ... CAA/SEF
Chaplains Assistant (SAUS) ... Chap Asst
Chaplains' Relevance to the Emerging Drug Order [*Navy*] ... CREDO
Chapleau [*Canada*] [*Airport symbol*] (OAG) ... YLD
Chapleau, ON [*ICAO location identifier*] (ICLI) ... CYLD
Chapleau Public Library, Ontario [*Library symbol*] [*National Library of Canada*] (NLC) ... OCHAP
Chapleau Resources Ltd. [*Vancouver Stock Exchange symbol*] ... CHI
Chaplin [*Connecticut*] [*Seismograph station code, US Geological Survey*] [*Closed*] (SEIS) ... CPL
Chaplin General (SAUS) ... Chap Gen
Chapman [*One who sells in a cheaping or market*] [*Said to be origin of "chap," meaning "fellow"*] ... CHAP
Chapman & Cutter, Law Library, Chicago, IL [*Library symbol*] [*Library of Congress*] (LCLS) ... ICChC
Chapman & Hall (SAUO) ... ISBN 0-412
Chapman Chemical Co., Memphis, TN [*Library symbol*] [*Library of Congress*] (LCLS) ... TMCC
Chapman College Library, Orange, CA [*OCLC symbol*] (OCLC) ... CCX
Chapman College, Orange, CA [*Library symbol*] [*Library of Congress*] (LCLS) ... COrC
Chapman Freeborn [*British*] [*FAA designator*] (FAAC) ... CFO
Chapman. Practice of the Court of King's Bench [*2nd ed.*] [*1831*] [*A publication*] (DLA) ... Cha Pr
Chapman Research Station (SAUO) ... CRS
Chapman University (GAGS) ... Chapman U
Chapman-Jouquet [*Pressures*] (MCD) ... CJ
Chapman's Addenda [*A publication*] (DLA) ... Cha Add
Chappaqua Library, Chappaqua, NY [*Library symbol*] [*Library of Congress*] (LCLS) ... NChap
Chappell [*Record label*] [*Great Britain*] ... Chap
Chappell and Shoard. Copyright [*1863*] [*A publication*] (DLA) ... Chap & Sh
Chappell, NE [*Location identifier*] [*FAA*] (FAAL) ... CNP
Chappel-Perry Medium [*Microbiology*] ... CP
Chapter ... C
Chapter (AAGC) ... Ch
Chapter (WDMC) ... ch
Chapter ... CH
Chapter (AFM) ... CHAP
Chapter (WDMC) ... chap
Chapter (PROS) ... Chap
chapter (SAUO) ... chap
Chapter (VRA) ... chpt
Chapter ... CHPTR
Chapter ... CP
Chapter Director ... CD
Chapter House [*British*] (ROG) ... CH
Chapter House [*British*] (ROG) ... CHAP HO
Chapter House (VRA) ... chpt hs
Chapter Illuminators of Sweden [*Freemasonry*] (ROG) ... CHAP I of S
Chapter Liaison Officer ... CLO
Chapter Relations Committee [*American Library Association*] ... CRC
Chapters (WGA) ... CC
Chapters of Instruction [*Freemasonry*] (ROG) ... CI
Chara Corallina Virus [*Plant pathology*] ... CCV
Charabanc [*Bus used for sightseeing trips*] [*Slang*] [*British*] (DSUE) ... CHARA
Characato [*Formerly, Arequipa*] [*Peru*] [*Later, FRD*] [*Geomagnetic observatory code*] ... ARE
Character (BUR) ... C
Character [*Computer science*] (BUR) ... CH
Character ... CHAR
Character [*or Characteristic*] [*Computer science*] (IAA) ... CHARAC
Character (BUR) ... CHR
Character (SAUS) ... Chr
Character Address Module [*Computer science*] (PDAA) ... CAM
Character Alignment (SAUS) ... CA
Character Allocated Transfer Channel [*Computer science*] (IAA) ... CATCH
Character and Pattern Telephone Access Information Network (RALS) ... CAPTAIN
Character and Pattern Telephone Access Information Network System [*Viewdata system*] [*Japan*] ... CAPTAINS
Character Assemble/Disassemble ... CAD
Character Assembler and Distributor (SAUS) ... CAD
Character Assignment (SAUS) ... CA
Character Assignment Table [*Computer science*] (IAA) ... CAT
Character Background Generator [*Television*] (WDMC) ... Dubner CBG
Character Bitmap Distribution Format [*Computer science*] (VERA) ... CBDF
Character Block Transfer (BYTE) ... CBLT
Character Buffer Unit [*Computer science*] (ECII) ... CBU
Character, Capacity, Capital [*Accounting*] ... 3C's
Character, Capacity, Capital, Collateral, and Conditions [*Credit evaluation*] [*Banking*] ... 5C's
Character Change (SAUS) ... CC
Character Code Translation (SAUS) ... CCT
Character Coding (SAUS) ... CC
Character Constant (SAUS) ... CC
Character Control Block [*Computer science*] (IBMDP) ... CCB
Character Controlled Protocol (HGAA) ... CCP
Character Count [*Typography*] ... CC
Character Count Protocol (HGAA) ... CCP
Character Counter (SAUS) ... CC
Character Data (SAUS) ... CDATA
Character Data Representation Architecture [*Computer science*] (VERA) ... CDRA
Character Delete [*Computer science*] (WDMC) ... char del
Character Density (SAUS) ... CD
Character Disorder Sign [*Psychology*] ... CdS
Character Display (SAUS) ... Ch Dis

Character Early (SAUS) .... Ch E
Character Education Inquiry (DB) .... CEI
Character Education Institute (EA) .... CEI
Character Education Partnership [*An association*] .... CEP
Character Error Rate (CCCA) .... CER
Character Error Rate Test .... CERT
Character Error Rate Tester (or Testing) (SAUS) .... CERT
Character Fill (SAUS) .... CF
Character Form for the Representation and Exchange of Data (SAUS) .... CREX
Character Generation Module Identifier (SAUS) .... CGMID
Character Generator [*Telecommunications*] .... CG
Character Generator (SAUS) .... CGEN
Character Generator (SAUS) .... CHARGEN
Character Generator [*Computer science*] (NITA) .... CHRGN
Character Generator Read Only Memory [*Computer science*] .... CGROM
Character Guidance [*Army*] (AABC) .... CHARGUID
Character Identifier (SAUS) .... CID
Character Imaging System (SAUS) .... CIS
Character Instruction Set (IEEE) .... CIS
Character Large Object (SAUS) .... CLOB
Character Late (SAUS) .... Ch L
Character Manipulation Procedures .... CHAMP
Character Mode (SAUS) .... CHARM
Character Mode Communications Adapter .... CMCA
Character Multiplexer [*Telecommunications*] .... CMX
Character Organized Memory (SAUS) .... COM
Character Organized Store (SAUS) .... COS
Character Orientated Windows [*Computer science*] (VERA) .... COW
Character per Column (SAUS) .... CPC
Character Position in Frame .... CPIF
Character Printer [*Computer science*] .... CP
Character Reader [*Computer science*] (IAA) .... CR
Character Reading Device (SAUS) .... CRD
Character Recognition (SAUS) .... CR
Character Recognition Circuit (IAA) .... CRC
Character Recognition Logic (SAUS) .... CRL
Character Recognition System (SAUS) .... CRS
Character Recognition Terminal (SAUS) .... CRT
Character Register (SAUS) .... Ch R
Character Register .... CHR
Character Research Project (SAUO) .... CRP
Character Role Playing Game (SAUS) .... CRPG
Character Scan Command [*Computer science*] .... CSCN
Character Scan or Alternate [*Computer science*] .... CSA
Character Scan or Fail [*Computer science*] .... CSF
Character Selection (SAUS) .... CS
Character Sensing (SAUS) .... CS
Character Sensing System (SAUS) .... CSS
Character Sequence (SAUS) .... CS
Character Sequence Detector (MCD) .... CSD
Character Set Computer Development .... CSCD
Character Shape Player (PCM) .... CSP
Character Shape Recorder (SAUS) .... CSR
Character Speed (SAUS) .... CS
Character Start-Stop .... CSS
Character String Scanner [*Computer program*] .... CSS
Character To Decimal (SAUS) C2D
Character To Hexadecimal (SAUS) C2X
Character Translate Table (SAUS) .... CTT
Character Translation Table [*Computer science*] (VERA) .... CTT
Character Translator (SAUS) .... CT
Character User Interface [*Computer science*] (VERA) .... CUI
Character Variable (SAUS) CV
Character Width Table [*Computer science*] (VERA) .... CWT
Character-Based User Interface [*Computer science*] .... CUI
Character/Common User Interface (SAUS) .... CUI
Character-Error Correcting Convolutional Self-Orthogonal Code (PDAA) .... CCSOC
Characteres [*of Theophrastus*] [*Classical studies*] (OCD) .... Char
Character-Generated [*Refers to electronically produced text*] (WDMC) .... CG
Character-Handling Interface Processor (SAUS) .... CHIP
Characteristic (SAUS) .... CH
Characteristic (ADWA) .... char
Characteristic (AABC) .... CHAR
Characteristic (MSA) .... CHRST
Characteristic (SAUS) .... Chrst
Characteristic (SAUS) .... Chrtc
Characteristic Distortion Compensation [*Telecommunications*] (TEL) .... CDC
Characteristic Equation System (SAUS) .... CES
Characteristic Event Hypothesis [*For earthquake occurence*] .... CEH
Characteristic Frequencies (SAUS) .... CFs
Characteristic Frequency [*Acoustics*] .... CF
Characteristic Function Estimator .... CFE
Characteristic Impedance (IDOE) .... Z
Characteristic Independence CI
Characteristic Information (SAUS) .... CHIN
Characteristic Instants of Restitution [*Telecommunications*] (OA) .... CIR
Characteristic Item Description (MCD) .... CID
Characteristic Loss Spectroscopy .... CLS
Characteristic Orange Luminescence (AAEL) .... COL
Characteristic Relief .... CR
Characteristic Slope .... CS
Characteristic Standard .... CS
Characteristic Statistical Value .... CSV
Characteristic Storage and Retrieval (EDAC) .... CSAR
Characteristics and Requirements of Information Systems based on Traffic Data in an Integrated Network (SAUO) .... CHRISTINE
Characteristics of Business Owners [*Bureau of the Census*] (GFGA) .... CBO
Characteristics of Business Owners survey (SAUS) .... CBO
Characteristics of Materials (KSC) .... COMAT
Characteristics of Transportation Resources [*Environmental science*] (COE) .... CHSTR
Characteristics of Transportation Resources File .... CHSTR
Characteristics of Transportation Resources Report [*Environmental science*] (COE) .... CHSTREP
Characteristics of Urban Transportation Demand (MCD) .... CUTD
Characteristics Properties Code [*NASA*] (NASA) .... CPC
Characterization and Assessment Division [*Environmental Protection Agency*] (GFGA) .... CAD
Characterization of Neurospora Circadian Rhythms (SAUS) .... CNCR
Character-Mode Data Terminal Equipment [*Computer science*] (PDAA) .... C-DTE
Character-Oriented Input-Output Processor [*Computer science*] (IAA) .... CHIO
Character-Oriented Message (RDA) .... COM
Character-Oriented Protocol [*Computer science*] (VERA) .... COP
Character-Oriented User Interface (SAUS) .... CUI
Characters (SAUS) .... CHARs
Characters in 19th Century Literature [*A publication*] .... CNCL
Characters in Twentieth-Century Literature [*A publication*] .... CTCL
Characters per Column [*Typesetting*] .... CPC
Characters per Hour [*Computer science*] .... CPH
Characters Per Hour (WDMC) .... cph
Characters per Inch [*Computer science*] (CMD) .... CHPI
Characters per Inch [*Typesetting*] .... CPI
Characters Per Inch [*Typesetting*] (WDMC) .... cpi
Characters Per Line [*Typesetting*] (WDMC) .... cpl
Characters per Line [*Typesetting*] .... CPL
Characters per Millimeter [*Typesetting*] (IAA) .... CPMM
Characters per Minute [*Computer science*] .... CPM
Characters Per Minute [*Typesetting*] (WDMC) .... cpm
Characters Per Pica [*Typesetting*] (WDMC) .... CPP
Characters per Second [*Computer science*] (IAA) .... CHARSEC
Characters per Second [*Computer science*] (CMD) .... CHPS
Characters per Second [*Computer science*] (IAA) .... CHS
Characters per Second [*Computer science*] (IAA) .... CHSEC
Characters per Second [*Computer science*] .... CPS
Characters Per Second [*Computer science*] (WDMC) .... cps
Character-to-Date [*Microsoft Corp. FoxPro function*] (PCM) .... CTOD
Charactron Tube [*Electronics*] .... CHT
Charactron Tube [*Electronics*] .... CRT
Charagua [*Bolivia*] [*ICAO location identifier*] (ICLI) .... SLCG
Charan Industries, Inc. [*Toronto Stock Exchange symbol*] .... CHN
Charana [*Bolivia*] [*ICAO location identifier*] (ICLI) .... SLCN
Charbonneau Connection (EA) CC
Charburjak [*Afghanistan*] [*ICAO location identifier*] (ICLI) .... OACB
Charcoal [*Automotive advertising*] .... CH
Charcoal .... CHAR
Charcoal (SAUS) .... CharC
Charcoal (VRA) .... chl
Charcoal .... CHRCL
Charcoal Accumulation Rate [*Ecology*] .... CHAR
Charcoal Canister (GNE) CC
Charcoal Hemoperfusion [*Medicine*] .... CH
Charcoal Hemoperfusion (DB) .... CHP
Charcoal Inhalation Tester (PDAA) .... CIT
Charcoal, Ink, Oil, Pencil, and Watercolor [*Acronym is used as title of 1931 volume containing art works by e.e. cummings*] .... CIOPW
Charcoal Treated .... CT
Charcoal Viral Transport [*Medium*] [*Microbiology*] .... CVTR
Charcoal Yeast Extract [*Agar medium*] [*Microbiology*] .... CYE
Charcot Joint (MELL) .... CJ
Charcot-Erb [*Disease*] [*Medicine*] (DB) .... CE
Charcot-Marie Tooth 1B [*Medicine*] CMT1B
Charcot-Marie-Tooth [*Atrophy*] [*Medicine*] .... CMT
Charcot-Marie-Tooth Association (EA) .... CMTA
Charcot-Marie-Tooth Disease [*Medicine*] (DB) .... CMTD
Charcot-Marie-Tooth International (EA) .... CMTI
Charcot-Marie-Tooth Syndrome [*Medicine*] (DMAA) .... CMTS
Charcot-Marie-Tooth, X-Linked [*Medicine*] [*Syndrome*] (DMAA) .... CMTX
Charcot-Weiss-Baker [*Syndrome*] [*Medicine*] (DB) .... CWB
Chardon du Dol et de la Fraude [*A publication*] (DLA) .... Chard
Chardon, OH [*Location identifier*] [*FAA*] (FAAL) .... CXR
Chardon, OH [*AM radio station call letters*] .... WATJ
Chardonnay (ADWA) .... chard
Charette, Fortier, Hawey, Touche, Ross, Centre de Documentation, Montreal, PQ, Canada [*Library symbol*] [*Library of Congress*] (LCLS) .... CaQMCFH
Charge (ROG) C
Charge .... CGE
Charge (SAUS) .... Char
Charge (KSC) .... CHG
Charge (WDAA) .... chg
Charge .... CHGE
Charge .... CHRG
Charge Account Bankers Association [*Later, ABA*] .... CABA
Charge Air-Temperature Sensor [*Automotive engineering*] .... CAS
Charge Amplifier (NRCH) .... CA
Charge and Discharge [*Environmental science*] (COE) .... C&D
Charge Capacitance Probe (NASA) .... CCP
Charge Composition Explorer [*Spacecraft*] .... CCE
Charge Conjugation [*Atomic physics*] C

Charge Conjugation - Parity - Time-Reversal [*Theorem*] [*Atomic physics*] ...... CPT
Charge Control Ring (SAUS) .... CyR
Charge Controlled Negative Capacitance (SAUS) .... CCNC
Charge Conveyor [*Electronics*] (EECA) CC
Charge Coupled (IAA) CC
Charge Coupled Diode Array [*Liquid chromatography*] .... CCDA
Charge Coupled Imager (SAUS) CCI
Charge Coupled Ring (SAUS) .... CyR
Charge Crueze (SAUS) CC
Charge d'Affaires [*Foreign Service*] .... CA
Charge d'Affaires [*Foreign Service*] .... CHG
Charge Data System [*Equal Employment Opportunity Commission*] (GFGA) .... CDS
Charge, Element and Isotope Analysis System (SAUS) .... CELIAS
Charge Exchange .... CEX
Charge Exchange Cross Section .... CECS
Charge Exchange Excitations [*Physics*] .... CXE
Charge Exchange Neutralo Analyzer (MCD) .... CENA
Charge for Service .... CS
Charge Generation Layer (MCD) .... CGL
Charge Imaging Matrix [*Electronics*] .... CIM
Charge Injected Device Imager (SAUS) .... CID Imager
Charge Injection Device Module (SAUS) .... CID Module
Charge Injection Devices (SAUS) .... CIDs
Charge Injection Transistor (SAUS) .... CHINT
Charge Injection Transistor Memory [*Electronics*] (NITA) .... CITM
Charge Linear Cutting (SAUS) CLC
Charge Material Allocation Processor .... CMAP
Charge Memory (SAUS) .... CM
Charge Motion Oriented Process .... CMOP
Charge Number (ACAE) .... CN
Charge Number Grouping (MCD) .... CNG
Charge Number of a Cell Reaction [*Symbol*] [*Electrochemistry*] .... z
Charge Nurse [*Medicine*] .... CN
charge of electron (SAUS) .... e
charge of positron (SAUS) .... e
Charge of Quarters [*Army*] .... CQ
Charge on Delivery (SAUS) .... COD
Charge One Site Only (SAUS) .... COSO
Charge Paid (SAUS) .... Cge Pd
Charge Parity [*Atomic physics*] .... CP
Charge, Parity, and Time Coordinates [*Physics*] .... CPT
Charge Priming Device [*Video technology*] .... CPD
Charge Pumping Logic (IAA) .... CPL
Charge Routing Network (IAA) .... CRN
Charge Sensitive Amplifier .... CSA
Charge Spotting Bomb Unit .... CXU
Charge Storage Junction Field Effect Transistor (IAA) .... CSJFET
Charge Television (SAUS) .... Chargtel
Charge Temperature (SAUS) .... CH Temp
Charge Time-of-Flight (ADWA) .... CTOF
Charge Transfer Efficiency [*In photodetectors*] .... CTE
Charge Transfer Inefficiency [*in Photodetectors*] (IAA) .... CTI
Charge Transfer Light Modulator [*Instrumentation*] .... CTLM
Charge Transfer Spectrum (SAUS) .... CTS
Charge Transfer State (SAUS) .... CTS
Charge Transforming Operator (IEEE) .... CTO
Charge Transforming Parameter (IEEE) .... CTP
Charge Transport Layer (MCD) .... CTL
Chargeable Downtime [*Navy*] .... CDT
Chargeable Time (DGA) .... CT
Chargeable Time Clock [*Telecommunications*] (NITA) .... CTC
Chargeable to Accidents (MCD) .... CA
Chargeable to Crew (MCD) CC
Chargeable to Hardware .... CH
Chargeable to Manuals (MCD) .... CM
Chargeable to Support Equipment (MCD) .... CSE
Charge-Air Cooling [*Automotive engineering*] .... CAC
Charge-Amplified Sample and Hold (PDAA) .... CASH
Charge-Coupled Area Image Sensor (SAUS) .... CCAIS
Charge-Coupled Area Imaging Device (PDAA) .... CCAID
Charge-Coupled Device [*Data storage device*] .... CCD
Charge-Coupled Imager CCI
Charge-Coupled Infrared Information Device (PDAA) .... CCIRID
Charge-Coupled Line-Imaging Device (SAUS) .... CCLID
Charge-Coupled Memories (SAUS) .... CCMs
Charge-Coupled Memory [*Computer science*] (IAA) .... CCM
Charge-Coupled Photodiode (CIST) .... CCPD
Charge-Coupled Photodiode Array .... CCPD
Charge-Coupled Random Access Memory (SAUS) C2RAM
Charge-Coupled Random Access Memory (SAUS) C3RAM
Charged (ADWA) .... chgd
Charged (ROG) .... CHGD
Charged Coupled Device Detector (ACAE) .... CCDD
Charged Current [*Physics*] CC
Charged Droplet Scrubber .... CDS
Charged in Full (WDAA) .... CIF
Charged Liquid Cluster Beam (ROAS) .... CLCB
Charged Particle Activation .... CPA
Charged Particle Activation Analysis [*Analytical chemistry*] .... CPAA
Charged Particle Analysis (AAEL) .... CPA
Charged Particle Analyzer .... CPA
Charged Particle Beam [*Weapon*] [*DoD*] .... CPB
Charged Particle Beam Weapon [*Computer science*] (PDAA) .... CPBW
Charged Particle Cross-section (SAUS) .... CPX
Charged Particle Electrostatic Thruster .... CPET

Charged Particle Equilibrium (DEN) .... CPE
Charged Particle Lunar Environment Experiment [*NASA*] .... CPLEE
Charged Particle Nuclear Data (SAUS) .... CPND
Charged Particle Telescope .... CPT
Charged Particles Information Center [*ORNL*] .... CPIC
Charged Particles Research Laboratory (SAUO) .... CPRL
Charged Pigment Xerography (IEEE) .... CPX
Charged Tape Detection [*Fuel-failure monitor*] [*Nuclear energy*] (NRCH) .... CTD
Charged-Drop Precipitator (PDAA) .... CDP
Charge-Density Wave [*Physics*] .... CDW
Charge/Discharge (IAA) .... CD
Charge/Discharge (SAUS) .... C/D
Charge-exchange Scattering (SAUS) .... CS
Charge-Flow Transistor (PDAA) .... CFT
Charge-Free Anticontamination System .... CFAS
Charge-Induced Voltage Alteration [*Electronics*] .... CIVA
Charge-Injected (or Injection Device) (SAUS) .... CID
Charge-Injection Device [*Electronics*] .... CID
Charger (MSA) .... CHGR
Charger Battery Relay (MCD) .... CBR
Charger Battery Relay Module (SAUS) .... CBRM
Charger Resources Ltd. [*Vancouver Stock Exchange symbol*] .... CHJ
Charger-Battery-Regulator Module [*NASA*] .... CBRM
Charge-Recombination [*Physical chemistry*] .... CR
Charges (EBF) .... Chgs
Charges .... CHGS
Charges Collect [*Business term*] CC
Charges Forward (DS) .... Ch Fwd
Charges Forward (SAUS) .... Ch/Fwd
Charges Prepaid (SAUS) .... Ch/Ppd
Charges Prepaid (WDAA) .... CH PPD
Charges Prepaid (EBF) .... Ch ppd
Charge-Separation [*Physical chemistry*] .... CS
Charge-Sweep Device (SAUS) .... CSD
Charge-Transfer [*Intermolecular electron transfer*] .... CT
Charge-Transfer Device [*Electronics*] .... CTD
Charge-Transfer Photography .... CTP
Charge-Transfer Spectrum .... CTS
Charge-Voltage (SAUS) .... Q-V
Charging (SAUS) .... CHG
Charging (SAUS) .... CRG
Charging Electrical Effects Analyzer (MCD) .... CEEA
Charging Message (SAUS) .... CHG Message
Charging Order (DCTA) .... CO
Charging Pump (IEEE) .... CHGP
Charging Pump (NRCH) .... CP
Charging Resistor (SAUS) .... CR
Charing Cross, Euston & Highgate (Underground) Railway [*British*]
(ROG) .... CCE & HR
Charing Cross Station [*England*] (ROG) CX
Charismatic Renewal Services (EA) .... CRS
Charitable .... CHRTBL
Charitable / Employee Stock Ownership Plan [*Tax plan*] (MHDW) .... CHEPSOP
Charitable Lead Trust .... CLT
Charitable Organizations of the US [*A publication*] .... COUS
Charitable Remainder Annuity Trust (NFD) .... CRAT
Charitable Remainder Trust .... CRT
Charitable Remainder Unitrust (NFD) .... CRUT
Charitable Trust for Vietnam War Art (EA) .... CTVWA
Charitable/Employee Stock Ownership Plan [*Tax plan*] .... CHESOP
Charities Aid Foundation [*Information service or system*] (IID) .... CAF
Charities Aid Fund [*British*] .... CAF
Charities Aid Fund (SAUO) .... CAF
Charities Deposit Fund [*Finance*] [*British*] .... CDF
Charities Information Bureaux [*British*] (CB) .... CIB
Charities Official Investment Fund [*Finance*] [*British*] .... COIF
Chariton Herald-Patriot, Chariton, IA [*Library symbol*] [*Library of Congress*]
(LCLS) .... IaChHP
Chariton, IA [*Location identifier*] [*FAA*] (FAAL) .... CNC
Chariton, IA [*FM radio station call letters*] .... KELR
Chariton Leader, Chariton, IA [*Library symbol*] [*Library of Congress*]
(LCLS) .... IaChL
Charity .... CHAR
Charity .... CHY
Charity Christmas Card Council [*British*] (DI) CCCC
Charity Commission [*British*] CC
Charity Commission (SAUO) CC
Charity Commissioners for England and Wales (SAUO) .... CCEW
[*The*] Charity Forum [*British*] (EAIO) .... TCF
Charity Organization Society [*British*] .... COS
Charity Organization Society (SAUO) .... COS
Charlemagne Resources [*Vancouver Stock Exchange symbol*] .... CHG
Charleroi, PA [*AM radio station call letters*] .... WESA
Charleroi, PA [*FM radio station call letters*] .... WESA-FM
Charleroi, PA [*FM radio station call letters*] (BROA) .... WZKT-FM
Charleroi/Gosselies [*Belgium*] [*ICAO location identifier*] (ICLI) .... EBCI
Charles A. Janeway Child Health Centre, St. John's, NF, Canada [*Library symbol*] [*Library of Congress*] (LCLS) .... CaNfSCJ
Charles A. Lindbergh Association [*Defunct*] (EA) .... CALA
Charles A. Lindbergh Collectors Club (EA) .... CALCC
Charles A. Lindbergh Collectors Club (EA) LCC
Charles A. Lindbergh Fund [*An association*] (EA) .... CALF
Charles A. Ransom Public Library, Plainwell, MI [*Library symbol*] [*Library of Congress*] (LCLS) .... MiPl
Charles Babbage Foundation (RALS) .... CBF

Charles Babbage Institute (CIST) .... CBI
Charles Babbage Institute for the History of Information Processing (EA).... CBI
Charles Bonnet Syndrome (SAUS) .... CBS
Charles Brown & Co., Inc. (SAUO) .... CBC
Charles Bruning Reproduction Processes .... CB
Charles Camsell Hospital, Peter Wilcock Library, Edmonton, AB, Canada
[Library symbol] [Library of Congress] (LCLS) .... CaAECCH
Charles City, IA [Location identifier] [FAA] (FAAL) .... CCY
Charles City, IA [AM radio station call letters] .... KCHA
Charles City, IA [FM radio station call letters] .... KCHA-FM
Charles City Press, Charles City, IA [Library symbol] [Library of Congress]
(LCLS) .... IaChcP
Charles City Public Library, Charles City, IA [Library symbol] [Library of
Congress] (LCLS) .... IaChc
Charles City, VA [FM radio station call letters] (BROA) .... WAUQ-FM
Charles City Western Railway Co. [AAR code] .... CCW
Charles County Community College [La Plata, MD] CCCC
Charles County Community College, La Plata, MD [Library symbol] [Library
of Congress] (LCLS) .... MdLapC
Charles Crane Memorial Library, University of British Columbia,
Vancouver, British Columbia [Library symbol] [National Library of
Canada] (NLC) .... BVAUCC
Charles Curtis [Genotype of Phlox paniculata] C
Charles Curtis Memorial Hospital, International Grenfell Association, St.
Anthony, Newfoundland [Library symbol] [National Library of Canada]
(NLC) .... NFSAIC
Charles Curtis Memorial Hospital, International Grenfell Association, St.
Anthony, NF, Canada [Library symbol] [Library of Congress]
(LCLS) .... CaNfSaIC
Charles Darwin Foundation for the Galapagos Islands (SAUO) .... CDFGI
Charles Darwin Foundation Research Station (SAUO) .... CDFRS
Charles Darwin Foundation Research Station, Academy Bay, Santa Cruz,
Gal pagos (SAUS) .... CDFRS
Charles Darwin Research Station [Santa Cruz, Galapagos Islands] .... CDRS
Charles De Gaulle Airport [France] .... CDG
Charles E. Drew Postgraduate Medical School (SAUS) .... Drew
Charles E. Frosst & Co., Montreal, PQ, Canada [Library symbol] [Library of
Congress] (LCLS) .... CaQMCF
Charles E. Merriam Center for Public Administration, Merriam Center
Library, Chicago, IL [Library symbol] [Library of Congress] .... ICMer
Charles E. Schwarting Elementary School, Massapequa, NY [Library
symbol] [Library of Congress] (LCLS) .... NMassSE
Charles E. Stevens American Atheist Library and Archives (SAUS) ...... CESAALA
Charles E. Stevens American Atheist Library and Archives, Inc., Austin
(SAUS) .... TxAuA
Charles E. Stevens American Atheist Library and Archives, Inc., Austin, TX
[Library symbol] [Library of Congress] (LCLS) .... TxAuA
Charles E Turtles books (SAUS) .... Tut Books
Charles Edison Memorial Youth Fund [Later, FAS] (EA) .... CEMYF
Charles Evans Hughes High School (SAUS) .... CEHHS
Charles F. Kettering Foundation, Dayton, OH [OCLC symbol] (OCLC) .... OKK
Charles F. Kettering Foundation, Kettering, OH [Library symbol] [Library of
Congress] (LCLS) .... OKetK
Charles F. Kettering Foundation, Research Laboratory Library, Yellow
Springs, OH [Library symbol] [Library of Congress] (LCLS) .... OYesK
Charles, [J. W.] Financial Services [Associated Press] (SAG) .... CharlsFS
Charles, [J. W.] Financial Services [NASDAQ symbol] (SAG) .... KORP
Charles G. Chandler .... CGC
Charles H. Roth High School Library, Henrietta, NY [OCLC symbol]
(OCLC) .... RVW
Charles H. Stone Memorial Library, Pilot Mountain, NC [Library symbol]
[Library of Congress] (LCLS) .... NcPm
Charles H. Taylor Memorial Library, Hampton, VA [Library symbol] [Library of
Congress] (LCLS) .... ViHa
Charles Homer Haskins Society (EA) .... CHHS
Charles Howard & Associates, Winnipeg, Manitoba [Library symbol]
[National Library of Canada] (NLC) .... MWCHA
Charles Howard & Associates, Winnipeg, MB, Canada [Library symbol]
[Library of Congress] (LCLS) .... CaMWCHA
Charles Ives Society (EA) .... CIS
Charles J. Colgan & Associates, Inc. [FAA designator] (FAAC) .... CJC
Charles (JW) Finl Svcs [NASDAQ symbol] (TTSB) .... KORP
Charles Lamb Society [British] .... CLS
Charles Lamb Society (SAUO) .... CLS
Charles Lathrop Pack Forestry Foundation (SAUO) .... CLPFF
Charles Lindbergh Elementary School, Little Falls, MN [Library symbol]
[Library of Congress] (LCLS) .... MnLfCL
Charles M. Russell National Wildlife Range (SAUS) .... CMRNWR
Charles M. Shields Centennial Library, South Porcupine, Ontario [Library
symbol] [National Library of Canada] (BIB) .... OSPCS
Charles Patterson Van Pelt Library (SAUS) .... CPVPL
Charles Pfizer & Co. [Research code symbol] .... CP
Charles Rennie Mackintosh Society (EAIO) .... CRMS
Charles River Associates Library, Boston, MA [OCLC symbol] (OCLC) .... CRA
Charles River Breeding Laboratories .... CRBL
Charles River Data Systems, Inc. (NITA) .... CRDS
Charles River Labs. [NYSE symbol] .... CRL
Charles S. Peirce Society (EA) .... CPS
Charles Scribners Sons (SAUS) .... Scribner
Charles Sheldon National Antelope Refuge (SAUS) .... CSNAR
Charles Simkins and Rachel Hawthorne Family Association (EA) .... CSRHFA
Charles Stark Draper Laboratory (SAUS) .... CSDL
Charles Stark Draper Laboratory, Inc. [MIT] [Research center] (NASA) .... CSDL
Charles Stark Draper Laboratory, Inc., Technical Information Center,
Cambridge, MA [Library symbol] [Library of Congress] (LCLS) .... MCCSD

Charles Stewart Mott Community College [Formerly, Genesee Community
College] [Flint, MI] .... CSMCC
Charles Stuart Calverley [19th-century British parodist] .... CSC
Charles Sturt University - Mitchell at Bathurst [Australia] .... CSU-MB
Charles Sturt University - Murray, at Albury Wodonga [Australia] .... CSU-MAW
Charles Town, WV [AM radio station call letters] (BROA) .... WMRE
Charles Town, WV [AM radio station call letters] .... WXVA
Charles Town, WV [FM radio station call letters] .... WXVA-FM
Charles University University of Prague (SAUO) .... Charl
Charles Williams Society (SAUO) .... CWRU
Charles Williams Society [British] (EAIO) .... CWS
Charlesbourg [Quebec] [Seismograph station code, US Geological Survey]
(SEIS) .... CHQ
Charleston [Diocesan abbreviation] [South Carolina] (TOCD) .... CHR
Charleston [South Carolina] [Airport symbol] .... CHS
Charleston [West Virginia] [Airport symbol] (AD) .... CHW
Charleston [West Virginia] [Airport symbol] (OAG) .... CRW
Charleston Air Force Base [South Carolina] .... CAFB
Charleston Air Force Base (SAUO) .... ChastAFB
Charleston & Western Carolina Railway Co. [Seaboard Coast Line
Railroad] .... C & WC
Charleston & Western Carolina Railway Co. [Seaboard Coast Line Railroad]
[AAR code] .... CWC
Charleston Area Cooperative Film Library, Charleston, IL [Library symbol]
[Library of Congress] (LCLS) .... ICharF
Charleston Army Depot [South Carolina] [Closed] (AABC) .... CHAD
Charleston Carnegie Public Library, Charleston, IL [Library symbol] [Library
of Congress] (LCLS) .... IChar
Charleston Community Memorial Hospital, Charleston, IL [Library symbol]
[Library of Congress] (LCLS) .... ICharH
Charleston Community Unit School District, Charleston, IL [Library symbol]
[Library of Congress] (LCLS) .... ICarSD
Charleston Community Unit School District, Charleston, IL [Library symbol]
[Library of Congress] (LCLS) .... ICharSD
Charleston County Library, Charleston (SAUS) .... ScCF
Charleston County Library, Charleston, SC [Library symbol] [Library of
Congress] (LCLS) .... ScCF
Charleston Diocesan Archives, Roman Catholic Church, Charleston, SC
[Library symbol] [Library of Congress] (LCLS) .... ScCRC
Charleston General Hospital, Charleston, WV [Library symbol] [Library of
Congress] (LCLS) .... WvCGH
Charleston, IL [AM radio station call letters] .... WEIC
Charleston, IL [FM radio station call letters] .... WEIU
Charleston, IL [Television station call letters] .... WEIU-TV
Charleston, IL [FM radio station call letters] .... WHQQ
Charleston Library Society, Charleston, SC [Library symbol] [Library of
Congress] (LCLS) .... ScC
Charleston, MO [Location identifier] [FAA] (FAAL) .... CHQ
Charleston, MO [AM radio station call letters] .... KCHR
Charleston, MO [FM radio station call letters] .... KWKZ
Charleston, MS [FM radio station call letters] .... WTGY
Charleston Museum [South Carolina] .... CHM
Charleston Museum Library, Charleston (SAUS) .... ScCMu
Charleston Museum Library, Charleston, SC [Library symbol] [Library of
Congress] (LCLS) .... ScCMu
Charleston Naval Shipyard [South Carolina] (DNAB) .... CHANSY
Charleston Naval Shipyard [South Carolina] .... CHASNAVSHIPY
Charleston Naval Shipyard [South Carolina] .... CHNSY
Charleston Naval Shipyard (DOGT) .... CNS
Charleston Naval Shipyard [South Carolina] .... CNSY
Charleston Naval Shipyard [South Carolina] .... CNSYD
Charleston Naval Station [South Carolina] .... CNAVSTA
Charleston Naval Weapons Annex [South Carolina] .... CNWA
Charleston, NC [AM radio station call letters] .... WQSC
Charleston Public Library (SAUS) .... CPL
Charleston Resources [Vancouver Stock Exchange symbol] .... CNJ
Charleston, SC [Location identifier] [FAA] (FAAL) CCI
Charleston, SC [Location identifier] [FAA] (FAAL) .... JZI
Charleston, SC [Location identifier] [FAA] (FAAL) .... NAO
Charleston, SC [FM radio station call letters] (BROA) .... WALC-FM
Charleston, SC [Television station call letters] (RBYB) .... WBNU
Charleston, SC [Television station call letters] .... WCBD
Charleston, SC [Television station call letters] .... WCIV
Charleston, SC [Television station call letters] .... WCSC
Charleston, SC [FM radio station call letters] .... WEZL
Charleston, SC [FM radio station call letters] .... WFCH
Charleston, SC [Television station call letters] .... WITV
Charleston, SC [FM radio station call letters] (RBYB) .... WJZK-FM
Charleston, SC [FM radio station call letters] (BROA) .... WLLC-FM
Charleston, SC [Television station call letters] (BROA) .... WMMP
Charleston, SC [AM radio station call letters] .... WPAL
Charleston, SC [AM radio station call letters] (RBYB) .... WQNT-AM
Charleston, SC [FM radio station call letters] .... WSCI
Charleston, SC [FM radio station call letters] .... WSSX
Charleston, SC [FM radio station call letters] .... WSUY
Charleston, SC [Television station call letters] .... WTAT
Charleston, SC [AM radio station call letters] .... WTMA
Charleston, SC [AM radio station call letters] .... WUJM
Charleston, SC [AM radio station call letters] .... WXTC
Charleston, SC [FM radio station call letters] .... WXTC-FM
Charleston Storage Activity (SAUO) .... CSA
Charleston Submarine Training Center [South Carolina] .... CSTC
Charleston Training Center [South Carolina] .... CTC
Charleston, WV [Location identifier] [FAA] (FAAL) .... CRW
Charleston, WV [AM radio station call letters] .... WCAW

Charleston, WV [AM radio station call letters] ... WCHS
Charleston, WV [Television station call letters] ... WCHS-TV
Charleston, WV [AM radio station call letters] ... WCZR
Charleston, WV [Television station call letters] ... WKRP
Charleston, WV [FM radio station call letters] ... WKWS
Charleston, WV [Television station call letters] (BROA) ... WLPX-TV
Charleston, WV [AM radio station call letters] ... WQBE
Charleston, WV [FM radio station call letters] ... WQBE-FM
Charleston, WV [AM radio station call letters] (BROA) ... WSWW-AM
Charleston, WV [AM radio station call letters] ... WVAF
Charleston, WV [Television station call letters] ... WVAH
Charleston, WV [FM radio station call letters] ... WVPN
Charleston, WV [AM radio station call letters] ... WVSR
Charleston, WV [FM radio station call letters] ... WVSR-FM
Charleston/Municipal and Air Force Base [South Carolina] [ICAO location identifier] (ICLI) ... KCHS
Charlestown, IN [FM radio station call letters] (BROA) ... WBLO-FM
Charlestown, IN [FM radio station call letters] (BROA) ... WLVX-FM
Charlestown Township Public Library, Charlestown, IN [Library symbol] [Library of Congress] (LCLS) ... InCha
Charlestown/Newcastle [Nevis Island] [ICAO location identifier] (ICLI) ... TKPN
Charleswood Public Library, Winnipeg, Manitoba [Library symbol] [National Library of Canada] (NLC) ... MWCHD
Charleswood Public Library, Winnipeg, MB, Canada [Library symbol] [Library of Congress] (LCLS) ... CaMWCHD
Charleville [Australia] [ICAO location identifier] (ICLI) ... ABCV
Charleville [Australia] [Airport symbol] (OAG) ... CTL
Charleville/Mezieres [France] [ICAO location identifier] (ICLI) ... LFQV
Charlevoix, MI [Location identifier] [FAA] (FAAL) ... CVX
Charlevoix, MI [FM radio station call letters] ... WKHQ
Charlevoix, MI [AM radio station call letters] ... WMKT
Charlevoix Public Library, Charlevoix, MI [Library symbol] [Library of Congress] (LCLS) ... MiChv
Charley [Nevada] [Seismograph station code, US Geological Survey] [Closed] (SEIS) ... NYC
Charley Pride Fan Club (EA) ... CPFC
Charley-Horse [Spasm] (MELL) ... CH
Charley's Chamber Cases [1875-76] [England] [A publication] (DLA) ... Char Cham Cas
Charley's Chamber Cases [1875-76] [England] [A publication] (DLA) ... Charl Cha Cas
Charley's Chamber Cases [1875-76] [England] [A publication] (DLA) ... Charley Ch Cas
Charley's Pleading under the Judicature Acts [A publication] (DLA) ... Charl Pl
Charley's Practice Cases [1875-81] [England] [A publication] (DLA) ... Charley Pr Cas
Charley's Practice Cases [1875-81] [England] [A publication] (DLA) ... Charl Pr Cas
Charley's Practice Cases [1875-81] [England] [A publication] (DLA) ... Char Pr Cas
Charley's Real Property Statutes [A publication] (DLA) ... Charl RP Stat
Charlie [Phonetic alphabet] [International since 1956] (DSUE) ... C
Charlie Daniels Band ... CDB
Charlie Daniels Fan Club (EA) ... CDFC
Charlie Daniels Fan Club Volunteers (EA) ... CDFCV
Charlie Foxtrot (SAUS) ... CF
Charlie Hammonds Flying Service, Inc. [FAA designator] (FAAC) ... HMD
Charlie Hodge Fan Club Internationale (EA) ... CHFCI
Charlie O Beverage [Vancouver Stock Exchange symbol] ... CJV
Charlie Rich Fan Club (EA) ... CRFC
Charlie/Victor/Yankee [Military] (CAAL) ... CVY
Charlim Explorations [Vancouver Stock Exchange symbol] ... CHO
Charlo [Canada] [Airport symbol] (OAG) ... YCL
Charlo, NB [ICAO location identifier] (ICLI) ... CYCL
Charlotte [North Carolina] [Mint mark, when appearing on US coins] ... C
Charlotte [Diocesan abbreviation] [North Carolina] (TOCD) ... CHL
Charlotte [North Carolina] [Airport symbol] (OAG) ... CLT
Charlotte Amalie, St. Thomas, VI [Location identifier] [FAA] (FAAL) ... TMN
Charlotte Amalie, VI [Location identifier] [FAA] (FAAL) ... STT
Charlotte Amalie, VI [FM radio station call letters] (BROA) ... WARD-FM
Charlotte Amalie, VI [AM radio station call letters] ... WGOD
Charlotte Amalie, VI [FM radio station call letters] ... WGOD-FM
Charlotte Amalie, VI [FM radio station call letters] ... WIVI
Charlotte Amalie, VI [FM radio station call letters] ... WIYC
Charlotte Amalie, VI [AM radio station call letters] ... WSTA
Charlotte Amalie, VI [Television station call letters] ... WTJX
Charlotte Amalie, VI [FM radio station call letters] ... WVGN
Charlotte Amalie, VI [FM radio station call letters] (BROA) ... WVJZ-FM
Charlotte Amalie, VI [FM radio station call letters] ... WVNX
Charlotte Amalie, VI [FM radio station call letters] (BROA) ... WVPI-FM
Charlotte Amalie, VI [FM radio station call letters] ... WVWI
Charlotte Amalie, VI [Television station call letters] ... WVXF
Charlotte County Historical Society, Inc., St. Andrews, NB, Canada [Library symbol] [Library of Congress] (LCLS) ... CaNBACCH
Charlotte County Historical Society, Inc., St. Andrews, New Brunswick [Library symbol] [National Library of Canada] (NLC) ... NBACCH
Charlotte Junior/Senior High School Library, Rochester, NY [OCLC symbol] (OCLC) ... RVX
Charlotte, MI [AM radio station call letters] ... WLCM
Charlotte, MI [FM radio station call letters] ... WMMQ
Charlotte, MI [FM radio station call letters] (BROA) ... WVIC-FM
Charlotte Motor Speedway [Auto racing] ... CMS
Charlotte, NC [Location identifier] [FAA] (FAAL) ... BQC
Charlotte, NC [Location identifier] [FAA] (FAAL) ... DQG
Charlotte, NC [Location identifier] [FAA] (FAAL) ... PEP
Charlotte, NC [AM radio station call letters] ... WBAV
Charlotte, NC [AM radio station call letters] (BROA) ... WBHE

Charlotte, NC [AM radio station call letters] ... WBT
Charlotte, NC [Television station call letters] ... WBTV
Charlotte, NC [Television station call letters] (BROA) ... WBTV-DT
Charlotte, NC [Television station call letters] ... WCCB
Charlotte, NC [Television station call letters] (BROA) ... WCCB-DT
Charlotte, NC [Television station call letters] ... WCNC
Charlotte, NC [FM radio station call letters] ... WEDJ
Charlotte, NC [FM radio station call letters] ... WFAE
Charlotte, NC [AM radio station call letters] (RBYB) ... WFNZ
Charlotte, NC [AM radio station call letters] (BROA) ... WGFY
Charlotte, NC [AM radio station call letters] (BROA) ... WGIV-AM
Charlotte, NC [AM radio station call letters] ... WGSP
Charlotte, NC [AM radio station call letters] ... WHVN
Charlotte, NC [AM radio station call letters] ... WIST
Charlotte, NC [FM radio station call letters] (BROA) ... WLNK-FM
Charlotte, NC [FM radio station call letters] (RBYB) ... WNKS-FM
Charlotte, NC [AM radio station call letters] (RBYB) ... WNMX-AM
Charlotte, NC [AM radio station call letters] ... WOGR
Charlotte, NC [FM radio station call letters] ... WSOC
Charlotte, NC [Television station call letters] (BROA) ... WSOC-DT
Charlotte, NC [Television station call letters] ... WSOC-TV
Charlotte, NC [FM radio station call letters] ... WSSS
Charlotte, NC [AM radio station call letters] (BROA) ... WTLT-AM
Charlotte, NC [Television station call letters] ... WTVI
Charlotte, NC [FM radio station call letters] (RBYB) ... WWSN
Charlotte, NC [AM radio station call letters] ... WYFQ
Charlotte, NC [FM radio station call letters] ... WYHC
Charlotte, NC Air National Guard [FAA designator] (FAAC) ... CGD
Charlotte Ordnance Missile Plant ... COMP
Charlotte Public Library (SAUS) ... CPL
Charlotte Public Library, Charlotte, MI [Library symbol] [Library of Congress] (LCLS) ... MiChar
Charlotte-Glades Library System, Port Charlotte, FL [Library symbol] [Library of Congress] (LCLS) ... FPoCG
Charlotte-Mecklenburg School District ... CMS
Charlotte-Mecklenburg Schools, Staff Development Center, Charlotte, NC [Library symbol] [Library of Congress] (LCLS) ... NcCS
Charlottesville [Virginia] [Airport symbol] (OAG) ... CHO
Charlottesville [Virginia] [Seismograph station code, US Geological Survey] [Closed] (SEIS) ... CLT
Charlottesville [Virginia] [Seismograph station code, US Geological Survey] [Closed] (SEIS) ... CTV
Charlottesville [Virginia] [Seismograph station code, US Geological Survey] (SEIS) ... CVV
Charlottesville, VA [Location identifier] [FAA] (FAAL) ... AZS
Charlottesville, VA [AM radio station call letters] ... WCHV
Charlottesville, VA [Television station call letters] ... WHTJ
Charlottesville, VA [AM radio station call letters] ... WINA
Charlottesville, VA [AM radio station call letters] ... WKAV
Charlottesville, VA [FM radio station call letters] ... WLJL
Charlottesville, VA [FM radio station call letters] (RBYB) ... WNRN-FM
Charlottesville, VA [FM radio station call letters] ... WQMZ
Charlottesville, VA [FM radio station call letters] ... WTJU
Charlottesville, VA [FM radio station call letters] (BROA) ... WUMX-FM
Charlottesville, VA [FM radio station call letters] ... WUVA
Charlottesville, VA [Television station call letters] ... WVIR
Charlottesville, VA [FM radio station call letters] ... WVTU
Charlottesville, VA [FM radio station call letters] (RBYB) ... WVTW-FM
Charlottesville, VA [FM radio station call letters] ... WWWV
Charlottetown [Canada] [Airport symbol] (OAG) ... YYG
Charlottetown Area Tourism Industry Association (AC) ... CATIA
Charlottetown, PE [Television station call letters] ... CBCT
Charlottetown, PE [FM radio station call letters] ... CBCT-FM
Charlottetown, PE [AM radio station call letters] ... CFCY
Charlottetown, PE [FM radio station call letters] ... CHLQ
Charlottetown, PE [AM radio station call letters] ... CHTN
Charlottetown, PE [FM radio station call letters] (RBYB) ... CIMN
Charlottetown, PE [Television station call letters] ... CKCW-1
Charlottetown, PE [ICAO location identifier] (ICLI) ... CYYG
Charlton Kings [Urban district in England] ... CHARL
Charlton, MA [FM radio station call letters] ... WBPV
Charm (ADWA) ... C
Charm [Jewelry] (ROG) ... CHM
Charm Bracelet Polymer [Organic chemistry] ... CBP
Charmed (Quark) [Atomic physics] ... c
Charmides [of Plato] [Classical studies] (OCD) ... Chrm
Charming Shoppes [NASDAQ symbol] (TTSB) ... CHRS
Charming Shoppes, Inc. [Associated Press] (SAG) ... ChmSh
Charming Shoppes, Inc. [Associated Press] (SAG) ... ChrmSh
Charming Shoppes, Inc. [NASDAQ symbol] (NQ) ... CHRS
Charnes Organizational Diagnosis Survey [Medicine] (DMAA) ... CODS
Charnwood Forest [England] [Seismograph station code, US Geological Survey] (SEIS) ... CWF
Charoen Pokphand [Thai business conglomerate] (ECON) ... CP
Char-Oil-Energy-Development [Process] [Project of Office of Coal Research] ... COED
Charolais Society of Australia ... CSA
Charpy V-Notch [Nuclear energy] (NRCH) ... CVN
Charring Ablation Program [NASA] ... CHAP
Charriot Resources [Vancouver Stock Exchange symbol] ... CIO
Char-Swiss Breeders Association (EA) ... CSBA
Chart ... CH
Chart ... CT
Chart Comparison Unit ... CCU
Chart Datum ... CD

Chart Distribution Data ... CDD
Chart Dynamic Flow (SAUS) ... CDF
Chart House Enterprises [*NYSE symbol*] (SPSG) ... CHT
Chart House Enterprises [*Associated Press*] (SAG) ... ChtHou
Chart Industries [*Associated Press*] (SAG) ... Chart
Chart Industries [*NYSE symbol*] (SPSG) ... CTI
Chart Information Network (WDAA) ... CIN
Chart Maker [*Computer Design*] [*Software package*] (NCC) ... CM
Chart Not Available [*Medicine*] (DAVI) ... CNA
Chart Standardization Committee (SAUS) ... CSC
Chart Updating Manual [*Air Force*] ... CHUM
Charta [*Paper*] [*Pharmacy*] ... CHART
Charta Bibula [*Blotting Paper*] [*Latin*] ... CHART BIB
Charta Cerata [*Waxed Paper*] [*Pharmacy*] ... CHART CERAT
Charta de Foresta [*Charter of the Forest*] [*Latin*] [*A publication*] (DLA) ... Chart Forest
Charta de Foresta [*Charter of the Forest*] [*Latin*] [*A publication*] (DLA) ... Chart Foresta
Charta Mercatoria [*Latin*] [*A publication*] (DLA) ... Char Merc
Chartae Antiquae [*A publication*] (DLA) ... Chart Antiq
Chartair, Inc. [*ICAO designator*] (FAAC) ... SJN
Charted Visual Flight Procedure (PIPO) ... CVFP
Charted Visual Flight Procedure Approach [*FAA*] (TAG) ... CVFP
Charter ... CHAR
Charter ... CHRTR
Charter [*Travel industry*] (TRID) ... CHTR
Charter Air Ges. MbH & Co. Kg [*Austria*] [*FAA designator*] (FAAC) ... CHW
Charter Bancshares [*NASDAQ symbol*] (SPSG) ... SAIL
Charter Bancshares, Inc. [*Associated Press*] (SAG) ... ChtBnc
Charter Bank SB [*Associated Press*] (SAG) ... ChrtBk
Charter Bank Shares, Inc. [*NASDAQ symbol*] (SAG) ... CBSB
Charter Change [*Manila, Philippines*] ... cha cha
Charter Cruise Air Ltd. [*Australia*] ... CCA
Charter Federal Savings & Loan Virginia [*Associated Press*] (SAG) ... ChartFdl
Charter Federal Savings & Loan Virginia [*NASDAQ symbol*] (NQ) ... CHFD
Charter Financial [*NQS*] (TTSB) ... CBSB
Charter Group (SAUO) ... CG
Charter Long Term ... CHLT
Charter Medical Corp. [*Associated Press*] (SAG) ... ChrtMed
Charter Medical Corp. [*AMEX symbol*] (SPSG) ... CMD
Charter Muni Mtg Acceptance [*AMEX symbol*] (SG) ... CHC
Charter New York Corp. (SAUO) ... CN
Charter Oak Times, Charter Oak, IA [*Library symbol*] [*Library of Congress*] (LCLS) ... IaChoT
Charter of Economic Rights and Duties of States [*United Nations*] ... CERDS
Charter of the United Nations (SAUS) ... UN Charter
Charter Oil Co. Ltd. [*Toronto Stock Exchange symbol*] ... CHR
Charter One Financial, Inc. [*Associated Press*] (SAG) ... ChtOneF
Charter One Financial, Inc. [*NASDAQ symbol*] (SAG) ... COFI
Charter One Finl [*NASDAQ symbol*] (TTSB) ... COFI
Charter Party [*Transportation*] ... CP
Charter Party (SAUO) ... CP
Charter Party (SAUO) ... C Py
Charter Power Systems [*Associated Press*] (SAG) ... ChtPwr
Charter Power Systems [*NASDAQ symbol*] (SAG) ... CHTR
Charter Rolls [*British*] ... CH
Charter, Rural, and Intercity Bus Survey [*Bureau of the Census*] (GFGA) ... CRIBS
Charter Yacht Brokers Association (TRID) ... CYBA
Charterair [*ICAO designator*] (AD) ... HO
Chartered ... CHRTRD
Chartered Account Executive [*Canada*] (ASC) ... CAE
Chartered Account Executive [*Canada*] (ASC) ... cae
Chartered Accountant ... CA
Chartered Accountant ... CHARTAC
Chartered Accountant in Australia [*A publication*] ... Ch Acc Aust
Chartered Accountant in Australia [*A publication*] ... Chart Acc Aust
Chartered Accountant Students' Society [*Australia*] ... CASS
Chartered Accountants Students Association of Ontario (SAUO) ... CASAO
Chartered Administrator (DD) ... CAdm
Chartered Agent [*Business term*] ... C/A
Chartered Appraiser (SAUO) ... C App
Chartered Association Executive (SAUO) ... CAE
Chartered Association of Certified Accountants (COBU) ... ACCA
Chartered Association of Certified Accountants [*British*] (EAIO) ... CACA
Chartered Auctioneers and Estate Agents (SAUO) ... CAEA
Chartered Auctioneers' and Estate Agents' Institute [*British*] (BI) ... CAEAI
Chartered Auctioneers and Estate Agents Institute (SAUS) ... CAEAI
Chartered Automobile Engineer (SAUS) ... CAE
Chartered Building Societies Institute [*British*] (DBA) ... CBSI
Chartered Building Societies Intitute (SAUO) ... CBSI
Chartered Business Valuator [*Canada*] (ASC) ... CBV
Chartered Cartographer ... CC
Chartered Chemist [*British*] ... CChem
Chartered Chemist [*British*] (WA) ... C Chem
Chartered Colorist (DD) ... CCol
Chartered Colourist [*British*] (DBQ) ... CCol
Chartered Electrical Engineer [*British*] (DAS) ... CEE
Chartered Electronics Industries Pte Ltd. (SAUO) ... CEI
Chartered Engineer [*British*] ... CE
Chartered Engineer [*British*] ... C Eng
Chartered Engineer [*A publication*] ... Chart Engr
Chartered Engineering Institutes (WDAA) ... CEI
Chartered Financial Analyst [*Institute of Chartered Fi nancial Analysts*] [*Designation awarded by*] ... CFA
Chartered Financial Consultant (MHDB) ... CFC
Chartered Financial Consultant [*The American College*] [*Designation awarded by*] ... ChFC
Chartered Financial Counselor (DFIT) ... CFC
Chartered Financial Planner ... CFP
Chartered Financial Planner [*Insurance*] ... ChFP
Chartered Financial Underwriter ... CFU
Chartered Firearms Industries Pte Ltd. (SAUO) ... CFI
Chartered Industries of Singapore (SAUO) ... CIS
Chartered Institute of Arbitrators [*British*] (DBA) ... CIArb
Chartered Institute of Bankers [*London, England*] (EAIO) ... CIB
Chartered Institute of Building [*British*] [*Research center*] (DI) ... CIOB
Chartered Institute of Loss Adjusters [*British*] (BI) ... CILA
Chartered Institute of Management Accountants [*British*] (EAIO) ... CIMA
Chartered Institute of Marine Engineers ... CIME
Chartered Institute of Marketing [*British*] (EAIO) ... CIM
Chartered Institute of Marketing Management of Ontario (AC) ... CIMMO
Chartered Institute of Patent Agents [*British*] (BI) ... CIPA
Chartered Institute of Patent Agents (SAUO) ... CIPA
Chartered Institute of Public Finance and Accountancy [*Formerly, IMTA*] [*British*] ... CIPFA
Chartered Institute of Purchasing & Supply (WDAA) ... CIPS
Chartered Institute of Secretaries [*British*] (BI) ... CIS
Chartered Institute of Transport (EAIO) ... CIT
Chartered Institute of Transport in Australia ... CITA
Chartered Institute of Transport in Canada [*Institut Agree des Transports du Canada*] (AC) ... CIT in Canada
Chartered Institution of Building Service (EAIO) ... CIBS
Chartered Institution of Building Services Engineers (EAIO) ... CIBSE
Chartered Insurance Broker ... CIB
Chartered Insurance Institute [*British*] ... CII
Chartered Insurance Institute (SAUO) ... CII
Chartered Investment Counsel (MHDB) ... CIC
Chartered Investment Counsellor [*Canada*] (DD) ... CIC
Chartered Land Agents Society (SAUO) ... CLAS
Chartered Librarian [*British*] ... CL
Chartered Life Underwriter [*Solomon S. Huebner School of CLU Studies, The American College*] [*Designation awarded by*] ... CLU
Chartered Life underwriters of Canada (SAUO) ... CLC
Chartered Loss Adjuster (DD) ... CLA
Chartered Patent Agent ... CPA
Chartered Property and Casualty Underwriter [*Designation awarded by American Institute for Property and Liability Underwriters*] ... CPCU
Chartered Psychologist ... CPsychol
Chartered Public Accountant ... CPA
Chartered Quantity Surveying Association (COBU) ... CQSA
Chartered Secretary [*A publication*] ... Chart Secretary
Chartered Secretary [*A publication*] ... Ch Sec
Chartered Shorthand Reporters' Association of Ontario (AC) ... CSRAO
Chartered Society of Designers [*British*] [*England*] (EAIO) ... CSD
Chartered Society of Designers (SAUS) ... SIAD
Chartered Society of Massage and Medical Gymnastics (DAVI) ... CSMMG
Chartered Society of Massage and Medical Gymnastics (SAUO) ... CSMMG
Chartered Society of Physiotherapists (SAUO) ... CSP
Chartered Society of Physiotherapy [*British*] ... CSP
Chartered Society of Physio-Therapy (SAUO) ... CST
Chartered Stenographic Reporter ... CSR
Chartered Surveyor (WDAA) ... CS
Chartered Surveyors' Institution [*British*] (DAS) ... CSI
Chartered Union of Taxpayers (SAUO) ... Cut
Charterer (SAUS) ... Ch
Charterers (SAUS) ... Chrs
Charterers Agent (SAUS) ... Ch Agt
Charterers Option (SAUS) ... Ch Opt
Charterers' Option (RIMS) ... CHOPT
Charterers Pay Dues (WGA) ... CPD
Charterers Stevedors (SAUS) ... Ch Stev
Charterhall Oil Canada [*Vancouver Stock Exchange symbol*] ... CHL
Charterhouse J. Rothschild (SAUO) ... CJF
Charterhouse J. Rothschild (SAUO) ... CJR
Charters Towers [*Australia*] [*Seismograph station code, US Geological Survey*] (SEIS) ... CTA
Charters Towers [*Australia*] [*Seismograph station code, US Geological Survey*] (SEIS) ... CTAO
Charters Towers [*Australia*] [*Airport symbol*] (OAG) ... CXT
Chartier Family Association (EA) ... CFA
Charting (AFM) ... CHTG
Charting and Geodetic Services Office [*National Oceanic and Atmospheric Administration*] (PDAA) ... C & GS
Charting by Exception ... CBE
Chartres/Champhol [*France*] [*ICAO location identifier*] (ICLI) ... LFOR
Chartula [*A Small Paper*] [*Pharmacy*] ... CHARTUL
Chartwell Leisure, Inc. [*Associated Press*] (SAG) ... ChartwellL
Chartwell Leisure, Inc. [*NASDAQ symbol*] (SAG) ... CHRT
Chartwell Re [*NYSE symbol*] (SG) ... CWL
Chartwell Re Corp. [*Associated Press*] (SAG) ... ChartwllRe
Chartwell Re Corp. [*NYSE symbol*] (SAG) ... CWL
Chartwell Re Corp. [*NASDAQ symbol*] (TTSB) ... CWLR
Charwoman [*Slang*] [*British*] (DSUE) ... CHAR
Charybdotoxin [*Biochemistry*] ... CTX
Chase (WDAA) ... C
Chase Aircraft Co. ... CAC
Chase Automated Clearing House, Inc. (TBD) ... CHASE ACH
Chase Brass Indus [*NYSE symbol*] (TTSB) ... CSI
Chase Brass Industries, Inc. [*Associated Press*] (SAG) ... ChaseBr
Chase Brass Industries, Inc. [*Associated Press*] (SAG) ... ChaseBrs

Chase Brass Industries, Inc. [*NYSE symbol*] (SAG) .... CSI
Chase City, VA [*Location identifier*] [*FAA*] (FAAL) .... CXE
Chase City, VA [*FM radio station call letters*] .... WFXQ
Chase City, VA [*AM radio station call letters*] .... WMEK
Chase Corp. [*AMEX symbol*] (SAG) .... CCF
Chase Corp. [*Associated Press*] (SAG) .... ChaseCp
Chase Econometrics Associates, Inc. [*Information service or system*] (IID) .... CEAI
Chase Econometrics/Interactive Data Corp. [*Database vendor*] .... CE/IDC
Chase Federal Bank [*NASDAQ symbol*] (TTSB) .... CHFB
Chase Industries [*NYSE symbol*] (SG) .... CSI
Chase Manhattan [*NYSE symbol*] (TTSB) .... CMB
Chase Manhattan 10 1/2%'A'Pfd [*NYSE symbol*] (TTSB) .... CMBPrA
Chase Manhattan 10.84%'C'Pfd [*NYSE symbol*] (TTSB) .... CMBPrC
Chase Manhattan 10.96% Pfd [*NYSE symbol*] (TTSB) .... CMBPrG
Chase Manhattan 7.50% Dep Pfd [*NYSE symbol*] (TTSB) .... CMBPfK
Chase Manhattan 7.58% Dep Pfd [*NYSE symbol*] (TTSB) .... CMBPrJ
Chase Manhattan 7.92% Dep Ptd [*NYSE symbol*] (TTSB) .... CMBPrI
Chase Manhattan 8.32%'F'Pfd [*NYSE symbol*] (TTSB) .... CMBPrF
Chase Manhattan 8.375% Pfd [*NYSE symbol*] (TTSB) .... CMBPrH
Chase Manhattan 8.40% M Pfd [*NYSE symbol*] (TTSB) .... CMBPrM
Chase Manhattan 8.50%'E'Pfd [*NYSE symbol*] (TTSB) .... CMBPrE
Chase Manhattan 9.08%'D'Pfd [*NYSE symbol*] (TTSB) .... CMBPrD
Chase Manhattan 9.76%'B'Pfd [*NYSE symbol*] (TTSB) .... CMBPrB
Chase Manhattan Adj N Pfd [*NYSE symbol*] (TTSB) .... CMBPrN
Chase Manhattan Adj Rt'L'Pfd [*NYSE symbol*] (TTSB) .... CMBPrL
Chase Manhattan Bank (SAUO) .... CHAMANBANK
Chase Manhattan Bank Corp. (SAUO) .... CMB
Chase Manhattan Bank, New York, NY [*OCLC symbol*] (OCLC) .... ZCB
[*The*] **Chase Manhattan Corp.** [*Associated Press*] (SAG) .... Chase
[*The*] **Chase Manhattan Corp.** [*Associated Press*] (SAG) .... Chse
[*The*] **Chase Manhattan Corp.** [*New York, NY*] [*NYSE symbol*] (SPSG) .... CMB
Chase Manhattan Mortgage & Realty Trust (SAUO) .... CMR
Chase Manhattan Wrrt [*NYSE symbol*] (TTSB) .... CMB.WS
Chase on Stephens' Digest of Evidence [*A publication*] (DLA) .... Chase Steph Dig Ev
Chase Preferred Capital Corp. [*Associated Press*] (SAG) .... ChsePC
Chase Preferred Capital Corp. [*NYSE symbol*] (SAG) .... CMB
Chase Public Library, Chase, MI [*Library symbol*] [*Library of Congress*] (LCLS) .... MiCha
Chase Ranch [*California*] [*Seismograph station code, US Geological Survey*] (SEIS) .... CSR
Chase Resources [*Vancouver Stock Exchange symbol*] .... CQS
Chase, Shields, Lambert, Baker & Shillito, Small Business Financing (SAUS) .... SBF
Chase World Information Corp. [*Information service or system*] (IID) .... CWIC
Chase's Blackstone [*A publication*] (DLA) .... Chase's Bl
Chase's Blackstone [*A publication*] (DLA) .... Ch Black
Chase's Statutes at Large [*Ohio*] [*A publication*] (DLA) .... Chase's St
Chase's Trial (Impeachment) by the United States Senate [*A publication*] (DLA) .... Chase Tr
Chase's United States Circuit Court Decisions [*A publication*] (DLA) .... Chase
Chase's United States Circuit Court Decisions [*A publication*] (DLA) .... Chase Dec
Chase's United States Circuit Court Decisions, Edited by Johnson [*A publication*] (DLA) .... John
Chase's United States Circuit Court Decisions, Edited by Johnson [*A publication*] (DLA) .... Johns
Chasing (VRA) .... cha
Chasmogamous [*Botany*] .... CH
Chassahowitzka National Wildlife Refuge (SAUS) .... CNWR
Chassemaree [*Ship's rigging*] (ROG) .... CH
Chassis .... CHA
Chassis (MSA) .... CHAS
Chassis Compound-Control System [*Automotive engineering*] .... CCS
Chassis Marking Kit .... CMK
Chassis Plug (SAUS) .... CHAS PL
Chasti Osobogo Naznacheniia [*Elements of Special Designation*] [*Political police units attached to the armed forces (1918-1924)*] [*Former USSR*] .... ChON
Chasuble (VRA) .... chsbl
Chat Fruit Virus (SAUS) .... CFV
Chataugua National Wildlife Refuge (SAUS) .... CNWR
Chatauqua National Wildlife Refuge (SAUS) .... CNWR
ChatCom [*NASDAQ symbol*] (SAG) .... CHAT
ChatCom [*Associated Press*] (SAG) .... ChatCom
ChatCom Inc. [*NASDAQ symbol*] (TTSB) .... CHAT
Chateau [*New Zealand*] [*Seismograph station code, US Geological Survey*] (SEIS) .... CNZ
Chateau Communities [*NYSE symbol*] (SG) .... CPJ
Chateau Properties [*Associated Press*] (SAG) .... ChateauP
Chateau Properties [*NYSE symbol*] (SPSG) .... CPJ
Chateau Stores of Canada Ltd. [*Toronto Stock Exchange symbol*] .... CTU
Chateau-Arnoux/Saint-Auban [*France*] [*ICAO location identifier*] (ICLI) .... LFMX
Chateaugay, NY [*FM radio station call letters*] .... WYUL
Chateauguay Valley English-Speaking Peoples' Association (AC) .... CVESPA
Chateauneuf-Sur-Cher [*France*] [*ICAO location identifier*] (ICLI) .... LFFU
Chateauquay, PQ [*FM radio station call letters*] (RBYB) .... CHAI-FM
Chateauroux Air Depot (SAUO) .... CHAD
Chateauroux/Deols [*France*] [*ICAO location identifier*] (ICLI) .... LFLX
Chateauroux/Villers [*France*] [*ICAO location identifier*] (ICLI) .... LFEJ
Chateau-Thierry-Belleau [*France*] [*ICAO location identifier*] (ICLI) .... LFFH
Chatelaine [*Jewelry*] (ROG) .... CHATNE
Chatellerault/Targe [*France*] [*ICAO location identifier*] (ICLI) .... LFCA
Chatfield Applied Research Laboratories (SAUO) .... CARL
Chatfield College, St. Martin, OH [*Library symbol*] [*Library of Congress*] (LCLS) .... OStmaC
Chatfield Elementary School, Clifton, CO [*Library symbol*] [*Library of Congress*] (LCLS) .... CoCfCE
Chatham [*Canada*] [*Airport symbol*] (OAG) .... YCH
Chatham, AK [*Location identifier*] [*FAA*] (FAAL) .... CYM
Chatham Canadian Forces Base, NB [*ICAO location identifier*] (ICLI) .... CYCH
Chatham College, Pittsburgh, PA [*OCLC symbol*] (OCLC) .... HHC
Chatham College, Pittsburgh, PA [*Library symbol*] [*Library of Congress*] (LCLS) .... PPiCC
Chatham Courier, Chatham, NJ [*Library symbol*] [*Library of Congress*] (LCLS) .... NjCC
Chatham Division Royal Marines (SAUO) .... CDRM
Chatham Division Royal Marines [*Military unit*] [*British*] .... CDRM
Chatham Division, Royal Marines (SAUO) .... Chat
Chatham, Hotel-Dieu Hospital, New Brunswick (SAUS) .... NBCHD
Chatham House (DAS) .... CH
Chatham House Foundation (EA) .... CHF
Chatham Islands [*New Zealand*] [*Seismograph station code, US Geological Survey*] (SEIS) .... CIZ
Chatham Island/Tuuta [*New Zealand*] [*ICAO location identifier*] (ICLI) .... NZCI
Chatham Island/Waitangi [*New Zealand*] [*ICAO location identifier*] (ICLI) .... NZWA
Chatham, MA [*Location identifier*] [*FAA*] (FAAL) .... CHH
Chatham, MA [*FM radio station call letters*] .... WFCC
Chatham, NJ [*Location identifier*] [*FAA*] (FAAL) .... CAT
Chatham, ON [*AM radio station call letters*] .... CFCO
Chatham, ON [*Television station call letters*] CICO-59
Chatham, ON [*FM radio station call letters*] .... CKSY
Chatham Public General Hospital, Chatham, ON, Canada [*Library symbol*] [*Library of Congress*] (LCLS) .... CaOChaH
Chatham Public General Hospital, Ontario [*Library symbol*] [*National Library of Canada*] (NLC) .... OCHAH
Chatham Public Library, Chatham, NJ [*Library symbol*] [*Library of Congress*] (LCLS) .... NjC
Chatham Public Library, Chatham, NY [*Library symbol*] [*Library of Congress*] (LCLS) .... NCha
Chatham Public Library, Chatham, ON, Canada [*Library symbol*] [*Library of Congress*] (LCLS) .... CaOCha
Chatham Public Library, Chatman, NY [*Library symbol*] [*Library of Congress*] (LCLS) .... NChaL
Chatham Public Library, Ontario [*Library symbol*] [*National Library of Canada*] (NLC) .... OCHA
Chatham Railway (SAUO) .... CR
Chatham Society (SAUO) .... CS
Chatham Township Echoes, Chatham, NJ [*Library symbol*] [*Library of Congress*] (LCLS) .... NjCE
Chatham, VA [*AM radio station call letters*] .... WKBY
Chatham-Kent Museum, Chatham, ON, Canada [*Library symbol*] [*Library of Congress*] (LCLS) .... CaOChaK
Chatham-Kent Museum, Chatham, Ontario [*Library symbol*] [*National Library of Canada*] (NLC) .... OCHAK
Chatillon-Sur-Seine [*France*] [*ICAO location identifier*] (ICLI) .... LFQH
Chatom, AL [*FM radio station call letters*] (RBYB) .... WFOW-FM
Chator-Lea Sidecar [*Early motorcars*] (ROG) CL
Chatra [*Nepal*] [*Seismograph station code, US Geological Survey*] (SEIS) .... CHA
Chatsworth, GA [*Television station call letters*] .... WCLP
Chatsworth, GA [*FM radio station call letters*] .... WQMT
Chattahoochee, FL [*FM radio station call letters*] .... WBCD
Chattahoochee, FL [*AM radio station call letters*] .... WTCL
Chattahoochee Industrial Railroad [*AAR code*] .... CIRR
Chattahoochee Valley Railway Co. [*AAR code*] .... CHV
Chattahoochee Valley Regional Library, Columbus, GA [*OCLC symbol*] (OCLC) .... GCV
Chattanooga [*Tennessee*] [*Airport symbol*] .... CHA
Chattanooga Public Library (SAUS) .... CPL
Chattanooga State Technical Community College, Chattanooga, TN [*Library symbol*] [*Library of Congress*] (LCLS) .... TCST
Chattanooga State Technical Institute [*Tennessee*] .... CSTI
Chattanooga, TN [*Location identifier*] [*FAA*] (FAAL) .... CGW
Chattanooga, TN [*Location identifier*] [*FAA*] (FAAL) .... CQN
Chattanooga, TN [*AM radio station call letters*] .... WDEF
Chattanooga, TN [*FM radio station call letters*] .... WDEF-FM
Chattanooga, TN [*Television station call letters*] .... WDEF-TV
Chattanooga, TN [*AM radio station call letters*] .... WDOD
Chattanooga, TN [*FM radio station call letters*] .... WDOD-FM
Chattanooga, TN [*Television station call letters*] .... WDSI
Chattanooga, TN [*FM radio station call letters*] .... WDYN
Chattanooga, TN [*AM radio station call letters*] .... WGOW
Chattanooga, TN [*AM radio station call letters*] .... WJOC
Chattanooga, TN [*AM radio station call letters*] .... WLMR
Chattanooga, TN [*FM radio station call letters*] .... WMBW
Chattanooga, TN [*AM radio station call letters*] .... WNOO
Chattanooga, TN [*Television station call letters*] .... WRCB
Chattanooga, TN [*FM radio station call letters*] .... WSKZ
Chattanooga, TN [*Television station call letters*] .... WTCI
Chattanooga, TN [*Television station call letters*] .... WTVC
Chattanooga, TN [*Television station call letters*] .... WUTC
Chattanooga-Hamilton County Bicentennial Library, Chattanooga, TN [*Library symbol*] [*Library of Congress*] (LCLS) .... TC
Chattanooga-Hamilton County Bicentennial Library, Chattanooga, TN [*Library symbol*] [*Library of Congress*] (LCLS) .... TCHCB
Chattanooga-Hamilton County Bicentennial Library, Chattanooga, TX [*OCLC symbol*] (OCLC) .... TCH
Chattanooga/Lovell [*Tennessee*] [*ICAO location identifier*] (ICLI) .... KCHA
Chattel [*Legal shorthand*] (LWAP) .... CHAT
Chattel Mortgage [*Legal term*] (DLA) .... C/M

Chattem Drug and Chemical Co., Chattanooga, TN [Library symbol] [Library of Congress] (LCLS) .... TCCDC
Chattem, Inc. [Associated Press] (SAG) .... Chattm
Chattem, Inc. [NASDAQ symbol] (NQ) .... CHTT
Chatterbox Recording Club [British] (EAIO) .... CRC
Chatteris [Urban district in England] .... CHATT
Chatterji's Non-Language Preference [Vocational guidance test] .... CNPR
Chatterton Elementary School, Merrick, NY [Library symbol] [Library of Congress] (LCLS) .... NMerk CE
Chatto, Bodley Head, and Jonathan Cape Group [Publishers] [British] .... CBC
Chatwood Resources [Vancouver Stock Exchange symbol] .... CHW
Chaucer [Fourteenth century English poet] (ROG) .... CHAUC
Chaudiere Branch, Departmental Library, Environment Canada [Succursale Chaudiere, Bibliotheque du Ministere, Environnement Canada] Ottawa, Ontario [Library symbol] [National Library of Canada] (NLC) .... OOPAC
Chauffair Ltd. [British] [ICAO designator] (FAAC) .... CFR
Chauffeur [Army] .... Cfr
Chauffeur (SAUS) .... Chauf
Chauffeur (DSUE) .... CHAUFF
Chauffeur .... CHFFR
Chaumont-La Vendue [France] [ICAO location identifier] (ICLI) .... LFSY
Chauncey, GA [FM radio station call letters] .... WQIL
Chaurjahari [Nepal] [Airport symbol] (OAG) .... CJR
Chaus [Bernard], Inc. [Associated Press] (SAG) .... Chaus
Chaus [Bernard], Inc. [NYSE symbol] (SPSG) .... CHS
Chaussee (SAUS) .... Ch
Chaussure .... CHSSR
Chautauqua Airlines [ICAO designator] (FAAC) .... CHQ
Chautauqua County Board of Cooperative Educational Services, Fredonia, NY [Library symbol] [Library of Congress] (LCLS) .... NFredCB
Chautauqua County Historical Society, Westfield, NY [Library symbol] [Library of Congress] (LCLS) .... NWefHi
Chautauqua Literary and Scientific Circle (EA) .... CLSC
Chautauqua Literary and Scientific Society (SAUO) .... CLSS
Chautauqua-Cattaraugus Library System [Library network] .... CCLS
Chautauqua-Cattaraugus Library System, Jamestown, NY [Library symbol] [Library of Congress] (LCLS) .... NJamC
Chautauqua-Cattaraugus Library System, Jamestown, NY [OCLC symbol] (OCLC) .... VXU
Chauvco Resources Ltd. [Toronto Stock Exchange symbol] .... CHA
Chauvigny [France] [ICAO location identifier] (ICLI) .... LFDW
Chauvin Municipal Library, Alberta [Library symbol] [National Library of Canada] (BIB) .... ACHM
Chavenay/Villepreux [France] [ICAO location identifier] (ICLI) .... LFPX
Chaves [Portugal] [ICAO location identifier] (ICLI) .... LPCH
Chavin of Canada [Vancouver Stock Exchange symbol] .... CHX
Chavis, KY [Location identifier] [FAA] (FAAL) .... DUF
Chazuta [Peru] [ICAO location identifier] (ICLI) .... SPZT
CHC Helicopter [NASDAQ symbol] (SAG) .... FLYA
CHC Helicopter Cl'A' [NASDAQ symbol] (TTSB) .... FLYAF
CHC Helicopter Corp. [Associated Press] (SAG) .... CHCHel
CHC Helicopter Corp. [Toronto Stock Exchange symbol] .... FLY
Cheap Access Terminal [Computer science] (MHDI) .... CHAT
Cheap Access To Space (SAUO) .... CATS
Cheap Analyzer of Demographic Data [Term coined by William F. Doescher, publisher of "D & B Reports"] .... Cadd
Cheap Array of Obsolete Systems (SAUS) .... CHAOS
Cheap Money [Banking] .... CM
Cheap Personal Computer (ADWA) .... CPC
Cheap Reprint (DGA) .... CH RPT
Cheap Tickets [NASDAQ symbol] (SG) .... CTIX
Cheap Trick International (EA) .... CTI
Cheapest to Deliver (ADWA) .... CTD
Cheapest to Deliver (NUMA) .... ctd
Cheasapeake, VA [FM radio station call letters] .... WFOS
Cheatham Dam [TVA] .... CD
Cheb [Eger] [Czechoslovakia] [Seismograph station code, US Geological Survey] [Closed] (SEIS) .... CHE
Cheboygan Area Public Library, Cheboygan, MI [Library symbol] [Library of Congress] (LCLS) .... MiChe
Cheboygan, MI [AM radio station call letters] .... WCBY
Cheboygan, MI [FM radio station call letters] .... WGFM
Cheboygan, MI [Television station call letters] .... WTOM
Chebycheff Polynomial Discriminant Method (SAUS) .... CPDM
Chebychev Trajectory Optimization Program (SAUS) .... CHEBYTOP
Chebyshev Filter (SAUS) .... CHEB Filter
Chechen [MARC language code] [Library of Congress] (LCCP) .... che
Check .... CH
Check (WDMC) .... chk
Check .... CHK
Check (WDMC) .... ck
Check (AFM) .... CK
Check Addition (SAUS) .... CA
Check and Analysis System for Errors (SAUS) .... CHASE
Check and Store .... CHST
Check Area Airports (FAAC) .... CARA
Check Authorization Method .... CAM
Check Authorization Record (IBMDP) .... CAR
Check Bit (SAUS) .... Ch Bit
Check Bit .... CHKB
Check Bits (SAUS) .... Cbs
Check Bits (SAUS) .... CK Bits
Check Brushes (SAUS) .... Ch B
Check Channel (SAUS) CC
Check Code (SAUS) CC

Check Coil .... CHC
Check Collectors Round Table [Later, ASCC] (EA) .... CCRT
Check Computation (SAUS) CC
Check Correct (ECII) .... CD
Check Digit [IRS] .... CD
Check Digit [Computer science] (EECA) .... CKDIG
Check Digit Procedure (SAUS) .... CDP
Check Digit Verification (CMD) .... CDV
Check Digit Verifier .... CDG
Check Disk [Computer science] .... CHKDSK
Check Engine Light [Automotive term] .... CEL
Check Entry (SAUS) .... CHE
Check Express, Inc. [Associated Press] (SAG) .... ChckExp
Check Express, Inc. [Associated Press] (SAG) .... ChkEx
Check Express, Inc. [NASDAQ symbol] (SAG) .... CHXS
Check Fixture (MCD) .... CKF
Check Following Numbers (SAUS) .... CFN
Check Form [Tool] (AAG) .... CKFM
Check Gauge [Tool] (AAG) .... CKGA
Check Handling Executive Control System (CIST) .... CHECS
Check In (SAUS) CI
Check Indicator (SAUS) CI
Check Information (SAUS) CI
Check Issued .... CKI
Check Label Field (SAUS) .... CLF
Check List of Social Science Serials (SAUS) .... CLOSSS
Check List Question (CAAL) .... CLQ
Check Not OK [Telecommunications] (TEL) .... CN
Check Number (SAUS) .... CHKNO
Check OK [Telecommunications] (TEL) .... CO
Check Okay (FAAC) .... CHOK
Check Open [Nuclear energy] (NRCH) .... CO
Check Operator (DEN) .... CKO
Check Out [Medicine] (DAVI) .... C/O
Check Parity (SAA) .... CP
Check Plotter (GEOI) .... CK-PL
Check Plus Minus Subroutine .... CPMS
Check Point (SAUS) .... Ch Pt
Check Point (SAUS) .... Ck Pt
Check Point Recovery Routine (SAUS) .... CPRR
Check Point Software Tech [NASDAQ symbol] (SG) .... CHKP
Check Point Software Technologies Ltd. [NASDAQ symbol] (SAG) .... CHKP
Check Point Software Technologies Ltd. [Associated Press] (SAG) .... ChkPnt
Check Problem (SAUS) .... Chk Prob
Check Problem (SAUS) .... CP
Check Processing Control System [IBM Corp.] (BUR) .... CPCS
Check Protection (SAUS) .... CP
Check Received .... CKR
Check Register (SAUS) .... CR
Check Register Against Bounds [Computer science] .... CHK
Check Reporting Service .... CRS
Check Routine (SAUS) .... CR
Check Run (SAUS) .... CR
Check Signal Return (NASA) .... CSR
Check Signal Unit [Telecommunications] (TEL) .... CSU
Check Sorter .... CS
Check Status Reply (KSC) .... CSR
Check Sum (SAUS) .... CS
Check Surface (IAA) .... CS
Check Tape (SAUS) .... CT
Check Technology [NASDAQ symbol] (TTSB) .... CTCO
Check Technology [NASDAQ symbol] (SG) .... CTCQ
Check Technology Corp. [Associated Press] (SAG) .... ChkTch
Check Technology Corp. [NASDAQ symbol] (NQ) .... CTCQ
Check Template .... CKT
Check Template (SAUS) .... CKTP
Check Template (MCD) .... CT
Check Test (MCD) .... CT
Check Value (SAUS) CV
Check Valve (KSC) .... CHV
Check Valve (SAUS) .... CKVLV
Check Valve CV
Check Visit (HEAS) CV
Check Your Keying [Amateur radio shorthand] (WDAA) .... ZCK
Checked Operation (SAUS) .... CO
Checked Output (SAUS) .... CO
Checked Punching (SAUS) .... CP
Checked Statement (SAUS) .... CS
Checker (MSA) .... CHKR
Checker Car Club of America (EA) .... CCCA
Checker Club (EA) CC
Checker Motors Corporation (SAUO) .... CHC
Checker Redundant Scheme (SAUS) .... CRS
Checkerboard Immunoblotting Technique [Immunology] .... CBIB
Checkered (WGA) .... CH
Checkered [Navigation markers] .... CHEC
Checkered (SAUS) .... Chec
Checkers Drive In Restaurants [Associated Press] (SAG) .... Checkers
Checkers Drive-In Restaurants [NASDAQ symbol] (SPSG) .... CHKR
Checkers Drive-In Restr [NASDAQ symbol] (TTSB) .... CHKR
Checkfree Corp. [Associated Press] (SAG) .... Chkfree
Checkfree Corp. [NASDAQ symbol] (SAG) .... CKFR
Checkfree Holdings [NASDAQ symbol] [Formerly, Checkfree Corp.] (SG) .... CKFR
Checking .... CHKG

Checking, Accounting and Reporting for Member Firm [*Banking*] (IAA) ... CHARM
Checking, Accounting, and Reporting for Member Firms [*London Stock Exchange*] (MHDW) ... CHARM
Checking Automation Language (SAUS) ... CAL
Checking Document (SAUS) ... CD
Checking Operation (SAUS) ... CKO
Checking Operator (SAUS) ... CKO
Checking Sequence (SAUS) ... CS
Checking Subroutine (SAUS) ... CS
Checking System (SAUS) ... CS
Checking Unit (SAUS) ... CU
Checklist (KSC) ... C/L
Check-list of the Fishes of the Eastern Tropical Atlantic (SAUS) ... CLOFETA
Check-list of the Fishes of the North-Eastern Atlantic and of the Mediterranean (SAUS) ... CLOFNAM
Check-list of the Freshwater Fishes of Africa (SAUS) ... CLOFFA
Checklist Question (CAAL) ... CQ
Checkmate ... CHM
Checkmate (ADWA) ... chm
Checkmate Electronics [*NASDAQ symbol*] (TTSB) ... CMEL
Checkmate Electronics, Inc. [*Associated Press*] (SAG) ... Checkmte
Checkmate Electronics, Inc. [*NASDAQ symbol*] (SAG) ... CMEL
Checkmate Resources [*Vancouver Stock Exchange symbol*] ... CKM
Checkout ... CKOUT
Checkout (SAUS) ... CO
Checkout and Automatic Monitoring (MSA) ... CAM
Checkout and Fault Isolation [*NASA*] (KSC) ... COFI
Checkout and Maintenance ... CAM
Checkout Atmospheric Science Experiment Set (SAUS) ... CASES
Checkout Command Decoder (NASA) ... CCD
Checkout Control and Monitor Subsystem [*NASA*] (NASA) ... CCMS
Checkout, Control and Monitor Subsystem (SAUS) ... CCMS
Checkout, Control, and Monitor Subsystem (NAKS) ... ccms
Checkout Data Processor [*RADAR*] ... CDP
Checkout Equipment for Onboard Automatic Maintenance ... CEFOAM
Checkout Interpreter Module (MCD) ... COIM
Checkout Language [*NASA*] (NASA) ... COL
Checkout Operating System ... COSY
Checkout Operations Manual (AAG) ... COM
Check-Out Procedure (CAAL) ... CHOP
Checkout, Servicing, and Maintenance [*Airlock equipment*] (SSD) ... COSM
Checkout Station (ACAE) ... COS
Checkout Station (MCD) ... CS
Checkout Station (NAKS) ... cs
Checkout Tape [*Computer science*] (IAA) ... CT
Checkout Techniques Test Bed (NASA) ... CTTB
Checkout Test Language [*Computer science*] ... CTL
Checkout Test Set (AAG) ... COTS
Checkout Time ... COT
Checkout Valve ... COV
Checkout/Control and Monitor Subsystem Interface [*NASA*] (NASA) ... CMSI
Checkout-Oriented Language [*Computer science*] (IEEE) ... COOL
Checkpoint [*A publication*] ... Check
Checkpoint [*Computer science*] (BUR) ... CHKPT
Checkpoint (MCD) ... CKPT
Checkpoint ... CP
Checkpoint Certified Security Administrator (SAUO) ... CCSA
Checkpoint Sys [*NYSE symbol*] (TTSB) ... CKP
Checkpoint Systems, Inc. [*Associated Press*] (SAG) ... ChkPt
Checkpoint Systems, Inc. [*NYSE symbol*] (SAG) ... CKP
Checks (SAUS) ... Chs
Checks (NAKS) ... CKS
Checks Anonymous ... CA
Checks Fragmentation [*Computer science*] (PCM) ... CHKFRAG
Checksum (SAUS) ... CKSM
Checksum Error (MCD) ... CS
Checkup X-Ray [*Radiology*] (DAVI) ... CUX
Checkwriting Redemptions [*Business term*] ... CWR
Chediak-Higashi Disease [*Medicine*] ... CHD
Chediak-Higashi Syndrome [*Medicine*] (DMAA) ... CH
Chediak-Higashi Syndrome [*Medicine*] ... CHS
Chediak-Higasht Syndrome (SAUS) ... C-H S
Chedong [*South Korea*] [*ICAO location identifier*] (ICLI) ... RKPD
Cheektowaga, NY [*AM radio station call letters*] ... WECK
Cheers International [*Vancouver Stock Exchange symbol*] ... CHR
Cheese (ROG) ... CH
Cheese ... CHES
Cheese Bureau of England (SAUS) ... CBE
Cheese Importers Association of America (EA) ... CIAA
Cheese Whey Powder ... CWP
Cheesecake Factory [*NASDAQ symbol*] (TTSB) ... CAKE
[*The*] **Cheesecake Factory, Inc.** [*NASDAQ symbol*] (SAG) ... CAKE
[*The*] **Cheesecake Factory, Inc.** [*Associated Press*] (SAG) ... Cheeseck
Cheever's Medical Jurisprudence for India [*A publication*] (DLA) ... Cheev Med Jur
Chef der Zivilverwaltung [*Chief of Civil Affairs Section*] [*German military - World War II*] ... CDZ
Chef des Generalstabs des Heeres [*Chief of General Staff of the Army*] [*German military - World War II*] ... CGS
Chefornak [*Alaska*] [*Airport symbol*] (OAG) ... CYF
Chefornak, AK [*Location identifier*] [*FAA*] (FAAL) ... CFZ
Chefornak, AK [*Location identifier*] [*FAA*] (FAAL) ... CYF
Chefs de Cuisine Association of America (EA) ... CCAA
Chefs de Cuisine Association of America ... CDCA
Chefs de Cuisine Association of America (NTPA) ... CdCAA
Chefs International, Inc. [*NASDAQ symbol*] (NQ) ... CHEF
Chefs International, Inc. [*Associated Press*] (SAG) ... ChefsInt
Chefs Intl. [*NASDAQ symbol*] (TTSB) ... CHEF
Cheguitti [*Mauritania*] [*Airport symbol*] (OAG) ... CGT
Chehalis, WA [*Location identifier*] [*FAA*] (FAAL) ... CLS
Chehalis, WA [*FM radio station call letters*] ... KACS
Cheju [*South Korea*] [*Airport symbol*] (OAG) ... CJU
Cheju/International [*South Korea*] [*ICAO location identifier*] (ICLI) ... RKPC
Cheju/Mosulpo [*South Korea*] [*ICAO location identifier*] (ICLI) ... RKPM
Chekiang Province [*China, Mainland*] [*MARC geographic area code*] [*Library of Congress*] (LCCP) ... a-cc-ch
Chekok [*Alaska*] [*Seismograph station code, US Geological Survey*] (SEIS) ... CKK
Chelan Butte [*Washington*] [*Seismograph station code, US Geological Survey*] (SEIS) ... CBW
Chelan Resources, Inc. [*Vancouver Stock Exchange symbol*] ... CJN
Chelan, WA [*AM radio station call letters*] ... KOZI
Chelan, WA [*FM radio station call letters*] ... KOZI-FM
Chelating Agent - Diethylenetriaminepentaacetic Acid (PDAA) ... Ca-DTPA
Chelation-Enhanced Fluorescence [*Chemistry*] ... CHEF
Chelation-Enhanced Quenching [*Chemistry*] ... CHEQ
Chelik Resources, Inc. [*Vancouver Stock Exchange symbol*] ... CKV
Chelinda [*Malawi*] [*ICAO location identifier*] (ICLI) ... FWCD
Chelkar [*Former USSR*] [*ICAO location identifier*] (ICLI) ... UATR
Chelles/Le Pin [*France*] [*ICAO location identifier*] (ICLI) ... LFPH
Chelmsford [*City in England*] ... CHELM
Chelmsford [*City in England*] (ROG) ... CHELMSF
Chelmsford (ODBW) ... CM
Chelmsford Branch, Rayside-Balfour Public Library, Chelmsford, Ontario [*Library symbol*] [*National Library of Canada*] (NLC) ... OCHERB
Chelmsford Library, Chelmsford, United Kingdom [*Library symbol*] [*Library of Congress*] (LCLS) ... UkCh
cheloniologist (SAUS) ... cheloniol
Cheloniology Chelons Chelonians (SAUS) ... Cheloniol
Chelsea [*A publication*] (BRI) ... Chel
Chelsea Against Nuclear Destruction United (SAUO) ... CANDU
Chelsea College of Science and Technology (SAUS) ... CCST
Chelsea GCA Realty [*NYSE symbol*] (TTSB) ... CCG
Chelsea GCA Realty [*Associated Press*] (SAG) ... ChelGCA
Chelsea GCA Realty [*NYSE symbol*] (SAG) ... COG
Chelsea, London, Islington, Office [*Denoting a location where a manuscript was written*] [*Acronym used as pseudonym of Joseph Addison, British author, 1672-1719*] ... CLIO
Chelsea Public Library, Chelsea, MA [*Library symbol*] [*Library of Congress*] (LCLS) ... MChels
Chelsea Resources [*Vancouver Stock Exchange symbol*] ... CHD
Chelsea Royal Hospital (SAUO) ... CRH
Chelsea Vocational High School (SAUS) ... CVHS
Cheltenham [*Typeface*] (DGA) ... CHELT
Cheltenham [*City in England*] ... CHELT
Cheltenham [*City in England*] (ROG) ... CHELTM
Cheltenham [*Maryland*] [*Seismograph station code, US Geological Survey*] [*Closed*] (SEIS) ... CLH
Cheltenham and Gloucester [*A British Building Society*] (ECON) ... C & G
Cheltenham Annex [*Military*] (DNAB) ... CAX
Cheltenham, Glos. (SAUO) ... Chelm
Cheltenham Ladies' College [*England*] (WDAA) ... CLC
Cheltenham-Gloucester [*England*] [*Airport symbol*] (AD) ... GLO
Chelyabinsk Air Enterprise [*Former USSR*] [*FAA designator*] (FAAC) ... CHB
Chem. Fabr. Tempelhof [*Germany*] [*Research code symbol*] ... CFT
Chem International, Inc. [*Associated Press*] (SAG) ... ChemIntl
Chem International, Inc. [*Associated Press*] (SAG) ... ChmInt
Chem International, Inc. [*NASDAQ symbol*] (SAG) ... CXIL
CHEM Singly Indexed Substances [*DIALOG Information Services, Inc.*] [*Database*] ... CHEMSIS
Chem. Werke Albert [*Germany*] [*Research code symbol*] ... HA
Chemagro, Kansas City, MO [*Library symbol*] [*Library of Congress*] (LCLS) ... MoKChe
Chemcell Ltd., Montreal, PQ, Canada [*Library symbol*] [*Library of Congress*] (LCLS) ... CaQMCh
Chemdex Corp. [*NASDAQ symbol*] (SG) ... CMDX
Chemech Aviation Ltd. [*Pakistan*] [*FAA designator*] (FAAC) ... CMC
Chemed Corp. [*NYSE symbol*] (SPSG) ... CHE
Chemed Corp. [*Associated Press*] (SAG) ... Chemed
Chemehuevi Mountains [*California*] [*Seismograph station code, US Geological Survey*] (SEIS) ... CMH
Chemeketa Community College, Salem, OR [*OCLC symbol*] (OCLC) ... CHK
Chemeketa Community College, Salem, OR [*Library symbol*] [*Library of Congress*] (LCLS) ... OrSaC
Chemeketa Cooperative Regional Library Service [*Library network*] ... CCRLS
Chemetics International Ltd., Vancouver, BC, Canada [*Library symbol*] [*Library of Congress*] (LCLS) ... CaBVaCl
Chemetics International Ltd., Vancouver, British Columbia [*Library symbol*] [*National Library of Canada*] (NLC) ... BVACI
Chemetron Corporation (SAUO) ... CTN
Chemfab Corp. [*NYSE symbol*] (SG) ... CFA
Chemfab Corp. [*Associated Press*] (SAG) ... Chmfab
Chemfab Corp. [*NASDAQ symbol*] (NQ) ... CMFB
ChemFirst, Inc. [*NYSE symbol*] (SG) ... CEM
Chemi Trol Chem [*NASDAQ symbol*] (TTSB) ... CTRL
Chemical (NFPA) ... C
Chemical [*or Chemistry*] (AFM) ... CHEM
Chemical ... CHEML
Chemical [*Freight*] ... CHM
Chemical (AABC) ... CML
Chemical Abstract Nummer (SAUS) ... CAS-Nr

Chemical Abstract Searching Terminal (NITA) ... CAST
Chemical Abstract Series (SAUO) ... CAS
Chemical Abstracts [*A publication*] (MEC) ... CA
Chemical Abstracts ... ChemAb
Chemical Abstracts Condensates [*A publication*] (IID) ... CAC
Chemical Abstracts Condensates [*Database*] ... CACON
Chemical Abstracts, Even-Numbered Issue ... CAE
Chemical Abstracts Integrated Subject File [*Chemical Abstracts Service*] [*Database*] [*A publication*] (IID) ... CAISF
Chemical Abstracts (journ.) (SAUS) ... Chem Abstr
Chemical Abstracts, Odd-Numbered Issue ... CAO
Chemical Abstracts, Ohio State University, Columbus, OH [*Library symbol*] [*Library of Congress*] (LCLS) ... OUCA
Chemical Abstracts Reference (NITA) ... CR
Chemical Abstracts Registry Service (SAUS) ... CAS
Chemical Abstracts Selective Dissemination of Information (NITA) ... CHEMSDI
Chemical Abstracts Service [*American Chemical Society*] [*Columbus, OH*] [*Database producer*] ... CAS
Chemical Abstracts Service, Columbus, OH [*OCLC symbol*] (OCLC) ... CAS
Chemical Abstracts Service Condensates (journ.) (SAUS) ... CASCON
Chemical Abstracts Service Document Delivery Service [*American Chemical Society*] (NITA) ... CAS DDS
Chemical Abstracts Service (journ.) (SAUS) ... CAS
Chemical Abstracts Service Registry Number [*Medicine*] (DMAA) ... CAS-REGN
Chemical Abstracts Service Registry Number ... CASRN
Chemical Abstracts Service Source Index [*American Chemical Society*] [*Information service or system*] ... CASSI
Chemical Abstracts Subject Index Alert [*Database*] [*A publication*] ... CASIA
Chemical Abuse Addiction Treatment Outcome Registry ... CATOR
Chemical Accident/Incident Control (MCD) ... CAIC
Chemical Accident/Incident Control Officer [*Military*] (AABC) ... CAICO
Chemical Activity (SAUS) ... A
Chemical Activity Status Report [*Chemical Information Systems, Inc.*] [*Information service or system*] (CRD) ... CASR
Chemical Addiction Certification (BARN) ... CAC
Chemical Addition and Sampling System [*Nuclear energy*] (NRCH) ... CA
Chemical Addition Tank (NRCH) ... CAT
Chemical Advertisers Group of New York [*Inactive*] (EA) ... CAGNY
Chemical Age of India (journ.) (SAUS) ... Chem Age India
Chemical Age Project File [*Pergamon ORBIT InfoLine Inc.*] [*Information service or system*] ... CAPF
Chemical Agent Alarm ... CAA
Chemical Agent Casualty Assessment System (MCD) ... CACAS
Chemical Agent Decontamination Simulant (MCD) ... CADS
Chemical Agent Detection Network ... CADNET
Chemical Agent Detection System (SAUS) ... CADS
Chemical Agent Disclosure Solution [*Toxicology*] ... CADS
Chemical Agent Identification Training Set ... CAITS
Chemical Agent Monitor [*Military*] (RDA) ... CAM
Chemical Agent Munition (SAUS) ... CAM
Chemical Agent Munition Disposal System [*Army*] ... CAMDS
Chemical Agent Munitions Dispersal System (SAUS) ... CAMDS
Chemical Agent, Nonpersistent (SAUS) ... G-NP
Chemical Agent, Persistent (SAUS) ... G-P
Chemical Agent Remote Monitor System (SAUS) ... CARMS
Chemical Agent Resistant Coated (SAUS) ... CARC
Chemical Agent Resistant Coating [*A paint*] ... CARC
Chemical Agent Resistant Material (SAUS) ... CARM
Chemical Agent T (SAUS) ... T
Chemical Agent Training Dispenser (SAUS) ... CAT-D
Chemical Agent Training Mixture (SAUS) ... CATM
Chemical Agent/Arsine (SAUS) ... SA
Chemical Agent/Nerve Gas Persistent Toxic (SAUS) ... VX
Chemical Agent/Plastized (SAUS) ... PWP
Chemical Agents Sensor (SAUS) ... CHASE
Chemical Agents Tracer (SAUS) ... CAT
Chemical Agent/Soman (SAUS) ... GD
Chemical Agent/Tear Gas, Chloropicrin (SAUS) ... PS
Chemical Agent/Thermate (SAUS) ... TH
Chemical Algorithm for Reticulation Linearization (NITA) ... CARL
Chemical Ammunition Storage Specialist (SAUS) ... Cml Ammo Stor Sp
Chemical Ammunition Train (SAUS) ... Cml Am Tn
Chemical Analysis (SAUS) ... Chemanal
Chemical Analysis by Microwave Spectroscopy (SAUS) ... CAMSPEC
Chemical Analysis Detection Instrumentation Control ... CADIC
Chemical Analysis Facility (NRCH) ... CAF
Chemical and Allied Industries [*Department of Employment*] [*British*] ... CAI
Chemical and Biological [*Warfare*] [*Formerly, CBR, CEBAR*] [*Military*] ... CB
Chemical and Biological Accident and Incident Control [*Army*] (AABC) ... CBAIC
Chemical and Biological Accident and Incident Control Plan [*Army*] (AABC) ... CBAICP
Chemical and Biological Agent Delivery System (MCD) ... CBADS
Chemical and Biological Agent Protection System (ACAE) ... CABAPS
Chemical & Biological Defence Establishment (SAUS) ... CBDE
Chemical and Biological Defense Command [*Army*] ... CBCCOM
Chemical and Biological Defense Command [*Army*] (RDA) ... CBDCOM
Chemical and Biological Information Handling [*National Institutes of Health*] ... CBIH
Chemical and Biological Medical Treatment Symposia (ADWA) ... CBMTS
Chemical and Biological Oxygen Demand (LDT) ... CBOD
Chemical and Biological Warfare [*Military*] ... CBW
Chemical and Biological Weapons [*Military*] ... CBW
Chemical and Coating Laboratory [*Army*] (MCD) ... CCL
Chemical and Engineering News (MEC) ... Chem Eng News
Chemical and Engineering News (journ.) (SAUS) ... CAEN
Chemical and Engineering News (journ.) (SAUS) ... C&EN
Chemical and Industrial Consultants Association (DBA) ... CICA
Chemical and Insulating ... C + I
Chemical and Metallurgical Engineering (journ.) (SAUS) ... Chem&Met Eng
Chemical and Mixed Waste Operations (SAUS) ... CMWO
Chemical & Petroleum Division (ACII) ... CHEMPID
Chemical and Petroleum Engineering (journ.) (SAUS) ... Chem Pet Eng
Chemical and Process Engineering (journ.) (SAUS) ... Chem Process Eng
Chemical and Radiological Laboratories (SAUO) ... C&RL
Chemical and Radiological Laboratories (SAUS) ... CARL
Chemical and Radiological Laboratories [*Army*] ... CRLR
Chemical and Radiological Laboratory (SAUO) ... CARL
Chemical and Statistical Policy Division [*Environmental Protection Agency*] (GFGA) ... CSPD
Chemical & Thermal Engineering Ltd. (SAUS) ... CTE Ltd
Chemical and Transport Systems (SAUS) ... CTS
Chemical and Volume Control [*Nuclear energy*] (NRCH) ... CVC
Chemical and Volume Control System [*Nuclear energy*] (NRCH) ... CVCS
Chemical Applications of Nuclear Explosions (PDAA) ... CANE
Chemical Asphyxiants [*Medicine*] (MELL) ... Ca
Chemical Assembly Fuel Element Exchange (NUCP) ... CAFEE
Chemical Assessments and Related Activities (AUEG) ... CARA
Chemical Attack Warning Transmission System (MCD) ... CAWTS
Chemical Automated Search Terminal [*Computer Corp. of America*] [*Information service or system*] (IID) ... CAST
Chemical Awareness and Emergency Response [*Program for handling hazards*] ... CAER
Chemical Awareness and Emergency Response Program (SAUS) ... CAER
Chemical, Bacteriological, and Radiation (WDAA) ... CBR
Chemical, Bacteriological, Nuclear (SAUS) ... CBN
Chemical Banking Corp. [*Associated Press*] (SAG) ... ChBk
Chemical Banking Corp. [*NYSE symbol*] (SPSG) ... CHL
Chemical Banking Corp. [*Associated Press*] (SAG) ... ChmBnk
Chemical Beam Epitaxy [*Solid state physics*] ... CBE
Chemical Binding Effect ... CBE
Chemical Biological (COE) ... C-B
Chemical, Biological and Radiation Laboratories (SAUS) ... CBRL
Chemical, Biological, and Radiological Center [*Military*] ... CBRC
Chemical, Biological, and Radiological Element [*Military*] (AABC) ... CBRE
Chemical, Biological and Radiological Integrated Reconnaissance System [*Army*] ... CBRIDS
Chemical, Biological, and Radiological Protection (DNAB) ... CBRP
Chemical, Biological, and Radiological Section [*Military*] ... CBRS
Chemical, Biological and Radiological Selection (SAUS) ... CBRS
Chemical, Biological and Radiological Warfare (SAUS) ... CBRW
Chemical, Biological and Radiological Warfare (SAUS) ... CEBAR Warfare
Chemical Biological Defense Agency [*Army*] ... CBDA
Chemical, Biological, Protected Shelter ... CBPS
Chemical, Biological, Radiological (SAUS) ... CBR
Chemical, Biological, Radiological Agency [*Military*] ... CBRA
Chemical, Biological, Radiological, and Nuclear [*Army*] (AABC) ... CBRN
Chemical, Biological, Radiological Control Center [*Military*] (AABC) ... CBRCC
Chemical, Biological, Radiological Officer [*Army*] ... CBRO
Chemical, Biological, Radiological Operations Center (SAUO) ... CBROC
Chemical, Biological, Radiological Warfare (SAUS) ... CBRW
Chemical, Biological, Radiological Warfare [*Later, CB*] [*Military*] ... CEBAR
Chemical Biological Weaponry (SAUS) ... CBW
Chemical Blowing Agent [*Plastics technology*] ... CBA
Chemical Board (SAUS) ... Cml Bd
Chemical Bond Approach ... CBA
Chemical Bond Approach Study ... CBAS
Chemical Bottle Storage [*Area*] (AAEL) ... CBS
Chemical Burns (MELL) ... CB
Chemical Business News Service (SAUO) ... CBNS
Chemical Business NewsBase [*Royal Society of Chemistry*] [*Information service or system*] ... CBNB
Chemical Carcinogenesis Research Information System [*National Library of Medicine*] [*Information service or system*] ... CCRIS
Chemical Cleaning Building [*Nuclear energy*] (NRCH) ... CCB
Chemical Closet ... CC
Chemical Coaters Association (EA) ... CCA
Chemical Coaters Association International (NTPA) ... CCAI
Chemical Collection System (SAUS) ... CCS
Chemical Collection System / Request Tracking [*Online database*] [*Environmental Protection Agency*] ... CCS/RTS
Chemical Collection/Request Tracking System [*Environmental Protection Agency*] (ERG) ... CC/RTS
Chemical Comments of the General Metallurgical and Chemical Company (SAUO) ... GEMEC
Chemical Communications (MEC) ... Chem Commun
Chemical Communications Association (EA) ... CCA
Chemical Company (SAUO) ... Cml Co
Chemical Composition [*Of precious stones*] ... CC
Chemical Composition Distribution ... CCD
Chemical Compound Registry (System) (DIT) ... CCR(S)
Chemical Control Division [*Environmental Protection Agency*] (GFGA) ... CCD
Chemical Control Order (SAUS) ... CCO
Chemical Control Procedure [*Nuclear energy*] (NRCH) ... CCP
Chemical Coordination Staff [*Environmental Protection Agency*] (GFGA) ... CCS
Chemical Corporation of Singapore (SAUO) ... CCS
Chemical Corps (SAUO) ... C
Chemical Corps [*Army*] (GFGA) ... CC
Chemical Corps [*Army*] (RDA) ... CM
Chemical Corps (AAGC) ... CML
Chemical Corps (SAUO) ... Cml

Chemical Corps (SAUS) .... Cml C
Chemical Corps [Army] .... CMLC
Chemical Corps Association (SAUS) .... CCA
Chemical Corps Association, Inc. (SAUO) .... CCA
Chemical Corps Biological Laboratories [Army] .... CMLCBL
Chemical Corps Decontamination Company (SAUO) .... Cml Decon Co
Chemical Corps Engineering Agency (SAUO) .... CCEA
Chemical Corps Engineering Command (SAUS) .... CmlCEnCom
Chemical Corps Engineering Command [Army] .... CMLCENCOM
Chemical Corps Engineering Command (SAUS) .... CMLCENGRCOM
Chemical Corps Engineering Command (SAUS) .... Cml C Engr Comd
Chemical Corps Enlisted Reserve (SAUO) .... CCER
Chemical Corps Historical Office [Army] .... CMLHO
Chemical Corps Material Command [Army] .... CMLCMATCOM
Chemical Corps Materiel Command (SAUS) .... Cml C Mat Comd
Chemical Corps Proving Ground [Army] .... CCPG
Chemical Corps Research and Development Command (SAUS) .... CCRC
Chemical Corps Research and Development Command [Army] (AAG) .... CCRDC
Chemical Corps Research and Development Command [Army] .... CMLCRDCOM
Chemical Corps Research and Development Command (SAUS) .... Cml CRD Com
Chemical Corps Research and Development Command (SAUS) .... Cml C Res&Dev Comd
Chemical Corps Research and Engineering Command [Army] .... CMLCRECOM
Chemical Corps Research and Engineering Command (SAUO) .... CMLRECOM
Chemical Corps School (SAUO) .... CMLCSCH
Chemical Corps School (SAUS) .... Cml C Sch
Chemical Corps Technical Command [Army] (MCD) .... CCTC
Chemical Corps Training Command [Army] .... CMLCTNGCOM
Chemical Data Base Directory (SAUS) .... CDBD
Chemical Data Center, Inc. [Information service or system] (IID) .... CDC
Chemical Data System .... CDS
Chemical Decontamination (SAUS) .... Cml Decon
Chemical Decontamination Centre (SAUS) .... CDC
Chemical Decontamination Training Facility [Military] .... CDTF
Chemical Defence Committee (SAUS) .... CDC
Chemical Defence Establishment [British] .... CDE
Chemical Defence Experimental Station [British] [World War II] .... CDES
Chemical Defence Research Department (SAUO) .... CDRD
Chemical Defence System (SAUS) .... CDS
Chemical Defense .... CMLDEF
Chemical Defense Equipment [Military] (INF) .... CDE
Chemical Defense Experimental Establishment (SAUS) .... CDEE
Chemical Defense Multipurpose Mask (ACAE) .... CDMM
Chemical Defense Planning Document (SAUO) .... CDPD
Chemical Defense Program (MCD) .... CDP
Chemical Defense Research Establishment (SAUS) .... CDRE
Chemical Delivery System [Medicine] .... CDS
Chemical Demilitarization [Military] (RDA) .... CHEM DEMIL
Chemical Demilitarization and Installation Restoration (MCD) .... CDIR
Chemical Demilitarization Program [Army] .... CDP
Chemical Department (SAUS) .... CD
Chemical Department (SAUO) .... CD
Chemical Dependence Profile [Medicine] (MELL) .... CDP
Chemical Dependency (MELL) .... CD
Chemical Dependency (OICC) .... ChemDep
Chemical Dependency Unit (SAUS) .... CDU
Chemical Depot (SAUO) .... Cml Dep
Chemical Depot Company (SAUO) .... Cml Dep Co
Chemical Detection (SAUS) .... CHEM DET
Chemical Detection and Alarm Training Simulator (MCD) .... CDATS
Chemical Development Corp. [Geneva, Switzerland] .... CDC
Chemical Dictionary On-Line [National Library of Medicine] [Bethesda, MD] [Database] .... CHEMLINE
Chemical dictionary Online (SAUS) .... CHEMLINE
Chemical Discriminator System .... CDS
Chemical Distribution Institute (SAUO) .... CDI
Chemical Distribution Room (AAEL) .... CDR
Chemical Diversion and Trafficking Act [1988] .... CDTA
Chemical Division Council (SAUO) .... CDC
Chemical Downstream Etch (AAEL) .... CDE
Chemical Downwind Message [Military] (INF) .... CDM
Chemical Dry Etching (SAUS) .... CDE
Chemical Economic Services (SAUS) .... Chem Econ
Chemical Economics Handbook [SRI International] [Database] .... CEH
Chemical Economy & Engineering Review (journ.) (SAUS) .... CEER
Chemical Education (MEC) .... Chem Educ
Chemical Education for Public Understanding Program [University of California, Berkley] .... CEPUP
Chemical Education Material Study (SAUS) .... CEMS
Chemical Education Material Study [American Chemical Society] (AEE) .... CHEMS
Chemical Education Planning and Coordinating Committee [American Chemical Society] .... CEPACC
Chemical Education Publishing Co (SAUS) .... Chem Educ
Chemical Education Publishing Company (SAUO) .... Chem Ed
Chemical Effects Information Center [Department of Energy] (IID) .... CEIC
Chemical Effects Information Task Group [Department of Energy] [Information service or system] (IID) .... CEITG
Chemical Eingineering (journ.) (SAUS) .... Chem Engng
Chemical Element Balance (GFGA) .... CEB
Chemical Elements Publishing Co (SAUS) .... Chem Elements Pub
Chemical Emergency Planning and Response Commission .... CEPRC
Chemical Emergency Preparedness and Prevention Office (SAUO) .... CEPPO
Chemical Emergency Preparedness Plan (GNE) .... CEPP
Chemical Emergency Preparedness Program [Environmental Protection Agency] .... CEPP

Chemical Energy .... CE
Chemical Engineer .... CE
Chemical Engineer .... Ch E
Chemical Engineer .... Chem E
Chemical Engineer .... Chem Eng
[The] Chemical Engineer [A publication] .... TCE
Chemical Engineering (SAUS) .... CHEG
Chemical Engineering Abstracts [Royal Society of Chemistry] [Information service or system] .... CEA
Chemical Engineering and Biotechnology Abstracts [A publication] .... CEABA
Chemical Engineering and Mining Review [A publication] .... Chem Engng Mining Rev
Chemical Engineering Catalog [A publication] .... CEC
Chemical Engineering Database .... CHERUB
Chemical Engineering Information Processing System .... CHIPS
Chemical Engineering Investigation of Reaction Paths [Computer science] .... CHIRP
Chemical Engineering (journ.) (SAUS) .... Chem Engng
Chemical Engineering Laboratory (ABAC) .... CEL
Chemical Engineering Modular Instruction [Project] .... CHEMI
Chemical Engineering News (journ.) (SAUS) .... Chem Eng News
Chemical Engineering Operations [MIT] (MCD) .... CEO
Chemical Engineering Optimization System (SAUS) .... CHEOPS
Chemical Engineering Organization .... CEO
Chemical Engineering Progress (journ.) (SAUS) .... CEP
Chemical Engineering Progress, Symposium Series (journ.) (SAUS) .... Chem Eng Progr Symp Ser
Chemical Engineering Science (journ.) (SAUS) .... Chem Eng Sci
Chemical Engineering Simulation System (SAUS) .... CHESS
Chemical Engineering World (journ.) (SAUS) .... Chem Eng World
Chemical Engineering-California Institute of Technology (SAUS) .... CHE-CIT
Chemical Etching (SAUS) .... Chem Etch
Chemical Evaluation Search and Retrieval System [Michigan Department of Natural Resources] [Information service or system] (CRD) .... CESARS
Chemical Exchange Directory SA [Information service or system] (IID) .... CED
Chemical Explosive (SAUS) .... CE
Chemical Explosive Ordnance Disposal (SAUS) .... CEOD
Chemical Fabrics and Film Association (EA) .... CFFA
Chemical Field Effect Transistor (ACAE) .... CHEMFET
Chemical Field Emission Transistor (ABAC) .... Chem-FET
Chemical Field Laboratory (SAUO) .... Cml F Lab
Chemical Financial [NASDAQ symbol] (TTSB) .... CHFC
Chemical Financial Corp. (EFIS) .... CFC
Chemical Financial Corp. [NASDAQ symbol] (NQ) .... CHFC
Chemical Financial Corp. [Associated Press] (SAG) .... ChmFin
Chemical Flux Cutting (SAUS) .... FOC
Chemical Foaming Agent (SAUS) .... CFA
Chemical Force Microscope .... CFM
Chemical Force Microscopy (SAUS) .... CFM
Chemical Gas (MCD) .... CG
Chemical Geology (SAUS) .... Chem Geol
Chemical Graphics Programming Language (SAUS) .... CGP Language
Chemical Group (SAUO) .... Cml Gp
Chemical Hazard Alert Notices (HEAS) .... CHAN
Chemical Hazard Assessment System (ACAE) .... CHAS
Chemical Hazard Communication Policy [Stanford University] .... CHCP
Chemical Hazard Information Profile [Environmental Protection Agency] .... CHIP
Chemical Hazard Information Profile System [Environmental science] (COE) .... CHIPS
Chemical Hazard Response Information System (SAUO) .... CHRIS
Chemical Hazards .... CH
Chemical Hazards and Emergency Management Unit [Queensland] [Australia] .... CHEMU
Chemical Hazards Communications Society (HEAS) .... CHCS
Chemical Hazards Emergency Management System [Environmental science] (COE) .... CHEMS
Chemical Hazards in Industry [Royal Society of Chemistry] [Information service or system] .... CHI
Chemical Hazards Response Information System [Coast Guard] [Information service or system] .... CHRIS
Chemical Hazards Response Information System/Hazard Assessment Computer System [Coast Guard] (ERG) .... CHRIS/HACS
Chemical Health & Safety (SAUS) .... CH&S
Chemical Heat Pipe [Energy storage] .... CHP
Chemical Heritage Foundation [Formerly, NFHC] .... CHF
Chemical Hygiene Officer (SARE) .... CHO
Chemical Hygiene Plan [Occupational Safety and Health Administration] .... CHP
Chemical Identification (SAUO) .... CHEMID
Chemical Identification File [National Library of Medicine] [Information service or system] (IID) .... ChemID
Chemical Importers and Exporters Council of Australia (SAUO) .... CIEGA
Chemical Incident Unit (WDAA) .... CIU
Chemical Index [Database] .... CHEMDEX
Chemical Industries Association .... CIA
Chemical Industries Association's Safety and Health Council [British] .... CISHEC
Chemical Industry Advisory Board (SAUO) .... CIAB
Chemical Industry Council CIC
Chemical Industry Data Exchange [Computer science] (ACRL) .... CIDX
Chemical Industry Emergency Mutual Aid Network (EEVL) .... CHEMNET
Chemical Industry for Minorities in Engineering (EA) .... ChIME
Chemical Industry in Basle .... CIBA
Chemical Industry Institute of Technology (SARE) .... CIIT
Chemical Industry Institute of Toxicology (EA) .... CIIT
Chemical Industry institute of Toxicology, Durham, NC [Library symbol] [Library of Congress] (LCLS) .... NcDurIT

Chemical Industry of Canada (SAUO) CIC
Chemical Industry Safety and Health (SAUS) .... CISHEC
Chemical Industry Safety and Health Council (SAUO) .... CISHEC
Chemical Industry Scheme for Assistance in Freight (HEAS) .... CHEMSAFE
Chemical Information and Data System [*Army*] .... CIDS
Chemical Information and Tracking System (GNE) .... CHEMTRACK
Chemical Information Center [*Indiana University*] CIC
Chemical Information Management, Inc. [*Information service or system*] (IID) .... CIMI
Chemical Information On-Line [*Ministry of Labour*] [*Hamilton, ON*] [*Information service or system*] (IID) .... CIOL
Chemical Information Resources Directory (SAUS) .... CIRD
Chemical Information Retrieval System [*Army*] (IID) .... CIRS
Chemical Information Services [*Stanford Research Institute*] (IID) .... CIS
Chemical Information System [*Environmental science*] (COE) .... CIS
Chemical Information Systems, Inc. [*Fein-Marquart Associates*] [*Information service or system*] (IID) .... CIS
Chemical Information Systems Operators [*Later, EUSIDIC*] .... CHEOPS
Chemical Injection [*Nuclear energy*] (NRCH) CI
Chemical Injection (System) [*Nuclear energy*] (NRCH) .... CI(S)
Chemical Injection System (SAUS) .... CIS
Chemical Inspectorate (SAUO) CI
Chemical Inspectorate [*British*] CI
Chemical Institute of Canada CIC
Chemical Instrumentation (journ.) (SAUS) .... Chem Instrum
Chemical Instrumentation Test and Evaluation [*NASA*] (USDC) .... CITE
Chemical International Finance & Consulting [*Belgium*] .... CHEMFICO
Chemical International Information Center CIIC
Chemical Inventory System (SAUS) .... CISR
Chemical Ion Generator (AAG) .... CIG
Chemical Ionization [*Spectrometry*] CI
Chemical Ionization Mass Spectrometer (or Spectrometry) (SAUS) .... CIMS
Chemical Ionization Mass Spectroscopy (ACAE) .... CIM
Chemical Ionization/Electron Impact [*Spectroscopy*] .... CI/EI
Chemical Journal of the Association of Official Analytical Chemists [*Association of Official Analytical Chemists*] [*Information service or system*] (CRD) .... CJAOAC
Chemical Journals of John Wiley & Sons [*John Wiley & Sons, Inc.*] [*Information service or system*] (CRD) .... CJWILEY
Chemical Journals of the American Chemical Society [*Information service or system*] (CRD) .... CJACS
Chemical Journals of the Royal Society of Chemistry [*British*] [*Information service or system*] (CRD) .... CJRSC
Chemical Journals Online [*American Chemical Society*] [*Database*] .... CJO
Chemical Kinetics Information Center [*National Institute of Standards and Technology*] .... CKIC
Chemical Laboratory CL
Chemical Laboratory (SAUO) .... Cml Lab
Chemical Laboratory Analysis and Scheduling System [*Computer science*] .... CLASS
Chemical Laboratory Company (SAUO) .... Cml Lab Co
Chemical Laboratory, Mobile (SAUS) .... Cml Lab Mbl
Chemical Laboratory Technician [*or Technology*] [*Navy*] .... LBT
Chemical LASER (MCD) CL
Chemical Laser Advanced Diffuser/Ejector (ACAE) .... CLADE
Chemical LASER Analysis Program (MCD) .... CLAP
Chemical LASER Analytical System Program (MCD) .... CLASP
Chemical LASER Mode Control .... CLMC
Chemical LASER Study [*or System*] .... CLS
Chemical LASER System Code (MCD) .... CLASYC
Chemical Library, Canadian National Railways [*Bibliotheque Chimique, Chemins de fer Nationaux du Canada*] **Montreal, Quebec** [*Library symbol*] [*Obsolete*] [*National Library of Canada*] (NLC) .... QMCNC
Chemical List and Information Pointer System (SAUS) .... CLIPS
Chemical List Index and Processing System [*Environmental Protection Agency*] (ERG) .... CLIPS
Chemical Literature [*A publication*] CL
Chemical Literature Data Extraction .... CLIDE
Chemical Low-Altitude Missile [*Air Force program*] .... CLAM
Chemical Low-Altitude Missile Puny [*Air Force program*] (MCD) .... CLAMP
Chemical Machining [*Factory automation*] (BTTJ) .... CHM
Chemical Machining Template (MCD) .... CMT
Chemical Machining Template Line (MCD) .... CMTL
Chemical Maintenance Company (SAUO) .... Cml Maint Co
Chemical Management and Resources Association (NTPA) .... CMRA
Chemical Management System (ABAC) .... CMS
Chemical Manufacture [*Department of Employment*] [*British*] .... CM
Chemical Manufacturers Association (EA) .... CMA
Chemical Manufacturing Association (SAUO) .... CMA
Chemical Manufacturing Process Unit (EEVL) .... CMPU
Chemical Market Associates, Inc. [*Information service or system*] (IID) .... CMAI
Chemical Market Research Association (SAUS) .... CMRA
Chemical Marketing and Economics .... CM & E
Chemical Marketing and Economics .... CMEC
Chemical Marketing Reporter (journ.) (SAUS) .... OPD
Chemical Marketing Research Association (EA) .... CMRA
Chemical Markup Language (TELE) .... CML
Chemical Mass Balance [*Environmental science*] (COE) .... CMB
Chemical Material Study Model [*Military*] (AFIT) .... CMSM
Chemical Materials Catalog .... CMC
Chemical Mechanical Polishing [*Engineering*] .... CMP
Chemical Metallizing System (SAUS) .... CMS
Chemical, Metallurgical and Mining Society of South Africa (SAUO) .... CMMSSA
Chemical Metallurgical Reporting .... CMR
Chemical Micro Milling Company (SAUO) .... CMMC
Chemical Milling (SAUS) .... Chem Mill
Chemical Milling (SAUS) .... CHM
Chemical Milling (MSA) .... CM
Chemical Milling Machine .... CMM
Chemical Modeling Laboratory [*NIH/EPA Chemical Information System*] [*Database*] .... CHEMLAB
Chemical Modeling project (SAUS) .... CM
Chemical Monograph Referral Center [*Consumer Product Safety Commission*] [*Information service or system*] (IID) .... CHEMRIC
Chemical Mortar Battalion (SAUO) .... Cml Mtr Bn
Chemical Name Dictionary [*Dialog Information Services, Inc.*] [*Database*] .... CHEMNAME
Chemical Network [*Chemical Transportation Emergency Center*] (ERG) .... CHEMNET
Chemical Neutron Activation Analysis .... CNAA
Chemical Nomenclature Advisory Service (PDAA) .... CNAS
Chemical Noncommissioned Officer (SAUS) .... Ch NCO
Chemical Notation Association (SAUO) .... CNA
Chemical of Highest Concern (EEVL) .... CHC
Chemical Officer (SAUS) .... Chem O
Chemical Officer (SAUS) .... Cml O
Chemical On-Line Data Analyzer [*Interactive Elements, Inc.*] .... CODA
Chemical On-Line Retrieval Experiment (TELE) .... CORE
Chemical Operations [*Army*] (AABC) .... CMLOPS
Chemical Operations System .... CHEOPS
Chemical Operations System Study (ACAE) .... CHEOPS
Chemical Orbit-to-Orbit Shuttle [*NASA*] .... COOS
Chemical Oxygen Consumption (SAUS) .... COC
Chemical Oxygen Demand .... COD
Chemical Oxygen Iodine LASER (MCD) .... COIL
Chemical Physics (MEC) .... Chem Phys
Chemical Physics Letters (MEC) .... Chem Phys Lett
Chemical Physics Letters (journ.) (SAUS) .... Chem Phys Lett
Chemical Pigment Co., Metals Division, Baltimore, MD [*Library symbol*] [*Library of Congress*] (LCLS) .... MdBCPM
Chemical Polish .... CP
Chemical Power Augmented Projectile (SAUS) .... CPAP
Chemical Practitioner (DAS) .... CP
Chemical Preparation (OA) .... CP
Chemical Process Industries (SAUS) .... CPIs
Chemical Process Industry .... CPI
Chemical Process Quantitative Risk Assessment [*Chemical engineering*] .... CPQRA
Chemical Process Synthesis [*Chemical engineering*] .... CPS
Chemical Processing and Engineering (journ.) (SAUS) .... Chem Process Eng
Chemical Processing Cell [*Nuclear energy*] (NUCP) .... CPC
Chemical Processing Facility [*Nuclear energy*] (NUCP) .... CPF
Chemical Processing (journ.) (SAUS) .... Chem Process
Chemical Processing Plant (SAUS) .... CPP
Chemical Processors, Inc. (EFIS) .... CHEMPRO
Chemical Producers and Distributors Association (NTPA) .... CPDA
Chemical Product (SAUS) .... CP
Chemical Propulsion .... CP
Chemical Propulsion Abstracts [*Database*] [*Chemical Propulsion Information Agency*] [*Information service or system*] (CRD) .... CPA
Chemical Propulsion Division [*NASA*] (KSC) .... CPD
Chemical Propulsion Information Agency [*Laurel, MD*] [*DoD*] .... CPIA
Chemical Propulsion Rocket (SAUS) .... CPR
Chemical Propulsion Technology Reviews [*Chemical Propulsion Information Agency*] (MCD) .... CPTR
Chemical Protective Clothing .... CPC
Chemical Protective Overgarment [*Army*] (DOMA) .... CPO
Chemical Protective Overgarment [*Military*] (INF) .... CPOG
Chemical Public Relations Association [*Later, CCA*] (EA) .... CPRA
Chemical Publishing Company (SAUO) .... Chem Pub
Chemical Pulp .... CP
[*A*] **Chemical Radical** (DOG) .... R
Chemical, Radiological, Biological Warfare [*NATO*] (NATG) .... CRB
Chemical Reaction Engineering .... CRE
Chemical Reaction in Colloidal solution (SAUS) .... CRC
Chemical Reaction Interface Mass Spectrometry .... CRIMS
Chemical Reactions Documentation Service [*Derwent Publications Ltd.*] [*Bibliographic database*] (IID) .... CRDS
Chemical Records and Grading System (SAUS) .... CRAGS
Chemical Recovery Association [*British*] (DBA) .... CRA
Chemical Referral Center (EA) .... CRC
Chemical Regulations and Guidelines System [*CRC Systems, Inc.*] [*Information service or system*] (IID) .... CRGS
Chemical Release and Radiation Effects Satellite [*NASA*] .... CRRES
Chemical Release Module (MCD) .... CRM
Chemical Releasing Factor (SAUS) .... CRF
Chemical Remanent Magnetization [*Geophysics*] .... CRM
Chemical Replacement Training Center (SAUS) .... Cml RTC
Chemical Replacement Training Center (SAUO) .... CmlRTC
Chemical Report .... CR
Chemical Research and Development Center [*Aberdeen Proving Ground, MD*] [*Army*] (RDA) .... CRDC
Chemical Research and Development Laboratories [*Edgewood Arsenal, MD*] [*Army*] .... CRDL
Chemical Research and Environmental Needs (SAUO) .... CREN
Chemical Research Applied to World Need [*IUPAC*] .... CHEMRAWN
Chemical Research Applied to World Needs (SAUS) .... CHEMRAWN
Chemical Research Consultants, Inc. .... CRC
Chemical Research, Development, and Engineering Center [*Aberdeen Proving Ground, MD*] [*Army*] (RDA) .... CRDEC

Chemical Research Laboratory (SAUO) .... CRL
Chemical Research Laboratory, CIL, Inc., Mississauga, Ontario [*Library symbol*] [*National Library of Canada*] (NLC) .... OMCILCR
Chemical Research Project [*Military*] .... CRP
Chemical Resistant Coating .... CRC
Chemical Resources, Inc. (EFIS) .... CRI
Chemical Reviews (MEC) .... Chem Rev
Chemical Reviews (journ.) (SAUS) .... Chem Rev
Chemical Rubber Company (SAUO) .... CRC
Chemical Rust Inhibiting Germicide (SAUS) .... CRI Germicide
Chemical Rust Inhibitor (SAUS) .... CRI
Chemical Rust-Inhibiting .... CRI
Chemical Safety Abstracts (COE) .... CSA
Chemical Safety and Hazard Investigation Board .... CSB
Chemical Safety and Hazardous Investigation Board [*Environmental Protection Agency*] .... CSHIB
Chemical Safety Board (COE) .... CSB
Chemical Safety Data Sheet .... CSDS
Chemical Sampling Information .... CH
Chemical Science and Technology Laboratory [*National Institute of Standards and Technology*] .... CSTL
Chemical Screening Battery (DAVI) .... CSB
Chemical Section (SAUS) .... Chem Sec
Chemical Section (SAUS) .... Cml Sec
Chemical Selection Working Group [*National Cancer Institute*] .... CSWG
Chemical Self-funded Technical Advocacy and Research (SAUS) .... CHEMSTAR
Chemical Service Truck (SAUS) .... Cml Sv Trc
Chemical Shielding Anisotropy [*Physics*] .... CSA
Chemical Shift [*Physical chemistry*] .... CS
Chemical Shift Anisotropy [*Physical chemistry*] .... CSA
Chemical Shift Selective [*Medicine*] (DMAA) .... CHESS
Chemical Short-Range Order (MCD) .... CSRO
Chemical Smoke Generator (SAUS) .... Cml Smoke Genr
Chemical Smoke Generator (SAUS) .... CSG
Chemical Smoke Generator Battalion (SAUO) .... Cml Smoke Genr Bn
Chemical Societies of the Nordic Countries (EAIO) .... CSNC
Chemical Society (SAUO) .... CS
Chemical Society [*Later, RSC*] [*British*] .... CS
Chemical Society Information Services (SAUO) .... CSIS
Chemical Society, London, United Kingdom [*Library symbol*] [*Library of Congress*] (LCLS) .... UkLC
Chemical Society of Japan .... CSJ
Chemical Society of Japan (SAUO) .... CS of J
Chemical Society of Japan (SAUO) .... CS of J
Chemical Society of London (SAUO) .... CSL
Chemical Society Research Unit in Information Dissemination and Retrieval [*British*] (DIT) .... CSRUIDR
Chemical Society/Royal Institute of Chemistry (SAUO) .... CS/RIC
Chemical Solution (SAUS) .... CHEMSOL
Chemical Sources Association (EA) .... CSA
Chemical Special Emphasis Program [*Occupational Safety and Health Administration*] .... ChemSEP
Chemical Specialities Manufacturers Association, Inc. (SAUO) .... CSMA
Chemical Specialties Manufacturers Association (EA) .... CSMA
Chemical Species Balance (GFGA) .... CSB
Chemical Spray Deposition (PDAA) .... CSD
Chemical Stable Oxide (SAUS) .... CSO
Chemical Stimulation of the Brain (WGA) .... CSB
Chemical Stockpile Disposal [*Military*] (RDA) .... CSD
Chemical Stockpile Disposal Program [*Military*] (DOMA) .... CSDP
Chemical Stockpile Emergency Preparedness [*Military*] (RDA) .... CSEP
Chemical Stockpile Emergency Preparedness Program (ABAC) .... CSEPP
Chemical Storage and Transfer Facility (SAUS) .... LSL A
Chemical Storage Area (NRCH) .... CSA
Chemical Structure Analysis Routine .... ChemSTAR
Chemical Structure and Nomenclature System [*Environmental Protection Agency*] .... CSNS
Chemical Structure Association (EAIO) .... CSA
Chemical Substances Information Network [*No longer exists*] [*Environmental Protection Agency*] [*Information service or system*] .... CSIN
Chemical Substances Inventory [*Environmental Protection Agency*] (GFGA) .... CSI
Chemical Substructure Index [*Trademark*] .... CSI
Chemical Supply Point (SAUO) .... Cml Sup Pt
Chemical Surety Material (MCD) .... CSM
Chemical Sympathectomy [*Neurology*] (DAVI) .... CS
Chemical System Laboratory, Aberdeen Proving Grounds, MD [*OCLC symbol*] (OCLC) .... ADE
Chemical Systems Division [*NASA*] (NASA) .... CSD
Chemical Systems Laboratory [*Later, CRDC*] [*Army*] (RDA) .... CSL
Chemical Tariff Harmonization Agreement (SAUS) .... CDHA
Chemical Tariff Harmonization Agreement (SAUS) .... CTEA
Chemical Technical Intelligence Detachment (SAUS) .... Cml Tech Intel Det
Chemical Technicians Curriculum (SAUS) .... CHEMTEC
Chemical Technicians Curriculum [*Project*] .... ChemTeC
Chemical Technology (MEC) .... Chemtech
Chemical Technology Division (SAUO) .... CTD
Chemical Technology (journ.) (SAUS) .... Chem Technol
Chemical Temperature Resistant [*Automotive engineering*] .... CTR
Chemical Test (MCD) .... CT
Chemical Testing and Assessment Research Commission (GNE) .... CTARC
Chemical Therapy [*or Chemotherapy*] [*Pharmacology*] (DAVI) .... Kemo Tx
Chemical Thermodynamics and Energy Hazard Appraisal (SAUS) .... CHETA
Chemical Thermodynamics and Energy Hazard Evaluation (SAUS) .... CHETAEH Evaluation

Chemical Thermodynamics and Energy Hazard Evaluation [*American Society for Testing and Materials*] .... CHETAH
Chemical Thermodynamics Data Center [*National Institute of Standards and Technology*] .... CTDC
Chemical Titles (journ.) (SAUS) .... CT
Chemical Toilet Association (EA) .... CTA
Chemical Transfer (MCD) .... CT
Chemical Transport and Analysis Program (EEVL) .... CTAP
Chemical Transport and Deposition (MCD) .... CTD
Chemical Transport Model .... CTM
Chemical Transport Reaction .... CTR
Chemical Transportation Emergency Center [*Chemical Manufacturers Association*] .... CHEMTREC
Chemical Transportation Emergency Center (SAUS) .... CTEC
Chemical Transportation Industry Advisory Committee .... CTIAC
Chemical Treatment Pond (IEEE) .... CTP
Chemical Underwater Explosive (PDAA) .... CUE
Chemical Unions Council (SAUO) .... CUC
Chemical Unit Record Estimates Data Base (SAUS) .... CURE
Chemical Update System [*Environmental science*] (COE) .... CUS
Chemical Vapor Cleaning (AAEL) CVC
Chemical Vapor Deposition [*Coating technology*] .... CVD
Chemical Vapor Infiltration [*Materials science*] CVI
Chemical Vapor Phase Oxidization (EECA) .... CVPO
Chemical Vapor Plating .... CVP
Chemical Vapor Transport .... CVT
Chemical Vapor Transport Equipment (SAUS) .... CVTE
Chemical Vapor Transport Experiment (SAUS) .... CVTE
Chemical Vehicle Vulnerability Analysis Model (MCD) .... CHEMVVAM
Chemical Vocabulary (EEVL) CV
Chemical Warfare (SAUS) .... Cml Wfare
Chemical Warfare .... CW
Chemical Warfare - Bacteriological Warfare .... CWBW
Chemical Warfare Agent (ABAC) .... CWA
Chemical Warfare Committee (SAUS) .... CWC
Chemical Warfare Defense .... CWD
Chemical Warfare Defense Equipment .... CWDE
Chemical Warfare Directional Detector [*Military*] (CAAL) .... CWDD
Chemical Warfare Laboratories [*Army Chemical Center, MD*] (MCD) .... CWL
Chemical Warfare Laboratory (SAUS) .... CW Laby
Chemical Warfare Officer (SAUS) .... CWO
Chemical Warfare Protective Equipment (SAUS) .... CWPE
Chemical Warfare Research Department (SAUO) .... CWRD
Chemical Warfare Reserve (SAUS) .... CWRes
Chemical Warfare School (SAUO) .... CW Sch
Chemical Warfare Section (SAUS) .... CWS
Chemical Warfare Service [*Army*] .... CWS
Chemical Warfare Service (SAUO) .... CWS
Chemical Warfare Service, Army (SAUO) .... CWSA
Chemical Warfare Service Officer [*Army*] .... CWSO
Chemical Warfare Service Reserve (SAUS) .... CWSRes
Chemical Warfare Service Reserve (SAUO) .... CWS Res
Chemical Warfare Specialist, Medical [*Navy rating*] .... CWT
Chemical warfare tear agent (SAUS) .... CNB
Chemical warfare tear agent (SAUS) .... CNC
Chemical warfare tear agent (SAUS) .... CNS
Chemical Warfare Technical Committee .... CWTC
Chemical Warfare Training Regiment (SAUS) .... CWTR
Chemical Warfare Training Regiment (SAUO) .... CWTR
Chemical Warfare Treaty (SAUS) .... CWT
Chemical Warfare-Biological Warfare .... CWBW
Chemical Warfare/Chemical Biological Defense (RDA) .... CW/CBD
Chemical Warfare/Chemical Biological Defense Information Analysis Center [*DoD*] .... CBIAC
Chemical Warfare/Nuclear, Biological, and Chemical (RDA) .... CW/NBC
Chemical Warhead (SAUS) .... CW
Chemical Warning .... CHEMWARN
Chemical Warning Scanning Alarm (ACAE) .... CWSA
Chemical Waste Disposal Request (SAUS) .... CWDR
Chemical Waste Program [*Stanford University*] .... CWP
Chemical Waste Storage Facility (SAUO) .... CWSF
Chemical Waste Transportation Council [*Washington, DC*] (EA) .... CWTC
Chemical Waste Transportation Institute .... CWTI
Chemical Wavelength (CCCA) .... CW
Chemical Wavelength Laser (CCCA) .... CWL
Chemical Weapon Free Zone (ACAE) .... CWFZ
Chemical Weapons .... CW
Chemical Weapons & Civil Defence (SAUS) .... CWCD
Chemical Weapons Convention [*Proposed treaty*] .... CWC
Chemical Weapons Working Group [*A coalition of groups living near chemical weapons incinerators*] .... CWWG
Chemical Week (journ.) (SAUS) .... CW
Chemical Wood [*Paper*] (DGA) .... CW
Chemical Workers' Union .... CWU
Chemical World Index Key .... CWIK
Chemical-Atomic-Biological (BARN) .... CAB
Chemical/Bacterial/Nuclear [*Military*] (MCD) .... CBN
Chemical-Biological Activities [*Information service or system*] [*A publication*] .... CBAC
Chemical-Biological Computer System .... CBCS
Chemical-Biological Coordination Center [*NAS/NRC*] .... CBCC
Chemical-Biological Defense [*Military*] .... CBD
Chemical/Biological Incident Response Force [*Marine Corps*] .... CBIRF
Chemical/Biological Munitions (AFM) .... CBM
Chemical/Biological Unit (DWSG) .... CBU

Chemical-Biological-Radiological Engineering Group [*Army*] (MCD) .... CBREG
Chemically [*Freight*] .... CHEMLY
Chemically (SAUS) .... Chemly
Chemically Active Fluidized Bed [*Fuel gas*] .... CAFB
Chemically Active Material Ejected in Orbit (MCD) .... CAMEO
Chemically Amplified Positive resist (SAUS) .... CAMP
Chemically and Biologically Protected Shelter [*Army*] .... CBPS
Chemically Assembled Electronic Nanocomputers .... CAEN
Chemically Benign [*Medicine*] .... CB
Chemically Bonded Ceramic [*Materials science*] .... CBC
Chemically Contaminated Biological Mask (MCD) .... CCBM
Chemically Crosslinked Collagen (DB) CCLC
Chemically Defined Medium [*Microbiology*] .... CDM
Chemically Diabetic [*Endocrinology*] .... CD
Chemically Enhanced Primary Treatment [*Water treatment*] .... CEPT
Chemically Etched (or Etching) (SAUS) .... Chem Etch
Chemically Induced Dynamic Electron Polarization [*Spectrometry*] .... CIDEP
Chemically Induced Dynamic Nuclear Polarization [*Spectrometry*] .... CIDNP
Chemically Initiated Electron Exchange Luminescence .... CIEEL
Chemically Malignant [*Medicine*] .... CM
Chemically Milled (SAUS) .... Chem Mill
Chemically Modified Electrode [*Electrochemistry*] .... CME
Chemically Perturbed Region [*Meteorology*] .... CPR
Chemically Polished (SAUS) .... CP
Chemically Prepared and Oxygen Hot Pressed (SAUS) .... CP-OX-HP
Chemically Pure (SAUS) .... Chempure
Chemically Pure [*Chemistry*] .... CP
Chemically Pure (STED) .... cp
Chemically Pure Ethylamine (PDAA) .... CPEA
Chemically Recuperated Intercooled Steam-Injected Gas Turbine .... CRISTIG
Chemically Rigidized Space Structure .... CRSS
Chemically Sensitive Field Effect Transistor .... CHEMFET
Chemically sensitive Field-Effect Transistor (SAUS) .... ChemFET
Chemically Sensitive Semiconductor Devices .... CSSD
Chemically Stable Oxide .... CSO
Chemically Treated Steel (DICI) .... CTS
Chemically-Assisted Field Evaporation [*Materials science*] .... CAFE
Chemically-Assisted Ion Beam Etching (MCD) .... CAIBE
Chemically-Bound Residue [*Medicine*] (DMAA) .... CBR
Chemically-Induced Mutants [*Genetics*] .... CM
Chemically-Modified Carbon Paste [*Electrode*] .... CMCP
Chemically-Powered Interorbital Space Shuttle (MCD) .... CIS
Chemically-Stimulated Rubber (PDAA) .... CSR
Chemical/Petroleum Engineering (DD) .... Chem/PetEng
Chemical-Related Data Estimation Subroutines [*Environmental science*] .... CRDES
Chemical-Resistant Coating (SAUS) .... CRC
Chemicals (SAUS) .... Chem
Chemicals and Minerals Requirements Board (SAUO) .... CMRB
Chemicals and Polymers Group [*British*] .... C & P
Chemicals Consultative Committee (SAUO) CCC
Chemicals Control Order [*Australia*] .... CCO
Chemicals in Agriculture Advisory Group (HEAS) .... CHEMAG
Chemicals in Commerce Information System [*Environmental Protection Agency*] .... CICIS
Chemicals Notation Association [*British*] .... CNA
Chemicals on Reporting Rules Database [*Environmental Protection Agency*] .... CORR
Chemicals, Plastic Research .... CPR
Chemicals, Runoff, and Erosion from Agricultural Management Systems [*Agricultural Research Service*] .... CREAMS
Chemicals, Runoff and Erosion from Agricultural Management Systems (SAUS) .... CREAMS
Chemicals Selected for Equal, Analogous, or Related Character (DIT) .... CHEMSEARCH
Chemical-Vapour-Deposited .... CVD
Chemic-Ionization Detector (SAUS) .... CID
Chemico-Biological Interactions (SAUS) .... Chem Biol Interact
Chemico-Viscous Remanent Magnetization [*Geophysics*] .... CVRM
Chemie Gruenenthal GmbH [*Germany*] [*Research code symbol*] .... CG
Chemie-Information und Dokumentation Berlin [*Chemical Information and Documentation - Berlin*] [*Information service or system*] [*German*] (IID) .... CIDB
Chemiewerke Homburg [*Germany*] [*Research code symbol*] .... D
Chemiluminescence CL
Chemiluminescence Depletion [*Chemical kinetics*] .... CD
Chemiluminescence Detector .... CLD
Chemiluminescence Immunoassay (OA) .... CIA
Chemi-Mechanical Pulp .... CMP
Chemin [*Road*] [*French*] (ASC) .... ch
Chemi-Nuclear Systems Inc., Bellevue (SAUO) .... CNSI
Chemisch Thermische Prozeßtechnik (SAUS) .... CTP
Chemische Technik [*A database*] (NITA) .... CT
Chemischer Ingenieur [*Chemical Engineer*] [*German*] .... Chem Ing
Chemisches Untersuchungsamt Speyer (SAUS) .... ChUA
Chemisch/Physikalische Behandlungsanlage (SAUS) .... CPB
Chemist (SAUS) .... Chem
Chemist .... CHEM
Chemist and Druggist .... C & D
Chemist and Druggist (SAUS) .... C&D
Chemistry [*Secondary school course*] [*British*] C
Chemistry (DD) .... Chem
Chemistry (NTIO) .... chem
Chemistry and Biology [*A publication*] (MEC) .... Chem & Biol
Chemistry and Biology Research Institute [*Agriculture Canada Research Branch*] [*Research center*] (RCD) .... CBRI
Chemistry and Circulation Spectroscopy Mission (SAUO) .... CCOSM
Chemistry and Health Physics (GFGA) .... C & HP
Chemistry and Industry (journ.) (SAUS) .... Chem Ind
Chemistry and Laser Sciences (SAUS) .... CLS
Chemistry and Materials Science .... C&MS
Chemistry and Metallurgy Research (SAUS) .... CMR
Chemistry and Physics Laboratory [*Environmental science*] (COE) .... CPL
Chemistry and Physics on Stamps Study Unit [*An association*] (EA) .... CPOSSU
Chemistry and Physics Study Unit (EA) .... CPSU
Chemistry and Technology of Fuels and Oils (journ.) (SAUS) .... Chem Technol Fuels Oils
Chemistry Associates [*Australia*] .... CA
Chemistry, Bachelor of (SAUS) .... Ch B
Chemistry Consortium (EA) CC
Chemistry Department, St. Francis Xavier University, Antigonish, Nova Scotia [*Library symbol*] [*National Library of Canada*] (NLC) .... NSASC
Chemistry Division (CARB) .... CD
Chemistry, Doctor of (SAUS) .... Ch D
Chemistry in Britain (MEC) .... Chem Brit
Chemistry in Britain (journ.) (SAUS) .... Chem Br
Chemistry in Canada (journ.) (SAUS) .... Chem Can
Chemistry Information Center (SAUS) CIC
Chemistry Library, Canada Institute for Scientific and Technical Information [*Division de Chimie, Institut Canadien de l'Information Scientifique et Technique*] **Ottawa, Ontario** [*Library symbol*] [*National Library of Canada*] (NLC) .... OONC
Chemistry of High Elevation Fog Project [*Environment Canada*] .... CHEF
Chemistry Online Retrieval Experiment .... CORE
Chemistry Operations Support Laboratory (SAUS) .... COSL
Chemistry Records and Grading System [*Computer science*] .... CRAGS
Chemistry Screening Batteries I and II (STED) .... CSB I&II
Chemistry Study Unit [*Later, CPSU*] (EA) .... CSU
Chemistry Teaching Information Processing System .... CHEMTIPS
Chemistry Test Item Collection (ADA) .... CHEMTIC
Chemistry/Transport Models (SAUS) .... CTM
Chemists Club (SAUO) CC
Chemists' Club [*New York*] (SRA) CC
Chemists' Club [*Formerly, Mining Club*] (EA) .... MC
Chemists' Club - of New York (EA) .... CCNY
Chemists' Club, New York, NY [*Library symbol*] [*Library of Congress*] (LCLS) .... NNCC
Chemists' Defence Association [*British*] (BI) .... CDA
Chemists Federation (SAUO) .... CF
Chemist's Personal Software Series .... CPSS
Chemithermomechanical Pulp [*Papermaking*] .... CTMP
Chemi-Trol Chemical Co. [*Associated Press*] (SAG) .... ChemTrl
Chemi-Trol Chemical Co. [*NASDAQ symbol*] (SAG) .... CTRL
Chemoglobulin [*Biochemistry*] (DAVI) .... cg
Chemogram (VRA) .... CHGR
Chemohormonal Therapy [*Medicine*] (MELL) .... CHT
Chemonuclear (SAUS) .... Chemonuc
Chemonucleolysis [*Surgery*] .... CNL
Chemoprophylaxis [*Medicine*] (MELL) .... CP
Chemoreceptor [*Medicine*] (MELL) .... CR
Chemoreceptor Trigger Zone .... CTZ
Chemoreceptor Trigger Zone (SAUS) .... CT Zone
chemosensory (SAUS) .... chemosens
chemosphere (SAUS) .... chemos
chemosterilant (SAUS) .... chemoste
chemosterilization (SAUS) .... chemoste
chemosurgery (SAUS) .... chemosurg
Chemotactic Activity [*Medicine*] (MELL) .... CTA
Chemotactic Agent [*Medicine*] (MELL) .... CTA
Chemotactic Factor [*Immunology*] .... CF
Chemotactic Factor Inactivator [*Immunology*] .... CFI
Chemotactic Index [*Immunology*] .... CMI
Chemotaxis (DB) .... CTX
Chemotaxis-Generating Factor .... CGF
chemotaxonomist (SAUS) .... chemotax
chemotaxonomy (SAUS) .... chemotax
Chemotherapeutic Index [*Medicine*] CI
chemotherapist (SAUS) .... chemo
Chemotherapy [*Medicine*] (MAE) .... Chem
Chemotherapy [*Medicine*] (WDAA) .... CHEMO
Chemotherapy (NTIO) .... chemo
chemotherapy (SAUS) .... chemo
chemotherapy (SAUS) .... chemoth
Chemotherapy [*Medicine*] .... CT
Chemotherapy Foundation (EA) .... CF
Chemotherapy of Leprosy Program [*World Health Organization*] (BABM) .... THELEP
Chemotherapy Research Bulletin .... CRIB
Chemotherapy-Induced Nausea and Emesis [*Medicine*] (DMAA) .... CINE
Chempower, Inc. [*NASDAQ symbol*] (NQ) .... CHEM
Chempower, Inc. [*Associated Press*] (SAG) .... Chmpwr
Chemring Limited (SAUO) .... Chemring
Chemstrand Research Center, Inc., Durham, NC [*Library symbol*] [*Library of Congress*] (LCLS) .... NcDurCR
ChemTrak, Inc. [*Associated Press*] (SAG) .... ChmTrk
Chemtrak, Inc. [*NASDAQ symbol*] (SAG) .... CMTR
Chemtronics, Inc., Swannanoa, NC [*Library symbol*] [*Library of Congress*] (LCLS) .... NcSwC
Chemung County Historical Society, Elmira, NY [*Library symbol*] [*Library of Congress*] (LCLS) .... NEImHi
Chemurgic Council (SAUO) CC

Chemurgy Society (SAUO) .... CS
Chemway Corporation (SAUO) .... CMY
Chena Hot Springs, AK [*Location identifier*] [*FAA*] (FAAL) .... CEX
Chenango Bridge, NY [*FM radio station call letters*] (RBYB) .... WYOS-FM
Cheney, WA [*FM radio station call letters*] .... KEWU
Cheney, WA [*FM radio station call letters*] .... KEYF
Chengchow [*China*] [*Airport symbol*] (AD) .... CGO
Chengdu [*Republic of China*] [*Seismograph station code, US Geological Survey*] (SEIS) .... CNU
Chengdu [*China*] [*Airport symbol*] (OAG) .... CTU
Chengdu [*China*] [*ICAO location identifier*] (ICLI) .... ZUUU
Chengdu Aircraft Industry Corp. (SAUO) .... CAC
Cheni Gold Mines, Inc. [*Toronto Stock Exchange symbol*] [*Vancouver Stock Exchange symbol*] .... CZG
Chenodeoxycholic Acid [*Biochemistry*] (DB) .... CCA
Chenodeoxycholic Acid [*Also, CDC, CDCA, CHENIC*] [*Biochemistry*] .... CDA
Chenodeoxycholic Acid [*Also, CDA, CDCA, CHENIC*] [*Biochemistry*] .... CDC
Chenodeoxycholic Acid [*Also, CDA, CDC, CHENIC*] [*Biochemistry*] .... CDCA
Chenodeoxycholic Acid [*Also, CDA, CDC, CDCA*] [*Biochemistry*] .... CHENIC
Cheongokri [*South Korea*] [*ICAO location identifier*] (ICLI) .... RKSC
Chepes [*Argentina*] [*ICAO location identifier*] (ICLI) .... SACP
Cheque (WDAA) .... Ch
Cheque [*British*] (ROG) .... CHE
Cheque [*British*] (ROG) .... CHEQ
Cheque [*British*] .... CHQ
Cheque (WDAA) .... Chq
Cheque (SAUS) .... Chq
Cheque (WDAA) .... Cq
Cheque Account [*British*] [*Banking*] (ADA) .... C/A
Cheque Book [*British*] (DAS) .... C Bk
Cheque Book (SAUS) .... CBK
Cheque Reconciliation and Information System [*Australia*] .... CHRIS
Cheque Returned (SAUS) .... CR
Chequemate, Intl. [*AMEX symbol*] .... DDD
Cheques [*British*] (ROG) .... CHEX
Cheragas [*Algeria*] [*ICAO location identifier*] (ICLI) .... DAAX
Cheraw, SC [*Location identifier*] [*FAA*] (FAAL) .... CQW
Cheraw, SC [*AM radio station call letters*] .... WCRE
Cheraw, SC [*FM radio station call letters*] .... WJMX
Cherbourg [*France*] [*Airport symbol*] (OAG) .... CER
Cherbourg [*France*] [*ICAO location identifier*] (ICLI) .... LFRY
Cherbourg Sub-Area Channel (SAUO) .... CHERCHAN
Cherbourg/Maupertus [*France*] [*ICAO location identifier*] (ICLI) .... LFRC
Cher'd Interest [*Fan club*] (EA) CI
Cherenkov Array at Themis (SAUS) .... CAT
Cherished Numbers Dealers Association [*British*] (DBA) .... CNDA
Chernobyl Project Bibliographic Data Base (SAUS) .... CHERN
Chernofski Harbor, AK [*Location identifier*] [*FAA*] (FAAL) .... KCN
Chernovtsy [*Former USSR*] [*Seismograph station code, US Geological Survey*] [*Closed*] (SEIS) .... CRA
Chernovtsy [*Former USSR*] [*Seismograph station code, US Geological Survey*] [*Closed*] (SEIS) .... CRB
Cherokee [*MARC language code*] [*Library of Congress*] (LCCP) .... chr
Cherokee Case [*A publication*] (DLA) .... Cher Ca
Cherokee County Courthouse, Cherokee, IA [*Library symbol*] [*Library of Congress*] (LCLS) .... IaCheCoC
Cherokee County Historical Society, Cherokee, IA [*Library symbol*] [*Library of Congress*] (LCLS) .... IaCheCHi
Cherokee County Public Library, Gaffney, SC [*Library symbol*] [*Library of Congress*] (LCLS) .... ScGa
Cherokee Group [*NASDAQ symbol*] (NQ) .... CHKE
Cherokee, IA [*Location identifier*] [*FAA*] (FAAL) .... CKP
Cherokee, IA [*AM radio station call letters*] .... KCHE
Cherokee, IA [*FM radio station call letters*] .... KCHE-FM
Cherokee, Inc. [*Associated Press*] (SAG) .... Cheroke
Cherokee Inc. [*NASDAQ symbol*] (TTSB) .... CHKE
Cherokee Leasing, Inc. [*ICAO designator*] (FAAC) .... CBM
Cherokee National Historical Society (EA) .... CNHS
Cherokee Nuclear Station (NRCH) .... CNS
Cherokee, OK [*Location identifier*] [*FAA*] (FAAL) .... CKA
Cherokee Pilots Association [*Commercial firm*] (EA) .... CPA
Cherokee Public Library, Cherokee, IA [*Library symbol*] [*Library of Congress*] (LCLS) .... IaChe
Cherokee Village, AR [*Location identifier*] [*FAA*] (FAAL) .... CVK
Cherokee Village, AR [*FM radio station call letters*] .... KFCM
Cherokee, WY [*Location identifier*] [*FAA*] (FAAL) .... CKW
Cherquered (SAUS) .... CHEQ
Cherry (VRA) .... che
Cherry .... CHRY
Cherry Central Cooperative (EA) CCC
Cherry Corp. [*NASDAQ symbol*] (NQ) .... CHER
Cherry Corp. [*Associated Press*] (SAG) .... Cherry
Cherry Corp. 'A' [*NASDAQ symbol*] (TTSB) .... CHERA
Cherry Corp.'B' [*NASDAQ symbol*] (TTSB) .... CHERB
Cherry Creek Schools, Englewood, CO [*Library symbol*] [*Library of Congress*] (LCLS) .... COEnCS
Cherry European Rusty Mottle Virus (SAUS) .... ERMV
Cherry Growers and Industries Foundation (EA) .... CGIF
Cherry Hill Free Public Library, Cherry Hill, NJ [*OCLC symbol*] (OCLC) .... CHF
Cherry Hill Free Public Library, Cherry Hill, NJ [*Library symbol*] [*Library of Congress*] (LCLS) .... NjCh
Cherry Hill Medical Center, Cherry Hill, NJ [*Library symbol*] [*Library of Congress*] (LCLS) .... NjChM
Cherry Hill, NJ [*FM radio station call letters*] (RBYB) .... WSJI-FM
Cherry Hospital, Learning Resource Center, Goldsboro, NC [*Library symbol*] [*Library of Congress*] (LCLS) .... NcGoCH
Cherry Lane Elementary School, Carle Place, NY [*Library symbol*] [*Library of Congress*] (LCLS) .... NCpCE
Cherry Lane Fashion [*Vancouver Stock Exchange symbol*] .... CFG
Cherry Leafroll Virus [*Plant pathology*] .... CLRV
Cherry Marketing Institute (EA) .... CMI
Cherry Point [*North Carolina*] [*Seismograph station code, US Geological Survey*] [*Closed*] (SEIS) .... CPC
Cherry Point Marine Corps Air Station [*North Carolina*] [*ICAO location identifier*] (ICLI) .... KNKT
Cherry Point, NC [*Location identifier*] [*FAA*] (FAAL) .... NJF
Cherry Point, NC [*Location identifier*] [*FAA*] (FAAL) .... NKT
Cherry Point, North Carolina [*Marine Corps Air Station*] .... CPNC
Cherry Processors' Cooperative [*Australia*] .... CPC
Cherry Public School, Iron, MN [*Library symbol*] [*Library of Congress*] (LCLS) .... MnIrCS
Cherry Rasp Leaf Virus [*Plant pathology*] .... CRLV
Cherry Red Spot Myoclonus [*Medicine*] (DMAA) .... CRSM
Cherry School District 92, Cherry, IL [*Library symbol*] [*Library of Congress*] (LCLS) .... ICherSD
Cherry Valley Elementary School, Cherry Valley, IL [*Library symbol*] [*Library of Congress*] (LCLS) .... IChevE
Cherry Valley, NY [*FM radio station call letters*] .... WJIV
Cherry-Burrel Corporation (SAUO) .... CHY
Cherry-Crandall Unit (MAE) .... CCU
Cherry-Red (SAUS) .... CR
Cherry-Red Spot [*Tay's sign*] [*Medicine*] (MELL) .... CRS
Cherryville, NC [*AM radio station call letters*] .... WCSL
Cherryville, OR [*FM radio station call letters*] (BROA) .... KLVP-FM
Chervonets [*Monetary unit; 1922-1947*] [*Russian*] .... ch
Cheryl Hale Fan Club [*Defunct*] (EA) .... CHFC
Cheryl K. Warner Fan Club (EA) .... CKWFC
Cheryl Resources, Inc. [*Vancouver Stock Exchange symbol*] .... CYU
Cheryl Roth International Fan Club (EA) .... CRIFC
Chesaning Public Library, Chesaning, MI [*Library symbol*] [*Library of Congress*] (LCLS) .... MiChes
Chesapeake Air Services [*ICAO designator*] (FAAC) .... CAB
Chesapeake & Ohio - Baltimore & Ohio (SAUO) .... C&O-B&O
Chesapeake and Ohio Canal National Monument .... CHOH
Chesapeake and Ohio Historical Society (EA) .... COHS
Chesapeake & Ohio Railroad (SAUO) .... CO
Chesapeake & Ohio Railroad Co. (SAUO) .... C&ORy
Chesapeake and Ohio Railway (SAUO) .... COR
[*The*] **Chesapeake & Ohio Railway Co.** [*Later, Chessie System, Inc.*] .... C & O
[*The*] **Chesapeake & Ohio Railway Co. (Pere Marquette District)** [*AAR code*] .... PM
Chesapeake & Potomac Telephone Co. (SAUO) .... C&P
Chesapeake Automotive Wholesalers Association (SRA) .... CAWA
Chesapeake Bay [*Virginia and Maryland*] .... CHES
Chesapeake Bay Agreement (GNE) .... CBA
Chesapeake Bay Annex [*Navy*] .... CBA
Chesapeake Bay Basin (COE) .... CBB
Chesapeake Bay Bridge Tunnel (SAUS) .... CBBT
Chesapeake Bay Center for Environmental Studies [*Smithsonian Institution*] .... CBCES
Chesapeake Bay Detachment [*Washington, DC*] [*Navy*] (GRD) .... CBD
Chesapeake Bay Foundation [*Marine science*] (OSRA) .... CBF
Chesapeake Bay Group [*Navy*] (DNAB) .... CHESBAYGRU
Chesapeake Bay Institute [*Johns Hopkins University*] .... CBI
Chesapeake Bay Observing System [*Marine science*] (OSRA) .... CBOS
Chesapeake Bay Program (COE) .... CBP
Chesapeake Bay Project (SAUO) .... CBP
Chesapeake Bio Labs 'A' [*ECM, Symbol*] (TTSB) .... PHD.EC
Chesapeake Biological Laboratories [*University of Maryland*] .... CBL
Chesapeake Biological Laboratories, Inc. [*Associated Press*] (SAG) .... ChesBio
Chesapeake Biological Laboratories, Inc. [*AMEX symbol*] (SAG) .... PHD
Chesapeake Computer [*Vancouver Stock Exchange symbol*] .... CKR
Chesapeake Conference (PSS) .... CHEC
Chesapeake Corp. [*Associated Press*] (SAG) .... Chspk
Chesapeake Corp. [*NYSE symbol*] (SPSG) .... CSK
Chesapeake Corporation of Virginia (SAUO) .... CSK
Chesapeake Division (SAUO) .... CHESDIV
Chesapeake Division Naval Facilities Engineering Command (DNAB) .... CHESDIVNAVFACENGCOM
Chesapeake Division Naval Facilities Engineering Command [*Washington, DC*] .... CHES/NAVFAC
Chesapeake Division Naval Facilities Engineering Command [*Washington, DC*] .... CHESNAVFACENGCOM
Chesapeake Division Naval Facilities Engineering Command .... DIRCHESDOCKS
Chesapeake Division Support Facility [*Navy*] (DNAB) .... CHESDIVSUPPAC
Chesapeake Energy [*NYSE symbol*] (SG) .... CHK
Chesapeake Energy Corp. [*Associated Press*] (SAG) .... ChesEn
Chesapeake Energy Corp. [*NYSE symbol*] (SAG) .... CHK
Chesapeake Highway Advisories Routing Traffic .... CHART
Chesapeake Information Retrieval Service (IID) .... CIRS
Chesapeake, OH/Huntington, WV [*Location identifier*] [*FAA*] (FAAL) .... HTW
Chesapeake Physics Association (SAUO) .... CPA
Chesapeake Public Library, Chesapeake, VA [*Library symbol*] [*Library of Congress*] (LCLS) .... ViChe
Chesapeake Research Consortium .... CRC
Chesapeake Seafood Packers Association (EA) .... CSPA
Chesapeake Utilities [*NYSE symbol*] (SPSG) .... CPK
Chesapeake Utilities Corp. [*Associated Press*] (SAG) .... ChesUtl
Chesapeake, VA [*AM radio station call letters*] (BROA) .... WCPK-AM

Chesapeake, VA [*AM radio station call letters*] ... WJQI
Chesapeake, VA [*FM radio station call letters*] (RBYB) ... WKOC
Chesapeake Western Railway [*AAR code*] ... CHW
Chesapeake Western Railway (IIA) ... CW
Chesbar Resources, Inc. [*Toronto Stock Exchange symbol*] ... CBI
Chesbro Reservoir [*California*] [*Seismograph station code, US Geological Survey*] (SEIS) ... CBO
Chesham [*Urban district in England*] ... CHES
Cheshire [*County in England*] ... CHES
Cheshire [*County in England*] (ODBW) ... Ches
Cheshire [*County in England*] (ROG) ... CHESH
Cheshire Achievement of Scientific Skills in Schools [*British*] (AIE) ... CHASSIS
Cheshire Air Training School [*British*] [*ICAO designator*] (FAAC) ... CHZ
Cheshire Experiment in Educational Software [*British*] (AIE) ... CHEESE
Cheshire Field Squadron, Royal Engineers (SAUO) ... Ch Sq RE
Cheshire Lines (SAUO) ... CL
Cheshire Lines Committee (SAUO) ... CLC
Cheshire Lines Committee Railway [*British*] (ROG) ... CLC
Cheshire Lines Committee Railway [*British*] (ROG) ... CLCR
Cheshire Regiment (SAUO) ... Che
Cheshire Regiment (SAUO) ... Che R
Cheshire Regiment (SAUO) ... CHESHIRE
Cheshire Regiment (SAUO) ... Ches R
Cheshire Regiment (SAUO) ... Ch R
Cheshire Regiment (SAUO) ... CR
Cheshire School of Agriculture (SAUO) ... CSA
Cheshire School of Agriculture (SAUS) ... CSA
Cheshire Yeomanry (SAUO) ... Ches Y
Cheshire Yeomanry (SAUO) ... Ch Y
Chesley Branch, Bruce County Public Library, Ontario [*Library symbol*] [*National Library of Canada*] (NLC) ... OCH
Chesnut Fencing Manufacturers Society [*British*] (DBA) ... CFRMS
Chess ... CHSS
Chess Association of New South Wales [*Australia*] ... CANSW
Chess Association of Queensland [*Australia*] ... CAQ
Chess Club ... CC
Chess Club (SAUO) ... CC
Chess Collectors Association [*Defunct*] (EA) ... CCA
Chess Collectors International (EA) ... CCI
Chess Federation of Canada ... CFC
Chess Journalists of America (EA) ... CJA
Chess Life [*A publication*] ... Chess L
Chess on Stamps Unit [*Defunct*] (EA) ... CSU
Chessminster Group Ltd. [*Vancouver Stock Exchange symbol*] ... CRG
Chest [*Tea trade*] (ROG) ... C
Chest [*Medicine*] ... C
Chest (DMAA) ... ch
Chest [*Medicine*] ... CH
Chest [*Shipping*] ... CHT
Chest [*Anatomy*] (DAVI) ... V
Chest and Heart Association [*British*] (BI) ... CHA
Chest and Left Arm [*Cardiology*] ... CL
Chest and Right Arm [*Cardiology*] ... CR
Chest Circumference [*Neonatology and pediatrics*] (DAVI) ... cc
Chest Complaint [*Medicine*] (ADA) ... CC
Chest, Heart and Stroke Association (SAUO) ... CHSA
Chest Incision [*Medicine*] ... CI
Chest of Drawers ... CDWR
Chest Pain [*Medicine*] (MAE) ... CP
Chest Pain Emergency Room ... CPER
Chest Pain of Undetermined Etiology [*Medicine*] (MELL) ... CPUE
Chest Pain of Unknown Etiology [*Medicine*] ... CPUE
Chest Pain Syndrome [*Medicine*] (MELL) ... CPS
Chest Percussion and Postural Drainage [*Medicine*] (STED) ... CP & PD
Chest Percussion and Postural Drainage [*Medicine*] (STED) ... CPPD
Chest Physiotherapy [*Medicine*] ... CPT
Chest Physiotherapy and Physical Drainage [*Medicine*] ... CPPD
Chest Pysician (BABM) ... ChP
Chest Roentgenogram [*Radiology*] ... CR
Chest Roentgenogram [*Medicine*] (MELL) ... CRG
Chest Strap [*Medicine*] ... CS
Chest, Training [*Parachute*] ... CT
Chest Training (SAUS) ... CT
Chest Tube [*Medicine*] ... CT
Chest Tube Drainage [*Medicine*] (DAVI) ... CTD
Chest Tube Out [*Medicine*] ... CTO
Chest Tube Under Water-Seal Drainage [*Medicine*] (MEDA) ... CTUWSD
Chest Wall [*Medicine*] ... CW
Chest Wall Compliance [*Medicine*] (DMAA) ... CWC
Chest Wall Pain (MELL) ... CWP
Chest Wall Stimulation [*Medicine*] ... CWS
Chest X-Ray [*Medicine*] ... CX
Chest X-Ray [*Medicine*] ... CXR
Chest X-Ray (DMAA) ... CxR
Chestatee Regional Library [*Library network*] ... NGAL
Chestatee Regional Library System, Gainsville, GA [*Library symbol*] [*Library of Congress*] (LCLS) ... GGaCL
Chest-Back [*Medicine*] ... CB
Chester [*England*] [*Airport symbol*] (AD) ... CEG
Chester [*British*] (WA) ... Cestr
Chester [*City in England*] (ROG) ... CHEST
Chester [*British depot code*] ... CHS
Chester Alan Arthur [*US president, 1829-1886*] ... CAA
Chester & Holyhead Railway Co. (SAUO) ... CHR
Chester and North Wales Medical Society (SAUO) ... CNWMS
Chester Archaeological Society (SAUO) ... CAS
Chester Bancorp, Inc. [*Associated Press*] (SAG) ... ChestrBc
Chester Bancorp, Inc. [*NASDAQ symbol*] (SAG) ... CNBA
Chester Beatty Research Institute [*Great Britain*] [*Research code symbol*] ... CB
Chester Beatty Research Institute (SAUS) ... CBRI
Chester, CA [*Location identifier*] [*FAA*] (FAAL) ... CBD
Chester, CA [*FM radio station call letters*] (BROA) ... KBNF-FM
Chester, CA [*FM radio station call letters*] ... KCMT
Chester County District Library Center, Exton, PA [*OCLC symbol*] (OCLC) ... PWC
Chester County District Library Center, West Chester, PA [*Library symbol*] [*Library of Congress*] (LCLS) ... PWcC
Chester County Historical Society, West Chester, PA [*Library symbol*] [*Library of Congress*] (LCLS) ... PWcHi
Chester County Library, Chester, SC [*Library symbol*] [*Library of Congress*] (LCLS) ... ScCh
Chester County Reports [*Pennsylvania*] [*A publication*] (DLA) ... Ches Co
Chester County Reports [*Pennsylvania*] [*A publication*] (DLA) ... Ches Co Rep
Chester County Reports [*Pennsylvania*] [*A publication*] (DLA) ... Chest Co
Chester County Reports [*Pennsylvania*] [*A publication*] (DLA) ... Chest Co (PA)
Chester County Reports [*Pennsylvania*] [*A publication*] (DLA) ... Chest Co Rep
Chester County Reports [*Pennsylvania*] [*A publication*] (DLA) ... Chester
Chester County Reports [*Pennsylvania*] [*A publication*] (DLA) ... Chester Co (PA)
Chester County Reports [*Pennsylvania*] [*A publication*] (DLA) ... Chester Co Rep
Chester Free Public Library, Chester, NJ [*Library symbol*] [*Library of Congress*] (LCLS) ... NjChe
Chester Hldgs Ltd [*NASDAQ symbol*] (TTSB) ... CHES
Chester, IL [*AM radio station call letters*] ... KSGM
Chester, MA [*Location identifier*] [*FAA*] (FAAL) ... CTR
Chester Music [*Publisher*] ... CH
Chester, PA [*FM radio station call letters*] ... WDNR
Chester, PA [*AM radio station call letters*] ... WPWA
Chester, PA [*AM radio station call letters*] ... WVCH
Chester Palatine Courts [*1811*] [*England*] [*A publication*] (DLA) ... Booth
Chester Park Elementary School, Duluth, MN [*Library symbol*] [*Library of Congress*] (LCLS) ... MnDuCPE
Chester, SC [*Location identifier*] [*FAA*] (FAAL) ... DCM
Chester, SC [*FM radio station call letters*] (RBYB) ... WBT-FM
Chester, SC [*AM radio station call letters*] (BROA) ... WGCD-AM
Chester Society of Natural Sciences, Literature and Art (SAUO) ... CSNSLA
Chester, VA [*FM radio station call letters*] ... WDYL
Chester, VA [*AM radio station call letters*] ... WGGM
Chester Valley Bancorp [*Associated Press*] (SAG) ... ChestrV
Chester Valley Bancorp [*NASDAQ symbol*] (TTSB) ... CVAL
Chester Valley Bancorp, Inc. [*NASDAQ symbol*] (SAG) ... CVAL
Chester White Swine Record Association (EA) ... CWSRA
Chesterfield County Library, Chesterfield, SC [*Library symbol*] [*Library of Congress*] (LCLS) ... ScChf
Chesterfield Inlet, NT [*ICAO location identifier*] (ICLI) ... CYCS
Chesterfield Kings [*An association*] (EA) ... CK
Chesterfield, SC [*Location identifier*] [*FAA*] (FAAL) ... CTF
Chesterfield, SC [*FM station call letters*] (RBYB) ... WVSZ-FM
Chesterfield, VA [*Location identifier*] [*FAA*] (FAAL) ... CFU
Chesterfield, VA [*Location identifier*] [*FAA*] (FAAL) ... HYU
Chesterfield-Marlboro Technical College, Cheraw (SAUS) ... ScChwC
Chesterfield-Marlboro Technical College, Cheraw, SC [*Library symbol*] [*Library of Congress*] (LCLS) ... ScChwC
Chesterton [*England*] ... CHEST
Chesterton, IN [*FM radio station call letters*] (RBYB) ... WAJW
Chesterton, IN [*FM radio station call letters*] ... WDSO
Chesterton Tribune, Chesterton, IN [*Library symbol*] [*Library of Congress*] (LCLS) ... InCheT
Chestertown, MD [*AM radio station call letters*] ... WCTR
Chesterville Branch, Stormont, Dundas, and Glengarry County Public Library, Ontario [*Library symbol*] [*National Library of Canada*] (BIB) ... OCHSDG
Chestnut [*Horse racing*] ... CH
Chestnut (ROG) ... CHES
Chestnut [*Philately*] ... chnt
Chestnut [*Horse racing*] ... CHSTNT
Chestnut (VRA) ... chstnt
Chestnut Hill College [*Pennsylvania*] ... CHC
Chestnut Hill College, Philadelphia, PA [*OCLC symbol*] (OCLC) ... CHE
Chestnut Hill College, Philadelphia, PA [*Library symbol*] [*Library of Congress*] (LCLS) ... PPCCH
Chestnut Hills College (SAUO) ... CHC
Chestnut Ridge Railway Co. [*AAR code*] ... CHR
Cheswick & Harmar [*AAR code*] ... CHH
Cheswick Historical Society (EA) ... CHS
Chet Atkins Appreciation Society (EA) ... CAAS
Chet Atkins Guitar Society [*British*] (EAIO) ... CAGS
Chetco Community Public Library, Brookings, OR [*Library symbol*] [*Library of Congress*] (LCLS) ... OrBroo
Chete Game Reserve (SAUS) ... CGR
Chetek, WI [*FM radio station call letters*] (BROA) ... WATQ-FM
Chetek, WI [*FM radio station call letters*] ... WVXD
Cheticamp, NS [*Television station call letters*] ... CBHFT-4
Cheticamp, NS [*Television station call letters*] ... CBIT-2
Cheticamp, NS [*FM radio station call letters*] (RBYB) ... CKJM-FM
Chetumal [*Mexico*] [*Airport symbol*] (OAG) ... CTM
Chetumal [*Mexico*] [*ICAO location identifier*] (ICLI) ... MMCM
Chetwynd [*British Columbia*] [*Seismograph station code, US Geological Survey*] [*Closed*] (SEIS) ... CTC
Chetwynd Public Library, British Columbia [*Library symbol*] [*National Library of Canada*] (NLC) ... BCHE
Cheung Chau [*Hong Kong*] [*ICAO location identifier*] (ICLI) ... VHCH

Cheung Kong Infrastructure .... CKI
Chevak [Alaska] [Airport symbol] (OAG) .... VAK
Chevak, AK [FM radio station call letters] .... KCUK
Chevalier [Knight title] .... CHEV
Chevalier (DD) .... Chev
Cheval-Vapeur [Horsepower] [French] .... CH-V
Cheval-Vapeur [Horsepower] [French] CV
Cheveley [England] .... CHEV
Cheves' South Carolina Equity Reports [1839-1940] [A publication]
(DLA) .... Chev Ch
Cheves' South Carolina Equity Reports [1839-1940] [A publication]
(DLA) .... Chev Eq
Cheves' South Carolina Equity Reports [1839-1940] [A publication]
(DLA) .... Cheves Eq (SC)
Cheves' South Carolina Equity Reports [1839-1940] [A publication]
(DLA) .... Cheves L (SC)
Cheves' South Carolina Law Reports [1839-1940] [A publication] (DLA) .... Chev
Cheves' South Carolina Law Reports [1839-1940] [A publication] (DLA) .... Cheves
Chevet (VRA) .... chvt
Chevrolet [Automotive engineering] .... CHEV
Chevrolet .... CHEVY
Chevrolet Car Club of Victoria [Australia] CCCV
Chevrolet Motor Division [General Motors Corp.] .... CMD
Chevrolet Nomad Association (EA) .... CNA
Chevrolet-Pontiac-Canada Group [General Motors Corp.] .... CPC
Chevron .... CHEV
Chevron Canada Resources Ltd., Calgary, Alberta [Library symbol] [National
Library of Canada] (NLC) .... ACHS
Chevron Corp. [Associated Press] (SAG) .... Chevron
Chevron Corp. [Vancouver Stock Exchange symbol] [NYSE symbol]
(SPSG) .... CHV
Chevron Oil Field Research Co. .... COFRC
Chevron Oil Field Research Co., La Habra, CA [Library symbol] [Library of
Congress] (LCLS) .... CLhC
Chevron Research Co., Technical Information Center, Richmond, CA
[Library symbol] [Library of Congress] (LCLS) .... CRicC
Chevron Standard Ltd., Calgary, AB, Canada [Library symbol] [Library of
Congress] (LCLS) .... CaACHS
Chevy Chase Preferred Capital Corp. [NYSE symbol] (SAG) .... CCP
Chevy Chase Preferred Capital Corp. [Associated Press] (SAG) .... ChevyC
Chevy Development Corp. [Vancouver Stock Exchange symbol] .... CDY
Chevy Oil Corp. [Vancouver Stock Exchange symbol] .... CVO
Chewable Tablet (SAUS) .... CTB
Chewing, Sucking, Swallowing [Medicine] .... CSS
Chewings Fescue and Creeping Red Fescue Commission (EA) .... CFCRFC
Chewings Fescue and Creeping Red Fescue Committee (SAUO) .... CFCRFC
Chewore Game Reserve (SAUS) .... CGR
CHExchange Network [An association] (EA) .... CN
Cheyenne [City in Wyoming] (ROG) .... CHEY
Cheyenne [MARC language code] [Library of Congress] (LCCP) .... chy
Cheyenne [Diocesan abbreviation] [Wyoming] (TOCD) .... CHY
Cheyenne [Wyoming] [Airport symbol] (OAG) .... CYS
Cheyenne [Wyoming] [ICAO location identifier] (ICLI) .... KCYS
Cheyenne Airways, Inc. [ICAO designator] (FAAC) .... CYA
Cheyenne Mountain Air Force Base (ACAE) .... CMAFB
Cheyenne Mountain Air Force Software Support [Army] .... CMAFSS
Cheyenne Mountain Air Force Station .... CMAFS
Cheyenne Mountain Complex [NORAD] (MCD) .... CMC
Cheyenne Mountain National Command Center (ACAE) .... CMNCC
Cheyenne Mountain Upgrade .... CMU
Cheyenne, OK [Television station call letters] .... KWET
Cheyenne Petroleums [Vancouver Stock Exchange symbol] .... CYP
Cheyenne Software [AMEX symbol] (TTSB) .... CYE
Cheyenne Software, Inc. (MHDW) .... CHEY
Cheyenne Software, Inc. [Associated Press] (SAG) .... CheySoft
Cheyenne Software, Inc. [AMEX symbol] (SPSG) .... CYE
Cheyenne, WY [Location identifier] [FAA] (FAAL) .... CYS
Cheyenne, WY [Location identifier] [FAA] (FAAL) .... FEW
Cheyenne, WY [AM radio station call letters] .... KFBC
Cheyenne, WY [FM radio station call letters] .... KFBQ
Cheyenne, WY [Television station call letters] .... KGWN
Cheyenne, WY [FM radio station call letters] (RBYB) .... KIGN-FM
Cheyenne, WY [AM radio station call letters] (RBYB) .... KJJL-AM
Cheyenne, WY [FM radio station call letters] .... KKAZ
Cheyenne, WY [Television station call letters] .... KKTU
Cheyenne, WY [FM radio station call letters] .... KLEN
Cheyenne, WY [Television station call letters] .... KLWY
Cheyenne, WY [FM radio station call letters] (BROA) .... KOLZ-FM
Cheyenne, WY [AM radio station call letters] .... KRAE
Cheyenne, WY [FM radio station call letters] (RBYB) .... KRRR-FM
Cheyenne, WY [AM radio station call letters] .... KSHY
Cheyenne, WY [FM radio station call letters] (BROA) .... KZCY-FM
Cheyne-Stokes Breathing [Medicine] (STED) .... CSB
Cheyne-Stokes Respiration [Medicine] .... CSR
Cheyney State College, Cheyney, PA [OCLC symbol] (OCLC) .... PCH
Cheyney State College, Cheyney, PA [Library symbol] [Library of Congress]
(LCLS) .... PCheS
Chi (SAUS) X
Chi Square .... CS
Chian Federation of America (EA) .... CFA
Chiang Ching-kuo [Son of Nationalist Chinese leader Chiang Kai-shek] .... CCK
Chiang Kai-shek .... CKS
Chiang Mai [Thailand] [Seismograph station code, US Geological Survey]
(SEIS) .... CHG

Chiang Mai [Thailand] [Seismograph station code, US Geological Survey]
(SEIS) .... CHTO
Chiang Mai [Thailand] [Airport symbol] (OAG) .... CNX
Chiang Mai [Thailand] [ICAO location identifier] (ICLI) .... VTCC
Chiang Mai University (SAUO) .... CMU
Chiang Rai [Thailand] [Airport symbol] (OAG) .... CEI
Chiang Rai [Thailand] [ICAO location identifier] (ICLI) .... VTCR
Chiang Rai/Ban Chiang Kham [Thailand] [ICAO location identifier] (ICLI) .... VTCB
Chiang Rai/Chiang Khong [Thailand] [ICAO location identifier] (ICLI) .... VTCA
Chiao, Garmire and Townes Solution (SAUS) .... CGT Solution
Chiari Osteotomy [Medicine] (MELL) .... CO
Chiari-Frommel (Syndrome) [Medicine] .... CF
Chiaroscuro (VRA) .... chiaro
Chiasma [Genetics] (AAMN) .... Xa
Chiasma [Anatomy] (DAVI) .... Xta
Chiavari [Italy] [Seismograph station code, US Geological Survey] [Closed]
.... CHV
Chiayi [Republic of China] [Seismograph station code, US Geological Survey]
(SEIS) .... CHY
Chiayi [Taiwan] [Airport symbol] (OAG) .... CYI
Chibcha [MARC language code] [Library of Congress] (LCCP) .... chb
Chibougamau [Canada] [Airport symbol] (OAG) .... YMT
Chibougamau, PQ [AM radio station call letters] .... CJMD
Chic By HIS, Inc. [Associated Press] (SAG) .... ChicBy
Chic by HIS, Inc. [NYSE symbol] (SPSG) .... JNS
Chicaco Sun Book Week (journ.) (SAUS) .... CSBW
Chicago [Illinois] (ROG) .... CH
Chicago [Illinois] .... CHGO
Chicago (NTIO) .... Chgo
Chicago (ADWA) .... Chi
Chicago [Illinois] [Airport symbol] (OAG) .... CHI
Chicago [Illinois] .... CHIC
Chicago [Illinois] [Seismograph station code, US Geological Survey] [Closed]
(SEIS) .... CHK
Chicago [Branch in the Federal Reserve regional banking system] (BARN) .... G
Chicago [Illinois] [ICAO location identifier] (ICLI) .... KRGC
Chicago - Loyola [Illinois] [Seismograph station code, US Geological Survey]
(SEIS) .... CHI
Chicago Academic Library Council [Library network] .... CALC
Chicago Academy of Fine Arts .... CAFA
Chicago Academy of Science .... CAS
Chicago Academy of Sciences, Matthew Laflin Memorial Library, Chicago,
IL [Library symbol] [Library of Congress] (LCLS) .... ICCAS
Chicago Access Support Module (SAUS) .... CHASM
Chicago Air Defense Sector (SAUS) .... CHADS
Chicago Air, Inc. [ICAO designator] (FAAC) .... CGO
Chicago Air Shower Array (SAUS) .... CASA
Chicago Alliance of Businessmen (SAUO) .... CAB
Chicago Amateur Radio Club (SAUO) .... CARC
Chicago and Alton Railroad (SAUO) .... C&ARR
Chicago and Alton Railroad Co. (SAUO) .... C&A
Chicago & Alton Railroad Co. [Also known as Alton] .... C & A
Chicago & Eastern Illinois Railroad Co. [Absorbed into Missouri Pacific
System] .... C & EI
Chicago & Eastern Illinois Railroad Co. [Absorbed into Missouri Pacific
System] .... CEI
Chicago & Eastern Illinois Railroad Co. (SAUO) .... CEIRR
Chicago & Eastern Illinois Railroad Co. (SAUO) .... CGE
Chicago and Erie Railroad Co. (SAUO) .... C&E
Chicago and Erie Railroad Co. .... C & E
Chicago & Great Western Railway (SAUO) .... C&GWRY
Chicago & Great Western Railway (SAUO) .... CGW
Chicago & Illinois Midland Railway Co. .... C & IM
Chicago & Illinois Midland Railway Co. [AAR code] .... CIM
Chicago & Illinois Western Railroad [AAR code] .... CIW
Chicago and Midwest Envelope Manufacturers Association [Defunct] .... CMEMA
Chicago & North Western Railway (SAUS) .... NW
Chicago & North Western Railway Co. (SAUO) .... C&NWR
Chicago & Northern Pacific Railroad .... C & NPRR
Chicago & Northwestern Railway (EFIS) .... C&NW
Chicago and Northwestern Railway Co. .... CNW
Chicago and South Consortium [Library network] .... C & SC
Chicago & Southern Airlines (SAUO) .... C&S
Chicago and Southern Airlines (SAUO) .... CHI
Chicago & West Michigan Railroad .... C & WM
Chicago & Western Indiana Railroad Co. [AAR code] .... CWI
Chicago Architecture Foundation (SAUO) .... CAF
Chicago Area Computer Hobbyist Exchange .... CACHE
Chicago Area Computer Information Centers (SAUS) .... CACIC
Chicago Area Draft Resisters (SAUO) .... CADRE
Chicago Area Geographic Information Study [University of Illinois at
Chicago] [Also, an information service or system] (IID) .... CAGIS
Chicago Area Radio Club Council (SAUO) .... CARCC
Chicago Area Teleprinter Society (SAUO) .... CATS
Chicago Area Transportation Study .... CATS
Chicago Association of Commerce and Industry (SAUO) .... CACI
Chicago Association of Consulting Engineers (SAUO) .... CACE
Chicago Assyrian Dictionary [A publication] (BJA) .... CAD
Chicago, Aurora [Illinois] [ICAO location identifier] (ICLI) .... KZAU
Chicago, Aurora & Elgin Railroad Corp. [AAR code] .... CAE
Chicago Bar Association. Record [A publication] (DLA) .... Chi BA Rec
Chicago Bar Record [A publication] (DLA) .... Chi B Record
Chicago Bears [National Football League] [1922-present] (NFLA) .... Chi
Chicago Board of Options Exchange (ROAS) .... CBOE
Chicago Board of Trade .... CB

Chicago Board of Trade [*Chicago, IL*] (EAIO) .... CBOT
Chicago Board of Trade [*A futures exchange*] [*Investment term*] .... CBT
Chicago Board of Trade, Chicago, IL [*OCLC symbol*] (OCLC) .... IEY
Chicago Board Options Exchange .... CBO
Chicago Board Options Exchange [*Chicago, IL*] (EA) .... CBOE
Chicago Book Clinic .... CBC
Chicago Botanic Gardens, Glencoe, IL [*Library symbol*] [*Library of Congress*] (LCLS) .... IGlcB
Chicago Bridge & Iron Co. [*Later, CBI Industries*] .... CB & I
Chicago Bridge & Iron Co., Oak Brook, IL [*Library symbol*] [*Library of Congress*] (LCLS) .... IObC
Chicago Bridge & Iron N.V. [*NYSE symbol*] (SG) .... CBI
Chicago, Burlington & Quincy Railroad [*Also known as Burlington Route*] .... CB & Q
Chicago, Burlington & Quincy Railroad [*Also known as Burlington Route*] [*AAR code*] .... CBQ
Chicago, Burlington & Quincy Railroad [*Also known as Burlington Route*] [*Slang*] .... Q
Chicago Cardinals [*National Football League*] [*1920-59*] (NFLA) .... ChC
Chicago, Cincinnati & Louisville Railway .... CC & L
Chicago City Ballet .... CCB
Chicago City College [*Illinois*] (AEBS) CCC
Chicago City Junior College [*Illinois*] .... CCJC
Chicago Clinical Chemist [*A publication*] CCC
Chicago Cluster of Theological Schools [*Library network*] .... CCTS
Chicago College of Chiropody and Pedic Surgery (SAUS) .... CCCPS
Chicago College of Osteopathic Medicine .... CCOM
Chicago College of Osteopathic Medicine, Chicago, IL [*Library symbol*] [*Library of Congress*] (LCLS) .... ICCO
Chicago College of Osteopathy (SAUO) .... CCO
Chicago Council on Foreign Relations (SAUO) .... CCFR
Chicago Daily Tribune, Chicago, IL [*Library symbol*] [*Library of Congress*] (LCLS) .... ICDT
Chicago Dance Arts Coalition .... CDAC
Chicago Dental Society (SAUO) .... CDS
Chicago District Electric Generating Corporation (SAUO) .... CDEG
Chicago Dock & Canal Trust [*Associated Press*] (SAG) .... ChDock
[*The*] Chicago Dock & Canal Trust [*NASDAQ symbol*] (NQ) .... DOCK
Chicago Dock & Canal Trust [*NASDAQ symbol*] (TTSB) .... DOCKS
Chicago Envelope Manufacturers Association (SAUO) .... CEMA
Chicago Evangelistic Institute .... CEI
Chicago Fan Club (EA) .... CFC
Chicago Gorilla [*Slang for a desperado gunman*] .... CHICAGORILLA
Chicago Great Western Railroad (IIA) .... CGW
Chicago Great Western Railway .... C & GWRY
Chicago Heights Free Public Library, Chicago Heights, IL [*Library symbol*] [*Library of Congress*] (LCLS) .... ICh
Chicago Heights Free Public Library, Chicgo Heights, IL [*Library symbol*] [*Library of Congress*] (LCLS) .... IChL
Chicago Heights, IL [*Location identifier*] [*FAA*] (FAAL) .... CGT
Chicago Heights, IL [*AM radio station call letters*] .... WCFJ
Chicago Heights, IL [*AM radio station call letters*] .... WCGO
Chicago Heights Terminal Transfer Railroad Co. [*AAR code*] .... CHTT
Chicago Helicopter Airways (SAUO) .... CHP
Chicago Helicopter Airways, Inc. [*ICAO designator*] [*Obsolete*] .... CH
Chicago Helicopter Airways, Inc. .... CHA
Chicago Helicopter Airways, Inc. [*Air carrier designation symbol*] .... CHP
Chicago Historical Society (SAUO) .... CHS
Chicago Historical Society, Chicago, IL [*Library symbol*] [*Library of Congress*] (LCLS) .... IChi
Chicago Housing Authority (SAUO) .... CHA
Chicago Hydrometeorological Area Project (SAUS) .... CHAP
Chicago, IL [*Location identifier*] [*FAA*] (FAAL) .... FJU
Chicago, IL [*Location identifier*] [*FAA*] (FAAL) .... HKH
Chicago, IL [*Location identifier*] [*FAA*] (FAAL) .... HNA
Chicago, IL [*Location identifier*] [*FAA*] (FAAL) .... IAC
Chicago, IL [*Location identifier*] [*FAA*] (FAAL) .... IDN
Chicago, IL [*Location identifier*] [*FAA*] (FAAL) .... JAV
Chicago, IL [*Location identifier*] [*FAA*] (FAAL) .... LQQ
Chicago, IL [*Location identifier*] [*FAA*] (FAAL) .... MED
Chicago, IL [*Location identifier*] [*FAA*] (FAAL) .... MXT
Chicago, IL [*Location identifier*] [*FAA*] (FAAL) .... NOH
Chicago, IL [*Location identifier*] [*FAA*] (FAAL) .... OHA
Chicago, IL [*Location identifier*] [*FAA*] (FAAL) .... PHA
Chicago, IL [*Location identifier*] [*FAA*] (FAAL) .... PYN
Chicago, IL [*Location identifier*] [*FAA*] (FAAL) .... RVG
Chicago, IL [*Location identifier*] [*FAA*] (FAAL) .... RXZ
Chicago, IL [*Location identifier*] [*FAA*] (FAAL) .... TSL
Chicago, IL [*AM radio station call letters*] .... WBBM
Chicago, IL [*Television station call letters*] (BROA) .... WBBM-DT
Chicago, IL [*FM radio station call letters*] .... WBBM-FM
Chicago, IL [*Television station call letters*] .... WBBM-TV
Chicago, IL [*FM radio station call letters*] .... WBEZ
Chicago, IL [*FM radio station call letters*] .... WBHI
Chicago, IL [*Television station call letters*] .... WCFC
Chicago, IL [*Television station call letters*] .... WCIU
Chicago, IL [*Television station call letters*] (BROA) .... WCPX
Chicago, IL [*AM radio station call letters*] .... WCRW
Chicago, IL [*AM radio station call letters*] .... WCRX
Chicago, IL [*FM radio station call letters*] .... WCYC
Chicago, IL [*AM radio station call letters*] .... WEDC
Chicago, IL [*AM radio station call letters*] .... WEJM
Chicago, IL [*Television station call letters*] .... WFLD
Chicago, IL [*Television station call letters*] (BROA) .... WFLD-DT
Chicago, IL [*FM radio station call letters*] .... WFMT

Chicago, IL [*AM radio station call letters*] .... WGCI
Chicago, IL [*FM radio station call letters*] .... WGCI-FM
Chicago, IL [*AM radio station call letters*] .... WGN
Chicago, IL [*Television station call letters*] .... WGN-TV
Chicago, IL [*FM radio station call letters*] .... WHPK
Chicago, IL [*AM radio station call letters*] (BROA) .... WIDB-AM
Chicago, IL [*AM radio station call letters*] .... WIND
Chicago, IL [*AM radio station call letters*] .... WJJD
Chicago, IL [*FM radio station call letters*] .... WJMK
Chicago, IL [*FM radio station call letters*] .... WKKC
Chicago, IL [*AM radio station call letters*] .... WKQX
Chicago, IL [*FM radio station call letters*] (RBYB) .... WKXK-FM
Chicago, IL [*AM radio station call letters*] .... WLIT
Chicago, IL [*AM radio station call letters*] .... WLS
Chicago, IL [*Television station call letters*] (BROA) .... WLS-DT
Chicago, IL [*FM radio station call letters*] .... WLS-FM
Chicago, IL [*Television station call letters*] .... WLS-TV
Chicago, IL [*FM radio station call letters*] .... WLUP
Chicago, IL [*FM radio station call letters*] .... WLUW
Chicago, IL [*FM radio station call letters*] (RBYB) .... WLXX
Chicago, IL [*AM radio station call letters*] .... WMAQ
Chicago, IL [*Television station call letters*] .... WMAQ-TV
Chicago, IL [*AM radio station call letters*] .... WMBI
Chicago, IL [*FM radio station call letters*] .... WMBI-FM
Chicago, IL [*FM radio station call letters*] .... WMVP
Chicago, IL [*FM radio station call letters*] .... WNIB
Chicago, IL [*FM radio station call letters*] (BROA) .... WNND-FM
Chicago, IL [*FM radio station call letters*] .... WNUA
Chicago, IL [*FM radio station call letters*] .... WOUI
Chicago, IL [*FM radio station call letters*] .... WPNT
Chicago, IL [*FM radio station call letters*] .... WRCX
Chicago, IL [*FM radio station call letters*] (BROA) .... WRTE-FM
Chicago, IL [*AM radio station call letters*] .... WSBC
Chicago, IL [*AM radio station call letters*] .... WSCR
Chicago, IL [*Television station call letters*] .... WSNS
Chicago, IL [*FM radio station call letters*] .... WSSD
Chicago, IL [*Letters stand for "Windows to the World"*] [*Television station call letters*] .... WTTW
Chicago, IL [*FM radio station call letters*] .... WUSN
Chicago, IL [*FM radio station call letters*] (BROA) .... WXCD-FM
Chicago, IL [*FM radio station call letters*] .... WXRT
Chicago, IL [*Television station call letters*] .... WYCC
Chicago, IL [*AM radio station call letters*] (BROA) .... WYPA-AM
Chicago, IL [*FM radio station call letters*] .... WZRD
Chicago, IL [*Location identifier*] [*FAA*] (FAAL) .... ZAU
Chicago, Indianapolis & Louisville [*Louisville & Nashville Railroad Co.*] [*AAR code*] CIL
Chicago, Indianapolis & Louisville Railway (SAUO) .... CI&LRy
Chicago Industrial Communications Association (SAUO) .... CICA
Chicago Institute for the Study of Learning Disabilities [*Research center*] (RCD) .... CHILD
Chicago International Antiques Show (ITD) .... CIAS
Chicago International Art Exhibition (ITD) .... CIAE
Chicago International Boat Show (ITD) .... CIBS
Chicago, Kalamazoo & Saginaw Railway [*AAR code*] .... CKS
Chicago LASER Systems, Inc. (NITA) .... CLS
Chicago Law Bulletin [*A publication*] (DLA) .... Chicago LB
Chicago Law Bulletin [*A publication*] (DLA) .... Chic LB
Chicago Law Bulletin [*A publication*] (DLA) .... Chi LB
Chicago Law Enforcement Week (SAUS) .... CLEW
Chicago Law Institute, Chicago, IL [*Library symbol*] [*Library of Congress*] (LCLS) .... ICLaw
Chicago Law Journal [*A publication*] (DLA) .... Chicago LJ
Chicago Law Journal [*A publication*] (DLA) .... Chic LJ
Chicago Law Journal [*A publication*] (DLA) .... Chi LJ
Chicago Law Journal [*A publication*] (DLA) .... CLJ
Chicago Law Record [*Illinois*] [*A publication*] (DLA) .... Chicago L Rec
Chicago Law Record [*Illinois*] [*A publication*] (DLA) .... Chicago L Record (III)
Chicago Law Record [*Illinois*] [*A publication*] (DLA) .... Chic LR
Chicago Law Record [*Illinois*] [*A publication*] (DLA) .... Chi LR
Chicago Law Times [*A publication*] (DLA) .... Chicago LT
Chicago Law Times [*A publication*] (DLA) .... Chic LT
Chicago Law Times [*A publication*] (DLA) .... Chi LT
Chicago Legal News [*Illinois*] [*A publication*] (ILCA) .... Chicago Leg News
Chicago Legal News [*Illinois*] [*A publication*] (DLA) .... Chicago Leg News (III)
Chicago Legal News [*Illinois*] [*A publication*] (DLA) .... Chic Leg N
Chicago Legal News [*Illinois*] [*A publication*] (DLA) .... Chi Leg N
Chicago Legal News [*Illinois*] [*A publication*] (DLA) .... CLN
Chicago Library Services for the Blind and Physically Handicapped (Subregional),Chicago Public Library, Chicago, IL [*Library symbol*] [*Library of Congress*] (LCLS) .... IC-CBPH
Chicago Library System [*Chicago Public Library*] [*Chicago, IL*] [*Library network*] .... CLS
Chicago Linear Music Language .... CLML
Chicago Livestock Exchange .... CLE
Chicago Lutheran Theological Seminary .... CLTS
Chicago Lying-In Hospital .... CLIH
Chicago Map Society (EA) .... CMS
Chicago Mean Time (SAUS) .... CMT
Chicago Medical School .... CMS
Chicago Medical School Quarterly (journ.) (SAUS) .... Chicago Med Sch Quart
Chicago [*Illinois*] Meigs Field [*Airport symbol*] (OAG) .... CGX
Chicago Mercantile Exchange (EA) .... CME
Chicago Mercantile Exchange (SAUO) .... Merc
Chicago Mercantile Exchange (EBF) .... MERC

Chicago Mercantile Exchange, Chicago, IL [*Library symbol*] [*Library of Congress*] (LCLS) .... ICMen

Chicago Mercantile Exchange, Chicago, IL [*OCLC symbol*] (OCLC) .... IHU

Chicago [*Illinois*] Midway [*Airport symbol*] (OAG) .... MDW

Chicago Midway Laboratory [*Army*] (MCD) .... CML

Chicago, Milwaukee & Gary Railroad [*Nickname: Cold, Miserable, and Grouchy*] .... CM & G

Chicago, Milwaukee, and Gray Railroad (SAUO) .... CM&G

Chicago, Milwaukee & Puget Sound Railroad .... CM & PS

Chicago, Milwaukee & St. Paul Railway .... CM & StP

Chicago Milwaukee Corp. (SAUO) .... CHG

Chicago, Milwaukee, St. Paul & Pacific Railroad (IIA) .... CMSP & P

Chicago, Milwaukee, St. Paul and Pacific Railroad Co. (SAUO) .... CMSPP

Chicago, Milwaukee, St. Paul & Pacific Railroad Co. .... CM ST P & P

Chicago, Milwaukee, St. Paul & Pacific Railroad Co. [*AAR code*] .... MILW

Chicago Miniature Lamp [*NASDAQ symbol*] (TTSB) .... CHML

Chicago Miniature Lamp, Inc. [*Associated Press*] (SAG) ...... ChiMini

Chicago Miniature Lamp, Inc. [*NASDAQ symbol*] (SAG) .... CHML

Chicago Municipal Reference Library, Chicago, IL [*OCLC symbol*] (OCLC) .... IBF

Chicago Municipal Reference Library, Chicago, IL [*Library symbol*] [*Library of Congress*] (LCLS) .... ICMR

Chicago Museum of Natural History (SAUS) .... ChMNH

Chicago Natural History Museum .... CNHM

Chicago North Shore & Milwaukee R. R. [*AAR code*] .... CNSM

Chicago Nurses Association (SAUO) .... CNA

Chicago [*Illinois*] O'Hare Airport [*Derived from former name: Orchard Field*] [*Airport symbol*] .... ORD

Chicago Open Board of Trade [*Later, MIDAM*] .... COBT

Chicago Operations and Regional Office [*Department of Energy*] (GRD) ..... CORO

Chicago Operations Office [*Energy Research and Development Administration*] .... COO

Chicago Operations Office Clearing House (SAUO) .... CH

Chicago Osteopathic Medical Center .... COMC

Chicago Outer Belt R. R. [*AAR code*] .... EJE

Chicago Pile [*Nuclear reactor*] .... CP

Chicago Pile-5 [*Nuclear heavy-water-research reactor*] CP-5

Chicago Piza & Brewery, Inc. [*Associated Press*] (SAG) ...... ChiPizza

Chicago Pizza & Brewery, Inc. [*NASDAQ symbol*] (SAG) ...... CHGO

Chicago Pizza & Brewery, Inc. [*Associated Press*] (SAG) ...... ChiPza

Chicago Playing Card Collectors (EA) .... CPCC

Chicago Pneumatic Tool Company (SAUO) .... CGG

Chicago Press Association (SAUO) .... CPA

Chicago Printed String Co. (SAUO) .... CPS

Chicago Procurement District (SAUS) .... CHIPDIS

Chicago Produce Terminal Co. [*Later, CPTC*] [*AAR code*] ..... CPT

Chicago Produce Terminal Co. [*Formerly, CPT*] [*AAR code*] ..... CPTC

Chicago Public Library (SAUS) .... CPL

Chicago Public Library, Chicago, IL [*OCLC symbol*] (OCLC) ... CGP

Chicago Public Library, Chicago, IL [*Library symbol*] [*Library of Congress*] (LCLS) IC

Chicago Publishers Association (SAUO) .... CPA

Chicago Quartermaster Depot (SAUO) .... CQD

Chicago Radio Traffic Association (SAUO) .... CRTA

Chicago Railroad Terminal Information System [*Pronounced "Curtis"*] .... CRTIS

Chicago Rawhide Manufacturing Co. (SAUO) .... CM

Chicago Reactor (NRCH) .... CR

Chicago Regional Port District (SAUS) .... CRPD

Chicago Religious Task Force on Central America (EA) ..... CRTFCA

Chicago Research & Trading Bank (ECON) .... CRT

Chicago Resource Guide (SAUO) .... CRG

Chicago Review Press [*Publisher*] .... CRP

Chicago Rice and Cotton Exchange (EA) .... CRCE

Chicago Ridge Public Library, Chicago Ridge, IL [*Library symbol*] [*Library of Congress*] (LCLS) .... ICr

Chicago River and Indiana Railroad Co. (SAUO) .... CRI

[*The*] Chicago River & Indiana Railway Co. [*Absorbed into Consolidated Rail Corp.*] .... CR & I

[*The*] Chicago River & Indiana Railway Co. [*Absorbed into Consolidated Rail Corp.*] [*AAR code*] .... CRI

Chicago Rivet & Mach [*AMEX symbol*] (TTSB) .... CVR

Chicago Rivet & Machine Co. [*Associated Press*] (SAG) .... ChiRv

Chicago Rivet & Machine Co. [*AMEX symbol*] (SPSG) .... CVR

Chicago, Rock Island & Pacific Railroad Co. [*Nickname: The Baby Road*] .... CRI & P

Chicago, Rock Island and Pacific Railroad Co. (SAUO) .... CRIP

Chicago, Rock Island & Pacific Railroad Co. (MHDB) .... RI

Chicago School of Professional Psychology, Chicago, IL [*Library symbol*] [*Library of Congress*] (LCLS) .... ICCSP

Chicago School of Professional Psychology, Chicago, IL [*OCLC symbol*] (OCLC) .... JAX

Chicago Sewage Disposal System (SAUS) .... CSDS

Chicago Short Line Railway Co. [*AAR code*] .... CSL

Chicago Society of Clinical Hypnosis (SAUO) .... CSCH

Chicago Software Association (SAUO) .... CSA

Chicago South Shore & South Bend Railroad [*AAR code*] .... CSS

Chicago South Suburban Mass Transit District (SAUO) .... CSSMTD

Chicago, St. Paul & Kansas City Railway .... CStP & KC

Chicago, St. Paul, Minneapolis & Omaha R. R. [*AAR code*] ..... CMO

Chicago, St. Paul, Minneapolis & Omaha Railway .... CStPM & O

Chicago, St. Paul, Minneapolis & Omaha Railway Co. (SAUO) .... CSTPM&O

Chicago Staleys [*National Football League*] [*1921*] (NFLA) ...... ChS

Chicago Standbys Fan Club (EA) .... CSFC

Chicago State University (GAGS) .... Chicago St U

Chicago State University, Chicago, IL [*OCLC symbol*] (OCLC) ..... IAA

Chicago State University, Chicago, IL [*Library symbol*] [*Library of Congress*] (LCLS) .... ICSU

Chicago Steel Tape Co. (SAUO) .... CST

Chicago Stock Exchange, Inc. .... CHX

Chicago Suburban Motor Carriers Association, Inc., Homewood IL [*STAC*] .... CHS

Chicago Suburban Radio Association (SAUO) .... CSRA

Chicago Sun-Times and Chicago Daily News, Chicago, IL [*Library symbol*] [*Library of Congress*] (LCLS) .... ICSN

Chicago Symphony Orchestra .... CSO

Chicago Teachers College [*Later, Chicago State University*] ..... CTC

Chicago Teachers Union (SAUO) .... CTU

Chicago Technical College (SAUO) .... CTC

Chicago Technical College .... CTC

Chicago Technology Park .... CTP

Chicago Telephone Supply Corp. (SAUO) .... CTS

Chicago, Terre Haute & Southeastern R. R. [*AAR code*] .... CTSE

Chicago Theological Seminary .... CTS

Chicago Theological Seminary, Chicago, IL [*Library symbol*] [*Library of Congress*] (LCLS) .... ICT

Chicago Theological Seminary, Chicago, IL [*OCLC symbol*] (OCLC) ..... IDG

Chicago Title [*NYSE symbol*] (SG) .... CTZ

Chicago Transit Authority .... CTA

Chicago Transit Authority, Chicago, IL [*OCLC symbol*] (OCLC) ..... IBB

Chicago Transit Authority, Chicago, IL [*Library symbol*] [*Library of Congress*] (LCLS) .... ICTA

Chicago Tribune [*A publication*] (BARN) .... Chi Trib

Chicago Tribune [*A publication*] .... CT

Chicago Union Station Co. [*AAR code*] .... CUST

Chicago, West Pullman & Southern Railroad Co. [*AAR code*] ..... CWP

Chicago White Sox [*Baseball team*] .... CHISOX

Chicago World Trade Conference (SAUO) .... CWTC

Chicago Yellow Cab Co., Inc. (SAUO) .... CYC

Chicago Zoological Park (SAUS) .... CZP

Chicago-Argonne Resonant Ionization Spectrometer for Microanalysis [*Astronomy*] .... CHARISMA

Chicago/Chicago Midway [*Illinois*] [*ICAO location identifier*] (ICLI) .... KMDW

Chicago-Joliet Livestock Marketing Center (EA) .... CJLMC

Chicago-Kent College of Law .... CKCL

Chicagoland Collegiate Athletic Conference (PSS) .... CCAC

Chicago/Metropolitan Area [*Illinois*] [*ICAO location identifier*] (ICLI) .... KCHI

Chicago/O'Hare [*Illinois*] [*ICAO location identifier*] (ICLI) .... KORD

Chicago-Pittsburgh [*Proposed name for possible "super-city" formed by growth and mergers of other cities*] .... CHIPITTS

Chicago-University of Illinois [*RADAR system*] .... CHILL

Chicago/West Chicago, IL [*Location identifier*] [*FAA*] (FAAL) ..... DPA

Chicago/Wheeling, IL [*Location identifier*] [*FAA*] (FAAL) ...... PWK

Chicana Research and Learning Center (EA) .... CRLC

Chicana Rights Project [*Defunct*] (EA) .... CRP

Chicano Education Project [*Defunct*] (EA) .... CEP

Chicano Employment Committee (DICI) .... CEC

Chicano Family Center (EA) .... CFC

Chicano Humanities and Arts Council (EDAC) .... CHAC

Chicano Press Association (EA) .... CPA

Chicano Studies Research Center [*University of California, Los Angeles*] [*Research center*] (RCD) .... CSRC

Chicano Training Center (EA) .... CTC

Chicanos Against Military Intervention in Latin America [*Promotes understanding between Mexico and the US at the grassroots level*] (CROSS) .... CAMILA

Chichen Itza [*Mexico*] [*Airport symbol*] (OAG) .... CZA

Chichester [*City in England*] (ROG) .... CESTR

Chichester [*City in England*] (ROG) .... CHICH

Chichester [*British*] (WA) .... Cicestr

Chichester/Goodwood [*British*] [*ICAO location identifier*] (ICLI) ..... EGHR

Chichibu [*Japan*] [*Seismograph station code, US Geological Survey*] (SEIS) .... CHJ

Chichijima [*Bonin Islands*] [*Seismograph station code, US Geological Survey*] (SEIS) .... CBI

Chichijima [*Japan*] [*ICAO location identifier*] (ICLI) .... RJAO

Chick Cell Agglutination [*Vaccine potency test*] .... CCA

Chick Cell Agglutination Test (DMAA) .... CCAT

Chick Embryo Extract [*Culture media*] .... CEE

Chick Embryo Fibroblast .... CEF

Chick Embryo Kidney [*Medicine*] (DMAA) .... CEK

Chick Embryo Origin .... CEO

Chick Embryonic Skin .... CES

Chick Fibroblast [*Cytology*] .... CF

Chick Heart Fibroblast [*Cytology*] .... CHF

Chick Infective Dose (MAE) .... CID

Chick Infective Dose (SAUS) .... cid

Chick Muscle Extract [*Embryology*] .... CMX

Chick Neurotropic Factor [*Neurochemistry*] .... CNTF

Chick Red Blood Cells .... CRBC

Chick Syncytial Virus [*Veterinary science*] (DB) .... CSV

Chickamauga and Chattanooga National Military Park .... CHCH

Chickamauga Dam [*TVA*] .... CMD

Chickasaw, AL [*FM radio station call letters*] .... WDLT

Chickasaw County Historical Society, Ionia, IA [*Library symbol*] [*Library of Congress*] (LCLS) .... IaIonCHi

Chickasaw County Historical Society, Nashua, IA [*Library symbol*] [*Library of Congress*] (LCLS) .... IaNasCHi

Chickasaw Horse Association (EA) .... CHA

Chickasaw Library System, Ardmore, OK [*OCLC symbol*] (OCLC) ..... CKL

Chickasaw Library System, Ardmore, OK [*Library symbol*] [*Library of Congress*] (LCLS) .... OkArC

Chickasha Cotton Oil Company (SAUO) .... CIK
Chickasha, OK [Location identifier] [FAA] (FAAL) .... CHK
Chickasha, OK [FM radio station call letters] (BROA) .... KTUZ-FM
Chickasha, OK [AM radio station call letters] .... KWCO
Chickasha, OK [FM radio station call letters] .... KXXK
Chicken .... CHICK
Chicken .... CHKN
Chicken, AK [Location identifier] [FAA] (FAAL) .... CKX
Chicken Anaemia Agent [Australia] .... CAA
Chicken Cell Agglutination Unit (SAUS) .... CCA Unit
Chicken Embryo .... CE
Chicken Embryo Bursal (SAUS) .... CEB
Chicken Embryo Fibroblast [Cell line] .... CEF
Chicken Embryo Fibroblast [Cytology] .... CHEF
Chicken Embryo Kidney (SAUS) .... CEK
Chicken Embryo Lethal Dose (SAUS) .... CELD
Chicken Embryo Lethal Orphan [Virus] .... CELO
Chicken Erythrocyte (DB) .... CRBC
Chicken Gamma-Globulin [Immunology] .... CGG
Chicken Hepatic Lectin .... CHL
Chicken Kidney .... CK
Chicken Kidney Cell (SAUS) .... CKC
Chicken Lactose-Lectin [Biochemistry] CLL
Chicken Meat Industry Committee [Queensland] [Australia] ..... CMIC
Chicken Meat Research and Development Council [Australia] .... CMRDC
Chicken Neural Cell Adhesion Molecule .... ChNCAM
Chicken Ovalbumin Upstream Promoter [Genetics] .... COUP
Chicken Ovalbumin Upstream Promoter Transcription Factor
[Genetics] .... COUP-TF
Chicken Progesterone Receptor [Genetics] .... CPR
Chicken Red Blood Cell [Medicine] (DMAA) .... ChRBC
Chicken Red Blood Cell (STED) .... CRBC
Chicken Thymidine Kinase [An enzyme] .... ChTK
Chicken Vitellogenin .... cVit
Chickenpox [Also, Cp] [Medicine] .... CHPX
Chickenpox [Also, CHPX] [Medicine] .... Cp
Chickering House, Dover, MA [Library symbol] [Library of Congress]
(LCLS) .... MDovC
Chick-Martin [Test] [Microbiology] .... CM
Chiclayo [Peru] [Airport symbol] (OAG) CIX
Chiclayo/Cap. Jose Abelardo Quinones Gonzalez [Peru] [ICAO location
identifier] (ICLI) .... SPHI
Chico [California] [Seismograph station code, US Geological Survey] (SEIS).... CCO
Chico [California] [Airport symbol] (OAG) CIC
Chico, CA [FM radio station call letters] .... KCHO
Chico, CA [Television station call letters] .... KCPM
Chico, CA [FM radio station call letters] .... KFMF
Chico, CA [FM radio station call letters] .... KHAP
Chico, CA [Television station call letters] .... KHSL-TV
Chico, CA [FM radio station call letters] .... KLRS
Chico, CA [FM radio station call letters] (RBYB) .... KMXI
Chico, CA [AM radio station call letters] (RBYB) .... KNSN
Chico, CA [Television station call letters] (BROA) .... KNVN
Chico, CA [AM radio station call letters] .... KPAY
Chico, CA [FM radio station call letters] .... KZFR
Chico Public Library, Chico, CA [Library symbol] [Library of Congress]
(LCLS) .... CChi
Chicopee Falls, MA [Location identifier] [FAA] (FAAL) .... CEF
Chicopee Falls, MA [Location identifier] [FAA] (FAAL) .... GWJ
Chicopee Falls, MA [Location identifier] [FAA] (FAAL) .... GWT
Chicopee Falls/Westover Air Force Base [Massachusetts] [ICAO location
identifier] (ICLI) .... KCEF
Chicopee, MA [AM radio station call letters] .... WACE
Chicopee Public Library, Chicopee, MA [Library symbol] [Library of
Congress] (LCLS) .... MChi
Chicory Yellow Mottle Virus [Plant pathology] .... CHYMV
Chico's FAS [NASDAQ symbol] (TTSB) .... CHCS
Chicos Fas, Inc. [NASDAQ symbol] (SAG) .... CHCS
Chicos Fas, Inc. [Associated Press] (SAG) .... Chicos
Chicoutimi, PQ [AM radio station call letters] .... CBJ
Chicoutimi, PQ [FM radio station call letters] .... CBJE-FM
Chicoutimi, PQ [Television station call letters] .... CBJET
Chicoutimi, PQ [FM radio station call letters] .... CBJ-FM
Chicoutimi, PQ [Television station call letters] CIVV
Chicoutimi, PQ [FM radio station call letters] .... CJAB
Chicoutimi, PQ [Television station call letters] .... CJPM
Chido [Antibodies] [Immunology] (DAVI) .... Ch
Chidren's Wonderland Unit [NASDAQ symbol] (TTSB) ..... CWICU
Chief C
Chief (WDMC) .... ch
Chief (AFM) .... CH
Chief (TBD) .... Ch
Chief .... CHF
Chief (PHSD) .... Chf
Chief Accountant .... CA
Chief Accountant Officer [RAF] [British] .... CAO
Chief Activation Engineer .... CAE
Chief Administrative Engineer .... CAE
Chief Administrative Law Judge (DHP) .... CALJ
Chief Administrative Medical Officer [British] .... CAMO
Chief Administrative Officer .... CAO
Chief Advisor .... CA
Chief Advisor, International District Office (SAUS) .... CAIDO
Chief Advisor, International Field Office (SAUS) .... CAIFO

Chief, Aerial Reconnaissance Coordination, All Hurricanes [National
Hurricane Center] .... CARCAH
Chief Aerographer [Navy rating] [Obsolete] .... CAER
Chief Aerographer [Navy rating] [Obsolete] .... CHAER
Chief Aerographer's Mate [Navy rating] [Obsolete] .... CAERM
Chief Agency Officer [Insurance] .... CAO
Chief, Air Doctrine and Operations (MCD) .... CADO
Chief Air Fitter [British military] (DMA) .... CAF
Chief, Air Force Advisory Group .... CHAFAG
Chief, Air Force Modernization Coordination Office (MCD) ... CAFMCO
Chief, Air Force Section (CINC) .... CHAFSEC
Chief Aircraft Artificer [British military] (DMA) .... CAA
Chief Aircraft Communicator [British military] (IAA) ..... CACOM
Chief, Aircraft Maintenance .... CAM
Chief Aircraft Mechanician [British military] (DMA) ...... CAMN
Chief Aircrew Survival Equipmentman [Formerly, Chief Parachute Rigger]
[Navy rating] .... PRC
Chief, Airport District Office (SAUO) .... CADO
Chief Airship Rigger [Navy rating] [Obsolete] .... CAR
Chief Airways Technical District Office .... CATDO
Chief Airways Technical Field Office .... CATFO
Chief Ancient Philosophies [A publication] .... CAP
Chief and Assistant Chief Fire Officers' Association [British] .... CACFOA
Chief, Army Reserve (AABC) .... CAR
Chief, Army Reserve and Reserve Officers Training Corps Affairs ... CARROTC
Chief Army Staff Netherlands (SAUO) .... CAS The Hague
Chief Artificer Engineer [Navy] [British] (ROG) .... CH AE
Chief Artillery Controller (NATG) .... CAC
Chief Auditor (SAUS) .... CA
Chief Aviation Boatswain's Mate, Handler [Navy rating] (DNAB) .... ABHC
Chief Aviation Machinist's Mate (Reciprocating) [Navy rating] ..... ADC
Chief Aviation Maintenance Technician (DNAB) .... CHAVMAINTECH
Chief Aviation Pilot [Navy, Coast Guard] .... CAP
Chief Banking Officer (TBD) .... CBO
Chief Baron [British] .... CB
Chief Baron of the Exchequer [British] (ROG) .... CB EX
Chief Baron of the Exchequer [British] (DLA) .... Ch B Ex
Chief Benefits Director [Department of Veterans Affairs] .... CBD
Chief Boatswain [Navy rating] [Obsolete] .... CHBOSN
Chief Boatswain (SAUS) .... Ch Bosn
Chief Boatswains Mate (SAUS) .... CBM
Chief Boatswain's Mate [Navy rating] [Obsolete] .... CBM
Chief Boatswain's Mate, A [Master-at-Arms] [Navy rating] [Obsolete] .... CBMM
Chief Boatswain's Mate, Acting [Navy rating] [Obsolete] .... CBMA
Chief Boatswain's Mate, Construction Battalion, Boatswain [Navy rating]
[Obsolete] .... CBMCBB
Chief Boatswain's Mate, Construction Battalion, Stevedore [Navy rating]
[Obsolete] .... CBMCBS
Chief Boatswain's Mate, Ship Repair, Canvasman [Navy rating]
[Obsolete] .... CBMSRS
Chief Boatswain's Mate, Ship Repair, Crane Operator [Navy rating]
[Obsolete] .... CBMSRC
Chief Boatswain's Mate, Ship Repair, Rigger [Navy rating] [Obsolete] .... CBMSRR
Chief Boilermaker [Navy rating] [Obsolete] .... CB
Chief Boilermaker [Coast Guard] .... CBMKR
Chief Boilermaker, Ship Repair [Navy] .... CBSR
Chief Bombardment Liaison Officer [Navy] .... CBLO
Chief Buglemaster [Navy] .... CBgmstr
Chief Bug-O-Nay-Ge-Shig Library, Cass Lake, MN [Library symbol] [Library of
Congress] (LCLS) .... MnCasCB
Chief Builder [Navy rating] .... BUC
Chief Cable Censor [Navy rating] [Obsolete] CCC
Chief Carpenter [Navy rating] [Obsolete] .... CHCARP
Chief Carpenter's Mate [Navy rating] [Obsolete] .... CCM
Chief Carpenters Mate (SAUS) .... CCM
Chief Carpenter's Mate, Construction Battalion, Builder [Navy rating]
[Obsolete] .... CCMCBB
Chief Carpenter's Mate, Construction Battalion, Draftsman [Navy rating]
[Obsolete] .... CCMCBD
Chief Carpenter's Mate, Construction Battalion, Excavation Foreman [Navy
rating] [Obsolete] .... CCMCBE
Chief Carpenters Mate, Construction Battalion, Excavation Foreman
(SAUS) .... CCMCBEF
Chief Carpenter's Mate, Construction Battalion, Surveyor [Navy rating]
[Obsolete] .... CCMCBS
Chief Carpenter's Mate, Ship Repair, Boatbuilder, Wood [Navy rating]
[Obsolete] .... CCMSRB
Chief Carpenter's Mate, Ship Repair, Joiner [Navy rating] [Obsolete] ..... CCMSRJ
Chief Central Security Service .... CHCSS
Chief, Chemical Corps (SAUO) .... CCMLC
Chief Chemical Officer (SAUO) .... CCmlO
Chief Chemical Officer [Army] .... CCMLO
Chief Chemical Officer [Army] .... CCO
Chief, Chemical War Service (SAUO) .... CCWS
Chief Chemist (SAUS) .... Chf Chem
Chief Cipher Officer (SAUO) .... CCO
Chief Civil Affairs Officer [Navy] .... CCAO
Chief Civil Affairs Officer (Burma) [British] .... CCAO(B)
Chief Clerk CC
Chief Clerk (BARN) .... Ch Clk
Chief Clerk of the Admiralty [British] .... CCA
Chief, Command Naval Air Systems [Later, NAVAIR] ...... CHCOMNAVAIRSYS
Chief Commanding Officer .... CCO
Chief Commissary Steward [Navy rating] [Obsolete] ...... CCS
Chief Commissary Steward [Navy rating] [Obsolete] ...... CCSTD

Chief Commissaryman [*Later, MSC*] [*Navy rating*] ... CSC
Chief Commissioner of Police (DAS) ... CCP
Chief Commissioner of Police (SAUO) ... CCP
Chief, Communications Section (SAUS) ... Ch Comm Sect
Chief Communications Yeoman [*British military*] (DMA) ... CCY
Chief Complaint [*Medicine*] ... CC
Chief Conservation Officer (SAUO) ... CCO
Chief Consol Mining [*NASDAQ symbol*] (TTSB) ... CFCM
Chief Consolidated Mining Co. [*NASDAQ symbol*] (NQ) ... CFCM
Chief Consolidated Mining Co. [*Associated Press*] (SAG) ... ChfCon
Chief Constable [*Scotland Yard*] ... CC
Chief, Construction and Properties, Library, Department of National Defence [*Bibliotheque, Chef - Construction et Immeubles, Ministere de le Defense Nationale*] **Ottawa, Ontario** [*Library symbol*] [*National Library of Canada*] (NLC) ... OONDCP
Chief Construction Engineer (OA) ... CCE
Chief Constructor (SAUS) ... CC
Chief, Contracting Office (AAGC) ... CCO
Chief Control Electrical Artificer [*British military*] (DMA) ... CCEA
Chief Control Electrical Mechanician [*British military*] (DMA) ... CCEMN
Chief Control Electrician [*British military*] (DMA) ... CCEL
Chief Controller (NATG) ... CC
Chief Controller ... CCNT
Chief Controller (FAAC) ... CCTLR
Chief Cook [*Navy rating*] [*Obsolete*] ... CCK
Chief Cook [*Navy rating*] [*Obsolete*] ... CHCK
Chief Cook (Baker) [*Navy rating*] [*Obsolete*] ... CCK(B)
Chief Cook (Commissary) [*Navy rating*] [*Obsolete*] ... CCK(C)
Chief, Corps of Engineers [*Army*] ... CCE
Chief Counsel (KSC) ... CC
Chief Counsel (NAKS) ... cc
Chief Court [*Freemasonry*] (ROG) ... CC
Chief Court of Cochin, Select Decisions [*A publication*] (DLA) ... Coch Ch Ct
Chief Credit Officer [*Banking*] (TBD) ... CCO
Chief Damage Controlman [*Navy*] ... DCC
Chief Data Processing Technician [*Formerly, MAC*] [*Navy rating*] ... DPC
Chief Decision Makers ... CDM
Chief Decontamination Officer (SAUS) ... CDO
Chief, Defense Liaison Group (CINC) ... CHDLG
Chief, Defense Liaison Group-Indonesia (DNAB) ... CHDLG-INDO
Chief Design Engineer (SAUS) ... Chf Des Engr
Chief Development Officer (NFD) ... CDO
Chief Directorate of the Aviation Industry (SAUO) ... GUAP
Chief Directorate to the Council of Ministries for the Utilisation of Atomic Energy [*British*] (NUCP) ... GLAVATOM
Chief Draftsman (MCD) ... CD
Chief Draftsman Office Memorandum (SAA) ... CDOM
Chief Draftsman's Instructions (MCD) ... CDI
Chief Duty Signal Officer (SAUS) ... CDSO
Chief Economist (SAUS) ... CECON
Chief Education Officer [*British*] (DET) ... CEO
Chief Elected Official (OICC) ... CEO
Chief Electoral Officer [*Canada*] ... CEO
Chief Electrical Artificer [*British military*] (DMA) ... CEA
Chief Electrical Mechanician [*British military*] (DMA) ... CELMN
Chief Electrician [*Navy rating*] [*Obsolete*] ... CHELEC
Chief Electrician (Air) [*British military*] (DMA) ... CEL(A)
Chief Electrician (Air Weapon) [*British military*] (DMA) ... CEL(AW)
Chief Electrician's Mate [*Navy rating*] [*Obsolete*] ... CEM
Chief Electricians Mate, Construction Battalion (SAUS) ... CEMCB
Chief Electrician's Mate, Construction Battalion, Communications [*Navy rating*] [*Obsolete*] ... CEMCBC
Chief Electrician's Mate, Construction Battalion, Draftsman [*Navy rating*] [*Obsolete*] ... CEMCBD
Chief Electrician's Mate, Construction Battalion, General [*Navy rating*] [*Obsolete*] ... CEMCBG
Chief Electrician's Mate, Construction Battalion, Line and Station [*Navy rating*] [*Obsolete*] ... CEMCBL
Chief Electrician's Mate, Ship Repair, General Electrician [*Navy rating*] [*Obsolete*] ... CEMSRG
Chief Electrician's Mate, Ship Repair, IC Repairman [*Navy rating*] [*Obsolete*] ... CEMSRT
Chief Electrician's Mate, Ship Repair, Shop Electrician [*Navy rating*] [*Obsolete*] ... CEMSRS
Chief Electronics Technician (DNAB) ... CHELECTECH
Chief Engine Room Artificer [*British military*] (DMA) ... CERA
Chief Engine Room Artificer (SAUS) ... Ch ERA
Chief Engineer [*Navy*] ... CE
Chief Engineer [*British military*] (DMA) ... Ch E
Chief Engineer and Superintendent of Armaments Design [*British military*] (DMA) ... CEAD
Chief Engineer Officer (SAUS) ... CEO
Chief Engineer Port Construction [*British military*] (DMA) ... CEPC
Chief Engineer's Office (SAA) ... CEO
Chief Enlisted Manager ... CEM
Chief Executive ... CE
Chief Executive Dockyard [*Navy*] [*British*] ... CED
Chief Executive Officer ... CEO
Chief Executive Officer (PROS) ... ceo
Chief Executive Officer [*Also, CEO*] ... Ch Ex Off
Chief Executive/Highest Elected Official (SAUS) ... CE-HEO
Chief Executives Forum [*Later, CEO*] ... CEF
Chief Executives of Large Public Libraries of Ontario (AC) ... CELPLO
Chief Executives Organization (EA) ... CEO
Chief Financial Officer [*Business term*] ... CFO
Chief Financial Officer (PROS) ... cfo
Chief Financial Officer Act of 1990 ... CFOA
Chief Financial Officers Act (SAUO) ... CFO
Chief Financial Officers Act (SAUS) ... CFO Act
Chief Financial Officers Council ... CFOC
Chief Financial Official (AAGC) ... CFO
Chief Fire Controlman [*Navy rating*] [*Obsolete*] ... CFC
Chief Fire Controlman, Operator [*Navy rating*] [*Obsolete*] ... CFCO
Chief Fire Controlman, Submarines [*Navy rating*] [*Obsolete*] ... CFCS
Chief Fire Officer [*British*] (ADA) ... CFO
Chief Flight Operator (AAGC) ... CFO
Chief Flying Instructor [*RAF*] [*British*] ... CFI
Chief Gas Officer (SAUS) ... CGO
Chief Ground Instructor [*British military*] (DMA) ... CGI
Chief Growth Officer ... CGO
Chief Gunner [*Navy rating*] [*Obsolete*] ... CHGUN
Chief Gunner (SAUS) ... CH GUN
Chief Gunner's Mate [*Navy rating*] [*Obsolete*] ... CGM
Chief Gunners Mate, Construction Battalion, Armorer (SAUS) ... CGMCBA
Chief Gunner's Mate, Construction Battalion, Armorer [*Navy rating*] [*Obsolete*] ... CGMCBG
Chief Gunner's Mate, Construction Battalion, Powderman [*Navy rating*] [*Obsolete*] ... CGMCBP
Chief Gunner's Mate, Technician [*Navy rating*] ... GMTC
Chief Gunnery Instructor [*British military*] (DMA) ... CGI
Chief Hospital Corpsman (SAUS) ... HMC
Chief Hull Maintenance Technician (SAUS) ... HTC
Chief Hydrologist (GEOI) ... CH
Chief Illustrator Draftsman [*Navy rating*] ... DMC
Chief Immigration Officer (DS) ... CIO
Chief in Finance (SAUS) ... C Fin
Chief Income Producer (SAUS) ... CIP
Chief Income Spender (SAUS) ... CIS
Chief Industrial Property ... CIP
Chief Information Officer [*Business term*] ... CIO
Chief Information Officer (SAUO) ... CIO
Chief Inspecting Armorer (SAUS) ... CIA
Chief Inspecting Artificer (SAUS) ... CIA
Chief Inspecting Ordnance Officer (SAUS) ... CIOO
Chief Inspector ... CI
Chief Inspector, Engineer and Signal Stores (SAUO) ... CIESS
Chief Inspector, Mechanical Transport (SAUO) ... CIMT
Chief Inspector of Agriculture (HEAS) ... CIAg
Chief Inspector of Ancient Monuments (SAUO) ... CIAM
Chief Inspector of Armaments ... CIA
Chief Inspector of Clothing (SAUS) ... CIC
Chief Inspector of Constabularies [*British*] (WDAA) ... CIC
Chief Inspector of Engineering and Signal Stores [*Military*] [*British*] ... CIESS
Chief Inspector of Factories (HEAS) ... CIF
Chief Inspector of Factories (SAUO) ... CIF
Chief Inspector of Fighting Vehicles (SAUO) ... CIFV
Chief Inspector of Land Service Ammunition (NATG) ... CILSA
Chief Inspector of Machinery [*Navy*] [*British*] (ROG) ... CHIM
Chief Inspector of Machinery [*Navy*] [*British*] (ROG) ... CIM
Chief Inspector of Mechanical Transport (SAUS) ... CIMT
Chief Inspector of Naval Ordnance [*British*] ... CINO
Chief Inspector of Royal Engineer Stores [*British military*] (DMA) ... CIRES
Chief Inspector of Small Arms (SAUO) ... CISA
Chief Inspector of Stores (SAUS) ... CIS
Chief Inspector of Subsidized (or Supplementary) Transport (SAUO) ... CIST
Chief Inspector of Supplement Transport (SAUS) ... CIST
Chief Inspector of Supplementary Transport [*British military*] (DMA) ... CIST
Chief Inspector of Taxes (SAUO) ... CIT
Chief Inspector Officer (SAUO) ... CIO
Chief Inspectorate Electric and Mechanical Equipment (SAUS) ... CIEME
Chief Inspectorate, Electrical and Mechanical Equipment (SAUO) ... CIEME
Chief Inspector's Management Meeting (HEAS) ... CIMM
Chief Inspector's Memo (HEAS) ... CIM
Chief Inspector's Specialist Management Meeting (HEAS) ... CISMM
Chief Instructor ... CI
Chief Instrumentman [*Navy rating*] ... IMC
Chief, Intelligence Corps ... CINTC
Chief Intelligence Specialist (SAUS) ... ISC
Chief Intendent-General [*Freemasonry*] (ROG) ... CIG
Chief Intercept Director ... CIND
Chief Interior Communications Electrician (SAUS) ... ICC
Chief Investment Officer [*Banking*] (TBD) ... CIO
Chief Japanese Maritime Staff Office (CINC) ... CMSO
Chief, Joint United States Military Advisory Group [*Followed by name of country*] (CINC) ... CHJUSMAG
Chief Journalist [*Navy rating*] ... JOC
Chief Judge [*Sports*] ... CJ
Chief Judge in Bankruptcy (DLA) ... CJB
Chief Judicial Officer (EEVL) ... CJO
Chief Justice [*British*] (ROG) ... CHJ
Chief Justice [*Various supreme courts*] ... CJ
Chief Justice of the Common Pleas [*British*] (DLA) ... CHCP
Chief Justice of the Common Pleas [*British*] (ROG) ... CHJCP
Chief Justice of the Common Pleas (DLA) ... CJCP
Chief Justice of the Common (Upper) Bench (DLA) ... CJUB
Chief Justice of the King's Bench (DLA) ... CJKB
Chief Justice of the Queen's Bench (DLA) ... CHQB
Chief Justice of the Queen's Bench (DLA) ... CJQB
Chief Justice of the Upper Bench [*British*] (ROG) ... CHJUB
Chief Justices Law Reform Committee, Victoria (SAUS) ... VCJC

Chief Knowledge Officer ... CKO
Chief, Korea Military Assistance Group ... CHKMAG
Chief Labour Management Officer [*Ministry of Supply*] [*British*] ... CLMO
Chief Land Agent Valuer (SAUO) ... CLAV
Chief Launch Vehicle Test Conductor [*NASA*] (KSC) ... CLTC
Chief Learning Officer ... CLO
Chief Leisure Officers Association [*British*] (DBA) ... CLOA
Chief Liaison Officer (SAUS) ... CLO
Chief Lithographer [*Navy rating*] ... LIC
Chief Loan Officer [*Banking*] (TBD) ... CLO
Chief, Logistics Data Management Office [*Army*] ... C/LDMO
Chief Machine Accountant [*Later, DPC*] [*Navy rating*] ... MAC
Chief Machinist [*Navy rating*] [*Obsolete*] ... CHMACH
Chief Machinist (SAUS) ... Ch Mach
Chief Machinist's Mate [*Navy rating*] [*Obsolete*] ... CMM
Chief Machinist's Mate, Construction Battalion, Equipment Operator [*Navy rating*] [*Obsolete*] ... CMMCBE
Chief Machinist's Mate, Industrial Gas Generating Mechanic [*Navy rating*] [*Obsolete*] ... CMMG
Chief Machinist's Mate, Refrigeration [*Navy rating*] [*Obsolete*] ... CMMR
Chief Machinist's Mate, Ship Repair, Outside Machinist [*Navy rating*] [*Obsolete*] ... CMMSRO
Chief Machinist's Mate, Shop [*Navy rating*] [*Obsolete*] ... CMMS
Chief Mailman [*Navy rating*] [*Obsolete*] ... CMAM
Chief Maintenance Officer ... CMO
Chief Marine Engineering Artificer [*British military*] (DMA) ... CMEA
Chief Marine Engineering Mechanic [*British military*] (DMA) ... CMEM
Chief Marine Gunner [*Navy rating*] ... CMG
Chief Marine Surveyor (SAUO) ... CMS
Chief Marketing Officer [*Insurance*] ... CMO
Chief Master at Arms [*Navy rating*] ... CMAA
Chief Master Sergeant ... CMSGT
Chief Master Sergeant (SAUO) ... CMSgt
Chief Master Sergeant [*Air Force*] ... E9
Chief Master Sergeant of the Air Force (AFM) ... CMSAF
Chief Mechanic ... CM
Chief Mechanical and Electrical Engineer (SAUS) ... CM&EE
Chief Mechanical and Electrical Engineer (SAUO) ... CMEE
Chief Mechanical and Electrical Engineer [*Air Force*] [*British*] ... CMEE
Chief Mechanical Engineer [*Military*] [*British*] ... CME
Chief Mechanical Engineer, Electrical Branch (SAUO) ... CME
Chief Medical Adviser ... CMA
Chief Medical Director [*Department of Veterans Affairs*] ... CMD
Chief Medical Officer (SAUS) ... Ch Med O
Chief Medical Officer [*Military*] ... CMO
Chief Medical Technician [*British military*] (DMA) ... CMT
Chief Merchanist's Mate [*Navy*] [*British*] ... CMM
Chief Mess Management Specialist [*Formerly, CSC, CST, SDC*] [*Navy rating*] ... MSC
Chief Metalsmith [*Navy rating*] [*Obsolete*] ... CM
Chief Metalsmith, Ship Repair, Blacksmith [*Navy rating*] [*Obsolete*] ... CMSRB
Chief Metalsmith, Ship Repair, Coppersmith [*Navy rating*] [*Obsolete*] ... CMSRC
Chief Metalsmith, Ship Repair, Sheet Metal Worker [*Navy rating*] [*Obsolete*] ... CMSRS
Chief, Military Assistance Advisory Group [*Followed by name of country*] (CINC) ... CHMAAG
Chief, Military Equipment Delivery Team (CINC) ... CHMEDT
Chief Military Physician (SAUS) ... CMP
Chief, Military Planning Office (CINC) ... CHMPO
Chief, Military Technical Advisory Group (CINC) ... CHMILTAG
Chief Minister's Department [*Australian Capital Territory*] [*Australia*] ... CMD
Chief Motor Boatman [*British military*] (DMA) ... CMB
Chief Motor Machinist's Mate [*Navy rating*] [*Obsolete*] ... CMOMM
Chief Motor Machinists Mate, Ship Repair, Diesel Engineering Mechanic (SAUS) ... CMOMMSRD
Chief Motor Machinist's Mate, Ship Repair, Diesel Engineering Mechanic [*Navy rating*] [*Obsolete*] ... CMOMSRD
Chief Motor Machinists Mate, Ship Repair, Gasoline Engineering Mechanic (SAUS) ... CMOMMSRG
Chief Motor Machinist's Mate, Ship Repair, Gasoline Engineering Mechanic [*Navy rating*] [*Obsolete*] ... CMOMSRG
Chief Motor Mechanic [*British military*] (DMA) ... CMM
Chief Moulder [*Navy rating*] [*Obsolete*] ... CML
Chief Musician [*Navy rating*] [*Obsolete*] ... CMUS
Chief, National Guard Bureau [*Army*] ... CNGB
Chief, Naval Advanced Air Training ... CNAAT
Chief Naval Adviser [*British*] ... CNA
Chief, Naval Advisory Group ... CHNAVADGP
Chief, Naval Advisory Group [*Followed by name of country*] (CINC) ... CHNAVADGRU
Chief, Naval Advisory Group ... CHNAVGP
Chief [*or Commander*], **Naval Advisory Group** (DNAB) ... CNAG
Chief, Naval Advisory Group (SAUO) ... CNAG
Chief, Naval Air Advanced Training (SAUS) ... Ch Nav Air Adv Tra
Chief, Naval Air Basic Training (SAUS) ... Ch NAB Tra
Chief, Naval Air Basic Training (SAUO) ... ChNABTra
Chief, Naval Air Basic Training (SAUS) ... Ch Nav Air Basic Tra
Chief, Naval Air Basic Training ... CNABT
Chief, Naval Air Basic Training (DNAB) ... CNABTRA
Chief, Naval Air Reserve Training (SAUO) ... CHNAVAIRRESTRA
Chief, Naval Airships Training ... CHNAVAIRSHIPTRA
Chief Naval Architect (SAUO) ... CNA
Chief Naval Censor [*Navy rating*] [*Obsolete*] ... CNC
Chief Naval Engineering Officer (SAUS) ... CNEngO
Chief Naval Engineering Officer [*British*] ... CNEO
Chief Naval Judge Advocate [*British*] ... CNJA
Chief, Naval Mission ... CHNAVMIS
Chief, Naval Ordnance Management Information System Office (DNAB) ... CHNOMISO
Chief Naval Representative [*British*] ... CNR
Chief Naval Representative (SAUO) ... CNR
Chief, Naval Reserve Forces ... CNRF
Chief, Naval Reserve Training ... CNRT
Chief Naval Secretary (SAUS) ... Ch Nav Sec
Chief, Naval Section (SAUO) ... CHNAVSEC
Chief Naval Signal Officer (SAUS) ... CNSO
Chief Naval Supply and Secretariat Officer [*British*] ... CNSSO
Chief, Naval Training Support (SAUO) ... CHNAVTRASUPP
Chief Navy Disbursing Officer ... CNDO
Chief, Navy Section (CINC) ... CHNAVSEC
Chief, Navy Section, Joint United States Military Advisory Group, Thailand (DNAB) ... CHNAVSECJUSMAGTHAI
Chief, Navy Section, Military Assistance Advisory Group ... CHNAVSECMAAG
Chief, Navy Section, Military Training Mission (DNAB) ... CHNAVSECMTM
Chief, Navy Section, United States Military Group (DNAB) ... CHNAVSECUSMILGP
Chief Navy Staff, Netherlands (SAUO) ... CNS The Hague
Chief, Navy-Marine Corps Military Affiliate Radio Station (DNAB) ... CHNAVMARCORMARS
Chief Nursing Officer [*British*] ... CNO
Chief, Nursing Services (DAVI) ... CNS
Chief Observer [*Navy*] (NVT) ... CHOBS
Chief of Aeronautical Engineering (SAUS) ... CAE
Chief of Air Corps [*World War II*] ... CAC
Chief of Air Corps [*World War II*] ... C of AC
Chief of Air Defense ... CAD
Chief of Air Force Chaplains ... C of AFCH
Chief of Air Force Chaplains ... COFAFCH
Chief of Air Force Chaplains (SAUS) ... CofAFCH
Chief of Air Operations (SAUS) ... CAOps
Chief of Air Service (SAUO) ... C of AS
Chief of Air Staff [*World War II*] ... CAS
Chief of Air Staff [*World War II*] ... C of AS
Chief of Amphibious Warfare (SAUS) ... CAW
Chief of Army Audit Agency ... CAAA
Chief of Army Aviation ... CAA
Chief of Artillery (SAUS) ... C of A
Chief of Budget and Finance Division [*Supreme Headquarters Allied Powers Europe*] (NATG) ... CBUDFIN
Chief of Budget and Finance Division [*Supreme Headquarters Allied Powers Europe*] (NATG) ... CCM
Chief of Bureau of Insular Affairs (SAUO) ... C of BIA
Chief of Cavalry ... C of CAV
Chief of Chaplains [*Later, CCH*] [*Army*] ... CC
Chief of Chaplains [*Formerly, CC, C of CH, COFCH*] [*Army*] (AABC) ... CCH
Chief of Chaplains (SAUO) ... CCH
Chief of Chaplains [*Navy*] ... COC
Chief of Chaplains [*Later, CCH*] [*Army*] ... COFCH
Chief of Chaplains [*Later, CCH*] [*Army*] ... C of CH
Chief of Civil Affairs [*Army*] ... CCA
Chief of Civil Engineers [*Army*] (DNAB) ... CHCIVENG
Chief of Civil Engineers [*Army*] ... CHCIVENGS
Chief of Coast Artillery ... C of CA
Chief of Combat Operations (SAUO) ... CCO
Chief of Combined Operations [*British Army*] [*World War II*] ... CCO
Chief of Combined Operations (SAUO) ... COCOS
Chief of Communications - Electronics ... CCE
Chief of Communications Electronics (SAUS) ... CC-E
Chief of Communications-Electronics (SAUO) ... CC-E
Chief of Construction Engineering (SAUO) ... CCE
Chief of Defence Equipment Collaboration (SAUS) ... CDEC
Chief of Defence Intelligence (SAUS) ... CDI
Chief of Defence (or Defense) (SAUO) ... CHOD
Chief of Defence Procurement [*British*] (RDA) ... CDP
Chief of Defence Staff [*British*] (NATG) ... CDS
Chief of Defence Staff Norway (SAUO) ... CODS NORWAY
Chief of Defense (SAUO) ... COD
Chief of Defense Force Staff (MCD) ... CDFS
Chief of Department of Nonresident Instruction (SAUS) ... C/NRI
Chief of Detail (SAUS) ... C of Det
Chief of Detectives ... CD
Chief of Division ... CD
Chief of Doctrine (SAUS) ... C/Doc
Chief of Electronics (SAUS) ... C of E
Chief of Engineers [*Later, COE*] [*Army*] ... CE
Chief of Engineers [*Formerly, CE, C of E, C of ENGRS, COFENGS*] [*Army*] (AABC) ... COE
Chief of Engineers [*Later, COE*] [*Army*] ... C of E
Chief of Engineers (SAUO) ... C of E
Chief of Engineers (MCD) ... COFENGRS
Chief of Engineers [*Later, COE*] [*Army*] ... C of ENGRS
Chief of Engineers [*Army*] (SAA) ... C of Engs
Chief of Engineers [*Later, COE*] [*Army*] ... COFENGS
Chief of Engineers (Assistant Chief of Engineers) [*Military*] ... COE(ACE)
Chief of Establishments and Research [*British*] ... CER
Chief of Field Artillery ... CFA
Chief of Field Artillery (SAUO) ... C of FA
Chief of Finance [*Army*] ... CF
Chief of Finance [*Army*] ... C of F
Chief of Finance [*Army*] ... COFF
Chief of Finance and Accounting [*Army*] (AABC) ... CF & A

Chief of Finance and Accounting (SAUO) ... CF&A
Chief of Fleet Support [*Navy*] [*British*] ... CFS
Chief of Government ... COG
Chief of Industrial Relations (SAUS) ... CIR
Chief of Information [*Also, CINFO*] [*Navy*] ... CHINFO
Chief of Information [*Army*] ... CI
Chief of Information [*Also, CHINFO*] [*Navy*] ... CINFO
Chief of Information (SAUO) ... COFI
Chief of Information and Education (SAUO) ... CINFOE
Chief of Legislative Liaison [*Army*] ... CLL
Chief of Logistics Support (SAUS) ... CLS
Chief of Marine Air (SAUS) ... C of MAir
Chief of Material (SAUS) ... C Mat
Chief of Military History [*Army*] ... CMH
Chief of Military History (SAUS) ... GMH
Chief of Mission [*Foreign service*] ... CM
Chief of Mission Operations [*NASA*] ... CMO
Chief of Naval Air ... CNA
Chief of Naval Air Advanced Training [*Also, CNAVANTRA*] [*Formerly, CNAOPTRA, CNAOT*] ... CNAADTRA
Chief of Naval Air Advanced Training (SAUS) ... CNAATRA
Chief of Naval Air Advanced Training (SAUO) ... CNAVADTRA
Chief of Naval Air Advanced Training [*Also, CNAADTRA*] ... CNAVANTRA
Chief of Naval Air Basic Training ... CNABATRA
Chief of Naval Air Basic Training (SAUS) ... CNABTra
Chief of Naval Air Intermediate Training [*Later, CNABATRA*] ... CNAINTERMTRA
Chief of Naval Air Intermediate Training [*Later, CNABATRA*] ... CNAIT
Chief of Naval Air Operational Training [*Later, CNAADTRA, CNAVANTRA*] ... CNAOPTRA
Chief of Naval Air Operational Training [*Later, CNAADTRA, CNAVANTRA*] ... CNAOT
Chief of Naval Air Pacific (MCD) ... CNAP
Chief of Naval Air Primary Training (SAUS) ... CNAPIMTRA
Chief of Naval Air Primary Training [*Later, CNARFSTRA*] ... CNAPRIMTRA
Chief of Naval Air Primary Training [*Later, CNARFSTRA*] ... CNAPT
Chief of Naval Air Primary Training ... CNARFSTRA
Chief of Naval Air Reserve Training ... CNARESTRA
Chief of Naval Air Reserve Training (SAUO) ... CNART
Chief of Naval Air Reserve Training (SAUS) ... CNAVAIRRESTRA
Chief of Naval Air Services (SAUO) ... CNAS
Chief of Naval Air Services [*British*] ... CNAS
Chief of Naval Air Technical Training (SAUO) ... CNATechTr
Chief of Naval Air Technical Training ... CNATECHTRA
Chief of Naval Air Technical Training ... CNATT
Chief of Naval Air Training ... CNAT
Chief of Naval Air Training ... CNATRA
Chief of Naval Air Training (SAUO) ... CNATra
Chief of Naval Airship Training (SAUS) ... Ch Nav Airship Tra
Chief of Naval Airships Training and Experimentation ... CNATE
Chief of Naval Aviation Logistics (MCD) ... CNAL
Chief of Naval Aviation Training ... CNATRA
Chief of Naval Communications (SAUO) ... CHACOM
Chief of Naval Communications [*Formerly, DNC*] ... CNC
Chief of Naval Development (DNAB) ... CHNAVDEV
Chief of Naval Development ... CND
Chief of Naval Education and Training (MCD) ... CNET
Chief of Naval Education and Training Support (SAUO) ... CNETS
Chief of Naval Group (SAUO) ... CNG
Chief of Naval Information (SAUO) ... CNI
Chief of Naval Information [*Obsolete*] [*British*] ... CNI
Chief of Naval Intelligence ... CNI
Chief of Naval Material (MCD) ... CHNAVMAT
Chief of Naval Material ... CNM
Chief of Naval Material Emergency Relocation Site Commander (DNAB) ... CHNAVMAT ERS
Chief of Naval Mission (SAUS) ... Ch Nav Mis
Chief of Naval Operational Requirement and Plans ... CNORP
Chief of Naval Operations [*Also, CNO*] ... CNAVOP
Chief of Naval Operations [*Also, CNAVOP*] [*Washington, DC*] ... CNO
Chief of Naval Operations (AAGC) ... OPNAV
Chief of Naval Operations Budget Office ... CNOBO
Chief of Naval Operations Command (SAUO) ... CNOCOM
Chief of Naval Operations Command/Management Information System ... CNOCOM/MIS
Chief of Naval Operations Communications Center (MCD) ... CNOCC
Chief of Naval Operations Memorandum ... CNOM
Chief of Naval Operations Memorandum and Commandant of the Marine Corps Memorandum [*Joint*] ... CNOM/CMCM
Chief of Naval Operations Reserve Affairs Advisory Board (DNAB) ... CNO/RAAB
Chief of Naval Personnel (NVT) ... CHNAVPERS
Chief of Naval Personnel [*The Second Sea Lord*] [*British*] ... CNP
Chief of Naval Personnel (SAUO) ... CNP
Chief of Naval Personnel (SAUS) ... CNP
Chief of Naval Research (SAUO) ... CHNAVRSCH
Chief of Naval Research ... CNR
Chief of Naval Reserve (DOMA) ... CHNAVRES
Chief of Naval Reserve (DOMA) ... CNR
Chief of Naval Staff, Turkey (SAUO) ... CNS Turkey
Chief of Naval Technical Services [*Canada*] ... CNTS
Chief of Naval Technical Training (NVT) ... CNTT
Chief of Naval Training ... CHNAVTRA
Chief of Naval Training (AAGC) ... CNATRA
Chief of Naval Training ... CNT
Chief of Naval Transportation Service ... CNTS
Chief of Navy Technical Training (DNAB) ... CNTECHTRA
Chief of Office of Research and Inventions [*Navy*] ... CHORI
Chief of Operational Requirements (SAUS) ... COR
Chief of Operations ... CHOPS
Chief of Operations (SAUS) ... C Ops
Chief of Operations Analysis (MCD) ... COA
Chief of Ordnance [*Army*] ... CO
Chief of Ordnance (SAUO) ... C of O
Chief of Ordnance [*Army*] ... COFORD
Chief of Ordnance [*Army*] ... C of ORD
Chief of Ordnance (SAUO) ... COO
Chief of Ordnance [*Army*] ... CORD
Chief of Organization and Management (SAUS) ... C Org M
Chief of Outpost [*CIA officer in charge of a field office*] ... COO
Chief of Overseas Supply Division (SAUS) ... COSD
Chief of Personnel (SAUO) ... C Pers
Chief of Personnel and Logistics [*Navy*] [*British*] ... CPL
Chief of Personnel Services (SAUS) ... CPS
Chief of Plans and Intelligence (SAUS) ... C Plans I
Chief of Police ... COP
Chief of Police ... CP
Chief of Public Affairs (AABC) ... CPA
Chief of Public Information [*Army*] ... CPI
Chief of Public Information Division [*NATO*] (NATG) ... CPUBINFO
Chief of Regulation Staff (SAUS) ... CRS
Chief of Research and Development [*Army*] ... CR & D
Chief of Research and Development [*Army*] ... CRD
Chief of Research, Development, and Acquisition [*Army*] (RDA) ... CRDA
Chief of Reserve Components (SAUS) ... CORC
Chief of Reserve Components [*Army*] ... CRC
Chief of Rocket Troops and Artillery (MCD) ... CRTA
Chief of Section ... C of S
Chief of Section ... COS
Chief of Section ... CS
Chief of Service (SAUS) ... C of S
Chief of Special Services (SAUS) ... C of SpS
Chief of Special Services (SAUO) ... COFSPS
Chief of Staff [*Military*] ... C of S
Chief of Staff [*Military*] ... COFS
Chief of Staff [*Military*] ... COS
Chief of Staff [*Medicine*] (DAVI) ... COS
Chief of Staff (SAUO) ... COS
Chief of Staff [*Military*] ... CS
Chief of Staff Air Force Memorandum (AFM) ... CSAFM
Chief of Staff, Army Memorandum [*Air Force*] ... CSAM
Chief of Staff Civil Administration Division (SAUO) ... CSCAD
Chief of Staff, Civil Administration Division (SAUS) ... CSCAD
Chief of Staff Memorandum [*Military*] (AABC) ... CSM
Chief of Staff, Military Intelligence Committee (NATG) ... COSMIC
Chief of Staff Office (SAUS) ... Ch Staff Off
Chief of Staff Regulations ... CSR
Chief of Staff Supreme Headquarters [*British*] ... CSSH
Chief of Staff Supreme Headquarters (SAUO) ... CSSH
Chief of Staff to Supreme Allied Commander [*Europe*] [*World War II*] ... COSSAC
Chief of Staff, United States Air Force (NATG) ... COFSAF
Chief of Staff, United States Air Force ... CSAF
Chief of Staff, United States Air Force (SAUO) ... CSUSAF
Chief of Staff, United States Army [*Later, CSA*] ... C of SA
Chief of Staff, United States Army [*Later, CSA*] ... COFSA
Chief of Staff, United States Army [*Formerly, COFSA, C of SA*] ... CSA
Chief of Staff, United States Army (SAUO) ... CSUSA
Chief of State ... COS
Chief of Station [*CIA country team*] ... COS
Chief of Supplies and Transport (SAUO) ... CST
Chief of Supplies and Transport [*Navy*] [*British*] ... CST
Chief of Supply Depot (SAUS) ... CSD
Chief of Support Services (SAUS) ... CofSptS
Chief of Support Services [*Army*] (AABC) ... C of SptS
Chief of Support Services [*Army*] ... COFSPTS
Chief of Support Services [*Army*] ... CSS
Chief of Tariff Bureau ... CTB
Chief of Telecommunications (SAUS) ... CTEL
Chief of Telecommunications (SAUO) ... C Tel
Chief of the Army Air Forces [*World War II*] ... CAAF
Chief of the Army Air Forces [*World War II*] ... C of AAF
Chief of the Bureau of Aeronautics (SAUS) ... CbBuAer
Chief of the Bureau of Aeronautics [*Obsolete*] [*Navy*] ... CHBUAER
Chief of the Bureau of Docks (SAUS) ... ChBuDocks
Chief of the Bureau of Medicine (SAUS) ... ChBuMed
Chief of the Bureau of Medicine and Surgery [*Navy*] ... CHBUMED
Chief of the Bureau of Medicine and Surgery (SAUS) ... ChBuMedSurg
Chief of the Bureau of Naval Personnel ... CHBUPERS
Chief of the Bureau of Ordnance [*Obsolete*] [*Navy*] ... CHBUORD
Chief of the Bureau of Ordnance (SAUS) ... ChBuOrd
Chief of the Bureau of Ships (SAUS) ... ChBuShips
Chief of the Bureau of Ships [*Obsolete*] [*Navy*] ... CHBUSHIPS
Chief of the Bureau of Supplies and Accounts [*Obsolete*] [*Navy*] ... CHBUSANDA
Chief of the Bureau of Supplies and Accounts (SAUS) ... ChBuSandA
Chief of the Bureau of Weapons (SAUS) ... ChBuWeps
Chief of the Bureau of Yards and Docks [*Obsolete*] [*Navy*] ... CHBUDOCKS
Chief of the Canadian Naval Staff (SAUS) ... CCNS
Chief of the Canadian Naval Staff (SAUO) ... CCNS
Chief of the Chemical Warfare Service [*World War II*] ... CCWS
Chief of the Chemical Warfare Service [*World War II*] ... C of CWS
Chief of the Corps (SAUS) ... C of C
Chief of the Defence Force (SAUS) ... CDF

Chief of the General Staff [*in the field*] [*Formerly, CIGS*] [*Military*] [*British*] ..... CGS
Chief of the General Staff (ACAE) ..... COGS
Chief of the Imperial General Staff [*Later, CGS*] [*British*] ..... CIGS
Chief of the Joint General Staff [*Vietnam*] ..... CJGS
Chief of the Naval Staff [*Canada*] ..... CNS
Chief of the Purchasing Office (AAGC) ..... CPO
Chief of the Regulating Staff (SAUS) ..... CORS
Chief of the Royal Naval Scientific Service (SAUS) ..... CRNSS
Chief of the Royal Naval Scientific Service (SAUO) ..... CRNSS
Chief of the Tabernacle [*Freemasonry*] (ROG) ..... C of T
Chief of the United States Army Air Force (SAUS) ..... CUSAAF
Chief of Training (SAUO) ..... C Train
Chief of Transportation [*Army*] ..... C of T
Chief of Transportation [*Army*] ..... COFT
Chief of Transportation (SAUO) ..... COT
Chief of Transportation [*Army*] ..... CT
Chief, Office of Personnel Operations [*Army*] ..... COPO
Chief, Office of Reserve Components [*Army*] (AABC) ..... CORC
Chief Officer (SAUS) ..... Ch Off
Chief Officer (SAUS) ..... CO
Chief Officer [*Women's Royal Naval Service*] [*British*] ..... C/O
Chief Officer, Shore Signal Service (SAUS) ..... COSSS
Chief Officer, Shore Signal Service (SAUO) ..... COSSS
Chief Officer, Shore Wireless Service (SAUO) ..... COSWS
Chief Officers of State Library Agencies (EA) ..... COSLA
Chief Operating Area Coordinator (DNAB) ..... COAC
Chief Operating Officer ..... COO
Chief Operating Officer (PROS) ..... coo
Chief Operating Officer of Business Affairs [*Proposed alternative to the hiring of a baseball commissioner*] ..... COOBA
Chief Operation Officer (SAUS) ..... COO
Chief, Operations & Maintenance (SAUO) ..... CO&M
Chief Operations Manager (SAUS) ..... COM
Chief Operator (NVT) ..... CHOP
Chief Operator (NRCH) ..... CO
Chief Opticalman [*Navy rating*] ..... OMC
Chief Ordnance Electrical Artificer [*British military*] (DMA) ..... COEA
Chief Ordnance Electrical Mechanician [*British military*] (DMA) ..... COEMN
Chief Ordnance Electrician [*British military*] (DMA) ..... COEL
Chief Ordnance Mechanical Engineer [*British*] (ADA) ..... COME
Chief Ordnance Officer ..... COO
Chief Ordnance Officer ..... CORDO
Chief Painter [*Navy rating*] [*Obsolete*] ..... CPTR
Chief Painter, Aircraft [*Navy rating*] [*Obsolete*] ..... CPTRV
Chief Parachute Rigger [*Navy*] ..... CPR
Chief Parliamentary Counsel's Office [*Victoria*] [*Australia*] ..... CPCO
Chief Patriarch ..... CP
Chief Patrol Inspector [*Immigration and Naturalization Service*] ..... CPI
Chief Patternmaker [*Navy rating*] [*Obsolete*] ..... CPM
Chief Patternmaker [*Navy rating*] ..... PMC
Chief Pay Clerk [*Navy rating*] [*Obsolete*] ..... CHPCLK
Chief Pay Clerk [*Navy rating*] [*Obsolete*] ..... CPC
Chief, Perry, IA [*Library symbol*] [*Library of Congress*] (LCLS) ..... IaPerC
Chief, Personnel Division (SAUS) ..... Ch Pers Div
Chief Personnelman [*Navy rating*] ..... PNC
Chief Petty Officer [*Navy*] ..... CPO
Chief Petty Officer [*Navy*] E7
Chief Petty Officer Air Technical Aircraft [*Military*] [*Australia*] ..... CPO ATA
Chief Petty Officer Air Technical Communication [*Military*] [*Australia*] ..... CPO ATC
Chief Petty Officer, Aircrewman [*British military*] (DMA) ..... CPOACMN
Chief Petty Officer, Caterer [*British military*] (DMA) ..... CPOCA
Chief Petty Officer Clearance Diver [*Military*] [*Australia*] ..... CPO CD
Chief Petty Officer, Cook [*British military*] (DMA) ..... CPOCK
Chief Petty Officer Coxswain [*Military*] [*Australia*] ..... CPO COX
Chief Petty Officer Dental [*Military*] [*Australia*] ..... CPO DEN
Chief Petty Officer Electrical Technical Power [*Military*] [*Australia*] ..... CPO ETP
Chief Petty Officer Electrical Technical Weapons [*Military*] [*Australia*] ..... CPO ETW
Chief Petty Officer Electronic Technical Communications [*Military*] [*Australia*] ..... CPO ETC
Chief Petty Officer Electronic Warfare [*Military*] [*Australia*] ..... CPO EW
Chief Petty Officer Fire Control [*Military*] [*Australia*] ..... CPO FC
Chief Petty Officer Firefighter [*Military*] [*Australia*] ..... CPO FF
Chief Petty Officer, First Class [*Canadian*] [*Navy*] C1
Chief Petty Officer Marine Technical Hull [*Military*] [*Australia*] ..... CPO MTH
Chief Petty Officer Marine Technical Propulsion [*Military*] [*Australia*] ..... CPO MTP
Chief Petty Officer, Master [*Navy*] (WGA) ..... CPOM
Chief Petty Officer Medical [*Military*] [*Australia*] ..... CPO MED
Chief Petty Officer, Medical Assistant [*British military*] (DMA) ..... CPOMA
Chief Petty Officer Meteorology [*Military*] [*Australia*] ..... CPO MET
Chief Petty Officer Mine Warfare [*Military*] [*Australia*] ..... CPO MW
Chief Petty Officer Motor Transport Driver [*Military*] [*Australia*] ..... CPO MTD
Chief Petty Officer Musician [*Military*] [*Australia*] ..... CPO MUSN
Chief Petty Officer of the Command [*Navy*] (DNAB) ..... CPOC
Chief Petty Officer of the Watch [*Navy*] ..... CPOW
Chief Petty Officer Photography [*Military*] [*Australia*] ..... CPO PH
Chief Petty Officer, Physical Trainer [*British military*] (DMA) ..... CPOPT
Chief Petty Officer Quartermaster Gunner [*Military*] [*Australia*] ..... CPO QMG
Chief Petty Officer Radio Operator [*Military*] [*Australia*] ..... CPO RO
Chief Petty Officer Radio Plotter [*Military*] [*Australia*] ..... CPO RP
Chief Petty Officer, Second Class [*Canadian*] [*Navy*] C2
Chief Petty Officer, Senior [*Navy*] (WGA) ..... CPOS
Chief Petty Officer Signalman [*Military*] [*Australia*] ..... CPO SIG
Chief Petty Officer, Steward [*British military*] (DMA) ..... CPOSTD
Chief Petty Officer, Stores Accountant [*British military*] (DMA) ..... CPOSA
Chief Petty Officer Stores Naval [*Military*] [*Australia*] ..... CPO SN
Chief Petty Officer Stores Victualling [*Military*] [*Australia*] ..... CPO SV
Chief Petty Officer Survey Recorder [*Military*] [*Australia*] ..... CPO SR
Chief Petty Officer Survival Equipment [*Military*] [*Australia*] ..... CPO SE
Chief Petty Officer Underwater Control [*Military*] [*Australia*] ..... CPO UC
Chief Petty Officer Work Study [*Military*] [*Australia*] ..... CPO WS
Chief Petty Officer, Writer [*British military*] (DMA) ..... CPOWTR
Chief Petty Officer-in-Charge [*Navy*] (DNAB) ..... CPOIC
Chief Petty Officers Association (NTPA) ..... CPOA
Chief Pharmacist [*Navy rating*] [*Obsolete*] ..... CHPHAR
Chief Pharmacist's Mate [*Navy rating*] [*Obsolete*] ..... CPHM
Chief Pharmacist's Mate, Dental Prosthetic Technician [*Navy rating*] [*Obsolete*] ..... CPHMDP
Chief Pharmacists Mate Radium Plaque Adaptometer (SAUS) ..... CPHM RPA
Chief Pharmacist's Mate (Radium Plaque Adaptometer Operator) [*Navy rating*] [*Obsolete*] ..... CPHM(RPA)
Chief Photographer [*Navy rating*] [*Obsolete*] ..... CHPHOT
Chief Photographer [*Navy rating*] [*Obsolete*] ..... CPHO
Chief Photographer's Mate [*Navy rating*] [*Obsolete*] ..... CPHOM
Chief Photographer's Mate [*Navy rating*] ..... PHC
Chief Photographic Intelligenceman [*Navy rating*] ..... PTC
Chief Pilot ..... CP
Chief Pilot Inspector (SAUS) ..... CPI
Chief Planning and Control Staff [*Coast Guard*] ..... CPC
Chief Planning Engineer (SAUS) ..... Chf Plan Engr
Chief Plumber [*British military*] (DMA) ..... CPLMB
Chief Pointer (SAUS) ..... CPTR
Chief Polaris Executive [*Missiles*] ..... CPE
Chief Political Officer [*British Military Administration*] ..... CPO
Chief Post Office [*British*] (ADA) ..... CPO
Chief Postal Censor (SAUO) ..... CPC
Chief Postal Clerk [*Navy rating*] ..... PCC
Chief Postal Inspector [*US Postal Service*] ..... CPI
Chief Preventive Officer [*Customs*] [*British*] (ROG) ..... CPO
Chief Printer [*Navy rating*] [*Obsolete*] ..... CPRTR
Chief Printer, Lithographer [*Navy rating*] [*Obsolete*] ..... CPRTRL
Chief Printer, Offset Process [*Navy rating*] [*Obsolete*] ..... CPRTRM
Chief Privacy Officer ..... CPO
Chief Procurement Officer (AAGC) ..... CPO
Chief Program Engineer [*NASA*] (NASA) ..... CPE
Chief Programmer Organization (SAUS) ..... CPO
Chief Programmer Team [*Computer science*] ..... CPT
Chief Programmer Team Organization [*Computer science*] (MHDI) ..... CPTO
Chief Publications Engineer (SAUS) ..... Chf Publn Engr
Chief Quality Officer [*Business term*] (ECON) ..... CQO
Chief Quartermaster [*Navy rating*] [*Obsolete*] ..... CQM
Chief Quartermaster [*Navy rating*] ..... QMC
[*The*] **Chief Quartermaster** [*Military*] ..... TCQM
Chief Quartermaster Clerk [*Coast Guard*] ..... CHQMCLK
Chief Quartermaster Clerk [*Navy rating*] [*Obsolete*] ..... CQMC
Chief RADARman [*Navy rating*] [*Obsolete*] ..... CRDM
Chief RADARman [*Navy rating*] ..... RDC
Chief Radio Electrical Artificer [*British military*] (DMA) ..... CREA
Chief Radio Electrical Mechanician [*British military*] (DMA) ..... CREMN
Chief Radio Electrician [*Navy rating*] [*Obsolete*] ..... CHRELE
Chief Radio Electrician [*Navy rating*] [*Obsolete*] ..... CRE
Chief Radio Electrician [*British military*] (DMA) ..... CREL
Chief Radio Supervisor (Special) [*British military*] (DMA) ..... CRS(S)
Chief Radio Supervisor (Warfare) [*British military*] (DMA) ..... CRS(W)
Chief Radio Technician [*Navy rating*] [*Obsolete*] ..... CRT
Chief Radioman [*Navy rating*] [*Obsolete*] ..... CRM
Chief Radioman [*Navy rating*] ..... RMC
Chief Railway Construction Engineer [*British military*] (DMA) ..... CRCE
Chief Ranger ..... CR
Chief Recruiting Officer [*British military*] (DMA) ..... CRO
Chief Recruiting Officer (SAUO) ..... CRO
Chief Regional Officer (SAUO) ..... CRO
Chief Registrar's Reports [*England*] [*A publication*] (DLA) ..... CRR
Chief Regulating Officer [*Southwest Pacific Area, World War II*] [*Army*] ..... CREGO
Chief, Research and Development [*Department of National Defence*] [*Canada*] ..... CRAD
Chief, Reserve Division (SAUS) ..... Ch Res Div
Chief Resident (STED) ..... CR
Chief Resource Officer ..... CRO
Chief Royal Engineers Stores Officer (SAUO) ..... CRESO
Chief Sailmaker [*British military*] (DMA) ..... CSLMR
Chief Satellite Officer (ACAE) ..... CSO
Chief School Administrator ..... CSA
Chief Scientific Adviser [*British*] (RDA) ..... CSA
Chief Scientific Officer [*Also, CSO*] [*Ministry of Agriculture, Fisheries, and Food*] [*British*] ..... CScO
Chief Scientific Officer [*Also, CScO*] [*Ministry of Agriculture, Fisheries, and Food*] [*British*] ..... CSO
Chief Scientist [*National Oceanic and Atmospheric Administration*] (USDC) ..... CS
Chief Scientist (Royal Air Force) [*British*] ..... CS(RAF)
Chief Scientist's Directorate [*Nature Conservancy Council*] [*British*] ..... CSD
Chief, SEATO [*Southeast Asia Treaty Organization*] **Military Planning Office** (CINC) ..... CMPO
Chief Secretary (ADA) ..... CS
Chief Sector Control [*Aviation*] (OA) ..... CSC
Chief, Security Assistance Management and Staff [*Military*] (DNAB) ..... CHSAMS
Chief Shipfitter [*Navy rating*] [*Obsolete*] ..... CSF
Chief Shipfitter [*Navy rating*] ..... SFC
Chief Shipfitter, Construction Battalion, Mechanical Draftsman [*Navy rating*] [*Obsolete*] ..... CSFCBM

Chief Shipfitter, Construction Battalion, Pipe Fitter and Plumber [Navy rating] [Obsolete] .... CSFCBP
Chief Shipfitter, Construction Battalion, Rigger [Navy rating] [Obsolete] .... CSFCBR
Chief Shipfitter, Construction Battalion, Steel Worker [Navy rating] [Obsolete] .... CSFCBS
Chief Shipfitter, Construction Battalion, Welder [Navy rating] [Obsolete] .... CSFCBW
Chief Shipfitter, Ship Repair [Navy rating] [Obsolete] .... CSFSR
Chief Shipfitter, Ship Repair, Pipe Fitter and Plumber [Navy rating] [Obsolete] .... CSFSRP
Chief Shipfitter, Ship Repair, Welder [Navy rating] [Obsolete] .... CSFSRW
Chief Ship's Clerk [Navy rating] [Obsolete] .... CHSCLK
Chief Ship's Clerk [Navy rating] [Obsolete] .... CSCLK
Chief Ship's Service Man [Navy rating] [Obsolete] .... CSSM
Chief Ship's Service Man, Barber [Navy rating] [Obsolete] ...... CSSMB
Chief Ship's Service Man, Cobbler [Navy rating] [Obsolete] ..... CSSMC
Chief Ship's Service Man, Laundryman [Navy rating] [Obsolete] ... CSSML
Chief Ship's Service Man, Tailor [Navy rating] [Obsolete] .... CSSMT
Chief Ships Serviceman (SAUS) .... SHC
Chief Ship's Serviceman [Navy rating] .... SHC
Chief Sick Berth Attendant [British military] (DMA) .... CSBA
Chief Signal Boatswain [Navy] [British] (ROG) .... CHSB
Chief Signal Boatswain (SAUS) .... Ch SB
Chief, Signal Corps [Army] .... CSIGC
Chief Signal Officer [Army] .... CSIGO
Chief Signal Officer (SAUO) .... CSigO
Chief Signal Officer (SAUO) .... CSO
Chief Signal Officer [Army] .... CSO
Chief Signalman [Navy rating] [Obsolete] .... CSM
Chief Signalman [Navy rating] .... SMC
Chief Skipper [Navy] [British] .... ChSkr
Chief Skipper (SAUS) .... Ch Skr
Chief SONAR Technician [Navy rating] .... STC
Chief SONARman [Navy rating] [Obsolete] .... CSOM
Chief SONARman [Navy rating] [Obsolete] .... SOC
Chief SONARman, Harbor Defense [Navy rating] [Obsolete] ... CSOMH
Chief Special Artificer [Navy rating] [Obsolete] .... CSA
Chief Special Artificer, Instruments [Navy rating] [Obsolete] ... CSAI
Chief Special Artificer, Instruments, Typewriter and Office Equipment Repairman [Navy rating] [Obsolete] .... CSAITR
Chief Special Artificer, Instruments, Watch Repairman [Navy rating] [Obsolete] .... CSAIWR
Chief Special Artificer, Optical [Navy rating] [Obsolete] .... CSAO
Chief Special Artificer, Synthetic Training Devices [Navy rating] [Obsolete] .... CSAD
Chief Specialist [Navy rating] [Obsolete] .... CSP
Chief Specialist, All Designators [Navy rating] [Obsolete] .... CSPX
Chief Specialist, Chaplain's Assistant [Navy rating] [Obsolete] ... CSPW
Chief Specialist, Control Tower Operator [Navy rating] [Obsolete] ... CSPY
Chief Specialist, Identification [Navy rating] [Obsolete] .... CSPR
Chief Specialist, Laboratory [Navy rating] [Obsolete] .... CSPPLB
Chief Specialist, Link Trainer Instructor [Navy rating] [Obsolete] ... CSPTLT
Chief Specialist, Motion Picture Production [Navy rating] [Obsolete] ... CSPMP
Chief Specialist, Personnel Supervisor [Navy rating] [Obsolete] ... CSPS
Chief Specialist, Petroleum Inspector [Navy rating] [Obsolete] ... CSPO
Chief Specialist, Photogrammetry [Navy rating] [Obsolete] ...... CSPPPG
Chief Specialist, Physical Training Instructor [Navy rating] [Obsolete] ... CSPA
Chief Specialist, Recruiter [Navy rating] [Obsolete] .... CSPR
Chief Specialist, Shore Patrol and Security [Navy rating] [Obsolete] ... CSPS
Chief Specialist, Teacher [Navy rating] [Obsolete] .... CSPT
Chief Specialist, Transport Airman [Navy rating] [Obsolete] .... CSPV
Chief Specialist, V-Mail [Navy rating] [Obsolete] .... CSPPVM
Chief Specification Engineer (SAUS) .... Chf Spec Engr
Chief Staff Officer .... CSO
Chief Staff Officer, Reserves (SAUS) .... CSO
Chief State School Officer (AEE) .... CSSO
Chief Steelworker [Navy rating] .... SWC
Chief Steward [Later, MSC] [Navy rating] .... CST
Chief Steward [Later, MSC] [Navy rating] .... SDC
Chief Storekeeper [Navy rating] [Obsolete] .... CSK
Chief Storekeeper, Aviation [Navy rating] [Obsolete] .... CSKV
Chief Storekeeper, Construction Battalion, Stevedore [Navy rating] [Obsolete] .... CSKCB
Chief Storekeeper, Disbursing [Navy rating] [Obsolete] .... CSKD
Chief Storekeeper, Technical [Navy rating] [Obsolete] .... CSKT
Chief Stores Officer (SAUO) .... CSO
Chief Strategic Systems Executive (SAUS) .... CSSE
Chief Student Affairs Officer (DHP) .... CSAO
Chief Superintendent (ADA) .... CS
Chief Superintendent National Guard Bureau (SAUO) .... CSNGB
Chief Superintendent Naval Meteorology (SAUO) .... CSNM
Chief Superintendent of Armament Supply (SAUS) .... CSAS
Chief Superintendent of Hydrographic Supplies .... CSHS
Chief Superintendent of Juvenile Templars [Order of Good Templars] [Freemasonry] (ROG) .... CS of JT
Chief Superintendent of Naval Meteorology [British] .... CSNM
Chief Superintendent of Ordnance Factories [British] [World War II] ... CSOF
Chief, Superintendent Range Operations [NASA] (KSC) .... CSRO
Chief Superintendent, Research Department [British military] (DMA) ... CSRD
Chief Supply and Transport Officer (SAUS) .... CSTO
Chief Supply Clerk (SAUS) .... Ch Sup Clk
Chief Supply Officer (SAUO) .... CSO
Chief Surgeon (SAUS) .... Chf Surg
Chief Surgeon (SAUS) .... CS

Chief Surgeon (SAUS) .... CTO
Chief Systems Engineer (SSD) .... CSE
Chief Technical Adviser (SAUS) .... CTA
Chief Technical Examiner of Works (SAUS) .... CTEW
Chief Technical Examiner of Works (SAUO) .... CTEW
Chief Technical Officer [British] (ADA) .... CTO
Chief Technical Offices (SAUO) .... CTO
Chief, Technical Services .... CTS
Chief Technical Services Officer (SAUO) .... CTSO
Chief Technology Officer (SAUO) .... CTO
Chief Telegrapher [Navy rating] [Obsolete] .... CT
Chief Test Conductor (NASA) .... CTC
Chief Test Pilot (SAUO) .... CTP
Chief Testboard Man [Telecommunications] (TEL) .... CTBM
Chief, Topographic Division (GEOI) .... CTD
Chief Torpedoman [Navy rating] [Obsolete] .... CHTORP
Chief Torpedoman [Navy rating] [Obsolete] .... CTORP
Chief Torpedoman's Mate [Navy rating] [Obsolete] .... CTM
Chief Torpedoman's Mate [Navy rating] .... TMC
Chief Torpedoman's Mate, Aviation [Navy rating] [Obsolete] .. CTMV
Chief Torpedoman's Mate, Electrical [Navy rating] [Obsolete] .. CTME
Chief TRADEVMAN [Training Devices Man] [Navy rating] ...... TDC
Chief Transport & Movements Officer (SAUO) .... CTMO
Chief Transport Officer (SAUO) .... CTO
Chief Transportation Officer (SAUO) .... CTO
Chief Treasury Officer (SAUO) .... CTO
Chief Turret Captain [Obsolete] [Navy] .... CTC
Chief, United States Army Overseas Supply Agency, San Francisco (CINC) .... CHUSAOSASF
Chief, United States Army Reserve and Reserve Officers Training Corps Affairs .... CUSARROTC
Chief, United States Defense Liaison Group (DNAB) .... CHUSDLG
Chief, United States Military Supply Mission, India (CINC) ..... CHUSMSI
Chief, United States Naval Mission (DNAB) .... CHUSNAVMIS
Chief, United States Naval Mission (SAUS) .... ChUSNavMis
Chief, U.S. Naval Mission (SAUO) .... CHNAVMIS
Chief US Naval Section (SAUO) .... CHINAVSEC
Chief Value CV
Chief Veterinary Officer [Ministry of Agriculture, Fisheries, and Food] [British] .... CVO
Chief Warrant and Warrant Officers Association, United States Coast Guard (EA) .... CW & WOA
Chief Warrant and Warrant Officers Association, United States Coast Guard .... CWOA
Chief Warrant Officer [Military rank] .... CW
Chief Warrant Officer [Army] (GPO) .... CWO
Chief Warrant Officer 2 [Army] CW2
Chief Warrant Officer 3 [Army] CW3
Chief Warrant Officer 4 [Army] CW4
Chief Warrant Officer, W-2 [Army] (AABC) CWO-2
Chief Warrant Officer, W-3 [Army] (AABC) CWO-3
Chief Warrant Officer, W-4 [Army] (AABC) CWO-4
Chief Watch Officer [Navy] .... CWO
Chief Water Tender [Navy rating] [Obsolete] .... CWT
Chief, Western Pacific Transportation Office (CINC) .... CHWTO
Chief WREN [Women's Royal Naval Service] Air Fitter [British military] (DMA) .... CWRENAF
Chief WREN [Women's Royal Naval Service] Cinema Operator [British military] (DMA) .... CWRENCINE
Chief WREN [Women's Royal Naval Service] Cook [British military] (DMA) .... CWRENCK
Chief WREN [Women's Royal Naval Service] Dental Hygienist [British military] (DMA) .... CWRENDHYG
Chief WREN [Women's Royal Naval Service] Dental Surgery Assistant [British military] (DMA) .... CWRENDSA
Chief WREN [Women's Royal Naval Service] Education Assistant [British military] (DMA) .... CWRENEDUC
Chief WREN [Women's Royal Naval Service] Meteorological Observer [British military] (DMA) .... CWRENMET
Chief WREN [Women's Royal Naval Service] Photographer [British military] (DMA) .... CWRENPHOT
Chief WREN [Women's Royal Naval Service] Quarters Assistant [British military] (DMA) .... CWRENQA
Chief WREN [Women's Royal Naval Service] (RADAR) [British military] (DMA) .... CWREN(R)
Chief WREN [Women's Royal Naval Service] Radio Electrician [British military] (DMA) .... CWRENREL
Chief WREN [Women's Royal Naval Service] Radio Supervisor (Morse) [British military] (DMA) .... CWRENRS(M)
Chief WREN [Women's Royal Naval Service] Regulating [British military] (DMA) .... CWRENREG
Chief WREN [Women's Royal Naval Service] Steward [British military] (DMA) .... CWRENSTD
Chief WREN [Women's Royal Naval Service] Stores Accountant [British military] (DMA) .... CWRENSA
Chief WREN [Women's Royal Naval Service] Stores Assistant (Clothes) [British military] (DMA) .... CWRENS(C)
Chief WREN [Women's Royal Naval Service] Stores Assistant (Victualling) [British military] (DMA) .... CWRENS(V)
Chief WREN [Women's Royal Naval Service] Telephonist [British military] (DMA) .... CWRENTEL
Chief WREN [Women's Royal Naval Service] Training Support Assistant [British military] (DMA) .... CWRENTSA
Chief WREN [Women's Royal Naval Service] Weapon Analyst [British military] (DMA) .... CWRENWA

Chief WREN [Women's Royal Naval Service] Welfare Worker [British military] (DMA) .... CWRENWW
Chief WREN [Women's Royal Naval Service] Writer (General) [British military] (DMA) .... CWRENWTR(G)
Chief WREN [Women's Royal Naval Service] Writer (Pay) [British military] (DMA) .... CWRENWTR(P)
Chief Yeoman [Navy rating] [Obsolete] .... CY
Chiefland, FL [AM radio station call letters] .... WLQH
Chiefland, FL [FM radio station call letters] .... WLQH-FM
Chiefland, FL [FM radio station call letters] .... WTBH
Chief-of-the-Boat [Navy] (MUSM) .... COB
Chiefs of Defence Staff (SAUO) .... CHODs
Chiefs of Staff Committee (SAUO) .... Ch of StC
Chiefs of Staff Committee (SAUO) .... COSC
Chiefs of Staff Committee [Australia] .... CSC
Chiefs of Staff, Mediterranean [Military] .... COSMED
Chiefs of Staff Secretariat (SAUO) .... COSSEC
Chiefs of Staff, Washington [Military] .... COS(W)
Chieftain (ROG) .... CHFTN
Chieftain Airways PLC [British] [ICAO designator] (FAAC) .... PQC
Chieftain Aviation PC [South Africa] [ICAO designator] (FAAC) .... LNP
Chieftain International [Associated Press] (SAG) .... Chief
Chieftain International [AMEX symbol] [Toronto Stock Exchange symbol] (SPSG) .... CID
Chieftain International Fund [Associated Press] (SAG) .... ChfInt
Chieftain International Fund [AMEX symbol] (SPSG) .... GSS
Chieftain Intl. [AMEX symbol] (TTSB) .... CID
Chieftain Intl Fd $1.8125 Cv Pfd [AMEX symbol] (TTSB) .... GSSPr
Chievres [Belgium] [ICAO location identifier] (ICLI) .... EBCV
Chifeng [China] [Airport symbol] (OAG) .... CIF
Chiffonier .... CH
Chiffre (SAUS) .... Ch
Chignik, AK [Location identifier] [FAA] (FAAL) .... KCG
Chignik, AK [Location identifier] [FAA] (FAAL) .... KCL
Chigorodo [Colombia] [Airport symbol] (OAG) .... IGO
Chigwell [Urban district in England] .... CHIGW
Chihuahua [Mexico] [Seismograph station code, US Geological Survey] (SEIS) .... CHH
Chihuahua [Mexico] (BARN) .... Chic
Chihuahua [Mexico] [Airport symbol] (OAG) .... CUU
Chihuahua Club of America (EA) .... CCA
Chihuahua/Internacional [Mexico] [ICAO location identifier] (ICLI) .... MMCU
Chihuahuan Desert Research Institute (EA) .... CDRI
Chikrassy Timber (SAUS) .... CHI Timber
Chikungunya Virus CV
Chilas [Pakistan] [ICAO location identifier] (ICLI) .... OPCL
Chilchota Taxi Aereo SA de CV [Mexico] [ICAO designator] (FAAC) .... CCH
Chilcotin Caribou Aviation [Canada] [ICAO designator] (FAAC) .... DES
Child C
Child (DMAA) .... ch
Child [or Children] .... CH
Child (ROG) .... CHD
Child (ADA) .... CHIL
Child Abuse (DIPS) .... CA
Child Abuse Accountability Act (WDAA) .... CAAA
Child Abuse and Maltreatment Reporting Center (SAUO) .... CAMRC
Child Abuse and Neglect .... CA/N
Child Abuse and Neglect Database Instrument System (SAUO) .... CANDIS
Child Abuse and Neglect Reprint and Inquiry Systems (EDAC) .... CANRIS
Child Abuse Institute of Research (EA) .... CAIR
Child Abuse Listening Mediation (EA) .... CALM
Child Abuse Prevention, Adoption, and Family Services Act of 1988 .... CAPAFSA
Child Abuse Prevention and Treatment Act .... CAPTA
Child Abuse Protection Board [Tasmania] [Australia] .... CAPB
Child Abuse Register (WDAA) .... CAR
Child Abuse Unit for Studies, Education and Services (SAUO) .... CAUSES
Child Abuse Victims' Rights Act of 1986 .... CAVRA
Child Adult Mist [Medicine] (MELL) .... CAM
Child Amputee Program [Canada] .... CHAMP
Child and Adolescent Adjustment Profile [Child development test] [Psychology] .... CAAP
Child and Adult Care Food Program (SAUO) .... CACFP
Child and Family Policy Center (EA) .... CFPC
Child and Youth Centered Information Systems .... CYCIS
Child Anxiety Scale [Child development test] [Psychology] .... CAS
Child Attitudes Survey [Education] .... CAS
Child Behavior and Characteristics .... CBC
Child Behavior Checklist .... CBCL
Child Behavior Rating Scale [Devereaux] [Psychology] .... CBRS
Child Behavior Therapy Special Interest Group [Defunct] (EA) .... CBTSIG
Child Care (ADA) CC
Child Care Action Campaign (EA) .... CCAC
Child Care Advocacy Association of Canada [Association Canadienne pour la Promotion des Services de Garde a l'Enfance] [Formerly, Canadian Day Care Advocacy Association] (AC) .... CCAAC
Child Care and Development Block Grant (SAUO) .... CCDBG
Child Care Assistance .... CCA
Child Care Association of Illinois (SRA) .... CCA
Child Care Centres Association, Victoria [Australia] .... CCCAV
Child Care Employee Project (EA) .... CCEP
Child Care Food Program [Washington, DC] .... CCFP
Child Care Food Programs (SAUO) .... CCFP
Child: Care, Health and Development (SAUS) .... Child Care Health Dev
Child Care Law Center (EA) CCLC
Child Care Officer (SAUO) .... CCO

Child Care Resource and Referral Program (WYGK) .... CCR&R
Child Care Worker .... CCW
Child Development Associate [National certificate] (OICC) .... CDA
Child Development Associate Consortium [CDANCP] [Superseded by] (EA) .... CDAC
Child Development Associate National Credentialing Program (EA) .... CDANCP
Child Development Center .... CDC
Child Development Center Q-Sort [Personality development test] [Psychology] .... CDCQ
Child Development Consultant .... CDC
Child Development Group of Mississipi (SAUO) .... CDGM
Child Development Inventory [Test] (TMMY) .... CDI
Child Development Programme [British] .... CDP
Child Development Questionnaire (EDAC) .... CDQ
Child Development Research (BARN) .... CDR
Child Development Research Unit [Nigeria] .... CDRU
Child Education Foundation, New York, NY [Library symbol] [Library of Congress] [Obsolete] (LCLS) .... NNCEF
Child Evacuation Bureau (SAUO) .... CEB
Child Evangelism Fellowship (EA) .... CEF
Child Evangelism Fellowship International [Later, CEF] (EA) .... CEFI
Child Evangelism Fellowship of Australia .... CEFA
Child Exploitation and Obscenity Section .... CEOS
Child Find [Later, CFA] [An association] (EA) .... CF
Child Find Alberta [Formerly, Friends of Child Find Society] (AC) .... CFA
Child Find of America (EA) .... CFA
Child Find PEI Inc. (AC) .... CEPEI
Child Growth Foundation [British] (DBA) .... CGF
Child Health Assessment Program .... CHAP
Child Health Associate Program (SAUO) .... CHAP
Child Health Bulletin (journ.) (SAUS) .... Child Health Bul
Child Health Centre [Australia] .... CHC
Child Health Clinic (WDAA) .... CHC
Child Health Foundation [Formerly, International Child Health Foundation] (EA) .... ICHF
Child Health Magazine (journ.) (SAUS) .... Child Health M
Child Health Services Research .... CHSR
Child [or Children] in Need of Service [Pediatrics and social services] (DAVI) .... CHINS
Child Keyppers' International (EA) .... CKI
Child Labor Bulletin (journ.) (SAUS) .... Child Labor Bul
Child Language Ability Measures [Child development test] .... CLAM
Child Life Council (EA) CLC
Child Migrants Trust .... CMT
Child Neurology .... CHN
Child Neurology Society (EA) .... CNS
Child Neuropsychological Questionnaire [Psycholoy] (DHP) .... CNQ
Child Nutrition .... CN
Child Nutrition Act (SAUO) .... CNA
Child Nutrition Division (SAUO) .... CND
Child Nutrition Forum (EA) .... CNF
Child Nutrition Programs (SAUO) .... CNP
Child Of [Genealogy] .... CH/O
Child of a Deaf Adult .... CODA
Child of a Substance Abuser .... COSA
Child of Upwardly Mobile Professionals [Lifestyle classification] .... Chump
Child Online Protection Act .... COPA
Child Personality Scale [Medicine] (MELL) .... CPS
Child Poverty Action Group (SAUO) .... CPAG
Child Poverty Action Group [British] (BI) .... CPAG
Child Protection and Family Crisis Service [New South Wales] [Australia] .... CPFCS
Child Protection Case Management Team (SAUO) .... CPCMT
Child Protection Council [New South Wales] [Australia] .... CPC
Child Protection Register (SAUO) .... CPR
Child Protection Report [A publication] .... CPR
Child Protection Services (SAUO) .... CPS
Child Protective Services [Public human service program] (PHSD) .... CPS
Child Psychiatry [Medical specialty] (DHSM) .... CHP
Child Psychiatry .... CP
Child Psychology .... CP
Child Quest International [An association] (EA) .... CQI
Child Rearing Study (SAUS) .... CRS
Child Report of Parent Behavior Inventory (EDAC) .... CRPBI
Child Resistant .... CR
Child Resistant Container (STED) .... CRC
Child Resistant Device (MELL) .... CRD
Child Restraint and Air Bag Information [Automotive safety] .... CRABI
Child Restraint System (SAUO) .... CRS
Child Safety Council [Later, NCSC] (EA) .... CSC
Child Safety Seat Questionnaire [Auto safety research] .... CSSQ
Child Service Demonstration Center [Department of Education] .... CSDC
Child Sexual Abuse (MELL) .... CSA
Child Sexual Abuse Accommodation Syndrome .... CSAAS
Child Sexual Assault Program [Australia] .... CSAP
Child Study Association of America (BARN) .... CSA
Child Study Association of America [Defunct] (EA) .... CSAA
Child Study Association of America, New York, NY [Library symbol] [Library of Congress] (LCLS) .... NNCS
Child Study Center [Brown University] [Research center] (RCD) .... CSC
Child Study Society (SAUO) .... CSS
Child Study Team [Education] .... CST
Child Support Agency [British] (ECON) .... CSA
Child Support Enforcement [Department of Health and Human Services] .... CSE
Child Support Network [Defunct] (EA) .... CSN

Child Support Recovery Act (SAUS) .... CSRA
Child Support Resistance (EA) .... CSR
Child Support Rulings [Australian Taxation Office] [A publication] .... CS
Child Support Services (SAUO) .... CSS
Child Survival (SAUO) .... CS
Child Survival and Disease (SAUO) .... CSD
Child Survival and Disease Fund (SAUO) .... CSD
Child Survival Assistance Program [Agency for International Development] .... CSAP
Child Trends (EA) .... CT
Child Welfare (SAUS) .... Child Welfare
Child Welfare .... CW
Child Welfare Center [British] (DAS) .... CWC
Child Welfare Centre (SAUO) .... CWC
Child Welfare Information Services/Non-Profit Computer Services [Information service or system] (IID) .... CWIS/NPC
Child Welfare Institute (EA) .... CWI
Child Welfare League (BARN) .... CWL
Child Welfare League of America (EA) .... CWLA
Child Welfare League of Canada [La Ligue pour la Protection de l'Enfance du Canada] (AC) .... CWLC
Child Welfare Service (SAUO) .... CWRU
Child Welfare Service .... CWS
Child Workers In Nepal (SAUS) .... CWIN
Child, Youth, and Family Education Network [Online resource] (PAZ) .... CYFERNET
Childbearing Age (MELL) .... CBA
Childbearing Hips .... CBH
Childbirth and Parenting Association of Victoria [Australia] .... CPAV
Childbirth Education Association (SAUO) .... CEA
Childbirth Education Association of Australia .... CEAA
Childbirth Education Foundation (EA) .... CEF
Childbirth without Pain .... CWOP
Childbirth without Pain (MAE) .... CWP
Childbirth without Pain Education Association [Also known as Lamaze Birth without Pain Education Association] (EA) .... CWPEA
Child-Centered Experience-Based Learning [An association] [Canada] .... CEL
Child-Focused Network (SAUO) .... CFN
Childhelp USA, Inc. (EA) .... CUI
Childhood .... CHILDHD
Childhood Aphasia, Neurological Disorders, Landau-Klefner, and Epilepsy .... CANDLE
Childhood Autism Rating Scale [Medicine] (DB) .... CARS
Childhood Brain Tumor Foundation (SAUO) .... CBTF
Childhood Celiac Disease [Medicine] (DMAA) .... CCD
Childhood Disability Benefits [Social Security Administration] (OICC) .... CDB
Childhood Disease (HGAA) .... CD
Childhood Disease [Medicine] .... CHD
Childhood Education [A publication] (BRI) .... CE
Childhood Epileptic Encephalopathy [Medicine] (MELL) .... CEE
Childhood in Poetry [A publication] .... CIP
Childhood in Poetry Supplement [A publication] .... CIPS
Childhood Language Disorder (MELL) .... CLD
Childhood Muscular Dystrophy .... CMD
Childhood Polycystic Disease (PAZ) .... CPD
Childhood Polycystic Kidney Disease [Medicine] .... CPKD
Childhood Rheumatic Disease (STED) .... CRD
Childhood Sensuality Circle (EA) .... CSC
Childhood Sexual Abuse (MELL) .... CSA
Childless by Choice [An association] .... CBC
Child-Operated Mobile Electric Transport .... COMET
Children (GEAB) .... ch
Children (AL) .... Ch
Children (SAUS) .... CH
Children (ROG) .... CHDN
Children .... CHLD
Children (GEAB) .... chldn
Children [Genealogy] .... CHN
Children Affected with Lymphatic Malformations (SAUO) .... CALM
Children Against Smoking [British] .... CAS
Children and Adults with Attention Deficit Disorder (PAZ) .... CHADD
Children and Families World Community Chest (SAUO) .... CFWCC
Children and Young Persons Act [British] .... CYPA
Children and Youth .... C & Y
Children as the Peacemakers [An association] (EA) .... CATP
Children as the Peacemakers (EA) .... CTP
Children Assistance Programme (SAUO) .... CAP
Children at Risk Screener: Kindergarten and Preschool [Test] (TMMY) .... CARS
Children Awaiating Parents [An association] .... CAP
Children before Dogs (EA) .... CBD
Children Before Dogs (SAUO) .... CBD
Children by Choice [Australia] .... CBC
Children Have a Potential [Program for handicapped or disturbed children of Air Force personnel] (AFM) .... CHAP
Children Helped in Litigated Divorce (SAUO) .... CHILD
Children in Crisis (SAUO) CIC
Children in Especially Difficult Circumstances (SAUO) .... CEDC
Children in Hospitals (EA) .... CIH
Children in Libraries-Improving Multimedia Virtual Library Access and Information Skills (TELE) .... CHILIAS
Children in Libraries-improving multimedia virtual library access and information skills (SAUS) .... CHILIAS
Children in Need of Assistance (OICC) .... CHINA
Children in Need of Supervision [Classification for delinquent children] (OICC) .... CHINS

Children in Need of Supervision .... CINS
Children in Residential Institutions Program [Australia] .... CRI
Children, Inc. [An association] (EA) CI
Children, Incorporated (SAUO) CI
Children of Aging Parents Society (SAUO) .... CAPS
Children of Alcoholic .... COA
Children of Alcoholic Parents [An association] (EA) .... CAP
Children of Alcoholic Parents [An association] (EA) .... CAPS
Children of Alcoholics .... CoA
Children of Alcoholics Foundation (EA) .... CAF
Children of Auschwitz - Nazis' Deadly Lab Experiments Survivors [Acronym is used as name of associaton] (EA) .... CANDLES
Children of Deaf Adults (EA) .... CODA
Children of Gay Parentage (EA) .... CGP
Children of Gays/Lesbians [Later, CGP] (EA) .... CGL
Children of God (SAUO) .... COG
Children of High Intellectual Potential .... CHIP
Children of High Intellectual Potential Foundation [Australia] .... CHIPF
Children of Lesbians and Gays Everywhere [An association] (EA) .... CLGE
Children of Light [Freemasonry] (ROG) .... C of L
Children of Prisoners Support Group [Australia] .... CPSG
Children of the Americas (EA) .... CA
Children of the Americas (EA) .... COA
Children of the Confederacy (EA) .... C of C
Children of the Green Earth (EA) .... CGE
Children of the Night (EA) .... CN
Children of the Universe [Defunct] (EA) .... CU
Children of War [An association] (EA) .... CW
Children Today [A publication] (BRI) .... CT
Children with Attention-Deficit Disorders (EA) .... ChADD
Children with Behavioral and Emotional Difficulty (EA) .... CBED
Children with Learning Disabilities .... CLD
Children with Retarded Mental Development (SAUS) .... CRMD
Children with Special Health Care Needs .... CSHCN
Children's .... CHILD
Children's Academic Intrinsic Motivation Inventory [Test] (TES) .... CAIMI
Children's Action Network [Defunct] (EA) .... CAN
Children's Adaptive Behavior Report [Child development test] [Psychology] .... CABR
Childrens Adaptive Behavior Scale (SAUS) .... CABS
Children's Advocacy Center (EA) .... CAC
Children's Affective Reading Scale .... CARS
Children's Aid International (EA) .... CAI
Children's Aid Society (BARN) .... CAS
Children's Aid Society of Ottawa-Carleton, Ottawa, Ontario [Library symbol] [National Library of Canada] (NLC) .... OOCAS
Children's Aid Society, Ottawa, ON, Canada [Library symbol] [Library of Congress] (LCLS) .... CaOOCAS
Children's Alliance for Protection of the Environment (EA) .... CAPE
Children's and Adults' Library, St. John's, Newfoundland [Library symbol] [National Library of Canada] (NLC) .... NFSCA
Children's and Adults' Library, St. John's, NF, Canada [Library symbol] [Library of Congress] (LCLS) .... CaNfSCA
Children's and Young Adult Services .... CAYAS
Children's Apparel Manufacturers' Association [Canada] .... CAMA
Children's Apperception Test [Psychology] .... CAT
Children's Apperception Test [Child development test] [Psychology] .... CAT-A
Children's Apperception Test - Human Figures [Child development test] [Psychology] .... CAT-H
Children's Apperception Test - Supplement [Child development test] [Psychology] .... CAT-S
Children's Apperceptive Story-Telling Test (TES) .... CAST
Children's Art Foundation (EA) .... CAF
Children's Assertiveness Behavior Scale .... CABS
Children's Associative Responding Test (EDAC) .... CART
Children's Asthma Research Institute and Hospital [Denver, CO] .... CARIH
Children's Attitude toward Reading Test (EDAC) .... CHART
Children's Attribution of Responsibility and Locus of Control (EDAC) .... CARALOC
Children's Attributional Style Questionnaire .... CASQ
Children's Authors and Illustrators [A publication] .... CAI
Children's Behavior Checklist .... CBC
Children's Behavior Inventory [Medicine] (DB) .... CBI
Children's Blood Foundation (EA) .... CBF
Children's Book Action Group [National Book League] [British] .... CBAG
Children's Book Circle [British] .... CBC
Children's Book Council (EA) .... CBC
Children's Book News [A publication] (BRI) .... Ch Bk News
Children's Book of the Year [British] .... CBY
Children's Book Review Service [A publication] (BRI) .... CBRS
Children's Book Week .... CBW
Children's Book Writers' Group [Australia] .... CBWG
Children's Bookwatch [A publication] (BRI) .... Ch BWatch
Children's Brittle Bone Foundation .... CBBF
Children's Broadcast Institute [Canada] .... CBI
Children's Broadcasting [NASDAQ symbol] (SG) .... FILM
Childrens Broadcasting Corp. [NASDAQ symbol] (SAG) .... AAHS
Childrens Broadcasting Corp. [Associated Press] (SAG) .... ChldBrd
Children's Bureau [of SSA] .... CB
Children's Campaign for a Positive Future (EA) .... CCPF
Children's Campaign for Nuclear Disarmament (EA) .... CCND
Children's Cancer Fund of America [Defunct] (EA) .... CCFA
Childrens Cancer Group .... CCG
Children's Cancer Research Group [England] .... CCRG
Children's Cancer Study Group [National Institutes of Health] .... CCSG

Children's Category Test (TMMY) ... CCT
Children's Checking Test (EDAC) ... CCT
Children's Cognitive Style Assessment Instrument (EDAC) ... CCSA
Children's Committee 10 (EA) ... CC
Children's Comp Svcs [NASDAQ symbol] (TTSB) ... KIDS
Childrens Comprehensive Services [Associated Press] (SAG) ... ChldCmp
Children's Comprehensive Services [NASDAQ symbol] (SAG) ... KIDS
Children's Computer Workshop ... CCW
Children's Country Holiday Fund [British] ... CCHF
Children's Court [Australia] ... CC
Children's Court (DLA) ... Child Ct
Children's Court Advisory Committee [Australia] ... CCAC
Children's Craniofacial Association (EA) ... CCA
Children's Creative Response to Conflict Program (EA) ... CCRC
Children's Creative Writing Campaign, Inc. ... CCWC
Children's Defense Fund (EA) ... CDF
Children's Depression Inventory [Personality development test] [Psychology] ... CDI
Children's Depression Rating Scale ... CDRS
Children's Depression Rating Scale for Classrooms (EDAC) ... CDRSC
Children's Depression Scale ... CDS
Children's Diagnostic Inventory ... CDI
Childrens Discovery Centers of America [Associated Press] (SAG) ... ChildDis
Children's Discovery Centers of America, Inc. [NASDAQ symbol] (NQ) ... CDCR
Children's Embedded Figures Test [Psychology] ... CEFT
Children's Emotions Anonymous (EA) ... CEA
Children's Environmental Health Network (ADWA) ... CEHN
Children's Environments Advisory Service, Canada Mortgage and Housing Corp. [Service Consultatif sur l'Environnement de l'Enfant, Societe Canadienne d'Hypotheques et de Logement] Ottawa, Ontario [Library symbol] [National Library of Canada] (NLC) ... OOCMC
Childrens Evaluation and Rehabilitation Center (SAUS) ... CERC
Children's Express Foundation (EA) ... CEF
Children's Eye Care Foundation [Later, NCECF] (EA) ... CECF
Childrens Fashion Group [British] (BI) ... CFG
Children's Fear Survey Schedule [Psychology] (EDAC) ... CESS
Children's Film and Television Center of America (EA) ... CFTCA
Children's Film and Television Foundation [British] ... CFTF
Children's Film Theatre [Later, Media Center for Children] ... CFT
[The] Children's Foundation (EA) ... TCF
Children's Friendship Project for Northern Ireland (EA) ... CFPNI
[The] Children's Garland [A publication] ... CG
Children's Health and Fitness Fund ... CHeaFF
Children's Health, Education, and Safety Services [Australia] ... CHESS
Children's Health Information about Liver Disease ... CHILD
Children's Health Insurance Program [Public human service program] (PHSD) ... CHIP
Children's Health Services Division [HEW] ... CHSD
Children's Healthcare Is a Legal Duty (EA) ... CHILD
Children's Heart Association for Support & Education (AC) ... CHASE
Children's Heart Fund (EA) ... CHF
Children's Heartlink (EA) ... CHL
Children's Home of Kingston, Kingston, NY [Library symbol] [Library of Congress] (LCLS) ... NKiC
Children's Home-Based Education Association [British] (DBA) ... CHEA
Children's Hospice International (EA) ... CHI
Children's Hospital [Philadelphia, PA] ... CH
Children's Hospital Automated Medical Program (DMAA) ... CHAMP
Children's Hospital, Buffalo, NY [Library symbol] [Library of Congress] (LCLS) ... NBuCH
Children's Hospital, Los Angeles, CA ... CHLA
Children's Hospital Medical Center [Ohio] ... CHMC
Childrens Hospital Medical Center (SAUS) ... CHMC
Children's Hospital, Medical Library, Denver, CO [Library symbol] [Library of Congress] (LCLS) ... CoDCH-M
Children's Hospital of Eastern Ontario [Hopital pour Enfants de l'Est de l'Ontario] Ottawa, Ontario [Library symbol] [National Library of Canada] (NLC) ... OOCHEO
Children's Hospital of Michigan ... CHM
Children's Hospital of Michigan, Detroit, MI [Library symbol] [Library of Congress] (LCLS) ... MiDCh
Children's Hospital of Philadelphia (HGEN) ... CHOP
Children's Hospital of Pittsburgh, Pittsburgh, PA [OCLC symbol] (OCLC) ... PHC
Children's Hospital, Ottawa, ON, Canada [Library symbol] [Library of Congress] (LCLS) ... CaOOCH
Children's Hospital Research Foundation [Research center] (RCD) ... CHRF
Childrens Hospital Research Foundation, Research Library, Cincinnati (SAUS) ... OCCH
Children's Hospital Research Foundation, Research Library, Cincinnati, OH [Library symbol] [Library of Congress] (LCLS) ... OCCH
Children's Hospital Society, Doctor's Library, Los Angeles, CA [Library symbol] [Library of Congress] (LCLS) ... CLCH
Children's Hospital, St. Paul, MN [Library symbol] [Library of Congress] (LCLS) ... MnSCH
Children's Hypnotic Susceptibility Scale [Psychology] ... CHSS
Children's Intensive Care Unit (ADA) ... CICU
Children's Interaction Matrix [Child development test] [Psychology] ... CIM
Children's Interests Bureau [South Australia] ... CIB
Childrens International Summer Village (SAUS) ... CISV
Children's International Summer Villages International Association [Newcastle-Upon-Tyne, England] (EAIO) ... CISV
Children's Legal Centre (EAIO) ... CLC
Children's Legal Foundation (EA) ... CLF
Children's Legal Rights Information and Training [An association] (EA) ... CLRIT
Children's Legal Rights Journal [A publication] (DLA) ... Child Legal Rts J
Children's Leukemia and Cancer Foundation [Australia] ... CLCF
Children's Leukemia Research Association [Formerly, National Leukemia Association] (EA) ... NLA
Children's Literature [A publication] (BRI) ... Child Lit
Children's Literature Association (EA) ... ChLA
Children's Literature Association Quarterly [A publication] (BRI) ... ChLAQ
Children's Literature in Education [A publication] (BRI) ... Ch Lit Ed
Children's Liver Alliance (ADWA) ... CLA
Children's Liver Foundation (EA) ... CLF
Children's Magazine Guide ... CMG
Children's Manifest Anxiety Scale [Psychology] (AEBS) ... CMAS
Children's Medical Center of Israel [Tel Aviv] ... CMCI
Children's Medical Relief International [Defunct] ... CMRI
Children's Medical Research ... CMR
Childrens Medical Research Foundation (SAUO) ... CMRF
Children's Medical Research Institute [Australia] ... CMRI
Children's Memorial Hospital, Joseph Brennemann Medical Library, Chicago, IL [Library symbol] [Library of Congress] (LCLS) ... ICChH
Children's Memory Scale [M. Cohen] (DIPS) ... CMS
Children's Mercy Hospital, Kansas City, MO [Library symbol] [Library of Congress] (LCLS) ... MoKCH
Children's Miracle Network [Medicine] ... CMN
Children's Miracle Network Telethon ... CMNT
Children's Miracle Network Television ... CMNT
Children's Museum of Indianapolis, Indianapolis, IN [OCLC symbol] (OCLC) ... IIM
Children's Museum of Indianapolis, Indianapolis, IN [Library symbol] [Library of Congress] (LCLS) ... InICM
Children's Nutrition Laboratory [Baylor College of Medicine] ... CNL
Children's Oncology Care of Ontario Inc. [Also, Ronald McDonald House] (AC) ... COCO
Children's Online Privacy Protection Act ... COPPA
Children's Organ Replacement Program Special Medical Alert Network ... CORPSMAN
Children's Organ Transplant Association ... COTA
Children's Organization for Peace and Brotherhood [Defunct] (EA) ... COPB
Children's Orientation and Amnesia Test [Medicine] (DMAA) ... COAT
Children's Orthopedic Hospital and Medical Center, Seattle, WA [Library symbol] [Library of Congress] (LCLS) ... WaSCO
Children's Own Garden International [See also BjBI] (EAIO) ... COGI
Children's Peace Union [Defunct] (EA) ... CPU
Children's Perceived Self-Control Scale ... CPSCS
Children's Perceived Self-Control Scale - Usually That's Me ... CPSCS-UTM
Children's Personality Questionnaire [Psychology] ... CPQ
Children's Picture Information Test [Psychology] (AEBS) ... CPIT
Children's PKU [Phenylketonuria] Network (PAZ) ... CPN
Children's Place Retail Stores [NASDAQ symbol] (SG) ... PLCE
Children's Play Activities Ltd. [British] (BI) ... CPA
Children's Plea for Peace [Later, World Pen Pals] ... CPP
Children's Psychiatric Rating Scale (DB) ... CPRS
Children's Psychiatric Research Institute, Ontario Ministry of Community and Social Services, London, Ontario [Library symbol] [National Library of Canada] (NLC) ... OLCSSCP
Children's Public Policy Network [Later, CAN] (EA) ... CPPN
Children's Radio Network (NTCM) ... CRN
Children's Reading Round Table ... CRRT
Children's Reading Service (AEBS) ... CRS
Children's Record Guild [Record label] ... CRG
Children's Rehabilitation Centre, St. John's, Newfoundland [Library symbol] [National Library of Canada] (NLC) ... NFSCR
Children's Rehabilitation Centre, St. John's, NF, Canada [Library symbol] [Library of Congress] (LCLS) ... CaNfSCR
Children's Reinforcement Survey Schedule ... CRSS
Children's Relief International [British] (BI) ... CRI
Children's Research Unit [Market research company] [British] ... CRU
Children's Rights Council (EA) ... CRC
Children's Rights Group [Defunct] (EA) ... CRG
Children's Rights, Inc. [CFC] [Superseded by] (EA) ... CRI
Children's Rights of America (EA) ... CRA
Children's Rights Report [A publication] (DLA) ... Chil Rts Rep
Children's Role Inventory [Test] (TMMY) ... CRI
Children's Safety Network (ADWA) ... CSN
Children's Self-Conceptions Test ... CSC
Childrens Self-Conceptions Test (SAUS) ... CSC Test
Children's Service Council [Australian Capital Territory] ... CSC
Children's Services Division [American Library Association] [Later, ALSC] (EA) ... CSD
Children's Services Planning Committee [Australia] ... CSPC
Children's Services Support Unit of Western Australia ... CSSUWA
Children's Special Health Care Needs Program [Social Security Administration (SSA)] (PAZ) ... CSHCN
Children's Special Service Mission [British] ... CSSM
Children's Strategies Assessment System (EDAC) ... CSAS
Children's Stressful Life Events Scale ... CSLES
Children's Supplementary Educational Publishing [Division of Torstar Corp.] ... CSEP
Children's Television Workshop (EA) ... CTW
Children's Theatre Association of America [Formerly, CTC] (EA) ... CTA
Children's Theatre Association of America [Formerly, CTC] (EA) ... CTAA
Children's Theatre Conference (EA) ... CTC
Children's Transplant Association (EA) ... CTA
Children's Treatment Center, Madison, WI [Library symbol] [Library of Congress] (LCLS) ... WMaCT
Children's Vaccine Initiative [Coalition of international donors] ... CVI

Children's Version/Family Environment Scale [*Child development test*] [*Psychology*] .... CV/FES
Children's Village, USA [*of International Orphans Inc.*] [*Later, CVC*] (EA) .... CVUSA
Children's Ward [*of a hospital*] .... CW
Children's Wear Association (EA) .... CWA
Children's Wish Foundation International (EA) .... CWFI
Children's Wonderland [*NASDAQ symbol*] (TTSB) .... CWIC
Childrens Wonderland, Inc. [*Associated Press*] (SAG) .... ChldWn
Childrens Wonderland, Inc. [*Associated Press*] (SAG) .... ChldWon
Childrens Wonderland, Inc. [*NASDAQ symbol*] (SAG) .... CWIC
Children's Wonderland Wrrt [*NASDAQ symbol*] (TTSB) .... CWICW
Childrenswear Manufacturers Association (EA) .... CMA
Child-Resistant Closure [*Medicine containers, etc.*] .... CRC
Child-Resistant Packaging (EPAT) .... CRP
Childress [*Texas*] [*Seismograph station code, US Geological Survey*] (SEIS) .... CEC
Childress [*Texas*] [*Seismograph station code, US Geological Survey*] (SEIS) .... CNE
Childress [*Texas*] [*Seismograph station code, US Geological Survey*] (SEIS) .... CNO
Childress [*Texas*] [*Seismograph station code, US Geological Survey*] (SEIS) .... CNW
Childress [*Texas*] [*Seismograph station code, US Geological Survey*] (SEIS) .... CSE
Childress [*Texas*] [*Seismograph station code, US Geological Survey*] (SEIS) .... CSW
Childress [*Texas*] [*Seismograph station code, US Geological Survey*] (SEIS) .... CWT
Childress [*Texas*] [*ICAO location identifier*] (ICLI) .... KCDS
Childress, TX [*Location identifier*] [*FAA*] (FAAL) .... CDS
Childress, TX [*AM radio station call letters*] .... KCTX
Childress, TX [*FM radio station call letters*] .... KSRW
Childrobics, Inc. [*Associated Press*] (SAG) .... Childr
Childrobics, Inc. [*Associated Press*] (SAG) .... Childrbc
Childrobics, Inc. [*NASDAQ symbol*] (SAG) .... CHLD
Childrobics Inc. Wrrt [*NASDAQ symbol*] (TTSB) .... CHLDW
Childs Apperception Test (SAUS) .... CAT
Child's Fare [*Airline fare code*] .... CH
Child's Meal [*Travel industry*] (TRID) .... CSML
Childs Nervous System (SAUS) .... Childs Nerv Syst
Child's Report of the Impact of Separation by Parents (EDAC) .... CRISP
[*A*] **Child's Wish Come True** (EA) .... CWCT
Childsave Project [*Defunct*] (EA) .... CP
Childtime Learning Centers [*NASDAQ symbol*] (TTSB) .... CTIM
Childtime Learning Centers, Inc. [*Associated Press*] (SAG) .... Chldtime
Childtime Learning Centers, Inc. [*NASDAQ symbol*] (SAG) .... CTIM
Chile .... CHIL
Chile [*ANSI three-letter standard code*] (CNC) .... CHL
Chile (MILB) .... Chl
Chile [*MARC country of publication code*] [*Library of Congress*] (LCCP) cl
Chile [*ANSI two-letter standard code*] (CNC) CL
Chile [*International vehicle registration*] (ODBW) .... RCH
Chile [*MARC geographic area code*] [*Library of Congress*] (LCCP) .... s-cl-
Chile [*IYRU nationality code*] (IYR) X
Chile Alert [*Defunct*] (EA) .... CA
Chile Chico [*Chile*] [*Airport symbol*] (AD) .... CCH
Chile Chico/Chile Chico [*Chile*] [*ICAO location identifier*] (ICLI) .... SCCC
Chile Committee for Human Rights [*Institute for Policy Studies*] (EA) .... CCHR
Chile Democratico (EA) .... ChD
Chile Fund, Inc. [*NYSE symbol*] (SPSG) .... CH
Chile Fund, Inc. [*Associated Press*] (SAG) .... Chile
Chile Legislative Center [*An association*] (EA) CLC
Chile Resource Center and Clearinghouse (EA) .... CRCCH
Chile Solidarity Campaign (EAIO) .... CSC
Chile-American Association (EA) .... CAA
Chilean Communist Party [*Political party*] .... CCP
Chilean Current (SAUS) .... Chil Cur
Chilean Directorate of National Intelligence (SAUS) .... DINA
Chilean Institute for Cooperative Education (SAUO) .... ICECOOP
Chilean Iodine Educational Bureau [*Defunct*] (EA) .... CIEB
Chilean National Committee for Pacific Economic Cooperation .... CHILPEC
Chilean National Committee of the International Association on Water Pollution Research and Control (EAIO) .... CNCIAWPRC
Chilean National Union for the Enviornment (SAUS) .... PNUMA
Chilean Nuclear Energy Commission (SAUO) .... CChEN
Chilean Odeon [*Record label*] .... ChOd
Chilean Space Studies Committee (SAUO) .... CEE
Chilean Victor [*Record label*] .... ChV
Chilecito [*Argentina*] [*Seismograph station code, US Geological Survey*] [*Closed*] (SEIS) .... CCT
Chilecito [*Argentina*] [*ICAO location identifier*] (ICLI) .... SANO
Chileka [*Malawi*] [*Seismograph station code, US Geological Survey*] (SEIS) .... CLK
Chiles [*Ecuador*] [*ICAO location identifier*] (ICLI) .... SECL
Chiles Offshore, Inc. [*AMEX symbol*] .... COD
Chilford [*England*] .... CHILF
Chilgener SA [*NYSE symbol*] (SAG) .... CHR
Chilgener S.A. ADS [*NYSE symbol*] (TTSB) .... CHR
Chilhood-Onset Insomnia [*Medicine*] (MELL) .... COI
Chili Appreciation Society International (EA) .... CASI
Chilianus Koenig [*Deceased, 1526*] [*Authority cited in pre-1607 legal work*] (DSA) .... Chilian
Chilianus Koenig [*Deceased, 1526*] [*Authority cited in pre-1607 legal work*] (DSA) .... Chil Kon
Chilik [*Former USSR*] [*Seismograph station code, US Geological Survey*] [*Closed*] (SEIS) .... CHL
Chill Adventures into the Unknown (SAUS) .... CHI
Chillagoe [*Australia*] [*Airport symbol*] [*Obsolete*] (OAG) .... LLG
Chillan/Gral, Bernardo O'Higgins [*Chile*] [*ICAO location identifier*] (ICLI) .... SCCH
Chilldown [*NASA*] (KSC) .... CD
Chilldown Flow Meter .... CFM
Chill-down Flow Meter (SAUS) .... CFM
Chilled (MSA) .... CHLD
Chilled Drinking Water [*Aerospace*] (AAG) .... CDW
Chilled Drinking Water Return [*Aerospace*] .... CDWR
Chilled Foods Association (EA) .... CFA
Chilled Sea Water [*Pisciculture*] .... CSW
Chilled Water [*Aerospace*] (AAG) .... CHW
Chilled Water [*Aerospace*] (DNAB) .... CW
Chilled Water Supply [*Aerospace*] (AAG) .... CWS
Chilled-Mirror Dew Point hygrometer (SAUS) .... CMDEWP
Chillicothe and Ross County Public Library, Chillicothe, OH [*Library symbol*] [*Library of Congress*] (LCLS) .... OCh
Chillicothe, IL [*FM radio station call letters*] (BROA) .... WFXF-FM
Chillicothe, IL [*FM radio station call letters*] (RBYB) .... WKZW
Chillicothe, MO [*Location identifier*] [*FAA*] (FAAL) .... CHT
Chillicothe, MO [*AM radio station call letters*] .... KCHI
Chillicothe, MO [*FM radio station call letters*] .... KCHI-FM
Chillicothe, MO [*FM radio station call letters*] .... KRNW
Chillicothe, OH [*Location identifier*] [*FAA*] (FAAL) .... RZT
Chillicothe, OH [*AM radio station call letters*] .... WBEX
Chillicothe, OH [*AM radio station call letters*] .... WCHI
Chillicothe, OH [*FM radio station call letters*] .... WFCB
Chillicothe, OH [*FM radio station call letters*] .... WKKJ
Chillicothe, OH [*FM radio station call letters*] .... WOHC
Chillicothe, OH [*FM radio station call letters*] .... WOUH
Chillicothe, OH [*FM radio station call letters*] .... WVXC
Chillicothe, OH [*Television station call letters*] .... WWHO
Chillicothe Township Free Public Library, Chillicothe, IL [*Library symbol*] [*Library of Congress*] (LCLS) .... IChil
Chillicothe Township Free Public Library, Chillicothe, IL [*OCLC symbol*] (OCLC) .... ISI
Chilliwack Aviation Ltd. [*Canada*] [*ICAO designator*] (FAAC) .... CAD
Chilliwack, BC [*Television station call letters*] (RBYB) CHAN-1
Chilliwack, BC [*AM radio station call letters*] .... CHWK
Chilliwack, BC [*FM radio station call letters*] .... CKSR
Chilliwack, BC [*ICAO location identifier*] (ICLI) .... CYCW
Chilliwack Museum, British Columbia [*Library symbol*] [*National Library of Canada*] (NLC) .... BCHM
Chilliwack Public Library, British Columbia [*Library symbol*] [*National Library of Canada*] (NLC) .... BCH
Chilliwack Public Library, Chilliwack, BC, Canada [*Library symbol*] [*Library of Congress*] (LCLS) .... CaBCh
Chills and Fever (MELL) .... C & F
Chills, Fever, Night Sweats (SAUS) .... CFNS
Chilpancingo [*Mexico*] [*ICAO location identifier*] (ICLI) .... MMCH
[*The*] **Chilswell Book of English Poetry** [*A publication*] .... CBE
Chiltern Airways [*British*] [*ICAO designator*] (FAAC) .... CHA
Chilton, WI [*AM radio station call letters*] .... WMBE
Chilworth Research Centre (SAUO) .... CRC
Chilworth Technology Ltd. [*British*] (IRUK) .... CTL
Chimachoy [*Guatemala*] [*Seismograph station code, US Geological Survey*] (SEIS) .... CIM
Chimaeric Virus Particles [*Biochemistry*] .... CVP
Chimbote [*Peru*] [*Airport symbol*] [*Obsolete*] (OAG) .... CHM
Chimbote [*Peru*] [*ICAO location identifier*] (ICLI) .... SPEO
Chimera Resources Ltd. [*Vancouver Stock Exchange symbol*] .... CMZ
Chimeric Receptor .... CR
Chimes .... chm
Chimkent [*Former USSR*] [*Seismograph station code, US Geological Survey*] [*Closed*] (SEIS) .... CHM
Chimkent [*Former USSR*] [*ICAO location identifier*] (ICLI) .... UAII
Chimney [*Technical drawings*] (DAC) .... Chim
Chimney .... CHMNY
Chimney .... CHY
Chimney Safety Institute of America (EA) .... CSIA
Chimney Sweep Guild [*Later, NCSG*] (EA) .... CSG
Chimney Sweeps Cancer [*Medicine*] (MELL) .... CSC
Chimney Tray (EEVL) .... CT
Chimoio [*Mozambique*] [*ICAO location identifier*] (ICLI) .... FQCH
Chimpanzee Astronaut (SAUS) .... Chimponaut
Chimpanzee Coryza Agent [*A virus*] .... CCA
Chimpanzee Infectious Dose for Half the Population .... CID_{50}
Chimpanzee Leucocyte Antigen (SAUS) .... ChlA
Chin National Army [*Myanmar*] [*Political party*] (EY) .... CNA
Chin National Front [*Myanmar*] [*Political party*] (EY) .... CNF
Chin National Organization [*Burma*] .... CNO
China [*IYRU nationality code*] (ROG) .... CH
China .... CHI
China (SAUS) .... Chi
China .... CHIN
China [*ANSI three-letter standard code*] (CNC) .... CHN
China [*ANSI two-letter standard code*] (CNC) .... CN
China Academy of Telecommunication Technology (SAUO) .... CATT
China Accreditation Committee for Environmental management system certification Bodies (SAUS) .... CACEB
China Aeronautics Airline Corporation (SAUO) .... CAAC
China Aero-Space Corp. (ECON) .... CASC
China Air Cargo [*ICAO designator*] (FAAC) .... CHY
China Air Transport Command (SAUO) .... CATC
China Airlines [*Taiwan*] [*ICAO designator*] (FAAC) .... CAL
China Airlines [*Airline flight code*] (ODBW) CI
China Airlines Ltd. (SAUO) .... CAL
China American Petrochemical Co. Ltd. [*Taiwan*] .... CAPCO

China and Glass Retailers Association [*British*] (DBA) ... CGRA
China and Japan (SAUS) ... C&J
China Association (SAUO) ... CA
China Association for Science and Technology ... CAST
China Association of Plant Engineering (EAIO) ... CAPE
China Association of Standardization [*INFOTERM*] ... CAS
China Book Information Letter [*A publication*] ... CBIL
China Broadcasting Satellite (SAUS) ... CBS
China Building Technology Development Centre [*Beijing*] [*Information service or system*] (IID) ... CBTDC
China, Burma, India (ADWA) ... CBI
China Burma India Theatre of Operations (SAUO) ... CBI
China Business Resources Co. Ltd. (ECON) ... CBR
China Business Review [*A publication*] ... CBR
China Campaign Committee (SAUO) ... CCC
China Center for Advanced Science and Technology ... CCAST
China Central Television [*The national Chinese network*] ... CCTV
China Christian Council ... CCC
China Classification Society (SAUO) ... CCS
China Clay Producers Association (NTPA) ... CCPA
China Clay Producers Trade Association (EA) ... CCP
China Coast Time (VERA) ... CCT
China Commission for GCOS (SAUO) ... CCGCOS
China Committee (SAUO) ... ChinCom
China Construction Machinery Corporation (SAUO) ... CCMC
China Container Holdings ... CCHL
China Council [*An association*] (EA) ... CC
China Council for the Promotion of International Trade (PDAA) ... CCPIT
China Council for the Quality System of the Export Manufacturers (SAUO) ... CCQSEM
China Defence Supplies Incorporated (SAUO) ... CDSI
China Defense Supplies, Inc. ... CDS
China Democratic League (SAUO) ... CDL
China Democratic Socialist Party [*Political party*] (EY) ... CDSP
China Development Corporation (SAUO) ... CDC
China Eastern Airlines [*ICAO designator*] (FAAC) ... CES
China Eastern Airlines [*ICAO designator*] (AD) ... MU
China Eastern Airlines ADS [*NYSE symbol*] (SG) ... CEA
China Economic & Technology Alliance [*Sponsored by international chemical firms*] ... CETA
China Education and Research Network [*Computer science*] ... CERnet
China Energy Resources [*AMEX symbol*] (SG) ... CHG
China Environmental Research Network ... CERN
China Europe International Business School ... CEIBS
China Expeditionary Force (SAUO) ... CEF
China External Trade Development Council [*Taiwan*] ... CETDC
China External Trade Development Council ... CETRA
China First Capital [*Vancouver Stock Exchange symbol*] ... CWF
China Flying Dragon Aviation Co. [*FAA designator*] (FAAC) ... CFA
[*The*] **China Fund** [*Associated Press*] (SAG) ... ChinaFd
China Fund [*NYSE symbol*] (SPSG) ... CHN
China General Aviation Corp. [*ICAO designator*] (FAAC) ... CGAC
China General Aviation Corp. [*ICAO designator*] (FAAC) ... CTH
China, Glass, and Giftware Association (EA) ... CGGA
China, Glass, and Pottery Association of America [*Later, CGGA*] (EA) ... CGPAA
China, Glass, Giftware Board of Trade [*Later, CGGA*] (EA) ... CGGBT
China Grove, NC [*AM radio station call letters*] ... WRNA
China, India, Burma ... CIB
China Industrial Group [*Associated Press*] (SAG) ... ChinaIndl
China Industrial Group [*Associated Press*] (SAG) ... ChinI
China Industrial Group [*NASDAQ symbol*] (SAG) ... CIND
China Industrial Grp Wrrt'A' [*NASDAQ symbol*] (TTSB) ... CINDW
China Industrial Grp Wrrt'B' [*NASDAQ symbol*] (TTSB) ... CINDZ
China Inland Mission ... CIM
China Inland Mission (SAUO) ... CIM
China Inland Mission Overseas Missionary Fellowship [*Later, Overseas MissionaryFellowship*] (EA) ... CIM-OMF
China Institute in America (EA) ... CI
China Institute in America (EA) ... CIA
China Institute of New Jersey, Montclair State College, Upper Montclair, NJ [*Library symbol*] [*Library of Congress*] (LCLS) ... NjUpM-C
China International Center for Technical and Economic Exchange ... CICTEE
China International Cultural Exchange Organization ... CICEO
China International Foundation [*Later, TIF*] (EA) ... CIF
China International Travel Service ... CITS
China International Trust and Investment Corporation (SAUO) ... CITIC
China International Trust Investment Corp. ... CITIC
China Investment & Trust Company, Ltd. (SAUO) ... CITC
China Investment Bank ... CIB
China Lake [*California*] [*Seismograph station code, US Geological Survey*] (SEIS) ... CLC
China Lake, CA [*FM radio station call letters*] ... KSSI
China Law and Business Update [*A publication*] ... CLBU
China Law Review [*A publication*] (DLA) ... China Law Rev
China Law Review [*A publication*] (DLA) ... China L Rev
China Liberated Areas Relief Association (SAUO) ... CLARA
China Light and Power Company Ltd (SAUO) ... CLP
China, Mainland [*MARC geographic area code*] [*Library of Congress*] (LCCP) ... a-cc-
China Man-Made Fiber Corp. [*Taiwan*] ... CMFC
China Man-Made Fiber Corporation (SAUO) ... CMFC
China Market Intelligence [*National Council for US-China Trade*] [*A publication*] ... CMI
China Medical Board (SAUO) ... CMB
China Medical Board of New York (EA) ... CMBNY
China Medical Informatics Association (VERA) ... CMIA
China Merchant Holdings (ECON) ... CMH
China Merchant Steamship Navigation Company (SAUO) ... CMSNC
China Metallurgical Import and Export Corporation (SAUO) ... CMIEC
China Meteorological Administration ... CMA
China Meteorological Agency (SAUO) ... CMA
China National Accreditation Committee for Laboratories (SAUS) ... CNACL
China National Accreditation Council for Product Certification Bodies (SAUO) ... CNACP
China National Accreditation Council for Registrars (SAUO) ... CNACR
China National Aero-Technology Import & Export Corp. (SAUS) ... CATIC
China National Aero-Technology Import and Export Corporation (SAUO) ... CATIC
China National Aviation Corporation (SAUO) ... CNAC
China National Aviation Corps ... CNAC
China National Cereals Oils & Foodstuffs Import & Export Corp. ... COFCO
China National Chartering Corporation (SAUS) ... SINO-CHART
China National Chemicals Import and Export Corporation (SAUO) ... CNCIEC
China National Committee for Pacific Economic Cooperation ... CNCPEC
China National Complete Plant Export Corp. (SAUO) ... CNCPEC
China National Electronics Import & Export Corp. (SAUO) ... CEIEC
China National Import and Export Corporation (SAUO) ... CNIEC
China National Machinery and Equipment Import and Export Corporation (SAUO) ... CMEC
China National Oceanographic Data Center [*Marine science*] (OSRA) ... CNODC
China National Petroleum Corp. ... CNPC
China National Publications Import Corporation (SAUO) ... CNPIC
China National Rice Research Institute (SAUO) ... CNRRI
China National Software Corporation (SAUO) ... CNSC
China National Technical Import Corporation (SAUO) ... CNTIC
China Netcom Corporation (SAUO) ... CNC
China News Service ... CNS
China Northern Airlines [*FAA designator*] (FAAC) ... CBF
China Northwest Airlines [*ICAO designator*] (FAAC) ... CNW
China Northwest Airlines [*ICAO designator*] (AD) ... WH
China Nuclear Energy Industry Corporation (SAUO) ... CNEIC
China Ocean Helicopter Corp. [*ICAO designator*] (FAAC) ... CHC
China Ocean Helicopter Corp. [*ICAO designator*] (FAAC) ... COHC
China Ocean Mineral Resources Research and Development Association (SAUS) ... COMRA
China Ocean Shipping Co. ... COSCO
China Pacific [*NASDAQ symbol*] (TTSB) ... CHNA
China Petrol & Chem ADS [*NASDAQ symbol*] ... SNP
China Petroleum Company (SAUO) ... CPC
China Philatelic Study Group [*Defunct*] (EA) ... CPSG
China Policy Study Group [*British*] ... CPSG
China Pottery and Glassware Association (EA) ... CPGA
China Precision Machinery Import & Export Corp. (SAUO) ... CPMIEC
China Productivity and Trade Center (SAUO) ... CPTC
China Productivity Center (SAUO) ... CPC
China Relief Mission (SAUO) ... CRM
China, Republic of [*Taiwan*] [*MARC geographic area code*] [*Library of Congress*] (LCCP) ... a-ch-
China, Republic of [*Taiwan*] [*MARC country of publication code*] [*Library of Congress*] (LCCP) ... ch
China Research Associates ... CRA
China Resource Dvlmt [*NASDAQ symbol*] (TTSB) ... CHRB
China Resources Development, Inc. [*Associated Press*] (SAG) ... ChinRs
China Resources Development, Inc. [*NASDAQ symbol*] (SAG) ... CHRB
China Review International [*A publication*] (BRI) ... Ch Rev Int
China Review (journ.) (SAUS) ... China R
China Sea Resources Corp. [*Vancouver Stock Exchange symbol*] ... CHQ
China Securities Regulatory Commission (ECON) ... CSRC
China Service Medal [*Military decoration*] ... CHSM
China Shipbuilding Corp. ... CSBC
China Society for International Professionals Exchange and Development (EAIO) ... CSRIPPED
China Society of America (EA) ... CSA
China Solidarity Committee [*An association*] [*Defunct*] (EA) ... CSC
China Southern Airlines [*FAA designator*] (FAAC) ... CSN
China Southern Airlines'H' ADS [*NYSE symbol*] (SG) ... ZNH
China Southwest Airlines [*ICAO designator*] (FAAC) ... CXN
China Southwest Airlines [*ICAO designator*] (AD) ... SZ
China Spring (EA) ... CS
China Stamp Society (EA) ... CSS
China Surface-to-Surface Experimental Number 4 [*Rocket*] ... CSS-X-4
China Technical Consultants, Inc. ... CTCI
China Telecom Hong Kong ADS [*NYSE symbol*] (SG) ... CHL
China Television Co. (EY) ... CTV
China Theater [*World War II*] ... CT
China Theater of Operations [*World War II*] ... CTO
China Tire Holdings Ltd. [*Associated Press*] (SAG) ... ChinTire
China Tire Holdings Ltd. [*NYSE symbol*] (SPSG) ... TIR
China Today [*A publication*] ... China T
China Tourist Hotel Association (EAIO) ... CTHA
China Travel Service (ECON) ... CTS
China Travel Service (SAUO) ... CTS
China Treasure, Inc. [*Associated Press*] (SAG) ... ChinaTr
China Treasure, Inc. [*NASDAQ symbol*] (SAG) ... CHNA
China Unicom ADS [*NYSE symbol*] ... CHU
China United Airlines [*ICAO designator*] (FAAC) ... CUA
China Weekly Review (journ.) (SAUS) ... China W R
China Xinhua Airlines [*FAA designator*] (FAAC) ... CXH
China Yuchai International Ltd. [*Associated Press*] (SAG) ... ChiYuc
China Yuchai International Ltd. [*NYSE symbol*] (SAG) ... CYD

China Yuchai Intl. [*NYSE symbol*] (TTSB) ... CYD
China/Brazil Earth Resources Satellite (SAUS) ... CBERS
China-Burma-India Hump Pilots Association (EA) ... CBIHPA
China-Burma-India Theater [*World War II*] ... CBI
China-Burma-India Theater [*World War II*] ... CBIT
China-Burma-India Veterans Association (EA) ... CBIVA
Chinachona Products Institute (SAUO) ... CPI
China.com Corp. [*NASDAQ symbol*] (SG) ... CHINA
China-Europe Management Institute ... CEMI
Chinandega/German Pomares [*Nicaragua*] [*ICAO location identifier*] (ICLI) ... MNCH
China's Travel Information Database [*Information service or system*] (IID) ... CTIDB
China-United States Physics Examination and Application Program ... CUSPEA
Chinch Bug [*Entomology*] ... CB
Chincha [*Peru*] [*ICAO location identifier*] (ICLI) ... SPHA
Chinchilla [*Australia*] [*Airport symbol*] ... CCL
Chinchilla (SAUS) ... CHIN
Chinchilla Fur Breeders' Association [*British*] (BI) ... CFBA
Chinchilla Pelt Marketing Association Ltd. [*British*] (BI) ... CPMA
Chinchina [*Colombia*] [*Seismograph station code, US Geological Survey*] (SEIS) ... CHN
Chincoteague Island, VA [*Location identifier*] [*FAA*] (FAAL) ... VWU
Chincoteague National Wildlife Refuge (SAUS) ... CNWR
Chincoteague, VA [*Location identifier*] [*FAA*] (FAAL) ... WAL
Chinese ... Ch
Chinese [*MARC language code*] [*Library of Congress*] (LCCP) ... chi
Chinese [*Language, etc.*] (ROG) ... CHIN
Chinese (WDAA) ... Chin
Chinese Academy of Agricultural and Forestry Sciences (SAUO) ... CAAFS
Chinese Academy of Geological Science ... CAGS
Chinese Academy of Meteorological Science (SAUS) ... CAMS
Chinese Academy of Science and Technology (SAUO) ... CAST
Chinese Academy of Sciences ... CAS
Chinese Academy of Space Technology ... CAST
Chinese Access Method (SAUS) ... CAM
Chinese Advanced Very High Resolution Radiometer (SAUS) ... CAVHRR
Chinese Agricultural Technical Group (SAUO) ... CATG
Chinese Agricultural Technical Mission to Vietnam (SAUO) ... CATM
Chinese Air Force [*Nationalist*] ... CAF
Chinese Air Task Force ... CATF
Chinese Alliance for Democracy (EA) ... CS
Chinese American Arts Council (EA) ... CAAC
Chinese American Association of Commerce (EA) ... CAAC
Chinese American Citizens Alliance (EA) ... CACA
Chinese American Civic Council (EA) ... CACC
Chinese American Food Society (EA) ... CAFS
Chinese American Forum (EA) ... CAF
Chinese American Medical Society (EA) ... CAMS
Chinese American Restaurant Association (EA) ... CARA
Chinese Army (CINC) ... CA
Chinese Army (SAUO) ... Ch A
Chinese Army in India ... CAI
Chinese Art Society of America [*Later, AS*] (EA) ... CASA
Chinese Association for the Advancement of Science ... CAAS
Chinese Association of Science and Technology (SAUO) ... CAST
Chinese Association of Victoria [*Australia*] ... CAV
Chinese Astronomical Society (SAUO) ... CAS
Chinese Atmospheric Nuclear Test (MCD) ... CANT
Chinese Banknote Collectors Society [*Defunct*] (EA) ... CBCS
Chinese Binary Code (SAUS) ... CBC
Chinese Biopharmaceutical Association ... CBA
Chinese Brazilian Earth Resources Satellite (SAUS) ... CBERS
Chinese Broadcasting Satellite Corporation (SAUO) ... CBSC
Chinese Canadian Information Processing Professionals (EAIO) ... CCIPP
Chinese Canadian National Council [*Conseil National des Canadiens Chinois*] [*Also, Chinese Canadian National Council for Equality*] (AC) ... CCNC
Chinese Canadian National Council for Equality ... CCNCE
Chinese Central News Agency (SAUO) ... CN
Chinese Chamber of Commerce of Hawaii (SRA) ... CCCH
Chinese Chamber of Commerce of New York (SAUO) ... CCCNY
Chinese Chamber of Commerce of San Francisco (SAUO) ... CCCSF
Chinese Character Code for Information Exchange (SAUS) ... CCCIE
Chinese Christian Mission (EA) ... CCM
Chinese Classification Society (SAUO) ... CCS
Chinese Communist ... ChiCom
Chinese Communist ... CHICOM
Chinese Communist Air Force ... CCAF
Chinese Communist Army (CINC) ... CCA
Chinese Communist Forces ... CCF
Chinese Communist Navy (CINC) ... CCN
Chinese Communist Party [*Political party*] (PD) ... CCP
Chinese Communist Party (SAUO) ... CPC
Chinese Communist Party [*Political party*] ... KKP
Chinese Consolidated Benevolent Association (EA) ... CCBA
Chinese Coordination Centre of World Evangelism (EA) ... CCCOWE
Chinese Coordination Centre of World Evangelism (North America) (EA) ... CCCOWE-NA
Chinese Cultural and Trade Center (SAUS) ... CCTC
Chinese Culture Association (EA) ... CCA
Chinese Culture Foundation of San Francisco (EA) ... CCFSF
Chinese Development Council (EA) ... CDC
Chinese Dictionary (SAUS) ... ChiDic
Chinese Digital Seismograph Network ... CDSN
Chinese Eastern Railway (SAUO) ... CER
Chinese Ecological Research Network (QUAC) ... CERN
Chinese Economic Area or Council of Economic Advisors (SAUO) ... CEA
Chinese Educational Resources Information System [*Database*] [*National Taiwan Normal University Library*] [*Information service or system*] (CRD) ... CERIS
Chinese Exclusion Act ... CEA
Chinese Expeditionary Force ... CEF
Chinese Export Commodities Fair ... CECF
Chinese Federation of Industrial Associations (SAUO) ... CFIA
Chinese Federation of Labor [*Nationalist China*] ... CFL
Chinese for Affirmative Action (EA) ... CAA
Chinese Foreign Missionary Union (EA) ... CFMU
Chinese Forestry Association (SAUO) ... CFA
Chinese Freedom Party [*Political party*] (EY) ... CFP
Chinese Geodetical Star Catalogue (SAUO) ... CGSC
Chinese Geophysical Socitey (SAUO) ... CGS
Chinese Government Information Office (SAUO) ... CGIO
Chinese Government Radio Administration (SAUO) ... CGRA
Chinese Hamster [*Medicine*] (DMAA) ... CHN
Chinese Hamster Embryo Fibroblast [*Cytology*] ... CHEF
Chinese Hamster Lung [*Cell line*] ... CHL
Chinese Hamster Ovarian [*or Ovary*] [*Cytology*] ... CHO
Chinese Hamster Ovarian Tumor (SAUS) ... CHO Tumor
Chinese Hamster Ovary ... CHO
Chinese Historical Society of America (SAUO) ... ChHS
Chinese Historical Society of America (EA) ... CHSA
Chinese Industrial Cooperatives (SAUO) ... CIC
Chinese Industrial Standards ... CIS
Chinese Information Processing System (SAUS) ... CHIPS
Chinese Institute of Electronics (CARB) ... CIE
Chinese Institute of Engineers - USA (EA) ... CIE-USA
Chinese Institute of Mining and Metallurgical Engineers (SAUO) ... CIMME
Chinese, Japanese, and Korean [*Library of Congress computer system*] ... CJK
Chinese Journal of Physics (journ.) (SAUS) ... Chin J Phys
Chinese Labour Corps (SAUO) ... CLC
Chinese Lake Status Data Base (SAUS) ... CLSDB
Chinese Language Computer Society (EA) ... CLCS
Chinese Language Encoder ... CHICODER
Chinese Language Teachers Association (EA) ... CLTA
Chinese Laundry Association (EA) ... CLA
Chinese Librarians Association (EA) ... CLA
Chinese Linguistics Bibliography on Computer [*Cambridge University Press*] [*England*] ... CLIBOC
Chinese Literature (journ.) (SAUS) ... ChinL
Chinese Literature Monthly (journ.) (SAUS) ... CLM
Chinese Liver Fluke [*Medicine*] (MELL) ... CLF
Chinese Loess Plateau (SAUS) ... CLP
Chinese Masonic Society [*Australia*] ... CMS
Chinese Materials and Research Aids Service Center, Inc., Taipei, Taiwan, China [*Library symbol*] [*Library of Congress*] (LCLS) ... CiTCM
Chinese Medicine & Acupunture Association Canada [*L'Association de Medecine Chinoise et d'Acupuncture du Canada*] (AC) ... CMAAC
Chinese Merchants Association (EA) ... CMA
Chinese Music Society of North America (EA) ... CMSNA
Chinese Musical and Theatrical Association (EA) ... CMTA
Chinese National Accreditation Board (SAUS) ... CNAB
Chinese National Bureau of Standards (SAUO) ... CNS
Chinese National Committee on Oceanic Research (SAUO) ... CNCOR
Chinese National Import and Export Corporation (SAUO) ... CHIEC
Chinese National Laboratory Accreditation (SAUS) ... CNLA
Chinese National Relief and Rehabilitation Administration (SAUO) ... CNRRA
Chinese National Standard (SAUS) ... CNS
Chinese Nationalist ... CHINAT
Chinese Nationalist Air Force ... CNAF
Chinese Navy (CINC) ... CN
Chinese Operational Earth Resources Satellite (SAUO) ... COFRS
Chinese Overseas Mission (SAUO) ... COM
Chinese People's Political Consultative Conference ... CPPCC
Chinese People's Republic ... CPR
Chinese Petroleum Corp. (SAUO) ... CPC
Chinese Pharmacopoeia [*A publication*] ... Chin P
Chinese Procurement Mission (ACAE) ... CPM
Chinese Proficiency Test (TMMY) ... CPT
Chinese Public Packet switching data network (SAUO) ... CHINAPAC
Chinese Refugee Relief [*Defunct*] (EA) ... CRR
Chinese Remainder Theorem (RALS) ... CRT
Chinese Republican Party [*Political party*] (EY) ... CRP
Chinese Restaurant Asthma [*Medicine*] ... CRA
Chinese Restaurant Syndrome [*Monosodium glutamate sensitivity*] [*Medicine*] ... CRS
Chinese School of Table Tennis [*France*] (EAIO) ... CSTT
Chinese Scientific and Technological Periodical Abstracts [*Information service or system*] (IID) ... STADB
Chinese Shar-Pei Club of America (EA) ... CSPCA
Chinese Society for European Community Studies (SAUO) ... CESECS
Chinese Society for European Community Studies (SAUO) ... CSECS
Chinese Society of Astronautics (CARB) ... CSA
Chinese Society of Chemical Engineering (SAUO) ... CSCE
Chinese Society of Geophysics (SAUO) ... CGS
Chinese Solar-Geophysical Data (SAUO) ... CSGD
Chinese Speaking Test [*Center for Applied Linguistics*] (TES) ... CST
Chinese Speaking Test, 1995 Edition (TMMY) ... CST
Chinese Surface-to-Surface missile (SAUS) ... CSS
Chinese Taipei [*IYRU nationality code*] (IYR) ... TA
Chinese Taipei Pacific Economic Cooperation Committee ... CTPECC

Chinese Television System (EY) .... CTS
Chinese University Language Translation [Human-aided machine translation]
    [Hong Kong] (NITA) .... CULT
Chinese University of Hong Kong (SAUO) .... CUHK
Chinese Urban Professional [Hong Kong Yuppie] [Lifestyle
    classification] .... Chuppie
Chinese Women's Association (EA) .... CWA
Chinese Women's Benevolent Association (EA) .... CWBA
Chinese World, San Francisco, CA [Library symbol] [Library of Congress]
    (LCLS) .... CSfCWL
Chinese Youth Council [Later, CDC] (EA) .... CYC
Chinese-American Composite Wing [Air Force] .... CACW
Chinese-American Educational Foundation (EA) .... CAEF
Chinese-American Librarians Association (EA) .... CALA
Chinese-English Translation Assistance Group (EA) .... CETA
Chinese-Oriented Antiballistic Missile System (AABC) ..... C-ABM
Ching Chuan Kang Air Base [Vietnam] .... CCK
Chinguacousy Township Public Library, Bramalea, ON, Canada [Library
    symbol] [Library of Congress] (LCLS) .... CaOBram
Chinguacousy Township Public Library, Bramalea, Ontario [Library symbol]
    [National Library of Canada] (NLC) .... OBRAM
Chinhae [South Korea] [ICAO location identifier] (ICLI) ...... RKPE
Chinin-Oxidase (SAUS) .... CO
Chinle, AZ [FM radio station call letters] (RBYB) .... KFXR
Chinle High School Library, Chinle, AZ [Library symbol] [Library of
    Congress] (LCLS) .... AzCH
Chino, CA [Location identifier] [FAA] (FAAL) .... CHJ
Chino, CA [Location identifier] [FAA] (FAAL) .... CNO
Chino Valley, AZ [FM radio station call letters] (BROA) ...... KAKP-FM
Chinoiserie (VRA) .... Chino
Chinook Jargon [MARC language code] [Library of Congress] (LCCP) ..... chn
Chinook, MT [FM radio station call letters] .... KRYK
Chinook Regional Library, Swift Current, Saskatchewan [Library symbol]
    [National Library of Canada] (NLC) .... SCR
Chinook Regional Library, Swift Current, SK, Canada [Library symbol]
    [Library of Congress] (LCLS) .... CaSCR
Chin-Rex (SAUS) .... Ch Rex
Chinsali [Zambia] [ICAO location identifier] (ICLI) .... FLCS
Chintheche [Malawi] [ICAO location identifier] (ICLI) .... FWCC
Chios [Greece] [Airport symbol] (OAG) .... JKH
Chios Societies of America (EA) .... CSA
Chios Societies of America & Canada .... CSA
Chip (SAUS) .... CHI
Chip Carrier [Electronics] (EECA) CC
Chip Design System (SAUS) .... CDS
Chip Detector Sensor (MCD) .... CDS
Chip Enable [Computer science] (NITA) .... CE
Chip Enable [Computer science] (MHDI) .... CHE
Chip Enable Input [Computer science] (MHDI) .... CEI
Chip Enable Output [Computer science] .... CEO
Chip Enable Pulse (SAUS) .... CE Pulse
Chip Fracture (MELL) .... CF
Chip Hermeticity in Plastic [Electronics] (MDG) .... CHIP
Chip Mounting Technology [Electronics] (AAEL) .... CMT
Chip on Module Evaluation Tester (SAUS) .... COMET
Chip on Module Parameter Tester (SAUS) .... COMPT
Chip Operational Multifunction Auxiliary Computer (MCD) ... COMFAX
Chip Performance Index [Computer science] .... CPI
Chip Place (AAEL) .... CP
Chip Placement Machine (SAUS) .... CPM
Chip Scale Package (AAEL) .... CSP
Chip Select .... CSE
Chip Select Input [Computer science] .... CS
Chip Selection [Electronics] (ECII) .... CS
Chip Size Packaging (SAUS) .... CSP
Chipata [Zambia] [Airport symbol] (OAG) .... CIP
Chipata [Zambia] [ICAO location identifier] (ICLI) .... FLCP
Chip-Carrying Card (SAUS) CCC
Chipewyan Lake School, Wabasca, Alberta [Library symbol] [National Library
    of Canada] (BIB) .... AWACS
Chipinge [Zimbabwe] [ICAO location identifier] (ICLI) .... FVCH
Chipley, FL [AM radio station call letters] .... WBGC
Chipman on the Law of Contracts [A publication] (DLA) ...... Chip Cont
Chipman's New Brunswick Manuscript Reports [A publication] (DLA) ..... Chip Ms
Chipman's New Brunswick Reports [1825-35] [A publication] (DLA) ..... Chip
Chipman's New Brunswick Reports [1825-35] [A publication] (DLA) ..... Chip W
Chipman's New Brunswick Reports [1825-35] [A publication] (DLA) ..... NBR Chip
Chipmans New Brunswick Reports (SAUS) .... NBR Chip
Chipman's Principles of Government [A publication] (DLA) ..... Chip Gov
Chip-Matched Filter (SAUS) .... CMF
Chipola Junior College [Marianna, FL] .... CJC
Chipola Junior College, Marianna, FL [Library symbol] [Library of Congress]
    (LCLS) .... FMaC
Chip-On-Board [Computer science] (CIST) .... COB
Chippewa Air Commuter, Inc. [ICAO designator] (FAAC) ...... CPW
Chippewa County Library System, Montevideo, MN [Library symbol] [Library
    of Congress] (LCLS) .... MnMov
Chippewa County-Montevideo Hospital, Montevideo, MN [Library symbol]
    [Library of Congress] (LCLS) .... MnMovCH
Chippewa Falls Public Library, Chippewa Falls, WI [Library symbol] [Library
    of Congress] (LCLS) .... WCf
Chippewa Falls Public Library, Chippewa Falls, WI [Library symbol] [Library
    of Congress] [Obsolete] (LCLS) .... WCh
Chippewa Falls, WI [AM radio station call letters] .... WAYY
Chippewa Falls, WI [FM radio station call letters] .... WCFW

Chippewa Falls, WI [Television station call letters] .... WEUX
Chippewa Library League [Library network] CLL
Chippewa Library League, Mt. Pleasant, MI [Library symbol] [Library of
    Congress] (LCLS) .... MiMtpC
Chippewa Resource Center, Muncey, ON, Canada [Library symbol] [Library
    of Congress] (LCLS) .... CaOMuCR
Chippewa Resource Centre, Muncey, Ontario [Library symbol] [National
    Library of Canada] (NLC) .... OMCR
Chippewa Valley Museum, Eau Claire, WI [Library symbol] [Library of
    Congress] (LCLS) .... WECV
Chippewa-Ottawa Treaty Fishery Management Authority ...... COTFMA
Chipping (SAUS) C
Chipping Sodbury [England] .... CHIPSODB
Chips and Technologies (SAUS) .... C&T
Chips & Technologies (VERA) .... CT
Chips and Technologies, Inc. [Associated Press] (SAG) ...... ChipsTc
Chips & Technologies, Inc. [NASDAQ symbol] (NQ) .... CHPS
Chips per Second (CCCA) .... CPS
Chips/Technologies [NASDAQ symbol] (TTSB) .... CHPS
Chiquita Br Intl $2.875 Cv'A'Pfd [NYSE symbol] (TTSB) ..... CQBPrA
Chiquita Brands International [Associated Press] (SAG) ...... Chiq
Chiquita Brands International [Associated Press] (SAG) ...... Chiquta
Chiquita Brands International [NYSE symbol] (SPSG) .... CQB
Chiquita Brands Intl. [NYSE symbol] (TTSB) .... CQB
Chiral Chromatography CC
Chiral Ligand Exchange Chromatography (DB) .... CLEC
Chiral Solid Phase (SAUS) .... CSP
Chiral Stationary Phase [Chemical separation technique] ..... CSP
Chirat [Pakistan] [ICAO location identifier] (ICLI) .... OPCT
Chiredzi [Rhodesia] [Seismograph station code, US Geological Survey]
    (SEIS) .... CIR
Chiredzi/Buffalo Range [Zimbabwe] [ICAO location identifier] (ICLI) ..... FVCV
ChiRex, Inc. [Associated Press] (SAG) .... ChiRex
ChiRex Inc. [NASDAQ symbol] (TTSB) .... CHRX
Chiricahua National Monument (SAUS) .... CNM
Chiricahua National Monument and Fort Bowie National Historic Site ...... CHIR
ChiroClec Resolves .... CR
Chirography (SAUS) .... CHIRO
Chiron Corp. [NASDAQ symbol] (NQ) .... CHIR
Chiron Corp. [Associated Press] (SAG) .... Chiron
Chiropodists' Registration Board of Victoria [Australia] ...... CRBV
Chiropody (SAUS) .... CHIR
Chiropody Bibliographical Research Society .... CBRS
Chiropody Board of South Australia [Medicine] .... CBSA
Chiropractic (SAUS) .... CHIRO
Chiropractic .... CHIROPRCTC
Chiropractic Advancement Association [British] .... CAA
Chiropractic Association of Louisiana (SRA) .... CAL
Chiropractic Association of Oklahoma (SRA) .... CAO
Chiropractic Association of Oregon (SRA) .... CAO
Chiropractic Board of the Australian Capital Territory [Medicine] ..... CBACT
Chiropractic Foundation for Spinal Research (SAUO) .... CFSR
Chiropractic Information Centre Ltd. [British] (CB) CIC
Chiropractic Information Network-Board Action Databank (SAUO) ..... CIN-BAD
Chiropractic Journal of Australia (SAUS) .... CJA
Chiropractic Library Consortium (ADWA) .... CLIBCON
Chiropractic Research Abstracts Collection (SAUO) .... CRAC
Chiropractic Research Journal (SAUS) .... CRJ
Chiropractor .... CHIRO
Chiropractors' and Osteopaths' Board of Queensland [Australia] ..... COBQ
Chiropractors' Association of Australia .... CAA
Chiropractors' Association of Australia, Australian Capital Territory ..... CAAACT
Chiropractors' Board of South Australia [Medicine] .... CBSA
Chiropractors' Registration Board [Australia] .... CRB
Chiropractors'and Osteopaths' Registration Board [Victoria] [Australia] ..... CORB
Chiroptical Discrimination [Steroisomeric chemistry] .... CD
Chiro-Xylographic [Type of block book] .... CHX
Chirp (IAA) C
Chirp Duration [Entomology] .... CD
Chirp Fourier Transform (SAUS) .... CFT
Chirp Period [Entomology] .... CP
Chirp Rate [Entomology] .... CR
Chirped Pulse Amplification [Physics] .... CPA
Chirp-Z-Transform .... CZT
Chirurgia [Surgery] [Latin] .... CH
Chirurgiae Baccalaureus [Bachelor of Surgery] .... CB
Chirurgiae Baccalaureus [Bachelor of Surgery] .... Ch B
Chirurgiae Baccalaureus [Bachelor of Surgery] [Latin] (BARN) ..... Chit B
Chirurgiae Doctor [Doctor of Surgery] .... ChD
Chirurgiae Doctor [Doctor of Surgery] [Latin] (NADA) .... ChirDoc
Chirurgiae Doctor [Doctor of Surgery] .... Chir Doct
Chirurgiae Doctor [Doctor of Surgery] .... D Ch
Chirurgiae Magister [Master of Surgery] .... Ch M
Chirurgiae Magister [Master of Surgery] [Latin] .... CM
Chirurgical (SAUS) .... chir
Chirurgicalis [Surgical] [Pharmacy] .... CHIRURG
Chirurgiese Navorsingsvereniging van Suidelike Afrika [Surgical Research
    Society of Southern Africa] (EAIO) .... CNSA
Chirurgische Klinik und Poliklinik (SAUS) .... CUK
Chisago Lakes Area Junior High School, Lindstrom, MN [Library symbol]
    [Library of Congress] (LCLS) .... MnLiJ
Chisago Lakes Primary School, Chisago City, MN [Library symbol] [Library
    of Congress] (LCLS) .... MnCgP
Chisago Lakes Senior High School, Lindstrom, MN [Library symbol] [Library
    of Congress] (LCLS) .... MnLiS

Chisana [*Alaska*] [*Airport symbol*] (OAG) .... CZN
Chisana, AK [*Location identifier*] [*FAA*] (FAAL) .... CZN
Chisholm Junior High School, Chisholm, MN [*Library symbol*] [*Library of Congress*] (LCLS) .... MnChiJ
Chisholm Public Library, Chisholm, MN [*Library symbol*] [*Library of Congress*] (LCLS) .... MnChi
Chisholm Resources [*Vancouver Stock Exchange symbol*] .... CHZ
Chisholm Senior High School, Chisholm, MN [*Library symbol*] [*Library of Congress*] (LCLS) .... MnChiSH
Chi-Square Automatic Interaction Detection (SAUS) .... CHAID
Chi-Square Test (MELL) .... CST
Chi-Squared Automatic Interaction Detector .... CHAID
Chi-Squared Function .... CSF
Chi-Squared Test [*Statistics*] (DAVI) .... X_2t
Chistochina, AK [*Location identifier*] [*FAA*] (FAAL) .... CZO
Chita [*USSR*] [*Airport symbol*] (AD) .... CHT
Chita [*Former USSR*] [*Seismograph station code, US Geological Survey*] (SEIS) .... CIT
Chitaavia [*Former USSR*] [*FAA designator*] (FAAC) .... CHF
Chita/Kadala [*Former USSR*] [*ICAO location identifier*] (ICLI) .... UIAA
Chitarrone [*Large Guitar*] [*Music*] .... CHIT
Chitato [*Angola*] [*ICAO location identifier*] (ICLI) .... FNCH
Chitato [*Angola*] [*Airport symbol*] [*Obsolete*] (OAG) .... PGI
Chitina, AK [*Location identifier*] [*FAA*] (FAAL) CXC
Chitipa [*Malawi*] [*Airport symbol*] (AD) CII
Chitipa [*Malawi*] [*ICAO location identifier*] (ICLI) .... FWCT
Chitral [*Pakistan*] [*Airport symbol*] [*Obsolete*] (OAG) .... CJL
Chitral [*Pakistan*] [*ICAO location identifier*] (ICLI) .... OPCH
Chittagong [*Bangladesh*] [*Airport symbol*] (OAG) .... CGP
Chittagong [*Bangladesh*] [*Seismograph station code, US Geological Survey*] (SEIS) .... CHT
Chittagong [*Bangladesh*] [*ICAO location identifier*] (ICLI) .... VGEG
Chittagong Hill Tracks National Park (SAUS) .... CHTNP
Chittenden Corp. [*Associated Press*] (SAG) .... Chittend
Chittenden Corp. [*NYSE symbol*] (SG) .... CHZ
Chittenden Corp. [*NASDAQ symbol*] (NQ) .... CNDN
Chitty and Hulme on Bills of Exchange [*A publication*] (DLA) .... Chit & H Bills
Chitty and Mew's Supplement to Fisher's English Digest [*A publication*] (DLA) .... Chit & M Dig
Chitty and Patell's Supreme Court Appeals [*India*] [*A publication*] (DLA) .... Chitt & Pat
Chitty and Temple on Carriers [*A publication*] (DLA) .... Chit & T Car
Chitty, Junior, on Bills [*A publication*] (DLA) .... Chit Jun B
Chitty. Law of Nations [*1812*] [*A publication*] (DLA) .... Chit L of N
Chitty. Law of Nations [*1812*] [*A publication*] (DLA) .... Chit Nat
Chitty on Bills [*A publication*] (DLA) .... Ch Bills
Chitty on Bills [*A publication*] (DLA) .... Chit Bills
Chitty on Bills [*A publication*] (DLA) .... Chitty
Chitty on Commercial Law [*A publication*] (ILCA) .... Chit Com L
Chitty on Commercial Law [*A publication*] (DLA) .... Chit Com Law
Chitty on Commercial Law [*A publication*] (DLA) .... Chitty Com Law
Chitty on Contracts [*A publication*] (DLA) .... Chit Con
Chitty on Contracts [*A publication*] (DLA) .... Chit Cont
Chitty on Medical Jurisprudence [*A publication*] (DLA) .... Chit Med Jur
Chitty on Pleading [*A publication*] (DLA) .... Chit Pl
Chitty on Pleading [*A publication*] (DLA) .... Ch Pl
Chitty on the Game Laws [*A publication*] (DLA) .... Chit GL
Chitty on the Law of Descents [*A publication*] (DLA) .... Chit Des
Chitty's Commercial and General Lawyer [*A publication*] (DLA) .... Chit Lawy
Chitty's Criminal Law [*A publication*] (DLA) .... Ch Cr L
Chitty's Criminal Law [*A publication*] (DLA) .... Chit Crim Law
Chitty's Criminal Law [*A publication*] (DLA) .... Chit Cr L
Chitty's Criminal Law [*A publication*] (DLA) .... Chit Cr Law
Chitty's Edition of Archbold's Practice [*A publication*] (DLA) .... Chit Archb Pr
Chitty's Edition of Archbold's Practice [*A publication*] (DLA) .... Chit Arch Pr
Chitty's Edition of Blackstone's Commentaries [*A publication*] (DLA) .... Ch Black
Chitty's Edition of Blackstone's Commentaries [*A publication*] (DLA) .... Chi Black
Chitty's Edition of Blackstone's Commentaries [*A publication*] (DLA) .... Chit Bl
Chitty's Edition of Blackstone's Commentaries [*A publication*] (DLA) .... Chit Bl Comm
Chitty's Edition of Blackstone's Commentaries [*A publication*] (DLA) .... Chitty Bl Comm
Chitty's Edition of Burn's Justice [*A publication*] (DLA) .... Ch Burn's J
Chitty's Edition of Burn's Justice [*A publication*] (DLA) .... Chit Burn's J
Chitty's English Bail Court Reports [*1770-1822*] [*A publication*] (DLA) .... Chit
Chitty's English Bail Court Reports [*1770-1822*] [*A publication*] (DLA) .... Chit BC
Chitty's English Bail Court Reports [*1770-1822*] [*A publication*] (DLA) .... Chit R
Chitty's English Bail Court Reports [*1770-1822*] [*A publication*] (DLA) .... Chitt
Chitty's English Bail Court Reports [*1770-1822*] [*A publication*] (DLA) .... Chitty BC
Chitty's English Bail Court Reports [*1770-1822*] [*A publication*] (DLA) .... Chitty BC (Eng)
Chitty's English King's Bench Forms [*A publication*] (DLA) .... Chit F
Chitty's English King's Bench Practice Reports [*1819-20*] [*A publication*] (DLA) .... Chit
Chitty's English King's Bench Reports [*A publication*] (DLA) .... Ch R
Chitty's Equity Digest [*A publication*] (DLA) .... Chit Eq Dig
Chitty's Equity Index [*A publication*] (DLA) .... Chit Eq Ind
Chitty's Equity Index [*A publication*] (DLA) .... Chitty Eq Ind
Chitty's General Practice [*A publication*] (DLA) .... Chit Gen Pr
Chitty's General Practice [*A publication*] (DLA) .... Chit Pr
Chitty's Law Journal [*A publication*] (DLA) .... Chitt LJ
Chitty's Law of Apprentices [*A publication*] (DLA) .... Chit Ap
Chitty's Precedents in Pleading [*A publication*] (DLA) .... Chit Prec
Chitty's Prerogatives of the Crown [*A publication*] (DLA) .... Chit Prer
Chitty's Stamp Act [*A publication*] (DLA) .... Chit St A
Chitty's Statutes of Practical Utility [*1235-1948*] [*England*] [*A publication*] (DLA) .... Chit St
Chitty's Statutes of Practical Utility [*1235-1948*] [*England*] [*A publication*] (DLA) .... Chit Stat
Chitty's Summary of the Practice of the Superior Courts [*A publication*] (DLA) .... Chit Sum P
Chitty's Treatise on Carriers [*A publication*] (DLA) .... Chit Car
Chitwan District Development Committee (SAUS) .... CDDC
Chivalry (ROG) .... CHIV
Chivalry & Sorcery (SAUS) .... C&S
Chivenor [*British*] [*ICAO location identifier*] (ICLI) .... EGDC
Chivenor FTU [*British*] [*ICAO designator*] (FAAC) .... CHV
Chizaria Game Reserve (SAUS) .... CGR
chlamydia (SAUS) .... chlamy
Chlamydia Antigen Detection [*medicine*] (MELL) .... CAD
Chlamydia Trachomatis [*Medicine*] .... CT
Chlamydia Transport Media (STED) .... CTM
Chloracetophenone (SAUS) .... CN
Chloracetophenone Solution (SAUS) .... CHS
Chloral Hydrate [*Pharmacology*] (DAVI) .... HYDRAT
Chlor-Alkali-Market Model .... CAMM
Chlorambucil [*Also, CHL, CMB*] [*Antineoplastic drug*] C
Chlorambucil (DB) .... CB
Chlorambucil [*Antineoplastic drug*] .... CHL
Chlorambucil [*Antineoplastic drug*] (CDI) .... CLB
Chlorambucil [*Antineoplastic drug*] .... CMB
Chlorambucil and Prednisone [*Antineoplastic drug regimen*] (DAVI) .... CHL + PRED
Chlorambucil, Vinblastine, Procarbazine, Prednisone [*Antineoplastic drug regimen*] .... CHL VPP
Chlorambucil, Vinblastine, Procarbazine, Prednisone [*Antineoplastic drug regimen*] .... CIVPP
Chlorambucil, Vinblastine, Vincristine, Prednisone [*Antineoplastic drug regimen*] (DAVI) .... LVVP
Chloramphenical (SAUS) .... CAM
Chloramphenicol [*Antimicrobial compound*] C
Chloramphenicol [*Antimicrobial compound*] .... CAM
Chloramphenicol [*Antimicrobial compound*] .... CAP
Chloramphenicol [*Antimicrobial compound*] (MAE) .... CHL
Chloramphenicol [*Antimicrobial compound*] .... CM
Chloramphenicol [*Antimicrobial compound*] .... CMC
Chloramphenicol [*Antimicrobial compound*] .... CMP
Chloramphenicol Acetyltransferase [*An enzyme*] .... CAT
Chloramphenicol Transferase (SAUS) .... CAT
Chloramphenicol-Amended Potato Dextrose Agar [*Microbiology*] .... CPDA
Chloramphenicol-Sensitive Microsomal Protein [*Biochemistry*] (DB) .... CSMP
Chloramphetamine [*Neurochemistry*] .... CA
Chloranil [*Organic chemistry*] .... CA
Chloraromatic Compound [*Organic chemistry*] .... CAP
Chlorate Oxygen Candle .... COC
Chlordan [*or Chlordane*] [*Insecticide*] .... CD
Chlordecone (Kepone) [*Pesticide*] .... CD
Chlordiazepoxide [*Librium*] [*Sedative*] .... CDE
Chlordimeform [*Insecticide*] .... CDF
Chlordimeform [*Expectorant*] .... CDM
Chlorella International Union [*Later, MIU*] .... CIU
Chlorendic Acid [*Organic chemistry*] .... CA
Chlorendic Aldehyde [*Organic chemistry*] .... CEA
Chlorendic Anhydride [*Also, CAN*] [*Organic chemistry*] .... CA
Chlorendic Anhydride [*Also, CA*] [*Organic chemistry*] .... CAN
Chlorfenvinphos (LDT) .... CVP
Chlorfluorkohlenstoffe (SAUS) .... CFK
chlorhexidine (SAUS) .... chx
Chloriazepoxide [*Medicine*] (MELL) .... CDX
Chloricum (SAUS) .... Chloric
Chloride [*Chemistry*] (ADA) .... CHLO
Chloride [*Chemistry*] (ROG) .... CHLOR
Chloride (DAVI) Cl
Chloride (SAUS) CL
Chloride Channel (DMAA) .... CLCN
Chloride Industrial Batteries [*Manufacturer*] [*British*] .... CIB
Chloride Leak Detector (IEEE) .... CLD
Chloride Silent Power Ltd. (SAUO) .... CSP
Chloride Test [*Dentistry*] (BABM) .... CLR
Chloride Test (SAUS) .... CLR Test
Chlorid-Ion (SAUS) .... Cl-
Chlorinated [*Freight*] .... CHLOR
Chlorinated Aromatic Compound [*Organic chemistry*] .... CAC
Chlorinated Biphenyl (EDCT) .... CBP
Chlorinated Dibenzofuran (COE) .... CD
Chlorinated Dibenzofuran [*Organic chemistry*] (FFDE) .... CDBF
Chlorinated Dibenzofuran [*Organic chemistry*] .... CDF
Chlorinated Dibenzo-para-dioxin [*Organic chemistry*] .... CDD
Chlorinated Flour Oil (SAUS) .... CFO
Chlorinated Fluorocarbon (GAAI) .... CFC
Chlorinated Hydrocarbon .... CHC
Chlorinated HydroCarbon (SAUS) .... CHC
Chlorinated Hydrocarbon Solvents .... CHS
Chlorinated Methane [*Organic chemistry*] .... CM
Chlorinated Naphthalene [*Organic chemistry*] .... CN
Chlorinated Organics in Wastewater .... COW
Chlorinated Paraffin [*Organic chemistry*] .... CP
Chlorinated Paraffins Industry Association (EA) .... CPIA
Chlorinated Pesticide [*Toxicology*] (LDT) .... Cl-PEST
Chlorinated Polyethylene [*Organic chemistry*] .... CPE
Chlorinated Polyethylene (SAUS) .... PEC

Chlorinated Polypropylene (SAUS)	PPC
Chlorinated Poly(vinyl Chloride) [Organic chemistry]	CPVC
Chlorinated Rubber (EDCT)	CR
Chlorinated Synthetic Rubber	CSR
Chlorination (SAUS)	Chlor
Chlorine (SAUS)	Chlor
Chlorine [Chemical element]	Cl
Chlorine	CL
Chlorine Chemistry Council (SAUO)	CCC
Chlorine Chemisty Council (NTPA)	C3
Chlorine Demand (SAUS)	CD
Chlorine Dioxide (MELL)	ClO
Chlorine Dioxide (SAUS)	OClO
Chlorine Efficiency Factor	CEF
Chlorine Emergency Plan [Chlorine Institute]	CHLOREP
Chlorine Gas (SAUS)	Cl
Chlorine Institute (EA)	Cl
Chlorine Institute, Inc.	CHI
Chlorine Monoxide (EOSA)	ClO
Chlorine Nitrate	ClNO3
Chlorine Pentafluoride [Inorganic chemistry] (MCD)	ClPF
Chlorine Pentafluoride [Inorganic chemistry]	CPF
Chlorine Resistant (SAUS)	CR
Chlorine Scrubber (EEVL)	CLS
Chlorine Trifluoride [Inorganic chemistry]	CTF
Chlorine-Catalyzed Oxidative-Pyrolysis [Chemical engineering]	CCOP
Chloris Striate Mosaic Virus [Plant pathology]	CSMV
Chlorite (SAUS)	Ch
Chlorite [A mineral]	CHL
Chlorite (VRA)	chlr
Chlorite [A mineral]	Cl
Chlorite-Iodide-Malonic-Acid [Chemical reaction]	CIMA
Chlormadinone Acetate (SAUS)	CA
Chlormerodrin Accumulation Test [Medicine] (MAE)	CAT
Chlormethyl Ether (SAUS)	BCME
Chlornaltrexamine [Narcotic antagonist] [Pharmacochemistry]	CNA
Chloro [As substituent on nucleoside] [Biochemistry]	cl
Chloroacetaldehyde Diethyl Acetal [Organic chemistry]	CADEA
Chloroacetaldehyde Dimethyl Acetal [Organic chemistry]	CADMA
Chloroacetaldehydedinitrophenylhydrazone [Fungicide]	CADNPH
Chloroacetate Esterase [An enzyme]	CAE
Chloroacetophenone [Also, CN] [Tear gas]	CAP
Chloroacetophenone [Also, CAP] [Tear gas] [Army symbol] (AAG)	CN
Chloroacetophenone in a chlorine solution (SAUS)	CNC
Chloroacetophenone in a solution of benzine and chloroform (SAUS)	CNB
Chloroacetophenone in Chloroform (PDAA)	CNbr
Chloroacetyl (SAUS)	ChAc
Chloroacetyl [Organic chemistry] (DAVI)	ClAc
Chloroacetyl Chloride [Organic chemistry]	CAC
Chloroallyl Diethyldithiocarbamate [Herbicide]	CDEC
Chlorobenzalmalononitrile [Tear gas] [Army symbol]	CS
Chlorobenzine Producers Association (EA)	CPA
Chlorobenzoic Acid [Organic acid]	CBA
Chlorobenzotrifluoride [Organic chemistry]	CBTF
Chlorobiphenyl [Chemistry]	CB
Chlorobiphenyls (DB)	CBP
Chlorobromide Print Process (VRA)	CHBR
Chlorobromoethane [Organic chemistry]	CBE
Chlorobromomethane [Also, CBM] [Organic chemistry] (MCD)	CB
Chlorobromomethane [Also, CB] [Organic chemistry]	CBM
Chlorobromomethane (SAUS)	CBM
Chlorobutanol (SAUS)	CHLB
Chlorobutanol [Pharmacology] (DAVI)	Chlb
Chlorobutyronitrile (EDCT)	CBN
Chlorocetophenone Solution (AAG)	CNS
Chlorocholine Chloride [Organic chemistry]	CCC
Chlorodeoxyadenosine [Biochemistry]	CDA
Chlorodeoxycellulose (SAUS)	CDC
Chloro-deoxy-glucose [Biochemistry]	CDG
Chlorodeoxylincomycin (MAE)	CDL
Chlorodiallylacetamide [Herbicide]	CDAA
Chlorodifluoroethylene [Organic chemistry]	CDF
Chlorodihydroxybenzopyranone [Organic chemistry]	CDBP
Chlorodinitrobenzene [Organic chemistry]	CDNB
Chloroethane Phosphoric Acid [Organic chemistry] (DAVI)	CEPA
(Chloroethyl)cyclohexylnitrosourea [Lomustine] [Antineoplastic drug regimen]	CCNU
Chloroethyl-Cyclohexyl-Nitrosoures [Also called Lomustine] [Antineoplastic drug] (DAVI)	CEENU
(Chloroethyl)deoxycytidine [Antiviral]	CEDC
(Chloroethyl)deoxyuridine [Biochemistry]	CEDU
Chloroethylnitrosourea [A class of antineoplastic agents]	CENU
Chloroethylphosphonic Acid [Maturation compound for fruits]	CEPA
Chlorofluorocarbon [Organic chemistry]	CFC
Chlorofluoromethane [Propellant]	CFM
Chloroform [Organic chemistry] (WGA)	CHL
Chloroform (ADWA)	chl
Chloroform [Organic chemistry] (ADA)	CHLO
Chloroform [Organic chemistry] (ROG)	CHLOR
Chloroform and Ether [Mixture]	CE
Chloroform Fumigation-Incubation Technique	CFI
Chlorogenic Acid [Organic chemistry]	CA
Chlorogenic Acid [Organic chemistry]	CGA
Chloroisatoic Anhydride [Organic chemistry]	CIA
Chloroisobutene Isoprene Rubber	CIIR
Chloromercuri Benzoate (SAUS)	CMB
Chloromercuribenzoate [Biochemistry]	ClHgBzO
Chloromercuribenzoic [Organic chemistry]	CMB
Chloromethyl Chloroformate [Organic chemistry] (DAVI)	K stoff
Chloromethyl Ether [Organic chemistry]	CME
Chloromethyl Ketone [Medicine] (DMAA)	CMK
Chloromethyl Methyl Ether [Organic chemistry]	CMME
Chloromethyldimethylchlorosilane [Organic chemistry]	CMDMS
Chloromethyldioxolane [Organic chemistry]	CMDO
Chloromethylfurfuraldehyde [Organic chemistry]	CMF
Chloro(methyl)phenol [Organic chemistry]	CMP
((Chloro(methyl)phenoxy))propionic Acid [Herbicide]	CMPP
Chloro(methyl)(ribityl)isoalloxazine [Biochemistry]	CMRI
Chloronitroaniline [Organic chemistry]	CNA
Chloro(nitro)phenol [Organic chemistry]	CNP
Chloroperbenzoic Acid [Organic acid]	CPBA
Chlorophenoxyacetic Acid [Plant growth hormone]	CPA
(Chlorophenoxy)butanoic Acid [Biochemistry]	CPBA
Chlorophenoxyisobutyrate [Pharmacology]	CPIB
(Chlorophenoxy)propionic Acid [Biochemistry]	CPPA
Chlorophenyl Red [A dye]	CPR
Chlorophenylalanine [Biochemistry]	CPA
Chlorophenyldimethylurea [Herbicide]	CMU
(Chlorophenyl)methylcarbamate [Organic chemistry]	CPMC
Chlorophyll	ChL
Chlorophyll A (SAUS)	Chl A
Chloropicolinic Acid [Organic chemistry]	CPA
Chloropicrin [Poison gas] [Army symbol]	PS
Chloropicrin Stannic Chloride [Inorganic chemistry]	NC
Chloroplast DNA [Deoxyribonucleic Acid] [Genetics] (DOG)	chDNA
Chloroplasts, Ferredoxin, and Hydrogenase [Photoreactant system]	CFH
Chloroplasts to Nuclei per Cell [Botany]	C/N
Chloroprene (SAUS)	CHLORO
Chloroprene Rubber (EDCT)	CR
Chloroprene Rubbers (SAUS)	CRs
Chloroprocaine [A local anesthetic]	CP
(Chloropropyl)deoxyuridine [Antiviral]	CPDU
Chloropurine [Antineoplastic drug] (AAMN)	CP
Chloroquine [Antimalarial drug]	CQ
Chloroquine and Primaquine [Medicine] (MELL)	C & P
Chloroquine and Primaquine [Antimalarial drugs] (AAMN)	CP
Chloroquine Mustard (MAE)	CQM
Chloroquine, Pyrimethamine, Sulfisoxazole (MAE)	CPS
Chloroquine Resistance [Chemoprophylaxis]	CQR
Chloroquine-Mepacrine [Antimalarial drugs] (MAE)	CM
Chloroquine-Quinine [Antimalarial drug] [Pharmacology] (DAVI)	CQ
Chloroquine-Resistant [Genetics]	CQR
Chloroquine-Resistant Plasmodium Falciparum [Chemoprophylaxis]	CRPF
Chloroquine-Susceptible [Genetics]	CQS
Chloroquinol [Medicine] (DMAA)	CHQ
Chloroquinoxaline Sulfonamide [Antineoplastic drug]	CQS
Chlorosulfonic Acid [Organic chemistry]	CSA
Chlorosulfonyl Isocyanate [Organic chemistry]	CSI
(Chlorosulfonyl)dicyclohexylamine [Antineoplastic drug]	CSD
Chlorosulfopolyethylene Rubber (SAUS)	CSER
Chlorosulphonated Polyethylene	CSP
Chlorosulphonated Polyethylene	CSPE
Chlorosulphonated Polyethylenes (SAUS)	CSPs
Chlorothiazide [Diuretic]	CHTZ
Chlorothiazide [Diuretic]	CT
Chlorothiazide [Diuretic] (MAE)	CTZ
Chlorotic Necrotic Ring Virus (SAUS)	CNRV
Chlorotic Ringspot Virus (SAUS)	CRV
Chlorotic Spot Virus (SAUS)	CSV
Chlorotluoromethane (SAUS)	CFM
Chlorotrifluoroethylene [Organic chemistry]	CFE
Chlorotrifluoroethylene [Organic chemistry]	CTFE
Chlorotriflurorethane [Organic chemistry]	CTF
Chloroxymorphamine [Narcotic agonist] [Pharmacochemistry]	COA
Chlorozotocin [Antineoplastic drug] (CDI)	CLZ
Chlorozotocin [Antineoplastic drug]	CZT
Chlorozotocin [Organic chemistry] (DAVI)	DCNU
Chlorpheniramine [Pharmacology]	CH
Chlorpheniramine Maleate [Antihistamine]	CPM
chlorpheniramine polistirex (SAUS)	cpm pol
chlorpheniramine tannate (SAUS)	cpm tan
Chlorpromazine [Sedative]	CPZ
Chlorpropamide (MELL)	CPA
Chlorpropamide-Alcohol Flushing [Medicine]	CPAF
Chlorprothixene (SAUS)	CPT
Chlorprothixene (SAUS)	CPX
Chlorsulphonic Acid Mixture (SAUS)	CSAM
Chlortetracycline [Antibiotic]	CTC
Chlorthalidone [Diuretic]	CHLT
Chlorthalidone (DMAA)	CTHD
Chlorthalidone [Diuretic and antihypertensive agent] [Medicine] (STED)	CTLD
Chlortrimeton [Antihistamine] [Trademark of Schering-Plough Corp.]	CTM
Chlorus (SAUS)	Chloro
Chlorzotocin [Organic chemistry] (DAVI)	CZN
Choay [France] [Research code symbol]	CY
Chocha [Zambia] [ICAO location identifier] (ICLI)	FLCO
Chochma, Bina, Daat [Wisdom, Understanding, Knowledge] [Philosophy of the Lubavitch Movement, a Hasidic sect]	CHABAD
Chock Full O'Nuts Corp. [Wall Street slang name: "Nuts"] [NYSE symbol] (SPSG)	CHF

Chock Full O'Nuts Corp. [*Wall Street Slang Name: "Nuts"*] [*Associated Press*] (SAG) .... ChkFull
Chocktaw, Oklahoma & Gulf Railroad .... CO & G
Chocolate .... ch
Chocolate .... CHOC
Chocolate Blood [*Agar*] [*Biochemistry*] (MAE) .... CB
Chocolate Manufacturers Association of the USA (EA) .... CMA
Chocolate Milk Foundation [*Defunct*] (EA) .... CMF
Chocolate-Coated [*Pharmacy*] CC
Chocolate-Coated [*or Covered*] Tablet [*Pharmacy*] .... CCT
Chocolate-Colored Tablet (SAUS) .... CCT
Choctaw [*MARC language code*] [*Library of Congress*] (LCCP) .... cho
Choctaw Nation Multi-County Library, McAlester, OK [*OCLC symbol*] (OCLC) .... OKI
Choctaw Nation Multi-County Library, McAlester, OK [*Library symbol*] [*Library of Congress*] (LCLS) .... OkMcC
Choctawhatchee Regional Library [*Library network*] .... CRL
Choephori [*of Aeschylus*] [*Classical studies*] (OCD) .... Cho
Chofu [*Japan*] [*ICAO location identifier*] (ICLI) .... RJTF
Choice (SAUS) .... ch
Choice (ADA) .... CH
Choice .... CHCE
Choice Drug Systems, Inc. [*NASDAQ symbol*] (NQ) .... DOSE
Choice Hotels International, Inc. [*NYSE symbol*] (SAG) .... CHH
Choice Hotels International, Inc. [*Associated Press*] (SAG) .... ChoiceH
Choice in Dying .... CID
Choice Magazine Listening [*An "aural magazine" for the blind and visually handicapped*] .... CML
Choice of Programming Languages (SAUS) .... CPL
Choice Old Marsala .... COM
Choice Reaction (STED) .... CR
Choice Reaction Time (PDAA) .... CRT
Choice-in-Currency Research Institute (EA) .... CNCRI
ChoicePoint, Inc. [*NYSE symbol*] (SG) .... CPS
Choir (SAUS) .... Ch
Choir (ROG) .... CH
Choir .... CHOR
Choir Organ .... CH
Choir Organ (ROG) .... CO
Choir Screen (VRA) .... chr scrn
Choirmaster (SAUS) .... Chm
Choirmaster [*Music*] .... Choirm
Choirmaster [*Music*] .... CM
Choiseul Bay [*Solomon Islands*] [*Airport symbol*] (OAG) .... CHY
Choke (MSA) .... CH
Choke Breaker [*Automotive engineering*] .... CB
Choke Coil CC
Choke Coil (AAG) .... CHC
Choke Coil (SAUS) .... ChC
Choke Oil (SAUS) .... CHO
Choke Packet (SAUS) .... CP
Choking Gas [*US Chemical Corps symbol*] .... CG
Chokio-Alberta High School, Alberta, MN [*Library symbol*] [*Library of Congress*] (LCLS) .... MnAlbeCH
Chokio-Alberto Elementary School, Chokio, MN [*Library symbol*] [*Library of Congress*] (LCLS) .... MnChoE
Choky Gas (SAUS) .... CG
Chol Chol Foundation for Human Development (EA) .... CCFHD
Cholame Valley [*California*] [*Seismograph station code, US Geological Survey*] (SEIS) CVC
(Cholamidopropyl)dimethylammonio(hydroxy) Propanesulfonate [*Organic chemistry*] .... CHAPSO
((Cholamidopropyl)dimethylammonio)propanesulfonate [*Biochemistry*] .... CHAPS
Cholamine (PDAA) .... CA
Chole Packet (ACRL) .... CHO
Cholecalciferol (SAUS) CC
Cholecalciferol [*Organic chemistry*] (DAVI) .... D
Cholecalciferol [*Medicine*] (MELL) D3
Cholecystectomy [*Medicine*] (MAE) .... chole
Cholecystogram [*Radiology*] (DAVI) .... CCG
Cholecystokinin [*Also, PZ*] [*Endocrinology*] .... CCK
Cholecystokinin Octapeptide [*Biochemistry*] (DAVI) .... CCK-OP
Cholecystokinin-Brain Type Receptor .... CCK-B
Cholecystokinin-Gallbladder [*Medicine*] (MEDA) .... CCK-GB
Cholecystokinin-Pancreozymin [*Endocrinology*] .... CCK-PZ
Cholecystokinin-Pankreozymin (SAUS) .... CCK-PZ
Cholecystokinin-Releasing Peptide [*Biochemistry*] .... CCKRP
Choledochoduodenal Junction [*Anatomy*] .... CDJ
Choledocwo-Caval Shunt [*Medicine*] .... CCS
Cholelithiasis (MELL) CL
Cholera (SAUS) .... Chol
Cholera Research Laboratory [*Bangladesh*] .... CRL
Cholera Toxin [*Medicine*] .... CT
Cholera Toxin [*Medicine*] .... ctx
Cholera Toxin B [*Medicine*] .... CHB
Cholera Toxin B [*Medicine*] .... CTB
Cholera Vaccine [*Medicine*] .... CHO/VAC
Cholera Vaccine Immunization [*Medicine*] CVI
Cholestatic Liver Disease [*Medicine*] .... CLD
Cholestech Corp. [*Associated Press*] (SAG) .... Cholest
Cholestech Corp. [*NASDAQ symbol*] (SAG) .... CTEC
Cholesteric Analysis Profile Test [*Thermography*] [*Radiology*] (DAVI) .... CAP
Cholesteric Liquid Crystal (PDAA) CLC
Cholesteric-Nematic Transition (SAUS) .... CNT
Cholesterol [*Also, Ch, Cho, CHOL*] [*Biochemistry*] (AAMN) C

Cholesterol [*Also, C, Cho, CHOL*] [*Biochemistry*] .... Ch
Cholesterol [*Also, C, Ch, CHOL*] [*Biochemistry*] .... Cho
Cholesterol [*Also, C, Ch, Cho*] [*Biochemistry*] .... CHOL
Cholesterol (ADWA) .... chol
Cholesterol (SAUS) .... Chol
Cholesterol Binding Protein [*Biochemistry*] .... CBP
Cholesterol Epoxide [*Biochemistry*] .... CAE
Cholesterol Ester (SAUS) .... CE
Cholesterol Ester [*Clinical chemistry*] (MAE) .... Chol Est
Cholesterol Ester Hydrolase (DB) .... CEH
Cholesterol Ester Ratio [*Medicine*] (MELL) .... CER
Cholesterol Ester Storage Disease [*Medicine*] .... CESD
Cholesterol Ester Transport Protein [*Biochemistry*] .... CETP
Cholesterol Esters [*Organic chemistry*] (MAH) .... CHOL E
Cholesterol Esters [*Clinical chemistry*] (CPH) .... chol est
Cholesterol Esters (SAUS) .... CHOLEST
Cholesterol Gallstones [*Medicine*] .... CGS
Cholesterol Lowering Lipid [*Biochemistry*] CLL
Cholesterol Oxidase [*An enzyme*] .... CHOD
Cholesterol Saturation Index [*Clinical chemistry*] .... CSI
Cholesterol Total (SAUS) .... CT
Cholesterol-Esterifying Activity [*Biochemistry*] [*Medicine*] (DMAA) .... CEA
Cholesterol-Lecithin Flocculation [*Biochemistry*] (DAVI) .... CLF
Cholesterol-Lecithin Test [*Medicine*] (MAE) CL
Cholesterol-Lowering Atherosclerosis Study [*National Heart, Lung, and Blood Institute - NHLBI*] .... CLAS
Cholesterol-Lowering Therapy [*Medicine*] (MELL) .... CLT
Cholesterol/Phospholipid Ratio [*Clinical chemistry*] .... C/P
Cholesterol/Triglyceride Ratio [*Clinical chemistry*] (AAMN) .... C/TG
Cholesteryl Erucyl Carbonate (PDAA) .... CEC
Cholesteryl Ester Transfer Protein [*Biochemistry*] .... CETP
Cholesteryl Iopanoate [*Biochemistry*] CI
Cholesteryl Nonanoate (SAUS) .... CN
Cholesteryl Oleate-Triglyceride [*Biochemistry*] .... COT
Cholesteryl Oleyl Carbonate (SAUS) .... COC
Cholet/Le Pontreau [*France*] [*ICAO location identifier*] (ICLI) .... LFOU
Cholic Acid [*Biochemistry*] (AAMN) .... CA
Choline [*Also, Cho*] [*Biochemistry*] .... Ch
Choline [*Also, Ch*] [*Biochemistry*] .... Cho
Choline Acetyl Transferase [*Also, ChA, ChAc, ChAT*] [*An enzyme*] .... CAT
Choline Acetylase [*Also, CAT, ChAc, ChAT*] [*An enzyme*] .... ChA
Choline Acetylase [*Also, CAT, ChA, ChAT*] [*An enzyme*] .... ChAc
Choline Acetyl-Transferase [*Also, CAT, ChA, ChAc*] [*An enzyme*] .... ChAT
Choline Dehydrogenase (SAUS) .... CDH
Choline Dehydrogenase (DB) .... CLDH
Choline Glycerophosphatide (MAE) .... CGP
Choline Kinase [*An enzyme*] .... CK
Choline Magnesium Trisalicylate [*Pharmacy*] .... CMT
Choline Oxidase [*An enzyme*] .... CO
Choline-Adrenalin [*Test*] [*Medicine*] .... CA
Choline-O-Acetyltransferase (SAUS) .... CAT
Cholinergic Blocking Agent [*Medicine*] (MELL) .... CBA
Cholinergic Receptor Site [*Medicine*] (MELL) .... CRS
Cholinesterase (SAUS) .... CHE
Cholinesterase [*An enzyme*] .... ChE
Cholinesterase [*An enzyme*] .... CHS
Cholorquinine-Resistant Malaria .... CRPM
Choluteca [*Honduras*] [*ICAO location identifier*] (ICLI) .... MHCH
Choma [*Zambia*] [*ICAO location identifier*] (ICLI) .... FLCH
Chomsky Normal Form (SAUS) .... CNF
Chon Buri/Bang Phra [*Thailand*] [*ICAO location identifier*] (ICLI) .... VTBT
Chon Buri/Sattahip [*Thailand*] [*ICAO location identifier*] (ICLI) .... VTBS
Chonco [*Nicaragua*] [*Seismograph station code, US Geological Survey*] (SEIS) .... CNR
Chondrite-Normalized (SAUS) .... CN
Chondritic Porous [*Aggregate*] [*Inorganic chemistry*] .... CP
Chondritic Uniform Reservoir [*Geology*] .... CHUR
Chondrocalcinosis [*Orthopedics*] (DAVI) CC
Chondrocyte Growth Factor [*Biochemistry*] .... CGF
Chondrodysplasia Punctata [*Medicine*] (MELL) .... CDP
Chondrodysplasia Punctata, Rhizomelic [*Medicine*] (DMAA) .... CDPR
Chondrodysplasia Punctata, X-Linked Dominant [*Medicine*] (DMAA) .... CPXD
Chondrodysplasia Punctata, X-Linked Recessive [*Medicine*] (DMAA) .... CPXR
Chondrodystrophia Foetalis [*Medicine*] (DMAA) .... CDF
Chondrodystrophic Myotonia [*Medicine*] (MELL) .... CDM
Chondroectodermal Dysplasia [*Medicine*] (DMAA) .... CED
Chondroitin Sulfate [*Biochemistry*] .... CS
Chondroitin Sulfate A [*Biochemistry*] .... CSA
Chondroitin Sulfate Protein (MELL) .... CSP
Chondroitinsulfat-Proteine (SAUS) .... CSP
Chondromalacia [*Medicine*] (MAE) .... CM
Chondromalacia Patella [*Orthopedics*] (DAVI) .... CP
Chondromalacia Patellae [*Orthopedics*] (DAVI) .... CMP
Chondromalacia/Patella [*Medicine*] .... CH/P
Chondromyxoid Fibroma [*Medicine*] .... CMF
Chondrosoma Permeation Pattern [*Oncology*] .... CPP
Chone [*Ecuador*] [*ICAO location identifier*] (ICLI) .... SECH
Chongqing [*China*] [*Airport symbol*] (OAG) .... CKG
Chongqing [*China*] [*ICAO location identifier*] (ICLI) .... ZUCK
Chopart Amputation [*Medicine*] (MELL) .... CA
Chopart Joint (MELL) .... CJ
Chopin Cultural Center (SAUS) CCC
Chopp Computer Corp. [*Vancouver Stock Exchange symbol*] .... CRP
Chopped (SAUS) .... CHOP
Chopped Meat [*Medium*] [*Microbiology*] .... CM

Chopped Meat Carbohydrate [*Medium*] [*Microbiology*] ... CMC
Chopped Meat Glucose [*Medium*] [*Microbiology*] ... CMG
Chopped Meat Glucose Broth with Digoxin [*Medium*] [*Microbiology*] ... CMCD
Chopped Meat-Glucose-Starch Medium [*Medicine*] (DMAA) ... CMGS
Chopped Nylon Phenolic (SAA) ... CNP
Chopped Strand Mat (PDAA) ... CSM
Chopper (MSA) ... CHP
Chopper Circuitized Module (SAUS) ... CCM
Chopper Mines Ltd. [*Vancouver Stock Exchange symbol*] ... COR
Chopper Stabilized Amplifier ... CSA
Choppy, Short, or Cross Sea [*Navigation*] ... C
Choral ... CHO
Choral ... CHOR
Choral Conductors Guild (EA) ... CCG
Chorale Book [*Music*] (ROG) ... CB
Chord ... CD
Chord (KSC) ... CHD
Chord (SAUS) ... CRD
Chord Length (SAUS) ... C
Chord Plane Line (MCD) ... CPL
Chorda Chirurgicalis [*Surgical Catgut*] [*Pharmacy*] ... CHORD CHIRURG
Chorda Equina of Spinal Cord [*Medicine*] (MELL) ... CESC
Chorda Tympani [*Neuroanatomy*] ... CT
Chore [*Pakistan*] [*ICAO location identifier*] (ICLI) ... OPKE
Choreograph ... CHOR
Choreographed By (ADWA) ... chor
Choreographers Guild (EA) ... CG
Choreographers Theatre (EA) ... CT
Choreography ... CHGPH
Choreography (SAUS) ... Chor
Choreography ... Choreog
Choreti [*Bolivia*] [*ICAO location identifier*] (ICLI) ... SLCT
Chorioallantoic Membrane [*Embryology*] [*Assay for chemical irritability*] ... CAM
Chorioallantoic Sac (SAUS) ... CAS
Choriocarcinoma [*Oncology*] ... CC
Choriocarcinoma [*Oncology*] ... CCA
Choriogenic Gynecomastia (DB) ... CG
Chorion (MELL) ... C
Chorionic Biopsy [*Also, Chorionic Villus Sampling*] [*Medicine*] (PAZ) ... CVS
Chorionic Gonadotrophic Hormone (SAUS) ... CGH
Chorionic Gonadotrophin [*Endocrinology*] ... CG
Chorionic Gonadotrophin Hormone [*Endocrinology*] (AAMN) ... CGH
Chorionic Gonadotrophin, Human [*Endocrinology*] ... CGH
Chorionic Gonadotropin [*Endocrinology*] (DAVI) ... APL
Chorionic Gonadotropin [*Endocrinology*] (MAE) ... CGT
Chorionic Gonadotropin in Pregnant Mare's Serum [*Veterinary medicine*] (DAVI) ... PMS
Chorionic Growth Hormone - Prolactin [*Also, HCS, HPL*] [*Endocrinology*] ... CGP
Chorionic Somatomammotrophin [*Endocrinology*] ... CS
Chorionic Villi [*Medicine*] (MELL) ... CV
Chorionic Villi Biopsy [*Medicine*] ... CVB
Chorionic Villi Sampling [*Medicine*] ... CVS
Chorionic Villus Sampling (ADWA) ... CVS
chorioretinal (SAUS) ... c-r
Chorioretinal Degeneration (STED) ... CRD
Chorioretinopathy and Pituitary Dysfunction [*Medicine*] ... CPD
Chorismic Acid [*Biochemistry*] ... Chr
Choristers Guild (EA) ... CG
Choroid Plexus Papilloma [*Medicine*] ... CPP
Choroidal Neovascular Membrane (SAUS) ... CNVM
Choroidal Neovascularization [*Opthalmology*] ... CNV
Choroideremia [*Ophthalmology*] ... CHM
Chorus [*Music*] ... Cho
Chorus ... CHOR
Chorus Object-Oriented Layer [*Computer science*] ... COOL
Chorzow [*Poland*] [*Seismograph station code, US Geological Survey*] (SEIS) ... CHZ
Chose ... CHS
Chosen (SAUS) ... Cho
Chosen Coefficient of Variation [*Statistics*] ... CCV
Chosen People Ministries (EA) ... CPM
Chosen Point (SAUS) ... CP
Choshi [*Japan*] [*Seismograph station code, US Geological Survey*] (SEIS) ... CHO
Chosin Few (EA) ... CF
Chosmadal [*Argentina*] [*ICAO location identifier*] (ICLI) ... SAHC
Chota [*Peru*] [*ICAO location identifier*] (ICLI) ... SPCT
Chota Nagpur Regiment [*British military*] (DMA) ... CN Regt
Choteau, MT [*Location identifier*] [*FAA*] (FAAL) ... CHX
Chouteau County Free Library, Fort Benton, MT [*Library symbol*] [*Library of Congress*] (LCLS) ... MtFb
Chow Chow Club (EA) ... CCC
Chowan College, Murfreesboro, NC [*Library symbol*] [*Library of Congress*] (LCLS) ... NcMfC
Chowchilla, CA [*FM radio station call letters*] (RBYB) ... KLVN
Chowchilla, CA [*FM radio station call letters*] (BROA) ... KSKD-FM
Chowiet Island [*Alaska*] [*Seismograph station code, US Geological Survey*] (SEIS) ... CHW
Choya [*Argentina*] [*Seismograph station code, US Geological Survey*] (SEIS) ... CYA
Choyce's Cases in Chancery [*1557-1606*] [*England*] [*A publication*] (DLA) ... CCC
Choyce's Cases in Chancery [*1557-1606*] [*England*] [*A publication*] (DLA) ... Ch Ca Ch
Choyce's Cases in Chancery [*1557-1606*] [*England*] [*A publication*] (DLA) ... Ch Cas Ch
Choyce's Cases in Chancery [*1557-1606*] [*England*] [*A publication*] (DLA) ... Ch Cas in Ch
Choyce's Cases in Chancery [*1557-1606*] [*England*] [*A publication*] (DLA) ... Cho Ca Ca
Choyce's Cases in Chancery [*1557-1606*] [*England*] [*A publication*] (DLA) ... Cho Ca Ch
Choyce's Cases in Chancery [*1557-1606*] [*England*] [*A publication*] (DLA) ... Choyce Cas Ch
Choyce's Cases in Chancery [*1557-1606*] [*England*] [*A publication*] (DLA) ... Choyce Cas (Eng)
Chr. Robinsons English Admiralty reports (SAUS) ... Robinson
Chr. Robinsons Reports, Ontario (SAUS) ... Robinson Chr
Chr. Robinsons Upper Canada Reports (SAUS) ... Rob
Chreod International, Ottawa, Ontario [*Library symbol*] [*National Library of Canada*] (NLC) ... OOCHI
Chreschtlech-Sozial Vollekspartei [*Christian Social Party*] [*Luxembourg*] [*Political party*] (PPW) ... CSV
Chrestomathy (BARN) ... chr
Chretiens pour la Liberation du Peuple Guadeloupeen [*Guadeloupe*] (PD) ... CLPG
Chretiens pour Une Eglise Populaire [*Christians for One Common Church*] [*Canada*] ... CEP
Chrezvychainaya Komissiya po Borbe s Kontrrevolutisiei i Sabotazhem [*Extraordinary Commission for Combating Counterrevolution and Sabotage; Soviet secret police organization, 1917-1921*] ... CHEKA
Chripa [*Costa Rica*] [*Seismograph station code, US Geological Survey*] (SEIS) ... AR6
Chris LeDoux International Fan Club (EA) ... CLIFC
Chris-Craft Antique Boat Club (EA) ... CCABC
Chris-Craft Ind,$1 Pr Pfd [*NYSE symbol*] (TTSB) ... CCNPrA
Chris-Craft Ind,$1.40 Cv Pfd [*NYSE symbol*] (TTSB) ... CCNPrB
Chris-Craft Indus [*NYSE symbol*] (TTSB) ... CCN
Chris-Craft Industries ... CCN
Chris-Craft Industries, Inc. [*NYSE symbol*] (SPSG) ... CCN
Chris-Craft Industries, Inc. [*Associated Press*] (SAG) ... ChCft
Chris-Craft Industries, Inc. [*Associated Press*] (SAG) ... ChrisCr
Chrisitian Anti-Defamation League (SAUO) ... CADL
Chrisman Public Library, Chrisman, IL [*Library symbol*] [*Library of Congress*] (LCLS) ... IChr
Christ (WDAA) ... C
Christ ... CH
Christ [*or Christian*] ... CHR
Christ ... CHRST
Christ (GEAB) ... Xt
Christ ... XT
Christ Alongside (EA) ... CA
Christ Church (SAUO) ... CHC
Christ Church (SAUO) ... ChCh
Christ Church College [*Oxford University*] (ROG) ... C CH COLL
Christ for the Nations (EA) ... CFN
Christ Hospital Institute of Medical Research, Research Library, Cincinnati, OH [*Library symbol*] [*Library of Congress*] (LCLS) ... OCCIM
Christ Hospital, Oak Lawn, IL [*Library symbol*] [*Library of Congress*] (LCLS) ... IOIC
Christ in Action Ministries (EA) ... CAM
Christ Seminary-Seminex, St. Louis, MO [*Library symbol*] [*Library of Congress*] (LCLS) ... MoSCEx
Christ the King ... CHK
Christ the King Foundation [*Defunct*] (EA) ... CKF
Christ the King School, Browerville, MN [*Library symbol*] [*Library of Congress*] (LCLS) ... MnBvC
Christ the King Seminary, East Aurora, NY [*Library symbol*] [*Library of Congress*] (LCLS) ... NEAuC
Christ the King Seminary, East Aurora, NY [*OCLC symbol*] (OCLC) ... VYK
Christ Truth Ministries (EA) ... CTM
Christadelphian Auxiliary Lecturing Society [*British*] (BI) ... CALS
Christchurch [*New Zealand*] [*Airport symbol*] (OAG) ... CHC
Christchurch [*New Zealand*] [*Later, EYR*] [*Geomagnetic observatory code*] ... CHR
Christchurch [*New Zealand*] [*ICAO location identifier*] (ICLI) ... NZCO
Christchurch [*New Zealand*] [*ICAO location identifier*] (ICLI) ... NZZC
Christchurch Chromosome [*Genetics*] (DAVI) ... CH
Christchurch Chromosome ... Ch^1c
Christchurch/International [*New Zealand*] [*ICAO location identifier*] (ICLI) ... NZCH
Christchurch/International [*New Zealand*] [*ICAO location identifier*] (ICLI) ... NZDF
Christel, Bean & Linihan, Buffalo, NY [*Library symbol*] [*Library of Congress*] (LCLS) ... NBuCBL
Christelijke Bond voor de Ondergrondse Kerk/Action Chretienne pour l'Eglise du Silence [*Belgium*] ... CBOK-ACES
Christelijke Vervoerarbeiders en Diamantbewerkers [*Christian Trade Union of Transport and Diamond Workers*] [*Belgium*] (EAIO) ... CVD
Christelijke Volkspartij [*Christian Social Party*] [*Also, PSC*] [*Belgium*] [*Political party*] (PPW) ... CVP
Christelijk-Historische Unie [*Christian-Historical Union*] [*Netherlands*] [*Political party*] (PPW) ... CHU
Christen Democratisch Appel [*Christian Democratic Appeal*] [*Netherlands*] [*Political party*] (PPW) ... CDA
Christened (GEAB) ... chr
Christened ... CHR
Christened (SAUS) ... Chr
Christened (ADA) ... CHRIS
Christensen Canadian African Line [*Steamship*] (MHDW) ... CCAL
Christensen Dietary Distress Inventory (TMMY) ... CDDI
Christentum und Wissenschaft [*A publication*] (BJA) ... ChrW
Christentum und Wissenschaft [*A publication*] (BJA) ... CHuW
Christian ... C

Christian	Chr
Christian (SAUS)	Chris
Christian	CHRSTN
Christian (VRA)	Xian
Christian	XN
Christian (GEAB)	Xr
Christian (GEAB)	Xtian
Christian	XTIAN
Christian (ROG)	XTN
Christian Action Council (EA)	CAC
Christian Action for Development in the Caribbean [Caribbean Conference of Churches]	CADEC
Christian Action for Development in the Eastern Caribbean (SAUO)	CADEC
Christian Action for the Abolition of Torture [Defunct] (EA)	ACAT
Christian Action Ministry (SAUO)	CAM
Christian Action Party (SAUO)	CAP
Christian Action, Research, and Education [British]	CARE
Christian Addiction Rehabilitation Association (EA)	CARA
Christian Aid (SAUO)	CA
Christian Aid for Romania (EA)	CAR
Christian Aid Ministries (EA)	CAM
Christian Aid Mission (EA)	CAM
Christian AIDS Services Alliance (EA)	CASA
Christian Airmen's Fellowship International [Defunct] (EA)	CAS
Christian Alliance of Women and Girls [British] (BI)	CAWG
Christian Amateur Radio Fellowship [Defunct] (EA)	CARF
Christian Amendment Movement [Later, CGM] (EA)	CAM
Christian Americans for Life (EA)	CAFL
Christian and Missionary Alliance	CMA
Christian Anti-Communism Crusade (EA)	CACC
Christian Anti-Communist Crusade (SAUO)	CA-CC
Christian Anti-Jewish Party (BJA)	CAJP
Christian Anti-Narcotic Association [Later, SFM]	CANA
Christian Appalachian Project	CAP
Christian Army (ROG)	CA
Christian Assembly of New South Wales [Australia]	CANSW
Christian Association for Adult and Continuing Education [British]	CAACE
Christian Association for Psychological Studies (EA)	CAPS
Christian Association of Business Executives [British]	CABE
Christian Beacon, Collingswood, NJ [Library symbol] [Library of Congress] (LCLS)	NjCoB
Christian Blind Mission (WDAA)	CBM
Christian Blind Mission International [Bensheim, Federal Republic of Germany] (EAIO)	CBMI
Christian Boaters Association (EA)	CBA
Christian Bodybuilding Association (EA)	CBA
Christian Book Distributors [An association]	CBD
Christian Book Selling Association of Australia	CBSAA
Christian Booksellers Association (EA)	CBA
Christian Bookstall Managers Association (EA)	CBMA
Christian Brethren Assemblies [Australia]	CBA
Christian Brethren Church in the Province of Quebec [l'Eglise des Freres Chretiens dans la Province du Quebec] [Also, Plymouth Brethren] (AC)	CBCPQ
Christian Brethren Schools [Australia]	CBS
Christian Brethren Youth Hostel [Australia]	CBYH
Christian Broadcasting Association (EA)	CBA
Christian Broadcasting Network [Cable-television system]	CBN
Christian Brothers (SAUO)	CB
Christian Brothers' Association of Australia	CBA
Christian Brothers Boys Association (EA)	CBBA
Christian Brothers College [Tennessee]	CBC
Christian Brothers College, Memphis, TN [Library symbol] [Library of Congress] (LCLS)	TMCBC
Christian Brothers Conference (EA)	CBC
Christian Brothers Education Association [Later, RECCB] (EA)	CBEA
Christian Brothers School [Ireland]	CBS
Christian Business Men of Canada	CBMC
Christian Business Men's Committee International [Later, CBMC] (EA)	CBMCI
Christian Business Men's Committee of USA (EA)	CBMC
Christian Business Men's Committees Australia	CBMCA
Christian Businessman [Christian Business Men's Committee of United States of America] [A publication]	CB
Christian Businessman's Committees [Australia]	CBC
Christian Camping International [Later, CCI/USA] (EA)	CCI
Christian Camping International/USA (EA)	CCI/USA
Christian Century [A publication] (BRI)	CC
Christian Century Foundation (EA)	CCF
Christian Chamber of Commerce (EA)	CCC
Christian Chaplain Services (EA)	CCS
Christian Children's Fund (EA)	CCF
Christian Children's Fund, Richmond, VA [Library symbol] [Library of Congress] (LCLS)	ViRCCF
Christian Chiropractors Association (EA)	CCA
Christian Church (Disciples of Christ) in Canada [Formerly, All-Canada Committee of the Christian Church (Disciples of Christ)] (AC)	DISCAN
Christian Churches, International Convention (SAUO)	Disciples of Christ
Christian Circuit (SAUS)	CC
Christian Citizens' Crusade (EA)	CCC
Christian City Church [Australia]	CCC
Christian Classic Bikers Association [Later, ICCM] (EA)	CCBA
Christian Classic Bikers Association International [Later, ICCM] (EA)	CCBAI
Christian Coalition (EA)	CC
Christian College Coalition (EA)	CCC

Christian College, Columbia, MO [Library symbol] [Library of Congress] (LCLS)	MoCoC
Christian College Consortium (EA)	CCC
Christian College of the Southwest, Dallas, TX [Library symbol] [Library of Congress] (LCLS)	TxDaCC
Christian Comic Arts Society (EA)	CCAS
Christian Commission (SAUO)	CC
Christian Committee for Human Rights in Latin America [Canada] (EAIO)	CCHRLA
Christian Communications, Inc. (EA)	CCI
Christian Community (SAUO)	CC
Christian Community Church [Australia]	CCC
Christian Community Concern [Australia]	CCC
Christian Community High School [Australia]	CCHS
Christian Community School, Willmar, MN [Library symbol] [Library of Congress] (LCLS)	MnWilCS
Christian Community Schools [Australia]	CCS
Christian Computer Users [Defunct] (EA)	CCU
Christian Computer Users Association (EA)	CCUA
Christian Computing Magazine (SAUS)	CCM
Christian Conference in/of Asia (SAUO)	CCA
Christian Conference of Asia (EA)	CCA
Christian Crusade (SAUO)	CC
Christian Dance Federation of Australia	CDFA
Christian Defense League (EA)	CDL
Christian Democrat International (EAIO)	CDI
Christian Democrat Party [Australia] [Political party]	CDP
Christian Democratic Action for Social Justice [Namibia] [Political party] (EY)	CDA
Christian Democratic Labour Party [Grenada] [Political party] (EY)	CDLP
Christian Democratic Movement [Former Czechoslovakia] [Political party] (EY)	CDM
Christian Democratic Organisation of America [Venezuela] (EAIO)	CDOA
Christian Democratic Party [Italy] [Political party]	CDP
Christian Democratic People's Party [Hungary] [Political party] (EY)	CDPP
Christian Democratic Union [Czechoslavakia] [Political party] (ECON)	KDU
Christian Democratic Union of Central Europe [Former Czechoslovakia] (EAIO)	CDUCE
Christian Democratic World Union (EA)	CDWU
Christian Democrats [European political movement] (ECON)	CD
Christian Democrats (EY)	ChrDem
Christian Dental Society (EA)	CDS
Christian Dior [Couturier]	CD
Christian Doctors Sodality (EA)	CDS
Christian Economic and Social Research Foundation [British] (DI)	CESRF
Christian Education Movement [British]	CEM
Christian Education Publications [Australia]	CEP
Christian Educators Association International (EAIO)	CEAI
Christian Educators Fellowship [Later, CEAI] (EA)	CEF
Christian Endeavor (IIA)	CE
Christian Endeavor International (EA)	CEI
Christian Endeavor Union	CEU
Christian Endeavour Holiday Homes (SAUO)	CEHH
Christian Endeavour Society (SAUO)	CES
Christian Endeavour Union (SAUO)	CEU
Christian Endeavour Union of Great Britain and Ireland (SAUO)	CEUGBI
Christian era (SAUS)	CE
Christian Era	CE
Christian European Visual Media Association (EAIO)	CEVMA
Christian Evidence Society [British] (DBA)	CES
Christian Evidence Society (SAUO)	CES
Christian Family Life (EA)	CFL
Christian Family Movement (EA)	CFM
Christian Family Renewal (EA)	CFR
Christian Farmers Federation of Ontario [Federation des Agriculteurs Chretien de l'Ontario] (AC)	CFFO
Christian Feminists (EA)	CF
Christian Film Distributors Association (NTCM)	CFDA
Christian Focus on Government (EA)	CFG
Christian Forum Research Foundation [Later, CC] (EA)	CFRF
Christian Foundation for Children and Aging (EA)	CFCA
Christian Freedom Foundation (EA)	CFF
Christian Friends of Israel [British] (BI)	CFI
Christian Frontier Council (SAUO)	CFC
Christian Government Movement [Defunct] (EA)	CGM
Christian Herald Association (EA)	CHA
Christian Heritage Center (EA)	CHC
Christian Heritage College [El Cajon, CA]	CHC
Christian Heritage Library, El Cajon, CA [Library symbol] [Library of Congress] (LCLS)	CEcajC
Christian Heritage Party of Canada [Parti d'Heritage du Canada] (AC)	CHP
Christian Heritage Year [1984] [British]	CHY
Christian Holiness Association (EA)	CHA
Christian Home Educators Association (EA)	CHEA
Christian Homesteading Movement (EA)	CHM
Christian Instrumental Directors Association (EA)	CIDA
Christian Instrumentalists and Directors Association (EA)	CIDA
Christian Ireland Ministries (EA)	CIM
Christian Israelite Church [Australia]	CIC
Christian Jail Workers (EA)	CJW
Christian Knowledge Society [Also known as Society for Promoting Christian Knowledge]	CKS
Christian Labor Association of the United States of America (NTPA)	CLA-USA
Christian Labor Association of the United States of America (SAUO)	CLAUSA
Christian Labor Association of the USA (EA)	CLA

Christian Labour Association of Canada .... CLAC
Christian Law Association (EA) .... CLA
Christian Law Institute (EA) CLI
Christian Leaders for Responsible Television (NTCM) .... CLeaR-TV
Christian League for the Handicapped (EA) .... CLH
Christian Learning Materials Centre, Nairobi (SAUO) .... CLMC
Christian Legal Society (EA) .... CLS
Christian Librarians' Fellowship (EA) .... CLF
Christian Life and Ministry [*Canada*] .... CLM
Christian Life Centre [*Australia*] CLC
Christian Life Commission of the Southern Baptist Convention (EA) ..... CLCSBC
Christian Life Communities [*English Canada*] (AC) CLC
Christian Life Movement .... CLM
Christian Literacy Associates (EA) .... CLA
Christian Literature and Bible Center (EA) .... CLBC
Christian Literature Crusade [*British*] CLC
Christian Literature Crusade (International) [*Australia*] .... CLC(I)
Christian Literature Society for India and Africa (SAUO) .... CLS
Christian Macintosh Users Group (EA) .... CMUG
Christian Management Association (EA) .... CMA
Christian Management Report [*Christian Ministries Management Association*] [*A publication*] .... CMR
Christian Maternity Home Association (EA) .... CMHA
Christian Medical and Dental Society (EA) .... CMDS
Christian Medical Commission (EA) .... CMC
Christian Medical Council [*Defunct*] (EA) .... CMC
Christian Medical Fellowship [*British*] (DAVI) .... CMF
Christian Medical Foundation International (EA) .... CMF
Christian Medical Society [*Later, CMDS*] (EA) .... CMS
Christian Methodist Episcopal Church .... CME
Christian Methodist Episcopal Church .... CMEC
Christian Michelson Institute (SAUS) .... CMI
Christian Military Fellowship (EA) .... CMF
Christian Ministries Management Association [*Later, CMA*] (EA) .... CMMA
Christian Ministry Centre [*Australia*] .... CMC
[*A*] **Christian Ministry in the National Parks** (EA) .... ACMNP
Christian Mission (EA) .... CM
Christian Mission for the Deaf (EA) .... CMD
Christian Mission for the Deaf (EA) .... CMFD
Christian Mission to Buddhists [*See also NKB*] [*Arhus, Denmark*] (EAIO) ..... CMB
Christian Mission to the Communist World [*Australia*] .... CMCW
Christian Mission to the Communist World [*Australia*] .... CMTTCW
Christian Missionary Fellowship (EA) .... CMF
Christian Missions in Many Lands (EA) .... CMML
Christian Missions in Many Lands (SAUO) .... CMML
Christian Missions to the Communist World (EA) .... CMCW
Christian Mothers Association (SAUO) .... CMA
Christian Motorcyclist Association (EA) .... CMA
Christian Movement for Peace [*See also MCP*] [*Brussels, Belgium*] (EAIO) .... CMP
Christian National Education (SAUO) .... CNE
Christian National Party (SAUO) .... CNP
Christian Nationals' Evangelism Council [*Australia*] .... CNEC
Christian Observer (journ.) (SAUS) .... Chr Obs
Christian Organisation for Relief and Rehabilitation (SAUO) .... CORR
Christian Organisations Research and Advisory Trust [*Church of England*] .... CORAT
Christian Outdoorsman Association (EA) .... COA
Christian Overcomers [*An association*] (EA) .... CO
Christian Palestinian Aramaic (BJA) .... CPA
Christian Parent-Controlled Schools [*Australia*] .... CPCS
Christian Patriot Association (EA) .... CPA
Christian Peace Conference [*See also CCP*] [*Prague, Czechoslovakia*] (EAIO) .... CPC
[*The*] **Christian People's Party - Progressive and Fishing Industry Party** [*Kristiligi Folkaflokkurin, Foroya Framburds- og Fiskivinnuflokkurin*] [*The Faroe Islands*] [*Political party*] (EY) .... CPP-PFIP
Christian Periodical Index [*A publication*] .... CPI
Christian Pharmacists Fellowship International (EA) .... CPFI
Christian Pilots Association (EA) .... CPA
Christian Preaching Conference [*Defunct*] (EA) .... CPC
Christian Projects [*Australia*] .... CP
Christian Psychological Services [*Australia*] .... CPS
Christian Publicity Organisation [*British*] .... CPO
Christian Quarterly (journ.) (SAUS) .... Chr Q
Christian Quarterly Spectator (journ.) (SAUS) .... Chr Q Spec
Christian Record Benevolent Association (SAUO) .... CRB
Christian Record Benevolent Association [*Later, CRBF*] .... CRBA
Christian Record Braille Foundation [*Later, CRS*] (EA) .... CRBF
Christian Record Services (EA) .... CRS
Christian Reformed Church .... CRC
Christian Reformed Church in North America (AC) .... CRCNA
Christian Reformed Church World Literature Ministries (EA) .... CRCWLM
Christian Reformed World Relief Committee (EA) .... CRWRC
Christian Relief and Development Agency (SAUO) .... CRDA
Christian Relief and Development Association [*Ethiopia*] .... CRDA
Christian Renewal Ministry (EA) .... CRM
Christian Renewal Outreach [*Australia*] .... CRO
Christian Republican Party [*Bulgaria*] [*Political party*] .... CRP
Christian Rescue Effort for the Emancipation of Dissidents [*Acronym now used as organization name*] (EA) .... CREED
Christian Research (EA) .... CR
Christian Research Association (WDAA) .... CRA
Christian Research Institute (EA) .... CRI
Christian Research Institute International (EA) .... CRI
Christian Response International (EA) .... CRI
Christian Restoration Association (EA) .... CRA
Christian Revival Fellowship [*Australia*] .... CRF
Christian Road Safety League [*British*] (BI) .... CRSL
Christian Rural Fellowship [*Defunct*] (EA) .... CRF
Christian Rural Fellowship of East Africa (SAUO) .... CREFA
Christian Rural Overseas Program [*Acronym is now the official name of organization*] (EA) .... CROP
Christian Schools' Association [*Australia*] .... CSA
Christian Schools International (EA) .... CSI
Christian Science .... CS
Christian Science (SAUO) .... CS
Christian Science Bachelor (SAUO) .... CSB
Christian Science Committee on Publications (SAUS) .... CSCP
Christian Science Journal (journ.) (SAUS) .... CSJ
Christian Science Monitor (SAUO) .... CSM
Christian Science Monitor [*A publication*] (BRI) .... CSM
Christian Science Monitor Section (journ.) (SAUS) .... CSMMS
Christian Science Organisation (SAUO) .... CSO
Christian Science Publishing Society (EA) .... CSPS
Christian Science Reading Room, Cleveland, OH [*Library symbol*] [*Library of Congress*] (LCLS) .... OClCh
Christian Science Reading Room, Montreal, PQ, Canada [*Library symbol*] [*Library of Congress*] (LCLS) .... CaQMCS
Christian Science Reading Room, Montreal, Quebec [*Library symbol*] [*National Library of Canada*] (NLC) .... QMCS
Christian Science Visiting Nurse Service New South Wales [*Australia*] .... CSVNSNSW
Christian Scientist (SAUS) .... CS
Christian Scientist .... SC
Christian Service Brigade (EA) .... CSB
Christian Service Club (EA) .... CSC
Christian Service Corps [*Defunct*] (EA) .... CSC
Christian Services for the Blind [*Australia*] .... CSB
Christian Services for the Hearing Impaired [*Australia*] .... CSHI
[*The*] **Christian Sisters (Pious Union)** (TOCD) .... CS
Christian Social Council (SAUO) .... CSC
Christian Social Union [*Germany*] .... CSU
Christian Social-Democratic Party (SAUO) .... CSDP
Christian Socialist (EY) .... ChrSoc
Christian Solidarity International [*Zurich, Switzerland*] (EAIO) .... CSI
Christian Solidarity International, U.S.A. (EA) .... CSIUSA
Christian Syndrome [*Medicine*] (DMAA) .... CHRS
Christian Television Association of New South Wales [*Australia*] .... CTVANSW
Christian Television Association of South Australia .... CTASA
Christian Television Mission (EA) .... CTM
Christian Temperance Council for the Nordic Countries (EA) .... CTCNC
Christian Theological Seminary, Indianapolis, IN [*Library symbol*] [*Library of Congress*] (LCLS) .... InIT
Christian Theological Seminary, Indianapolis, IN [*OCLC symbol*] (OCLC) ...... IXT
Christian Union [*University student group*] [*British*] .... CU
Christian Urgent Action Network for Emergency Support-Philippines (SAUO) .... CUANES-Philippines
Christian Veterinary Mission (GVA) .... CVM
Christian Veterinary Missions of Canada (GVA) .... CVMC
Christian Voice (EA) CV
Christian Volunteer Ministries (EA) .... CVM
Christian Welfare and Social Relief Organization [*Sierra Leone*] (EAIO) .... CWASRO
Christian Welfare Hospital, East St. Louis, IL [*Library symbol*] [*Library of Congress*] (LCLS) .... IEsCH
Christian Witness International [*British*] .... CWI
Christian Women's Fellowship (EA) .... CWF
Christian Women's Movement [*Bulgaria*] [*Political party*] .... CWM
Christian Women's National Concerns [*Defunct*] (EA) .... CWNC
Christian Workers Fellowship [*Sri Lanka*] (EAIO) .... CWF
Christian Workers Party [*Malta*] [*Political party*] (PPE) .... CWP
Christian World Communion Executives Conference (SAUO) .... CWC
Christian Yellow Pages [*A publication*] .... CYP
Christian Youth Travel Association [*Australia*] .... CYTA
Christiana [*City in South Africa*] (ROG) .... CR
Christiana Companies, Inc. [*Associated Press*] (SAG) .... Christn
[*The*] **Christiana Companies, Inc.** [*NYSE symbol*] (SPSG) .... CST
Christiana, DE [*FM radio station call letters*] .... WXHL
Christian-Albrechts-Universitat Kiel, Kiel, Germany [*Library symbol*] [*Library of Congress*] (LCLS) .... GyKiU
Christianburg, VA [*FM radio station call letters*] .... WBNK
Christianburg, VA [*FM radio station call letters*] (BROA) .... WBZV-FM
Christiane Fabre de Morlhon [*Information service name CFM Documentazione*] (IID) .... CFM
Christianity .... XNTY
Christianity .... XTY
Christianity (GEAB) .... Xty
Christianity Today [*A publication*] (BRI) .... Ch Today
Christian-Muslim Dialogue Committee (EA) .... CMDC
Christians (SAUS) .... Xians
Christians Associated for Relationships with Eastern Europe (EA) .... CAREE
Christian's Bankrupt Law [*A publication*] (DLA) .... Chris BL
Christian's Charges to Grand Juries [*A publication*] (DLA) .... Chr Ch
Christians Concerned for Israel [*Superseded by NCLCI*] (EA) CCI
Christians for Peace in El Salvador (EA) .... CRISPAZ
Christians for Socialism in the United States (EA) .... CFS
Christians for the Upliftment of the Poor (SAUO) .... CUP International
Christians Heeding Righteousness Instead of Satanic Tyranny .... CHRIST
Christians in Crisis (EA) CC
Christians in Futures [*Defunct*] (EA) .... CF

Christians in Government (EA) ... CG
Christians in Government [*An association*] (EA) ... CIG
Christians in the Arts Networking (EA) ... CAN
Christians' Israel Public Action Campaign (EA) ... CIPAC
Christians United for Responsible Entertainment (EA) ... CURE
Christiansburg, VA [*AM radio station call letters*] (RBYB) ... WNNI
Christiansburg, WA [*AM radio station call letters*] (BROA) ... WWVT
Christianshab [*Greenland*] [*ICAO location identifier*] (ICLI) ... BGCH
Christianskii Wostok [*A publication*] (BJA) ... ChrWo
Christiansted National Historic Site ... CHRI
Christiansted, St. Croix, VI [*Location identifier*] [*FAA*] (FAAL) ... STX
Christiansted, VI [*FM radio station call letters*] ... WAVI
Christiansted, VI [*Television station call letters*] (BROA) ... WCVI-TV
Christiansted, VI [*FM radio station call letters*] ... WIVH
Christiansted, VI [*FM radio station call letters*] ... WJKC
Christiansted, VI [*FM radio station call letters*] (BROA) ... WMNG-FM
Christiansted, VI [*AM radio station call letters*] ... WSTX
Christiansted, VI [*FM radio station call letters*] ... WSTX-FM
Christiansted, VI [*Television station call letters*] ... WSVI
Christiansted, VI [*FM radio station call letters*] ... WVIQ
Christiansted, VI [*FM radio station call letters*] ... WVIS
Christian-Weber [*Disease*] [*Medicine*] (DB) ... CW
Christic Institute (EA) ... CI
Christie, Atkins, Munch-Peterson Test [*Bacteriology*] ... CAMP
Christie Home Historical Society, Long Prairie, MN [*Library symbol*] [*Library of Congress*] (LCLS) ... MnLpCHi
Christie Township Public Library, Parry Sound, Ontario [*Library symbol*] [*National Library of Canada*] (NLC) ... OPSCT
Christie's Contemporary Art [*Reproductions*] [*London, England*] ... CCA
Christie's Precedents of Wills [*A publication*] (DLA) ... Chr Pr W
Christina Exploration [*Vancouver Stock Exchange symbol*] ... KRX
Christlich Demokratische Union/Christlich Soziale Union [*Christian Democratic Union/Christian Social Union*] [*Germany*] [*Political party*] (PPE) ... CDU/CSU
Christlich Soziale Partei [*Christian Social Party*] [*Liechtenstein*] [*Political party*] (PPW) ... CSP
Christlich-Demokratische Union [*Christian Democratic Union*] [*Germany*] [*Political party*] (PPW) ... CDU
Christlichdemokratische Volkspartei der Schweiz [*Christian Democratic Party of Switzerland*] [*Political party*] (PPE) ... CVP
Christliche Bayerische Volkspartei - Bayerische Patriotenbewegung [*Christian Bavarian People's Party - Movement of Bavarian Patriots*] [*Germany*] [*Political party*] (PPW) ... CBV
Christliche Volkspartei [*Christian People's Party*] [*Pre-1945 Germany*] [*Political party*] (PPE) ... CVP
Christliche Waehlerunion Bayern [*Christian Voters' Union of Bavaria*] [*Germany*] [*Political party*] (PPW) ... CWU
Christliche-Sozialistische Arbeitsgemeinschaft [*Christian Social-Workers' Community*] [*Lithuania*] [*Political party*] (PPE) ... CSA
Christlich-Nationaler Gewerkschaftsbund der Schweiz [*Swiss Federation of National-Christian Trade Unions*] ... CNGS
Christlich-Soziale Union [*Political party in Bavaria connected with the CDU*] [*West Germany*] ... CSU
Christlich-Soziale Waehler Union im Saarland [*Christian Social Voters' Union in Saarland*] [*Germany*] [*Political party*] (PPW) ... CSWU
Christman Air System [*ICAO designator*] (FAAC) ... CAS
Christman Air System [*ICAO designator*] (AD) ... SX
Christmas (SAUS) ... Christ
Christmas ... XM
Christmas ... XMAS
Christmas and Easter [*Refers to Church of England members who attend church only on those days*] (DSUE) ... C and E
Christmas Bird Count [*National Audubon Society*] ... CBC
Christmas Club (EA) ... CC
Christmas Factor [*Also, PTC*] [*Hematology*] ... CF
Christmas Factor (SAUS) ... X-mas Factor
Christmas, FL [*AM radio station call letters*] ... WORL
Christmas Interational House (SAUS) ... CIH
Christmas Island [*Australia*] [*ICAO location identifier*] (ICLI) ... APXM
Christmas Island (SAUS) ... CI
Christmas Island [*ANSI two-letter standard code*] (CNC) ... CX
Christmas Island [*Kiribati*] [*Airport symbol*] (OAG) ... CXI
Christmas Island [*ANSI three-letter standard code*] (CNC) ... CXR
Christmas Island [*Indian Ocean*] [*MARC geographic area code*] [*Library of Congress*] (LCCP) ... i-xa-
Christmas Island [*Indian Ocean*] [*MARC country of publication code*] [*Library of Congress*] (LCCP) ... xa
Christmas Island [*Airport symbol*] ... XCH
Christmas Island [*Seismograph station code, US Geological Survey*] (SEIS) ... XMI
Christmas Island Administration and Assembly [*Australia*] ... CIAA
Christmas Island Arbitrator ... CIA
Christmas Island Services Corp. ... CISC
Christmas Island Station [*Military*] (SAA) ... CIS
Christmas Philatelic Club (EA) ... CPC
Christmas Seal and Charity Stamp Society (EA) ... CS & CSS
Christmas Seal and Charity Stamp Society (SAUO) ... CS&CSS
Christmas Study Unit [*American Topical Association*] (EA) ... CSU
[*A*] **Christmas Trains and Trucks Program** [*Marine Corps program in Vietnam*] ... ACTT
Christmas Tree Pattern ... CTP
Christopher Burns, Inc. [*Also, an information service or system*] (IID) ... CBI
Christopher Columbus High School (SAUS) ... CCHS
Christopher Columbus Philatelic Society (EA) ... CCPS
Christopher Davies [*Publisher*] [*British*] ... CD
Christopher, IL [*FM radio station call letters*] ... WUEZ
Christopher Morley Knothole Association (EA) ... CMKA
Christopher Newport College, Newport News, VA [*OCLC symbol*] (OCLC) ... VCN
Christopher Newport College, Newport News, VA [*Library symbol*] [*Library of Congress*] (LCLS) ... ViNeC
Christopher Robinson's English Admiralty Reports [*165 English Reprint*] [*A publication*] (DLA) ... Chr Rob
Christopher Robinson's English Admiralty Reports [*165 English Reprint*] [*A publication*] (DLA) ... C Rob
Christopher Robinson's English Admiralty Reports [*165 English Reprint*] [*A publication*] (DLA) ... C Rob Adm
Christopher Robinson's English Admiralty Reports [*165 English Reprint*] [*A publication*] (DLA) ... C Rob (Eng)
Christophorus Lanfranchinus [*Deceased, 1490*] [*Authority cited in pre-1607 legal work*] (DSA) ... Christ Lanfran
Christos Lavatus [*An association*] (EA) ... CL
Christ's College [*Cambridge University*] (ROG) ... CH COLL
Christ's College (Cambridge University) (ROG) ... CCC
Christschall [*Record label*] [*Austria*] ... Chr
Christ-Siemens-Touraine [*Syndrome*] [*Medicine*] (DB) ... CST
Christus [*Christ*] [*Latin*] ... X
Christus [*Christ*] [*Latin*] ... XPC
Christus [*Christ*] [*Latin*] ... XS
Christus Dominus [*Decree on the Bishops' Pastoral Office in the Church*] [*Vatican II document*] ... CD
Chritiania Bank og Kreditkasse [*Bank*] [*Norway*] ... K
Chrom Vanadium (SAUS) ... CR VAN
Chroma Sweep Signal (SAUS) ... CSS
Chroma Time Compressed Multiplex (NTCM) ... CTCM
Chromacom Proof Recorder (DGA) ... CPR
Chromaffin Granule Amine Transporter [*Biochemistry*] ... CGAT
Chromalloy American Corp. (SAUO) ... CRO
Chromate (MSA) ... CRMT
Chromate Sensitivity [*Immunology*] ... CS
Chromated Copper Arsenate [*Wood preservative*] ... CCA
Chromated Zinc Chloride [*Wood preservative*] ... CZC
Chromatic Aberration-Free [*Optics*] ... CF
Chromaticity Color Triangle with Hue and Saturation (SAUS) ... CCTHS
Chromatics Color Sci Wrrt [*NASDAQ symbol*] (TTSB) ... CCSIW
Chromatics Color Sciences [*NASDAQ symbol*] (TTSB) ... CCSI
Chromatics Color Sciences International, Inc. [*NASDAQ symbol*] (SAG) ... CCSI
Chromatics Color Sciences International, Inc. [*Associated Press*] (SAG) ... ChmCS
Chromatics Color Sciences International, Inc. [*Associated Press*] (SAG) ... ChromCS
Chromatid Breaks (SAUS) ... CB
Chromatid Gaps (SAUS) ... CG
Chromatid Interchange (PDAA) ... CI
Chromatin Assembly Factor [*Genetics*] ... CAF
Chromatin Protein [*Biochemistry*] ... CP
Chromatin-Accessibility Complex [*Genetics*] ... CHRAC
Chromatofocusing [*Analytical biochemistry*] ... CRF
Chromatogram Automatic Soaking, Scanning and Digital Recording Apparatus (SAUS) ... CASSANDRA
Chromatographia [*A publication*] ... Chromia
Chromatographic Optimization Function [*Analytical chemistry*] ... COF
Chromatographic Response Factor ... CRF
Chromatographic Separation ... CGS
Chromatographic Specialties Ltd., Brockville, ON, Canada [*Library symbol*] [*Library of Congress*] (LCLS) ... CaOBCS
Chromatographic Specialties Ltd., Brockville, Ontario [*Library symbol*] [*National Library of Canada*] (NLC) ... OBCS
Chromatography Control Module [*Instrumentation*] ... CCM
Chromatography Laboratory Automatic Software ... CLAS
Chromatography Signal Interface ... CSI
Chromatopyrography [*for polymer characterization*] ... CPG
Chromcraft Revington [*NYSE symbol*] (TTSB) ... CRC
Chromcraft Revington, Inc. [*Associated Press*] (SAG) ... Chrcft
Chromcraft Revington, Inc. [*NYSE symbol*] (SAG) ... CRC
Chrome (ROG) ... CHR
Chrome (VRA) ... chr
Chrome (MSA) ... CRM
Chrome and Nickel Plating Logistics Automated Test Electronics System (MCD) ... CANPLATES
Chrome Card Collectors Club [*Later, D of A*] (EA) ... CCCC
Chrome Molybdenum (SAUS) ... CR MOLY
Chrome Oxide (SAUS) ... Cr O
Chrome Plated (SAUS) ... Chro Pltd
Chrome Plated [*Freight*] ... CHRO PLTD
Chrome Plated ... CP
Chrome Tanned Leather (SAUS) ... cr tan lthr
Chrome Vanadium ... CRV
Chrome Vanadium ... CRVAN
Chrome Wire Wheels [*Automotive accessory*] ... CWW
Chromemoly ... CroMo
Chromex Nickel Mines Ltd. [*Vancouver Stock Exchange symbol*] ... CXN
Chromic Acid [*Inorganic chemistry*] (OA) ... CA
Chrominance [*Video monitor*] ... C
Chrominance Time-Compression Multiplexing (SAUS) ... CTCM
Chromite [*CIPW classification*] [*Geology*] ... cm
Chromite (SAUS) ... Cr
Chromium [*Chemical symbol is Cr*] (MSA) ... CHR
Chromium [*Chemical symbol is Cr*] ... CHROM
chromium (SAUS) ... chrom
Chromium [*Chemical element*] ... Cr
Chromium Oxalate [*Organic chemistry*] ... CROX

Chromium Plate [*Metallurgy*] .... CRPL
Chromium Release Assay [*Clinical chemistry*] .... CRA
Chrom-Moly (MCD) .... CM
Chrom-Molybdenum (SAUS) .... CM
Chromobacterium (SAUS) .... CHR
Chromobacterium (MAE) .... Chr
Chromogenic (WGA) .... CH
Chromogenic Systems Analyzer .... CSA
Chromogranin [*Biochemistry*] .... Cg
Chromogranin A [*Biochemistry*] .... CGA
Chromographic Mode Sequencing [*Chromatography*] .... CMS
Chromolithograph (VRA) .... chlith
Chromolithograph (DSUE) .... CHRO
Chromolithograph (ROG) .... CHROMO
Chromolithograph (SAUS) .... Chromo
Chromophore-Assisted LASER Inactivation [*Analytical biochemistry*] .... CALI
Chromosomal Expression Vector [*Genetics*] .... CEV
Chromosomal Fraction .... CF
Chromosomal Gonadal Dysgenesis [*Genetics*] (AAMN) .... CGD
Chromosomal In Situ Suppression [*Genetics*] .... CISS
Chromosomal Ribonucleic Acid (STED) .... cRNA
Chromosomal Ribonucleid Acid (SAUS) .... CRNA
Chromosomally-Mediated Resistant Neisseria Gonorrhoeae [*Medicine*] .... CMRNG
Chromosome [*Genetics*] .... Chrom
Chromosome and Plant Cell Division in Space (SAUS) .... CHROMEX
Chromosome Coordinating Meeting (HGEN) .... CCM
Chromosome Distribution Pattern [*Genetics*] .... CDP
Chromosome Eight Trisomy Syndrome [*Medicine*] (MELL) .... CETS
Chromosome Eighteen Trisomy Syndrome [*Medicine*] (MELL) .... CETS
Chromosome Information System [*Genetics*] .... CIS
Chromosome Interphase Staining [*Medicine*] .... CHIPS
Chromosome Mapping [*Medicine*] (MELL) .... CM
Chromosome Modification Site [*Genetics*] (DAVI) .... CMS
Chromosome Number (SAUS) .... CN
Chromosome-Doubled Haploid (SAUS) .... DH
Chromosome-Mediated Gene Transfer [*Biochemistry*] .... CMGT
Chromosomes and Plant Cell Division in Space Experiment (SAUO) .... CHROMEX
Chromospheric Hel Imaging Photometer (SAUS) .... CHIP
Chromospheric Variability Monitor (SAUS) .... CVM
Chromotropic Acid (MAE) .... CTA
Chrondroitin Sulfate Proteoglycans [*Biochemistry*] .... CSPG
Chrondroitin Sulphuric Acid (DB) .... CHS
Chronic [*Medicine*] .... CH
Chronic [*Medicine*] (DMAA) .... ch
Chronic [*Medicine*] .... CHR
chronic (SAUS) .... chr
Chronic [*Medicine*] (AAMN) .... chron
Chronic Abdominal Tympany [*Medicine*] (AAMN) .... CAT
Chronic, Acquired, Pure Red Cell Aplasia [*Medicine*] (DMAA) .... CAPRCA
Chronic Active Autoimmune Hepatitis [*Medicine*] (DMAA) .... CAAH
Chronic Active Hepatitis [*Medicine*] .... CAH
Chronic Active Hepatitis Type B [*Medicine*] .... CAHB
Chronic Active Liver Disease [*Medicine*] .... CALD
Chronic Adrenal Insufficiency [*Medicine*] (MELL) .... CAI
Chronic Affliction Serum Hepatitis [*Medicine*] .... CASH
Chronic Aggressive Hepatitis [*Medicine*] (MEDA) .... CAH
Chronic Airflow Limitation [*Medicine*] .... CAL
Chronic Airway Obstruction [*Medicine*] .... CAO
Chronic Alcoholic Pancreatitis [*Medicine*] (MELL) .... CAP
Chronic Ambulatory Peritoneal Dialysis [*Medicine*] .... CAPD
Chronic Anovulation Syndrome [*Medicine*] (MEDA) .... CAS
Chronic Articular Rheumatism [*Medicine*] (DB) .... CAR
Chronic Atrophic Gastritis [*Medicine*] .... CAG
Chronic Bacterial Prostatitis [*Medicine*] (MELL) .... CBP
Chronic Bed Rest [*Medicine*] .... CBR
Chronic Benign Mucous Membrane Pemphigoid [*Medicine*] .... CBMMP
Chronic Benign Neutropenia [*Hematology*] (DAVI) .... CBN
Chronic Beryllium Disease [*Medicine*] (MCD) .... CBD
Chronic Biological False-Positive (SAUS) .... CBFP
Chronic Brain Syndrome [*Medicine*] .... CBS
chronic brain syndrome (SAUS) .... ch br syn
Chronic Brain Syndrome [*Medicine*] .... CHRBRSYN
Chronic Bronchitis [*Medicine*] .... CB
Chronic Bronchitis and Asthma [*Medicine*] .... CBA
Chronic Bullous Disease of Children [*Medicine*] (DMAA) .... CBDC
Chronic Calcific Pancreatitis [*Medicine*] .... CCP
Chronic Calculous Cholecystitis [*Medicine*] (MAE) CCC
Chronic Cardiac Failure (SAUS) .... CCF
Chronic Catarrhal Colitis [*Medicine*] (MELL) CCC
Chronic Catarrhal Tonsillitis [*Medicine*] (MELL) .... CCT
Chronic Cerebellar Stimulation [*Medicine*] .... CCS
Chronic Cerebrovascular Disease [*Medicine*] (DMAA) .... CCVD
Chronic Cholestatic Liver Disease [*Medicine*] .... CCLD
Chronic Cigarette Cough (MELL) CCC
Chronic Complainer [*Medicine*] (DMAA) CC
Chronic Constrictive Pericarditis [*Medicine*] (MELL) .... CCP
Chronic Coronary Insufficiency [*Medicine*] CCI
Chronic Cutaneous (Discoid) Lupus Erythematosus [*Medicine*] .... CCLE
Chronic Daily Headache [*Neurology*] (DAVI) .... CDH
Chronic Daily Intake (SAUS) .... CDI
Chronic Degenerative Disease [*Medicine*] (DB) .... CDD
Chronic Destructive Periodontitis [*Medicine*] (MELL) .... CDP
Chronic Dialysis [*Medicine*] (MELL) .... CD
Chronic Diarrhea [*Medicine*] (MELL) .... CD
Chronic Diffuse Interstitial Lung Disease [*Medicine*] (DMAA) .... CDILD
Chronic Disabling Dermatoses [*Medicine*] .... CDD
Chronic Discoid Lupus Erythematosus [*Medicine*] (DMAA) .... CDLE
Chronic Disease Facility [*Medicine*] .... CDF
Chronic Disease Notes and Reports (SAUO) .... CDNR
Chronic Diseases in Canada (SAUS) .... CDIC
Chronic Dislocating Shoulder [*Medicine*] (MELL) .... CDS
Chronic Disseminated Candidiasis [*Medicine*] (MELL) .... CDC
Chronic Ectopic Atrial Tachycardia [*Medicine*] (DMAA) .... CEAT
Chronic Electrophysiological Study [*Medicine*] (DB) .... CES
Chronic Endstage Renal Disease [*Nephrology*] .... CERD
Chronic Enthusiasm Disorder [*Medicine*] (MEDA) .... CED
Chronic Eosinophilic Pneumonia [*Medicine*] (MELL) .... CEP
Chronic Epstein-Barr Virus [*Medicine*] .... CEBV
Chronic Ethanolism [*Chemical dependency*] (DAVI) .... Chr Etoh
Chronic Exertional Compartment Syndrome [*Medicine*] .... CECS
Chronic False Positive [*Test*] [*Medicine*] .... CFP
Chronic Fatigue and Immune Dysfunction Syndrome (SAUS) .... CFIDS
Chronic Fatigue and Immune Dysfunction Syndrome Association of America (SAUO) .... CFIDS
Chronic Fatigue Immune Disfunction Syndrome Activation Network (EA) .... CAN
Chronic Fatigue Immune Dysfunction Syndrome [*Medicine*] .... CFIDS
Chronic Fatigue Immune Dysfunction Syndrome Association (EA) .... CFIDSA
Chronic Fatigue Syndrome [*Medicine*] .... CFS
Chronic Fatigue Syndrome Society (SAUO) .... CFSS
Chronic Fatigue Syndrome Society, International (EA) .... CFSS
Chronic Fibrous Thyroiditis [*Medicine*] (MELL) .... CFT
Chronic Follicular Gastritis [*Medicine*] (MELL) .... CFG
Chronic Foot Dermatitis [*Medicine*] (MELL) .... CFD
Chronic Freshwater Toxicity Level (ABAC) .... CFWTL
Chronic Gastrointestinal [*Tract*] **Bleeding** [*Gastroenterology*] (DAVI) .... CGB
Chronic Glomerulonephritis [*Medicine*] .... CG
Chronic Glomerulonephritis [*Medicine*] .... CGN
Chronic Glomerulonephritis [*Nephrology*] (DAVI) .... Ch GN
Chronic Gonadotropin, Beta-Unit [*Medicine*] (DMAA) .... CGB
Chronic Graft-Versus-Host Disease [*Medicine*] .... CGVHD
Chronic Granulocytic Leukemia [*Medicine*] .... CGL
Chronic Granulomatous Disease [*Medicine*] .... CGD
Chronic Granulomatous Disorder (SAUO) .... CGD
Chronic Granulomatous Inflammation [*Medicine*] (DB) .... CGI
Chronic Granumalatous Disease (SAUS) .... CGD
Chronic Heart Failure [*Cardiology*] (DAVI) .... CHF
Chronic Hemodialysis [*Nephrology*] .... CHD
Chronic Hemolytic Anemia [*Medicine*] .... CHA
Chronic Hepatic Encephalopathy [*Medicine*] (MELL) .... CHE
Chronic Hepatitis (MELL) .... CH
Chronic Hepatitis B [*Medicine*] (DMAA) .... CHB
Chronic Hypertension (MELL) .... CH
Chronic Hypertrophic Emphysema [*Medicine*] (MELL) .... CHE
Chronic Hypoxic Lung Disease [*Medicine*] (DMAA) .... CHLD
Chronic Idiopathic Anhidrosis [*Medicine*] (DAVI) .... CIA
Chronic Idiopathic Intesinal Pseudo-Obstruction Syndrome [*Medicine*] (DMAA) .... CIIPS
Chronic Idiopathic Megacolon [*Medicine*] (MELL) .... CIM
Chronic Idiopathic Thrombocytopenic Purpura [*Medicine*] .... CITP
Chronic Idiopathic Ulcerative Colitis [*Gastroenterology*] .... CIUC
Chronic Idiopathic Urticaria [*Dermatology*] (DAVI) .... CIU
Chronic Infantile Neurological Cutaneous and Auricular [*Syndrome*] [*Medicine*] (DMAA) .... CINCA
Chronic Infectious Neuropathic Agents [*Medicine*] .... CHINA
Chronic Inflammatory Bowel Disease [*Medicine*] .... CIBD
Chronic Inflammatory Cell [*Medicine*] (MELL) CIC
Chronic Inflammatory Demyelinating Polyradiculoneuropathy [*Neurology*] (DAVI) .... CIDP
Chronic Inflammatory Polyneuropathy [*Medicine*] (DMAA) .... CIPN
Chronic Intermittent Peritoneal Dialysis [*Medicine*] (MELL) .... CIPD
Chronic Interstitial Nephritis [*Medicine*] (MAE) .... CIN
Chronic Intestinal Ischemia [*Medicine*] (MELL) CII
Chronic Intestinal Pseudoobstruction [*Medicine*] (MELL) .... CIP
Chronic Intractable Benign Pain [*Medicine*] (DMAA) .... CIBP
Chronic Intractable Benign Pain Syndrome [*Medicine*] (DMAA) .... CIBPS
Chronic Intractable Shoulder Pain (MELL) .... CISP
Chronic Irritant Contact Dermatitis (MELL) .... CICD
Chronic Ischemic Heart Disease [*Medicine*] (MELL) .... CIHD
Chronic Leukemia [*Hematology and oncology*] (DAVI) CL
Chronic Liver Disease [*Medicine*] .... CLD
Chronic Lobular Hepatitis [*Medicine*] (MAE) .... CLH
Chronic Low Back Pain [*Medicine*] (DMAA) .... CLBP
Chronic Lung Disease [*Medicine*] .... CLD
Chronic Lyme Disease .... CLD
Chronic Lymphatic [*or Lymphocytic*] **Leukemia** [*Medicine*] CLL
Chronic Lymphocytic Leukemia Foundation (SAUO) .... CLL Foundation
Chronic Lymphocytic Thyroiditis [*Medicine*] .... CLT
Chronic Lymphosarcoma Cell Leukemia [*Medicine*] (MAE) .... CLSL
Chronic Lymphosarcoma Leukemia (SAUS) .... CLSL
Chronic Maxillary Sinusitis [*Medicine*] (MELL) .... CMS
Chronic Megakaryocytic Granulocytic Myelosis [*Medicine*] .... CMGM
Chronic Membranoproliferative Glomerulonephritis [*Immunology*] .... CMPGN
Chronic Membranous Glomerulonephritis [*Medicine*] (MAE) .... CMGN
Chronic Mental Defective [*British*] (ADA) .... CMD
Chronic Mental Patient (SAUS) .... Cmp
Chronic Mesenteric Ischemia [*Medicine*] .... CMI
Chronic Metabolic Acidosis (STED) .... CMA

Chronic Minamata Disease [*Medicine*] ..... CMD
Chronic Monoblastic Leukemia [*Hematology and oncology*] (DAVI) ..... CMoL
Chronic Monocytic Leukemia [*Medicine*] (MAE) ..... CMoL
Chronic Monocytic Leukemia [*Medicine*] (MELL) ..... CMOL
Chronic Motor (STED) ..... CMT
Chronic Mucocutaneous Candidiasis [*Medicine*] ..... CMC
Chronic Mucocutaneous Candidiasis [*Medicine*] (DMAA) ..... CMCC
Chronic Mucocutaneous Moniliasis [*Medicine*] (DAVI) ..... CMC
Chronic Mucopurulent Bronchitis [*Medicine*] (MELL) ..... CMPB
Chronic Myelocytic [*or Myeloid or Myelogenous*] **Leukemia** [*Oncology*] ..... CML
Chronic Myelodysplastic Syndrome [*Medicine*] (MELL) ..... CMS
Chronic Myelogenous Leukemia [*Medicine*] ..... CML
Chronic Myeloid Leukemia in Blast Crisis [*Medicine*] (DB) ..... CML-BC
Chronic Myelomonocytic Leukemia [*Oncology*] ..... CMML
Chronic Myelomonocytic Leukemia in Transition [*Oncology*] ..... CMMLIT
Chronic Myeloproliferative Disorder [*Medicine*] (DMAA) ..... CMPD
Chronic Narrow Angle Glaucoma (MELL) ..... CNAG
Chronic Nerve Irritation [*Medicine*] (DMAA) ..... CNI
Chronic Nervous Exhaustion [*Medicine*] ..... CNE
Chronic Nervous Exhaustion Syndrome [*Medicine*] (DMAA) ..... CNES
Chronic Neutrophilic Leukemia [*Medicine*] (MELL) ..... CNL
Chronic Nodular Fibrositis [*Medicine*] (DMAA) ..... CNF
Chronic Nonspecific Diarrhea [*Medicine*] ..... CNSD
Chronic Nonspecific Diarrhea of Childhood [*Medicine*] (MELL) ..... CNDC
Chronic Nonspecific Lung Disease (CPH) ..... CNSLD
Chronic Nonvalvular Atrial Fibrillation [*Medicine*] (DMAA) ..... CNAF
Chronic Obstruction of Biliary Tract [*Medicine*] ..... COBT
Chronic Obstructive Airflow Limitation [*Medicine*] (DMAA) ..... COAL
Chronic Obstructive Airway Disease [*Medicine*] ..... COAD
Chronic Obstructive Arterial Disease [*Cardiology*] (DAVI) ..... COAD
Chronic Obstructive Bronchitis [*Medicine*] (DMAA) ..... COB
Chronic Obstructive Lung Disease [*Medicine*] ..... COLD
Chronic Obstructive Outflow Disease [*Medicine*] ..... COOD
Chronic Obstructive Pulmonary Disease [*Medicine*] ..... COPD
Chronic Obstructive Pulmonary Emphysema [*Medicine*] ..... COPE
Chronic Obstructive Respiratory Disease [*Medicine*] ..... CORD
Chronic Obstructive Uropathy [*Medicine*] (MELL) ..... COU
Chronic Open Angle Glaucoma [*Ophthalmology*] ..... COAG
Chronic Open Angle Glaucoma (STED) ..... coag
Chronic Opioid Medication [*Medicine*] (MELL) ..... COM
Chronic Organic Brain Syndrome [*Medicine*] ..... COBS
Chronic Osteomyelitis [*Medicine*] (MELL) ..... COM
Chronic Otitis Media [*Medicine*] ..... COM
Chronic Pain (DAVI) ..... CP
Chronic Pain Anonymous [*Self-help program*] ..... CPA
Chronic Pain Center (MELL) ..... CPC
Chronic Pain Disorder (MELL) ..... CPD
Chronic Pain Support Group (EA) ..... CPSG
Chronic Pancreatic Insufficiency [*Medicine*] ..... CPI
Chronic Pancreatitis [*Medicine*] (PDAA) ..... CP
Chronic Paroxysmal Hemicrania [*Medicine*] (MELL) ..... CPH
Chronic Passive Congestion [*Medicine*] ..... CPC
Chronic Pelvic Inflammatory Disease [*Gynecology*] (DAVI) ..... CPID
Chronic Pelvic Pain (MELL) ..... CPP
Chronic Peritoneal Dialysis [*Medicine*] (MELL) ..... CPD
Chronic Persistent Hepatitis [*Medicine*] ..... CPH
Chronic Pharyngitis [*Medicine*] (MELL) ..... CP
Chronic Pigmented Purpura [*Medicine*] (MELL) ..... CPP
Chronic Pleurisy (MELL) ..... CP
Chronic Polyarthritis [*Medicine*] (MELL) ..... CP
Chronic Polyneuropathy [*Medicine*] (AAMN) ..... CPN
Chronic Post-Traumatic Headache [*Neurology*] (DAVI) ..... CPTH
Chronic Progressive [*Medicine*] ..... CP
Chronic Progressive Coccidioidal Pneumonitis [*Medicine*] ..... CPCP
Chronic Progressive External Ophthalmoplegia [*Ophthalmology*] ..... CPEO
Chronic Progressive Multiple Sclerosis [*Medicine*] (DMAA) ..... CPMS
Chronic Progressive Myelopathy [*Medicine*] (MELL) ..... CPM
Chronic Progressive Renal Disease [*Medicine*] (CPH) ..... CPRD
Chronic Proliferative Glomerulonephritis [*Immunology*] ..... CPGN
Chronic Prostatitis Syndrome [*Medicine*] (MELL) ..... CPS
Chronic Protein Deprivation [*Medicine*] (MELL) ..... CPD
Chronic Pulmonary Disease (BARN) ..... CPD
Chronic Pulmonary Emphysema [*Medicine*] ..... CPE
Chronic Pulmonary Insufficiency of Prematurity [*Medicine*] (DMAA) ..... CPIP
Chronic Pyelonephritis [*Urology*] ..... CP
Chronic Pyelonephritis [*Urology*] ..... CPN
Chronic Pyrophosphate Arthropathy (STED) ..... CPA
Chronic Radiodermatitis [*Medicine*] (MELL) ..... CRD
Chronic Reactive Lymphadenopathy Syndrome [*Medicine*] ..... CRLS
Chronic Rejection [*Medicine*] ..... CR
Chronic Relapsing Demyelinating Inflammatory Polyneuropathy [*Medicine*] (MELL) ..... CRDIP
Chronic Relapsing Pancreatitis [*Medicine*] (STED) ..... CRP
Chronic Renal Disease [*Medicine*] ..... CRD
Chronic Renal Failure [*Medicine*] ..... CRF
Chronic Respiratory Alkalosis [*Medicine*] (MELL) ..... CRA
Chronic Respiratory Disease [*Medicine*] ..... CRD
Chronic Respiratory Failure [*Medicine*] (DAVI) ..... CRF
Chronic Respiratory Insufficiency [*Medicine*] (MELL) ..... CRI
Chronic Respiratory Questionnaire (ADWA) ..... CRQ
Chronic Restrictive Pulmonary Disease [*Medicine*] (DMAA) ..... CRPD
Chronic Rheumatoid Arthritis (MELL) ..... CRA
Chronic Rheumatoid Nodular Fibrositis [*Medicine*] (DB) ..... CRNF
Chronic Schizophrenia (AAMN) ..... CS
Chronic Serous Otitis Media [*Otorhinolaryngology*] (DAVI) ..... CSOM
Chronic Simple Glaucoma [*Ophthalmology*] (CPH) ..... CSG
Chronic Smoke Inhalation (MELL) ..... CSI
Chronic Spinal Muscular Atrophy [*Medicine*] (DMAA) ..... CSMA
Chronic Stasis Leg Ulcer [*Medicine*] (AAMN) ..... CSLU
Chronic Subclinical Scurvy [*Medicine*] ..... CSS
Chronic Subdural Hematoma [*Medicine*] (MELL) ..... CSDH
Chronic Subdural Hematoma [*Medicine*] ..... CSH
Chronic Suppurative Otitus Media [*Otolaryngology*] ..... CSOM
Chronic Symptomatic Maladjustment (SAUS) ..... CSM
Chronic Syndrome Disorder [*Medicine*] (WDAA) ..... CSD
Chronic Tension Headache (MELL) ..... CTH
Chronic Thrombotic Pulmonary Vascular Obstruction [*Medicine*] (MELL) ..... CTPVO
Chronic Tic Disorder (SAUS) ..... CTD
Chronic Toxicity Endpoint (EEVL) ..... CTE
Chronic Ulcerative Colitis [*Medicine*] ..... CUC
Chronic Ulcerative Stomatitis [*Medicine*] ..... CUS
Chronic Undifferentiated Schizophrenia [*Psychiatry*] (DAVI) ..... CUS
Chronic Urticaria [*Immunology*] ..... CU
Chronic Uterine Inflammation [*Medicine*] ..... CUI
Chronic Valvular Heart Disease [*Medicine*] (MELL) ..... CVHD
Chronic Venous Insufficiency [*Medicine*] (DMAA) CVI
Chronic Villous Arthritis [*Medicine*] (DMAA) ..... CVA
Chronic Wasting Disease (SAUS) ..... CWD
Chronica [*of St. Jerome*] [*Classical studies*] (OCD) ..... Chron
Chronica Juridicalia [*A publication*] (DLA) ..... Chron Jur
Chronically Mentally Ill [*Medicine*] ..... CMI
Chronicity Factor (LDT) ..... CF
Chronicle ..... CHRNCL
Chronicle ..... CHRON
Chronicle of Higher Education [*A publication*] (BRI) ..... CHE
Chronicles [*Old Testament book*] (BJA) ..... Ch
Chronicles [*Old Testament book*] ..... Chr
Chronicles [*Old Testament book*] ..... Chron
Chronicles Concerning Early Babylonian Kings [*A publication*] (BJA) ..... CCEBK
Chronicles of Oklahoma (journ.) (SAUS) ..... OklaChronicles
Chronicles of the Divorce Courts [*A publication*] (DLA) ..... Chron Div Cts
Chronik der Christlichen Welt [*A publication*] (BJA) ..... ChChW
Chronimed, Inc. [*NASDAQ symbol*] (SAG) ..... CHMD
Chronimed, Inc. [*Associated Press*] (SAG) ..... Chronimd
Chronium (ROG) C
Chronoc Passive Congestion (SAUS) ..... CPC
Chronocoulometry [*Electrochemistry*] CC
chronogram (SAUS) ..... chron
chronological (SAUS) ..... chr
Chronological (ADWA) ..... chron
Chronological ..... CHRON
Chronological (AFM) ..... CHRONO
Chronological (ADWA) ..... chronol
chronological (SAUO) ..... chronol
Chronological Age [*Psychology*] ..... CA
Chronologically (SAUS) ..... Chrono
Chronology ..... chron
chronology (SAUO) ..... chronol
Chronology of African-American History [*A publication*] ..... CAAH
Chronology of Hispanic-American History [*A publication*] ..... CHAH
Chronology of Native North American History [*A publication*] ..... CNNAH
Chronology of Twentieth-Century Eastern European History [*A publication*] ..... CTCEEH
Chronology of Womens's History [*A publication*] ..... CWH
Chronometer ..... CHRON
Chronometer (ROG) ..... CHRONTER
Chronometer ..... CRNMTR
Chronometer Correction [*Navigation*] CC
Chronometer Error [*Navigation*] ..... CE
Chronometer Time [*Navigation*] C
Chronometer Time [*Navigation*] (IAA) ..... CT
Chronometer Time Minus Watch Time [*Navigation*] ..... C-W
Chronometric (SAUS) ..... Crnmtc
Chronometric ..... CRNMTC
Chronometry (SAUS) ..... Chron
Chronopotentiometric Stripping Analysis [*Analytical electrochemistry*] ..... CPSA
Chronotherapeutics (MELL) ..... CT
Chronotropic Dose (SAUS) ..... CD
Chrostwaite's Pennsylvania Municipal Law Reporter [*A publication*] (DLA) ..... Mun L Rep
Chrysanthemum [*Horticulture*] (DSUE) ..... CHRYSANT
Chrysanthemum [*Horticulture*] ..... Mum
Chrysanthemum Chlorotic Mottle Viroid ..... ChCMV
Chrysanthemum Stunt Viroid ..... CSV
Chrysanthemum Virus B [*Plant pathology*] ..... CVB
Chrysene (SAUS) ..... CHY
Chrysler (SAUS) ..... Chrys
Chrysler ..... CHRYSLR
Chrysler Art Museum, Jean Outland Chrysler Library, Norfolk, VA [*Library symbol*] [*Library of Congress*] (LCLS) ..... ViNC
Chrysler Car Club Council (EA) CCCC
Chrysler Collision Detection [*Automotive safety and electronics*] C2D
Chrysler Corp. [*NYSE symbol*] [*Toronto Stock Exchange symbol*] (SPSG) C
Chrysler Corp. CC
Chrysler Corp. ..... CHRY
Chrysler Corp. [*Associated Press*] (SAG) ..... Chryslr
Chrysler Corp., Engineering Division, Detroit, MI [*Library symbol*] [*Library of Congress*] (LCLS) ..... MiDChryE
Chrysler Corporation (SAUO) CC

Chrysler Corporation Missile Division (MCD) .... CCMD
Chrysler Corporation Space Division (KSC) .... CCSD
Chrysler Data Visualizer .... CDV
Chrysler de Mexico SA [Chrysler Corp.] .... CdM
Chrysler Financial Corp. .... CFC
Chrysler Historical Foundation .... CHF
Chrysler Improved Numerical Differencing Analyzer [Computer science] .... CINDA
Chrysler Improved Numerical Differencing Analyzer for Third-Generation Computers [Computer science] CINDA-3G
Chrysler Information Resources Center [Pronounced "serk"] .... CIRC
Chrysler Institute of Engineering (SAUS) .... CIE
Chrysler LASER Atlas Satellite System [Automotive engineering] .... CLASS
Chrysler Military Sales Corporation (SAUO) .... CMSC
Chrysler Optical Processing Scanner .... COPS
Chrysler Pentastar Aviation, Inc. [FAA designator] (FAAC) .... CYL
Chrysler Performance Parts Association (EA) .... CPPA
Chrysler Product Owners Club (EA) .... CPOC
Chrysler Products Restorers Club [Later, CRC] (EA) .... CPRC
Chrysler Restorers Club [Formerly, CPRC] (EA) .... CRC
Chrysler Technologies (SAUS) .... CT
Chrysler Technologies Airborne Systems Inc (SAUS) .... CTAS
Chrysler Town and Country Owners Registry (EA) .... CTCOR
Chrysler Town and Country Owners Registry (EA) .... CTCR
Chrysler Town and Country Owners Registry (EA) .... TCOR
Chrysoberyl [Jewelry] (ROG) .... CHRS
Chrysoberyl [Jewelry] (ROG) .... CS
Chrysolite [Jewelry] (ROG) .... CRY
CHS Aviation Ltd. [Kenya] [ICAO designator] (FAAC) .... HSA
CHS Electronics [NASDAQ symbol] (TTSB) .... CHSE
CHS Electronics [NYSE symbol] .... HS
CHS Electronics, Inc. [NASDAQ symbol] (SAG) .... CHSE
CHS Electronics, Inc. [Associated Press] (SAG) .... CHS EI
Chu Itoh Techno Science Company (SAUO) .... CTC
Chualar, CA [FM radio station call letters] .... KHDC
Chuan Hup Canada [Vancouver Stock Exchange symbol] .... CJU
Chub Cay [Bahamas] [Airport symbol] (OAG) .... CCZ
Chub Cay, Berry Island [Bahamas] [ICAO location identifier] (ICLI) .... MYBC
[The] Chubb Corp. [NYSE symbol] (SPSG) .... CB
[The] Chubb Corp. [Associated Press] (SAG) .... Chubb
Chubbuck, ID [AM radio station call letters] .... KRCD
Chubbuck, ID [FM radio station call letters] .... KRSS
Chubbuck, ID [AM radio station call letters] (BROA) .... KRTK
Chuchupate [California] [Seismograph station code, US Geological Survey] [Closed] (SEIS) .... CHP
Chuck Jaws [Tools] .... CCJW
Chuck Jennings Fan Club [Defunct] (EA) .... CJFC
Chuck Norris International Fan Club (EA) .... CNIFC
Chuian-Garon [Former USSR] [Seismograph station code, US Geological Survey] [Closed] (SEIS) .... CGT
Chukchi Sea Circulation Study [Marine science] (OSRA) .... CSCS
Chukyo University [UTLAS symbol] .... CUL
Chula Vista Public Library, Chula Vista, CA [Library symbol] [Library of Congress] (LCLS) .... CChu
Chulman [Former USSR] [ICAO location identifier] (ICLI) .... UELL
CHUM Ltd. [Toronto Stock Exchange symbol] .... CHM
Chumleigh [England] .... CHUM
Chumpon [Thailand] [ICAO location identifier] (ICLI) .... VTSD
Chums, Inc. [An association] (EA) CI
Chunchon [South Korea] [ICAO location identifier] (ICLI) .... RKNC
Chung Shan Institute of Science and Technology (SAUO) .... CSIST
Chung Wah Association [Australia] .... CWA
Chung Wah Society [Northern Territory] [Australia] .... CWS
Chung-Hau Min Kuo [Republic of China] .... CHMK
Chungju [South Korea] [ICAO location identifier] (ICLI) .... RKTC
Chungking [China] [Airport symbol] (AD) .... CKG
Chunya [Tanzania] [ICAO location identifier] (ICLI) .... HTCH
Chun-ying [Leung] [Hong Kong politician] .... CY
Chuo Electric Computer (SAUS) .... CEC
Chur [Coire] [Switzerland] [Seismograph station code, US Geological Survey] [Closed] (SEIS) .... CHU
Church C
Church (VRA) .... ch
Church .... CH
Church [Alaska] [Seismograph station code, US Geological Survey] (SEIS) .... CHB
Church (ROG) .... CHCH
church (SAUO) .... chh
Church (MCD) .... CHR
Church (BEE) .... chr
Church .... CHU
Church Action with the Unemployed [Church of England] .... CAWTU
Church Aircraft Ltd. [ICAO designator] (FAAC) .... CHU
Church & Dwight [NYSE symbol] (TTSB) .... CHD
Church & Dwight Co., Inc. [NYSE symbol] (SPSG) .... CHD
Church & Dwight Co., Inc. [Associated Press] (SAG) .... ChrDwt
Church and Peace [Schoeffengrund, Federal Republic of Germany] (EAIO) .... CaP
Church and Synagogue Library Association (EA) .... CSLA
Church Architectural Guild of America [Later, IFRAA] (EA) .... CAGA
Church Army [An association] (EA) .... CA
Church Army (SAUO) .... CA
Church Army Society (EA) .... CAS
Church Assembly (SAUO) .... CA
Church Assembly Measure (DLA) .... CAM
Church Association (SAUO) .... CA
Church Association [British] .... CA

Church Association for Seamen's Work [Later, SCI] (EA) .... CASW
Church Building Society [British] .... CBS
Church Building Society (SAUO) .... CBS
Church Center for the United Nations (EA) .... CCUN
Church Coalition for Human Rights in the Philippines (EA) .... CCHRP
Church Committee for Human Rights in Asia (EA) .... CCHRA
Church Committee of War Damage (SAUO) .... CCWD
Church Council on Justice and Correction [Conseil des Eglises pour la Justiceet la Criminologie], Ottawa, Ontario [Library symbol] [National Library of Canada] (BIB) .... OOCCJ
Church Council on Justice & Corrections [Conseil des Eglises pour la Justice et la Criminologie] (AC) .... CCJC
Church Defence Institution [British] .... CDI
Church Defence Institution (SAUO) .... CDI
Church Education Corporation (SAUO) .... CEC
Church Elementary School, Rockford, IL [Library symbol] [Library of Congress] (LCLS) .... IRoChE
Church Employed Women (EA) .... CEW
Church Estates Commissioners (SAUO) .... CEC
Church Estates Development and Improvement Company (SAUO) .... CEDIC
Church Evangelical Board (SAUO) .... CEB
Church Evangelism Association [Later, Masterkey Association] (EA) .... CEA
Church Executive Development Board .... CEDB
Church Extension Association [British] .... CEA
Church Extension Association (SAUO) .... CEA
Church Family Newspaper [A publication] (ROG) .... CFN
Church Fenton [British] [ICAO location identifier] (ICLI) .... EGXG
Church Furniture Manufacturers Association [Defunct] (EA) .... CFMA
Church Growth Center (EA) .... CGC
Church Guilds Union [British] .... CGU
Church Heritage [A publication] (APTA) .... CH
Church Hill, TN [AM radio station call letters] .... WMCH
Church Historical Society [Later, HSEC] (EA) .... CHS
Church Historical Society, Austin, TX [Library symbol] [Library of Congress] (LCLS) .... TxAuCH
Church History [A publication] (BRI) .... CH
Church House (SAUO) .... CH
Church Information Office [British] .... CIO
Church Jesus Christ of Latter-Day Saints, Genealogical Society Library, Cleveland Branch, Westlake, OH [Library symbol] [Library of Congress] (LCLS) .... OWIGS
Church Lads and Church Girls Brigade [British] [An association] (DBA) .... CL & CGB
Church Lads' Brigade [Church of England] .... CLB
Church League of America [Defunct] (EA) .... CLA
Church League of Industrial Democracy (SAUO) .... CLID
Church Literature Association [British] (BI) .... CLA
Church Missionary (IIA) .... CM
Church Missionary College (SAUO) .... CMC
Church Missionary College [Church of England] .... CMCOLL
Church Missionary Society [British] .... CMS
Church Missionary Society of Australia .... CMSA
Church Missionary Union [British] .... CMU
Church Monuments Society (EA) .... CMS
Church Music Association [British] .... CMA
Church Music Association of America (EA) .... CMAA
Church Music Publishers Association (EA) .... CMPA
Church Music Publishers of America (SAUO) .... CMPA
Church Music Trust [British] (BI) .... CMT
Church of Christ CC
Church of Christ, Scientist .... CCS
Church of England .... CE
Church of England (SAUO) .... CE
Church of England (SAUO) .... Ch of Eng
Church of England .... COE
Church of England .... C of E
Church of England (WDAA) .... CofE
Church of England (SAUO) .... C of E
Church of England Advisory Council of Empire Settlement (SAUO) .... CEACES
Church of England and Roman Schools Department (SAUO) .... CERSD
Church of England Boys' School in Tasmania [Australia] .... CEBST
Church of England Children's Society .... CECS
Church of England Education Society (SAUO) .... CEES
Church of England Girls Grammar School (SAUS) .... CEGGS
Church of England Grammar School (SAUO) .... CEGS
Church of England Historical Society (ADA) .... CEHS
Church of England Historical Society [Australia] .... COEHS
Church of England Hospital and Sick Nursing Association (SAUO) .... CEHSNA
Church of England in South Africa (SAUO) .... CESA
Church of England Men's Society .... CEMS
Church of England Newspaper .... CEN
Church of England School [British] .... E
Church of England Soldiers', Sailors', and Airmen's Club .... CESSA
Church of England Soldiers', Sailors', and Airmen's Clubs .... CESSAC
Church of England Sunday School Institute .... CESSI
Church of England Temperance Society .... CETS
Church of England Temperance Society (SAUO) .... CETS
Church of England Women's Help Society [British] .... CEWHS
Church of England Working Men's Society .... CEWMS
Church of England Young Men's Society .... CEYMS
Church of England Young People's Assembly [British] .... CEYPA
Church of England Youth Council (BI) .... CEYC
Church of England Zenana Missionary Society [British] .... CEZMS
Church of England Zenana Missionary Society (SAUO) .... CEZMS
Church Of God In Christ (SAUS) .... COGIC

Church of God, Men International (EA) .... CGMI
Church of God Peace Fellowship (EA) .... CGPF
Church of Good Peace Fellowship (SAUO) .... CGPF
Church of India, Pakistan, Burma and Ceylon (SAUO) .... CIPBC
Church of Ireland (SAUO) .... C of I
Church of Ireland .... C of I
Church of Ireland .... C of IRE
Church of Ireland Young Men's Society .... CIYMS
Church of Jesus Christ and Latter Day Saints (SAUO) .... LDS
Church of Jesus Christ of Latter-Day Saints, Genealogical Society Library (SAUO) .... GDunGS
Church of Jesus Christ of Latter-Day Saints, Genealogical Society Library, Adelaide Stake Branch, Firle, SA, Australia [*Library symbol*] [*Library of Congress*] (LCLS) .... AuFirGS
Church of Jesus Christ of Latter-Day Saints, Genealogical Society Library, AftonBranch, Afton, WY [*Library symbol*] [*Library of Congress*] (LCLS) .... WyAGS
Church of Jesus Christ of Latter-Day Saints, Genealogical Society Library, Albany New York Stake Branch, Loudonville, NY [*Library symbol*] [*Library of Congress*] (LCLS) .... NLouvGS
Church of Jesus Christ of Latter-Day Saints, Genealogical Society Library, Albuquerque Branch, Albuquerque, NM [*Library symbol*] [*Library of Congress*] (LCLS) .... NmAGS
Church of Jesus Christ of Latter-Day Saints, Genealogical Society Library, Anaheim Branch, Anaheim, CA [*Library symbol*] [*Library of Congress*] (LCLS) .... CAnaGS
Church of Jesus Christ of Latter-Day Saints, Genealogical Society Library, Anchorage Branch, Anchorage, AK [*Library symbol*] [*Library of Congress*] (LCLS) .... AkAGS
Church of Jesus Christ of Latter-Day Saints, Genealogical Society Library, Annandale Branch, Annandale, VA [*Library symbol*] [*Library of Congress*] (LCLS) .... ViAnGS
Church of Jesus Christ of Latter-Day Saints, Genealogical Society Library, Arvada Branch, Arvada, CO [*Library symbol*] [*Library of Congress*] (LCLS) .... CoArGS
Church of Jesus Christ of Latter-Day Saints, Genealogical Society Library, Auckland Branch, Auckland, New Zealand [*Library symbol*] [*Library of Congress*] (LCLS) .... NzAGS
Church of Jesus Christ of Latter-Day Saints, Genealogical Society Library, Augusta Branch, Farmingdale, ME [*Library symbol*] [*Library of Congress*] (LCLS) .... MeFarGS
Church of Jesus Christ of Latter-Day Saints, Genealogical Society Library, Austin Branch, Austin, TX [*Library symbol*] [*Library of Congress*] (LCLS) .... TxAuGS
Church of Jesus Christ of Latter-Day Saints, Genealogical Society Library, Bakersfield Branch, Bakersfield, CA [*Library symbol*] [*Library of Congress*] (LCLS) .... CBaGS
Church of Jesus Christ of Latter-Day Saints, Genealogical Society Library, Barstow Branch, Barstow, CA [*Library symbol*] [*Library of Congress*] (LCLS) .... CBarGS
Church of Jesus Christ of Latter-Day Saints, Genealogical Society Library, Baton Rouge (SAUO) .... LBrGS
Church of Jesus Christ of Latter-Day Saints, Genealogical Society Library, BatonRouge Branch, Baton Rouge, LA [*Library symbol*] [*Library of Congress*] (LCLS) .... LBrGS
Church of Jesus Christ of Latter-Day Saints, Genealogical Society Library, Bear Lake Branch, Montpelier, ID [*Library symbol*] [*Library of Congress*] (LCLS) .... IdMonGS
Church of Jesus Christ of Latter-Day Saints, Genealogical Society Library, Beaumont Branch, Vidor, TX [*Library symbol*] [*Library of Congress*] (LCLS) .... TxVidGS
Church of Jesus Christ of Latter-Day Saints, Genealogical Society Library, Beaver Branch, Beaver, UT [*Library symbol*] [*Library of Congress*] (LCLS) .... UBeGS
Church of Jesus Christ of Latter-Day Saints, Genealogical Society Library, Beaverton Branch, Beaverton, OR [*Library symbol*] [*Library of Congress*] (LCLS) .... OrBGS
Church of Jesus Christ of Latter-Day Saints, Genealogical Society Library, Bellevue Branch, Bellevue, WA [*Library symbol*] [*Library of Congress*] (LCLS) .... WaBGS
Church of Jesus Christ of Latter-Day Saints, Genealogical Society Library, Billings Branch, Billings, MT [*Library symbol*] [*Library of Congress*] (LCLS) .... MtBilGS
Church of Jesus Christ of Latter-Day Saints, Genealogical Society Library, Blackfoot West Branch, Stake Center, Blackfoot, ID [*Library symbol*] [*Library of Congress*] (LCLS) .... IdBfGS
Church of Jesus Christ of Latter-Day Saints, Genealogical Society Library, Bloomfield Hills Branch, Bloomfield Hills, MI [*Library symbol*] [*Library of Congress*] (LCLS) .... MiBloGS
Church of Jesus Christ of Latter-Day Saints, Genealogical Society Library, Boston Branch, Weston, MA [*Library symbol*] [*Library of Congress*] (LCLS) .... MWestonGS
Church of Jesus Christ of Latter-Day Saints, Genealogical Society Library, Boulder Stake Branch, Boulder, CO [*Library symbol*] [*Library of Congress*] (LCLS) .... CoBGS
Church of Jesus Christ of Latter-Day Saints, Genealogical Society Library, Brigham City South Branch, Brigham City, UT [*Library symbol*] [*Library of Congress*] (LCLS) .... UBcGS
Church of Jesus Christ of Latter-Day Saints, Genealogical Society Library, Burley Branch, Burley, ID [*Library symbol*] [*Library of Congress*] (LCLS) .... IdBurGS
Church of Jesus Christ of Latter-Day Saints, Genealogical Society Library, ButteStake Branch, Dillon Chapel, Dillon, MT [*Library symbol*] [*Library of Congress*] (LCLS) .... MtDiGS
Church of Jesus Christ of Latter-Day Saints, Genealogical Society Library, CacheBranch, Logan, UT [*Library symbol*] [*Library of Congress*] (LCLS) .... ULGS
Church of Jesus Christ of Latter-Day Saints, Genealogical Society Library, Caldwell Branch, Summit, NJ [*Library symbol*] [*Library of Congress*] (LCLS) .... NjSGS
Church of Jesus Christ of Latter-Day Saints, Genealogical Society Library, Calgary Branch, Calgary, AB, Canada [*Library symbol*] [*Library of Congress*] (LCLS) .... CaACCJC
Church of Jesus Christ of Latter-Day Saints, Genealogical Society Library, Canterbury Branch, Christchurch, New Zealand [*Library symbol*] [*Library of Congress*] (LCLS) .... NzCGS
Church of Jesus Christ of Latter-Day Saints, Genealogical Society Library, Cardston Branch, Cardston, AB, Canada [*Library symbol*] [*Library of Congress*] (LCLS) .... CaACaCJC
Church of Jesus Christ of Latter-Day Saints, Genealogical Society Library, Casper Branch, Casper, WY [*Library symbol*] [*Library of Congress*] (LCLS) .... WyCaGS
Church of Jesus Christ of Latter-Day Saints, Genealogical Society Library, Champaign Stake Branch, Champaign, IL [*Library symbol*] [*Library of Congress*] (LCLS) .... IChamGS
Church of Jesus Christ of Latter-Day Saints, Genealogical Society Library, Charlotte North Carolina Branch, Charlotte, NC [*Library symbol*] [*Library of Congress*] (LCLS) .... NcCGS
Church of Jesus Christ of Latter-Day Saints, Genealogical Society Library, Cheyenne Branch, Cheyenne, WY [*Library symbol*] [*Library of Congress*] (LCLS) .... WyCGS
Church of Jesus Christ of Latter-Day Saints, Genealogical Society Library, Chicago Heights Branch, Chicago Heights, IL [*Library symbol*] [*Library of Congress*] (LCLS) .... IChGS
Church of Jesus Christ of Latter-Day Saints, Genealogical Society Library, ChicoBranch, Stake Center, Chico, CA [*Library symbol*] [*Library of Congress*] (LCLS) .... CChiGS
Church of Jesus Christ of Latter-Day Saints, Genealogical Society Library, Cincinnati Branch, Cincinnati, OH [*Library symbol*] [*Library of Congress*] (LCLS) .... OCGS
Church of Jesus Christ of Latter-Day Saints, Genealogical Society Library, Cleveland Branch, Westlake, OH [*Library symbol*] [*Library of Congress*] (LCLS) .... OWlGS
Church of Jesus Christ of Latter-Day Saints, Genealogical Society Library, Cody Branch, Cody, WY [*Library symbol*] [*Library of Congress*] (LCLS) .... WyCoGS
Church of Jesus Christ of Latter-Day Saints, Genealogical Society Library, Colonia Juarez Branch, Chihuahua, Mexico [*Library symbol*] [*Library of Congress*] (LCLS) .... MxChGS
Church of Jesus Christ of Latter-Day Saints, Genealogical Society Library, Colorado Springs Branch, Colorado Springs, CO [*Library symbol*] [*Library of Congress*] (LCLS) .... CoCGS
Church of Jesus Christ of Latter-Day Saints, Genealogical Society Library, Columbia Branch, Columbia, SC [*Library symbol*] [*Library of Congress*] (LCLS) .... ScCoGS
Church of Jesus Christ of Latter-Day Saints, Genealogical Society Library, Columbia Missouri Branch, Columbia, MO [*Library symbol*] [*Library of Congress*] (LCLS) .... MoCoGS
Church of Jesus Christ of Latter-Day Saints, Genealogical Society Library, Columbus Branch, Columbus, OH [*Library symbol*] [*Library of Congress*] (LCLS) .... OCoGS
Church of Jesus Christ of Latter-Day Saints, Genealogical Society Library, Coos Bay Stake Branch, North Bend, OR [*Library symbol*] [*Library of Congress*] (LCLS) .... OrNbGS
Church of Jesus Christ of Latter-Day Saints, Genealogical Society Library, Corpus Christi Branch, Corpus Christi, TX [*Library symbol*] [*Library of Congress*] (LCLS) .... TxCcGS
Church of Jesus Christ of Latter-Day Saints, Genealogical Society Library, Corvallis Branch, Corvallis, OR [*Library symbol*] [*Library of Congress*] (LCLS) .... OrCGS
Church of Jesus Christ of Latter-Day Saints, Genealogical Society Library, Covina Branch, Covina, CA [*Library symbol*] [*Library of Congress*] (LCLS) .... CCovGS
Church of Jesus Christ of Latter-Day Saints, Genealogical Society Library, Dallas Branch, Dallas, TX [*Library symbol*] [*Library of Congress*] (LCLS) .... TxDaGS
Church of Jesus Christ of Latter-Day Saints, Genealogical Society Library, Dayton Ohio Branch, Dayton, OH [*Library symbol*] [*Library of Congress*] (LCLS) .... ODaGL
Church of Jesus Christ of Latter-Day Saints, Genealogical Society Library, Dearborn Stake Branch, LDS Chapel, Dearborn, MI [*Library symbol*] [*Library of Congress*] (LCLS) .... MiDbGS
Church of Jesus Christ of Latter-Day Saints, Genealogical Society Library, Denver Branch, Stake Center, Denver, CO [*Library symbol*] [*Library of Congress*] (LCLS) .... CoDGL
Church of Jesus Christ of Latter-Day Saints, Genealogical Society Library, Denver North Branch, Northglenn, CO [*Library symbol*] [*Library of Congress*] (LCLS) .... CoNgGS
Church of Jesus Christ of Latter-Day Saints, Genealogical Society Library, Des Moines Branch, West Des Moines, IA [*Library symbol*] [*Library of Congress*] (LCLS) .... IaWdmGS
Church of Jesus Christ of Latter-Day Saints, Genealogical Society Library, Driggs Branch, Driggs, ID [*Library symbol*] [*Library of Congress*] (LCLS) .... IdDrGS
Church of Jesus Christ of Latter-Day Saints, Genealogical Society Library, Duchesne Branch, Stake Center, Duchesne, UT [*Library symbol*] [*Library of Congress*] (LCLS) .... UDucGS

Church of Jesus Christ of Latter-Day Saints, Genealogical Society Library, Durango Stake Branch, Cortez, CO [Library symbol] [Library of Congress] (LCLS) .... CoCoGS

Church of Jesus Christ of Latter-Day Saints, Genealogical Society Library, East Brunswick Stake Branch, East Brunswick, NJ [Library symbol] [Library of Congress] (LCLS) .... NjEbGS

Church of Jesus Christ of Latter-Day Saints, Genealogical Society Library, Edmonton Branch, Edmonton, AB, Canada [Library symbol] [Library of Congress] (LCLS) .... CaAECJC

Church of Jesus Christ of Latter-Day Saints, Genealogical Society Library, El Paso Branch, El Paso, TX [Library symbol] [Library of Congress] (LCLS) .... TxEGS

Church of Jesus Christ of Latter-Day Saints, Genealogical Society Library, Ely Branch, Ely, NV [Library symbol] [Library of Congress] (LCLS) .... NvElGS

Church of Jesus Christ of Latter-Day Saints, Genealogical Society Library, Eugene Branch, Eugene, OR [Library symbol] [Library of Congress] (LCLS) .... OrEGS

Church of Jesus Christ of Latter-Day Saints, Genealogical Society Library, Eureka Branch, Eureka, CA [Library symbol] [Library of Congress] (LCLS) .... CEGS

Church of Jesus Christ of Latter-Day Saints, Genealogical Society Library, Evanston Branch, Evanston, WY [Library symbol] [Library of Congress] (LCLS) .... WyEvGS

Church of Jesus Christ of Latter-Day Saints, Genealogical Society Library, Everett, Washington Stake Branch, Everett, WA [Library symbol] [Library of Congress] (LCLS) .... WaEGS

Church of Jesus Christ of Latter-Day Saints, Genealogical Society Library, Fairbanks Alaska District Branch, Fairbanks, AK [Library symbol] [Library of Congress] (LCLS) .... AkFGS

Church of Jesus Christ of Latter-Day Saints, Genealogical Society Library, Fallon Branch, Fallon, NV [Library symbol] [Library of Congress] (LCLS) .... NvFGS

Church of Jesus Christ of Latter-Day Saints, Genealogical Society Library, Farmington Branch, Farmington, NM [Library symbol] [Library of Congress] (LCLS) .... NmFGS

Church of Jesus Christ of Latter-Day Saints, Genealogical Society Library, Flagstaff Branch, Flagstaff, AZ [Library symbol] [Library of Congress] (LCLS) .... AzFGS

Church of Jesus Christ of Latter-Day Saints, Genealogical Society Library, Fort Collins Branch, Fort Collins, CO [Library symbol] [Library of Congress] (LCLS) .... CoFGS

Church of Jesus Christ of Latter-Day Saints, Genealogical Society Library, Fort Wayne Branch, Fort Wayne, IN [Library symbol] [Library of Congress] (LCLS) .... InFwGS

Church of Jesus Christ of Latter-Day Saints, Genealogical Society Library, Fort Worth Branch, North Richland Hills, Fort Worth, TX [Library symbol] [Library of Congress] (LCLS) .... TxFGS

Church of Jesus Christ of Latter-Day Saints, Genealogical Society Library, Fresno Branch, Fresno, CA [Library symbol] [Library of Congress] (LCLS) .... CFGS

Church of Jesus Christ of Latter-Day Saints, Genealogical Society Library, Gettysburg Branch, York, PA [Library symbol] [Library of Congress] (LCLS) .... PYGS

Church of Jesus Christ of Latter-Day Saints, Genealogical Society Library, GrandJunction Branch, Stake Center, Grand Junction, CO [Library symbol] [Library of Congress] (LCLS) .... CoGjGS

Church of Jesus Christ of Latter-Day Saints, Genealogical Society Library, GreatFalls Branch, Great Falls, MT [Library symbol] [Library of Congress] (LCLS) .... MtGrGS

Church of Jesus Christ of Latter-Day Saints, Genealogical Society Library, Gresham Branch, Gresham, OR [Library symbol] [Library of Congress] (LCLS) .... OrGrGS

Church of Jesus Christ of Latter-Day Saints, Genealogical Society Library, Gridley Branch, Gridley, CA [Library symbol] [Library of Congress] (LCLS) .... CGrlGS

Church of Jesus Christ of Latter-Day Saints, Genealogical Society Library, Hartford Branch, Manchester, CT [Library symbol] [Library of Congress] (LCLS) .... CtManGS

Church of Jesus Christ of Latter-Day Saints, Genealogical Society Library, Helena Branch, Helena, MT [Library symbol] [Library of Congress] (LCLS) .... MtHGS

Church of Jesus Christ of Latter-Day Saints, Genealogical Society Library, Holbrook Branch, Holbrook, AZ [Library symbol] [Library of Congress] (LCLS) .... AzHGS

Church of Jesus Christ of Latter-Day Saints, Genealogical Society Library, Houston Branch, Houston, TX [Library symbol] [Library of Congress] (LCLS) .... TxHGS

Church of Jesus Christ of Latter-Day Saints, Genealogical Society Library, Houston East Branch, Houston, TX [Library symbol] [Library of Congress] (LCLS) .... TxHGS-E

Church of Jesus Christ of Latter-Day Saints, Genealogical Society Library, Huntsville Branch, Huntsville, AL [Library symbol] [Library of Congress] (LCLS) .... AHGS

Church of Jesus Christ of Latter-Day Saints, Genealogical Society Library, IdahoFalls Branch, Idaho Falls, ID [Library symbol] [Library of Congress] (LCLS) .... IdIfGS

Church of Jesus Christ of Latter-Day Saints, Genealogical Society Library, Indianapolis Branch, Indianapolis, IN [Library symbol] [Library of Congress] (LCLS) .... InIGS

Church of Jesus Christ of Latter-Day Saints, Genealogical Society Library, Ithaca Branch, Vestal, NY [Library symbol] [Library of Congress] (LCLS) .... NVeGS

Church of Jesus Christ of Latter-Day Saints, Genealogical Society Library, Jacksonville Branch, Jacksonville, FL [Library symbol] [Library of Congress] (LCLS) .... FJGS

Church of Jesus Christ of Latter-Day Saints, Genealogical Society Library, Kalispell Branch, Kalispell, MT [Library symbol] [Library of Congress] (LCLS) .... MtKGS

Church of Jesus Christ of Latter-Day Saints, Genealogical Society Library, KanabBranch, Stake Center, Kanab, UT [Library symbol] [Library of Congress] (LCLS) .... UKaGS

Church of Jesus Christ of Latter-Day Saints, Genealogical Society Library, Kaneohe Stake Branch, Kaneohe, HI [Library symbol] [Library of Congress] (LCLS) .... HKGS

Church of Jesus Christ of Latter-Day Saints, Genealogical Society Library, Kansas City Branch, Kansas City, MO [Library symbol] [Library of Congress] (LCLS) .... MoKGS

Church of Jesus Christ of Latter-Day Saints, Genealogical Society Library, Knoxville Branch, Knoxville, TN [Library symbol] [Library of Congress] (LCLS) .... TKGS

Church of Jesus Christ of Latter-Day Saints, Genealogical Society Library, La Grande Branch, La Grande, OR [Library symbol] [Library of Congress] (LCLS) .... OrLgGS

Church of Jesus Christ of Latter-Day Saints, Genealogical Society Library, Laie Branch, Laie, HI [Library symbol] [Library of Congress] (LCLS) .... HLaGS

Church of Jesus Christ of Latter-Day Saints, Genealogical Society Library, LaJara Branch, Stake Center, LaJara, CO [Library symbol] [Library of Congress] (LCLS) .... CoLjaGS

Church of Jesus Christ of Latter-Day Saints, Genealogical Society Library, Lansing Branch, Stake Center, Lansing, MI [Library symbol] [Library of Congress] (LCLS) .... MiLGS

Church of Jesus Christ of Latter-Day Saints, Genealogical Society Library, Las Vegas Branch, Las Vegas, NV [Library symbol] [Library of Congress] (LCLS) .... NvLGS

Church of Jesus Christ of Latter-Day Saints, Genealogical Society Library, Lethbridge Branch, Stake Center, Lethbridge, AB, Canada [Library symbol] [Library of Congress] (LCLS) .... CaALCJC

Church of Jesus Christ of Latter-Day Saints, Genealogical Society Library, Lewiston Branch, Stake Center, Lewiston, ID [Library symbol] [Library of Congress] (LCLS) .... IdLGS

Church of Jesus Christ of Latter-Day Saints, Genealogical Society Library, Littleton Branch, Littleton, CO [Library symbol] [Library of Congress] (LCLS) .... CoLiGS

Church of Jesus Christ of Latter-Day Saints, Genealogical Society Library, Long Beach East Branch, Stake Center, Long Beach, CA [Library symbol] [Library of Congress] (LCLS) .... CLobGS

Church of Jesus Christ of Latter-Day Saints, Genealogical Society Library, Longview Branch, Gilmer, TX [Library symbol] [Library of Congress] (LCLS) .... TxGilGS

Church of Jesus Christ of Latter-Day Saints, Genealogical Society Library, Longview Stake Branch, Longview, WA [Library symbol] [Library of Congress] (LCLS) .... WaLoGS

Church of Jesus Christ of Latter-Day Saints, Genealogical Society Library, Los Angeles East Branch, Los Angeles, CA [Library symbol] [Library of Congress] (LCLS) .... CLGLE

Church of Jesus Christ of Latter-Day Saints, Genealogical Society Library, Los Angeles Temple, Los Angeles, CA [Library symbol] [Library of Congress] (LCLS) .... CLGL

Church of Jesus Christ of Latter-Day Saints, Genealogical Society Library, Lovell Branch, Lovell, WY [Library symbol] [Library of Congress] (LCLS) .... WyLoGS

Church of Jesus Christ of Latter-Day Saints, Genealogical Society Library, MaconBranch, Columbus, GA [Library symbol] [Library of Congress] (LCLS) .... GColuGS

Church of Jesus Christ of Latter-Day Saints, Genealogical Society Library, MaladStake Branch, Malad City, ID [Library symbol] [Library of Congress] (LCLS) .... IdMaGS

Church of Jesus Christ of Latter-Day Saints, Genealogical Society Library, Medford Branch, Medford, OR [Library symbol] [Library of Congress] (LCLS) .... OrMeGS

Church of Jesus Christ of Latter-Day Saints, Genealogical Society Library, Melbourne Branch, Northcote, V, Australia [Library symbol] [Library of Congress] (LCLS) .... AuNocGS

Church of Jesus Christ of Latter-Day Saints, Genealogical Society Library, Memphis Branch, Memphis, TN [Library symbol] [Library of Congress] (LCLS) .... TMGS

Church of Jesus Christ of Latter-Day Saints, Genealogical Society Library, Mesa Branch, Mesa, AZ [Library symbol] [Library of Congress] (LCLS) .... AzMGS

Church of Jesus Christ of Latter-Day Saints, Genealogical Society Library, Mexico City Branch, Mexico City, Mexico [Library symbol] [Library of Congress] (LCLS) .... MxMGS

Church of Jesus Christ of Latter-Day Saints, Genealogical Society Library, MiamiBranch, Miami, FL [Library symbol] [Library of Congress] (LCLS) .... FMGS

Church of Jesus Christ of Latter-Day Saints, Genealogical Society Library, Midland Stake Branch, Midland, MI [Library symbol] [Library of Congress] (LCLS) .... MiMidGS

Church of Jesus Christ of Latter-Day Saints, Genealogical Society Library, Milwaukee Branch, Hales Corners, WI [Library symbol] [Library of Congress] (LCLS) .... WHcGS

Church of Jesus Christ of Latter-Day Saints, Genealogical Society Library, Minneapolis Branch, Minneapolis, MN [Library symbol] [Library of Congress] (LCLS) .... MnMGS

Church of Jesus Christ of Latter-Day Saints, Genealogical Society Library, Missoula Branch, Missoula, MT [Library symbol] [Library of Congress] (LCLS) .... MtMisGS

Church of Jesus Christ of Latter-Day Saints, Genealogical Society Library, Modesto, CA [Library symbol] [Library of Congress] (LCLS) .... CMG

Church of Jesus Christ of Latter-Day Saints, Genealogical Society Library, Monterey Branch, Seaside, CA [*Library symbol*] [*Library of Congress*] (LCLS) .... CSeaGS

Church of Jesus Christ of Latter-Day Saints, Genealogical Society Library, MooreBranch, Lost River Stake Center, Moore, ID [*Library symbol*] [*Library of Congress*] (LCLS) .... IdMoGS

Church of Jesus Christ of Latter-Day Saints, Genealogical Society Library, MosesLake Branch, Moses Lake, WA [*Library symbol*] [*Library of Congress*] (LCLS) .... WaMlGS

Church of Jesus Christ of Latter-Day Saints, Genealogical Society Library, MountPleasant Branch, Stake Center, Mount Pleasant, UT [*Library symbol*] [*Library of Congress*] (LCLS) .... UMpGS

Church of Jesus Christ of Latter-Day Saints, Genealogical Society Library, MountVernon Branch, Mount Vernon, WA [*Library symbol*] [*Library of Congress*] (LCLS) .... WaMtvGS

Church of Jesus Christ of Latter-Day Saints, Genealogical Society Library, Naperville Branch, Naperville, IL [*Library symbol*] [*Library of Congress*] (LCLS) .... INapGS

Church of Jesus Christ of Latter-Day Saints, Genealogical Society Library, New York Branch, New York, NY [*Library symbol*] [*Library of Congress*] (LCLS) .... NNGS

Church of Jesus Christ of Latter-Day Saints, Genealogical Society Library, Norfolk Virginia Stake Branch, Virginia Beach, VA [*Library symbol*] [*Library of Congress*] (LCLS) .... ViVbGS

Church of Jesus Christ of Latter-Day Saints, Genealogical Society Library, NyssaBranch, Nyssa, OR [*Library symbol*] [*Library of Congress*] (LCLS) .... OrNyGS

Church of Jesus Christ of Latter-Day Saints, Genealogical Society Library, Oakland Branch, Oakland, CA [*Library symbol*] [*Library of Congress*] (LCLS) .... COGS

Church of Jesus Christ of Latter-Day Saints, Genealogical Society Library, Odessa Stake Branch, Odessa, TX [*Library symbol*] [*Library of Congress*] (LCLS) .... TxOGS

Church of Jesus Christ of Latter-Day Saints, Genealogical Society Library, OgdenBranch, Ogden, UT [*Library symbol*] [*Library of Congress*] (LCLS) .... UOGS

Church of Jesus Christ of Latter-Day Saints, Genealogical Society Library, Oklahoma City Branch, Oklahoma City, OK [*Library symbol*] [*Library of Congress*] (LCLS) .... OkOkGS

Church of Jesus Christ of Latter-Day Saints, Genealogical Society Library, Olympia Branch, Olympia, WA [*Library symbol*] [*Library of Congress*] (LCLS) .... WaOGS

Church of Jesus Christ of Latter-Day Saints, Genealogical Society Library, OmahaBranch, Omaha, NE [*Library symbol*] [*Library of Congress*] (LCLS) .... NbOGS

Church of Jesus Christ of Latter-Day Saints, Genealogical Society Library, Orlando Branch, Orlando, FL [*Library symbol*] [*Library of Congress*] (LCLS) .... FOGS

Church of Jesus Christ of Latter-Day Saints, Genealogical Society Library, PascoBranch, Pasco, WA [*Library symbol*] [*Library of Congress*] (LCLS) .... WaPaGS

Church of Jesus Christ of Latter-Day Saints, Genealogical Society Library, Pensacola Branch, Pensacola, FL [*Library symbol*] [*Library of Congress*] (LCLS) .... FPeGS

Church of Jesus Christ of Latter-Day Saints, Genealogical Society Library, Philadelphia Branch, Broomall, PA [*Library symbol*] [*Library of Congress*] (LCLS) .... PBroGS

Church of Jesus Christ of Latter-Day Saints, Genealogical Society Library, Phoenix Arizona North Branch, Phoenix, AZ [*Library symbol*] [*Library of Congress*] (LCLS) .... AzPhGS

Church of Jesus Christ of Latter-Day Saints, Genealogical Society Library, Phoenix Arizona West Branch, Phoenix, AZ [*Library symbol*] [*Library of Congress*] (LCLS) .... AzPhWGS

Church of Jesus Christ of Latter-Day Saints, Genealogical Society Library, Plainview Branch, Plainview, NY [*Library symbol*] [*Library of Congress*] (LCLS) .... NPlGS

Church of Jesus Christ of Latter-Day Saints, Genealogical Society Library, Pocatello Branch, Pocatello, ID [*Library symbol*] [*Library of Congress*] (LCLS) .... IdPGS

Church of Jesus Christ of Latter-Day Saints, Genealogical Society Library, Portland Branch, Portland, OR [*Library symbol*] [*Library of Congress*] (LCLS) .... OrPGS

Church of Jesus Christ of Latter-Day Saints, Genealogical Society Library, Portland East Branch, Portland, OR [*Library symbol*] [*Library of Congress*] (LCLS) .... OrPGSE

Church of Jesus Christ of Latter-Day Saints, Genealogical Society Library, Prescott Branch, Prescott, AZ [*Library symbol*] [*Library of Congress*] (LCLS) .... AzPrGS

Church of Jesus Christ of Latter-Day Saints, Genealogical Society Library, PriceBranch, Price, UT [*Library symbol*] [*Library of Congress*] (LCLS) .... UPrGS

Church of Jesus Christ of Latter-Day Saints, Genealogical Society Library, Quincy Branch, Quincy, WA [*Library symbol*] [*Library of Congress*] (LCLS) .... WaQGS

Church of Jesus Christ of Latter-Day Saints, Genealogical Society Library, Raleigh Branch, Raleigh, NC [*Library symbol*] [*Library of Congress*] (LCLS) .... NcRGS

Church of Jesus Christ of Latter-Day Saints, Genealogical Society Library, Redding Branch, Redding, CA [*Library symbol*] [*Library of Congress*] (LCLS) .... CRedGS

Church of Jesus Christ of Latter-Day Saints, Genealogical Society Library, Reno Branch, Reno, NV [*Library symbol*] [*Library of Congress*] (LCLS) .... NvRGS

Church of Jesus Christ of Latter-Day Saints, Genealogical Society Library, Richfield Branch, Richfield, UT [*Library symbol*] [*Library of Congress*] (LCLS) .... URifGS

Church of Jesus Christ of Latter-Day Saints, Genealogical Society Library, Richland Branch, Richland, WA [*Library symbol*] [*Library of Congress*] (LCLS) .... WaRiGS

Church of Jesus Christ of Latter-Day Saints, Genealogical Society Library, Richmond Stake Branch, Richmond, VA [*Library symbol*] [*Library of Congress*] (LCLS) .... ViRGS

Church of Jesus Christ of Latter-Day Saints, Genealogical Society Library, Riverside Branch, Riverside, CA [*Library symbol*] [*Library of Congress*] (LCLS) .... CRivGS

Church of Jesus Christ of Latter-Day Saints, Genealogical Society Library, Riverside West Branch, Riverside, CA [*Library symbol*] [*Library of Congress*] (LCLS) .... CRivGS-W

Church of Jesus Christ of Latter-Day Saints, Genealogical Society Library, Rochester Branch, Rochester, NY [*Library symbol*] [*Library of Congress*] (LCLS) .... NRGS

Church of Jesus Christ of Latter-Day Saints, Genealogical Society Library, Sacramento Branch, Sacramento, CA [*Library symbol*] [*Library of Congress*] (LCLS) .... CSGS

Church of Jesus Christ of Latter-Day Saints, Genealogical Society Library, Safford Branch, Safford, AZ [*Library symbol*] [*Library of Congress*] (LCLS) .... AzSafGS

Church of Jesus Christ of Latter-Day Saints, Genealogical Society Library, SalemBranch, Salem, OR [*Library symbol*] [*Library of Congress*] (LCLS) .... OrSaGS

Church of Jesus Christ of Latter-Day Saints, Genealogical Society Library, Salmon Branch, Salmon River Stake Center, Salmon, ID [*Library symbol*] [*Library of Congress*] (LCLS) .... IdSulGS

Church of Jesus Christ of Latter-Day Saints, Genealogical Society Library, Salt Lake City, UT [*Library symbol*] [*Library of Congress*] (LCLS) .... USlGS

Church of Jesus Christ of Latter-Day Saints, Genealogical Society Library, San Antonio Branch, San Antonio, TX [*Library symbol*] [*Library of Congress*] (LCLS) .... TxSaGS

Church of Jesus Christ of Latter-Day Saints, Genealogical Society Library, San Bernardino Branch, San Bernardino, CA [*Library symbol*] [*Library of Congress*] (LCLS) .... CSbGS

Church of Jesus Christ of Latter-Day Saints, Genealogical Society Library, San Diego Branch, San Diego, CA [*Library symbol*] [*Library of Congress*] (LCLS) .... CSdGS

Church of Jesus Christ of Latter-Day Saints, Genealogical Society Library, San Jose Branch, San Jose, CA [*Library symbol*] [*Library of Congress*] (LCLS) .... CSjGS

Church of Jesus Christ of Latter-Day Saints, Genealogical Society Library, San Luis Obispo Branch, San Luis Obispo, CA [*Library symbol*] [*Library of Congress*] (LCLS) .... CSluGS

Church of Jesus Christ of Latter-Day Saints, Genealogical Society Library, SandySprings Georgia Branch, Dunwoody, GA [*Library symbol*] [*Library of Congress*] (LCLS) .... GDunGS

Church of Jesus Christ of Latter-Day Saints, Genealogical Society Library, SantaBarbara Branch, Goleta, CA [*Library symbol*] [*Library of Congress*] (LCLS) .... CGoGS

Church of Jesus Christ of Latter-Day Saints, Genealogical Society Library, SantaClara Branch, Santa Clara, CA [*Library symbol*] [*Library of Congress*] (LCLS) .... CStclGS

Church of Jesus Christ of Latter-Day Saints, Genealogical Society Library, SantaMaria Branch, Lompoc, CA [*Library symbol*] [*Library of Congress*] (LCLS) .... CLomGS

Church of Jesus Christ of Latter-Day Saints, Genealogical Society Library, Santaquin Stake Branch, Santaquin, UT [*Library symbol*] [*Library of Congress*] (LCLS) .... USanGS

Church of Jesus Christ of Latter-Day Saints, Genealogical Society Library, Seattle North Branch, Seattle, WA [*Library symbol*] [*Library of Congress*] (LCLS) .... WaSGS

Church of Jesus Christ of Latter-Day Saints, Genealogical Society Library, Show Low Branch, Show Low, AZ [*Library symbol*] [*Library of Congress*] (LCLS) .... AzShGS

Church of Jesus Christ of Latter-Day Saints, Genealogical Society Library, Silver Spring Branch, Silver Spring, MD [*Library symbol*] [*Library of Congress*] (LCLS) .... MdSsGS

Church of Jesus Christ of Latter-Day Saints, Genealogical Society Library, Snowflake Branch, Snowflake, AZ [*Library symbol*] [*Library of Congress*] (LCLS) .... AzSnGS

Church of Jesus Christ of Latter-Day Saints, Genealogical Society Library, Spokane Branch, Spokane, WA [*Library symbol*] [*Library of Congress*] (LCLS) .... WaSpGL

Church of Jesus Christ of Latter-Day Saints, Genealogical Society Library, Springville Branch, Springville, UT [*Library symbol*] [*Library of Congress*] (LCLS) .... USpGS

Church of Jesus Christ of Latter-Day Saints, Genealogical Society Library, St. David Arizona Stake Branch, St. David, AZ [*Library symbol*] [*Library of Congress*] (LCLS) .... AzStdGS

Church of Jesus Christ of Latter-Day Saints, Genealogical Society Library, St. George Branch, St. George, UT [*Library symbol*] [*Library of Congress*] (LCLS) .... UStgGS

Church of Jesus Christ of Latter-Day Saints, Genealogical Society Library, St. Johns Branch, Stake Center, St. Johns, AZ [*Library symbol*] [*Library of Congress*] (LCLS) .... AzSjGS

Church of Jesus Christ of Latter-Day Saints, Genealogical Society Library, St. Louis Branch, St. Louis, MO [*Library symbol*] [*Library of Congress*] (LCLS) .... MoSGS

Church of Jesus Christ of Latter-Day Saints, Genealogical Society Library, Stockton Branch, Stockton, CA [*Library symbol*] [*Library of Congress*] (LCLS) .... CStoGS

Church of Jesus Christ of Latter-Day Saints, Genealogical Society Library, Sydney Branch, Sydney, NSW, Australia [*Library symbol*] [*Library of Congress*] (LCLS) ... AuSGS
Church of Jesus Christ of Latter-Day Saints, Genealogical Society Library, Sydney South Branch, Sutherland Ward Chapel, Kirrawee, NSW, Australia [*Library symbol*] [*Library of Congress*] (LCLS) ... AuKirGS
Church of Jesus Christ of Latter-Day Saints, Genealogical Society Library, Tacoma Branch, Tacoma, WA [*Library symbol*] [*Library of Congress*] (LCLS) ... WaTGS
Church of Jesus Christ of Latter-Day Saints, Genealogical Society Library, TampaBranch, Tampa, FL [*Library symbol*] [*Library of Congress*] (LCLS) ... FTGS
Church of Jesus Christ of Latter-Day Saints, Genealogical Society Library, Temple View Branch, Temple View, New Zealand [*Library symbol*] [*Library of Congress*] (LCLS) ... NzTvGS
Church of Jesus Christ of Latter-Day Saints, Genealogical Society Library, Tennessee South District Branch, Tullahoma, TN [*Library symbol*] [*Library of Congress*] (LCLS) ... TTuGS
Church of Jesus Christ of Latter-Day Saints, Genealogical Society Library, Toronto Branch, Etobicoke, ON, Canada [*Library symbol*] [*Library of Congress*] (LCLS) ... CaOTCJC
Church of Jesus Christ of Latter-Day Saints, Genealogical Society Library, Tucson Branch, Tucson, AZ [*Library symbol*] [*Library of Congress*] (LCLS) ... AzTGS
Church of Jesus Christ of Latter-Day Saints, Genealogical Society Library, TulsaBranch, Tulsa, OK [*Library symbol*] [*Library of Congress*] (LCLS) ... OkTGS
Church of Jesus Christ of Latter-Day Saints, Genealogical Society Library, Twin Falls Branch, Twin Falls, ID [*Library symbol*] [*Library of Congress*] (LCLS) ... IdTfGS
Church of Jesus Christ of Latter-Day Saints, Genealogical Society Library, Uintah Basin Branch, Vernal, UT [*Library symbol*] [*Library of Congress*] (LCLS) ... UVGS
Church of Jesus Christ of Latter-Day Saints, Genealogical Society Library, Utah Valley Branch, Provo, UT [*Library symbol*] [*Library of Congress*] (LCLS) ... UPGS
Church of Jesus Christ of Latter-Day Saints, Genealogical Society Library, Vancouver Branch, Stake Center, Burnaby, Vancouver, BC, Canada [*Library symbol*] [*Library of Congress*] (LCLS) ... CaBBCJC
Church of Jesus Christ of Latter-Day Saints, Genealogical Society Library, Ventura Branch, Ventura, CA [*Library symbol*] [*Library of Congress*] (LCLS) ... CVtGS
Church of Jesus Christ of Latter-Day Saints, Genealogical Society Library, Wellington Stake Branch, Wellington, New Zealand [*Library symbol*] [*Library of Congress*] (LCLS) ... NzWGS
Church of Jesus Christ of Latter-Day Saints Genealogical Society Library, Wichita Branch (SAUO) ... KWiGS
Church of Jesus Christ of Latter-Day Saints, Genealogical Society Library, Wichita Branch, Wichita, KS [*Library symbol*] [*Library of Congress*] (LCLS) ... KWiGS
Church of Jesus Christ of Latter-Day Saints, Genealogical Society Library, Wilmette Branch, Wilmette, IL [*Library symbol*] [*Library of Congress*] (LCLS) ... IWilGS
Church of Jesus Christ of Latter-Day Saints, Genealogical Society Library, Wisconsin East District Branch, Shawano, WI [*Library symbol*] [*Library of Congress*] (LCLS) ... WShawGS
Church of Jesus Christ of Latter-Day Saints, Genealogical Society Library, Yakima Branch, Yakima, WA [*Library symbol*] [*Library of Congress*] (LCLS) ... WaYGS
Church of Jesus Christ of Latter-Day Saints, Genealogical Society Library, Yuma Branch, Yuma, AZ [*Library symbol*] [*Library of Congress*] (LCLS) ... AzYGS
Church of Jesus Christ of Latter-Day Saints, Historian's Office, Salt Lake City,UT [*Library symbol*] [*Library of Congress*] (LCLS) ... USIC
Church of Jesus Christ of Latter-Day-Saints, Genealogical Society Library, Ridgecrest [*Library symbol*] [*Library of Congress*] (LCLS) ... CRidGS
Church of Monday Night Football (EA) ... CMNFB
Church of Scientology ... CoS
Church of Scientology of California (EA) ... CSC
Church of Scotland ... C of S
Church of Scotland (WDAA) ... CofS
Church of Scotland ... C of SCOT
Church of Scotland (SAUO) ... CS
Church of Scotland and Free Churches [*British military*] (DMA) ... CSFC
Church of Scotland and Free Churches Chaplain [*Navy*] [*British*] ... CSFCh
Church of Scotland Chaplain [*British military*] (DMA) ... C of S Ch
Church of Scotland Mission (SAUO) ... CSM
Church of South India (SAUO) ... CSI
Church of South India ... CSI
Church of Spiritual Discovery (EA) ... CSD
Church of the Brethren General Board World Ministries Commission (EA) ... WMC
[*The*] **Church of the Brethren Homes and Hospitals Association** [*Later, BHOAM*] (EA) ... CBHHA
Church of the Lutheran Confession ... CLC
Church of the Movement for Spiritual Inner Awareness (ECON) ... MSIA
Church of What's Happening Now (EA) ... CWHN
Church Office for International Relations and News Analysis (SAUO) ... CONTAK Philippines
Church Organization Research and Advisory Trust of Africa (SAUO) ... CORAT AFRICA
Church Organization Research and Advisory Trust of Africa (SAUO) ... CORATAFRICA
Church Pastoral Aid Society (SAUO) ... CPAS
Church Pastoral Aid Society [*British*] ... CPAS
Church Pastoral-Aid Society (SAUO) ... CPA
Church Patronage Society (SAUO) ... CPS
Church Peace Union [*Later, CRIA*] ... CPU
Church Penitentiary Association [*British*] ... CPA
Church Pennant [*Navy*] [*British*] ... CH
Church Pension Fund (EA) ... CPF
Church Pensions Conference (EA) ... CPC
Church Periodical Club (EA) ... CPC
Church Planting International (EA) ... CPI
Church Quarterly Review [*A publication*] (ODCC) ... CQR
Church Record [*Genealogy*] ... CR
Church Records Archives (GEAB) ... CRA
Church Research and Information Projects ... CRIPS
Church Resource Ministries (SAUO) ... CRM
Church Scene [*A publication*] (APTA) ... CS
Church Schools Company Ltd. [*British*] (BI) ... CSC
Church Slavic [*MARC language code*] [*Library of Congress*] (LCCP) ... chu
Church Society for College Work (EA) ... CSCW
Church Sunday School Union (SAUO) ... CSSU
Church Sunday School Union [*British*] ... CSSU
Church Union [*British*] (DAS) ... CU
Church Universal and Triumphant (EA) ... CUT
Church Women United (EA) ... CWU
Church Women's Missionary Association [*Episcopalian*] ... CWMA
Church World Service (SAUO) ... CWRU
Church World Service (SAUO) ... CWS
Church World Service [*Later, CWSW*] (EA) ... CWS
Church World Service Aids for the Horn of Africa (EA) ... CWSAHA
Church World Service and Witness (EA) ... CWSW
Church World Service, Immigration and Refugee Program (EA) ... CWSIRP
Church Youth Fellowship Association (SAUO) ... CYFA
Church Youth Research (SAUO) ... CYR
Churches at Bosra and Samaria-Sebaste [*A publication*] (BJA) ... CBSS
Churches' Center for Theology and Public Policy (EA) ... CCTPP
Churches Commission on Overseas Students (EAIO) ... CCOS
[*The*] **Churches' Committee for Supplementing Religious Education Among Men in HM Forces** [*British military*] (DMA) ... CCMF
Churches' Committee for Voter Registration-Education (EA) ... CCVRE
Churches Committee for Work Among Women Serving with HM Forces [*British military*] (DMA) ... CWWF
Churches Committee on Migrant Workers (SAUO) ... CCMW
Churches' Committee on Migrants in Europe (EAIO) ... CCME
Churches' Conservation Trust [*British*] (WDAA) ... CCT
Churches' Council on Alcohol and Drugs [*Church of England*] ... CCOAD
Churches' Initiative in Musical Education (WDAA) ... CHIME
Churches' National Housing Coalition (WDAA) ... CNHC
Churches Speak [*A publication*] ... CHU
Churches Speak [*A publication*] ... CS
Churchill [*Canada*] [*Airport symbol*] (OAG) ... YYQ
Churchill and Bruce. Office and Duties of Sheriff [*2nd ed.*] [*1882*] [*A publication*] (DLA) ... Church & Br Sh
Churchill College, Cambridge (SAUS) ... Chur
Churchill Downs, Inc. [*NASDAQ symbol*] (SAG) ... CHDN
Churchill Downs, Inc. [*Associated Press*] (SAG) ... ChrchllD
Churchill Elementary School, Cloquet, MN [*Library symbol*] [*Library of Congress*] (LCLS) ... MnClCE
Churchill Falls [*Canada*] [*Airport symbol*] (OAG) ... ZUM
Churchill Falls, NF [*FM radio station call letters*] ... CFLC
Churchill Falls Public Library, Churchill Falls, NF, Canada [*Library symbol*] [*Library of Congress*] (LCLS) ... CaNfCF
Churchill Falls Public Library, Newfoundland [*Library symbol*] [*National Library of Canada*] (NLC) ... NFCF
Churchill, MB [*AM radio station call letters*] ... CHFC
Churchill, MB [*ICAO location identifier*] (ICLI) ... CYYQ
Churchill Public Library, Churchill, MB, Canada [*Library symbol*] [*Library of Congress*] (LCLS) ... CaMCh
Churchill Public Library, Manitoba [*Library symbol*] [*National Library of Canada*] (NLC) ... MCH
Churchill Research Range [*Air Force*] ... CRR
Churchill Technology [*Associated Press*] (SAG) ... ChchTch
Churchill Technology, Inc. [*NASDAQ symbol*] (NQ) ... CHUR
Churchman Associates (EA) ... CA
Churchman Publishing [*British*] ... CP
Churchman's Library [*A publication*] ... CL
Churchmen's Commission for Decent Publications [*Defunct*] (EA) ... CCDP
ChurchNews International [*Database*] [*Resources for Communication*] [*Information service or system*] (CRD) ... CNI
Church-Related Educational Development Organization (SAUO) ... CREDO
Church's Ministry among Jews [*Church of England*] ... CMJ
Churchville, VA [*FM radio station call letters*] ... WBOP
Churchville, VA [*AM radio station call letters*] ... WNLR
Churchville-Chili Senior High School Library, Rochester, NY [*OCLC symbol*] (OCLC) ... RVY
Churchwarden ... C
Churchwarden ... CHWDN
Churchwarden ... CW
Churchyard ... CHYD
Churdan City Library, Churdan, IA [*Library symbol*] [*Library of Congress*] (LCLS) ... IaChu
Churg-Strauss Syndrome [*Medicine*] (STED) ... CSS
Churn Analysis, Modeling, and Prediction (IDAI) ... CHAMP
Churn Drill Hole (SAUS) ... CDH
Churubusco, IN [*FM radio station call letters*] (RBYB) ... WEJE
Chusal [*Former USSR*] [*Seismograph station code, US Geological Survey*] [*Closed*] (SEIS) ... CHS

Chute [KSC] .... CH
Chute [KSC] .... CHT
Chute's Equity under the Judicature Act [A publication] [DLA] .... Chute Eq
Chutine Resources Ltd. [Vancouver Stock Exchange symbol] .... CHS
Chutty [Chewing gum] [Slang] [British] [DSUE] .... CHUT
Chutz La'aretz [BJA] .... CHTr
Chutzpah [SAUS] .... CH-factor
Chuvash [MARC language code] [Library of Congress] [LCCP] .... chv
Chylomicron Remnant [Physiology] .... CR
Chylomicrons [MELL] .... CM
Chymase Heart [DMAA] .... CYH
Chymohelizyme [Biochemistry] .... CHZ
Chymotrypsin [An enzyme] .... ChTr
Chymotrypsin [An enzyme] .... CT
Chymotrypsin Inhibitor Activity .... CIA
Chymotrypsin Unit .... CU
Chymotrypsin Units Inhibited .... CUI
Chymotrypsin-Like [Protease] [DMAA] .... CTRL
Chymotrypsin-Like Protein [STED] .... CLP
Chymotrypsinogen [Biochemistry] .... ChTg
Chymotrypsinogen [DB] .... CTG
Chymotrypsinogen B [Biochemistry] .... CTRB
Chyron Corp. [NYSE symbol] [SPSG] .... CHY
Chyron Corp. [Associated Press] [SAG] .... Chyron
CI Realty Investors SBI [SAUO] CIX
Ciao Cucina Corp. [Associated Press] [SAG] .... CiaoCuc
Ciao Cucina Corp. [NASDAQ symbol] [SAG] .... CIAU
Ciatti's, Inc. [NASDAQ symbol] [NQ] .... CIAT
Ciatti's, Inc. [Associated Press] [SAG] .... Ciattis
Ciba Co. Ltd., Montreal, PQ, Canada [Library symbol] [Library of Congress] [LCLS] .... CaQMCi
Ciba Foundation Symposium [SAUO] .... Ciba Found Symp
Ciba Pharmaceutical Co., Research Library, Summit, NJ [Library symbol] [Library of Congress] [LCLS] .... NjSC
Cibachrome [VRA] .... CIBCH
Cibachrome Print [SAUS] .... CCP
Cibachrome-Print [Color photography] .... CCP
Ciba-Geigy [France] [Research code symbol] .... AP
Ciba-Geigy AG [Switzerland] [Research code symbol] .... Ba
Ciba-Geigy AG [Switzerland] [Research code symbol] C
Ciba-Geigy AG [Switzerland] [Research code symbol] .... G
Ciba-Geigy AG [Switzerland] [Research code symbol] .... GP
Ciba-Geigy Canada Ltd., Dorval, PQ, Canada [Library symbol] [Library of Congress] [LCLS] .... CaQMCG
Ciba/Geigy Canada Ltd., Mississauga, ON, Canada [Library symbol] [Library of Congress] [LCLS] .... CaOMCG
Ciba/Geigy Canada Ltd., Mississauga, Ontario [Library symbol] [National Library of Canada] [NLC] .... OMCG
Ciba-Geigy Corp. [Research code symbol] .... GPA
Ciba-Geigy Corp. [Research code symbol] .... Su
Ciba-Geigy Corp., Biotechnology Library, Durham, NC [Library symbol] [Library of Congress] [LCLS] .... NcDurCG
CIBA-GEIGY Corp., Corporate Library, Ardsley, NY [Library symbol] [Library of Congress] [LCLS] .... NArdCG
Ciba-Geigy Corp., Technical Information Service, Greensboro, NC [Library symbol] [Library of Congress] [LCLS] .... NcGCG
CIBER, Inc. [NYSE symbol] [SG] .... CBR
Ciber, Inc. [Associated Press] [SAG] .... CIBER
Ciber, Inc. [NASDAQ symbol] [SAG] .... CIBR
Ciborium [VRA] .... cibr
Cibus [Meal] [Latin] C
Cibus [Meal] [Latin] .... CIB
CICAR [Cooperative Investigation of the Caribbean and Adjacent Regions] Data Inventory [Marine science] [MSC] .... CICARDI
CICAR [Cooperative Investigation of the Caribbean and Adjacent Regions] Intercalibration Experiment [Marine science] [MSC] .... CINTEX
Cicatricial Ocular Pemphigoid [Ophthalmology] [DAVI] .... COP
Cicatricial Pemphigoid [Medicine] .... CP
Cicero [Marcus Tullius, Roman orator and author, 106-43BC] [Classical studies] CIC
Cicero [of Plutarch] [Classical studies] [OCD] Cic
Cicero, IL [AM radio station call letters] .... WCEV
Cicero, IL [AM radio station call letters] .... WVON
Cicero Public Library, Cicero, IL [Library symbol] [Library of Congress] [LCLS] ICic
Cicero's De Oratore [A publication] [DLA] .... De Orat
Cicia [Fiji] [Airport symbol] [OAG] ICI
Ciclopirox Olamine [Antifungal agent] .... CO
CICS [Customer Information Control System] Queue Command Facility [Computer science] [HGAA] .... CQCF
Cicutoxin [SAUS] .... CT
CID [Consortium on International Development] Information Network .... CIDNET
Cidco, Inc. [NASDAQ symbol] [SAG] .... CDCO
Cidco, Inc. [Associated Press] [SAG] .... Cidco
Cider Association of North America [EA] .... CANA
Cidra, PR [FM radio station call letters] .... WBRQ
CIE color space [SAUS] .... XYY
CIE color space [SAUS] .... XYZ
CIE color space, Laboratory [SAUS] .... LAB
Cie. Internationale des Wagons-Lits et du Tourisme [International Sleeping Car Co.] .... CIWLT
CIE [Communications Interface Equipment] Test Unit .... CTU
Ciego de Avila [Cuba] [ICAO location identifier] [ICLI] .... MUCA
Ciego De Avila Norte [Cuba] [ICAO location identifier] [ICLI] .... MUCN
Ciena [Stock market symbol] .... CIEN

CIENA Corp. [NASDAQ symbol] [SG] .... CIEN
Cienfuegos [Cuba] [Airport symbol] [Obsolete] [OAG] .... CFG
Cienfuegos [Cuba] [ICAO location identifier] [ICLI] .... MUCF
Cierics Regular of Somasca [SAUO] .... CRS
Ciesta Gold Exploration Ltd. [Vancouver Stock Exchange symbol] CI
Ciga Hotels Aviation SpA [Italy] [ICAO designator] [FAAC] .... CHO
Cigar .... CG
Cigar Association of America [EA] .... CAA
Cigar Box Makers' and Paperers' Trade Union [British] .... CBMPTU
Cigar Box Manufacturers [Defunct] [EA] .... CBM
Cigar Institute of America [Later, CAA] [EA] .... CIA
Cigar Makers International Union of America [SAUO] .... CMIU
Cigar Makers' International Union of America [EA] .... CMIU of A
Cigar Makers' Mutual Association [A union] [British] .... CMMA
Cigar Manufacturers Association of America [Later, CAA] [EA] .... CMA
Cigar Manufacturers Association of America [Later, CAA] .... CMAA
Cigar Manufacturers Association of Tampa [SAUO] .... CMAT
Cigar Smokers of America [Defunct] [EA] .... CSA
Cigarette .... CIG
Cigarette Advertising Code, Inc. [EA] .... CAC
Cigarette Advertising Normally Directed to Youth [Student legal action organization] .... CANDY
Cigarette [or Cigar] Lighter [Automotive engineering] .... C/LTR
Cigarette Lighter Manufacturers Association [EA] .... CLMA
Cigarette Machine Operators' Society [A union] [British] .... CMOS
Cigarette Makers' and Tobacco Cutters' Union [British] .... CMTCU
Cigarette Pack Collectors Association [EA] .... CPCA
Cigarette Smoke [or Smoker] [DAVI] .... CS
Cigarette Smoke Condensate .... CSC
Cigarettes per Day [Medicine] .... C/d
Cigna Corp. [EFIS] .... CG
CIGNA Corp. [NYSE symbol] [SPSG] CI
CIGNA Corp. [Associated Press] [SAG] .... CIGNA
CIGNA High Income Shares [Associated Press] [SAG] .... CIGHi
CIGNA High Income Shares [NYSE symbol] [SPSG] .... HIS
Ciguatera Fish Poisoning [Medicine] .... CFP
Ciguatoxin .... CT
Ciguatoxin [Agent in fish poisoning] .... CTX
C-I-L, Inc. [Toronto Stock Exchange symbol] CIL
Cilacap/Tunggul Wulung [Indonesia] [ICAO location identifier] [ICLI] .... WIIL
Cilag-Chemie AG [Switzerland] [Research code symbol] C
Cilag-Chemie AG [Switzerland] [Research code symbol] .... R
Cilco, Sanford, NC [Library symbol] [Library of Congress] [LCLS] .... NcSaCi
Cilcorp [NYSE symbol] [SAG] .... CER
CILCORP ,Inc. [NYSE symbol] [TTSB] .... CER
Cilcorp., Inc. [Associated Press] [SAG] .... Cilcorp
Cilgener SA [Associated Press] [SAG] .... Chilgener
Cilia-Associated Respiratory Bacillus [Medicine] [MELL] .... CARB
Ciliary Body [SAUS] .... CB
Ciliary Dyskinesia Activity [PDAA] .... CDA
Ciliary Ganglion [Neurology] .... CG
Ciliary Neurotrophic Factor [Biochemistry] .... CNTF
Ciliary Particle Transport Activity .... CPTA
Ciliated Epithelial Cells [Medicine] .... CEC
Ciliated Groove to Mouth .... CGM
Ciliated Groove to Ventral Sac .... CGVS
Ciliated Grove to Ventral Sac [SAUS] .... CGVS
Cilicap [Indonesia] [Airport symbol] [OAG] .... CXP
Ciliocytopathoria [Medicine] .... CCP
Cilium [MELL] C
Cilium [Zoology] CL
Cilla's Circle of Fans [EAIO] .... CCF
CIM Applications Architecture [SAUS] .... CAA
CIM architecture [SAUS] .... CA
CIM High Yield Sec [AMEX symbol] [TTSB] .... CIM
CIM High Yield Securities [Associated Press] [SAG] .... CIM
CIM Systems Architecture [SAUS] .... CSA
CIM Systems Technology [SAUS] .... CST
CIMA Labs [NASDAQ symbol] [TTSB] .... CIMA
CIMA Labs, Inc. [NASDAQ symbol] [SAG] .... CIMA
CIMA Labs, Inc. [Associated Press] [SAG] .... CIMA Lb
Cima Resources Ltd. [Vancouver Stock Exchange symbol] .... CIU
Cimarron, NM [Location identifier] [FAA] [FAAL] .... CIM
Cimarron Petroleum Ltd. [Toronto Stock Exchange symbol] .... CIR
Cimatron Ltd [NASDAQ symbol] [TTSB] .... CIMTF
Cimbalom [Music] .... CIMB
Cimbalom .... cimb
Cimber Air [ICAO designator] [AD] .... QI
Cimber Air, Sonderjyllands Flyveselskab [Denmark] [ICAO designator] [FAAC] .... DQI
Cimbr Air, AS [Denmark] [FAA designator] [FAAC] .... CIM
CIMCO, Inc. [NASDAQ symbol] [NQ] .... CIMC
Cimco, Inc. [Associated Press] [SAG] .... Cimco
Cimel Sunphotometer [SAUS] .... CSPHOT
Cimetidine [Pharmacology] C
Cimetidine [Pharmacology] CI
Cimex [Genus of microorganisms] [MAH] C
CIMIC Exercise [SAUO] .... CIMICEX
Cimitarra [Colombia] [Airport symbol] [OAG] .... CIM
Cimon [of Plutarch] [Classical studies] [OCD] .... Cim
CIM-Oncologie [SAUO] .... CIM-O
Cinar Films CI'B' [NASDAQ symbol] [TTSB] .... CINRF
Cinar Films, Inc. [Associated Press] [SAG] .... CinarF
Cinar Films, Inc. [NASDAQ symbol] [SAG] .... CINR
CINC [Commander in Chief] Command Center [DOMA] CCC

CINC [*Commander-in-Chief*] **Initiative Fund** [*DoD*] ... CIF
CINC Mobile Alternate Headquarters (SAUO) ... CMAH
CINC Mobile Command Center (SAUO) ... CMCC
CINC [*Commander in Chief*] **Strategic Preparedness Assessment Report** (DOMA) ... CSPAR
CINCENT Airlift Coordination Staff (SAUO) ... CACS
CINCFLEETWOC [*British*] [*ICAO location identifier*] (ICLI) ... EGWX
Cinchona [*Quinine*] [*Pharmacology*] (ROG) ... Cinch
Cinchona Products Institute (SAUS) ... CPI
Cincinnati [*Ohio*] ... CIN
Cincinnati [*Ohio*] (WGA) ... Cinn
Cincinnati [*Ohio*] [*Seismograph station code, US Geological Survey*] [*Closed*] (SEIS) ... CNN
Cincinnati [*Ohio*] [*Airport symbol*] (OAG) ... CVG
Cincinnati [*Ohio*] **- Covington** [*Kentucky*] [*Airport symbol*] ... CVG
Cincinnati Accounting Operations Office (COE) ... CAOO
Cincinnati Area Health Sciences Library Association [*Library network*] ... CAHSLA
Cincinnati Art Museum, Cincinnati, OH [*Library symbol*] [*Library of Congress*] (LCLS) ... OCA
Cincinnati Bar Association. Journal [*A publication*] (DLA) ... Cin B Ass'n J
Cincinnati Bell [*NYSE symbol*] (TTSB) ... CSN
Cincinnati Bell, Inc. (EFIS) ... CBIS
Cincinnati Bell, Inc. [*Associated Press*] (SAG) ... CinnBel
Cincinnati Bell, Inc. [*NYSE symbol*] (SPSG) ... CSN
Cincinnati Bell Information Systems (ROAS) ... CBIS
Cincinnati Bell Long Distance (SAUS) ... CBLD
Cincinnati Bengals [*National Football League*] [*1968-present*] (NFLA) ... Cin
Cincinnati Bible Seminary, Cincinnati, OH [*OCLC symbol*] (OCLC) ... BSC
Cincinnati Bible Seminary, Cincinnati, OH [*Library symbol*] [*Library of Congress*] (LCLS) ... OCB
Cincinnati Board of Trade [*Defunct*] (EA) ... CBT
Cincinnati Electronics Corp. [*Information service or system*] [*Defunct*] (IID) ... CE
Cincinnati Electronics Corporation, Cincinnati, OH [*Library symbol*] [*Library of Congress*] (LCLS) ... OCEleC
Cincinnati Financial [*NASDAQ symbol*] (TTSB) ... CINF
Cincinnati Financial Corp. [*NASDAQ symbol*] (NQ) ... CINF
Cincinnati Financial Corp. [*Associated Press*] (SAG) ... CinnFin
Cincinnati Financial Management Center (SAUO) ... CFMC
Cincinnati G & E,4% Pfd [*NYSE symbol*] (TTSB) ... CINPrA
Cincinnati G & El 4 3/4% Pfd [*NYSE symbol*] (TTSB) ... CINPrB
Cincinnati G&E 7.375% Pfd [*NYSE symbol*] (TTSB) ... CINPrG
Cincinnati G&E 7.875% Pfd [*NYSE symbol*] (TTSB) ... CINPrI
Cincinnati G&E8.28%JrSubDebs [*NYSE symbol*] (TTSB) ... JRL
Cincinnati Gas and Electric (SAUS) ... CGAE
Cincinnati Gas & Electric [*NYSE symbol*] (SAG) ... JRL
Cincinnati Gas and Electric Co. (SAUO) ... CG&E
Cincinnati Gas & Electric Co. [*NYSE symbol*] (SPSG) ... CIN
Cincinnati Gas & Electric Co. [*Associated Press*] (SAG) ... CinG
Cincinnati Gas & Electric Co. (SAUO) ... CinGE
Cincinnati Gear Co. (SAUO) ... CINTI
Cincinnati Gear Company (ACAE) ... CGCO
Cincinnati Gear Company (SAUS) ... CINTI
Cincinnati General Hospital, Medical Library, Cincinnati, OH [*Library symbol*] [*Library of Congress*] (LCLS) ... OCG
Cincinnati Historical Society, Cincinnati, OH [*Library symbol*] [*Library of Congress*] (LCLS) ... OCHP
Cincinnati, Indiana & Western Railway ... CI & W
Cincinnati Law Bulletin [*A publication*] (DLA) ... Cinc L Bul
Cincinnati Law Bulletin [*A publication*] (DLA) ... Cin Law Bul
Cincinnati Law Bulletin [*A publication*] (DLA) ... Cin L Bull
Cincinnati Law Library Association, Cincinnati, OH [*Library symbol*] [*Library of Congress*] (LCLS) ... OCLaw
Cincinnati Masonic Temple, Cincinnati, OH [*Library symbol*] [*Library of Congress*] (LCLS) ... OCM
Cincinnati Microwave [*NASDAQ symbol*] (TTSB) ... CNMW
Cincinnati Microwave, Inc. [*Associated Press*] (SAG) ... CinMic
Cincinnati Microwave, Inc. ... CMI
Cincinnati Microwave, Inc. [*NASDAQ symbol*] (NQ) ... CNMW
Cincinnati Microwave Wrrt [*NASDAQ symbol*] (TTSB) ... CNMWW
Cincinnati Milacron [*NYSE symbol*] (TTSB) ... CMZ
Cincinnati Milacron, Inc. [*Associated Press*] (SAG) ... CinMil
Cincinnati Milacron, Inc. [*NYSE symbol*] (SPSG) ... CMZ
Cincinnati Milacron, Inc., Corporate Information Center, Cincinnati, OH [*OCLC symbol*] (OCLC) ... CML
Cincinnati Milacron, Inc., Corporate Information Center, Cincinnati, OH [*Library symbol*] [*Library of Congress*] (LCLS) ... OCMilC
Cincinnati Milacron, Inc., Research Library, Cincinnati, OH [*Library symbol*] [*Library of Congress*] (LCLS) ... OCMil
Cincinnati Milacron, Inc., Technical Information Center, Cincinnati, OH [*Library symbol*] [*Library of Congress*] (LCLS) ... OCMil-T
Cincinnati Municipal Decisions [*A publication*] (DLA) ... Cin Mun Dec
Cincinnati Museum (SAUS) ... CM
Cincinnati, New Orleans & Texas Pacific Railroad (MHDB) ... CNO & TPR
Cincinnati, New Orleans & Texas Pacific Railway Co. ... CNO & TP
Cincinnati, New Orleans & Texas Pacific Railway Co. [*AAR code*] ... CNTP
Cincinnati Northern [*AAR code*] ... CNOR
Cincinnati Numerical Automatic Programming (SAUS) ... CINAP
Cincinnati, OH [*Location identifier*] [*FAA*] (FAAL) ... LUK
Cincinnati, OH [*Location identifier*] [*FAA*] (FAAL) ... MDE
Cincinnati, OH [*FM radio station call letters*] ... WAKW
Cincinnati, OH [*AM radio station call letters*] ... WAOZ
Cincinnati, OH [*FM radio station call letters*] (RBYB) ... WAZU-FM
Cincinnati, OH [*Television station call letters*] ... WCET
Cincinnati, OH [*AM radio station call letters*] ... WCIN
Cincinnati, OH [*AM radio station call letters*] ... WCKY
Cincinnati, OH [*Television station call letters*] ... WCPO
Cincinnati, OH [*Television station call letters*] (BROA) ... WCPO-DT
Cincinnati, OH [*FM radio station call letters*] ... WEBN
Cincinnati, OH [*FM radio station call letters*] ... WGUC
Cincinnati, OH [*FM radio station call letters*] ... WJVS
Cincinnati, OH [*AM radio station call letters*] (BROA) ... WKRC
Cincinnati, OH [*Television station call letters*] ... WKRC-TV
Cincinnati, OH [*FM radio station call letters*] ... WKRQ
Cincinnati, OH [*AM radio station call letters*] ... WLW
Cincinnati, OH [*Television station call letters*] ... WLWT
Cincinnati, OH [*Television station call letters*] (BROA) ... WLWT-DT
Cincinnati, OH [*FM radio station call letters*] ... WRRM
Cincinnati, OH [*AM radio station call letters*] ... WSAI
Cincinnati, OH [*Television station call letters*] ... WSTR
Cincinnati, OH [*AM radio station call letters*] ... WTSJ
Cincinnati, OH [*AM radio station call letters*] ... WUBE
Cincinnati, OH [*FM radio station call letters*] ... WUBE-FM
Cincinnati, OH [*FM radio station call letters*] (BROA) ... WVMX-FM
Cincinnati, OH [*FM radio station call letters*] ... WVXU
Cincinnati, OH [*FM radio station call letters*] ... WWNK
Cincinnati Public Library (SAUS) ... CPL
Cincinnati Reds [*National Football League*] [*1933-34*] (NFLA) ... CiR
Cincinnati Service Center [*IRS*] ... CSC
Cincinnati Society of Natural History (SAUO) ... CSNH
Cincinnati Stock Exchange ... CI
Cincinnati Stock Exchange [*Ohio*] ... CSE
Cincinnati Superior Court Decisions [*Ohio*] [*A publication*] (DLA) ... Hosea's Rep
Cincinnati Superior Court Reporter [*Ohio*] [*A publication*] (DLA) ... Cinc Sup Ct Rep
Cincinnati Superior Court Reporter [*Ohio*] [*A publication*] (DLA) ... Cinc Super
Cincinnati Superior Court Reporter [*Ohio*] [*A publication*] (DLA) ... Cin Sup Ct R
Cincinnati Superior Court Reporter [*Ohio*] [*A publication*] (DLA) ... Cin Super Ct
Cincinnati Superior Court Reporter [*Ohio*] [*A publication*] (DLA) ... CSCR
Cincinnati Superior Court Reports [*Ohio*] [*A publication*] (DLA) ... Cinc (Ohio)
Cincinnati Superior Court Reports [*Ohio*] [*A publication*] (DLA) ... Cin R
Cincinnati Superior Court Reports [*Ohio*] [*A publication*] (DLA) ... Cin Rep
Cincinnati Superior Court Reports [*Ohio*] [*A publication*] (DLA) ... Cin SCR
Cincinnati Superior Court Reports [*Ohio*] [*A publication*] (DLA) ... Cin SC Rep
Cincinnati Superior Court Reports [*Ohio*] [*A publication*] (DLA) ... Cin Sup Ct
Cincinnati Superior Court Reports [*Ohio*] [*A publication*] (DLA) ... Cin Sup Ct Rep
Cincinnati Superior Court Reports [*Ohio*] [*A publication*] (DLA) ... Cin Super Ct Rep'r
Cincinnati Superior Court Reports [*Ohio*] [*A publication*] (DLA) ... Cin Super (Ohio)
Cincinnati Symphony Orchestra (BARN) ... CSO
Cincinnati Technical College, Cincinnati, OH [*Library symbol*] [*Library of Congress*] [*OCLC symbol*] (LCLS) ... OCT
Cincinnati Testing and Research Laboratories (SAUO) ... CTL
Cincinnati Testing Laboratories (SAUS) ... CTL
Cincinnati Uplink, Inc. [*Cincinnati, OH*] [*Telecommunications*] (TSSD) ... CUI
Cincinnati, Washington & Baltimore Railroad ... CW & B
Cincinnati Weekly Law Bulletin (SAUS) ... Weekly Cin Law Bull
Cincinnati Weekly Law Bulletin [*A publication*] (DLA) ... Weekly Cin Law Bull
Cincinnati/Greater Cincinnati [*Ohio*] [*ICAO location identifier*] (ICLI) ... KCVG
Cincinnati/Municipal-Lunken Field [*Ohio*] [*ICAO location identifier*] (ICLI) ... KLUK
Cincinnati/New Orleans City Ballet ... C/NOCB
Cincinnatus Society [*Defunct*] (EA) ... CS
CINCLANT Command Center Automation System (SAUO) ... CCACS
CINCPAC [*Commander-in-Chief, Pacific*] **Operation Center** (CINC) ... COC
CINCPAC [*Commander-in-Chief, Pacific*] **Route Slip** (CINC) ... CPRS
CINCPAC [*Commander-in-Chief, Pacific*] **Supplement to DoD Basic Planning** [*Department of Defense*] (CINC) ... CSBPD
CINCPAC [*Commander-in-Chief, Pacific*] **Supplement to the Military Assistance Manual** (CINC) ... CSMAM
CINCPAC Support Group (SAUO) ... CSG
CINCPAC [*Commander-in-Chief, Pacific*] **Teletype Automated Net** (NVT) ... CTAN
CINCPAC Voice Alert Net (MCD) ... CVN
CINCPAC [*Commander-in-Chief, Pacific*] **Voice Automated Net** (NVT) ... CVAN
CINCPACAF [*Commander-in-Chief, Pacific Air Force*] **Integrated Decision Support System** ... CIDSS
CINC's [*Commander in Chief's*] **Strategic Priorities Assessment** (DOMA) ... CSPA
Cinder-Block on Concrete Slab [*Construction*] ... CBS
Cinderella Softball Leagues (EA) ... CSL
Cinders [*Quality of the bottom*] [*Nautical charts*] ... Cn
C-Index Sequential Access Method (SAUS) ... C-ISAM
Cine [*Turkey*] [*Seismograph station code, US Geological Survey*] (SEIS) ... CIN
Cine Coronary Arteriography [*Medicine*] (MELL) ... CCA
Cine Target Range Projection System (SAUS) ... CTRPS
Cine Video Recording (SAUS) ... CVR
Cinegraphic Scoring System (MCD) ... CSS
Cinema (SAUS) ... Cine
Cinema (WDMC) ... cine
Cinema ... CINE
Cinema Advertising Association [*British*] ... CAA
Cinema and Television Benevolent Fund [*British*] ... CTBF
Cinema Board [*Tasmania*] [*Australia*] ... CB
Cinema Center Films ... CCF
Cinema Digital Sound ... CDS
Cinema Industry Benevolent Fund of Victoria [*Australia*] ... CIBFV
Cinema International Corporation (SAUO) ... CIC
Cinema Organ Society [*British*] ... COS
Cinema Ride [*Associated Press*] (SAG) ... CineRide
Cinema Ride [*Associated Press*] (SAG) ... CinRd
Cinema Ride Inc. [*NASDAQ symbol*] (TTSB) ... MOVE
Cinema Ride Wrrt [*NASDAQ symbol*] (TTSB) ... MOVEW
Cinema Television Digest ... CTVD
Cinema Theatre Association [*British*] ... CTA

Cinemas [*Public-performance tariff class*] [*British*] ... C
Cinemascope ... CS
Cinemastar Luxry Theaters Wrrt [*NASDAQ symbol*] (TTSB) ... LUXYW
Cinemastar Luxury Theaters [*NASDAQ symbol*] (TTSB) ... LUXY
CinemaStar Luxury Theaters, Inc. [*Associated Press*] (SAG) ... CinStar
CinemaStar Luxury Theaters, Inc. [*Associated Press*] (SAG) ... CinStr
CinemaStar Luxury Theaters, Inc. [*NASDAQ symbol*] (SAG) ... LUXY
Cinema-Televivion, Ltd. (SAUO) ... CINTEL
Cinematheque Quebecoise, Montreal, Quebec [*Library symbol*] [*National Library of Canada*] (BIB) ... QMCQ
Cinematheque Scientifique Internationale [*International Scientific Film Library*] ... CSI
Cinematografia [*Ministerio de Cultura*] [*Spain*] [*Information service or system*] (CRD) ... CINE
Cinematograph Exhibitioners' Association of Great Britian and Ireland ... CEA
Cinematograph Exhibitors' Association [*Australia*] ... CEA
Cinematograph Exhibitors Association of Great Britain and Ireland (SAUO) ... CEA
Cinematograph Films Council [*British*] ... CFC
Cinematograph Operators' Board [*Victoria*] [*Australia*] ... COB
Cinematograph Trade Benevolent Fund (SAUO) ... CTBF
Cinematographic (MSA) ... CINE
Cinematographic Films Council (SAUO) ... CFC
Cinematography (SAUS) ... Cine
Cinematography (ADWA) ... cinemat
Cinemax [*Cable television channel*] ... MAX
Cinemists 63 (EA) ... C63
Cineplex Odeon Corp. [*Associated Press*] (SAG) ... CineOd
Cineplex Odeon Corp. [*NYSE symbol*] [*Toronto Stock Exchange symbol*] ... CPX
Cinequity Corp. [*Toronto Stock Exchange symbol*] ... CEQ
Cinergi Pictures Entertain [*NASDAQ symbol*] (TTSB) ... CINE
Cinergi Pictures Entertainment, Inc. [*NASDAQ symbol*] (SAG) ... CINE
Cinergi Pictures Entertainment, Inc. [*Associated Press*] (SAG) ... Cinergi
CINergy Corp. [*NYSE symbol*] (SAG) ... CIN
CINergy Corp. [*Associated Press*] (SAG) ... CINergy
Cinetheodolite (SAUS) ... CINE
Cinetheodolite Orientation Target Array ... COTA
Cingulate Gyrus (DB) ... CG
Cingulate Motor Area [*Part of brain's cortex*] ... CMA
Cingulate Sulcus (DB) ... CiS
Cinnabar Resources Ltd. [*Vancouver Stock Exchange symbol*] ... CBS
Cinnamic Acid [*Organic chemistry*] (OA) ... CA
Cinnaminson Little Paper, Cinnaminson, NJ [*Library symbol*] [*Library of Congress*] (LCLS) ... NjCiL
Cinnamomum [*Cinnamon*] [*Pharmacology*] (ROG) ... Cinnam
Cinnamon Rabbit Breeders Association (EA) ... CRBA
Cinnamyl Alcohol Dehydrogenase [*An enzyme*] ... CAD
Cinque Ports Artillery Volunteers [*British military*] (DMA) ... CPAV
Cinque Ports Rifle Volunteers [*British military*] (DMA) ... CPRV
Cinram Ltd [*NASDAQ symbol*] (TTSB) ... CNRMF
Cinram Ltd. [*Toronto Stock Exchange symbol*] ... CRW
Cintas Corp. [*Associated Press*] (SAG) ... Cintas
Cintas Corp. [*NASDAQ symbol*] (NQ) ... CTAS
Cintered Tungsten-Tantalum Emitter (SAUS) ... CTTE
Cinus de Pistoia [*Deceased, 1336*] [*Authority cited in pre-1607 legal work*] (DSA) ... Ci
CIP Research Ltd., Hawkesbury, Ontario [*Library symbol*] [*National Library of Canada*] (NLC) ... OHKC
CIP3 Editing Library (SAUS) ... CEL
CIP3 Parser Library (SAUS) ... CPL
Cipher and Telephony Equipment [*Military*] ... CIPHONY
Cipher Block Chaine (or Chaining) (SAUS) ... CBC
Cipher Block Chaining [*Computer science*] (HGAA) ... CBC
Cipher Feedback ... CFB
Cipher Telegram (SAUS) ... CT
Cipher Text [*Telecommunications*] (MCD) ... CT
Cipher Text Auto Key [*Computer science*] ... CTAK
Cipher Text Stealing [*Cryptography*] (VERA) ... CTS
Cipher Type Byte (SAUS) ... CTB
Ciphergen Biosystems [*NASDAQ symbol*] ... CIPH
Ciphertext Auto Key (SAUS) ... CAK
Cipolletti [*Argentina*] [*Seismograph station code, US Geological Survey*] [*Closed*] (SEIS) ... CIP
Ciprico, Inc. [*Associated Press*] (SAG) ... Ciprico
Ciprico, Inc. [*NASDAQ symbol*] (NQ) ... CPCI
Ciprofloxacin [*Oral antibiotic*] [*Medicine*] (TAD) ... Cipro
CIPSCO, Inc. [*NYSE symbol*] (SPSG) ... CIP
CIPSCO, Inc. [*Associated Press*] (SAG) ... CIPSCO
CIRC [*Central Information Reference and Control*] **Online Experiment** ... COLEX
Circa [*or Circiter or Circum*] [*About (used with dates denoting approximate time)*] [*Latin*] (GPO) ... c
Circa [*or Circiter or Circum*] [*About (used with dates denoting approximate time)*] [*Latin*] ... ca
Circa [*About, Approximately*] [*Latin*] ... cca
Circa (GEAB) ... cir
Circa [*or Circiter or Circum*] [*About (used with dates denoting approximate time)*] [*Latin*] ... CIR
Circa [*or Circiter or Circum*] [*About (used with dates denoting approximate time)*] [*Latin*] ... CIRC
circadiamy (SAUS) ... circad
circadian (SAUS) ... circad
Circadian Data System (MCD) ... CDS
Circadian Pacemaker [*Neurophysiology*] ... CP
Circadian Periodicity Experiment [*Skylab*] [*NASA*] ... CPE
Circadian Quotient (MAE) ... CQ
Circadian Rhythm (MELL) ... CR
Circadian Rhythm Disorder [*Medicine*] (MELL) ... CRD
Circadian Time [*Physiology*] ... CT
circadic (SAUS) ... circad
Circeo [*Italy*] [*ICAO location identifier*] (ICLI) ... LIQT
Circimus [*Constellation*] ... Cir
Circimus [*Constellation*] ... Circ
Circle [*Freemasonry*] (ROG) ... C
Circle (WDMC) ... cir
Circle ... CIR
Circle (TBD) ... Cir
Circle ... CIRC
Circle (WDMC) ... circ
Circle [*Commonly used*] (OPSA) ... CIRCL
Circle [*Commonly used*] (OPSA) ... CIRCLE
Circle (ROG) ... CR
Circle [*Commonly used*] (OPSA) ... CRCL
Circle [*Commonly used*] (OPSA) ... CRCLE
Circle [*Alaska*] [*Airport symbol*] (OAG) ... IRC
Circle, AK [*Location identifier*] [*FAA*] (FAAL) ... CRC
Circle Analysis System (SAUS) ... CIRCALS
Circle Bed [*Medicine*] ... CB
Circle Card Test [*For syphilis*] ... CT
Circle Cutting ... CCT
Circle Digit Identification (SAUS) ... CDI
Circle End Point ... CEP
Circle Financial Corp. [*Associated Press*] (SAG) ... CircFn
Circle Financial Corp. [*NASDAQ symbol*] (SAG) ... CRCL
Circle Finl [*NASDAQ symbol*] (TTSB) ... CRCL
Circle Hot Springs [*Alaska*] [*Airport symbol*] [*Obsolete*] (OAG) ... CHP
Circle Income Shares [*Associated Press*] (SAG) ... CircInc
Circle Income Shares, Inc. [*NASDAQ symbol*] (NQ) ... CINS
Circle International Group [*NASDAQ symbol*] (SG) ... CRCL
Circle K Corp. [*Associated Press*] (SAG) ... CircleK
Circle K Corp. [*NYSE symbol*] (SAG) ... CRK
Circle K International (EA) ... CKI
Circle, MT [*Location identifier*] [*FAA*] (FAAL) ... CRR
Circle of Companions [*Defunct*] (EA) ... COC
Circle of Equal Probability ... CEP
Circle of Equivalent Vulnerability Radius (ACAE) ... CEVR
Circle of Position [*Boating*] ... COP
Circle of State Librarians [*British*] ... CSL
Circle of Willis [*Medicine*] (MELL) ... COW
Circle Repertory Theater Company ... CRTC
Circle Track [*A publication*] ... CT
Circle Trip [*Travel industry*] (TRID) ... CT
Circle Trip Minimum [*Travel industry*] (TRID) ... CTM
Circle Wire & Cable Corp. (SAUO) ... CWX
Circle/Dashed Circle (MCD) ... CIR/CIRD
Circles [*Commonly used*] (OPSA) ... CIRCLES
Circles [*Postal Service standard*] (OPSA) ... CIRS
Circles Effect Research Group [*British*] (DBA) ... CERES
Circles of Exchange [*Later, COE*] [*An association*] (EA) ... CE
Circles of Exchange (EA) ... COE
Circleville, OH [*Location identifier*] [*FAA*] (FAAL) ... CYO
Circleville, OH [*FM radio station call letters*] ... WAHC
Circleville, OH [*FM radio station call letters*] (BROA) ... WAZU-FM
Circleville, OH [*AM radio station call letters*] ... WNRJ
Circleville, OH [*Location identifier*] [*FAA*] (FAAL) ... XUB
Circling [*Approach and landing charts*] [*Aviation*] ... C
Circling Guidance Light [*Aviation*] (FAAC) ... CGL
Circling the Drain [*Medical slang describing patient who is dying*] ... CTD
Circo Craft Co., Inc. [*Toronto Stock Exchange symbol*] ... CCC
CircOlectric Bed [*A trademark*] [*Medicine*] ... COL
Circon Corp. [*NASDAQ symbol*] (NQ) ... CCON
Circon Corp. [*Associated Press*] (SAG) ... Circon
Circuit ... C
Circuit (NATG) ... CCT
Circuit (NTIO) ... cir
Circuit (AFM) ... CIR
Circuit ... CIRC
Circuit (ADWA) ... circ
Circuit (DD) ... Circt
Circuit (ADWA) ... ckt
Circuit (AAG) ... CKT
Circuit (KSC) ... CRCT
Circuit ... CT
Circuit Access Point [*Telecommunications*] (TEL) ... CAP
Circuit Activation Order ... CAO
Circuit Administration Center (SAUS) ... CAC
Circuit Algebra (SAUS) ... CA
Circuit Allocation Order (SAUS) ... CAO
Circuit Analysis (SAUS) ... CA
Circuit Analysis (SAUS) ... Circal
Circuit Analysis [*Computer science*] ... CIRCAL
Circuit Analyzer - Fault Isolation Generator (PDAA) ... CAFIG
Circuit Assembly and Processing System [*Electronics*] (AAEL) ... CCAPS
Circuit Associated Signaling (SAUS) ... CAS
Circuit Assurance Block (SSD) ... CAB
Circuit Board (DWSG) ... CB
Circuit Board [*Automotive engineering*] ... C/BRD
Circuit Board (SAUS) ... Ckt Bd
Circuit Board Assembly (MCD) ... CBA
Circuit Board Card ... CBC
Circuit Board Card Tester ... CBCT

Circuit Board Design System [*IBM Corp.*] ... CBDS
Circuit Board Extractor ... CBE
Circuit Board Holder ... CBH
Circuit Board Rack ... CBR
[*The*] **Circuit Board Thermometer** [*Computer science*] ... TCBT
Circuit Break/Alternating Current ... CB/ac
Circuit Breaker (NTCM) ... BKR
Circuit Breaker ... CB
Circuit Breaker [*Technical drawings*] (DAC) ... CIR BKR
Circuit Breaker (SAUS) ... Cir Bkr
Circuit Breaker (SAUS) ... Ckt Bkr
Circuit Breaker (MSA) ... CKT BKR
Circuit Breaker and Primary Guidance Navigation Control System (SAUS) ... CB&PGNCS
Circuit Breaker/Direct Current ... CB/dc
Circuit Card (SAUS) ... CC
Circuit Card (SAUS) ... Circard
Circuit Card Assembly (MCD) ... CCA
Circuit Card Design Automation (SAUS) ... CCDA
Circuit Cards (SAUS) ... Circards
Circuit Cellar Intelligent Serial EPROM Programmer [*Computer science*] ... CCSP
Circuit Characteristic Function (SAUS) ... CCF
Circuit Check [*Electronics*] (IAA) ... CK
Circuit City Stores [*NYSE symbol*] (TTSB) ... CC
Circuit City Stores, Inc. [*NYSE symbol*] (SPSG) ... CC
Circuit City Stores, Inc. [*Associated Press*] (SAG) ... CirCty
Circuit City Strs-CarMx Grp [*NYSE symbol*] (SG) ... KMX
Circuit City Strs-CrctCty Grp [*NYSE symbol*] (SG) ... CC
Circuit Closing ... CC
Circuit Closing (SAUS) ... Cir Cl
Circuit Closing (SAUS) ... Ckt Cl
Circuit Concentration Bay (IEEE) ... CCB
Circuit Condition Indicator ... CCI
Circuit Continuity Tester [*Electronics*] (IAA) ... CCT
Circuit Control ... C/C
Circuit Control Office [*Automatic Digital Information Network*] (CET) ... CCO
Circuit Court ... CC
Circuit Court (SAUO) ... CC
Circuit Court (DLA) ... Cir
Circuit Court Decisions [*A publication*] (DLA) ... Cir Ct Dec
Circuit Court Decisions [*Ohio*] [*A publication*] (DLA) ... Cir Ct Dec (Ohio)
Circuit Court Library, Birmingham, AL [*Library symbol*] [*Library of Congress*] (LCLS) ... ABCC
Circuit Court of Appeal (SAUO) ... CCA
Circuit Court of Appeals (GPO) ... CCA
Circuit Court of Appeals (DLA) ... Cir
Circuit Court of Appeals (DLA) ... Cir Ct App
Circuit Court of Appeals (United States) [*A publication*] (DLA) ... CCA (US)
Circuit Court of the United States (DLA) ... CCUS
Circuit Court Reports [*A publication*] (DLA) ... CCR
Circuit Court Reports [*Ohio*] [*A publication*] (DLA) ... Cir Ct R
Circuit Data Sheet ... CDS
Circuit Decisions [*A publication*] (DLA) ... CD
Circuit Defense Counsel ... CDC
Circuit Description (MSA) ... CD
Circuit Descriptive Language ... CDL
Circuit Design Engineer (SAUS) ... Cir Des Eng
Circuit Design Fabrication (NASA) ... CDF
Circuit Design, Fabrication, and Test Data Systems (NASA) ... CDF & TDS
Circuit Design, Fabrication and Test Data Systems (SAUS) ... CDF&TDS
Circuit Design System (MCD) ... CDS
Circuit Diagrams ... CD
Circuit Directory Maintenance (IAA) ... CDM
Circuit Distribution Assembly [*Ground Communications Facility, NASA*] ... CDA
Circuit Distribution Assembly [*Ground Communications Facility, NASA*] ... CDSA
Circuit Edges [*Bookbinding*] (DGA) ... CE
Circuit Edges [*Bookbinding*] (DGA) ... CIRC E
Circuit Emulation Service [*Electronics*] (ACRL) ... CES
Circuit Failure Simulation (SAUS) ... CFS
Circuit Feasibility Model (SAUS) ... CFM
Circuit Finder ... CF
Circuit Finder (MSA) ... CKTF
Circuit Group [*Telecommunications*] (TEL) ... CGRP
Circuit Group Blocking (SAUO) ... CGB
Circuit Group Blocking Acknowledgement (SAUO) ... CGBA
Circuit Group Congestion [*Telecommunications*] (TEL) ... CGC
Circuit Group Congestion Signal [*Telecommunications*] (IAA) ... CGS
Circuit Group Reset Receipt (SAUO) ... CGRR
Circuit Group Reset Sending (SAUO) ... CGRS
Circuit Group Set (SAUO) ... CGSET
Circuit Group Unblocking (SAUO) ... CGU
Circuit Group Unblocking Acknowledgement (SAUO) ... CGUA
Circuit Group Unblocking Acknowledgement Message (SAUS) ... UAG
Circuit Group Unblocking Message (SAUS) ... UBG
Circuit Group-supervision Message (SAUO) ... CGM
Circuit Identification [*Telecommunications*] (TEL) ... CKT-ID
Circuit Identification Code (SAUS) ... CIC
Circuit Information Display Board (SAUS) ... CIDB
Circuit Interrupter (MCD) ... CI
Circuit Judge (DLA) ... CJ
Circuit Layout [*AT & T*] ... CL
Circuit Layout, Automated Scheduling and Production (PDAA) ... CLASP
Circuit Layout Record Card [*Telecommunications*] (TEL) ... CLRC
Circuit Line Up ... CLU
Circuit Load Logic (SAUS) ... CLL
Circuit Logic (SAUS) ... CL
Circuit Maintenance System [*AT & T*] ... CMS
Circuit Mask Translator (SAUS) ... CMAT
Circuit Master (MSA) ... CM
Circuit Master Tape [*Computer science*] (IAA) ... CMT
Circuit Merit (SAUS) ... CM
Circuit Micrologic (SAUS) ... CML
Circuit Mode Data (SAUS) ... CMD
Circuit Mode Voice ... CMV
Circuit Modeller [*Seasim Engineering Software Ltd.*] [*Software package*] (NCC) ... CM
Circuit Modeller Plus [*Seasim Engineering Software Ltd.*] [*Software package*] (NCC) ... CMP
Circuit Module (SAUS) ... CM
Circuit Multiplication System (SAUS) ... CMS
circuit net loss (SAUS) ... cnl
Circuit Net Loss ... CNL
Circuit Noise Power Referred to Zero Transmission Level (SAUS) ... dBaO
Circuit Observation Patrol car (SAUS) ... COP car
Circuit Opening (SAUS) ... Cir Op
Circuit Opening (SAUS) ... Ckt Op
Circuit Order Control (SAUS) ... COC
Circuit Order Layout Record [*Telecommunications*] (TEL) ... COLR
Circuit Order Preparation [*or Processing*] **System** [*AT & T*] ... COPS
Circuit Order Processing System (SAUS) ... COPS
Circuit Package (MSA) ... CP
Circuit Package Schematic (MSA) ... CPS
Circuit Parameter Analysis (SAUS) ... CPA
Circuit Protection Device ... CPD
Circuit Provision System [*AT & T*] ... CPS
Circuit Provisioning Center (SAUS) ... CPC
Circuit Quality Monitoring System ... CQMS
Circuit Reliability Improvement ... CRI
Circuit Requirement Table (MSA) ... CRT
Circuit Research [*Associated Press*] (SAG) ... CircRsh
Circuit Research Laboratories, Inc. [*NASDAQ symbol*] (NQ) ... CRLI
Circuit Reset (SAUS) ... CRS
Circuit Resh Labs [*NASDAQ symbol*] (TTSB) ... CRLI
Circuit Rule Master Tape (SAUS) ... CRMT
Circuit Science, Incorporated (SAUO) ... CSI
Circuit Simulation [*Electronics*] (IAA) ... CCTSIM
Circuit Simulator (MHDB) ... CIRCUS
Circuit State Sequence Number (SAUS) ... CSSN
Circuit Switched Data [*Telecommunications*] ... CSD
Circuit Switched Data Network (NITA) ... CSDN
Circuit Switched Data Service (SAUS) ... CSDS
Circuit Switched Digital Capability [*AT & T*] ... CSDC
Circuit Switched Digital Network (SAUS) ... CSDN
Circuit Switched Line [*Telecommunications*] (MCD) ... CSL
Circuit Switched Multiplexer [*Telecommunications*] ... CS-MUX
Circuit Switched Public Data Network [*Telecommunications*] ... CSPDN
Circuit Switched Voice [*Telecommunications*] ... CSV
Circuit Switching [*Telecommunications*] ... CS
Circuit Switching Center [*Telecommunications*] (TEL) ... CSC
Circuit Switching Magnetic Tape [*Telecommunications*] (AFM) ... CSMT
Circuit Switching Multiplexer (SAUS) ... CSMUX
Circuit Switching Network [*Telecommunications*] ... CSN
Circuit Switching Station [*Telecommunications*] (CET) ... CSS
Circuit Switching Unit [*Telecommunications*] (CET) ... CSU
Circuit Systems [*NASDAQ symbol*] (TTSB) ... CSYI
Circuit Systems, Inc. [*Associated Press*] (SAG) ... CircSy
Circuit Systems, Inc. [*NASDAQ symbol*] (NQ) ... CSYI
Circuit Technology (IAA) ... CT
Circuit Technology (SAUS) ... CTA
Circuit Technology Incorporated (ACAE) ... CTI
Circuit Terminal Unit [*Mercury Communications Ltd.*] [*British*] ... CTU
Circuit Terminating Arrangement ... CTA
Circuit Test Set [*Electricity*] ... CTS
Circuit Theory [*Electricity*] (MCD) ... CT
Circuit Transient Analysis Program (IAA) ... CTAP
Circuit Trial Counsel ... CTC
Circuit under Test [*Electricity*] (IEEE) ... CUT
Circuit Unit Assembly ... CUA
Circuit-Card Assembly and Processing System (SAUS) ... CCAPS
Circuit-Group-Congestion Signal (SAUO) ... CGC Signal
Circuitless Electron Beam Amplifier (MCD) ... CEBA
Circuitry Adapter [*Electronics*] (IAA) ... CA
Circuits (SAUS) ... CKTS
Circuits and Systems [*IEEE*] (MCD) ... CAS
Circuits Master Tape (SAUS) ... CMT
Circuits to Specifications Corp. (SAUO) ... CTS
Circuit-Switched Digital [*or Data*] **Network** [*Telecommunications*] (IAA) ... CSDN
Circuit-Switched Digital Services [*Telecommunications*] (HGAA) ... CSDS
Circuit-Switched Exchange [*Telecommunications*] (IAA) ... CSE
Circuit-to-Pin Ratio (SAUS) ... CP Ratio
Circuit-to-Specification (IAA) ... CTS
CircuitWriter Network [*Information service or system*] (IID) ... CWN
Circuity Upgrade ... CU
Circular ... C
Circular (WDMC) ... cir
Circular (AABC) ... CIR
Circular (WDMC) ... circ
Circular ... CIRCL
Circular (SAUS) ... CR
Circular ... CRCLR

Circular 175 (SAUS) C-175
Circular Active Reflector Antenna (PDAA) .... CARA
Circular Antenna [*Electromagnetism*] (IAA) .... CIRANT
Circular Aperture Aerial (SAUS) .... CAA
Circular Aperture Antenna .... CAA
Circular Arc [*Aviation*] .... CA
Circular Arc .... CIRCARC
Circular Area Method .... CAM
Circular Average Error (SAUS) .... CAE
Circular Capacitor (SAUS) .... CIRCAP
Circular Clip (SAUS) .... Circlip
Circular Crystal Facet .... CCF
Circular Cylindrical Shell .... CCS
Circular Date Stamp [*Postmark of a stamp cancellation*] .... CDS
Circular Dichroism [*Optics*] .... CD
Circular Diffraction Grating .... CDG
Circular Dispersion .... CD
Circular Electric Mode .... CEM
Circular Electric Wire .... CEW
Circular Error [*Military*] .... CE
Circular Error Average [*Military*] .... CEA
Circular Error Probability [*Military*] .... CEP
Circular Error Probability [*Military*] (DNAB) .... CIREP
Circular Error Probable (AAGC) .... CEP
Circular Exhaust Cloud (PDAA) .... CEC
Circular Grate (SAUS) .... circ g
Circular Hollow Section [*Metal industry*] .... CHS
Circular Intensity Difference [*Spectrometry*] .... CID
Circular Letter .... CILET
Circular Letter [*Military*] .... CIRCLTR
Circular Letter CL
Circular Letter of Credit (SAUS) CLC
Circular Magnetic Wave .... CMW
Circular Mail (NTIO) .... cm
Circular Map Accuracy Standard (PDAA) .... CMAS
Circular Measure .... CM
Circular Mil (IDOE) .... cir mil
Circular Mil [*Wire measure*] (IAA) .... CIRMIL
Circular Mil [*Wire measure*] .... CM
Circular Mil [*Wire measure*] (MSA) .... CMIL
Circular Mil .... cmil
Circular Mil Area .... CMA
Circular Mil Foot .... CMF
Circular Mils, Thousands .... MCM
Circular Minute (HEAS) .... CM
Circular Muscle [*Anatomy*] .... CM
Circular Note [*Business term*] .... CN
Circular of Requirements .... COR
Circular Order (SAUS) .... Cr O
Circular Orders, Northwestern Provinces [*India*] [*A publication*] (ILCA) .... Cir Od NWP
Circular Orders, Northwestern Provinces [*India*] [*A publication*] (DLA) .... Cir Ord NWP
Circular Outlet Gas Duct (SAUS) .... COGD
Circular Parking Orbit [*Aerospace*] (AAG) .... CPO
Circular Permutation Analysis [*Genetics*] .... CPA
Circular Pitch [*Technical drawings*] .... CP
Circular Polarization [*Optics*] .... CP
Circular Polarization Ratio [*Physics*] .... CPR
Circular Polarized Light [*Physics*] .... CPL
Circular Probable Error .... CPE
Circular Radio Beacon .... RC
Circular Reference (SAUS) .... CIRC
Circular Research (journ.) (SAUS) .... Circ Res
Circular Sequential Access Memory .... CSAM
Circular Standard Deviation [*Statistics*] .... CSD
Circular Tank System [*Pisciculture*] .... CT
Circular Terminal Orbit [*Aerospace*] (AAG) .... CTO
Circular Variable Filter [*Instrumentation*] .... CVF
Circular Variable Filter Spectrometer .... CVFS
Circular Vection [*Optics*] CV
Circular Velocity VC
Circular-Arc-Toothed Cylindrical (PDAA) .... CATC
Circularization Burn [*Orbital Maneuvering Subsystem 2*] [*NASA*] (NASA) .... CIRC
Circularly Disposed Antenna Array [*Radio receiver*] .... CDAA
Circularly Polarized Antenna [*or Array*] .... CPA
Circularly Polarized Fluorescence [*Physics*] .... CPF
Circularly Polarized Luminescence [*Spectroscopy*] .... CPL
Circularly Polarized-Electron Nuclear Double Resonance [*Spectroscopy*] .... CP-ENDOR
Circulate (NAKS) .... CIR
Circulate (SAUS) .... CIRC
Circulate (MSA) .... CRCLT
Circulate (FAAC) .... CRLC
Circulating (AL) .... Circ
Circulating (SAUS) .... CIRG
Circulating Anticoagulant [*Medicine*] (MEDA) .... CAC
Circulating Beam (SAUS) .... CB
Circulating Blood Lymphocyte [*Medicine*] (DB) .... CBL
Circulating Blood Volume [*Medicine*] .... CBV
Circulating Copy CC
Circulating Fluid Bed [*Chemical engineering*] .... CFB
Circulating Fluidized Bed (SAUS) .... CFB
Circulating Fuel Reactor Experiment [*Nuclear energy*] .... CFRE
Circulating Granulocyte Pool [*Hematology*] .... CGP
Circulating Immune Complex Content (DB) CICC
Circulating Immune Complexes [*Medicine*] CIC
Circulating Immune-Complex Disease [*Medicine*] (MELL) .... CICD
Circulating Library (SAUS) .... C-Library
Circulating Nurse (HGAA) .... CN
Circulating Plasma Volume [*Hematology*] .... CPV
Circulating Platelet Aggregate [*Hematology*] .... CPA
Circulating Reflux [*Chemical engineering*] .... CR
Circulating Shift Register (IAA) .... CSR
Circulating Store (SAUS) .... CS
Circulating System (SAUS) .... CS
Circulating Time (SAUS) .... CT
Circulating Water [*Nuclear energy*] (NRCH) .... CW
Circulating Water Pump .... CWP
Circulating Water Pumphouse [*Nuclear energy*] (NRCH) .... CWPH
Circulating Water System [*Nuclear energy*] (NRCH) .... CWS
Circulation (ADA) .... CIR
Circulation (WDMC) .... cir
Circulation (NTIO) .... circ
Circulation (EY) .... CIRC
Circulation (AL) .... Circ
Circulation and Finding System (SAUS) .... CFS
Circulation and Retrieval On-Line [*James Cook University, Australia*] (CIST) .... CAROL
Circulation Audit Board (SAUO) .... CAB
Circulation Bed Combustor [*Chemical engineering*] .... CBC
Circulation Control Point (AABC) .... CCP
Circulation Control Rotor [*Navy*] .... CCR
Circulation Control System (SAUS) .... CIRC System
Circulation Control Updating Program (SAUS) .... CIRCUP
Circulation Control Wing (MCD) .... CCW
Circulation Controlled Rotor (SAUS) .... CC Rotor
Circulation Council of DMA [*Direct Marketing Association*] [*New York, NY*] (EA) CC
Circulation Input Recording (SAUS) .... CIRC
Circulation Input Recording Center [*Data processing system*] .... CIRC
Circulation Input Recording Center System (SAUS) .... CIRC System
Circulation Library Automated System for Inventory Control [*Cincinnati Electronics Corp.*] [*Discontinued*] [*Information service or system*] (IID) .... CLASSIC
Circulation Lift Limit CLL
Circulation Manager (IIA) .... CM
Circulation, Motion, and Sensation (HGAA) .... CMS
Circulation, Motor Ability, Sensation, and Swelling [*Medicine*] .... CMSS
Circulation Pump .... CP
Circulation Research of East Asian Marginal Seas (SAUS) .... CREAMS
Circulation, Sensation [*or Sensory*], **Movement** [*or Motion*] [*Neurology and orthopedics*] (DAVI) .... CSM
Circulation Shift Register (SAUS) .... CSR
Circulation System [*Computer science*] (NITA) .... CIRC
Circulation System (ADA) .... CIRSYS
Circulation Time [*Cardiology*] .... CT
Circulation Time Descending (SAUS) .... CTD
Circulation Time Distribution [*Chemical engineering*] .... CTD
Circulator Outlet Gas Duct (OA) .... COGD
Circulatory [*Medicine*] (DAVI) .... Circ
Circulatory Assist Device (PDAA) .... CAD
Circulatory Collapse [*Cardiology*] CC
Circulo de Escritores y Poetas Iberoamericanos [*An association*] (EA) .... CEPI
Circulo Espanol de Amigos de Europa [*Spanish Circle of Friends of Europe*] (PD) .... CEDADE
Circum C
Circum Lunar Mission (SAUS) .... CLM
Circumambulation [*Freemasonry*] (ROG) .... CIRCUM
Circumarctic Active Layer Monitoring (SAUO) .... CALM
Circumarctic Vegetation Map (SAUO) .... CAVM
Circum-Atlantic Project [*Marine science*] (OSRA) .... CAO
Circum-Atlantic Project (SAUS) .... CAP
Circumbentricular Organs (STED) .... CVO
Circumcaribbean [*MARC geographic area code*] [*Library of Congress*] (LCCP) .... cr---
Circumcised (ADWA) .... circ
Circumcision [*Medicine*] .... CIRC
Circumcision (MELL) .... Circ
Circumcision [*Urology*] (DAVI) .... circum
Circumcision Information and Resource Pages (SAUO) .... CIRP
Circumcision Information Network (SAUO) .... CIN
Circumference (ADWA) c
Circumference C
Circumference (WDMC) .... cir
Circumference (WDMC) .... circ
Circumference .... CIRC
Circumference (ROG) .... CIRCFCE
Circumference .... CIRCM
Circumference (KSC) .... CIRCUM
Circumference (NTIO) .... circum
Circumference (MSA) .... CRCMF
Circumference (SAUS) .... Crcmf
Circumference of Head [*Medicine*] .... C of H
Circumferential Pneumatic Compression [*Medicine*] .... CPC
Circumferential Pneumatic Compression Suit [*Medicine*] (DMAA) .... CPCS
Circumferential Selectable Aim Warhead .... CSAW
Circumflex [*Coronary artery*] [*Cardiology*] (DAVI) .... CFX
Circumflex [*Coronary artery*] [*Medicine*] (DB) Cx
Circumflex Branch of Left Coronary Artery [*Medicine*] (MELL) .... CBLCA

Circumflex Coronary Artery [*Medicine*] (MEDA) ... CCA
Circumflex Coronary Artery [*Anatomy*] ... CIRC
Circumjacent (ROG) ... CIRCUMJAC
Circumlocution [*Used in correcting manuscripts, etc.*] ... C
Circumlunar Mission (KSC) ... CLM
Circumnavigators Club (EA) ... CC
Circum-Pacific Council for Energy and Mineral Resources (EA) ... CPCEMR
Circum-Pacific Energy and Mineral Resources Conference ... CPEMRC
Circum-Pacific Map Project (SAUO) ... CPMP
Circum-Pacific Project (SAUS) ... CPP
Circumpolar (SAUS) ... CP
Circum-polar Active Layer Monitoring (SAUS) ... CALM
Circumpolar Active Layer Monitoring Program (SAUO) ... CALM
Circumpolar Arctic Paleo Environments (QUAC) ... CAPE
Circumpolar Deep Water [*Oceanography*] ... CDW
Circumpolar Deep Water [*Also, CDW*] [*Oceanography*] ... CPDW
Circumpolar Intermediate Water (SAUS) ... CPIW
Circumpolar Protected Area Network (SAUO) ... CPAN
Circumpolar Seabird Working Group (SAUO) ... CSWG
Circumpolar Water [*Oceanography*] ... CPW
Circumscribing Circle Diameter (MCD) ... CCD
Circumsolar Radiation (SAUS) ... CSR
Circumsporozoite [*Protozoology*] ... CS
Circumsporozoite Precipitation [*Clinical chemistry*] ... CSP
Circumsporozoite Precipitin (DB) ... CSP
Circumstance (AABC) ... CIRC
Circumstance ... CIRCE
Circumstance (SAUS) ... Circe
Circumstances [*Slang*] (DSUE) ... CIRCS
Circumstances Not Known (SAUS) ... CNK
Circumstances Undetermined Pending Police Investigation ... CUPPI
Circumstellar Imaging Telescope ... CIT
Circumstellar Matter [*Astrophysics*] ... CSM
Circumvallate Papilla [*Medicine*] (MELL) ... CVP
Circumventricular Organs [*Medicine*] (DB) ... CVO
Circus (WDAA) ... C
Circus ... CIR
Circus (WDAA) ... CIRC
Circus ... CRCS
Circus Circus Enterp [*NYSE symbol*] (TTSB) ... CIR
Circus Circus Enterprises, Inc. [*NYSE symbol*] (SPSG) ... CIR
Circus Circus Enterprises, Inc. [*Associated Press*] (SAG) ... Circus
Circus Clown Friends Club [*British*] ... CCFC
Circus Education Specialists [*In association name, CES, Inc.*] (EA) ... CES
Circus Fans Association of America (EA) ... CFA
Circus Fans Association of Great Britain (SAUO) ... CFA
Circus Historical Society (EA) ... CHS
Circus Model Builders, International (EA) ... CMB
Circus Movement Tachycardia [*Medicine*] (DMAA) ... CMT
Circus Saints and Sinners Club of America (EA) ... CSSCA
Circus World Museum, Baraboo, WI [*Library symbol*] [*Library of Congress*] (LCLS) ... WBaraC
Circuses [*Public-performance tariff class*] [*British*] ... K
Circut Cards (SAUS) ... Circards
Cirebon [*Indonesia*] [*Airport symbol*] (OAG) ... CBN
Cirebon/Panggung [*Indonesia*] [*ICAO location identifier*] (ICLI) ... WIIC
Cirencester [*Urban district in England*] ... CIRENC
Ciro Alegria [*Peru*] [*ICAO location identifier*] (ICLI) ... SPAC
Cirque ... CRQ
Cirque Energy Ltd. [*NASDAQ symbol*] (SAG) ... CIRQ
Cirque Energy Ltd [*NASDAQ symbol*] (TTSB) ... CIRQF
Cirque Energy Ltd. [*Associated Press*] (SAG) ... CirqueE
Cirrhosis [*Medicine*] ... Ci
Cirrhosis [*Medicine*] ... CIR
Cirrhosis of Liver [*Medicine*] (MELL) ... CL
Cirripedia [*Quality of the bottom*] [*Nautical charts*] ... Cir
Cirrocumulus [*Meteorology*] ... CC
Cirrocumulus (SAUS) ... Cc
Cirrocumulus (SAUS) ... Ci-Cu
Cirrocumulus [*Meteorology*] ... CICU
Cirrocumulus Cloud (WEAT) ... Cc
Cirrocumulus Standing Lenticular Cloud (WEAT) ... CCSL
Cirrostratus [*Meteorology*] ... CS
Cirrostratus (SAUS) ... Cs
Cirrostratus Cloud (WEAT) ... Cs
Cirrus [*Meteorology*] ... C
Cirrus [*Meteorology*] ... CI
Cirrus Air, Inc. [*ICAO designator*] (FAAC) ... NTS
Cirrus Cloud (WEAT) ... Ci
Cirrus Logic [*NASDAQ symbol*] (TTSB) ... CRUS
Cirrus Logic, Inc. [*Associated Press*] (SAG) ... Cirrus
Cirrus Logic, Inc. [*NASDAQ symbol*] (NQ) ... CRUS
Cirrus Test (CARB) ... CIRT
Ciruelas [*Costa Rica*] [*ICAO location identifier*] (ICLI) ... MRCI
Cis Anti-Repression Sequence [*Genetics*] ... CAR
C/IS Communications/Information Systems (SAUO) ... C/IS
CIS Integration Services (SAUS) ... CIS
Cis Repressor Sequence [*Genetics*] ... CRS
C.I.S. Technologies [*NASDAQ symbol*] (TTSB) ... CISI
CIS Technologies, Inc. [*Vancouver Stock Exchange symbol*] ... CIH
CIS Technologies, Inc. [*NASDAQ symbol*] (NQ) ... CISI
CIS Technologies, Inc. [*Associated Press*] (SAG) ... CIS Tch
Cis-1,2-Dichlorethen (SAUS) ... Cis
CISA Export Trade Group, Inc. (NTPA) ... CETGI
cis-Aconityl [*Organic radical*] ... CA
Cis-Acting Repression [*Effect*] (DB) ... CRS
cis-Acting REV-Responsive Sequence [*Genetics*] ... CAR
Cis-Air [*Czechoslovakia*] [*ICAO designator*] (FAAC) ... CSR
Cisco Certified Internetwork Expert (CDE) ... CCIE
Cisco Educational Archive (VERA) ... CEARCH
Cisco Enterprise Accounting [*Computer science*] ... CEA
Cisco Information Online (VERA) ... CIO
Cisco Internetwork Operating System (SAUS) ... Cisco IOS
Cisco Junior College [*Texas*] ... CJC
Cisco Junior College, Cisco, TX [*Library symbol*] [*Library of Congress*] (LCLS) ... TxCiC
Cisco Resources [*Vancouver Stock Exchange symbol*] ... CCO
Cisco Router Module [*Cisco Systems, Inc.*] [*Computer science*] ... CRM
Cisco Systems [*NASDAQ symbol*] (SAG) ... CSCO
Cisco Systems, Inc. [*Associated Press*] (SAG) ... Cisco
Ciscorouter Modell (SAUS) ... AGS
cis-Diamminadichloroplatinum [*Cisplatin*] [*Also, cis-DDP, CPDD, CPT, DDP, P*] [*Antineoplastic drug*] ... CDDP
cis-Diamminodichloroplatinum [*Cisplatin*] [*Also, CDDP, CPDD, CPT, DDP, P*] [*Antineoplastic drug*] ... cis-DDP
Ciskei Defence Force (SAUS) ... CDF
Ciskei International Airways Corp. [*South Africa*] [*ICAO designator*] (FAAC) ... COK
Ciskei People's Rights Protection Party [*South Africa*] [*Political party*] (EY) ... CPRP
Cislunar Interorbital Transportation (SAUS) ... CIT
Cislunar Space ... CLS
Cislunar Swing Station (SAUS) ... CSS
Cisplatin [*Antineoplastic drug*] (DAVI) ... CACP
Cisplatin [*or Cis-platinum*] [*Antineoplastic drug*] (DAVI) ... CP
Cisplatin [*Also, cis-DDP, CDDP, CPDD, DDP, P*] [*Antineoplastic drug*] ... CPT
Cisplatin [*Antineoplastic drug*] (DAVI) ... DDP
Cisplatin, Adriamycin, Cyclophosphamide, CCNU [*Lomustine*], **Oncovin** [*Vincristine*] [*Antineoplastic drug regimen*] ... PACCO
Cisplatin, Cyclophosphamide, Adriamycin [*Antineoplastic drug regimen*] ... CISCA
Cisplatin, Fluorouracil [*Antineoplastic drug*] (CDI) ... CF
Cisplatin, Fluorourncil, Leucovorin Calcium [*Antineoplastic drug*] (CDI) ... CFL
Cisplatin, Methotrexate, and Vinblastine (STED) ... CMV
Cisplatin, Methotrexate, Bleomycin, Oncovin (Vincristine) [*Antineoplastic drug regimen*] ... CABO
Cisplatin, Oncovin [*Vincristine*], **Bleomycin** [*Antineoplastic drug regimen*] (DAVI) ... COB
Cisplatin, Oncovin, Bleomycine [*Antineoplastic drug*] (CDI) ... COB
Cisplatin, VePesid [*Antineoplastic drug*] (CDI) ... CV
Cisplatin, Vinblastine, Etoposide, Bleomycin [*Antineoplastic drug*] (CDI) ... CVEB
Cisplatin, Vindesine, Dacarbazine [*Antineoplastic drug regimen*] ... CiViDiC
cis-Platinum [*Cisplatin*] [*Also, cis-DDP, CDDP, CPDD, CPT, DDP*] [*Antineoplastic drug*] ... P
cis-Platinum [*Cisplatin*], **Adriamycin, Cyclophosphamide** [*Antineoplastic drug regimen*] ... PAC
cis-Platinum Diammine Dichloride [*Cisplatin*] [*Also, CDDP, cis-DDP, CPT, DDP, P*] [*Antineoplastic drug*] ... cPDD
Cis-Platinum, Methotrexate, Bleomycin [*Antineoplastic drug regimen*] (DAVI) ... PMB
Cis-Platinumdiamminedichloride [*Also called Cisplatin and Platinol*] [*Antineoplastic drug*] (DAVI) ... CPE
Cisplatis, VePesid, Ifosfamide [*Antineoplastic drug*] (CDI) ... CVI
Cissna Park Community Unit School District, Cissna Park, IL [*Library symbol*] [*Library of Congress*] (LCLS) ... ICipSD
Cistellaria [*of Plautus*] [*Classical studies*] (OCD) ... Cist
Cistercian Fathers (TOCD) ... ocist
Cistercian Fathers (TOCD) ... OCist
Cistercian Monks of the Strict Observance (TOCD) ... socist
Cistercian Monks of the Strict Observance (TOCD) ... SOCist
[*The*] **Cistercians Order of the Strict Observance, Trappists** (TOCD) ... ocso
Cisterdan Nuns (TOCD) ... OCist
Cistern Cay, Berry Island [*Bahamas*] [*ICAO location identifier*] (ICLI) ... MYBT
Cisterna Chyli [*Medicine*] (MELL) ... CC
CISTI [*Canada Institute for Scientific and Technical Information*] **Serials** [*Information service or system*] (CRD) ... CISTISER
CIT Financial Corporation (SAUO) ... CIT
CIT Group 'A' [*NYSE symbol*] (SG) ... CIT
Citadel (SAUS) ... Cit
Citadel (ROG) ... CIT
Citadel Capital Corp. [*Toronto Stock Exchange symbol*] ... CZJ
Citadel, Charleston, SC [*Library symbol*] [*Library of Congress*] (LCLS) ... ScCCit
Citadel Communications [*NASDAQ symbol*] (SG) ... CITC
Citadel, Daniel Library, Charleston, SC [*OCLC symbol*] (OCLC) ... SCN
Citadel Gold Mines, Inc. [*Toronto Stock Exchange symbol*] ... CIG
Citadel Holding Corp. [*AMEX symbol*] (SPSG) ... CDL
Citadel Holding Corp. [*Associated Press*] (SAG) ... Citadel
Citation (AFM) ... CIT
Citation (WDMC) ... cit
Citation (AABC) ... CITA
Citation Abstract Procurement ... CAP
CITATION Computer Sys [*NASDAQ symbol*] (TTSB) ... CITA
Citation Computer Systems [*NASDAQ symbol*] (SAG) ... CITA
Citation Computer Systems [*Associated Press*] (SAG) ... CitatnCpt
Citation Corp. [*NASDAQ symbol*] (TTSB) ... CAST
Citation Corp. Alabama [*NASDAQ symbol*] (SAG) ... CAST
Citation Corp. Alabama [*Associated Press*] (SAG) ... Citation
Citation in Examiner's Decision [*Legal term*] (DLA) ... Ex
Citation Insurance [*NASDAQ symbol*] (TTSB) ... CITIN
Citation Number [*Database terminology*] (NITA) ... CN
Citations and Delivery service from RLG (SAUS) ... CITADEL

Citations to Statutes at large (SAUS) .... STAT
Citato [*Cited*] [*Latin*] (ADA) .... CIT
Citator [*or Cited In or Citing*] [*Legal term*] (DLA) .... cit
Citator and Indian Law Journal [*1908-14*] [*A publication*] (DLA) .... Cit
Citatus [*Cited*] [*Latin*] (EES) .... cit
Citco Growth Investment [*Vancouver Stock Exchange symbol*] .... CGW
CITE Augmentation Support System (MCD) .... CASS
Cite de la Sante de Laval, Laval, PQ, Canada [*Library symbol*] [*Library of Congress*] (LCLS) .... CaQLACS
Cite de la Sante de Laval, Quebec [*Library symbol*] [*National Library of Canada*] (NLC) .... QLACS
Cited (DLA) C
Cited (WDMC) .... cit
Cited (SAUS) .... Cit
Cited Authors [*Database terminology*] (NITA) .... CA
Cited Pages [*Database terminology*] (NITA) .... CP
Cited Reference [*Online database field identifier*] .... CR
Cited Volume [*Database terminology*] (NITA) CV
Citfed Bancorp [*NASDAQ symbol*] (TTSB) .... CTZN
CitFed Bancorp, Inc. [*Associated Press*] (SAG) .... CitFed
CitFed Bancorp, Inc. [*NASDAQ symbol*] (SAG) .... CTZN
Citi Bancshares, Inc. [*Associated Press*] (SAG) .... CitiBnc
Citi Bancshares, Inc. [*NASDAQ symbol*] (SAG) .... CNBL
Citi-Bancshares [*NASDAQ symbol*] (TTSB) .... CNBL
Citibank Economic Database [*Citibank, NA*] [*New York, NY*] [*Information service or system*] (IID) .... CITIBASE
Citibank NA [*ICAO designator*] (FAAC) XCX
CITIBASE-Weekly [*Citicorp Database Services*] [*Information service or system*] (IID) .... CBW
Citicasters, Inc. [*NASDAQ symbol*] (SAG) .... CITI
Citicasters, Inc. [*Associated Press*] (SAG) .... Citicast
Citicasters Inc.'A' [*NASDAQ symbol*] (TTSB) .... CITI
Citicorp [*NYSE symbol*] (SPSG) CCI
Citicorp [*Associated Press*] (SAG) .... Citcp
Citicorp [*Associated Press*] (SAG) .... Citicorp
Citicorp [*Toronto Stock Exchange symbol*] .... CTI
Citicorp 7.50% Dep Pfd [*NYSE symbol*] (TTSB) .... CCIPrF
Citicorp 7.75% Dep Sr 22 Pfd [*NYSE symbol*] (TTSB) .... CCIPrK
Citicorp 8.00% Dep Pfd [*NYSE symbol*] (TTSB) .... CCIPrE
Citicorp 8.30% Dep Pfd [*NYSE symbol*] (TTSB) .... CCIPrI
Citicorp 8.50% Dep Pfd [*NYSE symbol*] (TTSB) .... CCIPrJ
Citicorp 9.08% Dep Pfd [*NYSE symbol*] (TTSB) .... CCIPrD
Citicorp Adj Rt 2nd Pfd [*NYSE symbol*] (TTSB) .... CCIPr
Citicorp Adj Rt 3rd Pfd [*NYSE symbol*] (TTSB) .... CCIPrA
Citicorp Adj Rt Dep Pfd [*NYSE symbol*] (TTSB) .... CCIPrG
Citicorp Adj Rt Dep'H'Pfd [*NYSE symbol*] (TTSB) .... CCIPrH
Citicorp Economic Report [*Database*] [*Citicorp Information Services*] [*Information service or system*] (CRD) .... CER
Citicorp Economic Services [*Information service or system*] (IID) .... CES
Citicorp Information Technology Industries Limited .... CITIL
Citicorp International (SAUO) .... Citicorp
Citicorp Investment Bank Ltd. [*England*] .... CIBL
Citicorp Scrimgeour Vickers [*Commercial firm*] [*British*] (ECON) .... CSV
Citicorp Venture Capital Fund [*Investment term*] .... CVCF
Cities in Schools (EA) .... CIS
Cities in Schools [*An association*] (EA) .... CS
Cities of London and Westminster Society of Architects (SAUO) .... CLAWSA
[*The*] **Cities of the Eastern Roman Provinces** [*A publication*] (OCD) .... Cities E Rom Prov
Cities of the United States [*A publication*] .... CUS
Cities of the World [*A publication*] .... CIW
Cities of the World [*A publication*] .... CW
Cities Service Co., Corporate Library, New York, NY [*Library symbol*] [*Library of Congress*] (LCLS) .... NNCit
Cities Service Co., Energy Resources Group, E & P Library, Tulsa, OK [*Library symbol*] [*Library of Congress*] (LCLS) .... OkTCS
Cities Service Co., Technical Center - Energy Resources Group, Research Library,Tulsa, OK [*OCLC symbol*] (OCLC) .... OCS
Cities Service Company (SAUO) .... CS
Cities-Aerospace Industry Coalition (SAUO) .... CAIC
Citigroup, Inc. [*NYSE symbol*] (SG) C
CitiSave Financial [*AMEX symbol*] (TTSB) .... CZF
Citisave Financial Corp. [*Associated Press*] (SAG) .... Citisave
Citisave Financial Corp. [*AMEX symbol*] (SAG) .... CZF
Citiz Util Tr 5%'EPPICS' [*NYSE symbol*] (TTSB) .... CZNPr
Citizen (AFM) .... CIT
Citizen (NTIO) .... cit
Citizen .... CITZN
Citizen Act (COE) .... CA
Citizen Action Fund (EA) .... CAF
Citizen Action Group [*Defunct*] (EA) .... CAG
Citizen Air Force (SAUO) .... CAF
Citizen Ambassador Program of People to People International (SAUS) .... CAPPPI
Citizen Diplomacy (EA) .... CD
Citizen Education Association [*Defunct*] (EA) .... CEA
Citizen Education Project .... CEP
Citizen Exchange Corps (SAUO) .... CEC
Citizen Exchange Council (EA) .... CEC
Citizen Forum on Self Government [*National Municipal League*] (COE) .... CFSG
Citizen Initiated Nongovernmental Organization (SAUO) .... CINGO
Citizen Initiated Referendum Alliance [*Australia*] [*Political party*] .... CIRA
Citizen Initiated Referendums [*Political party*] [*Australia*] .... CIR
Citizen Involvement Training Program (EA) .... CITP
Citizen Kane [*Film title*] (WDAA) .... CK
Citizen Military Forces [*New Guinea*] .... CMF
Citizen Mobilization Campaign [*Defunct*] (EA) .... CMC
Citizen of Morris County, Denville, NJ [*Library symbol*] [*Library of Congress*] (LCLS) .... NjDeC
Citizen Radio [*Telecommunications*] (IAA) .... CR
Citizen Radio Service [*Telecommunications*] (IAA) .... CRS
Citizen Soldier (EA) .... CS
Citizen Utility Board (SAUO) .... CUB
Citizen Utility Board Campaign [*Defunct*] (EA) .... CUBC
Citizen/Labor Energy Coalition [*Defunct*] (EA) .... C/LEC
Citizens Action League (SAUO) .... CAL
Citizens' Advice Bureau [*British*] .... CAB
Citizens' Advice Bureau, Adelaide [*Australia*] .... CABA
Citizen's Advice Bureau, Australian Capital Territory .... CABACT
Citizens' Advice Bureau, Brisbane [*Australia*] .... CABB
Citizens' Advice Bureaux [*British*] (ILCA) .... CABx
Citizens' Advice Notes [*British*] (DI) .... CANS
Citizen's Advisory Board (OICC) .... CAB
Citizens Advisory Committee on Environmental Quality .... CACEQ
Citizens' Advisory Council on the Status of Women .... CACSW
Citizens Advocacy .... CA
Citizens Advocate Center [*Antipoverty organization*] [*Defunct*] .... CAC
Citizens Against a Radioactive Environment [*An association*] (ECON) .... CARE
Citizens Against Airport Environment Association .... CAAEA
Citizens Against Bad Law (AC) .... CABL
Citizens Against Crime Association [*Australia*] .... CACA
Citizens Against Foreign Control of America (EA) .... CAFCA
Citizens Against Government Waste (EA) .... CAGW
Citizens Against Lawyer Abuse (EA) .... CALA
Citizens Against Legalized Murder [*Opposes death penalty for criminals*] [*Defunct*] .... CALM
Citizens Against Military Injustice [*Defunct*] (EA) .... CAMI
Citizens Against Noise .... CAN
Citizens Against Nuclear Trash [*An association*] .... CANT
Citizens Against Nuclear War [*Defunct*] (EA) .... CAN
Citizens Against PAC's [*Political Action Committees*] [*Defunct*] (EA) .... CAP
Citizens Against Pornography (EA) .... CAP
Citizens Against Radioactive Dumping (SAUS) .... CARD
Citizens Against Rationing Health [*An association*] .... CARH
Citizens Against Route Twenty (SAUO) .... CART
Citizens Against the Concorde Here .... CATCH
Citizens Against Tobacco Smoke (EA) .... CATS
Citizens Against UFO [*Unidentified Flying Object*] **Secrecy** (EA) .... CAUS
Citizens Against Unneccessary Tax Increases and Other Nonsense [*St. Louis organization*] .... CAUTION
Citizens Against Virtually Everything [*An association*] (PA) .... CAVE
Citizens Air Force (SAUS) .... CAF
Citizens Alarm System (MCD) .... CAS
Citizens Alliance for Self-Help (EA) .... CASH
Citizens Alliance for VD [*Venereal Disease*] **Awareness** (EA) .... CAVDA
Citizens and Scientists Concerned About Dangers to the Environment (SAUS) .... CASCADE
Citizens & Southern Corp. .... C & S
Citizens and Southern Realty Investors (SAUO) .... CZS
Citizens Armed Forces Geographical Unit (SAUS) .... CAFGU
Citizens Assessment Administration .... CAA
Citizens Association for Racial Equality (SAUO) .... CARE
Citizens Association for Sound Energy (EA) .... CASE
Citizens Association for the Care of Animals (EA) .... CACA
Citizens Bancorp [*NASDAQ symbol*] (NQ) .... CIBC
Citizens Bancorp [*Associated Press*] (SAG) .... CtzBcp
Citizens Bancshares [*NASDAQ symbol*] (TTSB) .... CICS
Citizens Bancshares, Inc. [*NASDAQ symbol*] (SAG) .... CICS
Citizens Bancshares, Inc. [*Associated Press*] (SAG) .... CtzBnch
Citizens Band [*A radio frequency band for limited-range, two-way voice communications by persons without technical training or standard operator licenses*] .... CB
Citizens Band Operating Area .... CBOA
Citizens Band Radio (IAA) .... CBR
Citizens Band Radio Service (SAUS) .... CBRS
Citizens Band Receiver (SAUS) .... CB RCVR
Citizens Bander (SAUS) .... CBER
Citizens Banking [*NASDAQ symbol*] (TTSB) .... CBCF
Citizens Banking Corp. [*NASDAQ symbol*] (NQ) .... CBCF
Citizens Banking Corp. [*Associated Press*] (SAG) .... CitizBkg
Citizens Bar Association (EA) .... CBA
Citizen's Call (EA) CC
Citizen's Choice [*Defunct*] (EA) CC
Citizens' Civic Action Association [*Canada*] (BARN) .... CCAA
Citizen's Clearinghouse for Hazardous Wastes (EA) .... CCHW
Citizens Clearinghouse for Hazardous Wastes (SAUO) .... CCHW
Citizens' Clearinghouse on Waste Management (AC) .... CCWM
Citizens Coalition for Rational Traffic Laws [*Later, NMA*] (EA) .... CCRTL
Citizens' Commission on AIDS [*Acquired Immune Deficiency Syndrome*] (EA) .... CCA
Citizens' Commission on Civil Rights (EA) .... CCCR
Citizens Committee for a Free Cuba .... CCFC
Citizens' Committee for Children of New York (EA) CCC
Citizens Committee for Constitutional Liberties [*Defunct*] CCCL
Citizens' Committee for Immigration Reform [*Defunct*] (EA) .... CCIR
Citizens Committee for the Right to Keep and Bear Arms (SAUS) .... CCRI
Citizens Committee for the Right to Keep and Bear Arms (EA) .... CCRKBA
Citizens Committee for Victim Assistance (EA) .... CCVA
Citizens Committee on Future Directions for the Peace Corps [*Defunct*] (EA) .... CCFDPC

Citizens Committee on Natural Resources [Defunct] (EA) .... CCNR
Citizens Committee on the El Salvador Crisis (EA) .... CCESC
Citizens Committee on the Fair Labor Standards Act (EA) .... CCFLSA
Citizens Communication Center (NTCM) CCC
Citizens Communication Center of the Institute for Public Representation [Later, CCCPIPR] (EA) .... CCCIPR
Citizens Communications Center Project of the Institute for Public Representation (EA) .... CCCPIPR
Citizens Concerned About Free Trade [Canadian organization opposed to the US/Canadian free trade agreement] (CROSS) .... CCAFT
Citizens concerned About Radiation Pollution (SAUS) .... CARP
Citizens Conference on State Legislatures [Later, Legis 50/The Center for Legislative Improvement] (EA) .... CCSL
Citizens Corp. [Associated Press] (SAG) .... CtznCp
Citizens Corp. [NYSE symbol] (SPSG) .... CZC
Citizens Council for Land Use Research and Education (SAUO) .... CLURE
Citizens' Council Forum [Defunct] (EA) .... CCF
Citizens' Council of America for Segregation [Defunct] (EA) .... CCAS
Citizens' Council on Civic Development [Canada] .... CCCD
Citizens' Councils of America (EA) .... CCA
Citizens Crusade Against Poverty [Absorbed by Center for Community Change] (EA) .... CCAP
Citizens Defense Corps (SAUO) .... CDC
Citizens Democracy Corps [An association] (EA) .... CDC
Citizens Educational Advisory Committee .... CEAC
Citizens Electoral Council [Political party] [Australia] .... CEC
Citizens Energy Corp. [Nonprofit] .... CEC
Citizen's Energy Council (EA) .... CEC
Citizens' Energy Project [Defunct] (EA) .... CEP
Citizens Environment Alliance of Southwestern Ontario (AC) .... CEA
Citizens Federal Bank, a Federal Savings Bank [NASDAQ symbol] (SAG) .... CFBK
Citizens Federal Bank, FSB [Associated Press] (SAG) .... CtzFBk
Citizens Fidelity Corp. (EFIS) .... CFC
Citizens Financial Corp. [Associated Press] (SAG) .... CitzFnCp
Citizens Financial Corp. [NASDAQ symbol] (SAG) .... CNFL
Citizens Finl Kentucky [NASDAQ symbol] (TTSB) .... CNFL
Citizens First Financial Corp. [AMEX symbol] (SAG) .... CBK
Citizens First Financial Corp. [Associated Press] (SAG) .... CitFFin
Citizens First Finl [AMEX symbol] (TTSB) .... CBK
Citizens' Flag Alliance [An association] .... CFA
Citizens for a Balanced Budget (EA) .... CBB
Citizens for a Better America (EA) .... CBA
Citizens for a Better Environment (EA) .... CBE
Citizens for a Competitive America (EA) .... CCA
Citizens for a Debt Free America (EA) .... CDFA
Citizens for a Drug Free America (EA) .... CDFA
Citizens for a Lakeshore Greenway (AC) .... CFLAG
Citizens for a Lebanon-Grenada National Memorial [Defunct] (EA) .... CLGNM
Citizens for a Nuclear Freeze [Defunct] (EA) .... CNF
Citizens for a Quieter City [New York City] [Defunct] (EA) .... CQC
Citizens for a Safe Environment (AC) .... CSE
Citizens for a Sound Economy [Washington, DC] (EA) .... CSE
Citizens for a Tobacco Free Society (EA) .... CATS
Citizens for Alternatives to Trident and ELF [Extremely Low Frequency System] [Defunct] (EA) .... CATE
Citizens for America [Later, CFAEF] (EA) .... CFA
Citizens for America Educational Foundation (EA) .... CFAEF
Citizens for an Alternative Tax System (EA) .... CATS
Citizens for Animals [Defunct] (EA) .... CA
Citizens for Animals, Resources, and Environment (EA) .... CARE
Citizens for Better Care (SAUO) .... CBC
Citizens for Better Care in Nursing Homes (SAUO) .... CBC
Citizens for Better Care in Nursing Homes, Homes for the Aged, and Other After-Care Facilities .... CBC
Citizens for Better Driving Records [Later, CSD] (EA) .... CBDR
Citizens for Cable Awareness (NTCM) .... CCA
Citizens for Civil Justice Reform (EA) .... CCJR
Citizens for Clean Air .... CCA
Citizens for Common Sense [Defunct] (EA) .... CCS
Citizens for Constitutional Concerns (EA) CCC
Citizens for Decency through Law [Later, CLF] (EA) .... CDL
Citizens for Decent Literature [Later, Citizens for Decency through Law] (EA) .... CDL
Citizens for Educational Freedom (EA) .... CEF
Citizens for Energy Conservation and Solar Development .... CECSD
Citizens for Eye Research (EA) .... CER
Citizens for Eye Research to Prevent Blindness [Defunct] (EA) .... CERPB
Citizens for Farm Labor [Defunct] (EA) .... CFL
Citizens for Foreign Aid Reform [Canada] .... CFAR
Citizens for Foreign Aid Reform Inc. (AC) .... C-FAR
Citizens for Free Kuwait [Defunct] (EA) .... CFK
Citizens for Good Government [Political fund of Ling-Temco-Vought, Inc.] .... CITIGO
Citizens for Governmental Restraint (EA) .... CGR
Citizens for Health .... CFH
Citizens for Highway Safety [Defunct] (EA) .... CHS
Citizens for Improved Education .... CIE
Citizens for Informed Choices on Marijuana (EA) .... CICOM
Citizens for Law and Order (DICI) .... CLO
Citizens for Media Responsibility without Law (EA) .... CMRWL
Citizens for Ocean Law (EA) .... COL
Citizens for Proportional Representation (EA) .... CPR
Citizens for Public Action on Blood Pressure and Cholesterol (EA) .... CPABPC
Citizens for Public Justice (AC) .... CPJ

Citizens for Quieter Cities (SAUS) .... CQCs
Citizens for Reagan (EA) .... CFR
Citizens for Safe Drivers [Formerly, CBDR] (EA) .... CSD
Citizens for Sensible Control of Acid Rain [Defunct] (EA) .... CSCAR
Citizens for Sensible Safeguards [An association] (EA) .... CSS
Citizens for Social Justice (EA) .... CSJ
Citizens for Social Reponsibility [Citoyen pour la Conscience Sociale] [Formerly, Citizens for Nuclear Responsibility] (AC) .... CFSR
Citizens for Space Demilitarization (EA) .... CFSD
Citizens for Tax Justice (EA) .... CTJ
Citizens for the Republic (EA) .... CFTR
Citizens for the Treatment of High Blood Pressure (EA) .... CTHBP
Citizens Foreign Aid Committee [Defunct] (EA) .... CFAC
Citizens Forum on Self-Government/National Municipal League [Information service or system] (IID) .... CF/NML
Citizens Forum on Self-Government/National Municipal League [Information service or system] (IID) .... CFSG/NML
Citizens Freedom Foundation (EA) .... CFF
Citizens Global Action (EA) .... CGA
Citizens Guild for Civil Defence (SAUO) .... CGCD
Citizens Honest Elections Foundation .... CHEF
Citizens in Defense of Civil Liberties [Defunct] (EA) .... CDCL
Citizens in Politics [Defunct] (EA) .... CIP
Citizens, Inc. [AMEX symbol] (SAG) .... CIA
Citizens, Inc. [Associated Press] (SAG) .... CitizInc
Citizens Inc.'A' [AMEX symbol] (TTSB) .... CIA
Citizen's Internet Empowerment Coalition [Sponsored by CDT - Center for Democracy and Technology] .... CIEC
Citizens Law and Research Association [Defunct] (EA) .... CLARA
Citizens Leadership Foundation [Defunct] (EA) .... CLF
Citizens League Against the Sonic Boom [Defunct] .... CLASB
Citizens Legal Protective League [Defunct] (EA) .... CLPL
Citizen's Library of Economics [A publication] .... CLE
Citizens Library, Washington, PA [Library symbol] [Library of Congress] (LCLS) .... PW
Citizen's Library, Washington, PA [OCLC symbol] (OCLC) .... WWC
Citizens Medical Reference Bureau (SAUO) .... CMRB
Citizens Military Training Camp (SAUS) .... CMTC
Citizens Military Training Corps (AABC) .... CMTC
Citizens Mortgage Investment Trust (SAUO) .... CZM
Citizens National Bank (EFIS) .... CNB
Citizens Network for Foreign Affairs (EA) .... CNFA
Citizens Network on Waste Management (AC) .... CNWM
Citizens of the United Kingdom and Commonwealth .... CUKC
Citizens' Organisation for a Sane World [British] (DI) .... COSW
Citizens Organized to Defend the Environment .... CODE
Citizens Organized to Restore an Effective Corporate Tax (EA) .... CORECT
Citizens' Parliamentary Club [Poland] [Political party] .... OKP
Citizens Participation Project/the Missing Half [Defunct] (EA) .... CPP/TMH
Citizen's Party (EA) .... CIP
Citizen's Party [Defunct] (EA) .... CP
Citizens Protection Society [British] .... CPS
Citizens Radio Operations Organization (SAUO) .... CROO
Citizens Radio Service (SAUO) .... CRS
Citizens Radio UFO [Unidentified Flying Object] Network .... CRUFON
Citizens Research and Investigative Committee [California] .... CRIC
Citizens' Research Foundation .... CRF
Citizens Responsible Action for Safety on the Highways .... CRASH
Citizens' Rights Movement [Israel] [Political party] (ECON) .... CRM
Citizens' Scholarship Foundation of America (EA) .... CSFA
Citizens Security Group, Inc. [NASDAQ symbol] (NQ) .... CSGI
Citizens Security Group, Inc. [Associated Press] (SAG) .... CtzSec
Citizens Security Grp [NASDAQ symbol] (TTSB) .... CSGI
Citizens' Service Corps .... CSC
Citizens' Stamp Advisory Committee [US Postal Service] (EA) .... CSAC
Citizens to Bring Broadway Back (SAUO) .... CBBB
Citizens to End Animal Suffering and Exploitation (EA) .... CEASE
Citizens to Reduce Airline Smoking Hazards [Student legal action organization] .... CRASH
Citizens Training Camp (SAUO) .... CTC
Citizens' Training Corps .... CTC
Citizens United for Bear .... CUB
Citizens United for Racial Equality .... CURE
Citizens United for Rehabilitation of Errants (EA) .... CURE
Citizens United for Research and Education (EA) .... CURE
Citizens United for Responsible Energy (EA) .... CURE
Citizens United for Safety and Justice [Canada] .... CUSJ
Citizens Util 'B' [NYSE symbol] (TTSB) .... CZN.B
Citizens Util'A' [NYSE symbol] (TTSB) .... CZN.A
Citizens Utilities [Associated Press] (SAG) .... CitzUt
Citizens Utilities Co. [NYSE symbol] (SAG) .... CZN
Citizens Utilities Trust [Associated Press] (SAG) .... CitzUt
Citizens Utility Board .... CUB
Citizens Welfare Service, Drummond Street Centre [Australia] .... CWSDSC
Citizens Welfare Service of Victoria [Australia] .... CWSV
Citizenship Automated System [Australia] .... CAS
Citizenship Clearing House .... CCH
Citizenship of British Dependent Territories .... CBDT
CITL [Crew-in-the-Loop] Encapsulated Methodology [Army] .... CEM
CITL [Crew-in-the-Loop] Encapsulation Template [Army] .... CET
CitnIns [NASDAQ symbol] (SAG) .... CITN
CitnIns [Associated Press] (SAG) .... CitnIns
Cito Dispensetur [Dispense Quickly] [Pharmacy] .... CITO DISP
Citraconic Anhydride [Organic chemistry] .... CTA
Citrate .... CIT

Citrate (SAUS) .... CITR
Citrate Synthase [An enzyme] .... CS
Citrated Calcium Carbimide (SAUS) CCC
Citrated Calcium Cyanamide (IIA) CCC
Citrated Normal Rabbit Serum (STED) .... CNRS
Citrated Whole Human Blood (DMAA) .... CWHB
Citrate-Extractable Heavy Metal .... cxHM
Citrate-Phosphate-Dextrose [Anticoagulant] [Hematology] .... CPD
Citrate-Phosphate-Dextrose-Adenine [Anticoagulant] [Hematology] .... CPDA
Citrat-Synthetase (SAUS) .... CS
Citric Acid (SAUS) .... CITA
Citric Acid (SAUS) .... Cit Acid
Citric Acid Cycle [Medicine] (MELL) .... CAC
Citric Acid Esters of Mono/Diglycerides .... CMG
Citric Acid Fermentation (DMAA) .... CAF
Citric Acid Fermenter [Microbiology] .... CAF
Citriculture .... CITRIC
Citriculture (SAUS) .... Citricult
Citrix Systems [NASDAQ symbol] (TTSB) .... CTXS
Citroen Car Club (EA) CCC
Citroen Quarterly Car Club (EA) .... CQCC
Citron [Philately] .... cit
Citronelle, AL [FM radio station call letters] .... WHXT
Citronelle, AL [FM radio station call letters] (BROA) .... WQUA-FM
Citrovorum Factor [Biochemistry] .... CF
Citrovorum Rescue Factor [Medicine] (MEDA) ...... CRF
Citrovorum-Factor Rescue [Cancer treatment] ...... CFR
Citrulline [An amino acid] .... Cit
Citrus .... CTRS
Citrus Administrative Committee [Florida] (SRA) .... CAC
Citrus & Canned Products Association (SAUO) ..... CPA
Citrus Bacterial Canker Disease [Plant pathology] .... CBCD
Citrus Board of South Australia .... CBSA
Citrus College, Azusa, CA [Library symbol] [Library of Congress] (LCLS) .... CAzC
Citrus College, Azusa, CA [OCLC symbol] (OCLC) CCI
Citrus Crinkly Leaf Virus [Plant pathology] CICLV
Citrus Exocortis Viroid .... CEV
Citrus Junior College [California] .... CJC
Citrus Label Society (EA) .... CLS
Citrus Leaf Rugose Virus [Plant pathology] .... CILRV
Citrus Marketing Board of Israel (SAUO) .... CMBI
Citrus Mealybug [Plant pest] .... CMLB
Citrus Tatter Leaf Virus [Plant pathology] .... CITLV
Citrus Tristeza Virus .... CTV
Citrus Variegation Virus [Plant pathology] CVV
Citrus Vitamin P (SAUS) .... CVP
CITS Expert Parameters System (SAUS) .... CEPS
Citty Taxi Aereo Nacional SA de CV [Mexico] [ICAO designator] (FAAC) .... CCT
City [Maps and charts] C
City .... CTY
City (MCD) .... CY
City Administration Center (SAUO) .... CAC
City Administrative Office .... CAO
City Air Bus Ltd. [British] [FAA designator] (FAAC) .... CYB
City Air Defense Evaluation Tool .... CADET
City Air Ltd. [British] [ICAO designator] (FAAC) .... ISY
City Air Material Area (SAUO) .... CAMA
City Air Terminal (IAA) .... CAT
City and Borough Architects Society (SAUO) .... CBAS
City & Guilds [British] (WDAA) .... C&G
City and Guilds College (SAUO) .... CGC
City and Guilds Institute (SAUO) .... CGI
City and Guilds [of London] Institute (BARN) .... CGI
City and Guilds of London [British] .... C & G
City and Guilds of London Insignia Award [British] .... CGIA
City & Guilds of London Institute (ACII) .... C&GLI
City & Guilds of London Institute [British] (WDAA) .... CGLI
City and Guilds of London Institute (SAUO) .... CGLI
City and Regional Magazine Association (EA) .... CRMA
City and South London Railway (SAUO) .... C&SL
City and South London Railway ["The Tube"] (ROG) .... C & SLR
City and South London Railway ["The Tube"] (ROG) .... CSLR
City and State Directories in Print [A publication] .... C & S DIP
City and State Directories in Print [A publication] .... CSDIP
City & Suburban Homes Co. (SAUO) .... CBU
City Art Museum (SAUO) .... CAM
City Art Museum of St. Louis, St. Louis, MO [Library symbol] [Library of Congress] (LCLS) .... MoSR
City Art Workshop New York (SAUO) .... CAW
City Attorney (SAUS) .... CA
City Bank, North America, New York, NY [Library symbol] [Library of Congress] (LCLS) .... NNCBN
City Business System [British Telecom] (NITA) ..... CBS
City Center Arts [A publication] .... CCA
City Center Arts (journ.) (SAUS) .... CCA
City [or County] Civil Defense Director .... CCD
City Collection Center (ACAE) CCC
City College of Chicago (SAUO) CCC
City College of City University of New York .... CCCUNY
City College of City University of New York, New York, NY [Library symbol] [Library of Congress] (LCLS) .... NNR
City College of New York [Later, City University of New York] .... CCNY
City College of New York [New York] [Seismograph station code, US Geological Survey] (SEIS) .... CNY
City College of New York, New York, NY [OCLC symbol] (OCLC) .... ZXC

City College of San Francisco [California] .... CCSF
City College of San Francisco, San Francisco, CA [OCLC symbol] (OCLC) .... CCS
City College of San Francisco, San Francisco, CA [Library symbol] [Library of Congress] (LCLS) .... CSfCiC
City College of The City University of New York (GAGS) .... CCNY (CUNY)
City Communications Centre [British] (CB) CCC
City Company Law Committee (SAUO) CCLC
City Corp. [of London] CC
City Council [or Councillor] CC
City Council (SAUO) CC
City Court (DLA) CC
City Court (DLA) .... City Ct
City Court Reports [A publication] (DLA) .... CCR
City Court Reports [New York] [A publication] (DLA) .... City Ct R
City Court Reports [New York] [A publication] (DLA) .... City Ct Rep
City Court Reports, Supplement [New York] [A publication] (DLA) .... CC Supp
City Court Reports, Supplement [New York] [A publication] (DLA) .... City Ct Rep Supp
City Court Reports, Supplement [New York] [A publication] (DLA) .... City Ct R Supp
City Court Reports, Supplement [New York] [A publication] (DLA) .... City Ct Supp (NY)
City Demonstration Agency (SAUO) .... CD
City Demonstration Agency .... CDA
City Development Board (OICC) .... CDB
City Electrical Factors (SAUO) .... CEF
City Express [ICAO designator] (AD) .... OU
City Facts and Abstracts [EDIC] [Ringmer Near Lewes, East Sussex, England] [Information service or system] (IID) .... CFA
City Flug [ICAO designator] (AD) .... VG
City Graphic (GEOI) .... CITYG
City Hall Branch, Gloucester Public Library, Ontario [Library symbol] [National Library of Canada] (NLC) .... OGO
City Hall Recorder [New York City] [A publication] (DLA) .... City Hall Rec (NY)
City Hall Recorder (Rogers) [New York City] [A publication] (DLA) .... CH Rec
City Hall Reporter (Lomas) [New York City] [A publication] (DLA) .... CH Rep
City Hall Reporter (Lomas) [New York City] [A publication] (DLA) .... City Hall Rep
City Hall Reporter (Lomas) [New York City] [A publication] (DLA) .... City Hall Rep (NY)
City Hall Reporter (Lomas) [New York City] [A publication] (DLA) .... City H Rep
City Holding [NASDAQ symbol] (TTSB) .... CHCO
City Holding Co. [NASDAQ symbol] (NQ) .... CHCO
City Holding Co. [Associated Press] (SAG) .... CtyHld
City Hospital at Elmhurst, Elmhurst, NY [Library symbol] [Library of Congress] (LCLS) .... NElmhC
City Hostess International (EA) .... CHI
City Imperial Volunteers [Military unit] [British] CIV
City Industry Task Force [Confederation of British Industry] .... CITF
City Investing Co. (EFIS) CI
City Investing Co. Liquidating Trust [NASDAQ symbol] (NQ) .... CNVL
City Investing Co. Liquidating Trust [Associated Press] (SAG) .... CtyLTr
City Investing Company (SAUO) .... CNV
City Investing Liq Tr [NASDAQ symbol] (TTSB) ..... CNVLZ
City Investment Centres [British] CIC
City Jet [Ireland] (FAAC) .... BCY
City Kids Foundation (EA) .... CKF
City Limits [In outdoor advertising] (WDMC) .... C/
City Livery Club (SAUO) CLC
City Merchant Developers [British] .... CMD
City Merchant Developers Development Coordination [British] .... CMDDC
City National [NYSE symbol] (TTSB) .... CYN
City National Corp. [Associated Press] (SAG) .... CityNC
City National Corp. [NYSE symbol] (SPSG) .... CYN
City Normal School, Syracuse, NY [Library symbol] [Library of Congress] [Obsolete] (LCLS) .... NSyN
City of Adelaide Planning Commission [Australia] .... CAPC
City of Alamosa-Southern Peaks Library, Alamosa, CO [Library symbol] [Library of Congress] (LCLS) .... CoAl
City of Bangor, Maine [FAA designator] (FAAC) ..... XBG
City of Birmingham Symphony Orchestra [British] .... CBSO
City of Calgary Electric System, Resource Centre, Calgary, AB, Canada [Library symbol] [Library of Congress] (LCLS) .... CaACES
City of David Archaeological Project .... CODAP
City of Edmonton Archives, Alberta [Library symbol] [National Library of Canada] (NLC) .... AEEA
City of Edmonton Archives, Edmonton, AB, Canada [Library symbol] [Library of Congress] (LCLS) .... CaAEEA
City of Etobicoke Archives, Etobicoke, ON, Canada [Library symbol] [Library of Congress] (LCLS) .... CaOEA
City of Hope (EA) .... CH
City of Hope [An association] (EA) .... COH
City of Hope Medical Center, Duarte, CA [Library symbol] [Library of Congress] (LCLS) .... CDuH
City of Hope Medical Center, Duarte, CA [OCLC symbol] (OCLC) .... CHM
City of Houston Legal Department, Houston, TX [Library symbol] [Library of Congress] (LCLS) .... TxHLD
City of Lincoln Public Library, Lincoln, United Kingdom [Library symbol] [Library of Congress] (LCLS) .... UkLin
City of Liverpool College of Technology (SAUS) .... CLCT
City of London [British] CL
City of London [British] .... C of L
City of London (SAUO) .... C of L
City of London Engineers [British military] (DMA) .... CLE
City of London General Pension Society (SAUO) .... CLGPS

City of London National Guard [*British military*] (DMA) .... CLNG
City of London Police (ROG) .... CLP
City of London Rifles [*British*] .... CLR
City of London Rifles (SAUO) .... CLR
City of London Yeomanry (SAUO) .... C of LY
City of London Yeomanry [*Military*] [*British*] (ROG) .... C of LY
City of London Yeomanry (SAUO) .... COLY
City of Memphis Hospital, Memphis, TN [*Library symbol*] [*Library of Congress*] (LCLS) .... TMCH
City of Ottawa Archives, Ontario [*Library symbol*] [*National Library of Canada*] (NLC) .... OOOA
City of Portland Bureau of Planning [*Oregon*] (GEOI) .... COP/BOP
City of Prineville Railway [*AAR code*] .... COP
City of Refuge National Historic Park .... CIRE
City of Savannah, Municipal Research Library, Savannah, GA [*Library symbol*] [*Library of Congress*] (LCLS) .... GSM
City of Sydney Cultural Centre [*Australia*] .... CSCC
City of Sydney Public Library, Sydney, NSW, Australia [*Library symbol*] [*Library of Congress*] (LCLS) .... AuS
City of Toronto, Division of Records and Archives, Toronto, ON, Canada [*Library symbol*] [*Library of Congress*] (LCLS) .... CaOTCTAR
City of Tucson, Department of Planning, Tucson, AZ [*Library symbol*] [*Library of Congress*] (LCLS) .... AzTDP
City of White Rock Museum and Archives, British Columbia [*Library symbol*] [*National Library of Canada*] (NLC) .... BWRM
City of Winnipeg Metro Planning Division, Manitoba [*Library symbol*] [*National Library of Canada*] (NLC) .... MWMP
City of York Community & Agency Social Planning Council (AC) .... Y-CASP
City of York Public Library, Toronto, Ontario [*Library symbol*] [*National Library of Canada*] (NLC) .... OTYP
City Planning Commission (WDAA) .... CPC
City Police Commissioner (DAS) .... CPC
City Police Court [*British*] (DAS) .... CPC
City Police Court (SAUO) .... CPC
City Products Corporation (SAUO) .... CY
City Projects Council (SAUO) .... CPC
City Public Service Board (SAUO) .... CPSB
City Real Property Database (GEOI) .... CRPD
City Reference File [*Bureau of the Census*] (GFGA) .... CRF
City Resources (Canada) Ltd. [*Vancouver Stock Exchange symbol*] [*Toronto Stock Exchange symbol*] .... CIZ
City Stipendiary Magistrate (SAUO) .... CSM
City Stores Company (SAUO) .... CSS
City Surveyor (SAUS) .... CS
City Technology Colleges [*British*] .... CTC
City Technology Holdings (WDAA) .... CTH
City Ticket Office [*Travel industry*] (TRID) .... CTO
City University (SAUO) .... CU
City University Business School [*London, England*] .... CUBS
City University Library Resource Center, Bellevue, WA [*Library symbol*] [*Library of Congress*] (LCLS) .... WaBC
City University of New York (CDAI) .... CUNY
City University of New York Athletic Conference (PSS) .... CUNY
City University of New York, Central Office, New York, NY [*Library symbol*] [*Library of Congress*] (LCLS) .... NNCU-C
City University of New York, Division of Teacher Education, New York, NY [*Library symbol*] [*Library of Congress*] (LCLS) .... NNCU-T
City University of New York (Graduate Center) (GAGS) .... CUNY (Grad Cent)
City University of New York, Graduate Center, New York, NY [*Library symbol*] [*Library of Congress*] (LCLS) .... NNCU-G
City University of New York, Graduate School (SAUS) .... ZGM
City University of New York, Law School, Flushing, NY [*Library symbol*] [*Library of Congress*] (LCLS) .... NNCU-L
City Urban Renewal Management Corp. [*New York City*] .... CURMCO
City Urban Renewal Management Corporation (SAUO) .... CURMCO
City Vehicle System (SAUS) .... CVS
City View .... c/v
City Wide Centrex (SAUS) .... CWC
City Women's Network (WDAA) .... CWN
City-County Memorial Library, Bay St. Louis, MS [*Library symbol*] [*Library of Congress*] (LCLS) .... MsBs
City-County Public Library, Moundsville, WV [*Library symbol*] [*Library of Congress*] (LCLS) .... WvMo
Cityflyer Express [*British*] [*ICAO designator*] (FAAC) .... CFE
City-Jet Luftverklehrsges, GmbH [*Austria*] [*ICAO designator*] (FAAC) .... CIT
City-Jet Luftverklehrsges, MBH [*Austria*] [*FAA designator*] (FAAC) .... CIT
City-Link Airlines Ltd. [*Nigeria*] [*FAA designator*] (FAAC) .... CRG
Cityscape Financial [*NASDAQ symbol*] (TTSB) .... CTYS
Cityscape Financial Corp. [*NASDAQ symbol*] (SAG) .... CTYS
Cityscape Financial Corp. [*Associated Press*] (SAG) .... Ctyscape
Ciudad Acuna [*Mexico*] [*ICAO location identifier*] (ICLI) .... MMCC
Ciudad Bolivar [*Venezuela*] [*Airport symbol*] (OAG) .... CBL
Ciudad Bolivar, Bolivar [*Venezuela*] [*ICAO location identifier*] (ICLI) .... SVCB
Ciudad de Valles [*Mexico*] [*Airport symbol*] (AD) .... VAE
Ciudad Del Carmen [*Mexico*] [*Airport symbol*] (OAG) .... CME
Ciudad Del Carmen [*Mexico*] [*ICAO location identifier*] (ICLI) .... MMCE
Ciudad Juarez [*Mexico*] [*Airport symbol*] (OAG) .... CJS
Ciudad Juarez, Mexico [*Television station call letters*] (BROA) .... XHIJ
Ciudad Juarez/Abraham Gonzalez Internacional [*Mexico*] [*ICAO location identifier*] (ICLI) .... MMCS
Ciudad Mante [*Mexico*] [*Airport symbol*] (AD) .... MMC
Ciudad Mante [*Mexico*] [*ICAO location identifier*] (ICLI) .... MMDM
Ciudad Obregon [*Mexico*] [*Airport symbol*] (OAG) .... CEN
Ciudad Obregon [*Mexico*] [*ICAO location identifier*] (ICLI) .... MMCN
Ciudad Presidente Stroessner [*Paraguay*] [*ICAO location identifier*] (ICLI) .... SGPS
Ciudad Victoria [*Mexico*] [*Airport symbol*] (OAG) .... CVM
Ciudad Victoria [*Mexico*] [*ICAO location identifier*] (ICLI) .... MMCV
Civic CVC
Civic Action .... CA
Civic Action Centers [*Military*] (CINC) .... CAC
Civic Action Detachment (SAUO) .... CAD
Civic Action Group [*Military*] (CINC) .... CAG
Civic Action Group [*Military*] (CINC) .... CIVACTGP
Civic Action Institute [*Defunct*] (EA) .... CAI
Civic Action Team [*Navy*] (VNW) .... CATS
Civic Administration Center (SAUO) .... CAC
Civic Affairs Mobile Training Team (SAUO) .... CAMTT
Civic Bancorp [*NASDAQ symbol*] (SAG) CIVC
Civic Bancorp [*Associated Press*] (SAG) .... CivicBc
Civic Catering Association [*British*] (BI) .... CCA
Civic Club of Philadelphia, Philadelphia, PA [*Library symbol*] [*Library of Congress*] [*Obsolete*] (LCLS) .... PPCiC
Civic Democratic Alliance [*Former Czechoslovakia*] [*Political party*] (EY) .... CDA
Civic Democratic Alliance [*Czech Republic*] [*Political party*] (BUAC) .... ODA
Civic Democratic Party [*Former Czechoslovakia*] [*Political party*] (EY) .... CDP
Civic Democratic Party - Public Against Violence [*Former Czechoslovakia*] [*Political party*] (EY) .... CDU-PAV
Civic Development Movement [*Sierra Leone*] [*Political party*] (EY) .... CDEM
Civic Entertainment Officers' Association [*British*] (BI) .... CEOA
Civic Information & Techniques Exchange [*Citizens Forum on Self-Government/National Municipal League*] [*Information service or system*] (IID) .... CIVITEX
Civic Instruction (WDAA) CI
Civic Issues Voluntary Information Council [*Michigan*] CIVIC
Civic Leaders for Ecological Action and Responsibility (SAUO) .... CLEAR
Civic Movement [*Former Czechoslovakia*] [*Political party*] (EY) .... CM
Civic Square, Information and Reference, Sudbury Public Library, Ontario [*Library symbol*] [*National Library of Canada*] (NLC) .... OSUCS
Civic Trust (DCTA) .... CT
Civic Trust (SAUO) .... CT
Civic United Front [*Tanzania*] [*Political party*] .... CUF
Civil [*Legal term*] (DLA) c
Civil (GEAB) civ
Civil (AFM) CIV
Civil (MSA) CVL
Civil Action Detachment [*Military*] (DNAB) .... CAD
Civil Action Team [*Military*] .... CAT
Civil Administration (SAUO) .... CA
Civil Administration Commission (SAUO) .... CAC
Civil Administration Committee [*US Military Government, Germany*] .... CAC
Civil Administration Division (SAUO) .... CAD
Civil Administrator (CINC) .... CIVAD
Civil Advanced Gas-Cooled Reactor (NUCP) .... CAGR
Civil Aeromedical Agricultural Research Institute (SAUS) .... CARI
Civil Aeromedical Institute [*FAA*] .... CAI
Civil Aeromedical Institute [*FAA*] .... CAMI
Civil Aeromedical Research Institute [*FAA*] .... CARI
Civil Aeronautical Regulation (MCD) .... CAR
Civil Aeronautics Administration [*Later, part of FAA*] .... CAA
Civil Aeronautics Administration Manual .... CAAM
Civil Aeronautics Administration Type Certificate .... CAATC
Civil Aeronautics Administration-Type-Certificate (SAUS) .... CAATC
Civil Aeronautics and Development Policy Study (SAUO) .... CARD
Civil Aeronautics Authority (AAGC) .... CAA
Civil Aeronautics Authority Journal [*A publication*] (AAGC) .... CAAJ
Civil Aeronautics Authority Manual (SAUS) .... CAAM
Civil Aeronautics Authority Opinions [*A publication*] (DLA) .... CAA Op
Civil Aeronautics Authority Reports [*A publication*] (DLA) .... CAA
Civil Aeronautics Board [*Independent government agency*] [*Terminated, 1984, functions transferred to Department of Transportation*] .... CAB
Civil Aeronautics Board Air Transport Mobilization Standby Order .... CAB-ATM
Civil Aeronautics Board Reports [*A publication*] (DLA) .... CAB
Civil Aeronautics Bulletin .... CAB
Civil Aeronautics Bulletin (SAUS) .... CAB
Civil Aeronautics Manual .... CAM
Civil Aerospace Medical Association (SAUO) .... CAMA
Civil Affairs (DOMA) .... CA
Civil Affairs Agency (SAUO) .... CAA
Civil Affairs Association (EA) .... CAA
Civil Affairs Branch (SAUO) .... CAB
Civil Affairs Committee (SAUO) .... CAC
Civil Affairs Division [*Military*] .... CAD
Civil Affairs Group [*Military*] (DNAB) .... CAG
Civil Affairs Inland Depot [*for relief supplies to liberated territory*] [*British*] [*World War II*] .... CAID
Civil Affairs Liquidating Agency (SAUO) .... CALA
Civil Affairs Mission (SAUO) .... CAM
Civil Affairs Mobile Training Team [*Military*] (CINC) .... CAMTT
Civil Affairs Officer [*Navy*] .... CAO
Civil Affairs Officer [*Army*] (AABC) S5
Civil Affairs Police Officer [*British*] [*World War II*] .... CAPO
Civil Affairs Section .... CAS
Civil Affairs Section [*of an Army division or brigade general staff; the officer in charge of this section*] G-5
Civil Affairs Service (SAUO) .... CAS
Civil Affairs Service (Burma) [*British*] .... CAS(B)
Civil Affairs Service (Malaya) [*British*] .... CAS(M)
Civil Affairs Staff Center (SAUO) .... CASC
Civil Affairs Staff Center [*Wimbledon, England*] .... CCSC
Civil Affairs Staff Officer [*British*] .... CASO

Civil Affairs Staging Area [*World War II*] ..... CASA
Civil Affairs Summary [*Navy*] ..... CASUM
Civil Affairs Team ..... CAT
Civil Affairs Training Center [*World War II*] ..... CATC
Civil Affairs Training School [*Navy*] ..... CATS
Civil Affairs Unit [*British*] ..... CAU
Civil Affairs Unit (SAUO) ..... CA Unit
Civil Affairs/Military Government ..... CA/MG
Civil Agency ..... CA
Civil Air Attache [*British*] ..... CAA
Civil Air Branch [*Air Force*] ..... CAB
Civil Air Carrier Turbojet (FAAC) ..... CACT
Civil Air Defense Identification Zone (MCD) ..... CADIZ
Civil Air Defense Services ..... CADS
Civil Air Defense Warning [*System*] ..... CADW
Civil Air Guard [*British*] ..... CAG
Civil Air Manual (SAUS) ..... CAM
Civil Air Movement ..... CAM
Civil Air Operations Officers Association of Australia (SAUO) ..... CAOOAA
Civil Air Patrol (EA) ..... CAP
Civil Air Patrol Coastal Patrol [*Wartime*] ..... CAPCP
Civil Air Patrol Guard ..... CAPG
Civil Air Publication [*British*] (DEN) ..... CAP
Civil Air Regulation [*FAA*] ..... CAR
Civil Air Rescue Emergency Services (AC) ..... CARES
Civil Air Rescue Emergency Services - AAC Project [*Also, Alberta Aviation Council Project*] (AC) ..... CARES
Civil Air Reserve (AAG) ..... CAR
Civil Air Search & Rescue Association (AC) ..... CASARA
Civil Air Service (SAUO) ..... CAS
Civil Air Surgeon [*of FAA*] ..... CAS
Civil Air Traffic Control (ACAE) ..... CATC
Civil Air Traffic Operations (AIA) ..... CATO
Civil Air Training Academy [*Australia*] ..... CATA
Civil Air Transport [*Free China's international airline*] ..... CAT
Civil Air Transport (SAUO) ..... CT
Civil Air Transport Industry Training Board (MCD) ..... CATITB
Civil Aircraft Airworthiness Data Recording Program [*British*] (MCD) ..... CAADRP
Civil Aircraft Control Advisory Committee [*British*] (AIA) ..... CACAC
Civil Aircraft for Remote sensing and In-Situ Measurement of the Troposphere andLower Stratosphere Based on the Instrument Container Concept ..... CARIBIC
Civil Aircraft Inspection Procedure (DA) ..... CAIP
Civil Aircraft Notification Procedure (PDAA) ..... CANP
Civil Aircraft Research and Technology Demonstration Program (SAUO) ..... CARAD
Civil Airworthiness Regulation (SAUS) ..... CAR
Civil and Commercial Code [*A publication*] (DLA) ..... C Com C
Civil and Commercial Code [*A publication*] (DLA) ..... C Comm C
Civil and Construction Engineering (SAUS) ..... CCE
Civil and Criminal Law Series [*India*] [*A publication*] (DLA) ..... Civ & Cr LS
Civil and Defense Mobilization Board [*Military*] (SAA) ..... CDMB
Civil and Environmental Engineering ..... CEE
Civil and Environmental Engineering Development Office [*Tyndall Air Force Base, FL*] ..... CEEDO
Civil and Mechanical Engineers Society (SAUO) ..... CMES
Civil and Mining Engineer (SAUS) ..... C&ME
Civil and Mining Engineer ..... C & ME
Civil and Public Services Association [*British*] ..... CPSA
Civil and Public Services Association (SAUO) ..... CPSA
Civil and Sanitary Engineering (MCD) ..... CSE
Civil Anti-Gas School (SAUO) ..... CAGS
Civil Appeals [*A publication*] (DLA) Civ
Civil Appeals, Texas [*A publication*] (DLA) ..... CA TX
Civil Assistant Personal Services [*Navy*] [*British*] ..... CAPS
Civil Assistant Personal Services (SAUO) ..... CAPS
Civil Assistant to Medical Director-General [*Navy*] [*British*] ..... CAMDG
Civil Authorities ..... CA
Civil Authorities [*Army*] ..... C Auth
Civil Authorities (OTD) CIV
Civil Aviation ..... CA
Civil Aviation (SAUS) ..... Civ Avn
Civil Aviation Administration (SAUO) ..... CAA
Civil Aviation Administration [*Marine science*] (OSRA) ..... CAA
Civil Aviation Administration of China (SAUO) ..... CA
Civil Aviation Administration of China ..... CAAC
Civil Aviation Administration of Korea [*North Korea*] ..... CAAK
Civil Aviation Administration of Vietnam ..... CAAV
Civil Aviation Advisory [*or Assistance*] **Group** [*FAA*] ..... CAAG
Civil Aviation Authorities (CTAS) ..... CAA
Civil Aviation Authority [*British*] ..... CAA
Civil Aviation Authority (SAUO) ..... CAA
Civil Aviation Authority - War Training Service ..... CAA-WTS
Civil Aviation Authority Flying Unit (PIAV) ..... CAAFU
Civil Aviation Authority of China (GAVI) ..... CAAC
Civil Aviation Authority of New Zealand [*ICAO designator*] (FAAC) CIV
Civil Aviation Board (SAUO) ..... CAB
Civil Aviation Branch (SAUO) ..... CAB
Civil Aviation Branch, Canadian Air Transportation Administration, Transport Canada [*Direction Generale de l'Aviation Civile, Administration Canadienne des Transports Aeriens, Transports Canada*] **Edmonton, Alberta** [*Library symbol*] [*National Library of Canada*] (NLC) ..... AEMTCA
Civil Aviation Caretaker Authority for Somalia (SAUO) ..... CACAs
Civil Aviation Chaplains International (EAIO) ..... CACI
Civil Aviation Communication Center [*Canada*] ..... CACC
Civil Aviation Council of Arab States (SAUO) ..... CACAS
Civil Aviation Development Committee (SAUO) ..... CADC
Civil Aviation Flying Unit [*British*] (AIA) ..... CAFU
Civil Aviation Historical Society [*Australia*] ..... CAHS
Civil Aviation Information Circular [*British*] (AIA) ..... CAIC
Civil Aviation Inspectorate of the Czech Republic [*ICAO designator*] (FAAC) ..... CBA
Civil Aviation Licensing Act (DLA) ..... CALA
Civil Aviation Medical Association (EA) ..... CAMA
Civil Aviation Medical Institute (MCD) ..... CAMI
Civil Aviation Medicine (SAUS) ..... CAM
Civil Aviation Meteorological Facsimile Network (PDAA) ..... CAMFAX
Civil Aviation Navigational Services Group (SAUO) ..... CANSG
Civil Aviation Notification Procedure (PIAV) ..... CANP
Civil Aviation Order ..... CAO
Civil Aviation Packet Switching Integrated Network (DA) ..... CAPSIN
Civil Aviation Planning Committee (AFM) ..... CAPC
Civil Aviation Planning Committee (SAUS) ..... VAPC
Civil Aviation Purchasing Service [*ICAO*] (DA) ..... CAPS
Civil Aviation Research and Development [*NASA*] ..... CARD
Civil Aviation Rules (SAUS) ..... CAR
Civil Aviation Safety Agency (SAUO) ..... CASA
Civil Aviation Signal Training Establishment (IAA) ..... CASTE
Civil Aviation Signals Training Establishment (SAUO) ..... CASTE
Civil Aviation Statistics Programme [*ICAO*] [*United Nations*] (DUND) ..... CASP
Civil Aviation Training Centre (SAUO) ..... CATC
Civil Aviation Wireless Association (SAUO) ..... CAWA
Civil Budget Committee [*NATO*] (NATG) ..... CBC
Civil Catering Department (SAUO) ..... CCD
Civil Censorship Department (or Detachment, or Division (SAUO) ..... CCD
Civil Censorship Division [*US Military Government, Germany*] ..... CCD
Civil Censorship Study Group (EA) ..... CCSG
Civil Code [*A publication*] (DLA) CC
Civil Code of Louisiana [*A publication*] (DLA) ..... Code LA
Civil Code of Practice [*A publication*] (DLA) ..... Civ Code Prac
Civil Code of Quebec [*A publication*] (DLA) ..... CCQ
Civil Commotion CC
Civil Communication Planning Committee [*Military*] (NATG) ..... CCPC
Civil Communication Service (SAUO) ..... CCS
Civil Communications Element [*Military*] (NATG) ..... CCE
Civil Communications Planning Committee (SAUO) ..... CCEP
Civil Communications-Electronics Working-Group [*Military*] (NATG) ..... CCEWG
Civil Contingency Unit [*Cabinet Office*] [*British*] (DI) ..... CCU
Civil Cooperation Bureau [*South African covert-operations team*] (ECON) ..... CCB
Civil Coordination Detachment [*General Air Traffic Element at Operational Traffic and Defense Centers*] [*NATO*] ..... CCD
Civil Coordination Detachment General [*NATO*] (NATG) ..... CCDG
Civil Court CC
Civil Court (SAUO) CC
Civil Court (DLA) ..... Civ Ct
Civil Court of Record (DLA) ..... Civ Ct Rec
Civil Damage Assessment Program [*Army*] (AABC) ..... CDAP
Civil Data Management System (SAUS) ..... CDMS
Civil Defence ..... CIVDEF
Civil Defence Ambulance Service (SAUO) ..... CDAS
Civil Defence Force [*British military*] (DMA) ..... CDF
Civil Defence Legion [*British military*] (DMA) ..... CDL
Civil Defence Regional Commission (SAUO) ..... CDRC
Civil Defence Regional Commissioner (SAUS) ..... CDRC
Civil Defence Rescue Service (SAUO) ..... CDRS
Civil Defence Services (SAUO) ..... CDS
Civil Defence Volunteers (SAUO) ..... CDV
Civil Defense ..... CD
Civil Defense Administration (SAUO) ..... CDA
Civil Defense Adult Education [*Program*] ..... CDAE
Civil Defense Adult Education Program ..... CDAEP
Civil Defense Advisory Council ..... CDAC
Civil Defense Agency ..... CDA
Civil Defense Ambulance Service (WDAA) ..... CDAS
Civil Defense and Emergency Response (SAUO) ..... CD&ER
Civil Defense Bulletin (SAUS) ..... Civ Def Bull
Civil Defense Career Development Program ..... CDCDP
Civil Defense Committee (NATG) ..... CDC
Civil Defense Coordinator (AAG) ..... CDC
Civil Defense Countermeasures System ..... CDCS
Civil Defense Director/Coordinator ..... CD D/C
Civil Defense Education Program ..... CDEP
Civil Defense Emergency Operations System ..... CDEOS
Civil Defense Exercise ..... CDEX
Civil Defense Management ..... CDM
Civil Defense National Telephone System (SAUO) ..... CDNTS
Civil Defense Officer (SAUS) ..... CDO
Civil Defense Organization [*United Nations*] ..... CDO
Civil Defense Quality Check Program [*Military*] (DNAB) ..... CDQCP
Civil Defense Receiver ..... CDR
Civil Defense Report ..... CIDERE
Civil Defense Research Associates ..... CDRA
Civil Defense Support Detachment (SAUO) ..... CDSD
Civil Defense, United States of America [*Home study course*] ..... CD-USA
Civil Defense University Extension Program ..... CDUEP
Civil Defense Warning ..... CDW
Civil Defense Warning System ..... CDWS
Civil Direction of Shipping (NVT) ..... CDS
Civil Direction of Shipping Organization (MCD) ..... CDSORG
Civil Director of Economics ..... CDE

Civil Disobedience ... CD
Civil Disobedience Unit (SAUS) ... CDU
Civil District Court (DLA) ... Civ D Ct
Civil Disturbance Group [*Department of Justice intelligence unit*] ... CDG
Civil Disturbance Readiness Conditions [*Army*] (AABC) ... CIDCON
Civil Disturbance Status report (SAUS) ... CIDSTAT report
Civil Disturbance Status Reporting [*Army*] (AABC) ... CIDSTAT
Civil Earth Remote Sensing System (SAUS) ... CERSS
Civil Effects Exercise [*NASA*] (KSC) ... CEX
Civil Effects Experiments [*DASA and AEC*] ... CEX
Civil Effects Test Group [*DASA and AEC*] ... CETG
Civil Effects Test Operations [*DASA and AEC*] ... CETO
Civil Emergency Coordinating Committee (SAUO) ... CECC
Civil Emergency Information Room [*NATO*] (NATG) ... CEIR
Civil Emergency Message [*Telecommunications*] (OTD) ... CEM
Civil Emergency Planning [*NATO*] (NATG) ... CEP
Civil Emergency Planning Bureau [*NATO*] (NATG) ... CEPB
Civil Emergency Planning Committee [*US/Canada*] ... CEPC
Civil Engineer ... CE
Civil Engineer (FAAC) ... CENGR
Civil Engineer Automated Specification Retrieval System [*Air Force*] ... CEASRS
Civil Engineer Combat AFSC Simulation (SAUO) ... CECAS
Civil Engineer Construction Operations Group [*Air Force*] (AFM) ... CECOGp
Civil Engineer Corps [*Army*] ... CEC
Civil Engineer Corps, Engineer-in-Training [*Army*] (DNAB) ... CEC EIT
Civil Engineer Corps Officer's School [*Army*] (DNAB) ... CECOFFSCOL
Civil Engineer Corps Officer's School [*Army*] (DNAB) ... CECOS
Civil Engineer Corps Officers School (SAUO) ... CECOS
Civil Engineer Corps, Professional Engineer [*Army*] (DNAB) ... CEC PE
Civil Engineer Corps, Registered Architect [*Army*] (DNAB) ... CEC RA
Civil Engineer Management System (AFM) ... CEMS
Civil Engineer, Officer-In-Change (SAUS) ... CEOINC
Civil Engineer Operational Project List (SAUO) ... CEOPL
Civil Engineer Preventive Maintenance [*Air Force*] ... CEPM
Civil Engineer Support Equipment [*Army*] ... CESE
Civil Engineer Support Management Information System [*Military*] (DNAB) ... CESMIS
Civil Engineer Support/ Management Information System (SAUO) ... CES/MIS
Civil Engineer Support Office [*Navy*] ... CESO
Civil Engineer Support Plan ... CESP
Civil Engineering (NAKS) ... CE
Civil Engineering ... CIVENG
Civil Engineering and Evaluation Laboratory [*Navy*] (MCD) ... CEREL
Civil Engineering and Public Works Review (journ.) (SAUS) ... Civ Eng&PWR
Civil Engineering and Services Management Evaluation Team [*Military*] ... CESMET
Civil Engineering College (SAUO) ... CECOL
Civil Engineering Computer Laboratory [*MIT*] (MCD) ... CECL
Civil Engineering Computing Center at Lund Institute of Technology (SAUS) ... VDC
Civil Engineering Computing System (PDAA) ... CECS
Civil Engineering Construction Conciliation Board (SAUO) ... CECCB
Civil Engineering Contract Reporting System (SAUO) ... CECORS
Civil Engineering Data ... CED
Civil Engineering Field Activities Center ... CEFAC
Civil Engineering File (DOMA) ... CEF
Civil Engineering Flight [*Military*] ... CEF
Civil Engineering Flight, Heavy Repair [*Military*] ... CEFHR
Civil Engineering Group [*Air Force*] ... CEG
Civil Engineering Laboratory [*Also, CIVENGRLAB*] [*Port Hueneme, CA*] [*Navy*] (MCD) ... CEL
Civil Engineering Laboratory [*Navy*] (DNAB) ... CIVENGLAB
Civil Engineering Laboratory [*Also, CEL*] [*Navy*] (MUGU) ... CIVENGRLAB
Civil Engineering Maintenance, Inspection, Repair, and Training Team [*Air Force*] ... CEMIRT
Civil Engineering Materials Acquisition System (ACAE) ... CEMAS
Civil Engineering Office at Vandenberg (SAUS) ... DECS
Civil Engineering Operational Planning System (SAUO) ... CESPS
Civil Engineering Operations Squadron [*Air Force*] ... CEOS
Civil Engineering Package (IEEE) ... CEP
Civil Engineering Plan (SAUO) ... CEP
Civil Engineering Problems (SAUS) ... CEPs
Civil Engineering Problems ... CEPS
Civil Engineering Program Applications (MCD) ... CEPA
Civil Engineering Program Association (SAUO) ... CEPA
Civil Engineering Project Information System (SAUO) ... CEPIS
Civil Engineering Report ... CER
Civil Engineering Report of Performance (AFM) ... CERP
Civil Engineering Research Association ... CERA
Civil Engineering Research Foundation (SAUO) ... CERF
Civil Engineering Research Laboratory (SAUO) ... CERL
Civil Engineering School at Lund Institute of Technology, Lund University (SAUS) ... V-LTH
Civil Engineering Squadron [*Air Force*] ... CES
Civil Engineering Squadron [*Air Force*] ... CIVENGSq
Civil Engineering Squadron, Heavy Repair [*Air Force*] ... CESHR
Civil Engineering Standard Method of Measurement (SAUS) ... CESMM
Civil Engineering Support Flight [*Military*] ... CESF
Civil Engineering Support Plan (SAUO) ... CESP
Civil Engineering Support Plan Generator (DOMA) ... CESPG
Civil Engineering Support Program (SAUO) ... CESP
Civil Engineering Support Squadron [*Air Force*] ... CESS
Civil Engineering Systems Laboratory [*University of Illinois*] ... CESL
Civil Engineering Technologies for Automatic Roadmaking (SAUO) ... CENTAUR
Civil Engineers Corps Officers School [*Navy*] ... CECOS
Civil Enterprise [*Publishing program*] ... CE
Civil Fast Reactor (PDAA) ... CFR
Civil GPS Service (SAUO) ... CGS
Civil GPS Service Interface Committee (SAUO) ... CGSC
Civil GPS Service Interface Committee (SAUO) ... CGSIC
Civil GPS Service Interface Committee (SAUO) ... CGSICO
Civil Guard [*Air Force*] (MCD) ... CG
Civil Imprisonment ... CI
Civil Industrial Technologies Cooperation Plan [*Framework agreement for conducting cooperative global research*] ... CITCP
Civil Information and Education (SAUO) ... CIE
Civil Information and Education Section of Allied Headquarters [*World War II*] ... CIANDE
Civil Institute of Electrical Engineers (SAUO) ... CIEE
Civil Internment Camp (SAUO) ... CIC
Civil Investigative Demand [*Department of Justice*] ... CID
Civil Jet Transport ... CJT
Civil Justice Quarterly [*A publication*] (DLA) ... Civ Just Q
Civil Justice Quarterly [*A publication*] ... CJQ
Civil Labour Control Unit [*British*] ... CLCU
Civil Law ... CL
Civil Liability Convention [*British*] ... CLC
Civil Liability for Oil Pollution Damage (SAUS) ... CLC
Civil Liaison Division [*Army*] ... CLD
Civil Liaison Officer [*Army*] (AABC) ... CLO
Civil Liberties (ILCA) ... CL
Civil Liberties Action Security Project [*Canada*] ... CLASP
Civil Liberties and Police [*Germany*] ... CILIP
Civil Liberties Bureau [*Forerunner of the American Civil Liberties Union*] ... CLB
Civil Liberties Defense Committee (SAUS) ... GICLDC
Civil Liberties Docket (DLA) ... Civ Lib Dock
Civil Liberties Educational Foundation [*Defunct*] (EA) ... CLEF
Civil Liberties Legal Defense Fund (EA) ... CLLDF
Civil Liberties Union (IIA) ... CLU
Civil Liberties Union of Massachusetts (SAUO) ... CLUM
Civil Liberty (DLA) ... CIV LIB
Civil Litigation Reporter [*A publication*] (DLA) ... Civ Litigation Rep
Civil Lord (SAUS) ... CL
Civil Lord of the Admiralty (SAUS) ... CLA
Civil Mediator Organisation [*British*] (DA) ... CASOR
Civil Member for Development and Production [*British*] ... CMDP
Civil Military Exercise (MCD) ... CIMEX
Civil Military Operations Center ... CMOC
Civil Military Operations Team ... CMOT
Civil Military Relations Exercise (SAUO) ... CIMIREX
Civil Monetary Penalties [*Medicaid program*] (GFGA) ... CMP
Civil Navigation Aids System ... CNAS
Civil Number [*Docket number*] (AAGC) ... Civ No
Civil Nursing Reserve (DAVI) ... CNR
Civil Nursing Reserve (SAUO) ... CNR
Civil Operations for Rural Development Support [*Army*] ... CORDS
Civil Operations Revolutionary Development Support [*Army*] (AABC) ... CORDS
Civil Parish [*British*] ... CP
Civil Personnel (SAUS) ... Civ Per
Civil Pilot Training Program (SAUS) ... CPTP
Civil Pilots for Regulatory Reform (EA) ... CPRR
Civil, Police, Military activities (SAUS) ... CPM
Civil Post Office (AFM) ... CPO
Civil Power ... CP
Civil Practice Act [*New York*] (DLA) ... CPA
Civil Practice Law and Rules [*A publication*] (DLA) ... Civ Prac
Civil Practice Law and Rules [*New York, NY*] ... CPLR
Civil Preparedness Guide [*Civil Defense*] ... CPG
Civil Procedure [*Legal term*] (DLA) ... Civ Proc
Civil Procedure [*Legal term*] ... CP
Civil Procedure Reports [*New York*] [*A publication*] (DLA) ... Civil Pro R
Civil Procedure Reports [*New York*] [*A publication*] (DLA) ... Civ Pr
Civil Procedure Reports [*New York*] [*A publication*] (DLA) ... Civ Pro
Civil Procedure Reports [*New York*] [*A publication*] (DLA) ... Civ Proc R
Civil Procedure Reports [*New York*] [*A publication*] (DLA) ... Civ Proc Rep
Civil Procedure Reports [*New York*] [*A publication*] (DLA) ... Civ Pro R
Civil Procedure Reports [*New York*] [*A publication*] (DLA) ... Civ Pro Reports
Civil Procedure Reports [*New York*] [*A publication*] (DLA) ... Civ Pr Rep
Civil Procedure Reports [*New York*] [*A publication*] (DLA) ... CP
Civil Procedure Reports [*New York*] [*A publication*] (DLA) ... NY Civ Proc Rep
Civil Procedure Reports [*New York*] [*A publication*] (DLA) ... NYCP
Civil Procedure Reports, New Series [*1908-13*] [*New York*] [*A publication*] (DLA) ... Civ Proc (NS)
Civil Procedure Reports, New Series [*1908-13*] [*New York*] [*A publication*] (DLA) ... Civ Proc Rep NS
Civil Procedure Reports, New Series [*1908-13*] [*New York*] [*A publication*] (DLA) ... Civ Proc R (NS)
Civil Procedure Reports, New Series [*1908-13*] [*New York*] [*A publication*] (DLA) ... Civ Pro R (NS)
Civil Procedure Reports, New Series [*1908-13*] [*New York*] [*A publication*] (DLA) ... CPRC (NS)
Civil Procedure Reports, New Series [*1908-13*] [*New York*] [*A publication*] (DLA) ... CPR (NS)
Civil Procedures, Quebec ... CPQ
Civil Rail Lines Important to National Defense [*BTS*] (TAG) ... CRLIND
Civil Readjustment Officer [*Military*] ... CRO
Civil Relief in Korea (SAUO) ... CRIK
Civil Reserve Air Field [*Department of Commerce*] (MCD) ... CRAF
Civil Reserve Air Fleet [*Department of Commerce*] ... CRAF
Civil Reserve Air Fleet Summary Report [*Department of Commerce*] ... CRAFREP

Civil Reserve Air Tanker [*Department of Commerce*] (MCD)	CRAT
Civil Reserve Aircraft Fleet [*OST*] (TAG)	CRAF
Civil Reserve Airlift Fleet (DOMA)	CRAF
Civil Reserve Auxiliary Fleet Ships (DOMA)	CRAFTS
Civil Reserve Information Service (SAUS)	CRIS
Civil Resettlement Unit (SAUO)	CRU
Civil Resettlement Unit [*British*] (DAS)	CRU
Civil Rights (DLA)	CIV R
Civil Rights	CR
Civil Rights Act [*1957, 1964, 1968*]	CRA
Civil Rights Act Compliance Log (OICC)	CRACL
Civil Rights and Law Reform [*Australia*]	CRLR
Civil Rights Commission [*Federal government*]	CRC
Civil Rights Commission (SAUO)	CRC
Civil Rights Congress (SAUO)	CRC
Civil Rights Division [*Department of Justice*]	CRD
Civil Rights Documentation Project (SAUO)	CRDP
Civil Rights Movement (SAUO)	CRM
Civil Rights of Institutionalized Persons Act of 1980 (EDAC)	CRIPA
Civil Rights Office, Education Department (OICC)	CROED
Civil Rights Party [*South Korea*] [*Political party*] (PPW)	CRP
Civil Rights-Civil Liberties (DLA)	CR-CL
Civil Rotorcraft IFR [*Instrument Flight Rules*] Terminal-Area Technology Enhancement Research (GAVI)	CRITTER
Civil Rules for Courts of Limited Jurisdiction (SAUO)	CRLJ
Civil Secret Service (SAUO)	CSS
Civil Servant (DLA)	CS
Civil Service (DLA)	CIV S
Civil Service (DLA)	Civ Serv
Civil Service (SAUO)	CivServ
Civil Service (SAUO)	CS
Civil Service	CS
Civil Service and Cooperation Office for Developing Countries (SAUO)	CISCOD
Civil Service and Post Office Sanitorium Society [*British*] (DI)	CSSS
Civil Service Arbitration Awards (DLA)	CSAA
Civil Service Arbitration Awards (DLA)	CSAB
Civil Service Arbitration Tribunal [*British*]	CSAT
Civil Service Arbitration Tribunal (SAUO)	CSAT
Civil Service Assembly of the United States and Canada (SAUO)	CSA
Civil Service Association of Canada	CSAC
Civil Service Benevolent Fund [*British*]	CSBF
Civil Service Benevolent Fund (SAUO)	CSBF
Civil Service Board (AAG)	CSB
Civil Service Building Society [*British*]	CSBS
Civil Service Cadet Battalion [*British military*] (DMA)	CSCB
Civil Service Catering Organization [*British*]	CISCO
Civil Service Clerical Association [*Later, CPSA*] [*British*] (DI)	CSCA
Civil Service Club [*British*]	CSC
Civil Service College [*British*]	CSC
Civil Service Commission [*Later, MSPB*]	CSC
Civil Service Commission - Investigations	CSC-I
Civil Service Commission of Canada (BARN)	CSCC
Civil Service Commission of Canada (SAUO)	CSCC
Civil Service Commission of Ontario, Toronto, ON, Canada [*Library symbol*] [*Library of Congress*] (LCLS)	CaOTCSC
Civil Service Commission of Ontario, Toronto, Ontario [*Library symbol*] [*National Library of Canada*] (NLC)	OTCSC
Civil Service Co-operative Society (SAUO)	CSCS
Civil Service Cooperative Society [*British*]	CSCS
Civil Service Co-operative Stores (SAUO)	CSCS
Civil Service Council for Further Education [*British*]	CSCFE
Civil Service Department (SAUO)	CSC
Civil Service Department [*British*]	CSD
Civil Service Educational Council (SAUO)	CSEC
Civil Service Employees (EFIS)	CSE
Civil Service Employees Association (EA)	CSEA
Civil Service Foreign Service Allowances Committee [*British*]	CSFSAC
Civil Service Forum (EA)	CSF
Civil Service Housing Association [*British*]	CSHA
Civil Service Insurance Society [*British*]	CSIS
Civil Service Legal Society [*British*]	CSLS
Civil Service Motoring Association [*British*] (BI)	CSMA
Civil Service National Whitley Council [*British*]	CSNWC
Civil Service National Whitley Council (SAUO)	CSNWC
Civil Service of Pakistan (SAUO)	CSP
Civil Service Organization (SAUO)	CSO
Civil Service Pay Research Unit (DLA)	CSPRU
Civil Service Pensioners Alliance [*British*]	CSPA
Civil Service Reform Act [*1978*] (RDA)	CSRA
Civil Service Requirement (SAUS)	CSR
Civil Service Reserve [*British*] (ROG)	CSR
Civil Service Retirement	CSR
Civil Service Retirement and Disability Fund	CSRDF
Civil Service Retirement Fellowship [*British*]	CSRF
Civil Service Retirement System (MCD)	CSRS
Civil Service Rifle Volunteers [*British*]	CSRV
Civil Service Rifle Volunteers (SAUO)	CSRV
Civil Service Rule	CSR
Civil Service Sailing Association (SAUO)	CSSA
Civil Service Sanatorium Society (SAUO)	CSSS
Civil Service Selection Board (SAUO)	CSSB
Civil Service Selection Board [*Pronounced "sissby"*] [*British*]	CSSB
Civil Service Sports Association (SAUO)	CSSA
Civil Service Sports Council (SAUO)	CSSC

Civil Service Sports Council [*British*] (DI)	CSSC
Civil Service Staff Association (SAUO)	CSSA
Civil Service Supply Association [*British*]	CSSA
Civil Service Supply Association, Ltd. (SAUO)	CSSA
Civil Service Survivor Benefit Plan	CSSBP
Civil Service Typists' Association [*A union*] [*British*]	CSTA
Civil Service Union [*British*]	CSU
Civil Service Working Party [*US Military Government, Germany*]	CSWP
Civil Situation Reporting System (NATG)	CIVSITREP
Civil Society (EA)	CS
Civil Space Technology Initiative [*NASA*] (GFGA)	CSTI
Civil Surgeon (DAS)	CS
Civil Technical Corps (SAUO)	CTC
Civil Tilt Rotor [*Aviation*] (DA)	CTR
Civil Transport Development Corporation (SAUO)	CTDC
Civil Trust (SAUO)	CT
Civil War (GEAB)	CW
Civil War Centennial Association	CWCA
Civil War Centennial Commission [*Terminated, 1966*]	CWCC
Civil War Philatelic Society [*Later, AHPS*] (EA)	CWPS
Civil War Press Corps (EA)	CWPC
Civil War Round Table Associates (EA)	CWRTA
Civil War Round Table of New York (SAUO)	CWRTNY
Civil War Society (EA)	CWS
Civil War Times Illustrated [*A publication*]	CWTI
Civil War Token Society (EA)	CWTS
Civil Work Requirements (SAUS)	CWR
Civil Works [*Assistant Secretary of the Army*]	CW
Civil Works Administration [*1933-1934*]	CWA
Civil Works Policy Review and Analysis Division (SAUO)	CWPRAD
Civil Works Program	CWP
Civil Works Service (SAUO)	CWRU
Civile [*Civil*] [*Latin*] (DLA)	Civ
Civilian (AFM)	CIV
Civilian (NTIO)	civ
Civilian Acquired Skills Program [*Military*]	CASP
Civilian Acquisition Management Branch [*Army*] (RDA)	CAMB
Civilian Acquisition Position List [*Army*] (RDA)	CAPL
Civilian Actress Technician [*Term for professional actresses who worked under Army Special Services Division in soldier shows*] [*World War II*]	CAT
Civilian Address Technician Service (SAUO)	CATS
Civilian Advisory Group (SAUO)	CAG
Civilian Affairs Officer (SAUS)	CAO
Civilian Affairs Supports for Echelon above Corps [*Military*]	CASEAC
Civilian Agency Acquisition Council (AAGC)	CAAC
Civilian Air Navigation School	CANS
Civilian Air Transport	CAT
Civilian Anti-Aircraft Co-Operation Unit [*British military*] (DMA)	CAACU
Civilian Appellation Review Agency [*Army*] (MCD)	CARA
Civilian Application of the Results of Military Research and Development (PDAA)	CARMAND
Civilian Application of the Results of Military Research and Development (SAUO)	CARMRAND
Civilian Armed Force Geographical Units [*Paramilitary security force*] [*Philippines*] (ECON)	CAGFU
Civilian Authority for the Protection of Everybody, Regardless [*Crime-fighting unit in TV series "The Kids From C.A.P.E.R."*]	CAPER
Civilian Aviation Advisory Committee [*Air Defense Planning Board*] (AAG)	CAAC
Civilian Aviation Board (SAUS)	CAB
Civilian Bachelor Quarters [*Air Force*] (AFM)	CBQ
Civilian Budgeting System [*Military*]	CBS
Civilian Career Management Center [*Military*] (DNAB)	CCMC
Civilian Career Management Field Agency (MCD)	CCMFA
Civilian Casualty Fund (EA)	CCF
Civilian Censorship Service (SAUO)	CCS
Civilian Clothing	CIVCLO
Civilian Clothing Maintenance Allowance [*Army*] (AABC)	CCMA
Civilian Complaint Review Board	CCRB
Civilian Confinement [*Military*] (DNAB)	CIV CONF
Civilian Congress (EA)	CC
Civilian Conservation Centers [*Job Corps*]	CCC
Civilian Conservation Corps [*Created, 1937; liquidated, 1943*]	CCC
Civilian Control Agency	CCA
Civilian Control Commission (SAUO)	CCC
Civilian Defence Fire Service (SAUO)	CDFS
Civilian Defence Forces (SAUO)	CDF
Civilian Defence General Services (SAUO)	CDGS
Civilian Defense Volunteer Office	CDVO
Civilian Duty (SAUS)	CD
Civilian Education Level [*Military*] (INF)	CEL
Civilian Electronics Technician Afloat [*Navy*] (NVT)	CETA
Civilian Employee (MCD)	CIVEMP
Civilian Employee Health Service	CEHS
Civilian Employee Welfare and Recreation Committee [*Military*] (DNAB)	CEWRC
Civilian Employment Level Plan [*DoD*]	CELP
Civilian Employment Projection (MCD)	CEP
Civilian Engineering Technical Service [*Navy*] (NVT)	CETS
Civilian Enterprise	CE
Civilian Establishment and Pay Officer (SAUS)	CEPO
Civilian Executive Management Board [*Military*] (DNAB)	CEMB
Civilian Extraction [*Nuclear energy*]	CIVEX
Civilian Goods (Supply) Committee [*British*] [*World War II*]	CG(S)C

Civilian Health and Medical Program of the Uniformed Services [*Military*] ... CHAMPUS
Civilian Health and Medical Program of the Veterans Administration [*Military*] ... CHAMPVA
Civilian Hood Mask (SAUS) ... CHM
Civilian Industrial Technology Program (SAUS) ... CITP
Civilian Information Center (SAUO) ... CIC
Civilian Information Management System (AFIT) ... CIMS
Civilian Information Manpower Management System [*Navy*] ... CIMMS
Civilian Information Manpower System (SAUS) ... CIMS
Civilian Institutions Programs Directorate (SAUO) ... CIPD
Civilian Instruction Program (MUGU) ... CIP
Civilian Instructor/Trainer (WDAA) ... CIT
Civilian International (SAUO) ... CI
Civilian Internee (SAUS) ... Ci
Civilian Internee [*Military*] (INF) ... CI
Civilian Irregular Defense Group [*Military*] ... CIDG
Civilian Jeep ... CJ
Civilian Labor Force [*DoD*] ... CLF
Civilian Labor Group (MCD) ... CLG
Civilian Labor Group Center [*Army*] (AABC) ... CLGC
Civilian Labor Group Special Orders [*Army*] (AABC) ... CLGSO
Civilian Labour Control Unit (SAUO) ... CLCU
Civilian Labour Employment Office (SAUO) ... CLEO
Civilian Maimed and Limbless Association of Western Australia ... CMLAWA
Civilian Manpower & Funding Extract (SAUO) ... CMFE
Civilian Manpower & Funding Extract (SAUO) ... CMFESIS
Civilian Manpower Management Guides [*Navy*] (NG) ... CMMG
Civilian Manpower Management Instruction [*Navy*] (NG) ... CMMI
Civilian Manpower Management Letters [*Navy*] (NG) ... CMML
Civilian Man-Years [*Military*] (AABC) ... CMY
Civilian Marine Emergency Volunteers ... CMEV
Civilian Marine Personnel Instructions [*Navy*] ... CMPI
Civilian Marksmanship Program (MCD) ... CMP
Civilian Material Assistance (EA) ... CMA
Civilian Medical Personnel (SAUS) ... CMP
Civilian Military Cooperation (NATG) ... CIMIC
Civilian Military Institute (SAUS) ... CMI
Civilian Military Training Camp (DNAB) ... CMTC
Civilian Mixed Labour Organization (SAUO) ... CMLO
Civilian Mixed Watchman Service (SAUO) ... CMWS
Civilian Mobilization Manpower Allocation/Requirements Plan ... CIV-M-MARP
Civilian Modification Committee (SAUO) ... CMC
Civilian National Commission on Space Activities (SAUO) ... CONAE
Civilian Occupational Specialty ... COS
Civilian Orientation Cruise (DNAB) ... COC
Civilian Payroll Circular ... CPRC
Civilian Personnel (ACAE) ... CP
Civilian Personnel Accounting System [*Military*] (MCD) ... CPAS
Civilian Personnel Administration Services Record System [*Military*] (DNAB) ... CIVPERSADMSYS
Civilian Personnel Advisor [*Military*] ... CPA
Civilian Personnel Advisory Center [*Army*] ... CPAC
Civilian Personnel and Payroll Letter [*Military*] ... CPPL
Civilian Personnel Branch [*BUPERS*] ... CPB
Civilian Personnel Career Plan [*Air Force*] ... CPCP
Civilian Personnel Circular [*Army*] ... CPC
Civilian Personnel Coordinating Committee (SAUO) ... CPCC
Civilian Personnel Directorate [*Military*] (GFGA) ... CPD
Civilian Personnel Division (SAUO) ... CPD
Civilian Personnel Division [*Coast Guard*] ... PC
Civilian Personnel Information System [*Army*] ... CIVPERSINS
Civilian Personnel Letter ... CPL
Civilian Personnel Letters and Dispatches ... CPL & D
Civilian Personnel Management Center [*Air Force*] (DOMA) ... CPMC
Civilian Personnel Management Information System (MCD) ... CPMIS
Civilian Personnel Management Services ... CPMS
Civilian Personnel Manual [*A publication*] (COE) ... CPM
Civilian Personnel Modernization Project [*Military*] ... CPMP
Civilian Personnel Occupational Standards [*Military*] (AABC) ... CPOS
Civilian Personnel Office [*or Officer*] ... CPO
Civilian Personnel Pamphlet [*Military*] ... CPP
Civilian Personnel Policy (ACAE) ... CPP
Civilian Personnel Procedures Manual [*Military*] ... CPPM
Civilian Personnel Records [*Military*] ... CPR
Civilian Personnel Reduction Plan (MCD) ... CPRP
Civilian Personnel Regulation [*Military*] ... CPR
Civilian Personnel Section (SAUO) ... CPS
Civilian Personnel/Equal Employment Opportunity Directives System [*Military*] (DNAB) ... CIVPERS/EEODIRSYS
Civilian Pilot Training [*Became War Training Service*] [*World War II*] ... CPT
Civilian Police (MILB) ... civ pol
Civilian Population (MCD) ... CP
Civilian Position Control Number ... CPCN
Civilian Position File (MCD) ... CPF
Civilian Production Administration [*Became part of Office of Temporary Controls, 1946*] ... CPA
Civilian Products Administration (SAUO) ... CPA
Civilian Property Agent ... CPA
Civilian Public Service ... CPS
Civilian Radioactive Waste Management [*Department of Energy*] (NUCP) ... CRWM
Civilian Radioactive Waste Management, Office of (SAUS) ... RW
Civilian Radioactive Waste Management System-Management and Operating [*Contractor*] (GAAI) ... CRWMS-M&O
Civilian Repair Organisation (SAUO) ... CRO
Civilian Repair Organization [*Aircraft*] ... CRO
Civilian Repair Unit [*British military*] (DMA) ... CRU
Civilian Research and Development Foundation [*An organization formed to retain former FSU scientists in civilian research*] ... CRDF
Civilian Research and Development Foundation for the Independent States of the FSU [*former Soviet Union*] ... CRDF
Civilian Research, Interplanetary Flying Objects ... CRIFO
Civilian Saucer Intelligence of New York (SAUO) ... CSI
Civilian Science Systems Administration [*Proposed for National Science Foundation*] ... CSSA
Civilian Screening Center ... CSC
Civilian Service Group (SAUO) ... CSG
Civilian Service Unit (AFM) ... CSU
Civilian Skill Code (MCD) ... CSC
Civilian Society Development Centre (SAUO) ... CSDC
Civilian Space Technology Initiative (SAUS) ... CSTI
Civilian Sreening Center (SAUO) ... CSC
Civilian Steering Center (SAUS) ... CSB
Civilian Substitution Program [*Navy*] (NVT) ... CIVSUB
Civilian Supervisory Selection Battery [*Military*] (AFM) ... CSSB
Civilian Supply Administration (SAUO) ... CSA
Civilian Supply Branch [*Army Service Forces*] [*World War II*] ... CSB
Civilian Supply Division [*Allied Military Government*] [*World War II*] ... CSD
Civilian Support Group (SAUO) ... CSG
Civilian Support Operation [*Military*] (INF) ... CSO
Civilian Technology Corporation (AAGC) ... CTC
Civilian Training, Education, and Development (MCD) ... CTED
Civilian War Casualties (VNW) ... CWC
Civilian War Dead ... CWD
Civilian Wartime Injuries ... CWTI
Civilian Welfare and Recreation Association (SAUO) ... CWRA
Civilian Welfare and Recreation Committee (MUGU) ... CWRC
Civilian Welfare Fund (AABC) ... CWF
Civilian-Based Defense Association (EA) ... CBDA
Civilian-Military Contingency Hospital System [*DoD*] ... CMCHS
Civilian/Military Liaison Committee ... CMLC
Civilians in Foreign Communications Operations [*Military*] ... CIFCO
Civilisations [*A publication*] ... CIV
Civilisations. International Institute of Differing Civilizations. Bruxelles (SAUS) ... IIDC/C
Civilization (SAUS) ... Civ
Civilization (ROG) ... CIV
Civilization As We Know It [*An association*] [*British*] ... CAWKI
Civilize (SAUS) ... CIV
Civil-Military Affairs ... CMA
Civil-Military Integration (AAGC) ... CMI
Civil-Military Operations (AABC) ... CMO
Civil-Society Organizations ... CSOs
Civis Romanus [*Roman Citizen*] [*Latin*] ... CR
Civitan International (EA) ... CI
Civitavecchia [*Italy*] [*ICAO location identifier*] (ICLI) ... LIQJ
CKE Restaurants [*Associated Press*] (SAG) ... CKE Rst
CKE Restaurants [*NYSE symbol*] (TTSB) ... CKR
CKE Restaurants Ltd. [*Formerly, Carl Karcher Enterprise*] [*NYSE symbol*] (SAG) ... CKR
CKF Bancorp [*NASDAQ symbol*] (TTSB) ... CKFB
CKF Bancorp, Inc. [*NASDAQ symbol*] (SAG) ... CKFB
CKF Bancorp, Inc. [*Associated Press*] (SAG) ... CKF Bc
CKS Group [*NASDAQ symbol*] (TTSB) ... CKSG
CKS Group, Inc. [*NASDAQ symbol*] (SAG) ... CKSG
CKS Group, Inc. [*Associated Press*] (SAG) ... CKS Gr
CL & P Capital LP [*Associated Press*] (SAG) ... CL & P
C.L. Organization (SAUS) ... CLO
Clackamas Community College Library, Oregon City, OR [*OCLC symbol*] (OCLC) ... CCK
Clackamas Community College, Oregon City, OR [*Library symbol*] [*Library of Congress*] (LCLS) ... OrOCC
Clackamas Cooperative County-Wide Library Services [*Library network*] ... CCCLS
Clackamas County Public Library, Oregon City, OR [*Library symbol*] [*Library of Congress*] (LCLS) ... OrOC
Clackamas High School, Media Center, Milwaukie, OR [*Library symbol*] [*Library of Congress*] (LCLS) ... OrMiCHS
Clackamas, OR [*Location identifier*] [*FAA*] (FAAL) ... CWY
Clackmannan [*Town and county in Scotland*] (ROG) ... CLC
Clackmannanshire [*County in Scotland*] ... CLACK
Clad Aluminum Alloy (SAUS) ... ALCLAD
Clad Controlled Expansion ... CCEX
Clad Failure Detection [*Nuclear energy*] (NUCP) ... CFD
Cladding Hull Waste (ABAC) ... CHW
Cladding Removal Waste (ABAC) ... CRW
Cladosporium [*A fungus*] ... Clad
Cladosporium Herbarum [*A fungus*] ... Ch
Clafkin University (SAUO) ... CU
Claflin College, Orangeburg, SC [*OCLC symbol*] (OCLC) ... CFC
Claflin College, Orangeburg, SC [*Library symbol*] [*Library of Congress*] (LCLS) ... ScOrC
Claiborne [*Liz*], **Inc.** [*Associated Press*] (SAG) ... LizClab
Claiborne Industries Ltd. [*Toronto Stock Exchange symbol*] ... CIB
Claim (WGA) ... CL
Claim ... CLM
Claim Account Number [*Social Security Administration*] (GFGA) ... CAN
Claim Agent [*Insurance*] ... CA
Claimant (WGA) ... CLT

Claimant Advisory Service Program [*Unemployment insurance*] .... CLASP
Claimant Procurement Planning Officer .... CPPO
Claimants and Unemployed Workers' Union (AIE) .... CUWU
Claimer Resources [*Vancouver Stock Exchange symbol*] .... CJL
Claiming (WGA) .... CLMG
Claiming Race [*Horse racing*] .... CLM
Claims (DLA) .... Clms
Claims (DLA) .... Cls
Claims and Records Office (SAUO) .... CRO
Claims Commission (SAUO) CC
[*United States*] **Claims Court** [*Now Court of Federal Claims*] (AAGC) .... Cl Ct
Claims Court Reporter [*West*] [*A publication*] (AAGC) .... Cl Ct
Claims, Defense (CAAL) .... CD
Claims Inquiry Form (MEDA) .... CIF
Claims Manual [*Social Security Administration*] (OICC) .... CM
Claims Payable Abroad [*Insurance*] (MARI) .... CPA
Claims Representative Exam for Social Security [*Federal job exam*] .... CRESS
Clairborne Parish Library, Homer, LA [*Library symbol*] [*Library of Congress*] (LCLS) .... LHoC
Claircolle and Whiten (SAUS) .... C&W
Claire's Stores [*Associated Press*] (SAG) .... ClairStr
Claire's Stores [*NYSE symbol*] (TTSB) .... CLE
Claire's Stores, Inc. [*Associated Press*] (SAG) .... ClairSt
Claire's Stores, Inc. [*NYSE symbol*] (SPSG) .... CLE
Clairton Organizers to Keep Employment (SAUO) .... COKE
Clallam Bay Correctional Center, Clallam Bay, WA [*Library symbol*] [*Library of Congress*] (LCLS) .... WaCbC
Clamp (SAUS) .... CLA
Clamp (SAUS) .... CLM
Clamp (MSA) .... CLP
Clamp Insulation (SAUS) .... CLP INS
Clamp Lamp (SAUS) CL
Clamp Screw (SAUS) .... CLP SCR
Clamped (SAUS) .... CLMD
Clamped Dielectric Constant .... CDC
Clamped Homogeneous Electric Field .... CHEF
Clamped Speed Register (SAUS) .... CSR
Clamped Speed Regulator .... CSR
Clamping Fixture (MCD) .... CF
Clamshell Alliance (EA) .... CA
Clan Cunning Association (EA) .... CCA
Clan Forrester Society (EA) .... CFS
Clan Grant No. 17, Order of Scottish Clans (EA) .... OSC
Clan Maitland Society of North America (EA) .... CMSNA
Clan McGillivray Society, Australia .... CMcGSA
Clan Napier in North America [*An association*] .... CNNA
Clan Rose Society of America (EA) .... CRSA
Clan Sinclair Association (USA) (EA) .... CSAUSA
Clancy's Treatise of the Rights, Duties, and Liabilities of Husband and Wife [*A publication*] (DLA) .... Clancy Husb & W
Clancy's Treatise of the Rights, Duties, and Liabilities of Husband and Wife [*A publication*] (DLA) .... Clancy Rights
Clandestine Fission Explosive [*Nuclear energy*] (NRCH) .... CFE
Clandestine Intelligence (LAIN) CI
Clandestine Lodges [*Freemasonry*] (ROG) CL
Clandestine Underwater Nuclear Explosion .... CUNE
CL&P Capital LP.9.30%'MIPS' [*NYSE symbol*] (TTSB) .... CPMPrA
C-language for the analysis and display of gridded numerical data (SAUS) .... Candis
C-Language Integrated Production System (SAUS) .... CLIPS
Clann Ltd., Sydney, NSW, Australia [*OCLC symbol*] (OCLC) .... CLN
Clans and Scottish Societies of Canada .... CSSC
Clansman Radio Control Harness (SAUS) .... CRCH
Clanton, AL [*Location identifier*] [*FAA*] (FAAL) .... GGY
Clanton, AL [*FM radio station call letters*] .... WEZZ
Clanton, AL [*AM radio station call letters*] .... WKLF
Clanwilliam [*South Africa*] [*ICAO location identifier*] (ICLI) .... FACW
Clapeyron-Clausius Equation [*Physics*] .... CCE
Clapham [*England*] .... CLAP
Clapham Notre Dame Association [*British*] (BI) .... CNDA
Clapper [*Electricity*] .... CLPR
Clara Barton Vocational High School (SAUS) .... CBVHS
Clara Cell-Specific Protein (DMAA) .... CCSP
Clara City Public Library, Clara City, MN [*Library symbol*] [*Library of Congress*] (LCLS) .... MnClc
Clara City Public Schools, Clara City, MN [*Library symbol*] [*Library of Congress*] (LCLS) .... MnClcPS
Clara H. Carlson Elementary School, Elmont, NY [*Library symbol*] [*Library of Congress*] (LCLS) .... NElmoCCE
Clara Peak [*New Mexico*] [*Seismograph station code, US Geological Survey*] (SEIS) .... CLP
Clara Rios [*Bolivia*] [*ICAO location identifier*] (ICLI) .... SLCI
Clarcor, Inc. [*Associated Press*] (SAG) .... Clarcor
CLARCOR Inc. [*NYSE symbol*] (TTSB) CLC
Clare College (SAUO) .... Cla
Clare College (SAUS) .... Cla
Clare College (SAUO) .... ClColl
Clare [*C.P.*] **Corp.** [*Associated Press*] (SAG) .... Clare
Clare [*C.P.*] **Corp.** [*NASDAQ symbol*] (SAG) .... CPCL
Clare Hall [*Cambridge University*] (ROG) .... CL H
Clare, MI [*FM radio station call letters*] .... WCFX
Claremont & Concord Railway Co., Inc. [*AAR code*] .... CLCO
Claremont, CA [*FM radio station call letters*] .... KSPC
Claremont Economics Institute [*Information service or system*] (IID) .... CEI
Claremont Graduate School (GAGS) .... Claremont Grad Sch
Claremont Men's College [*California*] .... CMC
Claremont Men's College, Claremont, CA [*OCLC symbol*] (OCLC) .... HDC
Claremont, NC [*AM radio station call letters*] .... WCXN
Claremont, NH [*Location identifier*] [*FAA*] (FAAL) .... CNH
Claremont, NH [*FM radio station call letters*] .... WHDQ
Claremont, NH [*AM radio station call letters*] .... WTSV
Claremont Public Library, Claremont, SD [*Library symbol*] [*Library of Congress*] (LCLS) .... SdCla
[*The*] **Claremont Ras Shamra Tablets** [*A publication*] (BJA) .... CRST
Claremont Technology Group, Inc. [*Associated Press*] (SAG) .... ClareTch
Claremont Technology Group, Inc. [*NASDAQ symbol*] (SAG) .... CLMT
Claremont, VA [*AM radio station call letters*] (RBYB) .... WVNS
Claremore, OK [*Television station call letters*] .... KRSC
Claremore, OK [*FM radio station call letters*] (RBYB) .... KRSC-FM
Claremore, OK [*FM radio station call letters*] .... KTFR
Claremore, OK [*AM radio station call letters*] .... KTRT
Clarence Bain, Andros Island [*Bahamas*] [*ICAO location identifier*] (ICLI) .... MYAB
Clarence Rhode National Wildlife Range (SAUS) .... CRNWR
Clarence W. Mills, Laurel MD (SAUO) .... MCW
Clarenden Press (DAS) .... CP
Clarendon [*Type*] (ROG) .... CLAR
Clarendon (SAUO) .... ISBN 0-19
Clarendon and Pittsford Railroad Co. (SAUO) .... CLP
[*The*] **Clarendon & Pittsford Railroad Co.** [*AAR code*] .... CLP
Clarendon College, Clarendon, TX [*Library symbol*] [*Library of Congress*] (LCLS) .... TxClaC
Clarendon County Public Library, Manning, SC [*Library symbol*] [*Library of Congress*] (LCLS) .... ScMan
Clarendon Hills Public Library, Clarendon Hills, IL [*Library symbol*] [*Library of Congress*] (LCLS) .... IClh
Clarendon Hills Public Library, Clarendon Hills, IL [*Library symbol*] [*Library of Congress*] (LCLS) .... IClhP
Clarendon Junior College (SAUO) .... CJC
Clarendon Laboratory [*Oxford University*] (MCD) CL
Clarendon, PA [*FM radio station call letters*] (RBYB) .... WKNB
Clarendon Press (SAUO) .... CP
Clarendon, TX [*Location identifier*] [*FAA*] (FAAL) .... CNZ
Clarendon, TX [*FM radio station call letters*] (BROA) .... KEFH-FM
Clarendon-Miller Branch, Frontenac County Library, Plevna, Ontario [*Library symbol*] [*National Library of Canada*] (NLC) .... OPFRC
Clarendon's Parliamentary Chronicle [*A publication*] (DLA) .... Clar Parl Chr
Clarent Corp. [*NASDAQ symbol*] (SG) .... CLRN
Clarenville, NF [*FM radio station call letters*] (RBYB) .... CJKK-FM
Clarenville, NF [*FM radio station call letters*] .... CKCV
Clarenville, NF [*AM radio station call letters*] .... CKVO
Clarenville Public Library, Clarenville, NF, Canada [*Library symbol*] [*Library of Congress*] (LCLS) .... CaNfCl
Clarenville Public Library, Newfoundland [*Library symbol*] [*National Library of Canada*] (NLC) .... NFCL
Clarepine Industries, Inc. [*Toronto Stock Exchange symbol*] .... DRS
Claresholm Public Library, Alberta [*Library symbol*] [*National Library of Canada*] (NLC) .... ACLAR
Claret [*Philately*] cl
Claretian Fathers Library, Washington, DC [*Library symbol*] [*Library of Congress*] (LCLS) .... DCF
Claretian Missionaries (TOCD) .... CMF
Claretian Missionaries, Missionary Sons of the Immaculate Heart of Mary (TOCD) .... cmf
Claretian Missionary Sisters (TOCD) .... RMI
Clarification [*or Clarify*] (AFM) .... CLAR
Clarification Request (AAGC) .... CR
Clarify (FAAC) .... CFY
Clarify (SAUS) .... CLAR
Clarify, Inc. [*Associated Press*] (SAG) .... Clarify
Clarify, Inc. [*NASDAQ symbol*] (SAG) .... CLFY
Clarinda Herald-Journal, Clarinda, IA [*Library symbol*] [*Library of Congress*] (LCLS) .... IaCladHJ
Clarinda, IA [*Location identifier*] [*FAA*] (FAAL) ICL
Clarinda, IA [*FM radio station call letters*] .... KKBZ
Clarinda Public Library, Clarinda, IA [*Library symbol*] [*Library of Congress*] (LCLS) .... IaClad
Clarinet CL
Clarinet cl
Clarinet .... CLAR
Clarinet (SAUS) .... Clar
Clarinet (WDAA) .... clt
Clarinetist (BARN) .... Clst
Clarinette Basse [*Bass Clarinet*] [*Music*] .... Cl B
Clarinette Contre Basse [*Contrabass Clarinet*] [*Music*] .... Cl CB
Clarinetto [*Clarinet*] [*Music*] (ROG) .... CLARTTO
Clarino [*Clarion*] [*Music*] (ROG) .... CLAR
Clarino [*Clarion*] [*Music*] .... CLARO
Clarion Commercial Hldgs'A' [*NYSE symbol*] (SG) .... CLR
Clarion Free Library, Clarion, PA [*Library symbol*] [*Library of Congress*] (LCLS) .... PCl
Clarion, IA [*Location identifier*] [*FAA*] (FAAL) .... CAV
Clarion, IA [*FM radio station call letters*] .... KIAQ
Clarion Music Society (EA) .... CMS
Clarion, PA [*Location identifier*] [*FAA*] (FAAL) .... CIP
Clarion, PA [*FM radio station call letters*] .... WCCR
Clarion, PA [*FM radio station call letters*] .... WCUC
Clarion, PA [*AM radio station call letters*] .... WWCH
Clarion Public Library, Clarion, IA [*Library symbol*] [*Library of Congress*] (LCLS) .... IaCla

Clarion State College, Clarion, PA [*Library symbol*] [*Library of Congress*] (LCLS) .... PCIS
Clarion State College, Clarion, PA [*OCLC symbol*] (OCLC) .... REC
Clarion State College, Oil City, PA [*Library symbol*] [*Library of Congress*] (LCLS) .... POC
Clarion State College, School of Library Media, Clarion, PA [*OCLC symbol*] (OCLC) .... CSI
Clarion University of Pennsylvania (GAGS) .... Clarion U
Claris Dynamic Markup Language [*Computer science*] .... CDML
Clarissa Elementary School, Clarissa, MN [*Library symbol*] [*Library of Congress*] (LCLS) .... MnClaE
Clarissa High School, Clarissa, MN [*Library symbol*] [*Library of Congress*] (LCLS) .... MnCLaH
Clarissima Femina [*Most Illustrious Woman*] [*Latin*] .... CF
Clarissima Puella [*Most Illustrious Maiden*] [*Latin*] .... CP
Clarissimi Viri [*Illustrious Men*] [*Latin*] (BARN) CCVV
Clarissimus Vir [*Most Illustrious Man*] [*Latin*] CLV
Claritas Corp. [*Information service or system*] (IID) CLC
Clarity, Brevity, Sharpness [*Objectives of good editing, as set forth in Barry Tarshis' book "How to Write without Pain"*] .... CBS
Clark Air Base, Pampanga [*Philippines*] [*ICAO location identifier*] (ICLI) .... RPMK
Clark Air Force Base (SAUO) .... CAFB
Clark and Finnelly's English House of Lords Cases [*1831-46*] [*A publication*] (DLA) .... Cl & F
Clark and Finnelly's English House of Lords Cases [*1831-46*] [*A publication*] (DLA) .... Cl & Fin
Clark and Finnelly's English House of Lords Cases [*1831-46*] [*A publication*] (DLA) .... Clark & Fin
Clark and Finnelly's English House of Lords Cases, New Series [*A publication*] (DLA) .... Clark & F (NS) Eng
Clark and Finnelly's English House of Lords Reports [*6-8 English Reprint*] [*A publication*] (DLA) .... C & F
Clark and Finnelly's English House of Lords Reports [*6-8 English Reprint*] [*A publication*] (DLA) .... Clark & F
Clark and Finnelly's English House of Lords Reports [*6-8 English Reprint*] [*A publication*] (DLA) .... Clark & F (Eng)
Clark and Finnelly's English House of Lords Reports, New Series [*9-11 English Reprint*] [*1847-66*] [*A publication*] (DLA) .... Clark & Fin (NS)
Clark and Finnelly's English House of Lords Reports, New Series [*9-11 English Reprint*] [*1847-66*] [*A publication*] (DLA) .... Clark & F (NS)
Clark Atlanta University (GAGS) .... Clark Atl U
Clark Aviation Corp. [*ICAO designator*] (FAAC) .... CLK
Clark, Cobb, and Irwin's Code [*Georgia*] [*A publication*] (DLA) .... Irwin's Code
Clark, Cobb and Irwins Code (journ.) (SAUS) .... Irwins Code
Clark College, Atlanta, GA [*OCLC symbol*] (OCLC) CLC
Clark College, Atlanta, GA [*Library symbol*] [*Library of Congress*] (LCLS) .... GAC
Clark College, Library, Vancouver, WA [*OCLC symbol*] (OCLC) CCV
Clark College, Vancouver, WA [*Library symbol*] [*Library of Congress*] (LCLS) .... WaVC
Clark. Colonial Law [*1834*] [*A publication*] (ILCA) .... Clark Col Law
Clark County Community College, North Las Vegas, NV [*Library symbol*] [*Library of Congress*] (LCLS) .... NvNolC
Clark County Department of Health (SAUS) .... CCDH
Clark County Library, Las Vegas, NV [*Library symbol*] [*Library of Congress*] (LCLS) .... NvLC
Clark County Public Library, Winchester, KY [*Library symbol*] [*Library of Congress*] (LCLS) .... KyWn
Clark County Technical Institute, Springfield, OH [*Library symbol*] [*Library of Congress*] (LCLS) .... OSC
Clark Dietz Engineers, Urbana, IL [*Library symbol*] [*Library of Congress*] (LCLS) .... IUrCD
Clark Equipment Co. (MCD) .... CEC
Clark Equipment Company (SAUO) .... CEC
Clark Equipment Company (SAUO) .... CKL
Clark Free Public Library, Clark, NJ [*Library symbol*] [*Library of Congress*] (LCLS) .... NjCl
Clark Hill Reservoir [*Georgia*] [*Seismograph station code, US Geological Survey*] (SEIS) CH5
Clark Hill Reservoir [*Georgia*] [*Seismograph station code, US Geological Survey*] (SEIS) CH6
Clark Lake Radio Observatory [*University of Maryland*] [*Research center*] (RCD) .... CLRO
Clark Memorial College [*Mississippi*] .... CMC
Clark Oil & Refining Corp. (SAUO) .... CKO
Clark Public Library, Clark, SD [*Library symbol*] [*Library of Congress*] (LCLS) .... SdCl
Clark Road Secondary School, London, ON, Canada [*Library symbol*] [*Library of Congress*] (LCLS) .... CaOLCR
Clark Road Secondary School, London, Ontario [*Library symbol*] [*National Library of Canada*] (NLC) .... OLCR
Clark Technical College, Library Resource Center, Springfield, OH [*OCLC symbol*] (OCLC) .... CLT
Clark University (GAGS) .... Clark U
Clark University (SAUO) .... Cl Univ
Clark University (SAUO) .... CU
Clark University, Worcester, MA [*OCLC symbol*] (OCLC) .... CKM
Clark University, Worcester, MA [*Library symbol*] [*Library of Congress*] (LCLS) .... MWC
Clarke and Hall's Cases of Contested Elections in Congress [*1789-1834*] [*United States*] [*A publication*] (DLA) .... C & H Elec Cas
Clarke and Hall's Cases of Contested Elections in Congress [*1789-1834*] [*United States*] [*A publication*] (DLA) .... Cl & H
Clarke and Hall's Cases of Contested Elections in Congress [*1789-1834*] [*United States*] [*A publication*] (DLA) .... Clarke & H Elec Cas
Clarke and Scully's Drainage Cases [*Canada*] [*A publication*] (DLA) .... C & S
Clarke and Scully's Drainage Cases [*Canada*] [*A publication*] (DLA) .... Cl & Sc Dr Cas
Clarke and Scully's Drainage Cases [*Canada*] [*A publication*] (DLA) .... Clarke & S Dr Cas
Clarke College (GAGS) .... Clarke C
Clarke College, Dubuque, IA [*Library symbol*] [*Library of Congress*] (LCLS) .... IaDuCl
Clarke College, Dubuque, IA [*OCLC symbol*] (OCLC) .... IOC
Clarke County Courthouse, Osceola, IA [*Library symbol*] [*Library of Congress*] (LCLS) .... IaOscCoC
Clarke Courier, Dubuque, IA [*Library symbol*] [*Library of Congress*] (LCLS) .... IaDuCo
Clarke Institute of Psychiatry [*Research center*] (RCD) .... CIP
Clarke Institute of Psychiatry, University of Toronto, Ontario [*Library symbol*] [*National Library of Canada*] (NLC) .... OTUDP
Clarke Memorial College, Newton, MS [*Library symbol*] [*Library of Congress*] (LCLS) .... MsNeC
Clarke Memorial Museum, Eureka, CA [*Library symbol*] [*Library of Congress*] (LCLS) .... CECM
Clarke, Nichols & Co. [*British*] (ROG) .... CLARNICO
Clarke on Bills and Notes [*Canada*] [*A publication*] (DLA) .... Clarke B
Clarke on Bills and Notes [*Canada*] [*A publication*] (DLA) .... Cl Bills
Clarke on Extradition [*A publication*] (DLA) .... Clarke Extr
Clarke on Extradition [*A publication*] (DLA) .... Cl Extr
Clarke on Law of Insurance [*Canada*] [*A publication*] (DLA) .... Cl Ins
Clarke, W. H., New York NY [*STAC*] .... CWH
Clarke-Hadfield [*Syndrome*] [*Medicine*] (DB) .... CH
Clarke's Admiralty Practice [*A publication*] (DLA) .... Clarke Adm Pr
Clarke's Bibliotheca Legum [*A publication*] (DLA) .... Clarke Bib Leg
Clarke's Canada Insolvent Acts [*A publication*] (DLA) .... Cl Can Ins
Clarke's Constable's Manual [*Canada*] [*A publication*] (DLA) .... Clarke Const
Clarke's Criminal Law [*Canada*] [*A publication*] (DLA) .... Clarke Cr L
Clarke's Early Roman Law [*A publication*] (DLA) .... Clarke Rom L
Clarke's Early Roman Law [*A publication*] (DLA) .... Cl RL
Clarke's Edition of 1-8 Iowa [*A publication*] (DLA) .... Clarke
Clarke's Edition of 1-8 Iowa [*A publication*] (DLA) .... Clarke (IA)
Clarke's Insolvent Acts [*Canada*] [*A publication*] (DLA) .... Clarke Insol
Clarke's Insurance Law [*Canada*] [*A publication*] (DLA) .... Clarke Insur
Clarke's New York Chancery Reports [*A publication*] (DLA) .... Clarke
Clarke's New York Chancery Reports [*A publication*] (DLA) .... Clarke Ch
Clarke's New York Chancery Reports [*A publication*] (DLA) .... Clarke Ch (NY)
Clarke's New York Chancery Reports [*A publication*] (DLA) .... Clarke CR
Clarke's New York Chancery Reports [*A publication*] (DLA) .... Clarke's Chy (NY)
Clarke's New York Chancery Reports [*A publication*] (DLA) .... Cl Ch
Clarke's New York Chancery Reports [*A publication*] (DLA) .... Cl R
Clarke's Notes of Cases [*Bengal*] [*A publication*] (DLA) .... Clarke
Clarke's Notes of Cases, in His "Rules and Orders" [*Bengal*] [*A publication*] (DLA) .... Clarke Not
Clarke's Notes of Cases, in His "Rules and Orders" [*Bengal*] [*A publication*] (DLA) .... Clarke R & O
Clarke's Pennsylvania Reports [*5 vols.*] [*A publication*] (DLA) .... Clarke
Clarke's Pennsylvania Reports [*5 vols.*] [*A publication*] (DLA) .... Clarke (PA)
Clarke's Reports [*19-22 Michigan*] [*A publication*] (DLA) .... Clarke
Clarke's Reports [*19-22 Michigan*] [*A publication*] (DLA) .... Clarke (Mich)
Clarkesville, GA [*AM radio station call letters*] .... WCHM
Clarkesville, GA [*FM radio station call letters*] .... WMJE
Clarkia District Library, Clarkia, ID [*Library symbol*] [*Library of Congress*] (LCLS) .... IdCl
Clark's Appeal Cases, House of Lords [*England*] [*A publication*] (DLA) .... Cl App
Clark's Appeal Cases, House of Lords [*England*] [*A publication*] (DLA) .... Clark App
Clark's Colonial Laws [*A publication*] (DLA) .... Cl Col
Clark's Digest, House of Lords Reports [*A publication*] (DLA) .... Clark Dig
Clarks Fork Wild and Scenic Designation Act of 1990 (COE) .... CFWRDA
Clark's House of Lords Cases [*1847-66*] [*England*] [*A publication*] (DLA) .... Ho L Cas
Clark's House of Lords Cases [*1847-66*] [*England*] [*A publication*] (DLA) .... Ho Lords C
Clark's House of Lords Cases [*1847-66*] [*England*] [*A publication*] (DLA) .... Ho Lords Cas
Clark's Pennsylvania Law Journal Reports [*A publication*] (DLA) .... Clark (PA)
Clark's Pennsylvania Law Journal Reports [*A publication*] (DLA) .... PA LJR
Clarks Point [*Alaska*] [*Airport symbol*] (OAG) .... CLP
Clarks Point, AK [*Location identifier*] [*FAA*] (FAAL) .... CLP
Clark's Reports [*58 Alabama*] [*A publication*] (DLA) .... Clark
Clark's Reports [*58 Alabama*] [*A publication*] (DLA) .... Clark (Ala)
Clark's Summary of American Law [*A publication*] (DLA) .... Clark's Summary
Clark's Treatise on Elections [*A publication*] (DLA) .... Cl Elec
Clarksburg [*West Virginia*] [*Airport symbol*] (OAG) .... CKB
Clarksburg Public Library, Clarksburg, WV [*Library symbol*] [*Library of Congress*] (LCLS) .... WvCl
Clarksburg, WV [*Location identifier*] [*FAA*] (FAAL) .... CKB
Clarksburg, WV [*Television station call letters*] .... WBOY
Clarksburg, WV [*FM radio station call letters*] (RBYB) .... WFBY-FM
Clarksburg, WV [*AM radio station call letters*] .... WHAR
Clarksburg, WV [*FM radio station call letters*] .... WKJL
Clarksburg, WV [*FM radio station call letters*] .... WKKW
Clarksburg, WV [*Television station call letters*] .... WLYJ
Clarksburg, WV [*AM radio station call letters*] .... WOBG
Clarksburg, WV [*AM radio station call letters*] .... WPDX
Clarksburg, WV [*FM radio station call letters*] .... WPDX-FM
Clarksburg, WV [*Television station call letters*] (BROA) .... WVFX
Clarksburg, WV [*FM radio station call letters*] .... WVHF
Clarksdale, MS [*Location identifier*] [*FAA*] (FAAL) .... CKM
Clarksdale, MS [*FM radio station call letters*] .... WAID

Clarksdale, MS [*FM radio station call letters*] ..... WKDJ
Clarksdale, MS [*AM radio station call letters*] ..... WROX
Clarksdale, MS [*FM radio station call letters*] ..... WWUN
Clarkson College of Technology [*Potsdam, NY*] ..... CCT
Clarkson College of Technology, Potsdam, NY [*Library symbol*] [*Library of Congress*] (LCLS) ..... NPotC
Clarkson College of Technology, Potsdam, NY [*OCLC symbol*] (OCLC) ..... VYT
Clarkson, Gordon & Co.: Woods, Gordon & Co., Toronto, ON, Canada [*Library symbol*] [*Library of Congress*] (LCLS) ..... CaOTCGW
Clarkson Gordon Library, Calgary, Alberta [*Library symbol*] [*National Library of Canada*] (BIB) ..... ACCG
Clarkson Gordon, London, Ontario [*Library symbol*] [*National Library of Canada*] (BIB) ..... OLCG
Clarkson, Gordon, Woods, Gordon, Montreal, Quebec [*Library symbol*] [*National Library of Canada*] (NLC) ..... QMCGW
Clarkson, Gordon, Woods, Gordon, Toronto, Ontario [*Library symbol*] [*National Library of Canada*] (NLC) ..... OTCGW
Clarkson University (GAGS) ..... Clarkson U
Clarkson University Transmission control protocol Communication Package (SAUS) ..... CUTCP
Clarkston University Terminal Emulator (SAUO) ..... CUTE
Clarkston, WA [*FM radio station call letters*] ..... KCLK
Clarkston, WA [*FM radio station call letters*] (RBYB) ..... KNWV-FM
Clarkston, WA [*FM radio station call letters*] (RBYB) ..... KVAB-FM
Clarksville [*Tennessee*] [*Airport symbol*] (OAG) ..... CKV
Clarksville, AR [*Location identifier*] [*FAA*] (FAAL) ..... CZE
Clarksville, AR [*AM radio station call letters*] ..... KLYR
Clarksville, AR [*FM radio station call letters*] ..... KLYR-FM
Clarksville, AR [*FM radio station call letters*] ..... KXIO
Clarksville Branch Office [*AEC*] ..... CBO
Clarksville, IN [*FM radio station call letters*] (BROA) ..... WQSH-FM
Clarksville Memorial Hospital (SAUS) TC1H
Clarksville Memorial Hospital, Clarksville, TN [*Library symbol*] [*Library of Congress*] (LCLS) ..... TCIH
Clarksville Star, Clarksville, IA [*Library symbol*] [*Library of Congress*] (LCLS) ..... IaCkvS
Clarksville Star, Clarksville, IA [*Library symbol*] [*Library of Congress*] (LCLS) ..... IaClvS
Clarksville, TN [*Location identifier*] [*FAA*] (FAAL) ..... CKV
Clarksville, TN [*FM radio station call letters*] ..... WAPX
Clarksville, TN [*AM radio station call letters*] ..... WCTZ
Clarksville, TN [*AM radio station call letters*] ..... WDXN
Clarksville, TN [*AM radio station call letters*] ..... WJZM
Clarksville, TX [*AM radio station call letters*] ..... KCAR
Clarksville, TX [*FM radio station call letters*] ..... KGAP
Clarksville, VA [*FM radio station call letters*] ..... WLCQ
Claro [*Light-colored cigar*] CCC
Clarsach Society (EAIO) ..... CS
Clasp ..... CLP
Class [*Used with number for Navy rating as: 1c; i.e., first class*] C
Class (SG) Cl
Class (WDMC) cl
Class (AFM) CL
Class [*Freight*] ..... CLA
Class ..... CLAS
Class 1 Price/Percentage (SAUS) CL1PP
Class 2 (SAUO) CL2
Class A Airspace [*Aviation*] (FAAC) ..... CAAS
Class "A" Preferred or Common Stock [*Investment term*] ..... A
Class Action Reports [*A publication*] (DLA) ..... Class Act Rep
Class Action Study and Survey [*Student legal action organization*] ..... CLASS
Class Activities Questionnaire [*Teacher evaluation test*] ..... CAQ
Class and Kind Made in Canada [*Business term*] ..... CKMIC
Class and Kind Not Made in Canada [*Business term*] ..... CKNMIC
Class, Architecture, Topology and Homologous superfamily (SAUS) ..... CATH
Class, Architecture, Topology, Homology [*Database of protein structures*] ..... CATH
Class Association Diagram (SAUO) ..... CAD
Class Attendance Verification (SAUS) ..... CAV
Class B Airspace [*Aviation*] (FAAC) ..... CBAS
Class "B" Preferred or Common Stock [*Investment term*] ..... B
Class B Surface Area [*Aviation*] (FAAC) ..... CBSA
CLass Based Queuing [*Computer science*] ..... CBQ
Class C Airspace [*Aviation*] (FAAC) ..... CCAS
Class "C" Preferred or Common Stock [*Investment term*] C
Class C Surface Area [*Aviation*] (FAAC) ..... CCSA
Class Code [*Database terminology*] (NITA) CC
Class Code, Assignee, Index Method, Search [*IFI/Plenum Data Co.*] [*Patent database*] (NITA) ..... CLAIMS
Class Code, Assignee, Index Method, Search/Chemistry [*Patent database*] [*IFI/Plenum Data Co.*] [*Arlington, VA*] ..... CLAIMS/CHEM
Class Code, Assignee, Index Method, Search/Classification [*Patent database*] (NITA) ..... CLAIMS/CLASS
Class Code, Assignee, Index Method, Search/General [*IFI/Plenum Data Co.*] [*Patent database*] (NITA) ..... CLAIMS/GEN
Class Code, Assignee, Index, Method, Search/General, Electrical, Mechanical [*Patent database*] [*IFI/Plenum Data Co.*] [*Arlington, VA*] ..... CLAIMS/GEM
Class Code, Assignee, Index Method, Search/US Patent Abstracts (NITA) ..... CLAIMS/US Pats Abs
Class Communication Diagram (SAUS) ..... CCD
Class Convening ..... CLCON
Class Convening ..... CLCVN
Class D Airspace [*Aviation*] (FAAC) ..... CDAS
Class D Surface Area [*Aviation*] (FAAC) ..... CDSA
Class Determination and Finding ..... CD & F
Class Determination and Finding ..... CDF
Class E Airspace [*Aviation*] (FAAC) ..... CEAS
Class E Surface Area [*Aviation*] (FAAC) ..... CESA
Class Featuring Information Compression (PDAA) ..... CLAFIC
Class for Retarded in Mental Development ..... CRMD
Class G Airspace [*Aviation*] (FAAC) ..... CGAS
Class Identifier (GEOI) ..... CLID
Class Identifier [*Computer science*] (VERA) ..... CLSID
Class II-Associated Invariant Chain Peptides [*Biochemistry*] ..... CLIP
Class Improvement Plan [*Navy*] ..... CIP
Class Interval (DIPS) ci
Class Interval [*Statistics*] i
Class IX Study ..... CLIXS
Class Life Asset Depreciation Range [*Insurance*] (DICI) ..... CLADR
Class Marks [*Telecommunications*] (TEL) ..... CM
Class Mask Table (SAUS) ..... CMT
Class Music Teaching (AIE) ..... CMT
Class of Blue Copper Proteins [*Crystallography*] ..... CBP
Class of Interface (SAUS) ..... COI
Class of Material (MCD) ..... CM
Class of Property (SAUS) ..... CO-OP
Class of Restriction [*AT&T*] (CIST) ..... COR
Class of Service [*Telecommunications*] (TEL) ..... COS
Class of Service [*Telecommunications*] (TEL) ..... CS
Class of Subscriber (SAUS) ..... COS
Class of Supply [*Military*] ..... CS
Class On-Line Reference Services (SAUO) ..... COLRS
Class Queue Management (IAA) ..... CQM
Class Quotient (SAUS) ..... CQ
Class Rate [*Business term*] ..... CR
Class, Responsibility, Collaboration (SAUS) ..... CRC
Class Responsibility Collaboration Card (CDE) ..... CRC card
Class Room ..... CR
Class Size Reduction ..... CSR
Class Work Planning Document [*Navy ship overhauls*] ..... CWPD
Classic (ROG) ..... CLASS
Classic (WDMC) ..... class
Classic [*Record label*] [*France*] Clc
Classic ..... CLSC
Classic Air AG [*Switzerland*] [*ICAO designator*] (FAAC) CLC
Classic Air Ltd. [*New Zealand*] [*FAA designator*] (FAAC) ..... CLS
Classic AMX Club International (EA) ..... CACI
Classic Bancshares [*NASDAQ symbol*] (TTSB) ..... CLAS
Classic Bicycle and Whizzer Club (EA) ..... CBWCA
Classic Bicycle and Whizzer Club of America (EA) ..... CBWCA
Classic Car Club of America (EA) ..... CCCA
Classic Chevy Club International (EA) CCCI
Classic Chevy Club International (EA) CCI
Classic Comet Club of America (EA) ..... CCA
Classic Comet Club of America (EA) ..... CCCA
Classic Desk Accessories [*Apple Computer, Inc.*] [*Utility program*] [*Computer science*] ..... CDA
Classic Editions [*Record label*] ..... CEd
Classic English Detective Novel ..... CEDN
Classic Form of Kaposi Sarcoma [*Medicine*] (DMAA) ..... CKS
Classic Jaguar Association (EA) ..... CJA
Classic Motorcycle Club of Victoria [*Australia*] ..... CMCV
Classic Press International (SAUO) ..... CPI
Classic Racing Motorcycle Club [*Defunct*] (EA) ..... CRMC
Classic Record Club [*Record label*] ..... ACC
Classic Stage Company ..... CSC
Classic Technique [*Surgery*] (DAVI) ..... CT
Classic Thunderbird Association (EA) ..... CTA
Classic Thunderbird Club International (EA) ..... CTCI
Classic Vehicle Club's Committee [*British*] (DBA) CVCC
Classic Yacht Association (EA) ..... CYA
Classical C
Classical CL
Classical ..... class
Classical America (EA) ..... CA
Classical Analytic Technique ..... CAT
Classical Anaphylatoxin [*Immunology*] ..... CAT
Classical and Medieval Literature Criticism [*A publication*] ..... CMLC
Classical and Medieval Numismatic Society (SAUS) ..... CMNS
Classical and Modern Literature [*A publication*] (BRI) ..... CML
Classical Association (EAIO) ..... CA
Classical Association of Canada [*See also SCEC*] ..... CAC
Classical Association of New England (EDAC) ..... CANE
Classical Association of Scotland (SAUO) ..... CAS
Classical Association of Southern Africa (SAUO) ..... CASA
Classical Association of the Atlantic States (SAUO) ..... CAAS
Classical Association of the Middle West and South (SAUO) ..... CAMWS
Classical Association of the Pacific Northwest (SAUO) ..... CAPN
Classical Association of Victoria [*Australia*] ..... CAV
Classical Association of Virginia (SAUO) ..... CAV
Classical Association of Western New York (SAUO) ..... CAWNY
Classical Conditioning CC
Classical Factor Analysis Regression (SAUO) ..... CFAR
Classical General Linear Model [*Statistics*] ..... CGLM
Classical IP over ATM (SAUS) ..... CIP
Classical Journal [*A publication*] (BRI) ..... CJ
Classical Journal (SAUS) ..... ClassJ
Classical Latin (BARN) Cl
Classical Latin [*Language, etc.*] (ROG) ..... CL L

Classical Latin (BARN) ... Cl Lat
Classical Mechanics [*Physics*] ... CM
Classical Music [*Radio station format*] (WDMC) ... CL
Classical Music [*Radio station format*] (WDMC) ... Clas
Classical Music Lovers' Exchange (EA) ... CMLE
Classical Outlook [*A publication*] (BRI) ... Class Out
Classical Philology [*A publication*] (OCD) ... CPhil
Classical Philology (journ.) (SAUS) ... Class Phiol
Classical Philology (journ.) (SAUS) ... CPH
Classical Philosophy ... CP
Classical Receptive Field [*Biochemistry*] ... CRF
Classical Review [*A publication*] (BRI) ... Class R
Classical Scattering Aerosol Spectrometer [*Aerosol measurement device*] ... CSASP
Classical Scattering Spectrometer Probe [*Aerosol measurement device*] ... CSSP
Classical Society of the American Academy of Rome (SAUO) ... CSAAR
Classical Strain [*Of RNA*] ... Cl
Classical Swine Fever Virus ... CSFV
Classical T Tauri Stars [*Astronomy*] ... CTTS
Classical World [*A publication*] (BRI) ... CW
Classical Writers [*A publication*] ... CW
Classics (SAUS) ... Cl
Classics (ADA) ... CL
Classics International Entertainment, Inc. [*NASDAQ symbol*] (SAG) ... ClEI
Classics International Entertainment, Inc. [*Associated Press*] (SAG) ... Classics
Classics Intl. Entertainment [*NASDAQ symbol*] (TTSB) ... ClEI
Classics of Art [*A publication*] ... CA
Classification (WDMC) ... cl
Classification ... CL
Classification [*or Classified*] (DNAB) ... CLAS
Classification (AFM) ... CLASS
Classification (WDMC) ... class
Classification (SAUS) ... Class
Classification ... CLASSIF
Classification ... CLASSN
Classification Act of 1949 (COE) ... CA
Classification and Audit (AFM) ... C & A
Classification and Audit (SAUS) ... C&A
Classification and Classified List of Occupations ... CCLO
Classification and Compensation Society (NTPA) ... C&CS
Classification and Compensation Society (EA) ... CCS
Classification and Index [*Air Force*] (AFM) ... C & I
Classification and Labelling of Explosives Regulations ... CLER
Classification and Placement Examination (SAUS) ... CAPE
Classification and Rating Administration [*For movies*] ... CARA
Classification and Ratings Administration [*Motion Picture Association of America*] (WDMC) ... CARA
Classification and Regression Tree Technique [*Statistics*] ... CART
Classification and Regression Trees ... CART
Classification and Research Support Information System (AAGC) ... CASSIS
Classification and Search Support Information System [*Patent and Trademark Office*] [*Information service or system*] ... CASSIS
Classification and Technical Information Division (SAUO) ... CTID
Classification and Testing [*Air Force*] (AFM) ... C & T
Classification by Computer (SAUS) ... CBC
Classification Change Notice (KSC) ... CCN
Classification Code [*IRS*] [*Online database field identifier*] ... CC
Classification Code (NITA) ... CL
Classification Code (SAUS) ... CLC
Classification Decimale Universelle [*Universal Decimal Classification*] ... CDU
Classification, Discrimination & Identification (SAUS) ... CDI
Classification Document Index (DNAB) ... CDI
Classification Group [*Database terminology*] (NITA) ... CL
Classification, Hazard Information and Packaging [*British*] ... CHIP
Classification Internationale des Handicaps (SAUS) ... CIH
Classification Inventory [*Military*] ... CI
Classification Keyboard (SAUS) ... CK
Classification List [*Military*] ... CL
Classification Management (DNAB) ... CLAM
Classification of Characteristics [*Navy*] (NG) ... CC
Classification of Defects (AAG) ... CD
Classification of Documents (SAUS) ... ClofD
Classification of Finite Simple Groups (SAUO) ... CFSG
Classification of Galactic Nebulae Between Elliptical and Spiral Types Having a Bright Nucleus and Dark Bands of Matter But No Distinguishable Arms [*Astronomy*] (BARN) ... SBO
Classification of Identification of Covert Satellites ... CLASSICS
Classification of Instructional Disciplines (SAUS) ... CID
Classification of Instructional Programs [*Department of Education*] (OICC) ... CIP
Classification of Library and Information Science (SAUS) ... CLIS
Classification of Library Science (SAUS) ... CLS
Classification of Mental Disorders (DIPS) ... CMD
Classification of Occupations and Directory of Occupational Titles [*Formerly, MOLOC*] [*British*] ... CODOT
Classification of Outlays of Industry by Purpose (SAUS) ... COIP
Classification of Publications Board [*South Australia*] ... CPB
Classification of Secondary School Courses [*National Center for Education Statistics*] (EDAC) ... CSSC
Classification of the Functions of Government (SAUS) ... COFOG
Classification on Science and Technology ... CST
Classification Order Watch Service [*Research Publications, Inc.*] ... COWS
Classification, Packaging and Labelling [*Toxicology*] ... CPL
Classification Research ... CR
Classification Research Group [*British*] ... CRG
Classification Research Study Group (SAUO) ... CRSG
Classification Review Area [*Environmental Protection Agency*] (GFGA) ... CRA
[*The*] **Classification Society** (EA) ... TCS
Classification Society Bulletin (journ.) (SAUS) ... Class Soc Bull
Classification Society of North America (EA) ... CSNA
Classification Test Battery [*Aptitude and skills test*] ... CTB
Classification Type pour le Commerce International [*Standard International Trade Classification*] [*French*] ... CTCI
Classified (WDMC) ... class
Classified Abstract Archive of the Alcohol Literature ... CAAAL
Classified Advertisement Management Program [*British*] (DGA) ... CAMP
Classified Advertising Manager (IIA) ... CAM
Classified Anaphylatoxin [*Pharmacology*] (DAVI) ... CAT
Classified and Search Support Information System (SAUO) ... CASSIS
Classified Area Term Pass (AAG) ... CATP
Classified by Association (DNAB) ... CBA
Classified Control Clerk [*Army*] ... CCC
Classified Control Officer ... CCO
Classified Defense Information [*Military*] ... CDI
Classified Document Control ... CDC
Classified Energy On-line (SAUS) ... CLEO
Classified Entries in Lateral Transposition [*Indexing*] ... CELT
Classified Image Editor (GEOI) ... CIE
Classified Information Procedures Act [*1980*] ... CIPA
Classified Information-Handling System [*Department of State*] (GFGA) ... CIHS
Classified Intelligence Handling Environment (SAUS) ... CHIVE
Classified Job Accountability Record (MCD) ... CJAR
Classified Layout System (SAUS) ... CLS
Classified List of Army Forms and Books (SAUS) ... CLAFB
Classified Mail Address ... CMA
Classified Material Control Officer (AFIT) ... CMCO
Classified Material Receipt ... CMR
Classified Materials System (LAIN) ... CMS
Classified Matter Control Center (AAG) ... CMCC
Classified Message ... CM
Classified Military Information (MCD) ... CMI
Classified Ministry Lists of Types of Educational Establishments [*British*] ... CMLTEE
Classified Register (AAG) ... CR
Classified Restricted Data (DNAB) ... CRD
Classified Scientific and Technical Aerospace Reports [*NASA*] ... CSTAR
Classified Telephone Directory (SAUS) ... CTD
Classifier Overflow (IAA) ... CO
Classify (AFM) ... CLAS
Classify (SAUS) ... Clas
Classify (WDMC) ... class
Classify (MSA) ... CLS
Classify, Locate, and Avoid Wind Shear [*National Center for Atmospheric Research*] ... CLAWS
Classifying (SAUS) ... Classg
Classless Inter-Domain Routing (CDE) ... CIDR
Classless Internet Domain Routing [*Computer science*] (VERA) ... CIDIR
Classless Internet Domain Routing (SAUS) ... CIDR
Class-Oriented Ring-Associative Language [*Computer science*] ... CORAL
Class-Responsibility-Collaboration (RALS) ... CRC
Classroom (BARN) ... Clrm
Classroom (SAUS) ... CLRM
Classroom (SAUO) ... CR
Classroom Adjustment Code ... CAC
Classroom Adjustment Rating Scale ... CARS
Classroom Business Venture (EDAC) ... CBV
Classroom Climate Questionnaire (EDAC) ... CCQ
Classroom Communication Skills Inventory: A Listening and Speaking Checklist (TMMY) ... CCSI
Classroom Environment Index [*Student attitude test*] ... CEI
Classroom Environment Scale [*Teacher evaluation test*] ... CES
Classroom Instruction Program [*Dialog Information Services, Inc.*] ... CIP
Classroom Interactive Computer (SAUS) ... CLASSIC
Classroom Management Improvement Study (EDAC) ... CMIS
Classroom Management Observation Scale (EDAC) ... CMOS
Classroom Observation System for Analyzing Depression (SAUS) ... COSAD
Classroom Observations Keyed for Effectiveness Research (EDAC) ... COKER
Classroom Of The Future (SAUS) ... COTF
Classroom Periodical Publishers Association [*Later, CPA*] (EA) ... CPPA
Classroom Publishers Association (EA) ... CPA
Classroom Reading Inventory (EDAC) ... CRI
Classroom Teacher Network ... CTN
Classroom Teaching (OICC) ... C/T
Classroom Test Support System (SAUS) ... CTSS
Classroom Trainer (MCD) ... CRT
Classroom Trainer (MCD) ... CT
Classroom-Aided Dynamic Educational Time-Sharing System (IEEE) ... CADETS
Classroom-Aided Dynamic Educational Time-Sharing System (SAUS) ... CADETS System
Clastogenic Factor [*Medicine*] ... CF
Clathan Literary Institute [*British*] ... CLT
Clathrin Heavy Chain [*Genetics*] ... CHC
Clathrin-Associated Protein [*Cytology*] ... CAP
Clatsop Community College, Astoria, OR [*Library symbol*] [*Library of Congress*] (LCLS) ... OrAstC
Claude Dornier [*German aircraft designer, 1884-1969*] ... CD
Claude Resources, Inc. [*Toronto Stock Exchange symbol*] ... CRJ
Claude, TX [*FM radio station call letters*] ... KARX
Claudianus [*Fourth century AD*] [*Classical studies*] (OCD) ... Claud
Claus Oxygen-Based Process Expansion [*Petroleum technology*] ... COPE
Clause ... CL

Clause (MARI) ... Cl
Clause (WDMC) ... cl
Clause Interconnectivity Graph (SAUS) ... CIG
Clausen, Miller, Gorman, Caffrey & Witous, Chicago, IL [*Library symbol*] [*Library of Congress*] (LCLS) ... ICCMG
Clausen, Miller, Gorman, Caffrey & Witous, Chicago, IL [*OCLC symbol*] (OCLC) ... ILP
Clauses (ADA) ... CLL
Clauses (DLA) ... Cls
Clauson Rolling Platform ... CRP
Clausthal [*Federal Republic of Germany*] [*Seismograph station code, US Geological Survey*] (SEIS) ... CLZ
Claustrum [*Neuroanatomy*] ... Clau
Clavering [*England*] ... CLAV
Clavibacter Xyli Cynodontis [*Microbiology*] ... Cxc
Clavichord [*Music*] ... Clav
Clavichord [*Music*] ... Clavi
Clavichord [*Music*] ... CLVCHD
Clavichord [*Music*] ... CLVD
Clavicle [*Anatomy*] ... CL
Clavicle [*Anatomy*] (DHSM) ... CLAV
Clavicle [*Medicine*] (DMAA) ... clav
Clavicular [*Medicine*] (ROG) ... CLAVR
Clavier [*Keyboard*] [*Music*] ... CLAV
Clavieruebung [*Music*] ... CU
Clavis Patrum Graecorum (BJA) ... CPG
Clavis Patrum Latinorum (BJA) ... CPL
Claw Hand Deformity (MELL) ... CHD
Claw Plate [*Technical drawings*] ... CP
Claw Resources Ltd. [*Vancouver Stock Exchange symbol*] ... KLW
Claxton, GA [*AM radio station call letters*] ... WCLA
Claxton, GA [*FM radio station call letters*] ... WCLA-FM
Clay [*Quality of the bottom*] [*Nautical charts*] ... Cl
Clay & Abraham Ltd., Manufacturing Chemists (SAUO) ... C&A
Clay Bernard Systems International (EFIS) ... CBSI
Clay Bird Shooting Association (SAUO) ... CBSA
Clay Bird Shooting Association [*British*] (DI) ... CBSA
Clay Brick and Paver Association of New South Wales [*Australia*] ... CBPANSW
Clay Brick and Paver Institute of South Australia ... CBPISA
Clay Brick Association of Canada [*Association Canadienne de Brique d'Argile Cuite*] [*Formerly, Canadian Structural Clay Asssociation*] (AC) ... CBAC
Clay Brick Association of Queensland [*Australia*] ... CBAQ
Clay Brick Manufacturers' Association of Western Australia ... CBMAWA
Clay Center, KS [*Location identifier*] [*FAA*] (FAAL) ... CYW
Clay Center, KS [*FM radio station call letters*] ... KCLY
Clay City News, Clay City, IN [*Library symbol*] [*Library of Congress*] (LCLS) ... InClcN
Clay County Historical Society, Brazil, IN [*Library symbol*] [*Library of Congress*] (LCLS) ... InBraCHi
Clay County Historical Society, Library and Archives, Moorhead, MN [*Library symbol*] [*Library of Congress*] (LCLS) ... MnMohHi
Clay County Public Library, Green Cove Springs, FL [*Library symbol*] [*Library of Congress*] (LCLS) ... FGcC
Clay County Public Library, Manchester, KY [*Library symbol*] [*Library of Congress*] (LCLS) ... KyMan
Clay Flue Lining Institute [*Defunct*] (EA) ... CFLI
Clay Minerals (SAUS) ... Clay Miner
Clay Minerals Society (EA) ... CMS
Clay or Terra Cotta [*Freight*] ... CLY T C
Clay Pigeon Shooting Association [*British*] ... CPSA
Clay Pigmented Organic Coating ... CPOC
Clay Pipe [*Technical drawings*] ... CP
Clay Pipe Development Association [*British*] (DBA) ... CPDA
Clay Pipe Institute (EA) ... CPI
Clay Products Association (EA) ... CPA
Clay Products Haulers Bureau, Inc., Worthington OH [*STAC*] ... CPH
Clay Products Technical Bureau [*British*] ... CPTB
Clay Roofing Tile Council [*British*] (DBA) ... CRTC
Clay Sewer Pipe Association (EA) ... CSPA
Clay Shoveler's Fracture [*Medicine*] (MELL) ... CSF
Claydon [*England*] ... CLAY
Claydon. Landlord and Tenant [*A publication*] (DLA) ... Clay L & T
Clay-Filled (SAUS) ... Cl Fd
Clay-Mill Technical Systems, Inc. [*Toronto Stock Exchange symbol*] ... CLY
Claymont Public Library, Claymont, DE [*Library symbol*] [*Library of Congress*] (LCLS) ... DeC
Claymore Resources [*Vancouver Stock Exchange symbol*] ... CYA
Claypool, AZ [*FM radio station call letters*] ... KIKO
Clays and Clay Minerals (journ.) (SAUS) ... Clays Clay Miner
Clay's Digest of Laws of Alabama [*A publication*] (DLA) ... Clay's Dig
Clay-Sized Sediment (SAUS) ... CSS
Clayton College, Denver, CO [*Library symbol*] [*Library of Congress*] (LCLS) ... CoDC
Clayton County Register, Elkader, IA [*Library symbol*] [*Library of Congress*] (LCLS) ... IaElkCR
Clayton, GA [*AM radio station call letters*] ... WGHC
Clayton, GA [*FM radio station call letters*] ... WQXJ
Clayton, GA [*FM radio station call letters*] (BROA) ... WRBN-FM
Clayton Homes [*Associated Press*] (SAG) ... ClaytH
Clayton Homes [*NYSE symbol*] (TTSB) ... CMH
Clayton Homes, Inc. [*Associated Press*] (SAG) ... ClaytHm
Clayton Homes, Inc. [*NYSE symbol*] (SPSG) ... CMH
Clayton Junior College, Morrow, GA [*Library symbol*] [*Library of Congress*] (LCLS) ... GMorC
Clayton, LA [*FM radio station call letters*] (BROA) ... KFGA-FM
Clayton, MO [*AM radio station call letters*] ... KFUO
Clayton, MO [*FM radio station call letters*] ... KFUO-FM
Clayton, MO [*AM radio station call letters*] ... KSIV
Clayton, MO [*FM radio station call letters*] ... KWUR
Clayton, NC [*AM radio station call letters*] (RBYB) ... WHPY
Clayton, NM [*Location identifier*] [*FAA*] (FAAL) ... CAO
Clayton, NM [*AM radio station call letters*] (RBYB) ... KLMX-AM
Clayton on Conveyancing [*A publication*] (DLA) ... Clay Conv
Clayton, W. G., III, Buffalo NY [*STAC*] ... CWG
Clayton Williams Energy [*NASDAQ symbol*] (TTSB) ... CWEI
Clayton Williams Energy, Inc. [*Associated Press*] (SAG) ... ClayEng
Clayton Williams Energy, Inc. [*NASDAQ symbol*] (SAG) ... CWEI
Clayton's English Reports, York Assizes [*A publication*] (DLA) ... Clay
Clayton's English Reports, York Assizes [*A publication*] (DLA) ... Clayt
Clayton's English Reports, York Assizes [*A publication*] (DLA) ... Clayton
Clayton's English Reports, York Assizes [*A publication*] (DLA) ... Clayton (Eng)
Clayton's English Reports, York Assizes [*A publication*] (DLA) ... Rep Ass Y
Clayton's English Reports, York Assizes [*A publication*] (DLA) ... Rep York Ass
Clayton's English Reports, York Assizes [*A publication*] (DLA) ... York Ass
Claytons Pleas of Assize at York (SAUS) ... Rep York Ass
Claytons Reports of Assizes at Yorke (SAUS) ... Rep Ass Y
Claytons Reports, Yorke Assizes (SAUS) ... Yorke Ass
Clean ... C
Clean (EBF) ... c
Clean (SAUS) ... CL
Clean (ADWA) ... cln
Clean (MSA) ... CLN
Clean Air ... CA
Clean Air Act [*1963, 1990*] ... CAA
Clean Air Act Amendment ... CAAA
Clean Air Act Amendments of 1990 (WPI) ... CAAA
Clean Air Car Race ... CACR
Clean Air Council (SAUO) ... CAC
Clean Air Delivery Rate [*of air purifiers*] ... CADR
Clean Air Dot Angle (SAUS) ... CADA
Clean Air Facility (CARB) ... CAF
Clean Air Movement ... CAM
Clean Air Package ... CAP
Clean Air Projector ... CAP
Clean Air Scientific Advisory Committee [*Environmental Protection Agency*] [*Washington, DC*] ... CASAC
Clean Air Society [*Australia*] ... CAS
Clean Air. Special Edition (journ.) (SAUS) ... KSTKBO
Clean Air Station (ACAE) ... CLAS
Clean Air Status and Trends Network ... CASTNet
Clean Air System (SAUS) ... CAS
Clean Air Transport [*Commercial firm*] [*Sweden*] ... CAT
Clean Air Turbulence (SAUS) ... CAT
Clean Air Working Group [*An association*] [*Defunct*] (EA) ... CAWG
Clean Alternative Fuels (COE) ... CAF
Clean Alternative Fuels Program [*Environmental science*] (COE) ... CAFP
Clean and Recycling (SAUS) ... CR
Clean and Sober (SAUS) ... C&S
Clean and Sober [*Slang*] ... C and S
Clean and Tight [*Publishing*] ... C/T
Clean Annapolis River Project (AC) ... CARP
Clean Arithmetic with Decimal Base and Controlled Precision (MCD) ... CADAC
Clean Assembly Facility ... CAF
Clean Ballast Tanks [*Transportation*] ... CBT
Clean Bill of Lading (EBF) ... ClB/L
Clean Bill of Lading (SAUS) ... Clean B/L
Clean Car Initiative ... CCI
Clean Catch [*of urine*] [*Medicine*] ... CC
Clean Catch Midstream Urine [*Medicine*] ... CCMS
Clean Catch Midstream Urine [*Medicine*] ... CCMSU
Clean Catch Urinalysis [*Medicine*] (MELL) ... CCUA
Clean Coal Coalition [*Defunct*] (EA) ... CCC
Clean Coal Technology Demonstration Program [*Department of Energy*] ... CCTDP
Clean Coal Technology Program (GNE) ... CCTP
Clean Community System [*Waste management program*] ... CCS
Clean Development Mechanism ... CDM
Clean Diesel Technologies [*NASDAQ symbol*] (TTSB) ... CDTI
Clean Draft (EBF) ... DFT/c
Clean Draft (EBF) ... dft/c
Clean Draft [*Business term*] ... DFT/C
Clean Dry Air (AAEL) ... CDA
Clean Energy Research Institute [*University of Miami*] [*Research center*] ... CERI
Clean Fleet Vehicle [*VDOT*] (TAG) ... CFV
Clean Fuel Fleet [*VDOT*] (TAG) ... CFF
Clean Fuel Oil Tank (MSA) ... CFT
Clean Fuel Vehicle ... CFV
Clean Fuels Development Coalition (EA) ... CFDC
Clean Gulf of Mexico Associates (SAUO) ... CGA
Clean Harbors [*NASDAQ symbol*] (TTSB) ... CLHB
Clean Harbors Cooperative (EA) ... CHC
Clean Harbors, Inc. [*Associated Press*] (SAG) ... CleanH
Clean Harbors, Inc. [*NASDAQ symbol*] (NQ) ... CLHB
Clean Intermittent Catherization [*Medicine*] ... CIC
Clean Lakes Clearinghouse (AUEG) ... CLC
Clean Lakes Database (SAUO) ... LAKE
Clean Letter of Credit [*Banking*] ... CLOC
Clean Liquid Radioactive Waste System (NRCH) ... CLRWS
Clean Liquid RADwater [*Nuclear energy*] (IEEE) ... CLR
Clean Lube Oil (AAG) ... CLO

Clean Midstream Urinalysis [*Medicine*] (DAVI) .... CMSUA
Clean Midstream Urine [*Specimen*] [*Medicine*] (MELL) .... CMSU
[*The*] Clean Nova Scotia Foundation (AC) .... CNSF
Clean Ocean Action (GNE) .... COA
Clean RADWASTE [*Radioactive waste*] [*Nuclear energy*] (NRCH) .... CRW
Clean Report of Findings [*Societe Generale de Surveillance SA*] (DS) .... CRF
Clean Room Kit .... CRK
Clean Shelter Area [*Army*] (ADDR) .... CSA
Clean Sites, Inc. (EA) .... CSI
Clean Suppressed Radiation (SAUS) .... CSR
Clean Sweep Generator (NVT) .... CSG
Clean Tanks, Gas Free (NVT) .... CTGF
Clean Up Buck (MCD) .... CUB
Clean Up TV Campaign [*Defunct*] (EA) .... CUTVC
Clean Urban River Environment Project (SAUS) .... CURE Project
Clean Urban River Environments [*Project*] .... CURE
Clean Urban Vehicle .... CUV
Clean Voided [*Specimen*] [*Biochemistry*] (DAVI) .... CL VOID
Clean Voided Specimen [*Medicine*] .... CVS
Clean Water (IEEE) .... CW
Clean Water Act [*Environmental Protection Agency*] .... CWA
Clean Water Act Project (SAUO) .... CWAP
Clean Water Action [*An association*] (EA) .... CWA
Clean Water Action Project [*Later, CWA*] (EA) .... CWAP
Clean Water Action Project (SAUO) .... CWAP
Clean Water Fund [*An association*] (EA) .... CWF
Clean Water Restoration Act (MELL) .... CWRA
Clean Waters Advisory Committee [*New South Wales*] [*Australia*] .... CWAC
Clean Work Area [*NASA*] (NASA) .... CWA
Clean World International [*Brighton, East Sussex, England*] (EAIO) .... CWI
Clean-Catch-Midstream Urinalysis [*Medicine*] (MEDA) .... CCMSUA
Cleaned in Transit .... CIT
Cleaner [*Automotive engineering*] CL
Cleaner .... CLNR
Cleaner Air Package (SAUS) .... CAP
Cleaner Air System [*Automotive engineering*] .... CAS
Cleaner Technologies Subsitutes Assessment (SAUO) .... CTSA
Cleaner-Burning Gasoline (SAUS) .... CBG
Cleaner/Lubricant/Preservation [*for firearms*] (MCD) .... CLP
Cleaners and Solvents Council (SAUO) .... C&SC
Cleaning .... CLNG
Cleaning and De-Icing System (MCD) .... CDS
Cleaning and Support Services Association [*British*] (EAIO) .... CSSA
Cleaning Arm (SAUS) .... CA
Cleaning Contractors' Association of Western Australia .... CCAWA
Cleaning, Decontamination Request (MCD) .... CDR
Cleaning Equipment Manufacturers Association [*Later, CETA*] (EA) .... CEMA
Cleaning Equipment Trade Association (EA) .... CETA
Cleaning Gear Locker .... CGLKR
Cleaning Gear Locker (SAUS) .... CGLkr
Cleaning, Lubrication, and Adjustment [*Camera repair*] .... CLA
Cleaning Management Institute (EA) .... CMI
Cleaning Management Station .... CMS
Cleaning-in-Place [*Microbiology*] .... CIP
Cleanliness Identification [*Label*] [*Aerospace*] (AAG) .... CID
Cleanly Designed Cigar .... CDC
Cleanout (AAG) .... CO
Clean-Out Door (OA) .... COD
Cleanout Flush with Finished Floor .... FCO
Cleanroom Interface Chamber (AAEL) CIC
Cleanser .... CLNSR
Cleansing Officers' Guild [*British*] (BI) .... COG
Cleanup (SAUS) .... CU
Clean-Up Information [*Environmental Protection Agency*] (AEPA) .... CLU-IN
Clean-Up System (IEEE) .... CUS
Clear [*Calculators*] C
Clear CL
Clear [*Biochemistry*] (DAVI) .... CLER
Clear [*Alaska*] [*Airport symbol*] (AD) .... CLF
Clear (WDMC) .... clr
Clear [*Alaska*] [*BMEWS Site 1*] (MCD) .... CLR
Clear [*Wood industry*] (WPI) .... Clr
Clear [*Alaska*] [*ICAO location identifier*] (ICLI) .... PACL
Clear Above [*Aviation*] (FAAC) .... CA
Clear Accumulator (SAUS) .... CLA
Clear Add (SAUS) .... CAD
Clear Air Dot Angle .... CADA
Clear Air Mass .... CLAM
Clear Air Mass Anti Aircraft Fire Control System (ACAE) .... CAMAAFCS
Clear Air Mass Systems (ACAE) .... CLAM
Clear Air Mass Systems (ACAE) .... CLAMS
Clear Air Temperature .... CAT
Clear Air Turbulence [*Aviation*] .... CAT
Clear, AK [*Location identifier*] [*FAA*] (FAAL) .... CLF
Clear All Channels .... CAC
Clear An Operand (SAUS) .... CLR
Clear and Add .... CA
Clear and Add (SAA) .... CAD
Clear and Add .... CLA
Clear and Add Clock (SAA) .... CAC
Clear and Add Magnitude (IAA) .... CAM
Clear and Secure [*Military*] (VNW) .... C and S
Clear and Smooth [*NWS*] (FAAC) .... CLRS
Clear and Subtract (IEEE) .... CLS
Clear and Subtract .... CS

Clear and Subtract (IAA) .... CSU
Clear and Subtract Magnitude (SAUS) .... CSM
Clear and Write (SAUS) .... CW
Clear Aperture (MSA) .... CA
Clear Aperture Antenna (ACAE) .... CAA
Clear Back [*Telecommunications*] (TEL) .... CB
Clear Both [*Computer science*] .... CLB
Clear, Cancel, or Complete (MCD) CCC
Clear Carry CLC
Clear Cell Adenocarcinoma [*Medicine*] (MELL) .... CCA
Clear Cell Adenocarcinoma [*Medicine*] (MELL) .... CCAC
Clear Cell Carcinoma [*Medicine*] (MELL) CCC
Clear Channel Broadcasting Service (EA) .... CCBS
Clear Channel, Inc. [*NYSE symbol*] (SAG) .... CCU
Clear Channel, Inc. [*Associated Press*] (SAG) .... ClearC
Clear Channel, Inc. [*Associated Press*] (SAG) .... ClearCh
Clear Chill (SAUS) CC
Clear Confirmation (SAUS) CLC
Clear Confirmation Delay (SAUS) .... CLCD
Clear, Creamy Layer at Top [*Biochemistry*] (DAVI) .... CCT
Clear Creek Butte [*Alaska*] [*Seismograph station code, US Geological Survey*] [*Closed*] (SEIS) .... CCB
Clear Daylight (SAUS) .... DCL
Clear Direction Flag (SAUS) .... CLD
Clear Flight Level .... CFL
Clear Forward [*Telecommunications*] (TEL) .... CLF
Clear Forward Signal [*Telecommunications*] (NITA) .... CLF
Clear Glased (or Glazed) Structural Unit Base (SAUS) .... CLGSUB
Clear Glass .... CG
Clear Glazed Structural Facing Units [*Technical drawings*] .... CLGSFU
Clear Glazed Structural Unit Base [*Technical drawings*] .... CLGSUB
Clear Ice [*Aviation*] (DA) .... CLA
Clear Indicating Lamp (SAUS) CIL
Clear Indicating Light (MSA) CIL
Clear Indication (SAUS) CLI
Clear Interrupt [*PC instruction*] (PCM) CLI
Clear Lake City [*Texas*] [*Airport symbol*] (OAG) CLC
Clear Lake City, TX [*Location identifier*] [*FAA*] (FAAL) CLC
Clear Lake, IA [*FM radio station call letters*] .... KLKK
Clear Lake Public Library, Clear Lake, IA [*Library symbol*] [*Library of Congress*] (LCLS) .... IaCll
Clear Lake, SD [*FM radio station call letters*] (BROA) .... KBGV-FM
Clear Lamp (SAUS) CL
Clear Lane Marking System [*Army*] (RDA) .... CLAMS
Clear Language for Expressing Orders [*Computer science*] (IEEE) .... CLEO
Clear Line-of-Sight (MCD) .... CLOS
Clear Link (SAUS) CLL
Clear Liquid [*Medicine*] CL
Clear Liquid (BABM) .... Cl liq
Clear Liquid [*Dietetics*] (DAVI) .... cl liq
Clear Memory (IAA) .... CM
Clear Message (SAUS) .... Clr Msg
Clear Mews [*Alaska*] [*Seismograph station code, US Geological Survey*] [*Closed*] (SEIS) .... CMA
Clear Mines Ltd. [*Vancouver Stock Exchange symbol*] .... CEE
Clear, No Creamy Layer [*Biochemistry*] (DAVI) .... CNC
Clear of Clouds [*Aviation*] (FAAC) .... CCLDS
Clear Only if Known [*Buzz words, acronyms, etc., that are clear in context only if already known to the reader*] .... COIK
Clear or Scattered Clouds and Visibility Greater than Ten, Remainder of Report Missing [*NWS*] (FAAC) .... DCAVU
Clear over Base [*System of paint finishing*] [*Automotive engineering*] .... COB
Clear Record [*Telecommunications*] (TEL) .... CR
Clear Round [*Show jumping*] (ADA) .... CR
Clear Screen [*Computer science*] .... CLS
Clear Status (MCD) .... CS
Clear Stream Avenue Elementary School, Valley Stream, NY [*Library symbol*] [*Library of Congress*] (LCLS) .... NVsCSE
Clear Task Switch Flag (SAUS) .... CLTS
Clear Text Reading (SAUS) .... CTP
Clear to Auscultation [*Medicine*] (DAVI) .... CTA
Clear to Send [*Modem status information light*] [*Computer science*] (IGQR) .... CTR
Clear to Send [*Telecommunications*] .... CTS
Clear to Send/Request to Send .... CTSRTS
Clear To Stand [*Telecommunications*] (EECA) .... CTS
Clear to Zero [*Computer science*] .... CLR
Clear Wire Glass [*Technical drawings*] .... CLWG
Clear Word Identifier (SAUS) .... CWI
Clear Write Condition .... CWC
Clear Zone (SAUS) .... CZ
Clearance C
Clearance [*Broadcasting*] (WDMC) cl
Clearance (MSA) CL
Clearance (KSC) .... CLN
Clearance (AFM) .... CLNC
Clearance (SAUS) .... CLR
Clearance [*Physiology*] Cx
Clearance Array (MSA) .... CLA
Clearance Delivery [*Aviation*] (PIPO) .... CD
Clearance Delivery (PIPO) .... CLNCDEL
Clearance Distance (SAUS) .... CLDIST
Clearance Divers Breathing Apparatus (SAUS) .... CDBA
Clearance Diving [*Navy*] [*British*] .... CD
Clearance Diving Tender .... CDT
Clearance Dock Club [*A union*] [*British*] .... CDC

Clearance Group [*Customs*] (DS) ... CG
Clearance Hot Delivered (SAUS) ... N
Clearance Plane (SAUS) ... CLEARP
Clearance Rate [*Renal*] [*Nephrology*] (DAVI) ... C
Clearance Required [*Civil Service*] ... CR
Clearance Surface (SAUS) ... CLRSRF
Clearance Void if Not Off [*Aviation*] (FAAC) ... CVINO
Clear-and-Gate Operation (SAUS) ... CGO
Clear-Back Signal (SAUS) ... CBK Signal
Clearbrook Public School, Clearbrook, MN [*Library symbol*] [*Library of Congress*] (LCLS) ... MnCleS
Clear-Cell Carcinoma of Endometrium [*Medicine*] ... CCE
Clear-Channel Station [*Telecommunications*] (LAIN) ... CCS
Cleared ... CLD
Cleared (EBF) ... Cld
Cleared (SAUS) ... CLR
Cleared Altitude (IAA) ... CALT
Cleared as Field (SAUS) ... CAF
Cleared As Filed [*Aviation*] (PIPO) ... CAF
Cleared as Planned (FAAC) ... CLRAP
Cleared Bidder's List ... CBL
Cleared Customs (FAAC) ... CCUS
Cleared for Approach [*Aviation*] ... CFA
Cleared for Approach [*Aviation*] (FAAC) ... CFAP
Cleared Land Explosion Widening and Proofing (MCD) ... CLEWP
Cleared Lane Explosive Widening Path Charge (SAUS) ... CLEWP
Cleared Through for Landing and Takeoff (SAUS) ... T
Cleared to Land (SAUS) ... L
Cleared to the Outer Marker (SAUS) ... O
Cleared V-8 Juice Agar [*Microbiology*] ... CV-8A
Cleared V-8 Juice Broth [*Microbiology*] ... CV-8B
Cleared without Examination [*Business term*] ... CWE
Clearence Diver (SAUS) ... CD
Clear-Entry [*Calculators*] ... CE
Clearfield Chronicle, Clearfield, IA [*Library symbol*] [*Library of Congress*] (LCLS) ... IaClfC
Clearfield, PA [*AM radio station call letters*] ... WCPA
Clearfield, PA [*Television station call letters*] ... WPSX
Clearfield, PA [*FM radio station call letters*] ... WQYX
Clear-Forward Signal (SAUS) ... CLF Signal
Clearing (SAUS) ... CLG
Clearing (SAUS) ... CLR
Clearing (MSA) ... CLRG
Clearing ... CLRNG
Clearing Banks Union (SAUO) ... CBU
Clearing Company (SAUO) ... Clr Co
Clearing House (SAUO) ... CH
Clearing House (SAUS) ... CH
Clearing House Accession Number [*Online database field identifier*] ... CHAN
Clearing House and Laboratory for Census Data (SAUO) ... CLCD
Clearing House Automated Payment System (SAUO) ... CHAPS
Clearing House Catalogue (CIST) ... CHCAT
Clearing House Code [*Database terminology*] (NITA) ... CH
Clearing House Electronic Subregister System [*Australian Stock Exchange*] ... CHESS
Clearing House for Education and Social Studies/Social Science [*Department of Education*] (NITA) ... ChESS
Clearing House Interbank Payment System (BUR) ... CHIPS
Clearing House Interbank Payments System (SAUS) ... CHIPS
Clearing House Mechanism (SAUO) ... CHM
Clearing Key (SAUS) ... CK
Clearing Machine Corporation (SAUO) ... CMC
Clearing Processing System [*British*] (NUMA) ... CPS
Clearing Station (SAUO) ... Clr Sta
Clearinghouse [*Banking*] ... CH
Clearinghouse and Laboratory for Census Data [*Defunct*] ... CLCD
Clearinghouse Announcements in Science and Technology [*of CFSTI*] [*Later, WGA*] ... CAST
Clearinghouse Automated Payments System [*Banking*] [*London*] ... CHAPS
Clearinghouse Committee for Information on the Arts and Humanities ... CCIAH
Clearinghouse database on disability-related information (SAUO) ... Clear
[*The*] **Clearinghouse Directory** [*A publication*] ... CD
Clearinghouse for Applied Performance Testing (SAUO) ... CAPT
Clearinghouse for Augmenting Resources for Training [*DoD*] ... CHART
Clearinghouse for Community Based Free Standing Educational Institutions (EA) ... CBFSEI
Clearinghouse for Federal Scientific and Technical Information (SAUO) ... CFESTI
Clearinghouse for Federal Scientific and Technical Information [*Later, NTIS*] [*National Institute of Standards and Technology*] ... CFSTI
Clearinghouse for Innovation in Scientific Communication ... CISC
Clearinghouse for Inventories and Emission Factors [*Environmental Protection Agency*] (AEPA) ... CHIEF
Clearinghouse for Library and Information Resources (SAUS) ... CLIR
Clearinghouse for Library and Information Sciences ... CLIS
Clearinghouse for Network Information and Discovery and Retrieval [*Computer science*] ... CNIDR
Clearinghouse for Occupational Safety and Health Information [*HEW*] (IID) ... COSHI
Clearinghouse for Research in Child Life [*Federal Security Administration*] ... CRCL
Clearinghouse for Scientific and Technical Information [*Later, NTIS*] [*National Institute of Standards and Technology*] ... CSTI
Clearing-House for Specialized Media and Technology ... CSMT
Clearinghouse for Subject Orientated Internet Resource Guides (SAUO) ... CSOIRG
Clearinghouse for Subject Orientated Resource Guides (SAUO) ... CSORG
Clearinghouse for Volunteer Accounting Services (SAUO) ... CVAS
Clearinghouse Information System (SAUS) ... CHIS
Clearinghouse International of the Women's Forum (EA) ... CIWF
Clearinghouse on Business Coalitions for Health Action [*Defunct*] (EA) ... CBCHA
Clearinghouse on Child Abuse and Neglect Information (EA) ... CCANI
Clearinghouse on Computer Accommodation [*General Services Administration*] ... COCA
Clearinghouse on Counseling and Personnel Services [*ERIC*] ... CAPS
Clearinghouse on Development Communication (EA) ... CDC
Clearinghouse on Disability Information (EA) ... CDI
Clearinghouse on Early Childhood Education (SAUS) ... ECE
Clearinghouse on Educational Administration [*ERIC*] ... CEA
Clearinghouse on Educational Facilities [*ERIC*] ... CEF
Clearinghouse on Election Administration [*Federal Election Commission*] ... CEA
Clearinghouse on Elementary and Early Childhood Education (SAUS) ... EEC
Clearinghouse on Environmental Carcinogens (EEVL) ... CEC
Clearinghouse on Health Indexes [*Public Health Service*] [*Information service or system*] (IID) ... CHI
Clearinghouse on Information Resources (SAUS) ... CIR
Clearinghouse on Languages and Linguistics (SAUO) ... CLL
Clearinghouse on Rural Education and Small Schools [*ERIC*] ... CRESS
Clearinghouse on Women's Issues (EA) ... CWI
Clearinghouse on Women's Issues in Congress [*Later, CWI*] (EA) ... CWIC
Clearinghouse on Women's Studies (EA) ... CWS
Clearinghouse Review [*A publication*] (AAGC) ... Clearinghouse Rev
Clearlink Network Control System [*AT & T Tridom*] ... CNCS
Clearly Canadian Beverage [*NASDAQ symbol*] (TTSB) ... CLCDF
Clearly Canadian Beverage Corp. [*NASDAQ symbol*] (SAG) ... CLCD
Clearly Canadian Beverage Corp. [*Associated Press*] (SAG) ... ClerCd
Clearnet Communic 'A' [*NASDAQ symbol*] (TTSB) ... CLNTF
Clearnet Communications, Inc. [*Associated Press*] (SAG) ... Clearnet
Clearnet Communications, Inc. [*NASDAQ symbol*] (SAG) ... CLNT
Clearport Petroleum Ltd. [*Vancouver Stock Exchange symbol*] ... CPR
Clear-Type Exterior Trim [*Weyerhaeuser Co.*] ... CTX
Clearview Elementary School, Clear lake, MN [*Library symbol*] [*Library of Congress*] (LCLS) ... MnClkE
Clearwater, BC [*AM radio station call letters*] ... CHNL-1
Clearwater Christian College, Clearwater, FL [*Library symbol*] [*Library of Congress*] (LCLS) ... FClCC
Clearwater Correctional Center, Resident Library, Forks, WA [*Library symbol*] [*Library of Congress*] (LCLS) ... WaForC-R
Clearwater Correctional Center, Staff Library, Forks, WA [*Library symbol*] [*Library of Congress*] (LCLS) ... WaForC
Clearwater, FL [*Location identifier*] [*FAA*] (FAAL) ... CLW
Clearwater, FL [*Television station call letters*] ... WCLF
Clearwater, FL [*FM radio station call letters*] ... WMTX
Clearwater, FL [*FM radio station call letters*] (BROA) ... WSSR-FM
Clearwater, FL [*AM radio station call letters*] ... WTAN
Clearwater, FL [*FM radio station call letters*] ... WXTB
Clearwater, KS [*FM radio station call letters*] (BROA) ... KAYY-FM
Clearwater, KS [*FM radio station call letters*] ... KSPG
Clearwater Memorial Public Library, Orofino, ID [*Library symbol*] [*Library of Congress*] (LCLS) ... IdOr
Clearwater Public Library, Clearwater, FL [*Library symbol*] [*Library of Congress*] (LCLS) ... FCl
Clearwater Publishing Co., Inc., New York, NY [*Library symbol*] [*Library of Congress*] (LCLS) ... CpCo
Clearwater, SC [*FM radio station call letters*] ... WSLT
Clearwater-St. Petersburg [*Florida*] [*Airport symbol*] (AD) ... PIE
Clearway [*Aviation code*] ... CWY
ClearWorks.net, Inc. [*AMEX symbol*] ... CLW
Cleary College, Ypsilanti, MI [*Library symbol*] [*Library of Congress*] (LCLS) ... MiYCC
Cleary's Registration Cases [*England*] [*A publication*] (DLA) ... Cleary RC
Cleary's Registration Cases [*Ireland*] [*A publication*] (DLA) ... Cleary Reg Cas
Cleat ... CLT
Cleaton & Workington Junction Railway Co. (SAUO) ... CWJR
Cleavage and Polyadenylation Specificity Factor [*Biochemistry*] ... CPSF
Cleavage of Lateral Epitaxial Film for Transfer [*Photovoltaic energy systems*] ... CLEFT
Cleaved Coupled Cavity Laser (SAUS) ... C3 Laser
Cleaved Edge Overgrowth [*Materials science*] ... CEO
Cleaveland on the Banking System [*A publication*] (DLA) ... Cleve Bank
Cleaveland's Banking Laws of New York [*A publication*] (DLA) ... Cleav Bank L
Clebsch-Gordan Coefficients [*Mathematics*] ... CGC
Cleburne Public Library, Cleburne, TX [*Library symbol*] [*Library of Congress*] (LCLS) ... TxCle
Cleburne, TX [*AM radio station call letters*] ... KCLE
Cleco Corp. [*NYSE symbol*] [*Formerly, Central La Elec.*] ... CNL
Cleft Lip (MELL) ... CL
Cleft Lip and Cleft Palate [*Medicine*] (MAE) ... CL/CP
Cleft Lip and Palate [*Medicine*] (DAVI) ... CL & P
Cleft Lip and Palate Association [*British*] (DI) ... CLAPA
Cleft Palate [*Medicine*] ... CL PAL
Cleft Palate [*Medicine*] ... CP
Cleft Palate and Lip Society [*Australia*] ... CPLS
Cleft Palate Foundation (ADWA) ... CPF
Cleft Palate-Craniofacial Journal (SAUO) ... CPCJ
Cleft Palate-Lateral Synechia Syndrome [*Medicine*] (DMAA) ... CPLS
Cleft Uvula [*Medicine*] (MELL) ... CU
Cleidocranial Dysostosis [*Medicine*] (DMAA) ... CLCD

Cleidocranial Dysplasia [*Medicine*] .... CCD
Cleistogamous [*Botany*] CL
CLEM [*Closed-Loop Ex-Vessel Machine*] **Maintenance Pit** [*Nuclear energy*] (NRCH) .... CMP
CLEM [*Closed-Loop Ex-Vessel Machine*] **Transporter** [*Nuclear energy*] (NRCH) .... CT
Clemency Review Board [*for Vietnam War draft dodgers and defectors*] .... CRB
Clemens Alexandrinus [*First century AD*] [*Classical studies*] (OCD) .... Clem Al
Clemens and August Breeninkmeyers international house of fashion (SAUS) .... C&A
Clemens on Corporate Securities [*A publication*] (DLA) .... Clem Corp Sec
Clemens' Reports [*57-59 Kansas*] [*A publication*] (DLA) .... Clem
Clement of Alexandria (BJA) .... Clem
Clemente Global Gr [*NYSE symbol*] (TTSB) .... CLM
Clemente Global Growth Fund, Inc. [*Associated Press*] (SAG) .... ClemGlb
Clemente Global Growth Fund, Inc. [*NYSE symbol*] (SPSG) .... CLM
Clementina [*Ecuador*] [*ICAO location identifier*] (ICLI) .... SECM
Clementinae Constitutiones [*A publication*] (DSA) .... Cle
Clementinae Constitutiones [*A publication*] (DSA) .... Clem
Clemson Hydraulics Laboratory [*Clemson University*] [*Research center*] (RCD) .... CHL
Clemson, SC [*Location identifier*] [*FAA*] (FAAL) .... CEU
Clemson, SC [*AM radio station call letters*] (BROA) .... WAHT-AM
Clemson, SC [*AM radio station call letters*] .... WCCP
Clemson, SC [*FM radio station call letters*] .... WCCP-FM
Clemson, SC [*FM radio station call letters*] .... WSBF
Clemson University (GAGS) .... Clemson U
Clemson University (SAUS) .... ScCleU
Clemson University, Clemson, SC [*Library symbol*] [*Library of Congress*] (LCLS) .... ScCleU
Clemson University, Clemson, SC [*OCLC symbol*] (OCLC) .... SEA
Cleobury, Mortimer, and Ditton Prior Light Railway [*Wales*] .... CMDP
Cleomenes [*of Plutarch*] [*Classical studies*] (OCD) .... Cleom
Cleopatra [*Queen of Egypt, 69-30BC*] (ROG) .... CLEOP
Clerestory (VRA) .... clst
Clerfield, Utah (SAUO) .... CLFD
Clergy CL
Clergy .... CLER
Clergy Against Nuclear Arms [*British*] [*An association*] (DBA) .... CANA
Clergy and Laity Concerned (EA) .... CALC
Clergy and Laity Concerned About Vietnam [*An association*] (VNW) CLCV
Clergy and Laymen Concerned about Vietnam [*Later, CALC*] (EA) .... CALCAV
Clergy and Laymen Concerned About Vietnam (SAUO) .... CLCAV
Clergy Augmentation Fund (SAUO) .... CAF
Clergy Counseling Service for Problem Pregnancies [*Defunct*] (EA) .... CCSPP
Clergy Couples of the Presbyterian Family [*Defunct*] (EA) .... CCPF
Clergy Economic Education Foundation [*Later, EEFC*] .... CEEF
Clergy Friendly Society (SAUO) .... CFS
Clergy Mutual Assurance Society (SAUO) .... CMAS
Clergy Mutual Assurance Society [*British*] .... CMAS
Clergy Orphan Corp. [*British*] .... COC
Clergy Orphan Corporation (SAUO) .... COC
Clergy Orphan Schools [*British*] (ROG) .... CO
Clergy Pensions Institution [*Church of England*] .... CPI
Clergyman .... CLERG
Cleric (BARN) Cl
Clerical .... CLER
Clerical (SAUS) .... Cler
Clerical Administration .... CLAD
Clerical, Administrative, and Fiscal [*Used with number, as, CAF-6, to indicate grade of position*] [*Civil Service*] .... CAF
Clerical Administrative Class (ADA) .... CAC
Clerical and Administrative Workers Union [*British*] .... CAWU
Clerical and Allied Service Employees (DICI) .... CASE
Clerical Aptitude [*Test*] .... CA
Clerical Aptitude Area (AABC) CL
Clerical Aptitude Test .... CAT
Clerical Assistant [*Civil Service*] [*British*] .... CA
Clerical Medical [*Insurance firm*] [*British*] .... CM
Clerical, Medical & General Life Assurance Society (WDAA) .... CM&GLAS
Clerical Medical International [*British*] .... CMI
Clerical Officer [*Civil Service*] [*British*] .... CO
Clerical Perception [*On General Aptitude Test Battery*] (DAVI) .... Q
Clerical Support .... CLS
Clerical Support Staff (COE) .... CSS
Clerical Technician, Medical [*Navy*] .... CLT
Clerical Test [*Military*] .... CLER
Clerical Work Data (MHDI) .... CWD
Clerical Work Evaluation [*British*] .... CWE
Clerical Work Improvement Program [*British*] .... CWIP
Clerical Work Improvement Programme (SAUO) .... CWIP
Clerical Work Measurement (MHDI) .... CWM
Clerici Regulares Congregationis Somaschae [*Somaschi Fathers*] [*Roman Catholic religious order*] .... CRCS
Clerici Regulares Matris Dei [*Clerics Regular of the Mother of God*] [*Roman Catholic religious order*] .... CRMD
Clerici Regulares Ministrantes Infirmis [*Clerics Regular Attendant on the Sick, Camillini, Camilliani*] [*Roman Catholic religious order*] .... CRMI
Clerici Regulares Minores [*Clerics Regular Minor*] [*Adorno Fathers*] [*Roman Catholic religious order*] .... CRM
Clerici Regulares Pauperum Matris Dei Scholarum Piarum [*Clerics Regular of the Poor Men of the Mother of God for Pious Schools*] [*Piarists*] [*Roman Catholic religious order*] .... CRSP
Clerici Regulares Sancti Pauli [*Clerics Regular of St. Paul*] [*Barnabites*] [*Also, Barn*] [*Roman Catholic men's religious order*] .... CRSP
Clerici Regulares Theatini [*Theatines*] [*Roman Catholic religious order*] .... CRT
Clerici Sancti Viatoris [*Clerics of St. Viator*] [*Viatorian Fathers*] [*Roman Catholic religious order*] .... CSV
Clericorum Regularium Somaschensium [*Clerics Regular of Somasca*] [*Somascan Fathers*] [*Roman Catholic religious order*] .... CRS
Clerics of St. Viator (TOCD) .... CSV
Clerics of St. Vistor, Viatorian Fathers (TOCD) .... csv
Clerics Regular of St. Paul (SAUO) .... Barnabites
Clerics Regular of St. Paul (TOCD) .... CRSP
Clerics Regular of St. Paul, Barnabite Fathers (TOCD) .... crsp
Clericus Parliamentariorum [*Clerk of Parliaments*] [*British*] (ROG) .... CLER PARL
Clerk (ROG) .... CK
Clerk CL
Clerk (WDAA) cl
Clerk (AFM) .... CLK
Clerk (GEAB) .... clk
Clerk (GEOI) .... Clk
Clerk .... CLRK
Clerk and Steward [*British*] .... C & S
Clerk Home's Decisions, Scotch Court of Session [*1735-44*] [*A publication*] (DLA) .... C Home
Clerk Home's Decisions, Scotch Court of Session [*1735-44*] [*A publication*] (DLA) .... Clerk Home
Clerk Home's Decisions, Scotch Court of Session [*1735-44*] [*A publication*] (DLA) .... Home (Cl)
Clerk Home's Scotch Session Cases [*A publication*] (DLA) .... Cl Home
Clerk in Orders [*Church of England*] .... CLKO
Clerk of Monmouth County, Freehold, NJ [*Library symbol*] [*Library of Congress*] (LCLS) .... NjFrCoC
Clerk of Petty Sessions [*British*] (ADA) .... CPS
Clerk of Sessions [*British*] (ROG) .... CS
Clerk of State Papers [*British*] (ROG) .... CSP
Clerk of the Chapel [*Unions*] [*British*] (DGA) CC
Clerk of the Chapel [*Unions*] [*British*] (DGA) .... COC
Clerk of the Council (SAUO) CC
Clerk of the Crown [*British*] CC
Clerk of the House of Commons (SAUS) .... CHC
Clerk of the House of Commons [*British*] (ROG) .... CL HO COM
Clerk of the House of Lords [*British*] (ROG) .... CL HL
Clerk of the Peace [*British*] (ROG) .... CL of P
Clerk of the Peace [*British*] .... CP
Clerk of the Privy Council [*British*] CC
Clerk of the Privy Council [*British*] .... CPC
Clerk of the Works (DAC) .... C/W
Clerk of Works (SAUS) .... CW
Clerk (Pay and Records) [*British military*] (DMA) .... CPR
Clerk to Guardians [*British*] (ROG) .... C to G
Clerk to Magistrates [*British*] (ROG) .... CL to MAGS
Clerk to the House of Commons (DLA) .... CHC
Clerk to the Signet [*British*] .... CS
Clerk to Vestry [*British*] (ROG) .... CL to VEST
Clerke and Brett on Conveyancing, Etc. [*A publication*] (DLA) .... Clerke & Br Conv
Clerke's American Law and Practice [*A publication*] (DLA) .... Clerke Am L
Clerke's Digest [*New York*] [*A publication*] (DLA) .... Clerke Dig
Clerke's Praxis Curiae Admiralitatis [*A publication*] (DLA) .... Clerke Pr
Clerke's Praxis Curiae Admiralitatis [*A publication*] (DLA) .... Clerke Prax
Clerks and Officers of the House of Commons (SAUO) .... COHC
Clerks and Officers of the House of Parliament (SAUO) .... COHP
Clerk's Magazine [*A publication*] (DLA) .... Clk's Mag
Clerks of Court [*Legal term*] (DLA) .... CLK CT
Clerks of Works Association of Great Britain (SAUO) .... CWAGB
Clerks Regular, Ministers of the Sick [*Rome, Italy*] (EAIO) .... CRMS
Clerks Regular of the Poor Men of the Mother of God for Pious Schools (SAUO) .... CRSP
Clerkship Directors in Internal Medicine (ADWA) .... CDIM
Clerk-Typist (SAUS) .... Clk-Typ
Clermont [*Australia*] [*Airport symbol*] (OAG) .... CMQ
Clermont County Public Library, Batavia, OH [*Library symbol*] [*Library of Congress*] (LCLS) .... OBat
Clermont, FL [*Television station call letters*] .... WKCF
Clermont, FL [*FM radio station call letters*] (RBYB) .... WLAZ-FM
Clermont, FL [*AM radio station call letters*] (BROA) .... WWFL-AM
Clermont General and Technical College, Batavia, OH [*Library symbol*] [*Library of Congress*] (LCLS) .... OBatC
Clermont Mercy Hospital, Batavia, OH [*Library symbol*] [*Library of Congress*] (LCLS) .... OBatH
Clermont-Ferrand [*France*] [*Airport symbol*] (OAG) .... CFE
Clermont-Ferrand [*France*] [*Seismograph station code, US Geological Survey*] (SEIS) .... CFF
Clermont-Ferrand/Aulnat [*France*] [*ICAO location identifier*] (ICLI) .... LFLC
CLEU Library, British Columbia Ministry of Attorney General, Victoria, British Columbia [*Library symbol*] [*National Library of Canada*] (NLC) .... BVIAGC
Cleve [*Australia*] [*Seismograph station code, US Geological Survey*] (SEIS) CLV
Cleve Trust Realty SBI [*NASDAQ symbol*] (TTSB) .... CTRIS
Cleveland [*Ohio*] [*Airport symbol*] .... CLE
Cleveland [*Ohio*] [*Seismograph station code, US Geological Survey*] (SEIS) .... CLE
Cleveland [*District in Yorkshire, England*] (ROG) .... CLEV
Cleveland (BARN) .... Cleve
Cleveland (BARN) CLV
Cleveland [*Branch in the Federal Reserve regional banking system*] (BARN) .... D
Cleveland [*Postcode*] (ODBW) .... TS
Cleveland Area Interlibrary Network (SAUS) .... CAIN
Cleveland Area Metropolitan Library System [*Library network*] .... CAMLS

Cleveland Bay Association of America [*Later, Cleveland Bay Society of America*] (EA) ... CBAA
Cleveland Bay Association of America (SAUO) ... CBAA
Cleveland Bay Horse Society of America (EA) ... CBHSA
Cleveland Bay Horse Society of North America (NTPA) ... CBHSNA
Cleveland Bay Society of America (EA) ... CBSA
Cleveland Browns [*National Football League*] [*1999-present*] (NFLA) ... CIB
Cleveland Browns [*National Football League*] [*1950-95*] (NFLA) ... Cle
Cleveland [*Ohio*] **Burke Lakefront** [*Airport symbol*] (OAG) ... BKL
Cleveland, Cincinnati, Chicago & St. Louis Railway ... CCC & StL
Cleveland, Cincinnati, Chicago and St. Louis Railway (SAUO) ... CCC&StLR
Cleveland, Cincinnati, Chicago & St. Louis Railway [*AAR code*] ... CCCL
Cleveland Cliffs, Inc. Holding Co. [*NYSE symbol*] (SAG) ... CLF
Cleveland Cliffs, Inc. Holding Co. [*Associated Press*] (SAG) ... ClvClf
Cleveland Clinic Educational Foundation, Cleveland, OH [*Library symbol*] [*Library of Congress*] (LCLS) ... OCIC
Cleveland Clinic Foundation (SAUO) ... CCF
Cleveland Clinic Journal of Medicine (SAUS) ... CCJM
Cleveland Clinic Quarterly (journ.) (SAUS) ... Cleve Clin Quart
Cleveland Contract Management District (SAUS) ... CLCMD
Cleveland County Memorial Library, Shelby, NC [*Library symbol*] [*Library of Congress*] (LCLS) ... NcSh
Cleveland County Technical Institute, Shelby, NC [*Library symbol*] [*Library of Congress*] (LCLS) ... NcShC
Cleveland Crane + Engineering S.A. (SAUO) ... CC+E
Cleveland Department of Water (SAUO) ... CDW
Cleveland Diesel Engine Division [*GM Corp.*] ... CDED
Cleveland Elec Ill $7.56 Pfd [*NYSE symbol*] (TTSB) ... CVXPrB
Cleveland Elec Ill Adj L Pfd [*NYSE symbol*] (TTSB) ... CVXPrL
Cleveland Elec Ill'93 Sr'A'Dep Pfd [*NYSE symbol*] (TTSB) ... CVXPrT
Cleveland Electric Illuminating Co. (SAUO) ... CEI
Cleveland Electric Illuminating Co. [*Associated Press*] (SAG) ... ClvEl
Cleveland Electric Illuminating Co. [*NYSE symbol*] (SAG) ... CVX
Cleveland Electronic Conference (SAUS) ... CECON
Cleveland Elementary School, Fergus Falls, MN [*Library symbol*] [*Library of Congress*] (LCLS) ... MnFfCE
Cleveland Engineering Society (SAUO) ... CES
Cleveland, GA [*FM radio station call letters*] ... WAZX
Cleveland, GA [*AM radio station call letters*] ... WRWH
Cleveland Graphite [*American Cleveland Graphite Corp.*] [*Automotive parts supplier*] ... CLEVITE
Cleveland Health Museum (SAUS) ... CHM
Cleveland Health Sciences Library (SAUO) ... CHSL
Cleveland Health Sciences Library, Cleveland, OH [*OCLC symbol*] (OCLC) ... CHS
Cleveland Heights, OH [*AM radio station call letters*] ... WJMO
Cleveland Heights, OH [*FM radio station call letters*] ... WZJM
Cleveland Heights-University Heights Public Library, Cleveland Heights, OH [*Library symbol*] [*Library of Congress*] (LCLS) ... OClh
Cleveland Heights-University Heights Public Library, Cleveland Heights, OH [*OCLC symbol*] (OCLC) ... OZC
Cleveland Hockey Booster Club (EA) ... CHBC
Cleveland Industrial Archaeology Society (SAUO) ... CIAS
Cleveland Institute of Art, Cleveland, OH [*OCLC symbol*] (OCLC) ... OAC
Cleveland Institute of Art, Cleveland, OH [*Library symbol*] [*Library of Congress*] (LCLS) ... OCISA
Cleveland Institute of Electronics [*Ohio*] ... CIE
Cleveland Institute of Engineers (SAUO) ... CIE
Cleveland Institute of Music [*Record label*] ... CIM
Cleveland Institute of Music, Cleveland, OH [*Library symbol*] [*Library of Congress*] (LCLS) ... OCICIM
Cleveland International Program for Youth Leaders and Social Workers (SAUO) ... CIP
Cleveland Law Record [*Ohio*] [*A publication*] (DLA) ... Cleve Law Rec
Cleveland Law Record [*Ohio*] [*A publication*] (DLA) ... Cleve L Rec
Cleveland Law Record [*Ohio*] [*A publication*] (DLA) ... Cleve L Rec (Ohio)
Cleveland Law Record [*Ohio*] [*A publication*] (DLA) ... Clev L Rec
Cleveland Law Record [*Ohio*] [*A publication*] (DLA) ... CLR
Cleveland Law Record [*Ohio*] [*A publication*] (DLA) ... CL Rec
Cleveland Law Register [*Ohio*] [*A publication*] (DLA) ... Cleve Law Reg
Cleveland Law Register [*Ohio*] [*A publication*] (DLA) ... Cleve L Reg
Cleveland Law Register [*Ohio*] [*A publication*] (DLA) ... Cleve L Reg (Ohio)
Cleveland Law Register [*Ohio*] [*A publication*] (DLA) ... Clev L Reg
Cleveland Law Register [*Ohio*] [*A publication*] (DLA) ... CL Reg
Cleveland Law Reporter [*Ohio*] [*A publication*] (DLA) ... Cleve Law R
Cleveland Law Reporter [*Ohio*] [*A publication*] (DLA) ... Cleve Law Rep
Cleveland Law Reporter [*Ohio*] [*A publication*] (DLA) ... Cleve L Rep
Cleveland Law Reporter [*Ohio*] [*A publication*] (DLA) ... Clev L Rep
Cleveland Law Reporter [*Ohio*] [*A publication*] (DLA) ... CL Rep
Cleveland Law Reporter (Ohio) [*A publication*] (ILCA) ... Cleve LR (Ohio)
Cleveland Law Reporter (Reprint) [*Ohio*] [*A publication*] (DLA) ... Cleve Rep
Cleveland Law Reporter (Reprint) [*Ohio*] [*A publication*] (DLA) ... Clev Law Rep
Cleveland Law Reporter (Reprint) [*Ohio*] [*A publication*] (DLA) ... Clev R
Cleveland Marshall Law School (SAUS) ... CMLS
Cleveland Metal Abrasive Co. (SAUO) ... CMA
Cleveland Metropolitan General Hospital, Cleveland, OH [*Library symbol*] [*Library of Congress*] (LCLS) ... OCIMGH
Cleveland, MS [*Location identifier*] [*FAA*] (FAAL) ... RNV
Cleveland, MS [*AM radio station call letters*] ... WCLD
Cleveland, MS [*AM radio station call letters*] (RBYB) ... WCLD-AM
Cleveland, MS [*FM radio station call letters*] ... WCLD-FM
Cleveland, MS [*FM radio station call letters*] ... WDFX
Cleveland, MS [*AM radio station call letters*] (RBYB) ... WDSK
Cleveland, MS [*FM radio station call letters*] ... WDTL
Cleveland, MS [*Television station call letters*] (BROA) ... WMAI
Cleveland, MS [*FM radio station call letters*] ... WMJW
Cleveland Museum of Art (SAUO) ... CMA
Cleveland Museum of Art, Cleveland, OH [*Library symbol*] [*Library of Congress*] (LCLS) ... OCIMA
Cleveland Museum of Natural History (SAUO) ... CMNH
Cleveland Museum of Natural History, Cleveland, OH [*Library symbol*] [*Library of Congress*] (LCLS) ... OCIMN
Cleveland National Forest (SAUS) ... CNF
Cleveland National Park (SAUS) ... CNP
Cleveland, Oberlin [*Ohio*] [*ICAO location identifier*] (ICLI) ... KZOB
Cleveland, OH [*Location identifier*] [*FAA*] (FAAL) ... BFT
Cleveland, OH [*Location identifier*] [*FAA*] (FAAL) ... CEE
Cleveland, OH [*Location identifier*] [*FAA*] (FAAL) ... CGF
Cleveland, OH [*Location identifier*] [*FAA*] (FAAL) ... DJB
Cleveland, OH [*Location identifier*] [*FAA*] (FAAL) ... HPI
Cleveland, OH [*Location identifier*] [*FAA*] (FAAL) ... LVJ
Cleveland, OH [*Location identifier*] [*FAA*] (FAAL) ... SQF
Cleveland, OH [*AM radio station call letters*] ... WABQ
Cleveland, OH [*FM radio station call letters*] ... WCLV
Cleveland, OH [*FM radio station call letters*] ... WCPN
Cleveland, OH [*FM radio station call letters*] ... WCRF
Cleveland, OH [*FM radio station call letters*] ... WCSB
Cleveland, OH [*FM radio station call letters*] ... WDOK
Cleveland, OH [*FM radio station call letters*] ... WENZ
Cleveland, OH [*AM radio station call letters*] ... WERE
Cleveland, OH [*Television station call letters*] ... WEWS
Cleveland, OH [*Television station call letters*] (BROA) ... WEWS-DT
Cleveland, OH [*FM radio station call letters*] ... WGAR
Cleveland, OH [*AM radio station call letters*] ... WHK
Cleveland, OH [*Television station call letters*] ... WJW
Cleveland, OH [*AM radio station call letters*] ... WKNR
Cleveland, OH [*Television station call letters*] ... WKYC
Cleveland, OH [*Television station call letters*] (BROA) ... WKYC-DT
Cleveland, OH [*FM radio station call letters*] ... WLTF
Cleveland, OH [*AM radio station call letters*] (RBYB) ... WMIH
Cleveland, OH [*FM radio station call letters*] ... WMJI
Cleveland, OH [*FM radio station call letters*] ... WMMS
Cleveland, OH [*FM radio station call letters*] (BROA) ... WMVX-FM
Cleveland, OH [*FM radio station call letters*] ... WNCX
Cleveland, OH [*FM radio station call letters*] ... WQAL
Cleveland, OH [*Television station call letters*] ... WQHS
Cleveland, OH [*AM radio station call letters*] ... WRMR
Cleveland, OH [*FM radio station call letters*] ... WRUW
Cleveland, OH [*AM radio station call letters*] (RBYB) ... WTAM-AM
Cleveland, OH [*Television station call letters*] ... WVIZ
Cleveland, OH [*AM radio station call letters*] ... WWWE
Cleveland, OH [*FM radio station call letters*] ... WZAK
Cleveland, OH [*Location identifier*] [*FAA*] (FAAL) ... ZOB
Cleveland, OK [*Location identifier*] [*FAA*] (FAAL) ... EVL
Cleveland Open Cup [*Flash point determination*] ... COC
Cleveland Plain Dealer (SAUS) ... PD
Cleveland Procurement District (SAUS) ... CLEVPDIS
Cleveland Public Library (SAUS) ... CPL
Cleveland Public Library (SAUS) ... Ocl
Cleveland Public Library (SAUS) ... Tcle
Cleveland Public Library, Cleveland, OH [*OCLC symbol*] (OCLC) ... CLE
Cleveland Public Library, Cleveland, OH [*Library symbol*] [*Library of Congress*] (LCLS) ... OCl
Cleveland Public Library, Cleveland, TN [*Library symbol*] [*Library of Congress*] (LCLS) ... TCle
Cleveland Public [*Charles O. Austin Memorial*] **Library, Cleveland, TX** [*Library symbol*] [*Library of Congress*] (LCLS) ... TxClv
Cleveland Rams [*National Football League*] [*1937-45*] (NFLA) ... CIR
Cleveland Regional Sewer District (SAUS) ... CRSD
Cleveland School of Welding (SAUO) ... CSW
Cleveland Scientific and Technical Institution (SAUO) ... CSTI
Cleveland Society of Professional Engineers (SAUO) ... CSPE
Cleveland State Community College (SAUS) ... TC1eC
Cleveland State Community College, Cleveland, TN [*Library symbol*] [*Library of Congress*] (LCLS) ... TCleC
Cleveland State Law Journal [*A publication*] (DLA) ... Cleveland SLJ
Cleveland State University (GAGS) ... Cleve St U
Cleveland State University, Cleveland, OH [*OCLC symbol*] (OCLC) ... CSU
Cleveland State University, Cleveland, OH [*Library symbol*] [*Library of Congress*] (LCLS) ... OCIU
Cleveland Teachers' Union ... CTU
Cleveland, TN [*Location identifier*] [*FAA*] (FAAL) ... HDI
Cleveland, TN [*FM radio station call letters*] ... WALV
Cleveland, TN [*AM radio station call letters*] ... WBAC
Cleveland, TN [*AM radio station call letters*] ... WCLE
Cleveland, TN [*Television station call letters*] ... WFLI
Cleveland, TN [*FM radio station call letters*] ... WUSY
Cleveland Transport Action Program (SAUO) ... CTAP
Cleveland Trust Co. ... CTC
Cleveland, TX [*FM radio station call letters*] (BROA) ... KKTL-FM
Cleveland, TX [*FM radio station call letters*] (RBYB) ... KOND-FM
Cleveland, WI [*FM radio station call letters*] ... WKTT
Cleveland/Cleveland-Hopkins International [*Ohio*] [*ICAO location identifier*] (ICLI) ... KCLE
Cleveland-Cliffs [*NYSE symbol*] (TTSB) ... CLF
Cleveland-Cliffs, Inc. [*NYSE symbol*] (SPSG) ... CLF
Cleveland-Cliffs, Inc. [*Associated Press*] (SAG) ... ClvClf
Cleveland-Cliffs Iron Co. (SAUO) ... CLF
Cleveland-Columbus-Cincinnati Highway (SAUS) ... CCC Highway
ClevelandElec $7.40 cm A Pfd [*NYSE symbol*] (TTSB) ... CVXPr

Cleveland-Marshall College of Law, Cleveland, OH [*OCLC symbol*]
(OCLC) .... LMC
Cleveland-Marshall College of Law, Cleveland State University, Cleveland,
OH [*Library symbol*] [*Library of Congress*] (LCLS) .... OCIU-L
Clevenger's Medical Jurisprudence of Insanity [*A publication*]
(DLA) .... Clev Insan
Clever Fellows Innovation Consortium .... CFIC
Cleverness Factor [*Psychology*] C
Cleverness Factor (SAUS) .... C Factor
Clevetrust Realty [*NASDAQ symbol*] (SAG) .... CTRI
Clevetrust Realty Investors [*Associated Press*] (SAG) .... ClevtRt
Clevis [*Metal shackle*] (KSC) CLV
Clewiston, FL [*AM radio station call letters*] .... WAFC
Clewiston, FL [*FM radio station call letters*] .... WAFC-FM
Cliche Verre (VRA) .... CLVR
Click Commerce [*NASDAQ symbol*] .... CKCM
Click2Send Safe Deposit Box [*Digital storage*] .... CSDB
Client (DHP) CL
Client (ROG) .... CLT
Client Access License (SAUS) .... CAL
Client Access to Systems and Services (SAUS) .... CLASS
Client Application Enabler (SAUS) .... CAE
Client Assessment Package (SAUS) .... CAP
Client Assistance Program [*Department of Education*] [*Department of Health
and Human Services*] (GFGA) .... CAP
Client Behavior Inventory [*Psychology*] (AEBS) .... CBI
Client Information Control System (ECII) .... CICS
Client Information Server (SAUS) .... CIS
Client Information System (SAUS) .... CIS
Client Liaison Officer .... CLO
Client Library Interface (SAUS) CLI
Client Oriented Data Acquisition Program (DHP) .... CODAP
Client Owned and Maintained (ECII) .... COAM
Client Server Architecture (CDE) .... CSA
Client Service Agent (OSI) .... CSA
Client Services Review [*Australia*] .... CSR
Client-Centered Counseling Progress Record [*Psychology*] ...... CCCPR
Client-Employee Management Information System (MHDB) ..... CEMIS
Client-Oriented Data Acquisition Process [*FDA*] .... CODAP
Clients Lifetime Advisory Service Program [*Insurance*] .... CLASP
Client/Server [*Computer science*] (VERA) .... CS
Client-Server Application Development Environment (SAUS) .... CADE
Client-Server Environment (SAUS) .... CSE
Client-Server Interface [*Computer science*] (CIST) .... CSI
Client/Server Open Development Environment [*Computer architecture*]
(PCM) .... CODE
Client-Server Systems Management (SAUS) .... CSSM
Client-Server-System (SAUS) .... CSS
Client-Systems Computer Access Networks (SAUS) .... C-SCANS
Client-To-Client-Protocol (SAUS) .... CTCP
CLIF Commonwealth Land Information Forum (SAUS) .... CLI-COM
Cliff (ROG) C
Cliff .... CLF
Cliff [*Commonly used*] (OPSA) .... CLIFF
Cliff Leader [*British military*] (DMA) CL
Cliff Resources Corp. [*Toronto Stock Exchange symbol*] .... CFK
Cliff Richard Fan Club of America (EA) .... CRFCA
Cliff Richard Movement - USA [*Later, CRFCA*] (EA) .... CRM-USA
Clifford and Richard's English Locus Standi Reports [*1873-84*]
[*A publication*] (DLA) .... C & R
Clifford and Richard's English Locus Standi Reports [*1873-84*]
[*A publication*] (DLA) .... Clif & R
Clifford and Richard's English Locus Standi Reports [*1873-84*]
[*A publication*] (DLA) .... Clif & Rich
Clifford and Richard's English Locus Standi Reports [*1873-84*]
[*A publication*] (DLA) .... Cliff & Rich
Clifford and Stephens' English Locus Standi Reports [*1867-72*]
[*A publication*] (DLA) .... C & S
Clifford and Stephens' English Locus Standi Reports [*1867-72*]
[*A publication*] (DLA) .... Clif & St
Clifford and Stephens' English Locus Standi Reports [*1867-72*]
[*A publication*] (DLA) .... Clif & Steph
Clifford and Stephens' English Locus Standi Reports [*1867-72*]
[*A publication*] (DLA) .... Cliff & Steph
Clifford and Stephens' English Locus Standi Reports, Appendix
[*A publication*] (ILCA) .... C & S App
Clifford & Wills [*Commercial firm*] .... CW
Clifford, Arlington, Buckingham, Ashley, Lauderdale [*Ministers of Charles II
of England*] [*Some claim that the word "cabal" is derived from this acronym;
others, that it comes from the Hebrew "cabala"*] .... CABAL
Clifford's English Southwick Election Cases [*1796-97*] [*A publication*]
(DLA) .... Clif El
Clifford's English Southwick Election Cases [*1796-97*] [*A publication*]
(DLA) .... Clif El Cas
Clifford's English Southwick Election Cases [*1796-97*] [*A publication*]
(DLA) .... Cliff
Clifford's English Southwick Election Cases [*1796-97*] [*A publication*]
(DLA) .... Cliff El Cas
Clifford's English Southwick Election Cases [*1796-97*] [*A publication*]
(DLA) .... Clif South El
Clifford's English Southwick Election Cases [*1796-97*] [*A publication*]
(DLA) .... Clif South El Cas
Clifford's Probate Guide [*A publication*] (DLA) .... Clif Prob
Clifford's United States Circuit Court Reports, First Circuit [*A publication*]
(DLA) .... Clif

Clifford's United States Circuit Court Reports, First Circuit [*A publication*]
(DLA) .... Cliff
Clifford's United States Circuit Court Reports, First Circuit [*A publication*]
(DLA) .... Cliff (CC)
Cliffs (MCD) .... CLFS
Cliffs [*Commonly used*] (OPSA) .... CLIFFS
Cliffs Drilling [*NASDAQ symbol*] (TTSB) .... CLDR
Cliffs Drilling Co. [*NASDAQ symbol*] (NQ) .... CLDR
Cliffs Drilling Co. (MHDW) .... CLDRV
Cliffs Drilling Co. [*Associated Press*] (SAG) .... ClfDr
Cliffs Drilling Co. [*Associated Press*] (SAG) .... ClifDr
Cliffside [*Montana*] [*Seismograph station code, US Geological Survey*]
[*Closed*] (SEIS) .... CFM
Cliffside Park Public Library, Cliffside Park, NJ [*Library symbol*] [*Library of
Congress*] (LCLS) .... NjClp
Cliffside Railroad Co. [*AAR code*] .... CLIF
Clifton Assessment Procedures for the Elderly [*Personality development
test*] [*Psychology*] .... CAPE
Clifton, AZ [*AM radio station call letters*] .... KCUZ
Clifton, AZ [*FM radio station call letters*] (RBYB) .... KWRQ
Clifton Elementary School, Clifton, CO [*Library symbol*] [*Library of
Congress*] (LCLS) .... CoCfCfE
Clifton Forge, VA [*AM radio station call letters*] .... WXCF
Clifton Forge, VA [*FM radio station call letters*] .... WXCF-FM
Clifton Herbarium [*British*] .... CFN
Clifton Hills [*Australia*] [*Airport symbol*] [*Obsolete*] (OAG) ...... CFH
Clifton Independent Prospector, Clifton, NJ [*Library symbol*] [*Library of
Congress*] (LCLS) .... NjClifl
Clifton Leader, Clifton, NJ [*Library symbol*] [*Library of Congress*] (LCLS) ..... NjClifL
Clifton Park, NY [*FM radio station call letters*] (BROA) .... WDCD-FM
Clifton Park, NY [*FM radio station call letters*] .... WWCP
Clifton Precision Products Co. Inc. (SAUO) .... CPPC
Clifton Public Library, Clifton, NJ [*Library symbol*] [*Library of Congress*]
(LCLS) .... NjClif
Clifton Publishing Co., Clifton, NJ [*Library symbol*] [*Library of Congress*]
(LCLS) .... NjClifP
Clifton Resources Ltd. [*Vancouver Stock Exchange symbol*] .... CLF
Clifton Shakespeare Society (SAUO) .... CSS
Clifton Star Resources, Inc. [*Vancouver Stock Exchange symbol*] ...... CFD
Clifton, TX [*FM radio station call letters*] .... KWOW
Clifton-Essex-Franklin Library [*Library network*] .... C-E-F L
Clifton-Morenci, AZ [*Location identifier*] [*FAA*] (FAAL) .... CFT
Clift's Entries [*1719*] [*England*] [*A publication*] (DLA) .... Clift
Clima Commerce International (SAUO) CCI
Climate (SAUS) .... CLIM
Climate .... CLIMAT
Climate - Altitude Chamber .... CAC
Climate Action Network [*An alliance of groups that includes Greenpeace, the
World Wide Fund for Nature, and The Natural Resources Defense
Council*] .... CAN
Climate Air-Sea Interaction Drifter (SAUS) .... CASID
Climate Alert Bulletin (SAUS) .... BAC
Climate Analysis Center [*National Weather Service*] .... CAC
Climate Analysis Section (SAUS) .... CAS
Climate and Environmental Data Retrieval and Archive (SAUO) ...... CERA
Climate and Global Change .... CGC
Climate and Global Change Impacts of the Maghreb Countries
(SAUS) .... CLIMAGH
Climate and Global Change Program (USDC) .... C&GC
Climate and Global Change Program [*National Oceanic and Atmospheric
Administration*] (USDC) .... CGCP
Climate and Global Dynamics Division (SAUS) .... CGD
Climate and Globe Change Program [*Marine science*] (OSRA) ...... C&GC
Climate and Remote Sensing Group [*University of California, San Diego*]
[*Research center*] (RCD) .... CARS
Climate Applications Project (SAUS) .... CLIMAP
Climate Applications Referral System (CARB) .... CARS
Climate Assessment Data Base [*National Meteorological Center*]
[*Database*] .... CADB
Climate Assistance Service (SAUS) .... CLASS
Climate Change Action Fund (SAUO) .... CCAF
Climate Change Action Plan [*Environmental Protection Agency*] (EPAT) .... CCAP
Climate Change and Carrying Capacity (SAUS) .... CCCC PICES-GLOBEC
Climate Change Detection Project [*Marine science*] (OSRA) .... CCDP
Climate Change Experiment (SAUS) .... CLIMEX
Climate Change Information Exchange CCIX
Climate Change Information Exchange Programme (SAUS) ...... CCInfo
Climate Change Training Programme (SAUS) .... CCTrain
Climate Computing [*Marine science*] (OSRA) .... CLICOM
Climate Computing Project (SAUS) .... CLICOM
Climate Control International [*Auto industry supplier*] CCI
Climate Data Assimilation System (SAUS) .... CDAS
Climate Data Referral System (SAUS) .... INFOCLIMA
Climate Data Service for West Africa [*Marine science*] (OSRA) ..... WACLIM
Climate Diagnostics Center [*Environmental Research Laboratories*]
(USDC) .... CDC
Climate Diagnostics Center Laboratory (SAUO) .... CDCL
Climate Dynamics (SAUS) .... Clim Dyn
Climate Dynamics and Experimental Prediction (SAUS) .... CDEP
Climate Impact and Response Strategies Network (SAUS) ...... CIRSNet
Climate Impact Assessment Division [*National Enviromental Satellite, Data,
and Information Service*] (USDC) .... CIAD
Climate Impact Assessment Program (SAUS) .... CIAP
Climate Impacts Assessment and Management Program for
Commonwealth Countries (SAUO) .... COMCIAM

Climate Impacts Centre (SAUO) CIC
Climate Information and Prediction Services (SAUO) .... CLIPS
Climate Interest Group (GEOI) .... CIG
Climate Inventory and Catalog (SAUO) CLIC
Climate: Long-Range Investigation, Mapping, and Prediction [National Science Foundation] .... CLIMAP
Climate Mapping (SAUS) .... CLIMAP
Climate Modeling and Analysis Program (SAUS) .... CMAP
Climate Modeling Experiment (SAUS) .... CME
Climate Modeling Prediction (USDC) .... CLIMAP
Climate Modeling Section (SAUS) .... CMS
Climate Modeling Programme (SAUO) .... CMP
Climate Monitoring and Diagnostics Laboratory [National Oceanic and Atmospheric Administration] .... CMDL
Climate Monitoring Bulletin (SAUO) .... CMB
Climate Observing System Fund (SAUS) .... COSF
Climate (or Climatic) Impact Assessment Program (SAUO) .... CIAP
Climate Pay [British military] (DMA) .... CP
Climate Prediction Center .... CPC
Climate Research (SAUS) .... Clim Res
Climate Research Centre (SAUO) .... CRC
Climate Research Committee (CARB) .... CRC
Climate Research Data Center [Project] [Marine science] (OSRA) .... CRDC
Climate Research Data Tools (USDC) .... CRDtools
Climate Research Data Tools [Marine science] (OSRA) .... CRDTools
Climate Research Institute [Oklahoma State University] (CARB) .... CRI
Climate Research Program (SAUO) .... CRP
Climate Research Project [Boulder, CO] [Department of Commerce] (GRD) .... CRP
Climate Sensitivity and CO2 Research Group (SAUO) .... CSCORG
Climate Services (SAUO) .... CS
Climate Simulation Laboratory (ARMP) .... CSL
Climate Simulation Laboratory Allocation Panel (SAUS) .... CSLAP
Climate System Laboratory (SAUS) .... CSL
Climate System Model (SAUS) .... CSM
Climate System Modeling Program (SAUS) .... CSMP
Climate System Monitoring [Marine science] (OSRA) .... CSM
Climate Systems Modeling and Information Program (SAUS) .... CSMIP
Climate Systems Modeling Initiative (SAUS) .... CSMI
Climate Test Chamber .... CTC
Climate Variability .... CLIVAR
Climate Variability and Predictability (ARMP) .... CLIVAR
Climate Variability and Predictability Study .... CLIVAR
Climate Variability and Prediction [Program] [Marine science] (OSRA) .... CLIVAR
Climate Variability and Prediction Research Programme (SAUO) .... CLIVAR
Climate Variability Study (SAUS) .... CLIVAR
Climate, Vegetation, Productivity .... CVP
Climate-Hydrology-Ecosystems Interrelations in Mountainous Regions (SAUS) .... CHESMO
Climates and Environments of the Last Interglacial in the Arctic (SAUS) .... CELIA
Climates of the Past (SAUS) .... CLIP
Climates of the States [A publication] .... C of S
Climatic .... Clim
Climatic (AFM) .... CLIM
Climatic Change (SAUS) .... Clim Chang
Climatic Data Analysis Program .... CDAP
Climatic Data for the World [A publication] .... W
Climatic Data for the World (journ.) (SAUS) .... W
Climatic Extremes of the Past (SAUO) .... CLIMEX
Climatic Impact Assessment Program [for high altitude aircraft] .... CIAP
Climatic Impact Committee [National Academy of Sciences - National Academy of Engineering] CIC
Climatic Impacts Centre CIC
Climatic Implications of Atmospheric Pollution .... CIAP
Climatic Laboratory [Military] CL
Climatic Laboratory Instrumentation System (MCD) .... CLINS
Climatic Mapping of Australia and New Zealand (SAUS) .... CLIMANZ
Climatic Research Unit .... CRU
Climatic Variation Analysis (SAUS) .... CVA
Climatic Wind Tunnel [Automotive testing] .... CWT
Climatographer (SAUS) .... Cltgr
Climatological (SAUS) .... Climat
Climatological (SAUS) .... Cltgl
Climatological (AABC) .... CLTGL
Climatological Aerological Reference Data Set (SAUS) .... CARDS
Climatological and Historical Analysis of Clouds for Environmental Simulations (SAUO) .... CHANCES
Climatological Data (EEVL) .... CD
Climatological Data, National Summary (NOAA) .... CDNS
Climatological Data Sheet [Air Force] .... CDS
Climatological Dispersion Model [Environmental Protection Agency] (GFGA) .... CDM
Climatological Dispersion Model with Calibration and Source Contribution (SAUO) .... CDMQC
Climatological Prediction by Model Statistics (SAUS) .... CPMS
Climatologist (SAUS) .... Climat
Climatology .... CLIMATOL
Climatology and Persistence .... CLIPER
Climatology Mission Success Indicators (MCD) .... CMSI
Climax Mine [Nevada] [Seismograph station code, US Geological Survey] [Closed] (SEIS) .... NYM
Climax Molybdenum Co., Technical Library, Climax, CO [Library symbol] [Library of Congress] (LCLS) .... CoCxC
Climax Public Library, Climax, MN [Library symbol] [Library of Congress] (LCLS) .... MnClim

Climax Stock Quartz Monsonite (SAUS) .... CSQM
Climax-Shelly School, Climax, MN [Library symbol] [Library of Congress] (LCLS) .... MnClimS
Climb (FAAC) .... CLB
Climb [or Climbing] [Aviation] (FAAC) .... CMB
Climb and Cross [Aviation] (FAAC) .... CATX
Climb and Cruise [Aviation] (FAAC) .... CCRZ
Climb at Pilot's Discretion [Aviation] (FAAC) .... CAPD
Climb Detent of the Thrust Levers (GAVI) .... CLB
Climb en Route [Aviation] (FAAC) .... CER
Climb Enroute (SAUS) .... CER
Climb Immediately [Aviation] (FAAC) .... CLBI
Climb on Course [Aviation] (FAAC) .... COC
Climb so as to Cross (SAUS) .... CSATC
Climb So as to Cross [Aviation] (FAAC) .... CSATX
Climb So as to Reach [Aviation] (FAAC) .... CSATR
Climb to and Cross [Aviation] (FAAC) .... CTAX
Climb to and Maintain [Aviation] (FAAC) .... CTAM
Climb Well to Right [Aviation] (FAAC) .... CWTR
Climb Well to Right of Course [Aviation] (FAAC) .... CWRC
Climbing Fiber [Cytology] .... CF
Climbing Power (SAUS) .... CL Pow
Climbing Sport (SAUO) CC
Clin-Byla [France] [Research code symbol] .... CB
Clin-Byla [France] [Research code symbol] .... FH
Clincal (CMD) .... Clin
Clinch River Breeder Reactor .... CRBR
Clinch River Breeder Reactor Plant [Department of Energy] .... CRBRP
Clinch River Breeder Reactor Program Office [Nuclear Regulatory Commission] (GFGA) .... CRBRPO
Clinch River Breeder Reactor Project [Department of Energy] (NUCP) .... CRBRP
Clinch River Mile [Energy Research and Development Administration] .... CRM
Clinch Valley College of the University of Virginia, Wise, VA [OCLC symbol] (OCLC) VCV
Clinch Valley College of the University of Virginia, Wise, VA [Library symbol] [Library of Congress] (LCLS) .... ViWisC
Clinchco, VA [AM radio station call letters] .... WDIC
Clinchco, VA [FM radio station call letters] .... WDIC-FM
Clinchfield Railroad (SAUO) .... CRR
Clinchfield Railroad Co. [AAR code] .... CCO
Clinchfield Railroad Company (SAUO) .... CCO
Clindamycin [Antibacterial compound] CC
Cline Development Corp. [Vancouver Stock Exchange symbol] .... CND
Cling Peach Advisory Board (SAUO) .... CPAG
Clinic CI
Clinic [Medicine] (WDAA) .... CLIN
Clinic .... CLNC
Clinic Without Walls (ADWA) .... CWW
Clinical .... CLIN
Clinical (ADWA) .... clin
Clinical .... CLINIC
Clinical Academic Staff Salaries Committee [Committee of Vice Chancellors and Principals] (AIE) .... CASSC
Clinical Administrative Data Service (ADWA) .... CADS
Clinical Analysis Questionnaire .... CAQ
Clinical Anatomy Interactive Lesson (SAUO) .... CLASS
Clinical and Administrative Record [System] .... CARE
Clinical and Administrative Record System (SAUS) .... CARE System
Clinical and Administrative Research (SAUS) .... CARE
Clinical and Diagnostic Laboratory Immunology (SAUS) .... CDLI
Clinical and Experimental Immunology (journ.) (SAUS) .... Clin Exp Immunol
Clinical and Experimental Pharmacology and Physiology (SAUS) .... Clin Exp Pharmacol Physiol
Clinical and Investigative Medicine (SAUS) .... CIM
Clinical Applications and Prevention Program [Bethesda, MD] [National Heart, Lung, and Blood Institute] [Department of Health and Human Services] (GRD) .... CAPP
Clinical Articulation Profile [Speech evaluation test] .... CAP
Clinical Assessment of the Reliability of the Examination (SAUO) .... CARE
Clinical Attending, Psychiatry Clerkship (SAUS) .... CAPC
Clinical Behavior Therapy Review [A publication] .... CBTR
Clinical Breast Examination [Medicine] (DMAA) .... CBE
Clinical Bulletin of Myofascial Therapy [A publication] (ADWA) .... CBMT
Clinical Care Management System [Medicine] (DMAA) .... CCMS
Clinical Center [National Institutes of Health] (GRD) CC
Clinical Center Blood Bank .... CCBB
Clinical Chemistry (MEC) .... Clin Chem
Clinical Chemistry Data Communication Group (SAUO) .... CCDCG
Clinical Chemistry (journ.) (SAUS) .... Clin Chem
Clinical Chemistry Lookout [Medical Information Centre] [Defunct] [Information service or system] (CRD) CCL
Clinical Computing Limited (SAUO) CCL
Clinical Course [Medicine] CC
Clinical Cytometry Society (SAUO) .... CCS
Clinical Data Abstraction Center [Medicine] (DMAA) .... CDAC
Clinical Data Acquisition System (SAUS) .... CLDAS
Clinical Death (MELL) .... CD
Clinical Death (SAUS) .... CLIN/D
Clinical Decision Making [Medicine] (DMAA) .... CDM
Clinical Decision Support System (MAE) .... CDSS
Clinical Dementia Rating .... CDR
Clinical Ecological Illness (MELL) .... CEI
Clinical Education and Assessment Center [Medicine] (DMAA) .... CEAC
Clinical Efficacy Assessment Project [Medicine] (DMAA) .... CEAP
Clinical Emphysema [Medicine] (MAE) .... CE

Clinical Evaluation Exercise [*Medicine*] (DMAA) .... CEX
Clinical Evaluation of Language Functions [*Speech evaluation test*] .... CELF
Clinical Experience Abstracts (SAUS) .... CEA
Clinical Fellow Year (BARN) .... CFY
Clinical Full-Time [*Medicine*] (MAE) .... CFT
Clinical Gene Therapy Branch .... CGTB
Clinical General Impression [*Psychiatric testing*] .... CGI
Clinical Genetical Society [*British*] .... CGS
Clinical Global Impression (SAUS) .... CGI
Clinical Global Impression of Change .... CGIC
Clinical Global Impression [*Scale*] PY (DAVI) .... CGI
Clinical Hyaline Membrane Disease [*Medicine*] (AAMN) .... CHMD
Clinical Immunology Society (EA) .... CIS
Clinical Infectious Diseases (SAUO) .... CID
Clinical Information (SAUS) .... CLINFO
Clinical Information Access Project (SAUO) .... CIAP
Clinical Information System (MCD) .... CIS
Clinical Information Was Not Provided [*Medicine*] .... CIWNP
Clinical Investigation [*Medicine*] (MAE) CI
Clinical Investigation Center [*Oakland, CA*] CIC
Clinical Investigation Control Center [*Military*] (DNAB) CICC
Clinical Investigation Program (SAUO) .... CIP
Clinical Journal [*A publication*] (ROG) .... CLIN JL
Clinical Laboratory (DAVI) CL
Clinical Laboratory Assistant (American Society of Clinical Pathologists) (DAVI) .... CLA(ASCP)
Clinical Laboratory Automated System (PDAA) .... CLAS
Clinical Laboratory Data Acquisition System (SAUS) .... CLADS
Clinical Laboratory Data Acquisition System [*Computer science*] .... CLDAS
Clinical Laboratory for Evaluation and Assessment of Noxious Substances [*Environmental Protection Agency*] (GFGA) .... CLEANS
Clinical Laboratory for Evaluation and Validation of Epidemiologic Research [*Environmental Protection Agency*] (GFGA) .... CLEVER
Clinical Laboratory Improvement Act (CLIA) .... CLIA
Clinical Laboratory Improvement Amendments of 1988 .... CLIA
Clinical Laboratory Management Association (EA) .... CLMA
Clinical Laboratory Management Review (SAUO) .... CLMR
Clinical Laboratory Management System [*Computer science*] .... CLMS
Clinical Laboratory Monitoring System (SAUS) .... CLMS
Clinical Laboratory News (SAUO) .... CLN
Clinical Laboratory of Evaluation and Assessment of Tox Substances (GNE) .... CLEATS
Clinical Laboratory Reference (SAUS) .... CLR
Clinical Laboratory Scientist (MAE) .... CLS
Clinical Laboratory Scientist (STED) .... CS
Clinical Laboratory Specialist (MEDA) .... CLSP
Clinical Laboratory Technician .... CLT
Clinical Laboratory Test Database [*Computer science*] .... CLTDB
Clinical Ligand Assay Society (EA) .... CLAS
Clinical Literature Untoward Effects [*Service published by International Information Institute*] .... CLUE
Clinical Magnetic Resonance Society (ADWA) .... CMRS
Clinical Medical Librarian .... CML
Clinical Medical Officer [*British*] .... CMO
Clinical Medicine (journ.) (SAUS) .... Clin Med
Clinical Micro Sensors .... CMS
Clinical Microbiology Laboratory .... CML
Clinical Microbiology Procedures Handbook [*A publication*] (ADWA) .... CMPH
Clinical Microbiology Reviews (SAUO) .... CMR
Clinical Modification .... CM
Clinical Neurology Information Center .... CNIC
Clinical Notes On-Line [*IRCS Medical Science*] [*Ceased operation*] [*Information service or system*] (IID) .... CNOL
Clinical Nurse Consultant (NUJO) .... CNC
Clinical Nurse Specialist .... CNS
Clinical Nursing .... CN
Clinical Nursing Research (SAUS) .... CNR
Clinical Nutrition Certification Board (ADWA) .... CNCB
Clinical Nutrition Research Unit [*Medical College of Georgia*] [*Research center*] (RCD) .... CNRU
Clinical Nutrition Research Unit [*Birmingham, AL*] [*Department of Health and Human Services*] (GRD) .... CNRU
Clinical Obstetrics and Gynecology (journ.) (SAUS) .... Clin Obstet Gynecol
Clinical Orthopaedics and Related Research (ADWA) .... CORR
Clinical Orthopedic Society (EA) .... COS
Clinical Orthopedics and Related Research (journ.) (SAUS) .... Clin Orthop Related Res
Clinical Outcomes Assessment Program (SAUO) .... COAP
Clinical Pastoral Education .... CPE
Clinical Pathology (DAVI) .... Clin Path
Clinical Pathology (SAUS) .... Clin Path
Clinical Pathology [*Medicine*] (DMAA) .... CIP
Clinical Pathology .... CP
Clinical Pathology Conference .... CPC
Clinical Pathology Data Processing System (SAUS) .... CPDPS
Clinical Pathway Database (ADWA) .... CPDB
Clinical Pediatrics (journ.) (SAUS) .... Clin Pediat
Clinical Performance Score [*Medicine*] (MAE) .... CPS
Clinical Pharmacokinetics Team [*Pharmacology*] (DAVI) .... CPT
Clinical Pharmacology and Therapeutics (SAUS) .... CP&T
Clinical Pharmacology and Therapeutics (journ.) (SAUS) .... Clin Pharmacol Ther
Clinical Pharmacy (SAUS) .... CP
Clinical Practice Guidelines .... CPG
Clinical Practice of Medicine (SAUS) .... CPM
Clinical Probes of Articulation Consistency [*Speech evaluation test*] .... C-PAC

Clinical Procedure [*Medicine*] (DAVI) .... Clin Proc
Clinical Procedures (SAUS) .... Clin Proc
Clinical Protocols [*National Cancer Institute*] [*Information service or system*] .... CLINPROT
Clinical Record [*Medicine*] .... CR
Clinical Record Cover Sheet [*Army medical*] .... CRCS
Clinical Reference Library (SAUO) .... CRL
Clinical Research [*Medicine*] (DAVI) .... CR
Clinical Research Assistant (SAUS) .... CRA
Clinical Research Center [*University of Tennessee*] [*Research center*] (RCD) .... CRC
Clinical Research Center [*Medical Research Institute of Delaware*] [*Research center*] .... CRC
Clinical Research Center [*Case Western Reserve University*] [*Research center*] (RCD) .... CRC
Clinical Research Center [*University of Rochester*] [*Research center*] (RCD) .... CRC
Clinical Research Center [*University of Utah*] [*Research center*] (RCD) .... CRC
Clinical Research Center [*UCLA*] [*Research center*] .... CRC
Clinical Research Center [*Massachusetts Institute of Technology*] [*Research center*] (RCD) .... CRC
Clinical Research Center for Periodontal Disease [*University of Minnesota*] .... CRCPD
Clinical Research Center for Periodontal Disease [*University of Florida*] [*Research center*] (RCD) .... PDRC
Clinical Research Centre [*British*] (CB) .... CRC
Clinical Research Institute of Montreal [*University of Montreal*] [*Research center*] (RCD) .... CRIM
Clinical Research Nurses Association (SAUO) .... CRNA
Clinical Research Unit .... CRU
Clinical Research Unit for Anxiety Disorders (ADWA) .... CRUFAD
Clinical Science (journ.) (SAUS) .... Clin Sci
Clinical Sleep Society [*Neurology*] (DAVI) .... CCS
Clinical Social Work Federation (SAUO) .... CSWF
Clinical Society of Genito-Urinary Surgeons (EA) .... CSGUS
Clinical Sociology Association [*Later, SPA*] (EA) .... CSA
Clinical Specialist (PGP) .... CS
Clinical Staging [*Oncology*] .... CS
Clinical Standards Advisory Group [*Medicine*] (WDAA) .... CSAG
Clinical State .... CS
Clinical Studies Trust Fund (GVA) .... CSTF
Clinical Supplies and Inventory System [*Medicine*] (DMAA) .... CSIS
Clinical Target Volume [*Medicine*] (DMAA) .... CTV
Clinical Text Inquiry System (SAUS) .... CTIS
Clinical Theological Association (SAUO) .... CTA
Clinical Toxicology and Commercial Products (MELL) .... CTCP
Clinical Toxicology (journ.) (SAUS) .... Clin Toxicol
Clinical Treatment Failure .... CTF
Clinical Trial Certificate [*Medicine*] (DMAA) .... CTC
Clinical Trial Exemption [*Medicine*] (DB) .... CTE
Clinical Trial Exemption [*Medicine*] (DB) .... CTX
Clinical Trials and Treatments Advisory Committee [*Australia*] .... CTTAC
Clinical Trials Monitoring System .... CTMS
Clinical Trials Office [*Medicine*] .... CTO
Clinical Trials Supplies .... CTS
Clinical Unit .... CU
Clinical Unit Coordinator .... CUC
Clinical Vascular Laboratory (STED) CVL
Clinical-Diagnostic Staging of Cancer [*Oncology*] (DAVI) .... cTNM
Clinically (SAUS) .... Clin
Clinically Definite Multiple Sclerosis (SAUS) .... CDMS
Clinically Observed Seizure [*Medicine*] (STED) .... COS
Clinically Significant Macular Edema (SAUS) .... CSME
Clinically Undetectable Primary Malignancy [*Oncology*] .... CUPM
Clinician Administered Postraumatic Stress [*Disorder*] (MELL) .... CAPS
Clinician Full Time [*Chiropody*] [*British*] .... CF
Clinician in Management (SAUS) .... CIM
Clinician Interview Based Impression .... CI-BI
Clinician's Interview Based Impression of Change .... CIBIC
Clinico-Pathologic Conference (STED) .... CPC
Clinicorp, Inc. [*AMEX symbol*] (SPSG) .... BAK
Clinics Without Walls (SAUO) .... CWW
Clinique d'Aide a l'Enfance, Ste.-Foy, PQ, Canada [*Library symbol*] [*Library of Congress*] (LCLS) .... CaQSFCAE
Clinique d'Aide a l'Enfance, Ste.-Foy, Quebec [*Library symbol*] [*National Library of Canada*] (NLC) .... QSFCAE
Clinitest [*Miles Inc.*] [*Endocrinology*] (DAVI) .... clini
Clinitest and Acitest [*Trademarked clinical laboratory tests*] .... C & A
Clinitron Air Fluidized Therapy [*Medicine*] (DAVI) .... CAFT
Clinoenstatite [*A mineral*] .... CE
Clinohypersthene [*Inorganic chemistry*] .... Chp
Clinometer (SAUS) .... Clin
Clinometer [*Engineering*] .... CLN
Clinopyroxene [*A mineral*] .... CPX
Clint Ritchie Official Fan Club [*Defunct*] (EA) .... CROFC
Clinton [*Iowa*] [*Airport symbol*] (OAG) .... CWI
Clinton, AR [*AM radio station call letters*] .... KGFL
Clinton, AR [*FM radio station call letters*] .... KHPQ
Clinton Community College, Clinton, IA [*Library symbol*] [*Library of Congress*] (LCLS) .... IaCliCC
Clinton Community College, Plattsburgh, NY [*Library symbol*] [*Library of Congress*] (LCLS) .... NPlaCC
Clinton Community College, Plattsburgh, NY [*OCLC symbol*] (OCLC) .... YLC
Clinton Corn Processing Co., Clinton, IA [*Library symbol*] [*Library of Congress*] (LCLS) .... IaCliC

Clinton Corners Reading Center, Clinton Corners, NY [*Library symbol*] [*Library of Congress*] (LCLS) .... NClinc
Clinton County Historical Society, Clinton, IA [*Library symbol*] [*Library of Congress*] (LCLS) .... IaCliCHi
Clinton Engineer Works (SAA) .... CEW
Clinton Gas Systems, Inc. [*NASDAQ symbol*] (NQ) .... CGAS
Clinton Gas Systems, Inc. [*Associated Press*] (SAG) .... ClintGs
Clinton Health Security Plan [*Medicine*] .... CHSP
Clinton Herald, Clinton, IA [*Library symbol*] [*Library of Congress*] (LCLS) .... IaCliH
Clinton, IA [*Location identifier*] [*FAA*] (FAAL) .... CWI
Clinton, IA [*Location identifier*] [*FAA*] (FAAL) .... FNO
Clinton, IA [*FM radio station call letters*] .... KCLN
Clinton, IA [*AM radio station call letters*] .... KLNT
Clinton, IA [*FM radio station call letters*] .... KMXG
Clinton, IA [*AM radio station call letters*] .... KROS
Clinton, IA [*FM radio station call letters*] (BROA) .... KZEG-FM
Clinton, IL [*AM radio station call letters*] .... WHOW
Clinton, IL [*FM radio station call letters*] .... WHOW-FM
Clinton, IN [*FM radio station call letters*] (BROA) .... WPFR-FM
Clinton Junior College, Rock Hill, SC [*Library symbol*] [*Library of Congress*] (LCLS) .... ScRhM
Clinton, KY [*FM radio station call letters*] (BROA) .... WCBF-FM
Clinton, LA [*FM radio station call letters*] .... WQCK
Clinton Memorial Hospital, Health Resource Center, Wilmington, OH [*Library symbol*] [*Library of Congress*] (LCLS) .... OWilmH
Clinton, MO [*Location identifier*] [*FAA*] (FAAL) .... GLY
Clinton, MO [*AM radio station call letters*] .... KDKD
Clinton, MO [*FM radio station call letters*] .... KDKD-FM
Clinton, MO [*FM radio station call letters*] .... KLRQ
Clinton, MS [*FM radio station call letters*] .... WHJT
Clinton, MS [*AM radio station call letters*] .... WTWZ
Clinton Museum, British Columbia [*Library symbol*] [*National Library of Canada*] (NLC) .... BCLM
Clinton Museum, Clinton, BC, Canada [*Library symbol*] [*Library of Congress*] (LCLS) .... CaBCLM
Clinton, NC [*Location identifier*] [*FAA*] (FAAL) .... CTZ
Clinton, NC [*AM radio station call letters*] .... WCLN
Clinton, NC [*FM radio station call letters*] .... WCLN-FM
Clinton, NC [*AM radio station call letters*] .... WRRZ
Clinton Nuclear Power Plant (NRCH) .... CNPP
Clinton, NY [*FM radio station call letters*] .... WHCL
Clinton, OK [*Location identifier*] [*FAA*] (FAAL) .... BFV
Clinton, OK [*Location identifier*] [*FAA*] (FAAL) .... BZF
Clinton, OK [*Location identifier*] [*FAA*] (FAAL) .... CLK
Clinton, OK [*Location identifier*] [*FAA*] (FAAL) .... CSM
Clinton, OK [*FM radio station call letters*] .... KCLI
Clinton, OK [*AM radio station call letters*] (RBYB) .... KCLI-AM
Clinton, OK [*FM radio station call letters*] (RBYB) .... KQMX-FM
Clinton, OK [*FM radio station call letters*] .... KSWR
Clinton, OK [*AM radio station call letters*] .... KXOL
Clinton Point, NT [*ICAO location identifier*] (ICLI) .... CYUH
Clinton Power Station [*Nuclear energy*] (GFGA) .... CPS
Clinton Public Library, Clinton, IA [*Library symbol*] [*Library of Congress*] (LCLS) .... IaCli
Clinton Public Library, Clinton, IN [*Library symbol*] [*Library of Congress*] (LCLS) .... InCli
Clinton Public Library, Clinton, MI [*Library symbol*] [*Library of Congress*] (LCLS) .... MiClin
Clinton Public Library, Clinton, OK [*Library symbol*] [*Library of Congress*] (LCLS) .... OkCl
Clinton, SC [*AM radio station call letters*] .... WPCC
Clinton, TN [*FM radio station call letters*] .... WDVX
Clinton, TN [*FM radio station call letters*] .... WYFC
Clinton, TN [*AM radio station call letters*] .... WYSH
Clinton-Essex-Franklin Library, Plattsburgh, NY [*OCLC symbol*] (OCLC) .... VZC
Clinton-Essex-Franklin Library System, Plattsburgh, NY [*Library symbol*] [*Library of Congress*] (LCLS) .... NPlaCEF
Clinton-Graceville High School, Graceville, MN [*Library symbol*] [*Library of Congress*] (LCLS) .... MnGraCHS
Clinton's Digest [*New York*] [*A publication*] (DLA) .... Clin Dig
Clintonville, WI [*Location identifier*] [*FAA*] (FAAL) CLI
Clintonville, WI [*AM radio station call letters*] .... WFCL
Clintonville, WI [*FM radio station call letters*] .... WJMQ
Clintrials Research [*NASDAQ symbol*] (SAG) .... CCRO
Clintrials Research, Inc. [*Associated Press*] (SAG) .... Clintrials
Clio: A Journal of Literature, History and the Philosophy of History [*A publication*] (BRI) .... Clio
Clip (MSA) CL
Clip Joint (SAUS) .... CJ
Clip on Socket [*Computer science*] (VERA) .... COS
Clipboard (SAUS) .... CLP
Clip-On Unit (DCTA) .... COU
Clip-on-Board [*Instrumentation*] .... COB
Clipped [*Ecology*] C
Clipped and Ash [*Ecology*] .... CA
Clipped and Burned [*Ecology*] .... CB
Clipped and Nitrogen Added [*Ecology*] .... CN
Clipped, Torched [*Ecology*] .... CT
Clipper .... CLPPR
Clipper Club [*Pan American Airlines' club for frequent flyers*] (EA) CC
Clipper Cross-Correlation (SAUS) CCC
Clipper Negative .... CLN
Clipper Positive .... CLP
Clipping [*Medicine*] .... Clip
Clipping (SAUS) .... Clpg
Clipping Amplifier .... CA
Clipping Circuit (SAUS) CC
Clipping Injury Fracture (MELL) .... CIF
Clips per Day [*Photocopying, microfilming*] .... CPD
Clips per Year [*Photocopying, microfilming*] .... CPY
CLIRA [*Closed-Loop In-Reactor Assembly*] **Backup Plug Tool** [*Nuclear energy*] (NRCH) .... CBPT
CLIRA [*Closed-Loop In-Reactor Assembly*] **Holddown Assembly Tool** [*Nuclear energy*] (NRCH) .... CHAT
Clitoria Yellow Vein Virus [*Plant pathology*] .... CYVV
CLIVAR/WOCE Surface Velocity Programme Planning Committee (SAUS) .... CWSVPPC
CLIVAR/WOCE XBT/XCDT Programme Planning Committee (SAUS) .... CWXXPPC
Clive Public Library, Alberta [*Library symbol*] [*National Library of Canada*] (NLC) .... ACLI
Cloak and Suit Trucking Association (EA) .... CSTA
Clock C
Clock .... CK
Clock .... CLCK
Clock (AAG) .... CLK
Clock Actuated Readout (SAUS) .... CARO
Clock and Simulation tape Maintenance (SAUS) .... CSM
Clock and Tone Module (SAUS) .... CTM
Clock and Tones Distribution (SAUS) .... CLTD
Clock and Watch Manufacturers Association of America [*Defunct*] .... CWMAA
Clock Assemblers and Importers Association (EA) .... CAIA
Clock Card (SAUS) CC
Clock Coercion .... C/C
Clock Coercion Signal .... CCS
Clock Control (IAA) CC
Clock Controlled Readout (SAUS) .... CCRO
Clock Delay .... CDL
Clock Distribution Circuit (SAUS) .... CDC
Clock Driver .... CD
Clock Enable Pulse (ACAE) .... CEP
Clock Frequency (SAUS) .... CF
Clock Generation & Support (SAUS) .... CGS
Clock Generator (SAUS) .... CG
Clock Generator Random-Access Memory [*Computer science*] (OA) .... CGRAM
Clock Hour (KSC) .... CH
Clock In (SAUS) .... CLKIN
Clock Manufacturers and Marketing Association (EA) .... CMMA
Clock Master (SAUS) .... Ck Master
Clock Module (SAUS) .... CLM
Clock Oscillator .... CO
Clock Out (CIST) .... CLKOUT
Clock Per Instruction (SAUS) .... CPI
Clock Phase .... CP
Clock, Programming, and Timing [*NASA*] (KSC) .... CPT
Clock Pulse .... CP
Clock Pulse (IAA) .... CPS
Clock Pulse Enable (SAUS) .... CPEN
Clock Pulse Generator .... CPG
Clock Pulse Interval .... CPI
Clock Pulse Repeater .... CPR
Clock Pulse Width Modulation (SAUS) .... CPWM
Clock Pulsed Control .... CPC
Clock Start Command .... CSC
Clock Subsystem (CET) .... CSS
Clock Synchronization .... CS
Clock Synchronization Unit (SAUS) .... CSU
Clock Synchronous Random Access Memory (SAUS) .... CSRAM
Clock Time .... CT
Clock Track Number (SAUS) .... CTN
Clock Unit (SAUS) .... CU
Clock-Cycle Proportional-Pulse (SAUS) .... CCPP
Clocked CMOS [*Complementary Metal-Oxide Semiconductor*] **Logic** [*Electronics*] (IAA) CCL
Clocked Complementary Metal Oxide Semiconductor [*Electronics*] (IAA) .... CCMOS
Clocked Logic Simulation (SAUS) .... CLSIM
Clocking (SAUS) .... Clkg
Clock-Sync Receiver Assembly [*Deep Space Instrumentation Facility, NASA*] .... CSR
Clockwise C
Clockwise (ADWA) .... ckw
Clockwise (ADA) .... CKW
Clockwise (ADA) .... CLKW
Clockwise .... CLKWS
Clockwise (AFM) .... CLKWZ
Clockwise (IAA) .... CLW
Clockwise (SAUS) .... Clw
Clockwise .... CLWS
Clockwise (STED) .... cw
Clockwise .... CW
Clockwise (AAG) .... CWS
Clockwise Bottom Angular Down (OA) .... CWBAD
Clockwise Bottom Angular Up (OA) .... CWBAU
Clockwise Down Blast (OA) .... CWDB
Clockwise Orbit [*Aviation*] (FAAC) .... CLKOB
Clockwise Top Angular Down (OA) .... CWTAD
Clockwise Top Angular Up (OA) .... CWTAU
Clockwise Top Horizontal (OA) .... CWTH
Clockwise Up Blast (OA) .... CWUB
Clode's Martial Law [*A publication*] (DLA) .... Clode ML

Clodius [of Scriptores Historiae Augustae] [Classical studies] (OCD) .... Clod
Clofibrate (DMAA) .... CLOF
Clogher [Town in Northern Ireland] (ROG) .... CLOGH
Clogs & Shawls [Literary genre] (WDAA) .... C&S
Cloisonne (VRA) .... clois
Cloisonne Collectors Club (EA) CCC
Cloister (DSUE) .... CLOI
Cloister (VRA) .... clstr
Clomiphene Challenge Test (ADWA) .... CCT
Clomiphene Citrate [Fertility drug] CC
Clomiphene Citrate Challenge Test (ADWA) .... CCCT
Clomipramine [Medicine] (DMAA) CI
Clomipramine [An antidepressant] [Medicine] .... CMI
Clonal Apple Rootstock Liner .... CRL
Clonal Seed Orchard .... CSO
Clonazepam [Antiepileptic drug] .... CZP
Cloncurry [Australia] [Airport symbol] (OAG) .... CNJ
Clone CI
Clonfert [Village in Ireland] (ROG) .... CLONF
Clonidine (DMAA) .... CLON
Clonidine Displacing Substance [Biochemistry] .... CDS
Cloning Inhibiting Factor .... CIF
Cloning Inhibitory Factor [Medicine] (DMAA) .... CLIF
Clonorchis [A liver fluke] [Gastroenterology] (DAVI) .... Clon
Clonus C
Clonus Index (MAE) CI
Clopay Corporation (SAUO) .... CPY
Cloquet Middle School, Cloquet, MN [Library symbol] [Library of Congress] (LCLS) .... MnCIM
Cloquet, MN [Location identifier] [FAA] (FAAL) .... COQ
Cloquet, MN [AM radio station call letters] .... WKLK
Cloquet, MN [FM radio station call letters] .... WKLK-FM
Cloquet, MN [FM radio station call letters] .... WSCN
Cloquet Public Library, Cloquet, MN [Library symbol] [Library of Congress] (LCLS) .... MnCI
Cloquet Senior High School, Cloquet, MN [Library symbol] [Library of Congress] (LCLS) .... MnCISH
Cloquet's Lymph Node [Medicine] (MELL) .... CLN
Clorinda [Argentina] [ICAO location identifier] (ICLI) .... SATC
Clorine Demand (SAUS) .... CD
Clorox Chemical Company (SAUO) CXC
Clorox Co. [Associated Press] (SAG) .... Clorox
Clorox Co. [NYSE symbol] (SPSG) CLX
Close (WDAA) C
Close (AAG) CL
Close .... CLO
Close [Computer science] (BUR) .... CLS
Close Air Picture (SAUS) .... CLAP
Close Air Support .... CAIRS
Close Air Support [Military] .... CAS
Close Air Support Aircraft [Military] .... CASA
Close Air Support Aircraft (SAUS) .... CAS Aircraft
Close Air Support Aircraft Design Alternative [Military] .... CASADA
Close Air Support Aircraft Design Alternatives study (SAUS) .... CASADA
Close Air Support Cargo Dispenser (SAUS) .... CASCAD
Close Air Support Communication Exercise (SAUO) .... CASCOMEX
Close Air Support Communications Exercise (SAUS) .... CASCOMEX
Close Air Support Control [Military] (NVT) .... CASCON
Close Air Support Evaluation (SAUS) .... CASE
Close Air Support Exercise [Military] (NVT) .... CASEX
Close Air Support Gun Program [Military] (MCD) .... CASGP
Close Air Support Gun System [Military] (MCD) .... CASGS
Close Air Support Missile [Military] (MCD) .... CASM
Close Air Support Mission Area Review Group (SAUO) .... CASMARG
Close Air Support Mission Card (ACAE) .... CASMC
Close Air Support Request Processing [Military] .... CASRP
Close Air Support Standoff Munition (MCD) .... CASSCM
Close Air Support Survivability Enhancement System [Military] (MCD) ..... CASSE
Close Air Support System (SAUS) .... CASS
Close Air Support System [Military] .... CLASS
Close Air Support Weapon [Military] (MCD) .... CASW
Close Air Support Weapon [Military] (MCD) .... CLAW
Close Air Support Weapon System [Military] (MCD) .... CASWS
Close Air Support/Battlefield Air Interdiction (DOMA) .... CAS/BAI
Close Air Support/Battlefield Air Interdiction .... CAS/BAT
Close Annealed [Metal industry] .... CA
Close Annealed (SAUS) .... C/A
Close Approach Indicator (IEEE) .... CAI
Close Assault Weapon (INF) .... CAW
Close Boundary Sentry [Military] (AFM) .... CBS
Close Combat (SAUS) CC
Close Combat Anti-Armor Task Force (SAUO) .... CCAATF
Close Combat Antiarmor Task Force (MCD) .... CCAATF
Close Combat Antiarmor Weapon System (MCD) .... CCAAWS
Close Combat Anti-Armor Weapon System [Army] (RDA) .... CCAWS
Close Combat Armament Center [Dover, NJ] [Army] (GRD) .... CCAC
Close Combat, Engineering, and Mine Warfare Directorate [Army] .... CCEMWD
Close Combat Force (SAUO) .... CCF
Close Combat, Heavy .... CCH
Close Combat Helicopter (SAUS) .... CCH
Close Combat LASER Assault Weapon .... C-CLAW
Close Combat LASER Assault Weapon [Military] (PDAA) .... C-LAW
Close Combat Leadership Exercise [Military] .... CCLEx
Close combat Light Armor Weapon System (SAUS) .... CLAWS
Close Combat Optics .... CCO

Close Combat Tactical Trainer .... CCTT
Close Combat Training System [Army] .... CCTS
Close Combat Vehicle [Military] CCV
Close Combat Vehicle - Light [Army] CCVL
Close Combat Vehicle Integration Diagnostic [Army] (RDA) .... CCVID
Close Combat Vehicle, Light (SAUS) .... CCV-L
Close Combat Weapon System [Army] (MCD) .... CCW
Close Combat Weapon System [Marine Corps] .... CCWS
Close Confinement Mesa [Electronics] (NITA) .... CCM
Close Contact Annealing (MCD) .... CCA
Close Control (SAUS) CC
Close Control Bombing [Air Force] .... CCB
Close Copper Nailing (SAUS) .... CCN
Close Defence Relations (SAUS) .... CDR
Close Doublet (SAA) .... CD
Close Encounter [with a UFO] .... CE
Close Encounters of the Third Kind [Movie title] CE3
Close Focus Lens .... CFL
Close Light Assault Weapon (SAUS) .... CLAW
Close Lunar Satellite .... CLS
Close Medium Shot [A photograph or motion picture sequence taken from a relatively short distance] .... CMS
Close Observation Platoon (SAUS) .... COP
Close of Business [With date] .... COB
Close Order Drill (DNAB) .... COD
Close Packed (MSA) .... CP
Close Protection (SAUS) .... CP
Close Quarter Battle Range (SAUS) .... CQBR
Close Quarter Engagements (SAUS) .... CQE
Close Quarters (SAUS) .... C Quart
Close Range Analytical Bundle System (PDAA) .... CRABS
Close Range Missile System (PDAA) .... CRMS
Close Range Unmanned Aerial Vehicle (SAUS) .... CLOSE UAV
Close Ratio [Automotive engineering] .... CR
Close Reconnaissance Zone [Army] (AABC) .... CRZ
Close Rolls [British] CL
Close Shot [Photography] .... CS
Close Space Vapor Transport [Photovoltaic energy systems] .... CSVT
Close Station March Order (MCD) .... CSMO
Close Stowing (SAUS) .... CS
Close Supervision (STED) .... CS
Close Support [Army] .... CS
Close Support Area [Military] (CAAL) .... CSA
Close Support Artillery Rocket System (MCD) .... CSARS
Close Support Artillery Weapon System (MCD) .... CSAWS
Close Support Assault Weapon [Obsolete] [Navy] (MCD) .... CSAW
Close Support Bridge (SAUS) .... CSB
Close Support Gun (DNAB) .... CSG
Close Support Missile [Air Force] (MCD) .... CSM
Close Support Mission (SAUS) .... CSM
Close Supportive Fire (ACAE) .... CSF
Close Surveillance Contractor List [DoD] .... CSCL
Close Talking Microphone .... CTM
Close this Office (SAUS) .... CLOTO
Close This Office (FAAC) .... CLOTO
Close to Fire (ACAE) .... CTF
Close to Shoulder (MSA) .... CTS
Close Tolerance .... CT
Close Triplet (SAA) .... CT
Close Type Control Circuit Contact (MSA) .... CTCCC
Close Wound (SAUS) .... C-W
Close-Air Defence Weapon System (SAUS) .... CADWS
Close-Assault Weapon System .... CAWS
Close-Binding-Intimate [Biochemistry] .... CBI
Close-Coupled [Electricity] CC
Closed C
Closed (AAG) .... CLSD
Closed Angle Glaucoma [Medicine] (MELL) .... CAG
Closed Angle Glaucoma [Ophthalmology] (CPH) .... COG
Closed Area Security System (MCD) .... CASS
Closed at All Times (Except When in Actual Use) [Ship's fittings classification] X
Closed at Sea (for High Degree of Emergency Readiness) [Ship's fittings classification] .... Y
Closed Bladder Drainage [Medicine] .... CBD
Closed Bomb Data Reduction Program (MCD) .... CBRED
Closed Brayton Cycle [Thermodynamics] .... CBC
Closed Breech Scavenging System (MCD) .... CBSS
Closed Building Syndrome (MELL) .... CBS
Closed Captioned [Refers to captioning of television programs for the deaf] CC
Closed Cerebral Trauma (MELL) .... CCT
Closed Chest Cardiac Massage and Mouth-to-Mouth Resuscitation [Medicine] (AABC) .... CCCMMM
Closed Chest Cardiac Resuscitation [Medicine] .... CCCR
Closed Chest Massage [Medicine] (MELL) .... CCM
Closed Circuit [Transmission] (DEN) CC
Closed Circuit Breathing Apparatus (SAUS) .... CCBA
Closed Circuit Loop (MCD) CCL
Closed Circuit Radio Transmitter (NTCM) .... CCRT
Closed Circuit Television Manufacturers Association (EA) .... CCTMA
Closed Circuit Test [Telecommunications] (OTD) .... CCT
Closed Circuit Voltage (SAUS) CCV
Closed Condensation Nuclei (MCD) .... CCN
Closed Cone at Maturity [Botany] .... CLCONE
Closed Container [Packaging] (DCTA) CC

Closed Cooling Water [*Nuclear energy*] (NRCH) .... CCW
Closed Cooling Water System [*Nuclear energy*] (NRCH) .... CCWS
Closed Corporation [*Business term*] (MHDB) .... CO LTD
Closed Craniocerebral Trauma [*Medicine*] (DMAA) .... CCCT
closed cup (SAUS) cc
Closed Cup CC
Closed Cup Test [*Flammability*] CC
Closed Cycle ADCAP [*Advanced Capability*] **Propulsion System** [*Mk48 torpedo improvement*] (DOMA) .... CCAPS
Closed Cycle Cooler (SAUS) CCC
Closed Cycle Fluid Supply System (ACAE) .... CCFS
Closed Cycle Vaporization Cooling System (ACAE) .... CCVCS
Closed Drainage System [*Medicine*] (MELL) .... CDS
Closed Ecological Life Support System [*NASA*] .... CELSS
Closed Ecological System .... CES
Closed End .... CLE
Closed Entry Socket Insulation (or Insulator) (SAUS) .... CESI
Closed Flux Memory [*Computer science*] .... CFM
Closed Hard Access Device (SAUS) .... CHA Device
Closed Head Injury [*Medicine*] .... CHI
Closed Head Trauma [*Emergency medicine*] (DAVI) .... CHT
Closed Head Unit [*Neurology*] (DAVI) .... CHU
Closed Intramedullary Pinning [*Medicine*] (MELL) .... CIMP
Closed Line Assembly for Single Particles (IEEE) .... CLASP
Closed Loop (KSC) CL
Closed Loop (SAUS) .... C/L
Closed Loop Accounting for Stores Sales (IEEE) .... CLASS
Closed Loop Aeronautical Management Program (SAUO) .... CLAMP
Closed Loop Aerospace Management Program (ACAE) .... CLAMP
Closed Loop Artillery Simulation System [*Army*] .... CLASS
Closed Loop Congestion Control (SAUS) CLCC
Closed Loop Control Logic (NAKS) CL
Closed Loop Cover and Administration System (SAUS) .... CLCAS
Closed Loop Fire Control System (ACAE) .... CLFCS
Closed Loop Infrared Countermeasures (ACAE) .... CLIRCM
Closed Loop Jumper Assembly (SAUS) .... CLJA
Closed Loop Telemetry (SAUS) .... CLT
Closed Loop Television Camera (SPST) .... CTVC
Closed Loop Test (SAUS) .... CLT
Closed Mouth [*Doll collecting*] .... CM
Closed Numbering Area [*Telecommunications*] .... CNA
Closed Observation Room (MELL) .... COR
Closed Olivocochlear Potential (SAUS) .... COCP
Closed Open Switch (SAUS) .... CO Switch
Closed Orbit (SAUS) .... CO
Closed Pack Ice Zone [*Oceanography*] .... CPIZ
Closed Pore Insulation .... CPI
Closed Position [*Dancing*] .... CP
Closed Reduction [*Osteology*] (AAMN) .... CR
Closed Reduction and Cast (STED) .... CR & C
Closed Roller Chock [*Shipfitting*] .... CRC
Closed Routine (SAA) .... CR
Closed Shell .... CS
Closed Shelter Deck [*Shipping*] (DS) .... CSD
Closed Subroutine (SAUS) .... CS
Closed System Respirator Evaluator (KSC) .... CSRE
Closed Thoracotomy [*Medicine*] (MELL) .... CT
Closed Throttle [*Automotive engineering*] .... CT
Closed Timelike Curve [*Time travel*] .... CTC
Closed Tracheal Suction System [*Medicine*] (DMAA) .... CTSS
Closed Transaction File (SAUS) .... CTF
Closed Transition Transfer Switch .... CTTS
Closed Urinary Drainage System [*Medicine*] (MELL) .... CUDS
Closed User Group [*Communications*] .... CUG
Closed User Group with Outgoing Access (SAUO) .... CUGOA
Closed Vitrectomy [*Ophthalmology*] (DAVI) CV
Closed Waveguide .... CWG
Closed, Well-Formed Formula [*Logic*] .... CWFF
Closed World Assumption (RALS) .... CWA
Closed-Circuit Cable Television (CIST) .... CCTV
Closed-Circuit Radio .... CCR
Closed-Circuit Saturation Diving System [*Navy*] (CAAL) .... CCSDS
Closed-Circuit Television .... CCTV
Closed-Circuit Television System (IAA) .... CCTVS
Closed-Circuit Television/Large-Screen Display (SAUS) .... CCTV/LSD
Closed-Cycle Cooler CCC
Closed-Cycle Cryogenic Equipment .... CCCE
Closed-Cycle Diesel engine technology (SAUS) .... CCD
Closed-Cycle Gas Turbine (PDAA) .... CCGT
Closed-Cycle Gas-Cooled Reactor (DEN) .... CCGCR
Closed-Cycle Refrigerator .... CCR
Closed-Cycle Thermal System (SAUS) .... CCTS
Closed-End Fund [*Investment term*] .... CEF
Closed-End Investment Company [*Business term*] .... CEIC
Closed-Fist Injury .... CFI
Closed-form Ray Analysis (SAUS) .... CLORA
Closed-Form Solutions Applied to a Mesh-Point-Field [*Mathematics*] .... CLAMP
Closed-In-Bottom Hole Pressure (SAUS) .... CIBHP
Closed-Loop Adaptive Single Parameter (MCD) .... CLASP
Closed-Loop Aiming Mechanism Prototype .... CLAMP
Closed-Loop Approach Control .... CLAC
Closed-Loop Bandwidth .... CLBW
Closed-Loop Boresight Alignment (MCD) .... CLBA
Closed-Loop Condensate [*Nuclear energy*] (NRCH) CLC
Closed-Loop Conjugate Point (SAUS) .... CLCP
Closed-Loop Continuity Check [*Aerospace*] (AAG) CLCC
Closed-Loop Control [*Automotive engineering*] CLC
Closed-Loop Control and Instrumentation System [*Nuclear energy*] (NRCH) .... CLCIS
Closed-Loop Control System [*Nuclear energy*] (IAA) .... CLCS
Closed-Loop Cooling Water [*Nuclear energy*] (NRCH) .... CLCW
Closed-Loop Cover Gas Monitor [*Nuclear energy*] (NRCH) .... CLCGM
Closed-Loop Dynamic Stability Test (NASA) .... CLDST
Closed-Loop Ecological Cycle [*Aerospace*] (AAG) .... CLEC
Closed-Loop Environmental Control System .... CECS
Closed-Loop Evaluation and Reporting System (MCD) .... CLEAR
Closed-Loop Ex-Vessel Machine [*Formerly, EVHM*] [*Nuclear energy*] (NRCH) .... CLEM
Closed-Loop Fire Control [*Army*] (MCD) .... CLFC
Closed-Loop Flight Test Language (SAUS) .... CLFT Language
Closed-Loop Gain .... CLG
Closed-Loop In-Reactor Assembly [*Nuclear energy*] (NRCH) .... CLIRA
Closed-Loop Intensity Control (AAEL) CLIC
Closed-Loop Jumper Assembly [*Nuclear energy*] (NRCH) .... CLJA
Closed-Loop, Lock-In Compensation CLIC
Closed-Loop Operation Test (SAUS) .... CLOT
Closed-Loop Stripping Analysis [*Analytical chemistry*] .... CLSA
Closed-Loop Support [*Army*] (AABC) .... CLS
Closed-Loop Support Extended [*Army*] (AABC) .... CLSX
Closed-Loop System [*Chemical engineering*] [*Nuclear energy*] (NRCH) .... CLS
Closed-Loop System Melt-Down Accident [*Nuclear energy*] (NRCH) .... CLSMDA
Closed-Loop Telemetry .... CLT
Closed-Loop Television .... CLTV
Closed-Loop Test (NASA) .... CLT
Closed-Loop Trainer Aid (MCD) .... CLA
Closed-Open (SAUS) .... CO
Closed-Queuing Network (AAEL) .... CQN
Close-Fitting Mask [*Medicine*] (DMAA) .... CFM
Close-In CI
Close-in Air Defence (SAUS) .... CAD
Close-In Automatic Route Restoral System [*NORAD*] .... CARRS
Close-In Fire Support (SAUS) .... CIFS
Close-In Improvement Program [*to increase torpedo effectiveness*] (MCD) .... CLIP
Close-In Jamming (SAUS) .... CIJ
Close-In Support [*Military*] (AFM) .... CIS
Close-In Weapon System (NATG) .... CIWS
Closely Spaced Basing [*Proposed plan for protecting MX missiles from enemy attack*] .... CSB
Closely Spaced Objects (ACAE) .... CSO
Close-Open .... CO
Close-Open-Close (NASA) .... COC
Closeout Door System (MCD) .... CDS
Closeout System Installation (NASA) .... COSI
Close-Packed Hexagonal [*Metallography*] .... CPH
Close-Packed Structure .... CPS
Close-Pair Interstitial Atom .... CPIA
Close-Quarter Battle [*British military*] (DMA) .... CQB
Close-Quarter Marksmanship .... CQM
Closer Economic Relations (ADA) .... CER
Close-range Surveillance system (SAUS) .... CSV
Closest Approach [*Aerospace*] .... CA
Closest Approach Time (SAA) .... CAT
Closest Point of Approach [*Navigation*] .... CPA
Closet CL
Closet (MSA) .... CLO
Closet .... CLOS
Closet (ADWA) .... CLST
Closet Accordion Players of America .... CAPA
Closet Approach Point (SAUS) .... CAP
Closet Distance to Approach (SAUS) .... CDA
Closet User Group (SAUS) .... CUG
Close-Up [*A photograph or motion picture sequence taken from a short distance*] .... CU
Close-Up (WDMC) .... cu
Close-Up Europe (SAUO) .... CUE
Close-up Stereo Camera (SAUS) .... CSC
Closing (AAG) .... CLSG
Closing .... CLSNG
Closing Abductory Wedge Osteotomy [*Orthopedics*] (DAVI) .... CAWA
Closing Agreement Program (WYGK) .... CAP
Closing Capacity CC
Closing Coil CC
Closing Date .... CD
Closing Date .... CLODA
Closing Down [*Amateur radio shorthand*] (WDAA) CL
Closing of Business London (RIMS) .... COBLDN
Closing Order (ROG) .... CO
Closing Pressure [*Medicine*] .... CP
Closing Price [*Business term*] .... CP
Closing Purchase [*Business term*] .... CP
Closing Sale [*Business term*] .... CS
Closing the Gap [*An association*] (PAZ) .... CTG
Closing Volume [*Physiology*] CV
Clostridium [*Genus of microorganism*] (CPH) C
Clostridium [*Genus of microorganisms*] Cl
Clostridium [*Medicine*] (DMAA) .... Clostr
Clostridium Difficile (DB) .... CD
Clostridium Difficile Disease [*Medicine*] .... CDD
Clostridium Difficile-Associated Diarrhea [*Medicine*] .... CDAD
Closure [*Medicine*] C

Closure [*Physiology*] CL
Closure (MSA) .... CLOS
Closure [*Technical drawings*] .... CLS
Closure (AAG) .... CLSR
Closure (SAUS) .... Clsr
Closure Covering (SAUS) CC
Closure Manufacturers Association (EA) .... CMA
Closure Medical Corp. [*Associated Press*] (SAG) .... ClosMed
Closure Medical Corp. [*NASDAQ symbol*] (SAG) .... CLSR
Closure of Semilunar Valves [*Gastroenterology*] (DAVI) .... SC
Closure/Post-Closure .... C/PC
Clot Dissolving Drug [*Medicine*] (MELL) .... CDD
Clot Lysis [*Hematology*] (DAVI) .... CL LYS
Clot Lysis Time [*Hematology*] .... CLT
Clot Reaction (SAUS) .... CR
Clot Retraction (STED) .... CLOT R
Clot Retraction [*Medicine*] .... CR
Clot to Hold [*Medicine*] (STED) .... CTH
Cloth CL
Cloth (SAUS) Cl
Cloth [*Bookbinding*] (ROG) .... CLO
Cloth (VRA) .... cth
Cloth Assistance Factor [*Textiles*] .... CAF
Cloth Boards [*Bookbinding*] (ROG) .... CL BDS
Cloth Both Sides (SAUS) .... CBS
Cloth Elongation Factor [*Textiles*] .... CEF
Cloth Extra [*Bookbinding*] (ROG) .... CL EX
Cloth Gilt [*Bookbinding*] (ROG) .... CL GT
Cloth Limp [*Bookbinding*] (ROG) .... CL LP
Cloth Pressers' Society [*A union*] [*British*] (DCTA) .... CPS
Cloth, Rollers, and Varnished [*Maps*] (ROG) .... CRV
Cloth Sides [*Bookbinding*] .... CS
Cloth Wrapping System (SAUS) .... CW System
Clothes .... CLTH
Clothes .... CLTHS
Clothes Closet (REAL) cc
Clothes Drier .... CD
Clothes Time, Inc. [*Associated Press*] (SAG) .... Cloth
Clothes Time Inc. [*NASDAQ symbol*] (TTSB) .... CTMEO
Clothes Washer .... CW
Clothespin Manufacturers of America (EA) .... CMA
Clothestime, Inc. [*NASDAQ symbol*] (NQ) .... CTME
Clothier .... CLTHR
Clothing (AABC) .... CLO
Clothing (SAUS) .... Clo
Clothing .... CLOTH
Clothing (MSA) .... CLTHG
Clothing .... CLTHNG
Clothing Allowance [*British military*] (DMA) .... CA
Clothing and Allied Products Industry Training Board (AIE) .... CAPITB
Clothing and Equipage .... C & E
Clothing and Equipage Department (SAUO) .... C&E
Clothing and Equipment Development Branch [*Army Natick Laboratories, MA*] .... C/ED
Clothing and Equipment Physiological Research Establishment (SAUO) .... CEPRE
Clothing & Equipment Physiological Research Establishment (SAUS) .... CEPRE
Clothing and Equipment Test Facility [*Army*] (RDA) .... CETF
Clothing and Footwear [*Department of Employment*] [*British*] .... CF
Clothing and Footwear Institute [*British*] (EAIO) .... CFI
Clothing and Housing Research Division [*of ARS, Department of Agriculture*] .... CH
Clothing and Individual Equipment [*Army*] (RDA) .... CIE
Clothing and Life Support Equipment [*Military*] .... C & LSE
Clothing and Organic Materials [*Army*] (MCD) .... C & OM
Clothing and Organic Materials (SAUS) .... C&OM
Clothing and Organic Materials Division (SAUO) .... CM
Clothing and Organic Materials Laboratory [*Army Natick Laboratories, MA*] .... C/OM
Clothing and Personal Life Support Equipment Laboratory [*Army Natick Laboratories, MA*] .... C/PLSEL
Clothing and Personal Life Support Equipment Laboratory (SAUO) .... C/PLSELd
Clothing and Small Stores [*Military*] (DNAB) .... C & SS
Clothing and Small Stores (SAUO) .... CSS
Clothing and Small Stores Account [*Military*] .... CSSA
Clothing and Small Stores Fund [*Military*] .... CSSF
Clothing and Survival Equipment Bulletin (MCD) .... CSEB
Clothing and Survival Equipment Change [*Naval Air Systems Command*] (NG) .... CSC
Clothing and Survival Equipment Change [*Naval Air Systems Command*] .... CSEC
Clothing and Textile (SAUO) .... CT
Clothing and Textile Materiel [*Army*] (AABC) .... C & TM
Clothing and Textiles .... C & T
Clothing Articles Require Explanation [*Student legal action organization*] .... CARE
Clothing Depot (SAUS) .... CD
Clothing Depot (SAUO) .... CD
Clothing, Equipment, and Materials Engineering Laboratory [*Army Natick Research and Development Laboratories, MA*] (RDA) .... CEMEL
Clothing Exchange Store (WDAA) .... CES
Clothing Export Council [*British*] (DS) .... CEC
Clothing Export Council of Great Britain (SAUO) .... CEC
Clothing Initial Issue Point [*Military*] (AABC) .... CIIP
Clothing Maintenance Allowance [*Military*] .... CMA
Clothing Maintenance [*or Monetary*] Allowance, Basic [*Army*] .... CMAB
Clothing Maintenance Allowance, Initial (SAUS) .... CMAI

Clothing Maintenance Allowance, Standard [*Air Force*] .... CMAS
Clothing Maintenance Allowance System [*Military*] .... CMAS
Clothing Manufacturers Association of the United States of America (NTPA) .... CMA-USA
Clothing Manufacturers Association of the USA (EA) .... CMA
Clothing Monetary Allowance .... CLMA
Clothing Monetary Allowance, Basic (SAUS) .... CMAB
Clothing Monetary Allowance, Initial Issue [*Army*] .... CMAIISS
Clothing Monetary Allowance, Initial (Women's Army Corps) .... CMAIWAC
Clothing Monetary Allowance List [*Military*] (AFM) .... CMAL
Clothing Monetary Allowance, Standard [*Army*] .... CMAS
Clothing Monetary Maintenance Allowance [*Military*] (AABC) .... CMMA
Clothing Pattern Repository [*DoD*] .... CPR
Clothing Regulations (SAUS) .... CR
Clothing Sales Store (AABC) .... CSS
Clothing Store Operating Budgets [*Air Force*] (AFIT) .... CSOB
Clothing Store Operating Programs [*Air Force*] (AFIT) .... CSOP
Clothing Supply Office [*Military*] .... CSO
Clothing Supply Officer (SAUS) .... CSO
Cloting Time (SAUS) .... CLT
Clot-Promoting Factor (MAE) .... CPF
Clotrimazole [*Antifungal agent*] .... CT
Clottable Protein [*Medicine*] (MAE) .... CP
Clotted [*Biochemistry*] (DAVI) .... CLT
Clotting Assay [*Medicine*] (DB) .... CA
Clotting Factor [*Medicine*] (MELL) .... CF
Clotting Time [*Medicine*] (MELL) .... CLT
Clotting [*or Coagulation*] Time [*Hematology*] .... CT
Cloud .... CLD
Cloud Absorption Anomaly (SAUS) .... CAA
Cloud Absorption Radiometer (SAUS) .... CAR
Cloud Altitude Radiometer (SAUS) .... CAR
Cloud and Aerosol Remote Sensing Radiometer (SAUS) .... CARSR
Cloud and Radiation (or Radiative) Testbed (SAUS) .... CART
Cloud and Radiation Testbed [*Network*] [*Department of Energy*] (OSRA) .... CART
Cloud and Radiation Testbed Network [*Department of Energy*] (USDC) .... CART
Cloud and the Earth's Radiant Energy System .... CERES
Cloud and Visibility Okay [*NWS*] (FAAC) .... CAVOK
Cloud Base Height (ARMP) .... CBH
Cloud Base Recorder (PDAA) .... CBR
Cloud Camera Multiplexer .... CCM
Cloud Ceiling Height (WEAT) .... CIG
Cloud Chamber [*Physics*] CC
Cloud Chamber Analysis .... CCA
Cloud Chamber Photographic Analysis .... CCPA
Cloud Climate Interactions Group (SAUO) .... CCIG
Cloud Condensation Nuclei [*Fog*] .... CCN
Cloud Cover (KSC) CC
Cloud Cover Radiometer (ADWA) .... CCR
Cloud Depiction and Forecast System [*Marine science*] (OSRA) .... CDFC
Cloud Depiction and Forecast System (SAUO) .... CDFS
Cloud Detection Lidar (ARMP) .... CDL
Cloud Drop Number Concentration (CARB) .... CDNC
Cloud Droplet Nuclei [*Climatology*] .... CDN
Cloud Ensemble Model (ARMP) .... CEM
Cloud Experiment Oberpfaffenhofen and Transports (SAUS) .... CLEOPATRA
Cloud Fraction (SAUS) .... CF
Cloud Height And Motion Experiment (SAUS) .... CHAMEX
Cloud Height Indicator (ACAE) .... CHI
Cloud Height Remote Indicating System (PDAA) .... CHRIS
Cloud in Cell CIC
Cloud Information Reference Archive and Library (SAUS) .... CIRLA
Cloud Interstitial Aerosol (SAUS) .... CIA
Cloud Layer Experiment (ARMP) .... CLEX
Cloud Lidar and Radar Exploratory Test (SAUS) .... CLARET
Cloud Lidar and Radar Exploratory Test (SAUS) .... CLARET II
Cloud LIDAR System (MCD) .... CLS
Cloud Mean (SAUS) .... CM
Cloud Model with Explicit Microphysics [*Marine science*] (OSRA) .... CM-XMP
Cloud Nine [*Manufacturer of remote control devices for home electronics*] [*Company founded by Stephen Wozniak*] CL9
Cloud Photopolarimeter (CARB) .... CPP
Cloud Physics (SAUS) .... CP
Cloud Physics Observatory [*University of Hawaii*] .... CPO
Cloud Physics Radar (SAUS) CP-2
Cloud Physics Radar (SAUS) .... CPR
Cloud Physics Radiometer .... CPR
Cloud Physics Studies in Israel (SAUS) .... CPSI
Cloud Point [*Petroleum characteristic*] .... CP
Cloud Processing Equipment (AABC) .... CPE
Cloud Profiling Radar System (ARMP) .... CPRS
Cloud Radiation Feedback [*Marine science*] (OSRA) .... CRF
Cloud Radiation Spectrometer (SAUS) .... CRS
Cloud Radiative Forcing [*Climatology*] .... CRF
Cloud Shadow (DNAB) .... CS
Cloud Systems Division (SAUS) .... CSD
Cloud to Air Lightning (WEAT) .... CA
Cloud to Cloud Lightning (WEAT) CC
Cloud to Ground [*Marine science*] (OSRA) .... CG
Cloud Top Scanner (MCD) .... CTS
Cloud Water Project [*A cooperative ecosystem study*] .... CWP
Cloud-Croft Radiation Measurement .... CRM
Cloud-Free Line of Sight .... CFLOS
Cloudiness Index (SAUS) CI
Cloudiness-Temperature [*Hypothesis*] [*Meteorology*] .... C-T

Cloud-Resolving Convection Parameterization (SAUS) .... CRCP
Cloud-Resolving Model (SAUS) .... CRM
Clouds (SAUS) .... Clds
Clouds and Climate Program (SAUS) .... CCPR
Clouds and Visibility Okay (SAUS) .... CAVOK
Clouds from AVHRR (SAUS) .... CLAVR
Clouds in Climate Program (SAUS) .... CCP
Clouds, Storms, and Regional Meteorology .... CSRM
Cloudscope (ARMP) .... CS
Cloud-to-Ground Lightning [*Meteorology*] .... CG
Cloud-to-Ground Lightning [*Meteorology*] (KSC) .... CGLTG
Cloud-Top Altitude Radiometer .... CAR
Cloud-Topped Boundary Layer [*Meterology*] .... CTBL
Cloud-Topped Marine Boundary Layer [*Marine science*] (OSRA) .... CTMBL
Cloudy [*Meteorology*] C
Cloudy [*Biochemistry*] (DAVI) cl
Cloudy .... CLDY
Cloudy (ADWA) .... cldy
Cloudy Cornea Syndrome [*Medicine*] (DMAA) .... CCS
Clove [*Seven pounds*] [*Unit of weight*] [*British*] (ROG) CL
Clover Bar Branch, Alberta Research Council, Edmonton, Alberta [*Library symbol*] [*National Library of Canada*] (NLC) .... AERC
Clover Blotch Virus [*Plant pathology*] .... CBV
Clover Primary Leaf Necrosis Virus [*Plant pathology*] .... CPLNV
Clover Yellow Mosaic Virus [*Plant pathology*] .... CLYMV
Clover Yellow Mosaic Virus .... CYMV
Clover Yellow Vein Virus [*Plant pathology*] .... CLYVV
Clover Yellow Vein Virus .... CYVV
Clover Yellows Virus [*Plant pathology*] .... CYV
Cloverdale Public Library, Cloverdale, CA [*Library symbol*] [*Library of Congress*] (LCLS) CCl
Cloverland Processing Center, Escanaba, MI [*OCLC symbol*] (OCLC) .... EZB
Clovis [*New Mexico*] [*Airport symbol*] (OAG) .... CVN
Clovis, CA [*AM radio station call letters*] (BROA) .... KBEG
Clovis, CA [*Television station call letters*] .... KGMC
Clovis, CA [*AM radio station call letters*] (BROA) .... KOOR
Clovis, CA [*AM radio station call letters*] .... KOQO
Clovis, NM [*Location identifier*] [*FAA*] (FAAL) .... CRY
Clovis, NM [*Location identifier*] [*FAA*] (FAAL) .... CVN
Clovis, NM [*Location identifier*] [*FAA*] (FAAL) .... CVS
Clovis, NM [*Location identifier*] [*FAA*] (FAAL) .... GLO
Clovis, NM [*FM radio station call letters*] (RBYB) .... KAQF-FM
Clovis, NM [*AM radio station call letters*] .... KCLV
Clovis, NM [*FM radio station call letters*] .... KCLV-FM
Clovis, NM [*AM radio station call letters*] .... KICA
Clovis, NM [*FM radio station call letters*] (BROA) .... KKYC-FM
Clovis, NM [*FM radio station call letters*] (RBYB) .... KSMX
Clovis, NM [*FM radio station call letters*] .... KTQM
Clovis, NM [*Television station call letters*] .... KVIH
Clovis, NM [*AM radio station call letters*] .... KWKA
Clovis, NM [*FM radio station call letters*] .... KWUA
Clovis/Cannon Air Force Base [*New Mexico*] [*ICAO location identifier*] (ICLI) .... KCVS
Clovis-Carver Public Library, Clovis, NM [*OCLC symbol*] (OCLC) CVC
Clovis-Carver Public Library, Clovis, NM [*Library symbol*] [*Library of Congress*] (LCLS) .... NmCl
Clown Care Unit .... CCU
Clown Club of America [*Later, CAI*] (EA) .... CCA
Clown Club of America (SAUO) .... CCA
Clowns of America [*Later, CAI*] (EA) .... CA
Clowns of America International (EA) .... CAI
Clowns of America, International (NTPA) .... COAI
Clow's Leading Cases on Torts [*A publication*] (DLA) .... Clow LC on Torts
Cloyne Branch, Frontenac County Library, Ontario [*Library symbol*] [*National Library of Canada*] (BIB) .... OCFC
Clozapine [*Organic chemistry*] .... CLOZ
Clozapine [*A drug*] .... CLZ
CLSC Albert Samson, Coaticook, Quebec [*Library symbol*] [*National Library of Canada*] (NLC) .... QCCL
CLSC de Hull, Centre de Documentation, Hull, PQ, Canada [*Library symbol*] [*Library of Congress*] (LCLS) .... CaQHCL
Club C
Club .... CLB
Club [*Commonly used*] (OPSA) .... CLUB
Club Air Europe Ltd. [*British*] [*ICAO designator*] (FAAC) .... CLU
Club & Institute Union Ltd. [*British*] (BI) .... CIU
Club and Society Union (SAUO) .... CSU
Club Anri [*Commercial firm*] (EA) .... CA
Club Aquarius (EA) .... CA
Club Cricket Conference [*British*] (BI) CCC
Club de las Americas [*Defunct*] (EA) .... CLA
Club de Petanque d'Adelaide [*Australia*] .... CdePA
Club Delahaye [*An association*] [*France*] (EAIO) .... CD
Club d'Electricite du Quebec Inc. (AC) .... CEleQ
Club der Luftfahrt (SAUS) .... CdL
Club des Ornithologues de Quebec Inc. (AC) .... COQ
Club Elite of North America (EA) .... CE
Club for Philately in Gerontology [*Defunct*] (EA) .... CPG
Club for Young Friends of Animals (SAUO) .... CYFA
Club Ford [*Class of racing cars*] .... CF
Club Francais d'Amerique (EA) .... CFA
Club Francais du Disque [*Record label*] [*France*] .... CFD
Club Francais du Livre [*French Book Club*] .... CFL
Club International des Jeunes Naturistes [*Paris, France*] (EAIO) .... CIJN
Club Magazine [*Generic term for a publication covering the activities of a science-fiction fan club*] .... CLUBZINE
Club Management [*Club Managers Association of America*] [*A publication*] .... CM
Club Managers' Association [*Australia*] .... CMA
Club Managers Association of America (EA) .... CMAA
Club Med, Inc. (EFIS) .... CMI
Club Mediterranee (EA) .... CM
Club National du Disque [*Record label*] [*France*] .... CND
Club of Channel Islands Collectors (EA) CCIC
Club of Printing Women of New York (EA) .... CPW
Club of the Friends of Ancient Smoothing Irons (EA) .... CFASI
Club Royale d'Automobile du Canada [*Royal Automobile Club of Canada*] .... CRAC
Club Safety Officer (DNAB) .... CSO
Club Zoologico [*Universiti Putra Malaysia*] [*University student group*] (GVA) .... CZ
Clubair [*ICAO designator*] (AD) .... CG
Clubbing, Cyanosis, or Edema [*Medicine*] .... CCE
Clubhouse .... CLBHS
Clublink Corp. [*Toronto Stock Exchange symbol*] (SG) .... LNK
Clubs [*Public-performance tariff class*] [*British*] .... J
CluckCorp International, Inc. [*Associated Press*] (SAG) .... ClkCorp
CluckCorp International, Inc. [*NASDAQ symbol*] (SAG) .... ROTI
Clue Computing Co. [*British*] CCC
Cluett, Peabody & Co., Inc. (SAUO) .... CLU
Cluj [*Kolozvar*] [*Romania*] [*Seismograph station code, US Geological Survey*] [*Closed*] (SEIS) .... CLU
Cluj-Napoca [*Romania*] [*Airport symbol*] (OAG) .... CLJ
Cluj-Napoca/Someseni [*Romania*] [*ICAO location identifier*] (ICLI) .... LRCL
Clumber Spaniel Club of America (EA) .... CSCA
Clumped (STED) .... clmp
Clumped [*Biochemistry*] (DAVI) .... CLMP
Clumping Inducing Agent [*Bacteriology, genetics*] .... CIA
Cluny [*Queensland*] [*Airport symbol*] (AD) .... CZY
Cluskey's Political Text Book [*A publication*] (DLA) .... Clusk Pol TB
Cluster (NASA) CL
Cluster [*Programming language*] [*1973*] (CSR) .... CLU
Cluster Activation Systems Specialist [*NASA*] .... CAS
Cluster Activation Systems Specialist [*NASA*] (KSC) .... CASS
Cluster Activator Systems Specialist (SAUS) .... CASS
Cluster Analysis [*Data analysis*] .... CA
Cluster Analysis (SAUS) .... CLUSAN
Cluster Analysis and Regression Program (SAUS) .... CARP
Cluster Bomb [*Military*] .... CLSTBB
Cluster Bomb Unit [*Military*] .... CBU
Cluster Coding Algorithm (SAUS) .... CCA
Cluster Compression Algorithm (MCD) .... CCA
Cluster Control Unit .... CCU
Cluster Controller CC
Cluster Controller Node (IAA) .... CCN
Cluster Designation [*Immunology*] .... CD
Cluster Environmental Protection Specialist (SARE) .... CEPS
Cluster F (SAUS) .... CF
Cluster Headache [*Neurology*] (DAVI) .... CH
Cluster Maintenance Facility [*Military*] .... CMF
Cluster Mission Simulator [*NASA*] (KSC) .... CLMS
Cluster Munition (SAUS) .... CM
Cluster of Differentiation [*Immunology*] .... CD
Cluster of Orthologous Group [*Genetics*] .... COG
Cluster of Stones [*Jewelry*] (ROG) .... CLUS
Cluster of Working Nodes (SAUS) .... CLOWN
Cluster of Workstations (RALS) .... COW
Cluster Process (ACAE) .... CP
Cluster Significance Analysis [*Data Analysis*] .... CSA
Cluster Systems Description Document (KSC) .... CSDD
Cluster Tool Controller (AAEL) .... CTC
Cluster Tool Modular Communications (AAEL) .... CTMC
Cluster Variation Method [*Physics*] .... CVM
Cluster-Bethe-Lattice Method (MCD) .... CBLM
Cluster-Catalyzed Reactivity [*Physics*] .... CCR
Clustered Air Technology (ACAE) .... CAT
Clustered Airfield Defeat Munition (MCD) .... CADM
Clustered Airfield Depot Munition (MCD) .... CADM
Clustered Airfield Dispersed Munition (SAUS) .... CADM
Clustered Atomic Warhead .... CLAW
Clustered Bomb Units (SAUS) .... CBUs
Clustered File Migration (SAUS) .... CFM
Clusterin (DMAA) .... CLU
Clustering Identification (SAUS) .... CLID
Cluster-Ion Spectroscopy (SAUS) .... CIS
Cluster-Limited. Journal Cross-Citing Matrix (SAUS) .... CLJCC Matrix
Clutch (MSA) CL
Clutch .... CLTCH
Clutch (SAUS) .... CLU
Clutch Drive [*on a ship*] (DS) .... CD
Clutch Hitting Index (SAUS) .... chi
Clutch Pitching Index (SAUS) .... cpi
Clutch Release Bearing .... CRB
Clutter (MSA) .... CLTR
Clutter (SAUS) .... Clut
Clutter Acquisition .... CLA
Clutter Attenuation (ACAE) .... CA
Clutter Automatic Gain Control (SAUS) .... CACC
Clutter Automatic Gain Control .... CAGC
Clutter Discriminating Fuze (MCD) .... CDF
Clutter Doppler Error (MCD) .... CDE

Clutter Gate .... CG
Clutter Gate Amplifier (MCD) .... CGA
Clutter Map (MSA) .... CLTRM
Clutter Map Update [*Military*] .... CMUP
Clutter Mapper Card .... CMC
Clutter on Target (MCD) .... COT
Clutter Reject Band (MCD) .... CRB
Clutter Rejection Factor (ACAE) .... CRF
Clutter Rejection RADAR .... CRR
Clutter Suppression Interferometry (SAUS) .... CSI
Clutter Threshold Detector (CET) .... CTD
Clutter-Locked Airborne Moving Target Indicator [*Air Force*] .... CLAMTI
Clutter-Operated Anticlutter .... COAC
Clutter-to-Noise Ratio (SAUS) .... CNR
Clyde Bowling Fan Club [*Defunct*] (EA) .... CBFC
Clyde Cablevision [*Commercial firm*] [*British*] (NITA) CCV
Clyde Mood Scale [*Psychology*] .... CMS
Clyde, NY [*FM radio station call letters*] .... WECQ
Clyde, NY [*FM radio station call letters*] (RBYB) .... WLLW-FM
Clyde, OH [*FM radio station call letters*] .... WHVT
Clyde, OH [*FM radio station call letters*] .... WNCG
Clyde Operational Headquarters (SAUS) .... COH
Clyde Port Authority (SAUO) .... CPA
Clyde River [*Canada*] [*Airport symbol*] (OAG) .... YCY
Clyde River, NT [*ICAO location identifier*] (ICLI) .... CYCY
Clyde Shipping Co. (MHDW) .... CSC
Clyde Surveys Ltd. [*British*] [*ICAO designator*] (FAAC) .... CLY
Clyde Yacht Clubs Association [*British*] (DBA) .... CYCA
Clyde Yacht Clubs Association (SAUO) .... CYCA
Clydebank (SAUS) .... Cly
Clydesdale [*Valley in Scotland*] (ROG) .... CLD
Clydesdale Bank [*British*] .... CB
Clydesdale Breeders Association of the United States [*Later, CBUS*] (EA) .... CBA
Clydesdale Breeders of the United States (EA) .... CBUS
Clydesdale Horse Society [*British*] (DBA) .... CHS
Clydesdale Horse Society of Great Britain and Ireland (SAUO) .... CHSGBI
Clydesdale Runner's Association [*Defunct*] (EA) .... CRA
Clyidyl Methacrylate (SAUS) .... GMA
Clymer System .... CS
CM: A Reviewing Journal of Canadian Materials for Young People [*A publication*] (BRI) .... Can Mat
CM Preference Corp. [*Toronto Stock Exchange symbol*] .... ZCM
CMAC Computer Systems Ltd. [*Vancouver Stock Exchange symbol*] .... CMB
CMAC Investment [*NYSE symbol*] (TTSB) .... CMT
CMAC Investment Corp. [*Associated Press*] (SAG) .... CMAC
CMAC Investment Corp. [*NYSE symbol*] (SPSG) .... CMT
CMC Industries [*NASDAQ symbol*] (TTSB) .... CMCI
CMC Industries, Inc. [*NASDAQ symbol*] (NQ) .... CMCI
CMC Industries, Inc. [*Associated Press*] (SAG) .... CMC Ind
CME Capital, Inc. [*Toronto Stock Exchange symbol*] .... CME
CME Information Services (SAUO) .... CMEIS
C-Methylene-Bisphenol-Isocyanate (SAUS) .... MDI
CMG Computer Management Group Ltd. (SAUO) .... CMG
CMG Info Services [*NASDAQ symbol*] (TTSB) .... CMGI
CMG Information Services [*NASDAQ symbol*] (SAG) .... CMGI
CMG Information Services [*Associated Press*] (SAG) .... CMG Inf
CMGI, Inc. [*NASDAQ symbol*] (SG) .... CMGI
CMI Commodity Management International (SAUO) .... CMI
CMI Corp. [*Associated Press*] (SAG) .... CMI Cp
CMI Corp. [*NYSE symbol*] (SAG) .... CMX
CMI Corp. Cl'A' [*NYSE symbol*] (SG) .... CMI
CMI Corp. Cl'A' [*NYSE symbol*] (TTSB) .... CMX
CMI Investment (SAUO) .... CML
C-minus (SAUS) .... C-
CML Group [*NYSE symbol*] (TTSB) .... CML
CML Group, Inc. [*NYSE symbol*] (SPSG) .... CML
CML Group, Inc. [*Associated Press*] (SAG) .... CML Gp
CML Industries Ltd. [*Toronto Stock Exchange symbol*] .... CNO
CMOS [*Complementary Metal Oxide Semiconductor*] **Compact Cell Logic** [*Electronics*] (NITA) CCCL
CMOS Idustrial Microcomputer (NITA) .... CIM
CMOS PLDs programmed with EyPROM switching arrays (SAUS) .... EyPLD
CMOS Programmable Logic Device (SAUS) .... CPLD
CMOS Random Access Memory (SAUS) .... SCRAM
CMP Group [*Formerly, Central Maine Power*] [*NYSE symbol*] .... CTP
CMS Energy [*Associated Press*] (SAG) .... CMS
CMS Energy [*NYSE symbol*] (SAG) .... CPG
CMS Energy Cl'G' [*NYSE symbol*] (TTSB) .... CPG
CMS Energy Corp. [*NYSE symbol*] (SPSG) .... CMS
CMS Energy Corp. [*Associated Press*] (SAG) .... CMS Eng
CMV [*Cucumber Mosaic Virus*] **Associated Ribonucleic Acid** [*Biochemistry, genetics*] .... CARNA
CMX Company (SAUO) .... CMX
CN Biosciences, Inc. [*NASDAQ symbol*] (SAG) .... CNBI
CN Biosciences, Inc. [*Associated Press*] (SAG) .... CN Biosc
CNA Financial [*NYSE symbol*] (TTSB) .... CNA
CNA Financial Corp. (SAUO) .... CAF
CNA Financial Corp. [*NYSE symbol*] (SPSG) .... CNA
CNA Financial Corp. [*Associated Press*] (SAG) .... CNA Fn
CNA Financial Corp., Chicago, IL [*Library symbol*] [*Library of Congress*] (LCLS) .... ICCNA
CNA Financial Corp., Library, Chicago, IL [*Inactive*] [*OCLC symbol*] (OCLC) .... IBG
CNA Income Shares [*NYSE symbol*] (TTSB) .... CNN
CNA Income Shares, Inc. [*Associated Press*] (SAG) .... CNAI
CNA Income Shares, Inc. [*NYSE symbol*] (SPSG) .... CNN
CNA Larwin Investment Co. (SAUO) .... CNL
CNA Surety [*NYSE symbol*] (SG) .... SUR
CNARESTRA [*Chief of Naval Air Reserve Training*] **Fleet Operating Squadrons** .... CFOS
CNB Bancshares, Inc. [*NYSE symbol*] (SAG) .... BNK
CNB Bancshares, Inc. [*Associated Press*] (SAG) .... CNB
CNB Bancshares, Inc. [*Associated Press*] (SAG) .... CNB Bcsh
CNB Bancshares, Inc. [*NASDAQ symbol*] (NQ) .... CNBE
CNB Financial Corp. [*New York*] [*NASDAQ symbol*] (SAG) .... CNBF
CNB Financial Corp NY [*Associated Press*] (SAG) .... CNB Fn
CNB Financial(NY) [*NASDAQ symbol*] (TTSB) .... CNBF
Cneius (ABBR) .... CN
Cnel. Suarez [*Argentina*] [*ICAO location identifier*] (ICLI) .... SAZC
CNES Gravity Satellite (SAUO) .... GRADO
CNET, Inc. [*NASDAQ symbol*] (SG) .... CNET
CNF Transportation [*NYSE symbol*] (SG) .... CNF
CNI-Computer Networks International Ltd. [*Vancouver Stock Exchange symbol*] .... CUW
CNN Financial News .... CNNFn
CNO [*Chief of Naval Operations*] **Advisory Board** .... CAB
CNO [*Chief of Naval Operations*] **Executive Board** .... CEB
CNO [*Chief of Naval Operations*] **Industry Advisory Committee for Telecommunications** [*DoD*] (EGAO) .... CIACT
CNO [*Chief of Naval Operations*] **Policy and Planning Guidance** .... CPPG
CNO [*Chief of Naval Operations*] **Program Analysis Memorandum** .... CPAM
CNO [*Chief of Naval Operations*] **Program Fiscal Guidance** [*Navy*] (CAAL) .... CPFG
CNP Resource Centre, Energy, Mines, and Resources Canada [*Centre d'Information EESP, Energie, Mines, et Ressources Canada*] **Ottawa, Ontario** [*Library symbol*] [*National Library of Canada*] (NLC) .... OOCNP
CNR [*Christian News Report*] **Ministries** (EA) .... CNRM
CNS Applications Research & Development (SAUO) .... CARD II
CNS Bancorp, Inc. [*NASDAQ symbol*] (SAG) .... CNSB
CNS Bancorp, Inc. [*Associated Press*] (SAG) .... CNS Bcp
CNS, Inc. [*Associated Press*] (SAG) .... CNS
CNS, Inc. [*NASDAQ symbol*] (NQ) .... CNXS
Cntrolled Slip Clutch .... CSC
CNW Corp. [*NYSE symbol*] (SPSG) .... CNW
Co. Counsel Inc. Wrrt [*NASDAQ symbol*] (TTSB) .... LEGIW
Co Sine Communications [*NASDAQ symbol*] .... COSN
CO_2 LASER Technology [*Military*] .... COLT
Coach .... CH
Coach [*Airline fare code*] .... Y
Coach and Bus First Aid Association [*British*] (DBA) .... CABFAA
Coach and Independent Bus Sector [*British*] (DI) .... CIBS
Coach Builder (ROG) .... CB
Coach House .... CH
Coach, Inc. [*NYSE symbol*] .... COH
Coach Lace Institute [*Defunct*] (EA) CLI
Coach USA [*NYSE symbol*] (SG) .... CUI
Coach USA [*NASDAQ symbol*] (TTSB) .... TOUR
Coachella [*California*] [*Seismograph station code, US Geological Survey*] (SEIS) .... COA
Coachella, CA [*AM radio station call letters*] .... KCLB
Coachella, CA [*FM radio station call letters*] .... KCLB-FM
Coachella Municipal Public Library, Coachella, CA [*Library symbol*] [*Library of Congress*] (LCLS) .... CCoac
Coaches [*Freight*] .... COCH
Coaches Association of PEI (AC) .... CAPEI
Coaching Association of Canada .... CAC
Coaching Club (EA) CC
Coaching Club (SAUO) CC
Coaching Club American Oaks (SAUO) .... CCAO
Coaching Process Questionnaire (TMMY) .... CPQ
Coachmen Indus [*NYSE symbol*] (TTSB) .... COA
Coachmen Industries, Inc. [*NYSE symbol*] (SPSG) .... COA
Coachmen Industries, Inc. [*Associated Press*] (SAG) .... Coachm
Coadjutor (ROG) .... COAD
Coadjutor (ROG) .... COADJ
Coadjutor Bishop (ROG) .... COADJ BP
Coady International Institute (AC) CII
Coagulant (SAUS) .... COAG
Coagulant (SAUS) .... vit K
Coagulase [*An enzyme*] C
Coagulase [*An enzyme*] .... coag
Coagulase-Negative Staphylococci [*Medicine*] (DMAA) .... CNST
Coagulase-Reacting Factor [*Biochemistry*] (MAE) .... CRF
Coagulation [*Test*] .... CA
Coagulation .... CoA
Coagulation .... COAG
Coagulation Profile - Diagnosis [*Hematology*] (DAVI) .... COAG PD
Coagulation Profile - Presurgery [*Hematology*] (DAVI) .... COAG PP
Coagulation Screen (STED) .... COAGSC
Coagulation Time (DB) .... CT
Coahoma Junior College [*Clarksdale,MS*] .... CJC
Coahoma, TX [*FM radio station call letters*] .... KBYG
Coahuila & Zacatecas Railway [*AAR code*] .... CZ
Coal and Allied Industries Ltd. (SAUS) .... CAIL
Coal and Coke .... C & C
Coal and Metalliferous Mines Fatigue Board (SAUO) .... CMMFB
Coal and Mining (SAUS) .... C&M
Coal and Mining .... C & M
Coal and Petroleum Products [*Department of Employment*] [*British*] .... CPP
Coal and Shale Mine Workers' Superannuation Tribunal [*Australia*] .... COSMWST

Coal and Slurry Technology Association (NTPA)	CSTA
Coal and Steel (NATG)	CS
Coal and Steel Community (SAUO)	CSC
Coal and Steel Planning Committee [NATO] (NATG)	CSPC
Coal and Technology Export Program (AAGC)	CTEP
[The] Coal Association of Canada (AC)	CAC
Coal Aston [British] [ICAO location identifier] (ICLI)	EGCA
Coal Bed Methane (SAUS)	CBM
Coal Board (SAUO)	CB
Coal Bug One [Microbe used to remove sulfur from coal]	CB1
Coal Charges Fund (SAUO)	CCF
Coal City, IL [FM radio station call letters] (BROA)	WBVS-FM
Coal City, IL [FM radio station call letters]	WKBM
Coal Combustion Technology	CCT
Coal Commission (SAUO)	CC
Coal Commission (SAUS)	CC
Coal Committee of the Combined Raw Materials Board (SAUS)	CCCRMB
Coal Committee of the Combined Raw Materials Board (SAUO)	CCCRMB
Coal, Conservation, and Nuclear [Energy substitutes for oil] [British]	Co-Co-Nuke
Coal Consumers Protective Association (SAUO)	CCPA
Coal Container (SAUS)	Cooltainer
Coal Contractors Ltd. [British]	CCL
Coal Corporation of Victoria [Australia] [Commercial firm]	CCV
Coal Data Base [International Energy Agency] [British] (NITA)	CDB
Coal Development Establishment [British] (BI)	CDE
Coal Division, Denison Mines Ltd., Vancouver, British Columbia [Library symbol] [National Library of Canada] (BIB)	BVADC
Coal Employment Project (EA)	CEP
Coal Energy Research Committee	CERC
Coal Equivalent	CE
Coal Experts Committee [Allied German Occupation Forces]	CEC
Coal Exporters Association of the United States (EA)	CEA
Coal Extraction and Utilization Research Center [Southern Illinois University at Carbondale] [Research center] (RCD)	CEURC
Coal Fired Combined Cycle (SAUS)	CFCC
Coal Fluid Flow Facility	CFFF
Coal Fuel Mixtures Association (EA)	CFMA
Coal [into] Gas [Process]	COGAS
Coal Grove, OH [FM radio station call letters]	WBVB
Coal Handling Plant	CHP
Coal India Limited (CARB)	CIL
Coal Industry Advisory Board	CIAB
Coal Industry National Consultative Council (HEAS)	CINCC
Coal Industry Social Welfare Organisation [British]	CISWO
Coal Industry Society [British] (BI)	CIS
Coal Industry Society (SAUO)	CIS
Coal Industry Tripartite Group (SAUO)	CITG
Coal into Gas Process (SAUS)	COGAS Process
Coal Laboratory Analyses (SAUO)	CLA
Coal Merchants Federation [British] (DBA)	CMF
Coal Mine Maps (SAUO)	CMM
Coal Mine Roof Rating [US Bureau of Mines]	CMRR
Coal Mine Workers' Pension Tribunal [Victoria] [Australia]	CMWPT
Coal Miners' Industrial Union of Workers [Australia]	CMIUW
Coal Miners of North America (SAUO)	CMNA
Coal Mines Administration (SAUO)	CMA
Coal Mines Authority Ltd. (SAUO)	CMAL
Coal Mines Board (DAS)	CMB
Coal Mines Department (SAUO)	CMD
Coal Mines Department (SAUS)	CMD
Coal Mines Research Station (SAUO)	CMRS
Coal Mining Act (SAUO)	CMA
Coal Mining and Quarrying	CMAQ
Coal Mining Institute of America [Later, PCMIA] (EA)	CMIA
Coal Mining Qualifications Board [New South Wales] [Australia]	CMQB
Coal Mining Research Centre [Canada]	CMRC
Coal Operators' Industrial Organisation of Employers, Queensland [Australia]	COIOEQ
Coal Preparation Plant Association [British] (EAIO)	CPPA
Coal Production Committee (SAUO)	COPROD
Coal Research Association (SAUO)	CRA
Coal Research Association of New Zealand (SAUO)	CRANZ
Coal Research Board (SAUO)	CRB
Coal Research Establishment [British] (IRUK)	CRE
Coal Research Program (SAUO)	CRP
Coal Research Projects [IEA Coal Research] [Database]	COALPRO
Coal Research Series Titles (SAUO)	CRST
Coal Reserves Data Base	CRDB
Coal Samples Analyses (SAUO)	CSA
Coal Store (OA)	CS
Coal Supply and Transportation Model [Department of Energy] (GFGA)	CSTM
Coal Tar Pitch Emulsion Council [Defunct] (EA)	CTPEC
Coal Tar Pitch Volatile [Organic chemistry]	CTPV
Coal Tar Research Association [British] (BI)	CTRA
Coal Tar Research Association (SAUO)	CTRA
Coal Technology Information Centre [Alberta Research Council] [Information service or system] (IID)	CTIC
Coal to Oil to Gas (SAUS)	C-O-G
Coal Trade Benevolent Association (SAUO)	CTBA
Coal Trade Conciliation Board (SAUO)	CTCB
Coal Trading Association (SAUO)	CTA
Coal Traffic Manager	CTM
Coal Transport (SAUS)	CT
Coal Utilisation Council [British]	CUC
Coal Utilization Joint Council (SAUO)	CUJC
Coal Workers' Pneumoconiosis [Black lung] [Medicine]	CWP
Coaldale, NV [Location identifier] [FAA] (FAAL)	OAL
Coaldale Public Library, Alberta [Library symbol] [National Library of Canada] (NLC)	ACO
Coalesce	CLSC
Coalescence Progress (SAUS)	COPROG
Coal-Fired Power Plant	CFPP
Coal-Gas Atmosphere (MCD)	CGA
Coalgate, OK [FM radio station call letters] (BROA)	KAZE-FM
Coalicion de Liberacion Nacional [Panama] [Political party] (EY)	COLINA
Coalicion del Centro Democratico [Nicaragua] [Political party] (EY)	CD
Coalicion Democratica [Democratic Coalition] [Spain] [Political party] (PPE)	CD
Coalicion Galega [Spain] [Political party] (EY)	CG
Coalicion Institucionalista Democratica [Democratic Institutional Coalition] [Ecuador] [Political party] (PPW)	CID
Coalicion Nacional Republicana [Ecuador] [Political party] (EY)	CNR
Coalicion Nacionalista [Spain] [Political party] (ECED)	CN
Coalicion Popular [Popular Coalition] [Spain] [Political party] (PPW)	CP
Coaling Station [As part of a symbol]	CS
Coalinga, CA [Location identifier] [FAA] (FAAL)	CLG
Coalinga, CA [FM radio station call letters] (BROA)	KAZB-FM
Coalinga, CA [AM radio station call letters]	KKFO
Coalinga, CA [FM radio station call letters]	KNGS
Coalinga Unified School District Library, Coalinga, CA [Library symbol] [Library of Congress] (LCLS)	CCoa
Coaliquid, Inc. (MCD)	CLI
Coalition (ADA)	COAL
Coalition (SAUS)	Coal
Coalition Advocating for Disability Refoerm in Education	CADRE
Coalition Against Anti-Asian Violence (EA)	CAAAV
Coalition Against Black Exploitation (EA)	CABE
Coalition Against Dangerous Exports	CADE
Coalition Against Double Taxation [Defunct] (EA)	CADT
Coalition Against Noneffective Lightning Protection Technologies (EA)	CANT
Coalition Against On-Line Forms	CAOF
Coalition Against Pipeline Pollution (EA)	CAP
Coalition Against Regressive Taxation (EA)	CART
Coalition Against Sexist-Racist Hiring [Student legal action organization]	CASH
Coalition Against Unsolicited Commercial Email [An association] [Computer science]	CAUCE
Coalition Canadienne pour les Droits des Lesbiennes et des Gais [Canadian Lesbian and Gay Rights Coalition]	CCDLG
Coalition Concerned with Developmental Disabilities [American Occupational Therapy Association]	CCDD
Coalition, Coordination, Communications, and Integration Center (DOMA)	C³IC
Coalition de l'Opposition Democratique [Togo] [Political party] (EY)	COD
Coalition des Gauches [Left Unity] [Transnational party group in the European Parliament] (ECED)	CG
Coalition des Organismes Communautaires Quebecois de Lutte Contre le Sida (AC)	COCQ-SIDA
Coalition for a Decent USA [Defunct] (EA)	CDUSA
Coalition for a Democratic Majority (EA)	CDM
Coalition for a National Health System (EA)	CNHS
Coalition for a New Foreign Policy [Defunct] (EA)	CNFP
Coalition for a Non-Nuclear World [Defunct] (EA)	CNNW
Coalition for a Nuclear Free Harbor (EA)	CNFH
Coalition for Academic Supercomputer Centers (SAUS)	CASC
Coalition for Advancement in Jewish Education (SAUO)	CAJE
Coalition for Advertising Supported Information and Entertainment	CASIE
Coalition for Affordable Health Care	CAHC
Coalition for Alternatives in Jewish Education (EA)	CAJE
Coalition for an Undercharge Relief Bill (WPI)	CURB
Coalition for Asian Peace and Security (EA)	CAPS
Coalition for Auto Repair Choice [Defunct] (EA)	CARC
Coalition for Auto Repair Equality [Automotive aftermarket parts lobbying group]	CARE
Coalition for Better Television (SAUO)	CBT
Coalition for Better Television	CBTV
Coalition for Biomedical & Health Research (SAUO)	CBHR
[The] Coalition for Brand Equity [An organization of advertisers, agencies, and media]	CBE
Coalition for Children and Youth [American Occupational Therapy Association]	CCY
Coalition for Christian Colleges and Universities (NTPA)	CCCU
Coalition for Common Courtesy [Defunct] (EA)	CCC
Coalition for Common Sense in Government Procurement [Later, CGP] [Washington, DC] (EA)	CCSGP
Coalition for Constitutional Justice and Security (EA)	CCJS
Coalition for Consumer Health and Safety (EA)	CCHS
Coalition for Consumer Justice [Defunct] (EA)	CCJ
Coalition for Corporate Responsibility [Defunct] (EA)	CCR
Coalition for Decency [Later, NFF] (EA)	CFD
Coalition for Drug-Free Horse Racing (EA)	CDFHR
Coalition for Earth Science Education (SAUO)	CESE
Coalition for Economic Growth (SAUS)	CEG
Coalition for Economic Survival (EA)	CES
Coalition for Education in the Life Sciences (SAUO)	CELS
Coalition for Energy Efficiency and Renewable Technologies (EA)	CEERT
Coalition for Environmentally-Responsible Economies (EA)	CERES
Coalition for Excellence in Science Education (SAUO)	CESE
Coalition for Food Irradiation [Defunct] (EA)	CFI
Coalition for Free and Open Elections (EA)	COFOE
Coalition for Government Procurement (EA)	CGP
Coalition for Handicapped Children's Education (DAVI)	CHANCE

Coalition for Harmony of Races in the US (EA) .... CHORUS
Coalition for Health and the Environment (EA) .... CHE
Coalition for Health Funding (EA) .... CHF
Coalition for Healthier Cities and Communities (SAUO) .... CHCC
Coalition for Heritable Disorders of Connective Tissue (SAUO) .... CHDCT
Coalition for Hypertension Education and Control .... CHEC
Coalition for Indian Education (EA) .... CIA
Coalition for Information Access for Print Handicapped Readers [An association] .... CIAPHR
Coalition for Intelligent Manufacturing Systems (SAUS) .... CIMS
Coalition for International Cooperation and Peace (EA) .... CICP
Coalition for International Trade Equity .... CITE
Coalition for Jobs, Peace, and Freedom in America (EA) .... CJPFA
Coalition for Justice in the Maquiladoras (CROSS) .... CJM
Coalition for Lesbian & Gay Right in Ontario [Coalition pour les Droits des Lesbiennes et Personnes Gaies en Ontario] [Formerly, Coalition for Gay Rights in Ontario] (AC) .... CLGRO
Coalition for Life for All Mollusks .... CLAM
Coalition for Literacy (EA) CL
Coalition for Manufacturing Performance through Technology .... COMPETE
Coalition for National Dance Week (EA) .... CNDW
Coalition for National Science Funding (SAUS) .... CNSF
Coalition for Networked Information [Computer science] (TNIG) .... CNI
Coalition for Networked Information Directories (SAUO) .... CNIDIR
Coalition for Non-Violent Food (EA) .... CNVF
Coalition for Non-Violent Food (EA) .... CONF
Coalition for Patient Rights (SAUO) .... CPR
Coalition for Peace through Strength [Later, CCNS] (EA) .... CPTS
Coalition for Pesticide Reform (COE) .... CPR
Coalition for Positive Sexuality (SAUO) .... CPS
Coalition for Prompt Pay (EA) .... CPP
Coalition for Public Information (AC) .... CPI
Coalition for Religious Freedom (EA) .... CRF
Coalition for Responsible Genetic Research (HGAA) .... CRGR
Coalition for Responsible Mining Law [Defunct] .... CRML
Coalition for Responsible Waste Incineration (EA) .... CRWI
Coalition for Retirement Income Security (EA) .... CRIS
Coalition for Safe and Efficient Transportation [MTMC] (TAG) .... CSET
Coalition for Safe Energy (SAUS) .... CASE
Coalition for Safe Food [Defunct] (EA) .... CSF
Coalition for Safety of Abortion Clinics [Defunct] (EA) .... CSAC
Coalition for Scenic Beauty [Later, SA] (EA) .... CSB
Coalition for Sensible Pesticide Policy (WPI) .... CSPP
Coalition for Sound Money (EA) .... CSM
Coalition for State Prompt Pay (EA) .... CSPP
Coalition for Strategic Stability in the Middle East (EA) .... CSSME
Coalition for the Abolition of Marijuana Prohibition (EA) .... CAMP
Coalition for the Advancement of Foreign Languages and International Studies .... CAFLIS
Coalition for the Advancement of Jewish Education (EA) .... CAJE
Coalition for the Apostolic Ministry [Later, ECM] .... CAM
Coalition for the Defense of Human Rights Under Islam .... CDHRUI
Coalition for the Education and Support of Attention Deficit Disorder (PAZ) .... Co-ADD
Coalition for the Medical Rights of Women (SAUO) .... CDRR
Coalition for the Medical Rights of Women [Defunct] .... CMRW
Coalition for the Peaceful Uses of Space (EA) .... CPUS
Coalition for the Strategic Defense Initiative (EA) .... CSDI
Coalition for Travel Industry Parity (TRID) .... CTIP
Coalition for Uniform Product Liability Law (EA) .... CUPLL
Coalition for Urban Transport Sanity (SAUO) .... CUTS
Coalition for Vehicle Choice (SAUS) CVC
Coalition for Vocational Home Economics Education (EA) .... CVHEE
Coalition for Women in International Development (EA) .... CWID
Coalition for Women in the Humanities and Social Sciences [Defunct] (EA) .... CWHSS
Coalition for Women's Appointments (EA) .... CWA
Coalition for Workplace Technology [Defunct] (EA) .... CWT
coalition government (SAUO) .... coalgovt
Coalition Government of Democratic Kampuchea .... CGDK
Coalition in the Use of Learning Skills (SAUS) .... CULS
Coalition Internationale pour l'Action au Developpement [International Coalition for Development Action - ICDA] (EAIO) .... CIAD
Coalition Mondiale pour l'Abolition de la Vivisection [World Coalition for the Abolition of Vivisection] .... CMAV
Coalition Nationale pour les Droits des Homosexuals [National Gay Rights Coalition] [Canada] .... CNDH
Coalition of Adult Education Organizations (EA) .... CAEO
Coalition of America to Save the Economy (EA) .... CASE
Coalition of American Pro-Life University Students [Later, ACL] (EA) .... CAMPUS
Coalition of American Public Employees .... CAPE
Coalition of Apparel Industries in California (SRA) .... CAIC
Coalition of Asians to Nix Charlie Chan (EA) .... CAN Charlie Chan
Coalition of Automotive Associations [Defunct] (EA) .... CAA
Coalition of Black Trade Unionists (EA) .... CBTU
Coalition of Digestive Disease Organizations (EA) .... CDDO
Coalition of Eastern Native Americans [Defunct] (EA) .... CENA
Coalition of Essential Schools .... CES
Coalition of Ethiopian Forces .... COEDF
Coalition of Higher Education Assistance Organizations (EA) .... CHEAO
Coalition of Higher Education Assistance Organizations (EA) .... COEAO
Coalition of Higher Education Assistance Organizations (NTPA) .... COHEAO
Coalition of Holistic Health Organizations [Defunct] (EA) .... CHHO
Coalition of Indian Controlled School Boards (EDAC) .... CICSB

Coalition of Labor Union Women (EA) .... CLUW
Coalition of Labor Union Women Center for Education and Research (EA) .... CLUWCER
Coalition of Minority Policy Professionals (EA) .... CoMPP
Coalition of Minority Women in Business [Washington, DC] (EA) .... CMWB
Coalition of Municipalities to Ban Animal Trafficking (EA) .... COMBAT
Coalition of National Agreement [Croatia] [Political party] .... CNA
Coalition of National Voluntary Organizations (DICI) .... CONVO
Coalition of National Voluntary Organizations [Also, National Voluntary Organizations] (AC) .... NVO
Coalition of Non-Postal Media [Defunct] (EA) .... CNPM
Coalition of Northeastern Governors (EPA) .... CNG
Coalition of Northeastern Governors .... CONEG
Coalition of Public Employee Organizations (EA) .... CPEO
Coalition of Publicly Traded Limited Partnerships [Later, CoPTP] (EA) .... CPTLP
Coalition of Publicly Traded Partnerships (EA) .... CoPTP
Coalition of Publicly Traded Partnerships (NTPA) .... CPTP
Coalition of Service Industries [Washington, DC] (EA) .... CSI
Coalition of Spanish Speaking Mental Health Organizations [Later, NCHHHSO] (EA) .... COSSMHO
Coalition of Steel-Using Manufacturers .... CASUM
Coalition of Women in National and International Business [Boston, MA] (EA) .... CWNIB
Coalition of Women's Art Organizations (EA) .... CWAO
Coalition on Block Grants and Human Needs (EA) .... CBGHN
Coalition on Government Information (EA) .... CGI
Coalition on Human Needs (EA) .... CHN
Coalition on Political Assassinations (EA) .... COPA
Coalition on Resource Recovery and the Environment (EA) .... CORRE
Coalition on Sensible Transport .... COST
Coalition on Sexuality and Disability (EA) .... CSD
Coalition on Smoking or Health (EA) .... CSH
Coalition on Southern Africa (EA) .... CSA
Coalition on Temporary Shelter .... COTS
Coalition on Women and Religion (EA) .... CWR
Coalition on Women and the Budget [Defunct] (EA) .... CWB
Coalition Opposed to Signal Theft (EA) .... COST
Coalition Sida des Sourds du Quebec (AC) .... CSSQ
Coalition Task Force (SAUS) .... CTF
Coalition to Abolish the Draize Rabbit Blinding Tests (EA) .... CADRBT
Coalition to Cease Ocean Dumping (SAUS) .... CCOD
Coalition to End Grand Jury Abuse [Later, CPR] (EA) .... CEGJA
Coalition to Free Petkus and Gajauskas [Defunct] (EA) .... CFPG
Coalition to Free Soviet Jews (EA) .... CFSJ
Coalition to Halt Auto Theft (EA) .... CHAT
Coalition to Keep Alaska Oil (EA) .... CKAO
Coalition to Preserve the American Copyright [Defunct] (EA) .... CPAC
Coalition to Promote America's Trade [Washington, DC] (EA) .... CPAT
Coalition to Protect Animals in Entertainment (EA) .... CPAE
Coalition to Protect Animals in Parks and Refuges (EA) .... CPAPR
Coalition to Protect Social Security (EA) .... SOS
Coalition to Save America's Music (EA) .... CSAM
Coalition to Save Our Documentary Heritage [Defunct] (EA) .... CSDH
Coalition to Stop Draize Rabbit Blinding Tests [Later, CADRBT] (EA) .... CSDRBT
Coalition to Stop Food Irradiation [Later, NCSFWI] (EA) .... CSFI
Coalition to Stop Government Waste (EA) .... CSGW
Coalition to Stop Gun Violence (EA) .... CSGV
Coalition to Support Cuban Detainees [Defunct] (EA) .... CSCD
Coalition United for Bear .... CUB
Coalition Unity Party [British] .... CoU
Coalitions for America (EA) .... CA
Coalitions for Health Care (EA) .... CHC
Coalitive Pareto Optimal (SAUS) .... CPO
Coal-Methane Mixture .... CMM
Coal-Methanol-Water [Fuel] .... CMW
Coalmont, TN [FM radio station call letters] .... WSGM
Coal-Oil Dispersion [Fuel technology] .... COD
Coal-Oil Mixture .... COM
Coal-Oil-Gas [Fuel mixture] .... COG
Coal-Oil-Water [Fuel mixture] .... COW
Coal-Oil-Water Mixture [Fuel] .... COWM
Coalville, UT [FM radio station call letters] .... KCUA
Coal-Water [Fuel mixture] .... CW
Coal-Water Mixture Fuel .... CWF
Coal-Water Mixture Fuel .... CWM
Coal-Water Slurry [Fuel] .... CWS
Coal-Water Slurry Fuel .... CWSF
Coaming [Naval architecture] .... COAM
Coamo [Puerto Rico] [Seismograph station code, US Geological Survey] (SEIS) .... CCA
Coamo, PR [AM radio station call letters] .... WCPR
COAR [Comunidad Oscar A. Romero] Peace Mission (EA) .... COAR
Coarctation [Cardiology] .... COARC
Coarctation of Aorta [Medicine] (STED) .... coarc
Coarctation of the Aorta [Medicine] (DMAA) .... CA
Coarctation of the Aorta [Cardiology] (DAVI) .... CoA
Coari [Brazil] [Airport symbol] (AD) .... CZA
Coariolanus [Shakespearean drama] (BARN) .... Coriol
Coarse [Appearance of bacterial colony] C
Coarse [Agronomy] C
Coarse (AAG) .... CRS
Coarse Acquisition Code [Computer science] (RDA) .... C/A
Coarse Aim Positioning .... CAP
Coarse Alignment .... CA
Coarse Alignment Servo .... CAS

Coarse Alignment Subsystem	CASS
Coarse Alignment Unit	CAU
Coarse Bearing Servo	CBS
Coarse Concrete (SAUS)	CC
Coarse Control [Nuclear energy] (NRCH)	CC
Coarse Control Damper [Nuclear energy] (NRCH)	CCD
Coarse Crushed Aggregate (SAUS)	CCA
Coarse Diffraction Pattern Analysis (MCD)	CDPA
Coarse Element Refinement (IAA)	CER
Coarse Erection	CE
Coarse Glass Frit	CGF
Coarse Grain (DAC)	CG
Coarse Gravel Aggregate (SAUS)	CGA
Coarse Optical Alignment Sight (NASA)	COAS
Coarse Particulate Matter [Pisciculture]	CPM
Coarse Particulate Organic Matter	CPOM
Coarse Pointing System (SSD)	CPS
Coarse Pumice Concrete (SAUS)	CPC
Coarse Rales [On chest ausculation] [Medicine] (DAVI)	RL
Coarse Sand Aggregate (SAUS)	CSA
Coarse Slag Aggregate (SAUS)	CSA
Coarse Sun Pointing Attitude Anomaly Detection (ADWA)	CSPAAD
Coarse Sun Sensor (SAUS)	CSS
Coarse Sun Sensor Assembly (SAUS)	CSSA
Coarse Tar Concrete (SAUS)	CTC
Coarse Turned (SAUS)	CT
Coarse/Acquisition	C/A
Coarse-Fine/Pulse Code Modulator	C-F/PCM
Coarse-Grained (SAUS)	C Gr
Coarse-Grained Material (MCD)	CGM
Coarsely Granular [Organic chemistry] (DAVI)	CGRN
Coarsening in Solid-Liquid Mixtures (SAUS)	CSLM
Coarticulation Assessment in Meaningful Language [Speech evaluation test]	CAML
Coast (SAUS)	C
Coast	CO
Coast	CST
Coast African People's Union [Kenya]	CAPU
Coast Air KS [Norway] [ICAO designator] (FAAC)	CST
Coast Air Ltd. [Kenya] [ICAO designator] (FAAC)	CQA
Coast Alliance [Defunct] (EA)	CA
Coast and Antiaircraft Experimental Establishment [British] [World War II]	CAAEE
Coast and Anti-Aircraft Experimental Establishment (SAUO)	CAEE
Coast and Geodetic Magnetic Observatory	CGMO
Coast and Geodetic Survey [Later, NOAA] [Rockville, MD]	C & GS
Coast and Geodetic Survey (SAUO)	C&GS
Coast and Geodetic Survey [Later, NOAA] [Rockville, MD] (AFM)	CGS
Coast and Geodetic Tide Station	CGTS
Coast and Shelf-Ecology of the Antarctic Sea Ice Zone (SAUO)	CS-EASIZ
Coast and Wetlands Society [New South Wales] [Australia]	CWS
Coast Artillery (SAUO)	CA
Coast Artillery	CA
Coast Artillery Antiaircraft	CAAA
Coast Artillery Cooperation Unit (SAUS)	CACU
Coast Artillery Corps [Army]	CAC
Coast Artillery Corps Reserve (SAUO)	CA-Res
Coast Artillery District (SAUO)	CA Dist
Coast Artillery Drill Regulations (SAUS)	CADR
Coast Artillery Field Manual (SAUS)	CAFM
Coast Artillery Memorandum (SAUS)	CAM
Coast Artillery Replacement Training Center (SAUO)	CARTC
Coast Artillery Reserve Corps	CARC
Coast Artillery School [British]	CAS
Coast Artillery School (SAUO)	CAS
Coast Artillery School (SAUO)	CA Sch
Coast Artillery Training (SAUS)	CAT
Coast Artillery Training Battalion	CATB
Coast Artillery Training Battalion (SAUO)	CATBn
Coast Artillery Training Centre [British military] (DMA)	CATC
Coast Community College District, Orange Coast College, Costa Mesa, CA [OCLC symbol] (OCLC)	CRG
Coast Conference (PSS)	COC
Coast Defence Artillery (SAUO)	CDA
Coast Defence Command (SAUO)	CDC
Coast Defence (or Defense) Battery (SAUO)	CD Bty
Coast Defense	CD
Coast Defense and Antiaircraft (SAUS)	CD&AA
Coast Defense Artillery	CDA
Coast Defense Battery (SAUS)	CD Bty
Coast Defense Study Group (EA)	CDSG
Coast Distribution Sys [AMEX symbol] (TTSB)	CRV
Coast Distribution Systems [Associated Press] (SAG)	CoastD
Coast Distribution Systems [AMEX symbol] (SPSG)	CRV
Coast Earth Station [INMARSAT]	CES
Coast for Orders [Chartering]	CFO
Coast Garrison Force (SAUO)	CGF
Coast Geodetic Survey (SAUS)	Co Geo Surv
Coast Guard (SAUO)	C
Coast Guard	CG
Coast Guard (SAUO)	CG
Coast Guard (SAUO)	CoGard
Coast Guard	COGARD
Coast Guard Academy	CGA
Coast Guard Achievement Medal [Military decoration]	CGAM

Coast Guard Activities Europe	CGACTEUR
Coast Guard Administrative Management Division (SAUO)	CAM
Coast Guard Aids to Navigation Facility (DNAB)	COGARDANFAC
Coast Guard Aids to Navigation Team (DNAB)	COGARDANT
Coast Guard Air Base	CGAB
Coast Guard Air Detachment (SAUO)	CGAD
Coast Guard Air Detachment	CGAIRDET
Coast Guard Air Service (SAUO)	CAS
Coast Guard Air Station	CGAS
Coast Guard Aircraft Program Office (DNAB)	COGARDACFTPROGOFF
Coast Guard Aircraft Repair and Supply Center (DNAB)	COGARDARSC
Coast Guard Assistance Instruction Data	COGAID
Coast Guard Auxiliary	CGA
Coast Guard Aviation (SAUO)	CGA
Coast Guard Aviation Depot (SAUO)	CGAD
Coast Guard Aviation Detachment (DNAB)	COGARDAVDET
Coast Guard Aviation Technical Training Center (DNAB)	COGARDAVTECHTRACEN
Coast Guard Aviation Training Center (DNAB)	COGARDAVTC
Coast Guard Base	CGBASE
Coast Guard Board of Contract Appeals [A publication] (AAGC)	CGBCA
Coast Guard Boating Safety Team (DNAB)	COGARDBST
Coast Guard Capabilities Plan (COE)	CGCAP
Coast Guard Captain of the Port Office (DNAB)	COGARDCOTP
Coast Guard Coastal Search and Rescue Facility (DNAB)	COGARDCOSARFAC
Coast Guard Combat Veterans Association (EA)	CGCVA
Coast Guard Command (SAUO)	CGC
Coast Guard Commandant	COMDTCOGARD
Coast Guard Commendation Medal [Military decoration]	CGCM
Coast Guard Communications Station (DNAB)	COGARDCOMMSTA
Coast Guard Court Martial (SAUO)	CGCM
Coast Guard Court-Martial Manual [A publication] (DLA)	CGCMM
Coast Guard Cutter	CGC
Coast Guard Depot (SAUS)	CGD
Coast Guard Depot (DNAB)	COGARDEP
Coast Guard Detachment National Data Buoy Office (DNAB)	COGARDETNDBO
Coast Guard District	CGD
Coast Guard District	CGDIST
Coast Guard District Office	CGDO
Coast Guard Docket	CGD
Coast Guard Electronic Shop (DNAB)	COGARDES
Coast Guard Electronic Shop Minor (DNAB)	COGARDESM
Coast Guard Electronics Engineering Center (DNAB)	COGARDEECEN
Coast Guard Electronics Shop Major Telephone and Teletype (DNAB)	COGARDEST
Coast Guard Electronics Shop Minor Telephone and Teletype (DNAB)	COGARDESMT
Coast Guard Fire and Safety Test Detachment (DNAB)	COGARDFSTD
Coast Guard Good Conduct Medal	CGGCM
Coast Guard Institute (DNAB)	COGARDINST
Coast Guard International Ice Patrol (NOAA)	CGIIP
Coast Guard Law Bulletin [A publication] (DLA)	CGL Bull
Coast Guard League (EA)	CGL
Coast Guard Liaison Officer (SAUO)	CGLNO
Coast Guard Liaison Officer, Commander Fleet Training Group (DNAB)	COGARDLOCOMFLETRAGRU
Coast Guard Liaison Officer, Eastern Pacific Intelligence Center (DNAB)	COGARDLOEPIC
Coast Guard Liaison Officer Representative (DNAB)	COGARDLOREP
Coast Guard Lifeboat Station	CGLBSTA
Coast Guard Light Attendant Station	CGLASTA
Coast Guard Light Station	CGLTSTA
Coast Guard Light Station (DNAB)	COGARDLTSTA
Coast Guard Logistic Support and Mobilization Plan (COE)	CGLSMP
Coast Guard LORAN [Long-Range Aid to Navigation] Monitor Station (DNAB)	COGARDLORMONSTA
Coast Guard LORAN [Long-Range Aid to Navigation] Station	CGLS
Coast Guard LORAN Station (SAUS)	CGLS
Coast Guard LORAN [Long-Range Aid to Navigation] Station (DNAB)	COGARDLORSTA
Coast Guard LORAN [Long-Range Aid to Navigation] Transmitting Station	CGLORSTA
Coast Guard LORAN Transmitting Station (SAUS)	CGLORSTA
Coast Guard Maintenance Repair Detachment (DNAB)	COGARDMRDET
Coast Guard Marine Inspection Detachment (DNAB)	COGARDMID
Coast Guard Marine Inspection Office (DNAB)	COGARDMIO
Coast Guard Marine Safety Detachment (DNAB)	COGARDMSD
Coast Guard Marine Safety Office (DNAB)	COGARDMSO
Coast Guard National Data Buoy Office (DNAB)	COGARDNDBO
Coast Guard National Motor Lifeboat School (DNAB)	COGARDNMLBS
Coast Guard National Strike Force (DNAB)	COGARDNSF
Coast Guard National Strike Force, Atlantic (DNAB)	COGARDNSFLANT
Coast Guard National Strike Force, Pacific (DNAB)	COGARDNSFPAC
Coast Guard Oceanographic Unit	CGOU
Coast Guard Officer (SAUS)	CGO
Coast Guard Oil Identification Laboratory [Groton, CT]	COIL
Coast Guard Omega Navigation Systems Office Detachment (DNAB)	COGARDONSOD
Coast Guard Omega Station (DNAB)	COGARDOMSTA
Coast Guard Operating Base	CGOB
Coast Guard Operations Computer Center (DNAB)	COGARDOCC
Coast Guard Operations Data Analysis Center (DNAB)	COGARDOPDAC
Coast Guard Ordnance Support Facility (DNAB)	COGARDORDSUPPFAC
Coast Guard Patrol Cutter	CGPC
Coast Guard Pension [British] (ROG)	CGP

Coast Guard Port Safety Detachment (DNAB) .... COGARDPSDET
Coast Guard Port Safety Station (DNAB) .... COGARDPSSTA
Coast Guard Procurement Regulations .... CGPR
Coast Guard Publication [*Formerly, NCG*] .... NAVCG
Coast Guard Publication [*Later, NAVCG*] .... NCG
Coast Guard Radio (NOAA) .... CGRDO
Coast Guard Radio Liaison Station (PDAA) .... CRLS
Coast Guard Radio Station .... CGRADSTA
Coast Guard Radio Station (DNAB) .... COGARDRADSTA
Coast Guard Records Depot (DNAB) .... COGARDRECDEP
Coast Guard Recruiting Office (DNAB) .... COGARDCRUITOFF
Coast Guard Recruiting Station .... CGCRUITSTA
Coast Guard Recruiting Station (SAUS) .... CGRUITSTA
Coast Guard Regulations [*A publication*] (DLA) .... CGR
Coast Guard Representative, Naval Regional Medical Center (DNAB) .... COGARDREPNAVREGMEDCEN
Coast Guard Representative, Student Records (DNAB) .... COGARDREPSTUDREC
Coast Guard Representative, Tripler Army Medical Center (DNAB) .... COGARDREPTAMC
Coast Guard Representative, United States Air Force Hospital (DNAB) .... COGARDREPUSAFH
Coast Guard Representative, United States Public Health Service Hospital (DNAB) .... COGARDREPUSPHS
Coast Guard Research and Development Center [*Groton, CT*] .... CGR/DC
Coast Guard Reserve .... CGR
Coast Guard Reserve (SAUO) .... CGR
Coast Guard Reserve Center (DNAB) .... COGARDRESCEN
Coast Guard Reserve Training Center (DNAB) .... COGARDRESTRACEN
Coast Guard Resident Inspecting Officer (DNAB) .... COGARDRIO
Coast Guard, Shelburne, Nova Scotia [*Library symbol*] [*National Library of Canada*] (NLC) .... NSSCO
Coast Guard, Shelburne, NS, Canada [*Library symbol*] [*Library of Congress*] (LCLS) .... CaNSSheCO
Coast Guard Ship (SAUS) .... CGS
Coast Guard Ship [*When precedes vessel classification*] [*Navy symbol*] .... W
Coast Guard Ship Introduction Unit (DNAB) .... COGARDSIU
Coast Guard Specification .... CGS
Coast Guard Station (SAUO) .... CGS
Coast Guard Station .... CGSTA
Coast Guard Station (DNAB) .... COGARDSTA
Coast Guard Station, Washington [*District of Columbia*] [*ICAO location identifier*] (ICLI) .... KNMH
Coast Guard Stock Inventory Control Point (DNAB) .... COGARDSICP
Coast Guard Supplement to Manual for Courts-Martial [*A publication*] (DLA) .... CGSMCM
Coast Guard Supply Center (SAUO) .... CGSC
Coast Guard Supply Center .... CGSUPCEN
Coast Guard Supply Center (DNAB) .... COGARDSUPCEN
Coast Guard Support Center (DNAB) .... COGARDSUPRTCEN
Coast Guard Support Facility (DNAB) .... COGARDSUPRTFAC
Coast Guard Teletype (NOAA) .... CGTEL
Coast Guard Training Center (DNAB) .... COGARDTRACEN
Coast Guard Training Station .... CGTRASTA
Coast Guard Training Station .... CGTS
Coast Guard Training Station (SAUO) .... COGARDTRASTA
Coast Guard Vessel Traffic System (DNAB) .... COGARDVTS
Coast Guard Yard .... CGYD
Coast Independent Hi-Tech [*Vancouver Stock Exchange symbol*] .... KIH
Coast Lines [*Steamship*] (MHDW) CL
Coast of Scotland (SAUS) .... C o S
Coast Orbital Insertion (MCD) .... COI
Coast Orbital Insertion (NAKS) .... COL
Coast Phase Control System [*Army*] (AABC) .... CPCS
Coast Protection Act [*Town planning*] [*British*] .... CPA
Coast Protection Board [*South Australia*] .... CPB
Coast RADAR Station [*Maps and charts*] .... RA
Coast Range Resources Ltd. [*Vancouver Stock Exchange symbol*] .... CSG
Coast Regiment, Royal Artillery (SAUO) .... CRRA
Coast Savings Financial, Inc. [*Associated Press*] (SAG) .... CoastSv
Coast Savings Financial, Inc. [*NYSE symbol*] (SPSG) .... CSA
Coast Star, Manasquan, NJ [*Library symbol*] [*Library of Congress*] (LCLS) .... NjManS
Coast Station [*ITU designation*] (CET) .... FC
Coast Survey Marine Observation System .... COSMOS
Coast Svgs Finl [*NYSE symbol*] (TTSB) .... CSA
Coast Torpedo Boat [*Navy symbol*] [*Obsolete*] .... CTB
Coast Waiter [*Coast Guard*] [*British*] (ROG) .... CW
Coast Watch Post (SAUS) .... CWP
Coastair [*Denmark*] [*ICAO designator*] (FAAC) .... CSX
Coastal .... CSTL
Coastal Aerial Photo-LASER Survey (PDAA) .... CAPS
Coastal Air Defense Identification Zone (SAUS) .... CADIZ
Coastal Air Force (SAUO) .... CAF
Coastal Air Force [*British*] .... CAF
Coastal Air Navigation Supplement (MCD) .... CANS
Coastal Air Transport [*St. Croix*] [*ICAO designator*] (FAAC) .... CXT
Coastal Air Transport [*ICAO designator*] (AD) .... DQ
Coastal Airways [*ICAO designator*] (FAAC) .... CNG
Coastal Airways [*ICAO designator*] (AD) .... PN
Coastal America Partnership [*US Army Corps of Engineers*] .... CAP
Coastal AMOS [*Automated Meteorological Observing Station*] **Experiment** .... CAMEX
Coastal and Antiaircraft Training Centre (SAUO) .... C&AATC
Coastal and Anti-aircraft Training Centre (SAUS) .... C&AATC
Coastal and Arctic Research Division [*Formerly, Marine Services Research Division*] [*Marine science*] (OSRA) .... CARD
Coastal and Continental Shelf Zone [*Oceanography*] .... CCSZ
Coastal and Estuarine Oceanography Branch (SAUS) .... CEOB
Coastal and Estuarine Oceanography Branch (SAUO) .... COEB
Coastal and Estuarine Regimes [*Oceanography*] (MSC) .... CER
Coastal and Hydraulics Laboratory [*U.S. Army Engineer Waterways Experiment Station*] .... CHL
Coastal and Marine Research (SAUO) .... COMAR
Coastal and Marine Resources Information System (SAUO) .... CANRIS
Coastal Antimissile System (MCD) .... CAMS
Coastal Anti-Pollution League [*British*] .... CAPL
Coastal Area Management Act [*1974*] (MSC) .... CAMA
Coastal Area Management Plan (SAUO) .... CAMP
Coastal Areas Management Programme (SAUO) .... CAMP
Coastal Artillery Anti-Aircraft Regiment, Royal Artillery (SAUO) .... CA AA Reg RA
Coastal Artillery Computer (SAUS) .... CAC
Coastal Artillery Co-operation Unit (SAUO) .... CACU
Coastal Artillery Mine Planter (SAUS) .... CAMP
Coastal Athletic Conference (PSS) .... COAC
Coastal Ballast Water Guidelines Working Group (SAUO) .... CBWGWG
Coastal Bancorp [*NASDAQ symbol*] (SAG) .... CBSA
Coastal Bancorp [*Associated Press*] (SAG) .... CstBn
Coastal Bancorp [*Associated Press*] (SAG) .... CstBncp
Coastal Bancorp 9% 'A' Pfd [*NASDAQ symbol*] (TTSB) .... CBSAP
Coastal Barrier Improvement Act of 1990 (COE) .... CBIA
Coastal Barrier Resources Act (COE) .... CBRA
Coastal Barrier Resources System [*Department of the Interior*] .... CBRS
Coastal Base Section [*Name changed to Continental Advance Section*] [*World War II*] .... CBS
Coastal Border Surveillance System (SAUS) .... CBSS
Coastal Building Zone (DEMM) .... CBZ
Coastal Buoy Tender [*Coast Guard symbol*] (DNAB) .... WLM
Coastal Buoy Tender Replacement Vessel [*USCG*] (TAG) .... WLMR
Coastal California Conference (PSS) .... CCALC
Coastal Carolina Community College, Jacksonville, NC [*Library symbol*] [*Library of Congress*] (LCLS) .... NcJaC
Coastal Change Analysis Program (ROAS) .... CCAP
Coastal Change Analysis Project (QUAC) .... CCAP
Coastal Command [*Air Force*] [*British*] CC
Coastal Command (SAUO) CC
Coastal Command [*Air Force*] [*British*] (DMA) .... C Cmd
Coastal Command (SAUS) .... COSCOM
Coastal Command Defence Unit (SAUO) .... CCDU
Coastal Command Defence Unit [*British*] .... CCDU
Coastal Command Development Unit [*British*] .... CCDU
Coastal Command Fighter Affiliation Training Unit [*British military*] (DMA) .... CCFATU
Coastal Command Flying Instructors School [*British military*] (DMA) .... CCFIS
Coastal Confluence Region (DNAB) .... CCR
Coastal Confluence Zone [*Aviation*] (DA) .... CCZ
Coastal Conservation Association (EA) .... CCA
Coastal Construction Control Line (DEMM) CCCL
Coastal Coordination Council [*Texas*] CCC
[*The*] **Coastal Corp.** [*Formerly, Coastal States Gas Producing Co.*] [*NYSE symbol*] (SPSG) .... CGP
[*The*] **Coastal Corp.** [*Formerly, Coastal State Gas Producing Co.*] [*Associated Press*] (SAG) .... Coastal
[*The*] **Coastal Corp.** [*Formerly, Coastal State Gas Producing Co.*] [*Associated Press*] (SAG) .... Coastl
[*The*] **Coastal Corp.** [*Formerly, Coastal State Gas Producing Co.*] [*Associated Press*] (SAG) .... Cstl
Coastal Corp. $1.19 Cv A Pfd [*NYSE symbol*] (TTSB) .... CGPPrA
Coastal Corp. $1.83 Cv B Pfd [*NYSE symbol*] (TTSB) .... CGPPrB
Coastal Corp.$2.125 cm Pfd [*NYSE symbol*] (TTSB) .... CGPPrH
Coastal Courier, Glace Bay, Nova Scotia [*Library symbol*] [*National Library of Canada*] (NLC) .... NSGCC
Coastal Courier, Glace Bay, NS, Canada [*Library symbol*] [*Library of Congress*] (LCLS) .... CaNSGbCC
Coastal Current Radar (SAUS) .... CCR
Coastal Defence Force (SAUO) .... CDF
Coastal Defense Base (SAUS) .... CDB
Coastal Defense Exercise (SAUS) .... CDX
Coastal Defense Radar (SAUS) .... CDR
Coastal Defense Ship (SAUS) .... CDS
Coastal Defense Unit (SAUS) .... CDU
Coastal District Surveillance Center [*Military*] .... CDSC
Coastal Division [*Navy*] (DNAB) .... COSDIV
Coastal Ecology Laboratory [*Louisiana State University*] [*Research center*] (RCD) .... CEL
Coastal Education and Research Foundation (SAUO) .... CERF
Coastal Energy Impact Program [*National Oceanic and Atmospheric Administration*] .... CEIP
Coastal Energy Impact Program (USDC) .... CIEP
Coastal Engineering Data Retrieval System .... CEDRS
Coastal Engineering Education Program [*U.S. Army Engineer Waterways Experiment Station*] .... CEEP
Coastal Engineering Information Analysis Center [*Vicksburg, MS*] [*DoD*] (GRD) .... CEIAC
Coastal Engineering Manual [*A publication*] [*Army*] .... CEM
Coastal Engineering Research Board [*Vicksburg, MS*] [*Army*] (AABC) .... CERB
Coastal Engineering Research Center [*Vicksburg, MS*] [*Army*] (AABC) .... CERC
Coastal Engineering Research Council (EA) .... CERC
Coastal Engineering Research Laboratories (SAUO) .... CERL
Coastal Engineering Research Laboratory (SAUS) .... CERL

Coastal Engineering Research Office (SAA)	CERO
Coastal Environment Research Demonstration Areas (SAUO)	CERDA
Coastal Environmental Assessment Studies (SAUS)	CEAS
Coastal Environmental Management Plan [Advisory Committee on Pollution of the Sea]	CEMP
Coastal Escort [Ship symbol] (NATG)	PC
Coastal Escort Medium [200-500 tons] [Ship symbol] (NATG)	PCM
Coastal Financial Corp. [NASDAQ symbol] (SAG)	CFCP
Coastal Financial Corp. [Associated Press] (SAG)	CstlFncl
Coastal Finl Del [NASDAQ symbol] (TTSB)	CFCP
Coastal Fisheries Institute [Louisiana State University]	CFI
Coastal Flotilla [Navy] (DNAB)	COSFLOT
Coastal Forces Material (or Materiel) Department (SAUO)	CFMD
Coastal Frontier (SAUS)	Cf
Coastal Frontier [Military]	CF
Coastal Frontier [Coast Guard]	COFRON
Coastal Geology Program (SAUO)	CGP
Coastal Georgia Historical Society, St. Simons Island, GA [Library symbol] [Library of Congress] (LCLS)	GSsiHi
Coastal Habitat Assessment Research and Mensuration Program (SAUS)	CHARM
Coastal Habitat Fisheries Assessment Research Mensuration [National Oceanic and Atmospheric Administration]	CHARM
Coastal Harbor [Telecommunications] (TEL)	CH
Coastal, Harbor, and Inland [Waterways] (MCD)	CHI
Coastal Harbour (SAUS)	CH
Coastal Health Library Information Consortium (SAUS)	CHLIC
Coastal Healthcare Group, Inc. [NYSE symbol] (SAG)	DR
Coastal Helicopter Aircraft Carrier [Ship symbol] (NATG)	CVHC
Coastal High Hazard Area (DEMM)	CHHA
Coastal Intrusion & Detection System (SAUS)	CIDS
Coastal Lagoons of Latin America (SAUS)	COSALC-II
Coastal Management and Coordination Committee [Victoria] [Australia]	CMCC
Coastal Management Programs [Marine science] (OSRA)	CMP
Coastal Mapping Program (GEOI)	CMP
Coastal Marine Area (SAUO)	CMA
Coastal Marine Automated Network [National Weather Service] (USDC)	C-MAN
Coastal Marine Information System (SAUO)	COMARIS
Coastal Marine Programme (SAUO)	COMAR
Coastal Marine Project (USDC)	COMAR
Coastal Marine Research and Training in Africa (SAUO)	COMARAF
Coastal Minehunter (SAUS)	MHC
Coastal Minelayer [Navy symbol]	CMC
Coastal Modeling System [Army]	CMS
Coastal Motorboat [Obsolete] [British]	CMB
Coastal Observation and Simulation with Topography [Marine science] (OSRA)	COAST
Coastal Observation Program, Engineering (SAUO)	COPE
Coastal Observations and Simulations with Topography (USDC)	COAST
Coastal Ocean Dynamics Applications RADAR [Marine science] (OSRA)	CODAR
Coastal Ocean Dynamics Experiment [National Oceanic and Atmospheric Administration]	CODE
Coastal Ocean Management, Planning, and Assessment System (GEOI)	COMPAS
Coastal Ocean Observing System (SAUO)	COOS
Coastal Ocean Prediction Systems Program [Marine science] (OSRA)	COPS
Coastal Ocean Probing Experiment [Marine science] (OSRA)	COPE
Coastal Ocean Processes (SAUS)	CoOP
Coastal Ocean Program [National Oceanic and Atmospheric Administration] (USDC)	COP
Coastal Ocean Reponse Experiment (SAUS)	CORE
Coastal Ocean Surface RADAR	COSR
Coastal Patrol and Interdiction [Navy] (DOMA)	CP & I
Coastal Patrol and Interdiction Craft [Navy symbol]	CPIC
Coastal Patrol Boat [Navy symbol]	CPC
Coastal Patrol Service (SAUO)	Cosps
Coastal Physician Grp [NYSE symbol] (TTSB)	DR
Coastal Physician Group [Associated Press] (SAG)	CstlPhys
Coastal Plains Commuter [ICAO designator] (AD)	KA
Coastal Plains Experiment Station, Tifton, GA [Library symbol] [Library of Congress] (LCLS)	GTiE
Coastal Plains Regional Library, Tifton, GA [Library symbol] [Library of Congress] (LCLS)	GTi
Coastal Plains Sands	CPS
Coastal Radar Integration Segment (ACAE)	CRIS
Coastal RADAR Integration System (MCD)	CRIS
Coastal Radio Station (SAUS)	CRS
Coastal Regions and Small Islands (SAUO)	CSI
Coastal Research Amphibious Buggy [Army] (MSC)	CRAB
Coastal Research Center (GNE)	CRC
Coastal Resources Center (SAUO)	CRC
Coastal Resources Inventory (SAUO)	CRI
Coastal Resources Management Council [United Nations]	CRMC
Coastal Resources Management Programme [Canada] (EAIO)	CRMP
Coastal Restoration Technology (SAUO)	CRT
Coastal River Squadron [Navy] (NVT)	COSRIVRON
Coastal River Squadron Mobile Support Team [Navy] (DNAB)	COSRIVRON MST
Coastal Security Zone (MCD)	CSZ
Coastal Sentry (SAUS)	SCQ
Coastal Sentry Quebec	CSQ
Coastal Shelf Oceanography Program [Marine science] (MSC)	CSOP
Coastal Shipping Commission (SAUO)	ACSC
[The] Coastal Society (EA)	CS
[The] Coastal Society (EA)	TCS
Coastal Squadron (SAUO)	COCRON
Coastal Squadron [Navy] (DNAB)	COSRON
Coastal State (SAUS)	CS
Coastal States Gas Producing Co. (SAUO)	CGP
Coastal States Organization (EA)	CSO
Coastal Structure Acoustic Raster Scanner (RDA)	CSARS
Coastal Studies Institute [Louisiana State University] [Research center]	CSI
Coastal Submarine [Navy symbol]	SSC
Coastal Surveillance Center	CSC
Coastal Surveillance RADAR (MCD)	CSR
Coastal Survey Ship [Marine science] (MSC)	CSS
Coastal Surveying Ship	AGSC
Coastal Telegraph Station [ITU designation] (CET)	CT
Coastal Transition Zone (SAUS)	CTZ
Coastal Transport Ltd. [Steamship] (MHDW)	CTL
Coastal Upwelling Ecosystems Analysis [Marine science] (MSC)	CUEA
Coastal Upwelling Experiment [Marine science] (MSC)	CUE
Coastal Watching RADAR (NATG)	CWR
Coastal Zone (SAUO)	CZ
Coastal Zone Act Reauthorization Amendments [1990]	CZARA
Coastal Zone as a Resource in its own Right (SAUS)	CZAR
Coastal Zone Authority (COE)	CZA
Coastal Zone Color Scanner	CZCS
Coastal Zone Conservation Act (SAUS)	CZCA
Coastal Zone Information Center (GNE)	CZIC
Coastal Zone Management	CZM
Coastal Zone Management Act [1972]	CZMA
Coastal Zone Management Act Reauthorization Amendments (SAUO)	CZARA
Coastal Zone Management Advisory Committee [Department of Commerce] (MSC)	CZMAC
Coastal Zone Management Centre (SAUS)	CZMC
Coastal Zone Management Program (GNE)	CZMP
Coastal-Nonrigid Airship [Royal Naval Air Service] [British]	C
Coastal/Oceans Monitoring Satellite System (PDAA)	COMSS
Coastal-Research Amphibious Buggy (SAUS)	CRAB
Coastcast Corp. [Associated Press] (SAG)	Coastcst
Coastcast Corp. [NYSE symbol] (SPSG)	PAR
Coastguards Radio Liaison Station (SAUO)	CRLS
Coasting Drive	CD
Coasting Flight	CF
Coasting Group (SAUO)	CG
Coast-in-Point (NVT)	CIP
Coastline Resources [Vancouver Stock Exchange symbol]	CSY
Coastoro Resources [Vancouver Stock Exchange symbol]	COQ
Coast-Out Point (NVT)	COP
Coasts and Clean Seas (SAUO)	CCS
Coastwatchers' Association [Australia]	CA
Coastwide Energy Services [NASDAQ symbol] (SAG)	CNRG
Coastwide Energy Services [Associated Press] (SAG)	CstEngy
Coastwide Summary Data Base (SAUO)	CSDB
Coastwise-Great Lakes and Inland Hull Association [Defunct] (EA)	CGLIHA
Coat Cupboard [Classified advertising] (ADA)	CC
Coat Hook	CH
Coat of Arms (AABC)	C/A
Coat Protein	COP
Coat [or Capsid] Protein [Cytology]	CP
Coated (KSC)	CTD
Coated Abrasive Manufacturers' Association [British] (BI)	CAMA
Coated Abrasives Fabricators Association [Defunct] (EA)	CAFA
Coated Abrasives Manufacturers Institute (EA)	CAMI
Coated Aluminium Coated Steel, Polyethylene (SAUS)	CACSP
Coated and Processed Paper Association [Defunct]	CPPA
Coated Back [Paper] (WDMC)	cb
Coated Cargo Tank (DNAB)	CCT
Coated Cartridge [Paper] (DGA)	CC
Coated Cartridge [Paper] (DGA)	C/CDGE
Coated Compressed Tablet [Pharmacy]	CCT
Coated Electrodes International [British]	CEI
Coated Foam Tape	CFT
Coated Front and Back [Carbonless paper]	CFB
Coated Front Paper (SAUS)	CF Paper
Coated Metal (AAG)	CMET
Coated on the Back Side [Carbonless paper]	CB
Coated on the Front Side [Carbonless paper]	CF
Coated One Side [Paper] (WDMC)	c1s
Coated One Size [Paper]	C1S
Coated Open Tabular (SAUS)	COT
Coated Paper Copier [Reprography]	CPC
Coated Polycarbonate Visor	CPV
Coated Powder Cathode	CPC
Coated Power Cathode (SAUS)	CPC
Coated Solid-State Device [Sensor]	CSSD
Coated Tablet [Pharmacy]	CT
Coated Wire Electrode [Sensor]	CWE
Coated-Front Paper (WDMC)	cf
Coated-Paper Copier (SAUS)	CPC
Coatepeque [Guatemala] [ICAO location identifier] (ICLI)	MGCT
Coatesville, PA [Location identifier] [FAA] (FAAL)	CVE
Coatesville, PA [Location identifier] [FAA] (FAAL)	MQS
Coatesville, PA [Location identifier] [FAA] (FAAL)	VZO
Coatesville, PA [AM radio station call letters]	WCOJ
Coatesville Public Library, Coatesville, IN [Library symbol] [Library of Congress] (LCLS)	InCoa
Coating (MSA)	CTG
Coating Ageing-Resistant Aluminum Technology [Materials science]	CARAT

Coating and Chemical Laboratory [*Aberdeen Proving Ground, MD*] [*Army*] (RDA) ... C & CL
Coating and Chemical Laboratory [*Aberdeen Proving Ground, MD*] [*Army*] ... CCL
Coating & Filter Design (SAUS) ... C&FD
Coating for Infra-red and Light Reflection (SAUS) ... CIRALR
Coatings, Adhesives, Sealants, and Elastomers [*Polyurethanes*] ... CASE
Coatings and Surfaces Technology [*National Centre for Tribology*] [*British*] ... CAST
Coats (SAUS) ... HQT
Coats, NC [*Location identifier*] [*FAA*] (FAAL) ... HQT
Coax to Twisted Pair Adapter (SAUS) ... CTPA
Coaxial (AAG) ... CA
Coaxial (AAG) ... COAX
Coaxial Adapter Waveguide ... CAWG
Coaxial Cable (ADWA) ... coax
Coaxial Cable Information System (NTCM) ... CCIS
Coaxial Cavity Resonator (IAA) ... CCR
Coaxial Diode Limiter ... CDL
Coaxial Directional Coupler ... CDC
Coaxial Hybrid (SAUS) ... COBRID
Coaxial Injection Combustion (MCD) ... CIC
Coaxial Injection Combustion Model (MCD) ... CICM
Coaxial Line Attenuator ... CLA
Coaxial Machine Gun ... COAX
Coaxial Output Printer (IAA) ... COP
Coaxial Plug (SAUS) ... Coax Pl
Coaxial Power Divider ... CPD
Coaxial Single-Pole Relay ... CSR
Coaxial Slotted Line ... CSL
Coaxial Socket (SAUS) ... Coax SKT
Coaxial Subscriber System (SAUS) ... CSy
Coaxial Switch and Alternator Panel ... COSWAP
Coaxial Switching Matrix ... CSM
Coaxial Terminal Switch (SAUS) ... CTS
Coaxial Thermal Converter (IAA) ... CTC
Coaxial Thermal Voltmeter ... CTV
Coaxial to Twisted Pair Adapter (HGAA) ... ctpa
Coaxial Transceiver Interface ... CTI
Coaxial Triple-Stud Tuner ... CTST
Cobalamin [*Biochemistry*] ... Cbl
Cobalamin-Binding Protein [*Biochemistry*] (DB) ... CBP
Cobalt [*Chemical symbol is Co*] ... C
Cobalt [*Chemical element*] ... Co
Cobalt [*Philately*] ... cob
Cobalt Base Alloy Foil ... CBAF
Cobalt Bomb [*Nuclear*] (AAG) ... CB
Cobalt Bomb [*Nuclear*] ... C (Bomb)
Cobalt Development Institute (EAIO) ... CDI
Cobalt Gray Equivalent [*Radiology*] ... CGE
Cobalt Information Center [*Battelle Memorial Institute*] [*Information service or system*] (IID) ... CIC
Cobalt Public Library, Cobalt, ON, Canada [*Library symbol*] [*Library of Congress*] (LCLS) ... CaOCob
Cobalt Public Library, Ontario [*Library symbol*] [*National Library of Canada*] (BIB) ... OCOB
Cobalt Thiocyanate Active Substance [*Organic analysis*] ... CTAS
Cobalt-60 ... Co-60
Cobalt-Chrome ... COBCRM
Cobaltiprotoporphyrin [*Medicine*] ... COPP
Cobaltite (SAUS) ... CB
Cobamide [*Biochemistry*] ... Cba
Coban [*Guatemala*] [*ICAO location identifier*] (ICLI) ... MGCB
Cobancorp, Inc. [*Associated Press*] (SAG) ... Cobancp
Cobancorp, Inc. [*NASDAQ symbol*] (SAG) ... COBI
Cobar [*Australia*] [*Airport symbol*] (OAG) ... CAZ
Cobb [*New Zealand*] [*Seismograph station code, US Geological Survey*] (SEIS) ... COB
Cobb County-Marietta Public Library (SAUS) ... GMarC
Cobb County-Marietta Public Library, Marietta, GA [*Library symbol*] [*Library of Congress*] (LCLS) ... GMarC
Cobb Elementary Library, Duluth, MN [*Library symbol*] [*Library of Congress*] (LCLS) ... MnDuCE
Cobb Memorial Library, North Truro,MA [*Library symbol*] [*Library of Congress*] (LCLS) ... MNot
Cobb on Slavery [*A publication*] (DLA) ... Cobb Slav
Cobbett on Pawns and Pledges [*A publication*] (DLA) ... Cobb P & Pl
Cobbett's Parliamentary History [*A publication*] (DLA) ... Cobb Parl Hist
Cobbett's Political Register [*A publication*] (DLA) ... Cobb Pol Reg
Cobbett's [*later, Howell's*] **State Trials** [*1163-1820*] [*England*] [*A publication*] (DLA) ... Cobb St Tr
Cobbett's [*later, Howell's*] **State Trials** [*1163-1820*] [*England*] [*A publication*] (DLA) ... Cob St Tr
Cobbey's Annotated Statutes [*Nebraska*] [*A publication*] (DLA) ... Cobbey's Ann St
Cobbey's Practical Treatise on the Law of Replevin [*A publication*] (DLA) ... Cobbey Repl
Cobbler ... COBB
Cobbler Shop ... CBSHP
Cobbly [*Agronomy*] ... C
Cobb's Digest of Statute Laws [*Georgia*] [*A publication*] (DLA) ... Cobb Dig
Cobb's New Digest, Laws of Georgia [*1851*] [*A publication*] (DLA) ... Cobb
Cobb's Reports [*121 Alabama*] [*A publication*] (DLA) ... Cobb
Cobb's Reports [*4-20 Georgia*] [*A publication*] (DLA) ... Cobb
Cobden Airways [*ICAO designator*] (AD) ... XF
Cobden Club (SAUO) ... CC
Cobden Public Library, Cobden, ON, Canada [*Library symbol*] [*Library of Congress*] (LCLS) ... CaOCoBD
Cobden Public Library, Ontario [*Library symbol*] [*National Library of Canada*] (BIB) ... OCOBD
Cobe Laboratories, Denver, CO [*Library symbol*] [*Library of Congress*] (LCLS) ... CoDCo
Cobelda RADAR Automatic Preflight Analyzer (IEEE) ... CORAPRAN
Cobequid Resources Ltd. [*Vancouver Stock Exchange symbol*] ... KQR
Cobi Foods, Inc. [*Toronto Stock Exchange symbol*] ... CFJ
Cobija [*Bolivia*] [*Airport symbol*] (OAG) ... CIJ
Cobija [*Bolivia*] [*ICAO location identifier*] (ICLI) ... SLCO
Cobinamide [*Biochemistry*] ... Cbi
Coblentz Society (EA) ... CS
Cobleskill, NY [*AM radio station call letters*] (RBYB) ... WDCS
Cobleskill, NY [*AM radio station call letters*] (RBYB) ... WLAL-AM
Cobleskill, NY [*FM radio station call letters*] ... WQBJ
Cobleskill, NY [*AM radio station call letters*] (BROA) ... WXBH
COBOL [*Common Business-Oriented Language*] [*Computer science*] (IAA) ... CO
COBOL Abbreviation Expander (SAUS) ... COAX
COBOL [*Common Business-Oriented Language*] **Automatic Language Modifier** [*Computer science*] ... CALM
COBOL Automatic Translator (SAUS) ... CAT
COBOL [*Common Business-Oriented Language*] **Communications Facility** (IAA) ... CCF
COBOL Compiler Validation System (SAUS) ... CCVS
COBOL Compiler-Oriented Language (SAUS) ... COCOL
COBOL Conversion (SAUS) ... CCONV
COBOL [*Common Business-Oriented Language*] **Conversion** [*Computer science*] (MCD) ... COCO
COBOL Data Communication Philips (SAUS) ... CODACOP
COBOL [*Common Business-Oriented Language*] **Element Subtype** [*Computer science*] ... COB
COBOL [*Common Business-Oriented Language*] **File Handler** (IAA) ... CFH
COBOL File Handler (SAUS) ... CFH
COBOL Indexing (SAUS) ... COIN
COBOL Information Bulletin (SAUS) ... CIB
COBOL [*Common Business-Oriented Language*] **Information Bulletin** [*Air Force*] ... CIB
COBOL [*Common Business-Oriented Language*] **Instrumentation Package** [*Computer science*] ... CIP
COBOL [*Common Business-Oriented Language*] **Library** [*Computer science*] (MCD) ... COBLIB
COBOL Macro Processor (SAUS) ... CMP
COBOL Object Orientated Language (SAUS) ... COOL
COBOL [*Common Business-Oriented Language*] **Performance Monitor** [*Computer science*] (IAA) ... CPM
COBOL Program Generator (NITA) ... CPG
COBOL Sampler EDP Program [*DCAA*] [*Also DCAM*] (AAGC) ... COSAM
COBOL [*Common Business-Oriented Language*] **Shared Access Method** [*Pertec*] ... COSAM
COBOL Shared-Access Method (SAUS) ... COSAM
COBOL Structured Facility [*IBM Corp.*] (NITA) ... COBOL/SF
COBOL to COBOL (SAUS) ... CTC
COBOL [*Common Business-Oriented Language*] **Tuner** ... COTUNE
COBOL Update and Test Environment (SAUS) ... CUTE
COBOL Utility (SAUS) ... COBILITY
COBOL [*Common Business-Oriented Language*] **Virtual Machine** ... CVM
COBOL [*Common Business-Oriented Language*]**-to-COBOL Translator** (IEEE) ... COTRAN
Cobourg, ON [*FM radio station call letters*] ... CFMX
Cobourg, ON [*AM radio station call letters*] ... CHUC
Cobourg Peninsula Reserve (SAUS) ... CPR
Cobourg Public Library, Cobourg, ON, Canada [*Library symbol*] [*Library of Congress*] (LCLS) ... CaOCo
Cobourg Public Library, Ontario [*Library symbol*] [*National Library of Canada*] (NLC) ... OCO
Cobra Club [*Later, SAAC*] (EA) ... CC
Cobra Club (SAUO) ... CC
Cobra Dane System Modernization (DWSG) ... CDSM
Cobra Electronics [*NASDAQ symbol*] (TTSB) ... COBR
Cobra Electronics Corp. [*NASDAQ symbol*] (SAG) ... COBR
Cobra Electronics Corp. [*Associated Press*] (SAG) ... CobraEl
Cobra Enterprises [*Vancouver Stock Exchange symbol*] ... CBB
Cobra Factor ... CoF
Cobra Fleet Life Extension Program [*Military*] ... C-FLEX
Cobra Golf, Inc. [*NASDAQ symbol*] (SAG) ... CBRA
Cobra Golf, Inc. [*Associated Press*] (SAG) ... CobraG
Cobra Jet [*Automotive engineering*] ... CJ
Cobra Night Fire Control System [*Military*] ... CONFICS
Cobra Night Fire Control System (SAUS) ... Confics
Cobra Owners Club of America (EA) ... COCOA
Cobra Toxin (DB) ... CT
Cobra Toxin ... CTX
Cobra Venom Factor [*Immunochemistry*] ... CoVF
Cobra Venom Factor [*Immunochemistry*] ... CVF
Coburg/Brandensteinsebene [*Germany*] [*ICAO location identifier*] (ICLI) ... EDQC
Coburg/Steinrucken [*Germany*] [*ICAO location identifier*] (ICLI) ... EDQY
Cobyric Acid [*Biochemistry*] ... Cby
Coca [*Ecuador*] [*Airport symbol*] (OAG) ... OCC
Coca [*Ecuador*] [*ICAO location identifier*] (ICLI) ... SECO
Coca Cola Femsa SA de CV [*Commercial firm*] [*Associated Press*] (SAG) ... CCFem
Coca Cola Femsa SA de CV [*Associated Press*] (SAG) ... CCFemsa
Coca Cola South Pacific [*Commercial firm*] ... CCSP
Coca-Cola & Schweppes Beverages [*British*] ... CCSB
Coca-Cola Bott Consol [*NASDAQ symbol*] (TTSB) ... COKE

Coca-Cola Bottling Co. Consolidated [*Associated Press*] (SAG) ... CocaBtl
Coca-Cola Bottling Co. Consolidated [*NASDAQ symbol*] (NQ) ... COKE
[*The*] **Coca-Cola Co.** [*Associated Press*] (SAG) ... CocaCl
[*The*] **Coca-Cola Co.** [*NYSE symbol*] (SPSG) ... KO
Coca-Cola Co., Business Information, Atlanta, GA [*OCLC symbol*] (OCLC) ... GCC
Coca-Cola Co., Law Library, Atlanta, GA [*OCLC symbol*] (OCLC) ... GCW
Coca-Cola Co., Marketing Information Center, Atlanta, GA [*Library symbol*] [*Library of Congress*] (LCLS) ... GACo
Coca-Cola Co., Technical Information Services, Atlanta, GA [*Library symbol*] [*Library of Congress*] (LCLS) ... GACCC
Coca-Cola Co., Technical Information Services, Atlanta, GA [*OCLC symbol*] (OCLC) ... GCT
Coca-Cola Collectors Club International (EA) ... CCCI
Coca-Cola Enterprises [*NYSE symbol*] (TTSB) ... CCE
Coca-Cola Enterprises, Inc. [*NYSE symbol*] (SPSG) ... CCE
Coca-Cola Enterprises, Inc. [*Associated Press*] (SAG) ... CocaCE
Coca-Cola FEMSA [*NYSE symbol*] (SPSG) ... KOF
Coca-Cola FEMSA ADS [*NYSE symbol*] (TTSB) ... KOF
Cocaine [*Slang*] ... C
Cocaine (DAVI) ... COCAIN
Cocaine [*Slang*] (DSUE) ... COKE
Cocaine- and Amphetamine-Regulated Transcript [*Physiology*] ... CART
Cocaine and Heroin (SAUS) ... C&H
Cocaine and Heroin ... C & H
Cocaine and Morphine (MAE) ... C & M
Cocaine and Morphine (SAUS) ... C&M
Cocaine Anonymous (EA) ... CA
Cocaine Anonymous World Services (SAUO) ... CA
Cocaine Anonymous World Services (EA) ... CAWS
Cocaine Hydrochloride [*Medicine*] (MELL) ... CHCl
Cocaine-Induced Respiratory Failure [*Medicine*] (MELL) ... CIRF
Coccidioidomycosis [*Bacteriology*] (DAVI) ... cocci
Coccidioidomycosis [*Medicine*] (MELL) ... COCCID
Coccygeal [*Anatomy*] (DAVI) ... Cd
Coccygeal [*Anatomy*] ... COC
coccygeal (SAUS) ... coc
Cocensys, Inc. [*NASDAQ symbol*] (SAG) ... COCN
Cocesna [*ICAO designator*] (FAAC) ... COC
Cochabamba [*Bolivia*] [*Airport symbol*] (OAG) ... CBB
Cochabamba [*Bolivia*] [*Seismograph station code, US Geological Survey*] (SEIS) ... CCH
Cochabamba/Jorge Wilsterman [*Bolivia*] [*ICAO location identifier*] (ICLI) ... SLCB
Co-Chair of the Board (DD) ... cochr
Co-Channel Interface [*Telecommunications*] (NITA) ... CCI
Co-Channel Interference (NTCM) ... CCI
Cochin [*Region in India*] (ROG) ... COCH
Cochin [*India*] [*Airport symbol*] (OAG) ... COK
Cochin [*India*] [*ICAO location identifier*] (ICLI) ... VOCC
Cochin, India (ILCA) ... Coch Ind
Cochin Law Journal [*A publication*] (DLA) ... Cochin LJ
Cochin Law Journal [*A publication*] (DLA) ... Co LJ
Cochin Law Reports [*1909-48*] [*India*] [*A publication*] (DLA) ... Cochin
Cochin Law Reports [*1909-48*] [*India*] [*A publication*] (DLA) ... Cochin LR
Cochise Airlines [*ICAO designator*] (AD) ... DP
Cochise, AZ [*Location identifier*] [*FAA*] (FAAL) ... CIE
Cochise College, Douglas, AZ [*Library symbol*] [*Library of Congress*] (LCLS) ... AzDC
Cochise County Library District, Bisbee, AZ [*Library symbol*] [*Library of Congress*] (LCLS) ... AzBC
Cochise Resource Center (SAUO) ... CRC
Cochise Resource Center for Environmental Education (SAUO) ... CRCEE
Cochiti [*New Mexico*] [*Seismograph station code, US Geological Survey*] (SEIS) ... COH
Cochlea (MELL) ... C
Cochlear Implant [*Otorhinolaryngology*] (DAVI) ... CI
Cochlear Implant Club International (EA) ... CICI
Cochlear Microphonics [*Response*] [*Auditory testing*] ... CM
Cochlear Nuclei [*Brain anatomy*] ... CN
Cochlear Occlusion [*Medicine*] (MELL) ... CO
Cochlear Ossification [*Medicine*] (MELL) ... CO
Cochlear Potential [*Otolaryngology*] ... CP
Cochleare [*Spoonful*] [*Pharmacy*] ... COCH
Cochleare [*Spoonful*] [*Pharmacy*] ... COCHL
Cochleare Amplum [*A tablespoonful*] [*Pharmacy*] ... Coch Apm
Cochleare Amplum [*Heaping spoonful*] [*Pharmacy*] (MAH) ... COCHL AMP
Cochleare Amplum [*Tablespoonful*] [*Pharmacy*] (ROG) ... COCHL AMPL
Cochleare Infantum [*Teaspoonful*] [*Pharmacy*] ... COCH INFANT
Cochleare Infantum [*Teaspoonful*] [*Pharmacy*] ... COCHL INFANT
Cochleare Magnum [*Tablespoonful*] [*Pharmacy*] (ROG) ... COCHL MAG
Cochleare Magnum [*Tablespoonful*] [*Pharmacy*] ... COCH MAG
Cochleare Maximum [*Tablespoonful*] [*Pharmacy*] ... COCH MAX
Cochleare Medium [*Dessertspoonful*] [*Pharmacy*] (ROG) ... COCHL MED
Cochleare Medium [*Dessertspoonful*] [*Pharmacy*] ... COCH MED
Cochleare Minimum [*Teaspoonful*] [*Pharmacy*] ... COCH MIN
Cochleare Modicum [*Dessertspoonful*] [*Pharmacy*] (ROG) ... COCHL MOD
Cochleare Modicum [*Dessertspoonful*] [*Pharmacy*] ... COCH MOD
Cochleare Parvum [*Teaspoonful*] [*Pharmacy*] (ROG) ... COCHL PARV
Cochleare Parvum [*Teaspoonful*] [*Pharmacy*] ... COCH PARV
Cochleare Plenum [*Tablespoonful*] [*Pharmacy*] ... COCH PLEN
Cochleatim [*Spoonfuls*] [*Pharmacy*] (ROG) ... COCHLEAT
Cochleopalpebral Reflex (STED) ... CPR
Cochran, GA [*FM radio station call letters*] ... WDCO
Cochran, GA [*Television station call letters*] ... WDCO-TV
Cochran, GA [*AM radio station call letters*] ... WVMG
Cochran, GA [*FM radio station call letters*] ... WVMG-FM
Cochrane [*Canada*] [*Airport symbol*] (OAG) ... YCN
Cochrane Controlled Trials Register (ADWA) ... CCTR
Cochrane Database of Systematic Reviews (SAUO) ... CDSR
Cochrane Ecological Institute (SAUO) ... CEI
Cochrane Municipal Library, Alberta [*Library symbol*] [*National Library of Canada*] (NLC) ... ACOM
Cochrane Municipal Library, Cochrane, AB, Canada [*Library symbol*] [*Library of Congress*] (LCLS) ... CaACoM
Cochrane Musculoskeletal Review Group (SAUO) ... CMSG
Cochrane Public Library, Cochrane, ON, Canada [*Library symbol*] [*Library of Congress*] (LCLS) ... CaOCoc
Cochrane Public Library, Ontario [*Library symbol*] [*National Library of Canada*] (NLC) ... OCOC
Cochrane Review Methodology Database (SAUO) ... CRMD
Cochrane/Cochrane [*Chile*] [*ICAO location identifier*] (ICLI) ... SCHR
Cochrane's Hindu Law [*A publication*] (DLA) ... Cochr Hind L
Cochran's Nova Scotia Reports [*1859*] [*A publication*] (DLA) ... Coch
Cochran's Nova Scotia Reports [*1859*] [*A publication*] (DLA) ... Coch N Sc
Cochran's Nova Scotia Reports [*1859*] [*A publication*] (DLA) ... Cochr
Cochran's Nova Scotia Reports [*1859*] [*A publication*] (DLA) ... NSR Coch
Cochrans Nova Scotia Reports (SAUS) ... NSR Coch
Cochran's Reports [*3-10 North Dakota*] [*A publication*] (DLA) ... Cochr
Cochran's Reports [*3-10 North Dakota*] [*A publication*] (DLA) ... Cochran
Cock (WDAA) ... C
Cockatiel [*Bird*] ... Tiel
Cockatoo [*Bird*] ... Too
Cockayne's Syndrome [*Medicine*] ... CS
Cockburn and Rowe's English Election Cases [*1833*] [*A publication*] (DLA) ... C & R
Cockburn and Rowe's English Election Cases [*1833*] [*A publication*] (DLA) ... Cock & R
Cockburn and Rowe's English Election Cases [*1833*] [*A publication*] (DLA) ... Cock & Rowe
Cockburn and Rowe's English Election Cases [*1833*] [*A publication*] (DLA) ... Cockb & R
Cockburn and Rowe's English Election Cases [*1833*] [*A publication*] (DLA) ... Cockb & Rowe
Cockburn on Nationality [*A publication*] (DLA) ... Cock Nat
Cockburn Sound Conservation Council [*Western Australia*] ... CSCC
Cockburn Town, San Salvador Island [*Bahamas*] [*ICAO location identifier*] (ICLI) ... MYSM
Cockburn's Charge in the Tichborne Case [*A publication*] (DLA) ... Cock Tich Ca
Cockcroft-Walton Accelerator [*Physics*] ... CWA
Cockcroft-Walton Experiment [*Physics*] ... CWE
Cocke. Reports [*14, 15 Florida*] [*A publication*] (DLA) ... Cocke
Cocke. Reports [*16-18 Alabama*] [*A publication*] (DLA) ... Cocke
Cockerill Mechanical Industries (SAUS) ... CMI
Cocke's Common and Civil Law Practice of the US Courts [*A publication*] (DLA) ... Cocke US Pr
Cocke's Constitutional History of the United States [*A publication*] (DLA) ... Cocke Const Hist
Cockfield Brown, Inc. [*Toronto Stock Exchange symbol*] ... CFD
Cockpit ... CCKPT
Cockpit ... CKPT
Cockpit Alerting and Warning System (MCD) ... CAWS
Cockpit Area Microphone (MCD) ... CAM
Cockpit Assessment of Reach [*Aviation*] (PDAA) ... CAR
Cockpit Automation Technology [*Air Force*] ... CAT
Cockpit Avionics System (ACAE) ... CAS
Cockpit Control System (DWSG) ... CCS
Cockpit Control Unit (SAUS) ... CCU
Cockpit Display of Traffic Information (SAUS) ... CDTI
Cockpit Display System ... CDS
Cockpit Display Unit (SAUS) ... CDU
Cockpit Dynamic Simulator (SAUS) ... CDS
Cockpit Emergency & Procedures Trainer (SAUS) ... CEPT
Cockpit Familiarization Trainer (MCD) ... CFT
Cockpit Geometry Evaluation [*Computer program*] [*Boeing Co.*] ... CGE
Cockpit Interface Computer (ACAE) ... CIC
Cockpit Kill Indicator [*Military*] ... CKI
Cockpit Laser Designation System (SAUS) ... CLDS
Cockpit Management System [*Aviation*] ... CMS
Cockpit Motor Yacht ... CMY
Cockpit Operating Manual (GAVI) ... COM
Cockpit Orientation Trainer [*Aviation*] (MCD) ... COT
Cockpit Orientation Trainer [*Aviation*] (NG) ... COTR
Cockpit Procedures Trainer [*Air Force*] (AFM) ... CPT
Cockpit Resource Management (MCD) ... CRM
Cockpit Systems Simulator [*Aviation*] ... CSS
Cockpit Television Sensor (MCD) ... CTV
Cockpit Television Sensor ... CTVS
Cockpit TV Sensor (SAUS) ... CTVS
Cockpit Voice & Flight Data Recorder (SAUS) ... CVFDR
Cockpit Voice Recorder ... CVR
Cockpit Weapons Emergency Procedural Trainer [*Military*] ... CWEPT
Cockpit-Angle Measure (SAUS) ... CAM
Cockrell Hill, TX [*AM radio station call letters*] ... KRVA
Cockroach Antigen [*Immunology*] ... CR
Cocksfoot Mottle Virus [*Plant pathology*] ... COMV
Cocksfoot Streak Virus [*Plant pathology*] ... CSV
Coco Island [*Myanmar*] [*ICAO location identifier*] (ICLI) ... VBCI
Coco Solo, Canal Zone ... CS
Cocoa ... CCO
Cocoa Beach Apollo [*NASA*] (MCD) ... CBA

Cocoa Beach, FL [*FM radio station call letters*] ... WJRR
Cocoa Beach, FL [*FM radio station call letters*] ... WTKS
Cocoa Beach, FL [*AM radio station call letters*] ... WXXU
Cocoa Beach Public Library, Cocoa Beach, FL [*Library symbol*] [*Library of Congress*] (LCLS) ... FCb
Cocoa, Chocolate, and Confectionary Alliance [*British*] ... CCCA
Cocoa Consultative Committee (SAUO) ... CCC
Cocoa, FL [*Location identifier*] [*FAA*] (FAAL) ... COF
Cocoa, FL [*Location identifier*] [*FAA*] (FAAL) ... COI
Cocoa, FL [*Location identifier*] [*FAA*] (FAAL) ... IHR
Cocoa, FL [*Location identifier*] [*FAA*] (FAAL) ... PKC
Cocoa, FL [*Location identifier*] [*FAA*] (FAAL) ... PPU
Cocoa, FL [*Location identifier*] [*FAA*] (FAAL) ... RDX
Cocoa, FL [*Television station call letters*] ... WBCC
Cocoa, FL [*FM radio station call letters*] ... WLRQ
Cocoa, FL [*FM radio station call letters*] ... WMIE
Cocoa, FL [*AM radio station call letters*] (BROA) ... WMMV-AM
Cocoa, FL [*AM radio station call letters*] ... WMYM
Cocoa, FL [*AM radio station call letters*] ... WRFB
Cocoa, FL [*Television station call letters*] ... WTGL
Cocoa, FL [*AM radio station call letters*] ... WWBC
Cocoa Merchants' Association of America (EA) ... CMAA
Cocoa Producers' Alliance ... COPAL
Cocoa Producers' Alliance (EAIO) ... CPA
Cocoa Public Library, Cocoa, FL [*Library symbol*] [*Library of Congress*] (LCLS) ... FCoa
Cocoa Scientific Advisory Committee (SAUO) ... CSAC
Cocoa/Patrick Air Force Base [*Florida*] [*ICAO location identifier*] (ICLI) ... KCOF
Cocobeach [*Gabon*] [*ICAO location identifier*] (ICLI) ... FOOC
Coconut Cadang-Cadang Viroid [*Also, CCV*] ... CCCV
Coconut Cadang-Cadang Viroid [*Also, CCCV*] ... CCV
Coconut Fatty Alcohol [*Organic chemistry*] ... CFA
Coconut Grove [*Florida*] ... CG
Coconut Grove and Coral Gables [*Florida*] ... CG^2
Coconut Oil (PDAA) ... CCO
Coconut-oil-extended Ethanol (SAUS) ... COCOHOL
COCORP Extended Research Project [*Geology*] ... CERP
Cocos Island [*Keeling Islands, Australia*] [*Airport symbol*] (AD) ... CCK
Cocos Island Animal Quarantine Station (SAUO) ... CIAQS
Cocos Islands [*Australia*] [*ICAO location identifier*] (ICLI) ... APCC
Cocos Islands [*Australia*] [*ICAO location identifier*] (ICLI) ... APOS
Cocos [*Keeling*] **Islands** [*ANSI two-letter standard code*] (CNC) ... CC
Cocos [*Keeling*] **Islands** [*Seismograph station code, US Geological Survey*] [*Closed*] (SEIS) ... CCK
Cocos [*Keeling*] **Islands** [*ANSI three-letter standard code*] (CNC) ... CCK
Cocos [*Keeling*] **Islands** [*MARC geographic area code*] [*Library of Congress*] (LCCP) ... i-xb-
Cocos [*Keeling*] **Islands** [*MARC country of publication code*] [*Library of Congress*] (LCCP) ... xb
Cocos (Keeling) Islands Administration and Council [*Australia*] ... C(K)IAC
Co-Counsel, Inc. [*Associated Press*] (SAG) ... CoCou
Co-Counsel, Inc. [*Associated Press*] (SAG) ... CoCounsl
Co-Counsel, Inc. [*NASDAQ symbol*] (SAG) ... LEGL
Coctio [*Boiling*] ... COCT
Cod and Climate Change (SAUS) ... CCC
Cod Liver Oil ... CLO
Coda Energy, Inc. [*NASDAQ symbol*] (NQ) ... CODA
Coda Energy, Inc. [*Associated Press*] (SAG) ... CodaEn
Coda Music Tech [*NASDAQ symbol*] (TTSB) ... COMT
Coda Music Technology, Inc. [*Associated Press*] (SAG) ... CodaMu
Coda Music Technology, Inc. [*NASDAQ symbol*] (SAG) ... COMT
CODAP [*Control Data Assembly Program*] **Language Block-Oriented Compiler** (MCD) ... COBLOC
Coddair Air East [*ICAO designator*] (AD) ... JJ
Coddington's Digest of the Law of Trade Marks [*A publication*] (DLA) ... Codd Tr M
Codd-Rennie [*Boundary condition*] [*Nuclear energy*] (NRCH) ... C-R
Code (DLA) ... C
Code (MCD) ... CD
Code ... CDE
Code Actuated Random Load Apparatus (MCD) ... CARLA
Code Address [*Telecommunications*] (ECII) ... CADD
Code Address Identification (ACAE) ... CAI
Code Alarm [*NASDAQ symbol*] (TTSB) ... CODL
Code Amendments [*A publication*] (DLA) ... Code Am
Code Analysis Recording by Letters (PDAA) ... CARL
Code and Climate Change Programme (SAUS) ... CCC ICES-GLOBEC
Code and Unit Test ... CUT
Code and Visual Entry Authorization Technique [*Closed-circuit TV*] (MCD) ... CAVEAT
Code Applications and Maintenance Program (SAUO) ... CAMP
Code Behind Form [*Computer science*] (VERA) ... CBF
Code Blue [*Emergency hospital code*] (DAVI) ... CB
Code Book (AFM) ... CB
Code Chain (SAUS) ... CC
Code Character (SAUS) ... CC
Code Chart (SAUS) ... CC
Code Checking Time (SAUS) ... CCT
Code Civil Annote, Dalloz [*A publication*] (ILCA) ... C Civ Ann
Code Clock Transfer Loop ... CCTL
Code Combination (SAUS) ... CC
Code Control (AFM) ... CC
Code Control Number Identifier [*Department of Health and Human Services*] (GFGA) ... CCNI
Code Conversion (SAUS) ... CC
Code Converter ... CC
Code Converter (IAA) ... CCV
Code Coordination and Information Center (SAUS) ... CIC
Code de Commerce [*Commercial Code*] [*French*] ... C COM
Code de Commerce [*Commercial Code*] (DLA) ... Code de Com
Code de Commerce Belge (DLA) ... CCB
Code de Justice Militaire [*A publication*] (DLA) ... Code de JM
Code Definition ... CD
Code des Faillites et Canqueroutes [*A publication*] (DLA) ... Code des F
Code Digit (SAUS) ... CD
Code d'Instruction Criminelle [*Code of Criminal Procedure*] [*A publication*] (ILCA) ... CIC
Code d'Instruction Criminelle [*Code of Criminal Procedure*] [*A publication*] (ILCA) ... C Inst Crim
Code d'Instruction Criminelle [*Code of Criminal Procedure*] (DLA) ... C Instr Cr
Code d'Instruction Criminelle [*Code of Criminal Procedure*] [*A publication*] (ILCA) ... C Instr Crim
Code Directing Character [*Computer science*] ... CDC
Code Division Modulation (SAUO) ... CDM
Code Division Multiple Access Development Group (CGWS) ... CDG
Code Division Testbed (SAUS) ... CODIT
Code du Travail [*Labor Code*] [*A publication*] (ILCA) ... C Trav
Code Equipment (SAUS) ... CE
Code Excited Linear Prediction [*Computer science*] (ACRL) ... CELP
Code Fiels Address (SAUS) ... CFA
Code Figure (SAUS) ... CF
Code for Dangerous Goods (SAUS) ... CDG
Code for Extended Nonlinear Transient Analysis of Extraterrestrial Reactors (SAUS) ... CENTAR
Code for High Resolution Accelerated Radiative Transfer with Scattering (SAUS) ... CHARTS
Code for Magnetic Characters (IEEE) ... CMC
Code for One-Dimensional Reactor Analysis (PDAA) ... CORA
Code for the Construction and Equipment of Mobile Offshore Drilling Units (SAUO) ... MODU Code
Code Fragment Manager [*Computer science*] ... CFM
Code Francais Annote [*A publication*] (DLA) ... Code Fr An
Code Generating Routine (SAUS) ... CGR
Code Generating Unit (SAUS) ... CGU
Code Generator (IAA) ... CG
Code Group (SAUO) ... CG
Code Holes (SAUS) ... CH
Code Identification Number (MSA) ... CIN
Code Impulse Modulation (IAA) ... CIM
Code Information (SAUS) ... CI
Code Inserter Verifier [*Air Force*] ... CIV
Code Instruction (SAUS) ... Cde Insn
Code Interface Module (CAAL) ... CIM
Code Inverter Verifier (SAUS) ... CIV
Code Language Telegram (IAA) ... CLT
Code Learning Machine (SAUS) ... CLEM
Code Line (SAUS) ... CL
Code List (SAUS) ... CL
Code List (SAUS) ... COD
Code Management System [*Computer science*] (VERA) ... CMS
Code Maritime International (SAUS) ... CMI
Code Mark Inversion [*Telecommunications*] (TEL) ... CMI
Code Matching Technique ... CMT
Code Matrix Block (DNAB) ... CMB
Code Matrix Reader (PDAA) ... CMR
Code Modulation (SAUS) ... CM
Code Modulus Generator (SAUS) ... CMG
Code Municipal [*Quebec*] [*A publication*] (DLA) ... Code M
Code Names Dictionary [*A publication*] ... CND
Code Napoleon [*Napoleonic Code*] [*French*] [*Legal term*] ... CN
Code Not Allocated ... CNA
Code Number (SAUS) ... CODEN
Code of Advertising Practices [*British*] ... CAP
Code of Alabama [*A publication*] (DLA) ... Ala Code
Code of Arms (SAUS) ... C/A
Code of Canon Law ... CC
Code of Civil and Commercial Procedure (DLA) ... CC Com Proc
Code of Civil Procedure [*A publication*] (DLA) ... CCP
Code of Civil Procedure [*A publication*] (DLA) ... CC Proc
Code of Civil Procedure [*A publication*] (DLA) ... Code Civ Pro
Code of Civil Procedure [*A publication*] (DLA) ... Code Civ Proc
Code of Civil Procedure [*A publication*] (DLA) ... Code of Civ Proc
Code of Civil Procedure [*Quebec*] [*A publication*] (DLA) ... CPC
Code of Civil Procedure [*India*] [*A publication*] (DLA) ... India Code Civ P
Code of Colorado Regulations [*A publication*] ... CCR
Code of Colorado Regulations [*A publication*] (DLA) ... Colo Admin Code
Code of Conduct [*Military*] (AFM) ... COC
Code of Criminal Procedure [*A publication*] (DLA) ... C Crim Proc
Code of Criminal Procedure (SAUS) ... CCrP
Code of Criminal Procedure [*A publication*] (DLA) ... C Cr Pr
Code of Criminal Procedure [*A publication*] (DLA) ... Code Crim Proc
Code of Criminal Procedure [*A publication*] (DLA) ... Code Cr Pro
Code of Criminal Procedure [*A publication*] (DLA) ... Code Cr Proc
Code of Criminal Procedure [*India*] [*A publication*] (DLA) ... India Code Crim P
Code of Fair Labor Practices (NOAA) ... CFLP
Code of Federal Regulation (DOMA) ... CFR
Code of Federal Regulations [*Department of Energy*] ... CFR
Code of Federal Regulations Supplement [*A publication*] (GFGA) ... CFR Supp
Code of General Laws [*A publication*] (DLA) ... Code Gen Laws
Code of Georgia [*A publication*] (DLA) ... GA Code

Code of Iowa [*A publication*] (AAGC)	Iowa Code
Code of Judicial Conduct (SAUO)	CJC
Code of Judicial Procedure [*A publication*] (DLA)	C Jud Proc
Code of Justinian [*A publication*] (DSA)	CJ
Code of Justinian [*A publication*] (DLA)	Code
Code of Justinian [*A publication*] (DLA)	Jus Code
Code of Justinian (journ.) (SAUS)	Jus Code
Code of Laws of South Carolina [*A publication*] (DLA)	SC Code
Code of Laws of South Carolina, Annotated [*A publication*] (DLA)	SC Code Ann
Code of Maine Rules (AAGC)	CMR
Code of Maine Rules [*Also CMR*] [*A publication*] (AAGC)	Code Me R
Code of Maryland Regulations [*A publication*]	COMAR
Code of Maryland Regulations [*A publication*] (DLA)	MD Admin Code
Code of Massachusetts Regulations [*A publication*]	CMR
Code of Massachusetts Regulations [*A publication*] (DLA)	Mass Admin Code
Code of Military Justice	CMJ
Code of Practice [*Legal term*] (DLA)	Code Prac
Code of Practice [*Telecommunications*] (TEL)	COP
Code of Practice [*Legal term*]	CP
Code of Procedure [*Legal term*] (DLA)	Code Pro
Code of Procedure [*Legal term*] (DLA)	Code Proc
Code of Procedure [*Legal term*]	CP
Code of Procedure [*Legal term*] (DLA)	C Pr
Code of Professional Conduct (SAUS)	ET
Code of Professional Responsibility [*American Bar Association*]	CPR
Code of Public General Laws [*A publication*] (DLA)	Code Pub Gen Laws
Code of Public Local Laws [*A publication*] (DLA)	Code Pub Loc Laws
Code of Rhode Island Rules [*A publication*] (AAGC)	CRIR
Code of Safe Practice for Ships Carrying Timber Deck Cargoes (SAUS)	TD
Code of Safe Practice for Solid Bulk Cargoes (SAUS)	BC
Code of Safe Working Practices for Merchant Seamen (SAUS)	CoSWP
Code of Safe Working Practices For Merchant Seamen (SAUO)	CoSWP
Code of Safety for Diving Systems (SAUS)	DS
Code of Safety for Dynamically Supported Craft (SAUS)	DSC
Code of Safety for Special Purpose Ships (SAUS)	SPS
Code of Shipmanagement Standards (SAUO)	CSS
Code of Theodosius [*Roman law*] [*A publication*] (DLA)	Code Theod
Code of Theodosius [*Roman law*] [*A publication*] (DSA)	C Th
Code of Virginia (SAUS)	Va Code
Code Operations Coordinator (MUGU)	COC
Code Parasite Autopropageable (SAUS)	CPA
Code Pattern (SAUS)	CP
Code Penal [*Penal Code*] [*French*] (BARN)	C Pen
Code Position (SAUS)	CP
Code Practice Oscillator	CPO
Code Proficiency [*Amateur radio*]	CP
Code Reader	CR
Code Receiver [*Computer science*] (IAA)	CR
Code Red (MELL)	CR
Code Regeneration (SAUS)	CR
Code Relations Index	CRI
Code Reporter [*New York*] [*A publication*] (DLA)	Code NY Rep
Code Reporter [*New York*] [*A publication*] (DLA)	Code R
Code Reporter [*New York*] [*A publication*] (DLA)	Code Rep
Code Reporter [*New York*] [*A publication*] (DLA)	Co R
Code Reporter [*New York*] [*A publication*] (DLA)	Co Rep
Code Reporter [*New York*] [*A publication*] (DLA)	Co R (NY)
Code Reporter [*New York*] [*A publication*] (DLA)	CR
Code Reports [*New York*] [*A publication*] (DLA)	Code R (NY)
Code Reports, New Series [*New York*] [*A publication*] (DLA)	Code RNS
Code Reports, New Series [*New York*] [*A publication*] (DLA)	Code RNS (NY)
Code Reports, New Series [*New York*] [*A publication*] (DLA)	Co R NS
Code Reports, New Series [*New York*] [*A publication*] (DLA)	CRNS
Code Rule Violation [*Telecommunications*] (CIST)	CRV
Code Segment [*Computer science*]	CS
Code Segment Descriptor Cache [*Computer science*] (VERA)	CSDC
Code Segment Table [*Computer science*]	CST
Code Segment:Instruction Pointer [*Computer science*]	CS:IP
Code Selection Language [*Computer science*] (BUR)	CSL
Code Sensor (SAUS)	CS
Code Sequential Pulse Generator (IAA)	CSPG
Code Set Map (SAUS)	CSM
Code Ship Parametric Model (MCD)	CSPM
Code Signal (SAUS)	CS
Code Sort Optical Character Recognition [*Computer science*]	CSOCR
Code Storage Segment (SAUS)	CSS
Code Storage Unit	CSU
Code Symbol (SAUS)	CS
Code System (SAUS)	CS
Code Table (IAA)	CT
Code Table Buffer	CTB
Code Telegram	CT
Code Telegram (SAUS)	TC
Code to Analyze Mutual Interface from Nuclear Bursts (ACAE)	CAIN
Code to Handle Angular Data (IEEE)	CHAD
Code Tone Call Selective Signalling [*Telecommunications*] (PDAA)	CTCSS
Code Transcription (SAUS)	CT
Code Transfer Logic	CTL
Code Translation Data System [*Air Force*]	CTDS
Code Translator (SAUS)	CT
Code Universel de Produit [*Universal Product Code*] [*French*]	CUP
Code Variante [*Codification*] (NATG)	CV
Code Verification (SAUS)	CODEFER
Code Verification (IEEE)	CODEVER
Code Verification (SAUS)	COVE
Code Violations (ADWA)	CV
Code Walk-Through (CTAS)	CWT
Code Walk-Through Report (SAUS)	CWTR
Code Wave (BARN)	CW
Code Word (IAA)	CW
Code Word for Greenwich mean time (SAUS)	Zulu
Code-Alarm, Inc. [*Associated Press*] (SAG)	CodeAI
Code-Alarm, Inc. [*NASDAQ symbol*] (NQ)	CODL
Coded (IAA)	CDD
Coded (SAUS)	Cdd
Coded Acoustic Interrogator	CAI
Coded Address [*NATO*]	CODRESS
Coded Address Private Radio Intercom (SAUS)	CAPRI
Coded Address Private Radio Intercommunication (MCD)	CAPRI
Coded Analysis [*Navy*]	CODAN
Coded Armaments System	CAS
Coded Automatic Gain Control	CAGC
Coded Automatic Reading Device	CARD
Coded Biphase	COBI
Coded Block Pattern (ROAS)	CBP
Coded Character Set Identification [*IBM Corp*] (VERA)	CCSID
Coded Command	CCMD
Coded Current Block (SAUS)	CCB
Coded Decimal Digit	CDD
Coded Decimal Notation	CDN
Coded Description Pattern (AFIT)	CDP
Coded Digital Facsmile (SAUS)	CDF
Coded Discharge (DNAB)	CODIS
Coded Doppler RADAR Command	CODORAC
Coded Fuzzy Language (SAUS)	CFL
Coded Identification (SAUS)	CI
Coded Information (SAUS)	CI
Coded Integrated Armament Control System (MCD)	CIACS
Coded Label Additional Security and Protection System (SAUS)	CLASPS
Coded Mark Inversion (SAUS)	CMI
Coded Modulator-Demodulator (PDAA)	CODEM
Coded Optical Character [*Computer science*] (BUR)	COC
Coded Orthogonal Frequency Division Multiplex (AAEL)	COFDM
Coded Parts List (SAUS)	CPL
Coded Print File (SAUS)	CPF
Coded Pulse Anticlutter System (CET)	CPACS
Coded Signal (SAUS)	CS
Coded Switch System [*To permit or deny the ability to arm nuclear weapons in strategic aircraft*]	CSS
Coded Tape (SAUS)	CT
Coded Telemetry Processor	CTP
Coded Time Sequence (MCD)	CTS
Coded Virtual Channel Data Units (SAUS)	CVCDU
Coded Voice System Digitization (NITA)	CVSD
Coded Wire Tagging [*Pisciculture*]	CWT
Coded-Access Teleconferencing System [*Telecommunications*]	CATS
Coded-Bias Mosaic (MCD)	COBM
Coded-Impulse Modulation (SAUS)	CIM
Code-Division Multiple Access [*Navigation systems*]	CDMA
Co-Defendant [*Legal term*] (WDAA)	Co-D
Codeine (AAMN)	Cod
Codeine [*Pharmacology*] (DAVI)	CODEIN
Codeine Tablet [*Slang*] (DSUE)	CODI
Coden [*Online database field identifier*]	CD
Coden [*Online database field identifier*]	CO
Codependency (SAUS)	COD
Co-Dependents Anonymous (EA)	CoDA
Co-Dependents of Sexual Addicts [*Acronym is now organization's official name*] (EA)	COSA
Coder and Random Access Switch (AAG)	CRAS
Coder, Filter, Decoder (SAUS)	COFIDEC
Coder Sequential Pulse	CSP
Coder-Decoder [*Telecommunications*] (MCD)	CODEC
Coder-Decoder [*Telecommunications*]	codec
Coder-Decoder Control (SAUS)	CDC
Coder/Decoder Device	CODEC Device
Coder-Decoder Group [*Army*] (AABC)	CDG
Codes and Paging (NRCH)	CAP
Codes of Practice Committees (SAUS)	CPC
Codes, Standards, and Regulations [*Environmental science*] (COE)	CS&R
Code-View [*Computer software*] (PCM)	CV
CodeView for Windows [*Program debugger*] [*Computer science*] (PCM)	CVW
Codewarrior Analysis Tools (SAUS)	CATS
Codeword, Nickname and Exercise Term System (SAUS)	NICKA
Codex	C
Codex	COD
Codex (WDAA)	cod
Codex (SAUS)	Cod
Codex Aleppensis (BJA)	CA
Codex Alexandrinus (BJA)	A
Codex Alimentarius Commission [*United Nations*] (PDAA)	CAC
Codex Alimentarius Commission (SAUO)	CODEX
Codex Bezae (BJA)	D
Codex Committee on Food Hygiene (SAUO)	CCFH
Codex Committee on Pesticide Residues [*Australia*]	CCPR
Codex Committee on Residues of Veterinary Drugs in Food [*Australia*]	CCRVDF
Codex Diplomaticus [*A publication*] (ILCA)	Cod Dip
Codex Ephaemi [*Ephraem the Syrian*] [*A publication*] (ROG)	CE
Codex Hammurabi (BJA)	CH

Codex Iuris Canonici [*Code of Canon Law*] [*Latin*] CIC
Codex Iustinianus [*Classical studies*] (OCD) .... Cod Iust
Codex Juris Civilis [*A publication*] (ILCA) C
Codex Juris Civilis [*Latin*] [*A publication*] (DLA) .... Cod Jur Civ
Codex Justinianus (BJA) .... CJ
Codex Justinianus [*Code of Justinian*] [*Latin*] [*A publication*] (DLA) .... Code
Codex Justinianus (BJA) .... CodJust
Codex Leningradensis (BJA) CL
Codex Marchalianus (BJA) .... Q
Codex Membranacius [*A book written on vellum or skins*] [*Latin*]
  (ROG) .... COD MEMB
Codex Petropolitanus (BJA) .... CP
Codex Prophetarum Cairensis (BJA) CC
Codex Reuchlinianus (BJA) .... CR
Codex Sinaiticus (BJA) .... S
Codex Theodosianus [*Theodosian Code*] [*438AD*] [*Latin*] [*Legal term*]
  (DLA) .... Code Theodos
Codex Theodosianus [*Theodosian Code*] [*438AD*] [*Latin*] [*Legal term*]
  (OCD) .... Cod Theod
Codex Theodosianus [*Theodosian Code*] [*438AD*] [*Latin*] [*Legal term*]
  [*A publication*] (DLA) .... Cod Theodos
Codex Theodosianus [*Theodosian Code*] [*438AD*] [*Latin*] [*Legal term*] (BJA) .... CT
Codex Theodosianus [*Theodosian Code*] [*438AD*] [*Latin*] [*A publication*]
  (DLA) .... C Theod
Codex Vaticanus (BJA) .... B
Codex Vector Sum Excited Linear Prediction [*Algorithm*] (VERA) .... CVSELP
Codice Civile [*Civil Code*] [*Italian*] (ILCA) CC
Codice Commerciale [*Commercial Code*] [*A publication*] (ILCA) .... C Comm
Codices (VRA) .... cod
Codices (ROG) .... CODD
Codices (SAUS) .... Codd
Codices Latini Antiquiores [*A publication*] (OCD) .... Codd Lat Ant
Codices Palatini (BJA) .... CPal
Codicil .... COD
Codicil .... CODL
Codification [*Legal term*] (ILCA) .... Cod
Codification File (MCD) .... CODFIL
Codified Statutes [*A publication*] (DLA) .... Cod St
Codifying Act of Sederunt (DLA) .... CAS
Coding (SAUS) .... Cdg
Coding (SAUS) .... Cod
Coding (MSA) .... COD
Coding Board Officer .... CBO
Coding Decoder Device (SAUS) .... CODEC
Coding Delay (SAUS) .... CD
Coding Field (SAUS) .... CF
Coding Language (SAUS) CL
Coding Line (SAUS) CL
Coding Memory (SAUS) .... CM
Coding Modulation (ACAE) .... CM
Coding Printer (SAUS) .... CP
Coding Recorder (SAUS) .... CR
Coding Room Watch Officer [*Navy*] .... CRWO
Coding Section (SAUS) .... CS
Coding Sequence [*Genetics*] .... CDS
Coding Specification .... CS
Coding Speed Test (DNAB) .... CST
Coding Store (SAUS) .... CS
Coding Symbols for Thesaurus of Adverse Reaction Terms (SAUO) .... COSTART
Coding/Decoding (SAUS) .... CODEC
Coding/Decoding Device .... CODEC
Coding/Decoding Device (SAUS) .... CODEC Device
Codling Moth Granulosis Virus .... CMGV
Codon Adaptation Index [*Genetics*] .... CAI
Codon Usage Tabulated from Genbank (SAUO) .... CUTG
Codrington [*Barbuda Island*] [*ICAO location identifier*] (ICLI) .... TAPH
Codrington College (SAUS) .... Cdrngtn C
Codroy Valley Public Library, Upper Ferry, Newfoundland [*Library symbol*]
  [*National Library of Canada*] (NLC) .... NFUF
Codroy Valley Public Library, Upper Ferry, NF, Canada [*Library symbol*]
  [*Library of Congress*] (LCLS) .... CaNfUF
Cody [*Wyoming*] [*Airport symbol*] (OAG) .... COD
Cody, WY [*Location identifier*] [*FAA*] (FAAL) .... COD
Cody, WY [*AM radio station call letters*] .... KODI
Cody, WY [*FM radio station call letters*] .... KTAG
Cody, WY [*FM radio station call letters*] .... KYDZ
Coe College, Cedar Rapids, IA [*Library symbol*] [*Library of Congress*]
  (LCLS) .... IaCrC
Coe College, Cedar Rapids, IA [*OCLC symbol*] (OCLC) .... ION
COE Engineering System (SAUS) .... COEES
Coe. Practice of the Judges' Chambers [*1876*] [*A publication*] (DLA) ..... Coe Ch Pr
Coe Ranch [*California*] [*Seismograph station code, US Geological Survey*]
  (SEIS) .... COE
Coe Township Library, Shepherd, MI [*Library symbol*] [*Library of Congress*]
  (LCLS) .... MiShep
COEA [*Cost and Operational Effectiveness Analysis*] Cost Advisory Group
  [*Military*] .... CCAG
Coeburn, VA [*FM radio station call letters*] .... WZQK
Co-Editor .... CO-ED
Co-Editor (SAUS) .... CoEd
Coeducational .... COED
Co-Educational (AIE) .... CoEd
Coefficient C
Coefficient (ADWA) .... coef
Coefficient (KSC) .... COEF

Coefficient .... COEFF
Coefficient (ADWA) .... coeff
Coefficient Association (DIPS) .... CA
Coefficient of Alienation [*Psychology*] .... k
Coefficient of Association (SAUS) .... q
Coefficient of Association [*Statistics*] .... Q
Coefficient of Beam Utilization [*Floodlighting*] .... CBU
Coefficient of Concordance (DIPS) .... W
Coefficient of Contingency (DIPS) C
Coefficient of Contingency [*Statistics*] CC
Coefficient of Correlation [*Statistics*] CC
coefficient of determination (SAUS) .... $r2$
coefficient of determination (SAUS) .... ry
Coefficient of Drag (SAUS) .... Cd
Coefficient of Drag (MCD) .... CD
Coefficient of Drag-Area .... CDA
Coefficient of Elasticity (SAUS) .... CofE
Coefficient of Fat Retention (AAMN) .... CR
Coefficient of Friction [*Physics*] (BARN) .... CF
Coefficient of Friction [*Physics*] .... COF
Coefficient of Haze [*Environment*] .... COH
Coefficient of Haze (DB) .... CoH
Coefficient of Heat Transfer [*Symbol*] [*Thermodynamics*] .... h
Coefficient of Impact (SAUS) .... e
Coefficient of Induced Drag [*Aviation*] (DA) .... C_{Di}
Coefficient of Intelligence CI
Coefficient of Intensity, Luminous (SAUS) CIL
Coefficient of Lift CL
Coefficient of Linear Extensibility .... COLE
Coefficient of Linear Thermal Expansion .... CLTE
Coefficient of Luminous Intensity CLI
Coefficient of Mean Square Contingency (DIPS) C
Coefficient of Merit [*Electronics*] (IAA) .... COM
Coefficient of Multiple Determination (DIPS) R2
Coefficient of Nondetermination (DIPS) K2
Coefficient of Octanolwater Partition (GNE) .... Kow
Coefficient of Organic Carbon Partition (GNE) .... Koc
Coefficient of Overestimation .... CO
Coefficient of Oxygen Delivery .... COD
Coefficient of Performance .... COP
Coefficient of Performance (IEEE) .... CP
Coefficient of Physics [*Physics*] (DAVI) L
Coefficient of Profile Drag [*Aviation*] (DA) .... C_{Dp}
Coefficient of Protection [*Against insects*] .... CP
Coefficient of Relative Variation .... CRV
Coefficient of Resilience (SAUS) .... e
Coefficient of Restitution (SAUS) .... COR
Coefficient of Restitution (SAUS) .... e
Coefficient of Retention (SAUS) .... CR
Coefficient of Retraction .... CR
Coefficient of Scleral Rigidity [*Ophthalmology*] (DAVI) .... K
Coefficient of Sliding Friction (SAUS) .... f
Coefficient of Soil-Water Absorption (GNE) .... Kd
Coefficient of Stability (DIPS) .... W
Coefficient of Temperature (DAVI) .... Q_{10}
Coefficient of Thermal Expansion .... CTE
Coefficient of Utilization .... CU
Coefficient of Variation [*Mathematics*] .... COV
Coefficient of Variation [*Mathematics*] CV
Coefficient of Variation [*Statistics*] (BARN) V
Coefficient of Vibration (SAUS) V
Coefficient Z-Axis [*Downforce on a racing car*] [*Aerodynamics*] .... CZ
Coeliac Axis (BABM) .... CA
Coeliac Society of Australia .... CSA
Coeliac Society of the United Kingdom (EAIO) .... CSUK
Coelieac [*or Celiac*] Axis [*Gastroenterology*] (DAVI) .... CA
Coelliptic Rendezvous Sequence [*Aerospace*] .... CRS
Coelliptic Sequence Initiation [*Aerospace*] .... CSI
Co-elliptic Sequence initiation (SAUS) .... CSI
Coelliptic Sequence Initiation (NAKS) .... csi
Coen [*Australia*] [*Airport symbol*] (OAG) .... CUQ
Coenzyme [*Biochemistry*] .... Co
Coenzyme A [*Biochemistry*] .... CoA
Coenzyme A ester (SAUS) .... acyl-Co A
Coenzyme A-Cholesterol Acyltransferase (DB) .... ACAT
Coenzyme A-Synthetizing Protein Complex [*Medicine*] (DMAA) .... CoA-SPC
Coenzyme Community Organization (STED) .... CO
Coenzyme M .... CoM
Coenzyme Q [*Ubiquinone*] [*Also, Q, U, UQ*] [*Biochemistry*] .... CoQ
Coenzyme Q [*Ubiquinone*] [*Also, CoQ, U, UQ*] [*Biochemistry*] .... Q
Coercion (MSA) .... CORCN
Coeroeni [*Surinam*] [*ICAO location identifier*] (ICLI) .... SMCI
Coeur D'Alene [*Idaho*] [*Airport symbol*] (OAG) .... COE
Coeur D'Alene, ID [*Location identifier*] [*FAA*] (FAAL) .... AUC
Coeur D'Alene, ID [*Location identifier*] [*FAA*] (FAAL) .... COE
Coeur D'Alene, ID [*Location identifier*] [*FAA*] (FAAL) .... HYD
Coeur d'Alene, ID [*FM radio station call letters*] (BROA) .... KBIH-FM
Coeur D'Alene, ID [*FM radio station call letters*] .... KCDA
Coeur D'Alene, ID [*Television station call letters*] (TTSB) .... KCDT
Coeur D'Alene, ID [*AM radio station call letters*] .... KVNI
Coeur D'Alene Mines Corp. [*NYSE symbol*] (SPSG) .... CDE
Coeur D'Alene Mines Corp. [*Associated Press*] (SAG) .... Coeur
Coeur d'Alene Mines 'MARCS' [*NYSE symbol*] (TTSB) .... CDEPr
Coeur D'Alene Public Library, Coeur D'Alene, ID [*Library symbol*] [*Library of
  Congress*] (LCLS) .... IdC

Coeur d'Alene Public Library, Coeur d'Alene, ID [Library symbol] [Library of Congress] (LCLS) .... IdCL
Coexisting Illness (MELL) .... CEI
Coextrusion Welding .... CEW
Cofactor [Laboratory] (DAVI) .... CoF
Cofer's Kentucky Digest [A publication] (DLA) .... Cof Dig
Coffee .... COF
Coffee Association of Canada [Association du Cafe du Canada] (AC) .... CAC
Coffee Berry Disease .... CBD
Coffee Brewing Center (SAUO) .... CBC
Coffee Brewing Institute (SAUO) .... CBI
Coffee Commission of the Inter-American Economic and Social Council [United States] .... CCIAESC
Coffee Development Group (EA) .... CDG
Coffee from Council (SAUO) .... CPC
Coffee Growers' Association of El Salvador [Defunct] (EA) .... CGAES
Coffee House (ROG) .... CO HO
Coffee Information Institute (SAUS) CII
Coffee Marketing Board (SAUO) .... CMB
Coffee Mill .... COFML
Coffee People, Inc. [Associated Press] (SAG) .... CoffPeop
Coffee People, Inc. [NASDAQ symbol] (SAG) .... MOKA
Coffee Promotion Council Ltd. (SAUO) .... CPC
Coffee Ringspot Virus [Plant pathology] .... CRV
Coffee, Sugar, and Cocoa Exchange (EA) .... CSCE
Coffee Table Book [Large, extensively illustrated book designed for display and browsing] .... CTB
Coffee Trade Federation [British] (DBA) .... CTF
Coffee Worker's Lung (MELL) .... CWL
Cofferdam [Engineering] .... COFF
Coffey's California Probate Decisions [A publication] (DLA) .... Cof
Coffey's California Probate Decisions [A publication] (DLA) .... Coffey
Coffey's California Probate Decisions [A publication] (DLA) ...... Coffey Probate Dec
Coffey's California Probate Decisions [A publication] (DLA) ...... Coffey Prob Dec
Coffey's California Probate Decisions [A publication] (DLA) .... Coffey's Prob Dec
Coffey's California Probate Decisions [A publication] (DLA) ...... Coff Prob
Coffey's California Probate Decisions [A publication] (DLA) ...... Cof Pro
Coffey's California Probate Decisions [A publication] (DLA) ...... Cof Prob
Coffey's California Probate Decisions [A publication] (DLA) ...... Cof Prob Dec (Cal)
Coffeyville, KS [Location identifier] [FAA] (FAAL) .... CFV
Coffeyville, KS [AM radio station call letters] .... KGGF
Coffeyville, KS [FM radio station call letters] .... KUSN
Coffin [Missile launch environment symbol] C
Coffin Furniture and Cerement Making Trade Board (SAUO) .... CFCMTB
Coffin Ground-Attack Missile .... CGM
Coffin Intercept Missile .... CIM
Coffin Strategic Missile .... CSM
Coffin Texts (BJA) .... CT
Coffin-Lowry Syndrome [Medicine] .... CLS
Coffin-Lowry Syndrome Foundation (SAUO) .... CLSF
Coffman Cove, AK [Location identifier] [FAA] (FAAL) .... KCC
Coffs Harbour [Australia] [ICAO location identifier] (ICLI) .... ASCH
Coffs Harbour [Australia] [Airport symbol] (OAG) .... CFS
Cofield, NC [Location identifier] [FAA] (FAAL) CVI
Co-Fired, Multilayer Ceramic [Materials science] .... CMC
Coflexip [NASDAQ symbol] (SAG) .... CXIP
Coflexip ADS [NASDAQ symbol] (TTSB) .... CXIPY
Coflexip & Services, Inc. [Associated Press] (SAG) .... Coflexip
Coformycin [Biochemistry] .... CF
Cogdean [England] .... COGD
Cogeco, Inc. [Toronto Stock Exchange symbol] .... CGO
Cogeneration and Independent Power Coalition of America (EA) .... CIPCA
Cogeneration Coalition [Later, CIPCA] (EA) CIC
Cogeneration Coalition of America [Later, CIPCA] (EA) .... CICA
Cogeneration of Heat and Power .... CHP
Cogenital Virilizing Adrenal Hyperplasia [Medicine] (STED) .... CVAH
Cogesco Mining Resources [Toronto Stock Exchange symbol] .... COJ
Coggan Monitor, Coggan, IA [Library symbol] [Library of Congress] (LCLS) .... IaCogM
Coggeshall [England] .... COGG
Coghlan Island, AK [Location identifier] [FAA] (FAAL) .... CGL
Coghlan's Epitome of Hindu Law Cases [A publication] (DLA) .... Cogh Epit
Cogitive Style (EDAC) .... CS
COGLA [Canada Oil and Gas Lands Administration] Ocean Mining Resource Centre , Ottawa, Ontario [Centre de Ressources sur l'Extraction de Minerais Oceaniques, Administration du Petrole et du Gaz des Terres du Canada] [Library symbol] [National Library of Canada] (NLC) .... OOCOG
COGLA [Canada Oil and Gas Lands Administration] Ocean Mining Resource Centre, APGTC , Ottawa, ON, Canada [Administration du Petrole et du Gaz des Terres du Canada] [Library symbol] [Library of Congress] (LCLS) .... CaOOCOG
Cognac (ADA) .... COG
Cognac Information Bureau [Commercial firm] (EA) .... CIB
Cognac Information Centre [British] (CB) CIC
Cognac/Chateau Bernard [France] [ICAO location identifier] (ICLI) .... LFBG
Cognate C
Cognate (ADWA) .... cog
Cognate (ROG) .... COG
Cognate With (ROG) .... COGN W
Cognex Corp. [NASDAQ symbol] (NQ) .... CGNX
Cognex Corp. [Associated Press] (SAG) .... Cognex
Cognition Disorder (MELL) .... CD
Cognitive C
Cognitive [Function tests] [Psychology] (DAVI) .... COG
Cognitive Abilities Screening Instrument [Medicine] (DMAA) .... CASI

Cognitive Abilities Test [Education] .... CAT
Cognitive Abilities Test [Academic achievement and aptitude test] .... COGAT
Cognitive Abilities Test (TMMY) .... CogAT
Cognitive Academic Language Proficiency (SAUO) .... CALP
Cognitive Acceleration through Science Education (AIE) .... CASE
Cognitive Acceleration through Science Education Project (AIE) .... CASEP
Cognitive and Affective Learning Model [Psychology] .... CALM
Cognitive Avoidance [Medicine] (MELL) .... Ca
Cognitive Behavioral Therapy .... CBT
Cognitive Capacity Screening Examination [Psychology] .... CCSE
Cognitive Complexity (SAUS) CC
Cognitive Diagnostic Battery [Test] .... CDB
Cognitive Dysfunction Syndrome [Medicine] .... CDS
Cognitive Enhancement Research Institute (SAUO) .... CERI
Cognitive Environmental Stimulation [Medicine] (DAVI) .... CES
Cognitive Failure Questionnaire [Education] (AIE) .... CFQ
Cognitive Hybrid Intelligent Learning Device .... CHILD
Cognitive Laterality Quotient (SAUS) .... CLQ
Cognitive Levels Matching [Psychology] (EDAC) .... CLM
Cognitive, Linguistic, and Social-Communicative Scales [Speech evaluation test] .... CLASS
Cognitive Operating System [NASA] .... COGNOSYS
Cognitive Processing System [Education] (WDAA) .... COPS
Cognitive Processing Therapy (DIPS) .... CPT
Cognitive Research Trust [British] (DI) .... CORT
Cognitive Research Trust (WDAA) .... CRT
Cognitive Restructuring (SAUS) .... C-R
Cognitive Science Society (EA) .... CSS
Cognitive Skills Assessment Battery (EDAC) .... CSAB
Cognitive Skills Program (WDAA) .... CSP
Cognitive Stimulation [Experimental psychology] .... CS
Cognitive Strategies Questionnaire (MELL) .... CSQ
Cognitive Style Mapping Inventory (EDAC) .... CSMI
Cognitive Therapy (SAUS) .... CT
Cognitive-Behavior Modification [Psychology] .... CBM
Cognitronics Corp. [AMEX symbol] (SPSG) .... CGN
Cognitronics Corp. [Associated Press] (SAG) .... Cognitr
Cognizance Symbol .... CS
Cognizant (NG) .... COG
Cognizant Controlling Custodian (ACAE) CCC
Cognizant Development Engineer .... CDE
Cognizant Engineer .... CE
Cognizant Federal Agency (COE) .... CFA
Cognizant Field Activity .... CFA
Cognizant Government Inspector (SAA) .... CGI
Cognizant Operating Authority (MUGU) .... COA
Cognizant Operations Engineer .... COE
Cognizant Operations Engineer's Parts List .... COEPL
Cognizant Quality Engineer (NRCH) .... CQE
Cognizant Security Authority [Military] .... CSA
Cognizant Security Office [Controls industrial security at government facilities] [Military] .... CSO
Cognizant Security Officer (AAGC) .... CSO
Cognizant Sustaining Engineer .... CSE
Cognizant Technical Manager .... CTM
Cognizant Transportation Office [or Officer] [Air Force] (AFM) .... CTO
Cognizant User Engineer [Deep Space Network, NASA] .... CUE
Cognomen (SAUS) .... Cogn
Cognos, Inc. [NASDAQ symbol] (NQ) .... COGN
Cognos Inc. [NASDAQ symbol] (TTSB) .... COGNE
Cognos, Inc. [Associated Press] (SAG) .... Cognos
Cognos, Inc. [Toronto Stock Exchange symbol] .... CSN
Cognos, Inc., Ottawa, Ontario [Library symbol] [National Library of Canada] (BIB) .... OOCOI
Cognos International Users' Group (AC) .... CIUG
Cogswell Family Association (EA) .... CFA
Cogswell Polytechnical College (SAUS) .... CPC
Cogwheel [Respiration] [Medicine] .... sacc
Cohasset School, Cohasset, MN [Library symbol] [Library of Congress] (LCLS) .... MnCohS
Coheir [Joint heir] [Genealogy] .... COH
Cohen and Lee's Maryland Digest [A publication] (DLA) .... C & L Dig
Cohen & Steers Realty Income Fund [Associated Press] (SAG) .... CohenStr
Cohen & Steers Realty Income Fund [Formerly, Real Estate Securities Income Fund, Inc.] (CTT) .... RIF
Cohen & Steers Rlty Inc. Fd [AMEX symbol] (TTSB) .... RIF
Cohen & Steers Total Return Realty Fund [Associated Press] (SAG) ...... CohenST
Cohen & Steers Total Return Rt. Realty Fund [NYSE symbol] (SPSG) .... RFI
Cohen & Steers Total Rt Rty Fd [NYSE symbol] (TTSB) .... RFI
Cohen's Admiralty Jurisdiction, Law, and Practice [A publication] (DLA) .... Cohen Adm Law
Cohen's Criminal Appeals Reports [England] [A publication] (DLA) .... Crim App Rep
Cohen's Nova Scotia Reports [A publication] (DLA) .... NSR Coh
Coherence [Statistics] .... COH
Coherence (SAUS) .... Coher
Coherence Enhanced Radiation Rejection (ACAE) .... CERR
Coherence Function (SAUS) .... CF
Coherency (SAUS) .... Coher
Coherent (SAUS) .... Coh
Coherent (IAA) .... COH
Coherent Acceleration and Velocity Observations in Real Time .... CAVORT
Coherent Acoustic Torpedo System (MCD) .... CATS
Coherent Acquisition System (MCD) .... CAS
Coherent Active Source Experiment (SAUS) .... CASE

Coherent Advanced Solid State Phased Array System (ACAE) .... CASPAR
Coherent Airborne Moving Target Indication (ACAE) .... CAMTI
Coherent Airborne Moving Target Track (ACAE) .... CAMTT
Coherent All Radio Band Sensing (SAUS) .... CARABAS
Coherent Amplitude Detector (ACAE) .... CAD
Coherent Antarctic Radar Depth Sounder (SAUS) .... CARDS
Coherent Antistokes Raman (ACAE) .... CAR
Coherent Anti-Stokes Raman Scattering (SAUS) .... CARS
Coherent Anti-Stokes Raman Spectroscopy (SAUS) .... CARS
Coherent Anti-Stokes Resonance Raman Scattering [Spectrometry] .... CARRS
Coherent Array RADAR (MSA) .... COAR
Coherent Backscatter Opposition Effect [Physics] .... CBOE
Coherent Carrier Keying [Computer science] (IAA) .... CCK
Coherent Cloud Physics RADAR .... CCPR
Coherent Cloud Physics Radar (SAUS) .... CCPR
Coherent Communic Sys [NASDAQ symbol] (TTSB) .... CCSC
Coherent Communications Systems Corp. [NASDAQ symbol] (SAG) .... CCSC
Coherent Communications Systems Corp. [Associated Press] (SAG) .... CoherC
Coherent Countermeasures Processor (SAUS) .... CCP
Coherent Crystal Radiation (PDAA) .... CCR
Coherent Detection Phase Shift Keying (ACAE) .... CPSK
Coherent Detector [Electronics] (OA) .... CD
Coherent Digital Exciter (ADWA) .... CoDE
Coherent Digital Phased Array System [ARPA] .... CODIPHASE
Coherent Display Analyzing and Recording (SAUS) .... CODAR
Coherent Doppler Measurement System .... CDMS
Coherent Echo Modulation and Detection (MCD) .... CEMAD
Coherent Electromagnetic Energy Transmission .... COMET
Coherent Emitter Location Testbed (IEEE) .... CELT
Coherent Emitter Locator Targeting System (ACAE) .... CELTS
Coherent Event [Trademark] .... COHVENT
Coherent File Distribution Protocol (SAUS) .... CFDP
Coherent Forward Scattering [Spectrometry] .... CFS
Coherent Frequency Multiplexed Radar (ACAE) .... CFMR
Coherent Frequency Shift Keying .... CFSK
Coherent Frequency Synthesizer .... CFS
Coherent Frequency-Hopping Signal .... CFHS
Coherent Ground Moving Target Indication (ACAE) .... CGMTI
Coherent Ground Moving Target Tracking (ACAE) .... CGMTT
Coherent Heterodyne Receiver (PDAA) .... CHR
Coherent High-Intensity Photon Source (SAUS) .... CHIPS
Coherent Imaging RADAR .... CIR
Coherent, Inc. [Associated Press] (SAG) .... Cohernt
Coherent, Inc. [NASDAQ symbol] (NQ) .... COHR
Coherent Infrared Energy (AAG) .... CIE
Coherent Interpretation Time (MCD) .... CIT
Coherent Jammer Simulator (SAUS) .... COJAS
Coherent LASER Illumination CLI
Coherent Laser radar Airborne Shear Sensor (SAUS) .... CLASS
Coherent Light Detecting and Ranging [RADAR] [Hughes Aircraft] .... COLIDAR
Coherent Light Detector .... COLD
Coherent Light Detector System (MCD) .... COLIDS
Coherent Linear Frequency Modulated (IAA) .... CLFM
Coherent Local Oscillator (ACAE) .... COLO
Coherent Master Oscillator (NG) .... COMO
Coherent Memory Filter .... CMF
Coherent Memory Filter (SAUS) .... COMEF
Coherent Microwave Memory .... CMM
Coherent Monopulse Doppler RADAR .... CMDR
Coherent Moving Target Indication (ACAE) .... CMTI
Coherent Multi-Channel (IAA) .... CMC
Coherent Multichannel Communication .... CMC
Coherent Multiple Frequency Signature (ACAE) .... CMFS
Coherent Optical Adaptive Techniques .... COAT
Coherent Optical Array .... COA
Coherent Optical Array Techniques .... COAT
Coherent Optical Device .... COD
Coherent Optical Fingerprint Identification System (MCD) .... COFIDS
Coherent Optical LASER .... COL
Coherent Optical Processing System .... COPS
Coherent Optical Processor .... COP
Coherent Optical RADAR Laboratory .... CORAL
Coherent Optical Receiver .... COR
Coherent Optical System of Modular Imaging Collectors .... COSMIC
Coherent Oscillator [RADAR] .... COHO
Coherent Phase Shift Keyed [System] [Computer science] .... CPSK
Coherent Phase Shift Keying (NITA) .... CPSK
Coherent Potential (OA) .... CP
Coherent Potential Approximation [Physics] .... CPA
Coherent Processing Interval [Computer science] .... CPI
Coherent RADAR Array .... CORA
Coherent RADAR Seeker Investigation (MCD) .... CORSI
Coherent Raman Spectroscopy (MCD) .... CRS
Coherent Receiver/Transmitter (SAUS) .... CORT
Coherent Sidelobe Cancellation (ACAE) .... CSC
Coherent Side-Lobe Cancellation .... CSLC
Coherent Signal Processing System [Army] (AABC) .... CSPS
Coherent Signal Processor .... CSP
Coherent Signal Simulator (SAUS) .... CSS
Coherent Space Mirror Complex .... COSMIC
Coherent Stokes Raman Scattering (SAUS) .... CSRS
Coherent Stokes Raman Spectroscopy (SAUS) .... CSRS
Coherent Synthetic Aperture RADAR (MCD) .... CSAR
Coherent Tilted Superlattice [Solid state physics] .... CTSL
Coherent Transient Spectroscopy (MCD) .... CTS

Coherent-on-Receive .... CORE
Coherent-on-Receive Doppler System [RADAR] .... CORDS
Coherent-Pulse Radar (SAUS) .... CPR
coherer (SAUS) .... coher
cohering (SAUS) .... coher
Cohesant Technologies [NASDAQ symbol] (TTSB) .... COHT
Cohesant Technologies, Inc. [Associated Press] (SAG) .... Cohes
Cohesant Technologies, Inc. [Associated Press] (SAG) .... Cohesant
Cohesant Technologies, Inc. [NASDAQ symbol] (SAG) .... COHT
Cohesant Technologies Wrrt [NASDAQ symbol] (TTSB) .... COHTW
Cohesion, Operational Readiness, and Training [Army] .... COHORT
Cohesion, Organization, Resourcefulness and Energy Model (EDAC) .... CORE
Cohesive Energy Density [Solubility parameter] .... CED
Cohesive Energy Ratio (MCD) .... CER
Cohesive Intermolecular Force .... CIF
Cohesive Unit Program [Army] .... CUP
Cohlmia Aviation [ICAO designator] (FAAC) .... CHL
Coho Energy [NASDAQ symbol] (TTSB) .... COHO
Coho Energy, Inc. [NASDAQ symbol] (SAG) .... COHO
Coho Energy, Inc. [Associated Press] (SAG) .... CohoEn
Cohort Analysis of Increased Risks of Deaths Model (SAUS) .... CAIRD
Cohort Production Intervals .... CPI
Cohort Research Development Program (SAUO) .... CORD
COHR, Inc. [NASDAQ symbol] (SAG) .... CHRI
COHR, Inc. [Associated Press] (SAG) .... COHR
COHU Electronics, Inc. (SAUO) .... COHU
Cohu, Inc. [NASDAQ symbol] (SAG) .... COHU
Coiffeur .... CFFR
Coiffeuse .... CFFS
Coiffure .... COIFF
Coil [Genetics] C
Coil CL
Coil Finish (MSA) .... CF
Coil Former (SAUS) .... CF
Coil Planet Centrifuge (DB) .... CPC
Coil Power Programmer [Nuclear energy] (NRCH) .... CPP
Coil Predriver (IAA) .... CPD
Coil Sketch (MSA) .... CS
Coil Spring Brace [Medicine] (MELL) .... CSB
Coil Spring Federation Research Organisation (SAUO) .... CSFRO
Coil Spring-loaded Beveled-edge Ring [Automotive engineering] .... CSBR
Coil Stock Cradle .... CSC
Coil Test (DB) .... CT
Coil Winding Equipment .... CWE
Coil Winding International Exhibition [British] (ITD) .... CWI
Coil Winding Machine .... CWM
Coiled [Freight] .... COIL
Coiled Coil (SAUS) CC
Coiled Information [Computer science] (VERA) CI
Coils [Freight] .... CLS
Coils per Slot [Technical drawings] .... CPS
Coimbatore [India] [Airport symbol] (OAG) .... CJB
Coimbatore [India] [ICAO location identifier] (ICLI) .... VOCB
Coimbra [Portugal] [Seismograph station code, US Geological Survey]
(SEIS) .... COI
Coimbra [Portugal] [ICAO location identifier] (ICLI) .... LPCO
Coin and Fee Checking [Telecommunications] (TEL) .... CFC
Coin Bill Validator [NASDAQ symbol] (TTSB) .... CBVI
Coin Bill Validator, Inc. [NASDAQ symbol] (SAG) .... CBVI
Coin Bill Validator, Inc. [Associated Press] (SAG) .... CoinBill
Coin Box [Telecommunications] (TEL) .... CB
Coin Box Adapter [Computer science] (ECII) .... CBA
Coin Box Telephone [Telecommunications] .... CBT
[The] Coin Coalition (EA) .... TCC
Coin Collect [Telecommunications] (TEL) CC
Coin Collecting Box [Telecommunications] (TEL) .... CCB
Coin Collecting Box, Pay Station [Telecommunications] (TEL) CX
Coin Completing [Telecommunications] (TEL) CC
Coin Detection and Announcement [Telecommunications] (TEL) .... CDA
Coin First payphone (SAUS) .... CF
Coin Lake Gold Mines Ltd. [Toronto Stock Exchange symbol] .... COI
Coin Laundry Association (EA) .... CLA
Coin L-Band Ranging and Homing System [Military] .... COBRAH
Coin Lesion (MELL) CL
Coin Level Indicator [Telephone communications] CLI
Coin Machine Industries Association (NTPA) .... CMIA
Coin Operated Telephone System (SAUS) .... COTS
Coin Phone Operational and Information Network System
[Telecommunications] (TEL) .... COIN
Coin Phones, Inc. (SAUS) .... OPER
Coin Return (SAUS) .... CR
Coin Supervising Link (SAUS) .... CSL
Coin Trunk [Telecommunications] (TEL) .... CN
Coin World [A publication] .... Coin W
Coinage (SAUS) .... Coin
[The] Coinage of the Roman Republic [A publication] (OCD) .... CRR
Coinbox Line [Telecommunications] (TEL) .... CO
Coinbox Set [Telecommunications] (TEL) CX
Coincidence (SAUS) .... Coin
Coincidence Adjusting Scale (SAUS) .... CAS
Coincidence Circuit (SAUS) CC
Coincidence Counts .... COINCNT
Coincidence Detection Program (SAA) .... CDT
Coincidence Detector [Cytology] .... CD
Coincidence Element (SAUS) .... CE

Coincidence Gate .... CG
Coincidence Guidance .... C/G
Coincidence Memory (SAUS) .... CM
Coincidence Moessbauer Spectroscopy (OA) .... CMS
Coincidence Register (SAUS) .... CR
Coincidence Site Lattice (MCD) .... CSL
Coincidence Store (SAUS) .... CS
Coincidence-Ledge-Dislocation (PDAA) .... CLD
Coincident Current Core Storage (SAUS) .... CCCS
Coincident Light Information Photographic Strips .... CLIPS
Coincident-Current (IAA) CC
Coincident-Current Magnetic Core .... CCMC
Coincident-Current Memory .... CCM
Coinmach Laundry Corp. [*Associated Press*] (SAG) .... Coinmch
Coinmach Laundry Corp. [*NASDAQ symbol*] (SAG) .... WDRY
Coin-Operated (ADWA) .... coin-op
Coin-Operated (SAUS) .... COIN-OP
Coin-Operated Amusement Device .... COAD
Coin-Operated Car Wash Association (SAUO) .... COCWA
Coin-phone Operational and Information Network (SAUS) .... COIN
COINS Network Control Center (SAUO) .... CNCC
Coins on Stamps Unit [*American Topical Association*] (EA) .... COSSU
Coinsurance .... CO
Coinsurance .... COINS
COINTELPRO [*FBI Counterintelligence Program*] **Survivors** [*Defunct*] (EA) .... CS
Coinvestigator .... Co-I
Coismic Ray Produced (SAUS) .... CRP
Cokato Elementary School, Media Center, Cokato, MN [*Library symbol*] [*Library of Congress*] (LCLS) .... MnCoE
Cokato Museum, Cokato, MN [*Library symbol*] [*Library of Congress*] (LCLS) .... MnCoM
Cokato Public Library, Cokato, MN [*Library symbol*] [*Library of Congress*] (LCLS) .... MnCo
Coke (SAUS) .... Ck
Coke on Courts [*or Fourth Institute*] [*England*] [*A publication*] (DLA) .... Co Cts
Coke on Courts [*or Fourth Institute*] [*England*] [*A publication*] (DLA) .... Co on Courts
Coke on Littleton [*England*] [*A publication*] (DLA) .... Coke Lit
Coke on Littleton [*England*] [*A publication*] (DLA) .... Co Lit
Coke on Littleton [*England*] [*A publication*] (DLA) .... Co Litt
Coke on Littleton [*England*] [*A publication*] (DLA) .... Co Litt (Eng)
Coke on Regenerated Catalyst [*Chemical engineering*] .... CRC
Coke Oven .... CO
Coke Oven Gas .... COG
Coke Oven Managers' Association [*British*] (BI) .... COMA
Coke Oven Production Technology .... COPT
Coker College, Hartsville, SC [*Library symbol*] [*Library of Congress*] (LCLS) .... ScHaC
Coker Gas Oil .... CGO
Coke's Bankrupt Law [*A publication*] (DLA) .... Co BL
Coke's Book of Entries [*1614*] [*England*] [*A publication*] (DLA) .... Co Ent
Coke's Book of Entries [*1614*] [*England*] [*A publication*] (DLA) .... Coke Ent
Coke's Book of Entries [*1614*] [*England*] [*A publication*] (DLA) .... Ent
Coke's Compleat Copyholder [*5 eds.*] [*1630-73*] [*England*] [*A publication*] (DLA) .... Co Cop
Coke's English King's Bench Reports [*1572-1616*] [*A publication*] (DLA) .... Co
Coke's English King's Bench Reports [*1572-1616*] [*A publication*] (DLA) .... Coke
Coke's English King's Bench Reports [*1572-1616*] [*A publication*] (DLA) .... Coke (Eng)
Coke's English King's Bench Reports [*1572-1616*] [*A publication*] (DLA) .... Co Rep
Coke's English King's Bench Reports [*1572-1616*] [*A publication*] (DLA) .... Rep
Coke's English King's Bench Reports [*1572-1616*] [*A publication*] (DLA) .... Reports
Coke's Institutes [*England*] [*A publication*] (DLA) .... Co
Coke's Institutes [*England*] [*A publication*] (DLA) .... Co Inst
Coke's Institutes [*England*] [*A publication*] (DLA) .... Co Inst (Eng)
Coke's Institutes [*England*] [*A publication*] (DLA) .... Coke Inst
Coke's Institutes [*England*] [*A publication*] (DLA) .... Inst
Coke's Magna Charta [*or Second Institute*] [*A publication*] (DLA) .... Co MC
Coke's Pleadings [*Sometimes published separately*] [*A publication*] (DLA) .... Co Pl
Coke's Pleas of the Crown [*or Third Institute*] [*A publication*] (DLA) .... Co PC
Cokesbury Satellite Television Network [*United Methodist Publishing House*] [*Telecommunications service*] (TSSD) .... CSTN
Col [*With The*] [*Music*] C
Col Basso [*With the Bass*] [*Italian*] [*Music*] (WDAA) .... Cb
Col Basso [*With the Bass*] [*Music*] .... CB
Col Canto [*With the Melody*] [*Music*] .... COL C
Col Legno [*With the Back of the Bow*] [*Music*] CL
Cola [*or Colatus*] [*Strain*] [*See also COLAT*] [*Pharmacy*] .... COL
[*The*] **Cola Clan** [*Later, Coca-Cola Collectors Club International*] (EA) .... TCC
Colatitude [*Navigation*] .... CO-L
Colatus [*Strained*] [*See also COL*] [*Pharmacy*] .... COLAT
Colborne Public Library, Ontario [*Library symbol*] [*National Library of Canada*] (BIB) .... OCOLB
Colbphon (BARN) .... col
Colby College, Waterville, ME [*OCLC symbol*] (OCLC) .... CBY
Colby College, Waterville, ME [*Library symbol*] [*Library of Congress*] (LCLS) .... MeWC
Colby Community College, Colby, KS [*Library symbol*] [*Library of Congress*] (LCLS) .... KColC
Colby Junior College (SAUS) .... CJC
Colby Junior College for Women [*Later, CSC*] [*New Hampshire*] .... CJCW
Colby Junior College for Women [*Later, CSC*], **New London, NH** [*Inactive*] [*OCLC symbol*] (OCLC) .... CYC
Colby Junior College for Women [*Later, CSC*], **New London, NH** [*Library symbol*] [*Library of Congress*] (LCLS) .... NhNelC
Colby, KS [*Location identifier*] [*FAA*] (FAAL) .... CBK
Colby, KS [*Television station call letters*] .... KLBY
Colby, KS [*FM radio station call letters*] .... KQLS
Colby, KS [*FM radio station call letters*] .... KTCC
Colby, KS [*FM radio station call letters*] (BROA) .... KWGB-FM
Colby, KS [*AM radio station call letters*] .... KXXX
Colby on Mortgage Foreclosures [*A publication*] (DLA) .... Col Mort
Colby Resources Corp. [*Vancouver Stock Exchange symbol*] .... CY
Colby's Criminal Law and Practice [*New York*] [*A publication*] (DLA) .... Col Crim Law
Colby's Massachusetts Practice [*A publication*] (DLA) .... Col Mass Pr
Colby's Massachusetts Practice [*A publication*] (DLA) .... Co Mass Pr
Colby's Practice [*A publication*] (DLA) .... Colb Pr
Colby-Sawyer College [*Formerly, CJCW*] [*New London, NH*] .... CSC
Colcemid [*Demecolcine*] [*Antineoplastic drug*] .... CMD
Colchester [*Municipal borough in England*] .... COLCH
Colchester [*Vermont*] [*Seismograph station code, US Geological Survey*] (SEIS) .... COV
Colchester - East Hants Regional Library, Truro, Nova Scotia [*Library symbol*] [*National Library of Canada*] (NLC) .... NSTC
Colchester English Study Centre (SAUO) .... CESC
Colchester Historical Society, Truro, Nova Scotia [*Library symbol*] [*National Library of Canada*] (BIB) .... NSTCH
Colchester, VT [*FM radio station call letters*] .... WWPV
Colchester-East Hants Regional Library, Truro, NS, Canada [*Library symbol*] [*Library of Congress*] (LCLS) .... CaNSTC
Colchicine [*Biochemistry*] .... CCH
Colchicine Binding Site on Tubulin [*Biochemistry*] .... CBST
Colchicine Sensitivity [*Medicine*] (DMAA) .... CLCS
Colchicine-Binding Protein [*Biochemistry*] .... CBP
Colchicine-Blocked Meiosis [*Biology*] (DOG) .... C-meiosis
Colchicine-Blocked Metaphase [*Biology*] (DOG) .... C-metaphase
Colchicine-Blocked Mitosis [*Biology*] (DOG) .... C-mitosis
Colchis Resources Ltd. [*Vancouver Stock Exchange symbol*] .... CLK
Cold C
Cold Acclimated [*Physiology*] .... CA
Cold Adapted (SAUS) .... CA
Cold Agglutination [*Test*] [*Clinical chemistry*] .... CA
Cold Agglutinin (SAUS) .... CA
Cold Agglutinin Disease [*Medicine*] (DMAA) .... CAD
Cold Agglutinin Syndrome [*Medicine*] (DMAA) .... CAS
Cold Air .... CA
Cold Air Induction .... CAT
Cold Air Mass [*Meteorology*] (BARN) .... k
Cold Air Turbine Drive (MCD) .... CATD
Cold and Clammy (MELL) .... C & C
Cold and Hot (SAUS) .... C&H
Cold and Hot Isostatic Pressing [*Materials science and technology*] .... CHIP
Cold and Hot Water .... CHW
Cold Arctic Mesopause Project (SAUS) .... CAMP
Cold Asphalt Association (SAUO) .... CAA
Cold Bay [*Alaska*] [*Seismograph station code, US Geological Survey*] [*Closed*] (SEIS) .... CBA
Cold Bay [*Alaska*] [*ICAO location identifier*] (ICLI) .... PACD
Cold Bay, AK [*Location identifier*] [*FAA*] (FAAL) .... CDB
Cold Brine Pump .... CBPMP
Cold Canvassing [*Business term*] CC
Cold Cathode Discharge .... CCD
Cold Cathode Electron Beam LASER (MCD) .... CCEBL
Cold Cathode Fluorescent Technology .... CCFT
Cold Cathode Fluorescent Tube .... CCFT
Cold Cathode Gauge Experiment [*Apollo*] [*NASA*] .... CCGE
Cold Cathode Ion Gauge .... CCIG
Cold Cathode Ion Source .... CCIS
Cold Chemi-Excited Infra-red Simulation Experiment (SAUS) .... COCHISE
Cold Cloud Duration (SAUS) .... CCD
Cold, Cough, Allergy, Bronchodilator, and Antiasthmatic [*Medicine*] (DB) .... CCABA
Cold Cranking Ampere .... CCA
Cold Cranking Simulator Test [*for petroleum products*] .... CCS
Cold Crucible Melter (ABAC) .... CCM
Cold Cup Biopsy [*Medicine*] (MELL) .... CCB
Cold Cure Foam (SAUS) .... CC Foam
Cold Dark Matter [*Astronomy*] .... CDM
Cold Drawn Seamless (SAUS) .... CDS
Cold Drawn Steel (SAUS) .... CDS
Cold Filament Resistance .... CFR
Cold Filter Plugging Point .... CFPP
Cold Finished Seamless (SAUS) .... CFS
Cold Finished Steel Bar Institute (EA) .... CFSBI
Cold Flow Development Test System [*AEC*] .... CFDTS
Cold Flow Electric LASER (MCD) .... CFEL
Cold Flow Facility (SAUS) .... CFF
Cold Flow Laboratory [*Martin Marietta Corp.*] .... CFL
Cold Flow Test .... CFT
Cold Fluctuating Temperature .... CFT
Cold Fluid (DICI) .... CF
Cold Fog Dissipation System .... CFD
Cold Front [*NWS*] (FAAC) .... CDFNT
Cold Front [*Meteorology*] .... CF
Cold Front Passage [*NWS*] (FAAC) .... CFP
Cold Fusion Markup Language [*Computer science*] (PCM) .... CFML
Cold Heading Wire .... CHW

Cold High Pressure Separator [Chemical engineering] ...... CHPS
Cold, Hungry, and Dry [Slang] ...... CH and D
Cold Insoluble Globulin (SAUS) ...... CIG
Cold Intermediate Layer [Oceanography] CIL
Cold Iron (SAUS) CI
Cold Isostatic Pressing (SAUS) ...... CIP
Cold Isostatically Pressed [Materials processing] ...... CIP
Cold Joint (SAUS) ...... CJ
Cold Junction ...... CJ
Cold Junction Box (MHDI) ...... CJB
Cold Junction Compensator (SAUS) ...... CJC
Cold Knife Conization [Gynecology] (DAVI) ...... CKC
Cold Lake [Canada] [Airport symbol] (OAG) ...... YOD
Cold Lake Canadian Forces Base, AB [ICAO location identifier] (ICLI) ...... CYOD
Cold Lake Municipal Library, Alberta [Library symbol] [National Library of Canada] (NLC) ...... ACLM
Cold Lake Municipal Library, Cold Lake, AB, Canada [Library symbol] [Library of Congress] (LCLS) ...... CaACLM
Cold Leg [Nuclear energy] ...... COLG
Cold Leg Check Valve [Nuclear energy] (NRCH) CLCV
Cold Leg Isolation Valve [Nuclear energy] (NRCH) CLIV
Cold Leg Temperature [Nuclear energy] (NRCH) ...... TC
Cold Maritime Polar Air Mass [Meteorology] (BARN) ...... mPK
Cold Metal Products [NYSE symbol] (SAG) ...... CLQ
Cold Metals Products [Associated Press] (SAG) ...... ColdMtl
Cold Molded Thermoforming [Fiberglass production] ...... COMOFORM
Cold Molecular Weld ...... CMW
Cold Month Mean Temperture [Climatology] ...... CMMT
Cold Neutron Research Facility [Physics] ...... CNRF
Cold Ocean-Warm Land [Climatology] ...... COWL
Cold Pack [Medicine] ...... CP
Cold Pipe [Nuclear energy] (NRCH) ...... CP
Cold Plate (SAUS) ...... CP
Cold Plate Support Structure (MCD) ...... CPSS
Cold Presors [or Pressure] Test [Cardiology] (DAVI) ...... CPT
Cold Press [Metallurgy] (IAA) ...... CP
Cold Press Molding ...... PM
Cold Press or Recovery Index (SAUS) ...... CPRI
Cold Pressor Recovery Index (PDAA) ...... CPRI
Cold Pressor Response Test [Medicine] ...... CPR
Cold Pressor Response Test [Medicine] ...... CPRT
Cold Pressure Test (SAUS) ...... CP-Test
Cold Protective Response [Physiology] ...... CPR
Cold Receptors (SAUS) ...... CR
Cold Region Automatic Weather Stations (SAUO) ...... CRAWS
Cold Regions Bibliography Project (SAUO) ...... CRBP
Cold Regions Engineering Laboratory ...... CREL
Cold Regions Research and Engineering Laboratory [Hanover, NH] [Army] [Also, an information service or system] (IID) ...... CRREL
Cold Regions Research Co. (MCD) ...... CRRC
Cold Regions Science and Technology (SAUS) ...... Cold Reg Sci Technol
Cold Regions Science & Technology Bibliography (SAUO) ...... COLD
Cold Regions Science and Technology Information Analysis Center [DoD] (MSC) ...... CRSTIAC
Cold Regions Test Center [Seattle, WA] [Army] (RDA) ...... CRTC
Cold Rocket Instrument Carrying Kit ...... CRICKET
Cold Rocket Instrument Carrying Kit (SAUS) ...... CRI CKIT
Cold Rolled Half Hard (SAUS) ...... CRHH
Cold Rolled Sections Association [British] (DBA) ...... CRSA
Cold Rubber (SAUS) ...... CR
Cold Running Intelligibility [Test for hearing continuous speech] (BABM) ...... CRI
Cold Shutdown [Nuclear energy] (NRCH) ...... CSD
Cold Side ...... CSD
Cold Splice Miter-Joint ...... CSM
Cold Spring Community Library, Cold Spring, MN [Library symbol] [Library of Congress] (LCLS) ...... MnCls
Cold Spring Elementary/Rocori Junior School, Cold Spring, MN [Library symbol] [Library of Congress] (LCLS) ...... MnClsE
Cold Spring Harbor Biological Laboratory, Cold Spring Harbor, NY [Library symbol] [Library of Congress] (LCLS) ...... NCshB
Cold Spring Harbor Laboratory [Cold Spring Harbor, NY] ...... CSH
Cold Spring Harbor Laboratory (HGEN) ...... CSHL
Cold Spring Harbor Public Library, Cold Spring Harbor, NY [Library symbol] [Library of Congress] (LCLS) ...... NCsh
Cold Spring Harbor Public Library, Cold Spring Harbor, NY [Library symbol] [Library of Congress] (LCLS) ...... NCshL
Cold Spring Harbor Symposia on Quantitative Biology (journ.) (SAUS) ...... Cold Spring Harbor Symp Quant
Cold Spring Harbor Whaling Co. (SAUO) ...... CSH
Cold Spring, MN [FM radio station call letters] ...... KMXK
Cold Stabilized [Automotive engineering] ...... CS
Cold Start Entry [Computer science] ...... CSE
Cold Start Injector [Automotive engineering] ...... CSI
Cold Start Spark Advance [Automotive engineering] ...... CSSA
Cold Start Spark Hold [Automotive engineering] ...... CSSH
Cold Storage ...... CS
Cold Storage and Ice Association of Victoria [Australia] ...... CSIAV
Cold Storage Association of Queensland [Australia] ...... CSAQ
Cold Storage Association of Tasmania [Australia] ...... CSAT
Cold Storage Association of the Northern Territory [Australia] ...... CSANT
Cold Storage Association of Western Australia ...... CSAWA
Cold Temperature Carbon Monoxide Test Procedure [Exhaust emissions testing] [Automotive engineering] ...... CTCOTP
Cold to the Opposite and Warm to the Same Side [Audiometry] ...... COWS
Cold Tongue (SAUS) ...... CT

Cold Transient [Automotive engineering] ...... CT
Cold Type Composition [Selection of Printing Industries of America] ...... CTC
Cold Vapor Atomic Absorption Spectrometry [Also, CVAAS] ...... CVAA
Cold Vapor Atomic Absorption Spectrometry [Also, CVAA] ...... CVAAS
Cold Wall ...... CW
Cold War (CINC) ...... CW
Cold War Activities Group [Military] (CINC) ...... CWAG
Cold War Council ...... CWC
Cold War International History Project [Woodrow Wilson International Center for Scholars] [Internet resource] ...... CWIHP
Cold Water [Technical drawings] ...... CW
Cold water component of Watercolors (SAUS) ...... ICECOLORS
Cold Water Reactor Test Assembly ...... CWTA
Cold Water Rinse (SAUS) ...... CWR
Cold Water Soluble (SAUS) ...... CWS
Cold Water Supply (SAUS) ...... CWS
Cold Water Tank ...... CWT
Cold Water Temperature ...... CWT
Cold Water Treatment [Medicine] ...... CWT
Cold Weather Clothing and Individual Equipment [Military] ...... CWCE
Cold Weather Exercise [Military] (NVT) ...... COWEAEX
Cold Weather Injury [Military] ...... CWINJ
Cold Weather Landing Exercise [Military] (NVT) ...... COWLEX
Cold Weather Materiel Test Unit [Military] ...... CWMTU
Cold Weather Modulator [Automotive engineering] ...... CWM
Cold Weather Operations [Military] ...... CWOP
Cold Weather Training Center (SAUO) ...... CWTC
Cold Weld [Mechanics] (BARN) ...... CW
Cold Weld Evaluation Device (OA) ...... CWED
Cold Welding ...... CW
Cold Working Pressure (SAUS) ...... CWP
Cold-Cathode Fluorescent Lamp (PCM) ...... CCFL
Cold-Cathode Fluorescent Lamp ...... CFL
Cold-Drawn [Metal] ...... CD
Cold-Drawn Copper (MSA) ...... CDC
Cold-drawn Electric-resistance Welded (SAUS) ...... CEW
Cold-Drawn Tube (SAUS) ...... CDT
Cold-Extractable Copper ...... cxCu
Cold-Finished [Metal] (MSA) ...... CF
Cold-Finished Steel (MSA) ...... CFS
Cold-Finished Steel Bar ...... CFSB
Coldfoot, AK [Location identifier] [FAA] (FAAL) ...... CXF
Cold-Induced Vasodilation ...... CIVD
Cold-Insoluble Fibrinogen [Hematology] ...... CIF
Cold-Insoluble globulin [Cytochemistry] ...... CIg
Cold-Iron Soldered Joint (IAA) CI
Coldplate (KSC) ...... CP
Coldplate Clamp ...... CPC
Cold-Punched [Metal] ...... CP
Cold-Rolled [Metal] ...... CR
Cold-Rolled and Tempered [Metal] ...... CRT
Cold-Rolled Close-Annealed [Metal] ...... CRCA
Cold-Rolled Half Hard [Metal] ...... CRHH
Cold-Rolled Non-Oriented [Metallurgy] ...... CRNO
Cold-Rolled Steel ...... CRS
Cold-Rolled Steel (IAA) ...... CRST
Coldset Offset [Printing] (DGA) ...... CO
Cold-Shock Domain [Genetics] ...... CSD
Cold-Shock Protein [Biochemistry] ...... CSP
Coldspring Resources [Vancouver Stock Exchange symbol] ...... CGB
Coldstream Guards [British military] ...... CG
Coldstream Guards [British military] (DMA) ...... Cm Gds
Coldstream Guards (SAUO) ...... COLDM GDS
Coldstream's Scotch Court of Session Procedure [A publication] (DLA) ...... Colds Pr
Cold-Temperature-Actuated Vacuum [Automotive engineering] ...... CTAV
Coldwater Creek [NASDAQ symbol] (SG) ...... CWTR
Cold-Water Detergent ...... CWD
Coldwater Memorial Public Library, Ontario [Library symbol] [National Library of Canada] (BIB) ...... OCOLD
Coldwater, MI [FM radio station call letters] ...... WNWN
Coldwater, MI [AM radio station call letters] ...... WTVB
Coldwater, MS [FM radio station call letters] ...... WVIM
Coldwater Public Library, Coldwater, MI [Library symbol] [Library of Congress] (LCLS) ...... MiCw
Cold-Water Soluble ...... CWS
Coldwell Banker & Co. (EFIS) ...... CB
Coldwell, Banker & Company (SAUO) ...... CBC
Coldwell's Reports [41-47 Tennessee] [A publication] (DLA) ...... Col
Coldwell's Reports [41-47 Tennessee] [A publication] (DLA) ...... Cold (Tenn)
Coldwell's Reports [41-47 Tennessee] [A publication] (DLA) ...... Coldw
Coldwell's Reports [41-47 Tennessee] [A publication] (DLA) ...... Coldwell
Coldwell's Reports [41-47 Tennessee] [A publication] (DLA) ...... Coldw (Tenn)
Coldwell's Tennessee Supreme Court Reports [1860-70] [A publication] (DLA) ...... Cold
Cold-Worked [Nuclear energy] (NRCH) ...... CW
Cole Country Band Fan Club (EA) ...... CCBFC
Cole. Criminal Informations [1843] [A publication] (DLA) ...... Cole Cr Inf
Cole. Ejectment [1857] [A publication] (DLA) ...... Cole Ejec
Cole. Ejectment [1857] [A publication] (DLA) ...... Cole Eject
Cole National [NYSE symbol] (TTSB) ...... CNJ
Cole National Corp. [Associated Press] (SAG) ...... ColeNatl
Cole. Particulars and Conditions of Sale [1879] [A publication] (DLA) ...... Cole Cond
Cole Taylor Financial Group, Inc. [Associated Press] (SAG) ...... CTaylor
Cole Taylor Financial Group, Inc. [NASDAQ symbol] (SAG) ...... CTFG

Cole Taylor Financial Grp [*NASDAQ symbol*] (TTSB) ... CTFG
Coleambally Irrigation Area (SAUO) ... CIA
Colebrooke's Digest of Hindu Law [*A publication*] (DLA) ... Cole Dig
Coleco Industries (SAUO) ... CLO
Colectivo Latinoamericano de Trabajo Psico-Social [*Belgium*] ... COLAT
Coleford Nature Reserve (SAUS) ... CNR
Colegio de Mexico, Mexico, Mexico City, Mexico [*Library symbol*] [*Library of Congress*] (LCLS) ... MxMCM
Colegio Ibero-Latino-Americano de Dermatologia [*Ibero Latin American College of Dermatology - ILACD*] (EA) ... CILAD
Colegio Universitario de Cayey, Cayey, PR [*Library symbol*] [*Library of Congress*] (LCLS) ... PrCaC
Colegio Universitario del Sagrado Corazon [*College of the Sacred Heart*], **Santurce, PR** [*Library symbol*] [*Library of Congress*] (LCLS) ... PrSaC
Colel Hibath Jerusalem [*Society of the Devotees of Jerusalem*] (EA) ... CHJ
Coleman [*Alberta*] [*Seismograph station code, US Geological Survey*] [*Closed*] (SEIS) ... CLM
Coleman [*Germany*] [*ICAO location identifier*] (ICLI) ... EDOR
Coleman and Caines' Cases [*New York*] [*A publication*] (DLA) ... C & C
Coleman and Caines' Cases [*New York*] [*A publication*] (DLA) ... Col & Cai
Coleman and Caines' Cases [*New York*] [*A publication*] (DLA) ... Col & Cai Cas
Coleman and Caines' Cases [*New York*] [*A publication*] (DLA) ... Col & Caines Cas (NY)
Coleman and Caines' Cases [*New York*] [*A publication*] (DLA) ... Col & C Cas
Coleman and Caines' Cases [*New York*] [*A publication*] (DLA) ... Cole & Cai Cas
Coleman and Caines' Cases [*New York*] [*A publication*] (DLA) ... Colem & C Cas
Coleman Area Library, Coleman, MI [*Library symbol*] [*Library of Congress*] (LCLS) ... MiCole
Coleman Art Library (SAUS) ... MiCole
Coleman Co. [*NYSE symbol*] (TTSB) ... CLN
Coleman Co., Inc. [*NYSE symbol*] (SPSG) ... CLN
Coleman Co., Inc. [*Associated Press*] (SAG) ... Colemn
Coleman Collieries [*Vancouver Stock Exchange symbol*] ... CMN
Coleman, MI [*FM radio station call letters*] ... WPRJ
Coleman Research Corp. (SAUO) ... CRC
Coleman Research Corporation (ACAE) ... CRC
Coleman, TX [*Location identifier*] [*FAA*] (FAAL) ... COM
Coleman, TX [*AM radio station call letters*] ... KSTA
Coleman, TX [*FM radio station call letters*] ... KSTA-FM
Coleman's Cases [*New York*] [*A publication*] (DLA) ... CC
Coleman's Cases [*New York*] [*A publication*] (DLA) ... Cole Cas
Coleman's Cases [*New York*] [*A publication*] (DLA) ... Cole Cases
Coleman's Cases [*New York*] [*A publication*] (DLA) ... Cole Cas Pr
Coleman's Cases [*New York*] [*A publication*] (DLA) ... Colem
Coleman's Cases [*New York*] [*A publication*] (DLA) ... Coleman
Coleman's Cases [*New York*] [*A publication*] (DLA) ... Colem Cas
Coleman's Cases of Practice [*New York*] [*A publication*] (DLA) ... Col Cas
Coleman's Cases of Practice [*New York*] [*A publication*] (DLA) ... Col Cas (NY)
Coleman's Reports [*99, 101-106, 110-129 Alabama*] [*A publication*] (DLA) ... Col
Coleman's Reports [*99, 101-106, 110-129 Alabama*] [*A publication*] (DLA) ... Cole
Colentur [*Let Them Be Strained*] [*Pharmacology*] (DAVI) ... colen
Colentur [*Let Them Be Strained*] [*Pharmacy*] (ROG) ... COLENT
Coleoptera [*Entomology*] ... Col
Coleopterists' Society (EA) ... CS
Coleoptile Node-Tillers of Wheat [*Plant pathology*] ... CNT
Coleraine, MN [*FM radio station call letters*] ... KGPZ
Coleraine Public Library, Coleraine, MN [*Library symbol*] [*Library of Congress*] (LCLS) ... MnCol
Coleridge [*England*] ... COLER
Coler's Law of Municipal Bonds [*A publication*] (DLA) ... Col Mun B
Coles Associates Ltd., Charlottetown, PE, Canada [*Library symbol*] [*Library of Congress*] (LCLS) ... CaPCCOA
Coles Associates Ltd., Charlottetown, Prince Edward Island [*Library symbol*] [*National Library of Canada*] (NLC) ... PCCOA
Cole's Edition of Iowa Reports [*A publication*] (DLA) ... Cole
Coles Elementary School, Glen Cove, NY [*Library symbol*] [*Library of Congress*] (LCLS) ... NGlcCE
Coles Myer Ltd. [*NYSE symbol*] (CTT) ... CM
Coles Myer Ltd. [*Australia*] ... CML
Coles Myer Ltd. [*Associated Press*] (SAG) ... ColeMyr
Coles Myer Ltd ADR [*NYSE symbol*] (TTSB) ... CM
Coles Signal Laboratory [*Army*] (MCD) ... CSL
Colesburg [*South Africa*] [*ICAO location identifier*] (ICLI) ... FACB
Coletur [*Let It Be Strained*] [*Pharmacy*] ... COLET
Colfax Energy [*Vancouver Stock Exchange symbol*] ... CFX
Colfax Free Public Library, Colfax, IA [*Library symbol*] [*Library of Congress*] (LCLS) ... IaCol
Colfax, IL [*FM radio station call letters*] (RBYB) ... WAPU-FM
Colfax, IL [*FM radio station call letters*] (BROA) ... WSNI-FM
Colfax Public Library, Colfax, IN [*Library symbol*] [*Library of Congress*] (LCLS) ... InColf
Colfax, WA [*AM radio station call letters*] ... KCLX
Colfax, WA [*FM radio station call letters*] ... KRAO
Colgan Airways [*ICAO designator*] (AD) ... CJ
Colgate, SK [*Television station call letters*] ... CKCK-1
Colgate University (GAGS) ... Colgate U
Colgate University (SAUO) ... CU
Colgate University, Hamilton, NY [*Library symbol*] [*Library of Congress*] (LCLS) ... NHC
Colgate University, Hamilton, NY [*OCLC symbol*] (OCLC) ... VVC
Colgate-Palmolive [*NYSE symbol*] (TTSB) ... CL
Colgate-Palmolive Co. [*NYSE symbol*] (SPSG) ... CL
Colgate-Palmolive Co. [*Associated Press*] (SAG) ... ColgP
Colgate-Palmolive Co. [*Associated Press*] (SAG) ... ColgPal
Colgate-Palmolive Co. (SAUO) ... CP
Colgate-Palmolive Co., Technical Information Center, Piscataway, NJ [*Library symbol*] [*Library of Congress*] (LCLS) ... NjPwC
Colgate-Palmolive,$4.25 Pfd [*NYSE symbol*] (TTSB) ... CLPr
Colgate-Rochester Divinity School [*Rochester, NY*] ... CRDS
Colgate-Rochester Divinity School, Library, Rochester, NY [*OCLC symbol*] (OCLC) ... VQE
Colgate-Rochester Divinity School, Rochester, NY [*Library symbol*] [*Library of Congress*] (LCLS) ... NRCR
Coli Genetic Stock Center ... CGSC
Colibri Aviation Reg'd. [*Canada*] [*FAA designator*] (FAAC) ... CAE
Colicin (DB) ... Col
Colicin Factor (SAUS) ... CF
Colicine Factor [*Immunology*] ... CF
Colicinogenic (DB) ... Col
Colicinogenic Factor E 1 (SAUS) ... Col E 1
Colidyspepsie (SAUS) ... CD
Coliform Count [*Microbiology*] (OA) ... CC
Coliform Growth Response [*Bioassay*] ... CGR
Coligacao Democratico Social [*Portugal*] [*Political party*] (ECED) ... CDU
Colima [*Mexico*] [*ICAO location identifier*] (ICLI) ... MMIA
Colima Resources Ltd. [*Vancouver Stock Exchange symbol*] ... CJA
Colin Energy Corp. [*Toronto Stock Exchange symbol*] ... CN
Colistimethate-Nystatin-Vancomycin [*Antibiotic mixture*] ... CNV
Colistin [*Also, CO*] [*Generic form*] [*An antibiotic*] ... CL
Colistin [*Also, CL*] [*Generic form*] [*An antibiotic*] ... CO
Colistin [*or Colimycin*] **- Nalidixic Acid** [*Antibacterial combination*] [*Clinical chemistry*] ... CNA
Colla [*With The*] [*Music*] (ROG) ... C
Colla Destra [*With the Right Hand*] [*Music*] ... CD
Colla Parte [*With the Solo Part*] [*Music*] (ROG) ... COL P
Colla Parte [*With the Solo Part*] [*Music*] ... CP
Colla Sinistra [*With the Left Hand*] [*Music*] ... CS
Colla Sinistra [*With the Left*] [*Italian*] [*Music*] (WDAA) ... cs
Colla Voce [*With the Voice*] [*Music*] ... COL VO
Colla Voce [*With the Voice*] [*Music*] (ROG) ... COL VOCE
Colla Voce [*With the Voice*] [*Music*] ... CV
Colla Voce [*With the Voice*] [*Music*] ... C VOC
Collaborate [*or Collaborator*] (ROG) ... COLLAB
Collaborating Centre (SAUS) ... CC
Collaborating on Drug Education (SAUS) ... CODE
Collaboration (VRA) ... colab
Collaboration (WDAA) ... collab
Collaboration (SAUS) ... CRC
Collaboration Data Object (RALS) ... CDO
Collaboration in Science and Technology between Australia and Indonesia (SAUO) ... COSTAI
Collaboration Market Interest (SAUS) ... LMI
Collaboration of Australia and Nippon for a Gamma Ray Observatory in the Outback (SAUS) ... CANGAROO
Collaboration on Drug Development Improvement [*Drug evaluation*] ... CDDI
Collaboration on Repair Discoveries (SAUO) ... CORD
Collaboration Partners Acquired (SAUS) ... LPA
Collaboration Planning Forecasting Replenishment ... CPFR
Collaboration Programme (SAUS) ... LPG
Collaboration Programme Interest (SAUS) ... LPI
Collaboration Research Interest (SAUS) ... LRI
Collaboration Research Level (SAUS) ... LRL
Collaboration Type (SAUS) ... LTY
Collaboration Type Details (SAUS) ... LTD
Collaboration Validity Date (SAUS) ... LVD
Collaborative ... CLLBRTV
Collaborative Access Team ... CAT
Collaborative Advanced Interagency Research Network (SAUS) ... CAIRN
Collaborative Arrival Planning (CTAS) ... CAP
Collaborative Atmospheric Boundary Layer Experiment (PDAA) ... CABLE
Collaborative Authoring Production and Transmission of Interactive Video for Education (AIE) ... CAPTIVE
Collaborative Clinical Research, Inc. [*NASDAQ symbol*] (SAG) ... CCLR
Collaborative Clinical Research, Inc. [*Associated Press*] (SAG) ... CollbClin
Collaborative Computational Projects [*Daresbury Laboratory*] [*British*] (IRUK) ... CCP
Collaborative Computing Environment ... CCE
Collaborative Corneal Transplantation Studies ... CCTS
Collaborative Decisionmaking (COE) ... CDM
Collaborative Environment ... CE
Collaborative Forecasting and Replenishment [*Computer science*] ... CFAR
Collaborative Health Informatics Centre (SAUO) ... CHIC
Collaborative Hypertext of Radiology (SAUO) ... CHORUS
Collaborative International Pesticides Analytical Council Ltd. [*See also CIMAP*] [*Wageningen, Netherlands*] (EAIO) ... CIPAC
Collaborative Library System Development ... CLSD
Collaborative Longitudinal Evaluation of Keratoconus (ADWA) ... CLEK
Collaborative Model for Multiscale Atmospheric Simulation (SAUS) ... COMMAS
Collaborative Ocular Melanoma Study [*Medicine*] ... COMS
Collaborative Perinatal Project ... CPP
Collaborative Pesticide Analytical Committee (DICI) ... CPAC
Collaborative Pesticides Analytical Committee (SAUO) ... CPAG
Collaborative Radar Acquisition Field Test (SAUS) ... CRAFT
Collaborative Radiological Health Laboratory [*Colorado State University*] [*Department of Health and Human Services*] [*Research center*] (RCD) ... CRHL
Collaborative Research and Development Agreement ... CRADA
Collaborative Research Grant (SAUO) ... CRG
Collaborative Research Group [*Of scientific institute*] ... CRG
Collaborative Research, Inc. ... CR
Collaborative Research Into Small Arms Technology (SAUS) ... CRISAT

Collaborative Research Support Program [*Agency for International Development*] ... CRSP
Collaborative Resource Information Database (SAUO) ... CRID
Collaborative Science, Technology and Applied Research (SAUS) ... CSTAR
Collaborative Solar-Terrestrial Research (ADWA) ... COSTR
Collaborative Special Project and Programme (SAUS) ... CSPP
Collaborative Study on the Genetics of Alcoholism [*National Institute of Alcohol Abuse and Alcoholism*] ... COGA
Collaborative System (RALS) ... CS
Collaborative Testing Services, Inc. (SAUO) ... CTS
Collaborative UK Twin Location Auroral Sounding System [*A radar interferometer with antennae in Finland and Iceland*] ... CUTLASS
Collaborative Virtual Environment (SAUS) ... CVE
Collage (VRA) ... col
Collagen (MELL) ... C
Collagen [*Biochemistry*] ... COL
Collagen [*Biochemistry*] ... COLL
Collagen Antigen [*Immunology*] (DAVI) ... CA
Collagen Corp. [*NASDAQ symbol*] (NQ) ... CGEN
Collagen Corp. [*Associated Press*] (SAG) ... Colagen
Collagen Matrix Support [*Cell culture*] ... CMS
Collagen Replacement Therapy [*Medicine*] (MELL) ... CRT
Collagen Sponge Contraceptive ... CSC
Collagen Synthesis Inhibitory Factor [*Biochemistry*] ... CSIF
Collagen Vascular Disease [*Medicine*] ... CVD
Collagenase (SAUS) ... COL
Collagenase Soluble Glomerular Basement Membrane [*Medicine*] (STED) ... CSGBM
Collagenase-Digestible Protein ... CDP
CollaGenex Pharmaceuticals, Inc. [*NASDAQ symbol*] (SAG) ... CGPI
CollaGenex Pharmaceuticals, Inc. [*Associated Press*] (SAG) ... ColGenx
Collagen-Glycosaminoglycan [*Physiology*] ... CG
Collagen-Induced Arthritis [*Medicine*] ... CIA
Collagen-Induced Autoimmune Ear Disease [*Immunology and otorhinolaryngology*] (DAVI) ... CIAED
Collapse ... COLPS
collapsed (SAUS) ... colspd
Collapsible Airborne Military Equipment Lifter ... CAMEL
Collapsible Container (SAUS) ... Coltainer
Collapsible Maintenance Hangar (MCD) ... CMH
Collapsible Maintenance Shelter (MCD) ... CMS
Collapsible Mobile Hangar (MCD) ... CMH
Collapsible Mobile Shelter (MCD) ... CMS
Collapsible Rollup Antenna Mast ... CRAM
Collapsible Tube Manufacturers' Association [*British*] (BI) ... CTMA
Collar (MSA) ... CLR
Collar ... COL
Collar Button Abscess [*Medicine*] (MELL) ... CBA
Collar Pricing [*Investment term*] ... CP
Collar Tie ... CT
Coll'arco [*With the Bow*] [*Music*] ... CA
Collarette [*Horticulture*] ... Coll
Collate ... COL
Collate (WGA) ... COLL
Collated (ROG) ... COLD
Collated (ROG) ... COLLD
Collated and Perfect (ADA) ... C & P
Collateral ... C
Collateral ... CLLTRL
Collateral (WGA) ... COL
Collateral ... COLL
Collateral (WDMC) ... coll
Collateral (EBF) ... Coll
Collateral (ADWA) ... collat
Collateral [*Finance*] ... COLLAT
Collateral Action Officer [*Army*] (AABC) ... CAO
Collateral Branches [*Genealogy*] (ROG) ... COLLS
Collateral Circulation [*Medicine*] (MELL) ... CC
Collateral Damage Distance (AABC) ... CDD
Collateral Duty Alcoholism Counselor [*Navy*] (NVT) ... CODAC
Collateral Duty Inspector (MCD) ... CDI
Collateral Information Display Station (SAUS) ... CIDS
Collateral Loan Brokers Association of New York (EA) ... CLBANY
Collateral Mortgage Bond (EBF) ... CMB
Collateral Recurring Document Listing [*Defense Intelligence Agency*] (DNAB) ... CRDL
Collateral Trust [*Bond*] ... CLT
Collateral Trust (DLA) ... Coll Tr
Collateral Trust [*Bond*] ... CT
Collateral Trust Bond [*Investment term*] ... CTB
Collateralized Automobile Receivable Security ... CARS
Collateralized Bond Obligation [*Investment term*] (DFIT) ... CBO
Collateralized Depository Receipt [*Finance*] (EMRF) ... CDR
Collateralized Lease Equipment (EBF) ... CLEO
Collateralized Loan Obligation (TDOB) ... CLO
Collateralized Mortgage Obligation [*Federal Home Loan Mortgage Corp.*] ... CMO
Collating and Binding ... CAB
Collating and Binding (SAUS) ... C&B
Collatio [*Novels of Justinian*] [*A publication*] (DSA) ... Coll
Collation [*Online database field identifier*] ... CLLT
Collation [*Online database field identifier*] ... CO
Collation [*Library science*] (WDMC) ... COL
Collation Sequence (SAUS) ... CS
Collationes Brugenses (BJA) ... CBrug
Collationes Gandavenses (BJA) ... CGand
Collatis Pecuniis Poni Curaverunt [*They Collected the Money and Had Put in Position*] [*Latin*] ... CPPC
Collato [*Collated*] [*Latin*] ... COLL
Collator (SAUS) ... CLTR
Collator ... COLL
Collator Counting Device (SAUS) ... CCD
Collbran Public Library, Collbran, CO [*Library symbol*] [*Library of Congress*] (LCLS) ... CoCol
Colle Del Gigante [*Italy*] [*ICAO location identifier*] (ICLI) ... LIMI
Colleague (WGA) ... COL
Colleague ... COLL
Colleague (SAUS) ... Coll
Collect ... COL
Collect (WDMC) ... col
Collect (WDMC) ... coll
Collect [*or Collection*] (AFM) ... COLL
Collect Adapter ... CLAD
Collect and Transmit (DNAB) ... CAT
Collect Bill of Lading (AAGC) ... CBL
Collect Call [*Telecommunications*] (TEL) ... CC
Collect on Delivery (DFIT) ... COD
Collectable ... CLLCTABL
Collectanea Alexandrina [*A publication*] (OCD) ... Coll Alex
Collectanea Juridica [*England*] [*A publication*] (DLA) ... Co Jurid
Collectanea Juridica [*England*] [*A publication*] (DLA) ... Coll Jurid
Collecte Selective Quebec (AC) ... CSQ
Collected (ROG) ... COLLD
Collected Algorithm for Learning Machines [*Computer science*] ... CALM
Collected Algorithms for Learning Machines (SAUS) ... CALM
Collected Alongside Ship [*Shipping*] ... CAS
Collected and Delivered (SAUS) ... C&D
Collected [*or Delivered*] **by Barge** [*Shipping*] ... C by B
Collected [*or Delivered*] **by Truck** [*Shipping*] ... C by T
Collected Least Squares [*Statistics*] ... CLS
Collected Localization Satellites (SAUS) ... CLS
Collected or Delivered by Truck or Barge [*Shipping*] ... C or D by T or B
Collected Original Resources in Education [*Carfax Publishing*] (NITA) ... CORE
Collected Volatile Condensable Materials (AAEL) ... CVCM
Collectible ... CLLCTIBL
Collectibles and Platemakers Guild (NTPA) ... CPG
Collectif de Defense des Usagers de l'Acupuncture (AC) ... CODUA
Collectif de Recherche et d'Information Sociales [*Collective of Research and Social Information*] [*Canada*] ... CRIS
Collectif d'Information et de Travail Anti-Imperialiste [*Collective of Information and Anti-Imperialist Labour*] [*Canada*] ... CITA
Collectif d'Informations Sexuelles et Sexologiques [*Collective of Sexual Information and Sexology*] [*Canada*] ... CISS
Collecting (MSA) ... CLTG
Collecting (SAUS) ... Cltg
Collecting (SAUS) ... Coll
Collecting Battalion (SAUO) ... Coll Bn
Collecting Center (or Centre) (SAUS) ... CC
Collecting Company (SAUO) ... Coll Co
Collecting Point for Prisoners of War (SAUO) ... Coll Pt PW
Collecting Station (SAUO) ... Coll Sta
Collecting Tubule (MAE) ... CT
Collection (AL) ... Clln
Collection (WDAA) ... COL
Collection (VRA) ... coll
Collection (TBD) ... Coll
Collection ... COLLECT
Collection ... COLLN
Collection Activity Reports [*IRS*] ... CAR
Collection Advisory Center (MCD) ... CAC
Collection Agencies Association [*British*] (DBA) ... CAA
Collection Agency Practices ... CAP
Collection Agency Project [*Student legal action organization*] (EA) ... CAP
Collection Agent System for Hospitals [*Navy*] (GFGA) ... CASH
Collection Analysis Support Subsystem (MCD) ... CASS
Collection and Credit Agency (DLA) ... COLL & CR A
Collection and Delivery [*Shipping*] ... C & D
Collection and Delivery (EBF) ... c&d
Collection and Distribution [*Transportation*] ... C & D
Collection and Forwarding System (SAUO) ... CFS
Collection and Jamming ... C & J
Collection and Update (ACAE) ... COLUP
Collection Center [*FAA designator*] (FAAC) ... YPY
Collection, Classification, Cannibalization, and Field Expedients [*Military*] ... C3FE
Collection, Control & Dissemination Section (SAUO) ... CC&DS
Collection Control File [*Bureau of the Census*] (GFGA) ... CCF
Collection Control System (SAUS) ... CCS
Collection, Co-ordination & Intelligence Requirements Management (SAUS) ... CCIRM
Collection Coordination Facility (MCD) ... CCF
Collection Coordination Facility Support System (MCD) ... CCF-SS
Collection County Memorial Library, Walterboro, SC [*Library symbol*] [*Library of Congress*] (LCLS) ... ScW
Collection De Clercq. Catalogue Methodique et Raisonne: Antiquites Assyriens [*A publication*] (BJA) ... ColldeClercq
Collection des Tablettes Cuneiformes du Musee d'Art et d'Histoire de Geneve (BJA) ... MAH
Collection Development and Evaluation Section [*Reference and Adult Services Division*] [*American Library Association*] ... CODES
Collection Development Policy [*Libraries*] ... CDP

Collection District (SAUS) ... CD
Collection Entry [*Banking*] ... CL
Collection, Holding, Transfer [*Shipboard waste disposal*] (MCD) ... CHT
Collection, Inquiry, Reporting and Communication (SAUS) ... CIRC
Collection Insertion Map (GEOI) ... CIM
Collection Intelligence Requirements (NVT) ... CIR
Collection Letter [*Business term*] (MHDB) ... Coll L
Collection Letter (SAUS) ... Coll/L
Collection Management [*A publication*] ... CM
Collection Management and Development Section [*ALCTS*] (AL) ... CMDS
Collection, Management and Dissemination Section (SAUO) ... CDMS
Collection, Management and Dissemination Section (SAUO) ... CM&D
Collection, Management, and Dissemination Section ... CMDS
Collection Management Authority (MCD) ... CMA
Collection Management Branch (SAUO) ... CMB
Collection Management Center (SAUO) ... CMC
Collection Management Information System (SAUS) ... COLMIS
Collection Management Information System (MCD) ... COMIS
Collection Management Office (SAUO) ... CMO
Collection Management Support Tool (SAUS) ... CMST
Collection Management System [*IRS*] ... CMS
Collection Nationale de Cultures des Microorganismes [*France*] (DB) ... CNCM
Collection Nelson Rockefeller [*Identifying mark on art reproductions from the collection of Nelson Rockefeller*] ... CNR
Collection Node (SAUS) ... CN
Collection of Abstracts of Acts of Parliament [*A publication*] (DLA) ... Smee
Collection of Abstracts of Acts of Parliament (journ.) (SAUS) ... Smee
[*A*] **Collection of English Poems** [*A publication*] ... CEP
Collection of Indexable Data (SAUS) ... CID
Collection of Labor by Serial System (MCD) ... CLASS
Collection of LAMA Affiliates (AL) ... COLA
Collection of Scientific Works. Faculty of Medicine. Charles University (journ.) (SAUS) ... SVLKAO
Collection of the National Museum of Antiquities at Leiden (BJA) ... CNM
Collection on Wheels [*Shipping*] (DS) ... COW
Collection Operation Potential Yield System [*IRS*] ... COPYS
Collection Operations Management [*Environmental science*] (COE) ... COM
Collection Opportunity (MCD) ... COLOP
Collection Opportunity Requirements List (MCD) ... CORL
Collection Post (SAUS) ... CP
Collection, Repair, Evacuation (MCD) ... CRE
Collection Statute Expiration Date [*IRS*] ... COLSED
Collection Statute Expiration Date [*IRS*] ... CSED
Collection Voucher ... CV
Collection/Classification/Cannibalization [*Military*] ... CCC
Collection/Requirements ... C/R
Collective ... CLLCTV
Collective (MSA) ... CLTV
Collective (SAUS) ... Coll
Collective Address (SAUS) ... CAD
Collective Address Directory [*Navy*] (NVT) ... CAD
Collective address for NOTAM and SNOWTAM [*Switzerland*] [*ICAO location identifier*] (ICLI) ... LSZZ
Collective Address Group [*Navy*] (NVT) ... CAG
Collective Analysis Only (IAA) ... CAO
Collective Art Technology ... CAT
Collective Bancorp, Inc. [*NASDAQ symbol*] (NQ) ... COFD
Collective Bancorp, Inc. [*Associated Press*] (SAG) ... ColctBcp
Collective Bargaining (DCTA) ... CB
Collective Bargaining Institute [*New York, NY*] ... CBI
Collective Bargaining Negotiations and Contracts [*Bureau of National Affairs*] [*Information service or system*] ... CBNC
Collective Bargaining Organization ... CBO
Collective Bargaining Unit (MCD) ... CBU
Collective Black Artists (EA) ... CBA
Collective Call Sign [*Radio*] ... CCS
Collective Catalogue Belgium (SAUS) ... CCB
[*The*] **Collective Catalogue of Belgium** [*Database*] (IID) ... CCB
Collective Consciousness Society [*Vocal and instrumental group*] ... CCS
Collective Emitter Voltage (SAUS) ... VCE
Collective Employment Contract (SAUO) ... CEC
Collective Front-End Analysis (MCD) ... CFEA
Collective Investment Institution (MHDW) ... CII
Collective Linear Ion Accelerator (SAUS) ... CLIA
Collective Measures Commission [*United Nations*] (DLA) ... CMC
Collective Negotiations ... CN
Collective Notebook (SAUS) ... CNB
Collective Nuclear, Biological, and Chemical Protection [*Environmental science*] (COE) ... CNBCP
Collective of Self Help Groups [*Australia*] ... CSHG
Collective Pitch Lever ... CPL
Collective Protection [*from NBC contaminants*] [*Military*] (RDA) ... CP
Collective Protection Enclosure [*NBC contamination*] [*Military*] (RDA) ... CPE
Collective Protection Equipment ... CPE
Collective Protection Shelter [*Army*] ... CPS
Collective Protection Unit (IEEE) ... CPU
Collective Protective System [*Navy*] ... CPS
Collective Reserve Unit [*International finance*] ... CRU
Collective Routing Indicator (CCCA) ... CRI
Collective Security [*Army*] (MCD) ... COLSEC
Collective Stick Grip (MCD) ... CSG
Collective Subscription Agency (SAUO) ... CSA
Collective Television Reception (OA) ... CTR
Collective Trademark (MCD) ... CTM
Collective Training [*Army*] ... CT
Collective Training Facility [*Army*] (INF) ... CTF
Collective Training Plan [*Army*] ... CTP
Collective Training Range (MCD) ... CTR
Collective Volume (SAUS) ... Coll Vol
Collective Volume [*Medicine*] (DAVI) ... coll vol
Collective-Bargaining Agreement ... CBA
Collective-Electronic Oscillator [*Physics*] ... CEO
Collective-Focusing Ion Accelerator (MCD) ... CFIA
Collectively (ROG) ... COLLECT
Collect-Localization-Satellites (SAUS) ... CLS
Collector [*Electronics*] ... C
Collector (IDOE) ... c
Collector [*Freight*] ... CLCT
Collector (DLA) ... Coll
Collector ... COLL
Collector [*Business term*] ... COLLR
Collector Capacitance (IDOE) ... C_c
Collector Capacitance (SAUS) ... CC
Collector Car Appraisers Association (EA) ... CCAA
Collector Car Appraisers International (NTPA) ... CCAI
Collector Circle [*Defunct*] (EA) ... CC
Collector Coupled Structure (IAA) ... CCS
Collector Coupled Transistor Logic (SAUS) ... CCTL
Collector Diffusion Isolation [*Electronics*] ... CDI
Collector, Diffusion, Isolation, Bipolar [*Electronics*] (NITA) ... CDIB
Collector Field Effect Register [*Electronics*] (OA) ... CFER
Collector Field-Effect Resistor (SAUS) ... CFER
Collector Implanted Technology (SAUS) ... CI Technology
Collector Lens Assembly (ACAE) ... CLA
Collector Mesh (SAUS) ... COLM
Collector Module with Memory (SAUS) ... CM/M
Collector of Public Moneys ... CPM
Collector Platemakers Guild (EA) ... CPG
Collector Ring [*Electricity*] ... CLRG
Collector Voltage (IDOE) ... V_C
Collector-Base (DNAB) ... CB
Collector-Base Junction (SAUS) ... CBJ
Collector-Diffusion-Isolated Transistor-Transistor Logic (SAUS) ... CDI-TTL
Collector-Emitter (SAUS) ... CE
Collector-Region Width (IDOE) ... W_C
Collectors, Artists, and Dealers for Responsible Equity ... CADRE
Collector's Chronicle [*A publication*] ... CC
Collectors Club (EA) ... CC
Collectors Club, New York, NY [*Library symbol*] [*Library of Congress*] (LCLS) ... NNCo
Collector's Edition ... Coll Ed
Collectors Music Shop [*Record label*] ... CMS
Collectors of American Art (EA) ... CAA
Collectors of Numismatic Errors ... CONE
Collectors of Religion on Stamps (EA) ... COROS
Collectors of Religion on Stamps Society (SAUO) ... CRSS
Collectors of Unusual Data - International (EA) ... COUD-I
Collectors Record Club (EA) ... CRC
Collectors Record Society [*Record label*] ... CRS
Collectors Service Bureau (EA) ... CSB
Collectors Vehicle Specialists Association [*British*] (DBA) ... COVESA
Collector-Substrate (SAUS) ... C-S
Collector-Voltage Supply (IDOE) ... V_{CC}
Collects No Revenue [*Humorous interpretation for Canadian National Railways*] ... CNR
Colleen Casey Fan Club [*Defunct*] (EA) ... CCFC
College ... C
College (VRA) ... clg
College (MCD) ... CLG
College ... COL
College (WDMC) ... col
college (SAUO) ... col
college (SAUO) ... colg
College ... COLG
College [*Army*] ... Colg
College [*or Collegiate*] ... COLL
College (WDMC) ... coll
College (AL) ... Coll
college (SAUO) ... coll
College - Fairbanks [*Alaska*] [*Seismograph station code, US Geological Survey*] [*Closed*] (SEIS) ... CMO
College - University Resource Institute (EA) ... CURI
College Ability Test ... CAT
College Adjustment Scales [*Test*] (TMMY) ... CAS
College Admission Test (DIPS) ... CAT
College Admissions Assistance Center [*Defunct*] ... CAAC
College Admissions Center (EA) ... CAC
College Admissions System (SAUO) ... CAS
College Advanced Technology [*British technical colleges*] ... CAT
College, AK [*FM radio station call letters*] ... KSUA
College & Research Libraries (AL) ... C&RL
College & Research Libraries [*A publication*] (BRI) ... CRL
College & Research Libraries News (AL) ... C&RL News
College & Seminary Library, Inc., Naperville, IL [*Library symbol*] [*Library of Congress*] [*Obsolete*] (LCLS) ... INapC
College and University [*A publication*] (BRI) ... C & U
College and University [*A publication*] (DLA) ... Coll & U
College and University Affiliations Program ... CUAP
College and University Booksellers' Group [*British*] ... CUBG

College and University Business Administration, Administrative Service [*National Association of College and University Business Officers*] [*A publication*] .... CUBA
College and University Business (journ.) (SAUS) .... CAUB
College and University Business (journ.) (SAUS) .... CUBS
College and University Computer Users Conference (EA) .... CUCUC
College and University Environment Scales [*Psychology*] .... CUES
College and University Library Division [*Texas Library Association*] .... CULD
College and University Machine Records Conference [*Later, CUCUC*] (EA) .... CUMREC
College and University Personnel Association (EA) .... CUPA
College and University Systems Exchange [*Acronym is now used as name of association*] .... CAUSE
College Andre Grasset, Montreal, PQ, Canada [*Library symbol*] [*Library of Congress*] (LCLS) .... CaQMCAG
College Andre Grasset, Montreal, Quebec [*Library symbol*] [*National Library of Canada*] (NLC) .... QMCAG
College Applicant Information System (SAUS) .... CAIS
College Applicant Status Report [*Honeywell, Inc.*] [*Computer science*] .... CASTOR
College Art Association (EA) .... CAA
College Art Association of America [*Later, CAA*] (EA) .... CAAA
College Assistance Migrant Program .... CAMP
College Association for Public Events and Services (SAUO) .... CAPES
College Athletic Business Management Association (EA) .... CABMA
College Athletic Business Managers Association (SAUO) .... CABMA
College Band Directors National Association (EA) .... CBDNA
College Basic Academic Subjects Examination [*Steven F. Osterlind and Center for Educational Assessment Staff*] (TES) .... CBASE
College Bibliocentre, Scarborough, Ontario [*Library symbol*] [*National Library of Canada*] (BIB) .... OSCB
[*The*] **College Board** (EA) .... TCB
College Board Admission Test (WDAA) .... CBAT
[*The*] **College Board, New York, NY** [*Library symbol*] [*Library of Congress*] (LCLS) .... NNCB
College Bois-De-Boulogne, Montreal, PQ, Canada [*Library symbol*] [*Library of Congress*] (LCLS) .... CaQMBB
College Bois-De-Boulogne, Montreal, Quebec [*Library symbol*] [*National Library of Canada*] (NLC) .... QMBB
[*The*] **College Book of Verse** [*A publication*] .... CBOV
College Bourgchemin (CEGEP) [*College d'Enseignement General et Professionnel*], **Drummondville, PQ, Canada** [*Library symbol*] [*Library of Congress*] (LCLS) .... CaQDCE
College Bourgchemin (CEGEP), Drummondville, Quebec [*Library symbol*] [*National Library of Canada*] (NLC) .... QDCE
College Bourget, Rigaud, PQ, Canada [*Library symbol*] [*Library of Congress*] (LCLS) .... CaQRCB
College Bourget, Rigaud, Quebec [*Library symbol*] [*National Library of Canada*] (NLC) .... QRCB
College Canadien des Enseignants [*Canadian College of Teachers - CCT*] .... CCE
College Cataloguing (ADA) .... COLCAT
College Caterers Association [*British*] (DBA) .... CCA
College Center of the Finger Lakes, Corning, NY [*Library symbol*] [*Library of Congress*] (LCLS) .... NCorniFL
College Certificate in Physical Education [*British*] .... CCPE
College Characteristics Analysis .... CCA
College Characteristics Index [*A questionnaire*] CCI
College Chemistry Consultants Service C3S
College Chips, Luther College, Decorah, IA [*Library symbol*] [*Library of Congress*] (LCLS) .... IaDCC
College Communautaire du New Brunswick, Bathurst, NB, Canada [*Library symbol*] [*Library of Congress*] (LCLS) .... CaNBBCC
College Communautaire du New Brunswick, Bathurst, New Brunswick [*Library symbol*] [*National Library of Canada*] (NLC) .... NBBCC
College Composition and Communication [*A publication*] (BRI) .... Col Comp
College Conference of Illinois and Wisconsin (PSS) .... CCIW
College Cooperative Engineering Training Program (SAUO) .... CCETP
College Corner News, Liberty, IN [*Library symbol*] [*Library of Congress*] (LCLS) .... InLibCN
College Curriculum Support Project [*Bureau of the Census*] (GFGA) .... CCSP
College d'Alma, Lac St.-Jean, PQ, Canada [*Library symbol*] [*Library of Congress*] (LCLS) .... CaQALC
College d'Alma, Lac St.-Jean, Quebec [*Library symbol*] [*National Library of Canada*] (NLC) .... QALC
College de France, Paris, France [*Library symbol*] [*Library of Congress*] (LCLS) .... FrPCF
College de Joliette, Joliette, PQ, Canada [*Library symbol*] [*Library of Congress*] (LCLS) .... CaQJC
College de Joliette, Quebec [*Library symbol*] [*National Library of Canada*] (NLC) .... QJC
College de Jonquiere, Jonquiere, PQ, Canada [*Library symbol*] [*Library of Congress*] (LCLS) .... CaQJoC
College de Jonquiere, Quebec [*Library symbol*] [*National Library of Canada*] (NLC) .... QJOC
College de la Gaspesie, Gaspe, PQ, Canada [*Library symbol*] [*Library of Congress*] (LCLS) .... CaQGC
College de la Gaspesie, Gaspe, Quebec [*Library symbol*] [*National Library of Canada*] (NLC) .... QGC
College de la Prevention des Risques Technologiques [*College for the Preven tion of Technological Risks*] [*France*] .... CPRT
College de la Region de l'Amiante (CEGEP), Thetford-Mines, Quebec [*Library symbol*] [*National Library of Canada*] (NLC) .... QTMC
College de l'Abitibi-Temiscamingue, Rouyn, Quebec [*Library symbol*] [*National Library of Canada*] (NLC) .... QRCN
College de l'Assomption, L'Assomption, PQ, Canada [*Library symbol*] [*Library of Congress*] (LCLS) .... CaQLASC
College de l'Assomption, Quebec [*Library symbol*] [*National Library of Canada*] (NLC) .... QLASC
College de Levis, Levis, PQ, Canada [*Library symbol*] [*Library of Congress*] (LCLS) .... CaQLeC
College de Levis, Quebec [*Library symbol*] [*National Library of Canada*] (NLC) .... QLC
College de Maisonneuve, Montreal, PQ, Canada [*Library symbol*] [*Library of Congress*] (LCLS) .... CaQMCDM
College de Maisonneuve, Montreal, Quebec [*Library symbol*] [*National Library of Canada*] (NLC) .... QMCDM
College de Matane, Quebec [*Library symbol*] [*National Library of Canada*] (NLC) .... QMATC
College de Montreal, Montreal, PQ, Canada [*Library symbol*] [*Library of Congress*] (LCLS) .... CaQMC
College de Montreal, Quebec [*Library symbol*] [*National Library of Canada*] (NLC) .... QMC
College de Rimouski, Rimouski, PQ, Canada [*Library symbol*] [*Library of Congress*] (LCLS) .... CaQRiC
College de Rouyn, Rouyn, PQ, Canada [*Library symbol*] [*Library of Congress*] [*Obsolete*] (LCLS) .... CaQRC
College de Sainte-Anne, La Pocatiere, PQ, Canada [*Library symbol*] [*Library of Congress*] (LCLS) .... CaQPC
College de Shawinigan, Quebec [*Library symbol*] [*National Library of Canada*] (NLC) .... QSC
College de Sherbrooke (CEGEP) [*College d'Enseignement General et Professionnel*], **Quebec** [*Library symbol*] [*National Library of Canada*] (NLC) .... QSHERE
College de Sherbrooke (CEGEP) [*College d'Enseignement General et Professionnel*], **Sherbrooke, PQ, Canada** [*Library symbol*] [*Library of Congress*] (LCLS) .... CaQSherE
College de St. Boniface, St. Boniface, MB, Canada [*Library symbol*] [*Library of Congress*] (LCLS) .... CaMSC
College de St.-Boniface, Manitoba [*Library symbol*] [*National Library of Canada*] (NLC) .... MSC
College de Ste.-Anne, La Pocatiere, Quebec [*Library symbol*] [*National Library of Canada*] (NLC) .... QPC
College de Victoriaville, Ecole du Meuble et du Bois Ouvre, Victoriaville, PQ, Canada [*Library symbol*] [*Library of Congress*] (LCLS) .... CaQVCEMBO
College de Victoriaville, Quebec [*Library symbol*] [*National Library of Canada*] (NLC) .... QVC
College de Victoriaville, Victoriaville, PQ, Canada [*Library symbol*] [*Library of Congress*] (LCLS) .... CaQVC
College Democrats of America (EA) .... CDA
College d'Enseignement General et Professionnel [*College of General and Professional Instruction*] [*Canada*] .... CEGEP
College d'Enseignement General et Professionnel de l'Outaouais, Hull, PQ, Canada [*Library symbol*] [*Library of Congress*] (LCLS) .... CaQHC
College d'Enseignement General et Professionnel de Regional Cote Nord, Hauterive, PQ, Canada [*Library symbol*] [*Library of Congress*] (LCLS) .... CaQHaC
College d'Enseignement, Ste.-Foy, PQ, Canada [*Library symbol*] [*Library of Congress*] (LCLS) .... CaQSFC
College d'Enseignement, Ste.-Foy, Quebec [*Library symbol*] [*National Library of Canada*] (NLC) .... QSFC
College des Medecins de Famille du Canada (EAIO) .... CMFC
College Descriptive Index (EDAC) .... CDI
College Diploma (SAUS) .... CD
College Diploma in Agriculture [*British*] (DI) .... CDA
College Diploma of Horticulture (SAUS) .... CDH
College Discovery [*Educational project for disadvantaged youngsters*] (EA) .... CD
College Discovery and Development Program [*New York City*] (EDAC) .... CDDP
College Dominicain de Philosophie et de Theologie, Ottawa, ON, Canada [*Library symbol*] [*Library of Congress*] (LCLS) .... CaOOCDP
College Dominicain de Philosophie et de Theologie, Ottawa, Ontario [*Library symbol*] [*National Library of Canada*] (NLC) .... OOCDP
College du Nord Ouest, Rouyn, PQ, Canada [*Library symbol*] [*Library of Congress*] (LCLS) .... CaQRCN
College du Sacre-Coeur, Sherbrooke, PQ, Canada [*Library symbol*] [*Library of Congress*] (LCLS) .... CaQSherSC
College du Sacre-Coeur, Sherbrooke, Quebec [*Library symbol*] [*National Library of Canada*] (NLC) .... QSHERSC
College Edouard-Montpetit, Longueuil, PQ, Canada [*Library symbol*] [*Library of Congress*] (LCLS) .... CaQLoCE
College Edouard-Montpetit, Longueuil, Quebec [*Library symbol*] [*National Library of Canada*] (NLC) .... QLOCE
College Employers Links Project (AIE) .... CELP
College English Association (EA) .... CEA
College English (journ.) (SAUS) .... CE
College Entrance Examination Board [*Known as The College Board; acronym no longer used*] (EA) .... CEEB
College Entry Examination Board (ADWA) .... CEEB
College Environmental Stress Index (DHP) .... CESI
College Extension Course Program (SAUO) .... CECP
College Eye Data Processing System [*Air Force*] (MCD) .... CEDPS
College Fiord [*Alaska*] [*Seismograph station code, US Geological Survey*] (SEIS) .... CFI
College Food Service Association (SAUO) .... CFSA
College Football Association (EA) .... CFA
College for Human Services [*Formerly, WTC*] .... CHS
College Fraternity Editors Association (EA) .... CFEA
College Fraternity Scholarship Officers Association .... CFSOA
College Fraternity Secretaries Association [*Later, FEA*] (EA) .... CFSA
College Heights Secondary School, Guelph, ON, Canada [*Library symbol*] [*Library of Congress*] (LCLS) .... CaOGCH

College Heights Secondary School, Guelph, Ontario [*Library symbol*] [*National Library of Canada*] (NLC) ...... OGCH
College Information System (SAUS) ...... CIS
College Institute Educators' Association of BC (AC) ...... CIEA
College International de Podologie [*International College of Podology*] ...... CIP
College International de Recherches Implantaires et Lariboisiere [*Rouen, France*] (EAIO) ...... CIRIL
College International de Recherches pour la Production [*Later, CIESTPM*] (EAIO) ...... CIRP
College International pour l'Etude Scientifique des Techniques de Production Mecanique [*International Institute for Production Engineering Research*] (EAIO) ...... CIESTPM
College Inventory of Academic Adjustment [*Psychology*] ...... CIAA
College Jean-De-Brebeuf, Montreal, PQ, Canada [*Library symbol*] [*Library of Congress*] (LCLS) ...... CaQMDB
College Jean-De-Brebeuf, Montreal, Quebec [*Library symbol*] [*National Library of Canada*] (NLC) ...... QMDB
College Jesus-Marie de Sillery, Quebec [*Library symbol*] [*National Library of Canada*] (NLC) ...... QSILC
College Jesus-Marie de Sillery, Sillery, PQ, Canada [*Library symbol*] [*Library of Congress*] (LCLS) ...... CaQSilC
College Lafleche, Trois-Rivieres, PQ, Canada [*Library symbol*] [*Library of Congress*] (LCLS) ...... CaQTCL
College Lafleche, Trois-Rivieres, Quebec [*Library symbol*] [*National Library of Canada*] (NLC) ...... QTCL
College Language Association (EA) ...... CLA
College Law Bulletin [*A publication*] (DLA) ...... Coll L Bull
College Law Digest [*A publication*] (DLA) ...... Coll L Dig
College Letter [*British*] CL
College Level Academic Skills Project [*Florida*] (EDAC) ...... CLASP
College Level Academic Skills Test ...... CLAST
College Libraries Section [*Association of College and Research Libraries*] ...... CLS
College Library Access and Storage System [*Xerox*] (TELE) ...... CLASS
College Library Center (SAUS) ...... Ohio
College Library Information Packet (SAUS) ...... CLIP
College Lionel Groulx, Ste-Therese, Quebec [*Library symbol*] [*National Library of Canada*] (NLC) ...... QMCLG
College Literature [*A publication*] (BRI) ...... Col Lit
College Marguerite d'Youville, Ste.-Foy, PQ, Canada [*Library symbol*] [*Library of Congress*] (LCLS) ...... CaQSFCM
College Marguerite d'Youville, Ste.-Foy, Quebec [*Library symbol*] [*National Library of Canada*] (NLC) ...... QSFCM
College Mathematics Journal [*A publication*] ...... CMJ
College Mathieu, Gravelbourg, Saskatchewan [*Library symbol*] [*National Library of Canada*] (NLC) ...... SGM
College Mathieu, Gravelbourg, SK, Canada [*Library symbol*] [*Library of Congress*] (LCLS) ...... CaSGM
College Media Advisers (EA) ...... CMA
College Media Journal [*A publication*] [*Alternative music*] (WDMC) ...... CMJ
College Merici, Quebec, PQ, Canada [*Library symbol*] [*Library of Congress*] (LCLS) ...... CaQQCM
College Merici, Quebec, Quebec [*Library symbol*] [*National Library of Canada*] (NLC) ...... QQCM
College Militaire Royal [*Canada*] ...... CMR
College Militaire Royal de Saint-Jean [*UTLAS symbol*] ...... CMR
College Militaire Royal de Saint-Jean, Quebec [*Library symbol*] [*National Library of Canada*] (NLC) ...... QSTJ
College Militaire Royal de Saint-Jean, Saint-Jean, PQ, Canada [*Library symbol*] [*Library of Congress*] (LCLS) ...... CaQStJ
College Misericordia, Dallas, PA [*Library symbol*] [*Library of Congress*] (LCLS) ...... PDalCM
College Music Society (EA) ...... CMS
College Occupational Programs Educational System (SAUS) ...... COPES
College of Advanced Education [*Australia*] (WDAA) ...... CAE
College of Advanced Science (SAUS) ...... TCAS
College of Advanced Technology (SAUO) ...... CAT
College of Aeronautics (SAUO) ...... COA
College of Aeronautics [*British*] ...... COA
College of Aeronautics ...... C of A
College of Aerospace Doctrine, Research, and Education [*Air Force*] ...... CADRE
College of African Wildlife Management (SAUS) ...... CAWM
College of Agriculture and Forestry (AIE) ...... CAF
College of Agriculture and Horticulture [*British*] (DI) ...... CAH
College of Air Traffic Control (SAUO) ...... CATC
College of Air Warfare (SAUS) ...... CAW
College of American Pathologists (EA) ...... CAP
College of American Pathology ...... CAP
College of Applied Arts and Technology ...... CAAT
College of Architecture and Urban Planning ...... CAUP
College of Arms (SAUO) ...... COA
College of Art and Technology (AIE) ...... CAT
College of Arts, Science and Technology (SAUO) ...... CAST
College of Boca Raton, Boca Raton, FL [*Library symbol*] [*Library of Congress*] (LCLS) ...... FBoC
College Of Business (SAUS) ...... COB
College of Cape Breton, Archives and General Library, Sydney, NS, Canada [*Library symbol*] [*Library of Congress*] (LCLS) ...... CaNSSXA
College of Cape Breton, Sydney, NS, Canada [*Library symbol*] [*Library of Congress*] (LCLS) ...... CaNSSX
College of Chaplains (NTPA) ...... COC
College of Chaplains [*of APHA*] (EA) ...... COC-APHA
College of Charleston, Charleston (SAUS) ...... SBM
College of Charleston, Charleston (SAUS) ...... ScCC
College of Charleston, Charleston, SC [*OCLC symbol*] (OCLC) ...... SBM

College of Charleston, Charleston, SC [*Library symbol*] [*Library of Congress*] (LCLS) ...... ScCC
College of Commerce (AIE) CC
College of Commerce and Technology (AIE) ...... CCT
College of Creative Studies [*University of California, Santa Barbara*] ...... CCS
College of Dieticians of Ontario [*L'Ordre des Dietetistes de l'Ontario*] (AC) ...... CDO
College of Diplomates of the American Board of Orthodontics (EA) ...... CDABO
College of Distance Education, Papua New Guinea (SAUO) ...... CODE
College of Du Page, Glen Ellyn, IL [*OCLC symbol*] (OCLC) ...... IBI
College of Du Page, Glen Ellyn, IL [*Library symbol*] [*Library of Congress*] (LCLS) ...... IGleD
College of Earth and Mineral Sciences (SAUO) ...... CEMS
College of Earth and Minerals (SAUO) ...... CEM
College of Eastern Utah, Price, UT [*Library symbol*] [*Library of Congress*] (LCLS) ...... UPrE
College of Economics and Management (SAUO) ...... CEM
College of Emmanuel and St. Chad, Saskatoon, Saskatchewan [*Library symbol*] [*National Library of Canada*] (NLC) ...... SSESC
College of Emmanuel and St. Chad, Saskatoon, SK, Canada [*Library symbol*] [*Library of Congress*] (LCLS) ...... CaSSESC
College of Emporia, Emporia, KS [*Library symbol*] [*Library of Congress*] (LCLS) ...... KEmC
College of Engineering ...... CoE
College of Engineering and Agro-Industrial Technology (SAUO) ...... CEAT
College of Engineering and Applied Sciences (SAUO) ...... CEAS
College of Engineers of Puerto Rico ...... CEPR
College of English Studies (SAUO) ...... CES
College of Environmental Science and Forestry [*SUNY*] ...... CESF
College of Estate Management [*British*] (BI) ...... CEM
College of Extended Studies (SAUS) ...... CES
College of Family Physicians of Canada (EAIO) ...... CFPC
College of Fisheries, St. John's, NF, Canada [*Library symbol*] [*Library of Congress*] (LCLS) ...... CaNfSCF
College of Further & Higher Education (WDAA) ...... CF&HE
College of Further and Higher Education (AIE) ...... CFHE
College of Further Education (WDAA) ...... CFE
College of Future Education [*British*] ...... F
College of General Practitioners [*British*] (BI) ...... CGP
College of General Practitioners (SAUO) ...... CGP
College of Geographic Sciences (SAUS) ...... COGS
College of Great Falls [*Montana*] ...... CGF
College of Great Falls, Great Falls, MT [*Library symbol*] [*Library of Congress*] (LCLS) ...... MtGrCF
College of Health Sciences [*Iran*] ...... CHS
College of Healthcare Information Management Executives (SAUO) ...... CHIME
College of Human Ecology (SAUO) ...... CHE
College of Idaho, Caldwell, ID [*Library symbol*] [*Library of Congress*] (LCLS) ...... IdCaC
College of Insurance (GAGS) ...... C Insurance
College of Insurance, New York, NY [*Library symbol*] [*Library of Congress*] (LCLS) ...... NNCI
College of Lake County, Grayslake, IL [*Library symbol*] [*Library of Congress*] (LCLS) ...... IGralC
College of Law, University of Utah (DLA) ...... CLUU
College of Letters and Science (SAUS) ...... L&S
College of Librarianship Wales [*British*] (NITA) ...... CLW
College of Library and Information Services (SAUS) ...... CLIS
College of Marin, Kentfield, CA [*Library symbol*] [*Library of Congress*] (LCLS) ...... CKenM
College of Marin, Kentfield, CA [*OCLC symbol*] (OCLC) ...... CMK
College of Marine Studies (SAUO) ...... CMS
College of Massage Therapists of Ontario (AC) ...... CMTO
College of Medical Evangelists [*Los Angeles, CA*] ...... CME
College of Medical Laboratory Technologists of Ontario (AC) ...... CMLTO
College of Medicine and Dentistry of New Jersey [*Newark*] ...... CMDNJ
College of Medicine and Dentistry of New Jersey, Newark, NJ [*OCLC symbol*] (OCLC) ...... NJN
College of Mineral and Energy Resources [*West Virginia University*] (PDAA) ...... COMER
College of Mines and Earth (SAUO) ...... CME
College of Mount Saint Vincent, New York, NY [*Library symbol*] [*Library of Congress*] (LCLS) ...... NNMtSV
College of Mount Saint Vincent, New York, NY [*OCLC symbol*] (OCLC) ...... VZV
College of Mount St. Joseph-On-The-Ohio, Mount St. Joseph, OH [*OCLC symbol*] (OCLC) ...... CMJ
College of Mount St. Joseph-On-The-Ohio, Mount St. Joseph, OH [*Library symbol*] [*Library of Congress*] (LCLS) ...... OMtsjC
College of New Caledonia Library [*UTLAS symbol*] ...... NCA
College of New Caledonia, Prince George, BC, Canada [*Library symbol*] [*Library of Congress*] (LCLS) ...... CaBPGC
College of New Caledonia, Prince George, British Columbia [*Library symbol*] [*National Library of Canada*] (NLC) ...... BPGC
College of New Rochelle [*New York*] ...... CNR
College of New Rochelle (GAGS) ...... C N Rochelle
College of New Rochelle, New Rochelle, NY [*Library symbol*] [*Library of Congress*] (LCLS) ...... NNerC
College of New Rochelle, New Rochelle, NY [*OCLC symbol*] (OCLC) ...... VZN
College of Notre Dame (GAGS) ...... C Notre Dame
College of Notre Dame, Belmont, CA [*Library symbol*] [*Library of Congress*] (LCLS) ...... CBelmN
College of Nurses of Ontario (SAUO) ...... CNO
College of Optometrists in Vision Development (EA) ...... COVD
College of Optometry of Ontario ...... COO
College of Osteopathic Healthcare Executives (EA) ...... COHE
College of Osteopathic Medicine (DAVI) ...... COM

College of Osteopathic Medicine and Surgery (OICC) ... COMS
College of Osteopathic Medicine and Surgery, Des Moines, IA [Library symbol] [Library of Congress] (LCLS) ... IaDmS
College of Osteopathic Medicine of the Pacific (SAUS) ... COMP
College of Osteopathic Physicians and Surgeons ... COPS
College of Our Lady of Mount Carmel, Washington, DC [Library symbol] [Library of Congress] (LCLS) ... DOLM
College of Our Lady of the Elms [Chicopee, MA] ... COLE
College of Our Lady of the Elms, Chicopee, MA [Library symbol] [Library of Congress] (LCLS) ... MChiL
College of Petroleum and Energy Studies [British] ... CPS
College of Petroleum and Minerals [Dhahran, Saudi Arabia] ... CPM
College of Physical Education (SAUS) ... CPE
College of Physical Education (SAUO) ... CPE
College of Physical Therapists of Alberta (AC) ... CPTA
College of Physicians and Surgeons, and School of Dentistry, San Francisco, CA [Library symbol] [Library of Congress] (LCLS) ... CSfCPS
College of Physicians and Surgeons of New Brunswick (SAUO) ... CPSNB
College of Physicians and Surgeons of Nova Scotia (SAUO) ... CPSNS
College of Physicians & Surgeons of Ontario [Canada] (CMD) ... CPSO
College of Physicians and Surgeons-Columbia University (SAUO) ... CPSCU
College of Physicians of Philadelphia (SAUO) ... CPP
College of Physicians of Philadelphia, Philadelphia, PA [Library symbol] [Library of Congress] [OCLC symbol] (LCLS) ... PPC
College of Physicians of Philadelphia, Philadelphia, PA [Library symbol] [Library of Congress] (LCLS) ... PPCP
College of Police Science, New York, NY [Library symbol] [Library of Congress] (LCLS) ... NNCPL
College of Preceptors (SAUO) ... CP
College of Preceptors [British] ... CP
College of Psychic Studies [London] ... CPS
College of Radiographers (SAUO) ... COR
College of Radiologists of Australia (SAUS) ... CRA
College of Saint Elizabeth, Convent Station, NJ [OCLC symbol] (OCLC) ... CSE
College of Saint Elizabeth, Convent Station, NJ [Library symbol] [Library of Congress] (LCLS) ... NjConC
College of Saint Francis [Joliet, IL] ... CSF
College of Saint Francis, Joliet, IL [OCLC symbol] (OCLC) ... ICD
College of Saint Francis, Joliet, IL [Library symbol] [Library of Congress] (LCLS) ... IJolStF
College of Saint Gertrude, Library, Cottonwood, ID [Library symbol] [Library of Congress] (LCLS) ... IdCoStG
College of Saint Mary [Omaha, NE] ... CSM
College of Saint Mary of the Springs [Ohio] ... CSMS
College of Saint Mary-of the-Wasatch, Salt Lake City (SAUS) ... USlStM
College of Saint Mary-of-the-Wasatch, Salt Lake City, UT [Library symbol] [Library of Congress] [Obsolete] (LCLS) ... USlStM
College of Saint Rose [Albany, NY] ... CSR
[The] **College of Saint Rose** (GAGS) ... C St Rose
College of Saint Rose, Albany, NY [Library symbol] [Library of Congress] (LCLS) ... NAlCSR
College of Saint Scholastica [Duluth, MN] ... CSS
College of Saint Scholastica, Duluth, MN [Library symbol] [Library of Congress] (LCLS) ... MnDuStS
College of Saint Scholastica Library, Duluth, MN [OCLC symbol] (OCLC) ... MNS
College of Saint Teresa [Winona, MN] ... CST
College of Saint Teresa, Winona, MN [Library symbol] [Library of Congress] (LCLS) ... MnWinoCT
College of Saint Teresa, Winona, MN [OCLC symbol] (OCLC) ... MNZ
College of Saint Thomas (SAUO) ... CST
College of San Mateo [California] ... CSM
College of San Mateo Library, San Mateo, CA [OCLC symbol] (OCLC) ... CMT
College of San Mateo, San Mateo, CA [Library symbol] [Library of Congress] (LCLS) ... CSmatC
College of Santa Fe, Santa Fe, NM [Library symbol] [Library of Congress] (LCLS) ... NmSC
College of Santa Fe, Santa Fe, NM [Library symbol] [Library of Congress] (LCLS) ... NmSCS
College of Science (SAUO) ... CS
College of Science and Technology (SAUO) ... CST
College of Southern Idaho, Twin Falls, ID [Library symbol] [Library of Congress] (LCLS) ... IdTfSI
College of Speech Therapists [British] ... CST
College of St. Benedict [St. Joseph, MN] ... CSB
College of St. Benedict, St. Joseph, MN [OCLC symbol] (OCLC) ... MNF
College of St. Benedict, St. Joseph, MN [Library symbol] [Library of Congress] (LCLS) ... MnStjoS
College of St. Catherine [St. Paul, MN] ... CSC
College of St. Catherine, St. Paul, MN [OCLC symbol] (OCLC) ... MNE
College of St. Catherine, St. Paul, MN [Library symbol] [Library of Congress] (LCLS) ... MnSSC
College of St. Scholastica (GAGS) ... C St Scholastica
College of St. Thomas [St. Paul, MN] ... CST
College of St. Thomas, St. Paul, MN [Library symbol] [Library of Congress] (LCLS) ... MnSST
College of St. Thomas, St. Paul, MN [OCLC symbol] (OCLC) ... MNT
College of Staten Island [New York] ... CSI
[The] **College of Staten Island of The City University of New York** (GAGS) ... C Staten Island (CUNY)
College of Staten Island, St. George Campus Library, Staten Island, NY [OCLC symbol] (OCLC) ... VSI
College of Staten Island, St. George Campus, Staten Island, NY [Library symbol] [Library of Congress] (LCLS) ... NSiCS
College of Steubenville, Steubenville, OH [Library symbol] [Library of Congress] (LCLS) ... OSteC
College of Teachers of the Blind (SAUO) ... CTB
College of Technologists (SAUO) ... CT
College of Technology (SAUO) ... COT
College of Technology (SAUO) ... CT
College of Technology and Art (AIE) ... CTA
College of the Albemarle, Dare County Center Library, Manteo, NC [Library symbol] [Library of Congress] (LCLS) ... NcManA
College of the Albemarle, Elizabeth City, NC [Library symbol] [Library of Congress] (LCLS) ... NcElcA
College of the Holy Cross [Worcester, MA] ... CHC
College of the Holy Cross, Worcester, MA [OCLC symbol] (OCLC) ... HCD
College of the Holy Cross, Worcester, MA [Library symbol] [Library of Congress] (LCLS) ... MWH
College of the Holy Names (SAUO) ... CHN
College of the Mainland, Texas City (SAUS) ... TxTCM
College of the Mainland, Texas City, TX [Library symbol] [Library of Congress] (LCLS) ... TxTCM
College of the Ozarks, Clarksville, AR [Library symbol] [Library of Congress] (LCLS) ... ArClC
College of the Sacred Heart [Puerto Rico] ... CSH
College of the Sea (SAUO) ... COS
College of the Sequoias, Visalia, CA [Library symbol] [Library of Congress] (LCLS) ... CViCS
College of the Siskiyous Library, Weed, CA [OCLC symbol] (OCLC) ... CIS
College of the Siskoyous, Weed, CA [Library symbol] [Library of Congress] (LCLS) ... CWeeC
College of the Southwest, Hobbs, NM [Library symbol] [Library of Congress] (LCLS) ... NmHoSW
College of the Virgin Islands ... CVI
College of the Virgin Islands, St. Thomas, VI [Library symbol] [Library of Congress] (LCLS) ... VnStC
College of Trades and Technology [St. John's, NF] ... CTT
College of Trades and Technology, Medical Sciences Library, St. John's, NF, Canada [Library symbol] [Library of Congress] (LCLS) ... CaNfSCTM
College of Trades and Technology, St. John's, NF, Canada [Library symbol] [Library of Congress] (LCLS) ... CaNfSCT
College of Universal Knowledge (SAUO) ... KUK
College of Veterinarians of Ontario (AC) ... CVO
College of Veterinary Medicine [University of Florida] [Research center] (RCD) ... CVM
College of White Plains, White Plains, NY [Library symbol] [Library of Congress] (LCLS) ... NWhpG
College of White Plains, White Plains, NY [OCLC symbol] (OCLC) ... VZW
College of William and Mary (GAGS) ... C Wm & Mary
College of William and Mary (SAUS) ... W&M
College of William and Mary, Law School, Williamsburg, VA [Library symbol] [Library of Congress] (LCLS) ... ViW-L
College of William and Mary, Law School, Williamsburg, VA [OCLC symbol] (OCLC) ... VWL
College of William and Mary, Williamsburg, VA [Library symbol] [Library of Congress] (LCLS) ... ViW
College of William and Mary, Williamsburg, VA [OCLC symbol] (OCLC) ... VWM
College of Wooster (SAUS) ... W
College of Wooster, Wooster, OH [Library symbol] [Library of Congress] (LCLS) ... OWoC
College of Wooster, Wooster, OH [OCLC symbol] (OCLC) ... WOO
College on Problems of Drug Dependence (SAUO) ... CPDD
College on Research and Development (HGAA) ... COLRAD
College on the Practice of Management Science ... CPMS
College Ouest Africaine des Chirurgiens [West African College of Surgeons - WACS] (EAIO) ... COAC
College Outcome Measures Program [American College Testing Program] (TES) ... COMP
College Outpost [Alaska] [Seismograph station code, US Geological Survey] (SEIS) ... COL
College Park, MD [Location identifier] [FAA] (FAAL) ... CGS
College Park, MD [FM radio station call letters] ... WMUC
College Physical Education Association [Later, NAPEHE] ... CPEA
College Place, WA [FM radio station call letters] ... KGTS
College Placement Council (EA) ... CPC
College Placement Services [Later, CCDM] (EA) ... CPS
College Plaza Resource Centre, Alberta Public Works, Supply and Services, Edmonton, Alberta [Library symbol] [National Library of Canada] (NLC) ... AEPW
College Press Service (EA) ... CPS
College Proficiency Examination (WGA) ... CPE
College Publishers Group [Defunct] (EA) ... CPG
College Qualification (SAUS) ... CQU
College Qualification Test (WGA) ... CQT
College Qualification Test ... CQU
College Reading and Learning Association (NTPA) ... CRLA
College Reading and Study Skills Inventory (EDAC) ... CRSS
College Recruitment Database [Executive Telecom System, Inc.] [Information service or system] (CRD) ... CRD
College Republican National Committee (EA) ... CRNC
College Retirement Equities Fund [New York, NY] (EA) ... CREF
College Sainte-Croix, Montreal, PQ, Canada [Library symbol] [Library of Congress] (LCLS) ... CaQMStC
College Sainte-Marie, Montreal, PQ, Canada [Library symbol] [Library of Congress] (LCLS) ... CaQMSM
College Saint-Jean-Sur-Richelieu, Saint-Jean, PQ, Canada [Library symbol] [Library of Congress] (LCLS) ... CaQStJC
College Saint-Jean-Sur-Richelieu, Saint-Jean, Quebec [Library symbol] [National Library of Canada] (NLC) ... QSTJC

College Saint-Louis-Maillet, Edmundston, NB, Canada [*Library symbol*] [*Library of Congress*] (LCLS) .... CaNBESLM
College Scholarship Service [*Service mark of the College Entrance Examination Board*] .... CSS
College Science Improvement Program [*National Science Foundation*] [*Defunct*] .... COSIP
College Selection Service [*Peterson's Guides*] [*Information service or system*] (IID) .... CSS
College Self-Expression Scale .... CSES
College Senior Engineering Program [*Air Force*] .... CSEP
College Service Bureau (EA) .... CSB
College Sports Information Directors of America (EA) .... CoSIDA
College Station [*Texas*] [*Airport symbol*] (OAG) CLL
College Station, TX [*Location identifier*] [*FAA*] (FAAL) CLL
College Station, TX [*FM radio station call letters*] .... KAMU
College Station, TX [*Television station call letters*] .... KAMU-TV
College Station, TX [*AM radio station call letters*] (BROA) .... KAZW-AM
College Station, TX [*FM radio station call letters*] (RBYB) .... KEOS
College Station, TX [*FM radio station call letters*] .... KTSR
College Station, TX [*AM radio station call letters*] .... WTAW
College Station/Easterwood Field [*Texas*] [*ICAO location identifier*] (ICLI) .... KCLL
College Stores Association .... CSA
College Stores of New England (SRA) .... CSNE
College Student Experinces Questionnaire .... CSEQ
College Student Personnel (DHP) .... CSP
College Student Personnel Institute [*Defunct*] .... CSPI
College Student Questionnaires [*Psychology*] .... CSQ
College Student Satisfaction Questionnaire (DHP) .... CSSQ
College Swimming Coaches Association of America (EA) .... CSCAA
College Theology Society (EA) .... CTS
College Training Detachment .... CTD
College Training Plan (SAUS) .... CTP
College Universitaire de Hearst, Ontario [*Library symbol*] [*National Library of Canada*] (NLC) .... OHCU
College, University and Research Libraries (or Library) Section (SAUS) .... CURLS
College, University and Research Libraries Section (SAUO) .... CURLS
College Women's Assertion Sample (EDAC) .... CWAS
College Women's Volunteer Service [*World War II*] .... CWVS
College Work-Study [*Program*] .... CW-S
College Work-Study Program .... CWSP
College World Series [*Baseball*] (NDBD) .... CWS
College Young Democrats of America (EA) .... CYD
Collegedale, TN [*FM radio station call letters*] .... WSMC
College-Industry Committee on Material Handling Education (SAUO) .... CICMHE
College-Level and State Services .... CLSS
College-Level Examination Program [*Trademark/service mark of the College Entrance Examination Board*] .... CLEP
CollegeLink.com, Inc. [*AMEX symbol*] (SG) .... APS
Colleges & Institutes of Further Education (WDAA) .... CIFE
Colleges and Universitites, Ontario Ministry of Education, Toronto, Ontario [*Library symbol*] [*National Library of Canada*] (NLC) .... OTECU
Colleges, Institutes, and Schools in Education (AIE) .... CISE
Colleges, Institutes and Schools of Education (SAUO) .... CISE
Colleges of Education Learning Programme Project [*British*] .... CELPP
Colleges of Education Learning Programmes Information Service (SAUS) .... CELPIS
Colleges of Mid-America (EA) .... CMA
Colleges of Technology and Further Education (SAUS) .... CTFE
Collegeville, MN [*FM radio station call letters*] .... KNSR
Collegeville, MN [*FM radio station call letters*] .... KSJR
Collegial Association for the Development and Renewal of Educators (EDAC) .... CADRE
Collegiate .... COLGT
Collegiate (SAUS) .... Coll
Collegiate (ROG) .... COLLEG
Collegiate Anti-Protest Organization Group (SAUO) .... CAPOG
Collegiate Assessment of Academic Proficiency [*American College Testing Program*] (TES) .... CAAP
Collegiate Association for Research of Principle (EA) .... NCARP
Collegiate Association for the Research of Principles (SAUO) .... CARP
Collegiate Association for the Research of Principles (DICI) .... CARP
Collegiate Basketball Officials Bureau [*Later, Eastern College Basketball Association*] (EA) .... CBOB
Collegiate Commissioners Association (EA) .... CCA
Collegiate Conference of Central Illinois (PSS) CCCI
Collegiate Coordinator for Disability Students (DHP) .... CCDS
Collegiate Council for the United Nations (EA) .... CCUN
Collegiate Council of Women's Athletic Administrators (EA) .... CCWAA
Collegiate Dictionary of Botany (SAUS) .... CDB
Collegiate Dictionary of Zoology (SAUS) .... CDZ
Collegiate Gymnastics Association (EA) .... CGA
Collegiate Microcomputer (SAUS) .... CM
Collegiate Pacific [*AMEX symbol*] .... BOO
Collegiate Soaring Association (EA) .... CSA
Collegiate Track Conference (PSS) .... CTC
Collegiate Video Counseling Network (SAUS) .... CVCN
Collegium (ROG) .... COL
Collegium Academicum (SAUS) .... CA
Collegium International Neuro-Psychopharmacologicum .... CINP
Collegium Internationale Activitatis Nervosae Superioris [*Milan, Italy*] (EAIO) .... CIANS
Collegium Internationale Activitatis Nervosae Superioris .... CINS
Collegium Internationale Allergologicum [*Berne, Switzerland*] (EA) .... CIA
Collegium Internationale Chirurgiae Digestivae [*Rome, Italy*] (EAIO) .... CICD
Collegium Internationale Neuro-Psychopharmacologicum (EA) .... CINP
Collegium Medicorum Theatri (EA) .... COMET
Colles' English Parliamentary Cases [*1697-1714*] [*A publication*] (DLA) .... Coll
Colles' English Parliamentary Cases [*1697-1714*] [*A publication*] (DLA) .... Colles
Colles' English Parliamentary Cases [*1697-1714*] [*A publication*] (DLA) .... Colles (Eng)
Colles' English Parliamentary Cases [*1697-1714*] [*A publication*] (DLA) .... Colles PC
Colles' English Parliamentary Cases [*1697-1714*] [*A publication*] (DLA) .... Coll PC
Collet, Dickinson, Pearce (SAUO) .... CDP
Collet on Torts and Measure of Damages [*A publication*] (DLA) .... Coll Tor
Collet-Sicard [*Syndrome*] [*Otorhinolaryngology and neurology*] (DAVI) .... CS
Collett Dickenson Pearce [*British advertising agency*] .... CDP
Collider Detector at Fermilab [*Particle physics*] .... CDF
Collidge Elementary School, Baldwin, NY [*Library symbol*] [*Library of Congress*] (LCLS) .... NBaldCE
Colliding Beam Accelerator [*High-energy physics*] .... CBA
Colliding Beam Fusion Reactor [*Nuclear physics*] .... CBFR
Colliding Beams (SAUS) .... CB
Colliding Electron-Beam Storage Ring [*Nuclear energy*] (NRCH) .... CESR
Colliding-Pulse-Mode [*LASER*] .... CPM
Collie Club of America (EA) .... CCA
Collie Federated School of Mines (SAUO) .... CFSM
Collier [*Navy symbol*] [*Obsolete*] .... AC
Collier and Eaton's American Bankruptcy Reports [*A publication*] (DLA) .... Coll & E Bank
Collier and Eaton's American Bankruptcy Reports [*A publication*] (DLA) .... Collier & E Am Bankr
Collier and Eaton's American Bankruptcy Reports [*A publication*] (DLA) .... Collier Bank
Collier and Miller on Bills of Sale [*A publication*] (DLA) .... C & M Bills
Collier and Miller on Bills of Sale [*A publication*] (DLA) .... Coll & Mil BS
Collier County Free Public Library, Naples, FL [*Library symbol*] [*Library of Congress*] (LCLS) .... FNaC
Collier de Perles, Carre de Hermes [*Pearl Necklace, Silk Scarf from the boutique Hermes*] [*French Yuppie garb*] .... CPCH
Collier Macmillan Library Service (SAUS) .... Collier Macmillan
Collier on Patents [*A publication*] (DLA) .... Coll Pat
Collier's Bankruptcy Cases [*A publication*] (DLA) .... CBC
Collier's Bankruptcy Cases [*A publication*] (DLA) .... Collier Bankr Cas
Colliers Encyclopedia (SAUS) .... CollEncy
Collier's Law of Bankruptcy [*A publication*] (DLA) .... Coll Bank
Collier's Law of Contribution [*1875*] [*A publication*] (DLA) .... Coll Contr
Collier's Law of Mines [*A publication*] (DLA) .... Coll Min
Collier's Law of Mines [*A publication*] (DLA) .... Col Mines
Collierville, TN [*AM radio station call letters*] .... WCRV
Colliery .... COLL
Colliery (ROG) .... COLLY
colliery (SAUO) .... colly
Colliery Information System (HEAS) .... CIS
Colliery Mazdoor Union [*India*] .... CMU
Colliery Screened (ROG) .... C/S
Colliery Screened (SAUS) .... CS
Colliery Screened Coal (SAUS) .... CS Coal
Colliery Under-Managers (SAUO) .... CU-M
Collimated Holes Structure (PDAA) .... CHS
Collimated Ion Resonance Cannon, Ephermal (SAUS) .... CIRCE
Collimated Monochromatic Light .... CML
Collimated Photon Scattering (MCD) .... CPS
Collimated Proportional Counter (PDAA) .... CPC
Collimated Slit Radiography (MCD) .... CSR
Collimation Test Module [*Nuclear energy*] (GFGA) .... CTM
Collimator (MSA) .... COLIM
Collimator Target (MCD) .... CT
Collin County Community College District, McKinney, TX [*Library symbol*] [*Library of Congress*] (LCLS) .... TxMckC
Collinear Exact Quantum Bend [*Kinetics*] .... CEQB
Colling Fan (SAUS) .... CF
Collingswood Free Public Library, Collingswood, NJ [*Library symbol*] [*Library of Congress*] (LCLS) .... NjCo
Collingswood Publishing Co., Collingswood, NJ [*Library symbol*] [*Library of Congress*] (LCLS) .... NjCoC
Collingwood Air Services Ltd. [*Canada*] [*ICAO designator*] (FAAC) .... BLE
Collingwood & District Information Centre (AC) .... CDIC
Collingwood Energy [*Vancouver Stock Exchange symbol*] .... CIW
Collingwood, ON [*AM radio station call letters*] .... CKCB
Collingwood, ON [*FM radio station call letters*] (BROA) .... CKCB-FM
Collingwood Public Library, Collingwood, ON, Canada [*Library symbol*] [*Library of Congress*] (LCLS) .... CaOCol
Collingwood Public Library, Ontario [*Library symbol*] [*National Library of Canada*] (NLC) .... OCOL
Collingwood Township Public Library, Brockville, ON, Canada [*Library symbol*] [*Library of Congress*] (LCLS) .... CaOCCT
Collingwood Township Public Library, Clarksburg, Ontario [*Library symbol*] [*National Library of Canada*] (NLC) .... OCCT
Collins Adaptive Processing System (SAUS) .... CAPS
Collins & Aikman [*NYSE symbol*] (TTSB) .... CKC
Collins & Aikman Corp. (SAUO) .... CK
Collins & Aikman Holdings Corp. [*NYSE symbol*] (SAG) .... CKC
Collins & Aikman Holdings Corp. [*Associated Press*] (SAG) .... CollAik
Collins Birmingham University International Language Database .... COBUILD
Collins Canada Division, Rockwell International, Toronto, Ontario [*Library symbol*] [*National Library of Canada*] (NLC) .... OTRIC
Collins English Dictionary [*A publication*] [*British*] .... CED
Collins Foods International, Inc. (SAUO) .... CF

Collins Industries [*NASDAQ symbol*] (TTSB) .... COLI
Collins Industries, Inc. [*NASDAQ symbol*] (SAG) .... COLL
Collins Industries, Inc. [*Associated Press*] (SAG) .... Collins
Collins Industries, Inc. (SAUO) .... GO
Collins Industries, Inc. (SAUS) .... GOR
Collins Motor Corp. [*Alternative engine technology*] .... CMC
Collins, MS [*FM radio station call letters*] .... WKNZ
Collins Public Library, Collins, IA [*Library symbol*] [*Library of Congress*] (LCLS) .... IaColn
Collins Radio Co. (KSC) .... CRC
Collins Radio Co. (SAUO) .... CRI
Collins Radio Co., Dallas, TX [*Library symbol*] [*Library of Congress*] (LCLS) .... TxDaCR
Collins Resources Ltd. [*Vancouver Stock Exchange symbol*] .... CR
Collin's Solution (MAE) .... C₃
Collinson on the Law of Idiots and Lunatics [*A publication*] (DLA) .... Coll Id
Collinson on the Law of Idiots and Lunatics [*A publication*] (DLA) .... Coll Lun
Collinson on the Stamp Laws [*A publication*] (DLA) .... Coll St L
Collinsville [*Australia*] [*Airport symbol*] (OAG) .... KCE
Collinsville Community Unit 10, Collinsville, IL [*Library symbol*] [*Library of Congress*] (LCLS) .... IColCU
Collinsville, OK [*FM radio station call letters*] (BROA) .... KMRX-FM
Collinsville Public Library, Collinsville, IL [*Library symbol*] [*Library of Congress*] (LCLS) .... ICol
Collinsville, VA [*AM radio station call letters*] .... WFIC
Collique [*Peru*] [*ICAO location identifier*] (ICLI) .... SPOL
Collision .... CLLSN
Collision (DS) .... Col
Collision [*Insurance*] .... COLL
Collision Alert [*Air traffic control*] .... CACA
Collision and Contamination Avoidance Maneuver (ADWA) .... CCAM
Collision and Obstacle/Terrain Avoidance Warning System .... COTAWS
Collision Avoidance Aid .... CAA
Collision Avoidance and Navigation System (ACAE) .... CAANS
Collision Avoidance Maneuver (ACAE) .... CAM
Collision Avoidance, Proximity Warning, Station Keeping Equipment [*Military*] (NG) .... CAPWSK
Collision Avoidance RADAR and Navigation System [*Military*] .... CARNS
Collision Avoidance RADAR Simulator [*Maritime*] .... CARS
Collision Avoidance RADAR Trainer (PDAA) .... CART
Collision Avoidance System [*Aviation*] .... CAS
Collision Avoidance System / Pilot Warning Indicator [*Aviation*] (PDAA) .... CAS/PWI
Collision Avoidance System Proximity Warning Indicator [*Aviation*] (IAA) .... CASPWI
Collision Avoidance System Proximity Warning indicator (SAUS) .... CAS/PWI
Collision Avoidance System Technical Evaluation [*Aviation*] (MCD) .... CASTE
Collision Avoidance System Using Baseband Reflectrometry [*Aviation*] (PDAA) .... CASBAR
Collision Avoidance System/Pilot Warning Instrument (SAUS) .... CAS/PWI
Collision Bulkhead (SAUS) .... COLBH
Collision, Caldera Open Linux (SAUS) .... COL
Collision Computer Oriented Language (SAUS) .... COL
Collision Damage Classification [*Insurance*] .... CDC
Collision Damage Waiver [*Insurance*] .... CDW
Collision Detect [*Computer science*] .... CD
Collision Detection [*Telecommunications*] (ACRL) .... CD
Collision Detector System (NASA) .... CDS
Collision Detector/Multiple Access [*Computer science*] .... CD/MA
Collision Diameter of a Molecule [*Symbol*] [*IUPAC*] .... d
Collision Elimination [*Wiring hub*] [*Computer science*] (PCM) .... CE
Collision Force Method (SAUS) .... CFM
Collision Number [*Symbol*] [*IUPAC*] .... Z
Collision Parts Journal [*A publication*] (EAAP) .... CPJ
Collision Prevention Advisory Group [*US*] .... COPAG
Collision Prevention Advisory Group (SAUO) .... CPAG
Collision Probability (OA) .... CP
Collision Risk Model [*Aviation*] (DA) .... CRM
Collision Threat Assessment .... CTA
Collision Warning System [*Automotive safety*] .... CWS
Collision-Activated Dissociation [*Spectrometry*] .... CAD
Collisional Mode (MCD) .... CMODE
Collisional Radiation Damage Sticking (SAUS) .... CRDS
Collisionally Activated Dissociation .... CAD
Collision-Dominated Quiescent Discharge .... CDQD
Collision-Force Method (PDAA) .... CFM
Collision-Imparted Velocity Method .... CIVM
Collision-Induced Absorption (MCD) .... CIA
Collision-Induced Decomposition [*or Dissociation*] [*Spectrometry*] .... CID
Collision-Induced Dissocation (SAUS) .... CID
Collision-Induced Light Scattering (MCD) .... CILS
Collmberg [*German Democratic Republic*] [*Seismograph station code, US Geological Survey*] (SEIS) CLL
Collocated CL
Collocated Operating Bases (MCD) .... COB
Collocation [*Computer software package*] [*University of Birmingham*] [*British*] (NITA) .... CLOC
Collocation Flutter Analysis .... CFA
Collocation Flutter Analysis .... COFA
Collodion Glass Negative (VRA) .... CGNG
Collodion Print (VRA) .... CLPT
Colloid .... COLL
Colloid (SAUS) .... Coll
Colloid Antigen [*Immunology*] .... CA
Colloid Droplet (SAUS) .... CD

Colloid Journal (SAUS) .... Colloid J
Colloid Microthruster Experiment .... CME
Colloidal .... COL
Colloidal (SAUS) .... Coll
Colloidal Array Filters [*for LASER applications*] .... CAF
Colloidal Bismuth Subcitrate [*Pharmacy*] .... CBS
Colloidal Disorder-Order Transitions (SAUS) .... CDOT
Colloidal Gas Aphron [*Physical chemistry*] .... CGA
Colloidal Gelatin (SAUS) .... CGEL
Colloidal Gold [*Chemistry*] .... CG
Colloidal Iron (OA) CI
Colloidal Iron Hydroxide .... CIH
Colloidal Organic Carbon [*Environmental chemistry*] .... COC
Colloidal Osmotic Pressure [*Analytical biochemistry*] .... COP
Colloidal Silicon Dioxide (DB) .... CSD
Colloidal Suspension (SAUS) .... CSN
Colloidal System Test .... CST
Colloidal Thorium (OA) .... CT
Colloque International de Droit Compare [*A publication*] (DLA) .... Col Int'l Dr Comp
Colloque International de Marketing Gazier [*International Colloquium about Gas Marketing - ICGM*] (EA) .... CIMG
Colloque sur le Traitement Automatique des Textes [*Colloquium on the Computer Processing of Textual Data - CCPTD*] .... CTAT
Colloquia for Presidents and Academic Administrators [*Formerly, ICUA*] (EA) .... CPAA
Colloquial .... COLL
Colloquial (WDMC) .... coll
Colloquial .... COLLOQ
Colloquial (NTIO) .... colloq
Colloquialism (SAUS) .... Coll
Colloquium (SAUS) .... Colloq
Colloquium on the Computer Processing of Textural Data (SAUO) .... CCPTD
Colloquium Spectroscopicum Internationale .... CSI
Colloquium: The Australian and New Zealand Theological Review [*A publication*] (APTA) .... Coll
Colloredo [*Italy*] [*Seismograph station code, US Geological Survey*] (SEIS) .... COLI
Collostyle (SAUS) .... COL
Coll'Ottava [*With the Octave*] [*Music*] (ROG) .... C 8VA
Coll'Ottava [*With the Octave*] [*Music*] .... Coll'Ott
Coll'Ottava [*With the Octave*] [*Music*] .... COLL'OTTA
Coll'Ottava [*With the Octave*] [*Music*] (ROG) .... COL OTTA
Collotype (VRA) .... COLTY
Collpa [*Bolivia*] [*ICAO location identifier*] (ICLI) .... SLCY
Collpani [*Bolivia*] [*ICAO location identifier*] (ICLI) .... SLCL
Collum Corpus (SAUS) CC
Collum Diaphysen (SAUS) .... CD
Collunarium [*Nose Wash*] [*Pharmacy*] .... COLLUN
Collurania [*Italy*] [*Seismograph station code, US Geological Survey*] [*Closed*] (SEIS) .... CLR
Collutorium [*Mouthwash*] [*Pharmacy*] .... COLLUT
Collyer's Chancery Cases Tempore Bruce, V-C [*63 English Reprint*] [*1844-45*] [*A publication*] (ILCA) .... Coll CC
Collyer's Chancery Cases Tempore Bruce, V-C [*63 English Reprint*] [*1844-45*] [*A publication*] (DLA) .... Coll NC
Collyer's English Chancery Cases [*1845-47*] [*A publication*] (DLA) .... Col CC
Collyer's English Chancery Cases [*1845-47*] [*A publication*] (DLA) .... Coll
Collyer's English Chancery Cases [*1845-47*] [*A publication*] (DLA) .... Colly Ch Cas (Eng)
Collyer's English Chancery Reports [*A publication*] (DLA) .... Coll CR
Collyer's English Vice Chancellors' Reports [*1845-47*] [*A publication*] (DLA) .... Colly
Collyer's Law of Partnership [*A publication*] (DLA) .... Coll Part
Collyer's Law of Partnership [*A publication*] (DLA) .... Colly Part
Collyer's Law of Partnership [*A publication*] (DLA) .... Col Part
Collyrium [*Eye Wash*] [*Pharmacy*] (ROG) .... COLL
Collyrium [*Eye Wash*] [*Pharmacy*] .... COLLYR
Colman, Prentis & Varley Export Ltd. (SAUO) .... CPV
Colmar [*France*] [*Airport symbol*] .... CMR
Colmar/Houssen [*France*] [*ICAO location identifier*] (ICLI) .... LFGA
Colmar/Meyenheim [*France*] [*ICAO location identifier*] (ICLI) .... LFSC
Colmenar Viejo [*Spain*] [*ICAO location identifier*] (ICLI) .... LECV
Colocasia Bacilliform Virus [*Plant pathology*] .... CoBV
Colocasia Bobone Disease Virus [*Plant pathology*] .... CBDV
Colocated Automatic Intercept System (SAUS) .... CAIS
Colocation Flutter Analysis (ACAE) .... COFA
Colocynthus [*Bitter Apples*] [*Pharmacy*] (ROG) .... COLOCYNTH
Coloforma, Heart Disease, Arrested Growth or Development, Genital Hypoplasia, and Ear Abnormalities [*Medicine*] .... CHARGE
Cologarithm [*Mathematics*] .... COLOG
Cologarithm (ADWA) .... colog
Cologne [*West Germany*] [*Seismograph station code, US Geological Survey*] (SEIS) .... CLG
Cologne Air Transport [*Germany*] [*FAA designator*] (FAAC) .... GAG
Cologne/Bonn [*Germany*] [*Airport symbol*] (OAG) .... CGN
Cologne/Bonn-Main RR [*Germany*] [*Airport symbol*] (OAG) .... QKL
Coloma Public Library, Coloma, MI [*Library symbol*] [*Library of Congress*] (LCLS) .... MiCol
Colomb Bechar [*Algeria*] [*Airport symbol*] (AD) .... CBH
Colombia [*IYRU nationality code*] (IYR) .... CB
Colombia [*ucu (United States Miscellaneous Caribbean Islands) used in records cataloged before January 1978*] [*MARC country of publication code*] [*Library of Congress*] (LCCP) .... ck
Colombia [*ANSI two-letter standard code*] (CNC) .... CO
Colombia (MILB) .... Co
Colombia [*ANSI three-letter standard code*] (CNC) .... COL

Reverse Acronyms, Initialisms & Abbreviations Dictionary • 29th Edition

Colombia (NTIO)	Col
Colombia	Colom
Colombia [MARC geographic area code] [Library of Congress] (LCCP)	s-ck-
Colombia Human Rights Information Committee (EA)	CHIBCHA
Colombia National Committee for Pacific Economic Cooperation	COLPECC
Colombia Press (SAUO)	CP
Colombia, SC [Location identifier] [FAA] (FAAL)	VYK
Colombian American Association (EA)	CAA
Colombian Government Trade Bureau (EA)	CGTB
Colombian National Oceanographic Data Centre (SAUS)	CECOLDO
Colombian-American Chamber of Commerce (EA)	CACC
Colombian-American Chamber of Commerce (EA)	COL-AMCHAM
Colombian-American Culture Foundation (SAUO)	CACF
Colombo [Sri Lanka] [Airport symbol] (OAG)	CMB
Colombo [Sri Lanka] [Seismograph station code, US Geological Survey] (SEIS)	COC
Colombo Law Journal [A publication] (DLA)	Colombo LJ
Colombo National Museum (SAUS)	CNM
Colombo Plan	CP
Colombo Tea Traders Association (SAUO)	CTTA
Colombo/Katunayake [Sri Lanka] [ICAO location identifier] (ICLI)	VCBI
Colombo/Ratmalana [Sri Lanka] [ICAO location identifier] (ICLI)	VCCC
Colombus Air Force Base [Mississippi] [ICAO location identifier] (ICLI)	KCBM
Colome Public Library, Colome, SD [Library symbol] [Library of Congress] (LCLS)	SdCo
Colon [Monetary unit] [Costa Rica, El Salvador]	C
Colon (AABC)	CLN
Colon (SAUS)	Cln
Colon [City in Panama] (ROG)	CO
Colon (WDAA)	COL
Colon [Panama] [ICAO location identifier] (ICLI)	MPCO
Colon [Cuba] [ICAO location identifier] (ICLI)	MUCO
Colon [Panama] [Airport symbol] (OAG)	ONX
Colon Adenocarcinoma [Medicine] (MELL)	CAC
Colon and Rectal [or Colorectal] Surgery [Medicine]	CRS
Colon and Rectal Surgery Educational Program (SAUO)	CARSEP
Colon Cancer [Medicine] (DB)	CC
Colon Cancer Alliance (SAUS)	CCA
Colon Classification [Library science]	CC
Colon Mucoprotein Antigen [Immunochemistry]	CMA
Colon Resection [Medicine]	CR
Colon Township Library, Colon, MI [Library symbol] [Library of Congress] (LCLS)	MiColo
Colona, CO [AM radio station call letters] (BROA)	KAVP-AM
Colonel (ROG)	C
Colonel (GEAB)	col
Colonel [Military] (AABC)	COL
Colonel (WDAA)	Col
Colonel (SAUO)	Col
Colonel [Air Force, Army, Marine Corps]	O6
Colonel By Campus, Algonquin College of Applied Arts and Technology, Ottawa, Ontario [Library symbol] [National Library of Canada] (NLC)	OOACC
Colonel By Secondary School, Ottawa, ON, Canada [Library symbol] [Library of Congress] (LCLS)	CaOOCB
Colonel By Secondary School, Ottawa, Ontario [Library symbol] [National Library of Canada] (NLC)	OOCB
Colonel Coon Collectors Club (EA)	CCCC
Colonel Hill, Crooked Island [Bahamas] [ICAO location identifier] (ICLI)	MYCI
Colonel, Royal Artillery Training [British]	CRAT
Colonel-Commandant (SAUS)	Col-Comdt
Colonel-in-Chief (SAUS)	Col-in-Ch
Colonels International, Inc. (The) [NASDAQ symbol] (SAG)	COLO
Colonels International, Inc. (The) [Associated Press] (SAG)	Colonels
Colonel's Intl. [NASDAQ symbol] (TTSB)	COLO
Colonel's Island [AAR code]	COLI
Colonia [Uruguay] [Airport symbol]	CYR
Colonia Sabana [Puerto Rico] [Seismograph station code, US Geological Survey] (SEIS)	CSB
Colonia Sarmiento [Argentina] [Airport symbol] (AD)	OLN
Colonia/Aeropuerto Deptal. [Uruguay] [ICAO location identifier] (ICLI)	SUCA
Colonial	CL
Colonial	CLNL
Colonial (ADWA)	Col
Colonial (ROG)	COL
Colonial	COLON
Colonial Administration Service (SAUO)	CAS
Colonial Air Lines	CAL
Colonial Air Lines, Inc. (SAUO)	CAL
Colonial Aircraft Co.	CAC
Colonial Aircraft Company (SAUO)	CAC
Colonial Airlines (SAUO)	CAI
Colonial Allowance [British military] (DMA)	CA
Colonial Ammunition Company (SAUO)	CAC
Colonial [or Commonwealth] and Continental Church Society [British]	CCCS
Colonial and Continental Church Society (SAUO)	CCCS
Colonial and Dominions Offices (SAUO)	CDO
Colonial and Local Troops (SAUO)	CLT
Colonial Athletic Association (PSS)	CAA
Colonial Audit Department (SAUO)	CAD
Colonial BancGroup [NYSE symbol] (TTSB)	CNB
Colonial Bankgroup [NYSE symbol] (SAG)	CNB
Colonial Bankgroup [Associated Press] (SAG)	ColBgp
Colonial Beach, VA [FM radio station call letters]	WGRQ
Colonial Bird Register [Cornell University] [Information service or system] (IID)	CBR

Colonial Bishoprics' Fund [British]	CBF
Colonial Coml [NASDAQ symbol] (TTSB)	CCOM
Colonial Commercial Corp. [NASDAQ symbol] (NQ)	CCOM
Colonial Commercial Corp. [Associated Press] (SAG)	ColCm
Colonial Commercial Corp. [Associated Press] (SAG)	ColCmc
Colonial Comml Cv Pfd [NASDAQ symbol] (TTSB)	CCOMP
Colonial Corporation of America (SAUO)	CLA
Colonial Dames [An association] (IIA)	CD
Colonial Dames of America (EA)	CDA
Colonial Data Tech [NASDAQ symbol] (TTSB)	CDTX
Colonial Data Technologies Corp. [AMEX symbol] (SPSG)	CDT
Colonial Data Technologies Corp. [Associated Press] (SAG)	ColData
Colonial Development and Welfare (SAUS)	CD&W
Colonial Development Corp.	CDC
Colonial Economic Advisory Committee (SAUO)	CEAC
Colonial, Fish-Eating Water Bird	CFEWB
Colonial Forces (SAUO)	CF
Colonial Forest Resources Development Department (SAUO)	CFRDD
Colonial Forest Resources Development Department (SAUS)	CFRDD
Colonial Gas [NASDAQ symbol] (TTSB)	CGES
Colonial Gas [NYSE symbol] (SG)	CLG
Colonial Gas Co. [NASDAQ symbol] (NQ)	CGES
Colonial Gas Co. [Associated Press] (SAG)	ColnlGas
Colonial Heights, TN [FM radio station call letters]	WLJQ
Colonial Heights, TN [AM radio station call letters] (RBYB)	WPWT-AM
Colonial Heights, TN [FM radio station call letters] (BROA)	WRZK-FM
Colonial Heights, TN [AM radio station call letters]	WZMC
Colonial Heights, VA [AM radio station call letters] (BROA)	WDZY
Colonial Heights, VA [FM radio station call letters]	WKHK
Colonial Heights, VA [FM radio station call letters]	WSTK
Colonial Heights, VA [AM radio station call letters] (BROA)	WZOD-AM
Colonial High Income Muni [NYSE symbol] (TTSB)	CXF
Colonial High Income Municipal Trust [Associated Press] (SAG)	ColHln
Colonial High Income Municipal Trust [NYSE symbol] (SPSG)	CXE
Colonial Insecticide Research unit (SAUO)	CIR
Colonial Insecticide Research Unit (SAUO)	CIRU
Colonial Insecticide Research Unit (SAUS)	CIR Unit
Colonial Interim Hi Income [NYSE symbol] (TTSB)	CIF
Colonial Intermarket Income Trust [Associated Press] (SAG)	ColIntIn
Colonial Intermarket Income Trust I [NYSE symbol] (SPSG)	CMK
Colonial Intermediate High Income Fund [NYSE symbol] (SPSG)	CIF
Colonial Intermediate High Income Fund [Associated Press] (SAG)	ColIHI
Colonial InterMkt Inc. Tr I [NYSE symbol] (TTSB)	CMK
Colonial Inv Grade Muni [NYSE symbol] (TTSB)	CXH
Colonial Investment Grade Municipal [NYSE symbol] (SPSG)	CXH
Colonial Investment Grade Municipal Trust [Associated Press] (SAG)	ColInvG
Colonial Law Journal [A publication] (DLA)	Co LJ
Colonial Law Journal [A publication] (DLA)	Col LJ
Colonial Law Journal (New Zealand) [A publication] (DLA)	Col LJNZ
Colonial Law Journal Reports [A publication] (DLA)	CLJ
Colonial Life Co. [Trinidad]	CLICO
Colonial Medical Department [British]	CMD
Colonial Medical Department (SAUO)	CMD
Colonial Medical Service (SAUO)	CMS
Colonial Military Forces (SAUO)	CMF
Colonial Military Forces [British]	CMF
Colonial Monthly [A publication]	Col Mon
Colonial Muni Inc. Tr [NYSE symbol] (TTSB)	CMU
Colonial Municipal Income Trust [NYSE symbol] (SPSG)	CMU
Colonial Municipal Income Trust [Associated Press] (SAG)	ColMu
Colonial National Historic Park	COLO
Colonial National Park (SAUS)	CNP
Colonial Office [British]	CO
Colonial Office Scrub Typhus Research Unit, Institute for Medical Research (SAUO)	COSTRU
Colonial Officer (SAUS)	CO
Colonial Oil & Gas Ltd. [Toronto Stock Exchange symbol]	COO
Colonial Order of the Acorn (SAUO)	COA
Colonial Penn Group, Inc., Marketing Research Library, Philadelphia, PA [Library symbol] [Library of Congress] (LCLS)	PPColP
Colonial Plant and Animal Products (SAUS)	Colon Plant Anim Prod
Colonial Police Medal [British]	CPM
Colonial Police Meritorious Service Medal [British]	CPMSM
Colonial Police Service (SAUO)	CPS
Colonial Products Council (SAUO)	CPC
Colonial Products Laboratory (SAUO)	CPL
Colonial Products Laboratory (SAUS)	CPL
Colonial Properties Tr [NYSE symbol] (TTSB)	CLP
Colonial Properties Trust [NYSE symbol] (SPSG)	CLP
Colonial Properties Trust [Associated Press] (SAG)	ColonPT
Colonial Secretary [British] (ADA)	CS
Colonial Service (SAUO)	CS
Colonial Social Sciences Research Committee (SAUO)	CSSRC
Colonial Society of Massachusetts (EA)	CSM
Colonial Society of Pennsylvania (EA)	CSP
Colonial States Athletic Conference (PSS)	CSAC
Colonial Stores, Incorporated (SAUO)	CSI
Colonial Sugar Refining Co. [Australia] (WDAA)	CSR
Colonial Sugar Refining Co. (SAUO)	CSR
Colonial Treasure Hunters Association (EA)	CTHA
Colonial Warriors United (EA)	CWU
Colonial Waterbird Group [Later, CWS] (EA)	CWG
Colonial Waterbird Society (EA)	CWS
Colonial Waterbirds (SAUS)	Colon Waterbirds
Colonial Welfare and Development Fund (SAUO)	CWDF

Colonial Welfare Committee (SAUO)	CWC
Colonial Williamsburg, Inc. (CDAI)	CW
Colonial Williamsburg, Inc., Williamsburg, VA [Library symbol] [Library of Congress] (LCLS)	ViWC
Colonialism and Indigenous Minorities Research and Action [British] (DI)	CIMRA
Colonic Adenomatous Polyp [Medicine] (MELL)	CAP
Colonic Intestinal Metaplasia [Oncology]	CIM
Colonic Polyposis [Medicine] (MELL)	CP
Colonie Interim Storage Site [Department of Energy]	CISS
Colonies per Milliliter [Measurement] (DAVI)	col/ml
Colonist	Col
Colonization (SAUS)	Col
Colonization Factor (DB)	CF
Colonization Factor Antigen [Analytical biochemistry]	CFA
Colonize (SAUS)	col
Colonizing Efficiency Ratio [Forestry]	CER
Colonnade (VRA)	colnd
Colonpouch-anale Anastomose (SAUS)	CPAA
Colon-Rectal Surgery (SAUS)	CRS
Colon-Specific Antigen [Biochemistry] (DAVI)	CSA
Colon-Specific Antigen Protein [Biochemistry] (DAVI)	CSAP
Colony	CLNY
Colony (BEE)	col
Colony	COL
Colony [or Colonies] [Bacteriology] (DAVI)	Col
colony (SAUO)	col
Colony (VRA)	colo
Colony Count and Culture [Bacteriology] (DAVI)	CC & C
Colony Count for Diarrhea [Medicine] (MELL)	CCD
Colony Forming [Cytology]	CF
Colony Forming Unit-Granulocyte [Cytology]	CFU-G
Colony Overlay Test [Microbiology]	COT
Colony Pacific Explorations Ltd. [Toronto Stock Exchange symbol] [Vancouver Stock Exchange symbol]	CYX
Colony-Forming Ability [Microbiology]	CFA
Colony-Forming Assay [Medicine] (MELL)	CFA
Colony-Forming Cell [Cytology]	CFC
Colony-Forming Efficiency [Cytology]	CFE
Colony-Forming Unit [Cytology]	CFU
Colony-Forming Unit - Culture [Cytology]	CFU-C
Colony-Forming Unit - Eosinophil [Cytology]	CFU-Eo
Colony-Forming Unit - Granulocyte-Erythrocyte-Monocyte-Megakaryocyte [Cytology]	CFU-GEMM
Colony-Forming Unit - Megakaryocyte [Cytology] (DAVI)	CFU_{MEG}
Colony-Forming Unit - Single Cell [Cytology]	CFU-S
Colony-Forming Unit - Spleen [Cytology]	CFUS
Colony-Forming Unit Eosinophil [Cytology] (MAE)	CFUeos
Colony-Forming Unit Neutrophil-Monocyte [Cytology] (MAE)	CFUnm
Colony-Forming Unit per Milliliter [Cytology] (DAVI)	CFU_{-mL}
Colony-Forming Unit/Erythroid [Cytology]	CFU-E
Colony-Forming Unit/Granulocyte Macrophage [Cytology]	CFU-GM
Colony-Forming Unit/Lymphoid [Cytology]	CFU-L
Colony-Forming Unit/Megakaryocyte [Cytology]	CFU-M
Colony-Inhibiting Activity (DB)	CIA
Colony-Stimulating Activity [Genetics]	CSA
Colony-Stimulating Factor [Hematology]	CSF
Colony-Stimulating Factor [Medicine] (TAD)	CSF-1
Colophon [Publishing] (WGA)	COLO
Colophon [Printing] (DGA)	COLOPH
Colophon (SAUS)	Coloph
Colophon Society [Australia]	CS
Color	C
Color	CLR
Color (VRA)	clr
Color (WDMC)	col
Color	COL
Color Adjusted Transmission [Optical coating to facilitate use of binoculars in low light] [Steiner-Optik of West Germany]	CAT
Color Allergy Screen Test	CAST
Color and Temperature [Medicine] (MELL)	C & T
Color and Temperature Normal, Both Lower Extremities [Medicine] (STED)	C & TN BLE
Color Appearance Monitoring System [Automotive quality control]	CAMS
Color Association of the United States	CA
Color Association of the United States (EA)	CAUS
Color Blindness, Blue Monocone-Monochromatic Type [Medicine] (DMAA)	CBBM
Color Business Graphics (HGAA)	CBG
Color Calibration System (SAUS)	CCS
Color Center LASER (PDAA)	CCL
Color Changing Unit [Medical technology]	CCU
Color Code [as, for types of wire] [Technical drawings]	CC
Color Compensation [Photography]	CC
Color Computer	COCO
Color Contrast	CC
Color Contrast Value	CCV
Color Correction [Color printing]	CC
Color Data Display	CDD
Color Data System	CDS
Color Depth Enhancement (SAUS)	CODE
Color Detail [Rorschach] [Psychology]	C
Color Developer System [Canon, Inc.]	CD
Color Developing Unit (NITA)	CDU
Color Diaposition Plate	CDP
Color Difference Computer (MUGU)	CODIC
Color Difference Meter	CDM
Color Difference Signal	CDS
Color Display (ROAS)	CD
Color Electronic Prepress System (SAUS)	CEPS
Color Electronic Prepress Systems [Printing technology]	CEPS
Color Enhancement Technology	CET
Color Evaluation Program	CEP
Color Excess [Astronomy]	E
Color Exterior Film (MCD)	CX
Color Filter Array (IAA)	CFA
Color Forming Ability [Food technology]	CFA
Color Frame Buffer (SAUS)	CFB
Color Graphics (MHDI)	CG
Color Graphics Converter [Computer science]	CGC
Color Graphics Indicator (HGAA)	CGI
Color Graphics Interface (SAUS)	CGI
Color Graphics Printer	CGP
Color Graphics Terminal (MCD)	CGT
Color Graphics Workstation	CGW
Color Guild Associates (EA)	CGA
Color Image Assembly [Graphic arts] (DGA)	CIA
Color Image Assembly and Manipulation System [Graphic arts] (DGA)	CIAMS
Color Imaging Systems (GEOI)	CIS
Color Index	C
Color Index	CI
Color Infrared [Image]	CIR
Color Interior Film (MCD)	CI
Color Laser Copier (SAUS)	CLC
Color Layout Programmer (DGA)	CLP
Color Line [Illustration] (DGA)	CL
Color Lithograph (SAUS)	Colograph
Color Look-Up Table [Computer graphics]	CLUT
Color Magnitude Diagrams	CMD
Color Management Method [Computer science] (VERA)	CMM
Color Management Module (SAUS)	CMM
Color Management System [Computer science]	CMS
Color Marketing Group [Washington, DC] (EA)	CMG
Color Mat Processor	CMP
Color Matrix Display (ACAE)	CMD
Color Mixture Curve	CMC
Color Mixture Function	CMF
Color Modulation (SAUS)	c/m
Color Multifunction Display	CMFD
Color Naming System (SAUS)	CNS
Color Orographic Seeding Experiment (SAUS)	COSE
Color Pack Camera	CPC
Color Page [Printing] (DGA)	COL P
Color Perception [Medicine]	CP
Color Phase Alternation	CPA
Color Photographic Association of Canada	CPAC
Color Picture Signal	CPS
Color Picture Tube [Electronics] (EECA)	CPT
Color Pigments Manufacturing Association	CPMA
Color Print [Publishing]	C (Print)
Color Printer (SAUS)	CP
Color Printing [Filter] [Photography]	CP
Color Prints [Not tinted] (VRA)	CLRP
Color Purple Educational Fund Foundation (EA)	CPSF
Color Pyramid Test [Psychology]	CPT
Color Rendering Dictionary (VERA)	CRD
Color Rendition [or Rendering] Index [Measure of Color distortion]	CRI
Color Reproduction Indices (SAUS)	CRI
Color Response [Used in Rorschach tests] (DIPS)	C
Color Response [Psychology] (BARN)	CR
Color Reversal Intermediate [Photography] (NTCM)	CRI
Color Scanner (GEOI)	CS
Color Science Association of Japan (SAUO)	CSAJ
Color Sense (AAMN)	C
Color Separation Overlay	CSO
Color Shaded Relief Map Images (SAUO)	CSRMI
Color Shadow Mask [Type of cathode ray tube] (NITA)	CSM
Color Slow Scan Television (ACAE)	CSSTV
Color Space (SAUS)	YCC
Color Specification	CS
Color Stabilizer (SAUS)	CS
Color Strength [Dye technology]	CS
Color Sync Signal	CSS
Color System Support Group (SAUO)	CSS
Color Television (DEN)	CTV
Color Television Committee (SAUS)	CTC
Color Television Committee (SAUO)	CTC
Color Television Incorporated (SAUO)	CTI
Color Temperature (NTCM)	CT
Color Trace Tube (IAA)	CTT
Color Transparency (WDMC)	C/T
Color Uniformity Recognition Equipment [Quality control]	CURE
Color Unit (MAE)	CU
Color Video Graphics Array (SAUS)	CVGA
Color Video Printer (SAUS)	CVP
Color Video Tape (MCD)	CVT
Color Vision [Ophthalmology]	CV
Color Vision [Ophthalmology]	VC
Color Vision Constant Speed [Physiology] (IAA)	CCS
Color Vision Deviate [Ophthalmology]	CVD

Color Vision Test (SAUS) CV
Color, Warmth, Movement Sensation [Medicine] (DMAA) ...... CWMS
Color Word Test .... CWT
Color You See Is What You Get [Computer science] .... CYSIWIG
Color Your World, Inc. [Toronto Stock Exchange symbol] .... CYW
Colorado [Dark-colored cigar] C
Colorado [Postal code] .... CO
Colorado .... COL
Colorado (AFM) .... COLO
Colorado (ODBW) .... Colo
Colorado [MARC country of publication code] [Library of Congress] (LCCP) ...... cou
Colorado [MARC geographic area code] [Library of Congress] (LCCP) .... n-us-co
Colorado Academy, Englewood, CO [Library symbol] [Library of Congress] (LCLS) .... CoEnCA
Colorado Academy of Family Physicians (SRA) .... CAFP
Colorado Academy of Physician Assistants (SRA) .... CAPA
Colorado Advanced Technology Institute .... CATI
Colorado Advanced Technology Institute .... CATT
Colorado Air National Guard (ACAE) .... COANG
Colorado Allergy and Respiratory Disease Institute (SAUS) .... CARDI
Colorado Alliance of Research Libraries [Denver, CO] [Library network] ..... CARL
[The] Colorado & Southern Railway Co. .... C & S
[The] Colorado & Southern Railway Co. [AAR code] .... CS
Colorado & Southern Railway Co. (SAUS) .... CS
Colorado & Southern Railway Co. (SAUO) CX
Colorado & Southern Railway Company (SAUO) .... C&SRyCo
Colorado & Wyoming Railway Co. (SAUO) .... C&W
[The] Colorado & Wyoming Railway Co. [AAR code] .... CW
Colorado Appeals Reports [A publication] (DLA) .... Col App
Colorado Appellate Reports [A publication] (AAGC) .... Colo App
Colorado Area Research Libraries (AEPA) .... CARL
Colorado Asphalt Pavement Association (SRA) .... CAPA
Colorado Assessors' Association (SRA) .... CAA
Colorado Associated University Press (SAUO) .... Colo Assoc
Colorado Association of Campgrounds, Cabins, and Lodges (SRA) .... CACCL
Colorado Association of Commerce and Industry (SRA) .... CACI
Colorado Association of Community Centered Boards (SRA) .... CACCB
Colorado Association of D.A.R.E. [Drug Abuse Resistance Education] Officers (SRA) .... CADO
Colorado Association of Distributors (SRA) .... CAD
Colorado Association of Home Builders (SRA) .... CAHB
Colorado Association of Homes and Services for the Aging (SRA) .... CAHSA
Colorado Association of Life Underwriters (SRA) .... CALU
Colorado Association of Medical Equipment Services (SRA) .... CAMES
Colorado Association of Mortgage Brokers (SRA) .... CAMB
Colorado Association of Nonprofit Organizations (SRA) .... CANPO
Colorado Association of Public Employees (SRA) .... CAPE
Colorado Association of Realtors (SRA) .... CAR
Colorado Association of Research Libraries (SAUO) .... CAR
Colorado Association of Research Libraries (AUEG) .... CARL
Colorado Association of School Boards (SRA) .... CASB
Colorado Association of School Executives (SRA) .... CASE
Colorado Association of Soil Conservation Districts (SRA) .... CASCD
Colorado Association of Transit Agencies (SRA) .... CASTA
Colorado Association of Wheat Growers (SRA) .... CAWG
Colorado Athletic Conference (PSS) .... COLAC
Colorado Automatic Single Crystal Analysis Diffraction Equipment (SAUS) .... CASCADE
Colorado Automobile Dealers Association (SRA) .... CADA
Colorado Bankers Association (SRA) .... CBA
Colorado Bar Association (SRA) .... CBA
Colorado Basin River Forecast Office (SAUS) .... STR
Colorado Beef Council (SRA) .... CBC
Colorado Casino Resorts [NASDAQ symbol] (TTSB) .... CCRI
Colorado Casino Resorts, Inc. [NASDAQ symbol] (SAG) .... CCRI
Colorado Casino Resorts, Inc. [Associated Press] (SAG) .... ColoCas
Colorado Cattle Feeders Association (SRA) .... CCFA
Colorado Cattlemen's Association (SRA) .... CCA
Colorado Center for Astrodynamics Research [University of Colorado at Boulder] [Research center] (RCD) .... CCAR
Colorado Center for Educational Assistance, Denver, CO [Library symbol] [Library of Congress] (LCLS) .... CoDEA
Colorado Chiropractic Association (SRA) .... CCA
Colorado City, AZ [FM radio station call letters] .... KCCA
Colorado City, TX [FM radio station call letters] .... KAUM
Colorado City, TX [AM radio station call letters] .... KVMC
Colorado College, Colorado Springs, CO [OCLC symbol] (OCLC) .... COC
Colorado College, Colorado Springs, CO [Library symbol] [Library of Congress] (LCLS) .... CoCC
Colorado College, Colorado Springs, CO [Library symbol] [Library of Congress] (LCLS) .... CoCCC
Colorado Committee for Environmental Information (SAUS) .... CCEI
Colorado Community Health Network (SRA) .... CCHN
Colorado Computational Science Fair (SAUS) .... CCSF
Colorado Congress of Foreign Language Teachers (EDAC) .... CCFLT
Colorado Constitution [A publication] (DLA) .... Colo Const
Colorado Contractors Association (SRA) .... CCA
Colorado Cooperative Council (SRA) CCC
Colorado Corn Growers Association (SRA) .... CCGA
Colorado Court of Appeals Reports [A publication] (DLA) .... CO A
Colorado Court of Appeals Reports [A publication] (DLA) .... Colo App
Colorado Court Reporters Association (SRA) .... CCRA
Colorado Credit Union League (SRA) .... CCUL
Colorado Creek, AK [Location identifier] [FAA] (FAAL) .... KCR
Colorado Decisions [A publication] (DLA) .... Colo Dec

Colorado Decisions, Federal [A publication] (DLA) .... Colo Dec Fed
Colorado Decisions Supplement [A publication] (DLA) .... Colo Dec Supp
Colorado Dental Association (SRA) .... CDA
Colorado Department of Agriculture (GEOI) .... CDA
Colorado Department of Education (EDAC) .... CDE
Colorado Department of Education, Resource Center, Denver, CO [Library symbol] [Library of Congress] (LCLS) .... CoDDE
Colorado Department of Forestry (SAUS) .... CDF
Colorado Department of Health (SAUS) .... CDH
Colorado Department of Public Health and Environment (COE) .... CDPH&E
Colorado Department of Public Health and Environment (DOGT) .... CDPHE
Colorado Division of Planning (GEOI) .... CDP
Colorado Division of State Archives, Denver, CO [Library symbol] [Library of Congress] (LCLS) .... CoDAr
Colorado Division of Wildlife (GEOI) .... CDOW
Colorado Division of Wildlife (journ.) (SAUS) .... TPCWDL
Colorado Dude/Guest Ranch Association (SRA) .... CDGRA
Colorado Education Association (SRA) .... CEA
Colorado Educational Interest Indicator [Whetstone and Taylor] (TES) .... CEII
Colorado Educational Media Association .... CEMA
Colorado Electronic Community College .... CECC
Colorado Energy and Minerals (SAUO) .... CEM
Colorado Energy Research Institute (SAUO) .... CERI
Colorado Engineering Laboratories (ACAE) .... CEL
Colorado Forestry and Horticulture Association (SAUO) .... CFHA
Colorado Foundation for Medical Care (SAUO) .... CFMC
Colorado Foundation for Research in Tuberculosis (SAUO) .... CFRT
Colorado Front Range (SAUS) .... CFR
Colorado Fuel & Iron (SAUS) .... CF
Colorado Fuel & Iron Co. (SAUO) .... CF&I
Colorado Fuel & Iron Co., Pueblo, CO [Library symbol] [Library of Congress] (LCLS) .... CoPC
Colorado Fuel & Iron Corp. (SAUO) .... CF
Colorado Genealogical Society (EA) .... CGS
Colorado General Hospital, Residents' Library, Denver, CO [Library symbol] [Library of Congress] (LCLS) .... CoDGH
Colorado Geological Survey (SAUO) .... CGS
Colorado Grain and Feed Association (SRA) .... CGFA
Colorado Greenhouse Growers Association (SRA) .... CGGA
Colorado Health Care Association (SRA) .... CHCA
Colorado High School Coaches Association (SRA) .... CHSCA
Colorado Hospital Association (SRA) .... CHA
Colorado Hotel and Lodging Association (SRA) .... CH&LA
Colorado Human Resource Association (SRA) .... CHRA
Colorado Industrial Commission Report [A publication] (DLA) .... Colo IC
Colorado Institute for Conflict Resolution and Creative Leadership (SAUO) .... CICRCL
Colorado Institute for Research in Biotechnology (HGEN) .... CIRB
Colorado Law Reporter [A publication] (DLA) .... Col Law Rep
Colorado Law Reporter [A publication] (DLA) .... Col L Rep
Colorado Law Reporter [A publication] (DLA) .... Colo LR
Colorado Law Reporter [A publication] (DLA) .... Colo L Rep
Colorado libraries electronic system (SAUO) .... MARMOT
Colorado Library Association .... CLA
Colorado Library Network [Colorado State Library] [Denver, CO] [Library network] .... COLONET
Colorado Medtech [NASDAQ symbol] (TTSB) .... CMED
Colorado MEDtech, Inc. [NASDAQ symbol] (SAG) .... CMED
Colorado MEDtech, Inc. [Associated Press] (SAG) .... ColoMED
Colorado Midland .... CM
Colorado Migrant Education Resource Center (EDAC) .... CoMERC
Colorado Mining Association (EA) .... CMA
Colorado Motor Carriers' Association, Denver CO [STAC] .... COA
Colorado Motor Tariff Bureau, Inc., Denver CO [STAC] .... COB
Colorado Mountain College, Eastern Campus, Leadville, CO [Library symbol] [Library of Congress] (LCLS) .... CoLeC
Colorado Mountain College, Western Campus, Glenwood Springs, CO [Library symbol] [Library of Congress] (LCLS) .... CoGsC
Colorado National Guard (SAUO) .... ColoNG
Colorado National Monument (SAUS) .... CNM
Colorado National Monument .... COLM
Colorado Natural Areas Inventory [Colorado State Department of Natural Resources] [Denver] [Information service or system] (IID) .... CNAI
Colorado Natural Areas Program [Colorado State Department of Natural Resources] [Information service or system] (IID) .... CNAP
Colorado Nisi Prius Decisions [A publication] (DLA) .... Col NP
Colorado Nisi Prius Decisions [A publication] (DLA) .... Colo NP Dec
Colorado Northwestern Community College, Rangely, CO [Library symbol] [Library of Congress] (LCLS) .... CoRaC
Colorado Nursery Association (SRA) .... CNA
Colorado Nurses Association (SRA) .... CNA
Colorado Optometric Association (SRA) .... COA
Colorado Outfitters Association (SRA) .... COA
Colorado Plateau Field Station (GEOI) .... CPFS
Colorado Plateau-Land Use History Northern Arizona (SAUS) .... CP-LUHNA
Colorado Podiatric Medical Association (SRA) .... CPMA
Colorado Potato Beetle .... CPB
Colorado Potato Beetle Spiroplasma [Insect pathogen] .... CPBS
Colorado Professional Electronics Association (SAUO) .... CPEA
Colorado Psychiatric Hospital, Residents' Library, Denver, CO [Library symbol] [Library of Congress] (LCLS) .... CoDPH
Colorado Psychiatric Society (SRA) .... CPS
Colorado Public Utilities Commission Decisions [A publication] (DLA) .... Colo PUC

Colorado Public Utilities Commission Report [*A publication*] (DLA) ... Colo PUC Rep
Colorado Ranger Horse Association (EA) ... CRHA
Colorado Register [*A publication*] (AAGC) ... CR
Colorado Reports [*A publication*] (DLA) ... CO
Colorado Reports [*A publication*] (DLA) ... Col
Colorado Reports [*A publication*] (DLA) ... Colo
Colorado Reports [*A publication*] (DLA) ... Col Rep
Colorado Research Corp. (AAG) ... CRC
Colorado Resources Development Council (SAUO) ... CRDC
Colorado Revised Statutes [*A publication*] (DLA) ... Col Rev Stat
Colorado Revised Statutes Annotated [*West*] [*A publication*] (AAGC) ... Colo Rev Stat Ann
Colorado River Aqueduct (SAUS) ... CRA
Colorado River Association (EA) ... CRA
Colorado River Authority (SAUS) ... CRA
Colorado River Basin Project ... CRBP
Colorado River Board of California, Los Angeles, CA [*Library symbol*] [*Library of Congress*] (LCLS) ... CLCol
Colorado River Dam Fund [*Department of the Interior*] (GFGA) ... CRDF
Colorado River Ecology Alliance (SAUO) ... CREA
Colorado River Indian Tribes Public Library, Parker, AZ [*Library symbol*] [*Library of Congress*] (LCLS) ... AzPa
Colorado River Municipal Water District ... CRMWD
Colorado River Storage Project [*Department of the Interior*] ... CRSP
Colorado Rudimentary Operating Nucleus for Intelligent Controllers (SAUS) ... CRONIC
Colorado School for the Deaf and Blind, Colorado Springs, CO [*Library symbol*] [*Library of Congress*] (LCLS) ... CoCD
Colorado School of Mines (GAGS) ... Colo Sch Mines
Colorado School of Mines [*Golden, CO*] ... CSM
Colorado School of Mines, Golden, CO [*Library symbol*] [*Library of Congress*] (LCLS) ... CoG
Colorado School of Mines, Golden, CO [*OCLC symbol*] (OCLC) ... COP
Colorado School of Mines Research Institute (SAUS) ... CSMRI
Colorado Scientific Society (SAUO) ... CSS
Colorado Society of Certified Public Accountants (SRA) ... CSCPA
Colorado Society of Engineers (SAUO) ... CSE
Colorado Society of Osteopathic Medicine (SRA) ... CSOM
Colorado Speech-Language-Hearing Association (SRA) ... CSHA
Colorado Spg-Peterson Field (SAUO) ... COS
Colorado Springs [*Colorado*] [*Airport symbol*] (OAG) ... COS
Colorado Springs, CO [*Location identifier*] [*FAA*] (FAAL) ... AFF
Colorado Springs, CO [*Location identifier*] [*FAA*] (FAAL) ... COS
Colorado Springs, CO [*AM radio station call letters*] ... KCMN
Colorado Springs, CO [*FM radio station call letters*] ... KEPC
Colorado Springs, CO [*FM radio station call letters*] ... KILO
Colorado Springs, CO [*AM radio station call letters*] ... KKCS
Colorado Springs, CO [*FM radio station call letters*] ... KKCS-FM
Colorado Springs, CO [*FM radio station call letters*] ... KKFM
Colorado Springs, CO [*Television station call letters*] ... KKTV
Colorado Springs, CO [*FM radio station call letters*] ... KRCC
Colorado Springs, CO [*AM radio station call letters*] ... KRDO
Colorado Springs, CO [*FM radio station call letters*] ... KRDO-FM
Colorado Springs, CO [*Television station call letters*] ... KRDO-TV
Colorado Springs, CO [*FM radio station call letters*] ... KSPZ
Colorado Springs, CO [*FM radio station call letters*] ... KTLF
Colorado Springs, CO [*AM radio station call letters*] ... KTWK
Colorado Springs, CO [*AM radio station call letters*] ... KVOR
Colorado Springs, CO [*AM radio station call letters*] ... KWYD
Colorado Springs, CO [*Television station call letters*] ... KXRM
Colorado Springs, CO [*Location identifier*] [*FAA*] (FAAL) ... LPI
Colorado Springs, CO [*Location identifier*] [*FAA*] (FAAL) ... SFC
Colorado Springs Fine Arts Center (SAUS) ... CSFAC
Colorado Springs Fine Arts Center, Fine Arts and Anthropology of the Southwest, Library, Colorado Springs, CO [*Library symbol*] [*Library of Congress*] (LCLS) ... CoCF
Colorado Springs Maintenance and Operations System [*Space Defense Center*] ... COSMOS
Colorado Springs Mineralogical Society ... CSMS
Colorado Springs/Peterson Field [*Colorado*] [*ICAO location identifier*] (ICLI) ... KCOS
Colorado State (SAUS) ... CSL
Colorado State Bar Association Report [*A publication*] (DLA) ... Colo St BA
Colorado State College [*Later, University of Northern Colorado*] ... CSC
Colorado State Department of Highways, Denver, CO [*Library symbol*] [*Library of Congress*] (LCLS) ... CoDCDH
Colorado State Department of Social Services, Denver, CO [*Library symbol*] [*Library of Congress*] (LCLS) ... CoDSS
Colorado State Forest Service (GEOI) ... CSFS
Colorado State Historical Society, Denver, CO [*Library symbol*] [*Library of Congress*] (LCLS) ... CoHi
Colorado State Home and Training School, Grand Junction, CO [*Library symbol*] [*Library of Congress*] (LCLS) ... CoGjT
Colorado State Home and Training School, Medical Library, Wheatridge, CO [*Library symbol*] [*Library of Congress*] (LCLS) ... CoWeT-M
Colorado State Home and Training School, Residents' Library, Pueblo, CO [*Library symbol*] [*Library of Congress*] (LCLS) ... CoPT
Colorado State Home and Training School, Staff Library, Grand Junction, CO [*Library symbol*] [*Library of Congress*] (LCLS) ... CoGjTS
Colorado State Home and Training School, Staff Library, Pueblo, CO [*Library symbol*] [*Library of Congress*] (LCLS) ... CoPTS
Colorado State Home and Training School, Wheatridge, CO [*Library symbol*] [*Library of Congress*] (LCLS) ... CoWeT
Colorado State Home for the Aged, Trinidad, CO [*Library symbol*] [*Library of Congress*] (LCLS) ... CoTA
Colorado State Hospital, Children's Center, Pueblo, CO [*Library symbol*] [*Library of Congress*] (LCLS) ... CoPCS-C
Colorado State Hospital, Hospital Community Library, Pueblo, CO [*Library symbol*] [*Library of Congress*] (LCLS) ... CoPCS
Colorado State Hospital, Professional Library, Pueblo, CO [*Library symbol*] [*Library of Congress*] (LCLS) ... CoPCS-M
Colorado State Library, Denver, CO [*Library symbol*] [*Library of Congress*] (LCLS) ... Co
Colorado State Library, Denver, CO [*OCLC symbol*] (OCLC) ... COZ
Colorado State Library for the Blind and Physically Handicapped, Denver, CO [*Library symbol*] [*Library of Congress*] (LCLS) ... Co-B
Colorado State Library, Western Slope Clearinghouse, Grand Junction, CO [*Library symbol*] [*Library of Congress*] (LCLS) ... CoGjW
Colorado State Medical Society (SAUO) ... CSMS
Colorado State Penitentiary, Canon City, CO [*Library symbol*] [*Library of Congress*] (LCLS) ... CoCcP
Colorado State Penitentiary, Colorado Women's Correctional Institution, Law Library, Canon City, CO [*Library symbol*] [*Library of Congress*] (LCLS) ... CoCcPWL
Colorado State Penitentiary, Colorado Women's Correctional Institution, Residents' Library, Canon City, CO [*Library symbol*] [*Library of Congress*] (LCLS) ... CoCcPW
Colorado State Penitentiary, Colorado Women's Correctional Institution, Staff Library, Canon City, CO [*Library symbol*] [*Library of Congress*] (LCLS) ... CoCcPWS
Colorado State Penitentiary, Law Library, Canon City, CO [*Library symbol*] [*Library of Congress*] (LCLS) ... CoCcPL
Colorado State Penitentiary, Medium Security Law Library, Canon City, CO [*Library symbol*] [*Library of Congress*] (LCLS) ... CoCcPML
Colorado State Penitentiary, Medium Security Residents' Library, Canon City, CO [*Library symbol*] [*Library of Congress*] (LCLS) ... CoCcPM
Colorado State Penitentiary, Medium Security Staff Library, Canon City, CO [*Library symbol*] [*Library of Congress*] (LCLS) ... CoCcPMS
Colorado State Penitentiary, Staff Library, Canon City, CO [*Library symbol*] [*Library of Congress*] (LCLS) ... CoCcPS
Colorado State Publications Depository and Distribution Center, Denver, CO [*OCLC symbol*] (OCLC) ... DDB
Colorado State Reformatory, Buena Vista, CO [*Library symbol*] [*Library of Congress*] (LCLS) ... CoBueR
Colorado State Reformatory, Law Library, Buena Vista, CO [*Library symbol*] [*Library of Congress*] (LCLS) ... CoBueRL
Colorado State Reformatory, Staff Library, Buena Vista, CO [*Library symbol*] [*Library of Congress*] (LCLS) ... CoBueRS
Colorado State University (GAGS) ... Colo St U
Colorado State University [*Fort Collins*] ... CSU
Colorado State University Dual Doppler Radar (SAUO) ... CSU-CHILL
Colorado State University. Experiment Station. Progress Report (journ.) (SAUS) ... Prog Rep Exp Stn Colorado State Univ
Colorado State University, Fort Collins, CO [*OCLC symbol*] (OCLC) ... COF
Colorado State University, Fort Collins, CO [*Library symbol*] [*Library of Congress*] (LCLS) ... CoFS
Colorado State University Research Foundation [*Research center*] (RCD) ... CSURF
Colorado State Veterans Center, Homelake, CO [*Library symbol*] [*Library of Congress*] (LCLS) ... CoHlV
Colorado State Veterans Nursing Home, Florence, CO [*Library symbol*] [*Library of Congress*] (LCLS) ... CoFloV
Colorado Student Assessment Program ... CSAP
Colorado Supreme Court, Denver, CO [*Library symbol*] [*Library of Congress*] (LCLS) ... Co-SC
Colorado Supreme Court Library, Denver, CO [*OCLC symbol*] (OCLC) ... DVJ
Colorado Technical Reference Center [*University of Colorado - Boulder*] [*Information service or system*] (IID) ... CTRC
Colorado Tick Fever [*Hematology*] (DAVI) ... CTF
Colorado Tick Fever Virus (MELL) ... CTFV
Colorado Tick fever Virus (SAUS) ... CTV
Colorado Tracking Station (ACAE) ... CTS
Colorado Union Catalog, Denver Public Library, Denver, CO [*OCLC symbol*] (OCLC) ... CLF
Colorado University (PDAA) ... CU
Colorado University Long Term Ecological Research (SAUO) ... CULTER
Colorado Video, Inc. ... CVI
Colorado Water Data Bank System (SAUS) ... CWDBS
Colorado Weights and Measures Laboratory [*National Institute of Standards and Technology*] ... CWML
Colorado Women's College [*Formerly, Temple Buell College*] ... CWC
Colorado Women's College, Denver, CO [*Library symbol*] [*Library of Congress*] (LCLS) ... CoDCW
Colorado Youth Center, Denver, CO [*Library symbol*] [*Library of Congress*] (LCLS) ... CoDYC
Colorado-Amudarya Rivers Project (SAUS) ... CARP
Colorado-Claro [*Medium-colored cigar*] ... CC
Colorado-Maduro [*Very dark-colored cigar*] ... CM
Colorado-Utah-Wyoming Committee, Chicago IL [*STAC*] ... CUW
Colorant Mixer Computer (SAUS) ... COMIC
Colorant Mixture Computer [*Du Pont trademark*] ... COMIC
Coloratura ... col
Color-Control Unit (SAUS) ... CCU
Colorectal Cancer [*Oncology*] (DAVI) ... CRC
Colorectal Carcinoma [*Oncology*] ... CRC
Colorectal Surgery [*Medicine*] (MELL) ... CRS
Colo-Rectal Surgical Society ... CRSS
Colored (SAUS) ... C

Colored .... CLD
Colored .... COL
Colored (ROG) .... COLD
Colored Digital Panel Meter (EECA) .... CDPM
Colored Electronic Attitude Director Indicator (MCD) .... CEADI
Colored Female .... C-F
Colored Methodist Episcopal Church (IIA) .... CME
Colored Movie Software produced by Brigham Young University (SAUO) .... MOVIEBYU
Colored People's Time [*Slang*] .... CPT
Colored Plate [*Printing*] (DGA) .... COL PL
Colored-Bordered [*Paper*] (DGA) .... CB
Coloretur [*Let It Be Colored*] [*Pharmacy*] (ROG) .... COLOR
Color-Forming Units [*Biochemistry*] (DAVI) .... CFU
Color/Graphics Adapter [*Computer technology*] .... CGA
coloriert (SAUS) .... col
Colorimetric Solution .... CS
Colorimetry [*Biochemistry*] (MAE) .... color
Coloring Book .... clrb
colorless (SAUS) c
Colorless [*Laboratory*] (DAVI) .... coll
Color-Resolution Enhancement Technology (VERA) .... CRET
Colortech Corp. [*Toronto Stock Exchange symbol*] .... CLR
Color-to-Color Register [*Graphic arts*] (DGA) .... CCR
Color-Word Interference Test .... CWIT
Colossal .... CLSSL
Colossal .... Col
Colossal Energy, Inc. [*Vancouver Stock Exchange symbol*] .... COY
Colossal Magnetoresistance [*Physics*] .... CMR
Colossal Resources [*NASDAQ symbol*] (TTSB) .... CLPZF
Colosseum [*Record label*] .... Csm
Colosseum of Motion Picture Salesmen (EA) .... CMPS
Colossians [*New Testament book*] .... Col
Colossians [*New Testament book*] (ROG) .... COLOSS
Colossus Resources [*Vancouver Stock Exchange symbol*] .... CZK
Colostomy and Ileostomy Association [*Medicine*] .... CIA
Colostomy Welfare Group [*British*] .... CWG
Colostrum-Free Bovine Serum .... CFBS
Colour (SAUS) .... Clr
Colour (SAUS) .... Col
Colour Additive Viewing In Agriculture (SAUS) .... CAVIA
Colour Cathode Ray Tube (SAUS) .... CCRT
Colour Code (SAUS) CC
Colour Compact (SAUS) CC
Colour Compensation (SAUS) CC
Colour Correction (SAUS) CC
Colour External (SAUS) .... CEX
Colour Film Recorder (SAUS) .... CFR
Colour Filter Array (SAUS) .... CFA
Colour Framing (SAUS) .... CF
Colour Graphics Printer (SAUS) .... CGP
Colour Image Processor [*Computer science*] (NITA) .... CIP
Colour Image Recorder (SAUS) .... CIR
Colour Index [*Used in the dye industry*] (DAVI) CI
Colour Internal (SAUS) .... CIN
Colour Killer (SAUS) .... CK
Colour Mobile Control Room (SAUS) .... CMCR
Colour Mobile Video Tape Recorder (SAUS) .... CMVTR
Colour Modulation (SAUS) .... CM
Colour Picture Signal (SAUS) .... CPS
Colour Preference Index (SAUS) .... CPI
Colour Printed Pottery Collectors Association (EA) .... CPPCA
Colour Pyramid Technics (SAUS) .... CPT
Colour Rendering (SAUS) .... CR
Colour Rendering Capacity (SAUS) .... CRC
Colour Rendering Index (SAUS) .... CRI
Colour Sergeant (SAUS) .... Col-Sgt
Colour Specification (SAUS) .... CS
Colour Stabilizer (SAUS) .... CS
Colour Sub Carrier [*Telecommunications*] (NITA) .... CSC
Colour Subcarrier (SAUS) .... CSC
Colour Synchronization Signal (SAUS) .... CSS
Colour Tactical Display (SAUS) .... CTD
Colour Television (SAUS) .... CTV
Colour Television Monitor (SAUS) .... CTVM
Colour Trace Tube (SAUS) .... CTT
Colour Users' Association [*British*] (BI) .... CUA
Colour Vision Deviant (SAUS) .... CVD
Colour Word Test (SAUS) .... CWT
Coloured (SAUS) .... Cld
Coloured Dissolved Organic Matter (SAUS) .... CDOM
Coloured Progressive Matrices .... CPM
Coloured Workers' Welfare Association [*British*] (BI) .... CWWA
Colour-Graphic Monitor (SAUS) .... CGM
Colouring (SAUS) .... COL
Colour/Monochrome Attributes Controller (SAUS) .... CMAC
Colour-Sergeant [*Army*] [*British*] .... COL-SERGT
Colour-Sergeant [*Army*] [*British*] (DMA) .... Col-Sgt
Colour-Sergeant [*Army*] [*British*] (DMA) .... C/Sgt
Colour-Word Interference Test (SAUS) .... CWIT
Colpocystourethropexy [*Medicine*] .... CCUP
Colposcopy [*Gynecology*] (DAVI) .... colpo
Colquechaca [*Bolivia*] [*ICAO location identifier*] (ICLI) .... SLHT
Colquhoun on Roman Civil Law [*A publication*] (DLA) .... Colq Civ Law
Colquhoun on Roman Civil Law [*A publication*] (DLA) .... Colq CL
Colquhoun on Roman Civil Law [*A publication*] (DLA) .... Colq Rom Civ Law
Colquhoun on Roman Civil Law [*A publication*] (DLA) .... Colq Rom Law
Colquhoun on the Judicature Acts [*A publication*] (DLA) .... Colq Jud A
Colquit's Reports [*1 Modern*] [*England*] [*A publication*] (DLA) .... Colq
Colquit's Reports [*1 Modern*] [*England*] [*A publication*] (DLA) .... Colquit
Colquitt-Thomas Regional Library, Moultrie, GA [*Library symbol*] [*Library of Congress*] (LCLS) .... GMoC
Colray Resources, Inc. [*Toronto Stock Exchange symbol*] .... CJR
Colson Canyon [*California*] [*Seismograph station code, US Geological Survey*] (SEIS) .... BCC
Colstrip Bicentennial Library, Colstrip, MT [*Library symbol*] [*Library of Congress*] (LCLS) .... MtCol
Colt [*Thoroughbred racing*] C
Colt Automatic Pistol Hammerless (DICI) .... CAPH
Colt Car Co. [*British*] [*ICAO designator*] (FAAC) .... CEA
COLT Computer Unit (SAUS) .... CCU
Colt Industries, Inc. (SAUO) .... COT
COLT Measurement Unit (SAUS) .... CMU
COLT Telecom Group ADS [*NASDAQ symbol*] (SG) .... COLT
Coltec Industries, Inc. [*Associated Press*] (SAG) .... Coltec
Coltec Industries, Inc. [*NYSE symbol*] (SPSG) .... COT
Coltishall [*British*] [*ICAO location identifier*] (ICLI) .... EGYC
Coltman's Registration Appeal Cases [*1879-85*] [*England*] [*A publication*] (ILCA) .... Colt
Coltman's Registration Appeal Cases [*1879-85*] [*England*] [*A publication*] (DLA) .... Coltm
Coltman's Registration Appeal Cases [*1879-85*] [*England*] [*A publication*] (DLA) .... Colt (Reg Ca)
Coltman's Registration Appeal Cases [*1879-85*] [*England*] [*A publication*] (DLA) .... Colt Reg Cas
Colton High School, Colton, OR [*Library symbol*] [*Library of Congress*] (LCLS) .... OrColHS
Colton Public Library, Colton, CA [*Library symbol*] [*Library of Congress*] (LCLS) .... CCol
Colts Neck, NJ [*Location identifier*] [*FAA*] (FAAL) .... COL
Columba [*Constellation*] .... Col
Columba [*Constellation*] .... Colm
Columba House Fund [*Later, CIM*] (EA) .... CHF
Columbia [*Record Label*] [*Great Britain, Europe, Australia, etc.*] C
Columbia [*South Carolina*] [*Airport symbol*] .... CAE
Columbia [*Italy*] [*ICAO designator*] (FAAC) .... CLA
Columbia (SAUO) .... Col
Columbia (ROG) .... COLUM
Columbia (ROG) .... COLUMB
Columbia [*Missouri*] [*Airport symbol*] (OAG) .... COU
Columbia [*South Carolina*] [*Seismograph station code, US Geological Survey*] [*Closed*] (SEIS) .... CSC
Columbia Airlines Ltd. [*Canada*] [*ICAO designator*] (FAAC) .... COL
Columbia & Cowlitz Railway Co. [*AAR code*] CLC
Columbia & Cowlitz Railway Company (SAUO) CLC
Columbia & Millstadt R. R. [*AAR code*] .... COML
Columbia Appletalk Package (SAUS) .... CAP
Columbia Artists Management, Inc. .... CAMI
Columbia Astrophysics Laboratory (ACAE) .... CAL
Columbia Bancorp [*NASDAQ symbol*] (SAG) .... CBMD
Columbia Bancorp [*Associated Press*] (SAG) .... ColumBc
Columbia Banking System [*NASDAQ symbol*] (TTSB) .... COLB
Columbia Banking Systems [*NASDAQ symbol*] (SAG) .... COLB
Columbia Banking Systems [*Associated Press*] (SAG) .... ColBnk
Columbia Basin Agricultural Research Center [*Oregon State University*] [*Research center*] (RCD) .... CBARC
Columbia Basin College, Pasco, WA [*Library symbol*] [*Library of Congress*] (LCLS) .... WaPaC
Columbia Basin Collegesso (SAUS) .... WaPaC
Columbia Basin Inter-Agency Committee [*Department of Commerce*] (NOAA) .... CBIAC
Columbia Bible College [*South Carolina*] .... CBC
Columbia Bible College (SAUS) .... SBI
Columbia Bible College (SAUS) .... ScCoB
Columbia Bible College, Clearbrook, British Columbia [*Library symbol*] [*National Library of Canada*] (BIB) .... BCCB
Columbia Bible College, Columbia, SC [*OCLC symbol*] (OCLC) .... SBI
Columbia Bible College, Columbia, SC [*Library symbol*] [*Library of Congress*] (LCLS) .... ScCoB
Columbia Bible College, Columbia, SC [*Library symbol*] [*Library of Congress*] (LCLS) .... ScCoBC
Columbia Broadcasting Corporation (SAUO) .... CBC
Columbia Broadcasting System [*Later, CBS, Inc.*] .... CBS
Columbia Broadcasting System, Inc., New York, NY [*Library symbol*] [*Library of Congress*] (LCLS) .... NNCBS
Columbia, CA [*Location identifier*] [*FAA*] (FAAL) .... CUF
Columbia, CA [*FM radio station call letters*] (RBYB) .... KTDO
Columbia Carbon Co. (SAUO) .... CBN
Columbia Carbon Company (SAUS) .... CBN
Columbia Cellulose [*Company*] [*Canada*] .... COLCEL
Columbia Christian College, Portland, OR [*Library symbol*] [*Library of Congress*] (LCLS) .... OrPCol
Columbia City, IN [*FM radio station call letters*] .... WDJB
Columbia City, IN [*FM radio station call letters*] .... WJHS
Columbia City, IN [*FM radio station call letters*] (BROA) .... WSHI-FM
Columbia College (SAUS) .... ScCoC
Columbia College, Chicago, IL [*Inactive*] [*OCLC symbol*] (OCLC) .... IBZ
Columbia College, Chicago, IL [*Library symbol*] [*Library of Congress*] (LCLS) ICCC

Columbia College, Columbia, SC [*Library symbol*] [*Library of Congress*] (LCLS) ScCoC
Columbia College Library, Columbia, CA [*OCLC symbol*] (OCLC) CCY
Columbia Computing Services Ltd. [*Toronto Stock Exchange symbol*] CUP
Columbia County Historical Library, Valatie, NY [*Library symbol*] [*Library of Congress*] (LCLS) NValHi
Columbia County Historical Society, Bloomsburg, PA [*Library symbol*] [*Library of Congress*] (LCLS) PBbCHi
Columbia County, New York Official Historian, Hudson, NY [*Library symbol*] [*Library of Congress*] (LCLS) NHudHi
Columbia District Hospital, Medical Library, St. Helens, OR [*Library symbol*] [*Library of Congress*] (LCLS) OrSthDH
Columbia Encyclopedia (SAUS) Col Ency
Columbia Encylopedia [*A publication*] CE
Columbia Energy Group [*NYSE symbol*] (SG) CG
Columbia Falls, MT [*FM radio station call letters*] KCWX
Columbia Falls, MT [*FM radio station call letters*] (BROA) KKMT-FM
Columbia First Federal Savings & Loan Association (MHDW) COAS
Columbia Football Association (PSS) COLFA
Columbia Gas Service Corporation (SAUO) CGSC
Columbia Gas System [*NYSE symbol*] (TTSB) CG
Columbia Gas System, Inc. [*NYSE symbol*] [*Toronto Stock Exchange symbol*] (SPSG) CG
Columbia Gas System Service Corp. [*of Columbia Gas System, Inc.*] CGSSC
Columbia Gay and Lesbian Alliance (EA) CGLA
Columbia Growth [*Mutual fund ticker symbol*] (SG) CLMBX
Columbia Gulf Transmission Co., Houston, TX [*Library symbol*] [*Library of Congress*] (LCLS) TxHCG
Columbia HCA Healthcare Corp. [*NYSE symbol*] (SAG) COL
Columbia HCA Healthcare Corp. [*Formerly, Columbia Healthcare*] [*Associated Press*] (SAG) ColHCA
Columbia Healthcare [*NYSE symbol*] (SPSG) COL
Columbia Helicopters, Inc. [*ICAO designator*] (FAAC) WCO
Columbia Historical Society [*Later, HSWDC*] (EA) CHS
Columbia Historical Society, Washington, DC [*Library symbol*] [*Library of Congress*] (LCLS) DCHi
Columbia Homogeneous Parallel Processor (SAUS) CHoPP
Columbia Homogenous Parallel Processor CHOPP
Columbia Hospital School of Nursing, Milwaukee, WI [*Library symbol*] [*Library of Congress*] (LCLS) WMCH
Columbia, IL [*FM radio station call letters*] (BROA) KMJM-FM
Columbia, IL [*FM radio station call letters*] WCBW
Columbia International Affairs Online [*Computer science*] Ciao
Columbia Journal of International Affairs [*A publication*] (DLA) Colum J Int'l Aff
Columbia Journalism Review [*A publication*] [*Columbia University*] [*New York, NY*] (WDMC) CJR
Columbia Junior College, Columbia, CA [*Library symbol*] [*Library of Congress*] (LCLS) CColumC
Columbia Jurist [*A publication*] (DLA) Colum Jr
Columbia Jurist [*A publication*] (DLA) Colum Jur
Columbia, KY [*AM radio station call letters*] WAIN
Columbia, KY [*FM radio station call letters*] WAIN-FM
Columbia, LA [*Television station call letters*] (BROA) KAQY
Columbia, LA [*AM radio station call letters*] KCTO
Columbia, LA [*FM radio station call letters*] KCTO-FM
Columbia Laboratories [*AMEX symbol*] (TTSB) COB
Columbia Laboratories, Inc. [*AMEX symbol*] (SPSG) COB
Columbia Laboratories, Inc. [*Associated Press*] (SAG) COILB
Columbia Law Review [*A publication*] (BRI) CLR
Columbia Law Review [*A publication*] (ILCA) Col Law Rev
Columbia Law Review [*A publication*] Col LR
Columbia Law Times [*A publication*] (DLA) Colum LT
Columbia Leisure [*Vancouver Stock Exchange symbol*] COF
Columbia Lesbian, Bisexual and Gay Coalition (EA) LBGC
Columbia Libraries Information Online (SAUS) CLIO
Columbia Mental Maturity Scale [*Psychology*] CMMS
Columbia Mental Maturity Test [*Psychology*] (DAVI) CMMT
Columbia, MO [*Location identifier*] [*FAA*] (FAAL) CBI
Columbia, MO [*Location identifier*] [*FAA*] (FAAL) COU
Columbia, MO [*FM radio station call letters*] KBIA
Columbia, MO [*FM radio station call letters*] KCMQ
Columbia, MO [*FM radio station call letters*] KCOU
Columbia, MO [*FM radio station call letters*] KFMZ
Columbia, MO [*AM radio station call letters*] KFRU
Columbia, MO [*Television station call letters*] KMIZ
Columbia, MO [*Television station call letters*] KOMU
Columbia, MO [*FM radio station call letters*] KOPN
Columbia, MO [*FM radio station call letters*] KOQL
Columbia, MO [*FM radio station call letters*] (RBYB) KPLA
Columbia, MO [*AM radio station call letters*] KTGR
Columbia, MO [*FM radio station call letters*] KWWC
Columbia, MS [*Location identifier*] [*FAA*] (FAAL) FOH
Columbia, MS [*AM radio station call letters*] WCJU
Columbia, MS [*AM radio station call letters*] WFFF
Columbia, MS [*FM radio station call letters*] WFFF-FM
Columbia National Fisheries Research Laboratory [*Later, NFCRC*] [*Department of the Interior*] [*Columbia, MO*] (GRD) CNFRL
Columbia National Fisheries Research Laboratory, Columbia, MO [*OCLC symbol*] (OCLC) FZX
Columbia National Wildlife Refuge (SAUS) CNWR
Columbia, NC [*FM radio station call letters*] WRSF
Columbia, NC [*Television station call letters*] WUND
Columbia, Newberry & Laurens Railroad Co. [*AAR code*] CNL
Columbia, PA [*AM radio station call letters*] WNZT
Columbia, PA [*AM radio station call letters*] (BROA) WVZN-AM
Columbia Pictures Industries (SAUO) CPS
Columbia Public Library, Columbia, IL [*Library symbol*] [*Library of Congress*] (LCLS) IColu
Columbia Radiation Laboratory (SAUO) CRL
Columbia Region Association of Governments (GEOI) CRAG
Columbia Research and Development Corp. (MCD) CRDC
Columbia River and Tributaries Study (NOAA) CR & T
Columbia River Basalt Group [*Geology*] CRBG
Columbia River Basalts [*Geology*] CRB
Columbia River Basin Treaty (NOAA) CRBT
Columbia River Comprehensive Impact Assessment (ABAC) CRCIA
Columbia River Conservation League (EA) CRCL
Columbia River Datum CRD
Columbia River Estuary Data Development Program (SAUO) CREDDP
Columbia River Fisheries Development Program CRFDP
Columbia River Gorge National Scenic Area Act (COE) CRGNSA
Columbia River Maritime Museum, Astoria, OR [*Library symbol*] [*Library of Congress*] (LCLS) OrAstM
Columbia River Operational Hydromet Management System (NOAA) CROHMS
Columbia River Salmon and Tuna Packers Association (EA) CRSTPA
Columbia, SC [*Location identifier*] [*FAA*] (FAAL) CUB
Columbia, SC [*Location identifier*] [*FAA*] (FAAL) EOV
Columbia, SC [*Location identifier*] [*FAA*] (FAAL) MMT
Columbia, SC [*Television station call letters*] WACH
Columbia, SC [*FM radio station call letters*] WARQ
Columbia, SC [*AM radio station call letters*] WCOS
Columbia, SC [*FM radio station call letters*] WCOS-FM
Columbia, SC [*AM radio station call letters*] WCTG
Columbia, SC [*Television station call letters*] WIS
Columbia, SC [*AM radio station call letters*] (RBYB) WISW
Columbia, SC [*FM radio station call letters*] WLTR
Columbia, SC [*Television station call letters*] WLTX
Columbia, SC [*FM radio station call letters*] WMHK
Columbia, SC [*FM radio station call letters*] WNOK
Columbia, SC [*AM radio station call letters*] WOIC
Columbia, SC [*Television station call letters*] WOLO
Columbia, SC [*FM radio station call letters*] WOMG-FM
Columbia, SC [*AM radio station call letters*] WQXL
Columbia, SC [*Television station call letters*] WRLK
Columbia, SC [*FM radio station call letters*] WUSC
Columbia, SC [*AM radio station call letters*] WVOC
Columbia Scholastic Press Advisers Association (EA) CSPAA
Columbia Scholastic Press Association (EA) CSPA
Columbia Sheep Breeders Association of America (EA) CSBA
Columbia Society of International Law. Bulletin [*A publication*] (DLA) Colum Soc'y Int'l L Bull
Columbia Sportswear [*NASDAQ symbol*] (SG) COLM
Columbia State Community College, Columbia, TN [*Library symbol*] [*Library of Congress*] (LCLS) TCoC
Columbia Survey of Human Rights Law [*A publication*] (DLA) Colum Survey Human Rights L
Columbia Survey of Human Rights Law [*A publication*] (DLA) Colum Surv Hum Rts L
Columbia Technical Translations (SAUS) CTT
Columbia Theological Seminary, Decatur, GA [*OCLC symbol*] (OCLC) GCL
Columbia Theological Seminary, Decatur, GA [*Library symbol*] [*Library of Congress*] (LCLS) GDC
Columbia, TN [*FM radio station call letters*] WAYM
Columbia, TN [*FM radio station call letters*] WKOM
Columbia, TN [*AM radio station call letters*] WKRM
Columbia, TN [*AM radio station call letters*] WMCP
Columbia, TN [*AM radio station call letters*] WMRB
Columbia Township Library, Unionville, MI [*Library symbol*] [*Library of Congress*] (LCLS) MiUnv
Columbia Union College, Takoma Park, MD [*OCLC symbol*] (OCLC) CUC
Columbia Union College, Takoma Park, MD [*Library symbol*] [*Library of Congress*] (LCLS) DColU
Columbia Unit District 4, Columbia, IL [*Library symbol*] [*Library of Congress*] (LCLS) IColuD
Columbia University (GAGS) Columbia U
Columbia University (SAUO) Col Univ
Columbia University [*New York, NY*] CU
Columbia University, American Typefounders' Library, New York, NY [*Library symbol*] [*Library of Congress*] (LCLS) NNC-Typ
Columbia University, Avery Library of Architecture, New York, NY [*Library symbol*] [*Library of Congress*] (LCLS) NNC-A
Columbia University, Biological Sciences Library, New York, NY [*Library symbol*] [*Library of Congress*] (LCLS) NNC-B
Columbia University, Business-Economic Library, New York, NY [*Library symbol*] [*Library of Congress*] (LCLS) NNC-BE
Columbia University, College of Pharmacy, New York, NY [*Library symbol*] [*Library of Congress*] (LCLS) NNC-P
[*The*] **Columbia University College of Physicians and Surgeons Complete HomeMedical Guide** [*A publication*] CHMG
Columbia University, Division of War Research CUDWR
Columbia University, East Asiatic Library, New York, NY [*Library symbol*] [*Library of Congress*] (LCLS) NNC-EA
Columbia University Electronic Research Laboratory (SAA) CUERL
Columbia University Electronics Research Laboratories CUERL
Columbia University Forum (journ.) (SAUS) CUF
Columbia University Germanic Studies (journ.) (SAUS) CUGS
Columbia University Hudson Laboratory CUHL
Columbia University, International Institute for the Study of Human Reproduction, Center for Population and Family Health, New York, NY [*Library symbol*] [*Library of Congress*] (LCLS) NNC-Pop

Columbia University (journ.) (SAUS) ... Column Univ Q
Columbia University, Lamont-Doherty Geological Observatory, Palisades, NY [*Library symbol*] [*Library of Congress*] (LCLS) ... NNC-G
Columbia University, Law Library, New York, NY [*Library symbol*] [*Library of Congress*] (LCLS) ... NNC-L
Columbia University Library (SAUO) ... CUL
Columbia University, Medical Library, New York, NY [*Library symbol*] [*Library of Congress*] (LCLS) ... NNC-M
Columbia University, New York (SAUS) ... NNC
Columbia University, New York, NY [*Library symbol*] [*Library of Congress*] (LCLS) ... NNC
Columbia University Press ... CUP
Columbia University, Psychology Library, New York, NY [*Library symbol*] [*Library of Congress*] (LCLS) ... NNC-Ps
Columbia University Quarterly (journ.) (SAUS) ... Columbia U Q
Columbia University School of Medicine (SAUO) ... CUSM
Columbia University, Teachers College, New York, NY [*Library symbol*] [*Library of Congress*] (LCLS) ... NNC-T
Columbia Valley Authority ... CVA
Columbia Viking Desk Encyclopedia (SAUS) ... CVDE
Columbia, Yale, Harvard [*Used to refer to a project involving the medical libraries of these universities*] ... COLYAHAR
Columbia-Barnard Athletic Consortium (PSS) ... CBAC
Columbia-Greene Community College, Athens, NY [*Library symbol*] [*Library of Congress*] (LCLS) ... NAtC
Columbia-Greene Community College, Hudson, NY [*Library symbol*] [*Library of Congress*] (LCLS) ... NHudC
Columbia/HCA Hlthcare [*NYSE symbol*] (TTSB) ... COL
Columbia-Lafayette-Ouachita-Calhoun Regional Library, Magnolia, AR [*Library symbol*] [*Library of Congress*] (LCLS) ... ArMag
Columbia/Mt. Pleasant, TN [*Location identifier*] [*FAA*] (FAAL) ... MRC
Columbia/Mt. Pleasant, TN [*Location identifier*] [*FAA*] (FAAL) ... PBC
Columbian Carbon Company (SAUO) ... CCC
Columbian National Oceanographic Data Centre (SAUS) ... CECOLDO
Columbian Squires (EA) ... CS
Columbiana County Court House, Lisbon, OH [*Library symbol*] [*Library of Congress*] (LCLS) ... OLiC
Columbiana Public Library, Columbiana, OH [*Library symbol*] [*Library of Congress*] (LCLS) ... OCoa
Columbia-Presbyterian Medical Center ... CPMC
Columbine Elementary School, Grand Junction, CO [*Library symbol*] [*Library of Congress*] (LCLS) ... CoGjCoE
Columbite (SAUS) ... cl
Columbium [*A chemical element; modern name is niobium, see Nb*] ... Cb
Columbium (SAUS) ... Co
Columbus [*Ohio*] [*Airport symbol*] (OAG) ... CMH
Columbus (ROG) ... COL
Columbus (BEE) ... Colmbs
Columbus [*Georgia*] [*Airport symbol*] (OAG) ... CSG
Columbus [*Mississippi*] [*Airport symbol*] (OAG) ... GTR
Columbus [*Nebraska*] [*Airport symbol*] (OAG) ... OLU
Columbus [*Mississippi*] [*Airport symbol*] (AD) ... UBS
Columbus Air Force Base (SAUO) ... CAFB
Columbus Air Transport, Inc. [*ICAO designator*] (FAAC) ... KLR
Columbus & Greenville Railway Co. [*AAR code*] ... CAGY
Columbus & Greenville Railway Co. ... C & G
Columbus & Greenville Railway Co. (SAUO) ... C&G
Columbus & Greenville Railway Co. (SAUO) ... CLG
Columbus & Southern Ohio Electric Company (SAUO) ... COC
Columbus Army Depot [*Ohio*] (AABC) ... COAD
Columbus Avia [*Ukraine*] [*FAA designator*] (FAAC) ... CBS
Columbus City School, Columbus, OH [*OCLC symbol*] (OCLC) ... CSS
Columbus College (GAGS) ... Columbus C
Columbus College, Columbus, GA [*Library symbol*] [*Library of Congress*] (LCLS) ... GColuC
Columbus College, Library, Columbus, GA [*OCLC symbol*] (OCLC) ... GCO
Columbus: Countdown 1992 [*An association*] (EA) ... CC 1992
Columbus County Public Library, Whiteville, NC [*Library symbol*] [*Library of Congress*] (LCLS) ... NcWhC
Columbus Elementary School, Freeport, NY [*Library symbol*] [*Library of Congress*] (LCLS) ... NFreeCE
Columbus Elementary School, Grand Junction, CO [*Library symbol*] [*Library of Congress*] (LCLS) ... CoGjCsE
Columbus Energy [*AMEX symbol*] (TTSB) ... EGY
Columbus Energy Corp. [*Associated Press*] (SAG) ... ColuEng
Columbus Energy Corp. [*AMEX symbol*] (SPSG) ... EGY
Columbus [*Georgia*] **Fort Benning** [*Airport symbol*] (OAG) ... QFE
Columbus Fort Benning (SAUS) ... QFE
Columbus Free Flyer (SAUS) ... CFF
Columbus, GA [*Location identifier*] [*FAA*] (FAAL) ... AWS
Columbus, GA [*FM radio station call letters*] ... WCGQ
Columbus, GA [*AM radio station call letters*] ... WDAK
Columbus, GA [*AM radio station call letters*] ... WEAM
Columbus, GA [*FM radio station call letters*] ... WFRC
Columbus, GA [*FM radio station call letters*] ... WFXE
Columbus, GA [*Television station call letters*] ... WJSP
Columbus, GA [*Television station call letters*] ... WLTZ
Columbus, GA [*AM radio station call letters*] (BROA) ... WMLF
Columbus, GA [*AM radio station call letters*] ... WOKS
Columbus, GA [*Television station call letters*] ... WRBL
Columbus, GA [*AM radio station call letters*] ... WRCG
Columbus, GA [*FM radio station call letters*] ... WTJB
Columbus, GA [*AM radio station call letters*] ... WTMQ
Columbus, GA [*Television station call letters*] ... WTVM
Columbus, GA [*FM radio station call letters*] ... WVRK
Columbus, GA [*Television station call letters*] ... WXTX
Columbus, GA [*FM radio station call letters*] ... WYFK
Columbus, GA [*Location identifier*] [*FAA*] (FAAL) ... XLE
Columbus Gallery of Fine Arts (SAUS) ... CGFA
Columbus Gazette & Columbus Safeguard, Columbus Junction, IA [*Library symbol*] [*Library of Congress*] (LCLS) ... IaCjGS
Columbus General Depot (SAUO) ... CGD
Columbus High School, Columbus, MT [*Library symbol*] [*Library of Congress*] (LCLS) ... MtCoHS
Columbus Hospital, Health Sciences Library, Great Falls, MT [*Library symbol*] [*Library of Congress*] (LCLS) ... MtGrCH
Columbus, IN [*Location identifier*] [*FAA*] (FAAL) ... BAK
Columbus, IN [*AM radio station call letters*] ... WCSI
Columbus, IN [*FM radio station call letters*] ... WKKG
Columbus, IN [*FM radio station call letters*] ... WWWY
Columbus, KS [*FM radio station call letters*] (BROA) ... KJML-FM
Columbus, KS [*FM radio station call letters*] ... KOCD
Columbus McKinnon [*NASDAQ symbol*] (TTSB) ... CMCO
Columbus, MS [*Location identifier*] [*FAA*] (FAAL) ... CBM
Columbus, MS [*Location identifier*] [*FAA*] (FAAL) ... IGB
Columbus, MS [*Location identifier*] [*FAA*] (FAAL) ... TBB
Columbus, MS [*Location identifier*] [*FAA*] (FAAL) ... UBS
Columbus, MS [*AM radio station call letters*] ... WACR
Columbus, MS [*FM radio station call letters*] ... WACR-FM
Columbus, MS [*Television station call letters*] ... WCBI
Columbus, MS [*AM radio station call letters*] ... WJWF
Columbus, MS [*FM radio station call letters*] ... WKOR
Columbus, MS [*Television station call letters*] (BROA) ... WMAA
Columbus, MS [*FM radio station call letters*] ... WMBC
Columbus, MS [*FM radio station call letters*] ... WMUW
Columbus, NE [*AM radio station call letters*] ... KJSK
Columbus, NE [*FM radio station call letters*] ... KKOT
Columbus, NE [*FM radio station call letters*] ... KLIR
Columbus, NE [*FM radio station call letters*] ... KTLX
Columbus, NE [*AM radio station call letters*] ... KTTT
Columbus, NE [*Location identifier*] [*FAA*] (FAAL) ... PLT
Columbus News Index [*Public Library of Columbus and Franklin County*] [*Information service or system*] (IID) ... CNI
Columbus, NM [*Location identifier*] [*FAA*] (FAAL) ... CUS
Columbus, OH [*Location identifier*] [*FAA*] (FAAL) ... BUZ
Columbus, OH [*Location identifier*] [*FAA*] (FAAL) ... CBP
Columbus, OH [*Location identifier*] [*FAA*] (FAAL) ... DDV
Columbus, OH [*Location identifier*] [*FAA*] (FAAL) ... DKG
Columbus, OH [*Location identifier*] [*FAA*] (FAAL) ... IVX
Columbus, OH [*Location identifier*] [*FAA*] (FAAL) ... LCK
Columbus, OH [*Location identifier*] [*FAA*] (FAAL) ... OSU
Columbus, OH [*Location identifier*] [*FAA*] (FAAL) ... OYY
Columbus, OH [*AM radio station call letters*] ... WBNS
Columbus, OH [*Television station call letters*] (BROA) ... WBNS-DT
Columbus, OH [*FM radio station call letters*] (BROA) ... WBNS-FM
Columbus, OH [*Television station call letters*] ... WBNS-TV
Columbus, OH [*FM radio station call letters*] ... WBZX
Columbus, OH [*FM radio station call letters*] (BROA) ... WCBE-FM
Columbus, OH [*Television station call letters*] ... WCMH
Columbus, OH [*AM radio station call letters*] ... WCOL
Columbus, OH [*FM radio station call letters*] (BROA) ... WCOL-FM
Columbus, OH [*AM radio station call letters*] (BROA) ... WFII-AM
Columbus, OH [*FM radio station call letters*] ... WJZA
Columbus, OH [*FM radio station call letters*] ... WLVQ
Columbus, OH [*AM radio station call letters*] ... WMNI
Columbus, OH [*FM radio station call letters*] ... WNCI
Columbus, OH [*AM radio station call letters*] ... WOSU
Columbus, OH [*FM radio station call letters*] ... WOSU-FM
Columbus, OH [*Television station call letters*] ... WOSU-TV
Columbus, OH [*FM radio station call letters*] ... WSNY
Columbus, OH [*Television station call letters*] ... WSYX
Columbus, OH [*Television station call letters*] ... WTTE
Columbus, OH [*AM radio station call letters*] ... WTVN
Columbus, OH [*FM radio station call letters*] (RBYB) ... WUFM-FM
Columbus, OH [*AM radio station call letters*] ... WVKO
Columbus, Ohio Regional News Index [*Grandview Heights Public Library*] [*Information service or system*] (IID) ... CORNI
Columbus Orbital Facility [*Space technology*] ... COF
Columbus Polar Platform (SAUS) ... PPF
Columbus Public Library (SAUS) ... CPL
Columbus Public Library (SAUS) ... Oco
Columbus Public Library, Columbus, NE [*Library symbol*] [*Library of Congress*] (LCLS) ... NbCo
Columbus Public Library, Columbus, OH [*Library symbol*] [*Library of Congress*] (LCLS) ... OCo
Columbus Realty Trust [*NYSE symbol*] (SPSG) ... CLB
Columbus Realty Trust [*Associated Press*] (SAG) ... ColumRT
Columbus Republic, Columbus, IN [*Library symbol*] [*Library of Congress*] (LCLS) ... InColuR
Columbus Research Tool [*Control Data Corp.*] ... CRT
Columbus SoPwr 7.92% Sub Db [*NYSE symbol*] (SG) ... CJA
Columbus SoPwr 8.375% Sub Db [*NYSE symbol*] (TTSB) ... CSJ
Columbus Southern Power Co. [*Associated Press*] (SAG) ... ColSP25
Columbus Southern Power Co. [*NYSE symbol*] (SAG) ... CSJ
Columbus Southern Power Co. [*NYSE symbol*] (SAG) ... CSU
Columbus State Hospital, Columbus, OH [*Library symbol*] [*Library of Congress*] (LCLS) ... OCoSH
Columbus Technical Institute, Columbus, OH [*OCLC symbol*] (OCLC) ... CTI
Columbus Technical Institute, Columbus, OH [*Library symbol*] [*Library of Congress*] (LCLS) ... OCoCT

Columbus, TX [*FM radio station call letters*] ..... KULM
Columbus, WI [*FM radio station call letters*] (BROA) ..... WTLX-FM
Columbus, WI [*FM radio station call letters*] ..... WYKY
Columbus/Municipal [*New Mexico*] [*ICAO location identifier*] (ICLI) ..... KCUS
Columbus/Port Columbus International [*Ohio*] [*ICAO location identifier*] (ICLI) ..... KCMH
Columbus-Worthington, OH [*AM radio station call letters*] ..... WRFD
Columellar Muscle ..... CM
Column (IAA) ..... CLM
Column [*Typesetting*] (WDMC) ..... clm
Column (SAUS) ..... Cmn
Column (WDMC) ..... col
Column (AAG) ..... COL
Column (AFM) ..... COLM
Column ..... COLN
Column (SAUS) ..... Coln
column (SAUO) ..... coln
Column Address Generator (SAUS) ..... CAG
Column Address Select (SAUS) ..... CAS
Column Bandwidth (SAUS) ..... CBW
Column Base ..... CB
Column Binary Mode (SAUS) ..... CBM
Column Binary Read (SAUS) ..... CBR
Column Builder (GEOI) ..... CB
Column Capacity (SAUS) CC
Column Chromatography [*Analytical chemistry*] CC
Column Chromatography - High-Performance [*or Pressure*] **Liquid Chromatography** [*Analytical chemistry*] ..... CC-HPLC
Column Code Suppression [*Computer science*] (IAA) ..... CCS
Column Code Suppression (SAUS) ..... Col Cde Sup
Column Extractant [*Nuclear energy*] (NRCH) CX
Column Feed [*Nuclear energy*] (NRCH) ..... CF
Column Gap [*Army*] (AABC) ..... COLMGP
Column Grid Array ..... CGA
Column Indicating Device (SAUS) ..... CID
Column Indicator (SAUS) CI
Column Liquid Chromatography CLC
Column of Fornix (DB) ..... CF
Column Pitch (SAUS) ..... CP
Column Position Counter ..... CPC
Column Press (SAUS) ..... COL Press
Column Product [*Nuclear energy*] (NRCH) ..... CP
Column Purified Enzyme (SAUS) ..... CPE
Column Reference Centerline (SAUS) ..... CRC
Column Research Council [*Later, SSRC*] (EA) ..... CRC
Column Shock Protection [*Chromatography*] ..... CSP
Column Skipping Key (SAUS) ..... CSK
Column Spacing (SAUS) ..... CS
Column Split [*Computer science*] (IAA) ..... CS
Column Splitting (SAUS) ..... CS
Column, Sum, Row (SAUS) ..... COSUMR
Column Transition Matrix (SAUS) ..... CTM
Column Valve Diaphragm ..... CVD
Column Volume (ABAC) cv
Column Waste [*Nuclear energy*] (NRCH) ..... CW
Column-Address Strobe (IEEE) ..... CAS
Columnar Water Vapor (ARMP) ..... CWV
Columnar-Lined Lower Esophagus [*Gastroenterology*] (DAVI) ..... CLLE
Column-Digit Binary Network ..... CDBN
Columnea Latent Viroid [*Plant pathology*] ..... CLVd
Columns (ROG) ..... COLS
Columns per Card (SAUS) ..... Col/Card
Columns per Line (SAUS) ..... CPL
Colusa, CA [*FM radio station call letters*] ..... KKCY
Colusa, CA [*FM radio station call letters*] ..... KPPL
Colusa County Free Library, Colusa, CA [*Library symbol*] [*Library of Congress*] (LCLS) ..... CColu
Colusa County Genealogical Society, Colusa, CA [*Library symbol*] [*Library of Congress*] (LCLS) ..... CColuGS
Colville [*Washington*] [*Seismograph station code, US Geological Survey*] [*Closed*] (SEIS) ..... CLW
Colville River, AK [*Location identifier*] [*FAA*] (FAAL) CVL
Colville, WA [*FM radio station call letters*] ..... KCRK
Colville, WA [*AM radio station call letters*] ..... KCVL
Colvil's Manuscript Decisions, Scotch Court of Session [*A publication*] (DLA) ..... Colvil
Colvin Aviation, Inc. [*ICAO designator*] (FAAC) ..... NVE
Colwell Mortgage Trust (SAUO) ..... CLM
Colyar on Guarantees [*A publication*] (DLA) ..... Coly Guar (De)
Colyer & Southey (WDAA) ..... C&S
Com Dev Ltd., Cambridge, Ontario [*Library symbol*] [*National Library of Canada*] (NLC) ..... OCCD
Com21, Inc. [*NASDAQ symbol*] (SG) ..... CMTO
Coma Berenices [*Berenice's Hair*][*Constellation*] [*Latin*] (BARN) ..... Com
Coma Level Greater than 400 Milligrams per Liter [*Medicine*] (DAVI) COM3
Coma Recovery Association (EA) ..... CRA
Comac Condition Base Monitor Module [*Comac Systems Ltd..*] [*Software package*] (NCC) ..... CCBMM
Comair [*ICAO designator*] (AD) ..... OH
Comair Holdings [*NASDAQ symbol*] (TTSB) ..... COMR
Comair, Inc. [*ICAO designator*] (FAAC) ..... COM
Comair, Inc. [*Associated Press*] (SAG) ..... Comair
Comair, Inc. [*NASDAQ symbol*] (SAG) ..... COMR
Comalco Investments Europe S.A. (SAUO) ..... Comalco
Comanche Crew Support System [*Army*] (RDA) ..... CCSS
Comanche, OK [*FM radio station call letters*] ..... KDDQ
Comanche Petroleums [*Vancouver Stock Exchange symbol*] ..... COA
Comanche Portable Cockpit [*Army*] ..... CPC
Comanche, TX [*AM radio station call letters*] ..... KCOM
Comanche, TX [*FM radio station call letters*] (BROA) ..... KOXZ-FM
Comanding General, United States, Army, Atlantic ..... CGUSARLANT
Comando de Material - Fabrica Militar de Aviones [*Argentina*] [*ICAO aircraft manufacturer identifier*] (ICAO) ..... IA
Comando de Operacoes do Continente [*Continental Operations Command*] [*Portugal*] ..... COPCON
Comando de Resistencia Popular Javier Carrera [*Javier Carrera Popular Resistance Commando*] [*Chile*] (PD) ..... CRP
Comando Geral do Ar [*Brazilian Air Force*] ..... COMGAR
Comando Guerrilleros del Pueblo [*Guerrilla group*] [*Guatemala*] (EY) ..... CGP
Comando Urbano Revolucionario [*Guatemala*] [*Political party*] (EY) ..... CUR
Comandor Avia [*Ukraine*] [*FAA designator*] (FAAC) ..... CMD
Comandos Armados de Liberacion [*Armed Liberation Commandos*] [*Puerto Rico*] (PD) ..... CAL
Comandos Autonomos Anti-Capitalistas [*Spain*] [*Political party*] (EY) ..... CAA
Comandos Revolucionarios del Pueblo [*Peru*] [*Political party*] (EY) ..... CRP
Comaplex Resources International Ltd. [*Toronto Stock Exchange symbol*] ..... CXR
Comarapa [*Bolivia*] [*ICAO location identifier*] (ICLI) ..... SLCR
COMARC [*Cooperative Machine-Readable Cataloging Program*] [*Source file*] [*UTLAS symbol*] ..... CMC
Comarco ..... CMRO
COMARCO, Inc. [*NASDAQ symbol*] (NQ) ..... CMRO
Comarco, Inc. [*Associated Press*] (SAG) ..... Comrco
Comator Advanced Training System (SAUS) ..... CATS
Comayagua [*Honduras*] [*ICAO location identifier*] (ICLI) ..... MHCG
Comb Filter [*Military*] (CAAL) ..... CF
Combat [*In unit designations and symbols only*] C
Combat (MILB) ..... cbt
Combat (AABC) ..... CBT
Combat (AFM) ..... CMBT
Combat (CINC) ..... COMBT
Combat Action Ribbon [*Military decoration*] (VNW) ..... CAR
Combat Active and Passive RADAR Identification System (MCD) ..... CAPRIS
Combat Activity Report [*Navy*] ..... COACT
Combat Advice System (SAUS) ..... CAS
Combat Air Command (ACAE) ..... CAC
Combat Air Command & Control Centre (SAUS) ..... CACCC
Combat Air Crew ..... CAC
Combat Air Delivery Division [*Air Force*] (AFM) ..... CADD
Combat Air Division (SAUO) ..... CAD
Combat Air Forces Workstation (SAUS) ..... CAF-WS
Combat Air Operations (ACAE) ..... CAO
Combat Air Operations Center (CINC) ..... CAOC
Combat Air Patrol ..... CAP
Combat Air Patrol Mission [*Air Force*] ..... CPM
Combat Air Patrol Support [*Aircraft*] (PDAA) ..... CAPS
Combat Air Rescue Aircraft (SAUS) ..... CARA
Combat Air Surveillance Correlation and Display Equipment (SAUS) ..... CASCADE
Combat Air Traffic Controller [*Air Force*] (VNW) ..... CATC
Combat Air Vehicle Navigation and Vision ..... CAVNAV
Combat Aircraft Prototype (MCD) ..... CAP
Combat Aircraft Prototype programme (SAUS) ..... CAP
Combat Aircraft Recording and Data System ..... CARDS
Combat Aircraft Recovery Aircraft (SAUS) ..... CARA
Combat Aircraft Repair Team (SAUS) ..... CART
Combat Aircraft Service Unit [*Navy*] (MUGU) ..... CASU
Combat Aircraft Service Unit (Fleet) [*Navy*] (DNAB) ..... CASU(F)
Combat Aircraft Technology ..... CAT
Combat Aircrew [*or Aircrewman*] ..... CA
Combat Aircrew Recovery [*or Rescue*] **Aircraft** [*Later, ARRS, ARS*] ..... CARA
Combat Aircrew Refresher Training Unit (SAUO) ..... CARTU
Combat Aircrew Training System (SAUS) ..... CATS
Combat Aircrew Training Unit [*Navy*] ..... CATU
Combat Airlift Support Unit [*Air Force*] ..... CALSU
Combat Alert Aircrew [*Air Force*] ..... CAAC
Combat Alert Center (SAA) ..... CAC
Combat Ammunition Production (SAUS) ..... CAP
Combat Ammunition System (SAUS) ..... CAS
Combat Analysis Capability (MCD) ..... CAC
Combat Analysis Extended ..... COMANEX
Combat Analysis Group [*Joint Chiefs of Staff*] ..... CAG
Combat and Combat Support System (MCD) ..... CCSS
Combat and Liaison (CINC) CL
Combat and Training Development Management Information System ..... CTDMIS
Combat Applications Group (ACAE) ..... CAG
Combat Applications Squadron [*Air Force*] ..... CAS
Combat Aptitude Area (AABC) ..... CO
Combat Area Surveillance System (PDAA) ..... CASS
Combat Arms ..... CA
Combat Arms Division (INF) ..... CAD
Combat Arms Enlistment Bonus [*Military*] ..... CAEB
Combat Arms Group [*Army*] (AABC) ..... CAG
Combat Arms Maneuver Battalions Command (SAUO) ..... CAMBCOM
Combat Arms Regimental System [*Army*] ..... CARS
Combat Arms Regimented System [*Army*] ..... CARS
Combat Artist Team ..... CAT
Combat Assault ..... CA
Combat Assault Dory (SAUS) ..... CAD
Combat Assessment Capability (ACAE) ..... CAC
Combat Assessment of Readiness and Training (DOMA) ..... CART
Combat Assistance Team [*US military advisory team, Vietnam*] (VNW) ..... CAT

Combat Attrition and Intensity of War (MCD)	CATIWAR
Combat Augmentation Subsystem (MCD)	CBAS
Combat Aviation (SAUO)	CBT AVN
Combat Aviation Battalion [or Brigade]	CAB
Combat Aviation Brigade (SAUS)	CAB
Combat Aviation Group	CAG
Combat Aviation Management System (SAUS)	CAMS
Combat Aviation Squadron (SAUO)	CAS
Combat Body Armour (SAUS)	CBA
Combat Brigade Air Attack	CBAA
Combat Brigade Air Cavalry	CBAC
Combat Camera Group (SAUO)	CCG
Combat Capabilities (MCD)	COMCAP
Combat Capabilities Assessment Tool (SAUS)	DYNAMETRICS
[Readiness status][Fully] Combat Capable [Military] (DOMA)	C-1
Combat Car (SAUS)	C Car
Combat Cargo Command (SAUO)	CARCOM
Combat Cargo Command	CCC
Combat Cargo Group (CINC)	CCG
Combat Cargo Mission [Air Force]	CCM
Combat Cargo Officer [Military] (NVT)	CCO
Combat Cargo Service (SAUO)	CCS
Combat Cargo Task Force [British military] (DMA)	CCTF
Combat Center [Military]	CC
Combat Center Active [Military] (SAA)	CCA
Combat Center and Crosstell (SAA)	CC & T
Combat Center Director	CCD
Combat Center Duty Officer [Military] (SAA)	CCDO
Combat Center Function [Military] (SAA)	CCF
Combat Center Group [Military] (SAA)	CCG
Combat Center Programming Leader [Military] (SAA)	CCPL
Combat Center Remoted [Military]	CCR
Combat Center Simulation Generation System [Military] (SAA)	CSGS
Combat Center Standby [Military] (SAA)	CCS
Combat Center Status Indicator [Military] (SAA)	CCSL
Combat Clothing [NATO]	CC
Combat Clothing and Equipment Working Party [NATO]	CCEWP
Combat Coded (ACAE)	CC
Combat Coded Aircraft (ACAE)	CCA
Combat Command [Initialism may be followed by a number as, CC2, to indicate a specific, numbered command] [Army]	CC
Combat Command A	CCA
Combat Command B	CCB
Combat Command C	CCC
Combat Command D	CCD
Combat Command Group (SAUO)	CMBTCG
Combat Command L	CCL
Combat Command Post (SAUS)	CCP
Combat Command Reserve	CCR
Combat Command V	CCV
Combat Commandant [Military]	CC
Combat Communications Equipment [Military]	CCE
Combat Communications Flight	CCFT
Combat Communications Flight/Squadron/Group (SAUO)	CMBTC/F/S/G
Combat Communications Group (AFIT)	CCG
Combat Communications Group [Air Force]	CCGP
Combat Communications Squadron [Air Force] (AFIT)	CCS
Combat Configured Load [Military] (INF)	CCL
Combat Consumption [Military]	CC
Combat Consumption Support from D-Day to P-Day [Military] (AABC)	DPSPT
Combat Contingency Element (SAUS)	CCE
Combat Control [Army]	CC
Combat Control [Army]	COMCON
Combat Control Centre (SAUS)	CC
Combat Control Concept Evaluation System (SAUS)	CCCES
Combat Control Elements [Army]	CCE
Combat Control Group	CCG
Combat Control Squadron	CCS
Combat, Control, Support [Army]	COMCONSUP
Combat Control System [Military] (CAAL)	CCS
Combat Control System Mark 2 [Navy]	CCS MK2
Combat Control Systems Improvement Program [Military] (CAAL)	CCSIP
Combat Control Team [Australia]	CCT
Combat Control Unit (SAUS)	CCU
Combat Controller [Air Force] (VNW)	CCT
Combat Correspondent	CC
Combat Crew [Air Force] (AFM)	CCr
Combat Crew (SAUO)	CCR
Combat Crew Replacement Center [World War II]	CCRC
Combat Crew Standardization School (SAUO)	CCSS
Combat Crew Training [Air Force] (AFM)	CCT
Combat Crew Training Group (SAUO)	CCrTG
Combat Crew Training Group (SAUO)	CCTG
Combat Crew Training School [Air Force] (AFM)	CCTS
Combat Crew Training School [Air Force]	CCTSCH
Combat Crew Training Squadron (MCD)	CCTS
Combat Crew Training Squadron [Air Force]	CCTSq
Combat Crew Training Unit (SAUS)	CCTU
Combat Crew Training Wing (SAUS)	CCrTngWg
Combat Crew Training Wing [Air Force]	CCTW
Combat Crew Training Wing [Air Force] (AFM)	CCTWg
Combat Cryptological Support Console (MCD)	CCSC
Combat Damage Information Center [Military]	CDIC
Combat Damage Repair Assessment Team (SAUO)	CDRAT
Combat Damage Repair Time (ACAE)	CDRT

Combat Damage/Assessment Model (MCD)	CODAM
Combat Data Director [Military] (SAA)	CDD
Combat Data Information Center [Army]	CDIC
Combat Days of Supply (MCD)	CDOS
Combat Defense Force	CDF
Combat Deployable Radio (SAUO)	CDR
Combat Developer (AAGC)	Cbt Dev
Combat Developer	CBTDEV
Combat Developer Proponent (MCD)	CDP
Combat Development	CD
Combat Development and Experimentation Center (SAUS)	CDETC
Combat Development Branch	CDB
Combat Development Command [Terminated, 1973] [Army] (MCD)	CDC
Combat Development Command - Intelligence Agency [Terminated] [Army] (MCD)	CDC-INTA
Combat Development Command Division (SAUS)	CyDy
Combat Development Command Experimentation Center [Terminated] [Army] (MCD)	CDCEC
Combat Development Command Infantry Agency [Terminated] [Army]	CDCIA
Combat Development Command Maintenance Agency [Terminated] [Army]	CDCMA
Combat Development Command Transportation Agency [Terminated] [Army]	CDCTA
Combat Development Experimentation Center [Fort Ord, CA] (MCD)	CDEC
Combat Development Experimentation Center (SAUO)	CODEC
Combat Development Objective Guide [CDC]	CDOG
Combat Development Office	CDO
Combat Development Phase (or Plan, or Process, or Project) (SAUO)	CDP
Combat Development Support Facility	CDSF
Combat Development Support Manager [Army]	CDSM
Combat Development Technical Evaluation Center	CDTEC
Combat Development Test Center (CINC)	CDTC
Combat Development Test Center - Vietnam	CDTC-V
Combat Developments and Material Evaluation [Program] [Army]	CD & ME
Combat Developments Command Experimental Center (SAUS)	CDCEC
Combat Developments Command Intelligence Agency (SAUO)	CDCINTA
Combat Developments Evaluation Command (MCD)	CDEC
Combat Developments Experimentation Command [Army]	CDE
Combat Developments Experimentation Command [Army] (RDA)	CDEC
Combat Developments Planning Group (MCD)	CDPG
Combat Direction Center (NVT)	CDC
Combat Direction Center Officer [Navy] (DOMA)	CDCO
Combat Direction Finding (SAUO)	CDF
Combat Direction System (SAUO)	CDS
Combat Distribution Team Status Report (SAUO)	CODSTAT
Combat Documentation (AFM)	COMDOC
Combat Earthmover [Army]	CEM
Combat Effective Training Management (MCD)	CETRM
Combat Effectiveness Measure [Military] (CAAL)	CEM
Combat Effectiveness Report (NATG)	CER
Combat Effectiveness with Logistics Support (MCD)	CELOGS
Combat Effects Simulator (SAUS)	CES
Combat Efficiency Improvement (SAUS)	CEI
Combat Electromagnetic Environment Simulator (SAUS)	CEESIM
Combat Electronic Warfare and Intelligence O & S [Operations and Support] Concept Development	CEWISCON
Combat Electronic Warfare Intelligence	CEWI
Combat Element [Marine Corps] (DOMA)	CE
Combat Elevation Launch	CEL
Combat Emplacement Excavator	CEE
Combat Engineer (SAUS)	Cmbt Engr
Combat Engineer Battalion (DNAB)	CBTENGRBN
Combat Engineer Conference (SAUO)	CEC
Combat Engineer Mission Management Module [Software]	CEM3
Combat Engineer Party [Army] (VNW)	CEP
Combat Engineer Supply Vehicle (MCD)	CESV
Combat Engineer Team [Army] (VNW)	CET
Combat Engineer Tractor [British] (RDA)	CET
Combat Engineer Vehicle [Army]	CEV
Combat Enhancing Capability Aviation Team (SAUO)	CECAT
Combat Enhancing Team (SAUS)	CECAT
Combat Entry Point (SAUO)	CEP
Combat Equipment Battalion East (SAUO)	CEBE
Combat Equipment Battalion, North [Military]	CEBN
Combat Equipment Company (SAUO)	CEC
Combat Equipment Fighting Order (SAUS)	CEFO
Combat Equipment Group, Europe (SAUO)	CEG
Combat Equipment Group, Europe (MCD)	CEGE
Combat Equipment Marching Order (SAUS)	CEMO
Combat Essential Items List [Army]	CEIL
Combat Evaluation Group [Strategic Air Command] (SAA)	CEG
Combat Evaluation Group [Strategic Air Command]	CEVG
Combat Evaluation Model (MCD)	CEM
Combat Evaluation Squadron [Air Force]	CESq
Combat Excavator [Military]	CEX
Combat Exercises [Canadian Navy]	COMBATEX
Combat Exhaustion (SAUS)	CE
Combat Field Feeding System [Army] (INF)	CFFS
Combat File Maintenance (SAUS)	CFM
Combat Fitness Badge [Army] (INF)	CFB
Combat Fitness Retraining Unit	CFRU
Combat Flight Inspection & Navigation (SAUS)	C-FIN
Combat Follow-on Spares Support (SAUO)	CFDSS
Combat Force, Eastern Continental Region (SAUO)	CFECR
Combat Gap Crosser [Army]	CGC

Combat Group (SAUO)	CBT GP
Combat Group	CG
Combat Group (SAUO)	C Gp
Combat Gunnery Officers School [Army Air Forces]	CGOS
Combat History Analysis Study Effort (SAUO)	CHASE
Combat Identification [Army] (RDA)	CID
Combat Identification Dismounted Soldier System [Army] (INF)	CIDSS
Combat Identification System	CIS
Combat Identification System Program Officer (MCD)	CISPO
Combat Identification System-Indirect Subsystem (SAUS)	CIS-ISS
Combat Identification Systems Project Office [Army]	CISPO
Combat Identification Tank Force [Army]	CITF
Combat Identification Task Force [Army] (DOMA)	CITF
Combat Illumination (MCD)	COIL
Combat Indoctrination (MCD)	CI
Combat Ineffective [Military] (NVT)	CI
Combat Infantry Badge [Army]	CIB
Combat Infantryman's Badge [Military decoration]	CIB
Combat Information (SAUS)	CI
Combat Information and Detection (NVT)	CID
Combat Information Bureau (SAUO)	CIB
Combat Information Center [Navy]	CIC
Combat Information Center Office [or Officer] [Navy] (MUGU)	CICO
Combat Information Center (or Centre) (SAUO)	CIC
Combat Information Center Watch Officer [Navy]	CICWO
Combat Information Centre Procedure Trainer (SAUS)	CIC-PT
Combat Information Display System (SAUS)	CIDIS
Combat Information Message (SAUO)	CIM
Combat Information Net	CIN
Combat Information Systems Flight [Military]	CISF
Combat Information Systems Group (SAUO)	CISG
Combat Information Systems Squadron (SAUO)	CISS
Combat Intelligence	CBTI
Combat Intelligence Center	CIC
Combat Intelligence Co. (SAUO)	CBTI
Combat Intelligence Division (SAUO)	CID
Combat Intelligence Officer [Navy]	CIO
Combat Intelligence Operations Center (MCD)	CIOC
Combat Intelligence Plot (NATG)	CIP
Combat Intelligence Proficiency Course [Military] (INF)	CIPC
Combat Intelligence System (MCD)	CIS
Combat Intercept Control	CIC
Combat Interviews	CI
Combat Jamming/Communication Support System (SAUS)	COJACS
Combat Launch and Recovery Kit (AFM)	CLARK
Combat Leader's Guide (INF)	CLG
Combat Leadership Exercise (SAUS)	CLX
Combat Lessons Bulletin	CLB
Combat Lifesaver [Army]	CLS
Combat Logistic Support System (AABC)	CLSS
Combat Logistics Force [Navy] (GFGA)	CLF
Combat Logistics Network [DoD]	COMLOGNET
Combat Logistics Support Squadron [Air Force]	CLSS
Combat Logistics System [Air Force] (GFGA)	CLS
Combat Logistics System Computer Aided Load Manifesting (SAUO)	CLS/CALM
Combat Logistics Vehicle [Army]	CLV
Combat Loss	C/L
Combat Loss and Expenditure Data (MCD)	COLED
Combat Loss and Expenditure Data - Vietnam	COLED-V
Combat Maintenance Capability (MCD)	CMC
Combat Maintenance System (SAUS)	CMS
Combat Maneuver Battalion [Army]	CMB
Combat Maneuver Battalion [Army]	COMANBAT
Combat Maneuver Training Center (INF)	CMTC
Combat Maneuver Training Center - Instrumentation System [Army]	CMTC-IS
Combat Maneuver Training Command	CMTC
Combat Maneuver Training Complex [Hohenfels Training Area] [Germany]	CMTC
Combat Material	CM
Combat Material Research Laboratory [Army]	CMRL
Combat Materiel Exploitation Center [Military] (VNW)	CMEC
Combat Medical Badge [Military decoration] (AABC)	CMB
Combat Merchant Mariners World War II (EA)	CMMWWII
Combat Mission [Military]	CM
Combat Mission Failure (AABC)	CMF
Combat Mission Folder (AFM)	CMF
Combat Mission Scenario [Army]	CMS
Combat Mission Simulation (MCD)	CMS
Combat Mission Simulator (SAUS)	CMS
Combat Mission Trainer [Air Force]	CMT
Combat Mobility System [Army] (RDA)	CMSYS
Combat Mobility Vehicle [Army] (RDA)	CMV
Combat Monitoring System (SAUS)	CMS
Combat, Naval (SAUS)	CN
Combat Net Radio [Military]	CNR
Combat Net Radio Environment (SAUS)	CNRE
Combat Net Radio Interface (SAUS)	CNRI
Combat Observation and Lasing Teams [Army] (INF)	COLT
Combat Observation Lasing Team (SAUS)	COLT
Combat Operation (INF)	CO
Combat Operational Reserve Group (AAG)	CORG
Combat Operational Support Aircraft (NVT)	COSA
Combat Operational Support Group (SAUO)	COSG
Combat Operations Center [Air Force]	COC
Combat Operations Center Marine Air Ground Task Force (SAUO)	COCMAGTF
Combat Operations Division (SAUO)	CBTOPS
Combat Operations Division (SAUO)	COD
Combat Operations Group (SAA)	COG
Combat Operations Information Centre (SAUS)	COIC
Combat Operations Intelligence Center (MCD)	COIC
Combat Operations Intelligence Division (SAUO)	COID
Combat Operations, Naval Gunfire Activity	CONGA
Combat Operations Report	COR
Combat Operations Research Group [Technical Operations, Inc.] [Fort Belvoir, VA]	CORG
Combat Operations Section (SAUO)	COS
Combat Operations Section, Air Force (SAUO)	COS/AF
Combat Operations Specialist Course [Air Force] (AFM)	COSC
Combat Optimization and Analysis Program [Air Force]	COAP
Combat Organization Potential [DoD]	COP
Combat Outpost	COP
Combat Outpost Line (SAUS)	COMPL
Combat Outpost Line	COPL
Combat Personnel Control System [Air Force] (GFGA)	CPCS
Combat Photographer [Military] [Slang] (WDMC)	84 Charlie
Combat Pilots Association (SAUO)	CPA
Combat Plans Division (SAUO)	CBTPLANS
Combat Plans Division (SAUO)	CPD
Combat Potential Display [SAGE] [Air Force]	CPD
Combat Power [DoD]	CP
Combat Psychiatric Casualty [Military] (INF)	CPC
Combat Radio Dialler (SAUS)	CRD
Combat Radius Capability [Military]	COMRAC
Combat Rated Thrust [Navy] (NG)	CRT
Combat Rations [Military] (VNW)	Cs
Combat Reaction	CR
Combat Reaction Time	CRT
Combat Readiness Air Group (DNAB)	CRAG
Combat Readiness Air Wing	CRAW
Combat Readiness Analysis Team Effort (ACAE)	CREATE
Combat Readiness Assessment Exercise [Obsolete] [Navy] (NG)	CRAE
Combat Readiness by Electronic Service Testing [Army] (AABC)	CREST
Combat Readiness Categories [Navy] (NG)	CRCAT
Combat Readiness Electromagnetic Analysis and Measurement (MCD)	CREAM
Combat Readiness Evaluation [Army]	CRE
Combat Readiness Evaluation Criteria [Navy] (NG)	CREC
Combat Readiness Medal [Military decoration] (AFM)	CRM
Combat Readiness Rating System [Air Force]	CRRS
Combat Readiness Requirements [Canadian Navy]	CRR
Combat Readiness Trainer [or Training]	CRT
Combat Ready (AFM)	CR
Combat Ready Early Warning System (SAUS)	CREWS
Combat Ready Rate (MCD)	CRR
Combat Ready Storage Program (DOMA)	CRSP
Combat Reconnaissance Platoon	CRP
Combat Reporting Center (AFM)	CRC
Combat Reporting Post	CRP
Combat Reporting System [Air Force] (MCD)	CREST
Combat Required Operational Capability (AFIT)	CROC
Combat Rescue [Military] (MUSM)	CR
Combat Rescue Mission Analysis (SAUO)	CRMA
Combat Rescue Training Exercise (SAUS)	CRTE
Combat Reserve [Military]	CR
Combat Reserve Air Fleet [Military]	CRAFT
Combat Resource Allocation Model (MCD)	CRAM
Combat Results Table (SAUO)	CRT
Combat Rubber Raiding Craft (DOMA)	CRRC
Combat Sample Generator [Military]	COSAGE
Combat Search and Rescue [Aviation]	CSAR
Combat Search and Rescue [Aviation] (MCD)	CSR
Combat Search and Rescue Special Warfare Support Helicopter (SAUS)	HCS
Combat Security Police [Air Force] (VNW)	CSP
Combat Sequence Summary (SAUS)	CSS
Combat Service Group [Army]	CSG
Combat Service Readiness (DWSG)	CSR
Combat Service Support [DoD] (AABC)	CSS
Combat Service Support Area [Army]	CSSA
Combat Service Support Computer System (SAUS)	CSSCS
Combat Service Support Control System [Army]	CSSCS
Combat Service Support Detachment [Marine Corps] (DOMA)	CSSD
Combat Service Support Element [Marine Corps] (DOMA)	CSSE
Combat Service Support Group [Army]	CSSG
Combat Service Support Level [Military] (INF)	CS^2
Combat Service Support Precommand Course	CSS PCC
Combat Service Support System (SAUS)	CS 3
Combat Service Support System [Army]	CS3
Combat Service Support System [Army]	CSSS
Combat Service Support Training Simulator System [Army]	CSSTSS
Combat Serviceable (SAUS)	CS
Combat Simulation Test System (SAUS)	CSTS
Combat Store Ship [Navy symbol]	AFS
Combat Stress Control [Army]	CSC
Combat Stress Reaction [Army] (ADDR)	CSR
Combat Studies Institute [Command and General Staff College, Fort Leavenworth] [Army] (INF)	CSI
Combat Supplies [British]	CSUPS
Combat Supply System (ACAE)	CSS
Combat Support (SAUS)	COMSUP

Combat Support ... CS
Combat Support Air Traffic Management System (MCD) ... CSATMS
Combat Support Aviation Battalion [*Army*] ... CSAB
Combat Support Aviation Comp (SAUS) ... SCAC
Combat Support Aviation Company [*Army*] ... CSAC
Combat Support Boat (SAUS) ... CSB
Combat Support Capability Management System (MCD) ... CSCMS
Combat Support Center [*Army*] ... CSC
Combat Support Chemical Platoon (SAUO) ... CSCP
Combat Support Company [*Army*] ... CSC
Combat Support Coordination Center ... CSCC
Combat Support Force ... CSF
Combat Support Group [*Army*] ... CSG
Combat Support Group [*Air Force*] (AFM) ... CSGp
Combat Support Helicopter (SAUS) ... CSH
Combat Support Hospital (AABC) ... CSH
Combat Support Liaison (CINC) ... CSL
Combat Support Module (SAUS) ... CSM
Combat Support of the Army (AFIT) ... COSTAR
Combat Support Rearm and Refuel in Battalions [*Study*] [*Army Logistics Center*] ... COSRRIB
Combat Support Ship [*Military*] ... AFS
Combat Support Smoke Vehicle [*Army*] ... CSSV
Combat Support Squadron [*Air Force*] ... CMBTSPTSq
Combat Support Squadron [*Air Force*] ... CSS
Combat Support Trailer (SAUS) ... CST
Combat Support Training [*Military*] (AABC) ... CST
Combat Support Training System [*Military*] ... CSTS
Combat Support Units [*Army*] ... COMSUP
Combat Support Units [*Army*] ... CSU
Combat Support Vehicle (MCD) ... CSV
Combat Support Wing ... CSW
Combat Surveillance Agency [*Signal Corps*] ... CSA
Combat Surveillance and Target Acquisition [*Army*] ... CSTA
Combat Surveillance and Target Acquisition Equipment [*Army*] ... CS & TAE
Combat Surveillance and Target Acquisition Equipment (SAUS) ... CS&TAE
Combat Surveillance and Target Acquisition Laboratory (SAUO) ... CS&TAL
Combat Surveillance and Target Acquisition Laboratory [*Army*] (RDA) ... CSTAL
Combat Surveillance and Target Acquisition Training Command [*Army*] ... CSTATC
Combat Surveillance Laboratory ... CSL
Combat Surveillance Night Vision and Target Acquisition Laboratories [*Army*] (RDA) ... CSNVTAL
Combat Surveillance RADAR ... CSR
Combat Surveillance Radar (SAUS) ... CSR
Combat Surveillance Target Acquisition RADAR ... CSTAR
Combat Swimmer Mine Neutralization System (DOMA) ... CSMNS
Combat System (SAUS) ... COSYS
Combat System [*Military*] (CAAL) ... CS
Combat System Alignment Document (NVT) ... CSAD
Combat System Alignment Test ... CSAT
Combat System Architecture [*Military*] ... CSA
Combat System Configuration Matrix [*Military*] (CAAL) ... CSCM
Combat System Coordinator [*Military*] (CAAL) ... CSC
Combat System Design Requirement [*Military*] (CAAL) ... CSDR
Combat System Detection [*Military*] (CAAL) ... CSD
Combat System Engineer [*Military*] (CAAL) ... CSE
Combat System Engineering Agent (ACAE) ... CSEA
Combat System Engineering Authorization ... CSEA
Combat System Engineering Development [*Military*] (CAAL) ... CSED
Combat System Engineering Development Site ... CSEDS
Combat System Exercise (MCD) ... CYSTEX
Combat System Highway interface (SAUS) ... CSH
Combat System Initialization Procedure [*Military*] (CAAL) ... CSIP
Combat System Integration (MCD) ... CSI
Combat System Integration and Interface Control Group [*Military*] (CAAL) ... CSIICG
Combat System Integration Manager [*Military*] (CAAL) ... CSIM
Combat System Integration Test [*Military*] (CAAL) ... CSIT
Combat System Interface Test [*Military*] (CAAL) ... CSIT
Combat System Interface Test Tool (NVT) ... CSITT
Combat System Land-Based Test Site (CAAL) ... CSLBTS
Combat System Maintenance Central [*Navy*] (DOMA) ... CSMC
Combat System Management Plan [*Military*] (CAAL) ... CSMP
Combat System Manager [*Military*] (CAAL) ... CSM
Combat System Mission Demonstration [*Military*] (CAAL) ... CSMD
Combat System Operability Monitor [*Military*] (CAAL) ... CSOM
Combat System Operational Design [*Military*] (CAAL) ... CSOD
Combat System Operational Sequencing System [*Navy*] (DOMA) ... CSOSS
Combat System Requirements Analysis (SAUS) ... CSRA
Combat System Ship Interface Criteria [*Navy*] (CAAL) ... COMSSIC
Combat System Ship Qualification Trial [*Military*] (CAAL) ... CSSQT
Combat System Simulator (SAUS) ... CSS
Combat System Steering Group [*Military*] (CAAL) ... CSSG
Combat System Support Equipment [*Military*] (CAAL) ... CSSE
Combat System Tactical Operation Manual [*Navy*] (NVT) ... CSTOM
Combat System Team Operational Trainer [*Military*] (CAAL) ... CSTOT
Combat System Test Implementation Plan [*Military*] (CAAL) ... CSTIP
Combat System Test-Bed (SAUS) ... CSTB
Combat System Training Unit (NVT) ... CSTU
Combat System Working Group [*Military*] (CAAL) ... CSWG
Combat Systems Advisory Group [*NMC*] (DNAB) ... CSAG
Combat Systems Analysis Tool (SAUS) ... COSAT
Combat Systems Assessment [*Navy*] (DOMA) ... CSA
Combat Systems Assessment [*Navy*] (DOMA) ... CSAT
Combat Systems Certification Site [*Navy*] ... COMCERTS
Combat Systems Data Processing Project (SAUO) ... CSDPP
Combat Systems Division (SAUO) ... CSD
Combat Systems Equipment Training (MCD) ... CSET
Combat Systems Improvement Program [*Navy*] (PDAA) ... CSIP
Combat Systems Integration Department (SAUO) ... CSID
Combat Systems Mobile Training Team [*Navy*] (ANA) ... CSMTT
Combat Systems Multi-format Information Centre (SAUS) ... COSMIC
Combat Systems Operability Test (NVT) ... CSOT
Combat Systems Post-Overhaul Examination [*Navy*] (ANA) ... CSPOE
Combat Systems Readiness Review [*Navy*] (MCD) ... CSRR
Combat Systems Readiness Test (NVT) ... CSRT
Combat Systems Support [*Military*] (DNAB) ... CSS
Combat Systems Technical Aerospace Report ... CSTAR
Combat Systems Technical School Command ... CSTCS
Combat Systems Test Activity [*Aberdeen Proving Ground, MD*] [*Army*] (RDA) ... CSTA
Combat Systems Test and Support Facility [*Canadian Navy*] ... CSTSF
Combat Systems Test Development Director (DNAB) ... CSTDD
Combat Systems Text Agency [*Military*] ... CSTA
Combat Systems Training (NVT) ... CST
Combat Systems Training Exercise (DNAB) ... CSTEX
Combat Systems Training Team (SAUS) ... CSTT
Combat Tactics Trainer (SAUS) ... CTT
Combat Talon (SAUS) ... MC-130
Combat Targeting Center (SAUO) ... CTC
Combat Targeting Team [*Military*] ... CTT
Combat Team ... CT
Combat Terrain Information System [*Military*] ... CTIS
Combat Theater Communications (SAUO) ... CTC
Combat Theater Communications Program [*Air Force*] (MCD) ... CTCP
Combat to Support Balance Study ... CSBS
Combat Tracking [*or Tracker*] **Team** ... CTT
Combat Train (SAUS) ... C Tn
Combat Train (SAUO) ... CTn
Combat Training Center [*Army*] (INF) ... CTC
Combat Training Centers / Tactical Engagement Simulation ... CTC/TES
Combat Training Facilities [*DoD*] ... CTF
Combat Training Launch (AFM) ... CTL
Combat Training Launch Instrumentation [*Minuteman*] ... CTLI
Combat Training Program (SAUO) ... CTP
Combat Training Theater ... CTT
Combat Training Unit ... CTU
Combat Trains Command Post [*Army*] (INF) ... CTCP
Combat Unit Training Center [*Army*] (MCD) ... CUTC
Combat Using Price Incentives Doctrine ... CUPID
Combat Vehicle [*Army*] ... CV
Combat Vehicle [*Army*] (AABC) ... CVEH
Combat Vehicle - Heading Reference Unit ... CV-HRU
Combat Vehicle Armament System Technology [*Army*] ... CVAST
Combat Vehicle Armament Technology (ACAE) ... COMVAT
Combat Vehicle Command and Control [*Army*] (RDA) ... CVC2
Combat Vehicle Command and Control (RDA) ... CVCC
Combat Vehicle Commander [*Army*] ... CVC
Combat Vehicle Crew [*Army*] ... CVC
Combat Vehicle Crewman Uniform System [*Army*] (INF) ... CVCUS
Combat Vehicle Crewman's Protective Ensemble [*Army*] (RDA) ... CVCPE
Combat Vehicle Crewmen (MCD) ... CVC
Combat Vehicle Fire Control System (ACAE) ... CVFCS
Combat Vehicle Kill Indicator (MCD) ... CVKI
Combat Vehicle Kill Indicator Pyrotechnic Device (MCD) ... CVKI-PD
Combat Vehicle LASER Detector Assembly (MCD) ... CVLD
Combat Vehicle Maintenance Policy Study ... CVMP
Combat Vehicle Night Sight ... CVNS
Combat Vehicle Program Review ... CVPR
Combat Vehicle Ram Simulation (MCD) ... COVERS
Combat Vehicle Reconnaissance (SAUS) ... CVR
Combat Vehicle, Reconnaissance (Tracked) [*British military*] (MCD) ... CVR(T)
Combat Vehicle, Reconnaissance (Tracked) (Armoured Personnel Carrier) [*British military*] ... CVR(T)(APC)
Combat Vehicle, Reconnaissance (Tracked) (Recovery) [*British military*] ... CVR(T)(REC)
Combat Vehicle, Reconnaissance (Tracked)(Guided Weapon Carrier) [*British military*] ... CVR(T)(GW)
Combat Vehicle, Reconnaissance (Wheeled) [*British military*] (DMA) ... CVR(W)
Combat Vehicle Research & Development Establishment (SAUS) ... CVRDE
Combat Vehicle Research Development Establishment (SAUO) ... CVRDE
Combat Vehicle Self Protection System (ACAE) ... CVSPS
Combat Vehicle Signature Management Plan [*Army*] (RDA) ... CVSMP
Combat Vehicle Simulator (MCD) ... CVS
Combat Vehicle Thermal Targeting System (SAUS) ... CVTTS
Combat Vehicle Weapons System [*Army*] (AFIT) ... CBVWS
Combat Vehicle Weapons System [*Army*] ... CVWS
Combat Vehicle Weapons System (Long-Range) [*Army*] ... CVWS(LR)
Combat Visual Information Support Center [*DoD*] ... CVISC
Combat Water Survival Test [*Army*] (INF) ... CWST
Combat Wing Command Post ... CWCP
Combat Zone ... CZ
Combat Zone Distance (SAUS) ... CZD
Combat Zone Mobile Communication System (SAUS) ... CZMCS
Combat Zone Radius (SAUS) ... CZR
Combatant Command [*Military*] ... COCOM
Combatant Craft Passive Electronic Warfare [*Navy*] (CAAL) ... CCPEW
Combatant Ships Integrated Communications System (SAUS) ... CSICS
Combat-Capable Trainer (MILB) ... CCT

Combating Childhood Communicable Diseases Project [*Agency for International Development*] .... CCCD
Combat-Oriented General Support [*Army*] .... COGS
Combat-Oriented General Support Center (MCD) ...... COGSC
Combat-Oriented Maintenance Organization [*Army*] ...... COMO
Combat-Oriented Supply Organization (MCD) .... COSO
Combat-Service to the Army (KSC) .... CO-STAR
Combatting Communicable Childhood Diseases (SAUO) ...... CCCD
Combed Yarn Spinners Association [*Later, AYSA*] (EA) ...... CYSA
Comberbach's English King's Bench Reports [*1685-99*] [*A publication*] (DLA) .... Com
Comberbach's English King's Bench Reports [*1685-99*] [*A publication*] (DLA) .... Comb
Combika [*Sao Paulo, Brazil*] [*Airport symbol*] (AD) ...... CUK
Combinatio Nova [*New Combination*] [*Biology, taxonomy*] ...... comb nov
Combinatio Revivisco [*Combination Revived*] [*Latin*] (EES) ...... combrey
Combination [*or Combine*] (AFM) .... COMB
Combination (VRA) .... comb
Combination (BARN) .... combi
Combination Acknowledgement Reschedule Request (SAUS) ...... CARR
Combination and Dissemination of Experiment Data System [*Army*] (RDA) .... CADEX
Combination Block [*Engraving*] (DGA) .... CB
Combination Camcorder and Playback Machine; Sony (SAUO) CCD-V8
Combination Companies [*Insurance*] CC
Combination Die (MCD) .... CD
Combination Die .... CNDI
Combination Drug .... CD
Combination Drug Therapy (MELL) .... CDT
Combination Export Management [*Small Business Administration*] ...... CEM
Combination Fabrication and Assembly (SAA) .... CFA
Combination Flat Top and Typewriter (SAUS) .... FT&TW
Combination Inventory [*LIMRA*] CI
Combination Job Analysis Method (DIPS) .... C-JAM
Combination Network [*Graph theory*] .... CNW
Combination Neutron Source Rod [*Nuclear energy*] (NRCH) ...... CNSR
Combination of Forward Combustion and Waterflooding [*Commercial oil production process*] ...... COFCAW
Combination of Purpose [*JETDS nomenclature*] .... Q
Combination of Sequential Mutant Interaction Cycles [*Biochemistry*] ...... COSMIC
Combination of Steam and Gas (SAUS) .... COSAG
Combination Product [*Medicine*] (MAE) .... CP
Combination Publication Authority .... CPA
Combination Pump Valve (SAUS) .... CPV
Combination Tone (SAUS) .... CT
Combination Type Oral Contraceptive [*Medicine*] ..... COC
Combinational Array Test Generator (ACAE) .... CATGEN
Combinational Logic Network (SAUS) .... CLN
Combinations (SAUS) .... Combs
Combinations Not Allowed (SAUS) .... CNA
Combinatorial and Algebraic Machine-Aided Computation (WGA) ...... CAMAC
Combinatorial Geometry .... COM-GEOM
Combinatorial Optimization Problem (SAUS) .... COP
Combinatory Categorical Grammar [*Artificial intelligence*] ...... CCG
Combinatory Code (SAUS) CC
Combine (SAUS) .... COMB
Combine Regency Network - Flaming Arrow Network [*Military*] ...... CRN-FAN
Combined .... CMBD
Combined (NTIO) .... comb
Combined .... COMB
Combined Accelerated Program in Psychiatry (SAUO) ...... CAPP
Combined Acceleration Vibration Climatic Test System ...... CAVCTS
Combined Acceptance Trials .... CAT
Combined Accident Reduction Effort .... CARE
Combined Account Number File [*IRS*] .... CANF
Combined Acquisition and Tracking RADAR [*NASA*] (MCD) ...... CATRADAR
Combined Action Company (SAUO) .... CAC
Combined Action Company [*Formerly, Joint Action Co.*] [*Military*] ...... CAC
Combined Action Forces [*Military*] (DNAB) .... CAF
Combined Action Group [*Senior command of all Combined Action Companies*] [*Military*] ...... CAG
Combined Action Platoon [*Military*] .... CAP
Combined Action Program (SAUO) .... CAP
Combined Action Program Unit Veterans Association (EA) ...... CUVA
Combined Active/Passive Emitter Rangings .... CAPER
Combined Active/Passive RADAR .... CAPAR
Combined Activities System [*Vietnam*] [*Air Force*] ...... CAS
Combined Additional Coverage [*Insurance*] .... CAC
Combined Administrative Commission (SAUO) .... CADC
Combined Administrative Committee (SAUO) .... CAdC
Combined Administrative Committee .... CADC
Combined Administrative Liquidating Agency [*Microfilmed SHAEF documents for each participating country after SHAEF was disbanded*] [*Post-World War II*] ...... CALA
Combined Agencies Field Team [*US Military Government, Germany*] ...... CAFT
Combined Agency for Middle East Supplies [*World War II*] ...... CAMES
Combined Agricultural and Food Machinery Committee [*World War II*] ...... CAFMC
Combined Air Defense Systems (SAUS) .... CADS
Combined Air Documents Research Center .... CADRC
Combined Air Force Operating Base (CINC) .... CAFOB
Combined Air Operations [*Air Force*] (DOMA) .... COMAO
Combined Air Operations Center (ACAE) .... CAOC
Combined Air Operations Centre (SAUS) .... CAOC
Combined Air Operations Coordination Center (SAUO) ...... CAOCC
Combined Air Support [*Army*] (DOMA) .... CAS

Combined Air Transport Operations Room [*Allied office, World War II*] ...... CATOR
Combined Airborne Surveillance and Control for Aerospace Defense ...... CASCADE
Combined Aircraft Submarine Exercise [*NATO*] (NATG) ...... CASEX
Combined Aircraft Transfer and Release Assembly (MCD) ...... CATRA
Combined Air-Defense System [*Military*] (DOMA) ...... CADS
Combined Airglow Telescope Spectrometer (SAUS) ...... CATS
Combined Air-Warfare Course (SAUS) .... CAWC
Combined Allied Air Forces .... CAAF
Combined Allied Defence Experiment (SAUS) .... CADE
Combined Allied Defense Experiment [*Military*] (SDI) ...... CADE
Combined Allied Forces Information Center (SAUO) ...... CAFIC
Combined Allied Land Forces .... CALF
Combined Allied Naval Forces .... CANF
Combined Allied Naval Forces, Southwest Pacific Area ...... CANFSWPA
Combined Allied Naval Forces, Southwest Pacific Ocean Area Operating Plan ...... CANFSWPAOPPLAN
Combined Allowance for Logistics and Maintenance Support System [*Coast Guard*] (MCD) ...... CALMS
Combined Allowance for Logistics Management .... CALM
Combined Alternate Data/Voice (SAUS) .... CADV
Combined Altitude Radar Altimeter (SAUS) .... CARA
Combined Altitude RADAR Altimeter [*Electronic defense system*] ...... CARA
Combined Amphibious Task Force (NVT) .... CATF
Combined Amplitude Phase Shift Keying (MCD) .... CAPSK
Combined Analog-Digital Systems Simulator [*Computer science*] ...... CADSS
Combined Annual Wage Reporting [*IRS*] .... CAWR
Combined Antenna System (CAAL) .... CAS
Combined Antiaircraft Operations Room (SAUS) .... CAAOR
Combined Anti-Submarine Exercise (SAUS) .... CASEX
Combined Approach Control/International Station (FAAC) ...... CAP/IS
Combined Approach System Investigation (SAA) .... CASI
Combined Armed Armies (ACAE) .... CAA
Combined Arms (AABC) .... CA
Combined Arms & Command Post Trainer (SAUS) ...... CACPT
Combined Arms and Service Staff School (DOMA) ..... CAS³
Combined Arms and Services Staff School [*Army*] (RDA) CAS3
Combined Arms and Support [*Army*] (AABC) .... CAAS
Combined Arms and Support Research Office [*Fort Leavenworth, KS*] ...... CASRO
Combined Arms and Support Task Force Evaluation Model [*Army*] (RDA) ...... CASTFOREM
Combined Arms and Tactics Department [*Military*] (INF) ...... CATD
Combined Arms Army (MCD) .... CAA
Combined Arms Assessment Network [*DoD*] .... CAAN
Combined Arms Battalion (MCD) .... CAB
Combined Arms Battalions (Heavy) [*Army*] .... CAB(H)
Combined Arms Battalions (Light) [*Army*] .... CAB(L)
Combined Arms Center (AABC) .... CAC
Combined Arms Combat Development Activity [*Fort Leavenworth, KS*] [*Army*] (AABC) ...... CACDA
Combined Arms Combat Development Activity C3I [*Command, Control, Communications, and Intelligence*] Directorate [*Fort Leavenworth, KS*] [*Army*] CACDA/C3I
Combined Arms Command and Control [*Army*] (RDA) CAC2
Combined Arms Command-Training [*Fort Leavenwoth, KS*] [*Army*] (INF) ...... CAC-TNG
Combined Arms Exercise [*Marine Corps*] (DOMA) ..... CAX
Combined Arms Fighting Vehicle (MCD) .... CAFV
Combined Arms Group [*Army*] .... CAG
Combined Arms in a Nuclear/Chemical Environment [*Military*] (RDA) ...... CANE
Combined Arms Initiative [*Army*] .... CAI
Combined Arms Live Fire Exercises (INF) .... CALFEX
Combined Arms Maneuver Battalion [*Experiment*] [*Army*] (INF) ...... CAMB
Combined Arms Mission Area Analysis [*Army*] .... CAMAA
Combined Arms Modeling [*Military*] .... CAM
Combined Arms Multipurpose Missile System [*Army*] ...... CAMMS
Combined Arms Operations Research Activity [*Fort Leavenworth, KS*] ...... CAORA
Combined Arms Regiment [*Marine Corps*] (DOMA) ..... CAR
Combined Arms Research Library [*Military*] .... CARL
Combined Arms Research Office .... CARO
Combined Arms School (SAUO) .... CAS
Combined Arms Services Staff School (SAUO) .... CAS
Combined Arms Simulation (ACAE) .... CAS
Combined Arms Simulation Model (MCD) .... CASM
Combined Arms Staff Trainer (SAUS) .... CAST
Combined Arms Studies and Analysis Activity [*Fort Leavenworth, KS*] ...... CASAA
Combined Arms Support Command [*DoD*] (RDA) .... CASCOM
Combined Arms Systems Engineering .... CASE
Combined Arms Tactical Trainer [*Army*] (RDA) ...... CATT
Combined Arms Tactical Training Simulator [*Army*] (MCD) ...... CATTS
Combined Arms Team (MCD) .... CAT
Combined Arms Team/Lightweight Combat Vehicle (SAUS) ...... CAT/LCV
Combined Arms Training [*Military*] (NVT) .... CMBARMTNG
Combined Arms Training Activity [*Fort Leavenworth, KS*] (INF) ...... CATA
Combined Arms Training Board [*Military*] .... CATB
Combined Arms Training Center [*Army*] .... CATC
Combined Arms Training Developments Activity [*or Agency*] [*Army*] (RDA) ...... CATRADA
Combined Arms Training Integrated Evaluation System [*Military*] ...... CATIES
Combined Arms Training Strategy [*Army*] (DOMA) ..... CATS
Combined Army Air Transport Organization [*World War II*] ...... CAATO
Combined Army Group (SAUO) .... CAG
Combined Army Tactical Training [*System*] (DOMA) ... CATT
Combined Army Training Board (SAUO) .... CATB
Combined Artillery/Aviation Simulator (DWSG) .... CAAS

Combined Automated Resource System [*Department of Health and Human Services*] (GFGA) .... CARES
Combined Aviation Force .... CAF
Combined Balancing & Elevating (SAUS) .... CBE
Combined Black Publishers [*Defunct*] (EA) .... CBP
Combined Blood Count (WDAA) .... CBC
Combined Bomber Offensive [*World War II*] .... CBO
Combined Book Exhibit .... CBE
Combined Bureau, Middle East [*British military*] (DMA) .... CBME
Combined Cadet Force [*British equivalent of US ROTC*] .... CCF
Combined Cadet Force (SAUO) .... CCF
Combined Cadet Force Association [*British military*] (DMA) .... CCFA
Combined Carbon (SAUS) CC
Combined Carrier (SAUS) CC
Combined Case Control [*IRS*] CCC
Combined Center Radar Approach Control [*FAA*] (TAG) .... CERAP
Combined Center/Tower (SAUS) .... CC/T
Combined Chiefs of Staff [*DoD*] .... CCOS
Combined Chiefs of Staff [*DoD*] .... CCS
Combined Cipher Machine .... CCM
Combined Civil Affairs Committee [*World War II*] .... CCAC
Combined Civil Affairs Committee, London Subcommittee [*World War II*] .... CCAC/L
Combined Civil Affairs Committee, Supply Subcommittee [*World War II*] .... CCAC/S
Combined Civil Affairs Liquidating Agency [*World War II*] .... CCALA
Combined Civil Affairs Task Force (SAUS) .... CCATF
Combined Coal Control Group, Essen (SAUO) .... CCCG
Combined Coding Machine .... CCM
Combined Combat Center, Direction Center [*Military*] (SAA) .... CC/DC
Combined Command for Reconnaissance Activities in Korea .... CCRAK
Combined Command Post .... CCP
Combined Committee for North Africa [*World War II*] .... CCNA
Combined Committee on Air Training in North America .... CCATNA
Combined Communications (SAUO) .... CCA
Combined Communications Board [*World War II*] .... CCB
Combined Communications Board Publications .... CCBP
Combined Communications Electronics Boards (CIST) .... CCEB
Combined Communications Material Center (SAUO) .... COCOMAC
Combined Contaminants, Oxygen, and Humidity (MCD) .... CCOH
Combined Control Unit (SAUS) .... CCU
Combined Cooling Performance Factor .... CCPF
Combined Coordinating Committee (SAUO) CCC
Combined Cortical Thickness (DNAB) .... CCT
Combined Cryptographical Shore Support Activity (SAUS) .... CCSSA
Combined Currency and Interest Rate Swap (EBF) .... CIRCUS
Combined CUSUM [*Cumulative Sum*]/Stewart Method [*Laboratory analysis*] .... CCS
Combined Cycle (CARB) CC
Combined Defense Improvement Projects .... CDIP
Combined Deputy Military Governors (SAUO) .... CDMG
Combined Development Agency [*Anglo-American uranium procurement*] .... CDA
Combined Diesel and Diesel (SAUS) .... CODAD
Combined Diesel and Gas [*Turbine*] .... CODAG
Combined Diesel, Electric and Gas (SAUS) .... CODLAG
Combined Diesel Or Gas .... CODOG
Combined Diesel or Gas Turbine Propulsion .... CODOG
Combined Diesel-Electric And Gas [*Turbine*] (DOMA) .... CODELAG
Combined Diptheria and Tetanus [*Vaccine*] [*Medicine*] .... CDT
Combined Displaced Persons Executive [*World War II*] .... CDPX
Combined Distribution Frame [*RADAR*] .... CDF
Combined Distribution Function (MCD) .... CDF
Combined Documents Exploitation Center [*Saigon, Vietnam*] (VNW) .... CDEC
Combined Double Tee [*Engineering*] (IAA) .... CDT
Combined Economic Warfare Agencies .... CEWA
Combined Edible Nut Trade Association [*British*] (DBA) .... CENTA
Combined Effects Bomb (MCD) .... CEB
Combined Effects Bomblets (SAUS) .... CEB
Combined Effects Munition (MCD) .... CEM
Combined Effects Submissile (MCD) .... CES
Combined Effects Warhead (SAUS) .... CEW
Combined Electrolysis and Catalytic Exchange [*CANDU-reactor advantage*] .... CECE
Combined Electron Quench and Optical Masker (SAUS) .... CEQOM
Combined Electronic Display & Map .... CEDAM
Combined Electronic Warfare Control Center (SAUO) .... CEWCC
Combined Electronics Assembly (SAUS) .... CEA
Combined Elements and Integrated Systems (SSD) .... CE & IS
Combined Elements and Integration Systems (SAUS) .... CE&IS
Combined Emitter Locator Test-bed (SAUS) .... CELT
Combined Engineering Plant Exchange Record [*Telecommunications*] (TEL) .... CEPER
Combined English Stores [*Commercial firm*] [*British*] .... CES
Combined Environment Centrifuge (SAUS) .... CEC
Combined Environment Groups (SAUO) .... CEG
Combined Environmental Chamber (SAUS) .... CEC
Combined Environmental Data Information System (SAUS) .... CEDIS
Combined Environmental Reliability Testing [*Air Force*] (RDA) .... CERT
Combined Environmental Test (MCD) .... CET
Combined Environmental, Vibration, Acceleration, Temperature [*Aerospace*] (AAG) .... CEVAT
Combined Exercise [*Military*] (NVT) .... COMBEX
Combined Exercise Planning Staff [*Military*] (MCD) .... CEPS
Combined Exports Market Committee [*World War II*] .... CEMC
Combined Fates and Effects Model (SAUS) .... CFEM

Combined Federal Campaign [*Federal government*] (AABC) .... CFC
Combined Federal Services Campaign (SAUO) .... CFSC
Combined Field Army (MCD) .... CFA
Combined Field Command (MCD) .... CFC
Combined Field Maintenance Shop [*Army*] (AABC) .... CFMS
Combined File Search [*IBM program*] [*Computer science*] .... CFS
Combined File Search Strategy [*Computer science*] .... CFSS
Combined File Search System (SAUS) .... CFSS
Combined Filter and Plot (NATG) .... CFP
Combined Food Board [*United States, United Kingdom, and Canada*] [*World War II*] .... CFB
Combined Food Board (SAUO) .... CFB
Combined Forces Air Component (SAUS) .... CFAC
Combined Forces Command [*Korea*] (MCD) .... CFC
Combined Forces, Europe (SAUS) .... CFE
Combined Function (OA) .... CF
Combined Gas and Gas (PDAA) .... COGAG
Combined Gas or Gas (PDAA) .... COGOG
Combined Gas Turbine or Gas Turbine Propulsion .... COGOG
Combined Glass and Ceramic Research Institute (SAUO) .... CGCRI
Combined Ground Command Post (MCD) .... CGCP
Combined Headquarters (SAUO) .... CHQ
Combined Health Agencies Drive (ACAE) .... CHAD
Combined Health Appeal of America (EA) .... CHAA
Combined Health Information Database [*Public Health Service*] [*Information service or system*] (IID) .... CHID
Combined Heart and Power Association [*British*] (DBA) .... CHPA
Combined Heat and Power [*Generation*] .... CHP
Combined Heat and Power Group (SAUO) .... CHPG
Combined Heating Performance Factor .... CHPF
Combined Helicopter Outyear Procurement Package - Educational Requirement [*Army*] .... CHOPPER
Combined Helmholtz Integral Equation Formulation .... CHIEF
Combined High Frequency of Ventilation [*Medicine*] (DAVI) .... CHFV
Combined Higher Education Software Team (AIE) .... CHEST
Combined Hormonal Therapy [*Medicine*] (MELL) .... CHT
Combined Immunodeficiency Disease [*Immunology*] .... CID
Combined Industry Committee [*Australia*] CIC
Combined Influence Sweep (SAUS) .... CIS
Combined Information Storage and Retrieval System (SAUS) .... COMISARS
Combined In-Port Tactical Exercise [*Navy*] (NVT) .... CINTEX
Combined Instrument Panel .... CIP
Combined Intelligence Center (DOMA) CIC
Combined Intelligence Center, Iraq [*World War II*] CICI
Combined Intelligence Center, Vietnam CICV
Combined Intelligence Committee [*World War II*] CIC
Combined Intelligence Course (SAUO) CIC
Combined Intelligence Objectives Subcommittee [*World War II*] .... CIOS
Combined Intelligence Operations Section (SAUO) .... CIOS
Combined Intelligence Priorities Committee [*Later, CIU*] [*US and British*] [*London, World War II*] .... CIPC
Combined Intelligence Staff [*World War II*] .... CIS
Combined Intelligence Unit [*Formerly, CIPC*] [*RAF*] [*British*] .... CIU
Combined Intercept Valve [*Nuclear energy*] (NRCH) CIV
Combined Interest Rate and Currency Swap [*Finance*] .... CIRCUS
Combined Interim System Test (ACAE) .... CIST
Combined Intermediate Valve [*Nuclear energy*] (NRCH) CIV
Combined Intermittent Therapy (DAVI) .... CIT
Combined Interrogator-Transponder (SAUS) .... CIT
Combined Intracapsular Cataract Extraction [*Opthalmology*] (DAVI) .... CICE
Combined Jewish Philanthropies .... CJP
Combined Joint Maritime Operations Centre (SAUS) .... CJMOC
Combined Joint Task Forces [*NATO*] (ECON) .... CJTF
Combined Language Age [*of the hearing-impaired*] .... CLA
Combined LASER Instrumentation Package (NASA) .... CLIP
Combined Lease Plan .... CLP
Combined Liberated Areas Committee [*World War II*] .... CLAC
Combined Liberated Areas Committee, Supply Subcommittee [*World War II*] .... CLAC(S)
Combined Library Unions Committee [*Australia*] .... CLUC
Combined Life Assurance Co. (WDAA) .... CLAC
Combined Limit [*Insurance*] .... C/L
Combined Line and Recording Traffic (SAUS) .... CLR Traffic
Combined Line and Recording Trunk (IEEE) .... CLR
Combined Loads Orbiter Test (MCD) .... CLOT
Combined Logistics Stores Facility (DOMA) .... CLSF
Combined Logistics Support System (SAUO) .... CLSS
Combined Mailing [*Postal Service*] [*United States*] (WDMC) .... comailing
Combined Main Distributing Frame .... CMDF
Combined Maintenance Removal Interval (AFIT) .... CMRI
Combined [*Arms*] Maneuver Training Center [*Hohenfels, Germany*] [*Army*] (DOMA) .... CMTC
Combined Map and Electronic Display (MCD) .... COMED
Combined Marine Surcharge (SAUS) .... CMS
Combined Master File [*Computer science*] .... CMF
Combined Memory (SAUS) .... CM
Combined Meteorological Committee .... CMC
Combined Military Coordination Planning Staff (SAUO) .... CMCPS
Combined Military Exploitation Center (MCD) .... CMEC
Combined Military Hospital (SAUO) .... CMH
Combined Military Hospital (SAUS) .... GMH
Combined Military Interrogation Center .... CMIC
Combined Military Transportation [*British*] .... CMT
Combined Military Transportation Committee .... CMTC

Combined Miniature Deterrent Forces [*Organization in film "Fantastic Voyage"*] .... CMDF
Combined Mixer Settler [*Chemical engineering*] .... CMS
Combined Movement Center (SAUO) .... CMC
Combined Movements Control Center (SAUO) .... CMCC
Combined Multiplication (SAUS) .... CM
Combined Munitions Assignments Board [*World War II*] .... CMAB
Combined Munitions Board (SAUO) .... CMB
Combined Name and Address File [*IRS*] .... CNAF
Combined National Veterans Association of America (EA) .... CNVAA
Combined Navigation and Radar system (SAUS) .... NAVAR
Combined Neutral and Earth (SAUS) .... cne
Combined Neutral and Earth (PDAA) .... CNE
Combined New Australia Party [*Political party*] .... CNA
Combined New Australia Party [*Political party*] .... CNAP
Combined Nomenclature [*EC*] (ECED) .... CN
Combined Nuclear and Steam [*Propulsion*] (DOMA) .... CONAS
Combined Nuclear Steam and Gas (PDAA) .... CONAG
Combined Nuclear Steam or Gas (PDAA) .... CONOG
Combined Office Material Procurement and Distribution .... COMPAD
Combined Office Standard Environment (SAUO) .... COSE
Combined Officer of Merchant Navy Operations [*British*] .... COMNO
Combined Oil and Tanker Group (NATG) .... COT
Combined Operation Centre (SAUS) .... COC
Combined Operational Intelligence Center [*Navy*] .... COIC
Combined Operational Planning Committee [*Royal Air Force and US 8th Air Force*] [*World War II*] .... COPC
Combined Operational Service Command .... COSC
Combined Operations .... CO
Combined Operations [*Military*] .... Comops
Combined Operations Bombardment Battery (SAUO) .... COBB
Combined Operations Command [*British*] .... COC
Combined Operations Development Centre [*British military*] (DMA) .... CODC
Combined Operations Experimental Wing [*World War II*] .... COEW
Combined Operations Headquarters [*World War II*] .... COHQ
Combined Operations Headquarters (SAUO) .... COHQ
Combined Operations Headquarters, Zara [*Former Yugoslavia*] [*World War II*] .... COZA
Combined Operations Intelligence Center (SAUS) .... COIC
Combined Operations Lasing Team [*Army*] (INF) .... COLT
Combined Operations Material Department (SAUO) .... COMD
Combined Operations Material Liaison Officer .... COMLO
Combined Operations Nuclear Medical Evaluation Team (MCD) .... CONMET
Combined Operations Personnel [*Navy*] [*British*] .... COP
Combined Operations Pilotage Party .... COPP
Combined Operations Repair Organization [*For invasion of France*] [*World War II*] .... COREP
Combined Operations Scout Unit .... COSU
Combined Operations Signal Maintenance Depot .... COSMD
Combined Operations Signal Maintenance Officer .... COSMO
Combined Operations Signal Officer .... COSO
Combined Operations Supply Depot .... COSD
Combined Operations Support Depot (SAUO) .... COSD
Combined Operations Tug Organization [*For invasion of France*] [*World War II*] .... COTUG
Combined Opposition Parties [*Politics*] .... COP
Combined Opposition Party [*Pakistan*] [*Political party*] (FEA) .... COP
Combined Optical [*Photography*] .... COMOPT
Combined Optical (SAUS) .... COMPOT
Combined Orbital Maneuvering and Abort System [*NASA*] (NASA) .... COMAS
Combined Organic Movement for Education and Training [*British*] .... COMET
Combined Organizations of Numismatic Error Collectors of America (EA) .... CONECA
Combined Overload Repair Control (MCD) .... COREP
Combined Overseas Rehabilitation Relief Appeal (SAUO) .... CORRA
Combined Over-the-Beach Terminal Unit (NATG) .... COBTU
Combined Paging and Access (CGWS) .... CPA
Combined Passenger Check List (ADA) .... CPCL
Combined Passive Active Detection [*RADAR*] .... COMPACT
Combined Passive Active Detection (SAUS) .... COMPACT Detection
Combined Pensioners' Association of Victoria. News [*A publication*] .... Combined Pension Ass Vic News
Combined Personnel Recovery Center (CINC) .... CPRC
Combined Photographic Interpretation Center .... CPIC
Combined Photographic Reconnaisance Wing (SAUO) .... CPRW
Combined Pituitary Hormone Deficiency [*Medicine*] .... CPHD
Combined Planning Staff [*Military*] [*British*] .... CPS
Combined Policy Committee [*NATO*] (NATG) .... CPC
Combined Principles Simulator [*Nuclear engine*] .... CPS
Combined Processor and RAM Module [*Computer science*] (NITA) .... CPR
Combined Procurement Processing Series (MCD) .... CPPS
Combined Production and Resources Board [*World War II*] .... CPRB
Combined Programming Language [*Computer science*] .... CPL
Combined Protocol (SAUS) .... CP
Combined Pulsed Neutron Experiment (MCD) .... CPNE
Combined Quarantine Force [*US/Venezuela/Dominican Republic/Argentina*] .... COMBQUARFOR
Combined Radiation Effects Test Chamber (OA) .... CRETC
Combined Radiation Test .... CRT
Combined Radiation Treatment [*Oncology*] .... CRT
Combined Raw Materials Board [*US and Britain*] [*World War II*] .... CRMB
Combined Readiness Air Exercise (MCD) .... CRAE
Combined Receiving and Transmitting Unit .... CRTU
Combined Reconnaissance and Intelligence Platoon [*Military*] (VNW) .... CRIP
Combined Reentry Effort in Small Systems .... CRESS

Combined Reference Frequency System .... CRFS
Combined Refining Process (PDAA) .... CRP
Combined Registered Publication Memoranda .... CRPM
Combined Release and Radiation Effects Satellite [*NASA*] .... CRRES
Combined Removal Interval [*Engine*] .... CMRI
Combined Repatriation Executive (SAUO) .... CRX
Combined Rescue Coordination Center (SAUO) .... CRCC
Combined Resources Allocation Board [*World War II*] .... CRAB
Combined Retrospective Index Sets [*Information service or system*] (IID) .... CRIS
Combined Rocket Warhead (KSC) .... CROW
Combined Rotating Unit [*Nuclear energy*] .... CRU
Combined Rotation and Multiple-Pulse Spectroscopy [*Physics*] .... CRAMPS
Combined Rubber Committee (SAUO) .... CRC
Combined S-Band .... CSB
Combined Scottish Society of New South Wales [*Australia*] .... CSSNSW
Combined Sensor Program (ARMP) .... CSP
Combined Sensor Tracking Exercise [*Military*] (NVT) .... COMSENEX
Combined Server Overflow (SAUS) .... CSO
Combined Service Command (DOMA) .... CSC
Combined Service Forces (SAUO) .... CSF
Combined Service Territory [*Red Cross*] .... CST
Combined Services (SAUS) X
Combined Services Detailed Interrogation Center [*World War II*] .... CSDIC
Combined Services Detailed Interrogation Center - Nonoperational Intelligence [*World War II*] .... CSDICNOI
Combined Services Directorate (SAUO) .... DOCS
Combined Services Directorate and Economic Directorate (SAUO) .... DOCSECO
Combined Services Entertainment (SAUO) .... CSE
Combined Services Entertainment [*British military*] (DMA) .... CSE
Combined Services Entertainment Unit [*British military*] (DMA) .... CSEU
Combined Services Liaison Officer .... CSLO
Combined Services Support Program [*Navy*] (NG) .... CSSP
Combined Services Support Program School, Atlantic [*Navy*] (DNAB) .... COMBSVCSUPPSCOLANT
Combined Services Support Program School, Pacific [*Navy*] (DNAB) .... COMBSVCSUPPSCOLPAC
Combined Setter Clubs of America (EA) .... CSCA
Combined Sewer Overflow .... CSO
Combined Sewer System (ADWA) .... CSS
Combined Shaft Unit .... CSU
Combined Shipbuilding Committee [*World War II*] .... CSC
Combined Shipping Adjustment Board [*World War II*] .... CSAB
Combined Short Takeoff and Landing (SAUS) .... C-STOL
Combined Signal Board [*North Africa*] [*World War II*] .... CSB
Combined Single Limit [*Insurance*] .... CSL
Combined Sorting System (SAUS) .... COSOS
Combined Special Forces Operational Detachment (CINC) .... CSFOD
Combined Special Operations Area [*Military*] (DOMA) .... CSOA
Combined Staff Planners .... CSP
Combined Station/Tower [*Aviation*] .... CS/T
Combined Steam and Gas [*Propulsion*] (MCD) .... COSAG
Combined Steam and Nuclear [*Propulsion*] (DOMA) .... COSAN
Combined Steel Control Group (SAUO) .... CSCG
Combined Steel Group (SAUO) .... CStG
Combined Storage (SAUS) .... CS
Combined Strategic Targets Committee [*World War II*] .... CSTC
Combined Stratospheric Measuring Program [*Army*] .... COSMEP
Combined Stress Reliability Test (MCD) .... CSRT
Combined Studies Group [*Central Intelligence Agency operation in Southeast Asia*] .... CSG
Combined Supply Board (SAUO) .... CSB
Combined Support Division [*Canadian Navy*] .... CSD
Combined Support Maintenance Shop [*USNG*] (MCD) .... CSMS
Combined Surveillance and Foliage Penetration RADAR (MCD) .... COMSFOR
Combined Symbol Matching [*Fax compression technology*] [*Compression Labs, Inc.*] (PCM) .... CSM
Combined System Test Stand (IEEE) .... CSTS
Combined Systems Acceptance Test (MCD) .... CSAT
Combined Systems Test .... CST
Combined Systems Test Unit (MCD) .... CSTU
Combined Tab Vaccine plus Tetanus and Diphtheria Toxoid (SAUS) .... TABTD
Combined Tactical Trainer, Stage 5 feasibility study (SAUS) .... CTT 5
Combined Target Area .... CTA
Combined Task Force [*NATO*] (NATG) .... CTF
Combined Task Group [*NATO*] (NATG) .... CTG
Combined Test Force [*Military*] .... CTF
Combined Test Stand (SAUS) .... CTS
Combined Test Team (MCD) .... CTT
Combined Testicular Weight [*Medicine*] (DMAA) .... CTW
Combined Thermomechanical Treatment .... CTMT
Combined Tin Committee (MCD) .... CTC
Combined Total Loan-to-Value Ratio [*Business term*] (EMRF) .... CTLVR
Combined Traffic Center (SAUO) .... CTC
Combined Training Center .... CTC
Combined Training Exercise [*Military*] (ADDR) .... CTX
Combined Transcortical Aphasia (DIPS) .... CTA
Combined Transport [*Shipping*] .... CT
Combined Transport Bill of Lading (SAUS) .... CT-B/L
Combined Transport Document [*Shipping*] .... CTD
Combined Transport Operator [*Shipping*] .... CTO
Combined Transportation Equipment Committee [*Combined Production and Resources Board*] [*World War II*] .... CTEC
Combined Travel Board [*Allied German Occupation Forces*] .... CTB
Combined Travel Security Board [*Allied German Occupation Forces*] .... CTSB
Combined Trials [*Shipbuilding*] .... CT

Combined Unconventional Warfare Task Force (CINC) ... CUWTF
Combined Union and Shop Committee [*Australia*] ... CUSC
Combined Unit Record Tape (ACAE) ... CURT
Combined United Kingdom / Australian Long Range Weapons Committee ... CUKAC
Combined Universities Campaign for Nuclear Disarmament [*Canada*] ... CUCND
Combined Ventricular Hypertrophy (MAE) ... CVH
Combined VHF [*Very-High-Frequency*]**-Band** ... CVB
Combined Volume-Weighted Mean [*Statistics*] ... CVWM
Combined VOR and DME radio station (SAUS) ... VOR/DME
Combined VOR and TACAN Navigational Facility [*FAA*] (TAG) ... VORTAC
Combined VOR and Tacan system (SAUS) ... VORTAC
Combined Wage Claim [*Unemployment insurance*] ... CWC
Combined Welfare Administration Fund ... CWAF
Combined Wheat Control Secretariat (SAUO) ... CWCS
Combined Wheat Control Section [*Allied German Occupation Forces*] ... CWCS
Combined-Cycle Gas Turbines (ECON) ... CCGT
Combined-Heat-and-Power District Heating [*British*] (DI) ... CHPDH
Combined-Heat-and-Power Station [*Energy production*] ... CHP
Combining (ADWA) ... comb
Combining (SAUS) ... Comb
Combining Conditional Expectations and Residuals Plot ... CERES plot
Combining Power ... CP
Combining Power Test (AAMN) ... CPT
Comboni Missionaries of the Heart of Jesus (TOCD) ... mccj
Comboni Missionaries of the Heart of Jesus (Verona) (TOCD) ... MCCJ
Comboni Missionary Sisters (TOCD) ... CMS
Comborne School of Metalliferous Mining (SAUS) ... CSMM
Combustibility (SAUS) ... Comb
Combustible (MSA) ... COMBL
Combustible Augmented Plasma (SAUS) ... CAP
Combustible Cartridge Case (SAUS) ... CCC
Combustible Case Ammunition [*Weaponry*] [*Military*] (VNW) ... CBSS
Combustible Case Charge (SAUS) ... CCC
Combustible Charge Container (SAUS) ... CCC
Combustible Gas Tracer (SAUS) ... CGT
Combustible Limit Relay (IAA) ... CLR
Combustible Metals [*Fire classification*] ... D
Combustible Storage Building (AAG) ... CSB
Combustion (ADWA) ... com
Combustion (AAG) ... COMB
Combustion ... COMBN
Combustion ... COMBSTN
Combustion and Explosives Research (AAG) ... C & ER
Combustion and Explosives Research (SAUS) ... C&ER
Combustion and Flame (journ.) (SAUS) ... Combust Flame
Combustion Byproduct (EEVL) ... CBP
Combustion Chamber (KSC) ... CC
Combustion Chamber Deposits [*Fuels and lubricants testing*] ... CCD
Combustion Chemical Vapor Deposition ... CCVD
Combustion Control by Vortex Stratification [*Automotive engine design*] ... CCVS
Combustion Efficiency (CARB) ... CE
Combustion Efficiency ... COMB EFF
Combustion Engineering Association [*British*] ... CEA
Combustion Engineering Inc. (SAUO) ... CE
Combustion Engineering, Inc. (SAUO) ... CSP
Combustion Engineering Nuclear Division [*AEC*] (MCD) ... CEND
Combustion Engineering Safety Analysis Report [*Nuclear energy*] (IAA) ... CESAR
Combustion Engineering Standard Safety Analysis Report [*Nuclear energy*] (NRCH) ... CESSAR
Combustion Engineering Superheater Ltd., Ottawa, ON, Canada [*Library symbol*] [*Library of Congress*] (LCLS) ... CaOOCES
Combustion Engineering Superheater Ltd., Ottawa, Ontario [*Library symbol*] [*National Library of Canada*] (NLC) ... OOCES
Combustion Engineering Superheater Ltd., Ottawa, Ontario (SAUS) ... OOCFS
Combustion Equilibrium Calculation Computer Program (MCD) ... CECCP
Combustion Equipment Associates, Inc. (EFIS) ... CEA
Combustion Explosion and Shock Waves (journ.) (SAUS) ... Combust Explos Shock Waves
Combustion Gas Analyzer Program [*Nuclear energy*] (NRCH) ... COGAP
Combustion Gas Control System [*Nuclear energy*] (NRCH) ... CGCS
Combustion, Heat, and Mass (PDAA) ... CHAM
Combustion Institute (EA) ... CI
Combustion Integrated Rack (SAUS) ... CIR
Combustion Metamorphism [*Geology*] ... CM
Combustion Modified Highly Resilient (SAUS) ... CMHR
Combustion Module-1 (SAUS) ... CM-1
Combustion Research Facility [*Department of Energy*] [*Livermore, CA*] ... CRF
Combustion Space Monitor (SAUS) ... CSM
Combustion Stability Monitor ... CSM
Combustion Subcommittee [*Military*] ... CS
Combustion Systems Ltd. (SAUS) ... CSL
Combustion Turbine [*Type of cogenerator*] ... CT
Combustion Zone Temperature [*Fuel technology*] ... CZT
Combustor (MSA) ... CMBSTR
Combustor Exit Temperature (MCD) ... CET
Comcast Cl'A' [*NASDAQ symbol*] (TTSB) ... CMCSA
Comcast Cl'A'Spl(non-vtg) [*NASDAQ symbol*] (TTSB) ... CMCSK
Comcast Corp. [*NASDAQ symbol*] (NQ) ... CMCS
Comcast Corp. [*Associated Press*] (SAG) ... Comc
Comcast Corp. [*Associated Press*] (SAG) ... Comcast
Comcast UK Cable Partners Ltd. [*NASDAQ symbol*] (SAG) ... CMCA
Comcast UK Cable Partners Ltd. [*Associated Press*] (SAG) ... CmcstUK
Comcast UK Cable Partners'A' [*NASDAQ symbol*] (TTSB) ... CMCAF
Comdata Holding Corp. [*Associated Press*] (SAG) ... Comdata
Comdata Holdings Corp. [*NASDAQ symbol*] (NQ) ... CMDT
Comdial Corp. [*Associated Press*] (SAG) ... Cmdial
Comdial Corp. [*NASDAQ symbol*] (NQ) ... CMDL
Comdisco 8.75% cm Ser'A'Pfd [*NYSE symbol*] (TTSB) ... CDOPrA
Comdisco 8.75% cm Ser'B'Pfd [*NYSE symbol*] (TTSB) ... CDOPrB
Comdisco Disaster Recovery Services (HGAA) ... CDRS
Comdisco, Inc. [*NYSE symbol*] (SPSG) ... CDO
Comdisco, Inc. [*Associated Press*] (SAG) ... Comd
Comdisco, Inc. [*Associated Press*] (SAG) ... Comdis
Comdisco, Inc. [*Associated Press*] (SAG) ... Comdisco
Conditional Command (SAUS) ... CC
Come [*Like, As*] [*Music*] (ROG) ... CO
Come Hither [*A publication*] ... CH
Come, Let Us Reason Together [*Labor mediators' slogan*] ... CLURT
Come Off Your Old Tired Ethics [*Prostitutes' lobbying group*] ... COYOTE
Come Primo [*As at First*] [*Music*] ... Co Imo
Come Quick - Danger [*International distress signal, used before SOS*] ... CQD
Come Sopra [*As Above*] [*Music*] (ROG) ... CO SA
Come Sopra [*As Above*] [*Music*] ... CO SO
Come Sopra [*As Above*] [*Music*] ... CS
Come-All-Ye [*A publication*] (BRI) ... CAY
Comed Aviation Ltd. [*British*] [*FAA designator*] (FAAC) ... CDE
Comed Financial I [*NYSE symbol*] (SAG) ... CWE
ComEd Financing 1 8.48% 'TOPrS' [*NYSE symbol*] (TTSB) ... CWEPrT
Comed Financing I [*Associated Press*] (SAG) ... Comed
Comedian [*or Comedy*] (ROG) ... COM
Comedian Society for Amateurs and Professionals [*Defunct*] (EA) ... CSAP
Comedo (MELL) ... C
Comedy (WDMC) ... com
Comedy Central (ADWA) ... COM
[*The*] **Comedy Channel** ... TCC
[*The*] **Comedy of Errors** [*Shakespearean work*] ... C of E
Comedy of Errors [*Shakespearean drama*] (BARN) ... Com Err
[*The*] **Comedy of Errors** [*Shakespearean work*] ... Err
Comedy Prescription [*An association*] (EA) ... CP
Comedy Store [*Nightclub in which inexperienced comedians appear free in return for exposure to an audience*] ... CS
Comedy Television [*Cable-television system*] ... CTV
Comedy Writers Association (EA) ... CWA
Comence (FAAC) ... CMNC
Comenius Centre for Education and Democracy [*Praha 1, Czech Republic*] ... CCED
Comenius World Council (EA) ... CWC
Comercial Aerea SA de CV [*Mexico*] [*ICAO designator*] (FAAC) ... CRS
Comerica, Inc. [*NYSE symbol*] (SPSG) ... CMA
Comerica, Inc. [*Associated Press*] (SAG) ... Comeric
Comer's Forms of Writs [*A publication*] (DLA) ... Com Forms
Comerstone Natural Gas [*Formerly, Endevco, Inc.*] [*AMEX symbol*] (SPSG) ... CGA
Comet and Asteroid Rendezvous Docking (MCD) ... CARD
Comet Halley Active Monitoring Program ... CHAMP
Comet Halley American Southern-Hemisphere Expedition ... CHASE
Comet Industries [*Vancouver Stock Exchange symbol*] ... CMU
Comet Mesoscale Analysis and Prediction (SAUS) ... COMAP
Comet Nucleus Sample Return ... CNSR
Comet Nucleus Tour [*NASA's study of photochemical processes in comet comas*] ... CONTOUR
Comet Rendezvous and Asteroid Flyby [*Proposed NASA mission*] ... CRAF
Comet Rendezvous Mission ... CRM
Cometary Feasability Study Group (SAUO) ... CFSG
Cometary Feasibility Study Group [*European Space Research Organization*] (IEEE) ... CFSG
Cometary Kilometric Radiation [*Astrophysics*] ... CKR
Cometary-Mass-to-Planets [*Astronomy*] ... CMTP
Comet-Like Object ... CLO
Comets Equipment Performance Tracking (AAEL) ... CEPT
COMETS Equipment Performance Tracking (SAUS) ... CEPT
Come-Up ... C/U
Come-Up Time [*Time required for a retort to reach operating conditions*] ... CUT
Comex Clearing Association (SAUO) ... CCA
Comex Market of the NYSE (SAUS) ... CMX
Comfair Airwing Pacific (ACAE) ... CFAW
ComForce Corp. [*AMEX symbol*] [*Formerly, Lori Corp.*] (SG) ... CFS
Comforce Corp. [*Associated Press*] (SAG) ... Comforce
Comfort ... CMFRT
Comfort Cooling Tower [*Air conditioning*] ... CCT
Comfort Index ... CI
Comfort Measures Only [*Medicine*] (DAVI) ... CMO
Comfort Public Library, Comfort, TX [*Library symbol*] [*Library of Congress*] (LCLS) ... TxComf
Comfort Systems USA [*NYSE symbol*] (SG) ... FIX
Comfort, TX [*FM radio station call letters*] ... KRNH
Comfortable Interpersonal Distance Scale (EDAC) ... CID
Comfortable Interpersonal Distance Scale (DIPS) ... CIDS
Comfortable Recreation Vehicle ... CRV
Comfortable Walking Speed (STED) ... CWS
Comfortably Weird [*In the record business, refers to a successful performer who has retained his individuality*] ... CW
Comhairle Sabhailteacht Naisiunta [*National Safety Council*] [*Ireland*] (EAIO) ... CSN
Comhaltas Ceoltoiri Eireann [*Traditional Irish Singing and Dancing Society*] (EA) ... CCE
Comhaltas Peil Eitleoiga na Heireann [*Volleyball Association of Ireland*] [*See also VAI*] [*Ireland*] (EAIO) ... CPEH
Comhuriyet Halk Partisi [*Turkey*] ... CHP

Comic ... COM
Comic Book Retailers International [*An association*] (EA) ... CBRI
Comic Crusader [*A publication*] ... CC
Comicorum Atticorum Fragmenta [*A publication*] (OCD) ... CAF
Comicorum Graecorum Fragmenta [*A publication*] (OCD) ... CGF
Comicorum Romanum Fragmenta [*A publication*] (OCD) ... CRF
Comics Amateur Press Alliance ... CAPA
Comics Code Authority [*Regulatory body for comic book and comic magazine publishing industry*] ... CCA
Comics Magazine Association of America (EA) ... CMAA
Comilla [*Bangladesh*] [*Airport symbol*] (AD) ... CLA
Comilla [*Bangladesh*] [*ICAO location identifier*] (ICLI) ... VGCM
Cominco Ltd. [*AMEX symbol*] [*Toronto Stock Exchange symbol*] [*Vancouver Stock Exchange symbol*] (SPSG) ... CLT
Cominco Ltd. [*Associated Press*] (SAG) ... Cominc
Cominco Ltd., Toronto, ON, Canada [*Library symbol*] [*Library of Congress*] (LCLS) ... CaOTCom
Cominco Ltd., Toronto, Ontario [*Library symbol*] [*National Library of Canada*] (NLC) ... OTCOM
Cominco Ltd., Vancouver, BC, Canada [*Library symbol*] [*Library of Congress*] (LCLS) ... CaBVaCOM
Cominco Ltd., Vancouver, British Columbia [*Library symbol*] [*National Library of Canada*] (NLC) ... BVACOM
Cominco Resources International Ltd. [*Toronto Stock Exchange symbol*] [*Vancouver Stock Exchange symbol*] ... COR
Coming Off Pills Entirely ... COPE
COMINT [*Communications Intelligence*] **Receiver Test System** (MCD) ... CRTS
COMIREX [*Committee on Imagery Requirements and Exploitation*] **Advanced Exploitation System** (MCD) ... CADES
COMIREX [*Committee on Imagery Requirements and Exploitation*] **Automated Management System** (MCD) ... CAMS
Comisiãn Coordinadora del Servicio Social de las Instituciones de Educaciãn Superior (SAUO) ... COSSIES
Comisiãn Intersecretarial del Control del Proceso y uso de Plaguicidas, Fertilizantes y Sustancias Tãxicas (SAUO) ... CICOPLAFEST
Comisiãn Intersecretarial para el Control de Plaguicidas, Fertilazantes y Sustancias Tãxicas (SAUO) ... CICOPLAFEST
Comision Andina de Juristas [*Andean Commission of Jurists - ACJ*] (EAIO) ... CAJ
Comision Asesora Regional de Pesca para el Atlantico Sudoccidental [*Regional Fisheries Advisory Commission for the South-West Atlantic*] [*Inactive*] (EAIO) ... CARPAS
Comision Centroamericana de Energia [*Central American Energy Commission*] (EAIO) ... COMENER
Comision Centroamericana de Transporte Maritimo [*Central American Commission of Maritime Transport*] [*Organization of Central American States*] [*San Salvador, El Salvador*] (EAIO) ... COCATRAM
Comision de Derechos Humanos de El Salvador [*Spain*] ... CDHES
Comision de Estudios de Historia de la Iglesia en Latinoamerica [*Commission of the Studies of History of the Church in Latin America*] [*Mexico*] ... CEHILA
Comision de Estudios del Territorio Nacional [*Mexico*] (GEOI) ... CETENAL
Comision de Integracion Electrica Regional [*Commission of Regional Electrical Integration*] (EAIO) ... CIER
Comision de Pesca Continental para America Latina [*Commission for Inland Fisheries of Latin America*] [*FAO*] [*Italy*] (ASF) ... COPESCAL
Comision de Proteccion Fitosanitaria para el Caribe [*Caribbean Plant Protection Commission - CPPC*] (EAIO) ... CPFC
Comision de Solidaridad con las Familiares de Presos Politicos, Desaparecidos y Matados en Argentina ... COSOFAM
Comision Economica para America Latina y el Caribe [*Economic Commission for Latin America and the Caribbean - ECLAC*] [*Santiago, Chile*] [*United Nations*] (EAIO) ... CEPAL
Comision Economica y Social para Asia Occidental [*Economic and Social Commission for Western Asia*] [*Spanish*] [*United Nations*] (DUND) ... CESPAO
Comision Economica y Social para Asia y el Pacifico [*Economic and Social Commission for Asia and the Pacific*] [*Spanish*] [*United Nations*] (DUND) ... CESPAP
Comision Ejecutiva Permanente del Consejo Interamericano Economico y Social [*Permanent Executive Committee of the Inter-American Economic and Social Council*] (EA) ... CEPCIES
Comision Especial de Coordinacion Latinoamericana ... CECLA
Comision Especial de Expertos para el Estudio de las Necesidades Financieras quePlantea la Ejecucion de Planes de Reforma Agraria [*Consejo Interamericano Economico y Social*] [*Washington, DC*] ... CERA
Comision Femenil Mexicana Nacional (EA) ... CFM
Comision Femenil Mexicana Nacional [*An association*] [*Spanish*] (EA) ... CFMN
Comision Interamericana del Atun Tropical [*Interamerican Tropical Tuna Commission - IATTC*] ... CIAT
Comision Latinoamericana de Aviacion Civil [*Latin American Civil Aviation Commission - LACAC*] (EAIO) ... CLAC
Comision Latinoamericana de Trabajadores de la Educacion [*Venezuela*] ... CLATEC
Comision Nacional para el Conocimiento y uso de la Biodiversidad (SAUS) ... CONABIO
Comision Nacional Peruana de Cooperacion con la UNESCO [*Peruvian National Commission for the United Nations Educational, Scientific and Cultural Organization*] [*Peru*] (EAIO) ... CNPC
Comision Panamericana de Normas Tecnicas [*Pan American Standards Commission - PASC*] (EAIO) ... COPANT
Comision para la Defensa de los Derechos Humanos en Centroamerica [*Commission for the Defense of Human Rights in Central America - CDHRCA*] (EA) ... CODEHUCA
Comision Permanente de Derechos Humanos [*Managua, Nicaragua*] ... CPDH
Comision Permanente del Pacifico Sur [*Permanent Commission for the South Pacific - PCSP*] (EAIO) ... CPPS
Comision Tecnica de la Red Andina Telecomunicaciones [*Technical Commission for the Andean Telecommunication Network*] (PDAA) ... COMTEC/RAT
Comiso [*Italy*] [*Airport symbol*] (AD) ... CIY
Comiso [*Italy*] [*ICAO location identifier*] (ICLI) ... LICB
Comissao Democratica Eleitoral [*Democratic Electoral Committee*] [*Portugal*] [*Political party*] (PPE) ... CDE
Comissao Eleitoral Monarquica [*Monarchy Electoral Committee*] [*Portugal*] (PPE) ... CEM
Comissao Eleitoral para a Unidade Democratico [*Electoral Committee for Democratic Unity*] [*Portugal*] [*Political party*] (PPE) ... CEUD
Comissao Nacional de Energia Nuclear [*National Commission for Nuclear Energy*] [*Brazil*] [*Information service or system*] (IID) ... CNEN
Comission Internationale de l'Organisation Scientifique du Travail [*International Committee of Work Study and Labour Management in Agriculture*] (EAIO) ... IOSTA
Comitan [*Mexico*] [*Seismograph station code, US Geological Survey*] (SEIS) ... COM
Comitatis Causa [*For the County's Sake*] [*Latin*] (ROG) ... COMIT CAUS
Comitato Italiano Atlantico [*Italian Atlantic Committee*] (EAIO) ... CIA
Comitato per la Difesa della Repubblica [*Committee for the Defense of the Republic*] [*San Marino*] [*Political party*] (PPW) ... CDR
Comitatus [*County*] [*Latin*] (ROG) ... COM
Comite Administratif de Coordination [*Administrative Committee on Coordination - ACC*] [*United Nations*] [*French*] (ASF) ... CAC
Comite Administrativo de Coordinacion [*Administrative Committee on Coordination - ACC*] [*United Nations*] [*Spanish*] (MSC) ... CAC
Comite Arctique International [*International Arctic Committee*] [*Monte Carlo, Monaco*] (EAIO) ... CAI
Comite Associe du Code National du Batiment [*Associate Committee of the National Building Code*] [*National Research Council of Canada*] ... CACNB
Comite Canadien de la Classification Ecologique du Territoire [*Canadian Committee on Ecological (Biophysical) Land Classification - CCELC*] ... CCCET
Comite Canadien d'Oceanographie [*Canadian Committee on Oceanography - CCO*] ... CCO
Comite Canadien pour le Programme Biologique International [*Canadian Committee for the International Biological Programme - CCIBP*] ... CCPBI
Comite Canadien sur le Financement de la Recherche dans les Universites [*Canadian Committee on Financing University Research - CCFUR*] ... CCFRU
Comite Canadien sur les Services Socio-Economiques [*Canada Committee on Socio-Economic Services - CCSES*] ... CCSSE
Comite Catholique Contre la Faim et pour le Developpement [*France*] ... CCFD
Comite Catholique International de Coordination Aupres de l'UNESCO ... CCIC
Comite Central de la Propriete Forestiere [*Central Committee for Forest Ownership in the EEC - CCFOE*] (EAIO) ... CCPF
Comite Chretien pour les Droits Humains en Amerique Latine [*Christian Committee for Human Rights in Latin America*] [*Canada*] (EAIO) ... CCDHAL
Comite Commun pour la Promotion de l'Aide aux Cooperatives [*Joint Committee for the Promotion of Aid to Cooperatives*] [*UN Food and Agriculture Organization*] ... COPAC
Comite Comunista Unificado Marxista-Leninista [*Peru*] [*Political party*] (EY) ... CCUML
Comite Consultatif de la Radioprotection [*Advisory Committee on Radiological Protection*] [*Canada*] ... CCRP
Comite Consultatif de la Surete Nucleaire [*Advisory Committee on Nuclear Safety*] [*Canada*] ... CCSN
Comite Consultatif International des Radiocommunications [*International Radio Consultative Committee*] [*of the International Telecommunications Union*] [*Switzerland*] ... CCIR
Comite Consultatif International du Coton [*International Cotton Advisory Committee*] ... CCIC
Comite Consultatif International Telegraphique et Telephonique [*Consultative Committee on International Telegraphy and Telephony*] [*of the International Telecommunications Union*] [*Switzerland*] ... CCITT
Comite Consultatif International Telephonique des Frequences [*International Telephone Consultative Committee*] (NATG) ... CCIF
Comite Consultatif Mondial de la Societe des Amis [*World Consultative Committee of the Society of Friends*] [*British*] (EAIO) ... CCMSA
Comite Consultatif National des Recherches sur les Ressources Hydrauliques [*National Advisory Committee on Water Resources Research*] [*Canada*] ... CCNRRH
Comite Consultatif pour les Standards des Mesurement Radiations Ionizant [*Consultative Committee for the Standards of Measurement of Ionizing Radiations*][*International Standards Organization*] [*French*] (BARN) ... CCEMRI
Comite Contre la Torture [*Committee Against Torture - CAT*] [*Switzerland*] (EAIO) ... CCT
Comite d'Action de la Pomme de Terre [*Potato Action Committee*] [*Canadian Department of Agriculture*] ... CAP
Comite d'Action des Transports Publics des Communautes Europeennes [*Action Committee of Public Transport of the European Communities - ACPTEC*] (EAIO) ... CATPCE
Comite d'Action du Personnel Autochtone [*Native Employees Action Team*] [*Canada*] ... CAPA
Comite d'Action en France ... COMDAC
Comite d'Action et de Concertation du Conseil Democratique Revolutionnaire [*Chad*] [*Political party*] (EY) ... CAC-CDR
Comite d'Action Musulman [*Mauritian political party*] ... CAM
Comite d'Aide au Developpement [*OCDE*] ... CAD
Comite d'Appui au Peuple Espagnol [*Committee of Support for Spanish People*] [*Canada*] ... CAPE

Comite de Apoio de Reconstrucao do Partido Marxista-Leninista [*Support Committee for the Reconstruction of the Marxist-Leninist Party*] [*Portugal*] [*Political party*] (PPE) .... CARP M-L

Comite de Bourses de la Communaute Europeenne [*Committee of Stock Exchanges in the European Community - CSEE*] (EAIO) .... CBCE

Comite de Compradores de Material Aeronautico de America Latina (MCD) .... CCMA

Comite de Cooperacion Economica del Istmo Centroamericano [*Central American Economic Cooperation Committee*] .... CCE

Comite de Coordination de l'Assistance Technique [*ONU*] .... CCAT

Comite de Coordination des Associations de Constructeurs d'Appareillage [*Coordinating Committee for Common Market Associations of Manufacturers of Electrical Switchgear and Controlgear*] [*EC*] (ECED) .... CAPIEL

Comite de Coordination des Constructeurs des Machines Tournantes Electriques du Marche Commun [*Coordinating Committee for Common Market Associations of Manufacturers of Rotating Electric Machinery*] (EAIO) .... COMEL

Comite de Coordination des Experts Budgetaires Gouvernementaux [*Coordinating Committee of Government Budget Experts*] [*NATO*] (NATG) .... CCG

Comite de Coordination des Industries Textiles de la Communaute Economique Europeenne [*Coordination Committee for the Textile Industries in the European Economic Community*] [*Brussels, Belgium*] (EAIO) .... COMITEXTIL

Comite de Coordination des Plans Civils d'Urgence [*Civil Emergency Coordinating Committee*] [*NATO*] (NATG) .... CCPC

Comite de Coordination des Plans de Transport [*Coordinating Committee for Transport Planning*] [*NATO*] (NATG) .... CCPT

Comite de Coordination des Services Agricoles Canadiens [*Canadian Agricultural Services Coordinating Committee*] .... CCSAC

Comite de Coordination des Telecommunications [*Coordinating Committee for Communications*] [*NATO*] [*France*] (NATG) .... CCT

Comite de Coordination du Service Volontaire International [*Coordinating Committee for International Voluntary Service - CCIVS*] [*Paris, France*] (EA) .... CCSVI

Comite de Defense des Libertes Democratiques au Mali [*Committee for the Defense of Democratic Liberties in Mali*] (PD) .... CDLDM

Comite de Defense des Prisonniers en Indonesie [*France*] .... TAPOL

Comite de Defense du Peuple Canadien (Citoyens et Residents) [*Canadian People's (Citizens and Residents) Defence Committee*] .... CDPC

Comite de Fabricants Europeens d'Installations et de Distribution de Petrole [*Committee of European Manufacturers of Petroleum Measuring and Distributing Equipment*] [*EC*] (ECED) .... CECOD

Comite de Familiares de Presos Politicos Uruguayos [*Relatives' Committee for Uruguayan Political Prisoners*] [*Malmo, Sweden*] (EAIO) .... CFPPU

Comite de Formation et de Developpement Municipaux des Maritimes [*Maritime Municipal Training and Development Board*] [*Canada*] .... CFDMM

Comite de la Bibliographie et des Services d'Information en Sciences Humaines [*Committee on Bibliography and Information Services for the Social Sciences and Humanities - CBISSSH*] [*National Library of Canada*] .... CBSISH

Comite de la Science et de la Technologie dans les Pays en Voie de Developpement [*Committee on Science and Technology in Developing Countries*] .... COSTED

Comite de Liaison Commerce de Detail [*Liaison Committee of European Retail Trade Associations*] (EAIO) .... CLD

Comite de Liaison de la Construction Automobile [*Liaison Committee for the Motor Industry in the EEC Countries*] [*Brussels, Belgium*] (EAIO) .... CLCA

Comite de Liaison de la Construction de Carrosseries et de Remorques [*Liaison Committee of the Body- and Trailer-Building Industry*] (EAIO) .... CLCCR

Comite de Liaison de la Construction d'Equipements et de Pieces d'Automobiles [*Liaison Committee of Manufacturers of Motor Vehicle Parts and Equipment*] (EAIO) .... CLEPA

Comite de Liaison de l'Agrumiculture Mediterraneenne [*Liaison Committee for Mediterranean Citrus Fruit Culture - LCMCFC*] (EAIO) .... CLAM

Comite de Liaison de l'Industrie Europeenne des Tubes d'Acier [*Liaison Committee of the EEC Steel Tube Industry*] (EAIO) .... CLIETA

Comite de Liaison des Architectes de l'Europe Unie [*Liaison Committee of the Architects of United Europe*] [*EC*] (ECED) .... CLAEU

Comite de Liaison des Associations Europeennes de l'Industrie de la Parfumerie, des Produits Cosmetiques, et de Toilette [*European Federation of the Perfume, Cosmetics, and Toiletries Industry*] (EAIO).... COLIPA

Comite de Liaison des Fabricants de Bicyclettes (EA) .... COLIBI

Comite de Liaison des Fabricants de Motocyclettes [*Liaison Committee of European Motorcycle Manufacturers*] [*Belgium*] (EAIO) .... COLIMO

Comite de Liaison des Fabricants de Pieces et Equipements de Deux Roues des Paysde la CEE [*Liaison Committee of Manufacturers of Parts and Equipment for Two-Wheeled Vehicles*] (EAIO) .... COLIPED

Comite de Liaison des Industries Cimentieres de la CEE [*Liaison Committee of the Cement Industries in the EEC*] (ECED) CLC

Comite de Liaison des Industries Metalliques Europeennes .... COLIME

Comite de Liaison des Organisations Non-Gouvernmentales de Developpement aupres des Communautes Europeennes [*Liaison Committee of Development Non-Governmental Organizations to the European Communities*] (EAIO) .... CLONG-CE

Comite de Liaison des Organisations Non-Gouvernmentales de Developpement aupres des Communautes Europeennes [*Liaison Committee of Development Non-Governmental Organizations to the European Communities*] (EAIO) .... NCOS

Comite de Liaison des Organismes Chretiens de Cooperation Internationale (EAIO) .... CLOCCI

Comite de Liaison des OrganizationSs Non-Gouvernmentales de Volontariat [*Committee for the Liaison of Non-Governmental Voluntary Organizations*] [*France*] (EAIO) .... CLONGV

Comite de Liaison des Petites et Moyennes Entreprises Industrielles des Pays de la CEE [*Liaison Committee for Small and Medium-Sized Industrial Enterprises in the EEC*] [*Brussels, Belgium*] (EAIO) .... EUROPMI

Comite de Liaison des Podologues de la CE [*Liaison Committee of Podologists of the Common Market*] (ECED) .... CLPCE

Comite de Liaison Entr'Aide et Action [*Help and Action Coordinating Committee*] (EAIO) .... CLEAA

Comite de Liaison Europeen de la Distribution Independante de Pieces de Rechangeet Equipements pour Automobiles [*European Liaison Committee for the Independent Distribution of Spare Parts and Equipment for Motor Cars*] [*EC*] (ECED) .... CLEDIPA

Comite de Liaison Europeen des Commissionnaires et Auxiliaires de Transport [*European Liaison Committee of Forwarders*] (EAIO) .... CLECAT

Comite de Liaison Europeen des Osteopathes [*European Liaison Committee for Osteopaths - ELCO*] (EA) .... CLEO

Comite de Liaison International des Broderies, Rideaux, et Dentelles [*International Liaison Committee for Embroideries, Curtains, and Laces*] .... CELIBRIDE

Comite de Liaison International des Cooperatives d'Epargne et de Credit [*International Liaison Committee on Co-Operative Thrift and Credit - ILCCTC*] [*Paris, France*] (EA) .... CLICEC

Comite de Problemas de Productos Basicos [*Committee on Commodity Problems*] [*Italy*] (ASF) .... CPPB

Comite de Solidaridad con el Pueblo Argentino [*Spain*] .... COSPA

Comite de Solidarite avec les Prisonniers Politiques Arabes et du Proche Orient [*Solidarity Committee for Arab and Near-Eastern Political Prisoners*] .... CSPPA

Comite de Solidarite Tiers-Monde/Trois-Rivieres [*Third World Solidarity Committee/Trois-Rivieres*] (AC) .... CSTM-TR

Comite de Surveillance Ecologique des Pulverisations Seriennes [*Canada*] .... CSEPA

Comite de Travail des Malteries de la CEE [*Working Committee of European Economic Community Malters*] .... EUROMALT

Comite de Unidad Campesina [*Committee of Peasant Unity*] [*Guatemala*] [*Political party*] (PD) .... CUC

Comite des Amities Acadiennes [*Acadian Friendship Committee - AFC*] (EAIO) .... CAA

Comite des Associations Europeennes de Cafe [*Committee of European Coffee Associations*] [*EC*] (ECED) .... CAEC

Comite des Associations Europeennes de Fonderie [*Committee of European Foundry Associations*] (EA) .... CAEF

Comite des Bibliotheques Publiques de la Region de Quebec (AC) .... COBIPUQ

Comite des Constructeurs d'Automobiles du Marche Common [*Common Market Automobile Manufacturers Committee*] [*French*] .... CCMC

Comite des Constructeurs de Materiel Frigorifique de la CEE [*Committee of Manufacturers of Refrigeration Equipment of the EEC*] .... COMAF

Comite des Constructeurs Europeens de Materiel Alimentaire [*Committee of European Plant Manufacturers for the Food Industry*] [*Common Market*] .... COCEMA

Comite des Demenageurs du Marche Commun .... CODEMAC

Comite des Eglises Aupres des Migrants en Europe [*Churches' Committee on Migrants in Europe*] (EA) .... CEME

Comite des Fabricants d'Acide Glutamique de la CEE [*Committee of Glutamic Acid Manufacturers of the European Economic Community*] (EAIO) .... COFAG

Comite des Fabricants de Levure de Panification de la CEE [*Committee of Bread Yeast Manufacturers of the EEC*] .... COFALEC

Comite des Forces Vives - Hery Velona [*Madagascar*] [*Political party*] (EY).... CFV

Comite des Industries Cinematographiques des Communautes Europeennes [*Committee of the Cinematography Industries in the European Communities*] (EAIO) .... CICCE

Comite des Industries de la Moutarde de la CEE [*EEC Committee for the Mustard Industries*] .... CIMCEE

Comite des Industries des Mayonnaises et Sauces Condimentaires de la CEE [*Committee of the Industries of Mayonnaises and Table Sauces of the European Economic Community*] .... CIMSCEE

Comite des Industries du Coton et des Fibres Connexes de la CEE [*Committee of the Cotton Industries of the European Economic Community*] (PDAA) .... EUROCOTON

Comite des Industries Lainieres de la CEE [*Committee of the Wool Textile Industry in the EEC*] (EAIO) .... INTERLAINE

Comite des Normes Gouvernementales en Informatique [*Government Electronic Data Processing Standards Committee*] [*Canada*] .... CNGI

Comite des Organisations Commerciales des Pays de la CEE [*Committee of Commercial Organizations in the EEC Countries*] .... COCCEE

Comite des Organisations de la Boucherie-Charcuterie de la CEE [*Committee of Butchery and Cooked Meats Organizations of the EEC*] .... COBCCEE

Comite des Organisations Familiales aupres des Communautes Europeennes [*Committee of Family Organizations in the European Communities*] [*Common Market*] [*Belgium*] .... COFACE

Comite des Organisations Professionnelles Agricoles de la CEE [*Committee of Professional Agricultural Organizations in the EEC*] .... COPA

Comite des Paysans Africains [*African Farmers Committee - AFC*] (EAIO) .... CPA

Comite des Peches pour l'Atlantique Centre-Est [*Committee for the Eastern Central Atlantic Fisheries - CECAF*] [*Senegal*] (MSC) .... COPACE

Comite des Personnes Atteintes du VIH [*Committee of Persons Living with HIV*] (AC) .... CPAVIH

Comite des Petites et Moyens Enterprises Commerciales [*Committee of Small and Medium Commercial Enterprises*] [*EEC*] (PDAA) .... COPMEC

Comite des Semences du Marche Commun [*Seed Committee of the Common Market*] .... COSEMCO

Comite des Services Bibliographiques pour le Canada [*Committee on Bibliographical Services for Canada*] .... CSBC

Comite des Travaux Historiques et Scientifiques [*Ministere de l'Education Nationale*] [*Database*] .... CTHS
Comite d'Etude de la Corrosion et de la Protection des Canalisations [*Committee for the Study of Pipe Corrosion and Protection*] (EAIO) .... CEOCOR
Comite d'Etude des Droits des Autochtones [*Committee for Original Peoples' Entitlement*] [*Canada*] .... CEDA
Comite d'Etude des Producteurs de Charbon d'Europe Occidentale [*Association of the Coal Producers of the European Community*] (EAIO) .... CEPCEO
Comite d'Etude sur les Conditions du Logement [*Study Committee Study on Housing Conditions*] [*Canada*] .... CECL
Comite d'Information sur la Lutte Solidarite [*Portugal*] .... CILS
Comite d'Initiative pour le Congres du Peuple Europeen .... CICPE
Comite d'Organisation du Congres Mondial d'Implantologie des Biomateriaux [*Organizing Committee of the World Congress on Implantology and Bio-Materials - OCWCIB*] [*Rouen, France*] (EAIO) .... COCMIB
Comite du Commerce des Cereales et des Aliments du Betail de la Communaute Economique Europeenne [*Committee of the Cereals and Animal Feed Trade of the European Economic Community*] .... COCERAL
Comite du Patrimoine Mondial [*World Heritage Committee - WHC*] (EAIO) .... CPM
Comite Economique et Social [*Economic and Social Committee*] [*of CEE*] .... CES
Comite Ecumenico de Proyectos (SAUS) .... CEP
Comite Engine Repair Requirements Card (SAUS) .... CERRC
Comite Euro-International du Beton [*Euro-International Committee for Concrete*] .... CEB
Comite Europe-Amerique Latine [*Belgium*] .... CEAL
Comite European de Liaison du Commerce de Gros des Papiers et Cartons [*European Liaison Committee of Wholesalers of Paper and Cardboard*] (PDAA) .... COMEPA
Comite European de Normalisation Electrotechnique [*European Committee for Electrotechnical Standardization*] (EAIO) .... CENELEC
Comite Europeen de Controle Laitierbeurrier .... CECLB
Comite Europeen de Cooperation des Industries de la Machine Outil [*European Committee for Cooperation of the Machine Tool Industries*] [*EC*] (ECED) .... CECIMO
Comite Europeen de Cooperation Juridique [*French*] .... CCJ
Comite Europeen de Coordination des Normes [*European Committee for Coordination of Standards*] .... CEN
Comite Europeen de Coordination des Normes Electriques [*European Electrical Standards Coordinating Committee*] .... CENEL
Comite Europeen de Droit Rural [*France*] .... CEDR
Comite Europeen de la Chaudronnerie et de la Tolerie [*European Committee for Boilermaking and Kindred Steel Structures*] .... CECT
Comite Europeen de la Culture du Houblon [*European Hop Growers Committee*] .... CECH
Comite Europeen de l'Association Internationale de l'Ozone [*European Committee of the International Ozone Association*] (EAIO) .... CEAIO
Comite Europeen de l'Hospitalisation Privee [*European Committee of Private Hospitalization*] [*EC*] [*Belgium*] (ECED) .... CEHP
Comite Europeen de Liaison des Commerces Agro-Alimentaires [*European Liaison Committee for Agricultural and Food Trades*] (EAIO) .... CELCAA
Comite Europeen de Liaison des Industries de la Machine a Coudre [*European Liaison Committee for the Sewing Machine Industries - ELCSMI*] [*Defunct*] (EAIO) .... CELIMAC
Comite Europeen de Liaison des Negociants et Utilisateurs de Combustibles [*European Liaison Committee of Fuel Merchants and Users*] .... CELNUCO
Comite Europeen de l'Industrie de la Robinetterie [*European Committee for the Valves and Fittings Industry*] [*EC*] [*Germany*] (ECED) .... CEIR
Comite Europeen de l'Internationale du Personnel des Postes, Telegraphes et Telephones [*European Committee of the Postal, Telegraph and Telephone International*] [*EC*] (ECED) .... EPTT
Comite Europeen de l'Outillage [*European Tool Committee - ETC*] (EA) .... CEO
Comite Europeen de l'Outillage [*European Tool Committee*] [*France*] (EAIO) .... COE
Comite Europeen de l'Outillage Agricole et Horticole [*European Committee for Agricultural and Horticultural Tools and Implements - ECAHTI*] (EA) .... CEOAH
Comite Europeen de Normalisation [*European Committee for Standardization*] [*Belgium*] .... CEN
Comite Europeen de Reflexion sur les Retraites [*European Pension Committee*] [*Paris, France*] (EAIO) .... CERR
Comite Europeen de Rink Hockey [*European Committee for Rink Hockey*] (EAIO) .... CERH
Comite Europeen des Associations des Fabricants de Peinture, d'Encres d'Imprimerie, et de Couleurs [*European Committee of Paint, Printing Ink, and Artists' Colours Manufacturers Associations*] (EAIO) .... CEPE
Comite Europeen des Constructeurs de Broleurs [*European Committee of Manufacturers of Burners*] (EA) .... CEB
Comite Europeen des Constructeurs de Machines a Bois [*European Committee of Woodworking Machinery Manufacturers*] (EAIO) .... EUMABOIS
Comite Europeen des Constructeurs de Materiel Frigorifique [*European Committee of Manufacturers of Refrigeration Equipment*] (EAIO) .... CECOMAF
Comite Europeen des Constructeurs de Materiel Textile [*European Committee of Textile Machinery Manufacturers*] (EAIO) .... CEMATEX
Comite Europeen des Constructeurs de Materiels d'Incendie et de Secours [*European Committee of the Manufacturers of Fire Protection and Safety Equipment and Fire Fighting Vehicles*] (EAIO) .... EUROFEU
Comite Europeen des Constructeurs de Pompes [*European Committee of Pump Manufacturers*] (EAIO) .... EUROPUMP
Comite Europeen des Constructeurs d'Instruments de Pesage [*European Committee of Weighing Instrument Manufacturers - ECWIM*] (EAIO) .... CECIP
Comite Europeen des Cooperatives de Production et de Travail Associe [*European Committee of Workers' Cooperatives*] [*EC*] (ECED) .... CECOP
Comite Europeen des Equipements Techniques du Batiment [*European Committee for Building Technical Equipment - ECBTE*] (EAIO) .... CEETB
Comite Europeen des Fabricants d'Appareils de Chauffage en Fonte (PDAA) .... CEFACEF
Comite Europeen des Fabricants d'Appareils de Chauffage et de Cuisine Domestiques [*European Committee of Manufacturers of Domestic Heating and Cooking Appliances*] .... CEFACD
Comite Europeen des Fabricants de Sucre [*European Committee of Sugar Manufacturers*] [*Common Market*] .... CEFS
Comite Europeen des Federations Nationales de la Maroquinerie, Articles de Voyages, et Industries Connexes (EAIO) .... CEDIM
Comite Europeen des Groupements de Constructeurs du Machinisme Agricole [*European Committee of Associations of Manufacturers of Agricultural Machinery*] (EAIO) .... CEMA
Comite Europeen des Ingenieurs-Conseils [*European Committee of Consulting Engineers*] [*EC*] (ECED) .... CEDIC
Comite Europeen des Materiels de Genie Civil [*Committee for European Construction Equipment - CECE*] (EAIO) .... CEMGC
Comite Europeen des Materiels et Produits pour la Fonderie [*European Committee of Foundry Materials and Products*] (EAIO) .... CEMAFON
Comite Europeen des Services des Conseillers [*European Committee for Consultant Services - ECCS*] (EAIO) .... CESCE
Comite Europeen des Syndicats de l'Alimentation, du Tabac, et de l'Industrie Hoteliere [*European Trade Union Committee of Food and Allied Workers*] [*Common Market*] .... CESA
Comite Europeen d'Etude du Sel [*European Committee for the Study of Salt - ECSS*] (EA) .... CEES
Comite Europeen d'Etudes de Zoologie Agricole .... CEZA
Comite Europeen du Commerce des Produits Amylaces et Derives [*European Center for Trade in Starch Products and Derivatives*] [*Common Market*] .... CECPA
Comite Europeen du Commerce et de la Reparation Automobiles [*European Committee for Motor Trades and Repairs*] [*EC*] (ECED) .... CECRA
Comite Europeen du The [*European Tea Committee*] [*EC*] (ECED) .... CEDT
Comite Europeen Permanent de Recherches sur la Protection des Populations contreles Risques de Toxicite a Long Terme [*Permanent European Research Committee for the Protection of the Population against the Hazards of Chronic Toxicity*] .... EUROTOX
Comite Europeen pour le Mini-Basketball [*European Committee for Mini-Basketball - ECMB*] [*Munich, Federal Republic of Germany*] (EAIO) .... CEMB
Comite Europeen pour le Progres Economique et Social [*European Committee for Economic and Social Progress*] .... CEPES
Comite Europeen pour l'Enseignement Catholique [*European Committee for Catholic Education*] (EAIO) .... CEEC
Comite Europeen pour les Problemes Criminels [*Council of Europe*] .... CEPC
Comite Europeen pour les Relations Economiques .... CERE
Comite Francais de Liberation Nationale [*Algeria*] .... CFLN
Comite General de la Cooperation Agricole de la CE [*General Committee of Agricultural Cooperation in the EC*] (EAIO) .... COGECA
Comite Generale de la Cooperation Agricole de la CEE [*General Committee of Agricultural Cooperation of the European Economic Community*] (PDAA) .... GOGECA
Comite Guatemalteco de Unidad Patriotica [*Guatemalan Committee of Patriotic Unity*] (PD) .... CGUP
Comite Illusionniste d'Expertise des Phenomenes Paranormaux [*International PSI Committee of Magicians - IPSICM*] (EAIO) .... CIEPP
Comite Interafricain d'Etudes Hydrauliques [*Inter-African Committee for Hydraulic Studies - ICHS*] [*Ouagadougou, Burkina Faso*] (EAIO) .... CIEH
Comite Interallie des Officiers Medecins de Reserve [*Interallied Committee of Medical Reserve Officers*] .... CIOMR
Comite Interamericano de Desarrollo Agricola [*Inter-American Committee for Agricultural Development*] .... CIDA
Comite Interamericano de la Alianza para el Progreso [*Inter-American Committee of the Alliance for Progress*] .... CIAP
Comite Interamericano de Proteccion Agricola [*Interamerican Committee for Crop Protection*] .... CIPA
Comite Interamericano Permanente Antiacridiana .... CIPA
Comite Inter-Eglises des Droits Humains en Amerique Latine [*Inter-Church Committee on Human Rights in Latin America*] [*Canada*] (EAIO) .... CIEDHAL
Comite Intergouvernemental de Recherches Urbaines et Regionales [*Intergovernmental Committee on Urban and Regional Research*] [*Canada*] .... CIRUR
Comite Intergouvernemental du Droit d'Auteur [*Intergovernmental Copyright Committee - IGC*] [*UNESCO*] (EAIO) .... CIDA
Comite Intergouvernemental pour les Migrations Europeennes [*Intergovernmental Committee for European Migration*] .... CIME
Comite Interministeriel de la Gestion du Personnel [*Personnel Administration Interdepartmental Committee*] [*Canada*] .... CIGP
Comite Interministeriel des Terres [*Interdepartmental Committee on Land*] [*Canada*] .... CIT
Comite Inter-Mouvement Aupres des Evacues [*France*] .... CIMADE
Comite Internacional de la Cruz Roja [*Switzerland*] .... CIRC
Comite International Catholique des Aveugles (EAIO) .... CICA
Comite International Catholique des Infirmieres et Assistantes Medico-Sociales [*International Committee of Catholic Nurses - ICCN*] [*Vatican City, Vatican City State*] (EAIO) .... CICIAMS
Comite International Contre la Repression [*International Committee Against Repression*] [*Paris, France*] (EAIO) .... CICR
Comite International d'Aide aux Intellectuels .... CIAI
Comite International d'Auschwitz [*International Auschwitz Committee*] .... CIA
Comite International de Cooperation dans les Recherches Nationales en Demographie [*Committee for International Cooperation in National Research in Demography*] (EAIO) .... CICRED

Comite International de Coordination et d'Action des Groupements de Techniciens des Industries de Revetements de Surface [*International Committee to Coordinate Activities of Technical Groups in Coatings Industry - ICCATCI*] (EAIO) .... CICATIRS
Comite International de Coordination pour l'Initiation a la Science et le Developpement des Activites Scientifiques Extra-Scolaires [*International Coordinating Committee for the Presentation of Science and the Development of Out-of-School Scientific Activities - ICC*] (EAIO) CIC
Comite International de Dachau .... CID
Comite International de Geophysique [*International Geophysical Committee*] .... CIG
Comite International de la Conserve CIC
Comite International de la Croix-Rouge [*International Committee of the Red Cross*] .... CICR
Comite International de La Croix-Rouge [*Switzerland*] [*ICAO designator*] (FAAC) .... RED
Comite International de la Culture du Houblon [*International Hop Growers Convention - IHGC*] (EAIO) .... CICH
Comite International de la Rayonne et des Fibres Synthetiques [*International Rayon and Synthetic Fibres Committee - IRSFC*] (EAIO) .... CIRFS
Comite International de la Teinture et du Nettoyage [*International Committee for Dyeing and Dry Cleaning*] .... CITEN
Comite International de Liaison des Associations Feminines [*International Liaison Committee of Women's Organizations*] [*French*] .... CILAF
Comite International de Liaison des Gynecologues et Obstetriciens .... CILOPGO
Comite International de Liaison pour la Navigation de Plaisance [*Pleasure Navigation International Joint Committee - PNIC*] [*The Hague, Netherlands*] (EAIO) .... CINP
Comite International de Liaison pour la Reunification et la Paix en Coree [*International Liaison Committee for Reunification and Peace in Korea*] (EAIO) .... CILRECO
Comite International de l'Inspection Technique Automobile [*International Motor Vehicle Inspection Committee*] [*Verviers, Belgium*] (EAIO) .... CITA
Comite International de Medecine d'Assurances sur la Vie [*International Committee for Life Assurance Medicine*] [*France*] (EAIO) .... CIMAV
Comite International de Medecine et de Pharmacie Militaires [*International Committee of Military Medicine and Pharmacy - ICMMP*] [*Liege, Belgium*] (EA) .... CIMPM
Comite International de Medecine Militaire [*International Committee of Military Medicine*] [*Belgium*] (EAIO) .... CIMM
Comite International de Photobiologie [*International Committee of Photobiology*] .... CIP
Comite International de Photogrammetrie Architecturale [*International Committee of Architectural Photogrammetry*] (EAIO) .... CIPA
Comite International de Plastiques en Agriculture [*International Committee of Plastics in Agriculture*] (EAIO) .... CIPA
Comite International de Prevention des Accidents du Travail de la Navigation Interieure/International Committee for the Prevention of Work Accidents in Inland Navigation (EAIO) .... CIPA/ICPA
Comite International de Recherche et d'Etude de Facteurs de l'Ambiance [*International Committee for Research and Study on Environmental Factors*] .... CIFA
Comite International de Sociologie Clinique [*International Committee on Clinical Sociology - ICCS*] (EA) .... CISC
Comite International de Solidarite avec la Jeuness Algerienne .... CISJA
Comite International de Soutien aux Antifascistes Iberiques .... CISAI
Comite International de Standardisation en Biologie Humaine [*International Committee for Standardization in Human Biology*] .... CISBH
Comite International de Standardisation en Hematologie [*International Committee for Standardization in Haematology*] (EAIO) .... CISH
Comite International de Television [*International Television Committee*] .... CIT
Comite International de Thermodynamique et de Cinetique Electro-Chimiques [*International Committee of Electro-Chemical Thermodynamics and Kinetics*] .... CITCE
Comite International d'Enregistrement des Frequences [*International Frequency Registration Board*] .... CIEF
Comite International des Associations Techniques de Fonderie [*International Committee of Foundry Technical Associations*] (EAIO) .... CIATF
Comite International des Cooperatives de Production et Artisanales [*International Committee of Producers' Cooperatives*] (EAIO) .... CICOPA
Comite International des Derives Tensio-Actifs [*International Committee of Tensio-Active Derivatives*] .... CID
Comite International des Echanges pres la Chambre de Commerce Internationale .... CIE
Comite International des Entreprises a Succursales [*International Associationof Chain Stores*] [*Later, International Center for Companies of the Food Trade and Industry*] (EAIO) .... CIES
Comite International des Federations Theatrales d'Amateurs de Langue Francaise .... CIFTA
Comite International des Jeux Mediterraneens [*Athens, Greece*] (EAIO) .... CIJM
Comite International des Mouvements d'Enfants et d'Adolescents [*International Committee of Children's and Adolescents' Movements*] [*Budapest, Hungary*] (EAIO) .... CIMEA
Comite International des Organisateurs de Festivals de Folklore [*International Committee of Folklore Festival Organizers*] [*Canada*] .... CIOFF
Comite International des Pharmaciens Homeopathiques [*International Committee of Homeopathic Pharmacists*] [*Karlsruhe, Federal Republic of Germany*] (EAIO) .... CIPH
Comite International des Poids et Mesures [*International Committee on Weights and Measures*] .... CIPM
Comite International des Sciences Historiques [*International Committee of Historical Sciences*] .... CISH
Comite International des Sciences Onomastiques [*International Committee of Onomastic Sciences*] .... CISO
Comite International des Sports des Sourds [*International Committee of Sports for the Deaf*] (EAIO) .... CISS
Comite International des Telecommunications de Presse (EAIO) .... CIPT
Comite International des Telecommunications de Presse [*International Press Telecommunications Council - IPTC*] (EAIO) .... CITP
Comite International des Transports Ferroviaires [*International Rail Transport Committee*] (EAIO) .... CIT
Comite International d'Esthetique et de Cosmetologie [*International Committee for Esthetics and Cosmetology*] .... CIDESCO
Comite International d'Histoire de l'Art (EAIO) .... CIHA
Comite International d'Historiens et Geographes de Langue Francaise [*International Committee of French-Speaking Historians and Geographers - ICFHG*] (EAIO) .... CIHGLF
Comite International du Film Ethnographique .... CIFE
Comite International du Mini-Basketball [*International Committee for Mini-Basketball*] [*Munich, Federal Republic of Germany*] (EAIO) .... CIM
Comite International Olympique [*International Olympic Committee*] .... CIO
Comite International Permanent de la Conserve [*International Permanent Committee on Canned Foods*] .... CIPC
Comite International Permanent des Linguistes [*Permanent International Committee of Linguists*] (EAIO) .... CIPL
Comite International pour la Diffusion des Arts et des Lettres par le Cinema [*International Committee for the Diffusion of Arts and Literature through the Cinema*] (EAIO) .... CIDALC
Comite International pour la Metrologie Historique [*International Committee for Historical Metrology*] (EAIO) .... CIMH
Comite International pour la Sauveguarde de la Langue Bretonne [*International Committee for the Defense of the Breton Language - ICDBL*] (EAIO) .... CISLB
Comite International pour la Securite et la Cooperation Europeennes [*International Committee for European Security and Co-Operation - ICESC*] (EAIO) .... CISCE
Comite International pour le Controle de la Productivite Laitiere du Betail [*International Committee for Recording the Productivity of Milk Animals - ICRPMA*] (EAIO) .... CICPLB
Comite International pour le Fair Play [*International Fair Play Committee*] [*Paris, France*] (EAIO) .... CIFP
Comite International pour les Etudes Myceniennes [*Standing International Committee for Mycenaean Studies*] (EAIO) .... CIPEM
Comite International pour l'Etude et le Developpement de la Construction Tubulaire [*International Committee for the Study and Development of Tubular Construction*] [*Canada*] .... CIDECT
Comite International pour l'Information et Documentation des Sciences Sociales [*International Committee for Social Sciences Documentation*] .... CIDSS
Comite International Radio Maritime [*International Maritime Radio Association*] (EAIO) .... CIRM
Comite International Radioaeronautique .... CIRA
Comite International Special des Perturbations Radioelectriques [*International Special Committee on Radio Interference*] (EAIO) .... CISPR
Comite International sur l'Alcool, les Drogues et la Securite Routiere [*International Committee on Alcohol, Drugs, and Traffic Safety*] (EAIO) .... CIADSR
Comite International Technique d'Experts Juridiques Aeriens [*International Technical Committee of Aerial Legal Experts*] .... CITEJA
Comite International Tzigane [*International Gypsy Committee*] .... CIT
Comite Interregional des Bibliotheques Publiques [*Interregional Committee of Public Libraries*] [*Canada*] .... CIBP
Comite Juridique International de l'Aviation .... CJIA
Comite Latinoamericano de Textos Teologicos .... CLATT
Comite Liquidant ou Detournant les Ordinateurs [*Committee to Liquidate or Neutralize Computers*] [*France*] (PD) .... CLODO
Comite Maritime International [*International Maritime Committee - IMC*] [*Antwerp, Belgium*] (EAIO) .... CMI
Comite Marxista-Leninista Portugues [*Portuguese Marxist-Leninist Committee*] (PPE) .... CM-LP
Comite Meteorologique International .... CMI
Comite Nacional de Turismo [*National Committee on Tourism*] [*El Salvador*] (EY) .... CONATUR
Comite National d'Action sur la Situation de la Femme du Canada [*National Action Committee on the Status of Women*] [*Canada*] .... CNA
Comite National de Jumelage [*National Committee for Town/City Twinning*] [*France*] (EAIO) .... CNJ
Comite National pour la Liberation de la Cote d'Ivoire [*National Committee for the Liberation of the Ivory Coast*] .... CNLCI
Comite Nationale de Lutte Contre le SIDA [*National Committee on the Fight Against AIDS*] [*Mauritania*] (EAIO) .... CNLS
Comite Nationale de Lutte Contre le SIDA [*National Committee on the Fight Against AIDS*] [*Burkina Faso*] (EAIO) .... CNL-SIDA
Comite Nordique des Commissions des Sciences Humaines [*Nordic Committee of the Research Councils for the Humanities - NCRCH*] (EAIO) .... CNCSH
Comite Oceanografico Nacional [*Chile*] [*Marine science*] (OSRA) .... CONA
Comite Olimpico Boliviano [*Bolivian Olympic Committee*] (EAIO) .... COB
Comite Olimpico Hondureno [*Honduran Olympic Committee*] (EAIO) .... COH
Comite Olympique Hongrois [*Hungarian Olympic Committee*] (EAIO) .... COH
Comite Organisateur de Jeux Olympiques [*Organizing Committee of the Olympic Games (1976)*] [*Canada*] .... COJO
Comite Permanent Canadien des Noms Geographiques [*Canadian Permanent Committee on Geographical Names - CPCGN*] .... CPCNG
Comite Permanent de Liaison des Kinesitherapeutes de la CEE [*Standing Liaison Committee of Physiotherapists within the EEC - SLCP*] [*Copenhagen, Denmark*] (EAIO) .... CPLK
Comite Permanent des Congres Internationaux de Zoologie [*Permanent Committee of International Zoological Congresses*] [*France*] .... CPCIZ

Comite Permanent des Congres Internationaux pour l'Apostolat des Laics [*Permanent Committee of International Congresses for the Lay Apostolate*] [*Italy*] ... COPECIAL
Comite Permanent des Industries du Verre de la CEE [*Brussels, Belgium*] (EAIO) ... CPIV
Comite Permanent des Secretaires Generaux [*Standing Committee of Secretaries General*] [*NATO*] (NATG) ... CSG
Comite Permanent des Sous-Ministres [*Continuing Committee of Deputy Ministers - CCDM*] [*Canada*] ... CPSM
Comite Permanent du CE de l'Association Internationale de la Savonnerie et de laDetergence [*Standing EEC Committee of the International Association of the Soap and Detergent Industry - SEECCIASDI*] [*Brussels, Belgium*] (EAIO) ... CPCEAISD
Comite Permanent Interetats de Lutte Contre la Secheresse dans le Sahel [*Permanent Interstate Committee for Drought Control in the Sahel*] (EAIO) ... CILSS
Comite Permanent International des Techniques et de l'Urbanisme Souterrains [*Permanent and International Committee of Underground Town Planning and Construction*] ... CPITUS
Comite Permanent International du Vinaigre [*Permanent International Committee on Vinegar*] [*Common Market*] ... CPIV
Comite Permanent International d'Urbanisme Souterrain ... CPIUS
Comite pour le Developpement des Alternatives a l'Incarceration [*Committee for the Development of Alternatives to Incarceration*] [*Canada*] ... CODAI
Comite pour l'Utilisation des Resultats de l'Annee Geophysique Internationale [*IGY completion committee*] ... CURAGI
Comite pro Maria [*An association*] [*Belgium*] (EAIO) ... CPM
Comite Regional d'Afrique Centrale pour la Conservation et l'Utilisation du Sol ... CRACCUS
Comite Regional d'Education pour le Developpement International de la Region de Lanaudiere (AC) ... CREDIL
Comite Regional Intersyndical de Montreal [*Montreal Regional Inter-Trade Union Committee*] [*Canada*] ... CRIM
Comite Regional Ouest-Africain pour la Conservation et l'Utilisation du Sol ... CROACUS
Comite Revolucionario de Mocambique ... COREMO
Comite Scientifique Consultatif des Peches Canadiennes dans l'Atlantique [*Canadian Atlantic Fisheries Scientific Advisory Committee - CAFSAC*] (ASF) ... CSCPCA
Comite Scientifique International de Recherches sur les Trypanosomiases ... CSIRT
Comite Scientifique pour les Recherches Antarctiques [*Scientific Committee on Antarctic Research*] (MSC) ... CSRA
Comite Scientifique pour les Recherches Oceaniques [*Scientific Committee on Oceanic Research - SCOR*] [*France*] (MSC) ... CSRO
Comite Sida Aide Montreal (AC) ... CSAM
Comite Special de l'Annee Geophysique Internationale [*Special Committee for the International Geophysical Year*] [*Superseded by CIG*] ... CSAGI
Comite Special du Programme Biologique International [*Special Committee for the International Biological Program*] ... CSPBI
Comite Sportif International du Travail [*International Workers Sport Committee*] [*Brussels, Belgium*] (EAIO) ... CSIT
Comite Syndical Europeen des Personnels de l'Education [*European Teachers Trade Union Committee*] [*EC*] (ECED) ... CSEE
Comite Syndical International du Tourisme Social et des Loisirs [*International Trade Unions Committee of Social Tourism and Leisure - ITUCSTL*] (EA) ... CSITSL
Comite Technique International de Prevention et d'Extinction du Feu [*International Technical Committee for the Prevention and Extinction of Fire*] (EAIO) ... CTIF
Comiteco [*Race of maize*] ... COM
Comitel, Bedarfsfluge, KG [*Austria*] [*FAA designator*] (FAAC) ... COE
Comites Communistes pour l'Autogestion [*Communist Committees for Self-Management*] [*France*] [*Political party*] (PPW) ... CCA
Comites Comunistas Revolucionarios, Marxistas-Leninistas [*Marxist-Leninist Revolutionary Communist Committees*] [*Portugal*] [*Political party*] (PPE) ... CCR M-L
Comites Reunis de l'Industrie de l'Ennoblissement Textile dans le CE [*EC*] (ECED) ... CRIET
Comlevel Indicator (SAUS) ... CLI
COMLINE Business Analysis [*COMLINE International Corp.*] [*Japan*] [*Information service or system*] (CRD) ... CBA
COMLINE Industrial Monitor [*COMLINE International Corp.*] [*Japan*] [*Information service or system*] (CRD) ... CIM
Comlinear Corp. (SAUO) ... CLC
comma (SAUS) ... cma
Comma (FAAC) ... CMA
Comma (AABC) ... CMM
Comma (ROG) ... COM
Comma (WDMC) ... com
Comma Delimited Format (SAUS) ... CDF
Comma Separated Value [*Computer science*] (IGQR) ... CSV
Comma Separated Values File [*Computer science*] ... CSV
Commack Public Library, Commack, NY [*Library symbol*] [*Library of Congress*] (LCLS) ... NCo
Commanche Peak Steam Electric Station (NRCH) ... CPSES
Command (ROG) ... C
Command ... CD
Command ... CM
Command (EY) ... CMD
Command (WDAA) ... Cmd
Command (ADWA) ... cmd
Command ... CMND
Command (AAG) ... COM
Command (AFM) ... COMD
Command (MILB) ... comd
command (SAUO) ... comd
Command (WGA) ... COMM
Command Acceptance Pattern (ACAE) ... CAP
Command Access Keys ... CAK
Command Accountant [*Military*] [*British*] ... CA
Command Accounting and Finance Office (AFM) ... CAFO
Command Acknowledge (BUR) ... CAK
Command Acquisition Unit (NASA) ... CAU
Command Action (NATG) ... CA
Command Action Plan (NVT) ... CAP
Command Action Report [*Army*] ... CAR
Command Action Team (ACAE) ... CAT
Command Activated Multi-Beam Sonobuoy (SAUS) ... CAMBS
Command Activation Unit (MCD) ... CAU
Command Active Multi-Beam Sonobuoy (PDAA) ... CAMBS
Command Active Sonobuoy System [*Navy*] ... CASS
Command Actuated Bit (ACAE) ... CAB
Command Address [*Computer science*] (IAA) ... CAD
Command Address Change (SAUS) ... CAC
Command Adjusted Trajectory/Fire Control System (SAUS) ... CAT/FCS
Command ADP Modernization Program (SAUO) ... CAMP
Command Advisory Board ... CAB
Command Aerospace Maintenance Manpower Information System ... CAMMIS
Command Air Force Vehicle Integrated Management System (SAUO) ... CAFVIMS
Command Aircraft Maintenance and Manpower Information System (SAUO) ... CAMMIS
Command Aircraft Maintenance Manpower Information System (SAUS) ... CAMMIS
Command Airways [*South Africa*] [*ICAO designator*] (FAAC) ... CAH
Command Airways [*ICAO designator*] (AD) ... CT
Command Airways [*ICAO designator*] (AD) ... DD
Command Algorithmic Language [*Computer science*] (NITA) ... COMAL
Command Analysis [*Telecommunications*] (TEL) ... CANAL
Command Analysis Center ... CAC
Command Analysis of Office of Military Assistance Funding (MCD) ... CAOMAF
Command Analysis Pattern (KSC) ... CAP
Command and Administration ... C & A
Command and Administration (SAUS) ... C&A
Command and Administration System [*Army*] ... COADS
Command and Administrative Data System (SAUS) ... COADS
Command and Arithmetic Unit (SAUS) ... CAU
Command and Communications System [*or Subsystem*] [*NASA*] ... CCS
Command and Control (AAGC) ... C2
Command and Control (NVT) ... CAC
Command and Control ... C & C
Command & Control (CCCA) ... CC
Command and Control (SAUS) ... COC
Command and Control [*Pronounced "see-squared"*] ... C^2
Command and Control (SAUS) ... Cy
Command and Control - Division Air Defense (MCD) ... CC-DAD
Command and Control Agency (SAUO) ... CCA
Command and Control Alert/Conferencing Network (CINC) ... CCACN
Command and Control Battalion (SAUO) ... Comd & Con Bn
Command and Control Board (SAUS) ... CCB
Command and Control Boat [*Navy symbol*] ... CCB
Command and Control Center [*Air Force*] (AFM) ... CCC
Command and Control Center ... C^3
Command & Control Centre (SAUS) ... CDC
Command and Control, Communications and Computers (PDAA) ... C4
Command and Control Console (ACAE) ... C2C
Command and Control Defense Systems Office ... CCDSO
Command and Control Development Division [*Air Force*] ... CCDD
Command and Control Development Division (SAUS) ... CyDy
Command and Control Director [*Air Force*] ... CCD
Command & Control Display (SAUS) ... CCD
Command and Control Display Processing (ACAE) ... CCDP
Command and Control Division [*SHAPE Technical Center*] (NATG) ... CCD
Command and Control Electronics (ACAE) ... C&CE
Command & Control Element (SAUS) ... C2E
Command and Control Engineering Center [*Washington, DC*] ... CCEC
Command and Control Evaluation (SAUO) ... CCE
Command and Control Exercise ... C2X
Command and Control Information Exchange (SAUO) ... C2IE
Command and Control Information Processing [*Computer science*] (MHDI) ... CCIP
Command and Control Information Processing System (SAUO) ... C2IPS
Command & Control Information Processing System (SAUS) ... C2IPS
Command and Control Information System (SAUO) ... C2IS
Command and Control Information System [*Hughes Aircraft Co.*] ... CCIS
Command and Control Information System [*Military*] ... C^2IS
Command and Control Information Systems (SAUS) ... C2IS
Command and Control Information Systems Management Office (SAUO) ... C2ISMO
Command and Control Information Systems Manager (SAUO) ... C2ISM
Command and Control Initiatives Program (SAUO) ... C2IP
Command and Control Micro-Computer Users Group [*Fort Leavenworth, KS*] [*Army*] (INF) ... C^2MUG
Command and Control Modernization Methodology (SAUO) ... C2MS
Command & Control Processing & Display System (SAUS) ... CCPDS
Command & Control Processor (SAUS) ... C2P
Command and Control Reports (SAUO) ... COMCONS
Command and Control Research (SAUS) ... CCR

Command and Control Segment [*Air Force*] (DOMA) ... CCS
Command and Control Set (MCD) ... CCS
Command and Control Simulation System (MCD) ... CCSS
Command and Control Standardization and Evaluation Team [*Military*] ... CCSET
Command & Control Station (SAUS) ... CCS
Command and Control Steering Committee ... C2SC
Command and Control Subordinate System (SAUO) ... C2S2
Command and Control Subordinate System (SAUO) ... CCS2
Command and Control Subsystem (NASA) ... CCS
Command and Control Support Agency (ACAE) ... CCSA
Command and Control Switching System (DOMA) ... CCSS
Command and Control System (SAUO) ... C2S
Command and Control System ... C & CS
Command and Control System [*Army*] (RDA) ... CCS
Command and Control System (DOMA) ... C^{2}S
Command and Control System Interface Test [*Military*] (CAAL) ... C & CSIT
Command and Control Systems Center (SAUO) ... CCSC
Command and Control Systems Office [*Military*] ... CCSO
Command and Control Systems Organization [*Defense Communications Agency*] [*Washington, DC*] ... CCSO
Command and Control Systems Program Management Office (SAUO) ... C2SPMO
Command and Control Team Trainer (ACAE) ... CCTT
Command and Control Technical Center [*DoD*] ... CCTC
Command and Control Technical Center WWMCCS [*Worldwide Military Command and Control System*] **ADP Directorate** [*Automatic Data Processing*] [*DoD*] ... CCTC-WAD
Command and Control Test Facility ... CCTF
Command and Control Training Vehicles (MCD) ... CCTV
Command & Control Vehicle (SAUS) ... C2V
Command and Control Vehicle [*Army*] ... C^{2}V
Command and Control Voice Communications System [*Defense Supply Agency*] ... CCVCS
Command and Control Warfare [*Military*] ... C2W
Command and Control Warfare (ADWA) ... CCW
Command and Control Warfare (SAUS) ... CyW
Command and Control Zone (SSD) ... CCZ
Command and Coordination Set ... CCS
Command and Data Acquisition (NASA) ... CDA
Command and Data Acquisition Station [*Aerospace*] ... CDAS
Command and Data Handling (NASA) ... C & DH
Command and Data Handling (DEN) ... CDH
Command and Data Interface Simulator unit (SAUS) ... CDIS
Command and Data Processing Area (MCD) ... CDPA
Command and Data Simulator (NASA) ... CADS
Command and Data Simulator (NAKS) ... C&DS
Command and Data System (SAUS) ... CDDS
Command and Data-Handling Console ... CDC
Command and Data-Handling Console (KSC) ... CDHC
Command and Decision [*Military*] (CAAL) ... C & D
Command and Decision Sensor Interface Data System (MCD) ... CDSIDS
Command and Decision System (MCD) ... CDS
Command & Display Workstation (SAUS) ... CDW
Command and Edit Language (NITA) ... CANDE
Command and Edit Program [*Burroughs Corp.*] [*Computer science*] (BUR) ... CANDE
Command and Expenditure Report ... CER
Command & Fire Control System (SAUS) ... CFCS
Command and General Staff [*Military*] ... C & GS
Command and General Staff College [*Fort Leavenworth, KS*] [*Military*] ... C & GSC
Command and General Staff College [*Fort Leavenworth, KS*] [*Military*] ... CGSC
Command and General Staff Officer Course [*Military*] (INF) ... CGSOC
Command and General Staff School [*Army*] ... C & GSS
Command and General Staff School (SAUO) ... C&GSS
Command and General Staff School [*Army*] ... C & GS Sch
Command and Intelligence Support Indications Center (SAUO) ... CISIC
Command and Launch Subsystem (ACAE) ... CALS
Command and Launch Subsystem (MCD) ... CLS
Command and Management Presentation [*Marine Corps*] ... CAMP
Command and Navigation Equipment (SAUS) ... CANE
Command and Observation Post (SAUO) ... COP
Command and Reporting Center (SAUO) ... CRC
Command and Response Unit ... CRU
Command and Service Module [*NASA*] (IAA) ... CASM
Command and Service Module [*NASA*] (MCD) ... CSM
Command and Stability Augmentation System (MCD) ... CSAS
Command and Staff ... C & S
Command and Staff College (SAUO) ... C&SC
Command and Staff College [*Air Force*] ... CSC
Command & Staff Course (SAUS) ... CSC
Command and Telemetry Data Handling (IEEE) ... CTDH
Command and Telemetry System (AAG) ... CTS
Command and Training Launch Demonstration (ACAE) ... CTLD
Command and Triangulation ... CAT
Command Area Study and Mission Analysis Program [*Military*] (INF) ... CASMAP
Command Arithmetic Unit ... CAU
Command, Arming, Recording and Timing (SAUS) ... CARS System
Command, Arming, Recording, and Timing (PDAA) ... CART
Command Arrangement Agreement (COE) ... CAA
Command Assessment Review [*Air Force*] (AAGC) ... CAPCAR
Command Assessment Review (MCD) ... CAR
Command Assistance Team (SAUO) ... CAT
Command Augmentation System ... CAS
Command Authorization List ... CAL
Command Automated Budget Execution and Retrieval System (SAUO) ... CABERS
Command Automated Budget System [*Army*] ... CABS
Command Automated Procurement System (MCD) ... CAPS
Command Automated Support Network [*Marine Corps*] (DOMA) ... CASN
Command Automated System for Procurement [*Army*] ... CASPR
Command Automatic Card Tester ... CACT
Command Automation Master Plan (SAUO) ... CAMP
Command Aviation Net [*Military*] (INF) ... CAN
Command Battle Simulation (MCD) ... CBS
Command Budget Automated System [*Air Force*] (GFGA) ... CBAS
Command Budget Estimates [*Military*] (AABC) ... CBE
Command Byte (SAUS) ... CB
Command Cab (SAUO) ... CC
Command Cadet Team [*Military*] [*British*] ... CCT
Command Car (SAA) ... CC
Command Card (SAUS) ... CC
Command Career Program Management (MCD) ... CCPM
Command Center Automation (SAUO) ... CCA
Command Center Automation System (SAUO) ... CCAS
Command Center Complex (SAUO) ... CCC
Command Center Evaluation Facility (SAUO) ... CCEF
Command Center Evaluation System (SAUO) ... CCES
Command Center Information System (SAUO) ... CCIS
Command Center Operations Chief (MCD) ... CCOC
Command Center (or Centre) (SAUS) ... CC
Command Center Processing and Display Systems [*Air Force*] (MCD) ... CCPDS
Command Center Processing and Display Systems Replacement [*Military*] (GFGA) ... CCPDS-R
Command Center Support System (MCD) ... CCSS
Command Center Terminal System (MCD) ... CCTS
Command Center Upgrade (SAUO) ... CCU
Command Center Watch Officer (MCD) ... CCWO
Command Center Watch Station (SAUO) ... CCWS
Command Center Watch Teams (ACAE) ... CCWT
Command Centre Processing & Data System (SAUS) ... CCPDS
Command Chain [*Computer science*] ... CC
Command Channel Interface Unit (MHDI) ... CCIU
Command Chaplain [*AFSC*] ... HC
Command Chief Engineer (SAUS) ... CCE
Command Classified Control Register ... CCCR
Command Code [*IRS*] ... CC
Command Communication Systems (SAUS) ... CCS
Command, Communications and Control/Information Resource Management (SAUO) ... C3/IRM
Command Communications Boat ... CCB
Command Communications Console ... CCC
Command Communications Service Designator (CET) ... CCSD
Command Compiler (ACAE) ... CC
Command Comply Current Instructions ... PLYINST
Command Computer (AAG) ... CC
Command Computer Console ... CMDCC
Command Computer Input Multiplexer (MCD) ... CCIM
Command Conference [*Viking lander mission*] [*NASA*] ... CC
Command Confirmation ... CCN
Command Confirmation Buffer ... COMB
Command Console (IAA) ... CC
Command Console Processor [*Computer science*] (VERA) ... CCP
Command Contractor Data Management Review Board [*Air Force*] (AFIT) ... CCDMRB
Command Control (SAUS) ... CC
Command, Control & Alerting (SAUS) ... C2A
Command, Control, and Communications (AAGC) ... C3
Command, Control, and Communications [*Military*] ... C3I
Command, Control, and Communications [*Air Force*] ... CC & C
Command, Control, and Communications (ACAE) ... CCC
Command, Control, and Communications [*Pronounced "see-cubed"*] ... C^3
Command, Control, and Communications Agency Joint Test Organization [*Fort Huachuca, AZ*] ... C3A-JTO
Command, Control, and Communications Battle Management [*Military*] ... C^3/BM
Command, Control, and Communications Countermeasures [*Warfare*] ... C3CM
Command, Control, and Communications Countermeasures Joint Test Force [*Kirtland Air Force Base, NM*] ... C3CM-JTF
Command, Control, and Communications for Battle Management [*Military*] (DOMA) ... C^{3}BM
Command, Control, and Communications Master Plan (DOMA) ... C^{3}MP
Command, Control and Communications Order of Battle (SAUO) ... C3OB
Command Control and Communications Program [*Air Force*] ... CC & CP
Command, Control, and Communications System (NATG) ... CCCS
Command, Control, and Communications Systems (DOMA) ... C^{3}S
Command, Control and Communications Systems Directorate (SAUO) ... J-6
Command Control and Communications/Counter-Measures (SAUS) ... C3/CM
Command, Control, and Detection System [*Military*] ... CCDS
Command, Control, and Intelligence [*Military*] (RDA) ... C2I
Command, Control and Intelligence (SAUO) ... C2I
Command, Control, and Intelligence (ACAE) ... CCI
Command, Control and Intelligence Processor (SAUO) ... C2IP
Command Control and Monitor System (NAKS) ... ccms
Command Control and Monitor System [*NASA*] (NASA) ... CCMS
Command, Control & Status (SAUS) ... C2S
Command, Control, and Subordinate Systems [*Telecommunications*] (TEL) ... CCS^2
Command, Control and Subordinate Systems (SAUS) ... CCSy
Command, Control, and Systems Integration Directorate [*Army and NASA joint operation*] (RDA) ... C^2 SID

Command Control and Telemetry (ACAE) ... CCT
Command Control and Weather (SAA) ... CCW
Command Control Block [*Computer science*] (BUR) ... CCB
Command Control Center (SAUS) ... CCC
Command, Control Communication, and Computer Systems (USGC) ... C4
Command, Control, Communication, Information (SAUS) ... C3I
Command, Control, Communications, and Combat Service Support [*Military*] (INF) ... C^{4S2}
Command, Control, Communications, and Computer Systems (NVT) ... C^4
Command, Control, Communications, and Computer Systems (DOMA) ... C^4S
Command, Control, Communications, and Computers [*Military*] ... C4I
Command, Control, Communications, and Computers (ACAE) ... CCCC
Command, Control, Communications and Intelligence (SAUO) ... C3I
Command, Control, Communications, and Intelligence (USGC) ... C31
Command, Control, Communications, and Intelligence [*Telecommunications*] (TEL) ... CCCI
Command, Control, Communications, and Intelligence [*Pronounced "see-cubed eye"*] ... C^3I
Command, Control, Communications and Intelligence Acquisition Center [*Army*] (RDA) ... C3IAC
Command, Control, Communications and Intelligence Information Systems (SAUS) ... C3IIS
Command, Control, Communications and Intelligence Systems (AAGC) ... C31
Command, Control, Communications and Track (ACAE) ... CCCT
Command, Control, Communications, Computer and Information (SAUO) ... C4I
Command, Control, Communications, Computer, and Intelligence [*Army*] ... C4I
Command, Control, Communications Computer and Intelligence for the Warrior [*Army*] ... C_4IFTW
Command, Control, Communications, Computers, and Intelligence ... C4I
Command, Control, Communications, Computers, Intelligence, and Counter-Measures (DOMA) ... C^4ICM
Command, Control, Communications, Computers, Intelligence & Information (SAUS) ... C4I2
Command, Control, Communications, Computers, Intelligence, and Interoperability [*Marine Corps*] (DOMA) ... C^4I^2
Command, Control, Communications, Computers, Intelligence, Electronic Warfare, and Sensors [*Army*] ... C4IEWS
Command, Control, Communications, Computers, Intelligence, Surveillance, and Reconnaissance [*Military*] ... C4ISR
Command, Control, Communications, Computing/Information and Intelligence ... C^{4I2}
Command, Control, Communications Intelligence and Interoperability (SAUO) ... C3I2
Command, Control, Communications, Intelligence, and Interoperability ... C^{3I2}
Command Control Communications Laboratory Center (SAA) ... CCCLC
Command, Control, Communications Program Plan (SAUO) ... C3P2
Command, Control, Communications Systems Directorate (DOMA) ... C^3SYS DIR
Command Control Console (KSC) ... CCC
Command Control Destruct (SAUS) ... CCD
Command Control Destruct System (MUGU) ... CCDS
Command Control Dial Panel ... CCDP
Command Control Equipment (KSC) ... CCE
Command Control Group [*Air Force*] ... CCG
Command Control Handover and Keying (SAA) ... CCH
Command Control Information Requirements (SAUS) ... CCIR
Command Control Information System (SAUS) ... CCIS
Command Control Information Utility [*Military*] ... CCIU
Command, Control, Intelligence Support Squadron [*Air Force*] ... CCISS
Command, Control, Intelligence Support System (SAUO) ... CCISS
Command Control Interactive Display Experimentation System [*Army*] (MCD) ... CCIDES
Command Control Interface [*Army*] (AABC) ... CCI
Command Control Language (SAUS) ... CCL
Command Control Number [*Air Force*] (AFM) ... CCN
Command Control Operations Center [*Army*] (AABC) ... CCOC
Command Control Order ... CCO
Command Control Panel ... CCP
Command Control Post ... CCP
Command Control Receiver ... CCR
Command Control Room ... CCR
Command, Control Simulation Integration Language [*ARPA*] ... CCSIL
Command, Control, Support [*Army*] ... CCS
Command Control System (SAUS) ... CCS
Command Control Transmitter (MCD) ... CCT
Command Control Word (IAA) ... CCW
Command Control/Destruct (MUGU) ... CC/D
Command Counter (SAUS) ... CC
Command Cruiser-Destroyer Force, Pacific (DNAB) ... COMCRUDESPAC
Command Data Administration (ACAE) ... CDA
Command Data Base (SAUO) ... CDB
Command Data Buffer [*Air Force*] (MCD) ... CDB
Command Data Buffer [*Air Force*] (MCD) ... CDBFR
Command Data Buffer Program (SAUS) ... CDBP
Command Data Channel (SAUO) ... CDC
Command Data Format Control Handbook [*NASA*] (KSC) ... CDFCHB
Command Data Management Routine [*Computer science*] ... CDMR
Command, Data Processing, and Instrumentation [*NASA*] ... CDPI
Command, Data Processing, and Instrumentation System [*NASA*] (NASA) ... CDPIS
Command Data Processing Interface Equipment ... CDPIE
Command Data Processor ... CDP
Command Data System (ACAE) ... CDS
Command Data Word (MCD) ... CDW
Command Database Interface Language (MCD) ... CDIL
Command Decision and Movement Control Charts ... COMDEC
Command Decision Echelon (MCD) ... CDE
Command Decision Subsystem [*Military*] (CAAL) ... CDSS
Command Decoder ... CD
Command Decoder (GFGA) ... CMD DCDR
Command Decoder Coaxial (MCD) ... CDC
Command Decoder Coaxial Cable (SAUS) ... CDC Cable
Command Decoder Film (SAUS) ... CDF
Command Decoder Filter ... CDF
Command Definition Language [*Computer science*] (IAA) ... CDL
Command Delimiter (SAUS) ... CD
Command Delivering Orders Initiate Background Investigation [*Military*] (DNAB) ... DELCOMBI
Command Demodulator Decoder (ACAE) ... CDD
Command Dental Service Report [*Air Force*] ... COMD DSR
Command Descriptor Block (RALS) ... CDB
Command Descriptor Table (NASA) ... CDT
Command Designated Position List (MCD) ... CDPL
Command Destruct (AAG) ... C/D
Command Destruct Control (AAG) ... CDC
Command Destruct Decoder ... CDD
Command Destruct Receiver (AFM) ... CDR
Command Destruct System (MCD) ... CDS
Command Destruct Transmitter (AFM) ... CDT
Command Destruct Unit (AABC) ... CDU
Command Detector Unit (MCD) ... CDU
Command Device (SAUS) ... CD
Command Direct Support (SAUO) ... CDS
Command Director (ACAE) ... CD
Command Director of Administration (AAGC) ... CCTA
Command Disable System [*Air Force*] ... CDS
Command, Display & Control (SAUS) ... COMDAC
Command Display and Control Processor ... CDCP
Command Display Indicator (MCD) ... CDI
Command Display Unit (MCD) ... CDU
Command Distribution Rack ... CDR
Command Distribution Unit (IIA) ... CDU
Command Distributor Flip-Flop (SAA) ... CDFF
Command Document Capability List (IAA) ... CDCL
Command Document Control Number (AFIT) ... CDCN
Command Document Discard (IAA) ... CDD
Command Document End (IAA) ... CDE
Command Document Page Boundary (SAUS) ... CDPB
Command Document Resynchronization (IAA) ... CDR
Command Document Start (IAA) ... CDS
Command Document User Information (IAA) ... CDUI
Command Duty Officer [*Navy*] ... CDO
Command Education Officer [*Military*] [*British*] ... CEO
Command Electronic Operating Instruction (SAUO) ... CEOI
Command Element (SAUO) ... CE
Command Element Specific Program (SAUO) ... CESP
Command Entertainments Officer [*Military*] [*British*] ... CEO
Command Equipment Management Office [*Military*] (AFM) ... CEMO
Command Equipment Management Program Review [*Military*] (MCD) ... CEMPR
Command Equipment Management Team [*Military*] ... CEMT
Command Evaluation and Training (SAA) ... COMENT
Command Evaluation Teams (MCD) ... COMET
Command Excess Equipment Redistribution System (SAUO) ... CEERS
Command Execution Module (CIST) ... CEM
Command Execution Planning Group (SAUO) ... CEPG
Command Executioner (ACAE) ... CE
Command Executive Procedure [*Computer science*] (OA) ... CEP
Command Experience and Training (ACAE) ... COMET
Command Field (SAUS) ... CF
Command Field Exercise [*Military*] (INF) ... CFX
Command File (SAUS) ... CME
Command File (IAA) ... CMF
Command File (CDE) ... COM file
Command File System (SAUS) ... CFS
Command Flight Medical Officer (SAUS) ... CFMO
Command Flight Path Display (ACAE) ... CFPD
Command Flight Safety Officer (SAUS) ... CFSO
Command Forces ... CFOR
Command Fund Control System (SAUO) ... CFCS
Command Generation Program [*Mariner*] [*NASA*] ... COMGEN
Command Generator Tracker (MCD) ... CGT
Command, Ground Component Command (SAUO) ... CGCC
Command Ground Station [*Army*] (RDA) ... CGS
Command Group (MCD) ... CG
Command Group Training Support System (MCD) ... CGTSS
Command Guard List [*Navy*] (CAAL) ... CGL
Command Guidance [*Aerospace*] (AAG) ... CG
Command Guidance Computer (NASA) ... CGC
Command Guidance Test Vehicle ... CGTV
Command Guidance-Training Support System [*Military*] ... CGTSS
Command Guided Tactical Missile ... CGTM
Command Hardware System [*Army*] ... CHS
Command Hardware/Software [*Army*] ... CHS
Command Headquarters (SAUS) ... CHQ
Command Home All the Way [*Military*] (CAAL) ... CHAW
Command Indicator Performance Review (MCD) ... CIPR
Command Information (MCD) ... CI
Command Information (SAA) ... COIN
Command Information Bureau [*Military*] (CINC) ... CIB
Command Information Bureau/ Allied Press and Information Centers (SAUO) ... CIB/APIC

Command Information Center [*Military*] ... CIC
Command Information Division (MCD) ... CID
Command Information Flow [*Military*] (CAAL) ... CIF
Command Information Network (SAUO) ... CIN
Command Information Network System (SAUO) ... CINS
Command Information Program [*Military*] (AABC) ... CIP
Command Information Requirement Analysis (MCD) ... CIRA
Command Information System (SAUS) ... CIS
Command Information Systems [*Army*] ... CIS
Command Input Block [*Computer science*] ... CIB
Command Input Buffer [*Computer science*] (IBMDP) ... CIB
Command Input Coupler (CET) ... CIC
Command Inspection [*Military*] (NVT) ... CMDINSP
Command Inspection Program [*Army*] (INF) ... CIP
Command Inspection System Inspection (SAUS) ... CISI
Command Instrument System ... CIS
Command Instrument System Trainer [*Army*] ... CIST
Command Integrated Logistics Management Office ... CILSMO
Command Intelligence (MCD) ... CIC
Command Intelligence and Weather (SAA) ... CIW
Command Intelligence Architecture Plan [*Environmental science*] (COE) ... CIAP
Command Intelligence System (SAUS) ... CIS
Command Interface Control (MCD) ... CIC
Command Interface Port (SAUS) ... CIP
Command Interface Test (KSC) ... CIT
Command Interface Unit (KSC) ... CIU
Command Interpretation Table (SAUS) ... CIT
Command Interpreter (SSD) ... CI
Command Involvement Report [*Army*] ... CMD/INV
Command Issuing Office [*or Officer*] ... CIO
Command Job Language Interpreter [*Computer science*] [*Telecommunications*] ... CJLI
Command Language ... CL
[*The*] **Command Language** [*Computer science*] (PCM) ... TCL
Command Language for Interrogating Computers [*Royal RADAR Establishment*] [*British*] ... CLIC
Command Language Interface (RALS) ... CLI
Command Language Interpreter [*Computer science*] ... CLI
Command Language Processor ... CLP
Command Launch Computer (SAUS) ... CLC
Command Launch Computer (DWSG) ... CLCP
Command Launch Unit [*Military*] ... CLU
Command Level Maintenance Repair and Minor Construction Program Reporting System (SAUO) ... MARMIC
Command Liaison and Surveillance and Keying (SAA) ... CLS
Command Liaison Officer [*Military*] (DNAB) ... CLO
Command Line [*Military*] ... CL
Command Line Input Filter (SAUS) ... CLIF
Command Line Interface [*For Amiga computers*] ... CLI
Command Line Interpret [*Military*] (CAAL) ... CLI
Command Line Interpreter (SAUS) ... CLI
Command Line User Interface (SAUS) ... CLUI
Command Link Control Word (ADWA) ... CLCW
Command Link Transmission Unit (SAUS) ... CLTU
Command List [*Computer science*] (ITCA) ... CLIST
Command Load Acceptance Message ... CLAM
Command Load Controller ... CLC
Command Logic Unit (MCD) ... CLU
Command Logistics Information Improvement Program (SAUO) ... CLIIP
Command Logistics Review Program [*DoD*] ... CLRP
Command Logistics Review Team (MCD) ... CLRT
Command Logistics Review Teams Expanded (MCD) ... CLRTX
Command Maintenance [*Military*] (AABC) ... COMAINT
Command Maintenance Inspection [*Army*] ... CMI
Command Maintenance Management Inspection [*Army*] ... CMMI
Command Maintenance Readiness Inspection [*Army*] (AABC) ... CMRI
Command Management Center [*Military*] ... CMC
Command Management Control List ... CMCL
Command Management Engineering Team (ACAE) ... CMET
Command Management Facility (SAUS) ... CMF
Command Management Information System [*Air Force*] ... CMIS
Command Management Information System [*Air Force*] ... COMIS
Command Management Inventory Accounting [*Army*] ... CMIA
Command Management Review and Analysis [*Army*] ... CAMERA
Command Management System (MCD) ... CMS
Command Management Systems Engineer (ADWA) ... CMSE
Command Manpower Data System ... CMDS
Command Master Chief [*Navy*] (DOMA) ... CMC
Command Message ... CMDMSG
Command Message Formulator (SAUS) ... CME
Command Message Formulator (SAA) ... CMF
Command Meteorological Centre (SAUO) ... CMC
Command Military Training ... CMT
Command Mode Rejection Ratio (HGAA) ... CMMRR
Command Model for Analysis and Design (MCD) ... COMMAND
Command Modular Operation Room Equipment (PDAA) ... COMMODORE
Command Modulator Assembly [*NASA*] ... CMA
Command Module (SAUS) ... A/M
Command Module [*NASA*] ... CM
Command Module - Service Module [*Combined*] [*NASA*] (MCD) ... CM-SM
Command Module Computer [*NASA*] (MCD) ... CMC
Command Module Electrical Power System [*NASA*] ... CEPS
Command Module Multiple Docking Assembly [*NASA*] (KSC) ... CMMDA
Command Module Pilot [*Apollo*] [*NASA*] ... CMP
Command Module Procedures Simulator [*NASA*] ... CMPS
Command Module Reaction Control System (SAUS) ... CMRCS
Command Module Simulator [*NASA*] ... CMS
Command Module Technician (SAUS) ... CMT
Command Module/Service Module (SAUS) ... CM/SM
Command Money [*British military*] (DMA) ... CM
Command Monitor Panel (SSD) ... CMP
Command Munitions Management System (SAUO) ... CMMS
Command NODAL [*Network-Oriented Data Acquisition Language*] **Control Element** ... CNCE
Command Not Operationally Ready [*Navy*] (NVT) ... CNOR
Command Nuclear Target List (MCD) ... CNTL
Command Objective Plan [*Air Force*] ... COP
Command Observation Post (AABC) ... COP
Command of Camp [*Military*] (VNW) ... COC
Command of Naval Operations (SAUS) ... CNO
Command of Quarters [*Army*] (VNW) ... CQ
Command Off the Line of Sight [*Military*] [*British*] ... COLOS
Command On-line Accounting and Reporting System (SAUO) ... COARS
Command Operating Budget [*Army*] ... COB
Command Operating Budget Estimate/Execution (MCD) ... COBE
Command Operating Budget System (SAUO) ... COBS
Command Operating Program [*Army*] (AABC) ... COP
Command Operating Program/Budget [*DoD*] (MCD) ... COP/B
Command Operation Procedure (SAUS) ... COP
Command Operationally Ready [*Navy*] (NVT) ... COR
Command Operations [*Army*] (AABC) ... CO
Command Operations Center [*Military*] (NVT) ... COC
Command Operations Priority Requirements List [*Air Force*] (AFM) ... COPRL
Command Operations Simulation Model with Interrogation Control (SAA) ... COSMIC
Command Operator (SAUS) ... CO
Command Orders ... CO
Command Ordnance Depot (SAUO) ... Comm OD
Command Output ... CO
Command Paper ... C
Command Paper (SAUO) ... CMD
Command Papers [*A publication*] (DLA) ... Cd
Command Papers (DLA) ... Cmd
Command Papers [*A publication*] (DLA) ... Cmnd
Command Pass Through (or Thru) (SAUS) ... CPT
Command Patrol Plane Replacement Squadrons Pacific ... COMPATPLANEREPRONSPAC
Command Paymaster [*British military*] (DMA) ... CP
Command Performance Indicator (MCD) ... CPI
Command Performance Indicator Review (MCD) ... CPIR
Command Performance Review ... CPR
Command Personnel Management Inspections (AABC) ... CPMI
Command Personnel Management Team (SAUO) ... CPMT
Command Personnel Summary (AABC) ... CPS
Command Pilot (AFM) ... CP
Command Point (AFIT) ... CP
Command Point of Contact [*Navy*] (AFIT) ... CPC
Command Post [*Military*] ... CP
Command Post Alerting Network [*Military*] ... COPAN
Command Post Automated Staff Support System (SAUO) ... CPASS
Command Post Communication Network (SAUS) ... CPCN
Command Post Digital Display [*SAGE*] [*Air Force*] ... CPDD
Command Post Duty Controller [*Air Force*] ... CPDYCONTR
Command Post Exercise [*Military*] ... CPEx
Command Post Exercise [*Military*] ... CPX
Command Post Exercise-Field Training Exercise (SAUS) ... CPX-FTX
Command Post Experience [*Army*] [*British*] ... CPX
Command Post Modem/Processor (SAUS) ... CPM/P
Command Post Modern Processor (CCCA) ... CPMF
Command Post Officer [*Military*] ... CPO
Command Post Record Capability [*Military*] ... COPREC
Command Post Terminal (SAUS) ... CPT
Command Post Vehicle [*British military*] (DMA) ... CPV
Command Postal and Courier Communications Depot (SAUO) ... CPCCD
Command Post/Observation Post (SAUS) ... CPOP
Command Pouch [*Air Force*] (AFM) ... CP
Command Power Cruise Control [*Diesel engines*] [*Automotive engineering*] ... CPCC
Command Preparation (ACAE) ... CP
Command Processor [*Computer science*] ... COMPROC
Command Processor [*Computer science*] (BUR) ... CP
Command Processor Distributor (SAA) ... CPD
Command Processor Distributor Control (MCD) ... CPDC
Command Processor Distributor Storage (SAUS) ... CPDS
Command Processor Module ... CPM
Command Procurement System (SAUS) ... PROCURE
Command Programmer Unit (DWSG) ... CPU
Command Programming Language ... CPL
Command Pulse (MSA) ... CP
Command Pulse Output ... CPO
Command Qualification Examination (MCD) ... CQE
Command Quality and Productivity Board (SAUO) ... CQPB
Command Quality Team (DOMA) ... CQT
Command Radio Link ... CORAL
Command, Ranging and Telemetry (SAUS) ... CR&T
Command Read Pulse (KSC) ... CRP
Command Readiness Exercise System [*Air Force*] (GFGA) ... CRES
Command Readout Station [*Military*] ... CRS
Command Receiver (KSC) ... C/R
Command Receiver Equipment (KSC) ... CRE

Command Receiver Monitor (AAG) .... CRM
Command Reconnaissance (SAUS) .... COMRCN
Command Register .... CR
Command Register Not Operable (SAUS) .... CRNO
Command Reject (IAA) .... CMDR
Command Reject (SAUS) .... CRJ
Command Relationship Agreements [*Army*] (AABC) .... CRA
Command Relationship Study .... CRS
Command Relay Driver Unit (MCD) .... CRDU
Command Repeat (SAUS) .... CRP
Command Reporting Center .... CRC
Command Representative (CINC) .... CR
Command Response (SAUS) .... C/R
Command Retrieval Information System .... CRIS
Command Retrieval System (DEN) .... CRS
Command Review .... CR
Command Review Board [*Aerospace*] .... CRB
Command Review Council (SAUO) .... CRC
Command Scheduling Chain [*Computer science*] (IAA) .... CSC
Command Scheduling Control Block [*Computer science*] (BUR) .... CSCB
Command Secretary/ Headquarters, United Kingdom Land Forces (SAUS) .... Sec/HQUKLF
Command Secretary/Secretariat (SAUS) .... Comd Sec
Command Security [*NASDAQ symbol*] (TTSB) .... CMMD
Command Security Corp. [*NASDAQ symbol*] (SAG) .... CMMD
Command Security Corp. [*Associated Press*] (SAG) .... CmndSc
Command Security Service (MCD) .... CSS
Command Selection List [*Army*] .... CSL
Command Selection (or Selector) (SAUS) .... CS
Command Selector .... CS
Command Selector Control .... CSC
Command Selector Panel (DNAB) .... CSP
Command Selector Value (DNAB) .... CSV
Command Senior Chief [*Navy*] (DOMA) .... CSC
Command Sensor Unit (SAUS) .... CSU
Command Sequence Introducer (SAUS) .... CSI
Command Sergeant Major [*Army*] (AABC) .... COMDSGTMAJ
Command Sergeant Major [*Army*] .... CSM
Command Sergeant Major [*Army*] E9
Command Service Force, Pacific (MCD) .... COMSERPAC
Command Session Abort [*Computer science*] (IAA) .... CSA
Command Session Change Control (IAA) .... CSCC
Command Session End [*Computer science*] (IAA) .... CSE
Command Session Start [*Computer science*] (IAA) .... CSS
Command Session Typed Data (SAUS) .... CSTD
Command Session User Information (IAA) .... CSUI
Command Set 80 (SAUS) CS80
Command Ship [*Navy symbol*] [*Obsolete*] CC
Command Ship (MILB) .... CMDS
Command Ship Data System [*Navy*] (MUGU) .... CSDS
Command Signal Decoder .... CSD
Command Signal Generator .... CSG
Command Signal Limiter (MCD) .... CSL
Command Signals Officer (SAUS) .... CSO
Command Software Subsystem [*Space Flight Operations Facility, NASA*] .... CMDSW
Command Standard [*Program, Commissary*] (MCD) .... COST
Command Start Point [*Military*] .... CSPT
Command Statement (SAUS) .... CS
Command String Interpreter [*Digital Equipment Corp.*] .... CSI
Command Structure (SAUS) .... CS
Command Study Advisory Committee [*TRADOC*] (MCD) .... CSAC
Command Substitution System (NITA) .... CSS
Command Subsystem Group (MCD) .... CSG
Command Supply Depot [*British military*] (DMA) .... COSD
Command Supply Depot (SAUO) .... CSD
Command Supply Discipline Program [*Army*] .... CSDP
Command Supply Management Data Bank (SAUS) .... DBNK
Command Supply Support (MCD) .... CSS
Command Support Aircraft (SAUS) .... CSA
Command Support Center (MCD) .... CSC
Command Support Center Watch Officer (MCD) .... CSCWO
Command Support Control Console .... CSCC
Command Support System (SAUS) .... CSS
Command Support System Demonstrator (SAUS) .... CSSD
Command Surgeon [*AFSC*] .... SG
Command Surveillance and Weather .... CSW
Command Synchronizer Slave (MCD) .... CSS
Command System (NATG) .... CS
Command System Operations Analysis Group Area [*Space Flight Operations Facility, NASA*] .... CAG
Command Systems Operations Division (SAUO) .... CSOD
Command Systems Support Activity .... COSSACT
Command Table (ACAE) .... CT
Command Tactical [*Navy*] (NVT) .... COMTAC
Command Tactical Console (SAUS) .... CTC
Command Tactical Trainer (ACAE) .... CTT
Command Tank (SAUS) .... Comd Tk
Command Tape (SAUS) .... CT
Command Team Training (SAUS) .... CTT
Command Technical Inspection [*Army*] (AABC) .... CTI
Command Technical Library (SAUO) .... CTL
Command Telemetry Buoy .... CTB
Command Telemetry Unit (ACAE) .... CTU
Command Terminal (SAUS) .... CTERM
Command Terminator (SAUS) .... CT
Command Test Vehicle (IAA) .... CTV
Command to Line of Sight [*Military*] [*British*] .... CLOS
Command Track Receiver (ACAE) .... CTR
Command Training Team (DNAB) .... CTT
Command Translator and Programmer .... CTP
Command Transmitter (KSC) .... C/T
Command Transmitter (SAUS) .... CT
Command Trust Network (EA) .... CTN
Command Uplink [*NASA*] (KSC) .... CUL
Command Uplink Electronics (SAUS) .... CUE
Command Uplink Request [*NASA*] (KSC) .... CUR
Command Vehicle CV
Command Verification [*NASA*] CV
Command Verification .... CVR
Command Verification/Drop .... CVR/D
Command Verify/Transmit .... CVT
Command Video Prelaunch Distribution System (IAA) .... CVPDS
Command Voltage Regulator .... CVR
Command Weapon Carrier (SAA) .... COMD WC
Command Wire Improvised Explosive Device [*Military*] (LAIN) .... CWIED
Command Word [*Computer science*] (MCD) .... CW
Command Word Chaining (SAUS) .... CWC
Command Word Sequence (SAUS) .... CWS
Command Word Trap [*Computer science*] (IAA) .... CWT
Command Works Office [*British military*] (DMA) .... CWO
Command Workshop (SAUO) .... Comd Wksp
Commandable Acoustic Engine Ignition Detectors (MCD) .... CAEDETS
Commandable Audio Engine Detector (MCD) .... CAEDET
Commandable Manual Entry Panel (SAUS) .... CMEP
Commandable Microphone (SAUS) .... Commike
Commandant [*Coast Guard*] C
Commandant (WGA) .... CDT
Commandant .... CMDT
Commandant [*Military*] .... COM
commandant (SAUO) .... comd
commandant (SAUO) .... comdt
Commandant [*Air Force*] (AFM) .... COMDT
Commandant (WDAA) .... Comdt
Commandant .... COMMDT
Commandant .... COMT
Commandant, Armed Forces Staff College (DNAB) .... COMDTAFSC
Commandant Assistant [*Coast Guard*] .... CA
Commandant, Civil Affairs Branch [*British*] [*World War II*] .... CCAB
Commandant, Defense Intelligence School (SAUO) .... CDIS
Commandant, Eighth Naval District (SAUO) .... COMEIGHT
Commandant, Eleventh Naval District (MUGU) .... COMELEVEN
Commandant, Fifth Naval District (MUGU) .... COMFIVE
Commandant, First Naval District (MUGU) .... COMONE
Commandant Fourteenth Naval District (SAUO) .... COMFOURTEEN
Commandant Fourth Naval District (SAUO) .... COMFOUR
Commandant General [*British military*] (DMA) .... CG
Commandant General [*British military*] (DMA) .... Cmdt Gen
Commandant, Marine Corps Program Policy and Planning Guidance (MCD) .... CMCPPG
Commandant, Marine Corps Schools [*Quantico, VA*] .... CMCS
Commandant, Naval Base, San Diego .... COMNAVBASEDIEGO
Commandant, Naval District (SAUS) .... ComNavDis
Commandant, Naval District, Washington, DC .... COMNAVDIST WASHDC
Commandant, Naval District, Washington, DC .... COMNDW
Commandant, Naval Operating Base .... COMDTNOB
Commandant, Navy Yard (SAUO) .... CMDTNY
Commandant, Navy Yard .... COMDTNY
Commandant, Ninth Naval District (MUGU) .... COMNINE
Commandant, North Atlantic Treaty Organization Defense College (DNAB) .... COMNATODEFCOL
Commandant Nucleus Department [*Military*] [*British*] .... CND
Commandant of Cadets [*Military*] .... COC
Commandant of the Coast Guard .... CCG
Commandant of the Coast Guard (DNAB) .... COMDTCOGARD
Commandant of the Marine Corps .... CMC
Commandant of the Marine Corps .... COMDTMARCORPS
Commandant of the Marine Corps Memorandum .... CMCM
Commandant, Potomac River Naval Command (SAA) .... COMPRNC
Commandant, Second Naval District (SAUO) .... COMTWO
Commandant, Seventh Naval District (SAUO) .... COMSEVEN
Commandant, Severn River Naval Command (SAA) .... COMSRNC
Commandant, Sixth Naval District (SAUO) .... COMSIX
Commandant, Third Naval District (MUGU) .... COMTHREE
Commandant, Thirteenth Naval District (MUGU) .... COMTHIRTEEN
Commandant, Twelfth Naval District (MUGU) .... COMTWELVE
Commandant, United States Coast Guard .... COMDTUSCG
Commandant, United States Marine Corps .... COMDTUSMC
Commandants Committee (SAUO) .... Comd C
Commandant's Instruction .... COMDTINST
Commandant's Training Strategy [*Military*] .... CTS
Command/Control Disable (SAUS) .... C/CDSB
Command-Destruct Epoxy [*A plastic resin*] .... CDE
Commanded .... CMDD
Commanded Active Sonobuoy System (SAUS) .... CASS
Commandement Aerien des Forces de Defense Aerienne [*Air Defense Forces Air Command*] (NATG) .... CAFDA
Commandement Aerien Tactique [*French Tactical Air Command*] .... CATAC
Commandement Allie des Approches de la Baltique [*Baltic Approaches Allied Command*] [*NATO*] (NATG) .... CAAB

Commandement du Transport Aerien Militaire Francais [*France*] [*ICAO designator*] (FAAC) ... CTM
Commandement du Transport Aerien Militaire. Military Air (SAUS) ... COTAM
Commander [*Usually in combination, as: CNAB for Commander, Naval Air Bases*] ... C
Commander (SAUO) ... CC
Commander ... CDR
Commander (WDAA) ... Cdr
Commander (WDAA) ... Cmdr
Commander (EY) ... CMDR
Commander ... COM
Commander (WDAA) ... Com
Commander (GEAB) ... com
Commander (ADWA) ... comb
Commander (WGA) ... COMD
commander (SAUO) ... comd
Commander (AFM) ... COMDR
Commander (WDAA) ... Comdr
Commander ... COMM
Commander ... COMMDR
Commander [*Navy*] [*British*] ... Cr
Commander (SAUS) ... Cr
Commander [*Navy*] ... O5
Commander, Aegean Defense Sector (NATG) ... COMAEGEANBASE
Commander Air Carter Ltd. [*Canada*] [*ICAO designator*] (FAAC) ... CML
Commander Air Center ... CAC
Commander, Air Component Command (SAUO) ... CACC
Commander, Air Defense Command ... COMADC
Commander, Air, Early Warning Squadron (SAUS) ... COAEWRON
Commander, Air Early Warning Squadron (SAUO) ... COAEWRon
Commander, Air Force (SAUS) ... COM AF
Commander, Air Force, Atlantic Fleet ... COMAIRLANT
Commander, Air Force Center for Studies and Analysis (SAUS) ... AFCSA/CC
Commander, Air Force Forces (AABC) ... COMAFFOR
Commander Air Force Forces (SAUO) ... COMAFOR
Commander, Air Force Forces-Alaska (SAUO) ... COMAFFOR-AK
Commander, Air Force, Pacific Fleet ... COMAIRPAC
Commander, Air Force Special Operations Cmd (SAUO) ... COMAFSOC
Commander, Air Force Task Force ... COMAFTASKFOR
Commander Air Force Unconventional Warfare Forces, Europe (SAUO) ... COMAFUWFORCE
Commander, Air Forces [*Navy*] ... COMAIR
Commander, Air Forces, Gulf [*British military*] (DMA) ... CAFG
Commander, Air Forces, Solomons ... COMAIRSOLS
Commander, Air Forces, South Pacific Force ... COMAIRSOPAC
Commander Air Forces South Pacific Force (SAUO) ... ComAirSoPac
Commander Air Forces US Atlantic Fleet (SAUO) ... COMAIRLANT
Commander, Air Forces-Korea (SAUO) ... COMAFK
Commander, Air Group [*Navy*] ... CAG
Commander Air Materiel Command (SAUO) ... COMAMC
Commander, Air Materiel Command (SAUS) ... COMAMC
Commander, Air Support Command (SAUS) ... COM AS COM
Commander Air Support Command (SAUO) ... Com AS Com
Commander, Air Task Group (SAUS) ... CATG
Commander, Air Transport ... COMAIRTRANS
Commander, Air Transport Squadron ... COMAIRTRANSRON
Commander, Airborne Early-Warning Wing (DNAB) ... COMAEWW
Commander Aircraft [*NASDAQ symbol*] (TTSB) ... CMDR
Commander, Aircraft (SAUS) ... COMAIR
Commander Aircraft Co. [*NASDAQ symbol*] (SAG) ... CMDR
Commander Aircraft Co. [*Associated Press*] (SAG) ... ComndAr
Commander, Aircraft Ferry Squadron (SAUS) ... COMAIRFERON
Commander Aircraft Ferry Squadron (SAUO) ... ComAirFeRon
Commander, Aircraft Support Control Unit [*Navy*] ... CASCU
Commander Airlift Forces (SAUO) ... CAF
Commander, Airlift Forces-Europe (SAUO) ... COMALF-E
Commander, Airship Group ... COMAIRSHIPGR
Commander, Alameda Group ... COMALAMGRU
Commander Alameda Group (SAUO) ... COMALAMGRU
Commander, Alaskan Air Command (MCD) ... COMAAC
Commander Alaskan Air Command (SAUO) ... COMALAIRC
Commander, Alaskan Norad Region (SAUO) ... COMANR
Commander, Alaskan Sea Frontier (MUGU) ... COMALSEAFRON
Commander, Alaskan Sector ... COMALSEC
Commander, All Forces, Aruba-Curacao ... CAFAC
Commander, Allied Air Force Central Europe ... COMAAFACE
Commander Allied Air Forces (SAUO) ... COMAIR
Commander Allied Air Forces Atlantic (SAUO) ... COMAIRLANT
Commander, Allied Air Forces, Baltic Approaches (AABC) ... COMAIRBALTAP
Commander, Allied Air Forces Canadian Atlantic Subarea (SAUS) ... COMAIRCANLANT
Commander Allied Air Forces Central Europe [*NATO*] (PDAA) ... COMAAFCE
Commander, Allied Air Forces, Central Europe ... COMAIRCENT
Commander, Allied Air Forces Eastern Atlantic (SAUS) ... COMAIREASTLANT
Commander, Allied Air Forces, North Norway (NATG) ... COMAIRNON
Commander, Allied Air Forces Northern Atlantic (SAUS) ... COMAIRNORLANT
Commander, Allied Air Forces, Northern Europe ... COMAIRNORTH
Commander Allied Air Forces Northern Europe (SAUO) ... ComAlAirNorEur
Commander, Allied Air Forces, Northern Europe ... GOVTLAIRNOREUR
Commander, Allied Air Forces Plymouth Channel (SAUS) ... COMAIRPLYMCHAN
Commander, Allied Air Forces, South Norway (NATG) ... COMAIRSONOR
Commander, Allied Air Forces, Southern Europe ... COMAIRSOUTH
Commander Allied Forces Baltic Approaches (SAUO) ... COMBALTAP
Commander, Allied Forces, North Norway (NATG) ... COMNON
Commander, Allied Forces Southern Norway [*Navy*] (ANA) ... COMSONOR
Commander Allied Land Forces (SAUO) ... COMLAND
Commander, Allied Land Forces, Central Europe ... COMLANDCENT
Commander, Allied Land Forces, Denmark (SAUS) ... COMLANDDENMARK
Commander, Allied Land Forces, Denmark (NATG) ... COMLANDENMARK
Commander, Allied Land Forces, Denmark (AFM) ... COMLANDMARK
Commander, Allied Land Forces, Jutland (SAUS) ... COMLANDJUT
Commander, Allied Land Forces, Northern Europe (SAUS) ... COMLANDNORTH
Commander Allied Land Forces Northern Europe (SAUO) ... COMLANDNORTH
Commander, Allied Land Forces, Norway ... COMLANDNORWAY
Commander, Allied Land Forces, Schleswig-Holstein ... COMLANDSCHLESWIG
Commander, Allied Land Forces, Schleswig-Holstein and Jutland (AABC) ... COMLANDJUT
Commander, Allied Land Forces, South Norway (SAUS) ... COMLANDSONOR
Commander, Allied Land Forces, Southeastern Europe ... COMLANDSOUTHEAST
Commander, Allied Land Forces, Southern Europe ... COMLANDSOUTH
Commander, Allied Land Forces, Zealand (AABC) ... COMLANDZEALAND
Commander, Allied land Forces, Zealand (SAUS) ... COMLAND-ZEALAND
Commander, Allied Maritime Air Force Channel [*NATO*] ... COMMAIRCHAN
Commander, Allied Naval Forces, Baltic Approaches (AABC) ... COMNAVBALTAP
Commander, Allied Naval Forces, Central Army Group (SAUS) ... COMNAVCAG
Commander, Allied Naval Forces, Central Europe ... COMNAVCENT
Commander, Allied Naval Forces, North Norway (AABC) ... COMNAVNON
Commander, Allied Naval Forces, Northern Europe ... COMALNAVNOREUR
Commander Allied Naval Forces Northern Europe (SAUO) ... ComAlNavNorEur
Commander, Allied Naval Forces, Northern Europe ... COMNAVNORTH
Commander, Allied Naval Forces, Scandinavian Approaches (AABC) ... COMNAVSCAP
Commander, Allied Naval Forces, South Norway (NATG) ... COMNAVSONOR
Commander, Allied Tactical Air Force, North Norway (AABC) ... COMTAFNORNOR
Commander, Allied Tactical Air Force, South Norway (AABC) ... COMTAFSONOR
Commander Allied Tactical Air Forces (SAUO) ... COMATAF
Commander, Allied Tactical Air Forces, Southern Norway ... COMATAFSONOR
Commander, Allied Task Forces, North Norway (AFM) ... COMTASKFORNON
Commander, Amphibious Force ... COMPHIB
Commander, Amphibious Force ... COMPHIBFOR
Commander Amphibious Force, Atlantic (SAUO) ... COMPHIBFORLANT
Commander, Amphibious Force, Atlantic Fleet ... CAFAF
Commander, Amphibious Force, Atlantic Fleet ... COMPHIBLANT
Commander, Amphibious Force, Europe ... COMPHIBEU
Commander, Amphibious Force, Northwest African Waters ... COMPHIBNAW
Commander Amphibious Force, Pacific (SAUO) ... CPP
Commander, Amphibious Force, Pacific Fleet (DNAB) ... CAFPF
Commander, Amphibious Force, Pacific Fleet (MUGU) ... COMPHIBFORPAC
Commander, Amphibious Force, Pacific Fleet ... COMPHIBPAC
Commander Amphibious Group (SAUO) ... COMAMPHGR
Commander Amphibious Group (SAUO) ... ComAmphibGru
Commander, Amphibious Group (SAUO) ... ComPhibGru
Commander, Amphibious Group (CINC) ... COMPHIBGRU
Commander; Amphibious Group (SAUO) ... ComPhiGru
Commander Amphibious Group (SAUO) ... CPG
Commander, Amphibious Group Detachment (DNAB) ... COMPHIBGRUDET
Commander, Amphibious Group, Eastern Pacific (DNAB) ... COMPHIBGRUEASTPAC
Commander, Amphibious Ready Group [*Navy*] (NVT) ... CARG
Commander, Amphibious Squadron ... COMPHIBRON
Commander Amphibious Squadron (SAUO) ... CPR
Commander, Amphibious Task Force (NVT) ... CATF
Commander, Amphibious Task Force (AABC) ... COMATF
Commander, Amphibious Task Group (DNAB) ... CATG
Commander Amphibious Training (SAUO) ... ComAmphibTra
Commander, Amphibious Training (SAUS) ... COMAMPHIBTRA
Commander, Amphibious Training Command, Atlantic (SAUO) ... ComPhibTraLant
Commander, Amphibious Training Command, Atlantic ... COMPHIBTRALANT
Commander, Amphibious Training Command, Pacific ... COMPHIBTRAPAC
Commander, Amphibious Training Command, United States Atlantic Fleet ... CATCUSAF
Commander, Amphibious Troops ... CAT
Commander Amphibous Transportation Group (SAUO) ... COMAMPHTGP
Commander & Gunner Crew Station Simulator (SAUS) ... CGCSS
Commander and Staff Visualization Research Tool [*Army*] (RDA) ... CoVRT
Commander, Antarctic Support Activities [*Military*] (DNAB) ... CASA
Commander, Antarctic Support Activities ... COMANTARCTICSUPPACT
Commander, Antilles Defense Command (AABC) ... COMANTDEFCOM
Commander, Antisubmarine Defense, Atlantic Fleet (SAUS) ... COMANTISUBDEFLANT
Commander Antisubmarine Defense Atlantic Fleet (SAUO) ... ComAntiSubDefLant
Commander, Antisubmarine Warfare Force ... COMASWFOR
Commander, Antisubmarine Warfare Forces, Atlantic (MUGU) ... COMASWFORLANT
Commander, Antisubmarine Warfare Forces, Pacific (CINC) ... COMASWFORPAC
Commander Antisubmarine Warfare Forces, U.S. Pacific Fleet (SAUO) ... CAMASWFORPAC
Commander, Antisubmarine Warfare Group ... COMASWGRU
Commander, Antisubmarine Warfare Support Training Detachment (DNAB) ... COMASWSUPPTRADET
Commander, Arabian Sea and Persian Gulf (SAUS) ... COMAS
Commander, Area Antisubmarine Warfare Forces (DNAB) ... COMAREASWFOR
Commander, Army Forces ... COMARFOR
Commander, Army Forces-Alaska (SAUO) ... COMARFOR-AK
Commander, Army Group, Royal Artillery (SAUS) ... CAG RA
Commander, Army Group, Royal Artillery (SAUO) ... CAGRA
Commander, Army Group, Royal Engineers (SAUO) ... CAGRE
Commander, Army Group, Royal Engineers (SAUS) ... CAG RE
Commander, Army Group, Signals (SAUO) ... CAGSigs
Commander; Army Group; Signals (SAUO) ... CAG Sigs

Commander, Army Signals (SAUO) .... CA Sigs
Commander, Army Space Command (ACAE) .... COMARSPACE
Commander, ASW Strike Force (SAUS) .... COMASWSTRIKFOR
Commander at Arms [Navy] [British] .... CrAA
Commander, Atlantic Approaches Gibraltar (NATG) ...... COMGIBLANT
Commander, Atlantic Fleet Bases, Antilles .... COMFLTBASTILLES
Commander, Atlantic Fleet Weapons Range (DNAB) .... COMLANTFLTWPNRAN
Commander, Atlantic Fleet Weapons Range .... COMLANTFLTWPNRNGE
Commander Atlantic Reserve Fleet (SAUO) .... COMLANDRESFLT
Commander, Atlantic Reserve Fleet (SAUS) .... COMLANTRESFLT
Commander, Attack Carrier Air Wing .... COMATKCARAIRWING
Commander, Attack Carrier Striking Force ...... COMATKCARSTRIKEFOR
Commander, Australian Patrol Boat Force (SAUS) ...... COMAUSPABFOR
Commander, Auxiliaries Flotilla (SAUO) .... COMAUXFLOT
Commander, Barrier Forces, Atlantic (NATG) ...... COMBARFORCLANT
Commander Barrier Forces Atlantic (SAUO) .... COMBARLANT
Commander, Barrier Forces Atlantic (SAUS) .... COMBARLANT
Commander, Barrier Pacific (CINC) .... COMBARPAC
Commander Base Area Command [Australia] .... CBAC
Commander, Base Force (SAUS) .... COM BASE FOR
Commander Battleship Division .... COMBATDIV
Commander Battleship Force (SAUO) .... CBF
Commander, Battleship Force (SAUS) .... COMBATFOR
Commander, Battleships, Atlantic Fleet .... COMBATLANT
Commander, Battleships, Pacific Fleet .... COMBATPAC
Commander, Battleships, United States Fleet (SAUS) .... COMBATSUS
Commander Battleships United States Fleet (SAUO) .... COMBATSUS
Commander, Battleships-Cruisers, Atlantic Fleet (MUGU) ...... COMBATCRULANT
Commander, Bay of Biscay, Atlantic (SAUS) .... COMBISCLANT
Commander, Bay of Biscay Atlantic Subarea [NATO] ...... COMBISLANT
Commander Bay of Biscay Subarea (SAUO) .... COMBISCLANT
Commander Belgian Naval Rhine Squadron (SAUO) .... COMBELRHINE
Commander, Belgian Naval Rhine Squadron (SAUS) .... COMBELRHINE
Commander, BENELUX Subarea Channel .... COMBENECHAN
Commander, Black Sea Defense Sector (NATG) .... COMBLACKBASE
Commander Blue (Friendly) Force [Navy] (CAAL) ...... COMBLUE
Commander, Bombardment Squadron (SAUS) .... COMBOMSQ
Commander, Bombing Squadron .... COMBOMRON
Commander, Bosphorus Fortifications (NATG) .... COMBOSFORT
Commander, Boston Group .... COMBSNGRU
Commander, Bremerhaven Naval Group (NATG) .... COMNAVBREM
Commander, Bremerton Group .... COMBREMGRU
Commander, Brest Subarea Channel .... COMBRESTCHAN
Commander British Forces (SAUS) .... CBF
Commander, British Forces, Arabian Peninsula [British military] (DMA) ..... CBFAP
Commander, British Forces, Caribbean Area [NATO] (NATG) ...... CBFCA
Commander, British Forces, Gulf [British military] (DMA) .... CBFG
Commander, British Naval Elbe Squadron (NATG) .... COMBRITELBE
Commander, British Naval Rhine Squadron (NATG) .... COMBRITRHIN
Commander British Naval Rhine Squadron (SAUO) .... COMBRITRHINE
Commander British Naval Staff (SAUO) .... CBNS
Commander, British Naval Staff .... CBNS
Commander, Canadian Atlantic Subarea [NATO] .... COMCANLANT
Commander, Canadian Destroyers, Atlantic ...... CANCOMDESLANT
Commander, Canadian Destroyers, Far East ...... CANCOMDESFE
Commander, Canadian Destroyers, Pacific .... CANCOMDESPAC
Commander, Caribbean Sea Frontier .... CCSF
Commander, Caribbean Sea Frontier (NATG) ...... COMCARIBSEAFRON
Commander, Caribbean Sector Antisubmarine Warfare Group
(DNAB) .... COMCARIBSECASWGRU
Commander Carrier (CCCA) .... COMC
Commander Carrier Air Group (SAUO) .... ComCarAirGru
Commander, Carrier Air Group (SAUS) .... COMCARAIRGRU
Commander, Carrier Air Wing (SAUS) .... COMCAW
Commander, Carrier Air Wing [Navy] (NVT) .... COMCVW
Commander, Carrier Aircraft Service Unit .... COMCASU
Commander Carrier Antisubmarine Air Group (SAUO)..... COMCARANTISUBAIRGRU
Commander, Carrier Antisubmarine Air Group ...... COMCARASWAIRGRU
Commander, Carrier Division .... COMCARDIV
Commander, Carrier Division (SAUS) .... COM CAR DIV
Commander, Carrier Group (DNAB) .... COMCARGRU
Commander, Carrier Striking Force (AFM) ...... COMCARSTRIKFOR
Commander, Carrier Striking Group .... COMCARSTRIKGRU
Commander, Carrier Striking Group One (AFM) .... COMCARSTRIKGRUONE
Commander, Carrier Striking Group One (SAUO) .... COMCARSTRIKGRU ONE
Commander, Carrier Striking Group Two (AFM) .... COMCARSTRIKGRUTWO
Commander, Carrier Training Squadron, Pacific Fleet .... COMTRAINCARRONPAC
Commander, Central Army Group (SAUO) .... COMCENAG
Commander, Central Army Group (SAUS) .... COMCENAG
Commander, Central Army Group, Central Europe .... COMCENTAG
Commander, Central Atlantic Subarea [NATO] ...... COMCENTLANT
Commander Central European Air Forces (SAUO) .... CCEAF
Commander Central European Ground Forces (SAUO) .... CCEGF
Commander Central European Sea Forces (SAUO) ...... CCESF
Commander, Central Mediterranean .... COMEDCENT
Commander, Central Pacific .... COMCENPAC
Commander, Central Region SEATO Field Forces (Designate) .... CCRSFF(D)
Commander, Central Region SEATO [Southeast Asia Treaty Organization]
FieldForces (CINC) .... CCRSFF
Commander Central Section/Western Sea Frontier
(SAUO) .... COMCENSECT/WESTSEAFRON
Commander, Charleston Group .... COMCHASNGRU
Commander, Cherbourg Subarea Channel .... COMCHERCHAN
Commander, Clyde Area (SAUS) .... COMCLYDE
Commander, Coast Artillery (SAUS) .... CCA

Commander, Coast Defenses .... CCD
Commander, Coast Guard Activities, Europe (DNAB) .... COMCOGARDACTEUR
Commander, Coast Guard District .... CCGD
Commander, Coast Guard District .... COMCOGARD
Commander, Coast Guard Force, Atlantic (DNAB) ...... COMCOGARDLANT
Commander, Coast Guard Force, Europe (DNAB) ...... COMCOGARDEUR
Commander, Coast Guard Group (DNAB) .... COMCOGARDGRU
Commander, Coast Guard, Maritime Section (DNAB) .... COMCOGARDMARSEC
Commander, Coast Guard Section Office, Far East Section
(DNAB) .... COMCOGARDFESEC
Commander, Coast Guard Section Office, Guantanamo Section
(DNAB) .... COMCOGARDGANTSEC
Commander, Coast Guard Southeast Squadron (DNAB) .... COMCOGARDSERON
Commander, Coast Guard Squadron (DNAB) ...... COMCOGARDRON
Commander, Coast Guard World-Wide Military Command and Control
System, Atlantic (DNAB) .... COMCOGARDLANTWWMCCS
Commander, Coastal Division (DNAB) .... COMCOSDIV
Commander, Coastal Forces (SAUS) .... CCF
Commander Coastal Squadron (SAUO) .... COMCOSRON
Commander, Coastal Squadron (DNAB) .... COMCOSRON
Commander, Coastal Surveillance Force (DNAB) .... COMCOSURVFOR
Commander, Columbia River Group .... COMCOLUMGRU
Commander, Combat Force, Easten Continental Region (SAUO) .... ComCFECR
Commander, Combat Force, Eastern Continental Region (SAUS) ...... COMCFECR
Commander, Combined Amphibious Task Force [Military] (NVT) .... CCATF
Commander, Combined Unconventional Warfare Task Force
(SAUO) .... COMCUWTF
Commander, Composite Squadron .... COMCOMRON
Commander Concept of Operation (SAUS) .... CCO
Commander, Corps, Canadian Artillery (SAUS) .... CCCA
Commander, Corps, Coast Artillery (SAUS) .... CCCA
Commander, Corps Medium Artillery (SAUO) .... CCM
Commander Corps Medium Artillery [British] .... CCMA
Commander Corps Royal Artillery [British] .... CCRA
Commander, Corps, Royal Artillery (SAUS) .... CCRA
Commander Corps Royal Corps of Transport [Military] [British] ...... CCRCT
Commander Corps Royal Engineers [Military] [British] .... CCRE
Commander, Corps, Royal Engineers (SAUS) .... CCRE
Commander, Cruiser Division .... COMCRUDIV
Commander, Cruiser Force (SAUS) .... COMCRUFOR
Commander Cruiser Force (SAUO) .... COMCRUFOR
Commander, Cruiser Forces, Atlantic Fleet (MCD) ...... COMCRULANT
Commander, Cruiser Forces, Pacific Fleet .... COMCRUPAC
Commander, Cruiser Scouting Squadron .... COMCRUSCORON
Commander, Cruiser-Destroyer Flotilla [Acronym always followed by a
number] [Navy] .... COMCRUDESFLOT
Commander, Cruiser-Destroyer Force [Navy] (DNAB) .... CCD
Commander, Cruiser-Destroyer Force .... COMCRUDES
Commander Cruiser-Destroyer Force, Atlantic Fleet (SAUO) ...... CDDL
Commander Cruiser-Destroyer Force, Atlantic Support Group
(SAUO) .... COAMCRUDESLANTSUPPGRUCHAR
Commander Cruiser-Destroyer Force, Pacific Fleet (SAUO) ...... CDDP
Commander, Cruiser-Destroyer Forces, Atlantic (MCD) .... CCDL
Commander, Cruiser-Destroyer Forces, Atlantic [Navy]
(DNAB) .... COMCRUDESLANT
Commander, Cruiser-Destroyer Forces, Atlantic Support Group [Navy]
(DNAB) .... COMCRUDESLANTSUPPGRU
Commander, Cruiser-Destroyer Forces, Atlantic Support Group,
Charleston [South Carolina] [Navy] (DNAB) ...... COMCRUDESLANTSUPPGRUCHAR
Commander, Cruiser-Destroyer Forces, Atlantic Support Group, Mayport
[Florida] [Navy] (DNAB) .... COMCRUDESLANTSUPPGRUMPT
Commander, Cruiser-Destroyer Forces, Atlantic Support Group, Norfolk,
Virginia [Navy] (DNAB) ...... COMCRUDESLANTSUPPGRUNORVA
Commander, Cruiser-Destroyer Forces, Pacific [Navy] (DNAB) ...... CCDP
Commander, Cruiser-Destroyer Forces, Pacific [Navy] (MCD) .... COMCRUDESPAC
Commander, Cruiser-Destroyer Group [Navy] (DNAB) .... COMCRUDESGRU
Commander, Cruisers United States Fleet (SAUO) .... COMCRUSUS
Commander, Cruisers, United States Fleet (SAUS) .... COMCRUSUS
Commander, Dardanelles Fortifications (NATG) .... COMDARFORT
Commander, Destroyer Battle Force (SAUS) ...... COMDESBATFOR
Commander Destroyer Battle Force (SAUO) ...... COMDESBATFOR
Commander, Destroyer Development Group (SAUO) .... ComDesDevGru
Commander, Destroyer Development Group [Navy] ...... COMDESDEVGRU
Commander, Destroyer Development Group, Pacific [Navy] (MCD) .... CDDGP
Commander, Destroyer Division .... COMDESDIV
Commander, Destroyer Flotilla .... COMDESFLOT
Commander Destroyer Force (SAUO) .... COMDESFOR
Commander, Destroyer Force (SAUS) .... COMDESFOR
Commander, Destroyer Force (SAUS) .... COMDESTR
Commander, Destroyer Group .... COMDESGRU
Commander, Destroyer Squadron .... CDS
Commander, Destroyer Squadron .... COMDESRON
Commander, Destroyers .... COMDES
Commander, Destroyers, Atlantic Detachment (DNAB) .... COMDESLANTDET
Commander, Destroyers, Atlantic Fleet (SAUO) .... CDL
Commander, Destroyers, Atlantic Fleet .... COMDESLANT
Commander, Destroyers, Pacific Detachment (DNAB) ...... COMDESPACDET
Commander, Destroyers, Pacific Fleet .... COMDESPAC
Commander, Destroyers, United States Fleet (SAUS) .... COMDESUS
Commander, Disaster Control Element .... CDCE
Commander, Disaster Control Force .... CDCF
Commander, Disaster Control Group .... CDCG
Commander, Disaster-Preparedness Group [Military] (DNAB) ...... CDPG
Commander, Drill Squadron (SAUS) .... COMDRILLRON
Commander Drill Squadron (SAUO) .... COMDRILLRON

Commander East African Forces (SAUO) .... Cr EAF
Commander, East African Forces (SAUS) .... CREAF
Commander, Eastern Area, United States Coast Guard (SAUS) .... COMEASTAREA USCG
Commander, Eastern Atlantic Forces .... COMEASTLANT
Commander Eastern Continental Air Defense Region (SAUO) .... COMEASTCONRADREG
Commander, Eastern Mediterranean (AFM) .... COMEDEAST
Commander, Eastern Sea Frontier [*Navy*] .... CESF
Commander, Eastern Sea Frontier [*Navy*] (MUGU) .... COMEASTFRON
Commander, Eastern Sea Frontier [*Navy*] .... COMEASTSEAFRON
Commander, Emergency Recovery Force .... CERF
Commander, Emergency Recovery Group .... CERG
Commander, Emergency Recovery Section .... CERS
Commander, Emergency Recovery Unit .... CERU
Commander, Escort Division (DNAB) .... COMCORTDIV
Commander, Escort Squadron (DNAB) .... COMCORTRON
Commander, Experimental Division [*Navy*] .... COMEXDIV
Commander, Explosive Ordnance Disposal Group (DNAB) .... COMEODGRU
Commander Extended Link for Thermal Imaging Combat Sight (SAUS) .... CELTICS
Commander Far East Fleet (SAUO) .... COMFEF
Commander, Field Command, Defense Atomic Support Agency (AABC) .... COMFLDCOMDASA
Commander, Fifth Allied Tactical Air Force (AFM) .... COMFIVEATAF
Commander Fifth Allied Tactical Air Force Southern Europe (SAUO) .... COMFIVEATAF
Commander Fighter Wing (MCD) .... COMFITWING
Commander Fighter Wing One (ACAE) .... COMFITWINGONE
Commander, Fighting Squadron .... COMFIGHTRON
Commander, First Canadian Destroyer Flotilla .... CANCOMDESFLOT 1
Commander, [*US*] First Fleet .... COMFIRSTFLEET
Commander, [*US*] First Fleet (MUGU) .... COMFIRSTFLT
Commander, Fleet Activities (DNAB) .... COMFLEACT
Commander, Fleet Activities Detachment (DNAB) .... COMFLEACTDET
Commander Fleet Activity (SAUO) .... ComFltActy
Commander, Fleet Activity (SAUS) .... COMFLTACTY
Commander, Fleet Air .... COMFAIR
Commander, Fleet Air, Adak, Alaska .... COMFAIRADAK
Commander, Fleet Air, Alameda .... COMFAIRALAMEDA
Commander, Fleet Air, Bermuda .... COMFAIRBERMUDA
Commander, Fleet Air, Brunswick .... COMFAIRBRUNSWICK
Commander, Fleet Air Defense (NATG) .... CFAD
Commander, Fleet Air Detachment .... CFAD
Commander, Fleet Air, Eastern Atlantic and Mediterranean (NATG) .... COMFAIRELM
Commander, Fleet Air Force (SAUS) .... COMFAIR
Commander, Fleet Air Force, Atlantic Fleet (SAUS) .... COMFAIRLANT
Commander Fleet Air Force, Atlantic Fleet (SAUO) .... ComFAirLant
Commander, Fleet Air Force, Eastern Atlantic and Mediterranean (SAUS) .... COMFAIRELM
Commander, Fleet Air Force, Pacific Fleet (SAUS) .... COMFAIRPAC
Commander Fleet Air Force, Pacific Fleet (SAUO) .... ComFAirPac
Commander, Fleet Air, Hawaii (MUGU) .... COMFAIRHAWAII
Commander, Fleet Air, Jacksonville, Florida .... COMFAIRJAX
Commander, Fleet Air, Japan .... COMFAIRJAPAN
Commander, Fleet Air, Keflavik, Iceland .... COMFAIRKEFLAVIK
Commander, Fleet Air, Mediterranean .... COMFAIRMED
Commander, Fleet Air, Miramar (ACAE) .... COMFAIRMIR
Commander, Fleet Air, Norfolk, Virginia .... COMFAIRNORFOLK
Commander, Fleet Air, Quonset Point, Rhode Island .... COMFAIRQUONSET
Commander, Fleet Air, San Diego, California .... COMFAIRSANDIEGO
Commander, Fleet Air, Southwest Pacific (MUGU) .... COMFAIRSOWESTPAC
Commander, Fleet Air, Western Pacific .... COMFAIRWESTPAC
Commander, Fleet Air Wing .... CFAW
Commander, Fleet Air Wing .... COMFAIRWING
Commander, Fleet Air Wing (SAUS) .... COMFAIRWNG
Commander, Fleet Air Wing, Atlantic .... CFAWL
Commander, Fleet Air Wing, Atlantic (NATG) .... COMFAIRWINGLANT
Commander, Fleet Air Wing, Atlantic Fleet (SAUS) .... COMFAIRWNGLANT
Commander, Fleet Air Wing, Northern Atlantic (AABC) .... COMFAIRWINGNORLANT
Commander, Fleet Air Wing, Pacific .... CFAWP
Commander, Fleet Air Wing, Pacific Fleet (SAUS) .... COMFAIRWNGPAC
Commander Fleet Air Wings, Atlantic (SAUO) .... COMFAIRWINGSLANT
Commander Fleet Air Wings, Pacific (SAUO) .... COMFAIRWINGSPAC
Commander Fleet Aircraft Service Squadron (SAUO) .... COFASRON
Commander, Fleet Aircraft Service Squadron (SAUS) .... COFasron
Commander, Fleet Electronic Warfare Support Group (DNAB) .... COMFEWSG
Commander, Fleet Electronic Warfare Support Group Detachment (DNAB) .... COMFEWSGDET
Commander, Fleet Logistic Air Wing .... COMFLOGWING
Commander, Fleet Operational Training Command .... COTC
Commander, Fleet Operational Training Command, Atlantic Fleet .... COTCLANT
Commander, Fleet Operational Training Command, Pacific Fleet .... COTCPAC
Commander, Fleet Operational Training Command, Pacific Subordinate Command .... COTCPACSUBCOM
Commander Fleet Tactical Support Wing (SAUO) .... COMFLETACSUPPWING
Commander Fleet Tactical Support Wing (SAUO) .... COMTACSUPPWING
Commander, Fleet Train .... COFT
Commander, Fleet Training Group .... COMFLETRAGRU
Commander, Fleet Training Group and Underway Training Element (MUGU) .... COMFLETRAGRUWATE
Commander, Fleet Training Group, Atlantic (DNAB) .... COMFLETRAGRULANT
Commander, Fleet Training Group, Pacific (DNAB) .... COMFLETRAGRUPAC
Commander, Fleet Training Group, Western Pacific (DNAB) .... COMFLETRAGRUWESPAC
Commander, Florida Group .... COMFLAGRU
Commander, Flying [*British military*] (DMA) .... FLYCO
Commander, Forward Area (SAUS) .... COMFWDAREA
Commander, Forward Area (SAUO) .... ComFwdArea
Commander, Fourth Allied Tactical Air Force, Central Europe .... COMFOURATAF
Commander French Maritime Forces Morocco (SAUO) .... COMAR CASA
Commander, French Rhine River Squadron [*NATO*] .... COMSUFRHIN
Commander, German Naval Forces, Baltic (NATG) .... COMNAVGERBALT
Commander, German North Sea (SAUS) .... COMGRNORSEA
Commander, German North Sea Subarea (NATG) .... COMGERNORSEA
Commander, Gibraltar [*Navy*] (AABC) .... COMGIB
Commander, Gibraltar-Mediterranean Command (AFM) .... COMGIBMED
Commander, Greenland Patrol .... COMGREPAT
Commander, Guantanamo Bay, Cuba Sector, Antisubmarine Warfare Unit (DNAB) .... COMGTMOSECTASWU
Commander, Hawaiian Sea Frontier [*Navy*] .... COMHAWSEAFRON
Commander, Headquarters Squadron .... COMHEDRON
Commander Headquarters Support Acitivities (SAUS) .... COMHEDSUPPACT
Commander Headquarters Support Activities (SAUO) .... CHSA
Commander, Hunter-Killer Force, Atlantic Fleet .... COMHUKFORLAN
Commander, Iberian Atlantic Area (NATG) .... COMIBERLANT
Commander, Iceland Antisubmarine Warfare Group .... COMICEASWGRU
Commander, Iceland Defense Force .... COMICEDEFOR
Commander, Iceland Defense Force (DNAB) .... COMIDF
Commander, Iceland Defense Force/Commander Iceland Antisubmarine Warfare Group (DNAB) .... COMICEDEFOR/COMICEASWGRU
Commander in Chief (AAGC) .... CinC
Commander in Chief, Atlantic [*Military*] (DOMA) .... CINCANT
Commander in Chief, Atlantic Forces (AAGC) .... CINCLANT
Commander In Chief, Channel Command (SAUO) .... CINCCHAN
Commander in Chief, [*US*] Forces [*Command*] (DOMA) .... CINCFOR
Commander in Chief, Southern Command (AAGC) .... CINCSOUTH
Commander in Chief, [*US*] Space [*Command*] (DOMA) .... CINCSPACE
Commander in Chief, [*US*] Special Operations [*Command*] (DOMA) .... CINCSOC
Commander in Chief, [*US*] Strategic [*Command*] (DOMA) .... CINCSTRAT
Commander in Chief, Strategic Defense (ACAE) .... CINCSD
Commander in Chief, [*US*] Transportation [*Command*] (DOMA) .... CINCTRANS
Commander in Chief, US Army Forces, Readiness [*Command*] (DOMA) .... CINCUSARRED
Commander in Chief, US European Command (DOMA) .... CINCUSEUCOM
Commander in Chief, USA Command [*Established in 1993*] (DOMA) .... CINCUSACOM
Commander, Initial Training Group (SAUO) .... CITG
Commander, Inshore Fire Support Division (DNAB) .... COMIFSDIV
Commander Instructor (SAUS) CI
Commander, Intelligence Center, Pacific (DNAB) .... COMICPAC
Commander, International Ice Patrol [*Coast Guard*] .... CIIP
Commander International Ice Patrol (SAUO) .... COMINTICEPAT
Commander, Joint Expeditionary Force (SAUO) .... ComJEF
Commander, Joint Expeditionary Force .... COMJEF
Commander, Joint Military Postal Activity, Atlantic (DNAB) .... CDRJPAA
Commander, Joint Military Postal Activity, Atlantic (DNAB) .... CDRJPAALANT
Commander, Joint Special Operations Task Force (SAUO) .... COMJSOTF
Commander, Joint Task Element (DNAB) .... CDRJTE
Commander Joint Task Force (DOMA) .... CJTF
Commander, Joint Task Force (AABC) .... COMJTF
Commander, Joint Task Force-Alaska (SAUO) .... COMJTF-AK
Commander, Joint Task Group .... CJTG
Commander, Joint Unconventional Warfare Task Force (AABC) .... COMJUWATF
Commander, Joint Unconventional Warfare Task Force (DNAB) .... COMJUWTF
Commander Key West Force (SAUO) .... COMKWESTFOR
Commander Key West Test and Evaluation Detachment (SAUO) .... COMKWESTEVDET
Commander, Land Forces [*Army*] (AABC) .... COMLANDFOR
Commander, Land Forces, North Norway (NATG) .... COMLANDNON
Commander Landing Craft Utility Squadron (SAUO) .... ComLCURon
Commander, Landing Craft Utility Squadron (SAUS) .... COMLCURON
Commander, Landing Force [*Navy*] (NVT) .... CLF
Commander Landing Ship Flotilla (SAUO) .... COMLANSHIPFLOT
Commander Landing Ship Squadron (SAUO) .... COMLANSHIPRON
Commander, Landing Ship Tank Division (DNAB) .... COMLSTDIV
Commander Landing Ship Tank Squadron (SAUO) .... ComLSTRon
Commander, Landing Ship Tank Squadron (SAUS) .... COMLSTRON
Commander, Landing Ships Flotilla (SAUS) .... COMLANSHIPFLOT
Commander, Landing Ships Squadron (SAUS) .... COMLANSHIPRON
Commander, Light Attack Wing - Pacific Fleet (MCD) .... CLAWP
Commander, Local Air Defence (SAUS) .... COMLODEF
Commander, Local Defence (SAUO) .... ComLoDef
Commander, Logistics Group, Western Pacific (SAUO) .... COMLOG WESTPAC
Commander Logistics Rear Combat Zone (SAUO) .... COMLOG RCZ
Commander, Logistics Support Force (DNAB) .... COMLOGSUPPFOR
Commander, Long Beach Group .... COMLBEACHGRU
Commander, Mare Island Group .... COMAREGRU
Commander Mare Island-Vallejo Area, Naval Base (SAUO) .... COMARVALLEJOAREA
Commander, Marianas .... COMMARIANAS
Commander, Marine Air Reserve Training .... COMART
Commander, Marine Air Reserve Training (SAUO) .... ComMART
Commander, Marine Air Reserve Training (SAUS) .... COMMART
Commander Marine Basic Air Training (SAUO) .... COMBAT
Commander, Marine Corps Air Reserve Training (SAUS) .... COMART
Commander, Marine Forces .... COMMARFOR
Commander, Maritime Air Central Subarea [*NATO*] .... COMMAIRCENTLANT

Commander, Maritime Air Channel (SAUS) .... COMAIRCHAN
Commander, Maritime Air Eastern Atlantic Area [*NATO*] .... COMMAIREASTLANT
Commander, Maritime Air Forces Mediterranean (SAUS) .... COMARAIRMED
Commander Maritime Air Forces Mediterranean (SAUO) .... COMARAIRMED
Commander, Maritime Air Gibraltar Subarea [*NATO*] (NATG) .... COMMAIRGIBLANT
Commander Maritime Air Mediterranean (SAUO) .... COMMARAIRMED
Commander, Maritime Air Northeast Subarea Channel [*NATO*] .... COMMAIRNORECHAN
Commander Maritime Air Northern Atlantic Subarea (SAUO) .... COMMAIRNORLANT
Commander, Maritime Air Northern Subarea [*NATO*] .... COMMAIRNORLANT
Commander, Maritime Air Plymouth Subarea Channel [*NATO*] .... COMMAIRPLYMCHAN
Commander, Maritime Defense Zone (SAUO) .... COMMARDEZ
Commander, Maritime Forces, Morocco .... COMOROCLANT
Commander, Maritime Prepositioned Force [*Navy*] (ANA) .... CMPF
Commander, Maritime Rhine (NATG) .... COMARRHIN
Commander, Maritime Surveillance and Reconnaissance Force (DNAB) .... COMARSURV
Commander, Maritime Surveillance and Reconnaissance Force Detachment (DNAB) .... COMARSURVRECFORDET
Commander, Maritime Surveillance and Reconnaissance Force, Passive ASRAP [*Acoustic Sensor Range Prediction*] **Data** (DNAB) .... COMARSURVRECFORPASRAP
Commander, Marshalls-Carolines Area .... COMARCARAREA
Commander, Mediterranean Defense Sector (NATG) .... COMEDBASE
Commander, Mediterranean Occidental Area (SAUS) .... COMEDOC
Commander, Mediterranean Operations Center .... COMEDOC
Commander, Mediterranean Support Activities (SAUS) .... COMMEDSUPPACT
Commander, Mediterranean Support Activities (SAUO) .... ComMedSuppAct
Commander, Merchant Marine Atlantic (SAUO) .... COMMERMARLANT
Commander Mexicana SA de CV [*Mexico*] [*ICAO designator*] (FAAC) .... CRM
Commander, Middle East (SAUS) .... CR ME
Commander, Middle East Force (DOMA) .... CMEF
Commander, Middle East Force (AABC) .... COMIDEASTFOR
Commander, Middle East Force (SAUO) .... ComMidEastFor
Commander Military Air Transport Service (SAUO) .... COMATS
Commander, Military Air Transport Service [*Later, COMAC*] .... COMATS
Commander, Military Airlift Command [*Formerly, COMATS*] (AFM) .... COMAC
Commander, Military Assistance Group, Republic of China, Vietnam .... COMMAGROCV
Commander Military Sea Transport Service (SAUO) .... COMSTS
Commander Military Sea Transport Service, Pacific (SAUO) .... COMSTSPAC
Commander, Military Sea Transportation Service [*Obsolete*] .... COMSTS
Commander, Military Sea Transportation Service, Atlantic Area .... COMSTSLANTAREA
Commander, Military Sea Transportation Service, Eastern Atlantic and Mediterranean Area .... COMSTSELMAREA
Commander, Military Sea Transportation Service, Far East (CINC) .... COMSTSFE
Commander, Military Sea Transportation Service, Gulf Subarea .... COMSTSGULFSUBAREA
Commander, Military Sea Transportation Service, Management Information System .... COMSTS/MIS
Commander, Military Sea Transportation Service, Mid-Pacific Subarea .... COMSTSMIDPACSUBAREA
Commander, Military Sea Transportation Service, Northern Pacific Subarea .... COMSTSNORPACSUBAREA
Commander, Military Sea Transportation Service, Pacific Area .... COMSTSPACAREA
Commander, Military Sea Transportation Service, Southeast Asia (CINC) .... COMSTSSEA
Commander, Military Sea Transportation Service, West Pacific Area .... COMSTSWESTPACAREA
Commander, Military Sealift Command .... COMMSC
Commander, Military Sealift Command .... COMSC
Commander, Military Sealift Command, Atlantic .... COMSCLANT
Commander, Military Sealift Command, Eastern Atlantic and Mediterranean .... COMSCELM
Commander, Military Sealift Command, Europe (DNAB) .... COMSCEUR
Commander, Military Sealift Command, Far East .... COMSCFE
Commander, Military Sealift Command, Gulf Subarea .... COMSCGULF
Commander, Military Sealift Command, Mediterranean .... COMSCMED
Commander, Military Sealift Command, Pacific .... COMSCPAC
Commander, Military Sealift Command, Southeast Asia (DNAB) .... COMSCSEA
Commander, Mine Division (SAUO) .... ComMineDiv
Commander, Mine Flotilla .... COMINFLOT
Commander, Mine Force, Atlantic Fleet [*Navy*] .... COMINELANT
Commander, Mine Force, Atlantic Fleet [*Navy*] .... COMINLANT
Commander, Mine Force, Pacific Fleet [*Navy*] .... COMINEPAC
Commander, Mine Forces, Atlantic Fleet (SAUO) .... ComMineLant
Commander, Mine Group .... COMINGRP
Commander, Mine Group, Okinawa .... COMINGRPOK
Commander, Mine Squadron .... COMINRON
Commander, Mine Warfare Flotilla (SAUO) .... COMMINEWARFLOT
Commander, Mine Warfare Forces .... COMINEWARFOR
Commander, Mine Warfare/War vessels (SAUS) .... COMMW
Commander, Minecraft [*Navy*] .... COMIN
Commander, Minecraft [*Navy*] (DNAB) .... COMINE
Commander Minecraft, Atlantic (SAUO) .... COMINLANT
Commander, Minecraft Division [*Navy*] .... COMINDIV
Commander, Minecraft Division [*Navy*] (DNAB) .... COMINEDIV
Commander, Minecraft, Pacific Fleet [*Navy*] .... COMINPAC
Commander Minecraft Unites States Fleet (SAUO) .... COMINUS
Commander, Mobile Mine Assembly Group (DNAB) .... COMOMAG
Commander, Mobile Support Unit Detachment (DNAB) .... COMMOBSUPPUDET
Commander, Moroccan Sea Frontier Forces .... COMORSEAFRON
Commander, Motor Torpedo Boat Flotilla .... COMTBFLOT
Commander, Motor Torpedo Boat Squadron .... COMTBRON
Commander, Motor Torpedo Boat Squadron Training Center .... COMTBRONTRACENT
Commander, NATO Airborne Early Warning Force (SAUS) .... COMNAEWF
Commander, NATO Naval Baltic Forces (SAUO) .... COMNATONAVFORLANT
Commander, Naval Activities (DNAB) .... COMNAVACT
Commander, Naval Activities, Japan .... COMNAVJAP
Commander, Naval Activities, United Kingdom (DNAB) .... COMNAVACTUK
Commander Naval Air, Atlantic .... ComNavAirLant
Commander, Naval Air Bases .... CNAB
Commander, Naval Air Bases .... COMNAB
Commander, Naval Air Bases (SAUO) .... ComNAB
Commander, Naval Air Division (SAUO) .... COMNAVAIRDIV
Commander, Naval Air Force .... COMNAVAIR
Commander, Naval Air Force, Atlantic .... CNAL
Commander, Naval Air Force, Atlantic Fleet (MCD) .... COMNAVAIRLANT
Commander, Naval Air Force, Pacific Fleet (MCD) .... COMNAVAIRPAC
Commander, Naval Air Forces, Pacific (SAUS) .... CNAP
Commander, Naval Air Reserve (DNAB) .... CNAR
Commander Naval Air Reserve (SAUO) .... COMNAVAIRRES
Commander, Naval Air Reserve Force (DNAB) .... CNARF
Commander Naval Air Reserve Force (SAUO) .... COMNAVAIRRESFOR
Commander, Naval Air Station (SAUO) .... COMNAVAIRSTA
Commander, Naval Air Systems Command (MCD) .... COMNAVAIRSYSCOM
Commander Naval Air Systems Command Headquarters (SAUO) .... COMNAVAIRSYSCOMHQ
Commander, Naval Air Technical Training (SAUO) .... ComNavAirTechTra
Commander, Naval Air Technical Training (SAUS) .... COMNAVAIRTECHTRA
Commander, Naval Air Technical Training (Lighter Than Air) .... CNATEC (LTA)
Commander, Naval Air Technical Training Unit (SAUS) .... COMNAVAIRTECHTRAU
Commander, Naval Air Technical Training Unit (SAUO) .... ComNavAirTechTraU
Commander, Naval Air Test Center (SAUO) .... ComNavAirTestCen
Commander, Naval Air Test Center (SAUS) .... COMNAVAIRTESTCEN
Commander Naval Air Transport Wing (SAUO) .... COMNAVAIRTRANSWING
Commander Naval Air Transport Wing, Pacific (SAUO) .... COMNAVAIRTRANSWINGPAC
Commander, Naval Aviation Safety Center (SAUO) .... ComNavAvSafetyCen
Commander, Naval Aviation Safety Center (SAUS) .... COMNAVAVSAFETYCEN
Commander, Naval Base .... CNB
Commander, Naval Base (SAUO) .... ComNavB
Commander Naval Base (SAUO) .... ComNavBase
Commander, Naval Base .... COMNAVBASE
Commander, Naval Base, Los Angeles .... CNBLA
Commander, Naval Base, Los Angeles and Long Beach (SAUS) .... COMNAVBLOSALBEACH
Commander, Naval Beach Group (SAUS) .... COMNAVBEACHGRU
Commander, Naval Beach Group (SAUO) .... ComNavBeachGru
Commander, Naval Communications (NVT) .... COMNAVCOMM
Commander Naval Communications Command (SAUO) .... COMNAVCOMM
Commander, Naval Construction Battalion, Atlantic Fleet (SAUO) .... ComNavConstBnLant
Commander, Naval Construction Battalion, Atlantic Fleet (SAUS) .... COMNAVCONSTBNLANT
Commander, Naval Construction Battalion, Pacific Fleet (SAUO) .... ComNavConstBnPac
Commander, Naval Construction Battalions, Atlantic Detachment (DNAB) .... COMCBLANTDET
Commander, Naval Construction Battalions, Atlantic Fleet .... COMCBLANT
Commander, Naval Construction Battalions, Atlantic, Material Liaison Office (DNAB) .... COMCBLANT MLO
Commander, Naval Construction Battalions, Pacific Fleet .... COMCBPAC
Commander, Naval Data Automation Center (DNAB) .... COMNAVDAC
Commander, Naval Defense Forces, Eastern Pacific (MUGU) .... COMNAVDEFOREEASTPAC
Commander, Naval District (SAUO) .... ComNavDis
Commander, Naval Division Baltic (SAUO) .... COMNAVDIV BALT
Commander, Naval Division North Sea (SAUO) .... COMNAVDIV NORSEA
Commander Naval Education and Training Command (SAUO) .... CNET
Commander, Naval Education and Training Command, Representative Coordinator for Atlantic (DNAB) .... CNETLANTREP
Commander, Naval Education and Training Command, Representative Coordinator for Pacific (DNAB) .... CNETPACREP
Commander, Naval Electronic Systems Command (DNAB) .... COMNAVELEXSYSCOM
Commander, Naval Electronic Systems Command, Alternate Commander (DNAB) .... COMNAVELEXSYSCOM ALT
Commander, Naval Electronic Systems Command, Emergency Relocation Site Commander (DNAB) .... COMNAVELEXSYSCOM ERS
Commander, Naval Electronic Systems Command Headquarters (DNAB) .... COMNAVELEXSYSCOMHQ
Commander, Naval Facilities Engineering Command (DNAB) .... COMNAVFACENGCOM
Commander, Naval Facilities Engineering Command, Alternate Commander (DNAB) .... COMNAVFACENGCOM ALT
Commander, Naval Facilities Engineering Command Detachment (DNAB) .... COMNAVFACENGCOMDET
Commander, Naval Facilities Engineering Command, Emergency Relocation Site Commander (DNAB) .... COMNAVFACENGCOM ERS
Commander, Naval Facilities Engineering Command Headquarters (DNAB) .... COMNAVFACENGCOMHQ
Commander, [*US*] Naval Forces .... CNF
Commander Naval Forces (SAUO) .... COMNAV
Commander, [*US*] Naval Forces .... COMNAVFOR

Commander, [US] Naval Forces, Azores .... COMNAVZOR
Commander, Naval Forces, Central Army Group Area and Bremerhaven
  (NATG) .... COMNAVCAG
Commander, [US] Naval Forces, Continental Air Defense Command
  (MUGU) .... COMNAVFORCONAD
Commander, [US] Naval Forces, Eastern Atlantic and
  Mediterranean .... COMNAVEASTLANTMED
Commander, [US] Naval Forces, Europe .... COMNAVEU
Commander, [US] Naval Forces, Far East .... COMNAVFE
Commander, [US] Naval Forces, Germany (MCD) ...... COMNAVFORGER
Commander, [US] Naval Forces, Germany .... COMNAVGER
Commander Naval Forces Gulf (SAUO) .... CNFG
Commander, [US] Naval Forces, Iceland .... COMNAVFORICE
Commander, [US] Naval Forces, Iceland .... COMNAVICE
Commander, [US] Naval Forces, Japan (SAA) .... COMNAVFORJAP
Commander, [US] Naval Forces, Japan (AFM) .... COMNAVFORJAPAN
Commander, [US] Naval Forces, Korea .... COMNAVFORKOREA
Commander Naval Forces, Marianas (SAUO) .... CNM
Commander, [US] Naval Forces, Marianas .... COMNAVFMARIANAS
Commander, Naval Forces Marianas (SAUO) .... COMNAVFORCES MARIANAS
Commander, [US] Naval Forces, Marianas (CINC) ..... COMNAVMARIANAS
Commander, [US] Naval Forces, Northwest African Waters .... COMNAVNAW
Commander, [US] Naval Forces, Philippines .... COMNAVFORPHIL
Commander, Naval Forces, Philippines (SAUO) .... COMNAVPHIL
Commander Naval Forces Southern Europe (SAUO) ..... COMNAVSOUTH
Commander, Naval Forces, Southern Europe (NATG) ... COMNAVSOUTH
Commander, [US] Naval Forces, Vietnam .... COMNAVFORV
Commander, Naval Inshore Warfare Command, Atlantic .... COMNAVINSWARLANT
Commander, Naval Intelligence Command (DNAB) ...... CNIC
Commander, Naval Intelligence Command (DNAB) ...... COMNAVINTCOM
Commander, Naval Legal Service Command (DNAB) ..... COMNAVLEGSVCCOM
Commander, Naval Logistics Command, Pacific (DNAB) .... COMNAVLOGPAC
Commander, Naval, Los Angeles and Long Beach
  (SAUO) .... ComNavB LosA LBeach
Commander, Naval Missile Center (MUGU) .... COMNMC
Commander, Naval Oceanography Command (ACAE) ...... CNOC
Commander, Naval Operating Base .... CNOB
Commander, Naval Operations Control systems (SAUS) .... CNOCS
Commander, Naval Operations Support Group (DNAB) .... COMNAVOPSUPPGRU
Commander, Naval Operations Support Group, Atlantic
  (DNAB) .... COMNAVOPSUPPGRULANT
Commander, Naval Operations Support Group, Pacific
  (DNAB) .... COMNAVOSUPPGRUPAC
Commander Naval Ordnance [Military systems command] .... COMNAVORD
Commander, Naval Ordnance Systems Command (MCD) ..... COMNAVORDSYSCOM
Commander, Naval Reserve Construction Battalions, Pacific
  (DNAB) .... COMNRCBPAC
Commander, Naval Reserve Construction Force (DNAB) .... COMNRCF
Commander, Naval Reserve Construction Force Representative
  (DNAB) .... COMNRCFREP
Commander, Naval Reserve Inshore-Undersea Warfare Group
  (DNAB) .... COMNRIUWGRU
Commander, Naval Reserve Personnel Center (DNAB) .... COMNAVRESPERSCEN
Commander, Naval Reserve Personnel Center (DNAB) .... COMNRPC
Commander, Naval Reserve Security Group (DNAB) .... COMNAVRESSECGRU
Commander, Naval Reserves (NVT) .... CNAVRES
Commander Naval Sea Systems Command (SAUO) .... COMNAVSEASYSCOM
Commander, Naval Security Group (DNAB) .... COMNAVSECGRU
Commander Naval Ship Systems Command (SAUO) .... COMNAVSHIPSYSCOM
Commander, Naval Special Warfare Group (DNAB) ..... COMNAVSPECWARGRU
Commander, Naval Special Warfare Group Detachment
  (DNAB) .... COMNAVSPECWARGRUDET
Commander, Naval Special Warfare Task Group (NVT) .... CNSWTG
Commander, Naval Supply Systems Command (DNAB) .... COMNAVSUPSYSCOM
Commander, Naval Supply Systems Command, Emergency Relocation Site,
  Commander (DNAB) .... COMNAVSUPSYSCOM ERS
Commander, Naval Supply Systems Command Headquarters
  (DNAB) .... COMNAVSUPSYSCOMHQ
Commander, Naval Support Activity (AFM) .... COMNAVSUPPACT
Commander, Naval Support Force .... COMNAVSUPPFOR
Commander, Naval Support Force, Antarctic .... COMNAVSUPPFORANTARCTIC
Commander, Naval Surface Forces, Atlantic .... COMNAVSURFLA
Commander, Naval Surface Forces, Atlantic (DNAB) ...... COMNAVSURFLANT
Commander, Naval Surface Forces, Atlantic Detachment
  (DNAB) .... COMNAVSURFLANTDET
Commander, Naval Surface Forces, Atlantic Representative
  (DNAB) .... COMNAVSURFLANTREP
Commander, Naval Surface Forces, Pacific (DNAB) ... COMNAVSURFPAC
Commander, Naval Surface Forces, Pacific Automatic Data Processing
  (DNAB) .... COMNAVSURFPAC ADP
Commander, Naval Surface Forces, Pacific Detachment
  (DNAB) .... COMNAVSURFPAC DET
Commander, Naval Surface Forces, Pacific Distributed Information System
  for CASREP/UNIT Status (DNAB) ...... COMNAVSURFPAC DISCUS
Commander, Naval Surface Forces, Pacific, Emergency Relocation Site
  Commander (DNAB) .... COMNAVSURFPAC ERS
Commander, Naval Surface Forces, Pacific Representative
  (DNAB) .... COMNAVSURFPACREP
Commander, Naval Surface Group, Mediterranean
  (DNAB) .... COMNAVSURFGRUMED
Commander, Naval Surface Group, Mid-Pacific
  (DNAB) .... COMNAVSURFGRUMIDPAC
Commander, Naval Surface Group, Western Pacific
  (DNAB) .... COMNAVSURFGRUWESTPAC

Commander, Naval Surface Group, Western Pacific Detachment
  (DNAB) .... COMNAVSURFGRUWESTPACDET
Commander, Naval Surface Reserve Force (DNAB) ..... COMNAVSURFRES
Commander Naval Task Force (CCCA) .... CNTF
Commander, Naval Technical Training (SAUO) .... ComNavTechTra
Commander, Naval Technical Training (SAUS) .... COMNAVTECHTRA
Commander, Naval Telecommunications Command (ACAE) .... CNTC
Commander, Naval Telecommunications Command (NVT) ...... COMNAVTELCOM
Commander, Naval Test Center (SAUS) .... COMNAVTESTCEN
Commander, Navy Military Personnel Command (NVT) ...... COMNAVMILPERSCOM
Commander, Navy Recruiting Area (DNAB) .... CNRA
Commander Navy Recruiting Area (SAUO) .... COMNAVCRUITAREA
Commander, Navy Recruiting Command (DNAB) .... CNRC
Commander, Navy Recruiting Command (DNAB) .... COMNAVCRUITCOM
Commander, Navy Recruiting Command, Quality Assurance Team
  (DNAB) .... COMNAVCRUITCOM QAT
Commander, New London Group .... COMNEWLONGRU
Commander, New London [Connecticut] Test and Evaluation Detachment
  (DNAB) .... COMNLONTEVDET
Commander, New York Group .... COMNYKGRU
Commander, New Zealand Army Forces, Far East ...... COMNZAFFE
Commander, New Zealand Assistance Detachment, Vietnam .... COMNEWZEDV
Commander, Norfolk Group .... COMNORVAGRU
Commander, Norfolk, Virginia Test and Evaluation Detachment
  (DNAB) .... COMNORVATEVDET
Commander, North American Antisubmarine Defense Force, Atlantic
  [NATO] .... COMNORASDEFLANT
Commander, North American Defense Force, Atlantic [NATO] .... COMNADEFLANT
Commander, North Pacific Force .... COMNORPAC
Commander, North Sea Subarea, Central Europe (NATG) .... COMNORSEACENT
Commander, Northeast Atlantic (NATG) .... COMNEATLANT
Commander, Northeast Mediterranean (AABC) .... COMEDNOREAST
Commander, Northeast Subarea Channel .... COMNORECHAN
Commander, Northern Area Forces, Central Europe (NATG) .... COMNAVNORCENT
Commander, Northern Army Group, Central Europe .... COMNORTHAG
Commander, Northern Atlantic Subarea [NATO] .... COMNORLANT
Commander, Northern Group .... CNG
Commander, Northern Norway (SAUS) .... COMNON
Commander, Northern Section .... COMNORSECT
Commander Northern Section/Western Sea Frontier
  (SAUO) .... COMNORSECT/WESTSEAFRON
Commander, Northern Striking Force (DNAB) .... COMNORSTRIKFOR
Commander, Nuclear Power Training Group, Atlantic
  (DNAB) .... COMNUPWRTRAGRULANT
Commander, Nuclear Power Training Group, Pacific
  (DNAB) .... COMNUPWRTRAGRUPAC
Commander, Nuclear Weapons Training Group, Atlantic
  (DNAB) .... COMNUWPNTRAGRULANT
Commander, Nuclear Weapons Training Group, Pacific
  (DNAB) .... COMNUWPNTRAGRUPAC
Commander, Ocean Atlantic Subarea [NATO] .... COMOCEANLANT
Commander, Ocean Subarea .... COMOCEANSUBAREA
Commander Ocean Systems, Atlantic (DOMA) .... COSL
Commander Ocean Systems Pacific (DOMA) .... COSP
Commander, Oceanographic Surveillance Systems, Atlantic
  (MUGU) .... COMOCEANSYSLANT
Commander, Oceanographic Surveillance Systems, Pacific .... COMOCEANSYSPAC
Commander, Oceanographic System, Atlantic (SAUS) ..... COMOCEANSYSTLANT
Commander Oceanographic Systems, Atlantic (SAUO) ..... COMOCEANSYSTLANT
Commander of a Numbered Group .... COMGRU
Commander of Air Base (SAUO) .... COMAIRBASE
Commander of Airlift Forces [Air Force] (DOMA) .... COMALF
Commander of Base (SAUO) .... C of B
Commander of Central European Air Forces (SAUS) ... CCEAF
Commander of Central European Ground Forces (SAUS) .... CCEGF
Commander of Central European Sea Forces (SAUS) ... CCESF
Commander of Coast Defenses (SAUO) .... CCD
Commander of Destroyer force (SAUO) .... COMDESTR
Commander of Destroyers United States Fleet (SAUO) .... COMDESUS
Commander of Federal Republic of Nigeria .... CFR
Commander of Hunter-Killer Fleet, Atlantic (SAUS) ..... COMHUKLANT
Commander of Northern European Air Forces (SAUO) ..... CNEAF
Commander of Northern European Ground Forces (SAUO) .... CNEGF
Commander of Northern European Sea Forces (SAUO) ..... CNESF
Commander of Service Cross [British] (ROG) .... CSC
Commander of Southern European Air Forces (SAUO) ..... CSEAF
Commander of Southern European Ground Forces (SAUO) .... CSEGF
Commander of the Air Group (SAUO) .... CAG
Commander of the American Forces in the Pacific (SAUO) ..... CAFPAC
Commander of the [Order of the] British Empire [Facetious translation: Can't
  Be Everywhere] .... CBE
Commander of the Dockyard at [place] .... COMYARD
Commander of the Fleet (SAUO) .... ComFleet
Commander of the Fleet (SAUO) .... ComFlt
Commander of the Guard [Military] .... COG
Commander of the Most Excellent Order of the Bath [British] ..... CB
Commander of the North-West Territories (SAUO) .... CNWT
Commander of the Order of Distinction [Jamaica] ... CD
Commander of the Order of Leopold CL
Commander of the Order of Military Merit [Canada] (DD) .... CMM
Commander of the Order of St. Lazarus of Jerusalem .... CLJ
Commander of the Order of the Niger [Nigeria] ..... CON
Commander of the Royal Artillery (SAUO) .... CRA
Commander of the Royal Victorian Order [British] .. CVO
Commander of Troops [for a parade or review] [Military] ..... COT

Commander, Operational Control Center ... COMOPCONCEN
Commander, Operational Development Force [*Navy*] ... COMOPDEVFOR
Commander Operational Development Force, Atlantic Fleet (SAUO) ... ComOpDevForLant
Commander, Operational Forces, Denmark (SAUS) ... COFDEN
Commander, Operational Test and Evaluation Force [*Navy*] ... COMOPTEVFOR
Commander Operational Test and Evaluation Force [*Navy*] (CAAL) ... COTF
Commander, Operational Test and Evaluation Force, Atlantic [*Navy*] (DNAB) ... COMOPTEVFORLANT
Commander, Operational Test and Evaluation Force, Pacific [*Navy*] (DNAB) ... COMOPTEVFORPAC
Commander Orange (Aggressor) Force [*Navy*] (CAAL) ... COMORANGE
Commander, Orange, Texas, Group; Inactive Reserve Fleet, Atlantic ... COMORTEXGRU
Commander Orange, Texas Group, Inactive Reserve Fleet, Atlantic (SAUO) ... COMORTEXGRU
Commander, Order of St. John of Jerusalem [*British*] ... CStJ
Commander, Order of the British Empire (SAUS) ... CBE
Commander, Pacific Air Fleet ... COMPAF
Commander, Pacific Air Force (SAUO) ... ComPAF
Commander, Pacific Electronic Intelligence Center (DNAB) ... COMPACELINTCEN
Commander, Pacific Missile Range (MUGU) ... COMPACMISRAN
Commander, Pacific Missile Range (AAG) ... COMPMR
Commander, Pacific Missile Range Instruction (MUGU) ... COMPMRINST
Commander, Pacific Missile Range Notice (MUGU) ... COMPMRNOTE
Commander, Pacific Reserve Fleet (SAUO) ... COMPACRESFLT
Commander, Panama Sea Frontier ... COMPASEAFRON
Commander, Panama Section (DNAB) ... COMPASECT
Commander, Panama Section, Antisubmarine Warfare Group (DNAB) ... COMPASECTASWGRU
Commander Panama Section/Caribbean Sea Frontier (SAUO) ... COMPASECTCARIBSEAFRON
Commander Panama Section/Western Sea Frontier (SAUO) ... COMPASECT/WESTSEAFRON
Commander, Panama Sector (SAUS) ... COMPASECT
Commander, Panama Sector, Caribbean Sea Frontier (SAUS) ... COMPASECTCARIBSEAFRON
Commander, Patrol Aircraft Service Unit ... COMPASU
Commander, Patrol and Reconnaissance Force (DNAB) ... COMPATRECONFOR
Commander, Patrol Antisubmarine Warfare Development Group (DNAB) ... COMPATASWDEVGRU
Commander, Patrol Forces (NATG) ... COMPATFOR
Commander, Patrol Forces, Northern Subarea, Atlantic (NATG) ... COMPATFORNORLANT
Commander, Patrol Squadron ... COMPATRON
Commander, Patrol Squadron (SAUS) ... COPATRON
Commander, Patrol Wings Atlantic (SAUO) ... COMPATWINGSLANT
Commander, Philadelphia Group ... COMPHILAGRU
Commander, Philippine Military Assistance Group, Vietnam ... COMPHILMAGV
Commander, Plymouth Subarea Channel ... COMPLYMCHAN
Commander, [*US*] **Ports and Bases, France** ... COMBASFRANCE
Commander, Puerto Rico Section Antisubmarine Warfare Unit (DNAB) ... COMPRSECTASWU
Commander Puerto Rico Section/Caribbean Sea Frontier (SAUO) ... COMPUERTORICOSECT/ CARIBSEAFRON
Commander, Rapid Development Naval Force (DNAB) ... COMRDNAVFOR
Commander Readiness Attack Carrier Air Wing (SAUO) ... COMREDATKCARAIRWING
Commander, Rear Area Security (SAUO) ... COMRASC
Commander Reconnaissance Attack Wing (SAUO) ... COMRECONATKWING
Commander, Republic of Korea Forces, Vietnam ... COMROKFV
Commander, Republic of Korea Military Assistance Group, Vietnam ... COMROKMAGV
Commander, Reserve Destroyer Squadron ... COMRESDESRON
Commander, Reserve Escort Squadron (SAUO) ... ComResEscortRon
Commander, Reserve Escort Squadron (SAUS) ... COMRESESCORTRON
Commander, Reserve Flotilla (SAUO) ... COMRESFLOT
Commander, Reserve Naval Construction Battalions, Atlantic (DNAB) ... COMRNCBLANT
Commander, Reserve Naval Construction Force (DNAB) ... COMRNCF
commander, reserve squadron (SAUO) ... ComResRon
Commander, Reserve Squadron (SAUS) ... ComResRon
Commander Rhine River Naval Group, French II Corps Sector (SAUO) ... COMNOFRHIN
Commander, River Division ... COMRIVDIV
Commander, River Flotilla ... COMRIVFLOT
Commander, River Flotilla One ... COMRIVFLOTONE
Commander, River Patrol Force ... COMRIVPATFOR
Commander, River Support Squadron ... COMRIVSUPPRON
Commander, Riverine Division [*Navy*] ... COMRNDN
Commander, Riverine Flotilla [*Navy*] ... COMRNFLOT
Commander, Riverine Squadron [*Navy*] ... COMRNRON
Commander, Royal Armoured Corps [*British military*] (DMA) ... CRAC
Commander, Royal Army Ordnance Corps [*Military*] [*British*] ... CRAOC
Commander, Royal Army Service Corps [*British*] ... CRASC
Commander, Royal Army Service Corps (SAUO) ... CRASC
Commander, Royal Artillery [*Division level*] [*British*] ... CRA
Commander Royal Canadian Army Service Corps (SAUO) ... CRCASC
Commander, Royal Canadian Army Service Corps (SAUS) ... CRCASC
Commander, Royal Corps of Transport [*Military*] [*British*] ... CRCT
Commander, Royal Electrical and Mechanical Engineers [*Military*] [*British*] ... CREME
Commander, Royal Engineers [*British*] ... CRE
Commander, Royal Thai Military Assistance Group, Vietnam ... COMRTMAGV
Commander, San Diego Group ... COMDIEGOGRU
Commander, San Francisco Group ... COMSANFRANGRU
Commander, Scouting Squadron ... COMSCORON
Commander Sea Area South (SAUO) ... COMSARSOUTH
Commander, Sea Frontier ... COMSEAFRON
Commander Sea Training [*Canadian Navy*] ... CST
Commander, Search and Rescue (DNAB) ... COMSAR
Commander, SEATO [*Southeast Asia Treaty Organization*] **Field Forces** (CINC) ... CSFF
Commander, Second Allied Tactical Air Force ... COMTWOATAF
Commander, Second Fleet [*Atlantic*] (SAA) ... COMSECFLT
Commander, Second Fleet (MUGU) ... COMSECONDFLT
Commander, Second Fleet, Headquarters (MCD) ... COMSECFLTHQ
Commander, Security Command (SAUO) ... COMSECOM
Commander, Service Force ... COMSERV
Commander, Service Force (DNAB) ... COMSERVFOR
Commander, Service Force, Atlantic (DNAB) ... COMSERFORLANT
Commander, Service Force, Atlantic (DNAB) ... COMSERVLANT
Commander Service Force, Atlantic (MCD) ... CSL
Commander, Service Force, Atlantic Fleet ... COMSERVLANT
Commander, Service Force Group (DNAB) ... COMSERVGRU
Commander, Service Force Group Detachment (DNAB) ... COMSERVGRUDET
Commander Service Force, Pacific (SAUO) ... COMSERFORPAC
Commander Service Force, Pacific (SAUO) ... COMSERVPAC
Commander Service Force, Pacific (MCD) ... CSP
Commander, Service Force, Pacific Fleet ... COMSERVPAC
Commander Service Force, Pacific Petroleum School (SAUO) ... COMSERVPACETSCOL
Commander, Service Force, Pacific Petroleum School (DNAB) ... COMSERVPACPETSCOL
Commander, Service Force, Pacific Subordinate Command (SAUO) ... COMSERFORPACSUBCOM
Commander, Service Force, South Pacific Subordinate Command ... COMSERFORSOPACSUBCOM
Commander, Service Force, Southwest Pacific ... COMSERVSOWESPAC
Commander, Service Group Two [*Navy*] ... CSG2
Commander, Service Squadron ... COMSERVRON
Commander, Seventh Fleet (MUGU) ... COMSEVENTHFLT
Commander, Sixth Allied Tactical Air Force (AFM) ... COMSIXATAF
Commander Sixth Allied Tactical Air Force Southeastern Europe (SAUO) ... COMSIXATAF
Commander, Sixth Fleet (NATG) ... COMSIXFLT
Commander, Sixth Fleet (NATG) ... COMSIXTHFLT
Commander, South Atlantic Force ... COMSOLANT
Commander, South Atlantic Maritime Area ... CAMAS
Commander, South Pacific ... COMSOPAC
Commander, Southeast Mediterranean (AFM) ... COMEDSOUEAST
Commander, Southeast Pacific Force ... COMSOEASTPAC
Commander, Southern European Air Forces (SAUS) ... CSEAF
Commander, Southern European Ground Forces (SAUS) ... CSEGF
Commander, Southern European Sea Forces (SAUS) ... CSESF
Commander Southern European Sea Forces (SAUO) ... CSESF
Commander, Southern Norway (SAUS) ... COMSONOR
Commander, Southern Section (DNAB) ... COMSOSECT
Commander Southern Section/Western Sea Frontier (SAUO) ... COMSOSECT/WESTSEAFRON
Commander, Southern Sector, Western Sea Frontier (MUGU) ... COMSOSECWESTSEAFRON
Commander, Southwest Pacific Force ... COMSOWESPAC
Commander, Special Operating Forces Central Command [*Navy*] (ANA) ... COMSOCCENT
Commander, Special Operations Command (SAUO) ... COMSOC
Commander, Standing Naval Force Channel (SAUS) ... COMSTANAVFORCHAN
Commander, State Area Command (SAUO) ... COMSTARC
Commander, Stockton Group ... COMSTOCKGRU
Commander, Straits and Marmara Defense Sector (NATG) ... COMSAMAR
Commander, Strategic Reserve, Allied Land Forces, Central Europe (NATG) ... COMSTRATRESCENT
Commander, Strategic Submarine Force (DNAB) ... COMSTRATSUBFOR
Commander Strike Fleet, Atlantic (SAUO) ... COMSTRIKEFLTLANT
Commander, Strike Force Atlantic (SAUO) ... COMSTRKFORLANT
Commander, Striking and Support Forces, Southern Europe ... COMSTRIKFORSOUTH
Commander, Striking Fleet, Atlantic (MCD) ... CMSTRKFLT
Commander Striking Fleet Atlantic [*Military*] ... CMSTRKFLT-LANT
Commander, Striking Fleet, Atlantic (AABC) ... COMSTRIKFLANT
Commander, Striking Fleet, Atlantic (AFM) ... COMSTRIKFLTLANT
Commander, Striking Fleet, Atlantic Representative in Europe (NATG) ... COMSTRIKFLANTREPEUR
Commander Striking Fleet Atlantic Representative in Europe (SAUO) ... COMSTRIKFLTLANTREPEUR
Commander, Striking Fleet, Atlantic Representative in Europe (SAUS) ... COMSTRIKFLTLANTREPEUR
Commander, Striking Forces Southern Europe (SAUS) ... COMSTRIKFORSOUTH
Commander, Sub-Frontier Defense (DNAB) ... COMSUBFRONDEF
Commander Sub-Frontier Defense (SAUO) ... COMSUBFRONDESF
Commander, Sub-Frontier Defense/Delaware Group (DNAB) ... COMSUBFRONDEF/DELGRU
Commander, Sub-Frontier Defense/Southern Group (DNAB) ... COMSUBFRONDEF/SOGRU
Commander, Submarine Allied Command, Atlantic (AABC) ... COMSUBACLANT
Commander, Submarine Base ... COMSUBASE
Commander Submarine Base (SAUO) ... COMSUGBASE
Commander; Submarine Development Group (SAUO) ... ComSubDevGru
Commander, Submarine Development Group ... COMSUBDEVGRU

Commander, Submarine Development Group Detachment (DNAB) .... COMSUBDEVGRUDET
Commander, Submarine Development Group, Unmanned Vehicles (DNAB) .... COMSUBDEVGRU UMV
Commander, Submarine Development Squadron (DNAB) .... COMSUBDEVRON
Commander, Submarine Development Squadron Training Detachment (DNAB) .... COMSUBDEVRONTRADET
Commander, Submarine Division .... COMSUBDIV
Commander, Submarine Division (SAUS) .... CSD
Commander, Submarine Flotilla .... COMSUBFLO
Commander, Submarine Flotilla (MUGU) .... COMSUBFLOT
Commander, Submarine Force (SAUS) .... COMSUBFOR
Commander Submarine Force (SAUO) .... COMSUBFOR
Commander, Submarine Force, Atlantic .... COMSUBLANT
Commander Submarine Force, Atlantic Fleet (SAUO) .... COMSUBSLANT
Commander, Submarine Force, Atlantic Representative (DNAB) .... COMSUBLANTREP
Commander, Submarine Force, Eastern Atlantic .... COMSUBEASTLANT
Commander, Submarine Force, Mediterranean (AABC) .... COMSUBMED
Commander, Submarine Force, Northeast Mediterranean (AABC) .... COMSUBMEDNOREAST
Commander, Submarine Force, Pacific .... COMSUBPAC
Commander, Submarine Force, Pacific Command Center (DNAB) .... COMSUBPAC CC
Commander, Submarine Force, Pacific Emergency Command Center (DNAB) .... COMSUBPAC ECC
Commander, Submarine Force, Pacific, Over-the-Horizon Fleet Commander (DNAB) .... COMSUBPAC OTH
Commander, Submarine Force, Pacific Representative (DNAB) .... COMSUBPACREP
Commander, Submarine Force, Western Atlantic Area (AABC) .... COMSUBWESTLANT
Commander Submarine Forces, Atlantic Fleet (SAUO) .... COMSUBLANT
Commander Submarine Forces, Pacific Fleet (SAUO) .... COMSUBPAC
Commander Submarine Forces, United States Fleet (SAUO) .... COMSUBUS
Commander, Submarine Group (SAUO) .... COMSUBGRP
Commander, Submarine Group (SAUO) .... ComSubGru
Commander, Submarine Group (SAUS) .... COMSUBGRU
Commander Submarine Group 8 .... COMSUBGRU 8
Commander, Submarine Group Detachment (DNAB) .... COMSUBGRUDET
Commander, Submarine Sea Training (SAUS) .... CSST
Commander, Submarine Squadron .... COMSUBRON
Commander, Submarine Training Facilities .... COMSUBTRAFAC
Commander, Submarine Training Group (DNAB) .... COMSUBTRAGRU
Commander, Submarine Training Group, Northwest Area (DNAB) .... COMSUBTRAGRUNORWEST
Commander, Submarine Training Group, West Coast Area (DNAB) .... COMSUBTRAGRUWESCO
Commander, Submarines .... COMSUBS
Commander Submarines Force, Pacific Fleet (SAUO) .... COMSUBSPAC
Commander, Submarines, Northeast Mediterranean (NATG) .... COMSUBLEDNOREAST
Commander, Submarines, Southwest Pacific Force .... COMSUBSSOWESPAC
Commander, Subordinate Command, [*US*] Atlantic Fleet (NATG) .... COMSUCOMLANTFLT
Commander, Subordinate Command, [*US*] Naval Forces Eastern Atlantic and Mediterranean, Commander Headquarters Support Activities [*Said to be the longest English-language acronym*] .... COMSUBCOMNELMCOMHEDSUPPACT
Commander, Subordinate Command, [*US*] Naval Forces Eastern Atlantic and Mediterranean, Commander Headquarters Support Activities .... CSCN/CHSA
Commander, Subordinate Command, Service Force Pacific Fleet [*Navy*] .... CSFPSC
Commander, Subordinate Command, United States Naval Forces, Eastern Atlantic (SAUS) .... COMSUBCOMNELM
Commander Subordinate Command, United States Naval Forces, Eastern Atlantic and Mediterranean (SAUO) .... COMSUBCOMNELM
Commander Subordinate Command, United States Naval Forces Eastern Atlantic and Mediterranean (SAUO) .... CSCN
Commander Subordinate Command, United States Naval Forces Eastern Atlantic and Mediterranean/Commander Headquarters Cupport Acitivities (SAUO) .... COMSUBCOMNELM/COMHEDSUPPACT
Commander, Support Operations Task Force, Europe (AFM) .... COMSOTFE
Commander, Surface Forces, Pacific Fleet (SAUO) .... COMSURFPAC
Commander, Surface Squadron (DNAB) .... COMSURFRON
Commander Tacoma Group (SAUO) .... COMTACGRU
Commander, Tactical Air Command (AFM) .... COMTAC
Commander, Tactical Air Control Group .... COMTACGRU
Commander, Tactical Air Control Squadron .... COMTACRON
Commander, Tactical Air Force, Denmark (NATG) .... COMTAFDEN
Commander; Tactical Group (SAUO) .... ComTacGru
Commander, Tactical Group (SAUS) .... COMTACGRU
Commander, Tactical Wings, Atlantic Fleet (ACAE) .... COMTACWINGSLANT
Commander, Taiwan Defense Command (MUGU) .... COMTAIWANDEFCOMD
Commander, Taiwan Patrol Force (CINC) .... COMTAIWANPATFOR
Commander, Task Element .... CTE
Commander, Task Fleet (SAUO) .... CTF
Commander, Task Force .... CTF
Commander, Task Group .... CTG
Commander, Task Unit .... CTU
Commander, Texas Group .... COMTEXGRU
Commander Third Fleet Computer Assisted Search (SAUO) .... COMPASS
Commander, Tongue Point Group, Inactive Reserve Fleet, Pacific .... COMTONGRU
Commander, Torpedo Squadron .... COMTORPRON
Commander, Training Command, Atlantic .... COMTRALANT
Commander, Training Command, Pacific .... COMTRAPAC
Commander Training Squadron (SAUO) .... COMTRAINRON
Commander, Training Squadron (SAUS) .... COMTRAINRON
Commander, Transport Amphibious Squadron (SAUS) .... COMTRANSPHIBRON
Commander, Transport Amphibious Squadron (SAUO) .... ComTransPhibRon
Commander, Transport Division .... COMTRANSDIV
Commander, Transport Group .... COMTRANSGR
Commander, Transport Group, South Pacific Force .... COMTRANSGRSOPAC
Commander, Transportation Division .... CTD
Commander, Transports, Amphibious Force .... COMTRANSPHIB
Commander, Transports, Amphibious Force, Atlantic Fleet .... COMTRANSPHIBLANT
Commander, Transports, Amphibious Force, Pacific Fleet .... COMTRANSPHIBPAC
Commander UK Task Group (SAUO) .... COMUK TG
Commander, United Kingdom Air Defense Region (AFM) .... COMUKADR
Commander, United States Air Force Forces .... COMUSAFFOR
Commander, United States Air Force Southern Command (AFM) .... COMUSAFSO
Commander, United States Air Force Task Force (AABC) .... COMUSAFTF
Commander United States Army Europe (SAUS) .... USARUER
Commander, United States Army Forces (SAUO) .... COMUSAFROR
Commander, United States Army Forces .... COMUSARFOR
Commander, United States Army Forces Southern Command (AABC) .... COMUSARSO
Commander, United States Army, Japan (CINC) .... COMUSARJAPAN
Commander, United States Army Task Force .... COMUSARTF
Commander, United States Atlantic Subarea .... COMUSLANT
Commander, United States Facility (DNAB) .... COMUSFAC
Commander, United States Fleet Air Wing, Mediterranean (AABC) .... COMUSFAIRWINGMED
Commander, United States Force, Caribbean (DNAB) .... COMUSFORCARIB
Commander, United States Force, Caribbean Representative (DNAB) .... COMUSFORCARIBREP
Commander, United States Force, Iceland (DNAB) .... COMUSFORICE
Commander, United States Force, Marianas (DNAB) .... COMUSFORMAR
Commander, United States Forces (CINC) .... COMUS
Commander, United States Forces, Azores (AFM) .... COMUSFORAZ
Commander United States Forces, Japan (SAUO) .... COMUSFORJAPAN
Commander, United States Forces, Japan (MCD) .... COMUSJ
Commander, United States Forces, Japan (SAUS) .... COMUSJAP
Commander, United States Forces, Japan (AFM) .... COMUSJAPAN
Commander United States Forces, Korea (SAUO) .... COMUSFORKOREA
Commander, United States Forces, Korea (MCD) .... COMUSK
Commander, United States Forces, Korea (AFM) .... COMUSKOREA
Commander United States Forces, Marianas (SAUO) .... COMUSFORMARIANAS
Commander, United States Forces, Marianas .... COMUSMARIANAS
Commander, United States Forces, Southeast Asia (CINC) .... COMUSSEASIA
Commander, United States Joint Task Force (AABC) .... COMUSJTF
Commander, United States Joint Unconventional Warfare Task Force .... COMUSJUWTF
Commander, United States Land Forces .... COMUSLANDFOR
Commander, United States Marine Forces (AABC) .... COMUSMARFOR
Commander, United States Marine Task Force (AABC) .... COMUSMARTF
Commander, United States Military Assistance Command, Atlantic (SAUS) .... COMUSMACLANT
Commander, United States Military Assistance Command, Europe (SAUS) .... COMUSMACEUR
Commander, United States Military Assistance Command, Pacific (SAUS) .... COMUSMACPAC
Commander, United States Military Assistance Command, Thailand (AFM) .... COMUSMACTHAI
Commander, United States Military Assistance Command, Vietnam .... COMUSMACV
Commander, United States Military Group (AFM) .... COMUSMILGP
Commander, United States Naval Advanced Base [*Weser River, West Germany*] .... COUSNAB
Commander, United States Naval Forces (AABC) .... COMUSNAVFOR
Commander United States Naval Forces, Continental Air Defense Command (SAUO) .... COMUSNAVFORCONAD
Commander, United States Naval Forces, Southern Command (MUGU) .... COMUSNAVSO
Commander United States Naval Supply Force (SAUO) .... COUSNAVSUPPFOR
Commander United States Naval Support Force (SAUO) .... ComUSNavSuppFor
Commander, United States Naval Task Force (AABC) .... COMUSNAVTF
Commander, United States Ports and Bases, France .... COMUSBASFRANCE
Commander, United States Rhine River Patrol (NATG) .... COMUSRHIN
Commander, United States Special Advisory Group (AFM) .... COMUSSAG
Commander, United States Taiwan Defense Command (SAUS) .... COMUSTAIWANDEFCOM
Commander, United States Taiwan Defense Command (AFM) .... COMUSTDC
Commander, US Naval Forces, Azores (DNAB) .... CNFA
Commander U.S. Naval Forces, Azores (SAUO) .... COMNAVFORAZORES
Commander, US Naval Forces, Caribbean (DNAB) .... COMNAVFORCARIB
Commander, US Naval Forces, Caribbean Detachment (DNAB) .... COMNAVFORCARIBDET
Commander, US Naval Forces Central Command (ANA) .... COMUSNAVCENT
Commander, US Naval Forces, Far East (DNAB) .... COMNAVFORFE
Commander, US Naval Forces, Marianas (DNAB) .... CNM
Commander U.S. Naval Forces, Marianas (SAUO) .... COMNAVFORMARIANAS
Commander, US Naval Forces, Marianas (DNAB) .... COMNAVMAR
Commander, USMC Forces, Korea (SAUO) .... COMUSMARFORK
Commander, Utility Squadron .... COMUTRON
Commander, Utility Wing .... COMUTWING
Commander, Utility Wing, Service Force, Atlantic .... COMUTWINGSERVLANT

Commander, Utility Wing, Service Force, Pacific .... COMUTWINGSERVPAC
Commander, Venerable Order of St. John of Jerusalem [*Decoration*]
   (CMD) .... CStJ
Commander, Western Area, United States Coast Guard
   (SAUS) .... COMWESTAREA USCG
Commander Western Mediterranean Area (SAUO) .... COMEDOC
Commander, Western Sea Frontier (MUGU) .... COMWESTSEAFRON
Commander, Western Sea Frontier .... CWSF
Commander Western Sea Frontier (SAUO) .... CWSF
Commander, Western Transport Air Force [*Travis AFB*] (CINC) .... COMWESTAF
Commanderie de Bordeaux (EA) .... CB
Commanderie de Bordeaux (EA) .... CdB
Commanderie des Cordons Bleus de France (EA) .... CCBF
Commander-in-Charge (SAUS) .... COM-IN-CH
Commander-in-Chief [*Air Force*] CIC
Commander-in-Chief .... CINC
Commander-in-Chief [*US fleet*] .... COMINCH
commander-in-chief (SAUO) .... cominch
Commander-in-Chief Aerospace Defense Command (CCCA) .... CINCAD
Commander-in-Chief, Air Base (SAUO) .... CINCAIR
Commander-in-Chief, Air Force Atlantic Command (AFM) .... CINCAFLANT
Commander-in-Chief, Air Force Strike Command (AFM) ...... CINCAFSTRIKE
Commander-in-Chief, Air Forces, Europe (NATG) .... CINCAFE
Commander-in-Chief, Alaskan Command .... CINCAL
Commander-in-Chief, Allied Air Forces, Central Europe (MCD) .... CINCAIRCENT
Commander-in-Chief, Allied Air Forces, Central Europe .... CINCALAIRCENEUR
Commander-in-Chief, Allied Air Forces Central Europe
   (SAUO) .... CINCALAirCenEur
Commander-in-Chief, Allied Air Forces, Channel (SAUO) ...... CINCAirChan
Commander-in-Chief, Allied Air Forces, Channel (SAUS) .... CINCAIRCHAN
Commander-in-Chief, Allied Air Forces, Eastern Atlantic Area
   (SAUS) .... CINCAIREASTLANT
Commander-in-Chief, Allied Air Forces, Western Atlantic Area
   (SAUS) .... CINCAIRWESTLANT
Commander-in-Chief, Allied Air Forces Western Atlantic Area
   (SAUO) .... CINCAirWestLant
Commander-in-Chief, Allied Forces .... CINCAF
Commander-in-Chief, Allied Forces, Central Europe [*NATO*] .... CINCCENT
Commander-in-Chief, Allied Forces, Central Europe (MCD) .... CINCENT
Commander-in-Chief, Allied Forces, Mediterranean [*NATO*] .... CINCAFMED
Commander-in-Chief Allied Forces Mediterranean (SAUO) .... CINCAFMED
Commander-in-Chief, Allied Forces, Northern Europe [*NATO*] .... CINCNORTH
Commander-in-Chief Allied Forces Southern Europe .... CINCAFSOUTH
Commander-in-Chief, Allied Forces, Southern Europe [*NATO*] .... CINCSOUTH
Commander-in-Chief, Allied Land Forces, Central Europe
   (MCD) .... CINCLANDCENT
Commander-in-Chief, America West Indies Station [*British*] .... CINCAWI
Commander-in-Chief, [*US*] Army Forces, Atlantic (AABC) .... CINCARLANT
Commander-in-Chief, [*US*] Army Forces in the Pacific .... CINCAFPAC
Commander-in-Chief, [*US*] Army Forces, Pacific (AFM) .... CINCARPAC
Commander-in-Chief, Army Strike Command (AFM) .... CINCARSTRIKE
Commander-in-Chief, [*US*] Asiatic Fleet .... CINCAF
Commander-in-Chief, Asiatic Fleet (SAUS) .... CINC ASIATIC
Commander-in-Chief, Asiatic Fleet (SAUO) .... C-in-C Asiatic
Commander-in-Chief, Atlantic .... CINCATL
Commander-in-Chief, Atlantic .... CINCLANT
Commander-in-Chief, Atlantic Airborne Command Post
   (DNAB) .... CINCLANT ABNCP
Commander-in-Chief, Atlantic and Pacific (AFIT) .... CINCLANT/PAC
Commander-in-Chief, Atlantic and West Indies .... CINCA & WI
Commander-in-Chief, Atlantic and West Indies (SAUS) .... CINCA&WI
Commander-in-Chief, Atlantic Command (DEMM) .... CINCLANT
Commander-in-Chief, Atlantic Coordination of Atomic Operations
   (DNAB) .... CINCLANT CAO
Commander-in-Chief, Atlantic Fleet (SAUO) .... CICAF
Commander-in-Chief, Atlantic Fleet [*Navy*] .... CINCLANTFLT
Commander-in-Chief, Atlantic Representative (DNAB) .... CINCLANTREP
Commander-in-Chief Bomber Command (SAUO) .... CINC BOMBER COMMAND
Commander-in-Chief, British Pacific Fleet .... CINCBPF
Commander-in-Chief, Canadian Northwest Atlantic [*World War II*] ...... C in C CNA
Commander-in-Chief, Caribbean .... CINCARIB
Commander-in-Chief, Central Command (SAUO) .... CINCCENT
Commander-in-Chief, Channel & Eastern Atlantic Areas (SAUS) .... CINCHEL
Commander-in-Chief Channel and Southern North Sea .... CINCHAN
Commander-in-Chief Coastal Command (SAUO) .... CINC COASTAL COMMAND
Commander-in-Chief, Combined Forces Command (SAUO) .... CINCCFC
Commander-in-Chief, Continental Air Command (AFM) .... CINCAC
Commander-in-Chief, Continental Air Defense Command (SAUS) .... CINCCONAD
Commander-in-Chief, Continental Air Defense Command .... CINCONAD
Commander-in-Chief, [*US Fleet*], Convoy and Routing Section .... COMROUTE
Commander-in-Chief, East Indies Station [*British*] .... CINCEI
Commander-in-Chief, Eastern Atlantic Area [*NATO*] .... CINCEASTLANT
Commander-in-Chief Eastern Atlantic Area, Air Commander-in-Chief
   Eastern Atlantic Area (SAUO) .... JOINTCINCEASTLANT
Commander-in-Chief, Europe .... CINCEUR
Commander-in-Chief, European Command (SAUS) .... CINCEUR
Commander-in-Chief, European Theater of Operations (SAUO) ..... C-in-C ETOUSA
Commander-in-Chief, Far East .... CINCFE
Commander-in-Chief, Far East Station [*British*] .... CINCFES
Commander-in-Chief, Far East Station [*British*] .... CINCFESTA
Commander-in-Chief, Fleet (SAUS) .... CINCFLEET
Commander-in-Chief, Fleet [*British*] .... CINCFLT
Commander-in-Chief, German Fleet (SAUS) .... CINCGERFLT
Commander-in-Chief, German Naval Fleet (SAUO) .... CINCGERFLEET
Commander-in-Chief, Home Fleet (SAUS) .... C-IN-C HF

Commander-in-Chief, Home Forces [*British*] .... C-in-CHF
Commander-in-Chief, Iberian Atlantic Area (NATG) .... CINCIBERLANT
Commander-in-Chief, Iraq (SAUO) CiCI
Commander-in-Chief, Japan Area [*World War II*] .... CINCJAPA
Commander-in-Chief, Mediterranean .... CINCMED
Commander-in-Chief, Mediterranean (SAUS) .... C-IN-C MED
Commander-in-Chief Middle East Air Forces (SAUO) .... CINCMEAF
Commander-in-Chief, Middle East Land Forces (NATG) .... CINCMELF
Commander-in-Chief, Middle East/Southern Asia and Africa South of the
   Sahara [*Military*] .... CINCMEAFSA
Commander-in-Chief, Military Airlift Command .... CINCMAC
Commander-in-Chief, Naval Base (SAUO) .... CINCNAVBASE
Commander-in-Chief, Naval Forces, Eastern Atlantic and Mediterranean
   (SAUO) .... CINCNAVEASTLANT-MED
Commander-in-Chief, Naval Forces, Eastern Atlantic and
   Mediterranean .... CINCNAVEASTLANTMED
Commander-in-Chief, Naval Forces, Eastern Atlantic and
   Mediterranean .... CINCNELM
Commander-in-Chief Naval Forces Europe (SAUO) .... CINCNAVEUR
Commander-in-Chief Naval Forces Europe (SAUO) .... CINCNAVFOREUR
Commander-in-Chief, Naval Forces, Europe (SAUS) .... CINCNAVFOREUR
Commander-in-Chief, Naval Home Command (SAUS) .... CINCNAVHOME
Commander-in-Chief Naval Home Command (SAUO) .... CINCNAV HOME
Commander-in-Chief, Naval Surface Fleet, Atlantic (SAUO) .... CINCNAVSURFLANT
Commander-in-Chief, Netherlands Forces in the East .... CINCNEDE
Commander-in-Chief Netherlands Home Station
   (SAUO) .... CINCNETH HOME STATION
Commander-in-Chief North American Aerospace Defense Command
   (SAUO) .... CINCNORAD
Commander-in-Chief, North American Air Defense (SAUO) .... CINCNARAD
Commander-in-Chief, North American Air Defense .... CINCNORAD
Commander-in-Chief, [*US*] Northeast Command .... CINCNE
Commander-in-Chief, Northern Europe .... CINCNOREUR
Commander-in-Chief, Northern Naval Forces in Europe
   (SAUO) .... CINCNORNAVEUR
Commander-in-Chief, Norwegian Army (SAUO) .... CINC NA
Commander-in-Chief, Norwegian Army (SAUS) .... CINCNA
Commander-in-Chief of the Atlantic Fleet (SAUO) .... C-in-CAF
Commander-in-Chief, Pacific (SAUS) .... C-IN-C PAC
Commander-in-Chief, Pacific .... CINCPAC
Commander-in-Chief, Pacific Air Forces .... CINCPACAF
Commander-in-Chief, Pacific Fleet [*Navy*] .... CCPF
Commander-in-Chief, Pacific Fleet (SAUO) .... CiCPF
Commander-in-Chief, Pacific Fleet (SAUO) .... C-in-CPac
Commander-in-Chief, Pacific Fleet (SAUS) .... CINCPacFlt
Commander-in-Chief, Pacific Fleet [*Navy*] .... CINCPACFLT
Commander-in-Chief, Pacific Fleet [*Navy*] (VNW) .... COMCINCPACFLT
Commander-in-Chief, Pacific Fleet, Alternate Command Element
   Commander (DNAB) .... CINCPACFLT ACE
Commander-in-Chief, [*US*] Pacific Fleet and Pacific Ocean
   Areas .... CINCPAC-CINCPOA
Commander-in-Chief, Pacific Fleet, Emergency Command Center
   Commander (DNAB) .... CINCPACFLT ECC
Commander-in-Chief, Pacific Fleet, Emergency Relocation Site
   Commander (DNAB) .... CINCPACFLT ERS
Commander-in-Chief, [*US*] Pacific Fleet Headquarters, Pearl
   Harbor .... CINCPACHEDPEARL
Commander-in-Chief, Pacific Fleet, Oceanic Airspace Coordinator
   (DNAB) .... CINCPACFLT OAC
Commander-in-Chief, Pacific Fleet Representative (DNAB) .... CINCPACFLTREP
Commander-in-Chief, Pacific Ocean Areas .... CINCPOA
Commander-in-Chief, Pacific Ocean Areas Headquarters, Pearl
   Harbor .... CINCPOAHEDPEARL
Commander-in-Chief, Pacific Ocean (or Operation) Area (SAUS) .... CINCPOA
Commander-in-Chief, Pacific Representative (AABC) .... CINCPACREP
Commander-in-Chief, Pacific Representative, Philippines .... CINCPACREPPHIL
Commander-in-Chief, Pacific Staff Instruction (CINC) .... CINCPACSTAFFINSTR
Commander-in-Chief, Plymouth (SAUO) .... CINCPLYMOUTH
Commander-in-Chief, Portsmouth (SAUO) .... CINCPORTSMOUTH
Commander-in-Chief, Readiness Command .... CINCRED
Commander-in-Chief, Readiness Command .... CINCREDCOM
Commander-In-Chief Report (SAUO) .... CINC REPORT
Commander-in-Chief, Royal Danish Air Force (NATG) .... CINCRDAF
Commander-in-Chief Royal Danish Army (SAUO) .... CINCRDA
Commander-in-Chief Royal Danish Army (SAUS) .... CINCRDA
Commander-in-Chief Royal Danish Navy (NATG) .... CINCRDN
Commander-in-Chief Royal Norway Army (SAUO) .... CINCRNOA
Commander-in-Chief Royal Norway Force (SAUO) .... CINCRNOAF
Commander-in-Chief Royal Norway Navy (SAUO) .... CINCRNON
Commander-in-Chief, Royal Norwegian Air Force (SAUO) .... CINC RNAF
Commander-in-Chief, Royal Norwegian Air Force (NATG) .... CINCRNAF
Commander-in-Chief, Royal Norwegian Army (SAUS) .... CINCRNOA
Commander-in-Chief, Royal Norwegian Navy (SAUS) .... CINCRNorN
Commander-in-Chief, Royal Norwegian Navy (SAUO) .... CINC RNORN
Commander-in-Chief, Royal Norwegian Navy (NATG) .... CINCRNORN
Commander-in-Chief, South Atlantic Station [*British*] .... CINCSA
Commander-in-Chief, Southern Command (AFM) .... CINCSO
Commander-in-Chief, Southern Europe Command (SAUO) .... CINCSEURCOM
Commander-in-Chief, Southwest Pacific (SAUO) .... CINCSowesPac
Commander-in-Chief, Southwest Pacific (SAUS) .... CINCSOWESPAC
Commander-in-Chief, Southwest Pacific Area [*World War II*] .... CINCSWPA
Commander-in-Chief, Specified Command, Middle East .... CINCSPECOMME
Commander-in-Chief, Strategic Air Command .... CINCSAC
Commander-in-Chief, Strike Command .... CINCSTRIKE
Commander-in-Chief, Tactical Air Command .... CINCTAC

Commander-in-Chief, Turkish Navy (SAUO) ... CINCTURNAV
Commander-in-Chief, United Kingdom Air Force (NATG) ... CINCUKAIR
Commander-in-Chief United Kingdom Home Fleet (SAUO) ... CINCHEF
Commander-in-Chief, United Kingdom Home Fleet [*Also, CINCHOMEFLT*] (NATG) ... CINCHF
Commander-in-Chief, United Kingdom Home Fleet [*Also, CINCHF*] (NATG) ... CINCHOMEFLT
Commander-in-Chief, United Nations Command ... CINCUNC
Commander-in-Chief, United Nations Command (SAUO) ... CINCUNG
Commander-in-Chief, United Nations Command, Korea ... CINCUNCKOREA
Commander-in-Chief, United Nations Forces in Korea (MCD) ... CINCUNK
Commander-in-Chief, United States Air Force, Atlantic (AFM) ... CINCUSAFLANT
Commander-in-Chief, United States Air Force Strike (AFM) ... CINCUSAFSTRIKE
Commander-in-Chief, United States Air Forces in Europe ... CINCUSAFE
Commander-in-Chief, United States Army, Europe ... CINCUSAREUR
Commander-in-Chief, United States Army Forces, Naval Supply Center, Oakland [*California*] ... CINCUSAFNSCO
Commander-in-Chief, United States Army Forces-Europe Command (SAUO) ... CINCAREUR
Commander-in-Chief, United States Army Forces-Readiness (SAUO) ... CINCARRED
Commander-in-Chief, United States Army, Pacific (AABC) ... CINCUSARPAC
Commander-in-Chief, United States Atlantic Command ... USCINCLANT
Commander-in-Chief, United States Central Command ... USCINCCENT
Commander-in-Chief, United States Command (SAUO) ... CINCUS
Commander-in-Chief, United States Fleet [*Later, COMINCH*] ... CINCUS
Commander-in-Chief United States Fleet and Chief of Naval Operations (SAUO) ... COMINCH
Commander-in-Chief, United States Naval Forces, Europe ... CINCUSNAVEUR
Commander-in-Chief, United States Naval Forces, Europe, Emergency Relocation Site Commander (DNAB) ... CINCUSNAVEUR ERS
Commander-in-Chief, United States Naval Forces, Europe, Intelligence Data-Handling System (DNAB) ... CINCUSNAVEUR IDHS
Commander-in-Chief, United States Navy (SAUS) ... CINCUS
Commander-in-Chief, United States Pacific Command ... USCINCPAC
Commander-in-Chief, United States/Thai Forces ... CINCUSTAF
Commander-in-Chief, US Readiness Command (MCD) ... USCINCREDCOM
Commander-in-Chief, US Transportation Command (SAUS) ... CINCTRANSCOM
Commander-in-Chief, Vietnamese Navy ... CINCVNN
Commander-in-Chief, Western Approaches [*British*] [*World War II*] ... C in C WA
Commander-in-Chief, Western Atlantic Area [*NATO*] ... CINCWESTLANT
Commander-in-Chief, Western Pacific [*World War II*] ... CINCWESPAC
Commander-Instructor [*Navy*] [*British*] ... CI
Commanders Availability Report (CINC) ... CAR
Commander's Control and Monitoring Unit (DNAB) ... CCMU
Commander's Critical Information Requirement [*Army*] (INF) ... CCIR
Commander's Critical Item List [*Army*] (AABC) ... CCIL
Commanders Critical Item List (SAUS) ... CCIL
Commander's Distinguished Visitors [*Program*] [*Air Force*] ... CDV
Commanders Evaluation Report [*Army*] ... CER
Commander's Independent Thermal Viewer [*Military*] (RDA) ... CITV
Commander's Independent Viewer [*Army*] (INF) ... CIV
Commander's Information Network (ACAE) ... CIN
Commander's Integrated Display [*Military*] (RDA) ... CID
Commander's Intelligent Display [*Military*] (RDA) ... CID
Commanders' Internal Management Conference [*Air Force*] ... CIMC
Commanders' Internal Management Review [*Also known as Black Saturday*] [*Military*] (AAG) ... CIMR
Commander's Manual [*Military*] ... CM
Commander's Narrative Analysis [*Military*] ... CNA
Commander's Office Writer [*British military*] (DMA) ... CW
Commanders Operational Intelligence Requirements (MCD) ... COIR
Commander's Operations Security Support System (MCD) ... COSS
Commander's Organization Orientation Program [*Military*] (INF) ... COOP
Commander's Panoramic Sight (ACAE) ... CPS
Commanders Radar Bombing Familiarization (SAUS) ... CRBF
Commanders Research and Development Objective ... CR & DO
Commander's Statement and Budget Summary (AFIT) ... CSBS
Commander's Surveillance and Target Acquisition Information Needs (MCD) ... CSTAIN
Commanders Tactical Terminal (ACAE) ... CTT
Commanders' Target Criteria [*Army*] (ADDR) ... CTC
Commanders Training Management System [*DoD*] ... CTMS
Commander's Weapons Station (MCD) ... CWS
Commanders-in-Chief (SAUO) ... CinCs
Commanders-in-Chief (SAUO) ... CS-in-C
Commanders-in-Chief Committee (SAUO) ... CICC
Commandery of Knights Templar [*Freemasonry*] (ROG) ... CKT
Commandeur de l'Ordre de l'Empire Britannique [*French*] [*Commander of the Order of the British Empire*] (CPGU) ... CBE
Commandeur de l'Ordre du Merite Militaire [*French*] [*Commander of the Order of Military Merit*] (CPGU) ... CMM
Commandeur de l'Ordre Royal de Victoria [*French*] (CPGU) ... CVO
Commanding (ADWA) ... cdg
Commanding (ADWA) ... cmdg
Commanding ... CMDG
Commanding (AFM) ... COMDG
Commanding (WDAA) ... comdg
Commanding (SAUO) ... Comdg
Commanding ... COMMDG
Commanding Air Force (SAUO) ... Comg AF
Commanding Air Officer (SAUS) ... CAO
Commanding Army Audit Agency - Midwestern District ... CAAA-MWD
Commanding Artillery Officer (SAUS) ... CA
Commanding Chain (SAUS) ... CC
Commanding General ... CG
Commanding General ... COMDGEN
Commanding General ... COMGEN
Commanding General, Air Defense Command (NATG) ... CGADC
Commanding General, Aircraft, Fleet Marine Force, Atlantic (SAUS) ... CGAIRFMFLANT
Commanding General, Aircraft Fleet Marine Force, Atlantic (NATG) ... CGAIRFMLANT
Commanding General, Aircraft Fleet Marine Force, Pacific (MUGU) ... CGAIRFMFPAC
Commanding General, American Middle East Theater (SAUS) ... CG/AMET
Commanding General, Army Air Forces (SAUO) ... CG/AAF
Commanding General, Army Air Forces ... CGAAF
Commanding General, Army Forces, Mid-Pacific [*World War II*] ... COMGENAFMIDPAC
Commanding General, Army Ground Forces (SAUO) ... CG/AGF
Commanding General Continental Army Command (SAUO) ... CGCARC
Commanding General, Continental Army Command (NATG) ... CGCONARC
Commanding General, European Command (NATG) ... COMGENEUCOM
Commanding General, Fleet Marine Force (DNAB) ... CGFMF
Commanding General, Fleet Marine Force, Atlantic (NATG) ... CGFMFLANT
Commanding General, Fleet Marine Force, Pacific (MUGU) ... CGFMFPAC
Commanding General, Frankfurt Military Post (SAUS) ... CGFMP
Commanding General, Ground Forces [*World War II*] ... CCGN
Commanding General, India-Burma Theater [*World War II*] ... CGIBT
Commanding General India-Burma Theater (SAUS) ... CGIBT
Commanding General, Lines of Communication (SAUS) ... CGL of C
Commanding General, Marianna and Bonin Islands (SAUS) ... CGMARBO
Commanding General, Marine Aircraft Group ... CGMAG
Commanding General, Marine Aircraft Wing ... CGMAW
Commanding General, Marine Base ... CGMB
Commanding General, Marine Brigade ... CGMARBRIG
Commanding General, Mediterranean Theater of Operations [*World War II*] ... CGMTO
Commanding General, Mediterranean Theater of Operations [*World War II*] ... COMGENMED
Commanding General, Pacific Ocean Areas [*World War II*] ... COMGENPOA
Commanding General, South Pacific Area [*World War II*] ... COMGENSOPAC
Commanding General, Strategic Air Command (NATG) ... CGSAC
Commanding General, Tactical Air Command (NATG) ... CGTAC
Commanding General, Tenth Army ... COMGENTEN
Commanding General, Third Air Division (NATG) ... COMGENTHIRDAIR
Commanding General, Third Marine Air Wing (MUGU) ... CGTHIRDMAW
Commanding General, United States Air Forces, Europe (NATG) ... COMGENUSAFE
Commanding General, United States Armed Forces in Korea (SAUS) ... COMGENUSAFIK
Commanding General United States Armed Forces in Korea (SAUO) ... COMGENUSAFIK
Commanding General, United States Army (SAUS) ... CGUSAR
Commanding General, United States Army Air Defense Command (MUGU) ... CGARADCOM
Commanding General, United States Army Air Defense Command ... CGUSARADCOM
Commanding General, United States Army, Alaska (MUGU) ... CGUSARAL
Commanding General, United States Army Combat Developments Command ... CGUSADC
Commanding General, United States Army Combat Developments Command (MUGU) ... CGUSARCDC
Commanding General, United States Army Communications Zone, Europe (NATG) ... CGUSACOMZEUR
Commanding General, United States Army, Europe (NATG) ... COMGENUSAREUR
Commanding General, United States Army Forces (CINC) ... CGUSARF
Commanding General, United States Army in Alaska (SAUS) ... COMGENUSARAL
Commanding General United States Army in Alaska (SAUO) ... COMGENUSARAL
Commanding General United States Army in the Caribbean Sea Area (SAUO) ... COMGENUSARCARIB
Commanding General, United States Army in the Pacific (SAUS) ... CGUSAR PAC
Commanding General, United States Army Material Command ... CGUSAMC
Commanding General, United States Army Material Command (CINC) ... CGUSARMAC
Commanding General, United States Army Material Command (MUGU) ... CGUSARMC
Commanding General, United States Army, Ryukyu Islands (CINC) ... CGUSARYIS
Commanding General, United States Continental Army Command [*Obsolete*] ... CGUSCONARC
Commanding General, United States Forces, European Theater [*World War II*] ... CGUSFET
Commanding General's Management Information System [*Army*] ... CGMIS
Commanding Officer ... C
Commanding Officer ... CO
Commanding Officer [*Military*] [*British*] (ROG) ... COMDG
Commanding Officer ... COMDG OF
Commanding Officer [*Military slang*] ... KO
Commanding Officer, Air Base (SAUS) ... COAB
Commanding Officer, Air Evacuation Squadron ... COAIREVACRON
Commanding Officer, Area (SAUS) ... COA
Commanding Officer, Area (SAUO) ... COA
Commanding Officer, Atlantic Coast ... COAC
Commanding Officer, Base Command (SAUS) ... CO Ba Com
Commanding Officer, Landing Force Air Support Control Unit ... COLANFORASCU
Commanding Officer, Military Department (SAUS) ... COMILDEP
Commanding Officer, Military Departments (SAUO) ... COMILDEPT
Commanding Officer, Military Police (SAUS) ... COMP

Commanding Officer, Naval Advanced Base .... CONAB
Commanding Officer, Naval Air Base .... CONAB
Commanding Officer, Naval Air Station .... CONAS
Commanding Officer, Naval Air Wing .... CONAIR
Commanding Officer, Naval Divisions [Canada] .... COND
Commanding Officer, Naval Supply Depot (MCD) .... CONSD
Commanding Officer, Observation Squadron .... COOBSRON
Commanding Officer of Commodore Messenger Organisation (SAUS) .... CO CMO
Commanding Officer of Ship (SAUS) .... COS
Commanding Officer of Troops (SAUO) .... COT
Commanding Officer, Pacific Coast [Navy] [Canada] .... COPC
Commanding Officer, Panama Air Defense (SAUO) .... COPAD
Commanding Officer, Port of Embarkation .... COPOE
Commanding Officer, Research Operations Detachment (DNAB) .... CORSCHOPSDET
Commanding Officer Reserve Divisions [World War II] [Canada] .... CORD
Commanding Officer, Reserve Fleet (SAUS) .... CORF
Commanding Officer, Section Base [Navy] .... COSECTBASE
Commanding Officer, Submarine Chaser Training Center .... COSCTRACEN
Commanding Officer, United States Army Radio Station (SAUS) .... COUSARS
Commanding Officer, United States Navy Advanced Base Bremerhaven (SAUS) .... COUNABB
Commanding Officer, United States Ship .... COUSS
Commanding Officer, United States Special Forces (Provisional) (CINC) .... COUSSF(P)
Commanding Officer, US Army Radio Station (SAUO) .... COUSARS
Commanding Officer, US Navy Advanced Base (SAUO) .... COUNAB
Commanding Officers Cabin (SAUS) .... COC
Commanding Officer's Leave Listing (DNAB) .... COLL
Commanding Officer's Narrative Report .... CONAR
Commanding Officers Position Finder (SAUS) .... COPF
Commanding Officer's Punishment (DNAB) .... COP
Commanding Officers Qualifying Course (SAUS) .... COQC
Commanding Officer's Tactical Display System [Navy] (MCD) .... COTDS
Commanding Officer's Tactical Plan [or Plot] [Navy] (NG) .... COTP
Commanding Officer's Wife [Slang] (DNAB) .... COW
Commanding Postmaster (SAUS) .... Comd Ps
Commanding Ribbon (SAUS) .... CR
Commanding Scouting Force (SAUO) .... CSF
Commanding Signal Officer (SAUS) .... CSO
Commando (SAUO) .... Cdo
Commando (NATG) .... CDO
Commando (MILB) .... cdo
Commando (CINC) .... CMDO
Commando (SAUO) .... Cmdo
commando (SAUO) .... comdo
Commando (AFM) .... COMDO
Commando Anticomunista del Sur [Southern Anticommunist Commando] [Guatemala] (PD) .... CADS
Commando Association, Victoria [Australia] .... CAV
Commando Forces, Royal Marines [British] .... CdoFcsRM
Commando Logistics Regiment, Royal Marines [British] .... CdoLogRegtRM
Commando, Marine (SAUS) .... CDO MR
Commando School, Royal Marines (SAUS) .... Cdo Sch R M
Commando School, Royal Marines (SAUO) .... CdoSchRM
Commando Shackle Relay [Intelligence gathering] [Vietnam] (MCD) .... CSR
Commando Training Centre [British] .... CTC
Commando Training Centre, Royal Marines [British military] (DMA) .... CTCRM
Commandos Rouges [Military group] [Chad] (EY) .... Codos
Command/Response [Computer science] .... CR
Commands Interested Have by Mail [Military] (DNAB) .... COINT
Command-Unique (SAUO) .... C-U
Comma-Separated Variable (AAEL) .... CSV
Commelina Virus X [Plant pathology] .... COMVX
Commemorate .... COMMEM
Commemorating .... COMMEMG
Commemoratio Professorum Burdigalensium [of Ausonius] [Classical studies] (OCD) .... Prof Burd
Commemoration (SAUS) .... Com
Commemoration (ADA) .... COM
Commemoration (DSUE) .... COMMEM
Commemorative (SAUS) .... Commem
Commemorative Bucks of Michigan .... CBM
Commemorative Collectors Society [Long Eaton, Nottinghamshire, England] (EAIO) .... CCS
Commemorative Stamp Club [US Postal Service] .... CSC
Commemorative Stamp Posters .... CSP
Commence (ROG) .... COCE
Commence (ROG) .... COMMCE
Commence Exercise [Military] (NVT) .... COMEX
Commencement (ROG) .... COMM
Commencement .... COMMNCMNT
Commencement (ROG) .... COMMT
Commencement (SAUS) .... Commt
Commencement and Termination [British railroad term] .... C and T
Commencement of Deployment Date (SAUO) .... CDAY
Commencement of Rifling (SAUS) .... C of R
Commencement of Rifling (NATG) .... CR
Commencing .... COM'G
Commencing at a Point .... CAP
Commendation (AABC) .... CMD
Commendation List (SAUS) CL
Commendation Ribbon [Military decoration] .... CR
Commendation Ribbon with Medal Pendant [Military decoration] .... CRWMP

Commendation Ribbon with Metal Pendant [Military decoration] .... CRMPT
Comment (MSA) .... CMNT
Comment (AABC) .... CMT
Comment [Legal term] (DLA) .... Com
Comment and Data Integration and Printing (IAA) .... CADIAP
Comment Convention (SAUS) CC
Comment Issue CI
Comment Line (SAUS) CL
Comment Output (SAUS) .... CMO
Comment Recevez-Vous [French] .... CRV
Comment Statement (SAUS) .... CS
Commentaar op het Oude Testament [Kampen] [A publication] (BJA) .... ComOT
Commentaar op het Oude Testament [A publication] (BJA) .... CoOT
Commentaar op het Oude Testament [Kampen] [A publication] (BJA) .... COuT
Commentaire du Nouveau Testament [Neuchatel] [A publication] (BJA) .... CNT
Commentaries on Laws of Scotland [7 eds.] [1800-70] [A publication] (DLA) .... Bell's Comm Bell's
Commentaries upon Littleton, by Sir Edward Coke [A publication] (DLA) .... Co Litt
Commentario Biblico "San Jeronimo" [A publication] (BJA) .... ComBibSJeron
Commentarium pro Religionis et Missionariis [Rome] [A publication] (BJA) .... ComRelMiss
Commentary .... COM
Commentary (WDMC) .... com
Commentary (ROG) .... COME
Commentary .... COMM
Commentary [A publication] (BRI) .... Comt
Commentary [or Pesher on Habakkuk] from Qumran. Cave One (BJA) 1QpHab
Commentary on Hosea from Qumran. Cave One (BJA) 1QpHos
Commentary on the Mishnah [Maimonides] (BJA) .... CM
Commentated Phase Comparison Amplitude Monopulse (ACAE) .... COMPCAMP
Commentationes Humanorum Litterarum [A publication] (BJA) .... CHL
Commentator [MARC relator code] [Library of Congress] (LCCP) .... cmm
Commenti Spirituali dell'Antico Testamento/del Nuovo Testamento [Rome] [A publication] (BJA) .... ComSpirAT/NT
Comments (COE) .... CMTS
Commenwealth (SAUS) .... COM
Commerce [Legal shorthand] (LWAP) .... CMC
Commerce (ABBR) .... CMRC
Commerce .... COM
Commerce (WDAA) .... com
Commerce [or Commercial] .... COMM
Commerce (NTIO) .... comm
Commerce (AAGC) .... Comm
Commerce (ROG) .... COMMCE
Commerce .... COMMRCE
Commerce Acquisition Regulation [Department of Commerce] .... CAR
Commerce Acquisition Regulations (SAUS) .... CAR
Commerce Action Group for the Near East [Terminated, 1981] .... CAGNE
Commerce Administrative Management System (SAUS) .... CAMS
Commerce Administrative Management Systems Implementation Office (SAUS) .... CAMSIO
Commerce and Finance .... C & F
Commerce and Industry (SAUS) .... C&I
Commerce and Industry Association Institute (SAUO) .... CIAI
Commerce and Navigation (SAUS) .... Com&Nav
Commerce Bancorp [NYSE symbol] (SG) .... CBH
Commerce Bancorp [NASDAQ symbol] (TTSB) .... COBA
Commerce Bancorp New Jersey [NYSE symbol] (SAG) .... CBH
Commerce Bancorp New Jersey [Associated Press] (SAG) .... CmcBNJ
Commerce Bancorp New Jersey [NASDAQ symbol] (SAG) .... COBA
Commerce Bancshares [NASDAQ symbol] (TTSB) .... CBSH
Commerce Bancshares, Inc. [NASDAQ symbol] (NQ) .... CBSH
Commerce Bancshares, Inc. [Associated Press] (SAG) .... CmcBMO
Commerce Bank (Harrisburg) [Associated Press] (SAG) .... CmcBHb
Commerce Bank (Harrisburg) [NASDAQ symbol] (SAG) .... COBH
Commerce Bk Harrisburg PA [NASDAQ symbol] (TTSB) .... COBH
Commerce Building Daily [Marine science] (OSRA) .... CBD
Commerce Business Daily [A publication] (AAGC) .... CBD
Commerce City, CO [AM radio station call letters] (RBYB) .... KLDC
Commerce Clearing House (DFIT) .... CCH
Commerce Clearing House (EBF) .... CCh
Commerce Clearing House, Inc. [Publisher] [Chicago, IL] .... CCH
Commerce Clearing House, Washington, DC [Library symbol] [Library of Congress] (LCLS) .... DCCH
Commerce Control List (AAGC) CCL
Commerce Court (DLA) .... Comm Ct
Commerce Department C
Commerce Department .... CD
Commerce Department of the Office of Technical Services (SAUO) .... CDOTS
Commerce Department Procurement Regulations .... COMPR
Commerce Electronic Data Interchange (SAUO) .... COMEDI
Commerce, GA [AM radio station call letters] .... WJJC
Commerce Group [NASDAQ symbol] (TTSB) .... CGCO
Commerce Group Corp. [NASDAQ symbol] (NQ) .... CGCO
Commerce Group, Inc. [NYSE symbol] (SAG) .... CGI
Commerce Group, Inc. [Associated Press] (SAG) .... CmceG
Commerce Group, Inc. [Associated Press] (SAG) .... CmceGp
Commerce International Audio Visual .... CIAV
Commerce International Group Ltd. (SAUO) .... CIG
Commerce, Labor, Industry Corporation of Kings County (SAUO) .... CLICK
Commerce Laboratory [NASA] .... COMLAB
Commerce One [NASDAQ symbol] (SG) .... CMRC
Commerce Performance Review (SAUS) .... CPR
Commerce Procurement Data System [Marine science] (OSRA) .... CPDS

Commerce Productivity Center ... CPC
Commerce, Science, and Transportation (DLA) ... CST
Commerce Service Provider ... CSP
Commerce Solution Provider ... CSP
Commerce Technical Advisory Board [*Terminated, 1981*] [*Department of Commerce*] (EGAO) ... CTAB
Commerce Total Return Fund, Inc. (MHDW) ... CTO
Commerce, TX [*FM radio station call letters*] ... KEMM
Commerce, TX [*FM radio station call letters*] ... KETR
Commercial [*FCC*] (NTCM) ... C
Commercial [*Rate*] [*Value of the English pound*] ... CM
Commercial ... CML
Commercial (WDMC) ... cml
Commercial (SAUS) ... Cml
Commercial (SAUS) ... Cmrc
Commercial (ABBR) ... CMRCL
Commercial ... CO
Commercial (ROG) ... COM
Commercial ... com
Commercial (AFM) ... COML
Commercial (EBF) ... coml
Commercial (TBD) ... Coml
Commercial (ADWA) ... comm
Commercial (AAGC) ... Comm
Commercial (WDMC) ... comml
Commercial (ROG) ... COMML
Commercial ... COMRCL
Commercial Activities ... CA
Commercial Activities Management Information System (AAGC) ... CAMIS
Commercial Activities Program (AAGC) ... CAP
Commercial Activities Program Detachment [*Military*] (DNAB) ... CAPDET
Commercial Activities Program Detachment Regional Office [*Military*] (DNAB) ... CAPDETREGOFF
Commercial Ada Development Environment (SAUO) ... CADE
Commercial Advance Design [*Reports*] (MCD) ... CAD
Commercial Advanced Gas-Cooled Reactor (NUCP) ... CAGR
Commercial Advocacy Group (ACAE) ... CAG
Commercial Agent ... CA
Commercial Air ... CA
Commercial Air (NOAA) ... COMAIR
Commercial Air Freight Movement ... CAFM
Commercial Air Movement ... CAM
Commercial Air Services (SAUO) ... CAS
Commercial Air Transport (DA) ... CAT
Commercial Aircraft Requirements Committee (SAUO) ... CARC
Commercial Airlift Contract (SAUS) ... CAT
Commercial Airlift Review Board [*DOD*] (AAGC) ... CARB
Commercial Airplane Group (ACAE) ... CAG
Commercial Airways Ltd. [*South Africa*] [*FAA designator*] (FAAC) ... CAW
Commercial and Allied Workers' Union [*Somali Republic*] ... CAWU
Commercial and General Workers Union (SAUO) ... CGWU
Commercial and Government Entity (MCD) ... CAGE
Commercial and Industrial (GFGA) ... C & I
Commercial and Industrial Bulletin [*Ghana*] [*A publication*] (DLA) ... CIB
Commercial and Industrial-Type Activity (AABC) ... CITA
Commercial and Industrial-Type Functions [*Army*] (MCD) ... CITF
Commercial and Legal Reporter [*A publication*] (DLA) ... Com & Leg Rep
Commercial and Municipal Law Reporter [*A publication*] (DLA) ... Com & Mun L Rep
Commercial Announcement (NTCM) ... CA
Commercial Arbitration Centre [*Northern Territory*] [*Australia*] ... CAC
Commercial Art Program [*Association of Independent Colleges and Schools specialization code*] ... CA
Commercial Artists' Guild ... CAG
Commercial Asset Funding Company ... CAFCO
Commercial Assets [*AMEX symbol*] (SPSG) ... CAX
Commercial Assets, Inc. [*Associated Press*] (SAG) ... CmclAst
Commercial Assets Mobilization [*Navy*] (DOMA) ... CAM
Commercial Atomic Power Activities (SAUO) ... CAPA
Commercial Atomic Power Activity (SAUS) ... CAPA
Commercial Automatic Programming (SAUS) ... CAP
Commercial, Automatic Test System [*Military*] ... CATE
Commercial Automation Support of Technical Services (SAUS) ... CASTS
Commercial Aviation (IAA) ... CA
Commercial Aviation Association (SAUO) ... CAA
Commercial Aviation Association of South Africa (SAUO) ... CAASA
Commercial Aviation Sensing Humidity program (SAUS) ... CASH
Commercial Aviation Sensing of Humidity (SAUS) ... CASH
Commercial Aviation Systems (SAUO) ... CAS
Commercial Aviation Systems-Sensor Products Operation (SAUO) ... CAS-SPO
Commercial Bancshares [*NASDAQ symbol*] (TTSB) ... CLBK
Commercial Bancshares, Inc. [*AMEX symbol*] (SAG) ... CWV
Commercial Bank (ROG) ... C
Commercial Bank ... CB
Commercial Bank Address File [*IRS*] ... CBAF
Commercial Bank of Australia ... CBA
Commercial Bank of Australia (SAUO) ... CBA
Commercial Bank of Ethiopia. Market Report [*A publication*] ... CBEMR
Commercial Bank of Korea ... CBK
Commercial Bank of New York [*NASDAQ symbol*] (SAG) ... CBNY
Commercial Bank of New York [*Associated Press*] (SAG) ... CmcBNY
Commercial Banking Co. of Sydney [*Australia*] ... CBC
Commercial Bankshares, Inc. [*NASDAQ symbol*] (SAG) ... CLBK
Commercial Bankshares, Inc. [*Associated Press*] (SAG) ... CmclBsh
Commercial BASIC ... C-BASIC
Commercial Beginners All Purpose Symbolic Instruction Code [*Computer science*] (VERA) ... CBASIC
Commercial Best Practices Laboratory [*Army*] ... Comm BPL
Commercial Bill of Lading [*Shipping*] ... CBL
Commercial Bill of Lading [*Shipping*] (DNAB) ... CMBL
Commercial Bill of Landing (SAUS) ... CBL
Commercial Blanket Bond [*Insurance*] ... CBB
Commercial Breeder Reactor ... CBR
Commercial Building Energy Efficiency Program [*Australia*] ... CBEEP
Commercial Business (SAUS) ... COM
Commercial Business Management System (SAUS) ... CBMS
Commercial Cable Co. (MHDW) ... CC
Commercial Cable Co. ... COMCABCO
Commercial Cane Sugar ... CCS
Commercial Carrier ... CC
Commercial Cases [*1896-1941*] [*England*] [*A publication*] (DLA) ... Com Cas
Commercial Cases, Small Cause Court [*1851-60*] [*Bengal, India*] [*A publication*] (DLA) ... Com Cas SCC
Commercial Cases, Small Cause Court [*1851-60*] [*Bengal, India*] [*A publication*] (DLA) ... Rep Com Cas
Commercial Cases, Small Cause Court (SAUS) ... Rep Com Cas
Commercial Casualty Products [*Insurance*] ... CCP
Commercial Casualty Underwriting [*Insurance*] ... CCU
Commercial Change Proposal (MCD) ... CCP
Commercial Chemical Development Association [*Later, CDA*] (EA) ... CCDA
Commercial Code (DLA) ... Com C
Commercial Code (DLA) ... Comm C
Commercial Colour Development Ltd. (SAUO) ... CCD
Commercial Commodity Acquisition Program [*DoD*] (RDA) ... CCAP
Commercial Communications Satellite [*Japan*] ... CCS
Commercial Communications Work Order [*Air Force*] ... CCWO
Commercial Computer (SAUS) ... CC
Commercial Computer Documentation Set (MCD) ... CCDS
Commercial Computer Security Center [*British*] ... CCSC
Commercial COMSEC [*Communications Security*] **Endorsement Program** [*NASA*] ... CCEP
Commercial Construction and Selected Materials Handling Equipment (RDA) ... CCE/SMHE
Commercial Construction Equipment [*Plan*] [*Army*] ... CCE
Commercial Construction Equipment and Military Adaptation of Commercial Items (MCD) ... CCE/MACI
Commercial Consumables (CINC) ... CC
Commercial Continuity [*Broadcasting*] (NTCM) ... CC
Commercial Contract Change ... CCC
Commercial Contracting Officer ... CCO
Commercial Contractor-Furnished Equipment (AAG) ... CCFE
Commercial Credit Co. (SAUO) ... CC
Commercial Credit Co. (SAUO) ... Commercial
Commercial Credit Company (SAUO) ... CCC
Commercial Credit Corp. (MHDW) ... CCC
Commercial Customer-Furnished Equipment ... CCFE
Commercial Cut Flower Growers' Association of New South Wales [*Australia*] ... CCFGANSW
Commercial Data Management System [*Computer science*] (PDAA) ... CDMS
Commercial Data Masking Facility (SAUS) ... CDMF
Commercial Data Processing Center (IEEE) ... CDPC
Commercial Database Machine (SAUS) ... CDM
Commercial Demonstration Fast Reactor ... CDFR
Commercial Dental Laboratories of Indiana (SRA) ... CDLI
Commercial Development Association (EA) ... CDA
Commercial Dock [*Shipping*] ... CD
Commercial Driver's License ... CDL
Commercial Driver's License Information System [*FHWA*] (TAG) ... CDLIS
Commercial Driver's License Information System ... CDLS
Commercial Earth Station ... CES
Commercial Egg Producers' Association [*Australia*] ... CEPA
Commercial Electronic Equipment [*Military*] ... CEE
Commercial Engineer ... CE
Commercial Enterprise ... CE
Commercial Equipment ... CE
Commercial Equipment Requirement List ... CERL
Commercial Equivalent Equipment ... CEE
Commercial Exchange of Philadelphia [*Defunct*] (EA) ... CEP
Commercial Experiment Transporter [*BTS*] (TAG) ... COMET
Commercial Fast Reactor [*British*] ... CFR
Commercial Federal [*NYSE symbol*] (TTSB) ... CFB
Commercial Federal Corp. [*NYSE symbol*] (SAG) ... CFB
Commercial Federal Corp. [*Associated Press*] (SAG) ... CmcFdl
Commercial Finance (EBF) ... CF
Commercial Finance Association (NTPA) ... CFA
Commercial Finance Company [*Generic term*] ... CFC
Commercial Financial Corp. Ltd. [*Toronto Stock Exchange symbol*] ... CMF
Commercial Financial Services Inc. ... CFS
Commercial Fisheries Research and Development Act ... CFRDA
Commercial Fisheries Review (journ.) (SAUS) ... Commer Fish Rev
Commercial Fishing [*Type of water project*] ... CMF
Commercial Fishing Advisory Council (SAUS) ... CFAC
Commercial Food Equipment Service Agencies of America (SAUO) ... CFESA
Commercial Food Equipment Service Association (EA) ... CFESA
Commercial General Liability [*Insurance*] ... CGL
Commercial Generic Bioprocessing Apparatus (SPST) ... CGBA
Commercial Ground (IAA) ... CG
Commercial Ground High (IAA) ... CGH
Commercial High Level Waste [*Nuclear energy*] (NUCP) ... CHLW
Commercial Import Division [*Vietnam*] ... CID

Commercial Import Program .... CIP
Commercial Industrial Contract System (SAUO) .... CICS
Commercial Industrial Marine [*Automotive engineering*] .... CIM
Commercial Industrial Services Program [*Navy*] .... CIS
Commercial Industrial Trade Receivables .... CIESCO
Commercial Information Management System [*Department of Commerce*] .... CIMS
Commercial Instruction Processor [*Honeywell, Inc.*] .... CIP
Commercial Instruction Set .... CIS
Commercial Instrument Landing CIL
Commercial Instruments Conference (SAUO) CIC
Commercial Interest Reference Rate (RIMS) .... CIRR
Commercial International Corp. (EFIS) CIC
Commercial Internet Exchange .... CIE
Commercial Internet Exchange (PCM) CIX
Commercial Internet Exchange Association (SAUO) CIX
Commercial Internet Exchange Association (NTPA) .... CIXA
Commercial Intertech [*NYSE symbol*] (SAG) .... TEC
Commercial Intertech Corp. [*Associated Press*] (SAG) .... CmlTek
Commercial Investment Real Estate Journal [*Commercial-Investment Real Estate Council*] [*A publication*] .... CIREJ
Commercial Invoice (DS) .... Com/I
Commercial Invoice (SAUS) .... Coml
Commercial Item Description .... CID
Commercial Item Drawing (MCD) .... CID
Commercial Item Support Program [*DoD*] (RDA) .... CISP
Commercial Land Resource Information Group (SAUO) .... CLRIG
Commercial Language (HGAA) .... COML
Commercial Law [*Canada*] (DLA) .... Com L
Commercial Law (DLA) .... Com Law
Commercial Law Annual [*A publication*] (DLA) .... Com LA
Commercial Law Annual [*A publication*] (DLA) .... Com Law Ann
Commercial Law Association of Australia. Bulletin [*A publication*] .... CLAAB
Commercial Law Association of Australia. Bulletin [*A publication*] .... CLAA Bulletin
Commercial Law Bulletin [*Commercial Law League of America*] [*A publication*] .... CLB
Commercial Law Journal [*Commercial Law League of America*] [*A publication*] .... CLJ
Commercial Law League. Journal [*A publication*] (DLA) .... Com L League J
Commercial Law League of America [*Chicago, IL*] (EA) .... CLLA
Commercial Law Quarterly [*Australia*] [*A publication*] .... CLQ
Commercial Law Quarterly [*A publication*] .... Com LQ
Commercial Law Quarterly [*Australia*] [*A publication*] .... Comm LQ
Commercial Law Reports [*Canada*] [*A publication*] (DLA) .... Comm LR
Commercial Laws of the World [*A publication*] (DLA) .... CLW
Commercial Lending Newsletter [*Robert Morris Associates (National Association of Bank Loan and Credit Offices)*] [*A publication*] .... CLN
Commercial Liability Insurance [*International Risk Management Institute*] [*A publication*] CLI
Commercial Licensed Evaluation Facilities (SAUO) .... CLEF
Commercial Licensed Evaluation Facilities [*British*] .... CLEFS
Commercial Loan (EBF) CL
Commercial Loan Insurance Corp. CLIC
Commercial Loan System (SAUS) .... CLS
Commercial Mail Relay .... CMR
Commercial Manager (DCTA) .... CM
Commercial Manual [*DoD*] .... CM
Commercial Mariculture Council of Queensland [*Australia*] .... CMCQ
Commercial Market Appraisal .... CMA
Commercial Marketing Assistance International (SAUS) .... CMA INTL
Commercial Marketing Representative (AAGC) .... CMR
Commercial Materials Processing Laboratory (SPST) .... CMPL
Commercial Measuring Equipment (SAA) .... CME
Commercial Metals [*NYSE symbol*] (TTSB) .... CMC
Commercial Metals Co. [*NYSE symbol*] (SPSG) .... CMC
Commercial Metals Co. [*Associated Press*] (SAG) .... CmclMtl
Commercial Microwave Landing System Avionics (SAUS) .... CMLSA
Commercial Mission [*NASA*] .... COMM
Commercial Mobile Radio Service (OTD) .... CMRS
Commercial Mortgage Insurance, Inc. (EFIS) .... CMI
Commercial Motor Vehicle (ADA) .... CMV
Commercial Motor Vehicle Safety Act [*1986*] .... CMVSA
Commercial Multi-Engine [*Aviation*] (AIA) .... CME
Commercial Multi-Peril [*Insurance*] .... CMP
Commercial Museum, Philadelphia, PA [*Library symbol*] [*Library of Congress*] [*Obsolete*] (LCLS) .... PPComm
Commercial Net Lease Realty, Inc. [*Associated Press*] (SAG) .... CmclNL
Commercial Net Lease Realty, Inc. [*NYSE symbol*] (SAG) .... NNN
Commercial Net Lease Rlty [*NYSE symbol*] (TTSB) .... NNN
Commercial Nondevelopment Items [*Military*] (AABC) .... CNDI
Commercial Nondevelopment Items of Law Enforcement Equipment (MCD) .... CNDI-LEE
Commercial Nuclear Fuel Plant (NRCH) .... CNFP
Commercial Off the Shelf/Nondevelopmental Items .... COTS/NDI
Commercial Office of Spain (EA) .... COS
Commercial Off-the-Shelf [*Software*] .... COTS
Commercial Oil & Gas Ltd. [*Toronto Stock Exchange symbol*] .... CMO
Commercial Operating and Support Savings Initiative .... COSSI
Commercial Operating System (IAA) .... COS
Commercial Operation and Maintenance Manual [*Military*] .... COMM
Commercial Operational Requirements Document [*Military*] .... CORD
Commercial Operations and Support Savings Initiative [*Army*] .... COSSI
Commercial Operator License Examination Manager [*Telecommunications*] (OTD) .... COLEM
Commercial or Industrial and Control Service Data System .... CICS
Commercial or Industrial-Type Activities (AAGC) .... CITA
Commercial Orchid Growers' and Exporters' Association [*Australia*] .... COGEAA
Commercial Original Equipment Manufacturer (SAUS) .... COEM
Commercial Paper (EBF) .... Com'l Paper
Commercial Paper [*Banking*] (MHDW) .... Com'l Ppr
Commercial Paper [*Banking*] .... CP
Commercial Paper Note [*Banking*] .... CPN
Commercial Passenger Fishing Vessel .... CPFV
Commercial Performance Index (MHDW) .... CPI
Commercial Pilot's Licence [*British*] (DBQ) .... CPL
Commercial Plane (ACAE) .... CP
Commercial Practices Program [*Air Force*] .... CPP
Commercial Price List (SAUO) .... CPL
Commercial Printing and Publishing (SAUS) .... CPP
Commercial Printing Co., Trenton, NJ [*Library symbol*] [*Library of Congress*] (LCLS) .... NjTCP
Commercial Processing Workload (SAUS) .... CPW
Commercial Product Acquisition Team (EA) .... COMPACT
Commercial Product Acquisition Team [*Later, COMPACT*] [*An association*] [*Defunct*] (EA) .... CPAT
Commercial Product Development .... CPD
Commercial Production of Electronic Solid State Systems (MCD) .... COMPRESS
Commercial Products List (AFIT) .... CPL
Commercial Program Development .... CPD
Commercial Projected Window [*Technical drawings*] .... CPW
Commercial Property Coverage [*Insurance*] .... CPC
Commercial Property Products .... CPP
Commercial Property Underwriting [*Insurance*] .... CPU
Commercial Protein Crystal Growth (SAUS) .... CPCG
Commercial Quality .... CQ
Commercial Rabbit Association [*British*] (BI) .... CRA
Commercial Radio .... CR
Commercial Radio International Committee (SAUO) .... CRIC
Commercial Readinessor Commercially Ready (SAUS) .... CR
Commercial Receiver Test Program .... CRTP
Commercial Reference Room (SAUO) .... CRR
Commercial Refrigerator Incubator Module (SAUS) .... CRIM
Commercial Refrigerator Manufacturers Association (EA) .... CRMA
Commercial Relations and Exporters (SAUO) .... CRE
Commercial Relations and Exports (DS) .... CRE
Commercial Satellite Communications System .... COMSATCOM
Commercial Satellite Systems [*Berkeley, CA*] [*Telecommunications*] (TSSD) .... CSS
Commercial Satellite Terminal (CCCA) .... CST
Commercial Service Area [*Military*] (AFM) .... CSA
Commercial Service Authorization [*Military*] .... CSA
Commercial Service Provider (SAUO) .... CSP
Commercial Services Group, New South Wales [*Australia*] .... CSGNSW
Commercial Sex Worker [*Social science terminology for a prostitute*] .... CSW
Commercial Solvents Corp. .... CSC
Commercial Solvents Corp., Terre Haute, IN [*Library symbol*] [*Library of Congress*] [*Obsolete*] (LCLS) .... InTCS
Commercial Source Language (SAUS) .... CSL
Commercial Sovents Corporation (SAUO) CV
Commercial Space Centers .... CSC
Commercial Space Launch Act .... CSLA
Commercial Space Package .... CSP
Commercial Space Transportation Advisory Committee [*Department of Transportation*] [*Washington, DC*] (EGAO) .... COMSTAC
Commercial Spares Release .... CSR
Commercial Spent Fuel Management (ABAC) .... CSFM
Commercial Standard [*A publication*] .... CS
Commercial Steamship Company .... CSC
Commercial Subroutine Package [*IBM Corp.*] (BUR) .... CSP
Commercial Subsurface Transformer (IAA) .... CST
Commercial Synchronous Communication Satellite (NASA) .... CSCSAT
Commercial System [*Data General Corp.*] .... CS
Commercial Systems Division (ACAE) .... CSD
Commercial Technology and Industrial Base (AAGC) .... CTIB
Commercial Technology Integration Program .... CTIP
Commercial Telecommunications Corp. (SAUO) .... COMTEL
Commercial Telecommunications Network (SAUO) .... CTN
Commercial Telegraphers' Union [*Later, C/UBC*] (EA) .... CTU
Commercial Telegraphers Union (HGAA) .... CTUNA
Commercial Teleoperator Maneuvering System (SSD) .... CTMS
Commercial Television [*FCC*] (NTCM) .... CT
Commercial Television .... CTV
Commercial Test Equipment (MCD) .... CTE
Commercial Testing & Engineering (EFIS) .... CT&E
Commercial Text-Books [*A publication*] .... CTB
Commercial Traffic Bulletin .... CTB
Commercial Trailer Association [*British*] .... CTA
Commercial Trailer-Mounted Generator Set Assembly .... CTMGSA
Commercial Training Device .... CTD
Commercial Training Device Requirement .... CTDR
Commercial Transaction System [*Business term*] (MHDB) .... CTS
Commercial Translation (or Translator) (SAUS) .... COMTRAN
Commercial Translator (IEEE) .... CT
Commercial Transport Navigation Display System .... CTNDS
Commercial Transportation Officer .... CTO
Commercial Traveler .... CT
Commercial Travelers Insurance Federation [*Defunct*] .... CTIF
Commercial Travellers and Sales Representatives' Guild of Western Australia .... CTSRGWA
Commercial Travellers Association (SAUO) .... CTA

Commercial Travellers' Association of Queensland [*Australia*] .... CTAQ
Commercial Travellers' Association of Western Australia .... CTAWA
Commercial Tribunal [*South Australia*] .... CT
Commercial Tribunal, New South Wales [*Australia*] .... CTNSW
Commercial Tribunal of Western Australia .... CTWA
Commercial Truck Maintenance Association (MHDB) .... CTMA
Commercial Type Property .... CTP
Commercial Union Assurance Co. Ltd. [*British*] (ECON) .... CU
Commercial Union Assurance Company of Australia Ltd. .... CUA
Commercial Users Program for Index Data (PDAA) .... CUPID
Commercial Utilisation Area .... CUA
Commercial Utility Cargo Vehicle [*Army*] (RDA) .... CUCV
Commercial Utility Vehicle .... CUV
Commercial Value CV
Commercial Value Movement Order (DCTA) .... CVMO
Commercial Vehicle [*Automotive engineering*] CV
Commercial Vehicle and Road Transport Club [*British*] (BI) .... CVRTC
Commercial Vehicle Industry Association of South Australia .... CVIASA
Commercial Vehicle Industry Association of Victoria [*Australia*] .... CVIAV
Commercial Vehicle Information System and Network .... CVISN
Commercial Vehicle Maintenance Implications (MCD) .... CVMI
Commercial Vehicle Manufacturers' Association [*Australia*] .... CVMA
Commercial Vehicle Operations [*Highway safety*] .... CVO
Commercial Vehicle Repair Parts (MCD) .... CVRP
Commercial Vehicle Safety Alliance [*FHWA*] [*RSPA*] (TAG) .... CVSA
Commercial Vehicle Substitute .... C/S
Commercial Warehouse Field Officer [*Military*] .... CWFO
Commercial Waste and Spent Fuel Packaging Program (SAUS) .... CWSFPP
Commercial Waste Management Statement (ABAC) .... CWMS
Commercial Water Movement Number .... CWM
Commercial Weather Services Association (NTPA) .... CWSA
Commercial Weight .... CW
Commercial Weight (SAUS) .... CW
Commercial Wire Center Forecast Program [*Telecommunications*] (TEL) .... COMFOR
Commercial Zone (BARN) .... cmmz
Commercial Zone (SAUS) .... C Zone
Commercial-Accounts Receivable Management System (PDAA) .... C-ARMS
Commercial/Industrial Activities & Contract Services (SAUO) .... CICS
Commercial-Investment Real Estate Council (EA) .... CIREC
Commercial-Investment Real Estate Institute (NTPA) .... CIREI
Commercialism (ABBR) .... CMRCLSM
Commercialist (ABBR) .... CMRCLST
Commercialistic (ABBR) .... CMRCLSTC
Commercialization Model for Environmental Technologies (ABAC) .... ComMet
Commercialize (ABBR) .... CMRCLZ
Commercialized (ABBR) .... CMRCLZD
Commercializing (ABBR) .... CMRCLZG
Commercially Available (DNAB) .... CA
Commercially Available Organic Chemicals Index [*Chemical Notation Association*] [*Databank*] [*British*] .... CAOCI
Commercially Available/Fabricated Training Device .... CAFTD
Commercially Available/Fabricated Training Device Requirement .... CAFTDR
Commercially Available/Fabricated Training Device Requirement .... CAFTR
Commercially Developed Space Facility [*Proposed*] .... CDSF
Commercially Important Person .... CIP
Commercially Owned, Commercially Operated (AFIT) .... COCO
Commercially Owned, Government-Operated (AFIT) .... COGO
Commercial/Military Spares Release (MCD) .... CMSR
Commercial-off-the-shelf Affordable Near-term (SAUS) .... CANDO
Commercial-Type Product (AAGC) .... CIP
Commerical Bank of Wales [*British*] .... CBW
Commerical Control (SAA) CC
Commericial Air Services (Pty) Ltd. [*South Africa*] [*ICAO designator*] (FAAC) .... CAW
Commingled Real Estate Funds (MHDW) .... CREF
Commiserate (ABBR) .... CMSRA
Commiserated (ABBR) .... CMSRAD
Commiserating (ABBR) .... CMSRAG
Commiseration (ABBR) .... CMSRAN
Commiserative (ABBR) .... CMSRAV
Commiseratively (ABBR) .... CMSRAVY
Commiserator (ABBR) .... CMSRAR
Commision on Opticianry Accreditation (EA) .... COA
Commisioner of Metropolitan Police (BARN) .... CMP
Commissar (ABBR) .... CMSAR
Commissar (ABBR) .... CMSR
Commissar .... COMR
Commissariat .... COMRT
Commissariat a l'Energie Atomique [*Atomic Energy Commission - AEC*] [*France*] [*Research center*] .... CEA
Commissariat and Transport Corps [*British military*] (DMA) .... CTC
Commissariat for Montagnard Affairs .... CMA
Commissariat Staff Corps [*British military*] (DMA) .... CSC
Commissary [*Marine Corps*] C
Commissary (ABBR) .... CMSARY
Commissary (ABBR) .... CMSRY
Commissary .... COM
Commissary (ADA) .... COMM
Commissary .... COMMY
Commissary (SAUS) .... Commy
Commissary (SAUO) .... Comsry
Commissary .... COMSRY
Commissary [*Air Force*] (AFM) .... COMSY
commissary (SAUO) .... comsy
Commissary Accounting and Reporting System [*Army*] .... CARP
Commissary Accounting and Reporting System [*Army*] .... CARS
Commissary Automated Management Network [*Military*] (MUSM) .... CAMNET
Commissary Civilian Career Enhancement Program [*Air Force*] .... CCCEP
Commissary General (SAUO) .... CG
Commissary General (SAUS) .... CG
commissary general (SAUO) .... comgen
Commissary General of Subsistence (SAUO) .... CGS
Commissary Management Information system (SAUO) .... CMIS
Commissary of Subsistence [*Military*] [*British*] (HGAA) .... Com Sub
Commissary of Subsistence (SAUO) .... COS
Commissary of Subsistence (SAUO) .... CS
Commissary of Subsistence [*Military*] [*British*] (ROG) .... CS
Commissary Operating Manual (AABC) .... COM
Commissary Operating Program [*Air Force*] (AFM) .... COP
Commissary Privilege Card [*DoD*] .... CPC
Commissary Resale Division of the Army Stock Fund (AABC) .... CORDASF
Commissary Store [*Military*] (DNAB) .... COMSYSTO
Commissary Store [*Army*] (AABC) .... COMSYSTR
Commissary Store [*Navy*] .... CS
Commissary Store Region [*Military*] (DNAB) .... COMSYSTOREG
Commissary Store Region Detachment [*Military*] (DNAB) .... COMSYSTOREGDET
Commissary Store Reserve Fund [*Military*] (DNAB) .... CSRF
Commissary Store Reserve Fund Grant [*Military*] (DNAB) .... CSRFG
Commissary Technician, Medical .... CMT
Commissary-General [*British military*] (DMA) .... Com-Gen
Commissary-General of Subsistence [*Army*] [*British*] .... CGS
Commissaryman [*Navy rating*] .... CS
Commissaryman, First Class [*Navy rating*] CS1
Commissaryman, Master Chief [*Navy rating*] .... CSCM
Commissaryman, Second Class [*Navy rating*] CS2
Commissaryman, Ships Butcher (SAUS) .... CSB
Commissaryman, Third Class [*Navy rating*] CS3
Commissie voor Bibliografie en Documentatie [*Netherlands Bibliographical and Documentary Committee*] [*Information service or system*] (IID) .... COBIDOC
Commissie voor Internationaal Recht [*United Nations*] .... CIR
Commission [*Business term*] .... Cmm
Commission .... CMMN
Commission (DNAB) .... CMN
Commission (FAAC) .... CMSN
Commission (TBD) .... Cmsn
Commission (ABBR) .... CMSSN
Commission (SAUS) .... Co
Commission (SAUS) .... Com
Commission (GEOI) .... Com
Commission [*or Commissioner*] (AABC) .... COM
Commission (KSC) .... COMM
Commission (DD) .... comm
Commission (CMD) .... Comm
Commission (DLA) .... Commiss
Commission .... COMMN
Commission (PROS) .... commn
Commission .... COMMSN
Commission .... COMN
Commission (AFM) .... COMSN
Commission [*French*] [*Business term*] .... Con
Commission .... SOMM
Commission Africaine de l'Aviation Civile [*African Civil Aviation Commission - AFCAC*] (EAIO) .... CAFAC
Commission Against Discrimination (SAUO) .... CAD
Commission and Exchange (SAUS) .... C&E
Commission and Expenses (SAUS) .... Com&Exp
Commission and Warrant [*British military*] (DMA) .... CW
Commission Canadienne de l'Annee Internationale de l'Enfant [*Canadian Commission for the International Year of the Child*] .... CCAIE
Commission Canadienne de Pedologie [*National Soil Survey Committee*] [*Canadian Department of Agriculture*] .... CCP
Commission Canadienne des Droits de la Personne [*Canadian Human Rights Commission - CHRC*] .... CCDP
Commission Canadienne des Grains [*Canadian Grain Commission*] .... CCG
Commission Canadienne du Ble [*Canadian Wheat Board - CWB*] .... CCB
Commission Canadienne du Lait [*Canadian Dairy Commission - CDC*] CCL
Commission Canadienne pour la Theorie des Machines et des Mecanismes [*Canadian Committee for the Theory of Machines & Mechanisms*] (AC) .... CCTMM
Commission Centrale pour la Navigation du Rhin [*Central Commission for the Navigation of the Rhine*] .... CCR
Commission Certified [*Bacteriology*] CC
Commission d'Appel de l'Immigration [*Immigration Appeal Board - IAB*] [*Canada*] .... CAI
Commission de Controle de l'Energie Atomique [*Atomic Energy Control Board - AECB*] .... CCEA
Commission de Cooperation Technique en Afrique [*Commission for Technical Cooperation in Africa*] .... CCTA
Commission de la Carte Geologique du Monde [*Commission for the Geological Map of the World - GMW*] (EAIO) .... CCGM
Commission de la Fonction Publique du Canada [*Public Service Commission - PSC*] [*Canada*] .... CFPC
Commission de la Sante et de la Securite du Travail du Quebec [*Quebec Workers Health and Security Commission*] [*Montreal*] [*Information service or system*] (IID) .... CSST
Commission de la Sante et de la Securite du Travail du Quebec, Montreal [*Library symbol*] [*National Library of Canada*] (NLC) .... QMCAT
Commission de la Sante et de la Securite du Travail du Quebec, Quebec, Quebec [*Library symbol*] [*National Library of Canada*] (NLC) .... QQCAT

Commission de l'Acces a l'Information, Centre de Documentation, Quebec, PQ, Canada [*Library symbol*] [*Library of Congress*] (LCLS) .... CaQQCAI
Commission de l'Enseignement Superieur des Provinces Maritimes [*Maritime Provinces Higher Education Commission*] [*Canada*] .... CESPM
Commission de Paris [*Paris Commission - PARCOM*] (EAIO) .... CP
Commission de Police du Quebec, Ste.-Foy, PQ, Canada [*Library symbol*] [*Library of Congress*] (LCLS) .... CaQSFCP
Commission de Police du Quebec, Ste.-Foy, Quebec [*Library symbol*] [*National Library of Canada*] (NLC) .... QSFCP
Commission de Representants Permanents [*Committee of Permanent Representatives*] [*EEC*] .... COREPER
Commission de Toponymie du Quebec, Quebec, Quebec [*Library symbol*] [*National Library of Canada*] (NLC) .... QQCT
Commission de Toponymie, Quebec, PQ, Canada [*Library symbol*] [*Library of Congress*] (LCLS) .... CaQQCT
Commission de Transport de la Communaute Urbaine de Montreal, Montreal, PQ, Canada [*Library symbol*] [*Library of Congress*] (LCLS) .... CaQMCT
Commission de Transport de la Communaute Urbaine de Montreal, Quebec [*Library symbol*] [*National Library of Canada*] (NLC) .... QMCT
Commission d'Enquete pour le Crime Organise [*Organized Crime Investigating Commission*] [*Canada*] .... CECO
Commission des Accidents du Travail, Montreal, PQ, Canada [*Library symbol*] [*Library of Congress*] (LCLS) .... CaQMCAT
Commission des Champs de Bataille Nationaux [*National Battlefields Commission - NBC*] [*Canada*] .... CCBN
Commission des Communautes Europeennes [*Commission of the European Communities - CEC*] [*Belgium*] (EAIO) .... CCE
Commission des Droits de la Personne du Quebec, Montreal, Quebec [*Library symbol*] [*National Library of Canada*] (NLC) .... QMQDP
Commission des Droits de la Personne du Quebec, Quebec, Quebec [*Library symbol*] [*National Library of Canada*] (NLC) .... QQCDP
Commission des Episcopats de la Communaute Europeenne [*Association of Episcopacies of the European Community*] (EA) .... COMECE
Commission des Federations et Syndicats Nationaux des Entreprises de Recuperation de Ferrailles du Marche Commun [*Committee of the National Ferrous Scrap Federations and Associations of the Common Market - CNFSFACM*] (EAIO) .... COFENAF
Commission des Instruments et des Methodes d'Observation [*Commission for Instruments and Methods of Observation*] [*OMI*] .... CIMO
Commission des Nations Unies pour l'Inde et le Pakistan .... CNUIP
Commission des Nations Unies pour l'Unification et le Relevement de la Coree .... CNUURC
Commission des Operations de Bourse .... COB
Commission des Relations de Travail dans la Fonction Publique [*Public Service Staff Relations Board - PSSRB*] [*Canada*] .... CRTFP
Commission des Reparations [*Reparation Commission*] [*France*] .... CDR
Commission des Services Juridiques du Quebec, Montreal, Quebec [*Library symbol*] [*National Library of Canada*] (NLC) .... QMJSJ
Commission des Valeurs Mobilieres de Quebec, Quebec, PQ, Canada [*Library symbol*] [*Library of Congress*] (LCLS) .... CaQMCVM
Commission des Valeurs Mobilieres du Quebec, Montreal, Quebec [*Library symbol*] [*National Library of Canada*] (NLC) .... QMCVM
Commission d'Histoire de l'Historiographie [*Commission of the History of Historiography*] [*Ceret, France*] (EAIO) .... CHH
Commission du Codex Alimentarius [*Joint FAO-WHO Codex Alimentarius Commission*] (EA) .... CAC
Commission du Commerce International des Produits de Base [*United Nations*] .... CCIP
Commission du Danube [*Danube Commission - DC*] (EAIO) .... CD
Commission du Droit International [*United Nations*] .... CDI
Commission du Pacifique Sud [*South Pacific Commission - SPC*] (EAIO) .... CPS
Commission Dyers and Finishers' Association of Australia .... CDFAA
Commission Economique et Sociale pour l'Asie et le Pacifique [*Economic and Social Commission for Asia and the Pacific*] [*French*] [*United Nations*] (DUND) .... CESAP
Commission Economique et Sociale pour l'Asie Occidentale [*Economic and Social Commission for Western Asia - ESCWA*] (EAIO) .... CESAO
Commission Economique pour l'Afrique [*Economic Commission for Africa - ECA*] (EAIO) .... CEA
Commission Economique pour l'Europe [*Economic Commission for Europe - ECE*] [*French*] .... CEE
Commission Economique pour l'Europe/Organisation des Nations Unies [*Economic Commission for Europe/United Nations Organization*] (EAIO) .... CEE/ONU
Commission Electrotechnique Internationale [*International Electrotechnical Commission - IEC*] [*Switzerland*] (EAIO) .... CEI
Commission Episcopale de Cooperation Apostolique Canada-Amerique Latine .... CECAL
Commission Europeenne de Corrosion des Conduites Souterraines [*Brussels, Belgium*] (EAIO) .... CEOCOR
Commission Europeenne de la Corseterie [*European Corsetry Commission - ECC*] (EAIO) .... CEC
Commission Europeenne de l'Aviation Civile [*European Civil Aviation Conference - ECAC*] (EAIO) .... CEAC
Commission Europeenne de Marketing Industriel [*European Commission for Industrial Marketing*] [*Brixham, Devonshire, England*] (EAIO) .... CEMI
Commission Europeenne de Tourisme [*European Travel Commission - ETC*] [*Paris, France*] .... CET
Commission Europeenne des Constructeurs d'Appareillage Electrique d'Installations [*European Commission of Manufacturers of Electrical Installation Equipment*] (EAIO) .... CECAPI
Commission Europeenne des Droits de l'Homme [*European Commission of Human Rights - ECHR*] (EA) .... CEDH
Commission Europeenne des Forets .... CEF

Commission for Acceleration of Black Participation in Psychology .... CABPP
Commission for Accountability to the Public (EA) .... CAP
Commission for Aerology (SAUO) .... CAe
Commission for Aeronautical Meteorology [*WMO*] (MSC) .... CAeM
Commission for Agricultural Meteorology [*WMO*] (MSC) .... CAgM
Commission for Agricultural Meteorology [*WMO*] (ASF) .... CAM
Commission for Atmospheric Sciences [*WMO*] (MSC) .... CAS
Commission for Basic Systems [*WMO*] (MSC) .... CBS
Commission for Bibliography and Publications (SAUO) .... CBP
Commission for Catholic Missions among the Colored People and the Indians (EA) .... CCMACPI
Commission for Certification in Geriatric Pharmacy (SAUS) .... CCGP
Commission for Climatology [*Marine science*] (OSRA) CCl
Commission for Climatology [*WMO*] CCl
Commission for Climatology and Applications of Meteorology (SAUO) ..... CCAM
Commission for Controlling the Desert Locust in North-West Africa [*United Nations*] (EA) .... CCDLNWA
Commission for Controlling the Desert Locust in the Eastern Region of its Distribution Area in/on South West Asia (SAUO) .... DL/SWA
Commission for Controlling the Desert Locust in the Near East [*United Nations*] (EA) .... CCDLNE
Commission for Conventional Armaments (SAUO) .... CCA
Commission for Development and Exchange [*International Council of Scientific Unions*] .... CDE
Commission for Development Studies in Latin America (SAUO) .... CDSLA
Commission for Educational Exchange between the United States of America and Afghanistan (SAUO) .... CEEUSA
Commission for Environmental Cooperation [*Environmental Protection Agency*] (EPAT) .... CEC
Commission for Eritrean Refugee Affairs .... CERA
Commission for Fisheries Research in the West Pacific .... WPFC
Commission for Geographical Education (EA) .... GCE
Commission for Historical Architectural Preservation .... CHAP
Commission for Hydrology [*World Meteorological Organization*] (GFGA) .... CHy
Commission for Independent Colleges and Universities (SAUO) .... CICU
Commission for Independent Colleges and Universtties of Pennsylvania (SAUS) .... CICUP
Commission for Inland Fisheries of Latin America (SAUS) .... COPESCAL
Commission for International Development (EA) .... CID
Commission for International Due Process of Law (EA) .... CIDPL
Commission for International Educational Reconstruction .... CIER
Commission for Local Administration [*British*] (BARN) .... CLA
Commission for Marine Geology [*of the International Union of Geological Sciences*] (EAIO) .... CMG
Commission for Marine Meteorology [*Marine science*] (OSRA) .... CMM
Commission for Marine (or Maritime) Meteorology (SAUS) .... CMM
Commission for Maritime Meteorology [*World Meteorological Organization*] .... CMM
Commission for Organizing the Party of the Working People of Ethiopia (PD) .... COPWE
Commission For Our Common Future (SAUS) .... CFOCF
Commission for our Common Future (SAUO) .... CFOCF
Commission for Racial Equality [*British*] .... CRE
Commission for Racial Justice (EA) .... CRJ
Commission for Racial Justice (EA) .... MRSJ
Commission for Radical Justice (SAUO) .... CRJ
Commission for Relief in Belgium (SAUO) .... CRB
Commission for Social Justice (EA) .... CSJ
Commission for Special Applications of Meteorology and Climatology [*World Meteorological Organization*] .... CoSAMC
Commission for Synoptic Meteorology (SAUO) .... CMS
Commission for Synoptic Meteorology .... CSM
Commission for Synoptic Weather Information (SAUO) .... CSWI
Commission for Teacher Preparation and Licensing .... CTPL
Commission for Technical Cooperation for Africa .... CTCA
Commission for the Accreditation of Public Libraries [*Proposed*] .... CAPL
Commission for the Advancement of Public Interest Organizations (EA) .... CAPIO
Commission for the Blind and Visually Handicapped (SAUS) .... CBVH
Commission for the Conservation of Antarctic Marine Living Resources (SAUO) .... CCAMLR
Commission for the Conservation of the Antarctic Marine Living Resources [*Australia*] (EAIO) .... CCAMLR
Commission for the Defense of Human Rights in Central America (EA) .... CDHRCA
Commission for the European Defence Community (SAUO) .... CEDC
Commission for the Exploration and Utilization of Space [*Former USSR*] .... CEUS
Commission for the Future (SAUO) .... CFF
Commission For the Future (SAUS) .... CFF
Commission for the Geological Map of the World (SAUO) .... CGMW
Commission for the Geological Map of the World [*Marine science*] (OSRA) .... CGMW
Commission for World Christian Action .... CWCA
Commission Gastronomique, Vinicole, et Touristique (EA) .... CGVT
Commission Generale de l'Assurance du Risque Atomique [*Paris, France*] (EAIO) .... CGARA
Commission Geologique du Canada (GEOI) .... CGC
Commission Indo-Pacific des Peches [*Indo-Pacific Fishery Commission - IPFC*] (EAIO) .... CIPP
Commission Interamericaine d'Energie Nucleaire [*Inter-American Nuclear Energy Commission*] .... CIEN
Commission International d'Aeromodelisme [*International Aeromodelling Commission*] (PDAA) .... CIAM

Commission Internationale Catholique pour les Migrations [*International Catholic Migration Commission - ICMC*] [*Geneva, Switzerland*] (EAIO) ...... CICM
Commission Internationale Contre le Regime Concentrationnaire [*International Commission Against the Regime of Concentration Camps*] [*France*] ...... CICRC
Commission Internationale d'Analyses ...... CIA
Commission Internationale de Certification de Conformite de l'Equipement Electrique [*International Commission for Conformity Certification of Electrical Equipment*] [*French*] (EA) ...... CEE
Commission Internationale de Juristes [*International Commission of Jurists - ICJ*] [*Switzerland*] ...... CIJ
Commission Internationale de la Medecine du Travail [*International Commissionof Occupational Health - ICOH*] [*Information service or system*] (IID) ...... CIMT
Commission Internationale de la Navigation Aerienne [*International Air Navigation Commission*] ...... CINA
Commission Internationale de la Nomenclature Anatomique Veterinaire [*International Committee on Veterinary Anatomical Nomenclature - ICVAN*] [*Zurich, Switzerland*] (EAIO) ...... CINAV
Commission Internationale de l'Eclairage [*International Commission on Illumination*] [*Vienna, Austria*] (EA) ...... CIE
Commission Internationale de l'Enseignement de la Physique [*International Commission on Physics Education - ICPE*] (EAIO) ...... CIEP
Commission Internationale de l'Etat Civil [*International Commission on Civil Status - ICCS*] (EAIO) ...... CIEC
Commission Internationale de Lutte Biologique Contre les Ennemis des Cultures ...... CILB
Commission Internationale de Marketing [*International Marketing Commission - IMC*] [*Brixham, Devonshire, England*] (EAIO) ...... CIM
Commission Internationale de Meteorologie Aeronautique [*OMI*] ...... CIMAe
Commission Internationale de Nomenclature Zoologique [*International Commission on Veterinary Anatomical Nomenclature*] [*British*] (EAIO) ...... CINZ
Commission Internationale de Numismatique [*International Numismatic Commission*] [*Oslo, Norway*] (EA) ...... CIN
Commission Internationale de Reglementation en veu de l'Approbation de l'Equipement Electrique [*International Commission on Rules for the Approval of Electrical Equipment*] (PDAA) ...... CEE
Commission Internationale de Tourisme Aerien ...... CITA
Commission Internationale des Activites Commerciales [*International Commission on Commercial Activities*] (EAIO) ...... CAIC
Commission Internationale des Aumoniers Generaux des Prisons [*International Commission of Catholic Prison Chaplains - ICPC*] (EA) ...... CIAGP
Commission Internationale des Examens de Conduite Automobile [*International Driving Tests Committee*] (EAIO) ...... CIECA
Commission Internationale des Grands Barrages [*International Commission on Large Dams - ICOLD*] (EAIO) ...... CIGB
Commission Internationale des Industries Agricoles et Alimentaires [*International Commission for Food Industries*] (EAIO) ...... CIIA
Commission Internationale des Irrigations et du Drainage [*International Commission on Irrigation and Drainage - ICID*] (EAIO) ...... CIID
Commission Internationale des Methodes d'Analyse des Pesticides [*Collaborative International Pesticides Analytic Council - CIPAC*] (EAIO) ...... CIMAP
Commission Internationale des Peches de l'Atlantique Sud-Est [*International Commission for the Southeast Atlantic Fisheries - ICSEAF*] [*Madrid, Spain*] (EAIO) ...... CIPASE
Commission Internationale des Professionals de la Sante (EAIO) ...... CINPROS
Commission Internationale des Professionels de la Sante [*International Commission of Health Professionals for Health and Human Rights - ICHP*] (EA) ...... CINPROS
Commission Internationale d'Etudes de la Police de Circulation [*International Study Commission for Traffic Police*] ...... CIEPC
Commission Internationale d'Histoire Militaire [*International Commission of Military History*] (EAIO) ...... CIHM
Commission Internationale d'Optique [*International Commission for Optics - ICO*] (EAIO) ...... CIO
Commission Internationale du Chataignier CIC
Commission Internationale du Genie Rural [*International Commission of Agricultural Engineering*] [*ICSU*] (EAIO) ...... CIGR
Commission Internationale du Peuplier [*International Poplar Commission*] ...... CIP
Commission Internationale du Riz [*International Rice Commission - IRC*] [*United Nations*] (EAIO) ...... CIR
Commission Internationale du Verre [*International Commission on Glass - ICG*] (EAIO) CIV
Commission Internationale Medico-Physiologique [*International Medico-Physiological Commission*] (PDAA) ...... CIMP
Commission Internationale Permanente pour l'Epreuve des Armes a Feu [*Permanent International Commission for the Proof of Small-Arms - PICPSA*] (EAIO) ...... CIP
Commission Internationale pour la Conservation des Thonides de l'Atlantique [*International Commission for the Conservation of Atlantic Tunas - ICCAT*] ...... CICTA
Commission Internationale pour la Protection de la Moselle Contre la Pollution [*International Commission for the Protection of the Moselle Against Pollution - ICPMP*] (EA) ...... CIPMP
Commission Internationale pour la Protection des Regions Alpines [*International Commission for the Protection of Alpine Regions*] (EAIO) ...... CIPRA
Commission Internationale pour la Reglementation des Ascenseurs et Monte-Charge [*International Committee for Lift Regulations - ICLR*] (EAIO) ...... CIRA
Commission Internationale pour la Sauvegarde du Patrimoine Culturel Islamique [*International Commission for the Preservation of Islamic Cultural Heritage - ICPICH*] (EA) ...... CISPCI
Commission Internationale pour le Sauvetage Alpin [*International Commission for Alpine Rescue*] ...... CISA
Commission Internationale pour l'Enseignement des Mathematiques [*International Commission on Mathematical Instruction - ICMI*] (EA) ...... CIEM
Commission Internationale pour l'Etude Scientifique de la Famille [*International Scientific Commission on the Family*] ...... COMIFA
Commission Internationale pour l'Exploration Scientifique de la Mer Mediterranee[*International Commission for the Scientific Exploration of the Mediterranea n Sea - ICSEM*] [*Monaco*] [*Research center*] (IRC) ...... CIESM
Commission Internationale pour l'Organisation Scientifique du Travail en Agriculture [*International Committee of Scientific Management in Agriculture*] ...... CIOSTA
Commission Internationale Technique de Sucrerie [*International Commission of Sugar Technology*] (EAIO) ...... CITS
Commission Intersyndicale des Deshydrateurs Europeens [*European Dehydrators Association*] [*Common Market*] [*Paris, France*] ...... CIDE
Commission Issuance Posting System [*Department of Energy*] ...... CIPS
Commission Leaflets, American Telephone and Telegraph Cases [*A publication*] (DLA) CL
Commission Medicale Chretienne [*Christian Medical Commission*] [*Geneva, Switzerland*] (EA) ...... CMC
Commission Mixte Internationale pour les Experiences Relatives a la Protection des Lignes de Telecommunication et des Canalisations Souterraines [*Joint International Commission for the Protection of Telecommunication Lines and Underground Ducts*] [*Switzerland*] ...... CMI
Commission Mondiale d'Action Professionnelle [*World Committee for Trade Action - WCTA*] (EA) ...... CMAP
Commission Oceanographique Intergouvernementale [*Intergovernmental Oceanographic Commission - IOC*] (EAIO) ...... COI
Commission of Accreditation for Corrections (SAUO) ...... CAC
Commission of Accredited Truck Driving Schools (EA) ...... CATDS
Commission of Assembly of the Church of Scotland (DAS) ...... CAC
Commission of Assembly of the Church of Scotland (SAUO) ...... CACS
Commission of Editors of Biochemical Journals ...... CEBJ
Commission of European Communities (SAUO) ...... CEB
Commission of Fine Arts [*Independent government agency*] ...... CFA
Commission of Fluorite and Barite Deposits (SAUO) ...... COFAB
Commission of Foreign Students in Europe (SAUO) ...... CFSE
Commission of Formation and Properties of Glacial Deposits (SAUS) ...... INQUA
Commission of International Union of Crystallography [*British*] ...... CIUC
Commission of Overseas Chinese Affairs (SAUO) ...... COCA
Commission of Professors of Adult Education (EA) ...... CPAE
Commission of Science, Technology and Industry for National Defense (SAUS) ...... COSTIND
Commission of Support for Verification (SAUO) ...... CIAV
Commission of the Churches on International Affairs [*Switzerland*] (EAIO) ...... CCIA
Commission of the Churches on International Affairs (of the World Council of Churches) (EA) ...... CCIA/WCC
Commission of the European Communities [*See also CCE*] (EAIO) ...... CEC
Commission of the European Communities (SAUO) ...... EC
Commission of the Status and Role of Women (EA) ...... CSRW
Commission of United States Latin American Relations (EA) ...... CUSLAR
Commission of Voluntary Agencies (SAUO) ...... COVA
Commission of/on World Mission and Evangelism of the World Council of Churches (SAUO) ...... CWME
Commission on Accreditation/ Approval for Dietetics Education (SAUO) ...... CAADE
Commission on Accreditation for Law Enforcement Agencies (EA) ...... CALEA
Commission on Accreditation of Ambulance Services (SAUO) ...... CAAS
Commission on Accreditation of Medical Transport Systems (SAUO) ...... CAMTS
Commission on Accreditation of Rehabilitation Facilities (EA) ...... CARF
Commission on Accreditation of Service Experiences [*Later, OECC*] ...... CASE
Commission on Accreditations of Allied Health Education Programs (PGP) ...... CAAHEP
Commission on Administrative Review [*House of Representatives*] ...... CAR
Commission on Adult Basic Education (SAUO) ...... COABE
Commission on African Animal Trypanosomiasis (SAUO) ...... COAT
Commission on Agricultural Technology (SAUS) ...... CAT
Commission on Agricultural Workers (ECON) ...... CAW
Commission on Agriculture (SAUO) ...... COAC
Commission on Air Chemistry and Radioactivity (SAUS) ...... CACR
Commission on American Shipbuilding ...... CAS
Commission on Applied Quaternary Studies (SAUS) ...... INQUA
Commission on Archives and History of the United Methodist Church (EA) ...... CAHUMC
Commission on Art and Antiquities ...... CAA
Commission on Asian and Far Eastern Affairs of the International Chamber of Commerce ...... CAFEA-ICC
Commission on Asian and Pacific Affairs [*International Chamber of Commerce*] ...... CAPA
Commission on Asian and Pacific Affairs of the International Chamber of Commerce (SAUO) ...... ICC-CAPA
Commission on Atmospheric Chemistry and Global Pollution [*British*] ...... CACGP
Commission on Atmospheric Sciences (SAUS) ...... CAS
Commission on Behavioral & Social Sciences and Education (SAUS) ...... CBASSE
Commission on Biochemical Nomenclature [*IUPAC*] ...... CBN
Commission on Carbon (SAUO) ...... INQUA
Commission on Carbon (SAUO) ...... INQUA/C
Commission on Certification of Work Adjustment & Vocational Evaluation Specialists (NTPA) ...... CCWAVES
Commission on Chemical and Biological Warfare (SAUS) ...... CCBW
Commission on Chicago Historical and Architectural Landmarks ...... CCHAL
Commission on Civil Rights ...... CCR
Commission on Coastal Systems (SAUS) ...... CCS
Commission on College Geography (AEBS) ...... CCG

Commission on College Physics ... CCP
Commission on Critical Choices for Americans ... CCCA
Commission on Crystallographic Apparatus [*International Council of Scientific Unions*] ... CCA
Commission on Dental Accreditation (SAUO) ... CDA
Commission on Dietary Supplement Labels ... CDSL
Commission on Dietetic Registration (SAUO) ... CDR
Commission on Documentation (SAUO) ... CoD
Commission on Ecology (AUEG) ... COE
Commission on Ecosystem Management (SAUO) ... CEM
Commission on Education [*American Occupational Therapy Association*] ... COE
Commission on Education and Communication (SAUO) ... CEC
Commission on Education and Training (GEOI) ... CET
Commission on Education for Mission [*National Council of Churches*] (EA) ... CEM
Commission on Education in Agriculture and Natural Resources [*National Research Council*] [*Defunct*] ... CEANAR
Commission on Education of Teachers of Reading (EDAC) ... CETOR
Commission on Education of the World Leisure and Recreation Association (EAIO) ... CEWLRA
Commission on Elections [*Philippines*] ... COMELEC
Commission on Elections (SAUO) ... Comelec
Commission on Emergency Medical Services [*Defunct*] (EA) ... CEMS
Commission on Emotional and Learning Disorders in Children [*Canada*] ... CELDIC
Commission on Engineering and Technical Systems (SAUS) ... CETS
Commission on English of the College Entrance Examination Board (EA) ... CECEEB
Commission on Environment Policy, Law & Administration (SAUS) ... CEPLA
Commission on Environment Policy, Law and Administration (SAUO) ... CEPLA
Commission on Environmental, Economic and Social Policy (SAUO) ... CEESP
Commission on Environmental Economics, Strategy and Policy (SAUO) ... CEESP
Commission on Environmental Law (SAUO) ... CEL
Commission on Epidemiological Survey [*Armed Forces Epidemiological Board*] (DNAB) ... CES
Commission on Family Ministries and Human Sexuality (EA) ... CFMHS
Commission on Federal Paperwork [*Terminated, 1978*] ... CFP
Commission on Financial Structure and Regulation [*White House*] ... CFSR
Commission on Fisheries (SAUO) ... COFI
Commission on Folk Law and Legal Pluralism [*of the International Union of Anthropological and Ethnological Sciences*] (EAIO) ... CFLLP
Commission on Food, Environment, and Renewable Resources [*National Association of State Universities and Land-Grant Colleges*] (GVA) ... CFERR
Commission on Genetic Resources for Food and Agriculture (SAUO) ... CGRFA
Commission on Geography in Education (SAUS) ... CGE
Commission on Geological Sciences Environmental Planning (SAUO) ... CGSEP
Commission on Geology Teaching (SAUO) ... CGT
Commission on Glaciation (SAUO) ... INQUA
Commission on Glaciation (SAUO) ... INQUA/G
Commission on Global Continental (SAUO) ... INQUA
Commission on Global Continental Palaeohydrology (SAUO) ... INQUA/GLOCOPH
Commission on Government Procurement [*Terminated, 1973*] ... CGP
Commission on Government Procurement [*Terminated, 1973*] ... COGP
Commission on Government Security [*Terminated, 1957*] ... CGS
Commission on Graduates of Foreign Nursing Schools (EA) ... CGFNS
Commission on Health and Healing [*Formerly, CCMW*] (EA) ... CHH
Commission on Highway Beautification ... CHB
Commission on Human Ecology (SAUO) ... CHE
Commission on Human Evolution and Palaeoecology (SAUO) ... INQUA
Commission on Human Evolution and Palaeoecology (SAUO) ... INQUA/HEP
Commission on Human Resources [*National Research Council*] ... CHR
Commission on Human Rights [*Geneva, Switzerland*] (EAIO) ... CHR
Commission on Human Settlements (SAUO) ... Habitat
Commission on Igneous and Metamorphic Petrogenesis (SAUO) ... CIMP
Commission on Increased Industrial Use of Agricultural Products ... CIIUAP
Commission on Independent Colleges and Universities [*Pennsylvania*] ... CICU
Commission on Industrial Relations [*Department of Employment*] [*British*] ... CIR
Commission on Industry and Manpower (SAUO) ... CIM
Commission on Instructional Technology (EA) ... CIT
Commission on Insurance Technology (SAUS) ... CIT
Commission on Insurance Terminology of the American Risk and Insurance Association ... CIT
Commission on Intergovernmental Relations ... CIR
Commission on International Affairs (EA) ... CIA
Commission on International Commodity Trade ... CICT
Commission on International Peace and Reconciliation (SAUO) ... CIPAR
Commission on Judicial Conduct (SAUO) ... CJC
Commission on Land Carbon (SAUS) ... INQUA
Commission on Law and Public Affairs ... COLPA
Commission on Law Enforcement and Criminal Justice, Criminal Justice InformationSystem, Baton Rouge, LA [*Library symbol*] [*Library of Congress*] (LCLS) ... LBrCJIS
Commission on Life Sciences (SAUO) ... CLS
Commission on Loess (SAUO) ... INQUA
Commission on Loess (SAUO) ... INQUA/L
Commission on Man and Environment (SAUS) ... CME
Commission on Manganese (SAUO) ... COM
Commission on Map Use and Spatial Data Use (GEOI) ... CMSDU
Commission on Marine and Coastal Resources [*California*] ... CMC
Commission on Marine Science, Engineering and Research [*Stratton Commission*] [*Inactive*] [*Marine science*] (OSRA) ... COMSER
Commission on Marine Science, Engineering, and Resources ... CMSER
Commission on Marine Science, Engineering and Resources [*Stratton Commission*] [*Defunct*] (USDC) ... COMSER
Commission on Marriage and Family Life [*of NCC*] [*Defunct*] ... CMFL
Commission on Metamorphic Petrogenesis (SAUS) ... CIMP
Commission on Ministries in Specialized Settings [*Federal government*] ... COMISS
Commission on Missionary Education [*Later, Department of Education for Missions*] (EA) ... CME
Commission on Molecular Structure and Spectrometry (SAUO) ... CMSS
Commission on Molecular Structure and Spectroscopy ... CMSS
Commission on Money and Credit (SAUO) ... CMC
Commission on Narcotic Drugs (ADWA) ... CND
Commission on National and Regional Atlases (GEOI) ... CNRA
Commission on National Parks and Protected Areas [*of the International Union for Conservation of Nature and Natural Resources*] (EAIO) ... CNPPA
Commission on Natural Resources [*National Research Council*] ... CNR
Commission on Neotectonics (SAUO) ... INQUA
Commission on Neotectonics (SAUO) ... INQUA/N
Commission on New Minerals and Mineral Names [*Mineralogical Association*] ... CNMMN
Commission on New Technological Uses of Copyrighted Works (SAUO) ... CONTU
Commission on Nomenclature of Organic Chemistry (MEC) ... CNOC
Commission on Occupational Education Institutions (SAUO) ... COEI
Commission on Office Laboratory Accreditation (NTPA) ... COLA
Commission on Ore-Forming Fluid in Inclusions ... COFFI
Commission on Organization of the Executive Branch of the Government ... COEBG
Commission on Palaeoclimate (SAUO) ... INQUA
Commission on Palaeoclimate (SAUO) ... INQUA/PC
Commission on Paleopedology (SAUO) ... INQUA
Commission on Paleopedology (SAUO) ... INQUA/PP
Commission on Pastoral Research (EA) ... COMISS
Commission on Personnel Interchange [*Presidential*] ... CPI
Commission on Physical Sciences, Mathematics and Resources (SAUS) ... CPSMR
Commission on Plant Genetic Resources (SAUO) ... CPGR
Commission on Population Growth and the American Future [*Presidential commission*] ... CPGAF
Commission on Practice [*American Occupational Therapy Association*] ... COP
Commission on Present Day Geomorphic Process (SAUS) ... CPDGP
Commission on Preservation and Access ... CPA
Commission on Presidential Debates (EA) ... CPD
Commission on Private Philanthropy and Public Needs [*Defunct*] (EA) ... CPPPN
Commission on Professional and Hospital Activities (EA) ... CPHA
Commission on Professional Rights and Responsibilities of the NEA [*Defunct*] (EA) ... CPRR-NEA
Commission on Professionals in Science and Technology (EA) ... CPST
Commission on Public Ethics [*Australia*] ... COPE
Commission on Quantities and Units in Clinical Chemistry (DAVI) ... CQUCC
Commission on Quaternary Shorelines (SAUS) ... INQUA
Commission on Recent Crustal Movements [*Oceanography*] (MSC) ... CRCM
Commission on Reciprocal Deliveries (SAUO) ... CRD
Commission on Recognition of Postsecondary Accreditation (NTPA) ... CORPA
Commission on Reform Jewish Outreach (EA) ... CRJO
Commission on Reform of Undergraduate Education and Living [*University of Illinois*] ... CRUEL
Commission on Rehabilitation Counselor Certification (EA) ... CRCC
Commission on Rehabilitation Education [*American Occupational Therapy Association*] ... CORE
Commission on Religion in Appalachia (EA) ... CORA
Commission on Research Integrity [*Congressional group*] ... CRI
Commission on Research of the World Leisure and Recreation Association (EA) ... CRWLRA
Commission on Rules and Missions of the Armed Services (AAGC) ... CORM
Commission on Rural Water [*Defunct*] (EA) ... CRW
Commission on Science and Technology for Sustainable Development in the South (SAUS) ... COMSATS
Commission on Science Education ... CSE
Commission on Science, Technology & Industry for National Defence (SAUS) ... CSTIND
Commission on Sea Level Changes and Coastal Evolution (SAUO) ... INQUA
Commission on Sea Level Changes and Coastal Evolution (SAUO) ... INQUA/SLCCE
Commission on Security and Cooperation in Europe [*Washington, DC*] (EGAO) ... CSCE
Commission on Social Action of Reform Judaism (EA) ... CSARJ
Commission on Software Issues in the 80s [*Defunct*] (EA) ... COSIE
Commission on Soil Biology of the International Society of Soil Science (EAIO) ... CSBISSS
Commission on Soil Biology of the International Society of Soil Science [*Netherlands*] (EAIO) ... CSBUSSS
Commission on Soil Fertility and Plant Nutrition [*of the International Society of Soil Science*] (EA) ... CSFPN
Commission on Soil Genesis, Classification, and Cartography [*of the International Society of Soil Science*] (EA) ... CSGCC
Commission on Standardization of Biological Stains (SAUO) ... CSBS
Commission on Standards and Accreditation of Services for the Blind [*Superseded by NAC*] ... COMSTAC
Commission on Storage, Automatic Processing, and Retrieval of Geological Data (EAIO) ... COGEODATA
Commission on Storage, Automatic Processing and Retrieval of Geological Data (SAUS) ... IUGS/COGEODATA
Commission on Stratigraphy (SAUO) ... INQUA
Commission on Stratigraphy (SAUO) ... INQUA/S
Commission on Student Learning ... CSL
Commission on Sustainable Development ... CSD

Commission on Systematics in Petrology (SAUO) CSP
Commission on Tectonics (SAUO) COMTEC
Commission on Tectonics (SAUS) IUGS/COMTEC
Commission on Tectonics of Ore Deposits (SAUO) CTOD
Commission on Tephrochronology (SAUS) INQUA
Commission on Tephrochronology and Volcanism (SAUO) INQUA
Commission on Tephrochronology and Volcanism (SAUO) INQUA/TV
Commission on the Aging (OICC) COA
Commission on the Application of Science to Agriculture, Forestry and Aquaculture (SAUO) CASA
Commission on the Education of Teachers of Science (SAUS) CETS
Commission on the Holocene (SAUO) INQUA
Commission on the Holocene (SAUO) INQUA/H
Commission on the Isle Of Man Constitution. Report [*1959*] [*A publication*] (DLA) MacDermott Commission
Commission on the Limits of the Continental Shelf (SAUS) CLCS
Commission on the Mentally Disabled [*Formerly, Mental and Physical Disability Legal Research Services and Data Bases*] (EA) MPDLRSDB
Commission on the Nomenclature of Organic Chemistry [*IUPAC*] CON
Commission on the Paleoecology of Early Man (SAUS) INQUA
Commission on the Paleogeographic Atlas of the Quaternary (SAUS) INQUA
Commission on the Patent System CPS
Commission on the Quaternary of South America (SAUS) INQUA
Commission on the Status of Jewish War Orphans in Europe, American Section [*Defunct*] (EA) CSJWOE
Commission on the Status of Women [*Economic and Social Council of the UN*] [*Vienna, Austria*] (EAIO) CSW
Commission on the Status of Women in Adult Education [*Later, WISE*] (EA) CSWAE
Commission on the Study of Peace (EA) CSP
Commission on the Study of the Holocene (SAUS) INQUA
Commission on Thermal Physiology (SAUS) CTP
Commission on Transnational Corporations [*United Nations*] CTC
Commission on Transnational Corporations [*United Nations*] CTNC
Commission on Undergraduate Education in the Biological Sciences CUEBS
Commission on US-African Relations (EA) CUSAR
Commission on U.S.-Russian Relations (EA) CUSRR
Commission on US-Soviet Relations (EA) CUSSR
Commission on Visual Anthropology (SAUO) CVA
Commission on Voluntary Service and Action (EA) CVSA
Commission on World Mission and Evangelism (EAIO) CWME
Commission on World Mission and Evangelism of the World Council of Churches [*Later, CWME*] (EA) CWMEWCC
Commission on World Standards (SAUO) COWS
Commission (or Committee) on the Application of Science to Agriculture, Forestry and Aquaculture (SAUO) CASAFA
Commission Permanente de la Convention Internationale des Peches [*Permanent Commission of the International Fisheries Convention*] [*Political party*] (MSC) CPCIP
Commission Permanente du Pacifique Sud [*Permanent Commission for the South Pacific*] CPPS
Commission Permanente Internationale de l'Acetylene, de la Soudure Autogene, et des Industries qui S'y Rattachent [*Permanent International Committee on Acetylene, Oxy-Acetylene Welding, and Allied Industries*] CPI
Commission Permanente Internationale Europeenne des Gaz Industriels et du Carbure de Calcium [*Permanent International European Commission on Industrial Gases and Calcium Carbide*] (EAIO) CPI
Commission Phytosanitaire Interafricaine CPI
Commission pour le Marche Commun du Commerce International de Bulbes a Fleurs etde Plantes [*Common Market Commission for International Trade in Flower Bulbs and Plants*] CIBEP
Commission pour l'Etude des Nuages [*OMI*] CEN
Commission Preparatoire Europeenne de Recherches Spatiales [*European Preparatory Commission for Space Research*] COPERS
Commission Regionale de l'Utilisation des Terres et des Eaux au Proche-Orient [*Regional Commission on Land and Water Use in the Near East - RCLWUNE*] (EAIO) CRUTEPO
Commission Regionale Europeenne du Tourisme CRET
Commission Rochon, Centre de Documentation, Ste. Foy, PQ, Canada [*Library symbol*] [*Library of Congress*] (LCLS) CaQSFCRO
Commission Romande de Documentation (SAUO) CRD
Commission Scolaire de Sept-Iles, Quebec [*Library symbol*] [*National Library of Canada*] (NLC) OSICS
Commission Scolaire Regionale des Vieilles-Forges, Trois-Rivieres, PQ, Canada [*Library symbol*] [*Library of Congress*] (LCLS) CaQTCSRV
Commission Scolaire Regionale des Vieilles-Forges, Trois-Rivieres, Quebec [*Library symbol*] [*National Library of Canada*] (NLC) QTCSRV
Commission Seismologique Europeenne [*European Seismological Commission - ESC*] (EAIO) CSE
Commission Sericicole Internationale [*International Sericultural Commission - ISC*] (EAIO) CSI
Commission Sportive Internationale [*Auto racing*] CSI
Commission Telephone Cases Leaflets [*New York*] [*A publication*] (DLA) Comm Tel Cas
Commission to New Towns [*British*] CNT
Commission to Study the Organization of Peace (EA) CSOP
Commission Type Code (SAUS) CTCDE
Commissional (ABBR) CMSNL
Commissionary (ABBR) CMSNY
Commissione Nazionale per le Societa e la Borsa CONSOB
Commissioned CD
Commissioned CMMND
Commissioned CMSND
Commissioned (WGA) COMD
Commissioned (DLA) commd
Commissioned COMMND
Commissioned COMND
Commissioned (DA) COMSND
Commissioned Air Engineer (SAUS) Cd A Eng
Commissioned Alberta Land Surveyor [*Canada*] (ASC) ALS
Commissioned Armament Officer (SAUS) CAO
Commissioned Bandmaster (SAUS) Cd Bndr
Commissioned Boatswain (SAUS) Cd B
Commissioned Catering Officer (SAUS) CdCtO
Commissioned Communication Officer (SAUS) Cd CO
Commissioned Constructor (SAUS) Cd Con
Commissioned Corps Personnel Manual CCPM
Commissioned Electrical (or Electronic) Officer (SAUS) Cd ElO
Commissioned Engineer (SAUS) Cd Eng
Commissioned Engineer (SAUS) Comm Engr
Commissioned Engineer Officer (SAUS) CEO
Commissioned from the Ranks [*Canadian Navy*] CFR
Commissioned Gunner (SAUS) Cd Gr
Commissioned Gunner (SAUS) Cd Gunn
Commissioned Instructor Officer (SAUS) Cd In O
Commissioned Loss to Enlisted Status [*Revocation of an officer's appointment*] CLTE
Commissioned Master-at-Arms (SAUS) Cd MAA
Commissioned Observer (SAUS) Cd Obs
Commissioned Officer (SAUO) CO
Commissioned Officer (SAUS) Comoff
Commissioned Officer [*Military*] Com Off
Commissioned Officer Corps [*National Oceanic and Atmospheric Administration*] COC
Commissioned Officer Corps Advisory Group [*National Oceanic and Atmospheric Administration*] (NOAA) COCAG
Commissioned Officer Residency Deferment [*Program of Public Health Service*] CORD
Commissioned Officer Student Training and Extern Program [*Public Health Service*] COSTEP
Commissioned Officers Association (COE) COA
Commissioned Officers Association of the United States Public Health Service (EA) COA
Commissioned Officers Mess [*Navy*] COM
Commissioned Officers' Mess Open [*Navy*] (DNAB) COMO
Commissioned Ordnance Engineer (SAUS) Cd OE
Commissioned Ordnance Officer (SAUS) Cd OO
Commissioned Radio Officer (SAUS) Cd RadO
Commissioned Research CR
Commissioned Royal Marine Gunner [*British*] CdRMG
Commissioned Royal Marine Gunner (SAUS) Cd RMG
Commissioned Shipwright (SAUS) Cd Sh
Commissioned Signals Boatswain [*British*] CdSB
Commissioned Stores Officer (SAUS) Cd SO
Commissioned Supply Officer (SAUS) Cd SO
Commissioned Supply Officer [*British*] CdSO
Commissioned Vessel Liaison Inquiry (DNAB) CVLI
Commissioned Wardmaster (SAUS) Cd Wdr
Commissioned Warrant Officer CWO
Commissioned Warrant Officer Hospital Corps CWOHC
Commissioned Writer Officer (SAUS) Cd WO
Commissioner CMMNR
Commissioner Cmmr
Commissioner CMSNR
Commissioner (ABBR) CMSSNR
Commissioner (WGA) COMM
Commissioner (PHSD) Comm
Commissioner (ROG) COMMISR
Commissioner (PROS) commnr
Commissioner (DD) commr
Commissioner COMMR
Commissioner (AL) Commr
Commissioner COMMSNR
Commissioner (ROG) COMMSR
Commissioner COMR
Commissioner (ADWA) Comr
Commissioner COMS
Commissioner COMSNR
Commissioner, Chancery Court, County Palatine of Lancaster [*British*] (ROG) CCHCOPALLANC
Commissioner for Affidavits for Colonies [*British*] (ROG) C AFFS for COLS
Commissioner for Enterprise Agreements [*New South Wales*] [*Australia*] CEA
Commissioner for Northern Ireland (SAUS) CNI
Commissioner for Northern Ireland (SAUO) CNI
Commissioner for Oaths CO
Commissioner for Vocational Training [*New South Wales*] [*Australia*] CVT
Commissioner of Accounts CA
Commissioner of Appeals (DLA) COM APP
Commissioner of Crown Lands [*British*] CCL
Commissioner of Election Expenses [*Canada*] CEE
Commissioner of Internal Revenue (SAUS) CIR
Commissioner of Official Languages [*Canada*] COL
Commissioner of Official Languages, Ottawa, ON, Canada [*Library symbol*] [*Library of Congress*] (LCLS) CaOOCOL
Commissioner of Official Languages [*Commissaire aux Langues Officielles*] **Ottawa, Ontario** [*Library symbol*] [*National Library of Canada*] (NLC) OOCOL
Commissioner of Patents [*Legal term*] (DLA) COM PAT
Commissioner of Police for the Metropolis [*British*] (DI) CPM
Commissioner of Public Debt CPD
Commissioner of Soil Conservation [*Western Australia*] CSC

Commissioner of Taxation (ADA) ... C of T
Commissioner of Taxes [*Northern Territory*] [*Australia*] ... COT
Commissioner of the Great Seal [*British*] (ROG) ... COMGS
Commissioner of the Metropolitan Police (SAUS) ... CMP
Commissioner of Works Office (SAUO) ... CWO
Commissioner of Works Office, Supply Division (SAUO) ... CWOSD
Commissioner-General (SAUO) ... C-G
Commissioners (GEAB) ... comm
Commissioner's Adjusted Fair Market Value [*Business term*] (EMRF) ... CAFMV
Commissioner's Decisions [*US Patent and Trademark Office*] ... CD
Commissioners' Decisions [*US Patent and Trademark Office*] [*A publication*] (DLA) ... Com Dec
Commissioner's Delegation Order (DLA) ... Comm Del Order
Commissioners Disability Table [*Insurance*] ... CDT
Commissioners for the Conservancy of the River Mersey (SAUO) ... CCRM
Commissioners Industrial Extended Mortality Table [*Insurance*] ... CIET
Commissioners of Church Temporalities (SAUO) ... CCT
Commissioners of Customs and Excise (SAUO) ... CCE
Commissioners of Inland Revenue [*British*] ... CIR
Commissioners of Medical Services (SAUO) ... CMS
Commissioners of Sewers [*British*] (ROG) ... CS
Commissioners of the District of Columbia (SAUO) ... CDC
Commissioner's Office [*Scotland Yard*] ... CO
Commissioners Standard Industrial Mortality Table [*Insurance*] ... CSI
Commissioners Standard Ordinary Table [*Insurance*] ... CSO
Commissioning (ABBR) ... CMSNG
Commissioning Accession Management System [*Military*] (DNAB) ... CAMS
Commissioning and Advisory Team (SAUS) ... CAAT
Commissioning and Fitting Out ... CFO
Commissioning Detail ... COMMDET
Commissions and Warrants Department (SAUO) ... CW
Commissions Board of Trade ... CBOT
Commission's Yellowfin Regulatory Area [*Inter-American Tropical Tuna Commission*] (MSC) ... CYRA
Commissural and Association [*Anatomy*] ... CA
Commissural Ganglion [*Neurology*] ... COG
Commissural Gastric Driver [*Neurology*] ... CGD
Commit (MSA) ... CMT
Commit (AAG) ... COMT
Commit Sequence Summary (AAG) ... CSS
Commit Start (AAG) ... CST
Commit Stop (AAG) ... CS
Commited (ABBR) ... CMTD
Commiting (ABBR) ... CMTG
Commitment (ABBR) ... CMTMT
Commitment (MCD) ... COMM
Commitment Accounting and Management of Unit Supplies (MCD) ... CAMUS
Commitment and Payment System (MCD) ... CAPS
Commitment Authorization ... CA
Commitment, Concurrency and Recovery [*Computer science*] (TNIG) ... CCR
Commitment, Concurrency, and Recovery Element [*Computer science*] (TNIG) ... CCRE
Commitment Control System (NRCH) ... CCS
[*A*] **Commitment to Improve Our Nation** [*Canada*] ... ACTION
Commitment Unit (SAUS) ... CU
Commitments & Obligations Data Entry System (SAUS) ... CODES
Committal (ROG) ... COML
Committed Burst Size (SAUS) ... CBS
Committed Change Incorporation Record (KSC) ... CCIR
Committed Credit Line (SAUS) ... CCL
Committed Effective Dose Equivalent [*Radioactivity*] ... CEDE
Committed Information Rate [*Telecommunications*] ... CIR
Committed Interface Rate (SAUS) ... CIR
Committed out of Engineering ... COE
Committed Progenitor Cell (STED) ... CPC
Committed Quitters ... CQ
Committed Rate Measurement Interval (SAUS) ... CRMI
Committed Stem Cell [*Hematology*] ... CSC
Committed to Ride (SAA) ... CTR
Committed to Scheduled Programs [*Military*] (CINC) ... CSP
Committee ... CMMTE
Committee (SAUO) ... Cmt
Committee ... CMTE
Committee (TBD) ... Cmte
Committee ... CMTTEE
Committee (AABC) ... COM
Committee (WDMC) ... com
Committee (AL) ... Com
Committee (SAUO) ... Com
Committee (ROG) ... COME
committee (SAUO) ... comee
Committee (SAUO) ... Comm
Committee (PROS) ... comm
Committee ... COMM
Committee ... COMTE
committee (SAUO) ... comte
Committee (SAUO) ... Ctee
Committee ... CTEE
Committee (SAUO) ... Ctte
Committee (EY) ... CTTEE
Committee 51st State for Puerto Rico (EA) ... COMITE 51
Committee Against Academic Repression (SAUO) ... CAAR
Committee Against Government Waste (EA) ... CAGW
Committee Against Registration and the Draft (EA) ... CARD
Committee Against Repression in the Pacific and Asia [*Australia*] (EAIO) ... CARPA
Committee Against Revising Staggers [*Group opposed to changes in the Staggers Act*] ... CARS
Committee Against the Political Misuse of Psychiatry (EA) ... CAPMP
Committee Against Torture [*See also CCT*] [*Geneva, Switzerland*] (EAIO) ... CAT
Committee Charter (MCD) ... CC
Committee classification Research (SAUO) ... CR
Committee Code [*Database terminology*] (NITA) ... COCO
Committee Document (SAUO) ... CD
Committee Draft [*Telecommunications*] (OSI) ... CD
Committee Draft for Voting (SAUO) ... CDV
Committee Electrotechnical Rumanian (SAUO) ... CER
Committee European Mailorder (SAUO) ... CEM
Committee FID Education and Training (SAUO) ... ET
Committee for a Confrontation with Congress (SAUO) ... CWC
Committee for a Constitutional Presidency (SAUO) ... CCP
Committee for a Democratic Consensus (EA) ... CDC
Committee for a Free Afghanistan (EA) ... CFA
Committee for a Free Asia (SAUO) ... CFA
Committee for a Free China [*Defunct*] (EA) ... CFC
Committee for a Free Estonia [*Defunct*] (EA) ... CFE
Committee for a Free Europe (SAUO) ... CFE
Committee for a Free Gold Market (EA) ... CFGM
Committee for a Free Latvia (EA) ... CFL
Committee for a Free Lithuania [*Defunct*] (EA) ... CFL
Committee for a Free Mozambique [*Defunct*] (EA) ... CFM
Committee for a Free Namibia [*Defunct*] (EA) ... CFN
Committee for a National Peace Academy [*Later, N-PAC*] (EA) ... NPA
Committee for a National Trade Policy [*Defunct*] ... CNTP
Committee for a New Ireland [*Defunct*] (EA) ... CNI
Committee for a New Korea Policy (EA) ... CNKP
Committee for a Progressive Congress (EA) ... CPC
Committee for a Responsible Federal Budget (EA) ... CRFB
Committee for a Strong Peaceful America [*Defunct*] (EA) ... CSPA
Committee for a Voluntary Census (EA) ... CVC
Committee for Accuracy in Middle East Reporting in America (EA) ... CAMERA
Committee for Action for Rural Indians (EA) ... CARI
Committee for Agricultural Development [*Iowa State University*] [*Research center*] (RCD) ... CAD
Committee for American Principles (EA) ... CFAP
Committee for Ammunition Logistics Support [*Army*] (MCD) ... CALS
Committee for Amnesty and National Recognition (SAUO) ... CARN
Committee for an Extended Lifespan [*Defunct*] (EA) ... CEL
Committee for an Independent Canada ... CIC
Committee for an International Program in Atmospheric Sciences and Hydrology [*United Nations*] ... CIPASH
Committee for an Open Archives (EA) ... COA
Committee for Analytical Methods (SAUO) ... CAM
Committee for Anglophone Social Action [*Canada*] ... CASA
Committee for Aquatic Microbiology [*United Nations*] (ASF) ... CAM
Committee for Artistic and Intellectual Freedom in Iran (EA) ... CAIFI
Committee for Automated Weather Information Systems (SAUO) ... CAWIS
Committee for Automobile Reform ... CAR
Committee for Aviation & Space Industry Development (SAUS) ... CASID
Committee for Basic Services (ACAE) ... CBS
Committee for Better Transit (EA) ... CBT
Committee for Biological Pest Control (SAUS) ... Comm Bio Pest
Committee for Biotechnology (SAUS) ... COBIOTECH
Committee for Children (EA) ... CFC
Committee for Chilean Inquiry (EA) ... CCI
Committee for Collective Security [*Defunct*] (EA) ... CCS
Committee for Commerce and Distribution (SAUO) ... CCD
Committee for Common Security (EA) ... CCS
Committee for Common Sense Speed Laws [*California*] [*Defunct*] (EA) ... CCSSL
Committee for Competitive Television (NTCM) ... CCT
Committee for Computerized Library Networks (SAUO) ... CCLN
Committee for Congested Production Areas [*1943-1944*] ... CCPA
Committee for Conservation and Care of Chimpanzees (EA) ... CCCC
Committee for Constitutional Government (EA) ... CCG
Committee for Consumers No-Fault (EA) ... CCNF
Committee for Conventional Armaments ... CCA
Committee for Coordination and Liberalisation (SAUO) ... COCOLI
Committee for Coordination of Cathode Ray Tube Development (SAUO) ... CCRTD
Committee for Coordination of Emergency Economic Planning [*US/Canada*] ... CCEEP
Committee for Coordination of Environmental Health and Related Programs [*World Health Organization*] ... CCEHRP
Committee for Co-ordination of Imperial Telecommunications (SAUO) ... CCIT
Committee for Co-ordination of Joint Prospecting for Mineral Resources in Asian Offshore Areas (SAUO) ... CCCOP
Committee for Coordination of Joint Prospecting for Mineral Resources in Asian Offshore Areas, East Asia [*United Nations*] ... CCOPEA
Committee for Co-Ordination of Joint Prospecting for Mineral Resources in South Pacific Offshore Areas (EAIO) ... CCOP/SOPAC
Committee for Corporate Support of American Universities [*Later, Committee for Corporate Support of Private Universities*] (EA) ... CCSAU
Committee for Corporate Support of American Universities (SAUO) ... CCSAU
Committee for Corporate Support of Private Universities ... CCSPU
Committee for Crescent Observation International (EA) ... CCOI
Committee for Defense of Human Rights in Morocco (EA) ... CDHRM
Committee for Defense of Soviet Political Prisoners (EA) ... CDSPP
Committee for Development Planning (SAUO) ... CDP
Committee for Documentary and Legal Problems (SAUS) ... DC

Committee for Do-It-Yourself Household Moving (EA) .... DITY
Committee for Economic Defence (SAUO) .... CED
Committee for Economic Development (EA) .... CED
Committee for Education Funding (EA) .... CEF
Committee for Effective Capital Recovery [*Defunct*] (EA) .... CECR
Committee for Electrical Equipment for Use in Flammable Atmospheres (HEAS) .... CEFFA
Committee for Elimination of Death [*Later, CEL*] (EA) .... CFED
Committee for Energy Awareness [*Later, USCEA*] (EA) .... CEA
Committee for Energy Policy [*Organization for Economic Cooperation and Development*] (MCD) .... CEP
Committee for Energy Thrift in Industry (SAUO) .... CETI
Committee for Engineering Information (SAUS) .... CEI
Committee for Enlisted Classification Selection and Testing [*Navy*] (NVT) .... CECSET
Committee for Environmental Conservation (SAUO) .... CoEnCo
Committee for Environmental Information (IID) .... CEI
Committee for Environmental Monitoring of Forest Insect Control Operations .... EMOFICO
Committee for Environmentally Effective Packaging (EA) .... CEEP
Committee for Equality of Citizens Before the Courts (EA) .... CO-EQUAL
Committee for Equitable Access to Crude Oil (EA) .... CEACO
Committee for Equitable Compensation [*Defunct*] (EA) .... CEC
Committee for Establishing a National Testing Authority (SAUO) .... CENTA
Committee for European Airspace Coordination [*NATO*] .... CEAC
Committee for European Airspace Coordination [*NATO*] (NATG) .... CEASC
Committee for European Construction Equipment [*British*] (EAIO) .... CECE
Committee for European Co-operation in the Field of Science and Technology (SAUO) .... COST
Committee for European Development of Science and Technology (SAUS) .... CODEST
Committee for European Economic Cooperation [*Marshall Plan*] [*Post-World War II*] .... CEEC
Committee for European Marine Biological Symposia (SAUO) .... EMBS
Committee for European Standardization (SAUO) .... CEN
Committee for Evaluating the Feasibility of Space Rocketry [*Navy Bureau of Aeronautics*] [*Obsolete*] .... CEFSR
Committee for Exchange with Non-English Speaking Countries (AIE).... CENESC
Committee for Exploitation of the Oceans (SAUS) .... COMEXCO
Committee for Exploitation of the Oceans (BARN) .... COMEXO
Committee for Exports to Latin America (SAUO) .... CELA
Committee for Exports to Latin America and the Caribbean (SAUO) .... CELAC
Committee for Exports to the United States of America (SAUO) .... CEUSA
Committee for Fisheries (SAUS) .... RosCom-Rybolovstvo
Committee for Food and Shelter [*Later, NAEH*] (EA) .... CFS
Committee for Freedom of Choice in Cancer Therapy [*Later, CFCM*] (EA) .... CFCCT
Committee for Freedom of Choice in Medicine (EA) .... CFCM
Committee for Full Funding of Education Programs (EA) .... CFFEP
Committee for Geographical Names in Australia (SAUO) .... CGNA
Committee for Geology and Mineral Resources (SAUS) .... RosComNedra
Committee for Geophysical Data (SAUO) .... CGD
Committee for Graphic Arts Technologies Standards .... CGATS
Committee for Handgun Control (EA) .... CHC
Committee for Handicapable Dancers (EA) .... CHD
Committee for Handling European Automation Programmes (SAUS) .... CHEAP
Committee for Health in Southern Africa (SAUO) .... CHISA
Committee for Hispanic Arts and Research (EA) .... CHAR
Committee for Human Rights and Democracy in Turkey (EA) .... CHRDT
Committee for Human Rights in Argentina [*British*] .... CHRA
Committee for Human Rights in Rumania (EA) .... CHRR
Committee for Human Rights in Syria (EA) .... CHRS
Committee for Humane Legislation (EA) .... CHL
Committee for Immediate Nuclear War (EA) .... CINW
Committee for Imperial Defence [*British*] .... CID
Committee for Independent Political Action .... CIPA
Committee for Industrial Co-Operation [*European Economic Community/African, Caribbean, and Pacific States*] (DS) CIC
Committee for Industrial Development [*United Nations*] .... CID
Committee for Industrial Organization (SAUO) .... CIO
Committee for Industrial Technology (SAUO) .... CFIT
Committee for Information and Documentation in Science and Technology (SAUO) .... CIDST
Committee for Information and Documentation on Science and Technology [*EEC*] (PDAA) .... CIDST
Committee for Information, Computer and Communication Policy (SAUO) .... CICCP
Committee for Inland Fisheries of Africa [*UN Food and Agriculture Organization*] .... CIFA
Committee for Intercontinental Research Networks (SAUO) .... CCIRN
Committee for International Aeromodeling (SAUO) .... CIAM
Committee for International Collaborative Activities [*An association*] .... CICA
Committee for International Co-operation in Information Retrieval Among Examining Patent Offices .... CICIREPATO
Committee for International Coordination of National Research in Demography (SAUS) .... CICRED
Committee for International Economic Growth (SAUO) .... CIEG
Committee for International Human Rights Inquiry [*Formerly, Committee for Chilean Inquiry*] (EA) CCI
Committee for International Investment and Multinational Enterprises (SAUO) .... CIIME
Committee for International Justice and Peace of the Episcopal Conference of England and Wales (EAIO) .... CIJPECEW
Committee for International Municipal Cooperation (SAUO) .... CICM
Committee for International Municipal Cooperation .... CIMC
Committee for Italic Handwriting [*Defunct*] (EA) .... CIH
Committee for Italic Handwriting (SAUO) .... CIH
Committee for Justice and Liberty Foundation .... CJL
Committee for Justice for Domingo and Viernes [*Defunct*] (EA) .... CJDV
Committee for Land Resources and Management (SAUS) .... RosComZem
Committee for Latvian Song Festival in USA (SAUO) .... CLSF
Committee for Leaving the Environment of America Natural .... CLEAN
Committee for Liberation (SAUO) .... CFL
Committee for Library Advocacy and Student Success .... CLASS
Committee for Liquidation of German War Potential [*Allied German Occupation Forces*] .... CLWP
Committee for Maritime Unity (SAUO) .... CMU
Committee for Medical Aid to Central America (EA) .... COMACA
Committee for Modern Courts (EA) .... CMC
Committee for Monetary Research and Education, Inc. [*Research center*] (RCD) .... CMRE
Committee for Mother and Child Rights (EA) .... CMCR
Committee for National Accreditation of Environmental Laboratories (SAUO) .... CNAEL
Committee for National Arbor Day (EA) .... CNAD
Committee for National Health Insurance (EA) .... CNHI
Committee for National Land Development Policy [*Defunct*] .... CNLDP
Committee for National Security (EA) .... CNS
Committee for National Theatre Week (EA) .... CNTW
Committee for Nationalist Union [*British*] .... CNU
Committee for Nautical Archaeology (SAUO) .... CNA
Committee for Nonviolent Action [*Later, WRL*] (EA) .... CNVA
Committee for Nordic Universities of Journalism [*See also RNJ*] (EAIO) .... CNUJ
Committee for Nuclear Information [*Later, Committee for Environmental Information*] .... CNI
Committee for Nuclear Responsibility (EA) .... CNR
Committee for Oil Pipe Lines [*Later, AOPL*] .... COPL
Committee for Oil Shale Development [*Defunct*] (EA) .... COSHD
Committee for Open Debate on the Holocaust [*Defunct*] (EA) .... CODH
Committee for Operational Environmental Satellites (ACAE) .... COES
Committee for Operational Processing Centers (SAUO) .... COPC
Committee for Original People's Entitlement [*Eskimo claim to Canadian land*] .... COPE
Committee for Overseas Science and Technology [*British*] (PDAA) .... COST
Committee for OWSE-North America (SAUS) .... CONA
Committee for Peace Research (SAUO) .... CPR
Committee for Pedestrian Tolls [*Defunct*] (EA) .... CPT
Committee for Positive Education [*Defunct*] (EA) .... CPE
Committee for Presidents' Day [*Later, Presidents' Day National Committee*] (AEBS) .... CPD
Committee for Prisoner Humanity and Justice (EA) .... CPHJ
Committee for Private Offshore Rescue and Towing (EA) .... C-PORT
Committee for Privileges, House of Commons/Lords (DLA) .... C Priv
Committee for Production Sharing [*Defunct*] (EA) .... CPS
Committee for Promotion of International Trade (SAUO) .... CPIT
Committee for Proprietary Medicinal Products [*European Directorate*] .... CPMP
Committee for Public Education and Religious Liberty (EA) .... PEARL
Committee for Public Information (SAUO) .... CPI
Committee for Public Justice (EA) .... CPJ
Committee for Public Opinion Information (SAUS) .... KMSB
Committee for Purchase of Products and Services of the Blind and Other Severely Handicapped [*Later, Committee for Purchase from the Blind and Other Severely Handicapped*] .... CPPSBOSH
Committee for Radiation Protection and Public Health [*EURATOM*] (NUCP) .... CRPPH
Committee for Real Ale (EA) .... CRA
Committee for Reciprocity Information [*A federal government body*] .... CRI
Committee for Reciprocity Information (SAUO) .... CRI
Committee for Rejection of Obnoxious Commercials .... CROC
Committee for Religious Freedom (EA) .... CRF
Committee for Research and Development (SAUO) .... CRD
Committee for Research into Apparatus for the Disabled (SAUO) .... CRAD
Committee for Research into Teacher Education (AIE) .... CRITE
Committee for Restoration of Democracy in Burma (EA) .... CRDB
Committee for Restriction of Acronym Proliferation (SAUO) .... CRAP
Committee for Review of Our China Policy [*Defunct*] .... CROCP
Committee for Safe Bicycling [*Defunct*] (EA) .... CSB
Committee for Science, Engineering, and Public Policy .... COSEPP
Committee for Science, Engineering, and Public Policy [*Formerly, COSPUP*] [*National Academy of Sciences*] [*Washington, DC*] .... COSEPUP
Committee for Scientific and Technical Personnel (SAUO) .... CSTP
Committee for Scientific and Technological Policy (DMAA) .... CSTP
Committee for Scientific Research (SAUO) .... CSR
Committee for Single Adoptive Parents (EA) .... CSAP
Committee for Single Six-Year Presidential Term (EA) .... CSSYPT
Committee for Site Characterization (SAUO) .... CSCT
Committee for Small Business Exports (EA) .... COSBE
Committee for Small Business Exports (EA) .... CSBE
Committee for Social Responsibility in Engineering (SAUO) .... CSRE
Committee for Solidarity with the Bolivian People [*Defunct*] (EA) .... CSBP
Committee for Space Environment Forecasting (ACAE) .... CSEF
Committee for Stable Deterrence (EA) .... CSD
Committee for Standardization (SAUO) .... CSK
Committee for Standardizing Social Services Terminology (SAUO) .... COSST
Committee for State Security (SAUS) .... KGB
Committee for Statistics in the Physical Sciences (SAUO) .... CSPS
Committee for Sustainable Agriculture (EA) .... CSA
Committee for Systems Development (ACAE) .... CSD
Committee for the Absorption of Soviet Emigres .... CASE

Committee for the Accreditation of Canadian Medical Schools [*Canada*] (PGP) .... CACMS

Committee for the Advancement of Professional Practice (DIPS) .... CAPP

Committee for the Advancement of Role-Playing Games (EA) .... CAR=PGa

Committee for the Advancement of Role-Playing Games (EA) .... CARPG

Committee for the Advancemet of Virtue and Elimination of Sin (WDAA) .... CAVES

Committee for the Aid to West Papuan Refugees [*Netherlands*] (EAIO) .... CAWPR

Committee for the Alliance for Progress [*Department of Commerce*] .... COMAP

Committee for the Application of the Behavioral Sciences to the Strategies of Peace (SAUO) .... ABSSOP

Committee for the Application of the Behavioral Sciences to the Strategies of Peace (EA) .... ABSSOP

Committee for the Care of the Diabetic .... CCD

Committee for the Collegiate Education of Black Students .... CCEBS

Committee for the Communication of Conservative Policies (SAUO) .... CCCP

Committee for the Coordination of Joint Prospecting for Mineral Resources in Asian Offshore Areas (SAUS) .... CCOP

Committee for the Coordination of National Bibliographic Control [*Defunct*] (EA) .... CCNBC

Committee for the Co-Ordination of Patriotic and Democracy-Loving Forces [*Thailand*] (PD) .... CCPDF

Committee for the Coordination of Services to Displaced Persons in Thailand [*Australia*] .... CCSDPT

Committee for the Defence of Human and National Rights in Ukraine [*Australia*] .... CDHNRU

Committee for the Defence of the Unjustly Prosecuted (EAIO) .... CDUP

Committee for the Defense of Human Rights in India (EA) .... CoDHRI

Committee for the Defense of Legitimate Rights [*Saudi Arabia*] (ECON) ..... CDLR

Committee for the Defense of National Interest (SAUO) .... CDNI

Committee for the Defense of National Interests (SAUO) .... CDIN

Committee for the Defense of Persecuted Orthodox Christians [*Defunct*] (EA) .... CDPOC

Committee for the Defense of Persons Unjustly Persecuted [*Former Czechoslovakia*] [*Political party*] (PD) .... VONS

Committee for the Defense of Political Prisoners in Vietnam (EA) .... CDPPV

Committee for the Defense of the Revolution [*Cuba*] .... CDR

Committee for the Democratic Struggle [*Mexico*] .... COLUDE

Committee for the Development and Management of Fisheries in the South China Sea [*Thailand*] (EAIO) .... CDMSCS

Committee for the Development of Alternatives to Incarceration [*Canada*] .... CODAI

Committee for the Development of Art in Negro Colleges [*Later, CAA*].... CDANC

Committee for the Development of Art in Negro Colleges (SAUO) .... CDANC

Committee for the Development of Mycology in Asian Countries (SAUO) .... CDMAC

Committee for the Economic Growth of Israel (EA) .... CEG-I

Committee for the Elimination of Racial Discrimination .... CERD

Committee for the Employment of Disabled People (AIE) .... CEDP

Committee for the Eradication of Acronyms in Scientific Exchange (SAUO) .... CEASE

Committee for the Free World (EA) .... CFW

Committee for the Furtherance of Torah Observance (EA) .... CFTO

Committee for the Future of America (EA) .... CFA

Committee for the Game (EA) .... CG

Committee for the Global Atmospheric Research Program .... CGARP

Committee for the Implementation of Textile Agreements .... CITA

Committee for the Implementation of the Standardized Yiddish Orthography (EA) .... CISYO

Committee for the Jewish Idea (EA) .... CJI

Committee for the Maintenance of Jewish Standards (EA) .... CMJS

Committee for the Monument of Garibaldi (EA) .... CMG

Committee for the Mustard Industry of the European Communities [*Belgium*] (EAIO) .... CMI-EC

Committee for the National Institute for the Environment [*Lobby group*] ..... CNIE

Committee for the Preservation of the Tule Elk (EA) .... CPTE

Committee for the Promotion of Latin (SAUS) .... CPL

Committee for the Promotion of Temperance (SAUO) .... CPT

Committee for the Reception of Aid (SAUO) .... AIDRECEP

Committee for the Recovery of Archaeological Remains .... CRAR

Committee for the Reexamination of the History of the Second World War (EA) .... CRHSWW

Committee for the Reform of Animal Experimentation [*British*] .... CRAE

Committee for the Reform of Chinese Written Language (SAUO) .... CRCWL

Committee for the Reputation of Elizabeth Taylor (SAUO) .... CRET

Committee for the Restoration of the Republic [*Defunct*] (EA) .... CRR

Committee for the Restructuring and Progress of Equity [*Actors' Trade Union*] [*British*] (DI) .... CRAPE

Committee for the Reunification of the Cameroons (SAUO) .... CORECA

Committee for the Revision of the Criminal Code [*Allied German Occupation Forces*] .... CRICO

Committee for the Revolution in Oman and the Arabian Gulf [*Denmark*] .... KROAG

Committee for the Scientific Investigation of Claims of the Paranormal (EA) .... CSICOP

Committee for the Scientific Investigation of the Paranormal (SAUS) .... CSIP

Committee for the Scientific Survey of Air Defence [*British*] [*World War II*] .... CSSAD

Committee for the Scientific Survey of Air Offence [*British*] [*World War II*] .... CSSAO

Committee for the Scientific Survey of Air Warfare [*British*] [*World War II*] .... CSSAW

Committee for the Simplification of International Trade Procedures, London (SAUS) .... SITPRO

Committee for the Status of Women in Philosophy (EA) .... CSWP

Committee for the Study of Environmental Manpower [*National Research Council*] .... CSEM

Committee for the Study of Handgun Misuse (EA) .... CSHM

Committee for the Study of Scientific Problems of Peace and Disarmament (SAUO) .... CPD

Committee for the Study of the American Electorate (EA) .... CSAE

Committee for the Suit Against Government Misconduct (EA) .... CSAGM

Committee for the Survey of Chemistry [*National Academy of Sciences*] .... CSC

Committee for the Survival of a Free Congress .... CSFC

Committee for the Visual Arts [*Later, CVAAS*] (EA) .... CVA

Committee for the Visual Arts/Artists Space (EA) .... CVAAS

Committee for the Wool Industries of the EEC (SAUO) .... INTERLAINE

Committee for Thorough Agricultural Political Education [*Associated Milk Producers, Inc.*] .... C-TAPE

Committee for Time Uniformity [*Defunct*] .... CTU

Committee for Truth in Psychiatry (EA) .... CTIP

Committee for United States Action on Asylum Concern (SAUO) .... CUSAAC

Committee for University Assistance [*Military*] [*British*] .... CUA

Committee for Upgrading Environmental Radiation Data (SAUS) .... CUERD

Committee for Veterinary Medicinal Products [*European Community*] .... CVMP

Committee for Water Resources (SAUS) .... Ros ComVod

Committee for Western Civilization (EA) .... CWC

Committee for Whaling Statistics (SAUO) .... CWRU

Committee for Whaling Statistics (SAUS) .... CWS

Committee for Wildlife on the Last Frontier .... WOLF

Committee for Women in Geophysics [*Defunct*] (EA) .... CWG

Committee for Women in Public Administration (EA) .... CWPA

Committee for World Development and World Disarmament [*Defunct*] (EA) .... CWDWD

Committee for Youth Organizations (SAUO) .... CYO

Committee for Zero Automobile Growth (EA) .... CZAG

Committee for/of/on Inland Fisheries in/of Africa (SAUO) .... CIFA

Committee in Defense of the Palestinian and Lebanese Peoples [*Defunct*] (EA) .... CDPLP

Committee in Solidarity with Latin American Nonviolent Movements (EA) .... CISLANM

Committee in Solidarity with the People of Guatemala (EA) .... CSPG

Committee in Solidarity with the People of Iran (EA) .... CSPI

Committee in Support of Solidarity (EA) .... CSS

Committee in the Application of Computers in the Construction Industry (SAUS) .... CACCI

Committee Information for Industry (SAUO) II

Committee Insuring and Guaranteeing Anyone's Right to Smoke .... CIGARS

Committee International Radio Maritime (SAUS) .... CIRM

Committee Investigating Cartographic Entity, Definitions, and Standards (GEOI) .... CICAEDAS

Committee Meeting Information System (MCD) .... COMIS

Committee of 200 [*An association*] C200

Committee of Aeronautical Research (SAUO) .... CAR

Committee of Agricultural Organizations in the European Communities (EAIO) .... CAO-EC

Committee of American Steamship Lines [*Later, AIMS*] (EA) .... CASL

Committee of American Steamship Lines (SAUO) .... CASL

Committee of Americans for Peace in the Middle East [*Defunct*] (EA) ...... CAPME

Committee of an Advanced Nature (SAUO) .... CAN

Committee of Associations of Specialist Engineering Contractors (SAUO) .... CASEC

Committee of Atomic Bomb Survivors in the US (EA) .... CABSUS

Committee of Australian Museum Directors (SAUO) .... CAMN

Committee of Black Americans for Truth about the Middle-East [*Defunct*] .... COBATAME

Committee of Black Gay Men (EA) .... CBGM

Committee of Bomex Participants (SAUS) .... COB PANART

Committee of Butchery Organizations of the EEC (EAIO) .... CBOE

Committee of Catholics Who Care (EA) .... CCWC

Committee of Chiefs of Staff (SAUO) .... CCS

Committee of Chinese Correspondence (EA) CCC

Committee of Combined Boards .... COB

Committee of Commercial Organizations of the EEC Countries (SAUO) .... COCCEE

Committee of Common Market Automobile Constructors [*EEC*] .... CCMAC

Committee of Concern .... COC

Committee of Concern for Central America (EA) .... CCCA

Committee of Concerned Africans [*Defunct*] (EA) .... CCA

Committee of Concerned Artists and Professionals (EA) .... CCAP

Committee of Concerned Catholics [*Defunct*] (EA) CCC

Committee of Concerned Scientists (EA) .... CCS

Committee of Control of the International Zone of Tangier .... CCIZT

Committee of Corporate Finance [*of the National Association of Securities Dealers*] .... CCF

Committee of Corporate Telecommunications Users [*An association*] (EA) .... CCTU

Committee of County Court Judges (SAUO) .... CCCJ

Committee of Direction of Fruit Marketing [*Queensland*] [*Australia*] .... CDFM

Committee of Directors of Polytechnics [*British*] .... CDP

Committee of Directors of Research Associations (SAUO) .... CDRA

Committee of Directors of Textile Research Associations (SAUO) .... CDTRA

Committee of Ecological Research for the Interoceanic Canal [*National Academy of Science*] (MSC) .... CERIC

Committee of EEC [*European Economic Community*] Shipbuilders' Associations (EAIO) .... CESA

Committee of Engineering Professors' Conference (ACII) .... CEPC

Committee of European Associations of Manufacturers of Electronic Components [*EC*] [*Italy*] (ECED) .... CEMEC

Committee of European Associations of Manufacturers of Passive Electronic Components (SAUO) ... CEPEC
Committee of European Coffee Associations (EAIO) ... CECA
Committee of European Financial Executives Institutes [*EC*] (ECED) ... CEFEI
Committee of European Promotors of Exhibitions of Measurement and Automation (ACII) ... CEMA
Committee of Evidence (SAUS) ... CommEv
Committee of Experts (SAUO) ... COMEX
Committee of Experts for the Coordination of Scientific Terminology (SAUO) ... CECST
Committee of Experts for the Transfer of Information between Community Languages [*EEC*] (PDAA) ... CETIL
Committee of Experts for the Transfer of Information between European Languages (SAUO) ... CETIL
Committee of Experts on the Transport of Dangerous Goods of the United Nations Economic and Social Council [*RSPA*] (TAG) ... ECOSOC
Committee of Food and Nutrition (SAUO) ... CFNP
Committee of French American Wives [*Later, FAAC*] (EA) ... CFAW
Committee of French Speaking Societies (EA) ... CFSS
Committee of Glutamic Acid Manufacturers of the European Economic Community (EAIO) ... CGAMEEC
Committee of Good Officers (SAUO) ... CGO
Committee of Heads of Administration [*NATO*] (NATG) ... CHA
Committee of Heads of Architecture Schools of Australasia [*Australia*] ... CHASA
Committee of Heads of Drama Departments in Scotland (AIE) ... CHDDS
Committee of Housing, Building and Planning (SAUO) ... HBP
Committee of Housing, Building and Planning Seminar (SAUO) ... HBP/SEM
Committee of Housing, Building and Planning Working Party (SAUO) ... HBP/WP
Committee of Imperial Defence (SAUO) ... CID
Committee of Intellectuals for a Europe of Libertites (SAUO) ... CIEL
Committee of International Development Institutions for the Environment (SAUS) ... CIDIE
Committee of International Development Institutions on the Environment (ECON) ... CIDIE
Committee of Interns and Residents (EA) ... CIR
Committee of Labour Organizations (SAUO) ... CLO
Committee of Land Registry (SAUO) ... CLR
Committee of Liberal Exiles [*British*] (EAIO) ... CLE
Committee of Liner Operators - South America (SAUO) ... COMLOSA
Committee of London and Scottish Bankers [*British*] ... CLSB
Committee of London Clearing Bankers [*British*] ... CLCB
Committee of Manufacturers on Standarization of Pipe Fittings and Valves (SAUO) ... CMSPFV
Committee of Marketing Organizations [*British*] ... COMO
Committee of Middle East Trade [*British Overseas Trade Board*] (DS) ... COMET
Committee of Ministers on Energy Conservation (SAUO) ... MEC
Committee of National Armament Directors (SAUO) ... CNAD
Committee of National Institutes of Patent Agents [*Winchester, Hampshire, England*] (EA) ... CNIPA
Committee of National Liberation (SAUO) ... CNL
Committee of National Security Companies [*Memphis, TN*] (EA) ... CONSCO
Committee of Nuclear Regulatory Activities (SAUO) ... CNRA
Committee of Operations Analyst (SAUS) ... COA
Committee of Organizers of National Participations in International Economic Displays (SAUO) ... INTEREXPO
Committee of Permanent Representatives (SAUO) ... COREPER
Committee of Plastic Converter Associations of Western Europe (SAUS) ... EUTRAPLAST
Committee of Practitioners (SAUO) ... COP
Committee of Presidential Representatives (SAUO) ... CPR
Committee of Presidents of Statistical Societies (EA) ... COPSS
Committee of Presidents of Statistical Societies (EA) ... CPSS
Committee of Professors in Operational Research (AIE) ... COPIOR
Committee of Public Accounts (SAUO) ... CPA
Committee of Publicly Owned Companies (EA) ... COPOC
Committee of Purchasers of Aircraft Material (SAUO) ... CPAM
Committee of Religion and Art of America [*Later, FAAR*] (EA) ... CRAA
Committee of Religious Concern for Peace (EA) ... CRCP
Committee of Responsibility ... COR
Committee of Responsibility to save war-burned and war-injured Vietnamese children (SAUO) ... COR
Committee of Returned Volunteers [*Defunct*] (EA) ... CRV
Committee of Scottish Bank General Managers (SAUO) ... CSBGM
Committee of Scottish Higher Education Principals (AIE) ... COSHEP
Committee of Security Experts [*Military*] (CINC) ... CSE
Committee of Seismology [*National Academy of Sciences*] (USDC) ... CS
Committee of Senior Officers (SAUO) ... CSO
Committee of Singled-Out Taxpayers [*Later, American Council of Taxpayers*] (EA) ... COST
Committee of Small Magazine Editors and Publishers [*In association name COSMEP, The International Association of Independent Publishers*] (EA) ... COSMEP
Committee of Southern Churchmen (EA) ... CSC
Committee of Special Means [*British military*] (DMA) ... CSM
Committee of Sponsoring Organizations of the Treadway Commission (SAUO) ... COSO
Committee of Stock Exchanges in the European Community [*See also CBCE*] (EAIO) ... CSEE
Committee of Supply (SAUO) ... C/S
Committee of Ten Million (EA) ... COTM
Committee of Ten Thousand (ADWA) ... COTT
Committee of the Acta Endocrinologica Countries ... CAEC
Committee of the Associated Trades [*A union*] [*British*] ... CAT
Committee of the Association of Honey Importers and Packers of Europe (SAUO) ... CAHIPE
Committee of the Associations of Honey Importers and Packers of Europe (EAIO) ... CAHIPE
Committee of the Brick Industry (SAUO) ... CBI
Committee of the Cotton Industries of the European Economic Community (SAUO) ... EUROCOTON
Committee of the House [*British*] (ROG) ... COMH
Committee of the ICC and the Chambers of Commerce of Socialist Countries for the Development of East-West Trade and Economic Cooperation (SAUO) ... East-West Committee
Committee of the International Socialist Conference (SAUO) ... COMISCO
Committee of the International Union of Political Prisoners (SAUO) ... CIUPP
Committee of the National Ferrous Scrap Federations and Associations of the Common Market [*See also COFENAF*] (EAIO) ... CNFSFACM
Committee of the Regions [*Belgium*] (ECON) ... COR
Committee of the Russian Federation for Standardisation, Metrology, and Certification (BUAC) ... GOST
Committee of the Whole [*United Nations*] ... COW
Committee of the Whole House, House of Lords [*British*] (DLA) ... CWH
Committee of Tin Mill Products Producers (EA) ... CTMPP
Committee of Transylvania (EA) ... CT
Committee of United States Citizens Living in Nicaragua (EA) ... CUSCLN
Committee of University Industrial Relations Librarians ... CUIRL
Committee of Urban Program Universities ... CUPU
Committee of Vice-Chancellors and Principals of the Universities of the United Kingdom [*British*] ... CVCP
Committee of Ways and Means (SAUO) ... CWM
Committee of World Tensions (SAUO) ... COWT
Committee of Youth Hostel Organizations in the Nordic Countries (EA) ... CYHONC
Committee of/on Scientific and Technical (or Technological) Research (SAUS) ... CREST
Committee on a Multimedium Approach to Sludge Management [*National Research Council*] ... CMSM
Committee on Academic Science and Engineering [*Federal Council for Science and Technology*] ... CASE
Committee on Accounting Procedure (EBF) ... CAP
Committee on Accreditation [*American Library Association*] ... COA
Committee on Administration (SAUO) ... CA
Committee on Administrative Services of Hospitals ... CASH
Committee on Advanced Television Transmission Systems [*Australia*] ... CATTS
Committee on Aeronautical Meteorological Problems (SAUS) ... CAMP
Committee on Agricultural Policies (SAUO) ... CAP
Committee on Agriculture [*Food and Agricultural Organization*] [*United Nations*] ... COAG
Committee on Air and Water Conservation [*Later, Committee for Environmental Affairs*] [*American Petroleum Institute*] ... CAWC
Committee on Aircraft Engine Emissions [*ICAO*] (DA) ... CAEE
Committee on Aircraft Noise [*ICAO*] (DA) ... CAN
Committee on Allied Health Education and Accreditation (EA) ... CAHEA
Committee on American East Asian Relations [*Defunct*] (EA) ... AEAR
Committee on American Library Resources on South Asia [*Later, CORMOSE A*] (EA) ... CALROSA
Committee on American Library Resources on Southeast Asia [*Later, CORMOSEA*] (EA) ... CALROSEA
Committee on Amphibious Operations (SAA) ... CAO
Committee on Appeal for Human Rights ... COAHR
Committee on Application of Conventions and Recommendations (SAUO) ... CACR
Committee on Application of Polarized Headlights [*OECD*] ... CAPH
Committee on Arabic in Informatics (SAUS) ... COARIN
Committee on Army and Navy Religious Activities [*National Jewish Welfare Board*] ... CANRA
Committee on ASEAN Youth Cooperation (SAUO) ... CAYC
Committee on Assessing the Progress of Education [*Later, NAEP*] (EA) ... CAPE
Committee on Assessing the Progress of Education (SAUO) ... CAPE
Committee on Atlantic Studies (EA) ... CAS
Committee on Atmosphere and Oceans (SAUO) ... CAO
Committee on Atmospheric Chemistry (SAUO) ... CAC
Committee on Atmospheric Chemistry and Global Pollution (SAUS) ... CACGP
Committee on Atmospheric Problems of Aerospace Vehicles [*American Meteorological Society*] ... CAPAV
Committee on Atmospheric Sciences [*Marine science*] (OSRA) ... CAS
Committee on Autonomous Groups (EA) ... CAG
Committee on Auxiliary Language Study (SAUO) ... CALS
Committee on Aviation Medicine [*NAS/NRC*] ... CAM
Committee on Basic Research in Education ... COBRE
Committee on Bibliography and Information Services for the Social Sciences and Humanities [*National Library of Canada*] ... CBISSSH
Committee on Biological Information [*British*] (DIT) ... CBI
Committee on Biological Sciences Information [*NAS/NRC*] ... COBSI
Committee on Boarding Schools (EA) ... CBS
Committee on Canadian Labour History ... CCLH
Committee on Capacity Building in Science (SAUS) ... CCBS
Committee on Capital Movements and Invisible Transactions ... CMIT
Committee on Captured Enemy Electronic Equipment (SAUO) ... COCEE
Committee on Captured Enemy Electronics Equipment ... COCEEE
Committee on Carcinogenicity [*British*] ... COC
Committee on Cataloging: Description and Access [*Association for Library Collections and Technical Services*] ... CCDA
Committee on Certification (SAUO) ... CERTICO
Committee on Challenges of a Modern Society/North Atlantic Treaty Organization (SAUO) ... CCMS/NATO
Committee on Changing International Realities (EA) ... CIR
Committee on Chemical and Biological Warfare (SAUO) ... CCBW
Committee on Chemical Warfare (SAUO) ... CCW

Committee on Children's Television, Inc. (NTCM) .... CCTI
Committee on Christian Literature for Women and Children (EA) .... CCLWC
Committee on Christian Literature for Women and Children in Mission Fields (SAUO) .... CCLWCMF
Committee on Classical Articles and History of Statistics (SAUO) .... COCAAHOS
Committee on Climatic Changes and the Ocean [*Defunct*] [*Paris, France*] (EAIO) .... CCCO
Committee on Codes and Standards [*Defunct*] (EA) .... CCS
Committee on Commodity Problems [*Rome, Italy*] [*United Nations*] (ASF) .... CCP
Committee on Comparative Urban Economics (EA) .... CCUE
Committee on Computer Science in Electrical Engineering Education [*Military*] .... COSINE
Committee on Conformity Assessment (SAUO) .... CASCO
Committee on Conservation of Manpower in Industry (SAUO) .... CCMI
Committee on Constitutional and Legal Matters [*UN Food and Agriculture Organization*] .... CCLM
Committee on Consumer Policy [*ISO*] (DS) .... COPOLCO
Committee on Contamination of Extra-Terrestrial Exploration [*NASA*] .... CETEX
Committee on Continuing Education for School Personnel (EA) .... CCESP
Committee on Contracting Out [*Defunct*] (EA) .... COCO
Committee on Contributions for Elective State Officials .... CCESO
Committee on Cooperation in Latin America [*of The National Council of Churches of Christ in the USA*] (EA) .... CCLA
Committee on Cooperative Service and Research (SAUO) .... CCSR
Committee on Cosmic Humanism (EA) .... CCH
Committee on Crime Prevention and Control [*Economic and Social Council of the UN*] [*Vienna, Austria*] (EAIO) .... CCPC
Committee on Data for Science and Technology (EA) .... CODATA
Committee on Data Interchange and Data Centers (MSC) .... CDIDC
Committee on Data Management and Computation [*National Academy of Sciences*] .... CODMAC
Committee on Data Management and Computing (SAUS) .... CODMAP
Committee on Data Management, Archiving, and Computation (EOSA) .... CODMAC
Committee on Data Systems Languages (SAUO) .... CODASYL
Committee on Decentralization of Controls after V-E Day [*War Production Board*] .... CODCAVE
Committee on Defence Equipment Reliability & Maintainability (SAUS) .... CODERM
Committee on Defence Expenditure (SAUS) .... CDE
Committee on Dental and Surgical Materials [*British*] (BABM) .... CDSM
Committee on Desert and Arid Zones Research (SAUO) .... CODAZR
Committee on Diagnostic Reading Tests [*Defunct*] (EA) .... CDRT
Committee on Directives (SAUO) .... DICO
Committee on Disarmament (ACAE) .... CD
Committee on Disarmament, Europe (ACAE) .... CDE
Committee on Domestic Technology Transfer [*Federal Council for Science and Technology*] .... CDTT
Committee on Donor Enlistment [*Later, OR*] (EA) .... CODE
Committee on Donor Enlistment Code Blue (SAUS) .... CODE
Committee on Drugs and Alcohol .... CODA
Committee on Dynamic Measurement (SAUO) .... CODM
Committee on Earth and Envionmental Sciences [*Marine science*] (OSRA) .... CEES
Committee on Earth and Environmental Sciences (SAUO) .... CEES US
Committee on Earth Observations Satellites [*NASA*] .... CEOS
Committee on Earth Observing Sensors (SAUS) .... CEOS
Committee on Earth Observing Systems (SAUO) .... CEOS
Committee on Earth Sciences [*President's Office of Science & Technology Policy*] .... CES
Committee on East Asian Libraries .... CEAL
Committee on Economic Issues (SAUO) .... CEI
Committee on Economic Security [*Terminated as formal agency, 1936, but continued informally for some time thereafter*] .... CES
Committee on Economic, Social and Cultural Rights (SAUO) .... CECSR
Committee on Education [*American Library Association*] .... COE
Committee on Education for Central America and Panama (SAUO) .... CECAP
Committee on Education Needs for Teen-Age Unwed Mothers .... CENTAUM
Committee on Educational Policy in Agriculture [*National Academy of Sciences*] .... CEPA
Committee on Educational Reconstruction .... CER
Committee on Electrical and Electronic Items (SAUO) .... CEEI
Committee on Electronic Data (SAUS) .... CoE
Committee on Emergency Medical Identification (EA) .... CEMI
Committee on Energy and Commerce (COE) .... CEC
Committee on Energy and the Environment [*National Research Council*] .... CEE
Committee on Energy Research and Technology (SAUO) .... CERT
Committee on Engineering Laws (SAUO) .... CEL
Committee on Environment and Natural Resources [*National Science and Technology Council*] .... CENR
Committee on Environment and Public Works (COE) .... CEPW
Committee on Environmental Decision Making [*National Research Council*] .... CEDM
Committee on Environmental Protection [*Marine science*] (OSRA) .... CEP
Committee on Environmental Quality (SAUS) .... CEQ
Committee on Equal Opportunities in Science and Technology [*National Science Foundation*] .... CEOST
Committee on European Security (SAUO) .... CES
Committee on Evaluation and Information Systems (OICC) .... CEIS
Committee on Exchanges [*Military*] .... COMEX
Committee on Expenditure in Executive Departments (SAUO) .... CEED
Committee on Extension to the Standard Atmosphere .... COESA
Committee on Fair Employment Practices [*World War II*] .... CFEP
Committee on Fair Trade with China [*Medina, WA*] (EA) .... CFTC
Committee on Federal Laboratories [*Federal Council for Science and Technology*] [*Terminated, 1976*] .... CFL
Committee on Federal Laboratories [*Federal Council for Science and Technology*] [*Terminated, 1976*] (EGAO) .... COFL
Committee on Federalism and National Purpose [*Defunct*] (EA) .... CFNP
Committee on Fisheries [*Food and Agriculture Organization*] .... COFI
Committee on Food, Agriculture, and Forestry [*Association of South East Asian Nations*] [*Jakarta, Indonesia*] (EAIO) .... COFAF
Committee on Food Aid Policies and Programmes (SAUO) .... CFAPP
Committee on Food from the Sea [*National Council on Marine Resources and Engineering Development*] (GFGA) .... CFFS
Committee on Forecaster Training (SAUS) .... COMFORT
Committee on Foreign Correspondence [*Freemasonry*] .... CFC
Committee on Foreign Investment in the United States .... CFIUS
Committee on Foreign Resistance [*War Cabinet*] [*British*] [*World War II*] .... CFR
Committee on Foreign Resistance, Economic Policy [*Ministry of Supply*] [*British*] [*World War II*] .... CFR(EP)
Committee on Forest Development in the Tropics (SAUS) .... FDT
Committee on Forestry [*Food and Agricultural Organization*] [*United Nations*] .... COFO
Committee on Fort Churchill (SAUO) .... CFCC
Committee on Free Press and Fair Trial [*of the American Newspaper Publishers Association*] (EA) .... CFPFT
Committee on Friendly Relations among Foreign Students [*Later, ISS*] (EA) .... CFR
Committee on Genetic Experimentation (SAUO) .... CIGENE
Committee on Genetic Experimentation [*ICSU*] .... COGENE
Committee on Geological Sciences [*National Academy of Sciences*] (USDC) .... CGS
Committee on Geophysical Environmental Data (SAUO) .... CGED
Committee on Geostationary Meteorological Satellite System (SAUS) .... CGMS
Committee on Global Change (SAUO) .... CGC
Committee on Global Ecology Concern (SAUS) .... CGEC
Committee on Government Operations .... CGO
Committee on Government Statistics and Information Service (SAUO) .... COGSIS
Committee on Guided Missiles (SAUO) .... CGM
Committee on Health and Human Rights (EA) .... CHHR
Committee on Hearing and Bio Acoustics (SAUS) .... CHABA
Committee on Human Artificial Insemination. Report [*1960*] [*A publication*] (ILCA) .... Feversham Cttee
Committee on Human Rights for Nicaragua [*Later, CHRPN*] (EA) .... CHRN
Committee on Human Rights for the People of Nicaragua (EA) .... CHRPN
Committee on Human Rights in Malaysia and Singapore (EA) .... COHRIMS
Committee on Human Rights of the US National Academy of Sciences (EA) .... CHRUSNAS
Committee on Imagery Requirements and Exploitation [*United States Intelligence Board*] .... COMIREX
Committee on Improvement of National Statistics [*Inter-American*] .... COINS
Committee on Indoor Air Quality [*Environmental Protection Agency*] (GFGA) .... CIAQ
Committee on Information and Cultural Relations (EAIO) .... CICR
Committee on Information and Industry (SAUS) II
Committee on Information Needs .... COIN
Committee on Institutional Cooperation (EA) CIC
[*The*] **Committee on Institutional Cooperation Network** [*Computer science*] (TNIG) .... CICNet
Committee on Institutional Equity (SAUS) .... CIE
Committee on Instruction in the Use of Libraries [*Later, CUILL*] (EA) .... IULC
Committee on Integrity and Management Improvement [*Environmental Protection Agency*] (EPA) .... CIMI
Committee on Intellectual Property (SAUS) .... CIP
Committee on Interagency Radiation Research and Policy Coordination .... CIRRPC
Committee on Interest and Dividends [*Terminated, 1974*] [*Federal Reserve Board*] .... CID
Committee on Intergovernmental Science Relations (SAUS) .... CISR
Committee on Interior and Insular Affairs (COE) .... CIIA
Committee on International Cooperation (SAUS) CIC
Committee on International Education in Agricultural Sciences [*See also SVLB*] [*Deventer, Netherlands*] (EAIO) .... CIEAS
Committee on International Environmental Activities (SAUO) .... CIEA
Committee on International Environmental Affairs [*Department of State*] [*Washington, DC*] (EGAO) .... CIEA
Committee on International Exchange of Persons .... CIEP
Committee on International Exchange of Persons Conference Board of Associated Research Councils [*Later, Council for International Exchange of Scholars*] (EA) .... CIEPCBC
Committee on International Freedom to Publish (EA) .... CIFP
Committee on International Investment and Multinational Enterprises .... CIME
Committee on International Non-Theatrical Events (SAUO) .... CINE
Committee on International Nuclear Standards (SAUO) .... COINS
Committee on International Ocean Affairs (USDC) .... CIEA
Committee on International Ocean Affairs [*Department of State*] (NOAA) .... CIOA
Committee on International Policy in the Marine Environment [*National Council on Marine Resouces and Engineering Development*] (GFGA) .... CIPME
Committee on international programs of the USA standards institutes company Member Council (SAUO) .... CMC
Committee on International Reference Atmosphere .... CIRA
Committee on International Relations [*National Education Association*] (AEBS) .... CIR
Committee on International Science, Engineering, and Technology [*US government interagency committee*] [*Washington, DC*] .... CISET
Committee on International Scientific and Technical Information Programs [*National Academy of Sciences - National Research Council*] .... CISTIP

Committee on International Security and Arms Control [*National Academy of Sciences*] .... CISAC
Committee on International Standardization [*National Researh Council*] (NUCP) .... COIS
Committee on Interpretation of the Nation-Wide Marine Definition [*Later, COI*] (EA) .... CINWMD
Committee on Interstate and Foreign Commerce (COE) .... CIFC
Committee on Invisible Exports [*British*] (DS) .... CIE
Committee on Invisible Exports [*British*] (DS) .... COIE
Committee on Invisibles and Financing Related to Trade [*United Nations Conference on Trade and Development*] .... CIFT
Committee on Israeli Censorship (EA) CIC
Committee on Jobs, Environment, and Technology [*Defunct*] (EA) .... CJET
Committee on Joint Support of Air Navigation Services [*International Civil Aviation Organization*] .... CJSANS
Committee on Justice and the Constitution (EA) .... COJAC
Committee on Juvenile Delinquency (SAUO) .... JUDE
Committee on Latin American and Iberian Studies [*Harvard University*] [*Research center*] .... CLAIS
Committee on Legislation [*American Library Association*] .... COL
Committee on Lesbian and Gay History (NTPA) .... CLGH
Committee on Library Automation [*American Library Association*] .... COLA
Committee on Library Cooperation in Ireland (TELE) .... COLICO
Committee On Library Cooperation in Ireland (SAUS) .... COLICO
Committee on Life Sciences [*Federal interagency group*] .... CLS
Committee on Liguistic Information (SAUO) CLI
Committee on Local Radio Audience Measurement [*National Association of Broadcasters*] (NTCM) .... COLRAM
Committee on Local Television Audience Measurement [*National Association of Broadcasters*] (NTCM) .... COLTAM
Committee on Man and Radiation [*National Research Council*] (NUCP) ..... COMAR
Committee on Manpower Opportunities in Israel [*Later, IAC*] .... COMOI
Committee on Manpower Resources for Science and Technology .... CMR
Committee on Manpower Resources for Science and Technology [*British*] .... CMRST
Committee on Man's Underwater Activities (EA) .... CMU/WA
Committee on Marine Research, Education, and Facilities [*National Council on Marine Resources and Engineering Development*] (GFGA) .... CMREF
Committee on Marine Research Engineering and Facilities (SAUO) .... CMREP
Committee on Marine Research, Engineering and Facilities (SAUS) .... CMREP
Committee on Marine Science and Engineering [*Federal Council for Science and Technology*] (NOAA) .... COMSE
Committee on Marine Surveying and Mapping (GEOI) .... CMSM
Committee on Marine Technology [*British*] .... CMT
Committee on Materials [*Federal Council for Science and Technology*] ...... COMAT
Committee on Medical Aspects of Food Policy [*British*] .... CMAFP
Committee on Medical Aspects of Food Policy [*British*] .... COMA
Committee on Medical Aspects of Radiation in the Environment [*British*] .... COMARE
Committee on Medical Journalism (DAVI) .... CMJ
Committee on Medical Research [*Subdivision of OSRD*] [*World War II*] .... CMR
Committee on Medicine And Computers (SAUO) .... COMAC
Committee on Mediterranean Neogene Stratigraphy .... CMNS
Committee on Merchant Marine and Fisheries (COE) .... CMMF
Committee on Meteorological Analysis, Prediction and Research (SAUS) .... CMAPR
Committee on methods of strengthening International Cooperation (SAUO) CIC
Committee on Migration and Refugee Affairs (EA) .... CMRA
Committee on Migration and Resettlement [*Department of State*] [*World War II*] .... CMR
Committee on Migration, Refugees, and Demography (EA) .... CMRD
Committee on Militarism in Education [*Defunct*] (EA) .... CME
Committee on Military Affairs (SAUO) .... Com Mil Aff
Committee on Military Nutrition Research .... CMNR
Committee on Mineral Resources and the Environment [*National Research Council*] .... COMRATE
Committee on Missionary Evangelism (EA) .... COME
Committee on Motor Vehicle Emissions [*National Academy of Sciences*]..... CMVE
Committee on Multiple Use of the Coastal Zone [*National Council on Marine Resources and Engineering Development*] (GFGA) .... CMUCZ
Committee on Mutagenicity [*British*] .... COM
Committee on National Library and Information Systems (SAUS) .... CONIIS
Committee on National Library Information Systems .... CONLIS
Committee on National Statistics .... CNSTAT
Committee on National Student Citizenship in Every National Case of Emergency .... CONSCIENCE
Committee on Nationwide Television Audience Measurement (NTCM) .... CONTAM
Committee on Natural Gas Fluids Measurement (SAUO) .... COGM
Committee on Natural Resource Information Management [*Alaska*] (GEOI) .... CONRIM
Committee on Natural Resources (SAUO) .... CNR
Committee on New Alternatives in the Middle East [*Later, FOR*] (EA) .... CONAME
Committee on Non-discrimination and Integrity (SAUO) .... CANI
Committee on Nuclear and Alternative Energy Systems [*National Research Council*] [*Defunct*] .... CONAES
Committee on Nucleation and Atmospheric Aerosols (SAUO) .... CNAA
Committee on Ocean Exploration and Environmental Services [*National Council on Marine Resources and Engineering Development*] (GFGA) ..... COEES
Committee on Ocean Processes and Climate (SAUS) .... OPC
Committee on Office Systems and Technology [*Stanford University*] [*Stanford, CA*] (CSR) .... COST
Committee on Operational WWW Systems Evaluation for the North Atlantic (SAUS) .... CONA

Committee on Organization [*American Library Association*] .... COO
Committee on Overhead Reconnaissance [*Later, COMIREX*] .... COMOR
Committee on Paperless Entries [*Atlanta*] (MHDB) .... COPE
Committee on Parenthood Education [*Defunct*] (EA) .... COPE
Committee on Peaceful Uses of the Sea-Bed and Ocean Floor Beyond Limits of National Jurisdiction [*United Nations*] (EA) .... CPUSOFBLNJ
Committee on Period One [*US committee concerned with the period between the end of the German War and the end of the Japanese War*] [*World War II*] .... CPO
Committee on Persistent Pesticides (EA) .... CPP
Committee on Petroleum Measurement (SAUO) .... COPM
Committee on Physics and Society [*of American Institute of Physics*] ..... COMPAS
Committee on Planetary and Lunar Exploration [*National Research Council*] .... COMPLEX
Committee on Polar Research [*Later, PRB*] [*US*] .... CPR
Committee on Policy Implementation [*American Library Association*] .... COPI
Committee on Political Education [*AFL-CIO*] (EA) .... COPE
Committee on Political Parties .... CPP
Committee on Pollution Abatement and Control [*National Research Council*] (PDAA) .... COPAC
Committee on Power Plant Siting [*National Academy of Engineering*] .... COPPS
Committee on Prevention of Torture (SAUO) .... CPT
Committee on Principals and Directors of Central Institutions (AIE) .... COPADOCI
Committee on Procedure and Coordination for a possible Summit Conference (SAUO) .... CPC
Committee on Procedure and Valuation of Reparations (SAUO) .... CPV
Committee on Procedure and Valuation of Reparations [*Allied German Occupation Forces*] .... CPVR
Committee on Professional Ethics [*National Court Reporters Association*] .... COPE
Committee on Professional Ethics, Rights, and Freedom (EA) .... CPERF
Committee on Professional Standards [*American Psychological Association*] (DHP) .... COPS
Committee on Program Evaluation and Support [*American Library Association*] .... COPES
Committee on Propagation (SAA) .... COP
Committee on Propagation [*National Defense Research Committee*] .... CP
Committee on Prosthetics Research and Development [*National Research Council*] .... CPRD
Committee on Public Doublespeak (EA) .... CPD
Committee on Public Engineering Policy [*National Academy of Engineering*] .... COPEP
Committee on Public Engineering Policy [*National Academy of Engineering*] .... CPEP
Committee on Public Information (SAUO) .... CPI
Committee on Publication Ethics .... COPE
Committee on Publications and Communications [*International Council of Scientific Unions*] .... COPAC
Committee on Quaternary Economic Deposits (SAUO) .... INQUA
Committee on Quaternary Economic Deposits (SAUO) .... INQUA/QED
Committee on Radiation Oncology Studies [*National Cancer Institute*] .... CROS
Committee on Radio for Civil Aviation (SAUO) .... CRCA
Committee on Radio Frequencies [*National Academy of Sciences*] .... CORF
Committee on Radioactive Waste Management [*Later, BRWM*] (EA) .... CRWM
Committee on Radioactive Waste Management (SAUO) .... CRWM
Committee on Radiology (SAUS) .... CONRAD
Committee on Reactor Safety Technology .... CREST
Committee on Reciprocal Deliveries [*Allied German Occupation Forces*] ...... CRD
Committee on Reference Materials [*ISO*] (DS) .... REMCO
Committee on Remote Sensing Programs for Earth Resource Survey [*Formerly, COSPEAR*] [*National Academy of Sciences*] .... CORSPERS
Committee on Renewable Energy Commerce and Trade (AAGC) .... CORECT
Committee on Renewable Resources for Industrial Materials (SAUO) .... CORRIM
Committee on Research and Statistics [*American Library Association*] .... CORS
Committee on Research Evaluation [*US*] .... CORE
Committee on Research Expenditure (SAUO) .... CORE
Committee on Research in the Mathematical Sciences (SAUO) .... CORIMS
Committee on Research Materials on Southeast Asia (EA) .... CORMOSEA
Committee on Restrictions Against Disabled People (AIE) .... CORAD
Committee on Rhetoric, Administration, and Perspicacity [*Satirical bureaucracy term*] .... CRAP
Committee on Rural Economic and Social Trends .... CREST
Committee on Safety of Medicines [*British*] .... CSM
Committee on Sane Telephone Service .... COSTS
Committee on Scholarly Communications with the People's Republic of China .... CSCPRC
Committee on Scholarly Editions (EA) .... CSE
Committee on Science and Public Policy [*Later, COSEPUP*] [*National Academy of Sciences*] .... COSPUP
Committee on Science and Public Policy (SAUO) .... CSPP
Committee on Science and Technology in Developing Countries (ADWA) .... COSTED
Committee on Science and Technology Policy (SAUO) .... CSTP
Committee on Scientific and Technical Communication (SAUS) .... SAT COM
Committee on Scientific and Technical Information [*Federal Council for Science and Technology*] [*Defunct*] .... COSATI
Committee on Scientific and Technical Information (NITA) .... COST
Committee on Scientific and Technical Information (CIST) .... COSTI
Committee on Scientific and Technical Information [*Federal Council for Science and Technology*] [*Defunct*] (IEEE) .... CSTI
Committee on Scientific and Technical Information on Standardization (SAUO) .... INFCO
Committee on Scientific and Technical Research (SAUO) .... CREST
Committee on Scientific Information [*Federal Council for Science and Technology*] .... COSI

Committee on Seismology [*Marine science*] (OSRA) .... CS
Committee on Shipping Hydrography [*General Council of British Shipping*] (DS) .... COSH
Committee on Social Development and World Peace of the US Catholic Conference (EA) .... CSDWPUSCC
Committee on Social Implications of Technology (SAUO) .... CSIT
Committee on Social Implications of Technology (SAUS) .... C-SIT
Committee on Social Needs and Technology Assessment (SAUO) .... CSNTA
Committee on Societal Consequences of Transportation Noise Abatement [*National Research Council*] .... CTNA
Committee on Society, Development, and Peace [*of the Roman Catholic Church and the World Council of Churches*] [*Defunct*] (EA) .... SODEPAX
Committee on Sociological Research (SAUO) .... CSR
Committee on Solar and Space Physics (SAUS) .... CSSP
Committee on Solar Electromagnetic Radiation [*British*] (NUCP) .... CSER
Committee on Solar-Terrestrial Research [*National Academy of Sciences*] .... CSTR
Committee on SONAR Model Standards [*Navy*] .... COSMOS
Committee on South African War Resistance [*Defunct*] (EAIO) .... COSAWR
Committee on South Asian Women (EA) .... COSAW
Committee on Southern Map Libraries (GEOI) .... COSMI
Committee on Southern Map Libraries (SAUO) .... COSML
Committee on Southern Map Libraries (GEOI) .... CSML
Committee on Space Astronomy and Astrophysics (SAUS) .... CSAA
Committee on Space Programs for Earth Observations (EGAO) .... COSPEAR
Committee on Space Research [*of the International Council of Scientific Unions*] [*French*] .... COSPAR
Committee on Space Research (SAUO) .... COSR
Committee on Special Education .... CSE
Committee on Special Educational Needs [*Scotland*] (AIE) .... COSPEN
Committee on Special Educational Projects [*Cornell University*] .... COSEP
Committee on Standards (SAUO) .... COS
Committee on State and Local Government Cooperation .... CSLGC
Committee on State Prison (SAUO) .... ComSP
Committee on State Sovereignty [*Defunct*] (EA) .... CSS
Committee on State Taxation (NTPA) .... COST
Committee on Static Measurement (SAUO) .... COSM
Committee on Statistical Education (SAUO) .... CSE
Committee on Statistics of Drilling [*American Association of Petroleum Geologists*] (IID) .... CSD
Committee on Sugar Cane Diseases (EA) .... CSCD
Committee on Supply Questions in Liberated Areas (Official) [*World War II*] .... SLAO
Committee on Support and Financiel Affairs (SAUO) .... CSF
Committee on Support of Research in the Mathematical Sciences [*National Academy of Sciences*] .... COSRIMS
Committee on Surface Mining and Reclamation (DICI) .... COSMAR
Committee on Technology Transfer and Utilization (SAUO) .... COTTU
Committee on Temperance of the General Assembly (SAUO) .... CTGA
Committee on Terminology (SAUO) .... COT
Committee on the 1950 Census of the Americas (SAUO) .... COTA
Committee on the Acquisition and Use of Scientific and Technical Information in Pesticide Regulatory Decision Making at the Federal and State Levels [*National Research Council*] .... CPRDM
Committee on the Administration of Justice [*British*] (DBA) .... CAJ
Committee on the Application of Aerospace Technology to Society (SAUO) .... AATS
Committee on the Atlantic Salmon Emergency .... CASE
Committee on the Care of Children [*Defunct*] (EA) CCC
Committee on the Challenges of Modern Society [*Brussels, Belgium*] (EA) .... CCMS
Committee on the Conservation of Cultural Resources (SAUO) .... CCCR
Committee on the Conservation of Cultural Resources (SAUS) .... CCCR
Committee on the Constitutional System (EA) .... CCS
Committee on the Coordination of Antarctic Data (SAUS) .... CCAD
Committee on the Costs of Medical Care (DMAA) .... CCMC
Committee on the Development of Engineering Faculties .... CDEF
Committee on the Economic Impact of Defense and Disarmament (KSC) .... CEIDD
Committee on the Elimination of Discrimination Against Women [*United Nations*] .... CEDAW
Committee on the Exchange of Digital Data (GEOI) .... CEDD
Committee on the Exchange of Digital Data Spatial Transfer Format (SAUS) .... CEDD-STF
Committee on the Exercise of the Inalienable Rights of the Palestinian People (EA) .... CEIRPP
Committee on the Federal Procurement of Architect and Engineer Services (GEOI) .... COFPAES
Committee on the Formation of the National Biological Survey (SAUO) .... CFNBS
Committee on the Future of the American Physical Society (SAUO) .... FAPS
Committee on the Health Services Industry [*Cost of Living Council*] [*Abolished, 1973*] .... CHSI
Committee on the History of American Public Address (SAUO) .... CHAPA
Committee on the Human Environment (SAUO) .... CHEK
Committee on the Interplay of Engineering with Biology and Medicine (SAUS) .... CIEBM
Committee on the Medical Effects of Air Pollutants (SAUO) .... COMEAP
Committee on the Meteorological Effects of Stratospheric Aircraft .... COMESA
Committee on the Peaceful Uses of Outer Space [*United Nations*] (NITA) .... COPUOS
Committee on the Peaceful Uses of Outer Space [*United Nations*] (BARN) .... CPUOS
Committee on the Peaceful Uses of Outer Space [*United Nations*] (NTCM) .... CUPUOS
Committee on the Position of Modern Languages (SAUO) .... CPML
Committee on the Present Danger (EA) .... CPD
Committee on the Relationsship of Electricity to Agriculture (SAUO) .... CREA
Committee on the Reprocessing of Irradiated Nuclear Fuels (SAUO) .... CORECOM
Committee on the Safety of Machines [*British*] .... CSM
Committee on the Safety of Nuclear Installation [*Nuclear Regulatory Commission*] (NRCH) .... CSNI
Committee on the Standardization of Hospital Graphics [*Defunct*] .... CSHG
Committee on the Status of Endangered Wildlife in Canada (QUAC) .... COSEWIC
Committee on the Status of Women in Anthropology (EA) .... COSWA
Committee on the Status of Women in Librarianship [*American Library Association*] .... COSWL
Committee on the Status of Women in Linguistics (EA) .... CSWL
Committee on the Status of Women in Microbiology (EA) .... CSWM
Committee on the Status of Women in Sociology (EA) .... CSWS
Committee on the Status of Women in the Archival Profession (EA) .... CSWAP
Committee on the Status of Women in the Economics Profession (EA) .... CSWEP
Committee on the Status of Women in the Profession .... CSWP
Committee on the Survey of Materials Science and Engineering [*National Ac ademy of Sciences*] [*Obsolete*] .... COSMAT
Committee on the Teaching of Science [*ICSU*] (IRUK) .... CTS
Committee on the Teaching of Science of the International Council of Scientific Unions [*York, England*] (EAIO) .... ICSU-CTS
Committee on the Training of University Teachers (AIE) .... CTUT
Committee on the Undergraduate Program in Mathematics (SAUO) .... CUPM
Committee on the Unisex Military (EA) .... ComUnMil
Committee on the Unisex Military [*Defunct*] (EA) .... CUM
Committee on the World Food Crisis [*Defunct*] (EA) .... WFC
Committee on Thrombolytic Agents .... CTA
Committee on Tidal Hydraulics [*Army*] .... CTH
Committee on Toxicity [*British*] .... COT
Committee on Trade & the Environment [*World Trade Organization*] .... CTE
Committee on Tunneling and Underground Construction (EA) .... CTUC
Committee on Undersea Warfare .... CUW
Committee on Un-Filipino Activities (SAUO) .... CUFA
Committee on Uniform Crime Records (EA) .... UCR
Committee on Uniform Securities Identification Procedures (MHDB) .... CUSIP
Committee on Uniform Traffic Accident Statistics [*Later, Traffic Records Committee*] (EA) .... CUTAS
Committee on Vacuum Techniques, Inc. (SAUO) .... CVT
Committee on Valuation of Securities .... CVS
Committee on Value and Evaluation (SAUO) .... COVE
Committee on Veterans Medical Problems [*US*] .... CVMP
Committee on Water [*National Academy of Science*] (MSC) .... COW
Committee on Water Resources Research [*US*] .... COWRR
Committee on Women in Asian Studies (EA) .... CWAS
Committee on Women in Public Relations (NTCM) .... CWPR
Committee on Women's Employment and Related Social Issues (EA) .... CWERSI
Committee on Women's Employment and Related Social Issues (EA) .... WERSI
Committee on World Food Security [*United Nations*] (EA) .... CFS
Committee on World Literacy and Christian Literature [*Later, Intermedia*] (EA) .... LIT-LIT
Committee Program Review Council (AAGC) .... CPRC
Committee Substitute (WPI) .... CS
Committee Substitute House Bill (WPI) .... CSHB
Committee Substitute Senate Bill (WPI) .... CSSB
Committee to Abolish Sport Hunting (EA) .... CASH
Committee to Abolish the Fed (EA) .... CTAF
Committee to Aid Cold War Veterans (SAUO) .... CACW
Committee to Aid Cold War Veterans (EA) .... CACWV
Committee to Aid Democratic Dissidents in Yugoslavia [*Defunct*] (EA) .... CADDY
Committee to Assure the Availability of Casein [*Defunct*] (EA) .... CAAC
Committee to Award Miss Piggy the Oscar [*Defunct*] .... CAMPO
Committee to Bridge the Gap (EA) .... CBG
Committee to Cap the National Debt (EA) .... CCND
Committee to Combat Huntington's Disease [*Later, HDFA*] (EA) .... CCHD
Committee to Defend America by Aiding the Allies [*Active prior to US entry into World War II*] .... CDAAA
Committee to Defend America by Aiding the Allies (SAUO) .... CDAAA
Committee to Defend Reproductive Rights (EA) .... CDRR
Committee to Defend the First Amendment [*Later, FARI*] (EA) .... CDFA
Committee to Defend the US Constitution [*Defunct*] (EA) .... CDUSC
Committee to Eliminate Legal-Size Files [*Defunct*] (EA) .... CELSF
Committee to Eliminate Premature Christmas Advertising and Display [*Defunct*] (EA) .... CEPCAD
Committee to End Pay Toilets in America [*Defunct*] .... CEPTIA
Committee to End the Marion Lockdown (EA) .... CEML
Committee to Eradicate Syphilis [*Defunct*] (EA) .... CES
Committee to Establish the Gold Standard (EA) .... CEGS
Committee to Expose, Oppose, and Depose Patriarchy (EA) .... CEODP
Committee to Fight Microsoft Corporation (SAUO) .... CFMC
Committee to Form a US-Albania Friendship Association (EA) .... CFUSAFA
Committee to Halt Indoctrination and Demoralization in Education [*Group opposing sex education in schools*] .... CHIDE
Committee to Halt Useless College Killings [*Acronym is now organization's official name*] (EA) .... CHUCK
Committee to Investigate Assassinations .... CTIA
Committee to Investigate Copyright Problems .... CICP
Committee to Investigate Copyright Problems Affecting Communication in Science and Education (SAUO) .... CICP
Committee to Preserve American Color Television (EA) .... COMPACT
Committee to Promote Action [*Poverty program*] .... COMPACT
Committee to Promote Science and Technology .... CPST
Committee to Promote the Study of Austrian History (EA) .... CPSAH

Committee to Promote Uniformity in the Regulation of Motor Carriers .... CPURMC
Committee to Protect Journalists (EA) .... CPJ
Committee to Protect Our Children's Teeth [Defunct] (EA) .... CPCT
Committee to Re-Elect the President [Also, CRP] [1972] .... CREEP
Committee to Re-Elect the President [Also, CREEP] [1972] .... CRP
Committee to Remove Unnatural Deposits from the Environment [Student legal action organization] .... CRUDE
Committee to Rescue Italian Art .... CRIA
Committee to Resist Abortion (EA) .... CRA
Committee to Resist Acronym Proliferation .... CRAP
Committee to Resist the Efforts of the Ex-President [Opposed Richard Nixon's visit to Oxford University, 1978] .... CREEP
Committee to Restore the Constitution (EA) .... CRC
Committee to Retain Our Segregated Schools [Group in Arkansas, organized to oppose STOP] .... CROSS
Committee to Review Generic Requirements [Nuclear Regulatory Commission] .... CRGR
Committee to Save the Peace Symbol [Student legal action organization] .... CSPS
Committee to Stop Chemical Atrocities (EA) .... CSCA
Committee to Stop Children's Murder [Defunct] (EA) .... CSCM
Committee to Support Irish Political Prisoners (EA) .... CSIPP
Committee to Support Nicaragua [Defunct] (EA) .... CSN
Committee to Support the Antitrust Laws (EA) .... COSAL
Committee to Support the Antitrust Laws (EA) .... COSAT
[The] Committee to Unite America [Defunct] (EA) .... TCUA
Committee Urging Regulatory Reform for Efficient National Trucking [Later, BCIPT] (EA) .... CURRENT
Committee-Appointed Review Team (SAUO) .... CART
Committees of Correspondence [National Center for Science Education] .... C/C
Committees of Correspondence (EA) .... COC
Commmonwealth Weighlifting Federation (BUAC) .... WCF
CommNet Cellular [NASDAQ symbol] (TTSB) .... CELS
CommNet Cellular, Inc. [NASDAQ symbol] (SAG) .... CELS
CommNet Cellular, Inc. [Associated Press] (SAG) .... Commnet
Commode [Medicine] .... COM
Commodities - Coal and Steel (NATG) .... C/CS
Commodities - Food and Agriculture (NATG) .... C/FA
Commodities Data Information Service [MJK Associates] [Santa Clara, CA] [Information service or system] (IID) .... CDIS
Commodities Division (SAUO) .... COMMOD
Commodities Exchange Center [New York, NY] .... CEC
Commodities Import Program [Military] .... CIP
Commodities (or Commodity) Futures Trading Commission (SAUO) .... CFTC
Commodities Research Board (SAUS) .... CRB
Commodities Research Unit Ltd. [Originator and Databank] [Information service or system] (IID) .... CRU
Commodity (AABC) .... CMDTY
Commodity (SAUS) .... Cmdty
Commodity .... COM
Commodity .... COMMOD
Commodity (SAUS) .... Commod
Commodity Bookform Standard (MCD) .... CBS
Commodity Class Manager .... CCM
Commodity Classification Automated Tracking System .... CCATS
Commodity Classification Rates [British] (DS) .... CCR
Commodity Code (SAUS) .... COMCODE
Commodity Command Management Information System [Army] .... CCMIS
Commodity Command Standard System .... CCSS
Commodity Command Standard System - Modernization .... CCSS-MOD
Commodity Command Standard System Operating Instructions [Army] .... CCSSOI
Commodity Communication Agency (SAUO) .... CCA
Commodity Configuration Management System (AFIT) .... CCMS
Commodity Control List [Office of Export Administration] CCL
Commodity Coordinated Group Item (DNAB) .... CCGI
Commodity Coordination Group (SAUO) .... CCG
Commodity Coordination Groups .... CCG
Commodity Credit Corp. [Department of Agriculture] CCC
Commodity Credit Corporation (TDOB) .... CCO
Commodity Economics Division (SAUO) .... CED
Commodity Exchange [Investment term] .... CE
Commodity Exchange (EBF) .... COMEU
Commodity Exchange (EA) .... COMEX
Commodity Exchange Act .... CEA
Commodity Exchange Authority [Later, CFTC] [Department of Agriculture] .... CEA
Commodity Exchange Authority/Commodity Futures Trading Commission (SAUO) .... CEA/CFTC
Commodity Exchange Commission [Functions transferred to CFTC] .... CEC
Commodity Exchange Inc. (SAUO) .... Comex
Commodity Flow Survey [BTS] (TAG) .... CFS
Commodity Flow System .... CFS
Commodity Futures Law Reporter [Commerce Clearing House] [A publication] (DLA) .... Comm Fut L Rep
Commodity Futures Law Reporter [Commerce Clearing House] [A publication] (DLA) .... Commodity Futures L Rep
Commodity Futures Trading Commission [Formerly, CEA] [Independent government agency] .... CFTC
Commodity Futures Trading Commission, Washington, DC [Library symbol] [Library of Congress] (LCLS) .... DCFT
Commodity Information Services Co. (IID) .... CISCO
Commodity Integrated Materiel Manager .... CIMM
Commodity Letter of Credit .... CLOC
Commodity Management Master Plan (MCD) .... CMMP
Commodity Manager (SAUO) .... CM

Commodity Manager Code [Military] .... CMC
Commodity Manager Input Data (MCD) .... CMID
Commodity Master Plan [Army] .... CMP
Commodity Microanalysis, Inc. [Information service or system] (IID) .... CMI
Commodity News Services, Inc. [Information service or system] (IID) .... CNS
Commodity Options [I. P. Sharp Associates] [Database] .... COMOPTIONS
Commodity Oriented Digital Input Label System (SAUS) .... CODILS
Commodity Oriented General Support .... COGS
Commodity Policy Advisory Committee (SAUO) .... CPAC
Commodity Policy and Relief [British] .... CPR
Commodity Pool Operator .... CPO
Commodity Prices [A publication] .... CP
Commodity Production Statistics [United Nations Statistical Office] [Information service or system] (CRD) .... ICPDATA
Commodity Punched Card (SAUS) .... CPC
Commodity Put and Call Trading Data [Database] [Chronometrics] [Information service or system] (CRD) .... COMPACT
Commodity Quotations, Inc. (IID) .... CQI
Commodity Rate .... CR
Commodity Research Bureau .... CRB
Commodity Stabilization Service [Name changed to Agricultural Stabilization and Conservation Service, 1961] .... CSS
Commodity Standards Division (SAUO) .... CSD
Commodity Supplemental Food Program [Food and Nutrition Service] .... CSFP
Commodity Systems, Inc. [Information service or system] (IID) .... CSI
Commodity Trading Advisor .... CTA
Commodity Trading Services N.V. (SAUO) .... CTS
Commodity Transportation Survey [Census Bureau] .... CTS
Commodity World News Network [Later, Futures World News] [Information service or system] (IID) .... CWN
Commodity-Embedded Insurance .... COIN
Commodo [In an Easy Style] [Music] .... COM
Commodo [In an Easy Style] [Music] (ROG) .... COMO
Commodore [Navy] [British] (ROG) C
Commodore .... CDRE
Commodore (WDAA) .... Cdre
Commodore [British military] (DMA) .... Cmdre
Commodore .... COM
Commodore (WDAA) .... Com
Commodore (SAUO) .... Com
Commodore .... COMD
Commodore (ADA) .... COMDRE
Commodore .... COMM
Commodore .... COMMO
Commodore (ADWA) .... commo
Commodore .... COMO
Commodore (SAUS) .... Como
Commodore [Navy] O7
Commodore [ICAO designator] (AD) .... YJ
Commodore 128 [Computer] (VERA) C128
Commodore 64 [Computer] (VERA) C64
Commodore Air Train [Navy] .... COMAT
Commodore, Amphibious Forces [British military] (DMA) .... COMAF
Commodore Amphibious Warfare (SAUS) .... COMAW
Commodore Applied Technologies, Inc. [Associated Press] (SAG) .... CmdrA
Commodore Applied Technologies, Inc. [Associated Press] (SAG) .... CmdrAp
Commodore Applied Technologies, Inc. [AMEX symbol] (SAG) CXI
Commodore, Arabian Sea and Persian Gulf (SAUO) .... COMAS
Commodore Aviation [Australia] [ICAO designator] (FAAC) .... GAR
Commodore Business Machines [Commercial firm] (NITA) .... CBM
Commodore Command (SAUS) CC
Commodore Commanding New Zealand Force (SAUO) .... CCNZ
Commodore Commanding, New Zealand-Force (SAUS) .... CCNZ
Commodore Commanding Newfoundland Force [Navy] [Canada] [World War II] .... CCNF
Commodore, Contract-Built Ships [British military] (DMA) .... CCBS
Commodore Corp. (EFIS) CC
Commodore, (Destroyers) Western Approaches [British] .... COM(D) WA
Commodore Dynamic Total Vision [Interactive TV] .... CDTV
Commodore Hotel, Inc. (SAUO) .... COH
Commodore Information Network [Commodore Business Machines, Inc.] [Information service or system] (TSSD) .... CIN
Commodore Messangers Organisation (SAUS) .... CMO
Commodore National Life (EFIS) .... CNL
Commodore, Naval Air Stations, East Africa [British] .... COMNAS(EA)
Commodore Naval Ship Acceptance (SAUS) .... CNSA
Commodore, Royal Canadian Navy Barracks at [Place] .... COMBRAX
Commodore Superintendent (SAUS) .... CS
Commodore Superintendent, Atlantic Coast (SAUO) .... COMSUPTLANT
Commodore Superintendent Contract Built Ships [Navy] [British] .... CSCBS
Commodore Thomas ap Catesby Jones Society [Defunct] (EA) .... CTAPCJS
Commodore Training [Computer science] .... COMTRAIN
Commodus [of Scriptores Historiae Augustae] [Classical studies] (OCD) .... Comm
Common [Ecology] C
Common .... Cmmn
Common .... CMMN
Common .... CMN
Common .... COM
Common [Wood Industry] (WPI) .... Com
Common (BEE) .... com
Common .... COMM
Common [Commonly used] (OPSA) .... COMMON
Common .... COMN
Common Access Method [Computer programming] (BYTE) .... CAM
Common Access Model (SAUS) .... CAM

Common Access Security Terminal ... CAST
Common Access Switching Equipment (AAG) ... CASE
Common Access to Biotechnological Resources and Information (SAUO) ... CABR
Common Access to Libraries in Europe (SAUS) ... CALIBRE
Common Account Number [*Environmental Protection Agency*] (GFGA) ... CAN
Common Accounting Reporting System (ADA) ... CARS
Common Acute Lymphoblastic Leukemia Antigen [*or Antiserum*] [*Immunochemistry*] ... CALLA
Common Ada Interface Standard [*British*] ... CAIS
Common ADA Missile Packages (MCD) ... CAMP
Common Ada Missile Parts (SAUS) ... CAMP
Common Aerial (or Antenna) Television (SAUS) ... CATV
Common Aerial Working [*Telecommunications*] (TEL) ... CAW
Common Affordable Lightweight Fighter (SAUS) ... CALF
Common Agricultural Customs Transmission of Information (SAUO) ... CACTI
Common Agricultural Policy [*Common Market*] ... CAP
Common Air Interface [*Telecommunications*] ... CAI
Common Air Interference ... CAI
Common Algorithmic Language [*Computer science*] (HGAA) ... COMAL
Common ALL (SAUS) ... CALL
Common Allocation Table (SAUS) ... CAT
Common and Bulk Items List ... CBIL
Common and Standard (SAUS) ... C&S
Common and Standard [*Items*] (AAG) ... CS
Common Anode (SAUS) ... CA
Common Antenna Television (SAUS) ... CATV
Common Antenna Working (SAUS) ... CAW
Common Antigen [*Immunochemistry*] ... CA
Common Anti-Tank Helicopter (MCD) ... CATH
Common Aperture Electro Optical System (ACAE) ... CAEOS
Common Aperture Multifunction Array RADAR ... CAMAR
Common Aperture Multifunction Array Radar (SAUS) ... CAMAR
Common Aperture Multispectrum Seeker [*Army*] (MCD) ... CAMS
Common Aperture Technique for Imaging Electro-Optical Sensors (MCD) ... CATIES
Common Application Environment [*Computer science*] (BTTJ) ... CAE
Common Application Programmers Interface (SAUS) ... CAPI
Common Application Service Element [*Telecommunications*] (OSI) ... CASE
Common Applications (SAUS) ... CA
Common Applications and Tools Integration Services (SAUS) ... CATIS
Common Applications Environment [*Computer science*] (BARN) ... CAE
Common APSE [*Ada Program Support Environment*] **Interface Set** [*Computer science*] ... CAIS
Common APSE Interface Specification (SAUS) ... CAIS
Common Architecture for Next Generation Internet Protocol (VERA) ... CATNIP
Common Arterioventricular Canal [*Cardiology*] (DAVI) ... CAVC
Common Assembler Language [*Computer science*] (NITA) ... CAL
Common Assembly Language (MCD) ... CAL
Common Assembly Language for Electronic Warfare (MCD) ... CALEW
Common Assembly Language Scientific Subroutine Package [*Computer science*] (CIST) ... CALSSP
Common Assembly Language Scientific Subroutine Package [*Computer science*] (MHDI) ... CALSSR
Common Assembly Language Scientific Subroutine Package (SAUS) ... CARLSSP
Common Assessment Tasks ... CATS
Common Assessment Test [*Education*] ... CAT
Common ATCCS Support Software (SAUS) ... CASS
Common Atrioventricular Orifice [*Medicine*] (DMAA) ... CAVO
Common Attitude Pointing System (MCD) ... CAPS
Common Authentication Technology (VERA) ... CAT
Common Automatic Manifest Language (SAUS) ... CAMEL
Common Automatic Recovery System (SAUS) ... CARS
Common Automatic Test System (SAUS) ... CATS
Common Aviation Weather Sub-System (PIPO) ... CAWS
Common Avionics Baseline (SAUS) ... CAB
Common Base [*Computer science*] (MSA) ... CB
Common Basic Electronics Training (MCD) ... COBET
Common Batch Identification [*Computer science*] (EECA) ... CBI
Common Battery [*Electronics; technical drawings*] ... CB
Common Battery (SAUS) ... CB
Common Battery Signaling [*Telecommunications*] (TEL) ... CBS
Common Battery Signalling (SAUS) ... CBS
Common Battery Supply (SAUS) ... CBS
Common Battery System (MCD) ... CBA
Common Battery System ... CBS
Common Beam Former ... CBF
Common Bench [*Legal term*] (DLA) ... B
Common Bench [*Legal term*] ... CB
Common Bench (SAUO) ... CB
Common Bench, New Series [*A publication*] ... CBNS
Common Bench Reports [*A publication*] ... CB
Common Bench Reports (Manning, Granger, and Scott) [*1846-65*] [*England*] [*A publication*] (DLA) ... Com B
Common Bench Reports (Manning, Granger, and Scott) [*1846-65*] [*England*] [*A publication*] (DLA) ... Comm B
Common Bias (IAA) ... CB
Common Bias, Common Control ... CBCC
Common Bias, Single Control ... CBSC
Common Bile Duct [*Medicine*] ... CBD
Common Bile Duct Exploration [*Medicine*] (DAVI) ... CBDE
Common Bile Duct Ligation [*Medicine*] ... CDL
Common Bile Duct Stenosis [*Medicine*] ... CBDS
Common Bill (SAUS) ... CB
Common Bill of Material (MCD) ... CBM
Common Block (SAUS) ... CB
Common Bomb Rack (SAUS) ... CBR
Common Boundary [*An association*] (EA) ... CBI
Common Brick [*Construction*] (BARN) ... cb
Common Bulk Memory (SAUS) ... CBM
Common Bulkhead Joint ... CBJ
Common Business-Oriented Language [*1959*] [*Computer science*] ... COBOL
Common Carcinoembryonic Antigen (SAUS) ... CEA
Common Carier Line Pool (HGAA) ... CCLP
Common Carotid Artery [*Anatomy*] ... CCA
Common Carotid Artery Blood Flow [*Medicine*] ... CCABF
Common Carrier [*FCC*] (NTCM) ... C
Common Carrier ... CC
Common Carrier Bureau [*of FCC*] ... CCB
Common Carrier Interface (MCD) ... CCI
Common Carrier Line (HGAA) ... CCL
Common Carrier Motor Freight Association (SAUO) ... CCA
Common Carrier Motor Freight Association, Dallas TX [*STAC*] ... CCA
Common Carrier Special Application ... CCSA
Common Cathode (SAUS) ... CC
Common Cause (EA) ... CC
Common Cause Analysis (PDAA) ... COMCAN
Common Cause Failure [*Nuclear energy*] (NRCH) ... CCF
Common Cause Failure Analysis [*Nuclear energy*] (NRCH) ... CCFA
Common Centre of Research (SAUO) ... CCR
Common Channel Interoffice Signaling [*Telecommunications*] ... CCIS
Common Channel Module (SAUS) ... CCM
Common Channel Network Controller [*Telecommunications*] ... CCNC
Common Channel Signaling [*Telecommunications*] (TEL) ... CCS
Common Channel Signaling Network Control [*Telecommunications*] (ACRL) ... CCNC
Common Channel Signaling System [*Telecommunications*] (TEL) ... SSCC
Common Channel Signaling System No. 7 (CGWS) ... C7
Common Channel Signaling System Number 7 (CGWS) ... CCS7
Common Channel Signalling Arrangement [*Telecommunications*] (NITA) ... CCSA
Common Channel Signalling Device (SAUS) ... CCSD
Common Channel Signalling Network (SAUS) ... CCSN
Common Channel Signalling System [*Telecommunications*] (NITA) ... CCSS
Common Channel Terminal (SAUS) ... CCT
Common Chassis Advanced Technology Transition Demonstrator ... CCATTD
Common Chlorofluorocarbon (SAUS) ... CCF
Common Claims File [*Health insurance*] (GHCT) ... CCF
Common Client Interface (SAUS) ... CCI
Common Code (IAA) ... CC
Common Cold Foundation [*Defunct*] ... CCF
Common Cold Foundation (SAUO) ... CCF
Common Cold Research Unit [*British Medical Council*] ... CCRU
Common Cold-Virus (SAUS) ... CC-Virus
Common Collector [*Amplifier*] ... CC
Common Command Language [*Computer science*] (IT) ... CCL
Common Command Set [*Computer science*] ... CCS
Common Common-channel-signalling Receiver (SAUS) ... CCR
Common Communication Adapter [*Computer science*] ... CCA
Common Communications Adapter (SAUS) ... CCA
Common Communications Format [*International Standards Organization*] (NITA) ... CCF
Common Communications Services (RALS) ... CCS
Common Communications Support [*Computer science*] (PCM) ... CCS
Common Complaint [*Medicine*] (MELL) ... CC
Common Computer Language (SAUS) ... CCL
Common Configuration Method (SAUS) ... CCM
Common Control [*Telecommunications*] (TEL) ... CC
Common Control Channel (VERA) ... CCCH
Common Control Channel (CGWS) ... CCH
Common Control Circuit [*Telecommunications*] (IAA) ... CCC
Common Control Echo Suppressor [*Telecommunications*] (TEL) ... CCES
Common Control Interoffice Signaling ... CCIS
Common Control Language [*Computer science*] (NITA) ... CCL
Common Control Switching Arrangement [*AT & T*] [*Telecommunications*] ... CCSA
Common Control Unit [*Army*] (AABC) ... CCU
Common Control Vector (CIST) ... CCV
Common Core Character Set [*Computer science*] (TELE) ... CCCS
Common Core of Data [*National Center for Educational Statistics*] [*Department of Education*] (OICC) ... CCD
Common Core Task [*Army*] ... CCT
Common Council [*or Councilman*] ... CC
Common Council (SAUO) ... CC
Common Council of American Unity (SAUO) ... CCAU
Common Criteria (SAUS) ... CC
Common Cryptographic Architecture [*IBM encryption software*] (CDE) ... CCA
Common Cryptological Database (SAUS) ... CCDB
Common Cryptological Work Station (SAUS) ... CCWS
Common Customs Tariff [*Common Market*] ... CCT
Common Cycle ... CC
Common Damage Waiver ... CDW
Common Data Bank (or Base) (SAUS) ... CDB
Common Data Buffer (NASA) ... CDBFR
Common Data Bus [*Computer science*] ... CDB
Common Data Carrier (SAUS) ... CDC
Common Data Dictionary (MCD) ... CDD
Common Data Extraction Program (ACAE) ... CDEP
Common Data File (SAUS) ... CDF
Common Data Format [*Computer science*] ... CDF

Common Data Interface (SAUS) .... CDI
Common Data Pool (MCD) .... COMPOOL
Common Data Representation (SAUS) .... CDR
Common Data Security Architecture .... CDSA
Common Data Server (SAUS) .... CDS
Common Data Translation Language .... CDTL
Common Database Design .... CDBD
Common Data-Base in Computer Readable-form (SAUS) .... CDBCR
Common Database Server (SAUS) .... CDBS
Common Decking [*Lumber*] .... COMM DECK
Common Defense Exhibition & Seminar (SAUS) .... COMDEF
Common Defense Installation (AFM) .... CDI
Common Defense Market (SAUO) .... CDM
Common Denominator (AAG) .... CD
Common Depth Point [*Seismology*] .... CDP
Common Desktop Environment [*Graphical user interface*] (CDE) .... CDE
Common Destiny Alliance .... CoDA
Common Device Model (AAEL) .... CDM
Common Diagram System (IAA) .... CDS
Common Digital Exploitation System (ACAE) .... CODES
Common Digitizer [*FAA*] .... CD
Common Display Logic [*Computer science*] .... CDL
Common Display System (HLLA) .... CDS
Common Distributable Change (DNAB) .... CDC
Common Document Pool (SAUS) .... CDP
Common Dollar Accounting (ADA) .... CDA
Common Doppler System (MCD) .... CDS
Common Drain-Common Collector (SAUS) .... CD-CC
Common Drain-Common Emitter (SAUS) .... CD-CE
Common Duct [*Medicine*] .... CD
Common Duct Exploration [*Medicine*] (MAE) .... CDE
Common Effective Preferential Tariff .... CEPT
Common Electronic Parts .... CEP
Common Electronic Unit (ACAE) .... CEU
Common Emitter .... CE
Common Entrance [*Examination for entry into public school*] [*British*] C
Common Entrance [*Examination for entry into public school*] [*British*] .... CE
Common Entrance Examination (BARN) .... CEE
Common Equipment Card [*Telecommunications*] (MLOA) .... CEC
Common Equipment Group [*Environmental science*] (COE) .... CEG
Common Equipment Unit (SAUS) .... CEU
Common Equipment Voltage Indicator .... CEVI
Common Era .... CE
Common Error Analysis (MCD) .... CEA
Common European Demonstrator [*Automotive engineering*] .... CED
Common European Priority Areas (SAUS) .... CEPA
Common European Priority Areas (SAUS) .... CEPAS
Common European Research Project Information Format (SAUO) .... CERIF
Common Event Database System (SAUS) .... COEDS
Common Experiments Monitoring and Test Equipment (MCD) .... CEMTE
Common External Tariff [*for EEC countries*] [*Also, CXT*] .... CET
Common External Tariff [*EEC*] [*Also, CET*] .... CXT
Common Facilities Test [*NASA*] (NASA) .... CFT
Common Femoral Artery [*Anatomy*] (DAVI) .... CFA
Common Field Effect Transistor [*Computer science*] (ADA) .... CFET
Common File Control Unit (SAUS) .... CFCU
Common File System [*Computer science*] .... CFS
Common Fisheries Policy [*EEC*] .... CFP
Common Flash-Memory Interface .... CFI
Common Flash-memory Interface (SAUS) .... CFI
Common Foreign and Security Policy [*European Union*] .... CFSP
Common Forward Looking Infrared Test Sets (ACAE) .... C-FLIRTS
Common Functional Model (SAUS) .... CFM
Common Functions (SAUO) .... CF
Common Fund .... CF
Common Fund for Commodities .... CFC
Common Fund for Nonprofit Organizations [*Fairfield, CT*] (EA) .... CFNO
[*The*] **Common Fund for Nonprofit Organizations** [*Ford Foundation*] .... TCFNO
Common Gateway Interface [*Standard that extends the functionality of Web servers*] [*Computer science*] .... CGI
Common Gateway Interface-Binary (SAUS) .... CGI-BIN
Common Germanic (SAUS) .... CGmc
Common Graphic Interface (SAUS) .... CGI
Common Graphics Environment (SAUS) .... CGE
Common Graphics System (MCD) .... CGS
Common Ground - USA (EA) .... CGUSA
Common Ground Sensor (SAUS) .... CGS
Common Ground Station [*Military*] (RDA) .... CGS
Common Ground Support Element (SAUO) .... CGSE
Common Ground Support Equipment (MCD) .... CGSE
Common Ground Support Equipment List (NVT) .... CGSEL
Common Hardware (SAUO) .... CH
Common Hardware and Software [*Army*] .... CHS
Common Hardware Reference Platform [*Computer science*] .... CHRP
Common Hardware System (SAUS) .... CHS
Common Hepatic Duct [*Gastroenterology*] (DAVI) .... CHD
Common Heritage Institute (SAUO) .... CHI
Common Heritage Programme, Ottawa, Ontario [*Library symbol*] [*National Library of Canada*] (BIB) .... OOCHP
Common High Bandwith Data Link - Shipboard Terminal (DWSG) .... CHBDL-ST
Common High Order Language (SAUS) .... CHOL
Common High-Bandwidth Datalink (SAUS) .... CHBDL
Common ICAO [*International Civil Aviation Organization*] **Data Interchange Network** .... CIDIN
Common Iliac Artery [*Medicine*] (MELL) .... CIA
Common Iliac Catheter [*Medicine*] (MELL) CIC
Common Iliac Lymph Node [*Medicine*] (MELL) .... CILN
Common Indexing Protocol (SAUS) .... CIP
Common Information Carrier (SAUS) CIC
Common Information Exchange Glossary (SAUS) .... CIEG
Common Information Exchange Language (SAUS) .... CIEL
Common Information Model .... CIM
Common Information System (SAUS) .... CIS
Common Input Processor .... CIP
Common Input System (SAUS) .... CIS
Common Insecurity Fail Scrutiny (SAUS) .... CIFS
Common Instrument Flight Rules Room (SAUS) .... CIFRR
Common Integrated Processor [*Hughes Air Corp.*] .... CIP
Common Interactive Graphics Application Routine [*Army*] .... CIGAR
Common Interchange Format (SAUS) .... CIF
Common Interest Network (EA) .... CIN
Common Interest Seeker (SAUS) .... COINS
Common Interface Language (SAUS) CIL
Common Intermediate Format (CDE) .... CIF
Common Internal Iliac Artery [*Medicine*] (DMAA) .... CIIA
Common Internet File System [*Computer science*] (IGQR) .... CIFS
Common Internet Scheme Syntax (DMAA) .... CISS
Common Intersection Point [*Graphical representation*] .... CIP
Common Interswitch Rekeying Variable [*Environmental science*] (COE) .... CIRV
Common Intrusion Detection Framework (SAUS) .... CIDF
Common Ion Effect .... CIE
Common ISDN Application Programmable (or Programming) Interface (SAUS) .... CAPI
Common Item Order (AFM) .... CIO
Common Jammer (SAUS) .... COMJAM
Common Land Data Base (GEOI) .... CLDB
Common Language Equipment Identification (SAUS) .... CLEI
Common Language Equipment Order (SAUS) .... CLEO
Common Language Location Identification (SAUS) CLLI
Common Language location Identifier [*Telecommunications*] (TSSD) CLLI
Common Language System [*Computer science*] (BUR) .... CLS
Common Law CL
Common Law and Equity Reports [*1853-55*] [*A publication*] (DLA) .... Eq R
Common Law and Equity Reports [*1853-55*] [*A publication*] (DLA) .... Equity Rep
Common Law and Equity Reports, Published by Spottiswoode [*A publication*] (DLA) .... Spottis CL & Eq Rep
Common Law and Equity Reports, Published by Spottiswoode (journ.) (SAUS) .... Spottis CL&Eq Rep
Common Law Chamber Reports [*Ontario*] [*A publication*] (DLA) .... CL Ch
Common Law Chamber Reports [*Ontario*] [*A publication*] (DLA) .... CL Chamb
Common Law Chamber Reports [*Ontario*] [*A publication*] (DLA) .... CL Chamb Rep
Common Law Institute of Intellectual Property [*British*] (DBA) .... CLIP
Common Law Procedure [*England*] [*A publication*] (DLA) .... CLP
Common Law Procedure Acts (DLA) .... CLPA
Common Law Reports [*1853-85*] [*A publication*] (DLA) CL
Common Law Reports [*British*] .... CLR
Common Law Reports [*1835-55*] [*Canada*] [*A publication*] (DLA) .... CLR (Can)
Common Law Reports [*1853-85*] [*A publication*] (DLA) .... Com L Rep
Common Law Reports, Volume 3 [*England*] [*A publication*] (DLA) .... Das
Common Leaf Spot [*Plant pathology*] .... CLS
Common Leucocyte Antigen [*Immunology*] .... CLA
Common Line Receiver (IAA) .... CLR
Common LISP [*List Processing Language*] **Interface Management** [*Computer science*] .... CLIM
Common LISP Interface Manager (SAUS) .... CLIM
Common LISP Object System [*Computer science*] (BYTE) .... CLOS
Common LISP Operating Environment (SAUS) .... CLOE
Common Lodging House [*British*] (ROG) .... CLH
Common Lodging Houses Act [*1851*] [*British*] (ROG) .... CLHA
Common Log File [*Computer science*] .... CLF
Common Log Format (SAUS) .... CLF
Common Logarithm (SAUS) CL
Common Logic Unit (SAUS) .... CLU
Common Logistic Support Group [*Military*] .... CLSG
Common Los Alamos Mathematical Software (SAUS) .... CLAMS
Common Machine Language [*Computer science*] .... CML
Common Main Objective [*Stereomicroscope optical element*] .... CMO
Common Maintenance Trainer (MCD) .... CMT
[*The*] **Common Man in the Street** [*The average man*] [*See also MITS*] .... T C MITS
Common Management Bus (SAUS) .... CMB
Common Management Information Protocol (PCM) .... CMIP
Common Management Information Protocol Data Unit [*Telecommunications*] (OSI) .... CMIPDU
Common Management Information Service [*Computer science*] (VERA) .... CMIS
Common Management Information Service Element [*Telecommunications*] (OSI) .... CMISE
Common Management Information System (SAUS) .... CMIS
Common Manpower Standards (AFM) .... CMS
Common Manufacturing Accounting Control System (SAUS) .... COMACS
Common Manufacturing Information System (IAA) .... CMIS
Common Market (ADWA) .... CM
Common Market (DLA) .... Comm Mkt
Common Market Commission (SAUO) .... CMC
Common Market Computer (SAUS) .... CMC
Common Market Group of International Rayon and Synthetic Fibres Committee (EAIO) .... CIFRS
Common Market Law Review [*A publication*] (DLA) .... CMLR
Common Market Law Review [*A publication*] (DLA) .... CML Rev
Common Market Law Review [*A publication*] (DLA) .... Comm Market L Rev
Common Market Law Review [*A publication*] (DLA) .... Common Mkt L Rev

Common Market Liaison Bureau for the Ceramic Industries (SAUO) ... CERAME-UNIE
Common Market Nations (SAUS) ... CMN
Common Market Newspaper Publishers' Organization [*See also CAEJ*] [*Brussels, Belgium*] (EAIO) ... CMNPO
Common Market of the South ... MERCOSUR
Common Market Reporter [*Commerce Clearing House*] [*A publication*] (DLA) ... CMR
Common Market Reporter [*Commerce Clearing House*] [*A publication*] (DLA) ... Comm Mkt Rep
Common Market Reporter (Commerce Clearing House) [*A publication*] (DLA) ... CCH Comm Mkt Rep
Common Market Safeguards Campaign (SAUO) ... CMSC
Common Market Telephone Directory (SAUS) ... CMTD
Common Market Travel (SAUO) ... CMT
Common Market Travel Association (EAIO) ... CMT
Common Measure [*Music*] (IIA) ... CM
Common Measure Double (SAUS) ... CMD
Common Memory (SAUS) ... COMEM
Common Memory Manager (NITA) ... CMM
Common Mesonet Format (SAUS) ... CMF
Common Messaging Calls [*Computer science*] ... CMC
Common Meter [*Music*] ... C
Common Meter [*Music*] ... CM
Common Meter Double [*Music*] ... CMD
Common Migraine [*Neurology*] (DAVI) ... CM
Common Military Intelligence Skills (NVT) ... CMIS
Common Military Syllabus (SAUS) ... CMS
Common Missile Approach Warning System (ADWA) ... CMAWS
Common Missile Warning System (ADWA) ... CMWS
Common Mission Data Playback Support System (SAUS) ... CMDPSS
Common Mode (IAA) ... CM
Common Mode [*NASA*] (GFGA) ... COM-M
Common Mode (NAKS) ... com-m
Common Mode Error ... CME
Common Mode Failure [*Nuclear energy*] (NRCH) ... CMF
Common Mode Failure Analysis [*Nuclear energy*] (NRCH) ... CMFA
Common Mode Input Resistance ... CMIR
Common Mode Interface (IAA) ... CMI
Common Mode Interference (SAUS) ... CMI
Common Mode Logic ... CML
Common Mode Noise (SAUS) ... CMN
Common Mode Operation [*Telecommunications*] (TEL) ... CMO
Common Mode Processing System (CAAL) ... CMPS
Common Mode Rejection ... CMR
Common Mode Rejection Ratio ... CMRR
Common Mode Signal ... CMS
Common Mode Voltage ... CMV
Common Mode Voltage Range ... CMVR
Common Mode-to-Common Mode (IAA) ... CMTOCM
Common Mode-to-Common Mode (SAUS) ... CM-to-CM
Common Mode-to-Differential Mode (SAUS) ... CM-to-DM
Common Mode-to-Differential Mode (IAA) ... CMTODM
Common Modular Multimode RADAR ... CMMR
Common Module (SAUS) ... CM
Common Module Retrofit (ACAE) ... CMR
Common Mounting System (PDAA) ... CMS
Common Nacelle System/Engine Build-Up (MCD) ... CNS/EBU
Common Name (ACRL) ... CN
Common Network Architecture (IAA) ... CNA
Common Network Interface [*Computer science*] (VERA) ... CNI
Common Network Management System [*Unisys Corp.*] ... CNMS
Common Network Representation [*Telecommunications*] (OSI) ... CNR
Common New Generation Frigate (SAUO) ... CNGF
Common (Noun) [*Linguistics*] ... C
Common Noun Keywords (PDAA) ... CNK
Common Nozzle Assembly (MCD) ... CNA
Common Null Cell Acute Lymphoblastic Leukemia [*Medicine*] ... CALL
Common Number System (AAG) ... CNS
Common Object Facilities (SAUS) ... COFAC
Common Object Model [*Microsoft*] ... COM
Common Object Request Broken Architecture ... CORBA
Common Object Request Broker Architecture [*Computer science*] ... CORBA
Common Object Runtime (SAUS) ... COR
Common Object Service Specification [*Computer science*] (VERA) ... COSS
Common Occupational Classification System (ABAC) ... COCS
Common Olympic Algorithmic Language (SAUS) ... COOL ALGOL
Common On-Line Package [*Fujitsu Ltd.*] [*Japan*] ... COP
Common Open Policy Service (SAUO) ... COPS
Common Open Software Environment (PCM) ... COSE
Common Operating Environment ... COE
Common Operating System Control Language ... COSCL
Common Operating System Environment (SAUO) ... COSE
Common Operational Modeling Planning And Simulation Strategy (SAUS) ... COMPASS
Common Operational Research Equipment (NASA) ... CORE
[*A*] **Common Operational Software** (MCD) ... ACOS
Common Opto-electronic Laser Detection System (SAUS) ... COLDS
Common Optoelectronics LASER Detection System ... COLDS
Common Orders (DLA) ... CO
Common Organization of African, Malagasy, and Mauritian States (EBF) ... OCAM
Common Output Tape (SAUS) ... COT
Common Ownership Design and Construct [*British*] ... CODAC
Common Part Convergence Sublayer [*Electronics*] (ACRL) ... CPCS
Common Part Indicator (VERA) ... CPI
Common Particular Meter [*Music*] ... CPM
Common Payload Support Equipment [*NASA*] (NASA) ... CPSE
Common Peak Developed Isovolumic Pressure [*Cardiology*] (DAVI) ... CPIP
Common Performance Conditions (SAUO) ... CPC
Common Peripheral Channel (NITA) ... CPC
Common Personal Hygiene Equipment (KSC) ... CPHE
Common Picture Display (SAUS) ... CPD
Common Plane (SAUS) ... COPLANE
Common Pleas [*Legal term*] (DAS) ... Com Pl
Common Pleas [*Legal term*] ... CP
Common Pleas Division [*Legal term*] ... CPD
Common Pleas Division, English Law Reports [*1875-80*] [*A publication*] (DLA) ... Com P Div
Common Pleas Division, English Law Reports [*1875-80*] [*A publication*] (DLA) ... Com Pl
Common Pleas Division, English Law Reports [*1875-80*] [*A publication*] (DLA) ... Com Pl Div
Common Pleas Division, English Law Reports [*1875-80*] [*A publication*] (DLA) ... CP Div
Common Pleas Division, English Law Reports [*1875-80*] [*A publication*] (DLA) ... CP Div (Eng)
Common Pleas Division, English Law Reports [*1875-80*] [*A publication*] (DLA) ... CP (Eng)
Common Pleas Reporter [*Scranton, PA*] [*A publication*] (DLA) ... Com Pl Reptr
Common Pleas Reporter [*Scranton, PA*] [*A publication*] (DLA) ... Com Pl R (PA)
Common Pleas Reporter [*Scranton, PA*] [*A publication*] (DLA) ... Com P Reptr
Common Pleas Reporter [*Scranton, PA*] [*A publication*] (DLA) ... CP Rep
Common Pleas Reporter [*Scranton, PA*] [*A publication*] (DLA) ... CP Rept
Common Pleas Reports [*Upper Canada*] [*A publication*] (DLA) ... CPUC
Common Pleas Subpoena [*Legal*] [*British*] (ROG) ... CPSPA
Common Point of Trust (SAUS) ... CPT
Common Power Supply Group ... CPSG
Common Prayer ... CP
Common Price and Marketing Arrangement [*British*] ... CPMA
Common Procedural Terminology [*Human resources*] (WYGK) ... CPT
Common Procedure Coding System (SAUO) ... CPCS
Common Process [*Telecommunications*] (TEL) ... CP
Common Professional Examination (DLA) ... CPE
Common Program Control Station [*Emergency Broadcast System*] ... CPCS
Common Program Interface [*Computer science*] ... CPI
Common Program Language [*Computer science*] (AABC) ... CPL
Common Program Support System ... CPSS
Common Programming Interface for Communication [*Telecommunications*] (ACRL) ... CPI/C
Common Programming Interface for Communications (CDE) ... CPI-C
Common Programming Language (SAUS) ... CPL
Common Property and Environment (SAUO) ... COPE
Common Property Resource Management (SAUS) ... CPRM
Common Pulse Line ... CPL
Common Pulse-signalling Receiver (SAUS) ... CPR
Common Pulse-signalling Sender (SAUS) ... CPS
Common Query System [*Navy*] (DNAB) ... CQS
Common Queue Space (SAUS) ... CQS
Common RADAR Antenna Mount (DWSG) ... CRAM
Common Radio and Electronic Test Equipment [*Navy*] [*British*] (DEN) ... CRETE
Common Ragweed (MELL) ... CRW
Common Rail Launcher (SAUS) ... CRL
Common Random Number [*Mathematics*] (IAA) ... CRN
Common Real-Time Operating System (CAAL) ... CROS
Common Reference Platform [*Computer science*] (VERA) ... CRP
Common Reference Point [*Navigation*] (IAA) ... CRP
Common Register of Development Projects [*United Nations*] ... CORE
Common Release Processing System (SAUS) ... CRPS
Common Return [*Electronics*] (IAA) ... CR
Common Routing Connection Group [*Computer science*] (VERA) ... CRCG
Common Routing Output (SAUS) ... CROP
Common SAR Processor (SAUS) ... CSP
Common Secretarial Services (SAUO) ... COMSEC
Common Sense Algorithm (MCD) ... CSA
Common Sense for Drug Policy (EA) ... CSDP
Common Sense Initiative [*Environmental science*] (EPAT) ... CSI
Common Sense Media (EA) ... CSM
Common Serjeant [*British*] (ILCA) ... Com Serj
Common Serjeant [*British*] (ROG) ... CS
Common Service Area [*Computer science*] (BUR) ... CSA
Common Services Agency [*Scottish Health Service*] [*Research center*] ... CSA
Common Services Network [*Telecommunications*] (TEL) ... CSN
Common Services Rack [*Telecommunications*] (TEL) ... CSR
Common Services Subsystem [*Telecommunications*] (TEL) ... CSS
Common Services Unit [*Telecommunications*] (TEL) ... CSU
Common Set (MCD) ... CS
Common Set (NAKS) ... cs
Common Shell (SAUS) ... CS
Common Short Range Missile (ACAE) ... CSRM
Common Signal Processor [*Military*] (DOMA) ... CSP
Common Signaling Channel (IEEE) ... CSC
Common Skills Shop [*Military*] (DNAB) ... CSS
Common Slavic [*Language, etc.*] ... CS
Common Software (SAUS) ... CS
Common Source Data Base [*Computer science*] (CIST) ... CSDB
Common Source Noise Figure ... CSNF
Common Source Power Gain ... CSPG
Common Source Spot Noise ... CSSN
Common Source Spot Noise Figure ... CSSNF

Common Source-Common Collector (SAUS) .... CS-CC
Common Source-Common Emitter (SAUS) .... CS-CE
Common Specialist Training .... CST
Common Specification Language (NATG) .... CSL
Common Specifications Statements Generator (KSC) .... COMGEN
Common Spectrum Multiple Access (ACAE) .... CSMA
Common Speller Application Program Interface [Computer science] (VERA) .... CSAPI
Common Standards Revision Group (SAUO) .... CSRG
Common Statement (SAUS) .... CS
Common Steel [Projectile] .... CS
Common Stock [Investment term] .... CS
Common Strategic Doppler (MCD) .... CSD
Common Strategic Rotary Launcher .... CSRL
Common Subexpression Elimination (SAUS) .... CSE
Common Subnet Node [Telecommunications] (OSI) .... CSN
Common Supply Support [Military] (AABC) .... CSSPT
Common Supply Support Overseas [Military] .... COMSOS
Common Support Equipment (NASA) .... CSE
Common Support Module [NASA] (NASA) .... CSM
Common Support System (SAUS) .... CSS
Common Support System-Integrated Payload System (SAUS) .... CSS-IPS
Common Synchronous Interface (SAUS) .... CSI
Common System Area (IAA) .... CSA
Common Systems Main Interconnecting [Frame system] [Bell System] .... COSMIC
Common Table of Allowances [Army] (AABC) .... CTA
Common Tactical Grid (SAUS) .... CTG
Common Target Language (SAUS) .... CTL
Common Task Test [Army] (INF) .... CTT
Common Task Training [Military] (ADDR) .... CTT
Common Technical Interface Design Plan [Joint technical document developed by the US, UK, and Germany] [Military] (RDA) .... CTIDP
Common Technical Regulations (SAUS) .... CTR
Common Terminal RADAR Approach Control [Aviation] (FAAC) .... CTRAC
Common Terminating System (MCD) .... CTS
Common Termination System (SAUS) .... CTS
Common Test Data Collection System (MCD) .... CTDCS
Common Test Facility .... CTF
Common Test Subroutine [Computer science] .... CTS
Common Test/Support Equipment (MCD) .... CTSE
Common Time c
Common Time and Frequency Standard (ACAE) .... CTFS
Common Toxicity Criteria [Medicine] .... CTC
Common Track Stores Indicator (CAAL) .... CTSI
Common Traffic Advisory Frequency [FAA] (TAG) .... CTAF
Common Trailer Base (SAUS) .... CTB
Common Transmission Format (MCD) .... CTF
Common Transport Semantics (SAUS) .... CTS
Common University Fund [British] .... CUF
Common Update (SAUS) .... CU
Common Usage Equipment (NASA) .... CUE
Common Usage Item List (NASA) .... CUIL
Common Usage Radio Frequency Checkout Equipment (KSC) .... CURFCOE
Common Use (ROG) .... CU
Common Use Terminal Equipment [Travel industry] .... CUTE
Common User Access [Computer science] (BYTE) .... CUA
Common User Access Architecture [Computer science] (DOM) .... CUA Architecture
Common User Application [Computer science] (VERA) .... CUA
Common User Baseline for the Intelligence Community (MCD) .... CUBIC
Common User Contract (SAUO) .... CUC
Common User Data [Telecommunications] (TEL) .... CUDAT
Common User Data Network (ADA) .... CUDN
Common User Data Services (NITA) .... CUDS
Common User Data Terminal [Military] (AABC) .... CUDAT
Common User Digital Information Exchange [Satellite communication] (NVT) .... CUDIX
Common User Digital Information Exchange System [or Subsystem] [Satellite communication] (MCD) .... CUDIXS
Common User, Dynamic Allocation Multi-Media Network (MCD) .... CUDAMN
Common User Group [SAGE] .... CUG
Common User Installation Transport Network .... CUITN
Common User Interface [Computer science] .... CUI
Common User Interoffice Network [Telecommunications] (ECII) .... CUIN
Common User Land Transportation [Military] (NVT) .... CULT
Common User Products (SAUO) .... CUP
Common User Radio Transmission System (IAA) .... CURTS
Common User Subsystem (SAUO) .... CUS
Common User Support (SAUS) .... CUS
Common User System [Telecommunications] (TEL) .... CUS
Common Variable Hypogammaglobulinemia [Medicine] (MAE) .... CVH
Common Variable Immune Deficiency [Immunology] (DAVI) .... CVID
Common Variable Immunodeficiency [Medicine] CVI
Common Version [Bible] CV
Common Version of the Bible (BARN) .... Com Ver
Common Video System .... CVS
Common Wadden Sea Secretariat (SAUO) .... CWSS
Common Wart (MELL) .... CW
Common Wealth Movement (SAUO) .... CWM
Common Wealth Party (SAUO) .... CW
Common Weapon Control System [Military] .... CWCS
Common Weapon Control System Development Facility (MCD) .... CDF
Common Weapon Sight (SAUS) .... CWS
Common Welfare (SAUO) .... CW
Common X Interface [Computer science] CXI
Common X-Windows Interface [Unix] (VERA) CXI

Commonality and Standardization Effort (MCD) .... CASE
Commonality Candidate List [NASA] (NASA) CCL
Commonality Change Center (ACAE) CCC
Commonality Change Review Board (ACAE) .... CCRB
Commonality List (SAUS) CL
Commonality Usage Board (NASA) .... CUB
Commonality Usage Proposal (NASA) .... CUP
Common-Carrier Network (CIST) .... CCN
Common-Channel Interface Signaling (IDOE) .... CCIS
Common-Equipment System (IAA) .... CES
Common-Impression Cylinder CIC
Commonly Used Acronym .... CUA
Commonly Used System Programs [Digital Equipment Corp.] .... CUSP
Common-Metric Questionnaire (TMMY) .... CMQ
Common-Midpoint .... CMP
Common-Mode Rejection Ratio (AAEL) .... CMR
Common-Object-File Format [Computer science] .... COFF
Commons Expenditure Committee [British] .... CEC
Commons, Open Spaces, and Footpaths Preservation Society [British] (BARN) .... COSFPS
Commons, Open Spaces and Footpaths Preservation Society (SAUO) .... COSFPS
Commons Registration Act [Town planning] [British] .... CRA
Common/See Individual Components List (MCD) .... COMSICL
Common-Users Communication Program (ACAE) .... CCP
Commonweal [A publication] (BRI) .... Comw
Commonwealth C
Commonwealth .... CMNWLTH
Commonwealth .... COM
Commonwealth (ADWA) .... Com
Commonwealth (SAUO) .... Com
Commonwealth (SAUO) .... Commw
Commonwealth .... COMM
Commonwealth (DLA) .... Commonw
Commonwealth (DLA) .... Commw
Commonwealth (SAUO) .... COMWEL
Commonwealth (DLA) .... Com'w'th
Commonwealth (ADA) .... CTH
Commonwealth .... Cw
Commonwealth .... CWLTH
Commonwealth (WDAA) .... Cwlth
Commonwealth .... Cwth
Commonwealth Accreditation Agency [Australia] .... CAA
Commonwealth Act (DLA) .... Commonw Act
Commonwealth Acts (Australia) [A publication] (DLA) .... Austl C Acts
Commonwealth Advisory Aeronautical Research Council [British] (EAIO) .... CAARC
Commonwealth Agency Liaison Group on Regional Initiatives (SAUO) .... CALGRI
Commonwealth Agricultural Bureaux [Database producer] (EA) .... CAB
Commonwealth Agricultural Bureaux International [Research center] [British] (IRC) .... CABI
Commonwealth Air Force Telecommunications Network (IAA) .... CAFTN
Commonwealth Air Training Plan Museum, Inc., Brandon, Manitoba [Library symbol] [National Library of Canada] (NLC) .... MBCAM
Commonwealth Air Training Plan Museum, Inc., Brandon, MB, Canada [Library symbol] [Library of Congress] (LCLS) .... CaMBCAM
Commonwealth Air Transport Council [British] (EAIO) .... CATC
Commonwealth Aircraft Corp. Ltd. [Australia] [ICAO aircraft manufacturer identifier] (ICAO) CC
Commonwealth Aluminium Corporation Pty. Ltd. (SAUO) .... Comalco
Commonwealth Aluminum [NASDAQ symbol] (TTSB) .... CALC
Commonwealth Aluminum Corp. [NASDAQ symbol] (SAG) .... CALC
Commonwealth Aluminum Corp. [Associated Press] (SAG) .... CmwAl
Commonwealth and Continental Church Society (SAUO) .... CCCS
Commonwealth and Empire Conference on Radio for Civil Aviation (SAUO) .... CECRCA
Commonwealth and Empire Conference on Radio for Civil Aviation (SAUS) .... CECRCA
Commonwealth and Empire Conference on Radio for Civil Aviation (SAUO) .... CERCA
Commonwealth and Empire Radio for Civil Aviation [British] .... CERCA
Commonwealth Archivists Association [Later, ACARM] (EA) .... CAA
Commonwealth Arts Organization (EA) .... CAO
Commonwealth Association for Education and Training of Adults .... CAETA
Commonwealth Association for Education in Journalism and Communication (SAUO) .... CAEJAC
[The] Commonwealth Association for Education in Journalism & Communication (AC) .... CAEJC
Commonwealth Association of Architects [British] (EAIO) .... CAA
Commonwealth Association of Legislative Counsel (AC) .... CALC
Commonwealth Association of Mental Handicap and Developmental Disabilities (EA) .... CAMHDD
Commonwealth Association of Museums [Calgary, AB] (EAIO) .... CAM
Commonwealth Association of Planners [British] (EAIO) .... CAP
Commonwealth Association of Ploytechnics in Africa (SAUO) .... CAPA
Commonwealth Association of Polytechnics in Africa [Nairobi, Kenya] (EAIO) .... CAPA
Commonwealth Association of Science and Mathematics Educators [British] .... CASME
Commonwealth Association of Science, Technology, and Mathematics Educators [London, England] (EAIO) .... CASTME
Commonwealth Association of Scientific Agricultural Societies [Canada] .... CASAS

Commonwealth Association of Surveying and Land Economy [*British*] (EAIO) ... CASLE
Commonwealth Association of Tax Administrators [*British*] (EAIO) ... CATA
Commonwealth Banana Exporters Association [*Saint Lucia*] (EAIO) ... CBEA
Commonwealth Banking Corporation [*Australia*] ... CBC
Commonwealth Banking Corporation. Economic Newsletter [*A publication*] (ADA) ... CBEN
Commonwealth Board of Architectural Education [*British*] (EAIO) ... CBAE
Commonwealth Board of Surveying Education [*London, England*] (EAIO) ... CBSE
Commonwealth Broadcasting Association [*London, England*] (EAIO) ... CBA
Commonwealth Broadcasting Association. Handbook [*A publication*] ... CBA Handbook
Commonwealth Broadcasting Network [*British*] (NTCM) ... CBN
Commonwealth Bureau of Animal Breeding and Genetics. Technical Communication (journ.) (SAUS) ... TCBAAQ
Commonwealth Bureau of Animal Health [*British*] ... CBAH
Commonwealth Bureau of Animal Nutrition [*British*] ... CBAN
Commonwealth Bureau of Animal Nutrition. Technical Communication (journ.) (SAUS) ... TCANAQ
Commonwealth Bureau of Dairy Science and Technology [*British*] ... CBDST
Commonwealth Bureau of Helminthology (BI) ... CBH
Commonwealth Bureau of Horticulture and Plantation Crops [*British*] ... CBHPC
Commonwealth Bureau of Nutrition (SAUO) ... CAB
Commonwealth Bureau of Nutrition. Technical Communication (journ.) (SAUS) ... TCCND5
Commonwealth Bureau of Pastures and Field Crops [*British*] ... CBPFC
Commonwealth Bureau of Soils [*British*] ... CAB
Commonwealth Bureau of Soils [*British*] ... CBS
Commonwealth Bureau of Soils. Special Publication (journ.) (SAUS) ... SPCSDW
Commonwealth Cable Management Committee (SAUO) ... CCMC
Commonwealth Cable Network (SAUS) ... CCN
Commonwealth Centre Party (SAUO) ... CCP
Commonwealth Chess Association (EA) ... CCA
Commonwealth Club of California, San Francisco, CA [*Library symbol*] [*Library of Congress*] (LCLS) ... CSfCCL
Commonwealth Coast Conference (PSS) ... CCC
Commonwealth Code, Commonwealth of the Northern Mariana Islands [*A publication*] ... CNMI
Commonwealth Commercial Crime Unit (SAUO) ... CCU
Commonwealth Committee for Defence (Operational Clothing and Combat Equipment) (ADA) ... CCD(OCCE)
Commonwealth Committee for/of Foreign Ministers on Southern Africa (SAUO) ... CFMSA
Commonwealth Committee on Fuel Research [*British*] ... CCFR
Commonwealth Committee on Mineral Resources and Geology [*British*] ... CCMRG
Commonwealth Committee on Southern Africa (SAUO) ... CCSA
Commonwealth Communication of Army Networks (SAUS) ... COMCAN
Commonwealth Communications Council [*British*] [*World War II*] ... CCC
Commonwealth Communications Organization (SAUS) ... CCO
Commonwealth Consultative Group on Mineral Resources and Geology (SAUO) ... CCMRG
Commonwealth Consultative Group on Technology Management (SAUO) ... CCGTM
Commonwealth Copyright Office (DGA) ... CCO
Commonwealth Correspondents' Association (BI) ... CCA
Commonwealth Council for Educational Administration [*British*] (AIE) ... CCEA
Commonwealth Council for Educational Administration (SAUO) ... CEA
Commonwealth Countries' League [*Middlesex, England*] (EAIO) ... CCL
Commonwealth Court (DLA) ... Commw Ct
Commonwealth Defence Conference - Operational Clothing and Combat Equipment (EA) ... CDC-OCCE
Commonwealth Defence Science Organisation [*British*] ... CDSO
Commonwealth Department of Employment, Education, and Training [*Australia*] ... CDEET
Commonwealth Department of Health (SAUO) ... CDH
Commonwealth Development Bank of Australia ... CDBA
Commonwealth Development Corp. (ILCA) ... CDC
Commonwealth Development Finance Co. Ltd. [*Joint government and private agency in London established to aid businesses elsewhere in British Commonwealth*] ... CDFC
Commonwealth Development Finance Company (SAUO) ... COMDEV
Commonwealth Digital Boundaries database System (SAUO) ... CDBS
Commonwealth Division (SAUO) ... CD
Commonwealth Dried Vine Fruits Grade Fixing Committee [*Australia*] ... CDVFGFC
Commonwealth Economic Committee [*British*] ... CEC
Commonwealth Economic Conference (SAUO) ... CEC
Commonwealth Economic Consultative Council [*British*] ... CECC
Commonwealth Ed, $1.90 Pref [*NYSE symbol*] (TTSB) ... CWEPrC
Commonwealth Ed, $2.00 Pref [*NYSE symbol*] (TTSB) ... CWEPrD
Commonwealth Ed $8.40 Pvet [*NYSE symbol*] (TTSB) ... CWEPrJ
Commonwealth Ed,$2.425 Pref [*NYSE symbol*] (TTSB) ... CWEPrK
Commonwealth Ed,$7.24 Pref [*NYSE symbol*] (TTSB) ... CWEPrE
Commonwealth Ed,$8.38 Pref [*NYSE symbol*] (TTSB) ... CWEPrI
Commonwealth Ed,$8.40 Pref [*NYSE symbol*] (TTSB) ... CWEPrF
Commonwealth Edison Co. (MHDB) ... CEC
Commonwealth Edison Co. [*Associated Press*] (SAG) ... CwE
Commonwealth Edison Co. (SAUO) ... CWE
Commonwealth Edison Co., Chicago, IL [*Library symbol*] [*Library of Congress*] (LCLS) ... ICComE
Commonwealth Edison Company (SAUO) ... CECO
Commonwealth Edison Company (SAUO) ... CECo
Commonwealth Edison-Public Service (SAUO) ... CEPS
Commonwealth Education Conferences [*British*] ... CEC
Commonwealth Education Liaison Committee [*British*] ... CELC
Commonwealth Educational Media Co-operative/Centre for Asia (SAUO) ... CEMCA
Commonwealth Educational Media Resources Programme (SAUO) ... CEMREP
Commonwealth Electoral Act (SAUO) ... CEA
Commonwealth Employment Service Advisory Committee [*Australia*] ... CESAC
Commonwealth Energy Management Program ... CEMP
Commonwealth Energy Sys [*NYSE symbol*] (TTSB) ... CES
Commonwealth Energy System [*NYSE symbol*] (SPSG) ... CES
Commonwealth Energy System [*Associated Press*] (SAG) ... ComES
Commonwealth Engineer [*A publication*] ... Commonwealth Eng
Commonwealth Engineering Conference (MCD) ... CEC
Commonwealth Engineers Council [*See also CAICB*] [*British*] (EAIO) ... CEC
Commonwealth Environmental Services, Inc. (EFIS) ... CES
Commonwealth Exchange Commission (SAUO) ... CEC
Commonwealth Expedition [*British*] ... COMEX
Commonwealth Fishing Boat Licence (SAUO) ... CFBL
Commonwealth Forestry Association (SAUO) ... CFA
Commonwealth Forestry Association [*Oxford, England*] (EAIO) ... CFA
Commonwealth Forestry Bureau [*Oxford, England*] ... CFB
Commonwealth Forestry Bureau, Oxford (SAUO) ... CFB
Commonwealth Forestry Institute [*British*] ... CFI
Commonwealth Forestry Review (SAUS) ... Commonw For Rev
Commonwealth Foundation (EAIO) ... CF
Commonwealth Fund for Technical Co-Operation [*British*] (EAIO) ... CFTC
Commonwealth Fund, New York, NY [*Library symbol*] [*Library of Congress*] (LCLS) ... NNCF
[*The*] **Commonwealth Games Association of Canada Inc.** [*Association Canadienne des Jeux du Commonwealth Inc.*] (AC) ... CGAC
Commonwealth Games Federation [*British*] (EAIO) ... CGF
Commonwealth Geographical Bureau (EA) ... CGB
Commonwealth Gold [*Vancouver Stock Exchange symbol*] ... CWC
Commonwealth Government Directory [*Australia*] [*A publication*] ... CGD
Commonwealth government Railways (SAUO) ... CR
Commonwealth Hansard Editors Association (EAIO) ... CHEA
Commonwealth Headquarters (SAUO) ... CHQ
Commonwealth Heraldry Board [*Papatoetoe, New Zealand*] (EAIO) ... CHB
Commonwealth Higher Education Management Service (SAUO) ... CHEMS
Commonwealth Holiday Inns of Canada ... CHIC
Commonwealth Human Ecology Council [*British*] ... CHE
Commonwealth Human Ecology Council [*British*] (EAIO) ... CHEC
Commonwealth Industrial Training and Experience Programme (SAUO) ... CITEP
Commonwealth Institute (SAUO) ... CI
Commonwealth Institute [*British*] (DI) ... CI
Commonwealth Institute of Biological Control [*Trinidad*] ... CIBC
Commonwealth Institute of Entomology [*British*] (MCD) ... CIE
Commonwealth Institute of Health (SAUO) ... CIH
Commonwealth Institute of Helminthology [*St. Albans, England*] ... CIH
Commonwealth International Law Cases [*A publication*] (DLA) ... CILC
Commonwealth International Philatelic Society [*Defunct*] (EA) ... CIPS
Commonwealth Internet Reference Group [*Information service or system*] ... CIRG
Commonwealth Investigation Branch [*Australia*] ... CIB
Commonwealth Jam Preserving and Condiment Manufacturers' Association [*Australia*] ... CJPCMA
Commonwealth Jet Services, Inc. [*ICAO designator*] (FAAC) ... CJS
Commonwealth Joint Communication Board [*British military*] (DMA) ... CJCB
Commonwealth Joint Services Committee (SAUO) ... CJSC
Commonwealth Journalists Association [*British*] (EAIO) ... CJA
Commonwealth Judicial Journal [*A publication*] (DLA) ... Comm Jud J
Commonwealth Judicial Journal [*A publication*] (DLA) ... Commw Jud J
Commonwealth Land Party [*British*] (DAS) ... CLP
Commonwealth Land Party (SAUO) ... CLP
Commonwealth Law Enforcement Assistance Network [*Pennsylvania*] ... CLEAN
Commonwealth Law Reports [*A publication*] ... CLR
Commonwealth Law Review [*A publication*] ... Com LR
Commonwealth Law Review [*A publication*] (DLA) ... Commonw L Rev
Commonwealth Lawyers' Association [*British*] (EAIO) ... CLA
Commonwealth Legal Aid Commision [*Australia*] ... CLAC
Commonwealth Legal Education Association (EAIO) ... CLEA
Commonwealth Library Association ... CLA
Commonwealth Linking Trust (SAUO) ... CLT
Commonwealth Literacy Campaign (SAUO) ... CLC
Commonwealth Magistrates and Judges' Association (EAIO) ... CM & JA
Commonwealth Magistrates' Association [*British*] (EAIO) ... CMA
Commonwealth Management Information Centre (SAUS) ... CMIC
Commonwealth Medical Association [*British*] (EAIO) ... CMA
Commonwealth Medical Officers' Association [*Australia*] ... CMOA
Commonwealth Meteorology Research Centre (SAUO) ... CMRC
Commonwealth Microfilm Library Ltd., Calgary, AB, Canada [*Library symbol*] [*Library of Congress*] (LCLS) ... CmL
Commonwealth Microfilm Library Ltd., Calgary, AB, Canada [*Library symbol*] [*Library of Congress*] (LCLS) ... CmLL
Commonwealth Military Forces (SAUO) ... CMF
Commonwealth Military Forces [*British*] ... CMF
Commonwealth Minerals [*Vancouver Stock Exchange symbol*] ... CMY
Commonwealth Mining and Metallurgical Institution (SAUS) ... CMMI
Commonwealth Mining Investments (SAUS) ... CMI
Commonwealth Mycological Institute [*Research center*] [*British*] (IRC) ... CMI
Commonwealth Nation ... CN
Commonwealth National Library (DGA) ... CNL
Commonwealth National Library, Canberra (SAUO) ... CNL
Commonwealth National Library, Parliament House, Canberra, ACT, Australia [*Library symbol*] [*Library of Congress*] (LCLS) ... AuCNL

Commonwealth NGO Consortium for Agricultural Development Programmes (SAUO) .... ECAD
Commonwealth Nurses Federation (EA) .... CNF
Commonwealth of Australia .... COA
Commonwealth of Independent Nations (SAUO) .... CIN
Commonwealth of Independent Republics .... CIR
Commonwealth of Independent States [Formerly, Soviet Union] .... CIS
[The] Commonwealth of Learning (AC) .... COL
Commonwealth of Massachusetts (SAUS) .... MA
Commonwealth of Pennsylvania Air Monitoring System (SAUS) .... COPAMS
Commonwealth of Puerto Rico Rules and Regulations [A publication] (DLA) .... PRR & Regs
Commonwealth of Puerto Rico Rules and Regulations (journ.) (SAUS) .... PRR&Regs
Commonwealth of the Bahamas Trade Union Congress (SAUO) .... CBTUC
Commonwealth of Virginia Information Systems (GEOI) .... COVIS
Commonwealth of World Citizens .... CWC
Commonwealth Office [Formerly, CRO] [British] .... CO
Commonwealth Office of Local Government [Australia] .... COLG
Commonwealth Office of Space Science and Applications (SAUO) .... COSSA
Commonwealth Oil Refining Co., Inc. (SAUO) .... CWO
Commonwealth Ombudsman [Australia] .... CO
Commonwealth Open Systems Environment (SAUO) .... COSE
Commonwealth Pacific Cable (SAUS) .... COMPAC Cable
Commonwealth Palaeontological Collection (SAUO) .... CPC
Commonwealth Parliamentary Association [British] (EAIO) .... CPA
Commonwealth Party [Gibraltar] [Political party] (PPE) .... CP
Commonwealth Party (SAUO) .... CWP
Commonwealth Pharmaceutical Association [British] (EAIO) .... CPA
Commonwealth Preference Area .... CPA
Commonwealth Preference Standstill Area (PDAA) .... CPSA
Commonwealth Press Union [London, England] (EAIO) .... CPU
Commonwealth Procurement Circular [A publication] .... CPC
Commonwealth Professional [A publication] .... Com Prof
Commonwealth Program for the Promotion of Excellence in Research [Australia] .... CPPER
Commonwealth Public Library (SAUS) .... CPL
Commonwealth Public Service (SAUS) .... CPS
Commonwealth Radio Research Board (SAUO) .... CRRB
Commonwealth Reconstruction Training Scheme (SAUO) .... CRTS
Commonwealth Record [A publication] .... Commonw Rec
Commonwealth Record [Australia] [A publication] .... Comm Rec
Commonwealth Record [Australia] [A publication] .... CR
Commonwealth Refining Co. [Puerto Rico] .... CORCO
Commonwealth Regional Health Community Secretariat for East, Central and Southern Africa (SAUO) .... CRHCS
Commonwealth Regional Health Secretariat (EA) .... CRHS
Commonwealth Regional Renewable Energy Resources Information Service (IID) .... CRRERIS
Commonwealth Relations Office [Later, CO] [British] .... CRO
Commonwealth Research Centre .... CRC
Commonwealth Savings [NASDAQ symbol] (TTSB) .... CMSB
Commonwealth Savings Bank [NASDAQ symbol] (SAG) .... CMSB
Commonwealth Savings Bank [Associated Press] (SAG) .... CwltSav
Commonwealth Savings Bank of Australia .... CSBA
Commonwealth Scholarship Scheme [Australia] .... CSS
Commonwealth Science Council [London, England] (EAIO) .... CSC
Commonwealth Scientific and Industrial Research (SAUO) .... CSIR
Commonwealth Scientific and Industrial Research Automatic Computer [British] (IAA) .... CSIRAC
Commonwealth Scientific and Industrial Research Organisation (SAUO) .... CSIRO
Commonwealth Scientific and Industrial Research Organisation [Australia] [Information service or system] (NITA) .... CSIRO
Commonwealth Scientific and Industrial Research Organistion Divison of Information Technology (SAUS) .... CSIRODIT
Commonwealth Scientific and Industrial Research Organization Computing Network (SAUS) .... CSIRONET
Commonwealth Scientific and Industrial Research Organization Laboratory Craftsmen (SAUS) .... CSIROLCA
Commonwealth Scientific and Industrial Research Organization, Melbourne (SAUO) .... CSRIRO
[The] Commonwealth Scientific and Industrial Research Organization Network [Australia] [Computer science] (TNIG) .... CSIRONET
Commonwealth Scientific and Industrial Research Organization Technical Associati (SAUS) .... CSIROTA
Commonwealth Scientific and Research Organisation Network [Australia] [Information service or system] (NITA) .... CSIRONET
Commonwealth Scientific Committee (SAUO) .... CSC
Commonwealth Scientific Committee [British] .... CSC
Commonwealth Scientific Corporation (SAUO) .... CSC
Commonwealth Scientific Office (SAUO) .... CSO
Commonwealth Secondary Scholarship Scheme [Australia] .... CSSS
Commonwealth Secretariat (DLA) .... Comm Sec
Commonwealth Secretariat (DLA) .... Commw Sec
Commonwealth Secretariat [British] (EAIO) .... CS
Commonwealth Secretariat [Australia] .... CS
Commonwealth Service Corps [British] .... CSC
Commonwealth Society for the Deaf [British] (ADA) .... CSD
Commonwealth Society for the Deaf (SAUO) .... CSD
Commonwealth Society of Teachers of Dancing [Australia] .... CSTD
Commonwealth Sport Development Programme (SAUO) .... CSDP
Commonwealth Statutory Rules: Numbered (SAUS) .... NUMRUL
Commonwealth Steamship Owners' Association [Australia] .... CSOA
Commonwealth Steel Company (SAUO) .... CSC

Commonwealth Steel Company Ltd. (SAUS) .... Comsteel
Commonwealth Steel Company Ltd. [Australia] .... COMSTEEL
Commonwealth Steering Committee on Local and Regional Authorities (SAUO) .... CDRL
Commonwealth Students Children Society (SAUO) .... CSCS
Commonwealth Supply Council [British] [World War II] .... CSC
Commonwealth Taxation Board of Review [Australia] .... CTBR
Commonwealth Technical Consortium (SAUO) .... CTC
Commonwealth Technology, Inc. (EFIS) .... CTI
Commonwealth Tel Enterp [NASDAQ symbol] (SG) .... CTCO
Commonwealth Telecommunications Board [Later, CTO] [British] .... CTB
Commonwealth Telecommunications Organization [England] .... CTO
Commonwealth Tertiary Education Commission (SAUS) .... CTEC
Commonwealth Trade Union Council [British] (EAIO) .... CTUC
Commonwealth Trading Bank of Australia .... CTBA
Commonwealth Trans-Antarctic Expedition [1955-58] .... CTAS
Commonwealth Transpacific [Submarine cable in Pacific] .... COMPAC
Commonwealth Unit Trust Fund (SAUO) .... CUTF
Commonwealth United Corporation (SAUO) .... CUC
Commonwealth Veterinary Association .... CVA
Commonwealth Veterinary Emergency Plan (SAUO) .... COMVETPLAN
Commonwealth War Graves Commission [Maidenhead, Berkshire, England] (EAIO) .... CWGC
Commonwealth Weightlifting Federation [Ammanford, Dyfed, Wales] (EAIO) .... CWF
Commonwealth Workshop on Building and Planning in the Third World (SAUO) .... DW
Commonwealth Writers of Britain (BI) .... CWB
Commonwealth X-ray and Radium Laboratory (SAUS) .... CXRL
Commonwealth Year Book [A publication] .... CYB
Commonwealth Youth Exchange Council [British] .... CYEC
Commonwealth Youth Programme [British] .... CYP
Commonwealth-Pacific System (SAUS) .... COMPAC System
Commonwealth-State Advisory Group [Australia] .... CSAG
Commonwealth-State Consultative Committee (SAUO) .... CSCC
Commonwealth-State Housing Agreement (Service Personnel) [Australia] .... CSHA(SP)
Commonwealth/State Migration Committee [Australia] .... COSMIC
Commscope, Inc. [NYSE symbol] (SG) .... CTV
Commun Market Committee of the Nitrogenous and Phosphatic Fertilisers Industry (SAUO) .... CMC-ENGRAIS
Communal .... Comm
Communal Areas Management Program for Indigenous Resources .... CAMPFIRE
Communal Studies Association (EA) .... CSA
Communante des Associations d'Editeurs de Journaux [Community of Associations of Newspaper Publishers] [EEC] [Belgium] (PDAA) .... CAEJ
Communaute de Travail des Brasseurs du Marche Commun [Working Committee of Common Market Brewers] .... CBMC
Communaute de Travail des Regions Europeennes de Tradition Industrielle [Association of Traditional Industrial Regions of Europe] [Lille, France] (EAIO) .... RETI
Communaute des Associations d'Editeurs de Journaux de la CEE [Community of the Newspaper Publishing Associations of the EEC] [Belgium] (EAIO) .... CAEJ-CEE
Communaute des Chemins de Fer Europeens [Belgium] (EAIO) .... CCFE
Communaute des Radios Publiques de Langue Francaise (EAIO) .... CRPLF
Communaute Economique de l'Afrique de l'Ouest [West African Economic Community] .... CEAO
Communaute Economique des Etats de l'Afrique Centrale [Economic Community of Central African States - ECCAS] [Bangui, Central African Republic] (EAIO) .... CEEAC
Communaute Economique des Pays des Grands Lacs [Economic Community of the Great Lakes Countries - ECGLC] [Gisenye, Rwanda] (EAIO) .... CEPGL
Communaute Economique du Betail et de la Viande [Economic Community for Livestock and Meat - ECLM] (EAIO) .... CEBV
Communaute Economique Europeenne [European Economic Community] ..... CEE
Communaute EURAIL [EURAIL Community] [An association] [Netherlands] (EAIO) .... CE
Communaute Europeenne [European Community] .... CE
Communaute Europeenne de Credit Communal [European Municipal Credit Community] .... CECC
Communaute Europeenne de Defense [European Defense Community] .... CED
Communaute Europeenne de l'Energie Atomique .... CEEA
Communaute Europeenne des Associations du Commerce de Gros de Biere des Pays Membres de la CEE [European Community of Associations of the Wholesale Beer Trade of the EEC] .... CEGROB
Communaute Europeenne des Cooperatives de Consommateurs [European Consumers' Cooperation Committee] [Common Market] .... EURO COOP
Communaute Europeenne des Organisations de Publicitaires [European Community of Advertising Organizations] .... CEOP
Communaute Europeenne du Charbon et de l'Acier [European Coal and Steel Community] .... CECA
Communaute Financiere Africaine [Currency] (ECON) .... CFA
Communaute Internationale Baha'ie [Baha'i International Community] .... CIB
Communaute Internationale des Associations de la Librairie [International Community of Booksellers Associations] .... CIAL
Communaute Internationale des Obtenteurs de Plantes Ornementales et Fruitieres aReproduction Asexuee [International Community of Breeders of Asexually Reproduced Fruit Trees and Ornamental Varieties] [Geneva, Switzerland] (EAIO) .... CIOPORA
Communaute Mondiale de Vie Chretienne [World Christian Life Community] [Italy] (EAIO) CVX
Communaute Urbaine de Quebec [Library symbol] [National Library of Canada] (BIB) .... QQCUQ

commune (SAUS) c
Commune (ABBR) .... CMUN
Commune .... COM
Commune .... COMMN
Communed (ABBR) .... CMUND
Communes Network [*British*] (EAIO) .... CN
Communic Central [*NASDAQ symbol*] (TTSB) CCIX
Communic Sys [*NASDAQ symbol*] (TTSB) .... CSII
Communicability (ABBR) .... CMUNCBT
Communicable (ABBR) .... CMUNCB
Communicable [*Medicine*] .... commun
Communicable Disease [*or a patient with such a disease*] [*Medicine*] .... CD
Communicable Disease (DAVI) .... commun dis
Communicable Disease Center .... CDC
Communicable Disease Intelligence (SAUO) .... CDI
Communicable Disease Prevention & Control (SAUO) .... CDPC
Communicable Disease Report [*A publication*] .... CD
Communicable Disease Report (HEAS) .... CDR
Communicable Disease Surveillance Centre [*British*] .... CDSC
Communicableness (ABBR) .... CMUNCBNS
Communicably (ABBR) .... CMUNCBY
Communicant (ABBR) .... CMUNCNT
Communicant [*Religion*] (ROG) .... COM
Communicate (MDG) .... CMCT
communicate (SAUS) .... cmct
Communicate (ABBR) .... CMUNC
Communicate [*or Communications*] .... COM
Communicate .... COMMUN
Communicate Between Forces (SAUS) .... COMMS
Communicated (ABBR) .... CMUNCD
communicated (SAUS) .... com
Communicated Authenticity, Regard, Empathy [*Medicine*] (WDAA) .... CARE
Communicating (ABBR) .... CMUNCG
Communicating Alarm Response Equipment [*British Telecom*] .... CARE
Communicating Applications Specifications .... CAS
Communicating Hydrocele (DB) .... CH
Communicating Magnetic Card (HGAA) .... CMC
Communicating Magnetic Card Typewriter (AFIT) .... CMCT
Communicating NATO Intentions (MCD) .... CNI
Communicating Word Processing System .... CWPS
Communicating Word Processor .... CWP
Communication (SAUS) .... Cmn
Communication (ABBR) .... CMUNCN
Communication (IAA) .... CO
Communication (NTIO) .... com
Communication (AFM) .... COMM
Communication (BEE) .... comm
Communication (TBD) .... Comm
Communication .... COMMCTN
Communication (AL) .... Commun
Communication .... COMN
Communication Access Method (IAA) .... CAM
Communication Access System (IAA) .... CAS
Communication Accessories Company (SAUO) .... CAC
Communication Administration System (SAUS) .... CAS
Communication, Advertising, and Marketing Education Foundation [*British*] .... CAM
Communication, Advertising and Marketing Studies (SAUO) .... CAMS
Communication Advisors, Inc. [*Southfield, MI*] [*Telecommunications*] (TSSD) .... CAI
Communication Analysis Section .... CAS
Communication Analysis Tool for Space Station (MCD) .... CATSS
Communication and Access to information for Persons with Special needs (SAUO) .... CAPS
Communication and Cognition (EA) .... C & C
Communication and Cognition - Artificial Intelligence (EA) .... CC-AI
Communication and Command Control Requirements (AAG) .... CCCR
Communication and Consultation Unit (SAUO) .... CCU
Communication and Control (IAA) .... CAC
Communication and Control (SAUS) .... C&C
Communication and Data (IAA) .... CAD
Communication and Data Management System (SSD) .... CDMS
Communication and Data Processing Operation System (SAUS) .... CADPOS
Communication and Data Subsystem .... C & DSS
Communication and Information Systems [*Micro-Electronics Programme*] [*British*] (NITA) .... CAIS
Communication and Information Technology (SAUS) .... COINT
Communication and Instrumentation [*NASA*] (KSC) .... C & I
Communication and Instrumentation [*NASA*] (KSC) CI
Communication and Instrumentation Support Services [*NASA*] (KSC) .... CISS
Communication and Instrumentation System [*CIS is preferred*] [*NASA*] (KSC) .... C & IS
Communication and Instrumentation System [*Also, C & IS*] [*NASA*] .... CIS
Communication and Navigation (MCD) .... C & N
Communication and Navigation Laboratory (SAUO) .... C&N LAB
Communication and Navigation Research Laboratory (NASA) .... CNRL
Communication and Operating System Interface (SAUS) .... CaOS
Communication and RADAR Assignment Coordinating Committee .... CRACC
Communication and Reconnaissance (SAUS) .... C/R
Communication and Social Science Information Service [*Canadian research collection network*] .... CASSIS
Communication and Symbolic Behavior Scales (TMMY) .... CSBS
Communication and Tracking [*NASA*] (NASA) .... C & T
Communication and Tracking Subsystem (SAUS) .... C&TSS
Communication and Tracking Subsystem [*Military*] (IAA) .... CTS
Communication and Tracking Subsystem (MCD) .... CTSS
Communication Application Platform [*Computer science*] (PCM) .... CAP
Communication Application Program Interface [*Computer science*] (VERA) .... CAPI
Communication Application Software (SAUS) .... CAS
Communication Application Specification (SAUS) .... CAS
Communication Apprehension .... CA
Communication Arts .... CA
Communication Association of the Pacific [*Later, WCA*] (EA) .... CAP
Communication Automatic Processing Equipment .... CAPE
Communication Barge Receiver (SAUS) .... CBR
Communication Barge Transmitter (SAUS) .... CBT
Communication By Light (SAUS) .... CBL
Communication Cable, Inc. [*NASDAQ symbol*] (NQ) .... CABL
Communication Cable, Inc. (EFIS) CCI
Communication Cable, Inc. [*Associated Press*] (SAG) .... CmCbINC
Communication Capability Application Program (SAUS) .... CCAP
Communication Carrier Assembly [*Spaceship*] .... CCA
Communication Center CC
Communication Center (SAUS) .... Comcenter
Communication Center (SAUS) .... COMM CTR
Communication Center Console CCC
Communication Center Specialist (SAUS) .... COMM CTR SP
Communication Central Facility [*Air Force*] .... CCF
Communication Channel & Jammer Simulator (SAUS) .... CJS
Communication Check Point (DICI) .... CCP
Communication Check Point (SAUS) .... Comm Chk Pt
Communication Circuit Technical Control Facility (MCD) .... CCTCF
Communication Command (SAUO) CC
Communication, Command, Control, Computer, and Intelligence (USGC) C41
Communication Commission (EA) CC
Communication Comptroller CC
Communication Computer (SAUS) .... COC
Communication Computer Programming Center (AFM) .... CCPC
Communication Connect Time Monitor [*Computer science*] .... CCTM
Communication Control Aid System (SAUS) .... CCAS
Communication Control Application Program (SAUS) .... CCAP
Communication Control Block (SAUS) .... CCB
Communication Control Console (NAKS) ccc
Communication Control Number (AAG) .... CCN
Communication Control Program (BUR) .... CCP
Communication Control program (SAUS) .... COMCO program
Communication Control Record (SAUS) .... CCR
Communication Control System .... CCS
Communication Controller Node (SAUS) .... CUCN
Communication Countermeasures .... COMCM
Communication Countermeasures Evaluation Facility [*Air Force*] (MCD) .... CCEF
Communication, Culture, and Technology Program .... CCT
Communication Data (SAUS) .... CD
Communication Deception System (DWSG) .... CDS
Communication Department (SAUO) .... COM
Communication Desk (BUR) .... CDK
Communication Deviance (DIPS) .... CD
Communication Disorders Specialist .... CDS
Communication Driver (SAUS) .... CD
Communication Driver Maintenance System (SAUS) .... CDMS
Communication Effectiveness Centre [*Canada*] .... CEC
Communication, Electronic and Meteorological Equipment Status (SAUO) .... CEMES
Communication Electronic Equipment [*Military*] .... CEE
Communication Electronics and Meteorological (SAUS) .... CEM
Communication Electronics Element [*Army*] (AABC) .... CEE
Communication Electronics Staff Officer (MCD) .... CESO
Communication Engineering Standard .... CES
Communication Equipment Operator Trainer (SAUS) .... CEOT
Communication Equipment Room (SAUS) .... CER
Communication European Satellite Team (SAUO) .... COMEST
Communication Exercise [*Military*] (INF) .... COMEX
Communication Facilities Mediterranean and Middle East .... COMMFACMEDME
Communication Facilities Testing System (SAUS) .... COMFACTS
Communication Factor (SAUS) .... CF
Communication Format Tape (SAUS) .... CFT
Communication Foundation for Asia (SAUO) .... CFA
Communication Frequency and Facility Information System (SAUS) .... COFFI System
Communication Gateway (SAUO) .... CG
Communication Head (SAUS) .... COMMHD
Communication High-Accuracy Location System-Exploitable (SAUS) .... CHALS-X
Communication History Report (AAEL) .... CHR
Communication Identification Navigation .... CIN
Communication Identifier [*Computer science*] (IBMDP) .... CID
Communication Implementation Directive [*Air Force*] .... CID
Communication Improvement Augmentation Program (ACAE) .... CIAP
Communication Improvement Auxiliary Vessel (SAUS) .... CIMAV
Communication in Behavioral Biology (SAUS) .... CBB
Communication Indentification (ACAE) CI
Communication Industrial Services .... CIS
Communication Information CI
Communication Information Bulletin (DNAB) .... CIB
Communication Information System (IEEE) .... CIS
Communication Installation Squadron [*Air Force*] .... CISq
Communication Institute for Online Scholarship (SAUO) .... CIOS
Communication Instructions (SAUS) .... Comm Instn
Communication Instructions for Reporting Enemy Sightings [*Navy*] .... CIRES

Communication Instructions for Reporting Vital Intelligence Sightings [Army] .... CIRVIS
Communication Intelligence Corp. (PCM) CIC
Communication Intelligence Corp. [NASDAQ symbol] (SAG) CICI
Communication Intelligence Corp. [Associated Press] (SAG) .... CommIn
Communication Intelligence Security Regulation (MCD) .... CISR
Communication Intercept and Direction Finding (MCD) .... CIDF
Communication Interface (SAUS) CI
Communication Interface and Multiplexer Module (SAUS) .... CIMM
Communication Interface Control Unit (NAKS) .... CICU
Communication Interface Coordinator [NASA] CIC
Communication Interface Monitor .... CIM
Communication Interface System (SAUS) .... CIS
Communication Interface to fire direction system (SAUS) CCI
Communication Interface Unit (SAUS) .... CIU
Communication Interfaces (SAUS) .... CIs
Communication International [Vancouver Stock Exchange symbol] .... CUA
Communication Interrupt Analysis (SAUS) .... CIA
Communication Interrupt Control Program [Computer science] (IBMDP) .... CICP
Communication Jamming Processor (IEEE) .... CJP
Communication Liaison Facility (SAUO) .... COMLNOFAC
Communication Lieutenant [British military] (DMA) CL
Communication Lieutenant-Commander [British military] (DMA) .... CLCR
Communication Line Adapters .... CLA
Communication Line Adapters for Teletype .... CLAT
Communication Line Analyzer (SAUS) .... CLA
Communication Line Concentrator Module (MHDI) .... CLCM
Communication Line Interface (MCD) CLI
Communication Line Interface Computer (MCD) CLIC
Communication Line Processor .... CLP
Communication Line Terminal [Computer science] .... CLT
Communication Line Terminator [IBM Corp.] .... COLT
Communication Linear Integrated Circuit (IAA) CLIC
Communication Link Analyzer (IEEE) .... CLA
Communication Link Analyzer (or Adapter) (SAUS) .... CLA
Communication Link Subsystem .... CLSS
Communication Machinery Corporation (SAUO) .... CMC
Communication Maintenance Squadron (SAUO) .... COMMMAINTRON
Communication Management System [Computer science] .... CMS
Communication Manager /2 (SAUS) CM2
Communication Master Control (ACAE) .... CMC
Communication Measurements Laboratory (SAUS) .... CML
Communication Method SINIX (SAUS) .... CMX
Communication Mode Selector Control (SAUO) .... CMSC
Communication Module Terminal Controller (SAUS) .... CMTC
Communication Multiplexor Channel (DNAB) .... CMC
Communication Navigation (NFPA) .... CNI
Communication, Navigation, and Identification .... CNI
Communication, Navigation and Identification system (SAUO) .... CNI
Communication, Navigation, and Landing (ACAE) .... CNL
Communication, Navigation & Position Integration (SAUS) .... CNPI
Communication Navigation Surveillance (SAUO) .... CNS
Communication/ Navigation/Meteorological (SAUO) .... COM/NAV/MET
Communication Net Control Station [Navy] (NVT) .... NECOS
Communication Network .... CNET
Communication Network System (IAA) .... CNS
Communication Networks (SAUS) .... nets
Communication of Oita Amateur Research Association (SAUO) .... COARA
Communication Online Test System (IAA) .... COLTS
Communication On-Line Testing System (SAUS) .... COLTS
Communication Operating System (SAUS) .... COS
Communication Operation Station .... COS
Communication Optimization Program Translator [NASA] .... COPTRAN
Communication Oriented Application Analysis [Computer science] (VERA) .... CORAN
Communication Oriented Message System [IBM Corp.] .... CORMES
Communication Outlet (SAUS) .... CO
Communication Output Printer .... COP
Communication Personnel [Marine Corps] .... CP
Communication Physical Input Output Control System (SAUS) .... CPIOCS
Communication Physical Input/Output Control System (IAA) .... CPIOC
Communication Planning Corp. [Jacksonville, FL] [Telecommunications] (TSSD) .... CPC
Communication Pool (SAUS) .... COMPOOL
Communication Prediction Program [NASA] (KSC) .... CPPM
Communication Processing Definitions (SAUS) .... CPD
Communication Products Division (SAUS) .... CPD
Communication Radio and Teletype (Secure) System .... CRATTZ
Communication, Range, and Azimuth Unit [Computer science] .... COMRAZ
Communication Redirection (SAUS) .... CRD
Communication Registered Publication Memoranda .... CRPM
Communication Representative .... CR
Communication Research and Development Satellite [NASA] (NASA) .... COMR & DSAT
Communication Research and Development Satellite (SAUS) .... COMR&DSAT
Communication Research Center [University of Florida] [Research center] (RCD) .... CRC
Communication Research Center [Florida State University] [Research center] (RCD) .... CRC
Communication Research Center [Boston University] [Research center] (RCD) .... CRC
Communication Research Laboratory (SAUS) .... CRL
Communication Resources [Haddonfield, NJ] [Telecommunications] (TSSD) .... CR
Communication Satellite Planning Center [Stanford University] [Research center] (RCD) .... CSPC

Communication Scanner Base (IBMDP) .... CSB
Communication Science Research Center [Battelle Memorial Institute] (MCD) .... CSRC
Communication Sciences Laboratory [University of Florida] .... CSL
Communication Security (SAUS) .... Comm Scty
Communication Security Activity (SAUS) .... Comm Sec Act
Communication Security Activity .... COMMSECACT
Communication Security Publication Memorandum [Army] .... CSPM
Communication Segment (MCD) .... CS
Communication Sequential Process [Computer science] .... CSP
Communication Sergeant (SAUS) .... CS
Communication Service Facility (IAA) .... CSF
Communication Service Request .... CSR
Communication Serviceability Facilities (SAUS) .... CSF
Communication Services (SAUO) .... CS
Communication Services Ltd. [Hong Kong] [Telecommunications] .... CSL
Communication Services Manager [Novell, Inc.] .... CSM
Communication Setup (SAUS) .... CS
Communication Ship Quarters (SAUS) .... CSQ
Communication Signal Distribution System .... CSDS
Communication Simulator Console (SAUS) .... CSC
Communication Skills Corp. [British] .... CSC
Communication Skills Self-Assessment Exam (DMAA) .... CSSAE
Communication Standing Order .... CSO
Communication Station [Military] (CAAL) .... COMSTA
Communication Station .... CS
Communication Studies (AIE) .... CS
Communication Subnet Processor (OSI) .... CSNP
Communication Subsystem (MCD) .... COMS
Communication Subsystem For Interconnection (SAUS) .... CSFI
Communication Supplementary Activity .... COMMSUPACT
Communication Supplementary Detachment .... COMMSUPDET
Communication Support System (MCD) .... CSS
Communication System Control (SAUS) .... CSC
Communication System Control Element [of TCCF] (MCD) .... CSCE
Communication System Development (IAA) .... CSD
Communication System Discipline (IAA) .... COMSYSDISC
Communication System Monitor (ACAE) .... CSM
Communication, System, Results, Objectives, Exception, Participation, Motivation [Business term] (MHDB) .... CSROEPM
Communication System Simulation Language [Computer science] (IEEE) .... COMSL
Communication System Simulator (ACAE) .... CSS
Communication Systems Center (SAUS) .... CSC
Communication Systems Engineering Laboratory [NASA] (MCD) .... CSEL
Communication Systems Ltd. [London, England] [Telecommunications] (TSSD) .... COMSYS
Communication Systems Ltd. (SAUO) .... CSLtd
Communication Systems Research Ltd. [Ilkley, W. Yorkshire, England] (TSSD) .... CSR
Communication Systems Sector [or Segment] Replacement [Military] .... CSSR
Communication Systems Segment (ACAE) .... CSS
Communication Technical Evaluation Console (KSC) .... CTEC
Communication Terminal Asynchronous-International Standards Organization (SAUO) .... CTA-ISO
Communication Terminal Asynchronous-Standard (SAUO) .... CTA-STD
Communication Terminal Synchronous (SAUS) .... CTS
Communication Test Station (SAUS) .... CTS
Communication Theory (SAUS) .... COMTHEORY
Communication Training Consultants, Inc. [New York, NY] [Telecommunications] (TSSD) .... CTC
Communication Trench [Military] .... CT
Communication Valve Development [British] .... CVD
Communication Vector Table (BUR) .... CVT
Communication Watch Officer .... CWO
Communication with Extraterrestrial Intelligence [Later, SETI] [Radioastronomy] .... CETI
Communication Word Processor (SAUS) .... CWP
Communication Workers Alliance [Philippines] .... CWA
Communication Workers of Canada .... CWC
Communication Yeoman [Navy rating] [British] .... CY
Communication Zone (SAUS) .... Comm Z
Communication Zone [British military] (DMA) .... COMZONE
Communication-Electronic-Meteorological Board [Air Force] .... CEMB
Communication/Navigation/Instrument (ACAE) .... CNI
Communication-Quebec, Trois-Rivieres, PQ, Canada [Library symbol] [Library of Congress] (LCLS) .... CaQTCO
Communication-Quebec, Trois-Rivieres, Quebec [Library symbol] [National Library of Canada] (NLC) .... QTCO
Communications C
Communications (DOMA) .... COM
Communications (PIPO) .... COMM
Communications (NAKS) .... comm
Communications .... COMMS
Communications (MILB) .... comms
Communications .... COMMUN
Communications (DD) .... commun
Communications (SAUS) .... Comp
Communications (ROG) .... COMS
Communications (SAUS) .... CS
Communications / Air Traffic Service (SAA) .... COM/ATS
Communications - Electronics Deployment Report (MCD) .... CEDREP
Communications Access Device (CET) .... CAD
Communications Access Manager (MHDB) .... CAM
Communications Access Method (SAUS) .... CAM

Communications Access Processor (CCCA) ... CAP

Communications Acquisition Status and Assessment Report (MCD) ... CASAR

Communications Adapter ... CA

Communications Adaptor Board (NITA) ... CAB

Communications, Advertising and Marketing Studies (SAUS) ... CAMS

Communications Advisory Committee (SAUO) ... COMAC

Communications Advisory Team (OICC) ... CAT

Communications Aerial Sleeve (SAUS) ... CAS

Communications Afloat Program [*Military*] (DNAB) ... CAP

Communications Alert and Liaison System [*Office of Fisheries*] (MSC) ... CALL

Communications Allocation Order (CINC) ... CAO

Communications Alternative Provider (SAUS) ... CAP

Communications Analysis Corp. [*Framingham, MA*] [*Telecommunications*] (TSSD) ... CAC

Communications Analysis Package (SAUS) ... CAP

Communications, Analysis, Simulation, and Evaluation [*Army*] (MCD) ... CASE

Communications and Broadcasting Engineering Test Satellite ... COMETS

Communications and Configuration Console (MCD) ... CACC

Communications & Control Board (SAUS) ... CCB

Communications and Control Systems Laboratory ... CCSL

Communications and Data (SAUS) ... CAD

Communications and Data (SAUS) ... C&D

Communications and Data ... C & D

Communications and Data Centre (NITA) ... CDC

Communications and Data Handling (SAUO) ... CADH

Communications and Data Handling (SSD) ... C & DH

Communications and Data Handling (GEOI) ... CDH

Communications and Data Handling Subsystem (SAUO) ... C&DH

Communications and Data Link (KSC) ... CADL

Communications and Data Processing (ACAE) ... C&DP

Communications and Data Processing Exhibition (ADWA) ... Comdex

Communications and Data Processing Exposition ... COMDEX

Communications and Data Processing Operation ... CADPO

Communications and Data Processing Operations System (COE) ... CADPOS

Communications and Data Subsystem (IAA) ... CADSS

Communications and Data Subsystems ... CDS

Communications and Data Systems Integration (NASA) ... CADSI

Communications and Distributed Resources Report [*International Dat a Corp.*] [*Defunct*] [*Information service or system*] (CRD) ... CDR

Communications and Distributed Systems [*British*] ... CDS

Communications and Education Program Integration Working Group (SAUO) ... CEPIWG

Communications and Electronics (IAA) ... CAE

Communications and Electronics ... C & E

Communications and Electronics Command [*Formerly, ASC*] [*Army*] ... CEC

Communications and Electronics Division (SAUO) ... CANDE

Communications and Electronics Division (SAUO) ... CED

Communications and Electronics Engineering Library, Department of National Defence [*Bibliotheque du Genie Electronique et des Communications, Ministere de laDefense National*] **Ottawa, Ontario** [*Library symbol*] [*National Library of Canada*] (NLC) ... OONDC

Communications and Electronics Maintenance Squadron [*Air Force*] ... CEMS

Communications and Electronics Maintenance Squadron (AFM) ... CEMSq

Communications and Electronics Management Squadron (SAUO) ... CEMSq

Communications and Electronics Materiel Readiness Command [*Army*] ... CERCOM

Communications and Electronics Squadron (IAA) ... CAESQ

Communications and Electronics Squadron (SAUO) ... C&E Sq

Communications & Entertainment Corp. [*NASDAQ symbol*] (SAG) ... CECO

Communications & Entertainment Corp. [*Associated Press*] (SAG) ... ComEnt

Communications and Information Handling Equipment and Services ... CO IN HES

Communications and Information Policy Division (SAUO) ... CIPD

Communications and Information Processing Group [*Rensselaer Polytechnic Institute*] [*Research center*] (RCD) ... CIPG

Communications and Information Services - Communications ... CIS-COMMS

Communications and Information Systems (SAUO) ... CIS

Communications and Information Systems Committee [*NATO*] (EAIO) ... CCIS

Communications and Information Systems Division (ACAE) ... CISD

Communications and Information Technology Research [*British*] ... CIT

Communications and Instrumentation System (SAUS) ... CIS

Communications and Interface Group [*NASA*] (NASA) ... CIG

Communications & Measurement Technologies Ltd. (GEOI) ... C&MT

Communications and Media Law Association [*Australia*] ... CMLA

Communications and Navigation (SAUS) ... C&N

Communications and Navigation Airborne Radio Instrumentation [*Military*] (IAA) ... CANARI

Communications and Replenishment At Sea (SAUS) ... RAS

Communications and Signal Processing [*British*] ... CSP

Communications and Systems Management [*Software module*] [*Stratus Computer, Inc.*] ... CASM

Communications and Tactical [*Publications*] [*Navy*] (NVT) ... COMTAC

Communications and Technical Services (SAUS) ... C&TS

Communications and Telemetry ... CMTM

Communications and Tracking (NAKS) ... C&T

Communications and Tracking System [*or Subsystem*] ... CATS

Communications and Tracking System [*or Subsystem*] ... CTS

Communications Antenna Sleeve ... CAS

Communications Application Specification [*Computer science*] ... CAS

Communications Architecture (SAUS) ... CMA

Communications Architecture for Distributed Interactive Simulation (SAUS) ... CADIS

Communications Area Local Station (NVT) ... CALS

Communications Area Master Station (NVT) ... CAMS

Communications Assist Team (NVT) ... CAT

Communications Assistance for Law Enforcement Act ... CALEA

Communications Assistance for Law Enforcing Agencies (SAUO) ... CALEA

Communications Assistance for/to Law Enforcement Act (SAUO) ... CALEA

Communications Assistant [*Telecommunications*] (OTD) ... CA

Communications. Association for Computing Machinery ... CACM

Communications Authority of Zambia (DDC) ... CAZ

Communications Authorization Order (SAUS) ... CAO

Communications Branch, National Research Council ... CBNRC

Communications Buffer [*Computer science*] ... CB

Communications Buffer [*Air Force*] ... COMB

Communications Buffer Memory [*Computer science*] ... CBM

Communications Bus ... CB

Communications by Meteor Trails (SAUS) ... COMET

Communications Career Program [*Military*] ... CCP

Communications Carrier, Inc. [*Austin, TX*] [*Telecommunications*] (TSSD) ... CCI

Communications Carrier Umbilical (NAKS) ... CCU

Communications Carrier Unit (SAUS) ... CCU

Communications Center [*NATO*] (NATG) ... COMCEN

Communications Center ... COMMCEN

Communications Center (SAA) ... COMMCTR

Communications Center of Clarksburg [*Clarksburg, MD*] [*Telecommunications*] (TSSD) ... CCC

Communications Center (or Centre) (SAUS) ... CC

Communications Central [*Military*] ... CC

Communications Central [*NASDAQ symbol*] (SAG) ... CCIX

Communications Central [*Commercial firm*] [*Associated Press*] (SAG) ... ComCtrl

Communications Centre Officer (SAUO) ... CCO

Communications Change Group (SAA) ... CCG

Communications Change Initiation Request (IAA) ... CCIR

Communications Change Log (IAA) ... CCL

Communications Change Request (IAA) ... CCR

Communications Channel (NITA) ... CMC

Communications Channel Adapter (IAA) ... CCA

Communications Chief (SAUS) ... CC

Communications Chief (SAUS) ... Comm Ch

Communications Circular Letter [*Navy*] ... CCL

Communications Code (SAUS) ... CC

Communications Collection Standard System (MCD) ... CCSS

Communications, Command, and Control ... CCC

Communications, Command, and Telemetry Systems (MCD) ... CCATS

Communications, Command, Control, and Intelligence (PDAA) ... C3I

Communications Command Group [*Air Force*] ... COMCG

Communications Command Processor (SAUS) ... CCP

Communications Command Program (SAUS) ... CCP

Communications Command Technical Manual [*Army*] ... CCTM

Communications Compare (SAUS) ... COMP

Communications Computer (IAA) ... CC

Communications Concentrator Software Package [*Computer science*] ... CCSP

Communications Concepts, Inc. [*Newport Beach, CA*] [*Telecommunications*] (TSSD) ... CCI

Communications Construction Squadron (SAUO) ... CCS

Communications Construction Squadron (SAUO) ... COMMCONSTRON

Communications Consultants, Inc. [*Washington, NJ*] [*Telecommunications*] (TSSD) ... CCI

Communications Control (MCD) ... CC

Communications Control (NAKS) ... cc

Communications Control and Management Processor ... CCMP

Communications Control and Restoral Center (SAUO) ... CCRC

Communications Control Applications Program ... CCAP

Communications Control Architecture [*NAVY*] ... CCA

Communications Control Area (IAA) ... CCA

Communications Control Batches (SAUS) ... CCB

Communications Control Block [*Computer science*] ... CCB

Communications Control Centre (SAUS) ... CCC

Communications Control Console (MCD) ... CCC

Communications Control Equipment (MCD) ... CCE

Communications Control Facility [*Military*] ... CCF

Communications Control Field ... CCF

Communications Control Group Assembly [*Ground Communications Facility, NASA*] ... CCGA

Communications Control Interface (MCD) ... CCI

Communications Control Language ... CCL

Communications Control Link (DNAB) ... CCL

Communications Control Module [*Telecommunications*] (TEL) ... CCM

Communications Control Package ... CCP

Communications Control Panel ... CCP

Communications Control Processor ... CCP

Communications Control Program Initialization (MCD) ... CCPI

Communications Control Room (IAA) ... CCR

Communications Control Set (SAUS) ... CCS

Communications Control Team [*Military*] ... CCT

Communications Control Unit (SAUS) ... CCU

Communications Controller (SAUS) ... CCO

Communications Controller (MCD) ... COMC

Communications Controller Multichannel [*Computer science*] ... CCM

Communications Coordination Committee for the United Nations (EA) ... CCCUN

Communications Council (EA) ... CC

Communications Countermeasures [*Military*] (NVT) ... COMMCM

Communications Countermeasures (SAUS) ... Comm Cmeas

Communications Countermeasures Operator (SAUS) ... Comm Cmeas Op

Communications Coupling Unit (CET) ... CCU

Communications. CSIRO [*A publication*] ... COCO

Communications Cultural Promotion Foundation (SAUO) ... CCPF

Communications Data Base [*Canada*] [*Information service or system*] (IID) .... COMBASE
Communications Data Field (SAUS) .... CDF
Communications Data Formatter (MCD) .... CDF
Communications Data Network Controller (MCD) .... CDNC
Communications Data Processing System (NVT) .... CDPS
Communications Data Processor [*Electronics*] .... CDP
Communications Data Terminal (MCD) .... CDT
Communications Decency Act .... CDA
Communications Definition Language (SAUS) .... CODEL
Communications Degradation (SAUO) .... COMDEG
Communications Design Center [*Carnegie-Mellon University*] [*Research center*] (RCD) .... CDC
Communications Desk Reference [*A publication*] (TSSD) .... CDR
Communications Detachment (MCD) .... COMMDET
Communications Development Exposition (SAUS) ...... COMDEX
Communications Digital Control Unit .... CDCU
Communications Digital Switching System (ACAE) .... CDSS
Communications Direction and Coordination .... COMMDAC
Communications Direction-Finding Interface (SAUS) ...... CDFIF
Communications Display Terminal (IAA) .... CDT
Communications Distribution Amplifier (MCD) .... CDA
Communications, Distribution, and Switching Center [*NASA*] (KSC) .. CD & SC
Communications Distribution and Switching Center (SAUS) ...... CD&SC
Communications, Distribution, and Switching Center [*NASA*] (KSC) ..... CDSC
Communications Dual Access Controller (CIST) .... CDAC
Communications Duty Officer (FAAC) .... CDO
Communications Editing Unit (NOAA) .... COMED
Communications, Electronic, Technical, and Salaried Workers of Canada .... CWC
Communications Electronic Warfare System (SAUS) ...... CEWS
Communications Electronics (SAUO) .... CE
Communications Electronics Delivery and Retrieval System (ACAE) ...... CEDARS
Communications Electronics Engineering Installation Agency (SAUO) ...... CCEIA
Communications Electronics Evaluation and Test Agency (MCD) .... CEETA
Communications Electronics Facility Records (SAUO) ...... CEFR
Communications Electronics Management Center [*Air Force*] (AFIT) .... CEMC
Communications Electronics Management Systems .... CEMS
Communications Electronics Mission Order (MCD) .... CEMO
Communications Electronics Navigation [*Military*] .... CEN
Communications Electronics School [*Air Force*] .... CESCH
Communications Electronics Security Department (HEAS) ...... CESD
Communications Electronics Security Group (SAUO) .... GESG
Communications Electronics Special Account Code (SAUS) ...... CESAC
Communications, Energy & Paperworkers Union of Canada (AC) ...... CEP
Communications Engineering and Installation Agency .... CEIA
Communications Engineering and Installation Department [*Army*] .... CEI
Communications Engineering Department [*Military*] (DNAB) .... CED
Communications Engineering Research Satellite (NITA) ...... CERS
Communications Equipment .... CE
Communications Equipment Distributors Association (MHDI) ...... CEDA
Communications Equipment Information and Modelling System (SAUS) .... CEIMS
Communications Equipment List (SAUO) .... CEIS
Communications Equipment Logistics (MCD) .... COMLOG
Communications Equipment Manufacturers Association (SAUO) ...... CEMA
Communications Equipment Subcommittee (SAUO) .... CESC
Communications Equipment Support Element (MCD) .... CESE
Communications Equipment Support Group [*Environmental science*] (COE) .... CESG
Communications Era Task Force [*Defunct*] (EA) .... CERATF
Communications Errors Statistics (CMD) .... CES
Communications European Satellite Team (SAUS) .... COMEST
Communications Excellence to Black Audiences [*An award*] ...... CEBA
Communications Executive (CIST) .... COMX
Communications Exhibition [*Trade fair*] [*British*] .... COMEX
Communications Expansion Unit .... CEU
Communications Experiment (SAUS) .... COMEX
Communications Exploitation (MCD) .... COMMEX
Communications Facilities in Support of DA [*Department of the Army*] Continuity of Operations Plan (AABC) .... COOPCOMM
Communications Facility (IAA) .... CF
Communications Facility (ACAE) .... COMFAC
Communications Facility [*Control and Processing Co.*] ...... COMFAX
Communications Factor (IAA) .... CF
Communications Failure Detecting and Switching (SAUS) ...... Commstitch
Communications Field Exercise [*Military*] (NVT) .... COMMFEX
Communications for Online Systems [*Computer science*] (ODBW) ...... COLS
Communications for On-Line Systems (SAUS) .... COLS
Communications Fraud Control Association (EA) .... CFCA
Communications Frequency and Facility Information Systems [*ICAO databank*] (NITA) .... COFFI
Communications Front End (SSD) .... CFE
Communications Front-End Processor (SAUS) .... CFEP
Communications Group [*Air Force*] .... CG
Communications Group, Inc. [*Concord, MA*] [*Telecommunications*] (TSSD) ...... CGI
Communications Handler for Automatic Multiple Programs ...... CHAMP
Communications High-Accuracy Airborne Location System [*Military*] ...... CHAALS
Communications Identification Directory [*Air Force*] (CET) ...... CID
Communications III, Inc. [*Columbus, OH*] (TSSD) .... COM III
Communications, Implementation and Installation Working Group (SAUO) .... CIIWG
Communications Implementation Plan (SAUO) .... CIP
Communications Improvement Memorandum [*Military*] .... CIM
Communications Improvement Plan (CCCA) .... CIP

Communications in Mathematical Physics (journ.) (SAUS) ...... Commun Math Phys
Communications in Soil Science and Plant Analysis (SAUS) ...... Commun Soil Sci Plant Anal
Communications Individual Positioning Program (SAUO) ...... CIPP
Communications Industries Association of Japan [*Telecommunications*] ...... CIAJ
Communications Industries Group (SAUO) .... CIG
Communications Industries Report [*A publication*] (EAAP) ...... CIR
Communications Information System (SAUS) .... CIS
Communications Input and Output Control System (BUR) ...... CIOCS
Communications Input-Output Control System [*Computer science*] (ECII) .... CIOCS
Communications Input/Output Multiplexer .... CIOM
Communications Input/Output Processor [*Computer science*] (NITA) ...... CIOP
Communications Instructions [*Navy*] .... COMINST
Communications Instructions for Merchant Ships [*Navy*] ...... CIMS
Communications Instructions for Reporting Vital Intelligence Sightings [*Military*] .... CIRVIS
Communications Instructor Console (MCD) CIC
Communications Instruments Inc. (SAUO) CII
Communications Integrated Control Engineering, Reporting, and Operations (MCD) .... CICERO
Communications Integrated System Control Office (SAUO) ...... CISCO
Communications Integration Test Site [*Military*] (CAAL) ...... COMMITS
Communications Intelligence [*Military*] .... COMINT
Communications Intelligence (ACAE) .... COMIT
Communications Intelligence Channel CIC
Communications Intelligent Matrix Control (SAUS) .... CIMC
Communications Interface (MCD) CI
Communications Interface and Processing System (MCD) ...... CIP
Communications Interface Assembly [*Computer science*] ...... CIA
Communications Interface Coordinator (SAUS) .... CIE
Communications Interface Equipment (MCD) .... CIE
Communications Interface Modules [*Computer science*] ...... CIM
Communications Interface Processor (COE) .... CIP
Communications Interface System (MCD) .... CIS
Communications Interface Table (MCD) .... CIT
Communications Interface Terminal (ACAE) .... CIT
Communications Interface Unit .... CIU
Communications Interfaces and Data Exchange (SAUO) ...... CIDE
Communications. International Association of Theoretical and Applied Limnology (journ.) (SAUS) .... IVTMAS
Communications International, Inc. (SAUO) CII
Communications Interrupt Analysis [*Sperry UNIVAC*] (IEEE) ...... CIA
Communications Interrupt Program .... CIP
Communications Jamming [*Military*] .... COMJAM
Communications Jamming Operator [*Military*] .... CJO
Communications Junction Module Assembly [*Ground Control Facility, NASA*] .... CJMA
Communications Law Centre [*Australia*] CLC
Communications Liaison Officer (SAUO) .... CLO
Communications Line Adaptor (NITA) .... CLA
Communications Line Control CLC
Communications Line Expander [*Electrodata, Inc.*] [*Telecommunications*] ...... CLE
Communications Line Multiplexer .... CLM
Communications Line Switch .... CLS
Communications Link Analysis and Simulation System (MCD) ...... CLASS
Communications Link Analyzer (SAUS) .... CLA
Communications Link Analyzer System .... CLAS
Communications Link Characterization Experiment [*Communications Technology Satellite*] (MCD) .... CLCE
Communications Link Controller [*International Computers Ltd.*] [*Telecommunications*] CLC
Communications Link Interface Planning System (COE) ...... CLIPS
Communications Load Exercise [*Military*] (CAAL) ...... COMMLOADEX
Communications Logistics Depot (SAUS) .... CLD
Communications Logistics Network (IEEE) .... COMLOGNET
Communications [*Security*] Logistics Support Unit (DOMA) ...... CLSU
Communications Magnetic Card (SAUS) .... CMC
Communications Maintenance and Storage (NAKS) .... CM&S
Communications Maintenance and Storage (NASA) .... CM & S
Communications Maintenance Squadron [*Air Force*] .... CMSQ
Communications Maintenance Terminal .... CMT
Communications Management Agency .... CMA
Communications Management by Terrain Exploration (SAUS) ...... Comtex
Communications Management Configuration .... CMC
Communications Management Processor [*Information technology*] ...... CMP
Communications Management Subsystem .... COMMS
Communications Management Systems [*Military*] (RDA) ...... COMM MGT SYS
Communications Management Unit [*Aviation*] .... CMU
Communications Manager .... CM
Communications Manager/2 [*Software*] (CDE) CM/2
Communications Managers Association [*Bernardsville, NJ*] [*Telecommunications service*] (TSSD) .... CMA
Communications Managers Association of New York (SAUO) ...... CMANY
Communications Market Association (EA) .... CMA
Communications Measurements Laboratory, Inc. (SAUO) ...... CML
Communications Media Management Association (NTPA) ...... CMMA
Communications Message Processor (COE) .... CMP
Communications Message Traffic Control Unit [*Air Force*] (AFM) ...... CMTCU
Communications Mode Control .... CMC
Communications Mode Selection Control (MCD) .... CMSC
Communications Module [*AT&T*] (ACRL) .... CM
Communications Module Processor (ACRL) .... CMP
Communications Monitor (BTTJ) .... CM
Communications Monitor System (SAUS) .... CMS

Communications Monitoring and Control Subsystem (NVT) ...... CMCS
Communications Monitoring Report ...... CMR
Communications Moon Relay [*System*] [*NASA*] ...... CMR
Communications Multiplexer [*Computer science*] ...... CM
Communications Multiplexer (NITA) ...... COMM MUX
Communications Multiplexer Controller (SAUS) ...... CMC
Communications Multiplexer Module [*Computer science*] ...... CMM
Communications Naval Electronic Warfare System (SAUS) ...... CO-NEWS
Communications, Navigation, and Positioning [*Military*] ...... CNP
Communications, Navigation, and Surveillance ...... CNS
Communications Navigation Instrument (SAUS) ...... CNI
Communications Need ...... COMNEED
Communications Network ...... CN
Communications Network (AFM) ...... COMNET
Communications Network Application [*Computer science*] (VERA) ...... CNA
Communications Network Architects, Inc. [*Washington, DC*] [*Telecommunications service*] (TSSD) ...... CNA
Communications Network Architecture ...... CNA
Communications Network Center (SAUS) ...... CCNC
Communications Network Control (SAUS) ...... CNC
Communications Network Control Element (SAUO) ...... CNCE
Communications Network Control Processor (IAA) ...... CNCP
Communications Network Control Station (SAUO) ...... CNCS
Communications Network Controller (IAA) ...... CNC
Communications Network Design Program ...... CNDP
Communications Network Emulator ...... CNE
Communications Network for Manufacturing Application [*Computer science*] (TNIG) ...... CNMA
Communications Network International (SAUO) ...... CNI
Communications Network Management (SAUO) ...... CNM
Communications Network Management Interface ...... CNMI
Communications Network Manager (SAUS) ...... CNM
Communications Network Procedure [*Computer science*] (NITA) ...... CNP
Communications Network Processor ...... CNP
Communications Network Service [*Satellite Business Systems*] [*McLean, VA*] [*Telecommunications*] (TSSD) ...... CNS
Communications Network Services [*Virginia Polytechnic Institute and State University*] [*Blacksburg*] (TSSD) ...... CNS
Communications Network Simulation [*Computer science*] (NITA) ...... CNS
Communications Network Simulator (SAUS) ...... CNS
Communications Network System (SAUS) ...... CNS
Communications, Networks, and Information Processing Theory Group [*MIT*] (MCD) ...... CNIPTG
Communications NODAL [*Network-Oriented Data Acquisition Language*] Control Element ...... CNCE
Communications of the Association for Communicating Machinery (HGAA) ...... CACAM
Communications Office Building (NASA) ...... COB
Communications Officer [*Navy*] ...... CO
Communications Officer ...... COMMO
Communications Officer (WDAA) ...... Comm O
Communications Officer ...... COMO
Communications Officer School [*Air Force*] ...... COMMOSCH
Communications on Alternatives in Education [*Defunct*] (EA) ...... KOA
Communications on Pure an Applied Mathematics (journ.) (SAUS) ...... Commun Pure Appl Math
Communications On-Line Processor ...... COP
Communications Operating Directive (KSC) ...... COD
Communications Operating Module (SAUS) ...... COM
Communications Operating Requirement (CCCA) ...... COR
Communications Operating Summary (SAUO) ...... COMOPS
Communications Operational Planning System [*Environmental science*] (COE) ...... COPS
Communications, Operational Practices and Rules of the Air Committee (SAUS) ...... COM/OPS/RAC
Communications Operations Instructions [*Air Force*] ...... COI
Communications Operations Officer [*Air Force*] ...... COMMOPNSO
Communications Operations Report [*Air Force*] ...... COR
Communications Operations Squadron [*Air Force*] ...... COSQ
Communications Orbiter (ACAE) ...... CO
Communications Oriented Peripheral Equipment (SAUS) ...... COPE
Communications Oriented Processing Equipment (SAUS) ...... COPE
Communications Oriented Software ...... COS
Communications Outage Recorder [*NASA*] (SPST) ...... COR
Communications Outage Reporting System ...... COORS
Communications Outage Restoral Section [*ADC*] ...... COORS
Communications Outage Restoration Section (SAUS) ...... COORS
Communications Output Processor (CCCA) ...... COP
Communications, Participation, and Education [*Program*] (AAEL) ...... CPE
Communications Patching Panel ...... CPP
Communications Performance Monitoring and Assessment [*Military*] ...... CPMAS
Communications Plan ...... COMPLAN
Communications Planning and Development ...... CPD
Communications Plenum Cable (SAUS) ...... CMP
Communications Policy Branch, Saskatchewan Department of Justice, Regina, Saskatchewan (SAUS) ...... SRJC
Communications Policy Branch, Saskatchewan Department of Justice, Regina, Saskatchewan [*Library symbol*] [*National Library of Canada*] (NLC) ...... SRJC
Communications Port [*Computer science*] ...... COM
Communications Port [*Computer science*] (DDC) ...... COM port
Communications Privacy Equipment (SAUS) ...... CPE
Communications Procedure-Oriented Language [*Computer science*] ...... CPOL
Communications Procedures Management System (MCD) ...... CPMS
Communications Processing Center (CET) ...... CPC

Communications Processing Interface (MCD) ...... CPI
Communications Processing System ...... CPS
Communications Processing Unit (CET) ...... CPU
Communications Processor ...... COM
Communications Processor ...... CP
Communications Processor and Interface ...... CPI
Communications Processor Assembly [*Ground Control Facility, NASA*] ...... CPRA
Communications Processor Conversion Center ...... CPCC
Communications Processor Unit (SAUS) ...... CPU
Communications Processor Utility [*Telecommunications*] (TEL) ...... CPU
Communications Program Element ...... CPE
Communications Programs [*NASA*] ...... CP
Communications Project (EA) ...... CP
Communications Publishing Group, Inc. [*Boston, MA*] [*Information service or system*] [*Telecommunications*] (TSSD) ...... CPG
Communications Radar Exciter (SAUS) ...... CRE
Communications, Radio (SAUS) ...... CR
Communications Receiver (SAUS) ...... Com Rec
Communications Reconnaissance company (SAUO) ...... Comm Recon
Communications Register ...... CR
Communications Register Unit (IAA) ...... CRU
Communications Regulatory Commission ...... CRC
Communications Relay (ACAE) ...... CR
Communications Relay Center [*Air Force*] ...... CRC
Communications Relay Group (MCD) ...... CRG
Communications Relay Set (MCD) ...... CRS
Communications Requirements Systems Configuration and Equipment List (NVT) ...... CORESCEL
Communications Research Advisory Board [*Canada*] ...... CRAB
Communications Research and Development Command [*Fort Monmouth, NJ*] [*Army*] ...... CORADCOM
Communications Research Center [*University of Tennessee at Knoxville*] [*Research center*] (RCD) ...... CRC
Communications Research Center (HGAA) ...... CRS
Communications Research Center-Boston University (SAUO) ...... CRC-BU
Communications Research Center-University of Kansas (SAUO) ...... CRC-UK
Communications Research Center-University of Washington (SAUO) ...... CRC-UW
Communications Research Centre [*Defunct*] [*Canada*] ...... CRC
Communications Research Centre, Department of Communications [*Centre de Recherches sur les Communications, Ministere des Communications*] Ottawa, Ontario [*Library symbol*] [*National Library of Canada*] (NLC) ...... OORPL
Communications Research Division (SAUO) ...... CRD
Communications Research Establishment (NATG) ...... CRE
Communications Research Institute (MCD) ...... CRI
Communications Research Laboratories [*Information service or system*] (IID) ...... CRL
Communications Research Laboratory [*McMaster University*] [*Canada*] [*Research center*] (RCD) ...... CRL
Communications Research Machines, Inc. (SAUO) ...... CRM
Communications Resource Management System [*CHI/COR Information Management, Inc.*] ...... CRMS
Communications Resource Manager (SAUO) ...... CRM
Communications Resources Center (SAUS) ...... CRC
Communications Resources Data System [*Defense Communications Agency*] (MCD) ...... CREDATA
Communications Riser Cable (SAUS) ...... CMR
Communications Routing Indicator ...... COMRI
Communications Sales Results Measurement Plan (SAUS) ...... CSRMP
Communications Satellite (MUGU) ...... COMMUNICAT
Communications Satellite (EECA) ...... COMSAT
Communications Satellite [*Japan*] ...... CS
Communications Satellite Act (SAUS) ...... CSA
Communications Satellite Advanced Research [*AFSC*] ...... CSAR
Communications Satellite Corp. (DFIT) ...... COMSAT
Communications Satellite Corp. [*See also COMSAT*] ...... COMSATCORP
Communications Satellite Corp. (SAUO) ...... CQ
Communications Satellite Corp. [*See also COMSAT*] ...... CSC
Communications Satellite Corporation [*Washington, D.C.*] (WDMC) ...... COMSAT
Communications Satellite Corporation (ITCA) ...... COMSTAT
Communications Satellite Corporation (SAUO) ...... CSC
Communications Satellite Earth Station (ACAE) ...... CSES
Communications Satellite for Experimental Purposes [*Japan*] [*Telecommunications*] ...... CSE
Communications Satellite Program [*NASA*] ...... CSP
Communications Satellite Project Office ...... CSPO
Communications Satellite Relay (NG) ...... CSR
Communications Security (NAKS) ...... COMEC
Communications Security [*Military*] ...... COMSEC
Communications Security Analyst (SAUS) ...... Comm Scty Anal
Communications Security Association (EA) ...... COMSEC
Communications Security Control Group [*Navy*] (MCD) ...... CSCG
Communications Security Control Terminal (MCD) ...... CSCT
Communications Security Education Program (SAUO) ...... CSEP
Communications Security Equipment Engineering Bulletin (MCD) ...... CSEEB
Communications Security Equipment Systems Document [*National Security Agency*] (MCD) ...... CSESD
Communications Security Establishment [*Canada*] ...... CSE
Communications Security Establishment, Department of National Defence [*Centrede la Securite des Telecommunications, Ministere de la Defense Nationale*] Ottawa, Ontario [*Library symbol*] [*National Library of Canada*] (NLC) ...... OONDCS
Communications Security Interservice Depot Overhaul Standard (MCD) ...... CIDOS
Communications Security Logistics (MCD) ...... COMSECLOG
Communications Security Logistics Agency (MCD) ...... CSLA

Communications Security Material Sub-Issuing Office [*Military*] (NVT) .... CMSIO
Communications Security Material System [*Military*] (MCD) ...... CSMS
Communications Security Material Van-Issuing Office [*Military*] (NVT) ..... CMVIO
Communications Security Mobile Issuing Office [*Military*] (NVT) .... CMMIO
Communications Security, Phase 1 [*Course*] [*Military*] (DNAB) ... COMSEC 1
Communications Security Publication .... CSP
Communications Security System (MCD) .... CSS
Communications Selector Switch (CCCA) .... CSS
Communications Sergeant (SAUS) .... Com Sgt
Communications Server (SAUS) .... CS
Communications Service Authorization [*Obsolete*] .... CSA
Communications Service Industrial Fund (COE) .... CSIF
Communications Services (NITA) .... CS
Communications Services, Inc. [*Junction City, KS*] .... CSI
Communications Services Management Council (CIST) .... CSMC
Communications Services Manager (SAUS) .... CSM
Communications Signal Processor (CCCA) .... CSP
Communications Simulation Model (SAUS) .... COSMO
Communications Simulator (SAUS) .... COMSIM
Communications Simulator [*Sperry UNIVAC*] .... CS
Communications Simulator Console (IAA) .... CSC
Communications Society (CCCA) .... COMSOC
Communications Soft Hat [*NASA*] (KSC) .... CSH
Communications Software Developmental Package (ACAE) .... CSDP
Communications Solutions, Inc. [*San Jose, CA*] [*Information service or system*] [*Telecommunications*] (TSSD) .... CSI
Communications Spacecraft Operation Center [*NASA*] .... COMSOC
Communications Speaker .... COMSPK
Communications Squadron (SAUO) .... COMMRON
Communications Squadron (SAUO) .... Comm Sq
Communications Squadron [*Air Force*] .... COMMSq
Communications Squadron [*Marine Corps*] .... COMSQN
Communications Squadron [*Air Force*] .... CS
Communications Squadron, Theater Air Forces (SAUO) .... CSTAF
Communications Station (MCD) .... COMMSTA
Communications Status and Restoration Coordination Office .... CSRCO
Communications Status Report (MCD) .... COMSTAT
Communications Status Report [*Military*] (NVT) .... COMSTATRPT
Communications Storage Unit .... COMM-STOR
Communications Storage Unit (SAUS) .... COMM STOR Unit
Communications Strategic Rotary Launcher [*Military*] .... CSRL
Communications Study Group (SAUO) .... CSG
Communications Subcommittee [*Allied German Occupation Forces*] .... CSC
Communications Sub-Lieutenant (SAUS) .... CSL
Communications Subsystem .... CSS
Communications Supervisor (PDAA) .... COMSUP
Communications Supply Service Association (EA) .... CSSA
Communications Support .... COMS
Communications Support (SAUO) .... CONSTP
Communications Support (SAUO) .... CS
Communications Support Area .... CSA
Communications Support Control Element (MCD) .... CSCE
Communications Support Element [*Military*] (AFM) .... CSE
Communications Support Organization (COE) .... CSO
Communications Support Processor (SAUS) .... CSP
Communications Support Requirements (MCD) .... COMSR
Communications Surveillance Transistor .... CST
Communications Switch Operating System (MCD) .... CSOS
Communications Switchboard Console .... CSC
Communications Switcher .... CS
Communications Switching System [*Army*] (RDA) .... CSW
Communications Switching Unit (CAAL) .... CSU
Communications System (SAUS) .... Commun Syst
Communications System .... CS
Communications System Category Code [*Air Force*] (AFIT) .... CSCC
Communications System Control Console .... CSCC
Communications System Control Equipment .... CSCE
Communications System Language (NITA) .... COMSYL
Communications System Planning Element .... CSPE
Communications System Replacement [*Military*] (GFGA) .... CSR
Communications System Status Display (KSC) .... CSSD
Communications System User (SAUS) .... CSU
Communications System Working Group (SAUS) .... COSYWOG
Communications Systems Agency [*Fort Monmouth, NJ*] [*Army*] (RDA) .... CSA
Communications Systems Center (SAUS) .... CSB
Communications Systems Center .... CSC
Communications Systems Developing Element .... CSDE
Communications Systems Division (SAUS) .... CSD
Communications Systems Engineer (KSC) .... CSE
Communications Systems Engineering Program [*Army*] (RDA) .... CSEP
Communications Systems, Inc. [*Associated Press*] (SAG) .... ComSys
Communications Systems, Inc. .... CSI
Communications Systems, Inc. [*NASDAQ symbol*] (NQ) .... CSII
Communications Systems Industrial Funds (MCD) .... CSIF
Communications Systems Management Association (MCD) .... CSMA
Communications Systems Network Interoperability (SAUS) .... CSNI
Communications Systems Technician (MCD) .... CST
Communications Systems Working Group (SAUO) .... COSYWOG
Communications Systems Working Group (SAUO) .... CSWG
Communications Tag Pool .... COMPOOL
Communications Task Group [*CODASYL*] .... CTG
Communications Technical Operations Center [*Air Force*] .... CTOC
Communications Technician (MCD) .... COMT
Communications Technician [*Navy rating*] .... CT
Communications Technician, Chief [*Navy rating*] .... CTC

Communications Technician, First Class [*Navy rating*] CT1
Communications Technician Intercept [*Navy rating*] (IAA) .... CTI
Communications Technician, Master Chief [*Navy rating*] .... CTCM
Communications Technician, Second Class [*Navy rating*] CT2
Communications Technician, Senior Chief [*Navy rating*] .... CTCS
Communications Technician Special-devices-operator (SAUS) .... CTS
Communications Technician, Third Class [*Navy rating*] CT3
Communications Technology .... CT
Communications Technology, Incorporated (SAUO) .... CTI
Communications Technology Laboratory (CCCA) .... CTL
Communications Technology Management, Inc. [*McLean, VA*] [*Telecommunications*] (TSSD) .... CTM
Communications Technology Satellite .... CTS
Communications Technology Specialist [*International Communications Indust ries Association*] [*Designation awarded by*] (TSSD) .... CTS
Communications, Telemetry and Command (SAUS) .... CTC
Communications Terminal [*Computer science*] .... CT
Communications Terminal Modular Control Subsystem (SAUS) .... CTMC-Subsystem
Communications Terminal Module [*Computer science*] .... CTM
Communications Terminal Module Controller [*Computer science*] .... CTMC
Communications Terminal Multiplex Cabinet [*Computer science*] (CIST) .... CTMC
Communications Terminal, Synchronous [*Computer science*] .... CTS
Communications Terminal Unit (SAUS) .... CTU
Communications Test Facility [*Fort Huachuca, AZ*] [*United States Army Electronic Proving Ground*] (GRD) .... CTF
Communications Test Lab (SSD) .... CTL
Communications Test Laboratory (SAUO) .... CTL
Communications Test Station [*NASA*] .... CTS
Communications Theory and Systems Research Laboratory (SAUO) .... CTSRL
Communications Timing Procedure (NASA) .... CTP
Communications Toolbox (SAUS) .... CTB
Communications Trade Division (EA) .... CTD
Communications Training Centre (SAUS) .... CTC
Communications Training System (SAUS) .... CTS
Communications Transmission Group (SAUO) .... CTG
Communications Transmission Identifier (COE) .... CTID
Communications Union Canada .... CUC
Communications Unit (SAUO) .... CU
Communications Unit Executor .... CUE
Communications Unlimited [*Charlotte, NC*] [*Telecommunications*] (TSSD) .... CU
Communications User Emulated System for Traffic Analysis (MHDI) ..... CUESTA
Communications User Program [*Sperry UNIVAC*] .... CUP
Communications User Radio Transmission Sounding [*Navy*] .... CURTS
Communications Validating Office (CET) .... CVO
Communications Van (COE) .... COMVAN
Communications Vulnerability Analysis (ACAE) .... CVA
Communications Wing [*Air Force*] .... CW
Communications with and Service to the Public [*Army*] (AABC) .... CWSP
Communications Workers of America (EA) .... CWA
Communications Workers Union (WDAA) .... CWU
Communications Working Group (SAUS) .... CWG
Communications World International, Inc. [*Associated Press*] (SAG) .... ComW
Communications World International, Inc. [*Associated Press*] (SAG) .... ComWld
Communications World International, Inc. [*NASDAQ symbol*] (NQ) .... CWII
Communications World Intl. [*NASDAQ symbol*] (TTSB) .... CWII
Communications Wrld Intl. Wrrt [*NASDAQ symbol*] (TTSB) .... CWIIW
Communications Yeoman [*Navy rating*] .... CYN
Communications Zone (MUGU) .... COMMZ
Communications Zone .... COMZ
Communications Zone (MCD) .... CZ
Communications Zone, Europe (SAUS) .... COMZEUR
Communications Zone Indicator [*Air Force*] .... COZI
Communications/Aural Protective System (SAUS) .... CAPS
Communications-Automatic Data Processing (SAUS) .... COMM-ADP
Communications/Automatic Data Processing Center [*Fort Monmouth, NJ*] [*Army*] (GRD) .... COMM/ADP
Communications/Automatic Data Processing Laboratory [*Army Electronics Command*] [*Fort Monmouth, NJ*] .... CADPL
Communications/Automatic Data Processing Laboratory (SAUO) ...... Comm/ADP
Communications/Computer Link (COE) CCL
Communications-Computer System Program Plan (ACAE) .... CSPP
Communications-Computer Systems (SAUS) .... CCS
Communications-Computer Systems Requirements Document (SAUO) ..... CSRD
Communications/Data Manager (MCD) .... CDM
Communications-Electronics .... C-E
Communications-Electronics .... COMMEL
Communications-electronics Accommodation Program (SAUS) .... CAP
Communications-Electronics Agency (SAUO) .... CEA
Communications-Electronics Agency [*Army*] .... C-EA
Communications-Electronics Board (NATG) .... CEB
Communications-Electronics Command [*Fort Monmouth, NJ*] [*Army*] (GRD) .... CECOM
Communications-Electronics Committee (AFM) .... CEC
Communications-Electronics Consolidated Mobilization Reserve List .... CECMRL
Communications-Electronics Coordinating Section [*NATO*] .... CECS
Communications-Electronics Coordination Section, Standing Group (SAUO) .... CECS
Communications-Electronics Directive .... CED
Communications-Electronics Doctrinal Projects Office [*Air Force*] .... CEDPO
Communications-Electronics Doctrine [*Series of Air Force manuals*] .... CED
Communications-Electronics Document .... CED
Communications-Electronics Engineering Installation Agency [*DoD*] .... CEEIA

Communications-Electronics Engineering Installation Agency-National Communications Command [*DoD*] (RDA) .... CEEIA-NCC

Communications-Electronics Engineering Installation Agency-Western Hemisphere (SAUO) .... CEEIA-WH

Communications-Electronics Equipment Status Reporting (SAUO) .... C-E ESR

Communications-Electronics Facility Inoperative for Parts (MCD) .... CEFIP

Communications-electronics Implementation Directive (SAUO) .... CID

Communications-Electronics Implementation Document (SAUO) .... CEID

Communications-Electronics Implementation Plan [*For major air command requirements within the communications-electronics area*] [*Air Force*] .... CEIP

Communications-Electronics Implementation Plan Amendment [*See CEIP*] [*Air Force*] (AFM) .... CEIPA

Communications-Electronics Nomenclature Sub-Panel (SAUO) .... CENSP

Communications-Electronics Officer [*Air Force*] .... CEO

Communications-Electronics Operating Instruction (CINC) .... CEOI

Communications-Electronics Policy Directives [*NATO*] (NATG) .... CEPD

Communications-Electronics Post Deployment Requirement (SAUO) ...... CEPDR

Communications-Electronics Readiness Teams (SAUO) .... CERTs

Communications-Electronics Scheme Accounting and Control [*Air Force*] .... CESAC

Communications-Electronics Scheme Accounting and Distribution Control System (SAUO) .... CESAC

Communications-Electronics Section [*of a joint military staff; also, the officer in charge of this section*] J-6

Communications-Electronics Security Group [*British*] .... CESG

Communications-Electronics Standing Instruction (AABC) .... CESI

Communications-Electronics Survivability and Vulnerability .... CESV

Communications-Electronics War Readiness Materiel (SAA) .... CEWRM

Communications-Electronics-Meteorological [*Equipment*] .... CEM

Communications-Electronics-Meteorological Board (SAUO) .... CEMB

Communications-Electronics-Meteorological Program Aggregate Code [*Air Force*] (AFM) .... CEMPAC

Communications-Electronics-Meteorological Program Implementation Management System [*Air Force*] (CET) .... CEMPIMS

Communications-Failure Detecting and Switching Equipment (MDG) .... COMMSWITCH

Communications/Navigation Interface Unit (SAUS) .... CNIU

Communications-Oriented Automatic Test (MCD) .... COATS

Communications-Oriented Language .... COL

Communications-Oriented Multiple Terminal Executive (MHDI) .... COMTEX

Communications-Oriented Production Information and Control System [*IBM Corp.*] .... COPICS

Communications-Oriented Production Information and Control System Executive DataLink [*IBM Corp.*] .... COPICS EDL

Communications-Oriented Real-Time Executive .... CORTEX

Communications-Oriented User Programming Language .... COUPLE

Communications/Research/Machines, Inc. [*Publisher*] .... CRM

Communications/Symbiont Processor [*Sperry UNIVAC*] .... C/SP

Communications/Symbiont Processor (SAUS) .... CSP

Communicative (ABBR) .... CMUNCV

Communicative .... COMMUNV

Communicative Ability in Daily Living .... CADL

Communicative Disorders .... CD

Communicative Disorders Assistant (SAUO) .... CDA

Communicative Disorders Assistant Association of Canada (SAUO) .... CDAAC

Communicative Electronic Training System .... CETS

Communicative Technology Directorate [*Army Training Support Center*] [*Fort Eustis, VA*] .... CTD

Communicative Use of English as a Foreign Language (AIE) .... CUEFL

Communicatively (ABBR) .... CMUNCVY

Communicators for Agricultural and Rural Development (SAUO) .... CARD

Communicators for Nuclear Disarmament (EA) .... CFND

Communicators of Problem Solutions (ACAE) .... COPS

Communicatory (ABBR) .... CMUNCY

Communicavit [*Communicated*] [*Latin*] (EES) .... comm

Communing (ABBR) .... CMUNG

Communio Viatorum [*Prague*] [*A publication*] (BJA) .... ComViat

Communion (ABBR) .... CMUNN

Communion [*Service*] (ROG) .... COMM

Communique (ABBR) .... CMUNG

Communique .... COMMNQ

Communiquer a Toutes Adresses [*To Be Circulated to All Addresses*] [*Telecommunications*] [*French*] .... CTA

Communis [*Common*] [*Latin*] .... CS

Communism (ABBR) .... CMUNSM

Communist (ABBR) .... CMUNST

Communist .... COM

Communist (NTIO) .... com

Communist (WDAA) .... Com

Communist [*Slang*] .... commie

Communist Activities [*British*] .... CA

Communist Bloc Intelligence Service (NATG) .... CBIS

Communist Infiltration [*Name of 1960's FBI campaign against infiltrators*] .... COMINFIL

Communist Information .... COMINFORM

Communist International (SAUO) CI

Communist International (PPE) .... Comintern

Communist Labor Party (EA) .... CLP

Communist League Proletarian Left [*Netherlands*] [*Political party*] (PPW) ..... KBPL

Communist Party [*Political party*] .... COMM

Communist Party [*Political party*] .... CP

Communist Party [*Peru*] [*Political party*] (PD) .... PC

Communist Party (Bolsheviks) [*Political party*] .... CP (B)

Communist Party Congress (SAUO) .... CPC

Communist Party Marxist .... CPM

Communist Party of America [*Political party*] (CDAI) .... CPA

Communist Party of Arakan [*Myanmar*] [*Political party*] .... CPA

Communist Party of Argentina [*Political party*] .... CPA

Communist Party of Armenia [*Political party*] [*Defunct*] .... CPA

Communist Party of Australia [*Political party*] .... COM

Communist Party of Australia [*Political party*] (PPW) .... CPA

Communist Party of Azerbaidzhan [*Political party*] .... CPA

Communist Party of Belgium [*Political party*] .... CPB

Communist Party of Bohemia and Moravia [*Former Czechoslovakia*] [*Political party*] (EY) .... CPBM

Communist Party of Burma [*Political party*] (EY) .... CPB

Communist Party of Byelorussia [*Political party*] .... CPB

Communist Party of Canada [*Political party*] .... CPC

Communist Party of Canada (Marxist-Leninist) [*Political party*] .... CPC(M-L)

Communist Party of China [*Chung-Kuo Kung-Ch'an Tang*] [*Taiwan*] [*Political party*] (PPW) .... CPC

Communist Party of Colombia [*Political party*] (PPW) .... CPC

Communist Party of Czechoslovakia [*Political party*] (EY) .... CPCZ

Communist Party of Denmark [*Political party*] .... CPD

Communist Party of Ecuador [*Political party*] .... CPE

Communist Party of Egypt (SAUO) .... CPE

Communist Party of Estonia [*Political party*] .... CPE

Communist Party of Finland [*Political party*] .... CPF

Communist Party of Georgia [*Political party*] .... CPG

Communist Party of Germany [*Political party*] (EAIO) .... CPG

Communist Party of Great Britain [*Political party*] (DCTA) .... CPGB

Communist Party of Great Britain (SAUO) .... CPGB

Communist Party of India [*Political party*] (PPW) .... CPI

Communist Party of India - Marxist [*Political party*] (FEA) .... CPM

Communist Party of India (Marxist) [*Political party*] (PPW) .... CPI(M)

Communist Party of India (Marxist-Leninist) [*Political party*] (PD) .... CPI(ML)

Communist Party of Indo-China [*Political party*] (PPW) .... CPIC

Communist Party of Indonesia [*Political party*] (PD) .... CPI

Communist Party of Ireland [*Political party*] (PPW) .... CPI

Communist Party of Ireland (Marxist-Leninist) [*Political party*] (PPW) ...... CPI M-L

Communist Party of Japan (SAUO) .... CPJ

Communist Party of Kampuchea [*Political party*] (PD) .... CPK

Communist Party of Kazakhstan [*Former USSR*] [*Political party*] .... CPK

Communist Party of Kazakhstan [*Political party*] (BUAC) .... KPK

Communist Party of Latvia [*Political party*] .... CPL

Communist Party of Lesotho [*Political party*] (PD) .... CPL

Communist Party of Lithuania [*Political party*] .... CPL

Communist Party of Luxembourg [*Political party*] .... CPL

Communist Party of Malaya [*Political party*] (PD) .... CPM

Communist Party of Malaya - Marxist-Leninist [*Political party*] (PD) .... CPM-ML

Communist Party of Malaya - Revolutionary Faction [*Malaysia*] [*Political party*] (PD) .... CPM-RF

Communist Party of Malta [*Political party*] .... CPM

Communist Party of Moldavia [*Political party*] .... CPM

Communist Party of Nepal [*Political party*] (FEA) .... CPN

Communist Party of New Zealand [*Political party*] .... CPNZ

Communist Party of Northern Ireland (SAUO) .... CPNI

Communist Party of Norway [*Political party*] .... CPN

Communist Party of Pakistan (SAUO) .... CPP

Communist Party of Slovakia [*Political party*] .... CPS

Communist Party of Slovakia [*Former Czechoslovakia*] [*Political party*] (EY) .... CPSL

Communist Party of South Africa [*Political party*] (PD) .... CPSA

Communist Party of Sri Lanka [*Political party*] (FEA) .... CPSL

Communist Party of Syria and the Lebanon [*Political party*] (BJA) .... CPSL

Communist Party of Tadzhikistan [*Political party*] .... CPT

Communist Party of Thailand [*Political party*] (PD) .... CPT

Communist Party of the Philippines [*Political party*] .... CPP

Communist Party of the Philippines (SAUO) .... CPP

Communist Party of the Philippines/Marxist-Leninist [*Political party*] .... CPP/ML

Communist Party of the Soviet Union [*Political party*] (PPW) .... CPSU

Communist Party of the United States of America [*Political party*] (EA) ..... CPUSA

Communist Party of the United States of America (SAUO) .... CP-USA

Communist Party of the USA/Marxist Leninist [*Political party*] (EA) ..... CPUSA/ML

Communist Party of Turkey [*Political party*] (PD) .... CPT

Communist Party of Turkmenistan [*Political party*] .... CPT

Communist Party of Ukraine [*Political party*] .... CPU

Communist Party of Uzbekistan [*Political party*] .... CPUz

Communist Party of Venezuela [*Political party*] .... CPV

Communist Party of Yugoslavia .... CPY

Communist Rebel Combat Captives (CINC) .... CRCC

Communist Suppression Operations Command [*Thailand*] .... CSOC

Communist Sympathizer .... COMSYMP

Communist Terrorist .... CT

Communist University of London [*England*] (AIE) .... CUL

Communist Workers Group (SAUO) .... CWG

Communist Workers' Movement [*British*] (PPW) .... CWM

Communist Workers Party [*Political party*] .... CWP

Communist Youth Corps (SAUO) .... CYC

Communist Youth League .... CYL

Communist Youth League [*From the Russian*] .... KOMSOMOL

Communist Youth Union of Canada (Marxist-Leninist) .... CYUC (M-L)

Communistic (ABBR) .... CMUNSTC

Communistische Partij Holland [*Communist Party of Holland*] [*Netherlands*] (PPE) .... CPH

Communistische Partij van Nederland [*Communist Party of the Netherlands*] (PPE) .... CPN

Communitatis Europae Lex [*European Community Law*] [*Commission of the European Communities*] [*Information service or system*] (IID) .... CELEX

Communities in Economic Transition (SAUO) .... CET

Communities in Schools (SAUO) ... CIS
Communities of Common Concern (SAUO) ... Cas
Communities of Common Concern (SAUS) ... CCCs
Communities Organization of People ... COOP
Communities Organized for Public Service (DICI) ... COPS
Community (WDAA) ... C
Community ... CMNTY
Community (AL) ... Cmnty
Community (TBD) ... Cmty
Community ... CMTY
Community (ABBR) ... CMUNT
Community (AABC) ... COM
Community (SAUO) ... Com
Community (WGA) ... COMM
Community (ADWA) ... Comm
Community ... COMMUN
Community ... CTY
Community Access Library Line (SAUO) ... CALL
Community Access Producers and Viewers Association (EA) ... CAPVA
Community Access Television (WDAA) ... CATV
Community Action Agencies [*Community Services Administration*] ... CAA
Community Action Agency (SAUO) ... CAA
Community Action Association of Pennsylvania (SRA) ... CAAP
Community Action for Limited Learners (SAUO) ... CALL
Community Action for Post-War Jobs and Profits (SAUO) ... CAPWJP
Community Action Network (EA) ... CAN
Community Action on Latin America (EA) ... CALA
Community Action Party [*Thailand*] [*Political party*] (FEA) ... CAP
Community Action Program [*Community Services Administration*] ... CAP
Community Action Research Group (OICC) ... CARG
Community Action Team [*Department of Labor*] ... CAT
Community Action to Control High Blood Pressure [*HEW*] ... CATCH
Community Action to Reach the Elderly ... CARE
Community Activity Center (MCD) ... CAC
Community Adaptation Schedule [*Psychology*] ... CAS
Community Adjustment Profile System (DB) ... CAPS
Community Administration Council (SAUO) ... CAC
Community Advisory Committee (SAUO) ... CAC
Community Advisory Committee of the Murray-Darling Basin Ministerial Council [*Australia*] ... CACMDBMC
Community Aerodrome Radio Station (DA) ... CARS
Community Affairs (DLA) ... Com Affrs
Community Affairs and Regulatory Functions [*HUD*] (OICC) ... CARF
Community Affairs Officer ... CAO
Community Agriculture Centre (SAUO) ... CAC
Community AIDS Treatment Information Exchange [*Reseau Communautaire d'Infotraitement SIDA*] (AC) ... CATIE
Community Aids Worker (SAUO) ... CAW
Community Air Monitoring Program (SAUS) ... CAMP
Community Aircraft Activity Center (SAUO) ... CAC
Community Alert Patrol ... CAP
Community Alliance for Responsible Transport (SAUO) ... CART
Community Alternatives Program (SAUO) ... CAP
Community and Child Health (SAUO) ... CCH
Community and Child Health Service [*Australia*] ... CCHS
Community and District Nursing Association (SAUO) ... CDNA
Community and Economic Development Division (AAGC) ... CED
Community and Family Program Review Committee [*DoD*] ... CFRC
Community and Family Support Center [*Army*] ... CFSC
Community and Hospital Infection Control Association Canada (SAUO) ... CHICA
Community and Human Development Agency (SAUO) ... COHDA
Community and Junior College Libraries Section [*Association of College and Research Libraries*] ... CJCLS
Community & Legal Aid Services Program (AC) ... CLASP
Community and Mental Handicap Educational Research [*British*] (DBA) ... CMHERA
Community and Organization Research Institute [*Research center*] (RCD) ... CORI
Community and Public Sector Union [*Australia*] ... CPSU
Community and Race Relations Unit (SAUO) ... CRRU
Community and Special Broadcasting Agency [*British*] ... CSBA
Community and Technical College Libraries ... CTCL
Community and Youth Service Association (AIE) ... CYSA
Community & Youth Workers Union (WDAA) ... CYWU
Community Antenna Relay [*Service*] [*FCC*] ... CAR
Community Antenna Relay Service [*FCC*] [*Telecommunications*] ... CARS
Community Antenna Relay Station (SAUS) ... CARS
Community Antenna Relay System (SAUS) ... CARS
Community Antenna Television (SAUS) ... Cable TV
Community Antenna Television [*Later, CTV*] (IAA) ... CAT
Community Antenna Television [*Also, cable television*] (WDMC) ... CATV
Community Antenna Television Association (EA) ... CATA
Community Antenna Television System (IAA) ... CATVS
Community Anti-Drug Coalitions of America ... CADCA
Community Artists Residency Training (DICI) ... CART
Community Arts Council of Greater Victoria (AC) ... CACGV
Community Arts Councils, Inc. [*Later, American Council for the Arts*] (EA) ... CACI
Community Arts Network [*Australia*] ... CAN
Community Arts Teachers [*Australia*] ... CAT
Community Assistance Consultant (DEMM) ... CAC
Community Assistance Visit (DEMM) ... CAV
Community Association (SAUO) ... CA
Community Association for Riding for the Disabled (AC) ... CARD
Community Associations Institute (EA) ... CAI
Community Athenaeum Colleges of the Hellenic Advancement Council [*Australia*] ... CACHAC
Community Automated Counter-Terrorism Intelligence System (SAUS) ... CACTIS
Community Automatic Exchange [*Telephone*] (BUR) ... CAEX
Community Automatic Exchange [*Telephone*] ... CAX
Community Awareness and Emergency Response (SAUO) ... CAER
Community Awareness and Emergency Response Program [*Environmental Protection Agency*] (GFGA) ... CAER
Community Awareness and Emergency Response Program [*Environmental science*] (COE) ... CAERP
Community Bank & Trust (EFIS) ... CB&T
Community Bank League of New England (SRA) ... CBLNE
Community Bank Shares of Indiana, Inc. [*NASDAQ symbol*] (SAG) ... CBIN
Community Bank Shares of Indiana, Inc. [*Associated Press*] (SAG) ... CmBkIN
Community Bank Shares(Ind) [*NASDAQ symbol*] (TTSB) ... CBIN
Community Bank System [*NYSE symbol*] (SG) ... CBU
Community Bank System, Inc. [*NASDAQ symbol*] (NQ) ... CBSI
Community Bank System, Inc. [*Associated Press*] (SAG) ... CmtyBS
Community Bank Systems [*NASDAQ symbol*] (TTSB) ... CBSI
Community Bankers Association of Georgia (SRA) ... CBA
Community Bankers Association of Georgia (TBD) ... CBAG
Community Bankers Association of Illinois (TBD) ... CBAI
Community Bankers Association of Indiana (SRA) ... CBAI
Community Bankers Association of Kansas (TBD) ... CBAK
Community Bankers Association of Kansas (SRA) ... CBA-KS
Community Bankers Association of New Hampshire (TBD) ... CBNH
Community Bankers Association of New Jersey (TBD) ... CBNJ
Community Bankers Association of New York State (SRA) ... CBANYS
Community Bankers Association of Ohio (SRA) ... CBAO
Community Bankers Association of Oklahoma (SRA) ... CBAO
Community Bankers of Florida (SRA) ... CBF
Community Bankers of Indiana (TBD) ... CBI
Community Bankers of Kentucky (SRA) ... CBK
Community Bankers of Kentucky, Inc. (TBD) ... CBK
Community Bankers of Louisiana (TBD) ... CBL
Community Bankers of Oklahoma (TBD) ... CBOK
Community Bankers of Wisconsin (SRA) ... CBW
Community Banking Advisory Network (NTPA) ... CBAN
Community Banking Facilities (SAUO) ... CBF
Community Banks, Inc. [*NASDAQ symbol*] (NQ) ... CBKI
Community Banks, Inc. [*Associated Press*] (SAG) ... CmBkPa
Community Banks, Inc. [*AMEX symbol*] (SAG) ... CTY
Community Banks (PA) [*AMEX symbol*] (TTSB) ... CTY
Community Bankshares, Inc. [*NASDAQ symbol*] (NQ) ... CBNH
Community Bankshares, Inc. [*Associated Press*] (SAG) ... CmtyBn
Community Bankshares, Inc. [*Associated Press*] (SAG) ... CmtyBSC
Community Bankshares (NH) [*NASDAQ symbol*] (TTSB) ... CBNH
Community Bankshares S.C. [*AMEX symbol*] (SG) ... SCB
Community Base Station (GEOI) ... CBS
Community Based Corrections (OICC) ... CBC
Community Based Environmental Project (EPAT) ... CBEP
Community Based Public Health (SAUO) ... CBPH
Community Based Public Health Initiative (SAUO) ... CBPHI
Community Based Rehabilitation (SAUS) ... CBR
Community Breast Health Project (ADWA) ... CBHP
Community Broadcasters Association [*Defunct*] (EA) ... CBA
Community Broadcasters of America [*Defunct*] (EA) ... CBA
Community Bulletin Board System ... CBBS
Community Bureau of References (SAUO) ... CBR
Community Business Lothian [*British*] ... CBL
Community Business Scotland News [*A publication*] ... CB NEWS
Community Cancer Care Evaluation [*Department of Health and Human Services*] (GFGA) ... CCCE
Community Capital [*AMEX symbol*] (SG) ... CYL
Community Care Network [*Medicine*] ... CCN
Community Care of Amer [*NASDAQ symbol*] (TTSB) ... CCAL
Community Care of America [*NASDAQ symbol*] (SAG) ... CCAI
Community Care of America [*Associated Press*] (SAG) ... ComCare
Community Care of America [*Associated Press*] (SAG) ... ComCre
Community Care Services, Inc. [*NASDAQ symbol*] (SAG) ... CCSE
Community Care Services, Inc. [*Associated Press*] (SAG) ... CmtyCr
Community Care Unit (MAE) ... CCU
Community Careers Resource Center (EA) ... CCRC
Community Case Management Services ... CCMS
Community Charge Registration Officer [*British*] ... CCRO
Community Chemistry Transport Model (SAUS) ... CCTM
Community Child Care Cooperative [*Australia*] ... CCCC
Community Climate Model [*Meteorology*] ... CCM
Community Clinical Oncology Program [*Department of Health and Human Services*] (GFGA) ... CCOP
Community Code [*Database terminology*] (NITA) ... CM
Community Collaboration Office [*Veterans Administration*] (GFGA) ... CCO
Community College ... CC
Community College Activities Survey (EDAC) ... CCAS
Community College Assessment Program [*Academic achievement and aptitude test*] ... CCAP
Community College Association for Instruction and Technology (EA) ... CCAIT
Community College Business Officers (NTPA) ... CCBO
Community College General Education Association (EDAC) ... CCGEA
Community College Goals Inventory [*Test*] ... CCGI
Community College Humanities Association (EA) ... CCHA
Community College Journalism Association (EA) ... CCJA
Community College League of California (PSS) ... CCLA
Community College League of California (SRA) ... CCLC

Community College of Allegheny County, Boyce Campus, Monroeville, PA [*Ina ctive*] [*OCLC symbol*] (OCLC) ... AIB
Community College of Allegheny County, Boyce Campus, Monroeville, PA [*Library symbol*] [*Library of Congress*] (LCLS) ... PMvAC
Community College of Allegheny County, Center North, Pittsburgh, PA [*OCLC symbol*] (OCLC) ... AIN
Community College of Allegheny County, Pittsburgh, PA [*OCLC symbol*] (OCLC) ... AIC
Community College of Allegheny County, Pittsburgh, PA [*Library symbol*] [*Library of Congress*] (LCLS) ... PPiAC
Community College of Allegheny County, South Campus, West Mifflin, PA [*OCLC symbol*] (OCLC) ... AIS
Community College of Allegheny County, South Campus, West Mifflin, PA [*Library symbol*] [*Library of Congress*] (LCLS) ... PWesAC
Community College of Baltimore, Baltimore, MD [*Library symbol*] [*Library of Congress*] (LCLS) ... MdBBJC
Community College of Denver [*Colorado*] ... CCD
Community College of Denver, Auraria Campus, Denver, CO [*Library symbol*] [*Library of Congress*] (LCLS) ... CoDCC-A
Community College of Denver, Aurora Educational Learning Center, North Campus, Denver, CO [*Library symbol*] [*Library of Congress*] (LCLS) ... CoDCC-E
Community College of Denver, Denver, CO [*Library symbol*] [*Library of Congress*] (LCLS) ... CoDCC
Community College of Denver, North AEC Project, Westminster, CO [*OCLC symbol*] (OCLC) ... DVE
Community College of Denver, North Campus, Denver, CO [*Library symbol*] [*Library of Congress*] (LCLS) ... CoDCC-N
Community College of Denver, North Campus, Westminster, CO [*OCLC symbol*] (OCLC) ... DVC
Community College of Denver, North Campus, Westminster, CO [*OCLC symbol*] (OCLC) ... DVN
Community College of Denver, Red Rocks Campus, Golden, CO [*OCLC symbol*] (OCLC) ... DVR
Community College of Denver, Red Rocks Campus, Lakewood, CO [*Library symbol*] [*Library of Congress*] (LCLS) ... CoDCC-R
Community College of Philadelphia, Philadelphia, PA [*OCLC symbol*] (OCLC) ... PDC
Community College of Philadelphia, Philadelphia, PA [*Library symbol*] [*Library of Congress*] (LCLS) ... PPCoC
Community College of Rhode Island [*Formerly, RIJC*] ... CCRI
Community College of the Air Force (AFM) ... CCAF
Community College of the Finger Lakes, Canandaigua (SAUS) ... NCaaC
Community College of the Finger Lakes, Canandaigua, NY [*Library symbol*] [*Library of Congress*] (LCLS) ... NCanC
Community College of the Finger Lakes, Canandaigua, NY [*OCLC symbol*] (OCLC) ... ZFM
Community College Social Science Association (EA) ... CCSSA
Community College Unit [*Office of Education*] ... CCU
Community Colleges [*Educational Resources Information Center (ERIC) Clearinghouse*] [*University of California at Los Angeles (UCLA)*] (PAZ) ... JC
Community Colleges Data Base [*Information service or system*] (IID) ... COCO
Community Colleges for International Development (EA) ... CCID
Community Communications [*Independent Local Radio*] [*British*] ... CC
Community Concern for Senior Citizens [*Defunct*] (EA) ... CCSC
Community Conference Crew [*World online service referees*] ... CCC
Community Coordinated Child Care Program (SAUO) ... 4C
Community Coordinated Child Care Program (SAUO) ... 4C Programm
Community Coordinated Child Care Program (SAUO) ... CCCC
Community Council (SAUO) ... CC
Community Council Against Violence [*Australia*] ... CCAV
Community Council of Lancashire (SAUO) ... CCL
Community Counter Terrorism Board (COE) ... CCB
Community Creativity, Inc. [*Defunct*] (EA) ... CCI
Community Dental Health (SAUS) ... CDH
Community Design Center Directors Association (EA) ... CDCDA
Community Design Group [*North Carolina State University*] [*Research center*] (RCD) ... CDG
Community Development ... CD
Community Development - Data Information Analysis Laboratory (OICC) ... CD-DIAL
Community Development Action Plan (SAUO) ... CDAP
Community Development Administration [*HUD*] ... CDA
Community Development Agency (SAUO) ... CDA
Community Development Bank ... CDB
Community Development Block Grant (SAUO) ... CBDG
Community Development Block Grant [*HUD*] ... CDBG
Community Development Corp. [*Later, NCDC*] ... CDC
Community Development Employment Projects (SAUO) ... CDEP
Community Development Foundation [*SCF*] [*Absorbed by*] (EA) ... CDF
Community Development Fund (SAUO) ... CDF
Community Development Infrastructure Program [*Australia*] ... CDIP
Community Development Society (EA) ... CDS
Community Development Support [*Australia*] ... CDS
Community Development Trust (AIE) ... CDT
Community Development Venture Capital Association (NTPA) ... CDVCA
Community Development Work Study Program [*Department of Housing and Urban Development*] (GFGA) ... CDWSP
Community Dial Office [*Small switching system*] [*Telecommunications*] ... CDO
Community Dispute Services (EA) ... CDS
Community Dreamsharing Network (EA) ... CDN
Community Drug and Alcohol Assistance Center (SAUO) ... CDAAC
Community Drying-Out Centre [*British*] (DI) ... CDOC
Community Economic Development Act of 1981 ... CEDA
Community Economic Stabilization Corporation [*Member of FIRR*] (CROSS) ... CESCO
Community Economics, Inc. (EA) ... CEI
Community Education ... CE
Community Education Officer (ADA) ... CEO
Community Education Program (SAUO) ... CEP
Community Education Training Centre (SAUO) ... CETC
Community Educational Radio Fixed Service (MSA) ... CERFS
Community Educational Resources ... CER
Community Educational Services Foundation (IID) ... CESF
Community Electoral Assistant [*Australia*] ... CEA
Community Electronic Teller System ... COMETS
Community Elementary School (SAUO) ... CES
Community Emergency Care Association [*Defunct*] (EA) ... CECA
Community Emergency Coordinator [*Environmental science*] (COE) ... CEC
Community Emergency Drought Relief Act of 1977 ... CEDRA
Community Emergency Exposure Level (SARE) ... CEEL
Community Employment Development [*Department of Labor*] ... CED
Community Energy Action Network (SAUS) ... CEAN
Community Energy Program [*Office of Volunteer Liaison*] [*ACTION*] ... CEP
Community Engineering Corporation (SAUO) ... CECO
Community Enhancement & Economic Development Society (AC) ... CEEDS
Community Enterprise Program [*British*] ... CEP
Community Enterprise Trust (AIE) ... CET
Community Environmental Council (EA) ... CEC
Community Environmental Response Facilitation Act (BCP) ... CERFA
Community Environmental Service Teams (SAUO) ... CEST
Community Epidemiology Work Group (SAUO) ... CEWG
Community Equivalent Noise Level (PDAA) ... CENL
Community Express Airlines Ltd. [*BRT*] [*FAA designator*] (FAAC) ... UNI
Community Facilities Administration [*of HHFA*] [*Terminated*] ... CFA
Community, Family, and Soldier [*Support Command*] [*Korea*] (DOMA) ... CFS
Community, Family, and Soldier Support Command - Korea [*Army*] ... CFSSC-K
Community Federal Bancorp [*NASDAQ symbol*] (TTSB) ... CFTR
Community Federal Bancorp, Inc. [*NASDAQ symbol*] (SAG) ... CFTP
Community Federal Bancorp, Inc. [*Associated Press*] (SAG) ... ComFed
Community Fellows Program (EA) ... CFP
Community Financial Corp. [*NASDAQ symbol*] (SAG) ... CFFC
Community Financial Corp. [*Associated Press*] (SAG) ... ComtyFin
Community Financial Corp. (Illinois) [*NASDAQ symbol*] (SAG) ... CFIC
Community Financial Corp. (Illinois) [*Associated Press*] (SAG) ... CmFnIl
Community Financial Group [*NASDAQ symbol*] (SAG) ... CFGI
Community Financial Group [*Associated Press*] (SAG) ... CmtyF
Community Financial Group [*Associated Press*] (SAG) ... CmtyFncl
Community Financial Holding Corp. [*NASDAQ symbol*] (SAG) ... CMFH
Community Financial Holding Corp. [*Associated Press*] (SAG) ... CmtyFin
Community Financial (IL) [*NQS*] (TTSB) ... CFIC
Community Finl Group [*NASDAQ symbol*] (TTSB) ... CFGI
Community Finl Group Wrrt [*NASDAQ symbol*] (TTSB) ... CFGIW
Community Finl Hldg [*NASDAQ symbol*] (TTSB) ... CMFH
Community Finl VA [*NASDAQ symbol*] (TTSB) ... CFFC
Community First 7% Cv Dep Pfd [*NASDAQ symbol*] (TTSB) ... CFBXZ
Community First Bankshares [*NASDAQ symbol*] (SAG) ... CFBX
Community First Bankshares [*Associated Press*] (SAG) ... ComFB
Community First Bankshares [*Associated Press*] (SAG) ... ComFtBk
Community Fluorosis Index ... CFI
Community Food and Nutrition Programs [*Community Services Administration*] ... CFNP
Community for Creative Non-Violence (EA) ... CCNV
Community for Religious Research and Education (EA) ... CRRE
Community for Social Justice in the Middle East and North Africa (EA) ... CSJMENA
Community Forecast Model (SAUS) ... CFM
Community Foundation Silicon Valley ... CFSV
Community Framework Programme in Support of Culture (SAUO) ... CULTURE 2000
Community Free Library, Holley, NY [*Library symbol*] [*Library of Congress*] (LCLS) ... NHoll
Community General Hospital Library, Thomasville, NC [*Library symbol*] [*Library of Congress*] (LCLS) ... NcThCH
Community Guidance Service (EA) ... CGS
Community Health Accreditation and Standards Program (SAUO) ... CHASP
Community Health Accreditation Program (ADWA) ... CHAP
Community Health Action Planning Service ... CHAPS
Community Health Air Monitoring Program [*Environmental Protection Agency*] ... CHAMP
Community Health and Environmental Surveillance Studies (SAUS) ... CHESS
Community Health and Environmental Surveillance System [*Environmental Protection Agency project*] ... CHESS
Community Health Association ... CHA
Community Health Awareness Group ... C-HAG
Community Health Care Association of New York State (SRA) ... CHCANYS
Community Health Center ... CHC
Community Health Computing ... CHC
Community Health Council [*British*] ... CHC
Community Health Department, Lakeshore General Hospital [*Departement de SanteCommunautaire, Hopital General du Lakeshore*], **Pointe-Claire, Quebec** [*Library symbol*] [*National Library of Canada*] (NLC) ... QMLGC
Community Health Department, Montreal General Hospital [*Departement de Sante Communautaire, Hopital General de Montreal*], **Quebec** [*Library symbol*] [*National Library of Canada*] (NLC) ... QMGHC
Community Health Education Project ... CHEP
Community Health Information Classification and Coding (SAUO) ... CHIC
Community Health Information Network [*Library network*] ... CHIN
Community Health Information Partnerships (ADWA) ... CHIP
Community Health Information Technology Alliance (ADWA) ... CHITA
Community Health Management Information Systems (ADWA) ... CHMIS

Community Health Network (DHSM) ... CHN
Community Health Nurse (NUJO) ... CHN
Community Health Nurses Association of Canada (AC) ... CHNAC
Community Health Onsite Information Centers [*New York Public Library*] ... CHOICES
Community Health Program (MCD) ... CHP
Community Health Representative Program [*Department of Health and Human Services*] (GFGA) ... CHR
Community Health Research & Training Unit (SAUO) ... CHRTU
Community Health Service [*HEW*] ... CHS
Community Health Studies [*A publication*] ... Community Hlth Stud
Community Health Systems, Inc. [*Associated Press*] (SAG) ... ComHlSy
Community Health Systems, Inc. [*NYSE symbol*] (SAG) ... CYH
Community Health Worker (SAUO) ... CHW
Community Help and Improvement Program ... CHIP
Community Helps in Life Development (SAUO) ... CHILD
Community High School, Detroit Lakes, MN [*Library symbol*] [*Library of Congress*] (LCLS) ... MnDlH
Community Historical Society, Maxwell, IA [*Library symbol*] [*Library of Congress*] (LCLS) ... IaMaxHi
Community HIV and AIDS Prevention Strategy (SAUO) ... CHAPS
Community Hlth Sys [*NYSE symbol*] (TTSB) ... CYH
Community Homefinding, Relocation, and Referral Services [*US Army Corps of Engineers*] ... CHRRS
Community Hospital at Glen Cove, Glen Cove, NY [*Library symbol*] [*Library of Congress*] (LCLS) ... NGlcC
Community Hospital of Ottawa, Ottawa, IL [*Library symbol*] [*Library of Congress*] (LCLS) ... IOtCH
Community Hospital of Springfield, Springfield, OH [*Library symbol*] [*Library of Congress*] (LCLS) ... OSH
Community Housing and Infrastructure Program [*Australia*] ... CHIP
Community Housing Development Organization [*Department of Housing and Urban Development*] ... CHDO
Community Housing Improvement and Revitalization Program (SAUS) ... CHIRP
Community Human and Industrial Development (SAUS) ... CHID
Community Human and Industrial Development, Inc. [*Office of Economic Opportunity*] [*Terminated*] ... CHID
Community Hypertension Evaluation Clinic [*New Jersey*] ... CHEC
Community Improvement Program (EA) ... CIP
Community Improvement Scale [*Psychology*] ... CIS
Community Independent Bank [*AMEX symbol*] (SG) ... INB
Community Independent Living Service Delivery Systems (EDAC) ... CILSDS
Community, Industry, Accounting and Legal Consultants [*Database*] [*Australia*] ... CONSULT
Community Industry Scheme [*Department of Employment*] [*British*] ... CIS
Community Information ... CI
Community Information and Referral Service [*Library science*] ... CI & R
Community Information and Referral Service [*United Way/Crusade of Mercy*] [*Information service or system*] (IID) ... CIRS
Community Information and Services Center (SAUS) ... CISC
Community Information Network [*Cable TV programming service*] ... CIN
Community Information Section [*Public Library Association*] ... CIS
Community Information Services ... CIS
Community Information Sharing Service (SAUS) ... CISS
Community Information System (SAUS) ... CIS
Community information Utility (BUR) ... CIU
Community Infrastructure Training Program ... CITP
Community Integrated Service Systems (ADWA) ... CISS
Community Integrated Training and Education Program ... CITEP
Community Integrated Training Type Functions ... CITF
Community Intervention Trial for Smoking Cessation [*Department of Health and Human Services*] (GFGA) ... COMMIT
Community Investment Officer [*Federal Home Loan Bank Board*] ... CIO
Community Investors Bancorp, Inc. [*NASDAQ symbol*] (SAG) ... CIBI
Community Investors Bancorp, Inc. [*Associated Press*] (SAG) ... CmyIBc
Community Junior College ... CJC
Community Junior High School, Detroit Lakes, MN [*Library symbol*] [*Library of Congress*] (LCLS) ... MnDlJ
Community Land Bank (SAUO) ... CLB
Community Land Trust [*Agricultural economics*] ... CLT
Community Land Use Game [*Urban-planning game*] ... CLUG
Community Landcare Support Program (SAUO) ... CLSP
Community Landcare Technician (SAUO) ... CLT
Community Language in the Secondary Curriculum [*Project*] (AIE) ... CLSC
Community Language Learning (SAUS) ... CLL
Community Law Offices ... CLO
Community Leadership Workshop ... CLEW
Community Learning through America's Schools [*National Education Association*] ... CLASS
Community Legal Aid ... CLA
Community Legal Education Association (Manitoba) Inc. [*Association d'Education Juridique Communautaire (Manitoba) Inc.*] (AC) ... CLEA
Community Legal Education Ontario (AC) ... CLEO
Community Liaison Staff [*Environmental Protection Agency*] (GFGA) ... CLS
Community Library Association, Inc., Ketchem, ID [*Library symbol*] [*Library of Congress*] (LCLS) ... IdK
Community Library Information Center (SAUS) ... CLIC
Community Library, Roundup, MT [*Library symbol*] [*Library of Congress*] (LCLS) ... MtRd
Community Life Program (SAUO) ... CLP
Community Living Arrangement [*For the handicapped*] ... CLA
Community Living Fund ... CLF
Community Living Oakville (AC) ... CLO
Community Living Stormont County [*Integration Communautaire Comte de Stormont*] (AC) ... CLSC
Community Management Staff [*Environmental science*] (COE) ... CMS
Community Management Training Scheme [*Australia*] ... CMT
Community Management Training Service [*Australia*] ... CMTS
Community Market Catalog ... CM
Community Med Trans [*NASDAQ symbol*] (TTSB) ... CMTI
Community Med Trans Wrrt [*NASDAQ symbol*] (TTSB) ... CMTIW
Community Medical Transport, Inc. [*NASDAQ symbol*] (SAG) ... CMTI
Community Medical Transport, Inc. [*Associated Press*] (SAG) ... CmtyMd T
Community Medical Transport, Inc. [*Associated Press*] (SAG) ... CtyMT
Community Memorial Hospital, Health Science Library, Menomonee Falls, WI [*Library symbol*] [*Library of Congress*] (LCLS) ... WMenofH
Community Memorial Museum of Sutter County, Yuba City, CA [*Library symbol*] [*Library of Congress*] (LCLS) ... CYcM
Community Mental Health Activities ... CMHA
Community Mental Health Center [*or Clinic*] ... CMHC
Community Mental Health Center Program (SAUO) ... CMHCP
Community Mental Health Centers Act [*1975*] ... CMHCA
Community Mental Health Nurse (DAVI) ... CMHN
Community Mental Health Program ... CMHP
Community Modelling Effort [*Oceanography*] ... CME
Community Morale Support Fund (SAUO) ... CMSF
Community Noise Equivalent Level ... CNEL
Community Noise Rating ... CNR
Community Nurse Practitioner ... CNP
Community Nursing Center (DMAA) ... CNC
Community Nursing Home ... CNH
Community Nursing Organization (DMAA) ... CNO
Community Nutrition Institute (EA) ... CNI
Community of All Hallows [*Anglican religious community*] ... CAH
Community of Interest [*Telecommunications*] (TEL) ... CI
Community of Interest [*DoD*] ... COI
Community of Jesus of Nazareth [*Anglican religious community*] ... CJN
Community of Mediterranean Universities (SAUO) ... CMU
Community of Mediterranean University (SAUO) ... CUM
Community of Portuguese Language Countries (SAUO) ... CPLP
Community of Reparation to Jesus in the Blessed Sacrament [*Anglican religious community*] ... CRJBS
Community of Science, Inc. ... COS
Community of St. Clare [*Anglican religious community*] ... CSCl
Community of St. Denys [*Anglican religious community*] ... CSD
Community of St. Francis [*Anglican religious community*] ... CSF
Community of St. John the Baptist [*Anglican religious community*] ... CSJB
Community of St. John the Evangelist [*Anglican religious community*] ... CSJE
Community of St. Katharine of Egypt [*Anglican religious community*] ... CSK
Community of St. Laurence [*Anglican religious community*] ... CSL
Community of St. Mary the Virgin [*Anglican religious community*] ... CSMV
Community of St. Michael and All Angels [*Anglican religious community*] ... CSM and AA
Community of St. Peter [*Anglican religious community*] ... CSP
Community of St. Wilfrid [*Anglican religious community*] ... CSW
Community of the Blessed Virgin Mary [*Anglican religious community*] ... CBVM
Community of the Companions of Jesus the Good Shepherd [*Anglican religious community*] ... CJGS
Community of the Epiphany [*Anglican religious community*] ... CE
Community of the Glorious Ascension [*Anglican religious community*] ... CGA
Community of the Glorious Ascension (SAUO) ... CGA
Community of the Holy Cross [*Anglican religious community*] ... CHC
Community of the Holy Family [*Anglican religious community*] ... CHF
Community of the Holy Name of Jesus [*Anglican religious community*] ... CHN
Community of the Holy Rood [*Anglican religious community*] ... CHR
Community of the Holy Spirit (TOCD) ... CHS
Community of the Newspaper Publishing Associations of the European Economic Communities [*Belgium*] (EAIO) ... CNPA-EEC
Community of the Nursing Sisters of St. John the Divine [*Anglican religious community*] ... NSSJD
Community of the Presentation [*Anglican religious community*] ... CP
Community of the Resurrection [*Anglican religious community*] ... CR
Community of the Servants of the Cross [*Anglican religious community*] ... CSC
Community of the Sisters of the Church [*Anglican religious community*] ... CSC
Community of the Sisters of the Love of God [*Anglican religious community*] ... SLG
Community of the Whole Person (EA) ... CWP
Community of the Will of God [*Anglican religious community*] ... CWG
Community Office On-Line System (SAUS) ... COOLS
Community on Alcohol and Road Safety (SAUO) ... CARS
Community On-Line Intelligence Network System [*Computer network*] [*National Science Administration and Central Intelligence Agency*] ... COINS
Community Organization for Drug Abuse Control (SAUS) ... CODAG
Community Organization for Full Employment Economy ... COFFEE
Community Oriented Intelligence Network System (CCCA) ... COINS
Community Oriented Policing Services ... COPS
Community Outreach and Online Learning [*Awards*] ... COOL
Community Outreach Health Information System (SAUO) ... COHIS
Community Outreach Information Network ... COIN
Community Outreach Program (DIPS) ... COP
Community Partnership Against Crime Program (SAUO) ... COMPAC
Community Partnerships for the Advancement of Science in the Schools (SAUS) ... COMPASS
Community Patent Conference (SAUO) ... CPC
Community Patent Convention [*European Common Market*] ... CPC
Community Patrol Officer Program [*Police work*] ... CPOP
Community Perspectives on Land and Agrarian Reform [*South Africa*] (GEOI) ... CPLAR
Community Pharmacy Action Group (WDAA) ... CPAG
Community Physician (SAUS) ... CP

Community Placement .... CP
Community Planning and Design Center [*Information service or system*] (IID) .... CPDC
Community Planning and Development [*HUD*] (OICC) .... CPD
Community Planning and Management [*HUD*] .... CPM
Community Planning Association of Canada .... CPAC
Community Planning Association of Canada, Ottawa, ON, Canada [*Library symbol*] [*Library of Congress*] (LCLS) .... CaOOCP
Community Planning Association of Canada [*Association Canadienne d'Urbanisme*] **Ottawa, Ontario** [*Library symbol*] [*National Library of Canada*] (NLC) .... OOCP
Community Post Office .... CPO
Community Practitioners' Association (WDAA) .... CPA
Community Pre-School Employers' Association of Queensland [*Australia*] .... CPSEAQ
Community Pride Association (EA) .... CPA
Community Products, Inc. .... CPI
Community Program (WDAA) .... CP
Community Program Administrator (DEMM) .... CPA
Community Program for Clinical Research on AIDS [*FDA*] .... CPCRA
Community Program for Education and Training in Technology [*EC*] (ECED) .... COMETT
Community Programme in Education and Training for Technology [*British*] .... COMETT
Community Programs Branch [*Australian Capital Territory*] .... CPB
Community Progress Incorporated (SAUO) .... CPI
Community Projects Foundation [*British*] .... CPF
Community Psych Ctrs [*NYSE symbol*] (TTSB) .... CMY
Community Psychiatric Centers [*NYSE symbol*] (SPSG) .... CMY
Community Psychiatric Centers (EFIS) .... CPC
Community Psychiatric Centers [*Associated Press*] (SAG) .... CPsyc
Community Psychiatric Nurse (WDAA) .... CPN
Community Psychiatric Nursing Association [*British*] .... CPNA
Community Radio Association [*British*] .... CRA
Community Radio Watch .... CRW
Community Rating by Class .... CRC
Community Rating System [*National Flood Insurance Program*] .... CRS
Community Recreation and Skill Development Activities (AABC) .... CRSDA
Community Recreation Council [*Victoria*] [*Australia*] .... CRC
Community Redeployment Agency (SAUO) .... CRA
Community Redevelopment Agency .... CRA
Community Reference Bureau Databank [*European Atomic Energy Community*] (NITA) .... CRB
Community Refugee Settlement Scheme [*Australia*] .... CRSS
Community Regeneration [*Defunct*] (EA) .... CR
Community Reinvestment Act [*1977*] [*Requires banks to list credit facilities available to the communities they serve*] .... CRA
Community Relations [*Military*] (NVT) .... COMREL
Community Relations (AABC) .... CR
Community Relations Advisory Council [*Military*] .... CRAC
Community Relations Assessment (SAUO) .... CRA
Community Relations Commission [*British*] .... CRC
Community Relations Coordinator (EEVL) .... CRC
Community Relations Council (SAUO) .... CRC
Community Relations Director .... CRD
Community Relations Division [*Environmental Protection Agency*] (GFGA) .... CRD
Community Relations Manager (SAUO) .... CRM
Community Relations Officer (WDAA) .... CRO
Community Relations Plan .... CRP
Community Relations Service [*Department of Justice*] [*Terminated*] .... CRS
Community Relations Staff (SAUO) .... CRS
Community Release Program [*Australia*] .... CRP
Community Renewal Program .... CRP
Community Research Action Center (SAUS) .... CRAC
Community Research and Development Information Service (SAUO) .... CORDIS
Community Research Associates (EA) .... CRA
Community Research Bureau .... CRB
Community Research Center [*University of Illinois*] [*Research center*] (RCD) .... CRC
Community Research Group (SAUO) .... CRG
Community Research Initiative of Toronto [*Initiative de Recherche Communautaire de Toronto*] (AC) .... CRIT
Community Research Initiatives [*Community-based AIDS treatment organizations*] .... CRI's
Community Research Project .... CRP
Community Research Services [*Illinois State University*] [*Normal*] [*Information service or system*] (IID) .... CRS
Community Residences for the Developmentally Disabled (PA) .... CRDD
Community Residential Care [*Veterans Administration*] (GFGA) .... CRC
Community Residential Facility [*For the handicapped*] .... CRF
Community Residential Unit [*Victoria*] [*Australia*] .... CRU
Community Resource and Research Center [*University of Nebraska - Lincoln*] [*Research center*] (RCD) .... CRRC
Community Resource and Self Help (SAUS) .... CRASH
Community Resource and Self-Help, Inc. (SAUO) .... CRASH
Community Resources Against Street Hoodlums [*An association*] .... CRASH
Community Resources Information Service, Inc. [*Information service or system*] (IID) .... CRIS
Community Resources Workshop Association [*Later, NAIEC*] (EA) .... CRWA
Community Reuse Organization (BCP) .... CRO
Community Right to Know Code (SAUS) .... CRTK
Community Right-to-Know [*Environmental science*] (COE) .... CRTK
Community Rule, Rule of the Congregation [*or Manual of Discipline, Serekh ha-Yahad*] **from Qumran. Cave One** (BJA) 1QS
Community Savings FA [*NASDAQ symbol*] (SAG) .... CMSV
Community Savings FA [*Associated Press*] (SAG) .... CommSv
Community School District (SAUO) .... CSD
Community Security (NVT) .... COMSEC
Community Service [*An association*] (EA) .... CS
Community Service Activities [*AFL-CIO*] .... CSA
Community Service Announcement .... CSA
Community Service Council of Central Indiana [*United Way of Central Indiana*] [*Also, an information service or system*] (IID) .... CSC
Community Service Credit Union Council [*Defunct*] (EA) .... CSCUC
Community Service Employment for Older Americans [*Department of Labor*] .... CSEOA
Community Service Grant [*Corporation for Public Broadcasting*] .... CSG
Community Service Learning .... CSL
Community Service Obligation .... CSO
Community Service Order (WDAA) .... CSO
Community Service Organization (SAUO) .... CSO
Community Service Society (SAUO) .... CSS
Community Service Volunteers [*British*] .... CSV
Community Services Administration [*Superseded Office of Economic Opportunity*] [*HEW*] .... CSA
Community Services Block Grant .... CSBG
Community Services for Autistic Adults and Children (SAUO) .... CSAAC
Community Services Grants Program [*Australia*] .... CSGP
Community Services Program [*Canada*] .... CSP
Community Shelter Plan [*Civil Defense*] .... CSP
Community Shelter Planning Officer, State [*Civil Defense*] .... CSPOS
Community Skills Unit (AIE) .... CSU
Community Sports Leader Award (WDAA) .... CSLA
Community Standards Association [*British*] (DI) .... CSA
Community Station Resource Group (SAUO) .... CSRG
Community Support Framework [*EC*] (ECED) .... CSF
Community Support Program [*National Institute of Mental Health*] .... CSP
Community Supported Agriculture of North America .... CSANA
Community Surface Drainage Scheme (SAUO) .... CSDS
Community Sustainability Resource Institute (SAUO) .... CSRI
Community Systems Foundation (EA) .... CSF
Community Systems Foundation (Australia) .... CSF(A)
Community Task Force [*British*] .... CTF
Community Telecommunications Development Foundation [*Washington, DC*] (TSSD) .... CTDF
Community Telephone Plan (ADA) .... CTP
Community Television (NITA) .... CTV
Community Television Sydney [*Australia*] .... CTV
Community Trade Mark Office [*EC*] (ECED) .... CTMO
Community Training and Development [*An association*] (EA) .... CTD
Community Transit [*System*] [*Shipping*] [*EEC*] (DS) .... CT
Community Transportation Association of America [*ENO*] (TAG) .... CTAA
Community Transportation Coordinator [*MOCD*] (TAG) .... CTC
Community Trust Bancorp, Inc. [*Associated Press*] (SAG) .... CmtyTrBc
Community Trust Bancorp, Inc. [*NASDAQ symbol*] (SAG) .... CTBI
Community United Group Services [*British*] .... CUGS
Community Voice Mail [*Program providing the homeless with voice mail*] [*Telecommunications*] (ECON) .... CVM
Community Volunteer Services Commission of B'nai B'rith International (EAIO) .... CVS
Community Volunteer Services Commission of B'nai B'rith International (EA) .... CVSC
Community War Services (SAUO) .... CWRU
Community War Services [*of FSA*] [*World War II*] .... CWS
Community Water System [*Environmental Protection Agency*] .... CWS
Community Welfare Advisory Council [*New South Wales*] [*Australia*] .... CWAC
Community Welfare Planning Association, Social Research Library, Houston (SAUS) .... TxHCS
Community Welfare Planning Association, Social Research Library, Houston, TX [*Library symbol*] [*Library of Congress*] (LCLS) .... TxHCS
Community Wholistic Health Center (ADWA) .... CWHC
Community Wide Education and Information Services (SAUS) .... CWEIS
Community wide Information of the European Environment (SAUO) .... CORINE
Community Wide Information Service (SAUO) .... CWIS
Community Wide Information System (SAUO) .... CWIS
Community Work and Training Program [*Department of Labor*] .... CWTP
Community Youth Activities (SAUO) .... CYA
Community-Acquired Infection [*Medicine*] (MELL) .... CAI
Community-Acquired Meningitis [*Medicine*] (MELL) .... CAM
Community-Acquired Pneumonia .... CAP
Community/Airport Economic Development Model [*FAA*] .... CAEDM
Community-Based Clinical Trial [*Medicine*] .... CBCT
Community-Based Environmental Protection (GEOI) .... CBEP
Community-Based Order (ADA) .... CBO
Community-Based Organization [*Organization which provides employment and training services*] [*CETA*] .... CBO
Community-Based Residential Facility .... CBRF
Community-Based Teaching (SAUO) .... CBT
Community-Coordinated Child Care (SAUS) .... Four Cs
Community/Corridor Traffic Safety Program .... C/CTSP
Community-General Hospital, Staff Library, Syracuse, NY [*OCLC symbol*] (OCLC) .... ZUG
Community-General Hospital, Syracuse, NY [*Library symbol*] [*Library of Congress*] (LCLS) .... NSyGH
Community-Oriented Police .... COP
Community-Oriented Police Enforcement .... COPE
Community-Oriented Police Satellite (SAUS) .... COPS
Community-Oriented Police Station (SAUS) .... COPS
Community-Oriented Primary Care [*Medicine*] .... COPC

Community-Oriented Programs Environment Scale [*Psychosocial assessment test*] ... COPES
Community-Supported Agriculture ... CSA
Community-wide Coordination of Information on the Environment (SAUS) ... CORINE
Communization (ABBR) ... CMUNZN
Communize (ABBR) ... CMUNZ
Communized (ABBR) ... CMUNZD
Communizing (ABBR) ... CMUNZG
Commutability (ABBR) ... CMUTABT
Commutable (ABBR) ... CMUTAB
Commutate (ABBR) ... CMUTA
Commutated (ABBR) ... CMUTAD
Commutated Aerial Direction ... CAD
Commutated Aerial (or Antenna) Direction Finder (SAUS) ... CADF
Commutated Antenna Direction Finder (IEEE) ... CADF
Commutated Capacitor Filter (PDAA) ... CCF
Commutated Doppler Microwave Landing System (PDAA) ... CDMLS
Commutated Network (IAA) ... CN
Commutating (ABBR) ... CMUTAG
Commutating Auto Zero (SAUS) ... CAZ
Commutating Detection System ... CODES
Commutating Pole (SAUS) ... compole
Commutation [*Army*] ... Comtn
Commutation Factor ... CF
Commutation of Rations and Quarters [*Military*] ... CRQ
Commutation Rate (MCD) ... C/R
Commutative (ABBR) ... CMUTAV
Commutative Principle for Addition [*Mathematics*] ... CPA
Commutative Principle for Multiplication [*Mathematics*] ... CPM
Commutator (ABBR) ... CMUTAR
Commutator [*Electromagnetism*] (IAA) ... COM
Commutator ... COMM
Commutator [*Automotive engineering*] ... COMTR
Commutator Assemblies [*SONAR*] (MCD) ... CA
Commutator Bar (SAUS) ... COMBAR
Commutator End (MSA) ... CE
Commutatorless Motor (PDAA) ... CLM
Commute (ABBR) ... CMUT
Commuted (ABBR) ... CMUTD
Commuted Ration Allowance (SAUS) ... CRA
Commuted Rations [*Acronym refers to married Marine living off base and receiving these special pay dispensations*] ... COMRAT
Commuted Rations, Proceed Time [*Marine Corps*] (DNAB) ... COMRATS PT
Commuter (ABBR) ... CMUTR
Commuter ... COM
Commuter Aircraft Corporation (SAUO) ... CAC
Commuter Airline Association of America [*Later, RAA*] (EA) ... CAAA
Commuter Airlines [*Airline code*] ... CB
Commuter Services Corp. [*Formerly, ACSC*] ... CSC
Commuter Trip Reduction [*MOCD*] (TAG) ... CTR
Commuters Air Transport, Inc. ... CAT
Commuting (ABBR) ... CMUTG
Commuting Area Candidates [*Civil Service*] ... CAC
COMNAVMAR Environmental Quality Control (SAUO) ... CEQC
COMNAVOPSUPPGRU, Pacific (SAUO) ... COMNAVOPSUPPGRUPAC
COMNAVORDSYSCOM Headquarters (SAUO) ... COMNAVORDSYSCOMHQ
COMNAVSEASYSCOM Headquarters (SAUO) ... COMNAVSEASYSCOMHQ
COMNAVSHIPSYSCOM Headquarters (SAUO) ... COMNAVSHIPSYSCOMHQ
COMNAVSUPPFOR, Antarctic (SAUO) ... COMNAVSUPPFORCNATARCITIC
COMNET Corp. [*Formerly, Computer Network Corp.*] [*NASDAQ symbol*] (NQ) ... CNET
Comnet Corp. [*Associated Press*] (SAG) ... Comnet
Comodoro Rivadavia [*Argentina*] [*Airport symbol*] (OAG) ... CRD
Comodoro Rivadavia [*Argentina*] [*ICAO location identifier*] (ICLI) ... SAVF
Comodoro Rivadavia [*Argentina*] [*ICAO location identifier*] (ICLI) ... SAVU
Comodoro Rivadavia/Gral Mosconi [*Argentina*] [*ICAO location identifier*] (ICLI) ... SAVC
COMOPTEVFOR Acronym and Abbreviation List [*A publication*] (CAAL) ... CAAL
Comorbidity or Complication (SAUS) ... CC
Comorian Franc [*Monetary unit*] (ODBW) ... CF
Comoro Islands (SAUS) ... Com I
Comoro Islands [*MARC country of publication code*] [*Library of Congress*] (LCCP) ... cq
Comoro Islands [*MARC geographic area code*] [*Library of Congress*] (LCCP) ... i-cq-
Comoros [*ANSI three-letter standard code*] (CNC) ... COM
Comoros [*International civil aircraft marking*] (ODBW) ... D6
Comoros [*ANSI two-letter standard code*] (CNC) ... KM
Comoving Frame (SAUS) ... CMF
Comox [*Canada*] [*Airport symbol*] (OAG) ... YQQ
Comox Canadian Forces Base, BC [*ICAO location identifier*] (ICLI) ... CYQQ
Comox Resources Ltd. [*Vancouver Stock Exchange symbol*] ... CXO
Comox Valley Multicultural & Immigrant Support Society (AC) ... CVMISS
Comp Cervelaria Brahma Pfd ADS [*NYSE symbol*] (SG) ... BRH
Comp de Minas Buenaventura ADS [*NYSE symbol*] (TTSB) ... BVN
COMP Kernel Interface Package (SAUS) ... SKIPS
Comp Paranaense Energia'B' ADS [*NYSE symbol*] (SG) ... ELP
Comp Siderurgica Nacional ADS [*NYSE symbol*] (SG) ... SID
Comp. Tomkins & Jenckens Compendium of Modern Roman Law (SAUS) ... Tom&J
Comp Vale do Rio Doca ADS [*NYSE symbol*] ... RIOPr
Compact [*Car size*] ... C
Compact (FAAC) ... CMPCT
Compact (SAUS) ... Compt

Compact Air Supply Unit (SAUS) ... CASU
Compact Airborne Automatic Tracking System (SAUS) ... CAATS
Compact Airborne Spectrographic Imager (SAUS) ... CASI
Compact Air-Launched Ice Beacon (SAUS) ... CALIB
Compact All-Purpose Range Instrument [*RADAR*] (MCD) ... CAPRI
Compact Audio Disc (WDAA) ... CAD
Compact Automatic Retrieval Device [*Massachusetts Institute of Technology*] [*Computer science*] ... CARD
Compact Automatic Retrieval Display [*Computer science*] (IID) ... CARD
Compact Balancing Machine (SAUS) ... CBM
Compact Bipartite Committee (SAUO) ... CBC
Compact Blazing Combustion Axiom [*Auto engineering*] ... COMBAX
Compact Buoy System ... CBS
Compact Car (TRID) ... CCAR
Compact Cassette (IAA) ... CC
Compact Communication Products (SAUS) ... CCP
Compact Computers (SAUS) ... COCOS
Compact Data Disk Association [*Defunct*] (EA) ... CDDA
Compact Depth Sounder (SAUS) ... CDS
Compact Design [*Automotive engineering*] ... CD
Compact Detect ... CD
Compact Digital (SAUS) ... CD
Compact Digital Audio Disk (ADA) ... CDAD
Compact Dimension 2-Stroke Engine [*Automotive engineering*] ... CDS2
Compact Disc and Cathode Ray Tube Applied Format [*Automotive navigation systems*] ... CDCRAFT
Compact Disc Extra (SAUS) ... CD Extra
Compact Disc File Manager [*Computer science*] (NTCM) ... CD-FM
Compact Disc Group [*Defunct*] (EA) ... CDG
Compact Disc Mastering [*Dyna Tek Automation Systems, Inc.*] ... CDM
Compact Disc Packaging (SAUS) ... CD Pack
Compact Disc Plus (SAUS) ... CD Plus
Compact Disc Plus Graphics ... CD + G
Compact Disc Read and Write ... CD-RAW
Compact Disc Read-Only Memory Extended Architecture [*Computer science*] (PCM) ... CD-ROM XA
Compact Disc Rewriteable (AAEL) ... CDR
Compact Disc Universal Data Format [*Computer science*] (IGQR) ... CD UDF
Compact Disc Universal Disk Format ... CD-UDF
Compact Disc Write Only Read Many (SAUS) ... CD WORM
Compact Disc-Karaoke (SAUS) ... CD-K
Compact Disc-Read Only Memory [*Computer science*] (ACRL) ... CD-ROM
Compact Disc-Recordable/Erasable (RALS) ... CD-R/E
Compact Disc-Video (SAUS) ... CD-V
Compact Disk [*Audio/Video Technology*] [*Philips*] (ACRL) ... CD
Compact Disk and Graphics (SAUS) ... CDG
Compact Disk and Musical Instruments Digital Interface (SAUS) ... CDMIDI
Compact Disk Digital Audio [*Computer science*] ... CD-DA
Compact Disk File System [*Computer science*] (PCM) ... CDFS
Compact Disk Image Designer ... CDID
Compact Disk plus Graphics (SAUS) ... CD+G
Compact Disk Programmable Read-Only Memory [*Computer science*] ... CD-PROM
Compact Disk Television (BARN) ... CDTV
Compact Disk Video [*Audio/video technology*] ... CDV
Compact Disk Video Interactive [*Computer science*] ... CD-VI
Compact Disk-Audio ... CD-Audio
Compact Disk-Based Training (SAUS) ... CDBT
Compact Disk-Erasable (SAUS) ... CD-E
Compact Disk-Erasable (VERA) ... CDE
Compact Disk-Extended Architecture (ROAS) ... CD-XA
Compact Disk-Interactive (SAUS) ... CD-I
Compact Disk-Magneto Optical (SAUS) ... CD-MO
Compact Disk-Magneto Optical (VERA) ... CDMO
Compact Disk/Multimedia [*Computer science*] (TELE) ... CD/MM
Compact Disk-Read Only Data Exchange [*Computer science*] (TELE) ... CD-RDX
Compact Disk-Read Only Memory Data Exchange Standard (ROAS) ... CD-RDx
Compact Disk-Read Only Memory Extended Architecture [*Computer science*] (DDC) ... CD-ROM XA
Compact Disk-Read-Only Memory-Extended Architecture (SAUS) ... CD-ROM-XA
Compact Disk-Real Time Operating System (SAUS) ... CD-RTOS
Compact Disk-Recordable (SAUS) ... CD-R
Compact Disk-Rewritable ... CD-RW
Compact Disk-Re-writable (SAUS) ... CD-W
Compact Disk-Video (SAUS) ... CD-V
Compact Disk-Write Once (SAUS) ... CD-WO
Compact Disk-Write Once Read Many [*Computer science*] (TELE) ... CD-WORM
Compact Edition [*Windows*] [*Computer science*] (PCM) ... CE
Compact Electronic Components Inspection Laboratory ... CECIL
Compact Environment (RALS) ... CE
Compact Flash [*Computer science*] ... CF
Compact Floppy Disk [*Computer science*] (EECA) ... CFD
Compact Floppy Disk Drive [*Computer science*] (EECA) ... CFDD
Compact Fluorescent Lamp ... CFL
Compact Fluorescent Light ... CFL
Compact Font Format (SAUS) ... CFF
Compact for Responsive Electronic Writing (SAUS) ... CREW
Compact Gamma Ray Spectrometer ... CGRS
Compact Helicopter Approach Path Indicator (DA) ... CHAPI
Compact High-Energy Capacitor Module Advanced Technology Experiment (SAUS) ... CHECKMATE
Compact High-Energy Capacitor Module Advanced Technology Experiment [*For development of the rail gun*] ... CHECMATE
Compact High-Performance Aerial Gun (MCD) ... CHAG
Compact Ignition TOKAMAK [*Toroidal Kamera Magnetic*] [*Plasma physics*] ... CIT

Compact Indium Discharge (WDMC) ... CID
Compact Indium Discharge Lamp (SAUS) ... CID Lamp
Compact Infra-Red Television System (SAUS) ... CIRTEVS
Compact Interactive Standard (SAUS) ... CIS
Compact Interactive Standard for Common Business-Oriented Language [*Computer science*] (HGAA) ... CIS-COBOL
Compact Iodide Daylight (WDMC) ... CID
Compact Kinetic Energy Missile [*Military*] ... CKEM
Compact Laser Radar (SAUS) ... CLARA
Compact Machine Code (SAUS) ... CMC
Compact Meteorological & Oceanographic Drifter (SAUS) ... CMOD
Compact Molecular Cloud [*Chemistry*] (BARN) ... CMC
Compact Muon Solenoid ... CMS
Compact Nuclear Brayton System ... CONUBS
Compact Nuclear Power Source (SAUS) ... CNPS
Compact Operating System (IAA) ... COS
Compact Optronic Mast (SAUS) ... COM
Compact Orbital Gears Ltd. ... COG
Compact Periscope (MCD) ... COP
Compact Personal Computer (HGAA) ... CPC
Compact Power Plant (SAUS) ... CPP
Compact Programmed Airline Reservation System [*Computer science*] (PDAA) ... CPARS
Compact SIGINT Analysis Workstation (SAUS) ... CSAW
Compact Sodium-Cooled Nuclear Reactor Plant, Karlsruhe (SAUS) ... KNK
Compact Source Iodide (WDMC) ... CSI
Compact Source Iodide Lamp (SAUS) ... CSI Lamp
Compact Tactical Message Switch (SAUS) ... CTMS
Compact Tank Gun (SAUS) ... CTG
Compact Tension (SAUS) ... CT
Compact Tension-Probe (SAUS) ... CT-Probe
Compact Terrain Database (SAUS) ... CTDB
Compact Toroid (MCD) ... CT
Compact Transpiration Cooling ... CTC
Compact Very Low Frequency (SAUS) ... CVLF
Compact Very-Low-Frequency Equipment (DWSG) ... CVLFE
Compact Video ... CV
Compact Video Cassette (SAUS) ... CVC
Compact Video Cassette Recorder ... CVC
Compact Video Disk (SAUS) ... CVD
Compact Video-Rate Optical Scanner [*Instrumentation*] ... CVROS
Compact Watch Module (SAUS) ... CWM
Compact-Disc Player (SAUS) ... CD Player
Compact-Disc Technology (SAUS) ... CD Tec
Compacted Earth (PDAA) ... CE
Compacted Earth Sodium Treated (PDAA) ... CEST
Compacted Graphite Iron [*Metallurgical engineering*] ... CGI
Compact-Flake-Graphite [*Type of Iron*] ... CFG
Compacting Press (SAUS) ... COM Press
Compaction Ratio (SAUS) ... CR
Compactor Co., Inc. ... CCI
Compagnia Aeronautica Italiana SPA [*Italy*] [*ICAO designator*] (FAAC) ... CAI
Compagnia Generale Ripreseaeree, SPA [*Italy*] [*FAA designator*] (FAAC) ... CGR
Compagnie [*Company*] [*French*] ... Cie
Compagnie Aerienne du Languedoc [*ICAO designator*] (AD) ... FQ
Compagnie Aerienne du Languedoc [*France*] [*ICAO designator*] (FAAC) ... LGD
Compagnie Aeronautique Europeene [*France*] [*ICAO designator*] (FAAC) ... FEU
Compagnie Africaine des Ingenieurs-Conseils ... CADIC
Compagnie Air Mediterranee [*France*] [*ICAO designator*] (FAAC) ... MDT
Compagnie commune de Reassurance des Etats membres de la CICA (SAUO) ... CICA RE
Compagnie d'Assurance d'Hypotheques du Canada [*Mortgage Insurance Co. of Canada - MICC*] ... CAHC
Compagnie de Bauxites de Guinee [*Guinea*] [*ICAO designator*] (FAAC) ... GIC
Compagnie de Chemin de Fer Bas-Congo-Katanga [*Lower Congo-Katanga Railway*] [*Zaire*] ... BCK
Compagnie de Transport Aerien [*Switzerland*] [*ICAO designator*] (FAAC) ... CTA
Compagnie de Transports Aeriens [*Airline*] [*Switzerland*] ... CTA
Compagnie des Agents de Change [*French Stockbrokers Association*] [*Information Service or System*] (EAIO) ... CAC
Compagnie des Agents de Change-40 [*French stock index*] (NUMA) ... CAC-40
Compagnie des Jeunes Canadiens [*Company of Young Canadians*] [*Federal crown corporation to employ young people, 1966-75*] ... CJC
Compagnie des Pretres de St. Sulpice [*Society of the Priests of St. Sulpice - SPSS*] [*France*] (EAIO) ... CPSS
Compagnie Europeenne d'Automatisme [*Became part of Compagnie Internationale d'Informatique*] ... CAE
Compagnie Europeenne de la Jeunesse ... CEJ
Compagnie Francaise pour l'Assurance du Commerce Exterieur ... COFACE
Compagnie Generale d'Electricite [*General Electric Company*] [*France*] ... CGE
Compagnie Generale des Eaux ... CGE
Compagnie Generale d'Industrie et de Participations ... CGIP
Compagnie Generale Electrique du Canada [*Canadian General Electric Co. Ltd.*] ... CGE
Compagnie Genl Geophy ADS [*NYSE symbol*] (SG) ... GGY
Compagnie Industrielle de Telecommunication [*Computer manufacturer*] [*France*] ... CIT
Compagnie Industrielle du Disque [*Record label*] [*France*] ... CID
Compagnie Internationale de Papier du Canada [*Canadian International Paper Co.*] ... CIP
Compagnie Internationale de Services en Informatique [*Information service or system*] [*France*] (NITA) ... CISI-IAI
Compagnie Internationale de Services en Informatique-Electrical and Nuclear Energy [*France*] [*Information service or system*] (NITA) ... CISI-ELECNUL
Compagnie Internationale de Services et Informatique [*International Information Services Company*] [*Information service or system*] [*France*] (IID) ... CISI
Compagnie Internationale pour l'Informatique [*Formed by merger of SEA and CAE*] ... CII
Compagnie Maritime Camerounaise SA [*Shipping line*] (EY) ... CMC
Compagnie Nationale Air Gabon [*ICAO designator*] (FAAC) ... AGN
Compagnie Nationale Algerienne de Navigation [*Algerian National Shipping Company*] (AF) ... CNAN
Compagnie Nationale Naganagani [*Burkina Faso*] [*ICAO designator*] (FAAC) ... BFN
Compagnie Sans Fil (SAUS) ... CSF
Compagnie Senegalaise de Transports Aeriens [*Senegal*] [*ICAO designator*] (ICDA) ... DS
Compagnon (SAUS) ... Co
Compagnon de l'Ordre du Canada [*French*] [*Companion of the Order of Canada*] (CPGU) ... CC
Companded Delta Modulation [*Telecommunications*] (TEL) ... CDM
Companded Frequency Modulation (SAUS) ... CFM
Companding and Frequency Modulation [*Telecommunications*] (TEL) ... CFM
Companhia Brasileira ADS [*NYSE symbol*] (SG) ... CBD
Companhia Brasileira de Trens Urbanos [*Railway system*] [*Brazil*] (EY) ... CBTU
Companhia Danca Contemporanea [*Portugal*] ... CDC
Companhia de Navegacao do Norte [*Shipping company*] [*Brazil*] (EY) ... CONAN
Companhia Portuguesa Radio Marconi [*Portuguese Radio Marconi Co.*] [*Lisbon*] [*Information service or system*] (IID) ... CPRM
Companhia Vale do Rio Doce ... CVRD
Compania [*Company*] [*Spanish*] (DFIT) ... Cia
Compania [*Company*] [*Spanish*] ... CIA
Compania [*Company*] [*Spanish*] (BARN) ... Compa
Compania Aerea de Servicios Tur Air [*Spain*] [*ICAO designator*] (FAAC) ... TUU
Compania Aerea del Sur SA [*Uruguay*] [*ICAO designator*] (FAAC) ... ASU
Compania Aero Transportes Panamenos SA [*Panama*] [*ICAO designator*] (FAAC) ... AEP
Compania Aerotecnicas Fotograficas [*Spain*] [*ICAO designator*] (FAAC) ... ATF
Compania Anonima Nacional Telefonos de Venezuela [*Associated Press*] (SAG) ... CANTV
Compania Anonima Nacional Telefonos de Venezuela [*NYSE symbol*] (SAG) ... VNT
Compania Boliviana De Energia [*NYSE symbol*] (TTSB) ... BLP
Compania Boliviana de Energia Electrica [*Associated Press*] (SAG) ... CoBolv
Compania Boliviana de Energia Electrica SA [*NYSE symbol*] (SPSG) ... BLP
Compania Cervecerias ADS [*NASDAQ symbol*] (TTSB) ... CCUUY
Compania Cervecerias Unidas ADS [*NYSE symbol*] (SG) ... CU
Compania Cervecerias Unidas ADS [*NYSE symbol*] (SG) ... VNT
Compania Cervecerias Unides [*NASDAQ symbol*] (SAG) ... CCUU
Compania Cervecerias Unides [*Associated Press*] (SAG) ... Cervecer
Compania de Aviacion "Faucett" SA [*Peru*] [*ICAO designator*] (ICDA) ... CF
Compania de Aviacion Faucett SA [*Peru*] [*ICAO designator*] (FAAC) ... CFP
Compania de Aviacion Trans-Europa [*Spain*] [*ICAO designator*] (ICDA) ... TR
Compania de Minas Buenaventura SA [*NYSE symbol*] (SAG) ... BVN
Compania de Minas Buenaventura SA [*Associated Press*] (SAG) ... CoMBuen
Compania de Servicios Aereos SA [*Spain*] [*ICAO designator*] (FAAC) ... SAESA
Compania de Servicios Aereos SA [*Spain*] [*ICAO designator*] (FAAC) ... SSS
Compania de Servicios Aereos, TAVISA [*Spain*] [*ICAO designator*] (FAAC) ... TAV
Compania de Telecom Chile ADS [*NYSE symbol*] [*Formerly, Compania Tel de Chile ADS*] (SG) ... CTC
Compania de Telecommunicaciones de Chile SA [*Associated Press*] (SAG) ... ChileTel
Compania de Telecomunicaciones de Chile SA [*NYSE symbol*] (SAG) ... CTC
Compania de Telefonos de Chile SA [*Associated Press*] (SAG) ... ChileTel
Compania de Telefonos de Chile SA [*Santiago*] [*Telecommunications service*] ... CTC
Compania Dominicana de Aviacion SA [*ICAO designator*] (OAG) ... DO
Compania Dominicana de Aviacion SA [*Dominican Republic*] [*ICAO designator*] (FAAC) ... DOA
Compania Helicopteros de Transporte SA [*Spain*] [*ICAO designator*] (FAAC) ... HSO
Compania Helicopteros del Sureste SA [*Spain*] [*ICAO designator*] (FAAC) ... HSE
Compania Hispano Irlandesa de Aviacion [*Spain*] [*ICAO designator*] (FAAC) ... FUA
Compania Internacional Editora, Sociedad Anonima ... CIESA
Compania Internadia de Aviacion [*Colombia*] [*ICAO designator*] (FAAC) ... IAN
Compania Mexicana de Aeroplanos SA [*Mexico*] [*ICAO designator*] (FAAC) ... MDR
Compania Mexicana de Aviacion [*Mexican airline*] ... CMA
Compania Mexicana de Aviacion [*ICAO designator*] (OAG) ... MX
Compania Mexicana de Aviacion SA [*Mexico*] [*ICAO designator*] (FAAC) ... MXA
Compania Mexicana de Taxis Aereos SA [*Mexico*] [*ICAO designator*] (FAAC) ... CMX
Compania Nacional de Turismo Aereo [*Chilean airline*] ... CINTA
Compania Panamena de Aviacion SA [*Panama*] [*ICAO designator*] (FAAC) ... CMP
Compania Panamena de Aviacion, SA [*Panamanian airline*] ... COPA
Compania Peruana de Vapores [*Peruvian airline*] ... CPV
Compania Spantax [*Spain*] [*ICAO designator*] (FAAC) ... BXS
Compania SPANTAX (Servicios y Transportes Aereos Air Charter) [*Spain*] [*ICAO designator*] (ICDA) ... BX
Compania Sud America de Vapores [*Chilean airline*] ... CSAV
Compania Telefonica Nacional de Espana [*National Telephone Co. of Spain*] [*Telecommunications*] ... CTNE
Companies (ROG) ... COS
Companies Act (SAUO) ... CA
Companies, Agencies, Markets, Positions (IIA) ... CAMP
Companies and Their Brands [*Formerly, TND:CI*] [*A publication*] ... CTB

Companies Registration Office [*British*] (DS) ... CRO
Companies Update Bulletin [*National Companies and Securities Commission*] [*A publication*] ... CUB
Companion ... C
Companion (MSA) ... COMP
Companion (SAUS) ... Comp
Companion Animal Welfare Council (GVA) ... CAWC
Companion Dog [*Dog show term*] ... CD
Companion Dog [*Prefix*] ... U-CD
Companion Dog, Excellent [*Dog show term*] ... CDX
Companion Dog Excellent [*Prefix*] ... U-CDX
Companion, Institute of Radio Engineers ... CIRE
Companion Member of the Institution of Works and Highways Technician Engineers [*British*] (DBQ) ... CMIWHTE
Companion of Honour [*British*] ... CH
Companion of Honour of Barbados (SAUO) ... CHB
Companion of Literature [*Academic degree*] (WDAA) ... CL
Companion of Literature [*Royal Society of Literature award*] [*British*] ... CLit
Companion of Literature [*British*] (WA) ... C Lit
Companion of Literature [*Royal Society of Literature Award*] [*British*] (BARN) ... C Litt
Companion of the Association of Business Executives [*British*] (DBQ) ... CABE
Companion of the [*Order of the*] **Bath** [*British*] ... CB
Companion Of the Bath (SAUO) ... COB
Companion of the British Institute of Management (DBQ) ... CBIM
Companion of the Distinguished Service Order [*British*] ... CDS
Companion of the Distinguished Service Order [*British*] ... CDSO
Companion of the Distinguished Service Order [*Canada*] (DD) ... DSO
Companion of the [*Order of the*] **Indian Empire** [*British*] ... CIE
Companion of the Institute of Electrical Engineers (SAUS) ... CIEE
Companion of the Institute of Marine Engineers [*British*] ... CIMarE
Companion of the Institute of Mechanical Engineers (SAUS) ... CIMechn E
Companion of the Institute of Personnel Management [*Formerly, FIPM*] [*British*] ... CIPM
Companion of the Institute of Plumbing [*British*] (DBQ) ... CompIP
Companion of the Institution of Agricultural Engineers [*British*] ... CIAgrE
Companion of the Institution of Analysts and Programmers [*British*] (DBQ) ... CmpnIAP
Companion of the Institution of Analysts & Programmers (SAUS) ... Cmpn IAP
Companion of the Institution of Electrical Engineers [*British*] ... CIEE
Companion of the Institution of Electrical Engineers [*British*] (EY) ... CompIEE
Companion of the Institution of Electronic and Radio Engineers [*British*] ... CompIERE
Companion of the Institution of Gas Engineers [*British*] (DBQ) ... Companion IGasE
Companion of the Institution of Mechanical and General Technician Engineers [*British*] (DBQ) ... CIMGTechE
Companion of the Institution of Mechanical Engineers [*British*] ... CI Mech E
Companion of the Nautical Institute (SAUO) ... CNI
Companion of the Order of Canada ... CC
Companion of the Order of St. Michael and St. George [*Facetiously translated "Call Me God"*] [*British*] ... CMG
Companion of the Order of the British Empire (ADA) ... CBE
Companion of the order ofthe Star of Ghana (SAUO) ... CSG
Companion of the Society of Certified Professionals [*British*] (DBQ) ... CmpnSCP
Companion of the Society of Licensed Aircraft Engineers and Technologists [*British*] (DBQ) ... CompSLEAT
Companion of the [*Order of the*] **Star of India** [*British*] ... CSI
Companion of the Textile Institute [*British*] ... CompTI
Companion to the Authorized Daily Prayer Book [*A publication*] (BJA) ... CPB
Companion Trainer Aircraft ... CTA
Companions ... COM
Companions of Christ (TOCD) ... COC
Companions of Doctor Who Fan Club [*Defunct*] (EA) ... CODW
Companions of the Celtic Mission (EAIO) ... CCM
Companions of the Forest of America (EA) ... CFA
Companions of the Forest of America [*New York, NY*] (EA) ... COFOA
Company (SAUO) ... C
Company [*Business term*] (AAG) ... CO
Company (NTIO) ... co
Company (DD) ... Co
Company (SAUO) ... Co
Company (GEAB) ... comp
Company ... COMP
Company (ROG) ... COMPY
company (SAUO) ... compy
Company (MILB) ... coy
Company (WDAA) ... Coy
Company ... COY
Company (SAUO) ... Cy
Company A (SAUO) ... Co A
Company Ammunition Supply Point (SAUO) ... COASP
Company and Literature Information Center (SAUO) ... CLIC
Company and Securities Law Journal [*Australia*] [*A publication*] ... C & SLJ
Company and Securities Law Journal [*Australia*] [*A publication*] ... Co & Sec Law Journal
Company Average VOC [*Volatile Organic Compound*] **Emission** [*Environmental Protection Agency*] ... CAVE
Company B (SAUO) ... Co B
Company Buyer Study [*Life Insurance Management and Research Association*] ... CBS
Company C (SAUO) ... Co C
Company Cases [*India*] [*A publication*] (DLA) ... Com Cas
Company Cases [*India*] [*A publication*] (DLA) ... Comp Cas
Company Chemists' Association [*British*] ... CCA
Company Collection Point [*Army*] (INF) ... CCP
Company Commander ... CC
Company Commander (SAUO) ... Co Com
Company Commander (SAUO) ... Co Comdr
Company Conduct Book (SAUO) ... CCB
Company Credit Reports [*Teikoku DataBank Ltd.*] [*Japan*] [*Information service or system*] (CRD) ... CCR
Company D (SAUO) ... Co D
Company Data Coordinator ... CDC
Company Distributing Point [*Army*] ... CDP
Company Doctor [*NASDAQ symbol*] (TTSB) ... CDOC
Company Doctor (The) [*NASDAQ symbol*] (SAG) ... CDOC
Company Doctor (The) [*Associated Press*] (SAG) ... CDoctr
Company Doctor (The) [*Associated Press*] (SAG) ... CoDoctor
Company Doctor Wrrt [*NASDAQ symbol*] (TTSB) ... CDOCW
Company Document Distribution Center (ACAE) ... CDDC
Company Export Planning ... CEP
Company Facts and Addresses [*EDIC*] [*Ringmer Near Lewes, East Sussex, England*] [*Information service or system*] (IID) ... COAD
Company Fire Control [*Net*] (MCD) ... CFC
Company First [*A mealtime whimsicality for use when guests are present*] ... CF
Company Fiscal Year (NASA) ... CFY
Company Form Instruction (MCD) ... CFI
Company Grade Officer (ACAE) ... CGO
Company Grade Officer Council (ACAE) ... CGOC
Company Group (SAUO) ... CG
Company Headquarters [*British military*] (DMA) ... CHQ
Company Information System (SAUO) ... CIS
Company Integrated Telephony (SAUO) ... CIT
Company Law Journal [*A publication*] (DLA) ... Comp LJ
Company Level Field Feeding Kitchen [*Army's Combat System Test Activity*] (INF) ... CLFFK
Company Lightweight Mortar System [*Army*] ... CLMS
Company Lightweight Mortar System [*Army*] (MCD) ... CLWM
Company Maintenance Team (INF) ... CMT
Company Midshipman Officer-of-the-Watch [*Navy*] (DNAB) ... CMOOW
Company Name [*Database terminology*] (NITA) ... CN
Company Nuclear Review and Audit Group (NRCH) ... CNRAG
Company of American Dance ... CAD
Company of Engineers (SAUO) ... C of E
Company of Fifers and Drummers (EA) ... CFD
Company of Gold & Silver Wyre Drawers [*British*] (WDAA) ... CGSWD
Company of Mary [*Roman Catholic women's religious order*] ... ODN
Company of Master Mariners (SAUO) ... COMM
Company of Master Mariners of Australia ... CMMA
Company of Military Collectors and Historians [*Later, CMH*] (EA) ... CMCH
Company of Military Historians (EA) ... CMH
Company of Royal Engineers (SAUO) ... Co RE
Company of Saint Paul (EA) ... CSP
Company of the Daughters of Charity of St Vincent-de-Paul (SAUO) ... DC
Company of the Savior [*Roman Catholic women's religious order*] ... CS
Company of Veteran Motorists (SAUO) ... CVM
Company of Young Canadians [*Federal crown corporation to employ young people, 1966-75*] ... CYC
Company Operating Facility ... COF
Company Orders (SAUO) ... Co O
Company Organization Survey [*Bureau of the Census*] (GFGA) ... COS
Company Owned (NTCM) ... C-O
Company Pensions Information Centre [*British*] (CB) ... CPIC
Company Persistency Rater [*LIMRA*] ... CPR
Company Policy (MCD) ... CP
Company [*or Corporate*] **Policy Statement** ... CPS
Company Private (ACAE) ... CP
Company Program Manager (MCD) ... CPM
Company Quartermaster (SAUO) ... CQM
Company Quartermaster-Sergeant ... CQMS
Company Records Center (ACAE) ... CRC
Company Route (GAVI) ... CO ROUTE
Company, Royal Engineers (SAUO) ... CoyRE
Company Secretary ... CS
Company Sergeant Major (SAUS) ... CSM
Company Sergeant-Major [*Army*] [*British*] ... CSM
Company Sergeant-Major Instructor [*Army*] [*British*] ... CSMI
Company Services Advisory Committee [*British*] (GVA) ... CSAC
Company Skip List (SAUO) ... CSL
Company Source Inspection ... CSI
Company Stage Manager (SAUO) ... CSM
Company Standard Form Instruction ... CSFI
Company Standard Practice ... CSP
Company Tactics Course (SAUO) ... CTC
Company Team [*Combat Electronic Warfare Intelligence*] [*Army*] ... CT
Company Technical Document Center ... CTDC
Company Voluntary Arrangement [*Business term*] (ECON) ... CVA
Company Wide Quality Control (SAUO) ... CWQC
Company-Owned and Maintained (SAUO) ... COAM
Company's Risk [*Insurance*] ... CR
Company's Risk (EBF) ... cr
Company-to-Company Agreement (MCD) ... CCA
Company-Wide Quality Improvement (SAUO) ... CWQI
Compaq Computer Corp. [*Associated Press*] (SAG) ... Compaq
Compaq Computer Corp. [*NYSE symbol*] (SPSG) ... CPQ
Compaq Computer Corp., Component Engineering Library, Houston, TX [*Library symbol*] [*Library of Congress*] (LCLS) ... TxHCCo
Compaq Computer Corporation (SAUO) ... Compaq
Compaq Expanded Memory Manager (SAUS) ... CEMM

Compaq Extended Memory Manager [Software] .... CEMM
Compaq Networking Management Software [Computer science] .... CNMS
Compaq Telecommunications Corp. [Dallas, TX] .... CTC
Comparability Pay Increases (ACAE) .... CPI
Comparable Worth Project (EA) .... CWP
Comparably Efficient Interconnection [Telecommunications] .... CEI
Comparatio Aristophanis et Menandri [of Plutarch] [Classical studies]
(OCD) .... Comp Ar et Men
Comparative .... COMP
Comparative (ADWA) .... comp
Comparative (AAGC) .... Comp
Comparative (BEE) .... compar
Comparative .... COMPAR
Comparative .... COMPRTV
Comparative Administration Research Institute [Kent State University,
Ohio] .... CARI
Comparative Administrative Group (SAUO) .... CAG
Comparative Administrative Science Quarterly [A publication]
(DLA) .... Comp Admin Sci Q
Comparative and International Education Society (EA) .... CIES
Comparative and International Education Society of Canada .... CIESC
Comparative and International Law Journal of Southern Africa
[A publication] (DLA) .... CILJSA
Comparative Animal Research Laboratory [Department of Energy]
(GRD) .... CARL
Comparative Bantu On-Line Dictionary (SAUO) .... CBOLD
Comparative Biochemistry and Physiology (SAUS) .... Comp Biochem Physiol
Comparative Biochemistry and Physiology (journ.)
(SAUS) .... Comp Biochem Physiol
Comparative Biochemistry and Physiology. Part A, Physiology
(SAUS) .... Comp Biochem Physiol A Physiol
Comparative Biochemistry and Physiology. Part B, Biochemistry and
Molecular Biology (SAUS) .... Comp Biochem Physiol B Biochem Mol Biol
Comparative Biochemistry and Physiology. Part C, Pharmacology,
Toxicology and Endocrinology (SAUS) ....
Comp Biochem Physiol C Pharmacol Toxicol Endocrinol
Comparative Capital Cost (TEL) CCC
Comparative Construction Performance Working Party (SAUO) .... CCPWP
Comparative Crime Data File (SAUO) .... CCDF
Comparative Current Sinking Logic (SAUS) .... CCSL
Comparative Data (SAUS) .... CD
Comparative Distribution Analysis [Marketing] (WDMC) .... CDA
Comparative Drama [A publication] (BRI) .... Comp Dr
Comparative Education Review [A publication] .... Comp Ed Rev
Comparative Education Society [Later, CIES] (EA) .... CES
Comparative Education Society in Europe (EAIO) .... CESE
Comparative Educational Research Centre (SAUO) .... CERC
Comparative Estimating .... CE
Comparative Evaluation of the Different Radiating Cables and Systems
Technologies (SAUO) .... CERACS
Comparative Genomic Hybridization [Biochemistry] .... CGH
Comparative Guidance and Placement Program (EDAC) .... CGP
Comparative Guidance and Placement Program [College Entrance
Examination Board] .... CGPP
Comparative Immunology, Microbiology and Infectious Diseases
(SAUS) .... Comp Immunol Microbiol Infect Dis
Comparative Index of National and European Standards (SAUO) .... ICONE
Comparative Law Series. United States Bureau of Foreign and Domestic
Commerce. General Legal Bulletin [A publication] (DLA) .... Comp LS
Comparative Law Yearbook [A publication] (DLA) .... Comp L Yb
Comparative Library Organization Committee [American Library
Association] .... CLOC
Comparative Literature [A publication] (BRI) .... Comp L
Comparative Literature Association (EA) .... CLA
Comparative Literature Studies [A publication] (BRI) .... CLS
Comparative LOFAR Fixing [Military] (CAAL) .... CLF
Comparative Molecular Field Analysis [Software] .... CoMFA
Comparative Performance Exploratory Analysis .... CPEA
Comparative Planetology and the Early Earth (SAUS) .... CPEE
Comparative Postwar Recovery Analysis (MCD) .... COPRA
Comparative Respiratory Society (GVA) .... CRS
Comparative Soot Diagnostics (SAUS) .... CSD
Comparative Studies in Society and History (journ.) (SAUS) .... CSSH
Comparative Systems Laboratory .... CSL
Comparative Test Programme (SAUS) .... CTP
Comparative Testing .... CT
Comparative Tracking Index [Electronics] (EECA) .... CTI
Comparative Urban Research. International Sociological Association,
Committee for Community Research. College Park (SAUO) .... ISA/CUR
Comparative Wage Justice (ADA) .... CWJ
Comparator (CET) .... COMP
Comparator [Computer science] .... COMPTR
Comparator (SAUS) .... Comptr
Comparator Buffer [Computer science] (MUGU) .... CB
Comparator Chart-Tooling (MCD) .... CCT
Comparator Circuit (SAUS) CC
Comparator Sys [NASDAQ symbol] (TTSB) .... IDID
Comparator Systems Corp. [Associated Press] (SAG) .... Compartr
Comparator Systems Corp. [NASDAQ symbol] (SAG) .... IDID
Comparators [JETDS nomenclature] [Military] (CET) .... CM
Compare (DAVI) .... cf
Compare [Computer science] .... CMP
Compare (MSA) .... CMPR
Compare .... COMP
Compare (FAAC) .... COMPR

Compare .... CP
Compare (STED) .... cp
Compare Accumulator with Storage [Computer science] (IAA) .... CAS
Compare Alphabetic Equal [Computer science] (OA) .... CAE
Compare Alphabetic Unequal [Computer science] (OA) .... CAU
Compare and Difference Full Words (SAA) .... CDF
Compare and Difference Left Half Words (SAA) .... CDL
Compare and Difference of Masked BIT [Binary Digit] [Computer science]
(SAA) .... CDM
Compare and Difference Right-Half Words (SAA) .... CDR
Compare Binary (SAUS) .... CB
Compare Binary Immediate (SAUS) .... CBI
Compare Decimal (SAUS) .... CD
Compare Full Words (SAA) .... CMF
Compare Generiks [NASDAQ symbol] (TTSB) .... COGE
Compare Generiks, Inc [Associated Press] (SAG) .... CmpGen
Compare Generiks, Inc. [NASDAQ symbol] (SAG) .... COGE
Compare Generiks, Inc. [Associated Press] (SAG) .... CompG
Compare Generiks Unit [NASDAQ symbol] (TTSB) .... COGEU
Compare Generiks Wrrt'A' [NASDAQ symbol] (TTSB) .... COGEW
Compare Halfword (SAUS) .... CH
Compare Instruction (SAUS) CI
Compare Instruction (SAUS) .... CMP Instruction
Compare Left Half Words (SAA) .... CML
Compare Logical Characters (SAUS) CLC
Compare Logical Immediately (SAUS) CLI
Compare Long (SAUS) CL
Compare Mask (SAA) .... CMM
Compare Numeric Equal [Computer science] .... CNE
Compare Numeric Unequal [Computer science] .... CNU
Compare Right Half Words (SAA) .... CMR
Compare String with String [Computer science] (IAA) .... COMSS
Compare String with Word [Computer science] (IAA) .... COMSW
Compare Word String .... CMPS
Compare Zone Equal [Computer science] .... CZE
Compare Zone Unequal [Computer science] .... CZU
Compared .... CMPRD
Comparex Software Service (SAUS) .... CSS
Comparing (SAUS) .... Cmprg
Comparing (SAUS) .... Cpr
Comparing Element (IAA) .... CE
Comparing Feature (SAUS) .... CF
Comparing Political Experiences [National Science Foundation project] .... CPE
Comparing Reading Approaches in First Grade Teaching .... CRAFT
Comparing Storage Position (SAUS) .... CSP
Comparison (SAUS) .... Cmprn
Comparison (EBF) .... Comp
Comparison .... COMP
Comparison (VRA) .... comp
Comparison (SAUS) .... CP
Comparison Circuit [Telecommunications] (OA) CC
Comparison Group .... CG
Comparison Level (DIPS) CL
Comparison Level for Alternatives (DIPS) .... CLAlt
Comparison Measuring Circuit (PDAA) .... CMC
Comparison of Annual Growth Rate .... CAGR
Comparison of Mesoscale Prediction and Research Experiment Project
(SAUS) .... COMPARE
Comparison of Recognition Algorithms [US Postal Service] .... CORAL
Comparison Operator (SAUS) .... CO
Comparison Point Date [Social Security Administration] .... CPD
Comparison Point of Decision (DHP) .... CPD
Comparison Stimulus (DIPS) .... Co
Comparison Test (MCD) .... CPT
Comparison Voltage (SAUS) VC
Comparisons in Law and Monetary Comments [A publication]
(DLA) .... Comparisons in L & Monet Com
Compartment (NASA) .... CMPRT
Compartment (MCD) .... COMP
Compartment (FAAC) .... COMPRT
Compartment (KSC) .... COMPT
Compartment (ADWA) .... compt
Compartment (NITA) .... cpt
Compartment and Access (SAUS) .... C&A
Compartment and Access [Technical drawings] .... C & A
Compartment Checkoff List (DNAB) CCL
Compartment Checkoff List [Navy] (NVT) .... CCOL
Compartment for Peptide Loading [In antigen preventing cells]
[Immunology] .... CPL
Compartment Mode Workstation (SAUS) .... CMW
Compartment of Uncoupling Receptor and Ligand [Cytology] .... CURL
Compartment Testing (NITA) .... CT
Compartmental (ABBR) .... CMPRTL
Compartmental Knee Prosthesis (MELL) .... CKP
Compartmentalize (ABBR) .... CMPRTLZ
Compartmentalized (ABBR) .... CMPRTLZD
Compartmentalizing (ABBR) .... CMPRTLZG
Compartmented Consolidated Analysis Report Final (MCD) .... CARF
COMPAS [Computer Acquisition System] Online Interactive Language
(PDAA) .... COIL
Compass C
Compass (MSA) .... CMPS
Compass (SAUS) .... Cmps
Compass .... COMP
Compass Airlines of Australia [ICAO designator] (FAAC) .... CYM

Compass Altitude Heading Reference System (DWSG) ... CAHRS
Compass and Inclinometer (GEOI) ... CI
Compass Angle Measurement (SAUS) ... CAM
Compass Aviation [*British*] [*ICAO designator*] (FAAC) ... CPS
Compass Azimuth (SAUS) ... CZm
Compass Bancshares [*NASDAQ symbol*] (TTSB) ... CBSS
Compass Bancshares, Inc. [*NASDAQ symbol*] (SAG) ... CBSS
Compass Bancshares, Inc. [*Associated Press*] (SAG) ... CompBnc
Compass Bearing [*Navigation*] ... CB
Compass Compensating (SAUS) ... CPS CMPSG
Compass Control Alarm ... CCA
Compass Control System ... CCS
Compass Course ... CC
Compass Department [*British military*] (DMA) ... CD
Compass Department of the Admiralty (SAUO) ... CDA
Compass Diagnostic Test of Arithmetic (DIPS) ... CDTA
Compass Direction Indicator (PDAA) ... CDI
Compass Equal Target Acquisition System ... CETAS
Compass Error [*Navigation*] ... CE
Compass Failure Annunciator ... CFA
Compass Heading ... CH
Compass Integrated System Compiler (IEEE) ... CISCO
Compass Locator ... COMLO
Compass Locator [*Aviation*] (DA) ... COMO
Compass Locator of Inner Marker Site ... LIM
Compass North ... CN
Compass Operation Alarm ... COA
Compass Resources Ltd. [*Vancouver Stock Exchange symbol*] ... CPE
Compass Re-Transmission Unit (PDAA) ... CRU
Compass System Controller (MCD) ... CSC
Compass System Extensively Altered (SAA) ... COSEAL
Compass Test Language ... CTL
Compass: Theology Review [*A publication*] (APTA) ... Com
Compass Tilt Signal ... CTS
Compass Vertical Angular Measurement (RDA) ... C/VAM
Compass Voice Response (SAUO) ... CVR
Compassion in World Farming [*British*] ... CIWF
Compassion in World Farming (GVA) ... CWF
Compassion International (EA) ... CI
Compassionate [*Army*] (AABC) ... COMPATE
Compassionate Case [*Airline notation*] ... CM
Compassionate Friends [*British*] [*An association*] (DBA) ... CF
[*The*] **Compassionate Friends** (EA) ... TCF
Compassionate Posting Committee (SAUO) ... CPC
Compassionate Reassignment Not Favorably Considered [*Army*] (AABC) ... COMPATENFC
Compatibility (KSC) ... COMPAT
Compatibility ... CPT
Compatibility and Interoperability (RDA) ... C & I
Compatibility and Interoperability (SAUO) ... C&I
Compatibility and Interoperability (SAUO) ... C+I
Compatibility Basic Input Output System [*Computer science*] (VERA) ... CBIOS
Compatibility Class (SAUS) ... CC
Compatibility Engineering Change Proposal [*NASA*] (NASA) ... CECP
Compatibility Feature Initialize Mode (SAUS) ... CFIM
Compatibility Feature Load Constant (SAUS) ... CFLC
Compatibility Feature Load Variable (SAUS) ... CFLV
Compatibility Feature Mode Set (SAUS) ... CFMS
Compatibility Feature Store Constant (SAUS) ... CFSC
Compatibility Feature Store Variable (SAUS) ... CFSV
Compatibility Initialization Deck (IAA) ... CID
Compatibility List (SAUS) ... CL
Compatibility Mock-Up (KSC) ... CMU
Compatibility Modification Inference (IDAI) ... CMI
Compatibility of Materials (MCD) ... COMAT
Compatibility Operating System [*Computer science*] ... COS
Compatibility Processor-1 (SAUS) ... CP-1
Compatibility Test (MCD) ... CT
Compatibility Test Area [*NASA*] (KSC) ... CTA
Compatibility Test Capsule ... CTC
Compatibility Test Unit ... CTU
Compatibility Test Van [*Military*] ... CTV
Compatibility-Integration Mock-Up (MCD) ... CIMU
Compatible ... C
Compatible ... COMP
Compatible ... COMPTBL
Compatible ... COMPTBLE
Compatible Algebraic Compiler and Translator ... COMPACT
Compatible Communications Architecture [*Telecommunication protocol*] (CDE) ... CCA
Compatible Current Sourcing Logic (SAUS) ... CCSL
Compatible Current-Sinking Logic (MSA) ... CCSL
Compatible Duplex System ... CDS
Compatible Expansion [*Noise-reduction system for manufacturing phonograph records*] [*CBS*] ... CX
Compatible Extension (SAUS) ... CX
Compatible Hardware and Milestone Program for Integrating Organizational Needs (SAUO) ... CHAMPION
Compatible Hardware and Milestone Program for Integrating Organizational Needs [*AFSC*] ... CHAMPION
Compatible High-Density Bipolar Code [*Telecommunications*] (TEL) ... CHDB
Compatible Independent Peripherals (IEEE) ... CIP
Compatible Information Systems (SAUS) ... CIS
Compatible Instrument Landing System [*Aviation*] ... CILS
Compatible Land Use [*FAA*] (TAG) ... CLU
Compatible LASER System ... CLS
Compatible Laser System (SAUS) ... CLS
Compatible Materials (SAUS) ... CMAT
Compatible Materials List (NASA) ... CMAT
Compatible On-Board Ranging ... COBRA
Compatible Phase Multiplex (SAUS) ... CPM
Compatible Punched Tape (SAUS) ... CPT
Compatible Quadrature Amplitude Modulation [*Radio design*] [*Motorola, Inc.*] ... C-Quam
Compatible Residual Sideband (SAUS) ... CRSB
Compatible Sidelobe Suppression Technique (AAG) ... CSST
Compatible Single Sideband ... CSSB
Compatible Single Sideband Modulation (SAUS) ... CSSM
Compatible Time-Shared System ... CTSS
Compatible Time-Sharing System [*Massachusetts Institute of Technology*] [*Computer science*] ... CTSS
Compatible Vestigial Sideband (SAUS) ... CVSB
Compatible With (DAVI) ... C/W
Compatible With (STED) ... c/w
Compatible/Cray Time Sharing System [*Computer science*] (VERA) ... CTSS
Compazine [*Tranquilizer*] [*Trademark of Smith, Kline, & French Co.*] ... CPZ
Comp-Data International, Inc. [*Vancouver Stock Exchange symbol*] ... CPN
CompDent Corp. [*Associated Press*] (SAG) ... CompDnt
CompDent Corp. [*NASDAQ symbol*] (SAG) ... CPDN
Compelled Multi-Frequency (SAUS) ... CMF
COMPENDEX [*Computerized Engineering Index, Inc.*] [*Bibliographic database*] (NITA) ... CMPX
Compendious (SAUS) ... Compend
Compendium (SAUS) ... Compend
Compendium of Copyright Office Practices [*A publication*] ... CCP
Compendium of Laws of Armed Forces [*United States*] [*A publication*] (DLA) ... Comp Armed Forces
Compendium of Pharmaceuticals and Specialities [*A publication*] ... CPS
Compendium of Pharmaceuticals and specialties (SAUS) ... CP
Compendium of Plausible Materiel Options [*Army*] ... CPMO
Compensate [*or Compensating*] (KSC) ... COMP
Compensate [*or Compensator*] (AABC) ... COMPEN
Compensated Avalanche Diode ... CAD
Compensated Base [*Medicine*] (DAVI) ... CP
Compensated Character Recognition (SAUS) ... CCR
Compensated Gross Tons [*Measure of shipbuilding capacity*] ... CGT
Compensated Heart Disease (SAUS) ... CHD
Compensated Imaging System (MCD) ... CIS
Compensated Ion Chamber ... CIC
Compensated Ionization Chamber (SAUS) ... CIC
Compensated Laser Ultrasonic Evaluation (SAUS) ... CLUE
Compensated Linear Vector Dipole [*Seismology*] ... CLVD
Compensated Meatball Stabilization (PDAA) ... CMS
Compensated Pulsed Alternator (MCD) ... CPA
Compensated Twisted Nematic Display (CIST) ... CTN
Compensated Work Therapy ... CWT
Compensating (MSA) ... COMPSG
Compensating Air Supply ... CAS
Compensating Errors (SAUS) ... CE
Compensating Filter (SAUS) ... comp fil
Compensation ... CMPNSTN
Compensation (NTIO) ... comp
Compensation (ROG) ... COMPENSON
Compensation (ADA) ... COMPN
Compensation Act [*Forms*] ... CA
Compensation and Pension ... C & P
Compensation and Pension Service [*Veterans Administration*] ... CPS
Compensation Balance [*Watchmaking*] (ROG) ... COMPBAL
Compensation Booster Battery (SAUS) ... CBB
Compensation By Objectives (SAUS) ... CBO
Compensation Court [*Australia*] ... CC
Compensation, Employment, and Performance Management Staff [*Department of Agriculture*] (GFGA) ... CEPMS
Compensation Factor ... CF
Compensation Fee ... CF
Compensation, Pension, and Education (MAE) ... CPE
Compensation System Analyst ... CSA
Compensation System Review ... CSR
Compensation Unit ... CU
Compensator (SAUS) ... Comp
Compensator Design [*Computer science*] ... COMPDES
Compensator Group Adapter [*Military*] (CAAL) ... CGA
Compensators [*JETDS nomenclature*] [*Military*] (CET) ... CN
compensatory (SAUS) ... compen
Compensatory and Contingency Financing Facility [*International Monetary Fund*] ... CCFF
Compensatory Equipment Package (MCD) ... CEP
Compensatory Financing Facility [*International Monetary Fund*] ... CFF
Compensatory Ovarian Hypertrophy [*Endocrinology*] ... COH
Competative Cooperative Agreements Program (GEOI) ... CCAP
Competence Center Electronic Shopping (SAUO) ... CESH
Competence in Clearing Bacilli [*Test for leprosy bacilli*] ... CCB
Competence Level Unit [*Education*] ... CLU
Competence-Based Qualification [*Education*] (AIE) ... CBQ
Competency Based Education ... CBE
Competency Based Teaching (AIE) ... CBT
Competency Level ... CL
Competency Screening Test (EDAC) ... CST
Competency-Based Adult Education ... CBAE
Competency-Based Adult Vocational Education (EDAC) ... CBAVE

Competency-Based Career Education (OICC)	CBCE
Competency-Based Education and Training	CBET
Competency-Based Instruction	CBI
Competency-Based Instruments [Psychology] (DHP)	CBI
Competency-Based Learning [Education]	CBL
Competency-Based Teacher Education	CBTE
Competency-Based Teacher Preparation	CBTP
Competency-Based Teacher Training	CBTT
Competency-Based Testing [Psychology] (DHP)	CBT
Competent Authority	CA
Competent National Authority (SAUO)	CNA
Competent Reliability History Survey [Navy]	CRHS
Competent to Instruct [British military] (DMA)	CTI
Competetive Local Exchange Carrier (SAUS)	CLEC
Competing For Quality (SAUO)	CFQ
Competing Risks	CR
Competition	Comp
Competition [or Competitive]	COMPET
Competition Advocate (COE)	CA
Competition Advocate General [Army]	CAG
Competition and Credit Control [British]	CCC
Competition Engineering Program [Air Force]	CEP
Competition Evaluation Exercise	COMPEX
Competition Hot [In "Harley-Davidson XLCH"]	CH
Competition in Contracting Act (COE)	CCA
Competition in Contracting Act [1984]	CICA
Competition Law and Policy Committee (SAUO)	CLP
Competition of Agriculture and Management of Agricultural Resources (SAUO)	CAMAR
Competition Tribunal [Tribunal de la Concurrence], Ottawa, Ontario [Library symbol] [National Library of Canada] (BIB)	OOCOT
Competition with Confidence (AFIT)	CWC
Competition with Industrial Cooperation	CWIC
Competition-Sensitive Information [Military]	CSI
Competitive Access Provider [Telecommunications]	CAP
Competitive Access Provider	CAPS
Competitive Aircraft Data Summary Sheets (MCD)	COMPASS
Competitive Analysis Benchmarking (AAEL)	CAB
Competitive Analysis Group (AAEL)	CAG
Competitive Business Operation Fund (AAGC)	CBOF
Competitive Design	CD
Competitive Design (SAUS)	COMPDES
Competitive Design/Development (SAUO)	CDD
Competitive Development	CD
Competitive Development Group [Army] (RDA)	CDG
Competitive Development Phase	CDP
Competitive Engineering Definition (PDAA)	CED
Competitive Enterprise Institute (SAUS)	CEI
Competitive Enzyme-Linked Immunosorbent Assay	CELISA
Competitive Equality Banking Act [1987]	CEBA
Competitive Equilibrium [Mathematics]	CE
Competitive Evaluation Exercise (SAUO)	COMPEX
Competitive Events Guidelines [A publication] (EAAP)	CEG
Competitive Health and Medical Plan [Proposed]	CHAMP
Competitive Impulse, Non-Carcinogenic Hypergol	CINCH
Competitive in Situ Hybridization (DMAA)	CISH
Competitive Industrial Concept Formulation	CICF
Competitive Inhibition Enzyme Immunoassay [Analytical biochemistry]	CIEIA
Competitive Intelligence [Corporate libraries]	CI
Competitive Local Exchange Carrier (IGQR)	CLEC
Competitive Long Distance Coalition	CLDC
Competitive Market Analysis [Real estate]	CMA
Competitive Media Reporting [An association] [Broadcasting] (WDMC)	CMR
Competitive Medical Organization (MELL)	CMO
Competitive Medical Plans	CMP
Competitive Operational Readiness Evaluation [Air Force] (AFM)	CORE
Competitive Pipeline Price Index	CPPI
Competitive Placement Plan (SAUS)	CPP
Competitive Protein Binding [Clinical chemistry]	CPB
Competitive Protein-Binding Analysis [or Assay]	CPBA
Competitive Prototype Phase (MCD)	CPP
Competitive Prototyping Strategy (DOMA)	CPS
Competitive Research Grants Office [for federal research in agriculture]	CRGO
Competitive Sensitive (MCD)	CS
Competitive State Anxiety Inventory (EDAC)	CSAI
Competitive Statistical Analysis (IAA)	COMSTAT
Competitive Statistics (SAUS)	COMSTAT
Competitive Strategies [NATO]	CS
Competitive Strategies Initiative [Military] (DOMA)	CSI
Competitive Study Engineer	CSE
Competitive Technologies [AMEX symbol] (TTSB)	CTT
Competitive Technologies, Inc. [Formerly, University Patents] [Associated Press] (SAG)	CompTch
Competitive Technologies, Inc. [Formerly, University Patents] [AMEX symbol] (SAG)	CTT
Competitive Telecommunications Association (EA)	COMPTEL
Competitive Training Unit Exercise (ACAE)	COMTUEX
Competitive Voluntary Indefinite [Status] [Army] (INF)	CVI
Competitive-Binding Assay	CBA
Competitor (ADA)	COMP
Competitor (SAUS)	Comp
Compiegne/Margny [France] [ICAO location identifier] (ICLI)	LFAD
Compilable Abstract Ada Syntax (SAUS)	CAAS
Compilation (SAUS)	Cmpn
Compilation (ROG)	COMP
Compilation, Mission support, Integration & training facility (SAUS)	CMI
Compilation of the Federal Register	CFR
Compilation of Typed Logics (SAUS)	CTL
Compilation Stage (SAUS)	CS
Compile and Execute (SAUS)	C/E
Compile and Test (BUR)	CAT
Compile, Load, and Go [Computer science] (BUR)	CLG
Compile Online and Go [Computer science]	COLINGO
Compile Time (SAUS)	CT
Compile Time Diagnostic (SAUS)	CTD
Compile Time Expression (SAUS)	CTE
Compile Time Procedure (SAUS)	CTP
Compile Time Statement (SAUS)	CTS
Compile Time Variable (SAUS)	CTV
Compiled (SAUS)	Cmpld
Compiled (SAUS)	CPL
Compiled Laws [A publication] (DLA)	CL
Compiled Laws [A publication] (DLA)	Comp Laws
Compiled Statutes [A publication] (DLA)	Comp St
Compiled Statutes [A publication] (DLA)	Comp Stat
Compiled Statutes [A publication] (DLA)	CS
Compiler (IAA)	COM
Compiler	COMP
Compiler (WDAA)	comp
Compiler	COMPLR
Compiler and Assembler by General Electric	CAGE
Compiler and Generalized Translator [Argonne National Laboratory] [List processor] (IEEE)	COGENT
Compiler Declarative Statement (SAUS)	CDS
Compiler Description Language (SAUS)	CDL
Compiler Design Language (SAUS)	CDL
Compiler Directing Declarative (SAUS)	CDD
Compiler Directing Statement (SAUS)	CDS
Compiler, Executive Program, Assembler Routines	CLEAR
Compiler for Automatic Machine Programming (BUR)	CAMP
Compiler for Automatic Teaching Operation (IEEE)	CATO
Compiler for Writing and Implementing Compilers	CWIC
Compiler Generator (SAUS)	CG
Compiler Generator and Translator [Computer science] (NITA)	COGENT
Compiler Information File [Computer science]	CIF
Compiler Interpreter System (SAUS)	CIS
Compiler Language [Computer science] (DIT)	CL
Compiler Language for Information Processing [System Development Corp.] [Programming language]	CLIP
Compiler Language Utility Extension (SAUS)	CLUE
Compiler, Los Alamos Scientific Laboratories	COLASL
Compiler Method (SAUS)	CM
Compiler Monitor System (BUR)	CMS
Compiler Object Code [Telecommunications] (TEL)	COC
Compiler of Differentiable Expressions (PDAA)	CODEX
Compiler Operation (SAUS)	CO
Compiler Oriented for Multiprogramming and Multiprocessing Environments (IEEE)	COMMEN
Compiler System	COSY
Compiler Target Language [Computer science] (MHDB)	CTL
Compiler Writer's Virtual Machine	CWVM
Compiler Writing Language (SAUS)	XPL
Compiler Writing System (MCD)	CWS
Compiler-Assembler	COMPASS
Compiler-Compiler (RALS)	CC
Compiler/Massachusetts Institute of Technology (IEEE)	COMIT
Compile-time Reconfigurable Logic (SAUS)	CRL
Compiling Duration (SAUS)	CD
Compiling Routine (SAUS)	CR
Complainant (ROG)	COMPLAINT
Complainant	COMPLT
Complainant (SAUS)	Complt
Complainant (ROG)	COMPT
Complains Of [Medicine]	C/O
complains of (SAUS)	c/o
Complaint	COMP
Complaint (ROG)	COMPLT
Complaint (SAUS)	Complt
Complaint (DMAA)	Cx
Complaint Administration System [Office of Federal Contract Compliance] (GFGA)	CAS
Complaint Docket [Legal term] (DLA)	CD
Complaint Type Investigation [Army] (AABC)	CTI
Complaints Investigation Branch [Scotland Yard]	CIB
Comple Tel Europe NV [NASDAQ symbol] (SG)	CLTL
Compleat Health Corp. [Vancouver Stock Exchange symbol]	CLQ
Complement [Linguistics]	C
Complement [Immunochemistry]	C
Complement [Immunochemistry] (DAVI)	Cb
Complement (IAA)	CMPL
Complement (MSA)	CMPLM
Complement (MUGU)	COM
Complement (AFM)	COMP
Complement	COMPL
Complement (ADWA)	compl
Complement	CPL
Complement	CPLMT
Complement (SAUS)	Cplmt
Complement 3 Degradation Product [Immunology]	C3DP
Complement Accumulator	CMA

Complement Add (SAUS) .... CA
Complement and Increment Accumulator (SAUS) .... CIA
Complement Binding Antibody (SAUS) .... CBA
Complement Carry .... CMC
Complement Carry Flag (SAUS) .... CMF
Complement Component Three [Hematology] C3
Complement Factor H-Like [Protein] [Medicine] (DMAA) .... CFHL
Complement File (SAUS) .... COMP File
Complement Fixation (SAUS) .... CF
Complement Fixation [Immunochemistry] (DAVI) .... CMP-FX
Complement Fixation [Immunology] (DAVI) .... com fix
Complement Fixation Avian Leucosis Test (SAUS) .... COFAL-Test
Complement Fixation Inhibition [Test] [Immunology] .... CFI
Complement Fixation Reaction (SAUS) .... CFR
Complement Form (SAUS) .... CF
Complement Gate (SAUS) .... CG
Complement Hemolyzing 50 [Immunology] CH50
Complement Histolytica-Indirect Hemagglutination [Hematology] (DAVI) .... EH-IHA
Complement Link (SAUS) .... CML
Complement Lysis Inhibitor (DMAA) CLI
Complement Mediated Cell Lysis [Immunology] .... CML
Complement of Latitude .... Co-Lat
Complement Receptor [Immunology] .... CR
Complement Receptor Location (DB) .... CRL
Complement Receptor Lymphocyte [Immunology] .... CRL
Complement Receptor Type 1 [Medicine] (DMAA) CR1
Complement Regulatory Protein [Genetics] .... CRP
Complement Requiring Neutralizing .... CRN
Complement Restriction Factors [Biochemistry] .... CRF
Complement Storage (SAUS) .... CS
Complement-Activated Plasma [Medicine] (MELL) .... CAP
Complementarity-Determining Region [Immunology] .... CDR
Complementarity-Determining Residue [Genetics] .... CDR
Complementary (SAUS) .... Compl
Complementary Analysis Team [NASA] (KSC) .... CAT
Complementary and Alternative Medicine (SAUO) .... CAM
Complementary Binary-Coded Decimal (SAUS) .... CBCD
Complementary Bipolar Integrated Circuit [Telecommunications] (TEL) .... CBIC
Complementary Bipolar Transistor (SAUS) .... CBT
Complementary Coded Decimal [Computer science] (HGAA) .... CCD
Complementary Color Removal [Graphic arts] (DGA) .... CCR
Complementary Constant Current Logic (SAUS) C3L
Complementary Constant Current Logic [Computer science] (BUR) CCCL
Complementary Constant Current Logic [Computer science] (MCD) .... C³L
Complementary Cumulative Distribution Function [Mathematics] .... CCDF
Complementary Cumulative Distribution Function [Environmental science] (COE) .... CODF
Complementary Diode Transistor Logic (SAUS) .... CDTL
Complementary Distribution [Linguistics] .... CD
Complementary Emitter Follower .... CEF
Complementary Enhanced Metal Oxide Semiconductor [Electronics] (NITA) .... CEMOS
Complementary Error Function (SAUS) .... CERFC
Complementary Even Parity (PDAA) .... CEP
Complementary Expendable Launch Vehicle [Space technology] .... CELV
Complementary Function (ACAE) .... CF
Complementary Heterostructure Field Effect Transistor (ADWA) .... C-HFET
Complementary High-Performance Metal-Oxide Semiconductor .... CHMOS
Complementary Information System (SAUS) .... CIS
Complementary Instruction Book [Military] .... CIB
Complementary Insulated-Gate Field-Effect Transistor (PDAA) .... CIGFET
Complementary Magnetic Oxide on Silicone [Computer science] .... CMOS
Complementary Manual [Military] .... CM
Complementary Metal-Oxide Semiconductor (PCM) .... CMOS
Complementary Metal-Oxide Semiconductor Transistor [Electronics] .... CMOS
Complementary Metal-Oxide Semiconductor Transistor [Electronics] .... CMOST
Complementary Metal-Oxide Semiconductor/Silicon-on-Sapphire [Electronics] .... CMOS/SOS
Complementary Metal-Oxide Silicon (NASA) .... CMOS
Complementary Micrologic (SAUS) .... CML
Complementary Multi Role Fighter (ACAE) .... CMRF
Complementary Multirole Fighter (ACAE) .... CMF
Complementary Offset Binary (HGAA) .... COB
Complementary Pair Switch Element .... CPSE
Complementary Return to Bias (SAUS) .... CRB
Complementary Ribonucleic Acid (ADWA) .... cRNA
Complementary Semiconductor .... CSCR
Complementary Semiconductor Controlled Rectifier (MSA) .... CSCR
Complementary Silicon on Sapphire (MHDI) .... CSOS
Complementary Software House (VERA) .... CSH
Complementary Straight Binary [Computer science] (HGAA) .... CSB
Complementary Straight Binary Code (SAUS) .... CSB Code
Complementary Switching (IAA) .... COS
Complementary Symmetrically (SAUS) .... COS
Complementary Symmetry (IAA) .... COS
Complementary Symmetry [Electronics] (ECII) .... CS
Complementary Symmetry/Metal Oxide Semiconductor .... COS/MOS
Complementary Technical Report [Military] (AFM) .... COMTECHREP
Complementary Transistor Diode Logic (SAUS) .... CTDL
Complementary Transistor Logic [Computer science] .... CTL
Complementary Transistor Register [Computer science] (IAA) .... CTR
Complementary Transistor Register Logic (SAUS) .... CTRL
Complementary Transistor Switch .... CTS
Complementary Transistor-Transistor Logic .... CTTL

Complementary Under-Color Removal [Printing technology] .... CUCR
Complementary Unijunction Transistor (IEEE) .... CUJT
Complementary/Alternative Medicine [Medicine] .... CAM
Complementary-Transistor-Transistor Logic (SAUS) .... CTyL
Complement-Binding Antibody (DB) .... CBAB
Complement-Dependent Antibody (DB) .... CDA
Complement-Dependent Cytotoxicity [Immunology] .... CDC
Complement-Fixation [Immunology] .... CF
Complement-Fixation for Avian Leucosis Virus [Immunology] .... COFAL
Complement-Fixation for Murine Leukemia [Test] [Immunology] .... COMUL
Complement-Fixation Test [Immunology] .... CFT
Complement-Fixing Antibody [Immunology] .... CFA
Complement-Fixing Antibody Consumption [Immunology] (DAVI) .... CFAC
Complement-Fixing Islet Cell Antibodies [Immunochemistry] .... CF-ICA
Complement-Fixing-Inhibiting (SAUS) .... CFI
Complement-Free Reed Muller Canonical (SAUS) .... CFRMC
Complement-Mediated Neutrophil Activation [Medicine] (DMAA) .... CMNA
Complete (NASA) C
Complete (MUGU) .... CMPL
Complete .... CMPLT
Complete (ROG) .... COMP
Complete (NTIO) .... comp
Complete (AAG) .... COMPL
Complete (ADWA) .... cpl
Complete .... CPL
Complete (ROG) .... CPLT
Complete Active Space Self Consistent Field (MCD) .... CASSCF
Complete Address Constant .... CAC
Complete ADR [Applied Data Research, Inc.] Environment (EA) .... CADRE
Complete Affinity Server Enclosure [Computer science] .... CASE
Complete and Pain-Free (STED) .... C & P
Complete and Ready for Test (SAUS) .... CART
Complete Androgen Insensitivity Syndrome [Medicine] (DMAA) .... CAIS
Complete Answering Machine .... CAM
Complete Anthropomorphic Protective Enclosure (SAA) .... CAPE
Complete Area Network (SAUO) .... CAN
Complete Arena Networks [Computer science] (VERA) .... CAN
Complete Assembly for Ferry [Air Force] .... CAF
Complete Assembly for Strike .... CAS
Complete Atmospheric Energetics Experiment [Marine science] (OSRA) .... CAENEX
Complete Atrioventricular Block [Medicine] (DMAA) .... CAVB
[The] Complete Attorney [A publication] (DLA) .... C Atty
Complete Attorney [A publication] (DLA) .... Com Att
Complete Automatic Rating Technique (SAUS) .... CART
Complete Automatic Reliability (or Reliable) Testing (SAUS) .... CART
Complete Automatic Reliability Tester (SAUS) .... CART
Complete Automatic Reliable Testing .... CART
Complete Bachground Investigation (SAUS) .... CBI
Complete Background Investigation .... CBI
Complete Band Shape (MCD) .... CBS
Complete Basis of Issue [Military] (AABC) .... CBOI
Complete Basis of Issue Plan [Military] (AABC) .... CBOIP
Complete Bed Rest [Medicine] .... CBR
[The] Complete Bible, An American Translation [A publication] (BJA) .... AmTrans
Complete Blood Count [Medicine] .... CBC
Complete Breech Presentation [Medicine] (MELL) .... CBP
Complete Business Solutions [NASDAQ symbol] (SG) .... CBSI
Complete Calls To [Telecommunications] (TEL) .... CCT
Complete Cell Analysis [Medicine] .... CCA
Complete Cleft Palate (MELL) .... CCP
Complete Code (SAUS) CC
[A] Complete Computerized Examination System [Anatomy and physiology] .... ACCESS
Complete Controlled Quick Release .... CQR
Complete Correlation Matrix Memory [Computer science] (PDAA) .... CCMM
Complete Count Program [Bureau of the Census] (GFGA) .... CCP
Complete Crew .... CCRU
Complete Crew (SAUS) .... CCru
Complete Deal [Coupon redemption] .... C/D
Complete Depolarization .... DC
Complete Design Release [Navy] (NG) .... CDR
Complete Disk Checker [Compact disks] .... CDC
Complete Drawing [Animation] (NTCM) .... CD
Complete Effort Authorized (ACAE) .... CEA
Complete Element Matrix Analysis from Scatter [Spectrometry] .... CEMAS
Complete Engine Repair (NG) .... CER
Complete Engine Repair Requirements Card [DoD] .... CERRC
Complete Engineering Release .... CER
Complete Equipment Fighting Order [British military] (DMA) .... CEFO
Complete Equipment Schedule (SAUS) .... CES
Complete Fabrication .... CF
Complete Freuds Adjunct (SAUS) .... CFA
Complete Freund's Adjuvant [Immunology] .... CFA
Complete Games [Baseball] .... CG
Complete Health and Safety Evaluation Scheme (HEAS) .... CHASE
Complete Heart Block [Medicine] .... CHB
Complete Help and Assistance Necessary for College Education (SAUS) .... CHANCE
Complete Instruction (SAUS) CI
Complete Iridectomy [Ophthalmology] CI
Complete Isaiah Scroll from Qumran. Cave One (BJA) 1QIaIQIsa
Complete Isaiah Scroll from Qumran. Cave One (SAUS) 1QIaIQIsa
Complete Island Etch (SAUS) .... CIE
Complete Left Bundle Branch Block [Medicine] (MAE) .... CLBBB

Complete Line Interface Circuit (SAUS) CLIC
Complete Load and Go (SAUS) .... CLG
Complete Loss of Feedwater [Nuclear energy] (NRCH) .... CLOF
Complete Lower Motor Neuron [Lesion] [Neurology] (DAVI) .... CLMN
Complete Management [AMEX symbol] (TTSB) .... CMI
Complete Management, Inc. [AMEX symbol] (SAG) .... CMI
Complete Management, Inc. [Associated Press] (SAG) .... CmpMan
Complete Management Systems .... CMS
Complete Matched Set [Philately] .... CMS
Complete Medium [Microbiology] .... CM
Complete Meeting Package [Meetings industry] .... CMP
Complete Minimum Essential Medium .... CMEM
Complete Missile Container .... CMC
Complete Mixing Activated Sludge .... CMAS
Complete Neglect of Differential Overlap [Quantum mechanics] .... CNDO
Complete Network Centre (SAUO) .... CNC
Complete No-Good (SAUS) .... CNG
Complete Occupational Therapy Evaluation (MELL) .... COTE
Complete Operating Equipment .... COE
Complete Operating Information [Computer science] .... COIN
Complete Operational Capability .... COC
Complete Operational Software [Telecommunications] (TEL) .... OSC
Complete Operational System (MCD) .... COS
Complete Optoelectronic with Silicon High Efficiency Detectors
   (SAUS) .... COWSHED
Complete (or Complex) Atmospheric Energetics Experiment (SAUS) ..... CAENEX
Complete Parallel Activity and Security System (IAA) .... COMPASS
Complete Partitioning (SAUS) .... CP
Complete Physical [Medicine] (DAVI) .... CP
Complete Physical Examination (SAUS) .... CPE
Complete Physical Examination [Medicine] (DAVI) .... CPX
Complete Power Failure [Aviation] .... CPF
Complete Power Signalling Local Control System (SAUS) .... CPSLCS
Complete Provisions Only .... CPO
Complete Purchased Part (SAUS) .... CPP
Complete Quadratic Combination [Computer science] .... CQC
Complete Reaction of Degeneration [Physiology] .... CRD
Complete Reading-Writing Cycle (SAUS) .... CRWC
Complete Remission [Medicine] .... CR
Complete Remission Rate [Oncology] .... CRR
Complete Responders [to medication] .... CR's
Complete Response [Medicine] .... CR
Complete Right Bundle Branch Block [Cardiology] .... CRBBB
Complete Round [Technical drawings] .... CR
Complete Round Ammunition Shipment .... CRAMSHIP
Complete Round Chart .... CRC
Complete Sequence Number Packet [Computer science] (ACRL) .... CSNP
Complete Sequential Machine (SAUS) .... CSM
Complete Service Life .... CSL
Complete Service Supplier [Vendor operations] .... CSS
Complete Set of Detection Tests (SAUS) .... CSDTs
Complete Solicitor [A publication] (DLA) .... Comp Sol
Complete Solicitor [A publication] (DLA) .... C Sol
Complete State Coding (SAUS) .... CSC
Complete Statistical System .... CSS
Complete Store Cycle (SAUS) .... CSC
Complete Testicular Feminization Syndrome (MELL) .... CTFS
Complete Translation [Telecommunications] (TEL) .... CT
Complete Transposition of Great Arteries [Medicine] (DMAA) .... CTGA
Complete Treatment Module [Telecommunications] (TEL) .... CTM
Complete Utter Monumental Foul-Up [Military slang] [Bowdlerized
   version] .... CUMFU
Complete Utter Monumental Military Foul-Up [Slang] [Bowdlerized
   version] .... CUMMFU
Complete Vehicle Erector (SAA) .... CVE
Complete Verification Record (MCD) .... CVE
Complete With (MSA) .... C/W
Complete with Related Order [Telecommunications] (TEL) .... CRO
Completed .... CM
Completed (VRA) .... compl
Completed (NAKS) .... COMPL
Completed (SAUS) .... Compl
Completed Active Duty Requirements, Enlisted [Military] .... CADRE
Completed as Ordered (ECII) .... CAO
Completed Contract Method (AAGC) .... CCM
Completed Discharge .... CODIS
Completed Landing (SAUS) .... COLND
Completed Loading [Navy] .... COLOD
Completed Procedure Turn [Aviation] (FAAC) .... COPT
Completed Stroke [Neurology] (DAVI) .... CS
Completed Suicide [Psychiatry] (DAVI) .... CS
Completed Token Packet (SAUS) .... CTP
Completely Automated Operational System (SAUS) .... CAOS
Completely Automated Technique for Cataloguing and Acquisition of
   Literature forLibraries (NITA) .... CATCALL
Completely Automatic Operational System [UNIVAC] .... CAOS
Completely Built Up [Automotive manufacturing] .... CBU
Completely Controllable (SAUS) CC
Completely Denatured .... CD
Completely Denatured Alcohol .... CDA
Completely Finished Sets .... CFS
Completely Healed (MELL) .... CH
Completely Integrated Range Instrumentation System [NASA] .... CIRIS
Completely Integrated Reference Instrumentation System (SAUS) .... CIRIS
Completely Interconnected Computer (SAUS) CIC

Completely in-the-Canal [Audiology] CIC
Completely Knocked Down [i.e., disassembled, as a toy or piece of furniture
   which must be assembled before use] [Freight] .... CKD
Completely Knocked Down [i.e., disassembled, as a toy or piece of furniture
   which must be assembled before use] [Freight] .... COMKD
Completely Overlapped Subarray Antenna (MCD) .... COSA
Completely Randomized Design (STED) .... CRD
Completely Reliable Source for Intelligence Information .... A
Completely Ridiculous Anthropic Principle (SAUS) .... CRAP
Completely Self-Protected (SAUS) .... CSP
Completely Separating System (SAUS) .... CSS
Completely State Controllable (SAUS) .... CSC
Completely Symmetric Function (PDAA) .... CSF
Completely Universal Processor and I/O [Input/Output] Design [Computer
   science] .... CUPID
Completing (SAUS) .... CPLTG
Completion (SAUS) .... Compl
Completion (ROG) .... COMPLON
Completion and Ready for Test (MCD) .... CART
Completion, Arithmetic, Vocabulary, Directions [Psychology] .... CAVD
Completion Code (ECII) CC
Completion Fitting-Out Period .... CFP
Completion Flag [Computer science] (IAA) .... CF
Completion Guarantor [Motion picture financing] (NTCM) .... CG
Completion of Bed Occupancy Care [Veterans Administration] .... CBOC
Completion of Call on No Reply (SAUS) .... CCNR
Completion of Calls Meeting Busy [Telecommunications] (NITA) .... CCMB
Completion of Calls to Busy Subscriber [Telecommunications] (DOM) .... CCBS
Completion of Overhaul (DNAB) .... COH
Completion of Post Overhaul Availability (DNAB) .... CPOA
Completion Tour of Duty .... CTD
Completions .... COM
Complex C
Complex .... CMPX
Complex .... COMPLX
Complex .... CPLX
Complex (DMAA) Cx
Complex (KSC) CX
Complex Angle (PDAA) .... CA
Complex Arithmetic Unit (SAUS) .... CAU
Complex Arithmetic Vector Processor (RDA) .... CAVP
Complex Assessment Officer .... CAO
Complex Atmospheric Energetics Experiment [National Science Foundation
   and USSR] .... CAENEX
Complex Behavior Simulator .... CBS
Complex Carbohydrate Research Center [Athens, GA] .... CCRC
Complex Carbohydrate Structural Database [University of Georgia] .... CCSD
Complex Chemical Reaction .... CCR
Complex Coherence Function (PDAA) .... CCF
Complex Conjugate (MCD) CC
Complex Contrast Transmission Function (SAUS) .... CCTF
Complex Control Center (NAKS) ccc
Complex Control Center (KSC) CCC
Complex Control Equipment [NASA] (IAA) .... CCE
Complex Control Room [NASA] (KSC) .... CCR
Complex Control Set (NASA) .... CCS
Complex Coordination Test (AAG) .... CCT
Complex Data Entry (SAUS) .... CDE
Complex Effluent Toxicity Information System [Environmental Protection
   Agency] .... CETIS
Complex Effluent Toxicity Testing Program (EEVL) .... CETTP
Complex Electromechanical Device .... CEM
Complex Empirical Orthogonal Function [Mathematics] .... CEOF
Complex Energetics Experiment .... CENEX
Complex Equipment Contract (MCD) .... CEC
Complex Facility Console [Aerospace] (AAG) .... CFC
Complex Facility Control (SAUS) .... CFC
Complex Facility Operator [Aerospace] (AAG) .... CFO
Complex Field Amplitude .... CFA
Complex Fourier Transform .... CFT
Complex Geometry of Nature (SAUO) .... CGN
Complex Ginzburg-Landau Equation [Physics] [For study of spatio temporal
   chaos] .... CGLE
Complex Hazardous Air Release Model .... CHARM
Complex Hybrid Integrated Circuit [Electronics] (IAA) .... CHIC
Complex Impedance Spectroscopy .... CIS
Complex Information Processing (PDAA) .... CIP
Complex Inorganic Color Pigment [Chemistry] .... CICP
Complex Instruction Set Computer (MCD) .... CISC
Complex Integrated Circuit CIC
Complex Kohn Variation principle (SAUS) .... CKVA
Complex Layered Oxide [Physical chemistry] .... CLO
Complex Loading (SAUS) CL
Complex Logarithm (SAUS) .... CLOG
Complex Logical Operation (SAUS) .... CLO
Complex Maintenance Facility [Deep Space Instrumentation Facility,
   NASA] .... CMF
Complex Mode (SAUS) .... CM
Complex Modulus Apparatus .... CMA
Complex Motor Unit [Medicine] (HGAA) .... CMU
Complex Node Representation .... CNR
Complex Notophyll Vine Forest .... CNVF
Complex Optical Array (SAUS) .... COA
Complex Orbital Near-Earth Observations of the Solar Activity
   (SAUS) .... CORONAS

Complex Overhaul (NVT)	COH
Complex Partial Seizures [Medicine] (DMAA)	CPS
Complex Potential Model (SAUS)	CPM
Complex Problem-Solving Environment	CPSE
Complex Programmable Logic Device (AEBE)	CPLD
Complex Programming (SAUS)	CP
Complex Reaction Time [or Timer] [Neurology] (AAMN)	CRT
Complex Reduced-Instruction-Set Architecture [Intel Corp.]	CRISC
Complex Refraction Index (SAUS)	CRI
Complex Relation Object	ECO
Complex Repetitive Discharge [Neurophysiology]	CRD
Complex Safety Officer [Air Force] (AFM)	CSO
Complex Safety Technician [Air Force] (AFM)	CST
Complex Spikes	CS
Complex Support Controller [NASA] (KSC)	CSC
Complex Support Office [NASA] (KSC)	CSO
Complex Systems Research (SAUO)	CSR
Complex Systems Research Center [University of New Hampshire] [Research center] (RCD)	CSRC
Complex Targets Evaluation Model (MCD)	CTEM
Complex Terrain Data Base (SAUS)	CTM
Complex Terrain Deposition [Model] [Marine science] (OSRA)	COMPDEP
Complex Terrain Screening [Model] [Marine science] (OSRA)	CTSCREEN
Complex Terrain Screening Model (EEVL)	COMPLEX
Complex Utility Routine	CUR
Complex Variable Boundary Element Method (IAA)	CVBEM
Complex Vehicle Erector (KSC)	CVE
Complex Wiring System	CWS
Complex Working [Army]	CX
Complexant Concentrate (ABAC)	CC
Complexing Agent (SAUS)	CA
Complexity	C
Complexity & Artificial Life Research Concept for Self-Organizing Systems (SAUO)	CALResCo
Complex-Reduced Instruction Set Computer (VERA)	CRISC
Complex-Reduced Instruction Set Processor (VERA)	CRISP
Complex-Valued Non-Linear Discriminant Function (PDAA)	CNDF
Compliance [Volume change per unit of applied pressure] [Medicine] (DAVI)	C
Compliance	CMP
Compliance (TBD)	Cmpl
Compliance	COMPL
Compliance (KSC)	COMPLI
Compliance (SAUS)	Compli
Compliance Advisory Panel [Environmental Protection Agency]	CAP
Compliance Aid for Pharmaceuticals	CAP
Compliance and Investigations Group [U.S. Office of Personnel Management] (BARN)	CIG
Compliance and Law Enforcement (SAUS)	CLE
Compliance and Program Staff to the Deputy Assistant Administrator [Environmental Protection Agency] (GFGA)	CPSDAA
Compliance and Security (SAA)	CS
Compliance Assurance Agreement [Environmental Protection Agency] (GFGA)	CAA
Compliance Assurance Monitoring [Environmental Protection Agency]	CAM
Compliance Audit Program [Environmental technology]	CAP
Compliance Biomonitoring Inspection [Environmental Protection Agency] (GFGA)	CBI
Compliance Cost Assessments (HEAS)	CCA
Compliance Data System [Environmental Protection Agency] (MCD)	CDS
Compliance Division [Environmental Protection Agency] (GFGA)	CD
Compliance Evaluation Inspection [Environmental Protection Agency] (GFGA)	CEI
Compliance Index (DB)	CI
Compliance Level [Automotive emissions standards]	CL
Compliance Management Information System [FAA] (TAG)	CCMIS
Compliance Monitor Evaluation Log	CMEL
Compliance Officer [Department of Labor]	CO
Compliance Order Guidance [Environmental science] (COE)	COG
Compliance Order Guide	COG
Compliance Policy and Planning [Environmental Protection Agency] (GFGA)	CPP
Compliance Policy Guide [Food and Drug Administration]	CPG
Compliance Program and Schedule [Environmental Protection Agency] (GFGA)	CPS
Compliance Registered Options Principal (MHDB)	CROP
Compliance Report and Plan [Environmental science] (COE)	CRP
Compliance Review Commission (SAUO)	CRC
Compliance Review Information System [Office of Federal Contract Compliance] (GFGA)	CRIS
Compliance Review Unit (OICC)	CRU
Compliance Safety and Health Officer [Occupational Safety and Health Administration]	CSHO
Compliance Sampling Inspection [Environmental Protection Agency] (GFGA)	CSI
Compliance Schedule Approval (DOMA)	CSA
Compliance Schedule for Existing Sources [Environmental Protection Agency]	CSEC
Compliance Staff (EEVL)	CS
Compliance Test and Evaluation	CTE
Compliance Verification (SAUS)	CV
Compliance with Requirements (MCD)	CWR
Compliant Utilities and Applications [Computer science] (PCM)	CUA
Complicated Delivery [Obstetrics]	CD
Complicated Urinary Tract Infection [Medicine]	CUTI
Complication [Medicine] (DAVI)	CCX

Complication [Medicine] (AAMN)	CM
Complication [Medicine]	comp
Complication [Medicine]	COMPL
Complication [Medicine] (AAMN)	complic
Complications (STED)	cm
Complied With (AFIT)	CW
Compliment (ROG)	COMP
Compliment	COMPL
Compliment (SAUS)	Compl
Compliment (ROG)	COMPT
Complimentary (WDMC)	comp
Complimentary and Alternate Medicine (SAUS)	CAAM
Complimentary Copy	COMP
Complimentary Metal Oxide Semiconductor [Electronics] (ACRL)	CMOS
Complimentary Network Service [Telecommunications] (ACRL)	CNS
Complimentary symmetry Metal Oxide Semiconductor (SAUS)	CMOS
Complimentary Technical Manual	CTM
Compliments (ROG)	COMPTS
Compline	CP
Compline (WGA)	CPL
Complink Ltd. [NASDAQ symbol] (SAG)	CLNK
Complink Ltd. [Associated Press] (SAG)	Complnk
Complimentary Chromatic Adaptation [Plant Biology]	CCA
Component (DAVI)	C
Component (AFM)	CMPNT
Component (AAG)	CMPT
Component (AFM)	COMP
Component	COMPNNT
Component (SAUS)	Cpo
Component Acceptance Procedure (IAA)	CAP
Component Acceptance Test (IAA)	CAT
Component Acceptance Test System (SAUS)	CATS
Component Acquisition Executive (DOMA)	CAE
Component Action List [NASA] (KSC)	CAL
Component Advanced Technology Test Bed [US Army Tank-Automotive Command] (RDA)	CATTB
Component Advanced Technology Test-Bed (SAUS)	CATT-B
Component Analog Video (NTCM)	CAV
Component & Engine Structural Assessment Research programme (SAUS)	CAESAR
Component and Material Engineering Request	CMER
Component and Material Evaluation Loop [Nuclear energy] (NRCH)	CAMEL
Component and Network Testing (SAUS)	C/NT
Component Approval Process (SAUS)	CAP
Component Automatic Programmed Checkout Equipment (SAUS)	CAPChE
Component Automatic-Program Checkout Equipment [Aerospace] (AAG)	CAPCHE
Component Board (MSA)	CB
Component Board Assembly (MSA)	CBA
Component Broker (SAUS)	CB
Component Catalog Review (IAA)	CCR
Component Change Control [Navy] (NG)	CCC
Component Change Control Board [DoD]	CCCB
Component Change Order (MCD)	CCO
Component Change Request (MCD)	CCR
Component Characteristic File (DNAB)	CCF
Component Characteristics Record	CCR
Component Check [Nuclear energy] (NRCH)	CC
Component Check Test [Nuclear energy] (NRCH)	CC (Test)
Component Check Test (SAUS)	CC Test
Component Checkout Area (AAG)	CCA
Component Commander [Military]	CC
Component Configuration Control Board (AFIT)	CCCB
Component Control Committee [DoD]	CCC
Component Control Expediter Unit (ACAE)	CCEU
Component Control Index [Navy] (AFIT)	CCI
Component Control Issue Unit (DNAB)	CCIU
Component Control Section	CCS
Component Control Unit (DNAB)	CCU
Component Cooling [Nuclear energy] (NRCH)	CC
Component Cooling Heat Exchanger (IEEE)	CCHX
Component Cooling Service Water [Nuclear energy] (NRCH)	CCSW
Component Cooling System [Nuclear energy] (NRCH)	CCS
Component Cooling Water [Nuclear energy] (NRCH)	CCW
Component Cooling Water System [Nuclear energy] (NRCH)	CCWS
Component Cost Index	CCI
Component Data Bank (SAUS)	CDB
Component Description File (SAUS)	CDF
Component Description Operation Procedure (SAUS)	CDOP
Component Design Augmented by Computer (PDAA)	COMDAC
Component Design Confirmation	CDC
Component Design Document (SAUS)	CDD
Component Design Engineer (SAUS)	Comp Des Engr
Component Design Requirements Review (SAUS)	CDRR
Component Development and Integration Facility [Butte, MT] [Department of Energy]	CDIF
Component Disassembly Station [Nuclear energy] (NRCH)	CDS
Component Division Engineering Information System (SAUS)	CDEIS
Component Economic Area (OTD)	CEA
Component Encoding Stream Construction (SAUS)	CESC
Component End Item (ACAE)	CEI
Component Engineering and Support Laboratory (ACAE)	CESL
Component Engineering Request	CER
Component Error Propagation	CEP
Component Evaluation and Reliability Testing (ACAE)	CERT

Component Event Data Bank (SAUO) .... CEDB
Component Failure Analysis [*Electronics*] (AAEL) .... CFA
Component Failure Impact Analysis [*IBM Corp.*] .... CFIA
Component Failure Summary (KSC) .... CFS
Component Flow Analysis [*Business term*] (MHDW) .... CFA
Component Handling [*Environmental science*] (COE) .... CH
Component Handling and Cleaning Facility [*Energy Research and Development Administration*] .... CHCF
Component Handling Equipment (SAUS) .... CHE
Component Identification .... CID
Component Identification Designation (CAAL) .... CID
Component Identification Sheet (MCD) .... CIS
Component Improvement Program (ACAE) .... CIP
Component Improvement Testing .... CIP
Component Improvement Testing [*Military*] .... CIT
Component Information Management System (SAUS) .... CIMS
Component Integration Labs [*Sunnyvale, CA*] (CDE) .... CI Labs
Component Interface (SAUS) CI
Component Intergration Laboratories CIL
Component Item Manager [*Air Force*] (AFIT) .... CIM
Component Knocked Down (SAUS) .... CKD
Component Library Management System (SAUS) .... CLMS
Component Library Tape (SAUS) .... CLT
Component List [*DoD*] CL
Component Maintenance and Mock-Up Facility [*Nuclear energy*] (NRCH) .... CMMF
Component Maintenance Manual (MCD) .... CMM
Component Management Entity [*Computer science*] (VERA) .... CME
Component Management Interface [*Computer science*] .... CMI
Component Manufacturer [*Foundry Business Systems*] [*Software package*] (NCC) .... CM
Component Meantime Between Removals (MCD) .... CMBR
Component Metal Parts (MSA) .... CMP
Component Modification Cards [*Nuclear energy*] (NRCH) .... CMC
Component Object Model [*Computer science*] .... COM
Component of End Items (MCD) .... COEI
Component Open/Short Monitor .... COSMON
Component Operational Data Notice [*NASA*] (KSC) .... CODN
Component Overhaul/Repair Tracking Sheet (MCD) .... CORTS
Component Panel (SAUS) .... Cpo Pan
Component Part Number (SAUS) .... CPN
Component Parts (MCD) .... CP
Component Parts Clause (AIA) .... CPC
Component Parts manufacturer .... CPM
Component Percentage Shipment Schedule (NG) .... CPSS
Component Pilot Overhaul [*Navy*] (NG) .... CPO
Component Pilot Rework [*Navy*] (NG) .... CPR
Component Pilot Rework/Repair [*Navy*] (MCD) .... CPR/R
Component Placement System [*Electronics*] (EECA) .... COPS
Component Preparation Laboratory [*Oak Ridge*] [*Energy Research and Development Administration*] .... CPL
Component Processing Area (SAUS) .... CPA
Component Procurement Plan (ACAE) .... CPP
Component Quality Assurance .... CQA
Component Quality Assurance Program (SAUO) .... CQAP
Component Reclamation (AFIT) .... COMREC
Component Record Intensive Management .... CRIM
Component Release Reliability Analysis (SAUS) .... CRRA
Component Reliability History Survey (SAUS) .... CRHS
Component Reliability Prediction .... CRP
Component Repair (MSA) .... CR
Component Repair Data Sheets (NG) .... CRDS
Component Repair Program (ACAE) .... CRP
Component Repair Squadron (MCD) .... CRS
Component Repair Technologies Inc. (SAUO) .... CRT
Component Requirement Data Sheet (ACAE) .... CRDS
Component Requiring Intensive Management .... CRIM
Component Reword Analyst (MCD) .... CRA
Component Save List [*Military*] (AFIT) .... CSL
Component Scheduling Procedure .... CSP
Component Scheduling System (SAUS) .... CSS
Component Selection Board (SAUO) .... CSB
Component Selection Record .... CSR
Component Selection Review (SAUS) .... CSR
Component Sequencing and Insertion (PDAA) .... COMSEQIN
Component Sequencing and Insertion [*Computer science*] (MHDB) .... COMSEQUN
Component Services Framework (SAUS) .... CSF
Component Source List (IAA) .... CSL
Component Specification (AAG) .... CS
Component Supports (NRCH) .... CS
Component Test (KSC) .... CT
Component Test Area .... CTA
Component Test Equipment (KSC) .... CTE
Component Test Instruction (SAUS) .... CTI
Component Test Laboratory (KSC) .... CTL
Component Test Requirements Specifications (MCD) .... CTRS
Component Test Set (MCD) .... CTS
Component Test Stand [*Nuclear energy*] (NUCP) .... CTS
Component Test System (IAA) .... CTS
Component Time Control System (CIST) .... CTCS
Component to Part Record .... CPR
Component Tooling Gage (SAUS) .... COTG
Component Transaction Service [*Computer science*] .... CTS
Component Tree (SAUS) .... CT
Component Under Test (NITA) .... CUT
Component Utilization Effectiveness .... CUE
Component Verification Program (ACAE) .... CVP
Component/Equipment (MCD) .... C/E
Components (SAUS) .... COMPOs
Components and Materials Laboratory .... CML
Components Business Operations [*Chrysler campaign to increase sales*] .... CBO
Components Data File (SAUS) .... CDF
Components Data Representative (SAUS) .... CDR
Components Division Inventory Control (SAUS) .... CDIC
Components Division Technical Information System (SAUS) .... CDTIS
Components Evaluation Propulsion System (MCD) .... CEPS
Components Hybrids and Manufacturing Technology (MCD) .... CHMT
Components, Incorporated (SAUO) CI
Components Life Evaluation and Reliability .... CLEAR
Components Managed Laboratory (SAUS) .... CML
Components Material Organization Release (ACAE) .... CMOR
Components of End Items [*Military*] (INF) .... COEL
Components of End Items List (MCD) .... COEIL
Components of Inventory Change Survey [*Bureau of the Census*] (GFGA) .... CINCH
Components Only .... CO
Components Response Information Center (MCD) .... CRIC
Components Technology and Standardization (SAUS) .... CTS
Components Technology Group (SAUO) .... CTG
Components Test Unit (AAG) .... CTU
Compool Look-Up Memory Print .... CLUMP
Compose [*Typesetting*] (WDMC) .... comp
Compose .... COMPS
Composed Document Printing Facility [*IBM Corp.*] .... CDPF
Composed Document Viewing Utility [*IBM Corp.*] .... CDVU
Composer [*MARC relator code*] [*Library of Congress*] (LCCP) .... cmp
Composer (ROG) .... COMP
Composer (SAUS) .... Comp
Composer Recordings, Inc. [*Recording label*] .... CRI
Composers and Authors Union (SAUS) .... UKAM
Composers and Lyricists Guild of America (EA) .... CLGA
Composers Association of New Zealand (SAUO) .... CANZ
Composers, Authors, and Artists of America .... CAAA
Composers, Authors, and Publishers Association of Canada .... CAPAC
Composers' Autograph Publications [*Defunct*] (EA) .... CAP
Composers Cooperative Society [*Later, Composers Theatre*] .... CCS
Composers' Forum for Catholic Worship [*Defunct*] (EA) .... CFCW
Composers' Guild of Great Britain (EAIO) .... CGGB
Composers Theatre (EA) .... CT
Composers-Authors Guild (EA) .... CAG
Composing Reducing Camera [*Microfilm*] (NITA) .... CRC
Composing Room Chapel [*Unions*] [*British*] (DGA) .... CRC
Composite (ROG) C
Composite (ABBR) .... CMPSIT
Composite (MSA) .... CMPST
Composite (SAUS) .... Cmpst
Composite (AFM) .... COMP
Composite (EBF) .... Comp
Composite .... COMPST
Composite CX
Composite Aeronautical Load List .... CALL
Composite Air Defense Battalion (SAUS) .... CADB
Composite Air Operations (SAUS) .... COMAO
Composite Air Strike Force [*Air Force*] .... CASF
Composite Aircraft Program [*Military*] (RDA) .... CAP
Composite Aircraft Squadron [*Navy symbol*] VC
Composite Analog Video .... CAV
Composite Armored Vehicle [*Army*] (RDA) .... CAV
Composite Armored Vehicle Advanced Technology Demonstrator (RDA) .... CAV ATD
Composite Army-Marine .... CAM
Composite Assessment of Leverage (EDAC) .... CAL
Composite Auxiliary Boiler [*of a ship*] (DS) .... CAXB
Composite Auxiliary Boiler Survey [*of a ship*] (DS) .... CAXBS
Composite Boson [*Physics*] .... CB
Composite Can and Tube Institute (EA) .... CCTI
Composite Cell Logic CCL
Composite Checkout [*Aerospace*] (AAG) .... CC/O
Composite Clinical and Laboratory Index [*Medicine*] (DMAA) CCLI
Composite Command (SAUS) CC
Composite Concept Vehicle CCV
Composite Configuration List (ACAE) CCL
Composite Correction Plan [*Environmental Protection Agency*] (GFGA) .... CCP
Composite Cost Effectiveness Index (PDAA) .... CCEI
Composite Cross [*Genetics*] CC
Composite Current Conveyor (SAUS) CCC
Composite Cutoff [*Aerospace*] (AAG) .... CC-O
Composite Cyclic Therapy (MAE) .... CCT
Composite Damage Risk .... CDR
Composite Data Service Vendor (ACAE) .... CDSV
Composite Decompression Chamber (SAUS) .... CDC
Composite Double-Base [*Propellant*] .... CDB
Composite Educational Abilites Scale (AIE) .... CEAS
Composite Electrical Readiness Test (KSC) .... CERT
Composite Electro-chemical Materials (SAUS) .... CEM
Composite Engineering Change Memo [*NASA*] (KSC) .... CECM
Composite External Symbol Dictionary (or Directory) (SAUS) .... CESD
Composite Feed System .... CFS
Composite Flight Data Processing (FAAC) .... CFAD
Composite for the Lunar Excursion Module [*NASA*] (IEEE) .... CLEM

Composite Force Requirements and Development System (SAUO) .... CFDS
Composite Force Training (SAUS) .... CFT
Composite Ganglioneuroblastoma [Oncology] .... CGNB
Composite Group [Air Force] .... COMPG
Composite Health Care System [DoD] .... CHCS
Composite Healthcare System (MELL) .... CHS
Composite High Altitude Radiation Model (SAUS) .... CHARM
Composite Hospital System (SAUO) .... CHS
Composite HTGR [High-Temperature Gas-Cooled Reactor] Analysis Program
    [Nuclear energy] (NRCH) .... CHAP
Composite ID (SAUS) .... CPID
Composite Infantry Fighting Vehicle [Army] .... CIFV
Composite Infrared Spectrometer (ACAE) .... CIRS
Composite Interface Program (SAA) .... CIP
Composite International Diagnostic Interview [Test] (TMMY) .... CIDI
Composite Laminate Automated Sizing for Strength (MCD) .... CLASS
Composite Language Development Group (SAUO) .... CLDG
Composite Launch and Spacecraft Program System (MCD) .... CLASP
Composite Launch Sequence Plan (MCD) .... CLSP
Composite [or Consolidated] Limit Order Book [Stock exchange term] .... CLOB
Composite Lunar Excursion Vehicle (SAUS) .... CLEM
Composite Main Rotor Blade (MCD) .... CMRB
Composite Maintenance Group [Military] [British] .... CMG
Composite Maneuver Augmentation (MCD) .... COMMA
Composite Mechanized Information and Document Retrieval
    System .... COMEINDORS
Composite Medical Facility (AFM) .... CMF
Composite Medium Amplifier (SAUS) .... CMA
Composite Merge .... CM
Composite Military Police Strike Force (VNW) .... CMPSF
Composite Minimum Brightness (PDAA) .... CMB
Composite Mode Adjective Check List [FAA] .... CMACL
Composite Mood Adjective Check List (SAUS) .... CMACL
Composite Multiplex Signal (MCD) .... CMS
Composite Network Node .... CNN
Composite NFE Internal Network (SAUO) .... CNIN
Composite Noise Index (SAUS) .... CNI
Composite Noise Rating [Aviation] .... CNR
Composite Object Reference (AAEL) .... CORE
Composite Observing System for the North Atlantic (ADWA) .... COSNA
Composite Operational Mission Profiles (MCD) .... COMP
Composite Operational Reporting System (CAAL) .... CORS
Composite Optical/X-Ray LASER Microscope .... COXRALM
Composite Optics, Inc. (SAUO) .... COI
Composite Picture Signal (SAUS) .... CPS
Composite Primary Structures (MCD) .... CPS
Composite Professional Performance Score .... CPPS
Composite Quotation System (DICI) .... CQS
Composite RADAR Absorbing Structure (MCD) .... CRAS
Composite RADAR Data Processing (FAAC) .... CRAD
Composite Razor Blade (MCD) .... CRB
Composite Reactor Components Test Activity (NRCH) .... CRCTA
Composite Readiness Test .... CRT
Composite Rear Fuselage .... CRF
Composite Reentry Test Vehicle (MCD) .... CRTV
Composite Regiment (SAUO) .... CR
Composite Reporting System (MCD) .... COMPREP
Composite Research Aircraft .... CRA
Composite Resin Infusion Molding Process .... CRIMP
Composite Score (SAUS) .... CS
Composite Service [Army] (AABC) .... CS
Composite Signal Mixer .... CSM
Composite Signaling [Telecommunications] (TEL) CX
Composite Squadron .... COMPORON
Composite Squadron [Air Force] .... COMPS
Composite Standard Reference Section .... CSRS
Composite Standard Time Units .... CSTU
Composite Station Rate .... CSR
Composite Structures for Advanced Aircraft (MCD) .... CSAA
Composite Support Group [Air Force] .... COMPSG
Composite Support Group (SAUS) .... CSG
Composite Tail Section [Aviation] (MCD) .... CTS
Composite Tape Lay-Up [Engineering] .... CTL
Composite Tape Memory (SAUS) .... CTM
Composite Teacher Rating .... CTR
Composite Technology Ltd. (SAUO) .... CTL
Composite Tool Kit [Military] (AFIT) .... CTK
Composite Training School [British military] (DMA) .... CTS
Composite Training Squadron (SAUO) .... CTS
Composite Training Unit [Military] (NVT) .... COMPTU
Composite Training Unit Exercise [Military] (NVT) .... COMPTUEX
Composite Treatment Score [Medicine] (MEDA) .... CTS
Composite Utility .... CU
Composite Variability Study (ABAC) .... CVS
Composite Video (SAUS) CV
Composite Warfare Commander [Military] (NVT) .... CWC
Composite Warfare Concept (SAUS) .... CWC
Composite Warfare Oceanographic Support Module [Navy] (DOMA) .... CWOSM
Composite Wave [IEEE] .... CW
Composite Wave Filter .... CWF
Composite Weighted Work Unit (AFM) .... CWWU
Composite Wing (MCD) .... COMPW
Composite Wing (SAUS) .... Comp- Wg
Composite Wing (SAUS) .... CW
Compositech Ltd. [Associated Press] (SAG) .... Compt

Compositech Ltd. [Associated Press] (SAG) .... Comptch
Compositech Ltd. [NASDAQ symbol] (SAG) .... CTEK
Composite-Modified Double-Base [Propellant] .... CMDB
Composite-Rate Tax [British] .... CRT
Composites (SAUS) .... COMPOs
Composites Fabricators Association (NTPA) .... CFA
Composites Institute (EA) CI
Composites Institute .... CINS
Composites Institute of Australia .... CIA
Composites Manufacturing Association of the Society of Manufacturing
    Engineers (EA) .... CMA/SME
Composition (MSA) .... CMPSN
Composition (SAUS) .... Cmpsn
Composition .... COMP
Composition (ADWA) .... comp
Composition .... COMPN
Composition (ROG) .... COMPO
Composition (SAUS) .... Compo
Composition .... COMPOS
Composition (VRA) .... comps
Composition .... COMPSN
Composition and Editing Display [Later, MRTT] (MCD) .... COED
Composition and Make-Up .... CAM
Composition and Markup [Graphic arts] (DGA) .... CAM
Composition B (SAUS) .... Comp B
Composition Board (VRA) .... compbd
Composition Caster [Monotype] (DGA) CC
Composition Exploding (PDAA) .... CE
Composition Explosive (SAUS) .... CE
Composition Floor .... COMPF
Composition Information Services [Commercial firm] .... CIS
Composition Material (ADWA) .... compo
Composition Modulated Alloy (ACAE) .... CMA
Composition Node Design Method [For distillation] .... CNDM
Composition of Ending Inventory .... COEI
Composition Printing (SAUS) .... C/P
Composition Reduction Printing .... CRP
Composition Roof .... COMPR
Composition Storage and Retrieval (SAUS) .... COSTAR
Composition Support System (DGA) .... CSSYS
Composition Technology, Inc. .... CTI
Composition Technology Incorporated (SAUO) .... CTI
Composition with Creditors [A publication] (DLA) .... Comp Cred
Composition-4 [Explosive] C-4
Compositional Interdiffusion [Chemistry] (IAA) .... CID
Compositional Rule of Inference (IDAI) .... CRI
Compositions (SAUS) .... COMPOs
Compositor [MARC relator code] [Library of Congress] (LCCP) .... cmt
Compositor [Printers' term] (DSUE) .... COMP
Compositor (WDAA) .... comp
Compositor Hourly Rate (DGA) .... CHR
Compositus [Compound] [Pharmacy] C
Compositus [Compound] [Pharmacy] .... CO
Compositus [Compound] [Pharmacy] .... COMP
Compost (ABBR) .... CMPS
Compost (ABBR) .... CMPST
Composted (ABBR) .... CMPSTD
Composted Hardwood Barks .... CHB
COMPOSTELA Group of Universities (SAUO) .... COMPOSTELA Group
Composting (ABBR) .... CMPSTG
Composting Council (NTPA) CC
Composure (ABBR) .... CMPSU
Compound [Engines] [Lloyd's Register] [Shipping] C
Compound [Medicine] (DHSM) .... CMP
Compound .... CMPD
Compound [Medicine] (AAMN) .... CO
Compound .... COMP
Compound (EBF) .... Comp
Compound .... COMPD
Compound (VRA) .... compd
Compound [Medicine] .... CP
Compound .... CPD
Compound (ADWA) .... cpd
Compound Action Potential [Biology] .... APc
Compound Action Potential [Biology] .... CAP
Compound Animal Feeding Stuffs Manufacturers National Association
    [British] (BI) .... CAFSMNA
Compound Annual Growth Rate [Business term] .... CAGR
Compound Annual Return (WDAA) .... CAR
Compound Batch Identification [Computer science] .... CBI
Compound Carburetion [Automotive engineering] CC
Compound Card Terminal (CET) .... CCT
Compound Cathartic [Pills] CC
Compound Comminuted Fracture [Medicine] .... CCF
Compound Condition (SAUS) CC
Compound Correlated Bivariate Poison (SAUS) .... CCBVP
Compound Cycle Turbine Diesel Engine (MCD) .... CCTDE
Compound Cycle Turbofan Engine (PDAA) .... CCTE
Compound Cyclic Corrosion Test [Materials science] .... CCCT
Compound Department Architecture [Digital Equipment Corp.] [Computer
    science] .... CDA
Compound Diffraction Projector .... CDP
Compound Document Architecture .... CDA
Compound Document Framework [Compulter science] (VERA) .... CDF
Compound Document Interchange Format [Computer science] .... CDIF

Compound Document Management Program [*Computer science*] (CIST) .... CDMP
Compound Document Processor [*Computer science*] .... CDP
Compound Elliptic Concentrator (PDAA) .... CEC
Compound Expression (SAUS) .... CE
Compound Fracture [*Medicine*] .... FC
Compound Handling Machine .... CHM
Compound Hypermetropic Astigmatism [*Ophthalmology*] .... H + Hm
Compound Index File [*Computer science*] (PCM) .... CDX
Compound Induction Step Control (PDAA) .... CISC
Compound Inserting Machine .... CIM
Compound Interest Deposit [*Banking*] (DICI) .... CID
Compound Module (SAUS) .... CM
Compound Muscle Action Potential [*Neurophysiology*] .... CMAP
Compound Muscle/Motor Action Potential (STED) .... CMAP
Compound Myopic Astigmatism [*Medicine*] (MELL) .... CMA
Compound Myopic Astigmatism [*Ophthalmology*] .... M + Am
Compound Net Annual Rate (WDAA) .... CNAR
Compound OLAP Architecture (SAUS) .... COA
Compound Parabolic Concentrator [*Solar energy research*] .... CPC
Compound Phase-Locked Demodulator (SAUS) .... CPLD
Compound Pressure .... CPRESS
Compound Procedural Scientific Language (SAUS) .... COMPROSL
Compound Refractive Lens [*Optics*] .... CRL
Compound Sequential Probability Radio Test (SAUS) .... CSPRT
Compound Sequential Probability Ratio Test .... CSPRT
Compound Series Test [*Intelligence test*] .... CST
Compound Spectral Array .... CSA
Compound Statement (SAUS) .... CS
Compound Valve Hemispherical Head [*Engine*] .... CVH
Compound Vortex Combustion Chamber [*Auto engine*] CVCC
Compound-Cathartic Pill (SAUS) .... CC-Pill
Compounded Annual Rate [*Finance*] (ODBW) .... car
Compounded Interest [*Business term*] CI
Compounding (SAUS) .... Cmpd
Compounding .... COMPNDNG
Compounds (SAUS) .... Cpds
Compound-Specific Radiocarbon Analyses .... CSRA
Comprehending (ROG) .... COMPG
Comprehending Reflex Development, Attitude Formation, Memorizing, Procedural Learing (PDAA) .... CRAMP
Comprehension (SAUS) .... Comp
Comprehensive .... CMPRHNSV
Comprehensive .... COMP
Comprehensive (SAUS) .... Comp
Comprehensive Ability Battery [*Test*] .... CAB
Comprehensive Accreditation Manual for Hospitals (SAUO) .... CAMH
Comprehensive Achievement Monitoring (SAUS) .... CAM
Comprehensive, Adequate and Representative (SAUS) .... CAR
Comprehensive Adult Student Assessment System [*Test*] (TMMY) .... CASAS
Comprehensive Aerial Rainfall Program (SAUS) .... CARP
Comprehensive Aerological Reference Data Set (ARMP) .... CARDS
Comprehensive Agrarian Reform Programme [*Philippines*] (ECON) .... CARP
Comprehensive Agrimedia Measurement Study [*Database*] [*Doane Marketing Research, Inc.*] [*Information service or system*] (CRD) .... CAMS
Comprehensive AIDS Resources Emergency Act of 1990 [*For Ryan White*] [*Medicine*] (TAD) .... CARE
Comprehensive Aircraft Support Effectiveness Evaluation (MCD) .... CASEE
Comprehensive Airport Communications System (PDAA) .... CACS
Comprehensive Airship Sizing and Performance Computer Program .... CASCOMP
Comprehensive All-Purpose (SAUS) .... CAP
Comprehensive Analysis for Universal Scene Evaluation (SAUS) .... CAUSE
Comprehensive Analytical Method of Planning in the University Sphere [*Cost simulation technique*] .... CAMPUS
Comprehensive Analytical Method of Planning in the University Sphere (SAUO) .... CAMPUS
Comprehensive Analytical Methods for Planning in University Systems (SAUO) .... CAMPUS
Comprehensive Analytical Methods of Planning .... CAMP
Comprehensive Analytical Test System .... CATS
Comprehensive Antijam Equipment (MCD) .... CAJE
Comprehensive Approach for Reusable Defense Systems [*DoD*] .... CARDS
Comprehensive Area Service Plan .... CASP
Comprehensive Areal Rainfall Program [*British*] .... CARP
Comprehensive Asbestos Survey (COE) .... CAS
Comprehensive Assembler System [*Programming language*] [*1964*] [*Control Data Corp.*] .... COMPASS
Comprehensive Assembly System (SAUS) .... COMPASS
Comprehensive Assessment and Referral Evaluation [*Medicine*] (DMAA) .... CORE
Comprehensive Assessment Information Rule [*Environmental Protection Agency*] .... CAIR
Comprehensive Assessment of Information Rule (SAUO) .... CAIR
Comprehensive Assessment of Treatment Outcome Research (BARN) .... CATOR
Comprehensive Assessment Program [*Gatta and Valentin*] (TES) .... CAP
Comprehensive Assessment Program (SAUS) .... CAP
Comprehensive Assistance to Undergraduate Science Education [*National Science Foundation*] .... CAUSE
Comprehensive Automated Learning Resources System [*Elgin Community College*] [*Information service or system*] (IID) .... CALS
Comprehensive Automatic Test Equipment (SAUS) .... CATE
Comprehensive Automation of the Hydrometeorological Service .... CAHS
Comprehensive Automotive Release System [*3M Corp.*] [*Computer software*] .... CARS
Comprehensive Beacon RADAR .... CBR
Comprehensive Beacon Radar (SAUS) .... CBR
Comprehensive Behavior Rating Scale for Children (TMMY) .... CBRSC
Comprehensive Behavioral Services Model .... CBSM
Comprehensive Blast and Radiation Assessment System (MCD) .... COBRAS
Comprehensive Budget and Management Information System (MHDI) .... CBMIS
Comprehensive Business System (SAUS) .... CBS
Comprehensive Business Tax .... CBT
Comprehensive Cancer Center [*Ohio State University*] [*Research center*] (RCD) CCC
Comprehensive Cancer Center of Metropolitan Detroit [*National Cancer Institute*] [*Research center*] (RCD) .... CCCMD
Comprehensive Cancer Center Program [*National Cancer Institute*] .... CCCP
Comprehensive Capitol Complex Security Plan (DEMM) .... CCCSP
Comprehensive Carcinogen Policy (EEVL) .... CCP
Comprehensive Cardiac Care Unit [*Medicine*] (DMAA) .... CCCU
Comprehensive Care [*NYSE symbol*] (SPSG) .... CMP
Comprehensive Care [*Associated Press*] (SAG) .... CompCre
Comprehensive Care Clinic (MELL) CCC
Comprehensive Certificate of Origin [*Department of Commerce*] (BARN) .... CCO
Comprehensive Child Care Project (SAUS) .... CCCP
Comprehensive Clinical Evaluation Program [*For Gulf War veterans*] .... CCEP
Comprehensive Close Air Support [*Military*] .... CCAS
Comprehensive College Test .... CCT
Comprehensive Communications and Information System (ACAE) .... CCIS
Comprehensive Community Mental Health Centers Inventory [*Department of Health and Human Services*] (GFGA) .... CCMHC
Comprehensive Community Revitalization Project .... CCRP
Comprehensive Cooperative Agreement (MHDB) .... CCA
Comprehensive Core Medical Library [*Database*] [*BRS Information Technologies*] [*Information service or system*] (IID) .... CCML
Comprehensive Country Programming System [*Department of State*] .... CCPS
Comprehensive Crime Control Act [*1984*] (GFGA) .... CCCA
Comprehensive Data Entry Software (SAUS) .... CDES
Comprehensive Data Handling System [*Environmental Protection Agency*] .... CDHS
Comprehensive Data Management (GFGA) .... CDM
Comprehensive Data Systems (OICC) .... CDS
Comprehensive Day Care Programs [*An association*] (EA) .... CDCP
Comprehensive Developmental Evaluation Chart [*Child development test*] [*Psychology*] .... CDEC
Comprehensive Dishonesty, Disappearance, and Destruction Policy [*Insurance*] .... CDDD
Comprehensive Dishonesty, Disappearance, and Destruction Policy [*Insurance*] .... DDD
Comprehensive Display System .... CDS
Comprehensive Dissertation Abstracts [*University Microfilms International*] [*Information service or system*] .... CDA
Comprehensive Dissertation Database (SAUS) .... CDD
Comprehensive Dissertation Index [*University Microfilms International*] [*Ann Arbor, MI*] [*Bibliographic database*] [*A publication*] .... CDI
Comprehensive Drinker Profile [*Test*] [*Psychology*] .... CDP
Comprehensive Drug Abuse Prevention and Control Act (BARN) .... CDAPC
Comprehensive Drug Abuse Prevention and Control Act (MELL) .... CDAPCA
Comprehensive Drug Literature Computer Tape Service (SAUS) .... DRUGDOC
Comprehensive Dwelling Policies [*Insurance*] .... CDP
Comprehensive Economic Assessment (COE) .... CEA
Comprehensive Economic Data Atlas of China (GEOI) .... CEDAC
Comprehensive Education and Training Administration (SAUO) .... CETA
Comprehensive Educational Improvement and Financing Act .... CEIFA
Comprehensive Electronic Office [*Data General Corp.*] .... CEO
Comprehensive Electronic Office (SAUS) .... CEO
Comprehensive Emergency Assistance System .... CEAS
Comprehensive Emergency Management Plan (DEMM) .... CEMP
Comprehensive Emergency Response (AEPA) .... CERCLA
Comprehensive Emergency Response, Compensation, and Liability Information System (AEPA) .... CERCLIS
Comprehensive Employment and Training Act [*1973*] [*Formerly, MDTA*] [*Expired, 1982*] [*Department of Labor*] .... CETA
Comprehensive Employment and Training Plan [*Department of Labor*] .... CETP
Comprehensive Engine Management System .... CEMS
Comprehensive Envir'l Sys [*NASDAQ symbol*] (TTSB) .... COEV
Comprehensive Environmental Assessment and Response Program (COE) .... CEARP
Comprehensive Environmental Evaluation [*British Antarctic Survey*] .... CEE
Comprehensive Environmental Response, Compensation, and Liability Act [*1980*] .... CERCLA
Comprehensive Environmental Response, Compensation, and Liability Information System (COE) .... CERCLIS
Comprehensive Environmental Response, Compensation and Liability Information System (SAUO) .... CERCLIS
Comprehensive Environmental Responsibility, Compensation, and Liability System .... CERCLIS
Comprehensive Environmental Systems, Inc. [*Associated Press*] (SAG) .... CmpEnv
Comprehensive Environmental Systems, Inc. [*NASDAQ symbol*] (SAG) .... COEV
Comprehensive Epidemiologic Data Resource (ADWA) .... CEDR
Comprehensive Evaluation of Basic Living Skills .... CEBLS
Comprehensive Evaluation System (SAUO) .... CES
Comprehensive Export Schedule [*US*] .... CES
Comprehensive Extended Term Banker's Guarantee (DS) .... CXBG
Comprehensive External Trade Policy [*Export Credits Guarantee Department*] [*British*] .... CET
Comprehensive General and Automobile Liability [*Insurance*] .... CGAL
Comprehensive General Liability Insurance (SAUO) .... CGL
Comprehensive Geriatric Assessment [*Medicine*] (CPH) .... CGA
Comprehensive Grant Program (SAUO) .... CGP

Comprehensive (Ground Water) Monitoring Evaluation [*Environmental Protection Agency*] (ERG) .... CME
Comprehensive (Ground Water) Monitoring Evaluation Log [*Environmental Protection Agency*] (ERG) .... CMEL
Comprehensive Hazardous Material Management Programs (BCP) ...... CHAMMP
Comprehensive Health and Emergency Care [*Medicine*] .... CHEC
Comprehensive Health Assessments and Primary Care for Children [*Proposed*] .... CHAP
Comprehensive Health Care (MELL) .... CHC
Comprehensive Health Center [*Medicine*] .... CHC
Comprehensive Health Education Foundation (EA) .... CHEF
Comprehensive Health Insurance Act .... CHIA
Comprehensive Health Insurance Plan [*or Proposal*] .... CHIP
Comprehensive Health Manpower Training Act [*1971*] .... CHMA
Comprehensive Health Planning [*A requirement for HEW grants to local agencies*] .... CHP
Comprehensive Health Planning Service [*Federal government*] .... CHPS
Comprehensive Healthcare Analysis and Management Program (SAUO) .... CHAMP
Comprehensive Healthcare Clinic (MELL) .... CHCC
Comprehensive Homeless Assistance Plan [*Homeless Assistance Act*] (GFGA) .... CHAP
Comprehensive Hospital and Ambulatory Care Information Networking for Episode Linkage (SAUS) .... CHAINE
Comprehensive Hospital Drug Monitoring (SAUO) .... CHDM
Comprehensive Housing Affordability Strategy .... CHAS
Comprehensive Human Resources Data System (MCD) .... CHRDS
Comprehensive Identification Process [*Child development test*] .... CIP
Comprehensive Improvement Assistance Program [*HUD*] .... CIAP
Comprehensive Incomes and Prices Policy (DICI) .... CIPP
Comprehensive Index to the Publications [*A bibliographic publication*] .... CIP
Comprehensive Industry Distribution System (SAUS) .... CIDS
Comprehensive Industrywide Program of Communication [*Defunct*] (EA) .... CIPC
Comprehensive Information Service .... COMPIS
Comprehensive Information System and Data Base (SAUS) .... CIS&DB
Comprehensive Information System and Database .... CIS & DB
Comprehensive Inorganic Chemistry [*A publication*] CIC
Comprehensive Inorganic Chemistry (journ.) (SAUS) CIC
Comprehensive Integrated Planning Process (ABAC) .... CIPP
Comprehensive Integrated Remote Sensing (SAUS) .... CIRS
Comprehensive Lake Ecosystem Analyzer (SAUS) .... CLEAN
Comprehensive Land Use Plan .... CLUP
Comprehensive Language for Elegant Operating System and Translator Design (PDAA) .... CLEOPATRA
Comprehensive Language Program [*Test*] .... CLP
Comprehensive Logistics Automated Support Program (SAUS) .... CLASP
Comprehensive Long-Term Environmental Action-Navy .... CLEAN
Comprehensive Loss Management, Inc., of Minneapolis (SARE) .... CLMI
Comprehensive Mailing List System [*Library of Congress*] .... CMLS
Comprehensive Major Medical [*Health insurance*] (GHCT) .... CMM
Comprehensive Management Facility (IAA) .... CMF
Comprehensive Management Plan .... CMP
Comprehensive Manpower Planning (OICC) .... CMP
Comprehensive Manufacturing Control System .... CMCS
Comprehensive Medical Plan .... CMP
Comprehensive Medical Society [*Defunct*] (EA) .... CMS
Comprehensive Mental Health Assessment .... CMHA
Comprehensive Migrant Program [*Department of Labor*] .... CMP
Comprehensive Model .... COMO
Comprehensive Monitoring Evaluation .... CME
Comprehensive Nuclear-Test-Ban Treaty (SAUS) .... CTBT
Comprehensive Occupational Data Analysis Program [*Military*] (AABC) .... CODAP
Comprehensive Occupational Therapy Evaluation [*Scale*] .... COTE
Comprehensive Ocean Area Plan (SAUS) .... COAP
Comprehensive Ocean Atmosphere Data Set .... COADS
Comprehensive Ocean-Atmosphere Data Set (SAUO) .... COADS
Comprehensive Offender Program Effort [*Department of Labor*] .... COPE
Comprehensive Omnibus Budget Reconciliation Act (GFGA) .... COBRA
Comprehensive Online Manufacturing and Engineering Tracking System (NITA) .... COMETS
Comprehensive Option Stiffness Method of Structural Analysis (PDAA) .... COSMOS
Comprehensive Organic Chemistry [*A publication*] .... COC
Comprehensive Organometallic Chemistry [*A Publication*] .... COMC
Comprehensive Outpatient Rehabilitation Facility (MEDA) .... COR
Comprehensive Outpatient Rehabilitation Facility [*American Occupational Therapy Association*] .... CORF
Comprehensive Payroll Accounting System (MHDB) .... CPACS
Comprehensive Perl Archiving Network [*Computer science*] .... CPAN
Comprehensive Personal Liability [*Insurance*] .... CPL
Comprehensive Pharmacy Administrative Support System (SAUS) ..... COMPASS
Comprehensive Plan, South Vietnam (CINC) .... CPSVN
Comprehensive Planning Information System (SAUS) .... CPIS
Comprehensive Post Partum (SAUO) .... CPP
Comprehensive Power Management System [*Military*] (CAAL) .... CPMS
Comprehensive Procurement Guidelines [*EPA*] (AAGC) .... CPG
Comprehensive Program for Disarmament (SAUO) .... CPD
Comprehensive Psychopathological Rating Scale .... CPRS
Comprehensive Radar Effects Simulator Trainer (SAUS) .... CREST
Comprehensive Radiance Profile Synthesizer .... CORPS
Comprehensive Receptive and Expressive Vocabulary Test (TMMY) .... CREVT
Comprehensive Records Retention Schedule (SAUS) .... CRRS
Comprehensive Regional Assesment (SAUS) .... CRA
Comprehensive Regional Assessment (SAUO) .... CRA

Comprehensive Renal Scintillation Procedure [*Medicine*] (DMAA) .... CRSP
Comprehensive Reporting System (SAUS) .... CORE System
Comprehensive Research Injury Scale (PDAA) .... CRIS
Comprehensive Resource Inventory and Evaluation System (SAUO) .... CRIES
Comprehensive Respiratory Information System (SAUS) .... CRIS
Comprehensive Risk Assessment (SAUS) .... CRASH
Comprehensive Risk Evaluation and Management (ABAC) .... CREAM
Comprehensive Risk Information Structure Project (SAUO) .... CRISP
Comprehensive Scales of Student Abilities: Quantifying Academic Skills and School-Related Behavior Through the Use of Teacher Judgments (TMMY) .... CSSA
Comprehensive School [*British*] C
Comprehensive School Improvement Project (SAUO) .... CSIP
Comprehensive School Mathematics Program (EDAC) .... CSMP
Comprehensive School Reform Demonstration [*Program*] .... CSRD
Comprehensive Schools Committee (SAUO) .... CSC
Comprehensive Screening Tool for Determining Optimal Communication Mode [*Speech evaluation test*] .... CST
Comprehensive Self-Check [*Computer*] .... CSC
Comprehensive Service Delivery System (SAUO) .... CSDS
Comprehensive Sickle Cell Center [*Terminated, 1977*] [*HEW*] .... CSCC
Comprehensive Spending Review .... CSR
Comprehensive State Ground Water Protection Program [*Environmental science*] .... CSGWPP
Comprehensive Support Software [*Computer science*] (NITA) .... CSS
Comprehensive Supra Thermal and Energetic Particle (ADWA) .... COSTEP
Comprehensive System (SAA) .... CS
Comprehensive System of Personnel Development [*Education*] .... CSPD
Comprehensive System Readiness Tests (MCD) .... CSRT
Comprehensive System Test (ACAE) .... CST
Comprehensive Technologies International Inc. (SAUO) .... CTI
Comprehensive Test Ban [*Nuclear weapons*] .... CTB
Comprehensive Test Ban Treaty .... CTBT
Comprehensive Test of Nonverbal Intelligence (TMMY) .... CTONI
Comprehensive Testing Program [*Academic achievement and aptitude test*] .... CTP
Comprehensive Testing Program III (TMMY) .... CTPIII
Comprehensive Tests of Basic Skills [*Education*] .... CTBS
Comprehensive TeX Archive Network (SAUO) .... CTAN
Comprehensive Transportation Information & Planning System [*MTMC*] (TAG) .... CTIPS
Comprehensive Treatment and Management Plan [*Department of Energy*] .... CTMP
Comprehensive Treatment Plan [*Medicine*] (DAVI) .... CTP
Comprehensive Unified Land Data (SAUS) .... CULDATA
Comprehensive University of Dayton Online-information Service (SAUO) .... CUDOS
Comprehensive Water-quality Management Planning (SAUS) .... COWAMP
Comprehensive Weight Control System .... COMPWCS
Comprehensive Work Training Program [*Employment and Training Administration*] [*Department of Labor*] .... CWTP
Comprehensive Annual Financial Report .... CAFR
Compress (ABBR) .... CMPRS
Compress (NAKS) .... COMPR
Compress (MSA) .... CPRS
Compress .... SOMPRSS
Compress and/to Expand (SAUS) .... Compand
Compressed (ABBR) .... CMPRSD
Compressed .... COMP
Compressed (SAUS) .... CP
Compressed Aeronautical Chart (GEOI) .... CAAD
Compressed Aeronautical Chart (SAUO) .... CAC
Compressed Air (AAG) .... CA
Compressed Air .... COMPA
Compressed Air Accumulator Rocket .... CAAR
Compressed Air and Gas Institute (EA) .... CAGI
Compressed Air Breathing Apparatus .... CABA
Compressed Air Circuit Breaker (MSA) .... CACB
Compressed Air Disease [*Medicine*] (DB) .... CAD
Compressed Air Energy Storage (MCD) .... CAES
Compressed Air Equipment Distributors Association [*British*] (DBA) .... CAEDA
Compressed Air Institute (KSC) .... CAI
Compressed Air Loudspeaker .... CAL
Compressed Air Spraying .... CAS
Compressed Air Storage Power Plant (SAUS) .... CASPP
Compressed Air System (NUCP) .... CARS
Compressed Air System (NRCH) .... CAS
Compressed Air Tunnel [*British*] .... CAT
Compressed Analog [*Sound processing strategies*] .... CA
Compressed Binaries IBM PC (SAUS) .... CBIP
Compressed Binary Loader (SAUS) .... CBL
Compressed Citation File .... CCF
Compressed Coherency Detection [*RADAR technique*] .... COCODE
Compressed Data Mode [*Computer science.*] (VERA) .... CDM
Compressed Data Packet Data .... CDPD
Compressed Data Storage .... CDS
Compressed Data Storage System .... CDSS
Compressed database for homology searches and Multiple-aligned Sequence database (SAUO) .... CAMUS
Compressed Digital Terrain Elevation Data (GEOI) .... CDTED
Compressed Digital Video [*Telecommunications*] .... CDV
Compressed file (SAUS) .... Z
Compressed Gas (DNAB) .... CG
Compressed Gas (SAUS) .... Comp G
Compressed Gas Association (EA) .... CGA

Compressed Gas Association (SAUO) ... CGHA
Compressed Gas Association, Inc. (AAGC) ... CGA
Compressed Gas Insulation (SAUS) ... CGI
Compressed Gas Manufacturers Association (SAUO) ... CGMA
Compressed HTML (SAUS) ... CHTML
Compressed Index Sequential Access Method ... CISAM
Compressed International Trade Database [*United Nations*] ... COMTRADE
Compressed Limit Gauging Sampling (PDAA) ... CLGS
Compressed Liquid Fuel (EDCT) ... CLF
Compressed Medical Gas [*Food and Drug Administration*] ... CMG
Compressed Mortality File [*Medicine*] ... CMF
Compressed Mosiacked Image Data Record [*Geology*] ... CMIDR
Compressed Multisound (SAUS) ... COM
Compressed Natural Gas ... CNG
Compressed News Receive Via UUCP (SAUS) ... CNRCVUUCP
Compressed Pulse Altimeter ... CPA
Compressed Pulse RADAR Altimeter ... CPRA
Compressed Serial Line Interface Protocol (SAUS) ... CSLIP
Compressed Serial Line Internet Protocol (SAUS) ... CLIP
Compressed Serial Link Internet Protocol (SAUS) ... CSLIP
Compressed SLIP [*Serial Line Internet Protocol*] (CDE) ... CSLIP
Compressed Sources IBM PC (SAUS) ... CSIP
Compressed Spectral Array (SAUS) ... CSA
Compressed Spectral Assay (MAE) ... CSA
Compressed Symbolic [*Programming language*] [*Control Data Corp.*] ... COSY
Compressed Tablet [*Pharmacy*] ... CP
Compressed Tablet [*Pharmacy*] ... CT
Compressed Tablet Triturate [*Pharmacology*] ... CTT
Compressed Term (SAUS) ... CT
Compressed Volume File [*Computer science*] ... CVF
Compressed Work Schedule (COE) ... CWS
Compressed-Data Tape (SAUS) ... CDT
Compressed-Gas-Insulated Cable ... CGIC
Compressed-Gas-Insulated Transmission Line ... CGIT
Compressed-Gas-Insulated Tube (SAUS) ... CGIT
Compressed-impregnated (SAUS) ... Compreg
Compressed-Magnetic Field (SAUS) ... CMF
Compress/Expand (SAUS) ... CPX
Compressibility (ABBR) ... CMPRSBT
Compressible (ABBR) ... CMPRSB
Compressible Cell and Maker ... COMCAM
Compressible Flow Facility [*NASA*] ... CFF
Compressible Flow Wind Tunnel (MCD) ... CFWT
Compressible Navier-Stokes (ACAE) ... CNS
Compressibleness (ABBR) ... CMPRSBNS
Compressing (ABBR) ... CMPRSG
Compressing/Expanding [*Electronics*] (ACRL) ... Companding
Compression ... C
Compression (MUGU) ... CMP
Compression (ABBR) ... CMPRSN
Compression [*Automotive engineering*] ... COMP
Compression [*Automotive engineering*] ... COMPN
Compression (KSC) ... COMPR
Compression (MSA) ... CPRSN
Compression Active [*Modem status information light*] [*Computer science*] (IGQR) ... CA
Compression And Decompression of Imaging Sensor Signals (SAUS) ... CADISS
Compression Bonded (or Bonding) Encapsulation (SAUS) ... CBE
Compression Bonding Encapsulation ... CBE
Compression Control Protocol [*Computer science*] (VERA) ... CCP
Compression Engine ... CE
Compression Factor [*Symbol*] [*Thermodynamics*] ... Z
Compression Hip Screw [*System*] [*Orthopedics*] (DAVI) ... CHS
Compression Ignition [*Environmental science*] (COE) ... CI
Compression Ignition and Turbine Engine ... CITE
Compression Ignition Engine ... CI
Compression Ignition-Direct Injection ... CIDI
Compression in Transit ... CIT
Compression Labs [*NASDAQ symbol*] (TTSB) ... CLIX
Compression Labs, Inc. [*San Jose, CA*] [*Telecommunications*] (TSSD) ... CLI
Compression Labs, Inc. [*NASDAQ symbol*] (NQ) ... CLIX
Compression Labs, Inc. [*Associated Press*] (SAG) ... CmprsL
Compression Load Deflection (PDAA) ... CLD
Compression Mold Dies (MCD) ... CMD
Compression Ratio ... CR
Compression, Retrieval, and Maintenance [*of data*] (DNAB) ... CRAM
Compression Scanning Array RADAR [*Raytheon*] ... COSAR
Compression Switch ... CSW
Compression Yield Strength [*Engineering*] (BARN) ... CYS
Compressional Heating and Linear Injection Cusp Experiment ... CHALICE
Compression-Annealed Pyrolytic Boron Nitride (PDAA) ... CAPB
Compression-Annealed Pyrolytic Graphite (PDAA) ... CAPG
Compression/Decompression (SAUS) ... CODEC
Compression/Decompression Standard [*Computer science*] ... codec
Compressive (ABBR) ... CMPRSV
Compressive Load Cell ... CLC
Compressive Safety Index [*Engineering design*] ... CSI
Compressively (ABBR) ... CMPRSVY
Compressor (ABBR) ... CMPRSR
Compressor ... CMPSR
Compressor [*Automotive engineering*] ... COMP
Compressor (MSA) ... COMPR
Compressor (MSA) ... CPRSR
Compressor (SAUS) ... Cprsr
Compressor Decompressor [*Computer science*] (PCM) ... CODEC
Compressor Discharge Pressure ... CDP
Compressor Discharge Temperature (SAUS) ... CDT
Compressor End Seal ... CES
Compressor Endurance Loops (MCD) ... CEL
Compressor Expander [*Telecommunications*] (IEEE) ... COMPANDER
Compressor Inlet Pressure (MSA) ... CIP
Compressor Inlet Temperature (NG) ... CIT
Compressor Inlet Variable Vane (MCD) ... CIVV
Compressor Pressure Ratio (SAUS) ... CPR
Compressor Protect and Control System (SAUS) ... CPCS
Compressor Rear Frame (SAUS) ... CRF
Compressor Research Facility (IAA) ... CRF
Compressor-Expander (ADWA) ... compander
Compressor-Expander (SAUS) ... Compander
Compressor-Expandor (SAUS) ... Compandor
Compressor/Expandor [*Telecommunications*] ... compandor
Comprised (ROG) ... COMPRD
Comprising (WGA) ... COMP
Compromise (ADA) ... CMP
Compromise (ROG) ... COM
Compromise Approach to Compiler Design (SAUS) ... CACD
Compromise Sales Agreement [*Business term*] (EMRF) ... CSA
Compromised Container Caps [*Jerry Mason, 1995*] (SARE) ... CCC
Compromised Pulmonary Functions [*Medicine*] ... CPF
Compromising Emanations (AABC) ... CEM
Compromising Emanations Control (MCD) ... CEC
CompScript ... CPRX
CompScript, Inc. [*Associated Press*] (SAG) ... CmpScrpt
CompScript, Inc. [*NASDAQ symbol*] (SAG) ... CPRX
Compte [*Account*] [*French*] [*Business term*] (ROG) ... CTE
Compte Courant [*Current Account*] [*French*] [*Business term*] ... CC
Compte Ouvert [*Open Account*] [*French*] [*Business term*] ... c/o
Comptek Research, Inc. [*Associated Press*] (SAG) ... Comptek
Comptek Research, Inc. [*AMEX symbol*] (SPSG) ... CTK
Comptes Rendus. Academie des Inscriptions et Belles-Lettres [*A publication*] (OCD) ... CRAcad Inscr
Comptes Rendus Hebdomadaires des Seances de l'Academie des Science (MEC) ... C R Hebd Seance Acad Sci
Comptoir Commercial Franco-Africain [*Franco-African Trade Office*] [*Guinea*] (AF) ... CCFA
Comptoir du Livre [*Keren Hasefer*] [*A publication*] (BJA) ... CLKH
Comptoirs Francais du Pacifique (EBF) ... CFP
Compton Abbas [*British*] [*ICAO location identifier*] (ICLI) ... EGHA
Compton, CA [*Location identifier*] [*FAA*] (FAAL) ... CPM
Compton, CA [*FM radio station call letters*] ... KJLH
Compton College, Compton, CA [*Library symbol*] [*Library of Congress*] (LCLS) ... CComC
Compton County Historical and Museum Society [*Societe d'Histoire et du Musee du Comte de Compton*] **Eaton Corner, Quebec** [*Library symbol*] [*National Library of Canada*] (NLC) ... QECCH
Compton Edge (EDCT) ... CE
Compton Gamma Ray Observatory [*Satellite*] ... CGRO
Compton High-Altitude Pulse (SAUS) ... CHAP
Compton Junior College (SAUO) ... CJC
Compton, Meeson, and Roscoe's English Exchequer Reports [*1834-36*] [*A publication*] (DLA) ... CM & R
Compton Observatory Science Support Center (SAUO) ... COSSC
Compton Recoil Electron ... CRE
Compton Recoil Particle ... CRP
Compton Telescope [*NASA*] ... COMPTEL
Compton Telescope (SAUS) ... COMTEL
Compton's Multimedia Encyclopedia [*A publication*] ... CMME
Comptroller (SAUS) ... AC
Comptroller ... C
Comptroller (ABBR) ... CMPTR
Comptroller (ABBR) ... CMTRLR
Comptroller ... COMP
Comptroller (PHSD) ... Comp
Comptroller ... COMPT
Comptroller (DD) ... compt
Comptroller (AAGC) ... Compt
Comptroller ... COMPTLR
Comptroller (PROS) ... comptr
Comptroller (SAUS) ... Comt
Comptroller and Auditor General ... CAG
Comptroller and Auditor General (SAUO) ... CAG
Comptroller and Surveyor [*British*] (ROG) ... CS
Comptroller, Department of Defense (AAGC) ... CDOD
Comptroller Division (SAUO) ... CR
Comptroller General ... CG
Comptroller General ... COMPGEN
Comptroller General Decisions [*CCH*] [*A publication*] (AAGC) ... CGEN
Comptroller General Decisions [*Navy*] ... COMPGENDEC
[*The*] **Comptroller General of the United States** (AAGC) ... Comp Gen
Comptroller General Opinion ... CGO
Comptroller General Opinion [*A publication*] (DLA) ... Comp Gen Op
Comptroller Generals Decision (SAUS) ... CGD
Comptroller General's Decision (AAGC) ... CGDN
Comptroller General's Procurement Decisions [*A publication*] ... CPD
Comptroller of Accounts ... CA
Comptroller of Bureau of Supplies and Accounts (SAUS) ... COMT of BUSANDA
Comptroller of Stamps (SAUO) ... C of S
Comptroller of the Air Force (SAUO) ... AF Copmt
Comptroller of the Army ... CA
Comptroller of the Army ... COA

Comptroller of the Army (Director of the Army Budget) .... COA(DAB)
Comptroller of the Army Directorate of Cost Analysis [Washington, DC] .... COMPT-CA
Comptroller of the Currency .... COC
Comptroller of the Navy .... COMPT
Comptroller Office Automation Network (SAUO) .... COAN
Comptroller Office of the Future (SAUO) .... COOF
Comptroller Service Squadron [Air Force] .... CPTSq
Comptroller Service Squadron [Air Force] .... CPTSS
Comptroller Squadron [Air Force] .... CPTS
Comptroller Treasury Decisions [A publication] (DLA) .... Comptr Treas Dec
Comptroller-Director of Programs [Army] .... C-DP
Comptroller-General (SAUO) .... CompGenl
Comptroller-General of Patents, Designs and Trade Marks (SAUO) .... CGPDTM
Compucats' Computer Club [Defunct] (EA) CCC
CompuCoin Systems [NASDAQ symbol] (TTSB) .... CMPC
Compucom Speed Protocol (SAUS) .... CSP
Compucom Systems [NASDAQ symbol] (SAG) .... CMPC
Compucom Systems [Associated Press] (SAG) .... Cmpcm
Compucom Systems, Inc. [NASDAQ symbol] (SAG) .... CMPC
Compucom Systems, Inc. [Associated Press] (SAG) .... Cmpcm
CompuCredit Corp. [NASDAQ symbol] .... CCRT
Compudata, Inc. [Information service or system] (IID) .... CDI
Compuflight Operation Service, Inc. [ICAO designator] (FAAC) .... XCO
Compugraphic Corp. (SAUO) .... CPU
Compugraphic United Kingdom Users' Association (DGA) .... CUKUA
Compu/Graphics Users Association [Defunct] (EA) .... CGUA
Compugraphics Users Association [Bend, OR] (EA) .... CUA
Compu-Home Systems International, Inc. [Toronto Stock Exchange symbol] .... CPH
Compulaw Digest [A publication] (ADA) .... CLD
Compulink Information Exchange (SAUO) CIX
Compulsion (ABBR) .... CMPUL
Compulsive (ABBR) .... CMPULV
Compulsive Security Ritual (SAUS) .... CSR
Compulsive Stutterers Anonymous (EA) .... CSA
Compulsorily (ABBR) .... CMPULRY
Compulsorily Preserved Superannuation Benefit .... CPSB
Compulsory C
Compulsory (ABBR) .... CMPULR
Compulsory (DSUE) .... COMPUL
Compulsory Censorship [British] [World War II] CC
Compulsory Competitive Tendering [Australia] .... CCT
Compulsory Control (SAUS) CC
Compulsory Insurance CI
Compulsory Purchase Act [Town planning] [British] .... CPA
Compulsory Purchase Order [British] .... CPO
Compulsory Third Party [Australia] .... CTP
CompuMed, Inc. [NASDAQ symbol] (SAG) .... CMPD
CompuMed, Inc. [Associated Press] (SAG) .... CmpMd
CompuMed, Inc. [Associated Press] (SAG) .... CmpuMed
CompuMed Inc. Wrrt [NASDAQ symbol] (TTSB) .... CMPDW
Compunction (ABBR) .... CMPUN
Compunctiously (ABBR) .... CMPUNSY
CompuRAD, Inc. [Associated Press] (SAG) .... CmpRD
CompuRAD, Inc. [NASDAQ symbol] (SAG) .... COMD
Compurgation (ABBR) .... CMPUR
Compurhythm (SAUS) .... CR
Compuring Intelligent Character Recognition (SAUS) .... ICR
CompUSA, Inc. [Associated Press] (SAG) .... CompUSA
CompUSA, Inc. [NYSE symbol] (SPSG) .... CPU
CompuServe Corp. [Associated Press] (SAG) .... CmpuSrv
CompuServe Corp. [NASDAQ symbol] (SAG) .... CSRV
Compuserve Graphics Interchange Format (SAUS) .... GIF
CompuServe, Inc. [Commercial firm] .... CSI
CompuServe, Inc. [ICAO designator] (FAAC) .... XCS
CompuServe Information Manager [CompuServe, Inc.] (PCM) .... CIM
CompuServe Information Service [CompuServe, Inc.] (IID) .... CIS
CompuServe Information Service .... CompuServe
CompuServe Information Service B [Communications protocol] (CDE) .... CIS B
CompuServe Navigator [CompuServe, Inc.] [Telecommunications] (PCM) ..... CSNav
CompuServe Network Services [CompuServe, Inc.] [Columbus, OH] [Telecommunications] (TSSD) .... CNS
Compuserve Packet Network [Computer science] (VERA) .... CPN
COMPUSTAT Services, Inc. [Information service or system] (IID) .... C/S
computability (SAUS) .... compu
computable (SAUS) .... compu
Computable General Equilibrium model (SAUO) .... CGE
Computalog Gearhart Ltd. [Toronto Stock Exchange symbol] .... CGH
Computalog Ltd. [NASDAQ symbol] (SAG) .... CLTD
Computalog Ltd [NASDAQ symbol] (TTSB) .... CLTDF
Computalog Ltd. [Associated Press] (SAG) .... Computlg
Computation (ABBR) .... CMPUTAN
Computation (ABBR) .... CMPUTN
Computation (AFM) .... COMP
Computation and Analysis Division [NASA] (MCD) .... CAD
Computation and Analysis Section (SAUO) .... COMANSEC
Computation and Communication Trade-Off Study [ARPA] .... CACTOS
Computation and Data Flow Integrated Subsystem [Simulated flight tests] [NASA] .... CADFISS
Computation and Data Processing Branch (SAUS) .... CDPB
Computation and Data Processing Center (DIT) .... CDPC
Computation and Data Reduction Center [Military] (DNAB) .... CDRC
Computation and Research Evaluation System (SAUS) .... CARES
Computation Center CC

Computation Center-Advanced Graphics Laboratory [University of Texas at Austin] [Research center] (RCD) .... AGL
Computation Fluid Dynamics .... CFD
Computation Laboratory of Harvard University (SAUO) .... CLHU
Computation of Manpower Programs Using Linear Programming (MCD) .... COMPLIP
Computation of Miss Between Orbits [Air Force] (MCD) .... COMBO
Computation of Rendezvous Targeting (NAKS) .... COMP
Computation of Vulnerable Area and Repair Time (MCD) .... COVART
Computation Online of Network Chemical Engineering Process Technology (IAA) .... CONCEPT
Computation Structures Language (SAUS) .... CSL
Computation Subsystem [Space Flight Operations Facility, NASA] .... COMP
Computation Tree Logic (RALS) .... CTL
Computational (MDG) .... CMP
Computational Aeroacoustics [Laser technology] .... CAA
Computational and Information Sciences (SAUS) .... CIS
Computational Arithmetic Program .... CAP
Computational Component (MCD) CC
Computational Element (NITA) .... CE
Computational Engineering Research Institute, Inc. [Research center] (RCD) .... CERI
Computational Fluid Dynamics [Chemical engineering] .... CFD
Computational Fluid Dynamics Resources Online (SAUO) .... CFDRO
Computational Fluid Mechanics Laboratory [University of Arizona] [Research center] (RCD) .... CFML
Computational Fluids Dynamics [Organic chemistry] .... CFD
Computational Linguistics (IEEE) CL
Computational Map Processor (ACAE) .... CMP
Computational Physics Group Bibliographic Aid (SAUO) .... CPG BIBLIA
Computational Requirements for Engineering and Simulation, Training and Education [Time-sharing computer complex] [Air Force] .... CREATE
Computational Resources for Engineering and Training and Education (SAUS) .... CREATE
Computational Science and Engineering Research Center (RDA) .... ComSERC
Computational Support Section (SAUS) .... CSS
Computational Systems [NASDAQ symbol] (TTSB) .... CSIN
Computational Systems, Inc. [Associated Press] (SAG) .... Cmputa
Computational Systems, Inc. [Associated Press] (SAG) .... Computat
Computational Systems, Inc. [NASDAQ symbol] (SAG) .... CSIN
Computational Testbed for Industry (SAUS) .... CTI
Computational Transonic Aerodynamics (MCD) .... CTA
Computational Value (SAUS) CV
Computations and Data Reduction Division [NASA] (KSC) .... CDRD
Computations Incorporated (SAUO) CI
Computations Life Office Administrations System (NITA) .... CLOAS
Computations per Word (SAUS) .... CPW
Computation-Universal Cellular Space (PDAA) .... CUCS
Compute [or Computer] (MDG) C
Compute (ADWA) .... cmpt
Compute [or Computer] (AABC) .... CMPT
Compute (ABBR) .... CMPU
Compute Air-Trans Systems (SAUS) .... CATS
Compute Air-Trans Systems, Inc. .... CATS
Compute Clock Pulse (SAUS) .... CC Pulse
Compute Element (IAA) .... CE
Compute Parallel (IEEE) .... COMPEL
Compute Statement (SAUS) .... CS
Compute Topography (SAUS) .... CT
Computed .... CMPTD
Computed (ABBR) .... CMPUTD
Computed Air-Release Point .... CARP
Computed Axial Tomography (SAUS) .... CAT
Computed Body Tomography [Medicine] (CPH) .... CBT
Computed Ephemeris Position .... CEP
Computed Impact Point (ACAE) .... CIP
Computed Kill Point (SAUS) .... CKP
Computed Maximum Pressure (SAUS) .... CMP
Computed Mission Coverage Index (MCD) .... CMCI
Computed Point [Navigation] .... CP
Computed Radiosity (RALS) .... CR
Computed Slant Detection Range .... CSDR
Computed Thermography System [Computer science] .... CTS
Computed Tomographic Machine (SAUS) .... CT Machine
Computed Tomographic Metrizamide Myelography .... CTMM
Computed Tomography [Also, CAAT, CAT] [Roentgenography] .... CT
Computed Tomography Angiographic Portography [Medicine] (MELL) .... CTAP
Computed Tomography Dose Index (DB) .... CTDI
Computed Tomography Nominal Dose (DB) .... CTND
Computed Tomography with Multiplanar Reconstructions [Radiology] (DAVI) .... CT/MPR
Computed Transaxial Tomography [Later, CT] .... CTT
Computer (MUGU) .... CMP
Computer (KSC) .... CMPTR
Computer (TBD) .... Cmptr
Computer (ABBR) .... CMPUTR
Computer .... COM
Computer [or Computing] (AFM) .... COMP
Computer (DD) .... Comp
Computer (VRA) .... compr
Computer (IAA) .... CP
Computer (SAUS) .... CU
Computer [JETDS nomenclature] .... K
Computer Acceleration Control (SAUS) .... CAC
Computer Access (IAA) .... CA

Computer Access Corp. [*Information service or system*] (IID) .... CAC
Computer Access Device .... CAD
Computer Access Device Input (CET) .... CADI
Computer Access Device Output (CET) .... CADO
Computer Access Matrix (NITA) .... CAM
Computer Access Security System (NITA) .... CASS
Computer Access Technology Corp. (PCM) .... CATC
Computer Access Time (SAUS) .... CAT
Computer Access to Notation and Text in Music Libraries (TELE) .... CANTATE
Computer Access Unit (SAUS) .... CAU
Computer Accounting Ltd. (SAUS) .... CAL
Computer Accounting System [*Boole & Babbage, Inc.*] .... CAS
Computer Accounting System / Computer Performance Analysis (MHDB) .... CAS/CPA
Computer Accounting System for Office Expenditure (MHDB) .... CASOE
Computer Achievement Monitoring (MCD) .... CAM
Computer Acquisition System (PDAA) .... COMPAS
Computer Activity (NAKS) .... CMPTR ACTY
Computer Activity Monitor System (SAUS) .... CAMS
Computer Adaptive Control (SAUS) .... CAC
Computer Adaptive Language for Development of Structural Analysis Programs [*University of California at Berkeley*] (NITA) .... CAL/SAP
Computer Adaptive Test (SAUS) .... CAT
Computer Adaptive Testing .... CAT
Computer Adaptor Display .... CAD
Computer Address (ACAE) .... CA
Computer Address Bus (SAUS) .... CAB
Computer Address Decoder [*Navy Navigation Satellite System*] (DNAB) .... CAD
Computer Address Matrix .... CAM
Computer Address Panel (CAAL) .... CAP
Computer Address Panel (SAUS) .... CAP
Computer Addressed Memory (NITA) .... CAM
Computer Administrative Instruction (AABC) .... CADMINI
Computer Advanced Software Products [*Database producer*] (IID) .... CASPR
Computer Advisory Committee [*Marine science*] (OSRA) .... CAC
Computer Advisory Unit (SAUO) .... CAU
Computer, Aerial Reconnaissance .... COMAR
Computer Aid .... CAID
Computer Aid in the Physicians Office (SAUS) .... CAPO
Computer Aid System (NITA) .... CAS
Computer Aided Acquisition Logistic Support (ACAE) .... CAALS
Computer Aided Administration and Organization (SAUO) .... CAO
Computer Aided Animation (SAUS) .... CAA
Computer Aided Anthropometrics (SAUS) .... CAA
Computer Aided Art and Design (NITA) .... CAAD
Computer Aided Assembling (SAUS) .... CAA
Computer Aided Batch Searching (NITA) .... CABS
Computer Aided Breakfast (SAUS) .... CAB
Computer Aided Business Simulation (SAUS) .... CABS
Computer Aided Christmas (SAUS) .... CAC
Computer Aided Clamping system (SAUS) .... CAC
Computer Aided Community Oral Health Information System (SAUO) .... CACOHIS
Computer Aided Computing (SAUS) .... CAC
Computer Aided Computing Creativity (SAUS) .... CAC
Computer Aided Computing Crime (SAUS) .... CAC
Computer Aided Computing Detection (SAUS) .... CAC
Computer Aided Consulting (SAUS) .... CAC
Computer Aided Creativity (SAUS) .... CAC
Computer Aided Data Entry (SAUS) .... CADE
Computer Aided Design and Draughting (NITA) .... CADD
Computer Aided Design and Graphics Laboratory [*Purdue University*] [*Research center*] (RCD) .... CADLAB
Computer Aided Design and Numerical Analysis for Manufacture Group .... CADNAM
Computer Aided Design Center (SAUS) .... CADC
Computer Aided Design Centre [*Department of Trade and Industry*] [*British*] (NITA) .... CADC
Computer Aided Design for VLSI [*Very Large Scale Integration*] **in Europe** [*British*] .... CAVE
Computer Aided Design of Electronic Products (SAUS) .... CADEP
Computer Aided Design or Analysis (SAUS) .... CADA
Computer Aided Design Software, Incorporated (ACAE) .... CADSI
Computer Aided Detection (SAUS) .... CAD
Computer Aided Diagnostic Information (ACAE) .... CADI
Computer Aided Dinner (SAUS) .... CAD
Computer Aided Dispatch [*Police communications*] .... CAD
Computer Aided Document Engineering [*Computer software*] (PCM) .... CADE
Computer Aided Drug Design (SAUS) .... CADD
Computer Aided Education (ECII) .... CBE
Computer Aided Engineering Design System (NITA) .... CAEDS
Computer Aided Engineering Graphics [*FAA*] (TAG) .... CAEG
Computer Aided Engineering Support Office (NITA) .... CAESO
Computer Aided Estimating and Planning System (NITA) .... CAEPS
Computer Aided Facilities (or Facility) Management (SAUS) .... CAFM
Computer Aided Fishing (SAUO) .... CAF
Computer Aided Hausaufgaben (SAUO) .... CAH
Computer Aided Holidays (SAUO) .... CAH
Computer Aided Homework (SAUO) .... CAH
Computer Aided Inspection (SAUO) .... CAI
Computer Aided Inspection and Testing (SAUO) .... CAIT
Computer Aided Inspiration (SAUS) .... CAI
Computer Aided Instruction for Teacher Education (EDAC) .... CAITE
Computer Aided Instructional Training (SAUS) .... CAIT
Computer Aided Intuition Guided Programming (SAUS) .... CIP
Computer Aided Laboratory Automation System (SAUO) .... CALAS
Computer Aided Language Learning (SAUO) .... CALL
Computer Aided Learning (SAUO) .... CAL
Computer Aided Learning Centre [*Victoria University*] [*Australia*] .... CALC
Computer Aided Learning in Mathematics (AIE) .... CALM
Computer Aided Learning in Meteorology .... CALMET
Computer Aided Life (SAUO) .... CAL
Computer Aided Linguistic Analysis .... COALA
Computer Aided Locomotion by Implanted Electrical Stimulation (SAUO) .... CALIES
Computer Aided Logistics (SAUS) .... CAL
Computer Aided Lunch (SAUS) .... CAL
Computer Aided Management (SAUS) .... CAM
Computer Aided Management of Emergency Operations [*Marine science*] (OSRA) .... CAMEO
Computer Aided Manufacturing International (EA) .... CAM-I
Computer Aided Mapping (GEOI) .... CAM
Computer Aided Mathematical Analysis (SAUS) .... CAMA
Computer Aided Mission Planning System (SAUS) .... CAMPS
Computer Aided Molecular Design (SAUS) .... CAMD
Computer Aided Monitoring and Control (SAUS) .... CAMAC
Computer Aided Movement Analysis in a Rehabilitation Context (SAUO) .... CAMARC
Computer Aided Multimedia Courseware Engineering (SAUO) .... CAMCE
Computer Aided Part Planning (SAUS) .... CAPP
Computer Aided Personal Reference Index (SAUS) .... CAPRI
Computer Aided Personal Reference Index System [*Automic Energy Authority*] [*British*] (NITA) .... CAPRI
Computer Aided Photogrammetric Compilation And Drafting System (SAUS) .... CAPCADS
Computer Aided Planning System (HEAS) .... CAPS
Computer Aided Printing (SAUS) .... CAP
Computer Aided Problem Solving (NITA) .... CAPS
Computer Aided Process and Production Planning (SAUO) .... CAPPP
Computer Aided Production for Current Awareness Services [*Information service or system*] (IID) .... CAPCAS
Computer Aided Production Planning and Control (SAUO) .... CAPPC
Computer Aided Production Scheduling and Control (SAUS) .... CAPSC
Computer Aided Productivity (SAUS) .... CAP
Computer Aided Programming Software (SAUS) .... CAPS
Computer Aided Quality Control (ACAE) .... CAQ
Computer Aided Radio Amateur (SAUO) .... CARA
Computer Aided Real Language Orthographic System (SAUS) .... CARLOS
Computer Aided Reliability Estimation (SAUS) .... CARE
Computer Aided Reserve Engineering (SAUS) .... CARE
Computer Aided Resource Information Service (SAUS) .... CARIS
Computer Aided Retrieval (SAUS) .... CAR
Computer Aided Reverse Engineering (SAUS) .... CARE
Computer Aided Risc Simulation (SAUO) .... CARS
Computer Aided Service (SAUO) .... CAS
Computer Aided Software Engineering (ACAE) .... CASE
Computer Aided Subject Index System (SAUS) .... CASIN System
Computer Aided Support (ACAE) .... CAS
Computer Aided System for Circuit Analysis and Design (SAUS) .... CASCADE
Computer Aided System for Scheduling, Information and Operation of Public Transport in Europe (SAUO) .... CASSIOPE
Computer Aided Systems Construction and Documentation Environment (SAUS) .... CASCADE
Computer Aided Systems Engineering (SAUS) .... CASE
Computer Aided Tailoring of Software Programs (ACAE) .... CATSOP
Computer Aided Teaching of Applied Mathematics [*Cambridge University, England*] (EDAC) .... CATAM
Computer Aided Technical Publishing (SAUO) .... CATP
Computer Aided Technologies (SAUS) .... CAT
Computer Aided Telecommunications (SAUO) .... CAT
Computer Aided Telephone Interviewing (SAUO) .... CATI
Computer Aided Testing (SAUO) .... CAT
Computer Aided Three [*Dimensional*] **Interactive Application** .... CATIE
Computer Aided Tracking (ACAE) .... CAT
Computer Aided Training in Troubleshooting (SAUS) .... CATTS
Computer Aided User Oriented System Evaluation (SAUS) .... CAUSE
Computer Aided Verification (SAUS) .... CAV
Computer Aided Vision Engineering (SAUO) .... CAVE
Computer Aided-Fraud (NITA) .... CAF
Computer Aids Design of Systems (SAUS) .... CADOS
Computer Aids for Chemical Engineering Education [*National Academy of Engineering*] .... CACHE
Computer Aids for Human Translation [*Carnegie-Mellon University*] (NITA) .... CAHT
Computer Aids for Human Translations (SAUS) .... CAHT
Computer Air Navigation Unit (ACAE) .... CANU
Computer Air-Air Dispenser (MCD) .... CAAD
Computer Air-Trans Systems, Inc. (SAUO) .... CATS
Computer Algebra Information Network [*Computer science*] .... CAIN
Computer Algebra Systems (PDAA) .... CAS
Computer Amplifier Alarm .... CAA
Computer Analog Input .... CAI
Computer Analog Input/Output (DEN) .... CAI/O
Computer Analog Input/Output .... CAIOP
Computer Analysis (SAUS) .... CA
Computer Analysis (SAUS) .... COMPANAL
Computer Analysis and Design System (NITA) .... CADS
Computer Analysis and Programmer (or Programming) (SAUS) .... CAP
Computer Analysis and Simulation of Metaloxide Semiconductor Circuit (IAA) .... CASMOS

Computer Analysis Department (SAUS) .... CAD
Computer Analysis Group (SAUO) .... CAG
Computer Analysis of Images and Patterns [Conference] (VERA) .... CAIP
Computer Analysis of Library Postcards (SAUS) .... CALP
Computer Analysis of Maintenance Policies (MHDI) .... COAMP
Computer Analysis of Networks via Inversion of Network Equations
   (PDAA) .... CANINE
Computer Analysis of Networks with Design Orientation in the Frequency
   Domain (PDAA) .... CANDOFD
Computer Analysis of Nonlinear Circuits Excluding Radiation
   (SAUS) .... CANCER
Computer Analysis of Tape Signals (SAUS) .... CATS
Computer Analysis of Thermo-Chemical (SAUS) .... CATCH
Computer Analysis of Thermochemical Data Tables [University of Sussex]
   [Sussex, England] .... CATCH
Computer Analysis of Time-Varying Images (SAUS) .... CATVI
Computer Analysis of Transistors (IAA) .... CAT
Computer Analysis of Troubles on Trunk Circuits (PDAA) ... CANTOT
Computer Analysts & Programmers Ltd. [British] .... CAP
Computer Analysts and Programmers Ltd. Computer Programme
   Products (SAUO) .... CAP-CPP
Computer Analyzed Newspaper Data On-Line [Newspaper Advertising
   Bureau, Inc.] [Information service or system] (IID) ...... CAN DO
Computer and Academic Freedom (SAUO) .... CAF
Computer & Aerospace Components Ltd. [British] .... CACL
Computer and Automated Systems Association [Later, CASA/SME] .... CASA
Computer and Automated Systems Association (SAUO) .... CAS Association
Computer and Automated Systems Association of Society of
   Manufacturing Engineers (EA) .... CASA/SME
Computer and Automation (SAUS) .... CA
Computer and Business Equipment Manufacturers Association
   [Washington, DC] (EA) .... CBEMA
Computer and Business Equipment Manufacturers Association
   (SAUO) .... Cebema
Computer and Communications [Database] (IT) .... CMPCOM
Computer and Communications Access Device (AAGC) .... CCAD
Computer and Communications in Compact Size (SAUS) C3
Computer and Communications Industry Association (EA) .... CCIA
Computer and Communications Standards Board (SAUS) .... CCSB
Computer and Communications Technology Corporation (AAGC) .... CCT
Computer and Control Abstracts (journ.) (SAUS) .... CCA
Computer and Data Systems Unit (SAUO) .... CDSU
Computer & Engineering Bureau (EFIS) .... CEB
Computer and Human-Assisted Organization of a Technical Information
   Center (SAUO) .... CHAOTIC
Computer and Human-Assisted Organization of a Technical Information
   Center [National Institute of Standards and Technology] .... CHAOTIC
Computer and Information Science and Engineering (SAUS) .... CISE
Computer and Information Science and Engineering directorate (SAUO) .... CISE
Computer and Information Science Directorate (VERA) .... CISE
Computer and Information Science Research Center [Ohio State University]
   [Columbus, OH] .... CISRC
Computer and Information Sciences .... COINS
Computer and Information Sciences Research Laboratory [University of
   Alabama in Birmingham] [Research center] (RCD) .... CIS
Computer and Interactive Voice Response (SAUS) .... CIVR
Computer and Language Independent Modules for Automatic Test
   Equipment (MHDI) .... CLIMATE
Computer and Management Education Services (SAUS) .... CMES
Computer and Management Show for Contractors (TSPED) .... CMC
Computer and Network Services Division [Formerly, Computer Support
   Group] (USDC) .... CNSD
Computer and Peripherals Equipment Trade Association (MHDB) .... COMPETA
Computer and Peripherie GmbH (SAUS) .... Computer
Computer and Photographic Assisted Learning .... CAPAL
Computer and Science Network (SAUO) .... CSNet
Computer and System Engineering (IAA) .... CASE
Computer and Systems Engineering Ltd. (SAUO) .... CASE
Computer and Systems Research Laboratory (SAUO) .... CSRL
Computer and Telecommunications Acronyms [A publication] .... CTA
Computer Animation (VERA) .... CA
Computer Animation Language .... CAL
Computer Annunciation Matrix (MCD) .... CAM
Computer Antenna Pointing System (SAUS) .... CAPS
Computer Anti-Virus Research Organization (SAUO) .... CARO
Computer Anxiety Index (EDAC) .... CAIN
Computer Anxiety Scale [Oetting's] (TES) .... COMPAS
Computer Application (SAUS) .... CA
Computer Application Control Code .... CACC
Computer Application Digest (SAUS) .... CAD
Computer Application for Planning Manufacturing Engineering Costs
   (SAUS) .... CAPMEC
Computer Application Inc (SAUS) .... CAI
Computer Application Program (NASA) .... CAP
Computer Application Service (SAUS) .... CAPS
Computer Application Services, Inc. [Los Alamitos, CA]
   [Telecommunications] (TSSD) .... CASI
Computer Application Summary (IAA) .... CAS
Computer Application to Measurement and Control (SAUS) .... CAMAC
Computer Applications and Systems Technology (SAUS) .... CAST
Computer Applications for Military Problems (SAUS) .... CAMP
Computer Applications for Ministry Network (EA) .... CAMNET
Computer Applications for the Graphic Arts .... CAFGA
Computer Applications Group [Air Force] .... CAG

Computer Applications in Production and Engineering [Conference]
   (VERA) .... CAPE
Computer Applications in the Biosciences [A publication] .... CABIOS
Computer Applications in the Biosciences (SAUS) .... Comput Appl Biosci
Computer Applications, Inc. (MCD) .... CAI
Computer Applications Incorporated (SAUO) .... CAI
Computer Applications of Military Problems [Computer users' group] .... CAMP
Computer Applications Office (SAUO) .... CAO
Computer Applications Operating System (SAUS) .... CAOS
Computer Applications Support and Development Office [Navy] .... CASDO
Computer Applications to Manufacturing (SAUS) .... CAM
Computer Applied Systems Accounts Payable System (SAUS) .... CASAPS
Computer Aptitude, Literacy, and Interest Profile [Vocational guidance
   test] .... CALIP
Computer Aptitude Quotient (EDAC) .... CAQ
Computer Architecture (SAUS) .... CPA
Computer Architecture News [A publication] .... CAN
Computer Architecture Research Unit [York University] [Canada] [Research
   center] (RCD) .... CARU
Computer Architecture Specification Language (CSR) .... CASL
Computer Archive of Language Materials [Stanford University] (NITA) ...... CALM
Computer Archive of Modern English Text (SAUS) .... CAMET
Computer Arts Society (EAIO) .... CAS
Computer Assembly .... CA
Computer Assessment of Media (SAUS) .... CAM
Computer Assist Modification Radio Frequency Test (ACAE) .... CAM-RFTS
Computer Assistance for International Team Research (SAUS) .... CAITR
Computer Assistance Resource Exchange (SAUS) .... CARE
Computer Assistant to a Community Telephone Information Service
   (PDAA) .... CACTIS
Computer Assisted (ACAE) .... C/A
Computer Assisted (IAA) .... COMPASS
Computer Assisted Approach Sequencing (SAUS) .... CAAS
Computer Assisted Careers Guidance System (AIE) .... CACGS
Computer Assisted Clerical Coding (SAUS) .... CACC
Computer Assisted Command System (SAUS) .... CACS
Computer Assisted Continuous Infusion [Pharmacology] (DAVI) .... CACI
Computer Assisted Data Engineering (SAUS) .... CADE
Computer Assisted Decision Making for Image Understanding in
   Medicine (RALS) .... CADMIUM
Computer Assisted Depreciation and Life Analysis System [BTS]
   (TAG) .... CADLAS
Computer Assisted Diagnostic and Prescription Instruction (EDAC) .... CADPI
Computer Assisted Dial Access Video Retrieval System (SAUS) .... CADAVRS
Computer Assisted Distribution and Assignment (SAUS) .... CADA
Computer Assisted Document Drafting .... CADD
Computer Assisted Drawing Management and Control [Infodetics Co.]
   (NITA) .... CADMAC
Computer Assisted Education (SAUO) .... CAE
Computer Assisted Education Language (SAUS) .... CAMEL
Computer Assisted Indexing Program (NITA) .... CAIP
Computer Assisted Information Retrieval System (NITA) .... CAIRS
Computer Assisted Instruction (AIE) .... CAI
Computer Assisted Instruction and Support for the Handicapped
   (EDAC) .... CAISH
Computer Assisted Interviewing (SAUS) .... CAI
Computer Assisted Land Survey System (GEOI) .... CALS
Computer Assisted Land Use Planning (SAUS) .... CALUP
Computer Assisted Language Learning and Instruction Consortium
   (EA) .... CALICO
Computer Assisted Language Teaching (AIE) .... CALT
Computer Assisted Learning (AIE) .... CAL
Computer Assisted Learning and Education in Science and Engineering
   (SAUS) .... CALISE
Computer Assisted Legal Retrieval (NITA) .... CALR
Computer Assisted Library Instruction Co., Inc. [Information service or
   system] (IID) .... CALICO
Computer Assisted Maintenance Management System (SAUS) .... CAMMS
Computer Assisted Management and Emergency Operations (SAUS) ..... CAMEO
Computer Assisted Mapping (SAUS) .... CAM
Computer Assisted Mechanistic Evaluation of Organic Reactions [Data
   analysis] .... CAMEO
Computer Assisted Movie Production (SAUO) .... CAMP
Computer Assisted Network System (SAUO) .... CANS
Computer Assisted New Drug Application [Medicine] [Australia] .... CANDA
Computer Assisted New Drug Application [Food and Drug
   Administration] .... CANDA
Computer Assisted Optical Surfacing (SAUS) .... CAOS
Computer Assisted Physics Laboratory Instruction (SAUS) .... CAPLIN
Computer Assisted PLA [Product License Application] Review [FDA] .... CAPLAR
Computer Assisted Placement (SAUS) .... CAP
Computer Assisted Placing in the Areas of London (SAUS) .... CAPTAL
Computer Assisted Practice of Cardiology [Medicine] (MELL) .... CAPOC
Computer Assisted Radiology (SAUS) .... CAR
Computer Assisted Radiology and Surgery (SAUS) .... CARS
Computer Assisted Referee Selection (NITA) .... CARS
Computer Assisted Search Service (SAUO) .... CASS
Computer Assisted Simulation and Education System [Simulation of doctor's
   decision making] [Netherlands] (NITA) .... CASES
Computer Assisted Spanish English Transition Sequence (EDAC) .... CASETS
Computer Assisted Sperm Analyzer .... CASA
Computer Assisted Student Tutorial Learning Environment (EDAC) .... CASTLE
Computer Assisted Supervision of Transmission (SAUS) .... CAST
Computer Assisted Survey Information Collection Office (SAUS) .... CASIC
Computer Assisted Survey Research Office (SAUS) .... CASRO

Computer Assisted Synthetic Analysis Group (NITA) ... CASAG
Computer Assisted System for Image Interpretation (SAUS) ... CASYII
Computer Assisted Teaching System (SAUS) ... CATS
Computer Assisted Technique for Numerical Index Preparation (SAUS) ... CATNIP
Computer Assisted Televideo [*Commercial firm*] [*Netherlands*] (NITA) ... CAT
Computer Assisted Thermography (GEOI) ... CAT
Computer Assisted Traffic Engineering (SAUS) ... CATE
Computer Assisted Training System (SAUO) ... CATS
Computer Assisted Transcription (SAUS) ... CAT
Computer Assisted Typesetter (SAUS) ... CAT
Computer Assisted Virtual Environment ... CAVE
Computer Assoc Intl. [*NYSE symbol*] (TTSB) ... CA
Computer Associates [*A company*] [*Islandia, New York*] (WDMC) ... CA
Computer Associates Basic Language Extended [*Computer Associates International, Inc.*] (PCM) ... CABLE
Computer Associates Easy Access Report Language (SAUS) ... CA-Earl
Computer Associates International, Inc. [*NYSE symbol*] (SPSG) ... CA
Computer Associates International, Inc. [*Associated Press*] (SAG) ... CmpAsc
Computer Associates Job Accounting System for Performance Evaluation and Report (SAUS) ... CA-JASPER
Computer Associates-Visual Objects (VERA) ... CAVO
Computer Audio Interactive Video Manipulator [*Designed by Christopher Conley*] ... CAIVman
Computer Audio Research Laboratory [*Research center*] (RCD) ... CARL
Computer Audit Retrieval System [*Trade name for Sage Systems, Inc., computer software product*] ... CARS
Computer Audit Specialist [*IRS*] ... CAS
Computer Augmented Communication ... CAC
Computer Augmented Learning (CMD) ... CAL
Computer Augmented Resource System (SAUS) ... CARS
Computer Augmented Video Education [*US Naval Academy*] (NITA) ... CAVE
Computer Automated Cargo Documentation (IAA) ... CACD
Computer Automated Diameter Control (PDAA) ... CADC
Computer Automated Mailing System (SAUS) ... CAMS
Computer Automated Performance Data (ACAE) ... CAPD
Computer Automated Rapid Transit System (SAUS) ... CARTS
Computer Automated Reserved Track System (SAUS) ... CARTS
Computer Automated Software for the Total Library Environment (SAUS) ... CASTLE
Computer Automated Support Equipment (SAUS) ... CASE
Computer Automated Support System (ACAE) ... CASS
Computer Automated System (SAUS) ... CAS
Computer Automated Test System (SAUS) ... CATS
Computer Automated Vacuum Evaporator (SAUS) ... CAVE
Computer Automatic Branch Exchange (SAUS) ... CABEX
Computer Automatic Line Monitoring System (SAUS) ... CALMS
Computer Automatic Scheduling System ... CASS
Computer Automatic Virtual Environment [*Virtual reality system*] (CDE) ... CAVE
Computer Automation, Inc. [*Richardson, TX*] (TSSD) ... CA
Computer Automation, Inc. ... CAI
Computer Automation, Incorporated (SAUO) ... CAI
Computer Backing Store (SAUS) ... CBS
Computer Backup (SAUS) ... CB
Computer Bar Code (SAUS) ... CBC
Computer Based Conversation System (VERA) ... CBCS
Computer Based Educational Software System (ACAE) ... CBESS
Computer Based English Language Testing (AIE) ... CBELT
Computer Based Information System (SAUS) ... CBIS
Computer Based Instruction Training System (ACAE) ... CBITS
Computer Based Resource Units Project (SAUS) ... CBRU Project
Computer Basic Technology Research Association (SAUO) ... CBTRA
Computer Block Diagram (SAUS) ... CBD
Computer Book Review [*Comber Press*] [*Information service or system*] (CRD) ... CBR
Computer Brokers Exchange [*Information service or system*] (IID) ... CBE
Computer Buffer Store (SAUS) ... CBS
[*The*] **Computer Bulletin** (IAA) ... TCB
Computer Bulletin Board System ... CBBS
Computer Burst Order (AABC) ... CBO
Computer Business Services, Inc. ... CBSI
Computer Calculator ... CC
Computer Call Network [*Telemarketing*] ... CCN
Computer Campaign Services [*Data processing firm in field of politics*] ... CCS
Computer Capacity (SAUS) ... CC
Computer Carrier Interrupt (SAUS) ... CCI
Computer Center [*Telecommunications*] (TEL) ... CC
Computer Center ... CMPCTR
Computer Center [*Haverford College*] [*Research center*] (RCD) ... HCCC
Computer Center [*Vanderbilt University*] [*Research center*] (RCD) ... VUCC
Computer Center [*Yale University*] [*Research center*] (RCD) ... YCC
Computer Center at the University of Tokyo (SAUO) ... CCUT
Computer Center/ Communications Network Control Stations (SAUO) ... CC/CNCS
Computer Center Division (SAUO) ... CCD
Computer Center Management System (MHDB) ... CCMS
Computer Central Complex (ACAE) ... CCC
Computer Central Processing [*Telecommunications*] (TEL) ... CCP
Computer Channel (SAUS) ... CC
Computer Character Recognition ... CCR
Computer Checking Time (SAUS) ... CCT
Computer Chemical System ... CCS
Computer Chess Competition (SAUS) ... CCC
Computer Circuit Corporation (SAUO) ... CCC
Computer Circuit Protector (SAUS) ... CCP
Computer City System (SAUS) ... CCS
[*The*] **Computer Co.** [*Information service or system*] (IID) ... TCC
Computer Co., Richmond (SAUS) ... ViRCC
[*The*] **Computer Co., Richmond, VA** [*Library symbol*] [*Library of Congress*] (LCLS) ... TcC
[*The*] **Computer Co., Richmond, VA** [*Library symbol*] [*Library of Congress*] (LCLS) ... ViRCC
Computer Code (SAUS) ... CC
Computer Color Match Prediction ... CCMP
Computer Color Matching ... CCM
Computer Command Control [*General Motors Corp.*] ... CCC
Computer Command Engineer (MCD) ... CCE
Computer Command Engineer (NAKS) ... COMMAND
Computer Command Ride [*Automotive engineering*] ... CCR
Computer Command Subsystem [*NASA*] ... CCS
Computer Comment (ACAE) ... CC
Computer Communication (SAUS) ... COMPUNICATION
Computer Communication Centre, Europe (SAUS) ... CCCE
Computer Communication Optimization Program (ACAE) ... COPTRAN
Computer Communication Software (SAUS) ... CCS
Computer Communications Access Method (DNAB) ... CCAM
Computer Communications and Data Service (SAUS) ... CCDS
Computer Communications Console (AFM) ... CCC
Computer Communications Converter (MCD) ... CCC
Computer Communications Group [*Canada*] ... CCG
Computer Communications, Inc. ... CCI
Computer Communications Interface (IAA) ... CCI
Computer Communications Line Monitor (MCD) ... CCLM
Computer Communications Networks Group [*University of Waterloo*] [*Canada*] [*Information service or system*] [*Research center*] (IID) ... CCNG
Computer Communications Trouble Analysis Center (SAUS) ... CCTAC
Computer Community (IEEE) ... CC
Computer Company (SAUS) ... TCC
Computer Compatible Data Collection (SAUS) ... CCDC
Computer Competence Tests (TES) ... CCT
Computer Complex ... CC
Computer Components and System Group [*Massachusetts Institute of Technology*] ... CCSG
Computer Composition Corp. [*Also, an information service or system*] (IID) ... CCC
Computer Composition International [*Telecommunications*] (NITA) ... CCI
Computer Concepts [*NASDAQ symbol*] (TTSB) ... CCEE
Computer Concepts Corp. [*NASDAQ symbol*] (SAG) ... CCEE
Computer Concepts Corp. [*Associated Press*] (SAG) ... CptConc
Computer Concepts Trainer (SAUS) ... CCT
Computer Conference ... COMPCON
Computer Conferencing ... CC
Computer Conferencing System (RALS) ... CCS
Computer Consoles, Inc. (SAUS) ... CCI
Computer Consoles Leasing Corp. (EFIS) ... CCLC
Computer Consulting (IAA) ... CC
Computer Consulting Service (BUR) ... CCS
Computer Control and Display Panel (MCD) ... CCDP
Computer Control Center (ROAS) ... CCC
Computer Control Center (SAUO) ... COC
Computer Control Communication (BUR) ... CCC
Computer Control Company (SAUO) ... 3C
Computer Control Company (SAUO) ... CCC
Computer Control Company, Inc (SAUO) ... CCCI
Computer Control Complex ... CCC
Computer Control Corp. ... CCC
Computer Control Division (SAUO) ... CCD
Computer Control Group [*Military*] (CAAL) ... CCG
Computer Control Indicator (CAAL) ... CCI
Computer Control Language (SAUS) ... CCL
Computer Control Loading ... CCL
Computer Control Mode (SAUS) ... CCM
Computer Control Panel ... CCP
Computer Control Station (IAA) ... CCS
Computer Control System (SAUS) ... CCS
Computer Control Unit ... CCU
Computer Controlled (IAA) ... CC
Computer Controlled Automatic Rain Sampler (SAUS) ... CCARS
Computer Controlled Checkout Equipment (SAUS) ... CCCE
Computer Controlled Display (SAUS) ... CCD
Computer Controlled Inking [*Graphic arts*] (DGA) ... CCI
Computer Controlled Instruction (SAUS) ... CCI
Computer Controlled Manufacturing (SAUS) ... CCM
Computer Controlled Microform Search System (SAUS) ... CCMSS
Computer Controlled Microscope (SAUS) ... CCM
Computer Controlled Navigation System (SAUO) ... CCNS4
Computer Controlled Positioning Table (SAUS) ... CCPT
Computer Controlled Random-Access Cartridge Libraries (SAUS) ... CUERAC
Computer Controlled Retrieval (SAUS) ... CCR
Computer Controlled Scanning Electron Microscope (SAUS) ... CCSEM
Computer Controlled Simulator (ACAE) ... CCS
Computer Controlled Traffic Signal System (SAUS) ... CCTS System
Computer Controller Multiplexer Unit ... CCMU
Computer Controller Operation (SAUS) ... CCO
Computer Convention (IAA) ... COMPCON
Computer Core Segment (NASA) ... CCS
Computer Corp. (SAUS) ... COMPCORP
Computer Corp. of America ... CCA
Computer Cost Model ... COCOM
Computer Coupled Machines (NITA) ... CCM
Computer Coupling Unit (MCD) ... CCU

Computer Crime Digest (SAUS)	CCD
Computer Crime Research Laboratories (SAUS)	CCRL
Computer Cross-Select Unit (SAUS)	CCSU
Computer Curriculum Corp.	CCC
Computer Cycle (SAUS)	CC
Computer Data Entry Keyboard	CDEK
Computer Data Entry System (NITA)	CDES
Computer Data Package (SAUS)	CMP
Computer Data Recording System (KSC)	CDRS
Computer Data Switchboard	CDS
Computer Data System	CDS
Computer Data Systems [Associated Press] (SAG)	CmpData
Computer Data Systems, Inc. [Information service or system] (IID)	CDSI
Computer Data Transmission (SAUS)	CDT
Computer Data Transmitter (SAUS)	CDT
Computer Data Word (CET)	CDW
Computer Dealers and Lessors Association (EA)	CDLA
Computer Dealers Association [Later, CDLA]	CDA
Computer Dealers Association (SAUO)	CDA
Computer Dealer's Exposition	COMDEX
Computer Dealers Forum [Acronym represents organization's former name] [Later, NCDF] (EA)	CRF
Computer Description Language (BUR)	CDL
Computer Description Manual (SAUS)	CDM
Computer Design and Education System	CODES
Computer Design and Evaluation System (IEEE)	CODES
Computer Design Corp. (SAUO)	Compcorp
Computer Design Engineer (SAUS)	Comp Des Engr
Computer Design Language (CSR)	CDL
Computer Design of Armoured Cables (PDAA)	CODAC
Computer Design of Electronic Devices (SAUS)	CODED
Computer Desktop Encyclopedia	CDE
Computer Detector Test Console (DNAB)	CDTC
Computer Development Center (KSC)	CDC
Computer Development Center (KSC)	CDEVC
Computer Development Laboratory [Fujitsu Ltd., Hitachi Ltd., and Mitsubishi Corp.] [Japan]	CDL
Computer Development Personnel Association (SAUO)	CDPA
Computer Development System (SAUS)	CODELS
Computer Developments Limited Automatic Coding System (IEEE)	CODEL
Computer Devices, Inc.	CDI
Computer Diagram (SAUS)	CD
Computer Digest (journ.) (SAUS)	CD
Computer Digital Switching System (NITA)	CDSS
Computer Digital Test Station (ACAE)	C/DTS
Computer Diode Corporation (SAUO)	CDC
Computer Direct Input [Computer science] (DCTA)	CDI
Computer Direct to Telegraph	CODIT
Computer Directions Advisors, Inc. [Information service or system] (IID)	CDA
Computer Directions Corp.	CDC
Computer Directions Group, Inc. [Information service or system] (IID)	CDG
Computer Discount Warehouse (PCM)	CDW
Computer Display (SAUS)	CD
Computer Display and Exposition	COMDEX
Computer Display Channel	CDC
Computer Display Terminal (GEOI)	CDT
Computer Display Unit (MCD)	CDU
Computer Distribution System [FAA] (TAG)	CDS
Computer Drum (SAUS)	CD
Computer Dual Access Driver (MCD)	CDAD
Computer Duplex System (BUR)	CDS
Computer Economics Limited (SAUS)	CEL
Computer Economics Ltd. [British] (NITA)	CEL
Computer Education and Applied Research Center	CEARC
Computer Education for Management	CEM
Computer Education Group [British] (BI)	CEG
Computer Education in Schools (SAUS)	CES
Computer Election Systems, Inc.	CES
Computer Electrical System [Davy Computing Ltd.] [Software package] (NCC)	COMPELS
Computer Electroencephalogram	CEEG
Computer, Electronics, and Networking Technology	CENT
Computer Electronics Telecommunications Instruments Automation (ADA)	CETIA
Computer Electronics Unit (SAUS)	CEU
Computer Emergency Response Team	CERT
Computer Emulator Transfer Unit (ACAE)	CETU
Computer Energy Distribution and Automated Control (MHDB)	CEDAC
Computer Energy Storage (SAUS)	CES
Computer Energy Time Unit (MCD)	CETU
Computer Engineer	CE
Computer Engineer Console	CEC
Computer Engineering (DD)	CompEng
Computer Engineering (SAUS)	Comp Engr
Computer Engineering Associates, Inc. (SAUO)	CE
Computer Engineering Service	CES
Computer Enhanced Electronic Warfare Operations Centre [Military] [Canada]	CEEWOC
Computer Enhanced Language Instruction Archive (AIE)	CELIA
Computer Enhanced Radio Emission Surveillance System (SAUS)	CERES System
Computer Enhancement Process (SAUS)	CEP
Computer Entry and Read-Out Control [Computer science] (PDAA)	CERC
Computer Entry and Readout Equipment (KSC)	CERE
Computer Entry Device [Computer science] (PDAA)	CED

Computer Entry Keyboard	CEK
Computer Entry Punch	CEP
Computer Environment Energy Control System (SAUS)	CEECS
Computer Equipment Corporation (SAUO)	CEC
Computer Equipment Information Bureau [Information service or system] (IID)	CEIB
Computer Equipment News [A publication] (APTA)	CEN
Computer Equipment System for Surface-to-Air Missiles (MCD)	CESSAM
Computer Evaluation of Scanning Electron Microscope Image	CESEMI
Computer Event Marketing Association (NTPA)	CEMA
Computer Exchange, Incorporated (SAUO)	CEI
Computer Execute Function (KSC)	CEF
Computer Facilities Management (MCD)	CFM
Computer Facility for Mine Warfare (SAUS)	COFAM
Computer Family Architecture	CFA
Computer Fast Storage (SAUS)	CFS
Computer Fault Isolation (MCD)	CFI
Computer Feasibility Model (SAUS)	CFM
Computer Field Maintenance [British]	CFM
Computer File System (SAUS)	CFS
Computer Firmware Systems, Inc. (SAUS)	CFS
Computer Flight Plan	CFP
Computer Flight Testing (MCD)	CFT
Computer for Advanced Spare Systems (IAA)	COMPASS
Computer for Automatic Teaching Operations (DNAB)	CATO
Computer for Automatic Teaching Operations-Compiler (DNAB)	CATOCOMP
Computer for Automatic Teaching Operations-Resident (DNAB)	CATORES
Computer for Special Small Tactical Application	COSSTA
Computer for Uprange Point-of-Impact Determination [NASA] (KSC)	CUPID
Computer Form, Fit, and Function (MCD)	CF3
Computer Format Control Buffer	CFCB
Computer Forms Feeder (SAUS)	CFF
Computer Forms Printer (IAA)	CFP
Computer Forum and Exposition (SAUS)	COMFOR
Computer Fraud [A publication] (NITA)	CF
Computer, Freedom and Privacy (SAUO)	CFP
Computer Function Diagram (SAUS)	CFD
Computer Function Symbol (SAUS)	CFS
Computer Game Developers' Association (DDC)	CGDA
Computer Generated Forces [Army]	CGF
Computer Generated Letter	CGL
Computer Generation (SAUS)	CG
Computer Geoscience Section (SAUO)	CGS
Computer Graphic Aerodynamic Analysis (SAUS)	CGAA
Computer Graphics (MCD)	CG
Computer Graphics and Applications (journ.) (SAUS)	CG&A
Computer Graphics and Image Processing (MCD)	CGIP
Computer Graphics Arrangement Program (PDAA)	COGAP
Computer Graphics Display System [Army] (MCD)	CGDS
Computer Graphics for Aerodynamic Analysis (MCD)	CGAA
Computer Graphics Interface	CGI
Computer Graphics International (SAUS)	CGI
Computer Graphics Metafile [Image format] (AAEL)	CGM
Computer Graphics: Principles and Practise (SAUS)	CGPP
Computer Graphics Processing (HGAA)	CGP
Computer Graphics Reference Model (RALS)	CGRM
Computer Graphics Research Group [Ohio State University] [Research center] (RCD)	CGRG
Computer Graphics Society (SAUO)	CGS
Computer Graphics Structural Analysis	CGSA
Computer Graphics Unit (SAUS)	CGU
Computer Graphics World	CGW
Computer Group News (SAUO)	CGN
Computer Group News (journ.) (SAUS)	CGN
Computer Guidance Corporation (SAUO)	CGC
Computer Guided Optical Registration [VISCOM Optical Products, Inc.]	CGOR
Computer Handling of Reactor Data-Safety (SAUS)	CHORD-S
Computer Hardware Acquisition and Modernization Program [Department of Agriculture] (GFGA)	CHAMP
Computer Hardware, Advanced Mathematics and Model Physics (SAUS)	CHAMMP
Computer Hardware, Advanced Mathematics, and Model Physics Initiative [Department of Energy]	CHAMMP
Computer Hardware Consultants and Services (SAUS)	CHCS
Computer Hardware Consultants and Services, Inc. (SAUO)	CHCS
Computer Hardware Description Language	CHDL
Computer Hardware Services GmbH (SAUS)	CHS
Computer Having Intelligent Learning and Development (SAUS)	CHILD
Computer History and Maintenance Planning System (SAUS)	CHAMPS
Computer History Association of California	CHAC
Computer Horizons [NASDAQ symbol] (TTSB)	CHRZ
Computer Horizons Corp. [NASDAQ symbol] (NQ)	CHRZ
Computer Horizons Corp. [Associated Press] (SAG)	CmptHz
Computer Hostess (SAUS)	Comptess
Computer Hour	CHR
Computer Human Interaction (SAUS)	CHI
Computer Human Interface (SAUS)	CHI
Computer Identics Corp. [NASDAQ symbol] (NQ)	CIDN
Computer Identics Corp. [Associated Press] (SAG)	CmpIdn
Computer Image Generation System (ACAE)	CIGS
Computer Image Generation Unifying Device (ACAE)	CIGUD
Computer Image Generator [or Generation] (MCD)	CIG
Computer Image Processing (SAUS)	CIP
Computer in Control Logic (MCD)	CICL
Computer in Education Division (SAUS)	CoED

Computer Incident Advisory Capability [Department of Energy] [Computer science] ... CIAC
Computer Indentics [NASDAQ symbol] (TTSB) ... CIDN
Computer Independent Specification ... CIS
Computer Index for Neutron Data [Information service or system] (NITA) .... CINDA
Computer Index of Neutron Data [Atomic Energy Authority] [Databank] [British] ... CIND
Computer Index of Neutron Data [Brookhaven National Laboratory] [Information service or system] (CRD) ... CINDA
Computer Indicator (AFM) ... CI
Computer Indicator Test Console (DNAB) ... CITC
Computer Industries, Inc. (SAUO) ... CII
Computer Industry ... CI
Computer Industry Association [Later, CCIA] ... CIA
Computer Industry Coalition for Advanced Television Service ... CICATS
Computer Industry Council (EA) ... CIC
Computer Industry Daily [Zif-Davis] [A publication] (NITA) ... CID
Computer Industry Development Potential (IAA) ... CIDP
Computer Industry Software, Services, and Products [Information service or system] (IID) ... CISS
Computer Industry Training and Technology Corp., Inc. [Commercial firm] [Australia] ... CITTC
Computer Information Centre for Highway Engineering (SAUO) ... CICHE
Computer Information Control System/Enterprise Systems Architecture [IBM Corp.] (VERA) ... CICSESA
Computer Information Delivery Service (BARN) ... CIDS
Computer Information Network (SSD) ... CIN
Computer Information Processing (IAA) ... CIP
Computer Information Resources ... CIR
Computer Information Services [Corp. for Public Broadcasting - CPB] [Information service or system] (IID) ... CIS
Computer Information System (SAUO) ... CIS
Computer Information Systems Department (SAUO) ... CISD
Computer Innovations Distribution, Inc. [Toronto Stock Exchange symbol] CIC
Computer Input from Microfilm (ECII) ... CIM
Computer Input Matrix (KSC) ... CIM
Computer Input Media (SAUS) ... CIM
Computer Input Microfilming (MCD) ... CIM
Computer Input Multiplexer (KSC) ... CIM
Computer Input Quantity (SAUS) ... CIQ
Computer Input/Output Equipment (SAUS) ... CIOE
Computer Inquiries ... CI
Computer Inquiry (SAUS) ... CI
Computer Inquiry III [FCC] ... CI-III
Computer Installation Management Seminar (SAUO) ... CIMS
Computer Installation Management System (PDAA) ... CIMS
Computer Institute for Applications in Science and Engineering (MCD)..... CIASE
Computer Instruction (SAUS) ... CI
Computer Instruction and Training Assistance for the Blind ... CITAB
Computer Instruction Word (SAUS) ... CIW
Computer Instrumentation Limited (SAUS) ... CIL
Computer Instruments Corp. ... CIC
Computer Integrated Building (SAUS) ... CIB
Computer Integrated Bureaucracy (SAUO) ... CIB
Computer Integrated Business (VERA) ... CIB
Computer Integrated Command and Attack Systems (PDAA) ... CICAS
Computer Integrated Courtroom ... CIC
Computer Integrated Electron Design Series (SAUS) ... CIEDS
Computer Integrated Enterprise (SAUS) ... CIE
Computer Integrated Environment (SAUS) ... CIE
Computer Integrated Facilities (SAUS) ... CIF
Computer Integrated Flexible Manufacturing (NITA) ... CIFM
Computer Integrated Machinery (SAUS) ... CIM
Computer Integrated Manufacture (SAUO) ... CIM
Computer Integrated Manufacture/Data Collection System (NITA) ... CIM/DCS
Computer Integrated Manufacturing ... CIM
Computer Integrated Manufacturing Process Analysis and Control (SAUS) ... CIMPAC
Computer Integrated Manufacturing Techniques (ACAE) ... CIMT
Computer Integrated Manufacturing/Mechanical Engineering System (NITA) ... CIM/ME
Computer Integrated Measurement System (SAUS) ... CIMS
Computer Integrated Processing (SAUS) ... CIP
Computer Integrated Repair (SAUS) ... CIR
Computer Integrated Repair Facility (SAUS) ... CIRF
Computer Integrated Telephone (or Telephoning, or Telephony) (SAUS) ... CIT
Computer Integration Laboratories (VERA) ... CIL
Computer Integration of Requirements Procurement Logistics & Support (SAUS) ... CIRPLS
Computer Intelligence Corp. [Information service or system] (IID) ... CI
Computer Intelligence Corp. [Information service or system] (IID) ... CIC
Computer Interchange of Museum Information Committee ... CIMI
Computer Interconnect (ACRL) ... CI
Computer Interface (ACAE) ... CI
Computer Interface Adapter ... CIA
Computer Interface Conditioning Unit (MCD) ... CICU
Computer Interface Control [Part of digital television computer] ... CIC
Computer Interface Control Unit (NASA) ... CICU
Computer Interface Device (NASA) ... CID
Computer Interface Electronics (SAUS) ... CIE
Computer Interface for Television (MCD) ... CINTEL
Computer Interface Module [Computer science] ... CIM
Computer Interface Sub System (ACAE) ... CISS
Computer Interface Technology (IEEE) ... CIT
Computer Interface Terminal (CET) ... CIT

Computer Interface Unit ... CIU
Computer Intergrated Tooling (SAUS) ... CIT
Computer Interpreter Language (MHDB) ... CIL
Computer Interrogator ... CI
Computer Interrupt Equipment (MHDB) ... CIE
Computer Investment Group, Inc. (NITA) ... CIG
Computer Investments Ltd. [British] (NITA) ... CIL
Computer Investors Group, Inc. (SAUO) ... CIG
Computer Jobs Through Training (SAUS) ... CJTT
Computer Journal Abstracts (SAUS) ... CJA
Computer Laboratory (SAUS) ... CL
Computer Laboratory for Instruction in Psychological Research [University of Colorado - Boulder] [Research center] (RCD) ... CLIPR
Computer Laboratory of Harvard University ... CLHU
Computer Laboratory Systems Project (SAUO) ... CLASP
Computer Language (NITA) ... C
Computer Language (IAA) ... CL
Computer Language for Aeronautics and Space Programming [NASA] .... CLASP
Computer Language for Engineers and Technologists (MHDB) ... CLEAT
Computer Language for Information Processing (NITA) ... CLIP
Computer Language Magazine [Miller Freeman Publications] [Information service or system] (CRD) ... CLM
Computer Language One (SAUS) ... CL-1
Computer Language Recorder ... CLR
Computer Language Research (IEEE) ... CLR
Computer Language Research, Inc. [NASDAQ symbol] (SAG) ... CLRI
Computer Language Research, Inc. [Associated Press] (SAG) ... CmpLR
Computer Language Rsch [NASDAQ symbol] (TTSB) ... CLRI
Computer Language to Aid and Stimulate Scientific, Mathematical, and Technical Education ... CLASSMATE
Computer Language Translator ... CLT
Computer Language Utility Extension (PDAA) ... CLUE
Computer Languages for the Processing of Text (DGA) ... CLPT
Computer Launch and Separation Problem (MCD) ... CLASP
Computer Launch Interference Problems ... CLIP
Computer Launch Interference Problems (SAUS) ... CLIPS
Computer Law & Security Report [A publication] ... CLSR
Computer Law and Tax Report (SAUS) ... CLTR
Computer Law and Tax Report [A publication] (DLA) ... Computer L & Tax
Computer Law and Tax Report [A publication] (DLA) ... Computer L & T Rep
Computer Law Association (EA) ... CLA
Computer Law Service Reporter ... CLSR
Computer Law Service Reporter [A publication] (DLA) ... Computer L Serv Rep
Computer Layout Installation Planner (MHDB) ... CLIP
Computer Layout of Integrated Circuits (PDAA) ... CLIC
Computer League for Users in Education (EDAC) ... CLUE
Computer Learning Center (HGAA) ... CLC
Computer Learning Centers, Inc. [NASDAQ symbol] (SAG) ... CLCX
Computer Learning Centers, Inc. [Associated Press] (SAG) ... CptrLrn
Computer Learning Ctrs [NASDAQ symbol] (TTSB) ... CLCX
Computer Learning Under Evaluation (SAUS) ... CLUE
Computer Leasing and Remarketing Association (NTPA) ... CLRA
Computer Leasing Company (SAUO) ... CLC
Computer Leasing Ltd. (SAUS) ... CLL
Computer Lessors Association [Later, CDLA] (EA) ... CLA
Computer Letter Service (HGAA) ... CLS
Computer Liability Insurance Coverage (SAUS) ... CLIC
Computer Liaison Nurse (MEDA) ... CLN
Computer Library Applications Service ... CLAS
Computer Library Service, Inc. (SAUO) ... CLIS
Computer Library Services, Inc. [Wellesley Hills, MA] ... CLSI
Computer Line Terminal (HGAA) ... CLT
Computer Linguistics, Inc. (SAUS) ... CLI
Computer Linguistics, Incorporated (SAUO) ... CLI
Computer Link Corporation (SAUO) ... CLC
Computer Linked Information for Container Shipping (SAUS) ... CLICS
Computer Listing and Analysis of Maintenance Programs (MHDB) ... CLAMP
Computer Listing Service [Computer Listing Service, Inc.] [Information service or system] (IID) ... CLS
Computer Listings of Employment Opportunities [The Copley Press, Inc.] [Database] ... CLEO
Computer Literacy & Information Technology (WDAA) ... CLAIT
Computer Literacy and Studies in Schools (AIE) ... CLASS
Computer Literacy Council (EA) ... CLC
Computer Load and Resource Analysis (MCD) ... CLARA
Computer Load Simulator (SAUS) ... CLS
Computer Lock-On ... CLO
Computer Logging Unit and Editor (NITA) ... CLUE
Computer Logic Demonstrator ... CLD
Computer Logic Graphics (SAUS) ... CLOG
Computer Logic Unit Tester (MCD) ... CLUT
Computer Machinery Corp. Ltd. [Subsidiary of Microdata] (MCD) ... CMC
Computer Machinery Corporation (SAUO) ... CMC
Computer Magnetic Drum (SAUS) ... CMD
Computer Magnetic Tape (SAUS) ... CMT
Computer Main Memory [Telecommunications] (TEL) ... CMM
Computer Maintenance Corporation (SAUO) ... CMC
Computer Maintenance Test Set ... CMTS
Computer Managed Training (SAUS) ... CMT
Computer Management [British] [A publication] ... CM
Computer Management and Control (SAUS) ... CMAC
Computer Management and Development Services ... CMDS
Computer Management Association ... CMA
Computer Management Consultants, Inc. (SAUO) ... CMC
Computer Management Group [British] (NITA) ... CMG

Computer Management Learning (SAUS) .... CML
Computer Management Sciences, Inc. [*NASDAQ symbol*] (SAG) .... CMSX
Computer Management Sciences, Inc. [*Associated Press*] (SAG) .... CompMS
Computer Management System [*Burroughs Corp.*] (BUR) .... CMS
Computer Management Transaction Control System (SAUS) .... CMTCS
Computer Management/Computer-Assisted Instruction (MCD) .... CM/CAI
Computer Manufacture and Design (SAUS) .... CMAD
Computer Marked Assignment (SAUS) .... CMA
Computer Marketing [*Standard & Poor's*] .... COMPMARK
Computer Marketing Services [*Anaheim, CA*] [*Information service or system*] (IID) .... CMS
Computer Marketing/Mailing (SAA) .... CM/M
Computer Marketplace [*NASDAQ symbol*] (TTSB) .... MKPL
Computer Marketplace, Inc. [*Associated Press*] (SAG) .... CptM
Computer Marketplace, Inc. [*Associated Press*] (SAG) .... CptMk
Computer Marketplace, Inc. [*Associated Press*] (SAG) .... CptrMkt
Computer Marketplace, Inc. [*NASDAQ symbol*] (SAG) .... MKPL
Computer Marketplace Wrrt'A' [*NASDAQ symbol*] (TTSB) .... MKPLW
Computer Marketplace Wrrt'B' [*NASDAQ symbol*] (TTSB) .... MKPLZ
Computer Matching and Privacy Protection Amendments (COE) .... CMPPA
Computer Mathematics Corporation (ACAE) .... CMC
Computer Measurement and Evaluation .... CME
Computer Measurement Group (EA) .... CMG
Computer Measurement Group, Inc. (SAUO) .... CMG
Computer Measurements Company (SAUO) .... CMC
Computer Mechanisms Corporation (SAUO) .... CMC
Computer Mediated Communication .... CMC
Computer Mediated Communications (SAUO) .... CMC
Computer Mediated Drill and Educational Testing (SAUS) .... COMDET
Computer Mediated Interaction (SAUS) .... CMI
Computer Mediated Teleconferencing (SAUS) .... CMT
Computer Memories, Inc. (NITA) .... CMI
Computer Memory Divices, Inc (SAUO) .... CMD
Computer Memory Element .... CME
Computer Memory Interconnect (CIST) .... CMI
Computer Memory Tester .... CMT
Computer Memory Unit .... CMU
Computer Message Transmission .... COMET
Computer Method of Sequencing Operations for Assembly Lines (MCD) .... COMSOAL
Computer Methods Corporation (SAUO) .... CMC
Computer Methods for Automatic Diagnosis (PDAA) .... COMAD
Computer Mgmt Sciences [*NASDAQ symbol*] (TTSB) .... CMSX
Computer Micro Image Systems (SAUS) .... CMIS
Computer Microfilm Corp. [*Information service or system*] (IID) .... CMC
Computer Microfilm International Corp. [*Information service or system*] (IID) .... CMIC
Computer Microfilm Output (SAUS) .... CMO
Computer Micrographic Technology Users Group (SAUO) .... COMTEC
Computer Micrographics and Technology Group (NITA) .... COMTEC
Computer Micrographics Technology [*An association*] [*Defunct*] (EA) .... CMT
Computer Micrographics Technology (EA) .... COMtec
Computer Microtechnology (IAA) .... CM
Computer Misuse Detection System (SAUS) .... CMDS
Computer Model (MCD) .... COMO
Computer Model for Feasibility Analysis and Reporting [*United Nations*] (NITA) .... COMFAR
Computer Modeling Package (SAUS) .... CMP
Computer Modelling Group [*Research center*] (RCD) .... CMG
Computer Module .... CM
Computer Monitor Adapter .... CMA
Computer Monitor and Control (MCD) .... CMAC
Computer Monitor and Control Console (CAAL) .... CMCC
Computer Multi-Mini-Processor (SAUS) .... CMMP
Computer Multiple Listing Service [*Information service or system*] (IID) .... CMLS
Computer Musician Coalition (EA) .... CMC
Computer Negotiations Report (SAUS) .... CNREPORT
Computer Network (SAUS) .... COMNET
Computer Network Architecture (SAUS) .... CNA
Computer Network Center (SAUS) .... CCNC
Computer Network Corp. [*Information service or system*] (IID) .... COMNET
Computer Network Integrators (SAUS) .... CNI
Computer Network of Building Researchers (SAUO) .... CNBR
Computer Network of IFLA (SAUS) .... IFLANET
Computer Network Performance Symposium (SAUS) .... CNPS
Computer Network Security Response Team .... CNSRT
Computer Network System (SAUS) .... CNS
Computer Network Systems, Inc. (AAGC) .... CNSI
Computer Network Technology [*NASDAQ symbol*] (TTSB) .... CMNT
Computer Network Technology Corp. [*NASDAQ symbol*] (NQ) .... CMNT
Computer Network Technology Corp. [*Associated Press*] (SAG) .... CptNwk
Computer Networking and Communications Systems Program [*Georgia Institute of Technology, School of Information and Computer Science*] [*Atlanta*] [*Telecommunications service*] (TSSD) .... CNCS
Computer Networking Stand Alone Program .... COMPUNET
Computer Non Operational (SAUS) .... CNO
Computer Not Operational (IAA) .... CNO
Computer Numerical Control [*Computer science*] .... CNC
Computer Numerical Logic .... CNL
Computer Occupational Data Analysis Program .... CODAP
Computer of Average Transients [*Spectroscopy*] .... CAT
Computer On-Line Real-Time Applications Language [*Computer science*] (IEEE) .... CORAL
Computer Only Linofilm [*Graphic arts*] (DGA) .... COL
Computer Operated Automatic Test System (SAUS) .... COATS
Computer Operated Branch Recording and Acquisition System (ADA) .... COBRA
Computer Operated Electronics Display [*Program*] [*Computer science*] (ECII) .... COED
Computer Operated Instrument System (SAUS) .... COINS
Computer Operated Manufacturing and Test System (SAUS) .... COMATS
Computer Operated Peripheral Equipment (ACAE) .... COPE
Computer Operated Spectrophotometric Analysis of Cameras (NITA) .... COSAC
Computer Operated Spectrophotometric Analysis of Monitors (NITA) .... COSAM
Computer Operating and Programming Environment (DNAB) .... COPE
Computer Operating Instruction .... COI
Computer Operating Properly .... COP
Computer Operating System (SAUS) .... COOP System
Computer Operating Unit (SAUS) .... COU
Computer Operation (SAUS) .... CO
Computer Operation Code (SAUS) .... COC
Computer Operations, Audit and Security Technology (SAUO) .... COAST
Computer Operations Centre (SAUS) .... COC
Computer Operations Division (COE) .... COD
Computer Operations Europe (SAUO) .... COE
Computer Operations Facility .... COF
Computer Operations Group .... COG
Computer Operations Management Association .... COMA
Computer Operations Management Information Training (SAUS) .... COMIT
Computer Operations Procedures Manual .... COPM
Computer Operations Scheduling Accounting and Control System (SAUS) .... COSACS
Computer Operator (SAUS) .... Cmpt Op
Computer Operator Aptitude Battery [*Test*] .... COAB
Computer Operator Aptitude Test (SAUS) .... COAT
Computer Operator Console Training (SAUS) .... TELESPO
Computer Operator Handbook .... COH
Computer Operator Proficiency Examination (SAA) .... COPE
Computer Operators' Course .... COC
Computer Optimal Media Planning and Selection System (PDAA) .... COMPASS
Computer Optimization and Simulation Modelling for Operating Supermarkets (SAUS) .... COSMOS
Computer Optimization Package [*or Program*] [*General Electric Co.*] .... COP
Computer Optimized Experimental Design (AAEL) .... COED
Computer Optimized Fabrication [*Sheet metal*] [*Raytheon Co.*] .... COF
Computer Optimized Sheetmetal Technology [*Raytheon Co.*] .... COST
Computer or Computerized Acquisition System (NITA) .... CAS
Computer Oracle and Password System (SAUS) .... COPS
Computer Order Control Automated System (SAUS) .... COCAS
Computer Order Processing and Sales Accounting (IAA) .... COPSAC
Computer Orientated Reproducer Assembly (DGA) .... CORA
Computer Oriented Bearing Response Analysis (SAUS) .... COBRA
Computer Oriented Classicists (EA) .... COC
Computer Oriented Data Acquisition (SAUS) .... CODA
Computer Oriented Geological Society [*Database producer*] (IID) .... COGS
Computer Oriented Interactive Graphical Analysis and Design (SAUS) .... COINGRAD
Computer Oriented Management Planning and Scheduling System (SAUS) .... COMPASS
Computer Oriented Method for Payroll Accounting and Statistics (SAUS) .... COMPAS
Computer Oriented Music Materials Processed for User Transformation or Exchange (NITA) .... COMMPUTE
Computer Oriented Police Planning System (SAUS) .... COPPS
Computer Oriented Record Keeping System (NITA) .... CORKS
Computer Oriented Scheduling and Control System (SAUS) .... COSACS
Computer Oriented System And Newly Organized Storage-To-Retrieval Apparatus (SAUS) .... COSA NOSTRA
Computer Oriented System for Management Order Synthesis (SAUS) .... COSMOS
Computer Originated Document (SAUS) .... COD
Computer Output Committee (SAUS) .... COC
Computer Output Microfilm [*or Microfiche or Microform*] (BUR) .... COM
Computer Output Microfilm Equipment .... COME
Computer Output Microfilm Package .... COMPAC
Computer Output Microfilmer (SAUS) .... COM
Computer Output Microform Catalog .... COMCAT
Computer Output Micrographics (SAUS) .... COM
Computer Output to LASER Disk (PCM) .... COLD
Computer Outputer Microforms Program and Concept Study (MCD) .... COMPACS
Computer Outscoring Services [*NASDAQ symbol*] (SAG) .... COSI
Computer Outscoring Services [*Associated Press*] (SAG) .... CptOuts
Computer Owner Protection [*IDX Technologies, Inc.*] (PCM) .... COP
Computer Packages (MCD) .... COMPAC
Computer Packaging Committee (SAUS) .... CPC
Computer Packaging Engineer (SAUS) .... Comp Pkg Engr
Computer Paragraph .... CP
Computer Payroll (BUR) .... COMPAY
Computer People for Peace (SAUS) .... CPP
Computer Performance Analysis [*Boole & Babbage, Inc.*] .... CPA
Computer Performance Evaluation .... CPE
Computer Performance Evaluation Users Group [*Defunct*] (EA) .... CPEUG
Computer Performance Management .... CPM
Computer Performance Monitor (PDAA) .... CPM
Computer Performance Technical Center (SAUO) .... CPTC
Computer Peripheral Equipment (KSC) .... CPE
Computer Peripheral Manufacturers Association .... CPMA
Computer Peripheral Module (SAUS) .... CPM
Computer Peripheral Unit (IEEE) .... CPU
Computer Peripherals, Inc. (SAUS) .... CPI

Computer Peripherals, Small Computer and Systems Exhibition and Conference (SAUO) .... COMPEC
Computer Personnel Research Group [*Later, Special Interest Group for Computer Personnel Research*] .... CPRG
Computer Pete [*NASDAQ symbol*] (TTSB) .... CPCO
Computer Petroleum Corp. [*Information service or system*] (IID) .... CPC
Computer Petroleum Corp. [*NASDAQ symbol*] (SAG) .... CPCO
Computer Petroleum Corp. [*Associated Press*] (SAG) .... CptrPtl
Computer Planning and Control Technique (BUR) .... COMPACT
Computer Planning Corp. (SAUS) .... CPC
Computer Planning Corporation (SAUO) .... CPC
Computer Plotting Matrix System (PDAA) .... CPMS
Computer Pneumatic Input Panel .... CPIP
Computer Polarization Holography .... CPH
Computer Position Profile (PDAA) .... CPP
Computer Power Australia (SAUS) .... CPA
Computer Power Center .... CPC
Computer Power Supply .... CPS
Computer Power Support System .... CPSS
Computer Predicting and Automatic Course Tracking (PDAA) .... COMPACT
Computer Prepared Text (SAUS) .... COMPTEXT
Computer Prescribed Instruction (SAUS) .... CPI
Computer Press Association (EA) .... CPA
Computer Print Console .... CPC
Computer Print Control (SAUS) .... CPC
Computer Printer Unit (MCD) .... CPU
Computer Printing (SAUS) .... CP
Computer Printout (ADA) .... CPO
Computer Printout Processing (PDAA) .... CPP
Computer Private branch exchange Interface (SAUS) .... CPI
Computer Process Control .... CPC
Computer Processing Corporation for Economic and Industrial Research (SAUO) .... CEIR
Computer Processor Unit .... CPU
Computer Produced Drawing (SAUS) .... CPD
Computer Product News (MHDI) .... CPN
Computer Product Testing Service .... CPTS
Computer Production Control (SAUS) .... CPC
Computer Products [*NASDAQ symbol*] (TTSB) .... CPRD
Computer Products Directory [*Information service or system*] (IID) .... CPD
Computer Products, Inc. [*Associated Press*] (SAG) .... CmpPr
Computer Products, Inc. [*NASDAQ symbol*] (NQ) .... CPRD
Computer Professionals for Peace (SAUO) .... CPP
Computer Professionals for Social Responsibility (EA) .... CPSR
Computer Program (IEEE) .... COMPROG
Computer Program (MCD) .... CP
Computer Program Assistance Library (NITA) .... CPAL
Computer Program Associated Contractor .... CPAC
Computer Program Book .... CPB
Computer Program Change Instruction (NAKS) .... CPC
Computer Program Change Instruction (NASA) .... CPCI
Computer Program Change Library (NASA) .... CPCL
Computer Program Change Request (NASA) .... CPCR
Computer Program Components (MCD) .... CPC
Computer Program Configuration Identification .... CPCI
Computer Program Configured Item (MCD) .... CPCI
Computer Program Contract End Item .... CPCEI
Computer Program Control Library (MCD) .... CPCL
Computer Program Design Requirements (ACAE) .... CPDR
Computer Program Design [*or Development*] Specification [*NASA*] (NASA) .... CPDS
Computer Program Detail Design Specification (MCD) .... CPDDS
Computer Program Development and Management System .... CPDAMS
Computer Program Development Center [*Air Force*] (MCD) .... CPDC
Computer Program Development Plan .... CPDP
Computer Program Deviation Request (MCD) .... CPDR
Computer Program End Item (NASA) .... CPEI
Computer Program for Automatic Control .... COMPAC
Computer Program Functional Specification (CTAS) .... CPFS
Computer Program Identification Numbers (MCD) .... CPIN
Computer Program Implementation Process .... CPIP
Computer Program Information Center (MCD) .... COPIC
Computer Program Integrated Document (OA) .... CPID
Computer Program Integration Contractor .... CPIC
Computer Program Library (BUR) .... CPL
Computer Program Module (NASA) .... CPM
Computer Program Operational Flight Program (MCD) .... CPOFP
Computer Program Package (CAAL) .... CPP
Computer Program Product Specification (MCD) .... CPPS
Computer Program Products Ltd. (SAUO) .... CPP
Computer Program Specification (AFM) .... CPS
Computer Program Submodule (MCD) .... CPSM
Computer Program System [*Boeing Co.*] .... CPS
Computer Program Tapes (MCD) .... CPT
Computer Program Test and Evaluation .... CPT & E
Computer Program Test Plan .... CPTP
Computer Program Test Plan (CAAL) .... CPTPL
Computer Program Test Procedure .... CPTP
Computer Program Test Procedures (CAAL) .... CPTPR
Computer Program Test Report (MCD) .... CPTR
Computer Program Update .... CPU
Computer Program Users' Manual (ACAE) .... CPUM
Computer Program/Maintenance (AAEL) .... CP/M
Computer Programmer Aptitude Battery [*Test*] .... CPAB
Computer Programmer's Manual (MCD) .... CPM

Computer Programmes Information Center (SAUS) .... COSMIC
Computer Programming and Testing Activity (IEEE) .... CPTA
Computer Programming Concepts (BUR) .... CPC
Computer Programming Language [*for small computers*] (BARN) C
Computer Programming Performance Specification (MCD) .... CPPS
Computer Programming Service .... CPS
Computer Programming System (SAUS) .... CPS
Computer Programming Training (SAUS) .... CPT
Computer Programs in Science and Technology (SAUS) .... CPST
Computer Projects, Inc. [*Greensboro, NC*] [*Telecommunications*] (TSSD) .... CPI
Computer Projects Limited .... CPL
Computer Queue .... CQ
Computer Randomized Item Bank (SAUS) .... CRIB
Computer Readability Editing System (MCD) .... CRES
Computer Readable Magnetic Tape (SAUS) .... CR MT
Computer Readable Medium .... CRM
Computer Readable Output [*Computer science*] (PCM) .... CRO
Computer Readable System .... CRS
Computer Reader Enquiry Service System [*Automated library system*] (NITA) .... CRESS
Computer Readout Device (SAUS) .... CRD
Computer Ready Electronic Files (SAUS) .... CREF
Computer Realtime Access Method (IAA) .... CREAM
Computer Rearrangement of Subject Specialities (SAUS) .... CROSS
Computer Recognition Systems [*Commercial firm*] [*British*] (NITA) .... CRS
Computer Recognition Systems Ltd. [*British*] .... CRSL
Computer Reconstructed Images from Scene Photographs (SAUS) .... CRISP
Computer Recording of Defects in Sewerage Systems (SAUS) .... CRODISS
Computer Related Industries (SAUS) .... CRI
Computer Related Services (SAUS) .... CRS
Computer Remote Terminal (MCD) .... CRT
Computer Repair, Parts, and Tools (SAA) .... CR
Computer Report on Importance (PDAA) .... CRIMP
Computer Resale Brokers International Ltd. (SAUO) .... CRB
Computer Research and Education Network (SAUS) .... CREN
Computer Research Corporation of California (SAUO) .... CRC
Computer Research Education Network (SAUO) .... CREN
Computer Research Group, Inc. [*Information service or system*] (IID) .... CRG
Computer Research Laboratory (SAUO) .... CRL
Computer Research, Systems, and Software (IEEE) .... COMPRESS
Computer Reseller News (SAUS) .... CRN
Computer Reservation System .... CRS
Computer Reset Pulse (KSC) .... CRP
Computer Resident Automatic Instruction (MCD) .... CRAI
Computer Resident Planning (MCD) .... CRP
Computer Resource .... CR
Computer Resource acquisition course (SAUO) .... CR
Computer Resource Acquisition Course (SAUO) .... CRAC
Computer Resource Center (SAUO) .... CRC
Computer Resource Management [*Army*] (IAA) .... CRM
Computer Resource Management Plan [*Army*] (RDA) .... CRMP
Computer Resource Unit .... CRU
Computer Resource Utilization (SAUS) .... CRU
Computer Resources Board (SAUO) .... CRB
Computer Resources Council (SAUO) .... CRC
Computer Resources Development Plan [*NASA*] (NASA) .... CRDP
Computer Resources Integrated Support Data (MCD) .... CRISD
Computer Resources Integrated Support Document [*Military*] .... CRISD
Computer Resources Integrated Support Plan [*Military*] (AFIT) .... CRISP
Computer Resources International A/S (SAUS) .... CRI
Computer Resources Life Cycle Management Plan (SAUO) .... CRLCMP
Computer Resources Life-Cycle Management Plan .... CRLCMP
Computer Resources Management Data (MCD) .... CRMD
Computer Resources Management Program (SAUO) .... CRMP
Computer Resources Management Technology (SAUO) .... CRMT
Computer Resources Nucleus [*FAA*] (TAG) .... CORN
Computer Resources Support (ACAE) .... CRS
Computer Resources Working Group [*Military*] (AFIT) .... CRWG
Computer Response Corp. .... CRC
Computer Results Corp. [*Information service or system*] (IID) .... CRC
Computer Retailers Association [*British*] (NITA) .... CRA
Computer Retrieval Editor [*Used to manage CORKIPER file family*] .... COREDITOR
Computer Retrieval of Information on Scientific Projects [*National Institutes of Health*] [*Information service or system*] (IID) .... CRISP
Computer Retrieval of Kinetic Parameters of Electrode Reactions .... CORKIPER
Computer Retrieval of Organic Structures Based on Wiswesser .... CROSSBOW
Computer Review and Orientation Course .... CROC
Computer Room People (SAUS) .... CRP
Computer Routine for Evaluation of Simulation Tactics (SAUS) .... CREST
Computer Routine for Evaluation of Submarine Threats (MCD) .... CREST
Computer Run (SAUS) .... CR
Computer Run Report (NASA) .... CRR
Computer Sales and Services (SAUS) .... CSS
Computer Scatter Tomography (MELL) .... CST
Computer Scheduling System (IAA) .... CSS
Computer Science (DD) .... CompSc
Computer Science (VERA) .... CS
Computer Science Accreditation Board (RALS) .... CSAB
Computer Science and Electrical Engineering (SAUS) .... CSEE
Computer Science and Engineering .... CSE
Computer Science and Engineering Research Study (SAUS) .... COSERS
Computer Science & Information Laboratory (SAUS) .... CSIT
Computer Science and Technology Board (VERA) .... CSTB
Computer Science & Technology Board (SAUS) .... CTSB
Computer Science Association (SAUO) .... CSA

Computer Science Canada (SAUS) ... CSC
Computer Science Center [*North Carolina A & T State University*] [*Research center*] (RCD) ... CSC
Computer Science Center [*University of Maryland*] [*Research center*] (RCD) ... CSC
Computer Science Conference (SAUS) ... CSC
Computer Science Department (SAUO) ... CSD
Computer Science Division ... CSD
Computer Science for Environment Protection (SAUO) ... CSEP
Computer Science (journ.) (SAUS) ... CS
Computer Science Laboratory [*Sony*] [*Japan*] (ECON) ... CSL
Computer Science Lecturers' Association [*British*] ... CSLA
Computer Science Library (SAUO) ... CSL
Computer Science Network [*University Corp. for Atmospheric Research*] ... CSNET
Computer Science Press (SAUS) ... CSP
Computer Science Research Centre (SAUO) ... CSRC
Computer Science Research Laboratory (SAUO) ... CSRL
Computer Science Teleprocessing System (IAA) ... CSTS
Computer Science Time Sharing (SAUS) ... CSTS
Computer Science Time-Sharing System (IAA) ... CSTS
Computer Science-research Network (SAUS) ... CSNET
Computer Sciences [*NYSE symbol*] (TTSB) ... CSC
Computer Sciences Corp. [*Database originator*] [*Associated Press*] (SAG) ... CompSci
Computer Sciences Corp. [*El Segunda, CA*] [*Database originator*] [*NYSE symbol*] (SPSG) ... CSC
Computer Sciences Corp., Technical Library, El Segundo, CA [*Library symbol*] [*Library of Congress*] (LCLS) ... CEsC
Computer Sciences Corp., Technical Library, El Segundo, CA [*Library symbol*] [*Library of Congress*] (LCLS) ... CEsCS
Computer Sciences Corporation (NAKS) ... csc
Computer Sciences Information-France (SAUS) ... CSIF
Computer Sciences Information-Nederland (SAUS) ... CSIN
Computer Sciences of Australia (SAUS) ... CSA
Computer Sciences Teleprocessing System (PDAA) ... CSTS
Computer Search Center [*Illinois Institute of Technology Research Center*] [*Chicago, IL*] [*Defunct*] ... CSC
Computer Search International Corp. [*Database producer*] ... CSI
Computer Search Services ... CSS
Computer Security (MSA) ... CMPSCTY
Computer Security (COE) ... COMPUSEC
Computer Security Act [*1987*] ... CSA
Computer Security Center (SAUO) ... CSC
Computer Security Center Standard (SAUO) ... CSC-STD
Computer Security Education and Training Working Group (SAUO) ... CSETWG
Computer Security Evaluation (ACAE) ... CSE
Computer Security Evaluation Center ... CSEC
Computer Security for Acquisition Managers (COE) ... CSAM
Computer Security Institute (EA) ... CSI
Computer Security Officials (ADWA) ... CSO
Computer Security Program Office (SAUO) ... CSPO
Computer Security Program Office (SAUS) ... SCP
Computer Security Resource and Response Center ... CSRC
Computer Security Risk Analysis (SAUS) ... COMPUSEC RA
Computer Security Technical Vulnerability Reporting Program [*Army*] (ADDR) ... CSTVRP
Computer Security Technology Center (VERA) ... CSTC
Computer Security Vulnerability Reporting Program (ACAE) ... CSVRP
Computer Select and Cross Connect Unit (MCD) ... CSCCU
Computer Sensitive Language [*Programming language*] ... CSL
Computer Sentry Software ... CSS
Computer Sequence Number ... CSN
Computer series [*Digital Scientific*] ... META
Computer Service and Bureaux Association [*British*] ... COSBA
Computer Service Bureaux Association (SAUO) ... COBSA
Computer Service Center ... CSC
Computer Service Network (IAA) ... CSN
Computer Service Office (IAA) ... CSO
Computer Service Squadron [*Air Force*] ... COMPSERSq
Computer Services - Long Beach (MCD) ... CSLB
Computer Services and Systems Division [*Environmental Protection Agency*] (GFGA) ... CSSD
Computer Services Association [*British*] ... CSA
Computer Services Center (SAUO) ... CPSC
Computer Services Co. [*British*] (NITA) ... CSC
Computer Services Department (SAUO) ... CS
Computer Services Department (SAUO) ... CSD
Computer Services Division [*University of South Carolina at Columbia*] [*Research center*] (RCD) ... CSD
Computer Services Division (SAUS) ... CSvD
Computer Services for Motor-Freight Activities (PDAA) ... COSMA
Computer Services Industry Training Council [*British*] (NITA) ... COSIT
Computer Services Procedures Manual ... CSPM
Computer Services Squadron [*Air Force*] ... CPUSS
Computer Services Support and Evaluation Agency ... CSSEA
Computer Set Control (CAAL) ... CSC
Computer Sharing Services, Inc. [*Information service or system*] (IID) ... CSS
Computer Shopper Show (SAUO) ... CSS
Computer Sighting System (SAUS) ... CSS
Computer Signal Data Converter (ACAE) ... CSDC
Computer Simulated Clinical Exercise for Dental Hygiene (SAUO) ... CSCE
Computer Simulated Design (DGA) ... CSD
Computer Simulation (RDA) ... CS
Computer Simulation Language (BUR) ... CSL
Computer Simulation Model (MCD) ... CSM
Computer Simulation Pointing and Tracking System (ACAE) ... COSPOTS
Computer Simulation Program ... CSP
Computer Slave [*Computer science*] (DGA) ... CS
Computer Society (SAUO) ... CS
Computer Society International Conference (SAUO) ... COMCON
Computer Society of Canada ... CSC
Computer Society Press (SAUO) ... CSP
Computer Software (MCD) ... CS
Computer Software and Applications Conference ... COMPSAC
Computer Software and Peripheral Show (IEEE) ... COMPSO
Computer Software and Peripherals Shows and Conferences (SAUO) ... COMPSO
Computer Software and Services Group (IAA) ... CSSG
Computer Software and Services Industry (HGAA) ... CSSI
Computer Software and Services Industry Association [*Formerly, ADAPSO*] (NITA) ... CSSIA
Computer Software Co. (SAUS) ... TCSC
Computer Software Component (SSD) ... CSC
Computer Software Configuration Item [*Computer science*] ... CSCI
Computer Software Configuration Item (SAUS) ... SCSCI
Computer Software Configuration Management (SAUS) ... CSCM
Computer Software Data Tapes (MCD) ... CSDT
Computer Software Diagnostic Manual ... CSDM
Computer Software Documentation ... CSD
Computer Software Exchange Center (SAUS) ... COMSEC
Computer Software Management and Information Center [*University of Georgia*] [*NASA*] [*Research center*] (RCD) ... COSMIC
Computer Software Module (SAUS) ... CSM
Computer Software Operator's Manual ... CSOM
Computer Software Support Agency (SAUO) ... CSSA
Computer Software Trouble Report (MCD) ... CSTR
Computer Software Unit ... CSU
Computer Solutions (SAUS) ... CSL
Computer Solutions GmbH (SAUO) ... CSL
Computer Solutions, Incorporated (SAUO) ... CSI
Computer Sports World [*Information service or system*] (IID) ... CSW
Computer Status Lights (MCD) ... CSL
Computer Status Matrix (MCD) ... CSM
Computer Stock Inventory Control (MCD) ... CSIC
Computer Stock Timing and Analysis Technique ... COM-STAT
Computer Storage (SAUS) ... COMSTORE
Computer Store Matrix (SAUS) ... CSM
Computer Structure Language [*1974*] [*Computer science*] (CSR) ... CSL
Computer Subprogram Design Document (MHDI) ... CSDD
Computer Subroutine (SAUS) ... CS
Computer Subsystem (NASA) ... CSS
Computer Subsystem Controller ... CSC
Computer Subtraction Time (SAUS) ... CST
Computer Supervisory Control (SAUS) ... CSC
Computer Support Applications Manager [*Computer Support Corp.*] [*Computer science*] ... CSAM
Computer Support Base (AFIT) ... CSB
Computer Support Center (SAUS) ... CSC
Computer Support Equipment (MCD) ... CSE
Computer Support for Environmental Impact Assesment [*Conference*] (VERA) ... CSEIA
Computer Support Group (USDC) ... CSG
Computer Support in Military Psychiatry [*Project*] (RDA) ... COMPSY
Computer Support Program [*NASA*] (NASA) ... CSP
Computer Support Squadron (SAUO) ... CPUSS
Computer Support System (SAUS) ... CSS
Computer Supported (SAUS) ... CS
Computer Supported Collaborative Work (SAUS) ... CSCW
Computer Supported Network Analysis System (SAUS) ... CSNAS
Computer Supported Purchasing ... CSP
Computer Supported Telecommunications Applications (SAUS) ... CSTA
Computer Supported Telecommunications Standard (VERA) ... CSTS
Computer Supported Telephony Application (IGQR) ... CSTA
Computer Supported Telephony Standard (SAUS) ... CSTS
Computer Synthesised Image (SAUS) ... CSI
Computer Synthesized Imagery (MCD) ... CSI
Computer System Acceptance Review ... CSAR
Computer System Analyst (BUR) ... CSA
Computer System Architects Ltd. (SAUO) ... CSA
Computer System Center (SAUO) ... CSC
Computer System Command Support Group Europe (SAUO) ... CSCSGE
Computer System Design (IAA) ... CSD
Computer System Development Facility (MHDI) ... CSDF
Computer System for Crop Response to Fertilizers [*United Nations*] (NITA) ... CSCRF
Computer System for Main Frame Operations [*Bell System*] ... COSMOS
Computer System for Medical Information Services (DIT) ... COSMIS
Computer System Interface Circuits (IEEE) ... CSIC
Computer System Language ... CSL
Computer System Management Team (SAUS) ... CSMT
Computer System Manual ... CSM
Computer System Operators Manual ... CSOM
Computer System Science Training [*IBM Corp.*] ... CSST
Computer System Security Manager (DNAB) ... CSSM
Computer System Security Officer (SAUO) ... CSSC
Computer System Security Officer (DNAB) ... CSSO
Computer System Services, Inc. (SAUO) ... CSS
Computer System Simulator [*Programming language*] [*1969*] ... CSS
Computer System Support Center (SAUO) ... CSSC
Computer System Training (SAUS) ... CST

Computer System Working Group (SAUO) .... CSWG
Computer Systems Advisers (SAUO) .... CSA
Computer Systems Analyst and Programmer [*Air Force*] .... COMPSYSANLSTPGMR
Computer Systems and Electronics Requirements Board [*British*] .... CSERB
Computer Systems Association .... CSA
Computer Systems Command [*Also, ACSC*] [*Army*] .... CSC
Computer Systems Command Support Group, Fort Lee (MCD) .... CSCSGL
Computer Systems Development Ltd. [*Software supplier*] [*London, England*] (NCC) .... CSD
Computer Systems Director (KSC) .... CSD
Computer Systems Engineer (PGP) .... CSE
Computer Systems Engineering (SAUS) .... CSE
Computer Systems for Management Information and Control (PDAA) .... COSMIC
Computer Systems Group (SAUO) .... CSGP
Computer Systems Hardware/Software Integration (NAKS) .... CSIR
Computer Systems Information Network (GEOI) .... CSIN
Computer Systems Institute .... CSI
Computer Systems Integration (CIST) .... CSI
Computer Systems Integration Office (ACAE) .... CSIO
Computer Systems Integration Review (NASA) .... CSIR
Computer Systems International .... CSI
Computer Systems Laboratory [*Bethesda, MD*] [*Department of Health and Human Services*] (GRD) .... CSL
Computer Systems Management Institut Dr. Gerhard Maurer & Partner GmbH (SAUO) .... CSMI
Computer Systems News (SAUS) .... CSN
Computer Systems of America, Inc. (SAUO) .... CSA
Computer Systems Officer (ADA) .... CSO
Computer Systems Policy Project (BTTJ) .... CSPP
Computer Systems Requirements Board (SAUO) .... CSRB
Computer Systems Requirements Board Working Group (SAUO) .... CSRB-WG
Computer Systems Research Group (SAUO) .... CSRG
Computer Systems Research Institute [*University of Toronto*] [*Research center*] (RCD) .... CSRI
Computer Systems Research Project (SAUS) .... CSRP
Computer Systems Selection and Acquisition (ACAE) .... CSSA
Computer Systems Selection and Acquisition Agency [*Army*] (MCD) .... CSSAA
Computer Systems Simulator (SAUS) .... CSS
Computer Systems Squadron .... CSSQ
Computer Systems Suppliers Advisory Committee (SAUS) .... COSSAC
Computer Systems Support and Evaluation Command .... CSSEC
Computer Tape (SAUS) .... CT
Computer Tape Recorder .... CTR
Computer Task Group (HGAA) .... CTG
Computer Task Group [*NYSE symbol*] (TTSB) .... TSK
Computer Task Group, Inc. [*Associated Press*] (SAG) .... CmpTsk
Computer Task Group, Inc. [*NYSE symbol*] (SPSG) .... TSK
Computer Technologies [*Fair*] (VERA) .... COMTECH
Computer Technology (IEEE) .... CT
Computer Technology and Telecommunications Staff [*Department of Justice*] (GFGA) .... CTTS
Computer Technology Associates [*Goddard Spaceflight Center - Greenbelt, MD*] [*NASA*] (NASA) .... CTA
Computer Technology Center .... CTC
Computer Technology Division (ACII) .... COMPUTEC
Computer Technology, Incorporated (SAUO) .... CTI
Computer Technology Innovations (HGAA) .... CTI
Computer Technology Limited [*British*] (NITA) .... CTL
Computer Technology Research (SAUS) .... CRT
Computer Technology Research Corp. (SAUO) .... CRT
Computer Technology Research Corp. (IID) .... CTR
Computer Telegram System (SAUS) .... CTS
Computer Telephone Cl'1 [*NASDAQ symbol*] (TTSB) .... CPTI
Computer Telephone Corp. [*Associated Press*] (SAG) .... CmpTel
Computer Telephone Corp. [*NASDAQ symbol*] (NQ) .... CPTL
Computer Telephony (IGQR) .... CT
Computer Telephony Integration [*Telecommunications*] .... CTI
Computer Telephony Solution (SAUS) .... CTS
Computer Telewriter Systems (MCD) .... CTS
Computer TELEX Exchange [*RCA Corp.*] .... CTE
Computer Telex Exchange (SAUS) .... CTX
Computer Telex Exchange System (SAUS) .... CTES
Computer Terminal (SAUS) .... CT
Computer Test Console (ACAE) .... CTC
Computer Test Corporation (SAUO) .... CTC
Computer Test Sequences Document (MCD) .... CTSD
Computer Test Set .... CTS
Computer Test Stand (SAUS) .... CTS
Computer Test Unit (MCD) .... CTU
Computer Threat Research Association [*British*] (DBA) .... CoTRA
Computer Time Bookers .... CTB
Computer Time Brokers (SAUS) .... CTB
Computer Time Sharing Service (MHDI) .... CTSS
Computer Time-sharing Corp. (SAUS) .... CTC
Computer Timesharing Resource Control System (SAUS) .... RCS
Computer Timing and Costing Model (MHDB) .... CTCM
Computer to Assist Persons with Disabilities (SAUO) .... CAPD
Computer to Communications Interface Unit .... CCIU
Computer to PBX Interface [*Telecommunications*] (NITA) .... CPI
Computer to Plate (SAUS) .... CTP
Computer to Press (SAUS) .... CTP
Computer to Print (SAUS) .... CTP
Computer Town United Kingdom [*Computer literacy project*] (NITA) .... CTUK
Computer Trade Video [*British*] [*A publication*] (NITA) .... CTV
Computer Traders Association [*British*] (NITA) .... CTA
Computer Training System .... CTS
Computer Transceiver Systems, Inc. .... CTSI
Computer Transceiver Systems, Incorporated (SAUO) .... CTSI
Computer Transformer .... CT
Computer Translation (SAUS) .... Comtran
Computer Translation, Inc. [*Information service or system*] (IID) .... CTI
Computer Transmission Corporation (SAUO) .... CTC
Computer Transponder (MCD) .... CT
Computer Turnaround Time (SAUS) .... TURN
Computer Typesetting (SAUS) .... CTS
Computer Typewriter (SAUS) .... CT
Computer Typing System .... CTS
Computer UFO Network .... CUFON
Computer Under Test (SAUS) .... CUT
Computer Unit (EA) .... CU
Computer Unit Assembly (SAUS) .... cua
Computer Update Equipment .... CUE
Computer Usage Company (SAUO) .... CUC
Computer Usage Control (NASA) .... CUC
Computer Usage Development Corp. (SAUS) .... CUDC
Computer Usage Development Corporation (SAUO) .... CUDC
Computer Usage List Processor (IEEE) .... CULP
Computer Usage's Business-Oriented Language [*Computer science*] .... CUBOL
Computer Use in Social Sciences Network (SAUO) .... CUSSNET
Computer Use in Social Sciences Network (SAUS) .... CUSSNET
Computer Use in Social Services Network (EA) .... CUSSN
Computer Use in the Health Service [*British*] .... CUHS
Computer User Education [*An association*] .... CUE
Computer User Terminal Equipment [*Airport computer system*] .... CUTE
Computer Users Association .... CUA
Computer Users Associations Group (MHDB) .... CUAG
Computer Users committee (SAUS) .... CU
Computer Users for Social Responsibility (EA) .... CUSR
Computer Users in Speech and Hearing (EA) .... CUSH
Computer Users Replacement Equipment (SAUS) .... CURE
Computer Users Survival Electronic Magazine [*Information service or system*] (IID) .... CUSEM
Computer Users' Tape System (ODBW) .... CUTS
Computer Utilities for Education Systems (SAUS) .... CUES
Computer Utility Educational System (MCD) .... CUES
Computer Utilization Accounting System (IEEE) .... CUAS
Computer Utilization Efficiency (IAA) .... CUE
Computer Utilization Monitor (IAA) .... CUM
Computer Utilization Reporting System (IEEE) .... CURES
Computer Utilized Turning System [*Warner & Swasey*] .... CUTS
Computer Utilizing English (SAUS) .... CUE
Computer Validation Program (DNAB) .... CVP
Computer Variable (SAUS) CV
Computer Vehicle Erector (SAUS) .... CVE
Computer Video Instrument (NITA) CVI
Computer Virus as a Weapon [*DoD*] .... CVW
Computer Virus Industry Association (EA) .... CVIA
Computer Vision CV
Computer Vision and Image Processing .... CVIP
Computer Vision and Pattern Recognicer (or Recognition) (SAUS) .... CVPR
Computer Vision and Understanding .... CVIU
Computer Vision Graphics and Image Processing [*A publication*] .... CVGIP
Computer Vision Laboratory [*University of Maryland*] [*Research center*] (RCD) CVL
Computer Vision Syndrome .... CVS
Computer Voice Response .... CVR
Computer Weekly [*British*] [*A publication*] (NITA) .... CW
Computer Weekly (journ.) (SAUS) .... Computer Wkly
Computer with On-Line Remote Devices [*National Institute of Standards and Technology*] .... CORD
Computer Wizard [*Information service or system*] (IID) .... CW
Computer Word (SAUS) .... CW
Computer Word Processing (IAA) .... CWP
Computer World Trade Group [*British*] .... CWTG
Computer Zero Access Memory (SAUS) .... CZAM
Computer Zero Access Store (SAUS) .... CZAS
Computer-Accessed [*or-Aided*] **Telemetry System** .... CATS
Computer-Adjusted Spectrometry System .... COMPASS
Computer-Administered [*or Assisted*] **Instruction** (RDA) .... CAI
Computer-Administered Programmed Instruction (OA) .... CAPI
Computer-Aided [*or Assisted*] (HGAA) .... CA
Computer-Aided Abrasive Machining Oscillation Studies (PDAA) .... CAMOS
Computer-Aided Acquisition and Logistic Support/Concurrent Engineer (USGC) .... CALS/CE
Computer-Aided Acquisition and Logistics Support (MCD) .... CALS
Computer-Aided Acquisition and Logistics System (AAGC) .... CALS
Computer-Aided Adult Learning (HGAA) .... CAAL
Computer-Aided Alerting Subsystem (CAAL) .... CAAS
Computer-Aided Analysis (SSD) .... CAA
Computer-Aided Analysis and Information Recovery Systems (MCD) .... CAIRS
Computer-Aided Analytical Solution for Engineers .... CAASE
Computer-Aided Approach Spacing [*Aviation*] .... CAAS
Computer-Aided Architectural Design (MCD) .... CAAD
Computer-Aided Archiving and Change Accounting System (VERA) .... CARCAS
Computer-Aided Batch Scheduling .... CABS
Computer-Aided Building (PDAA) .... CAB
Computer-Aided Building Design (PDAA) .... CABD
Computer-Aided Building-Design System [*Computer science*] .... CABDS
Computer-Aided Calibration (ACII) .... CAC
Computer-Aided Chartroom .... COACH

Computer-Aided Circuit Analysis [Electronics] ..... CACA
Computer-Aided Circuit Design ..... CACD
Computer-Aided Classification ..... CAC
Computer-Aided [or -Assisted] Communication System ..... CACS
Computer-Aided Control System Design (PDAA) ..... CACSD
Computer-Aided Cost Estimating (BTTJ) ..... CACE
Computer-Aided Crime (VERA) ..... CAC
Computer-Aided [or Assisted] Data Entry (IAA) ..... CADE
Computer-Aided Data Management Procedure (MCD) ..... CADMP
Computer-Aided Data Retrieval and Evaluation Software (AUEG) ..... CADRE
Computer-Aided Design ..... CAD
Computer-Aided Design, Analysis, and Reliability (IEEE) ..... CADAR
Computer-Aided Design and Analysis ..... CADA
Computer-Aided Design and Computer-Aided Manufacture (NTIO) ..... CAD-CAM
Computer-Aided Design and Construction System (PDAA) ..... CADACS
Computer-Aided Design and Design Automation ..... CADDA
Computer-Aided Design and Drafting [Software package] (MCD) ..... CADD
Computer-Aided Design and Electrical Test ..... CADET
Computer-Aided Design and Engineering (MHDI) ..... CADAE
Computer-Aided Design and Engineering Group (SAUO) ..... CADE
Computer-Aided Design and Evaluation (MCD) ..... CADE
Computer-Aided Design and Evaluation Technology (MCD) ..... CADET
Computer-Aided Design and Fabrication (MCD) ..... CADF
Computer-Aided Design and Manufacturing ..... CADAM
Computer-Aided Design and Numerical Control (DNAB) ..... CADNC
Computer-Aided Design and Numerical Control Effort ..... CADANCE
Computer-Aided Design and System Analysis Tool (MCD) ..... CADSAT
Computer-Aided Design and Test [System] ..... CADAT
Computer-Aided Design and Test (MHDB) ..... CADTES
Computer-Aided Design Committee (SAUO) ..... CAD
Computer-Aided Design Development ..... CADD
Computer-Aided Design Drafting via Tektronix (MCD) ..... CADD/TEK
Computer-Aided Design Engineering (RDA) ..... CADE
Computer-Aided Design Engineering and Manufacturing (IAA) ..... CADEM
Computer-Aided Design Environment [Software system] (IEEE) ..... COMRADE
Computer-Aided Design Evaluation System (SAUS) ..... CADES
Computer-Aided Design Experiment Translator ..... CADET
Computer-Aided Design for Communications (PDAA) ..... CADCOM
Computer-Aided Design Framework Initiative (AAEL) ..... CFI
Computer-Aided Design Interactive System (IAA) ..... CADIS
Computer-Aided Design Laboratory [Pennsylvania State University]
[Research center] (RCD) ..... CAD-LAB
Computer-Aided Design, Manufacture, and Test (MCD) ..... CADMAT
Computer-Aided Design Manufacture and Testing (CIST) ..... CADMAT
Computer-Aided Design of Electronic Products (IEEE) ..... CADEP
Computer-Aided Design of Fire Escapes [Micro Core Ltd.] [Software
package] (NCC) ..... CAFE
Computer-Aided Design of Industrial Cabling Systems (PDAA) ..... CADICS
Computer-Aided Design of Information System (IAA) ..... CADIS
Computer-Aided Design of Integrated Circuits (MCD) ..... CADIC
Computer-Aided Design of Linear Integrated Circuits (MHDB) ..... CADLIC
Computer-Aided Design of Optical Character Recognition (MHDI) ..... CADOCR
Computer-Aided Design of Optical Systems [Energy Soft Computer Systems
Ltd.] [Software package] (NCC) ..... CADOS
Computer-Aided Design of Printed Circuit Artwork (PDAA) ..... CADOPCART
Computer-Aided Design Reliability ..... CADR
Computer-Aided Design System ..... CADS
Computer-Aided Design System (CIST) ..... CADSYS
Computer-Aided Design/Computer-Aided Manufacturing ..... CAD/CAM
Computer-Aided Design/Manufacturing [Army] (RDA) ..... CAD/M
Computer-Aided Design/Numerical Control (AABC) ..... CD/NC
Computer-Aided Detection ..... CAD
Computer-Aided Development and Evaluation System (MHDI) ..... CADES
Computer-Aided Dispatching [Vehicle fleet management] ..... CAD
Computer-Aided Document Management and Control System
(HGAA) ..... CADMAC
Computer-Aided Document Origination (MHDI) ..... CADO
Computer-Aided Drafting [or Drawing] ..... CAD
Computer-Aided Drafting, Mapping, and Photogrammetry (GEOI) ..... CADMAP
Computer-Aided Education (BUR) ..... CAE
Computer-Aided Electronic Warfare Information Systems [Air Force]
(GFGA) ..... CAEWIS
Computer-Aided Embarkation Management System [Navy] ..... CAEMS
Computer-Aided Emulation Design System ..... CAEDS
Computer-Aided Engineering ..... CAE
Computer-Aided Engineering and Architectural Design System (RDA) ..... CAEDS
Computer-Aided Engineering Center [University of Wisconsin - Madison]
[Research center] (RCD) ..... CAE
Computer-Aided Engineering Centre [Heriot-Watt University] [British] (CB) ..... CAE
Computer-Aided Engineering Laboratory [Lawrence Institute of Technology]
[Research center] (RCD) ..... CAE LAB
Computer-Aided Engineering Network (ADWA) ..... CAEN
Computer-Aided Environmental Control System (MCD) ..... CAECS
Computer-Aided Environmental Design Analysis and Realization
(MHDB) ..... CEDAR
Computer-Aided Exercise Facility (MCD) ..... CAEF
Computer-Aided Exploration (BTTJ) ..... CAEX
Computer-Aided Facility Management ..... CAFM
Computer-Aided Fault Finding (PDAA) ..... CAFF
Computer-Aided Film Editor ..... CAFE
Computer-Aided Flight Operations Center ..... CAFOC
Computer-Aided Force Management System (SAUS) ..... CAFMS
Computer-Aided Function Allocation and Evaluation System ..... CAFES
Computer-Aided Gear Changing [Automotive engineering] ..... CAG
Computer-Aided Genetic Engineering ..... CAGE

Computer-Aided Geometric Design (MCD) ..... CAGD
Computer-Aided Industrial Design (BTTJ) ..... CAID
Computer-Aided Industry (IAA) ..... CAI
Computer-Aided Information Logistics (IAA) ..... CAIL
Computer-Aided Inspection (BTTJ) ..... CAI
Computer-Aided [or -Assisted] Instruction ..... CAI
Computer-Aided Instruction (IEEE) ..... CAIS
Computer-Aided Instruction System (MHDB) ..... CAINS
Computer-Aided Instruction System [Programming language] [1971]
(CSR) ..... CAISYS
Computer-Aided Interactive Testing System (EDAC) ..... CAITS
Computer-Aided Laboratory Automation System (IAA) ..... CALAS
Computer-Aided Layout and Fabrication (MCD) ..... CALFAB
Computer-Aided Layout of Masks (PDAA) ..... CALM
Computer-Aided [or -Assisted] Learning (BUR) ..... CAL
Computer-Aided Lighting [Automotive engineering] ..... CAL
Computer-Aided Line Balance ..... CALB
Computer-Aided Livestock Marketing ..... CALM
Computer-Aided Loads Analysis (MCD) ..... CALA
Computer-Aided LOFT Lines (MCD) ..... CALL
Computer-Aided Logistics [Army] ..... CAL
Computer-Aided Logistics Support [Army] ..... CALS
Computer-Aided Logistics System [Air Force] (DOMA) ..... CALS
Computer-Aided Logistics/Technical Information Management System
[Military] (GFGA) ..... CAL/TIMS
Computer-Aided Machine Loading (MHDB) ..... CAMECEC
Computer-Aided Machining ..... CAM
Computer-Aided Magnetic Anomaly Detection (SAUS) ..... CAMAD
Computer-Aided Maintenance Management ..... CAMM
Computer-Aided Maintenance Project (SAUO) ..... CAMP
Computer-Aided Makeup [Graphic arts] ..... CAM
Computer-Aided Maneuver Evaluation, Reconstruction, and Analysis
[British] ..... CAMERA
Computer-Aided Manufacture (NTIO) ..... CAM
Computer-Aided Manufacturing ..... CAM
Computer-Aided Mask Preparation (DNAB) ..... CAMP
Computer-Aided Materials Management System [Canadian provincial
governments] ..... CAMMS
Computer-Aided Mathematics ..... CAM
Computer-Aided Measurement and Control [NASA] ..... CAMAC
Computer-Aided Mechanical Drafting ..... CAMD
Computer-Aided Message Processing (LAIN) ..... CAMP
Computer-Aided Milestone Schedule ..... CAMS
Computer-Aided Missile Synthesis [Army] (MCD) ..... CAMS
Computer-Aided Mission Preparation at Airbase Level (ACAE) ..... CAMPAL
Computer-Aided Munition Identification System (SAUS) ..... CAMIS
Computer-Aided Navigation Equipment (MCD) ..... CANE
Computer-Aided Office (IAA) ..... CAO
Computer-Aided Operations Research Facility [Kings Point, NY] [National
Maritime Research Center] [Department of Transportation] (MCD) ..... CAORF
Computer-Aided Optimization ..... CAO
Computer-Aided Parameter Design ..... CAPD
Computer-Aided Passive Ranging Indicator [Military] (CAAL) ..... CAPRI
Computer-Aided Patient Management ..... CAPM
Computer-Aided Pattern Evaluation and Recognition (KSC) ..... CAPER
Computer-Aided Personnel Scheduling ..... CAPS
Computer-Aided Pipe Sketching [System] [Du Pont] ..... CAPS
Computer-Aided Piping Design and Construction (MCD) ..... CAPDAC
Computer-Aided Placement and Routing System (PDAA) ..... CAPARS
Computer-Aided Planning ..... CAP
Computer-Aided Planning and Estimating [Marlow Microplan National
Engineering Laboratory] [Software package] (NCC) ..... CAPE
Computer-Aided Plant Management ..... CAPM
Computer-Aided Polymer Data System (IID) ..... CAPDAS
Computer-Aided Preparation of Electrical Routing (MCD) ..... CAPER
Computer-Aided Presentation (IAA) ..... CAP
Computer-Aided Process Design (MCD) ..... CAPD
Computer-Aided Process Engineering ..... CAPE
Computer-Aided Process Planning (MCD) ..... CAPP
Computer-Aided Process Synthesis ..... CAPS
Computer-Aided Processing and Terminal Access Information Network
[Rutgers University] [New Brunswick, NJ] [Library computer network] ..... CAPTAIN
Computer-Aided Processing of Industrial Cabling Systems (PDAA) ..... CAPICS
Computer-Aided Product Launch Application ..... CAPLA
Computer-Aided [or Assisted] Production ..... CAP
Computer-Aided Production Control (MHDB) ..... CAPC
Computer-Aided Production Management (IAA) ..... CAPM
Computer-Aided Production Planning and Control [John Yates &
Associates] [Software package] (NCC) ..... CAPPAC
Computer-Aided Program Simulator ..... CAPS
Computer-Aided Programming ..... CAP
Computer-Aided Programming System ..... CAPS
Computer-Aided Project Management (SAUS) ..... CAPM
Computer-Aided [or Assisted] Publishing ..... CAP
Computer-Aided Pulse Plating [Electrochemistry] ..... CAPP
Computer-Aided Purchasing (HGAA) ..... CAP
Computer-Aided [or Assisted] Quality ..... CAQ
Computer-Aided Quality Assurance ..... CAQA
Computer-Aided Question Answering [Computer science] (MHDB) ..... CQA
Computer-Aided RADAR Design (KSC) ..... CARD
Computer-Aided Radio Relay Frequency Assignment system (SAUS) ..... CARRFA
Computer-Aided Railway Engineering System (MCD) ..... CARES
Computer-Aided Rapid Prototyping ..... CARP
Computer-Aided Real Time Transcription [Medical records] (DAVI) ..... CART
Computer-Aided Redundant System Reliability Analysis (MCD) ..... CARSRA

Computer-Aided Reference Service [*University of Arizona Library, University of Utah*] [*Information service or system*] .... CARS
Computer-Aided Release Point (MCD) .... CARP
Computer-Aided Reliability and Design (MHDB) .... CARAD
Computer-Aided Reliability Data Analysis (MHDB) .... CARDA
Computer-Aided Reliability Data Systems [*Bell System*] .... CARDS
Computer-Aided Reliability Estimation .... CARE
Computer-Aided Reliability Model (MCD) .... CARM
Computer-Aided Remote Driving [*for robotic command vehicles*] (RDA) .... CARD
Computer-Aided Reorder Trap Analysis [*Bell Laboratories*] .... CARTA
Computer-Aided Repair (IAA) .... CAR
Computer-Aided Requirements Analysis (MCD) .... CARA
Computer-Aided Requirements Definition Software .... CARDS
Computer-Aided Research (AAEL) .... CAR
Computer-Aided Research into Stock Market Applications .... CARISMA
Computer-Aided Risk Evaluation (ODBW) .... CARE
Computer-Aided Routing System .... CARS
Computer-Aided Scantling Determination (PDAA) .... CASCADE
Computer-Aided Scheduling .... CAS
Computer-Aided Search Technique (SAUS) .... CAST
Computer-Aided Selling (IAA) .... CAS
Computer-Aided Service Handling (VERA) .... CASH
Computer-Aided Ship Design and Construction .... CASDAC
Computer-Aided Ship Design and Construction .... CASDC
Computer-Aided Software Development [*Computer science*] .... CASD
Computer-Aided Software Testing (MCD) .... CAST
Computer-Aided Stock Holdings (PDAA) .... CASH
Computer-Aided Structural Design (MCD) .... CASD
Computer-Aided Structural Detailing of Ships (DNAB) .... CASDS
Computer-Aided Structural Technology (MCD) .... CAST
Computer-Aided Styling .... CAS
Computer-Aided Supportability (SAUS) .... CAS
Computer-Aided System Design [*Programming language*] (BUR) .... CASD
Computer-Aided System Engineering (MCD) .... CASE
Computer-Aided System Evaluation .... CASE
Computer-Aided System for the Development of Aircrew Training (MCD) .... CASDAT
Computer-Aided System Hardware (MHDI) .... CASH
Computer-Aided Systems Analysis (MCD) .... CASA
Computer-Aided Tactical Information System (IEEE) .... CATIS
Computer-Aided Teaching .... CAT
Computer-Aided Teaching System (IEEE) .... CATS
Computer-Aided Technical Illustration (MCD) .... CATI
Computer-Aided Technical Management (DOMA) .... CATM
Computer-Aided Technology (MCD) .... CAT
Computer-Aided Telephony (VERA) .... CAT
Computer-Aided Telephony Performance Assessment (PDAA) .... CATPASS
Computer-Aided Test [*Telecommunications*] (TEL) .... CAT
Computer-Aided Test Development (CIST) .... CATD
Computer-Aided Test Engineering (CIST) .... CATE
Computer-Aided Test Equipment (MSA) .... CATE
Computer-Aided Test Generator (PDAA) .... CATGEN
Computer-Aided Testing [*Hoskyns Group Ltd.*] [*Software package*] (NCC) .... CAT
Computer-Aided Testing and Implementation (ITCA) .... CATI
Computer-Aided Text Processing (IAA) .... CATP
Computer-Aided Three-Dimensional Interactive Application .... CATIA
Computer-Aided Time Standard (PDAA) .... CATS
Computer-Aided Tomography (ACRL) .... CAT
Computer-Aided Trade (DS) .... COMPAT
Computer-Aided Training (RDA) .... CAT
Computer-Aided Training Evaluation and Scheduling (MCD) .... CATES
Computer-Aided Training System .... CATS
Computer-Aided Transceiver .... CAT
Computer-Aided Transcription .... CAT
Computer-Aided Translation (IEEE) .... CAT
Computer-Aided Travel Assistant .... CATA
Computer-Aided Tree (PDAA) .... CAT
Computer-Aided Troubleshooting .... CATS
Computer-Aided Typesetting (OA) .... CAT
Computer-Aided Typesetting Process .... CATP
Computer-Aided Victim Identification [*Computer software*] .... CAV-ID
Computer-Aided Weapons Stowage Planning System (SAUO) .... CAWSPS
Computer-Aided Work Sampling .... CAWS
Computer-Aided Writing .... CAW
Computer-Aided Written Communication .... CAWC
Computer-Animated Photographic Terrain View (MCD) .... CAPTV
Computer-Assisted Accounting (BUR) .... CAA
Computer-Assisted Acquisition System [*for libraries*] .... CAAS
Computer-Assisted Action Information System (CIST) .... CAAIS
Computer-Assisted Action Information System [*NATO*] .... CAIS
Computer-Assisted Area Source Emissions [*Environmental Protection Agency*] .... CAASE
Computer-Assisted Artillery Meteorology (SAUS) .... CAAM
Computer-Assisted Audit Techniques .... CAAT
Computer-Assisted Axial Tomography [*Also, CAT, CT*] [*Roentgenography*] .... CAAT
Computer-Assisted Bay-Area Law Enforcement (SAUO) .... CABLE
Computer-Assisted Bibliographic Service [*University of South Dakota*] (OLDSS) .... CABS
Computer-Assisted Circuit Engineering and Allocating System (SAUS) .... CACEAS
Computer-Assisted Classification and Assignment System (IEEE) .... COMPASS
Computer-Assisted Computer Language (SSD) .... CACL
Computer-Assisted Counseling [*Proposed for Air Force*] .... CAC
Computer-Assisted Data Entry (GFGA) .... CADE

Computer-Assisted Data Evaluation (ODBW) .... CADE
Computer-Assisted Decision Making System .... CDM
Computer-Assisted Densitometric Image Analysis [*Microbiology*] .... CADIA
Computer-Assisted Description of Patterns (PDAA) .... CADEP
Computer-Assisted Design .... CAD
Computer-Assisted Detailing of Ships .... CASDOS
Computer-Assisted Development Aids .... CADA
Computer-Assisted Diabetic Instruction [*System*] [*Endocrinology*] (DAVI) .... CADI
Computer-Assisted Diagnosis .... CAD
Computer-Assisted Dial Access Video Retrieval System (MHDI) .... CADAVRS
Computer-Assisted Dialog .... CAD
Computer-Assisted Dispatching System [*IBM Corp.*] .... CAD
Computer-Assisted Dispatching/Mapping .... CADMAP
Computer-Assisted Display Systems (MCD) .... CADS
Computer-Assisted Disposal Simulation [*Game*] .... CADISIM
Computer-Assisted Distribution and Assignment (NVT) .... CADA
Computer-Assisted Drug Design .... CADD
Computer-Assisted Dynamic Data Monitoring and Analysis System .... CADDMAS
Computer-Assisted Electron Microscope .... CEM
Computer-Assisted Enrollment [*IBM Corp.*] (IEEE) .... CAE
Computer-Assisted Entry .... CAE
Computer-Assisted Estimating .... CAE
Computer-Assisted Estimating and Management Information Systems .... CAE/MIS
Computer-Assisted Fault Isolation Test .... CAFIT
Computer-Assisted Force Management System [*Air Force*] (PDAA) .... CAFMS
Computer-Assisted Image .... CAI
Computer-Assisted Indexing and Categorizing [*or Classification*] .... CAIC
Computer-Assisted Industrial Simulation [*Army*] .... CAISIM
Computer-Assisted Information Retrieval Service [*Mississippi State University*] (OLDSS) .... CAIRS
Computer-Assisted Instruction Center .... CAIC
Computer-Assisted Instruction, Inc. (SAUO) .... CAI
Computer-Assisted Instruction Project [*Army-Signal Center and School*] [*Fort Monmouth, NJ*] .... CAI
Computer-Assisted Instruction Study Management System (MCD) .... CAISMS
Computer-Assisted Instruction with Voice Response (MHDI) .... CAIVR
Computer-Assisted Interactive Resources Scheduling System .... CAIRS
Computer-Assisted Interactive Video .... CAIV
Computer-Assisted Interrogation (IAA) .... CAINT
Computer-Assisted Interviewing (GFGA) .... CAI
Computer-Assisted Introduction System (SSD) .... CAIS
Computer-Assisted Job Evaluation [*Human resources*] (WYGK) .... CAJE
Computer-Assisted Language Analysis System (PDAA) .... CALAS
Computer-Assisted Language Learning (ADA) .... CALL
Computer-Assisted Learning and Teaching (RALS) .... CALT
Computer-Assisted Learning Network .... CALN
Computer-Assisted Legal Research (DLA) .... CALR
Computer-Assisted Legislative Liaison; On-Line Political Evaluation .... CALLIOPE
Computer-Assisted Library Mechanization .... CALM
Computer-Assisted Logic Design (PDAA) .... CALD
Computer-Assisted Logistics Simulation [*Navy*] .... CALOGSIM
Computer-Assisted Logistics Simulation [*Navy*] (MCD) .... CALS
Computer-Assisted Mailing (IAA) .... CAM
Computer-Assisted Maintenance .... CAM
Computer-Assisted Maintenance Planning and Control System .... CAMCOS
Computer-Assisted Maintenance Simulation [*Army*] .... CAMSIM
Computer-Assisted Makeup [*Graphic arts*] .... CAM
Computer-Assisted Makeup and Imaging Systems .... CAMIS
Computer-Assisted Management for Emergency Operations [*Database*] .... CAMEO
Computer-Assisted Management of Learning (PDAA) .... CAMOL
Computer-Assisted Management of Portfolios .... CAMP
Computer-Assisted Manpower Analysis System (MCD) .... CAMAS
Computer-Assisted Manufacturing (PCM) .... CAM
Computer-Assisted Map Maneuver Simulation (MCD) .... CAMMS
Computer-Assisted Map Maneuver System [*Military*] (INF) .... CAMMS
Computer-Assisted Mapping and Records Activities System (IEEE) .... CAMRAS
Computer-Assisted Match Program [*Military*] .... CAMP
Computer-Assisted Material Management (VERA) .... CAMM
Computer-Assisted Mathematics Program [*Scott, Foresman, 1968-1969*] [*Textbook series*] (BUR) .... CAMP
Computer-Assisted Menu Planning .... CAMP
Computer-Assisted Message Preparation Relay and Distribution (PDAA) .... CAMPRAD
Computer-Assisted Message Processing System (MCD) .... CAMPS
Computer-Assisted Messaging Services [*Electronic mail*] [*Computer science*] .... CAMS
Computer-Assisted Metabolic Prediction [*Biochemistry*] .... CAMP
Computer-Assisted Method Assembly [*Analytical method writing*] .... CAMA
Computer-Assisted Micrographic Retrieval (PDAA) .... CAMR
Computer-Assisted Mission Planner System (MCD) .... CAMPS
Computer-Assisted Molecular Design .... CAMD
Computer-Assisted Molecular Modeling [*Chemistry*] .... CAMM
Computer-Assisted Movie Production (IEEE) .... CAMP
Computer-Assisted Network Scheduling System (IEEE) .... CANS
Computer-Assisted Order Routing and Execution System [*Tokyo Stock Exchange*] [*Japan*] (ODBW) .... CORES
Computer-Assisted Paperless Automated Support System [*USPS*] (AAGC) .... COMPASS
Computer-Assisted Pathology Encoding and Reporting System [*Medicine*] (DHSM) .... CAPER
Computer-Assisted Pericardiac Surgery [*Cardiology*] (DMAA) .... CASPER
Computer-Assisted Personal Interviewing (GFGA) .... CAPI

Computer-Assisted Photo-Interpretation Research (MCD) .... CAPIR
Computer-Assisted Picking System (WDMC) .... CAPS
Computer-Assisted Placement Service [*British*] .... CAPS
Computer-Assisted Policy Evaluation (MCD) .... CAPE
Computer-Assisted Post Mortem Identification (RDA) .... CAPMI
Computer-Assisted Power System Engineering (MCD) .... CAPSE
Computer-Assisted Pricing Proposal System (MCD) .... CAPPS
Computer-Assisted Printing .... CAP
Computer-Assisted Prisoner Transportation Index Service [*National Sheriffs' Association*] .... CAPTIS
Computer-Assisted Problem Solving (IEEE) .... CAPS
Computer-Assisted Product Search [*Information service or system*] (IID) .... CAPS
Computer-Assisted Program Evaluation Review-Technique Simulation [*Army*] .... CAPERTSIM
Computer-Assisted Programming User Remotes (CIST) .... CAPUR
Computer-Assisted Prosthesis Selection [*Orthopedic surgery*] .... CAPS
Computer-Assisted Psychiatric Evaluation and Review System [*Medicine*] (DMAA) .... CAPERS
Computer-Assisted Psychosocial Evaluation .... CAPE
Computer-Assisted Public Safety System (SAUO) .... CAPSS
Computer-Assisted Radiology (VERA) .... CAR
Computer-Assisted Radiotherapy [*Medicine*] (DMAA) .... CART
Computer-Assisted Records Retrieval (ADA) .... CARR
Computer-Assisted Reference Center [*Information service or system*] (IID) .... CARC
Computer-Assisted Reference Service [*Indiana University Libraries*] (OLDSS) .... CARS
Computer-Assisted Regional Planning (SAUO) .... CARP
Computer-Assisted Reliability and Maintainability Simulation [*Game*] .... CARMSIM
Computer-Assisted Repair Simulation [*Game*] .... CARESIM
Computer-Assisted Reporting [*Journalism*] (WDMC) .... CAR
Computer-Assisted Reproduction (SAUS) .... CARS
Computer-Assisted Research (BUR) .... CAR
Computer-Assisted Research On-Line [*Information service or system*] (IID) .... CAROL
Computer-Assisted Research Services [*Brigham Young University*] [*Information service or system*] (IID) .... CARS
Computer-Assisted Retrieval .... CAR
Computer-Assisted Route Development (IAA) .... CARD
Computer-Assisted Scanning Techniques .... CAST
Computer-Assisted Search (CAAL) .... CAS
Computer-Assisted Search Planning (MCD) .... CASP
Computer-Assisted Self Assessment [*Medicine*] (DMAA) .... CASA
Computer-Assisted Sensory Examination .... CASE
Computer-Assisted Simulation of Supply and Related Systems .... CASSARS
Computer-Assisted Sonic Tomography [*Medicine*] (WDAA) .... CAST
Computer-Assisted Study Skills Improvement Program (EDAC) .... CASSIP
Computer-Assisted Subject Headings Programs [*University of California*] (CIST) .... CASH
Computer-Assisted Surveillance Subsystem (MCD) .... COMPASS
Computer-Assisted Surveillance System (SAUS) .... CASS
Computer-Assisted System for Theater Level Engineering [*Army*] (AABC) .... CASTLE
Computer-Assisted System Operation (PDAA) .... CASO
Computer-Assisted Tactical Intelligence System (MCD) .... CATIS
Computer-Assisted Teaching (RALS) .... CAT
Computer-Assisted Teaching and Learning System (PDAA) .... CATALYST
Computer-Assisted Technique for Numerical Indexing Purposes .... CATNIP
Computer-Assisted Telephone Inquiry .... CATI
Computer-Assisted Telephone Interviewing .... CATI
Computer-Assisted Terrain Mobility Analysis Techniques (MCD) .... CATMAT
Computer-Assisted Test Assembly [*Microcomputer program*] .... CATA
Computer-Assisted Test Construction (EDAC) .... CATC
Computer-Assisted Test Shop .... CATS
Computer-Assisted Testing (BUR) .... CAT
Computer-Assisted Threat Evaluation (SAUS) .... CATE
Computer-Assisted Three-Dimensional Interactive Application (ACRL) .... CATIA
Computer-Assisted Tomography .... CAT
Computer-Assisted Tomography Scanner [*Radiology*] (DAVI) .... CATSCAN
Computer-Assisted Total Value Assessment [*Army*] (MCD) .... CATVA
Computer-Assisted Tracking System (COE) .... CATS
Computer-Assisted Trading (WDAA) .... CAT
Computer-Assisted Trading System [*American Meat Exchange, Inc.*] [*Information service or system*] .... CATS
Computer-Assisted Training .... CAT
Computer-Assisted Training (IEEE) .... COMAT
Computer-Assisted Training System [*IRS*] .... CATS
Computer-Assisted Unit Data Acquisition/Reduction (PDAA) .... CAUDAR
Computer-Assisted Utility System Evaluation (MCD) .... CAUSE
Computer-Assisted War [*Slang*] (DNAB) .... CAW
Computer-Assisted Yeast Identification System [*AFRC Institute of Food Research*] [*Information service or system*] (IID) .... COMPASS
Computer-Assisted/Managed Instructional Language (CSR) .... CAMIL
Computer-Associated [*or -Assisted*] **Device** .... CAD
Computer-Associated Diagnostic and Evaluation Tests (CAAL) .... CADET
Computer-Associated [*or Assisted*] **Self-Assessment** [*British*] .... CASA
Computer-Augmented Block System (MHDB) .... CABS
Computer-Augmented Design and Manufacturing [*Trademark of Cadam, Inc.*] [*Aviation*] .... CADAM
Computer-Augmented Loft Lines [*Graphic arts*] (MCD) .... CALL
Computer-Augmented Oscilloscope System (PDAA) .... CAOS
Computer-Automated Frequency Control (MHDB) .... CAFC
Computer-Automated Laboratory System .... CALS
Computer-Automated Measurement and Control (MSA) .... CAMAC
Computer-Automated Real-Time Betting Information Network (IEEE) .... CARBINE
Computer-Automated Social Simulation .... CASS
Computer-Automated Speech Perception System (PDAA) .... CASPERS
Computer-Automated Structure Evaluator [*Database*] .... CASE
Computer-Automated Support Equipment .... CASE
Computer-Automated Test System [*AT & T*] .... CATS
Computer-Automated Transit Systems .... CATS
Computer-Automated Ultrasonic Inspecting Systems (MCD) .... CAUIS
Computer-Automated Ultrasonic System (MCD) .... CAUS
Computer-Based Accounting .... CBA
Computer-Based Analytical Chemistry [*Conference*] [*Munich, 1982*] .... COBAC
Computer-Based Automation .... CBA
Computer-Based Behavioral Studies (MCD) .... CBBS
Computer-Based Bibliographic Search Services .... CBBS
Computer-Based Bibliographic Search Services [*Washington State University Libraries*] (OLDSS) .... COBBS
Computer-Based Case Tracing [*Medicine*] .... COMTRAC
Computer-Based Conferencing (PDAA) .... CBC
Computer-Based Consultant (MCD) .... CBC
Computer-Based Education [*Project*] .... C-BE
Computer-Based Education and Training .... CBET
Computer-Based Education Research Laboratory [*University of Illinois*] [*Research center*] .... CERL
Computer-Based Electronic Mail (MCD) .... CBEM
Computer-Based Estimating Technique for Contractors .... COBESTCO
Computer-Based Examination .... CBX
Computer-Based Financial Management System [*Harper & Shuman, Inc.*] [*Cambridge, MA*] [*Information service or system*] (IID) .... CFMS
Computer-Based Information (SAUS) .... CBI
Computer-Based Information Center [*Free Library of Philadelphia*] (OLDSS) .... CBIC
Computer-Based Information Services [*Information service or system*] (IID) .... CIS
Computer-Based Instruction [*Education*] .... CBI
Computer-Based Instruction System (IEEE) .... CBIS
Computer-Based Instruction System (IEEE) .... COBIS
Computer-Based Instrumentation (CIST) .... CBI
Computer-Based Laboratory for Automated School Systems [*System Development Corp. project*] .... CLASS
Computer-Based Learning .... CBL
Computer-Based Loans System (MHDI) .... COBLOS
Computer-Based Maintenance Aid Presentation System (MCD) .... CMAS
Computer-Based Management Information System (MHDB) .... CBMIS
Computer-Based Management System (IAA) .... CBMS
Computer-Based Medical System .... CBMS
Computer-Based Message System [*Electronic mail*] .... CBMS
Computer-Based Operations Management System (MHDI) .... COMS
Computer-Based Optimization Routines and Techniques for Effective X (DIT) .... CORTEX
Computer-Based Patient Record Institute [*Medicine*] .... CPRI
Computer-Based Recruit Assignment (MCD) .... COBRA
Computer-Based Reference (CDE) .... CBR
Computer-Based Reference Assistance [*University of Northern Colorado*] (OLDSS) .... COBRA
Computer-Based Reference Service [*Information service or system*] .... CBRS
Computer-Based Resource Units [*Education*] .... CBRU
Computer-Based Terminal .... CBT
Computer-Based Training .... CBT
Computer-Based Training System (MCD) .... CBTS
Computer-Calculated (DAVI) CC
Computer-Chemistry-System [*Yokogawa Hewlett Packard Ltd.*] [*Japan*] .... CCS
Computer/Communications Network Center (VERA) .... CCNC
Computer-Compatible Tape .... CCT
Computer-Compatible Terminal (MCD) .... CCT
Computer-Controlled Action Entry Panel (DNAB) .... CCAEP
Computer-Controlled Area Sterilization Multisensor System .... CASMS
Computer-Controlled Automated Cargo Handling Envelope .... CACHE
Computer-Controlled Automatic Test Equipment .... CATE
Computer-Controlled Catalytic Converter [*Automotive engineering*] C-4
Computer-Controlled Catalytic Converter [*Automotive engineering*] CCCC
Computer-Controlled Coil Ignition [*Automotive engineering*] CCCI
Computer-Controlled Coil Ignition [*Automotive engineering*] .... C^3I
Computer-Controlled Dampers [*Automotive suspension feature*] .... CD
Computer-Controlled Display .... CCD
Computer-Controlled Information Readout .... CCIR
Computer-Controlled Interconnect System (MCD) .... CCIS
Computer-Controlled Launch Set [*NASA*] (KSC) .... CCLS
Computer-Controlled Machine Tool (MHDB) .... CCMT
Computer-Controlled Microfilm Search System (MCD) .... CCMSS
Computer-Controlled Monitor [*Philips Consumer Electronics Co.*] (PCM) .... CCM
Computer-Controlled Multiplexer (MCD) .... CCM
Computer/Controlled Operating System [*Computer science*] (PDAA) .... C/COS
Computer-Controlled Polisher [*Instrumentation*] .... CCP
Computer-Controlled Radiation Therapy [*Medicine*] (DMAA) .... CCRT
Computer-Controlled Range (SAUS) .... CCR
Computer-Controlled Receiving System (DNAB) .... CCRS
Computer-Controlled Scanning Electron Microscope .... CCSEM
Computer-Controlled Suspension [*Volvo*] [*Automotive engineering*] .... CCS
Computer-Controlled Teletext .... CCT
Computer-Controlled Test Management System [*Environmental science*] .... CTMS
Computer-Controlled Vehicle [*Public transit systems*] CCV
Computer-Controlled Vehicle System (IAA) .... CVS
Computer-Controlled X-Ray Diffractometer .... CCXD
Computer-Developed Instruction .... CDI
Computer-Directed Communication .... CODIC
Computer-Directed Drawing .... CDD

Computer-Directed Drawing Instrument .... CDDI
Computer-Directed Instrument .... CDI
Computer-Directed Training Lesson Building System .... CDTLBS
Computer-Directed Training System .... CDTS
Computer-Driven Simulation Environment [FAA] .... CDSE
Computer-Driven Tactical System (MCD) .... CDTS
Computer-Enhanced Instruction .... CEI
Computer-Enhanced Radio Emission Surveillance [British] .... CERES
Computer-Extended Instruction (IEEE) .... CEI
Computer-Generate Volume Hologram (PDAA) .... CGVH
Computer-Generated Acquisition Documents System (AAGC) ...... CGADS
Computer-Generated Hologram .... CGH
Computer-Generated Holographic Scanner [Instrumentation] ...... CGHS
Computer-Generated Image Visual System (MCD) .... CGIVS
Computer-Generated Imagery .... CGI
Computer-Generated Purchase Request .... CGPR
Computer-Generated Voice (SAUS) .... CGV
Computer-Generated Volume Hologram .... CGVH
Computer-Generated/Synthesized Imagery (MCD) .... CGSI
Computer-Graphics Aided Three-Dimensional Interactive Application
  System [IBM Corp.] .... CATIA
Computer-Graphics Language for Your Design Equations (PDAA) ...... CLYDE
Computer-Graphics-Augmented Design and Manufacturing (MCD) ...... CADAM
Computer-Graphics-Augmented Design and Manufacturing (IAA) ...... CODEM
Computer-Guided Instruction (IAA) .... CGI
Computer-Guided Teaching (EDAC) .... CGT
Computer-Harmonized, Application-Tailored (MCD) .... CHAT
Computer/Information/Library Sciences [Abstracts] .... C/I/L
Computer-Informationsdienst Graz [Graz Computer-Information Service]
  [Austria] (IID) .... CIG
Computer-Integrated Design .... CID
Computer-Integrated Design - Computer-Integrated Manufacturing
  (ADA) .... CIDCIM
Computer-Integrated Design - Manufacturing and Automation
  Center .... CID-MAC
Computer-Integrated Draughting [Terminal Display Systems Ltd.] [Software
  package] (NCC) .... CID
Computer-Integrated Engineering (AAEL) .... CIE
Computer-Integrated Enterprise (RALS) .... CIE
Computer-Integrated Environment (IAA) .... CIE
Computer-Integrated Factory .... CIF
Computer-Integrated Instruction (NVT) CII
Computer-Integrated Manufacturing Applications Architecture (AAEL) ...... CAA
Computer-Integrated Manufacturing Architecture (AAEL) .... CA
Computer-Integrated Manufacturing System .... CIMS
Computer-Integrated Manufacturing Systems Architecture (AAEL) ...... CSA
Computer-Integrated Manufacturing Systems Technology (AAEL) ...... CST
Computer-Integrated Manufacturing-Open Systems Architecture
  (SAUS) .... CIM-OSA
Computer-Integrated Processing (ECON) .... CIP
Computer-Integrated Research .... CIR
Computer-Integrated Telephony [Computer science] .... CIT
Computer-Integrated Test Equipment .... CITE
Computerintegrierte Logistik (SAUS) CIL
Computerised AIDS [Acquired Immune Deficiency Syndrome] Network
  [Medicine] [Australia] .... CAIN
Computerised Analysis for Planning Investments (SAUO) .... CAPRI
Computerised Bibliographic Records Actions (WDAA) .... COBRA
Computerised Information Retrieval in Schools [Project] (AIE) ...... CIRIS
Computerised Instrumented Residential Audit [Energy auditing] ...... CIRA
Computerised Legal Information Retrieval System [CLIRS Ltd.] [Information
  service or system] (IID) .... CLIRS
Computerised Personnel Information System [British] .... CPIS
Computerised Retrieval Information Service on Precision Engineering
  [Cranfield Institute of Technology] [A database] [British] (NITA) ...... CRISPE
Computerization and Mechanization of Local Office Tasks (MHDB) ...... CAMELOT
Computerization of Army Movement Schedules (CINC) .... COAMS
Computerization of Law Division (SAUO) .... COLD
Computerization of PAYE [Pay as You Earn] Taxation [Inland Revenue]
  [British] .... COP
Computerization of World Facts [Stanford Research Institute]
  [Databank] .... COMPACT
Computerize (ABBR) .... CMPUTRZ
Computerized (ABBR) .... CMPUTRZD
Computerized .... COMPTRZD
Computerized Academic Record-keeping System (SAUS) .... CARS
Computerized Access and Records Tracking System (SAUS) ...... CARTS
Computerized Accident Management Support system (SAUO) ...... CAMS
Computerized Accidental Release Planning System (SAUS) .... CARPS
Computerized Accident/Incident Reporting System (COE) .... CAIRS
Computerized Accommodated Percentage Evaluation (SAUS) ...... CAPE
Computerized Accounting System (SAUS) .... CAS
Computerized Accounting Tool Series (SAUO) .... CATS
Computerized Acquisition System (SAUS) .... CAS
Computerized Adaptive Screening Test (MCD) .... CAST
Computerized Adaptive Testing (ACAE) .... CAT
Computerized Administration of Patent Documents Reclassified According
  to the IPC [International Patent Classification] [INPADOC] [Information
  service or system] (ADA) .... CAPRI
Computerized Advance Personnel Requirements and Inventory
  (SAUS) .... CAPRI
Computerized Advance Personnel Requirements Information [or Inventory]
  [Navy] .... CAPRI
Computerized Aerospace Ground Equipment (MCD) .... CAGE
Computerized Agency Processing System (IAA) .... CAPS

Computerized Agricultural Research Information System (NITA) ...... CARIS
Computerized AIDS [Acquired Immune Deficiency Syndrome] Information
  Network [Los Angeles Gay and Lesbian Community Services Center]
  [Database] .... CAIN
Computerized AIDS Ministries (SAUO) .... CAM
Computerized Aircraft Maintenance Program .... CAMP
Computerized Aircraft Performance System (MCD) .... CAPS
Computerized Air-Launched Missile Management System (MCD) ...... CALMMS
Computerized Alarm Analysis System (SAUS) .... CAAS
Computerized Alert Monitor (LAIN) .... CAM
Computerized Algorithm for the Radar Range Equation (ACAE) ...... CARRE
Computerized Algorithmic Satellite Scheduler [NASA] .... CASS
Computerized Ambulance Location Logic (SAUS) .... CALL
Computerized Analysis for Programming Investments (MHDI) ...... CAPRI
Computerized Analytical Methods in Planning University System
  (SAUO) .... CAMPUS
Computerized Anatomical Man [NASA] .... CAM
Computerized Angular Indicator (SAUS) .... CAI
Computerized Annotated Bibliography System [Alberta University]
  [Canada] .... CABS
Computerized Applicant Search, Evaluation, and Selection (SAA) ...... CASES
Computerized Application and Reference System .... CARS
Computerized Area Pricing [Telecommunications] (TEL) .... CAPRI
Computerized Arrythmia Monitoring System [Medicine] (CPH) ...... CAMS
Computerized Assessment of Relative Risk Impacts (AAEL) ...... CARRI
Computerized Assignment of Personnel [Military] .... CAP
Computerized Attack/Defense System [Title of a science fiction novel by John
  Sievert] .... CADS
Computerized Audio Report Information and Status (IAA) .... CARIS
Computerized Audit and Record Evaluation System [Medical records]
  (DHSM) .... CARE
Computerized Audit and Reporting System (SAUS) .... CARS
Computerized Autodial System (VERA) .... CAS
Computerized Automated Blood Analysis System (SAUS) .... CABAS
Computerized, Automated, Bus Spacing and Dispatching System ...... CABSADS
Computerized Automated Psychophysiological Device .... CAP
Computerized Automatic Data Acquisition System (SAUS) ...... CADAS
Computerized Automatic Inertial Test Set (MCD) .... CAITS
Computerized Automatic Rating Technique (DEN) .... CART
Computerized Automatic Systems Tester (MCD) .... CAST
Computerized Automation and Robotics Information Center [Society of
  Manufacturing Engineers] [Information service or system] (IID) ...... CARIC
Computerized Automation by Electronic System with Automated
  Reservations (SAUS) .... CAESAR
Computerized Automotive Maintenance System [Buick's factory to dealership
  communication system] .... CAMS
Computerized Automotive Replacement Scheduling [Bell System] ...... CARS
Computerized Automotive Reporting Service (BUR) .... CARS
Computerized Automotive Reporting Service, Inc. (SAUO) .... CARS
Computerized Axial Tomography [Also, CAAT, CT] [Usually used in
  combination, as CATscan] [Roentgenography] .... CAT
Computerized Axial Tomography Scanner [Roentgenography] ...... CATscan
Computerized Axial Tomography Test (SAUS) .... CAT test
Computerized Battle Simulation .... COMBAT-SIM
Computerized Bibliographic Data Service (SAUS) .... COMBIDS
Computerized Bibliographic Network (SAUS) .... CBN
Computerized Bibliographic Record Action [Library science] (TELE) ...... CoBRA
Computerized Bibliographic Retrieval [Hope College] (OLDSS) ...... CBR
Computerized Biology Data and Program Bank at the University of Notre
  Dame [Information service or system] [Defunct] (IID) .... BIOBUND
Computerized Biomechanical Analysis Inc. (SAUO) .... CBA
Computerized Biomechanical Man Model (SAUS) .... COMBIMAN Model
Computerized Biomechanical Man-Model [Air Force] .... COMBIMAN
Computerized Boolean Reliability Analysis [Boeing] .... COBRA
Computerized [or Computer-Controlled] Branch Exchange
  [Telecommunications] .... CBX
Computerized Branch Exchange (SAUO) .... CBX
Computerized Brockerage Network (SAUS) .... COMBRONET
Computerized Bulletin Board .... CBB
Computerized Business Exchanges (SAUS) .... CBXs
Computerized Business Telephone System (CIST) .... CBTS
Computerized Cable Upkeep Administrative Program [Bell System] ...... CCUAP
Computerized Cataloguing System (SAUS) .... COCS
Computerized Central Information Bank (SAUS) .... CCIB
Computerized Clinical Information System [Micromedex, Inc.] [Database] ...... CCIS
Computerized Coffee Information Service System (SAUS) .... CCISS
Computerized Communcation Terminal (SAUS) .... CCT
Computerized Conferencing and Communications Center [New Jersey
  Institute of Technology] [Research center] (RCD) CCCC
Computerized Criminal History [FBI] .... CCH
Computerized Data Retrieval System for Documentation in the Social and
  Human Siences (SAUO) .... DARE
Computerized Deployment Execution System .... CODES
Computerized Design from Engineering Models (PDAA) .... CODEM
Computerized Digital Branch Exchange (SAUS) .... CDBX
Computerized Disease Vector Identification Keys (SAUS) .... CDVIK
Computerized Dispersive Spectroscopy .... CDS
Computerized Display of Deployment Considerations Subsystem
  (SAUO) .... COMDIS
Computerized Distribution and Control of Microfilm [American Motors
  Corp.] .... CODICOM
Computerized Documentation Service/Integrated Set of Information
  Systems [UNESCO] (IID) .... CDS/ISIS
Computerized Documentation System [UNESCO] (IID) .... CDS
Computerized Documentation Thesaurus (SAUS) .... CDTHES

Computerized Drawing Electrical Information (NG) .... CODEIN
Computerized Electro Neuro-Ophthalmograph .... CENOG
Computerized Electroneuroophthalmograph (SAUS) .... Cenog
Computerized Emission Tomogram (WGA) .... CET
Computerized Energy Distribution and Automated Control (SAUS) .... CEDAC
Computerized Engineering Index (SAUS) .... Compendex
Computerized Engineering Index [Engineering Index, Inc.] [New York, NY]
  [Bibliographic database] .... COMPENDEX
Computerized Environmental Legislative Data System [Army] .... CELDS
Computerized Environmental Resources Data System (SAUS) .... CERDS
Computerized Equipment Pricing System [Council of Petroleum Accountants
  Societies] [Information service or system] (CRD) .... CEPS
Computerized Evaluation of the Logistics System [Army] .... COMPELS
Computerized Exercise Machine .... CEM
Computerized Exploration and Technical Underwater Surveyor (PDAA).... CETUS
Computerized Facial Recognition .... CFR
Computerized Facilities Design (PDAA) .... COFAD
Computerized Fleet Analysis, Inc. .... CFA
Computerized Flight Test System (PDAA) .... CFTS
Computerized Forwarding System [US Postal Service] .... CFS
Computerized Freight Remittance System [Pronounced "coffers"] .... COFRS
Computerized Fuel Gauge (DWSG) .... CFG
Computerized Gas Chromatography .... CGC
Computerized Geographic Information System (SAUS) .... CGIS
Computerized Handheld Industrial Terminal (SAUS) .... CHIT
Computerized Harvest Bare Asset Management Prototype (SAUO) .... CHAMP
Computerized Head-End Access Information Network (HGAA) .... CHAIN
Computerized Health Education Assessment Program (SAUS) .... CHEAP
Computerized Heuristic Occupational Information and Career Exploration
  System (EDAC) .... CHOICES
Computerized Hierarchy and Relationship Table .... CHART
Computerized Homes Underwriting Management Systems [Department of
  Housing and Urban Development] (GFGA) .... CHUMS
Computerized Hospital Information System (MCD) .... CHICS
Computerized Hospital Information System .... CHIS
Computerized Image Processing System for Meteorological Applications
  (SAUS) .... CIPSMAP
Computerized Industrial Environmental Legislation [UNEP] [United
  Nations] (DUND) .... CIEL
Computerized Industrial Tomography [Nondestructive testing method] .... CIT
Computerized Information Network for Community Health (SAUS) .... CINCH
Computerized Information Research (IAA) .... CIR
Computerized Information Retrieval (SAUS) .... CIR
Computerized Information Retrieval and Contract Entry [Computer
  science] .... CIRCE
Computerized Information Retrieval and Current Awareness (MHDI) .... CIRCA
Computerized Information Retrieval Service [University of Houston
  Libraries] (OLDSS) .... CIRES
Computerized Information Retrieval Service [California State University,
  Fullerton] (OLDSS) .... CIRS
Computerized Information Service [Public Library of Columbus and Franklin
  County] (OLDSS) .... CIS
Computerized Information Storage System (SAUS) .... CISS
Computerized Information System for Nursing Educators (SAUS) .... CISNE
Computerized Information System for Pathology (SAUS) .... CISP
Computerized Information System of Organic Chemistry [Developed in
  China] [Computer science] .... CISOC
Computerized Information Transfer in English (SAUS) .... CITE
Computerized Informations System for Nursing Educators (SAUS) .... CISNE
Computerized Instruction (SAUS) CI
Computerized Integrated and Automated Manufacturing (IAA) .... CIAM
Computerized Interactive Graphics (MCD) .... CIG
Computerized Issue of Results and Certificates for Entries (PDAA) .... CIRCE
Computerized Laboratory Notebook .... CLN
Computerized Laser-Assisted Sight System [Military] (INF) .... CLASS
Computerized Legal Information Retrieval System (ADA) .... CLIRS
Computerized Lesson-Authoring System (EDAC) .... CLAS
Computerized Librarian-Assisted Search Service [Nicholls State University]
  (OLDSS) .... CLASS
Computerized Library Acquisitions System [Lukac Data Systems] [Lewis and
  Clark College] [Discontinued] [Information service or system] (IID) .... CLAS
Computerized Link Analysis System .... CLANS
Computerized Listing of Abnormal and Unusual Drug Effects
  (SAUS) .... CLAUDE
Computerized Literature Access Search Service [Colorado State University
  Libraries] [Information service or system] .... CLASS
Computerized Literature Searching Service .... CLSS
Computerized Litigation Support (HGAA) .... CLS
Computerized Loan Origination [for mortgages] .... CLO
Computerized Logging and Outage Control (SAUS) .... CLOC
Computerized Logic-Oriented Design System [Air Force] .... CLODS
Computerized Lubrication Control [Sun Oil Co.] CLC
Computerized Maintenance and Administration Support III
  [Telecommunications] (TEL) .... COMASIII
Computerized Maintenance Management Software (SAUS) .... CMMS
Computerized Maintenance Management System .... CMMS
Computerized Maintenance Test System (SAUS) .... CMTS
Computerized Management Account (SAUS) .... CMA
Computerized Management Network [For Agricultural Cooperative Extension
  Service Education] [Virginia Polytechnic Institute] [Database] .... CMN
Computerized Manufacturing System (MCD) .... CMS
Computerized Material Retrieval System (SAUS) .... CMRS
Computerized Materials Retrieval System [Computer science] (ECII) .... CMRS
Computerized Measurements for Safeguards and Accountability
  (PDAA) .... COMSAC

Computerized Medical Imaging Society (EA) .... CMIS
Computerized Medical Information (DB) .... CMI
Computerized Medical Information Support System [Veterans
  Administration] .... COMISS
Computerized Message Switching (SAUS) .... CMS
Computerized Message Transmission (SAUS) .... COMET
Computerized Microscopic Imaging System [Genetics] .... CMIS
Computerized Modular Monitoring (OA) .... CMM
Computerized Moment Stability System [Navy] .... CMSS
Computerized Movement Planning and Status System [Military]
  (AABC) .... COMPASS
Computerized Muscle Exerciser and Trainer [Bodylog, Inc.] .... COMET
Computerized National Range Documentation .... CONRAD
Computerized Natural Resources, Inc. (SAUO) .... CNR
Computerized Needs-Oriented Quality Measurement Evaluation System
  (ADWA) .... CONQUEST
Computerized Notation System (MEDA) .... CNS
Computerized Nuclear Morphometry (DB) .... CNM
Computerized Numerical Control [Computer science] .... CNC
Computerized Occupational Health Program (SAUO) .... COHP
Computerized Occupational Health Program Coronary Artery Risk
  Evaluation (SAUO) .... COHP/CARE
Computerized Office Layout (PDAA) .... COL
Computerized Officer Planning System [Navy] (NVT) .... COPS
Computerized Online System for the Management of Spares [Army] .... COSMOS
Computerized Online Testing .... COLT
Computerized Operating Room Information System .... CORIS
Computerized Operational Audit Routine .... COPAR
Computerized Optical Prescription Processing (SAUS) .... COPP
Computerized Optimization Model for Predicting and Analyzing Support
  Structures [Army] .... COMPASS
Computerized Optimization of Elastic Booster Autopilot .... COEBRA
Computerized Optimization of Microwave Passive and Active Circuits
  (SAUS) .... COMPACT Circuits
Computerized Optimization Procedure for Stabilators (PDAA) .... COPS
Computerized Outside Plant Records [Telecommunications] (TEL) .... COPR
Computerized Parcel Shipping System .... CPSS
Computerized Patient Record .... CPR
Computerized Performance and Analysis Response Evaluator
  (IEEE) .... COMPARE
Computerized Performance Monitoring System (DNAB) .... CPMS
Computerized Performance Rating [of a horse] .... CPR
Computerized Planar Motion Carriage (SAUS) .... CPMC
Computerized Preliminary Design System (SAUS) .... CPDS
Computerized Principles of Structures (ADA) .... COMPOST
Computerized Private Branch Exchange [Telecommunications] .... CPBX
Computerized Problem-Oriented Medical Record (SAUS) .... CPOMR
Computerized Process Control (SAUS) .... CPC
Computerized Production Control (SAUS) .... CPC
Computerized Production Operating System Extension (NITA) .... COMPOSE
Computerized Production Process Planning (MCD) .... CPPP
Computerized Publishing System (SAUS) .... CPS
Computerized Radiology Society [Later, CMIS] (EA) .... CRS
Computerized Reader Enquiry Service System .... CRESS
Computerized Real Estate Assessment and Land Records (MCD) .... CREALR
Computerized Rearrangements of Special Subjects [or Subject
  Specialties] .... CROSS
Computerized Recall Identification System [Automobile industry] .... CRIS
Computerized Reference and Bibliographic Services [University of Maryland
  at Baltimore] (OLDSS) .... CRABS
Computerized Reference Service [William Paterson College of New Jersey]
  (OLDSS) .... CRS
Computerized Register of Voice Research [No longer maintained] [Southern
  Illinois University at Carbondale] [Information service or system] (IID) .... CRVR
Computerized Registry Information System [UNIDO] [United Nations]
  (DUND) .... CORIS
Computerized Relalive Allocation of Facilities Technic (SAUS) .... CRAF
Computerized Relationship Layout Planning .... CORELAP
Computerized Relative Allocation of Facilities Technique [IBM Corp.] .... CRAFT
Computerized Reliability Analysis Method .... CRAM
Computerized Reliability Optimization (SAUS) .... CRO
Computerized Reliability Organization System .... CROS
Computerized Renal Tomography [Medicine] (MELL) .... CRT
Computerized Research Information Service [Colorado School of Mines]
  (OLDSS) .... CRIS
Computerized Reservation Systems (BTTJ) .... CRS
Computerized Reservations System Royal Dutch Airlines (SAUS) .... CORDA
Computerized Resources Information Bank [United States Geological
  Survey] [Later, MRDS] (IID) .... CRIB
Computerized Retrieval of Organic Structures Based on Wiswesser
  (SAUS) .... CROSSBOW
Computerized Retrieval Service .... CRS
Computerized River Information System (SAUO) .... CRIC
Computerized Routine for Observing and Testing the Channel Hardware
  (SAUS) .... CROTCH
Computerized Safety and Facility Design (PDAA) .... COSFAD
Computerized Scanner (SAUS) .... COMPSCAN
Computerized Scientific Management Planning System (AAG) .... CSMPS
Computerized Security System (SAUS) .... CSS
Computerized Self Administered Questionnaire (SAUS) .... CSAQ
Computerized Service for Motor Freight Activities (SAUS) .... COSMA
Computerized Severity Index (SAUS) .... CSI
Computerized Site Security Monitor & Response System (SAUS) .... CSSMRS
Computerized Specifications Management System (DNAB) .... CSMS

Computerized Spot Television Evaluation and Processing [*Advertising*] .... COM-STEP

Computerized Standard Data (SAUS) .... CSD

Computerized Static Automatic Restoring Equipment for Power System (PDAA) .... COMPSAP

Computerized Statistics (SAUS) .... COMPUSTAT

Computerized Status Accounting System (MCD) .... CSAS

Computerized Stress Inventory [*Personality development test*] [*Psychology*].... CSI

Computerized Structural Mechanics (ACAE) .... CSM

Computerized Telephone Number File [*FBI listing, begun in 1970, of political activists' telephone numbers*] [*Obsolete*] .... CTNF

Computerized Test of Spelling Errors (EDAC) .... CTSE

Computerized Text Management (SAUS) .... CTM

Computerized Tomoangiography [*Radiology*] (DAVI) .... CTA

Computerized Tomographic Scanning (SAUS) .... CT Scanning

Computerized Tomography (ECON) .... CT

Computerized Tomography [*Also, CATSCAN*] [*Medical test*] (PAZ) .... CT scan

Computerized Tomography Operating System (SAUS) .... CTOS

Computerized Tomography Scan (SAUS) .... CT Scan

Computerized Tomography Scanner (SAUS) .... CTS

Computerized Tomography Society [*Later, Computerized Radiology Society - CRS*] (EA) .... CTS

Computerized Topographic Scanner [*Medicine*] .... CTS

Computerized Trading Reconstruction [*System*] (NUMA) .... CTR

Computerized Training System [*Army Signal Center and School*] [*Fort Monmouth, NJ*] (RDA) .... CTS

Computerized Training Systems Directorate [*Army Training Support Activity*] [*Fort Gordon, GA*] .... CTSD

Computerized Transaxial Tomography .... CTAT

Computerized Transaxial Tomography (SAUS) .... CTT

Computerized Transverse Axial Tomography (SAUS) .... CTAT

Computerized Transverse Tomography (SAUS) .... CTT

Computerized Travel Aid [*Mobility device for the blind*] .... CTA

Computerized Type Setting (SAUS) .... CTS

Computerized Type System (SAUS) .... CTS

Computerized Ultrasonic Scan System (MCD) .... CUSS

Computerized Understanding of Morphology-Language Acquisition under Development (SAUS) .... CUM LAUDE

Computerized Understanding of Morphology-Language Acquisition Under Development in Education (PDAA) .... CUM LAUDE

Computerized Uniterm Search System (NITA) .... CUSS

Computerized Vocational Information System [*Guidance program*] .... CVIS

Computerizing (ABBR) .... CMPUTRZG

Computerizing Medical Examination [*IBM Corp.*] .... CME

Computerland Corp. (MHDW) .... CLD

Computer/LASER Access Systems for Information Exchange .... CLASIX

Computer-Linked Information for Container Shipping (IAA) .... CLIS

Computer-Managed Instruction .... CMI

Computer-Managed Laboratory .... CML

Computer-Managed Learning (ADA) .... CML

Computer-Managed Parts Manufacture .... CMPM

Computer-Managed Process Planning (MCD) .... CMPP

Computer-Managed Training (MHDI) .... CMT

Computer-Management Distributed Information Software (MHDI) .... CMDIS

Computer-Marked Assignment [*Education*] [*British*] .... CMA

Computer-Matching Privacy and Protection Act .... CMPPA

Computer-Mediated Communications System (RALS) .... CMCS

Computer-Mediated Conferencing (IT) .... CMC

Computer-Mediated Interaction (PDAA) .... CMI

Computer-Mediated Teleconferencing (MHDB) .... CMT

Computer-Modelling System [*Computer Modelling International Ltd.*] [*Software package*] (NCC) .... CMS

Computer-Operated [*or -Oriented*] Electronic Display .... COED

Computer-Operated Machine Evaluation Technique [*Air Force*] (MCD) ..... COMET

Computer-Operated Management Evaluation Technique [*AEC-Army*] .... COMET

Computer-Operated Marketing, Mailing and News Distribution System [*Computer science*] (MHDB) .... COMMANDS

Computer-Operated Micro-Program Automatic Commissioning Technique (PDAA) .... COMPACT

Computer-Operated Multifunction Electronic Test System (MCD) .... COMETS

Computer-Operated Transmission Measuring Set (PDAA) .... COTMS

Computer-Operated Universal Test .... COUNT

Computer-Operated Universal Test System (IAA) .... COUTS

Computer-Oriented Bearing Response Analysis [*Computer science*] (PDAA) .... COBRA

Computer-Oriented Design of Electronic Devices .... CODED

Computer-Oriented Language [*Programming language*] [*Computer science*] .... COL

Computer-Oriented Language Translator (IEEE) .... COLT

Computer-Oriented Managed Inventory Control System (MHDB) .... COMICS

Computer-Oriented Management Information System (IAA) .... CMIS

Computer-Oriented Manufacturing Production and Control System (IAA) .... COMPACS

Computer-Oriented Mechanical Design (MCD) .... COMMEND

Computer-Oriented Metering Planning and Advisory System [*Aviation*] (DA) .... COMPAS

Computer-Oriented Method of Program Analysis, Review, and Evaluation [*Computer science*] (MHDB) .... COMPARE

Computer-Oriented Microwaves Practices (PDAA) .... COMP

Computer-Oriented Modal Control and Appraisal System .... COMCAS

Computer-Oriented Notation Concerning Infrared Spectral Evaluation [*Programming language*] [*Analytical chemistry*] .... CONCISE

Computer-Oriented Partial Sum (NVT) .... COPS

Computer-Oriented Photo-Unit [*Linofilm*] (DGA) .... COPHU

Computer-Oriented Programmed Instruction (IEEE) .... COPI

Computer-Oriented Purchasing and Engineering System (MHDB) .... COPES

Computer-Oriented Reference System for Automatic Information Retrieval [*Forsvarets Forskningsamsalt*] [*Sweden*] .... CORSAIR

Computer-Oriented Reporting Efficiency (AFM) .... CORE

Computer-Oriented Retrieval of Auto Larcenists .... CORRAL

Computer-Oriented System - Newly Organized Storage-to-Retrieval Apparatus (KSC) .... COSNOSTRA

Computer-Oriented System for Management Order Synthesis [*IBM Corp.*] (BUR) .... COSMOS

Computerorientiertes Administrations- und Organisationssystem (SAUO) .... CADMOS

Computer-Output-Typesetting (PDAA) .... COT

Computer-Planning and Aircraft-Weighing Scales .... CPAWS

Computer-Prescribed Instruction (IEEE) .... CPI

Computer-Produced Drawing (IAA) .... CPD

Computer-Programmed Automatic Checkout and Test System .... COMPACT

Computer-Readable Databases [*A publication*] .... CRD

Computer-Readable Databases: a Directory and Data Sourcebook [*A publication*] .... CRDB

Computer-Reinforced Design (PDAA) .... CORD

Computer-Related Equipment (IAA) .... CORE

Computer-Related Systems Validation [*Engineering*] .... CRSV

Computers [*JETDS nomenclature*] [*Military*] (CET) .... CP

Computers Aided Pattern Evaluation and Recognition (SAUS) .... CAPER

Computers and Adult Basic Education [*Liverpool Institute of Higher Education*] [*British*] (AIE) .... CABE

Computers and Automation (BUR) .... CA

Computers and Automation (SAUS) .... CAA

Computers and Automation and People (journ.) (SAUS) .... CAP

Computers and Automation (journ.) (SAUS) .... C&A

Computers and Automation (journ.) (SAUS) .... COAU

Computers and Automation (journ.) (SAUS) .... Comput Automat

Computers and Automation (journ.) (SAUS) .... CPAU

Computers and Automation Universal Mailing List (IEEE) .... CAUML

Computers and Automations Universal Mailing List (SAUS) .... CAUML

Computers and Biomedical Research (journ.) (SAUS) .... ComputBiomedRes

Computers and Communications .... C & C

Computers and Communications (WDMC) .... c&c

Computers and Communications .... COMPUNICATIONS

Computers and Computing Information Resources Directory [*A publication*] .... CCIRD

Computers and Law [*Australia*] [*A publication*] .... Comp & L

Computers and Law [*A publication*] (DLA) .... Comp & Law

Computers and Law [*A publication*] (DLA) .... Comput & Law

Computers and Medicine (journ.) (SAUS) .... C&M

Computers and Medieval Data Processing [*Canada*] [*A publication*] (NITA) .... CAMDAP

Computers and Software Review Panel [*NASA*] (NASA) .... CSRP

Computers and Systems (IEEE) .... C & S

Computers and Systems (IAA) .... CAS

Computers and Systems (MCD) .... CS

Computers and the Humanities [*A publication*] (BRI) .... Compt & H

Computers and the Humanities (journ.) (SAUS) .... CHUM

Computers at Oregon State University, North Carolina Educational Computing Service, Dartmouth College, and the Universities of Iowa and Texas at Austin [*An educational consortium*] .... CONDUIT

Computers, Electronics and Control Symposium (MHDI) .... CEC

Computers Environment and Urban Systems (SAUO) .... CEUS

Computers for Advanced Space Transportation System (MCD) .... CASTS

Computers for the Advancement of Medicine & Science [*Information service or system*] (IID) .... CAMS

Computers in Aerospace Conference (SAUS) .... CAC

Computers in Chemistry, Logic Oriented Planning of Syntheses (SAUS) .... CICLOPS

Computers in Education as a Resource (SAUS) .... CEDAR

Computers in Higher Education Software Team (VERA) .... CHEST

[*The*] Computers in Manufacturing Show [*British*] (ITD) .... CIM

Computers in Mechanical Engineering [*American Society of Mechanical Engineers*] [*A publication*] (NITA) .... CIME

Computers in Mental Health (SAUO) .... CIMH

Computers in Nursing (MEDA) .... CIN

Computers in Nursing Interactive (SAUO) .... CINI

Computers in Teaching Initiative (AIE) .... CTI

Computers in Teaching Initiative Support Service (AIE) .... CTISS

Computers in the City Exhibition [*British*] (ITD) CIC

Computers in the Curriculum [*Education*] (AIE) CIC

Computers in the Undergraduate Curriculum Conference (SAUS) .... CUCC

Computers in the Undergraduate Science Curriculum (SAUS) .... CUCS

Computers in Training as a Resource (AIE) .... CITAR

Computers, Information Processing, and Office Machines .... CIPOM

Computers Interface Adaptor (SAUS) .... CIA

Computers Lawyers Association (EA) .... CLA

Computers, Learners, Users, Educators Association [*New Jersey*] (EDAC) .... CLUES

Computers, Systems and Electronics Division (SAUO) .... CSE

Computers Users' Committee [*United Nations Development Program*] .... CUC

Computers Utilities for Education Systems (SAUS) .... CUES

Computerservice and Software (SAUS) .... COSSO

Computer-Stored Ambulatory Record (MCD) .... COSTAR

Computer-Supported Cooperative Work [*Computer science*] .... CSCW

Computer-Supported Telecommunications Applications .... CSTA

Computer-to-Computer (NASA) .... C-to-C

Computer-to-Computer Network (SAUS) .... CCN

Computer-to-Computer Transfer Channel (ECII) .... CCTC

Computer-to-Plate [*Printing*] (DGA) .... CTP

ComputerTown, United States of America [*Defunct*] (EA) ... CTUSA
Computer-Using Educators of Kentucky (EDAC) ... CUE-KY
Computervision [*Commercial firm*] [*British*] ... CV
Computervision Automatic Design and Draughting System (SAUS) ... CADDS
Computervision Corp. [*Associated Press*] (SAG) ... Cmptvsn
Computervision Corp. [*NYSE symbol*] (SPSG) ... CVN
Computervision Graphics Operating System (MHDI) ... CGOS
Computervision Graphics Processor (CIST) ... CGP
Computerware Automated Total Systems-Account Payable (SAUS) ... CATS-A/P
Computerworld (journ.) (SAUS) ... CW
Computing (SAUS) ... Cmptg
Computing ... CMPTG
Computing (ABBR) ... CMPUG
Computing (ABBR) ... CMPUTG
Computing (SAUS) ... Comput
Computing Accounting Machine (SAUS) ... CAM
Computing Across America [*From book title, "Computing Across America: The Bicycle Odyssey of a High-Tech Nomad" by Steven K. Roberts*] ... CAA
Computing Advisory Group (SAUO) ... CAG
Computing Amplifier (SAUS) ... CA
Computing and Communications Services Office [*Telecommunications*] ... CCSO
Computing and Data Processing (ACAE) ... C&DP
Computing and Data Processing Services [*University of Maine*] [*Research center*] (RCD) ... CAPS
Computing and Data Processing Society (HGAA) ... CDPS
Computing and Data Processing Society of Canada (SAUO) ... CDPCA
Computing and Data Processing Society of Canada (SAUO) ... CDPSC
Computing and Information Resources Committee (SAUS) ... CIRC
Computing and Information Services [*McMaster University*] [*Canada*] (IRC) ... CIS
Computing & Information Systems [*East Carolina University*] [*Research center*] (RCD) ... CIS
Computing and Information Technology [*Princeton University*] [*Research center*] (RCD) ... CIT
Computing & Software, Inc. (SAUO) ... CSW
Computing and Software, Incorporated (SAUO) ... CSI
Computing and Telecommunications Division (SAUO) ... CTD
Computing and the Humanities (SAUS) ... CHUM
Computing Assistance Program [*Taylor University*] [*Information service or system*] (IID) ... CAP
Computing Attachment Machine (SAUS) ... CAM
Computing Australia Recruiting Directory [*A publication*] ... CARD
Computing Block (SAUS) ... CB
Computing Center [*Emory University*] [*Research center*] (RCD) ... EUCC
Computing Center [*University of Rochester*] [*Research center*] (RCD) ... UCC
Computing Center [*University of Cincinnati*] [*Research center*] (RCD) ... UCCC
Computing Center of Siberian Department of Academy of Sciences, Novosibirsk (SAUS) ... VTs SO AN SSSR
Computing Center (or Centre) (SAUO) ... CC
Computing Centre [*University of East Anglia*] [*British*] (IRUK) ... CPC
Computing Department, Loeb's MIS, Ottawa, Ontario [*Library symbol*] [*National Library of Canada*] (BIB) ... OOLM
Computing Development System (ACAE) ... CODES
Computing Device (SAUS) ... CD
Computing Devices Co. (SAUO) ... CD
Computing Devices Co. (SAUO) ... CDC
Computing Devices of Canada, Ltd. (SAUO) ... CDC
Computing Devices of Canada, Ottawa, ON, Canada [*Library symbol*] [*Library of Congress*] (LCLS) ... CaOOCDC
Computing Devices of Canada, Ottawa, Ontario [*Library symbol*] [*National Library of Canada*] (NLC) ... OOCDC
Computing Element (SAUS) ... CE
Computing Error (SAUS) ... CE
Computing for Analysis Project (SAUS) ... CAP
Computing in Distributed Networked Environments (SAUS) ... CODINE
Computing Index [*Computer analysis*] ... CI
Computing Information Center [*University of Washington*] [*Seattle*] [*Information service or system*] (IID) ... CIC
Computing Instrument (SAUS) ... CI
Computing Joint Academic Network (SAUS) ... JANET
Computing, Laser-Aided, Sight System (SAUS) ... CLASS
Computing Law (SAUS) ... CL
Computing Media ... CM
Computing Medium (SAUS) ... CM
Computing Memory (SAUS) ... CM
Computing Nodes (SAUS) ... CN
Computing Operation (SAUS) ... CO
Computing Power Index [*Computer science*] (PDAA) ... CPI
Computing Problem (SAUS) ... CP
Computing Research Association (NTPA) ... CRA
Computing Research Laboratory [*New Mexico State University*] [*Research center*] (RCD) ... CRL
Computing Research Station (SAUS) ... CRS
Computing Result (SAUS) ... CR
Computing Routine (SAUS) ... CR
Computing Science (SAUS) ... CS
Computing Sciences Accreditation Board (SAUS) ... CSAB
Computing Sequence (SAUS) ... CS
Computing Services Association [*British*] ... CSA
Computing Services Center [*Texas A & M University*] [*Research center*] (RCD) ... CSC
Computing Services Division [*Seton Hall University*] [*Research center*] (RCD) ... CSD
Computing Services Office [*Telecommunications*] ... CSO
Computing Speed (SAUS) ... CS
Computing Store (SAUS) ... CS
Computing Support Services [*California Institute of Technology*] [*Research center*] (RCD) ... CSS
Computing System for Air Cargo (DA) ... COSAC
Computing System, Massachusetts Institute of Technology (SAUS) ... COMIT
Computing Systems and Services A/S (SAUO) ... Computas
Computing Systems Technology Office (VERA) ... CSTO
Computing Technology Industry Association [*Lombard, IL*] [*An association*] (CDE) ... CompTIA
Computing Time (SAUS) ... CT
Computing To Assist Persons With Disabilities (SAUS) ... CAPD
Computing Unit (SAUS) ... CU
Computone Corp. [*NASDAQ symbol*] (SAG) ... CMPT
Computone Corp. [*Associated Press*] (SAG) ... Computne
Computrac, Inc. [*Associated Press*] (SAG) ... Cmptrc
Computrac, Inc. [*AMEX symbol*] (SPSG) ... LLB
Computrex Centres [*Vancouver Stock Exchange symbol*] ... CXC
Computron Software [*AMEX symbol*] (SG) ... CFW
Computron Software [*NASDAQ symbol*] (TTSB) ... CTRN
Computron Software, Inc. [*Associated Press*] (SAG) ... Cmputrn
Computron Software, Inc. [*NASDAQ symbol*] (SAG) ... CTRN
Compuware Corp. [*Associated Press*] (SAG) ... Compuwr
Compuware Corp. [*NASDAQ symbol*] (SAG) ... CPWR
CompX Intl.'A' [*NYSE symbol*] (SG) ... CIX
Comrade (ABBR) ... CMRD
COMRADE [*Computer-Aided Design Environment*] **Data Management System** ... CDMS
COMRADE [*Computer-Aided Design Environment*] **Data Storage Facility** ... CDSF
COMRADE [*Computer-Aided Design Environment*] **Permanent File Management System** ... CPFMS
Comrades of the Royal Air Force (SAUO) ... CRAF
Comrades of the Royal Air Force Association (SAUO) ... CRAFA
Comradeship (ABBR) ... CMRDSP
COMRESS, Inc. Computer Research Systems and Software (SAUO) ... COMRESS
Comrey Personality Scale ... CPS
COMSAT Capital 1 8.125%'MIPS' [*NYSE symbol*] (TTSB) ... CQPrA
Comsat Corp. [*Associated Press*] (SAG) ... Comsat
Comsat Corp. [*See also COMSAT*] [*NYSE symbol*] (SPSG) ... CQ
Comsat Corp. Capital [*Associated Press*] (SAG) ... CsatCap
COMSAT [*Communications Satellite Corp.*] **General Integrated System** (NITA) ... CGIS
COMSAT [*Communications Satellite Corp.*] **International Communications, Inc.** (TSSD) ... CICI
COMSAT [*Communications Satellite Corp.*] **Maritime Communications Satellite** (MCD) ... CMCS
COMSAT [*Communications Satellite Corp.*] **Nonreflecting** [*Solar cell*] ... CNR
COMSAT [*Communications Satellite Corp.*] **Video Enterprises** [*Washington, DC*] (TSSD) ... CVE
COMSAT [*Communications Satellite Corp.*], **Washington, DC** [*OCLC symbol*] (OCLC) ... CLD
COMSAT [*Communications Satellite Corp.*], **Washington, DC** [*OCLC symbol*] (OCLC) ... CMD
COMSEC [*Communications Security*] **Equipment Asset Reporting System** (MCD) ... CEARS
COMSEC [*Communications Security*] **Equipment Modification Application and Reporting System** [*Army*] (MCD) ... CEMARS
COMSEC Equipment Program (SAUO) ... CEP
COMSEC [*Communications Security*] **Field Office of Record** [*Army*] (AABC) ... CFOR
COMSEC [*Communications Security*] **Logistic Support Center** [*Army*] (AABC) ... CLSC
COMSEC [*Communications Security*] **Logistic Support Unit** [*Army*] (AABC) ... CLSU
COMSEC [*Communications Security*] **Logistics Data Center** (AABC) ... CLDC
COMSEC [*Communications Security*] **Material Issuing Office** [*Military*] (NVT) ... CMIO
COMSEC [*Communications Security*] **Material Management Center** (MCD) ... CMMC
COMSEC [*Communications Security*] **Mode Control Device** [*Army*] (DWSG) ... CMCD
COMSEC [*Communications Security*] **Priorities Field Evaluation** (MCD) ... CPFE
COMSEC [*Communications Security*] **Regional Issuing Office** [*or Officer*] [*Army*] (AABC) ... CRIO
COMSEC [*Communications Security*] **Repair Center** [*Army*] (NG) ... CRC
COMSEC [*Communications Security*] **Research and Engineering Coordinating Group** [*Army*] (AABC) ... CREC
COMSEC [*Communications Security*] **Resources Program** [*Army*] (AABC) ... CRP
COMSEC [*Communications Security*] **Wargaming** [*Simulation*] (MCD) ... CSWG
Comshare Communications Interface (IAA) ... CCI
Com-Share Communications Interface (SAUS) ... CCI
Comshare Development System (SAUS) ... CDS
Comshare, Inc. [*Associated Press*] (SAG) ... Comshr
Comshare, Inc. [*NASDAQ symbol*] (NQ) ... CSRE
Com-Shares Online Simulation System (SAUS) ... COSS
Comsource Independent Foodservice Companies (NTPA) ... ComSource
ComSouth Bankshares [*AMEX symbol*] (TTSB) ... CSB
Comsouth Bankshares, Inc. [*Associated Press*] (SAG) ... ComsthB
Comsouth Bankshares, Inc. [*AMEX symbol*] (SAG) ... CSB
Comstate Resources Ltd. [*Toronto Stock Exchange symbol*] ... CSR
Comstock Bank [*Associated Press*] (SAG) ... ComstBk
Comstock Bank [*NASDAQ symbol*] (SAG) ... LODE
Comstock Mealybug [*Plant pest*] ... CMB
Comstock on Executors [*A publication*] (DLA) ... Comp Ex
Comstock on Guardian and Ward [*A publication*] (DLA) ... Com G & W
Comstock Partners Capital Value Cl.A [*Mutual fund ticker symbol*] (SG) ... DRCVX

Comstock Resources [*NASDAQ symbol*] (TTSB) ... CMRE
Comstock Resources [*Associated Press*] (SAG) ... ComstkRs
Comstock Resources [*NYSE symbol*] (SAG) ... CRK
Comstock Resources, Inc. [*NASDAQ symbol*] (NQ) ... CMRE
Comstock Resources, Inc. [*Associated Press*] (SAG) ... CmstRs
Comstock Township Library, Comstock, MI [*Library symbol*] [*Library of Congress*] (LCLS) ... MiCom
Comstock's Digest of the Law of Dower [*A publication*] (DLA) ... Com Dow
Comstock's Reports [*1-4 New York Court of Appeals*] [*A publication*] (DLA) ... Com
Comstock's Reports [*1-4 New York Court of Appeals*] [*A publication*] (DLA) ... Coms
Comstock's Reports [*1-4 New York Court of Appeals*] [*A publication*] (DLA) ... Comst
COMSUBFRONDEF/ Chesapeake Bay Group (SAUO) ... COMSUBFRONDEF/CHESBAYGRU
COMSUBFRONDEF/Gulf Group (SAUO) ... COMSUBFRONDEF/GULFGRU
COMSUBFRONDEF/New England Group (SAUO) ... COMSUBFRONDEF/NEWENGRU
Comtec Cable Accessories Ltd. [*British*] (NITA) ... CCA
Com/Tech Commun Tech [*NASDAQ symbol*] (TTSB) ... CMTK
Com-Tech Communication Technologies, Inc. [*NASDAQ symbol*] (SAG) ... CMTK
Com-Tech Communication Technologies, Inc. [*Associated Press*] (SAG) ... ComTch
Com-Tech Communication Technologies, Inc. [*Associated Press*] (SAG) ... ComYch
Comtech Group International Ltd. [*Toronto Stock Exchange symbol*] ... CTG
Comtech Telecommns [*NASDAQ symbol*] (TTSB) ... CMIL
Comtech Telecommns [*NASDAQ symbol*] (SG) ... CMTL
Comtech Telecommunications Corp. [*NASDAQ symbol*] (NQ) ... CMTL
Comtech Telecommunications Corp. [*Associated Press*] (SAG) ... Comtch
Comtelburo, Ltd. (SAUO) ... Comtelburo
Comten Network Gateway [*NCR Corp.*] [*Computer science*] (NITA) ... CNG
Comterm, Inc. [*Toronto Stock Exchange symbol*] ... CMT
Comtrex Systems [*NASDAQ symbol*] (TTSB) ... COMX
Comtrex Systems Corp. [*Associated Press*] (SAG) ... Comtrx
Comtrex Systems Corp. [*NASDAQ symbol*] (NQ) ... COMX
Comunicacion, Intercambio, y Desarrollo Humano en America Latina ... CIDHAL
Comunication Foundation for Asia (SAUO) ... CFA
Comunidad Democratica Centroamericana [*Central American Democratic Community*] (EAIO) ... CDC
Comunidades Eclesiales de Base [*Spanish*] ... CEB
Comunity Care Plan [*Medicine*] ... CCP
Comunn na Clarsaich [*Clarsach Society*] (EAIO) ... CC
Comverse Technology [*NASDAQ symbol*] (TTSB) ... CMVT
Comverse Technology [*Associated Press*] (SAG) ... Comvers
Comverse Technology, Inc. [*NASDAQ symbol*] (NQ) ... CMVT
Comyn on Landlord and Tenant [*A publication*] (DLA) ... Com L & T
Comyn on the Law of Usury [*A publication*] (DLA) ... Com Us
Comyn's Digest of the Laws of England [*1762-1882*] [*A publication*] (ILCA) ... CD
Comyn's Digest of the Laws of England [*1762-1882*] [*A publication*] (DLA) ... Com Dig
Comyn's Digest of the Laws of England [*1762-1882*] [*A publication*] (DLA) ... Comyn's Dig
Comyn's English King's Bench Reports [*1695-1741*] [*A publication*] (DLA) ... Com
Comyn's English King's Bench Reports [*1695-1741*] [*A publication*] (DLA) ... Com Rep
Comyn's English King's Bench Reports [*1695-1741*] [*A publication*] (DLA) ... Comyn
Comyn's English King's Bench Reports [*1695-1741*] [*A publication*] (DLA) ... Comyns
Comyn's Law of Contracts [*A publication*] (DLA) ... Com Con
Con [*With*] [*Music*] (ROG) ... C
Con Anima [*With a Soulful Feeling*] [*Music*] (ROG) ... CON AN
Con Devotione [*With Devotion*] [*Music*] (ROG) ... CON DEVE
Con Dolore [*With Sadness*] [*Music*] (ROG) ... CON DOL
Con Espressione [*With Expression*] [*Music*] (ROG) ... C ESPR
Con Espressione [*With Expression*] [*Music*] ... CON ESP
Con Espressione [*With Expression*] [*Music*] ... CON ESPR
Con Fuoco [*With Force*] [*Music*] (ROG) ... CON FUO
Con Furia [*With Fury*] [*Music*] (ROG) ... CON FUR
Con Grazia [*With Grace*] [*Music*] (ROG) ... CON GRA
Con Gustoso [*With Taste*] [*Music*] (ROG) ... CON GUST
Con Moto [*With the Movement*] [*Music*] (ROG) ... CON MO
Con Ottava [*With the Octave*] [*Music*] (ROG) ... CON 8VA
Con Sordino [*With Mute*] [*Music*] ... CS
Con Tenerezza [*With Tenderness*] [*Music*] (ROG) ... CON TENA
CONAD [*Continental Air Defense Command*] **Operational Employment Concept** (AABC) ... COEC
CONAF [*Conceptual Design for the Army in the Field*] **Evaluation Model** ... CEM
ConAgra Cap L.C. 9% Pfd [*NYSE symbol*] (TTSB) ... CAGPrA
ConAgra Cap L.C.9.35% Pfd [*NYSE symbol*] (TTSB) ... CAGPrC
ConAgra Cap L.C.Adj Pfd'B' [*NYSE symbol*] (TTSB) ... CAGPrB
Conagra Capital [*NYSE symbol*] (SAG) ... CAG
ConAgra Capital [*Associated Press*] (SAG) ... CnCap
ConAgra, Inc. [*NYSE symbol*] (SPSG) ... CAG
ConAgra, Inc. [*Associated Press*] (SAG) ... ConAg
ConAgra, Inc. [*Associated Press*] (SAG) ... ConAgr
Conagra Trading Companies (EFIS) ... CTC
Conair AS [*Denmark*] [*ICAO designator*] (FAAC) ... OYC
Conair Aviation Ltd. [*Canada*] [*ICAO designator*] (FAAC) ... CRC
Conakry [*Guinea*] [*Airport symbol*] (OAG) ... CKY
Conakry/Gbessia [*Guinea*] [*ICAO location identifier*] (ICLI) ... GUCY
ConAm Inc. (SAUO) ... ConAm
CONARC [*Continental Army Command*] **Alternate Headquarters Plan** [*Obsolete*] ... CONALT
CONARC [*Continental Army Command*] **Automated System Support Agency** [*Obsolete*] (AABC) ... CASSA
CONARC [*Continental Army Command*] **Class One Automated System** [*Later, BASOPS*] (MCD) ... COCOAS
CONARC [*Continental Army Command*] **Education Data System** [*Obsolete*] (AABC) ... CONEDS
CONARC [*Continental Army Command*] **Emergency Relocation Plan** [*Obsolete*] ... CONREP
CONARC [*Continental Army Command*] **Intelligence Center** [*Obsolete*] (AABC) ... CONTIC
CONARC [*Continental Army Command*] **Logistics Operations - Streamline** [*Obsolete*] ... CONLOS
CONARC [*Continental Army Command*] **Operating Program** [*Obsolete*] (AABC) ... CONOPPR
CONARD Education Data System (SAUS) ... CONEDS
Conard [*Henry S.*] **Environmental Research Area** [*Grinnell College*] [*Research center*] (RCD) ... CERA
Conative Negative Variation (MAE) ... CNV
Conax Corp. (SAUO) ... CONAX
Concanamycin A [*Biochemistry*] ... CMA
Concanavalin [*Biochemistry*] ... CON
Concanavalin A [*Biochemistry*] ... Con A
Concanavalin A [*Biology*] (DOG) ... conA
Concanavalin A (SAUS) ... ConA
Concanavilin A-Horse-Radish Peroxidas [*Medicine*] (DMAA) ... Con A-HRP
Concatanated Network (SAUS) ... CATANET
Concatenate (SAUS) ... CAT
Concatenate (CDE) ... cat
Concave ... Cc
Concave (SAUS) ... CC
Concave (MSA) ... CNCV
Concave (SAUS) ... CV
Conceal (ABBR) ... CNCEL
Concealable (ABBR) ... CNCELB
Conceal-Control-Command-Instruction [*NATO*] ... CCCI
Concealed [*Ecology*] ... C
Concealed (ABBR) ... CNCELD
Concealed (MSA) ... CNCL
Concealed Figures Test (EDAC) ... CFT
Concealed Original Optical Locating System (PDAA) ... COOLS
Concealed Product Identification Number [*Automotive*] ... CPIN
Concealed Target Detection (MCD) ... CONTAD
Concealed Weapon Detector ... CWD
Concealed Weapons ... CW
Concealer (ABBR) ... CNCELR
Concealing (ABBR) ... CNCELG
Concealment (ABBR) ... CNCELT
Concealment Device [*Criminology*] (LAIN) ... CD
Concede (ABBR) ... CNCED
Conceded (ABBR) ... CNCEDD
Concededly (ABBR) ... CNCEDDY
Conceder (ABBR) ... CNCEDR
Conceding (ABBR) ... CNCEDG
Conceicao Do Araguaia [*Brazil*] [*Airport symbol*] (OAG) ... CDJ
Conceicao Do Araguaia [*Brazil*] [*ICAO location identifier*] (ICLI) ... SBAA
Conceit (ABBR) ... CNCET
Conceited (ABBR) ... CNCETD
Conceitedly (ABBR) ... CNCETDY
Conceiting (ABBR) ... CNCETG
Conceivability (ABBR) ... CNCEVBT
Conceivable (ABBR) ... CNCEVB
Conceivably (ABBR) ... CNCEVBY
Conceive (ABBR) ... CNCEV
Conceived (ABBR) ... CNCEVD
Conceiver (ABBR) ... CNCEVR
Conceiving (ABBR) ... CNCEVG
Concensys, Inc. [*Associated Press*] (SAG) ... Cocensys
Concentra Corp. [*Associated Press*] (SAG) ... Concntr
Concentra Corp. [*NASDAQ symbol*] (SAG) ... CTRA
Concentra Managed Care [*NASDAQ symbol*] [*Formerly, OccuSystems, Inc.*] (SG) ... CCMC
Concentracion de Fuerzas Populares [*Concentration of Popular Forces*] [*Ecuador*] [*Political party*] (PPW) ... CFP
Concentrate (ABBR) ... CNCEN
Concentrate (ABBR) ... CNCNTRA
Concentrate (SAUS) ... CNT
Concentrate [*or Concentration*] (AFM) ... CONC
Concentrate ... CONCNTRT
Concentrate Transfer System [*Nuclear energy*] (NRCH) ... CTS
Concentrated (ABBR) ... CNCED
Concentrated ... CONCD
Concentrated (DAVI) ... concentr
concentrated (SAUS) ... Concentr
Concentrated ... CONCTD
Concentrated (BABM) ... Cond
Concentrated Ammonia Liquor (SAUS) ... CAL
Concentrated Animal Feedlot (SAUS) ... CAFO
Concentrated Area Review [*US Postal Service*] ... CAR
Concentrated Boric Acid Storage Tank [*Nuclear energy*] (NRCH) ... CBAST
Concentrated Complete Fertiliser (or Fertilizer) (SAUS) ... CCF
Concentrated Complete Fertilizer [*Imperial Chemical Industries*] [*British*] ... CCF
Concentrated Data Set (SAUS) ... CDS

Concentrated Employment Program [Also known as CIEP] [Department of Labor] ... CEP
Concentrated Impact Employment Program [Also known as CEP] [Department of Labor] ... CIEP
Concentrated Liquor Discharge (DICI) ... CLD
Concentrated Liquor Outlet (DICI) ... CLO
Concentrated Oil of Vitriol ... COV
Concentrated Orange Juice for Manufacturing ... COJM
Concentrated Phosphate Export Association ... CPEA
Concentrated Range Extension with Gain [Telecommunications] (TEL) ... CREG
Concentrated Rust-Inhibiting [or Inhibitor] [Chemistry] ... CRI
Concentrated Sea Water ... CSW
Concentrated Solar Energy Imitator (PDAA) ... CSEI
Concentrated Solution (SAUS) ... concd soln
Concentrated Space (SAUS) ... CS
Concentrated Strength [of solutions] [Pharmacy] ... CS
Concentrated Super-Phosphate (OA) ... CSP
Concentrated Urban Enforcement [Bureau of Alcohol, Tobacco, and Firearms] ... CUE
Concentrated Urban Placement Service [Department of Labor] ... CUPS
Concentrated Volume [of solutions] (AAMN) ... CV
Concentrating (ABBR) ... CNCEG
Concentrating (ABBR) ... CNCNTRAG
Concentrating (SAUS) ... Conc
Concentrating ... CONCTG
Concentration [in the blood phase] [Medicine] (DAVI) ... C
Concentration (ABBR) ... CNCENN
Concentration (ABBR) ... CNCNTRN
Concentration ... CON
Concentration (EEVL) ... Conc
Concentration (ADWA) ... concn
Concentration ... CONCN
Concentration ... CONTRTN
Concentration - Dependent Regulation of Oxygen ... CDRO
Concentration by Volume [Chemistry] ... c
Concentration Camp ... CC
Concentration Camp (SAUO) ... CC
Concentration Camp Syndrome [Psychiatry] ... CCS
Concentration Factor [Nuclear energy] (NUCP) ... CF
Concentration Length ... CL
Concentration, minimal [Medicine] (DMAA) ... Cm
Concentration Module Extension [Telecommunications] (TEL) ... CMX
Concentration Module Main [Telecommunications] (TEL) ... CMM
Concentration of Adenosine Monophosphate [Medicine] (DMAA) ... CAMP
Concentration of Hydrogen (SAUS) ... CH
Concentration of Mechanical Transport (SAUS) ... ConcMe
Concentration of Respirable Dust (SAUS) ... CRD
Concentration of Total Carbon Dioxide [Medicine] (DAVI) ... $ctCO_2$
Concentration on Engineering Design (AAG) ... COED
Concentration Performance Test (SAUS) ... CPT
Concentration Product Value (SAUS) ... CP Value
Concentration Stress Test [Psychical stress] ... CST
Concentration to Control (SAUS) ... CTC
Concentration-Based Exemption Criteria [Environmental science] ... CBEC
Concentration/Exposure Time [Herbicides] ... CET
Concentration-Modulated Absorption Spectrometry ... COMAS
Concentrative (ABBR) ... CNCENV
Concentratively (ABBR) ... CNCENVY
Concentrator (ABBR) ... CNCENR
Concentrator (SAUS) ... CO
Concentrator Access Module (SAUS) ... CAM
Concentrator Access Unit (SAUS) ... CAU
Concentrator and Feed Make-Up-Tank (ABAC) ... CFMT
Concentrator Group Number ... CGN
Concentrator Isolation Working Subsystem [Telecommunications] (TEL) ... CIWS
Concentrator Network (SAUS) ... CONET
Concentrator Terminal Buffer [Computer science] (IBMDP) ... CTB
Concentrator Unit Control (SAUS) ... CUC
Concentrator-Identifier (SAUS) ... CI
Concentratus [Concentrated] [Pharmacy] (ROG) ... CONC
Concentric (SAUS) ... C/C
Concentric (ABBR) ... CNCENC
Concentric (ABBR) ... CNCNTRC
Concentric (MSA) ... CNCTRC
Concentric (SAUS) ... Cnctrc
Concentric (SAUS) ... Conc
Concentric ... CONC
Concentric ... CC
Concentric Cable (SAUS) ... CC
Concentric Coordinate Incident (SAUS) ... CCI
Concentric Flight Plan (KSC) ... CFP
Concentric Hemispherical Analyzer [Surface analysis] ... CHA
Concentric Line Oscillator ... CLO
Concentric Network [NASDAQ symbol] (SG) ... CNCX
Concentric Research Information Service (IID) ... CRIS
Concentric Rings [Botany] ... CR
Concentric Sequence Initiate (or Initiation) (SAUS) ... CSI
Concentric Sequence Initiation [Aerospace] ... CSI
Concentric Storage Rings (SAUS) ... CSR
Concentrically (ABBR) ... CNCENCY
Concentricity (ABBR) ... CNCENCT
Concentricity (SAUS) ... Concy
Concentric-Orbit Rendezvous [NASA] ... COR
Concepcion [Chile] [Airport symbol] (OAG) ... CCP
Concepcion [Bolivia] [Airport symbol] (OAG) ... CEP

Concepcion [Chile] [Seismograph station code, US Geological Survey] (SEIS) ... CON
Concepcion [Paraguay] [ICAO location identifier] (ICLI) ... SGCO
Concepcion [Bolivia] [ICAO location identifier] (ICLI) ... SLCP
Concepcion/Carriel Sur [Chile] [ICAO location identifier] (ICLI) ... SCIE
Concept ... CNCPT
Concept 90 Marketing, Inc. (SAUO) ... GYMS
Concept Alternative Selection [Automotive project management] ... CAS
Concept Analyser (SAUS) ... CONAN
Concept Analysis (MCD) ... CAA
Concept and Design Study (SAUS) ... CADS
Concept and Development Definition (ACAE) ... CDD
Concept and Objectives (SAUO) ... C&O
Concept and Requirements Definition Study (SAUO) ... CARDS
Concept Approval [Automotive project management] ... CA
Concept Assessment Kit [Child development test] ... CAK
Concept Chart (AFIT) ... CC
Concept Code [Database terminology] (NITA) ... CC
Concept Decision Model (ACAE) ... CDM
Concept Definition (MCD) ... CD
Concept Definition Proposal (MCD) ... CDP
Concept Demonstration Model ... CDM
Concept Demonstration/Validation Phase (AAGC) ... CD/V
Concept Development ... CD
Concept Development Associates, Inc. [Information service or system] (IID) ... CDA
Concept Development Group (ACAE) ... CDG
Concept Development Investigation ... CDI
Concept Development Phase (MCD) ... CDP
Concept Development Plan ... CDP
Concept Development Process (MCD) ... CDP
Concept Developments Talks ... CDT
Concept Developments Tasks (MCD) ... CDT
Concept Evaluation (SAUS) ... CE
Concept Evaluation Phase (SAUO) ... CEP
Concept Evaluation Plan (SAUO) ... CEP
Concept Evaluation Program [Army] ... CEP
Concept Evaluation Program Schedule and Review Committee (SAUO) ... CEPSARC
Concept Evaluation Technique [Psychometrics] ... CET
Concept Evaluation Test (MCD) ... CET
Concept Exploration ... CE
Concept Exploration and Definition [Military] ... CED
Concept Exploration and Technology Demonstration (SAUO) ... CETD
Concept Exploration Development Phase [DoD] ... CED
Concept Feasibility (AABC) ... CF
Concept Feasibility Analysis ... CFA
Concept Feasibility Report ... CFR
Concept for a Radiological Detection System (CINC) ... CCRDES
Concept for Low-Cost Air-to-Air Weapon (MCD) ... CLAW
Concept Formation Test [Psychology] ... CFT
Concept Former (SAUS) ... CF
Concept Formulation [DoD] ... CF
Concept Formulation Data Bank (DNAB) ... CFDB
Concept Formulation Package [Military] ... CFP
Concept Formulation Package - Technical Development Plan [Air Force] ... CFP/TDP
Concept Formulation Program Plan (SAUS) ... CFPP
Concept Formulation Studies ... CFS
Concept Formulation/Contract Definition [Procurement procedure] ... CF/CD
Concept Game [A war game] ... CONGA
Concept Identification [Psychology] ... CI
Concept Initiation [Automotive project management] ... CI
Concept Integration and Verification Laboratory [NASA] (SPST) ... CIVL
Concept Learning System [Computer science] (BUR) ... CLS
Concept Mastery Test (DHP) ... CMT
Concept Memory Test (EDAC) ... CMT
Concept of a Family of Army Divisions (AABC) ... CONFAD
Concept of Engineering (SAUO) ... COE
Concept of Maritime Operations (SAUS) ... CONMAROPS
Concept of Operations (DOMA) ... CONOP
Concept of Operations (DOMA) ... CONOPS
Concept of Operations (MCD) ... COO
Concept Oriented Programming System (SAUS) ... COPS
Concept Outline Plan (DOMA) ... COP
Concept Plan (NVT) ... CONPLAN
Concept Requirement [Automotive project management] ... CR
Concept Tech Group [Associated Press] (SAG) ... ConcpT
Concept Tech Group [Associated Press] (SAG) ... ConcT
Concept Tech Group [NASDAQ symbol] (SAG) ... TGSI
Concept to Customer ... CTC
Concept to Division [Automotive project management] ... CD
Concept Verification Test (NASA) ... CVT
Concept/International Programs Definitions [Military] ... C/IPD
Conception (ABBR) ... CNCPN
Conception Abbey and Seminary, Conception, MO [Library symbol] [Library of Congress] (LCLS) ... MoConA
Conception Assistee par Ordinateur [Computer-Assisted Design - CAD] [French] ... CAO
Conception Bay South Public Library, Manuels, Newfoundland [Library symbol] [National Library of Canada] (NLC) ... NFM
Conception Bay South Public Library, Manuels, NF, Canada [Library symbol] [Library of Congress] (LCLS) ... CaNfM
Conceptive (ABBR) ... CNCPTV
Conceptronic, Inc. [NASDAQ symbol] (SAG) ... CNCP

Conceptronic, Inc. [*Associated Press*] (SAG) ... Concept
Concepts About Print Test (EDAC) ... CAP
Concepts Analysis Agency [*Bethesda, MD*] [*Army*] (AABC) ... CAA
Concepts Analysis Agency, Bethesda, MD [*Library symbol*] [*Library of Congress*] (LCLS) ... MdBeCA
Concepts Analysis Group [*Army*] ... CAG
Concepts and Analysis Division [*US Army Engineer Topographic Laboratories*] ... CAD
Concepts Direct [*NASDAQ symbol*] (TTSB) ... CDIR
Concepts Direct, Inc. [*NASDAQ symbol*] (SAG) ... CDIR
Concepts Direct, Inc. [*Associated Press*] (SAG) ... ConcptD
Concepts, Doctrine, and Force [*Design*] ... CODAF
Concepts Evaluation Model [*Military*] ... CEM
Concepts of Postal Economics [*A series of newsletters of Mail Advertising Corp.*] ... COPE
Concepts Statements of the Financial Accounting Standards Board (SAUO) ... FASC
Concepts Statements of the Governmental Accounting Standards Board (SAUO) ... GASBC
Concepts, Trends, Relationships, Issues, Problems, Solutions ... CTRIPS
Concepts-Based Requirements System ... CBRS
Conceptual (ABBR) ... CNCPTL
Conceptual (VRA) ... concep
Conceptual Architecture Design Studies (SAUS) ... CARDS
Conceptual Armored Cavalry (MCD) ... CARCAV
Conceptual Communications Area [*Computer science*] (TNIG) ... CCA
Conceptual Data Store [*Telecommunications*] (OSI) ... CDS
Conceptual Design (ABAC) ... CD
Conceptual Design Activity (SAUO) ... CDA
Conceptual Design and Cost Review (CARB) ... CDCR
Conceptual Design and Rendering System [*Computer engineering*] ... CDRS
Conceptual Design for the Army in the Field ... CONAF
Conceptual Design Plan (ABAC) ... CDP
Conceptual Design Report (ABAC) ... CDR
Conceptual Design Requirement (NRCH) ... CDR
Conceptual Design Review (ABAC) ... CDR
Conceptual Design Review (SAUS) ... CoDR
Conceptual Design Study ... CDS
Conceptual Flight Profile (MCD) ... CFP
Conceptual Knowledge Markup Language (IDAI) ... CKML
Conceptual Learning of Science (SAUS) ... CoLoS
Conceptual Level (EDAC) ... CL
Conceptual Military Framework (SAUS) ... CMF
Conceptual Model of the Mission Space [*Army*] ... CMMS
Conceptual Modelling Language (SAUS) ... CML
Conceptual Network-Based Language [*NEC Corp.*] ... CL
Conceptual Operational System ... COS
Conceptual Organization [*Psychometrics*] ... CO
Conceptual Project Design Description (NRCH) ... CPDD
Conceptual Quotient [*Psychology*] ... CQ
Conceptual Recoilless Weapons (MCD) ... CRW
Conceptual Reference Mission [*NASA*] ... CRM
Conceptual Reference Repository Description (SAUS) ... CRRD
Conceptual Satellite Surveillance System ... CSSS
Conceptual Satellite Surveillance System ... CS^3
Conceptual Satellite System Studies (ACAE) ... CSSS
Conceptual Schema Definition Language [*Computer science*] (MHDI) ... CSDL
Conceptual Signaling and Status Store [*Telecommunications*] (OSI) ... CSS
Conceptual Site Treatment Plan [*Department of Energy*] ... CSTP
Conceptual System Design Description ... CSDD
Conceptual Systems Test ... CST
Conceptual Thought Random Net Simulation (SAUS) ... CONSTRANS
Conceptual Thought, Random Net Simulation (MUGU) ... CONTRANS
Conceptual Understanding through Blind Evaluation [*Educational test*] ... CUBE
Conceptualism (ABBR) ... CNCPTSM
Conceptualist (ABBR) ... CNCPTST
Conceptualize (ABBR) ... CNCPTLZ
Conceptualized (ABBR) ... CNCPTLZD
Conceptualizing (ABBR) ... CNCPTLZG
Conceptually (ABBR) ... CNCPTLY
Conceptually-Oriented Mathematics Program (SAUS) ... COMP
Conceptually-Oriented Program in Elementary Science [*New York University*] (AEBS) ... COPES
Conceptus, Inc. [*Associated Press*] (SAG) ... Concepts
Conceptus, Inc. [*NASDAQ symbol*] (SAG) ... CPTS
Concern (ABBR) ... CNCR
Concern (ABBR) ... CNCRN
Concern Against Nuclear Technology Organisations [*British*] (DI) ... CANTO
Concern Against Nuclear Technology Organization (SAUO) ... CANTO
Concern and Deficiency Reporting System (COE) ... CADRS
Concern for Dying (EA) ... CFD
Concern for Health Options: Information, Care and Education [*An association*] (EA) ... CHOICE
Concern for Helping Animals in Israel (EA) ... CHAI
Concern for the Health of Our Kids and the Environment [*Adelaide*] [*Australia*] ... CHOKE
Concern for the Kurds (SAUO) ... CFK
Concern, Inc. [*An association*] (EA) ... CI
CONCERN/America (EA) ... CA
Concerned (ABBR) ... CNCRND
Concerned about Trident [*Ecology group*] ... CAT
Concerned Agoraphobics Learning to Live [*An association*] (PAZ) ... CALI
Concerned American Indian Parents (EA) ... CAIP
Concerned Americans for Individual Rights (EA) ... CAIR
Concerned Americans for Military Improvements (EA) ... CAMI
Concerned Broadcasters Using Inter-City Video Transmission Facilities (EA) ... CBUIVTF
Concerned Broadcasters Using Inter-City Video Transmission Facilities (EA) ... CON-VID
Concerned Citizens for Charity (DICI) ... CCC
Concerned Citizens for Community Standards (SAUS) ... CCCS
Concerned Citizens for Nuclear Safety [*Advocacy group, New Mexico*] ... CCNS
Concerned Citizens for the Nuclear Breeder (EA) ... CCNB
Concerned Citizens for Universal Service [*Defunct*] (EA) ... CCUS
Concerned Citizens Information Council [*Group opposing sex education in schools*] ... CCIC
Concerned Citizens' Movement [*St. Christopher and Nevis*] [*Political party*] (EY) ... CCM
Concerned Citizens of America [*Defunct*] (EA) ... CCA
Concerned Educators Against Forced Unionism (EA) ... CEAFU
Concerned Educators Allied for a Safe Environment (EA) ... CEASE
Concerned Friends of Ontario Citizens in Care Facilities (AC) ... CFOCCF
Concerned Guatemala Scholars [*Defunct*] (EA) ... CGS
Concerned Neighbors in Action (EA) ... CNA
Concerned Persons for Adoption (EA) ... CPFA
Concerned Pet Owners' Association (EA) ... CPOA
Concerned Relatives of Nursing Home Patients (EA) ... CRNHP
Concerned Senators for the Arts (EA) ... CSA
Concerned Seniors for Better Government (EA) ... CSBG
Concerned South Africans Group (ECON) ... COSAG
Concerned United Birthparents (EA) ... CUB
Concerned Women for America (EA) ... CWA
Concerning (ABBR) ... CNCRG
Concerning (ABBR) ... CNCRNG
Concerning (ADA) ... CON
Concerning (ROG) ... CONC
Concerning (ADWA) ... conc
concerning (SAUS) ... conc
Concerning [*Legal term*] (ROG) ... CONCG
Concerns of Motherhood (EA) ... CM
Concerns of Police Survivors [*An association*] ... COPS
Concerns-Based Adoption Model (EDAC) ... CBAM
Concert (BEE) ... con
Concert Artist [*Record label*] [*Great Britain*] ... CA
Concert Artists Association [*British*] (BI) ... CAA
Concert Artists Guild (EA) ... CAG
Concert Dance Company ... CDC
Concert Growth Fund Cl.A [*Mutual fund ticker symbol*] (SG) ... CSGWX
Concert Hall Society [*Record label*] ... CHS
Concert Industry Ltd. [*Vancouver Stock Exchange symbol*] ... CNG
Concert Internet Plus (SAUS) ... CIP
Concert Multi-thread Architecture (SAUS) ... CMA
Concert Music Broadcasters Association (EA) ... CMBA
Concert Name [*Database terminology*] (NITA) ... CN
Concert Productions International [*Canada*] ... CPI
Concert Resources, Inc. [*Vancouver Stock Exchange symbol*] ... CCJ
Concertacion de los Partidos de la Democracia [*Chile*] [*Political party*] (EY) ... CPD
Concertacion Democratica Cubana [*Political party*] (EY) ... CDC
Concertation Unit for Biotechnology in Europe ... CUBE
Concerted Action for Research into Myopathies due to Enzyme deficiencies (SAUO) ... CARMEN
Concerted Action on Case Mix and Resource Management (SAUS) ... CAMIREMA
Concerted Action on Case Mix and Severity (SAUS) ... CAMISE
Concerted Action on Management Information for Libraries in Europe (TELE) ... CAMILE
Concerteum [*Record label*] [*France*] ... Cum
Concertina Wire (SAUS) ... CW
Concerto (ADWA) ... con
Concerto [*Music*] ... CON
Concerto [*Music*] ... CONC
Concerto (WDAA) ... conc
Concerto ... Conc
Concerto [*Music*] ... CTO
Concerto (ADWA) ... cto
Concerts and Recitals of Serious Music (Annual Licence) [*Public-performance tariff class*] [*British*] ... LA
Concerts and Recitals of Serious Music (Permits) [*Public-performance tariff class*] [*British*] ... L
Concession (MSA) ... CON
Concession (DD) ... Conc
Concession ... CONCSSN
Concession ... CSN
Concessional Finance Facility ... CFF
Conchological Society of Great Britain and Ireland (SAUO) ... CS
Conchological Society of Great Britain and Ireland (SAUO) ... CSGBI
Conchologists of America (EA) ... CA
Conchologists of America (EA) ... COA
Conchology (SAUS) ... Conch
Conchology ... CONCH
Conchology (WGA) ... CONCHOL
Conciencia de Patria [*Bolivia*] [*Political party*] (EY) ... Condepa
Conciertos Mexicanos [*Record label*] [*Mexico*] ... CM
Concil of European Industrial Federations (SAUO) ... CEIF
Conciliable (ABBR) ... CNCLAB
Conciliate (ABBR) ... CNCLA
Conciliated (ABBR) ... CNCLAD
Conciliating (ABBR) ... CNCLAG
Conciliation (ABBR) ... CNCLAN
Conciliation (ROG) ... CONCIL

Conciliation and Arbitration Board (SAUO) ... CAB
Conciliation and Arbitration Service (SAUO) ... CAS
Conciliation Commission for Palestine [*of the UN*] ... CCP
Conciliation Committees [*Australia*] ... CC
Conciliation Officer (Tribunal) [*British*] ... COT
Conciliator (ABBR) ... CNCLAR
Conciliatory (ABBR) ... CNCLARTRY
Conciliatory (ABBR) ... CNCLARY
Concilium [*Council*] [*Latin*] (WGA) ... CONC
Conciousness (STED) ... Cs
Concise (ABBR) ... CNCIS
Concise (ROG) ... CONC
Concise Australian Reference Book [*A publication*] (ADA) ... ARB
Concise Australian Reference Book (journ.) (SAUS) ... ARB
Concise Command Language [*Computer science*] (MHDI) ... CCL
Concise Dictionary of American Literary Biography [*A publication*] ... CDALB
Concise Handbooks of Art [*A publication*] ... CHA
Concise International Chemical Assessment Documents (SAUS) ... CICAD
Concise Oxford Dictionary [*A publication*] ... COD
Concise Oxford English Dictionary [*A publication*] ... COED
Concise Scots Dictionary [*Aberdeen University Press*] [*A publication*] ... CSD
Concise Tax Service [*Australia*] [*A publication*] ... CTS
Concisely (ABBR) ... CNCISY
Concision (ABBR) ... CNCISN
Concisus [*Cut*] [*Medicine*] ... C
Concisus [*Cut*] [*Medicine*] (ROG) ... CON
Concisus [*Cut*] [*Medicine*] ... CONCIS
Conclave (ABBR) ... CNCLAV
Conclave (ABBR) ... CNCLV
Conclave of Mystical Masons [*Freemasonry*] (ROG) ... CMM
Conclude (ABBR) ... CNCLD
Conclude (ABBR) ... CNCLU
Concluded (ABBR) ... CNCLUD
Concluder (ABBR) ... CNCLUR
Concluding (ABBR) ... CNCDG
Concluding (ABBR) ... CNCLUG
Conclusion (WGA) ... C
Conclusion [*Broadcasting*] (WDMC) ... CC
Conclusion (ABBR) ... CNCLSN
Conclusion (ABBR) ... CNCLUN
Conclusion (NTIO) ... con
Conclusion ... CON
Conclusion ... conc
Conclusion (MSA) ... CONCL
Conclusion (ADWA) ... concl
Conclusion (ROG) ... CONCLON
Conclusions, Recommendations, and Lessons Learned ... CRLL
Conclusive (ABBR) ... CNCLSV
Conclusive (ABBR) ... CNCLUV
Conclusively (ABBR) ... CNCLUVY
Concoct (ABBR) ... CNCOC
Concocted (ABBR) ... CNCOCD
Concocting (ABBR) ... CNCOCG
Concoction (ABBR) ... CNCOCN
Concoctive (ABBR) ... CNCOCV
Concoctor (ABBR) ... CNCOCR
Concomitance (ABBR) ... CNCOM
Concomitant (ABBR) ... CNCMTNT
Concomitant (ABBR) ... CNCOMT
Concora Medium Test ... CMT
Concord (ABBR) ... CNCRD
Concord [*City in California, Massachusetts, New Hampshire, and North Carolina*] (ROG) ... CON
Concord - Diablo Valley College [*California*] [*Seismograph station code, US Geological Survey*] [*Closed*] (SEIS) ... CNC
Concord Airlines Nigeria Ltd. [*ICAO designator*] (FAAC) ... CND
Concord, CA [*Location identifier*] [*FAA*] (FAAL) ... CCR
Concord, CA [*Television station call letters*] ... KFCB
Concord, CA [*AM radio station call letters*] ... KKIS
Concord, CA [*AM radio station call letters*] (RBYB) ... KRHT-AM
Concord, CA [*TV station call letters*] (RBYB) ... KTNC-TV
Concord, CA [*FM radio station call letters*] ... KVHS
Concord Camera Corp. [*Associated Press*] (SAG) ... CcdCam
Concord Camera Corp. [*NASDAQ symbol*] (NQ) ... LENS
Concord College, Athens, WV [*Library symbol*] [*Library of Congress*] (LCLS) ... WvAC
Concord Communications [*NASDAQ symbol*] (SG) ... CCRD
Concord Council [*Defunct*] (EA) ... CC
Concord EFS [*NASDAQ symbol*] (TTSB) ... CEFT
Concord EFS, Inc. [*NASDAQ symbol*] (NQ) ... CEFT
Concord EFS, Inc. [*Associated Press*] (SAG) ... CncEFS
Concord Energy [*Vancouver Stock Exchange symbol*] ... CCD
Concord Energy [*NASDAQ symbol*] (TTSB) ... CODE
Concord Energy, Inc. [*NASDAQ symbol*] (SAG) ... CODE
Concord Energy, Inc. [*Associated Press*] (SAG) ... ConcEgy
Concord Fabrics Cl'A' [*AMEX symbol*] (TTSB) ... CIS
Concord Fabrics, Inc. [*AMEX symbol*] (SPSG) ... CIS
Concord Fabrics, Inc. [*Associated Press*] (SAG) ... ConcdF
Concord Fabrics, Inc. [*Associated Press*] (SAG) ... ConcF
Concord Free Public Library, Concord, MA [*Library symbol*] [*Library of Congress*] (LCLS) ... MCo
Concord Grape Association (EA) ... CGA
Concord Health Group, Inc. [*NASDAQ symbol*] (SAG) ... CHGR
Concord Health Group, Inc. [*Associated Press*] (SAG) ... ConcH
Concord, MA [*AM radio station call letters*] ... WADN
Concord, MA [*FM radio station call letters*] ... WIQH
Concord, NC [*AM radio station call letters*] ... WEGO
Concord, NC [*FM radio station call letters*] ... WPEG
Concord, NC [*Television station call letters*] ... WUNG
Concord, NH [*Location identifier*] [*FAA*] (FAAL) ... CON
Concord, NH [*Location identifier*] [*FAA*] (FAAL) ... EPP
Concord, NH [*FM radio station call letters*] ... WEVO
Concord, NH [*FM radio station call letters*] ... WJYY
Concord, NH [*AM radio station call letters*] ... WKXL
Concord, NH [*FM radio station call letters*] ... WKXL-FM
Concord, NH [*Television station call letters*] (RBYB) ... WNBU
Concord, NH [*AM radio station call letters*] ... WNHA
Concord, NH [*FM radio station call letters*] ... WSPS
Concord, NH [*FM radio station call letters*] ... WVNH
Concord Public Library, Concord, NC [*Library symbol*] [*Library of Congress*] (LCLS) ... NcCo
Concord Scientific Corp., Downsview, Ontario [*Library symbol*] [*National Library of Canada*] (NLC) ... OTCOS
Concord Video and Film Council (EAIO) ... CVFC
Concordance (ABBR) ... CNCRDNC
Concordance (ROG) ... CONC
Concordance [*Computer software*] (NITA) ... CONCORD
Concordance Generation System [*A text editing system*] [*University of Toronto*] [*Canada*] (NITA) ... COGS
Concordance Words in Titles [*Indexing*] ... CWIT
Concordant (ABBR) ... CNCRDT
Concordant Memory Zone (SAUS) ... CMZ
Concordantly (ABBR) ... CNCRDTY
concordat (SAUS) ... conc
Concorde Engines Support Organisation Ltd. (SAUO) ... CESO
Concorde out, Concorde Home ... COCH
Concorde out, Tourist Class Home ... COTCH
Concordia [*Brazil*] [*Airport symbol*] [*Obsolete*] (OAG) ... CCI
Concordia [*Record label*] ... Cdia
Concordia [*Argentina*] [*Airport symbol*] (OAG) ... COC
Concordia [*Brazil*] [*ICAO location identifier*] (ICLI) ... SBCE
Concordia - Youth Service Volunteers (EAIO) ... CYSV
Concordia College, Bronxville, NY [*Library symbol*] [*Library of Congress*] (LCLS) ... NBronC
Concordia College, Conover, NC [*Library symbol*] [*Library of Congress*] [*Obsolete*] (LCLS) ... NcConC
Concordia College, Edmonton, AB, Canada [*Library symbol*] [*Library of Congress*] (LCLS) ... CaAEC
Concordia College, Edmonton, Alberta [*Library symbol*] [*National Library of Canada*] (NLC) ... AEC
Concordia College (Illinois) (GAGS) ... Concordia C (Ill)
Concordia College, Milwaukee, WI [*Library symbol*] [*Library of Congress*] (LCLS) ... WMC
Concordia College, Milwaukee, WI [*Library symbol*] [*Library of Congress*] (LCLS) ... WMCC
Concordia College, Moorhead, MN [*Library symbol*] [*Library of Congress*] (LCLS) ... MnMohC
Concordia College, Portland, OR [*Library symbol*] [*Library of Congress*] (LCLS) ... OrPCC
Concordia College, Seward, NE [*OCLC symbol*] (OCLC) ... NBC
Concordia College, St. Paul, MN [*OCLC symbol*] (OCLC) ... MNC
Concordia College, St. Paul, MN [*Library symbol*] [*Library of Congress*] (LCLS) ... MnSCC
Concordia Collegiate Institute [*New York*] ... CCI
Concordia Gospel Outreach [*An association*] (EA) ... CGO
Concordia Historical Institute (EA) ... CHI
Concordia Historical Institute, St. Louis, MO [*Library symbol*] [*Library of Congress*] (LCLS) ... MoSCH
Concordia Hospital, Winnipeg, Manitoba [*Library symbol*] [*National Library of Canada*] (NLC) ... MWCH
Concordia Hospital, Winnipeg, MB, Canada [*Library symbol*] [*Library of Congress*] (LCLS) ... CaMWCH
Concordia, KS [*Location identifier*] [*FAA*] (FAAL) ... CNK
Concordia, KS [*FM radio station call letters*] ... KCKS
Concordia, KS [*AM radio station call letters*] ... KNCK
Concordia, KS [*AM radio station call letters*] (BROA) ... KNCK-AM
Concordia, KS [*FM radio station call letters*] ... KVCO
Concordia Lutheran College, Ann Arbor, MI [*Library symbol*] [*Library of Congress*] (LCLS) ... MiAaC
Concordia Lutheran College, Austin, TX [*Library symbol*] [*Library of Congress*] (LCLS) ... TxAuC
Concordia Lutheran Seminary, Edmonton, Alberta [*Library symbol*] [*National Library of Canada*] (BIB) ... AECO
Concordia, MO [*FM radio station call letters*] (BROA) ... KYRV-FM
Concordia Mutual Life Association (EA) ... CML
Concordia Mutual Life Association (SAUO) ... CMLA
Concordia Paper Holding ADS [*NASDAQ symbol*] (TTSB) ... CPLNY
Concordia Paper Holding Ltd. [*Associated Press*] (SAG) ... ConcPap
Concordia Paper Holding Ltd. [*NASDAQ symbol*] (SAG) ... CPLN
Concordia Parish Library, Ferriday, LA [*Library symbol*] [*Library of Congress*] (LCLS) ... LFC
Concordia Seminary College (SAUO) ... CSC
Concordia Seminary, St. Louis, MO [*Library symbol*] [*Library of Congress*] (LCLS) ... MoSCS
Concordia Senior College, Fort Wayne, IN [*Library symbol*] [*Library of Congress*] (LCLS) ... InFwC
Concordia Teachers College [*Illinois, Nebraska*] ... CTC
Concordia Teachers College (Nebraska) (GAGS) ... Concordia Teachers C (Nebr)
Concordia Teachers College, River Forest, IL [*OCLC symbol*] (OCLC) ... ICE

Concordia Teachers College, River Forest, IL [Library symbol] [Library of Congress] (LCLS) .... IRivfT
Concordia Teachers College, Seward, NE [Library symbol] [Library of Congress] (LCLS) .... NbSeT
Concordia Theological Monthly (journ.) (SAUS) .... CTM
Concordia Theological Seminary [Later, Concordia Seminary] [Missouri] .... CTS
Concordia Theological Seminary, Fort Wayne, IN [Library symbol] [Library of Congress] (LCLS) .... InFwCT
Concordia Theological Seminary, Fort Wayne, IN [OCLC symbol] (OCLC) ..... ITC
Concordia Theological Seminary, Springfield, IL [Library symbol] [Library of Congress] [Obsolete] (LCLS) .... ISC
Concordia Tract Mission (EA) .... CTM
Concordia University (SAUO) .... CU
Concordia University Faculty Association [Association des Professeurs de l'Universite Concordia] (AC) .... CUFA
Concordia University Library [UTLAS symbol] .... CNC
Concordia University, Librry Studies Program, Montreal, PQ, Canada [Library symbol] [Library of Congress] (LCLS) .... CaQMGLS
Concordia University, Loyola Campus, Montreal, PQ, Canada [Library symbol] [Library of Congress] (LCLS) .... CaQML
Concordia University, Sir George Williams Campus, Department of Geography, Montreal, PQ, Canada [Library symbol] [Library of Congress] (LCLS) .... CaQMGG
Concordia University, Sir George Williams Campus, Department of Geography, University Map Collection, Montreal, PQ, Canada [Library symbol] [Library of Congress] (LCLS) .... CaQMGGM
Concordia University, Sir George Williams Campus, Montreal, PQ, Canada [Library symbol] [Library of Congress] (LCLS) .... CaQMG
Concordia/Commodoro Pierrest Egui [Argentina] [ICAO location identifier] (ICLI) .... SAAC
Concore Health Group, Inc. [Associated Press] (SAG) .... ConcHlth
Concors Latvian Air Service [FAA designator] (FAAC) .... COS
Concours (SAUO) .... Conc
Concours International de Musique de Montreal [Montreal International Music Competition] (AC) .... CIMM
Concourse (ABBR) .... CNCOR
Concourse .... CONCRS
Concourse Computer Center (SAUS) CCC
Concrete (SAUS) .... Cnrt
Concrete .... CON
Concrete .... CONC
Concrete .... CONCR
Concrete (VRA) .... concr
Concrete .... CONCRT
Concrete Additive (SAUS) .... CA
Concrete Admixture (SAUS) .... CA
Concrete Aggregate (SAUS) .... CA
Concrete and Steel Combination (SAUS) .... CSC
Concrete Arch [Bridges] .... KA
Concrete Articulated Production Tower (PDAA) .... CONAPT
Concrete Block .... CB
Concrete Block .... CCB
Concrete Block (SAUS) .... Conc B
Concrete Block Association (MHDB) .... CBA
Concrete Block Enclosed Elevator (GEOI) .... CBET
Concrete Block Stucco (SAUS) .... CBS
Concrete Brick Manufacturers Association [British] (DBA) .... CBMA
Concrete Cancer [Refers to disintegration caused by weathering and pollutants] CC
Concrete Ceiling CC
Concrete Ceiling CCC
Concrete Deep Water Structure [Oil platform] .... CONDEEP
Concrete Floor .... CCF
Concrete Floor [Technical drawings] .... CF
Concrete Floor (SAUS) .... Conc F
Concrete Forming Association of Ontario (AC) .... CFAO
Concrete Foundations Association (NTPA) .... CFA
Concrete Industries Council (EA) CIC
Concrete Industry Board .... CIB
Concrete Island Drilling System [Offshore oil exploration] .... CIDS
Concrete Joint Institute [Defunct] (EA) .... CJI
Concrete, lime, cinder .... C BR
Concrete, Lime, Cinder or Cement Brick (GEOI) .... CBR
Concrete Lintel Association [British] (DBA) .... CLASS
Concrete Masonry Association of Australia Cooperative .... CMAAC
Concrete Masonry Unit [Technical drawings] .... CMU
Concrete Median Barrier (OA) .... CMB
Concrete Missile Entry Warning System (MCD) .... CMEWS
Concrete Mixer Manufacturers' Association [British] (BI) .... CMMA
Concrete Mixing and Placing (SAUS) .... CMP
Concrete Modifications Contractors Association (NTPA) .... CMCA
Concrete Paver Project (SAUS) .... CPP
Concrete Paving Project (SAUS) .... CPP
Concrete Paviors' Association of New South Wales [Australia] .... CPANSW
Concrete Piercing .... CP
Concrete Pipe Association of Australia .... CPAA
Concrete Pipe Association of Great Britain (SAUO) .... CPA
Concrete Pipe Association of South Carolina (SRA) .... CPASC
Concrete Pipe Associations (SAUS) .... CPA
Concrete Plant Manufacturers Bureau (EA) .... CPMB
Concrete Polymer Data System (SAUS) .... COPODS
Concrete Pressure Vehicle (PDAA) .... CPV
Concrete Pressure Vessel (SAUS) .... CPV
Concrete Reinforcement Steel Association (SAUO) .... CRSA
Concrete Reinforcing Steel Institute (EA) .... CRSI

Concrete Repair Association [British] (DBA) .... CRA
Concrete Sawing and Drilling Association (EA) .... CSDA
Concrete Slab (OA) .... CS
Concrete Society [British] (EAIO) .... CS
Concrete Splash Block [Technical drawings] .... CSB
Concrete Technology Information Analysis Center [Army Corps of Engineers] [Vicksburg, MS] (IID) .... CTIAC
Concreted (SAUS) .... Conc
Concrete-Encased Ring Ground (SAUS) .... CERG
Concretely (SAUS) .... Concr
Concurrency Control Bus [Computer science] (NITA) .... C & B
Concurrency Control Unit (NITA) .... CCU
Concurrency Controller [Computer science] CC
Concurrency Update Group .... CUG
Concurrent C
Concurrent (AFM) .... CNCR
Concurrent (SAUS) .... Cncr
Concurrent Admission Program [DoD] .... CONAP
Concurrent Algorithmic Programming Language [Computer science] (CSR) .... CAP
Concurrent Art-to-Product Environment (SAUS) .... CAPE
Concurrent Budget Resolution (AAGC) .... CBR
Concurrent Care Concern [Medicine] CCC
Concurrent Computer [NASDAQ symbol] (TTSB) .... CCUR
Concurrent Computer [Associated Press] (SAG) .... ConcCm
Concurrent Computer Corp. [NASDAQ symbol] (NQ) .... CCUR
Concurrent Concession (MDG) CC
Concurrent Constraint Programming (SAUS) .... CCP
Concurrent Design (SAUS) .... CD
Concurrent Disk Operating System (ROAS) .... CDOS
Concurrent Engineering .... CE
Concurrent Engineering Directorate (SAUO) .... CED
Concurrent Engineering Europe (SAUS) .... CEE
Concurrent Engineering for Composites Materials Program [University of Delaware, Center for Composite Materials] (RDA) .... CECM
Concurrent Engineering in Costruction (SAUO) .... CIB TG33
Concurrent Engineering Network of excellence (SAUO) .... CE-NET
Concurrent Engineering Research Center (SAUS) .... CERC
Concurrent High-Level Language [Computer science] (MCD) .... CHLL
Concurrent Highspeed Advanced Operating System (SAUS) .... CHAOS
Concurrent Input/Output System [Computer science] (PCM) .... CIOSYS
Concurrent Language [Computer science] .... CLANG
Concurrent Machine Environment [International Computers Ltd.] [British] (NITA) .... CME
Concurrent Media Conversion (IAA) .... CMC
Concurrent Object Orientated Programming (SAUS) .... COOP
Concurrent Operating System [Sperry UNIVAC] [Computer science] (IEEE) .... COS
Concurrent Peripheral Operations (BUR) .... CPO
Concurrent Peripheral Processing (SAUS) .... CPP
Concurrent Photon Amplification [Air Force] .... CPA
Concurrent Planometric [A discrimination task] .... CP
Concurrent Processor Architecture Control (MCD) .... CPAC
Concurrent Product Development .... CPD
Concurrent Quality Assurance (STED) .... CQA
Concurrent Range Zone (SAUS) .... CRC
Concurrent Schedule of Reinforcement (DIPS) .... CONC
Concurrent Semiconductor Production and Equipment Development .... CSPED
Concurrent Spare Parts (AFM) .... CSP
Concurrent Stereometric [A discrimination task] .... CS
Concurrent Super Computing Consortium (VERA) .... CSCC
Concurrent Surface and Underground Mining (SAUO) .... CSAUM
Concurrent Versions System (SAUS) .... CVS
Concurrent With .... C/W
Concurrent with Aircraft Delivery (MCD) .... CWAD
Concurrent with Design Release (MCD) .... CWDR
Concurrently (FAAC) .... CNCNT
Concurring (ABBR) .... CNCRG
Concursos y Certamenes Culturales [Database] [Ministerio de Cultura] [Spanish] [Information service or system] (CRD) .... CECU
Concussion (DSUE) .... CONCUSS
Condaka Metals Corp. [Vancouver Stock Exchange symbol] .... CKA
Condamine [Queensland] [Airport symbol] (AD) .... ONM
Condat-Sur-Vezere [France] [ICAO location identifier] (ICLI) .... LFDZ
Condemn (MSA) .... CDM
Condemn at Depot (SAUO) .... CAD
Condemn Below Depot (SAUO) .... CBD
Condemnation [Legal term] (DLA) c
Condemnation [Legal shorthand] (LWAP) .... COMDN
Condemnation [Legal term] (DLA) .... Condem
Condemnation Rate .... CR
Condemned .... CD
Condemned (WGA) .... CD
Condemned (AABC) .... CND
Condemned [Prisoners'] Cell (IIA) CC
Condemned or Suppressed .... COS
Condemno [I Condemn] [Used by Romans in criminal trials] [Latin] C
Condensance (SAUS) .... Cond
Condensate (SAUS) .... Cnds
Condensate (KSC) .... CNDS
Condensate and Feedwater [Nuclear energy] (NRCH) .... CFW
Condensate and Feedwater Chemistry Control System [Nuclear energy] (NRCH) .... CFCCS
Condensate and Feedwater System [Nuclear energy] (NRCH) .... CFS
Condensate and Feedwater System [Nuclear energy] (NRCH) .... CFWS

Condensate and Refueling Water Storage System [Nuclear energy]
(NRCH) .... CRWSS
Condensate Booster Pump [Nuclear energy] (NRCH) .... CBP
Condensate Cleanup System [Nuclear energy] (NRCH) .... CCS
Condensate Cooling System [Nuclear energy] (NRCH) .... CCS
Condensate Demineralization Effluent [Nuclear energy] (NRCH) .... CDE
Condensate Demineralization Subsystem [Nuclear energy] (NRCH) .... CDS
Condensate Extraction Pump [Chemical engineering] .... CEP
Condensate Filter Demineralizer [Nuclear energy] (NRCH) .... CFR
Condensate Heat Exchanger (MCD) .... CH-X
Condensate Polishing System [Nuclear energy] (NRCH) .... CPS
Condensate Storage and Transfer System [Nuclear energy] (NRCH) .... CSTS
Condensate Storage Facility [Nuclear energy] (NRCH) .... CSF
Condensate Storage System [Nuclear energy] (NRCH) .... CSS
Condensate Storage Tank [Nuclear energy] (NRCH) .... CST
Condensate Transfer and Storage [Nuclear energy] (NRCH) .... CTS
Condensate Water Servicing Unit .... CWSU
Condensation [Physics] (BARN) .... S
Condensation Figure [Surface physical chemistry] .... CF
Condensation Nuclei .... CN
Condensation Nuclei Counter .... CNC
Condensation Nuclei Detector (MCD) .... CND
Condensation Nucleus [Marine science] (OSRA) .... CN
Condensation Nucleus Counter [Environmental science] (COE) .... CNC
Condensation Particle Counter [Marine science] (OSRA) .... CPC
Condensation Pressure Spread .... CPS
Condensation Trail [in the air] .... CONTRAIL
Condensation Trail (ADWA) .... contrail
Condensed .... COND
Condensed Chemical Dictionary [A publication] .... CCD
Condensed Ecclesiastical Reports [A publication] (DLA) .... Cond Eccl
Condensed Ecclesiastical Reports [A publication] (DLA) .... Cond Ecc R
Condensed English Chancery Reports [A publication] (DLA) .... Cond Ch R
Condensed English Chancery Reports [A publication] (DLA) .... Cond Eng Ch
Condensed Exchequer Reports [A publication] (DLA) .... Cond Exch R
Condensed Exchequer Reports [A publication] (DLA) .... Cond Ex R
Condensed Instruction Deck (SAUS) .... CID
Condensed Logic Diagram [Electronics] (IAA) .... CLD
Condensed Master File (SAUS) .... CMF
Condensed Matter Theory (SAUS) .... CMT
Condensed Nearest Neighbor [Mathematics] .... CNN
Condensed Negative Binomial Distribution [Statistics] .... CNBD
Condensed or Dried .... COD
Condensed Particulate Matter (SAUS) .... CPM
Condensed Random Access Memory (SAUS) .... CRAM
Condensed Strike Data Transmission System (MCD) .... CONTRAST
Condensed Tannin [Botany] .... CT
Condensed Tannin Leucoanthocyanin .... CTL
Condensed Tannin Proanthocyanidin .... CTP
Condenser c
Condenser (ADWA) .... cond
Condenser [Automotive engineering] .... COND
Condenser (SAUS) .... Cond
Condenser .... CONDR
Condenser Absolute Pressure .... CAP
Condenser Air Removal [Nuclear energy] (NRCH) .... CAR
Condenser Circulating Water [Nuclear energy] (NRCH) .... CCW
Condenser Cooling Water [Nuclear energy] (NRCH) .... CCW
Condenser Discharge Unit .... CDU
Condenser Heat Rejection (IAA) .... CHR
Condenser Load Compensation [Portable electric generators] CLC
Condenser Vacuum Pump Effluent Treatment System [Nuclear energy]
(NRCH) .... CVPETS
Condenser-Radiator Fan Module [Automotive cooling systems] .... CRFM
Condenset Nearest Neighbour Design Rule (SAUS) .... CNN Design Rule
Condensing (SAUS) .... Cond
Condensing .... CONDG
Condensing Vacuole (OA) CV
Conders. Highway Cases [A publication] (DLA) .... Cond HC
Conde-Sur-Noireau [France] [ICAO location identifier] (ICLI) .... LFAN
Condition [Automotive advertising] .... CD
Condition (MDG) .... CND
Condition (REAL) .... cond
Condition (AFM) .... COND
Condition [Legal term] (ROG) .... CONDON
Condition (MSA) .... CONDTN
Condition and Recommendation (AABC) .... CAR
Condition Assesment Programme Survey (SAUS) .... CAP
Condition Assessment Programme (RIMS) .... CAP
Condition Assessment Survey [Environmental science] (COE) .... CAS
Condition BIT [Binary Digit] [Computer science] .... CB
Condition Bit (SAUS) .... CB
Condition Code CC
Condition Code Register .... CCR
Condition Command (SAUS) CC
Condition Education Division [Department of Education] (GFGA) .... CED
Condition Flag (SAUS) .... CF
Condition Identification Work Authorization [Business term] (NRCH) .... CIWA
Condition Monitored Maintenance (NASA) .... CMM
Condition Monitoring (DS) .... CM
Condition Monitoring (MCD) .... COM
Condition Monitoring System (CAAL) .... CMS
Condition of Detail .... CD
Condition on Admission [Medicine] (ADA) .... COA
Condition on Discharge [Medicine] (DAVI) .... COD

Condition Precedent [Legal term] .... CP
Condition Recognition (SAUS) .... CR
Condition Reservation Code [Army] (AABC) .... CRC
Condition Response [Psychology] (DHP) .... CR
Condition Status [Computer science] .... CS
Condition Subsequent [Legal term] .... CS
Condition Unknown (SAUS) .... CU
Conditional (SAUS) .... Cndl
Conditional (ROG) .... CONDL
Conditional Access for Europe [An association] [Electronic Commerce] .... CAFE
Conditional Access System (SAUS) .... CAS
Conditional Addition (SAUS) .... CA
Conditional Amount of Sample Information [Statistics] .... CASI
Conditional Analysis for Random Networks [Electronics] (OA) .... CARN
Conditional Antimicrobial Reporting [Microbiology] .... CAR
Conditional Array Scaling (SAUS) .... CAS
Conditional Assembler Instruction (SAUS) .... CAI
Conditional Authorization [Environmental science] .... CA
Conditional Branch .... CB
Conditional Breakpoint Instruction .... CBI
Conditional Breakpoint Instruction .... CBPI
Conditional Command Processor [Computer science] (MHDI) .... CCP
Conditional Control Sequence Interruption (SAUS) .... CCSI
Conditional Control Transfer Instruction (SAUS) .... CCTI
Conditional Conventional Retaliation Capability (ACAE) .... CCRC
Conditional Critical Region (RALS) .... CCR
Conditional End Of Page (SAUS) .... CEOP
Conditional Exemption [Environmental science] .... CE
Conditional Expression .... CE
Conditional Forced Value (SAUS) .... CFV
Conditional Freedom (ADA) .... CF
Conditional Go-to-Statement (SAUS) .... CGS
Conditional Grant .... CG
Conditional Information Content (SAUS) CIC
Conditional Instability of the Second Kind .... CISK
Conditional Instability of the Third Kind (SAUS) .... CITHK
Conditional Instruction (SAUS) CI
Conditional Interrupt Request (SAUS) .... CIR
Conditional Jump (SAUS) .... CJ
Conditional Jump Instruction (SAUS) .... CJI
Conditional Jump Operation (SAUS) .... CJO
Conditional Jump Order (SAUS) .... CJO
Conditional Lease (ADA) CL
Conditional Mean Square Error [Statistics] .... CMSE
Conditional Move (SAUS) .... CMOV
Conditional Nonoperation [Computer science] .... CNOP
Conditional Open Probability Analysis [Mathematics] .... COPA
Conditional Order (SAUS) .... CO
Conditional Pardon (ADA) .... CP
Conditional Peak Flow [Biology] .... CPF
Conditional Prepayment Rate [for mortgages] .... CPR
Conditional Probability (SAUS) .... CP
Conditional Proof [Method in logic] .... CP
Conditional Purchase [Business term] (ADA) .... CP
Conditional Reflex (SAUS) .... CONFLEX
Conditional Reflex (SAUS) .... CR
Conditional Relaxation Analysis Method .... CRAM
Conditional Release [Nuclear energy] (NRCH) .... CR
Conditional Release Authorization (SAA) .... CRA
Conditional Release Violator [FBI standardized term] .... CRV
Conditional Response (SAUS) .... CR
Conditional Response Analog Machine .... CORA
Conditional Route (SAUS) .... CDR
Conditional Route Availability Message (SAUS) .... CRAM
Conditional Route System (SAUS) .... CRS
Conditional Sale [Legal shorthand] (LWAP) .... CS
Conditional Sale - Chattel Mortgage Reporter [Commerce Clearing House]
[A publication] (DLA) .... Condit Sale - Chat Mort Rep
Conditional Select Multiplexer .... CSM
Conditional Sentence .... CS
Conditional Statement (SAUS) .... CS
Conditional Symmetric Instability [Marine science] (OSRA) .... CSI
Conditional (Tense) [Linguistics] .... COND
Conditional Transfer of Control .... CTC
Conditional Use Permit (GNE) .... CUP
Conditional Value of Sample Information [Statistics] .... CVSI
Conditional Variable Incremental Computer (IEEE) CVIC
Conditional Variable Test (SAUS) .... CVT
Conditional Voluntary Indefinite [Status] [Army] (INF) CVI
Conditionally Accepted Tag (NRCH) .... CAT
Conditionally Exempt Generator (EEVL) .... CE
Conditionally Exempt Small Quantity Generator .... CESQG
Conditionally Exempt Specified Wastestream [Environmental science] .... CESW
Conditionally Qualified (AFM) .... CQ
Conditionally Streptomycin Dependent [Pharmacology] (DAVI) .... CSD
Conditional-Sum Addition (SAUS) .... CSA
Condition-Based Maintenance [Army] .... CBM
Conditioned (SAUS) .... Cond
Conditioned Abstinence (AAMN) .... CA
Conditioned Analog (ACAE) .... CA
Conditioned Avoidance Response [Psychometrics] .... CAR
Conditioned Bald Eagle Total Value .... CBETV
Conditioned Diphase (SAUS) .... CDP
Conditioned Diphase Modulation (SAUS) .... CDM
Conditioned Emotional Response [Psychology] .... CER

Conditioned Escape Response [*Medicine*] (MELL) .... CES
Conditioned Medium [*For growing microorganisms*] .... CM
Conditioned Medium Reconstituting Factor [*Immunochemistry*] .... CMRF
Conditioned Nausea and Vomiting [*Medicine*] .... CNV
Conditioned Orientation Reflex .... COR
Conditioned Orientation Reflex Audiometry [*Medicine*] (MAE) .... CORA
Conditioned Orienting Response [*Neurology*] (DAVI) .... COR
Conditioned Pitch Level (STED) .... CPL
Conditioned Place Preference [*Psychophysiology*] .... CPP
Conditioned Reflex (WGA) .... COND REF
Conditioned Reflex (SAUS) .... Cond Ref
Conditioned Reflex [*Machine*] (IEEE) .... CONFLEX
Conditioned Reflex [*or Response*] [*Psychometrics*] .... CR
Conditioned Reflex (DIPS) .... RC
Conditioned Reflex Analog (IEEE) .... CORA
Conditioned Response (WGA) .... COND RESP
Conditioned Response (SAUS) .... Cond Resp
Conditioned Response (SAUS) .... CR
Conditioned Stimulus [*Psychometrics*] .... CS
Conditioned Stimulus (DIPS) .... SC
Conditioned Taste Aversion (DB) .... CTA
Conditioned Wrinkle Recovery Angle [*Textile technology*] .... CWRA
Conditioner (SAUS) .... COND
Conditioner (NASA) .... CONDR
Conditioner .... CONDTR
Conditioning [*Neurophysiology*] C
Conditioning .... COND
Conditioning (SAUS) .... Cond
Conditioning [*Automotive engineering*] .... CONDTG
Conditioning Container (AAG) CC
Conditioning Thio Emulsion [*Roux Laboratories, Inc.*] .... CTE
Conditions [*Amateur radio shorthand*] (WDAA) .... CONDX
Conditions and Performance [*Report to Congress*] [*FHWA*] (TAG) .... C&P
Conditions, Covenants, and Restrictions [*On condominiums*] .... CC & R
Conditions of Assembly and Release Transfer .... CART
Conditions of Execution (MCD) .... COFE
Conditions of Participation [*Department of Health and Human Services*] (GFGA) .... COP
Conditions of Roads and Weather (SAUO) .... CROW
Conditions of Service (SAUS) .... C of S
Conditions of Service [*Engineering*] .... COS
Condobolin [*Australia*] [*Airport symbol*] (OAG) .... CBX
Condom Catheter Collecting System [*Medicine*] (DMAA) .... CCCS
Condominio .... COND
Condominium .... CONDO
Condominium (VRA) .... condo
Condominium [*Real estate*] (DLA) .... CONDOMIN
Condominium Research and Education Society .... CRES
Condominium Travel Associates (TRID) .... CTA
Condominium/Cooperative [*Real estate*] .... CONDOP
Condom-Valence-Sur-Baise [*France*] [*ICAO location identifier*] (ICLI) .... LFID
Condon, Kinzua & Southern Railroad Co. [*AAR code*] .... CKSO
Condon Public Library, Condon, OR [*Library symbol*] [*Library of Congress*] (LCLS) .... OrCon
Condor Aero Services, Inc. [*ICAO designator*] (FAAC) .... CNR
Condor Data Link .... CDL
Condor Data Link System .... CDLS
Condor Flugdienst GmbH [*Germany*] [*ICAO designator*] (FAAC) .... CFG
Condor Minerals and Energy Ltd. [*Australia*] .... CME
Condor Missile System .... CMS
Condor Services, Inc. [*NASDAQ symbol*] (NQ) .... COND
Condor Services, Inc. [*Associated Press*] (SAG) .... Condor
Condor Tech Solutions [*NASDAQ symbol*] (SG) .... CNDR
Condorcocha [*Ecuador*] [*ICAO location identifier*] (ICLI) .... SECC
Condoto [*Colombia*] [*Airport symbol*] (OAG) .... COG
Condoto/Mandinga [*Colombia*] [*ICAO location identifier*] (ICLI) .... SKCD
Conduct (AABC) .... CDT
Conduct (MSA) .... CNDCT
Conduct [*or Conductivity*] (ROG) .... COND
Conduct (SAUS) .... Cond
Conduct and Utilization of Research in Nursing .... CURN
Conduct Disorder (DIPS) .... CD
Conduct of Fire Trainer [*Army*] .... COFT
Conduct of Fire Trainer - Improved [*Army*] (MCD) .... COFTI
Conduct of Operations (SARE) .... COO
Conduct Sheet (SAUS) .... CS
Conductance .... cd
Conductance [*Symbol*] [*IUPAC*] .... G
Conductance and Metric (SAUS) .... Conductimetric
Conductance Increase Mechanism .... CIM
Conductance Measurement (SAUS) .... CM
Conductance of Upstream Segment [*Physics*] (DAVI) .... Gus
Conducted (SAUS) .... Cond
Conducted Electromagnetic Emissions (ACAE) .... CEE
Conducted Electromagnetic Interference .... CEI
Conducted Emission (IEEE) .... CE
Conducted Susceptibility (IEEE) .... CS
Conducting (SAUS) .... Cond
Conducting Channel (SAUS) CC
Conducting Composition (SAUS) CC
Conducting Furnace-black (SAUS) .... CF
Conduction Analysis Program Using Eigenvalues [*NASA*] .... CAPE
Conduction Analysis via Eigenvalues [*NASA*] (MCD) .... CAVE
Conduction Band [*Electronics*] .... CB
Conduction Band Minimum [*Electronics*] .... CBM
Conduction Electron Polarization .... CEP
Conduction Electron Spin Resonance .... CESR
Conduction Fingerprint Eletro-optic Search System (SAUS) .... CONFESS
Conduction Nerve Velocity [*Neurology*] (CPH) .... CNV
Conduction System Disease [*Medicine*] (MELL) .... CSD
Conduction Time (DIPS) .... CT
Conduction Velocity [*Neurology*] CV
Conduction Velocity of Slower Fibers (PDAA) .... CVSF
Conductive Anodic Filaments (SAUS) .... CAF
Conductive Channel (IAA) CC
Conductive Channel Black (SAUS) .... CC Black
Conductive Coating CC
Conductive Deafness (MELL) .... CD
Conductive Education Association (AIE) .... CEA
Conductive Furnace (SAUS) .... CF
Conductive Hearing Impairment Language Development Program (EDAC) .... CHILD
Conductive Hearing Loss (MELL) .... CHL
Conductive Plastic .... CP
Conductive Plastic Potentiometer .... CPP
Conductivity C
Conductivity (SAUS) .... Cndct
Conductivity (SAUS) .... Cond
Conductivity (MAE) .... cond
Conductivity Cell Volume [*Hematology*] CCV
Conductivity Detector .... CD
Conductivity Element [*Nuclear energy*] (NRCH) .... CE
Conductivity Indicator Transmitter [*Nuclear energy*] (NRCH) .... CIT
Conductivity Modulated Bipolar [*Computer science*] .... CMB
Conductivity Modulated Device (SAUS) .... CMD
Conductivity Recorder (SAUS) .... CR
Conductivity Recording Switch [*Nuclear energy*] (NRCH) .... CRS
Conductivity (Salinity)-Temperature-Depth [*Oceanography*] .... C/STD
Conductivity, Temperature, and Depth [*Oceanography*] .... CTD
Conductivity, Temperature, Depth Recorder (SAUS) .... CTD Recorder
Conductivity Temperature Depth Transmissometer [*Oceanography*] .... CTDT
Conductivity Transmitter (IAA) .... CT
Conductivity-Connected Charge-Coupled Device [*Electronics*] (EECA) .... C_4D
Conductivity-Connected Charge-Coupled Device [*Electronics*] (EECA) .... CCCCD
Conductivity-Controlled Transistor (SAUS) .... CCT
Conductivity-Modulated Field Effect Transistor (PDAA) .... COMFET
Conductivity-Recording Controller (IAA) .... CDRC
Conductivity-Temperature-Depth Probe [*Marine science*] (OSRA) .... CTD
Conductivity-Temperature-Depth Profiler [*Marine science*] (OSRA) .... CTD
Conductivity-Temperature-Depth-Oxygen Profiler (SAUS) .... CTDP
Conductometric .... Cond
Conductor C
Conductor (ADA) .... CDR
Conductor (SAUS) .... Cdr
Conductor [*MARC relator code*] [*Library of Congress*] (LCCP) .... cnd
Conductor (NTIO) .... Cond
Conductor (WDAA) .... cond
Conductor (KSC) .... COND
Conductor (AAG) .... CONDR
Conductor Generalis (DLA) .... COND GEN
Conductor Head (KSC) .... CH
Conductor, Insulator, Semiconductor (IAA) .... CIS
Conductor Oxide Diffusion (SAUS) .... COD
Conductor-Metal-Semiconductor-Resistor (SAUS) .... CMSR
Conductus, Inc. [*NASDAQ symbol*] (SAG) .... CDTS
Conductus, Inc. [*Associated Press*] (SAG) .... Conductu
Conduit (WDAA) C
Conduit .... CDT
Conduit (KSC) .... CND
Conduit [*Automotive engineering*] .... CONDT
Conduit [*Electronics*] (IAA) .... CT
Conduit Box (SAUS) .... CND BOX
Conduit Nuit, second generation, Helicopters (SAUS) CN2H
Condylar Blade Plate [*Medicine*] (MELL) .... CBP
Condylar Cartilage (SAUS) CL
Condylar Fracture (MELL) .... CF
Condylar Process of Mandible [*Medicine*] (MELL) .... CPM
Condylocephalic [*Medicine*] (DAVI) cc
Condylocephalic Nail (MELL) .... CCN
Condylomata Acuminata [*Medicine*] .... CA
Condy's Edition of Marshall on Insurance [*A publication*] (DLA) .... Cond Marsh
Cone .... CE
Cone .... CO
Cone Angle [*NASA*] (NASA) .... CA
Cone Length [*Botany*] .... COLGTH
Cone Mills [*NYSE symbol*] (TTSB) .... COE
Cone Mills Corp. [*NYSE symbol*] (SPSG) .... COE
Cone Mills Corp. [*Associated Press*] (SAG) .... ConeMl
Cone Mills Corp., Greensboro, NC [*Library symbol*] [*Library of Congress*] (LCLS) .... NcGCM
Cone of Depression [*Environmental science*] (COE) .... COD
Cone of Influence (ADWA) .... COI
Cone Peak [*Hawaii*] [*Seismograph station code, US Geological Survey*] (SEIS) .... CPK
Cone Penetrometer Tests [*Computer science*] .... CPT
Cone Point (MSA) .... CP
Cone Resistance Value [*Civil engineering*] (IAA) .... CRV
Conectiv, Inc. [*NYSE symbol*] (SG) CIV
Conejos County Public Library, La Jara, CO [*Library symbol*] [*Library of Congress*] (LCLS) .... CoLja

Conemaugh and Black Lick Railroad Co. (SAUO) .... CBL
Conemaugh & Black Lick Railroad Co. [*AAR code*] .... CBL
Cone-Rod Dystrophy (STED) .... CRD
Conesco Industries, Ltd. [*NASDAQ symbol*] (NQ) .... CNSC
Cone-Stabilised (SAUS) .... CS
Conestoga Bancorp [*NASDAQ symbol*] (TTSB) .... CONE
Conestoga Bancorp, Inc. [*NASDAQ symbol*] (SAG) .... CONE
Conestoga Bancorp, Inc. [*Associated Press*] (SAG) .... Conestga
Conestoga College of Applied Arts & Technology, Learning Resource Centre, Kitchener, ON, Canada [*Library symbol*] [*Library of Congress*] (LCLS) .... CaOKITC
Conestoga Enterprises [*NASDAQ symbol*] (TTSB) .... CENI
Conestoga Enterprises, Inc. [*NASDAQ symbol*] (SAG) .... CENI
Conestoga Enterprises, Inc. [*Associated Press*] (SAG) .... ConestEn
Conestoga Society (EA) .... CS
Conexant Systems [*NASDAQ symbol*] (SG) .... CNXT
Confabulate [*An informal meeting*] [*Slang*] (WDMC) .... confab
Confabulation (ADWA) .... confab
Confectio [*Confection*] [*Pharmacy*] .... CONF
Confectionary (SAUS) .... CONF
Confectionary .... CONFCTY
Confectioner (ROG) .... CONFEC
Confectioner, Tobacconist, and Newsagent [*British*] (DI) .... CTN
Confectioners Benevolent Fund [*British*] (BI) .... CBF
Confectionery .... CONF
Confectionery and Allied Trades Sports Association [*British*] (BI) .... CATSA
Confectionery and Mixed Business Association of Australia .... CMBA
Confectionery and Mixed Business Association of Australia and New Zealand .... CMBANZ
Confectionery Manufacturers Association of Canada [*Association Canadienne des Fabricants de Confiseries*] (AC) .... CMAC
Confectionery, Tobacco, and Newsagent [*British*] .... CTN
Confectionery Workers' Union of Australia .... CWUA
Confederaciān Interamericana de Ganaderos (SAUO) .... CIAGA
Confederacion de Organizaciones Turisticas de l' America Latina [*Confederation of Latin American Travel Organizations*] [*Spanish*] (BARN) .... COTAL
Confederacion de Trabajadores Cubanos [*Confederation of Cuban Workers*] .... CTC
Confederacion Democratica [*Democratic Confederation*] [*Chile*] [*Political party*] .... CODE
Confederacion Espanola de Derechas Autonomas [*Spanish Confederation of Autonomous Rightist Forces*] [*Political party*] (PPE) .... CEDA
Confederacion Evangelica Mundial [*World Evangelical Fellowship*] .... CEM
Confederacion Generale Trabajadores de Puerto Rico .... PRCGT
Confederacion Interamericana de Ganaderos .... CIAGA
Confederacion Internacional de Organizaciones Sindicales Libres [*International Confederation of Free Trade Unions*] .... CIOSL
Confederacion Laborista de Puerto Rico .... PRCL
Confederacion Latinoamericana de Asociaciones Cristianas de Jovenes [*Latin American Confederation of YMCAs - LACYMCA*] (EAIO) .... CLACJ
Confederacion Latinoamericana de Bioquimica Clinica [*Latin American Confederation of Clinical Biochemistry - LACCB*] (EAIO) .... CLBC
Confederacion Latinoamericana de Cooperativas de Ahorro y Credito [*Latin American Confederation of Savings and Loan Cooperatives*] (EAIO) .... COLAC
Confederacion Latinoamericana de Prensa Turistica [*Latin American Confederation of Touristic Press*] [*Medellin, Colombia*] (EAIO) .... CLAPTUR
Confederacion Norte, Centroamericana, y del Caribe de Futbol [*North and Central American and Caribbean Football Confederation*] (EAIO) .... CONCACAF
Confederacion Panamericana de Badminton [*Panamerican Badminton Conferation - PBC*] (EAIO) .... CPB
Confederacion Panamericana de Basketball [*Pan American Basketball Confederation - PABC*] (EAIO) .... CPB
Confederacion Sudamericana de Atletismo [*South American Athletic Confederation - SAAC*] (EAIO) .... CSA
Confederacion Universitaria Centroamericana [*Confederation of Central American Universities*] (EAIO) .... CSUCA
Confederate (NTIO) .... Confed
Confederate Action Party of Australia [*Political party*] .... CAP
Confederate Air Force (EA) .... CAF
Confederate Army .... CA
Confederate Army (SAUO) .... CA
Confederate High Command (SAUS) .... CHC
Confederate High Command, International (SAUO) .... CHC
Confederate High Command, International [*Later, AT*] [*An association*] (EA) .... CHC
Confederate Historical Society [*British*] .... CHS
Confederate Memorial Association .... CMA
Confederate Memorial Library, Hillsboro, NC [*Library symbol*] [*Library of Congress*] (LCLS) .... NcHil
Confederate Memorial Literary Society (EA) .... CMLS
Confederate National Congress (EA) .... CNC
Confederate Navy (SAUO) .... CN
Confederate Stamp Alliance (EA) .... CSA
Confederate States (HGAA) .... CS
Confederate States Army .... CSA
Confederate States Army (SAUO) .... CSA
Confederate States Navy (SAUO) .... CSN
Confederate States Navy .... CSN
Confederate States of America .... CSA
Confederate States of America (SAUO) .... CSA
Confederate States Ship .... CSS
Confederate White House (SAUO) .... CWH
Confederated .... CNFDRTD
Confederated (SAUS) .... Confd
Confederated Spanish Societies [*Defunct*] (EA) .... CSS
Confederated Unions of America [*Later, NFIU*] .... CUA
Confederation (SAUO) .... Cnfed
Confederation (WGA) .... CONF
Confederation (ADA) .... CONFD
Confederation (SAUO) .... Confd
Confederation (SAUO) .... Confed
Confederation (EY) .... CONFED
Confederation (ADWA) .... confed
confederation (SAUO) .... confedn
Confederation .... CONGDRTN
Confederation Africaine de Football [*African Football Confederation - AFC*] (EAIO) .... CAF
Confederation Arabe d'Athletisme [*Arab Amateur Athletic Federation - AAAF*] (EAIO) .... CAA
Confederation Art Gallery and Museum, Charlottetown, PE, Canada [*Library symbol*] [*Library of Congress*] (LCLS) .... CaPCCA
Confederation Art Gallery and Museum, Charlottetown, Prince Edward Island [*Library symbol*] [*National Library of Canada*] (NLC) .... PCCA
Confederation Centre Library, Charlottetown, PE, Canada [*Library symbol*] [*Library of Congress*] (LCLS) .... CaPCL
Confederation Centre Library, Charlottetown, Prince Edward Island [*Library symbol*] [*National Library of Canada*] (NLC) .... PCL
Confederation College of Applied Arts and Technology [*UTLAS symbol*] .... TBC
Confederation College, Thunder Bay, ON, Canada [*Library symbol*] [*Library of Congress*] (LCLS) .... CaOTBCC
Confederation College, Thunder Bay, Ontario [*Library symbol*] [*National Library of Canada*] (NLC) .... OTBCC
Confederation des Associations des Etudiants de l'Universite Laval (AC) .... CADEUL
Confederation des Associations et Societies Medicales d'Afrique [*Confederation of African Medical Associations and Societies - CAMAS*] [*Nigeria*] (EAIO) .... CASMA
Confederation des Associations Latino-Americaines (AC) .... CASA
Confederation des Associations Linguistiques et Culturelles du Quebec (AC) .... CALCQ
Confederation des Brasseurs du Marche Commun [*Belgium*] (EAIO) .... CBMC
Confederation des Caisses Populaires et d'Economie Desjardins du Quebec (AC) .... CCPEDQ
Confederation des Caisses Populaires et d'Economie Desjardins du Quebec, Levis, PQ, Canada [*Library symbol*] [*Library of Congress*] (LCLS) .... CaQLeCCP
Confederation des Compagnonnages Europeens [*European Companions - EC*] [*France*] (EAIO) .... CCE
Confederation des Educateurs Americains [*Confederation of American Educators*] .... CEA
Confederation des Educateurs Physiques du Qubec (AC) .... CEEP
Confederation des Industries Agro-Alimentaires de la CEE [*Confederation of the Food and Drink Industries of the ECC*] (EAIO) .... CIAA
Confederation des Industries Agro-Alimentaires de l'Union des Industries de la Communaute Europeenne [*Commission of the Agricultural and Food Industries of the Union of Industries of the European Community*] (EAIO) .... CIAA de l'UNICE
Confederation des Organismes Familiaux du Quebec Inc. (AC) .... COFAQ
Confederation des Organismes Provinciaux de Personnes Handicapees du Quebec (AC) .... COPHAN
Confederation des Sourds et des Malentendants du Canada (AC) .... CSMC
Confederation des Syndicats Canadiens [*Confederation of Canadian Unions - CCU*] .... CSC
Confederation des Syndicats Nationaux [*Confederation of National Trade Unions - CNTU*] [*Canada*] .... CSN
Confederation des Travailleurs Catholiques du Canada [*Catholic Federation of Labour, 1922-1960*] .... CTCC
Confederation Europe (SAUO) .... CO-EUR
Confederation Europeene dex Taxis [*Belgium*] (EAIO) .... CET
Confederation Europeenne de Baseball Amateur [*European Amateur Baseball Confederation - EABC*] (EA) .... CEBA
Confederation Europeenne de Billard .... CEB
Confederation Europeenne de l'Agriculture [*European Confederation of Agriculture*] (EAIO) .... CEA
Confederation Europeenne de l'Industrie de la Chaussure [*European Confederation of the Footwear Industry*] [*EC*] (ECED) .... CEC
Confederation Europeenne de l'Industrie de Pates, Papiers, et Cartons [*European Confederation of Pulp, Paper, and Board Industries*] (EAIO) .... CEPAC
Confederation Europeenne de Scoutisme [*European Confederation of Scouts - ECS*] (EAIO) .... CES
Confederation Europeenne des Cadres [*European Confederation of Managers*] [*EC*] (ECED) .... CEC
Confederation Europeenne des Categories Auxiliaires des Activites Viti-Vinicole [*European Confederation of Auxiliary Occupations in the Wine Trade*] [*Common Market*] .... CECAVI
Confederation Europeenne des Detaillants en Tabac [*European Federation of Tobacco Retail Organizations*] (EAIO) .... CEDT
Confederation Europeenne des Independants [*European Confederation of the Self Employed*] [*EC*] **Germany**] (ECED) .... CEDI
Confederation Europeenne des Industries du Bois [*European Confederation of Woodworking Industries*] .... CEIB
Confederation Europeenne des Industries du Bois [*European Confederation of Woodworking Industries*] (EAIO) .... CEI-BOIS
Confederation Europeenne des Relations Publiques [*European Confederation of Public Relations*] (EAIO) .... CERP
Confederation Europeenne d'Etudes Phytosanitaires [*European Confederation for Plant Protection Research*] .... CEP
Confederation Europeenne d'Organismes de Controle (EAIO) .... CEOC

Confederation Europeenne du Commerce de Detail [*European Federation for Retail Trade*] (EAIO) .... CECD

Confederation Europeenne du Jouet [*France*] (EAIO) .... CEJ

Confederation Europeenne Therapeutique Physique [*European Confederation for Physical Therapy*] (EAIO) .... CETP

Confederation Fiscale Europeenne [*European Fiscal Confederation*] (EAIO) .... CFE

Confederation for an Independent Poland (PD) .... KPN

Confederation for the Advancement of State Education .... CASE

Confederation Francaise de la Cooperation Agricole .... CFCA

Confederation Francaise Democratique du Travail [*French Democratic Confederation of Labor*] (BARN) .... CFDL

Confederation Generale de la Publicite (AC) .... COGEP

Confederation Generale Kamerounaise du Travail [*Cameroonian General Confederation of Workers*] .... CGKT

Confederation High School, Nepean, Ontario [*Library symbol*] [*National Library of Canada*] (NLC) .... ONC

Confederation Interalliee des Officiers de Reserve [*Interallied Confederation of Reserve Officers*] .... CIOR

Confederation Interamericaine d'Education Catholique [*Inter-American Confederation of Catholic Education*] .... CIEC

Confederation Internationale Catholique des Institutions Hospitalieres [*International Catholic Confederation of Hospitals*] .... CICIH

Confederation Internationale de Genealogie et d'Heraldique [*International Confederation of Genealogy and Heraldry - ICGH*] [*Paris, France*] (EAIO) .... CIGH

Confederation Internationale de la Boucherie et de la Charcuterie [*International Federation of Meat Traders' Associations*] .... CIBC

Confederation Internationale de la Coiffure [*International Conference of the Hairdressing Trade*] CIC

Confederation Internationale de la Representation Commerciale de la Communaute Europeenne [*International Confederation of Commercial Representation in the European Community*] .... CIRCCE

Confederation Internationale de Musique Electroacoustique [*International Confederation for Electroacoustic Music - ICEM*] (EAIO) .... CIME

Confederation Internationale des Accordeonistes [*International Confederation of Accordionists*] .... CIA

Confederation Internationale des Anciens Prisonniers de Guerre [*International Confederation of Former Prisoners of War*] [*Paris, France*] (EAIO) .... CIAPG

Confederation Internationale des Associations de Diplomes en Sciences Economiques et Commerciales [*International Confederation of Associations of Graduates in Economic and Commercial Sciences*] .... CIADEC

Confederation Internationale des Associations d'Experts et de Conseils [*International Confederation of Associations of Experts and Consultants*] .... CIDADEC

Confederation Internationale des Betteraviers Europeens [*International Confederation of European Sugar-Beet Growers*] (EAIO) .... CIBE

Confederation Internationale des Cadres [*International Confederation of Executive Staffs*] [*Paris, France*] (EAIO) CIC

Confederation Internationale des Cinemas d'Art et d'Essai [*International Experimental and Art Film Theatres Confederation*] [*France*] .... CICAE

Confederation Internationale des Corps de Fonctionnaires [*International Confederation of Public Service Officers*] .... CICF

Confederation Internationale des Fabricants de Tapis et de Tissus d'Ameublement [*International Confederation of Manufacturers of Carpets and Furnishing Fabrics*] (EAIO) .... CITTA

Confederation Internationale des Fonctionnaires [*International Confederation of Public Service Officers*] .... CIF

Confederation Internationale des Industries Techniques du Cinema .... CIITC

Confederation Internationale des Ingenieurs Agronomes [*International Confederation of Technical Agricultural Engineers*] .... CITA

Confederation Internationale des Ingenieurs et Techniciens de l'Agriculture [*International Confederation of Agricultural Engineers and Technicians*] [*Switzerland*] .... CITA

Confederation Internationale des Instituts Catholiques d'Education des Adultes Ruraux [*International Confederation of Catholic Rural People's Schools*] .... CIEPRC

Confederation Internationale des Negociants en Oeuvres d'Art [*International Confederation of Art Dealers*] (EAIO) .... CINOA

Confederation Internationale des Sages Femmes .... CISF

Confederation Internationale des Societes d'Auteurs et Compositeurs [*International Confederation of Societies of Authors and Composers*] .... CISAC

Confederation Internationale des Societes Musicales [*International Confederation of Societies of Music - ICSM*] (EA) .... CISM

Confederation Internationale des Societes Populaires de Musique .... CISPM

Confederation Internationale des Syndicats Chretiens [*International Federation of Christian Trade Unions*] .... CISC

Confederation Internationale des Syndicats Libres [*International Confederation of Free Trade Unions*] .... CISL

Confederation Internationale des Travailleurs Intellectuels [*International Confederation of Professional and Intellectual Workers*] .... CITI

Confederation Internationale du Commerce des Pailles, Fourrages, Tourbes et Derives [*International Straw, Fodder and Peat Trade Confederation*] [*EC*] (ECED) .... CIPF

Confederation Internationale du Commerce et des Industries des Legumes Secs [*International Pulse Trade and Industry Confederation*] [*EC*] (ECED) .... CICILS

Confederation Internationale du Credit Agricole [*International Confederation of Agricultural Credit*] [*Zurich, Switzerland*] (EAIO) .... CICA

Confederation Internationale du Credit Populaire [*International Federation of Popular Credit - ICPC*] [*Paris, France*] (EAIO) .... CICP

Confederation Internationale du Lin et du Chanvre [*International Linen and Hemp Confederation*] (EAIO) CILC

Confederation Internationale pour la Chirurgie Plastique et Reconstructive [*International Confederation for Plastic and Reconstructive Surgery*] (EAIO) .... CICPR

Confederation Internationale pour le Desarmement et la Paix [*International Confederation for Disarmament and Peace - ICDP*] [*London, England*] (EA) .... CIDP

Confederation Life Association, Toronto, ON, Canada [*Library symbol*] [*Library of Congress*] (LCLS) .... CaOTCLA

Confederation Life Association, Toronto, Ontario [*Library symbol*] [*National Library of Canada*] (NLC) .... OTCLA

Confederation Mondiale de Centres Communautaires Juifs [*World Confederation of Jewish Community Centers*] (EAIO) .... CMCCJ

Confederation Mondiale des Activites Subaquatiques [*World Underwater Federation - WUF*] [*ICSU*] [*Paris, France*] (EAIO) .... CMAS

Confederation Mondiale des Organisations de la Profession Enseignante [*World Confederation of Organizations of the Teaching Profession - WCOTP*] (EAIO) .... CMOPE

Confederation Mondiale du Travail [*World Confederation of Labour - WCL*] [*Brussels, Belgium*] (EAIO) .... CMT

Confederation Nationale de la Construction [*Civil Engineering, Road and Building Contractors, and Auxiliary Trades Confederation*] [*Brussels, Belgium*] (EY) .... CNC

Confederation Nationale des Cadres du Quebec (AC) .... CNCQ

Confederation Nordique des Cadres, Techniciens, et Autres Responsables [*Nordic Confederation of Supervisors, Technicians, and Other Managers*] (EAIO) .... NAU

Confederation of Aerial Industries [*British*] (DBA) .... CAI

Confederation of African Medical Associations and Societies [*Nigeria*] (EAIO) .... CAMAS

Confederation of All Type Canaries [*Defunct*] (EA) .... CATC

Confederation of American Educators (AE) .... CAE

Confederation of American Indians (EA) .... CAI

Confederation of American Public Employees (SAUO) .... CAPE

Confederation of Arab Trade Unions .... CATU

Confederation of Ariel Industries (NITA) .... CAI

Confederation of Art and Design Associations (AIE) .... CADA

Confederation of Asian-Pacific Chambers of Commerce and Industry [*Taipei, Taiwan*] (EAIO) .... CACCI

Confederation of Associations of Specialist Engineering Contractors (DBA) .... CASEC

Confederation of Australasian Performing Arts Presenters [*Australia*] .... CAPAP

Confederation of Australian Motor Sports (SAUO) .... CAMS

Confederation of Bank Staff Associations (SAUO) .... CBSA

Confederation of Brewers in the Common Market [*Belgium*] (EAIO) .... CBCM

Confederation of British Associations (DBA) .... CBA

Confederation of British Industry .... CBI

Confederation of British Industry (SAUO) .... CBI

Confederation of British Road Passenger Transport (ILCA) .... CBRPT

Confederation of British Wool Textiles (SAUO) .... CBWT

Confederation of Building Contractors [*British*] (DBA) .... CBC

Confederation of Canadian Unions .... CCU

Confederation of Canadian Unions/Confederation des Syndicats Canadiens (ASC) .... CCU/CSC

Confederation of Citizens Labor Unions (SAUO) .... CCLU

Confederation of Construction Professions [*British*] (DBA) .... CCP

Confederation of Construction Specialists [*British*] (DBA) .... CCS

Confederation of Dental Employers (SAUO) .... CODE

Confederation of Design and Technology Associations [*British*] .... CDTA

Confederation of Employee Organisations (SAUO) .... CEO

Confederation of Entertainment Unions [*British*] .... CEU

Confederation of Entertainment Unions [*British*] (DCTA) .... COEU

Confederation of Ethiopian Labour Unions (SAUO) .... CELU

Confederation of European Bath Manufacturers (EAIO) .... COFEB

Confederation of European Computer Users Associations (EAIO) .... CECUA

Confederation of European Soft Drinks Associations (SAUO) .... CESDA

Confederation of European Specialists in Pediatrics (EAIO) .... CESP

Confederation of European Union Shipmasters Associations (SAUO) .... CESMA

Confederation of Free Trade Unions [*India*] .... CFTU

Confederation of Health Service Employees (SAUO) .... CHSE

Confederation of Health Service Employees (SAUO) .... COHSE

Confederation of Health Service Employees [*Pronounced "cozy"*] [*A union*] [*British*] (DCTA) .... COHSE

Confederation of Health Service Employees [*British*] (ODBW) .... Cohse

Confederation of Importers and Marketing Organizations in Europe of Fresh Friut and Vegetables (SAUO) .... CIMO

Confederation of Importers and Marketing Organizations in Europe of Fresh Fruit and Vegetables [*Brussels, Belgium*] (EA) .... CIMO

Confederation of Importers and Marketing Organizations in Europe of Fresh Fruit and Vegetables (SAUO) .... CIPO

Confederation of Independent Orders, Ku Klux Klan (EA) .... CIOKKK

Confederation of Independent Trade Unions (EAIO) .... CITU

Confederation of Indian Industries (SAUO) CII

Confederation of Indian Organizations [*British*] (DBA) .... CIO

Confederation of Information Communication Industries [*British*] CICI

Confederation of Institute Directors (AIE) .... CID

Confederation of Insurance Trade Unions [*British*] (DCTA) .... COITU

Confederation of International Contractors' Associations [*Paris, France*] (EAIO) .... CICA

Confederation of International Contractors Associations (SAUO) .... CICA

Confederation of International Scientific and Technological Organizations for Development [*ICSU*] [*Paris, France*] [*Defunct*] (EAIO) .... CISTOD

Confederation of International Trading Houses Associations [*The Hague, Netherlands*] (EAIO) .... CITHA

Confederation of Iranian Students [*Germany*] (PD) .... CISNU

Confederation of Irish Industry (EAIO) CII

Confederation of Khmer Nationalists [*Cambodia*] (PD) ... CNK
Confederation of Latin American Teachers (SAUO) ... CLAT
Confederation of Medical Associations of Asia and Oceania (SAUO) ... CMAAO
Confederation of National Educational Associations ... CONEA
Confederation of National Trade Unions [*Canada*] ... CNTU
Confederation of Non-Governmental Organizations for Overseas Development ... CONGOOD
Confederation of North America (SAUO) ... CNA
Confederation of Oregon Foreign Language Teachers (SAUO) ... COFLT
Confederation of Photographic Industries [*British*] (DBA) ... CPI
Confederation of Regions [*Canada*] [*Political party*] ... COR
Confederation of Registered Gas Installers [*British*] (DI) ... CORGI
Confederation of Resident & Ratepayer Associations (AC) ... CORRA
Confederation of Roofing Contractors [*British*] (DBA) ... CRC
Confederation of Shipbuilding and Engineering Unions [*British*] ... CSEU
Confederation of Shipbuilding and Engineering Unions (SAUO) ... CSEU
Confederation of Socialist Parties of the European Community [*Belgium*] [*Political party*] (EAIO) ... CSPEC
Confederation of Tanners' Associations in the European Community [*Brussels, Belgium*] (EAIO) ... COTANCE
Confederation of the Canons Regular of Saint Augustine [*Italy*] (EAIO) ... CCRSA
Confederation of the National Hotel and Restaurant Associations in the EC (ECED) ... HOTREC
Confederation of Trade Unions (SAUO) ... COTU
Confederation of United Kingdom Indian Organizations (SAUO) ... CUKIO
Confederation of University Faculty/Associations of British Columbia (AC) ... CUFA/BC
Confederation of Western Australian Industry (SAUS) ... CWAI
Confederation of Western Australian Industry, Inc. [*Australia*] ... CWAI
Confederation Quebecoise des Centres d'Hebergement et de Readaptation (AC) ... CQCHR
Confederation Quebecoise des Cooperatives d'Habitation (AC) ... CQCH
Confederation Syndicale Mondiale des Enseignants [*World Confederation of Teachers - WCT*] [*Brussels, Belgium*] (EAIO) ... CSME
Confer (MEC) ... cf
Confer [*Compare, Consult*] [*Latin*] ... CF
Confer ... CNFR
Confer [*Compare*] [*Latin*] ... CONF
Conference ... CNFRNC
Conference (SAUO) ... CO
Conference (AFM) ... CONF
Conference (EBF) ... Conf
Conference (EBF) ... conf
Conference (ROG) ... CONFCE
conference (SAUO) ... confce
conference (SAUO) ... confer
Conference Administrative des Postes et Telecommunications des Etats de l'Afrique de l'Ouest [*Conference of Posts and Telecommunications Administrations of the States of West Africa*] ... CAPTEAO
Conference Administrative Regionale de Radiodiffusion a Ondes Hectometriques [*Regional Administrative FM Broadcasting Conference*] [*Canada*] ... CARR
Conference Aeronautique Internationale [*International Aeronautical Conference*] ... CAI
Conference and Exhibition on Computers in Engineering and Building Design (SAUO) ... CAD
Conference & Incentive Travel Bureau (SAUO) ... CITB
Conference and Laser Engineering and Applications (SAUS) ... CLEA
Conference Board (SAUO) ... CB
[*The*] **Conference Board** [*Formerly, National Industrial Conference Board*] ... CB
[*The*] **Conference Board** (EA) ... TCB
[*The*] **Conference Board Abstract Database** [*The Conference Board, Inc.*] [*Information service or system*] (CRD) ... CBABS
[*The*] **Conference Board Data Base** [*The Conference Board, Inc.*] [*Information service or system*] (CRD) ... CBDB
Conference Board in Canada, Ottawa, ON, Canada [*Library symbol*] [*Library of Congress*] (LCLS) ... CaOOCBC
Conference Board of Associated Research Councils (EA) ... CBARC
Conference Board of Canada ... CBC
Conference Board of Canada, Ottawa, Ontario [*Library symbol*] [*National Library of Canada*] (NLC) ... OOCBC
Conference Board of Major Printers [*Defunct*] (EA) ... CBMP
Conference Board of the Mathematical Sciences (EA) ... CBMS
Conference Bridge Unit (SAUO) ... CBU
Conference Canadienne des Administrateurs en Transport Motorise [*Canadian Conference of Transport Administrators*] ... CCATM
Conference Canadienne des Arts [*Canadian Conference of the Arts - CCA*] ... CCA
Conference Chretienne pour la Paix [*Christian Peace Conference - CPC*] [*Prague, Czechoslovakia*] (EAIO) ... CCP
Conference Committee for Refugee Rabbis (EA) ... CCRR
Conference Control Channel (SAUO) ... CCC
Conference Control Protocol (CCCA) ... CCP
Conference Control Unit (CCCA) ... CCU
Conference Coordinator (SAUS) ... CONCORD
Conference de la Haye de Droit International Prive [*Hague Conference on Private International Law*] (EA) ... CODIP
Conference de Solidarite des Pays Afro-Asiatiques ... CSPAA
Conference des Administrations des Postes et Telecommunications de l'Afrique Centrale [*Conference of Posts and Telecommunications Administrations of Central Africa*] (PDAA) ... CAPTAC
Conference des Communautes Ethniques de Langue Francaise [*Standing Committee of French-Speaking Ethnical Communities - SCFSEC*] (EA) ... CCELF
Conference des Cooperatives Forestieres du Quebec (AC) ... CCFQ
Conference des Directeurs des Bibliotheques Publiques de l'Ile de Montreal [*Conference of Public Library Directors of the Island of Montreal*] (AC) ... CDPIM
Conference des Eglises de Toute l'Afrique [*All Africa Conference of Churches - AACC*] (EAIO) ... CETA
Conference des Eveques de la Region Nord de l'Afrique [*North African Episcopal Conference*] (EAIO) ... CERNA
Conference des Juges du Quebec (AC) ... CJQ
Conference des Ministres de l'Education des Pays d'Expression Francaise ... CONFEMEN
Conference des Ministres Europeens du Travail [*Conference of European Ministers of Labour*] (EAIO) ... MTV
Conference des Nations Unies pour le Commerce et le Developpement [*United Nations Conference on Trade and Development - UNCTAD*] [*French*] ... CNUCD
Conference des Organismes Regionaux de Loisirs du Quebec (AC) ... CORLQ
Conference des Recteurs et des Principaux des Universites du Quebec [*Conference of Rectors & Principals of Quebec Universities*] (AC) ... CREPUQ
Conference des Recteurs et des Principaux des Universites du Quebec, Montreal, PQ, Canada [*Library symbol*] [*Library of Congress*] (LCLS) ... CaQMCRP
Conference des Recteurs et des Principaux des Universites du Quebec, Montreal, Quebec [*Library symbol*] [*National Library of Canada*] (NLC) ... QMCRP
Conference des Societes d'Ingenieurs de l'Europe Occidental et des Etats-Unis d'Amerique [*Conference of Engineering Societies of Western Europe and the United States of America*] ... EUSEC
Conference Director (CCCA) ... CD
Conference Euorpeenne des Horaires et des Services Directs [*European Conference of Time-tables and Direct Services*] (PDAA) ... CEH
Conference Europeenne des Administrations des Postes et des Telecommunications [*Conference of European Postal and Telecommunications Administrations*] [*Telecommunications*] (EAIO) ... CEPT
Conference Europeenne des Experts Meteorologistes de l'Aeronautique ... CEEMA
Conference Europeenne des Experts Radiotelegraphistes de l'Aeronautique ... CEERA
Conference Europeenne des Horaires des Trains de Marchandises [*European Freight Timetable Conference*] (EAIO) ... CEM
Conference Europeenne des Horaires des Trains de Voyageurs [*European Passenger Timetable Conference*] [*Switzerland*] ... CEH
Conference Europeenne des Ministres des Transports [*European Conference of Ministers of Transport - ECMT*] [*France*] ... CEMT
Conference Europeenne des Pouvoirs Locaux ... CEPL
Conference Europeenne des Telecommunications par Satellite [*European Conference on Satellite Communications*] ... CETS
Conference Europeenne des Telecommunications par Satellites [*Benelux*] ... CETS
Conference for Air Force Family Matters (SAUO) ... AFFAM
Conference for Basic Human Rights in the ASEAN [*Associaton of South East Asian Nations*] **Countries** [*British*] ... COBRA
Conference for Catholic Lesbians (EA) ... CCL
Conference for Chinese Oral and Performing Literature (EA) ... CHINOPERL
Conference for European Statistics (SAUO) ... CES
Conference for Health Council Work [*Later, Conference on Community Health Planning*] ... CHCW
Conference for Higher Education in Art and Design [*British*] ... CHEAD
Conference for Independent Further Education [*British*] ... CIFE
Conference for International Co-operation in Information Retrieval Among Examining Patent Offices (SAUO) ... CICIREPATO
Conference for Progressive Labor Action ... CPLA
Conference for Progressive Political Action ... CPPA
Conference for Reconciliation, Restitution Fund (EA) ... CONREC
Conference for Secondary School English Department Chairpersons (EA) ... CSSEDC
Conference for the Advancement of Private Practice [*in social work*] ... CAPP
Conference for the Advancement of Private Practice in Social Work (SAUO) ... CAPP
Conference for the Study of Political Thought (EA) ... CSPT
Conference for Universal Reason and Ethics [*Founded by motion picture actor Lew Ayres*] ... CURE
Conference for World Mission [*British Council of Churches*] ... CWM
Conference for/on Chinese Oral and Performing Literature (SAUO) ... CHINOPERL
Conference Group on French Politics and Society (EA) ... CGFPS
Conference Group on German Politics (EA) ... CGGP
Conference Group on Italian Politics (EDAC) ... CGIP
Conference Group on Italian Politics and Society (EA) ... CONGRIPS
Conference Internationale Administrative des Radiocommunications Aeronautiques ... CIARA
Conference Internationale Catholique du Guidisme [*International Catholic Conference of Guiding*] (EAIO) ... CICG
Conference Internationale de la Mutualite et des Assurances Sociales ... CIMAS
Conference Internationale de Liaison entre Producteurs d'Energie Electrique [*International Conference of Producers of Electrical Energy*] ... CILPE
Conference Internationale de Service Social [*International Conference of Social Service*] ... CISS
Conference Internationale de Sociologie Religieuse [*International Conference of Sociology of Religion*] ... CISR
Conference Internationale des Africanistes de l'Ouest ... CIAO
Conference Internationale des Associations d'Ingenieurs [*International Federatiio of Engineering Associations*] (PDAA) ... CIAI
Conference Internationale des Charites Catholiques [*International Conference of Catholic Charities*] ... CICC

Conference Internationale des Controles d'Assurances des Etats Africains [*International Conference of African States on Insurance Supervision*] (EAIO) ... CICA

Conference Internationale des Grands Reseaux Electriques a Haute Tension [*International Conference on Large High Voltage Electric Systems*] (EAIO) ... CIGRE

Conference Internationale des Trains Speciaux d'Agences de Voyages [*International Conference on Special Trains for Travel Agencies*] (EAIO) ... CITA

Conference Internationale du Goudron [*International Tar Conference - ITC*] (EAIO) ... CIG

Conference Internationale du Scoutisme Catholique [*International Conference of Catholic Scouting*] ... CISC

Conference Internationale Permanente de Directeurs d'Instituts Universitaires pour la Formation de Traducteurs et d'Interpretes [*Standing International Conference of the Directors of University Institutes for the Training of Translators and Interpreters*] (EAIO) ... CIUTI

Conference Internationale pour l'Enseignement Universitaire des Relations Publiques [*International Conference on University Education for Public Relations*] ... CIEURP

Conference Internationale pour l'Unite Technique des Chemins de Fer ... UT

Conference Internationale sur l'Assistance aux Refugies en Afrique [*International Conference on Assistance for Refugees in Africa - ICARA*] [*United Nations*] [*Geneva, Switzerland*] (EAIO) ... CIARA

Conference Letter Report (SAA) ... CLR

Conference Location (NITA) ... CL

Conference Lodges [*Freemasonry*] (ROG) ... CL

Conference Ministerielle des Etats d'Afrique de l'Ouest et du Centre sur les Transports Maritimes [*Ministerial Conference of West and Central African States on Maritime Transportation - MCWCS*] [*Abidjan, Ivory Coast*] (EAIO) ... CMEAOC

Conference Mondiale de l'Energie [*World Energy Conference - WEC*] (EAIO) ... CME

Conference Mondiale des Experts Radiotelegraphistes de l'Aeronautique ... CMERA

Conference Nationale des Veterinaires Specialises en Petits Animaux [*France*] (GVA) ... CNVSPA

Conference of Actuaries in Public Practice [*Itasca, IL*] (EA) ... CAPP

Conference of Administrators of College and University Counseling Services (EA) ... CACUCS

Conference of African Women (SAUO) ... CAW

Conference of American Renting and Leasing Associations (EA) ... CARALA

Conference of American Small Business Organizations [*AFSB*] [*Absorbed by*] (EA) ... CASBO

Conference of Americans of Central and Eastern European Descent [*Defunct*] (EA) ... CACEED

Conference of Asian and Pacific Accountants (SAUO) ... CAPA

Conference of Association Society Executives (EA) ... CASE

Conference of Baltic Oceanographers [*Germany*] (EAIO) ... CBO

Conference of Biological Editors (SAUS) ... CBE

Conference of Biology Editors (SAUO) ... CBE

Conference of British Studies (SAUO) ... CBS

Conference of Business Economists (EA) ... CBE

Conference of California Historical Societies ... CCHS

Conference of Casualty Insurance Companies [*Indianapolis, IN*] (EA) ... CCIC

Conference of Catholic Schools of Nursing (EA) ... CCSN

Conference of Central and East African States ... CCEAFS

Conference of Chaplains-General [*Australia*] ... CCHAPG

Conference of Chartering and Shipowning Organizations of CMEA Member Countries (SAUO) ... CCSO

Conference of Chief Executive Officers of Bulk Handling Authorities [*Australia*] ... CCEOBHA

Conference of Chief Justices (EA) ... CCJ

Conference of Church Workers Among the Deaf [*Later, ECD*] (EA) ... CCWAD

Conference of Churches of Western Australia [*Australia*] ... CCWA

Conference of Commissioners on Uniformity of Legislation in Canada (DLA) ... Conf Comm Uniformity Legis

Conference of Consulting Actuaries (NTPA) ... CCA

Conference of Consumer Organizations (EA) ... COCO

Conference of Defence Associations (SAUO) ... CDA

Conference of Defence Associations Institute [*Institut du Congres des Associations de la Defense*] (AC) ... CDA

Conference of Diocesan Executives [*Episcopalian*] ... CODE

Conference of Directors (SAUO) ... CD

Conference of Directors of Danube Lines [*Budapest, Hungary*] (EAIO) ... CDDL

Conference of Directors of National Libraries in Asia and Oceania [*Australia*] ... CDNLAO

Conference of Directors of State University Librarians of Illinois [*Library network*] ... CODSULI

Conference of Drama Schools [*British*] ... CDS

Conference of Eastern College Librarians ... CECL

Conference of Educational Administrators of Schools and Programs for the Deaf (NTPA) ... CEASD

Conference of Educational Associations (SAUO) ... CEA

Conference of Electrical Insulation and Dielectric Phenomena (SAUO) ... CEICP

Conference of Engineering Societies of Western Europe and the USA (SAUS) ... EUSEC

Conference of Engineering Trade Association (SAUO) ... CETA

Conference of European Churches (EA) ... CEC

Conference of European Computer User Associations (SAUO) ... CEDUA

Conference of European Ministers for Travel (SAUS) ... CEMT

Conference of European Soft Drinks Associations (SAUO) ... CESDA

Conference of Executives of State Associations of Counties [*Later, National Council of County Association Executives*] (EA) ... CESAC

Conference of Federal Environmental Engineers (COE) ... CFEE

Conference of Fire Protection Associations (SAUO) ... CFPA

Conference of Funeral Service Examining Boards of the United States (SAUO) ... CFSEB

Conference of Government Mining (SAUO) ... CGM

Conference of Governors (SAUO) ... CG

Conference of Independent African States (NATG) ... CIAS

Conference of Industrial Research Associations (DGA) ... CIRA

Conference of Insurance Legislators [*Later, NCOIL*] (EA) ... COIL

Conference of International Catholic Organizations [*Geneva, Switzerland*] (EAIO) ... CICO

Conference of International Catholic Organizations (SAUO) ... ICO

Conference of Internationally-Minded Schools ... CIS

Conference of Jesuit Student Personnel Administrators [*Later, JASPA*] (EA) ... CJSPA

Conference of Jesuit Student Personnel Administrators (SAUO) ... CJSPA

Conference of Jewish Communal Service (EA) ... CJCS

Conference of Jewish Organizations (BARN) ... COJO

Conference of Jewish Organizations (SAUO) ... COJO

Conference of LASER Engineering and Applications ... CLEA

Conference of Latin Americanist Geographers ... CLAG

Conference of Latin Bishops of Arab Regions [*Jersalem, Israel*] (EAIO) ... CELRA

Conference of Liberal Arts Colleges for Women ... CLACW

Conference of Local Environmental Health Administrators [*Later, NCLEHA*] (EA) ... CLEHA

Conference of Major Religious Superiors of Women's Institutes of the United States of America [*Later, LCWR*] ... CMSW

Conference of Major Superiors of Men (EA) ... CMSM

Conference of Major Superiors of Men of the United States of America (SAUO) ... CMSM

Conference of Major Superiors of Religious Brothers of Australia ... CMSRBA

Conference of Major Superiors of Women's Religious Institutes of Australia ... CMSWA

Conference of Mennonites in Canada (AC) ... CMC

Conference of Minister for Immigration and Ethnic Affairs [*Australia*] ... CMIEA

Conference of Ministers of Arab States responsible for the Application of Science and Technology to Development (SAUO) ... CASTARAB

Conference of Ministers of Asian Member States Responsible for the Application of Science and Technology to Development (SAUO) ... CASTASIA

Conference of Ministers of Education [*World War II*] ... CME

Conference of Ministers of Education and Those Responsible for Economic Planing in African Member States (SAUO) ... MINEDAF

Conference of Ministers of Education and Those Responsible for Economic Planning in Arab States (SAUO) ... MINEDARAB

Conference of Ministers of Education and those Responsible for Economic Planning in Latin America and Caribbean (SAUO) ... MINEDLAC

Conference of Ministers of Education and those Responsible for the Promotion of Science and Technology in Relation to Development in Latin American and the Caribbean (SAUO) ... MINESLA

Conference of Ministers of Education of Member States of the Europe Region (SAUO) ... MINEDEUROPE

Conference of Ministers Responsible for the Application of Science and Technology to Development in Africa (SAUO) ... CASTAFRICA

Conference of Ministers Responsible for the Application of Science and Technology to Development in Latin America and the Caribbean (SAUO) ... CASTALAC

Conference of Minority Public Administrators (EA) ... COMPA

Conference of Minority Transportation Officials (NTPA) ... COMTO

Conference of Municipal Public Health Engineers [*Later, NCLEHA*] (EA) ... CMPHE

Conference of Mutual Casualty Companies [*Later, CCIC*] (EA) ... CMCC

Conference of National Armaments Directors [*NATO*] ... CNAD

Conference of National Park Concessioners (EA) ... CNPC

Conference of National Park Cooperating Associations (NTPA) ... CNPCA

Conference of National Social Science Councils and Analogous Bodies ... CNSSC

Conference of New Emerging Forces [*Indonesia*] (CINC) ... CONEFO

Conference of New Emerging Forces (SAUO) ... Conefo

Conference of New Law Librarians ... CONELL

Conference of NGOs with Consultative Status to the UN (SAUS) ... CONGO

Conference of Non-Governemental Organizations in Consultative Status with the United Nations Economic and Social Council (SAUO) ... CONGO

Conference of Officers of Affiliated States and Territorial Associations ... COASTA

Conference of Peripheral Maritime Regions of the EEC (EAIO) ... CPMR

Conference of Pharmaceutical Ingredients ... CPhI

Conference of Philosophical Societies (EA) ... CPS

Conference of Podiatry Executives (EA) ... COPE

Conference of Presidents and Officers of State Medical Associations [*Later, FMA*] (EA) ... CPOSMA

Conference of Presidents of Major American Jewish Organizations (EA) ... COPMAJO

Conference of Presidents of Major American Jewish Organizations (EA) ... CPMAJO

Conference of Prince Hall Grand Masters (EA) ... CPHGM

Conference of Private Organizations (EA) ... CONPOR

Conference of Private Organizations [*Defunct*] (EA) ... CPO

Conference of Professional and Public Service Organisations (SAUO) ... COPPSO

Conference of Protestant Churches in the Latin Countries of Europe (SAUO) ... CEPPLE

Conference of Public Health Laboratorians (EA) ... COPHL

Conference of Public Health Laboratorians (SAUO) ... CPHL

Conference of Public Health Laboratory Directors [*Later, COPHL*] (EA) ... CPHLD

Conference of Public Health Veterinarians (EA) ... CPHV

Conference of Radiation Control Program Directors (EA) ... CRCPD

Conference of Rectors, Vice-Chancellors and Presidents of African Universities (SAUO) .... COREVIP
Conference of Repertory Theatre (SAUO) .... CORT
Conference of Representatives from European and United States Engineering Societies (SAUS) .... EUSEC
Conference of Research Workers in Animal Diseases (EA) .... CRWAD
Conference of Scottish Centrally Funded Colleges (AIE) .... CSCFC
Conference of Small Private Colleges [*Defunct*] [*Defunct*] (EA) .... CSPC
Conference of Societies for the History of Pharmacy [*Madrid, Spain*] (EAIO) .... CSHP
Conference of South African Students (SAUO) .... COSAS
Conference of South African Surveyors (SAUO) .... CONSAS
Conference of Speakers and Presiding Officers of Commonwealth Parliaments [*Canada*] (EAIO) .... CSPOCP
Conference of State and Provincial Health Authorities of North America (SAUO) .... CSPH
Conference of State and Provincial Health Authorities of North America [*Defunct*] (EA) .... CSPHA
Conference of State and Provincial Public Health Laboratory Directors (EA) .... CSPPHLD
Conference of State and Territorial Directors of Public Health Education (EA) .... CSTDPHE
Conference of State and Territorial Health Officers with Public Health Service (EA) .... CSTHOPHS
Conference of State Bank Supervisors [*Washington, DC*] (EA) .... CSBS
Conference of State Cable Agencies (EA) .... CSCA
Conference of State Cemetery Association Secretaries (EA) .... CSCAS
Conference of State Court Administrators (EA) .... COSCA
Conference of State Health and Environmental Managers (COE) .... CSHEM
Conference of State Health and Environmental Managers [*Conference of Stat e Sanitary Engineers*] [*Acronym is based on former name,*] [*Defunct*] (EA) .... CSSE
Conference of State Sanitary Engineers .... CSSE
Conference of State Societies [*Later, National Conference of State Societies*] (EA) .... CSS
Conference of State Utility Commission Engineers [*Later, NCRUCE*] (EA) .... CSUCE
Conference of the American Armies .... CAA
Conference of the Committee on Disarmament [*Formerly, ENDC*] [*NATO*] .... CCD
Conference of the Electronics Industry [*British*] (BI) .... CEI
Conference of the Information Ministers of Non-Aligned Countries (SAUO) .... COMINAC
Conference of the Labour Party [*British*] .... CLP
Conference of the Methodist Church in the Caribbean and the Americas (EAIO) .... CMCCA
Conference of the Methodist Church in the Caribbean and the Americas (EAIO) .... MCCA
Conference of the Parties [*Governments which have ratified UN climate change convention of 1992*] .... COP
Conference of UN Representatives, UNA [*United Nations Association*]**-USA** (EA) .... CUNR
Conference of Unions in Goverment Corporations (SAUO) .... CUGC
Conference of University Administrators [*British*] [*An association*] (DBA) .... CUA
Conference of Utility Commission Engineers (SAUO) .... CUCE
Conference of World Organizations Interested in the Handicapped (SAUO) .... CWOIH
Conference on Alternative State and Local Policies [*Later, CPA*] (EA) .... CASLP
Conference on Alternative State and Local Practices (SAUO) .... CASLP
Conference on Alternative State and Local Public Policies [*Later, CPA*] (EA) .... CASLPP
Conference on Application Development Systems (MHDI) .... COADS
Conference on Artificial Intelligence Application (ACAE) .... CAIA
Conference on Asian Affairs [*Later, AS*] (MCD) .... CAA
Conference on Asian History (EA) .... CAH
Conference on Baltic University Rectors (SAUO) .... CBUR
Conference on British Studies (EA) .... CBS
Conference on Charitable Foundations. Proceedings. New York University [*A publication*] (DLA) .... Conf on Char Found NYU Proc
Conference on Charitable Foundations. Proceedings. New York University [*A publication*] (DLA) .... NYU Conf on Char Found Proc
Conference on Charitable Foundations. Proceedings. New York University (journ.) (SAUS) .... NYU Conf on Char Found Proc
Conference on Christian Politics, Economics, and Citizenship (IIA) .... COPEC
Conference on Christianity and Literature (EA) CCL
Conference on College Composition and Communication (EA) CCCC
Conference on Computational Linguistics (SAUS) .... COLING
Conference on Computational Molecular Biology (HGEN) .... RECOMB
Conference on Computer Architecture for Pattern Analysis and Image Database Mana (SAUS) .... CAPAIDM
Conference on Computer Vision and Pattern Recognition (SAUS) .... CVPR
Conference on Computers in the Undergraduate Carricula (SAUS) .... CCUC
Conference on Computers in Undergraduate Science Education .... COMUSE
Conference on Conceptual and Terminological Analysis in the Social Sciences [*1981*] .... CONTA
Conference on Confidence and Security-Building Measures and Disarmament in Europe .... CDE
Conference on Consumer Finance Law (EA) .... CCFL
Conference on Co-ordination of Air Transport in Europe (SAUO) .... CATE
Conference on Critical Legal Studies (EA) .... CCLS
Conference on Current Theory and Practice in Human Resource Development (SAUO) .... HRD
Conference on Data Bases in the Humanities and Social Sciences (SAUS) .... CDBHSS
Conference on Data Mining (SAUO) .... CDM
Conference on Data Systems Languages [*Defunct*] (EA) .... CODASYL
Conference on Data Systems Languages (SAUO) .... CODASYSL
Conference on Disarmament .... CD
Conference on Disarmament in Europe (SAUO) .... CDE
Conference on Dual Distribution .... CDD
Conference on Early American History (EA) .... CEAH
Conference on Economic Progress [*Defunct*] (EA) .... CEP
Conference on Economic Progress (SAUS) .... ConfEcon Prog
Conference on Electrical Insulation and Dielectric Phenomena [*National Academy of Sciences*] .... CEIDP
Conference on English Education (EA) .... CEE
Conference on English Leadership (NTPA) .... CEL
Conference on European Security (SAUO) .... CES
Conference on European Security and Cooperation .... CESC
Conference on European Telecommunications Satellites (SAUS) .... CETS
Conference on Fair Use .... CONFU
Conference on Faith and History (EA) .... CFH
Conference on Forces in Europe .... CFE
Conference on Global Impacts of Applied Microbiology (SAUS) .... GIAM
Conference on Great Lakes Research (SAUO) .... CGLR
Conference on Industrial Robot Technology .... CIRT
Conference on Information Knowledge Management (GEOI) .... CIKM
Conference on Information Sciences and Systems (SAUS) .... CISS
Conference on Inter-American Telecommunications [*Organization of American States*] [*Telecommunications*] .... CITEL
Conference on Interlibrary Communications and Information Networks [*September 28 - October 2, 1970*] .... CICIN
Conference on International Economic Cooperation .... CIEC
Conference on Ionization Phenomena in Gases (SAUO) .... CIPIG
Conference on Jewish Material Claims Against Germany (EA) .... CJMCAG
Conference on Jewish Social Studies (EA) .... CJSS
Conference on LASER and Electro-Optical Systems .... CLEOS
Conference on Laser Engineering Applications (SAUO) .... CLEA
Conference on LASERs and Electro-Optics (MCD) .... CLEO
Conference on Latin American History (EA) .... CLAH
Conference on Local Computer Networks (SAUS) .... CLCN
Conference on Optical Fiber Communication [*Optical Society of America*] [*Washington, DC*] (TSSD) .... OFC
Conference on Oriental-Western Literary Relations [*Later, ALD*] (EA) .... COWLR
Conference on Personal Finance Law [*Later, CCFL*] (EA) .... CPFL
Conference on Politics, Economics and Christianity (SAUO) .... COPEC
Conference on Precision Electromagnetic Measurements (EA) .... CPEM
Conference on Protective Equipment (SAUO) .... COPE
Conference on Psychoanalytic Education and Research .... COPER
Conference on Remote Sensing Education (GEOI) .... CORSE
Conference on Research in Peace History (EA) .... CRPH
Conference on Safe Transportation of Hazardous Articles (EA) .... COSTHA
Conference on Science and Religion [*Later, UDC*] (EA) .... CSR
Conference on Science and Religion (SAUO) .... CSR
Conference on Science and World Affairs .... COSWA
Conference on Science, Philosophy, and Religion (EA) .... CSPR
Conference on Scientific Ocean Drilling [*JOIDES*] .... COSOD
Conference on Security and Cooperation in Europe (PD) .... CSCE
Conference on Security & Co-operation in the Mediterranean & Middle East (SAUS) .... CSCM
Conference on Security, Stability, Development, and Cooperation in Africa .... CSSDCA
Conference on Self-Operating Systems [*Computer science*] .... COSOS
Conference on Sustainable Development (SAUS) .... CSD
Conference on the Application of Science and Technology to the Development of Africa .... CASTAFRICA
Conference on the Application of Science and Technology to the Development of Asia (SAUO) .... CASTASIA
Conference on the Application of Science and Technology to the Development of Latin America .... CASTALA
Conference on the Atlantic Community (EA) .... CONTAC
Conference on the Development & Improvement of Urban Transport (SAUS) .... CODATU
Conference on the Development and the Planning of Urban Transport in Developing Countries (SAUO) .... CODATU
Conference on the Inhabitants of the Ocean (SAUO) .... CIO
Conference on the Problems of Standardization in the Developing Countries (SAUO) .... DEVCONF
Conference on the Public Service .... CPS
Conference on the Sociology of the Languages of American Women [*1976*] .... SLAW
Conference on Training Architects in Conservation [*London, England*] .... COTAC
Conference on Transportation Unity [*Defunct*] (EA) .... CTU
Conference on University Purchasing (AIE) .... COUP
Conference on Very Large Data Bases (SAUS) .... CVLB
Conference Order Wire (CCCA) .... COW
Conference Paper .... CP
Conference Papers Index [*A database*] (NITA) .... CONF
Conference Permanente de l'Europe de la Federation Internationale de Basketball [*Standing Conference for Europe of the International Basketball Federation*] (EAIO) .... CPEFIBA
Conference Permanente de l'Industrie Europeenne de Produits Emailles .... EUREMAIL
Conference Permanente des Recteurs, Presidents, et Vice Chanceliers des Universites Europeennes (EAIO) .... CRE
Conference Permanente des Recteurs, Presidents et Vice Chancellors (AIE) .... CRE
Conference Permanente d'Etudes sur les Civilisations du Monde Mediterraneen [*Standing Conference of Studies on the Civilisations of the Mediterranean World*] (EAIO) .... CPM

Conference Permanente Mediterraneenne pour la Cooperation Internationale [*Standing Mediterranean Conference for International Cooperation*] (EA) .... COPEMCI
Conference Permanente Mediterraneenne pour la Cooperation Internationale [*Standing Mediterranean Conference for International Cooperation - COPEMCI*] (EAIO) .... CPM
Conference Preparatory Meeting [*ITU/WARC*] .... CPM
Conference Proceedings (SAUS) .... Conf Proc
Conference Proceedings (ADA) .... CP
Conference Proceedings Index [*Database*] [*British Library*] [*Information service or system*] (CRD) .... CPI
Conference Proceedings. Inter-American Bar Association [*A publication*] (DLA) .... Conf Proc Inter-Amer Bar Assoc
Conference Publication (SAUS) .... CP
Conference Regionale du Service Volontaire International [*Regional Conference on International Voluntary Service*] (EAIO) .... CRSVI
Conference Reguliere sur les Problemes Universitaires [*Standing Conference on University Problems*] [*Council of Europe*] [*Strasbourg, France*] (EAIO) .... CC-PU
Conference Report (DLA) .... Conf Rept
Conference Report .... CR
Conference Reports [*North Carolina*] [*A publication*] (DLA) .... Conference (NC)
Conference Reports, by Cameron and Norwood [*North Carolina*] [*A publication*] (DLA) .... Conf
Conference Resource and Information Services (SAUS) .... CRIS
Conference Room (DNAB) .... CR
Conference Services Office [*American Library Association*] .... CSO
Conference Society of Alberta (AC) .... CSA
Conference Spatiale Europeenne [*European Space Conference*] .... CSE
Conference sur la Securite Europeene [*Conference on Security in Europe*] (NATG) .... CSE
Conference Terms (DS) .... CT
Conference Title [*Database terminology*] (NITA) .... CT
Conference to Explore Machine Readable Bibliographic Interchange .... CEMBI
Conference Upon Research and Education in World Government (EA) .... CURE
Conference Work Area (SAUS) .... CWA
Conference Year [*Database terminology*] (NITA) .... CY
Conferences in Energy, Physics, and Mathematics [*Fachinformationszentrum Karlsruhe GmbH*] [*Germany*] [*Information service or system*] (CRD) .... CONF
Conferences on Research on International Peace and Security [*Founded International Peace Research Association*] .... COROIPAS
Conferences Prop and Pulpwood Charter (SAUS) .... Propcon
Conferencia Interamericana de Bienestar Social [*Interamerican Social Welfare Conference*] .... CIBS
Conferencia Interamericana de Seguridad Social [*Inter-American Conference on Social Security - IACSS*] (EAIO) .... CISS
Conferencing System (SAUO) .... CoSy
Conferentia Episcopalis Pacifici [*Episcopal Conference of the Pacific*] (EAIO) .... CEPAC
Conferentia Episcopalis Scandiae [*Scandinavian Episcopal Conference - SEC*] (EAIO) .... CES
Conferred (ROG) .... CONFD
Conferred (GEAB) .... confer
Conferring (ROG) .... CONFG
Confessing Synod Ministries (EA) .... CSM
Confessions .... CF
Confessor C
Confessor (ROG) .... CONF
Confessor, Doctor [*Ecclesiastical*] (ROG) .... CD
Confessor Pontifex [*Confessor and Bishop*] [*Latin*] (ADA) .... CONFPONT
Confidence (ADA) .... CON
Confidence (NTIO) .... con
Confidence (FAAC) .... CONFDC
Confidence and Security-Building Measures .... CSBM
Confidence Building Measures (SAUS) .... CBM
Confidence Development Plan .... CDP
Confidence Firing Kit .... CFK
Confidence Game (ADWA) .... con
Confidence Game (ADWA) .... con game
Confidence Interval [*Statistics*] CI
Confidence Level [*Statistical mathematics*] CL
Confidence Limit (SAUS) CL
Confidence Limits CL
Confidence Man (ADWA) .... con man
Confidence Probability [*Mathematics*] .... CP
Confidence Range [*Statistics*] .... CR
Confidence Rulemaking (SAUS) .... CRM
Confidence Test (ACAE) .... CONT
Confidence Test (ACAE) .... CT
Confidence Test Program [*NASA*] (KSC) .... CTP
Confidence Training Launch .... CTL
Confidence Training Launching Instrumentation (SAUS) .... CTLI
Confidence-Building Measure .... CBM
Confidence-Building Measure [*for European military security*] .... CBM's
Confidencial (SAUS) .... Conf
Confident Disarming in Europe (SAUO) .... CDE
Confidential C
Confidential (ADWA) .... conf
Confidential (AFM) .... CONF
Confidential [*Security classification*] [*Military*] .... CONFD
Confidential (DSUE) .... CONFI
Confidential (ADA) .... CONFID
Confidential - Modified Handling [*Army*] .... CONF-MH
Confidential - Modified Handling Authorized [*Army*] (AFM) .... C-MHA
Confidential - Modified Handling Authorized [*Army*] .... CONFMOD

Confidential Admiralty Fleet Order [*British military*] (DMA) .... CAFO
Confidential Admiralty Merchant Ship Defense Instructions (SAUS) .... CAMDI
Confidential Admiralty Merchant Shipping Instructions .... CAMSI
Confidential Air Force Order [*British military*] (DMA) .... CAFO
Confidential and Secret Weekly Orders [*Naval Air Stations*] .... CASWO
Confidential Book [*Navy*] [*British*] .... CB
Confidential Books Office (SAUO) .... CB Office
Confidential Bulletin .... CB
Confidential Bulletin [*Navy*] .... CONFBUL
Confidential Business Information [*Government regulations*] .... CBI
Confidential Chemicals Identification System (GNE) .... CCID
Confidential Code Message (SAUS) .... CCM
Confidential Cover Sheet (AAG) .... CCS
Confidential Damage Level (SAA) .... CDL
Confidential Data (SAUS) .... CD
Confidential Document [*Navy*] .... CD
Confidential Employment Listing [*American Chemical Society*] .... CELACS
Confidential, Formerly Restricted Data .... CFRD
Confidential Human Incidents Reporting Programme [*British*] (WDAA) .... CHIRP
Confidential Hydrographic Office [*later, Naval Oceanographic Office*] **Reports - Atlantic** [*Navy*] .... CONHYDROLANT
Confidential Informant [*Department of Justice*] CI
Confidential Interim Order (SAUS) .... CIO
Confidential Letters of Map Amendment (GEOI) .... CLOMA
Confidential Material Control Officer (DNAB) .... CMCO
Confidential Measurement-Based Self-Evaluation [*Project*] (AIE) .... COMBSE
Confidential Memorandum .... CM
Confidential Monthly Order (SAUS) .... CMO
Confidential National Security Information (SAUS) .... CNSI
Confidential Restricted Data .... CRD
Confidential Statement of Formula (EEVL) .... CSF
Configurable Dynamic Memory Controller [*Computer science*] (CIST) .... CDMC
Configurable Function Block .... CFB
Configurable Gate Array (ACAE) .... CGA
Configurable Hardware Algorithm Mappable Preprocessor (SAUS) .... CHAMP
Configurable High Rate Processor (SAUS) .... CHRP
Configurable High Rate Processor System (SAUS) .... CHRPS
ConFigurable Interface (SAUS) .... CFI
Configurable Logic Block (AEBE) .... CLB
Configurable Long Instruction Word (SAUS) .... CLIW
Configurable Network Computing [*Software*] [*JD Edwards*] .... CNC
Configurable PostScript Interpreter [*Computer science*] (VERA) .... CPSI
Configurable Spread Spectrum Test Module (ACAE) .... CSSTM
Configurable Unified Search Engine [*Internet*] (DAVI) .... CUSI
Configurable Unified Search Index (SAUS) .... CUSI
Configurable Unified Search Interface [*Computer science*] (VERA) .... CUSI
Configural Frequency Analysis (SAUS) .... CFA
Configuration (SAUS) .... Cfg
Configuration (SAUS) .... CNF
Configuration .... CONF
Configuration (KSC) .... CONFIG
Configuration (ADWA) .... config
Configuration (FAAC) .... CONFIGN
Configuration Acceptance Inspection .... CAI
Configuration Accountability Systems, Aerospace .... CASA
Configuration Accountability Transmittal .... CAT
Configuration Accounting and Management Report (MCD) .... CAMR
Configuration Accounting Number .... CAN
Configuration Advisor (IAA) .... CONAD
Configuration Alternative (MCD) .... CA
Configuration Analysis and Performance (MCD) .... CAPER
Configuration Analysis Tool (MCD) .... CAT
Configuration and Acceptance Review (MCD) .... CAR
Configuration and Administration .... C & A
Configuration and Data Management (DNAB) .... CADM
Configuration and Data Management (ACAE) .... C&DM
Configuration and Data Management Department (ACAE) .... CDMD
Configuration and Data Management Support System .... CADMSS
Configuration and Product Definition Office (ACAE) .... C&PDO
Configuration and Switching Equipment Subsystem (MCD) .... CSES
Configuration and Trace System [*Military*] .... CTS
Configuration and Traceability (KSC) .... CAT
Configuration and Traceability Report (ACAE) .... CTR
Configuration and Tuning Module [*Computer science*] .... CTM
Configuration Assignment Unit (SAUO) .... CAU
Configuration Audit Inspection [*Army*] (AABC) .... CAI
Configuration Audit Plan .... CAP
Configuration Audit Review .... CAR
Configuration Baseline .... CB
Configuration Block Diagram [*Telecommunications*] (TEL) .... CBD
Configuration Breakdown List .... CBL
Configuration Budget Reviewion (SAUS) .... CBR
Configuration Card CC
Configuration Change Board [*NASA*] (MCD) .... CCB
Configuration Change Control Board [*NASA*] (KSC) .... CCCB
Configuration Change Directive (KSC) .... CCD
Configuration Change Notice (DOMA) .... CCN
Configuration Change Order .... CCO
Configuration Change Plan (KSC) .... CCP
Configuration Change Point (NASA) .... CCP
Configuration Change Proposal (MCD) .... CCP
Configuration Change Request .... CCR
Configuration Control (AAG) CC
Configuration Control Action (KSC) .... CCA
Configuration Control and Management (MCD) .... CC/M

Configuration Control and Sensing Unit (CET) .... CCSU
Configuration Control Board [*DoD*] .... CCB
Configuration Control Board Data [*or Directive*] [*DoD*] .... CCBD
Configuration Control Document (SAUS) .... CCD
Configuration Control Element (SAUS) .... CCE
Configuration Control Element (SAUS) .... CCF
Configuration Control Function [*Telecommunications*] (TEL) .... CCF
Configuration Control Group (SAUO) .... CCG
Configuration Control Identifier (ACAE) CCI
Configuration Control Logic (NASA) CCL
Configuration Control Number (AAG) .... CCN
Configuration Control Panel .... CCP
Configuration Control Phase (MCD) .... CCP
Configuration Control Plans (ACAE) .... CCP
Configuration Control Processor (ACAE) .... CCP
Configuration Control Register (SAUS) .... CCR
Configuration Control Reporting System [*Navy*] (MCD) .... CCRS
Configuration Control Review (SSD) .... CCR
Configuration Control Room [*Social Security Administration*] .... CCR
Configuration Control Secretariat (KSC) .... CCS
Configuration Control Sub-Board (SAUO) .... CCSB
Configuration Control Task Group (SAUO) .... CCTG
Configuration Control Test System (SAUS) .... CCTS
Configuration Control Unit (MCD) .... CCU
Configuration Control Verification List (MCD) CCVL
Configuration Coordinate Diagram .... CCD
Configuration Data Control (AAG) .... CDC
Configuration Data Management .... CDM
Configuration Data Package (DNAB) .... CDP
Configuration Data Processor (SAUS) .... CDP
Configuration Data Requirement (DNAB) .... CDR
Configuration Data Services, Inc. (SAUO) .... CDS
Configuration Data Set (SAUS) .... CDS
Configuration Data Table (MCD) .... CDT
Configuration Definition .... CD
Configuration Definition Phase (ACAE) .... CDP
Configuration Design Audit (MCD) .... CDA
Configuration Development of Advanced Fighters [*Military*] (MCD) .... CDAF
Configuration Development System (MCD) .... CDS
Configuration Deviation List (MCD) .... CDL
Configuration Element (AFIT) .... CE
Configuration End Item (AFIT) .... CEI
Configuration Engineering Office (SPST) .... CEO
Configuration Enhanced Radiation Rejection [*Space technology*] .... CERR
Configuration File (CDE) .... CFG file
Configuration Identification (MCD) CI
Configuration Identification Control and Accounting .... CICA
Configuration Identification Documentation .... CID
Configuration Identification Index CII
Configuration Identification Number [*Military*] .... CIN
Configuration Identification Package (SAA) .... CIP
Configuration Identification Tables (AABC) .... CIT
Configuration Indentification List (ACAE) CIL
Configuration Index CI
Configuration Index and Status Report (KSC) .... CISR
Configuration Index Document (MCD) .... CID
Configuration Information System .... CIS
Configuration Inspection (NASA) CI
Configuration [*or Contract*] Inspection Log CIL
Configuration Inspection Report (MCD) .... CIR
Configuration, Installation and Distribution (SAUS) .... CID
Configuration, Installation, and Distribution Architecture [*Computer science*] (PCM) .... CID
Configuration Interaction [*Quantum mechanics*] CI
Configuration Interaction including Double excitations (SAUS) .... CID
Configuration Interaction including only Single and Double excitations (SAUS) .... CISD
Configuration Interaction including Single (SAUS) .... CIS
Configuration Interface (SAUS) .... c/i
Configuration Item CI
Configuration Item Data List (NASA) .... CIDL
Configuration Item Development Specifications (MCD) .... CIDS
Configuration Item Product Fabrication Specification (MCD) .... CIPFS
Configuration Item Specification .... CIS
Configuration Item Specification (MCD) .... CISPEC
Configuration Item Validation [*or Verification*] Review .... CIVR
Configuration Management .... CM
Configuration Management (NAKS) .... cm
Configuration Management Accounting (NASA) .... CMA
Configuration Management and Change Control System [*Social Security Administration*] .... CMCCS
Configuration Management and Project Control Staff [*Social Security Administration*] .... CMPCS
Configuration Management Board .... CMB
Configuration Management Branch [*NASA*] (KSC) .... CMB
Configuration Management Capability (ACAE) .... CMC
Configuration Management Directive (ACAE) .... CMD
Configuration Management Division (SAUO) .... CMD
Configuration Management Facility (CTAS) .... CMF
Configuration Management Information System .... CMIS
Configuration Management Integrated Support Tool [*Marine science*] (OSRA) .... CMIST
Configuration Management Manual (DNAB) .... CMM
Configuration Management Office [*NASA*] (DNAB) .... CMO
Configuration Management Operating Plan (ACAE) .... CMOP

Configuration Management Operating System Manual (SAUS) .... CMOSM
Configuration Management Operating Systems Manual (MCD) .... CMOSM
Configuration Management Organization (CTAS) .... CMO
Configuration Management Panel (SAUS) .... CMP
Configuration Management Plan [*or Program*] .... CMP
Configuration Management Program (SAUO) .... CMP
Configuration Management Program Plan [*DoD*] .... CMPP
Configuration Management Requirements (ACAE) .... CMR
Configuration Management Review (AABC) .... CMR
Configuration Management Staff [*Social Security Administration*] .... CMS
Configuration Management Support Plan (ACAE) .... CMSP
Configuration Management System .... CMS
Configuration Management System Development Group (SAUO) .... CMSDG
Configuration Management Technology Organization (SAUS) .... CMTO
Configuration Management Tool (SSD) .... CMT
Configuration Management Version Control [*Computer science*] (PCM) .... CMVC
Configuration Management Working Group (SAUO) .... CMWG
Configuration Process [*Telecommunications*] (TEL) .... CONFG
Configuration Processor (SAUS) .... CONF PROC
Configuration Report and Accounting Program [*Military*] .... CORAP
Configuration Report Server (ACRL) .... CRS
Configuration Requirements Processing (MCD) .... CRP
Configuration Review (MCD) .... CR
Configuration Review Board (SAUO) .... CRB
Configuration Review Board Directive [*Military*] .... CRBD
Configuration Selection Register .... CSR
Configuration Standardization Document [*Deep Space Instrumentation Facility, NASA*] .... CSD
Configuration State Function (MCD) .... CSF
Configuration Status Accounting .... CSA
Configuration Status Accounting Data List (MCD) .... COSADL
Configuration Status Accounting Data Requirements (MCD) .... CSADR
Configuration Status Accounting Document (MCD) .... CSAD
Configuration Status Accounting Records (SAUS) .... SCAR
Configuration Status Accounting Report (KSC) .... CSAR
Configuration Status Accounting System .... CSAS
Configuration Sub Item (SAUS) .... CSI
Configuration Summary List (ACAE) .... CSL
Configuration Switch Controller (CET) .... CSC
Configuration Switching Equipment (MCD) .... CSE
Configuration Update Working Group (ACAE) .... CUWG
Configuration Usage Evaluator / Data Set Optimizer (PDAA) .... CUE/DSO
Configuration Utilization Efficiency (BUR) .... CUE
Configuration Utilization Evaluator (IAA) .... CUE
Configuratio Verification and Accounting System .... CVAS
Configuration Verification Index CVI
Configuration Verification List (MCD) CVL
Configuration Verification Review (MCD) .... CVR
Configuration Verification Test .... CVT
Configuration Word Package Item (SAUS) .... CWPI
Configuration Work Package Item [*Army*] (AABC) .... CWPI
Configuration/Data Management Division (SAUS) .... YVCB
Configuration-Installation-Distribution [*IBM Corp.*] (VERA) .... CID
Configured Article .... CA
Configured Article Identifier .... CAI
Configured Articles List (ACAE) .... CAL
Confine (FAAC) .... CFN
Confine (AABC) .... CNF
Confine (SAUS) .... Cnf
Confine [*or Confinement*] (AFM) .... CONF
Confine (SAUS) .... Confi
Confined Area Landing .... CAL
Confined Detonating Cord (MCD) .... CDC
Confined Detonating Fuse (SAUS) .... CDF
Confined Disposal Facilities .... CDF
Confined Space (SAUS) .... CS
Confined to Bed (SAUS) .... CTB
Confined to Camp [*Military*] CC
Confined to Post .... C to P
Confinement at Hard Labor [*Army*] (AABC) .... CHL
Confinement Factor [*Nuclear energy*] (NRCH) .... CF
Confinement Heat Removal [*Environmental science*] (COE) .... CHR
Confinement Physics Research Facility .... CPRF
Confinement Protection Limits [*Environmental science*] (COE) .... CPL
Confinement to Barracks [*A military punishment*] .... CB
Confirm (AAG) .... CFM
Confirm (SAUS) .... Cfm
Confirm (EBF) .... Conf
Confirm (EBF) .... conf
Confirmatio Chartarum [*Confirmation of the Charters*] [*Latin*] [*Legal term*] (DLA) .... Conf Chart
Confirmation [*Purchasing*] .... CONF
Confirmation (EBF) .... Conf
Confirmation (EBF) .... conf
Confirmation of Balance [*Banking*] .... C of B
Confirmation of Balance (SAUS) .... CofB
Confirmation of Broadcast Order (WDMC) .... CBO
Confirmation of Number of Order [*Purchasing*] (IAA) .... CONO
Confirmation of Receipt (SAUS) .... CofR
Confirmation Rolls (ROG) .... CONF R
Confirmation Study (BCP) .... CS
Confirmation to Receive [*Computer science*] .... CFR
Confirmatory Factor Analysis .... CFA
Confirmatory Test [*Army*] (AABC) .... CT
Confirmed (TRID) .... CFMD

Confirmed (SAUS) .... Cfmd
Confirmed (DAVI) .... conf
Confirmed and Compatible (MEDA) .... C & C
Confirmed and Made a Matter of Record [Army] (AABC) .... CMMR
Confirmed Exposure but Unconscious [Advertising] .... CEBUS
Confirming Design Layout Report Date [Bell System] (TEL) .... CDLRD
Confirming Engineering Information Report Date [Bell System] (TEL) .... CEIRD
Confirming Informal Order [Telecommunications] (TEL) .... CIO
Confirming Requisition Follows (FAAC) .... COREQ
Confirming Telephone [or message] **Authority Of** .... COTA
Conflagration Control (DNAB) .... CONFLAG
Conflict (MSA) .... CFL
Conflict Alert [Aviation] .... CA
Conflict Alert System [Aviation] .... CAS
Conflict Alert/Minimum Safe Altitude Warning [FAA] (TAG) .... CA/MSAW
Conflict and Peace Data Bank .... COPDAB
Conflict Archive on the Internet [Project] [British] (TELE) .... CAIN
Conflict Archive on the Internet Northern Ireland (SAUS) .... CAIN
Conflict Archives on the Internet [Multimedia database] .... CAIN
Conflict Management Group [An association] .... CMG
Conflict Management Survey [Interpersonal skills and attitudes test] .... CMS
Conflict of Interest [Legal term] .... COI
Conflict of Laws [Legal term] (DLA) .... CONF L
Conflict Prevention Centre (SAUS) .... CPC
Conflict Resolution .... CR
Conflict Resolution Advisory [FAA] (TAG) .... CRA
Conflict Resolution Center (EA) .... CRC
Conflict Resolution Inventory [Psychology] .... CRI
Conflict Resolution/Alternatives to Violence Training Center (EA) .... CR/AVTC
Conflict Tactics Scale (EDAC) .... CTS
Conflict-directed Backjumping (SAUS) .... CBJ
Conflict-Free Multi-Access (SAUS) .... CFMA
Conflicting-Use Writeback (SAUS) .... CUW
Confluence (GEOI) .... CNFL
Confluence (ROG) .... CON
Confluent Education Development and Research Center [Defunct] (EA) .... CEDARC
Confluent Reticulate Papillomatosis (STED) .... CRP
Confocal Flourescence Imaging Microscopy [Medicine] .... CFIM
Confocal LASER Scanning Microscope [or Microscopy] .... CLSM
Confocal Scanning LASER Microscope [or Microscopy] .... CSLM
Confocal Spherical Fabry-Perot .... CSFP
Confoederatio Internationalis ad Qualitates Plantarum Edulium Perquirendas [International Association for Quality Research on Food Plants] .... CIQ
Conform Tactical Array (SAUS) .... CONTACT Array
Conformal Array (CAAL) .... CFA
Conformal Countermeasures System (SAUS) .... CCS
Conformal Fuel Tank (MCD) .... CFT
Conformal Phased Array Antenna (SAUS) .... CPA Antenna
Conformal Solution Theory (MCD) .... CST
Conformal Space Projection (GEOI) .... CSP
Conformal Tactical Array (MCD) .... CONTACT
Conformal Wire Grating .... CWG
Conformal-array Aerial (SAUS) .... CA
Conformal-Array Antenna (PDAA) .... CAA
Conformal-Array Radar (SAUS) .... CAR
Conformance .... CONF
Conformance Inspection Record (SAA) .... CIR
Conformance Test (DDC) .... CT
Conformance Testing Service [Computer science] (TNIG) .... CTS
Conformational Analysis of Molecules in Solution by Empirical and Quantum Techniques .... CAMSEQ
Conforming Flush-plate Dipole (SAUS) .... CFD
Conforming Products List (SAUO) .... CPL
Conformist (WDAA) .... Con
Conformity Assessment and Product Marking (SAUS) .... CAPM
Conforms to Copyright Guidelines .... CCG
Conforms to Copyright Law CCL
Confortair, Inc. [Canada] [ICAO designator] (FAAC) .... COF
Confraternidad Evangelica Latinoamericana [Confraternity of Evangelicals in Latin America] [Argentina] (EAIO) .... CONELA
Confraternity (ROG) .... CFR
Confraternity New Testament [A publication] (BJA) .... CNT
Confraternity of Christian Doctrine (CCD) .... CCD
Confraternity of the Blessed Sacrament (EA) .... CBS
Confraternity Version (BJA) CV
Confrerie de la Chaine des Rotisseurs [France] (EAIO) .... CCR
Confrerie des Chevaliers du Goute Boudin [Brotherhood of Knights of the Black Pudding Tasters - BKBPT] (EA) .... CCGB
Confrerie des Chevaliers du Tastevin (EA) .... CCT
Confuse (MSA) .... CFS
Confused and Disabled Elderly Patient .... CADE
Confused Artificial Insemination .... CAI
Confused, Lacerated, Incised and Punctured (SAUS) .... CLIP
Confused Language Syndrome [Medicine] (DB) .... CLS
Confusion (MSA) .... CFSN
Confusion Reflector Material .... CRM
Confusion Signal (SAUS) .... COF Signal
Conga .... cga
Congdon Park Elementary School, Duluth, MN [Library symbol] [Library of Congress] (LCLS) .... MnDuCOE
Congdon's Digest [Canada] [A publication] (DLA) .... Cong Dig
Congdon's Mining Laws of California [A publication] (DLA) .... Cong Min L
Congenital [Medicine] (WGA) .... CONG

Congenital [Medicine] .... CONGEN
Congenital [Medicine] (DMAA) .... congen
Congenital Abduction Deficiency [Medicine] (MELL) .... CAD
Congenital Absence of Left Pericardium [Medicine] (DMAA) .... CALP
Congenital Absence of Vagina [Medicine] .... CAV
Congenital Adrenal Hyperplasia [Medicine] .... CAH
Congenital Adrenal Hyperplasia Support Association (SAUO) .... CAHSA
Congenital Adrenal Virilism [Medicine] .... CAV
Congenital Alcoholic Syndrome [Medicine] (DMAA) .... CAS
Congenital Anosmia [Medicine] (MELL) .... CA
Congenital Articular Dysplasia [Medicine] (MELL) .... CAD
Congenital Articular Rigidity [Medicine] (LDT) .... CAR
Congenital Atonic Sclerotic Muscular Dystrophy [Medicine] (DMAA) .... CASMD
Congenital Bilateral Absence of the Vas Deferens [Medicine] .... CBAVD
Congenital Cardiovascular Malformation [Medicine] (MELL) .... CCVM
Congenital Cataracts (MELL) CC
Congenital Central Hypoventilation Syndrome [Medicine] .... CCHS
Congenital Contracture Arachnodactyly [Medicine] .... CCA
Congenital Cystic Adenomatoid Malformation (SAUS) .... CCAM
Congenital Cytomegalovirus [Medicine] .... CMV
Congenital Dacryocystocele [Medicine] (MELL) .... CDC
Congenital Deafness (MELL) .... CD
Congenital Defect (MELL) .... CD
Congenital Diaphragmatic Hernia [Medicine] .... CDH
Congenital Dislocation of Knee (MELL) .... CDK
Congenital Dislocation [or Dysplasia] **of the Hip** [Medicine] .... CDH
Congenital Disorders of Neuromuscular Transmission (PAZ) .... CDNT
Congenital Dyserythropoietic Anemia [Hematology] .... CDA
Congenital Dysphagocytosis [Medicine] .... CDG
Congenital Dysplastic Hip (MELL) .... CDH
Congenital Ectropion Uveae [Medicine] (DMAA) .... CEU
Congenital Erythropoietic Porphyria [Medicine] .... CEP
Congenital Eyelid Tetrad [Medicine] (DMAA) .... CET
Congenital Facial Diplegia [Medicine] (MELL) .... CFD
Congenital Generalized Hypertrichosis [Werewolf syndrome] [Medicine] .... CGH
Congenital Glaucoma (MELL) .... CG
Congenital Heart Anomalies-Support, Education and Resources (SAUO) .... CHASER
Congenital Heart Block [Medicine] (DMAA) .... CHB
Congenital Heart Disease [Medicine] .... CHD
Congenital Heinz Body Hemolytic Anemia [Medicine] .... CHBA
Congenital Heinz Body Hemolytic Anemia [Medicine] (DMAA) .... CHBHA
Congenital Hemidysplasia with Ichthyosiform Erythroderma and Limb Defects Syndrome [Medicine] (DMAA) .... CHILD
Congenital Hepatic Fibrosis [Medicine] (DMAA) .... CHF
Congenital Hereditary Endothelial Dystrophy (SAUS) .... CHED
Congenital Hereditary Retinoschisis [Ophthalmology] (DAVI) .... CHRS
Congenital Hereditary Stromal Dystrophy (SAUS) .... CHSD
Congenital Hip Dislocation (SAUS) .... CHD
Congenital Hip Dysplasia .... CHD
Congenital Hip Subluxation [Medicine] (MELL) .... CHS
Congenital Hypertrophy of the Retinal Pigment Epithelium [Medicine] (DMAA) .... CHRPE
Congenital Hypertrophy of the RPE (SAUS) .... CHRPE
Congenital Hypomyelination [Medicine] .... CH
Congenital Hypoplastic Anemia [Hematology] .... CHA
Congenital Hypothyroidism [Medicine] .... CHT
Congenital Hypoventilation Syndrome [Medicine] (MELL) .... CHS
Congenital Ichtyosisform Erythroderma [Dermatology] .... CIE
Congenital Inclusion Body Hemolytic Anemia [Medicine] (AAMN) .... CIB HA
Congenital Inclusion-Body Hemolytic Anemia [Medicine] (DB) .... CIBHA
Congenital Intestional Aganglionosis [Medicine] (MELL) .... CIA
Congenital Lactase Deficiency [Medicine] (MELL) .... CLD
Congenital Lipoid Adrenal Hyperplasia [Medicine] (DMAA) .... CLAH
Congenital Lobar Emphysema [Medicine] (MELL) .... CLE
Congenital Lobar Overinflation .... CLO
Congenital Localized Absence of Skin [Medicine] (MAE) .... CLAS
Congenital Malformation [Medicine] .... CM
Congenital Malformation of Heart [Medicine] .... CMH
Congenital Multicystic Kidney [Nephrology] (DAVI) .... CMK
Congenital Muscular Dystrophy [Medicine] .... CMD
Congenital Myasthenia Gravis [Medicine] (MELL) .... CMG
Congenital Myocardial Sympathetic Dysinnervation [Medicine] (DMAA) .... CMSD
Congenital Myotonic Dystrophy [Medicine] .... CMD
Congenital Nephrogenic Diabetes Insipidus [Medicine] .... CNDI
Congenital Nephrosis [Medicine] (STED) .... CN
Congenital Nephrotic Syndrome [Medicine] (MELL) .... CNS
Congenital Nevocytic Nevus [Medicine] (STED) .... CNN
Congenital Nevomelanocytic Nevi [Medicine] .... CNN
Congenital Nonspherocytic Hemolytic Anemia [Medicine] (MELL) .... CNHA
Congenital Nonspherocytic Hemolytic Anemia [Medicine] .... CNSHA
Congenital Nonspherocytic Hemolytic Disease [Medicine] (MAE) .... CNHD
Congenital Nystagmus [Ophthalmology] (AAMN) .... CN
Congenital Palatopharyngeal Incompetence [Medicine] (STED) .... CPI
Congenital Phosphoruria [DB] .... CP
Congenital Polycystic Disease [Medicine] (MELL) .... CPD
Congenital Polyvalvular Disease [Medicine] (DMAA) .... CPVD
Congenital Portocaval Shunt [Medicine] .... C-PCS
Congenital Pulmonary Cystic Lymphangiectasis [Medicine] .... CPCL
Congenital Pulmonary Lymphangiectasia [Medicine] (DMAA) .... CPL
Congenital Red Cell Anemia [Medicine] (MELL) .... CRCA
Congenital Retinal Telangiectasia [Medicine] (MELL) .... CRT
Congenital Rubella [Medicine] (MELL) .... CR
Congenital Rubella Deafness [Medicine] (MELL) .... CRD
Congenital Rubella Syndrome [Medicine] .... CRS

Congenital Self-Healing Histiocytosis [*Medicine*] (DMAA) ... CSHH
Congenital Sensory Neuropathy [*Medicine*] (MELL) ... CSN
Congenital Sideroblastic Anemia [*Medicine*] ... CSA
Congenital Stationary Night Blindness ... CSNB
Congenital Syphilis [*Medicine*] ... CS
Congenital Thymic Dysplasia [*Medicine*] (MAE) ... CTD
Congenital Urinary Tract Deformity [*Medicine*] (AAMN) ... CUD
Congenital Vertical Talus [*Medicine*] (MELL) ... CVT
Congenital Virilizing Adrenal Hyperplasia [*Medicine*] (DB) ... CVAH
Congenital-Kyphosis [*Medicine*] (MELL) ... CK
Congenitally Corrected Transposition [*Of the great vessels*] [*Cardiology*] (DAVI) ... CCT
Congenitally Corrected Transposition of the Great Arteries [*Cardiology*] (DAVI) ... CCTGA
Congential (SAUS) ... Congen
Congential Inclusion Body Haemolytic Anaemia (SAUS) ... CIBHA
Congested Freeway Driving Schedule [*For vehicle emission measurements*] ... CFDS
Congestion (FAAC) ... CGSTN
Congestion [*Telecommunications*] (TEL) ... CONG
Congestion (SAUS) ... Cong
Congestion Avoidance and Reduction for Automobiles and Trucks [*FHWA*] (TAG) ... CARAT
Congestion Control (SAUS) ... CC
Congestion Indicator (VERA) ... CI
Congestion Management Systems [*VDOT*] (TAG) ... CMS
Congestion Mitigation and Air Quality [*Improvement program*] [*VDOT*] (TAG) ... CMAQ
Congestion Monitoring Period (SAUS) ... CMP
Congestion/Demand Management [*TXDOT*] (TAG) ... CDM
Congestive Cardiac Failure [*Medicine*] ... CCF
Congestive Cardiomyopathy [*Medicine*] (CPH) ... CCM
Congestive Cardiomyopathy [*Medicine*] (MELL) ... COCM
Congestive failure (SAUS) ... Cong fail
Congestive Heart Disease [*Cardiology*] (DAVI) ... CHD
Congestive Heart Failure [*Medicine*] ... CHF
Congestive Hepatomegaly [*Medicine*] (MELL) ... CHM
Congestive Mastitis [*Medicine*] (MELL) ... CM
Congestive Myocardiopathy [*Medicine*] ... CM
Congestive Right Ventricular Failure [*Medicine*] (DB) ... CRVF
Congius [*Gallon*] [*Pharmacy*] ... C
Congius [*Gallon*] [*Pharmacy*] ... CONG
Conglomerate [*Lithology*] ... CGL
Conglomerate (SAUS) ... Cgl
Conglomerate ... CONGL
Conglutinating Complement Absorption Test [*Immunochemistry*] ... CCAT
Conglutinating Complement Fixation (PDAA) ... CCF
Conglutinogen Activating Factor [*Medicine*] (MELL) ... KAF
Congo [*MARC country of publication code*] [*Library of Congress*] (LCCP) ... cf
Congo [*ANSI two-letter standard code*] (CNC) ... CG
Congo [*ANSI three-letter standard code*] (CNC) ... COG
Congo (NTIO) ... Con
Congo (WDAA) ... CON
Congo [*MARC geographic area code*] [*Library of Congress*] (LCCP) ... f-cf-
Congo African Grey [*Bird*] ... CAG
Congo Balolo Mission (SAUO) ... CBM
Congo Crimean Hemorrhagic Fever (SAUS) ... C-CHF
Congo Inland Mission (SAUO) ... CIM
Congo International Management Corporation (SAUO) ... CIMCO
Congo (Kinshasa) [*Zaire*] [*MARC country of publication code*] [*Library of Congress*] (LCCP) ... cg
Congo (Kinshasa) [*Zaire*] [*MARC geographic area code*] [*Library of Congress*] (LCCP) ... f-cg-
Congo Military Mission - United States ... COMISH-US
Congo Protestant Council (SAUO) ... CPC
Congo Protestant Relief Agency (SAUO) ... CPRA
Congo Protestant Relief Agency [*Defunct*] ... CPRA
Congo Red [*A dye*] ... CoR
Congo Red (STED) ... Cor
Congo River and Basin [*MARC geographic area code*] [*Library of Congress*] (LCCP) ... fg---
Congo Town, Andros Island [*Bahamas*] [*ICAO location identifier*] (ICLI) ... MYAK
Congolese ... Cong
Congolese National Army (SAUO) ... CNA
Congolese Progressive Students [*Zaire*] (PD) ... ECP
Congolese Socialist Party [*Zaire*] [*Political party*] (PD) ... PSC
Congoleum Corp. (SAUO) ... COG
Congoleum Corp. [*Associated Press*] (SAG) ... Conglm
Congoleum Corp.'A' [*NYSE symbol*] (TTSB) ... CGM
Congolomerate (SAUS) ... Cgl
Congo-Red Millipore Filter ... CRMF
Congou [*Tea trade*] (ROG) ... CONO
Congratulations (DSUE) ... CONGRATS
congratulations (SAUS) ... congrats
Congregate Housing Services Program [*HUD*] ... CHSP
Congregatie Broeders van Huybergen [*Brothers of the Immaculate Conception of the Mother of God - BICMG*] [*Huybergen, Netherlands*] (EAIO) ... CBH
Congregatio a Sacro Corde Jesu [*Congregation of the Priests of the Sacred Heart*] [*Roman Catholic religious order*] ... CCV
Congregatio a Sancta Cruce [*Congregation of Holy Cross*] [*Roman Catholic religious order*] ... CSC
Congregatio Caritatis Verbi Incarnati [*Congregation of the Sisters of Charity of the Incarnate Word*] [*Roman Catholic religious order*] ... CCVI
Congregatio Clericorum Regularium Marianorum sub titulo Immaculatae ConceptionisBeatae Mariae Virginis [*Marian Fathers*] [*Roman Catholic religious order*] ... MIC
Congregatio Filiarum Minimarum Mariae [*Minim Daughters of Mary Immaculate*] [*Roman Catholic religious order*] ... CFMM
Congregatio Filiorum Sacratissimi Cordis Jesu [*Sons of the Sacred Heart*] [*Verona Fathers*] [*Roman Catholic religious order*] ... FSCJ
Congregatio Fratrum Caritate [*Brothers of Charity*] [*Roman Catholic religious order*] ... FC
Congregatio Fratrum Cellitarum seu Alexianorum [*Alexian Brothers*] [*Roman Catholic religious order*] ... CFA
Congregatio Fratrum Immaculatae Conceptionis Beatae Mariae Virginis [*Brothers of the Immaculate Conception of the Blessed Virgin Mary*] (EAIO) ... FIC
Congregatio Fratrum Pauperum [*Brothers of the Poor of St. Francis*] [*Roman Catholic religious order*] ... CFP
Congregatio Fratrum Sancti Francisci Xaverii [*Brothers of St. Francis Xavier*] [*Xaverian Brothers*] [*Roman Catholic religious order*] ... CFX
Congregatio Immaculati Cordis Mariae [*Congregation of the Immaculate Heart of Mary*] [*Roman Catholic men's religious order*] ... CICM
Congregatio Iosephitarum [*Josephite Fathers*] [*Roman Catholic religious order*] ... CJ
Congregatio Jesu et Mariae [*Congregation of Jesus and Mary*] [*Eudist Fathers*] [*Roman Catholic religious order*] ... CJM
Congregatio Mariae [*Fathers of the Company of Mary*] [*Roman Catholic religious order*] ... CM
Congregatio Missionariorum a Sancta Familia [*Congregation of the Missionaries of the Holy Family*] [*Roman Catholic men's religious order*] ... MSF
Congregatio Missionariorum a Sancto Carlo [*Congregation of the Missionary Fathers of St. Charles*] [*Formerly, PSSC*] [*Roman Catholic religious order*] ... CS
Congregatio Missionariorum de Mariannhill [*Congregation of Mariannhill Missionaries*] [*Mariannhill Fathers*] [*Roman Catholic religious order*] [*Italy*] ... CMM
Congregatio Missionariorum Filiorum Immaculati Cordis Beatae Maria Virginia [*Congregation of Missionary Sons of the Immaculate Heart of the Blessed Virgin Mary*] [*Claretians*] [*Roman Catholic religious order*] ... CMF
Congregatio Missionis Sancti Vicentii a Paulo [*Congregation of the Mission of St. Vincent de Paul*] [*Vincentians*] [*Roman Catholic men's religious order*] ... CM
Congregatio Passionis [*Congregation of the Passion*] [*Passionists*] [*Roman Catholic religious order*] ... CP
Congregatio Pretiosissimi Sanguinis [*Society of the Most Precious Blood*] [*Roman Catholic religious order*] ... CPPS
Congregatio Reformatorium Praemonstratensium [*Premonstratensians*] [*Roman Catholic men's religious order*] ... CRP
Congregatio Resurrectionis [*Congregation of the Resurrection*] [*Roman Catholic religious order*] ... CR
Congregatio Sacerdotum a Corde Jesu [*Congregation of the Priests of the Sacred Heart of Jesus*] [*Roman Catholic religious order*] ... SCJ
Congregatio Sacratissimorum Cordium [*Missionaries of the Sacred Hearts of Jesus and Mary*] [*Roman Catholic religious order*] ... CSSCC
Congregatio Sancti Basilii [*Congregation of the Priests of St. Basil*] [*Basilians*] [*Roman Catholic men's religious order*] ... CSB
Congregatio Sancti Joseph [*Congregation of St. Joseph*] [*Roman Catholic religious order*] ... CSJ
Congregatio Sancti Pauli [*Paulists*] [*Roman Catholic men's religious order*] ... CSP
Congregatio Sancti Spiritus [*Congregation of the Holy Ghost*] [*Holy Ghost Fathers*] [*Roman Catholic religious order*] ... CSSP
Congregatio Sanctissimi Redemptoris [*Congregation of the Most Holy Redeemer*] [*Redemptionists*] [*Roman Catholic men's religious order*] ... CSSR
Congregatio Sororum Apostolatus Catholici [*Pallottine Sisters of the Catholic Apostolate*] [*Roman Catholic religious order*] ... CSAC
Congregatio Sororum Sacrae Familiae de Nazareth [*Sisters of the Holy Family of Nazareth*] [*Roman Catholic religious order*] ... CSFN
Congregation ... C
Congregation (BJA) ... Cngrn
Congregation ... cong
Congregation (BJA) ... Cong
congregation (SAUO) ... cong
Congregation (SAUS) ... Cong
Congregation (ROG) ... CONGN
Congregation (SAUO) ... Congreg
Congregation ... CONREG
Congregation de Hermanas Guadalupanas de la Salle (TOCD) ... HGS
Congregation de la Fraternite Sacerdotale [*Congregation of the Sacerdotal Fraternity*] [*Canada*] (EAIO) ... CFS
Congregation de la Mere du Carmel [*Congregation of Mother of Carmel*] [*Alwaye Kerala, India*] (EAIO) ... CMC
Congregation de Notre Dame de la Retraite au Cenacle [*Congregation of Our Lady of the Retreat in the Cenacle*] (EAIO) ... RC
Congregation des Soeurs Servantes du Coeur Immaculae de Marie [*Servants of the Immaculate Heart of Mary*] [*Good Shepherd Sisters*] [*Roman Catholic religious order*] ... SCIM
Congregation for Catholic Education (SAUO) ... CEC
Congregation for the Doctrine of the Faith ... CDF
Congregation of Augustinian Sisters Servants of Jesus and Mary (TOCD) ... OSA
Congregation of Bethlehemite Religious Women, Daughters of the Sacred Heart (BUAC) ... SCIF
Congregation of Bon Secours (TOCD) ... CBS
Congregation of Cellites (SAUO) ... Alexian Brothers
Congregation of Charity of the Most Sacred Heart of Jesus [*Roman Catholic religious order*] ... CCJ
Congregation of Christian Brothers [*Formerly, Christian Brothers of Ireland*] [*Roman Catholic religious order*] ... CFC

Congregation of Clerics Regular [*Theatine Fathers*] [*Roman Catholic religious order*] .... CR
Congregation of Daughters of Jesus [*Roman Catholic religious order*] .... FJ
Congregation of Humility of Mary [*Roman Catholic women's religious order*] .... CHM
Congregation of Incarnate Word and Blessed Sacrament (TOCD) CVI
Congregation of Jesus and Mary (TOCD) .... cjm
Congregation of Jesus and Mary, Eudist Fathers (TOCD) .... cjm
Congregation of Jesus Crucified (TOCD) .... OSB
Congregation of Josephites (SAUO) .... CJ
Congregation of Marianhill Missionaries Marianhill Fathers & Brothers (TOCD) .... CMM
Congregation of Mariannhill Missionaries, Mariannhill Fathers and Brothers (TOCD) .... cmm
Congregation of Marians of the Immaculate Conception (TOCD) .... mic
Congregation of Marians of the Immaculate Conception (TOCD) .... MIC
[*The*] Congregation of Maronite Lebanese Missionaries (TOCD) .... CMLM
Congregation of Maronite Monks (TOCD) .... omar
Congregation of Maronite Monks (TOCD) .... OMar
Congregation of Mary Queen (TOCD) .... CMR
Congregation of Missionary Catechists of the Sacred Heart of Jesus and Mary (TOCD) .... MCSJM
Congregation of Mother Coredemptrix (TOCD) .... cmc
Congregation of Mother Coredemptrix (TOCD) .... CMC
Congregation of Mother of Carmel (SAUO) .... CMC
Congregation of Notre Dame (TOCD) .... CND
Congregation of Notre Dame de Sion [*Roman Catholic women's religious order*] .... NDS
Congregation of Oblates of Bethany [*Roman Catholic women's religious order*] .... COB
Congregation of Our Lady, Help of the Clergy [*Roman Catholic women's religious order*] .... CLHC
Congregation of Our Lady of Mount Carmel (TOCD) .... OCarm
Congregation of Our Lady of the Holy Rosary [*Roman Catholic women's religious order*] .... RSR
Congregation of Our Lady of the Retreat in the Cenacle [*Roman Catholic women's religious order*] [*Italy*] .... RC
Congregation of Priests of Mercy [*Fathers of Mercy*] [*Roman Catholic religious order*] .... CPM
Congregation of Salesians [*Australia*] .... CS
Congregation of Salesius (SAUO) .... CS
Congregation of Sisters of Nazareth (TOCD) .... CSN
Congregation of Sisters of St. Thomas of Villanova [*Roman Catholic religious order*] .... SSTV
Congregation of St. Basil (SAUO) .... Basilian Fathers
Congregation of St. Basil (SAUO) .... CSB
Congregation of St. Brigid [*Roman Catholic women's religious order*] .... CSB
Congregation of St. John (TOCD) .... fj
Congregation of St. John (TOCD) .... FJ
Congregation of St. John the Baptist (TOCD) .... CSJB
Congregation of St. Joseph (TOCD) .... csj
Congregation of St. Joseph (TOCD) .... CSJ
Congregation of the Benedictine Sisters of Perpetual Adoration of Pontifical Jurisdiction (TOCD) .... OSB
Congregation of the Benedictine Sisters of the Sacred Heart (TOCD) .... OSB
Congregation of the Blessed Sacrament (TOCD) .... SSS
Congregation of the Blessed Sacrament (TOCD) .... sss
Congregation of the Divine Spirit [*Roman Catholic women's religious order*] .... CDS
Congregation of the Fathers of Mercy (TOCD) .... cpm
Congregation of the Holy Cross (TOCD) .... CHC
Congregation of the Incarnate Word and Blessed Sacrament (SAUO) .... IWBS
Congregation of the Incarnate Word and the Blessed Sacrament [*Roman Catholic women's religious order*] .... IWBS
Congregation of the Incarnate Word and the Blessed Sacrament [*Roman Catholic women's religious order*] .... SIW
Congregation of the Incarnate Word and the Blessed Sacrament [*Roman Catholic women's religious order*] VI
Congregation of the Marianites of the Holy Cross (TOCD) .... MSC
Congregation of the Mission [*Vincentians*] (DAS) .... CM
Congregation of the Mission, Vincentian Fathers (TOCD) .... cm
Congregation of the Missionary Fathers of St. Charles (SAUO) .... CS
Congregation of the Oblates of the Virgin Mary [*Rome, Italy*] (EAIO) .... OVM
Congregation of the Oratory [*Oratorians*] [*Roman Catholic men's religious order*] .... CO
Congregation of the Oratory [*Oratorians*] [*Roman Catholic men's religious order*] .... CongOrat
Congregation of the Oratory (SAUO) .... Cong Orat
Congregation of the Passion (TOCD) .... CP
Congregation of the Passion, Passionist Fathers (TOCD) .... cp
Congregation of the Priests of the Sacred Heart of Jesus (TOCD) .... scj
Congregation of the Religious Brothers of the Third Order Regular of St. Francis (TOCD) .... OSF
Congregation of the Resurrection, Resurrectionist Fathers (TOCD) .... cr
Congregation of the Resurrection Theatine Fathers (TOCD) .... CR
Congregation of the Sacerdotal Fraternity [*Canada*] (EAIO) .... CSF
Congregation of the Sacred Hearts and of Perpetual Adoration (TOCD) .... SSCC
Congregation of the Sacred Hearts of Jesus and Mary (TOCD) .... sscc
Congregation of the Sacred Hearts of Jesus and Mary [*Rome, Italy*] (EAIO) .... SSCC
Congregation of the Sacred Stigmata [*Stigmatine Fathers and Brothers*] [*Roman Catholic religious order*] .... CSS
Congregation of the Servants of Christ [*Anglican religious community*] .... SC
Congregation of the Sisters Marianites of Holy Cross [*Roman Catholic religious order*] .... MSC

Congregation of the Sisters of St. Felix [*Felician Sisters*] [*Roman Catholic religious order*] .... CSSF
Congregation of the Sisters of St John the Baptist (SAUO) .... CSJB
Congregation of the Sisters of St. Louis, Juilly-Monaghan (TOCD) .... SSL
Congregation of the Sisters of the Adoration of the Blessed Sacrament [*Kerala, India*] (EAIO) .... SABS
Congregation of the Sisters of the Family [*Roman Catholic religious order*] .... SSF
Congregation of the Sisters of the Holy Faith [*Australia*] .... CHF
Congregation of the Sisters of the Holy Family (TOCD) .... SSF
Congregation of the Sisters of the Holy Family of Nazareth [*Australia*] .... CSFN
Congregation of the Sisters of the Third Order of St. Francis Oldenburg, IN (TOCD) .... OSF
Congregation of the Third Order of St. Francis of Mary Immaculate, Joliet IL (TOCD) .... OSF
Congregation Organized by United Genial Hackers .... COUGH
Congregation Shaar Hashomayim Library-Museum, Westmount, PQ, Canad [*Library symbol*] [*Library of Congress*] (LCLS) .... CaQWsmSH
Congregation Shaar Hashomayim Library-Museum, Westmount, Quebec [*Library symbol*] [*National Library of Canada*] (NLC) .... QWSH
Congregation Sons of Israel and David, Temple Beth-El, Providence, RI [*Library symbol*] [*Library of Congress*] (LCLS) .... RPT
Congregational (SAUS) C
Congregational .... CONG
Congregational (NTIO) .... cong
Congregational .... CONGL
Congregational .... CONGR
Congregational .... CONGREGTNL
Congregational Christian Churches National Association (EA) .... CCCNA
Congregational Christian Historical Society (EA) .... CCHS
Congregational Christian Service Committee [*Superseded by UCBWM*] (EA) .... CCSC
Congregational Church Aid (SAUO) .... CCA
Congregational Church in England and Wales (BI) .... CCEW
Congregational Churches Fellowship [*Australia*] .... CCF
Congregational Council for World Mission (SAUO) .... CCWM
Congregational Historical Society (SAUO) .... CHS
Congregational Libraries Association of British Columbia (AC) .... CLABC
Congregational Publishing Society .... CPS
Congregational Publishing Society (SAUO) .... CPS
Congregational Union .... CU
Congregational Union of England and Wales (SAUO) .... CongU
Congregational Union of England and Wales (SAUO) .... CU
Congregational Union of England and Wales (SAUO) .... CUEW
Congregational Union of England and Wales (BARN) .... CUEW
Congregational Union of Scotland (SAUO) .... CUS
Congregational World Assembly of Youth (SAUO) .... C-WAY
Congregationalist [*Slang*] (DSUE) .... CONGO
Congregationalist Witchcraft Association Corporation (AC) .... CWA
Congregationis Missionum [*The Congregation of Lazarists*] (ROG) .... CM
Congregazione della Passione [*Congregation of the Passion*] (EAIO) .... CP
Congres Canadien pour la Promotion des Etudes chez la Femme [*Canadian Congress for Learning Opportunities for Women*] .... CCPEF
Congres des Psychanalystes de Langue Francaise [*Congress of Romance Language Psychoanalysts*] (EAIO) .... CPLF
Congres du Peuple Europeen .... CPE
Congres du Travail du Canada [*Canadian Labour Congress - CLC*] .... CTC
Congres Haitien Canada-Quebec (AC) .... CHCQ
Congres International des Editeurs [*International Congress of Publishers*] .... CIE
Congres International des Fabrications Mecaniques [*International Mechanical Engineering Congress*] .... CIM
Congres International des Sciences de l'Activite Physique [*International Congress of Physical Activity Sciences*] [*Canada*] .... CISAP
Congres International des Techniques de Vide en Recherche Spatiale [*International Congress for Vacuum Techniques in Space Research*] (PDAA) .... CIVRES
Congres Internationaux de Medecine Tropicale et de Paludisme [*International Congresses on Tropical Medicine and Malaria*] .... CIMTP
Congres Islamique Mondial .... CIM
Congres Juif Canadien [*Canadian Jewish Congress*] .... CJC
Congres Juif Mondial [*World Jewish Congress*] .... CJM
Congres Mondial Acadien (AC) .... CMA
Congres National d'Initiative Democratique [*Mali*] [*Political party*] (EY) .... CNID
Congres Panafricain du Cameroun [*Political party*] (EY) .... CPC
Congreso Nacional de Asuntos Colegiales (SAUO) .... CONAC
Congreso Nacional de Canarias [*Spain*] [*Political party*] (EY) .... CNC
Congreso Uniones Industriales de Puerto Rico .... PRCUI
Congress C
Congress (SAUO) C
Congress (SAUO) .... Cng
Congress .... CNGRS
Congress [*or Congressman*] .... CON
Congress (AFM) .... CONG
Congress (AAGC) .... Cong
Congress (SAUO) .... Cong
Congress (SAUO) .... Congr
Congress and Session Number (NITA) .... CS
Congress for Automotive Repair and Service .... CARS
Congress for Cultural Freedom [*British*] .... CCF
Congress for Cultural Freedom (SAUO) .... CCF
Congress for Democracy [*India*] .... CFD
Congress for Jewish Culture (EA) .... CJC
Congress for the Education of the Partially Seeing (AEBS) .... CEPS
Congress for the Unity of Black Students .... CUBS
Congress Liberation Party [*Nyasaland*] [*Political party*] .... CLP
Congress of African Peoples .... CAP

Congress of American Unions ... CAU
Congress of Arabic and Islamic Studies [*Madrid, Spain*] (EA) ... CAIS
Congress of Archaeological Society (SAUO) ... CAS
Congress of Astrological Organizations [*Defunct*] (EA) ... CAO
Congress of Cartographic Information Specialist Associations (GEOI) ... CCISA
Congress of County Medical Societies (EA) ... CCMS
Congress of Democratic Unions (AC) ... CDU
Congress of Democrats (SAUO) ... COD
Congress of Independent Unions (EA) ... CIU
Congress of Independent Unions ... COIU
Congress of Indian Trade Unions (SAUO) ... CITU
Congress of Industrial Organizations [*Later, AFL-CIO*] (GPO) ... CIO
Congress of Industrial Organizations, Political Action Committee [*Later, COPE*] ... CIOPAC
Congress of Industrial Organizations-Political Action Committee (SAUO) ... CIO-PAC
Congress of Irish Unions ... CIU
Congress of Italian-American Organizations ... CIAO
Congress of Joke-Abused Cities ... COJAC
Congress of Local and Regional Authorities of Europe (SAUO) ... CLARE
Congress of Lung Association Staff (EA) ... CLAS
Congress of National Black Churches (EA) ... CNBC
Congress of Neurological Surgeons (EA) ... CNS
Congress of Organizations of the Physically Handicapped (EA) ... COPH
Congress of Racial Equality (EA) ... CORE
Congress of racial Equality (SAUO) ... COrE
Congress of Russian Americans (EA) ... CRA
Congress of Scientists on Survival [*Inactive*] ... SOS
Congress of South African Trade Unions ... COSATU
Congress of Southeast Asian Librarians (EAIO) ... CONSAL
Congress of the International Theater Institute ... CITI
Congress of the People [*South Africa*] [*Political party*] (PPW) ... Cope
Congress of Unions of Employees in the Public and Civil Services [*Malaya*] ... CUEPACS
Congress of Unions of South Africa ... CUSA
Congress of Unrepresented People ... COUP
Congress of World Unity (EA) ... CWU
Congress on Ministry in Specialized Settings (NTPA) ... COMISS
Congress on Optimum Population and Environment (SAUO) ... COPE
Congress on Research in Dance (EA) ... CORD
Congress on Sedimentary Geology (SAUO) ... CSG
Congress Party [*India*] [*Political party*] ... CP
Congress Socialist Party (SAUO) ... CSP
Congress Task Force (EA) ... CTF
Congress Watch (EA) ... CW
Congressional (ROG) ... C
Congressional ... CNGRSNL
Congressional (AAGC) ... Cong
Congressional (ROG) ... CONG
Congressional ... CONGL
Congressional Action Fund (EA) ... CAF
Congressional Affairs Office (SAUS) ... CAO
Congressional Affairs Representative (SAUO) ... CAR
Congressional Agenda: 80's [*Later, CA: 90's*] (EA) ... CA: 80's
Congressional Agenda: 90's [*An association*] (EA) ... CA: 90's
Congressional Agricultural Committee (SAUO) ... CAC
Congressional Air Ltd. [*ICAO designator*] (FAAC) ... CGA
Congressional Alcohol Fuels Caucus (EA) ... CAFC
Congressional Arts Caucus (EA) ... CAC
Congressional Arts Caucus Education Program (EA) ... CACEP
Congressional Automotive Caucus (EA) ... CAC
Congressional Black Associates [*An association*] (EA) ... CBA
Congressional Black Caucus (EA) ... CBC
Congressional Border Caucus [*An association*] (EA) ... CBC
Congressional Budget Office [*Washington, DC*] ... CBO
Congressional Caucus for Women's Issues (EA) ... CC
Congressional Caucus for Women's Issues (EA) ... CCWI
Congressional Caucus on National Security (EA) ... CCNS
Congressional Clearinghouse on the Future (EA) ... CCF
Congressional Club (EA) ... CC
Congressional Coal Group (EA) ... CCG
Congressional Coalition for Soviet Jews (EA) ... CCSJ
Congressional Committee (SAUO) ... CONG
Congressional Committee on Atomic Energy (SAUO) ... CCAE
Congressional Committee on Science and Astronautics (SAUO) ... COMSAT
Congressional Committee Prints [*A publication*] (DLA) ... Comm Print
Congressional Competitiveness Caucus (EA) ... CCC
Congressional Crime Caucus [*Defunct*] (EA) ... CCC
Congressional Data Sheet (MCD) ... CDS
Congressional Debates [*United States*] [*A publication*] (DLA) ... Cong Deb
Congressional Delegate [*or Delegation*] (CINC) ... CODEL
Congressional Descriptive Summaries (RDA) ... CDS
Congressional Digest [*A publication*] (AAGC) ... Cong Dig
Congressional Digest, Washington, DC [*Library symbol*] [*Library of Congress*] (LCLS) ... DCD
Congressional District ... CD
Congressional District Data [*Bureau of the Census*] ... CDD
Congressional Economic Leadership Institute (EA) ... CELI
Congressional Education Associates [*Private, nonpartisan consulting group*] ... CEA
Congressional Election Cases [*United States*] [*A publication*] (DLA) ... Cong El Cas
Congressional Fact Paper [*Army*] ... CFP
Congressional Flying Service (SAA) ... CFS
Congressional Friends of Human Rights Monitors (EA) ... CFHRM
Congressional Globe [*A publication*] (DLA) ... Cong Gl
Congressional Globe [*A publication*] (DLA) ... Cong Globe
Congressional Hispanic Caucus (EA) ... CHC
Congressional Human Rights Caucus (EA) ... CHRC
Congressional Index (Commerce Clearing House) [*A publication*] (DLA) ... Cong Index (CCH)
Congressional Indexing Service (SAUO) ... CIS
Congressional Information Service [*Publisher*] (AAGC) ... CIS
Congressional Information Service, Bethesda, MD [*Library symbol*] [*Library of Congress*] (LCLS) ... MdBeCI
Congressional Information Service, Inc. [*Bethesda, MD*] [*Database producer*] [*Information service or system*] ... CIS
Congressional Information Sources, Inventories, and Directories (MCD) ... CISID
Congressional Information System (SAUO) ... CIS
Congressional Institute for the Future (EA) ... CIF
Congressional Interference ... CI
Congressional Liaison ... CL
Congressional Liaison Office ... CLO
Congressional Library (ROG) ... CONG LIB
Congressional Management Foundation (EA) ... CMF
Congressional Medal of Honor ... CMH
Congressional Medal of Honor Society (EA) ... CMHS
Congressional Monitoring Group on Southern Africa (EA) ... CMGSA
Congressional Office of Science and Technology ... COST
Congressional Office of Technology Assessment (SAUS) ... OTA
Congressional Office of the Budget ... COB
Congressional Presentation (SAUO) ... CP
Congressional Presentation Document ... CPD
Congressional Quarterly (AAGC) ... CQ
Congressional Quarterly, Inc. [*Washington, DC*] ... CQ
Congressional Quarterly, Inc. (SAUO) ... CQ
Congressional Quarterly Service [*A publisher*] [*Washington, D.C.*] (WDMC) ... CQ
Congressional Record [*A publication*] (AAGC) ... Cong Rec
Congressional Record (EEVL) ... CR
Congressional Record On-Line [*Capitol Services, Inc.*] [*Washington, DC*] [*Bibliographic database*] ... CRECORD
Congressional Relations (SAUO) ... CR
Congressional Relations Officer (SAUO) ... CRO
Congressional Report on Communications [*Arlington, VA*] [*A publication*] (TSSD) ... CRC
Congressional Reports Elimination Act ... CREA
Congressional Republicans (SAUO) ... CR
Congressional Research Center (SAUO) ... CICON
Congressional Research Service [*Formerly, Legislative Reference Service*] [*Washington, DC*] [*Library of Congress*] [*OCLC symbol*] ... CRS
Congressional Rural Caucus (EA) ... CRC
Congressional Session [*Online database field identifier*] ... CS
Congressional Space Caucus (EA) ... CSC
Congressional Staff Club (EA) ... CSC
Congressional Steel Caucus (EA) ... CSC
Congressional Textile Caucus (EA) ... CTC
Congressional Travel and Tourism Caucus (EA) ... CTTC
Congressional Underwater Explorers Club (EA) ... CUEC
Congressional Union (EA) ... CU
Congressional Wives for Soviet Jewry (EA) ... CWSJ
Congressionally Directed Medical Research Programs ... CDMRP
Congressionally Mandated Mobility Study [*DoD*] ... CMMS
Congressman ... Cong
Congressman ... CONGRSMAN
Congressus Internationalis Ornithologicus [*International Ornithological Congress - IOC*] (EA) ... CIO
Congruent (MSA) ... CONGR
Congruent Melting Point ... CMP
Conhairle Natsiunta Spoirt [*National Sports Council*] (EAIO) ... COSPOIR
Coniagas Mines Ltd. [*Toronto Stock Exchange symbol*] ... CO
Conic (ADA) ... CON
Conic Section (BARN) ... con sec
Conical (MSA) ... CONL
Conical Alignment Kit ... CAK
Conical Earth Sensor (SAUS) ... CES
Conical Fin ... COF
Conical Flow Field ... CFF
Conical Monopole Antenna ... CMA
Conical Monopole Antenna Kit ... CMAK
Conical Scan (NG) ... CONSCAN
Conical Scan Aerial (or Antenna) (SAUS) ... CSA
Conical Scan Antenna ... CSA
Conical Scanning Optical Microscope ... CSOM
Conical Scan-on-Receive Only (NG) ... COSRO
Conical Scan-on-Receive Only (CET) ... CSORO
Conical Shaped Charge (NASA) ... CSC
Conical Shaped Charge (NAKS) ... csc
Conical Shell Vibration ... CSV
Conical Shock Tube ... CST
Conical Side-Entry Sub (SAUS) ... CSES
Conical Tank [*Liquid gas carriers*] ... co
Conical-Monopulse Scan (SAUS) ... COMO Scan
Conico [*Race of maize*] ... CON
Conico Norteno [*Race of maize*] ... C-N
Coniectanea Biblica [*Lund*] [*A publication*] (BJA) ... ConBib
Coniectanea Neotestamentica [*Uppsala*] [*A publication*] (BJA) ... CnNT
Coniectanea Neotestamentica [*Uppsala*] [*A publication*] (BJA) ... ConiNT
Coniectanea Neotestamentica [*Uppsala*] [*A publication*] (BJA) ... ConNeot
Coniectanea Neotestamentica [*Uppsala*] [*A publication*] (BJA) ... ConNT
Conifair Aviation, Inc. [*Canada*] [*ICAO designator*] (FAAC) ... ROY

Coniferous (WDAA) ... C
Coniferous Forest Biome [*Ecological biogeographic study*] ... CFB
Coningsby [*British*] [*ICAO location identifier*] (ICLI) ... EGXC
Coningsby FTU [*British*] [*ICAO designator*] (FAAC) ... CBY
Coniston Branch, Nickel Centre Public Library, Ontario [*Library symbol*] [*National Library of Canada*] (NLC) ... OCNC
Coniunx [*Wife*] [*Latin*] (GPO) ... Con
Conization [*Of the cervix*] [*Gynecology*] (DAVI) ... cone
Conization [*Gynecology*] (DAVI) ... coniz
Conjectanea Neotestamentica [*A publication*] (BJA) ... CN
Conjectural (ADA) ... CJ
Conjecture (GEAB) ... conject
Conjoined Twins (MELL) ... CT
Conjoint Family Therapy (MELL) ... CFT
Conjoint Society of Massage and Medical Gymnastics [*British*] ... CSMMG
Conjugable Oxidation Product [*Fuel technology*] ... COP
conjugal (SAUS) ... conj
Conjugal Rights (MELL) ... CR
Conjugata Diagonalis [*Pelvic measurement*] [*Anatomy*] ... CD
Conjugata Vera [*Conjugate diameter of pelvic inlet*] [*Anatomy*] ... CV
Conjugata Vera Obstetrica [*Conjugate diameter of pelvic inlet*] [*Anatomy*] ... CVO
conjugate (SAUS) ... conj
Conjugate Acid-Base Pair [*Chemistry*] ... CABP
Conjugate (Counter) Base [*Chemistry*] ... CB
Conjugate Diameter (DB) ... CD
Conjugate Filter Data Link ... CONFIDAL
Conjugate Gradient (IAA) ... CG
Conjugate Gradient Method of Approximate Programming ... CGMAP
Conjugate Gradient Optimization Algorithm Program [*Lighting system design*] ... CGOAP
Conjugate Structure Algebraic Code Excited Linear Prediction (SAUS) ... CS-ACELP
Conjugated Bile Salts (MELL) ... CBS
Conjugated Bilirubin [*Chemistry*] ... Bc
Conjugated Bilirubin [*Gastroenterology and neonatology*] (DAVI) ... BILI-C
Conjugated Diene Hydroperoxide (SAUS) ... CDHP
Conjugated Equine Estrogen [*Endocrinology*] ... CEE
Conjugated Estrogen Substance [*Medicine*] (MELL) ... CES
Conjugated Estrogens [*Endocrinology*] ... CE
Conjugated Linoleic Acid [*Antineoplastic drug*] ... CLA
Conjugation (WGA) ... C
Conjugation ... CONJ
Conjugation (SAUS) ... Conj
Conjugation (ADA) ... CONJUG
Conjugation Factor [*Plant genetics*] ... CF
Conjugation-Parity [*Physics*] ... CP
Conjugation-Parity Asymmetry [*Physics*] ... CPA
Conjugi [*To My Spouse*] [*Latin*] ... COI
Conjugi Optimo [*To My Most Excellent Spouse*] [*Latin*] ... CO
Conjunction ... CJ
Conjunction [*Grammar*] (ROG) ... CON
Conjunction ... CONJ
Conjunction (VRA) ... conj
Conjunction (SAUS) ... Conj
Conjunctiva [*Ophthalmology*] (DAVI) ... conj
Conjunctiva [*Ophthalmology*] (DAVI) ... conjunc
Conjunctiva and Sclera [*Ophthalmology*] ... C & S
Conjunctival Intraepithelial Neoplasia [*Medicine*] (MELL) ... CIEN
Conjunctival Intraepithelial Neoplasia (SAUS) ... CIN
Conjunctival Secretion [*Ophthalmology*] (DAVI) ... CS
Conjunctival Secretions [*Medicine*] (MEDA) ... CS
Conjunctive (ADWA) ... conj
Conjunctive Alteration File ... CAF
Conjunctive Alteration Indicator ... CAI
Conjunctive Alterations File (SAUS) ... CAF
Conjunctive Normal Form (IDAI) ... CNF
Conjunctive Normal Formula ... CNF
Conjunctive Schedule of Reinforcement (DIPS) ... CONJ
Conjunctivitis [*Medicine*] (DMAA) ... CJ
Conjunctivitis [*Medicine*] ... CONJ
conjunctivitis (SAUS) ... conj
Conjux [*Consort, Spouse*] [*Genealogy*] ... CON
Conklin Community School, Alberta [*Library symbol*] [*National Library of Canada*] (BIB) ... ACONS
Conklin Elementary School, Rockford, IL [*Library symbol*] [*Library of Congress*] (LCLS) ... IRoCoE
Conklin, NY [*FM radio station call letters*] (BROA) ... WCDW-FM
Conklin, NY [*FM radio station call letters*] (RBYB) ... WMTT
Conkling's Admiralty [*A publication*] (DLA) ... Conk Adm
Conkling's Executive Powers [*A publication*] (DLA) ... Conk Ex Pow
Conkling's Iowa Justice of the Peace [*A publication*] (DLA) ... Conk JP
Conkling's Treatise on Jurisdiction and Practice of the United States Courts [*A publication*] (DLA) ... Conk Treat
Conkling's Treatise on Jurisdiction and Practice of the United States Courts [*A publication*] (DLA) ... Conk US Pr
CONMED Corp. [*NASDAQ symbol*] (NQ) ... CNMD
Conmed Corp. [*Associated Press*] (SAG) ... Conmed
Conn. State Board of Labor Relations (SAUS) ... SBLR
Connair [*ICAO designator*] (AD) ... CK
Connaissement [*Bill of Lading*] [*Legal term*] [*French*] ... CONNT
Connaitre la Bible [*Bruges*] [*A publication*] (BJA) ... CIB
Connaught Biosciences, Inc. [*Toronto Stock Exchange symbol*] ... CSE
Connaught Laboratories, Inc. ... CLI
Connaught Laboratories Ltd., Willowdale, Ontario [*Library symbol*] [*National Library of Canada*] (NLC) ... OTCL
Connaught Medical Research Laboratories, Toronto, ON, Canada [*Library symbol*] [*Library of Congress*] (LCLS) ... CaOTCL
Connaught Rangers [*Military*] [*British*] (DAS) ... Conn R
Connaught Rangers (SAUO) ... ConnR
Connaught Rangers [*Military*] [*British*] (ROG) ... CONN RANG
Connaught Rangers [*Military*] [*British*] ... CR
Connaught Rangers (SAUO) ... CR
Connaught Regional Airport [*Ireland*] [*ICAO location identifier*] (ICLI) ... EIKN
Conneaut Elementary School, Bowling Green, OH [*Library symbol*] [*Library of Congress*] (LCLS) ... OBgCE
Conneaut, OH [*FM radio station call letters*] ... WGOJ
Conneaut, OH [*AM radio station call letters*] ... WWOW
Connect (FAAC) ... CNCT
Connect (SAUS) ... Conn
Connect Acknowledge (SAUS) ... CA
Connect Acknowledge (SAUS) ... CONN ACK
Connect Confirmation (ACRL) ... CC
Connect Data Set to Line [*Computer science*] (IAA) ... CDSL
Connect, Inc. [*NASDAQ symbol*] (SAG) ... CNKT
Connect, Inc. [*Associated Press*] (SAG) ... Connct
Connect Request (ACRL) ... CR
Connectair [*ICAO designator*] (AD) ... AX
Connectair Charters Ltd. [*Canada*] [*ICAO designator*] (FAAC) ... BSN
Connected (ROG) ... CONN
Connected Case [*Different case from case cited but arising out of same subject matter or intimately connected therewith*] [*Used in Shepard's Citations*] [*Legal term*] (DLA) ... cc
Connected Client (SAUS) ... CC
Connected Family Environment (SAUS) ... CFE
Connected Internet Device (RALS) ... CID
Connected Line Identification Presentation (SAUS) ... COLP
Connected Line Identification Restriction (SAUS) ... CLIR
Connected Name Identification Presentation (SAUS) ... CONP
Connected Name Identification Restriction (SAUS) ... CNIR
Connected Network Backup [*Computer science*] ... CNB
Connected Network of Adaptive Processors System ... CNAPS
Connected Online Backup [*Computer science*] ... COB
Connected Replenishment [*Military*] (NVT) ... CONREP
Connected Speech Recognition (MCD) ... CSR
Connected Two-Color Simulated Photon Echo [*Spectroscopy*] ... C2CSE
Connected With (IAA) ... CW
Connecticut (ROG) ... CON
Connecticut ... CONN
Connecticut (ODBW) ... Conn
Connecticut [*Postal code*] ... CT
Connecticut [*MARC country of publication code*] [*Library of Congress*] (LCCP) ... ctu
Connecticut [*MARC geographic area code*] [*Library of Congress*] (LCCP) ... n-us-ct
Connecticut Academy of Arts and Sciences (SAUO) ... CAAS
Connecticut Academy of Family Physicians (SRA) ... CAFP
Connecticut Academy of Science and Engineering (SRA) ... CASE
Connecticut Advanced Nuclear Engineering Laboratory ... CANEL
Connecticut Aeronautical Historical Association (SAUO) ... CAHA
Connecticut Agricultural Experiment Station ... CAES
Connecticut Agricultural Experiment Station, New Haven, CT [*Library symbol*] [*Library of Congress*] (LCLS) ... CtNhAS
Connecticut Aircraft Nuclear Experiment (NRCH) ... CANE
Connecticut Ambulance Association (SRA) ... CAA
Connecticut Art Directors Club (SRA) ... CADC
Connecticut Artificial Breeding Association (SAUO) ... CABA
Connecticut Assessment of Educational Progress (EDAC) ... CAEP
Connecticut Association for Home Care (SRA) ... CAHC
Connecticut Association for Human Services (SRA) ... CAHS
Connecticut Association of Boards of Education (SRA) ... CABE
Connecticut Association of Child Caring Agencies (SRA) ... CACCA
Connecticut Association of Health Sciences Libraries [*Library network*] ... CAHSL
Connecticut Association of Independent Schools (SAUO) ... CAIS
Connecticut Association of Land Surveyors (SRA) ... CALS
Connecticut Association of Metal Finishers (SRA) ... CAMF
Connecticut Association of Not-for-Profit Providers for the Aging (SRA) ... CANPFA
Connecticut Association of Optometrists (SRA) ... CAO
Connecticut Association of Professional Accountants (SRA) ... CAPA
Connecticut Association of Public School Superintendents (SRA) ... CAPSS
Connecticut Association of Purchasing Management (SRA) ... CAPM
Connecticut Association of Realtors (SRA) ... CAR
Connecticut Association of Residential Facilities (SRA) ... CARF
Connecticut Association of Schools (SRA) ... CAS
Connecticut Association of Third Party Administrators (SRA) ... CATPA
Connecticut Audio-Visual Education Association (SAUO) ... CAVEA
Connecticut Automotive Trades Association (SRA) ... CATA
Connecticut Ballet Theatre ... CBT
Connecticut Bank & Trust Co. (MHDW) ... CBT
Connecticut Bankers Association (SRA) ... CBA
Connecticut Bar Association (SRA) ... CBA
Connecticut Board of Title Underwriters (SAUO) ... CBTU
Connecticut Botanical Society (SAUS) ... CBS
Connecticut Botanical Society, Inc. (SAUO) ... CBS
Connecticut Broadcasters Association (SRA) ... CBA
Connecticut Building Congress (SRA) ... CBC
Connecticut Business and Industry Association (SRA) ... CBIA
Connecticut Campground Owners Association (SRA) ... CCOA
Connecticut Catholic Hospital Council (SRA) ... CCHC
Connecticut Census Data Center [*Connecticut State Office of Policy and Management*] [*Information service or system*] (IID) ... CCDC

Connecticut Chemosensory Clinical Research Center [*University of Connecticut*] [*Research center*] (RCD) ...... CCCRC
Connecticut Christmas Tree Growers (SRA) ...... CCTGA
Connecticut Circuit Court Reports [*A publication*] (DLA) ...... Cir
Connecticut Circuit Court Reports [*A publication*] (DLA) ...... Conn Cir
Connecticut Circuit Court Reports [*A publication*] (DLA) ...... Conn Cir Ct
Connecticut Citizens Political Action Committee (SAUO) ...... CCPAAC
Connecticut College (SAUO) CC
Connecticut College (GAGS) ...... Conn C
Connecticut College, New London, CT [*OCLC symbol*] (OCLC) ...... CTL
Connecticut College, New London, CT [*Library symbol*] [*Library of Congress*] (LCLS) ...... CtNIC
Connecticut College of Emergency Physicians (SRA) ...... CCEP
Connecticut Community Bankers (TBD) ...... CCB
Connecticut Community Providers Association (SRA) ...... CCPA
Connecticut Community Tech College Athletic Association (PSS) ...... CCTCAA
Connecticut Compensation Commissioners, Compendium of Awards [*A publication*] (DLA) ...... Conn Comp Com
Connecticut Conference of Municipalities (SRA) ...... CCM
Connecticut Consolidated Industries (SAUO) CCI
Connecticut Constitution [*A publication*] (DLA) ...... Conn Const
Connecticut Construction Exposition [*Key Productions, Inc.*] (TSPED) ...... CONEX
Connecticut Construction Industries Association (SRA) ...... CCIA
Connecticut Credit Union League (SRA) ...... CCUL
Connecticut Decisions [*A publication*] (DLA) ...... Conn Dec
Connecticut Department of Environmental Protection ...... CTDEP
Connecticut Department of Forestry (SAUS) ...... CDF
Connecticut Education Association (SRA) ...... CEA
Connecticut Educational Media Association ...... CEMA
Connecticut Educators Computer Association ...... CECA
Connecticut Electric Association (SRA) ...... CEA
Connecticut Energy [*NYSE symbol*] (TTSB) ...... CNE
Connecticut Energy Corp. [*NYSE symbol*] (SPSG) ...... CNE
Connecticut Energy Corp. [*Associated Press*] (SAG) ...... ConnEn
Connecticut Farm Bureau Association (SRA) ...... CFBA
Connecticut Film Circuit [*Library network*] ...... CFC
Connecticut Florists Association (SRA) ...... CFA
Connecticut Food Association (SRA) ...... CFA
Connecticut Forest and Park Association, Inc. (SAUO) ...... CFPA
Connecticut General Mortgaging & Realty Investments (SAUO) ...... CGM
Connecticut General Statutes, Annotated [*A publication*] (DLA) ...... CGSA
Connecticut General Statutes, Annotated [*A publication*] (DLA) ...... Conn Gen Stat Ann
Connecticut Geological and Natural History Survey (GEOI) ...... CGNHS
Connecticut Guild of Craftsmen (SRA) ...... CGC
Connecticut Heating and Cooling Contractors Association (SRA) ...... CHCC
Connecticut Herpetological Society (SAUO) ...... CHS
Connecticut Historical Society (SAUO) ...... CHS
Connecticut Historical Society Bulletin (journ.) (SAUS) ...... CHSB
Connecticut Historical Society, Hartford, CT [*Library symbol*] [*Library of Congress*] (LCLS) ...... CtHi
Connecticut Horticultural Society (SAUO) ...... CHS
Connecticut Hospital Association (SRA) ...... CHA
Connecticut Industrial Arts Association (EDAC) ...... CIAA
Connecticut Institute of Water Resources [*Storrs, CT*] [*Department of the Interior*] (GRD) ...... IWR
Connecticut Irrigation Contractors (SRA) ...... CICA
Connecticut Law Journal [*Administrative Rules*] (AAGC) ...... Conn L J
Connecticut League for Nursing (SRA) ...... CLN
Connecticut Leather Co. [*Original name of Coleco Industries*] ...... COLECO
Connecticut Legislative Service (West) [*A publication*] (DLA) ...... Conn Legis Serv
Connecticut Library Association (SAUO) ...... CLA
Connecticut Light & Power Co. ...... CL & P
Connecticut Medicine (journ.) (SAUS) ...... Conn Med
Connecticut Mental Health Center, New Haven, CT [*Library symbol*] [*Library of Congress*] (LCLS) ...... CtNhMH
Connecticut Mutual Life Insurance Co. ...... CM
Connecticut Nat Gas [*NYSE symbol*] (TTSB) ...... CTG
Connecticut Natural Gas Corp. ...... CNG
Connecticut Natural Gas Corp. [*Associated Press*] (SAG) ...... ConnNG
Connecticut Natural Gas Corp. [*NYSE symbol*] (SPSG) ...... CTG
Connecticut Nurserymen's Association (SRA) ...... CNA
Connecticut Nurses Association (SRA) ...... CNA
Connecticut On-Line Law-Enforcement Communications and Teleprocessing [*Computer law-enforcement system*] ...... COLLECT
Connecticut Opticians Association (SRA) ...... COA
Connecticut Pharmaceutical Association (SAUO) ...... CPA
Connecticut Podiatric Medical Association (SRA) ...... CPMA
Connecticut Primary Care Association (SRA) ...... CPCA
Connecticut Psychiatric Society (SRA) ...... CPS
Connecticut Public Acts [*A publication*] (DLA) ...... Conn Pub Acts
Connecticut Public and Special Acts (DLA) ...... Conn Acts
Connecticut Public Expenditure Council (SAUO) ...... CPEC
Connecticut Reports [*A publication*] (DLA) ...... Connecticut R
Connecticut Reports [*A publication*] (DLA) ...... Connecticut Rep
Connecticut Reports [*A publication*] (DLA) ...... Connect Rep
Connecticut Reports [*A publication*] (DLA) ...... Conn R
Connecticut Reports [*A publication*] (DLA) ...... Conn Rep
Connecticut Reports [*A publication*] (DLA) ...... Conn Reports
Connecticut Reports [*A publication*] (DLA) ...... CT
Connecticut Reports, by Day [*1802-13*] [*A publication*] (DLA) ...... Day(Conn)
Connecticut Resources Recovery Authority (SAUS) ...... CRRA
Connecticut River Watershed Council (EA) ...... CRWC
Connecticut Society for Mental Hygiene Inc. (SAUO) ...... CSMH
Connecticut Society of Certified Public Accountants (SRA) ...... CSCPA

Connecticut Society of Civil Engineers, Inc. (SAUO) ...... CSCE
Connecticut Society of Emergency Medical Services Instructors (SAUO) ...... CSEMSI
Connecticut Society of Eye Physicians (SRA) ...... CSEP
Connecticut Society of Oral Surgeons (SRA) ...... CSOS
Connecticut Society of Professional Engineers (SRA) ...... CSPE
Connecticut Special Acts [*A publication*] (DLA) ...... Conn Spec Acts
Connecticut State Association of Life Underwriters (SRA) ...... CSALU
Connecticut State Dental Association (SRA) ...... CSDA
Connecticut State Department of Health, Hartford, CT [*Library symbol*] [*Library of Congress*] (LCLS) ...... Ct-H
Connecticut State Library, Hartford, CT [*Library symbol*] [*Library of Congress*] (LCLS) ...... Ct
Connecticut State Library, Hartford, CT [*OCLC symbol*] (OCLC) ...... CZL
Connecticut State Medical Society (SAUO) ...... CSMS
Connecticut State University (SAUO) ...... CSU
Connecticut Suburban and Shoreline Educational Computer Center (SAUO) ...... COSSECC
Connecticut Supplement [*A publication*] (DLA) ...... Conn S
Connecticut Supplement [*A publication*] (DLA) ...... Conn Sup
Connecticut Supplement [*A publication*] (DLA) ...... Conn Supp
Connecticut Supplement [*A publication*] (DLA) ...... CS
Connecticut Technical Council (SAUO) ...... CTC
Connecticut Track Conference (PSS) ...... CTTC
Connecticut Transportation Authority (SAUS) ...... CTA
Connecticut Treatment Corp. (EFIS) ...... CTC
Connecticut Union of Telephone Workers ...... CUTW
Connecticut United for Research Excellence (GVA) ...... CURE
Connecticut Valley Historical Museum, Springfield, MA [*Library symbol*] [*Library of Congress*] (LCLS) ...... MSCV
Connecticut Valley Power Exchange (SAUO) ...... CONVEX
Connecticut Water Service, Inc. [*Associated Press*] (SAG) ...... ConnWt
Connecticut Water Service, Inc. [*NASDAQ symbol*] (NQ) ...... CTWS
Connecticut Workmen's Compensation Decisions [*A publication*] (DLA) ...... Conn Comp Dec
Connecticut Wtr Svc [*NASDAQ symbol*] (TTSB) ...... CTWS
Connecticut Yankee Atomic Power Co. (SAUO) ...... CYAPC
Connecticut Yankee Station [*Nuclear energy*] (NUCP) ...... CY
Connecticutensis Academiae Socius [*Fellow of the Connecticut Academy of Arts and Sciences*] ...... CAS
Connecting (ECII) ...... CCTG
Connecting Arrangement [*Telecommunications*] ...... CA
Connecting Block [*Telecommunications*] (TEL) ...... CB
Connecting Card Perforator (SAUS) ...... CCP
Connecting Carrier CC
Connecting Circuit [*Electronics*] (IAA) ...... CCT
Connecting Circuit to Push-button-dialling Receiver (SAUS) ...... CCPR
Connecting Device (IAA) ...... CD
Connecting Devices, Incorporated (ACAE) ...... CDI
Connecting Line CL
Connecting Line Freight ...... CLF
Connecting Link for Application and Source Peripherals [*Computer science*] ...... CLASP
Connecting Machine (IAA) ...... CM
Connecting Post (SAUS) ...... CP
Connecting-Rod ...... CONNROD
Connecting-Rod ...... CONROD
Connection (NFPA) C
Connection ...... CON
Connection (AABC) ...... CONEC
Connection (SAUS) ...... Conn
Connection ...... CONNECT
Connection [*Technical drawings*] CX
Connection Activation (SAUS) ...... CA
Connection Admission Control [*Telecommunications*] (ACRL) ...... CAC
Connection Arrangement Unit (SAUS) ...... CAU
Connection Board (SAUS) ...... CONN BD
Connection Busy (SAUS) ...... CB
Connection Confirm (SAUS) CC
Connection Control Entity (SAUS) ...... CCE
Connection Control Function (VERA) ...... CCF
Connection Control Language [*Computer science*] CCL
Connection Conversion ...... CONVERS
Connection Co-Processor Application Manager [*Computer science*] ...... CCAM
Connection Diagram (SAUS) ...... conn diag
Connection Director (SAUS) ...... CD
Connection End Point (SAUS) ...... CEP
Connection Endpoint (VERA) ...... CE
Connection Endpoint Identifier [*Telecommunications*] (ACRL) ...... CEI
Connection Establishment (MCD) ...... CONESTAB
Connection Fitting Out [*Navy*] ...... CFO
Connection Identification (SAUS) ...... CID
Connection Information Distribution (SAUS) ...... CID
Connection Interface Module (SAUS) ...... CIM
Connection Less mode (SAUS) CL
Connection Machine [*Naval Research Laboratory*] (PS) ...... CM
Connection Machine 2 (SAUS) CM-2
Connection Machine 5 (SAUS) CM-5
Connection Machine 5 (VERA) CM5
Connection Machine Scientific Software Library (SAUS) ...... CMSSL
Connection Management [*Computer science*] (VERA) ...... CM
Connection Management (SAUS) ...... CMT
Connection Management System (SAUS) ...... CMS
Connection Manager (ACRL) ...... CM
Connection Manager Interface [*IBM Corp.*] (VERA) ...... CMI

Connection Matrix (SAUS) .... CM
Connection Mode Network Service (SAUS) .... CMNS
Connection Naval Air Reserve Training Program .... CONARESTRAPROG
Connection Naval Reserve Program (SAUO) .... CONAVRESPROG
Connection Network Simulator (SAUS) .... CNSIM
Connection Not Possible (SAUS) .... CNP
Connection Not Successful (SAUS) .... CNS
Connection Optimized Link Technology [*Computer science*] .... COLT
Connection Orientated Internet Packet eXchange (SAUS) .... COIPX
Connection Oriented Data [*Computer science*] (VERA) .... COD
Connection Oriented Networking Session (SAUS) .... CONS
Connection Pending [*Telecommunications*] (TEL) .... CP
Connection Point [*Computer science*] (IBMDP) .... CP
Connection Point Manager (SAUS) .... CPM
Connection Processor [*Computer science*] (VERA) .... CP
Connection Reactivation .... CONVATE
Connection Refused (SAUS) .... CREF
Connection Related Function Virtual Channel [*Computer science*] (VERA) .... CRFVC
Connection Related Function Virtual Path [*Computer science*] (VERA) .... CRFVP
Connection Request [*Computer science*] (TNIG) .... CR
Connection Request Mode (SAUS) .... CRM
Connection Switching (SAUS) .... CS
Connection Table to Coordinates [*Data analysis*] .... CONCORD
ConnectionLess (VERA) CL
Connectionless (SAUS) CL
Connectionless Acknowledged Information .... CAI
Connectionless Broadband Data Service [*Telecommunications*] .... CBDS
Connectionless Broadband Data Service (SAUS) .... CBMS
Connectionless Data Bearer Service (VERA) .... CDBS
Connectionless Data Transmission [*Telecommunications*] (OSI) .... CDT
Connectionless Layer [*Computer science*] (VERA) CLL
Connectionless Mode Network Protocol [*Telecommunications*] (OSI) .... CLNP
Connectionless Mode Network Service [*Telecommunications*] (OSI) .... CLNS
Connectionless Network Access Protocol [*Computer science*] (VERA) .... CLNAP
Connectionless Network Layer Protocol (SAUS) .... CNLP
Connectionless Network Protocol .... CLNP
Connectionless Network Service [*Telecommunications*] (ACRL) .... CLNS
Connectionless Server (SAUS) .... CLS
Connectionless Service (SAUS) CL
Connectionless Service Function [*Computer science*] (VERA) .... CLSF
Connectionless Transport Protocol [*Computer science*] (VERA) .... CLTP
Connectionless Transport Service [*Computer science*] (TNIG) .... CLTS
Connectionless-Mode Transport Service [*Telecommunications*] (ACRL) .... CLTS
Connection-Oriented (ACRL) .... CO
Connection-Oriented Network Protocol [*Computer science*] .... CONP
Connection-Oriented Network Service [*Telecommunications*] (OSI) .... CONS
Connection-Oriented Transport Protocol [*Computer science*] (VERA) .... COTP
Connection-Oriented Transport Service [*Computer science*] (VERA) .... COTS
Connection-Related Function [*Telecommunications*] .... CRF
Connections per Circuit per Hour [*Telecommunications*] (TEL) .... CCH
Connective (SAUS) .... Conn
Connective Instruction (SAUS) CI
Connective Operation (SAUS) .... CO
Connective Therapeutics [*NASDAQ symbol*] (TTSB) .... CNCT
Connective Therapeutics, Inc. [*NASDAQ symbol*] (SAG) .... CNCT
Connective Therapeutics, Inc. [*Associated Press*] (SAG) .... Connect
Connective Tissue .... CT
Connective Tissue Activating Peptide [*Medicine*] (MELL) .... CTAP
Connective Tissue Massage [*Medicine*] .... CTM
Connective Tissue Oncology Society (SAUO) .... CTOS
Connective-Tissue Disease [*Medicine*] .... CTD
Connective-Tissue Growth Factor [*Biochemistry*] .... CTGF
Connective-Tissue-Type Mast Cell [*Cytology*] .... CTMC
Connectivity Language/1 [*Apple*] (CDE) CL/1
Connectivity Table [*Computer science*] .... CT
Connector (KSC) .... CONN
Connector Backing Shell .... CBS
Connector Bracket Experiment (MCD) .... CBE
Connector Bracket (Power) (MCD) .... CBP
Connector Bracket Signal (MCD) .... CBS
Connector Circuit CC
Connector Data Base [*Aviation*] .... CDB
Connector Electronics (SAUS) .... CONNECTRONICS
Connector for Networked Information Transfer [*Massachusetts Institute of Technology*] [*Information service or system*] (IID) .... CONIT
Connector Panel .... CP
Connector Plug (SAUS) .... CON PL
Connector Position Assurance [*Automotive electronics*] .... CPA
Connector Register (SAUS) .... CR
Connector Replacement (MCD) .... CR
Connector Socket (SAUS) .... CON SKT
Connectorized Exchange Cable Splicing [*Telecommunications*] (TEL) .... CONECS
Connectors (SAUS) .... Conns
Connects [*Macintosh*] [*Computer science*] .... Ke:nx
Connel [*Washington*] [*Seismograph station code, US Geological Survey*] (SEIS) .... CNL
Connell on Parishes [*A publication*] (DLA) .... Con Par
Connellan Airways Ltd. .... CONN
Connellsville, PA [*Location identifier*] [*FAA*] (FAAL) .... COV
Connellsville, PA [*Location identifier*] [*FAA*] (FAAL) .... VVS
Connellsville, PA [*AM radio station call letters*] .... WCVI
Conner and Lawson's Irish Chancery Reports [*1841-43*] [*A publication*] (DLA) .... C & L
Conner Peripherals, Inc. (MHDW) .... CNNR
Conner Peripherals, Inc. [*NYSE symbol*] (SPSG) .... CNR
Conner Peripherals, Inc. [*Associated Press*] (SAG) .... ConrPr
Conners Teaching Rating Scale .... CTRS
Connersville, IN [*Location identifier*] [*FAA*] (FAAL) CV
Connersville, IN [*AM radio station call letters*] .... WCNB
Connersville, IN [*AM radio station call letters*] .... WIFE
Connersville, IN [*FM radio station call letters*] (BROA) .... WIFE-FM
Connersville News-Examiner, Connersville, IN [*Library symbol*] [*Library of Congress*] (LCLS) .... InCoNE
Connersville Public Library, Connersville, IN [*Library symbol*] [*Library of Congress*] (LCLS) .... InCo
Connetquot High School, Bohemia, NY [*Library symbol*] [*Library of Congress*] (LCLS) .... NBohCH
Connetquot Public Library, Bohemia, NY [*Library symbol*] [*Library of Congress*] (LCLS) .... NBoh
Connexin (DMAA) CX
Connexional Candidates Board (SAUO) .... CCB
Connie Causey Fan Club (EA) .... CCFC
Connie Francis Fan Club [*Defunct*] (EA) .... CFFC
Connie Stevens Fan Club (EA) .... CSFC
Conning Director [*Navy*] .... CD
Conning Tower [*Naval architecture*] .... CONTWR
Conning Tower (SAUS) .... CT
Connoisseur Country Range furniture (SAUS) .... CCR furniture
Connolly Elementary School, Glen Cove, NY [*Library symbol*] [*Library of Congress*] (LCLS) .... NGlcCoE
Connoly's New York Surrogate Reports [*A publication*] (DLA) .... Con
Connoly's New York Surrogate Reports [*A publication*] (DLA) .... Conn
Connoly's New York Surrogate Reports [*A publication*] (DLA) .... Connoly
Connoly's New York Surrogate Reports [*A publication*] (DLA) .... Connoly Sur Rep
Connoly's New York Surrogate Reports [*A publication*] (DLA) .... Connoly Surr Rep
Connoly's New York Surrogate Reports [*A publication*] (DLA) .... Conn Surr
Connoly's New York Surrogate Reports [*A publication*] (DLA) .... Conn Surr Rep
Connoly's New York Surrogate Reports [*A publication*] (DLA) .... Con Sur
Connoly's New York Surrogate Reports [*A publication*] (DLA) .... Cy
Connor and Lawson's Irish Chancery Reports [*1841-43*] [*A publication*] (DLA) .... Con & L
Connor and Lawson's Irish Chancery Reports [*1841-43*] [*A publication*] (DLA) .... Con & Law
Connor and Lawson's Irish Chancery Reports [*1841-43*] [*A publication*] (DLA) .... Connor & L
Connor and Simonton's South Carolina Digest [*A publication*] (DLA) .... C & S Dig
Connor and Simonton's South Carolina Equity Digest [*A publication*] (DLA) .... Con & Sim
Connor-Jasper Middle School, Bovey, MN [*Library symbol*] [*Library of Congress*] (LCLS) .... MnBovM
Connor's Irish Digest [*A publication*] (DLA) .... Con Dig
Connors State Agricultural College [*Oklahoma*] .... CSAC
Connot Find (SAUS) .... CF
Connotation .... CONN
Connotation (ADWA) .... conn
Connradh na Gaedhilge [*The Gaelic League, founded in 1893*] .... CG
Conoco, Inc., Law Library, Houston, TX [*Library symbol*] [*Library of Congress*] (LCLS) .... TxHCC-L
Conoco, Inc., North American Exploration Headquarters, Houston, TX [*Library symbol*] [*Library of Congress*] (LCLS) .... TxHCC-N
Conococheague District Library, Chambersburg, PA [*Library symbol*] [*Library of Congress*] (LCLS) .... PChCo
Conococheague District Library, Chambersburg, PA [*OCLC symbol*] (OCLC) .... PCO
Conodont Alteration Index (SAUS) .... CAI
Conolog Corp. [*NASDAQ symbol*] (SAG) .... CNLG
Conolog Corp. [*Associated Press*] (SAG) .... Conolg
Conolog Corp. [*Associated Press*] (SAG) .... Conolog
Conolog Corp. Unit [*NASDAQ symbol*] (TTSB) .... CNLGU
Conolog Corp. Wrrt'A' [*NASDAQ symbol*] (TTSB) .... CNLGW
Conoseal Pipe Joint .... CPJ
Conover's Digested Index [*Ohio, Indiana, and Illinois*] [*A publication*] (DLA) .... Con Dig Ind
Conover's Reports [*Wisconsin*] [*A publication*] (DLA) .... Con
Conover's Reports [*Wisconsin*] [*A publication*] (DLA) .... Conover
Conpac Resources Ltd. [*Vancouver Stock Exchange symbol*] .... CPQ
Conpak Seafoods, Inc. [*Toronto Stock Exchange symbol*] .... CPQ
Conquer [*or Conqueror*] (WDAA) .... CONQ
Conquering Hero [*British, for returning soldiers*] .... CH
Conquest (ROG) .... CONQ
Conquest Airlines Corp. [*ICAO designator*] (FAAC) .... CAC
Conquest Inds Wrrt [*NASDAQ symbol*] (TTSB) .... CAIRW
Conquest Industries Corp. [*NASDAQ symbol*] (SAG) .... CAIR
Conquest Industries Corp. [*Associated Press*] (SAG) .... Cngln
Conquest Industries Corp. [*Associated Press*] (SAG) .... Cnqln
Conquest Industries Corp. [*Associated Press*] (SAG) .... Conqlnd
Conquest of Cancer Act (SAUS) .... CCA
Conquest of Hunger Program [*Rockefeller Foundation*] (EA) .... CHP
Conqueyrac [*France*] [*ICAO location identifier*] (ICLI) .... LFNI
Conquista [*Brazil*] [*Airport symbol*] (OAG) .... COQ
Conquistador .... CONQUISDR
Conrac Corp. (SAUO) .... CAX
Conrad Grebel College Institute for Peace and Conflict Studies (SAUO) .... IPACS
Conrad, MT [*Location identifier*] [*FAA*] (FAAL) .... CRD
Conrad, MT [*FM radio station call letters*] (BROA) .... KEIN-FM
Conrad Public Library, Conrad, IA [*Library symbol*] [*Library of Congress*] (LCLS) .... IaCon
Conrad Public Library, Conrad, MT [*Library symbol*] [*Library of Congress*] (LCLS) .... MtCon

Conrad Record, Conrad, IA [*Library symbol*] [*Library of Congress*] (LCLS) .... IaConR
Conrad Technologies, Inc. .... CTI
Conrad Veidt Society (EA) .... CVS
Conradi-Huenermann [*Syndrome*] [*Medicine*] (DB) .... CH
Conradson Carbon Residue Test [*for petroleum products*] .... CCR
Conradson Carbon Test (SAUS) .... CCT
CONRAIL [*Consolidated Rail Corp.*] **Analysis Model** [*Computer science*] .... CRAM
Conrail, Inc. [*Associated Press*] (SAG) .... Conrail
Conrail, Inc. [*NYSE symbol*] (SPSG) .... CRR
Conrock Co. (SAUO) .... CRZ
Conroe Aviation Services, Inc. [*ICAO designator*] (FAAC) .... CXO
Conroe, TX [*Location identifier*] [*FAA*] (FAAL) .... CXO
Conroe, TX [*AM radio station call letters*] (BROA) .... KCHC
Conroe, TX [*FM radio station call letters*] (RBYB) .... KCHC-FM
Conroe, TX [*TV station call letters*] (RBYB) .... KHIM-TV
Conroe, TX [*AM radio station call letters*] .... KJOJ
Conroe, TX [*FM radio station call letters*] (RBYB) .... KKHT
Conroe, TX [*Television station call letters*] (BROA) .... KPXB
Conroe, TX [*AM radio station call letters*] .... KSSQ
Conroe, TX [*Television station call letters*] (BROA) .... KTBU
Conroe, TX [*Television station call letters*] .... KTFH
Conroller Area Network Bus (SAUS) .... CANBUS
Conrotatory [*Chemistry*] .... CON
Conroy's Custodian Reports [*1652-1788*] [*Ireland*] [*A publication*] (DLA) .... Con Cus
Conroy's Custodian Reports [*1652-1788*] [*Ireland*] [*A publication*] (DLA) .... Conr
Cons Westn & Pac Res [*NASDAQ symbol*] (TTSB) .... CWNPF
Consanguineous Donor [*Medicine*] .... CD
Consanguineous Marriage (MELL) .... CM
Conscience [*A publication*] .... Cons
Conscience and Military Tax Campaign - US (EA) .... CMTC
Conscientious Objector .... CO
Conscientious Objector .... CONOBJTR
Conscientious Objectors' News [*British*] .... CON
Conscious (DIPS) .... Cs
Conscious (SAUS) .... CS
Consciousness .... CON
Consciousness [*Neurology and psychiatry*] (DAVI) .... CS
Consciousness (STED) .... cs
Consciousness (SAUS) CX
Consciousness Research and Training Project (EA) .... CRTP
Consciousness-Raising .... CR
Conscot Resources Ltd. [*Vancouver Stock Exchange symbol*] .... CNU
Conscript Ratio in the Air Forces .... CRAF
ConSeal Private Desktop .... CPD
Conseco, Inc. [*NYSE symbol*] (SPSG) .... CNC
Conseco, Inc. [*Associated Press*] (SAG) .... Consc
Conseco, Inc. [*Associated Press*] (SAG) .... Conseco
Conseco Inc. 7%'PRIDES' [*NYSE symbol*] (TTSB) .... CNCPrE
Conseco Inc. Series'D'Cv Pfd [*NYSE symbol*] (TTSB) .... CNCPrD
Conseco Industries Ltd. [*Associated Press*] (SAG) .... Conesco
Consecrated (ROG) .... CON
Consecrated .... CONS
Consecrated (WDAA) .... cons
Consecrated (VRA) .... consr
Consecratione [*Decretum Gratiani*] [*A publication*] (DSA) .... Cons
Consecutive (ADA) .... CONS
Consecutive (SAUS) .... Cons
Consecutive (MSA) .... CONSEC
Consecutive (ADWA) .... consec
Consecutive Access Addresses (SAUS) .... CAA
Consecutive Blank Column (SAUS) .... CBC
Consecutive Blank Column (SAUS) .... Con Blk Col
Consecutive Case Conference (MAE) CCC
Consecutive Computer (SAUS) CC
Consecutive Days (SAUS) .... CD
Consecutive Duty Tour [*Air Force*] .... CDT
Consecutive Field (SAUS) .... CF
Consecutive Memory Words (SAUS) .... CMW
Consecutive Number Control (IAA) .... CNC
Consecutive Number Printer .... CNP
Consecutive Oversea Tour [*Military*] (AFM) .... COT
Consecutive Processing (SAUS) .... CP
Consecutive Punching (SAUS) .... CP
Consecutive Retrieval (SAUS) .... CR
Consecutive Sequential Storage (SAUS) .... CSS
Consecutive Store Organization (SAUS) .... CSO
Consecutive Voyage Charter (DNAB) CVC
Consecutive Voyage Charter Parly (SAUS) .... Shellconsec
Consecutive Voyages (SAUS) .... CVs
Consecutive-Valve Actuation [*Nuclear energy*] (NRCH) .... CVA
Consecutive-Weeks Discount [*Marketng*] (DOAD) .... CWD
Conseil [*Council*] [*French*] (DLA) .... Cons
Conseil Acadien de Cooperation Culturelle en Atlantique [*Acadian Council of Cultural Cooperation in Atlantic Canada*] .... CACC
Conseil Africain de l'Arachide [*African Groundnut Council*] (EAIO) .... CAA
Conseil Africain-Canadien (AC) .... CAC
Conseil Asiatique d'Analystes Financiers [*Asian Council of Securities Analysts - ASAC*] [*Tokyo, Japan*] (EAIO) .... CAAF
Conseil Canadien de Coordination de la Deficience Auditive [*Canadian Co-Ordinating Council on Deafness - CCCD*] .... CCCDA
Conseil Canadien de Developpement Social [*Canadian Council on Social Development*] (EAIO) .... CCDS
Conseil Canadien de la Documentation Juridique [*Canadian Law Information Council*] .... CCDJ
Conseil Canadien de la Main-d'Oeuvre en Genie [*Canadian Engineering Manpower Council*] .... CCMG
Conseil Canadien de la Medecine Sportive [*Canadian Academy of Sport Medicine - CASM*] .... CCMS
Conseil Canadien de la Musique [*Canadian Music Council*] (EAIO) .... CCM
Conseil Canadien de la Securite (AC) .... CCS
Conseil Canadien de Protection des Animaux [*Canadian Council on Animal Care*] .... CCPA
Conseil Canadien de Recherche en Sciences Sociales [*Social Sciences Research Council of Canada - SSRCC*] .... CCRSS
Conseil Canadien de Recherches sur les Humanites [*Humanities Research Council of Canada - HRCC*] .... CCRH
Conseil Canadien des Arpenteurs-Geometres [*Canadian Council of Land Surveyors - CLS*] .... CCAG
Conseil Canadien des Aveugles [*Canadian Council of the Blind*] (EAIO) .... CCA
Conseil Canadien des Droits des Personnes Handicapees (AC) .... CCDPH
Conseil Canadien des Eglises [*Canadian Council of Churches*] (EAIO) .... CCE
Conseil Canadien des Fabricants des Produits du Tabac [*Canadian Tobacco Manufacturers' Council*] .... CCFPT
Conseil Canadien des Ingenieurs [*Canadian Council of Engineers*] CCI
Conseil Canadien des Metiers d'Art (AC) .... CCMA
Conseil Canadien des Ministres des Ressources [*Canadian Council of Resource Ministers*] .... CCMR
Conseil Canadien des Ministres des Ressources et de l'Environnement [*Canadian Council of Resource and Environment Ministers - CCREM*] .... CCMRE
Conseil Canadien des Producteurs d'Oeufs [*Canadian Egg Producers Council*] .... CCPO
Conseil Canadien des Transformateurs d'Oeufs et de Volailles [*Formerly, Canadian Produce Council*] (AC) .... CCTOV
Conseil Canadien d'Experimentation des Jouets [*Canadian Toy Testing Council*] .... CCEJ
Conseil Canadien du Bois (AC) .... CCB
Conseil Canadien du Multiculturalisme [*Canadian Multicultural Council*] .... CCM
Conseil Canadien du Porc [*Formerly, Canadian Swine Council*] (AC) .... CCP
Conseil Canadien pour la Cooperation Internationale [*Canadian Council for International Cooperation - CCIC*] CCCI
Conseil Canadien pour la Readaptation des Handicapes [*Canadian Rehabilitation for the Disabled*] (EAIO) .... CCRH
Conseil Canadien pour la Recherche en Education [*Canadian Council for Research in Education*] .... CCRE
Conseil Canadien pour l'Education Multiculturelle et Interculturelle (AC) .... CCEMI
Conseil Canadien sur le Tabagisme et la Sante [*Canadian Council on Smoking and Health*] .... CCTS
Conseil Constitutionnel [*Constitutional Council*] [*French*] (DLA) .... Cons Const
Conseil Consultatif Canadien sur la Situation de la Femme (AC) .... CCSSF
Conseil Consultatif de la Politique du Personnel [*Advisory Council on Personnel Policy*] [*Canada Public Service Commission and Treasury Board*] .... CCPP
Conseil Consultatif de la Situation de la Femme [*Advisory Council on the Status of Women*] [*Canada*] .... CCSF
Conseil Consultatif des Athletes [*Athletes' Advisory Council*] [*Canada*] .... CCA
Conseil Cooperatif Acadien de la Nouvelle-Ecosse (AC) .... CCANE
Conseil d'Assistance Economique Mutuelle [*Council for Mutual Economic Assistance - CMEA*] [*French*] (AF) .... CAEM
Conseil de Commerce Canada-Arabe (AC) .... CCCA
Conseil de Cooperation Douaniere [*Customs Co-Operation Council - CCC*] (EAIO) .... CCD
Conseil de Developpement du Loisir Scientifique (AC) .... CDLS
Conseil de la Boulangerie du Quebec [*Quebec Bakery Council*] (AC) .... CBQ
Conseil de la Cooperation Culturelle du Conseil de l'Europe [*Council for Cultural Cooperation of the Council of Europe*] (EAIO) .... CCCCE
Conseil de la Cooperation d'Ontario (AC) .... CCO
Conseil de la Cooperation du Quebec (AC) .... CCQ
Conseil de la Culture des Laurentides (AC) CCL
Conseil de la Gravure du Quebec [*1978, founded 1971 as AGQ, CQE from 1984*] [*Canada*] (NGC) .... CGQ
Conseil de la Jeunesse d'Afrique [*African Youth Council*] [*Senegal*] .... CJA
Conseil de la Jeunesse de Cote d'Ivoire [*Ivory Coast Youth Council*] .... CJCI
Conseil de la Langue Francaise, Quebec, PQ, Canada [*Library symbol*] [*Library of Congress*] (LCLS) .... CaQQCLF
Conseil de la Langue Francaise, Quebec, Quebec [*Library symbol*] [*National Library of Canada*] (NLC) .... QQCLF
Conseil de la Peinture du Quebec [*1978, founded 1966 as SAPQ, SAVVQ from 1980, CAPQ from 1982*] [*Canada*] (NGC) .... CPQ
Conseil de la Politique Scientifique du Quebec, Quebec, PQ, Canada [*Library symbol*] [*Library of Congress*] (LCLS) .... CaQQCPS
Conseil de la Reine [*Canada*] (DD) .... CR
Conseil de la Sante et des Services Sociaux de la Region de Montreal Metropolitain, Service de Reference, Montreal, PQ, Canada [*Library symbol*] [*Library of Congress*] (LCLS) .... CaQMCSSS
Conseil de la Sculpture du Quebec [*1978, founded 1961 as ASQ*] [*Canada*] (NGC) .... CSQ
Conseil de la Vie Francaise en Amerique (AC) .... CVFA
Conseil de l'Entente [*Entente Council - EC*] (EAIO) .... CE
Conseil de l'Enveloppe du Batiment du Quebec (AC) .... CEBQ
Conseil de l'Europe [*Council of Europe*] (EAIO) .... CE
Conseil de l'Industrie Electronique du Quebec (AC) .... CIEQ
Conseil de l'Industrie Laitiere du Quebec Inc. [*Quebec Dairy Council Inc.*] (AC) .... CILQ
Conseil de Presse du Quebec (AC) .... CPQ
Conseil de Recherche Agricole du Canada [*Canadian Agricultural Research Council*] .... CRAC

Conseil de Recherches en Sciences Humaines du Canada [*Social Sciences and Humanities Research Council of Canada - SSHRCC*] ...... CRSHC

Conseil de Recherches Medicales [*Medical Research Council*] [*Canada*] ...... CRM

Conseil de Securite [*United Nations*] ...... CS

Conseil Democratique Revolutionnaire [*Democratic Revolutionary Council*] [*Chad*] (PD) ...... CDR

Conseil des Affaires Sociales et de la Famille, Quebec, PQ, Canada [*Library symbol*] [*Library of Congress*] (LCLS) ...... CaQQASF

Conseil des Affaires Sociales et de la Famille, Quebec, Quebec [*Library symbol*] [*National Library of Canada*] (NLC) ...... QQASF

Conseil des Agences de Securite et d'Investigation du Quebec Inc. (AC) ...... CASIQ

Conseil des Artistes Peintres du Quebec [*1982, founded 1966 as SAPQ*] [*Canada*] (NGC) ...... CAPQ

Conseil des Arts Textiles du Quebec (AC) ...... CATQ

Conseil des Associations d'Ingenieurs du Commonwealth Britannique [*Commonwealth Engineers Council*] (EAIO) ...... CAICB

Conseil des Assurances de Dommages (AC) ...... CAD

Conseil des Barreaux de la Communaute Europeenne [*Council of the Bars and Law Societies of the European Community*] (EAIO) ...... CCBE

Conseil des Bibliotheques du Gouvernement Federal (AC) ...... CBGF

Conseil des Bourses de Valeurs [*French*] (ECON) ...... CBV

Conseil des Communautes Musulmanes du Canada [*Council of Muslim Communities of Canada*] (EAIO) ...... CCMC

Conseil des Communes d'Europe [*Council of European Municipalities*] ...... CCE

Conseil des Directeurs Medias du Quebec (AC) ...... CDMQ

Conseil des Ecoles Francaises de la Communaute Urbaine de Toronto [*Metro Toronto French-Language School Council*] (AC) ...... CEFCUT

Conseil des Federations Commerciales d'Europe [*Council of European Commercial Federations*] ...... CFCE

Conseil des Federations Industrielles d'Europe [*Council of European Industrial Federations*] ...... CFIE

Conseil des Metiers d'Art du Quebec (AC) ...... SOMART

Conseil des Ministres Arabes de la Justice [*Council of Arab Ministers of Justice - CAMJ*] [*Rabat, Morocco*] (EAIO) ...... CMAJ

Conseil des Operations de Bourse [*French*] (ECON) ...... COB

Conseil des Organisations Internationales Directement Interessees a l'Enfance eta l'Adolescence [*Council of International Organizations Directly Interested in Children and Youth*] [*Geneva, Switzerland*] (EAIO) ...... COIDIEA

Conseil des Organismes Francophones du Toronto Metropolitain (AC) ...... COFTM

Conseil des Premiers Ministres des Maritimes [*Council of Maritime Premiers - CMP*] [*Canada*] ...... CPMM

Conseil des Provinces Atlantiques pour les Sciences (AC) ...... CPAS

Conseil des Regions d'Europe [*Council of European Regions - CER*] (EAIO) ...... CRE

Conseil des Syndicats Hospitaliers de Montreal Inc. [*Montreal Council of Hospital Syndicates Inc.*] (AC) ...... CSHM

Conseil des Travailleurs et Travailleuses de l'Estrie (AC) ...... CTTE

Conseil des Travailleurs et Travailleuses de l'Outaouais Quebecois (AC) ...... CTOQ

Conseil des Travailleurs et Travailleuses de Quebec (AC) ...... CTQ

Conseil des Travailleurs et Travailleuses des Laurentides-Lanaudiere (AC) ...... CTLL

Conseil des Travailleurs et Travailleuses du Montreal Metropolitain (AC) ...... CTM

Conseil des Universites du Quebec, Quebec, PQ, Canada [*Library symbol*] [*Library of Congress*] (LCLS) ...... CaQQCU

Conseil des Universites du Quebec, Ste.-Foy, Quebec [*Library symbol*] [*National Library of Canada*] (NLC) ...... QQCU

Conseil d'Etat [*Council of State*] [*French*] (ILCA) ...... CE

Conseil d'Expansion Economique [*Economic Expansion Council*] [*Canada*].... CEE

Conseil d'Intervention pour l'Acces des Femmes au Travail (AC) ...... CIAFT

Conseil du Patronat du Quebec (AC) ...... CPQ

Conseil du Salut du Peuple [*People's Salvation Council*] [*Burkina Faso*] (PD) ...... CSP

Conseil du Statut de la Femme, Quebec, PQ, Canada [*Library symbol*] [*Library of Congress*] (LCLS) ...... CaQQCSF

Conseil du Travails de l'Abitibi-Temiscaminque (AC) ...... CTAT

Conseil Economique et Social [*United Nations*] ...... CE et S

Conseil Economique et Social des Nations-Unies [*United Nations Economic and Social Council*] ...... CESNU

Conseil Europeen de Coordination pour le Developpement des Essais de Performancedes Combustibles et des Lubrifiants pour Moteurs [*Coordinating European Council for the Development of Performance Tests for Lubricants and Engine Fuels - CEC*] (EAIO) ...... CEC

Conseil Europeen de la Construction Electrodomestique [*European Committee of Manufacturers of Electrical Domestic Equipment*] (EA) ...... CECED

Conseil Europeen des Federations de l'Industrie Chimique [*European Council of Chemical Manufacturers Federations - ECCMF*] [*Belgium*] (EAIO) ...... CEFIC

Conseil Europeen des Jeunes Agriculteurs [*European Committee of Young Farmers*] [*Common Market*] ...... CEJA

Conseil Europeen du "Codex Alimentarius" ...... CODEXAL

Conseil Europeen du Comite International de l'Organisation Scientifique [*European Council of International Committee of Scientific Management*] ...... CECIOS

Conseil Europeen du Cuir Brut [*European Untanned Leather Council*] ...... CECB

Conseil Europeen pour la Construction de Lanceures d'Engins Spatiaux [*European Council for the Construction of Spacecraft Launching Areas*] [*France*] ...... CECLES

Conseil Europeen pour la Protection des Animaux [*European Council for Animal Welfare - ECAW*] (EA) ...... CEPA

Conseil General des Peches pour la Mediterranee [*General Fisheries Council for the Mediterranean*] ...... CGPM

Conseil Inter-Americain de Securite [*Inter-American Safety Council*] ...... CIAS

Conseil Interamericain du Commerce et de la Production ...... CICEP

Conseil Intergouvernemental des Pays Exportateurs de Cuivre [*Intergovernmental Council of Copper Exporting Countries - ICCEC*] (EAIO) ...... CIPEC

Conseil International de la Chasse et de la Conservation du Gibier [*International Council for Game and Wildlife Conservation*] (EAIO) CIC

Conseil International de la Langue Francaise [*International Council of the French Language - ICFL*] (EAIO) ...... CILF

Conseil International de la Musique [*International Music Council*] ...... CIM

Conseil International de la Musique Populaire [*International Folk Music Council*] ...... CIMP

Conseil International de la Philosophie et des Sciences Humaines [*International Council for Philosophy and Humanistic Studies*] (EAIO) ...... CIPSH

Conseil International de la Preparation a l'Enseignement [*International Council on Education for Teaching*] ...... CIPE

Conseil International de l'Action Sociale [*International Council on Social Welfare - ICSW*] [*Vienna, Austria*] (EA) ...... CIAS

Conseil International de l'Education Physique et Sportive [*International Council of Sport and Physical Education*] ...... CIEPS

Conseil International de l'Etain [*International Tin Council - ITC*] [*Defunct*] (EAIO) ...... CIE

Conseil International de Musique [*UNESCO*] [*Record label*] ...... CIDM

Conseil International d'Education des Adultes [*International Council for Adult Education*] [*Canada*] ...... CIEA

Conseil International d'Education Mesologique des Pays de Langue Francaise [*Established 1977*] [*Canada*] ...... CIEM

Conseil International des Agences Benevoles [*International Council of Voluntary Agencies - ICVA*] (EA) ...... CIAB

Conseil International des Archives [*International Council on Archives*] ...... CIA

Conseil International des Compositeurs [*International Council of Composers*] CIC

Conseil International des Economies Regionales [*International Council for Local Development*] (EAIO) ...... CIER

Conseil International des Employeurs du Commerce [*International Council of Commerce Employers*] ...... CIEC

Conseil International des Femmes [*International Council of Women - ICW*] [*Paris, France*] (EA) ...... CIF

Conseil International des Infirmieres [*International Council of Nurses - ICN*] [*Geneva, Switzerland*] (EA) CII

Conseil International des Machines a Combustion [*International Council on Combustion Engines*] [*Paris, France*] (EAIO) ...... CIMAC

Conseil International des Organisations de Festivals de Folklore et d'Arts Traditionnels [*International Council of Folklore Festival Organizations and Folk Art - ICFFO*] (EAIO) ...... CIOFF

Conseil International des Organismes de Travailleuses Familiales [*International Council of Home-Help Services*] ...... CIOTF

Conseil International des Praticiens du Plan Comptable International [*International Council of Practitioners of the International Plan of Accounts*] ...... CIPCI

Conseil International des Radios-Televisions d'Expression Francaise [*International Association of Broadcasting Manufacturers - IABM*] (EAIO) ...... CIRTEF

Conseil International des Ressources Phytogenetiques [*International Board for Plant Genetic Resources - IBPGR*] (EAIO) ...... CIRP

Conseil International des Sciences Sociales [*International Social Science Council - ISSC*] (EAIO) ...... CISS

Conseil International des Services d'Aide Familiale [*International Council of Homehelp Services - ICHS*] [*Driebergen-Rijsenburg, Netherlands*] (EAIO) ...... CISAF

Conseil International des Tanneurs [*International Council of Tanners - ICT*] (EAIO) ...... CIT

Conseil International des Unions Scientifiques [*International Council of Scientific Unions*] ...... CIUS

Conseil International d'Etudes Canadiennes [*International Council for Canadian Studies - ICCS*] ...... CIEC

Conseil International du Batiment pour la Recherche, l'Etude, et la Documentation [*International Council for Building Research, Studies, and Documentation*] (EAIO) ...... CIB

Conseil International du Ble [*International Wheat Council - IWC*] (EAIO) ...... CIB

Conseil International du Cinema et de la Television [*International Film and Television Council*] ...... CICT

Conseil International du Film d'Enseignement [*International Council for Educational Films*] ...... CIFE

Conseil International du Sport Militaire [*International Military Sports Council*] [*Belgium*] ...... CISM

Conseil International Formule 40 [*International F-40 Council*] [*Paris, France*] (EAIO) CIF40

Conseil International pour la Recherche en Agroforesterie [*International Council for Research in Agroforestry*] (EAIO) ...... CIRAF

Conseil International pour le Developpement du Cuivre [*International Copper Development Council*] (AF) ...... CIDEC

Conseil International pour le Recherche en Linguistique Fondamentale et Appliquee [*International Research Council on Pure and Applied Linguistics - IRCPAL*] (EA) ...... CIRELFA

Conseil International pour l'Education des Handicapes de la Vue [*International Council for Education of the Visually Handicapped - ICEVH*] (EAIO) ...... CIEHV

Conseil International pour l'Education Physique et la Science du Sport [*International Council of Sport Science and Physical Education - ICSSPE*] (EAIO) ...... CIEPSS

Conseil International pour l'Exploration de la Mer [*International Council for the Exploration of the Sea*] ...... CIEM

Conseil International pour l'Organization Scientifique [*World Management Council*] (EA) .... CIOS
Conseil Jeunesse Francophone de la Colombie-Britannique (AC) .... CJFCB
Conseil Jeunesse Provincial [*Manitoba*] (AC) .... CJP
Conseil Jeunesse Provincial [*Nouvelle-Ecosse*] (AC) .... CJP
Conseil Mondial de la Paix [*World Peace Council - WPC*] (EAIO) .... CMP
Conseil Mondial de l'Alimentation [*World Food Council*] [*French*] [*United Nations*] (DUND) .... CMA
Conseil Mondial d'Education [*World Council for Curriculum and Instruction*] .... CME
Conseil Mondial des Associations d'Education Comparee [*World Council of Comparative Education Societies - WCCES*] (EA) .... CMAEC
Conseil Mondial pour l'Assemblee Constituante des Peuples [*World Council for the Peoples World Convention*] .... CMACP
Conseil National Canadien du Travail [*National Council of Canadian Labour - NCCL*] .... CNCT
Conseil National de la Resistance Guadeloupeenne [*Political party*] (EY) .... CNRG
Conseil National de l'Industrie Laitiere du Canada [*National Dairy Council of Canada*] .... CNIL
Conseil National de l'Ordre des Medecins [*France*] .... CNOM
Conseil National de Recherche Scientifique [*International Council of Scientific Unions*] .... CNRS
Conseil National de Recherches Canada [*National Research Council Canada*] .... CNRC
Conseil Oecumenique de Jeunesse en Europe [*Ecumenical Youth Council in Europe*] [*Northern Ireland*] (EAIO) .... COJE
Conseil Oecumenique des Eglises [*World Council of Churches*] .... COE
Conseil Oleicole International [*International Olive Oil Council - IOOC*] (EAIO) .... COI
Conseil Parlementaire du Mouvement Europeen .... CPME
Conseil Pationa de Recherches [*Canada*] [*Marine science*] (OSRA) .... CNR
Conseil Pedagogique Interdisciplinaire du Quebec (AC) .... CPIQ
Conseil Permanent de la Convention Internationale de Stresa sur les Fromages (EAIO) .... CPCISF
Conseil pour la Liberation du Congo-Kinshasa [*Council for the Liberation of the Congo-Kinshasa*] [*Zaire*] (PD) CLC
Conseil pour l'Homologation des Etablissements Theologiques en Afrique [*Accrediting Council for Theological Education in Africa - ACTEA*] (EAIO) .... COHETA
[*Le*] **Conseil pour l'Unite Canadienne** [*The Council for Canadian Unity*] (AC) .... CUC
Conseil Provincial du Quebec des Metiers de la Construction (AC) .... CPQMC
Conseil Quebecois de l'Estampe [*1984, founded 1971 as AGQ, CGQ from 1978*] [*Canada*] (NGC) .... CQE
Conseil Quebecois de l'Estampe Inc. (AC) .... CQE
Conseil Quebecois des professionnels et Cadres (AC) .... CQPC
Conseil Quebecois du Commerce de Detail (AC) .... CQCD
Conseil Quebecois du Theatre (AC) .... CQT
Conseil Regional de Developpement, Trois-Rivieres, PQ, Canada [*Library symbol*] [*Library of Congress*] (LCLS) .... CaQTCRD
Conseil Regional de Developpement, Trois-Rivieres, Quebec [*Library symbol*] [*National Library of Canada*] (NLC) .... QTCRD
Conseil Regional de la Sante et des Services Sociaux, Chicoutimi, PQ, Canada [*Library symbol*] [*Library of Congress*] (LCLS) .... CaQCCRS
Conseil Regional de la Sante et des Services Sociaux, Chicoutimi, Quebec [*Library symbol*] [*National Library of Canada*] (NLC) .... QCCRS
Conseil Regional de la Sante et des Services Sociaux de la Region Cote-Nord, Hauterive, PQ, Canada [*Library symbol*] [*Library of Congress*] (LCLS) .... CaQHaCR
Conseil Regional de la Sante et des Services Sociaux de la Region Cote-Nord, Hauterive, Quebec [*Library symbol*] [*National Library of Canada*] (NLC) .... QHACR
Conseil Regional de la Sante et des Services Sociaux de la Region Outaouais-Hull, Hull, PQ, Canada [*Library symbol*] [*Library of Congress*] (LCLS) .... CaQHCRS
Conseil Regional de la Sante et des Services Sociaux de la Region Outaouais-Hull, Hull, Quebec [*Library symbol*] [*National Library of Canada*] (NLC) .... QHCRS
Conseil Regional de la Sante et des Services Sociaux des Cantons de l'Est, Sherbrooke, PQ, Canada [*Library symbol*] [*Library of Congress*] (LCLS) .... CaQSherCR
Conseil Regional de la Sante et des Services Sociaux des Cantons de l'Est, Sherbrooke, Quebec [*Library symbol*] [*National Library of Canada*] (NLC) .... QSHERCR
Conseil Regional de la Sante et des Services Sociaux Laurentides Lanaudiere, Saint-Jerome, ON, Canada [*Library symbol*] [*Library of Congress*] (LCLS) .... CaOStJeCR
Conseil Regional de la Sante et des Services Sociaux Laurentides-Lanaudiere, Saint-Jerome, Quebec [*Library symbol*] [*National Library of Canada*] (NLC) .... QSTJECR
Conseil Regional de la Sante et des Services Sociaux, Longueuil, PQ, Canada [*Library symbol*] [*Library of Congress*] (LCLS) .... CaQLoCRS
Conseil Regional de la Sante et des Services Sociaux, Longueuil, Quebec [*Library symbol*] [*National Library of Canada*] (NLC) .... QLCRS
Conseil Regional de la Sante et des Services Sociaux, Quebec, Quebec [*Library symbol*] [*National Library of Canada*] (NLC) .... QQCRS
Conseil Regional de la Sante et des Services Sociaux, Rimouski, PQ, Canada [*Library symbol*] [*Library of Congress*] (LCLS) .... CaQRCRS
Conseil Regional de la Sante et des Services Sociaux, Rimouski, Quebec [*Library symbol*] [*National Library of Canada*] (NLC) .... QRCRS
Conseil Regional de la Sante et des Services Sociaux Rouyn-Noranda, Noranda, PQ,Canada [*Library symbol*] [*Library of Congress*] (LCLS) .... CaQNCRS
Conseil Regional de la Sante et des Services Sociaux Rouyn-Noranda, Noranda, Quebec [*Library symbol*] [*National Library of Canada*] (NLC) .... QNCRS
Conseil Regional de la Sante et des Services Sociaux, Trois-Rivieres, PQ, Canada [*Library symbol*] [*Library of Congress*] (LCLS) .... CaQTCRS
Conseil Regional de la Sante et des Services Sociaux, Trois-Rivieres, Quebec [*Library symbol*] [*National Library of Canada*] (NLC) .... QTCRS
Conseil Regional des Travailleurs et Travailleuses Centre du Quebec (AC) .... CRTCQ
Conseil Scientifique pour l'Afrique au Sud de Sahara [*Scientific Council for Africa South of the Sahara*] .... CSA
Conseil Superieur de l'Audioviseul [*France*] (EY) .... CSA
Conseil Superieur de Livre [*Canada*] .... CSL
Conseil Superieur du Sport en Afrique [*Supreme Council for Sport in Africa - SCSA*] [*Yaounde, Cameroon*] (EAIO) .... CSSA
Conseil Universitaire des Directeurs de Biologie du Canada (AC) .... CUDBC
Conseiller [*Councillor, Judge*] [*French*] (ILCA) .... Cons
Conseiller de la Reine [*Queen's Counsel*] [*Canada*] .... CR
Conseiller Prive [*French*] (CPGU) .... CP
Conseillers en Gestion et Informatique [*Montreal, PQ*] [*Telecommunications service*] (TSSD) .... CGI
Conseillers en Gestion et Informatique CGI, Inc., Centre de Documentation, Quebec, PQ, Canada [*Library symbol*] [*Library of Congress*] (LCLS) .... CaQQCGI
Consejo de Defensa Centroamericana [*Central American Defense Council*] [*Guatemala, Guatemala*] (EAIO) .... CONDECA
Consejo de Educacion de Adultos de America Latina [*Santiago, Chile*] (EAIO) .... CEAAL
Consejo Empresarial Mexicano para Asuntos Internacionales [*The Mexican Business Council for International Affairs*] (CROSS) .... CEMAL
Consejo Episcopal Latinoamericano [*Latin American Episcopal Council*] (EAIO) .... CELAM
Consejo Interamericano de Comercio y Produccion [*Interamerican Council of Commerce and Production*] .... CICYP
Consejo Interamericano de Musica [*Inter-American Music Council*] (EA) .... CIDEM
Consejo Interamericano do Escultismo [*Inter-American Scout Committee - IASC*] [*San Jose, Costa Rica*] (EAIO) .... CIE
Consejo Interamericano Economico-Social [*Inter-American Economic and Social Council*] (EA) .... CIES
Consejo Interamericano para la Educacion, la Ciencia, y la Cultura [*Inter-American Council for Education, Science, and Culture*] (EA) .... CIECC
Consejo Internacional de Buena Vecindad, AC [*International Good Neighbor Council - IGNC*] [*Monterrey, Mexico*] (EAIO) .... CIBV
Consejo Internacional de la Pelicula de Ensenanza [*International Council for Educational Films*] .... CIPE
Consejo Internacional de Mujeres [*International Council of Women*] .... CIM
Consejo Internacional de Tratados Indios (SAUS) .... CITI
Consejo Internacional del Trigo [*International Wheat Council - IWC*] (EAIO) .... CIT
Consejo Latinoamericano de Ciencias Sociales [*Latin American Social Sciences Council - LASSC*] (EAIO) .... CLACSO
Consejo Latinoamericano de Iglesias [*Latin American Council of Churches*] (EAIO) .... CLAI
Consejo Latinoamericano de Mujeres Catolicas [*Latin American Council of Catholic Women*] (EAIO) .... CLAMUC
Consejo Latino-Americano de Radiacon Cosmica [*Latin-American Council on Cosmic Radiation*] [*Bolivia*] (PDAA) .... CLARC
Consejo Mundial de Artes y Oficios [*World Crafts Council*] .... CMAO
Consejo Mundial de Iglesias [*Switzerland*] .... CMI
Consejo Mundial de la Alimentacion [*World Food Council*] [*Spanish*] [*United Nations*] (DUND) .... CMA
Consejo Nacional de la Industria Maquiladora [*National Council of the Maquiladora Industry*] [*Mexican/US business organization*] (CROSS) .... CNIM
Consejo Nacional para la Prevenciãn y Control del S²ndrome de la Inmunodeficiencia Adquirida (SAUO) .... CONASIDA
Consejo Revolucionario Cubano [*Cuban Revolutionary Council*] .... CRC
Consejo Superior de Investigaciones Cientificas [*Spain*] (GEOI) .... CSIC
Consejo Universitario Inter-Americana para el Desarrollo Economico y Social [*Inter-American University Council for Economic and Social Development - IUCESD*] (EA) .... CUIDES
Conselho Federal de Medicina Veterinaria [*Brazil*] (GVA) .... CFMV
Conselho Regional de Medicina Veterinaria de Sao Paulo (GVA) .... CRMV-SP
Conselho Regional de Medicina Veterinaria do Rio de Janeiro (GVA) .... CRMV-RJ
Consensus .... Con
Consensus Language (RALS) .... CONLAN
Consensus Voluntary Reference Compound [*Environmental science*] .... CVRC
Consent (ROG) .... CONST
Consent Agreement/Final Order (GFGA) .... CAFO
Consent Decree (COE) .... CD
Consent Decree Tracking System (SAUS) .... CDETS
Consent Order and Compliance Agreement [*Environmental science*] (COE) .... COCA
Consent to Medical Treatment [*British Medical Association computer program*] .... COMET
Consep, Inc. [*Associated Press*] (SAG) .... Consep
Consep, Inc. [*NASDAQ symbol*] (SAG) .... CSEP
Consequence .... CONS
Consequence (SAUS) .... Cons
Consequence (ROG) .... CONSCE
Consequence [*Legal*] [*British*] (ROG) .... CONSEQCE
Consequence Counter (SAUS) .... CSC
Consequence Limiting Control System [*Nuclear energy*] (NRCH) .... CLCS
Consequence Management (DEMM) .... CoM
Consequences Assessment Tool Set (GEOI) .... CATS
Consequent [*Legal*] [*British*] (ROG) .... CONSEQT

Consequential Arc Back ... CAB
Consequential Loss Committee [*Insurance*] (MARI) ... CLC
Conserva [*Conserve*] [*Pharmacy*] ... CONS
Conservancy Advisory Scientist (SAUO) ... CAS
Conservandum [*Conserved*] [*Latin*] (EES) ... cons
Conservation (AABC) ... CON
Conservation ... CONSERV
Conservation ... CONSERVE
Conservation (AL) ... Consv
Conservation Act (SAUO) ... Cons Act
Conservation Administration News [*A publication*] ... CAN
Conservation Alliance of Zimbabwe (SAUO) ... CAZ
Conservation Analytical Laboratory [*Smithsonian Institution*] ... CAL
Conservation and Environment Library Information System ... CELIS
[*Department of*] **Conservation and Environment, Victoria** [*State*] (EERA) ... VDCE
Conservation and Extension Service (SAUO) ... CONEX
Conservation and Land Management (SAUS) ... CALM
Conservation and Natural Resources (SAUS) ... CNR
Conservation and Protection-Western and Northern Region, Environment Canada [*Conservation et Protection-Region de l'Ouest et du Nord, Environnement Canada*], **Edmonton, Alberta** [*Library symbol*] [*National Library of Canada*] (NLC) ... AEECW
Conservation and Renewable Energy ... CRE
Conservation and Renewable Energy Demonstration Program (SAUS) ... ENERDEMO
Conservation and Renewable Energy Inquiry and Referral Service [*Department ofEnergy*] [*Information service or system*] (IID) ... CAREIRS
Conservation and Renewable Energy Inquiry and Referral Service [*Database*] ... CEIRS
Conservation and Renewable Energy Office [*Canada*] ... CREO
Conservation and Renewable Energy Office, Energy, Mines, and Resources Canada [*Bureau de la Conservation de l'Energie et de l'Energie Renouvelable, Energie, Mines, et Ressources Canada*] **Toronto, Ontario** [*Library symbol*] [*National Library of Canada*] (NLC) ... OTEMR
Conservation and Renewable Energy Program [*Department of Energy*] ... C & RE
Conservation and Research Foundation (EA) ... CRF
Conservation and Wildlife Studies (SAUS) ... CAWS
Conservation Assessment and Management Planning (SAUS) ... CAMP
Conservation Association of Botanical Societies (DBA) ... CABS
Conservation Authority [*Canada*] ... CA
Conservation Biology (SAUS) ... Conserv Biol
Conservation Breeding Specialist Group (GVA) ... CBSG
Conservation Centre and Conservation Council of South Australia (SAUO) ... CCCSA
Conservation Certificate [*Hunting*] ... CC
Conservation, coal, nuclear energy (SAUO) ... Coconuc
Conservation Commission of the Northern Territory [*Australia*] ... CCNT
Conservation Committee of California Oil and Gas Producers (SRA) ... CCCOGP
Conservation Council for the South East Region and Canberra [*Australia*] ... CCSERC
Conservation Council of New Brunswick [*Conseil de la Conservation du Nouveu-Brunswick*] (AC) ... CCNB
Conservation Council of Ontario [*Le Conseil de Conservation de l'Ontario*] (AC) ... CCO
Conservation Council of the South East Region and Canberra (SAUO) ... CCSERV
Conservation Council of Victoria (SAUO) ... CCV
Conservation Data Center (or Centre) (SAUO) ... CDC
Conservation Dependent (EES) ... CD
Conservation Division (SAUO) ... CD
Conservation Division, Environment Canada [*Division de la Conservation, Environnement Canada*] **Ottawa, Ontario** [*Library symbol*] [*National Library of Canada*] (NLC) ... OOEOB
Conservation Education and Research Program (GNE) ... CERP
Conservation Education Association (EA) ... CEA
Conservation Education Diving Archeology Museums ... CEDAM
Conservation Environment and Historic Preservation [*Commercial firm*] ... CEHP
Conservation, Exploration, Diving, Archeology, Museums [*Acronym is used as name of an international organization interested in these five subjects*] (EA) ... CEDAM
Conservation Farming in the Tropical Uplands/Cornell International Institute for Food, Agriculture and Development (SAUO) ... CFTU/CIIFAD
Conservation for Development Centre (SAUO) ... CDC
Conservation, Forests and Land (SAUO) ... CF&L
[*Department of*] **Conservation, Forests and Lands of Victoria** [*State*] (EERA) ... VCF&L
Conservation Foundation (EA) ... CF
Conservation Fund [*An association*] (EA) ... CF
Conservation International (EA) ... CI
Conservation Law Foundation (ECON) ... CLF
Conservation Law Reform Act (SAUO) ... CIRA
Conservation Law Reform Act cluster (SAUO) ... CIRA
Conservation Law Society of America [*Defunct*] ... CLSA
Conservation League (EA) ... CL
Conservation Management Plan (SAUO) ... CMP
Conservation Management Strategy (SAUO) ... CMS
Conservation Materials and Services ... CMS
Conservation Monitoring Centre [*World trade of endangered species products*] ... CMC
Conservation Needs Inventory (SAUO) ... CNI
Conservation of Antarctic Marine Living Resources [*International agreement signed in 1982*] ... CAMLR
Conservation of Arctic Flora and Fauna (GEOI) ... CAFF
Conservation of Flora and Fauna (SAUS) ... CFF
Conservation Officer (SAUO) ... CO
Conservation OnLine [*Database collection*] [*Internet*] ... COOL
Conservation Options for Decision Analysis (SAUS) ... CODA
Conservation Organization Protesting Pollution (SAUS) ... COPP
Conservation Park (SAUO) ... CP
Conservation Policy Division (SAUO) ... CPD
Conservation Program Improvements Act ... CPIA
Conservation Reporting and Evaluation System [*Department of Agriculture*] ... CRES
Conservation Research Report [*A publication*] ... CRR
Conservation Reserve (SAUO) ... CR
Conservation Reserve Enhancement Program [*Michigan*] ... CREP
Conservation Reserve Program [*Department of Agriculture*] [*Department of Energy*] ... CRP
Conservation Society (SAUO) ... Con Soc
Conservation Society [*British*] (DCTA) ... CS
Conservation Strategy for Sustainable Land Management (SAUO) ... CSSLM
Conservation Technologies (SAUS) ... DRECT
Conservation Technology Information Center (WPI) ... CTIC
Conservation Terrestrial (SAUO) ... CT
Conservation Tillage Information Center ... CTIC
Conservation Tourism Liaison Group (SAUO) ... CTLG
Conservation Treaty Support Fund [*An association*] (EA) ... CTSF
Conservation Trust [*British*] (EAIO) ... CT
Conservation Voltage Reduction [*Public Utilities Commission*] ... CVR
Conservation World (SAUO) ... CW
Conservation Zone Advisory Committee [*Australia*] ... COZAC
Conservationist (AL) ... Consv
Conservatism-Radicalism Opinionaire [*Theodore F. Lentz*] (TES) ... C-R
Conservative [*Politics*] ... C
Conservative (WDAA) ... Con
Conservative (ADWA) ... Cons
Conservative ... CONS
Conservative Action for Electoral Reform [*British*] ... CAER
Conservative Action Foundation (EA) ... CAF
Conservative Action Foundation/Coalition Against Nuclear Annihilation [*Research center*] (RCD) ... CAF/CANA
Conservative Alliance (EA) ... CALL
Conservative and National Liberal Party [*British*] ... CNL
Conservative and Unionist Central Office [*British*] (DAS) ... CUCO
Conservative and Unionist Central Office (SAUO) ... CUCO
Conservative and Unionist Party [*British*] [*Political party*] ... CONS
Conservative Baptist Association of America (EA) ... CBAA
Conservative Baptist Foreign Mission Society (EA) ... CBFMS
Conservative Baptist Home Mission Society (EA) ... CBHMS
Conservative Baptist Theological Seminary, Denver, CO [*Library symbol*] [*Library of Congress*] (LCLS) ... CoDCB
Conservative Baptist Theological Seminary, Englewood, CO [*OCLC symbol*] (OCLC) ... CBS
Conservative Book Club ... CBC
[*The*] **Conservative Caucus** (EA) ... TCC
[*The*] **Conservative Caucus Research, Analysis, and Education Foundation** (EA) ... TCCRAEF
Conservative Central Council [*British*] ... CCC
Conservative Central Office (WDAA) ... CCO
Conservative Clubs of America (EA) ... CCA
Conservative Collegiate Forum (AIE) ... CCF
Conservative Democratic Forum (EA) ... CDF
Conservative Democratic Political Action Committee (EA) ... CDPAC
Conservative Evangelicals in Methodism (SAUO) ... CEIM
Conservative Leadership Political Action Committee (EA) ... CLPAC
Conservative Library Association [*Defunct*] ... CLA
Conservative Logic Element (CIST) ... CLE
Conservative Majority for Citizen's Rights (EA) ... CMCR
Conservative Mennonite Board of Missions and Charities [*Later, RMM*] (EA) ... CMBMC
Conservative Nationalist Party [*British*] ... CN
Conservative Nationalist Party [*Australia*] [*Political party*] ... ConsNP
Conservative Network (EA) ... CN
Conservative Opportunity Society (EA) ... COS
Conservative Orthopedics International Association (EA) ... COIA
Conservative Orthopedics International Association (EA) ... IACO
Conservative Party [*South Africa*] [*Political party*] ... CP
Conservative Party of Australia [*Political party*] ... CPA
Conservative Party of Australia [*Political party*] ... CVP
Conservative Party of Northern Ireland (SAUO) ... CPNI
Conservative Party of South Africa [*Konserwatiewe Party van Suid-Afrika*] [*Political party*] (PPW) ... CPSA
Conservative Party's Defense Committee [*British*] ... CPDC
Conservative Political Action Conference ... CPAC
Conservative Political Centre [*British*] ... CPC
Conservative Research Department (WDAA) ... CRD
Conservative Savings Corp. [*NASDAQ symbol*] (NQ) ... CONS
Conservative Savings Corp. [*Associated Press*] (SAG) ... ConsSv
Conservative Savings Corp. [*Associated Press*] (SAG) ... ConsvSv
Conservative Society [*British*] (DI) ... CONSOC
Conservative Society of America ... CSA
Conservative Trade Unionists [*British*] ... CTU
Conservative Victory Committee [*An association*] (EA) ... CVC
Conservative Way Forward [*British*] [*Political party*] ... CWF
Conservative Youth Federation [*Defunct*] (EA) ... CYF
Conservatives for a Constitutional Convention (EA) ... CCC
Conservatives for a Constitutional Convention (EA) ... ConConCon
Conservatoire [*Conservatory*] [*French*] ... Cons
Conservatoire d'Art Dramatique de Montreal, Quebec [*Library symbol*] [*National Library of Canada*] (NLC) ... QMCADQ

Conservatoire d'Art Dramatique de Quebec, Montreal, PQ, Canada [*Library symbol*] [*Library of Congress*] (LCLS) .... CaQMCADQ
Conservatoire d'Art Dramatique de Quebec, Quebec, PQ, Canada [*Library symbol*] [*Library of Congress*] (LCLS) .... CaQQCAD
Conservatoire d'Art Dramatique du Quebec, Quebec [*Library symbol*] [*National Library of Canada*] (NLC) .... QQCAD
Conservatoire de Musique de Montreal, Montreal, PQ, Canada [*Library symbol*] [*Library of Congress*] (LCLS) .... CaQMCOM
Conservatoire de Musique de Montreal, Quebec [*Library symbol*] [*National Library of Canada*] (NLC) .... QMCOM
Conservatoire de Musique du Quebec, Quebec, PQ, Canada [*Library symbol*] [*Library of Congress*] (LCLS) .... CaQQCMQ
Conservator (DLA) .... Cons
Conservator (AL) .... Consv
Conservatorium (ADA) .... CON
Conservatorium of Music in Melbourne (SAUO) .... CMM
Conservators of the River Lea (SAUO) .... CRL
Conservators of the River Lea (SAUS) .... CRL
Conservatorship (DLA) .... Consv
Conservatory (SAUO) .... Cons
Conservatory (SAUO) .... Conserv
Conservatory .... CONSERV
conservatory .... CONSRVTRY
Conservatory .... CONSV
Conservatory of Music (SAUO) .... ConsMus
Conserve (SAUS) .... Consv
Conserve (AABC) .... CONSV
Conserve, Preserve, and Restore (GNE) .... CPR
Conserved ATPase [*Adenosine Triphosphatase*] **Domain** [*Biochemistry*] .... CAD
Conserved DNA [*Deoxyribose Nucleic Acid*] **Element** [*Genetics*] .... CDE
Conserved Helix-Loop-Helix Ubiquitous Kinase [*An enzyme*] .... CHUK
Conserved Vector Current CVC
Conservez Taxe Payee [*Retain Charge Paid*] [*French*] [*Business term*] .... CTP
Consider (AABC) .... CONS
Consider (SAUS) .... Cons
Consider (ROG) .... CONSID
Consider (FAAC) .... CSDR
Consider (SAUS) .... Csid
Consider All Factors (BARN) .... caf
Consider Yourself Kissed [*Correspondence*] .... CYK
Considerable (FAAC) .... CSDRBL
considerable (SAUS) .... csidl
Considerable Conduct Disorder .... CCD
Considerable Damage (SAUS) .... Cons D
Considerant [*Whereas, In View*] [*French*] (ILCA) .... Cons
Consideration .... CON
Consideration (SAUS) .... Consid
Consideration .... CONSON
Consideration (SAUS) .... Csidn
Consideration of Alternatives [*Environmental science*] (COE) .... COA
Considered [*Legal*] [*British*] (ROG) .... CONSD
considered (SAUS) .... csidd
Consiel du Statut de la Femme, Quebec, Quebec [*Library symbol*] [*National Library of Canada*] (NLC) .... QQCSF
Consiglio Nazionale delle Ricerche [*National Research Council*] [*Italy*] [*Information service or system*] (IID) .... CNR
Consiglio Nazionale delle Ricerche, Rome, Italy [*Library symbol*] [*Library of Congress*] (LCLS) .... ItRC
Consiglio Nazionale Scienza Tecnologia [*Italy*] .... CNST
Consign .... CONS
Consign (SAUS) .... Csgn
Consigned (SAUS) .... Cons
Consigned (EBF) .... Cons
Consigned (ADWA) .... cons
Consigned (SAUS) .... Csgnd
Consignee [*Business term*] (DS) .... cnee
Consignee (SAUS) .... Con
Consignee [*Business term*] (ROG) .... CONSGEE
Consignees (SAUS) .... Cons
consigning (SAUS) .... csgng
Consignment (SAUS) .... Cnmt
Consignment [*Business term*] (DS) .... cnmt
Consignment (WDAA) .... cons
Consignment [*Business term*] .... CONS
Consignment (EBF) .... Cons
Consignment [*Business term*] .... CONSGT
Consignment [*Business term*] (ROG) .... CONST
Consignment (SAUS) .... Csgnmt
Consignment Item Request (MCD) .... CIR
Consignment Note [*Shipping*] .... CN
Consignment Note Control Label Number (DS) .... CCLN
Consilio et Prudentia [*By Counsel and Prudence*] [*Latin*] (ADA) .... CONS et PRUD
Consilium Conferentiarum Episcopalium Europae [*Council of European Bishops' Conferences*] (EAIO) .... CCEE
Consilium, Inc. [*Associated Press*] (SAG) .... Consilm
Consilium, Inc. [*NASDAQ symbol*] (NQ) .... CSIM
Consist (AABC) .... CONS
Consist (SAUS) .... Cons
Consist Of (MSA) .... C/O
Consistency .... CNSISTY
Consistency and Correction Software [*Bureau of the Census*] (GFGA) .... CONCOR
Consistency and Correction System (SAUS) .... CONCOR
Consistency Index [*Botany*] CI
Consistency Recording Controller .... CRC
Consistent .... CNSIST

Consistent (FAAC) .... CNSTNT
Consistent Payment Rate [*Finance*] (EMRF) .... CPR
Consistent With (ADWA) .... c/w
Consistent With (DAVI) .... C/W
Consisting Of [*Freight*] .... CON OF
Consistorial Decisions, Scotland, by George Ferguson, Lord Hermand [*A publication*] (DLA) .... Ferg
Consistorium (SAUO) .... Cons
Consistory of Masonic Magic [*Freemasonry*] (ROG) .... CMM
Conso Products [*NASDAQ symbol*] (TTSB) .... CNSO
Conso Products Co. [*NASDAQ symbol*] (SAG) .... CNSO
Conso Products Co. [*Associated Press*] (SAG) .... ConsoPd
Consociatio Internationalis Musicae Sacrae [*Rome, Italy*] (EAIO) .... CIMS
Consoer, Townsend & Associates, Chicago, IL [*Library symbol*] [*Library of Congress*] (LCLS) .... ICCT
Consol [*Navigation*] (AIA) .... CON
Consol Delivery & Logistics [*AMEX symbol*] (SG) .... CDV
Consol Ed NY,4.65% C Pfd [*NYSE symbol*] (TTSB) .... EDPrC
Consol Ed NY,$5 Pfd [*NYSE symbol*] (TTSB) .... EDPrA
Consol Ed NY,6% Cv B Pref [*NYSE symbol*] (TTSB) .... EDPPrB
CONSOL Energy [*NYSE symbol*] (SG) .... CNX
Consol Synthetic Fuel [*Coal liquefaction process*] .... CSF
Consolan Facility [*Aviation*] .... CONSO
Consolata Missionaries (TOCD) .... imc
Consolata Missionaries (TOCD) .... IMC
Consolata Missionary Sisters [*Roman Catholic religious order*] .... MC
Consolation .... CONSLTN
Console (KSC) .... CNSL
Console [*Computer science*] (IAA) .... CON
Console [*Computer science*] .... CONS
Console (AAG) .... CSL
Console Action Processor .... CAP
Console Address Register (SAUS) .... CAR
Console Command Language (SAUS) CCL
Console Command Processor [*Digital Research*] .... CCP
Console Command Program .... CCP
Console Communication System (MCD) .... CCS
Console Communications Equipment (MCD) .... CCE
Console Computer Interface Adapter .... CCIA
Console Control Circuit CCC
Console Control Package .... CCP
Console Control Processor (SAUS) .... CCP
Console Control Program (SAUS) .... CCP
Console Control Unit (SAUS) .... CCU
Console Digital Display Programmer (MUGU) .... CDDP
Console Electric Typewriter (SAUS) .... CET
Console File (SAUS) .... CF
Console for Optical Measurement and Precise Analysis of Radiation from Electronics .... COMPARE
Console Input (BTTJ) .... CONIN
Console Input/Output .... CONIO
Console Inquiry Station (SAUS) .... CIS
Console Inquiry Unit (SAUS) .... CIU
Console Intelligence Unit (MCD) .... CIU
Console Interface Board (SAUS) .... CIB
Console Interface Module (SAUS) .... CIM
Console Internally Generated and Refreshed Symbols (CAAL) .... CIGARS
Console Interrupt (SAUS) .... COIN
Console Interrupt Request (SAUS) .... CIR
Console Keyset (MCD) .... CK
Console Lighting Panel (MCD) .... CLP
Console Local Equipment (MCD) .... CLE
Console Manager (CIST) .... CONMAN
Console Message Processor [*Computer science*] .... CMP
Console Operating System (NASA) .... COS
Console Operator Proficiency Examination [*Computer Usage Co.*] .... COPE
Console Output (SAUS) .... CO
Console Output (BTTJ) .... CONOUT
Console Processor (NASA) .... CP
Console Programming System (IAA) .... CPS
Console Remote Equipment (MCD) .... CRE
Console Reply Queueing (SAUS) .... CRQ
Console Reply Queuing .... CRQ
Console Request Service (SAUS) .... CRS
Console Send/Receive [*Computer science*] (IAA) .... CSR
Console Set Group .... CSG
Console Simulator [*Computer science*] .... CONSIM
Console Teletype (SAUS) .... CTY
Console Terminal (SAUS) .... CST
Console to Computer Buffer (MUGU) .... CCB
Console Typewriter (IAA) .... CT
Console Typewriter (IAA) .... CTW
Console-Oriented Model Building [*Computer science*] .... COMB
Console-Oriented Statistical Matrix Operator System [*Computer science*] .... COSMOS
Consolidate (MSA) .... CNSLD
Consolidate (SAUS) .... Con
Consolidate .... CONS
Consolidate (EBF) .... Cons
Consolidate (TBD) .... Consol
Consolidate (AFM) .... CONSOL
Consolidate (FAAC) .... CSLDT
Consolidate Acquisition Directive [*DoD*] .... CAD
Consolidate Air Defense Order of Battle (MCD) .... CADOB
Consolidate Time Rate .... CTR

Consolidate-Cargo Container Service (DS) ... CCS
Consolidated [*Accounting*] ... CN
Consolidated ... CON
Consolidated (WDAA) ... cons
Consolidated ... CONS
Consolidated (DD) ... consol
Consolidated (ADA) ... CONSOLTD
Consolidated Accelerated Navy Documentation Organization ... CAN DO
Consolidated Acquistion Reporting System [*Army*] ... CARS
Consolidated Actuarial Data System [*Health insurance*] (GHCT) ... CADS
Consolidated Administrative Management Organization [*AID*] ... CAMO
Consolidated Advance Field Team [*Navy*] ... CAFT
Consolidated Aerospace Equipment List (MCD) ... CAEL
Consolidated Aerospace Ground Equipment List ... CAGEL
Consolidated Aerospace Supplier Equipment (ACAE) ... CASE
Consolidated Aerospace Supplier Evaluation (NRCH) ... CASE
Consolidated Afloat Requisitioning Guide (DNAB) ... CARGO
Consolidated AGE Ground Equipment List (MCD) ... CAGEL
Consolidated Air Mission Results Analysis (CINC) ... CAMRA
Consolidated Air Target Material Notices [*NOO*] ... CATMN
Consolidated Air Tour Manual [*Air travel term*] ... CATM
Consolidated Aircraft Corp. [*Later, General Dynamics Corp.*] (AAG) ... CAC
Consolidated Aircraft Corporation (SAUO) ... CONAIR
Consolidated Aircraft Maintenance ... CAM
Consolidated Aircraft Maintenance Group [*Air Force*] ... CAMG
Consolidated Aircraft Maintenance Squadron (SAUO) ... CAMRON
Consolidated Aircraft Maintenance Squadron [*Air Force*] ... CAMS
Consolidated Aircraft Maintenance Squadron [*Air Force*] ... CAMSq
Consolidated Aircraft Maintenance Training ... CAMT
Consolidated Aircraft Maintenance Wing [*Air Force*] ... CAMW
Consolidated Aluminum Corporation (SAUO) ... Conalco
Consolidated Aluminum Corporation (SAUO) ... CONALCO
Consolidated Amhawk Enterprise [*Vancouver Stock Exchange symbol*] ... CVK
Consolidated Ammunition Bulk Shippers (MCD) ... CABS
Consolidated Analysis Centers, Inc. ... CACI
Consolidated Andex Resources Ltd. [*Vancouver Stock Exchange symbol*] ... CON
Consolidated Annuities [*Insurance*] (DSUE) ... CONSOLS
Consolidated Annuities (WDAA) ... Consols
Consolidated Anti-Jam Equipment (MCD) ... CAJE
Consolidated Appeals Process (SAUO) ... CAP
Consolidated Aquanauts Vital Equipment ... CAVE
Consolidated Army System for Processing Entitlements to Reservists ... CASPER
Consolidated Ascot Petroleum [*Toronto Stock Exchange symbol*] [*Vancouver Stock Exchange symbol*] ... CSP
Consolidated Assistance and Relocation Efforts (MCD) ... CARE
Consolidated Athletic Commission (EA) ... CAC
Consolidated Atomic Time ... CAT
Consolidated Audio-Visual Coordinating Office [*Military*] (DNAB) ... CAVCO
Consolidated Automated Support Station (MCD) ... CASS
Consolidated Automatic Support System (SAUS) ... CASS
Consolidated Balance Sheet [*Accounting*] ... CBS
Consolidated Base Personnel Office [*Air Force*] ... CBPO
Consolidated Base Personnel Office Letter [*Air Force*] ... CBPOL
Consolidated Bel-Air [*Vancouver Stock Exchange symbol*] ... CBT
Consolidated Boulder Mountain [*Vancouver Stock Exchange symbol*] ... CBM
Consolidated Boundary Explorations [*Vancouver Stock Exchange symbol*] ... CBX
Consolidated Brinco Ltd. [*Toronto Stock Exchange symbol*] ... CBW
Consolidated BRX Mining & Petroleum Ltd. [*Vancouver Stock Exchange symbol*] ... CIX
Consolidated Business System (IAA) ... CBS
Consolidated Callinan Flin Flon Mines Ltd. [*Vancouver Stock Exchange symbol*] ... CFF
Consolidated Canarctic Industries Ltd. [*Vancouver Stock Exchange symbol*] ... CCA
Consolidated Cargo Service (SAUS) ... CCS
Consolidated Carma Corp. [*Toronto Stock Exchange symbol*] ... CVP
Consolidated Carriers Tariff Bureau ... CCTB
Consolidated Change Table (MCD) ... CCT
Consolidated Churchill Enterprises, Inc. [*Vancouver Stock Exchange symbol*] ... CHH
Consolidated Cigar Corporation (SAUO) ... CDR
Consolidated Cigar Holdings, Inc. [*NYSE symbol*] (SAG) ... CIG
Consolidated Cigar Holdings, Inc. [*Associated Press*] (SAG) ... CnCigar
Consolidated Cima Resources [*Vancouver Stock Exchange symbol*] ... CNA
Consolidated Cisco Resources [*Vancouver Stock Exchange symbol*] ... CSU
Consolidated Civilian Personnel Office [*Air Force*] ... CCPO
Consolidated Civilian Personnel Office Field Division [*Air Force*] (DNAB) ... CCPOFD
Consolidated Coal Company (SAUO) ... CSC
Consolidated Command Control and Communications Program (SAUO) ... CCCCP
Consolidated Command, Control, and Communications Program (MCD) ... CCCP
Consolidated Command Post [*Military*] ... CCP
Consolidated Communications Facilities [*NASA*] (SPST) ... CCF
Consolidated Communications Recording Facility (MCD) ... CCRF
Consolidated Companies (SAUS) ... TCD
Consolidated Component Usage File (SAUS) ... CCUF
Consolidated Computer (IAA) ... CC
Consolidated Computer and Control Center ... CCCC
Consolidated Computer Inc. (SAUO) ... CC
Consolidated Computer, Inc. (SAUS) ... CCI
Consolidated Computer Ltd. (SAUS) ... CCL
Consolidated Computer Security Program [*Military*] (GFGA) ... CCSP
Consolidated Container Processing System (MCD) ... CCPS
Consolidated Container Service (SAUS) ... CCS
Consolidated Containerization Point (SAUO) ... CCP
Consolidated Contingency Operations Center (SAUO) ... CCOC
Consolidated Contingency Steering Group (SAUO) ... CCSG
Consolidated contingency Steering Group (SAUO) ... COSG
Consolidated Contractor Repair Facility (ACAE) ... CCRF
Consolidated Controls Corporation (SAUO) ... CCCO
Consolidated Cryptologic Program [*DoD*] (AABC) ... CCP
Consolidated CSA Minerals, Inc. [*Vancouver Stock Exchange symbol*] ... CNV
Consolidated Customer Order Processing (IAA) ... CCOP
Consolidated Cyll Industry [*Vancouver Stock Exchange symbol*] ... CIY
Consolidated Data Base (PDAA) ... CDB
Consolidated Decision Package Set [*Military*] ... CDPS
Consolidated Defense Intelligence Program ... CDIP
Consolidated Defense Supply Material ... CDSM
Consolidated Deficiency and Improvement Data Systems ... CDIDS
Consolidated Delivery & Logistis, Inc. [*NASDAQ symbol*] (SAG) ... CDLI
Consolidated Delivery & Logistis, Inc. [*Associated Press*] (SAG) ... ConslDel
Consolidated Delivery Status Report (MCD) ... CDSR
Consolidated Delivery Status Report System (MCD) ... CDSRS
Consolidated Development Increment Package ... CDIP
Consolidated Diamond Mines of South West Africa (SAUO) ... CDM
Consolidated Diamond Mines of South-West Africa (SAUS) ... CDMSWA
Consolidated Diesel Electric Co. ... CONDEC
Consolidated Diesel Electric Corporation (SAUO) ... CDEC
Consolidated Diesel Electric Corporation (SAUO) ... CONDIESEL
Consolidated Duplicating Center (SAUO) ... CDC
Consolidated Ed 7.35%'PINES' [*NYSE symbol*] (SG) ... EPI
Consolidated Ed 7.75%'QUICS' [*NYSE symbol*] (TTSB) ... EDL
Consolidated Edison (MHDW) ... Con Ed
Consolidated Edison Co. (MHDB) ... CEC
Consolidated Edison Co., Inc., New York, NY [*Library symbol*] [*Library of Congress*] (LCLS) ... NNConE
Consolidated Edison Co. of New York, Inc. [*Associated Press*] (SAG) ... ConE
Consolidated Edison Co. of New York, Inc. [*Associated Press*] (SAG) ... ConEd
Consolidated Edison Co. of New York, Inc. [*NYSE symbol*] (SPSG) ... ED
Consolidated Edison Energy Control Center (SAUS) ... CEECC
Consolidated Edison Thorium Reactor ... CETR
Consolidated Edison Uranium (GAAI) ... CEU
Consolidated Edison Uranium Solidification Program [*Oak Ridge National Laboratory*] ... CEUSP
Consolidated Eglin Real-Time System (MCD) ... CERTS
Consolidated Electric Power Asia (ECON) ... CEPA
Consolidated Electrodynamics Corp. ... CEC
Consolidated Electronic Services (SAUS) ... CES
Consolidated Electronics Corp. ... CEC
Consolidated Electronics Industries Corp. (SAUO) ... CEI
Consolidated Energy Products Co. (EFIS) ... CONDEC
Consolidated Energy Services Inc. (SAUO) ... CES
Consolidated Engineering Corporation (SAUO) ... CEC
Consolidated Engineering Technology Corp. (MCD) ... CETEC
Consolidated Entry Level Training (MCD) ... CELT
Consolidated Environmental Technologies [*Commercial firm*] [*British*] (ECON) ... CET
Consolidated Exchange (SAUO) ... CE
Consolidated Explorer Petroleum Corp. [*Vancouver Stock Exchange symbol*] ... CEP
Consolidated Facilities Corp. [*Railroads*] ... CONFAC
Consolidated Federal Fund Report [*Bureau of the Census*] (GFGA) ... CFFR
Consolidated Federal Law Enforcement Training Center [*Later, FLETC*] [*Department of the Treasury*] ... CFLETC
Consolidated Fibres, Inc. (EFIS) ... CFI
Consolidated Film Industries [*Commercial firm*] ... CFI
Consolidated Film Manufacturers (SAUO) ... CFM
Consolidated Financial Statement (HGAA) ... CFS
Consolidated First Fund [*Vancouver Stock Exchange symbol*] ... FFP
Consolidated Five Star Resources [*Vancouver Stock Exchange symbol*] ... CFR
Consolidated Flight Record Custodian [*Air Force*] (AFM) ... CFRC
Consolidated Foods Corporation (SAUO) ... CFD
Consolidated Fredonia Resources Ltd. [*Vancouver Stock Exchange symbol*] ... CFN
Consolidated Free Library District, Athol Branch, Athol, ID [*Library symbol*] [*Library of Congress*] (LCLS) ... IdCC-A
Consolidated Free Library District, Coeur d'Alene, ID [*Library symbol*] [*Library of Congress*] (LCLS) ... IdCC
Consolidated Free Library District, Rathdrum Branch, Rathdrum, ID [*Library symbol*] [*Library of Congress*] (LCLS) ... IdCC-R
Consolidated Free Library District, Service Center, Couer d'Alene, ID [*Library symbol*] [*Library of Congress*] (LCLS) ... IdCC-SC
Consolidated Free Library District, Spirit Lake Branch, Spirit Lake, ID [*Library symbol*] [*Library of Congress*] (LCLS) ... IdCC-SL
Consolidated Freight Association (SAUO) ... CFA
Consolidated Freight Classification ... CFC
Consolidated Freightways [*NASDAQ symbol*] (SAG) ... CFWY
Consolidated Freightways [*NYSE symbol*] (TTSB) ... CNF
Consolidated Freightways [*Associated Press*] (SAG) ... CnsFrtC
Consolidated Freightways, Inc. ... CF
Consolidated Freightways, Inc. [*NYSE symbol*] (SPSG) ... CNF
Consolidated Freightways, Inc. [*Associated Press*] (SAG) ... CnsFrt
Consolidated Front End (ACAE) ... CFE
Consolidated Fuel Reprocessing Program [*Oak Ridge National Laboratory*] ... CFRP
Consolidated Function Ordinary [*IBM Corp.*] ... CFO
Consolidated Funds Ordinary [*Insurance*] ... CFO

Consolidated Gas, Electric Light and Power Company of Baltimore (SAUO) ... CGEL&PB
Consolidated Gas Supply Corp., Chelyan, WV [*Library symbol*] [*Library of Congress*] (LCLS) ... WvCheC
Consolidated Gas Supply Corp., Clarksburg, WV [*Library symbol*] [*Library of Congress*] (LCLS) ... WvClC
Consolidated Gas Supply Corporation (SAUO) ... CGSC
Consolidated General Orders in Chancery [*A publication*] (DLA) ... Consolid Ord
Consolidated General Orders in Chancery [*A publication*] (DLA) ... Cons Ord in Ch
Consolidated General Western Industries Ltd. [*Vancouver Stock Exchange symbol*] [*Toronto Stock Exchange symbol*] ... CVW
Consolidated Gold Fields [*British*] ... CGF
Consolidated Gold Fields [*British*] ... CONSGOLD
Consolidated Gold Fields Australia Ltd. (SAUO) ... CGFA
Consolidated Gold Fields of South Africa (SAUS) ... CGFSA
Consolidated Gold Standard Resources, Inc. [*Vancouver Stock Exchange symbol*] ... CGQ
Consolidated Goldwest [*Vancouver Stock Exchange symbol*] ... KGG
Consolidated Graphics [*NYSE symbol*] (SG) ... CGX
Consolidated Graphics [*NASDAQ symbol*] (TTSB) ... COGI
Consolidated Graphics, Inc. [*NASDAQ symbol*] (SAG) ... COGI
Consolidated Graphics, Inc. [*Associated Press*] (SAG) ... ConsGph
Consolidated Ground Support Equipment List (ACAE) ... CGSEL
Consolidated Ground Terminal (SAUS) ... CGT
Consolidated Group (SAUO) ... CG
Consolidated Group of Tribes and Organizations ... CGTO
Consolidated Guidance (RDA) ... CG
Consolidated Hazardous Item List (MCD) ... CHIL
Consolidated Hazardous Material Reutilization and Inventory Management Program (BCP) ... CHRIMP
Consolidated HCI Holdings Corp. [*Toronto Stock Exchange symbol*] ... CXA
Consolidated Headquarters Squadron [*Military*] ... CHS
Consolidated Health Care Associates, Inc. [*NASDAQ symbol*] (SAG) ... CHCA
Consolidated Health Care Associates, Inc. [*Associated Press*] (SAG) ... ConHCre
Consolidated Heron Resources [*Vancouver Stock Exchange symbol*] ... CNS
Consolidated Hlth Care Assoc [*NASDAQ symbol*] (TTSB) ... CHCA
Consolidated Housing & Community Development Plan (SAUO) ... HCD Plan
Consolidated Incineration Facility (SAUS) ... CIF
Consolidated Incinerator Facility [*Environmental science*] (COE) ... CIF
Consolidated Indescor Corp. [*Formerly, Indescor Hydrodynamics, Inc.*] [*Vancouver Stock Exchange symbol*] ... CIF
Consolidated Index of Translations into English ... CITE
Consolidated Industrial Relations Office (MUGU) ... CIRO
Consolidated Information Storage System (SAUS) ... CISS
Consolidated Inland Recovery [*Vancouver Stock Exchange symbol*] ... ILG
Consolidated Instrument Package [*Atmospheric research*] ... CIP
Consolidated Intelligence Communication Center (MCD) ... CICC
Consolidated Intelligence Periodic Summary ... CIPR
Consolidated Intelligence Program [*Military*] (AFM) ... CIP
Consolidated Intelligence Resource Information System [*Air Force*] (MCD) ... CIRIS
Consolidated Interchangeable and Substitute Item List ... CISIL
Consolidated Intermediate Repair Facility ... CIRF
Consolidated Knobby Lake Mines Ltd. [*Vancouver Stock Exchange symbol*] ... CKO
Consolidated Labor Union of the Philippines ... CLUP
Consolidated Leasing Corporation of America (SAUO) ... CLC
Consolidated Link Layer Management [*Telecommunications*] (ACRL) ... CLLM
Consolidated Listing (AFM) ... CL
Consolidated Load List (DNAB) ... CLL
Consolidated Logistics Information Planning and Programming Requirements ... CLIPPR
Consolidated Lone Star Resource Corp. [*Vancouver Stock Exchange symbol*] ... CQL
Consolidated Louanna Gold Mines Ltd. [*Toronto Stock Exchange symbol*] ... CLU
Consolidated Mail Room [*Air Force*] (AFM) ... CMR
Consolidated Maintenance Center (MCD) ... CMC
Consolidated Maintenance Squadron [*Air Force*] ... CMS
Consolidated Management Office [*Military*] ... CMO
Consolidated Manitou Resources [*Vancouver Stock Exchange symbol*] ... CSM
Consolidated Marbenor Mines Ltd. [*Toronto Stock Exchange symbol*] ... CBN
Consolidated Master Cross-Reference List [*Defense Supply Agency*] ... CMCRL
Consolidated Master Cross-Reference List [*Defense Supply Agency*] ... CMRL
Consolidated Material Distribution Objectives [*Air Force*] ... CMDO
Consolidated Material List (MCD) ... CML
Consolidated McKinney Resources, Inc. [*Vancouver Stock Exchange symbol*] ... CKY
Consolidated Mercantile [*NASDAQ symbol*] (TTSB) ... CSLMF
Consolidated Mercantile Corp. [*Toronto Stock Exchange symbol*] ... CMC
Consolidated Mercantile Corp. [*NASDAQ symbol*] (NQ) ... CSLM
Consolidated Mercatile Corp. [*Associated Press*] (SAG) ... CnsMerc
Consolidated Metal Industries (SAUS) ... CMI
Consolidated Metropolitan Area [*Later, CMSA*] [*Census Bureau*] (WDMC) ... CMA
Consolidated Metropolitan Statistical Area [*Census Bureau*] ... CMSA
Consolidated Midland Corp. (DAVI) ... CMC
Consolidated Mining & Smelting Co., Central Technical Library, Trail, BC, Canada [*Library symbol*] [*Library of Congress*] (LCLS) ... CaBTC
Consolidated Mission Support Center (SAUO) ... CMSC
Consolidated Nat Gas [*NYSE symbol*] (TTSB) ... CNG
Consolidated National Interveners [*An association*] (EA) ... CNI
Consolidated National Shoe Corp. (EFIS) ... CNS
Consolidated Natural Gas Co. [*NYSE symbol*] (SPSG) ... CNG
Consolidated Natural Gas Co. [*Associated Press*] (SAG) ... ConsNG
Consolidated Naval Telecommunications Program System (DNAB) ... CNTPS
Consolidated Navy Electronic Warfare School (PDAA) ... CNEWS
Consolidated Navy Electronic Warfare Test Plan (CAAL) ... CNEWTP
Consolidated Nev Goldfields [*NASDAQ symbol*] (TTSB) ... KNVCF
Consolidated Nevada Goldfields Corp. [*Associated Press*] (SAG) ... ConsNev
Consolidated Nevada Goldfields Corp. [*NASDAQ symbol*] (SAG) ... KNVC
Consolidated New Equipment Training Plan (MCD) ... CNETP
Consolidated Nord Resources Ltd. [*Vancouver Stock Exchange symbol*] ... CKN
Consolidated Norex Resources Corp. [*Toronto Stock Exchange symbol*] [*Vancouver Stock Exchange symbol*] ... CXK
Consolidated NRD Resources Ltd. (SAUS) ... NRDR
Consolidated Nuclear Steam Generator ... CNSG
Consolidated Omab Enterprises Ltd. [*Vancouver Stock Exchange symbol*] ... CEB
Consolidated Omnibus Budget Reconciliation Act of 1985 [*Health insurance law*] ... COBRA
Consolidated On-Line Intelligence System (ACAE) ... COINS
Consolidated Open Mess (SAUO) ... COM
Consolidated Operability Test [*or Trial*] (NG) ... COT
Consolidated Operability Trial (SAUS) ... COT
Consolidated Operating Base (CCCA) ... COB
Consolidated Operational Shipboard Allowance List (SAUS) ... COSAL
Consolidated Operations and Delay Analysis System [*FAA*] (TAG) ... CODAS
Consolidated Operations Steering Group (SAUO) ... COSG
Consolidated Ordnance Allowance List [*Navy*] ... COAL
Consolidated Pace II Industries Ltd. [*Vancouver Stock Exchange symbol*] ... CKP
Consolidated Package Store [*Military*] (DNAB) ... CPS
Consolidated Papers, Inc. [*NYSE symbol*] (SAG) ... CDP
Consolidated Papers, Inc. [*Associated Press*] (SAG) ... ConPap
Consolidated Parts List (ACAE) ... CPL
Consolidated Paymaster [*Vancouver Stock Exchange symbol*] ... CPY
Consolidated PCR Industries Ltd. [*Vancouver Stock Exchange symbol*] ... CTQ
Consolidated Pentagon Telecommunications Center (SAUO) ... CPTC
Consolidated Personal Property Shipping Office [*Military*] (DNAB) ... CPPSO
Consolidated Personnel Management Information System [*OST*] (TAG) ... CPMIS
Consolidated Petroquin [*Vancouver Stock Exchange symbol*] ... PQN
Consolidated Pilot Training Program [*Air Force*] ... CPT
Consolidated Pilot Training Program (SAUS) ... CPT Program
Consolidated Pipe Lines Co. [*Toronto Stock Exchange symbol*] ... CPP
Consolidated Plantations (SAUO) ... Consplant
Consolidated Plastic Industries (SAUS) ... CPI
Consolidated Products, Inc. [*Associated Press*] (SAG) ... ConPd
Consolidated Products, Inc. [*Associated Press*] (SAG) ... ConsPdts
Consolidated Products, Inc. [*NYSE symbol*] (SAG) ... COP
Consolidated Products, Inc. [*NASDAQ symbol*] (NQ) ... COPI
Consolidated Professor Mines Ltd. [*Toronto Stock Exchange symbol*] ... CPF
Consolidated Programming Document ... CPD
Consolidated Progress Record (SAUS) ... CPR
Consolidated Progress Report ... CPR
Consolidated Property Account (MCD) ... CPA
Consolidated Rail Corp. [*Also, CR, CRC*] ... CONRAIL
Consolidated Rail Corp. [*Also, CONRAIL, CRC*] [*AAR code*] ... CR
Consolidated Rail Corp. [*Also, CR, CONRAIL*] ... CRC
Consolidated Rail Corp. (Eastern District) [*AAR code*] ... CRE
Consolidated Rail Corporation (USGC) ... Conrail
Consolidated Rambler Mines Ltd. [*Toronto Stock Exchange symbol*] ... CRR
Consolidated Ramrod Gold Corp. [*Associated Press*] (SAG) ... ConRam
Consolidated Ramrod Gold Corp. [*Vancouver Stock Exchange symbol*] ... CYN
Consolidated Ramrod Gold Corp. [*NASDAQ symbol*] (SAG) ... CYNX
Consolidated Reactor Uranium [*Vancouver Stock Exchange symbol*] ... CRC
Consolidated Record Communications Center [*Army*] (AABC) ... CRCC
Consolidated Record of Uncontrolled Naval Calamitious Happenings ... CRUNCH
Consolidated Recreation (DNAB) ... CONSOLREC
Consolidated Regal Resources Ltd. [*Vancouver Stock Exchange symbol*] ... KRE
Consolidated Rehabilitation Programme (SAUS) ... CRP
Consolidated Remain-in-Place List (MCD) ... CRIPL
Consolidated Repair Parts List (MCD) ... CRPL
Consolidated Repairable Item List ... CRIL
Consolidated Report ... CR
Consolidated Reporting and Evaluating System, Tactical [*Computer program*] [*Air Force*] ... CREST
Consolidated Reporting of Earthquakes and Tsunamis [*National Oceanic and Atmospheric Administration*] ... CREST
Consolidated Reserve Components Reporting System (MCD) ... CORCAPS
Consolidated Reserve Personnel Office [*Air Force*] (AFM) ... CRPO
Consolidated Residual Undeleted Subordinated Tranches [*Finance*] ... CRUST
Consolidated Revenue ... CR
Consolidated Revenue Fund (SAUO) ... CRF
Consolidated Rexspar Minerals & Chemicals Ltd. [*Toronto Stock Exchange symbol*] ... CRM
Consolidated Rio Plata Resources [*Vancouver Stock Exchange symbol*] ... COP
Consolidated Rules of Practice [*Environmental Protection Agency*] (GFGA) ... CROP
Consolidated RVNAF [*Republic of Vietnam Armed Forces*] **Improvement and Modernization Program** (AABC) ... CRIMP
Consolidated Satellite Operations Center (CCCA) ... CSOC
Consolidated Satellite Test Center (ADWA) ... CSTC
Consolidated Schedule Technique ... CST
Consolidated Scientific Computing System [*Marine science*] (OSRA) ... CSCS
Consolidated Sea Gold Corp. [*Vancouver Stock Exchange symbol*] ... CDE
Consolidated Security Operations Center [*Military*] ... CSOC
Consolidated Serials Program (SAUS) ... CONSER Program
Consolidated Ships Allowance List ... COSAL
Consolidated Ships Electronic Design [*Navy*] (NG) ... CSED
Consolidated Shorebase Material Allowance List (AAGC) ... COSMAL
Consolidated Shore-Based Allowance List (MCD) ... COSBAL

Consolidated Short-Term Demand Simulation System [*Department of Energy*] (GFGA) ... CSTDSS
Consolidated Silver Butte Mines [*Vancouver Stock Exchange symbol*] ... CSB
Consolidated Silver Standard Mines Ltd. [*Vancouver Stock Exchange symbol*] ... CDS
Consolidated Site Base Loading ... CSBL
Consolidated Space Operations Center [*Colorado Springs, CO*] [*Military*] ... CSOC
Consolidated Space Test Center (ACAE) ... CSTC
Consolidated Special Information Dissemination Office [*Proposed for military intelligence gathering, late 1940's, but never activated*] ... CONSIDO
Consolidated Spot Buying [*Radio and TV advertising*] ... CSB
Consolidated Stainless [*NASDAQ symbol*] (TTSB) ... PIPE
Consolidated Stainless, Inc. [*Associated Press*] (SAG) ... CnStain
Consolidated Stainless, Inc. [*NASDAQ symbol*] (SAG) ... PIPE
Consolidated Standing Route Order [*Army*] (AABC) ... CSRO
Consolidated State Maintenance Shop [*USNB*] (MCD) ... CSMS
Consolidated States Racing Association [*Auto racing sanctioning organization*] ... CSRA
Consolidated Statutes [*A publication*] (DLA) ... Con St
Consolidated Statutes [*A publication*] (DLA) ... Con Stat
Consolidated Statutes [*A publication*] (DLA) ... CS
Consolidated Statutes of British Columbia [*A publication*] (DLA) ... CSBC
Consolidated Statutes of Canada [*A publication*] (DLA) ... CSC
Consolidated Statutes of Lower Canada [*A publication*] (DLA) ... CSLC
Consolidated Statutes of Manitoba [*A publication*] (DLA) ... CSM
Consolidated Statutes of New Brunswick [*A publication*] (DLA) ... CSNB
Consolidated Statutes of Upper Canada [*A publication*] (DLA) ... CSUC
Consolidated Steam Generator (PDAA) ... CSG
Consolidated Stikine Silver Ltd. [*Vancouver Stock Exchange symbol*] ... CKI
Consolidated Stock Status Report ... CSSR
Consolidated Stores [*NYSE symbol*] (TTSB) ... CNS
Consolidated Stores Corp. [*NYSE symbol*] (SPSG) ... CNS
Consolidated Stores Corp. [*Associated Press*] (SAG) ... CnStor
Consolidated Suntec Ventures [*Vancouver Stock Exchange symbol*] ... CQV
Consolidated Supply Contract [*Department of Housing and Urban Development*] (GFGA) ... CSC
Consolidated Supply Program [*Department of Housing and Urban Development*] (GFGA) ... CSP
Consolidated Supply Support Activity (MCD) ... CSS
Consolidated Support Equipment List (MCD) ... CSEL
Consolidated Support Model (MCD) ... CSM
Consolidated Support System ... CSS
Consolidated Surplus Sales Office [*Military - Merged with Defense Supply Agency*] ... CSSO
Consolidated Systems Corporation (SAUO) ... CSC
Consolidated Talcorp Ltd. [*Toronto Stock Exchange symbol*] ... CZZ
Consolidated Tape Association (EA) ... CTA
Consolidated Tape System [*Preferred name is Consolidated Transaction Reporting System*] [*Investment term*] ... CTS
Consolidated Target Program (ACAE) ... CTP
Consolidated Technology [*Commercial firm*] [*Associated Press*] (SAG) ... ConTech
Consolidated Technology Grp [*NASDAQ symbol*] (TTSB) ... COTG
Consolidated Telecommunications Center System (MCD) ... CTCS
Consolidated Telecommunications Program [*Military*] (GFGA) ... CTP
Consolidated Telemetry Checkout System [*Air Force*] ... CTCS
Consolidated Tenants League (EA) ... CTL
Consolidated Test Data System [*Military*] ... CTDS
Consolidated Textile Co. (SAUO) ... CTX
Consolidated Theater Target Services [*Military*] ... CTTS
Consolidated Thompson-Lundmark Gold Mines Ltd. [*Toronto Stock Exchange symbol*] ... TLG
Consolidated Tin Smelters (SAUO) ... CTS
Consolidated TOE Update [*DoD*] ... CTU
Consolidated Tomoka Land [*AMEX symbol*] (SPSG) ... CTO
Consolidated Tomoka Land Co. [*Associated Press*] (SAG) ... CnsTom
Consolidated Training Facility [*Army*] ... CTF
Consolidated Training Request [*Military*] ... CTR
Consolidated Training Support Work Group [*DoD*] ... CTSWG
Consolidated Translation Survey [*CIA*] ... CTS
Consolidated Treaty Series [*A publication*] (DLA) ... CTS
Consolidated TVX Mining Corp. [*Toronto Stock Exchange symbol*] ... CVX
Consolidated Undrained Shear with Pore Pressure Measurement [*Nuclear energy*] (NUCP) ... CAU
Consolidated Undrained Triaxial Test with Pore Pressure Measurements [*Nuclear energy*] (NUCP) ... CIU
Consolidated Unit Personnel Section ... CUPS
Consolidated Vacuum Corp., Rochester, NY [*Library symbol*] [*Library of Congress*] (LCLS) ... NRCV
Consolidated Vacuum Corporation (SAUO) ... CVC
Consolidated Vultee Aircraft Corp. (SAUO) ... CONVAIR
Consolidated Wellington Resources [*Vancouver Stock Exchange symbol*] ... CWG
Consolidated Western & Pacific Resources [*Associated Press*] (SAG) ... ConWPac
Consolidated Western & Pacific Resources [*NASDAQ symbol*] (SAG) ... CWNP
Consolidated Western Steel (SAUO) ... CWRU
Consolidated Western Steel (AAG) ... CWS
Consolidated Westrex Development [*Vancouver Stock Exchange symbol*] ... KWD
Consolidated Working Fund (OICC) ... CWF
Consolidated WWMCCS [*Worldwide Military Command and Control System*] **Program** [*DoD*] ... CWP
Consolidated Zinc Corporation Ltd. (SAUO) ... CZC
Consolidated-Bathurst, Inc. [*Toronto Stock Exchange symbol*] ... CB
Consolidated-Vultee Aircraft Corp. [*Later, General Dynamics Corp.*] ... CONVAIR
Consolidated-Vultee Aircraft Corp. [*Later, General Dynamics Corp.*] ... CVAC
Consolidating Station ... CSTA
Consolidating Station (SAUS) ... CSta
Consolidation ... CONSLDTN
Consolidation above Battalion Level [*Army*] (RDA) ... CABL
Consolidation Aerial Port System [*or Subsystem*] [*Air Force*] (MCD) ... CAPS
Consolidation and Management of Supply Consumption Rates (MCD) ... COMSCOR
Consolidation Coal - Bethlehem Steel - National Steel - Republic Steel [*Coke pellet process developed by four-company group of steel and coke producers*] ... CONSOL-BNR
Consolidation Exercise [*Military*] (NVT) ... CONSOLEX
Consolidation Incineration Facility ... CIF
Consolidation Loan Program [*Department of Education*] (GFGA) ... CLP
Consolidation Lodges [*Freemasonry*] (ROG) ... CL
Consolidation of Administration at Battalion Level [*Army*] ... CABLE
Consolidation of Basic Records Audit (SAUS) ... COBRA
Consolidation of [*Telecommunications*] **Center** (MCD) ... CC
Consolidation of Functions and Facilities Cutoff (MCD) ... COFF
Consolidation of Military Pay Services [*Strategic Air Command proposal*] ... COMPS
Consolidation of Military Personnel Activities at Fixed Installations (AABC) ... COMPACT
Consolidation of Pay and Personnel Functions [*Military*] ... COPPER
Consolidation of Serial Data Bases Project (SAUS) ... CONSER Project
Consolidation of Supply and Maintenance Regulations [*Military*] (AABC) ... COSAMREG
Consolidation of Telecommunications Center on Oahu (MCD) ... COTCO
Consolidation/Containerization Point ... CCP
Consolidator ... CONSLDTR
Consols [*Consolidateds*] ... CN
Consoltex Canada, Inc. [*Toronto Stock Exchange symbol*] ... CTX
Consommation et Corporations Canada [*Consumer and Corporate Affairs Canada-CCA*] ... CCC
Conson [*Viet Nam*] [*ICAO location identifier*] (ICLI) ... VVCS
Consonans [*Tinkling*] (DAVI) ... cons
Consonant [*Linguistics*] ... C
Consonant (NTIO) ... cons
Consonant ... CONS
Consonant Amplification (SAUS) ... CA
Consonant Nucleus Consonant (SAUS) ... CNC
Consonantal [*Linguistics*] ... K
Consonant-Consonant-Vowel-Consonant (SAUS) ... CCVC
Consonant-Vowel ... CV
Consonant-Vowel-Consonant [*Cuneiform sign*] (BJA) ... CVC
Consorcio G. Grupo Dina [*NYSE symbol*] (SPSG) ... DIN
Consorcio G Grupo Dina ADS [*NYSE symbol*] (TTSB) ... DIN
Consorcio G Grupo Dina SA de CV [*Commercial firm*] [*Associated Press*] (SAG) ... CGDina
Consorcio G Grupo Dina'L'ADS [*NYSE symbol*] (TTSB) ... DIN.L
Consort Art Graphics [*British*] ... CAG
Consort Aviation [*British*] [*ICAO designator*] (FAAC) ... CFL
Consort Coarse Servo ... CCS
Consort Energy Corp. [*Vancouver Stock Exchange symbol*] ... CEW
Consort Municipal Library, Alberta [*Library symbol*] [*National Library of Canada*] (NLC) ... ACONM
Consort Municipal Library, Consort, AB, Canada [*Library symbol*] [*Library of Congress*] (LCLS) ... CaAConM
Consort Observation Time ... COT
Consort Parallax Servo ... CXS
Consort Speed Servo ... CSS
Consortia of London Boroughs [*British*] ... CLB
Consortium ... C
Consortium ... CNSRTM
Consortium Communications International, Inc. [*New York, NY*] [*Telecommunications*] (TSSD) ... CCI
Consortium Data Network [*University of Michigan*] [*Ann Arbor*] [*Information service or system*] (IID) ... CDNET
Consortium Europeen de Transports Maritimes [*Shipping company*] [*France*] (EY) ... CETRAMAR
Consortium for Advanced Residential Buildings ... CARB
Consortium for an Advanced Silent Transport (MCD) ... CAST
Consortium for Assessment and Testing in Schools (AIE) ... CATS
Consortium for Atlantic Studies [*Arizona State University*] [*Research center*] ... CAS
Consortium for Continental Reconnaissance Using Seismic Techniques (SAUO) ... COCRUST
Consortium for Continental Reflection Profiling (SAUS) ... COCORD
Consortium for Continental Reflection Profiling [*Cornell University*] [*Ithaca, NY*] ... COCORP
Consortium for Continuing Higher Education - Librarians' Networking Committee [*Library network*] ... CCHENV-LNC
Consortium for Environmental Education in Medicine (SAUO) ... CEEM
Consortium for Equity in Standards and Testing ... CTEST
Consortium for Graduate Study in Business for Negroes [*Later, CGSM*] ... CGSBN
Consortium for Graduate Study in Management [*St. Louis, MO*] (EA) ... CGSM
Consortium for Health Information and Library Sciences [*Library network*] ... CHI
Consortium for Information Resources, Framingham, MA [*OCLC symbol*] (OCLC) ... CIR
Consortium for International Cooperation in Higher Education [*Defunct*] (EA) ... CICHE
Consortium for International Crop Protection (SAUO) ... CICP
Consortium for International Earth Science Information Network [*Information service or system*] (IID) ... CIESIN
Consortium for International Fisheries and Agricultural Development (SAUO) ... CIFAD
Consortium for International Studies Education (EA) ... CISE

Consortium for Legislative Development (SAUO) .... CLD
Consortium for Lexical Research (SAUO) .... CLR
Consortium for Library Automation in Mississipi (SAUS) .... CLAM
Consortium for Method Building (SAUO) .... CMB
[The] Consortium for Oceanographic Research and Education [A lobby group] .... CORE
Consortium for Peaceful Coexistence (EA) .... CPC
Consortium for Research in Elastic Wave Exploration Seismology (SAUS) .... CREWES Project
Consortium for Risk Evaluation with Stakeholder Participation (GEOI) .... CRESP
Consortium for School Networking [Internet] .... CoSN
Consortium for Scientific Computing (SAUS) .... CSC
Consortium for Sharing Instructional Materials [Library network] .... CSIM
Consortium for Slow Commotion Research (SAUO) .... CSCR
Consortium for Study of the California Crust (SAUS) .... CALCRUST
Consortium for Superconducting Electronics .... CSE
Consortium for the Advancement of Building Sciences [Pennsylvania State University] [Research center] (RCD) .... CABS
Consortium for the Advancement of Physics Education .... CAPE
Consortium for the Advancement of Private Higher Education (EA) .... CAPHE
Consortium for the Dissemination of Computer-based Curricular Materials (SAUO) .... CONDUIT
Consortium for the Education of Non-Traditional Students (BARN) .... CENTS
Consortium for the Study of Intelligence (EA) .... CSI
Consortium for the Sustainable Development of the Andean Ecoregion (SAUS) .... CONDESAN
Consortium Linking Universities of Science and Technology for Education and Research (SAUO) .... CLUSTER
Consortium of Academic and Special Libraries in Montana [Library network] .... CASLIM
Consortium of Academic Libraries in Manchester [British] (AIE) .... CALIM
Consortium of Aquariums, Universities, and Zoos (GVA) .... CAUZ
Consortium of Canadian Centres for Clinical Cognitive Research (SAUO) C5R
Consortium of Canadian Chiropractic Research Centres (SAUS) .... CCCRC
Consortium of Central Massachusetts Health Related Libraries [Library network] .... CCMHRL
Consortium of College and University Media Centers (NTPA) .... CCUMC
Consortium of Doctors (EA) .... COD
Consortium of East Slovakian Libraries (SAUO) .... KOLIN
Consortium of European Research Libraries (SAUS) .... CERL
Consortium of Evangelical Relief and Development Organizations (DICI) .... CERDO
Consortium of Fire Brigade Uniform Supplies [British] .... CFBUS
Consortium of Graduate Liberal Studies Programs (EA) .... CGLSP
Consortium of Institutions for Development & Research in Education in Europe (SAUO) .... CIDREE
Consortium of Jazz Organizations and Artists [Later, AJA] (EA) .... CJOA
Consortium of Latin American Studies Programs .... CLASP
Consortium of Local Authorities in Wales .... CLAW
Consortium of Local Authorities Special Programme [British] .... CLASP
Consortium of Local Education Authorities for the Provision of Science Equipment [British] .... CLEAPSE
Consortium of Multiple Sclerosis Centers (SAUO) .... CMSC
Consortium of National Hispanic Organizations [Defunct] (EA) .... CNHO
Consortium of North American Veterinary Interactive New Concept Education (ADWA) .... CONVINCE
Consortium of Professional Associations to Supervise Studies of Special Programs for the Improvement of Instruction in American Education (SAUO) .... CONPASS
Consortium of Publishers for Employment .... COPE
Consortium of Regional Environmental Education Councils .... CREEC
Consortium of Registered Nurses for Eye Acquisition [Later, ANET] (EA) .... CORNEA
Consortium of Rhode Island Academic and Research Libraries [Library network] .... CRIARL
Consortium of Social Science Associations (EA) .... COSSA
Consortium of Teachers in Genetics (HGEN) .... CONTIG
Consortium of Universities of the Metropolitan Washington Area .... CUMWA
Consortium of University Film Centers [Library network] (EA) .... CUFC
Consortium of University Research Libraries [British] (IID) .... CURL
Consortium on Advanced Biosensors (EA) .... CAB
Consortium on Automated Analytical Laboratory Systems [National Institute of Standards & Technology] .... CAALS
Consortium on Automated Standards (SAUS) .... CAALS
Consortium on Chemical Information [British] .... COCI
Consortium on Financing Higher Education (EA) .... COFHE
Consortium on International Development .... CID
Consortium on Peace Research, Education, and Development (EA) ...... COPRED
Consortium on Soils of the Tropics .... CST
Consortium Perfectae Caritatis [Association of Perfect Love] (EA) .... CPC
Consortium Research Development [Office of Education] .... CORD
Consortium Research on Indicators of System Performance (ADWA) .... CRISP
Consortium to Develop an Online Catalog [European Community] (MHDB) .... CONDOC
Consortium to Establish a Registry for Alzheimer's Disease .... CERAD
Consortium to Restructure Secondary Schools (SAUO) .... CRSS
Consorzio Interuniversitario Lombardo per l'Elaborazione Automatica [Lombard Interuniversity Consortium for Data Processing] [Information service or system] (IID) .... CILEA
Consorzio per il Sistema Informativo Piemonte [Piedmont Consortium for Information Systems] [Information service or system] (IID) .... CSI
Conspecific Sperm Precedence [Entomology] .... CSP
Conspectus of Workers' Compensation Legislation [Australia] [A publication] .... CWCL

Conspergere [Dust or Sprinkle] [Pharmacy] .... CONSPERG
Conspicuity Enhancement [Aviation] .... CE
Conspicuous .... conspic
Conspicuous Gallantry Cross [British] (WA) .... CGC
Conspicuous Gallantry Medal [British] .... CGM
Conspicuous Service Cross [Later, DSC] [British] .... CSC
Conspicuously .... CNSP
Conspiracy (ILCA) .... Consp
Constable C
Constable (NTIO) .... Cons
Constable .... CONS
Constable .... CONST
Constable (ADWA) .... const
Constable Art Club (SAUO) .... CAC
Constable on Patrol .... COP
Constable Point [Greenland] [ICAO location identifier] (ICLI) .... BGCO
Constabulary (SAUO) C
Constabulary (SAUO) .... Con
Constabulary (SAUO) .... Cons
Constabulary (AABC) .... CONSTAB
Constabulary Anti-Narcotics Unit (SAUO) .... CANU
Constabulary Brigade (SAUO) .... Con Bde
Constabulary Regiment (SAUO) .... CR
Constance-Lethbridge Rehabilitation Centre [Centre de Readaptation Constance-Lethbridge] Montreal, Quebec [Library symbol] [National Library of Canada] (NLC) .... QMLR
Constancy of Visual Direction (SAUS) .... CVD
Constant C
Constant (DNAB) .... CON
Constant (WEAT) .... CONS
Constant [Medicine] (DMAA) .... const
Constant .... CONST
Constant .... K
Constant Absolute Vorticity Trajectory .... CAVT
Constant Aerial Glide (SAUS) .... CAG
Constant Air Line (SAUS) .... Const AL
Constant Air Monitor [Nuclear energy] (NRCH) .... CAM
Constant Air Volume (SARE) .... CAV
Constant Alert Cycle .... CAC
Constant Altitude Glide .... CAG
Constant Altitude Plan Position Indicator (ACAE) .... CAPPI
Constant Altitude Z Log Range (SAUS) .... CAZLOR
Constant Amplitude .... CA
Constant Angular Velocity [Videodisk format] .... CAV
Constant Area Quantization (MCD) .... CAQ
Constant Attenuation (SAUS) .... CA
Constant Axial Offset Control (NRCH) .... CAOC
Constant Bandwidth (MCD) .... CB
Constant Bandwidth (MCD) .... CBW
Constant Bandwidth Frequency Modulation (MHDB) .... CBFM
Constant BIT [Binary Digit] Density [Control feature of magnetic tape recorders] [Computer science] .... CBD
Constant Bit Density (SAUS) .... CBD
Constant Bit Rate [Telecommunications] (CDE) .... CBR
Constant Blow Energy [Teledyne Roxon 400] [Hydraulics] .... CBE
Constant Boiling Mixture .... CBM
Constant Boiling Point .... CBP
Constant Capacitance - Deep Level Transient Spectroscopy (PDAA) ...... CC-DLTS
Constant Card Processing (SAUS) .... CCP
Constant Command (SAUS) CC
Constant Conditions CC
Constant Control Oil (IAA) .... CCO
Constant Control Oil Pressure (SAUS) .... CCO Pressure
Constant Cost Integer Code [Computer science] (IAA) CCIC
Constant Current [Electronics] (IAA) CC
Constant Current Flux Reset .... CCFR
Constant Current Fringes .... CDF
Constant Current Generator .... CCG
Constant Current Light Emitting Diode (DICI) .... CCLED
Constant Current Modulation .... CCM
Constant Current Operation (IAA) .... CCO
Constant Current Transformer .... CCT
Constant Delay Line .... CDL
Constant Delta Altitude (SAUS) .... CDA
Constant Delta Height [Aerospace] .... CDH
Constant Denaturing Gradient Electrophoresis [Analytical biochemistry] ..... CDGE
Constant Density Recording .... CDR
Constant Depression [Automotive engineering] .... CD
Constant Deviation Prism .... CDP
Constant Differential Height [Aerospace] (MCD) .... CDH
Constant [or Continuous] Distending Pressure (AAMN) .... CDP
Constant Dollar Accounting (ADA) .... CDA
Constant Dose Range [Radiation in atmosphere] .... CDR
Constant Drainage (WGA) .... CD
Constant Drive (ACAE) .... CD
Constant Elasticity of Substitution [Industrial production] .... CES
Constant Electric Contact (IAA) .... CEC
Constant Electric Field [Medicine] (DMAA) .... CEF
Constant Electric Field (SAUS) .... E
Constant Energy (SAUS) .... E
Constant Energy Differences .... CED
Constant Energy Synchronous Luminescence Spectroscopy .... CESLS
Constant Error [Psychology] .... CE
Constant Expression (SAUS) .... CE
Constant Extension Rate Tensile Test .... CERT

Constant Extinction Angle (IAA)	CEA
Constant False Alarm Probability [*Military*]	CFAP
Constant False Alarm Rate [*or Ratio*] [*Military*]	CFAR
Constant Feed Lubricator	CFL
Constant Final State Spectroscopy (MCD)	CFS
Constant Final State spectroscopy (SAUS)	CFS
Constant Flow Rate	CFR
Constant Flux (SAUS)	CF
Constant Fraction Discriminator [*Electronics*] (OA)	CFD
Constant Fraction Trigger (OA)	CFT
Constant Frequency [*Electronics*]	CF
Constant Frequency Generator (MCD)	CFG
Constant Frequency Variable Dot	CFVD
Constant Funding (MCD)	CF
Constant Gradient (SAUS)	CG
Constant Gradient Gel Electrophoresis [*Medicine*] (DMAA)	CGGE
Constant Hazard Ratio	CHR
Constant Heat Summation	CHS
Constant Hot Water [*British*]	CHW
Constant Human Immunoglobulin	Ch
Constant Impedance Mechanical Modulation (AAG)	CIMM
Constant Infusion Excretory Program (SAUS)	CIXA
Constant Infusion Excretory Urogram [*Medicine*] (DMAA)	CIXA
Constant Infusion Excretory Urogram [*Medicine*] (MAE)	CIXU
Constant Initial Concentration (DB)	CIC
Constant Initial State Spectroscopy (MCD)	CIS
Constant Injection System [*Automotive engineering*]	CIS
Constant Instruction (SAUS)	CI
Constant Level Balloon	CLB
Constant Level Discriminator [*Electronics*] (OA)	CLD
Constant Level Signalling (CCCA)	CLS
Constant Level Signals (SAUO)	CLS
Constant Level Speech	CLS
Constant Light Compensating (OA)	CLC
Constant Linear Time Velocity (SAUS)	CLTV
Constant Linear Velocity [*Videodisk format*]	CLV
Constant Load Rupture (OA)	CLR
Constant Load Tensile Test	CLT
Constant Magnetic Field (MHDB)	CMF
Constant Maturity Treasury (TDOB)	CMT
Constant Mean Curvature [*Mathematics*]	CMC
Constant Memory (SAUS)	CM
Constant Misery [*Slang*]	CM
Constant Miss Proportional Guidance	CMPG
Constant Momentum Transfer Average (MCD)	CMTA
Constant Multiplier Unit (SAUS)	CMU
Constant Net Loss [*Telecommunications*] (TEL)	CNL
Constant Offset Profile [*Seismology*]	COP
Constant Optimal Performance Theorem [*Physics*]	COPT
Constant Optimum Separation Lane [*Aviation*] (DA)	COS
Constant Output Level Adapter (SAUS)	COLA
Constant Parity [*Physics*]	CP
Constant Pattern Generator	CPG
Constant Percentage Resolution (SAUS)	CRP
Constant Phase Angle [*Electronics*] (BARN)	CPA
Constant Pitch (SAUS)	CP
Constant Point Calculation (SAUS)	CPC
Constant Position Mounting System (PDAA)	CPMS
Constant Positive Airway Pressure [*Medicine*]	CPAP
Constant [*or Continuous*] Positive-Pressure Breathing [*Medicine*] (DAVI)	CPPB
Constant Potential (DEN)	CP
Constant Potential Accelerator	CPA
Constant Power (DA)	CP
Constant Power Density (SAUS)	CPD
Constant Prepayment Rate [*Mortgage-backed securities*]	CPR
Constant Pressure (MSA)	CP
Constant Pressure Date (DNAB)	CPD
Constant Problem Size	CPS
Constant Product Curve [*Economics*]	CPC
Constant Property	CP
Constant Purchasing Power	CPP
Constant Rate (OA)	CR
Constant Rate Injector [*Instrumentation*]	CRI
Constant Rate of Heating	CRH
Constant Rate of Penetration (OA)	CRP
Constant Ratio Elasticity of Substitution (PDAA)	CRES
Constant Ratio Roll (SAUS)	CRR
Constant Ratio Rule (PDAA)	CRR
Constant Ratios of Elasticities of Substitution-Homothetic [*Statistics*]	CRESH
Constant Reflector Voltage (IAA)	CRV
Constant Region [*Immunochemistry*]	C
Constant Returns to Scale [*Econometrics*]	CRTS
Constant Ringing Drop [*Alarm system*]	CRD
Constant Ringing Relay [*Alarm system*]	CRR
Constant Routine	CR
Constant Scattering Length (OA)	CSL
Constant Security Surveillance [*Shipping*]	CSS
Constant Slew Rate Filter (SAUS)	CSRF
[*The*] Constant Society (EA)	TCS
Constant Speed Unit [*Aviation*] (ADA)	CSU
Constant Stimulus Difference [*Pair comparison*] [*Aircraft noise*]	CSD
Constant Stirred Reactor (EDCT)	CSTR
Constant Stress Rate (IAA)	CSR
Constant Tangential Velocity	CTV
Constant Temperature (SAUS)	CT

Constant Temperature Anemometer System	CTAS
Constant Temperature Circulator [*Instrumentation*]	CTC
Constant Temperature Sampling [*Automotive engineering*]	CTS
Constant Tension Band [*Mechanical clamping device*]	CTB
Constant Time Loci	CTL
Constant Torque Compensation	CTC
Constant Total Power (SAUS)	CTP
Constant Vacuum Control [*Automotive emissions*]	CVC
Constant Value	CV
Constant Velocity (SAA)	CONVEL
Constant Velocity	CV
Constant Velocity Alignment [*Drive system coupling*]	CVA
Constant Velocity Recording	CVR
Constant Velocity Transmission	CVT
Constant Viscosity (SAUS)	CV
Constant Voltage (IAA)	CV
Constant Voltage and Constant Frequency (BUR)	CVCF
Constant Voltage Current Limiting (IAA)	CVCL
Constant Voltage Reference	CVR
Constant Voltage Source	CVS
Constant Voltage Transformer	CVT
Constant Voltage Unit	CVU
Constant Voltage/Constant Current (IEEE)	CV/CC
Constant Voltage/Current Limiting (SAUS)	CV/CL
Constant Volume	CV
Constant Volume Drop Time	CVDT
Constant Volume Sampler (EEVL)	CVS
Constant Volume Sampling [*ACF Industries*]	CVS
Constant Wall Temperature [*Engineering*]	CWT
Constant Watch Network (SAUO)	CWNET
Constant Wattage Autotransformer (SAUS)	CWA
Constant Wattage Ballast (SAUS)	CWB
Constant Wear (KSC)	CW
Constant Weight (SAUS)	CW
Constant Word Length (SAUS)	CWL
Constanta [*Romania*] [*Airport symbol*] (OAG)	CND
Constant-Adjustment Matrix, Flexible-Accelerator Path [*Economic theory*]	CFAP
Constanta/M. Kogalniceau [*Romania*] [*ICAO location identifier*] (ICLI)	LRCK
Constant-Angle Mie Scattering [*Optics*]	CAMS
Constant-Angle Reflection Interference Spectroscopy	CARIS
Constant-Capacitance Deep-Level Transient Spectroscopy (SAUS)	CCDLTS
Constant-Choice Perceptual Maze Test	CCPM
Constant-Control Oil Pressure (MSA)	CCOP
Constant-Depth Temperature Sensor [*Oceanography*]	CDTS
Constant-Flow/High Pressure [*Oxygen system*]	CF/HP
Constant-Frequency Alternating Current (SAUS)	CFAC
Constantian Society (EA)	CS
Constantine [*Roman emperor, 272-337AD*] (ROG)	CONST
Constantine [*Algeria*] [*Airport symbol*] (OAG)	CZL
Constantine Order [*Freemasonry*] (ROG)	CO
Constantine/Ain El Bey [*Algeria*] [*ICAO location identifier*] (ICLI)	DABC
Constantinople [*Later, Istanbul*] [*Turkey*] (ROG)	CON
Constantinople [*Later, Istanbul*] [*Turkey*] (ROG)	CONST
Constantinople [*Later, Istanbul*] [*Turkey*] (DSUE)	CONSTANT
Constantinople [*Later, Istanbul*] [*Province in Turkey*]	CPLE
Constantinople Pentateuch (BJA)	CP
Constantinopolitana (ROG)	CPA
Constantinus Coptius [*Flourished, 16th century*] [*Authority cited in pre-1607 legal work*] (DSA)	Constan Copti
Constantius Rogerius [*Flourished, 16th century*] [*Authority cited in pre-1607 legal work*] (DSA)	Constan Roger
Constantly Operating	CO
Constant-Market-Shares (SAUO)	CMS
Constant-Output Amplifier (MUGU)	COA
Constant-Output Level Adapter	COLA
Constants Board Assembly	CBA
Constants Change Display (MCD)	CCD
Constant-Speed [*Propeller*] (PIAV)	CS
Constant-Speed Drive	CSD
Constant-Speed Drive/Starter (NG)	CSDS
Constant-Switch-Pace Symmetric Random Signal (PDAA)	CSRS
Constant-Viscosity [*Rubber*]	CV
Constant-Voltage Stress (SAUS)	CVS
Constant-Volume Feeder [*Nuclear energy*] (NUCP)	CVF
Constant-Wear Garment [*Apollo*] [*NASA*]	CWG
Constanza [*Dominican Republic*] [*ICAO location identifier*] (ICLI)	MDCZ
Constatine Township Library, Constatine, MI [*Library symbol*] [*Library of Congress*] (LCLS)	MiCon
Constellate Consultants (P) Ltd. [*Information service or system*] (IID)	CONCON
Constellation Communications, Inc.	CCI
Constellation Energy Group [*NYSE symbol*] (SG)	CEG
Constellation X-ray Mission (SAUS)	Constellation-X
Constipated (DSUE)	CONSTI
Constituency	CONST
Constituency (SAUS)	Const
Constituency	CONSTIT
Constituency Labour Party [*British*] (BARN)	CLP
Constituency Proportion Distribution	CPD
Constituency Relations Program (SAUO)	CRP
Constituent (SAUS)	Constit
Constituent (DAVI)	constit
Constituent Assembly [*Vietnam*]	CA
Constituent Concentration in a Waste Extract	CCWE

Constituent Concentrations in the Waste [*Environmental Protection Agency*] .... CCW
Constituent Electronic Mail System (SAUS) .... CEMS
Constitute (SAUS) .... Const
Constituted Soil Columns [*Agronomy*] .... CSS
Constitutio [*Point at Issue, Regulation, Settlement*] [*Latin*] (OCD) .... CONST
Constitutio Carolina Criminalis [*A publication*] (DSA) CCC
Constitution (NTIO) .... cons
Constitution .... CONS
Constitution [*or Constitutional*] .... CONST
Constitution (ADWA) .... Const
Constitution [*or Constitutional*] [*Medicine*] (DAVI) .... constit
Constitution .... CONSTN
Constitution (ROG) .... CONSTON
Constitution and Ancient Charges [*Freemasonry*] (ROG) .... CAC
Constitution Athletic Conference (PSS) .... CAC
Constitution Bancorp of New England, Inc. (MHDW) .... CBNEV
Constitution General Grand Chapter [*Freemasonry*] (ROG) .... CGGC
Constitution of the United States [*A publication*] (DLA) .... Const US
Constitution of the United States (SAUS) .... US Const
Constitution of Virginia [*A publication*] (DLA) CV
Constitution Parties of the United States [*An association*] (EA) .... CPUS
Constitutional (AAGC) .... Const
Constitutional [*Legal shorthand*] (LWAP) .... CONSTAL
Constitutional .... CONSTL
Constitutional (SAUS) .... Constl
Constitutional Acts of Canada [*Database*] [*Federal Department of Justice*] [*Information service or system*] (CRD) .... CAC
Constitutional and Legislative Policy Institute [*Budapest, Hungary*] .... COLPI
Constitutional and Parliamentary Information [*A publication*] (DLA) .... Const & Parliam Inf
Constitutional Aplastic Anemia [*Medicine*] .... CAA
Constitutional Commentary [*A publication*] (DLA) .... Const Commentary
Constitutional Commission [*An association*] (EA) CC
Constitutional Consultative Committee on the Political Future of Nigeria [*Political party*] CCC
Constitutional Convention .... CON-CON
Constitutional Court (SAUO) .... CCT
Constitutional Educational League .... CEL
Constitutional Hepatic Dysfunction (SAUS) .... CHD
Constitutional Officer (DNAB) .... CNO
Constitutional Psychopathic Inferior [*or Inferiority*] .... CPI
Constitutional Psychopathic State .... CPS
Constitutional Pure Red Cell Aplasia [*Medicine*] (DMAA) .... CPRCA
Constitutional Reform Centre [*British*] (CB) .... CRC
Constitutional Repeating Unit [*Organic chemistry*] .... CRU
Constitutional Reports [*South Carolina*] [*A publication*] (DLA) .... Const Rep
Constitutional Reports, New Series, Printed by Mills [*South Carolina*] [*A publication*] (DLA) .... Const NS
Constitutional Reports, New Series, Printed by Mills [*South Carolina*] [*A publication*] (DLA) .... Const SCNS
Constitutional Reports, Printed by Harper [*1 South Carolina*] [*A publication*] (DLA) .... Const
Constitutional Reports, Printed by Mills [*South Carolina*] [*A publication*] (DLA) .... Const
Constitutional Reports, Printed by Treadway [*South Carolina*] [*A publication*] (DLA) .... Const
Constitutional Reports, Printed by Treadway [*South Carolina*] [*A publication*] (DLA) .... Const RSC
Constitutional Reports, Printed by Treadway [*South Carolina*] [*A publication*] (DLA) .... Const SC
Constitutional Review [*A publication*] (DLA) .... Const Rev
Constitutional Revival (EA) .... CR
Constitutional Rights Foundation (EA) .... CRF
Constitutionalist Party [*Malta*] [*Political party*] (PPE) .... CP
Constitutionally Delayed Short Stature [*Medicine*] .... CDSS
Constitutiones Othoni [*At the end of Lyndewood's Provinciale*] [*A publication*] (DLA) .... Const Oth
Constitutiones Tiberii [*A publication*] (DLA) .... CT
Constitutions and Laws of the American Indian Tribes [*A publication*] (DLA) .... CLAIT
Constitutions of African States [*A publication*] (DLA) .... Const Afr States
Constitutions of Dependencies and Special Sovereignties [*A publication*] (DLA) .... Const Dep & Sp Sov
Constitutions of Nations [*A publication*] (DLA) .... Const Nations
Constitutive Androstane Receptor [*Endocrinology*] .... CAR
Constitutive Transcript [*Genetics*] .... CT
Constitutive Transcription Unit [*Genetics*] .... CTU
Constitutive Transport Element [*Biochemistry*] .... CTE
Conston Corp. (SAUO) .... KCS
Constrado Structural Analysis System [*Structures & Computers Ltd.*] [*Software package*] (NCC) .... CONSAS
Constrained and Unconstrained Testing Environment (SAUO) .... CUTE
Constrained Deconvolution Technique [*Computer science*] .... CD
Constrained Delaunay Triangulation (GEOI) .... CDT
Constrained Force Model (PDAA) .... CONFORM
Constrained Layer Damping (SAUS) .... CLD
Constrained Least Squares (PDAA) .... CLS
Constrained Least Squares Filter (SAUS) .... CLS Filter
Constrained Maximum Likelihood .... CML
Constrained Optimal Design [*Computer science*] (RDA) .... COD
Constrained Optimization (SAUS) .... Conopt
Constrained Optimization Procedure (MCD) .... COP
Constrained Procedure (AAG) .... CP
Constrained Resistor (SAUS) .... CR

Constrained Step Size (SAUS) .... CONSS
Constrained Structure Generation .... CONGEN
Constrained Vapor Bubble Heat Exchanger (SAUS) .... CVBT
Constrained Voltage Source (SAUS) .... CVS
Constraint (SAUS) .... Constr
Constraint (KSC) .... CONSTR
Constraint Based Diagnostic System (ROAS) .... CBDS
Constraint Control .... C/C
Constraint Handling in Industry and Commerce (SAUS) .... CHIC
Constraint Handling in Prolog [*A programming language*] [*Computer science*] .... CHIP
Constraint Handling Rules (SAUS) .... CHR
Constraint Imperative Programming (SAUS) .... CIP
Constraint Least Squares (SAUS) .... CLS
Constraint Logic Programming .... CLP
Constraint Qualification (DNAB) .... CQ
Constraint Satisfaction Problem [*Computer science*] .... CSP
Constraints and Restrictions Document (SAUS) .... CARD
Constricted Double Heterojunction (MCD) .... CDH
Constriction, Sclerosis, Hemorrhage, Exudate, Papilledema [*Ophthalmology*] .... CSHEP
Constrictive Pericarditis [*Medicine*] (MELL) .... CPC
Construcciones Aeronauticas SA [*Spain*] [*ICAO aircraft manufacturer identifier*] (ICAO) .... CS
Construcciones Agrometalicas Levante, S.A. (EFIS) .... CALSA
Construct (SAUS) .... Const
Construct [*or Construction*] (AFM) .... CONST
Construct State (BJA) .... Constr
Constructed (NTIO) .... cons
Constructed (SAUS) .... CONST
Constructed (SAUS) .... Constr
Constructed Double-Heterojunction Large Optical Cavity (SAUS) .... CDH-LOC
Constructeurs Europeens de Locomotives Thermiques et Electriques [*European Manufacturers of Thermal and Electric Locomotives*] (EAIO) .... CELTE
Constructing .... CONSTRCT
Constructing Contractor (AAG) CC
Constructing Quartermaster [*Army*] .... CQM
Construction .... CONS
Construction (DD) .... const
Construction (VRA) .... constr
Construction .... CONSTR
Construction (EBF) .... Constr
Construction .... CONSTRCTN
Construction .... CONSTRN
Construction (ROG) .... CONSTRON
Construction Acquisition Improvement Implementation Team (AAGC) .... CAITT
Construction Acquisition Work Group (AAGC) .... CAWG
Construction Advanced Planning and Sequencing [*Nuclear energy*] (NRCH) .... CAPS
Construction Aggregates Corporation (SAUO) .... CAC
Construction Analysis Workgroup (AAEL) .... CAW
Construction and Agricultural Film Manufacturers Film Association (NTPA) .... CAFMFA
Construction and Demolition waste (SAUS) .... C+D-waste
Construction and Development .... C & D
Construction and Equipment .... C & E
Construction and Industrial Machinery Technical Committee (SAUO) .... CIMTC
Construction and Machinery .... C & M
Construction and Machinery .... CM
Construction and Maintenance division (SAUO) .... C&M
Construction and Maintenance Unit (SAUO) .... CMU
Construction and Management of Distributed Office Systems [*ESPRIT*] (NITA) .... COMANDOS
Construction and Mining Equipment Association of Australia .... CMEAA
Construction and Operating License .... COL
Construction and Overhaul Testing .... COT
Construction and Repair [*Coast Guard*] .... C and R
Construction and Repair (SAUS) .... C&R
Construction and Repair, Alteration [*Coast Guard*] .... CONALT
Construction and Road Transport (ADA) .... CART
Construction and Startup/Turnover Surveillance Group [*Nuclear energy*] (NRCH) .... CSTS
Construction and Use (DCTA) .... C & U
Construction and Use Regulations (SAUS) .... CUR
Construction Appraisal Team (NRCH) .... CAT
Construction Apprentice (MUGU) .... CP
Construction Assistance Vehicle [*Navy*] (MCD) .... CAV
Construction Association of Michigan (SRA) .... CAM
Construction Association of New Brunswick Inc. (AC) .... CANB
Construction Authority (SAUO) .... CA
Construction Authorization (NRCH) .... CA
Construction Battalion [*SEABEE*] [*Navy*] .... CB
Construction Battalion [*Navy*] .... CBN
Construction Battalion (SAUO) .... ConBn
Construction Battalion [*CB*] [*Acronym is a phonetic reference to a member of this Naval unit*] .... SEABEE
Construction Battalion [*USNR classification*] .... VCB
Construction Battalion Base Unit [*Obsolete*] [*Navy*] .... CBBU
Construction Battalion Center [*Navy*] (MCD) .... CBC
Construction Battalion Center Management Information System [*Navy*] (DNAB) .... CBCMIS
Construction Battalion Center MIS (SAUO) .... CBC/MIS
Construction Battalion Detachment [*Navy*] .... CBD
Construction Battalion Detachment [*Navy*] (DNAB) .... CBNDET
Construction Battalion Maintenance Unit [*Navy*] .... CBMU

Construction Battalion Maintenance Unit Detachment [*Navy*] (DNAB) ... CBMUDET
Construction Battalion Replacement Depot [*Navy*] ... CBRD
Construction Battalion Unit [*Navy*] ... CBU
Construction Battalions, Atlantic [*Navy*] ... CBLANT
Construction Battalions, Pacific [*Navy*] ... CBPAC
[*The*] **Construction Briefing Collection** [*A publication*] (AAGC) ... CBC
Construction Briefing Paper [*A publication*] (AAGC) ... CB
Construction Briefing Paper [*A publication*] (AAGC) ... CBP
Construction Briefings [*A publication*] (AAGC) ... Constr Briefings
Construction Bureau (SAUO) ... KB
Construction Central Operations Unit (HEAS) ... CCOU
Construction Change Request ... CCR
Construction, Civil Engineering, Mining [*A publication*] ... CCEM
Construction Claims Monthly [*Business Publishers, Inc.*] [*A publication*] (AAGC) ... CCM
Construction Company (SAUO) ... Con Coy
Construction Completion Date (AFM) ... CCD
Construction Computer Applications Newsletter [*Database*] [*Construction Industry Press*] [*Information service or system*] (CRD) ... CCAN
[*The*] **Construction Contractor** [*A publication*] (AAGC) ... CC
Construction Contractor Appraisal Support System (AAGC) ... CCASS
Construction Coordination Group [*NASA*] (KSC) ... CCG
Construction Corp. [*Myanmar*] (DS) ... CONCORP
Construction Corps ... CC
Construction Corps (SAUO) ... CC
Construction Corps of the Philippines [*World War II*] ... CONCOR
Construction Cost Index ... CCI
Construction Criteria Base [*Information service or system*] (IID) ... CCB
Construction Defect ... CD
Construction Department (SAUO) ... CD
Construction Design and Management (HEAS) ... CDM
Construction Design and Management Regulations (HEAS) ... CONDAM
Construction Design Criteria [*Telecommunications*] (TEL) ... CDC
Construction Discrepancy Report ... CDR
Construction Dollar Control System [*AT & T*] ... CDCS
Construction Dollar Spreading [*System*] [*AT & T*] ... CDS
Construction Economics European Committee (EAIO) ... CEEC
Construction Education Foundation [*Formerly, Merit Shop Foundation*] (EA) ... MSF
Construction Electrician [*Navy rating*] ... CE
Construction Electrician [*Navy rating*] (DNAB) ... CONSTELEC
Construction Electrician, Chief [*Navy rating*] ... CEC
Construction Electrician, First Class [*Navy rating*] ... CE1
Construction Electrician, Master Chief [*Navy rating*] ... CECM
Construction Electrician, Power [*Navy rating*] ... CEP
Construction Electrician, Power, Construction Apprentice [*Navy rating*] (DNAB) ... CEPCA
Construction Electrician, Power, Constructionman [*Navy rating*] (DNAB) ... CEPCN
Construction Electrician, Power, First Class [*Navy rating*] (DNAB) ... CEP1
Construction Electrician, Power, Second Class [*Navy rating*] (DNAB) ... CEP2
Construction Electrician, Power, Third Class [*Navy rating*] (DNAB) ... CEP3
Construction Electrician, Second Class [*Navy rating*] ... CE2
Construction Electrician, Senior Chief [*Navy rating*] ... CECS
Construction Electrician, Shop [*Navy rating*] ... CES
Construction Electrician, Shop, Construction Apprentice [*Navy rating*] (DNAB) ... CESCA
Construction Electrician, Shop, Constructionman [*Navy rating*] (DNAB) ... CESCN
Construction Electrician, Shop, First Class [*Navy rating*] (DNAB) ... CES1
Construction Electrician, Shop, Second Class [*Navy rating*] (DNAB) ... CES2
Construction Electrician, Shop, Third Class [*Navy rating*] (DNAB) ... CES3
Construction Electrician, Telephone [*Navy rating*] ... CET
Construction Electrician, Telephone, Construction Apprentice [*Navy rating*] (DNAB) ... CETCA
Construction Electrician, Telephone, Constructionman [*Navy rating*] (DNAB) ... CETCN
Construction Electrician, Telephone, First Class [*Navy rating*] (DNAB) ... CET1
Construction Electrician, Telephone, Second Class [*Navy rating*] (DNAB) ... CET2
Construction Electrician, Telephone, Third Class [*Navy rating*] (DNAB) ... CET3
Construction Electrician, Third Class [*Navy rating*] ... CE3
Construction Electrician, Wiring [*Navy rating*] ... CEW
Construction Electrician, Wiring, Construction Apprentice [*Navy rating*] (DNAB) ... CEWCA
Construction Electrician, Wiring, Constructionman [*Navy rating*] (DNAB) ... CEWCN
Construction Electrician, Wiring, First Class [*Navy rating*] (DNAB) ... CEW1
Construction Electrician, Wiring, Second Class [*Navy rating*] (DNAB) ... CEW2
Construction Electrician, Wiring, Third Class [*Navy rating*] (DNAB) ... CEW3
Construction Engineer ... CONSTENGR
Construction Engineering (DD) ... ConstEng
Construction Engineering Research Laboratory [*Champaign, IL*] [*Army*] ... CERL
Construction Engineering Research Laboratory (SAUS) ... CREL
Construction Entrance (COE) ... CE
Construction Equipment Advertisers [*Later, CEA PRC*] (EA) ... CEA
Construction Equipment Advertisers and Public Relations Council [*Milwaukee, WI*] (EA) ... CEA PRC
Construction Equipment Advisers (SAUO) ... CEA
Construction Equipment and Materials Handling Equipment [*Military*] (RDA) ... CE/MHE
Construction Equipment Management System ... CEMS
Construction Exports Advisory Board (SAUO) ... CEAB
Construction Financial Management Association (EA) ... CFMA
Construction Forces (ABAC) ... CF
Construction, Forestry, Mining and Energy Union (SAUO) ... CFMEU
Construction Grants GICS (SAUS) ... CGGICS
Construction Grants Resource Model (SAUS) ... CGPRM
Construction Health and Safety Group (HEAS) ... CHSG
Construction Industries Association (SAUO) ... CIA
Construction Industries of Rhode Island (SRA) ... CIRI
Construction Industry Advisory Committee (SAUO) ... CIAC
Construction Industry Advisory Committee (HEAS) ... CONIAC
Construction Industry Advisory Council (SAUO) ... CIAC
Construction Industry Collective Bargaining Commission [*Terminated, 1978*] [*Department of Labor*] (EGAO) ... CICBC
Construction Industry Commission [*Canada*] ... CIC
Construction Industry Computing Association (EAIO) ... CICA
Construction Industry Development Council [*Canada*] ... CIDC
Construction Industry Federation (SAUO) ... CIF
Construction Industry Foundation [*Defunct*] (EA) ... CIF
Construction Industry Information Group (SAUO) ... CIIG
Construction Industry Information Group Bulletin (journ.) (SAUS) ... CIIG Bul
Construction Industry Institute [*Australia*] ... CII
Construction Industry Joint Conference (EA) ... CIJC
Construction Industry Management Board [*Defunct*] (EA) ... CIMB
Construction Industry Manufacturers Association (EA) ... CIMA
Construction Industry Marketing Group (SAUO) ... CIMG
Construction Industry Press [*Information service or system*] (IID) ... CIP
Construction Industry Reform Strategy ... CIRS
Construction Industry Research and Information Association [*Research center*] [*British*] (IRC) ... CIRIA
Construction Industry Sales (NTPA) ... CIS
Construction Industry Stabilization Committee [*Abolished, 1974*] ... CISC
Construction Industry Thesaurus (SAUS) ... CIT
Construction Industry Training Board (SAUO) ... CIBT
Construction Industry Training Board (MCD) ... CITB
Construction Industry Training Center (MCD) ... CITC
Construction Industry Training Centre (SAUO) ... CITC
Construction Industry Translation and Information Services [*Dublin, Ireland*] ... CITIS
Construction Industry Workforce Foundation (SAUO) ... CIWF
Construction Information Center Co. Ltd. [*Information service or system*] (IID) ... CIC
Construction Information Online Retrieval Network [*Information service or system*] (IID) ... CORNET
Construction Injury Liability Monthly [*Business Publishers, Inc.*] [*A publication*] (AAGC) ... CILM
Construction Inspection Procedure (SAUS) ... CIP
Construction Interface Surveillance Control Section (SAA) ... CISCS
Construction Joint [*Technical drawings*] ... CJ
Construction Keyed Lock (ADA) ... CK
Construction Labor Report (AAGC) ... CLR
Construction Labour Relations - An Alberta Association (AC) ... CLRA
Construction Law Reports (AAGC) ... CLR
Construction Lawyer [*ABA*] [*A publication*] (AAGC) ... Constr Law
Construction Litigation Reporter (AAGC) ... CLR
Construction Maintenance Center (SAUS) ... CMC
Construction Maintenance Supervisor (SAUS) ... CMS
Construction Management ... CM
Construction Management (DD) ... ConstMgmt
Construction Management Accounting System (MHDI) ... CMAS
Construction Management Agency Construction (SAUO) ... CMAC
Construction Management Association of America (EA) ... CMAA
Construction Management Control System [*General Services Administration*] ... CMCS
Construction Management General Contractor (SAUO) ... CMGC
Construction Management Plan (PA) ... CMP
Construction Management System (SAUS) ... CMS
Construction Manager (COE) ... CM
Construction Marketing Research Council (NTPA) ... CMRC
Construction Materials Testing (MHDI) ... CMT
Construction Mechanic [*Navy rating*] ... CM
Construction Mechanic, Automotive [*Navy rating*] ... CMA
Construction Mechanic, Chief [*Navy rating*] ... CMC
Construction Mechanic, Construction [*Navy rating*] ... CMH
Construction Mechanic, Construction Apprentice [*Navy rating*] (DNAB) ... CMCA
Construction Mechanic, First Class [*Navy rating*] ... CM1
Construction Mechanic, Master Chief [*Navy rating*] ... CMCM
Construction Mechanic, Second Class [*Navy rating*] ... CM2
Construction Mechanic, Senior Chief [*Navy rating*] ... CMCS
Construction Mechanic, Third Class [*Navy rating*] ... CM3
Construction Methods & Equipment (journ.) (SAUS) ... CM&E
Construction Notice (SAUS) ... CN
Construction Number (LAIN) ... C/N
Construction of Aircraft and Related Procurement ... CARP
Construction of Embedded Dedicated Real-Time System [*Computer science*] ... CEDAR
Construction of Facilities [*NASA*] (KSC) ... COF
Construction of Facilities ... C of F
Construction Period Recapture [*Nuclear power plant licensing*] ... CPR
Construction Permit [*FCC*] ... CP
Construction Permit Containment Support Fixture (NRCH) ... CPCSF
Construction Permit Power Reactor (NRCH) ... CPPR
Construction Permit Research Reactor (NRCH) ... CPRR
Construction Plant Association (SAUO) ... CPA
Construction Plant-Hire Association [*British*] (DBA) ... CPA
Construction Procedures [*Nuclear energy*] (NRCH) ... CP
Construction Productivity Advancement Research [*Military*] (RDA) ... CPAR
Construction Products Manufacturers Council [*Defunct*] (EA) ... CPMC

Construction Program Administration System [Telecommunications] (TEL) .... CPAS
Construction Programme Policy Group (SAUO) .... CPPG
Construction Progress Reporting Survey [Bureau of the Census] (GFGA) .... CPRS
Construction Project Alternative Selection Program [Bell System] .... CONPASP
Construction Project Control (IAA) .... CPC
Construction Quality Assurance (SAUS) .... COA
Construction Quality Assurance [Environmental science] .... CQA
Construction Quality Control [Environmental science] .... CQC
Construction Recruit [Navy] .... CR
Construction Report, Building Permits [A publication] .... CRBP
Construction Report, Construction Activity [A publication] .... CRCA
Construction Report, Housing Starts [A publication] .... CRHS
Construction Requirements Review Committee [Military] (AABC) .... CRRC
Construction Research Advisory Council (SAUO) .... CRAG
Construction Risk Management [International Risk Management Institute] [A publication] .... CRM
Construction Safety Association of Ontario, Toronto, Ontario [Library symbol] [National Library of Canada] (NLC) .... OTCSAO
Construction Safety Specialist (SAUO) .... CSS
Construction Scheduling and Coordination [AT & T] .... CSC
Construction Special Operations Center .... CSOC
Construction Specification (DAC) .... Con Spec
Construction Specification (SAUS) .... CON SPEC
Construction Specifications Canada [Toronto, ON] .... CSC
Construction Specifications Institute (EA) .... CSI
Construction Standards Board (SAUO) .... CSB
Construction Statistics Division [Washington, DC] [Department of Commerce] (OICC) .... CSD
Construction Surveyors Institute [Later, Architects and Surveyors Institute] (EA) .... CSI
Construction Systems Division (SAUO) .... CSD
Construction Tender [Coast Guard symbol] (DNAB) .... WLIC
Construction Test Procedure (NRCH) .... CTP
Construction Training Unit .... CTU
Construction Unit [Computer science] .... CU
Construction Unit Value (DCTA) .... CUV
Construction Verification Notification [Nuclear energy] (NRCH) .... CVN
Construction Work in Progress .... CWIP
Construction Workers Federation [San Marino] (EAIO) .... CWF
Construction Writers Association (EA) .... CWA
Constructional Engineering Union [British] .... CEU
Constructional Steel Research and Development Organization (SAUO) .... CONSTRADO
Construction-Differential Subsidy [Authorized by Merchant Marine Act of 1936] .... CDS
Construction/Inspection Procedure (NRCH) .... C/IP
Constructionman [Nonrated enlisted man] [Navy] .... CN
Constructionman, Apprentice [Navy rating] .... CA
Constructionman Apprentice, Builder, Striker [Navy rating] .... BUCA
Constructionman Apprentice, Construction Electrician, Striker [Navy rating] .... CECA
Constructionman Apprentice, Engineering Aid, Striker [Navy rating] .... EACA
Constructionman Apprentice, Equipment Operator, Striker [Navy rating] .... EOCA
Constructionman Apprentice, Steelworker, Striker [Navy rating] .... SWCA
Constructionman Apprentice, Utilitiesman, Striker [Navy rating] .... UTCA
Constructionman, Construction Electrician, Striker [Navy rating] .... CECN
Constructionman, Construction Mechanic, Striker [Navy rating] .... CMCN
Constructionman, Engineering Aid, Striker [Navy rating] .... EACN
Constructionman, Equipment Operator, Striker [Navy rating] .... EOCN
Constructionman Recruit [Navy] .... CR
Constructionman, Steelworker, Striker [Navy rating] .... SWCN
Constructionman, Utilitiesman, Striker [Navy rating] .... UTCN
Constructive Action, Inc. [Whittier, CA] (EA) .... CAI
Constructive Action, Incorporated (SAUO) .... CAI
Constructive Availability (CAAL) .... CA
Constructive Cost Model .... COCOMO
Constructive Dilemma [Rule of inference] [Logic] .... CD
Constructive Error Score (EDAC) .... CES
Constructive Error Source (SAUS) .... CES
Constructive Page Description (SAUS) .... CPD
Constructive Placement [Railcar] .... CP
Constructive Republican Alternative Programs [Position papers on legislative issues prepared for Republican House leaders during Lyndon Johnson administration] .... CRAP
Constructive Solid Geometry (VERA) .... CSG
Constructive Total Loss [Insurance] .... CTL
Constructive Total Loss Only [Insurance] .... CTLO
Constructive Variational Geometry [Computer science] .... CVG
Constructor [Freemasonry] (ROG) C
Constructor (ADA) .... CON
Constructor .... CONSTR
Constructor Captain (SAUS) .... Con C
Constructor Commander (SAUS) .... Con Cr
Constructor Lieutenant (SAUS) .... Con L
Constructor Lieutenant Commander (SAUS) .... Con L Cr
Constructor Sub-Lieutenant (SAUS) .... Con SL
Constructor Syntax (MHDI) .... CS
Construe (ROG) .... CONSTR
Const's Edition of Bott's Poor Law Cases [A publication] (DLA) ...... Bott PL Const
Const's Edition of Bott's Poor Law Cases [A publication] (DSA) .... Const
Const's Edition of Bott's Poor Law Cases [A publication] (DLA) ...... Const Bott
Consuelo, San Pedro De Macoris [Dominican Republic] [ICAO location identifier] (ICLI) .... MDCO

Consuetudines Feudorum [The Book of Feuds] [Latin] [A publication] (DLA) .... Consuet Feud
Consuetudines Feudorum [The Book of Feuds] [Latin] [A publication] (DLA) ...... F
Consul [License plate code assigned to foreign diplomats in the US] C
Consul (WDAA) .... Con
Consul [or Consulate] (AABC) .... CON
Consul .... CONS
Consul (EBF) .... Cons
Consul [Latin] (OCD) .... COS
Consul (ADWA) .... cos
Consul .... CS
Consul (SAUS) .... Cs
Consul General (SAUO) .... CG
Consul General .... CG
Consul General .... CGEN
Consul General .... CONGEN
Consul General (EY) .... CONSGEN
Consul General's Secretary .... CG SEC
Consul Suffectus [Latin] (OCD) .... COS SUFF
Consular Agent .... CA
Consular Certificate (EBF) .... Cons Cert
Consular Clerk [British] (ROG) CC
Consular Corps CC
Consular Corps College and International Consular Academy (EA) ...... CONSUL
Consular Declaration .... CD
Consular Department (SAUO) .... CD
Consular Invoice CI
Consular Invoice (ODBW) .... con inv
Consular Law Society (EA) .... CLS
Consular Liaison Officer .... CLO
Consular section (SAUO) .... CON
Consular Security Officer .... CSO
Consular Shipping Adviser .... CONSA
Consular Shipping Adviser .... CSA
Consulate (SAUO) .... Con
Consulate (SAUO) .... Cons
Consules [Consuls] [Latin] CC
Consules [Consuls] [Latin] .... COSS
Consulier Engineering [Associated Press] (SAG) .... Consulier
Consulier Engineering, Inc. [Associated Press] (SAG) .... Consulr
Consulier Engineering, Inc. [NASDAQ symbol] (NQ) .... CSLR
Consulier Engr [NASDAQ symbol] (TTSB) .... CSLR
Consult .... CON
Consult [or Consultation, Consultant] [Medicine] .... CONS
Consulta di i Cumitati Nationalisti [Corsica] (PD) .... CCN
Consultancy and Research Unit [Department of Information Studies, University of Sheffield] [British] (AIE) .... CRU
[The] Consultancy and Research Unit, University of Sheffield [England] [Information service or system] (IID) .... CRUS
Consultancy Services Wind Energy Developing Countries (SAUO) .... CWD
Consultant (SAUS) .... CN
Consultant (TBD) .... Cnslt
Consultant (DAVI) .... Cons
Consultant .... CONSLNT
Consultant (AABC) .... CONSLTNT
Consultant .... CONSULT
Consultant [Medicine] (DMAA) .... consult
Consultant (SAUS) .... Consult
Consultant (PROS) .... Consult
Consultant Agreement (MCD) .... CA
Consultant Dieticians in Health Care Facilities (NTPA) .... CDHCF
Consultant Dietitians in Health Care Facilities (EA) .... CDHCF
Consultant for Commercial Disease Control (WDAA) .... CCDC
Consultant in Dental Surgery [Medical Officer designation] [British] C
Consultant Orthodontists Group [British] (DBA) .... COG
Consultant Report (NATG) .... CR
Consultant-Adviser .... CA
Consultant-Initiated Activity [LIMRA] .... CIA
Consultants and Consulting Organizations Directory [A publication] .... CCO
Consultants and Consulting Organizations Directory [Gale Research Co.] [Detroit, MI] [Information service or system] [A publication] .... CCOD
Consultants Association for the Natural Industry .... CANI
Consultants (Computer & Financial) [Commercial firm] [British] .... CCF
Consultants Directory for Business and Industry [A publication] .... CDBI
Consultants' Network (EA) .... CN
Consultation [Medicine] C
Consultation .... CNSLTN
Consultation (DSUE) .... CON
Consultation [Legal] [British] (ROG) .... CONSN
Consultation .... CONSULTN
Consultation and Cooperation agreement (SAUS) .... C&C
Consultation and Education .... C & E
Consultation Distance (HEAS) .... CD
Consultation on Church Union (EA) .... COCU
Consultation Paper (DCTA) .... C/P
Consultation Zone (HEAS) .... CZ
Consultative Advisory Committee on Semi-Arid Food Grain Reasearch and Development (SAUS) .... SAFGRAD
Consultative Association of Guyanese Industry (SAUO) .... CAGI
Consultative Board for Diver Training (HEAS) .... CBDT
Consultative Committee for Exploratory Studies (SAUS) .... OCV
Consultative Committee for International Radio (SAUS) .... CCIR
Consultative Committee for International Telephone and Telegraph (SAUO) .... CCITT

Consultative Committee for Local Ecumenical Projects in England [Church of England] .... CCLEPE
Consultative Committee for Maritime Radio (SAUO) .... CCMR
Consultative Committee for Nuclear Research [EEC] (PDAA) .... CCNR
Consultative Committee for Photometry and Radiometry [International Committee on Weights and Measures] .... CCPR
Consultative Committee for Public Information [United Nations] .... CCPI
Consultative Committee for Space Data Systems (SSD) .... CCSDS
Consultative Committee for Standard Data Services (SAUO) .... CCSDS
Consultative Committee for the Definition of the Second .... CCDS
Consultative Committee for the Standards of Measurement of Ionizing Radiations [International Bureau of Weights and Measures] .... CCEDMRI
Consultative Committee for Units [International Bureau of Weights and Measures] .... CCU
Consultative Committee, International (SAUS) CCI
Consultative Committee International Telephony and Telegraphy .... CCITT
Consultative Committee of Accountancy Bodies [United Kingdom and Ireland] .... CCAB
Consultative Committee of the Bars and Law Societies of the European Community (ILCA) .... CCBE
Consultative Committee on Administrative Questions [United Nations] .... CCAQ
Consultative Committee on Electricity [International Bureau of Weights and Measures] .... CCE
Consultative Committee on Electronics for Civil Aviation (SAUO) .... CCECA
Consultative Committee on Exotic Animal Diseases [Australia] .... CCEAD
Consultative Committee on International Radio [Australia] .... CCIR
Consultative Committee on International Telephony [Later, CCITT] [ITU] .... CCIT
Consultative Committee on Programme and Operational Questions (SAUO) .... CCPOQ
Consultative Committee on Research (SAUS) .... CCR
Consultative Committee on Safety in the Offshore Petroleum Industry [Australia] .... CCOSOP
Consultative Committee on Statistical Matters (SAUO) .... CCSM
Consultative Committee on Substantive Questions [United Nations] .... CCSQ
Consultative Committee on the Curriculum [British] CCC
Consultative Committee on the Definition of the Meter [International Bureau of Weights and Measures] .... CCDM
Consultative Committee on the Ozone Layer (SAUO) .... CCOL
Consultative Committee on Thermometry [International Bureau of Weights and Measures] .... CCT
Consultative Council for Postal Studies [Universal Postal Union] (EY) .... CCPS
Consultative Council for Postal Studies (SAUO) .... CCPs
Consultative Council of Jewish Organizations (EA) .... CCJO
Consultative Council of Professional Management Organizations [British] (DBA) .... CCPMO
Consultative Council on Local Government Finance [British] .... CCLGF
Consultative Document (HEAS) .... CD
Consultative Environmental Review [Australia] .... CER
Consultative Examination [Social Security Administration] (OICC) .... CE
Consultative Group [NATO] .... CG
Consultative Group for Desertification Control (SAUO) .... DESCON
Consultative Group for/on International Agricultural Research (SAUO) .... CGIAR
Consultative Group on Biological Diversity (SAUO) .... CGBD
Consultative Group on Food Production and Investment (SAUO) .... CGFP
Consultative Group on Food Production and Investment in Developing Countries [United Nations] .... CGFPI
Consultative Group on International Agricultural Research (EA) .... CGIAR
Consultative Group on International Economic and Monetary Affairs (SAUO) .... CGIEMA
Consultative Group on Marine Industries Science and Technology (SAUO) .... CMIST
Consultative Group on Ocean Mapping (SAUO) .... CGOM
Consultative Group on Potentially Harmful Effects of Space Experiments (SAUO) .... CGOPHEOSE
Consultative Group on Potentially Harmful Effects of Space Experiments .... CGOPHEOSE
Consultative Group on Solar Energy Research and Application (SAUO) .... COSERA
Consultative Group-Coordinating Committee (SAUO) .... COCOM
Consultative Political Council [Laos] .... CPC
Consultative Program on Rice Mechanization (SAUO) .... CPRIME
Consultative Shipping Group (SAUO) .... CSG
Consultative sub-committee on Surplus Disposal (SAUO) .... CSD
Consultec Canada Ltd. [Vancouver, BC] [Telecommunications] (TSSD) CCL
Consulted (SAUS) .... Csuld
Consulting .... CNSLTNG
Consulting (DD) .... cons
Consulting (SAUS) .... Csulg
Consulting Chemists and Chemical Engineers .... CCCE
Consulting Committee on Educational Matters (AIE) .... CCEM
Consulting Communications Engineers, Inc. [Villanova, PA] (TSSD) .... CCE
Consulting Engineer .... CE
Consulting Engineer (SAUS) .... Cons Eng
Consulting Engineers and Land Surveyors of California (GEOI) .... CELSOC
Consulting Engineers Association of California (SAUO) .... CEAC
Consulting Engineers Council [Later, ACEC] (EA) .... CEC
Consulting Engineers Council of Florida (SAUO) .... CEC-F
Consulting Engineers Council of Ohio (SAUO) .... CECO
Consulting Engineers Council of Oregon (SAUO) .... CECO
Consulting Engineers Council of Pennsylvania (SAUO) .... CEC-PA
Consulting Engineers Council of Washington (GEOI) .... CECW
Consulting Engineers in the Nordic Countries (SAUS) .... RINORD
Consulting Engineers of British Columbia (AC) .... CEBC
Consulting Engineers of Indiana, Inc (SAUS) .... CEI
Consulting Engineers of New Brunswick (AC) .... CENB

Consulting Engineers of NWT (AC) .... CENT
Consulting Physician (ROG) .... CP
Consulting Psychologists Press, Inc. (DHP) .... CPP
Consulting Services Group (SAUO) .... CSG
Consulting Support Center (SAUO) .... CSC
Consulting Surgeon [British] (ROG) .... CS
Consulting Teacher .... CT
Consulting Traffic Bureau .... CTB
Consulting Traffic Manager .... CTM
Consumable Case Rocket .... CCR
Consumable Electrode Vacuum Melting .... CEVM
Consumable Maintenance and Overhaul List (MCD) .... CMOL
Consumable Maintenance and Overhaul Material List [Navy] (MCD) .... CMOML
Consumable Maintenance Overhaul Materials (ACAE) .... CMOM
Consumable Toroidal Igniter (MCD) .... CTI
Consumable Vacuum Melt [Steel] .... CVM
Consumable-Anode, Radial, One-Side, Electrolytic [Automotive engineering] .... CAROSEL
Consumable-Electrode Vacuum-Arc Remelt [Nuclear energy] (NRCH) .... CEVAR
Consumables Management (NASA) .... CM
Consumables Management (NAKS) .... cm
Consumables Status (NAKS) .... cs
Consumables Status (MCD) .... CS
Consummatum Est [It Is Finished] [Freemasonry] [Latin] (ROG) .... CE
Consumed Oxygen Demand (AAEL) .... COD
Consumer .... CNSMR
Consumer .... CNSR
Consumer (TBD) .... Cons
Consumer .... CONSMR
Consumer .... CONSUM
Consumer Action for Energy Conservation [British] .... CAFEC
Consumer Action Now (EA) .... CAN
Consumer Action Panels (SAUO) .... CAPs
Consumer Aerosol Products Council .... CAPCO
Consumer Affairs Advisory Committee of the Australian Capital Territory .... CAACACT
Consumer Affairs Bureau (SAUO) .... CAB
Consumer Affairs Clearinghouse .... CACH
Consumer Affairs Council .... CAC
Consumer Affairs Council, Northern Territory [Australia] .... CACNT
Consumer Affairs Medical Quality Assurance Board (SAUO) .... CAMQAB
Consumer Affairs Office [Federal Energy Administration] .... CAO
Consumer Aid Series [National Highway Traffic Safety Administration] .... CAS
Consumer Alert (EA) .... CA
Consumer and Commercial Credit (Prentice-Hall) [A publication] (DLA) .... Cons & Com Cred (P-H)
Consumer and Corporate Affairs Canada [UTLAS symbol] .... CCA
Consumer and Environmental Health Services Administration [HEW] .... CEHSA
Consumer and Food Economics Institute (SAUS) .... CFEI
Consumer and Marketing Service [Later, AMS] [Department of Agriculture] (IAA) .... CAMS
Consumer and Marketing Service [Later, AMS] [Department of Agriculture] .... C & MS
Consumer and Marketing Service (SAUO) .... C&MS
Consumer and Marketing Service [Later, AMS] [Department of Agriculture] .... CMS
Consumer and Marketing Service, Service and Regulatory Announcements [Later, AMS] [Department of Agriculture] .... C & MSSRA
Consumer and Marketing Service, Service and Regulatory Announcements (SAUO) .... C&MSSRA
Consumer and Patient Health Information Section (SAUS) .... CAPHIS
Consumer And Patient Health Information Section. Medical Library Association (SAUO) .... CAPHIS
Consumer and Producer Price Indexes [Department of Labor] [Database] .... CPI/PPI
Consumer and Professional Relations Division [of HIAA] [Washington, DC] (EA) .... CPRD
Consumer Assessment of Health Plans (SAUO) .... CAHPS
Consumer Attorneys of California (SRA) .... CAC
Consumer Bankers Association [Arlington, VA] (EA) .... CBA
Consumer Bulletin (journ.) (SAUS) .... Consumer Bul
Consumer Buying Expectations Survey [Formerly, Quarterly Survey of Intentions] [Bureau of the Census] .... CBE
Consumer Buying Expectations Survey (SAUS) .... CBE Survey
Consumer Choice Health Plan .... CCHP
Consumer Coalition for Health [Inactive] (EA) .... CCH
Consumer Commission on the Accreditation of Health Services [Defunct] (EA) .... CCAHS
Consumer Complaint Guide .... CCG
Consumer Computing Device (PCM) .... CCD
Consumer Confidence Index [Conference Board] CCI
Consumer Consortium on Assisted Living .... CCAL
Consumer Consultative Committee [British] CCC
Consumer Council [American National Standards Institute] CC
Consumer Credit Association [British] (EAIO) .... CCA
Consumer Credit Corporation CCC
Consumer Credit Counseling Services [Banking] .... CCCS
Consumer Credit Counselors [Banking] CCC
Consumer Credit Education Foundation (EA) .... CCEF
Consumer Credit Guide [Commerce Clearing House] [A publication] (DLA) .... Cons Cred Guide
Consumer Credit Guide (Commerce Clearing House) [A publication] (DLA) .... Consumer Cred Guide (CCH)
Consumer Credit Insurance CCI
Consumer Credit Insurance Association [Chicago, IL] (EA) .... CCIA

Consumer Credit Letter [*Business Publishers, Inc.*] [*Information service or system*] (CRD) ... CCL
Consumer Credit Project [*Defunct*] (EA) ... CCP
Consumer Credit Protection Act [*1969*] ... CCPA
Consumer Data Service (SAUS) ... CDS
Consumer Demographics, Inc. [*Information service or system*] (IID) ... CDI
Consumer Digital Subscriber Line [*Telecommunications*] ... CDSL
Consumer Discount Network ... CDN
Consumer Distribution Marketing ... CDM
Consumer Drug Information Fulltext [*American Society of Hospital Pharmacists*] [*Database*] [*Information service or system*] ... CDIF
Consumer Drug Information Service [*Australia*] ... CDIS
Consumer Economic Study Report [*Department of Agriculture*] ... CESR
Consumer Education Advisory Task Force (SAUS) ... Task Force
Consumer Education and Information Liaison [*Federal interagency group*] ... CEIL
Consumer Education Research Center (EA) ... CERC
Consumer Education Research Group [*Later, CERC*] (EA) ... CERG
Consumer Education Resource Network ... CERN
Consumer Electronic Bus (SAUS) ... CEBUS
Consumer Electronic Product Manufacturers Association (SAUO) ... CEPMA
Consumer Electronics (RALS) ... CE
Consumer Electronics Bus [*Residential wiring standard*] ... CEBus
Consumer Electronics Bus (SAUS) ... CE Bus
Consumer Electronics Group [*Education Industries Association*] (NTCM) ... CEG
Consumer Electronics (journ.) (SAUS) ... CE
Consumer Electronics Manufacturers Association (NTPA) ... CEMA
Consumer Electronics Show [*Computer industry*] ... CES
Consumer Energy Council of America (EA) ... CECA
Consumer Energy Council of America Research Foundation (EA) ... CECA/RF
Consumer Expenditure Survey [*Bureau of Labor Statistics*] (GFGA) ... CES
Consumer Federation of America (EA) ... CFA
Consumer Fraud Bureau (SAUO) ... CFB
Consumer Goods Standards (SAUS) ... CGS
Consumer Goods System [*Computer science*] ... COGS
Consumer Hazards Analytical Information Service [*Laboratory of the Government Chemist*] [*British*] (NITA) ... CHAIS
Consumer Health Care (MELL) ... CHC
Consumer Health Informatics (SAUO) ... CHI
Consumer Health Information (ADWA) ... CHI
Consumer Health Information Program and Services [*LSCA*] ... CHIPS
Consumer Health Information Resource Service ... CHIRS
Consumer Health Organization of Canada (AC) ... CHOC
Consumer Help on the Individual's Conservation of Energy [*Student legal action organization*] ... CHOICE
Consumer Housing Assistance Grants ... CHAG
Consumer Information ... CI
Consumer Information Association ... CIA
Consumer Information Catalog (AUEG) ... CIC
Consumer Information Center (EA) ... CIC
Consumer Information Regulation [*National Highway Traffic Safety Administration*] ... CIR
Consumer Information Series [*National Institute of Standards and Technology*] ... CIS
Consumer Information Service [*Electronic mail*] ... CIS
Consumer Information System ... CIS
Consumer Interests Foundation ... CIF
Consumer Interpol (EA) ... CI
Consumer Labelling Initiative (SAUO) ... CLI
Consumer Level Quality Audit Program [*Military*] ... COLQUAP
Consumer News and Business Channel [*A cable division of NBC*] ... CNBC
Consumer Organization of Diabled People of Newfoundland & Labrador (AC) ... COD
Consumer Pesticide Project (EA) ... CPP
Consumer Policy Committee (SAUO) ... COPOLCO
Consumer Portfolio Services [*Associated Press*] (SAG) ... ConPort
Consumer Portfolio Services [*NASDAQ symbol*] (SAG) ... CPSS
Consumer Premise Equipment (DOMA) ... CPE
Consumer Price Index [*Department of Labor*] [*Database*] ... CPI
Consumer Price Index for All Urban Consumers (OICC) ... CPI-U
Consumer Price Index for Services ... CPIS
Consumer Price Index for Urban Wage Earners and Clerical Workers (OICC) ... CPI-W
Consumer Product and Manufacturer Ratings [*A publication*] ... CPR
Consumer Product Information Center ... CPIC
Consumer Product Information Coordinating Center (SAUO) ... CPICC
Consumer Product Safety Act [*1972*] ... CPSA
Consumer Product Safety Act [*1972*] (DLA) ... CPS Act
Consumer Product Safety Commission (MELL) ... CPS
Consumer Product Safety Commission [*Federal agency*] ... CPSC
Consumer Product Safety Commission, Washington, DC [*OCLC symbol*] (OCLC) ... CPR
Consumer Product Safety Guide (Commerce Clearing House) [*A publication*] (DLA) ... Consumer Prod Safety Guide (CCH)
Consumer Products Department Committee (SAUO) ... CPDC
Consumer Products Division (SAUO) ... CPD
Consumer Products Information Index [*National Institute of Standards and Technology*] ... CPII
Consumer Protection Act ... CPA
Consumer Protection Advisory Committee (ODBW) ... CPAC
Consumer Protection Agency ... CPA
Consumer Protection and Environmental Health Service [*Later, Environmental Health Service*] [*US government*] ... CPEHS
Consumer Protection Association (SAUO) ... CPA
Consumer Protection Center (EA) ... CPC
Consumer Purchasing Service ... CPS
Consumer Pwr $2.08'A'Pfd [*NYSE symbol*] (TTSB) ... CMSPrI
Consumer Reports (journ.) (SAUS) ... Consumer Rep
Consumer Research and Action Foundation (SAUO) ... CRAF
Consumer Research Inc. (SAUO) ... CR
Consumer Safety Committee [*Queensland*] [*Australia*] ... CSC
Consumer Safety Glazing Committee ... CSGC
Consumer Safety Inspector [*Food and Drug Administration*] ... CSI
Consumer Safety Officer [*Food and Drug Administration*] ... CSO
Consumer Satisfaction Index ... CSI
Consumer Savings Alliance (EA) ... CSA
Consumer Service of New Zealand (SAUO) ... CSNZ
Consumer Services Organization (EA) ... CSO
Consumer Sounding-Board (IEEE) ... CSB
Consumer Sourcebook [*A publication*] ... CS
Consumer Sourcebook [*A publication*] ... CSB
Consumer Standards Advisory Committee (SAUO) ... CSAC
Consumer Subsidy Equivalent (SAUO) ... CSE
Consumer Survival Kit [*Program on public TV*] ... CSK
Consumer Technology Index [*Computer Intelligence InfoCorp*] (PCM) ... CTI
Consumer Transaction System (SAUS) ... CTS
Consumer Unity & Trust Society ... CUTS
Consumer Value Stores ... CVS
Consumer Video (NITA) ... CV
Consumer-Farmer Milk Cooperative (SAUS) ... CFMC
Consumers Action Movement (SAUO) ... CAM
Consumers' Advisory Board ... CAB
Consumer's Advisory Council ... CAC
Consumers and Taxpayers ... CONTAX
Consumers' Association (EAIO) ... CA
Consumers' Association of Canada ... CAC
Consumer's Association of Canada, Ottawa, Ontario [*Library symbol*] [*National Library of Canada*] (BIB) ... OOCOAC
Consumers' Association of Jamaica ... CAJ
Consumers' Association of Trinidad and Tobago ... CATT
Consumers' Association of Western Australia ... CAWA
Consumers' Consultative Committee [*EC*] (ECED) ... CCC
Consumers Cooperative Association [*Later, Farmland Industries*] (EA) ... CCA
Consumers Distributing Co. Ltd. [*Toronto Stock Exchange symbol*] ... CDG
Consumers Education and Protective Association International (EA) ... CEPA
Consumers Financial Corp. [*NASDAQ symbol*] (NQ) ... CFIN
Consumers Financial Corp. [*Associated Press*] (SAG) ... CnsFn
Consumers Financial Corp. [*Associated Press*] (SAG) ... ConsFn
Consumers Finl [*NASDAQ symbol*] (TTSB) ... CFIN
Consumers Finl 8.50% Cv Pfd [*NASDAQ symbol*] (TTSB) ... CFINP
Consumers for the Free Market [*Pittsburgh, PA*] (EA) ... CFM
Consumers for World Trade (EA) ... CWT
Consumers' Gas Co. Ltd. [*Toronto Stock Exchange symbol*] ... CGT
Consumers in the European Community Group ... CECG
Consumers' Law Reform Association [*Australia*] ... CLRA
Consumers' Law Reform Association, Queensland [*Australia*] ... CLRAQ
Consumers Opposed to Inflation in the Necessities (EA) ... COIN
Consumers Organization for the Hearing Impaired [*Defunct*] (EA) ... COHI
Consumers Packaging, Inc. [*Toronto Stock Exchange symbol*] ... CGC
Consumers Power Co. [*NYSE symbol*] (SAG) ... CMS
Consumers Power Co. [*Associated Press*] (SAG) ... CnP
Consumers Power Co. Financing I [*NYSE symbol*] (SAG) ... CMS
Consumers Power Co. Financing I [*Associated Press*] (SAG) ... CnPF
Consumers Power Co., Parnall Technical Library, Jackson, MI [*Library symbol*] [*Library of Congress*] (LCLS) ... MiJaCP
Consumers Public Power District ... CPPD
Consumers Pwr $4.16 Pfd [*NYSE symbol*] (TTSB) ... CMPSPrA
Consumers Pwr $4.50 Pfd [*NYSE symbol*] (TTSB) ... CMSPrB
Consumers Pwr $7.45cmPfd [*NYSE symbol*] (TTSB) ... CMSPrD
Consumers Pwr $7.68 Pfd [*NYSE symbol*] (TTSB) ... CMSPrH
Consumers Pwr $7.72 Pfd [*NYSE symbol*] (TTSB) ... CMSPrE
Consumers Pwr $7.76 Pfd [*NYSE symbol*] (TTSB) ... CMSPrG
Consumers Pwr Fin 1 8.36%'TOPrS' [*NYSE symbol*] (TTSB) ... CMSPrJ
Consumer's Reliability Risk ... CRR
Consumers' Research (EA) ... CR
Consumers Solar Electric Power Corporation, Culver City (SAUO) ... CSEP
Consumers Transport Council (SAUS) ... CTC
Consumers Union ... CU
Consumers Union of United States (EA) ... CU
Consumers United for Rail Equity (EA) ... CURE
Consumers United to Stop Food Irradiation (AC) ... CUSFI
Consumers Water [*NASDAQ symbol*] (TTSB) ... CONW
Consumers Water Co. [*NASDAQ symbol*] (SAG) ... CONW
Consumers Water Co. [*Associated Press*] (SAG) ... ConWat
Consumer-to-Consumer ... C2C
Consuming Interest [*A publication*] (ADA) ... CI
Consumnes River College, Sacramento, CA [*Library symbol*] [*Library of Congress*] (LCLS) ... CSCR
Consumption ... C
Consumption (ROG) ... CONSUMP
Consumption Data Exchange ... CDE
Consumption Entry [*Economics*] ... CE
Consumption Function [*Economics*] ... CF
Consumption Levels Enquiry [*British*] ... CLE
Consumption Variation (MCD) ... COVAR
Contact ... C
Contact (AABC) ... CNTC
Contact (NAKS) ... CON
Contact (KSC) ... CONT
Contact ... CTC

Contact (SAUS)	Ctc
Contact [Amateur Radio] (BARN)	QSO
Contact a Family Computer Assisted Learning (AIE)	CAFCAL
Contact Adhesive	CA
Contact Ammeter (SAUS)	CA
Contact Analog [Submarine instrumentation] (MCD)	CONALOG
Contact Analog Flight Display	CAFD
Contact and Cooperation (SAUS)	C&C
Contact and Repair Test Equipment (MCD)	CARTE
Contact Approach [Aviation] (DA)	CAP
Contact Approach [Aviation] (IAA)	CTAP
Contact Approach Control (FAAC)	CAC
Contact Area, Articular [Medicine]	CA
Contact Area Commander	CAC
Contact Area Summary Position Estimate Report [Military] (NVT)	CASPER
Contact Area Summary Position Report [Environmental science] (COE)	CASPER
Contact Back-Up (DNAB)	CBU
Contact Breaker	CB
Contact Center (EA)	CC
Contact Center (FAAC)	CTCEN
Contact Center Control (FAAC)	CTCC
Contact Charge Transfer (MCD)	CCT
Contact Children's Services [Australia]	CCS
Contact Clock (IAA)	CCL
Contact Closure (KSC)	CC
Contact Conversion Exercise [Military] (NVT)	CONVERSIONEX
Contact Dermatitis [Medicine]	CD
Contact Dermatitis (SAUS)	Contact Dermatitis
Contact End Resistance [Photovoltaic energy systems]	CER
Contact End Resistor (SAUS)	CER
Contact Equipment Handling Area [Nuclear energy] (NRCH)	CEHA
Contact Evaluation Plot (NVT)	CEP
Contact Flight Rules [Same as VFR] [Meteorology]	CFR
Contact Glow Discharge Electrolysis	CGDE
Contact Growing Index (SAUS)	CGI
Contact Handled	CH
Contact, Help, Advice, Information, Network for Effective Health Care (SAUO)	CHAIN
Contact Image Sensing [Reprography]	CIS
Contact Image Sensor	CIS
Contact Ion Thruster	CIT
Contact Ion-Pair [Physical chemistry]	CIP
Contact Karate	C-K
Contact Lens [Ophthalmology]	CL
Contact Lens [Ophthalmology] (DAVI)	ctl
Contact Lens Association for Optometry (EA)	CLAO
Contact Lens Association of Ophthalmologists (EA)	CLAO
Contact Lens Manufacturers Association (EA)	CLMA
Contact Lens Mirror (SAUS)	CLM
Contact Lens Practitioners (PDAA)	CLP
Contact Lens Registry Examination [National Contact Lens Examiners]	CLRE
Contact Lens Society of America (EA)	CLSA
Contact Lens Society of Australia (SAUO)	CLSA
Contact Lens Study Group (SAUO)	CLSG
Contact Lenses Quarterly (SAUO)	CLQ
Contact Limit Line [Technical drawings]	CLL
Contact Literacy Center (EA)	CLC
Contact Load Resistor (IAA)	CLR
Contact Loss (SAUS)	CL
Contact Lost [RADAR]	CL
Contact Maker	CM
Contact Making Ammeter (SAUS)	CMA
Contact Microradiography (DICI)	CMR
Contact Motion Analysis (CAAL)	CMA
Contact Operate (SAUS)	CO
Contact Party [Army]	CONPY
Contact Party [Army]	CP
Contact Personality Factor Test [Psychology]	CPFT
Contact Potential Difference	CPD
Contact Preclude (DNAB)	CP
Contact Print (VRA)	CONPR
Contact Process Cell [Nuclear energy] (GFGA)	CPC
Contact Proficiency (SAUS)	CP
Contact Publishers [Holland]	C
Contact Reconnaissance (SAUS)	Con R
Contact Resistance [Electricity] (IAA)	CR
Contact Resistance Variation [Telecommunications] (TEL)	CRV
Contact Sensitivity [Allergy and dermatology] (DAVI)	CS
Contact Settlements Office (ACAE)	CSO
Contact Signature Generator (SAUS)	CSG
Contact Soil Sampling Device [Aerospace]	CSSD
Contact Start-Stop (SAUS)	CSS
Contact Support Test Set (ACAE)	CSTS
Contact Team	CT
Contact Teleministries USA (EA)	CTUSA
Contact Tension	CT
Contact Test Set [Military]	CTS
Contact Test Set - Electro Optical Augmentation [Military] (DWSG)	CTS-EOA
Contact Trunk Module (SAUS)	CTM
Contact Urticaria [Medicine] (DMAA)	CU
Contact USA (EA)	CUSA
Contact Ventures [Vancouver Stock Exchange symbol]	CVU
Contact with Disabled Persons Scale (TES)	CDP
Contactair Flugdienst & Co. [Germany] [ICAO designator] (FAAC)	KIS
Contact-Bend-Stretch (PDAA)	C-B-S
Contacted (SAUS)	Ctcd
Contact-Free Syntactical Translator (SAUS)	CFST
Contacting (SAUS)	Ctcg
Contact-Lens-Induced Keratoconjunctivitis [Ophthalmology]	CLK
Contactless Vacuum Controller	CVC
Contact-Making Ammeter (KSC)	CMA
Contact-Making Clock	CMC
Contact-Making Voltmeter	CMV
Contact-Making Voltmeter	CMVM
Contactor (MSA)	CNTOR
Contactor (SAUS)	Cntor
Contactor (SAUS)	Con
Contactor Control Relay (MCD)	CCR
Contactor, Running	COR
Contactor, Starting	COS
Contactor, Starting (SAUS)	cos
Contacts (SAUS)	Conts
Contacts, Activities, Time [Computer science]	CAT
Contact's Business Phone (TRID)	CTCB
Contact's Home Phone (TRID)	CTCH
Contadora [Panama] [Airport symbol] (OAG)	OTD
Contadora Group	CG
Contagion [Medicine] (DMAA)	contag
Contagious	CONTAG
Contagious (SAUS)	Contag
Contagious Bovine Pleuropneumonia [Veterinary medicine]	CBPP
Contagious Disease (SAUS)	CD
Contagious Diseases Act [British]	CDA
Contagious Equine Metritis	CEM
Contagious Pustular Dermatitis [Dermatology]	CPD
Contagious Pustular Stomatitis [Medicine] (DB)	CPS
Contain (AABC)	CNTN
Contain (SAUS)	Cntn
Contain (ROG)	CONTN
Contained (MSA)	CNTD
Contained	CONTD
Contained Armament Test Set (ACAE)	CATS
Contained Disposal Facility	CDF
Contained-Liquid Membranes [Chemical engineering]	CLM
Container (DCTA)	C
Container [Shipping] (DS)	CNT
Container (MSA)	CNTNR
Container (KSC)	CNTR
Container	CO
Container (MCD)	CONT
Container	CONTNR
Container (KSC)	CONTR
Container Agreement (DNAB)	CA
Container Anchorage Terminal (NVT)	CAT
Container and Chassis Identification and Reporting System [Military] (MCD)	CCIRS
Container and Chassis Identification Reporting and Recording System [DoD] (PDAA)	CCIRRS
Container Automated Marking Systems	CAMS
Container Base (DS)	CB
Container Bomb Unit (SAUS)	CBU
Container Control (DCTA)	CC
Container Corp. of America [Later, Marcor, Inc.]	CCA
Container Corporation of America (SAUO)	CNR
Container Cost Data Reporting	CCDR
Container Delivery System [Military]	CDS
Container Deposit Legislation	CDL
Container Design Retrieval System (MCD)	CDRS
Container Discharge Facility (SAUO)	CDF
Container Distribution Center Toronto Port (SAUO)	CDC-Torport
Container Distribution System (MCD)	CDS
Container Express [Army] (AABC)	CONEX
Container for Export (NATG)	CONEX
Container Freight Station [Shipping]	CFS
Container Fumigated (ADA)	CF
Container Handling Equipment	CHE
Container Handling in Terminal Operations [Army study] (RDA)	CHITO
Container Inspection Training and Assistance Team [RSPA] (TAG)	CITAT
Container Lift Adapter for Helicopter (MCD)	CLAH
Container Load (SAUS)	CL
Container Load Trailer (SAUS)	CLT
Container Management Corp. (EFIS)	CMC
Container Marine Lines (SAUO)	CML
Container Master Information (SAUS)	CMI
Container Offloading and Transfer System (MCD)	COTS
Container on Flatcar [Shipping]	COFC
Container Operating Control System (PDAA)	COCS
Container Over-the-Shore	COTS
Container Products, Inc. (EFIS)	CPI
Container Recovery Service (SAUO)	CRS
Container Release System (SAUS)	CRS
Container Repair Building	CRB
Container Repair-Codes applied to Estimate/Survey Reports (SAUS)	R-Repair Codes
Container Research Corp. (SAUS)	CRC
Container Research Corporation (SAUO)	CRC
Container, Restrainer, Environment, Energy Absorption, Post-Crash Failure [Aviation] (PDAA)	CREEP
Container Safety Convention [ISO] (DS)	CSC

Container Service Port (SAUS) ... CSP
Container Service Tariff [*Shipping*] (DS) ... CST
Container Systems Corporation (SAUO) ... CSC
Container Systems Standardization Coordination Group (SAUO) ... CSSCG
Container Systems Standardization-Coordination Group (SAUS) ... CSSCG
Container Systems Standardization/Coordination Group ... CSS/CG
Container Tariff ... CT
Container Terminal [*Shipping*] ... CT
Container Terminal Operator [*Shipping*] (DS) ... CTO
Container Transport International, Inc. (SAUO) ... CTI
Container Transport System (SAUS) ... CTS
Container Unit (ACAE) ... CNU
Container Unit (SAUS) ... CU
Container Vessel (TRID) ... CV
Container, Weapon, Individual Equipment [*Army*] (ADDR) ... CWIE
Container Weapon System (MCD) ... CWS
Container Working Conference (SAUO) ... CWC
Container Yard [*Shipping*] (DCTA) ... CY
Containerboard and Kraft Paper Group (EA) ... CKPG
Containerization and Intermodal Institute (EA) ... CII
Containerization Institute [*Later, CII*] ... CI
Containerization Institute (SAUS) ... TCI
Containerized Ammunition Distribution System ... CADS
Containerized Ammunition Distribution System Van (DOMA) ... CADSVAN
Containerized Automated Rail-Highway Transportation (SAUS) ... CARS System
Containerized Automated Rail-Highway Transportation (SAUS) ... CART
Containerized Avionics Maintenance System (NG) ... CAMS
Containerized Hospital Emergency Mobile (PDAA) ... CHEM
Containerized Lighter Aboard Ship System (IAA) ... CLASS
Containerized Liquid Waste Sampler ... COLIWASA
Containerized Shipment and Storage of Ammunition (MCD) ... COSSA
Containerless Processing (SSD) ... CP
Containers ... cntrs
Containers in Barrels or Boxes [*Freight*] ... CNTRS BB
Containership Cargo Stowage Adapter [*Environmental science*] (COE) ... CCSA
Containership Strikeup System (ACAE) ... CSUS
Containerterminal (SAUS) ... Cont-Term
Containing (WDMC) ... cont
Containing ... CONT
Containing ... CONTG
Containing (ADWA) ... contg
Containing ... CTG
Containment (IEEE) ... CTMT
Containment (SAUS) ... Ctmt
Containment Air Recirculation and Cooling [*Environmental science*] (COE) ... CARC
Containment Air Removal [*Recirculation fan*] (IEEE) ... CAR
Containment and Meteorology for Radiation Exposure [*Nuclear energy*] (NRCH) ... COMRADEX
Containment and Reactor Vessel Isolation Control System (NRCH) ... CRVICS
Containment Atmosphere Control [*Monitor, or System*] [*Nuclear energy*] (IEEE) ... CAC
Containment Atmosphere Dilution [*Nuclear energy*] (NRCH) ... CAD
Containment Atmosphere Dilution System [*Nuclear energy*] (IEEE) ... CADS
Containment Atmosphere Heat Removal [*Environmental science*] (COE) ... CAHR
Containment Atmosphere Recirculation System [*Nuclear energy*] (NRCH) ... CARS
Containment Atmospheric Monitoring [*Nuclear energy*] (NRCH) ... CAM
Containment Building [*Nuclear energy*] (NRCH) ... CB
Containment Building Ventilation [*Nuclear energy*] (NRCH) ... CBV
Containment Combustion Gas Control System [*Nuclear energy*] (IEEE) ... CCGCS
Containment Control & Associates, Inc. (EFIS) ... CC&A
Containment Cooling Actuation Signal [*Nuclear energy*] (NRCH) ... CCAS
Containment Cooling System [*Nuclear energy*] (NRCH) ... CCS
Containment Cooling Unit [*Nuclear energy*] (NRCH) ... CCU
Containment Depressurization Actuation [*Nuclear energy*] (NRCH) ... CDA
Containment Depressurization Alarm [*Nuclear energy*] (IEEE) ... CDA
Containment Design Basis Accident [*Nuclear energy*] (NRCH) ... CDBA
Containment Environmental Control System [*Nuclear energy*] (NRCH) ... CECS
Containment Failure [*Environmental science*] (COE) ... CF
Containment Failure Mode [*Nuclear energy*] (NRCH) ... CFM
Containment Gaseous Radiation Monitor [*Nuclear energy*] (IEEE) ... CGRM
Containment Heat Removal System [*Nuclear energy*] (NRCH) ... CHRS
Containment Integrated Leak Rate Test [*Nuclear energy*] (NRCH) ... CILRT
Containment Integrity [*Nuclear energy*] (NRCH) ... CI
Containment Iodine Removal System [*Nuclear energy*] (NRCH) ... CIRS
Containment Isolation [*Nuclear energy*] (NRCH) ... CI
Containment Isolation A [*Nuclear energy*] (NRCH) ... CIA
Containment Isolation Actuation Signal [*Nuclear energy*] (NRCH) ... CIAS
Containment Isolation B [*Nuclear energy*] (NRCH) ... CIB
Containment Isolation Signal [*Nuclear energy*] (NRCH) ... CIS
Containment Isolation System [*Nuclear energy*] (NRCH) ... CIS
Containment Isolation Valve [*Nuclear energy*] (IEEE) ... CIV
Containment Leakage [*Nuclear energy*] (NRCH) ... CL
Containment Leakage Control [*Nuclear energy*] (IEEE) ... CLC
Containment Leakage System [*Nuclear energy*] (IEEE) ... CLS
Containment Person Air Lock [*Nuclear energy*] (IEEE) ... CPAL
Containment Pressure High Signal [*Nuclear energy*] (IEEE) ... CPHS
Containment Pressure Protection [*Nuclear energy*] (IEEE) ... CPP
Containment Purge [*Nuclear energy*] (NRCH) ... CP
Containment Purge System [*Nuclear energy*] (NRCH) ... CPS
Containment Radiation Monitor [*Nuclear energy*] (IEEE) ... CRM
Containment Radioactivity Removal [*Environmental science*] (COE) ... CNRR
Containment Recirculation Spray System [*Nuclear energy*] (NRCH) ... CRS
Containment Rupture [*Nuclear energy*] (NRCH) ... CR
Containment Rupture Signal [*Nuclear energy*] (IEEE) ... CRS
Containment Safety [*Nuclear energy*] (NRCH) ... CS
Containment Spray [*Nuclear energy*] (NRCH) ... CS
Containment Spray Actuating Signal [*Nuclear energy*] (NRCH) ... CSAS
Containment Spray Cooling [*Nuclear energy*] (NRCH) ... CSC
Containment Spray Heat Exchange [*Nuclear energy*] (NRCH) ... CSHX
Containment Spray Injection System [*Nuclear energy*] (NRCH) ... CSIS
Containment Spray Pump [*Nuclear energy*] (NRCH) ... CSP
Containment Spray Recirculation System [*Nuclear energy*] (NRCH) ... CSRS
Containment Spray System [*Nuclear energy*] (NRCH) ... CSS
Containment Spray System, Post-Accident Injection Phase [*Environmental science*] (COE) ... CSSI
Containment Spray System, Post-Accident Recirculation Phase [*Environmental science*] (COE) ... CSSR
Containment Steam Explosion [*Nuclear energy*] (IEEE) ... CSE
Containment Support Fixture [*Nuclear energy*] (NRCH) ... CSF
Containment Systems Experiment [*Nuclear energy*] ... CSE
Containment Vacuum Pump [*Nuclear energy*] (IEEE) ... CVP
Containment Vacuum Pump Valve [*Nuclear energy*] (NRCH) ... CVPV
Containment Vent Header [*Nuclear energy*] (NRCH) ... CVH
Containment Ventilation Isolation [*Nuclear energy*] (NRCH) ... CVI
Contains (ROG) ... CONTS
Contamana [*Peru*] [*ICAO location identifier*] (ICLI) ... SPCM
contaminant (SAUS) ... contam
Contaminant Analysis Automation ... CAA
Contaminant Collection Unit (OA) ... CCU
Contaminant Control Cartridge (MCD) ... CCC
Contaminant Control Cartridge (NAKS) ... ccc
Contaminant Control System (SAUS) ... CCS
Contaminate (SAUS) ... Contam
Contaminated (SAUS) ... Contam
Contaminated (KSC) ... CONTAM
Contaminated (SAUS) ... Contd
Contaminated Normal [*Statistics*] ... CN
Contaminated Oil Settling (PDAA) ... COS
Contaminated Oil Settling Tank (AAG) ... COST
Contaminated Small Bowel [*Medicine*] (DB) ... CSB
Contaminated Small Bowel Syndrome [*Medicine*] (DMAA) ... CSBS
Contaminated Surface Soil (ABAC) ... CSS
Contaminated Water Storage [*Environmental science*] (COE) ... CWS
Contamination (SAUS) ... Contn
Contamination by Extraterrestrial Exploration (SAUS) ... CETEX
Contamination Control Area [*Army*] (ADDR) ... CCA
Contamination Control Station (MCD) ... CCS
Contamination Control System (NASA) ... CCS
Contamination Free Manufacturing [*Semiconductor manufacturing*] ... CFM
Contamination Index [*Medicine*] ... CI
Contamination Investigation (ACAE) ... CONIN
Contamination Mode [*NASA*] (KSC) ... CM
Contamination Monitor Package (SAUS) ... CMD
Contamination Reduction Zone (SAUO) ... CRZ
Contamination Requirements Definition Group (SAUO) ... CRDG
Contamination Technology (SSD) ... CONT
Contamination-Decontamination Experiment [*Nuclear energy*] ... CDE
Contamination-Free Manufacturing (SAUS) ... CFM
Contamination-Free Manufacturing Research Center (AAEL) ... CFMRC
Contamination/Overpressure (MCD) ... C/O
[*Hyperbolic*] **Contangent** [*Mathematics*] (BARN) ... ctnh
Contango [*Premium or interest paid*] [*London Stock Exchange*] ... CGO
Contano [*Parts so marked to rest*] [*Music*] ... CONT
Conte (VRA) ... cnte
Conte Corrente [*Running Account*] ... C/C
Conte Crayon (VRA) ... cnte
Contecs Intl Ltd ADS [*NASDAQ symbol*] (TTSB) ... DLVRY
Contel ASC [*ICAO designator*] (FAAC) ... XCL
CONTEL [*Continental Telecom Corp.*] **Customer Support** [*Telecommunications service*] (TSSD) ... CCS
Contel Service Corp., Atlanta, GA [*Library symbol*] [*Library of Congress*] (LCLS) ... GACSC
Contemplate (SAUS) ... Contem
Contemplate (AABC) ... CONTEM
Contemplative Sisters of St. Benedict (TOCD) ... OSB
Contemplatives of Good Shepherd (TOCD) ... CGS
Contemporaneous Reserve Accounting [*Banking*] ... CRA
Contemporaneous Reserve Requirements [*Banking*] ... CRR
Contemporary (ADA) ... CONT
Contemporary (VRA) ... cont
Contemporary (NTIO) ... contemp
Contemporary ... CONTEMP
Contemporary Acapella Society of America (EA) ... CASA
Contemporary Agriculture (journ.) (SAUS) ... Contemp Agric
Contemporary American Business Leaders [*A publication*] ... CABL
Contemporary American Patriot Club (EA) ... CAP
Contemporary Archive on Latin America [*Defunct*] [*British*] ... CALA
Contemporary Art Centre of South Australia ... CACSA
Contemporary Art Society ... CAS
Contemporary Art Society (SAUO) ... CAS
Contemporary Authors [*A publication*] ... CA
Contemporary Authors Autobiography Series [*A publication*] ... CAAS
Contemporary Authors Bibliographical Series [*A publication*] ... CABS
Contemporary Authors First Revision Series [*A publication*] ... CAR
Contemporary Authors New Revision Series [*A publication*] ... CANR
Contemporary Authors: Permanent Series [*A publication*] ... CAP
Contemporary Books [*Publisher's imprint*] ... CB
Contemporary Christian [*Music*] (WDMC) ... CC

Contemporary Civilization [*University course*] ... CC
Contemporary Deep Rack Interior (MCD) ... CDRI
Contemporary Digital Services, Inc. [*New Rochelle, NY*] [*Telecommunications*] (TSSD) ... CDSI
Contemporary Education [*A publication*] (BRI) ... Cont Ed
Contemporary English Version [*Of the Bible*] ... CEV
Contemporary Entertainment Services [*Air carrier designation symbol*] ... CESX
Contemporary Evaluation Form [*Army*] ... CEF
Contemporary Force (OA) ... cf
Contemporary Games [*A publication*] ... CG
Contemporary Graphic Artists [*A publication*] ... CGA
Contemporary Heroes and Heroines [*A publication*] ... CHH
Contemporary Historical Examination Current Operations [*Air Force*] (AFM) ... CHECO
Contemporary Historical Vehicle Association (EA) ... CHVA
Contemporary Hit Radio ... CHR
Contemporary Issues Clearinghouse [*Defunct*] (EA) ... CIC
Contemporary Issues Criticism [*A publication*] ... CIC
Contemporary Issues in Science Program (EDAC) ... CIIS
Contemporary Jewish Learning Materials [*A publication*] (BJA) ... CJLM
Contemporary Law Review [*India*] [*A publication*] (DLA) ... Cont L Rev
Contemporary Literary Criticism [*Reference publication; often pronounced "click"*] ... CLC
Contemporary Men of Letters [*A publication*] ... CML
Contemporary Music Project [*Defunct*] (EA) ... CMP
Contemporary Music Society (EA) ... CMS
Contemporary Musicians [*A publication*] ... CM
Contemporary Newsmakers [*Later, Newsmakers*] [*A publication*] ... CN
Contemporary Pacific [*A publication*] (BRI) ... Cont Pac
Contemporary Physics (MEC) ... Contemp Physics
Contemporary Physics (journ.) (SAUS) ... Contemp Phys
Contemporary Psychology [*A publication*] (BRI) ... CP
Contemporary Records [*Los Angeles*] [*Record label*] ... Cty
Contemporary Records (New York) [*Record label*] ... CtyNY
Contemporary Review [*A publication*] (BRI) ... CR
Contemporary Rock (LAIN) ... CR
Contemporary Science Series [*A publication*] ... CSS
Contemporary Scientific Archives Centre (SAUO) ... CSAC
Contemporary Sociology [*A publication*] (BRI) ... CS
Contemporary Specialty Services [*Merchandiser*] [*Chicago, IL*] ... CSS
Contemporary Systems Design Ltd. (SAUO) ... CSD
Contemporary Theatre [*A publication*] ... CT
Contemporary Theatre, Film, and Television [*A publication*] ... CTFT
Contemporary World Writers [*A publication*] ... CWW
Contempory Comparison-Test (SAUS) ... CC-Test
Contempt [*FBI standardized term*] ... CMPT
Contempt of Court ... COC
Contemptuous (ADWA) ... contempt
Content [*of gas in blood phase*] (AAMN) ... C
Content Addressable Computing System ... CACS
Content Addressable File Store [*Computer science*] (PDAA) ... CADS
Content Addressable File Store [*Computer science*] (NITA) ... CAFS
Content Addressed File System (SAUS) ... CAFS
Content and Source of Cataloging Data for Local Use (PDAA) ... CASCADE
Content Dependent Information Language ... CODIL
Content Indication Codes (NG) ... CIC
Content Management Center (SAUS) ... CMC
Content of Thought [*Medicine*] (DMAA) ... COT
Content Replication Service [*Microsoft Corp.*] [*Computer science*] ... CRS
Content Scramble System [*Computer science*] ... CSS
Content Scrambling System (SAUS) ... CSS
Content Standard for Digital Geospatial Metadata (GEOI) ... CSDGM
Content Vectoring Protocol [*Computer science*] ... CVP
Content-Addressable Array Parallel Processor [*Computer science*] ... CAAPP
Content-Addressable Data Manager ... CADM
Content-Addressable Memory [*Computer science*] (IAA) ... CA
Content-Addressable Memory [*Computer science*] ... CAM
Content-Addressable Parallel Processor [*Computer science*] ... CAPP
Content-Addressable Random Access Memory [*Computer science*] (HGAA) ... CARAM
Content-Addressed Film System [*Computer science*] (PDAA) ... CAFS
Content-Based Image Retrieval (TELE) ... CBIR
Content-Based Retrieval ... CBR
Content/Format Selection Summaries (SAUS) ... SFSS
Contention Based Channel Reservation (SAUS) ... CBCR
Contention Priority Oriented Demand Assignment [*Protocol*] [*Computer science*] ... CPODA
Contention Procedure (SAUS) ... CP
Contents (SAUS) ... Cnt
Contents ... CONT
Contents (ODBW) ... cont
Contents, Abstracts, and Photocopies Services [*India*] [*Information service or system*] ... CAPS
Contents Addressable File Store (SAUS) ... CAFS
Contents Addressable Memory (SAUS) ... CAM
Contents Directory Entry [*Computer science*] (MHDI) ... CDE
Contents Listing (SAUS) ... CTL
Contents of Address Part of Register (RALS) ... CAR
Contents of Decrement Part of Register [*Computer science*] (NHD) ... CDR
Contents Unknown (SAUS) ... CU
Contere [*Rub Together*] [*Pharmacy*] ... CONTER
Conterminous United States Mineral Resource Assessment Program [*Department of the Interior*] ... CUSMAP
Conterminous U.S. Mineral Assessment Program (SAUS) ... CUSMAP
Contest ... CNTST
Contested ... CONT
Contested Election Cases [*United States*] [*A publication*] (DLA) ... Cont Elect Case
Context Addressed Segment Sequential Memory [*Computer science*] ... CASSM
Context Based Access Control (SAUS) ... CBAC
Context Control Object [*Telecommunications*] (OSI) ... CCO
Context Dependent File (SAUS) ... CDF
Context Dependent Information Language (SAUS) ... CODIL
Context Dependent Interchangeability (SAUS) ... CDI
Context Free (BUR) ... CF
Context Free Transduction Grammar (MHDI) ... CFTG
Context, Input, Process, Product [*Computer science*] ... CIPP
Context, Input, Process Product Model (SAUS) ... CIPP Model
Context Roll File (CIST) ... CRF
Context Sensitive Grammar [*Computer science*] (IAA) ... CSG
Context-Free Coded Fuzzy Grammar (SAUS) ... CFCFG
Context-Free Coded Fuzzy Language (SAUS) ... CFCFL
Context-Free Grammar [*Computer science*] ... CFG
Context-Free Graph Grammar (SAUS) ... CFGG
Context-Free Language [*Computer science*] ... CFL
Context-Free Phrase Structure Grammar [*Computer science*] (PDAA) ... CFPSG
Context-Free Picture Grammar (SAUS) ... CFPG
Context-Free Programmed Grammar (PDAA) ... CFPG
Context-Free Syntactical Translator ... CFST
Context-Free Transduction Grammer (SAUS) ... CFTG
Context-Sensitive (SAUS) ... CS
Context-Sensitive Language [*Computer science*] (IAA) ... CSL
Contextual Dependency (SAUS) ... CD
Contextual Enhancement Processor (SAUS) ... CEP
Contextual Indexing and Faceted Taxonomic Access System [*Computer science*] (BARN) ... CIFT
Contextual Indexing and Faceted Taxonomic System [*Modern Language Association of America*] [*A database*] (NITA) ... CIFT
Contextual Postprocessing System (SAUS) ... CPPS
ContiCurrency Foreign Exchange and Money Market Database [*No longer available online*] ... CCFX
ContiFinancial Corp. [*NYSE symbol*] (TTSB) ... CFN
Contifinancial Corp. [*Associated Press*] (SAG) ... Contifin
Conti-Flug Koln/Bonn [*Germany*] [*ICAO designator*] (FAAC) ... EPC
Contigency Gravity Gradient (SAUS) ... CGG
Contiguous (NASA) ... CONTIG
Contiguous Fisheries Zone [*Offshore*] ... CFZ
Contiguous Node Group Restoral Supervision and Switching ... CONGRESS
Contiguous United States ... CONUS
Contiguous-Disk File [*Computer science*] (PDAA) ... CDF
Continence Aids Assistance Scheme [*Australia*] ... CAAS
Continence Restored (EA) ... CR
Continence Restored, Inc. (EA) ... CRI
Continent ... CONT
Continent (ADWA) ... cont
Continent, Antwerp-Hamburg Range [*Shipping*] (DS) ... CONT (AH)
Continent between Bordeaux and Hamburg [*Business term*] ... CB & H
Continent between Havre and Hamburg [*Business term*] ... CH & H
Continent Between Havre and Hamburg (SAUS) ... CH&H
Continent, Bordeaux-Hamburg Range [*Shipping*] (DS) ... CONT (BH)
Continent, Britain & Asia [*Commercial firm*] (DS) ... COBRA
Continent, Havre-Hamburg Range [*Shipping*] (DS) ... CONT (HH)
Continent or Scandinavia (SAUS) ... C/S
Continent West Africa Conference (SAUO) ... COWAC
Continental [*Air mass*] ... C
Continental (AFM) ... CON
Continental ... Cont
Continental (ROG) ... CONTIN
Continental (AABC) ... CONTL
continental (SAUS) ... Contl
Continental ... CONTNTL
Continental Advance Section [*Originally called Coastal Base Section*] [*World War II*] ... CONAD
Continental Advertising Agency Network [*Later, Advertising and Marketing International Network*] (EA) ... CAAN
Continental Advertising and Marketing Agencies (SAUO) ... CAMA
Continental Aerospace Defense Command (SAUO) ... CONAD
Continental Africa Chamber of Commerce (EA) ... CACC
Continental Africa GATE Experiment (SAUS) ... CAGE
Continental Africa Project [*National Academy of Sciences*] ... CAP
Continental Air Command ... CAC
Continental Air Command ... CONAC
Continental Air Command (MCD) ... CONARC
Continental Air Defense (SAUS) ... Con AD
Continental Air Defense Command [*Discontinued, 1975*] ... CADC
Continental Air Defense Command [*Discontinued, 1975*] ... CONAD
Continental Air Defense Command Manual (SAUS) ... CONADM
Continental Air Defense Integration, North ... CADIN
Continental Air Defense Objectives Plan (AABC) ... CADOP
Continental Air Defense Study (ACAE) ... CADS
Continental Air Defense System ... CADS
Continental Air Forces ... CAF
Continental Air Services ... CAS
Continental Airborne Reconnaissance for Damage Assessment (SAUS) ... CARDA
Continental Aircraft Control and Warning (MUGU) ... CAC & W
Continental Airlines [*ICAO designator*] (AD) ... CO
Continental Airlines (MHDB) ... CONT
Continental Airlines, Inc. [*NYSE symbol*] (SPSG) ... CAI
Continental Airlines, Inc. (MCD) ... CAL
Continental Airlines, Inc. [*CAB official abbreviation*] ... CO

Continental Airlines, Inc. [*ICAO designator*] (FAAC) .... COA
Continental Airlines, Inc. [*Associated Press*] (SAG) .... CtlAir
Continental Airlines Reservation System (SAUS) .... CARS
Continental Airways (AAG) .... CA
Continental Airways and Communications Service [*Air Force*] .... CACS
Continental and Overseas Investments N.V. (SAUO) .... COIN
Continental Army .... CONAR
Continental Army and Major Overseas Commands Systems [*Later, ASMIS*] .... CARMOCS
Continental Army Command [*See CONARC*] .... CAC
Continental Army Command (SAUO) .... CARC
Continental Army Command [*Responsible for induction, processing, training of active duty personnel*] [*Superseded by FORSCOM*] .... CONARC
Continental Army Management Information System (RDA) .... CAMIS
Continental Army MIS (SAUO) .... CAMIS
Continental Association of CPA [*Certified Public Accountant*] **Firms** (EA) .... CACPAF
Continental Association of Funeral and Memorial Societies .... CAFMS
Continental Association of Resolute Employers [*Washington, DC*] (EA) .... CARE
Continental Assurance Co. .... CA
Continental Atlantic Tidewater and Cities (SAUS) .... CATC
Continental Aviation & Engineering Corp. .... CAE
Continental Aviation and Engineering Corp. (SAUO) .... CAE
Continental Aviation Ltd. [*Ghana*] [*ICAO designator*] (FAAC) CCL
Continental Baking Company (SAUO) CI
Continental Ballistic Missile .... CBM
Continental Bank Corp. (EFIS) .... CBC
Continental Bank of Canada [*Toronto Stock Exchange symbol*] .... CTL
Continental Baptist Mission (EA) .... CBM
Continental Base Section .... CBS
Continental Basketball Association (EA) .... CBA
Continental Breakfast .... CB
Continental Can [*Formerly, Viatech, Inc.*] [*NYSE symbol*] (SPSG) .... CAN
Continental Can Co., Inc. [*Associated Press*] (SAG) .... ContCan
Continental Can Company, Inc. (SAUO) CCC
Continental Car Ferry Centre [*British*] .... CCFC
Continental Carbon Co., Houston, TX [*Library symbol*] [*Library of Congress*] (LCLS) .... TxHCC
Continental Choice Care, Inc. [*NASDAQ symbol*] (SAG) CCCI
Continental Choice Care, Inc. [*Associated Press*] (SAG) .... CtlCC
Continental Choice Care, Inc. [*Associated Press*] (SAG) .... CtlCCare
Continental Choice Care Wrrt [*NASDAQ symbol*] (TTSB) .... CCCIW
Continental Circuits Corp. [*NASDAQ symbol*] (SAG) .... CCIR
Continental Circuits Corp. [*Associated Press*] (SAG) .... CntlCir
[*Tropical*] **Continental Cold Air Mass** (BARN) .... cTk
Continental Communications Division [*Military*] .... CCD
Continental Confederation of Adopted Indians (EA) .... CCAI
Continental Control Area [*FAA*] .... CCA
Continental Copper & Steel Industries (SAUO) .... CCS
Continental Copper & Steel Industries, Inc. (SAUO) CCX
Continental Corporation (SAUO) CIC
Continental Daily Parcels Express (SAUS) .... CDPE
Continental Datanet, Inc. [*Vancouver Stock Exchange symbol*] .... CDJ
Continental Defense Integrated Network [*DoD*] (CIST) .... CDIN
Continental Depositary Receipt [*Banking*] (MHDW) .... CDR
Continental Depository Receipts (SAUS) .... CDRs
Continental Divide (FAAC) .... CONTDVD
Continental Divide Trail Society (EA) .... CDTS
Continental Division, Military Air Transport Service (SAUO) .... CNTLDMATS
Continental Division, Transport Control Center [*Military*] .... CTCC
Continental Dorset Club (EA) .... CDC
Continental Early Warning (SAUS) .... CEW
Continental Electronic Security Division [*Military*] .... CESD
Continental Electronics Manufacturing Co. (AAG) .... CEMCO
Continental Entry Charts [*Air Force*] .... CEC
Continental Europe (SAUS) .... Cont Eur
Continental Europe and British Isles (SAUS) .... Cont Eur&Br I
Continental Exercise [*Military*] .... CONEX
Continental Flood Basalt [*Geology*] .... CFB
Continental Flood Basalt Province [*Geology*] .... CFBP
Continental Football League .... CFL
Continental Gas Company, Inc. (SAUO) .... CH
Continental Geographic Information System (SAUS) .... CGIS
Continental Gold Corp. [*Vancouver Stock Exchange symbol*] .... CUG
Continental Grain Company (SAUO) .... Contigrain
Continental Group Co., Inc., Chicago, IL [*Library symbol*] [*Library of Congress*] (LCLS) .... ICCon
Continental Group, Inc. [*Toronto Stock Exchange symbol*] .... CH
Continental Homes Holding Corp. [*NYSE symbol*] (SPSG) .... CON
Continental Homes Holding Corp. [*Associated Press*] (SAG) .... CtlHme
Continental Horsepower (IAA) .... CONTHP
Continental Horsepower (SAUS) .... CONT HP
Continental Hydrologic Processes (SAUS) .... CHP
Continental Illinois Corp. (SAUO) CIL
Continental Illinois National Bank and Trust Co., Research and Information Services, Chicago, IL [*Library symbol*] [*Library of Congress*] (LCLS) .... ICConB
Continental Illinois Properties (SAUO) .... CIE
Continental Illinois Realty (SAUO) .... CIR
Continental Indoor Soccer League (SAUO) .... CISL
Continental Info Sys [*NASDAQ symbol*] (TTSB) .... CISC
Continental Information Systems Corp. (SAUO) .... CIS
Continental Information Systems Corp. [*NASDAQ symbol*] (SAG) .... CISC
Continental Information Systems Corp. [*Associated Press*] (SAG) .... CntlInfo
Continental Insurance Co. (SAUO) .... CIS
Continental Intelligence Data Processing System (MCD) .... CIDPS
Continental Investment Corp. (SAUO) .... COI
Continental Kennel Club (GVA) .... CKC
Continental Land Masses Air Traffic Control [*NASA*] (MCD) .... COLM/ATC
Continental Limits of the United States (SAUS) .... CLUS
Continental Limits, United States .... CLUS
Continental Limits, United States of America [*Navy*] .... CLUSA
Continental Lithospheric Mantle [*Geology*] .... CLM
Continental Mains Transformer (SAUS) .... Cont Mains Tr
Continental Margin Environment and Mineral Resources Sub-programme (SAUS) .... COMEMIR
Continental Margin Sedimentology [*Oceanography*] (MSC) .... COMSED
Continental Margins Program [*Australia*] .... CMP
Continental Marines .... CM
Continental Mark II Owner's Association (EA) .... CMOA
Continental Materials Corp. [*Associated Press*] (SAG) .... ContMtl
Continental Materials Corp. [*AMEX symbol*] (SPSG) .... CUO
Continental Medical Systems [*NYSE symbol*] (SPSG) .... CNM
Continental Merchant Bank [*Nigeria*] .... CMB
Continental Meteorological Data System (SAUS) .... COMEDS
Continental [*United States*] **Meteorological Teletype System** [*Navy*] .... COMET
Continental Micronesia, Inc. [*Guam*] [*ICAO designator*] (FAAC) .... CMI
Continental Mortgage & Equity Trust [*NASDAQ symbol*] (NQ) .... CMET
Continental Mortgage & Equity Trust [*Associated Press*] (SAG) .... CtlMtg
Continental Mortgage Investors (SAUO) .... CMI
Continental Motors Corp. (SAUO) .... CO
Continental Motors Corporation (SAUO) .... CMR
Continental Motosport Club (EA) .... CMC
Continental National America [*Insurance group*] .... CNA
Continental National Assurance (SAUO) .... CNA
Continental NORAD Region [*Aviation*] (FAAC) .... CONR
Continental Offshore Stratigraphic Test [*Offshore oil technology*] .... COST
Continental Oil & Transportation Co. (EFIS) .... CONOCO
Continental Oil, Atlantic Refining, Tidewater Oil, and Cities Service [*Group of companies joined together for mutual drilling ventures*] .... CATC
Continental Oil, Atlantic Refining, Tidewater Oil, Cities Service (SAUO) .... CATC
Continental Oil Co. [*ICAO designator*] (FAAC) .... CON
Continental Oil Co. .... CONOCO
Continental Oil Co., R and D Technical Information Service, Ponca City, OK [*Library symbol*] [*Library of Congress*] (LCLS) .... OkPoC
Continental Oil Company (SAUO) CLL
Continental Oil Company (SAUS) .... Conoco
Continental Oil International Finance Corporation (SAUO) .... Conoco
Continental Operations Range (MCD) .... COR
Continental Organization of Distributor Enterprises, Inc. .... CODE
Continental Pacific [*Vancouver Stock Exchange symbol*] .... CXF
Continental Pharma [*Belgium*] [*Research code symbol*] .... CP
Continental Pharma Cryosan, Inc. [*Toronto Stock Exchange symbol*] .... CPM
Continental Plan [*Hotel rate*] .... CP
Continental Polar Air Mass .... CP
Continental Polar Air Mass (MSA) .... CPAM
Continental Polar Cold Air Mass (BARN) .... cPk
Continental Polluted Air Mass (QUAC) .... CPAM
Continental Program Marketing (SAUS) .... CPM
Continental Quilting Congress (EA) .... CQC
Continental Railway Circle (SAUO) .... CRC
Continental Scale Experiment (SAUS) .... CSE
Continental Scale International Project (GEOI) .... CSIP
Continental Scientific Drilling Committee [*National Academy of Science*] .... CSDC
Continental Scientific Drilling Program [*National Science Foundation, USGS, and Department of Energy*] .... CSDP
Continental Scientific Drilling Project (SAUS) .... CSDP
Continental Sediment [*Geology*] .... CS
Continental Service Corps (EA) .... CSC
Continental Shelf .... CONSHELF
Continental Shelf (SAUS) .... Conshelf
Continental Shelf (SAUS) .... CS
Continental Shelf Crawler .... CSC
Continental Shelf Discus [*Buoy system*] (MSC) .... CSD
Continental Shelf Drilling Program (SAUO) .... CSDP
Continental Shelf Mining .... CSM
Continental Shelf Sedimentology [*Oceanography*] (MSC) .... CONSED
Continental Shelf Submersible [*Undersea exploration vehicle*] (MCD) .... CONSUB
Continental Shelf Wave .... CSW
Continental Silver [*Vancouver Stock Exchange symbol*] .... CVR
Continental Sports Conference (SAUO) .... CSC
Continental Steel Corp. (SAUO) .... CTL
Continental Stratus Archive (ARMP) .... CSA
Continental Telecom, Inc. (EFIS) .... CONTEL
Continental Telecom, Inc. (EFIS) .... CTC
Continental Telephone Corporation (SAUO) .... CTC
Continental Tire System .... CTS
Continental Transportation Association [*Defunct*] (EA) .... CTA
Continental Tropical Air [*Meteorology*] (DA) .... CT
Continental Tropical Air (SAUS) .... CT Air
Continental Tropical Air Mass (MSA) .... CTAM
Continental Tyre Ltd. [*Vancouver Stock Exchange symbol*] .... CYH
Continental, Union, Shell, and Superior [*In CUSS I, ocean drilling barge named after oil companies that financed its development*] .... CUSS
Continental United States .... CONUS
Continental United States .... CUS
Continental United States and the Military District of Washington [*Refers to the numbered armies in that area*] (AABC) .... CONUSAMDW
Continental United States Army (DEMM) .... CONUSA
Continental United States Intelligence [*Domestic intelligence project*] [*Army*] .... CONUS INTEL

Continental United States Operations [*Army*] .... CONOPS
Continental United States Over-the-Horizon [*RADAR system*] .... CONUS OTH
Continental United States Over-the-Horizon-Backscatter [*RADAR system*] .... CONUS OTH-B
Continental U.S. [*Television news company*] [*St. Paul, MN*] (WDMC) .... Conus
Continental U.S. Digital Graphics System (SAUO) .... CONDIGS
Continental Wage Schedule [*Military*] (AABC) .... CWS
[*Tropical*] Continental Warm Air Mass (BARN) .... cTw
Continental Waste Industries [*NASDAQ symbol*] (SAG) .... CONT
Continental Waste Industries [*Associated Press*] (SAG) .... ContW
Continental Waste Industries [*Associated Press*] (SAG) .... ContWst
Continental-Oceanic [*Crust*] Boundary [*Geology*] .... COB
Continental-Scale Project (SAUS) .... GEWEX
Continent-Ocean Boundary [*Geology*] .... COB
Contingencies of the Army .... CA
Contingency (AABC) .... CNTGCY
Contingency (SAUS) .... Cntgcy
Contingency [*Type classification*] (MCD) .... CON
Contingency (MCD) .... CONT
Contingency (KSC) .... CONTG
Contingency (SAUS) .... Contg
Contingency Abort [*NASA*] (NASA) .... CA
Contingency Action/Limited Objective Warfare (DOMA) ..... CALOW
Contingency Airfield Logistic System (DWSG) .... CALS
Contingency Alternate Route Plan [*Environmental science*] (COE) .... CARP
Contingency Amphibious Plan [*NATO*] (NATG) .... CAP
Contingency Analysis Model (KSC) .... CAM
Contingency and Confidential Intelligence (CINC) .... C & CI
Contingency and Exercise Plan [*Environmental science*] (COE) .... CONEXPLAN
Contingency & Limited Objective Warfare (SAUS) .... CALOW
Contingency and Training [*Army*] (AABC) .... C & T
Contingency Capabilities Assessment [*Environmental science*] (COE) .... CCA
Contingency Coefficient (DIPS) C
Contingency Communication Element (ACAE) .... CCE
Contingency Communications Package (SAUS) .... CCP
Contingency Communications Team (SAUO) .... CCT
Contingency Contracting Officers [*Military*] (RDA) .... CCO
Contingency Extravehicular Transfer (SAUS) .... CEVIT
Contingency Extravehicular Transfer [*NASA*] (KSC) .... CEVT
Contingency Fee (COE) .... CF
Contingency Financing Mechanism [*International Monetary Fund*] .... CFM
Contingency for Movement [*Army*] .... CFM
Contingency Force Pool .... CFP
Contingency Intermediate-Level Maintenance Center (DOMA) .... CILMC
Contingency Landing Area [*NASA*] .... CLA
Contingency Landing Site [*NASA*] (NASA) .... CLS
Contingency Landing Support Officer (MCD) .... CLSO
Contingency Lines of Communication, Europe [*Military*] (AABC) .... CLOCE
Contingency MAGTF [*Marine Air Ground Task Force*] (DOMA) .... CMAGTF
Contingency Maintenance Allocation Chart (MCD) .... CMAC
Contingency Movement After-Effect (SAUO) .... CMAE
Contingency of Operations Planning (MCD) .... COOP
Contingency Operation Mobility Planning and Execution System [*Military*] .... COMPES
Contingency Operational Contracting Support Program [*Air Force*] (AAGC) .... COCSP
Contingency Operations (SAUS) .... CONOPS
Contingency Operations Plan (MCD) .... COP
Contingency Operations Plans Report (NVT) .... COPS
Contingency Operations Selection Techniques (MCD) ...... COST
Contingency Operations Space [*Army*] .... COPS
Contingency Orbit Insertion [*NASA*] (KSC) .... COI
Contingency Plan [*Military*] .... CONPLAN
Contingency Planning (MCD) .... CP
Contingency Planning Aid (NASA) .... CPA
Contingency Planning Facilites List [*Environmental science*] (COE) .... CFL
Contingency Planning Facilities Lists (CINC) .... CPFL
Contingency Planning Guidance (DOMA) .... CPG
Contingency Planning Support Capability (AFM) .... CPSC
Contingency Planning System (MHDB) .... CPS
Contingency Readiness System (SAUS) .... CONREDS
Contingency Rear Link (SAUS) .... CRL
Contingency Reference Book (MCD) .... CRB
Contingency Relief Force [*Military*] .... CRF
Contingency Remoting System [*Military*] (RDA) .... CRS
Contingency Rerouting of Communications [*NATO*] (NATG) .... CRDCS
Contingency Reserve (MCD) .... CR
Contingency Response Program [*DoD*] .... CORE
Contingency Retention Stock [*Military*] (AFIT) .... CRS
Contingency Sample [*NASA*] (KSC) .... CS
Contingency Special Airlift Mission [*Air Force*] .... C-SAM
Contingency Support Center (MCD) .... CSC
Contingency Support Center (NAKS) .... csc
Contingency Support Force [*Air Force*] (DOMA) .... CSF
Contingency Support Package (MCD) .... CSP
Contingency Support Staff (MCD) .... CSS
Contingency Support Stocks [*Military*] (AABC) .... CONSSTOCS
Contingency Support Stocks [*Military*] (NVT) .... CONSTOCS
Contingency TAC Automated Planning System (MCD) ...... CTAPS
Contingency Transfer System [*Aerospace*] .... CTS
Contingency Transportation Requirements System (MCD) .... CONTREQS
Contingent (SAUS) .... Cont
Contingent .... COT
Contingent After Effects (WDAA) .... CAEs
Contingent Aftereffects [*Visual*] .... CAE

Contingent Credit Lines CCL
Contingent Credit-Line CCL
Contingent Employee Liability Insurance .... CELI
Contingent Liability Ledger [*DoD*] CLL
Contingent Negative Variation [*Electrocortical measurement*] .... CNV
Contingent Security Element (ACAE) .... CSE
Contingent Valuation [*Environmental medicine*] CV
Contingent Value Method [*Pisciculture*] .... CVM
Contingent Value Right [*Finance*] .... CVR
Continous Electron Beam Accelerator [*Telecommunications*] (CIST) .... CEBA
Continous Printing (SAUS) .... CP
Continous Tone (SAUS) .... CT
Continuance .... CONTCE
Continuance [*Legal term*] (DLA) .... CONTIN
Continuation .... CONTN
Continuation (ADWA) .... contn
Continuation Address (SAUS) .... CA
Continuation Cards (SAUS) CC
Continuation Clause CC
Continuation Incentive Pay [*Proposed*] [*Army*] .... COIN
Continuation Line (SAUS) CL
Continuation of Message (ACRL) .... COM
Continuation of Pay (DNAB) .... COP
Continuation of Rolle's Reports [*2 Rolle*] [*A publication*] (DLA) .... Con
Continuation Operational Sea Training (SAUO) .... COST
Continuation Statement (SAUS) .... CS
Continuation-in-Part [*Patent application*] .... CIP
Continucare [*AMEX symbol*] (SAG) .... CNU
Continucare [*Associated Press*] (SAG) .... Continucre
Continucare Corp. [*AMEX symbol*] (SG) .... CNU
Continue (SAUS) .... Cnt
Continue [*or Continuing*] (AFM) .... CONT
Continue (DAVI) .... contin
Continue (SAUS) .... Ctin
Continue Calling (SAUS) .... CONCA
Continue Calling Until (FAAC) .... CONCA
Continue Operation (SAUS) .... CNT
Continue Present Duty (SAUS) .... CONPASP
Continue Present Duty [*Military*] .... CONPRESDU
Continue Present Management [*Medicine*] (DAVI) .... CPM
Continue Same [*Treatment*] [*Medicine*] (DAVI) .... CS
Continue Statement (SAUS) .... CS
Continue to Hold [*Aviation*] (FAAC) .... CONTH
Continue Treatment (SAUS) .... CONTREAT
Continue Treatment [*Medicine*] .... CT
Continue Treatment at Naval Hospital or Medical Facility Indicated .... CONTREAT
Continue With [*Medicine*] .... C/W
Continue-Any [*Mode*] [*Computer science*] (IBMDP) .... CA
Continued .... CON
Continued (ODBW) .... cont
Continued (WDMC) .... contd
Continued .... CONTD
Continued (ROG) .... CONTIND
Continued Addition (SAUS) .... CA
Continued Automated Multi-Baseline (MCD) .... CAMB
Continued Development .... CD
Continued Fraction Expansion (IAA) .... CFE
Continued Health Care Benefit Program [*DoD*] .... CHCBP
Continued Lymphocyte Culture [*Immunology*] CLC
Continued on Active Duty (AABC) .... COAD
Continued Quality Improvement (SAUO) .... CQI
Continued Skin Peeling Syndrome [*Dermatology*] .... CSPS
Continued Stay Review [*Medicine*] (MELL) .... CSR
Continue[d] (WDMC) .... cont
Continuentur [*Continue*] [*Pharmacy*] (ROG) .... CONT
Continuentur Remedia [*Continue the Medicines*] [*Pharmacy*] .... CONT REM
Continues to Improve (MELL) .... CTI
Continue-Specific [*Mode*] [*Computer science*] (IBMDP) .... CS
Continuetur [*Let It Be Continued*] [*Pharmacy*] .... CONTIN
Continuetur Remedium [*Let the Medicine Be Continued*] [*Pharmacy*] (ROG) .... CONTIN REM
Continuing .... CONTNG
Continuing Action Maintenance Instruction .... CAMI
Continuing Airworthiness Panel [*ICAO*] (DA) .... CAP
Continuing Balance System [*Army*] (MCD) .... CBS
Continuing Balance System - Expanded [*Army*] (AABC) .... CBS-X
Continuing Calibration CC
Continuing Calibration Blank [*Laboratory analysis*] ...... CCB
Continuing Calibration Verification [*Laboratory analysis*] CCV
Continuing Care [*Medicine*] (DAVI) CC
Continuing Care Accreditation Commission [*American Association of Homes for Aging*] .... CCAC
Continuing Committee of Deputy Ministers [*Canada*] .... CCDM
Continuing Committee of the National Women's Conference [*Later, NW*] (EA) .... CCNWC
Continuing Committee on Muslim-Christian Cooperation (EA) .... CCMCC
Continuing Community Care [*Psychology*] (DAVI) CCC
Continuing Criminal Enterprise .... CCE
Continuing Crown Allocation (SAUS) .... CCA
Continuing Dental Education .... CDE
Continuing Design Services (SAUS) .... CDS
Continuing Disability Investigation [*Social Security Administration*] (OICC) ..... CDI
Continuing Disability Review (MELL) .... CDR
Continuing Education .... CE
Continuing Education Achievement Unit (IEEE) .... CEAU

Continuing Education and Training (ACII) .... CET
Continuing Education Approval and Recognition Program (DMAA) .... CEARP
Continuing Education Books (SAUS) .... CEB
Continuing Education Center [*Veterans Administration*] (GFGA) .... CEC
Continuing Education Committee (SAUO) .... CEC
Continuing Education Council [*Later, CNCE*] (EA) .... CEC
Continuing Education Credit (DAVI) .... CEC
Continuing Education Delivery Systems .... CEDS
Continuing Education Field Unit [*Veterans Administration*] (GFGA) .... CEFU
Continuing Education for Laboratory Technicians [*Union Carbide Co.*] .... CELT
Continuing Education for Librarians in Staffs in the Southwest (SAUO) .... CELS
Continuing Education for Library and Information Management (SAUS) .... CELIM
Continuing Education for Library Staffs (SAUS) .... CELS
Continuing Education for Senior Citizens .... CESC
Continuing Education for Young Women .... CEYW
Continuing Education in Mental Retardation Program [*American Associaton on Mental Deficiency*] (EDAC) .... CEMR
Continuing Education of Librarians in the Southwest (SAUS) .... CELS
Continuing Education of the Bar (SAUS) .... CEB
Continuing Education Program [*State University of New York at Albany*] [*Research center*] .... CEP
Continuing Education Recognition Program [*For nurses*] .... CERP
Continuing Education Re-Education Program (DAVI) .... CERP
Continuing Education Service for State and Local Government Officials .... CESSLGO
Continuing Education Service for State and Local Government Officials (SAUO) .... CESSLGO
Continuing Education Standing Committee (AIE) .... CESC
Continuing Education Unit [*American Management Association*] .... CEU
Continuing Engineering Development (ACAE) .... CED
Continuing Evaluation Program (SAUO) .... CEP
Continuing Forestry Education (SAUO) .... CFE
Continuing Health Education (MCD) .... CHE
Continuing Improvement Council (SAUO) CIC
Continuing Intelligence Requirement (MCD) .... CIR
Continuing Legal Education .... CLE
Continuing Legal Education of the Bar, University of California Extension (DLA) .... CCEB
Continuing Legal Education, University of Kentucky College of Law (DLA) .... KCLE
Continuing Legal Education, University of Montana (DLA) .... CLEM
Continuing Legal Education, University of Oklahoma Law Center (DLA) .... OCLE
Continuing Library Education Network and Exchange [*American Library Association*] [*Information service or system*] (EA) .... CLENE
Continuing Library Education Network and Exchange Round Table (EA) .... CLENERT
Continuing Library Education Planning and Advisory Project .... COLEPAC
Continuing Medical Education .... CME
Continuing Medical Education Information Services (ADWA) .... CMEIS
Continuing Numerical Data Projects .... CNDP
Continuing Nursing Education (ADWA) .... CNE
Continuing Professional Development (PDAA) .... CPD
Continuing Professional Education .... CPE
Continuing Property Records .... CPR
Continuing Resolution .... CR
Continuing Resolution Authority [*Military*] (AFM) .... CRA
Continuing Revolution .... CR
Continuing Smoker (DAVI) .... CS
Continuing Survey of Food Intakes by Individuals [*Department of Agriculture*] (GFGA) .... CSFII
Continuing-Care Retirement Communities .... CCRC
Continuity (SAUS) .... Cont
Continuity [*Telecommunications*] (TEL) .... COT
Continuity Accept Limit .... CAL
Continuity and Logic Unit .... CONALOG
Continuity Cell (VERA) CC
Continuity Check .... CCHK
Continuity Check Request (SAUS) .... CCR
Continuity Data Area (SAUS) .... CDA
Continuity Irish Republican Army (SAUO) .... CIRA
Continuity Message [*Telecommunications*] (TEL) .... CM
Continuity of Government .... COG
Continuity of Government Emergency Management Team [*Environmental science*] (COE) .... COGEMT
Continuity of Operations (MCD) .... CONOPS
Continuity of Operations (CCCA) .... COO
Continuity of Operations, Alaskan Air Command .... COPAAC
Continuity of Operations Plan [*Army*] .... COOP
Continuity of Operations Plan [*Navy*] .... COOPLAN
Continuity of Operations Plan [*Military*] .... COP
Continuity of Operations Plan, Department of the Air Force (AFM) .... COPDAF
Continuity of Operations Plan of the Joint Chiefs of Staff .... COOP-JCS
Continuity of Service Set (MCD) .... CSS
Continuity Rambus Inline Memory Module (SAUS) .... CRIMM
Continuity Signal [*Telecommunications*] (NITA) .... COT
Continuity Test Current .... CTC
Continuity Tone Detector [*Telecommunications*] (TEL) .... CTD
Continuity Transceiver [*Telecommunications*] (TEL) .... CT
Continuity Transceiver Module [*Telecommunications*] (TEL) .... CTM
Continuity-Check (SAUS) CC
Continuity-Check Incoming (SAUS) CCI
Continuity-Check Indicator (SAUS) .... CCH Indicator
Continuity-Check Outgoing (SAUS) .... CCO
Continuity-Check-Request Signal (SAUS) .... CCR Signal
Continuity-Failure Signal (SAUS) .... CCF
Continuity-Recheck Incoming (SAUS) .... CRI
Continuity-Recheck Outgoing (SAUS) .... CRO
Continuo [*Thorough Bass*] [*Music*] .... CONT
Continuos Composite Servo (SAUS) .... CCS
Continuous [*Botany*] C
Continuous [*Aviation code*] .... CNS
Continuous (GAVI) .... CON
Continuous [*or Continuously*] (DAVI) .... CONT
Continuous (SAUS) .... Cont
Continuous .... CONTNS
Continuous (SAUS) .... Ctinus
Continuous Acceleration Device .... CAD
Continuous Accumulation of Coriolis Acceleration [*Bioscience*] .... CACA
Continuous Acquisition and Life-Cycle Support [*Military*] (RDA) .... CALS
Continuous Action [*Acronym is brand of decongestant capsule*] .... CONTAC
Continuous Address List (SAUS) .... CAL
Continuous Affinity Recycle Extraction [*Chemical engineering*] .... CARE
Continuous Aim Correction [*Military*] (CAAL) .... CAC
Continuous Air Borne Missle Alert (SAUS) .... CAMAL
Continuous Air Circulation (IIA) .... CAC
Continuous Air Monitor [*Nuclear energy*] (NRCH) .... CAM
Continuous Air Monitoring Program [*or Project*] [*Environmental Protection Agency*] .... CAMP
Continuous Air Monitoring System [*Environmental science*] (COE) .... CAMS
Continuous Air Patrol [*Proposed defense for missiles*] [*Military*] .... CAP
Continuous Air Resistance Tester (SAUS) .... CART
Continuous Aircraft Reliability Evaluation (PDAA) .... CARE
Continuous Airworthiness Visit .... CAV
Continuous Alarm Reporting Service [*Telecommunications*] (TEL) .... CARS
Continuous Ambulatory Peritoneal Dialysis [*Medicine*] .... CAPD
Continuous and Random Unwanted Deviations (SAUS) .... CRUD
Continuous Annealing and Processing Line [*Steel manufacture*] .... CAPL
Continuous Annealing Line (PDAA) .... CAL
Continuous Annular Chromatograph .... CAC
Continuous Area Pattern Mapping (GEOI) .... COMAP
Continuous Arteriovenous Hemodialysis [*Medicine*] (DMAA) .... CAVHD
Continuous Arteriovenous Hemofiltration [*Medicine*] .... CAVH
Continuous Arteriovenous Ultrafiltration [*Medicine*] (DMAA) .... CAVU
Continuous Atrial Fibrillation [*or Flutter*] [*Cardiology*] (DAVI) .... CAF
Continuous Audit Program [*Finance*] [*Computer science*] (IEEE) .... CAP
Continuous Automated Placement Survey [*Department of Labor*] .... CAPS
Continuous Automated Single Base Line [*Automated control system*] .... CASBL
Continuous Automatic Line Monitoring System .... CALMS
Continuous Automatic Multi-Base Propellant Line (MCD) .... CAMBL
Continuous Automatic Remote Display (SAUS) .... CARD
Continuous Automatic Train Control (SAUS) .... CATC
Continuous Beam [*Camutek*] [*Software package*] (NCC) .... CONTB
Continuous Beam Research Apparatus (SAUS) .... COBRA
Continuous Belt Xanthator [*Rayon technology*] .... CBX
Continuous Bit Rate (SAUS) .... CBR
Continuous Bladder Irrigation [*Urology*] .... CBI
Continuous Blowdown (AAG) .... CB
Continuous Boat Track [*Navy*] (CAAL) .... CBT
Continuous Boresight Correction (MCD) .... CBC
Continuous Breakdown (WDAA) .... CB
Continuous Bubbler [*Environmental science*] (COE) .... CB
Continuous Built-In Test Equipment (SAUS) .... C-BITE
Continuous Built-In-Test (SAUS) .... CBIT
Continuous Business Forms Manufacturers (DGA) .... CBFM
Continuous Butt-Weld [*Metal industry*] .... CBW
Continuous Card Feed (SAUS) .... CCF
Continuous Card Input (SAUS) CCI
Continuous Care Manikin [*Medical training*] [*Navy*] .... CCM
Continuous Cassette (SAUS) CC
Continuous Casting [*Metalworking*] CC
Continuous Casting Machine [*Metalworking*] .... CCM
Continuous Catalyst Regeneration [*Chemical engineering*] .... CCR
Continuous Clause (SAUS) CC
Continuous Coding Transformation (MCD) .... CCT
Continuous Color Sequence [*Telecommunications*] .... CCS
Continuous Commercial Service [*Equipment specifications*] .... CCS
Continuous Complete Remission [*Oncology*] (DAVI) .... CCR
Continuous Composite Servo [*Optical disc recording format*] (BYTE) .... CCS
Continuous Composite Write (CDE) .... CCW
Continuous Comprehensive Evaluation [*Army*] (RDA) .... C^2E
Continuous Contractor Field Service .... CCFS
Continuous Controller with Dead Zone (SAUS) .... CCDZ
Continuous Cooling Transformation .... CCT
Continuous Correlation Processing .... CCP
Continuous Countercurrent Ion-Exchange [*Chemistry*] CCIX
Continuous Current CC
Continuous Current-Monitoring Device .... CCMD
Continuous Cyclic Peritoneal Dialysis [*Medicine*] .... CCPD
Continuous Data Recording (COE) .... CDR
Continuous Deformation Monitoring System [*US Army Engineer Topographic Laboratories*] (RDA) .... CDMS
Continuous Deionization .... CDI
Continuous Disability History Sample [*Social Security Administration*] (GFGA) .... CDHS
Continuous Distending Airway Pressure [*Medicine*] (DMAA) .... CDAP
Continuous Document Feeding (SAUS) .... CDF
Continuous Dress Creep Feed (PDAA) .... CDCE
Continuous Drizzle (SAUS) .... DD
Continuous Duty (IAA) .... CD

Continuous Duty (MSA) .... CDTY
Continuous Duty Target .... CDT
Continuous Duty Target Source .... CDTS
Continuous Dynamical System .... CDS
Continuous Dynode Electron Multiplier [*Instrumentation*] .... CDEM
Continuous Edge Graphics [*Edson Laboratories*] [*Computer science*] .... CEG
Continuous Edge Graphics-Digital Signal Processor [*Edson Laboratories*] [*Computer science*] (PCM) .... CEG-DSP
Continuous Election Beam [*Accelerator facility*] .... CEB
Continuous Electrical Stimulation .... CES
Continuous Electrocardiogram in Ambulatory Patients [*Medicine*] .... CELIA
Continuous Electrocardiographic Monitoring [*Medicine*] (CPH) .... CEM
Continuous Electron Beam Accelerator Facility [*Physics*] .... CEBAF
Continuous Electro-Slag Melting (PDAA) .... CESM
Continuous Electroslag Powder Melting (SAUS) .... CESPM
Continuous Emission Monitoring [*Environmental Protection Agency*] (GFGA) .... CEM
Continuous Emission Rate Monitoring System [*Environmental science*] .... CERMS
Continuous Emission Reduction System [*Environmental science*] (COE) .... CERS
Continuous Emissions Monitor [*Environmental Protection Agency*] .... CEM
Continuous Emissions Monitoring Subset (SAUS) .... CEMS
Continuous Emissions Monitoring System .... CEMS
Continuous Estimation Program .... CEP
Continuous Estrus [*Endocrinology*] .... CE
Continuous Evaluation [*DoD*] .... CE
Continuous Explosion-Puffing System [*Food technology*] .... CEPS
Continuous Extravascular Infusion [*Medicine*] .... CEI
Continuous Fiber Reinforced Composites (ACAE) .... CFRC
Continuous Fiber Reinforcing Mat [*Fiberglass*] .... CFRM
Continuous Filament Mat .... CFM
Continuous Film Memory (SAUS) .... CFM
Continuous Film Store (SAUS) .... CFS
Continuous Fire Detection (SAUS) .... CFD
Continuous Flow [*Chemical engineering*] [*Nuclear energy*] (NRCH) .... CF
Continuous Flow Analysis .... CFA
Continuous Flow Diffusion (SSD) .... CFD
Continuous Flow Electrophoresis [*Physical chemistry*] .... CFE
Continuous Flow Electrophoresis [*Physical chemistry*] (SSD) .... CFEP
Continuous Flow Electrophoresis in Space [*Physical chemistry*] .... CFES
Continuous Flow Electrophoresis Separation (ACAE) .... CFES
Continuous Flow Electrophoresis System [*Chemical separation*] .... CFES
Continuous Flow Hypersonic Tunnel [*NASA*] .... CFHT
Continuous Flow Intersection [*Automated traffic management*] .... CFI
Continuous Flow Isoelectric Focusing [*Materials processing*] .... CFIF
Continuous Flow Isotope Ratio Mass Spectrometry (SAUS) .... CF-IRMS
Continuous Flow Manufacturing [*Automotive engineering*] .... CFM
Continuous Flow Stirred Tanks with Recycle (EDCT) .... CFSTR
Continuous Flow Ventilation [*Medicine*] (DMAA) .... CFV
Continuous Focusing (SAUS) .... CF
Continuous Forest Inventory (DICI) .... CFI
Continuous Form (SAUS) .... CF
Continuous Fourier Transform (SAUS) .... CFT
Continuous Fourier Transport .... CFT
Continuous Fuel Injection .... CFI
Continuous Function (SAUS) .... CF
Continuous Gas LASER .... CGL
Continuous Gradient Ray Tracing System .... CONGRATS
Continuous Grain Silicon (SAUS) .... CGS
Continuous Grinding Gage (SAUS) .... CGG
Continuous Grinding Gauge .... CGG
Continuous Heating Furnace (SAUS) .... CHF
Continuous Heating Transformation [*Chemical engineering*] .... CHT
Continuous Hepatic Artery Infusion [*Medicine*] (DAVI) .... CHAI
Continuous High Chair (SAUS) .... CHC
Continuous High Chair for Metal-deck (SAUS) .... CHCM
Continuous High Chair Upper (SAUS) .... CHCU
Continuous High Chair with Plate (SAUS) .... CHCP
Continuous High-Amplitude EEG [*Electroencephalogram*] **Rhythmical Synchronous Slowing** [*Medicine*] (DMAA) .... CHERSS
Continuous Hormones as Replacement Therapy [*Medicine*] .... CHART
Continuous Hyperfractionated Accelerated Radiotherapy (ADWA) .... CHART
Continuous Ideally Stirred Tank Reactor [*Chemical engineering*] .... CISTR
Continuous Image Microfilm (IEEE) .... CIM
Continuous Imprint Marking [*of medical linen*] (MCD) .... CIM
Continuous Improvement Process .... CIP
Continuous Improvement Program (AAEL) .... CIP
Continuous Improvement Team .... CIT
Continuous Inflating Pressure .... CIP
Continuous In-Flight Performance Recorder [*Aviation*] (PDAA) .... CIPR
Continuous Infrared (MCD) .... CIR
Continuous Injection [*Automotive engineering*] CI
Continuous Injection System [*Automotive engineering*] .... CIS
Continuous Input (SAUS) CI
Continuous Insulin Delivery System [*Endocrinology and pharmacology*] (DAVI) .... CIDS
Continuous Insulin Infusion [*Medicine*] (MELL) CII
Continuous Interleaved Sampling .... CIS
Continuous Interlock (MCD) CI
Continuous Intramuscular Insulin Infusion .... CIMII
Continuous Intrathecal Baclofen Infusion [*Medicine*] .... CIBI
Continuous Intravenous Infusion of Propranolol [*Medicine*] .... CIP
Continuous Intravenous Insulin Infusion [*Medicine*] (MELL) CIVII
Continuous Inventory of Stand Conditions (SAUS) .... CISC
Continuous Isoelectric Focusing [*Materials processing*] .... CIEF
Continuous Job Card (SAUS) .... CJC
Continuous LASER Argon-Age Microprobe .... CLAAMP
Continuous Level of Production Plan .... CLOPP
Continuous Lightweight Exterior CLX
Continuous Lightweight Exterior (SAUS) .... C-L-X
Continuous Line Bucket [*Deep mining system*] .... CLB
Continuous Line Plotter .... CLP
Continuous Linear Part (SAUS) .... CLP
Continuous Liner [*Fitting for a propeller shaft*] CL
Continuous Load (SAUS) cl
Continuous Log of Ongoing Events (PDAA) .... CLOOGE
Continuous Longitudinal Manpower Survey [*Department of Labor*] .... CLMS
Continuous Loop Tubular Reactor [*Chemical engineering*] .... CLTR
Continuous Lumbar Epidural [*Medicine*] (MELL) .... CLE
Continuous Mandatory Ventilation (MELL) .... CMV
Continuous Maximum Rate (or Rating) (SAUS) .... CMR
Continuous Maximum Rating [*of equipment*] (DEN) .... CMR
Continuous Measurable Improvement (ACAE) .... CMI
Continuous Measurement Office (SAUS) .... CMO
Continuous Measurement Survey [*US Census Bureau*] .... CMS
Continuous Mechanical Ventilation [*Medicine*] (DAVI) .... CMV
Continuous Melting, Casting and Rolling (MHDB) .... CMCR
Continuous Membrane Column [*Chemical engineering*] .... CMC
Continuous Memory Test (STED) .... CMT
Continuous Mining Machine (SAUO) .... CMM
Continuous Mixed Venous Oximetry (MELL) .... CMVO
Continuous Monitor .... CM
Continuous Motion Assembly Machine .... COMAM
Continuous Motor Unit Activity [*Medicine*] (DMAA) .... CMUA
Continuous Multibay Frames [*Jacys Computing Services*] [*Software package*] (NCC) .... CMF
Continuous Multiple Access Collator [*Proposed by Mortimer Taube, 1957*] [*Computer science*] .... COMAC
Continuous Multiple-Access Comparator (SAUS) .... COMAC
Continuous Murmur [*Cardiology*] (DAVI) .... CM
Continuous National Survey [*National Opinion Research Center*] .... CNS
Continuous Negative Pressure [*Medicine*] .... CNP
Continuous Negative Pressure Breathing [*Physiology*] .... CNPB
Continuous Negative Pressure Ventilation [*Medicine*] (DMAA) .... CNPV
Continuous Net Settlement .... CNS
Continuous Noise .... CN
Continuous Noise Condition (DB) .... CTN
Continuous Observation [*Nursing order*] (CPH) .... CO
Continuous Officer Professional Education (DNAB) .... COPE
Continuous Oil Analysis Treatment [*Automotive maintenance*] .... COAT
Continuous Online Trading System [*London Stock Exchange*] (NITA) .... COLT
Continuous Opacity Monitor [*Environmental Protection Agency*] (GFGA) .... COM
Continuous Opacity Monitoring System (EEVL) .... COMS
Continuous Operation during Hours Shown [*Broadcasting*] C
Continuous Operation Production Allocation and Control [*Computer science*] .... COPAC
Continuous Operation Program [*Computer science*] (MDG) .... COP
Continuous Operations [*Army*] .... CONOPS
Continuous Orbital Guidance Sensor (SAUS) .... COGS
Continuous Orbital Guidance System .... COGS
Continuous Oxygen Steel Making (SAUS) .... COS Making
Continuous Page Facsimile Recorder .... CPFR
Continuous Particle Electrophoresis .... CPE
Continuous Particle Electrophoresis Device (OA) .... CPED
Continuous Particle Monitor [*Environmental Protection Agency*] (GFGA) .... CPM
Continuous Passive Motion [*Medicine*] .... CPM
Continuous Path [*Robotics*] .... CP
Continuous Patrol Aircraft .... CPA
Continuous Performance Measure (MCD) .... CPM
Continuous Performance Task (SAUS) .... CPT
Continuous Performance Test [*Psychology*] .... CPT
Continuous Phase (OA) .... CP
Continuous Phase Frequency Shift Keying .... CPFSK
Continuous Phase Modulation (SAUS) .... CPM
Continuous Phase Shift Modulation [*Army*] .... CPSM
Continuous Plankton Recorder [*Oceanography*] (MSC) .... CPR
Continuous Plug Flow Reactor [*Chemical engineering*] .... CPFR
Continuous Positive Airway Pressure [*Resuscitation system*] [*Medicine*] .... CPAP
Continuous Positive Pressure Breathing [*Physiology*] .... CPPB
Continuous Positive Pressure Ventilation [*Medicine*] .... CPPV
Continuous Primary Test [*Psychiatry*] (DAVI) .... CPT
Continuous Process Control [*Design Software Ltd.*] [*Software package*] (NCC) .... CPC
Continuous Process Improvement [*Chemical engineering*] .... CPI
Continuous Process Plant Scheduling (SAUS) .... CPPS
Continuous Processing Machine (PDAA) .... CPM
Continuous Production Operation Sheet .... CPOS
Continuous Progress Center (SAUO) .... CPC
Continuous Progress Indicator [*Telecommunications*] (TEL) .... CPR
Continuous Progress Indicator (SAUS) .... CPR Indicator
Continuous Punching (SAUS) .... CP
Continuous Quality Improvement [*Quality control*] .... CQI
Continuous Radon (EPAT) .... CR
Continuous Radon Monitoring (SAUS) .... CR
Continuous Random Analog to Frequency Transmission .... CRAFT
Continuous Rating (SAUS) .... CR
Continuous Rating Permitting Overload (SAUS) .... CRPO
Continuous Rating Permitting Over-Load .... CRPO
Continuous Read-Out of Work Dimensions (SAUS) .... CROWD
Continuous Ream Discharge [*Papermaking*] .... CRD
Continuous Receiver On [*Electronic device*] .... CRO

Continuous Record of Personnel (ADA) .... CRP
Continuous Reflectometry for Radius Versus Time Experiment [*Nuclear testing verification*] .... CORRTEX
Continuous Reinforcement [*Psychometrics*] .... CRF
Continuous, Remote, Unobstructive Monitoring of Biobehavioral Systems .... CRUMBS
Continuous Ring Tone [*Telecommunications*] (TEL) .... CRT
Continuous Rod (NG) .... CR
Continuous Rod Warhead (MCD) .... CRW
Continuous Sampler Monitor [*Radioactivity*] .... CSM
Continuous Sampling Plan (IEEE) .... CSP
Continuous Sampling Run (DNAB) .... CSR
Continuous Scan [*Computer science*] (IAA) .... CS
Continuous Schedule of Reinforcement (DIPS) .... CRF
Continuous Seam Diffusion Bonding .... CSDB
Continuous Segregated Stirred Tank Reactor [*Chemical engineering*] .... CSSTR
Continuous Seismic Profiling (NUCP) .... CSP
Continuous Seismic Wave [*Radio transmission*] (IAA) ...... CSW
Continuous Self Mode Locking [*Electronics*] (OA) .... CSML
Continuous Service [*British military*] (DMA) .... CS
Continuous Service Certificate [*Navy*] .... CSC
Continuous Service Rating [*Engine technology*] .... CSR
Continuous Servo (SAUS) .... CS
Continuous Sheet Memory [*Computer science*] (BUR) ...... CSM
Continuous Sheet Music (MCD) .... CSM
Continuous Slope Delta Modulation [*Telecommunications*] ... CSDM
Continuous Slow Ultrafiltration [*Medicine*] (DMAA) .... CSUF
Continuous Slowing Down (SAUS) .... CSD
Continuous Slowing Down Models [*Physics*] .... CSM
Continuous Snow (SAUS) .... SS
Continuous Space-Discrete Time (PDAA) .... CSDT
Continuous Speech Recognizer [*ITT Corp.*] (NITA) .... CSR
Continuous Stationery [*Commercial firm*] [*British*] (DGA) ... CONT/S
Continuous Stationery [*Commercial firm*] [*British*] ...... CS
Continuous Stirred Tank Biological Reactor [*Chemical engineering*] ... CSTBR
Continuous Stirred Tank Fermentator (OA) .... CSTF
Continuous Stirred Tank Membrane Reactor [*Chemical engineering*] ... CSTMR
Continuous Stirred Tank Reactor [*Chemical engineering*] ... CSTR
Continuous Stirred Tank Reactor with an Ultrafiltration Membrane [*Chemical en gineering*] .... CSTR/UF
Continuous Stratification Profiler .... CSP
Continuous Strip Film (DNAB) .... CS
Continuous Stripping [*Surgery*] (DAVI) .... CS
Continuous Subcarrier Barrage (MCD) .... CSB
Continuous Subcutaneous Infusion [*Medicine*] (MELL) ... CSI
Continuous Subcutaneous Insulin Infusion [*Medicine*] .... CSII
Continuous Subcutaneous Insulin Infusion Pump [*Medicine*] (DMAA) ... CSIIP
Continuous Submarine Duty Incentive Pay (DNAB) .... CONSUB
Continuous Surveillance Service (MCD) .... CSS
Continuous Survey (DS) .... CS
Continuous Survey of Machinery .... CSM
Continuous Symmetry Measure [*Physical chemistry*] ...... CSM
Continuous System Modeling Program [*Computer science*] ... CSMP
Continuous System Simulator (SAUS) .... CSS
Continuous Systems Simulation Language [*Computer science*] ... CSSL
Continuous Thymus-Cell [*Cell line*] .... CTC
Continuous Tone [*Color printing*] .... CT
Continuous Tone-Coded Squelch System [*Telecommunications*] (PDAA) ... CTCSS
Continuous Tubular Reactor [*Chemical engineering*] ...... CTR
Continuous until Cancelled [*Insurance*] .... CUC
Continuous Update Memory Display .... CUMD
Continuous Variable Damper [*Automotive suspensions*] .... CVD
Continuous Variable Slope Delta (SAUS) .... CVSB
Continuous Variable Slope Delta (COE) .... CVSD
Continuous Velocity Joint [*Automotive engineering*] ...... CVJ
Continuous Velocity Log (SAUS) CVL
Continuous Venous Infusion [*Chemotherapy*] (DAVI) CVI
Continuous Veno-Veno Hemodialysis (NUJO) .... CVVHD
Continuous Veno-Venous Hemofiltration (NUJO) .... CVVH
Continuous Vent System (KSC) .... CVS
Continuous Vertical Retort [*Metallurgy*] [*Fuel technology*] ... CVR
Continuous Video Recorder (IAA) .... CVR
Continuous Vulcanization CV
Continuous Wage and Benefit History [*Unemployment insurance*] ... CWBH
Continuous Water Movement (SAA) .... CWM
Continuous Wave [*A form of radio transmission*] .... CW
Continuous Wave (STED) .... cw
Continuous Wave Acquisition and Track (MCD) .... CWAT
Continuous Wave Acquisition RADAR [*Military*] .... CWAR
Continuous Wave Broad (SAUS) .... CW BRD
Continuous Wave Detector (IAA) .... CWD
Continuous Wave Deuterium Demonstrator (SAUS) .... CWDD
Continuous Wave Deuterium Fluoride .... CWDF
Continuous Wave Fixed Frequency Electromechanical Modulation (IAA) ... CWFFEMM
Continuous Wave Frequency-Modulated (MSA) .... CWFM
Continuous Wave Gas .... CWG
Continuous Wave Illuminating Radar (SAUS) .... CWILL
Continuous Wave Illuminator (NG) .... CWI
Continuous Wave Illuminator RADAR [*Military*] .... CWIR
Continuous Wave Indicator (DWSG) .... CWI
Continuous Wave Intermediate Frequency .... CWIF
Continuous Wave Jammer (MCD) .... CWJ
Continuous Wave LASER .... CWL
Continuous Wave Narrow (SAUS) .... CW NRW

Continuous Wave Nuclear Magnetic Resonance .... CWNMR
Continuous Wave Oscillator .... CWO
Continuous Wave Radar (SAUS) .... CWR
Continuous Wave Separated Orbit Cyclotron (SAUS) ..... CWSOC
Continuous Wave Signal Generator (SAUS) .... CW SIG GEN
Continuous Wave Signal Generator (IAA) .... CWSIGGEN
Continuous Wave Space Duplexed .... CWSD
Continuous Wave Surface-to-Air Missile (MCD) .... CWSAM
Continuous Wave Tactical Detection Console (NATG) .... CWTDC
Continuous Wave Target Detection (NATG) .... CWTD
Continuous Wave Target Detection Console (SAUS) ...... CWTDC
Continuous Wave Target Detector (SAUS) .... CWTD
Continuous Wave Transmitter (CAAL) .... CWX
Continuous Wave Traveling Wave Tube (MCD) .... CWTWT
Continuous Wave Tunable (IAA) .... CWT
Continuous Wave Video .... CWV
Continuous Wave-Frequency Modulated (SAUS) .... CW/FM
Continuous Weather Watch (MCD) .... CWW
Continuous Window .... CONTW
Continuous Window (SAUS) .... Cont W
Continuous Work History Sample [*Department of Labor*] ... CWHS
Continuous Working Level Monitor (GNE) .... CWLM
Continuous Working-level monitoring (SAUS) .... CW
Continuous-Access Guided Communication [*Computer science*] (PDAA) ... CAGC
Continuous-Action [*Pharmacy*] .... CA
Continuous-Beam Analysis [*Jacys Computing Services*] [*Software package*] (NCC) ... CBA
Continuous-Descent Approach (PDAA) .... CDA
Continuous-Filament Ceramic Composite [*Materials science*] ... CFCC
Continuous-Flow Centrifuging [*Clinical chemistry*] .... CFC
Continuous-Flow Fast Atom Bombardment [*Spectroscopy*] ... CF-FAB
Continuous-Flow Stirred Tank Reactor [*Chemical engineering*] ... CFSTR
Continuous-Flow Tank Reactor [*Chemical engineering*] ... CTR
Continuous-Flow Tub .... CT
Continuous-Flow Zonal Centrifugation (DB) .... CFZC
Continuously Advertised Nutritionally Deficient Yummies [*In cookbook title, "The Taming of the CANDY Monster"*] ... CANDY
Continuously Annealed Processing Length (SAUS) .... CAPL
Continuously Charge-Coupled Random Access Memory [*Computer science*] (PDAA) ... C3RAM
Continuously Charge-Coupled Random Access Memory (SAUS) .... C3RA Memory
Continuously Charge-Coupled Random Access Memory [*Computer science*] (IAA) ... CCCRAM
Continuously Computed Impact Line (SAUS) CCIL
Continuously Computed Impact Point [*Type of bombing sighting system*] [*Air Force*] ... CCIP
Continuously Computed Release Point (MCD) .... CCRP
Continuously Contemporary Accounting (ADA) .... CCA
Continuously Contemporary Accounting (ADA) .... COCOA
Continuously Displayed Impact Point (MCD) .... CDIP
Continuously Expecting Transfer Interface [*IBM Corp.*] .. CETI
Continuously Fed Batch Reactor [*Chemical engineering*] ... CFBR
Continuously Habitable Zone (DICI) .... CHZ
Continuously Managed Data Base (SAUS) .... CMD
Continuously Offered Long-Term Securities [*Merrill Lynch & Co.*] [*Finance*] ... COLTS
Continuously Operated Reference Station (GEOI) .... CORS
Continuously Operating per Fluorocarbon Sniffer (CARB) ... COPS
Continuously Reinforced Concrete Pavement (OA) .... CRCP
Continuously Reinforced Concrete Paving (SAUS) .... CRCP
Continuously Stirred Tank .... CST
Continuously Stirred Tank Reactor [*Chemical engineering*] ... CSTR
Continuously Transposed Conductor (SAUS) .... CTC
Continuously Twisted, Structurally Chiral Medium (SAUS) ... CTSCM
Continuously Updated Dynamic Optimizing Systems (IEEE) ... CUDOS
Continuously Variable CV
Continuously Variable Accessory Drive .... CVAD
Continuously Variable Amplitude Carrier (ACAE) .... CVAC
Continuously Variable Filter [*Spectrometry*] .... CVF
Continuously Variable, for Emergency .... CVE
Continuously Variable Gearbox (PDAA) .... CVG
Continuously Variable Hydromechanical Transmission [*Engineering*] ... CVHT
Continuously Variable Mechanical Advantage Shifter ...... CVMAS
Continuously Variable Slope Delta Modulation [*Telecommunications*] ... CVSD
Continuously Variable Slope Delta Modulation [*Telecommunications*] (TEL) ... CVSDM
Continuously Variable Stroke [*Automotive engineering*] ... CVS
Continuously Variable Transaxle [*Automotive engineering*] ... CTX
Continuously Variable Transmission [*Of engines*] .... CVT
Continuously Varying Cell Constant [*Electrochemical instrumentation*] ... CVCC
Continuously Welded Rail (ADA) .... CWR
Continuously-Advancing Longwall Mining (PDAA) .... CALM
Continuously-Computed Optimum Release (PDAA) .... CCOR
Continuous-Moment Sum Rules (PDAA) .... CMSR
Continuous-Random-Network [*Noncrystalline structure*] ... CRN
Continuous-Reading Meter Relay .... CRMR
Continuous-Release [*Pharmacy*] .... CR
Continuous-Transmission Frequency-Modulated [*SONAR*] ... CTFM
Continuous-Wave Doppler [*Radiology*] (DAVI) .... CWD
Continuous-Wound (DEN) .... CW
Continuum [*A publication*] .... Cont
Continuum (SAUS) .... Cont
Continuum Co. [*NYSE symbol*] (SPSG) .... CNU
Continuum Co. [*Associated Press*] (SAG) .... Contin
Continuum Interpolated Band Ratio (SAUS) .... CIBR

Continuum Mechanics and Thermodynamics (SAUS) .... Contin Mech Thermodyn
ContiTire System [*German*] .... CTS
Contl Airlines'B' [*NYSE symbol*] (SG) .... CAL
Contl Can [*NYSE symbol*] (TTSB) .... CAN
Contl Choice Care [*NASDAQ symbol*] (TTSB) CCCI
Contl Circuits [*NASDAQ symbol*] (TTSB) .... CCIR
Contl Homes Hldg [*NYSE symbol*] (TTSB) .... CON
Contl Information Sys [*NASDAQ symbol*] (SG) .... CISC
Contl Materials [*AMEX symbol*] (TTSB) .... CUO
Contl Mtg & Eg Tr SBI [*NASDAQ symbol*] (TTSB) .... CMETS
Contol Unit Group [*Computer science*] .... CUG
Contolled Substance, Class Two [*Department of Health and Human Services*] (DAVI) CII
Contour (MSA) .... CTR
Contour (SAUS) .... ctr
Contour Analysis by Random Triangulation Algorithm (IAA) .... CARTA
Contour Blind & Shade (Canada) Ltd. [*Toronto Stock Exchange symbol*] .... CBM
Contour Center Adaptive Tracker (ACAE) .... CAT
Contour Check Template (MCD) .... CCT
Contour Check Template Set (MCD) .... CCTS
Contour Control System (IAA) .... CCS
Contour Interpolation Program (GEOI) .... CIP
Contour Interval (SAUS) CI
Contour Mapping On-Boresight (MCD) .... CMO
Contour Mapping RADAR System (MCD) .... COMAR
Contour Medical [*NASDAQ symbol*] (TTSB) .... CTMI
Contour Medical, Inc. [*Associated Press*] (SAG) .... ContMed
Contour Medical, Inc. [*NASDAQ symbol*] (SAG) .... CTMI
Contour Plotting System .... CPS
Contour RADAR Data (PDAA) .... CONRAD
Contour Rolls (AAG) .... CRRL
Contour Start Threshold (SAUS) .... CST
Contour Template (SAUS) .... CRTP
Contour Template .... CT
Contour to Grid (GEOI) .... CTOG
Contour-Adducted Trochanteric Controlled Alignment Method [*Medicine*] (MELL) .... CATCAM
Contour-Clamped Homogeneous Electric Field [*Instrumentation*] .... CHEF
Contoured Femoral Stem [*Total hip prosthesis*] [*Orthopedics*] (DAVI) .... CFS
Contra [*Against*] [*Latin*] C
contra (SAUS) c
Contra [*Against*] [*Latin*] .... CON
Contra [*Against*] [*Latin*] .... CONT
Contra [*Against*] [*Latin*] (ROG) .... CONTR
Contra Apionem [*Against Apion*] [*Josephus*] (BJA) .... Ap
Contra Apionem [*Against Apion*] [*Josephus*] (BJA) .... CAp
Contra Bonos Mores [*Contrary to Good Manners*] [*Latin*] .... CONT BON MOR
Contra Bonos Mores [*Contrary to Good Manners*] [*Latin*] (ROG) .... CONTR BON MOR
Contra Costa College, San Pablo, CA [*Library symbol*] [*Library of Congress*] (LCLS) .... CSpaW
Contra Costa County Library, Pleasant Hill, CA [*Library symbol*] [*Library of Congress*] (LCLS) .... CPlhC
Contra Costa Historical Society, Martinez, CA [*Library symbol*] [*Library of Congress*] (LCLS) .... CMartCH
Contra Credit [*Banking*] CC
Contra Credit [*Bookkeeping*] (ODBW) .... con cr
Contra Credit [*Banking*] (MHDW) .... Con Cr
Contra Invoice (WDAA) .... Con Inv
Contraband .... CONTBD
Contraband Control [*Navy*] .... CBC
Contraband Control Base [*Navy*] .... CCB
Contrabass [*Music*] .... CB
Contrabass [*Music*] .... CBs
Contrabass Clarinet .... cbcl
Contrabassoon .... cbn
Contraceptive (SAUS) .... Contra
Contraceptive Commodity Management Information System [*United Nations*] (ECON) .... CCMIS
Contraceptive Development and Research in Immunology Program (SAUO) .... CD&RI
Contraceptive Prevalence Rate (SAUO) .... CPR
Contraceptive Research and Development Program [*Research center*] (RCD) .... CONRAD
Contraceptive Social Marketing (SAUO) .... CSM
Contraceptive Technique [*Gynecology*] .... CT
Contraceptive Vaginal Ring [*Gynecology*] .... CVR
Contraceptives (SAUS) .... Contras
Contract .... CNT
Contract .... CNTRCT
Contract (ROG) .... CON
Contract .... CONT
Contract (ODBW) .... cont
Contract (GEAB) .... contr
Contract [*or Contractor*] (AFM) .... CONTR
Contract [*Legal term*] .... CONTT
Contract [*Legal shorthand*] (LWAP) .... K
Contract [*Navy*] .... KT
Contract Acceptance and Purchase Order .... CAPO
Contract Accounting Standard .... CAS
Contract Acquisition Cost Report (MCD) .... CACR
Contract Action Directive (MCD) .... CAD
Contract Addenda Committee .... CAC
Contract Adjustment Board (AAGC) .... CAB
Contract Administration [*or Administrator*] [*DoD*] .... CA
Contract Administration Advisory Board [*DoD*] .... CAAB
Contract Administration Automated Records Retrieval System (MCD) .... CAARRS
Contract Administration Control (DNAB) .... CAC
Contract Administration Data [*DoD*] .... CAD
Contract Administration Data File [*DoD*] (AFM) .... CADF
Contract Administration Function (DNAB) .... CAF
Contract Administration Office [*or Officer*] [*Navy*] .... CAO
Contract Administration Officer (SAUO) .... CAO
Contract Administration Panel [*Military*] .... CAP
Contract Administration Plan .... CAP
Contract Administration Report [*DoD*] .... CAR
Contract Administration Service Component (ACAE) .... CASC
Contract Administration Services [*DoD*] .... CAS
Contract Administration Southeast Area (Office of Naval Research) .... CASEAREA(ONR)
Contract Administration Subservice .... CASS
Contract Administrative Data File (SAUS) .... CADF
Contract Air (TAG) .... CA
Contract Air Cargo, Inc. [*FAA designator*] (FAAC) .... TSU
Contract Air Mail .... CAM
Contract Amendment (ACAE) .... CA
Contract Amendment Proposal .... CAP
Contract Analysis (ACAE) .... CA
Contract and Material .... C & M
Contract and Purchase (SAUS) .... CP
Contract and Purchase Department (SAUO) .... CP
Contract and Purchase Department (SAUO) .... CPD
Contract and Purchase Department [*British military*] (DMA) .... CPD
Contract Appeals [*Department of the Interior pre-1954*] (AAGC) .... CA
Contract Appeals Board [*Veterans Administration*] .... CAB
Contract Appeals Decision Reporter [*CCH*] [*A publication*] (AAGC) .... CADR
Contract Appeals Decisions [*CCH*] [*A publication*] (AAGC) .... Contr App Dec
Contract Appeals Decisions (Commerce Clearing House) [*A publication*] (DLA) .... Cont App Dec (CCH)
Contract Appraisal Report .... CAR
Contract Assistance Team (ACAE) .... CAT
Contract Audit Closing Statements (AAGC) .... CACS
Contract Audit Manual .... CAM
Contract Audit Services (SAUS) .... CAS
Contract Auditor Coordinator .... CAC
Contract Authorization .... CA
Contract Authorization Request (AAG) .... CAR
Contract Award .... CA
Contract Award Date (AAG) .... CAD
Contract Award Rates Delivery Study [*Army*] .... CARDS
Contract Baseline Report (MCD) .... CBR
Contract Brief .... CB
Contract Budget Baseline (MCD) .... CBB
Contract Budget Baselines (ACAE) .... CRB
Contract Budget Estimate (MCD) .... CBE
Contract Bulk Inclusive Tour [*Airline fare*] .... CBIT
Contract Carrier Conference [*Later, ICC*] (EA) CCC
Contract Cases, Federal (AFIT) .... CCF
Contract Cases, Federal [*A publication*] (DLA) .... Cont Cas Fed
Contract Change Authorization (KSC) .... CCA
Contract Change Board .... CCB
Contract Change Board Directive (SAA) .... CCBD
Contract Change Directive (DNAB) .... CCD
Contract Change Estimate .... CCE
Contract Change Identification (MCD) CCI
Contract Change Mass Estimate (NASA) .... CCME
Contract Change Negotiation (NASA) .... CCN
Contract Change Notice (MCD) .... CCN
Contract Change Notification (SAUS) .... CCN
Contract Change Order .... CCO
Contract Change Proposal (NAKS) .... CCP
Contract Change Release .... CCR
Contract Change Request .... CCR
Contract Change System (DNAB) .... CCS
Contract Cleaning and Maintenance Association [*British*] .... CCMA
Contract Clearance Approval Authority (AAGC) .... CCAA
Contract Closeout Extension (AFIT) .... CCE
Contract Completion Date [*Telecommunications*] (TEL) .... CCD
Contract Completion Notices [*DoD*] .... CCN
Contract Completion Studies (MCD) .... CCS
Contract Compliance Review (ACAE) .... CCR
Contract Configuration Process [*Telecommunications*] (TEL) .... CCP
Contract Cost Analysis Organization [*Navy*] (AFIT) .... CCAO
Contract Cost Data (ACAE) .... CCD
Contract Cost Data Reports (AAGC) .... CCDR
Contract Data (ACAE) .... CD
Contract Data Center (SAUO) .... CDC
Contract Data Change Notice (MCD) .... CDCN
Contract Data Coordinator (NG) .... CDC
Contract Data List .... CDL
Contract Data Management Officer (MCD) .... CDMO
Contract Data Management Officer (SAUO) .... DMO
Contract Data Package (AAGC) .... CDP
Contract Data Requirement (MCD) .... CDR
Contract [*or Contractor*] **Data Requirements List** .... CDRL
Contract Data Requirements Management System [*Computer science*] .... CDRMS
Contract Deficiency Listing (AFM) .... CDL
Contract Definition [*Military*] .... CD
Contract Definition .... CONDEF

Contract Definition Concept (DNAB)	CDC
Contract Definition Phase [*DoD*]	CDP
Contract Definition Test	CDT
Contract Delivery Order Tracking System (SAUS)	CDOTS
Contract Demonstration [*Army*] (AFIT)	CD
Contract Depot Maintenance Production and Cost System (SAUO)	CDMPCS
Contract Design	CD
Contract Design Exposition [*Atlanta Market Center*] (TSPED)	CONEXION
Contract Design Package (MCD)	CDP
Contract Direction (SPST)	CD
Contract Dispute Resolution Board [*States*] (AAGC)	CDRB
Contract Disputes Act of 1978 (AAGC)	CDA
Contract Document Change Notice (MCD)	CDCN
Contract Document Control List (SAUS)	CDCL
Contract Documentation Requirements Records [*NASA*] (NASA)	CDRR
Contract ELM Logistics Readiness Support (SAUO)	CELM
Contract Employment Program for Aboriginal People in Natural and Cultural Resource Management (SAUO)	CEPANCRM
Contract End Item (MCD)	CEI
Contract End Item Number	CEIN
Contract End Item Specification (ACAE)	CEIS
Contract End Item Specification (SAUO)	CEI SPEC
Contract Energy Managers [*British*]	CEM
Contract Engineering and Technical Services Personnel [*Air Force*] (AFIT)	CETSP
Contract Engineering Support Unit (SAUO)	CSU
Contract Engineers (MCD)	CE
Contract Estimating and Pricing (MCD)	CEP
Contract Execution Plan (SAUO)	CEP
Contract Exploration (MCD)	CE
Contract [*or Contractor*] Field Service (AFM)	CFS
Contract Field Service Representative (ACAE)	CFSR
Contract Field Support	CFS
Contract Field Technician	CFT
Contract Finance Committee [*Military*]	CFC
Contract Financial Reporting Manual	CFRM
Contract Financial Requirements Estimate [*NASA*] (KSC)	CFRE
Contract Financial Status (AFM)	CFS
Contract Financing Office (AAGC)	CFO
Contract Flooring Association [*British*] (DBA)	CFA
Contract for a Single Year (SAUS)	SYC
Contract Formulation	CF
Contract Formulation	CONFORM
Contract Fund Status Report [*Army*] (AABC)	CFSR
Contract Furnished (MCD)	CF
Contract Furnishings Council (EA)	CFC
Contract Furnishings Forum (EA)	CFF
Contract Heat Treatment Association [*British*] (DBA)	CHTA
Contract History File [*Military*] (AFIT)	CHF
Contract Identifier (ACAE)	CI
Contract Implementation Plan (MCD)	CIP
Contract Information Management System (SAUO)	CIMS
Contract Information Processor	CIP
Contract Information Reporting Groups [*Navy*] (AFIT)	CIRG
Contract Information Subsystem (MCD)	CISS
Contract Information System [*Environmental Protection Agency*] (GFGA)	CIS
Contract Item (SAUS)	CI
Contract Item Material List	CIML
Contract Item Number (MCD)	CIN
Contract Items Specification (MCD)	CIS
Contract Items Specification and Schedule (MCD)	CISS
Contract Laboratory Program [*Environmental Protection Agency*]	CLP
Contract Laboratory Program Analytical Results Database [*Environmental Protection Agency*] (AEPA)	CLP
Contract Laboratory Program Quality Assurance (SAUO)	CLPQA
Contract Laboratory System (SAUO)	CLPS
Contract Labour Branch [*Admiralty*] [*British*]	CLB
Contract Law	CL
Contract Letter [*DLA*] (AAGC)	CONTRLTR
Contract Liaison and Master Planning Office [*Military*]	CLIMPO
Contract Line Item Number [*Army*] (AABC)	CLIN
Contract Line Item Status (MCD)	CLIS
Contract Lineage Equivalent [*Formula used by certain publications for calculating number of lines of advertising copy*]	CLE
Contract Logistic Support Plan (MCD)	CLSP
Contract Machine Accessory (MCD)	CMA
Contract Maintenance Activity (AFM)	CMA
Contract Maintenance and Supply Support Operations (ACAE)	CMSSO
Contract Maintenance Data	CMD
Contract Maintenance Plan	CMP
Contract Maintenance Review Board (ACAE)	CMRB
Contract Maintenance Team (MCD)	CMT
Contract Management	CM
Contract Management [*NCMA*] [*A publication*] (AAGC)	Cont Mgmt
Contract Management Assistance Officer [*NASA*] (NASA)	CMAO
Contract Management District	CMD
Contract Management Group (SAUO)	CMG
Contract Management Information System (MCD)	CMIS
Contract Management Institute	CMI
Contract Management Network (MCD)	CMN
Contract Management Office [*Jet Propulsion Laboratory, NASA*]	CMO
Contract Management Plan [*Military*]	CMP
Contract Management Region	CMR
Contract Management Review [*DoD*]	CMR
Contract Manager (COE)	CM
Contract Managers' Association [*A union*] [*British*]	CMA
Contract Manufacturers Association (EA)	CMA
Contract Modification	CM
Contract Monitor of Progress [*Air Force*] (AFIT)	CMP
Contract Monitoring Point (AFM)	CMP
Contract Motor Vehicle Service	CMVS
Contract Note [*Banking*]	CN
Contract Note (SAUS)	C/N
Contract Number [*Computer science*]	CN
Contract Number Prefix [*Database terminology*] (NITA)	CP
Contract Nursing Home (DAVI)	CNH
Contract of Affreightment [*Shipping*]	COA
Contract of Affreightment Charter Party (RIMS)	COACP
Contract on Order (AFIT)	COO
Contract Operations Data [*DoD*]	COD
Contract Packager and/or Manufacturer [*Pharmaceutical distribution*]	CPM
Contract Packagers Association (NTPA)	CPA
Contract Parts Material Order	CPMO
Contract Payment System (SAUS)	CPS
Contract Pilot School	CPS
Contract [*or Contractor*] Plant Services (NG)	CPS
Contract Potential Difference (MCD)	CPD
Contract Price	C/P
Contract Price of Items Terminated [*Business term*]	CPIT
Contract Pricing Proposal (MCD)	CPP
Contract Pricing Report	CPR
Contract Procurement Request (MUGU)	CPR
Contract Program Manager (MCD)	CPM
Contract Progress Control (MCD)	CPC
Contract Property Administrator (SAUO)	CPA
Contract Provider Organization [*Information service or system*] (HCT)	CPO
Contract Purchasing System Review (DOMA)	CPSR
Contract Regarding an Interim Supplement to Tanker Liability for Oil Pollution [*Oil industry*]	CRISTAL
Contract Regulation Tribunal [*New South Wales*] [*Australia*]	CRT
Contract Repair Initial Support List (AFIT)	CRISL
Contract Repair Service (MCD)	CRS
Contract Repair Supply Procedure (SAUS)	CRSP
Contract Report (SAUS)	CR
Contract [*or Contractor*] Report	CR
Contract Required Detection Limits	CRDL
Contract Requirement	C/R
Contract Requirement Card	CRC
Contract Requirements Master Record [*Military*]	CRMR
Contract Requirements Package (ACAE)	CRP
Contract Requirements Review Board (SAUO)	CRRB
Contract Research and Development	CRAD
Contract Research and Development (SSD)	CR & D
Contract Review and Selection Criteria [*DoD*]	CRSC
Contract Review Board (SAUO)	CRB
Contract Revision Number (NASA)	CRN
Contract Serial Number (AFM)	CSN
Contract Service Rework Orders (NG)	CSRO
Contract Services Association (AAGC)	CSA
Contract Services Association of America (EA)	CSA
Contract Services Program [*General Services Administration*] (GFGA)	CSP
Contract Settlement Appeal Board [*United States*] (DLA)	CSAB
Contract Settlement Board [*Canada*] (AAGC)	CSB
Contract Specialist (GFGA)	CS
Contract Start Date (SSD)	CSD
Contract Stationers Forum (EA)	CSF
Contract Status File [*Military*] (AFIT)	CSF
Contract Status Report	CSR
Contract Strategy Paper	CSP
Contract Student Numbers (AIE)	CSN
Contract Subline Item Number (MCD)	CSLIN
Contract Summary Status Report (SAUS)	CSSR
Contract Supplemental Tooling (NASA)	CST
Contract Supply Facility	CSF
Contract Support Detachment	CSD
Contract Support Set (ACAE)	CSS
Contract Surgeon [*Military*]	CS
Contract Surgeon [*Military*] (AABC)	CSN
Contract Target Cost (MCD)	CTC
Contract Target Cost (SAUS)	CTV
Contract Task Change Proposal (AAG)	CTCP
Contract Task Charge (DNAB)	CTC
Contract Technical Compliance (MUGU)	CTC
Contract Technical Compliance Board (SAUS)	CTCB
Contract Technical Compliance Inspection	CTCI
Contract Technical Data File (AAGC)	CTDF
Contract Technical Instructor [*Army*] (AABC)	CTI
Contract Technical Manager	CTM
Contract Technical Personnel (ACAE)	CTP
Contract Technical Representative (NASA)	CTR
Contract [*or Contractor*] Technical Services [*Air Force*]	CTS
Contract Technical Services Personnel (AFM)	CTSP
Contract Termination and Completion (MCD)	CTC
Contract Termination Inventory [*DoD*]	CTI
Contract Termination Manual (AAG)	CTM
Contract Termination Settlement	CTS
Contract Trainer End Item (SAA)	CTEI
Contract Training Flight Services programme (SAUS)	CTFS
Contract War Service	CWS
Contract Work Breakdown Structure	CWBS

Contract Work Hours and Safety Standards Act .... CWHSSA
Contract Work Notification (KSC) .... CWN
Contract Work Statement (MCD) .... CWS
Contract Work Study Association (MHDB) .... CWSA
Contracted (SAUS) .... Contr
Contracted Advisory and Assistance Services [*DoD*] .... CAAS
Contracted Flight Training & Support (SAUS) .... CFTS
Contracted Gaussian-Type Orbital [*Atomic physics*] .... CGTO
Contracted Ground [*Personnel*] (OSRA) .... CG
Contracted Out Money-Purchase Schemes [*Pension plan*] [*British*] .... COMPS
Contracted Research Development (SAUS) .... CRAD
Contract-Furnished Aerospace Equipment (SAUS) .... CFAE
Contract/Grant Number [*Database terminology*] (NITA) .... CN
Contract/Grant Numbers [*Database terminology*] (NITA) .... CG
Contractile Element [*of skeletal muscle*] .... CE
Contractile Force [*Medicine*] .... CF
Contractile Pulse (PDAA) .... CP
Contracting .... CNTRCTNG
Contracting (WDMC) .... cont
Contracting (SAUS) .... Contg
Contracting Activity .... CA
Contracting and Acquisition Newsletter [*A publication*] .... CAAN
Contracting & Trading Co. (SAUO) .... CAT
Contracting Data Management System [*Military*] (MCD) .... CDMS
Contracting Information Data Base System (SAUO) .... CIDS
Contracting Information Data System [*Military*] (MUSM) .... CIDS
Contracting Lead Time (AAGC) .... CALT
Contracting Netherlands Military Agency, Den Haag (SAUO) .... CNMA
Contracting Officer (NAKS) .... Co
Contracting Officer [*Also, CONTRO, KO*] .... CO
Contracting Officer [*Also, CO, KO*] (KSC) .... CONTRO
Contracting Officer [*Also, CO, CONTRO*] .... KO
Contracting Officer .... KOR
Contracting Officer's Representative (TEL) .... COR
Contracting Officer's Technical Representative (DOMA) .... COTAR
Contracting Officers' Technical Representative [*Army*] .... COTR
Contracting Officer's Warrant Program (AAGC) .... COWP
Contracting Officer's Warrant System (AAGC) .... COWS
Contracting Operator Fast Fourier Transform Identification (PDAA) .... COFFTI
Contracting Party (SAUO) .... CP
Contracting Plasterers' and Lathers' International Association [*Later, IAWCC*] (EA) .... CPLIA
Contracting Squadron [*Air Force*] .... CONS
Contraction C
Contraction (WGA) .... CONTR
Contraction (SAUS) .... Contr
Contraction (MEDA) .... CONTRX
Contraction [*Obstetrics and orthopedics*] (DAVI) .... CTXN
Contraction [*Medicine*] .... Z
Contraction Augmenting Factor [*Medicine*] .... CAF
Contraction Mapping Analysis (SAUS) .... CMA
Contraction Mapping Theorem (SAUS) .... CMT
Contraction Peak Force [*Medicine*] (DMAA) .... CPF
Contraction Stress Test [*Obstetrics*] .... CST
Contraction Time (MAE) .... CT
Contractions (ADWA) .... Ctx
Contractions Handbook .... CTH
Contractor (SAUS) .... Cntor
Contractor .... CONTR
Contractor (ROG) .... CONTROR
Contractor .... COR
Contractor [*Navy*] .... KR
Contractor .... KTR
Contractor Acceptance Test (AABC) .... CAT
Contractor Alert List (AAGC) .... CAL
Contractor All Risk (AIA) .... CAR
Contractor All-Risk Incentive Contract [*Air Force*] .... CARIC
Contractor and Government Entity Code .... CAGE
Contractor Assessment Program (SAUS) .... CAP
Contractor Attention List .... CAL
Contractor Bonding Tape [*3M Co.*] .... CBT
Contractor Change Evaluation (AAG) .... CCE
Contractor Change Proposal (MCD) .... CCP
Contractor Change Request (NASA) .... CCR
Contractor Claims Settlement Program [*Military*] (DNAB) .... CCSP
Contractor Company Code [*Database terminology*] (NITA) CC
Contractor Cost Data Reporting (MCD) .... CCDR
Contractor Cost Reduction .... CCR
Contractor Critical Design Review (MCD) .... CCDR
Contractor Data Management Program [*Air Force*] (AFIT) .... CDMP
Contractor Data Requirements List (SAUS) .... CRDL
Contractor Deficiency Report (AAGC) .... CDR
Contractor Definition (SAUO) .... CD
Contractor Demonstration Test (ACAE) .... CDT
Contractor Depot Logistics Support (CTAS) .... CDLS
Contractor Design Freeze Baseline (MCD) .... CDFB
Contractor Design Review (DOMA) .... CDR
Contractor Developed Material .... CDM
Contractor Developed Specifications (MCD) .... CDS
Contractor Development Test and Evaluation .... CDT & E
Contractor Drawing Change Request (SAUS) .... CDCR
Contractor Employee Compensation System Review [*DoD*] .... CECSR
Contractor Employee Protection Program [*DOE*] (AAGC) .... CEPP
Contractor End Item (MCD) .... CEI
Contractor Engineer - Furnish and Install (AABC) .... CEFI
Contractor Engineering and Technical Services (AFM) .... CETS
Contractor Engineering and Technical Support .... CETS
Contractor Engineering Support (ACAE) .... CES
Contractor Establishment Code (AAGC) .... CEC
Contractor Estimating Methods Review [*DoD*] .... CEMR
Contractor Evidence Audit Team [*Environmental Protection Agency*] (ERG) .... CEAT
Contractor Experience List [*DoD*] .... CEL
Contractor Facilities and Capital Cost of Money .... CFCCOM
Contractor Field Maintenance Service [*Army*] .... CFMS
Contractor Field Services Personnel .... CFSP
Contractor Field Services Support .... CFSS
Contractor Field Team (MCD) .... CFT
Contractor Fin Opener Crank (NG) .... CFOC
Contractor Final Inspection (MCD) .... CFI
Contractor Financial Data Retrieval and Analysis System (SAUS) .... FINANDAS
Contractor Financial Management (DOMA) .... CFM
Contractor Fiscal Year (AAGC) .... CFY
Contractor Functional Demonstration (KSC) .... CFD
Contractor Furnish and Install (MSA) .... CF & I
Contractor Furnished Equipment (SAUO) .... CFE
Contractor Furnished Equipment Notice [*Military*] (DOMA) .... CFEN
Contractor Furnished Requirements .... CFR
Contractor Furnished Software (ACAE) .... CFS
Contractor Identification Data System (AAGC) .... CIDS
Contractor Improvement Program (AAGC) .... CIP
Contractor Independent Technical Effort [*DoD*] .... CITE
Contractor Independent Technical Effort (IEEE) .... CITEC
Contractor Independent Technical Evaluation (ACAE) .... CITE
Contractor Input to Total Performance [*DoD*] .... CITP
Contractor Installation Make for Buy Authorization (SAUS) .... CIMBA
Contractor Installation Make or Buy Association (SAUO) .... CIMBA
Contractor Installation Make or Buy Authorization (AAG) .... CIMBA
Contractor Insurance and Pension Review [*DoD*] .... CIPR
Contractor Integrated Technical Information Service (SAUS) .... CITIS
Contractor Integrated Technical Information Systems [*Military*] .... CITIS
Contractor Interface Guide .... CIG
Contractor Inventory CI
Contractor Inventory Redistribution System (MCD) .... CIRS
Contractor Inventory Utilization Group (MCD) .... CIUG
Contractor Involved in Litigation (AAGC) CIL
Contractor Line Item (MCD) CLI
Contractor Logistics Support [*DoD*] .... CLS
Contractor Logistics Support Services (MCD) .... CLSS
Contractor Logistics Support Services Management Information System (MCD) .... CLSS MIS
Contractor Maintenance and Logistics Support (CTAS) .... CMLS
Contractor Maintenance and Supply Services [*DoD*] .... CMSS
Contractor Maintenance Data Reporting System [*Department of State*] .... CMDRS
Contractor Maintenance Engineering Support (MCD) .... CMES
Contractor Maintenance Personnel (MCD) .... CMP
Contractor Maintenance Service [*or Support*] (MCD) .... CMS
Contractor Maintenance Supply and Support [*DoD*] .... CMSS
Contractor Maintenance Trainer [*Military*] .... CMT
[*A*] **Contractor Managed Account** (AAG) .... ACMA
Contractor Management Reserve (MCD) .... CMR
Contractor Material Review Board [*NASA*] (NASA) .... CMRB
Contractor Missile Installation .... CMI
Contractor Non-SECOMO [*Software Engineering Cost Model*] **Activity Factor** .... CNSAF
Contractor Obligation and Liquidation Tracking System [*Army*] .... COLTS
Contractor Operated and Maintained Base Supply (MCD) .... COMBS
Contractor Operated & Managed Base Supply (SAUS) .... COMBS
Contractor Operation and Maintenance Support (ACAE) .... COMS
Contractor Overhaul Facility .... COF
Contractor Packaging Capability Review [*DoD*] .... CPCR
Contractor Parts List .... CPL
Contractor Performance Assessment Report (SAUS) .... CPAR
Contractor Performance Assessment Reporting System (AAGC) .... CPARS
Contractor Performance Certification Program [*Army*] (RDA) CP2
Contractor Performance Certification Program (ACAE) .... CPCP
Contractor Performance Evaluation .... CPE
Contractor Performance Evaluation Group .... CPEG
Contractor Performance Evaluation Plan [*or Program*] [*Military*] (AABC) .... CPEP
Contractor Performance Evaluation Review Group (AAGC) .... CPERG
Contractor Performance Evaluation System .... CPES
Contractor Performance Factor [*DoD*] .... CPF
Contractor Performance Measurement (MCD) .... CPM
Contractor Performance Measurement Course [*DSMC*] (AAGC) .... CPMC
Contractor Performance Record [*DoD*] .... CPR
Contractor Performance Report .... CPR
Contractor Performance Review System (AAGC) .... CPRS
Contractor Performance Summary (AAGC) .... CPS
Contractor Personnel Employment Report (NG) .... CPER
Contractor Plant Services (ACAE) .... CPS
Contractor Preferred Parts List (ACAE) .... CPPL
Contractor Preliminary Inspection .... CPI
Contractor Procurement List (NATG) .... CPL
Contractor Procurement System Review [*DoD*] .... CPSR
Contractor Productivity Improvement (ACAE) .... CPI
Contractor Property Management System .... CPMS
Contractor Provided Training .... CPT
Contractor Quality Control (DNAB) .... CQC
Contractor Quality Control Plan (SAUO) .... CQCP
Contractor Recommend Support Plan [*Military*] .... CRSP

Contractor Recommended Change List (SAUS) .... CRCL
Contractor Recommended Code (SAUS) .... CRC
Contractor Registration System (AAGC) .... CRS
Contractor Relations Specialist [DoD] .... CRS
Contractor Repair Facility (ACAE) .... CRF
Contractor Report (SAUS) .... CR
Contractor Reports Register .... CRR
Contractor Required Shipment Date .... CRSD
Contractor Resident Office (AAG) .... CRO
Contractor Responsibility Review Program (SAUS) .... CRRP
Contractor Responsible Action (MCD) .... KRA
Contractor Review Board (AAGC) .... CRB
Contractor Risk Assessment Guide [Military] .... CRAG
Contractor Risk Assessment Guide (DOMA) .... CRSG
Contractor Risk Assessment Guides (SAUS) .... CRAG
Contractor Self-Evaluation Report [Environmental science] (COE) .... CSER
Contractor Sensitization (DNAB) .... CS
Contractor Source Inspection [Military] .... CSI
Contractor Special Security Officer (ACAE) .... CSSO
Contractor Standard Item (AAG) .... CSI
Contractor Standard Parts .... CSP
Contractor Standardization Plan (SAUO) .... CSP
Contractor State Code [Database terminology] (NITA) .... CS
Contractor Storage Site (AFM) .... CSS
Contractor Supply Center [Army] .... CSC
Contractor Supply Center List .... CSCL
Contractor Support .... CS
Contractor Support Area (KSC) .... CSA
Contractor Support Equipment Recommendation Data (MCD) .... CSERD
Contractor Support Facility (MCD) .... CSF
Contractor Support Material List (MCD) .... CSML
Contractor Support Milestone (DNAB) .... CSM
Contractor Support Plan .... CSP
Contractor Support Service (MCD) .... CSS
Contractor Technical Assistance (MCD) .... CTA
Contractor Technical Evaluation (CAAL) .... CTE
Contractor Technical Manual Plan [DoD] .... CTMP
Contractor Technical Meeting (AAG) .... CTM
Contractor Technical Organization (ACAE) .... CTO
Contractor Technical Support (MCD) .... CTS
Contractor Test and Evaluation (MCD) .... CTE
Contractor Traffic Management Association (SAUO) .... CTMA
Contractor Training Equipment (SAA) .... CTE
Contractor Training Instruction (DNAB) .... CTI
Contractor Training Program Coordinator (SAUO) .... CTPC
Contractor Transition Plan .... CTP
Contractor Turnaround Time .... CTAT
Contractor Using Price Incentive Doctrine (SAA) .... CUPID
Contractor Weighted Average Share .... CWAS
Contractor Weighted Average Share-Not Applicable (AAGC) .... CWAS-NA
Contractor Work Authorization (KSC) .... CWA
Contractor Work Plan (NRCH) .... CWP
Contractor-Acquired Materiel (AFM) .... CAM
Contractor-Acquired Operational Equipment .... CAOE
Contractor-Acquired Property (AFM) .... CAP
Contractor-Assisted .... CA
Contractor/Foreign Testing [Air Force] .... CFT
Contractor-Furnished Accessories (AFIT) .... CFA
Contractor-Furnished Aircraft Equipment (AFM) .... CFAE
Contractor-Furnished and Equipped .... CFAE
Contractor-Furnished Engineers (MCD) .... CFE
Contractor-Furnished Equipment / Contractor-Furnished Aircraft Equipment (SAA) .... CFE/CFAE
Contractor-Furnished Equipment - Repairable Items Support System (MCD) .... CFE-RISS
Contractor-Furnished Information (MCD) .... CFI
Contractor-Furnished Material (MCD) .... CFM
Contractor-Furnished Product (AAGC) .... CFP
Contractor-Furnished Property [Air Force] .... CFP
Contractor-Furnished Special Support Equipment (AFIT) .... CFSSE
Contractor-Furnished Technicians (MCD) .... CFT
Contractor-Held Air Force Property (AFM) .... CHAP
Contractor-Managed Base Supply [Facility] (MCD) .... COMBS
Contractor-Operated Civil Engineer Supply Store .... COCESS
Contractor-Operated Parts Stores [Military] .... COPARS
Contractor-Operated Storage Site (MCD) .... COSS
Contractor-Oriented Data Abstract Modules [Air Force] .... CODAM
Contractor-Owned, Contractor-Operated (AABC) .... COCO
Contractor-Prepared, Government-Approved .... CP/GA
Contractor-Recommended Change List .... CRCL
Contractor-Recommended Coding (MCD) .... CRC
Contractor-run Logistics System (SAUS) .... CLS
Contractors Accounting System (PDAA) .... CONACS
Contractor's Advisory Board (SAA) .... CAB
Contractors Association of West Virginia (SRA) .... CAWV
Contractors' Configuration Control Board (ACAE) .... CCCB
Contractor's Control Data Bank (DNAB) .... CCDB
Contractor's Current Fiscal Year (ROAS) .... CCFY
Contractor's Demonstration Inspection .... CDI
Contractor's Development Testing (MUGU) .... CDT
Contractor's Early Warning System (MCD) .... CEWS
Contractor's Identification Number .... CIDNO
Contractor's Information Submittal [or Submitted] (MCD) .... CIS
Contractor's Manual Prepared after Negotiated Authorization for Contract .... CMA

Contractors' Mechanical Plant Engineers [British] (BI) .... CMPE
Contractors Mutual Association [Defunct] (EA) .... CMA
Contractor's Operational Control Center (ACAE) .... COCC
Contractors' Operational Representative .... COR
Contractors Panel [Aerospace] (AAG) .... CN/PNL
Contractor's Preliminary Design Review (MCD) .... CPDR
Contractor's Profile System [Department of Health and Human Services] (GFGA) .... CPS
Contractors Pump Bureau (EA) .... CPB
Contractor's Satellite Control Site (ACAE) .... CSCS
Contractor's Summary Cost Breakdown (MCD) .... CSCB
Contractor's Training (MCD) .... CT
Contractor's Weighted Average Share in Cost Risk [Accounting] .... CWAS
Contractor's Work Estimate [Military] .... CWE
Contract-Relax, Antagonistic-Contract Method [Medicine] .... CRAC
Contract-Relax Method [Medicine] .... CR
Contract-Required Quantitation Limit (EEVL) .... CRQL
Contract-Research Organisations .... CROS
Contract-Research Organization (ECON) .... CRO
Contracts and Policy (ACAE) .... C&P
Contracts Compliance Regional Office [DoD] .... CCO
Contracts Division (SAUO) .... CD
Contracts Division .... CT
Contracts Equal Employment Opportunity Program (AAGC) .... CEEOP
Contracts Group Office .... CGO
Contracts Information System (SAUO) .... CIS
Contracts Maintenance Log (MCD) .... CML
Contracts Management Division [Environmental Protection Agency] (GFGA) .... CMD
Contracts Processing System (MCD) .... CPS
Contracts Station (AAG) .... CS
Contracts Termination Office (ACAE) .... CTO
Contractual Data Status Reporting System (MCD) .... CDSR
Contractual Engineering Project (AFIT) .... CEP
Contractual Nontechnical Report (AAG) .... CNR
Contractual Requirements, Recording, Analysis, and Management [Air Force] .... CRAM
Contractual Research and Development (MCD) .... CR & D
Contractual Technical Assistance (SAUO) .... CTA
Contractual Technical Evaluation (SAUS) .... CTE
Contractual Technical Report (AAG) .... CTR
Contracture [or Contraction] [Orthopedics] (DAVI) C
Contra-Current Distribution (SAUS) .... CCD
Contradiction (ADA) .... CONTR
Contraindicated [Medicine] .... CONTRA
Contralateral [Anatomy] C
Contralateral [Anatomy] CL
Contralateral [Anatomy] (MAE) .... contralat
Contralateral (SAUS) .... Controlat
Contralateral Axillary Metastasis [Medicine] (MAE) .... CAM
Contralateral Local Anesthesia [Medicine] (DMAA) .... CLA
Contralateral Optic Tectum [Medicine] .... COT
Contralateral Pyramidal Tract (PDAA) .... CPT
Contralateral Remote Masking (STED) .... CRM
Contralateral Renal Plasma Flow [Medicine] (DB) .... CRPF
Contralateral Routing of Offside Signals (SAUS) .... CROS
Contralateral Routing of Signal [Audiometry] .... CROS
Contralateral Threshold Shift (OA) .... CTS
Contralto [Music] C
Contralto [Music] .... CON
Contralto [Music] .... CONTR
Contrans Corp. [Toronto Stock Exchange symbol] .... CSS
Contrapposto (VRA) .... cntrps
Contrappunto [Counterpoint] [Music] (ROG) .... CP
Contrapuntist [Music] .... CPTST
Contrario [Opponent or Enemy] [Spanish] .... CONTRA
Contra-Rotating Propellers (SAUS) .... Contraprop
Contrary (SAUS) .... Cont
Contrary (WGA) .... CONT
Contrary .... CONTR
Contrary (ROG) .... CONTRY
Contrast (ADA) C
Contrast .... CONTR
Contrast .... CT
Contrast (MSA) .... CTRS
Contrast Baths [Physical therapy] (DAVI) .... CB
Contrast Contour Seeker .... CCS
Contrast Density/Appearance Time [of images on a film] .... CD/AT
Contrast Echocardiology [Cardiology] (DAVI) .... CE
Contrast Enhanced Lithography .... CEL
Contrast Enhancement Computed Tomography [Radiology] (DAVI) .... CECT
Contrast Enhancement Material [Photoprocessing] .... CEM
Contrast Gate (MCD) .... CG
Contrast Gate Amplifier .... CGA
Contrast Index [Photography] CI
Contrast Light Compensation (IAA) CLC
Contrast Media [Radiology] .... CM
Contrast Media Appearance Picture [Also known as coronary arteriography] [Radiology] .... CMAP
Contrast Media-Induced Acute Renal Insufficiency [Medicine] .... CM-ARI
Contrast Optical LASER Tracking Subsystem [Missile guidance] .... COLTS
Contrast Rendering Factor (PDAA) .... CRF
Contrast Rendition Factor (SAUS) .... CRF
Contrast Sensitivity Function [of the retina] .... CSF
Contrast Sensitivity test (SAUS) .... CS

Contrast Spatial Frequency [*Vision research*] ... CSF
Contrast Threshold (SAUS) ... CT
Contrast Transfer Function [*Video technology*] ... CTF
Contrast Transmission Function (SAUS) ... CTF
Contrast Value ... CV
Contrast Ventriculography [*Medicine*] (MELL) ... CV
Contrast Ventriculography (DB) ... CVG
Contrast-Enhancement Layer [*Photoprocessing*] ... CEL
Contrasting Color (SAUS) ... CC
Contraterrene [*Anti-matter in science fiction*] (BARN) ... CT
Contraves/Raytheon Air Defense System ... CRADS
Contre Complications Bronchiques [*Vaccine for "bronchial complaints"*] [*Medicine*] ... CCB
Contrepoint [*Record label*] [*France*] ... Cpt
Contre-Reforme Catholique [*In association name CRC Canada*] [*Catholic Counter-Reform Canada*] ... CRC
Contrexeville [*France*] [*ICAO location identifier*] (ICLI) ... LFXC
Contribute (SAUS) ... Cntr
Contribute (AABC) ... CNTR
Contributed (SAUS) ... Conbd
Contributed to Propagation Research (SAUS) ... CPR
Contributing (ADA) ... CONTBG
Contributing (AL) ... Contrib
Contributing (NTIO) ... contrib
Contributing (ADA) ... CTG
Contributing to Delinquency of Minor [*FBI standardized term*] ... C to D of M
Contributing Value [*Shipping*] ... CV
Contribution (WGA) ... CONTBN
Contribution ... CONTR
Contribution ... CONTRBTN
Contribution (WDMC) ... contrib
Contribution (MSA) ... CONTRIB
Contribution a l'Histoire Juridique de la Ire Dynastie Babylonienne [*A publication*] (BJA) ... CHJB
Contribution Margin [*Accounting*] ... CM
Contribution Record Reporting System (SAUS) ... CRRS
Contribution-Based Compensation and Appraisal System [*Army*] ... CCAS
Contributions from the Central Research Institute for Agriculture Bogor (SAUS) ... Contrib Cent Res Inst Agric Bogor
Contributions from the United States National Herbarium (SAUS) ... Contrib U S Natl Herb
Contributions Greater Than [*Database terminology*] (NITA) ... CG
Contributions in Aid of Construction [*IRS*] ... CIAC
Contributions. Institute of Geology and Paleontology. Tohoku University (journ.) (SAUS) ... TDRCAH
Contributions. Laboratory of Vertebrate Biology. University of Michigan (journ.) (SAUS) ... UNIVBA6
Contributions Less Than [*Database terminology*] (NITA) ... CL
Contributions. Museum of Paleontology. University of Michigan (journ.) (SAUS) ... UMMPA3
Contributions of Infantry to the Battle Test [*Combat Develolpments Experimentation Center*] [*Army*] (INF) ... CIBT
Contributions Record [*Database terminology*] (NITA) ... CR
Contributions to Mineralogy and Petrology (journ.) (SAUS) ... Contribut Mineral Petrol
Contributor (WGA) ... CONTBR
Contributor [*Publishing*] (WDMC) ... contrib
Contributor (SAUS) ... Contrib
Contributor (ROG) ... CONTRIBOR
Contributor (SAUS) ... CTP
Contributor (SAUS) ... Ctr
Contributor ... CTR
Contributory Employee Stock Ownership Plan ... CESOP
Contributory Negligence [*Legal shorthand*] (LWAP) ... CNEGL
Contributory Pension Fund (SAUO) ... CPF
Contributory Place (ROG) ... CP
Contritus [*Broken, ground*] [*Pharmacy*] (DAVI) ... contrit
[*A*] **Contrived Reduction of Nomenclature Yielding Mnemonics** [*Humorous interpretation of the term*] ... ACRONYM
Contro-Clusive Magnetism [*Pest control concept*] ... CCM
Control [*Officer's rating*] [*British Royal Navy*] ... C
Control [*Referring to a group in an experiment*] (DAVI) ... C
Control (IAA) ... CNL
Control (KSC) ... CNTL
Control ... CNTRL
Control (WDAA) ... Con
Control (AFM) ... CON
Control ... CONL
Control (MSA) ... CONT
Control (WDMC) ... cont
Control ... CONTL
Control ... CONTR
Control (TBD) ... Contr
Control (KSC) ... CONTRL
Control (AAG) ... CTL
Control (WGA) ... CTRL
Control [*Computer science*] ... Ctrl
Control (ADWA) ... ctrl
Control Accelerometer (IAA) ... CA
Control Access Manager (BUR) ... CAM
Control Access System (SAUS) ... CAS
Control Access Unit (SAUS) ... CAU
Control Accumulator ... C/A
Control Actuation System ... CAS
Control Adjustment Strap ... CAS
Control Advisory Board (ACAE) ... CAB
Control Advisory Release (NRCH) ... CAR
Control Air Centre (SAUO) ... CAC
Control Air Data System (MCD) ... CADS
Control Air Force Specialty Code ... CAFSC
Control Alarm Indicator (MCD) ... CAI
Control Alcohol and Drug Control (SAUS) ... A&D
Control and Acquisition Interface (KSC) ... CAI
Control and Action (SAUS) ... CONTACT
Control and Analysis Center (SAUO) ... CAC
Control and Analysis Centers [*ERADCOM*] (RDA) ... CAC
Control and Assessment Team [*Military*] (GFGA) ... CAT
Control & Audio Panel (SAUS) ... CAP
Control and Authorization Process (KSC) ... CAP
Control and Automation Manufacturers Association (CIST) ... CAMA
Control and Auxiliary Power Supply System ... CAPS
Control and Command Systems Support Agency [*NATO*] (NATG) ... CCSSA
Control & Communications Subsystem (SAUS) ... CCS
Control and Computation System [*or Subsystem*] [*Navy*] (MCD) ... CCS
Control and Coordination (SAUS) ... C2
Control and Coordination [*Army*] ... CAC
Control and Coordination (SAUS) ... C&C
Control & Correlation Processor (SAUS) ... CCP
Control and Data Acquisition System (MCD) ... CODAS
Control and Data Management System (ACAE) ... CDMS
Control and Data Retrieval System [*Formerly, DCDRS*] [*Air Force*] (MCD) ... CDRS
Control and Delay Channel (ACAE) ... CDC
Control and Diagnostic Unit [*Computer science*] ... CDU
Control and Display (IAA) ... CAD
Control and Display (NAKS) ... C&D
Control & Display of Infra-Red Reconnaissance System (SAUS) ... CDIRRS
Control and Display Panel (MCD) ... CDP
Control and Display Subsystem (MCD) ... CDS
Control and Display Unit (NASA) ... CADU
Control and Display Unit (NASA) ... CDU
Control and Evaluation ... C & E
Control and Guidance (MCD) ... C & G
Control and Guidance (SAUS) ... C&G
Control and Indicating Equipment ... CIE
Control and Indication (SAUS) ... CAI
Control and Indication (MCD) ... C & I
Control and Information Center (NASA) ... CIC
Control and Instrumentation (SAUS) ... CAI
Control and Instrumentation (NRCH) ... C & I
Control and Instrumentation (journ.) (SAUS) ... Contr Instrum
Control and Interrupt Register (SAUS) ... CIR
Control and Line (SAUS) ... C&L
Control and Line (AABC) ... C & L
Control and Monitor (SAUS) ... C&M
Control and Monitor Panel ... CAMP
Control and Monitoring (NAKS) ... C&M
Control and Monitoring (SAUS) ... C/M
Control and Monitoring Processor (IEEE) ... CAMP
Control and Monitoring System (SAUS) ... CAMS
Control and Navigation (SAUS) ... C and N
Control and Processing [*Company*] [*INSCOM*] ... C & P
Control and Processing Center (MCD) ... CPC
Control and Protection of Transoceanic Air Lanes of Communication ... CAPTALC
Control and Protection Panel ... CPP
Control and Protection System (SAUO) ... CPS
Control and Reporting (SAUS) ... C&R
Control and Reporting (NATG) ... C and R
Control and Reporting Center [*Air Force*] ... CRC
Control and Reporting Center/Post [*Air Force*] (MCD) ... CRC/P
Control and Reporting Post [*RADAR*] [*Air Force*] ... CRP
Control and Reporting System (NATG) ... CRS
Control and Reporting Unit ... CRU
Control and Reproducibility Monitor (IEEE) ... CRM
Control and Service Unit (SAUS) ... CSU
Control and Simulation Facility (MCD) ... CSF
Control and Simulation Language [*Computer science*] ... CSL
Control and Status Logic (KSC) ... CSL
Control and Status Register (SAUS) ... CSR
Control and Status System [*NASCOM*] (MCD) ... CSS
Control and Surveillance of Friendly Forces (MCD) ... CASOFF
Control and Switching Element (CCCA) ... CSE
Control and Switching Equipment [*RADAR*] ... CSE
Control and Switching Point (SAUS) ... CSP
Control and Timing (SAUS) ... C&T
Control and Timing Unit [*Computer science*] ... CTU
Control and Tracking System (SAUS) ... CATS
Control and Traffic Center ... CTC
Control and Warning (SAUS) ... CAW
Control and Warning Squadron (SAUO) ... C&W Sq
Control Anticipation Parameter (PDAA) ... CAP
Control Application Development Tool (AAEL) ... CADT
Control Application Link Layer Engieering (SAUS) ... CALLE
Control Architecture (SPST) ... CA
Control Area [*Computer science*] ... CA
Control Area [*ICAO <<[International Civil Aviation Organization]=>> Term*] (GAVI) ... CTA
Control Area (FAAC) ... CTLA
Control Area/Instrument Restricted (SAUS) ... CTA/IR

Control Area/Instrument Visual (SAUS) .... CTA/IV
Control Area/Visual Excepted (SAUS) .... CTA/VE
Control Arithmetic Unit (SAUS) .... CAU
Control Armourer [British military] (DMA) .... CA
Control Assembly .... CA
Control Assembly .... CONTA
Control Assembly Program (BUR) .... CAP
Control Assembly Set (MCD) .... CAS
Control Attenuator Timer (KSC) .... CAT
Control Augmentation .... CA
Control Augmentation System .... CAS
Control Automated System (SAUS) .... CAS
Control Automation System [IBM Corp.] .... CAS
Control Automation System Manufacturing Interface Tape (IAA) .... CASMIT
Control Beam Unit (SAUS) .... CBU
Control Block (SAUS) .... CB
Control Block Data Base (ECII) .... CBB
Control Blocks Configuration [Computer science] (ECII) .... CBC
Control Board .... CB
Control Board Operator [Lighting] (NTCM) .... CBO
Control Booth .... CB
Control Boundary (FAAC) .... CTLB
Control Branch [Military] .... CB
Control Break .... CB
Control Buffer [Computer science] (IAA) .... CB
Control Building [Nuclear energy] (NRCH) .... CB
Control Building Environmental Control System [Nuclear energy]
    (NRCH) .... CBECS
Control Bus (SPST) .... CB
Control Button .... CB
Control by Ship (NATG) .... CONSHIP
Control by Wire (MCD) .... CBW
Control Byte (SAUS) .... CB
Control Cabin CC
Control Cable Parallel Connector (SAUS) .... CCPC
Control Card Installation Card (SAUS) CCIC
Control Card Listing [Computer science] CCL
Control Center CC
Control Center Experimental Version (ACAE) .... CCEV
Control Center Mock-Up .... CCMU
Control Center Operations Manager (ADWA) .... CCOM
Control Center Programming Center [NASA] (KSC) .... CCPC
Control Center Rack (MCD) .... CCR
Control Center Systems Manager (ADWA) .... CCSM
Control Center/Security Monitor (SAUO) .... CC/SM
Control Central (SAUS) CC
Control Chamber [Diving apparatus] CC
Control Change (SAUS) CC
Control Channel Information Demodulator .... CCID
Control Character (SAUS) CC
Control Character [Keyboard] (CINC) .... CTRL
Control Check (SAUS) CC
Control Chief Hldgs [NASDAQ symbol] (TTSB) .... DIEM
Control Chief Holdings [Associated Press] (SAG) .... ContrCh
Control Chief Holdings [NASDAQ symbol] (SAG) .... DIGM
Control Circuit CC
Control Circuit Resistance .... CCR
Control Circuits (SAUS) .... Ctrl Ckts
Control Circuits Design Section .... CCDS
Control Civil and Military [British] (AIA) .... CCM
Control, Civil & Military (SAUS) .... CCM
Control Clause (SAUS) CC
Control Code (IAA) CC
Control Column (SAUS) CC
Control Command (SAUS) CC
Control Command Processor (IAA) .... CCP
Control Command Store (SAUS) .... CCS
Control Commission Court (SAUO) CCC
Control Commission for Germany [World War II] .... CCG
Control Commission Military Section [British] [World War II] .... CCMS
Control Commission Shipping Bureau [Allied German Occupation
    Forces] .... CCSB
Control, Communication, and Display Subsystem (MCD) .... CCDS
Control, Communication & Display Unit (MCD) .... CCDU
Control Communications Module [Telecommunications] (ECII) .... CCM
Control Communications Software (SAUS) .... COCOS
Control Communications Unit [Telecommunications] (ECII) .... CCU
Control Computer (KSC) CC
Control Computer Module (SAUS) .... CCM
Control Computer Subsystem (SAUS) .... CCS
Control Computer System [or Subsystem] (IAA) .... CCS
Control Configured Propulsion (MCD) .... CCP
Control Configured Vehicle [Air Force] CCV
Control Connector (IAA) CC
Control Console CC
Control Contactor (IEEE) .... CCR
Control Converter (MCD) CC
Control Core Cell (PDAA) CCC
Control Council (SAUO) CC
Control Council (SAUO) .... CONL
Control Counter [Computer science] CC
Control Creation Edition [Microsoft Corp.] [Computer science] (PCM) .... CCE
Control Current Impedance CCI
Control Cycle (SAUS) CC
Control Data .... CD

Control Data Assembly Program [Control Data Corp.] .... CODAP
Control Data Australia (SAUS) .... CDA
Control Data Center (SAUO) .... CDC
Control Data Communications Control Procedure [Telecommunications]
    (TEL) .... CDCCP
Control Data Company (SAUO) .... CDC
Control Data Computer (SAUS) .... CDC
Control Data Corp. [Information service or system] (IID) .... CDC
Control Data Corp. [Toronto Stock Exchange symbol] .... CTD
Control Data Corporation (SAUO) .... CDA
Control Data Corporation (NAKS) .... CDS
Control Data Corporation Distributed Communications Network
    [Telecommunications] .... CDCNET
Control Data Corporation, Inc. (SAUO) .... CDC
Control Data Education Institutes .... CDEI
Control Data Field (SAUS) .... CDF
Control Data Institute .... CDI
Control Data Link (SAUS) .... CONDAL
Control Data Ltd. (SAUS) .... CDL
Control Data Mathematic Program (IAA) .... CDM
Control Data Mathematical Programming (SAUS) .... CDM Programming
Control Data Panel .... CDP
Control Data Set (SAUS) .... CDS
Control Data Structural System (DNAB) .... CONSTRUCTS
Control Data System (NASA) .... CDS
Control Data Systems [NASDAQ symbol] (SAG) .... CDAT
Control Data Systems, Inc. [Associated Press] (SAG) .... CtrlDt
Control Data Terminal .... CDT
Control Data Unit .... CDU
Control Desk (SAUS) .... CD
Control Detonating Fuse (SAUS) .... CDF
Control Development Kit [Microsoft Corp.] (PCM) .... CDK
Control Device (SAUS) .... CD
Control Devices, Inc. [Associated Press] (SAG) .... ContDev
Control Devices, Inc. [NASDAQ symbol] (SAG) .... SNSR
Control Diagram Language [Computer science] (IEEE) .... CODIL
Control Diastolic Pressure [Cardiology] .... CDP
Control Dictionary (SAUS) .... CD
Control Diet .... CD
Control Differential Transformer .... CDT
Control Differential Transmitter .... CDX
Control Digit Test .... CDT
Control Direction Indicator (MCD) .... CDI
Control Director Intercept (CINC) .... CDI
Control Display Navigation Unit (SAUS) .... CDNU
Control Display System (SAUS) .... CDS
Control Distribution Center (AAG) .... CDC
Control Distribution System .... CDS
Control Drawing Change Request (AAG) .... CDCR
Control Electrical Artificer [Navy rating] [British] .... CEA
Control Electrical Mechanic [British military] (DMA) .... CEM
Control Electrical Mechanician [Navy rating] [British] .... CEMN
Control Electrician [British military] (DMA) .... CE
Control Electronics Assembly [Aerospace] .... CEA
Control Electronics Container (SAUS) .... CEC
Control Electronics Section [Apollo] [NASA] .... CES
Control Electronics Unit (MCD) .... CEU
Control Element (MCD) .... CE
Control Element Assembly [Nuclear energy] (NRCH) .... CEA
Control Element Assembly Calculator [Nuclear energy] (NRCH) .... CEAC
Control Element Drive Mechanism [Nuclear energy] (NRCH) .... CEDM
Control Element Drive Mechanism Control System [Nuclear energy]
    (NRCH) .... CEDMCS
Control Element Drive Motor (SAUS) .... CEDM
Control Element Drive System [Nuclear energy] (NRCH) .... CEDS
Control Element Test Stand [Nuclear energy] (NRCH) .... CETS
Control Encoder Coupler (NASA) .... CEC
Control Energy [Vancouver Stock Exchange symbol] .... CTY
Control Engineer, ship (SAUS) .... CE
Control Engineering .... CE
Control Engineering Approach to Management Systems (SAUS) .... CEATOMS
Control Engineering (journ.) (SAUS) .... CENG
Control Engineering (journ.) (SAUS) .... Contr Eng
Control Engineering (journ.) (SAUS) .... CTRL
Control Equipment (IAA) .... CE
Control Error (IAA) .... CE
Control Escort Ship (SAUS) .... DEC
Control Escort Vessel [Navy symbol] .... DEC
Control Execution Environment (AAEL) .... CEE
Control Facilities Area (SAUO) .... CFA
Control Facility (SAUO) .... CF
Control Feed Chart (SAUS) .... CFC
Control Field (SAUS) .... CF
Control Filter Post (NATG) .... CFP
Control Flag [Computer science] (IAA) .... CF
Control Flight Test Bed .... CFTB
Control Flow Analyzer (SAUS) .... CFA
Control Flow Diagram (MCD) .... CFD
Control Flow Expression (SAUS) .... CFE
Control Flow Jet (SAUS) .... CFJ
Control Flow Specification Diagram [Computer science] (VERA) .... CSD
Control flow Specification Diagram (SAUS) .... CSD
Control Footing .... CF
Control for Operations Programming and Systems (SAUS) .... COPS
Control for Submarine Discharge Torpedo (MCD) .... CSDT

Control for Surface Launched Torpedoes (SAUS) .... CSLT
Control for Surface-Launched Torpedoes (MCD) .... CSLT
Control for the Advanced Passenger Train (SAUS) .... CAPT
Control Format Item (SAUS) .... CFI
Control [*or Controlled*] **Fragmentation Munitions** (CINC) .... COFRAM
Control from Shore (NATG) .... CONSHORE
Control Function [*Computer science*] (IAA) .... CF
Control Function Memory (SAUS) .... CFM
Control Functional Diagram .... CFD
Control Functional Unit [*Data link*] (NG) .... CFU
Control Funds Status Report (SSD) .... CFSR
Control Gate (SAUS) .... CG
Control Grid .... CG
Control Group .... CG
Control Group Adapter (MCD) .... CGA
Control Group Level (SAUO) .... CGL
Control Guidance Subsystem (OA) .... CGS
Control Handling Aid for Increase Range (SAUS) .... CHAIR
Control Heading (BUR) .... CH
Control Hole (BUR) .... CH
Control in Information Systems .... COINS
Control Index File Europe [*Department of Defense*] (ACAE) .... CIFE
Control Indicator CI
Control Indicator Assembly (MCD) .... CIA
Control Indicator Power Distribution Unit [*Military*] (CAAL) .... CIPDU
Control Indicator Set (MCD) .... CIS
Control Indicator Unit (OA) .... CIU
Control Information (SAUS) CI
Control Inlet Panel [*Aerospace*] (AAG) .... CIP
Control Input Signal (SAUS) .... CIS
Control Input/Output (SAUS) .... CIO
Control Inquiry Card [*Computer science*] (IAA) CIC
Control Installation Code [*Air Force*] (AFIT) CIC
Control Instruction (SAUS) CI
Control Instruction Counter (SAUS) CIC
Control Instruction Register (SAUS) .... CIR
Control Instrument Company (SAUO) CIC
Control Interface (SAUS) CI
Control Interface Assembly (MCD) .... CIA
Control Interface Document .... CID
Control Interface Module [*Chemistry*] .... CIM
Control Interpreter Language (SAUS) CIL
Control Interval [*Computer science*] (ITCA) CI
Control Interval Definition Field [*Computer science*] (BUR) .... CIDF
Control Item Planners (ACAE) .... CIP
Control Joint (MCD) .... CJ
Control Joint [*Technical drawings*] .... CJT
Control Joint (AAG) .... CLJ
Control Joint (SAUS) .... clj
Control Key [*Electronics*] .... CNTRL
Control Key [*Computer science*] (DDC) .... CTRL
Control Keyboard (SAUS) .... CK
Control Language [*Computer science*] (BUR) CL
Control Language Services [*Computer science*] (IAA) .... CLS
Control Language Translator [*Computer science*] (IEEE) .... COLT
Control Launch Center (MUGU) CLC
Control Launch Subsystem (OA) .... CLS
Control Leader [*Computer science*] CL
Control Level Item CLI
Control Limit (SAUS) CL
Control Line Model (SAUS) .... CL Model
Control Line Platform (SAUS) .... CLP
Control Line Register .... CLR
Control Logic CL
Control Logic (SAUS) CL
Control Logic and Drive Assembly .... CLDA
Control Logic and Switching Assembly (ACAE) .... CLSA
Control Logic Array .... CLA
Control Logic Assembly (ACAE) .... CLA
Control Logic Diagram (SAUS) .... CLD
Control Logic Read Index [*Computer science*] (ECII) .... CLRNDX
Control Logistics Support (ACAE) .... CLS
Control Magnetization Curve .... CMC
Control Maintenance & Management Systems (ACII) .... CMMS
Control Maintenance Unit .... CMU
Control Mark (DEN) .... CM
Control Memory [*Telecommunications*] (TEL) .... CM
Control Memory Access Register [*Computer science*] (NITA) .... CMAR
Control Memory Address Register [*Computer science*] .... CMAR
Control Message Automation [*Aviation*] .... CMA
Control Methods and Technologies [*Environmental science*] (COE) .... CMT
Control Mode (MCD) .... CM
Control Module .... CM
Control Moment Gyro Assembly [*Aerospace*] .... CMGA
Control Moment Gyro Electrical Assembly [*Aerospace*] .... CMGEA
Control Moment Gyro Inverter Assembly [*Aerospace*] (MCD) .... CMGIA
Control Moment Gyro System [*or Subsystem*] [*Aerospace*] (KSC) .... CMGS
Control Moment Gyroscope [*Aerospace*] .... CMG
Control Monitor (MCD) .... CM
Control Monitor (NAKS) .... cm
Control Monitor and Isolation Subsystem (MCD) .... CMIS
Control Monitor Set (SAUS) .... CMS
Control Network System [*Chiefly British*] .... CNS
Control Network System of Receivers and Transmitters (SAUS) .... CONSORT
Control Number .... CN
Control of Advertisements Regulations [*Town planning*] [*British*] .... CAR
Control of Aircraft Maintenance and Servicing .... CAMS
Control of Asbestos at Work Regulations (HEAS) .... CAWR
Control of Banking (Prentice-Hall) [*A publication*] (DLA) .... Cont of Banking (P-H)
Control of Communicable Diseases in Man (ADWA) .... CCDM
Control of Destination of Ships .... CDS
Control of Diarrhoeal Diseases Program (SAUO) .... CDD
Control of Electromagnetic Radiation (NTIO) .... Conelrad
Control of Electromagnetic Radiations [*Purpose is to deny the enemy aircraft the use of electromagnetic radiations for navigation, while still providing essential services*] .... CONELRAD
Control of Engineering Material, Acquisition, Storage and Transport (IAA) .... CEMAST
Control of Illumination (SAUS) .... CONILLUM
Control of Industrial Major Accident Hazards [*British*] .... CIMAH
Control of Industrial Major Accident Hazards Regulations (HEAS) .... CIMAH
Control of Intensive Farming [*British*] .... COIF
Control of Logistics Expense [*USAREUR*] (MCD) .... COLEX
Control of Major Accident Hazards (HEAS) .... COMAH
Control of Material Planning Activities (PDAA) .... COMPACE
Control of Materials Planning and Isometric Drawings .... COMPAID
Control of Official Histories [*British*] .... COH
Control of Operation Programs .... COP
Control of Optimizing Series of Experiments (SAUS) .... COSX
Control of Panel Emulator .... CPE
Control of Pesticides Regulations [*British*] .... COPR
Control of Pollution Act [*1974*] [*British*] (DCTA) .... COPA
Control of Pollution Act [*1974*] [*British*] .... CPA
Control of Process (SAUS) .... COP
Control of Radio Transmission [*British*] [*World War II*] .... CRT
Control of Recombination [*Genetics*] .... CRE
Control of Rents and Furnished Lets [*British*] .... FRC
Control of Sea Ice Information (NATG) .... ICECON
Control of Substances Hazardous to Health [*British*] .... COSHH
Control of Transmission Test (SAUS) .... COTT
Control of Tropical Diseases (SAUO) .... CTD
Control of Unwanted Radiated Energy .... CURE
Control of Work in Confined Spaces (HEAS) .... CWCS
Control Officers' Console .... COC
Control only if Necessary (SAUS) .... COIN
Control Optimization (SAUS) .... COP
Control Orbitron Gauge .... COG
Control Order (MCD) .... CO
Control Ordered SONAR Hardware (PDAA) .... COSH
Control Organization Methods and Technique Studies (SAUS) .... COMATS
Control Panel .... CP
Control Panel [*Electronics*] (ECII) .... CTLPL
Control Panel Device [*Computer science*] (DOM) .... CDEV
Control Panel Subassembly .... CPS
Control Parameter Assembly Program .... CPAP
Control Part (SAUS) .... CP
Control Pascal [*Compiler*] [*Computer science*] .... CP
Control Pattern Generator .... CPG
Control Phasing Unit [*for aircraft*] (RDA) .... CPU
Control Platform (ACAE) .... CP
Control Point .... CP
Control Point Custodian [*Military*] (AFIT) .... CPC
Control Point Spanning Tree (SAUS) .... CPST
Control Position Indicator (IAA) .... CPI
Control Post [*RADAR*] .... CP
Control Power Supply .... CPS
Control Power Transformer (MSA) .... CPT
Control Pressure System (AAG) .... CPS
Control Print (SAUS) .... CP
Control Procedures (MCD) .... CP
Control Processes in Multicellular Organisms .... CPMO
Control Processing Module (SAUS) .... CPM
Control Processing Unit (MCD) .... CPU
Control Processor (IEEE) .... CP
Control Products Incorporated (SAUO) .... CPI
Control Program [*Computer science*] .... CP
Control Program - Real-Time [*Xerox Corp.*] .... CP-R
Control Program Assist [*IBM Corp.*] .... CPA
Control Program Facility (MCD) .... CPF
Control Program for Microcomputers (ACAE) .... CP/M
Control Program for Microprocessors [*Computer science*] .... CP/M
Control Program Services (IAA) .... CPS
Control Program-Five [*Operating system*] [*Xerox Corp.*] .... CP-V
Control Programme for Networks [*Computer science*] .... CP/NET
Control Programmer (SAUS) .... CP
Control Program/Monitor [*Computer science*] .... CP/M
Control Programs Development Division [*Environmental Protection Agency*] (GFGA) .... CPDD
Control Programs Support (IEEE) .... CPS
Control Purchasing Authority (NVT) .... CPA
Control Quality Monitor .... CQM
Control Question Test [*For lie detectors*] .... CQT
Control Radio Unit (SAUS) .... CRU
Control Rate Gyro [*Aerospace*] (KSC) .... CRG
Control Rating [*British military*] (DMA) .... CR
Control Rating (SAUS) .... CR
Control Ratio (SAUS) .... CR
Control Read-Only Memory [*Computer science*] .... CROM
Control Read/Write (MCD) .... CRW
Control Receiver (SAUS) .... CR

Control Recognition Character [*Computer science*] (ECII)	CRC
Control Reconfiguration Strategy (MCD)	CRS
Control Record Listing [*IRS*]	CRL
Control Red Bank Demand Indicator (IEEE)	CBDI
Control Register [*Computer science*] (IAA)	CR
Control Register (SAUS)	CTLR
Control Register Zero [*Computer science*] (PCM)	CRO
Control Relay	CR
Control Relay Automatic	CRA
Control Relay Forward	CRF
Control Relay Hand	CRH
Control Relay Latch	CRL
Control Relay Master	CRM
Control Relay Translator (IAA)	CRT
Control Relay Unlatch	CRU
Control Repeater Amplifier	CRA
Control Restrictive Instruction for Structural Programming (MCD)	CRISP
Control Review Board (SAUO)	CRB
Control Risks Information Services [*British*] [*Information service or system*] (IID)	CRIS
Control Rod [*Nuclear energy*] (NRCH)	CR
Control Rod Absorber [*Nuclear energy*] (NUCP)	CRA
Control Rod Analysis [*Nuclear energy*]	CORONA
Control Rod Assembly [*Nuclear energy*] (NRCH)	CRA
Control Rod Disconnect Driveline [*Nuclear energy*] (NRCH)	CRDD
Control Rod Drive [*Nuclear energy*] (IEEE)	CD
Control Rod Drive [*or Driveline*] [*Nuclear energy*] (NRCH)	CRD
Control Rod Drive Assembly [*Nuclear energy*] (IEEE)	CRDA
Control Rod Drive Control System [*Nuclear energy*] (NRCH)	CRDCS
Control Rod Drive Hydraulic System [*Nuclear energy*] (NRCH)	CRDHS
Control Rod Drive Mechanism [*Nuclear energy*] (GFGA)	CRDM
Control Rod Drive Mechanism Shroud [*Nuclear energy*] (NRCH)	CRDMS
Control Rod Drive Motor [*Nuclear energy*] (IEEE)	CRDM
Control Rod Drive System [*Nuclear energy*] (NRCH)	CRDS
Control Rod Drive Ventilating Fan [*Nuclear energy*] (NRCH)	CRDVF
Control Rod Drop Accident (SAUS)	CRDA
Control Rod Guide Tube [*Nuclear energy*] (NRCH)	CRGT
Control Rod Mechanism [*Nuclear energy*] (NUCP)	CRM
Control Rod Position Indication [*Nuclear energy*] (NRCH)	CRPI
Control Rod Scram Accumulator [*Nuclear energy*] (IEEE)	CRSA
Control ROM [*Read-Only Memory*] Address Register [*Computer science*]	CRAR
Control Room (MSA)	CR
Control Room [*Nuclear energy*] (NRCH)	CTRM
Control Room Air Conditioning System [*Nuclear energy*] (NRCH)	CRACS
Control Room Area Ventilation System [*Nuclear energy*] (NRCH)	CRAVS
Control Room Design Review/Audit [*Nuclear energy*] (NRCH)	CRDR/A
Control Room Emergency Ventilation System (IEEE)	CREVS
Control Room Isolation [*Nuclear energy*] (NRCH)	CRI
Control Room Operator [*Nuclear energy*] (NRCH)	CRO
Control Room Patching and Labeling	CORPAL
Control Route Tag (MCD)	CRT
Control Routine	CR
Control Scanner	CS
Control Science [*Vancouver Stock Exchange symbol*]	CLD
Control Section (IAA)	CS
Control Section (MCD)	CSECT
Control Section Report [*NATO*]	CSR
Control Section Tester (ACAE)	CST
Control Segment (MCD)	CS
Control Segment (NAKS)	cs
Control Selection Unit (SAUS)	CSU
Control Sequential Storage Organization (SAUS)	CSSO
Control Serum (DB)	CS
Control Servo Input (NASA)	CSI
Control Servo Input (NAKS)	csi
Control Set	CS
Control Setting Panel (IAA)	CSP
Control Shift Register (CET)	CSR
Control Signal	CS
Control Signal Generator Unit (ACAE)	CSGU
Control Signal Processor [*for spacecraft*]	CSP
Control Signaling Subsystem [*Telecommunications*] (TEL)	CSS
Control Signalling Code (SAUS)	CSC
Control Signalling Subsystem (SAUS)	CSS
Control Site Group (SAUO)	CSG
Control Slip (CINC)	CS
Control Software, Inc.	CSI
Control Staff Instructions [*Army*] (MCD)	COSIN
Control Station (MCD)	CS
Control Station Manual Operating Level (AAG)	CSMOL
Control Stations Maps (SAUO)	CMS
Control Status Register	CSR
Control Stick Assembly (MCD)	CSA
Control Stick Boost and Pitch Compensator (MCD)	CSBPC
Control Stick Maneuver (MCD)	CSM
Control Stick Sensor Assembly (MCD)	CSSA
Control Stick Steering [*Aviation*] (NG)	CSS
Control Stick Tie-In [*Aviation*] (MUGU)	CSTI
Control Storage Code (SAUS)	CSC
Control Store	CS
Control Store Address Register	CSAR
Control Store Data Register	CSDR
Control Strategy Development (SAUS)	CSD
Control Submarine Chaser [*136 feet*] [*Navy symbol*] [*Obsolete*]	PCSC
Control Subroutine Language [*Computer science*] (IEEE)	CONSUL
Control Subsystem	CSS
Control Surface Tie in (SAUS)	CSTI
Control Surveys Division (SAUO)	CSD
Control Switch (MSA)	CS
Control Switch (MSA)	CSW
Control Switching Arrangement Network (SAUS)	CORNET
Control Switching Assembly	CSA
Control Switching Module [*Electronics*] (ECII)	CSM
Control Switching Point (BUR)	CSP
Control Symbol Number (AFM)	CSN
Control Synthetic Gas [*Process*]	CSG
Control System Design Program	CSDP
Control System Development (MCD)	CSD
Control System for Plan Execution (SAUS)	CSPE
Control System Jet	CSJ
Control System Program [*Manufacturing engineering*] [*Computer science*]	CSP
Control System Simulation Equipment (MCD)	CSSE
Control System Test (AAG)	CST
Control System Test Vehicle (DNAB)	CSTV
Control Systems (MCD)	CS
Control Systems Analysis Program (MCD)	CSAP
Control Systems Character (SAUS)	CSC
Control Systems Development Division [*NASA*] (NASA)	CSDD
Control Systems Engineering	CSE
Control Systems Field Laboratory (SAUS)	CSFL
Control Systems Integration Group (SAA)	CSIG
Control Systems Laboratory [*University of Illinois*] (MCD)	CSL
Control Systems Procurement Office (SAA)	CSPO
Control Systems Science and Engineering Department (SAUO)	CSSE
Control Systems Society (EA)	CSS
Control Tag (MCD)	CT
Control Tag Vector (SAUS)	TVC
Control Techniques Guideline Document (SAUS)	CTGD
Control Techniques Guidelines [*Environmental Protection Agency*]	CTG
Control Technology and Application Training Series (ACII)	CTA
Control Technology Center [*Environmental Protection Agency*] (AEPA)	CTC
Control Technology Document [*Environmental Protection Agency*] (GFGA)	CTD
Control Technology Guidelines (WPI)	CTG
Control Technology Office [*Environmental Protection Agency*] (GFGA)	CTO
Control Terminal Unit (SAUS)	CTU
Control Termination Racks (SAUS)	CONTRX
Control Test Bed	CTB
Control Test Set (ACAE)	CTS
Control Test Vehicles	CTV
Control Tool Kits (SAUS)	CTK
Control Total (SAUS)	CT
Control Tower [*For chart use only*] [*Aviation*]	CT
Control Tower Operator [*Army*] (AABC)	CTO
Control Track Direction Computer (AABC)	CTDC
Control Transformer	CT
Control Translator [*Honeywell, Inc.*] [*Computer science*]	CONTRAN
Control Transmitter (SAUS)	CT
Control Transmitter (MUGU)	CX
Control Typewriter (SAUS)	CTW
Control Unit [*Computer science*]	CU
Control Unit / Control Block [*Computer science*] (IAA)	CUCB
Control Unit Bit Array (SAUS)	CUBA
Control Unit Busy (CMD)	CUB
Control Unit End (CMD)	CUE
Control Unit Error Insertion Generator (SAUS)	CUEING
Control Unit Group Input/Output Control Unit [*Computer science*]	CUG IOC
Control Unit Interface [*Computer science*] (IAA)	CUI
Control Unit Terminal [*Computer science*]	CUT
Control Unit Terminal Mode (CDE)	CUT mode
Control Unit Tester [*Sperry UNIVAC*] (BUR)	CUT
Control Users Handbook	CUH
Control, Utility, and Support (IAA)	CUS
Control Valve [*Computer science*] (ECII)	CV
Control Valve [*Automotive engineering*]	C/VAL
Control Valve Module (NASA)	CVM
Control Valve Primary Coolant (MCD)	CVPC
Control Valve Secondary Coolant (MCD)	CVSC
Control Van [*Diving apparatus*]	CV
Control Van Connecting Room (NATG)	CVCR
Control Variable Valve	CVV
Control Vision Unit [*Automotive engineering*]	CVU
Control Volume (SAUS)	CV
Control Volume Experiment (SAUS)	CONVEX
Control Wheel Steering (NG)	CWS
Control Withdrawal Prohibit [*Nuclear energy*] (NRCH)	CWP
Control Word (MCD)	CW
Control Word Address	CWA
Control Word Format (SAUS)	CWF
Control Word Mode (SAUS)	CW Mod
Control Word Modification (SAUS)	CWMOD
Control Word Transfer Cycle (SAUS)	CW Trf Cy
Control Zone [*Aviation*]	CTLZ
Control Zone [*Aviation*]	CTR
Control Zone [*Aviation*]	CTZ
Control Zone [*For chart use only*] [*Aviation*]	CZ
Control Zone/Instrument Visual (SAUS)	CTR/IV
Control Zone/Visual Exempted (SAUS)	CTR/VE
Controladora Comercial Mexicana SA de CV [*Associated Press*] (SAG)	ConCMx
Controladora Comercial Mexicana SA de CV [*NYSE symbol*] (SAG)	MCM

Controladora Comer'l Mex GDS [*NYSE symbol*] (SG) .... MCM
Control-Device Resource [*Computer science*] (BYTE) .... cdev
Control/Display Ratio [*Quality control*] .... C/D
Controles Nucleares del Norte, SA [*Spain*] .... NUCLENOR
Controllability and Observability .... C & O
Controllability, Observability, and Maintenance Engineering Technique (PDAA) .... COMET
Controllable and Reversible Pitch Propeller [*For ships*] (MCD) .... CRP
Controllable Liquid Artifical Dielectric (SAUS) .... CLAD
Controllable Pitch (SAUS) .... CP
Controllable Pitch Propeller [*For ships*] (MCD) .... CPP
Controllable RADAR Target Simulator .... CRTS
Controllable Radar Target Simulator (SAUS) .... CRTS
Controllable Twist Rotor [*Aviation*] .... CTR
Controllable-Displacement-Factor Frequency Changer (DICI) .... CDFFC
Controlled [*Currency exchange rate*] [*British*] C
Controlled .... CONTRLLD
Controlled (IAA) .... CTLD
Controlled (SAUS) .... Ctld
Controlled Acceleration Propulsion (SSD) .... CAP
Controlled Access Area (MCD) .... CAA
Controlled Access System (IAA) .... CAS
Controlled Access to Network Digital Libraries in Europe (TELE) .... CANDLE
Controlled Access Unit [*Computer science*] .... CAU
Controlled Adjustable Rate Preferred Stock (EBF) .... CARPS
Controlled Aerial Delivery System (SAUS) .... CADS
Controlled Air Incinerator (SAUS) .... CAI
Controlled Airspace .... CAS
Controlled Airspace (IAA) .... CTA
Controlled Airspace [*ICAO designator*] (FAAC) .... CTAS
Controlled Alternating Parachute Exit System (PDAA) .... CAPES
Controlled Ambient Facility (AAEL) .... CAF
Controlled American Source [*Military*] (CINC) .... CAS
Controlled Amortization Bond .... CAB
Controlled Approach (IAA) .... CA
Controlled Area Network [*Communication engineering*] .... CAN
Controlled Assembly Parts List [*Aerospace*] (AAG) .... CAPL
Controlled Atmosphere .... CA
Controlled Atmosphere Brazing [*Metallurgy*] .... CAB
Controlled Atmosphere Electron Microscopy .... CAEM
Controlled Atmosphere Packaging .... CAP
Controlled Atmosphere Protected [*Army*] (MCD) .... CONAP
Controlled Attenuator Timer (SAUS) .... CAT
Controlled Avalanche Diode (SAUS) .... CAD
Controlled Avalanche Transistor (IAA) .... CAT
Controlled Avalanche Transit Time [*Electronics*] .... CATT
Controlled Avalanche Transit-Time Triode [*Electronics*] (MED) .... CATT
Controlled Barrier System .... CBS
Controlled Batch Identification (SAUS) .... CBI
Controlled Blip Scan (CET) .... CBS
Controlled Canister Purge [*Automotive engineering*] .... CCP
Controlled Carrier Modulation (KSC) .... CCM
Controlled Carrier Modulation (NAKS) .... ccm
Controlled Circulation [*Newspaper and magazine distribution*] (NTCM) CC
Controlled Circulation Audit [*Name changed to Business Publications Audit of Circulation*] .... CCA
Controlled Clinical Trials (SAUS) .... Control Clin Trials
Controlled Collapse Chip Connection (SAUS) C-4
Controlled Collapse Component Connection [*Electronics*] (AAEL) C4
Controlled Collection Objective (MCD) .... CCO
Controlled Combustion System [*Antipollution device for automobiles*] .... CCS
Controlled Commodity .... COCOM
Controlled Communications Systems [*Chicago, IL*] [*Telecommunications*] (TSSD) .... CCS
Controlled Component Usage File (SAUS) .... CCUF
Controlled COMSEC [*Communications Security*] **Items** CCI
Controlled Configuration Explosive [*Military*] .... CCE
Controlled Cord Traction [*Medicine*] .... CCT
Controlled Current Distribution [*Telecommunications*] (OA) .... CCD
Controlled Current Feedback Transformer (MSA) .... CCFT
Controlled Data Analysis Workshops [*Magnetospheric physics*] .... CDAW
Controlled Date of Separation [*Military*] (AFM) .... CDOS
Controlled Decomposition/Oxidation (AAEL) .... CDO
Controlled Delivery System .... CDS
Controlled Demolition, Inc. (SAUO) .... CDI
Controlled Departure Time [*FAA*] (TAG) .... CDT
Controlled Deployment Specular Reflector [*Army*] (AABC) .... CDSR
Controlled Depth/Rapid Deployment Moored Sweep [*Navy*] (CAAL) .... CD/RDMS
Controlled Digital Simulator .... CODIS
Controlled Direct Injection [*Automotive engineering*] .... CDI
Controlled Dissemination (MCD) .... CD
Controlled Drinker-Control [*Medicine*] (DMAA) .... CD-C
Controlled Drinker-Experimental [*Chemical dependency*] (DAVI) .... CD-E
Controlled Droplet Application (PDAA) .... CDA
Controlled Drug .... CD
Controlled Ductility Forming (SAUS) .... CDF
Controlled Dynamic Range .... CDR
Controlled Ecological Life Support System .... CELSS
Controlled Ecosystem Pollution Experiment [*National Science Foundation project*] .... CEPEX
Controlled Element Computer .... CEC
Controlled Energy Flow Forming .... CEFF
Controlled Energy Relief Valve (MCD) .... CERV
Controlled Environment .... CE
Controlled Environment Agriculture .... CEA
Controlled Environment and Life Support System (ACAE) .... CELS
Controlled Environment and Life Support System (SAUS) .... CELSS
Controlled Environment Facilities .... CEF
Controlled Environment Gravity Tube System (PDAA) .... CEGTS
Controlled Environment Man Hole [*Telecommunications*] (ITD) .... CEMH
Controlled Environment Room [*Agricultural science*] (OA) .... CER
Controlled Environment Testing .... CET
Controlled Environmental Forestry .... CEF
Controlled Environmental System [*NASA*] .... CES
Controlled Environmental Vault (ACRL) .... CEV
Controlled Environments Ltd., Winnipeg, Manitoba [*Library symbol*] [*National Library of Canada*] (NLC) .... MWCE
Controlled Experimental Ecosystem [*Study technique*] .... CEE
Controlled Facility [*Aerospace*] (AAG) .... CF
Controlled Ferro Resonant (SAUS) .... CFR
Controlled Field Actuator [*Computer science*] (NITA) .... CFA
Controlled Firing Area [*Aviation*] (FAAC) .... CFA
Controlled Flash Evaporation .... CFE
Controlled Flight Into Terrain (SAUS) .... CFIT
Controlled Flight Toward Terrain (PDAA) .... CFTT
Controlled Flights into Terrain [*Aviation*] .... CFIT
Controlled Flow .... CONFLOW
Controlled Foods International Ltd. [*Toronto Stock Exchange symbol*] .... CFS
Controlled Force Circulation [*Boilers*] .... CFC
Controlled Foreign Company [*or Corporation*] .... CFC
Controlled Foreign Corporation (SAUO) .... CFC
Controlled Fragmentation (SAA) .... CF
Controlled Fuel Injection [*Engineering*] .... CFI
Controlled Fusion Atomic Data Center [*Department of Energy*] (IID) .... CFADC
Controlled Ground Landing (AAG) .... CGL
Controlled Handling of Internal Executive Functions [*UNIVAC*] .... CHIEF
Controlled Hardening [*Ferrous metallurgy*] .... CH
Controlled Heat & Air Limited (SAUO) .... CHAL
Controlled Helium Atmosphere Plant (PDAA) .... CHAP
Controlled High Flux Dialysis [*Medicine*] (DMAA) .... CHFD
Controlled Humidity (MCD) .... CH
Controlled Hypertension [*Medicine*] .... CH
Controlled Image Base (GEOI) .... CIB
Controlled Impact Demonstration [*FAA, NASA*] .... CID
Controlled Impact Reentry (MCD) .... CIR
Controlled Impulse (MCD) .... CIMP
Controlled Intact Reentry (IAA) .... CIR
Controlled Interceptor Trainer [*Aerospace*] (AAG) .... CIT
Controlled Internal Extension (MCD) .... CIE
Controlled Interval Inspection (MCD) CII
Controlled Ionization CI
Controlled Item CI
Controlled Item Code [*Air Force*] (AFIT) CIC
Controlled Items List CIL
Controlled Large Aperture Wavefront Sampling (MCD) .... CLAWS
Controlled Leakage System (SAA) .... CLS
Controlled Letter Contract Reduction (IEEE) .... CLCR
Controlled Library Environment and Resources (SAUS) .... CLEAR
Controlled Line of Sight (SAUS) .... CLOS
Controlled Low-Strength Material .... CLSM
Controlled Manual (ABAC) .... CM
Controlled Material Evaluation Request (ACAE) .... CMER
Controlled Materials Officer .... CMO
Controlled Materials Plan [*of War Production Board*] [*World War II*] .... CMP
Controlled Materials Plan Regulation (National Production) [*of War Production Board*] [*World War II*] (DLA) .... CMP Reg
Controlled Materials Production [*Nuclear energy*] .... CMP
Controlled Materiel Plan Priority (SAUS) .... CMPP
Controlled Materiels Plan (SAUS) .... CMP
Controlled Materiels Production (SAUS) .... CMP
Controlled Mechanical Ventilation .... CMV
Controlled Medical Assistance Drug List (MELL) .... CMADL
Controlled Minefield [*Navy*] .... CM
Controlled Mission Equipment (MCD) .... CME
Controlled Monitor Interface Calibrator (PDAA) .... CMIC
Controlled Multiple Address Letter (AFM) .... CMAL
Controlled Multispectral Image Base (GEOI) .... CMIB
Controlled Multivibrator .... CMV
Controlled Nucleation Thermochemical Deposition (MCD) .... CNTD
Controlled Object Deck Exploitation (PDAA) .... CODE
Controlled Oral Word Association Test [*Speech and language pathology*] (DAVI) .... COWAT
Controlled Orbital Decay and Input System (DNAB) .... CODIS
Controlled Ovarian Hyperstimulation (SAUS) .... COH
Controlled Overhead Management Performance and Standard System .... COMPASS
Controlled Oxygen Fugacity [*Apparatus*] .... COF
Controlled Partial Rebreathing Anesthesia Method [*Medicine*] (STED) .... CPRAM
Controlled Path System [*Computer science*] .... CPS
Controlled Plasma Glassification [*Of solid waste*] .... CPG
Controlled Precision Oscillator .... CPO
Controlled Process Serum Replacements [*Cell culture*] .... CPSR
Controlled Product Management (ACAE) .... CPM
Controlled Production Planning Officer .... CPPO
Controlled Production Unit [*Project sponsored by the Elder Craftsmen*] .... CPU
Controlled Products Area .... CPA
Controlled Pushdown Automaton (SAUS) .... CPA
Controlled Quality Established (SAUS) .... CONQUEST
Controlled Quick Release .... CQR
Controlled Radial Steering (PDAA) .... CRS

Controlled Radiation [or Reception] Pattern Antenna	CRPA
Controlled Range Air Burst Fuze (RDA)	CRAB
Controlled Range Network (MCD)	CORN
Controlled Recirculation Boiling Water Reactor	CRBR
Controlled Rectifier	CR
Controlled Referral Plan	CRP
Controlled Reflex [Neurology and psychiatry] (DAVI)	CR
Controlled Release [Neurology and psychiatry] (DAVI)	CR
Controlled Release Device (KSC)	CRD
Controlled Release Society (EA)	CRS
Controlled Release Time (DB)	CRT
Controlled Reluctance Eddy Current Generator (PDAA)	CREG
Controlled Rerouting Control (SAUS)	CRC
Controlled Residual Element [Nuclear energy]	CRE
Controlled Response [Neurology and psychiatry] (DAVI)	CR
Controlled Response in Maitland Emergencies	CRIME
Controlled Retracting Injection Port [System for underground coal burning]	CRIP
Controlled Rheology [Plastics technology]	CR
Controlled Rotary Vane [Compressor] [Automotive engineering]	CRV
Controlled Rupture Accuracy (MUGU)	CRA
Controlled Saturation Logic (IAA)	CSL
Controlled Scan Televideo (SAUS)	CSTV
Controlled Short Takeoff and Landing [Acronym used for a type of aircraft]	C-STOL
Controlled Silicon Rectifier [Electronics] (IAA)	CSR
Controlled Slip (SAUS)	CS
Controlled Slip Seconds (VERA)	CSS
Controlled Solder Process (SAUS)	CSP
Controlled Solid Rocket Motors (KSC)	CSRM
Controlled Space [Environmental science] (COE)	CS
Controlled Space-Charge Limited Resistor (SAUS)	CSCLR
Controlled Stock (SAA)	CS
Controlled Store (SAUS)	CS
Controlled Stress [Physiology]	CS
Controlled Substance Analog (STED)	CSA
Controlled Substance Sensing Device (AAGC)	CSSD
Controlled Substances Act [1970] (GFGA)	CSA
Controlled Supply Rate (AABC)	CSR
Controlled Surface Porosity (SAUS)	CSP
Controlled Surface Process (SAUS)	CSP
Controlled Swirl Scavenging [Automotive engine design]	CSS
Controlled Switch (SAUS)	CS
Controlled Takeoff and Landing (MCD)	CTOL
Controlled Target (SAUS)	CT
Controlled Temperature	CT
Controlled Temperature Bath	CTB
Controlled Temperature Furnace	CTF
Controlled Temperature Profile [Vapor trap] [Nuclear energy] (NRCH)	CTP
Controlled Term [Online database field identifier]	CT
Controlled Thermal Severity (OA)	CTS
Controlled Thermolytic Dissociation	CTD
Controlled Thermonuclear Fusion	CTF
Controlled Thermonuclear Fusion	CTNF
Controlled Thermonuclear Reaction [or Reactor] [National Institute of Standards and Technology]	CTR
Controlled Thermonuclear Research	CTR
Controlled Thrust Assembly (NASA)	CTA
Controlled Time of Arrival [FAA] (TAG)	CTA
Controlled Tornado Research (MCD)	CTR
Controlled Tuning Fork Oscillator	CTFO
Controlled Unmanned Recovery Vehicle (SAUS)	CURV
Controlled Variable [Psychology] (BARN)	CV
Controlled Variable Time [Fuze] (NVT)	CVT
Controlled Ventilation [Automotive engineering]	CV
Controlled Visual Flight	CVF
Controlled Visual Flight Rules [Military]	CVFR
Controlled Visual Rules [FAA]	CVR
Controlled Vortex Combustion Chamber (ROAS)	CVCC
Controlled Work Area (MCD)	CWA
Controlled Yeast Lysate	CYL
Controlled-Circulation [Boiler]	C/C
Controlled-Pore Ceramic [Organic chemistry]	CPC
Controlled-Pore Glass [Corning]	CPG
Controlled-Potential Coulometer [Nuclear energy] (NRCH)	CPC
Controlled-Potential Electrolysis	CPE
Controlled-Release Hydrocodone [An analgesic] [Pennwalt Corp.]	CRHC
Controlled-Release Tablet Corrected [Medicine] (MELL)	CRT
Controlled-Slip Differentials (IEEE)	CSD
Controlled-Source Audiofrequency Megnetotelllurics [Geophysics]	CSAMT
Controller (ECII)	C
Controller	CNTLR
Controller (NASA)	CNTRL
Controller	CNTRLLR
Controller (AFM)	CON
Controller (KSC)	CONT
Controller (TBD)	Cont
Controller (DD)	cont
Controller (ADWA)	Contr
Controller (PROS)	contr
Controller [Computer hardware] (NITA)	CONTROL
Controller (SAUS)	Ctrlr
Controller Access System (SAUS)	CAS
Controller Active State (IAA)	CACS
Controller Adaptor Unit [Computer science] (NITA)	CAU

Controller Administration Service, Europe [Air Force]	CASEUR
Controller and Auditor General	CAG
Controller & Communications Workstation (SAUS)	CCW
Controller Area Network (SAUO)	CAN
Controller Automated Spacing Aid [FAA] (TAG)	CASA
Controller Central Operating Authority (NATG)	CCOA
Controller Checkout Console (NASA)	CCC
Controller Checkout Console (NAKS)	ccc
Controller Decision Evaluation	CODE
Controller Defence Communications Network [Navy] [British]	CDCN
Controller Error (AFM)	CONE
Controller General, Inspection Services (SAUO)	CGIS
Controller General of Civil Aviation [British]	CGCA
Controller General of Economy [Military] [British]	CGE
Controller General of Machine Tools [Ministry of Supply] [British]	CGMT
Controller General of Munitions Production [Ministry of Supply] [British]	CGMP
Controller Input Test Equipment	CITE
Controller Interface Assembly (NAKS)	CIA
Controller Interface Unit (MCD)	CIU
Controller Military Accounts [British military] (DMA)	CMA
Controller of Accounts	CA
Controller of Aircraft (SAUS)	CA
Controller of American Supplies and Repair [Ministry of Aircraft Production] [British] [World War II]	CASR
Controller of Chemical Defence Department [Ministry of Supply] [British]	CCDD
Controller of Chemical Research and Development [Ministry of Supply] [British]	CCRD
Controller of Communication Services (SAUS)	CCS
Controller of Communications [RAF] [British]	C of C
Controller of Communications Equipment Overseas [British]	CCEO
Controller of Engineering and Equipment (SAUS)	CEE
Controller of Experimental Building Development (SAUS)	CEBD
Controller of Experimental Building Development (SAUO)	CEBD
Controller of Guided Weapons and Electronics (SAUS)	CGWL
Controller of Labour Allocation Supply (SAUO)	CLAS
Controller of Merchant Shipbuilding and Repair (SAUO)	CMSR
Controller of Merchant Shipbuilding and Repairs [Navy] [British]	CMSR
Controller of Military Accounts (SAUO)	CMA
Controller of Military Accounts (SAUS)	CMA
Controller of Office Services and Supplies (SAUS)	COSS
Controller of Ordnance (SAUS)	COO
Controller of Ordnance Accounting (SAUS)	COA
Controller of Ordnance Accounting (SAUO)	COA
Controller of Ordnance Services (SAUO)	COS
Controller of Ordnance Services (SAUS)	COS
Controller of Overseas Supplies (SAUS)	COS
Controller of Overseas Supplies (SAUO)	COS
Controller of Physical Research and Signals Development [Ministry of Supply] [British]	CPRSD
Controller of Projectile Development [Ministry of Supply] [British] [World War II]	CPD
Controller of Research and Development [Ministry of Aircraft Production] [British]	CRD
Controller of Research and Development Establishments and Research [British] (RDA)	CER
Controller of Royal Ordnance Factories (SAUO)	CROF
Controller of Stamps and Registrar of Companies (SAUO)	CSRC
Controller of the Navy (SAUS)	CofN
Controller of the Navy [British]	C of N
Controller Oriented Processor Series [Computer science] (PDAA)	COPS
Controller Overload Prediction Technique (PDAA)	COPTEC
Controller Pilot Datalink Communications (GAVI)	CPDLC
Controller Processor Signal (CAAL)	CPS
Controller Proficiency Unit (SAUS)	CPU
Controller Supply Rate (DOMA)	CSR
Controller Unit (SAUO)	CU
Controllerate Royal Ordnance Factories (PDAA)	CROF
Controller/Attitude-Direct Electronics (NASA)	CADE
Controller/Director Information File (AFM)	CDIF
Controller/Evaluator Group [Environmental science] (COE)	CEG
Controllers Council (EA)	CC
Controllers Institute of America [Later, FEI]	CIA
Controllers Institute Research Foundation (SAUO)	CIRF
Controllers' Operations and Procedures Committee (FAAC)	COPCOM
Controlling Directing Staff	DISCONSTAFF
Controlling Monitor Data Base System (SAUS)	COMDBS
Control-Oriented Computer (MCD)	CORC
Control-Oriented Language [Computer science]	COL
Control-Oriented Language [Computer science] (IEEE)	COOL
Control-Oriented Processor [Computer science] (PDAA)	COP
Controls [JETDS nomenclature] [Military] (CET)	C
Controls and Display Equipment (SAUS)	CDE
Controls and Displays (ACAE)	CD
Controls and Displays Subsystem (SAUS)	C&DS
Controls and Displays System [or Subsystem] [Aerospace]	C & DS
Controls and Displays Test Station (ACAE)	CDTS
Controls and Monitoring Processor (SAUS)	CAMP
Controls and Panel Arrangement by Logical Evaluation (PDAA)	CAPABLE
Controls Assembly Set	CAS
Controls Astrophysics Structures Experiment in Space (SAUS)	CASES
Controls Automation System (SAUS)	CAS
Controls Company of America (SAUO)	CC
Controls Company of America (SAUO)	CTC
Controls for Environmental Pollution, Inc. (EFIS)	CFEP
Controls Management (or Manufacturing) Information System (SAUS)	CMIS

Controls Mock-Up .... CMU
Controls-Displays-Doppler Filter Test Station (ACAE) .... CDDFTS
Controls-Instruments-Gas-Flaps-Trim-Prop-Run-up (SAUS) .... C-I-G-F-T-P-R
Controls-Structures Interactions (SAUS) .... CSI
Controversiae [*of Seneca the Elder*] [*Classical studies*] (OCD) .... Controv
Controversiarum Excerpta [*of Seneca the Elder*] [*Classical studies*] (OCD) .... Con Ex
Controversy (ROG) .... CONTROV
Controverted Elections Judges [*England*] (DLA) .... Cont El
Contruction Industry Council of California (SAUO) CICC
Contundere [*To Be Bruised, Pounded*] [*Pharmacy*] (ROG) .... CONTUND
Contusus [*Bruised*] [*Medicine*] C
Contusus [*Bruised*] [*Medicine*] .... CONT
Contusus [*Bruised*] [*Medicine*] .... CONTUS
Conurbation (SAUS) .... Conurb
Conurbation Transport Authority .... CTA
Conurbations (SAUS) .... Conurbs
CONUS [*Continental United States*] **Air Defense Effectiveness Model** (MCD) .... CADEM
CONUS [*Continental United States*] **Air Defense Engagement Simulation** .... CADENS
CONUS [*Continental United States*] **Air Defense Modernization** .... CADM
CONUS [*Continental United States*] **Airborne Reconnaissance for Damage Assessment** (MCD) .... CARDA
CONUS [*Continental United States*] **and Overseas Microfilm User Tests** .... COMUT
CONUS [*Continental United States*] **Army** (MCD) .... CONUSA
CONUS [*Continental United States*] **Army Installation Management Study** .... CAIMS
Conus Arteriosus [*Medicine*] (MELL) .... CA
Conus Branch [*Anatomy*] .... CB
CONUS [*Continental United States*] **Depot Equipment** [*Military*] .... CDE
CONUS Freight Management (SAUS) .... CFM
CONUS [*Continental United States*] **Freight Management System** [*DoD*] .... CFM
CONUS [*Continental United States*] **Ground Station** (MCD) .... CGS
CONUS Ground Station (SAUO) .... CGS
CONUS [*Continental United States*] **Installation Logistics Support** (MCD) .... COILS
CONUS [*Continental United States*] **Installation Maintenance Support** (MCD) .... COIMS
CONUS [*Continental United States*] **Installation Supply Support** (MCD) .... COISS
CONUS [*Continental United States*] **Installation Transportation System** (MCD) .... COITS
Conus Medullaris (MELL) .... CM
CONUS [*Continental United States*] **Meteorological Data System** [*or Distribution*] (MCD) .... COMEDS
CONUS Meteorological Environmental Distribution System (SAUO) .... COMEDS
CONUS [*Continental United States*] **Net Depot Method** .... CND
CONUS [*Continental United States*] **Replacement Center** [*Military*] (GFGA) .... CRC
CONUS [*Continental United States*] **Sustaining Increment** [*Army*] (AABC) .... CSI
CONUS Tactical Communications Team Conference (SAUO) .... CONTACCT
CONUS [*Continental United States*] **Telephone Modernization Program** .... CTMP
CONVAIR [*Consolidated-Vultee Aircraft Corp.*] **Astronautics Corp. Astronautics Corp.** [*Later, General Dynamics Corp.*] (AAG) .... CVA
Convair Automatic Test Equipment (SAUS) .... CATE
CONVAIR [*Consolidated-Vultee Aircraft Corp.*] **Daingerfield** [*Later, General Dynamics/Daingerfield*] (AAG) .... C-D
CONVAIR [*Consolidated-Vultee Aircraft Corp.*] **Fort Worth** [*Later, General Dynamics/Fort Worth*] (AAG) .... CFW
CONVAIR [*Consolidated-Vultee Aircraft Corp.; later, General Dynamics Corp.*] **Government-Owned Facilities and Equipment** (AAG) .... CGOFE
Convalescence [*Medicine*] (DAVI) .... conv
Convalescent [*Medicine*] (AFM) .... CONV
Convalescent (SAUS) .... Conv
Convalescent [*Medicine*] (ROG) .... CONVAL
Convalescent [*Medicine*] (ROG) .... CONVALESC
Convalescent and Additional Recovery Expenses Scheme (SAUS) .... CARE Scheme
Convalescent and Rehabilitation [*Military*] .... C & R
Convalescent Antidote for Nerve Agent (DOMA) .... CANA
Convalescent Camp (SAUO) .... Con Cp
Convalescent Camp (SAUS) CvC
Convalescent Camp [*Military*] CVC
Convalescent Depot (SAUS) .... CD
Convalescent Depot (SAUO) .... CD
Convalescent Depot (SAUO) .... Conv Dep
Convalescent Growing Nursery (MEDA) .... CGN
Convalescent Hospital (DAVI) .... CH
Convalescent Hospital (DAVI) .... Conv Hosp
Convalescent Hospital for Children, Library, Rochester (SAUS) .... VQF
Convalescent Status [*Medicine*] .... CS
Convalescent Training Depot (NATG) .... CTD
Convalescent Unit [*of a hospital*] .... CU
Convection (ADA) C
Convection .... CNV
Convection (MSA) .... CONVN
Convection and Moisture Experiment (SAUS) .... CAMEX
Convection and Precipitation/ Electrification (SAUS) .... CaPE
Convection and Precipitation/Experiment (SAUS) .... CaPE
Convection Instability of the Second Kind (SAUS) .... CISK
Convection Loss Cone (MCD) CLC
Convection Microthermal Oven .... CMT
Convection Storms: Evolution and Modification (SAUS) .... COSTEM
Convection Suppression Device [*for energy collectors*] .... CSD
Convection-Induced Turbulence (SAUS) .... CIT
Convective (FAAC) .... CNVTV
Convective Airspace Guidance (SAUS) .... CAG
Convective and Precipitation/Electrification [*Experiment*] [*Marine science*] (OSRA) .... CaPE
Convective Available Potential Energy .... CAPE
Convective Boundary Layer [*Marine science*] (OSRA) .... CBL
Convective Cloud (SAUS) CC
Convective Combustion (MCD) CC
Convective Condensation Level [*Meteorology*] CCL
Convective Heat Transfer .... CHT
Convective Heating and Ablation Program (SAUS) .... CHAP
Convective Heating and Ablative Program [*Army*] .... CHAP
Convective Infrared Satellite Technique (SAUS) .... CIST
Convective Inhibition (ARMP) .... CIN
Convective Initiation and Downburst Experiment (SAUS) .... CINDE
Convective Instability Base (PDAA) .... CIB
Convective Instability Top (PDAA) .... CIT
Convective Internal Boundary Layer (GFGA) .... CIBL
Convective Meteorology Section (SAUS) .... CMS
Convective precipitation over Land (SAUS) CL
Convective Precipitation Over Land (ARMP) CL
Convective Precipitation Over Water (ARMP) .... CW
Convective Scale (SAUS) .... D Scale
Convective Storms Division [*National Center for Atmospheric Research*] .... CSD
Convective Transport by Implicit Bouyant Elements (SAUS) .... CONTRIBE
Convector (DAC) .... Conv
Convector (MSA) .... CONVR
Convector Enclosure (SAUS) .... CONVENCL
Convectron-Microsyn Erection Circuit (SAA) .... CMEC
Convenant, Condition, and Restriction [*Business term*] (EMRF) .... CC & R
Convene (AABC) .... CVN
Convenience (MSA) .... CNVC
Convenience (ADA) .... CON
Convenience (TBD) .... Conv
Convenience .... CONV
Convenience .... CONVEN
Convenience Manufacturing Corp. (EFIS) .... CMC
Convenience of the Government .... C of G
Convenience of the Government .... COG
Convenience Store .... C-STORE
Convenience Store (WDMC) .... c-store
Convenience Store Association of Michigan (SRA) .... CSAM
Convenience, Value, Service .... CVS
Convenient .... CONV
Convenient (AABC) .... CONVN
Convenient .... CONVNT
Convenient (ROG) .... CONVT
Convenient Automotive Services Institute (EA) .... CASI
Convening Authority .... CA
Convenor .... Cvnr
Convent .... CNVNT
Convent .... CONV
Convent General of the Knights York Cross of Honour (EA) .... KYCH
Convent of Immaculate Conception Sisters of St. Benedict, Ferdinand, IN [*OCLC symbol*] (OCLC) XIC
Convent of the Holy Rood [*British*] (BI) .... CHR
Convention .... CNVNTN
Convention (NTIO) .... conv
Convention [*or Conventional*] .... CONV
Convention Africaine [*African Covenant*] .... CA
Convention and Visitors Bureau .... C & VB
Convention and Visitors Bureau (TRID) .... CVB
Convention Democratic Party [*Liberia*] [*Political party*] (EY) .... CDP
Convention des Institutions Republicaines [*Convention of Republican Institutions*] [*France*] [*Political party*] (PPE) .... CIR
Convention Europeenne de la Construction Metallique [*EC*] (ECED) .... CECM
Convention for Safe Containers (MCD) .... CSC
Convention for the Conservation of Antarctic Marine Living Resources (SAUS) .... CCAMLR
Convention for the Conservation of Antarctic Seals [*Australia*] .... CCAS
Convention for the Prevention of Marine Pollution from Ships (SAUS) .... MARPOL
Convention for the Prevention of Pollution of the Sea by Oil (SAUS) .... OILPOL
Convention for the Provention of Pollution of the Sea by Oil (SAUS) .... OILPOL
Convention for/on International Trade in Endangered Species of Wild Fauna and Flora (SAUO) .... CITES
Convention II (EA) CII
Convention Information System (IAA) .... CIS
Convention Internationale Concernant le Transport des Marchandises par Chemins de Fer [*International Convention Concerning the Carriage of Goods by Rail*] .... CIM
Convention Internationale Concernant le Transport des Voyageurs et des Bagages par Chemins de Fer [*International Convention Concerning the Carriage of Passengers and Luggage by Rail*] CIV
Convention Liaison Council (EA) CLC
Convention Liberale [*Cameroon*] [*Political party*] (EY) CL
Convention Magazine [*Generic term for a publication covering science-fiction fans' conventions*] .... CONZINE
Convention Nationale des Patriotes Progressistes-Parti Social-Democrate [*Burkina Faso*] [*Political party*] (EY) .... CNPP-PSD
Convention of American Instructors of the Deaf (EA) .... CAID
Convention of Dublin [*Freemasonry*] (ROG) .... C of D
Convention of Edinburgh [*Freemasonry*] (ROG) .... C of E
Convention of London [*Freemasonry*] (ROG) .... C of L
Convention of National Societies of Electrical Engineers of Western Europe (SAUO) .... CNSEE

Convention of National Societies of Electrical Engineers of Western Europe (EAIO) .... EUREL
Convention of Royal Burghs (SAUO) .... CRB
Convention of Scottish Local Authorities .... CoSLA
Convention of Scottish Local Authorities (EAIO) .... COSLA
Convention of the Estates of Scotland [A publication] (DLA) .... Conv Est
Convention of the Royal Burghs of Scotland (SAUO) .... CRBS
Convention of York [Freemasonry] (ROG) .... CY
Convention on a Code of Conduct for Liner Conferences (SAUS) .... UNCTAD Code
Convention on Biological Diversity [1992] [United Nations] [Marine science] (OSRA) .... CBD
Convention on Civil Liability for Oil Pollution Damage (DS) CLC
Convention on Early Notification of a Nuclear Accident (SAUO) .... CENNA
Convention on Facilitation of International Maritime Traffic (SAUO) .... FAL
Convention on International Trade in Endangered Species [Of wild fauna and flora] .... CITES
Convention on Limitation of Liability for Maritime Claims (SAUS) .... LLMC
Convention on Nature Protection and Wildlife Preservation (COE) .... CNPWP
Convention on the conservation of European wildlife and natural habitats (SAUO) .... Berne Convention
Convention on the Conservation of Migratory Species of Wild Animals (SAUO) .... CMS
Convention on the Conservation of Migratory Species of Wild Animals (ASF) .... CMSWA
Convention on the Continental Shelf (NOAA) .... CCS
Convention on the Contract for the International Carriage of Goods by Road [Geneva] [19 May 1956] (DLA) .... CMR
Convention on the contract for the international carriage of passengers and luggage by inland waterway (SAUO) .... CVN
Convention on the contract for the international carriage of passengers and luggage by road (SAUO) .... CVR
Convention on the International regulations for preventing collisions at sea (SAUO) .... COLREG
Convention on the Prevention of Marine Pollution (COE) .... CPMPDW
Convention on the Prevention of Marine Pollution by Dumping of Wastes and other Matter (SAUS) LC
Convention on the Prohibition of Military or any other Hostile use of Environmental Modification Techniques (SAUO) .... ENMOD
Convention on the protection of the marine environment of the Baltic Sea area (SAUO) .... Helsinki Convention
Convention on the Regulation of Antarctic Mineral Resource Activities (GNE) .... CRAMRA
Convention on the Territorial Sea and the Contiguous Zone (COE) .... CTSCZ
Convention on Wetlands of International Importance (SAUS) .... RAMSAR
Convention on Wetlands of International Importance Especially As Waterfowl Habitat (SAUS) .... Wetlands
Convention on Wetlands of International Importance, Especially as Waterfowl Habitat, Ramsar (SAUS) .... Ramsar
Convention on Wetlands of International Importance Especially as Waterfowl Habitats (SAUS) .... RAMSAR
Convention People's Party [1949-1966] [Ghana] .... CPP
Convention Record (SAUS) .... Conv Rec
Convention relating to the Limitation of the liability of owners of inland Navigation vessels (SAUO) .... CLN
Convention Relative au Contrat de Transport de Marchandises en Navigation Interieure [Convention on the Carriage of Goods by Inland Waterways] .... CMN
Convention Services Manager .... CSM
Conventional (SAUS) .... Cnv
Conventional .... CO
Conventional (SAUO) .... CONV
Conventional (AFM) .... CONVL
Conventional CV
Conventional (MSA) .... CVNTL
Conventional (SAUS) .... Cvntl
Conventional Addressing Machine (SAUS) .... CAM
Conventional Air Warfare Exercise (DNAB) .... CAWEX
Conventional Airfield Attack Missile (MCD) .... CAAM
Conventional Airfield Attack Munitions [Army] .... CAM
Conventional Airfield Attack System [Army] .... CAAS
Conventional Air-Launched Cruise Missile (MILB) .... CALCM
Conventional Alloy (OA) .... CA
Conventional Ammunition Integrated Management System .... CAIMS
Conventional Ammunition Integrated Management System (DNAB) .... CLAIMS
Conventional Ammunition Maintenance, Preservation, and Packaging Set (MCD) .... CAMPPS
Conventional Ammunition Working Capital Fund [DoD] .... CAWCF
Conventional and Alternative Transportation Systems Laboratory [University of Florida] [Research center] (RCD) .... CATS
Conventional Armaments Plan (SAUS) .... CAP
Conventional Armaments Planning System (DOMA) .... CAPS
Conventional Armed Forces and Conventional Armaments .... CAFCA
Conventional Armed Forces in Europe (ECON) .... CAFE
Conventional Armed Forces in Europe (SAUO) .... CFE
Conventional Arms Transfers .... CAT
Conventional Attack Missile (SAUS) .... CAM
Conventional, Bomb Triple Ejector (SAUS) .... CBTE
Conventional Boom Sprayer .... CBS
Conventional Buoy Mooring (DS) .... CBM
Conventional Catamaran (PDAA) .... CONCAT
Conventional Circuit Analysis Program (DNAB) .... CCAP
Conventional Color (OA) CC
Conventional Combustion Environmental Assessment [Environmental Protection Agency] (GFGA) .... CCEA

Conventional Core-Barrel Sampling (ABAC) .... CCBS
Conventional Cruise Missile (ACAE) .... CCM
Conventional Data Terrain Unit Cartridge (SAUO) .... CDTUC
Conventional Defense Improvements (DOMA) .... CDI
Conventional Defense Initiatives (SAUO) .... CDI
Conventional Defense Technology (SAUS) .... CDT
Conventional Diesel-Electric Submarine (SAUS) .... SSK
Conventional District [Church of England] .... CD
Conventional Engine Anti-Pollution System [Automotive engineering] .... CEAPS
Conventional Force Data Base [Model] .... CFDB
Conventional Forces (ACAE) .... CF
Conventional Forces Data Base (SAUS) .... CFDB
Conventional Forces in Europe [Military] .... CFE
Conventional Friend Virus .... CFV
Conventional Geometry Smart Projectile .... CGSP
Conventional Grain-Oriented Product (MCD) .... CGO
Conventional Inch of Water (SAUS) inH2O
Conventional Instruction (RDA) CI
Conventional Insulin Therapy (MELL) .... CIT
Conventional Insulin Treatment [Medicine] .... CIT
Conventional International Origin .... CIO
Conventional Land Attack Tomahawk Missile (MCD) .... CLAT
Conventional Landing (MCD) CL
Conventional Launch Sea Wolf (SAUS) .... CLSW
Conventional Mechanical Ventilation .... CMV
Conventional Military Fuels (RDA) .... CMF
Conventional Mission Planning Concept of Operations (SAUO) .... CMPCO
Conventional Mortgage Pass-Through Security (EBF) .... Connie Mac
Conventional Mortgage-Backed Security .... CMBS
Conventional Munition Disposal (PDAA) .... CMD
Conventional Munitions Master Plan (DOMA) .... CMMP
Conventional Munitions System [Military] .... CMS
Conventional Nonnuclear Weapons (SAUS) .... CNNR
Conventional Old Oil Prices .... COOP
Conventional Ordnance Release Computer (NG) .... CORC
Conventional Ordnance Status System (MCD) .... COSS
Conventional Oxidation Catalysis [of gasoline engine exhausts] .... COC
Conventional Polyethylene .... CPE
Conventional Solvent Extraction [Separation science and technology] .... CSX
Conventional Spin Hamiltonian (PDAA) .... CSH
Conventional Stability Talks [Arms control] .... CST
Conventional Standoff Capability (ACAE) .... CSC
Conventional Standoff Weapon .... CSW
Conventional Standoff Weapon System (ACAE) .... CSWS
Conventional System [Indexing] (NITA) .... CS
Conventional Systems Committee [DoD] (DOMA) .... CSC
Conventional Tactical Air Model (MCD) .... CONTACA
Conventional Takeoff [Aviation] (NATG) .... CTO
Conventional Take-off and Landing [Aircraft] .... CTOL
Conventional Terrestrial System (SAUO) .... CTS
Conventional Therapy [Medicine] .... CT
Conventional Tillage [Agroecosystem] .... CT
Conventional Transmission Electron Microscopy (SAUS) .... CTEM
Conventional Vehicle [Environmental science] CV
Conventional Ventilation [Medicine] CV
Conventional [Non-Nuclear] War Capability (AAG) .... CWC
Conventional Weapon Index (MCD) .... CWI
Conventional Weapon Technical Proficiency Inspection [Military] (CAAL) .... CTPI
Conventional Weapons Loading Exercise [Navy] (ANA) .... CONVWEPS LOADEX
Conventional Weapons Tactical Proficiency Inspection [Navy] (DOMA) .... CWTPI
Conventional Weapons Technology (MCD) .... CWT
Conventional Weighted Least Square .... CWLS
Conventional Wisdom [Professional political opinion] .... CW
Conventional Wisdom Watch [Newsweek Magazine] .... CW
Conventionally Armed Stand-Off Missile (SAUS) .... CASOM
Conventionally Armed Stand-Off Missiles (MILB) .... CASM
Conventionally Fueled Vehicle [Automotive engineering] .... CFV
Conventionally Refined Carrageenan [Food grade] .... CRC
Conventional-Transmission Electron Microscope .... CEM
Conventional-Transmission Electron Microscope .... CTEM
Conventions for the protection of the marine environment of the North-East Atlantic (SAUS) .... OSPENEA
Conventions, Meetings, Incentive Travel [Of CMI World, a publication aimed at those markets] .... CMI
Conventions Systems Committee (SAUS) .... CSC
Convention-Seminar Cassettes [Commercial firm] .... CSC
Conventry Health Care [NASDAQ symbol] [Formerly, Coventry Corp.] .... CVTY
Conventual (TOCD) .... conu
Conventual (ADWA) .... Conv
Conventual Franciscans (TOCD) .... OFMConv
Conventual Franciscans, Friars Minor (TOCD) .... ofm
Conventures Ltd. [Toronto Stock Exchange symbol] .... CVY
Converge (FAAC) .... CNVG
Convergence (IAA) .... CONV
Convergence [Medicine] (DMAA) .... converg
Convergence (MSA) .... CONVG
convergence (SAUS) CV
Convergence Insufficiency (SAUS) CI
Convergence Source-Image Distortion [Crystal] .... CSID
Convergence Sublayer [Electronics] (ACRL) .... CS
Convergence Sublayer Indication (VERA) .... CSI
Convergence Sublayer Protocol Data Unit [Computer science] (VERA) .... CSPDU
Convergence Zone [Military] (NVT) .... CZ
Convergence Zone Propagation [Military] .... CZP
Convergence Zone Range [Military] (CAAL) .... CZR

Convergence Zone Resolution Pattern [*Military*] (CAAL) ... CZRP
Convergence Zone Width [*Military*] (CAAL) ... CZW
Convergencia Democratica [*Democratic Convergence*] [*El Salvador*] [*Political party*] (EY) ... CD
Convergencia Democratica de Catalunya [*Democratic Convergence of Catalonia*] [*Spain*] [*Political party*] (PPE) ... CDC
Convergencia Democratica en Uruguay [*Democratic Convergence in Uruguay*] (PD) ... CDU
Convergencia i Unio [*Convergence and Union*] [*Spain*] [*Political party*] (PPE) ... CiU
Convergent (SAUS) ... Conv
Convergent Beam Diffraction ... CBD
Convergent Beam Electron Diffraction [*Analytical technique*] ... CBED
Convergent Communications [*NASDAQ symbol*] (SG) ... CONV
Convergent Exhaust Nozzle Control (MCD) ... CENC
Convergent Force Field [*Neuromechanics*] ... CFF
Convergent Stereoscopic [*Photography*] ... CS
Convergent Strabismus [*Ophthalmology*] (DAVI) ... conv strab
Convergent Technologies Expo [*Publications and Communications, Inc.*] (TSPED) ... CT
Convergent Technologies Operating System [*Computer science*] ... CTOS
Convergent-Divergent (SAUS) ... C-D
Convergent-Divergent Nozzle ... CDN
Converging Approach Standards Technical Working Group [*FAA*] (TAG) ... CASTWG
Converging Guide Accelerator (MCD) ... CGA
Converging Input, Converging Output (SAUS) ... CICO
Converging Runway Display Aid [*FAA*] (TAG) ... CRDA
Converging-Diverging (MCD) ... CD
Convergys Corp. [*NYSE symbol*] (SG) ... CVG
Conversation (AABC) ... CON
Conversation ... CONV
Conversation (ROG) ... CONVERS
Conversation Control Record (SAUS) ... CCR
Conversation Factor [*Computer science*] ... CF
Conversation Impossible (SAUS) ... CI
Conversation of Serial Records Program (SAUS) ... CONSER Program
Conversation Specifications and Work Requirements (DNAB) ... CSWR
Conversation System with On-Line Remote Terminals (SAUS) ... CONSORT
Conversational Algebraic Language [*Adaptation of JOSS language*] [*Computer science*] ... CAL
Conversational Analyzer and Drafting System (PDAA) ... CADS
Conversational and Interactive Project Evaluation and Control System [*IBM Corp.*] ... CIPREC
Conversational and Service Terminal (SAUS) ... CASTER
Conversational Circuit Analysis Program [*Computer science*] (PDAA) ... CONCAP
Conversational Communication Access Method ... CCAM
Conversational Compiling System [*Xerox Corp.*] (IEEE) ... CCS
Conversational Computation Project (SAUS) ... Concomp
Conversational Computer Information and Statistical System (SAUS) ... CCISS
Conversational Computer Statistical System (PDAA) ... CCSS
Conversational Data Entry System (SAUS) ... CDES
Conversational Design Information Network (SAUS) ... CODINE
Conversational English ... CE
Conversational Extensible Language [*Computer science*] (CSR) ... CEL
Conversational File Information Retrieval and Management System [*Computer science*] (MCD) ... CONFIRM
Conversational FORTRAN (SAUS) ... CFOR
Conversational Graphical Programming Language (PDAA) ... CGPL
Conversational Hypertext Access Technology (SAUS) ... CHAT
Conversational Interactive Digital/Analog Simulator [*IBM Corp.*] (IEEE) ... CIDAS
Conversational Job Facility (SAUS) ... CJF
Conversational Job Language (SAUS) ... CJL
Conversational Language for Input/Output [*Computer science*] ... CLIO
Conversational Language for Interactive Computing ... CLIC
Conversational Language Programming System (SAUS) ... COLAPS
Conversational Macro Package (PDAA) ... COMAP
Conversational Mode Terminal [*Friden, Inc.*] (IEEE) ... CMT
Conversational Modeling Language [*Computer science*] ... CML
Conversational Monitor System [*IBM Corp.*] [*Computer science*] ... CMS
Conversational On-Line Real-Time Algorithm Definition [*Computer science*] (MHDB) ... CONRAD
Conversational On-Line Storage and Retrieval [*Computer science*] (MHDB) ... COSTAR
Conversational Parts Programming Language [*Computer science*] (IEEE) ... CAPT
Conversational Planning Language (SAUS) ... CPL
Conversational Problem Solver (PDAA) ... COPS
Conversational Program Module [*Fujitsu Ltd.*] [*Japan*] ... CPM
Conversational Programming Language [*High-level language*] [*Digital Equipment Corp.*] [*Computer science*] ... CPL
Conversational Programming System [*Computer science*] ... CPS
Conversational Remote Batch Entry [*Computer science*] ... CRBE
Conversational Remote Job Entry [*Computer science*] ... CRJE
Conversational Software System [*National CSS, Inc.*] ... CSS
Conversational Statistical Analysis (MCD) ... COSAN
Conversational System (CIST) ... CVS
Conversational System with On-Line Remote Terminals [*Computer science*] (IEEE) ... CONSORT
Conversational Terminal System [*Computer science*] (BUR) ... CTS
Conversational Terminal System European Laboratories (SAUS) ... CTSEL
Conversational Time-Sharing [*Computer science*] (IEEE) ... CTS
Conversational Traffic Analysis (MCD) ... COTRAN
Conversational Utility Program for Information Display (PDAA) ... CUPID
Conversational Voice [*Medicine*] ... CV
Conversazione [*Conversation*] [*Italian*] (ROG) ... CONVERS
Converse ... CNV
Converse ... CONVRS
Converse College (GAGS) ... Converse C
Converse College, Spartanburg, SC [*OCLC symbol*] (OCLC) ... SCO
Converse College, Spartanburg, SC [*Library symbol*] [*Library of Congress*] (LCLS) ... ScSpC
Converse County Library, Douglas, WY [*Library symbol*] [*Library of Congress*] (LCLS) ... WyDo
Converse, Inc. [*Associated Press*] (SAG) ... Converse
Converse, Inc. [*NYSE symbol*] (SAG) ... CVE
Converse Jackson Township Public Library, Converse, IN [*Library symbol*] [*Library of Congress*] (LCLS) ... InCon
Conversion ... CNVRSN
Conversion (FAAC) ... CNVSN
Conversion ... CONV
Conversion (ROG) ... CONVERSN
Conversion (MSA) ... CVRSN
Conversion [*Legal shorthand*] (LWAP) ... CVSN
Conversion Adjustment Factor ... CAF
Conversion Aids Programming System (SAUS) ... CAPS
Conversion, Alteration, and Repair [*Navy*] ... CAR
Conversion and Check Limit (IAA) ... CCL
Conversion and Recording Equipment (MCD) ... CARE
Conversion Angle (SAUS) ... CA
Conversion Code (SAUS) ... CC
Conversion Complete (IAA) ... CCMP
Conversion Computer Unit ... CCU
Conversion Control Board (SAUO) ... CCB
Conversion Control Officer [*Army*] ... CCO
Conversion Electron Mossbauer Spectroscopy ... CEMS
Conversion Facility (SAUS) ... CF
Conversion Factor (MCD) ... CF
Conversion Factor ... CvF
Conversion for Reclaiming Earth in the Americas [*An association*] ... CREA
Conversion in Lieu of Procurement [*Military*] ... CILOP
Conversion in Place [*Aerospace*] (AAG) ... CIP
Conversion Industries, Inc. [*AMEX symbol*] (SPSG) ... CVD
Conversion Industries, Inc. [*Vancouver Stock Exchange symbol*] ... CVE
Conversion Kit (MCD) ... CK
Conversion Loss ... CL
Conversion Master Plan (CAAL) ... CMP
Conversion Matrix (SAUS) ... CM
Conversion, Memory and Fault Indication (SAUS) ... C/MFI
Conversion, Memory, and Fault Indication [*Telecommunications*] (TEL) ... C/MFI
Conversion of Production System [*Engineering Index, Inc.*] ... COPS
Conversion of Range Telemetry Systems (MCD) ... CORTS
Conversion of Serials (MCD) ... CONSER
Conversion of Serials Project [*Database project*] (NITA) ... CONSER
Conversion of the Federal Wage System (SAUS) ... CFWS
Conversion Operation (SAUS) ... CO
Conversion Operation Code (SAUS) ... COC
Conversion Process Controller System ... CPCS
Conversion Program System (NRCH) ... CPS
Conversion Programmer's Guide ... CPG
Conversion Ratio [*Endocrinology*] (DAVI) ... CR
Conversion Result Register (IAA) ... CRR
Conversion Routine (SAUS) ... CR
Conversion Tech Intl. [*NASDAQ symbol*] (TTSB) ... CTIX
Conversion Tech Intl.Wrrt'A' [*NASDAQ symbol*] (TTSB) ... CTIXW
Conversion Tech Intl.Wrrt'B' [*NASDAQ symbol*] (TTSB) ... CTIXZ
Conversion Technologies International, Inc. [*Associated Press*] (SAG) ... ConvT
Conversion Technologies International, Inc. [*Associated Press*] (SAG) ... ConvTch
Conversion Technologies International, Inc. [*NASDAQ symbol*] (SAG) ... CTIX
Conversion to Full-Time Manning ... CFTM
Conversion Unit [*British military*] (DMA) ... CU
Conversional File Information Retrieval and Management System (SAUS) ... CONFIRM System
Conversional FORTRAN [*Formula Translating System*] (IAA) ... CFOR
Convert (FAAC) ... CNVRT
Convert (ECII) ... CNVT
Convert (BARN) ... Cnvt
Convert (ADWA) ... cnvt
Convert (AABC) ... CONVT
Convert (EBF) ... Cvt
Convert ... CVT
Convert Acquisition Tracking System (ACAE) ... CATS
Convert Byte to Word (SAUS) ... CBW
Convert Character Code (OA) ... CCC
Convert Clock Input [*Computer science*] (IAA) ... CCI
Convert Enable (SAUS) ... CE
Convert Gray to Binary ... CGB
Convert Makers of America [*Later, CMOA*] (EA) ... CMA
Convert Makers of America (SAUO) ... CMOA
Convert Movement Our Apostolate (EA) ... CMOA
Convert Out (SAUS) ... CO
Convert Range Telemetry System (SAUS) ... CORTS
Convert Source Information (SAUS) ... COSINF
Convert to Binary (IAA) ... CVB
Convert to Decimal (IAA) ... CVD
Convert Word to Double word (SAUS) ... CWD
Converted (DCTA) ... CONV
Converted (SAUS) ... Convd
Converted Aerial Targets (NG) ... CAT
Converted Battalion Anti-Tank [*Military*] (PDAA) ... CONBAT

Converted Destroyer	CONVDD
Converted Fund International S.A. (SAUO)	CFI
Converted Gallery Range (SAUS)	CGR
Converted Prelease (ADA)	CPL
Converter [*Electronics*] (ECII)	CNVT
Converter (IAA)	CON
Converter (KSC)	CONV
Converter	CONVRTR
Converter (SAUS)	CV
Converter Amplifier Unit (MCD)	CAU
Converter, Analog to Analog (ACAE)	CAA
Converter Clutch Override [*Automotive engineering*]	CCO
Converter Compressor Facility (KSC)	CCF
Converter Display Group	CDG
Converter Enhanced, Electronically Managed Automatic Transmission	CEEMAT
Converter, Frequency to DC [*Direct Current*] Voltage (MCD)	CFD
Converter, Frequency to DC Voltage (SAUS)	CFD
Converter Instruction Register (SAUS)	CIR
Converter Multiplexer (CAAL)	CMUX
Converter, Pulse to DC [*Direct Current*] Voltage (NASA)	CPD
Converter Regulator Unit (MCD)	CRU
Converter Remote Off (SAUS)	ROFF
Converter Remote On (SAUS)	RON
Converter Simulator Signal Unit (MCD)	CSSU
Converter, Variable Resistance, to DC [*Direct Current*] Voltage (NASA)	CVRD
Converter, Voltage, AC [*Alternating Current*] to DC [*Direct Current*] (MCD)	CVAD
Converter, Voltage Discrete, AC [*Alternating Current*] (NASA)	CVDA
Converter/Programmer (MCD)	C/P
Converters [*Electronic*] [*JETDS nomenclature*] [*Military*] (CET)	CV
Convertible [*Rate*] [*Value of the English pound*]	CN
Convertible (ADWA)	CNVRT
Convertible (ADWA)	CNVRTBL
Convertible	CONV
Convertible (EBF)	Conv
Convertible	CONVRTBL
Convertible [*Classified advertising*]	CONVT
Convertible (ADWA)	cv
Convertible [*Stock exchange term*] (SPSG)	CV
Convertible [*Automotive engineering*]	CV
Convertible (EBF)	Cv
Convertible (EBF)	Cvt
Convertible [*Stock exchange term*]	CVT
Convertible (ADWA)	cvt
Convertible Adjustable Preferred (EBF)	CAP
Convertible Adjustable Preferred Stock [*Investment term*] (DFIT)	CAPS
Convertible Adjustable Rate Preferred Stock (MHDB)	CAP
Convertible Bond Option [*Finance*] (EMRF)	CBO
Convertible Circuit Breaker	CCB
Convertible Hldgs [*NYSE symbol*] (TTSB)	CNV
Convertible Hldgs Inc Shrs [*NYSE symbol*] (TTSB)	CNVPr
Convertible Holdings [*NYSE symbol*] (SPSG)	CNV
Convertible Holdings [*Associated Press*] (SAG)	ConvHld
Convertible Holdings [*Associated Press*] (SAG)	CvHd
Convertible Laser Designation Pod (SAUS)	CLDP
Convertible Lens [*Photography*]	CL
Convertible Money Market Preferred Stock [*Investment term*]	CMMP
Convertible Note	CN
Convertible Note	CVNT
Convertible Preferred Stock [*Investment term*]	CPS
Convertible Report (PDAA)	CR
Convertible Rotor (SAUS)	CR
Convertible Security [*Investment term*] (DFIT)	CV
Convertible Security [*Business term*] (MHDW)	CVC
Convertible Slip Knot (MELL)	CSK
Convertible Unsecured Loan Stock [*Finance*]	CULS
Convertible Wraparound Mortgage [*Banking*]	CWM
Converting Enzyme	CE
Converting Equipment Manufacturers Association (EA)	CEMA
Converting Machinery and Materials (DGA)	CMM
Converting-Enzyme Inhibitor [*Biochemistry*]	CEI
ConVest Energy Corp. [*Associated Press*] (SAG)	CnvstE
ConVest Energy Corp. [*AMEX symbol*] (SPSG)	COV
ConVest Energy Partners Ltd. (MHDW)	CEP
Convex (MSA)	CVX
Convex	CX
Convex (MELL)	Cx
Convex Computer [*Associated Press*] (SAG)	Convex
Convex Computer Corp. (MHDW)	CNVX
Convex Computer Corp. [*NYSE symbol*] (SPSG)	CNX
Convex Set Stochastic Dominance [*Statistics*]	CSD
Convexity, Symmetry, Maximum [*Statistics*]	CSM
Convexity Symmetry, Maximum Test (SAUS)	CSM Test
Convexo-Concave [*Replacement heart valves*] [*Cardiology*]	C-C
Convey [*Legal shorthand*] (LWAP)	COVY
Conveyance (SAUS)	Cnvc
Conveyance [*Transportation*] (DCTA)	CONV
Conveyance	CONVCE
Conveyance (SAUS)	Convce
Conveyance [*Legal shorthand*] (LWAP)	COVCE
Conveyancer [*or Conveyancing*] [*Legal term*] (DLA)	Conv
Conveyancer [*Legal term*] (DLA)	Convey
Conveyancer, Conveyancer & Property Lawyer [*A publication*]	Conv
Conveyancers' Year Book [*1940-51*] [*A publication*] (DLA)	Conv YB
Conveyances (SAUS)	Convs

Conveyancing [*Legal shorthand*] (LWAP)	COVNG
Conveyancing Review [*1957-63*] [*Scotland*] [*A publication*] (DLA)	Conv Rev
Conveyancing Review [*1957-63*] [*Scotland*] [*A publication*] (DLA)	CR
Conveyed (ROG)	CONVD
Conveyed by Air (SAUS)	Convair
Conveying	CNVYG
Conveyor (KSC)	CNVR
Conveyor (SAUS)	Cnvr
Conveyor	CNVYR
Conveyor (SAUS)	Conv
Conveyor	CONVYR
Conveyor Control System	CCS
Conveyor Equipment Manufacturers Association (EA)	CEMA
Conveyor Equipment Manufacturers Association	ConEMA
Conveyor Section of the Material Handling Institute (EA)	CS
Conveyorized Automatic Tube Tester [*Computer science*]	CATT
Convict (ADA)	C
Convict (AABC)	CNVT
Convict (SAUS)	Cnvt
Convict (SAUS)	Con
Convict (WDAA)	con
Convict (ADA)	CON
Convict	CONV
Convict Prison (SAUO)	CP
Convicted Poacher [*Legal*] [*British*] (ROG)	CP
Conviction by Civil Court	CBCC
Convicts' Association for a Good Environment [*Defunct*]	CAGE
Convivium Septem Sapientium [*of Plutarch*] [*Classical studies*] (OCD)	Conv Sept Sap
Convocation	CONV
Convocation (ADWA)	conv
Convocation	CONVOC
Convolution (SAUS)	CVM
Convolution Back-Projection (SAUS)	CBP
Convolutional Coding Unit	CCU
Convolutional Decoder Assembly	CDA
Convolutional Encoding/Sequential Decoding (SAUS)	CE/SD
Convolve-Multiply-Convolve (SAUS)	CMC
Convolvulus Jalapa [*Jalap Plant*] [*Pharmacology*] (ROG)	CONVOLV JAP
Convoy (NVT)	CONV
Convoy (SAUS)	Cv
Convoy and Routing (SAUS)	C&R
Convoy and Routing [*Section*] [*US Fleet*]	C & R
Convoy and Routing [*Section*] [*US Fleet*]	CONROUTE
Convoy Commodore [*Navy*] (NVT)	CC
Convoy Commodore [*Navy*]	CONCOMO
Convoy Control Center (SAUO)	CCC
Convoy Control Officer [*Navy*]	CCO
Convoy Escort Vessel [*Navy*]	CEV
Convoy Exercise [*Navy*] (NVT)	CONVEX
Convoy Exercise (SAUS)	Convex
Convoy, Routing, and Scheduling System [*USAREUR*]	CRASS
Convoy Service Center (SAUO)	CSC
Convoy Support Center (SAUO)	CSC
Convulsant Antidote for Nerve Agent	CANA
Convulsive Disorder [*Medicine*]	CD
Convulsive Dose [*Medicine*]	CD
Convulsive Shock Therapy [*Medicine*]	CST
Conway, AR [*Location identifier*] [*FAA*] (FAAL)	CWS
Conway, AR [*FM radio station call letters*] (BROA)	KASR-FM
Conway, AR [*AM radio station call letters*]	KCON
Conway, AR [*AM radio station call letters*]	KFCA
Conway, AR [*FM radio station call letters*]	KHDX
Conway, AR [*FM radio station call letters*]	KMJX
Conway, AR [*AM radio station call letters*]	KTOD
Conway, AR [*FM radio station call letters*]	KUCA
Con-Way Central Express	CCX
Con-way Intergrated Services	CIS
Conway, NH [*AM radio station call letters*]	WBNC
Conway, NH [*FM radio station call letters*] (RBYB)	WBNC-FM
Conway, NH [*FM radio station call letters*]	WMWV
Conway, SC [*Location identifier*] [*FAA*] (FAAL)	HYW
Conway, SC [*FM radio station call letters*]	WHMC
Conway, SC [*Television station call letters*]	WHMC-TV
Conway, SC [*AM radio station call letters*]	WJXY
Conway, SC [*FM radio station call letters*]	WJXY-FM
Conway, SC [*AM radio station call letters*]	WPJS
Conway, SC [*FM radio station call letters*]	WYAV
Con-Way Southern Express	CSE
Con-way Truckload Services	CWT
Conway Twitty Fan Club [*Defunct*] (EA)	CTFC
Con-way Western Express	CWX
Conwest Exploration Co. Ltd. [*Toronto Stock Exchange symbol*]	CEX
Conwest Exploration Company Ltd. [*NASDAQ symbol*] (SAG)	CEXC
Conwest Exploration Company Ltd. [*Associated Press*] (SAG)	Conwst
Conwood Corp. (SAUO)	CWD
Conyers, GA [*AM radio station call letters*]	WPBS
Conzinc Rio Tinto Australia Ltd. (SAUO)	CRA
Coober Pedy [*Australia*] [*Airport symbol*] (OAG)	CPD
Cooch Behar [*India*] [*Airport symbol*] (AD)	COH
Cooch-Behar [*India*] [*ICAO location identifier*] (ICLI)	VECO
Coode on the Written Law [*A publication*] (DLA)	Coode Wr L
Cooder Brown Band Fan Club (EA)	CBBFC
Coode's Legislative Expression [*A publication*] (DLA)	Coode Leg Exp

Coodinating Committee of South-East Asian Senior Officials on Transport and Communications (SAUO) .... COORDCOM
Cook [*Ranking title*] [*British Women's Royal Naval Service*] C
Cook [*Navy*] [*British*] .... CK
Cook College Remote Sensing Center (SAUS) .... CCRSC
Cook [*N. B.*] Corp. Ltd. [*Toronto Stock Exchange symbol*] [*Vancouver Stock Exchange symbol*] .... NBC
Cook County Clerk's Office, Chicago, IL [*Library symbol*] [*Library of Congress*] (LCLS) ICC
Cook County High School, Grand Marais, MN [*Library symbol*] [*Library of Congress*] (LCLS) .... MnGmH
Cook County Hospital, Dr. Frederick Tice Memorial Library, Chicago, IL [*Library symbol*] [*Library of Congress*] (LCLS) .... ICCH
Cook County Junior College (SAUS) .... CCJC
Cook County Law Library, Chicago, IL [*Library symbol*] [*Library of Congress*] (LCLS) ICCL
Cook County School of Nursing, Chicago, IL [*Library symbol*] [*Library of Congress*] (LCLS) .... ICCN
Cook Inlet Aviation, Inc. [*ICAO designator*] (FAAC) .... CKA
Cook Inlet Housing Authority (SAUO) .... CIHA
Cook Inlet Native Association [*Defunct*] (EA) .... CINA
Cook Inlet Region Inc. (SAUO) .... CIRI
Cook Island [*MARC geographic area code*] [*Library of Congress*] (LCCP) .... pocw-
Cook Island Airways Ltd. (SAUO) .... KH
Cook Island Islandair [*ICAO designator*] (AD) .... KH
Cook Islands [*ANSI two-letter standard code*] (CNC) .... CK
Cook Islands [*ANSI three-letter standard code*] (CNC) .... COK
Cook Islands [*MARC country of publication code*] [*Library of Congress*] (LCCP) .... cw
Cook Islands Department of Survey (GEOI) .... CISD
Cook Islands International [*New Zealand*] [*ICAO designator*] (FAAC) CII
Cook Islands International [*ICAO designator*] (AD) .... KC
Cook Islands Party [*Political party*] (PPW) .... CIP
Cook Memorial Public Library District, Libertyville, IL [*Library symbol*] [*Library of Congress*] (LCLS) .... ILib
Cook on Corporations [*A publication*] (DLA) .... Cook Corp
Cook on Stock, Stockholders, and General Corporation Law [*A publication*] (DLA) .... Cook Stock Stockh & Corp Law
Cook Paint & Varnish Co (SAUO) .... COK
Cook Public Library, Cook, MN [*Library symbol*] [*Library of Congress*] (LCLS) .... MnCoo
Cook Public School, Cook, MN [*Library symbol*] [*Library of Congress*] (LCLS) .... MnCooS
Cook Research Laboratories (SAUS) .... CRL
Cook Transit R. R. [*AAR code*] .... COOK
Cook United, Inc. (SAUO) .... CCF
Cookbook .... ckb
Cooke. Act Book of the Ecclesiastical Court of Whalley [*A publication*] (DLA) .... Cooke
Cooke. Agricultural Tenancies [*3rd ed.*] [*1882*] [*A publication*] (DLA) ..... Coo Agr T
Cooke. Agricultural Tenancies [*3rd ed.*] [*A publication*] (DLA) .... Cooke Agr T
Cooke Air Force Base [*Later, VAFB*] (AAG) .... CAFB
Cooke and Alcock's Great Britain Reports [*Ireland*] [*A publication*] (DLA) .... Co & Al
Cooke and Alcock's Irish King's Bench Reports [*1833-34*] [*A publication*] (DLA) .... C & A
Cooke and Alcock's Irish King's Bench Reports [*1833-34*] [*A publication*] (DLA) .... Coo & Al
Cooke and Alcock's Irish King's Bench Reports [*1833-34*] [*A publication*] (DLA) .... Cooke & Al (Ir)
Cooke and Alcock's Reports [*Ireland*] [*A publication*] (DLA) .... Cooke & A
Cooke and Alcock's Reports [*Ireland*] [*A publication*] (DLA) .... Cooke & Al
Cooke and Alcock's Reports [*Ireland*] [*A publication*] (DLA) .... Cooke & Alc
Cooke and Harwood's Charitable Trusts [*2nd ed.*] [*1867*] [*A publication*] (DLA) .... C & H Char Tr
Cooke and Harwood's Charitable Trusts Acts [*A publication*] (DLA) .... Coo & H Tr
Cooke and Harwood's Charitable Trusts Acts [*A publication*] (DLA) .... Cooke & H Ch Tr
Cooke County Junior College, Gainsville, TX [*Library symbol*] [*Library of Congress*] (LCLS) .... TxGaiC
Cooke on Life Insurance [*A publication*] (DLA) .... Cooke Ins
Cooke on the Agricultural Holdings Act [*A publication*] (DLA) .... Cooke Agr Hold
Cooked .... CKD
Cooked Cured-Meat Pigment [*Food technology*] .... CCMP
Cooked Potato Weight [*Food technology*] (OA) .... CPW
Cooked Therapeutic Inflight Meal (DNAB) .... CTIM
Cooker C
Cooker Control Unit .... CCU
Cooker Restaurant [*NYSE symbol*] (TTSB) .... CGR
Cooker Restaurant, Inc. [*NYSE symbol*] (SAG) .... CGR
Cooker Restaurant, Inc. [*Associated Press*] (SAG) .... Cooker
Cookerville, TN [*Television station call letters*] (BROA) .... WNPX
Cookery (SAUS) .... Cook
Cookery and Food Association [*British*] (BI) .... CFA
Cookery Officer [*Navy*] [*British*] .... CK
Cooke's Admiralty Cases [*Quebec*] [*A publication*] (DLA) .... Cook Adm
Cooke's Bankrupt Laws [*A publication*] (DLA) .... Coo Bankr
Cooke's Bankrupt Laws [*A publication*] (DLA) .... Cooke BL
Cooke's Cases of Practice [*125 English Reprint*] [*A publication*] (DLA) .... Cooke (Eng)
Cooke's Cases of Practice, English Common Pleas [*A publication*] (DLA) .... Cooke
Cooke's Enfranchisement of Copyholds [*2nd ed.*] [*1853*] [*A publication*] (DLA) .... Coo Cop

Cooke's Enfranchisement of Copyholds [*2nd ed.*] [*1853*] [*A publication*] (DLA) .... Cooke Cop
Cooke's English Common Pleas Reports [*1706-47*] [*A publication*] (DLA) .... Cooke CP
Cooke's Inclosure Acts [*A publication*] (DLA) .... Coo IA
Cooke's Inclosure Acts [*A publication*] (DLA) .... Cooke IA
Cooke's Inclosure Acts [*A publication*] (DLA) .... Cooke Incl Acts
Cooke's Law of Defamation [*A publication*] (DLA) .... Coo Def
Cooke's Law of Defamation [*A publication*] (DLA) .... Cooke Def
Cooke's New York Highway Laws [*A publication*] (DLA) .... Cooke High
Cooke's Practical Register of the Common Pleas [*A publication*] (DLA) .... Cooke Pr Reg
Cooke's Practice Cases [*1706-47*] [*England*] [*A publication*] (DLA) .... Ca Prac CP
Cooke's Practice Cases [*1706-47*] [*England*] [*A publication*] (DLA) .... Rep Cas Pr
Cookes Practice Cases (SAUS) .... Rep Cas Pr
Cooke's Practice Reports, English Common Pleas [*A publication*] (DLA) .... Cooke Pr Cas
Cooke's Tennessee Reports [*A publication*] (DLA) .... Cooke
Cooke's Tennessee Reports [*A publication*] (DLA) .... Cooke's Rep
Cooke's Tennessee Reports [*A publication*] (DLA) .... Cooke (Tenn)
Cookeville General Hospital, Stephen Farr Health Sciences Library, Cookeville, TN [*Library symbol*] [*Library of Congress*] (LCLS) .... TCooH
Cookeville, TN [*Location identifier*] [*FAA*] (FAAL) .... CJE
Cookeville, TN [*Television station call letters*] .... WCTE
Cookeville, TN [*FM radio station call letters*] (BROA) .... WGIC-FM
Cookeville, TN [*FM radio station call letters*] .... WGSQ
Cookeville, TN [*FM radio station call letters*] (RBYB) .... WHRS-FM
Cookeville, TN [*AM radio station call letters*] .... WHUB
Cookeville, TN [*FM radio station call letters*] .... WHUB-FM
Cookeville, TN [*Television station call letters*] .... WKZX
Cookeville, TN [*AM radio station call letters*] .... WPTN
Cookeville, TN [*AM radio station call letters*] .... WTTU
Cookeville, TN [*FM radio station call letters*] .... WWOG
Cookham [*England*] .... COOK
Cookhouse [*South Africa*] [*ICAO location identifier*] (ICLI) .... FACH
Cookie .... CK
Cookie and Snack Bakers Association (EA) .... CSBA
Cookie Cutter Collectors Club (EA) CCCC
Cooking Advancement Research and Education Foundation (EA) .... CAREF
Cooking for Survival Consciousness (EA) .... CSC
Cook's Lower Canada Admiralty Court Cases [*A publication*] (DLA) .... Co A
Cook's Penal Code [*New York*] [*A publication*] (DLA) .... Cook's Pen Code
Cook's Vice-Admiralty Reports [*Canada*] [*A publication*] (DLA) .... Cook Adm
Cook's Vice-Admiralty Reports [*Canada*] [*A publication*] (DLA) .... Cook V Adm
Cook's Vice-Admiralty Reports [*Canada*] [*A publication*] (DLA) .... Cook Vice-Adm
Cookstown Public Library, Ontario [*Library symbol*] [*National Library of Canada*] (BIB) .... OCOO
Cooktown [*Australia*] [*Airport symbol*] (OAG) .... CTN
Cookware Manufacturers Association (EA) .... CMA
Cool Container (SAUS) .... Cooltainer
Cool Dehumidified Air (PDAA) .... CDA
Cool Down (AAG) .... CLDWN
Cool Light (SAUS) .... CLT
Cool Mist Vaporizer [*Medicine*] (DMAA) .... CMV
Cool Room .... CLRM
Cool Science Site of the Day (SAUO) .... CSSD
Cool Site of the Day (SAUO) .... CSD
Cool Thermal Energy Storage [*Air-conditioning*] (PS) .... CTES
Cool Water Coal Gasification [*Fuel technology*] .... CWCG
Cool White (DAC) .... CW
Cool White Deluxe (DAC) .... CWX
Coolah [*New South Wales*] [*Airport symbol*] (AD) .... CLH
Coolangatta [*Australia*] [*ICAO location identifier*] (ICLI) .... ABCG
Coolangatta [*Queensland*] [*Airport symbol*] (AD) .... OOL
Coolant (AAG) .... CLNT
Coolant (MSA) .... COOL
Coolant Boiling and Rod Arrays [*Nuclear energy*] (NRCH) .... COBRA
Coolant Boiling in Rod Arrays code (SAUS) .... CoBRA-TF
Coolant Contamination Test Set (ACAE) .... CCTS
Coolant Control Assembly (NASA) .... CCA
Coolant Control Engine Vacuum Switch [*Automotive engineering*] .... CCEVS
Coolant Control Valve CCV
Coolant Distribution Unit [*Computer science*] .... CDU
Coolant Fan Control [*Automotive engineering*] .... CFC
Coolant Flow and Pressure Test Station (ACAE) .... CFPTS
Coolant Level Sensor [*Automotive engineering*] .... COLS
Coolant Override Valve [*Automotive engineering*] .... COV
Coolant Pump [*Nuclear energy*] (NRCH) .... CP
Coolant Pump Power Inverters (MCD) .... CPPI
Coolant Recovery System [*Automotive engineering*] .... CRS
Coolant Reserve System [*Automotive engineering*] .... CRS
Coolant Return Tank [*Environmental science*] (COE) .... CRT
Coolant Sampling (DNAB) .... CS
Coolant Spark Control [*Automotive engineering*] .... CSC
Coolant Temperature Override [*Automotive engineering*] .... CTO
Coolant Temperature Sensor [*Automotive engineering*] .... CTS
Coolant Vacuum Switch Cold Closed [*Automotive engineering*] .... CVSCC
Coolant-Controlled Exhaust Gas Recirculation [*Automotive engineering*] .... CCEGR
Cooldown [*Nuclear energy*] (NRCH) .... C/D
Cool-Down Facility (NASA) .... CDF
Cooled (MSA) .... CLD
Cooled (ADWA) .... cld
Cooled (SAUS) .... Cld
Cooled Atmospheric Spectrometer (SAUS) .... CATMOS

Cooled High-Energy Firing Unit ..... CHEFU
Cooled Infrared Radiometer (PDAA) ..... CIR
Cooled Spectral Shared Aperture Concepts (ACAE) ..... COSSAC
Cooled-Anode Transmitting (DEN) ..... CAT
Cooled-Anode Transmitting Tube ..... CATT
Cooled-Anode Transmitting Valve (IAA) ..... CATV
Cooled-Grating Array Spectrometer [*Instrumentation*] ..... CGAS
Cooler (MSA) ..... CLR
Cooler, Air Evaporative (SAUS) ..... CAE
Cooler Control Unit (SAUS) ..... CCU
Cooler Flusher Tank Cell [*Nuclear energy*] (NRCH) ..... CFTC
Cooler Flusher Tank Equipment [*Nuclear energy*] (NRCH) ..... CFTE
Cooler Liquid Electron Tube ..... CLET
Coolest Ultra Tiny Individuals on Earth [*Toy figures*] [*Mattel, Inc.*] ..... CUTIE
Cooley Electronics Laboratory [*University of Michigan*] [*Research center*] (RCD) ..... CEL
Cooley Family Association of America (EA) ..... CFA
Cooley Law Review [*A publication*] (DLA) ..... Cooley L Rev
Cooley on Constitutional Limitations [*A publication*] (DLA) ..... Cooley Const Lim
Cooley on Constitutional Limitations [*A publication*] (DLA) ..... Cooley Const Limit
Cooley on Taxation [*A publication*] (DLA) ..... Cooley Tax
Cooley on Taxation [*A publication*] (DLA) ..... Cooley Tax'n
Cooley on Taxation [*A publication*] (DLA) ..... Cool Tax
Cooley on Torts [*A publication*] (DLA) ..... Cool Torts
Cooley Programming System (SAUS) ..... CPS
Cooley's Anemia Foundation (EA) ..... CAF
Cooley's Constitutional Law [*A publication*] (DLA) ..... Cool Con Law
Cooley's Constitutional Law [*A publication*] (DLA) ..... Cooley Const Law
Cooley's Constitutional Limitations [*A publication*] (DLA) ..... Cool Con Lim
Cooley's Edition of Blackstone's Commentaries [*A publication*] (DLA) ..... Cool Black
Cooley's Edition of Blackstone's Commentaries [*A publication*] (DLA) ..... Cooley Bl Comm
Cooley's Michigan Digest [*A publication*] (DLA) ..... Cool Mich Dig
Cooley's Reports [*5-12 Michigan*] [*A publication*] (DLA) ..... Cooley
Coolidge, AZ [*FM radio station call letters*] (RBYB) ..... KBZR
Coolidge, AZ [*AM radio station call letters*] ..... KCKY
Coolidge Center for Environmental Leadership (EA) ..... CCEL
Coolidge High School Library, Sioux Falls, SD [*Library symbol*] [*Library of Congress*] (LCLS) ..... SdSifH
Coolidge Public Library, Coolidge, AZ [*Library symbol*] [*Library of Congress*] (LCLS) ..... AzCo
Coolimation Test Module [*Nuclear energy*] (NRCH) ..... CTM
Cooling (PS) C
Cooling (MSA) ..... CLG
Cooling ..... COOL
Cooling ..... COOLG
Cooling Coil (AAG) CC
Cooling Effect Detection and Control ..... CEDAC
Cooling Effect Detection and Control (SAUS) ..... Cedac
Cooling Fan (MSA) ..... CF
Cooling Tower [*Nuclear energy*] (NRCH) ..... CT
Cooling Tower Institute (EA) ..... CTI
Cooling Water [*Nuclear energy*] (NRCH) ..... CW
Cooling Water Association (SAUO) ..... CWA
Cooling Water Gamma Monitor [*Environmental science*] (COE) ..... CWGM
Cooling Water Return [*Nuclear energy*] (NRCH) ..... CWR
Cooling Water System [*Nuclear energy*] (NRCH) ..... CWS
Cooling Water/Hot Water Return [*Nuclear energy*] (NRCH) ..... CHR
Cooling Water/Hot Water Return [*Nuclear energy*] (NRCH) ..... CHWR
Cooling-Induced Luminescence [*In glass containing rare earth salts*] CIL
Coolullah [*Australia*] [*Airport symbol*] (AD) ..... WCO
Cooma [*Australia*] [*ICAO location identifier*] (ICLI) ..... ASCM
Cooma [*Australia*] [*Airport symbol*] (OAG) ..... OOM
Coomassie Brilliant Blue [*A stain*] ..... CBB
Coomb [*Combe*] [*British*] (ROG) ..... CB
Coombs' Test [*for the presence of globulin on the surface of red cells*] [*Hematology*] ..... CT
Coomutator End (SAUS) ..... CE
Coon Peak [*Utah*] [*Seismograph station code, US Geological Survey*] (SEIS) ..... CPU
Coon Rapids Enterprise, Coon Rapids, IA [*Library symbol*] [*Library of Congress*] (LCLS) ..... IaCoon
Coonabarabran [*Australia*] [*Airport symbol*] (OAG) ..... COJ
Coonamble [*Australia*] [*Airport symbol*] (OAG) ..... CNB
Cooney Tunnel [*Armidale*] [*Australia*] [*Seismograph station code, US Geological Survey*] (SEIS) ..... COO
Coooa Research Institute. Council for Scientific and Industrial Research. Annual Report (journ.) (SAUS) ..... WACRAX
Co-op Action Action Plan [*Advertising*] (WDMC) ..... CAP Rate
Cooper Aerial Surveys Ltd. [*British*] [*FAA designator*] (FAAC) ..... SVY
Cooper & Chyan Technology, Inc. [*NASDAQ symbol*] (SAG) ..... CCTI
Cooper & Chyan Technology, Inc. [*Associated Press*] (SAG) ..... CoopChy
Cooper Cameron [*NYSE symbol*] (SG) ..... CAM
Cooper Cameron [*NYSE symbol*] (TTSB) ..... RON
Cooper Cameron Corp. [*Associated Press*] (SAG) ..... Coop Ca
Cooper Cameron Corp. [*NYSE symbol*] (SAG) ..... RON
Cooper Canada Ltd. [*Toronto Stock Exchange symbol*] ..... CPC
[*The*] **Cooper Companies, Inc.** [*NYSE symbol*] (SPSG) ..... COO
[*The*] **Cooper Companies, Inc.** [*Associated Press*] (SAG) ..... CoopCo
Cooper Cos. [*NYSE symbol*] (TTSB) ..... COLL
Cooper Cos. [*NYSE symbol*] (SG) ..... COO
Cooper Development Co. [*NASDAQ symbol*] (NQ) ..... COOL
Cooper Development Co. [*Associated Press*] (SAG) ..... CooprD
Cooper Ind 6.00%'DECS'1998 [*NYSE symbol*] (TTSB) ..... CXW
Cooper Indus [*NYSE symbol*] (TTSB) ..... CBE
Cooper Industries [*NYSE symbol*] (SAG) ..... CXW
Cooper Industries, Inc. [*Formerly, Cooper-Bessemer Corp.*] [*NYSE symbol*] (SPSG) ..... CBE
Cooper Industries, Inc. [*Formerly, Cooper-Bessemer Corp.*] [*Associated Press*] (SAG) ..... Cooper
Cooper Landing, AK [*Location identifier*] [*FAA*] (FAAL) ..... JLA
Cooper Life Sciences [*NASDAQ symbol*] (TTSB) ..... ZAPS
Cooper Life Sciences, Inc. [*Associated Press*] (SAG) ..... CooprL
Cooper Life Sciences, Inc. [*NASDAQ symbol*] (NQ) ..... ZAPS
Cooper Medical Center, Camden, NJ [*Library symbol*] [*Library of Congress*] (LCLS) ..... NjCaC
Cooper Mtn Networks [*NASDAQ symbol*] (SG) ..... CMTN
Cooper Nuclear Station (NRCH) ..... CNS
Cooper Ornithological Society (EA) ..... COS
Cooper River Bridge (SAUS) ..... CRB
Cooper Skybird Air Charters Ltd. [*Kenya*] [*ICAO designator*] (FAAC) ..... SKY
Cooper Tire & Rubber [*NYSE symbol*] (TTSB) ..... CTB
Cooper Tire & Rubber Co. [*Associated Press*] (SAG) ..... CooprTr
Cooper Tire & Rubber Co. [*NYSE symbol*] (SPSG) ..... CTB
Cooper Union for the Advancement of Science and Art, New York, NY [*Library symbol*] [*Library of Congress*] (LCLS) ..... NNCoo
Cooper Union Library (SAUO) ..... CUL
Cooperage [*Freight*] ..... COOPG
Cooperate ..... COOp
Cooperate (SAUS) ..... COOP
Cooperate Central File (SAUS) ..... CCF
Cooperated Atomic Operations (SAUO) ..... CAO
Cooperateurs Pariosslaux du Christ Rol (SAUO) ..... CPCR
Cooperating (AL) ..... Coop
Cooperating Administrator [*Education*] (AEE) ..... CA
Cooperating Agency (SAUO) ..... CA
Cooperating Agency Method for Event Reporting and Analysis (IAA) ..... CAMERA
Cooperating Individual [*FBI*] CI
Cooperating Libraries in Consortium [*St. Paul, MN*] [*Library network*] CLIC
Cooperating Libraries of Greater Springfield [*Library network*] ..... CLGS
Cooperating Space System (ACAE) ..... CSS
Cooperating Systems Architecture (SAUS) ..... CSA
Cooperating Teachers' Attitude Questionnaire ..... CTAQ
Cooperating Users' Exchange ..... CUE
Cooperating Users of Burroughs Equipment (EA) ..... CUBE
Cooperation and Coordination ..... CAC
Cooperation Application Satellite-A (SAUS) ..... CAS-A
Cooperation Application Satellite-C (SAUS) ..... CAS-C
Cooperation Canada Mozambique (AC) ..... COCAMO
Cooperation Centre for Scientific Research Relative to Tobacco (SAUO) ..... CORESTA
Cooperation Council for the Arab States of the Gulf (SAUO) ..... GCC
Cooperation Europeene dans la Domaine de la Recherche Scientifique et Technique [*European Cooperation in the Field of Scientific and Technical Research*] (MSC) ..... COST
Cooperation for American Relief Everywhere (SAUO) ..... CARE
Cooperation for Development [*British*] (EAIO) ..... CD
Cooperation for Mediterranean Architectural Heritage-ICOMOS (SAUO) ..... COPAM
Cooperation for Open Systems ..... COS
Cooperation for Open Systems Interconnection Networking in Europe (OSI) ..... COSINE
Co-operation for Reinforcing the Development of Education in Europe (SAUO) ..... CORDEE
Cooperation in Applied Science and Technology (SAUO) ..... CAST
Cooperation in Automation of Data and Documentation for Imports/Exports and Agriculture [*EC*] (ECED) ..... CADDIA
Cooperation in Bureau, Research and Administration (SAUS) ..... COBRA
Cooperation in Documentation and Communication (SAUS) ..... CoDoC
Cooperation in Documentation and Communication [*An association*] ..... CODOC
Co-operation in Library Automation (SAUO) ..... COLA
Cooperation in Library Automation (NITA) ..... COLA
Cooperation in Library Automation Project (SAUS) ..... COLA Project
Cooperation in Research and Development for Educational in South and South East Europe (SAUO) ..... CODIESEE
Cooperation in Space [*Former USSR*] ..... COSPAS
Cooperation Internationale en Matiere de Documentation sur l'Economie des Transports [*International Cooperation in the Field of Transport Economics Documentation*] [*France*] [*Information service or system*] (IID) ..... CIDET
Cooperation Internationale pour le Developpement et la Solidarite [*International Cooperation for Development and Solidarity*] [*Formerly, Cooperation Internationale pour le Developpement Socio-Economique*] (EAIO) ..... CIDSE
Co-Operation on International Traceability in Analytical Chemistry (SAUS) ..... CITAC
Cooperation project for all libraries (SAUS) ..... DANBIB
Cooperation via Televised Instruction in Education [*Colorado State University*] ..... CO-TIE
Cooperativa ..... COOP
Cooperativa Tecnico Scientifica di Base (SAUO) ..... COBASE
Cooperative (SAUO) ..... CO-OP
Cooperative (AABC) ..... COOP
Cooperative (AL) ..... Coop
Co-operative (TBD) ..... Co-op
Cooperative ..... COOPRTV
Co-Operative Action Programme [*UNESCO*] (EA) ..... CO-ACTION
Cooperative Activity Ion Printing Technology (SAUO) ..... IONPRINTEX
Cooperative Administrative Support Units (SAUS) ..... CASU

Cooperative Advanced Digital Research Experiment (MCD) ... CADRE
Cooperative Advertising (WDMC) ... co-op
Cooperative African Microfilm Project (SAUO) ... CAMP
Cooperative African Microform Project (SAUO) ... CAMP
Cooperative Africana Microform Project, Archives-Libraries Committee, African Studies Association, Center for Research Libraries, Chicago, IL [*Library symbol*] [*Library of Congress*] (LCLS) ... ICRL(CAMP)
Cooperative Agreement ... CA
Cooperative Agreement Notice ... CAN
Cooperative Agreement Officer [*Department of Housing and Urban Development*] (GFGA) ... CAO
Cooperative Agreements Program (GEOI) ... CAP
Cooperative Agricole des Producteurs de Cereales de la Region d'Arras ... CAPCRA
Cooperative Agricultural Pest Survey Program [*Information service or system*] (IID) ... CAPS
Cooperative Agricultural Research Program [*Tennessee State University*] [*Research center*] (RCD) ... CARP
Cooperative Air Defense System (MCD) ... CADS
Cooperative Air Transport System for Antarctica (SAUS) ... CATSA
Cooperative Alliance for Refuge Enhancement ... CARE
Cooperative Alumni Association (EA) ... CAA
Cooperative Analysis of Broadcasting [*Term used in TV rating*] ... CAB
Co-Operative and Commerce Bank [*Nigeria*] ... CCB
Cooperative and Rural Development Bank (SAUO) ... CRDB
Co-operative Angle Jammer (SAUS) ... CAJ
Cooperative Applications Satellite [*France*] [*NASA*] ... CAS
Cooperative Arctic Seismological Project (SAUO) ... COASP
Cooperative Area Manpower Planning System [*Environmental Protection Agency*] ... CAMPS
Cooperative Arid Lands Agriculture Research Program [*Established by Egypt, Israel, and the US at the University of San Diego in 1981*] ... CALAR
Cooperative Assessment of Experiential Learning Project (EDAC) ... CAEL
Cooperative Assistance Fund (EA) ... CAF
Cooperative Association for Internet Data Analysis ... CAIDA
Cooperative Association of Professional Salespeople [*Defunct*] (EA) ... CAPS
Cooperative Association of States for Scholarships (SAUO) ... CASS
Cooperative Association of Suez Canal Users (SAUO) ... CASCU
Co-operative Association of Suez Canal Users (SAUO) ... CASU
Cooperative Association of Tractor Dealers (EA) ... CATD
Cooperative Astrophysical and Technology SATellite (SAUS) ... CATSAT
Cooperative Astrophysics and Technology Satellite [*Sponsored by the University of New Hampshire*] ... CATsat
Cooperative Atmosphere Surface Exchange Study (SAUS) ... CASES
Cooperative Atomic Migration ... CAM
Cooperative Auto Research Program [*Department of Transportation*] ... CARP
Cooperative Automation Group [*British Library*] [*Information service or system*] [*Defunct*] (IID) ... CAG
Cooperative Autoworks Malaysia (SAUO) ... CAM
Cooperative Average Fuel Economy (BARN) ... CAFE
Cooperative Awards in Pure Science [*British*] ... CAPS
Cooperative Awards in Science and Engineering [*British*] ... CASE
[*The*] **Co-Operative Bank of Concord** [*NASDAQ symbol*] (NQ) ... COBK
Co-Operative Bank of Concord [*Associated Press*] (SAG) ... CoOpBk
Cooperative Bankshares [*NASDAQ symbol*] (SAG) ... COOP
Cooperative Bankshares [*Associated Press*] (SAG) ... CoopBk
Cooperative Base Network (GEOI) ... CBN
Cooperative Bibliographic Center for Indiana Libraries ... COBICIL
Cooperative Breast Cancer Tissue Resource [*National Cancer Institute*] ... CBCTR
Co-operative Bulk Handling (SAUO) ... CBH
Co-Operative Bulletin. Taiwan Forestry Research Institute (journ.) (SAUS) ... TLYYA4
Co-operative Bureau for Teachers (SAUO) ... CBT
Cooperative Bureau for Teachers [*Superseded by IES*] (EA) ... CBT
Cooperative Business Education (SAUO) ... CBE
Cooperative Business International [*Washington, DC*] (EA) ... CBI
Cooperative Cardiovascular Project ... CCP
Co-Operative, Career & Work Education Association of Canada [*Association Canadienne pour l'Alternance Travail-Etudes*] [*Also, National Co-Operative Education Centre*] (AC) ... CCWEAC
Cooperative Caring Network (SAUS) ... CCN
Co-Operative Central Bank [*Malaysia*] ... CCB
Cooperative Central Research Institute of Agriculture (SAUO) ... CCRIA
Cooperative Centre for Local Sustainable Development (SAUO) ... CCLSD
Cooperative College - School Service (OICC) ... CCSS
Cooperative College Ability Test (WGA) ... CCAT
Cooperative College Development Program ... CCDP
Cooperative College Library Center [*Atlanta, GA*] [*Library network*] ... CCLC
Cooperative College Library Center, Atlanta, GA [*OCLC symbol*] (OCLC) ... CCL
Cooperative College Library Center, Inc., Atlanta, GA [*Library symbol*] [*Library of Congress*] (LCLS) ... GACCLC
Co-Operative College of Canada, Saskatoon, Saskatchewan [*Library symbol*] [*National Library of Canada*] (NLC) ... SSC
Cooperative College of Canada, Saskatoon, SK, Canada [*Library symbol*] [*Library of Congress*] (LCLS) ... CaSSC
Cooperative College Registry [*Defunct*] ... CCR
Cooperative College-School Science [*Program*] [*Defunct*] [*National Science Foundation*] ... CCSS
Cooperative Committee on Interstate Air Pollution (SAUS) ... CCIAP
Co-operative Commonwealth Federation (SAUO) ... CCF
Cooperative Commonwealth Federation [*Later, New Democratic Party - NDP*] [*Political party*] [*Canada*] ... CCF
Cooperative Communicators Association (EA) ... CCA
Cooperative Compliance Program (SARE) ... CCP
Cooperative Computing Environment (CIST) ... CCE
Cooperative Computing System [*Echo detection*] ... CCS
Cooperative Computing System Program (SAUS) ... CCSY
Co-operative Confederation of the Caribbean (SAUO) ... CCC
Cooperative Contracts and Agreements [*Business term*] ... COCA
Cooperative Convection Precipitation Experiment [*Meteorology*] ... CCOPE
Cooperative Core Laboratories and Clinical Nutrition Research Unit [*Research center*] (RCD) ... CNRU
Cooperative Corporations (DLA) ... Coop Corp
Cooperative Council for Oklahoma School Administration (SRA) ... CCOSA
Co-operative Council of the Arab States of the Gulf (WDAA) ... CCASG
Cooperative Council of North Carolina (SRA) ... CCNC
Cooperative Credit Purchasing Co. [*Company that buys banks' bad debts*] [*Japan*] (ECON) ... CCPC
Cooperative Data Management Committee (SAUS) ... CDMC
Cooperative Database Building System (SAUS) ... CODABASE Building System
Cooperative database on serials (SAUS) ... CATBIB
Cooperative Defense Efforts (MCD) ... CDE
Cooperative Degree Program [*Army*] (INF) ... COOP
Cooperative Development Environment [*Computer science*] (PCM) ... CDE
Cooperative Development Organization (SAUO) ... CDO
Cooperative Development Program (SAUO) ... CDP
Cooperative Development Research program (SAUO) ... CDR
Cooperative Development Services [*British*] ... CDS
Co-Operative Digest, United States Reports [*A publication*] (DLA) ... Co-Op Dig
Cooperative d'Information et de Recherche Ecologiste du Quebec [*Environmental Information & Research Group*] (AC) ... CIREQ
Cooperative Distributed Interactive Atmospheric Catalog [*Marine science*] (OSRA) ... CODIAC
Cooperative Distributed Interactive Atmospheric Catolog (USDC) ... CODIAC
Cooperative Documents Network Project [*University of Guelph Library*] [*Information service or system*] ... CODOC
Cooperative Documents Project [*Ontario Universities Library Cooperative System*] [*Canada*] (NITA) ... CODOC
Cooperative Ecological Research Project (SAUS) ... CERP
Cooperative Economic Insect Report [*Department of Agriculture*] [*A publication*] ... CEIR
Cooperative Education (SAUO) ... CO-OP
Cooperative Education Association (EA) ... CEA
Cooperative Educational Enterprises ... CEE
Cooperative Educational Research Laboratory, Inc. ... CERLI
Cooperative Educational Service Agency [*National Science Foundation*] ... CESA
Cooperative Educational Services ... CES
Cooperative Energy Development Corp. [*Toronto Stock Exchange symbol*] ... COE
Cooperative Enforcement Agreement [*Environmental Protection Agency*] (GFGA) ... CEA
Co-operative Engagement (SAUS) ... CE
Co-operative Engagement Capability (SAUS) ... CEC
Cooperative Engagement Capability [*Military*] ... CEC
Cooperative Engineering Program [*Automotive industry*] ... CEP
Cooperative English Test ... CET
Cooperative Environmental Management (SAUS) ... CEM
Cooperative Expendable Jammer ... CEJ
Cooperative Export Financing Corp. (MHDW) ... CEFCO
Cooperative Extension Service [*Department of Agriculture*] ... CES
Cooperative Extension Service Telephone Network [*University of Illinois at Champaign-Urbana*] [*Telecommunications service*] (TSSD) ... TELENET
Cooperative Family Registry for Breast Cancer Studies [*National Cancer Institute*] ... CFRBCS
Cooperative Federee du Quebec (AC) ... CFQ
Cooperative Finance Association of America (EA) ... CFAA
Cooperative Finance Corp. [*of National Rural Utilities*] ... CFC
Cooperative Finance Corporation (SAUO) ... CFC
Cooperative Financing Facility [*Export-Import Bank*] ... CFF
Cooperative Fishery and Wildlife Research Unit (COE) ... CFWRU
Cooperative Florida Meteorological Experiment (SAUS) ... COFMEX
Cooperative Food Distributors of America [*Later, NGA*] (EA) ... CFDA
Cooperative for American Relief Everywhere [*Formerly, Cooperative for American Remittances Everywhere*] (AEBS) ... CARE
Co-operative for American Relief to Everywhere (SAUS) ... CARE
Cooperative for American Remittances to Europe (SAUO) ... CARE
Cooperative for American Remittances Everywhere [*Former name*] ... CARE
Co-operative for American Remittances to Europe (WDAA) ... CIRE
Cooperative for Assistance and Relief Everywhere, Inc. (SAUO) ... CARE
Cooperative for Information (SAUO) ... COI
Cooperative Forest Fire Prevention [*Forest Service, Department of Agriculture*] ... CFFP
Cooperative Forest Management (SAUS) ... CFM
Cooperative Fuel Research Council (SAUO) ... CFRC
Cooperative Fuels Research [*Committee*] ... CFR
Cooperative Generic Technology [*Centers for cooperative government and industry work*] ... COGENT
Cooperative Geographic Information System (SAUO) ... CoGIS
Cooperative Hazardous Materials Enforcement Development Program [*RSPA*] (TAG) ... COHMED
Cooperative Health Manpower Education Program [*Veterans Administration*] (GFGA) ... CHMEP
Cooperative Health Statistics System [*Medicine*] ... CHSS
Cooperative High-Performance Sequential Inference Machine [*NEC Corp.*] ... CHI
Co-operative Holidays Association (SAUO) ... CHA
Cooperative Holocene Mapping Project [*Geology*] ... COHMAP
Cooperative Home Care Associates ... CHOA
Cooperative Housing Association of Ontario Inc. [*L'Association de l'Habitation Co-Operative de l'Ontario*] [*Formerly, Ontario Co-Op Housing Committee*] (AC) ... CHAO

Cooperative Housing Bulletin [*A publication*] (EAAP) .... CHB
Cooperative Housing Federation of Nova Scotia (AC) .... CHFNS
Cooperative Housing Foundation (EA) .... CHF
Cooperative Housing Journal [*A publication*] (EAAP) .... CHJ
Cooperative Housing Societies Association of New South Wales [*Australia*] .... CHSANSW
Cooperative Human Linkage Center [*Genetics research*] .... CHLC
Cooperative Human Tissue Network .... CHTN
Cooperative Huntsville Meteorological Experiment (SAUS) .... COHMEX
Cooperative Hurricane Upper Air Station [*National Weather Service*] (NOAA) .... CHUAS
Cooperative Hypermedia (SAUS) .... CHM
Cooperative Immunoassay .... CIA
Cooperative Independent Surveillance (DA) .... CIS
Cooperative Industrial and Commercial Reference and Information Service .... CICRIS
Cooperative Information Network [*Library network*] .... CIN
Cooperative Information Network, Coeur d'Alene, ID [*Library symbol*] [*Library of Congress*] (LCLS) .... IdCCIN
Cooperative Information System (SAUO) .... COINS
Cooperative Information Systems Research Centre (SAUO) .... CISRC
Cooperative Institute fo Climate Studies [*Marine science*] (OSRA) .... CICS
Cooperative Institute for Aerospace Science and Terrestrial Applications [*University of Nevada*] [*Research center*] (RCD) .... CIASTA
Cooperative Institute for Applied Meteorology (SAUS) .... CIAM
Cooperative Institute for Applied Remote Sensing (SAUS) .... CIARS
Cooperative Institute for Arctic Research [*Marine science*] (OSRA) .... CIFAR
Cooperative Institute for Geodata Management and Applications (SAUS) .... CIGMA
Cooperative Institute for Geoscience Management and Applications (SAUO) .... CIGMA
Cooperative Institute for Limnology and Ecosystems Research [*Marine science*] (OSRA) .... CILER
Cooperative Institute for Marine and Atmospheric Studies [*Coral Gables, FL*] [*NOAA, Rosenstiel School of Marine and Atmospheric Science of the University of Miami*] (GRD) .... CIMAS
Cooperative Institute for Marine Resources Studies [*Marine science*] (OSRA) .... CIMRS
Cooperative Institute for Mesoscale Meteorological Studies [*University of Oklahoma, NOAA*] [*Research center*] (RCD) .... CIMMS
Cooperative Institute for Meteorological Satellite Studies (SAUO) .... CIMSS
Cooperative Institute for Meteorological Training and Applied Research (SAUS) .... CIMTAR
Cooperative Institute for Research in Environmental Sciences .... CIRES
Cooperative Institute for Research in the Atmosphere [*Colorado State University, NOAA*] [*Research center*] (RCD) .... CIRA
Cooperative Institute of Meteorology Satellite Studies [*Marine science*] (OSRA) .... CIMSS
Cooperative Institutional Research Program [*UCLA*] .... CIRP
Co-Operative Insurance Development Bureau [*Canada*] (EAIO) .... CIDB
Cooperative Insurance Society [*British*] .... CIS
Cooperative Intelligence Network System [*Proposed*] [*Navy*] .... COINS
Cooperative International GPS Network of IAG (SAUS) .... CIGNET
Cooperative International Pupil-to-Pupil Program (EA) .... CIPPP
Cooperative International Pupil-to-Pupil Program (EA) .... CIPTPP
Cooperative Internationale de Recherche et d'Action en Matiere de Communication (EAIO) .... CIRCOM
Cooperative Investigation of the Caribbean and Adjacent Regions [*UNESCO*] .... CICAR
Cooperative Investigation of the Mediterranean .... CIM
Cooperative Investigation of the Northern Central West Indian Ocean (SAUS) .... CINCWIO
Cooperative Investigation of the Northern Part of the Eastern Central Atlantic .... CINECA
Co-operative Investigations in the Mediterranean (SAUS) .... CIM
Cooperative Investigations of the Caribbean and Adjacent Regions (SAUO) .... CIGAR
Cooperative Investigations of Tropical Reef Ecosystems [*Smithsonian Institution*] (MSC) .... CITRE
Co-operative Laundry and Allied Trades Association (SAUO) .... CLATA
Cooperative League of the United States of America (EA) .... CLUSA
Co-Operative Legislation [*ILO*] [*United Nations*] [*Information service or system*] (DUND) .... COOPLEG
Cooperative Libraries in Central Connecticut [*Library network*] CLICC
Cooperative Library Agency for Systems and Services [*San Jose, CA*] [*Telecommunications*] (TSSD) .... CLASS
Cooperative Library Agency for Systems and Services, San Jose, CA [*Library symbol*] [*Library of Congress*] (LCLS) .... CSjCLA
Cooperative Library and Information Centre (SAUS) CLIC
Cooperative Library Information Program (SAUS) .... CLIP
Cooperative Library Network of Clackamas County, Oak Grove, OR [*Library symbol*] [*Library of Congress*] (LCLS) .... OrOgCL
Cooperative Logistic Supply Support Arrangement [*Military*] (AFIT) .... CLSSA
Cooperative Logistic Support Arrangement [*Military*] (AFM) .... CLSA
Cooperative Logistics CL
Cooperative [*or Coordinated*] **Logistics Support Program** [*Air Force*] (MCD) .... CLSP
Cooperative Logistics Support Program (SAUO) .... CLSP
Cooperative Machine-Readable Cataloging Program [*Library of Congress*] .... COMARC
Cooperative Management Housing Insurance Fund [*Federal Housing Administration*] .... CMHIF
Cooperative Marine Science Programme for the Black Sea (SAUS) .... COMSBLACK
Cooperative Marketing Agreement (SAUS) .... CMA
Cooperative Marketing Partner (VERA) .... CMP
Cooperative Marketing Program (CIST) .... CMP
Cooperative Medical Advertising Bureau (SAUO) .... CMAB
Cooperative Merchandising Agreement (DOAD) .... CMA
Cooperative Meteorological Rocket Network [*NASA*] .... CMRN
Cooperative National Park Resource Studies Unit, University of Hawaii [*Research center*] (RCD) .... CPSU/UH
Cooperative National Park Resources Studies Unit [*Research center*] (RCD) .... CPSU
Cooperative National Plant Pest Survey and Detection Program [*Department of Agriculture*] [*Hyattsville, MD*] [*Database*] .... CNPPSDP
Cooperative Network of In-Service Resources (OICC) .... CNIR
Cooperative North Scandinavian Enalapril Survival Study [*Medicine*] .... CONSENSUS
Cooperative Observational and Modeling Project for the Analysis of Severe Storms (SAUO) .... COMPASS
Cooperative Observational Week (MUGU) .... COW
Cooperative Observations of Polar Electrodynamics (SAUS) .... COPE
Cooperative Observations Program (SAUO) .... COOP
Co-operative Octane Requirements Committee (SAUO) .... CORP
Cooperative of Relief Agencies Licensed for Operation in Germany (SAUO) .... CRALOG
Cooperative Office Distributive Education (AEBS) .... CODE
Cooperative Oklahoma P3 Studies (SAUS) .... COPS
Cooperative Oklahoma Profiler Studies-1991 [*Marine science*] (OSRA) COPS-91
Cooperative Oncology Group [*National Cancer Institute*] .... COG
Cooperative Online Resource Catalog .... CORC
Cooperative Online Serials [*Library of Congress*] .... CONSER
Cooperative Online Serials Acquisition Project (NITA) .... COSAP
Cooperative Online Serials Program (AL) .... CONSER
Cooperative Operating System Environment [*Computer science*] .... COSE
Cooperative Opportunities Document (AAGC) .... COD
Cooperative Opportunity for NCEP Data Using IDD Technology (SAUS) .... CONDUIT
Co-operative Party (SAUO) .... COP
Cooperative Phantom Jamming (MCD) .... CPJ
Cooperative Planting Program (GNE) .... CPP
Co-operative Pollution Abatement Research (SAUO) .... CPAR
Cooperative Pollution Abatement Research (SAUS) .... CPAR
Cooperative Polygyny .... CP
Cooperative Power [*Later, SPG*] (EA) .... CP
Cooperative Power Association [*Nuclear energy*] (NRCH) .... CPA
Cooperative Preservation of Architectural Records [*Defunct*] (EA) .... COPAR
Co-operative Production Federation of Great Britain (SAUO) .... CPFGB
Co-operative Productive Federation (SAUO) .... CPF
Cooperative Program (WDMC) .... co-op
Cooperative Program for Educational Opportunity (EA) .... CPEO
Cooperative Program for Operational Meteorology, Education and Training [*National Center for Atmospheric Research*] (USDC) .... COMET
Cooperative Program for Operational Meteorology, Education and Training (SAUO) .... COMET
Cooperative Program in Educational Administration .... CPEA
Cooperative Program of Research on Aquaculture [*UN Food and Agriculture Organization*] .... COPRAQ
Co-operative Programme for Monitoring and Evaluation of the Long-Range Transboundary of Air Pollutants in Europe (SAUO) .... EMEP
Cooperative Programme in Europe for Research on Nature and Industry through Coordinated University Studies (SAUO) .... COPERNICUS
Cooperative Project for Educational Development [*Office of Education*] .... COPED
Cooperative Projects with Industry [*National Research Council, Canada*] .... COPI
Cooperative Publication Association (EA) .... CPA
Cooperative Radiation Effects Simulation Program [*Military*] (DNAB) .... CORES
Co-operative R&D Agreement (SAUS) .... CRDA
Cooperative Recreation Service [*Later, World Around Songs*] (EA) .... CRS
Cooperative Research [*in agriculture*] .... COR
Cooperative Research Act .... CRA
Cooperative Research Action for Technology .... CRAFT
Cooperative Research and Design Agreement (SAUO) .... CRADA
Cooperative Research and Development Agreement [*Department of Energy National Laboratories*] .... CRADA
Cooperative Research and Development Agreement [*Department of Energy National Laboratories*] .... CRDA
Cooperative Research and Development Program (SAUO) .... CR&DP
Cooperative Research and Service Division (SAUO) .... CRSD
Cooperative Research Centre for Catchment Hydrology (SAUO) .... CRCCH
Cooperative Research Centre for Freshwater Ecology (SAUO) .... CRCFE
Co-operative Research Centre for Legumes in Mediterranean Agriculture (SAUO) .... CLIMA
Cooperative Research Centre for Southern Hemisphere Meteorology (SAUO) .... CRCSHM
Cooperative Research Centre for Viticulture [*Australia*] .... CRCV
Cooperative Research Centres Committee [*Australia*] .... CRCC
Cooperative Research Council .... CRC
Cooperative Research Institute [*Defunct*] (EA) .... CORE
Cooperative Research Program [*Military and Office of Education*] .... CRP
Cooperative Research Service [*Kentucky State University*] [*Research center*] (RCD) .... CRS
Cooperative Research Support Projects (SAUO) .... CRSP
Co-Operative Retail Services [*British*] .... CRS
Cooperative Retail Society (ODBW) .... CRS
Cooperative Robot (ADWA) .... cobot
Cooperative School Program [*US Employment Service*] [*Department of Labor*] .... CSP
Cooperative Secretaries Diploma (SAUO) .... CSD
Cooperative Security System (ACAE) .... CSS

cooperative society (SAUO) .... co op
Co-operative Society (SAUO) .... CS
Cooperative Society .... CS
Cooperative State Research, Education, and Extension Service [US
    Department of Agriculture] .... CSREES
Cooperative State Research, Education and Extensive Service
    (SAUO) .... CSREES
Cooperative State Research Service [Department of Agriculture] [Washington,
    DC] .... CSRS
Cooperative Statistical Program [For IUD data] .... CSP
Cooperative Study in the Mediterranean [Intergovernmental Oceanographic
    Commission Coordination Group] (USDC) .... CSM
Cooperative Study of the Kuroshio [UNESCO] .... CSK
Cooperative Study of the Kuroshio and Adjacent Regions
    [Intergovernmental Oceanographic Commission Coordination Group]
    (USDC) .... CSK
Co-operative Supply Association of Tanzania (SAUO) .... COSATA
Cooperative Survey of the Eastern Tropical Pacific (MSC) .... EASTROPIC
Cooperative Survey of the Pacific Equatorial Zone (SAUS) ...... EQUAPAC
Cooperative Threat Reduction [Military] (RDA) .... CTR
Cooperative Tracking System (MCD) .... CTS
Co-operative Union (SAUO) .... Co-OpU
Cooperative Union (SAUO) .... CU
Co-operative Union (SAUO) .... CU
Cooperative Union of Canada .... CUC
Cooperative Union Serials System .... CUSS
Cooperative Upper-Air Station [National Weather Service] (NOAA) .... CUAS
Cooperative Upper-Air Unit [National Weather Service] .... CUA
Cooperative Users of Equimatics Financial Systems (CSR) ...... CUEFS
Cooperative Users of FICS and MARS [Atlanta, GA] (CSR) ...... CUFAM
Co-operative War Industry (SAUO) .... CWI
Cooperative Weapon Delivery (MCD) .... CWD
Cooperative Weapon Delivery Aircraft (ACAE) .... CWDA
Cooperative Weapons Data Indexing Committee [AEC and DoD] ..... CWDIC
Cooperative Whole Grain Education Association (EA) .... CWGEA
Cooperative Wholesale Committee (SAUO) .... CWC
Cooperative Wholesale Society (SAUO) .... CWRU
Cooperative Wholesale Society [British] .... CWS
Cooperative Wildlife Research Laboratory [Southern Illinois University at
    Carbondale] [Research center] (RCD) .... CWRL
Cooperative Wind Tunnel .... CWT
Cooperative Work Experience Education Association (EA) ...... CWEEA
Cooperative Youth Initiative [British] .... CYI
Cooperative Youth Movement (SAUO) .... CYM
Cooperatively Assembled Virginia Low Intensity Educational Reactor
    (NRCH) .... CAVALIER
Cooperatives Research Unit [British] .... CRU
Cooper-Harper Rating [NASA] (NASA) .... CHR
Cooper-Hewitt Museum (SAUS) .... C-H M
Cooper-Johnson, Yellowknife, Northwest Territories [Library symbol]
    [National Library of Canada] (BIB) .... NWYCJ
Coopers Allied Water Committee (SAUO) .... CAWF
Coopers' and Allied Workers' Federation of Great Britain [A union] .... CAWFGB
Coopers & Lybrand Accounting and Distributive Inventory System
    (MHDB) .... CLAUDIUS
Coopers & Lybrand Consulting Group, Ottawa, Ontario [Library symbol]
    [National Library of Canada] (BIB) .... OOCLCG
Coopers & Lybrand USA [New York, NY] [Telecommunications] (TSSD) ...... C & L
Coopers Appreciation [An association] (EA) .... CA
Cooper's Chancery and Practice Reporter [Upper Canada] [A publication]
    (DLA) .... Coop C & PR
Cooper's Comprehensive Environmental Desk Reference [A publication]
    (COE) .... CCEDR
Cooper's Equity Digest [A publication] (DLA) .... Coop Eq Dig
Cooper's Equity Pleading [A publication] (DLA) .... Coop Eq Pl
Coopers' Federation of Great Britain and Ireland [A union] .... CFGBI
Cooper's Florida Reports [21-24 Florida] [A publication] (DLA) ..... Cooper
Cooper's Institutes of Justinian [A publication] (DLA) ...... Cooper Just Inst
Cooper's Institutes of Justinian [A publication] (DLA) .... Coop Inst
Coopers' International Union of North America .... CIU
Coopers' International Union of North America (EA) .... CIUNA
Cooper's Judgment [A publication] (DLA) .... Coop Judg
Coopers Lake [Montana] [Seismograph station code, US Geological Survey]
    [Closed] (SEIS) .... CKM
Cooper's Law of Libel [A publication] (DLA) .... Coop Lib
Cooper's Medical Jurisprudence [A publication] (DLA) ..... Coop Med Jur
Cooper's Public Records of Great Britain [A publication] (DLA) .... Coop Rec
Cooper's Reports [21-24 Florida] [A publication] (DLA) .... Coop
Coopers Select Cases tempore Brougham (SAUS) .... Sel CastBr
Cooper's Select Early Cases [Scotland] [A publication] (DLA) ..... Coop Sel EC
Cooper's Tennessee Chancery Reports [A publication] (DLA) .... Coop
Cooper's Tennessee Chancery Reports [A publication] (DLA) ..... Coop Ch
Cooper's Tennessee Chancery Reports [A publication] (DLA) ..... Cooper
Cooper's Tennessee Chancery Reports [A publication] (DLA) ..... Cooper Ch
Cooper's Tennessee Chancery Reports [A publication] (DLA) .... Coop Ten Chy
Cooper's Tennessee Chancery Reports [A publication] (DLA) ..... Coop Tenn Ch
Coopers Tennessee Chancery Reports [A publication] (DLA) .... Tenn Ch
Coopers Tennessee Chancery Reports (SAUS.) .... Tenn Ch
Coopers Tennessee Chancery Reports (journ.) (SAUS) .... Tenn Ch
Coopersmith Self-Esteem Inventory [Psychometrics] .... CSEI
Coopersmith Self-Esteem Scale (DHP) .... CSE
Cooperstown & Charlotte Valley Railway Corp. [AAR code] .... CACV
Cooperstown, ND [Location identifier] [FAA] (FAAL) .... TOW
Cooperstown Public Library, Cooperstown, ND [Library symbol] [Library of
    Congress] (LCLS) .... NdCo

Coopersville District Library, Coopersville, MI [Library symbol] [Library of
    Congress] (LCLS) .... MiCoop
Coopworth Sheep Society of Australia .... CSAA
Co-Orbit Support System (SSD) .... COSS
Co-Orbital (ACAE) .... CO
Co-orbital Intercepter Scoring Technique (SAUS) .... CIST
Coorbital Interceptor Scoring Technique .... CIST
Co-Orbiting Platform (SSD) .... COP
Co-Orbiting Satellite (ACAE) .... COS
Coordinaciãn General del Plan Nacional de Zonas Deprimidas y Grupos
    Marginados (SAUO) .... COPLAMAR
Coordinaciãn Nacional para la Planeaciãn y Programaciãn de la Educaciãn
    Media Superior (SAUO) .... CONPPEMS
Coordinacion de Organismos Empresariales de Comercio Exterior
    [Mexican Business Coordinating Council for NAFTA] (CROSS) ...... COECE
Coordinacion Democratica [Democratic Coordination] [Spain] [Political
    party] (PPE) .... CD
Coordinacion Revolucionaria de las Masas [Revolutionary Coordination of
    the Masses] [El Salvador] (PD) .... CRM
Coordinador Nacional de Bases [National Coordination of Bases]
    [Colombia] (PD) .... CNB
Coordinadora Civilista Nacional [Panama] [Political party] (EY) .... COCINA
Coordinadora de Organizaciones Feministas [Coordination of Feminist
    Organizations] [Puerto Rico] (EAIO) .... COF
Coordinadora de Salud, Educaciãn, Desarrollo y Promociãn Sicoal de
    Jocotan (SAUO) .... COSEDEPSO
Coordinadora Democratica [Democratic Coordinating Board] [Nicaragua]
    (PPW) .... CD
Coordinadora Democratica Nicaraguense Ramiro Sacasa [Nicaragua]
    [Political party] (EY) .... CDN
Coordinadora Europea de Asociaciones de Emigrantes Espanoles
    (SAUO) .... CEAEE
Coordinadora Guerrillera Nacional [Colombia] (EY) .... CGN
Coordinadora Guerrillera Simon Bolivar [Colombia] [Political party] (EY) .... CGSB
Coordinadora Nacional de Organizaciones Cafetaleras [National network of
    small coffee producers] [Mexico] (CROSS) .... CNOC
Coordinamento delle Industrie Radiologiche ed Elettromedicali
    [Coordination Committee of the Radiological and Electromedical Industries]
    [EC] (ECED) .... COCIR
Coordinamento Uruguaiano di Solidarieta in Italia .... CUSI
Coordinate .... COOR
Coordinate [or Coordination] (AFM) .... COORD
Coordinate (TBD) .... Coord
Coordinate (ADWA) .... coord
Coordinate Adder (SAA) .... COAD
Coordinate, Anticipate, and Verify (MCD) .... CAV
Coordinate Conversion Computer (MCD) CCC
Coordinate Conversion Processor (ACAE) .... CCP
Coordinate Conversion Routine .... COCO
Coordinate Converter (AAG) CC
Coordinate Data Set .... CORDAT
Coordinate Data Terminal (MCD) .... CDT
Coordinate Data Transmission .... CDT
Coordinate Data Transmitter (SAUS) .... CDT
Coordinate Index CI
Coordinate Indexing Group [ASLIB] (DIT) .... CIG
Coordinate Indexing System (SAUS) .... CIS
Coordinate Light Information Photographic Strips (SAUS) .... CLIPS
Coordinate Measuring and Recording System (SAUS) .... COMARS
Coordinate Measuring Machine .... CMM
Coordinate Measuring System (AAEL) .... CMS
Coordinate Reader (SAUS) .... CR
Coordinate Rotation Digital Computer .... CORDIC
Coordinate Transformation System (MCD) .... CTS
Coordinated (SAUS) .... Coord
Coordinated Accident Rescue Endeavor-State of Mississippi
    (SAUS) .... CARE-SOM
Coordinated Activity Allowance List [Military] (NVT) .... COAAL
Coordinated Activity List [Navy] (NVT) .... COOAL
Coordinated Aerospace Supplier Evaluation (SAUO) .... CASE
Coordinated Agency for Supplier Evaluation (SAUO) .... CASE
Coordinated Agency-Wide Research Activities [National Science
    Foundation] .... CARA
Coordinated Aircraft/Stores Program [Obsolete] [Navy] (NG) ...... COASP
Coordinated Air-Sea Experiment [Marine science] (OSRA) .... CASE
Coordinated Allocation System (SAUS) .... CAS
Coordinated Analysis of the Thermosphere (SAUS) .... CAT
Coordinated Antisubmarine Exercise (SAUO) .... CASEX
Coordinated ASW [Antisubmarine Warfare] Services and Training [Navy]
    (NVT) .... CAST
Coordinated Atomic Operations (CINC) .... CAO
Coordinated Auroral Experiment Using Scatter And Rockets (SAUS) ..... CAESAR
Coordinated Bargaining Committee (DICI) .... CBC
Coordinated Building Communication (PDAA) .... CBC
Coordinated Care Program [Medicine] .... CCP
Coordinated Caribbean Transport [US shipping line] (IMH) .... CCT
Coordinated Cockpit Display (MCD) .... CCD
Coordinated Command, Control, Communications and Computing for
    Integrated Information and Intelligence [Military] C5I3
Coordinated Commentary Programming [Computer science] .... CCP
Coordinated Containerization Point .... CCP
Coordinated Design Data Required .... CDDR
Coordinated Eastern Arctic Experiment [Marine science] (OSRA) ..... CEAREX
Coordinated Eastern Arctic Experiment (SAUO) .... CLEAREX
Coordinated Ecosystem Research [Marine science] (OSRA) .... CER

Coordinated Eiscat and Balloon Observations (SAUS) .... CEBO
Coordinated Electronic Countermeasures Exercise [*Military*] (NVT) .... COREX
Coordinated Evaluation System [*National Institute of Standards and Technology*] .... CES
Coordinated Examination Program [*Internal Revenue Service*] .... CEP
Coordinated Experimental Research [*Program*] [*National Science Foundation*] .... CER
Coordinated Federal Lands Highways Technial Information Program [*MTMC*] (TAG) .... CTIP
Coordinated Federal Wage System (MCD) .... CFWS
Coordinated Financial Planning .... CFP
Coordinated Fire Line (AABC) .... CFL
Coordinated Firing Doctrine (ACAE) .... CFD
Coordinated Geometry [*Programming language*] [*1957*] (CSR) .... COGO
Coordinated Helps in Language Development (ADA) .... CHILD
Coordinated Human Resource Technology (MCD) .... CHRT
Coordinated Hungarian Relief [*Defunct*] (EA) .... CHR
Co-ordinated Information System on the State of the Environment and Natural Resources (SAUO) .... CORINE
Coordinated Information Transfer for Education (AEBS) .... CITE
Coordinated Instrument Package (SAUS) .... CIP
Coordinated Interagency Partnership Regulating International Students .... CIPRIS
Co-ordinated Inter-service Incident Management System (SAUS) .... CIMS
Coordinated Inventory-control System (SAUS) .... COINS
Coordinated Investigation of Micronesian Anthropology (SAUO) .... CIMA
Coordinated Joint Outline Emergency Plan [*Military*] (CINC) .... CJOEP
Coordinated Keysort Index (ADA) .... COOKI
Coordinated Library Information Program (SAUS) .... CLIP
Coordinated Logistics Support Program (SAUO) .... CLSP
Coordinated Management of Meaning [*Communications theory*] .... CMM
Coordinated Manual Control .... CMC
Coordinated Mediterranean Pollution Monitoring and Research Programme (SAUS) .... MEDPOL
Coordinated Navy Total Acquisition Control [*System*] .... CONTAC
Coordinated Observations of Polar Electrodynamics (SAUO) .... COPE
Coordinated Occupational Information Network [*COIN Educational Products*] [*Information service or system*] (IID) .... COIN
Coordinated Off-Campus Degree Program (SAUO) .... COCDP
Coordinated Operability Test .... COT
Coordinated Procurement Program Appraisal [*DoD*] .... COPPA
Coordinated Program of Research in Distributed Computing [*British*] (NITA) .... CPRDC
Coordinated Proposal Ice-Sheet Research with ERS-1 (SAUS) ISR-ERS-1
Coordinated Reconnaissance Plan (CINC) .... CRP
Coordinated Regional Allowance List (AFIT) .... CORAL
Coordinated Regional Assessment (SAUS) .... CRA
Coordinated Research and Environmental Surveillance Programme (SAUO) .... CRESP
Coordinated Research & Monitoring Program of Marine Contamination in the SE Pacific (SAUS) .... CONPACSE
Coordinated Resources Plan .... CRP
Coordinated Review Effort (SAUO) .... CRE
Co-ordinated Roland Air Defence (SAUS) .... CORAD
Coordinated Science Laboratory [*University of Illinois*] [*Research center*] .... CSL
Coordinated Ship Development Plan [*Navy*] .... CSDP
Coordinated Ship Electronics Device [*Navy*] .... CSED
Coordinated Shipboard [*or Shorebased*] **Allowance List** [*Navy*] .... COSAL
Coordinated Shipboard [*or Shorebased*] **Allowance List** [*Navy*] .... COSBAL
Coordinated Shore Maintenance Allowance List [*Navy*] (CAAL) .... COSMAL
Coordinated Shorebased Allowance List (SAUS) .... COSAL
Coordinated Shorebased Material Allowance List [*Air Force*] (AFIT) .... COSMAL
Coordinated Situation System .... CSS
Coordinated Studies in Polar Stratospheric Clouds (SAUO) .... COSPOC
Coordinated Test Plan [*Obsolete*] .... CTP
Coordinated Test Program [*Military*] (AABC) .... CTP
Coordinated Transfer Application System [*For medical students*] .... COTRANS
Coordinated Universal Time (NASA) .... CUT
Coordinated Universal Time (USDC) .... UTC
Coordinated Vocational Academic Education (SAUO) .... CVAE
Coordinated Vocational-Academic Education .... CVAE
Coordinates Computed (MUGU) CC
Coordinates, Definitions, and Notations (GEOI) .... CDN
Coordinate-Superordinate-Subordinate-Collateral-Relationship (SAUS) .... COSSCO-Relationship
Coordinateur Automatique de Traffic .... CAUTRA
Coordinating (AL) .... Coor
Coordinating (SAUS) .... Coord
Coordinating (SAUO) .... COORD
Coordinating Agency (SAUO) .... CA
Coordinating Agency for Supplier Evaluation .... CASE
Coordinating and Programming Authority (SAUO) .... CPA
Co-Ordinating Animal Welfare [*British*] .... CAW
Coordinating Area Production Urgency Committee .... CAPUC
Coordinating Authority (NATG) .... COORAUTH
Coordinating Board (SAUO) .... COORDBD
Coordinating Board of Jewish Organizations (EA) .... CBJO
Coordinating Board of Tobacco Trade Associations [*Later, NATD*] (EA) .... CBTTA
Co-Ordinating Body on the Seas of East Asia .... COBSEA
Coordinating Centre for Regional Information Training (SAUO) .... CRIT
Coordinating Commission for the Justice Sector (SAUO) .... CCJS
Coordinating Commitee for European Youth Exchange (SAUO) .... CC-EYE
Coordinating Committee (MCD) .... CDCOM
Coordinating Committee .... COCOM
Coordinating Committee (SAUO) .... CORP
Co-Ordinating Committee for Cancer Research (SAUO) .... CCCR
Co-ordinating Committee for East-West Trade Policy (SAUS) .... COCOM
Coordinating Committee for Ellis Island (EA) .... CCEI
Coordinating Committee for Export Control to Communist Countries (SAUS) .... COCOM
Coordinating Committee for Independant Staff Unions and Associations of the United Nations System (SAUO) .... CCISUA
Coordinating Committee for Intercontinental Research Networks (SAUS) .... CCIRN
Coordinating Committee for International Voluntary Service [*France*] (EAIO) .... CCIVS
Co-ordinating Committee for Manufacturers of Static Converters (SAUO) .... COCOS
Coordinating Committee for Multilateral Export Controls (SAUO) .... COCAM
Co-ordinating Committee for Oceanographic Research, Science Cooperating Division (SAUO) .... CCOR
Coordinating Committee for Satellite Communication [*Switzerland*] (NITA) .... CCSC
Coordinating Committee for Slavic and East European Library Resources (SAUO) .... COCOSEER
Coordinating Committee for Slavic and East European Library Resources .... COCOSEERS
Coordinating Committee for the Alligators River Region (SAUO) .... CCARR
Co-ordinating Committee for the Liberation of Africa (SAUO) LC
Coordinating Committee for the Moon and Planets (SAUO) .... CCMP
Coordinating Committee for the Societies of Orthopaedic and Traumatic Surgery of the European Common Market (SAUO) .... COCOMAC
Co-ordinating Committee for the Welfare of Evacuees from Uganda (SAUO) .... CCWEU
Coordinating Committee for the World Climate Program [*Marine science*] (OSRA) .... CCWCP
Coordinating Committee for/on Multilateral Export Controls (SAUO) .... COCOM
Coordinating Committee of Allied Control Authorities (SAUO) .... CCACA
Coordinating Committee of Christian Broadcasting (SAUO) .... CCCB
Co-ordinating Committee of Democratic Forces [*Ghana*] [*Political party*] (EY) .... CCDF
Coordinating Committee of Engineering Society Presidents (SAUO) .... CCESP
Coordinating Committee of Independent Trade Unions .... CCITU
Coordinating Committee of International Anti-Apartheid Year (SAUO) .... CCIAAY
Coordinating Committee of International Networks (SAUS) .... CCIRN
Coordinating Committee of Overseas Students Organization [*British*] .... CCOSO
Coordinating Committee of Technical Assistance .... CCTA
Coordinating Committee of the Societies of Mineral-Deposit Geologists (SAUO) .... CCSMDG
Coordinating Committee of Trade Union Organizations [*Ceylon*] .... CCTUO
Coordinating Committee on Agricultural Chemicals (SAUS) .... CCAC
Coordinating committee on atmospheric conditioning for testing (SAUO) .... ATCO
Coordinating Committee on Documentation in the Social Science (SAUO) .... CCDSS
Coordinating Committee on Export Controls [*From Western to Eastern bloc nations*] .... COCOM
Coordinating Committee on Export Controls (ACRL) .... CoCOM
Coordinating Committee on General Sciences (SAUO) .... CCGS
Coordinating Committee on Great Lakes Basic Hydraulic and Hydrologic Data (SAUO) .... CCGLBHHD
Co-Ordinating Committee on Health Aspects of Radiation Research (HEAS) .... CCHARR
Coordinating Committee on Materials Research and Development [*Executive Office of the President*] .... CCMRD
Coordinating Committee on Multilateral Export Controls (AAGC) .... COCOM
Coordinating Committee on Oceanography .... CCO
Coordinating Committee on Science and Technology [*Australia*] .... CCST
Coordinating Committee on Slavic and East European Library Services (SAUS) .... COCOSEER
Coordinating Committee on the Ozone Layer [*United Nations*] (OSRA) .... CCOL
Coordinating Committee on the Standardization of the Writing of Dates (SAUO) .... DATCO
Coordinating Committee on Toxics and Drugs (EA) .... CCTD
Coordinating Committee on Women in the Historical Profession [*Later, CCWHP/CGWH*] (EA) .... CCWHP
Coordinating Committee on Women in the Historical Profession/ Conference Group onWomen's History (EA) .... CCWHP/CGWH
Coordinating Council for Computers in Construction (EA) CCCC
Coordinating Council for Higher Education .... CCHE
Coordinating Council of Library Organizations (SAUO) .... CCLO
Coordinating Council of Literary Magazines [*Later, CLMP*] (EA) .... CCLM
Coordinating Council of National Archaeological Societies (EA) .... CCONAS
Coordinating Council of National Court Organizations [*Defunct*] (EA) .... CCNCO
Coordinating Council of Private Educational Associations .... COCOPEA
Coordinating Council of South African Trade Unions .... CCSATU
Coordinating Council on Manufactured Housing Finance [*Defunct*] (EA) .... CCMHF
Coordinating Council on Medical Education [*Superseded by CFMA*] (EA) .... CCME
Coordinating Council on Research Networks (SAUO) .... CCRN
Coordinating Draft [*of field manuals*] [*Military*] (INF) .... CD
Coordinating Equipment Research Committee .... CER
Coordinating European Council for the Development of Performance Tests for/of Lubricants and Engine Fuels (SAUO) .... CEC
Coordinating Fuel Research (MCD) .... CFR
Coordinating Group .... CG
Coordinating group for NCAR research (SAUO) .... CSMAC

Coordinating Group for the Composite Observing System for the North Atlantic (SAUO) .... CGC
Coordinating Group for the Harmonization of Chemical Classification Systems (SAUO) .... CG/HCCS
Coordinating Group for the Tactical Weather Net (SAUO) .... CGTWN
Coordinating Information for Texas Educators [Texas State Education Agency] [No longer available] [Information service or system] (IID) ...... CITE
Co-ordinating Installation Design Authority (SAUS) .... CIDA
Coordinating Installations (MCD) CI
Coordinating Investigator (SAUS) CI
Coordinating Justice for Cyprus Committee [Australia] .... CJCC
Coordinating Lubricant and Equipment Research Committee [Coordinating Research Council] .... CLR
Coordinating of Research and Development [Navy] .... CORD
Coordinating Office for Regional Resource Centers .... CORRC
Coordinating Organization Director (SAA) .... COD
Coordinating Organization for Personal Enrichment (SAUO) .... COPE
Coordinating Organization of Book Associations [Defunct] .... COBA
Coordinating Panel [NATO] .... CP
Coordinating Research Center (SAUO) .... CRC
Coordinating Research Council (EA) .... CRC
Coordinating Research Council of the Petroleum Industry .... CRCPI
Coordinating Research Council-Air Pollution Research Advisory Committee (SAUS) .... CRC-APRAC
Coordinating Research Council-Air Polluttion Research Advisory Commitee (SAUO) .... CRC-APRAC
Coordinating Research Council-Environmental Protection Agency (SAUO) .... CRC-EPA
Coordinating Scientific and Technical Council (SAUS) .... CSTC
Coordinating Secretariat of National Unions of Students [in Africa] .... COSEC
Co-ordinating Unit for the MAP (SAUO) .... MEDU
Coordinating Working Party on Atlantic Fishery Statistics .... CWP
Coordination [ICAO designator] (FAAC) .... CDN
Coordination [Channel] [Electronics] (ECII) .... CO-ORD
Coordination (SAUO) .... COORD
Coordination .... COORDN
Coordination and Contract Summary Sheet .... CCSS
Coordination and Control of Personnel Surveys [Military] (DNAB) .... CCOPS
Coordination and Equipment .... C & E
Coordination and Equipment (SAUS) .... C&E
Coordination and Information Center [Department of Energy] [Information service or system] (IID) CIC
Coordination and Interference Management System (ACAE) .... CIMS
Coordination and Training Team [Special Operations Force] [Military] (DOMA) .... CTT
Co-ordination & Warning System (SAUS) .... CWS
Coordination Center (SAUO) CC
Coordination Center for Repair Work in Power Stations (SAUO) .... Interenergoremont
Coordination committee (SAUO) .... Concom
Coordination Committee for Science and Technology (SAUO) .... CSST
Coordination Committee for Transport Planning [NATO] (NATG) .... CCTP
Coordination Control Board (MCD) .... CCB
Co-ordination, Control, Communications & Intelligence Center (SAUS) C3IC
Coordination Council for North American Affairs .... CCNAA
Coordination Council on Control of Liquor Abuse .... CCCLA
Co-ordination de l'Opposition Democratique [Gabon] [Political party] (EY) .... COD
Coordination Document .... CD
Coordination Drawing .... CD
Coordination Group for Meteorological Satellites (ADWA) .... CGMS
Coordination Group for Meteorological Studies (SAUO) .... CGMS
Co-ordination Group for the Composite Observing System for the North Atlantic (SAUS) .... CGC
Coordination Group for/on Meteorological Satellites (SAUO) .... CGMS
Coordination Group of Non Governmental Organizations in the Field of Man-Made Environment (SAUO) .... COG
Coordination Group on Drugs (SAUO) .... CELAD
Coordination in Development (SAUO) .... CD
Coordination in Development (EA) .... CODEL
Coordination in Development Consortium (SAUO) .... CODEL
Coordination in Development Inc. (SAUO) .... CODEL
Coordination in Direct Support (NVT) .... CIDS
Coordination Letter Report (SAA) .... CLR
Coordination Line (NVT) CL
Coordination Message [Aviation code] .... CDN
Coordination Number [Chemistry] .... CN
Coordination Number Invariance [Chemistry] .... CNI
Coordination of Allied Supplies [World War II] .... CAS
Coordination of Atomic Operations - Standard Operating Procedures .... CAO-SOP
Coordination of Atomic Operations Communications Net .... CAOCOMNET
Coordination of Atomic Operations-Standing Operating Procedures (SAUS) .... CAO SOP
Coordination of Benefits [Insurance] .... COB
Coordination of Geostationary Meteorological Satellites [National Oceanic and Atmospheric Administration] .... CGMS
Coordination of Hybrid and Integrated Circuit Operations (IAA) .... CHICO
Coordination of Maya Unity and Consensus (SAUO) .... IUCM
Coordination of Operating Data by Automatic Computer .... CODAC
Coordination of Recent and Projected System Efforts [DoD] .... CORPSE
Coordination of Record and Data Base System [Telecommunications] (TEL) .... CORDS
Coordination of Space Techniques for Geodesy and Geodynamics (SAUO) .... CSTG

Coordination of Space Techniques for Geodesy and Geophysics (SAUO) .... CSTGAG
Coordination of Systems, Integrated Goals, and Networks [DoD] .... COSIGN
Co-ordination of Valve Development (SAUS) .... CVD
Coordination of Valve Development (SAUS) .... CVD
Coordination of Valve Development Committee (SAUO) .... CVD
Coordination of/on Geostationary Meteorological Satellites (SAUO) .... CGMS
Coordination on Geostationary Meteorological Satellites (SAUS) .... CGMS
Coordination Point (SAUS) .... CP
Coordination Processor [Telecommunications] .... CP
Co-ordination Staff Foreign and Commonwealth Office (SAUO) .... CSFCO
Coordination Working Group (SAUO) .... COORDWG
Coordinative Retrieval of Selectively Sorted Permuted Analogue-Title Entries [Computer science] .... CROSSPATE
Coordinator (AL) .... Coor
Coordinator (PHSD) .... Coord
Coordinator (SAUS) .... COORD
Coordinator .... COORDNTR
Coordinator (DNAB) .... CORD
Coordinator and Liaison Maintenance Officer (SAUS) .... CLMO
Coordinator ASW [Antisubmarine Warfare] Services and Training (DOMA) .... CASTEX
Coordinator Defense Production Board (SAUO) .... CODP
Coordinator, Department of the Navy Studies and Analyses (DNAB) .... CDONSA
Coordinator for Army Studies (SAUO) .... CAS
Coordinator for Industrial Cooperation [Functions ceased, 1937] CIC
Coordinator for International Relations [Australia] .... CIR
Coordinator for Multi-lateral Development program (SAUO) .... CMD
Coordinator for Multi-lateral Development Program (SAUS) .... CMD
Coordinator for Narcotics Affairs [Department of State] .... CNA
Coordinator for Production and Logistics (SAUO) .... CPL
Coordinator General (ADA) .... COG
Coordinator of Army Studies (AABC) .... CAS
Coordinator of Chain Operations [Coast Guard] (DNAB) .... COCO
Coordinator of Commercial and Cultural Relations [New Deal] .... CCCR
Co-Ordinator of Health Education (HEAS) .... CHE
Coordinator of Information .... COI
Coordinator of Inter-American Affairs .... CIAA
Coordinator Surface Search [Environmental science] (COE) .... CSS
Coordinators of Data Processing Education (HGAA) .... CODE
Coordinators of Undergraduate Psychiatric Education (SAUS) .... COUPE
Co-oriented Information of the European Environment (SAUO) .... CORINE
Coorong Fauna Reserve (SAUS) .... CFR
Coors (Adolph)Cl'B' [NASDAQ symbol] (TTSB) .... ACCOB
Coors (Adolph)Cl'B' [NYSE symbol] (SG) .... RKY
Coors [Adolph] Co. [NASDAQ symbol] (NQ) .... ACCO
Coors [Adolph] Co. [Associated Press] (SAG) .... Coors
Coos Bay, OR [Television station call letters] .... KCBY
Coos Bay, OR [FM radio station call letters] (RBYB) .... KDCQ
Coos Bay, OR [AM radio station call letters] .... KHSN
Coos Bay, OR [AM radio station call letters] (BROA) .... KMHS-AM
Coos Bay, OR [Television station call letters] .... KMTZ
Coos Bay, OR [AM radio station call letters] .... KRSR
Coos Bay, OR [FM radio station call letters] .... KSBA
Coos Bay, OR [FM radio station call letters] (RBYB) .... KYSG
Coos Bay, OR [FM radio station call letters] .... KYTT
Coos Bay Public Library, Coos Bay, OR [OCLC symbol] (OCLC) .... BAY
Coos Bay Public Library, Coos Bay, OR [Library symbol] [Library of Congress] (LCLS) .... OrCb
Coos Bay Wagon Road [Lands] [Department of the Interior] .... CBWR
Coos County Library Association [Library network] .... CCLA
Coosa, GA [FM radio station call letters] .... WSRM
Coosa Valley Librarians Association [Library network] .... CVLA
Cootamundra [Australia] [Airport symbol] (OAG) .... CMO
Coote on Mortgages [A publication] (DLA) .... Coo Mort
Coote on Mortgages [A publication] (DLA) .... Coote
Coote on Mortgages [A publication] (DLA) .... Coote Mor
Coote. Practice of the Court of Probate [9th ed.] [1883] [A publication] (DLA) .... Coote Pro Pr
Coote. Practice of the Court of Probate, Edited by Tristram [A publication] (DLA) .... Coote & Tr Pr Pr
Coote's Admiralty Practice [A publication] (DLA) .... Coote Adm
Coote's Ecclesiastical Court Practice [A publication] (DLA) .... Coote Ecc Pr
Coote's Law of Landlord and Tenant [A publication] (DLA) .... Coote L & T
Cop (WDAA) C
Cop Shop (SAUS) .... CS
Copa Girls Alumnae Association (EA) .... CGAA
Copacabana [Record label] [Brazil] .... Cop
Copacabana [Record label] [Brazil] .... Copa
Copacabana [Bolivia] [ICAO location identifier] (ICLI) .... SLCC
COPA-COGECA Working Party for Non Edible Horticultural Products (SAUO) .... COPA-COGECA
Copaipo [Chile] [Airport symbol] (AD) .... CPO
Copaquilla [Bolivia] [ICAO location identifier] (ICLI) .... SLCQ
Copart, Inc. [Associated Press] (SAG) .... Copart
Copart, Inc. [NASDAQ symbol] (SAG) .... CPRT
Co-Partner (ROG) .... CO-PTR
Co-Payment Requirement Rider [Health insurance] (GHCT) .... CRI
Copconda-York [Vancouver Stock Exchange symbol] .... CYK
Copeland Corporation (SAUO) .... CRF
Copeland, KS [FM radio station call letters] (BROA) .... KHYM-FM
Copeland, KS [FM radio station call letters] .... KJIL
Copeland, KS [FM radio station call letters] .... KYBD
Copeland Resources [Vancouver Stock Exchange symbol] .... KPL
Copeland/Sewell Family Organization (EA) .... CSFO

Copene-Petroquimica ADS [NYSE symbol] (SG) .... PNE
Copenhagen [Denmark] [Later, RSV] [Geomagnetic observatory code] .... COP
Copenhagen [Denmark] [Airport symbol] (OAG) .... CPH
Copenhagen (BARN) .... Cpn
Copenhagen Airtaxi [Denmark] [ICAO designator] (FAAC) .... CAT
Copenhagen, Brussels, and Amsterdam [Refers to a group of expressionist
   artists based in these three cities] .... COBRA
Copenhagen Business School [Denmark] (ECON) .... CBS
Copenhagen Image Processing System (SAUS) .... CHIPS
Copenhagen Interbank Offered Rate (SAUO) .... CIBOR
Copenhagen, NY [FM radio station call letters] .... WWLF
Copenhagen Offshore Craft Conference (SAUS) .... COSCON
Copenhagen School of Economics and Business Administration -
   Language Department (SAUO) .... CEBAL
Copenhagen Stock Exchange and Guaranteed Fund for Danish Options
   and Futures (SAUS) .... FUTOP
Copenhagen Stock Exchange and Guaranteed Fund for Danish options
   and Futures (SAUO) .... FUTOP
Copernican (BEE) .... Cop
Copernicus (ROG) .... COP
Copernicus Common (DOMA) .... COPCOM
Cope's Reports [63-72 California] [A publication] (DLA) .... Cope
Copiague High School, Copiague, NY [Library symbol] [Library of Congress]
   (LCLS) .... NCopHS
Copiague Memorial Public Library, Copiague, NY [Library symbol] [Library of
   Congress] (LCLS) .... NCop
Copiah-Jefferson Regional Library, Hazelhurst, MS [Library symbol] [Library
   of Congress] (LCLS) .... MsHz
Copiah-Lincoln Junior College [Wesson, MS] .... CLJC
Copiapo [Chile] [Seismograph station code, US Geological Survey] (SEIS) ...... CPP
Copiapo/Chamonate [Chile] [ICAO location identifier] (ICLI) .... SCHA
Copi-Elgot-Wright [Electronics] .... CEW
Copier .... COPR
Copier Dealers Association (EA) .... CDA
Copies per Hour (SAUS) .... CPH
Co-Pilot (SAUS) .... COPI
Co-Pilot (SAUS) .... CP
Copilot .... CP
Copilot .... CPLT
Copilot (SAUS) .... Cplt
Copilot Time (DNAB) .... CPT
Copilot/Gunner (MCD) .... CPG
Co-Pilot/Gunner (SAUS) .... CPG
Copilot/Gunner Panel (MCD) .... CPGP
Copilot/Gunner Stabilized Sight (MCD) .... CGSS
Copilots Display, Direct View (ACAE) .... CDDV
Copilot's Display, Remote View (ACAE) .... CDRV
Copilots Instrument Power Panel (SAUS) .... CIPP
Copilot/Tactical Coordinator [In S-3 Viking] [Navy] (DOMA) .... COTAC
Coping in Tough Times (AC) .... CITT
Coping Operations Preference Enquiry [Personality development test]
   [Psychology] .... COPE
Coping Resources Inventory for Stress (TMMY) .... CRIS
Coping Strategies Questionnaire (DIPS) .... CSQ
Copinger. Copyright [11th ed.] [1971] [A publication] (DLA) .... Cop Cop
Copinger on Title Deeds [A publication] (DLA) .... Cop Tit D
Copinger's Index to Precedents [A publication] (DLA) .... Cop Ind Pr
Coplanar Waveguide .... CPW
Copley News Service .... CNS
Copley Newspapers, Inc., James S. Copley Library, La Jolla, CA [Library
   symbol] [Library of Congress] .... CLjC
Copley Pharmaceutical [NASDAQ symbol] (TTSB) .... CPLY
Copley Pharmaceutical, Inc. [Associated Press] (SAG) .... CopleyPh
Copley Pharmaceutical, Inc. [NASDAQ symbol] (SAG) .... CPLY
Copley Properties, Inc. [AMEX symbol] (SPSG) .... COP
Copley Properties, Inc. [Associated Press] (SAG) .... Copley
Copolar Attenuation [Telecommunications] (TEL) .... CPA
Co-Polar Attenuation (SAUS) .... CPA
Copolyamide (SAUS) .... COPA
Copolyester (SAUS) .... COP
Copolyester Elastomer [Plastics technology] .... COPE
Copolymer (SAUS) .... copo
Copolymer Composition Distribution (PDAA) .... CCD
Copolymerized With [Organic chemistry] .... co
Copper [Chemical symbol is Cu] C
Copper [Chemical symbol is Cu] (MSA) .... COP
Copper (SAUS) .... Cop
Copper [Chemical symbol is Cu] .... COPR
Copper [Chemical symbol is Cu] .... CPR
Copper (SAUS) .... Cpr
Copper (VRA) .... cu
Copper (GNE) .... cu
Copper Acetic Standard Solution Test (SAUS) .... Cass Test
Copper Alloy Tubing .... CAT
Copper Amine Oxidase [An enzyme] .... CAO
Copper and Brass Fabrications Council (SAUO) .... CBFC
Copper and Brass Fabricators Council (EA) .... CBFC
Copper and Brass Fabricators Foreign Trade Association [Later, CBFC]
   (EA) .... CBFFTA
Copper and Brass Information Centre (SAUO) .... CABIC
Copper and Brass Research Association [Later, CDA] (SAUO) .... CABRA
Copper and Brass Research Association [Later, CDA] .... CBRA
Copper and Brass Servicenter Association (EA) .... CBSA
Copper and Brass Warehouse Association (PDAA) .... CABWA
Copper and Brass Warehouse Association [Later, CBSA] (EA) .... CBWA

Copper and Iron (SAUS) .... Cofron
Copper Band [Dentistry] .... CuB
Copper Cable Steel-Reinforced (IAA) .... CCSR
Copper Center, AK [Location identifier] [FAA] (FAAL) .... CZC
Copper Chrome Arsenate (SAUS) .... CCA
Copper Chromite CC
Copper Citrate [Wood preservative] (WPI) CC
Copper Concentric Neutral (PDAA) .... CCN
Copper Constantan (SAUS) CC
Copper Cylinder and Boiler Manufacturers' Association [British] (BI) .... CCBM
Copper Data Center [Inactive] [Battelle Memorial Institute] [Information service
   or system] .... CDC
Copper Development Association (EA) .... CDA
Copper Distributed Data Interface [Computer science] (TNIG) .... CDDI
Copper Distributed Digital Interface [Computer science] .... CDDI
Copper Ethanolamine .... CEN
Copper Ethylenediamine (SAUS) .... CED
Copper Fastened .... CF
Copper, Indium, Gallium, and Selenium [Photovoltaics] .... CIGS
Copper Indium Selenide (SAUS) .... CIS
Copper Institute (SAUS) CI
Copper Jacketed Steel .... CJS
Copper Lake Explorations Ltd. [Vancouver Stock Exchange symbol] .... CKX
Copper, Lead, or Zinc [Freight] .... CLZ
Copper Mine [Northwest Territories] [Seismograph station code, US Geological
   Survey] [Closed] (SEIS) .... CMC
Copper Molly Copper (AAEL) .... CMC
Copper Mountain Networks [NASDAQ symbol] .... CMTN
Copper Nickel Alloy (MSA) .... CNA
Copper Nickel Jacket (IAA) .... CNJ
Copper Non-Staining (SAUS) .... CNS
Copper or Steel [Freight] .... CS
Copper Oxidation Corrosion Test (PDAA) .... COCT
Copper Oxide (KSC) .... CUO
Copper Oxide Modulator .... COM
Copper Oxide Read-Only Storage (SAUS) .... COROS
Copper Oxide Rectifier .... COR
Copper Pair [Telecommunications] .... CP
Copper Phthalocyanine [Colored pigment] .... CPC
Copper Plate (SAUS) .... Cop Pl
Copper Products Development Association [Later, INCRA] .... CPDA
Copper Queen Library, Bisbee, AZ [Library symbol] [Library of Congress]
   (LCLS) .... AzB
Copper Range Co. (SAUO) .... CPX
Copper Range R. R. [AAR code] .... COPR
Copper Range Railroad (IIA) .... CR
Copper Recovery Corp. .... CRC
Copper Reduction Test [Chemistry] (DAVI) .... CRT
Copper Refineries Ltd. [Australia] .... CRL
Copper Reverbatory Furnace Slag (PDAA) .... CRFS
Copper River Basin Regional Housing Authority (SAUO) .... CRBHA
Copper Shielding Braid .... CSB
Copper Smelters and Refiners Association [British] (DBA) .... CSRA
Copper Stack Resources Ltd. [Vancouver Stock Exchange symbol] .... CTK
Copper State Air Service, Inc. [FAA designator] (FAAC) .... COP
Copper, Steel, or Zinc [Freight] .... CSZ
Copper Stretch Metal (SAUS) .... CSM
Copper Sulfate (SAUS) .... Vitriol
Copper Sulfate Treated Sorbeads .... CSTS
Copper Sulfide Rectifier .... CSR
Copper T [An intrauterine contraceptive device] (DAVI) .... TCu
Copper Technical Data Centre [Australia] .... CTDC
Copper to the Curb (SAUS) .... CTTC
Copper to the Home (SAUS) .... CTTH
Copper Trade Association .... CTA
[The] Copper Treasure Inventory Scroll from Qumran. Cave Three
   (BJA) 3QInv
Copper Unit of Pressure (WGA) .... CUP
Copper Vapor Laser (SAUS) CVL
Copper Weld .... CW
Copper Weld Steel [Telecommunications] (TEL) .... CWS
Copper Wire Counterpoise Ground (SAUS) .... CWGC
Copper Wire Engineering Association (SAUO) .... CWEA
Copper-7 [A contraceptive device] [Gynecology] (DAVI) Cu-7
Copperas Cove, TX [FM radio station call letters] .... KOOV
Copper-Brazed Crosley [Engine] [Automotive engineering] .... COBRA
Copper-Chrome Arsenate [Wood preservative] (ADA) .... CCA
Copper-Clad Invar (SAUS) CCI
Copper-Clad Steel Wire (IAA) .... CCSW
Copper-Cored Ground Electrode [Automotive engineering] .... CCGE
Coppered C
Coppered .... COPD
Coppered (SAUS) .... Copd
Copperhead Priority Target (SAUS) .... CPT
Copperhill, TN [AM radio station call letters] .... WLSB
Copper-Indium-Diselenide [Inorganic chemistry] .... CIS
Coppermine [Canada] [Airport symbol] (OAG) .... YCO
Coppermine, NT [ICAO location identifier] (ICLI) .... CYCO
Copperopolis, CA [FM radio station call letters] (RBYB) .... KRVR
Copperplate (SAUS) .... Copp
Copperplate (VRA) .... cuplt
Coppersmith [British] .... CS
Coppersmith (KSC) .... CSMITH
Coppersmiths Society [A union] [British] .... CS
Copperton [South Africa] [ICAO location identifier] (ICLI) .... FACO

Copperwald Steel Co. (SAUO) ... COS
Copperweld (SAUS) ... CW
Coppin State College, Baltimore, MD [*Library symbol*] [*Library of Congress*] (LCLS) ... MdBCS
Coppin State College, Parlett L. Moore Library, Baltimore, MD [*OCLC symbol*] (OCLC) ... MDP
Coppin State Teachers College (SAUO) ... CSTC
Copp's Land Office Decisions [*A publication*] (DLA) ... Copp Land
Copp's Manual for Courts-Martial [*A publication*] (DLA) ... Copp Ct Mar
Copp's Public Land Laws [*A publication*] (DLA) ... Copp LL
Copp's Public Land Laws [*A publication*] (DLA) ... Copp Pub Land Laws
Copp's Public Land Laws [*A publication*] (DLA) ... Copp Pub LL
Copp's United States Mining Decision [*A publication*] (DLA) ... Copp Min Dec
Coprecipitation ... CO-PPT
Coprecipitation X-Ray Fluorescence Spectroscopy ... COPREX
COPRED Students Peace Network [*Later, COPRED-SPWG*] (EA) ... COPRED-SPN
COPRED [*Consortium on Peace Research, Education, and Development*] **StudentsPeace Working Group** (EA) ... COPRED-SPWG
Coprinus laniger [*A fungus*] ... Cl
Coprinus Micaceous [*A fungus*] ... Cm
Co-Processing Node Architecture for Parallel Systems (SAUS) ... CNAPS
Co-Production ... COPRO
Coproduction for Security Program [*US and Italy*] ... CSP
Coproporphyrin [*Also, CP*] [*Clinical chemistry*] ... COPRO
Coproporphyrin [*Also, COPRO*] [*Clinical chemistry*] ... CP
Coproporphyrinogen Oxidase (DMAA) ... CPO
Copsystem Interest Inventory [*Knapp and Knapp*] (TES) ... COPS
Copsystem Interest Inverntory Form R [*Knapp and Knapp*] (TES) ... COPS-R
Copsystem Intermediate Inventory [*Knapp & Knapp*] (TES) ... COPS II
Copsystem Professional Level Interest Inventory (TES) ... COPS-P
Coptic (ADWA) ... Cop
Coptic ... COP
Coptic [*MARC language code*] [*Library of Congress*] (LCCP) ... cop
Coptic ... COPT
Coptic (VRA) ... Copt
Copula Pyramidna [*Neuroanatomy*] ... CP
Copulate (SAUS) ... Copu
Copulation (SAUS) ... Copu
Copulative ... COP
Copulative (ROG) ... COPUL
Copulatory (SAUS) ... Copu
Copulatory Mechanism [*Medicine*] ... CM
COPUOS Scientific and Technical Subcommittee (SAUS) ... STSC
Copy ... C
Copy (ROG) ... CO
Copy (ADWA) ... cop
Copy (WGA) ... COP
Copy (MCD) ... CP
Copy (BUR) ... CPY
Copy (AABC) ... CY
Copy and Add Logical Word (CET) ... CAL
Copy Control Character [*Computer science*] (IAA) ... CCC
Copy Deoxyribonucleic Acid ... DNA
Copy Editor (WDMC) ... ce
Copy Editor (WDMC) ... CE
Copy Furnished [*Army*] (AABC) ... CF
Copy Generation Management System [*Computer science*] (VERA) ... CGMS
Copy In and Out (SAUS) ... CPIO
Copy Instruction (SAUS) ... CI
Copy Libraries ... COPYLIB
Copy Network [*Computer science*] (VERA) ... CN
Copy of Reply Be Furnished This Office [*Army*] (AABC) ... CORBFUS
Copy Payments Center [*for copyrighted material*] ... CPC
Copy Processing System [*Photocomposition*] ... CPS
Copy Protected (or Protection) (SAUS) ... CP
Copy, Punch, Print (SAUS) ... COPPR
Copy Research Council (EA) ... CRC
Copy Service for Microform (SAUS) ... CSM
Copy to Go (NTCM) ... CTG
Copyeditors instruction: Delete (SAUS) ... DELE
Copyhold [*British*] [*Legal term*] (ROG) ... C
Copyhold [*British*] [*Legal term*] (ROG) ... CO HO
Copying of Parts (ADA) ... COP
Copying Products and Inked Ribbon Association (EA) ... CPIRA
Copyright ... C
Copyright (ADWA) ... c
Copyright (WDMC) ... cop
Copyright (WDMC) ... copr
Copyright (TEL) ... COPR
Copyright ... COPT
Copyright (DLA) ... COPY
Copyright (WDMC) ... copy
Copyright [*Deltiology*] ... CPY
Copyright and Literary Property [*Legal term*] (DLA) ... COPY & LIT P
Copyright Bulletin [*A publication*] (DLA) ... Copy Bull
Copyright Clearance Center (EA) ... CCC
Copyright Collective of Canada (AC) ... CCC
Copyright Control Association (SAUO) ... CCA
Copyright Convergence Group [*Australia*] ... CCG
Copyright Copying Guidelines (EDAC) ... CCG
Copyright Decisions [*A publication*] (DLA) ... Copy Dec
Copyright Holder [*MARC relator code*] [*Library of Congress*] (LCCP) ... cph
Copyright in Transmitted Electronic Documents ... CITED
Copyright Law Reporter (Commerce Clearing House) [*A publication*] (DLA) ... Copyright L Rep (CCH)
Copyright Law Symposium. American Society of Composers, Authors, and Publishers (DLA) ... ASCAP Sympos
Copyright Law Symposium. American Society of Composers, Authors, and Publishers [*A publication*] (DLA) ... Copyright L Symp(ASCAP)
Copyright Licensing Agency [*Government body*] [*British*] ... CLA
Copyright Licensing Agency Rapid Clearance Service ... CLARCS
Copyright Licensing Organisation [*British*] (AIE) ... CLO
Copyright Office [*US*] ... CO
Copyright Office History Document (SAUS) ... COHD
Copyright Office History Monograph (SAUS) ... COHM
Copyright Office Publication and Interactive Cataloging System [*Library of Congress*] [*Washington, DC*] ... COPICS
Copyright Protection Technical Working Group (SAUO) ... CPTWG
Copyright Receipt Office [*British Library Automated Information Service*] (NITA) ... CRO
Copyright Royalty Tribunal [*Library of Congress*] ... CRT
Copyright Society of the USA (EA) ... CSUSA
Copyrighted ... COP
Copyrighted (SAUS) ... Copr
Copytele, Inc. [*NASDAQ symbol*] (NQ) ... COPY
CopyTele, Inc. [*Associated Press*] (SAG) ... Copytel
Copywriter's Council of America (EA) ... CCA
Copywriting ... CW
Coqualeetza Archives, Sardis, British Columbia [*Library symbol*] [*National Library of Canada*] (NLC) ... BSC
Coque [*Boil*] [*Pharmacy*] ... COQ
Coque ad Medietatis Consumptionem [*Boil to the Consumption of Half*] [*Pharmacy*] (ROG) ... COQ ad MED CONSUMPT
Coque in Sufficiente Aquae [*Boil in Sufficient Water*] [*Pharmacy*] (ROG) ... COQ in SA
Coque Secundum Artem [*Boil According to Rule*] [*Pharmacy*] ... Coq SA
Coque Simul [*Boil at the Same Time*] [*Pharmacy*] (DAVI) ... coq simul
Coquille, OR [*FM radio station call letters*] ... KSHR
Coquille, OR [*AM radio station call letters*] ... KWRO
Coquille Public Library, Coquille, OR [*Library symbol*] [*Library of Congress*] (LCLS) ... OrCo
Coquitlam Public Library, British Columbia [*Library symbol*] [*National Library of Canada*] (NLC) ... BC
Cor Anglais [*English Horn*] ... CA
Cor Pulmonale [*Medicine*] ... CP
Cor Therapeutics, Inc. [*NASDAQ symbol*] (SAG) ... CORR
Cor Therapeutics, Inc. [*Associated Press*] (SAG) ... CorTher
Cora P. Maloney College (SAUS) ... CPM
Coracoacromial [*Anatomy*] ... CA
Coracoclavicular [*Anatomy*] (MAE) ... CC
Coracohumeral Ligament (MELL) ... CHL
Coracoid Process [*Anatomy*] ... CP
Corair [*France*] [*ICAO designator*] (FAAC) ... COZ
Coral [*Quality of the bottom*] [*Nautical charts*] ... Co
Coral (SAUS) ... Co
Coral (ROG) ... COR
Coral [*Record label*] [*USA, Europe*] ... Crl
Coral Air [*ICAO designator*] (AD) ... VY
Coral Cay Conservation Ltd. (SAUO) ... CCC
Coral Cove, FL [*FM radio station call letters*] ... WYNF
Coral Energy Corp. [*Vancouver Stock Exchange symbol*] ... CGL
Coral Gables [*Florida*] ... CG
Coral Gables, FL [*FM radio station call letters*] ... WHQT
Coral Gables, FL [*AM radio station call letters*] ... WRHC
Coral Gables, FL [*AM radio station call letters*] ... WVCG
Coral Gables, FL [*FM radio station call letters*] ... WVUM
Coral Gold Corp. [*Vancouver Stock Exchange symbol*] ... CLH
Coral Harbour [*Canada*] [*Airport symbol*] (OAG) ... YZS
Coral Harbour, NT [*ICAO location identifier*] (ICLI) ... CYZS
Coral Head [*Quality of the bottom*] [*Nautical charts*] ... Co Hd
Coral Reef Alliance (SAUS) ... CORAL
Coral Reef and Demersal Fish Recruitment Project (SAUS) ... CORDERP
Coral Reef Initiative (SAUS) ... CRI
Coral Reef Management and Research (SAUO) ... CORMAR
Coral Reef Monitoring Program ... CRMP
Coral Reef Survey Assessment (SAUS) ... CRSA
Coral Sea Islands (SAUS) ... CSI
Coralline Lethal Orange Disease ... CLOD
Coralta Resources [*Vancouver Stock Exchange symbol*] ... COU
Coralville Courier, Coralville, IA [*Library symbol*] [*Library of Congress*] (LCLS) ... IaCorvC
Coralville Public Library, Coralville, IA [*Library symbol*] [*Library of Congress*] (LCLS) ... IaCorv
Coram [*Before*] [*Latin*] (ROG) ... COR
Coram Healthcare [*NYSE symbol*] (TTSB) ... CRH
Coram Healthcare Corp. [*Associated Press*] (SAG) ... CoramH
Coram Healthcare Corp. [*NYSE symbol*] (SAG) ... CRH
Coran Nobis and Allied Statutory Remedies [*A publication*] (DLA) ... Coran N
Coras Iompair Eireann [*Irish Transport Co.*] ... CIE
Corazon De Jesus [*Panama*] [*Airport symbol*] (OAG) ... CZJ
CORBA Interface Repository (RALS) ... CIR
Corbeil Branch, East Ferris Township Public Library, Ontario [*Library symbol*] [*National Library of Canada*] (NLC) ... OCEFT
Corben Club (EA) ... CC
Corbett and Daniell's English Election Cases [*1819*] [*A publication*] (DLA) ... C & D
Corbett and Daniell's English Election Cases [*1819*] [*A publication*] (DLA) ... Corb & D
Corbett and Daniell's English Election Cases [*1819*] [*A publication*] (DLA) ... Corb & Dan

Corbett National Park (SAUS) ... CNP
Corbin [*Virginia*] [*Seismograph station code, US Geological Survey*] (SEIS) ... CBN
Corbin, KY [*AM radio station call letters*] ... WCTT
Corbin, KY [*FM radio station call letters*] ... WCTT-FM
Corbin, KY [*AM radio station call letters*] ... WKDP
Corbin, KY [*FM radio station call letters*] ... WKDP-FM
Corbin Research [*An association*] (EA) ... CR
Corbit-Calloway Memorial Library, Odessa, DE [*OCLC symbol*] (OCLC) ... CRB
Corby Distilleries Ltd. [*Toronto Stock Exchange symbol*] [*Vancouver Stock Exchange symbol*] ... CDL
Corcom, Inc. [*NASDAQ symbol*] (NQ) ... CORC
Corcom, Inc. [*Associated Press*] (SAG) ... Corcom
Corcoran Art Gallery, Washington, DC [*Library symbol*] [*Library of Congress*] (LCLS) ... DCA
Corcoran, CA [*Location identifier*] [*FAA*] (FAAL) ... COR
Corcoran, CA [*Location identifier*] [*FAA*] (FAAL) ... CRO
Corcoran, CA [*FM radio station call letters*] ... KLCZ
Corcoran Gallery of Art (SAUO) ... CGA
Corcoran School of Art, Washington, DC [*Library symbol*] [*Library of Congress*] (LCLS) ... DCAS
Cord ... C
Cord ... CD
Cord and Rod Sounding (SAUS) ... C&R Sounding
Cord Around Neck [*Neonatology and obstetrics*] (DAVI) ... CAN
Cord [*Umbilical*] **Blood Leukocytes** [*Hematology*] ... CBL
Cord Compression [*Medicine*] ... CC
Cord on Legal and Equitable Rights of Married Women [*A publication*] (DLA) ... Cord Mar Wom
Cord Welt ... CDWT
Cordage (SAUS) ... CO
Cordage Institute (EA) ... CI
Cordage Manufacturers Institute [*British*] (DBA) ... CMI
Cordant Technologies [*NYSE symbol*] [*Formerly, Thiokol Corp.*] ... CDD
Cordax Measuring Machine (SAUS) ... CMM
Cordele, GA [*FM radio station call letters*] (BROA) ... WAEF-FM
Cordele, GA [*FM radio station call letters*] ... WKKN
Cordele, GA [*Television station call letters*] ... WSST
Cordele, GA [*AM radio station call letters*] ... WUWU
Cordell Hull Dam [*TVA*] ... CHD
Cordell Hull Foundation for International Education (EA) ... CHFIE
Cordell, OK [*FM radio station call letters*] ... KCDL
Cordery. Solicitors [*6th ed.*] [*1968*] [*A publication*] (DLA) ... Cord Sol
Cord-Foot (SAUS) ... Cd Ft
Cordi Marian Sisters (TOCD) ... MCM
Cordiale Resources, Inc. [*Vancouver Stock Exchange symbol*] ... COD
Cordiant Communic Grp ADS [*NYSE symbol*] (SG) ... CDA
Cordiant PLC [*Associated Press*] (SAG) ... Cordiant
Cordic Arithmetic Processor (IAA) ... CAP
Cordierite (SAUS) ... CO
Cordierite [*A mineral*] ... Crd
Cordillera [*A mountain chain*] (BARN) ... Cord
Cordillera People's Liberation Army [*Philippines*] [*Political party*] (EY) ... CPLA
Cordillo Downs [*South Australia*] [*Airport symbol*] (AD) ... ODL
Cordi-Marian Missionary Sisters [*Roman Catholic religious order*] ... MCM
Cordis Corp. [*NASDAQ symbol*] (NQ) ... CORD
Cordis Corp. [*Associated Press*] (SAG) ... Cordis
Cordis Corp. Library, Miami, FL [*Library symbol*] [*Library of Congress*] (LCLS) ... FMCC
Cordless Communication Network (SAUS) ... CCN
Cordless Switchboard Section [*Telecommunications*] (NITA) ... CSS
Cordless Switchboard System ... CSS
Cordless Telephone ... CT
Cordless Telephone-1st Generation (CGWS) ... CT1
Cordless Terminal Mobility (SAUS) ... CTM
Cordoba [*Monetary unit*] [*Nicaragua*] ... C
Cordoba [*Argentina*] [*Airport symbol*] (OAG) ... COR
Cordoba [*Spain*] [*ICAO location identifier*] (ICLI) ... LEBA
Cordoba [*Spain*] [*Airport symbol*] (OAG) ... ODB
Cordoba [*Argentina*] [*ICAO location identifier*] (ICLI) ... SACE
Cordoba [*Argentina*] [*ICAO location identifier*] (ICLI) ... SACF
Cordoba [*Argentina*] [*ICAO location identifier*] (ICLI) ... SACG
Cordoba [*Argentina*] [*ICAO location identifier*] (ICLI) ... SACO
Cordoba [*Argentina*] [*ICAO location identifier*] (ICLI) ... SACU
Cordoba Durchmusterung [*Star chart*] ... CD
Cordoba/Area de Material [*Argentina*] [*ICAO location identifier*] (ICLI) ... SACA
Cordon and Search [*Military*] ... C & S
Cordova [*Alaska*] [*Airport symbol*] (OAG) ... CDV
Cordova [*Alaska*] [*Seismograph station code, US Geological Survey*] (SEIS) ... CVA
Cordova [*Alaska*] [*ICAO location identifier*] (ICLI) ... PACV
Cordova Airlines, Inc. ... COA
Cordova, AK [*Location identifier*] [*FAA*] (FAAL) ... CKU
Cordova, AK [*AM radio station call letters*] ... KLAM
Cordova, AL [*FM radio station call letters*] ... WFFN
Cordova, KS [*FM radio station call letters*] (RBYB) ... KCDV-FM
Cordova Public Library, Cordova, AK [*Library symbol*] [*Library of Congress*] (LCLS) ... AkC
Corduroy Council of America [*Defunct*] (EA) ... CCA
Corduroy Trousers [*Slang*] (DSUE) ... CORDS
Core (IAA) ... C
Core ... CR
Core and Drum Corrector ... CADCO
Core and Payload Control Centers [*NASA*] (SPST) ... C&PCC
Core and Random Access Manager [*General Automation, Inc.*] ... CRAM
Core Aspects of the Link Access Procedure to Frame Mode Bearer Services (SAUS) ... LAPF-Core
Core Australian Specification for Management and Administrative Computing ... CASMAC
Core Automated Maintenance System (MCD) ... CAMS
Core Automated Management System (SAUS) ... CAMS
Core Automated Virtual Environment ... CAVE
Core Auxiliary Cooling System [*Nuclear energy*] (NRCH) ... CACS
Core Auxiliary Cooling Water [*Nuclear energy*] (NRCH) ... CACW
Core Auxiliary Cooling Water System [*Nuclear energy*] (NRCH) ... CACWS
Core Auxiliary Heat Exchanger [*Nuclear energy*] (NRCH) ... CAHE
Core Based Tree [*Computer science*] (VERA) ... CBT
Core Binding Factor Beta [*Genetics*] ... CBFB
Core Block Table [*Computer science*] (OA) ... CBT
Core College Curriculm (EDAC) ... CCC
Core Component Cleaning System [*Nuclear energy*] (NRCH) ... CCCS
Core Component Conditioning Station [*Nuclear energy*] (NRCH) ... CCCS
Core Component Pot [*Nuclear energy*] ... CCP
Core Component Receiving Container [*Nuclear energy*] (NRCH) ... CCRC
Core Component Test Loop [*Nuclear energy*] (NRCH) ... CCTL
Core Concrete (SAUS) ... CC
Core Conflictional Relationships Theme [*Psychology*] ... CCRT
Core Current Address (ACAE) ... CCA
Core Current Address Register (ACAE) ... CCAR
Core Current Driver ... CCD
Core Current Layer (OA) ... CCL
Core Curriculum Content Standards ... CCCS
Core Curriculum Content Standards Aid ... CCSA
Core Damage Frequency [*Nuclear energy*] (NRCH) ... CDF
Core Diode Logic ... CDL
Core Disruptive Accident [*Nuclear energy*] (NRCH) ... CDA
Core Division Multiplexing (IAA) ... CDM
Core Element Assembly Motion Inhibit [*Nuclear energy*] (IEEE) ... CMI
Core End Address (ACAE) ... CEA
Core End Address Register (ACAE) ... CEAR
Core File (IEEE) ... COFIL
Core Financial System (SAUS) ... CFS
Core Flood Alarm [*Nuclear energy*] (IEEE) ... CFA
Core Flood Isolation Valve Assembly [*Nuclear energy*] (IEEE) ... CFIA
Core Flood Tank [*Nuclear energy*] (NRCH) ... CFT
Core Flooding System [*Nuclear energy*] (NRCH) ... CF
Core Flooding System Isolation Valve Interlock [*Nuclear energy*] (NRCH) ... CFI
Core Fluid System [*Environmental science*] (COE) ... CFS
Core Fluid Tank [*Environmental science*] (COE) ... CFT
Core Former Structure [*Nuclear energy*] (NRCH) ... CFS
Core Height Logger (SAUS) ... CHL
Core Hole (SAUS) ... CH
Core Image Buffer (SAUS) ... CIB
Core Image Converter [*Computer science*] ... CIC
Core Image Dictionary [*Computer science*] (IAA) ... CID
Core Image Dump (SAUS) ... CID
Core Image Library (CMD) ... CIL
Core, Inc. [*NASDAQ symbol*] (SAG) ... CORE
Core, Inc. [*Associated Press*] (SAG) ... Core Inc
Core Indus [*NYSE symbol*] (TTSB) ... CRI
Core Industries, Inc. [*Associated Press*] (SAG) ... CoreIn
Core Industries, Inc. [*NYSE symbol*] (SPSG) ... CRI
Core Instrumentation Facility [*Army*] ... CIF
Core Instrumentation Subsystem (MCD) ... CIS
Core Insulation [*Nuclear energy*] ... CI
Core Laboratories, Inc., Dallas, TX [*Library symbol*] [*Library of Congress*] (LCLS) ... TxDaCL
Core Laboratories NV [*Associated Press*] (SAG) ... CoreLab
Core Laboratories NV [*NASDAQ symbol*] (SAG) ... CRLB
Core Laboratories N.V. [*NASDAQ symbol*] (TTSB) ... CRLBF
Core Labortories N.V. [*NYSE symbol*] (SG) ... CLB
Core Load Overlay Builder [*General Automation, Inc.*] ... CLOB
Core Local Area Network (SSD) ... CLAN
Core Logic Intervalometer ... CLI
Core Logic Intervalometer ... CLIV
Core Materials [*AMEX symbol*] (SG) ... CME
Core Materials Corp. [*AMEX symbol*] (SAG) ... CME
Core Materials Corp. [*Associated Press*] (SAG) ... CoreMatl
Core Matrix (SAUS) ... CM
Core Maximum Fraction of Limiting Power Density [*Nuclear energy*] (NRCH) ... CMFLPD
Core Maximum Power Fraction [*Nuclear energy*] (IEEE) ... CMPF
Core Measurement Table (IAA) ... CMT
Core Mechanical Mock-Up [*Nuclear energy*] (NRCH) ... CMM
Core Melt [*Environmental science*] (COE) ... CM
Core Melt Review Group [*Nuclear energy*] (NRCH) ... CMRG
Core Melt Technology [*Metal casting*] ... CMT
Core Melt Through [*Nuclear energy*] (IEEE) ... MT
Core Memory ... CM
Core Memory Byte (SAUS) ... CMB
Core Memory Cycle (SAUS) ... CMC
Core Memory Driver ... CMD
Core Memory Shift Register (SAUS) ... CMSR
Core Memory Stack (SAUS) ... CMS
Core Memory Unit (MCD) ... CMU
Core Module Integration Facility (SAUS) ... CMIF
Core Module Integration Simulator (SAUS) ... CMIS
Core Monitoring Computer [*Nuclear energy*] (NRCH) ... CMC
Core Nodal Switching Subsystems [*Electronics*] (ACRL) ... CNSS
Core Operating Limit Supervisory System [*Nuclear energy*] (NRCH) ... COLSS
Core Operating Limit Support System [*Nuclear energy*] (NRCH) ... COLSS
Core Operating System [*Computer science*] (NITA) ... COS

Core Performance Log [*Nuclear energy*] (IEEE) .... CPL
Core Planning Group (SAUO) .... CPG
Core Prime (SAA) .... CP
Core Project (SAUS) .... CP
Core Project 1, the Global Description of the world ocean (SAUS) CP1
Core Project 2, the Southern Ocean Experiment (SAUS) CP2
Core Project 3, the Gyre Dynamics Experiment (SAUS) CP3
Core Project Office (SAUS) .... CPO
Core Project Planning Committee (SAUO) .... CPPC
Core Protection Calculator [*or Computer*] [*Nuclear energy*] (NRCH) .... CPC
Core Protection Computer (SAUS) .... CPC
Core Removal Coding (DNAB) .... CRC
Core Research for Evolutional Science and Technology [*Japan*] .... CREST
Core Restraint Mechanism [*Nuclear energy*] (NRCH) .... CRM
Core Restraint Test Facility [*Nuclear energy*] (NRCH) .... CRTF
Core Sample Vacuum Container [*NASA*] .... CSVC
Core Segment (NASA) .... CS
Core Segment (NAKS) .... cs
Core Segment Development Facility [*Nuclear energy*] (NRCH) .... CSDF
Core Segment Interface Unit (NASA) .... CSIU
Core Segment Processing Unit (NASA) .... CSPU
Core Segment Simulator (NASA) .... CSS
Core Sharing [*Computer science*] (IAA) .... CS
Core Shift .... CS
Core Shift Driver (CET) .... CSD
Core Special Assembly [*Nuclear energy*] (NRCH) .... CSA
Core Spray [*Nuclear energy*] (NRCH) .... CS
Core Spray Injection System [*Nuclear energy*] (IAA) .... CSIS
Core Stability Monitoring System (SAUS) .... COSMOS
Core Standby Cooling [*Nuclear energy*] (IEEE) .... CSC
Core Standby Cooling System [*Nuclear energy*] (NRCH) .... CSCS
Core States Financial [*NYSE symbol*] (SAG) .... CFL
Core States Financial [*Associated Press*] (SAG) .... CoreStF
Core Storage Element .... CSE
Core Storage Terminal Table [*Computer science*] .... CSTT
Core Storage Unit (SAUS) .... CSU
Core Store Allocation (SAUS) .... CSA
Core Store Control (SAUS) .... CSC
Core Store Dump (SAUS) .... CSD
Core Store Effective Address (SAUS) .... CSEA
Core Store Location (SAUS) .... CSL
Core Store Matrix (SAUS) .... CSM
Core Store Operand (SAUS) .... CSO
Core Store Print-Out (SAUS) .... CSPO
Core Store Technique (SAUS) .... CST
Core Structure Accident [*Nuclear energy*] (NRCH) .... CSA
Core Support Barrel [*Nuclear energy*] (NRCH) .... CSB
Core Support Cylinder [*Nuclear energy*] (NRCH) .... CSC
Core Support Structure [*Nuclear energy*] (NRCH) .... CSS
Core Tactical Operation Center (SAUS) .... GTOC
Core Technologies [*NASDAQ symbol*] (TTSB) .... CTXR
Core Temperature [*Medicine*] .... Tc
Core Test Facility .... CTF
Core Transistor Logic [*Computer science*] .... CTL
Core Transistor Register .... CTR
Core Transmission Logic (SAUS) .... CTL
Core Values Task Force .... CVTF
Core Ventures [*Vancouver Stock Exchange symbol*] .... CYR
Core Water-Recycling System (SAUS) .... CWRS
Coreceptor Skewed [*Immunology*] .... CRS
Core-Dominated Quasar [*Astronomy*] .... CDQ
Corel Clipart Image Format (AAEL) .... CMX
Corel Corp. [*Associated Press*] (SAG) .... CorelCp
Corel Corp. [*NASDAQ symbol*] (SG) .... CORL
Corel Corp. [*NASDAQ symbol*] (SAG) .... COSF
Corel Corp. [*NASDAQ symbol*] (TTSB) .... COSFF
Corel Draw (SAUS) .... CDR
Corel Draw Template (SAUS) .... CDT
Corel Photopaint [*Computer science*] .... cpt
Core-Mantle Boundary [*Geology*] .... CMB
Core-Mark International, Inc. [*Toronto Stock Exchange symbol*] [*Vancouver Stock Exchange symbol*] .... CMK
Corepressor Binding Domain [*Genetics*] .... CBD
Co-Respondent (DSUE) .... CO-RE
Co-Responsibility Levy [*Cereal production tax*] [*British*] .... CR
CoreStaff, Inc. [*Associated Press*] (SAG) .... CreStaff
CoreStaff, Inc. [*NASDAQ symbol*] (SAG) .... CSTF
CoreStates Financial Corp. [*NYSE symbol*] (SPSG) .... CFL
Core-Support Capability (ACAE) .... CSC
Corey-Pauling-Koltun [*Molecular models*] .... CPK
CorFile on Disc, Corporate and Industry Research Reports (IID) .... CIRR
Corfu [*Greece*] [*Airport symbol*] (OAG) .... CFU
Corfu [*Washington*] [*Seismograph station code, US Geological Survey*] (SEIS) .... CRF
Corfu Free Library, Corfu, NY [*Library symbol*] [*Library of Congress*] (LCLS) .... NCorf
Corimon ADS [*NYSE symbol*] (TTSB) .... CRM
Corimon CA [*NYSE symbol*] (SPSG) .... CRM
Corimon CA SACA [*Associated Press*] (SAG) .... Corimon
Corinaldo [*Italy*] [*Seismograph station code, US Geological Survey*] (SEIS) .... CRN
Coring Technician (SAUS) .... CT
Corinth & Counce Railroad (SAUO) .... CRC
Corinth and Counce Railroad Co. (SAUO) .... CCR
[*The*] Corinth & Counce Railroad Co. [*AAR code*] .... CCR
Corinth, MS [*Location identifier*] [*FAA*] (FAAL) .... CRX

Corinth, MS [*FM radio station call letters*] .... WADI
Corinth, MS [*AM radio station call letters*] .... WCMA
Corinth, MS [*AM radio station call letters*] .... WKCU
Corinth, MS [*FM radio station call letters*] .... WXRZ
Corinth Resources Ltd. [*Vancouver Stock Exchange symbol*] .... CTH
Corinthian (VRA) .... Corin
Corinthian Colleges [*NASDAQ symbol*] (SG) .... COCO
Corinthian Yacht Club (SAUO) .... CYC
Corinthians [*New Testament book*] (BJA) C
Corinthians [*New Testament book*] .... Cor
Coriolanus [*Shakespearean work*] .... Cor
Coriolis (SAUS) .... Cor
Coriolis Absorber .... CA
Coriolis Acceleration Platform .... CAP
Coriolis Correction .... Z
Coriolis Sickness Susceptibility Index [*Orientation*] .... CSSI
Corixa Corp. [*NASDAQ symbol*] (SG) .... CRXA
Cork (MSA) .... CK
Cork .... CRK
Cork [*Ireland*] [*ICAO location identifier*] (ICLI) .... EICK
Cork [*Ireland*] [*Airport symbol*] (OAG) .... ORK
Cork and Macroom Railway (SAUO) .... C&M
Cork, Bandon and South-East Coast Railway (SAUO) .... CB&SEC
Cork Base .... CKB
Cork Board (AAG) .... CKBD
Cork Floor (AAG) .... CKF
Cork Historical and Archaeological Society (SAUO) .... CHAS
Cork Historical and Archaeological Society (SAUS) .... CHAS
Cork Institute of America [*Defunct*] (EA) .... CIA
Cork Insulation Material .... CIM
Cork Leather and Celastic [*Orthotic*] [*Orthopedics*] (DAVI) CLC
Cormack Public Library, Cormack, NF, Canada [*Library symbol*] [*Library of Congress*] (LCLS) .... CaNfCo
Cormack Public Library, Newfoundland [*Library symbol*] [*National Library of Canada*] (NLC) .... NFCO
Corn, Beans, Miami [*Tongue-in-cheek description of a crop rotation system, allowing farmers to spend winter in Florida*] .... CBM
Corn Belt Library System [*Library network*] .... CBLS
Corn Belt Library System, Bloomington, IL [*Library symbol*] [*Library of Congress*] (LCLS) .... IBloC
Corn Belt Library System, Normal, IL [*OCLC symbol*] (OCLC) .... JAF
Corn Belt Livestock Feeders Association (SAUO) .... CBLFA
Corn Belt Livestock Feeders Association [*Later, NCA*] .... CBLFA
Corn Blight Watch Experiment (GEOI) .... CBWE
Corn, Corn, Oats, Meadow, Meadow [*Crop rotation*] .... CCOMM
Corn Exchange Bank (SAUO) .... CEX
Corn Flour (OA) .... CF
Corn Gluten Meal .... CGM
Corn Growers Association of North Carolina (SRA) .... CGANC
Corn Industries Research Foundation [*Later, CRA*] (EA) .... CIRF
Corn Island [*Nicaragua*] [*ICAO location identifier*] (ICLI) .... MNCI
Corn Items Collectors Association (EA) CIC
Corn Meal Agar [*Growth medium*] .... CMA
Corn Oil .... CO
Corn Products Intl. [*NYSE symbol*] (SG) .... CPO
Corn Products Refining Corporation (SAUO) .... CPC
Corn Refiners Association (EA) .... CRA
Corn Refiners Association, Inc. .... CR
Corn Residue Equivalents [*Environmental science*] .... CRE
Corn, Soybean, and Milk Products [*Main ingredients of a formulated food*] .... CSM
Corn Soybean Mixture (SAUS) .... CSM
Corn Stunt [*Plant pathology*] .... CS
Corn Stunt Organism [*Plant pathology*] .... CSO
Corn Stunt Spiroplasma [*Plant pathology*] .... CSS
Corn Syrup Solids .... CSS
Corn Trade Clauses [*Shipping*] .... CTC
Cornea (SAUS) .... K
Cornea, Conjunctiva, and Sclera [*Ophthalmology*] (DAVI) .... CC & S
Cornea, Sclera, Conjunctiva [*Ophthalmology*] (DAVI) .... CSC
Corneal Dystrophy [*Medicine*] (DMAA) .... CD
Corneal Endothelial Cell [*Medicine*] (CPH) .... CEC
Corneal Grafting (MELL) .... CG
Corneal Opacity [*Medicine*] (MAE) .... CO
Corneal Thickness [*Ophthalmology*] (DAVI) .... CT
Corneal Transplant [*Medicine*] .... CT
Corneal-Retinal Potential (STED) .... CRP
Corneal-Retinael Potential (DB) .... CRP
Cornea-Retinal Potential (SAUS) .... CRP
Corned Beef [*Restaurant slang*] .... CB
Cornelia de Lange Parents Group [*Later, Cornelia de Lange Syndrome Foundation*] (EA) .... CLPG
Cornelia De Lange Syndrome [*Medicine*] .... CdLS
Cornelia De Lange Syndrome Foundation (EA) .... CdLSF
Cornelia, GA [*AM radio station call letters*] .... WCON
Cornelia, GA [*FM radio station call letters*] .... WCON-FM
Cornelio Procopio [*Brazil*] [*Airport symbol*] (OAG) .... CKO
Cornelius Court Elementary School, Uniondale, NY [*Library symbol*] [*Library of Congress*] (LCLS) .... NUnCCE
Cornelius Nepos [*Historian, 31-14BC*] (ROG) .... CORN NEP
Cornelius Public Library, Cornelius, OR [*Library symbol*] [*Library of Congress*] (LCLS) .... OrCor
Cornell (ROG) .... CORN
Cornell Aeronautical Laboratory (KSC) .... CAL
Cornell Aeronautical Laboratory (SAUO) .... CBQ

Cornell Aeronautical Laboratory, Buffalo, NY [*Library symbol*] [*Library of Congress*] (LCLS) .... NBuCA
Cornell Aeronautical Laboratory, Inc. (SAUO) .... CAL
Cornell Aeronautical Laboratory, Inc. (SAA) .... CALI
Cornell Aeronautical Laboratory Shock Tunnel (SAA) .... CALST
Cornell College, Mount Vernon, IA [*Library symbol*] [*Library of Congress*] (LCLS) .... IaMvC
Cornell College, Mount Vernon, IA [*OCLC symbol*] (OCLC) .... IMV
Cornell Compiler (SAUS) .... CORC
Cornell Computer Services [*Cornell University*] [*Information service or system*] (IID) .... CCS
Cornell Computing Language [*Computer science*] .... CORC
Cornell Corrections [*NYSE symbol*] (SG) .... CRN
Cornell Corrections, Inc. [*Associated Press*] (SAG) .... CornCor
Cornell Corrections, Inc. [*AMEX symbol*] (SAG) .... CRN
Cornell Critical Thinking Test (SAUS) .... CCTT
Cornell Dubilier Electronics (MUGU) .... CDE
Cornell Electron Storage Ring [*Atomic physics*] .... CESR
Cornell Electron-positron Storage Ring (SAUS) .... CESR
Cornell Feline Health Center [*Cornell University*] [*Research center*] (RCD) .... CFHC
Cornell Geological Sciences (SAUO) .... CGS
Cornell Guggenheim Aviation Safety Center (SAUO) .... CGASC
Cornell High Energy Synchrotron Source (SAUS) .... CHESS
Cornell High-Energy Synchrotron Source Laboratory [*Cornell University*] [*Research center*] .... CHESS
Cornell Hotel Administration Simulation Exercise [*Computer-programmed management game*] .... CHASE
Cornell Index [*Psychology*] CI
Cornell Information Technologies [*Information service or system*] (IID) .... CIT
Cornell Institute for Research in Chemical Ecology .... CIRCE
Cornell Institute for Social and Economic Research [*Cornell University*] [*Research center*] (RCD) .... CISER
Cornell International Institute for Food, Agriculture and Development (SAUO) .... CIIFAD
Cornell Laboratory for Environmental Applications of Remote Sensing [*Cornell University*] [*Information service or system*] (IID) .... CLEARS
Cornell Laboratory of Ornithology (SAUS) .... CLO
Cornell Law Journal [*A publication*] (DLA) .... Cornell LJ
Cornell Law Review [*A publication*] (ILCA) .... CLR
Cornell Law School (DLA) .... CLS
Cornell Learning and Recognizing Automaton .... CLARA
Cornell List Processor [*Computer science*] .... CLP
Cornell Local Roads Program [*Cornell University*] [*Research center*] (RCD) .... CLRP
Cornell Macintosh Terminal Emulator (SAUS) .... COMET
Cornell Manufacturing Engineering and Productivity Program [*Cornell University*] [*Research center*] (RCD) .... COMEPP
Cornell Maritime Press (DGA) .... CMP
Cornell Medical Community Computer Project (SAUS) .... CMCCP
Cornell Medical Index [*Psychology*] .... CMI
Cornell Mixing Zone Model [*Environmental Protection Agency*] (AEPA) .... CORMIX
Cornell National Supercomputer Facility [*Cornell University*] [*Research center*] (RCD) .... CNSF
Cornell Nutrition Surveillance Programme (SAUO) .... CNSP
Cornell Parent Behavior Description (EDAC) .... CPBD
Cornell Parent Behavior Inventory (EDAC) .... CPBI
Cornell Plantations (SAUS) .... Cornell Plant
Cornell Reconstruction of Accident Speeds on the Highway .... CRASH
Cornell Scale for Depression in Dementia (SAUS) .... CSDD
Cornell Theory Center (SAUS) .... CTC
Cornell University (SAUO) .... Corn
Cornell University [*Record label*] .... Corn
Cornell University (GAGS) .... Cornell U
Cornell University [*Ithaca, NY*] .... CU
Cornell University Department of Geological Sciences (SAUO) .... CUDGS
Cornell University, Ithaca, NY [*OCLC symbol*] (OCLC) .... COO
Cornell University, Ithaca, NY [*Library symbol*] [*Library of Congress*] (LCLS) .... NIC
Cornell University Laboratory of Ornithology (EA) .... CULO
Cornell University Library (SAUO) .... CUL
Cornell University, Medical College, New York, NY [*Library symbol*] [*Library of Congress*] (LCLS) .... NNCorM
Cornell University, Medical College, New York, NY [*OCLC symbol*] (OCLC) .... VYC
Cornell University, Medical College, Oskar Diethelm Historical Library, New York, NY [*Library symbol*] [*Library of Congress*] (LCLS) .... NNCorM-D
Cornell University, New York State School of Industrial and Labor Relations, Sanford V. Lenz Library, New York, NY [*Library symbol*] [*Library of Congress*] (LCLS) .... NNCorI
Cornell University Press (SAUO) .... Cornell U Pr
Cornell University Press (SAUO) .... CUP
Cornell University Press (SAUO) .... ISBN 0-8014
Cornell University Programming Language (SAUO) .... CUPL
Cornell University Research Laboratory .... CRL
Cornell University Research Laboratory for Diseases of Dogs .... CRLDD
Cornell University-Computer Science Department (SAUO) .... CU-CSD
Cornell Word Ford (DMAA) .... CWF
Cornell Word Form (DB) .... CWF
Cornell Word Form 2 [*Psychology*] CWF2
Cornellian, Mount Vernon, IA [*Library symbol*] [*Library of Congress*] (LCLS) .... IaMvCor
Cornelsen & Oxford University Press (SAUO) .... COUP
Corn-equivalent Feed Unit (SAUS) .... CFU
Corn-Equivalent Feed Unit .... CFU
Corner (WDAA) C
Corner (ADA) .... CNR
Corner (TBD) .... Cnr
Corner (KSC) .... COR
Corner (WDMC) .... cor
Corner [*Commonly used*] (OPSA) .... CORNER
Corner (VRA) .... crnr
Corner Bead [*Technical drawings*] (DAC) .... COR BD
Corner Bead (SAUS) .... CorBd
Corner Brook City Library, Corner Brook, NF, Canada [*Library symbol*] [*Library of Congress*] (LCLS) .... CaNfCB
Corner Brook City Public Library, Newfoundland [*Library symbol*] [*National Library of Canada*] (NLC) .... NFCB
Corner Brook City Public Library, Newfoundland (SAUS) .... NFCH
Corner Brook, NF [*AM radio station call letters*] .... CBY
Corner Brook, NF [*Television station call letters*] .... CBYT
Corner Brook, NF [*AM radio station call letters*] .... CFCB
Corner Brook, NF [*Television station call letters*] .... CJWN
Corner Brook, NF [*FM radio station call letters*] .... CKOZ
Corner Brook, NF [*AM radio station call letters*] .... CKXX
Corner Brook, NF [*FM radio station call letters*] (BROA) .... CKXX-FM
Corner Cube Retroflectors (SAUS) .... CCR
Corner Guard [*Technical drawings*] .... CG
Corner Wear [*Deltiology*] .... COR/WR
Cornerback [*Football*] .... CB
Corners [*Commonly used*] (OPSA) .... CORNERS
Corners [*Postal Service standard*] (OPSA) .... CORS
Corner's Forms of Writs on the Crown Side [*A publication*] (DLA) .... Corn Wr
Corner's Queen's Bench Practice [*A publication*] (DLA) .... Corn Pr
Cornerstone Bancorp [*AMEX symbol*] (SG) .... CBN
Cornerstone Bank [*AMEX symbol*] (SAG) .... CBN
Cornerstone Bank [*Associated Press*] (SAG) .... CornerBk
Cornerstone Bank [*Associated Press*] (SAG) .... CrnrB
Cornerstone Christian School Library, Grand Junction, CO [*Library symbol*] [*Library of Congress*] (LCLS) .... CoGjCS
Cornerstone Financial Corp. [*Associated Press*] (SAG) .... CrnrFn
Cornerstone Financial Corp. [*NASDAQ symbol*] (NQ) .... CSTN
Cornerstone Imaging [*NASDAQ symbol*] (TTSB) .... CRNR
Cornerstone Imaging, Inc. [*Associated Press*] (SAG) .... CorImag
Cornerstone Imaging, Inc. [*NASDAQ symbol*] (SAG) .... CRNR
Cornerstone Internet Solutions .... CNRS
Cornerstone Natural Gas [*Associated Press*] (SAG) .... CornNG
Cornerstone Propane Partners LP [*NYSE symbol*] (SAG) .... CNO
Cornerstone Propane Partners LP [*Associated Press*] (SAG) .... CornPrp
Cornerstone Properties [*NYSE symbol*] (SG) .... CPP
Cornerstone Realty Income Tr [*NYSE symbol*] (SG) .... TCR
Cornet .... cnt
Cornet (ADWA) .... cor
Cornet .... COR
Cornet (SAUS) .... Cor
Cornet .... CORT
Cornette Library Online Information Service [*West Texas State University*] (OLDSS) .... CLOIS
Cornhusker Army Ammunition Plant (AABC) .... CAAP
Cornhusks (VRA) .... crnhs
Cornice (DAC) .... Corn
Corning, AR [*FM radio station call letters*] .... KBKG
Corning, AR [*AM radio station call letters*] .... KCCB
Corning, CA [*FM radio station call letters*] .... KCEZ
Corning Community College, Corning, NY [*Library symbol*] [*Library of Congress*] (LCLS) .... NCorniCC
Corning Community College, Corning, NY [*OCLC symbol*] (OCLC) .... ZDG
Corning Del L.P. 6% 'MIPS' [*NYSE symbol*] (TTSB) .... GLWPrM
Corning Delaware LP [*NYSE symbol*] (SAG) .... GLW
Corning Delaware Ltd. [*Associated Press*] (SAG) .... CornD
Corning Free Public Library, Corning, IA [*Library symbol*] [*Library of Congress*] (LCLS) .... IaCorn
Corning Glass Works .... CGW
Corning Glass Works (SAUO) .... GLW
Corning Glass Works, Corning, NY [*Library symbol*] [*Library of Congress*] (LCLS) .... NCorniC
Corning, IA [*Location identifier*] [*FAA*] (FAAL) .... CRZ
Corning, Inc. [*Associated Press*] (SAG) .... CorningIn
Corning, Inc. [*Wall Street slang name: "Glow Worm"*] [*NYSE symbol*] (SPSG) .... GLW
Corning Museum of Glass (SAUS) .... CMG
Corning Museum of Glass (SAUS) .... Corning Mus
Corning Museum of Glass, Corning, NY [*Library symbol*] [*Library of Congress*] (LCLS) .... NCorniM
Corning Museum of Glass, Corning, NY [*OCLC symbol*] (OCLC) .... YKM
Corning, NY [*AM radio station call letters*] .... WCBA
Corning, NY [*FM radio station call letters*] .... WCBA-FM
Corning, NY [*FM radio station call letters*] .... WCEB
Corning, NY [*AM radio station call letters*] .... WCLI
Corning, NY [*FM radio station call letters*] .... WNKI
Corning, NY [*FM radio station call letters*] .... WSQE
Corning, NY [*Television station call letters*] .... WYDC
Corning Public Library, Corning, NY [*Library symbol*] [*Library of Congress*] (LCLS) .... NCorni
Corning Resources [*Vancouver Stock Exchange symbol*] .... CGU
Corning Uniformity Limit Level .... CULL
Corning-Elmira [*New York*] [*Airport symbol*] (AD) .... ELM
Cornish [*MARC language code*] [*Library of Congress*] (LCCP) .... cor
Cornish (ROG) .... CORN
Cornish and Devon Granite Masters Association (SAUO) .... CDGMA
Cornish Association of South Australia .... CASA

Cornish Engines Preservation Society (SAUO) .... CEPS
Cornish Methodist Historical Association (SAUO) .... CMHA
Cornish on Purchase Deeds [*A publication*] (DLA) .... Corn Deeds
Cornish on Purchase Deeds [*A publication*] (DLA) .... Cornish Purch Deeds
Cornish on Purchase Deeds [*A publication*] (DLA) .... Corn Pur D
Cornish on Remainders [*A publication*] (DLA) .... Corn Rem
Cornish on Uses [*A publication*] (DLA) .... Corn Us
Cornish Scottish Australia [*Mine*] .... CSA
Cornish Water Wheels Preservation Society (SAUO) .... CWWPS
Cornmeal .... CM
Corno [*Cornet or Horn*] [*Music*] (ROG) .... COR
Corn-Soya-Blend .... CSB
Corn-Soya-Milk .... CSM
Corn-Soybeans-Corn-Soybeans-Corn [*Crop rotation*] .... CBCBC
Cornstock Bk Carson City Nev [*NASDAQ symbol*] (TTSB) .... LODE
Cornu Ammonis [*Anatomy*] .... CA
Cornu Cervi [*Hartshorn*] [*Pharmacy*] (ROG) CC
Cornu Cervi Ustum [*Burnt Hartshorn*] [*Pharmacy*] (ROG) .... CCU
Cornu Double Prism .... CDP
Cornucopia of Disability Information [*Internet*] (PAZ) .... CODI
Cornucopia Resources Ltd. [*Toronto Stock Exchange symbol*] [*Vancouver Stock Exchange symbol*] .... CNP
Cornucopia Resources Ltd. [*NASDAQ symbol*] (NQ) .... CNPG
Cornucopia Resources Ltd [*NASDAQ symbol*] (TTSB) .... CNPGF
Cornucopia Resources Ltd. [*Associated Press*] (SAG) .... Cornucp
Cornu-Jellet Prism .... CJP
Cornwall (ADWA) .... Corn
Cornwall [*County in England*] .... CORN
Cornwall [*County in England*] (ROG) .... CORNW
Cornwall [*County in England*] .... CRNWL
Cornwall and Devon Miners Royal Garrison Artillery [*British military*] (DMA) .... C & DM RGA
Cornwall Archaeological Society (SAUO) .... CAS
Cornwall General Hospital, Cornwall, ON, Canada [*Library symbol*] [*Library of Congress*] (LCLS) .... CaOCGH
Cornwall General Hospital, Ontario [*Library symbol*] [*National Library of Canada*] (NLC) .... OCGH
Cornwall Information Service (SAUS) .... CIS
Cornwall Light Infantry [*British military*] (DMA) CLI
Cornwall, NY [*AM radio station call letters*] .... WRWD
Cornwall, NY [*AM radio station call letters*] (BROA) .... WWLE-AM
Cornwall, ON [*FM radio station call letters*] .... CFLG
Cornwall, ON [*FM radio station call letters*] (RBYB) .... CHOD
Cornwall, ON [*Television station call letters*] CJOH-8
Cornwall, ON [*AM radio station call letters*] .... CJSS
Cornwall Petroleum [*Vancouver Stock Exchange symbol*] .... COW
Cornwall Public Library, Cornwall, NY [*Library symbol*] [*Library of Congress*] (LCLS) .... NCorn
Cornwall Public Library, Cornwall, ON, Canada [*Library symbol*] [*Library of Congress*] (LCLS) .... CaOC
Cornwall Public Library, Ontario [*Library symbol*] [*National Library of Canada*] (NLC) .... OC
Cornwall R. R. [*AAR code*] .... CWL
Cornwall Railroad (SAUO) .... CWL
Cornwall Railway (SAUO) .... CR
Cornwall's Table of Precedents [*A publication*] (DLA) .... Cornw Tab
Cornwell Avenue School, West Hempstead, NY [*Library symbol*] [*Library of Congress*] (LCLS) .... NWhCE
Cornwell's Digest [*A publication*] (DLA) .... Corn Dig
Cornwell-Weisskopf Formula .... CWF
Coro [*Venezuela*] [*Airport symbol*] (OAG) .... CZE
Coro Foundation (EA) .... CF
Coroico [*Bolivia*] [*ICAO location identifier*] (ICLI) .... SLIC
Coro/Internacional, Falcon [*Venezuela*] [*ICAO location identifier*] (ICLI) .... SVCR
Corolla C
Corolla Resources Ltd. [*Vancouver Stock Exchange symbol*] .... CRA
Corollary .... COROL
Corollary (ADWA) .... corol
Corollary (NTIO) .... coroll
Corollary (ADA) .... COROLL
Corollary (SAUS) .... Coroll
Corollary Discharge Interneuron [*Neurology*] .... CDI
Corollary Discharge Neuron [*Neurophysiology*] .... CD
Corona [*A publication*] .... COR
Corona Australis [*Constellation*] .... CorA
Corona Australis [*Constellation*] .... CrA
Corona Borealis [*Constellation*] .... CorB
Corona Borealis [*Constellation*] .... CrB
Corona, CA [*Television station call letters*] .... KVEA
Corona, CA [*AM radio station call letters*] .... KWRM
Corona Current Detector .... CCD
Corona Diagnostic Mission (SSD) .... CDM
Corona, Eddy Current, Beta Ray, Microwave .... CEBM
Corona Extinction Voltage (IEEE) .... CEV
Corona Inception Voltage (PDAA) CIV
Corona Inspection Voltage (ACAE) CIV
Corona, NM [*Location identifier*] [*FAA*] (FAAL) .... CNX
Corona Onset Voltage .... COV
Corona Oxide Semiconductor (SAUS) .... COS
Corona Public Library, Corona, CA [*Library symbol*] [*Library of Congress*] (LCLS) .... CCoro
Corona Radiata [*Medicine*] (MELL) .... CR
Corona Starting Voltage .... CSV
Corona Test Voltage (ACAE) .... CTV
Coronado 15 Association (EA) .... CFA
Coronado 15 Class Racing Association (EA) .... CFCRA
Coronado Aerolineas Ltda. [*Colombia*] [*ICAO designator*] (FAAC) .... CRA
Coronado National Memorial .... CORO
Coronado Public Library (SAUS) .... CPL
Coronado Public Library, Coronado, CA [*Library symbol*] [*Library of Congress*] (LCLS) .... CCoron
Coronado Resources, Inc. [*Vancouver Stock Exchange symbol*] .... CRD
Coronae Borealis [*Astronomy*] .... CrB
Coronagraph Polarimeter .... CP
Coronal and Interplanetary Section (SAUS) .... CIP
Coronal Diagnostic Spectrometer .... CDS
Coronal Doppler Spectrometer (SAUS) .... CDS
Coronal Emission Line Polarimeter (SAUS) .... KELP
Coronal Helium Abundance Spacelab Experiment (SAUS) .... CHASE
Coronal Mass Ejection [*Astrophysics*] .... CME
Corona-Penetrating Enzyme (MAE) .... CPE
Coronary [*Cardiology*] (DAVI) .... cor
Coronary (SAUS) .... Coron
Coronary Angiography [*Cardiology*] (DMAA) .... CAG
Coronary Angioplasty Versus Excisional Atherectomy Trial [*Cardiology study*] .... CAVEAT
Coronary Arrhythmia Monitoring Unit [*Cardiology*] (DAVI) .... CAMU
Coronary Arterial Calcinosis [*Medicine*] (MELL) .... CAC
Coronary Arteriosclerotic Heart Disease .... CASHD
Coronary Arteriovenous Fistula [*Cardiology*] .... CAVF
Coronary Artery [*Medicine*] .... CA
Coronary Artery [*Medicine*] (MELL) .... Ca
Coronary Artery Aneurysm [*Cardiology*] .... CAA
Coronary Artery Bypass [*Medicine*] .... CAB
Coronary Artery Bypass Graft [*Medicine*] .... CABG
Coronary Artery Bypass Graft [*Cardiology*] (DMAA) .... CARB
Coronary Artery Bypass Graft Surgery [*Medicine*] .... CABGS
Coronary Artery Bypass Grafting [*Medicine*] .... CABG
Coronary Artery Bypass Surgery [*Medicine*] .... CABS
Coronary Artery Disease [*Medicine*] .... CAD
Coronary Artery Embolism [*Medicine*] (MELL) .... CAE
Coronary Artery Endarterectomy [*Medicine*] (MELL) .... CAE
Coronary Artery Graft Bypass [*Cardiology*] (DAVI) .... CAGB
Coronary Artery Heart Disease [*Cardiology*] (DAVI) .... CAHD
Coronary Artery Obstruction [*Cardiology*] (DMAA) .... CAO
Coronary Artery Occlusive Disease [*Medicine*] (DMAA) .... CAOD
Coronary Artery Risk Development in Young Adults [*Epidemiologic study*] .... CARDIA
Coronary Artery Risk Evaluation Program [*Air Force*] .... CARE
Coronary Artery Spasm [*Medicine*] (DB) .... CAS
Coronary Artery Stenosis (SAUS) .... CAS
Coronary Artery Surgery Study [*Medicine*] .... CASS
Coronary Artery Surgery Trial [*Medicine*] .... CAST
Coronary Artery Vein Graft [*Medicine*] (DMAA) .... CAVG
Coronary Atherosclerotic Heart Disease [*Medicine*] (MAE) .... CAHD
Coronary Balloon Angioplasty [*Medicine*] (MELL) .... CBA
Coronary Blood Flow [*Medicine*] .... CBF
Coronary Bypass Grafting [*Medicine*] (DB) .... CBG
Coronary Care Intensive Medical (SAUS) .... CCIM
Coronary Care Nurse (or Nursing) (SAUS) .... CCO
Coronary Care Nursing [*Medicine*] (MAE) .... CCN
Coronary Care Team [*Medicine*] .... CCT
Coronary Care Training Project [*Cardiology*] (DAVI) .... CCTP
Coronary Care Unit [*of a hospital*] .... CCU
Coronary Club (EA) CC
Coronary Collateral [*Medicine*] (AAMN) CC
Coronary Dilatation Catheter [*Medicine*] (MELL) .... CDC
Coronary Drug Project .... CDP
Coronary Drug Project Group [*Medicine*] (BABM) .... CDPG
Coronary Flow [*Medicine*] .... CF
Coronary Force (MELL) .... CF
Coronary Heart Disease [*Medicine*] .... CHD
Coronary Insufficiency [*Medicine*] CI
Coronary Intensive Care Unit [*of a hospital*] .... CICU
Coronary Perfusion Pressure [*Cardiology*] .... CPP
Coronary Prevention Group [*British*] .... CPG
Coronary Primary Prevention Trial [*National Heart, Lung, and Blood Institute*] .... CPPT
Coronary Prognostic Index [*Medicine*] (AAMN) .... CPI
Coronary Rehabilitation Program (STED) .... CRP
Coronary Reserve [*Cardiology*] .... CR
Coronary Resistance (SAUS) .... CR
Coronary Sclerosis [*Medicine*] .... CS
Coronary Sinus [*Cardiology*] .... CS
Coronary Sinus Blood Flow [*Cardiology*] .... CSBF
Coronary Sinus Flow [*Medicine*] (DB) .... CSF
Coronary Sinus Stimulation [*Medicine*] (STED) .... CSS
Coronary Status [*Cardiology*] .... CS
Coronary Thrombosis [*Medicine*] .... CT
Coronary Unit (IIA) .... CU
Coronary Vascular Resistance [*Medicine*] .... CVR
Coronary Vascular Resistance Index [*Cardiology*] (DAVI) .... CVRI
Coronary Vein Graft [*Medicine*] .... CVG
Coronation (ROG) .... CR
Coronation, AB [*Television station call letters*] CKRD-1
Coronation, AB [*ICAO location identifier*] (ICLI) .... CYCT
Coronation Public Library, Alberta [*Library symbol*] [*National Library of Canada*] (NLC) .... ACOR
Coronavirus CV

Coronel Fontana [Argentina] [Seismograph station code, US Geological Survey] (SEIS) .... CFA
Coronel Olmedo [Argentina] [ICAO location identifier] (ICLI) .... SACD
Coronene (SAUS) .... COR
Coroner (ROG) .... COR
Coroner (BEE) .... cor
Coroner (DLA) .... CORON
Coroners' Rolls [British] .... COR
Coroner's Society Cases [England] [A publication] (DLA) .... Cor Soc Cas
Coronet (ADA) .... COR
Coronet Carpets, Inc. [Toronto Stock Exchange symbol] .... RUG
Coronie [Surinam] [ICAO location identifier] (ICLI) .... SMCO
Coronoid Process of Mandible [Medicine] (MELL) .... CPM
Corotating Interaction Region [Planetary science] .... CIR
Corotation Eccentricity Resonance [Planetary science] .... CER
Corotation Inclination Resonance [Planetary science] .... CIR
Corotation Resonance [Planetary science] .... CR
Corowa [New South Wales] [Airport symbol] (AD) .... COW
Corozal [Belize] [Airport symbol] (OAG) .... CZH
Corozal [Colombia] [Airport symbol] (AD) .... CZU
Corozal, PR [FM radio station call letters] .... WORO
Corozal/Las Brujas [Colombia] [ICAO location identifier] (ICLI) .... SKCZ
Corp. de Developpement du Canada [Canada Development Corp. - CDC] .... CDC
Corpo de Tropas Paraquedistas [Paratroopers Corps] [Air Force] [Portugal] .... CTP
Corpora Alata [Insect anatomy] .... CA
Corpora Amylacea [Neurology] .... CA
Corpora Cardiaca [Endocrinology] CC
Corpora Cavernosa [Medicine] (MELL) CC
Corporacion Aereo Cencor SA de CV [Mexico] [ICAO designator] (FAAC) .... CNC
Corporacion Aereo Internacional SA de CV [Mexico] [ICAO designator] (FAAC) .... CAI
Corporacion Andina de Fomento [Commercial firm] [Colombia] (ECON) .... CAF
Corporacion Area Ejecutiva SA de CV [Mexico] [ICAO designator] (FAAC) .... CEJ
Corporacion Bancaria de Espana [NYSE symbol] (SAG) .... AGR
Corporacion Bancaria de Espana [Associated Press] (SAG) .... Argentar
Corporacion Bancaria de Espana [Spain] (ECON) .... CBE
Corporacion Centroamericana de Dervicios de Navagacion Aerea [Mexico] [FAA designator] (FAAC) .... YGD
Corporacion de Investigaciones Economicas para Latinoamerica .... CIEPLAN
Corporacion Dominicana de Aviacion [Dominican Aviation Corporation] [Airline] [Dominican Republic] .... CDA
Corporal (ADWA) .... Corp
Corporal (GEAB) .... corp
Corporal .... CORP
Corporal (SAUO) .... Corp
Corporal .... CORPL
Corporal (ADWA) .... Corpl
Corporal (WDAA) .... Cpl
Corporal [Military] (AABC) .... CPL
Corporal [Army, Marine Corps] E4
Corporal of Horse [British military] (DMA) .... COH
Corporal Punishment (WDAA) .... CP
Corporal Veno-Occlusive Dysfunction [Medicine] (MELL) .... CVOD
corporalis (SAUS) .... corp
Corporal-Major of Horse [British] .... CMH
Corporate (VRA) .... corp
Corporate (ROG) .... CORP
Corporate (EBF) .... Corp
Corporate .... CORPRT
Corporate Account Profitability (SAUS) .... CAP
Corporate Accountability Research Group [Formed by consumer-advocate Ralph Nader] .... CARG
Corporate Action Project [Defunct] (EA) .... CAP
Corporate Administrative Contracting Officer [DoD] .... CACO
Corporate Advisory Group (ACAE) .... CAG
Corporate Affairs Processing System .... CAPS
Corporate Affiliates Program (SAUS) .... CAP
Corporate Agents, Inc. [Information service or system] (IID) .... CAI
Corporate Air [ICAO designator] (FAAC) .... CPT
Corporate Air, Inc. [ICAO designator] (FAAC) .... CPR
Corporate Aircraft Co. [ICAO designator] (FAAC) .... CPO
Corporate Airlink [Canada] [FAA designator] (FAAC) .... COO
Corporate and Foundation Givers [A publication] .... CFG
Corporate and Industry Research Reports Index [JA Micropublishing, Inc.] [Database] .... CIRR
Corporate and Staff Development .... C & SD
Corporate Angel Network (EA) .... CAN
Corporate Asset Funding Unit .... CAF
Corporate Author Authority List .... CAAL
Corporate Average Fuel Economy [Automobile industry] .... CAFE
Corporate Average Fuel Efficiency [Automobile Industry] .... CAFE
Corporate Aviation Services, Inc. [ICAO designator] (FAAC) .... CKE
Corporate Backbone Network Switch (SAUS) .... CBNS
Corporate Bureaucrat (ADWA) .... corprcrat
Corporate Business Law Journal [A publication] .... CBLJ
Corporate Capital Charge (MCD) CCC
Corporate Communication (WDMC) CC
Corporate Communications Services (SAUS) .... CCS
Corporate Communications Switching Equipment (SAUS) .... CCSE
Corporate Communications System [Bell-Northern Research Ltd.] [Computer science] .... COCOS
Corporate Components Procurement Management Operating Procedures (SAUS) .... CCPMOP
Corporate Conservation Council (EA) CCC

Corporate Consolidated Data Network [IBM Corp.] [Telecommunications] .... CCDN
Corporate Consolidation System (SAUS) .... CCS
Corporate Consolidation System (SAUS) .... CCS
Corporate Consulting & Development Co. Ltd. (SAUO) .... CCDC
Corporate Contract Officer .... CCO
Corporate Control Procedure (MCD) .... CCP
Corporate Control Usage File (SAUS) .... CCUF
Corporate Conversions [Information service or system] (IID) CC
Corporate Council for the Liberal Arts [Defunct] (EA) .... CCLA
Corporate Counsel Review [A publication] (DLA) .... Corp Counsel Rev
Corporate Customer Order Control Program (IAA) .... CCOCP
Corporate Customer Satisfaction Monitor .... CCSM
Corporate Data Base (SAUO) .... CDB
Corporate Data Exchange (EA) .... CDE
Corporate Data Network (SAUS) .... CDN
Corporate Data Sciences [Commercial firm] (NITA) .... CDS
Corporate Democracy (SAUO) .... CD
Corporate Depository (DLA) .... Corp Dep
Corporate Design (SAUS) .... CD
Corporate Electronic Publishing (HGAA) .... CEP
Corporate Electronic Publishing Systems Exhibition [or Exposition] (ITD) .... CEPS
Corporate Emergency Response Center [Nuclear emergency planning] .... CERC
Corporate Engineering and Sales Directive .... CEASD
Corporate Engineering Laboratory (SAUO) .... CEL
Corporate Engineering List (SAUS) .... CEL
Corporate Engineering Standard (IAA) .... CES
Corporate Engineering Transfer and Obsoletion System (IAA) .... CETOS
Corporate Environmental Advisors, Inc. (EFIS) .... CEA
Corporate Environmental Management Program [University of Michigan] .... CEMP
Corporate Equity-Reducing Transaction .... CERT
Corporate Executive Board [NASDAQ symbol] (SG) .... EXBD
Corporate Experimental Research Vehicle [General Motors Corp.] [Automotive engineering] .... CERV
Corporate Express [NASDAQ symbol] (TTSB) .... CEXP
Corporate Express File (or Format) (SAUS) .... CEF
Corporate Express, Inc. [NASDAQ symbol] (SAG) .... CEXP
Corporate Express, Inc. [Associated Press] (SAG) .... CorpEx
Corporate Express, Inc. [Associated Press] (SAG) .... CorpExp
Corporate Express Transfer/Obsoletion System (SAUS) .... CET/OS
Corporate Finance Director .... CFD
Corporate Finance Partner .... CFP
Corporate Financial System (SAUS) .... CFS
Corporate Foods Ltd. [Toronto Stock Exchange symbol] .... CFL
Corporate Functional Integration Board (SAUS) .... CFIB
Corporate Fund for Dance .... CFD
Corporate Headquarters (ACAE) .... CH
Corporate Headquarters Office Technology System (SAUS) .... CHOTS
Corporate Health Dimensions .... CHD
Corporate High Yield Fd II [NYSE symbol] (TTSB) .... KYT
Corporate High Yield Fund, Inc. [Associated Press] (SAG) .... CorpHY
Corporate High Yield Fund, Inc. [NYSE symbol] (SAG) .... COY
Corporate High Yield II [Associated Press] (SAG) .... CpHYII
Corporate High Yield II [NYSE symbol] (SAG) .... KYT
Corporate Home Office Administrative Contracting Officer (AAGC) .... CACO
Corporate Home Office Auditor (AAGC) .... CHOA
Corporate Hospitality Association (COBU) .... CHA
Corporate Identity (SAUS) CI
Corporate Income Fund .... CIF
Corporate Income Tax [Economics] .... CIT
Corporate Industrial Preparedness Representative [Military] .... CIPR
Corporate Information, BC Rail, Vancouver, British Columbia [Library symbol] [National Library of Canada] (NLC) .... BVABCR
Corporate Information Center [Later, ICCR] CIC
Corporate Information Centre, Royal Trust, Toronto, Ontario [Library symbol] [National Library of Canada] (BIB) .... OTROT
Corporate Information Management [DoD] (RDA) .... CIM
Corporate Information Officer .... CIO
Corporate Information Processing Standards (MCD) .... CIPS
Corporate Information Resource Management (SAUO) .... CIRM
Corporate Information Service Department (CIST) .... CISD
Corporate Information System (MCD) .... CIS
Corporate Information Technology .... CIT
Corporate Information Technology Plan .... CITP
Corporate Information Technology Strategy .... CITS
Corporate Information Unit (SAUS) .... CIU
Corporate Instruction (SAUS) CI
Corporate Integrated Information System [Consumer and Corporate Affairs Canada] [Information service or system] (IID) .... CIIS
Corporate Interplant Status Record (SAUS) .... CISR
Corporate Jets, Inc. [FAA designator] (FAAC) .... CJI
Corporate Jobs Outlook [Information service or system] (IID) .... CJO
Corporate Language and Communication (SAUS) .... CLAC
Corporate Lawyers' Association of New South Wales [Australia] .... CLANSW
Corporate Library, Domglas, Inc., Mississauga, Ontario [Library symbol] [National Library of Canada] (NLC) .... OMDO
Corporate Library Information Centre (SAUS) CLIC
Corporate Library, Mutual Life of Canada, Waterloo, Ontario [Library symbol] [National Library of Canada] (BIB) .... OWTML
Corporate Library Update [A publication] .... CLU
Corporate Logic Tester (SAUS) .... CLT
Corporate Low Level Code (SAUS) CLLC
Corporate Machine Features Index (SAUS) .... CMFI
Corporate Machine Level Control (SAUS) .... CMLC
Corporate Management Committee [Australia] .... CMC
Corporate Management Group, Inc. (SAUS) .... CORP

Corporate Management Group, Inc. (SAUO) .... KORP
Corporate Management Information System (SAUS) .... CMIS
Corporate Management Report and Plan (COE) .... CMRP
Corporate Management Systems Report (COE) .... CMSR
Corporate Management Team (SAUO) .... CMT
Corporate Management Technical Assignment (SAUS) .... CMTA
Corporate Manufacturing Practice (IAA) .... CMP
Corporate Manufacturing Technology Assignment (SAUS) .... CMTA
Corporate Manufacturing Transfer System (IAA) .... COMATS
Corporate Member of the Institution of Electrical and Electronics Incorporated Engineers [*British*] (DBQ) .... MIElecIE
Corporate Membership (SAUS) .... CM
Corporate Memory Systems, Inc. [*Computer science*] (PCM) .... CMSI
Corporate Message Recovery (SAUS) .... CMR
Corporate Minimum Tax .... CMT
Corporate Mountaineers Cult .... CMC
Corporate Network (SAUO) .... CN
Corporate Network Group (SAUO) .... CNG
Corporate Network Products (VERA) .... CNP
Corporate Network Provider (SAUO) .... CNP
Corporate Office (AAG) .... CO
Corporate Office Interconnectivity Network [*Computer science*] (CIST) .... COIN
Corporate Office Prop Tr SBI [*NYSE symbol*] (SG) .... OFC
Corporate Oil & Gas [*Vancouver Stock Exchange symbol*] .... CPA
Corporate Ombudsman Association (EA) .... COA
Corporate Organization and Procedures Economy (SAA) .... COPE
Corporate Payment System .... CPS
Corporate Planning Group (ACAE) .... CPG
Corporate Planning Information System (SAUS) .... CORPIS
Corporate Planning Office [*AFSC*] CCX
Corporate Planning System (IAA) .... CPS
Corporate Practice Review [*A publication*] (DLA) .... Corp Prac Rev
Corporate Practice Review [*A publication*] (DLA) .... Corp Pract Rev
Corporate Pricing System (ACAE) .... CPS
Corporate Programming Bulletin (SAUS) .... CPB
Corporate Programming List (SAUS) .... CPL
Corporate Programming Standard (SAUS) .... CPS
Corporate Purchasing Agreements (MCD) .... COPA
Corporate Quality Assurance Regulations (MCD) .... CQAR
Corporate Record Practice (SAUS) .... CRP
Corporate Records List (SAUS) .... CRL
Corporate Records Management Office (ACAE) .... CRMO
Corporate Renaissance Group [*NASDAQ symbol*] (TTSB) .... CREN
Corporate Renaissance Group, Inc. [*Associated Press*] (SAG) .... CorpRen
Corporate Renaissance Group, Inc. [*NASDAQ symbol*] (SAG) .... CREN
Corporate Reorganization and American Bankruptcy Review [*A publication*] (DLA) .... Corp Reorg & Am Bank Rev
Corporate Reorganizations [*A publication*] (DLA) .... Corp Reorg
Corporate Research and Development .... CRD
Corporate Research and Information Centre, Nova Scotia Power Corp., Halifax, Nova Scotia [*Library symbol*] [*National Library of Canada*] (NLC) .... NSHPC
Corporate Research Information Service [*Frederick Research*] .... CRIS
Corporate Research Programme (SAUO) .... CRP
Corporate Resource and Allocation (MHDB) .... CORPORAL
Corporate Responsibility Task Force of the Business Roundtable (EA) .... CRTF
Corporate Search Code (SAUS) .... SC
Corporate Security Regulation Appendices .... CSRA
Corporate Services Administration Department [*Medicine*] (DMAA) .... CSAD
Corporate Shareholder System (IAA) .... CSS
Corporate Source [*Online database field identifier*] .... COR
Corporate Source [*Online database field identifier*] .... CS
Corporate Source List (SAUS) .... CSL
Corporate Source Name [*Database terminology*] (NITA) .... CN
Corporate Systems List (SAUS) .... CSL
Corporate Systems Practice (SAUS) .... CSP
Corporate Tax Administration, Alberta Treasury, Edmonton, Alberta [*Library symbol*] [*National Library of Canada*] (NLC) .... AETCT
Corporate Tax Association [*Australia*] .... CTA
Corporate Tax Association of Australia .... CTAA
Corporate Technical Education Center (ACAE) .... CTEC
Corporate Technical Information Center (DIT) .... CTIC
Corporate Technological Assignment (SAUS) .... CTA
Corporate Technology Database [*Corporate Technology Information Services, Inc.*] (CRD) .... CTD
Corporate Technology Group [*British*] .... CTG
Corporate Technology Information Services, Inc. [*Information service or system*] (IID) .... CorpTech
Corporate Telecommunication Network (SAUO) .... CTN
Corporate Telecommunications and Office Systems (SAUO) .... CTOS
Corporate Telecommunications Operation (SAUS) .... CTO
Corporate Terminal System (SAUS) .... CTS
Corporate Towers (ACAE) .... CT
Corporate Trade Exchange [*Automated Clearing House*] .... CTX
Corporate Trade Payment [*Automated Clearing House*] .... CTP
Corporate Transfer Agents Association [*New York, NY*] (EA) .... CTAA
Corporate Transfer Manufacturing File Update (SAUS) .... CTMFU
Corporate Travel Department (TRID) .... CTD
Corporate Travel Index [*A publication*] .... CTI
Corporate Trust [*Legal term*] (DLA) .... C Tr
Corporate Trustee (DLA) .... Corp Tr
Corporate Value Associates [*Commercial firm*] [*British*] .... CVA
Corporate Venturing [*Business term*] CV
Corporate Word [*Database terminology*] (NITA) .... CW
Corporate-Higher Education Forum [*Forum Entreprises-Universites*] (AC) .... C-HEF
Corporate-Owned Life Insurance (WYGK) .... COLI
Corporation (NTIO) .... corp
Corporation (AFM) .... CORP
Corporation (TBD) .... Corp
Corporation (SAUO) .... Corp
Corporation .... CORPN
corporation (SAUO) .... corpr
Corporation (ROG) .... CPN
Corporation [*Prentice-Hall, Inc.*] [*A publication*] (DLA) .... P-H Corp
Corporation Aircraft Owners Association (SAUO) .... CAOA
Corporation Commission CC
Corporation Consulting Group [*British*] .... CCG
Corporation des Bibliothecaires Professionnels du Quebec [*Corporation of Professsional Librarians of Quebec*] (AC) .... CBPQ
Corporation des Concessionnaires d'Automobiles du Quebec Inc. (AC) .... CCAQ
Corporation des Entrepreneurs en Maconnerie du Quebec (AC) .... CEMQ
Corporation des Entrepreneurs Specialises du Grand Montreal (AC) .... CESGM
Corporation des Maitres Electriciens du Quebec [*Corporation of Master Electricians of Quebec*] (AC) .... CMEQ
Corporation des Maitres Entrepreneurs en Refrigeration du Quebec [*Corporation of Air Treatment & Cold Processing Entreprises*] (AC) .... CETAF
Corporation des Maitres Mecaniciens en Tuyauterie du Quebec [*Corporation of Master Pipe Mechanics of Quebec*] (AC) .... CMMTQ
Corporation des Officiers Municipaux Agrees du Quebec [*Corporation of Chartered Municipal Officers of Quebec*] (AC) .... COMAQ
Corporation des Proprietaires Immobiliers du Quebec (AC) .... CORPIQ
Corporation des Secretaires Municipaux du Quebec Inc. (AC) .... CSMQ
Corporation des Services aux Etablissements Touristiques Quebecois (AC) .... CSETQ
Corporation des Thanatologues du Quebec (AC) .... CTQ
Corporation des Traducteurs, Traductrices, Terminologues et Interpretes du Nouveau-Brunswick [*Corporation of Translators, Terminologists & Interpreters of New Brunswick*] (AC) .... CTINB
Corporation for Economic and Industrial Research (SAUO) .... C-E-I-R
Corporation for Economic and Industrial Research (SAUS) .... C-E-I-R
Corporation for Economic Development in the Caribbean (SAUO) .... CODECA
Corporation for Economics and Industrial Research [*Subsidiary of Control Data Corporation*] .... CEIR
Corporation for Enterprise Development (EA) .... CFED
Corporation for Excellence in Public Education (SAUO) .... EXCEL
Corporation for Information Systems Research and Development (MCD) .... CIRAD
Corporation for Jefferson's Poplar Forest (EA) .... CJPF
Corporation for Laser Optics Research .... COLOR
Corporation for Maintaining Editorial Diversity in America (EA) .... C/MEDIA
Corporation for Menke's Disease (EA) .... CMD
Corporation for National Academic Awards (SAUO) .... CNAA
Corporation for National Research Initiatives (TELE) .... CNRI
Corporation for National Service (SAUO) .... CNS
Corporation for Open Systems [*Telecommunications*] (EA) .... COS
Corporation for Open Systems International (SAUO) .... COSI
Corporation for Public Broadcasting (EA) .... CPB
Corporation for Research and Educational Networking [*Internet*] .... CREN
Corporation for Research and Educational Networking [*Computer science*] (TNIG) .... CREN/BITNET
Corporation for Research and Enterprise Network (SAUO) .... CoREN
Corporation for Television Broadcasts (SAUO) .... CTB
Corporation Guide [*Prentice-Hall, Inc.*] [*A publication*] (DLA) .... Corp Guide
Corporation Index System [*Securities and Exchange Commission*] (GFGA) .... CIN
Corporation Network [*Telephone communications*] .... CORNET
Corporation of Certified Secretaries (AIE) .... CCS
Corporation of Foreign Bondholders (SAUO) .... CFB
Corporation of Insurance Agents (SAUO) .... CIA
Corporation of Insurance and Financial Advisers [*British*] .... CIFA
Corporation of Land Surveyors of the Province of British Columbia [*Also, BC Land Surveyors*] [*Formerly, Provincial Land Surveyors*] (AC) .... BCLS
Corporation of Lloyds [*Also, Lloyd's of London*] [*Insurance*] (DS) CL
Corporation of London [*The City of London as opposed to Greater London*] .... C of L
Corporation of Professional Engineers of Quebec (SAUO) .... CPEQ
Corporation of Secretaries (SAUO) .... CS
Corporation of Sons of the Clergy (SAUO) .... CSC
Corporation of the City of London Staff Association (SAUO) .... CCLSA
Corporation of Trinity House (SAUO) .... CTH
Corporation Pierre Boucher, Trois-Rivieres, Quebec [*Library symbol*] [*National Library of Canada*] (NLC) .... QTCPB
Corporation Pierre-Boucher, Trois-Rivieres, PQ, Canada [*Library symbol*] [*Library of Congress*] (LCLS) .... CaQTCPB
[*La*] **Corporation Professionnelle des Administrateurs Agrees du Quebec** [*The Order of Chartered Administrators of Quebec*] (AC) .... CPAAQ
Corporation Professionnelle des Conseillers en Relations Industrielles du Quebec (AC) .... CPCRIQ
Corporation Professionnelle des Conseilliers et Conseillieres d'Orientation du Quebec (AC) .... CPCCOQ
Corporation Professionnelle des Ergotherapeutes du Quebec (AC) .... CPEQ
Corporation Professionnelle des Medecins du Quebec [*Professional Corporation of Physicians of Quebec*] (AC) .... CPMQ
Corporation Professionnelle des Medecins Veterinaires du Quebec (AC) .... CPMVQ
Corporation Professionnelle des Orthophonistes et Audiologistes du Quebec (AC) .... CPOAQ
Corporation Professionnelle des Physiotherapeutes du Quebec (AC) .... CPPQ
Corporation Professionnelle des Psychologues du Quebec (AC) .... CPPQ
Corporation Professionnelle des Technologistes Medicaux du Quebec (AC) .... CPTMQ

Corporation Professionnelle des Technologues Professionnelles du Quebec (AC) .... CPTPQ
Corporation Professionnelle des Travailleurs Sociaux du Quebec (AC) .... CPTSQ
Corporation Professionnelle des Urbanistes du Quebec (AC) .... CPUQ
Corporation Research Education Network (SAUO) .... CREN
Corporation Source System Listing (SAUO) .... CSSL
Corporation Standard Practice (AAG) .... CSP
Corporation Tax [British] .... CT
Corporation-Management Edition (Prentice-Hall, Inc.) [A publication] (DLA) .... Corp-Mgmt Ed (P-H)
Corporations and Associations [A publication] (DLA) .... Corp & Ass'ns
Corporations and Labor Union Returns Act .... CALURA
Corporations Code [A publication] (DLA) .... Corp C
Corporative Programming Practice (SAUS) .... CPP
Corporeal Pin (SAUS) .... Corppin
Corporeal Pin [Method of tuberculin and histoplasmin testing] [Medicine] .... CORPPIN
Corpori [To the Body] [Pharmacy] .... CORP
Corps (SAUO) C
Corps C
Corps (SAUO) .... Co
Corps [Army] .... COR
Corps (SAUO) .... CPS
Corps Adjutant [British military] (DMA) .... CA
Corps Advisory Detachment .... CAD
Corps Airborne Stand-Off RADAR (MCD) .... CASTOR
Corps Airborne Stand-Off Radar (SAUS) .... CASTOR
Corps Airspace Management Element (MCD) .... CAME
Corps Ammunition Park (SAUO) .... CAP
Corps and Division Training Coordination Program [DoD] .... CORTRAIN
Corps Area [Army] .... CA
Corps Area Air Defense (SAUS) .... CAAD
Corps Area Communications Center [Army] .... CACC
Corps Area Communications System [Vietnam] (MCD) .... CACS
Corps Area Signal Center (MCD) .... CASC
Corps Artillery (SAUO) .... CORPS ARTY
Corps Artillery Intelligence Officer [British] .... CAIO
Corps Automated Management Data Operations Center (SAUO) .... CAMDOC
Corps Automation Requirements [Army] .... CAR
Corps Aviation Company [Army] (VNW) .... CAC
Corps Battle Simulation [Army] .... CBS
Corps Battle Simulation .... CORSIM
Corps Brandenburgia (EA) .... CB
Corps Camouflage Officer (SAUO) .... CCO
Corps Commander [British military] (DMA) CC
Corps Commander Coast Artillery [British] .... CCCA
Corps Communications (MCD) .... CORCOM
Corps Communications Support Requirement Simulations (MCD) .... CCOMSRS
Corps Contingency Force [Army] (AABC) .... CCF
Corps Counterattack Force (SAUO) .... CCF
Corps Counterbombardment Officer (SAUS) .... CCBO
Corps d'Afrique .... C d'A
Corps Diplomatique [Diplomatic Corps] .... CD
Corps Districts and Divisions (SAUO) .... CDD
Corps Division Evaluation Model [Army] (RDA) .... CORDIVEM
Corps Duty (SAUS) .... CD
Corps Education Officer (SAUS) .... CEO
Corps Eligible [Army] (RDA) .... CE
Corps Epidemiological Reference Office [Military] .... CERO
Corps Expeditionaire Francais .... CEF
Corps Field Dressing Station (SAUO) .... CFDS
Corps Front Luxembourgeois [Resistance organization in Luxembourg] [World War II] .... CFL
Corps Headquarters [Army] .... CHQ
Corps Interim Upgrade System (MCD) .... CIUS
Corps Maintenance Area .... CMA
Corps Master Control Center (SAUO) .... CMCC
Corps Material Direct Support Activity (MCD) .... CMDSA
Corps Material Management Center (MCD) .... CMMC
Corps Material Management System (MCD) .... CMMS
Corps Medical Centre (SAUO) .... CMC
Corps Military Intelligence Support Element (SAUS) .... CMISE
Corps Movement Control Organization [Royal Corps of Transport] [British] .... CMCO
Corps Observation .... CO
Corps of Armourers [British military] (DMA) .... C of A
Corps of Cadets .... COC
Corps of Chartered Secretaries (SAUO) .... CCS
Corps of Commissioners (SAUO) .... COC
Corps of Drivers Royal Artillery [British military] (DMA) .... CDRA
Corps of Engineers [Army] .... CE
Corps of Engineers [Army] (AAG) .... COE
Corps of Engineers (SAUS) .... CoE
Corps of Engineers [Army] .... C of E
Corps of Engineers [Army] (MUGU) .... COREN
Corps of Engineers [Army] (SAA) .... CORENG
Corps of Engineers Automation Plan [DoD] (GFGA) .... CEAP
Corps of Engineers Ballistic Missile Construction Agency [Army] .... CEBMCA
Corps of Engineers Ballistic Missile Construction Office [Army] .... CEBMCO
Corps of Engineers Board of Contract Appeals [Army] .... ENGBCA
Corps of Engineers (Civil Works) [Army] .... COE(CW)
Corps of Engineers, Colorado Citizens Coordinating Committee on Environmental Planning .... CECEP
Corps of Engineers Enlisted Reserve (SAUO) .... CEER

Corps of Engineers Guide Specials (SAUO) .... CEGS
Corps of Engineers Guide Specifications for Emergency Type Construction [Army] .... CE-E
Corps of Engineers, Lower Mississippi Valley Division, New Orleans Planning Division [Louisiana] .... COELMN/PD
Corps of Engineers Management Information System [DoD] (GFGA) .... COEMIS
Corps of Engineers Manual for Military Construction [Army] .... EMMC
Corps of Engineers National Energy Network (SAUO) .... CENEN
Corps of Engineers Office of Appalachian Studies [Army] (AABC) .... CEOAS
Corps of Engineers Reserve Fleet .... CERF
Corps of Engineers Technical Committee [Army] .... CETC
Corps of Engineers Waterborne Commerce Statistics Center [Army] (AABC) .... CEWCSC
Corps of Indian Electrical and Mechanical Engineers [British military] (DMA) .... IEME
Corps of Intelligence Police [Army] (DOMA) .... CIP
Corps of Interpreters CI
Corps of Military Accountants [British military] (DMA) .... CMA
Corps of Military Mounted Police [British military] (DMA) .... CMMP
Corps of Military Police [British] .... CMP
Corps of Military Police Enlisted Reserve (SAUO) .... CMPER
Corps of Military Police (India) [British military] (DMA) .... CMP(I)
Corps of Military Staff Clerks (SAUO) .... CMSC
Corps of Ordnance Artificers [British military] (DMA) .... COA
Corps of Permanent Instructors [British military] (DMA) .... CPI
Corps of Royal Military Police (SAUO) .... CRMP
Corps of Signals (SAUO) .... CS
Corps of Signals [British] (DAS) .... CS
Corps of Transportation [Army] .... CT
Corps of Volunteers Artillery Regiment [British military] (DMA) .... VAR
Corps Ordnance Maintenance Park (SAUO) .... COMP
Corps Paymaster (SAUS) .... C Pm
Corps Personnel Operations Center [Army] .... CPOC
Corps Phase Line .... CPL
Corps Reinforcement Group (SAUO) .... CRG
Corps Reinforcement Holding Unit (SAUS) .... CRHU
Corps Reinforcement Unit [British military] (DMA) .... CRU
Corps Rest Station (SAUO) .... CRS
Corps Routine Order (SAUS) .... CRO
Corps Royal Engineering Workshops (SAUO) .... CREWKS
Corps Service Area [Army] (AABC) .... COSA
Corps Service Area .... CSA
Corps Specifications Revision (AAG) .... CSR
Corps Storage Area [Military] (AABC) .... CSA
Corps Supply Area (SAUS) .... CSA
Corps Supply Depot (SAUO) .... CSD
Corps Supply Point (SAUO) .... CSP
Corps Support Brigade (SAUO) .... CSB
Corps Support Command [Army] (AABC) .... COSCOM
Corps Support Group (SAUO) .... CSG
Corps Support Missile System (MCD) .... CSMS
Corps Support Services [Military] .... CSS
Corps Support Squadron (SAUO) .... Corps Sp Sqn
Corps Support Weapon System .... CSWS
Corps Surface-to-Air Missile [Army] (DOMA) .... CORPSAM
Corps Surface-to-Air Missile [Army] (MUSM) .... Corps SAM
Corps Surface-to-Air Missile (SAUS) .... Corps-SAM
Corps Surface-to-Air Missile/Medium Extended Air Defense System [Military] (RDA) .... CSAM/MEADS
Corps Tactical Operations Center .... CTOC
Corps Tactical Operations Center Ground Station Module [Army] .... CORPS TOC GMS
Corps Tactical Operations Center Support Element (SAUO) .... CTOCSE
Corps Tactical Operations System (MCD) .... CTOS
Corps Tactical Zone [Military] .... CTZ
Corps Transportation Officer (SAUO) .... CTO
Corps Troops (SAUO) .... CT
Corps troops (SAUO) .... Ctps
Corps Troops Ammunition Company (SAUO) .... CTA Coy
Corps Troops Ammunition Company (SAUO) .... CT Amn Coy
Corps Troops Ammunition Park (SAUO) .... CT Amn Pk
Corps Troops Supply Column (SAUO) .... CTSC
Corps Vehicle Company (SAUO) CVC
Corpse (DSUE) .... CORP
Corps/Theater Automatic Data Processing Service Center [Military] .... CTASC
Corptech Industry, Inc. [Vancouver Stock Exchange symbol] .... CH
Corpulmonale (SAUS) C
Corpus [Body] [Latin] (DLA) C
Corpus [Referring to the uterus] [Gynecology] (DAVI) .... CO
Corpus [Body] [Latin] .... COR
Corpus - National Association for a Married Priesthood (EA) .... CORPUS
CORPUS [Corps of Reserve Priests United for Service] - National Association Resigned/Married Priests (EA) .... CORPUS
Corpus Albicans [Medicine] (MELL) .... CA
Corpus Allatum .... CA
Corpus Callosotomy [Medicine] (MELL) CC
Corpus Callosum [Brain anatomy] CC
Corpus Cardiacum (PDAA) CC
Corpus Christi (ROG) CC
Corpus Christi [Texas] [Airport symbol] (OAG) .... CRP
Corpus Christi Army Depot (AABC) .... CCAD
Corpus Christi Bancshares [Associated Press] (SAG) .... CCBncsh
Corpus Christi Bancshares [AMEX symbol] (SPSG) .... CTZ
Corpus Christi Campaign CCC
Corpus Christi College [Cambridge and Oxford] CCC

Corpus Christi College (SAUO) ... CCC
Corpus Christi College (SAUO) ... Corp
Corpus Christi College (SAUO) ... CorpChColl
Corpus Christi College, Cambridge (SAUO) ... CCCC
Corpus Christi College-Cambridge (SAUS) ... Cor Chr Col
Corpus Christi Geological Society (SAUO) ... CCGS
Corpus Christi Public Library (SAUS) ... CCPL
Corpus Christi Public Library, Corpus Christi, TX [*OCLC symbol*] (OCLC) ... CCA
Corpus Christi State University, Corpus Christi, TX [*OCLC symbol*] (OCLC) ... TXF
Corpus Christi, TX [*Location identifier*] [*FAA*] (FAAL) ... CUX
Corpus Christi, TX [*Location identifier*] [*FAA*] (FAAL) ... EKI
Corpus Christi, TX [*FM radio station call letters*] ... KBNJ
Corpus Christi, TX [*FM radio station call letters*] ... KBSO
Corpus Christi, TX [*AM radio station call letters*] ... KCCT
Corpus Christi, TX [*AM radio station call letters*] ... KCTA
Corpus Christi, TX [*FM radio station call letters*] ... KEDT
Corpus Christi, TX [*Television station call letters*] ... KEDT-TV
Corpus Christi, TX [*AM radio station call letters*] ... KEYS
Corpus Christi, TX [*FM radio station call letters*] ... KFGG
Corpus Christi, TX [*Television station call letters*] ... KIII
Corpus Christi, TX [*FM radio station call letters*] ... KLTG
Corpus Christi, TX [*FM radio station call letters*] ... KMXR
Corpus Christi, TX [*Television station call letters*] ... KORO
Corpus Christi, TX [*Television station call letters*] ... KRIS
Corpus Christi, TX [*AM radio station call letters*] ... KRYS
Corpus Christi, TX [*FM radio station call letters*] ... KRYS-FM
Corpus Christi, TX [*AM radio station call letters*] ... KSIX
Corpus Christi, TX [*AM radio station call letters*] ... KUNO
Corpus Christi, TX [*FM radio station call letters*] ... KZFM
Corpus Christi, TX [*Television station call letters*] ... KZTV
Corpus Christi, TX [*Location identifier*] [*FAA*] (FAAL) ... NCX
Corpus Christi, TX [*Location identifier*] [*FAA*] (FAAL) ... NGP
Corpus Christi, TX [*Location identifier*] [*FAA*] (FAAL) ... NGW
Corpus Christi, TX [*Location identifier*] [*FAA*] (FAAL) ... NHT
Corpus Christi, TX [*Location identifier*] [*FAA*] (FAAL) ... NPJ
Corpus Christi, TX [*Location identifier*] [*FAA*] (FAAL) ... OYC
Corpus Christianorum [*Turnhout*] (BJA) ... CChr
Corpus Christi/Corpus Christi Naval Air Station [*Texas*] [*ICAO location identifier*] (ICLI) ... KNGP
Corpus Christi/International [*Texas*] [*ICAO location identifier*] (ICLI) ... KCRP
Corpus Cultus Deae Syriae (BJA) ... CCDS
Corpus des Tablettes en Cuneiformes Alphabetiques Decouvertes a Ras Shamra-Ugarit de 1929 a 1939 (BJA) ... CTA
Corpus des Tablettes en Cuneiformes Alphabetiques Decouvertes a Ras Shamra-Ugarit de 1929 a 1939 (BJA) ... CTCA
Corpus Glossariorum Biblicorum (BJA) ... CGB
Corpus Glossariorum Latinorum (BJA) ... CGL
Corpus Inscriptionum Chaldaicarum (BJA) ... CICh
Corpus Inscriptionum Elamicarum [*A publication*] (BJA) ... CIE
Corpus Inscriptionum et Monumentorum Religionis Mithriacae [*A publication*] (BJA) ... CIMRM
Corpus Inscriptionum Himjariticarum (BJA) ... CIH
Corpus Inscriptionum Judaicarum [*A publication*] (BJA) ... CIJ
Corpus Inscriptionum Regni Bosporani (BJA) ... CIRB
Corpus Inscriptionum Semiticarum [*A publication*] (OCD) ... CISem
Corpus Juris [*Body of Law*] [*Latin*] ... CJ
Corpus Juris [*Body of Law*] [*Latin*] (ROG) ... CORP JUR
Corpus Juris Annotations [*A publication*] (DLA) ... CJ Ann
Corpus Juris Canonici [*The Body of the Canon Law*] [*Latin*] (DLA) ... CJ Can
Corpus Juris Canonici [*The Body of the Canon Law*] [*Latin*] [*A publication*] (DLA) ... Corp Jur Can
Corpus Juris Canonici [*The Body of the Canon Law*] [*Latin*] [*A publication*] (DLA) ... Corp Jus Canon
Corpus Juris Civilis [*The Body of the Civil Law*] [*Latin*] (DLA) ... CJC
Corpus Juris Civilis [*The Body of the Civil Law*] [*Latin*] (DLA) ... CJ Civ
Corpus Juris Civilis [*The Body of the Civil Law*] [*Latin*] [*A publication*] (DLA) ... Corp Jur Civ
Corpus Juris Secundum [*A publication*] ... CJS
Corpus Juris Secundum Supplement [*West*] [*A publication*] (AAGC) ... CJS Supp
Corpus Luteum [*Endocrinology*] ... CL
Corpus Luteum Cyst [*Medicine*] (MELL) ... CLC
Corpus Luteum Hormone [*Medicine*] (MELL) ... CLH
Corpus Luteum Insufficiency [*Medicine*] (DMAA) ... CLI
Corpus Luteum Stimulating Hormone (BARN) ... CLSH
Corpus Medicorum Graecorum [*A publication*] (OCD) ... CMG
Corpus Medicorum Latinorum [*A publication*] (OCD) ... CML
Corpus of Ancient Near Eastern Seals in North American Collections [*Washington, DC*] (BJA) ... CANES
Corpus of Dated Palestinian Pottery (BJA) ... CPP
Corpus of Palestinian Pottery (BJA) ... CPP
Corpus Papyrorum Judaicarum (BJA) ... CPJ
Corpus Poetarum Latinorum [*A publication*] (OCD) ... CPL
Corpus Reformatorum (BJA) ... CR
Corpus Scriptorum Christianorum Orientalium [*Louvain*] (BJA) ... CsChrO
Corpus Scriptorum Christianorum Orientalium [*A publication*] (ODCC) ... CSCO
Corpus Scriptorum Ecclesiasticorum Latinorum [*A publication*] (ODCC) ... CSEL
Corpus Scriptorum Historiae Byzantinae [*A publication*] (ODCC) ... CSH Byz
Corpus Striatum (MAE) ... CS
Corpus Tannaiticum (BJA) ... CorpTann
Corpuscle of Meissner [*Medicine*] (MELL) ... COM
Corpuscular Volume [*Hematology*] ... CV
Corrales, NM [*AM radio station call letters*] ... KIVA
Corrales, NM [*FM radio station call letters*] ... KSVA
Corrdinate Conversion Computer (SAUS) ... CCC
Correct [*In marking school papers*] (BARN) ... C
Correct (ROG) ... COR
Correct [*or Corrected or Correction*] (AFM) ... CORR
Correct (SAUS) ... Corr
Correct (ECII) ... COT
Correct ... CQ
Correct [*Computer science*] [*British*] ... CQT
Correct (MUGU) ... CRT
Correct (EBF) ... OK
Correct Acceptance Rate (SAUS) ... CAR
Correct Age Stocking and Height [*Inventory*] [*Forestry*] ... CASH
Correct Algorithm (SAUS) ... CA
Correct Calling Station Identifier [*Telecommunications*] (PCM) ... CSID
Correct Code (MCD) ... CC
Correct Copy [*A printing direction*] ... CX
Correct Corps Time (SAUS) ... CCT
Correct Delayed Reaction [*Medicine*] (DB) ... CDR
Correct End Item (KSC) ... CEI
Correct Fast Reaction (DB) ... CFR
Correct Me If I'm Wrong (ADWA) ... CMIIW
Correct Operation Factor [*Telecommunications*] (OA) ... COF
Correct [*an error*] **or Amplify** [*information*] [*US Copyright Office form*] ... CA
Correct, Pause, Recovery [*Automobile driving*] ... CPR
Correct Report [*Laboratory*] (DAVI) ... CORR
Correct Routing (SAUS) ... CR
Correct Seating Institute ... CSI
Correct Selection [*Statistics*] ... CS
Correct Time (IAA) ... CT
Correct Words per Minute [*Typewriting, etc.*] ... CWPM
Correct Zeroing Point (SAUS) ... CZP
Correctable Gate [*Computer science*] (MDG) ... CORREGATE
Corrected (STED) ... corr
Corrected (MSA) ... CRCTD
Corrected Adjusted Sinus Node Recovery Time [*Medicine*] (DMAA) ... CASRT
Corrected Blood Volume [*Medicine*] ... CBV
Corrected Copy ... CC
Corrected Copy (DNAB) ... CORCY
Corrected Count Increment [*Hematology*] ... CCI
Corrected Count Increment [*Hematology*] ... CI
Corrected Depth (SAUS) ... CD
Corrected Effective Temperature (IEEE) ... CET
Corrected Geomagnetic Latitude ... CGL
Corrected Geomagnetic Latitude and Geomagnetic Local Time (DICI) ... CGL/GLT
Corrected Geomagnetic Time ... CGM
Corrected Geomagnetic Time ... CGT
Corrected Head Count ... CHC
Corrected Infection Efficiency [*of plant pathogens*] ... CIE
Corrected Line Length (GEOI) ... CLL
Corrected Mean Temperature ... CMT
Corrected Outside Air Temperature ... COAT
Corrected Overall Reference Equivalent (SAUS) ... CORE
Corrected Receiving Reference Equivalent (SAUS) ... CRRE
Corrected Reference Equivalent (SAUS) ... CRE
Corrected Relative Net Protein Ratio [*Nutrition*] ... CRNPR
Corrected Report (WEAT) ... COR
Corrected Retention Time [*Medicine*] (DAVI) ... CRT
Corrected Sedimentation Rate [*Medicine*] ... CSR
Corrected Sending Reference Equipment (SAUS) ... CSRE
Corrected Series (SAUS) ... CS
Corrected Sinus Node Recovery Time [*Medicine*] (DMAA) ... CNRT
Corrected Sinus Node Recovery Time [*Medicine*] ... CSNRT
Corrected Transposition (MAE) ... CT
Corrected Unpostable [*IRS*] ... CU
CorRecTerm [*Mergenthaler typesetting*] ... CRT
Correcting Computer (MCD) ... CORCOM
Correctio Romana [*Edition of the Decretals*] [*A publication*] (DSA) ... Corr Rom
Correction ... CO
Correction (WDMC) ... cor
Correction ... COR
Correction (WDMC) ... corr
Correction ... CRRCT
Correction (MUGU) ... CRTN
Correction (SAUS) ... Cxn
Correction Action Committee ... CAC
Correction Action Reporting System ... CARS
Correction and Rehabilitation Group [*Air Force*] ... CRG
Correction and Rehabilitation Squadron [*Air Force*] ... CRS
Correction Bit (SAUS) ... CB
Correction Control Number [*Army*] ... CORCN
Correction Education Demonstration Project Act of 1978 ... CEDPA
Correction Factor ... CF
Correction Field (MCD) ... CF
Correction Fluid (SAUS) ... CORFLU
Correction Information System (SAUS) ... CIS
Correction List (SAUS) ... CL
Correction Memo (MCD) ... CM
Correction Notice (MCD) ... CN
Correction of Deficiencies (SAUS) ... COD
Correction of Deficiency (MCD) ... COD
Correction of the Moment (SAUS) ... C of M
Correction Processor ... CP
Correction Support Circuitry (SAUS) ... CSC
Correction System ... COSY
Correction System (SAUS) ... CS

Correction Table (SAUS) .... CT
Correction to Follow .... CTF
Correction Tracking and Ranging Station .... COTAR
Correction, Update, and Extension Software Program [*Department of Commerce*] (GFGA) .... CUE
Correction with Glasses [*Optometry*] (MAE) .... cgl
Correctional .... CRRCTNL
Correctional Administrators Association of America [*Later, ASCA*] (EA) ...... CAA
Correctional Administrators Association of America (SAUO) .... CAA
Correctional Association of New York (SAUO) .... CANY
Correctional Association of New York State (SRA) .... CANYS
Correctional Custody Facility [*Military*] (AABC) .... CCF
Correctional Custody Facillity (SAUO) .... CCF
Correctional Custody Unit [*Navy*] .... CCU
Correctional Decision Information Project (SAUS) .... CDIP
Correctional Education Association (EA) .... CEA
Correctional Facilities Association [*Defunct*] (EA) .... CFA
Correctional Health Care Program .... CHCP
Correctional Holding Detachment [*Military*] (AABC) .... CHD
Correctional Industries Association (EA) .... CIA
Correctional Institutions Environment Scale [*Personality development test*] [*Psychology*] .... CIES
Correctional Medical Systems (SAUS) .... CMS
Correctional Officer .... CO
Correctional Officers' Interest Blank [*Screening and placement test*] .... COIB
Correctional Program for Adults [*Public human service program*] (PHSD) .... CP
Correctional Properties Tr [*NYSE symbol*] (SG) .... CPV
Correctional Reporting System [*Army*] .... CRS
Correctional Service Associates .... CSA
Correctional Service Federation - USA (EA) .... CSF/USA
Correctional Service Foundation (SAUO) .... CSF
Correctional Services Advisory Council [*South Australia*] .... CSAC
Correctional Services Corp. [*Associated Press*] (SAG) .... CorrecSv
Correctional Services Corp. [*Associated Press*] (SAG) .... CrrcS
Correctional Services Corp. [*NASDAQ symbol*] (SAG) .... CSCQ
Correctional Services of Ontario, Toronto, ON, Canada [*Library symbol*] [*Library of Congress*] (LCLS) .... CaOTCS
Correctional Training Facility [*Army*] (AABC) .... CTF
Correction/Discrepancy (DNAB) .... C/D
Corrections Corp. Amer [*NYSE symbol*] (TTSB) CXC
Corrections Corp. of America .... CCA
Corrections Corp. of America [*Associated Press*] (SAG) .... CorCp
Corrections Corp. of America [*Associated Press*] (SAG) .... CorctCp
Corrections Corp. of America [*NYSE symbol*] (SAG) CXC
Corrections Cp Amer Wrrt [*NYSE symbol*] (TTSB) .... CXC.WS
Corrections to Applied Research Laboratories Ion-Sputtering Mass Analyzers [*Computer science*] .... CARISMA
Correction-Update-Extension [*Computer science*] (CIST) .... CUE
Correctionville News, Correctionville, IA [*Library symbol*] [*Library of Congress*] (LCLS) .... IaCorrN
Corrective (SAUS) .... COR
Corrective .... CORREC
Corrective Action (MCD) .... CA
Corrective Action Board .... CAB
Corrective Action Commission (SAUO) .... CAC
Corrective Action Control Section (SAUO) .... CACC
Corrective Action Data Center (SAUO) .... CADC
Corrective Action Directive [*or Disposition*] .... CAD
Corrective Action Disposition (SAUS) .... CAD
Corrective Action Effectiveness (MCD) .... CAE
Corrective Action Evaluation Team (SAUO) .... CAET
Corrective Action for Solid Waste Management Unit (EEVL) .... CAMU
Corrective Action Group (SAUO) .... CAG
Corrective Action Management Unit [*Environmental science*] .... CAMU
Corrective Action Order [*Environmental Protection Agency*] (ERG) .... CAO
Corrective Action Plan [*Department of Health and Human Services*] (GFGA) .... CAP
Corrective Action Problem System (SAUS) .... CAPS
Corrective Action Reply .... CAR
Corrective Action Report .... CAR
Corrective Action Reporting [*Environmental science*] (COE) .... CAR
Corrective Action Reporting System (AUEG) .... CARS
Corrective Action Request .... CAR
Corrective Action Team (ACAE) .... CAT
Corrective Action Tracking System [*Environmental Protection Agency*] (GFGA) .... CATS
Corrective Action Trigger [*Environmental science*] (COE) .... CAT
Corrective Eye Care Foundation [*Later, CLMA*] (EA) .... CECF
Corrective Lens [*Freight*] .... C LN
Corrective Lens (SAUS) .... CLN
Corrective Maintenance .... CM
Corrective Maintenance Action [*Military*] (CAAL) .... CMA
Corrective Maintenance Burden .... CMB
Corrective Maintenance Card (MCD) .... CMC
Corrective Maintenance Downtime (MCD) .... CMDT
Corrective Maintenance Report (ACAE) .... CMR
Corrective Maintenance Request (ACAE) .... CMR
Corrective Maintenance System (NVT) .... CMS
Corrective Maintenance/Preventive Maintenance (ACAE) .... CM/PM
Corrective Management (MCD) .... CM
Corrective Measure Study [*Environmental science*] .... CMS
Corrective Measures [*Environmental science*] (COE) .... CM
Corrective Measures Implementation (BCP) .... CMI
Corrective Optics Space Telescope Axial Replacement [*NASA*] .... COSTAR
Corrective Osteotomy [*Medicine*] (MELL) .... CO

Corrective Repair Maintenance [*Environmental science*] (COE) .... CRM
Corrective Septorhinoplasty [*Otorhinolaryngology*] (DAVI) .... CSR
Corrective Service Diskettes [*Computer science*] (VERA) .... CSD
Corrective Therapist [*or Therapy*] .... CT
Corrective Therapist (or therapy) (SAUS) .... CT
Corrective Therapy Department [*Medical rehabilitation*] (DAVI) .... CTD
Corrector [*MARC relator code*] [*Library of Congress*] (LCCP) .... crr
Corrector-Quadrupole-Sexupole (SAUS) .... CQS
Correctus [*Corrected*] [*Latin*] (EES) .... corr
Corregidor, Cavite [*Philippines*] [*ICAO location identifier*] (ICLI) .... RPXR
Corregidor-Bataan Memorial Commission [*Government agency*] [*Terminated, 1967*] .... CBMC
Correlatable Access Memory (SAUS) .... CAM
Correlate (MSA) .... CORRE
correlated (SAUS) .... correl
Correlated Color Temperature (IEEE) .... CCT
Correlated Data Processor .... CDP
Correlated Double Sampling .... CDS
Correlated Orientation Tracking and Ranging (MSA) .... COTAR
Correlated Orientation Tracking and Ranging System (SAUS) .... COTAR System
Correlated RADAR Data Printout [*Electronics*] (SAA) .... CORDP
Correlated RADAR Data Printout [*Electronics*] .... CORDPO
Correlated RADAR Data Printout - Separation of RADAR Data [*Electronics*] .... CORDPO-SORD
Correlated Radio Lines (SAUS) .... CORAL
Correlated Spectroscopy .... COSY
Correlates of War Project (SAUO) .... COW
Correlating Users Exchange (SAA) .... CUE
Correlation (KSC) .... CORR
Correlation Air Navigation .... CAN
Correlation Algorithm and Techniques Analysis (ACAE) .... CATA
Correlation Analysis (SAUS) .... CA
Correlation Bombing System [*Air Force*] (MCD) .... CBS
Correlation Cancellation System .... CCS
Correlation Coefficient (MCD) CC
Correlation Coefficient (DAVI) .... r
Correlation Coefficient [*Statistics*] (BARN) .... R
Correlation Control Unit (SAUS) .... CCU
Correlation Data Analyzer Recorder (CAAL) .... CODAR
Correlation Data Processing System (SAUS) .... CORDAPS
Correlation Detection and Ranging (MCD) .... CODAR
Correlation Display Analyzing and Recording .... CODAR
Correlation Echo Sound Processor [*Oceanography*] .... CESP
Correlation Factor (AABC) .... CF
Correlation Interferometer for the Measurement of Atmosphere Trace Species (SAUS) .... CIMATS
Correlation Matrix (SAUS) .... CM
Correlation Metric Construction [*Analysis of chemical reaction*] .... CMC
Correlation of the Recognition of Degradation with Intelligibility Measurements [*Telecommunications*] (TEL) .... CORODIM
Correlation Processor .... CP
Correlation Protected Instrument Landing System (SAUS) .... CPILS
Correlation Protected Integrated Landing System (SAUS) .... CPILS
Correlation RADAR .... CORAD
Correlation Radio Link (MUGU) .... CORAL
Correlation Radiometer (MCD) .... CR
Correlation Recognition (SAUS) .... CR
Correlation Routine (ACAE) .... CR
Correlation Spectrometer .... COSPEC
Correlation spectroscopy for Long-range Couplings (SAUS) .... COLOC
Correlation Track .... CT
Correlation Tracking and Ranging [*System*] [*Satellite and missile tracking term*] [*RADAR*] .... COTAR
Correlation Tracking and Ranging Angle Measuring Equipment [*RADAR*] .... COTAR-AME
Correlation Tracking and Ranging Data Acquisition System [*RADAR*] .... COTAR-DAS
Correlation Tracking and Ranging Data Measuring Equipment [*RADAR*] .... COTAR-DME
Correlation Tracking and Ranging System (SAUS) .... COTAR System
Correlation Tracking and Triangulation .... COTAT
Correlation Unit (SAUS) .... CU
Correlation Velocity Log (SAUS) CVL
Correlation-Protected Instrument Landing System .... CP-ILS
Correlative .... COR
Correlative .... CORR
Correlative .... CORREL
Correlative (ADWA) .... correl
Correlative Radiometer (SAUS) .... CR
Correlator Acquisition [*Military*] .... CA
Correspond (ROG) .... COR
Correspond (DLA) .... corr
Correspond (MSA) .... CORRES
Correspond (GEAB) .... crspd
Correspondances Judiciaires [*Canada*] [*A publication*] (DLA) .... Cor Jud
Correspondances Judiciaires [*Canada*] [*A publication*] (DLA) .... Correspondances Jud
Corresponded (SAUS) .... CORRES
Correspondence .... COR
Correspondence (WDMC) .... cor
Correspondence (WDMC) .... corr
Correspondence (AFM) .... CORR
Correspondence (EBF) .... Corr
Correspondence (WDMC) .... corres
Correspondence (ADWA) .... corresp

Correspondence [*or Corresponding*] ..... CORRESP
Correspondence Aid [*A publication*] ..... CA
Correspondence Analysis [*Statistical analysis*] ..... CA
Correspondence and Open Studies Institute (SAUO) ..... COSIT
Correspondence and Service Branch [*BUPERS*] ..... C & SB
Correspondence Chess League of America (EA) ..... CCLA
Correspondence Control Center (ACAE) CCC
Correspondence Control Unit [*Environmental Protection Agency*] (GFGA) ..... CCU
Correspondence Course CC
Correspondence Factor Analysis ..... CFA
Correspondence Management Staff (SAUS) ..... CMS
Correspondence Printer (MHDI) ..... CP
Correspondence Quality (IAA) ..... CQ
Correspondence Quality Control Program (MCD) ..... CQCP
Correspondence Review Group [*NASA*] (NASA) ..... CRG
Correspondence Routing Form (NRCH) ..... CRF
Correspondence Survey Officer (MCD) ..... CSO
Correspondence System (SAUO) ..... CS
Correspondence Tracking System (SAUS) ..... CTS
Correspondent (WDMC) ..... cor
Correspondent (DLA) ..... corr
Correspondent (AL) ..... Corr
Correspondent [*Journalism*] (WDMC) ..... corres
Correspondent ..... CORRSPNDNT
Correspondent Committee [*Defunct*] (EA) CC
Correspondent Validity File [*IRS*] ..... CVF
Corresponding (SAUS) ..... cor
Corresponding (VRA) ..... corr
Corresponding (EBF) ..... Corr
Corresponding ..... CORR
Corresponding (SAUS) ..... Crsg
Corresponding Fellow ..... CF
Corresponding Fellow (WGA) ..... Corr Fell
Corresponding Member ..... CM
Corresponding Member (BARN) ..... Corr Mem
Corresponding Member of the Academy of Arts (SAUS) ..... COMACA
Corresponding Member of the International Institute of Arts and Letters ..... CIAL
Corresponding Member of the Zoological Society [*British*] ..... CMZS
Corresponding Objects Grid [*Computer science*] ..... COG
Corresponding Onshore Area (EEVL) ..... COA
Corresponding Secretary (BARN) ..... Corr Sec
Corresponding Secretary (WDAA) ..... COR SEC
Corresponding Secretary (IIA) ..... CS
Corresponding States Equation [*Physics*] ..... CSE
Corresponding States Liquid Density [*Chemical engineering*] ..... COSTALD
Corresponding States Principle (SAUS) ..... CSP
Corresponding Studies Course [*DoD*] ..... CSC
Corrida Oils Ltd. [*Toronto Stock Exchange symbol*] ..... COL
Corridor (AABC) ..... COR
Corridor (DA) ..... CORR
Corridor [*Board on Geographic Names*] ..... CRDR
Corridor Aerogeophysics of the Southeastern Ross Transect Zone [*Geology*] ..... CASERTZ
Corridor Assignment [*Aviation*] (FAAC) ..... CORAS
Corridor Overlay District (PA) ..... COD
Corrie Resources [*Vancouver Stock Exchange symbol*] ..... CIE
Corriente Batllista Independiente [*Uruguay*] [*Political party*] (EY) ..... CBI
Corriente Critica [*Mexico*] [*Political party*] (EY) CC
Corriente Nacionalista de Unidad y Reconciliacion [*Nicaragua*] [*Political party*] (EY) ..... CNUR
Corrientes [*Argentina*] [*Airport symbol*] (OAG) ..... CNQ
Corrientes [*Argentina*] [*ICAO location identifier*] (ICLI) ..... SARC
Corrigenda (BJA) ..... corr
Corrigenda (SAUS) ..... Corrig
Corrigendum [*Publishing*] (WGA) ..... COR
Corrin [*Biochemistry*] ..... Crn
Corris, Machynlleth & River Dovey Tramway [*Wales*] ..... CM & RDT
Corris Railway [*Wales*] ..... COR R
Corrosion (KSC) ..... CORR
Corrosion (MSA) ..... CRSN
Corrosion (SAUS) ..... Crsn
Corrosion Advice Bureau [*British Steel Corp.*] (PDAA) ..... CAB
Corrosion and Cathodic Protection (IAA) ..... CACP
Corrosion and Protection Association ..... CAPA
Corrosion and Protection Centre, Industrial Services Unit (SAUO) ..... CAPCIS
Corrosion and Wear Control Program (SAUO) ..... CWCP
Corrosion Center of Excellence [*US Army Materials Technology Laboratory*] ..... CTX
Corrosion Control [*Lloyds Register*] (DS) CC
Corrosion Control Section (SAUO) ..... CCS
Corrosion Control Unit (DNAB) ..... CORCONU
Corrosion Evaluation and Test Area [*NASA*] ..... CETA
Corrosion Fatigue (PDAA) ..... CF
Corrosion Fatigue Crack Propagation (PDAA) ..... CFCP
Corrosion Interception Sleeve ..... CIS
Corrosion Magazine (SAUS) ..... CM
Corrosion of Reinforcing Steel in Concrete [*Rilem Technical Committee*] [*British*] ..... CRC
Corrosion Prevention Advisory Center (SAUS) ..... CPAC
Corrosion Prevention Panel ..... CPP
Corrosion Prevention/Deterioration Control ..... CP/DC
Corrosion Protection [*Telecommunications*] (TEL) ..... CP
Corrosion Research Council (SAUO) ..... CRC
Corrosion Research Station (SAUS) ..... CRS
Corrosion Resistant [*Material*] [*Manufacturing*] (DCTA) ..... CR
Corrosion Resistant (AAG) ..... CRE
Corrosion Resistant (MCD) ..... CRES
Corrosion Resistant Alloy [*Metallurgy*] ..... CRA
Corrosion Resisting (SAUS) ..... CRE
Corrosion Science (journ.) (SAUS) ..... Corros Sci
Corrosion Status Index [*Military*] (RDA) ..... CSI
Corrosion-Fatigue Crack Growth Rate (PDAA) ..... CFCGR
Corrosion-Resistant Cladding [*Nuclear energy equipment*] ..... CRC
Corrosion-Resistant Nebulizer ..... CRN
Corrosion-Resistant Steel [*Manufacturing*] ..... CRES
Corrosive ..... COR
Corrosive (SAUS) ..... Corros
Corrosive (SAUS) ..... Crsv
Corrosive (MSA) ..... CRSV
Corrosive Contaminants, Oxygen, and Humidity (MCD) ..... CCOH
Corrpro Co. [*NYSE symbol*] (TTSB) ..... CO
Corrpro Companies [*Associated Press*] (SAG) ..... Corrpro
Corrugated (WGA) ..... COR
Corrugated ..... CORR
Corrugated (ADWA) ..... corr
Corrugated ..... CORRGTD
Corrugated ..... CORU
Corrugated Asbestos ..... CA
Corrugated Asbestos Cement (ADA) ..... CAC
Corrugated Capacitor Cell (SAUS) CCC
Corrugated Case Materials Association [*British*] (DBA) ..... CCMA
Corrugated Container Institute [*Defunct*] (EA) CCI
Corrugated, Cupped, or Indented [*Freight*] CCI
Corrugated Fiberboard (SAUS) ..... CORR FBD
Corrugated Fibreboard (SAUS) ..... CFB
Corrugated Furnace (DS) ..... CF
Corrugated Galvanized Iron ..... CGI
Corrugated Metal Pipe [*Technical drawings*] ..... CMP
Corrugated or Cupped [*Freight*] CC
Corrugated Plate Inteceptor (PDAA) ..... CPI
Corrugated Stainless-Steel Tubing ..... CSST
Corrugated Steel Pipe (DICI) ..... CSP
Corrugated Steel Reinforcement (SAUS) ..... CSR
Corrugated Structural Plate Pipe (SAUS) ..... CSPP
Corrugated Teflon Tubing (SAUS) ..... CTT
Corrugated TEFLON Tubing ..... CTT
Corrugated Wire Glass [*Technical drawings*] ..... CWG
Corrugated-Laminated Coaxial [*Cable*] ..... CLOAX
Corrugated-Laminated Coaxial Cable (SAUS) ..... CLOAX Cable
Corrugating Medium Test [*For containerboard*] ..... CMT
Corrupt ..... COR
Corrupt ..... CORR
Corrupt Commissioners [*Federal operation investigating illegal practices by Oklahoma's county commissioners*] ..... CORCOM
Corrupted [*or Corruption*] ..... CORRUP
Corruption (ROG) ..... CORR
Corruption (ADWA) ..... corrupt
Corruption-Perception Index ..... CPI
Corry, PA [*Location identifier*] [*FAA*] (FAAL) ..... ORJ
Corry, PA [*AM radio station call letters*] ..... WWCB
Corsair Avionics Subsystems Tester (ACAE) ..... CAST
Corse Aero Service [*France*] [*ICAO designator*] (FAAC) ..... CSS
Corse Air International [*France*] [*ICAO designator*] (FAAC) ..... CRL
Corse Air International [*France*] [*ICAO designator*] (ICDA) ..... CS
Corse-Mediterranee Compagnie [*France*] [*ICAO designator*] (FAAC) ..... CCM
Corset and Brassiere Association of America [*Later, AAMA*] (EA) ..... CBAA
Corset and Brassiere Association of America (SAUO) ..... CBAA
Corset and Brassiere Council [*Defunct*] (EA) ..... CBC
Corset and Brassiere Women's Club [*Later, UC*] (EA) ..... CBWC
Corset Trade Board (SAUO) ..... CTB
Corsica (ROG) ..... COR
Corsica ..... CORS
Corsica (VRA) ..... Cors
Corsicana, TX [*Location identifier*] [*FAA*] (FAAL) ..... CGQ
Corsicana, TX [*Location identifier*] [*FAA*] (FAAL) ..... CRS
Corsicana, TX [*AM radio station call letters*] ..... KAND
Corsicana, TX [*FM radio station call letters*] (BROA) ..... KDXX-FM
Corsicana, TX [*FM radio station call letters*] (RBYB) ..... KICI
Corsica/Sardinia/Calabria Microplate [*Geology*] ..... CSC
Corson and Stoughton (LDT) ..... CS
Corson Family History Association (EA) ..... CCFHA
Corson/Colson Family History Association (EA) ..... CCFHA
[*A*] **Corsortium on Restorative Dentistry Education** [*Medicine*] (DMAA) ..... ACORDE
Cort Business Services [*NYSE symbol*] (TTSB) ..... CBS
Cort Business Services [*NYSE symbol*] (SG) ..... CBZ
Cort Business Services Corp. [*NASDAQ symbol*] (SAG) ..... CORT
Cort Business Services Corp. [*Associated Press*] (SAG) ..... CortBus
Cort Business Svcs Wrrt [*NASDAQ symbol*] (TTSB) ..... CORTW
CORTA (Orly Ouest) [*France*] [*ICAO location identifier*] (ICLI) ..... LFFA
Cortaro, AZ [*AM radio station call letters*] ..... KEVT
Corte [*France*] [*ICAO location identifier*] (ICLI) ..... LFKT
Corte Costituzionale [*Constitutional Court*] [*Italian*] (DLA) ..... C Cost
Corte di Cassazione [*Court of Appeal*] [*Italian*] (DLA) ..... Cass
Corte Internacional de Justicia [*International Court of Justice*] [*Spanish*] [*United Nations*] (DUND) ..... CIJ
Cortebert Watch Company ..... CWC
Cortech, Inc. [*Associated Press*] (SAG) ..... Cortech
Cortech, Inc. [*NASDAQ symbol*] (SAG) ..... CRTQ
Cortecs International Ltd. [*Associated Press*] (SAG) ..... Cortecs

Cortecs International Ltd. [*NASDAQ symbol*] (SAG) ... DLVR
Corten Steel (VRA) ... crtnstl
Cortex [*Anatomy*] ... C
Cortex (STED) ... cort
Cortex [*Bark*] [*Pharmacy*] ... CORT
Cortex (SAUS) ... CTX
Cortex Cinchonae [*Bark of Cinchona or Peruvian Bark*] [*Pharmacy*] (ROG) ... CORT CINCHON
Cortex Pharmaceuticals [*NASDAQ symbol*] (TTSB) ... CORX
Cortex Pharmaceuticals, Inc. [*Associated Press*] (SAG) ... Cortex
Cortex Pharmaceuticals, Inc. [*Associated Press*] (SAG) ... Cortx
Cortex Pharmaceuticals, Inc. [*NASDAQ symbol*] (NQ) ... CORX
Cortez [*Colorado*] [*Airport symbol*] (OAG) ... CEZ
Cortez, CO [*FM radio station call letters*] ... KISZ
Cortez, CO [*FM radio station call letters*] ... KRTZ
Cortez, CO [*FM radio station call letters*] ... KSJD
Cortez, CO [*AM radio station call letters*] ... KVFC
Cortez Public Library, Cortez, CO [*Library symbol*] [*Library of Congress*] (LCLS) ... CoCo
Cortical ... cort
Cortical (SAUS) ... Cort
Cortical Area/Total Area (Ratio) ... CA/TA
Cortical Auditory Evoked Potential [*Medicine*] (DMAA) ... CAEP
Cortical Blood Flow [*Urology*] ... CBF
Cortical Bone Graft [*Medicine*] (MELL) ... CBG
Cortical Cataract [*Medicine*] (MELL) ... CC
Cortical Collecting Tubule [*Anatomy*] ... CCT
Cortical Evoked Potential [*Neurophysiology*] ... CEP
Cortical Evoked Response [*Medicine*] (MELL) ... CER
Cortical Granule Exocytosis [*Cytology*] ... CGE
Cortical Magnification Factor ... CMF
Cortical Necrosis of Kidneys [*Medicine*] (DMAA) ... CNK
Cortical Plate [*Neuroanatomy*] ... CP
Cortical Plate Thickness [*Anatomy*] ... CT
Cortical Secretion Rate (SAUS) ... CSR
Cortical Segment of Middle Cerebral Artery [*Cardiology*] (DAVI) ... M_4
Cortical Spoking [*Ophthalmology*] (DAVI) ... CS
Cortical Spreading Depression [*Medicine*] ... CSD
Cortical Stromal Hyperplasia [*Medicine*] (MAE) ... CSH
Cortical-Binding Globulin [*Medicine*] (MELL) ... CBG
Cortically Induced Movement [*Medicine*] ... CIM
Cortically Originating Extra-Pyramidal System [*Physiology*] ... COEPS
Cortically Orignating Extrapyramidal Symptoms [*Neurology*] (DAVI) ... COEPS
Corticoadrenal Stimulating Hormone [*Medicine*] (MELL) ... CASH
Cortico-Cortical Connection [*Neurology*] ... CC
Corticoid Binding Globulin (SAUS) ... CBG
Corticoid Sensitive [*Laboratory*] (DAVI) ... CS
Corticoid Suppression Test (MELL) ... CST
Corticoid-Resistant (DB) ... CR
Corticoliberin-Like Immunoreactivity ... CLI
Corticomedial Amygdaloid Nucleus (STED) ... CMAmg
Corticosomatosensory Evoked Potential [*Electrophysiology*] ... CSEP
Cortico-Spinal Tract [*Anatomy*] ... CST
Corticosteroid [*Endocrinology*] ... CS
Corticosteroid-Binding Globulin [*Transcortin*] [*Endocrinology*] ... CBG
Corticosteroid-Binding Globulin Variant [*Medicine*] (DMAA) ... CBGv
Corticosterone [*A hormone*] ... CORT
Corticosterone [*A hormone*] ... CT
Corticosterone and Testosterone-controlled (SAUS) ... CC-CT
Corticosterone Methyl Oxidase [*An enzyme*] ... CMO
Corticosterone Side-Chain Isomerase (DMAA) ... CSCI
Corticosterone-Controlled (SAUS) ... CC
Corticostriatocerebellar (DB) ... CSC
Corticotrophin-Like Intermediate-Lobe Peptide [*Endocrinology*] ... CLIP
Corticotrophin-Releasing Factor [*Also, CRH*] [*Endocrinology*] ... CRF
Corticotrophin-Releasing Hormone [*Also, CRF*] [*Endocrinology*] ... CRH
Corticotropic Hormone [*Medicine*] (MELL) ... CTH
Corticotropin Releasing Factor [*Neurochemistry*] ... CRF
Corticotropin-Releaseing Factor Receptor [*Medicine*] (DMAA) ... CRFR
Corticotropin-Releasing Factor-Like Immunoreactivity [*Medicine*] ... CRF-LI
Corticotropin-Releasing Hormone [*Medicine*] (MELL) ... CPH
Cortina d'Ampezzo [*Italy*] [*Airport symbol*] (AD) ... CDF
Cortisol (LDT) ... COL
Cortisol [*Pharmacology*] (DAVI) ... CORTIS
Cortisol Glucose Tolerance Test [*Medicine*] (DAVI) ... CGTT
Cortisol Production Rate [*Medicine*] (MAE) ... CPR
Cortisol [*or Cortical*] **Secretion Rate** [*Medicine*] (MAE) ... CSR
Cortisone (LDT) ... CON
Cortisone [*Endocrinology*] ... COR
Cortisone [*Endocrinology*] ... cort
Cortisone Acetate [*Endocrinology*] ... CA
Cortisone Acetate (LDT) ... CONA
Cortisone Glucose Tolerance Test [*Medicine*] ... CGTT
Cortisone [*Primed*] **Oral Glucose Tolerance Test** [*Medicine*] ... COGTT
Cortisone-Glucose Tolerance Test (SAUS) ... C-GTT
Cortisone-Resistant (DB) ... CR
Cortisone-Resistant Thymocyte [*Biochemistry*] ... CRT
Cortland County Historical Society, Cortland, NY [*Library symbol*] [*Library of Congress*] (LCLS) ... NCortHi
Cortland Free Library (SAUS) ... NCort
Cortland Free Library, Cortland, NY [*Library symbol*] [*Library of Congress*] (LCLS) ... NCort
Cortland, NY [*FM radio station call letters*] ... WIII
Cortland, NY [*AM radio station call letters*] ... WKRT
Cortland, NY [*FM radio station call letters*] ... WSUC
Cortland, OH [*AM radio station call letters*] ... WKTX
Corumba Mato Grosso [*Brazil*] [*Airport symbol*] (OAG) ... CMG
Corumba/Internacional [*Brazil*] [*ICAO location identifier*] (ICLI) ... SBCR
Corundum [*CIPW classification*] [*Geology*] ... C
Corus Bankshares, Inc. [*NASDAQ symbol*] (SAG) ... CORS
Corus Bankshares, Inc. [*Associated Press*] (SAG) ... CorusBk
CORUS Entertainment 'B' [*NYSE symbol*] ... CJR
Corvair Model Group (EA) ... CMG
Corvair Society of America (EA) ... CORSA
Corvallis [*Oregon*] [*Seismograph station code, US Geological Survey*] (SEIS) ... COR
Corvallis Clinic, Corvallis, OR [*Library symbol*] [*Library of Congress*] (LCLS) ... OrCC
Corvallis Environmental Research Laboratory [*Oregon*] [*Environmental Protection Agency*] ... CERL
Corvallis Environmental Research Laboratory [*Corvallis, OR*] [*Environmental Protection Agency*] (GRD) ... ERL/COR
Corvallis Microtechnology, Inc. (GEOI) ... CMI
Corvallis Microtechnology, Inc. (GEOI) ... CMT
Corvallis, OR [*Location identifier*] [*FAA*] (FAAL) ... CVO
Corvallis, OR [*FM radio station call letters*] ... KBVR
Corvallis, OR [*FM radio station call letters*] ... KEJO
Corvallis, OR [*FM radio station call letters*] ... KFAT
Corvallis, OR [*FM radio station call letters*] ... KFLY
Corvallis, OR [*AM radio station call letters*] ... KLOO
Corvallis, OR [*FM radio station call letters*] (BROA) ... KLOO-FM
Corvallis, OR [*AM radio station call letters*] ... KOAC
Corvallis, OR [*Television station call letters*] ... KOAC-TV
Corvallis, OR [*Location identifier*] [*FAA*] (FAAL) ... LWG
Corvallis Public Library, Corvallis, OR [*Library symbol*] [*Library of Congress*] (LCLS) ... OrC
Corvallis Workstation Operation (HGAA) ... CWO
Corvanal Holiday AG (SAUO) ... CH
Corvas International [*NASDAQ symbol*] (TTSB) ... CVAS
Corvas International, Inc. [*Associated Press*] (SAG) ... Corvas
Corvas International, Inc. [*NASDAQ symbol*] (SAG) ... CVAS
Corvel Corp. [*Associated Press*] (SAG) ... Corvel
CorVel Corp. [*NASDAQ symbol*] (SPSG) ... CRVL
Corvette [*Navy symbol*] [*Obsolete*] ... DDC
Corvette Petroleum Corp. [*Vancouver Stock Exchange symbol*] ... CRV
, Corvettes [*Zwillenberg*] [*Department store chain name derived from the owner's name, a business parter, and a Canadian warship*] ... EJ Korvette
Corvinus. Elementa Juris Civilis [*A publication*] (DLA) ... Corvin El
Corvinus' Jus Feodale [*A publication*] (DLA) ... Corv Jus
Corvita Corp. [*Associated Press*] (SAG) ... Corvita
Corvita Corp. [*NASDAQ symbol*] (SAG) ... CVTA
Corvita Corp. [*NASDAQ symbol*] (TTSB) ... CVTAC
Corvus [*Constellation*] ... Corv
Corvus [*Constellation*] ... Crv
Corvus Data Analysis Software (SAUS) ... CORDAS
Corwith Herald, Corwith, IA [*Library symbol*] [*Library of Congress*] (LCLS) ... IaCorwH
Cory on Accounts [*A publication*] (DLA) ... Cory Acc
Corydon Democrat, Corydon, IN [*Library symbol*] [*Library of Congress*] (LCLS) ... InCorD
Corydon, IN [*FM radio station call letters*] ... WGZB
Corydon, IN [*FM radio station call letters*] ... WHKW
Corydon, IN [*AM radio station call letters*] ... WOCC
Corydon, IN [*FM radio station call letters*] (RBYB) ... WSFR-FM
Corydon Public Library, Corydon, IN [*Library symbol*] [*Library of Congress*] (LCLS) ... InCor
Corydon Times-Republican, Corydon, IA [*Library symbol*] [*Library of Congress*] (LCLS) ... IaCoryTR
Corynebacteria, Mycobacteria, Nocardiae [*Trehalose containing genera*] ... CMN
Corynebacterium [*Genus of microorganisms*] (MAH) ... C
Corynebacterium Parvum (DB) ... CP
Corynebacterium Pseudotuberculosis Phospholipase D [*An enzyme*] ... Cor-PLD
Coryton on Copyrights [*A publication*] (DLA) ... Cory Cop
Coryton on Patents [*A publication*] (DLA) ... Cor Pat
Coryton on Patents [*A publication*] (DLA) ... Cory Pat
Coryton on Stage Rights [*A publication*] (DLA) ... Cory St R
Coryton's Reports [*Bengal*] [*A publication*] (DLA) ... Cor
Coryton's Reports [*Calcutta*] [*A publication*] (DLA) ... Cory
Coryton's Reports, Calcutta High Court [*A publication*] (DLA) ... Coryton
Coryza [*Medicine*] ... CZ
COSAL [*Coordinated Shipboard Allowance List*] **Processing Point** ... COPP
Cosanti Foundation [*Later, Arcosanti*] (EA) ... CF
Cosby, Mason, and Martland Public Library, Noelville, Ontario [*Library symbol*] [*National Library of Canada*] (NLC) ... ONCMM
Coscan Development Corp. [*Toronto Stock Exchange symbol*] ... COT
Cosecant ... COSEC
Cosecant (ADWA) ... cosec
Cosecant (NTIO) ... csc
Cosecant [*Mathematics*] (GPO) ... CSC
Cosecant Computing Amplifier (SAUS) ... CSC
Cosecant Computing Amplifier (NAKS) ... csc
Cosecant, Hyperbolic [*Mathematics*] (ROG) ... COSECH
Cosecant, Hyperbolic [*Mathematics*] (GPO) ... CSCH
Coseka Resources Ltd. [*Toronto Stock Exchange symbol*] ... CKS
Co-Selector (SAUS) ... Co-Sel
Cosford [*British*] [*ICAO location identifier*] (ICLI) ... EGWC
Coshocton, OH [*FM radio station call letters*] (RBYB) ... WOSE-FM
Coshocton, OH [*AM radio station call letters*] ... WTNS
Coshocton, OH [*FM radio station call letters*] ... WTNS-FM

Cosiguina [*Nicaragua*] [*Seismograph station code, US Geological Survey*] (SEIS) ... COS
Cosine ... CN
Cosine (ABAC) ... cos
Cosine [*Mathematics*] (MCD) ... COS
Cosine Amplitude (SAUS) ... Cos Am
Cosine Emission Law [*Optics*] ... CEL
Cosine, Hyperbolic [*Mathematics*] ... COSH
Cosine Integral ... Ci
Cosine of the Amplitude (SAUS) ... CN
Cosine Project Management Team (SAUS) ... CPT
Cosine Tracking and Triangulation (SAA) ... COTAT
Cosine Trajectory Angle and Range (IAA) ... COTAR
Cosite Analysis Model [*Computer science*] ... COSAM
Co-Site Analysis Model (SAUS) ... COSAM
Co-Site Analytical Model (SAUS) ... COSAM
Cosmetic ... CSMTC
Cosmetic & Fragrance Concepts, Inc. (MHDW) ... COSF
Cosmetic and Perfumery Retail Association [*British*] ... COPRA
Cosmetic Career Women [*Later, CEW*] ... CCW
Cosmetic Center [*Formerly, Cosmetic & Fragrance Concept*] [*NASDAQ symbol*] (SPSG) ... COSC
Cosmetic Center Cl'A' [*NASDAQ symbol*] (TTSB) ... COSCA
Cosmetic Center Cl'B'(vtg) [*NASDAQ symbol*] (TTSB) ... COSCB
Cosmetic Center, Inc. [*Associated Press*] (SAG) ... CosCtr
Cosmetic Executive Women (EA) ... CEW
Cosmetic Group USA [*NASDAQ symbol*] (TTSB) ... CUSA
Cosmetic Group USA, Inc. [*Associated Press*] (SAG) ... Cosmetic
Cosmetic Group USA, Inc. [*Associated Press*] (SAG) ... Cosmtc
Cosmetic Group USA, Inc. [*NASDAQ symbol*] (SAG) ... CUSA
Cosmetic Group USA Wrrt [*NASDAQ symbol*] (TTSB) ... CUSAW
Cosmetic Industry Buyers and Suppliers (EA) ... CIBS
Cosmetic Industry Buyers and Suppliers Association (SAUO) ... CIBS
Cosmetic Ingredient Review (EA) ... CIR
Cosmetic Pharmaceutical ... Cosmoceutical
Cosmetic, Toiletry, and Fragrance Association (EA) ... CTFA
Cosmetic, Toiletry, and Fragrance Association, Inc. (SAUS) ... CTFA
Cosmetic, Toiletry, and Perfumery Association [*British*] (DBA) ... CTPA
Cosmetics (SAUS) ... Cosm
Cosmetics for the Community of Tomorrow [*Acronym used as brand name*] ... KOSCOT
Cosmetologist ... CSMTLGST
Cosmetology Accrediting Commission [*Later, NACCAS*] (EA) ... CAC
Cosmetology Program [*Association of Independent Colleges and Schools specialization code*] ... CS
Cosmic (SAUS) ... Cos
Cosmic and Solar Particle Investigation [*Astronomy*] ... COSPIN
Cosmic Anisotropy Telescope ... CAT
Cosmic Background Explorer [*NASA*] ... COBE
Cosmic Background Imager (SAUS) ... CBI
Cosmic Background Radiation ... CBR
Cosmic Background Radiation Anisotropy [*Astronomy*] (ECON) ... COBRA
Cosmic Background Radiation Anisotropy Satellite (SAUS) ... COBRAS
Cosmic Black-Body Radiation [*Astrophysics*] ... CBR
Cosmic Dust Collection Experiment (SAUS) ... CDCE
Cosmic Dust Collection Facility (SSD) ... CDCF
Cosmic Dust Detector ... CDD
Cosmic Exposure Dating (QUAC) ... CED
Cosmic Far-Infrared Background ... CFIRB
Cosmic Hot Interstellar Plasma Spectrometer [*Developed to study a gas cloud surrounding the solar system*] ... CHIPS
Cosmic Hot Interstellar Plasma Spectrometer Satellite (SAUS) ... CHIPSat
Cosmic Infrared Background [*Astrophysics*] ... CIRB
Cosmic Infrared Background Radiation ... CIB
Cosmic Microwave Background [*Of radiation*] ... CMB
Cosmic Microwave Background Radiation ... CMBR
Cosmic Noise Absorption ... CNA
Cosmic Radiation Effects and Activation Monitor (SAUS) ... CREAM
Cosmic Radiation Ionization Spectrographic Program (SAUS) ... CRISP
Cosmic Radiation Satellite (SAUS) ... CORSA
Cosmic Ray ... CR
Cosmic Ray Albedo Neutron Decay [*Geophysics*] ... CRAND
Cosmic Ray Altimeter ... CRA
Cosmic Ray Anti-Matter Detector (PDAA) ... CRAMD
Cosmic Ray Detector [*NASA*] ... CRD
Cosmic Ray Emulsion Plastic Equipment [*NASA*] (MCD) ... CREPE
Cosmic Ray Exposure [*Geophysics*] ... CRE
Cosmic Ray Flux ... CRF
Cosmic Ray Gas ... CRG
Cosmic Ray Ionization Program [*NASA*] ... CRISP
Cosmic Ray Isotope Experiment (MCD) ... CRIE
Cosmic Ray Logic Box (IAA) ... CRLB
Cosmic Ray Nuclear [*or Nuclei*] **Experiment** (MCD) ... CRANE
Cosmic Ray Nuclei Experiment (SAUS) ... CRN
Cosmic Ray Nuclei [*or Nuclear*] **Experiment** (SSD) ... CRNE
Cosmic Ray Observatory ... CRO
Cosmic Ray Particle ... CRP
Cosmic Ray Physics Laboratory (NASA) ... CRPL
Cosmic Ray Produced (SAUS) ... CRP
Cosmic Ray Radiation Facility (SAUS) ... CRRF
Cosmic Ray Satellite [*Japan*] ... CORSA
Cosmic Ray Satellite-B [*European Space Agency*] ... COS-B
Cosmic Ray Shower ... CRS
Cosmic Ray Telescope ... CRT
Cosmic rays and trapped radiation committee (SAUO) ... COS
Cosmic Scale Integration (CIST) ... CSI
Cosmic Top Secret (NATG) ... CTS
Cosmic Top Secret Atomal (SAUO) ... CTSA
Cosmic X-Ray Background ... CXB
Cosmic X-Ray Background Radiation ... CXBR
Cosmic-Ray Subsystem [*Astrophysics*] ... CRS
Cosmis Rays ... CR
Cosmo Communications Corp. [*NASDAQ symbol*] (NQ) ... CSMO
Cosmo Communictions [*Associated Press*] (SAG) ... CosmoCm
Cosmo Dog ... CD
Cosmogenic (IAA) ... CP
Cosmographical (SAUS) ... cosmog
Cosmography ... COSMOG
Cosmology (SAUS) ... Cos
Cosmonautics (SAUS) ... Cosmonaut
Cosmopolitan Area Network [*Telecommunications*] (ACRL) ... CAN
Cosmopolitan Associates [*Later, OC*] ... CA
Cosmopolitan Correspondence Club (SAUO) ... CCC
Cosmopolitan International (EA) ... CI
Cosmopolitan Magazine (SAUS) ... Cosmo
Cosmopolitan School of Music (SAUS) ... CSM
Cosmopolitan Soccer League (EA) ... CSL
Cosmos Club, Washington, DC [*Library symbol*] [*Library of Congress*] (LCLS) ... DCos
Cosmos Public School, Cosmos, MN [*Library symbol*] [*Library of Congress*] (LCLS) ... MnCosPS
Cosmos Resources, Inc. [*Vancouver Stock Exchange symbol*] ... CES
Cosne-Sur-Loire [*France*] [*ICAO location identifier*] (ICLI) ... LFGH
Coso Basin North [*California*] [*Seismograph station code, US Geological Survey*] (SEIS) ... CBHM
Coso Springs South [*California*] [*Seismograph station code, US Geological Survey*] (SEIS) ... CSSM
COSPAR [*Committee on Space Research*] **International R eference Atmosphere** ... CIRA
COSPAS-SARSAT-Council (SAUO) ... CSC
Cosponsor ... COSP
Cossack National Press Association [*Defunct*] (EA) ... CNPA
Cossack-American Citizens' Committee (EA) ... CACC
Cossor Instrument Landing System (SAUS) ... CILS
Cossor Interrogation & Reply Cryptographic Equipment (SAUS) ... CIRCE
Cossor Marine Radar (SAUS) ... CMR
Cost ... C
Cost About ... ca
Cost Account [*Accounting*] ... CA
Cost Account Authorization Document (ACAE) ... CAAD
Cost Account Code [*Accounting*] ... CAC
Cost Account Manager (MCD) ... CAM
Cost Account Managers ... CAM
Cost Account Number [*Accounting*] (NG) ... CAN
Cost Account Package [*Accounting*] (NASA) ... CAP
Cost Account Performance Measurement and Analysis Report (MCD) ... CAPMAR
Cost Account Performance Status Report [*Accounting*] (MCD) ... CAPSR
Cost Account Plan ... CAP
Cost Accountant [*Accounting*] (AABC) ... CA
Cost Accounting Code [*NASA*] (NASA) ... COSTA
Cost Accounting Schedule (MCD) ... CAS
Cost Accounting Standards [*Accounting*] (MCD) ... CAS
Cost Accounting Standards Board [*US*] [*Terminated*] ... CASB
Cost Accounting Standards Board's Cost of Money Factors [*Form*] (AAGC) ... CASB-CMF
Cost Accounting Standards Guide [*CCH*] [*A publication*] (AAGC) ... CASG
Cost Accounting Standards Guide [*Commerce Clearing House*] [*A publication*] (DLA) ... Cost Acc'g Stand Guide
Cost Accounting System (SAUS) ... COS
Cost Accounting Work Plan (ABAC) ... CAWP
Cost Accumulation System ... CAS
Cost Adjustment Factor ... CAF
Cost Advisory Group [*Army*] ... CAG
Cost Allocation Application Summary (ACAE) ... CAS
Cost Allocation Procedure [*Environmental Protection Agency*] (GFGA) ... CAP
Cost Allocation Report [*DoD*] ... CAR
Cost Allocation Review ... CAR
Cost Amount (SAUS) ... CSTAM
Cost Analysis (SAUO) ... CA
Cost Analysis Brief (MCD) ... CAB
Cost Analysis Data Base (ACAE) ... CADB
Cost Analysis Improvement Group [*DoD*] (DOMA) ... CAIG
Cost Analysis Information Report [*Air Force*] (MCD) ... CAIR
Cost Analysis Monthly Exchange [*Army*] ... CAME
Cost Analysis of LASER Investment, Production, Engineering, and Research Cost Mode (MCD) ... CALIPER
Cost Analysis of Maintenance Policies (ACAE) ... COAP
Cost Analysis of Maintenance Policy ... COAMP
Cost Analysis Office [*Army*] (RDA) ... CAO
Cost Analysis Organization (SAUO) ... CAO
Cost Analysis Organization (SAA) ... CAOS
Cost Analysis Plan ... CAP
Cost Analysis Scheduling and Schedule Analysis (ACAE) ... CASSE
Cost Analysis System (SAUS) ... CAST
Cost Analysis Task Force [*NASA*] (KSC) ... CATF
Cost Analysis Technical Manual ... CATEM
Cost and Charges (SAUS) ... CaC
Cost and Economic Analysis Center (DOMA) ... CEAC
Cost and Economic Assessment (EEVL) ... CEA

Cost and Economic Information System [*DoD*] (MCD) .... CEIS
Cost and Efficiency Adjustment Clause (SAUS) .... CEAC
Cost and Freight [*Shipping*] .... CAF
Cost and Freight [*Shipping*] .... C & F
Cost and Freight .... C and F
Cost and Freight (EBF) .... c&f
Cost and Freight [*Shipping*] .... CF
Cost and Freight [*"INCOTERM," International Chamber of Commerce official code*] [*Business term*] .... CFR
Cost and Freight (SAUS) .... CFR
Cost & Freight (SAUS) .... CFR
Cost and Insurance (SAUS) .... C and I
Cost and Insurance [*Shipping*] .... C & I
Cost and Insurance (EBF) .... c&i
Cost and Insurance (EBF) ci
Cost and Insurance [*Shipping*] CI
Cost and Material Position System (MCD) .... CAMPS
Cost and Operational Effectiveness Analysis (SAUS) .... COE
Cost and Operational Effectiveness Analysis [*Military*] (AABC) .... COEA
Cost & Operational Effectiveness Assessment (SAUS) .... COE
Cost and Performance .... CP
Cost and Performance Analysis [*Air Force*] (AFIT) .... CPA
Cost and Performance Effectiveness Ratios .... CAPERS
Cost and Performance Summary Report [*Army*] .... CPSR
Cost and Progress System (SAUS) .... CAPS
Cost and Schedule Planning and Control .... CSPC
Cost and Schedule Reporting (SAUS) .... CASR
Cost and Training Effectiveness Analysis .... COTA
Cost and Training Effectiveness Analysis .... CTEA
Cost as an Independent Variable (AAGC) .... CAIV
Cost Assignment to Telecommunication Services [*Telecommunications*] .... CATS
Cost, Assurance, Freight (EBF) .... CAF
Cost, Assurance, Freight (EBF) .... caf
Cost at Completion (ACAE) .... CAC
Cost Audit Board (NASA) .... CAB
Cost Avoidance to Total Investment Ratio .... CVIR
Cost Breakdown Structure (MCD) .... CBS
Cost Bulletin [*A publication*] .... Cost Bull
Cost Category Code (MCD) CCC
Cost Category Input (SAA) CCI
Cost Category Input Form (SAA) .... CCIF
Cost Category Reporting System (MCD) .... CCRS
Cost Center (AFM) CC
Cost Center (NAKS) cc
Cost Center Determination (AAG) .... CCD
Cost Center Performance Measurement System (AFM) .... CCPMS
Cost Change Commitment Notice .... CCCN
Cost Charge Number (MCD) .... CCN
Cost Code (MCD) CC
Cost Commitment Team (SAUS) .... CCT
Cost Committee Advisory Group .... CCAG
Cost Comparison Handbook [*A publication*] (MCD) .... CCH
Cost Contract Fee Appendix (SAA) .... CCFA
Cost Control and Action Group .... CCAG
Cost Control Item (MCD) CCI
Cost Control Program (NASA) .... CCP
Cost Control System .... CCS
Cost Data Bank Index .... CDBI
Cost Data Bank System (AFIT) .... CDBS
Cost Data Base Management System [*Air Force*] .... CDBMS
Cost Data Collection Format (ACAE) .... CDCF
Cost Data Plan .... CDP
Cost Data Sheet (MCD) .... CDS
Cost Development Management System (SAUO) .... CDMS
Cost Differential (MCD) .... COSDIF
Cost Document Library System [*Air Force*] (AFIT) .... CDLS
Cost Driver Attribute .... CDA
Cost Effective Surface Torpedo (MCD) .... CEST
Cost Effectiveness [*Accounting*] .... CE
Cost Effectiveness Analysis of Bonuses and Reenlistment Policies .... CEABREP
Cost Effectiveness Analysis of the Tactical Operations System [*Military*] (MCD) .... CEATOS
Cost Effectiveness and Reliability Technology for the Automotive Industry .... CERTAIN
Cost Effectiveness Index [*Economics*] .... CEI
Cost Effectiveness Study [*Economics*] .... CES
Cost Element (MCD) .... CE
Cost Element Monitor [*Air Force*] .... CEM
Cost Engineering Automated System Estimate (SAUS) .... CEASE
Cost Estimate (SAUS) .... CE
Cost Estimate and Updating Form (MCD) .... CEUF
Cost Estimate Change Order (NRCH) .... CECO
Cost Estimate Control Data Center (AABC) .... CECDC
Cost Estimate Dispersion (KSC) .... CED
Cost Estimate Error Report .... CEER
Cost Estimate Input Sheet [*Jet Propulsion Laboratory, NASA*] .... CEIS
Cost Estimate Request .... CER
Cost Estimated Work Sheets (ACAE) .... CEWS
Cost Estimating Data Center .... CEDC
Cost Estimating Relation [*or Relationship*] (AFM) .... CER
Cost Estimating Techniques for System Acquisition [*Army*] .... CETSA
Cost Evaluation Model (SAUS) .... CEM
Cost Evaluation Plan (AAGC) .... CEP
Cost Extension (SAUS) .... CSTEX
Cost, Freight, and Exchange [*Shipping*] .... CF and E
Cost, Freight and Insurance (EBF) .... cf
Cost, Freight and Insurance (EBF) .... cf&i
Cost, Freight, and Insurance [*Shipping*] .... CF & I
Cost, Freight, and Insurance [*Shipping*] .... CFI
Cost, Freight, Assurance [*Shipping*] .... CFA
Cost Growth (DNAB) .... CG
Cost Guard Oceanographic Unit (SAUS) .... CGOU
Cost Improvement (ACAE) CI
Cost Improvement Program .... CIP
Cost Improvement Proposal (MCD) .... CIP
Cost Index (GAVI) CI
Cost Indicator Code [*Army*] (AFIT) CIC
Cost Information Reports [*DoD*] .... CIR
Cost Information System .... CIS
Cost Information System Report Order (ACAE) .... CISRO
Cost Inspection Service [*Navy*] .... CIS
Cost Inspector CI
Cost, Insurance, and Freight [*Shipping*] [*"INCOTERM," International Chamber of Commerce official code*] .... CIF
Cost Insurance and Freight [*Shipping*] (WA) .... cif
Cost, Insurance, Freight (SAUO) .... CIF
Cost, Insurance, Freight, and Commission [*Shipping*] .... CIF & C
Cost, Insurance, Freight, and Commission [*Shipping*] .... CIFC
Cost, Insurance, Freight, and Exchange [*Shipping*] .... CIF & E
Cost, Insurance, Freight and Exchange (EBF) .... cif&e
Cost, Insurance, Freight, and Exchange [*Shipping*] .... CIFE
Cost, Insurance, Freight, and Interest [*Shipping*] .... CIF & I
Cost, Insurance, Freight, and Interest [*Shipping*] .... CIFI
Cost, Insurance, Freight and Interest (EBF) .... cifi
Cost, Insurance, Freight, Commission, and Exchange [*Shipping*] .... CIFCE
Cost, Insurance, Freight, Commission, and Interest [*Shipping*] .... CIFC & I
Cost, Insurance, Freight, Commission, and Interest [*Shipping*] .... CIFCI
Cost, Insurance, Freight, Commission, Exchange, and Interest [*Shipping*] .... CIFCE & I
Cost, Insurance, Freight, Free Out [*Shipping*] .... CIFFO
Cost, Insurance, Freight, Interest, and Exchange [*Shipping*] .... CIFI & E
Cost, Insurance, Freight, Interest and Exchange (EBF) .... cifi&e
Cost, Insurance, Freight, London Terms [*Shipping*] .... CIFLT
Cost Laid Down .... CLD
Cost, Lawsuits, On-Air Requirements, and Time Available .... CLOT
Cost, Life, Interchangeability, Function, and Safety [*Navy*] (NG) .... CLIFS
Cost Limit Review Board .... CLRB
Cost Management Group [*An association*] (EA) .... CMG
Cost Management Improvement Program .... CMIP
Cost Management System .... CMS
Cost Measurement Technique (AAG) .... COMET
Cost Modeling Users Group (AAEL) .... CMUG
Cost of Alternative Military Programs (SAA) .... CAMP
Cost of Analysis Organization [*Navy*] (NG) .... CAO
Cost of Arms [*Army*] (AABC) .... C/A
Cost of Attaining Personnel Requirement .... CAPER
Cost of Compliance [*Automotive emissions standards*] .... COC
Cost of Construction (SAUS) .... C of C
Cost of Consumables (AAEL) .... COC
Cost of Cracking Adjustment [*Cryptography*] (VERA) .... COCA
Cost of Electricity (MCD) .... COE
Cost of Facilities (NASA) .... C of F
Cost of Facilities (NAKS) .... CofF
Cost of Facilities Capital (AAGC) .... CFC
Cost of Failure (SAUS) .... COF
Cost of Funds [*Business term*] (EMRF) .... COF
Cost of Funds Index [*Banking*] .... COFI
Cost of Goods Sold (AAGC) .... CGS
Cost of Goods Sold .... COGS
Cost of Illness [*Environmental medicine*] .... COI
Cost of Knowing .... CoK
Cost of Living [*Economics*] (AAG) CL
Cost of Living [*Economics*] (AAG) .... C of L
Cost of Living [*Economics*] .... COL
Cost of Living Adjustment .... COLA
Cost of Living Allowance [*Economics*] .... COLA
Cost of Living Award (PDAA) .... COLA
Cost of Living Bonus (DGA) .... COLB
Cost of Living Council [*Also, COLC*] [*Terminated, 1974*] [*Pronounced "click"*] CLC
Cost of Living Council [*Also, CLC*] [*Terminated, 1974*] .... COLC
Cost of Living Increase (ACAE) CLI
Cost of Maintaining Product (SAUS) .... CMP
Cost of Money [*DoD*] .... COM
Cost of Money Factor (SSD) .... CMF
Cost of Ownership Luminator .... COOL
Cost of Ownership Model (ACAE) .... COM
Cost of Quality [*Engineering*] .... COQ
Cost of Sale [*Accounting*] .... C/S
Cost of Sales Adjustment [*Economics*] (DCTA) .... COSA
Cost of Service Indexing .... COSI
Cost of Social Security [*International Labor Organization*] [*Information service or system*] [*United Nations*] (DUND) .... COSS
Cost on Delivery (MCD) .... COD
Cost Operating Budget (NOAA) .... COB
Cost Operating Profits [*Accounting*] .... COP
Cost Optimization Analysis of Maintenance Policy (SAUS) .... COAMP
Cost Optimization Utilizing Reference Technique (PDAA) .... COURT
Cost Optimized Launch Vehicle (ACAE) .... COLV
Cost Optimizing System to Evaluate Reliability (MHDB) .... COSTER

Cost Oriented Systems Technique (SAUS) ... COST
Cost per Average Pound Saved ... CAPS
Cost per Click [*Computer science*] ... CPC
Cost Per Copy (SAUS) ... CPC
Cost per Entered Employment [*Job Training and Partnership Act*] (OICC) ... CEE
Cost per Flight [*NASA*] ... CPF
Cost per Gross Rating Point [*Advertising*] (NTCM) ... CPGRP
Cost per Hand Stitch [*Tailoring*] ... CPHS
Cost per Inquiry ... CPI
Cost Per Inquiry (WDMC) ... cpi
Cost per Instruction [*Computer science*] ... CPI
Cost per Interview [*Marketing*] (WDMC) ... CPI
Cost Per Interview (WDMC) ... cpi
Cost per Man-Hour (MCD) ... C/MH
Cost per Meal (SAUS) ... CPM
Cost per Minute (SAUS) ... CPM
Cost per Order [*Advertising*] (WDMC) ... CPO
Cost per Point [*Advertising*] (WDMC) ... CPP
Cost per Positive Termination [*Job Training and Partnership Act*] (OICC) ... CPPT
Cost per Region [*Agricultural economics*] ... CR
Cost per Reportable Result ... CPRR
Cost per Thousand [*Advertising*] ... CPM
Cost per Thousand (ODBW) ... CPT
Cost per Unit ... CPU
Cost per Unit (SAUS) ... CSTUN
Cost per Unit Requirement (MCD) ... CUR
Cost Performance (SAUS) ... COP
Cost Performance Index (MCD) ... CPI
Cost Performance Management (MCD) ... CPM
Cost Performance Report (MCD) ... CPR
Cost Plan (SAUS) ... CP
Cost, Planning and Appraisal (SAUS) ... CPA
Cost Planning and Appraisal [*Air Force Systems Command, Aeronautical Systems Division*] ... CPA
Cost Planning and Control System (MCD) ... CPCS
Cost Planning and Evaluations System ... COPES
Cost Plus [*Insurance*] ... CP
Cost Plus a Percentage of Cost ... CPPC
Cost Plus Award [*Military*] ... CPA
Cost Plus Award Fee [*Business term*] ... CPAF
Cost Plus Fixed Fee [*Business term*] ... CPFF
Cost Plus, Inc. [*Associated Press*] (SAG) ... CostPlus
Cost Plus, Inc. [*NASDAQ symbol*] (SAG) ... CPWM
Cost Plus Incentive [*Business term*] (MSA) ... CPI
Cost Plus Intended Fee (SAUS) ... CPIF
Cost Plus Interim Fee (SAUS) ... CPIF
Cost Plus No Fee [*Business term*] (MCD) ... CPNF
Cost Price [*Business term*] (ADA) ... CP
Cost Price (SAUS) ... CSTPC
Cost Price of the Items Canceled [*Business term*] ... CPIC
Cost Price of the Items Terminated (SAUS) ... CPIT
Cost Principles for Educational Institutions [*OMB Circular*] (AAGC) ... A-21
Cost Principles for State and Local Governments (AAGC) ... A-87
Cost Progress Evaluation (MCD) ... COPE
Cost Proposal ... CP
Cost Proposal Outline (AAG) ... CPO
Cost Proposal Requirement (MCD) ... CPR
Cost Quality Management System [*for hospitals*] ... CQMS
Cost Quote Request ... CQR
Cost Realism Committee (AAGC) ... CRC
Cost Reduction Alternative Study [*Economics*] (NASA) ... CRAS
Cost Reduction Curve [*Economics*] (NASA) ... CRC
Cost Reduction Early Decision Information Techniques [*Hughes Aircraft Co.*] ... CREDIT
Cost Reduction Journal ... CRJO
Cost Reduction Program [*Economics*] (AFM) ... CRP
Cost Reduction Report [*Economics*] ... CRR
Cost Reduction Representative (SAUS) ... CRR
Cost Reduction/Technical Excellence ... CR/TE
Cost Reimbursement [*Type of contract*] (AAGC) ... Cost
Cost Reimbursement ... CR
Cost Reimbursement Contract [*Government contracting*] ... CRC
Cost Reimbursement Incentive Contracting [*Government contracting*] ... CRIC
Cost Reimbursement Research and Development (ACAE) ... CRRD
Cost Reliability Index (SAUS) ... CRI
Cost Reporting Requirements ... CRR
Cost Savings Model (MCD) ... CSM
Cost Schedule Control System (MCD) ... CS2
Cost Schedule Control Systems Criteria (SAUS) ... CJSCSC
Cost Schedule Cost System Criteria (SAUS) ... CSCSC
Cost Schedule, Logistics, and NATO Standardization (MCD) ... CSLS
Cost Schedule Planning and Control System (SAUS) ... C/SPCS
Cost Schedule Status Report [*Military*] ... CSSR
Cost Schedule Technical Control System ... CSTCS
Cost, Scheduling, Reporting ... CSR
Cost Sensitivity Factor (NASA) ... CSF
Cost Sharing ... CS
Cost System Indicator (AFIT) ... CSI
Cost to Complete (SAUS) ... CTC
Cost to Date (SAUS) ... CTD
Cost to Manuacture ... CTM
Cost Travel Chargeable ... TRAVCHAR
Cost Variance (MCD) ... CV
Cost Variance Report (SAUS) ... CVR
Cost Volume Profit (SAUS) ... CVP
Costa [*Rib*] [*Anatomy*] ... C
Costa [*Entomology*] ... Co
Costa I [*First rib*] [*Costa II, second rib is C_2, etc., through C12*] [*Orthopedics*] (DAVI) ... C_1
Costa Mesa, CA [*AM radio station call letters*] (BROA) ... KGXL-AM
Costa Mesa, CA [*AM radio station call letters*] (RBYB) ... KNNZ
Costa Mesa Historical Society, Costa Mesa, CA [*Library symbol*] [*Library of Congress*] (LCLS) ... CCmHi
Costa Rica [*MARC country of publication code*] [*Library of Congress*] (LCCP) ... cr
Costa Rica [*ANSI two-letter standard code*] (CNC) ... CR
Costa Rica [*ANSI three-letter standard code*] (CNC) ... CRI
Costa Rica (VRA) ... C Rica
Costa Rica [*MARC geographic area code*] [*Library of Congress*] (LCCP) ... nccr-
Costa Rica International, Inc. [*Associated Press*] (SAG) ... CostaRica
Costa Rica International, Inc. [*NASDAQ symbol*] (SAG) ... RICA
Costa Rican Academic Network (SAUO) ... CRNet
Costa Rican-American Chamber of Commerce (EA) ... AmCham
Costal Cartilage [*Medicine*] (MELL) ... CC
Costal Margin [*Medicine*] ... CM
Costal Ocean Program [*Marine science*] (OSRA) ... COP
Costal-Marine Project (SAUS) ... COMAR
Cost/Benefit [*Accounting*] ... C/B
Cost-Benefit Analysis [*Accounting*] ... CBA
Cost/Burden Reduction ... C/BR
Costco Cos. [*NASDAQ symbol*] (SG) ... COST
Co-Steel, Inc. [*Toronto Stock Exchange symbol*] ... CEI
Cost-Effective Ratio [*Economics*] ... CER
Cost-Effective Shape Technology (MCD) ... CEST
Cost-Effectiveness Analysis [*Economics*] ... CEA
Cost-Effectiveness Analysis Methodology [*Economics*] (MCD) ... CEAM
Costermonger [*Fruit or vegetable seller*] [*British*] (DSUE) ... COSTER
Cost-Estimating System (ODBW) ... CES
Cost-Exchange Ratio [*DoD*] ... CER
Cost-Factoring System for Force Readiness Projection (MCD) ... COFACTS
Cost-Free Evaluation ... CFE
Costilla County Library, San Luis, CO [*Library symbol*] [*Library of Congress*] (LCLS) ... CoSl
Costilla Energy, Inc. [*NASDAQ symbol*] (SAG) ... COSE
Costilla Energy, Inc. [*Associated Press*] (SAG) ... CostEner
Costing and Assessing via Substantival History ... CASH
Costing and Data Management System ... CADMS
Costing Out Policy Systems (PDAA) ... COPS
Costing System (DGA) ... CS
Cost-No Fee [*Type of contract*] (AAGC) ... C-NF
Costo y Flete [*Cost and Freight*] [*Shipping*] [*Spanish*] ... C & F
Costochondral [*Anatomy*] ... CC
Costochondral Junction [*Medicine*] (DAVI) ... CCJ
Costoclavicular Maneuver [*Medicine*] (MELL) ... CCM
Costoclavicular Syndrome [*Medicine*] (DB) ... CCS
Cost-of-Living Adjustment (NTIO) ... cola
Cost-of-Living Index [*Economics*] ... CLI
Cost-of-Living Index [*Economics*] ... COLI
Cost-of-Ownership ... COO
Cost-of-Ownership Reduction Investment (MCD) ... COORI
Costophrenic Angle [*Medicine*] (DMAA) ... CPA
Cost-Oriented Models Built to Analyze Tradeoffs (MCD) ... COMBAT
Cost-Oriented Production and Inventory Loading Operations Technique Works (MHDB) ... COPILOT
Cost-Oriented Resource Estimating Model [*Air Force*] (GFGA) ... CORE
Cost-Oriented Systems Technique ... COST
Costovertebral [*Angle*] [*Anatomy*] (DAVI) ... CV
Costovertebral Angle [*Medicine*] ... CVA
Costo-Vertebral Angle (SAUS) ... CVA
Costovertebral Angle Tenderness [*Medicine*] (MAE) ... CVAT
Costovertebral Joint (MELL) ... CVJ
Cost-per-Million (SAUS) ... CPM
Cost-Plus-Incentive Fee [*Business term*] ... CIF
Cost-Plus-Incentive Fee [*Business term*] (AFM) ... CPIF
Cost-Plus-Incentive-Award Fee [*Business term*] (MCD) ... CPIAF
Cost/Pricing Data [*Military*] (DOMA) ... C/PD
Cost/Quality Management Assessment (ABAC) ... CQMA
Cost-Reimbursement Contracting (AAGC) ... CRC
Cost-Reimbursement Facilities Contract (AAGC) ... CRFC
Cost/Resource Model (AAEL) ... CRM
Costriction Band Syndrome [*Medicine*] (MELL) ... CBS
Costs and Productivity Scheme (SAUO) ... CAPS
Costs and Schedules (SAUS) ... C and S
Costs and Schedules (SAUS) ... C&S
Costs, Budgeting, and Economics ... CBE
Costs Chargeable to Fund Authorization [*Army*] ... CHGFA
Costs Chargeable to Purchase Authorization Advice ... CHGPAA
Costs of Control Exceed Benefits of Control [*Environmental science*] (COE) ... CExB
Costs of Hard Rock Tunnelling (PDAA) ... COHART
Costs of the Soviet Empire [*International economics*] ... CSE
Cost/Schedule ... C/S
Cost/Schedule Control (MCD) ... C/SC
Cost/Schedule Control System (MCD) ... CSCS
Cost/Schedule Control System Criteria ... C/SC2
Cost/Schedule Control System Criteria ... C/SCSC
Cost/Schedule Control Systems (SAUO) ... C/SCS
Cost/Schedule Planning and Control Specification [*Air Force*] ... C/SPCS
Cost/Schedule Reporting System (SSD) ... C/SRS
Cost/Schedule Status Report (SAUO) ... C/SSR
Cost-Schedule-Milestone [*Chart*] ... CSM

Cost-Stirling [*Antibodies*] [*Immunology*] (DAVI) ... C/S
Costume (ROG) ... COST
Costume (VRA) ... cstu
Costume Designers Guild (EA) ... CDG
Costume Jewelry Board of Trade of New York [*Inactive*] ... CJBT
Costume Jewelry Salesmen's Association (EA) ... CJSA
Costume Jewelry Trade Association [*Defunct*] ... CJTA
Costume Society of America (EA) ... CSA
Costumer Access Network (SAUS) ... CAN
Cost-Utility Analysis (DMAA) ... CUA
Cost-Volume-Power ... CVP
Cost-Volume-Profit [*Analysis*] (MCD) ... CVP
Cosumnes River College, Sacramento, CA [*OCLC symbol*] (OCLC) ... CCR
Cosworth Vega Owner's Association [*Defunct*] (EA) ... CVOA
Cosyntropin Stimulation Test (STED) ... CST
Co-Systems Operator (SAUS) ... CoSysOp
Cotabato [*Philippines*] [*Airport symbol*] (OAG) ... CBO
Cotabato, North Cotabato [*Philippines*] [*ICAO location identifier*] (ICLI) ... RPWC
Cotacachi [*Ecuador*] [*ICAO location identifier*] (ICLI) ... SEHI
cotangent (SAUS) ... cot
Cotangent (NTIO) ... cot
Cotangent [*Mathematics*] ... COT
Cotangent [*Mathematics*] (IAA) ... CTG
cotangent (SAUS) ... ctg
cotangent (SAUS) ... ctn
Cotangent [*Mathematics*] ... CTN
Cotangent (ADWA) ... ctn
Cotangent, Hyperbolic [*Mathematics*] ... COTH
Cotangent, Hyperbolic [*Mathematics*] ... CTGH
Cotati, CA [*Television station call letters*] ... KRCB-TV
Cote D'Ivoire [*Internet country code*] ... CI
Cote St. Luc Public Library, Quebec [*Library symbol*] [*National Library of Canada*] (NLC) ... QCSTL
Cotelligent Group [*NASDAQ symbol*] (TTSB) ... COTL
Cotelligent Group, Inc. [*Associated Press*] (SAG) ... CotellG
Cotelligent Group, Inc. [*NASDAQ symbol*] (SAG) ... COTL
Cotelligent, Inc. [*Formerly, Cotelligent Group*] [*NYSE symbol*] ... CGZ
Cotenancy and Joint Ownership [*Legal term*] (DLA) ... COTEN & JT O
Cotgrave's Dictionary [*A publication*] (ROG) ... Cotg
Cotgrave's Dictionary [*A publication*] (ROG) ... Cotr
Cothran's Annotated Statutes of Illinois [*A publication*] (DLA) ... Coth Stat
Coto 47 [*Costa Rica*] [*ICAO location identifier*] (ICLI) ... MRCC
Coto 47 [*Costa Rica*] [*Airport symbol*] (OAG) ... OTR
Cotonou [*Benin*] [*Airport symbol*] (OAG) ... COO
Cotonou [*Dahomey*] [*Airport symbol*] (AD) ... COO
Cotonou [*Benin*] [*ICAO location identifier*] (ICLI) ... DBBV
Cotonou/Cadjehoun [*Benin*] [*ICAO location identifier*] (ICLI) ... DBBB
Cotquean (DSUE) ... COT
Co-Transfer Agent (DLA) ... Co-T/Agt
Co-Trustee (DLA) ... Co-Tr
Cotswold [*England*] ... COTSW
Cotswold Executive Aviation [*British*] [*ICAO designator*] (FAAC) ... CWD
Cotswold Personality Assessment [*Psychology*] ... CPA
Cott Beverages Ltd. [*Toronto Stock Exchange symbol*] ... BCB
Cott Corp. [*NASDAQ symbol*] (SAG) ... COTT
Cott Corp. [*Associated Press*] (SAG) ... CottCp
Cott Corp. [*NASDAQ symbol*] (TTSB) ... COTTF
Cott Corp. (SAUO) ... CTT
Cottage [*Travel industry*] (TRID) ... cot
Cottage (ADA) ... COTT
Cottage ... CT
Cottage ... CTG
Cottage (ADA) ... CTGE
Cottage (SAUS) ... ctge
Cottage and Rural Enterprises [*British*] (DI) ... CARE
Cottage Garden Society [*British*] (DBA) ... CGS
Cottage Grove, OR [*FM radio station call letters*] ... KCGR
Cottage Grove, OR [*FM radio station call letters*] (BROA) ... KEUG-FM
Cottage Grove, OR [*AM radio station call letters*] ... KNND
Cottage Industry Miniaturists Trade Association (EA) ... CIMTA
Cottage Program International (EA) ... CPI
Cottages (SAUS) ... Cots
Cottages ... COTTS
Cottaging or Cruising (WDAA) ... COC
Cottbus [*Germany*] [*ICAO location identifier*] (ICLI) ... ETCO
Cottenham. Reports, Chancery [*1846-48*] [*England*] [*A publication*] (DLA) ... Cott
Cotter ... COT
Cottesloe [*England*] ... COTT
Cottesmore [*British*] [*ICAO location identifier*] (ICLI) ... EGXJ
Cottesmore TTTE [*British*] [*ICAO designator*] (FAAC) ... COT
Cottey College, Nevada, MO [*Library symbol*] [*Library of Congress*] (LCLS) ... MoNvC
Cottica [*Surinam*] [*ICAO location identifier*] (ICLI) ... SMCT
Cotton (AAG) ... C
Cotton (VRA) ... cot
Cotton (MSA) ... COT
Cotton (ROG) ... COTT
Cotton ... CTN
Cotton and Allied Textiles Industry Advisory Committee (HEAS) ... CATIAC
Cotton and Rayon Merchants Association [*British*] (BI) ... CRMA
Cotton Board (SAUO) ... CB
Cotton Board Commission (SAUO) ... CBC
Cotton Canvas Manufacturers Association [*British*] (BI) ... CCMA
Cotton, Climate, Cattle, and Citrus [*Traditional elements of Arizona's economy*] ... 4C's
Cotton Control Board (SAUO) ... CCB
Cotton Corporation of India (SAUO) ... CCI
Cotton Council International (EA) ... CCI
Cotton Covered [*Wire insulation*] (IAA) ... CC
Cotton Double Silk [*Wire insulation*] (IAA) ... CDS
Cotton Effect ... CE
Cotton Elastic Bandage (DAVI) ... CEB
Cotton Equalization Program ... CEP
[*New York*] **Cotton Exchange** (BARN) ... CTN
Cotton Experiment Station (SAUO) ... CES
Cotton Export Market Acreage Program ... CEMAP
Cotton Fire and Marine Underwriters Association ... CFMUA
Cotton Fracture (MELL) ... CF
Cotton History Group (SAUO) ... CHG
Cotton Importers Association (EA) ... CIA
Cotton Inc. [*An association*] (EA) ... CI
Cotton Industries Association (SAUO) ... CIA
Cotton Insurance Association [*Defunct*] (EA) ... CIA
Cotton, Jute, or Sisal [*Freight*] ... CJS
Cotton Leaf Crumple [*Plant pathology*] ... CLC
Cotton Management Expert [*Computer program to improve crop production*] ... COMAX
Cotton Marketing Board [*Australia*] ... CMB
Cotton Mather [*Initials used as pseudonym*] ... CM
Cotton or Wool [*Freight*] ... CW
Cotton Piece Goods ... CPG
Cotton Plant - Fargo Railway Co. [*AAR code*] ... CPF
Cotton Public School, Cotton, MN [*Library symbol*] [*Library of Congress*] (LCLS) ... MnCotS
Cotton Research and Development Corporation (SAUO) ... CRDC
Cotton Research Corp. ... CRC
Cotton Research Corporation (SAUO) ... CRC
Cotton Seed ... CS
Cotton Seeds (SAUS) ... C/S
Cotton Silk [*Wire insulation*] (IAA) ... CS
Cotton, Silk and Man-Made Fibres Research Association (SAUO) ... CSMFRA
Cotton Stabilization Corp. [*New Deal*] ... CSC
Cotton States Life Ins [*NASDAQ symbol*] (TTSB) ... CSLI
Cotton States Life Insurance [*NASDAQ symbol*] (SAG) ... CSLI
Cotton States Life Insurance [*Associated Press*] (SAG) ... CtnSLf
Cotton Technological Research Laboratory (SAUO) ... CTRL
[*The*] **Cotton Textiles Export Promotion Council of India** (ECON) ... TEXPROCIL
Cotton Trade Organization (SAUO) ... CTO
Cotton Valley [*Vancouver Stock Exchange symbol*] ... CLY
Cotton Warehouse Association of America (EA) ... CWAA
Cotton Warehouse Inspection Service [*Defunct*] (EA) ... CWIS
Cotton Waste Reclamation Trade Board (SAUO) ... CWRTB
Cotton Waste Reclamation Trade Board (SAUS) ... CWRTB
Cotton Webbing (SAUS) ... COT WEB
Cottonian Manuscripts [*British Museum*] [*A publication*] (DLA) ... Cott Mss
Cotton's Abridgment of the Records [*A publication*] (DLA) ... Cot Abr
Cottonseed [*Freight*] ... COTNSD
Cottonseed Flour ... CF
Cottonseed Meal ... CSM
Cottonseed Oil (OA) ... CSO
Cottonseed Oil Assistance Program [*Department of Agriculture*] ... COAP
Cottonseed Protein Isolate ... CI
Cotton-Spot Macular Edema [*Medicine*] (MELL) ... CSME
Cottontail Rabbit Herpes Virus [*Veterinary science*] (DB) ... CRHV
Cottontail Rabbit Papillomavirus ... CRPV
Cottonwood [*California*] [*Seismograph station code, US Geological Survey*] (SEIS) ... CWC
Cottonwood, AZ [*AM radio station call letters*] ... KVRD
Cottonwood, AZ [*FM radio station call letters*] ... KVRD-FM
Cottonwood, AZ [*AM radio station call letters*] (RBYB) ... KYBC-AM
Cottonwood, AZ [*FM radio station call letters*] ... KZGL
Cottonwood, ID [*FM radio station call letters*] ... KNWO
Cottonwood Mountains [*California*] [*Seismograph station code, US Geological Survey*] (SEIS) ... CTW
Cottonwood Public Library, Cottonwood, AZ [*Library symbol*] [*Library of Congress*] (LCLS) ... AzCot
Cottonwood Public School, Cottonwood, MN [*Library symbol*] [*Library of Congress*] (LCLS) ... MnCtwPS
Cotton-Wool Exudate [*Ophthalmology*] (DAVI) ... CWE
Cotton-Wool Spot [*Ophthalomology*] (DAVI) ... CWS
Cottonwool Spot (SAUS) ... CWS
Cottony Blight [*of turf grass*] ... CB
Cotuit Library, Cotuit, MA [*Library symbol*] [*Library of Congress*] (LCLS) ... MCot
Cotulla, TX [*Location identifier*] [*FAA*] (FAAL) ... COT
Cotulla/Municipal [*Texas*] [*ICAO location identifier*] (ICLI) ... KCOT
C-O-Two Fire Equipment Co. (SAUO) ... C-O-Two
Coty, Inc. (SAUO) ... COT
Coty International Corporation (SAUO) ... CYI
Cotyledon [*Botany*] ... C
Cotyledon [*Botany*] ... Ct
Couch ... COU
Couch Potatoes [*Defunct*] (EA) ... CP
Couchant [*Heraldry*] (ADA) ... COUCH
Couchiching Institue on Public Affairs (AC) ... CIPA
Coudersport & Port Allegany [*AAR code*] ... CPA
Coudersport, PA [*AM radio station call letters*] ... WFRM
Coudersport, PA [*FM radio station call letters*] ... WFRM-FM
Couer d'Alene High School, Couer d'Alene, ID [*Library symbol*] [*Library of Congress*] (LCLS) ... IdCHS
Cougar Air, Inc. [*Canada*] [*ICAO designator*] (FAAC) ... CAJ

Cougar Club of America (EA) .... CCA
Cougar Club of America (EA) .... CCOA
Cougar Helicopter, Inc. [*Canada*] [*ICAO designator*] (FAAC) .... CHI
Cough [*Medicine*] C
Cough [*Medicine*] .... CGH
Cough and Deep-Breathe [*Medicine*] .... C & DB
Cough and Expectoration (MELL) .... C & E
Cough Frequency (MELL) .... CF.
Cough, Turn, and Deep Breathe [*Medicine*] .... CT & DB
Couhe/Verac [*France*] [*ICAO location identifier*] (ICLI) .... LFDV
Could .... CD
Could (ADA) .... CLD
Could [*Amateur radio shorthand*] (WDAA) .... CUD
Could Not Duplicate (ACAE) .... CND
Could Not Duplicate/Retest OK (SAUS) .... CND/RTOK
Could Not Test [*Laboratory*] (DAVI) .... CNT
Couldn't Be Cuter [*Slang*] .... CBC
Coulee Dam National Recreation Area (SAUS) .... CDNRA
Coulee Dam National Recreation Area .... CODA
Coulomb [*Symbol*] [*SI unit of electric charge*] C
Coulomb [*Unit of electric charge*] .... CB
Coulomb (SAUS) .... Cb
Coulomb [*Unit of electric charge*] .... COUL
Coulomb [*Unit of quality*] [*Electronics*] (WDAA) .... Q
Coulomb Blockade [*Physics*] .... CB
Coulomb Excitation [*Nuclear physics*] (OA) .... CE
Coulomb Explosion Imaging [*Nuclear physics*] .... CEI
Coulomb Meter (SAUS) .... CM
Coulomb Mutual Scattering (SAUS) .... CMS
Coulomb-Blockade Oscillations (SAUS) .... CBO
Coulomb-Mohr Criterion (SAUS) .... CMC
Coulombs per Cubic Meter .... C/M^3
Coulombs per Kilogram .... C/KG
Coulombs per Kilogram (SAUS) .... C/Kg
Coulombs per Square Meter (or Metre) (SAUS) .... C/my
Coulombs per Volt .... C/V
Coulomb-Volt (SAUS) CV
Coulometric .... Coul
Coulommiers/Voisins [*France*] [*ICAO location identifier*] (ICLI) .... LFPK
Coulsdon Library, Croydon, United Kingdom [*Library symbol*] [*Library of Congress*] (LCLS) .... UkCrC
Coulston and Forbes on Waters [*6th ed.*] [*1952*] [*A publication*] (DLA) .... Coul & F Wat
Coulter Counter [*Medicine*] (DMAA) CC
Coulter Diagnostics, Inc., Hialeah, FL [*Library symbol*] [*Library of Congress*] (LCLS) .... FHiaC
Coulter Pharmaceutical [*NASDAQ symbol*] (SG) .... CLTR
Council [*Australia*] C
Council (ADA) CL
Council (SAUO) Cl
Council (SAUO) .... Cncl
Council .... CNCL
Council (TBD) .... Cncl
Council .... COUN
Council (ROG) .... COUNC
Council (PROS) .... Counc
Council Accepted [*Medicine*] .... CA
Council Against Building Industry Nationalization (SAUO) .... CABIN
Council Against Cigarette Bootlegging (SAUO) .... CACB
Council Against Communist Aggression [*Later, CDF*] (EA) .... CACA
Council against Intolerance in America (SAUO) .... CAIA
Council Against Poverty (IIA) .... CAP
Council Agenda (SAUS) .... CA
Council, AK [*Location identifier*] [*FAA*] (FAAL) CIL
Council and Court of Examiners (SAUO) .... CCE
Council and International Education of Scholars (SAUO) .... CIES
Council Bluffs Free Public Library, Council Bluffs, IA [*Library symbol*] [*Library of Congress*] (LCLS) .... IaCb
Council Bluffs Free Public Library, Council Bluffs, IA [*OCLC symbol*] (OCLC) .... IWB
Council Bluffs, IA [*Location identifier*] [*FAA*] (FAAL) .... CBF
Council Bluffs, IA [*Television station call letters*] .... KBIN
Council Bluffs, IA [*FM radio station call letters*] .... KIWR
Council Bluffs, IA [*AM radio station call letters*] .... KLNG
Council Bluffs, IA [*FM radio station call letters*] .... KQKQ
Council Chambers [*Freemasonry*] (ROG) .... CO CH
Council Committee on Consumer Matters (SAUO) .... CCCM
Council Deputies (SAUO) .... DEPS
Council District Library, Council, ID [*Library symbol*] [*Library of Congress*] (LCLS) .... IdCnL
Council for a Beautiful Israel (EA) .... CBI
Council for a Black Economic Agenda (EA) .... CBEA
Council for a Competitive Economy (EA) .... CCE
Council for a Department of Peace (EA) .... CODEP
Council for a Livable World (EA) .... CLW
Council for a Livable World Education Fund (EA) .... CLWEF
Council for a Liveable Language (SAUO) CLL
Council for a Nuclear Weapons Freeze [*Later, IFLN*] (EA) .... CNWF
Council for a Secure America (EA) .... CSA
Council for a Tobacco-Free Ontario (AC) .... CTFO
Council for a Volunteer Military [*Defunct*] (EA) .... CVM
Council for Academic Freedom and Democracy [*British*] .... CAFD
Council for Accreditation in Occupational Hearing Conservation (EA) .... CAOHC
Council for Accreditation of Counseling and Related Educational Programs (AEE) .... CACREP
Council for Acupuncture [*British*] (DBA) .... CFA
Council for Adult and Experiential Learning (EA) .... CAEL
Council for Advancement and Support of Education (EA) .... CASE
Council for Advancement of Secondary Education [*Defunct*] (EA) .... CASE
Council for Affordable and Rural Housing (NTPA) .... CARH
Council for Agricultural and Chemurgic Research (EA) .... CACR
Council for Agricultural Planning and Development (SAUO) .... CAPD
Council for Agricultural Science and Technology (EA) .... CAST
Council for Aid to Education [*Formerly the Council for Financial Aid to Education*] (NFD) .... CAE
Council for Alternatives to Stereotyping in Entertainment [*Defunct*] (EA) .... CASE
Council for American Private Education (EA) .... CAPE
Council for Arms Control [*British*] (DBA) .... CAC
Council for Art Education (NTPA) .... CAE
Council for Basic Education (EA) .... CBE
Council for Better Business Bureaus (SAUO) .... CBBB
Council for Better Hearing and Speech Month (EA) .... CBHSM
Council for Biology in Human Affairs .... CBHA
Council for British Archaeology .... CBA
Council for British Plastics in Agriculture and Horticulture (SAUO) .... CBPAH
Council for Business and the Arts in Canada .... CBAC
Council for Cable Information [*Defunct*] (EA) CCI
Council for Career Planning [*Defunct*] (EA) .... CCP
Council for Chemical Research (EA) .... CCR
Council for Children with Behavioral Disorders (EA) .... CCBD
Council for Children's Television and Media (EA) .... CCTM
Council for Christian Education in Schools [*Australia*] .... CCES
Council for Christian Medical Work [*Later, CHH*] (EA) .... CCMW
Council for Christian Social Action [*Later, OCIS*] [*United Church of Christ*] .... CCSA
Council for Civil Liberties in Western Australia .... CCLWA
Council for Clinical Training [*Later, ACPE*] (EA) .... CCT
Council for Colored Affairs (SAUO) .... CCA
Council for Complementary Alternative Medicine [*British*] .... CCAM
Council for Computer Development [*British*] (NITA) .... CCD
Council for Computerized Library Networks (IID) .... CCLN
Council for Continuous Improvement CCI
Council for Court Excellence (EA) .... CCE
Council for Cultural Co-Operation [*Council of Europe*] (EY) CCC
Council for Dance Education and Training [*British*] .... CDET
Council for Democracy in Korea [*Defunct*] (EA) .... CDK
Council for Democracy in the Americas [*Defunct*] (EA) .... CDA
Council for Democratic and Secular Humanism (EA) .... CODESH
Council for Democratic Government [*Japan*] (ECON) .... CDG
Council for Disabled Children (AIE) .... CDC
Council for Distributive Teacher Education .... CDTE
Council for Early Childhood Professional Recognition (EA) .... CECPR
Council for Economic Advisors (AAGC) .... CEO
Council for Economic and Environmental Development (BARN) .... CEED
Council for Economic Development (SAUO) .... CED
Council for Economic Growth and Security [*Defunct*] .... CEGS
Council for Economic Mutual Assistance [*Also known as CMEA, COMECON*] [*Communist-bloc nations: Poland, Russia, East Germany, Czechoslovakia, Romania, Bulgaria, Hungary*] [*Dissolved 1991*] .... CEMA
Council for Education and Training in Youth and Community Work (AIE) .... CETYCW
Council for Education in Music and Arts (SAUO) .... CEMA
Council for Education in the Commonwealth (EAIO) .... CEC
Council for Education in World Citizenship [*British*] .... CEWC
Council for Education in World Citizenship (SAUO) .... CEWO
Council for Education on Electronic Media (NTCM) .... CEEM
Council for Education, Recruitment and Training for the Hotel Industry (SAUO) .... CERT
Council for Education Technology (SAUO) .... CET
Council for Educational Advance (SAUO) .... CEA
Council for Educational Advance [*British*] .... CEA
Council for Educational Development and Research (EA) .... CEDaR
Council for Educational Development and Research (SAUO) .... CEDAR
Council for Educational Diagnostic Services [*Council for Exceptional Children*] .... CEDS
Council for Educational Freedom in America (EA) .... CEFA
Council for Educational Technology [*London, England*] [*Telecommunications*] [*Information service or system*] (TSSD) .... CET
Council for Educational Technology for the United Kingdom (SAUO) .... CET
Council for Educational Technology for the United Kingdom (SAUO) .... CETUK
Council for Electronic Revenue Communication Advancement (NTPA) .... CERCA
Council for Elementary Science International (EA) .... CESI
Council for Energy Awareness (SAUO) .... CEA
Council for Energy Efficiency Development (WDAA) .... CEED
Council for Environmental Conservation (EAIO) .... CoEnCo
Council for Environmental Education [*British*] .... CEE
Council for Equal Rights in Adoption .... CERA
Council for European Studies (EA) .... CES
Council for Excellence in Government (EA) .... CEG
Council for Exceptional Children (EA) .... CEC
Council for Export Trading Companies [*Washington, DC*] (EA) .... CETC
Council for Exports to Latin America (SAUO) .... CELA
Council for Financial Aid to Education (EA) .... CFAE
Council for Fishing Vessel Safety (EA) .... CFVS
Council for Foreign Economic Policy (SAUO) .... CFEP
Council for Further Education (SAUO) .... CFE
Council for Health and Human Services Ministries (EA) .... CHHSM
Council for Health and Welfare Services, United Church of Christ [*Later, CHHSM*] (EA) .... CHWS

Council for Higher Education [*US and Israel*] ... CHE
Council for Higher Education Accreditation ... CHEA
Council for Holocaust Survivors with Disabilities (EA) ... CHSD
Council for Independent Archaeology (SAUO) ... CIA
Council for Independent Distribution [*Later, CPDA*] ... CID
Council for Independent School Aid (EA) ... CISA
Council for Indian Education (EA) ... CIE
Council for Industrial Organization (SAUO) ... CIO
Council for Industrial Research (SAUS) ... CSIR
Council for Industry and Higher Education (AIE) ... CIHE
Council for Inter-American Cooperation [*Later, NFTC*] ... CIAC
Council for Inter-American Security (EA) ... CIS
Council for Inter-American Security Foundation (EA) ... CISF
Council for Intercultural Studies and Programs [*Defunct*] (EA) ... CISP
Council for Interdisciplinary Communication in Medicine ... CIDCOMED
Council for Interinstitutional Leadership (EA) ... CIL
Council for International Business Risk Management (EA) ... CIBRM
Council for International Congresses of Entomology [*London, England*] (EA) ... CICE
Council for International Cooperation for the Exploitation of the Cosmos (SAUO) ... INTERCOSMOS
Council for International Economic Cooperation and Development (SAUO) ... CIECD
Council for International Exchange of Scholars (EA) ... CIES
Council for International Organizations of Medical Sciences (SAUO) ... COIMS
Council for International Organizations on Medical Sciences [*Geneva, Switzerland*] (EA) ... CIOMS
Council for International Progress in Management (EA) ... CIPM
Council for International Progress-American Branch (SAUO) ... CIP
Council for International Understanding (EA) ... CIU
Council for International Urban Liaison (EA) ... CIUL
Council for Intersocietal Studies (EA) ... CIS
Council for Jewish Education (EA) ... CJE
Council for Languages and Other International Studies [*Later, NCLIS*] (EA) ... CLOIS
Council for Latin America [*Later, COA*] ... CLA
Council for Lay Life and Work ... CLLW
Council for Learning Disabilities (EA) ... CLD
Council for Learning Resources in Colleges [*British*] ... COLRIC
Council for Liberal Learning [*Defunct*] (EA) ... CLL
Council for Library Training in East Africa (SAUO) ... CLTEA
Council for Livestock Protection [*Defunct*] (EA) ... CLP
Council for Management Education and Development (AIE) ... CMED
Council for Marketing and Opinion Research (NTPA) ... CMOR
Council for Medical Affairs (EA) ... CFMA
Council for Microphotography and Document Reproduction [*British*] (DIT) ... CMDR
Council for Microphotography and Document Reproduction (SAUO) ... MICROD
Council for Microphotography and Document Reproduction [*British*] ... MICRODOC
Council for Middle Eastern Affairs [*Defunct*] (EA) ... CMEA
Council for Military Aircraft Propulsion Standards ... CMAPS
Council for Military Aircraft Standards ... CMAS
Council for Mineral Technology (SAUO) ... MINTEK
Council for Museum Anthropology (EA) ... CMA
Council for Mutual Economic Aid (SAUO) ... CMEA
Council for Mutual Economic aid (SAUO) ... COMECON
Council for Mutual Economic Assistance (SAUO) ... CIMEA
Council for Mutual Economic Assistance [*Also known as CEMA, COMECON*] [*Communist-bloc nations: Poland, Russia, East Germany, Czechoslovakia, Romania, Bulgaria, Hungary*] [*Dissolved 1991*] [*Former USSR*] ... CMEA
Council for Mutual Economic Assistance [*Also known as CEMA, CMEA*] [*Communist-bloc nations: Poland, Russia, East Germany, Czechoslovakia, Romania, Bulgaria, Hungary*] [*Dissolved 1991*] ... COMECON
Council for National Academic Awards [*British*] ... CNAA
Council for National Cooperation in Aquatics (EA) ... CNCA
Council for National Parks [*British*] ... CNP
Council for National Research Initiatives ... CNRI
Council for Native American Indian Progress (EA) ... CNAIP
Council for Noncollegiate Continuing Education (EA) ... CNCE
Council for Noncollegiate Continuing Education Units ... CN-CEU
Council for Nordic Dental Students (SAUO) ... CNDS
Council for Nursing Centers (SAUO) ... CNC
Council for Old World Archaeology [*Defunct*] (EA) ... COWA
Council for Opportunity in Graduate Management Education [*Defunct*] (EA) ... COGME
Council for Overseas Colleges of Art, Science and Technology (SAUS) ... COCAST
Council for Overseas Colleges of Arts, Sciences, and TETOC [*British*] ... COCAST
Council for Partnership on Rice Research in Asia [*A consortium of agricultural research institutes*] ... CORRA
Council for Periodical Distributors Associations (EA) ... CPDA
Council for Philosophical Studies (EA) ... CPS
Council for Postgraduate Medical Education [*British*] (DI) ... CPME
Council for Postgraduate Medical Education in England and Wales (SAUO) ... CPMEEW
Council for Professional Education for Business [*Later, AACSB*] ... CPEB
Council for Professions Supplementary to the Medicine Act (SAUO) ... CPSM
Council for Progresssive Political Action (SAUO) ... CPPA
Council for Promoting Christian Unity (SAUO) ... CPCU
Council for Religion in Independent Schools (EA) ... CRIS
Council for Research in Music Education (EA) ... CRME
Council for Research on Turkish History [*Defunct*] (EA) ... CRTH
Council for Responsible Genetics (EA) ... CRG
Council for Responsible Nutrition (EA) ... CRN
Council for Rural Housing and Development (EA) ... CRHD
Council for Science and Society [*British*] ... CSS
Council for Science and Technological Information (HGAA) ... COSHTI
Council for Science and Technology [*Buenas Aires, Argentina*] ... CONICET
Council for Scientific and Industrial Research (SAUO) ... COSIR
Council for Scientific and Industrial Research. Bulletin [*A publication*] ... CSIR Bull
Council for Scientific and Industrial Research of India (SAUO) ... CSIRI
Council for Scientific and Industrial Research Organization (SAUO) ... COSIRO
Council for Scientific and Industrial Research Organizations (SAUO) ... CSIRO
Council for Scientific Policy ... CSP
Council for Sex Information and Education (EA) ... CSIE
Council for Small Industries in Rural Areas [*British*] ... COSIRA
Council for Small Industries in Rural Areas (SAUO) ... CSIRA
Council for Social and Economic Studies (EA) ... CSES
Council for Standards in Human Service Education ... CSHSE
Council for Technical Advancement (SAUO) ... CTA
Council for Technical Education and Training for Overseas Countries (BARN) ... CTETOC
Council for Technical Education and Training for Overseas Countries [*British*] ... TETOC
Council for Technological Advancement (EA) ... CTA
Council for Technology Education Associations (EA) ... CTEA
Council for Television Development [*Defunct*] ... CTD
Council for Tertiary Education in Scotland (AIE) ... CTES
Council for Textile Recycling (EA) ... CTR
Council for the Accreditation of Correspondence Colleges [*British*] ... CACC
Council for the Accreditation of Teacher Education [*British*] (DET) ... CATE
Council for the Advancement and Support of Education ... CASE
Council for the Advancement of Arab-British Understanding [*London, England*] ... CAABU
Council for the Advancement of Citizenship (EA) ... CAC
Council for the Advancement of Consumer Policy (EA) ... CACP
Council for the Advancement of Experimental Learning (SAUO) ... CAEL
Council for the Advancement of Hospital Recreation [*Defunct*] (EA) ... CAHR
Council for the Advancement of Science Writing (EA) ... CASW
Council for the Advancement of Small Colleges [*Later, CIC*] (EA) ... CASC
Council for the Advancement of Standards for Student Services/ Development Programs (EA) ... CAS
Council for the Advancement of the African People [*British*] ... CAAP
Council for the Advancement of the Psychological Professions and Sciences [*Later, AAP*] ... CAPPS
Council for the British Societies for Relief Abroad (DAS) ... COBSRA
Council for the Care of Churches [*British*] ... CCC
Council for the Care of Churches (SAUO) ... CCC
Council for the Central Laboratory of the Research Councils (SAUO) ... CCLRC
Council for the Co-ordination of International Congresses of Medical Sciences (SAUO) ... CCICMS
Council for the Defense of Freedom (EA) ... CDF
Council for the Development of Economic and Social Research in Africa [*Dakar, Senegal*] (EAIO) ... CODESRIA
Council for the Development of French in Louisiana (SAUO) ... CODOFIL
Council for the Disposition of the Dead (SAUO) ... CDD
Council for the Education and Training of Health Visitors (SAUO) ... CETHV
Council for the Education of the Partially Seeing (SAUO) ... CEPS
Council for the Education of the Partially Seeing [*Later, Division for the Visually Handicapped*] (EA) ... CEPS
Council for the Encouragement of Music and the Arts [*Later, Arts Council*] ... CEMA
Council for the Investigation of Fertility Control [*Obstetrics*] (DAVI) ... CIFC
Council for the National Interest [*Australia*] ... CNI
Council for the National Register of Health Service Providers in Psychology (EA) ... CNRHSPP
Council for the Preservation of Rural America (SAUO) ... CPRA
Council for the Preservation of Rural England (SAUO) ... COPRE
Council for the Preservation of Rural Wales (SAUO) ... CPRW
Council for the Principality [*British*] ... CP
Council for the Promotion of Agricultural Policy Research for the European Communities (SAUO) ... CAPREC
Council for the Promotion of Field Studies (SAUO) ... CPFS
Council for the Protection of Rural England (EAIO) ... CPRE
Council for the Protection of Rural Wales (EAIO) ... CPRW
Council for the Securities Industry [*Stock exchange*] [*London, England*] ... CSI
Council for the Securities Industry [*Levy*] [*British*] ... SCI
Council for the Single Mother and Her Child [*Australia*] ... CSMHC
Council for the Study of Mankind [*Defunct*] (EA) ... CSM
Council for Tobacco Research ... CTR
Council for Tobacco Research - USA (EA) ... CTR-USA
Council for UHF Broadcasting (EA) ... CUB
Council for Understanding Mental Illness [*Defunct*] [*Defunct*] (EA) ... CUMI
Council for Unified Research and Education [*Defunct*] (EA) ... CURE
Council for University Classics Departments (AIE) ... CUCD
Council for Urban Affairs [*Terminated, 1970*] ... CUA
Council for Visual Education (SAUO) ... CVE
Council for Voluntary Service [*British*] (WDAA) ... CVS
Council for Voluntary Welfare Work (SAUO) ... CVWW
Council for Voluntary Youth Service (AIE) ... CVYS
Council for Women in Independent Schools (EA) ... CWIS
Council for Women War Workers (SAUO) ... CWWW
Council for/of Arab Economic Unity (SAUO) ... CAEU
Council for/of Economic Mutual Assistance (SAUO) ... CEMA
Council, ID [*Location identifier*] [*FAA*] (FAAL) ... CQI
Council Moslem League [*Pakistan*] [*Political party*] ... CML

Council of 1890 College Presidents (EA) ... CCP
Council of Academic Societies (DAVI) ... CAS
Council of Academies of Engineering and Technological Sciences [*National Academyof Engineers*] ... CAETS
Council of Active Independent Oil and Gas Producers (EA) ... CAIOGP
Council of Administrators of Large Urban Public Libraries [*Canada*] ... CALUPL
Council of Administrators of Special Education (EA) ... CASE
Council of Adult Stutterers [*Later, NCS*] (EA) ... CAS
Council of Adult Stutterers (SAUO) ... CAS
Council of Advanced Programming (SAUS) ... CAP
Council of Affiliated Associations of Jewelers of America (EA) ... CAAJA
Council of Affiliated Marriage Enrichment Organizations [*Defunct*] (EA) ... CAMEO
Council of Affiliated Regional Radiation Oncology Societies (SAUO) ... CARROS
Council of AFL-CIO Unions for Scientific, Professional and Cultural Employees (SAUS) ... SPACE
Council of African Affairs (SAUO) ... CAA
Council of African Affairs (IIA) ... CAA
Council of African Organisations (SAUO) ... CAO
Council of Agriculture [*Queensland*] [*Australia*] ... COA
Council of Agriculture, Queensland [*Australia*] ... CA(Q)
Council of Air-Conditioning and Refrigeration Industry (EA) ... CARI
Council of American Artist Societies (EA) ... CAAS
Council of American Building Officials (EA) ... CABO
Council of American Chambers of Commerce in Europe [*Later, European Council of American Chambers of Commerce*] (EA) ... CACCE
Council of American Embroiderers (EA) ... CAE
Council of American Flag-Ship Operators (EA) ... CASO
Council of American Forensic Entomologists ... CAFE
Council of American Homeowners (EA) ... CAH
Council of American Indian Artists (EA) ... CAIA
Council of American Jewish Museums (EA) ... CAJM
Council of American Kidney Societies (SAUO) ... CAKS
Council of American Maritime Museums (EA) ... CAMM
Council of American Master Mariners (EA) ... CAMM
Council of American Official Poultry Tests (EA) ... CAOPT
Council of American Overseas Research Centers (EA) ... CAORC
Council of American Survey Research Organisations (SAUO) ... CASRO
Council of American Survey Research Organizations (EA) ... CASRO
Council of Arab Economic Unity ... CAEU
Council of Arab Ministers of Justice [*See also CMAJ*] [*Rabat, Morocco*] (EAIO) ... CAMJ
Council of Archives and Research Libraries in Jewish Studies (EA) ... CARLJS
Council of Archives New Brunswick [*Conseil des Archives du Nouveau-Brunswick*] (AC) ... CANB
Council of Association Attorneys (EA) ... CAA
Council of Associations of Developing Countries Producers-Exporters of Raw Material (SAUO) ... APEC
Council of Australian Food Technology Associations (SAUO) ... CAFrA
Council of Australian Governments (SAUO) ... COAG
Council of Australian Humanist Societies ... CAHS
Council of Australian Machine Tool and Robotics Manufacturers ... CAMTRON
Council of Australian Power Lifting Associations ... CAPLO
Council of Australian Public Abattoir Authorities ... CAPAA
Council of Australian Public Library Associations ... CAPLA
Council of Ballroom Dancing (SAUO) ... CBD
Council of Basic Education (SAUO) ... CBE
Council of Better Business Bureaus [*Arlington, VA*] (EA) ... CBBB
Council of Bible Believing Churches (EA) ... CBBC
Council of Bible Believing Churches in U.S.A. (EA) ... CBBC
Council of Biology Editors (EA) ... CBE
Council of Biology Editors (SAUO) ... Coun Biology Eds
Council of Black Architectural Schools [*Defunct*] (EA) ... COBAS
Council of Black Federal Employees (EA) ... COBFE
Council of British Ceramic Sanitaryware Manufacturers ... CBCSM
Council of British Cotton Textiles (DBA) ... CBCT
Council of British Fire Protection Equipment Manufactures (SAUO) ... CBFPEM
Council of British Geography (GEOI) ... COBRIG
Council of British Manufacturers and Contractors serving the Petroleum and Process Industries (SAUO) ... CBMPE
Council of British Manufacturers of Petroleum Equipment ... CBMPE
Council of Building Materials Manufacturers (COE) ... CBMM
Council of Building Materials Manufacturers (SAUO) ... CBMM
Council of Canadian Film Makers (SAUO) ... CCFM
Council of Canadian Filmmakers ... CCFM
Council of Canadian Personnel Associations ... CCPA
Council of Canadian Studies Programme Administrators ... CCSPA
Council of Canadians [*An association*] ... COC
Council of Canadians with Disabilities (SAUO) ... CCD
Council of Canning Association Executives [*Later, CFPAE*] (EA) ... CCAE
Council of Capital City Lord Mayors (SAUO) ... CCCLM
Council of Car Care Centers (EA) ... CCCC
Council of Caribbean Institutions for Development (SAUO) ... COUNCARID
Council of Chemical Association Executives (SAUO) ... CCAE
Council of Chemical Associations [*Defunct*] (EA) ... CCA
Council of Chief State School Officers (EA) ... CCSSO
Council of Churches ... CC
Council of Churches for Britain and Ireland (EAIO) ... CCBI
Council of Churches in/of Namibia (SAUO) ... CCN
Council of Churches on Lutheran Foundation in Southern Africa (SAUO) ... CCLF
Council of Churches, South Australia ... CCSA
Council of Citizens with Low Vision (EA) ... CCLV
Council of Citizens with Low Vision International (SAUO) ... CCLVI
Council of City Research and Information Libraries [*British*] (NITA) ... COCRIL
Council of Civil Service Unions [*British*] ... CCSU
Council of Colleges of Acupuncture and Oriental Medicine (NTPA) ... CCAOM
Council of Colleges of Arts and Sciences (EA) ... CCAS
Council of Commodity Control (SAUO) ... CCC
Council of Communication Management (EA) ... CCM
Council of Communication Societies [*Defunct*] (EA) ... CCS
Council of Community Blood Centers (EA) ... CCBC
Council of Community Churches [*Later, National Council of Community Churches*] (EA) ... CCC
Council of Community Health Services (SAUO) ... CCHS
Council of Community Mental Health Centers (DHP) ... CCMHC
Council of Community Services of New York State (SRA) ... CCSNYS
Council of Conservationists (EA) ... CC
Council of Conservative Citizens (EA) ... CCC
Council of Conservative Citizens (EA) ... CofCC
Council of Construction Employers [*Defunct*] (EA) ... CCE
Council of Consulting Organizations (EA) ... CCO
Council of Consumer Advisers ... CCA
Council of Container Carriers ... CCC
Council of Copper Exporting Countries (EBF) ... CIPEC
Council of County Territorial Associations [*British military*] (DMA) ... CCTA
Council of Cultural Ministers [*Australia*] ... CCM
Council of Dance Administrators (EA) ... CODA
Council of Deans (DAVI) ... COD
Council of Defence ... COD
Council of Defense and Space Industry Associations (SAUO) ... CODIA
Council of Defense and Space Industry Associations (EA) ... CODSIA
Council of Deliberation [*Freemasonry*] (ROG) ... CD
Council of Deputies (SAUO) ... CD
Council of Development Finance Agencies ... CDFA
Council of Disabled Persons, Victoria [*Australia*] ... CDV
Council of Drama in Education (AC) ... CODE
Council of Eastern Orthodox Youth Leaders of the Americas [*Defunct*] (EA) ... CEOYLA
Council of Economic Advisers [*to the President*] ... CEA
Council of Education of the Deaf [*Australia*] ... CED
Council of Educational Facility Planners (EA) ... CEFP
Council of Educational Facility Planners, International (EA) ... CEFPI
Council of Educational Facility Planners International (SAUO) ... EFPI
Council of Emergency Medicine Residency Directors (ADWA) ... CORD
Council of Emperor of East and West [*Freemasonry*] (ROG) ... C of EE & W
Council of Energy Resource Tribes (EA) ... CERT
Council of Engineering and Scientific Society (CIST) ... CESSE
Council of Engineering and Scientific Society Executives (EA) ... CESSE
Council of Engineering and Scientific Society Secretaries (SAUO) ... CESSS
Council of Engineering Associations (SAUO) ... CEA
Council of Engineering Institutions [*British*] ... CEI
Council of Engineering Society Secretaries [*Later, CESSE*] (EA) ... CESS
Council of Engineers and Scientists Organizations ... CESO
Council of Engineers and Scientists Organizations-West (SAUO) ... CESO-W
Council of Estonian Societies in Australia ... CESA
Council of Europe (NUCP) ... CE
Council of Europe ... COE
Council of Europe (SAUO) ... CoE
Council of Europe (SAUO) ... C of E
Council of Europe, Debates of the Consultative Assembly [*A publication*] (DLA) ... Eur Conslt Ass Deb
Council of Europe Resettlement Fund ... CERF
Council of European and Japanese National Shipowners Associations [*England*] (EAIO) ... CENSA
Council of European Industrial Federations (SAUO) ... CEIE
Council of European Industrial Federations ... CEIF
Council of European Municipalities ... CEM
Council of European Municipalities and Regions ... CEMR
Council of European National Librarians (TELE) ... CENL
Council of European National Top level domain Registries (SAUO) ... CENTR
Council of European National Youth Centres (SAUO) ... CENYC
Council of European National Youth Committees (EA) ... CENYC
Council of European Professional Informatics Societies (VERA) ... CEPIS
Council of European Regions (EAIO) ... CER
Council of European-American Associations [*Later, FEAO*] ... CEAA
Council of Families with Visual Impairment (EA) ... CFVI
Council of Fashion Designers of America (EA) ... CFDA
Council of Federal Libraries (AC) ... CFL
Council of Federated Jewish Organizations [*Defunct*] (EA) ... CFJO
Council of Federated Organization (SAUO) ... COFO
Council of Federated Organizations [*Also, CFO*] [*Defunct*] ... COFO
Council of Film Organizations (EA) ... CFO
Council of Fleet Specialists (EA) ... CFS
Council of Food Processors Association Executives (EA) ... CFPAE
Council of Foreign Affairs (SAUO) ... CFA
Council of Foreign Ministers ... CFM
Council of Forest Industries (AC) ... COFI
Council of Forest Industries of British Columbia, Vancouver, BC, Canada [*Library symbol*] [*Library of Congress*] (LCLS) ... CaBVaCF
Council of Forest Industries of British Columbia, Vancouver, British Columbia [*Library symbol*] [*National Library of Canada*] (NLC) ... BVACF
Council of Free Czechoslovakia (EA) ... CFC
Council of General Motors Credit Unions [*Warren, MI*] (EA) ... CGMCU
Council of Georgist Organizations (EA) ... CGO
Council of Geriatric Cardiology (NTPA) ... CGC
Council of Governing Bodies of Australian Zoos ... COBAZ
Council of Governments [*Voluntary organizations of municipalities and counties*] ... COG
Council of Governors Policy Advisors (EA) ... CGPA

Council of Graduate Schools (EA) .... CGS
Council of Graduate Schools in the United States (EA) .... CGSUS
Council of Graphological Societies (EA) .... COGS
Council of Growing Companies (NTPA) .... CGC
Council of Health Organizations .... COHO
Council of Higher Education Management Associations (SAUO) .... CHEMA
Council of Home Health Agencies and Community Health Services [*Later, NAHC*] .... CHHA/CHS
Council of Hotel and Restaurant Trainers (EA) .... CHART
Council of Housing Producers [*Defunct*] (EA) .... CHP
Council of Hungarian Associations in South Australia .... CHASA
Council of Hungarian Associations in Western Australia .... CHAWA
Council of Independent Black Institutions (EA) .... CIBI
Council of Independent Colleges (EA) CIC
Council of Independent Colleges and Universities of New Mexico (SAUO) .... CICUNM
Council of Independent Colleges in Virginia (SAUO) CICV
Council of Independent Kentucky Colleges and Universities (SAUO) .... CIKCU
Council of Independent Managers [*Milwaukee, WI*] (EA) .... CIM
Council of Indian Nations [*An association*] .... CIN
Council of Industrial Boiler Owners (EA) .... CIBO
Council of Industrial Design [*British*] .... CID
Council of Industrial Design [*British*] .... COID
Council of Industrial Design (SAUO) .... CoID
Council of Industrial Engineering Academic Department Heads (SAUO) .... CIEADH
Council of Industrial Federation of EFTA (SAUO) .... CIFEFTA
Council of Industrial Health (SAUO) .... CIH
Council of Infrastructure Financing Authorities (NTPA) .... CIFA
Council of Institute of Telecommunication Engineers .... CITE
Council of Institutional Investors [*Washington, DC*] (EA) CII
Council of Insurance Agents and Brokers (NTPA) .... CIAB
Council of Insurance Company Executives (NTPA) .... CICE
Council of Intellectual Disability Agencies [*Victoria*] [*Australia*] .... CIDA
Council of Intergovernmental Coordinators (EA) CIC
Council of International Civil Aviation .... CICA
Council of International Fellowship (EA) .... CIF
Council of International Fellowship-U.S.A. (EA) .... CIF-USA
Council of International Investigators (EA) CII
Council of International Law Associations (SAUO) .... CILA
Council of International Lay Associations [*Defunct*] (EA) .... CILA
Council of International Programs (EA) .... CIP
Council of International Socialistic Leagues (SAUO) .... CISOL
Council of International Trade Union Cooperation [*Sweden*] (EAIO) .... CITUC
Council of Iron Foundry Associations .... CFA
Council of Iron Producers [*British*] (BI) .... CIP
Council of Ivy Group Presidents (EA) .... CIGP
Council of Jewish Federations (EA) .... CJF
Council of Jewish Federations and Welfare Funds [*Later, CJF*] (EA) .... CJFWF
Council of Jewish Organizations in Civil Service .... CJO
Council of Jewish Organizations in Civil Service (EA) .... CJOCS
Council of Jewish Theatres (NTPA) .... CJT
Council of Jews from Germany [*British*] (EAIO) .... CJG
Council of Justice to Animals and Humane Slaughter Association (EAIO) .... CJA & HSA
Council of Labour and Defence (SAUO) .... CLD
Council of Landscape Architectural Registration Boards (EA) .... CLARB
Council of Large Public Housing Authorities (EA) .... CLPHA
Council of Latin American Airlines (SAUO) .... CLAA
Council of Law Reporting [*Australia*] .... CLR
Council of Law Reporting of New South Wales [*Australia*] .... CLRNSW
Council of Lebanese American Organizations (EA) .... CLAO
Council of Legal Education [*British*] .... CLE
Council of Legal Education (SAUO) .... CLE
Council of Library Association Executives (EA) .... CLAE
Council of Life Insurance Consultants (EA) CLIC
Council of Literary Magazines and Presses (EA) .... CLMP
Council of Local Education Authorities [*British*] (DET) .... CLEA
Council of Local Education Authorities/School Teacher Committee (AIE) .... CLEA/ST
Council of Logistics Management .... CLM
Council of Lutheran Church Men [*Defunct*] (EA) .... CLCM
Council of Lutheran Churches in Central America and Panana (SAUO) .... CONCAP
Council of Maritime Premiers [*See also CPMM*] [*Canada*] .... CMP
Council of Masajid of United States (EA) .... CMUS
Council of Mechanical Specialty Contracting Industries [*Later, ASC*] (EA) .... CMSCI
Council of Medical Specialty Societies (EA) .... CMSS
Council of Medical Staffs (MEDA) .... CMS
Council of Mennonite Colleges (EA) .... CMC
Council of Michigan Foundations (SRA) .... CMF
Council of Military Organization .... COMO
Council of Mining and Metallurgical Institutions [*British*] (EAIO) .... CMMI
Council of Ministers (SAUO) .... CM
Council of Ministers [*European Economic Commission*] (DLA) .... COM
Council of Ministers of Education of Canada (SAUO) .... CMEC
Council of Ministers of the European Communities (SAUO) .... CM
Council of Mortgage Lenders [*British*] (DBA) .... CML
Council of Motion Picture Organizations (SAUO) .... CMPO
Council of Motion Picture Organizations [*Defunct*] (EA) .... COMPO
Council of Motorcycle Clubs .... CMC
Council of Musculoskeletal Specialty Societies (ADWA) .... COMSS
Council of Music and Drama [*Queensland*] [*Australia*] .... CMD
Council of Muslim Communities of Canada (EAIO) .... CMMC
Council of Mutual Economic Aid (SAUO) .... CEMA
Council of Mutual Economic Cooperation (SAUO) .... COMECON
Council of Mutual Savings Institutions [*New York, NY*] (EA) .... CMSI
Council of Name Studies [*British*] (DBA) .... CNS
Council of National Library and Information Associations (EA) .... CNLIA
Council of National Library Associations [*Later, CNLIA*] (EA) .... CNLA
Council of National Organizations for Adult Education (EA) .... CNO-AE
Council of National Organizations for Children and Youth [*Later, NCOCY*] (EA) .... CNOCY
Council of National Representatives [*Of the International Council of Nurses*] (DAVI) .... CNR
Council of Nature Conservation Ministers [*Australia*] .... CNCM
Council of Nephrology Nurses and Technicians (NTPA) .... CNNT
Council of Nephrology Nurses and Technicians of the National Kidney Foundation (SAUO) .... CNNT
Council of Nephrology Social Workers (NTPA) .... CNSW
Council of Nordic Master-Craftsmen [*Oslo, Norway*] (EAIO) .... CNMC
Council of Nordic Teachers' Associations [*Copenhagen, Denmark*] (EAIO) .... CNTA
Council of North American Shipping Association (WPI) .... CONASA
Council of North Atlantic Shipping Associations [*Also, CONASA*] .... CNASA
Council of North Atlantic Shipping Associations [*Also, CNASA*] .... CONASA
Council of Nova Scotia Archives (AC) .... CNSA
Council of Nurse Practitioners (SAUO) .... CNP
Council of Oil-Importing Nations .... COIN
Council of Ontario Construction Associations (AC) .... COCA
Council of Ontario Universities (EDAC) .... COU
Council of Ontario Universities, Toronto, ON, Canada [*Library symbol*] [*Library of Congress*] (LCLS) .... CaOTCOU
Council of Ontario Universities, Toronto, Ontario [*Library symbol*] [*National Library of Canada*] (NLC) .... OTCOU
Council of Organisations for Relief Services Overseas (WDAA) .... CORSO
Council of Organizations Serving the Deaf [*Defunct*] (EA) .... COSD
Council of Oriental Organizations .... COO
Council of Outdoor Educators of Ontario (AC) .... COEO
Council of Pennsylvania State College and University Library Directors [*Library network*] .... COPSCAULD
Council of Petroleum Accountants Societies (EA) .... COPAS
Council of Philatelic Organizations (EA) .... COPO
Council of Planning Librarians (SAUO) .... COPL
Council of Planning Librarians (EA) .... CPL
Council of Polish Jews in Great Britain (SAUO) .... CPJGB
Council of Pollution Control Financing Agencies [*Defunct*] (EA) .... CPCFA
Council of Polytechnic Librarians [*British*] (NITA) .... COPOL
Council of Post Office Unions (SAUO) .... CPOU
Council of Prairie & Pacific University Libraries [*Formerly, Council of Prairie University Libraries*] (AC) .... COPPUL
Council of Presidents (EA) .... CP
Council of Principals (AIE) .... CP
Council of Professional Associations (SAUO) .... CPA
Council of Professional Associations on Federal Statistics (EA) .... COPAFS
Council of Professional Technological Societies (SAUO) .... CPTS
Council of Professions, New South Wales [*Australia*] .... CPNSW
Council of Profit Sharing Industries [*Later, PSCA*] (EA) .... COPSI
Council of Progress Associations of Victoria [*Australia*] .... CPAV
Council of Protestant Colleges and Universities [*Defunct*] (EA) .... CPCU
Council of Protocol Executives (EA) .... COPE
Council of Psychoanalytic Psychotherapists (EA) .... CPP
Council of Public Education [*Victoria*] [*Australia*] .... CPE
Council of Quality Pig Producers Associations (SAUO) .... CQPPA
Council of Regional Groups [*Association for Library Collections and Technical Services*] .... CRG
Council of Regional IT Associations (SAUO) .... CRITA
Council of Regional Networks for Genetic Services (HGEN) .... CORN
Council of Regional School Accrediting Commissions (EA) .... CORSAC
Council of Registered Engineers in Nigeria (SAUO) .... COREN
Council of Registered Engineers of Nigeria (SAUO) .... CREN
Council of Registrars [*Internet group*] .... CORE
Council of Rehabilitation Specialists (EA) .... CRS
Council of Relief Agencies Licensed for Operation in Germany [*Post-World War II*] .... CRALOG
Council of Religious Jewish Workers of America [*Defunct*] (EA) .... CRJWA
Council of Religious Volunteer Agencies (EA) .... CRVA
Council of Repertory Theatres [*British*] .... CORT
Council of Reprographics Executives [*Defunct*] (EA) .... CORE
Council of Research and Academic Libraries [*Library network*] .... CORAL
Council of Resident Stock Theatres (SAUO) .... CORST
Council of Resident Summer Theatres [*Defunct*] (EA) .... CORST
Council of Retail Distributors (SAUO) .... CRD
Council of Review Board [*Army*] .... CRB
Council of Sales Promotion Agencies [*New York, NY*] (EA) .... CSPA
Council of Savings and Loan Financial Corporations (EA) .... CSLFC
Council of Scientific and Industrial Research (SAUO) .... CISR
Council of Scientific and Industrial Research [*Information service or system*] [*South Africa*] (IID) .... CSIR
Council of Scientific and Technical Institutes (SAUO) .... CSTI
Council of Scientific Society Presidents (EA) .... CSSP
Council of Scottish Chambers of Commerce (SAUO) .... CSCC
Council of Scottish Clan Associations [*Later, COSCA*] (EA) .... CSCA
Council of Scottish Clans and Associations .... COSCA
Council of Scottish Local Authorities (SAUO) .... CSLA
Council of Sections and Affiliates Land Survey Division (SAUO) .... COSA
Council of Social Science Data Archives [*Defunct*] .... CSSDA
Council of Social Service [*British*] .... CSS
Council of Social Service (SAUO) .... CSS

Council of Social Service, Tasmania [*Australia*] .... COSST
Council of Social Welfare Ministers, National Secretariat [*Australia*] ..... CSWMNS
Council of Societies for the Study of Religion (EA) .... CSSR
Council of Societies in Dental Hypnosis [*Defunct*] (EA) .... CSDH
Council of Specialized Accrediting Agencies [*Defunct*] (EA) .... CSAA
Council of Spokane Area Libraries [*Library network*] .... COSAL
Council of State Administrators of Vocational Rehabilitation (EA) .... CSAVR
Council of State and Territorial Epidemiologists (EA) .... CSTE
Council of State Chambers of Commerce (EA) .... CSCC
Council of State Community Affairs Agencies (EA) .... COSCAA
Council of State Community Development Agencies (SAUO) .... COSCD
Council of State Community Development Agencies (NTPA) .... COSCDA
Council of State Governments (SAUO) .... COSG
Council of State Governments (EA) .... CSG
Council of State Governments, Lexington, KY [*OCLC symbol*] (OCLC) .... KSC
Council of State Governments, State Information Center, Lexington, KY [*Library symbol*] [*Library of Congress*] (LCLS) .... KyLxCS
Council of State Housing Agencies (EA) .... CSHA
Council of State Planning Agencies (COE) .... CSPA
Council of State Policy and Planning Agencies [*Later, CGPA*] (EA) .... CSPA
Council of State School Officers (SAUO) .... CSSO
Council of State Science Supervisors (EA) .... CSSS
Council of States [*An association*] .... COS
Council of Stock Theatres .... COST
Council of Student Personnel Associations in Higher Education [*Defunct*] .... COSPA
Council of Subject Teaching Associations (AIE) .... COSTA
Council of Subject Teaching Associations (AIE) .... CSTA
Council of Sustainable Vegetation Management (SAUO) .... CSVM
Council of Teaching Hospitals (EA) .... COTH
Council of Teaching Hospitals and Health Systems (DMAA) .... COTH
Council of Technical Examining Bodies [*British*] .... CTEB
Council of the Academy of Professional Reporters [*National Court Reporters Association*] .... CAPR
Council of the Alleghenies (EA) .... CA
Council of the Alternative Forces for Peace and Democracy in Ethiopia .... CAFPDE
Council of the American (SAUO) .... COA
Council of the Americas (SAUO) .... Co A
Council of the Americas (EA) .... CoA
Council of the Americas United States Inter-American Council (SAUO) .... COA
Council of the Americas/Fund for Multinational Management Education .... CoA/FMME
Council of the Brass and Bronze Ingot Industry (EA) .... CBBII
Council of the British Societies for Relief Abroad (SAUO) .... CBSRA
Council of the City of Sydney .... CCS
Council of the Duchy of Lancaster (SAUO) .... CDL
Council of the Entente .... Entente
Council of the European Communities .... CEC
Council of the Great City Schools (EA) .... CGCS
Council of the Haida Nation (AC) .... CHN
Council of the Institution of Civil Engineers (SAUO) .... CICE
Council of the Knights of the Red Cross (SAUO) .... CKRA
Council of the Knights of the Red Cross [*Freemasonry*] (ROG) .... CKRC
Council of the Living Theatre [*Defunct*] (EA) .... CLT
Council of the Museum of Victoria [*Australia*] .... CMV
Council of the Organization of American States [*OAS*] .... COAS
Council of the Printing Industries of Canada (HGAA) .... CPI
Council of the Southern Mountains [*Defunct*] (EA) .... CSM
Council of the State Library of Victoria [*Australia*] .... CSLV
Council of the Stock Exchange (SAUO) .... CSE
Council of the Thirteen Original States (EA) .... CTOS
Council of the World Poultry [*British*] .... CWP
Council of Tobacco Manufacturers of Great Britain and Ireland (SAUO) .... CTMGBI
Council of Tourism Associations of British Columbia [*Formerly, Tourism Industry Association of BC*] (AC) .... COTA
Council of Translators and Interpreters of Canada (SAUO) .... CTIC
Council of Travel and Tourism [*British*] (DBA) .... CTT
Council of Tree and Landscape Appraisers (EA) .... CTLA
Council of Underground Machinery Manufacturers [*British*] .... CUMM
Council of United States Universities for Rural Development in India .... CUSURDI
Council of United States Universities for Soil and Water Development in Arid andSub-Humid Areas .... CUSUSWASH
Council of University Classics Departments (WDAA) .... CUCD
Council of University Institutes for Urban Affairs [*Later, UAA*] (EA) .... CUIUA
Council of University Teaching Hospitals [*Defunct*] (EA) .... CUTH
Council of Urban Health Providers [*Defunct*] (EA) .... CUHP
Council of Urban Rebuilding Enterprises .... CURE
Council of Vehicle Associations (NTPA) .... COVA
Council of Veteran, Vintage and Thoroughbred Motor Clubs [*Australia*] .... CVVTMC
Council of Western European Union (IIA) .... CWEU
Council of Wisconsin Libraries [*Information service or system*] (IID) .... COWL
Council of Women Chiropractors [*Defunct*] (EA) .... CWC
Council of Women Citizens .... CWC
Council of World Organizations Interested in the Handicapped [*Later, ICOD*] (EA) .... CWOIH
Council of Writers Organizations (EA) .... CWO
Council of Young Israel Rabbis (EA) .... CYIR
Council Officer [*British*] (ROG) .... CO
Council on Abandoned Military Posts (SAUO) .... CAMP
Council on Access, Prevention and Interprofessional Relations (SAUO) .... CAPIR
Council on Accreditation of Nurse Anesthetists Educational Programs (PGP) .... CANAEP
Council on Accreditation of Services for Families and Children (EA) .... COA
Council on Adoptable Children (EA) .... COAC
Council on Advanced Programming .... CAP
Council on Aging .... COA
Council on Agricultural and Rural Development (SAUO) .... CARD
Council on Alcohol Policy (EA) .... CAP
Council on Alternate Fuels (EA) .... CAF
Council on American-Islamic Relations .... CAIR
Council on America's Military Past (EA) .... CAMP
Council on Anthropology and Education (SAUO) .... CA&E
Council on Anthropology and Education (EA) .... CAE
Council on Anxiety Disorders (EA) .... CAD
Council on Approved Student Education [*National Court Reporters Association*] .... CASE
Council on Arteriosclerosis of the American Heart Association (EA) .... CAAHA
Council on Atmospheric Sciences .... COAS
Council on Atmospheric Studies .... CAS
Council on Biological Sciences Information (DIT) .... CBSI
Council on Biological Sciences Information (SAUO) .... COBSI
Council on Botanical and Horticultural Libraries (EA) .... CBHL
Council on Broadcast Education [*Later, CEEM*] (NTCM) .... COBE
Council on Career Development for Minorities (EA) .... CCDM
Council on Certification of Nurse Anesthetists (EA) .... CCNA
Council on Children, Media, and Merchandising (NTCM) .... CCMM
Council on Chiropractic Education (EA) .... CCE
Council on Chiropractic Orthopedics (EA) .... CCO
Council on Chiropractic Physiological Therapeutics (EA) .... CCPT
Council on Chiropractic Physiological Therapeutics and Rehabilitation (NTPA) .... CCPTR
Council on Christian Unity (EA) .... CCU
Council on Clinical Classifications (HCT) CCC
Council on Clinical Optometric Care (EA) .... CCOC
Council on Competitiveness (EA) CC
Council on Competitiveness (EA) .... CoC
Council on Compulsive Gambling of New Jersey (EA) .... CCGNJ
Council on Consumer Information [*Later, ACCI*] (EA) CCI
Council on Cooperation in Teacher Education [*Defunct*] .... CCTE
Council on Cooperative College Projects [*Later, CCP*] (EA) .... CCCP
Council on Cooperative College Projects (SAUO) .... CCCP
Council on Dental Therapeutics (SAUS) .... CDT
Council on Documentation Research [*Defunct*] .... CDR
Council on Drug Abuse (AC) .... CODA
Council on Economic and Cultural Affairs [*Later, ADC*] [*Rockefeller Brothers Fund, Ford Foundation activity*] .... CECA
Council on Economic Policy [*Inactive*] .... CEP
Council on Economic Priorities (EA) .... CEP
Council on Economic Priorities Accreditation Agency (SAUO) .... CEPAA
Council on Economics and National Security [*Defunct*] (EA) .... CENS
Council on Education for Foreign Medical Graduates (BABM) .... CEFMG
Council on Education for Public Health (EA) .... CEPH
Council on Education in Professional Responsibility [*Later, CLEPR*] (EA) .... CEPR
Council on Education in the Geological Sciences .... CEGS
Council on Education of the American Medical Record Association (DAVI) .... COEAMRA
Council on Educational Finance [*National Education Association*] (AEBS) .... CEF
Council on Electrolysis Education (EA) .... CEE
Council on Employee Benefits (EA) .... CEB
Council on Employees Benefit Plans (SAUO) .... CEBP
Council on Energy Policy [*Proposed Presidential council*] .... CEP
Council on Engineering Laws [*Defunct*] (EA) .... CEL
Council on Environment, Employment, Economy, and Development (COE) .... CEEED
Council on Environmental Alternatives (EA) .... CEA
Council on Environmental Pollutants .... CEP
Council on Environmental Quality [*of Federal Council on Science and Technology*] [*Washington, DC*] .... CEQ
Council on Environmental Remediation (AAGC) .... CER
Council on Family Health (EA) .... CFH
Council on Federal Health Programs (DMAA) .... CFHP
Council on Fertilizer Application [*Defunct*] .... CFA
Council on Fine Art Photography (EA) .... CFAP
Council on Foreign Economic Policy [*Functions transferred to Secretary of State, 1961*] .... CFEP
Council on Foreign Relations (EA) .... CFR
Council on Foreign Relations and Royal Institute of International Affairs [*British*] .... CFRRIIA
Council on Foreign Relations, New York, NY [*Library symbol*] [*Library of Congress*] (LCLS) .... NNCFR
Council on Forest Engineering (EA) .... COFE
Council on Foundations (EA) .... CF
Council on Foundations [*Formerly the National Committee on Foundations and Trusts for Community Welfare*] (NFD) .... COF
Council on Foundations, New York, NY [*Library symbol*] [*Library of Congress*] (LCLS) .... NNCFo
Council on Gift Annuities [*Informal name for the American Council on Gift Annuities*] (NFD) .... CGA
Council on Governmental Ethics Laws (EA) .... COGEL
Council on Governmental Relations (EA) .... COGR
Council on Graduate Education for Administration in Nursing (SAUO) .... CGEAN
Council on Graduate Medical Education [*Department of Health and Human Services*] .... COGME
Council on Health Information and Education (EA) .... CHIE

Council on Health Research for Development [*Switzerland*] (ECON) .... COHRED
Council on Hemispheric Affairs (EA) .... COHA
Council on Higher Education in the American Republics [*Later, ICHE*] .... CHEAR
Council on Homosexuality & Religion [*Conseil de l'Homosexualite et la Region*] (AC) .... CHR
Council on Hotel, Restaurant and Institutional Education (SAUO) .... CHRIE
Council on Indoor Air Quality [*Environmental Protection Agency*] (EPAT) .... CIAQ
Council on Industrial Relations (SAUO) .... CIR
Council on Information Management (SAUO) .... CIM
Council on International and Public Affairs Program (EA) .... CIPA
Council on International Cooperation in the Study and Utilization of Outer Spac e .... INTERCOSMOS
Council on International Economic Policy [*Terminated, 1977*] .... CIEP
Council on International Educational Exchange (EA) .... CIEE
Council on International Nontheatrical Events (EA) .... CINE
Council on International Scientific and Technological Cooperation .... CISTC
Council on Interracial Books for Children (EA) .... CIBC
Council on Ionizing Radiation Measurements and Standards [*National Institute of Standards and Technology*] .... CIRMS
Council on Islamic Affairs (EA) .... CIA
Council on Law Enforcement Education and Training [*An association*] ..... CLEET
Council on Legal Education for Professional Responsibility (EA) .... CLEPR
Council on Legal Education Opportunity (EA) .... CLEO
Council on Library and Information Services (SAUO) .... COLIS
Council on Library Research (SAUO) .... CLR
Council on Library Resources (EA) .... CLR
Council on Library Resources Incorporated (SAUO) .... CLRI
Council on Library Technology (NITA) .... COLT
Council on Library-Media Technical-Assistants (EA) .... COLT
Council on Library/Media Technicians (AL) .... COLT
Council on Licensure, Enforcement and Regulation (NTPA) .... CLEAR
Council on Marine Resources and Engineering Development .... CMRED
Council on Medical Education - of the American Medical Association (EA) .... CME-AMA
Council on Medical Student Education Education in Pediatrics (SAUO) .... COMSEP
Council on Medical Television [*Later, HESCA*] (EA) .... CMT
Council on Medication and Hospitals (SAUO) .... CMEH
Council on Mind Abuse [*Canada*] .... COMA
Council on Multiemployer Pension Security [*Defunct*] (EA) .... COMPS
Council on Municipal Performance .... CMP
Council on Municipal Performance [*Defunct*] (EA) .... COMP
Council on National Literatures (EA) .... CNL
Council on Naturopathic Medical Education (EA) .... CNME
Council on Naturopathic Medicine (PGP) .... CNME
Council on Northern Resources Information Management (SAUO) .... CONRIM
Council on Nutritional Anthropology (EA) .... CNA
Council on Occupational Licensing [*Later, NCOL*] (EA) .... COL
Council on Ocean Law (EA) .... COL
Council on Oceanograhic Laboratory Directors [*Marine science*] (OSRA) .... COLD
Council on Oceanographic Laboratory Directors (USDC) .... COLD
Council on Optical Radiation Measurement .... CORM
Council on Optometric Education (EA) .... COE
Council on Packaging in the Environment (NTPA) .... COPE
Council on Peace, Disarmament and Security (SAUO) .... CPDS
Council on Peace Research in History (EA) .... CPRH
Council on Physical Therapy (SAUO) .... CPT
Council on Physics in Education (SAUO) .... CPE
Council on Plastics and Packaging in the Environment (EA) .... COPPE
Council on Podiatric Medical Education (EA) .... CPME
Council on Podiatry Education [*Later, CPME*] (EA) .... CPE
Council on Pollution and Environment (SAUO) .... COPE
Council on Population and Environment (EA) .... COPE
Council on Postal Suppression .... COPS
Council on Postsecondary Accreditation (EA) .... COPA
Council on Postsecondary Accreditation (DAVI) .... CPA
Council on Professional Certification (EA) .... CPC
Council on Professional Standards in Speech-Language Pathology and Audiology (EA) .... COPS
Council on Radio and Television (SAUO) .... CORT
Council on Regulatory and Information Management (SAUO) .... CRIM
Council on Rehabilitation Education (PGP) .... CORE
Council on Rehabilitation Education (EA) .... CRE
Council on Religion and International Affairs [*Later, CCEIA*] (EA) .... CRIA
Council on Religion and Law [*Defunct*] (EA) .... CORAL
Council on Religion and the Homosexual [*Defunct*] (EA) .... CRH
Council on Renal Nutrition (NTPA) .... CRN
Council on Research and Technology (EA) .... CORETECH
Council on Research in Bibliography, Inc. (DIT) .... CRB
Council on Resident Education in Obstetrics and Gynecology (EA) .... CREOG
Council on Roentgenology of the American Chiropractic Association (EA) .... CRACA
Council on School Administration [*Canada*] (AEBS) .... CSA
Council on Security and Cooperation in the Asia-Pacific (SAUO) .... CSCAP
Council on Size and Weight Discrimination (EA) .... CSWD
Council on Social Work Education (EA) .... CSWE
Council on Soil Testing and Plant Analysis (EA) .... CSTPA
Council on Southern Africa (EA) .... CSA
Council on Standards for International Educational Travel (EA) .... CSIET
Council on Student Travel [*Later, CIEE*] (EA) .... CST
Council on Superconductivity for American Competitiveness .... CSAC
Council on Synthetic Fuels (EA) .... CSF
Council on Tall Buildings and Urban Habitat (EA) .... CTBUH
Council on Technology Teacher Education (EA) .... CTTE
Council on Thai Studies .... COTS
Council on the Aging, New South Wales [*Australia*] .... COTANSW
Council on the Conservation of Antarctic Marine Living Resources (SAUO) .... CCAMLR
Council on the Continuing Education Unit [*Later, IACET*] (EA) .... CCEU
Council on the Study of Religion (EA) .... CSR
Council on Tribunals (SAUO) .... CT
Council on Undergraduate Research (EA) .... CUR
Council on Vocational Education .... COVE
Council on Wage and Price Stability [*Also, CWPS*] [*Abolished, 1981*] .... COWPS
Council on Wage and Price Stability [*Also, COWPS*] [*Abolished, 1981*] .... CWPS
Council on Women and the Church [*Later, JFW*] (EA) .... COWAC
Council on World Tensions [*Later, Institute on Man and Science*] (EA) .... CWT
Council on Youth Opportunity [*Disbanded 1971; functions taken over by Domestic Council and OMB*] .... CYO
Council Operations & Executive Committee (SAUO) .... COEC
Council Operations and Exercise Committee [*NATO*] .... COEC
Council Recycling Debate [*Australia*] .... CRR
Council Rock High School, Newtown, PA [*Library symbol*] [*Library of Congress*] (LCLS) .... PNtC
Council Situation Room [*NATO*] (NATG) .... CSR
Council to Save the Postcard [*Defunct*] (EA) .... CSP
Counciling .... CNCLNG
Councillor (ROG) C
Councillor (ODBW) .... Cllr
Councillor (WDAA) .... cllr
Councillor .... CLLR
Councillor (ADA) .... CLR
Councillor .... CNCLR
Councillor (SAUO) .... Cnclr
Councillor (ROG) .... COR
Councillor (ADA) .... CR
Councilor (ABBR) .... CNCLR
Counsel [*or Counseling or Counselor*] (AFM) .... CNSL
Counsel (PHSD) .... Cnsl
Counsel .... COL
Counsel (ADWA) .... coun
Counsel .... COUN
Counsel (PROS) .... couns
Counsel (ROG) .... CSL
Counsel and Care for the Elderly [*British*] .... CCE
Counsel Corp. [*Associated Press*] (SAG) .... Counsl
Counsel Corp. [*Toronto Stock Exchange symbol*] .... CXS
Counsel Corp. [*NASDAQ symbol*] (SAG) .... CXSN
Counsel Corp. [*NASDAQ symbol*] (TTSB) .... CXSNF
Counsel for Procurement Reform (AAGC) .... CPR
Counseling .... CNSLNG
Counseling and Assistance Center [*Military*] (NVT) .... CAAC
Counseling and Assistance Director [*Military*] (DNAB) .... CAAD
Counseling and Human Services Specialist (PGP) .... CHSS
Counseling and Personnel Services [*Educational Resources Information Center*] [*Information retrieval*] (AEBS) .... CAPS
Counseling and Student Services [*Educational Resources Information Center (ERIC) Clearinghouse*] [*University of North Carolina at Greensboro*] (PAZ) .... CG
Counseling and Testing Site .... CTS
Counseling at the Local Level [*Small Business Administration*] .... CALL
Counseling Effectiveness Rating Scale (EDAC) .... CERS
Counseling Practice Beliefs Inventory (EDAC) .... CPBI
Counseling Satisfaction Inventory [*Education*] .... CSI
Counseling Services Assessment Blank [*Test for counseling centers*] .... CSAB
Counseling-Orientation Preference Scale (EDAC) .... COS
Counselling (SAUS) .... CNSL
Counselling and Career Development Organisation [*British*] (AIE) .... CCDO
Counselling and Diagnosis in Dementia (SAUO) .... CANDID
Counselling Assistance to Small Enterprises [*Canada*] .... CASE
Counsellor (SAUS) .... Cnclr
Counsellor .... CNSLLR
Counsellor .... Cnsllr
Counsellor (SAUS) .... Coun
Counsellor (GEAB) .... couns
Counsellor of the Incorporated Society of Organ Builders [*British*] (DI) .... CISOB
Counsellors' Magazine [*1796-98*] [*A publication*] (DLA) .... Couns Mag
Counsellors Tandem [*NYSE symbol*] (SPSG) .... CTF
Counsellors Tandem Securities Fund [*Associated Press*] (SAG) .... CTF
Counsellors-Developers (SAUO) .... CD
Counselor .... CNSLNR
Counselor .... COUNS
Counselor Activity Inventory [*Guidance*] .... CAI
Counselor Advisor University Summer Education [*Department of Labor program*] .... CAUSE
Counselor Assessment Questionnaire [*Psychology*] (DHP) .... CAQ
Counselor Association (EA) .... CA
Counselor Behavior Evaluation Form (EDAC) .... CBE
Counselor Education and Supervision [*A publication*] (DHP) .... CES
Counselor Interview Competence Scale (EDAC) .... CICS
Counselor of Embassy (SAUS) .... CE
Counselor of Real Estate .... CRE
Counselor Preparation Comprehensive Examination (SAUO) .... CPCE
Counselor Rating Form (DHP) .... CRF
Counselor Structured .... CS
Counselor-in-Training [*for summer camps*] .... CIT
Counselors Association of Alcohol and Drug Abuse (DHP) .... CAADA
Count C
Count .... CNT
Count (NTIO) .... Ct
Count .... CT

Count - Double Count (MUGU) ... CDC
Count Attribute (SAUS) ... CA
Count Back Order and Sample Select [*Computer science*] ... CBOSS
Count Bus (SAUS) ... CB
Count Clock [*NASA*] (KSC) ... CTCL
Count Data (SAUS) ... CD
Count Dracula Fan Club (EA) ... CDFC
Count Dracula Society (EA) ... CDS
Count Enable (SAUS) ... CE
Count Field (SAUS) ... CF
Count Forward [*Computer science*] ... CF
Count in Process (SAUS) ... CIP
Count Key Data (SAUS) ... CKD
Count Median Diameter (MAE) ... CMD
Count Number and Punch Machine (SAUS) ... CNP Machine
Count on Losing this Sunday [*Humorous interpretation of NFL team name*] ... COLTS
Count Oriented Protocol (SAUS) ... COP
Count per Minute (MSA) ... CT/M
Count per Second (MSA) ... CT/S
Count Question Resolution (SAUS) ... CQR
Count Rate Meter (SAUS) ... crm
Count Rate Meter ... CRM
Count Reduction Technique [*Food bacteriology*] ... CRT
Count Register [*IBM Corp.*] (CIST) ... CTR
Count Register [*Computer science*] ... CX
Count Reserve (SAUS) ... CR
Count Reverse [*Computer science*] ... CR
Count Routine Applied to Zero Input [*Computer program*] ... CRAZI
Count Store (SAUS) ... CS
Count Strength Product ... CSP
Count, Time Data System (SAUS) ... CTDS
Count Zero Refill Trigger (SAUS) ... CZRT
Countdown [*Aerospace*] (AAG) ... CD
Countdown [*Credit card*] [*British*] ... CD
Countdown [*NASA*] (KSC) ... CTDN
Countdown and Status Receiving Station [*or System*] [*NASA*] (KSC) ... CASRS
Countdown and Status Transmission System [*NASA*] (KSC) ... CASTS
Countdown Clock [*Aerospace*] ... CDC
Countdown Demonstration Test [*NASA*] ... CDDT
Countdown Demonstration Test [*NASA*] ... CDT
Countdown Deviation Request [*Aerospace*] (AAG) ... CDR
Countdown Modification Request [*Aerospace*] (AAG) ... CMR
Countdown Sequence Timer [*Aerospace*] (IAA) ... CST
Countdown Time [*Aerospace*] ... CDT
Countdown Working Group [*NASA*] (KSC) ... CDWG
Counted Thread Society of America (EA) ... CTSA
Counter ... C
Counter (MDG) ... CNT
Counter (MSA) ... CNTR
Counter ... CT
Counter (KSC) ... CTR
Counter (WDMC) ... ctr
Counter Accelerometer Unit (MCD) ... CAU
Counter Air (MCD) ... CA
Counter Air Fighter (ACAE) ... CAF
Counter Air Operations (SAUO) ... CAO
Counter Air Operations Center (DNAB) ... CAOC
Counter and Decoder (SAUS) ... CAD
Counter Angle Deception Jammer [*Military*] (CAAL) ... CADJ
Counter Anti-Submarine Warfare (PDAA) ... CASW
Counter Artillery and Mortar RADAR Acquisition Simulation (MCD) ... CAMRAS
Counter Battery ... CB
Counter Battery Radar (SAUS) ... CBR
Counter Battery Staff Officer [*World War I*] [*Canada*] ... CBSO
Counter Bombardment [*British military*] (DMA) ... CB
Counter Control [*Military*] ... CNCT
Counter Control System (SAUS) ... CCS
Counter Current Flow Limit [*Nuclear energy*] ... CCFL
Counter Current Scrubber (EEVL) ... CCS
Counter Development Center (SAUS) ... CDEVC
Counter Display Unit (MCD) ... CDU
Counter Electrode (SAUS) ... CE
Counter Electromotive Cell ... CEM
Counter Electromotive Cell (MCD) ... CEMC
Counter Electromotive Force (MCD) ... CEMF
Counter Filling System ... CFS
Counter Flashing (SAUS) ... CFLG
Counter Flip-Flop [*Computer science*] ... CFF
Counter for Input/Output Buffer (SAUS) ... CIO Buffer
Counter Force (MCD) ... CF
Counter Force/Counter Value (CCCA) ... CF/CV
Counter Group Selector Entry (SAUO) ... CGSE
Counter Group Selector Entry (SAUO) ... Ctr Gr Sel Ent
Counter Group Selector Entry (SAUO) ... Ctr Gr Selr Ent
Counter Group Selector Exit (SAUO) ... CGS EX
Counter Group Selector Exit (SAUO) ... Ctr Gr Sel Ex
Counter Group Selector Exit (SAUO) ... Ctr Gr Selr Ex
Counter Improvised Nuclear Device Emergency Response [*British*] ... CINDER
Counter Infiltration - Counter Guerilla Concept and Requirement Plan (CINC) ... CIGCOREP
Counter Information Services [*British*] ... CIS
Counter Intelligence (SAUS) ... CIC
Counter Intelligence Center Corps School, Fort Holabird, Baltimore (SAUS) ... MdBCIC
Counter Intelligence Center Corps School, Fort Holabird, Baltimore, MD [*Library symbol*] [*Library of Congress*] (LCLS) ... MdBCIC
Counter Intelligence, Combat [*World War II*] ... CIC
Counter List Entry (SAUS) ... CLE
Counter List Printing Exit (SAUS) ... CLPE
Counter Logic (IAA) ... CL
Counter Low Observables (SAUS) ... CLO
Counter Measure Receiver (ACAE) ... CMR
Counter, n Stages [*Electronics*] (DEN) ... CT/N
Counter Position Exit (IAA) ... CPE
Counter Position Exit (SAUS) ... Ctr Pos Ex
Counter Read Back (SAUS) ... CRB
Counter Recoil-Operated Weapon Launcher [*Military*] (VNW) ... CROW
Counter Recovery Time ... CRT
Counter Register ... CR
Counter Rotating [*Aviation*] (PIPO) ... C/R
Counter Rotation (PDAA) ... CR
Counter Shift Register [*Computer science*] (IAA) ... CSR
Counter Technical Intelligence Activities (MCD) ... CTIA
Counter Tenor [*Music*] ... CTEN
Counter Timer ... CT
Counter Total Exit (SAUS) ... CTE
Counter Tube [*Electronics*] (IAA) ... CT
Counter Value (CCCA) ... CV
Counter Voltage ... CV
Counteracting Chromatographic Electrophoresis ... CACE
Counter-Agency for Sabotage and Espionage [*Military*] (DNAB) ... CASE
Counter-Air and Interdiction ... CAINT
Counter-Assault Tactical [*In television movie "C.A.T. Squad"*] ... CAT
Counterattack ... C/A
Counterattack (SAUS) ... C ATC
Counterattack (AABC) ... CATK
Counterbalance (KSC) ... CBAL
Counterbattery ... CBTRY
Counter-Battery Fire ... CBF
Counterbattery Intelligence Officer [*Army*] (AABC) ... CBIO
Counter-Battery Officer ... CBO
Counterbattery RADAR [*Military*] ... COBRA
Counter-Bombardment (SAUS) ... CB
Counterbore (KSC) ... CBORE
Counterbore (SAUS) ... CBR
Counterbore (SAUS) ... Ctbore
Counterbore Arbor [*Tool*] ... CBAR
Counterbore Cutter [*Tool*] (AAG) ... CBCU
Counterbore Other (SAUS) ... CBORE-O
Counterbore Other Side ... CBOREO
Counter-C3 (SAUS) ... CC3
Counter-Cast Tunnel Lighting Principle (SAUS) ... CCTLP
Counterclaim [*Legal shorthand*] (LWAP) ... C/CL
Counterclaim [*Legal term*] (ROG) ... COCLM
Counterclaim [*Legal term*] (DLA) ... COUNTCL
Counterclaim [*Legal term*] (ROG) ... CTRCLM
Counterclockwise ... CC
Counterclockwise (WGA) ... CCKW
Counterclockwise (NTIO) ... cckw
Counterclockwise (FAAC) ... CCLKWS
Counterclockwise (IDOE) ... ccw
Counterclockwise ... CCW
Counterclockwise ... CNTCLKWS
Counterclockwise (AFM) ... CNTCLKWZ
Counterclockwise Bottom Angular Down (OA) ... CCWBAD
Counterclockwise Bottom Angular Up (OA) ... CCWBAU
Counterclockwise Bottom Horizontal (OA) ... CCWBH
Counterclockwise Down Blast (OA) ... CCWDB
Counterclockwise Orbit [*Aviation*] (FAAC) ... CCLKOB
Counterclockwise Top Angular Down (OA) ... CCWTAD
Counterclockwise Top Angular Up (OA) ... CCWTAU
Counterclockwise Top Horizontal (OA) ... CCWTH
Counterclockwise Up Blast (OA) ... CCWUB
Counter/Counter-Countermeasure [*Military*] ... C/CCM
Counter-Countermeasures [*Military*] ... CCM
Counter-C^3 [*Command, Control, and Communications*] [*Pronounced "see-see-cubed"*] ... CC^3
Countercurrent ... CC
Countercurrent Chromatography ... CCC
Countercurrent Cooling Crystallization [*Tsukishima Kikai Co., Tokyo*] [*Chemical engineering*] ... CCCC
Countercurrent Decantation [*Engineering*] ... CCD
Countercurrent Digestion [*Ore leach process*] ... CCD
Countercurrent Distribution [*Analytical chemistry*] ... CCD
Counter-Current Distribution (SAUS) ... CCD
Countercurrent Electrophoresis [*Also, CE*] [*Analytical chemistry*] ... CCE
Countercurrent Electrophoresis [*Also, CCE*] [*Analytical chemistry*] ... CE
Countercurrent Electrophoresis [*Analytical chemistry*] (DAVI) ... CEP
Countercurrent Immunoelectrophoresis (PDAA) ... CCIE
Countercurrent Immunoelectrophoresis [*Immunology*] (DAVI) ... CIE
Counter-Double-Current Distribution [*Analytical chemistry*] ... CDCD
Counterdrill ... CDRILL
Counterdrill Other Side ... CDRILLO
Counterdrug (COE) ... cd
Counterdrug (COE) ... CD
Counterelectrophoresis [*Analytical chemistry*] ... CEP
Counterespionage ... CE
Counterfeit [*FBI standardized term*] ... CTFT
Counterfeiting (DLA) ... COUNTERF

Counterfeiting [*FBI standardized term*] ..... CTFG
Counterfeiting Intelligence Bureau [*International Chamber of Commerce*] [*British*] (CB) ..... CIB
Counterfire [*Military*] (AFM) ..... CF
Counterfire and Air Defense (MCD) ..... CF & AD
Counterfire Center(or Centre) (SAUS) ..... CFC
Counterfire Reference Grid (AABC) ..... CRG
Counterflashing [*Technical drawings*] ..... CFL
Counterflashing (MSA) ..... CFLG
Counterflow (SAUS) ..... CF
Counterflow Centrifugal Elutriation [*Analytical biochemistry*] ..... CCE
Counterflow Film Cooling ..... CFFC
Counterflow Reactor [*Chemical engineering*] ..... CFR
Counterflow Virtual Impactor [*Instrumentation*] CVI
Counter-Force Autonomous Surveillance & Targeting programme (SAUS) ..... C-FAST
Counterimmunoelectrophoresis [*Also, CIEP*] [*Analytical biochemistry*] ..... CIE
Counterimmunoelectrophoresis [*Also, CIE*] [*Analytical biochemistry*] ..... CIEP
Countering Attack Helicopter (MCD) ..... CATCH
Counterinsurgency (CINC) CI
Counterinsurgency (SAUS) ..... CINCGCY
Counterinsurgency (AABC) ..... CINSGCY
Counterinsurgency ..... COIN
Counterinsurgency and Special Activities (SAUS) ..... C&SA
Counterinsurgency Gas (SAUS) ..... CS Gas
Counterinsurgency Information Analysis Center (SAUO) ..... CINFAC
Counterinsurgency Information Analysis Center (ACAE) ..... COIN
Counterinsurgency Operations ..... COINOPS
Counterinsurgency Plan (CINC) ..... CIP
Counterinsurgency Research and Development System (MCD) ..... CIRADS
Counterinsurgency Support Office [*Army*] (VNW) ..... CSO
Counterinsurgency/Survival, Evasion, Resistance, and Escape (DNAB) ..... CI/SERE
Counterintelligence (MCD) CI
Counter-Intelligence (SAUO) CI
Counterintelligence (SAUS) ..... Co-Intel
Counterintelligence Analysis Detachment (SAUO) ..... CIAD
Counterintelligence Analysis Division [*DoD*] ..... CIAD
Counterintelligence and Investigative Activities [*Military*] ..... C & IA
Counterintelligence Branch (SAUO) ..... CIB
Counter-Intelligence Center (SAUS) CIC
Counterintelligence Corps [*Military*] CIC
Counterintelligence Detachment (SAUO) ..... CID
Counterintelligence Group [*Military*] ..... CIG
Counterintelligence Interrogation Center [*Military*] CIIC
Counterintelligence Operational Liaison (SAUO) ..... COL
Counterintelligence Periodic Summary (MCD) ..... CIPS
Counterintelligence Program [*FBI program carried out against political activists from 1956 to 1971*] ..... COINTELPRO
Counterintelligence Records Information System [*Army*] ..... CRIS
Counterintelligence Specialist (SAUS) ..... CI Sp
Counterintelligence Team (NVT) ..... CIT
Counterintelligence Working Party [*US Military Government, Germany*] ..... CIWP
Counterirritants (MELL) ..... CIs
Counter-Lock-Cord [*Tennis shoe technology*] [*Autry Industries, Inc.*] CLC
Countermarked ..... CM
Countermeasure ..... CM
Countermeasure Office [*of Harry Diamond Laboratories*] [*Military*] (RDA) ..... CMO
Countermeasures (AABC) ..... CTMS
Countermeasures [*JETDS nomenclature*] L
Countermeasures against Active Radar Missile Engagement (SAUS) ..... CARMEN
Countermeasures, Airborne Infrared ..... CAIR
Countermeasures and Deception [*RADAR*] ..... CM & D
Countermeasures and Test Directorate [*Army*] (RDA) ..... CMTD
Countermeasures and Weapon Systems Engagement Model programme (SAUS) ..... CAWSEM
Countermeasures Dispenser (MCD) ..... CMD
Countermeasures Dispenser Pod (SAUS) ..... CDP
Countermeasures Dispenser Set (MCD) ..... CDS
Countermeasures Dispenser Set (MCD) ..... CMDS
Countermeasures Dispenser System (SAUS) ..... CMDS
Countermeasures Duties (SAUS) ..... CMD
Countermeasures Evaluation (CAAL) ..... CME
Countermeasures Evaluation - Infrared and Optical ..... CERFIRO
Countermeasures Homing (CET) ..... CMH
Counter-Measures Homing (SAUS) ..... CMH
Countermeasures Internal Management System (PDAA) ..... CIMS
Countermeasures Launcher Modular System [*Navy*] (CAAL) ..... CLAMS
Countermeasures Penetrating Antiarmor Munitions (MCD) ..... CPAM
Countermeasures Precursor (SAUS) ..... CMP
Countermeasures Receiver System (SAUS) ..... CMRS
Countermeasures Receiving Set ..... CRS
Countermeasures Receiving System ..... CMRS
Countermeasures Related to Alcohol Safety on the Highway (SAUO) ..... CRASH
Countermeasures Response Optimisation (SAUS) ..... CRO
Countermeasures Set (MCD) ..... CMS
Countermeasures Set, Acoustic (NVT) ..... CSA
Countermeasures Subsystem (DWSG) ..... CMS
Countermeasures/Counter Countermeasures [*Army*] (RDA) ..... CM/CCM
Countermilitary Potential ..... CMP
Countermine/Counterintrusion Department [*Army*] (RDA) ..... CCID
Countermission Analysis (MCD) ..... CMA
Countermortar ..... CM
Countermortar Fire ..... CMF
Countermortar Intelligence Officer (SAUS) ..... CMIO
Countermortar Officer (SAUS) ..... CMO
Countermortar Radar (SAUS) ..... CMR
Countermortar RADAR ..... CMR
Counternarcotics [*Military*] (DOMA) ..... CN
Counternarcotics Center [*CIA-operated facility*] (MUSM) ..... CNC
Counternarcotics Command Management System [*Army*] (RDA) ..... CN/CMS
Counter-Obstacle Team [*Army*] (INF) ..... COT
Counter-Obstacle Vehicle [*Military*] (RDA) ..... COV
Counteroffer [*Legal shorthand*] (LWAP) ..... C/OFF
Counter-Operating Voltage ..... COV
Counterpart ..... COPART
Counterpart (SAUS) ..... co-part
Counterpart (ROG) ..... COPT
Counterpart [*Legal term*] (ROG) ..... CTRPT
Counterpart Alliance for Partnership Program (SAUO) ..... CAP
Counterpoint [*Music*] (ROG) ..... COPT
Counterpoint [*Music*] ..... CP
Counterpoint [*Music*] ..... CPT
Counterpoint (ADWA) ..... cpt
Counterpoise [*Electricity*] (IAA) ..... CP
Counterpoise (MSA) ..... CPSE
Counterpoise Aerial (or Antenna) (SAUS) ..... CA
Counter-Propaganda Directorate [*British*] ..... CPD
Counterpunch (KSC) ..... CPUNCH
Counter-Racism, Equal Opportunity [*Military*] (NVT) ..... CREO
CounterRADAR Measures ..... CRM
CounterRADAR Missile ..... CRM
Counterreconnaissance [*Army*] (IAA) ..... CRCN
Counterreconnaissance [*Army*] ..... CRECON
Counterreconnaissance (SAUS) ..... CRecon
Counterrevolutionary Organization on Salvation and Service (SAUO) ..... CROSS
Counter-Revolutionary Warfare [*British military*] (DMA) ..... CRW
Counter-Revolutionary Wing [*Special Air Service*] [*Military*] [*British*] ..... CRW
Counter-RISTA (SAUS) ..... C-RISTA
Counter-Rotating (SAUS) ..... C/R
Counter-Rotating Optical Wedge ..... CROW
Counter-Rotation [*or Rotating*] **Platform** (MHDB) ..... CRP
Counter-Sabotage (AABC) ..... CS
Countershaft [*Automotive engineering*] ..... CO/SHFT
Countershaft (MSA) ..... CTSHFT
Counter/Shift Register (SAUS) ..... C/SR
Countershocks ..... CS
countersigned (SAUS) ..... C/SGND
Countersink (WGA) ..... CK
Countersink [*Technical drawings*] ..... CS
Countersink [*Engineering*] (IAA) ..... CSINK
Countersink (KSC) ..... CSK
Countersink (ADWA) ..... csk
Countersink Cutter ..... CSCU
Countersink Other Side (SAUS) ..... CKOS
Countersink Other Side (SAUS) ..... CSK-O
Countersink Other Side ..... CSKO
Countersink Other Side ..... Csk-OS
Countersink this Side (SAUS) ..... CKTS
Countersniper Team [*Army*] (INF) ..... CST
Counterstamped [*Numismatics*] ..... CS
Countersunk ..... CTSK
Countersunk Head ..... CSKH
Countersunk Wood Screw (SAUS) ..... CWS
Countersurge Missile Mortar System (MCD) ..... COSMMOS
Countersurge Mortar System (MCD) ..... COSMOS
Counter-Target-Acquisition (MCD) ..... CTA
Counter-Targeting [*Navy*] (DOMA) ..... CTTG
Counter-Tenor [*Music*] C
Countertenor ..... Ct
Countertenor [*Music*] ..... CT
Counter-Terrorism (SAUS) ..... CT
Counterterrorist (ADA) ..... CT
Counterterrorist Joint Task Force [*Military*] ..... CTJTF
Counter-Terrorist Warfare (LAIN) ..... CTW
Counter/Timer Circuit [*Computer science*] ..... CTC
Counter-Timer Control ..... CTC
Counter-timer Input/Output (SAUS) ..... CIO
Countertrade [*Economics*] (IMH) ..... CT
Countervailing Duty [*Customs*] (FEA) ..... CVD
Counterweight ..... CNTRWT
Counterweight (AAG) ..... CTW
Counterweight (KSC) ..... CTWT
Counterweight (AAG) ..... C/W
Counterweight [*Automotive engineering*] ..... C/WT
Countess ..... CTS
Countess ..... CTSS
Counties (SAUO) ..... COS
Counties (Wales) ..... CW
Counting (KSC) ..... CTG
Counting Code (SAUS) CC
Counting Device ..... CD
Counting Fingers [*Also, FC*] ..... CF
Counting Machine (SAUS) ..... CM
Counting Operation (SAUS) ..... CO
Counting Rate (SAUS) ..... CR
Counting Switch ..... CS
Count-Key-Data Device [*Computer science*] ..... CKD
Count-Lea Strength Product (SAUS) ..... CSP
Countries and Peoples [*A publication*] ..... CP

Countries of the World [*A publication*] .... CW
Countries of the World and Their Leaders Yearbook [*A publication*] .... COW
Country C
Country .... CNTRY
Country (COE) .... CNTY
Country .... CO
Country (ROG) .... COU
Country (SAUO) .... Ct
Country (VRA) .... ctry
Country [*Online database field identifier*] .... CY
Country Analysis and Strategy Paper (SAUS) .... CASP
Country Analysis Strategy Paper [*Bureau of Inter-American Affairs*] [*Department of State*] .... CASP
Country and Democratic League (SAUO) .... CDL
Country and New Town Properties [*British*] .... CNTP
Country and Regional Specialist [*Navy*] (MCD) .... CARS
Country and Western [*Music*] .... C & W
Country, Area, or Regional Staff Officer [*Military*] (DNAB) .... CARSO
Country Assistance Strategy Statement [*Military*] (CINC) .... CASS
Country Bill [*Banking*] .... CB
Country, Bluegrass, Blues [*New York nightclub*] [*Later, CMGB & OMFUG*] .... CBGB
Country, Bluegrass, Blues, and Other Music for Uplifting Gourmandizers [*Formerly, CBGB*] [*New York nightclub*] .... CNGB & OMFUG
Country Bound Connection [*An association*] (EA) .... CBC
Country Bread Manufacturers' Association [*Western Australia*] [*Australia*] .... CBMA
Country Bread Manufacturers of Western Australia .... CBMWA
Country Business Patterns (journ.) (SAUS) .... CBP
Country Centres Project [*Australia*] .... CCP
Country Cheque [*Banking*] [*British*] CC
Country Clearing CC
Country Clearing Office .... CCO
Country Clearing Office (SAUO) .... CCO
Country Club CC
Country Club Hills Public Library District, Country Club Hills, IL [*Library symbol*] [*Library of Congress*] (LCLS) .... ICch
Country Club Hills Public Library District, Country Club Hills, IL [*Library symbol*] [*Library of Congress*] (LCLS) .... ICchP
Country Club Hotels [*British*] .... CCH
Country Code (AFM) CC
Country Connection [*Airline code*] [*Australia*] XL
Country Court Rule Committee (SAUO) .... CCRC
Country Cricket Club [*British*] (WA) CCC
Country Damage (MARI) .... C/D
Country Damage (SAUS) .... CD
Country Dance and Song Society of America (EA) .... CDSSA
Country Dance Society of America [*Later, CDSSA*] (EA) .... CDSA
Country Day School Headmasters Association of the United States (SAUO) .... CDSHA
Country Development Strategy Statement [*Agency for International Development*] .... CDSS
Country Economic Profiles [*I. P. Sharp Association Pty. Ltd.*] [*Australia*] [*Information service or system*] (CRD) .... CEP
Country Edition Fan Club [*Defunct*] (EA) .... CEFC
Country Experimental Laboratory (SAUO) .... CEL
Country Fire Authority (SAUO) .... CFA
Country Fire Fan Club (EA) .... CFFC
Country Gentlemen's Association [*British*] .... CGA
Country Grammar School [*British*] .... CGS
Country Handbooks [*A publication*] .... CH
Country Indicator Code [*Computer science*] (ACRL) CIC
Country Information Package (MCD) .... CIP
Country Intelligence Study (MCD) .... CIS
Country Joe and His All Star Band [*Pop music group*] .... CJASB
Country Joe and the Fish [*Pop music group*] .... CJF
Country Landowners' Association [*British*] .... CLA
Country Liaison Officer (SAUS) .... CLO
Country Liberal Party [*Australia*] (ADA) .... CLP
Country Library Service (SAUS) .... CLS
Country Life in America (journ.) (SAUS) .... Ctry Life Am
Country Life Library of Sport [*A publication*] .... CLLS
Country Living [*A publication*] CL
Country Logistics Improvement Program [*Air Force*] .... CLIP
Country Logistics Readiness Centers (SAUO) .... CLRCs
Country Marine Profile Database (SAUS) .... MARPRO
Country Mayors' Association [*New South Wales*] [*Australia*] .... CMA
Country Meatworks Association of New South Wales [*Australia*] .... CMANSW
Country Music [*Radio station format*] (WDMC) c
Country Music Association (EA) .... CMA
Country Music Disk Jockeys Association [*Defunct*] (EA) .... CMDJA
Country Music Fan Club [*Defunct*] (EA) .... CMFC
Country Music Foundation (EA) .... CMF
Country Music Foundation Library and Media Center, Nashville, TN [*Library symbol*] [*Library of Congress*] (LCLS) .... TNC
Country Music Guild of Australasia [*Australia*] .... CMGA
Country Music Showcase International (EA) .... CMSI
Country Music Television [*Cable-television system*] (WDMC) .... CMT
Country Music Television [*Cable-television system*] .... CMTV
Country Name [*Database terminology*] (NITA) .... CN
Country Name to Country Code (SAUO) .... CNCC
Country National Party [*Political party*] [*Australia*] .... CN
Country Nationalist Party [*Australia*] [*Political party*] .... CNP
Country Note (SAUS) .... CN
Country of Commencement [*Travel industry*] (TRID) .... COC
Country of Destination [*International trade*] (DCTA) .... COD
Country of Origin [*International trade*] (DCTA) .... COO
Country Party [*Political party*] [*Australia*] (BARN) .... CP
Country Party (SAUO) .... CP
Country Policy Programme [*Foreign trade*] [*British*] .... CPP
Country Potash, Oil and Wheat Country (SAUS) .... POW
Country Press Association (DGA) .... CPA
Country Press Association of New South Wales [*Australia*] .... CPANSW
Country Press Association of South Australia .... CPASA
Country Press Association of Western Australia .... CPAWA
Country Profile (ADA) .... CP
Country Progressive National Party [*Australia*] [*Political party*] .... CPN
Country Projection and Policy Analysis (SAUO) .... CPPA
Country Public Affairs Officer (SAUS) .... CPAO
Country Public Libraries Association, New South Wales [*Australia*] .... CPLANSW
Country Radio Broadcasters (EA) .... CRB
Country Regional Councils' Association of Western Australia .... CRCAWA
Country Representative .... CR
Country Representative/Freight Forwarder (AAGC) .... CR/FF
Country Shire Councils Association (SAUO) .... CSCA
Country Shires Association of Western Australia .... CSAWA
Country Standard Technical Order (MCD) .... CSTO
Country Star Rest Cv'A' Pfd [*NASDAQ symbol*] (TTSB) .... CAFEP
Country Star Restaurants [*NASDAQ symbol*] (TTSB) .... CAFE
Country Star Restaurants, Inc. [*NASDAQ symbol*] (SAG) .... CAFE
Country Star Restaurants, Inc. [*Associated Press*] (SAG) .... CtryStr
Country Support Team [*United Nations*] .... CST
Country Team [*Military*] (CINC) .... CT
Country War Agricultural Executive Committee (SAUO) .... CWAEC
Country Western (ADWA) .... C/W
Country Whence Consigned [*Shipping*] (DS) .... CWC
Country Wide Trans Svcs [*NASDAQ symbol*] (TTSB) .... CWTS
Country Wide Transport Services, Inc. [*Associated Press*] (SAG) .... CtryWTr
Country Wide Transport Services, Inc. [*NASDAQ symbol*] (SAG) .... CWTS
Country Women's Association .... CWA
Country Women's Council USA (EA) .... CWC
Country Wool Merchants Association [*British*] (BI) .... CWMA
Country Workshops, Inc. [*An association*] (EA) .... CWI
CountryBaskets [*Associated Press*] (SAG) .... CB
CountryBaskets [*NYSE symbol*] (SAG) .... GXA
CountryBaskets [*NYSE symbol*] (SAG) .... GXF
CountryBaskets [*NYSE symbol*] (SAG) .... GXG
CountryBaskets [*NYSE symbol*] (SAG) .... GXH
CountryBaskets [*NYSE symbol*] (SAG) .... GXI
CountryBaskets [*NYSE symbol*] (SAG) .... GXJ
CountryBaskets [*NYSE symbol*] (SAG) .... GXK
CountryBaskets [*NYSE symbol*] (SAG) .... GXR
CountryBaskets [*NYSE symbol*] (SAG) .... GXU
Countrybkts Australia Index Fd [*NYSE symbol*] (TTSB) .... GXA
Countrybkts France Index Fd [*NYSE symbol*] (TTSB) .... GXF
Countrybkts Germany Index Fd [*NYSE symbol*] (TTSB) .... GXG
Countrybkts Hong Kong Index Fd [*NYSE symbol*] (TTSB) .... GXH
Countrybkts Italy Index Fd [*NYSE symbol*] (TTSB) .... GXI
Countrybkts Japan Index Fd [*NYSE symbol*] (TTSB) .... GXJ
Countrybkts S.Africa Index Fd [*NYSE symbol*] (TTSB) .... GXR
Countrybkts UK Index Fd [*NYSE symbol*] (TTSB) .... GXK
Countrybkts US Index Fd [*NYSE symbol*] (TTSB) .... GXU
Country-Product-Dummy Method (SAUO) .... CPD
[*The*] **Country's Best Yogurt** [*Store franchise*] .... TCBY
Countryside .... CNTRYSD
Countryside Act [*Town planning*] [*British*] .... CA
Countryside Commission [*British*] CC
Countryside Commission for Scotland .... CCS
Countryside Council for Wales (GVA) .... CCW
Countryside Recreation Research Advisory Group [*British*] .... CRRAG
Countrywide [*ICAO designator*] (AD) .... MB
Countrywide Credit Indus [*NYSE symbol*] (TTSB) .... CCR
Countrywide Credit Industries, Inc. [*NYSE symbol*] (SPSG) .... CCR
Countrywide Credit Industries, Inc. [*Associated Press*] (SAG) .... CntCrd
Countrywide Holidays Association [*British*] (DBA) .... CHA
Countrywood Elementary School, Huntington Station, NY [*Library symbol*] [*Library of Congress*] (LCLS) .... NHsCE
Counts Palatine [*Rulers of historical region now part of Germany*] .... CO PAL
Counts per Hour .... CPH
Counts Per Inch (CDE) .... cpi
Counts per Minute .... C/M
Counts per Minute .... C/MIN
Counts per Minute (ABAC) .... cpm
Counts per Minute .... CPM
Counts per Minute (IDOE) .... NPM
Counts per Roentgen (SAUS) .... C/R
Counts per Second (DEN) .... CPS
Counts per Second (NASA) .... C/S
Counts per Second (IDOE) .... NPS
Count/Time Data System (IEEE) .... C/TDS
Countway Library of Medicine, Boston, MA [*Library symbol*] [*Library of Congress*] (LCLS) .... MBCo
County C
County (SAUO) C
County .... CNTY
County (AL) .... Cnty
County (ADWA) .... Co
County (VRA) .... co
County (EY) .... CO
County (SAUO) .... Co

County ... CT
County [*Board on Geographic Names*] ... CTY
County (ADWA) ... Cty
County (ADWA) ... Cy
County ... CY
county (SAUO) ... cy
County Administration Center (SAUO) ... CAC
County Advisory Officer (SAUS) ... CAO
County Agricultural Adviser (SAUO) ... CAA
County Agricultural Committee (BARN) ... CAC
County Agricultural Officer (SAUS) ... CAO
County Air Services Ltd. [*British*] [*ICAO designator*] (FAAC) ... CAK
County Alderman [*British*] ... CA
County Alderman (SAUO) ... CA
County and City Data Book [*Bureau of the Census*] (GFGA) ... CCDB
County and Intermediate Unit Superintendents (SAUO) ... CIUS
County and Regional Municipality Librarians (SAUO) ... CARML
County & Regional Municipality Librarians of Ontario (AC) ... CARML
County and Rural Area Superintendents (SAUO) ... CRAS
County Architect [*British*] ... CA
County Architects Society [*British*] (BI) ... CAS
County Attorney ... CA
County Bank of Chesterfield [*Associated Press*] (SAG) ... CBChest
County Bank of Chesterfield [*NASDAQ symbol*] (SAG) ... CBDC
County Bank of Chesterfield [*NASDAQ symbol*] (TTSB) ... CBOC
County Borough ... CB
County Borough (SAUO) ... CB
county borough (SAUO) ... cobor
County Borough Council (SAUO) ... CBC
County Borough Council [*British*] (ROG) ... CBC
County Borough of Wigan Public Libraries, Central Library, Wigan, United Kingdom [*Library symbol*] [*Library of Congress*] (LCLS) ... UkWg
County Boundary File [*Bureau of the Census*] (GFGA) ... CBF
County Business Patterns [*Bureau of the Census*] [*Information service or system*] [*A publication*] ... CBP
County Chasers of America (EA) ... CCA
County Circuit [*As in "CC Rider," i.e., a traveling preacher*] ... CC
County Clerk [*British*] (ROG) ... CC
County College of Morris, Dover, NJ [*Library symbol*] [*Library of Congress*] (LCLS) ... NjDC
County Comforts Organization (SAUO) ... CCO
County Commissioner ... CC
County Commissioners Association of Ohio (SRA) ... CCAO
County Commissioners Association of Pennsylvania (SRA) ... CCAP
County Constituency [*British*] ... CC
County Council [*or Councillor*] [*British*] ... CC
County Council (SAUO) ... CC
County Council [*British*] (ROG) ... CO COUNC
County Council Cases [*Scotland*] [*A publication*] (DLA) ... County Cc Cas
County Council Cases [*Scotland*] [*A publication*] (DLA) ... County Co Cas
County Council for District Nursing of London (SAUO) ... CCDNL
County Councilor (SAUO) ... CC
County Councils Association (SAUO) ... CCA
County Councils Association [*British*] (BI) ... CCA
County Counseling Center [*Psychology*] (DAVI) ... CCC
County Court ... CC
County Court (SAUO) ... CC
County Court Appeals [*A publication*] (DLA) ... CCA
County Court Cases [*England*] [*A publication*] (DLA) ... Co Ct Cas
County Court Judge (DLA) ... CCJ
County Court Practice (ILCA) ... CCP
County Court Reports [*Pennsylvania*] [*A publication*] (DLA) ... Co Ct Rep (PA)
County Court Rules (ILCA) ... CCR
County Courts [*Legal*] [*British*] ... COCTS
County Courts and Bankruptcy Cases [*A publication*] (DLA) ... County Cts & Bankr Cas
County Courts Branch (SAUO) ... CCB
County Courts Chronicle [*1847-1920*] [*England*] ... CCCHRON
County Courts Chronicle [*1847-1920*] [*England*] [*A publication*] (DLA) ... C Cts Chr
County Courts Chronicle [*1847-1920*] [*England*] [*A publication*] (DLA) ... Co Ct Ch
County Courts Chronicle [*1847-1920*] [*England*] [*A publication*] (DLA) ... Co Ct Chr
County Courts Chronicle [*1847-1920*] [*England*] [*A publication*] (DLA) ... Count Cts Ch
County Courts Chronicle [*1847-1920*] [*England*] [*A publication*] (DLA) ... Count Cts Chron
County Courts Chronicle [*1847-1920*] [*England*] [*A publication*] (DLA) ... County Cts Chron
County Courts Chronicle [*1847-1920*] [*England*] [*A publication*] (DLA) ... Cty Ct Chron
County Courts Reporter [*in Law Journal*] [*London*] [*A publication*] (DLA) ... CC Rep
County Courts Reports [*1860-1920*] [*England*] [*A publication*] (DLA) ... CCR
County Courts Reports [*1860-1920*] [*England*] [*A publication*] (DLA) ... Co Ct R
County Courts Reports [*1860-1920*] [*England*] [*A publication*] (DLA) ... Co Ct Rep
County Courts Reports [*1860-1920*] [*England*] [*A publication*] (DLA) ... County Cts Rep
County Courts Reports [*1860-1920*] [*England*] [*A publication*] (DLA) ... Cty Ct R
County Cricket Club (SAUO) ... CCC
County Designated Mental Health Professional (ROAS) ... CDMHP
County Development (SAUS) ... CD
County Donegal Joint Committee (SAUO) ... CDJC
County Down (SAUS) ... DWN
County Education Authority (SAUO) ... CEA
County Education Authority ... CEA
County Education District ... CED
County Education Officers' Society [*British*] ... CEOS
County Emergency Centre (SAUS) ... CEC
County Emergency Operations Center (DEMM) ... CEOC
County Emergency Planning Officers Society [*British*] ... CEPO
County Engineers Association of Ohio (SRA) ... CEAO
County Experimental Station (SAUO) ... CES
County Extension Service [*Agriculture*] ... CES
County Federation of Women Institutes (SAUO) ... CFWI
County Fermanagh (SAUS) ... FMH
County House of Corrections (SAUO) ... CHOC
County Intermediate Unit Superintendents [*of NEA*] [*Later, AASA*] (EA) ... CIUS
County Judge (GEAB) ... CJ
County Law Enforcement Applied Regionally ... CLEAR
County Links Access to Information about Resources and Expertise [*Education*] (AIE) ... CLAIRE
County Londonderry [*Northern Ireland*] ... CO DERRY
County Londonderry (SAUS) ... LDR
County Louth Archaeological and Historical Society (SAUO) ... CLAHS
County Louth Archaeological and Historical Society (SAUO) ... CLAS
County Medical Association (SAUO) ... CMA
County Medical Services (SAUS) ... CMS
County Military Commander (SAUS) ... CMC
County Military Headquarters (SAUS) ... CMHQ
County Milk Regulations Officer (SAUS) ... CMRO
County Naturalist Trust (SAUS) ... CNT
County of Carleton Law Library, Ottawa, Ontario [*Library symbol*] [*National Library of Canada*] (NLC) ... OOCCL
County of Henrico Public Library, Richmond, VA [*OCLC symbol*] (OCLC) ... VHP
County of London Regiment (Volunteers) [*British military*] (DMA) ... CLRV
County of London Yeomanry (SAUO) ... CLY
County of Londonderry (SAUO) ... Derry
County of Los Angeles Public Library ... CoLAPL
County of Strathcona Library, Sherwood Park, AB, Canada [*Library symbol*] [*Library of Congress*] (LCLS) ... CaASpS
County of Strathcona Library, Sherwood Park, Alberta [*Library symbol*] [*National Library of Canada*] (NLC) ... ASPS
County Office Manager ... COM
County Placita [*British*] (ROG) ... CO PLAC
County Planning Officer (SAUO) ... CPO
County Public Health Unit (DEMM) ... CPHU
County Quality Bacon Federation (SAUO) ... CQBF
County Registrars Office (BARN) ... CRO
County Reports [*A publication*] (DLA) ... County R
County Road Board (SAUO) ... CRB
County Road Board (SAUS) ... CRB
County Road Safety Officers' Association [*British*] (DBA) ... CRSOA
County Seat (ACAE) ... CS
County Situation Report [*Department of Emergency Management*] (DEMM) ... Co-SITREP
County Solid Waste Management Plan [*California*] (SARE) ... CSWMP
County Statistics [*Bureau of the Census*] (GFGA) ... CO-STAT
County Surveyor (SAUS) ... CS
County Surveyors Society [*British*] (DCTA) ... CSS
County War Agricultural Executive Committee (SAUS) ... CWAEC
County Warning Area [*Department of Emergency Management*] (DEMM) ... CWA
County Water Authority (SAUS) ... CWA
County/Coverage Service [*ISI audience data*] (NTCM) ... C/CS
Couny ... CNT
Coup sur Coup [*In Small Doses at Short Intervals*] [*French*] ... CSC
Coupe [*Automotive*] ... CP
Coupe [*Automotive*] (WGA) ... CPE
Coupe ... Cpe
Coupe Automatic [*Model designation of an automobile*] ... CA
Coupe Concept Vehicle [*Austin Rover*] ... CCV
Coupe Einspritz [*Coupe Fuel-Injection*] [*German*] ... CE
Coupe Sport [*Automotive*] ... CS
Coupe Sport Injection [*Automobile designation*] ... CSI
Coupe Sport Injection Automatic [*Automobile designation*] ... CSIA
Coupe Sport Leicht [*Automobile model designation*] [*German*] ... CSL
Couper's Judiciary Cases [*1868-85*] [*Scotland*] [*A publication*] (DLA) ... CJC
Couper's Justiciary Reports [*1868-85*] [*Scotland*] [*A publication*] (DLA) ... Cou
Couper's Justiciary Reports [*1868-85*] [*Scotland*] [*A publication*] (DLA) ... Coup
Couper's Justiciary Reports [*1868-85*] [*Scotland*] [*A publication*] (DLA) ... Couper
Couper's Justiciary Reports [*1868-85*] [*Scotland*] [*A publication*] (DLA) ... Coup Just
Coupeville, WA [*Location identifier*] [*FAA*] (FAAL) ... NRA
Couple (KSC) ... CPL
Couple Output (SAUS) ... CO
Couple to Couple League (EA) ... CCL
Couple to Couple League for natural family planning (SAUS) ... CCL
Couple Years Protection (SAUO) ... CYP
Coupled (SAUS) ... Cpld
Coupled (MSA) ... CPLD
Coupled Atmosphere/Ocean GCM (SAUS) ... A/OGCM
Coupled Atrial Pacing [*Medicine*] (DB) ... CAP
Coupled Biquad [*Electronics*] (OA) ... CB
Coupled Breeding Superheating Reactor ... CBSR
Coupled Cavity Structure (SAUS) ... CCS
Coupled Cavity Travelling Wave Tube (PDAA) ... CCTWT
Coupled Channel [*Electronics*] ... CC
Coupled Chermosphere-Ionosphere-Plasmasphere [*Model*] (USDC) ... CTIP
Coupled Climate Systems Program (SAUS) ... CCSP
Coupled Cluster [*Physical chemistry*] ... CC
Coupled Cluster Approach (MCD) ... CCA
Coupled Cluster Singles Doubles and Triples [*Physical chemistry*] ... CCSDT
Coupled Diffusion Control (MCD) ... CDC

Coupled Electron Pair Approach (SAUS) .... CEPA
Coupled Electron Pair Approximation [Physics] .... CEPA
Coupled Fast Reactivity Measurement Facility [Idaho Falls, ID] [Department of Energy] (NRCH) .... CFRMF
Coupled Fuselage-Aiming Mode (MCD) .... CFAM
Coupled General Circulation Model .... CGCM
Coupled Global Climate Model .... CGCM
Coupled Hartree-Fock [Quantum mechanics] .... CHF
Coupled Hydrosphere Atmosphere Research Model [Marine science] (OSRA) .... CHARM
Coupled Impedance Synthesis .... CIS
Coupled Load Analysis (ACAE) .... CLA
Coupled Microwave Plasma [Spectrometry] .... CMP
Coupled Mode Theory (PDAA) .... CMT
Coupled Model Intercomparison Project [Marine science] (OSRA) .... CMIP
Coupled Monostable Trigger Circuit [Electronics] (OA) ... CMTC
Coupled Ocean Atmosphere Mesoscale Prediction System [Marine science] (OSRA) .... COAMPS
Coupled Ocean-Atmosphere Processes and their Effect on Climate ..... COAPEC
Coupled Ocean-Atmosphere Response Experiment [Tropical Ocean-Global Atmosphere] (USDC) .... COARE
Coupled Ocean-Land-Atmosphere 1-Dimensional [Model] (USDC) COLA1D
Coupled Ocean-Land-Atmosphere One-Dimensional [Model] [Marine science] (OSRA) .... COCAID
Coupled Oceanographic and Atmospheric Model (SAUO) .... COAMPS
Coupled Optics and Flow Field Integration (MCD) .... COFFI
Coupled Oscillator (DEN) .... CO
Coupled Oscillator (SAUS) .... C-O
Coupled Quantum Wells (SAUS) .... CQW
Coupled Range-Finders .... CR
Coupled States [Physics] .... CS
Coupled to a Differential Synchro (ACAE) .... CDS
Coupled Vibration Dissociation (IEEE) .... CVD
Coupled Vibration Dissociation Process .... CVDP
Coupled Vibration Dissociation Vibration (IEEE) .... CVDV
Coupled-Cluster Singles and Doubles [Quantum chemistry] ... CCSD
Coupled-Pair Functional (MCD) .... CPF
Coupler (AAG) .... CPLR
Coupler (SAUS) .... Cplr
Coupler Cut-Through .... CCT
Coupler Electronics Unit .... CEU
Coupler Interface Unit (MCD) .... CIU
Couplers [JETDS nomenclature] [Military] (CET) .... CU
Couples, Inc. [An association] (EA) CI
Coupling .... CP
Coupling (KSC) .... CPLG
Coupling Between Object Classes (SAUS) .... CBO
Coupling Capacitor Potential Device (IEEE) .... CCPD
Coupling Capacitor Voltage Transformer .... CCVT
Coupling Control Unit .... CCU
Coupling Data Unit (MCD) .... CDU
Coupling Display Manual Control-Optics (SAA) .... CDCO
Coupling Display Optical Hand Controller (KSC) .... CDOH
Coupling Display Unit .... CDU
Coupling Display Unit - IMU [Inertial Measurement Unit] (SAA) ..... CDUM
Coupling Display Unit Optic (IAA) .... CDUO
Coupling, Energetics and Dynamics of Atmospheric Regions (SAUS) ... CEDAR
Coupling Factor [Cytology] .... CF
Coupling Multiplier (SAUS) .... CM
Coupon C
Coupon (ROG) .... COUP
Coupon (EBF) .... CP
Coupon (EBF) .... Cp
Coupon (ADWA) .... cp
Coupon (ADA) .... CPN
[With] Coupon [Commerce] (BARN) .... cum cp
Coupon Bond [Investment term] .... CB
Coupon Exchange Club [Commercial firm] (EA) .... CEC
Coupon Preparation Requirement (MCD) .... CPR
Coupon Reading and Marking Machine (MHDI) .... CRAMM
Coupon Under Book-Entry Safekeeping (EBF) .... CUBES
Coupons Attached [Business term] .... CA
Cour Canadienne de l'Impot [Tax Review Board - TRB] ... CCI
Cour de Cassation [Court of Appeal] [French] (DLA) .... Cass
Cour de Cassation [Court of Appeal] [French] .... C de CASS
Cour de Cassation, Assemblee Pleniere [France] .... Cass Ass Plen
Cour de Cassation, Chambres Reunies [France] (ILCA) ... Cass Ch Reun
Cour de Cassation, Commerciale [French] (ILCA) .... Cass Civ Com
Cour de Cassation, Commerciale [French] (ILCA) .... Cass Com
Cour de Cassation, Deuxieme Section Civile [French] (ILCA) ... Cass Cive 2e
Cour de Cassation, Premiere Section Civile [French] (ILCA) ... Cass Civ 1re
Cour de Cassation, Sociale [French] (ILCA) .... Cass Civ Soc
Cour de Cassation, Troisieme Section Civile [French] (ILCA) ... Cass Civ 3e
Cour du Banc de la Reine [Court of Queen's Bench] [Quebec] [Canada] (ILCA) .... CBR
Cour Internationale de Justice [International Court of Justice] ... CIJ
Cour Permanente d'Arbitrage [Permanent Court of Arbitration - PCA] [Hague, Netherlands] (EAIO) .... CPA
Cour Permanente de Justice Internationale [Permanent Court of International Justice] [Later, CIJ] .... CPJI
Cour Supreme du Canada [Supreme Court of Canada] (DLA) ... Can CS
Courage Stroke Network (EA) .... CSN
Courant [Of the Current Month] [French] .... CT
Courant Alternatif [Alternating Current] [French] ...... CA
Courant Continu [Direct Current] [French] CC

Courant Institute of Mathematical Sciences [New York University] [Research center] (RCD) .... CIMS
Courant-Friedrichs-Lewy criterion (SAUS) .... CFECFL
Courant-Isaacson-Rees [Method] .... CIR
Courant-Isaacson-Rees Method (SAUS) .... CIR Method
Courant-Snyder (SAUS) .... CS
Courchevel [France] [Airport symbol] (OAG) .... CVF
Courchevel [France] [ICAO location identifier] (ICLI) ... LFLJ
Courier .... COUR
[The] Courier [Code name for Robert W. Owen, participant in the Iran-Contra affair during the Reagan Administration] ... TC
Courier (SAUS) .... TC
Courier Air Service .... CAS
Courier and Periodicals Division [Later, UNESCO Publications and Periodicals] .... CPD
Courier and Transport Service Ltd. [British] .... CATS
Courier Corp. [Associated Press] (SAG) .... Courer
Courier Corp. [NASDAQ symbol] (NQ) .... CRRC
Courier, Digby, Nova Scotia [Library symbol] [National Library of Canada] (NLC) .... NSDC
Courier, Digby, NS, Canada [Library symbol] [Library of Congress] (LCLS) .... CaNSDiC
Courier Mail [Brisbane] [A publication] .... C Mail
Courier, Middletown, NJ [Library symbol] [Library of Congress] (LCLS) ... NjMiC
Courier Post, Cherry Hill, NJ [Library symbol] [Library of Congress] (LCLS) .... NjChCP
Courier Services, Inc. [ICAO designator] (FAAC) ...... CSD
Courier Time Server (SAUS) .... CTS
Courier Transfer Office [or Officer] .... CTO
Courier Transfer Station .... CTS
Courier-Journal & Louisville Times Co., Inc., Louisville, KY [Library symbol] [Library of Congress] (LCLS) ... KyLoC
Courier-Mail (Brisbane) [A publication] .... BCM
Courma-Rharous [Mali] [ICAO location identifier] (ICLI) ... GAGR
Courrier de la Nouvelle-Ecosse, Yarmouth, Nova Scotia [Library symbol] [National Library of Canada] (NLC) ... NSYC
Courrier de la Nouvelle-Ecosse, Yarmouth, NS, Canada [Library symbol] [Library of Congress] (LCLS) ... CaNSYC
Course C
Course .... CO
Course [Commonly used] (OPSA) .... COURSE
Course (AABC) .... CRS
Course [Postal Service standard] (OPSA) .... CRSE
Course .... CSE
Course [Ships] (CINC) .... CUS
Course Acquisition (ACAE) .... C/A
Course Administrative Data [DoD] .... CAD
Course Alignment .... CA
Course Alignment Servo .... CAS
Course Alignment Subsystem .... CASS
Course Alignment Unit .... CAU
Course and Curriculum Development (SAUS) .... CCD
Course and Distance Calculator (SAUS) .... cdc
Course and Distance Calculator [or Computer] .... CDC
Course and Speed Calculator [or Computer] .... CSC
Course and Speed Made Good over the Ground [Military] (NATG) ... CSG
Course and Speed Made Good through the Water [Military] (NATG) ... CSW
Course Angle [Navigation] C
Course Approval and Monitoring Form [Inner London Education Authority] [British] (AIE) .... CAMF
Course Author Language [Computer science] .... CAL
Course Automatic Gain Control (ACAE) .... CAGC
Course Change (SAUS) .... C/C
Course Content Improvement CCI
Course Corrected Shell (SAUS) .... CCS
Course Development and Student Administration/Registrar Keeping System (SAUO) .... CDSAR
Course Development in the Field of Telecommunications (SAUO) ... CODEVTEL
Course Deviation Indicator [Aviation] .... CDI
Course Finder 2000 [Test] (TMMY) CF2000
Course Generator .... CG
Course Heading [Aviation] (PIPO) .... CH
Course in Advanced Trauma Nursing (SAUO) .... CATN
Course Indicator (IEEE) CI
Course Invalid (NAKS) CI
Course Made Good [Navy] .... CMG
Course Made Good over the Ground [Military] (NVT) ... COG
Course Made Good through the Water [Military] (NATG) ... CTW
Course Measuring Unit (SAUS) .... CMU
Course Monitoring Tire [Tire testing] .... CMT
Course of Action Analysis [Military] .... COAA
Course of Construction [Insurance] .... COC
Course of Construction .... C of C
Course of Instruction [Military] .... COI
Course Optical Alignment Sight (NAKS) .... COAS
Course Ordered Transmitter .... COT
Course Pennant [Navy] [British] .... CO
Course per Gyro Compass [Navigation] .... CPGC
Course per Standard Compass .... Cpac
Course per Steering Compass (SAUS) .... Cpstgc
Course Record Book [Education] (AIE) .... CRB
Course Selection Guide (SAUS) .... CSG
Course Setting Bombsight .... CSBS
Course Severity Adjustment Factor [Tire testing] .... CSAF
Course Status Report .... CSR

Course Technology, Inc. [*Publishing*] .... CTI
Course Training Standard [*Air Force*] (AFM) .... CTS
Course Winner [*Horse racing*] C
Course Writing Facility (SAUS) .... CWF
Course/Acquisition Code (SAUS) .... C/A Code
Course-Line Computer [*Aviation*] (MCD) CLC
Course-of-Action [*Military*] .... COA
Courses by Newspaper (EDAC) .... CbN
Courses, Diplomas & Degrees (WDAA) .... CDD
Courses in the United Kingdom (SAUS) .... CORSUK
Courseware Authoring Language Generator [*Computer science*]
(MCD) .... CALGEN
Courseware Authoring Tools [*Stanford University computer software project*] .... CAT
Courseware Development (SAUO) .... CWD
Coursewriter [*IBM Corp. programming language*] .... CW
Court C
Court (SAUO) C
Court (DLA) .... COT
Court [*Commonly used*] (OPSA) .... COURT
Court (DD) .... Crt
Court (ADWA) .... crt
Court .... CRT
Court (SAUO) .... Crt
Court (SAUO) .... Ct
Court (ASC) .... Ct
Court (VRA) .... ct
Court .... CT
Court Appointed Special Advocates [*In association name National CASA Association*] .... CASA
Court Decisions, National Labor Relations Act [*A publication*] (DLA) .... Ct D
Court Decisions, National Labor Relations Act [*A publication*]
(DLA) .... Ct Dec NLRA
Court Druggist [*Foresters*] [*British*] (ROG) .... CD
Court Employment Project (EA) .... CEP
Court House .... CH
Court House [*British*] (ROG) .... CO HO
Court House Library, West Point, MS [*Library symbol*] [*Library of Congress*]
(LCLS) .... MsWpCt
Court Information Service [*South Australia*] .... CIS
Court Interpreters and Translators Association (EA) .... CITA
Court Journal and District Court Record [*A publication*]
(DLA) .... Court J & Dist Ct Rec
Court Library, Department of Justice, Yellowknife, Northwest Territories
[*Library symbol*] [*National Library of Canada*] (BIB) .... NWYC
Court Management Journal [*A publication*] (DLA) .... Ct Mgmt J
Court Martial (SAUO) .... CM
Court Martial Reports, Air Force Cases [*A publication*] (DLA) .... ACM
Court Martial Reports, Army Cases [*United States*] [*A publication*] (DLA) .... CM
Court Martial Reports, Citators and Indexes [*A publication*]
(DLA) .... CMR Cit & Ind
Court Martial Reports, Coast Guard Cases [*New York*] [*A publication*]
(DLA) .... CGCM
Court Martial Reports, Judge Advocate General of the Air Force
[*A publication*] (DLA) .... CMR JAG AF
Court Martial Reports, Judge Advocate General of the Armed Forces and United States Court of Military Appeals [*A publication*]
(DLA) .... CMR JAG & US Ct of Mil App
Court Martial Reports, Navy Cases [*A publication*] (DLA) .... NCM
Court of Appeal .... CA
Court of Appeal (SAUO) .... CtApp
Court of Appeal in Chancery [*England*] (DLA) .... Ch App
Court of Appeal in Chancery = Chancery Appeals (SAUO) .... ChApp
Court of Appeal Judgements (SAUS) .... APPL
Court of Appeal Reports (SAUS) .... Rep in CA
Court of Appeal Reports [*New Zealand*] [*A publication*] (DLA) .... Rep in CA
Court of Appeals for the District of Columbia Circuit (AAGC) .... CADC
Court of Appeals for the Federal Circuit [*Highest US patent court*] .... CAFC
Court of Appeals for the Federal Circuit (AAGC) .... Fed Cir
Court of Appeals Reports [*New Zealand*] [*A publication*] (DLA) .... CA
Court of Appeals Reports [*New Zealand*] [*A publication*] (DLA) .... Ct App NZ
Court of Appeals Reports [*New Zealand*] [*A publication*] (DLA) .... Ct Rep NZ
Court of Arbitration of Sport [*See also TAS*] [*Lausanne, Switzerland*]
(EAIO) .... CAS
Court of Arches [*England*] (DLA) .... Arch
Court of Arches [*England*] (DLA) .... CA
Court of Bankruptcy, Undischarged [*British*] .... CBU
Court of Chancery [*New Jersey*] (DLA) .... Ch
Court of Chancery (SAUO) .... Ch
Court of Civil Appeals, Dallas, TX [*Library symbol*] [*Library of Congress*]
(LCLS) .... TxDaCiA
Court of Claims .... CCLS
Court of Claims [*Renamed CAFC in 1992*] (AAGC) .... Ct Cl
Court of Claims .... CTCLS
Court of Claims Act (DLA) .... Ct Cl Act
Court of Claims Reports [*United States*] [*A publication*] (DLA) .... C Cl
Court of Claims Reports .... CCLSR
Court of Claims Reports [*New York*] [*A publication*] (DLA) .... Ct Cl NY
Court of Claims Rules [*A publication*] (DLA) .... Ct Cl R
Court of Claims Trial Division [*Defunct*] (AAGC) .... Ct Cl Trial Div
Court of Claims Trial Judge Opinion (AAGC) .... Ct Cl TJ Op
Court of Common Pleas .... CCP
Court of Common Pleas (SAUO) .... CCP
Court of Common Pleas (SAUO) .... CP
Court of Common Pleas (DLA) .... CP

Court of Common Pleas (DLA) .... Ct Com Pl
Court of Criminal Appeal (DLA) .... CCA
Court of Criminal Appeals [*England*] (DLA) .... Crim App
Court of Crown Cases Reserved [*England*] (DLA) .... CCR
Court of Customs and Patent Appeals .... CCPA
Court of Customs and Patent Appeals (DLA) .... Ct Cust & Pat App
Court of Customs and Patent Appeals Reports [*A publication*] (DLA) .... CA
Court of Customs Appeals (DLA) .... Ct Cust App
Court of Customs Appeals Reports [*1919-29*] [*A publication*] (DLA) .... CA
Court of Customs Appeals Reports [*1919-29*] [*A publication*] (DLA) .... Ct Cust App
Court of Divorce and Matrimonial Causes [*England*] (DLA) .... D
Court of Error [*Legal term*] (DLA) .... CT ERR
Court of Errors and Appeals [*New Jersey*] (DLA) .... Ct Err & App
Court of Errors and Appeals [*New Jersey*] (DLA) .... Ct Errors and App
Court of Errors and Appeals [*New Jersey*] (DLA) .... Ct of Er and Appeals
Court of Exchequer [*Scotland*] (DLA) .... CES
Court of Exchequer [*England*] [*Legal term*] (DLA) .... Ex
Court of Exchequer [*England*] [*Legal term*] (DLA) .... Exch
Court of Federal Claims (AAGC) .... CFC
Court of Federal Claims [*Formerly Claims Court*] (AAGC) .... COFC
Court of First Instance (BARN) .... CFI
Court of General Sessions (SAUO) .... CGS
Court of Honor [*Boy Scouts of America*] .... COH
Court of Industrial Relations [*Philippines*] .... CIR
Court of Industrial Relations (SAUO) .... CIR
Court of Inquiry (SAUO) .... COFI
Court of International Trade. Reports [*A publication*] (DLA) .... CIT
Court of International Trade. Rules [*A publication*] (DLA) .... CITR
Court of Justice .... COJ
Court of Justice of the European Communities .... CJ
Court of Justice of the European Communities (DLA) .... CJEC
Court of Justice of the European Communities (DLA) .... ECJ
Court of Justiciary (DLA) .... Ct Just
Court of Justiciary Cases (SAUS) .... SCJ
Court of Military Appeals .... CMA
Court of Military Appeals .... COMA
Court of Military Appeals Reports [*A publication*] (DLA) .... CMA
Court of Military Review (AFM) .... CMR
Court of Military Review (AFM) .... COMR
Court of Petty Sessions [*Australia*] .... CPS
Court of Probate .... CP
Court of Probate (SAUO) .... CP
Court of Quarter Sessions (SAUO) .... CQS
Court of Quarter Sessions [*Legal*] [*British*] (ROG) .... CQS
Court of Restitution Appeals (SAUO) .... CoRA
Court of Review Decisions, Ratcliffe and McGrath, New South Wales
(SAUS) .... R&McG Ct of Rev
Court of Session (WDAA) .... CS
Court of Session [*Scotland*] [*A publication*] (DLA) .... C Sess
Court of Session Cases [*Scotland*] [*A publication*] (DLA) .... C of S Ca
Court of Session Cases [*Scotland*] [*A publication*] (DLA) .... Court Sess Ca
Court of Session Cases [*Scotland*] [*A publication*] (DLA) .... CSC
Court of Session Cases [*Scotland*] [*A publication*] (DLA) .... Ct Sess Cas
Court of Session Cases [*Scotland*] [*A publication*] (DLA) .... SC
Court of Session Cases, Fifth Series [*Scotland*] [*A publication*]
(DLA) .... C of S Ca 5th Series
Court of Session Cases, First Series, by Shaw, Dunlop, and Bell [*Scotland*]
[*A publication*] (DLA) .... C of S Ca 1st Series
Court of Session Cases, Fourth Series, by Rettie, Crawford, and Melville
[*Scotland*] [*A publication*] (DLA) .... C of S Ca 4th Series
Court of Session Cases, House of Lords [*Scotland*] [*A publication*] (DLA) .... HHL
Court of Session Cases, House of Lords [*Scotland*] [*A publication*] (DLA) .... SCHL
Court of Session Cases House of Lords (SAUS) .... SCHL
Court of Session Cases (journ.) (SAUS) .... SC
Court of Session Cases, Second Series, by Dunlop, Bell, and Murray
[*Scotland*] [*A publication*] (DLA) .... C of S Ca 2d Series
Court of Session Cases, Third Series, by Macpherson, Lee, and Bell
[*Scotland*] [*A publication*] (DLA) .... C of S Ca 3rd Series
Court of Special Sessions [*Legal term*] (DLA) .... CT SPEC SESS
Court of Summary Jurisdiction [*British*] (ROG) .... CSJ
Court of the Lord Lyon (SAUO) CLL
Court Order (DLA) .... Ct/O
Court Physician (ROG) .... CP
Court Reporter (AABC) .... CTREPTR
Court Reporting Program [*Association of Independent Colleges and Schools specialization code*] .... CR
Court Reporting Typist .... CRT
Court Reports (SAUS) .... Sc LR
Court Rolls [*British*] .... CT
Court Rolls [*British*] (ROG) .... CT R
Court Rolls of Ramsey Abbey [*1928*] [*England*] [*A publication*] (DLA) .... Ault
Court Services Department [*South Australia*] .... CSD
Court Trust [*Includes executor, administrator, guardian*] [*Legal term*] (DLA) .... CT
Court Welfare Service (SAUO) .... CWRU
Courtauld's All-Purpose Simulator (IEEE) .... CAPS
Courtaulds Ltd. [*AMEX symbol*] (SPSG) .... COU
Courtaulds Ltd. [*Associated Press*] (SAG) .... Courtld
Courtaulds Ltd., Cornwall, ON, Canada [*Library symbol*] [*Library of Congress*]
[*Obsolete*] (LCLS) .... CaOCC
Courtaulds, plc ADR [*AMEX symbol*] (TTSB) .... COU
Courtauld's Rapid Extract, Sort, and Tabulate System (IEEE) .... CRESTS
Courtelary [*Switzerland*] [*ICAO location identifier*] (ICLI) .... LSZJ
Courtenay and District Museum, Courtenay, BC, Canada [*Library symbol*]
[*Library of Congress*] (LCLS) .... CaBCoM

Courtenay and District Museum, Courtenay, British Columbia [*Library symbol*] [*National Library of Canada*] (NLC) .... BCOM
Courtenay, BC [*AM radio station call letters*] .... CFCP
Courtenay, BC [*Television station call letters*] CHAN-4
Courtesy (CMD) .... Court
Courtesy .... CRTSY
Courtesy Announcement (NTCM) .... CA
Courtesy Copy (RALS) CC
Courtesy Flight (SAUS) .... CFLT
Courtesy Lamp [*Automotive engineering*] .... C/LP
Courtesy Motorboat Examination [*Coast Guard*] (IIA) .... CME
Courtesy Return Envelope (NFD) .... CRE
Courthouse (SAUS) .... CH
Courthouse .... Ct Ho
Courthouse (VRA) .... cths
Courthouse (SAUS) .... Cthse
Courtier .... CRTR
Court-Martial .... CM
Court-Martial Appeal Court of Canada .... CMAC
Court-Martial Appointing Order .... CMAO
Court-Martial, European Theater of Operations [*United States*] (DLA) .... CM-ETO
Court-Martial Forfeiture .... CMF
Court-Martial Index and Summary (DNAB) .... CMIS
Court-Martial Officer .... CMO
Court-Martial Orders [*Navy*] .... CMO
Court-Martial Report (AFM) .... CMR
Court-Material Orders .... CMO
Courtnay and Maclean's Scotch Appeals [*6, 7 Wilson and Shaw*] [*A publication*] (DLA) .... Cour & Macl
Courtnay and Maclean's Scotch Appeals [*6, 7 Wilson and Shaw*] [*A publication*] (DLA) .... Court & Macl
Courtney Foundation for the Welfare of Mother and Babies [*British*] .... WOMB
Court-Ordered Examination [*Medicine*] (MELL) .... COE
Courtroom Administrative Data Input [*National Court Reporters Association*] .... CADI
Courtroom Of The Future .... COTF
Courts [*Commonly used*] (OPSA) .... COURTS
Courts [*Postal Service standard*] (OPSA) .... CTS
Courts of London Sessions [*British*] (BARN) .... CLS
Courts of Survey (SAUO) .... C of S
Courtship Analysis [*Psychology*] .... CA
Courts-Martial Appeal Rules [*British military*] (DMA) .... CMAR
Courts-Martial (Appeals) Act [*British military*] (DMA) .... CMAA
Courtyard (VRA) .... ctyd
Courtyard .... c/y
Courvan Mining Co. Ltd. [*Toronto Stock Exchange symbol*] .... CVN
Courvoisier-Terrier [*Syndrome*] [*Medicine*] (DB) .... CT
Cous Creek Copper Mines [*Vancouver Stock Exchange symbol*] .... COK
Coushatta, LA [*AM radio station call letters*] .... KRRP
Coushatta, LA [*FM radio station call letters*] .... KSBH
Cousin (GEAB) c
Cousin C
Cousin (GEAB) .... cous
Cousin .... COUS
Cousin (ROG) .... COZ
Cousin [*Genealogy*] .... CSN
Cousins Mortgage and Equity Investors (SAUO) .... CUZ
Cousins Properties [*NYSE symbol*] (TTSB) .... CUZ
Cousins Properties, Inc. [*Associated Press*] (SAG) .... CousPr
Cousins Properties, Inc. [*NYSE symbol*] (SPSG) .... CUZ
Cousteau Society [*Established to Fund Marine Research*] (GNE) .... CS
[*The*] Cousteau Society (EA) .... TCS
Cout, Assurance, Fret [*Cost, Insurance, Freight - CIF*] [*Shipping*] [*French*] .... CAF
Cout et Fret [*Cost and Freight*] [*Shipping*] [*French*] .... C & F
Couterpoise Procedure [*Physical chemistry*] .... CP
Coutlee's Digest, Canada Supreme Court [*A publication*] (DLA) .... Cout Dig
Coutlee's Unreported Cases [*1875-1907*] [*Canada*] [*A publication*] (DLA) .... Cout
Coutlee's Unreported Cases [*1875-1907*] [*Canada*] [*A publication*] (DLA) .... Coutlee
Coutlee's Unreported Cases [*1875-1907*] [*Canada*] [*A publication*] (DLA) .... Coutlee Unrep (Can)
Coutts Public Library, Alberta [*Library symbol*] [*National Library of Canada*] (NLC) .... ACOU
Couvent des Ursulines, Quebec, PQ, Canada [*Library symbol*] [*Library of Congress*] (LCLS) .... CaQQU
Couvent des Ursulines, Quebec, Quebec [*Library symbol*] [*National Library of Canada*] (NLC) .... QQU
Covad Communications Grp [*NASDAQ symbol*] (SG) .... COVD
Coval Air Ltd. [*Canada*] [*ICAO designator*] (FAAC) CVL
Covalently Closed Circular [*Configuration of DNA*] [*Microbiology*] CCC
Covalently Closed Circular DNA [*Deoxyribonucleic Acid*] [*Genetics*] (DOG) .... cccDNA
Covance, Inc. [*NYSE symbol*] (SG) .... CVD
Covariance (DMAA) .... COV
Covariance (SAUS) CV
Covariance Analysis Describing-function Technique (SAUS) .... CADET
Covariance Analysis Program for the Study of Augmented Inertial Navigators (MCD) .... CAPTAIN
Covariance Structure Analysis (SAUS) .... CSA
Cove [*Maps and charts*] C
Cove CV
Cove Palisade State Park (SAUS) .... CPSP
Cove Resources [*Vancouver Stock Exchange symbol*] .... COV
Covefort [*Utah*] [*Seismograph station code, US Geological Survey*] (SEIS) .... CFU
Covenant .... COV

Covenant (GEAB) .... coven
Covenant (ROG) .... COVT
Covenant .... CVNNT
Covenant Bank for Savings [*NASDAQ symbol*] (SAG) .... CNSK
Covenant Bank for Savings [*Associated Press*] (SAG) .... CoventBk
Covenant Bank for Savings [*Associated Press*] (SAG) .... CovnB
Covenant Fellowship of Presbyterians (EA) .... CFP
Covenant House [*An association*] (EA) .... CH
Covenant of the Goddess (EA) .... COG
Covenant, the Sword and Arm of the Lord [*An association*] (EA) .... CSA
Covenant Theological Seminary, St. Louis, MO [*Library symbol*] [*Library of Congress*] (LCLS) .... MoSCT
Covenant Transport, Inc. [*Associated Press*] (SAG) .... Covenant
Covenant Transport, Inc. [*NASDAQ symbol*] (SAG) .... CVTI
Covenant Transport'A' [*NASDAQ symbol*] (TTSB) .... CVTI
Covenant Young Adults [*Defunct*] (EA) .... CYA
Covenanted [*Legal term*] (ROG) .... COVTD
Covenantee [*Legal term*] (ROG) .... COVTEE
Covenantor [*Legal term*] (ROG) .... COVTOR
Covenants, Conditions, and Restrictions (ROAS) .... CCR
Covenants, Conditions, Restrictions, and Reservations (MHDB) .... CCR & R
Covendo [*Bolivia*] [*ICAO location identifier*] (ICLI) .... SLVD
Covent Garden [*Royal Opera or Royal Ballet*] [*British*] .... CG
Covent Garden (SAUS) .... Cvt Gdn
Covent Garden Opera Company (SAUO) .... CGOC
Coventry [*City in England*] .... COV
Coventry [*England*] [*Airport symbol*] (OAG) .... CVT
Coventry [*British*] [*ICAO location identifier*] (ICLI) .... EGBE
Coventry and District Archaeological Society [*British*] (DBA) .... CADAS
Coventry and District Archaeological Society (SAUO) .... CADAS
Coventry and District Information Group (SAUO) .... CADIG
Coventry and Hughes' Digest of the Common Law Reports [*A publication*] (DLA) .... C & H Dig
Coventry and Hughes' Digest of the Common Law Reports [*A publication*] (DLA) .... Cov & H Dig
Coventry Climax [*Auto racing engine manufacturer*] [*British*] CC
Coventry. Common Recoveries [*1820*] [*A publication*] (DLA) .... Cov Rec
Coventry. Conveyancers' Evidence [*1832*] [*A publication*] (DLA) .... Cov Conv Ev
Coventry Corp. [*Associated Press*] (SAG) .... Coventry
Coventry Corp. [*NASDAQ symbol*] (SPSG) .... CVTY
Coventry Corp., Coventry, United Kingdom [*Library symbol*] [*Library of Congress*] (LCLS) .... UkCov
Coventry Health and Safety Movement (SAUO) .... CHASM
Coventry Management Training Centre (SAUO) .... CMTC
Coventry. Mortgage Precedents [*1827*] [*A publication*] (DLA) .... Cov Mort
Coventry Ordnance Works [*British military*] (DMA) .... COW
Coventry Radiator and Presswork Co. Ltd. (SAUO) .... Covrad
Coventry, RI [*FM radio station call letters*] .... WCVY
Coventry Ventures [*Vancouver Stock Exchange symbol*] .... CVQ
Cover (VRA) .... bv
Cover [*of a magazine*] C
Cover (MSA) .... COV
Cover (SAUS) .... Cov
Cover .... CVR
Cover (ADWA) .... cvr
Cover Aft .... CA
Cover and Deception (CINC) .... C & D
Cover and Deception, Direction, and Coordination .... C & DDAC
Cover and Deception, Direction, and Coordination (MCD) .... CDDAC
Cover and Removal Mechanism (ACAE) .... CRM
Cover, Artillery Protection [*Military*] (PDAA) .... CAP
Cover Collectors Circuit Club (EA) CCCC
Cover Collectors Club (EA) .... CoCo
Cover Forward .... CF
Cover Gas Clean-Up System [*Nuclear energy*] (NUCP) .... CGCS
Cover Gas Evaluation Loop [*Nuclear energy*] (NRCH) .... CGEL
Cover Gas Monitoring Subsystem [*Nuclear energy*] (NRCH) .... CGMS
Cover Layer Assembly (KSC) .... CLA
Cover Layer Automated Design (MHDI) .... CLAD
Cover Note [*Insurance*] .... CN
Cover Page (SAUS) .... CPE
Cover Paper and Board [*Printing*] (DGA) .... CP & B
Cover Plate (SAUS) .... CovPl
Cover Point [*Cricket*] (ROG) .... COV PT
Cover Point [*Lacrosse position*] .... CP
Cover Screen [*Medicine*] (DAVI) .... CS
Cover Test [*Ophthalmology*] .... CT
Cover Your Anatomy [*Military, government slang*] [*Bowdlerized version*] .... CYA
Cover Your Anatomy with Paper [*Military, government slang*] [*Bowdlerized version*] .... CYAWP
Coverage .... CVGE
Coverage Analysis (SAUS) .... CA
Coverage Evaluation (SAUS) .... COVEVL
Coverage Exercise (MUGU) .... COVEX
Coverage Factor [*Environmental science*] (COE) .... CF
Coverage Improvement (SAUS) .... COVIMP
Coverage Line Inventory Profile (SAUS) .... CLIP
Cover-All Technologies [*Associated Press*] (SAG) .... CoverAll
Cover-All Technologies [*NASDAQ symbol*] (SAG) .... COVR
Covered (VRA) .... bv
Covered (WDAA) C
Covered (SAUS) .... COV
Covered .... COVD
Covered Button Association of New York (EA) .... CBANY
Covered Carriage Trucks [*British railroad term*] .... CCT

Covered Conductors Association [*British*] (BI) .... CCA
Covered Conductors Association (SAUO) .... CCA
Covered Hopper [*Freight*] .... CVRD HPR
Covered Lighter [*Self-propelled*] [*Navy symbol*] .... YF
Covered Lighter [*Non-self-propelled*] [*Navy symbol*] .... YFN
Covered Lighter (Range Tender) [*Self-propelled*] [*Navy symbol*] .... YFRT
Covered Lighter (Repair) [*Navy symbol*] [*Obsolete*] .... YRL
Covered Lighter (Special Purpose) [*Later, YFNX*] [*Navy symbol*] .... YFNG
Covered Lighters (SAUS) .... YF
Covered Option [*Investment term*] .... CO
Covered Option Securities (EBF) .... COPS
Covered Pedestrian Space .... CPS
Covered Radio Teletype (NVT) .... CRATT
Covered Threads Association [*Defunct*] (EA) .... CTA
Covered-Back Paper (SAUS) .... CB-paper
Covered-Front Paper (SAUS) .... CF-Paper
Covering .... COVER
Covering Fire Mine (MCD) .... CFM
Covering Force (MCD) .... CF
Covering Force Area (AABC) .... CFA
Covering-Fire Mine (SAUS) .... CFM
Coverings, Facing, or Floor [*Freight*] .... COVFF
Coverplate (SAUS) .... Cov Pl
Covers [*JETDS nomenclature*] [*Military*] (CET) .... CW
Coversed Sine [*Mathematics*] .... Covers
Covert Active Modular Electro-Optical System (MCD) .... CAMEO
Covert All-Weather Gun System .... CAWGS
Covert & Operational Procurement Exhibition (SAUS) .... COPEX
Covert Camera Spy [*System*] .... CCS
Covert Communications .... COCO
Covert Communications Radio System (ACAE) .... COCORADS
Covert Elementary School, Elmont, NY [*Library symbol*] [*Library of Congress*] (LCLS) .... NElmoCE
Covert Entrepreneurial Organization [*Term used by Carl S. Taylor in his book on street gangs, Dangerous Society*] .... CEO
Covert Family Association (EA) .... CFA
Covert Investigation [*Police term*] CI
Covert Local Area Sensor System for Intrusion Classification (LAIN) .... CLASSIC
Covert Passive Air Defense Sensors (ACAE) .... CPADS
Covert Penetration Radar (SAUS) .... CPR
Covert Penetration System (SAUS) .... CPS
Covert Programmable Authentication Signaling System (ACAE) .... COPASS
Covert Strike Radar (SAUS) .... CSR
Covert Submarine Transmitter and Receiver (MCD) .... CO-STAR
Covert Survivable in Weather Reconnaissance and Strike [*Military*] (DOMA) .... COSIRS
Covert Viewing System .... CVS
Coves [*Commonly used*] (OPSA) .... COVES
Coves .... CVS
Covilha [*Portugal*] [*ICAO location identifier*] (ICLI) .... LPCV
Covina Public Library, Covina, CA [*Library symbol*] [*Library of Congress*] (LCLS) .... CCov
Covina Public Library, Covina, CA [*OCLC symbol*] (OCLC) .... CVP
Covington [*Diocesan abbreviation*] [*Kentucky*] (TOCD) .... COV
Covington & Burling, Washington, DC [*OCLC symbol*] (OCLC) .... DCO
Covington & Burling, Washington, DC [*Library symbol*] [*Library of Congress*] (LCLS) .... DCov
Covington Friend, Attica, IN [*Library symbol*] [*Library of Congress*] (LCLS) .... InAttCF
Covington, GA [*Location identifier*] [*FAA*] (FAAL) .... VOF
Covington, GA [*AM radio station call letters*] .... WGFS
Covington, IN [*FM radio station call letters*] .... WCDV
Covington, IN [*FM radio station call letters*] .... WFOF
Covington, IN [*FM radio station call letters*] (BROA) .... WKZS-FM
Covington, KY [*AM radio station call letters*] .... WCVG
Covington, KY [*Television station call letters*] .... WCVN
Covington, KY/Cincinnati, OH [*Location identifier*] [*FAA*] (FAAL) .... CVG
Covington, LA [*AM radio station call letters*] .... WASO
Covington, PA [*FM radio station call letters*] .... WDKC
Covington Public Library, Covington, IN [*Library symbol*] [*Library of Congress*] (LCLS) .... InCov
Covington, TN [*Location identifier*] [*FAA*] (FAAL) .... COO
Covington, TN [*AM radio station call letters*] .... WKBL
Covington, TN [*FM radio station call letters*] .... WKBL-FM
Covington, VA [*FM radio station call letters*] .... WIQO
Covington, VA [*AM radio station call letters*] .... WKEY
Covington/Cincinnati, OH [*Location identifier*] [*FAA*] (FAAL) .... JDP
Covington/Cincinnati, OH [*Location identifier*] [*FAA*] (FAAL) .... SIC
Covington/Cincinnati, OH [*Location identifier*] [*FAA*] (FAAL) .... URN
Cow Castle Creek [*South Carolina*] [*Seismograph station code, US Geological Survey*] (SEIS) .... COW
Cow Head Public Library, Cow Head, NF, Canada [*Library symbol*] [*Library of Congress*] (LCLS) .... CaNfCH
Cow Head Public Library, Newfoundland [*Library symbol*] [*National Library of Canada*] (NLC) .... NFCH
Cow Lung Lavage (STED) CLL
Cow Observers Worldwide [*An association*] (EA) .... COW
Cow Parsnip Mosaic Virus [*Plant pathology*] .... COPMV
Cowan. Land Rights in Scotland [*A publication*] (ILCA) .... Cow LR
Cowan, TN [*AM radio station call letters*] .... WZYX
Cowart Family (EA) .... CF
Cowater International, Inc., Ottawa, Ontario [*Library symbol*] [*National Library of Canada*] (BIB) .... OOCOW
Cowboy .... CWBY
Cowboy Artists of America (EA) .... CAA
Cowboy Artists of America Museum Foundation (EA) .... CAAMF
Cowboy Television Network .... CTN
Cowboys for Christ (EA) .... CFC
Cowdery's Law Encyclopaedia [*California*] [*A publication*] (DLA) .... Cowd L Enc
Cowell's East India Digest [*A publication*] (DLA) .... Cow Dig
Cowell's Institutiones Juris Anglicani [*A publication*] (DLA) .... Cow Inst
Cowell's Interpreter [*A publication*] (DLA) .... Cowell
Cowell's Interpreter [*A publication*] (DLA) .... Cow Int
Cowell's Law Dictionary [*A publication*] (DLA) .... Cow Dic
Cowell's Law Dictionary [*A publication*] (DLA) .... Cow Dict
Cowell's Law Dictionary [*A publication*] (DLA) .... Cowell
Cowen on Warrants of Attachment [*A publication*] (DLA) .... Cow Att
Cowen Opportunity Cl.A [*Mutual fund ticker symbol*] (SG) .... CWNOX
Cowen's Criminal Digest [*A publication*] (DLA) .... Cow Cr Dig
Cowen's Criminal Law [*New York*] [*A publication*] (DLA) .... Cow Cr L
Cowen's Criminal Reports [*New York*] [*A publication*] (DLA) .... Cow Cr
Cowen's Criminal Reports [*New York*] [*A publication*] (DLA) .... Cow Crim (NY)
Cowen's Criminal Reports [*New York*] [*A publication*] (DLA) .... Cow Cr R
Cowen's Criminal Reports [*New York*] [*A publication*] (DLA) .... Cow Cr Rep
Cowen's New York Reports [*A publication*] (DLA) .... Cow
Cowen's New York Reports [*A publication*] (DLA) .... Cow NY
Cowen's New York Reports [*A publication*] (DLA) .... Cow R
Cowen's New York Treatise on Justices of the Peace [*A publication*] (DLA) .... Cow JP
Cowen's New York Treatise on Justices of the Peace [*A publication*] (DLA) .... Cow Just
Cowen's New York Treatise on Justices of the Peace [*A publication*] (DLA) .... Cow Tr
Cowethas Lacha Sten Cernow (SAUO) .... CIC/SLS
Cowichan Valley Association for Community Living [*Formerly, Duncan & District Association for the Mentally Handicapped*] (AC) .... CVACL
Cowichan Valley Intercultural & Immigrant Society (AC) .... CVIIAS
Cowichan Valley Museum, Duncan, BC, Canada [*Library symbol*] [*Library of Congress*] (LCLS) .... CaBDUCVM
Cowichan Valley Museum, Duncan, British Columbia [*Library symbol*] [*National Library of Canada*] (NLC) .... BDUCVM
Cowles Communications, Inc. (SAUO) .... CWL
Cowles Communications, Inc., New York, NY [*Library symbol*] [*Library of Congress*] (LCLS) CcI
Cowley/Lovell/Byron, WY [*Location identifier*] [*FAA*] (FAAL) .... HCY
Cowl-Flap Angle [*Air Force*] .... CFA
Cowling (SAUS) .... Cowl
Cowling Number [*IUPAC*] .... Co
Cowlitz, Chehalis & Cascade Railroad (IIA) .... CC & C
Cowpea .... CP
Cowpea Aphid-Borne Mosaic Virus [*Plant pathology*] .... CABMV
Cowpea Aphid-Borne Mosaic Virus .... CAMV
Cowpea Chloretic Mottle Virus .... CCMV
Cowpea Chlorotic Mottle Virus (SAUS) .... CCMV
Cowpea Mild Mottle Virus [*Plant pathology*] .... CPMMV
Cowpea Mosaic Virus [*Plant pathology*] .... CPMV
Cowpea Mottle Virus [*Plant pathology*] .... CPMOV
Cowpea Ringspot Virus [*Plant pathology*] .... CPRSV
Cowpea Severe Mosaic Virus [*Plant pathology*] .... CPSMV
Cowpea Trypsin Inhibitor [*Biochemistry*] .... CpTI
Cowpens National Battlefield Site .... COWP
Cowper Greens [*Political party*] [*Australia*] .... CG
Cowper's Cases [*Third volume of Reports in Chancery*] [*A publication*] (DLA) .... Cowp Cas
Cowper's English King's Bench Reports [*1774-78*] [*A publication*] (DLA) .... Cow
Cowper's English King's Bench Reports [*1774-78*] [*A publication*] (DLA) .... Cowp
Cowper's English King's Bench Reports [*1774-78*] [*A publication*] (DLA) .... Cowp (Eng)
Cowra [*Australia*] [*Airport symbol*] (OAG) .... CWT
Cow's Milk .... CM
Cow's Milk Allergy [*Medicine*] (DMAA) .... CMA
Cow's Milk Base Formula .... CMBF
Cow's Milk Protein (MELL) .... CMP
Cow's Milk, Protein-Free (MELL) .... CMPF
Cowsills Fan Club (EA) .... CFC
Cox. Advocate [*1852*] [*A publication*] (DLA) .... Cox Adv
Cox and Atkinson's Registration Appeal Cases [*1843-46*] [*England*] [*A publication*] (DLA) .... Cox & Atk
Cox and Saunders' Criminal Law Consolidation Acts [*3rd ed.*] [*1870*] [*A publication*] (DLA) .... Cox & S Cr L
Cox Broadcasting Corp. (SAUO) .... COX
Cox Communications, Inc. [*NYSE symbol*] (SAG) .... COX
Cox Communications, Inc. [*Associated Press*] (SAG) .... CoxCm
Cox Communications'A' [*NYSE symbol*] (TTSB) .... COX
Cox Coronary Heart Institute, Dayton, OH [*Library symbol*] [*Library of Congress*] (LCLS) .... ODaCox
Cox. Law and Science of Ancient Lights [*1871*] [*A publication*] (ILCA) .... Cox Anc L
Cox, Macrae, and Hertslet's English County Court Cases [*1847-58*] [*A publication*] (DLA) .... Cox & M'C
Cox, Macrae, and Hertslet's English County Court Reports [*1847-58*] [*A publication*] (DLA) .... CM & H
Cox, Macrae, and Hertslet's English County Court Reports [*1847-58*] [*A publication*] (DLA) .... Cox M & H
Cox, Macrae, and Hertslet's English County Court Reports [*1847-58*] [*A publication*] (DLA) .... Cox Mc & H
Cox, Macrae, and Hertslet's Reports, Crown Cases [*1847-58*] [*England*] [*A publication*] (DLA) .... Mac & H
Cox Radio 'A' [*NYSE symbol*] (SG) .... CXR
Cox Radio, Inc. [*Associated Press*] (SAG) .... CoxRad

Cox Radio, Inc. [*NYSE symbol*] (SAG) ... CXR
Coxa Vera [*Medicine*] (MELL) ... CV
Coxe's Reports [*1 New Jersey Law*] [*A publication*] (DLA) ... Coxe
Coxe's Translation of Guterbach's Bracton [*A publication*] (DLA) ... Coxe Bract
Coxheath Gold Holdings Ltd. [*Toronto Stock Exchange symbol*] ... CXG
Cox's American Trade-Mark Cases [*A publication*] (DLA) ... Am Tr M Cas
Cox's American Trade-Mark Cases [*A publication*] (DLA) ... Cox Am T Cas
Cox's American Trade-Mark Cases [*A publication*] (DLA) ... Cox Am TM Cas
Cox's American Trade-Mark Cases [*A publication*] (DLA) ... Cox Tr M Ca
Cox's American Trade-Mark Cases [*A publication*] (DLA) ... Cox Tr M Cas
Cox's Bazar [*Bangladesh*] [*Airport symbol*] (OAG) ... CXB
Cox's Bazar [*Bangladesh*] [*ICAO location identifier*] (ICLI) ... VGCB
Cox's Chancery Practice [*A publication*] (DLA) ... Cox Ch Pr
Cox's Common Law Practice [*A publication*] (DLA) ... Cox CL Pr
Cox's County Court Cases [*1860-1919*] [*England*] [*A publication*] (DLA) ... Cox CC
Cox's County Court Cases [*1860-1919*] [*England*] [*A publication*] (DLA) ... Cox Cty Ct Ca
Cox's County Court Cases [*1860-1919*] [*England*] [*A publication*] (DLA) ... Cox Cty Ct Cas
Cox's Criminal Law Digest [*A publication*] (DLA) ... Cox Cr Dig
Cox's Crown Cases [*A publication*] (DLA) ... Cox CC
Cox's Edition of Peere Williams' Reports [*England*] [*A publication*] (DLA) ... Cox PW
Cox's English Chancery Cases [*A publication*] (DLA) ... Cox Ch
Cox's English Chancery Cases [*A publication*] (DLA) ... Cox Ch Cas (Eng)
Cox's English Chancery Reports [*1783-96*] [*A publication*] (DLA) ... Cox
Cox's English Criminal Cases [*A publication*] (DLA) ... CCC
Cox's English Criminal Cases [*A publication*] (DLA) ... Cox
Cox's English Criminal Cases [*A publication*] (DLA) ... Cox CC
Cox's English Criminal Cases [*A publication*] (DLA) ... Cox Cr Ca
Cox's English Criminal Cases [*A publication*] (DLA) ... Cox Cr Cas
Cox's English Criminal Cases [*A publication*] (DLA) ... Cox Crim Cas
Cox's Equity Cases [*England*] [*A publication*] (DLA) ... Cox Eq
Cox's Equity Cases [*England*] [*A publication*] (DLA) ... Cox Eq Cas
Cox's Institutions of the English Government [*A publication*] (DLA) ... Cox Gov
Cox's Institutions of the English Government [*A publication*] (DLA) ... Cox Inst
Cox's Joint Stock Company Cases [*1864-72*] [*England*] [*A publication*] ... Cox JS Cas
Cox's Joint Stock Company Cases [*1864-72*] [*England*] [*A publication*] (DLA) ... Cox JS Comp
Cox's Joint Stock Company Cases [*1864-72*] [*England*] [*A publication*] (DLA) ... Cox Jt Stk
Cox's Magistrates' Cases [*1859-1919*] [*England*] [*A publication*] (DLA) ... Cox Mag Ca
Cox's Magistrates' Cases [*1859-1919*] [*England*] [*A publication*] (ILCA) ... Cox Mag Cas
Cox's Magistrates' Cases [*1859-1919*] [*England*] [*A publication*] (DLA) ... Cox MC
Cox's Manual of Trade-Mark Cases [*A publication*] (DLA) ... Cox Man Tr M
Cox's Manual of Trade-Mark Cases [*A publication*] (DLA) ... Cox Tr M
Cox's Principles of Punishment [*1877*] [*A publication*] (DLA) ... Cox Pun
Cox's Questions for the Use of Students [*A publication*] (DLA) ... Cox Ques
Cox's Registration and Elections [*14th ed.*] [*1885*] [*A publication*] (DLA) ... Cox Elect
Cox's Registration and Elections [*14th ed.*] [*1885*] [*A publication*] (DLA) ... Cox Reg
Cox's Reports [*25-27 Arkansas*] [*A publication*] (DLA) ... Cox
Coxsackie [*Virus*] (MAE) ... C
Coxsackie Virus [*Medicine*] (STED) ... Cvirus
Coxswain ... COX
Coxswain [*British military*] (DMA) ... Coxn
Coxswain, Construction Battalion, Stevedore ... COXCBS
Coxswain, Ship Repair, Canvasman (SAUS) ... COXSRC
Coxswain, Ship Repair, Canvasman ... COXSRS
Coxswain, Ship Repair, Rigger ... COXSRR
Coyhaique [*Chile*] [*Airport symbol*] (AD) ... GXQ
Coyhaique/Teniente Vidal [*Chile*] [*ICAO location identifier*] (ICLI) ... SCCY
Coyle, NJ [*Location identifier*] [*FAA*] (FAAL) ... CYN
Coyote Hills [*California*] [*Seismograph station code, US Geological Survey*] (SEIS) ... CYH
Coyotepe [*Nicaragua*] [*Seismograph station code, US Geological Survey*] (SEIS) ... CYN
Cozad, NE [*Location identifier*] [*FAA*] (FAAL) ... CZD
Cozad, NE [*AM radio station call letters*] ... KAMI
Cozad, NE [*FM radio station call letters*] ... KAMI-FM
Cozumel [*Mexico*] [*Airport symbol*] (OAG) ... CZM
Cozumel/Internacional [*Mexico*] [*ICAO location identifier*] (ICLI) ... MMCZ
Cozzo Spadaro [*Italy*] [*ICAO location identifier*] (ICLI) ... LICO
C.P. Clare [*NASDAQ symbol*] (TTSB) ... CPCL
C.P. Clare & Co. (SAUO) ... CLA
CP National Network Services [*Concord, CA*] [*Telecommunications*] (TSSD) ... CPNS
CP1 [*Nevada*] [*Seismograph station code, US Geological Survey*] (SEIS) ... CPX
CP-17 [*Nevada*] [*Seismograph station code, US Geological Survey*] [*Closed*] (SEIS) ... CPN
CPA [*Certified Public Accountant*] **Associates** (EA) ... CPAA
CPA Associates International (NTPA) ... CPAAI
CPA Auto Dealer Consultants Association (NTPA) ... CADCA
CPA Cesar Augusto de la Cruze Lepe [*Mexico*] [*ICAO designator*] (FAAC) ... AUG
CPA [*Canadian Psychological Association*] **Interest Group on Women and Psychology** ... IGWAP
CPAC, Inc. [*Associated Press*] (SAG) ... CPAC
CPAC, Inc. [*NASDAQ symbol*] (SAG) ... CPAK
CPAC Voice Alerting Network (SAUO) ... CVANCIN
CPAs Structured Glossary of Technical Terms (SAUS) ... CPAG
CPB, Inc. [*Associated Press*] (SAG) ... CPB
CPB, Inc. [*NASDAQ symbol*] (NQ) ... CPBI
CPC International, Inc. (SAUO) ... CFG
CPC International, Inc. [*Formerly, Corn Products Co.*] [*NYSE symbol*] (SPSG) ... CPC
CPC International, Inc., Argo, IL [*Library symbol*] [*Library of Congress*] (LCLS) ... IArgoC
CPC Intl. [*NYSE symbol*] (TTSB) ... CPC
CPG Cyclic Stick Trigger (MCD) ... CCST
CPG Missile Control Panel (MCD) ... CMCP
CPG Missile Selection (MCD) ... CMSL
CPG Rocket Selection (MCD) ... CRKT
C-Phone Corp. [*NASDAQ symbol*] (SG) ... CFON
CPI Aerostructures [*NASDAQ symbol*] (TTSB) ... CPIA
CPI Aerostructures [*AMEX symbol*] ... CVU
CPI Aerostructures, Inc. [*NASDAQ symbol*] (SAG) ... CPIA
CPI Aerostructures, Inc. [*Associated Press*] (SAG) ... CPI Aero
CPI Corp. [*Associated Press*] (SAG) ... CPI
CPI Corp. [*NYSE symbol*] (SPSG) ... CPY
C-plus (SAUS) ... C+
C-Polysaccharide [*Clinical chemistry*] ... CPS
CPR Institute for Dispute Resolution (EA) ... CPR
CPS Systems [*AMEX symbol*] (SG) ... SYS
CPS [*Itek Copy Processing System*] **User Group** [*Defunct*] (EA) ... CPSUG
CPU Power Calibration Instrument ... CPCI
CR [*Christian Rovsing*] **Computer Systems, Inc.** [*Los Angeles, CA*] [*Telecommunications*] (TSSD) ... CRCS
CRA [*Conzinc Riotinto of Australia*] **Exploration Ltd.** ... CRAE
CRA Managed Care [*NASDAQ symbol*] (TTSB) ... CRAA
CRA Managed Care, Inc. [*Associated Press*] (SAG) ... CRA
CRA Managed Care, Inc. [*NASDAQ symbol*] (SAG) ... CRAA
Crab Angle Sensing System (MCD) ... CASS
Crab Apple [*Defunct*] (EA) ... CA
Crab Lice (MELL) ... CL
Crab Orchard & Egyptian Railroad [*American Rail Heritage Ltd.*] ... CO & E
Crab Orchard & Egyptian Railroad [*American Rail Heritage Ltd.*] [*AAR code*] ... COER
Crab Orchard National Wildlife Refuge (SAUS) ... CONWR
Crabb on the Common Law [*A publication*] (DLA) ... Crabb CL
Crabb on the Common Law [*A publication*] (DLA) ... Crabb Com Law
Crabb on the Law of Real Property [*A publication*] (DLA) ... Crabb Real Prop
Crabb on the Law of Real Property [*A publication*] (DLA) ... Crabb RP
Crabbe's United States District Court Reports [*A publication*] (DLA) ... Crab
Crabbe's United States District Court Reports [*A publication*] (DLA) ... Crabbe
Crabb's Digest of Statutes [*A publication*] (DLA) ... Crabb Dig Stat
Crabb's English Synonyms [*A publication*] (DLA) ... Crabb Eng
Crabb's History of the English Law [*A publication*] (DLA) ... Crabb Eng L
Crabb's History of the English Law [*A publication*] (ILCA) ... Crabb Eng Law
Crabb's History of the English Law [*A publication*] (DLA) ... Crabb Hist Eng Law
Crabb's Precedents in Conveyancing [*A publication*] (DLA) ... Crabb Prec
Crabb's Technological Dictionary [*A publication*] (DLA) ... Crabb Technol Dict
Crabb's Technological Dictionary [*A publication*] (DLA) ... Techn Dict
Crabbs Technological Dictionary (journ.) (SAUS) ... Techn Dict
Crabb's Treatise on Conveyancing [*A publication*] (DLA) ... Crabb Conv
Crab-Oriented Gyro (SAA) ... COG
Crabtree-Horsham Affective Trait Scale (EDAC) ... CHATS
Crack Arrest Temperature [*Nuclear energy*] (NRCH) ... CAT
Crack Initiation Temperature (PDAA) ... CIT
Crack Opening Displacement ... COD
Crack Opening Displacement Application (PDAA) ... CODA
Crack Opening Stress (SAUS) ... COS
Crack Propagation (AAG) ... CP
Crack Resources Ltd. [*Vancouver Stock Exchange symbol*] ... CCR
Crack Surface Displacement (PDAA) ... CSD
Crack Surface Opening Displacement ... CSOD
Crack Tip-Opening Angle (MCD) ... CTOA
Crack Tip-Opening Displacement (MCD) ... CTOD
Crack-Cocaine (SAUS) ... Crac-Coc
Cracked Lap Shear (SAUS) ... CLS
Cracker Barrel Old Country Store [*NASDAQ symbol*] (SAG) ... CBRL
Cracker Barrel Old Country Store, Inc. [*Associated Press*] (SAG) ... CrkrBrl
Cracker Brl Old Ctry [*NASDAQ symbol*] (TTSB) ... CBRL
Crackle (VRA) ... ckcl
Crack-Opening Angle (MCD) ... COA
Crack-Opening Interferometry (SAUS) ... COI
Craddock [*City in South Africa*] (ROG) ... CRA
Cradle (MSA) ... CRDL
Cradle Driver Interface Unit (ACAE) ... CDIU
Cradle Heater Electronics Unit (ACAE) ... CHEU
Cradle Mountain Lake Saint Clair National Park (SAUS) ... CMLSCNP
Cradle of Democracy Award (SAUS) ... CDA
Cradle Release Mechanism (ACAE) ... CRM
Cradock [*South Africa*] [*ICAO location identifier*] (ICLI) ... FACD
Craft (AABC) ... CFT
Craft (DNAB) ... CRA
Craft ... CRFT
Craft and Amphibious Material Department [*British military*] (DMA) ... CAMD
Craft & Design: Metalwork (SAUO) ... CDM
Craft Association of Queensland (SAUO) ... CAQ
Craft Council of Victoria [*Australia*] ... CCV
Craft, Design, Technology (WDAA) ... CDT
Craft Digital Assistant [*Computer science*] ... CDA
Craft Dispatch System (SAUS) ... CDS
Craft Inclination [*Aerospace*] (AAG) ... CI
Craft, Landing, Vehicle-Personnel (SAUS) ... CLVP
Craft Landing Zone [*Military*] (DOMA) ... CLZ

Craft Life Improvement Program (SAUS) .... CLIP
Craft Loss (SAUS) CL
Craft Loss [Shipping] .... C/L
Craft Masonry [Freemasonry] (ROG) .... CM
Craft Member of the British Horological Institute (DBQ) .... CMBHI
Craft of Opportunity Program [Minesweeper] (DOMA) .... COOP
Craft Union Department [AFL-CIO] .... CUD
Craft Yarn Council of America (EA) .... CYCA
Craft-Access Terminal [Computer science] .... CAT
Craftech Manufacturing, Inc. [Toronto Stock Exchange symbol] .... CTH
Crafted with Pride in USA Council (EA) .... CPUSAC
Crafter .... CFTR
Craftmade International, Inc. [NASDAQ symbol] (SAG) .... CRFT
Craftmade International, Inc. [Associated Press] (SAG) .... Crftmde
Craftmade Intl. [NASDAQ symbol] (TTSB) .... CRFT
Craft-of-Opportunity (SAUS) .... COOP
Crafts Advisory Committee (SAUO) .... CAC
Crafts, Protective and Custodial [Military] (DNAB) .... CPC
Crafts Training Centre (SAUO) .... CTC
Craftsman (SAUS) .... Cfn
Craftsman [Military] [British] .... CFN
Craftsman .... CFT
Craftsman (MUGU) .... CFTMN
Craftsman [Military] [British] (DMA) .... Cftn
Craftsman Homeowner Club (EA) .... CHC
Craftsman of the Incorporated British Institute of Certified Carpenters
    (DI) .... CIBICC
Craftsman of the Institute of Carpenters [British] (DBQ) .... CIOC
Craftsmen .... CFTMN
Craftsmen Potters Association [British] (DBA) .... CPA
Cragar Industries, Inc. [Associated Press] (SAG) .... CragrInd
Cragar Industries, Inc. [NASDAQ symbol] (SAG) .... CRGR
Cragar Industries, Inc. [Associated Press] (SAG) .... CrgrInd
Craig [Alaska] [Airport symbol] (OAG) .... CGA
Craig [Colorado] [Seismograph station code, US Geological Survey] [Closed]
    (SEIS) .... CGC
Craig and Phillips' English Chancery Reports [1840-41] [A publication]
    (DLA) .... C & P
Craig and Phillips' English Chancery Reports [1840-41] [A publication]
    (DLA) .... Craig & P
Craig and Phillips' English Chancery Reports [1840-41] [A publication]
    (DLA) .... Craig & Ph
Craig and Phillips' English Chancery Reports [1840-41] [A publication]
    (DLA) .... Craig & Ph (Eng)
Craig and Phillips' English Chancery Reports [1840-41] [A publication]
    (DLA) .... Cr & Ph
Craig, CO [Location identifier] [FAA] (FAAL) .... CAG
Craig, CO [AM radio station call letters] .... KRAI
Craig, CO [FM radio station call letters] .... KRAI-FM
Craig Consumer Electronics [Associated Press] (SAG) .... CraigCE
Craig Consumer Electronics [NASDAQ symbol] (SAG) .... CREG
Craig Corp. [Associated Press] (SAG) .... Craig
Craig Corp. [NYSE symbol] (SAG) .... CRG
Craig Corp. Cl 'A' [NYSE symbol] (TTSB) .... CRGPr
Craig Cove [Vanuatu] [Airport symbol] (OAG) CCV
Craig Heritage Park, Parksville, British Columbia [Library symbol] [National
    Library of Canada] (NLC) .... BPCH
Craig House Technoma Workshop, Pittsburgh, PA [OCLC symbol]
    (OCLC) .... PIC
Craig Mountain Railway [AAR code] .... CMT
Craigie, Stewart, and Paton's House of Lords Appeals from Scotland
    [1726-1857] [A publication] (DLA) .... Pat App
Craigie, Stewart, and Paton's Scotch Appeal Cases [1726-1821]
    [A publication] (DLA) .... Craig & St
Craigie, Stewart, and Paton's Scotch Appeal Cases [1726-1821]
    [A publication] (DLA) .... Craig S & P
Craigie, Stewart, and Paton's Scotch Appeal Cases [1726-1821]
    [A publication] (DLA) .... Craig St & Pat
Craigie, Stewart, and Paton's Scotch Appeal Cases [1726-1821]
    [A publication] (DLA) .... Cr & St
Craigie, Stewart, and Paton's Scotch Appeal Cases [1726-1821]
    [A publication] (DLA) .... Cr S & P
Craigie, Stewart, and Paton's Scotch Appeal Cases [1726-1821]
    [A publication] (DLA) .... CS & P
Craigie, Stewart, and Paton's Scotch Appeal Cases [1726-1821]
    [A publication] (DLA) .... Paton
Craigius Jus Feudale [A publication] (DLA) .... Craigius Jus Feud
Craigius Jus Feudale [A publication] (DLA) .... Craig Jus Feud
Craig-Moffat County Public Library, Craig, CO [Library symbol] [Library of
    Congress] (LCLS) .... CoCra
Craigmont Mines [Toronto Stock Exchange symbol] [Vancouver Stock
    Exchange symbol] .... CRI
Craig's Etymological, Technological, and Pronouncing Dictionary
    [A publication] (DLA) .... Craig Dict
Craig's Practice [A publication] (DLA) .... Craig Pr
Craik-Leibovich [Physics] CL
Craik's English Causes Celebres [A publication] (DLA) .... Craik CC
Crailsheim [Germany] [ICAO location identifier] (ICLI) .... EDER
Crain, Inc. [Toronto Stock Exchange symbol] .... CRL
Crainfield Institute of Technology [British] [ICAO designator] (FAAC) .... CFD
Craiova [Romania] [Airport symbol] (OAG) .... CRA
Craiova [Romania] [ICAO location identifier] (ICLI) .... LRCV
Cramahe Township Public Library, Castleton, Ontario [Library symbol]
    [National Library of Canada] (BIB) .... OCCR
Cramer - von Mises Test [Statistics] .... CVM

Cramer-Rao Lower Bound (SAUS) .... CRLB
Cramption & Knowles Corp. (SAUO) .... CNK
Cranberries (SAUS) .... Crans
Cranberry (SAUS) .... Cran
Cranberry .... CRNBRRY
Cranberry Institute (EA) CI
Cranborne [England] .... CRANB
Cranbrook [Canada] [Airport symbol] (OAG) .... YXC
Cranbrook Academy of Art (GAGS) .... Cranbrook Acad Art
Cranbrook Academy of Art, Bloomfield Hills, MI [Library symbol] [Library of
    Congress] (LCLS) .... MiBloA
Cranbrook, BC [Television station call letters] CBUBT-7
Cranbrook, BC [AM radio station call letters] .... CKEK
Cranbrook, BC [FM radio station call letters] (RBYB) .... CKKR
Cranbrook, BC [ICAO location identifier] (ICLI) .... CYXC
Cranbrook Eductional Community, Archives and Historical Collections,
    Bloomfield Hills, MI [Library symbol] [Library of Congress] (LCLS) ..... MiBloCAr
Cranbrook Institute of Science (SAUO) .... CIS
Cranbrook Institute of Science, Bloomfield Hills, MI [Library symbol] [Library
    of Congress] (LCLS) .... MiBloC
Cranbrook Public Library, British Columbia [Library symbol] [National Library
    of Canada] (NLC) .... BCR
Cranbury Press, Cranbury, NJ [Library symbol] [Library of Congress]
    (LCLS) .... NjCrbP
Cranch. Circuit Court Reports [United States] [A publication] (DLA) .... Cr
Cranch. Circuit Court Reports [United States] [A publication] (DLA) .... Cra
Cranch. Circuit Court Reports [United States] [A publication] (DLA) .... Cra CC
Cranch. Circuit Court Reports [United States] [A publication] (DLA) ...... Cranch CC
Cranch. Circuit Court Reports [United States] [A publication] (DLA) .... Cr CC
Cranch's Decisions on Patent Appeals [A publication] (DLA) .... Cr Pat Dec
Cranch's District of Columbia Reports [1-5 District of Columbia] [1801-40]
    [A publication] (DLA) .... Cranch
Cranch's Patent Decisions [United States] [A publication] (DLA) ..... Cranch Pat Dec
Crandall Library, Glens Falls, NY [Library symbol] [Library of Congress]
    (LCLS) .... NGlf
Crandell Feline Kidney [Cytology] .... CRFK
Crane (WDAA) C
Crane (RIMS) .... Cr
Crane [Shipping] (DS) .... CR
Crane .... CRN
Crane, Aircraft Maintenance (MCD) .... CAM
Crane Army Ammunition Activity (AABC) .... CAAA
Crane Attachment Lorry Mounted (PDAA) .... CALM
Crane Certification Association of America (NTPA) .... CCAA
Crane Co. [NYSE symbol] (TTSB) .... CR
Crane Co. [Associated Press] (SAG) .... Crane
Crane Co., Chicago, IL [Library symbol] [Library of Congress] (LCLS) ...... ICCra
Crane Control Room (SAUS) .... CCR
Crane Drip Pan Monitor [Environmental science] (COE) .... CDPM
Crane Engines [Trains] [British] C
Crane, Field, Medium (SAUS) .... CFM
Crane Load CL
Crane Manufacturers Association of America (EA) .... CMAA
Crane on Deck (MCD) .... COD
Crane Oral Dominance Test [English and Spanish test] .... CODT
Crane Ship [Navy symbol] [Obsolete] .... AB
Crane Specialised Representation Ltd. (SAUO) .... CSR Ltd
Crane Stores Lighter (SAUS) .... CSL
Crane, TX [AM radio station call letters] .... KXOI
Crane, TX [FM radio station call letters] .... KXXL
Crane-Load Moment-Indicator (PDAA) .... CLM
Cranenburgh's Criminal Cases [India] [A publication] (DLA) .... Crane CC
Crane's Reports [22-29 Montana] [A publication] (DLA) .... Crane
Cranfield [British] [ICAO location identifier] (ICLI) .... EGTC
Cranfield Aerospace Motion Cue Seat [Aviation] .... CAMCS
Cranfield Fluidics Conference (SAUO) .... CFC
Cranfield Institute of Technology [British] (ARC) .... CIT
Cranfield Institute of Technology [California] .... CIT
Cranfield Institute of Technology, Cranfield, Bedfordshire, United Kingdom
    [Library symbol] [Library of Congress] (LCLS) .... UkCraT
Cranfield Motion Systems (SAUS) .... CRANMOS
Cranfield Product Engineering Centre [Cranfield Institute of Technology]
    [Research center] [British] (CB) .... CPEC
Cranfield Robotics and Automation Group [British] .... CRAG
Cranfield Robotics and Automation Group (SAUO) .... Crag
Cranfield Unit for Precision Engineering [British] .... CUPE
Cranford Citizen & Chronicle, Cranford, NJ [Library symbol] [Library of
    Congress] (LCLS) .... NjCrC
Cranford Historical Society, Cranford, NJ [Library symbol] [Library of
    Congress] (LCLS) .... NjCrHi
Cranford Public Library, Cranford, NJ [Library symbol] [Library of
    Congress] (LCLS) .... NjCr
Cranial [Anatomy] .... CR
Cranial [Anatomy] .... cran
Cranial Academy (EA) .... CA
Cranial Computed Tomography [Medicine] (DMAA) .... CCT
Cranial Electrical Stimulation [Medicine] (MELL) .... CES
Cranial Nerve [Anatomy] .... CN
Cranial Nerve (DIPS) .... N
[First] Cranial Nerve [Second cranial nerve is NII, etc., through NVIII]
    [Medicine] (DAVI) .... NI
Cranial Nerve I [Olfactory nerve] [Medicine] (MELL) .... cranial I
Cranial Nerve II [Optic nerve] [Medicine] (MELL) .... cranial II
Cranial Nerve III [Oculomotor nerve] [Medicine] (MELL) .... cranial III
Cranial Nerve IV [Trochlear nerve] [Medicine] (MELL) .... cranial IV

Cranial Nerve IX [*Glossopharyngeal nerve*] [*Medicine*] (MELL) .... cranial IX
Cranial Nerve number 10 (SAUS) .... CNX
Cranial Nerve number 5 (SAUS) .... CNV
Cranial Nerve Palsy [*Medicine*] (STED) .... CNP
Cranial Nerve Syndrome [*Medicine*] (MELL) .... CNS
Cranial Nerve V [*Trigeminal nerve*] [*Medicine*] (MELL) .... cranial V
Cranial Nerve VI [*Abducent nerve*] [*Medicine*] (MELL) .... cranial VI
Cranial Nerve VII [*Facial nerve*] [*Medicine*] (MELL) .... cranial VII
Cranial Nerve VIII [*Vestibulocochlear nerve*] [*Medicine*] (MELL) .... cranial VIII
Cranial Nerve X [*Vagus nerve*] [*Medicine*] (MELL) .... cranial X
Cranial Nerves [*Neurology*] (DAVI) .... CrN
Cranial Nerves [*Neurology*] (DAVI) .... cr nn
Cranial Nerves [*Medicine*] (STED) .... crns
Cranial Radiotherapy .... CRT
Cranial Sector Scan [*Medicine*] (STED) .... CSS
Cranial Spinal Irradiation [*Medicine*] (MELL) .... CSI
Craniocaudal [*Anatomy*] CC
Craniocerebral Trauma [*Medicine*] .... CCT
Craniocervical [*Anatomy*] (HGAA) CC
Craniofacial Biology Group of the International Association for Dental Research (EA) .... CBG
Craniofacial Dysostosis [*Medicine*] (MELL) .... CFD
Craniofacial Dyssynostosis [*Medicine*] (DMAA) .... CFDS
Craniofacial Foundation of America (SAUO) .... CFA
Craniofacial Microsomia [*Medicine*] (DMAA) .... CFM
Craniofacial Pattern Profile [*Medicine*] (DMAA) .... CFPP
Craniofrontonasal Dysostosis [*Medicine*] (DMAA) .... CFND
Craniologist (SAUS) .... Craniol
Craniology .... CRAN
Craniology (ROG) .... CRANIOL
Craniomandibular Joint [*Anatomy*] .... CMJ
Craniomandibular Orthepedic Repositioning Device [*Dentistry and oral surgery*] (DAVI) .... CMOR
Craniomandibulofacial (DB) .... CMF
Craniometry (ROG) .... CRANIOM
Craniometry (SAUS) .... Craniom
Craniospinal [*Anatomy*] (AAMN) .... CrSp
Craniospinal Defect [*Medicine*] (MELL) .... CSD
Craniosynostosis, Boston Type [*Medicine*] (DMAA) .... CSB
Craniotomy (ROG) .... CRANIOT
Cranium (SAUS) .... Cran
Crank (KSC) .... CRK
Crank Angle (MCD) .... CA
Crankcase [*Automotive engineering*] .... C/C
Crankcase .... CRK
Crankcase (KSC) .... CRKC
Crankcase Depression Regulator [*AC Spark Plug Co.*] [*Automotive engineering*] .... CDR
Crankcase Depression Regulator Valve [*Emissions*] [*Automotive engineering*] .... CDRV
Cranking Amperes [*Battery*] [*Automotive engineering*] .... CA
Crankpin (MSA) .... CPIN
Crankpin (SAUS) .... CPin
Crank-radius to connecting-rod-length radio (SAUS) .... R/L
Crankshaft .... CRKSFT
Crankshaft .... CRNKSHFT
Crankshaft [*Automotive engineering*] .... C/S
Crankshaft .... CSHAFT
Crankshaft Information Element (SAUS) .... Crankshaft IE
Crankshaft Position [*Automotive engineering*] .... CP
Crankshaft Position Sensor [*Automotive engineering*] .... CPS
Crankshaft Rate (NVT) .... CSR
Crankshaft Revolutions per Minute (SAUS) .... CRPM
Cranksheave (MSA) .... CRKSHV
Cranwell [*British*] [*ICAO location identifier*] (ICLI) .... EGYD
Cranwell FTU [*British*] [*ICAO designator*] (FAAC) .... CWL
Crary's New York Practice, Special Pleading [*A publication*] (DLA) .... Cra NY Pr
Crary's New York Practice, Special Pleading [*A publication*] (DLA) .... Crar Pr
Cras [*Tomorrow*] [*Pharmacy*] .... CR
Cras Mane [*Tomorrow Morning*] [*Pharmacy*] .... CM
Cras Mane Sumendus [*To Be Taken Tomorrow Morning*] [*Pharmacy*] .... CMS
Cras Nocte [*Tomorrow Night*] [*Pharmacy*] .... CN
Cras Nocte Sumendus [*To Be Taken Tomorrow Night*] [*Pharmacy*] .... CNS
Cras Vespere [*Tomorrow Evening*] [*Pharmacy*] .... CR VESP
Cras Vespere [*Tomorrow Evening*] [*Pharmacy*] CV
Crash Avoidance Research Data File [*NHTSA*] (TAG) .... CARD
Crash Boat .... CB
Crash Damage (MCD) .... CD
Crash Damage Material List (MCD) .... CDML
Crash Damage Overhaul (MCD) .... CDOVHL
Crash Damage Rate (MCD) .... CDR
Crash Data Position Indication Recorder (MCD) .... CDPIR
Crash Data Position Indicator Recorder Subsystem (PDAA) .... CDPIRS
Crash Data Recorder (ACAE) .... CDR
Crash Data Recorder Subsystem (ACAE) .... CDRS
Crash Finish [*of paper*] [*Graphic arts*] (DGA) .... CF
Crash Impact Absorbing Structure [*Automotive safety*] .... CIAS
Crash Injury Research & Engineering Network [*Federal program*] .... CIREN
Crash Injury Research Organization [*Cornell University*] .... CIRO
Crash Injury Scale Intermediate Level Investigation (PDAA) .... CISILI
Crash Locator Beacon [*Aviation*] (AFM) .... CLB
Crash Locator Beacon [*Aviation*] (FAAC) .... CLBN
Crash Outcome Data Evaluation System [*BTS*] (TAG) .... CODES
Crash Phone Activated [*Aviation*] (FAAC) .... CPA
Crash Position Indicator [*Aviation*] (AFM) .... CPI
Crash Position Indicator Recorder (ACAE) .... CPIR
Crash Position Indicator/Flight Data Recorder [*Aviation*] (MCD) .... CPI/FDR
Crash Survivable Memory Unit (SAUS) .... CSMU
Crash Test Rating Index (ACAE) .... CTRI
Crash Vehicle Simulator .... CVS
Crashed Aircraft Transit Centre (SAUO) .... CATC
Crash/Maintenance Recorder System (SAUS) .... CMRS
Crash-Resistant Fuel System (RDA) .... CRFS
Crash-Survivable Flight Data Recorder (MCD) .... CSFDR
Crashworthiness Data System [*NHTSA*] (TAG) .... CDS
Crashworthy Fuel Systems [*Aviation*] .... CWFS
Crassulacean Acid Metabolism [*Biochemistry*] .... CAM
Crassus [*of Plutarch*] [*Classical studies*] (OCD) .... Crass
Crastinus [*Of Tomorrow*] [*Pharmacy*] .... CRAST
Crate .... CR
Crate .... CRT
Crate .... crt
Crate Controller (SAUS) CC
Crateaudun [*France*] [*ICAO location identifier*] (ICLI) .... LFOC
Crated - Rocket Unit [*Military*] .... CRU
Crater [*Costa Rica*] [*Seismograph station code, US Geological Survey*] (SEIS) A10
Crater (ROG) .... CRA
Crater [*Constellation*] .... Crat
Crater [*Constellation*] .... Crt
Crater (GEOI) .... CRTR
Crater Lake National Park (SAUS) .... CLNP
Crater Lake National Park .... CRLA
Crater Production Rate [*Geology*] .... CPR
Cratering and Related Effects Simulation (SAUS) .... CARES
Cratering Demolition Device .... CDD
Cratering Munition Dispenser (SAUS) .... CMD
Crater-Lamp Recorder .... CLR
Craters of the Moon National Monument (SAUS) .... CMNM
Craters of the Moon National Monument .... CRMO
Crates .... CTS
Crateus [*Brazil*] [*Airport symbol*] (AD) .... CTH
Crating (MSA) .... CTG
C-Rating Overall [*Military*] (CAAL) .... CROVL
Crating, Packaging Instructions .... CPI
Crato [*Brazil*] [*Airport symbol*] (AD) .... CQQ
Craton, Lodge and Knight [*British*] .... CLK
Cratylus [*of Plato*] [*Classical studies*] (OCD) .... Cra
Cravath, Swaine & Moore, New York, NY [*Library symbol*] [*Library of Congress*] (LCLS) .... NNCAM
Craven Community College, Havelock Learning Center, Havelock, NC [*Library symbol*] [*Library of Congress*] (LCLS) .... NcHavCr
Craven Resources Ltd. [*Vancouver Stock Exchange symbol*] .... CNI
Craven Technical Institute, New Bern, NC [*Library symbol*] [*Library of Congress*] (LCLS) .... NcNbC
Craven-Pamlico-Carteret Regional Library [*Library network*] .... C-P-C
Craven-Pamlico-Carteret Regional Library, New Bern, NC [*Library symbol*] [*Library of Congress*] (LCLS) .... NcNbCP
Cravo Norte [*Colombia*] [*Airport symbol*] (OAG) .... RAV
Crawford & Co. (MHDW) .... CRAW
Crawford & Co. [*Associated Press*] (SAG) .... Crwfd
Crawford & Co. Cl'B' [*NYSE symbol*] (TTSB) .... CRD.B
Crawford and Dix's Irish Abridged Cases [*A publication*] (DLA) .... Ab Ca
Crawford and Dix's Irish Abridged Cases [*A publication*] (DLA) .... Abr Cas
Crawford and Dix's Irish Abridged Cases [*A publication*] (DLA) .... C & DAC
Crawford and Dix's Irish Abridged Cases [*A publication*] (DLA) .... Cr & Dix Ab Ca
Crawford and Dix's Irish Abridged Cases [*A publication*] (DLA) .... Cr & Dix Ab Cas
Crawford and Dix's Irish Abridged Cases [*A publication*] (DLA) .... Craw & D Ab Cas
Crawford and Dix's Irish Abridged Cases [*A publication*] (DLA) .... Craw & D Abr Cas
Crawford and Dix's Irish Abridged Cases [*A publication*] (DLA) .... Craw & D (Ir)
Crawford and Dix's Irish Abridged Cases [*A publication*] (DLA) .... Crawf & D Abr Cas
Crawford and Dix's Irish Circuit Court Cases [*A publication*] (DLA) .... C & D
Crawford and Dix's Irish Circuit Court Cases [*A publication*] (DLA) .... C & DCC
Crawford and Dix's Irish Circuit Court Cases [*A publication*] (DLA) .... Cr & Dix
Crawford and Dix's Irish Circuit Court Cases [*A publication*] (DLA) .... Cr & Dix CC
Crawford and Dix's Irish Circuit Court Cases [*A publication*] (DLA) .... Craw & D
Crawford and Dix's Irish Circuit Court Cases [*A publication*] (DLA) .... Craw & DCC (Ir)
Crawford and Dix's Irish Circuit Court Cases [*A publication*] (DLA) .... Craw & Dix
Crawford and Dix's Irish Circuit Court Cases [*A publication*] (DLA) .... Crawf & D
Crawford and Dix's Irish Circuit Court Cases [*A publication*] (DLA) .... Crawf & Dix
Crawford and Dix's Irish Circuit Court Cases [*A publication*] (DLA) .... Ir Cir Cas
Crawford and Dix's Irish Criminal Cases [*A publication*] (DLA) .... Crawf & Dix
Crawford Bay, BC [*FM radio station call letters*] .... CBTE
Crawford Bay, BC [*FM radio station call letters*] .... CKKC-FM
Crawford Community Library, Crawford, CO [*Library symbol*] [*Library of Congress*] (LCLS) .... CoCfC
Crawford Community Library, Crawford, CO [*Library symbol*] [*Library of Congress*] (LCLS) .... CoCfCL
Crawford County Democrat, English, IN [*Library symbol*] [*Library of Congress*] (LCLS) .... InEngD
Crawford County Historical Society, Meadville, PA [*Library symbol*] [*Library of Congress*] (LCLS) .... PMCHi
Crawford County Legal Journal [*Pennsylvania*] [*A publication*] (DLA) .... Craw Co Leg J (PA)
Crawford County Legal Journal [*Pennsylvania*] [*A publication*] (DLA) .... Crawford Co Leg Jour

Crawford County Library, Grayling, MI [*Library symbol*] [*Library of Congress*] (LCLS) .... MiGray
Crawford County Public Library, English, IN [*Library symbol*] [*Library of Congress*] (LCLS) .... InEng
Crawford Fund for International Agricultural Research (SAUO) .... CFIAR
Crawford, GA [*FM radio station call letters*] .... WGMG
Crawford Small Parts Dexterity Test [*Education*] .... CSPDT
Crawford W. Long Memorial Hospital, Atlanta, GA [*Library symbol*] [*Library of Congress*] (LCLS) .... GACL
Crawford&Co. Cl'A'non-vtg [*NYSE symbol*] (TTSB) .... CRD.A
Crawford's Reports [*53-69, 72-101 Arkansas*] [*A publication*] (DLA) .... Craw
Crawford's Reports [*53-69, 72-101 Arkansas*] [*A publication*] (DLA) .... Craw (Ark)
Crawfordsville District Public Library, Crawfordsville, IN [*Library symbol*] [*Library of Congress*] (LCLS) .... InC
Crawfordsville, IN [*Location identifier*] [*FAA*] (FAAL) .... CFJ
Crawfordsville, IN [*AM radio station call letters*] .... WCVL
Crawfordsville, IN [*FM radio station call letters*] .... WIMC
Crawfordsville, IN [*FM radio station call letters*] .... WNDY
Crawfordsville, IN [*FM radio station call letters*] (BROA) .... WVXI-FM
Crawfordsville Journal and Review, Crawfordsville, IN [*Library symbol*] [*Library of Congress*] (LCLS) .... InCJR
Crawfordville, FL [*FM radio station call letters*] .... WAKU
Crawler (SAUS) .... CRAW
Crawler/Transporter [*Aerospace*] (KSC) .... C/T
Crawler/Transporter Intercom System [*Aerospace*] (KSC) .... CTIS
Crawler/Transporter/Mobile Service Structure [*Aerospace*] (KSC) .... CT/MSS
Crawlerway [*NASA*] (KSC) .... CW
Cray Assembly Language (SAUS) .... CAL
Cray C library (SAUO) .... LIBC
Cray Charging Unit (SAUS) .... CCU
Cray Computer Corporation (SAUO) CCC
Cray Computer Corporation (SAUO) .... CRAY
Cray Fish Co. ADS [*NASDAQ symbol*] (SG) .... CRFH
Cray Fortran [*Programming language*] (NITA) .... CFT
Cray FORTRAN 77 compiler (SAUS) CFT77
Cray Fortran compiler (SAUS) .... CFR
Cray Fortran Compiler (SAUS) .... CFT
Cray Operating System [*Computer science*] .... COS
Cray Research (SAUS) .... CR
Cray Research [*NYSE symbol*] (TTSB) .... CYR
Cray Research Adaptive FORTRAN (SAUS) .... CRAFT
Cray Research, Inc. [*Associated Press*] (SAG) .... CrayRs
Cray Research, Inc. .... CRI
Cray Research, Inc. [*NYSE symbol*] (SPSG) .... CYR
Cray Research Incorporated (SAUO) .... CRI
Cray Time Sharing System (ACAE) .... CTSS
Cray User Group (SAUO) .... CUG
Cray Valley Products (SAUO) .... CVP
Crayfish (DSUE) .... CRAY
Crayon (VRA) .... cray
Crayon, Water Color, and Craft Institute (EA) .... CWCCI
Craze Opening Displacement (SAUS) .... COD
Crazy .... CRZY
Crazy Horse Memorial Foundation (EA) .... CHMF
Crazy Woman Creek Bancorp, Inc. [*Associated Press*] (SAG) .... CrazyW
Crazy Woman Creek Bancorp, Inc. [*NASDAQ symbol*] (SAG) .... CRZY
Crazy Woman Creek Bncp [*NASDAQ symbol*] (TTSB) .... CRZY
Crazy Woman, WY [*Location identifier*] [*FAA*] (FAAL) .... CZI
CRC Press [*Boca Raton, FL*] .... CRC
CRC World Literature Ministries [*Formerly, Christian Reformed Church World Literature Ministries*] (EA) .... CRCWLM
C-Reactive Protein [*Clinical chemistry*] .... CRP
C-Reactive Protein Antiserum [*Clinical chemistry*] .... CRPA
Cream [*Philately*] .... cr
Cream [*Pharmacy*] (DAVI) .... CR
Cream (SAUS) .... CRE
Cream (ADA) .... CRM
Cream Laid [*Paper*] (DGA) CL
Cream of Tartar Substitute .... CTS
Cream Received in Separating Cottonseed Oil .... CRISCO
Cream Ridge Fruit Research Center [*Rutgers University*] [*Research center*] (RCD) .... CRRC
Cream Shade [*Paper*] .... CS
Cream Silver Mines Ltd. [*Vancouver Stock Exchange symbol*] .... CEM
Cream Wove [*Paper*] (DGA) .... CW
Cream Wove Large Post [*Paper*] (DGA) .... CWP
Creamery .... CRMRY
Creamware (VRA) .... crmwr
Crease [*Deltiology*] .... CR
Crease .... crs
Crease Clinic Library, Essondale, BC, Canada [*Library symbol*] [*Library of Congress*] (LCLS) .... CaBEC
Crease Recovery Angle [*Textile technology*] .... CRA
Creasy on International Law [*A publication*] (DLA) .... Creas Int L
Creasy's Ceylon Reports [*A publication*] (DLA) .... Creasy
Creasy's Colonial Constitutions [*A publication*] (DLA) .... Creas Col Const
Creasy's Rise and Progress of the English Constitution [*A publication*] (DLA) .... Creas Eng Cons
Create Occurrence Table [*University of Minnesota*] (NITA) .... COT
Create Test File (IAA) .... CRTF
Create Test Files (SAUS) .... CRTF
Create, Update, Interrogate, and Display [*Computer science*] (MHDI) .... CUPID
Create Your Own Newspaper (SAUS) .... CRAYON
Created C
Created [*or Creation*] .... CR

Create-Retrieve-Update-Delete (RALS) .... CRUD
Creatine (MELL) C
Creatine [*Biochemistry*] .... creat
Creatine Kinase [*Also, CPK*] [*An enzyme*] .... CK
Creatine Kinase B [*An enzyme*] .... CKB
Creatine Kinase MB Band (SAUS) .... CK-MB
Creatine Kinase, Muscle Type (DMAA) .... CKM
Creatine Kinase Myocardial Band .... CK-MB
Creatine Phosphate [*Phosphocreatine; see PC*] [*Biochemistry*] .... CP
Creatine Phosphate [*or Phosphocreatine*] [*Biochemistry*] (DAVI) .... CrP
Creatine Phosphokinase [*Biochemistry*] (DAVI) .... CP
Creatine Phosphokinase [*Preferred form is CK*] [*An enzyme*] .... CPK
Creatine Phosphokinase Depleted [*Medicine*] .... CPKD
Creatine Phosphokinase Isoenzyme [*Biochemistry*] (DAVI) .... CPKI
Creatine Phosphokinase Isoenzyme [*Biochemistry*] (DAVI) .... CPKISO
Creating a More Efficient Office (HEAS) .... CAMEO
Creating an Automatic Design .... CAD
Creatinine [*Biochemistry*] .... Cr
Creatinine [*Biochemistry*] (DAVI) .... CREA
Creatinine [*Biochemistry*] .... creat
Creatinine Clearance [*Clinical chemistry*] CC
Creatinine Clearance [*Clinical chemistry*] (MAE) .... Ccr
Creatinine Clearance (STED) CrC1
Creatinine Clearance [*Biochemistry*] (DAVI) .... CrCl
Creatinine Height Index [*Biochemistry*] (DAVI) .... CHI
Creatinine Phosphate [*Biochemistry*] (AAMN) .... Cr P
Creatinine Urine [*Test*] [*Biochemistry*] (DAVI) .... CREA-U
Creatinine Urine Spot [*Test*] [*Biochemistry*] (DAVI) .... CREA-S
Creation (SAUS) C
Creation .... CREAT
Creation Facilities Program [*Computer science*] (IBMDP) .... CFP
Creation Health Foundation (EA) .... CHF
Creation of New Enterprises [*British*] (DI) .... CONE
Creation Research .... CR
Creation Research Service (SAUO) .... CRS
Creation Research Society (EA) .... CRS
Creation Science Legal Defense Fund (EA) .... CSLDF
Creation Science Movement [*British*] .... CSM
Creation Science Research Center (SAUS) .... Creation Sci
Creation Sheet (SAA) .... CS
Creation Social Science and Humanities Society (EA) .... CSSHS
Creation-Evolution .... CREVO
Creative (SAUS) C
Creative .... CREATV
Creative and Performing Arts [*Education*] .... CAPA
[*The*] Creative and Supportive Trust [*British*] (DI) .... CAST
Creative Application Laboratories (SAUS) .... CAL
Creative Art Group [*Australia*] .... CAG
Creative Artists Agency .... CAA
Creative Artists Public Service Program (EA) .... CAPS
Creative Audio and Music Electronics Organization (EA) .... CAMEO
Creative BioMolecules [*NASDAQ symbol*] (TTSB) .... CBMI
Creative BioMolecules, Inc. [*NASDAQ symbol*] (SAG) .... CBMI
Creative BioMolecules, Inc. [*Associated Press*] (SAG) .... CrBioMol
[*The*] Creative Coalition .... TCC
Creative Computer Applications, Inc. [*AMEX symbol*] (SAG) .... CAP
Creative Computer Applications, Inc. [*Associated Press*] (SAG) .... CreatC
Creative Computer Solutions (SAUO) .... CCS
Creative Computers [*NASDAQ symbol*] (TTSB) .... MALL
Creative Computers, Inc. [*Associated Press*] (SAG) .... CreaCpt
Creative Computers, Inc. [*NASDAQ symbol*] (SAG) .... MALL
Creative Computing Services [*Information service or system*] (IID) .... CCS
Creative Decision Stimulation Systems (VERA) .... CDSS
Creative Development Unit [*Australian Film Commission*] .... CDU
Creative Director (DOAD) .... CD
Creative Editing (SAUS) .... CE
Creative Education Foundation (EA) .... CEF
Creative Electronic Systems .... CES
Creative Imagination Scale [*Psychology*] (EDAC) .... CIS
Creative Incentive Coalition CIC
Creative Industries Group, Inc. [*Auburn Hills, MI*] (TSSD) .... CIG
Creative Industries of Detroit, Inc. [*Warren, MI*] [*Telecommunications*] (TSSD) .... CID
Creative Initiative [*Later, BWF*] (EA) CI
Creative Learning Products [*NASDAQ symbol*] (TTSB) .... CLPI
Creative Learning Products, Inc. [*NASDAQ symbol*] (NQ) .... CLPI
Creative Learnings Products [*Associated Press*] (SAG) .... CreatLrn
Creative List Services, Inc. [*Information service or system*] (IID) .... CLS
Creative Management Technologies (AAGC) .... CMT
Creative Med Dev [*NASDAQ symbol*] (TTSB) .... CMDI
Creative Modern Design .... CMD
Creative Multimedia Corp. [*Database producer*] (IID) .... CMC
Creative Music Format (SAUS) .... CMF
Creative Music Foundation (EA) .... CMF
Creative Playthings Foundation [*Defunct*] .... CPF
Creative Printers of America .... CPA
Creative Problem-Solving (PDAA) .... CPS
Creative Problem-Solving Institute (EDAC) .... CPSI
Creative Progm Tech Venture [*NASDAQ symbol*] (TTSB) .... CPTV
Creative Programing & Technology [*Associated Press*] (SAG) .... CrePrg
Creative Programming & Technology [*NASDAQ symbol*] (SAG) .... CPTV
Creative Protein (SAUS) .... CRP
Creative Research Systems [*Information service or system*] (IID) .... CRS
Creative Resources Guild (EA) .... CRG
Creative Services Association [*British*] (DBA) .... CSA

Creative Strategies International (HGAA) .... CSI
Creative Strategies Research International [Information service or system]
  (IID) .... CSRI
Creative Styles Inventory [Test] (TMMY) .... CSI
Creative Technologies [NASDAQ symbol] (TTSB) .... CRTV
Creative Technologies Corp. [Associated Press] (SAG) .... CreTch
Creative Technologies Corp. [NASDAQ symbol] (SAG) .... CRTV
Creative Technology [NASDAQ symbol] (TTSB) .... CREAF
Creative Technology Ltd. [NASDAQ symbol] (SAG) .... CREA
Creative Technology Ltd. [Associated Press] (SAG) .... CreTcLtd
Creative Time (EA) .... CT
Creative Times Project [Later, CT] (EA) .... CTP
Creative Tour Operators Association .... CTOA
Creative Tourist Agents' Conference [British] (BI) .... CTAC
Creative Use of Leisure Time under Restrictive Environments [Federally
  funded prison program] .... CULTURE
Creative Visual Dynamics (OA) .... CVD
Creative Voice (SAUS) .... VOC
Creative Writing (SAUS) .... WRIT
Creativity Attitude Survey [Educational test] .... CAS
Creativity Checklist [Educational test] .... CCH
Creativity Quotient [Testing term] .... CQ
Creativity Tests for Children [Child development test series] .... CT
Creators' Copyright Coalition CCC
Creche and Kindergarten Association of Queensland [Australia] .... CKAQ
Credcor Bank Ltd. (SAUO) .... Credcor
Credence Systems [NASDAQ symbol] (TTSB) .... CMOS
Credence Systems Corp. [NASDAQ symbol] (SAG) .... CMOS
Credence Systems Corp. [Associated Press] (SAG) .... CredSys
Credentialing Commission (EA) CC
Credentialing Verification Organization (DMAA) .... CVO
Credentials Verification Organization (ADWA) .... CVO
Credicorp Ltd. [NYSE symbol] (SG) .... BAP
Credicorp Ltd. [Associated Press] (SAG) .... Credicp
Credit (AFM) .... CR
Credit (NTIO) .... cr
Credit (WDAA) .... Cr
Credit .... CRDT
Credit (AABC) .... CRED
Credit [or Creditor] (ROG) .... CT
Credit Acceptance [NASDAQ symbol] (TTSB) .... CACC
Credit Acceptance Corp. [NASDAQ symbol] (SAG) .... CACC
Credit Acceptance Corp. [Associated Press] (SAG) .... CrdAcp
Credit Account [Business term] .... CA
Credit Account Voucher (DCTA) .... CAV
Credit Accumulation and Transfer Scheme [British] (DET) .... CATS
Credit Accumulation and Transfer System (SAUO) .... CATS
Credit Agricole [France] .... CA
Credit and Load Management System [Software] [British] .... CALMS
Credit Associate [Society of Certified Consumer Credit Executives]
  [Designation awarded by] .... CA
Credit Authorization Terminal .... CAT
Credit Balance .... CB
Credit Card [Business term] (ADA) CC
Credit Card Asset Backed Security (EBF) .... CCABS
Credit Card Authorisation and Fund Transfer System [British] .... CRAFTS
Credit Card Purchase (AFM) .... CCP
Credit Card Reader .... CCR
Credit Card Reading System (SAUS) .... CCR System
Credit Card Register (SAUS) .... CCR
Credit Card Return Notice (TRID) .... CCRN
Credit Card Service Bureau .... CCSB
Credit Card Service Bureau of America (SAUO) .... CCSB
Credit Card Service Bureau of America [Later, CCSB] .... CCSBA
Credit Card Users of America [Beverly Hills, CA] (EA) .... CCUA
Credit Card Verification (SAUS) CCV
Credit Clearing Outward (DCTA) .... CCO
Credit Code (DNAB) .... CDC
Credit Control Act [1969] .... CCA
Credit Control Board (SAUO) .... CCB
Credit de la Cote-D'Ivoire [Credit Bank of the Ivory Coast] CCI
Credit Depot [NASDAQ symbol] (TTSB) .... LEND
Credit Depot Corp. [Associated Press] (SAG) .... CrdDept
Credit Depot Corp. [NASDAQ symbol] (SAG) .... LEND
Credit Factoring International [Commercial firm] [British] .... CFI
Credit Foncier de France [France] .... CFF
Credit for Exports [Bank] [British] .... CFX
Credit Given for (SAUS) .... CGF
Credit Information Bureau (SAUO) .... CIB
Credit Information Bureau, Incorporated (SAUO) .... CIBI
Credit Insurance Logistics Automated (PDAA) .... CRILA
Credit Licensing Authority [Victoria] [Australia] .... CLA
Credit Limit (DCTA) CL
Credit Limit Code (SAUS) .... CRLCD
Credit Lyonnais Bank Nederland [Credit Lyonnais' Dutch subsidiary]
  (ECON) .... CLBN
Credit Memo .... CM
Credit Note (WDAA) CC
Credit Note [Business term] .... CN
Credit Officers Group (EA) .... COG
Credit Populaire d'Algerie [People's Credit Bank of Algeria] (IMH) .... CPA
Credit Professionals International (EA) .... CPI
Credit Protection Association [British] (DBA) .... CPA
Credit Rating [Business term] (ADA) .... CR
Credit Reference Agency (SAUO) .... CRA

Credit Reference Association of Australia .... CRAA
Credit Report [Business term] .... CR
Credit Requisition (MCD) .... CR
Credit Research Center [Purdue University] [Research center] (RCD) .... CRC
Credit Research Foundation [Lake Success, NY] (EA) .... CRF
Credit Suisse [Bank] .... CS
Credit Suisse Financial Products [British] (ECON) .... CSFP
Credit Suisse First Boston [Banking] (ECON) .... CSFB
Credit Systems Inc. .... CSI
Credit Transfer .... CT
Credit Transfer Fee [Business term] .... CTF
Credit Tribunal [Victoria] [Australia] .... CT
Credit Union .... CRU
Credit Union .... CU
Credit Union Australia Ltd. .... CUA
Credit Union Central of Manitoba, Winnipeg, Manitoba [Library symbol]
  [National Library of Canada] (NLC) .... MWCU
Credit Union Central of Manitoba, Winnipeg, MB, Canada [Library symbol]
  [Library of Congress] (LCLS) .... CaMWCU
Credit Union Central, Regina, Saskatchewan [Library symbol] [National
  Library of Canada] (NLC) .... SRCU
Credit Union Central, Regina, SK, Canada [Library symbol] [Library of
  Congress] (LCLS) .... CaSRCU
Credit Union Executives Society .... CUES
Credit Union League of Great Britain (DI) .... CULGB
Credit Union National Association (EA) .... CUNA
Credit Union Office (DNAB) .... CUO
Credit Union Share Draft .... CUSD
Credit Union Stabilisation Board [South Australia] .... CUSB
Credit Valley Hospital, Mississauga, Ontario [Library symbol] [National
  Library of Canada] (NLC) .... OMCVH
Credit Voucher (SAUS) CV
Credit Women - International [Later, CPI] (EA) .... CW-I
Credit Women's Breakfast Clubs of North America [Later, CPI] (EA) .... CWBCNA
Creditable Record .... CR
Credithrift Financial Corp. (SAUO) .... CRD
Crediton [England] .... CRED
Creditor (ROG) .... CR
Creditor (EBF) .... cr
Creditor [Legal shorthand] (LWAP) .... CROR
Creditors' Bill [Legal term] (DLA) .... CRED B
Creditors' Voluntary Agreement (WDAA) .... CVA
Creditpoint (SAUS) .... CP
Creditreform Databank [Verband der Vereine Creditreform eV] [Information
  service or system] (IID) VC
Credo [Creed] [Latin] .... CR
Credo Pete [NASDAQ symbol] (TTSB) .... CRED
Credo Petroleum Corp. [NASDAQ symbol] (NQ) .... CRED
Credo Petroleum Corp. [Associated Press] (SAG) .... CredoPt
Cree [MARC language code] [Library of Congress] (LCCP) .... cre
Cree Airways Corp. [Canada] [ICAO designator] (FAAC) .... CRE
Cree Questionnaire [Psychology] .... CQ
Cree Regional Authority, Grand Council of the Crees (of Quebec)
  [Administration Regionale Crie, Grand Conseil des Cris (du Quebec)] Val
  D'Or, Quebec [Library symbol] [National Library of Canada] (NLC) .... QVGCCQ
Cree Research [NASDAQ symbol] (TTSB) .... CREE
Cree Research, Inc. [NASDAQ symbol] (SAG) .... CREE
Cree Research, Inc. [Associated Press] (SAG) .... CreeRsh
Cree School Board, Chisasibi, James Bay, Quebec [Library symbol]
  [National Library of Canada] (BIB) .... QCCS
Creed Taylor, Inc. [Recording label] .... CTI
Creede Public Library, Creede, CO [Library symbol] [Library of Congress]
  (LCLS) .... CoCre
Creedence Clearwater Revival [Rock music group] .... CCR
Creedmoor, TX [AM radio station call letters] (BROA) .... KNEZ-AM
Creedmoor, TX [AM radio station call letters] (BROA) .... KQQA
Creedmore Psychiatric Center, Queens Village, New York, NY [Library
  symbol] [Library of Congress] (LCLS) .... NNCre
Creek (WDAA) C
Creek (ADA) .... CK
Creek [Maps and charts] .... CR
Creek (ADWA) .... cr
Creek (NTIO) .... Cr
Creek [Commonly used] (OPSA) .... CREEK
Creek (MCD) .... CRK
Creek Chub [Ichthyology] Cc
Creek Indian Memorial Association (EA) .... CIMA
Creel Associates, Inc. [Oak Brook, IL] (TSSD) .... CA
Creemore Public Library, Ontario [Library symbol] [National Library of
  Canada] (BIB) .... OCR
Creep Form Block (MCD) .... CFB
Creep Form Block Template (MCD) .... CFBT
Creep in Axisymmetric Shells .... CRASH
Creep Isostatic Pressing .... CRISP
Creep strength and low-cycle fatigue test (SAUS) .... Z-LCF-L
Creeping [Horticulture] .... CR
Creeping Environmental Problems (SAUS) .... CEP
Creepy Crawlers Fan Club (EA) .... CCFC
[The] Creighton University (GAGS) .... Creighton U
Creighton University (SAUO) .... CU
Creighton University, Alumni Library, Omaha, NE [Library symbol] [Library of
  Congress] (LCLS) .... NbOC-A
Creighton University, Alumni Library, Omaha, NE [OCLC symbol] (OCLC) .... OCA
Creighton University, Health Sciences Library, Omaha, NE [Library symbol]
  [Library of Congress] (LCLS) .... NbOC-H

Creighton University, Health Sciences Library, Omaha, NE [*OCLC symbol*] (OCLC) .... OCM
Creighton University, Law Library, Omaha, NE [*OCLC symbol*] (OCLC) CLL
Creighton University, Omaha, NE [*Library symbol*] [*Library of Congress*] (LCLS) .... NbOC
Creighton University, School of Dentistry, Omaha, NE [*Library symbol*] [*Library of Congress*] (LCLS) .... NbOC-D
Creighton University, School of Law, Omaha, NE [*Library symbol*] [*Library of Congress*] (LCLS) .... NbOC-L
Creighton University, School of Medicine and School of Pharmacy, Omaha, NE [*Library symbol*] [*Library of Congress*] (LCLS) .... NbOC-M
Creil [*France*] [*ICAO location identifier*] (ICLI) .... LFPC
Cremaster Reflex [*Medicine*] (MELL) .... CR
Cremate [*or Crematorium*] (DSUE) .... CREM
Cremation Association of America [*Later, CANA*] (EA) .... CAA
Cremation Association of North America (EA) .... CANA
Cremation Society of Great Britain .... CSGB
Crematory .... CRMTRY
Cremona Public Library, Alberta [*Library symbol*] [*National Library of Canada*] (NLC) .... ACRE
Crenated [*Red blood cells*] [*Hematology*] (DAVI) .... CREN
Crenated Red Cell (DB) .... CRC
Crendon [*England*] .... CREN
Crenellation (VRA) .... crnltn
Crenshaw, MS [*FM radio station call letters*] (BROA) .... WHKL-FM
Creo Society [*Defunct*] (EA) .... CS
Creole Petroleum Corporation (SAUO) .... CPC
Creole-American Genealogical Society (EA) .... CAGS
Creoles and Pidgins [*MARC language code*] [*Library of Congress*] (LCCP) .... crp
Creosote [*Telecommunications*] (TEL) C
Creosote .... CRE
Creosote Bushes [*Ecology*] .... C/B
Creosote Coal Tar (SAUS) .... CCT
Creosoted Wood Duct [*Telecommunications*] (TEL) .... CWD
Crepe .... CRP
Crepitation (ADWA) .... crep
Crepitus [*Crepitation*] [*Medicine*] .... CREP
Cresap, McCormick and Paget (SAUO) .... CMP
Crescendo [*Music*] (ROG) .... CR
Crescendo [*Music*] .... CRES
Crescendo [*Music*] .... CRESC
Crescendo [*Music*] (ODBW) .... cresc
Crescendo [*Music*] .... CRESO
Crescendo Murmur [*Medicine*] (MELL) .... CM
Crescent [*Commonly used*] (OPSA) .... CRECENT
Crescent (MCD) .... CRES
Crescent (ASC) .... Cres
Crescent .... CRESC
Crescent [*Commonly used*] (OPSA) .... CRESCENT
Crescent [*Commonly used*] (OPSA) .... CRESENT
Crescent (ADA) .... CRS
Crescent [*Commonly used*] (OPSA) .... CRSCNT
Crescent (ROG) .... CRSCT
Crescent [*Commonly used*] (OPSA) .... CRSENT
Crescent [*Commonly used*] (OPSA) .... CRSNT
Crescent Air Transport (SAUS) .... KJ
Crescent City [*California*] [*Airport symbol*] (OAG) .... CEC
Crescent City, CA [*FM radio station call letters*] .... KCRE
Crescent City, CA [*AM radio station call letters*] .... KFVR
Crescent City, CA [*FM radio station call letters*] (BROA) .... KHSR-FM
Crescent City, CA [*AM radio station call letters*] .... KPOD
Crescent City Public Library, Crescent City, CA [*Library symbol*] [*Library of Congress*] (LCLS) CCc
Crescent City Public Library, Crescent City, CA [*Library symbol*] [*Library of Congress*] (LCLS) CCcL
Crescent Heights High School, Medicine Hat, AB, Canada [*Library symbol*] [*Library of Congress*] (LCLS) .... CaAMCH
Crescent Heights High School, Medicine Hat, Alberta [*Library symbol*] [*National Library of Canada*] (NLC) .... AMCH
Crescent Lake National Wildlife Refuge (SAUS) .... CLNWR
Crescent Medical Aid (SAUO) .... CMA
Crescent Mines Ltd. [*Vancouver Stock Exchange symbol*] .... CRS
Crescent North, CA [*FM radio station call letters*] .... KPOD-FM
Crescent Petroleum Corporation (SAUO) .... CRC
Crescent Real Estate Eq [*NYSE symbol*] (TTSB) .... CEI
Crescent Real Estate Equities [*Associated Press*] (SAG) .... CresRE
Crescentic .... CR
Crescit sub Pondere Virtus [*Virtue Increases under a Burden*] [*Latin*] .... Cres sub Pond Virt
Cresco, IA [*Location identifier*] [*FAA*] (FAAL) .... CJJ
Cresco, IA [*FM radio station call letters*] .... KCZQ
Cresco Public Library, Cresco, IA [*Library symbol*] [*Library of Congress*] (LCLS) .... IaCre
Cresco Public Library, Cresco, IA [*Library symbol*] [*Library of Congress*] (LCLS) .... IaCresco
Cresco Times-Plain Dealer, Cresco, IA [*Library symbol*] [*Library of Congress*] (LCLS) .... IaCrescoTP
Cresco Times-Plain Dealer, Cresco, IA [*Library symbol*] [*Library of Congress*] (LCLS) .... IaCreTP
Crescomm Transmission Services, Inc. [*Fairfield, NJ*] [*Telecommunications*] (TSSD) .... CTS
Cresol Formaldehyde .... CF
Cresol Red [*Acid-base indicator*] (AAMN) .... CR
Cresol-Formaldehyde Resin (EDCT) .... CF
Cresolphthalein Complexone [*Analytical chemistry*] .... CPC

Cressent [*A publication*] (BRI) .... Cres
Cresson, PA [*FM radio station call letters*] .... WBXQ
Cresswell's Insolvency Cases [*1827-29*] [*England*] [*A publication*] (DLA) ...... Cress
Cresswell's Insolvency Cases [*1827-29*] [*England*] [*A publication*] (ILCA) .... Cress Ins Ca
Cresswell's Insolvency Cases [*1827-29*] [*England*] [*A publication*] (DLA) .... Cress Ins Cas
Cresswell's Insolvency Cases [*1827-29*] [*England*] [*A publication*] (DLA) .... Cress Insolv Cas
Crest [*Commonly used*] (OPSA) .... CREST
Crest [*Postal Service standard*] (OPSA) .... CRST
Crest Aviation (SAUS) .... JF
Crest Factor (SAUS) .... cf
Crest Factor [*Physics*] (IAA) .... CF
Crest Hill, IL [*FM radio station call letters*] .... WCCQ
Crest Resources Ltd. [*Vancouver Stock Exchange symbol*] .... CQR
Crest Time (MAE) .... CT
Crest Working Voltage [*Electronics*] (IAA) .... CWV
Crestar Energy [*Toronto Stock Exchange symbol*] (SG) .... CRS
Crestar Financial [*NYSE symbol*] (TTSB) .... CF
Crestar Financial Corp. [*Associated Press*] (SAG) .... Crestar
Crestbrook Forest Industries Ltd. [*Toronto Stock Exchange symbol*] [*Vancouver Stock Exchange symbol*] .... CFI
Crested Butte, CO [*FM radio station call letters*] .... KBUT
Crested Corp. [*NASDAQ symbol*] (SAG) .... CBAG
Crested Corp. [*Associated Press*] (SAG) .... CrstCp
Crested Fowl Club of America [*Later, CFFA*] (EA) .... CFCA
Crested Fowl Fanciers' Association (EA) .... CFFA
Crestline Capital [*NYSE symbol*] (SG) .... CLJ
Crestline, OH [*FM radio station call letters*] .... WAPQ
Crestline, OH [*FM radio station call letters*] (RBYB) .... WYXZ-FM
Creston, BC [*AM radio station call letters*] .... CFKC
Creston, IA [*Location identifier*] [*FAA*] (FAAL) .... CSQ
Creston, IA [*FM radio station call letters*] .... KITR
Creston, IA [*AM radio station call letters*] .... KSIB
Creston, IA [*FM radio station call letters*] (BROA) .... KSIB-FM
Creston News-Advertiser, Creston, IA [*Library symbol*] [*Library of Congress*] (LCLS) .... IaCresNA
Creston Public Library, British Columbia [*Library symbol*] [*National Library of Canada*] (NLC) .... BCRE
Creston Valley Museum, Creston, British Columbia [*Library symbol*] [*National Library of Canada*] (NLC) .... BCVM
Crestview, FL [*Location identifier*] [*FAA*] (FAAL) .... CEW
Crestview, FL [*FM radio station call letters*] .... WAAZ
Crestview, FL [*AM radio station call letters*] .... WCNU
Crestview, FL [*AM radio station call letters*] .... WJSB
Crestview/Bob Sikes [*Florida*] [*ICAO location identifier*] (ICLI) .... KCEW
Crestwood Elementary School, East Grand Forks, MN [*Library symbol*] [*Library of Congress*] (LCLS) .... MnEgfCE
Crestwood Library District, Crestwood, IL [*Library symbol*] [*Library of Congress*] (LCLS) .... ICw
Crestwood Library District, Crestwood, IL [*Library symbol*] [*Library of Congress*] (LCLS) .... ICwL
Crestwood, MO [*FM radio station call letters*] .... KSHE
Creswell, OR [*FM radio station call letters*] (RBYB) .... KNRQ-FM
Cresyl Diphenyl Phosphate (SAUS) .... CDP
Cresyl Glycidyl Ether [*Organic chemistry*] .... CGE
Cresyl Red [*Chemistry*] (DAVI) .... CR
Cresyl Violet [*Biological stain*] CV
Cresyl Violet Acetate (STED) .... CVA
Creta Praeparata [*Prepared Chalk*] [*Pharmacy*] (ROG) .... CRET PP
Cretaceous [*Geology*] .... CRET
Cretaceous [*Period, era, or system*] [*Geology*] .... K
Cretaceous and Tertiary [*Geology*] .... C-T
Cretaceous Normal Superchron [*Geology*] .... CNS
Cretaceous-Tertiary .... K-T
Cretaceous-Tertiary [*Geology*] .... KT
Cretaceous/Tertiary boundary (SAUO) .... K/T
Cretan Airlines SA [*Greece*] [*ICAO designator*] (FAAC) .... KRT
Cretans' Association "Omonoia" (EA) .... CAO
Crete, IL [*FM radio station call letters*] .... WEMG
Crete, IL [*FM radio station call letters*] (BROA) .... WYAA-FM
Crete, NE [*FM radio station call letters*] .... KDNE
Crete, NE [*FM radio station call letters*] .... KKNB
Crete Public Library, Crete, IL [*Library symbol*] [*Library of Congress*] (LCLS) .... ICre
Crete Public Library, Crete, NE [*Library symbol*] [*Library of Congress*] (LCLS) .... NbCr
Creusot Loire, Uddelhom Process (SAUS) .... CLU Process
Creutzfeldt-Jakob Disease [*Neurological disorder*] .... CJ
Creutzfeldt-Jakob Disease [*Neurological disorder*] .... CJD
Crew (MSA) .... CR
Crew Accommodations and Support Equipment (SSD) .... CASE
Crew Activities Scheduling Program [*NASA*] (KSC) .... CASP
Crew Activity Plan (MCD) .... CAP
Crew Activity Planning System (SSD) .... CAPS
Crew Altitude Protection Suit (SAUS) .... CAPS
Crew Altitude Protection System (NAKS) .... CAPS
Crew and Administrative Management System (SAUS) .... CAMS
Crew and Equipment Translation Aids [*NASA*] .... CETA
Crew and Equipment Translation Techniques and Routing [*NASA*] (SPST) .... CETTR
Crew and Passenger Support Equipment [*Military*] (AFIT) .... CPSE
Crew and Thermal Systems Division (SAUO) .... CTSD
Crew Assignment Program (SAUS) .... CAP

Crew Augmented Stability Factor [Boating] .... CASF
Crew Ballistic Shelter (MCD) .... CBS
Crew Boat .... CB
Crew Cargo Module [NASA] (KSC) .... CCM
Crew Certified (MCD) CC
Crew Certified (NAKS) cc
Crew Chief (MCD) CC
Crew Chief .... CRC
Crew Chief .... CRCH
Crew Chief (FAAC) .... CRCHF
Crew Chief Junction Box (ACAE) .... CCJB
Crew Command Input Device .... CCID
Crew [or Crewman] Communications Umbilical [Apollo] [NASA] .... CCU
Crew Communications Unit (NAKS) .... CCU
Crew Compartment (NAKS) cc
Crew Compartment (MCD) CC
Crew Compartment Cooling Unit [NASA] (KSC) .... CCCU
Crew Compartment Fit and Function [NASA] (KSC) C2F2
Crew Compartment Fit and Function [NASA] .... CCFF
Crew Compartment Test & Alarm Panel (SAUS) .... CCTAP
Crew Conditioning Calibration Unit (SAUS) .... CCCU
Crew Cooling System (SAUS) .... CCS
Crew Correctable Maintenance Action (MCD) .... CCMA
Crew Duty Time (SAUO) .... CDT
Crew Emergency Reentry Vehicle (ACAE) .... CERV
Crew Emergency Vehicle (MCD) .... CERV
Crew Environment Requirements (SAA) .... CER
Crew Equipment Compartment (MCD) .... CEC
Crew Equipment Integration [or Interface] Test (MCD) .... CEIT
Crew Equipment Integration Test (SAUS) .... CEIT
Crew Equipment Interface Test (SAUS) .... CEIT
Crew Escape and Rescue Techniques (SAUS) .... CREST
Crew Escape System (MCD) .... CES
Crew Escape Technologies [Air Force] .... CREST
Crew Escape Technology (SAUS) .... CREST
Crew Evaluation Launcher (SAA) .... CEL
Crew Evaluator [Military] (INF) .... CE
Crew Factor (SAUO) .... CF
Crew Factor (SSD) .... CFT
Crew Gunnery Simulator (PDAA) .... CGS
Crew Habitability and Protection [NASA] (KSC) .... CH & P
Crew Habitability and Protection (SAUS) .... CH&P
Crew Health Care System (SAUS) .... CHeCS
Crew Interface (MCD) CI
Crew Interface Coordinator (SAUO) CIC
Crew Leader (SAUS) CL
Crew Leader District (SAUS) .... CLD
Crew Life-Support Monitor [NASA] (KSC) .... CLSM
Crew Loads Instrumental Panel [NASA] (SPST) .... CLIP
Crew Loose Equipment [Aerospace] (MCD) .... CLE
Crew Loose Equipment Nomenclature [Aerospace] (MCD) .... CLENOM
Crew Maintenance Time (SAUS) .... CMT
Crew Medical Restraint System (SAUO) .... CMRS
Crew Member (SAUS) .... Cr/M
Crew Member .... CR/M
Crew Member Communications Selector (ACAE) .... CCS
Crew Member Identification .... CM-ID
Crew Member Trainee (DNAB) .... CMT
Crew Module [NASA] (NASA) .... CM
Crew Module (NAKS) .... cm
Crew Module Computer (MCD) .... CMC
Crew Natural Resources [Vancouver Stock Exchange symbol] .... CWT
Crew [or Crewman] Optical Alignment Sight [or Subsystem] [NASA] .... COAS
Crew Optical Alignment Subsystem (SAUS) .... COAS
Crew Overboard [Boating] .... COB
Crew Passive Dosimeter [NASA] (KSC) .... CPD
Crew Personal Equipment .... CPE
Crew Personal Hygiene Equipment .... CPHE
Crew Procedures Change Request (MCD) .... CPCR
Crew Procedures Control Board [NASA] (NASA) .... CPCB
Crew Procedures Division [NASA] (NASA) .... CPD
Crew Procedures Documentation System (MCD) .... CPDS
Crew Procedures Evaluation Simulator (MCD) .... CPES
Crew Procedures Laboratory (SAUS) .... CPL
Crew Procedures Management Plan [NASA] (NASA) .... CPMP
Crew Procedures Simulator .... CPS
Crew Procedures Trainer .... CPT
Crew Procedures Trainer / Combat Training Launch (SAA) .... CPT/CTL
Crew Provisioning Report .... CPR
Crew Public Library, Salem, IA [Library symbol] [Library of Congress] (LCLS) .... IaSal
Crew Quarters (KSC) .... CQ
Crew Reception Area [Apollo] [NASA] .... CRA
Crew Requirements Data Base [NASA] (SPST) .... CRDB
Crew Research Laboratory [Randolph Air Force Base, TX] .... CRL
Crew Research Management (GAVI) .... CRM
Crew Reserve Status [Military] (AFM) .... CRS
Crew Resource Management [FAA] (TAG) .... CRM
Crew Rest [Military] (AFM) .... CR
Crew Safety System .... CSS
Crew Safety Vehicle (SAUS) .... CSV
Crew Scheduling and Training Plan (NVT) .... CSTP
Crew Software Interface (MCD) .... CSI
Crew Software Interface (NAKS) .... csi
Crew Software Training Aid (MCD) .... CSTA

Crew Station [NASA] (KSC) .... CS
Crew Station (NAKS) .... cs
Crew Station Automated Technology (ACAE) .... CSAT
Crew Station Automation Technology (SAUS) .... CSAT
Crew Station Design Facility (MCD) .... CSDF
Crew Station Maintenance Manual [Navy] (CAAL) .... CSMM
Crew Station Research and Development Facility [Ames Research Center] .... CSRDF
Crew Station Review [NASA] (NASA) .... CSR
Crew Station Trainer [NASA] .... CST
Crew Station Unit (ACAE) .... CSU
Crew Support Equipment (SAUS) .... CSE
Crew System Ergonomics Information Analysis Center [DoD] (IID) .... CSERIAC
Crew Systems .... CS
Crew Systems Division [NASA] .... CSD
Crew Systems Laboratory [NASA] (NASA) .... CSL
Crew Systems Operating Procedures (MCD) .... CSOP
Crew Systems Trainer [NASA] (NASA) .... CST
Crew Task Demand .... CTD
Crew Task Detail .... CTD
Crew Training Air Force .... CREWTAF
Crew Training Air Force .... CTAF
Crew Training and Procedures Division [Johnson Space Center] [NASA] (NASA) .... CTPD
Crew Training Officer (SAA) .... CTO
Crew Transfer Tunnel [NASA] .... CTT
Crew Weapons Sight .... CWS
Crew/Cargo Module (NAKS) .... ccm
Crew-Compartment Fit and Function (SAUS) .... CCFF
Crewcuts Fan Club (EA) .... CFC
Crewe, VA [FM radio station call letters] (RBYB) .... WBZU
Crewe, VA [FM radio station call letters] (BROA) .... WKJS-FM
Crewe, VA [AM radio station call letters] .... WSVS
Crew-Initiated Automatic Test .... CIAT
Crew-in-the-Loop .... CITL
Crew-Loading Analysis (DNAB) .... CLA
Crewman (KSC) .... CM
Crewman (NASA) .... CMN
Crewman (AABC) .... CRMN
Crewman (SAUS) .... Crmn
Crew-Operated (SAA) .... C-O
Crew-Served Weapon .... C/S
Crew-Served Weapon Sight .... CSWS
Crew-Served Weapon Thermal Sight [Army] (INF) .... CSWTS
Crew-Served Weapons Captured .... CSWC
Crew-Served Weapons Qualification [Military] .... CWQ
Crewstation Evaluation Facility [Warminster, PA] [Naval Air Development Center] (GRD) .... CREST
Crew-Station Integration Program (ACAE) .... CSIP
Crew-Vehicle Simulation Research Facility [National Aeronautics and Space Administration Ames] (GAVI) .... CVSRF
CRH, Ltd. [NASDAQ symbol] (NQ) .... CRHC
CRH PLC [Associated Press] (SAG) .... CRH
CRH plc [NASDAQ symbol] (TTSB) .... CRHCY
CRI IMI MAE [Formerly, Insured Mortgage Association] [NYSE symbol] (SPSG) .... CMM
CRI Liquidating Real Estate Investment Trust [NYSE symbol] (SPSG) .... CFR
CRI Liquidating Real Estate Investment Trust [Associated Press] (SAG) .... CRI Liq
CRI Liquidating REIT [NYSE symbol] (TTSB) .... CFR
Crichton Behavioral Rating Scale (SAUS) .... CBRC
Criciuma [Brazil] [ICAO location identifier] (ICLI) .... SBCM
Cricket Association .... CA
Cricket Club CC
Cricket Club (SAUO) CC
Cricket Club of India (SAUO) CCI
Cricket Union of Victoria [Australia] .... CUV
Cricoid Cartilage [Medicine] (MELL) CC
Cricothyroid Lymph Node [Medicine] (MELL) .... CTLN
Cricothyroid Muscle (DB) .... CTM
Crigler-Najjar [Syndrome] [Medicine] (STED) .... CN
Crigler-Najjar Syndrome [Medicine] .... CNS
Criimi Mae, Inc. [NYSE symbol] (SAG) .... CMM
Criimi Mae, Inc. [Associated Press] (SAG) .... Criimi
Criimi Mae, Inc. [Associated Press] (SAG) .... CriimiMa
Crikey [An exclamation] [British] (DSUE) .... CRI
Crim Elementary School, Bowling Green, OH [Library symbol] [Library of Congress] (LCLS) .... OBgCrE
Crime .... CRI
Crime Abatement Team (SAUO) .... CAT
Crime Aboard Aircraft .... CAA
Crime and Delinquency [A publication] (DLA) .... Crime & Del
Crime and Delinquency Abstracts [A publication] .... CDAB
Crime and Delinquency Abstracts [A publication] (DLA) .... Crime & Delin'cy Abst
Crime and Delinquency Literature [A publication] (DLA) .... Crime & Delin'cy Lit
Crime and Justice Bulletin [A publication] .... C & J
Crime and Social Justice [Australia] [A publication] .... CSJ
Crime Control CC
Crime Intelligence [British] (DI) CI
Crime on Government Reservation .... CGR
Crime on High Seas .... CHS
Crime on Indian Reservation .... CIR
Crime Prevention Unit [British] .... CPU
Crime, Racketeering, Influence, Money and Politicians (SAUO) .... CRIMP
Crime Report Information System [Metropolitan Police database] [British] .... CRIS

Crime Reporters Association [*British*] (DBA) .... CRA
Crime Reporting Information System [*British*] (NITA) .... CRIS
Crime Scene Unit (LAIN) .... CSU
Crime Stoppers International (EA) .... CSI
Crime Stoppers USA [*Later, CSI*] (EA) .... CS
Crime Victims Research and Treatment Center [*Medical University of South Carolina*] [*Research center*] (RCD) CVC
Crime Writers' Association (EAIO) .... CWA
Crimea Air [*Ukraine*] [*FAA designator*] (FAAC) .... CRF
Crimean .... CRI
Crimean Astrophysical Observatory .... CAO
Crimean Hemorrhagic Fever [*Medicine*] (DB) .... CHD
Crimean Hemorrhagic Fever [*Medicine*] (PDAA) .... CHF
Crimean-Congo Hemorrhagic Fever [*Medicine*] .... CCHF
Crime-Free America [*An association*] (EA) .... CFA
Crimes Compensation Tribunal [*Victoria*] [*Australia*] .... CCT
Criminal (DLA) .... Cr
Criminal (AFM) .... CRIM
Criminal (ADWA) .... crim
Criminal (ROG) .... CRIML
Criminal .... CRMNL
Criminal Act (DLA) .... Cr Act
Criminal Appeal Court (SAUO) .... CAC
Criminal Appeal Reports [*England*] [*A publication*] (DLA) .... C App R
Criminal Appeal Reports [*England*] [*A publication*] (DLA) .... CAR
Criminal Appeal Reports [*England*] [*A publication*] (DLA) .... Cr App R
Criminal Appeal Reports [*England*] [*A publication*] (DLA) .... Cr App Rep
Criminal Appeal Reports [*England*] [*A publication*] (DLA) .... Crim App
Criminal Appeal Reports [*England*] [*A publication*] (DLA) .... Crim App (Eng)
Criminal Appeal Reports [*England*] [*A publication*] (DLA) .... Crim App R
Criminal Appeal Reports (Sentencing) [*England*] [*A publication*] (DLA) .... Cr App R(S)
Criminal Appeals (DLA) .... Cr App
Criminal Bar Association [*British*] (DBA) .... CBA
Criminal Case and Comment [*A publication*] (DLA) .... Crim Case & Com
Criminal Code [*A publication*] (DLA) .... Cr Code
Criminal Code [*A publication*] (DLA) .... Crim Code
Criminal Code and Code of Criminal Procedure [*Kansas*] [*A publication*] (DLA) .... Kan Crim Code & Code of Crim Proc
Criminal Code of Practice [*A publication*] (DLA) .... Cr Code Prac
Criminal Conversation [*Adultery*] [*Slang*] (DSUE) .... CRIM CON
Criminal Department (SAUO) .... CriDep
Criminal Deportee (ADA) .... CD
Criminal Docket System (SAUO) .... CRIMDOCK
Criminal Enforcement Division [*Office of Enforcement and Compliance Monitoring*] [*Environmental Protection Agency*] (EPA) .... CED
Criminal Evidence (LAIN) .... CE
Criminal Headquarters for Underworld Master Plan [*Organization in TV series "Lancelot Link"*] .... CHUMP
Criminal Identification and Investigation CII
Criminal, Immoral, and Narcotic .... CIN
Criminal Informant CI
Criminal Injuries Compensation Appeals Board (WDAA) .... CICAB
Criminal Injuries Compensation Board [*British*] .... CICB
Criminal Injuries Compensation Board [*British*] (DLA) .... Crim Inj Comp Bd
Criminal Intelligence [*Branch of the Metropolitan Police, London*] CI
Criminal Intelligence Bureau .... CIB
Criminal Investigation [*or Investigator*] [*Military*] CI
Criminal Investigation Agency (SAUO) .... CIA
Criminal Investigation Branch (SAUO) .... CIB
Criminal Investigation Branch (WDAA) .... CIB
Criminal Investigation Command (MCD) CIC
Criminal Investigation Command [*Army*] (DOMA) .... CIDC
Criminal Investigation Court (SAUO) CIC
Criminal Investigation Department [*Often loosely referred to as Scotland Yard*] [*Facetious translation: Copper in Disguise*] [*British*] .... CID
Criminal Investigation Detachment .... CID
Criminal Investigation Division [*Army*] .... CID
Criminal Investigation Field Office [*Military*] .... CIFO
Criminal Investigation Index (SAUS) CII
Criminal Investigations Policy and Oversight (AAGC) .... CIPO
Criminal Jurisprudence, Doctor of (SAUS) .... CJD
Criminal Justice and Behavior [*A publication*] (BRI) .... Crim J & B
Criminal Justice Archive and Information Network [*Department of Justice*] (GFGA) .... CJAIN
Criminal Justice Information System .... CJIS
Criminal Justice Institute (BARN) .... CJI
Criminal Justice Journal [*A publication*] (DLA) .... Crim JJ
Criminal Justice Legal Foundation .... CJLF
Criminal Justice Planning Agency (SAUO) .... CJPA
Criminal Justice Policy Foundation (EA) .... CJFP
Criminal Justice Quarterly [*A publication*] (DLA) .... Crim Just Q
Criminal Justice Reference Library [*University of Texas*] .... CJRL
Criminal Justice Review [*A publication*] (DLA) .... Crim Just Rev
Criminal Justice Statistic Association (SAUO) .... CJSA
Criminal Justice Statistics Association (EA) .... CJSA
Criminal Justice System .... CJS
Criminal Law (DLA) .... Crim Law
Criminal Law and Procedure .... CLP
Criminal Law Education and Research Center (SAUO) .... CLEAR
Criminal Law Journal [*A publication*] .... Crim Law J
Criminal Law Journal Reports [*India*] [*A publication*] (DLA) .... India Crim LJR
Criminal Law Magazine [*A publication*] (DLA) .... Crim L Mag
Criminal Law Magazine [*A publication*] (DLA) .... Cr Law Mag
Criminal Law Magazine [*A publication*] (DLA) .... Cr L Mag
Criminal Law Magazine and Reporter [*A publication*] (DLA) .... Criminal L Mag & Rep
Criminal Law Quarterly [*A publication*] .... Crim LQ
Criminal Law Recorder [*A publication*] (DLA) .... Crim L Rec
Criminal Law Recorder [*A publication*] (DLA) .... Cr Law Rec
Criminal Law Reports [*A publication*] .... CRIM LR
Criminal Law Reports, by Green [*United States*] [*A publication*] (DLA) .... Crim Law Reps (Green)
Criminal Law Reports, by Green [*United States*] [*A publication*] (DLA) .... Green Crim Reports
Criminal Law Reports, by Green [*United States*] [*A publication*] (DLA) .... Green Cr Rep
Criminal Law Review [*A publication*] .... Crim LR
Criminal Law Review Division [*New South Wales*] [*Australia*] .... CLRD
Criminal Law Revision Committee (SAUO) .... CLRC
Criminal Lawyer [*India*] [*A publication*] (DLA) .... Cr L
Criminal Matters .... CM
Criminal Offence [*British*] .... CO
Criminal Office .... CO
Criminal Office (SAUO) .... CO
Criminal Procedure [*Legal term*] (DLA) .... Crim Pro
Criminal Procedure [*Legal term*] (DLA) .... Crim Proc
Criminal Procedure [*Legal term*] (DLA) .... Cr P
Criminal Procedure (SAUS) .... Cr P
Criminal Procedure Law [*New York, NY*] [*A publication*] .... CPL
Criminal Procedures (SAUO) .... CCP
Criminal Record Office [*Scotland Yard*] .... CRO
Criminal Recorder [*A publication*] (DLA) .... Crim Rec
Criminal Records Directorate [*Army*] (ADDR) .... CRD
Criminal Rules for Courts of Limited Jurisdiction (SAUO) .... CrRLJ
Criminal Rulings [*Bombay, India*] [*A publication*] (DLA) .... Cr Rg
Criminal Sexual Conduct .... CSC
Criminal Sexual Psychopath .... CSP
Criminalism (SAUS) .... CRIM
Criminalist (SAUS) .... CRIM
Criminalistic Laboratory Information Systems [*FBI*] .... CLIS
Criminally Receiving Stolen Property .... CRSP
Criminally Uttering and Publishing False [*or Forged*] **Check** [*Legal term*] .... CU & PFC
Criminologica [*A publication*] (DLA) .... Criminol
Criminologie [*Criminology*] [*French*] (DLA) .... Criminol
Criminologist (WDAA) .... CRIM
Criminologist (DLA) .... Criminol
Criminologist (ADWA) .... criminol
Criminology (ADA) .... CRIMINOL
Criminology Research Council [*Australia*] .... CRC
Criminology Research Unit [*Australia*] .... CRU
Criminology Series [*A publication*] .... CSA
Crimp [*Engineering*] .... CRP
Crimping Tool Kit .... CTK
Crimp-On Snap-In Contacts (MUGU) .... COSI-KON
Crimson (ROG) .... CR
Crimson (ROG) .... CRIM
Crimson Clover Latent Virus [*Plant pathology*] CCLV
[*The*] **Crimson Group** [*Cambridge, MA*] [*Telecommunications*] (TSSD) .... TCG
Crimsonstar Resources [*Vancouver Stock Exchange symbol*] .... KRQ
Crinkled Single Aluminized Mylar (NASA) .... CSAM
Crip Flow Management Facility [*NASA*] (GFGA) .... CFMF
Crip Flow Management Facility [*NASA*] .... CFMS
Cripple Creek Public Library, Cripple Creek, CO [*Library symbol*] [*Library of Congress*] (LCLS) .... CoCri
Crippled and Other Health Impaired [*Obsolete*] .... COHI
Crippled Children's Seaside Home Society [*Australia*] .... CCSHS
Crippled Children's Services .... CCS
Crippled Children's Society (DAVI) .... CCS
Cripples' Help Society [*British*] (BI) .... CHS
Cripp's Church and Clergy Cases [*1847-50*] [*England*] [*A publication*] (DLA) .... Ch & Cl Cas
Cripp's Church and Clergy Cases [*1847-50*] [*England*] [*A publication*] (DLA) .... Cripp Ch Cas
Cripp's Church and Clergy Cases [*1847-50*] [*England*] [*A publication*] (DLA) .... Cripps
Cripp's Church and Clergy Cases [*1847-50*] [*England*] [*A publication*] (DLA) .... Cripps Cas
Cripp's Church and Clergy Cases [*1847-50*] [*England*] [*A publication*] (DLA) .... Cripp's Ch Cas
Cripp's Church and Clergy Cases [*1847-50*] [*England*] [*A publication*] (DLA) .... Cripps Church Cas
Cripp's Compulsory Acquisition of Land [*11th ed.*] [*1962*] [*A publication*] (DLA) .... Cripp Comp
Cripp's Law Relating to Church and Clergy [*8th ed.*] [*1937*] [*A publication*] (DLA) .... Cripp Ch L
Crisan Resources Ltd. [*Vancouver Stock Exchange symbol*] .... CRU
Crisciuma [*Brazil*] [*Airport symbol*] (OAG) .... CCM
Crisfield, MD [*FM radio station call letters*] (RBYB) .... WBEY
Crisis Action Management System .... CAMS
Crisis Action Package (AAGC) .... CAP
Crisis Action Planning [*Environmental science*] (COE) .... CAP
Crisis Action System (MCD) .... CAS
Crisis Action Team (MCD) .... CAT
Crisis Action Team Director (SAUO) .... CATD
Crisis Action Team Report (SAUO) .... CATREP
Crisis Action Weather Support System (MCD) .... CAWSS
Crisis Assessment Group [*NATO*] (NATG) .... CAG
Crisis Basic Imagery File (MCD) .... CRBIF

Crisis Condition (MCD) ... CRISCON
Crisis Confrontation ... CRICON
Crisis Coordination Center (SAUO) ... CCC
Crisis Coordination Group [*Environmental science*] (COE) ... CCG
Crisis Counseling Assistance and Training Program (SAUO) ... CCP
Crisis Deployment Management System (SAUO) ... CDMS
Crisis Environments Training Initiative (SAUO) ... CETI
Crisis Home Alert Technique ... CHAT
Crisis Intervention Center (MELL) ... CIC
Crisis Intervention Clinic (HGAA) ... CIC
Crisis Management (SAUO) ... CM
Crisis Management (DEMM) ... CrM
Crisis Management ADP System (SAUS) ... CMAS
Crisis Management Automation System (ACAE) ... CMAS
Crisis Management Center (SAUO) ... CMC
Crisis Management Council (SAUO) ... CMC
Crisis Management Exercise (SAUS) ... CMX
Crisis Management Facility (SAUO) ... CMF
Crisis Management Information Report ... CRIMREP
Crisis Management Information Reporting System (SAUO) ... CRIMREP
Crisis Management INTERCOM System (MCD) ... CMIS
Crisis Management Organization [*DoD*] ... CMO
Crisis Management Plan (MCD) ... CRIMP
Crisis Management Support System (SAUO) ... CMSS
Crisis Management System ... CMS
Crisis Management Team [*Army*] (INF) ... CMT
Crisis Manager [*Environmental science*] (COE) ... CM
Crisis on Location [*Psychological test*] ... COL
Crisis Operations Procedures Analysis (SAUO) ... COPA
Crisis Relocation (MCD) ... CR
Crisis Relocation Plans [*Federal Emergency Management Agency*] ... CRP
Crisis Resolution Center [*Psychiatry*] (DAVI) ... CRC
Crisis Resolution Center [*Psychiatry*] (DAVI) ... CRU
Crisis Resource Manager (SAUO) ... CRM
Crisis Response [*A publication*] ... CR
Crisis Staffing Procedures (MCD) ... CSP
Crisis Support Manager [*Environmental science*] (COE) ... CSM
Crisis Support Team [*Environmental science*] (COE) ... CST
Crisis Task Force (MCD) ... CTF
Crisis-Oriented Program ... COP
Crisp Uncirculated [*Numismatic term*] ... CrUnc
Crisped, Rolled and Stitched (SAUS) ... CR&S
CRISTA Ministries [*Later, CRISTA*] (EA) ... CM
Crista Ministries [*An association*] (EA) ... CRISTA
Crista Terminalis [*Cardiology*] ... CT
Cristalandia [*Brazil*] [*Airport symbol*] (AD) ... CLZ
Cristalandia/Santa Isabel do Morro [*Brazil*] [*ICAO location identifier*] (ICLI) ... SBSY
Cristalerias de Chile ADS [*NYSE symbol*] (SPSG) ... CGW
Cristalerias de Chile SA [*Associated Press*] (SAG) ... CristChile
Cristalerias de Chile SA [*Associated Press*] (SAG) ... CristChle
[*The*] **Cristian & Missionary Alliance in Canada** [*Alliance Chretienne et Missionaire au Canada*] [*Also, The Alliance Church*] (AC) ... C&MA
Cristo Redentor [*Argentina*] [*ICAO location identifier*] (ICLI) ... SAMC
Cristobal High School (SAUS) ... CHS
Cristobalite [*A mineral*] ... CR
Cristobalite-Tridymite [*A form of silica*] ... CT
Criswell Bible College, Dallas, TX [*Library symbol*] [*Library of Congress*] (LCLS) ... TxDaCB
Critchfield's Reports [*5-21 Ohio State*] [*A publication*] (DLA) ... Critch
Critchfield's Reports [*5-21 Ohio State*] [*A publication*] (DLA) ... Critch (Ohio St)
Criteria (SAUS) ... CRIT
Criteria Air Pollutant [*Environmental Protection Agency*] (GFGA) ... CAP
Criteria Air Pollutants (SAUS) ... CAP
Criteria and Indicators (SAUS) ... C&I
Criteria and Macrobudget Accounting (SAUS) ... CRTMBA
Criteria and Standards Division [*Environmental Protection Agency*] (GFGA) ... CSD
Criteria Continuous Concentration (EEVL) ... CCC
Criteria for Preparation and Evaluation of Radiological Regulations and Guides (SAUS) ... NUREG
Criteria Maximum Concentration (EEVL) ... CMC
Criteria of Teacher Selection [*Project*] (AIE) ... CATS
Criteria Reference Information Bank (SAUO) ... CRIB
Criterion [*Theatre and restaurant at Piccadilly Circus*] [*London*] (DSUE) ... CRI
Criterion (AABC) ... CRIT
Criterion Action Element [*Army*] (ADDR) ... CAE
Criterion Document (EEVL) ... CD
Criterion Strategy Controller (SAUS) ... CSC
Criterion-Referenced English Syntax Test (EDAC) ... CREST
Criterion-Referenced Instruction ... CRI
Criterion-Referenced Measurement [*Education*] ... CRM
Criterion-Referenced Test [*or Testing*] [*Education*] ... CRT
Critias [*of Plato*] [*Classical studies*] (OCD) ... Criti
Critic (NTIO) ... crit
Critical (WDAA) ... crit
Critical [*Telecommunications*] (TEL) ... CRIT
Critical Acquisition Position [*Military*] (RDA) ... CAP
Critical Aeronautical Material and Equipment List ... CAMEL
Critical Aggregation Concentration [*Electrolyte induced aggregation of dispersed species*] ... CAC
Critical Agricultural Materials Act [*1984*] ... CAMA
Critical Air Blast [*Test*] ... CAB
Critical Angle Prism Sensor (KSC) ... CAPS
Critical Angle Towed Array System (SAUS) ... CATAS
Critical Appraisal for Medical Students (SAUO) ... CAMS
Critical Appraisal Skills Programme (SAUO) ... CASP
Critical Aquifer Protection Area [*Environmental Protection Agency*] (FFDE) ... CAPA
Critical Area Flag ... CAF
Critical Assembly [*Nuclear energy*] (NRCH) ... CA
Critical Assembly Fuel Element Exchange [*Nuclear energy*] ... CAFEE
Critical Assessment of Methods of Protein Structure Prediction ... CASP
Critical Assignment Development Program (SAUS) ... CADP
Critical Bandwidth [*of noise*] ... CBW
Critical Bibliography to Religion in America [*A publication*] (BJA) ... CBRA
Critical Carbohydrate Level [*Nutrition*] ... CCL
Critical Care [*Medicine*] ... CC
Critical Care Manual ... CCM
Critical Care Medical Unit (DMAA) ... CCMU
Critical Care Nurse (NUJO) ... CCN
Critical Care Nursing (MELL) ... CCN
Critical Care Recovery Unit [*Medicine*] (DAVI) ... CCRU
Critical Care Registered Nurse ... CCRN
Critical Care Unit [*Medicine*] ... CCU
Critical Care Ventilator (MELL) ... CCV
Critical Care Workstation [*Medicine*] (DMAA) ... CCW
Critical Coagulation Concentration [*Colloidal chemistry*] ... CCC
Critical Collection Problems Committee [*United States Intelligence Board*] [*Obsolete*] ... CCPC
Critical Color Flicker Frequency (PDAA) ... CCFF
Critical Commodities List [*Department of Commerce*] ... CCL
Critical Communication (SAUO) ... CRITICOM
Critical Communications System [*Military*] (AABC) ... CRITCOM
Critical Community Size [*For disease persitence*] ... CCS
Critical Component Demonstration (SAUS) ... CCD
Critical Component Temperature (ACAE) ... CCT
Critical Components List ... CCL
Critical Compression Pressure ... CCP
Critical Compression Ratio ... CCR
Critical Condition [*Medicine*] ... CC
Critical Control Circuit ... CCC
Critical Control Point [*Food technology*] ... CCP
Critical Crevice Solution (PDAA) ... CCS
Critical Damping Resistance External ... CDRX
Critical Decision Point ... CDP
Critical Demulsification Temperature (PDAA) ... CDF
Critical Design and Qualification Review (NASA) ... CDQR
Critical Design Audit (MCD) ... CDA
Critical Design Review (AFM) ... CDR
Critical Design Review Commercial (MCD) ... CDRC
Critical Design Review Meeting (SAA) ... CDRM
Critical Design Review Work Sheets (ACAE) ... CDRWS
Critical Design Walk-through (SAUS) ... CDW
Critical Difference (SAUS) ... CD
Critical Dimension (AAEL) ... CD
Critical Dimension Overlay (AAEL) ... CD/OL
Critical Dimension Scanning Electron Microscopes ... CD-SEM
Critical Dissolution Time [*Chemistry*] ... CDT
Critical Employment Indicator (COE) ... CEI
Critical Emulsification Temperature (PDAA) ... CET
Critical End Item (ACAE) ... CEI
Critical Engine Inoperative (MCD) ... CEI
Critical Equipment Monitoring System (SAUS) ... CEMS
Critical Error Detection (MCD) ... CED
Critical Evaluation Task Force (SAUS) ... CETF
Critical Event Discrimination Experiment (ACAE) ... CEDE
Critical Examination (CAAL) ... CE
Critical Experiment Laboratory ... CEL
Critical Experiment Pulsed Fast Reactor ... CEPFR
Critical Experiment Reactor (NRCH) ... CER
Critical Experiment Station [*Nuclear energy*] (GFGA) ... CES
Critical Experiment Tank ... CET
Critical Experiments Facility [*Nuclear energy*] (OA) ... CEF
Critical Field Length (MCD) ... CFL
Critical Field Strength (AAG) ... CFS
Critical Flashover [*Voltage*] (IEEE) ... CFO
Critical Flash-Over (SAUS) ... CFO
Critical Flicker Frequency [*Optics*] (AAMN) ... CFF
Critical Flicker Frequency (DIPS) ... cff
Critical Flicker Fusion [*Ophthalmology*] ... CFF
Critical Flicker Fusion Threshold [*Ophthalmology*] (PDAA) ... CFFT
Critical Flocculation Concentration [*Electrolyte induced flocculation of dispersed species*] ... CFC
Critical Flow Model (MCD) ... CFM
Critical Flow Orifice [*Engineering*] ... CFO
Critical Flow Venture-Constant Volume Sampler (ERG) ... CFV-CVS
Critical Flow Venturi [*Engineering*] ... CFV
Critical Fluid Light Scattering Experiment (SAUS) ... CFLSE
Critical Fluid Scattering Experiment (SAUS) ... ZENO
Critical Fluid Thermal Equilibration (SAUS) ... CFTE
Critical Fluid Viscosity Measurement Experiment (SAUS) ... CFVME
Critical Frequency (MSA) ... CRITF
Critical Frequency (CET) ... FC
Critical Friendly Zone [*Army*] (ADDR) ... CFZ
Critical Functions Avionics Control Unit (SAUS) ... CFACU
Critical Fusion Frequency [*Optics*] (IAA) ... CF
Critical Fusion Frequency [*Optics*] ... CFF
Critical Grid Current ... CGC
Critical Grid Voltage ... CGV

Critical Health Manpower Shortage Areas	CHMSA
Critical Heat Flux [Nuclear energy]	CHF
Critical Heat Flux Ratio [Nuclear energy] (NRCH)	CHFR
Critical Height (DA)	CH
Critical Height [Aviation] (DA)	HC
Critical Hours [Broadcasting term]	CH
Critical Housing Shortage At [named place] [Army]	CRITHOUS
Critical Human Performance and Evaluation, (IEEE)	CHPAE
Critical Impact Velocity (MCD)	CIV
Critical Incident Debriefing for General Aviation Pilots	CIDGAP
Critical Incident Detection (HEAS)	CID
Critical Incident Stress Debriefing	CISD
Critical Incident Technique [Department of Health and Human Services] (GFGA)	CIT
Critical Incidents Reporting System (SAUO)	CIRS
Critical Index Management (HGAA)	CIM
Critical Influence	CI
Critical Information [Environmental science] (COE)	CRITIC
Critical Information Requirement (SAUO)	CIR
Critical Infrastructure Assurance Office	CIAO
Critical Infrastructure Protection (DEMM)	CIP
Critical Initial Flaw Size (SAUS)	CIFS
Critical Innovation Potential (SAUS)	CIP
[A] Critical Insight into Israel's Dilemmas [Jewish student newspaper]	ACIID
Critical Inspection of Bearings for Life Extension (MCD)	CIBLE
Critical Intelligence	CI
Critical Intelligence [Army]	CRITIC
Critical Intelligence Communication	CRITICOMM
Critical Intelligence Communications System [DIN/DSSCS]	CRITICOM
Critical Intelligence Parameter (CAAL)	CIP
Critical Intelligence Report (CINC)	CRITIC
Critical Intermediate Design Review (NASA)	CIDR
Critical Inventory Parts File (SAUS)	CIP File
Critical Ionization Velocity (SAUS)	CIV
Critical Isotope Reactor, General Atomics	CIRGA
Critical Issues Council [Defunct] (EA)	CIC
Critical Issues Demonstration (MCD)	CID
Critical Issues Fund [National Trust for Historic Preservation]	CIF
Critical Item	CI
Critical Item Code	CIC
Critical Item Development Specification (CAAL)	CIDS
Critical Item Inspection [California Highway Patrol's accident inspection program]	CII
Critical Item List (MCD)	CIL
Critical Item Review Committee [Air Force] (AFIT)	CIRC
Critical Item Tag (MCD)	CIT
Critical Items and Residual Hazards List (MCD)	CIRHS
Critical Job Element (GFGA)	CJE
Critical Joint Duty Assignment (COE)	CJDA
Critical Labor Level (ADA)	CLL
Critical Laboratory Evaluation Roast [Food technology]	CLER
Critical Legal Studies Philosophy	CLS
Critical Line Item (CCCA)	CLI
Critical Link Factor	CLF
Critical List [Medicine]	CL
Critical Load Cycle (SAUS)	CLC
Critical Load Level	CLL
Critical Mass [Later, CMEP] [An association] (EA)	CM
Critical Mass Energy Project (EA)	CMEP
Critical Mass Energy Project of Public Citizen (EA)	CMEP
Critical Mass Laboratory	CML
Critical Materials Parts List (MCD)	CMPL
Critical Micelle Concentration	CMC
Critical Micelle Concentration (ADWA)	cmc
Critical Military Target	CMT
Critical Minimum Weight (SAUS)	CMW
Critical Mission Function [Army] (RDA)	CMF
Critical Node Recognizer (ACAE)	CNR
Critical Nuclear Defense Weapon Information (SAUO)	CNDWI
Critical Nuclear Material	CNM
Critical Nuclear Weapons Design Information (MCD)	CNWDI
Critical Occupational Specialty [Military] (INF)	COS
Critical Officer Personnel Requirement [Air Force]	COPR
Critical Off-Time [Medicine] (MAE)	COT
Critical Operational Issues Testing [DoD]	COI
Critical Optics Technology Development (ACAE)	COTD
Critical Outcome Data Evaluation System [Auto safety research]	CODES
Critical Outcomes Data Evaluation System [Automobile accident reporting]	CODES
Critical Oxygen Index (HEAS)	COI
Critical Packing Pressure (SAUS)	CBP
Critical Parent (DHP)	CP
Critical Parts Centralized Forecast Computation (SAUS)	CPCFC
Critical Path	CP
Critical Path [NASDAQ symbol] (SG)	CPTH
Critical Path Analysis [Computer science] (CIST)	CPA
Critical Path Bar (PDAA)	CPB
Critical Path Length	CPL
Critical Path Method [Graph theory] [Telecommunications] (TEL)	CPM
Critical Path Network	CPN
Critical Path Planning	CPP
Critical Path Planning and Scheduling	CPPS
Critical Path Programming Method (SAUS)	CPPM
Critical Path Programming Model (SAUS)	CPPM
Critical Path Schedule (SAUS)	CPS

Critical Path Scheduling [or System]	CPS
Critical Path Scheduling Method [Management]	CPSM
Critical Path System (SAUS)	CPS
Critical Path Technique	CPT
Critical Performance Weight (SAA)	CPW
Critical Period	CP
Critical Phase Matching (SAUS)	CPM
Critical Phase System Software [NASA] (NASA)	CPSS
Critical Pigment Volume Concentration [Paint technology]	CPVC
Critical Pitting Temperature [Metallurgy]	CPT
Critical Point (SAUS)	CP
Critical Point Drying (MELL)	CPD
Critical Point Facility (SISD)	CPF
Critical Power [Nuclear energy] (NRCH)	CP
Critical Power Ratio [Nuclear energy] (NRCH)	CPR
Critical Problem Report [NASA] (NASA)	CPR
Critical Process Team (AAGC)	CPT
Critical Processing Unit	CPU
Critical Qualification Design Review (NASA)	CQDR
Critical Quality Element (NRCH)	CQE
Critical Quarterly [A publication] (BRI)	Crit Q
Critical Ratio	CR
Critical Ratio of the Difference	CRD
Critical Reactor Component (NRCH)	CRC
Critical Reactor Experiments (SAUS)	CRITS
Critical Reasoning Test Battery	CRTB
Critical Reflection Activation Analysis	CRAA
Critical Relatice Humidity (SAUS)	RHc
Critical Relative Humidity	CRH
Critical Reliability Action Report (AAG)	CRAR
Critical Requirements Review (NASA)	CRR
Critical Resolved Shear Stress	CRSS
Critical Resource Allocation Method (PDAA)	CRAM
Critical Review [A publication] (BRI)	Crit R
Critical Reviews In Biochemistry and Molecular Biology (SAUS)	Crit Rev Biochem Mol Biol
Critical Reviews in Oncology/Hematology (SAUS)	Crit Rev Oncol Hematol
Critical Reviews in Oral Biology and Medicine (MEC)	Crit Rev Oral Biol Med
Critical Rule Curve (NOAA)	CRC
Critical Safety Item [Military]	CSI
Critical Safety Item Program [Army]	CSIP
Critical Sector Detector [FAA] (TAG)	CSD
Critical Sensitive	CS
Critical Serum Chemistry Value (DMAA)	CSCV
Critical Shear Stress	CSS
Critical Shortage Report (AAG)	CSR
Critical Sliding Velocity [Automotive safety, vehicle rollover]	CSV
Critical Solution Temperature	CST
Critical Solution Temperature (SAUS)	cst
Critical Solvent De-Ashing [Coal processing]	CSD
Critical Specifications Element (DNAB)	CSE
Critical Speed Formula	CSF
Critical Stress of Dislocation Generation (SAUS)	CSDG
Critical Subsystems Development (MCD)	CSD
Critical Success Factor [Management tool]	CSF
Critical Success Index (SAUS)	CSI
Critical Supersaturation Model (SAUS)	CSM
Critical Surface Tension [Physical chemistry]	CST
Critical Sustainability Item [Environmental science] (COE)	CSI
Critical Systems Advisory Group (SAUO)	CSAG
Critical Systems Support (SAUS)	CSS
Critical Technical Issue (ACAE)	CTI
Critical Technical Parameters (RDA)	CTP
Critical Technologies Institute [Federally funded research and development center]	CTI
Critical Temperature	CT
Critical Temperature (SAUS)	Tc
Critical Temperature Ratio [Environmental science] (COE)	CTR
Critical Temperature Resistor (SAUS)	CTR
Critical Temperature Threshold [Chemical technology]	CTT
Critical Terrain; Obstacles; Cover and Concealment; Observation and Fields of Fire; Avenues of Approach [Military]	COCOA
Critical Thermal Maximum	CTM
Critical Time Slice (SAUS)	CTS
Critical Tolerance Factor (MCD)	CTF
Critical Tool Service	CTS
Critical Tracking Task [System for preventing drunken driver from starting car]	CTT
Critical Transportation Item (MCD)	CTI
Critical Trauma Care [Medicine] (BARN)	CTC
Critical Trends Assessment (SAUO)	CTA
Critical Trends Assessment Project (SAUO)	CTAP
Critical Turning Distance Add (SAA)	CTDA
Critical Value	CV
Critical Water Temperature (OA)	CWT
Criticality	CRTL
Criticality, Accessibility, Recuperability, Vulnerability, Effect, Recognizability [Environmental science] (COE)	CARVER
Criticality Analysis (KSC)	CA
Criticality Experiment [Nuclear energy] (NRCH)	CX
Criticallity Data Center	CDC
Critically (SAUS)	Crit
Critically Alarm Annunciators (ABAC)	CAA
Critically Appraised Topic (SAUO)	CAT
Critically Sensitive	CS

Critically Sensitive Level 3 [*Information*] ... CS3
Critically Sensitive Level 4 [*Information*] ... CS4
Critical-Path Management ... CPM
Critical-Size Defect [*Medicine*] ... CSD
Critical-Temperature-Resistor (SAUS) ... Critesistor
Criticare Systems [*NASDAQ symbol*] (TTSB) ... CXIM
Criticare Systems, Inc. [*Associated Press*] (SAG) ... Criticre
Criticare Systems, Inc. [*NASDAQ symbol*] (NQ) ... CXIM
Criticised [*Soundness of decision or reasoning in cited case criticised for reasons given*] [*Used in Shephard's Citations*] [*Legal term*] (DLA) ... c
Criticism (NTIO) ... crit
Criticism ... CRIT
Criticism (SAUS) ... Crit
Criticism [*A publication*] (BRI) ... Critm
Criticized (ADWA) ... crit
Critique [*A publication*] (BRI) ... Critiq
Crito [*of Plato*] [*Classical studies*] (OCD) ... Cri
CrO2 chromium dioxide (SAUS) ... CRO
Croatia (MILB) ... Cr
Croatia (ECON) ... CRO
Croatia ... Croat
Croatia [*Internet country code*] ... HR
Croatia Airlines [*ICAO designator*] (FAAC) ... CTN
Croatian (ADWA) ... Croat
Croatian Academy of America (EA) ... CAA
Croatian Australian Association ... CAA
Croatian Catholic Union of the USA and Canada (EA) ... CCU
Croatian Catholic Union of United States of America and Canada ... CCUAC
Croatian Christian Democratic Party [*Political party*] (EY) ... CCDP
Croatian Christian Democratic Party [*Political party*] ... HKDS
Croatian Defence Council (SAUO) ... HVO
Croatian Defense Association [*Political party*] ... HOS
Croatian Democratic Community [*Political party*] ... CDC
Croatian Democratic Party [*Political party*] (EY) ... CDP
Croatian Democratic Union [*Political party*] (EY) ... CDU
Croatian Democratic Union [*Political party*] (BUAC) ... HDZ
Croatian Democratic Union of Bosnia-Herzegovina [*Political party*] (EY) ... CDU-BH
Croatian Ethnic School [*Australia*] ... CES
Croatian European Community Studies Association (SAUO) ... CESA
Croatian Fraternal Union of America (EA) ... CFU
Croatian Genealogical Society (EA) ... CGS
Croatian Liberation Movement [*Australia*] ... CLM
Croatian Male Choir, Melbourne [*Australia*] ... CMCM
Croatian National Congress (EA) ... CNC
Croatian Numismatic Society (SAUO) ... HND
Croatian Party of Law [*Political party*] ... CPL
Croatian Party of Rights [*Political party*] ... CPR
Croatian Peasant Party (EA) ... CPP
Croatian Peasants Party [*Political party*] (EY) ... CPP
Croatian Philatelic Society (EA) ... CPS
Croatian Revolutionary Brotherhood [*Former Yugoslavia*] (PD) ... HRB
Croatian Serbian Slovene Genealogical Society (EA) ... CSSGS
Croatian Social-Liberal Party [*Political party*] ... CSLP
Croatian Workers Association of America (EA) ... CWAA
Croatica Chemica Acta (MEC) ... Croatica Chem Acta
Croce Rossa Italiana [*Italian Red Cross*] ... CRI
Crochet ... CR
Crochet Association International (EA) ... CAI
Crocker National Bank, San Francisco, CA [*Library symbol*] [*Library of Congress*] (LCLS) ... CSfCAB
Crocker National Corp. (SAUO) ... CKN
Crocker National Corp. (EFIS) ... CNC
Crocker on Sheriffs and Constables [*A publication*] (DLA) ... Crock Sh
Crocker on the Duties of Coroners in New York [*A publication*] (DLA) ... Crock Cor
Crocker Realty Investors, Inc. [*AMEX symbol*] (SAG) ... CKT
Crocker Realty Investors, Inc. [*Associated Press*] (SAG) ... Crockr
Crocker Realty Trust [*AMEX symbol*] (TTSB) ... CKT
Crocker Realty Trust, Inc. [*Associated Press*] (SAG) ... CrckrRT
Crocker's Notes on Common Forms [*Massachusetts*] [*A publication*] (DLA) ... Crock Forms
Crocker's Notes on the Public Statutes of Massachusetts [*A publication*] (DLA) ... Crock Notes
Crockery ... CKRY
Crockery Township Library, Nunica, MI [*Library symbol*] [*Library of Congress*] (LCLS) ... MiNun
Crockett Public Library, Crockett, TX [*Library symbol*] [*Library of Congress*] (LCLS) ... TxCr
Crockett, TX [*Location identifier*] [*FAA*] (FAAL) ... CCP
Crockett, TX [*FM radio station call letters*] ... KBHT
Crockett, TX [*AM radio station call letters*] ... KIVY
Crockett, TX [*FM radio station call letters*] ... KIVY-FM
Crocodile (ADWA) ... croc
Crocodile (DSUE) ... CROC
crocodiliologist (SAUS) ... crocodiliol
Crocus Saffron [*Pharmacy*] (ROG) ... CROC
Croes Newydd [*Welsh depot code*] ... CNYD
Croesus Resources, Inc. [*Vancouver Stock Exchange symbol*] ... CWV
Croft (WDAA) ... C
Croft Readiness Assessment in Comprehension Kit [*Child development test*] ... CRAC-KIT
Croghan [*New York*] [*Seismograph station code, US Geological Survey*] (SEIS) ... CROG
Crohn's and Colitis Foundation of America (EA) ... CCFA
Crohn's and Colitis Foundation of America, Inc. (PAZ) ... CCFA
Crohn's Colitis [*Medicine*] (MELL) ... CC
Crohn's Disease [*Gastroenterology*] (DAVI) ... CD
Crohn's Disease Activity Index [*Medicine*] ... CDAI
Croion Agency (SAUO) ... CA
Croissant (DD) ... crois
Croix de Guerre [*French military decoration*] ... C de G
Croke's English King's Bench Reports [*1582-1641*] [*A publication*] (DLA) ... Cro
Croke's English King's Bench Reports [*1582-1641*] [*A publication*] (DLA) ... Croke
Croke's English King's Bench Reports Tempore Charles I [*1625-41*] [*A publication*] (DLA) ... Cro Car
Croke's English King's Bench Reports Tempore Charles I [*1625-41*] [*A publication*] (DLA) ... Cro Car (Eng)
Croke's English King's Bench Reports Tempore Charles I [*1625-41*] [*A publication*] (DLA) ... Cro Cas
Croke's English King's Bench Reports Tempore Charles I [*1625-41*] [*A publication*] (DLA) ... R3 Cro
Croke's English King's Bench Reports Tempore Elizabeth [*1582-1603*] [*A publication*] (DLA) ... Cro Eliz
Croke's English King's Bench Reports Tempore Elizabeth [*1582-1603*] [*A publication*] (DLA) ... Cro Eliz (Eng)
Croke's English King's Bench Reports Tempore Elizabeth [*1582-1603*] [*A publication*] (DLA) ... R1 Cro
Croke's English King's Bench Reports Tempore James [*Jacobus*] **I** [*A publication*] (DLA) ... R2 Cro
Croke's English King's Bench Reports Tempore James (Jacobus) I [*A publication*] (DLA) ... Cro Jac
Croke's English King's Bench Reports Tempore James (Jacobus) I [*A publication*] (DLA) ... Cro Jac (Eng)
Crole Investment Cooperation (SAUO) ... CIC
Cro-Magnon (VRA) ... CrMg
Cromaine Library, Hartland, MI [*Library symbol*] [*Library of Congress*] (LCLS) ... MiHal
Cromemco Local Area Network [*Cromemco, Inc.*] [*Mountain View, CA*] [*Telecommunications*] (TSSD) ... C-NET
Cromolyn Sodium [*Pharmacology*] ... CS
Crompton and Jervis' English Exchequer Reports [*1830-32*] [*A publication*] (DLA) ... C & J
Crompton and Jervis' English Exchequer Reports [*1830-32*] [*A publication*] (DLA) ... Cromp & J
Crompton and Jervis' English Exchequer Reports [*1830-32*] [*A publication*] (DLA) ... Cromp & J (Eng)
Crompton and Jervis' English Exchequer Reports [*1830-32*] [*A publication*] (DLA) ... Cromp & Jer
Crompton and Jervis' English Exchequer Reports [*1830-32*] [*A publication*] (DLA) ... Cromp & Jerv
Crompton & Knowles [*NYSE symbol*] (TTSB) ... CNK
Crompton & Knowles Corp. [*NYSE symbol*] (SPSG) ... CNK
Crompton & Knowles Corp. [*Associated Press*] (SAG) ... CrmpKnl
Crompton and Meeson's English Exchequer Reports [*1832-34*] [*A publication*] (DLA) ... C & M
Crompton and Meeson's English Exchequer Reports [*1832-34*] [*A publication*] (DLA) ... Cr & M
Crompton and Meeson's English Exchequer Reports [*1832-34*] [*A publication*] (DLA) ... Cromp & M
Crompton and Meeson's English Exchequer Reports [*1832-34*] [*A publication*] (DLA) ... Cromp & Mees
Crompton and Meeson's English Exchequer Reports [*1832-34*] [*A publication*] (DLA) ... Cromp & M (Eng)
Crompton, Meeson, and Roscoe's English Exchequer Reports [*1834-36*] [*A publication*] (DLA) ... Cr M & R
Crompton, Meeson, and Roscoe's English Exchequer Reports [*1834-36*] [*A publication*] (DLA) ... Cromp M & R
Crompton, Meeson, and Roscoe's English Exchequer Reports [*1834-36*] [*A publication*] (DLA) ... Cromp M & R (Eng)
Crompton's English Exchequer Reports [*A publication*] (DLA) ... Cromp Exch R
Crompton's English Exchequer Reports [*A publication*] (DLA) ... Cromp Ex R
Crompton's Jurisdiction of Courts [*A publication*] (DLA) ... Cromp Cts
Crompton's Jurisdiction of Courts [*A publication*] (DLA) ... Cromp JC
Crompton's Jurisdiction of Courts [*A publication*] (DLA) ... Cromp Jur
Crompton's Office of a Justice of the Peace [*1637*] [*A publication*] (DLA) ... Crom
Crompton's Office of a Justice of the Peace [*1637*] [*A publication*] (DLA) ... Cromp Just
Crompton's Rules and Cases of Practice [*A publication*] (DLA) ... Cromp R & C Pr
Cromwell [*New Zealand*] [*Airport symbol*] (AD) ... CWE
Cromwell Association (EA) ... CA
Cromwell High School, Cromwell, MN [*Library symbol*] [*Library of Congress*] (LCLS) ... MnCrwHS
Cromwell Hospital (SAUO) ... CH
Cronar Dot Litho [*Du Pont*] ... CDL
Cronar Halftone Litho [*Du Pont*] ... CHL
Cronholm-Ottosson Rating Scale [*Psychopathology*] ... CORS
Cronos Group [*NASDAQ symbol*] (SG) ... CRNS
Cronos Group [*NASDAQ symbol*] (TTSB) ... CRNSF
Cronos Group [*Associated Press*] (SAG) ... CronosG
Cronus Airlines [*Greece*] [*FAA designator*] (FAAC) ... CUS
Cronus Industries, Inc. (MHDW) ... CRNS
Crook Community Library, Crook, CO [*Library symbol*] [*Library of Congress*] (LCLS) ... CoCroo
Crook County Library, Prineville, OR [*Library symbol*] [*Library of Congress*] (LCLS) ... OrPr
Crook County Library, Prineville, OR [*Library symbol*] [*Library of Congress*] (LCLS) ... OrPrC
Crooked Creek [*Alaska*] [*Airport symbol*] (OAG) ... CKD
Crooked Creek, AK [*Location identifier*] [*FAA*] (FAAL) ... CKD

Crooked Creek Colony School, Alberta [Library symbol] [National Library of Canada] (BIB) .... ACCCS
Crooked Island [Bahamas] [Airport symbol] (OAG) .... CRI
Crooks Michell Peacock Stewart Pty Ltd. (SAUO) .... CMPS
Crookston [Diocesan abbreviation] [Minnesota] (TOCD) .... CR
Crookston, MN [Location identifier] [FAA] (FAAL) .... CKN
Crookston, MN [FM radio station call letters] .... KQHT
Crookston, MN [AM radio station call letters] .... KROX
Crookston, MN [FM radio station call letters] .... KYCK
Crookston, NE [FM radio station call letters] .... KINI
Crookston Public Library, Crookston, MN [Library symbol] [Library of Congress] (LCLS) .... MnCr
Crooksville, OH [FM radio station call letters] .... WYBZ
Crop and Food Supply Assessment (SAUO) .... CFSA
Crop Condition Assessment .... CCA
Crop Development Centre [University of Saskatchewan] [Canada] (IRC) .... CDC
Crop Dryer Manufacturers Council (EA) .... CDMC
Crop End Control (SAUS) .... CEC
Crop Environment Resource Synthesis (SAUS) .... CERES
Crop Estimation through Resource and Environment Synthesis (SAUS) .... CERES
Crop Evolution Laboratory [University of Illinois] .... CEL
Crop Forecasting and Early Warning Unit (SAUS) .... CFEWU
Crop Growers [NASDAQ symbol] (TTSB) .... CGRO
Crop Growers Corp. [NASDAQ symbol] (SAG) .... CGRO
Crop Growers Corp. [Associated Press] (SAG) .... CropGrw
Crop Growth Rate (OA) .... CGR
Crop Husbandry Adviser [Ministry of Agriculture, Fisheries, and Food] [British] .... CHA
Crop Husbandry Officer (SAUS) .... CHO
Crop Identification Technology Assessment for Remote Sensing [NASA] .... CITARS
Crop Insurance Research Bureau [Indianapolis, IN] (EA) .... CIRB
Crop Moisture Index (SAUS) .... CMI
Crop Protection Chemical .... CPC
Crop Protection Chemicals Reference .... CPCR
Crop Protection Institute (EA) .... CPI
Crop Protection Product (SAUS) .... CPP
Crop Quality Council (EA) .... CQC
Crop Reporting Board .... CRB
Crop Research Division (SAUS) .... CRD
Crop Research Division (SAUO) .... CRD
Crop Reserve Program (ADWA) .... CRP
Crop Resources Management Network (SAUO) .... CREMNET
Crop Science Society of America (EA) .... CSSA
Crop Science Society of South Australia .... CSSSA
Crop Simulation Model .... CSM
Crop Water Stress Index [Agronomy] .... CWSI
Crop Year (SAUO) .... CY
Crop-Condition Assessment (SAUS) .... CCA
Crop-Hail Insurance Actuarial Association [Later, NCIS] (EA) .... CHIAA
Cropland Adjustment Program .... CAP
Cropland Conversion Program .... CCP
Cropper and Burgess [Bank in "He Knew He Was Right" by Anthony Trollope] .... C and B
Cropping Index CI
Cropping Systems Network (SAUO) .... CSN
Crops Estimating Memorandum [Department of Agriculture] (GFGA) .... CEM
Crops Research Division [of ARS, Department of Agriculture] .... CR
Crops Research Division Agricultural Research Service [Washington, DC] [Department of Agriculture] .... CR-ARS
Crops Research Institute for the Semi-Arid-Tropics (SAUO) .... CRISAT
Croquet Association [British] .... CA
Croquet Association (SAUO) .... CA
Croquet Association of Ireland (EAIO) .... CAI
Croquet Club [British] CC
Croquet Club (SAUO) CC
Croquet Foundation of America (EA) .... CFA
Croquet Players' Association of New South Wales [Australia] .... CPANSW
Crosby Memorial Library, Picayune, MS [Library symbol] [Library of Congress] (LCLS) .... MsPi
Crosby, MN [FM radio station call letters] .... KTCF
Crosby, Stills, and Nash [Rock music group] [Later, CSN & Y] .... CSN
Crosby, Stills, Nash, and Young [Rock music group] [Formerly, CSN] .... CSN & Y
Crosby-Ironton Elementary School, Crosby, MN [Library symbol] [Library of Congress] (LCLS) .... MnCroE
Crosby-Ironton High School, Crosby, MN [Library symbol] [Library of Congress] (LCLS) .... MnCroH
Crosfield Users Group (EA) .... CUG
Crosier Fathers' Library, Hastings, NE [Library symbol] [Library of Congress] (LCLS) .... NbHCro
Crosier Heritage Association [Defunct] (EA) .... CHA
Crosier Missions (EA) .... CM
Crosier Seminary Library, Onamia, MN [Library symbol] [Library of Congress] (LCLS) .... MnOnC
Crosier Theological Seminary [Onamia, MN] .... CTS
Crosley Automobile Club (EA) .... CAC
Crosley on Wills [1828] [A publication] (DLA) .... Cros Wills
Cross (ADA) C
Cross .... CR
Cross (DAC) .... Cr
Cross (ADA) .... CRS
Cross [Referring to sections] [Pathology] (DAVI) X
Cross [As in X-roads] X
Cross Air AG [Switzerland] [ICAO designator] (FAAC) .... CRX

Cross Angle .... CR
Cross Appalachian Tracer Experiment (SAUS) .... CAPTEX
Cross Arm (AAG) .... XARM
Cross Assembler (SAUS) .... CRAS
Cross Assembler [Computer science] (MHDI) .... XASM
Cross Bar (SAUS) .... CB
Cross Bar [Automotive engineering] .... C/BAR
Cross Border Humanitarian Assistance (DOMA) .... CBHA
Cross Bracing (MSA) .... XBRA
Cross Bracing (SAUS) .... X-Bracing
Cross Branch Data Link (MCD) .... CBDL
Cross Cancer Institute [Alberta Cancer Board] [Canada] (IRC) CCI
Cross Cancer Institute, Edmonton, AB, Canada [Library symbol] [Library of Congress] (LCLS) .... CaAECCI
Cross Cancer Institute, Edmonton, Alberta [Library symbol] [National Library of Canada] (NLC) .... AECCI
Cross Channel CC
Cross Channel (SAUS) XC
Cross Channel Coordinating Committee (SAUO) CCCC
Cross Channel Co-ordination Centre (SAUS) CCCC
Cross Channel Special Rules Area (SAUS) .... XCSRA
Cross Charter (SAUS) .... X C/P
Cross CI'A' [AMEX symbol] (SG) .... ATX
Cross City, FL [Location identifier] [FAA] (FAAL) .... CTY
Cross City, FL [AM radio station call letters] .... WDFL
Cross City, FL [FM radio station call letters] .... WDFL-FM
Cross Claim [Legal shorthand] (LWAP) XCL
Cross [A. T.] Co. [AMEX symbol] (SPSG) .... ATX
Cross, [A. T.] Co. [Associated Press] (SAG) .... Cross
Cross Connect (MLOA) XC
Cross Connect Node (SAUS) XC
Cross Connection .... XCO
Cross Connection .... XCONN
Cross Connection Point [Telecommunications] (TEL) .... CCP
Cross Connector (VERA) CC
Cross Correlation CC
Cross Correlation Function (SAUS) .... CCF
Cross Corsen [France] [ICAO location identifier] (ICLI) .... LFIC
Cross Country [Also, XCY] XC
Cross Country [Also, XC] .... XCY
Cross Country Award (SAUS) .... CCA
Cross Country Club (SAUO) CCC
Cross Country Ski Areas Association (EA) .... CCSAA
Cross County Leasing (SAUS) XCL
Cross Couple (or Coupling) (SAUS) CC
Cross Creeks National Wildlife Refuge (SAUS) .... CCNWR
Cross Cultural Communication Centre, Toronto, ON, Canada [Library symbol] [Library of Congress] (LCLS) .... CaOTCCC
Cross Cultural Communication Centre, Toronto, Ontario [Library symbol] [National Library of Canada] (NLC) .... OTCCC
Cross Cultural Health Care Program (SAUS) .... CCHCP
Cross Cultural Medicine .... CCM
Cross Deck Pendant (MCD) .... CDP
Cross Direction .... CD
Cross Domain Resource Manager (VERA) .... CDRM
Cross Dresser (DHP) .... CD
Cross Ecosystems Research Program (SAUO) .... CE
Cross Etel [France] [ICAO location identifier] (ICLI) .... LFIE
Cross Factor (SAUS) .... CF
Cross Fade (SAUS) .... CF
Cross Feed .... CRSFD
Cross Field Closing Switch (SAUS) .... CFCS
Cross File Search Database [Information service or system] (IID) .... CROS
Cross Front [Photography] .... CF
Cross Grain [Technical drawings] .... CRG
Cross Gris-Nez [France] [ICAO location identifier] (ICLI) .... LFIN
Cross Hair (IEEE) .... XHAIR
Cross Hatch Generator (SAUS) .... CHG
Cross Head Speed (MCD) .... CHS
Cross Hill, SC [FM radio station call letters] (BROA) .... WBDQ-FM
Cross, Iddings, Pirsson, and Washington [Norms] [Geology] .... CIPW
Cross Impact Simulation Method (SAUO) .... CISM
Cross in Front of Left Foot [Dance terminology] .... XfL
Cross Industry Standard .... CIS
Cross Industry Working Team .... XIWT
Cross Information Co. [Boulder, CO] [Telecommunications] (TSSD) CIC
Cross Interface Switch (SAUS) .... XIS
Cross Interleave Solomon Code .... CIRSC
Cross Interleaved Reed Solomon Code (SAUS) .... CIRC
Cross Jobourg [France] [ICAO location identifier] (ICLI) .... LFIJ
Cross La Garde [France] [ICAO location identifier] (ICLI) .... LFJG
Cross Lake [Canada] [Airport symbol] (OAG) .... YCR
Cross Lake, MB [AM radio station call letters] .... CFNC
Cross Lake Minerals [Vancouver Stock Exchange symbol] .... CRN
Cross Launcher Assign [Navy] (CAAL) .... CLA
Cross Leg (STED) .... X-leg
Cross Leg Flap (MELL) .... CLF
Cross. Lien and Stoppage in Transitu [1840] [A publication] (DLA) .... Cross Lien
Cross Linkage (SAUS) XL
Cross Linking by Activated Species of Inert Gases (MCD) .... CASING
Cross Matching (SAUS) .... X Matching
Cross Media Publishing (SAUS) .... CMP
Cross Member [Automotive engineering] .... C/MBR
Cross Member [Automotive engineering] .... X/MBR
Cross Metal Oxide Semiconductor (NITA) .... XMOS

Cross Modulation [*Telecommunications*] (OA) ... CM
Cross Modulation Product (SAUS) ... CMP
Cross Modulation/Intermodulation (SAUS) ... CM/IM
Cross of Honour [*British military*] (DMA) ... HC
Cross of the Legion of Honour (CPGU) ... CLH
Cross of the Order of the Niger ... CON
Cross of Valour [*Military award*] [*Canada*] ... CV
Cross Office Check (SAUS) ... COC
Cross Over (SAUS) ... X-Over
Cross Pointer Indicator (MCD) ... CPI
Cross Polarization [*Atomic physics*] ... CP
Cross Polarization-Magic Angle Spinning (SAUS) ... CP/MAS
Cross Pollinated [*Genetics*] ... CP
Cross Products [*Statistics*] ... CP
Cross Program Auditor [*Applied Data Research, Inc.*] ... CPA
Cross Reactance (SAUS) ... X
Cross Reference (AFM) ... CREF
Cross Reference ... CRREF
Cross Reference (MCD) ... XR
Cross Reference (NG) ... X-REF
Cross Reference (SAUS) ... XREF
Cross Reference Code (SAUS) ... CRC
Cross Reference Generator (SAUS) ... CRG
Cross Reference List (SAUS) ... XREF List
Cross Reference Listing ... CRL
Cross Section ... CS
Cross Section ... XS
Cross Section ... XSECT
Cross Section (VRA) ... xsect
Cross Section (IDOE) ... X-section
Cross Section Information Storage and Retrieval System [*National Neutron Cross Section Center*] (NITA) ... CSISAS
Cross Sectional Transmission Electron Microscopy (AAEL) ... XTEM
Cross Servicing Working Group (SAUO) ... CSWG
Cross Shaft [*Automotive engineering*] ... C/SHFT
Cross Spectral Density [*Physics*] (IAA) ... CDS
Cross Spectral Density (SAUS) ... CSD
Cross System Product (BTTJ) ... CSP
Cross Tabulation of Frequencies ... CTAB
Cross Talk (IEEE) ... XT
Cross Talk [*Aviation*] (CIST) ... XTLK
Cross Tell (IEEE) ... XTEL
Cross Timbers Oil [*NYSE symbol*] (TTSB) ... XTO
Cross Timbers Oil Co. [*Associated Press*] (SAG) ... CrosTmb
Cross Timbers Oil Co. [*NYSE symbol*] (SPSG) ... XTO
Cross Timbers Royalty Tr [*NYSE symbol*] (TTSB) ... CRT
Cross Timbers Royalty Trust [*Associated Press*] (SAG) ... CrosTim
Cross Timbers Royalty Trust [*NYSE symbol*] (SAG) ... CRT
Cross Type (SAUS) ... X Type
Cross Utilization File (MCD) ... CUF
Cross Utilization Training ... CUT
Cross Wind Force (SAUS) ... CWF
Crossability Indices [*Botany*] ... CI's
Crossair [*ICAO designator*] (AD) ... LX
Cross-Assembler [*Computer science*] (CIST) ... XA
Crossbar (SAUS) ... CB
Crossbar [*Bell System*] ... XB
Crossbar ... XBAR
Crossbar Switch (NITA) ... XB
Crossbar Tandem [*Telecommunications*] (TEL) ... XBT
Cross-Bar Technology (SAUS) ... CBT
Crossbow Archery Development Association (EAIO) ... CADA
CROSSBOW [*Computer Retrieval of Organic Structures Based on Wiswesser*] **Subcommittee Working Group** ... CSWG
Cross-Bridge Kelvin Resistor (SAUS) ... CBKR
Cross-chain Loran Atmospheric Sounding System (SAUS) ... CLASS
Cross-Chain LORAN [*Long-Range Navigation*] **Atmospheric Sounding System** (USDC) ... CLASS
Cross-Channel Coordination Center [*NATO*] (NATG) ... CCCC
Cross-Channel Data Link (MCD) ... CCDL
Cross-Channel Rejection ... CCR
Cross-Charm LORAN [*Longe-Range Navigation*] **Atmospheric Sounding System** [*Marine science*] (OSRA) ... CLASS
Cross-Check Procedure (NG) ... CCP
Cross-Clamp [*of carotid artery*] ... XC
CrossCom Corp. [*Associated Press*] (SAG) ... CrosCom
CrossCom Corp. [*NASDAQ symbol*] (SAG) ... XCOM
CrossComm Corp. [*NASDAQ symbol*] (TTSB) ... XCOM
Cross-Commodity Forecasting System (SAUO) ... CCFS
Cross-Connect (ACAE) ... C
Crossconnect (SAUS) ... CC
Cross-Connect Data Conflict (SAUS) ... XDC
Cross-Connect Multiplexer (SAUS) ... CCM
Cross-Connection Point (SAUS) ... CCP
Cross-Content Workplace Readiness ... CCWR
Cross-Continent Auto Retailers, Inc. [*Associated Press*] (SAG) ... CrosCAu
Cross-Continent Auto Retailers, Inc. [*NYSE symbol*] (SAG) ... XC
Crosscorrelation (SAUS) ... Crosscorrel
Cross-Correlation Function ... CCF
Cross-Correlation Histogram [*Statistics*] ... CCH
Cross-Correlation-Average Magnitude Difference Function (SAUS) ... CC-AMDF
Cross-Country Movement [*Maps*] ... CCM
Cross-Country Skiing ... XCS
Cross-Cultural Cognitive Examination (DMAA) ... CCCE
Cross-Cultural Dance Resources (EA) ... CCDR
Cross-Cultural Shamanism Network (EA) ... CCSN
Crosscurrents International Institute (EAIO) ... CCII
Crosscurrents International Institute (EA) ... CII
Crosscut (SAUS) ... C/CUT
Crosscut (SAUS) ... XCUT
Crosscutting (SAUS) ... CC
Crossdressers International [*An association*] (EA) ... CDI
Crossed [*Stereo images*] ... C
Crossed [*Telecommunications*] (TEL) ... XD
Crossed Diagonal [*Medicine*] (DMAA) ... CD
Crossed Electroimmunodiffusion [*Analytical biochemistry*] ... CEID
Crossed Electrophoresis (MCD) ... CEP
Crossed Field Closing Switch (MCD) ... CFCS
Crossed Field Discharge (SAUS) ... XFD
Crossed Field Plasma Sheath (SAUS) ... CFPS
Crossed Grid Charge Detector (SAUS) ... CGCD
Crossed Immunoaffinoelectrophoresis [*Analytical biochemistry*] ... CIAE
Crossed Immunoelectrophoresis [*Analytical biochemistry*] ... CIE
Crossed Molecular Beam [*Instrumentation*] ... CMB
Crossed Olivocochlear Bundles [*Audiology*] ... COCB
Crossed Olivocochlear Potential [*Audiology*] ... COCP
Crossed Radioimmunoelectrophoresis [*Analytical biochemistry*] ... CRIE
Crossed Straight Leg Raising [*Sign*] [*Neurology*] (DAVI) ... XSLR
Crossed With (DAVI) ... X
Crossed-Field Acceleration (SAUS) ... XFA
Crossed-Field Amplifier [*Air Force*] ... CFA
Crossed-Field Output Tube ... CFOT
Crossed-Field Photomultiplier (IAA) ... CFPM
Crossed-Field Tube ... CFT
Crossed-Film Cryotron ... CFC
Crossed-Plane Polarized Light (SAUS) ... CPPL
Crossett, AR [*Location identifier*] [*FAA*] (FAAL) ... CRT
Crossett, AR [*AM radio station call letters*] ... KAGH
Crossett, AR [*FM radio station call letters*] ... KAGH-FM
Cross-Examination Debate Association (EA) ... CEDA
Cross-Fade (WDAA) ... XF
Crossfeed (NASA) ... XFD
Cross-Field Acceleration ... XFA
Cross-Field Jammer ... CFJ
Crossfield Municipal Library, Alberta [*Library symbol*] [*National Library of Canada*] (NLC) ... ACRM
Crossfield Municipal Library, Crossfield, AB, Canada [*Library symbol*] [*Library of Congress*] (LCLS) ... CaACrM
Crossfield Plasma Sheath (SAUS) ... CPS
Crossfire (MSA) ... CFR
Crossfire Injection [*Automotive engineering*] ... CFI
Crossflow Engine [*Automotive engineering*] ... XFLO
Crossflow Filtration [*Process engineering*] ... CFF
Cross-Frequency Statistical Deconvolution Algorithm (SAUS) ... CFSDA
Cross-Functional Analysis (ADA) ... CFA
Cross-Guide Coupler ... CGC
Crosshatch Generator ... CHG
Crosshead (MSA) ... CRSHD
Crossing (SAUS) ... Cross
Crossing [*Commonly used*] (OPSA) ... CROSSING
Crossing (VRA) ... crsg
Crossing [*Commonly used*] (OPSA) ... CRSSING
Crossing [*Commonly used*] (OPSA) ... CRSSNG
Crossing ... XG
Crossing (MCD) ... XING
Crossing [*Aviation*] (FAAC) ... XNG
Crossing Protective Device ... CPD
Crossing Restrictions (CTAS) ... CR
Cross-Interleaved Reed-Solomon Code [*Computer science*] ... CIRC
Cross-Lamination (SAUS) ... CL
Crossland Industries Corp. [*Vancouver Stock Exchange symbol*] ... CD
Cross-Latitudinal Measurement (SAUS) ... CLM
Cross-Leveling, Redistribution, Replenishment, and Excessing (MCD) ... CRRE
Crossley and Porter Orphan Home for Fatherless Children (SAUO) ... CPOHFC
Cross-Lines Alternative School ... CLAS
Crosslinked (SAUS) ... X-LINKED
Cross-Linked Biotinylated Microtubule [*Biochemistry*] ... CBMT
Cross-Linked Dextran Polymer [*Organic chemistry*] ... CDP
Cross-Linked Double Base (SAUS) ... XLDB
Cross-Linked Enzyme Crystal ... CLEC
Crosslinked Fibrin Degradation (SAUS) ... XDP
Cross-Linked Fibrin Degradation Products (DAVI) ... XLFDP
Cross-Linked Polyethylene [*Organic chemistry*] ... CLP
Cross-Linked Polyethylene [*Organic chemistry*] (MCD) ... CLPE
Cross-Linked Polyethylene [*Organic chemistry*] (NRCH) ... XLPE
Cross-Linked Polyethylene (SAUS) ... XLT
Cross-Linked Polyethylene Cable (SAUS) ... XLPE Cable
Crosslinked Protein [*Biochemistry*] (DB) ... CP
Cross-Linked Smectites [*Inorganic chemistry*] ... CLS
Cross-Linking Agent ... CLA
Cross-linking by Activated Species of Inert Gases (SAUS) ... CASING
Cross-linking Electron Resist (PDAA) ... CER
Crossman Communities, Inc. [*NASDAQ symbol*] (SAG) ... CROS
Crossman Communities, Inc. [*Associated Press*] (SAG) ... Crossman
Crossmann Communities [*NASDAQ symbol*] (TTSB) ... CROS
Crossmatch [*Hematology*] (DAVI) ... X
Crossmatch (MAE) ... XM
Crossmatch [*Hematology*] (DAVI) ... X-mat
Cross-Match (STED) ... X-match
Crossmatch: Transfusion ... CT

Cross-Media Analysis Staff [*Environmental science*] (COE) .... CMAS
Cross-Modality Matching (MELL) .... CMM
Cross-Modulation Factor (DEN) .... CMF
Cross-National Project in Social and Political Change (SAUO) .... CPSPC
Cross-Office (SAUS) .... XO
Cross-Office Highway [*Telecommunications*] (TEL) .... XON
Cross-Office Slot [*Telecommunications*] (TEL) .... XOS
Cross-Organizational Program Analysis [*Department of Commerce*] (GFGA) .... COPA
Cross-Out Test (SAUS) .... X-O Test
Crossover [*Genetics*] .... CO
Crossover [*Technical drawings*] (MSA) .... CRSVR
Crossover (IDOE) .... xover
Cross-over Connector (SAUS) .... COC
Crossover Electrophoresis (SAUS) .... COE
Cross-Over Electrophoresis (PDAA) .... COE
Crossover Value [*Genetics*] .... COV
Crossplot (SAUS) .... CP
Cross-Point (SAUS) .... XPT
Crosspoint [*Switching element*] (MSA) .... XPT
Crosspoint Control Unit (NITA) .... XCU
Crosspoint Switching Element (SAUS) .... XPT
Crosspoint Switching Matrix (IAA) .... CSM
Cross-Pointer Course Indicator (MCD) .... CPCI
Cross-Polarization (SAUS) .... CP
Cross-Polarization Discrimination [*Telecommunications*] .... XPD
Cross-Polarization Evaluation Radio Echo System (PDAA) .... CERES
Cross-Polarization Interference [*in radio transmission*] .... XPI
Cross-Polarization Magic Angle Spinning [*Spectroscopy*] .... CPMAS
Cross-Polarization Nuclear Magnetic Resonance [*Physics*] .... CPNMR
Cross-Power Spectral Density .... CPSD
Cross-Question [*Transcripts*] .... XQ
Cross-Range Error .... CRE
Cross-Range Error Function .... CEF
Cross-Range Velocity Correlator (MUGU) .... CRVC
Cross-Reacting Cannabinoids (STED) .... CRC
Cross-Reacting Determinant [*Immunochemistry*] .... CRD
Cross-Reacting Material [*Immunology*] .... CRM
Crossreaction (SAUS) .... XR
Cross-Reactive Idiotype [*Genetics*] .... CRI
Cross-Reference (WDMC) .... cf
Cross-Reference File .... CRF
Cross-Reference List XL
Cross-Reference Project .... CRP
Cross-Reference Utility [*Computer science*] .... CULL
Cross-Registration (SAUS) .... XREG
Cross-relaxation Appropriate for Minimolecules Emulated by Locked SPINs (SAUS) .... CAMELSPIN
Crossroad [*Commonly used*] (OPSA) .... CROSSROAD
Crossroad [*Postal Service standard*] (OPSA) .... XRD
Crossroad .... XROAD
Crossroads [*Maps and charts*] .... CR
Crossroads .... XRDS
Crossroads Center, Mount Airy, NC [*Library symbol*] [*Library of Congress*] (LCLS) .... NcMtaC
Crossroads Conference (PSS) .... CXRC
Crossroads Joint Task Force [*Atomic weapons testing*] .... CJTF
Crossroads Technical Instrumentation [*Atomic weapons testing*] .... CTI
Cross-Scan Ground Map Pencil (DNAB) .... CSGMP
Cross-Scan Terrain Avoidance (DNAB) .... CSTA
Cross-Scan Terrain-Avoidance Displays .... CRAN
Cross-Scan Terrain-Following radar mode (SAUS) .... CSTF
Cross-Section .... CRS
Cross-Section Data Reduction .... CSDR
Cross-Section Echocardiography (DAVI) .... CSE
Cross-Section Evaluation Working Group (SAUO) .... CSEWG
Cross-Section Information Storage and Retrieval System [*Brookhaven National Laboratory*] [*Information service or system*] .... CSISRS
Cross-Section Measurement System .... CMS
Cross-Sectional and Special Studies Branch [*Department of Education*] (GFGA) .... CSSB
Cross-Sectional Area .... CSA
Cross-Sectional Area [*Cardiology*] .... XSA
Cross-Sectional Point (SAUS) .... XSP
Cross-Service Agreement [*Obsolete*] [*Military*] .... CSA
Cross-Service Order [*Military*] (AFM) .... CSO
Cross-Species Mapping [*Zoology*] .... CSM
Cross-Spin Stabilization Systems .... CSSS
Cross-Stratification (SAUS) .... CS
Cross-Stratified (SAUS) .... XStrat
Cross-Strike Discontinuity [*Tectonics*] .... CSD
Cross-Strike Profile (SAUS) .... CSP
Cross-System Coupling Facility (SAUS) .... XCF
Crosstalk [*Telecommunications*] (MSA) .... XTALK
Crosstalk (IDOE) .... xtalk
Crosstalk Application Script Language [*Programming language*] [*1987*] [*Computer science*] .... CASL
Crosstalk Communicator [*Computer software*] [*Digital Communications Associates*] (PCM) .... CCM
Cross-Talk Unit .... CU
Crosstalk Unit (SAUS) .... CU
Crosstell Input CXI
Crosstell Input (SAUS) .... XTI
Crosstell Output .... CXO
Cross-Tell Simulator (IEEE) .... XTS
Crosstelling Technician (SAA) .... CTT
Cross-Tongued (SAUS) .... Xtgd
Crosstrack [*Cross track error*] (GAVI) .... XTK
Cross-Track Contiguous .... CTC
Cross-Track Distance [*Aerospace*] .... CTD
Cross-Track Error .... CTE
Cross-Track Noncontiguous .... CTNC
Crosstrail [*Military*] .... CT
Crossville, TN [*Location identifier*] [*FAA*] (FAAL) .... CSV
Crossville, TN [*Location identifier*] [*FAA*] (FAAL) .... HCH
Crossville, TN [*AM radio station call letters*] .... WAEW
Crossville, TN [*Television station call letters*] (BROA) .... WBXX-TV
Crossville, TN [*AM radio station call letters*] .... WCSV
Crossville, TN [*FM radio station call letters*] .... WEGE
Crossville, TN [*Television station call letters*] .... WINT
Crossville, TN [*FM radio station call letters*] (RBYB) .... WMKW-FM
Crossville, TN [*FM radio station call letters*] (BROA) .... WOWF-FM
Crossville, TN [*FM radio station call letters*] .... WXVL
Crosswalk/Air Toxic Emission Factor [*Environmental Protection Agency*] (AEPA) .... XATEF
Crosswind [*Aviation*] (FAAC) .... XW
Crosswind (HLLA) .... X/WIND
Crosswind Force .... CWF
Crossword Association [*British*] (DBA) .... CA
Crossword Club [*Romsey, Hampshire, England*] (EAIO) CC
Croswell's Collection of Patent Cases [*United States*] [*A publication*] (DLA) .... Crosw Pat Ca
Croswell's Collection of Patent Cases [*United States*] [*A publication*] (DLA) .... Crosw Pat Cas
Crosyton, TX [*Location identifier*] [*FAA*] (FAAL) .... CZX
Crotalus Adamanteus Venom .... CAV
Croton Free Library, Croton-On-Hudson, NY [*Library symbol*] [*Library of Congress*] (LCLS) .... NCroh
Croton Public Library, Newaygo, MI [*Library symbol*] [*Library of Congress*] (LCLS) .... MiNew-C
Crotonaldehyde (PDAA) .... CA
Crotone [*Italy*] [*Airport symbol*] (AD) .... CTW
Crotone [*Italy*] [*ICAO location identifier*] (ICLI) .... LIBC
Crotonylidene Diurea [*Fertilizer*] .... CDU
Crotonyloxymethyl(trihydroxy)cyclohexene [*Antineoplastic drug*] .... CROTCE
Crotty Family Organization (EA) .... CFO
Crounse's Reports [*3 Nebraska*] [*A publication*] (DLA) .... Crounse
Croup-Associated [*Virus*] .... CA
Croup-Associated Virus [*Medicine*] (DB) .... CAV
Croupy Cough [*Medicine*] (MELL) CC
Crouse-Hinds Co. .... CHC
Crouse-Hinds Co. (SAUO) .... CHI
Crouse-Irving Hospital, School of Nursing, Library, Syracuse, NY [*OCLC symbol*] (OCLC) .... ZUZ
Crouse-Irving Hospital, Syracuse, NY [*Library symbol*] [*Library of Congress*] (LCLS) .... NSyCH
Crow Canyon [*California*] [*Seismograph station code, US Geological Survey*] (SEIS) .... CYC
Crow Executive Air, Inc. [*FAA designator*] (FAAC) .... CCG
Crow River Regional Library, Willmar, MN [*Library symbol*] [*Library of Congress*] (LCLS) .... MnWilRL
Crow Valley Microwave System (ACAE) .... CVMS
Crowd, Lift, Actuate, Swing [*Backhoe controls for tractors*] .... CLAS
Crowder Communications Corp. [*Vancouver Stock Exchange symbol*] .... CWD
Crowding Effect LASER (IAA) .... CEL
Crowell-Collier & Macmillan, Inc. [*Later, Macmillan, Inc.*] [*Publishers*] .... CCM
Crowell-Collier & Macmillan Inc. (SAUO) .... CRW
Crowfoot (MSA) .... CRFT
Crowl Name Association (EA) .... CNA
Crowley, LA [*FM radio station call letters*] .... KAJN
Crowley, LA [*AM radio station call letters*] .... KPWS
Crowley, LA [*AM radio station call letters*] .... KSIG
Crowley, Milner & Co. [*AMEX symbol*] (SPSG) .... COM
Crowley, Milner & Co. [*Associated Press*] (SAG) .... CrowlMil
Crowley Ridge Regional Library, Jonesboro, AR [*Library symbol*] [*Library of Congress*] (LCLS) .... ArJCR
Crown (SAUS) .... Cr
Crown [*Paper size*] .... CR
Crown [*Dentistry*] (DAVI) .... CR
Crown (MSA) .... CRN
Crown .... CRWN
Crown Agent .... CA
Crown Agents Department (SAUO) .... CAD
Crown Agents for Oversea Governments and Administrations (SAUO) .... CAOGA
Crown Agents for Overseas Governments [*British*] .... CAOG
Crown Agents for the Colonies (SAUO) .... CAC
Crown Agents for the Colonies [*British*] .... CAC
Crown Air Systems [*ICAO designator*] (FAAC) .... CKR
Crown Airways, Inc. [*ICAO designator*] (FAAC) .... CRO
Crown Amer Realty Tr [*NYSE symbol*] (TTSB) .... CWN
Crown American Realty Trust [*Associated Press*] (SAG) .... CrwnAm
Crown American Realty Trust [*NYSE symbol*] (SPSG) .... CWN
Crown and Bridge [*Dentistry*] (DAVI) .... C & B
Crown and Bridge [*Dentistry*] (DAVI) .... Cr & Br
Crown and Sleeve Coping Prosthesis [*Dentistry*] .... CSC
Crown Andersen, Inc. [*NASDAQ symbol*] (NQ) .... CRAN
Crown Andersen, Inc. [*Associated Press*] (SAG) .... CrwnAn
Crown Appointments Commission (SAUO) .... CAC
Crown Asset Disposal Corp. [*Canada*] .... CADC
Crown Aviation [*ICAO designator*] (AD) CC

Crown Aviation, Inc. (SAUO) .... HPS
Crown Books [*NASDAQ symbol*] (TTSB) .... CRWN
Crown Books Corp. [*NASDAQ symbol*] (NQ) .... CRWN
Crown Books Corp. [*Associated Press*] (SAG) .... CwnBk
Crown Bute Resources Ltd. [*Vancouver Stock Exchange symbol*] .... CBL
Crown Cases CC
Crown Cases Reserved .... CCR
Crown Cases Reserved (DLA) .... Cr Cas Res
Crown Casino [*NASDAQ symbol*] (TTSB) .... DICE
Crown Casino Corp. [*Associated Press*] (SAG) .... CwnCas
Crown Casino Corp. [*NASDAQ symbol*] (SAG) .... DICE
Crown Cassette Communications Ltd. (SAUO) CCC
Crown Castle Intl. [*NASDAQ symbol*] (SG) .... TWRS
Crown Cat Fanciers Federation [*Defunct*] (EA) .... CCFF
Crown Centl Pet'A' [*AMEX symbol*] (TTSB) .... CNP.A
Crown Central Cl'B' [*AMEX symbol*] (TTSB) .... CNP.B
Crown Central Petroleum Corp. [*AMEX symbol*] (SPSG) .... CNP
Crown Central Petroleum Corp. [*Associated Press*] (SAG) .... CrnCP
Crown Circuit Assistant [*Legal term*] (DLA) .... CRCA
Crown Circuit Companion [*Ireland*] [*A publication*] (DLA) .... Cr Cir Comp
Crown Clerk [*British*] (ROG) CC
Crown Colony CC
Crown Colony (SAUO) CC
Crown Colony (SAUO) .... CrCol
Crown Companies Monitoring and Advisory Unit (SAUO) .... CCMAU
Crown Competition Factor (PDAA) .... CCF
Crown Cork & Seal [*NYSE symbol*] (TTSB) .... CCK
Crown Cork & Seal Co., Inc. [*NYSE symbol*] (SPSG) .... CCK
Crown Cork & Seal Co., Inc. [*Associated Press*] (SAG) .... CwnCork
Crown Cork & Seal Co., Inc. [*Associated Press*] (SAG) .... CwnCrk
Crown Cork Manufacturers' Technical Council [*British*] (BI) .... CCMTS
Crown Cork&Seal 4.50% Cv Pfd [*NYSE symbol*] (TTSB) .... CCKPr
Crown Court (ILCA) CC
Crown Crafts [*NYSE symbol*] (TTSB) .... CRW
Crown Crafts, Inc. [*NYSE symbol*] (SAG) .... CRW
Crown Crafts, Inc. [*Associated Press*] (SAG) .... CwnCr
Crown Estate Commissioner [*British*] .... CEC
Crown Estate Commissioner [*British*] .... CREST
Crown Flint (SAUS) .... CF
Crown Folio (SAUS) .... Cr Fol
Crown Forest Industries Ltd. [*Toronto Stock Exchange symbol*] [*Vancouver Stock Exchange symbol*] .... CRF
Crown Group [*NASDAQ symbol*] [*Formerly, Crown Casino*] (SG) .... CNGR
Crown International Airlines [*ICAO designator*] (AD) .... RL
Crown Laboratories [*ECM, exchange symbol*] (TTSB) .... CLLEC
Crown Laboratories, Inc. [*AMEX symbol*] (SAG) CLL
Crown Laboratories, Inc. [*Associated Press*] (SAG) .... CrwnL
Crown Land Reports, Queensland [*A publication*] (DLA) .... CLQ
Crown Lands Law Report-Queensland (SAUS) .... Queensl Cr Lands LR
Crown Law Department [*Western Australia*] .... CLD
Crown Law Office (SAUO) .... CLO
Crown Life Insurance Co. [*Toronto Stock Exchange symbol*] .... CLA
Crown Life Properties, Inc. [*Toronto Stock Exchange symbol*] .... CFM
Crown Metro Salchi SpA (SAUS) .... CMS
Crown Mine [*Nevada*] [*Seismograph station code, US Geological Survey*] [*Closed*] (SEIS) .... CMN
Crown Minerals Act (SAUO) .... CMA
Crown Octavo [*Book size*] .... Cr 8vo
Crown Office [*British*] .... CO
Crown Office (SAUO) .... CO
Crown Office Digest [*A publication*] .... COD
Crown Office in Chancery (SAUO) .... COC
Crown Office Rules [*A publication*] (DLA) .... COR
Crown Pac Partners L.P. [*NYSE symbol*] (TTSB) .... CRO
Crown Pacific Partners Ltd. [*NYSE symbol*] (SAG) .... CRO
Crown Pacific Partners Ltd. [*Associated Press*] (SAG) .... CwnPac
Crown Pleas [*Legal term*] (DLA) .... CP
Crown Point Center Public Library, Crown Point, IN [*Library symbol*] [*Library of Congress*] (LCLS) .... InCrp
Crown Point Community Schools, Crown Point, IN [*Library symbol*] [*Library of Congress*] (LCLS) .... InCrpCS
Crown Point Community Schools, Crown Point, IN [*OCLC symbol*] (OCLC) .... IPO
Crown Point, IN [*FM radio station call letters*] .... WWJY
Crown Point, IN [*FM radio station call letters*] (BROA) .... WXRD-FM
Crown Point, IN [*FM radio station call letters*] (RBYB) .... WZCO-FM
Crown Prosecution Service [*British*] (ECON) .... CPS
Crown Research Institute [*New Zealand*] .... CRI
Crown Resource Corp. [*Associated Press*] (SAG) .... CrwnRs
Crown Resources Corp. [*NASDAQ symbol*] (NQ) .... CRRS
Crown Side [*Records*] [*British*] (ROG) .... CS
Crown Solicitor [*Australia*] .... CS
Crown Solicitor's Office [*British*] (ADA) .... CSO
Crown Television Productions [*Commercial firm*] [*British*] .... CTV
Crown Theological Library [*A publication*] .... CTL
Crown Trust Co. [*Toronto Stock Exchange symbol*] .... CRT
Crown Valley Measurement & Debriefing System (SAUS) .... CVMDS
Crown Vantage [*NASDAQ symbol*] (TTSB) .... CVAN
Crown Vantage, Inc. [*Associated Press*] (SAG) .... CrwnVn
Crown Vantage, Inc. [*NASDAQ symbol*] (SAG) .... CVAN
Crown Victoria Association (EA) .... CVA
Crown Zellerbach Corp. .... CZ
Crown Zellerbach Corp., San Francisco, CA [*Library symbol*] [*Library of Congress*] (LCLS) .... CSfCZ
Crown Zellerbach, Paper & Paper Products (SAUO) .... CP
Crownair [*Canada*] [*ICAO designator*] (FAAC) .... CRW
Crown-Andersen [*NASDAQ symbol*] (TTSB) .... CRAN
Crowncap Collectors Society International (EA) .... CCSI
Crown-Crisp Experimental Index [*Personality development test*] [*Psychology*] .... CCEI
Crowned C
Crown-Heel [*Length of fetus*] [*Medicine*] .... CH
Crown-Heel Length (ADWA) .... CHL
Crown-Rump (SAUS) .... CR
Crown-Rump Distance [*Of fetus*] [*Medicine*] (DAVI) .... CRD
Crown-Rump Length [*of fetus*] [*Medicine*] .... CR
Crown-Rump Length [*of fetus*] [*Medicine*] .... CRL
Crown-Rump Length (SAUS) .... C-R Length
Crown-Rump Measurement (STED) .... CRM
Crownsville State Hospital, Crownsville, MD [*Library symbol*] [*Library of Congress*] (LCLS) .... MdCvH
Crown/Treasury of Relevant Quotations [*A publication*] .... CTRQ
Crownx, Inc. [*Toronto Stock Exchange symbol*] .... CRX
Crows Landing, CA [*Location identifier*] [*FAA*] (FAAL) .... NRC
Crowsnest Public Library, Coleman, Alberta [*Library symbol*] [*National Library of Canada*] (NLC) .... ACOL
Crowther's Ceylon Reports [*A publication*] (DLA) .... Crow
Crowther's Ceylon Reports [*A publication*] (DLA) .... Crowth
Crowther's Ceylon Reports [*A publication*] (DLA) .... Crowther
Crowthorne and Minety [*England*] .... CROWT & MIN
Croydon [*Australia*] [*Airport symbol*] [*Obsolete*] (OAG) .... CDQ
Croydon [*Borough of London*] .... CROYD
Croydon Advertiser, Croydon, United Kingdom [*Library symbol*] [*Library of Congress*] (LCLS) .... UkCrA
Croydon Library, Croydon, United Kingdom [*Library symbol*] [*Library of Congress*] (LCLS) .... UkCr
Croydon Library Internet Project [*British*] (TELE) .... CLIP
Croydon Natural History and Scientific Society (SAUO) .... CNHSS
Croydon Precision Instrument Company (SAUO) .... CROPICO
Crozet, VA [*FM radio station call letters*] .... WCYK
Crozet, VA [*FM radio station call letters*] (RBYB) .... WCYK-FM
Crozet, VA [*FM radio station call letters*] (RBYB) .... WMRY
CRREL [*Cross-Leveling, Redistribution, Replenishment, and Excessing*] **Instrumented Vehicle** [*Automobile traction testing*] CIV
CRT Controller (SAUS) .... CRTC
CRT [*Cathode-Ray Tube*] **Display Unit** (MCD) .... CDU
CRT [*Cathode-Ray Tube*] **Readout** (CAAL) .... CRO
Crucell N.V. ADS [*NASDAQ symbol*] .... CRXL
Cruciate Ligament [*Medicine*] (MELL) CL
Crucible and Tool Steel Association [*British*] (BI) .... CTSA
Crucible Institute [*Formerly, CMA*] (EA) CI
Crucible Manufacturers Association [*Later, CI*] .... CMA
Crucible Materials Research Center (MCD) .... CMRC
Crucible Melt Extraction [*Metal fiber technology*] .... CME
Crucible Steel (SAUS) .... CS
Crucible Steel (SAUS) .... XA
Crucible Swell Number .... CSN
Cruciform Ligament [*Medicine*] (MELL) CL
Cruciform Monument (BJA) .... CM
Cruciform Wing Module (MCD) .... CWM
Cruciform Wing Weapon (MCD) .... CWW
Crude (BARN) .... crd
Crude Barrel Equivalent [*Oil*] .... CBE
Crude Birth Rate [*Medicine*] .... CBR
Crude Coal Tar [*Medicine*] (CPH) .... CCT
Crude Coal Tar in Petroleum [*Pharmacology*] (DAVI) .... CCT in PET
Crude Death Rate [*Medicine*] .... CDR
Crude Distillation Unit [*Petroleum technology*] .... CDU
Crude Fiber .... CF
Crude Magazine [*Generic term for a one-person science-fiction fan magazine, produced by an inexperienced publisher*] .... CRUDZINE
Crude Marijuana Extract .... CME
Crude Marriage Rate .... CMR
Crude Mortality Ratio (MAE) .... CMR
Crude Myosin [*Food technology*] .... CM
Crude Oil Analyses File [*Petroleum Information Corp.*] [*Information service or system*] (CRD) .... COIL
Crude Oil Analysis System [*National Institute for Petroleum and Energy Research*] (CRD) .... COASYS
Crude Oil Equalization Tax [*Proposed, 1978*] .... COET
Crude Oil Equivalent (PDAA) .... COE
Crude Oil Processing Plant .... COPP
Crude Oil Production [*Database*] [*Petroleum Intelligence Weekly*] [*Information service or system*] (CRD) .... COP
Crude Oil Washing [*of cargo tank*] .... COW
Crude Palm Kernel Oil .... CPKO
Crude Protein .... CP
Crude Protein (SAUS) .... CP
Crude Sulfate Turpentine .... CST
Crude Tall Oil [*Industrial chemistry*] .... CTO
Cruelty to Animals Inspectorate (SAUO) .... CAI
Cruise (WDAA) .... CR
Cruise .... CRUS
Cruise [*Automotive advertising*] .... CRUZ
Cruise [*ICAO*] (FAAC) .... CRZ
Cruise .... CSE
Cruise Altitude [*Aviation*] .... CA
Cruise America [*AMEX symbol*] (TTSB) .... RVR
Cruise America, Inc. [*Associated Press*] (SAG) .... CruisAm
Cruise America, Inc. [*AMEX symbol*] (SPSG) .... RVR

Cruise and Maintain [*Aviation*] ... CAM
Cruise and Maintain [*Aviation*] (FAAC) ... CRZAM
Cruise Ballistic Missile (MCD) ... CBM
Cruise Control [*Automotive term*] ... CC
Cruise Guidance Control [*Aviation*] ... CGC
Cruise Guide Indicator [*Aviation*] ... CGI
Cruise Lines International Association (EA) ... CLIA
Cruise Mach Change (SAUS) ... CRMCH
Cruise Missile (MCD) ... CM
Cruise Missile (BARN) ... CRM
Cruise Missile Advanced Guidance (SAUS) ... CMAG
Cruise Missile Alarm System (MCD) ... CMAS
Cruise Missile Association (SAUO) ... CMA
Cruise Missile Carrier Aircraft ... CMC
Cruise Missile Carrier Aircraft (MCD) ... CMCA
Cruise Missile Defense (ACAE) ... CMD
Cruise Missile Engagement System Technology (SAUS) ... CMEST
Cruise Missile Guidance Set (MCD) ... CMGS
Cruise Missile Guidance System (MCD) ... CMGS
Cruise Missile Integration ... CMI
Cruise Missile Integration Kit (SAUS) ... CMIK
Cruise Missile Interface (SAUS) ... CMI
Cruise Missile Mission Control Aircraft (MCD) ... CMMCA
Cruise Missile Planning (MCD) ... CMP
Cruise Missile Project (SAUS) ... CMP
Cruise Missile Project Office (AAGC) ... CMPO
Cruise Missile Radar Altimeter (SAUS) ... CMRA
Cruise Missile Support Activity (DOMA) ... CMSA
Cruise Missile Surveillance Technology (ACAE) ... CMST
Cruise Missile Tactical Qualification Team (SAUS) ... CMTQT
Cruise Missile-Advanced Guidance (MCD) ... CMAG
Cruise on Dignities [*A publication*] (DLA) ... Cru Dign
Cruise on Titles of Honor [*A publication*] (DLA) ... Cru Titl
Cruise on Uses [*A publication*] (DLA) ... Cru Us
Cruise Passengers Club International (EA) ... CPCI
Cruise Power (ACAE) ... CP
Cruise Speed [*Aviation*] ... VC
Cruise Summary Report (SAUS) ... CSR
Cruise, Transition, Hover, Bob-Up (MCD) ... CTHB
Cruise Vehicle [*Military*] (AFM) ... CV
Cruise Well to Right (SAUS) ... CRWTR
Cruise Well to Right [*Aviation*] (FAAC) ... CRZWTR
Cruise/Entry Data Acquisition Unit [*NASA*] ... CEDAU
Cruiser ... C
Cruiser ... CR
Cruiser [*Navy*] ... CRU
Cruiser Base (SAUS) ... Cru Base
Cruiser Division [*Navy*] ... CRUDIV
Cruiser Flag [*Navy*] [*British*] ... CR
Cruiser Force (SAUO) ... CruFor
Cruiser Force, Atlantic (SAUO) ... CruForLant
Cruiser, Guided Missile [*NATO*] ... CG
Cruiser, Guided Missile and Command [*NATO*] ... CGC
Cruiser, Light [*British military*] (DMA) ... CL
Cruiser Minelayer ... CM
Cruiser Minerals [*Vancouver Stock Exchange symbol*] ... CUE
Cruiser Olympia Association (EA) ... COA
Cruiser, Scout ... CS
Cruiser Squadron [*Navy*] ... CS
Cruiser Submarine [*Navy symbol*] [*Obsolete*] ... SC
Cruiser Submarine [*Navy symbol*] [*Obsolete*] ... SSC
Cruiser Tank (SAUS) ... CT
Cruiser, United States Fleet (SAUO) ... CRUSUS
Cruiser-Destroyer Flotilla [*Navy symbol*] ... CRUDESFLOT
Cruiser-Destroyer Force (SAUO) ... CruDesFor
Cruiser-Destroyer Force, Atlantic Fleet [*Navy symbol*] ... CRUDESLANT
Cruiser-Destroyer Force, Pacific Fleet [*Navy symbol*] ... CRUDESPAC
Cruiser-Destroyer Group [*Navy*] (MUSM) ... CRUDESGRU
Cruiser-Destroyerman [*A publication*] (DNAB) ... CDDMAN
Cruisermen's Association (EA) ... CA
Cruisers (NATG) ... CC
Cruisers, Atlantic Fleet [*Navy*] ... CRULANT
Cruisers, Atlantic Fleet [*Navy*] ... CRULANTFLT
Cruisers, Battle Force [*Navy*] ... CRUBATFOR
Cruisers, Pacific Fleet [*Navy*] ... CRUPAC
Cruisers, Pacific Fleet [*Navy*] ... CRUPACFLT
Cruiser-Scouting Aircraft Squadron [*Navy symbol*] ... VCS
Cruiser-Scouting Force [*Navy*] ... CRUSCOFOR
Cruiser-Scouting Squadron [*Navy*] ... CRUSCORON
Cruise's Digest of the Law of Real Property [*1804-35*] [*England*] [*A publication*] (DLA) ... Cru
Cruise's Digest of the Law of Real Property [*1804-35*] [*England*] [*A publication*] (DLA) ... Cru Dig
Cruise's Digest of the Law of Real Property [*1804-35*] [*England*] [*A publication*] (DLA) ... Cruise Dig
Cruise's Digest of the Law of Real Property [*1804-35*] [*England*] [*A publication*] (DLA) ... Cruise's Dig
Cruise's Fines and Recoveries [*A publication*] (DLA) ... Cru Fin
Cruising (KSC) ... CRUIS
Cruising Association (SAUO) ... CA
Cruising Association [*British*] (EAIO) ... CA
Cruising Boats of America, Inc. (SAUO) ... CBA
Cruising Boost (SAUS) ... CB
Cruising Club (SAUO) ... CC
Cruising Club [*British*] ... CC
Cruising Club of America (EA) ... CCA
Cruising Speed ... CSPD
Cruising Speed [*Aviation code*] (AIA) ... VNO
Crum & Forster (EFIS) ... C&F
Crump on Marine Insurance [*A publication*] (DLA) ... Crump Ins
Crump on Marine Insurance [*A publication*] (DLA) ... Crump Mar Ins
Crump. Practice under the Judicature Acts [*A publication*] (DLA) ... Crump Jud Pr
Crump. Sale and Pledge [*A publication*] (DLA) ... Crump S & Pl
Crumrine's Reports [*116-146 Pennsylvania*] [*A publication*] (DLA) ... Crumrine
Crus Cerebri [*Medicine*] (DMAA) ... CC
Crusade ... CRSD
Crusade Against Corruption (EA) ... CAC
Crusade for a Cleaner Environment [*Defunct*] (EA) ... CCE
Crusade for Decency (EA) ... CD
Crusade to Abolish War and Armaments by World Law (EA) ... CAWAWL
Crusader ... CRSDR
Crusader (ROG) ... XDR
Crusader (SAUS) ... Xdr
Crusader Armaments [*Army*] (RDA) ... CR ARM
Crusader Concept Experimentation Program [*Army*] ... CEP
Crusader Mobility [*Army*] (RDA) ... CR MOB
Crusader Munitions/Resupply [*Army*] (RDA) ... CR MUN/RES
Crusader S-wire Container Service (SAUS) ... CSCS
Crusaders for Christ (EA) ... CC
Crush Kidney [*Medicine*] (MELL) ... CK
Crush Syndrome [*Medicine*] (MELL) ... CF
Crush, Tear, Curl [*Tea processing*] ... CTC
Crushed Aggregate (SAUS) ... CA
Crushed Brick Concrete (SAUS) ... CBC
Crushed Brock Aggregate (SAUS) ... CBA
Crushed or Ground ... CG
Crushed Rock Industries (SAUO) ... CRI
Crushed Stone (BARN) ... crst
Crushed Stone Producers' Association of Queensland [*Australia*] ... CSPAQ
Crusher and Portable Plant Association [*Defunct*] (EA) ... CAPPA
Crusher and Portable Plant Association ... CPPA
Crustacean Cardioactive Peptide [*Biochemistry*] ... CCAP
Crustacean Society (EA) ... CS
[*The*] **Crustacean Society** (EA) ... TCS
Crustal Accretion-Differentiation Supervent [*Geology*] ... CADS
Crustal Dynamics Data Information System (ARMP) ... CDDIS
Crustal Dynamics Project [*NASA*] ... CDP
Crustal Evolution Education Project [*National Association of Geology Teachers*] (EDAC) ... CEEP
Crutch Training [*Orthopedics*] (DAVI) ... CrTr
Crutch Walking [*Medicine*] ... CW
Crutch Walking (STED) ... c/w
Crutchfield [*Kentucky*] [*Seismograph station code, US Geological Survey*] (SEIS) ... CRU
Cruveilheir-Baumgarten Murmur [*Medicine*] (MELL) ... CBM
Cruveilhier-Baumgarten [*Syndrome*] [*Medicine*] (DB) ... CB
Crux [*Constellation*] ... Cru
Cruz Alta [*Brazil*] [*Airport symbol*] (OAG) ... CZB
Cruz Alta/Carlos Ruhl [*Brazil*] [*ICAO location identifier*] (ICLI) ... SBCL
Cruz Bay, VI [*FM radio station call letters*] ... WDCM
Cruz Bay, VI [*FM radio station call letters*] (RBYB) ... WWKS-FM
Cruzada Civica Nacionalista [*Nationalist Civic Crusade*] [*Venezuela*] [*Political party*] (PPW) ... CCN
Cruzada Civilista Nacional [*Panama*] [*Political party*] (EY) ... CCN
Cruzeiro [*Monetary unit*] [*Brazil*] ... CR
Cruzeiro [*Monetary unit*] [*Brazil*] ... Cruz
Cruzeiro Do Sul [*Brazil*] [*Airport symbol*] (OAG) ... CZS
Cruzeiro do Sul [*ICAO designator*] (AD) ... SC
Cruzeiro Do Sul/Internacional [*Brazil*] [*ICAO location identifier*] (ICLI) ... SBCZ
CRW Financial [*NASDAQ symbol*] (TTSB) ... CRWF
CRW Financial, Inc. [*NASDAQ symbol*] (SAG) ... CRWF
CRW Financial, Inc. [*Associated Press*] (SAG) ... CRW Fn
Cryderman Air Service [*Air carrier designation symbol*] ... CASX
Cryderman Air Service [*ICAO designator*] (FAAC) ... CTY
Cryderman Gold, Inc. [*Vancouver Stock Exchange symbol*] ... KGI
CRYENCO Cryogenic Engineering Co. (SAUO) ... CRYENCO
Cryenco Sciences [*NASDAQ symbol*] (TTSB) ... CSCI
Cryenco Sciences, Inc. [*Associated Press*] (SAG) ... Cryenco
Cryenco Sciences, Inc. [*NASDAQ symbol*] (SAG) ... CSCI
Crying Like A Baby (SAUS) ... CLAB
Crying My Eyes Out [*Online dialog*] ... CMEO
Crying Vital Capacity [*Medicine*] (AAMN) ... CVC
cryobiologist (SAUS) ... cryobio
cryobiology (SAUS) ... cryobio
Cryocautery [*Medicine*] (MELL) ... CC
cryoelectronicist (SAUS) ... cryoelectro
cryoelectronics (SAUS) ... cryoelectro
Cryofixation [*Electron microscopy*] ... CF
Cryogen Management Electronics (SAUS) ... CME
Cryogen Tank (SPST) ... CRYT
Cryogenic ... CRYGNC
Cryogenic ... CRYO
Cryogenic (KSC) ... CRYOG
Cryogenic Acoustic Microscopy (MCD) ... CAM
Cryogenic Aerosol Wafer Cleaning (AAEL) ... CAWC
Cryogenic Associative Processor (SAUS) ... CAP
Cryogenic Continuous Film Memory [*Computer science*] (DIT) ... CCFM
Cryogenic Dark Matter Search [*Astrophysics*] ... CDMS
Cryogenic Data (SAUS) ... CRYDAT
Cryogenic Data Center [*National Institute of Standards and Technology*] ... CDC

Cryogenic Distillation (MCD) ... CD
Cryogenic Electrically Suspended Gyroscope ... CESG
Cryogenic Engineering Conference (EA) ... CEC
Cryogenic Engineering Laboratory [*National Institute of Standards and Technology*] ... CEL
Cryogenic Explosive Valve ... CEV
Cryogenic Expulsive Bladder ... CEB
Cryogenic Fluid Management Experiment (MCD) ... CFME
Cryogenic Fluid Management Facility (MCD) ... CFMF
Cryogenic Fluid Storage ... CFS
Cryogenic Fluid Storage Container ... CFSC
Cryogenic Focusing [*Instrumentation*] ... CF
Cryogenic Gas Chromatography ... CGC
Cryogenic Gas Storage Subsystem (NAKS) ... CGSS
Cryogenic Gas Storage System (MCD) ... CGSS
Cryogenic Inertial Navigating System ... CINS
Cryogenic Information and Data Section (SAUS) ... CIDC
Cryogenic Infrared Radiance Instrument for Shuttle [*NASA*] ... CIRRIS
Cryogenic Infrared Radiance Instrumentation for Shuttle (ACAE) ... CIRRIS
Cryogenic Infrared Spectrometers and Telescopes for the Atmosphere ... CRISTA
Cryogenic In-Ground (OA) ... CIG
Cryogenic Instrumentation System ... CIS
Cryogenic Interferometer Spectrometer (MCD) ... CIS
Cryogenic Limb Array Etalon Spectrometer (MCD) ... CLAES
Cryogenic Limb Scanning Interferometer Radiometer (MCD) ... CLSIR
Cryogenic Limb scanning Interferometer-spectrometer and Radiometer (SAUS) ... CLIR
Cryogenic Linear Temperature Sensor (SAUS) ... CLTS
Cryogenic Memory (SAUS) ... CM
Cryogenic Noise Standard (SAUS) ... CNS
Cryogenic on Orbit Liquid Depot Storage, Acquisition, Transfer (SAUS) ... COLD-SAT
Cryogenic Positive Expulsion Bladder ... CPEB
Cryogenic Pressure Transducer ... CPT
Cryogenic Quartz Crystal Microbalance ... CQCM
Cryogenic Rare Event Search with Superconducting Thermometers [*Astrophysics*] ... CRESST
Cryogenic Refrigerator Maintenance Test Set (ACAE) ... CRMTS
Cryogenic Refrigerator Program (SAUS) ... CRP
Cryogenic Refrigerator Test Station (ACAE) ... CRTS
Cryogenic Society of America (EA) ... CSA
Cryogenic Storage and Transfer System (MCD) ... CSTS
Cryogenic Storage Container ... CSC
Cryogenic Storage System [*Apollo project*] [*NASA*] ... CSS
Cryogenic Store (SAUS) ... CS
Cryogenic Surgery [*Medicine*] (MELL) ... CGS
Cryogenic Switching by Avalanche and Recombination (SAUS) ... CRYOSAR
Cryogenic Temperature Sensor [*or Source*] ... CTS
Cryogenic Temperature Source (SAUS) ... CTS
Cryogenic Transmission Electron Microscopy ... CTEM
Cryogenic Upper Atmosphere Limb Emission Radiometer (MCD) ... CULER
Cryogenic Vacuum Calorimeter ... CVC
Cryogenic Whole Air Sampler [*Instrumentation*] ... CWAS
Cryogenics (SSD) ... CRY
Cryogenics (SAUS) ... CRYOG
Cryogenics (SAUS) ... CS
Cryogenics and Industrial Gases (journ.) (SAUS) ... Cryog Ind Gases
Cryogenics Engineering Laboratory (SAUS) ... CEL
Cryoglobulin [*Clinical medicine*] ... CG
Cryoglobulin [*Biochemistry*] (DAVI) ... CRYO
CryoLife, Inc. [*NYSE symbol*] (SG) ... CRY
Cryolife, Inc. [*NASDAQ symbol*] (SAG) ... CRYL
Cryolife, Inc. [*Associated Press*] (SAG) ... Cryolife
Cryomedical Sciences [*NASDAQ symbol*] (TTSB) ... CMSI
Cryomedical Sciences, Inc. [*NASDAQ symbol*] (NQ) ... CMSI
Cryomedical Sciences, Inc. [*Associated Press*] (SAG) ... Cryomed
Cryonic Rare Event Search with Superconducting Thermometers (SAUS) ... CRESST
Cryonics (SAUS) ... CRYON
Cryonics Association of Australia ... CAA
Cryophylactic Agent (SAUS) ... CPA
Cryoprecipitate [*Laboratory*] (DAVI) ... CPP
Cryosphere Research on Qingzang Plateau (SAUO) ... CREO
Cryospheric Data Management System (SAUS) ... CDMS
Cryospheric Imaging Microwave Radiometer (SAUS) ... CIMR
Cryospheric System (EOSA) ... CRYSYS
Cryostatic Switching-Avalanche and Recombination (MCD) ... CRYOSAR
cryosurgeon (SAUS) ... cryosurg
Cryosurgery [*Medicine*] (DAVI) ... cryo
cryosurgery (SAUS) ... cryosurg
Cryosurgical Unit [*Medicine*] (DB) ... CSU
Cryotherapy [*Medicine*] (DAVI) ... cryo
Cryotherapy [*Medicine*] (MELL) ... CT
Cryotron Associative Processor (IEEE) ... CAP
Cryotron Memory (SAUS) ... CM
Cryotron Store (SAUS) ... CS
Crypt Cell Production Rate [*Medicine*] ... CCPR
Cryptanalysis [*Air Force*] (AFM) ... CRYPTA
Cryptanalyst (SAUS) ... Crypta
Cryptic Masonry [*Freemasonry*] (ROG) ... CM
Crypto Access Authorization [*Military*] (AABC) ... CAA
Crypto Ancillary Unit (SAUS) ... CAU
Crypto Centre (SAUO) ... CRYPCEN
Crypto Equipment for Low speed Telegraphy (SAUS) ... CELT
Crypto Interface Unit (CCCA) ... CIU
Crypto Operating System (SAUS) ... COS
Crypto Operator (SAUS) ... CTO
Crypto Radio Service ... CRS
Crypto Remote Control Unit (SAUS) ... CRCU
Cryptoancillary Unit (AABC) ... CAU
Cryptocenter Watch Officer ... CCWO
Cryptococcal Antibody [*Immunology*] (DAVI) ... CRY-AB
Cryptococcal Antigen [*Immunology*] (DAVI) ... CRY-AG
Cryptococcal Pneumonitis [*Medicine*] (MELL) ... CCP
Cryptococcus [*Genus of microorganism*] (CPH) ... C
Cryptococcus [*Immunology*] (DAVI) ... CRYPTO
Cryptococcus Neoformans (SAUS) ... CN
Crypto-Communication Network (MDG) ... CRYPTONET
Cryptofacility Security Questionnaire [*Army*] ... CSQ
Cryptogamic Botany (SAUS) ... Cryptogam Bot
Cryptogenic Fibrosing Alveolitis [*Medicine*] ... CFA
Cryptogram (SAUS) ... CRYPTO
Cryptograph (SAUS) ... Crypto
Cryptograph (MSA) ... CTGH
Cryptograph Ancillary Unit (CCCA) ... CAU
Cryptographer [*Navy rating*] ... CR
Cryptographer (SAUS) ... Crypto
Cryptographic [*or Cryptography*] (AFM) ... CRYPTO
Cryptographic Aid, General Publication (CET) ... KAG
Cryptographic Bureau (SAUO) ... CB
Cryptographic Equipment Facility (MCD) ... CEF
Cryptographic File System (SAUS) ... CFS
Cryptographic Net Control Station (CCCA) ... CNCS
Cryptographic Repair Facilities ... CRF
Cryptographic Service Message [*Telecommunications service*] ... CSM
Cryptographic Service Provider (SAUO) ... CSP
Cryptographic Supplement to the Industrial Security Manual [*DoD*] ... CSISM
Cryptographic System (SAUS) ... CS
Cryptographic Unit (CCCA) ... CU
Cryptographic Variable (SAUS) ... CV
Cryptographic-Handshake Authentication Protocol (SAUS) ... CHAP
Cryptography (SAUS) ... Crypt
Cryptography (SAUS) ... Crypto
Cryptography (ADWA) ... crypto
Cryptography Application Programming Interface [*Computer science*] (VERA) ... CAPI
Cryptograpy API (SAUS) ... CAPI
Cryptologic Program [*Military*] (GFGA) ... CCP
Cryptologic Readiness Group [*Military*] (DOMA) ... CRG
Cryptologic Shore Support Activity (SAUO) ... CSSA
Cryptologic Support Center [*Military*] ... CSC
Cryptologic Support Group [*Military*] (NVT) ... CSG
Cryptologic Technician [*Navy*] (MUSM) ... CT
Cryptologic Technician, Administrative, Chief [*Navy rating*] (DNAB) ... CTAC
Cryptologic Technician, Administrative, First Class [*Navy rating*] (DNAB) ... CTA1
Cryptologic Technician, Administrative, Master Chief [*Navy rating*] (DNAB) ... CTACM
Cryptologic Technician, Administrative, Second Class [*Navy rating*] (DNAB) ... CTA2
Cryptologic Technician, Administrative, Senior Chief [*Navy rating*] (DNAB) ... CTACS
Cryptologic Technician, Administrative, Third Class [*Navy rating*] (DNAB) ... CTA3
Cryptologic Technician, Interpretative, Chief [*Navy rating*] (DNAB) ... CTIC
Cryptologic Technician, Interpretative, First Class [*Navy rating*] (DNAB) ... CTI1
Cryptologic Technician, Interpretative, Master Chief [*Navy rating*] (DNAB) ... CTICM
Cryptologic Technician, Interpretative, Second Class [*Navy rating*] (DNAB) ... CTI2
Cryptologic Technician, Interpretative, Senior Chief [*Navy rating*] (DNAB) ... CTICS
Cryptologic Technician, Interpretative, Third Class [*Navy rating*] (DNAB) ... CTI3
Cryptologic Technician, Maintenance, Chief [*Navy rating*] (DNAB) ... CTMC
Cryptologic Technician, Maintenance, First Class [*Navy rating*] (DNAB) ... CTM1
Cryptologic Technician, Maintenance, Master Chief [*Navy rating*] (DNAB) ... CTMCM
Cryptologic Technician, Maintenance, Second Class [*Navy rating*] (DNAB) ... CTM2
Cryptologic Technician, Maintenance, Senior Chief [*Navy rating*] (DNAB) ... CTMCS
Cryptologic Technician, Maintenance, Third Class [*Navy rating*] (DNAB) ... CTM3
Cryptologic Technician O (Communications), Chief [*Navy rating*] (DNAB) ... CTOC
Cryptologic Technician O (Communications), First Class [*Navy rating*] (DNAB) ... CTO1
Cryptologic Technician O (Communications), Master Chief [*Navy rating*] (DNAB) ... CTOCM
Cryptologic Technician O (Communications), Second Class [*Navy rating*] (DNAB) ... CTO2
Cryptologic Technician O (Communications), Senior Chief [*Navy rating*] (DNAB) ... CTOCS
Cryptologic Technician O (Communications), Third Class [*Navy rating*] (DNAB) ... CTO3
Cryptologic Technician R (Collection), Chief [*Navy rating*] (DNAB) ... CTRC
Cryptologic Technician R (Collection), First Class [*Navy rating*] (DNAB) ... CTR1
Cryptologic Technician R (Collection), Master Chief [*Navy rating*] (DNAB) ... CTRCM
Cryptologic Technician R (Collection), Second Class [*Navy rating*] (DNAB) ... CTR2

Cryptologic Technician R (Collection), Senior Chief [*Navy rating*] (DNAB) .... CTRCS
Cryptologic Technician R (Collection), Third Class [*Navy rating*] (DNAB) CTR3
Cryptologic Technician, Seaman Apprentice [*Navy*] (DNAB) .... CTSA
Cryptologic Technician, Technical, Chief [*Navy rating*] (DNAB) .... CTTC
Cryptologic Technician, Technical, First Class [*Navy rating*] (DNAB) CTT1
Cryptologic Technician, Technical, Master Chief [*Navy rating*] (DNAB) .... CTTCM
Cryptologic Technician, Technical, Second Class [*Navy rating*] (DNAB) CTT2
Cryptologic Technician, Technical, Senior Chief [*Navy rating*] (DNAB) .... CTTCS
Cryptologic Technician, Technical, Third Class [*Navy rating*] (DNAB) CTT3
Cryptologic Training Committee (SAUO) .... CTC
Cryptologic Van Junction Box [*Navy*] (ANA) .... CVJB
Cryptological Unified Build (SAUS) .... CUB
Cryptopathic Effect .... CPE
Crypto-Room Watch Officer (SAUS) .... CRWO
CRYPTOsporidiosis (SAUS) .... Crypto
cryptozoology (SAUS) .... cryptozool
Crysler Branch, Stormont, Dundas, and Glengarry County Library, Ontario [*Library symbol*] [*National Library of Canada*] (BIB) .... OCRSDG
Crystal [*or Crystallize*] (IAA) .... CR
Crystal [*or Crystallography*] .... CRY
Crystal .... CRYS
Crystal (VRA) .... crys
Crystal [*or Crystalline or Crystallize or Crystallography*] .... CRYST
Crystal .... CRYSTL
Crystal .... CTAL
Crystal XL
Crystal .... XTAL
Crystal (IDOE) .... xtal
Crystal Ball .... CB
Crystal Beach, TX [*FM radio station call letters*] (RBYB) .... KSTB-FM
Crystal Beach, TX [*FM radio station call letters*] .... KTKX
Crystal Can Relay .... CCR
Crystal City, TX [*FM radio station call letters*] .... KHER
Crystal Colloidal Array [*Chemistry*] .... CCA
Crystal Control CC
Crystal Controlled Receiver (SAUS) .... XCR
Crystal Current CC
Crystal Cut [*Symbol*] (DEN) X
Crystal Cut (SAUS) .... X-CUT
Crystal Data Center [*National Institute of Standards and Technology*] .... CDC
Crystal Defect Free (SAUS) .... CDF
Crystal Detector (SAUS) .... XD
Crystal Diffraction Spectrometer (MCD) .... CDS
Crystal Diffusion Reflection .... CDR
Crystal Diode .... CD
Crystal Document Management System [*Printer technology*] .... CDMS
Crystal Driver .... CD
Crystal Electric Field [*Electronics*] (AAEL) .... CEF
Crystal Examination Screen [*Medicine*] (DAVI) .... CRYST
Crystal Exploration & Production Co. (EFIS) .... CEPCO
Crystal Falls Community Library, Crystal Falls, MI [*Library symbol*] [*Library of Congress*] (LCLS) .... MiCf
Crystal Falls, MI [*FM radio station call letters*] (BROA) .... WAQJ-FM
Crystal Falls, MI [*FM radio station call letters*] (BROA) .... WOBE-FM
Crystal Field [*Ionic Model*] .... CF
Crystal Field Stabilization Energy .... CFSE
Crystal Field Surface Orbital-Bond Energy Bond Order [*Model for chemisorption*] .... CFSO-BEBO
Crystal Field Theory [*Chemistry*] .... CFT
Crystal Filter (IAA) .... CF
Crystal Flashover Voltage (SAUS) .... CFO Voltage
Crystal Frequency Indicator .... CFI
Crystal Frequency Multiplier .... CFM
Crystal Gas Storage [*AMEX symbol*] (SG) .... COR
Crystal Gayle Fan Club [*Defunct*] (EA) .... CGFC
Crystal Growth Facility (SAUO) .... CGF
Crystal Growth Furnace (SAUS) .... CGF
Crystal Holder [*JETDS nomenclature*] [*Military*] (CET) .... HC
Crystal Impedance CI
Crystal Impedance Meter .... CIM
Crystal Kit .... CK
Crystal Lake [*New York*] [*Seismograph station code, US Geological Survey*] (SEIS) .... CLY
Crystal Lake, IL [*AM radio station call letters*] .... WAIT
Crystal Lattice Dislocation (PDAA) .... CLD
Crystal Ligand Field (DB) .... CLE
Crystal Mall (SAUS) .... CM
Crystal Marker Oscillator .... CMO
Crystal Methamphetamine Capital (SAUS) .... C stal Meth Capital
Crystal Mountain [*Vancouver Stock Exchange symbol*] .... CYM
Crystal Number [*On urinalysis*] [*Biochemistry*] (DAVI) .... CRY N
Crystal Oil [*AMEX symbol*] (TTSB) .... COR
Crystal Oil Co. [*Associated Press*] (SAG) .... CrystOil
Crystal Oil Corp. [*AMEX symbol*] (SPSG) .... COR
Crystal Oscillator .... CO
Crystal Oscillator (IEEE) .... XO
Crystal Oscillator .... XTLO
Crystal Palace (SAUS) .... C Pal
Crystal Palace National Recreation Centre (SAUS) .... CPNRC
Crystal Palace National Sports Centre [*British*] .... CPNSC
Crystal Palace, Sydenham [*British*] .... CP
Crystal Pressure Transducer .... CPT
Crystal Quartz (SAUS) .... XTAL
Crystal Quartz Modem (SAUS) .... CQM
Crystal Quartz Modern .... CQM
Crystal Rectifier (AAG) .... CR
Crystal River, FL [*FM radio station call letters*] (BROA) .... WAQV-FM
Crystal River, FL [*FM radio station call letters*] .... WKTK
Crystal River, FL [*FM radio station call letters*] .... WXJC
Crystal River Plant (NRCH) .... CRP
Crystal Shamrock [*ICAO designator*] (FAAC) .... CYT
Crystal Size Distribution .... CSD
Crystal Springs Library, Crystal Springs, MS [*Library symbol*] [*Library of Congress*] (LCLS) .... MsCs
Crystal Springs Mining Company (SAUO) .... CSMC
Crystal Springs Resort (SAUO) .... CSR
Crystal Stabilized Oscillator (SAUS) .... XSO
Crystal Unit [*Piezoelectricity*] .... CU
Crystal Unit Cell .... CUC
Crystal Video Receiver .... CVR
Crystal Violet [*An indicator*] [*Chemistry*] CV
Crystal Violet Lactone [*Organic chemistry*] CVL
Crystal Violet Tetrazolium (OA) .... CVT
Crystal Violet-Pectate [*Microbiological medium*] .... CVP
Crystal-Controlled Oscillator .... CCO
Crystal-Controlled Transmitter .... CCT
Crystal-Induced Chemotactic Factor [*Immunology*] .... CCF
Crystallex Intl. [*AMEX symbol*] (SG) .... KRY
Crystalline C
Crystalline (SAUS) .... XLN
Crystalline (SAUS) .... XTL
Crystalline Amino Acid [*Biochemistry*] (DAVI) .... CAA
Crystalline Colloidal Array [*Chemistry*] .... CCA
Crystalline Egg Albumin (MAE) .... CEA
Crystalline Insulin CI
Crystalline or Powdered .... CP
Crystalline Overthrust Structures on the Platform Localizing Unconventional Me thane .... COSPLUM
Crystalline Rock Project Office (SAUS) .... CRPO
Crystalline Silicotitanate [*Materials science*] .... CST
Crystalline Style .... CST
Crystalline Sucrose Unit [*i.e., sugar cube*] [*Slang*] .... CSU
Crystalline Transitional Material (NASA) .... CTM
Crystalline Zinc Insulin [*Medicine*] .... CZI
Crystallinity Index (SAUS) CI
Crystallite Orientation Distribution Function (MCD) .... CODF
Crystallization .... CRYSTN
Crystallization Index (SAUS) CI
Crystallized .... CRYSTD
Crystallized (SAUS) .... XTAL
Crystallized Information Processing (SAUS) .... CIP
Crystallized Polyethylene Terephthalate [*Plastics technology*] .... CPET
Crystallizing (SAUS) .... Crystg
Crystallographic [*Origin*] [*Of precious stones*] .... CRST
Crystallographic Computing Network [*AEC*] (IID) .... CRYSNET
Crystallographic Data Centre (SAUS) .... CDC
Crystallographic Information File (SAUS) .... CIF
Crystallographic Laboratory [*MIT*] (MCD) CL
Crystallographic Shear [*Crystallography*] .... CS
Crystallographic Shear Plane .... CSP
Crystallographic Structural Database [*University of Cambridge*] [*British*] [*Information service or system*] (CRD) .... CSD
Crystallography (IAA) .... CR
Crystallography (ROG) .... CRYSTAL
Crystallography (ROG) .... CRYSTALLOG
Crystallume Inc. [*NASDAQ symbol*] (TTSB) .... CRYS
Crystalonics, Incorporated (SAUO) CI
Crystal-Originated Pits (SAUS) .... COP
Crystals [*JETDS nomenclature*] [*Military*] (CET) .... CR
Crystals (SAUS) .... XLS
Crystals, Monomers, Deposition and Separation Facility (SAUO) .... CMDSF
Crytallization (SAUS) .... crys
CS Chemical Hazards Response Information System/Hazard Communication System (SAUS) .... CHRIS/HA
CS Owner's Association (EA) .... CSOA
CSA Air, Inc. [*ICAO designator*] (FAAC) .... IRO
CSA Fraternal Life [*Acronym represents organization's former name*] (EA) .... CSA
CSA Management Ltd. [*Toronto Stock Exchange symbol*] .... CSA
CSAID Binding Protein [*Biochemistry*] .... CSBP
CSB [*Chemical Species Balance*] **Existing Chemicals Assessment Tracking System** [*Environmental Protection Agency*] (EPA) .... CECATS
CSB Financial [*NASDAQ symbol*] (TTSB) .... CSBF
CSB Financial Corp. [*NASDAQ symbol*] (SAG) .... COSB
CSB Financial Corp. [*Associated Press*] (SAG) .... CSB Fn
CSB Financial Group, Inc. [*NASDAQ symbol*] (SAG) .... CSBF
CSB Financial Group, Inc. [*Associated Press*] (SAG) .... CSBFin
CSC Clearing Corp. (EA) .... CSCCC
C-Scale sound level in decibels (SAUS) .... dBC
CSE Aviation Ltd. [*British*] [*FAA designator*] (FAAC) .... CSE
CSE Aviation Ltd. (SAUS) .... NR
C-Section (SAUS) .... CS
CSF Holdings, Inc. [*NASDAQ symbol*] (SAG) .... CSFC
CSF Holdings, Inc. [*Associated Press*] (SAG) .... CSF Hd
CSG Systems International, Inc. [*NASDAQ symbol*] (SAG) .... CSGS
CSG Systems International, Inc. [*Associated Press*] (SAG) .... CSGSys
CSG Systems Intl. [*NASDAQ symbol*] (TTSB) .... CSGS
C-shaped tube (SAUS) .... C-tube
CSI Computer Specialists [*Associated Press*] (SAG) .... CSI
CSI Computer Specialists [*NASDAQ symbol*] (SAG) .... CSIS

CSI Computer Specialists Wrrt'A' [*NASDAQ symbol*] (TTSB) ... CSISW
CSIRO [*Commonwealth Scientific and Industrial Research Organisation*] **Activities Archive** [*Database*] ... ACTC
CSIRO [*Commonwealth Scientific and Industrial Research Organisation*] **Activities File** [*Database*] ... ACTF
CSIRO Division of Atmospheric Research (SAUS) ... CSIRO/DAR
CSIRO Division of Entomology (SAUO) ... ENTO
CSIRO Division of Wildlife and Ecology (SAUS) ... W&E
CSIRO [*Commonwealth Scientific and Industrial Research Organisation*] **Films** [*Database*] ... FILM
CSIRO Forestry Databae (SAUS) ... TREDAT
CSIRO [*Commonwealth Scientific and Industrial Research Organization*] **Infolink News** [*Database*] ... CINS
CSIRO Institute of Farth Resources. Technical Communication (SAUS) ... Tech Commun CSIRO Inst Earth Resour
CSIRO Land-wetness Model (SAUS) ... TOPOG
CSIRO Mathematical and Information Services (SAUO) ... CMIS
CSIRO Minerals Research Laboratories. Technical Communication (SAUS) ... Tech Commun CSIRO Miner Res Lab
CSIRO News Releases (SAUS) ... NREL
CSIRO Office of Space Science and Applications (SAUO) ... COSSA
CSIRO Office of Space Science and Applications (SAUS) ... CSIRO OSSA
CSIRO Program on cost effective restoration technologies (SAUS) ... LANDREST
CSIRO Program on management improvement to prevent degradation (SAUS) ... LANDCARE
CSIRO Program to assess land degradation (SAUS) ... LANDASSESS
CSIRO Research in Progress (SAUS) ... SIRO
CSIRO Tree Seed Centre, Canberra, database (SAUS) ... TREES
C.S.I.S. [*Canadian Security Intelligence Service*], **Information Centre , Montreal, PQ, Canada** [*Library symbol*] [*Library of Congress*] (LCLS) ... CaQMRS
CSIS [*Canadian Security Intelligence Service*] **Open Information Centre Ontario** [*Bibliotheque du SCRS (Service Canadien du Renseignement de Securite), Ottawa*] [*Library symbol*] [*National Library of Canada*] (NLC) ... OORSS
CSK Auto [*NYSE symbol*] (SG) ... CAO
CSK Corp. [*Associated Press*] (SAG) ... CSK
CSK Corp. [*NASDAQ symbol*] (NQ) ... CSKK
CSK Corp. ADS [*NASDAQ symbol*] (TTSB) ... CSKKY
CSL Lighting Manufacturing [*Associated Press*] (SAG) ... CSL Lgt
CSL Lighting Manufacturing [*NASDAQ symbol*] (SAG) ... CSLX
CSL Lighting Mfg [*NASDAQ symbol*] (TTSB) ... CSLX
CSM [*Command and Service Module*] **and ATM Communications Specialist** [*Apollo Telescope Mount*] [*NASA*] ... CATCO
CSM [*Command and Service Module*] **Environmental and Electrical Systems Engineer** [*NASA*] ... EECOM
CSM [*Command and Service Module*] **Navigation Update** [*NASA*] ... CNU
CSM Steering Committee (SAUS) ... CSMSC
C(Sound)-Multiple Analogue Component [*Telecommunications*] ... C-MAC
CSP, Inc. [*Associated Press*] (SAG) ... CSP
CSP Inc. [*NASDAQ symbol*] (NQ) ... CSPI
CSS Industries [*NYSE symbol*] (TTSB) ... CSS
CSS Industries [*Associated Press*] (SAG) ... CSS Inds
CSS Industries, Inc. [*NYSE symbol*] (SPSG) ... CSS
CSS Training Simulation System (SAUS) ... CSSTST
C.S.S.M.M. [*Centre de Services Sociaux du Montreal Metropolitan*], **Mon treal, PQ, Canada** [*Library symbol*] [*Library of Congress*] (LCLS) ... CaQMCSSMM
CSSMM [*Centre de Services Sociaux du Montreal Metropolitain*], **Montreal, Quebec** [*Library symbol*] [*National Library of Canada*] (NLC) ... QMCSSMM
CST Entertainment [*AMEX symbol*] [*Formerly, CST Entertainment Imaging*] (SG) ... CLR
CST Entertainment Imaging [*Formerly, Color Systems Technology, Inc.*] [*AMEX symbol*] (SPSG) ... CLR
CST Entertainment Imaging, Inc. [*Associated Press*] (SAG) ... CSTEnt
CSU Regional Atmospheric Modeling System (USDC) ... CSU-RAMS
C^3[*Command, Control, and Communications*] **Countermeasures** [*Pronounced "see-cubed see-m"*] ... C^{3}CM
CSX Corp. [*Formed by merger of Chessie System, Inc. and Seaboard Coast Line Railroad*] [*Formerly, CO*] [*NYSE symbol*] (SPSG) ... CSX
CT Communications [*NASDAQ symbol*] (SG) ... CTCI
CT Financial Services [*Formerly, Canada Trustco Mortgage Co.*] [*Vancouver Stock Exchange symbol*] ... CT
CT Financial Services, Inc. [*Toronto Stock Exchange symbol*] ... CFS
CT Fini Services [*TS Symbol*] (TTSB) ... CFS
CTC Air, SA [*Spain*] [*FAA designator*] (FAAC) ... CTC
CTC Communications [*NASDAQ symbol*] (SG) ... CPTL
CTC Information Retrieval from Keywords (SAUS) ... CIRK
CTEC Corp. [*Associated Press*] (SAG) ... CTEC
C-TEC Corp. [*NASDAQ symbol*] (NQ) ... CTEX
C-TEC Corp.'B' [*NASDAQ symbol*] (TTSB) ... CTEXB
Ctenidial Analog [*Biology*] ... CA
Ctenidial Nerve [*Biology*] ... CTN
Ctenidial Sinus [*Biology*] ... CS
Ctenocephalides [*A genus of fleas*] [*Entomology*] (DAVI) ... Ct
Ctenocephalides (SAUS) ... Cteno
Ctenophora (SAUS) ... Cten
C-Terminal Parathyroid Hormone [*Endocrinology*] (DAVI) ... CPTH
CTF Central Trade Finance Corp. (SAUO) ... CTF
CTG Compression Technology Group, Inc. [*Vancouver Stock Exchange symbol*] ... CGN
CTG Resources [*NYSE symbol*] (SG) ... CTG
CTI Leveland Tramrail International S.A. (SAUO) ... CTI
CTI Technologies Corp. [*Vancouver Stock Exchange symbol*] ... CJT
CTL Credit [*NASDAQ symbol*] (TTSB) ... CTLI
CTL Credit, Inc. [*Associated Press*] (SAG) ... CTL Cr
CTL Credit, Inc. [*NASDAQ symbol*] (SAG) ... CTLI
CTM Access Profile (SAUS) ... CAP
CTS Corp. [*NYSE symbol*] (SPSG) ... CTS
CTS Information Resource Centre, Ontario Ministry of Government Services, Toronto [*Library symbol*] [*National Library of Canada*] (BIB) ... OTGSI
CTV News Research Library, CTV Television Network, Toronto, Ontario [*Library symbol*] [*National Library of Canada*] (NLC) ... OTCTVN
CTV Television Network, CTV News Research Library, Toronto, ON, Canada [*Library symbol*] [*Library of Congress*] (LCLS) ... CaOTCTVN
CTV Television Network Ltd. (SAUO) ... CTV
CU Bancorp [*NASDAQ symbol*] (SPSG) ... CUBN
CU Bancorp. [*Associated Press*] (SAG) ... CU Bnc
Cuadra Associates, Inc. [*Information service or system*] (IID) ... CA
Cuajimalpa [*Mexico*] [*Later, TEO*] [*Geomagnetic observatory code*] ... CUA
Cuamba [*Mozambique*] [*ICAO location identifier*] (ICLI) ... FQCB
Cub Koda Fan Club [*Defunct*] (EA) ... CKFC
Cub Master [*Scouting*] ... CM
Cuba ... C
Cuba [*ANSI two-letter standard code*] (CNC) ... CU
Cuba [*MARC country of publication code*] [*Library of Congress*] (LCCP) ... cu
Cuba (SAUS) ... Cu
Cuba [*ANSI three-letter standard code*] (CNC) ... CUB
Cuba [*License plate code assigned to foreign diplomats in the US*] ... DC
Cuba [*MARC geographic area code*] [*Library of Congress*] (LCCP) ... nwcu
Cuba [*IYRU nationality code*] (IYR) ... RC
Cuba Hill Elementary School, Huntington, NY [*Library symbol*] [*Library of Congress*] (LCLS) ... NHuCE
Cuba Library, Cuba, NY [*Library symbol*] [*Library of Congress*] (LCLS) ... NCu
Cuba Library, Cuba, NY [*Library symbol*] [*Library of Congress*] (LCLS) ... NCuL
Cuba, MO [*AM radio station call letters*] ... KFXE
Cuba, MO [*FM radio station call letters*] (BROA) ... KFXE-FM
Cuba, MO [*AM radio station call letters*] ... KGNN
Cuba, MO [*FM radio station call letters*] (RBYB) ... KGNN-FM
Cuba, MO [*Location identifier*] [*FAA*] (FAAL) ... UBX
Cuba Resource Center [*Defunct*] (EA) ... CRC
Cuban American Foundation (EA) ... CAF
Cuban American Legal Defense and Education Fund (EA) ... CALDEF
Cuban American National Council (EA) ... CANC
Cuban American National Council (EA) ... CNC
Cuban American National Foundation (EA) ... CANF
Cuban American Sugar Company (SAUO) ... CASC
Cuban Association for the United Nations (EAIO) ... CAUN
Cuban Cane Molasses (SAUS) ... CCM
Cuban Chamber of Commerce in the United States (SAUO) ... CCCUS
Cuban Committee for Peace Research (SAUO) ... CCPR
Cuban Communist Party [*Political party*] ... CCP
Cuban Communist Party [*Political party*] ... KKP
Cuban Expeditionary Force ... CEF
Cuban Liberty & Democratic Solidarity Act (WDAA) ... CuL De SAc
Cuban National Planning Council [*Later, CANC*] (EA) ... CNPC
Cuban Nationalist Movement ... CNM
Cuban Navy ... CN
Cuban Peso [*Monetary unit*] (ODBW) ... CUP
Cuban Philatelic Society of America (EA) ... CPSA
Cuban Refugee Program [*HEW*] ... CRP
Cuban Refugee Program Staff [*HEW*] ... CRPS
Cuban Representation of Exiles [*Also known as Representacion Cubana del Exilio*] (EA) ... RECE
Cuban Victor [*Record label*] ... CubV
Cuban Women's Club (EA) ... CWC
Cubana Airlines [*ICAO designator*] (AD) ... CU
Cubana Airways (DS) ... CU
Cuban-American Committee for Normalization of Relations with Cuba (EA) ... CACNRWC
Cuban/Haitian Entrant Program [*Department of Health and Human Services*] (GFGA) ... CHEP
Cube ... CU
Cube Alignment Kit ... CAK
Cube Connected Computer (SAUS) ... CCC
Cube Connected Computer (SAUS) ... CC Computer
Cube Corner Holder ... CCH
Cube Corner Reflector ... CCR
Cube Order Index Rule ... COI
Cube Resources [*Vancouver Stock Exchange symbol*] ... CUB
Cube-Connected Cycle (MCD) ... CCC
Cube-On-Edge [*Metal grain structure*] ... COE
Cubi Naval Air Station, Bataan [*Philippines*] [*ICAO location identifier*] (ICLI) ... RPMB
Cubic (NTIO) ... c
Cubic ... C
Cubic (IAA) ... CB
Cubic (SAUS) ... Cb
Cubic (EY) ... CU
Cubic (DB) ... cu
Cubic ... CUB
Cubic Air Capacity (WDAA) ... CAC
Cubic Boron Nitride [*Cutting tool edges*] ... CBN
Cubic Capacity (DS) ... CC
Cubic Capacity (COE) ... CU
Cubic Capacity of Bales (SAUS) ... CCBI
Cubic Capacity of Bunkers [*British*] (ADA) ... CCB
Cubic Capacity of Grain (SAUS) ... CCG
Cubic Capacity of Holds [*British*] (ADA) ... CCH
Cubic Capacity of Tank (SAUS) ... CCTk
Cubic Capacity Tonnage (SAUS) ... CCT

Cubic Centimeter	cc
Cubic Centimeter (ROG)	CCM
Cubic Centimeter (ROG)	CMR₃
Cubic Centimeter (AAMN)	cm³
Cubic Centimeter (STED)	cu cm
Cubic Centimeter	CUCM
Cubic Centimeter (or Centimetres) (SAUS)	cbcm
Cubic Centimeter (or Centimetres) (SAUS)	cc
Cubic Centimeter (or Centimetres) (SAUS)	ccm
Cubic Centimeter (or Centimetres) (SAUS)	cm3
Cubic Centimeter (or Centimetres) (SAUS)	cu cm
Cubic Centimeter per Liter [Measurement] (DAVI)	cc/l
Cubic Centimeter Per Minute (IAA)	CCPM
Cubic Centimeters at Standard Temperature and Pressure [Also, CSTP]	CCSTP
Cubic Centimeters at Standard Temperature and Pressure [Also, CCSTP]	CSTP
Cubic Centimeters (or Centimetres) per Minute (SAUS)	CCM
Cubic Centimeters (or Centimetres) per Minute (SAUS)	CC/min
Cubic Centimeters (or Centimetres) per Second (SAUS)	CC/sec
Cubic Centimeters (or Centimetres) per Second (SAUS)	cu cm/s
Cubic Chain-of-Rotators [Equation of state]	CCOR
Cubic Close Packing [Crystallography]	CCP
cubic cm (SAUS)	ccm
Cubic Contents	CC
Cubic Corp. [AMEX symbol] (SPSG)	CUB
Cubic Corp. [Associated Press] (SAG)	Cubic
Cubic Corp., San Diego, CA [Library symbol] [Library of Congress] (LCLS)	CSdCu
Cubic Decameters per Day	DAM³/D
Cubic Decimeter (IAA)	CUDM
Cubic Decimeter (ROG)	Dm³
Cubic Decimeter (or Decimetre) (SAUS)	cdm
Cubic Decimeter (or Decimetre) (SAUS)	cu dm
Cubic Decimeter (or Decimetre) (SAUS)	dm3
Cubic Decimetre per Hour (SAUS)	dm3/h
Cubic Dekameter	DAM³
Cubic Dekameter	Dkm³
Cubic Dekameter (or Dekametre) (SAUS)	dkm3
Cubic Feet (RIMS)	CBFT
Cubic Feet (AFM)	CF
Cubic Feet (SAUS)	cf
Cubic Feet [or Foot] (MSA)	CUFT
Cubic Feet	Cu Ft
Cubic Feet (IDOE)	cu ft
Cubic Feet	ft3
Cubic Feet (EG)	FT³
Cubic Feet of Gas (SAUS)	CFG
Cubic Feet of Gas per Day (SAUS)	CFGD
Cubic Feet of Gas per Hour (SAUS)	CFGH
Cubic Feet of Gas per Minute (SAUS)	CFGM
Cubic Feet per Day (ADWA)	cfd
Cubic Feet per Day	CFD
Cubic Feet per Foot Day	FT³/(FT D)
Cubic Feet per Hour	CFH
Cubic Feet per Hour (EEVL)	cfh
Cubic Feet per Minute (ABAC)	cfm
Cubic Feet per Minute	CFM
Cubic Feet per Minute (SAUS)	cu ft min
Cubic Feet per Minute (SAUS)	ft3/min/min
Cubic Feet per Minute/Second (DEN)	CFM/S
Cubic Feet per Month (SAUS)	CF/M
Cubic Feet per Second	CFS
Cubic Feet per Second (SAUS)	cuftsec
Cubic Feet per Second	CUSEC
Cubic Feet per Second (SAUS)	ft3/sec
Cubic Feet per Second	FT³/S
Cubic Feet per Second per Square Mile (ADWA)	cfsm
Cubic Foot (SAUS)	CF
Cubic Foot (DAS)	CFT
Cubic Foot (IDOE)	cu ft
Cubic Foot per Day (SAUS)	cfd
Cubic Foot per Minute (SAUS)	ft3/min
Cubic Foot per Minute (WDAA)	FT³/MIN
Cubic Foot per Second (SAUS)	CFS
Cubic Foot per Second [Marine science] (OSRA)	cfs
Cubic Hectometer (WDAA)	HM³
Cubic Inch (MCD)	CI
Cubic Inch	CUIN
Cubic Inch (IDOE)	cu in
Cubic Inch	Cu In
Cubic Inch (SAUS)	in3
Cubic Inch	IN³
Cubic Inch Displacement [in engines]	CID
Cubic Inch per Pound (SAUS)	cu in/lb
Cubic Inch per Pound (SAUS)	in3/lb
Cubic Inches (IDOE)	cu in
Cubic Inches per Minute (IAA)	CIM
Cubic Inches per Revolution (MCD)	CIPR
Cubic Kilometer	KM³
Cubic Meter (ROG)	CBM
Cubic Meter	CUM
Cubic Meter	m3
Cubic Meter (or Metre) (SAUS)	cu m
Cubic Meter (or Metre) per Second (SAUS)	cum/sec
Cubic Meter (or Metre) per Second (SAUS)	m3/s
Cubic Meter per (or Metre) Day (SAUS)	cum/d
Cubic Meters per Day	M³/D
Cubic Meters per Joule	M³/J
Cubic Meters per Kilogram	M³/KG
Cubic Meters per Meter Day	M³/(M D)
Cubic Meters per Meter Year	M³/(M A)
Cubic Meters per Minute	M³/MIN
Cubic Meters per Second	CUMECS
Cubic Meters per Second	M³/S
Cubic Metre (or Metre) per Hour (SAUS)	cu m/h
Cubic Micrometer (WDAA)	MU M³
Cubic Micron (IAA)	CUMN
Cubic Micron	CUMU
Cubic Mile (HGAA)	CUMI
Cubic Millimeter	CMM
Cubic Millimeter	CUMM
Cubic Millimeter	MM³
Cubic Millimeter (or Millimetre) (SAUS)	cmm
Cubic Millimeter (or Millimetre) (SAUS)	cu mm
Cubic Millimeter (or Millimetre) (SAUS)	mm3
Cubic Millimeters per Second [Measurement] (DAVI)	cmm/s
Cubic Root (IAA)	CURT
Cubic Spline Regression [Statistics]	CRS
Cubic Splines (SAUS)	CS
Cubic Stabilized Zirconia	CSZ
Cubic Tonnage [Shipping]	CT
Cubic Weight	CW
Cubic Yard	CUYD
Cubic Yard	cu yd
Cubic Yard (KSC)	CY
Cubic Yard (SAUS)	cy
Cubic Yard (ADA)	CYD
Cubic Yard (SAUS)	yd3
Cubic Yard	YD³
Cubic Yard Bank Measurement (DAC)	Cybm
Cubic Yard Compacted Measurement (DAC)	CYCM
Cubic Zirconia [Simulated diamonds]	CZ
Cubical (SAUS)	c
Cubical Expansion (SAUS)	cub exp
Cubicle (MSA)	CUB
Cubicle (VRA)	cub
Cubicle	CUBE
Cubicle (ADWA)	cube
Cubist Pharmaceuticals, Inc. [NASDAQ symbol] (SAG)	CBST
Cubist Pharmaceuticals, Inc. [Associated Press] (SAG)	CubistPh
Cubitainer (MCD)	CU
Cubital Fossa [Medicine] (MELL)	CF
Cubital Tunnel Syndrome [Medicine] (DMAA)	CuTS
Cubitron Memory Cell (SAUS)	CMC
CUBUS Management Ltd. (SAUO)	CUBUS
CUC International [Associated Press] (SAG)	CUC Intl
CUC International, Inc. [Formerly, Comp-U-Card International] [NYSE symbol] (SPSG)	CU
CUC Intl. [NYSE symbol] (TTSB)	CU
Cucos, Inc. [NASDAQ symbol] (NQ)	CUCO
Cucos, Inc. [Associated Press] (SAG)	Cucos
Cucui [Brazil] [Airport symbol] (AD)	CBZ
Cucui [Brazil] [ICAO location identifier] (ICLI)	SBKU
Cucumber [Slang] (DSUE)	CU
Cucumber [Slang] (DSUE)	CUE
Cucumber [Slang] (DSUE)	CUKE
Cucumber Green Mottle Mosaic Virus [Plant pathology]	CGMMV
Cucumber Mosaic Virus	CMV
Cucumber Pale Fruit Viroid	CPFV
Cucumber Soilborne Virus	CSBV
Cucumber Virus 4 [Plant pathology]	CV4
Cucumber Yellows Virus [Plant pathology]	CUYV
Cucurbita Cruenta [Cupping Glass] [Pharmacy]	CC
Cucurbitula Cruenta [Cupping Glass with Scarificator] [Pharmacy] (ROG)	CUCURB CRUENT
Cucuta [Colombia] [Airport symbol] (OAG)	CUC
Cucuta/Camilo Daza [Colombia] [ICAO location identifier] (ICLI)	SKCC
Cudahy Co. (SAUO)	CUD
Cudahy Public Library, Cudahy, WI [Library symbol] [Library of Congress] (LCLS)	WC
Cuddapah [India] [ICAO location identifier] (ICLI)	VOCP
Cuddapan [Queensland] [Airport symbol] (AD)	UDD
Cuddesdon Theological College [Later, Rippon College, Cuddesdon] [Oxford] [British] (ROG)	CUDD
Cuddon. Copyhold Acts [1865] [A publication] (ILCA)	Cudd Copyh
Cue Indexing System (IEEE)	CIS
Cue Room (SAUS)	Q-room
CUEA Synthesis and Publication Segment [Marine science] (MSC)	SYNAPSE
Cued Speech Center (EA)	CSC
Cueing L-band Rugged Search Track & Acquisition Radar (SAUS)	CLRSTAR
Cuenca [Ecuador] [Airport symbol] (OAG)	CUE
Cuenca [Ecuador] [ICAO location identifier] (ICLI)	SECU
Cuenta Abierta [Open Account] [Spanish] [Business term]	CA
Cuenta y Riesgo [For Account and Risk Of] [Spanish] [Business term]	C/R
Cuernavaca [Mexico] [ICAO location identifier] (ICLI)	MMCB
Cuero, TX [AM radio station call letters] (RBYB)	KTXC
Cuero, TX [FM radio station call letters] (RBYB)	KVCQ
Cuers/Pierrefeu [France] [ICAO location identifier] (ICLI)	LFTF
Cuesta (SAUS)	CUET

Cuesta College, San Luis Obispo, CA [*Library symbol*] [*Library of Congress*] (LCLS) ... CSluCu
Cufar [*Guinea-Bissau*] [*ICAO location identifier*] (ICLI) ... GGCF
CUG [*Control Unit Group*] **Interrupt Inhibit** ... CII
CUG Selection and Validation Response (SAUS) ... CSVR
Cuglieri [*Italy*] [*Seismograph station code, US Geological Survey*] (SEIS) ... CUG
Cuiaba [*Brazil*] [*Airport symbol*] (OAG) ... CGB
Cuiaba/Marechal Rondon [*Brazil*] [*ICAO location identifier*] (ICLI) ... SBCY
Cuirassed [*Numismatics*] ... CUIR
Cuisine ... CSN
Cuito Cuanavale [*Angola*] [*ICAO location identifier*] (ICLI) ... FNCV
Cujus [*Of Which*] [*Latin*] ... CUJ
Cujus Libet [*Of Any You Please*] [*Pharmacy*] ... CUJ LIB
Cujus Libet [*Of Any You Please*] [*Pharmacy*] (ROG) ... CUJUSL
Culbro Corp. [*NYSE symbol*] (SPSG) ... CUC
Culbro Corp. [*Associated Press*] (SAG) ... Culbro
Cul-de-Sac [*Medicine*] (MAE) ... CDS
Culdrose [*British*] [*ICAO location identifier*] (ICLI) ... EGDR
Culebra [*Puerto Rico*] [*Airport symbol*] (OAG) ... CPX
Culebra [*Puerto Rico*] [*Seismograph station code, US Geological Survey*] (SEIS) ... CUP
Culebra [*Puerto Rico*] [*ICAO location identifier*] (ICLI) ... TJCP
Culebra, PR [*FM radio station call letters*] (RBYB) ... WJVP-FM
Culebra, PR [*FM radio station call letters*] (RBYB) ... WXZX-FM
Culex [*Genus of microorganisms*] (MAH) ... C
Culex [*Classical studies*] (OCD) ... Cul
Culham Conceptual Tokamak Reactor [*Nuclear energy*] [*British*] (NUCP) ... CCTR
Culham Laboratory (SAUO) ... CLM
Culham Laboratory Reports [*United Kingdom Atomic Energy Authority*] ... CLM
Culham Language for System Development (SAUS) ... CLSD
Culham On-Line Single Experimental Console [*Computer science*] (OA) ... COSEC
Culiacan [*Mexico*] [*Airport symbol*] (OAG) ... CUL
Culiacan [*Mexico*] [*Seismograph station code, US Geological Survey*] [*Closed*] (SEIS) ... CUL
Culiacan [*Mexico*] [*ICAO location identifier*] (ICLI) ... MMCL
Culinary (ADA) ... CUL
Culinary (ADWA) ... cul
Culinary and Fine Arts Club [*Later, Culinary Arts Club*] (EA) ... C & FA
Culinary Arts Institute (SAUO) ... CAI
Culinary Arts Program [*Association of Independent Colleges and Schools specialization code*] ... CU
Culinary Institute of America [*Hyde Park, NY*] ... CIA
Cull and Print (SAUS) ... CULPRIT
Cullage (SAUS) ... CULL
Cullboard (SAUS) ... Cull
Cullen Frost Bankers [*NASDAQ symbol*] (TTSB) ... CFBI
Cullen/Frost Bankers [*NYSE symbol*] (SG) ... CFR
Cullen/Frost Bankers, Inc. [*NASDAQ symbol*] (NQ) ... CFBI
Cullen-Frost Bankers, Inc. [*Associated Press*] (SAG) ... CullnFr
Cullen's Bankrupt Law [*A publication*] (DLA) ... Cull BL
Culligan International Co. (SAUO) ... CUL
Culligan Water Tech [*NYSE symbol*] (TTSB) ... CUL
Culling (SAUS) ... CULL
Cullman, AL [*Location identifier*] [*FAA*] (FAAL) ... CPP
Cullman, AL [*AM radio station call letters*] ... WFMH
Cullman, AL [*FM radio station call letters*] ... WFMH-FM
Cullman, AL [*FM radio station call letters*] ... WKUL
Cullman, AL [*AM radio station call letters*] ... WXXR
Cullman County Library [*Library network*] ... CCPL
Cullompton [*England*] ... CULL
Cullowhee, NC [*Location identifier*] [*FAA*] (FAAL) ... HQL
Cullowhee, NC [*FM radio station call letters*] ... WWCU
Culminating Demonstration ... CD
Culp, Inc. [*NYSE symbol*] (SG) ... CFI
Culp, Inc. [*NASDAQ symbol*] (NQ) ... CULP
Culp, Inc. [*Associated Press*] (SAG) ... Culp Inc
Culpeper, VA [*FM radio station call letters*] ... WCUL
Culpeper, VA [*AM radio station call letters*] ... WCVA
Culpeper, VA [*FM radio station call letters*] ... WPVB
Culpepper, VA [*FM radio station call letters*] (BROA) ... WARN-FM
Culpepper, VA [*FM radio station call letters*] (BROA) ... WPER-FM
Cult Awareness Network (EA) ... CAN
Cult of the Dead Cow (SAUO) ... CDC
Cult of the Virgin (EA) ... CV
Cultists Anonymous [*British*] (DBA) ... CA
Cultivar [*Cultural Variety*] [*Biology*] ... cv
Cultivar (LDT) ... CV
Cultivated [*Botany*] ... cult
Cultivated (SAUS) ... Cult
Cultivated Mushroom Institute of America ... CMIA
Cultivation (SAUS) ... cult
Cultivation (ROG) ... CULTIVON
Cultivator ... CULTVR
Cultural ... CLTRL
Cultural ... CULT
cultural (SAUS) ... cult
Cultural / Ethnic Diversity (MEDA) ... CED
Cultural Action Committee ... CAC
Cultural Affairs Library, Nova Scotia Department of Tourism and Culture, Halifa x, Nova Scotia [*Library symbol*] [*National Library of Canada*] (NLC) ... NSHDR
Cultural Affairs Officer [*United States Information Service*] ... CAO
Cultural and Recreational Education Achieved through Investigations Ordinarily Neglected [*University course*] ... CREATION
Cultural and Recreational Education Achieved Through Investigations Ordinarily Neglected (SAUS) ... CREATION
Cultural Association of Bengal (EA) ... CAB
Cultural Attitudes Repertory Technique (EDAC) ... CART
Cultural Auction of Many Extraordinary Lots of Treasure [*St. Louis, Missouri*] ... CAMELOT
Cultural Awareness Program ... CAP
Cultural Centre [*Centre Culturel*] **Verdun, Quebec** [*Library symbol*] [*National Library of Canada*] (NLC) ... QVEC
Cultural Council [*Australia*] ... CC
Cultural Deprivation [*Psychology*] (AEBS) ... CD
Cultural Disadvantage ... CD
Cultural Exchange Officer [*United States Information Service*] ... CEO
Cultural Exchange Society of America (EA) ... CESA
Cultural Expression in the Navy Workshop (DNAB) ... CEN
Cultural Groups (SAUO) ... ARTS
Cultural Information Analysis Center (SAA) ... CIAC
Cultural [*formerly, Counterinsurgency*] **Information Analysis Center** [*Discontinued*] (MCD) ... CINFAC
Cultural Information Service (EA) ... CIS
Cultural Integration Fellowship (EA) ... CIF
Cultural Pollution Index ... CPI
Cultural Practices (ADWA) ... CP
Cultural Property Implementation Act ... CPIA
Cultural Resource Management [*Archaeology*] ... CRM
Cultural Resources Information System (SAUO) ... CRIS
Cultural Resources Protection on the Outer Continental Shelf [*Oceanography*] (MSC) ... CRPOCS
Cultural Survival (EA) ... CS
Cultural Technical (SAUS) ... CULTECH
Cultural Tourism Advisory Group [*Australia*] ... CTAG
Cultural Travel Organizations International (EA) ... CTOI
Cultural Work, Inc. [*An association*] (EA) ... CWI
Culture [*Microbiology*] ... CULT
Culture (ADWA) ... cult
Culture [*Biochemistry*] (DAVI) ... Cx
Culture and Animals Foundation (EA) ... CAF
Culture and Life [*A publication*] ... C & L
Culture and Nature Visitor (SAUO) ... CNV
Culture and Sensitivity (SAUS) ... C&S
Culture and Sensitivity ... C & S
Culture and Susceptibility [*Medicine*] (MEDA) ... C & S
Culture Centre of Algae and Protozoa [*Freshwater Biological Association*] [*British*] (CB) ... CCAP
Culture Collection [*Medicine*] (DB) ... CC
Culture Collection of Entomogenous Bacteria (MELL) ... CCEB
Culture Collection of the Commonwealth Mycological Institute (DB) ... CMI-CC
Culture Collections (SAUS) ... CC
Culture Filtrate [*Analytical biochemistry*] ... CF
Culture Media [*Bacteriology*] (DAVI) ... CM
Culture, Medicine and Psychiatry (SAUS) ... Cult Med Psychiatry
Culture Midvoid Specimen [*Medicine*] (STED) ... CMVS
Culture Ministers Council (SAUO) ... CMC
Culture Mutant Tuebingen (DB) ... CMT
Culture Shock Inventory [*Interpersonal skills and attitudes test*] ... CSI
Culture Supernatant [*Microbiology*] ... CS
Culture Supply Room [*Microbiology*] ... CSR
Culture, Understanding and Enrichment (SAUS) ... CUE
Cultured Macrophages (STED) ... CMA
Cultured Marble Institute (EA) ... CMI
Cultured Pearl Association of America (EA) ... CPAA
Cultured Thymic Epithelium [*Immunochemistry*] ... CTE
Culture-Fair Intelligence Test (DIPS) ... CFIT
Culture-Free Intelligence Test (DIPS) ... CFIT
Culture-Free/Self-Esteem Inventories for Children and Adults [*Psychology*] (DHP) ... CF/SEI
Culture-Negative Neutrocytic Ascite [*Bacteriology*] ... CNNA
Culture-Positive Toxin-Positive [*Medicine*] (DMAA) ... CPTP
Culture-Postive Toxin-Negative [*Medicine*] (DMAA) ... CPTN
Cultuur-en Ontspanningscentrum [*Center for Culture and Recreation*] [*Netherlands*] ... COC
Cultwatch Response [*An association*] (EA) ... CR
Culver City (ACAE) ... CC
Culver City, CA [*Location identifier*] [*FAA*] (FAAL) ... CVR
Culver Club (EA) ... CC
Culver, IN [*Location identifier*] [*FAA*] (FAAL) ... CPB
Culver Public Library, Culver, IN [*Library symbol*] [*Library of Congress*] (LCLS) ... InCu
Culver Senior High School, Culver, OR [*Library symbol*] [*Library of Congress*] (LCLS) ... OrCuHS
Culver Stockton College (SAUO) ... CSC
Culver-Stockton College [*Canton, MO*] ... CSC
Culver-Stockton College, Canton, MO [*Library symbol*] [*Library of Congress*] (LCLS) ... MoCanC
Culvert (WDAA) ... C
Culvert (SAUS) ... Cul
Culvert ... CULV
Culvert Analysis and Design (MHDB) ... CANDE
Cum [*With*] [*Latin*] ... C
cum (SAUS) ... c
Cum Correction [*With lenses*] [*Ophthalmology*] ... cc
Cum Dividend [*With Dividend*] [*Latin*] [*Stock exchange term*] ... Cum Div
Cum Dividendo [*With Dividend*] [*Latin*] [*Stock exchange term*] ... CD
Cum Dividendo [*With Dividend*] [*Stock exchange term*] (ADA) ... CDIV
Cum Entitlement [*With Entitlement*] [*Latin*] [*Legal term*] (ADA) ... CE

Cum Laude Approbatur [Latin] cl
Cum Laude Society (EA) .... CLS
Cum Omnibus Bonis Quiescat [May He, or She, Repose with All Good Souls]
  [Latin] .... COBQ
Cum Rights [With Rights] (ADA) .... CR
Cum Tanto [With the Same Amount Of] [Pharmacy] .... C TANT
Cum Testamento Annexo [With the Will Annexed] [Latin] .... CTA
Cumana [Venezuela] [Seismograph station code, US Geological Survey]
  (SEIS) .... CUM
Cumana [Venezuela] [Airport symbol] (OAG) .... CUM
Cumana, Sucre [Venezuela] [ICAO location identifier] (ICLI) .... SVCU
Cumann Cheol Tire Eireann [Folk Music Society of Ireland] (EAIO) .... CCTE
Cumann Cluiche Corr na hEireann [Rounders Association of Ireland]
  (EAIO) .... CCCE
Cumann Inneáltoiri Comhairle na hEirann [Association of Consulting
  Engineers of Ireland] (EAIO) .... CICE
Cumann Leabharann na hEireann [Library Association of Ireland] (EAIO) ..... CLNh
Cumann Luthchleas Gael [Gaelic Athletic Association] (EAIO) .... CLG
Cumann Muinteoiri Eireann [Irish National Teachers' Organization] (EAIO) ..... CME
Cumann Peile na Heireann [Football Association of Ireland] [Ireland] (EAIO) .... CPE
Cumberland [Maryland] [Airport symbol] (OAG) .... CBE
Cumberland [County in England] .... CUMB
Cumberland [England] (BARN) .... CumbId
Cumberland Airlines [ICAO designator] (AD) .... NQ
Cumberland & Pennsylvania Railroad (IIA) .... C & P
Cumberland and Westmorland Antiquarian and Archaeological Society
  (SAUO) .... CWAAS
Cumberland College of Tennessee (SAUS) .... CCT
Cumberland College of Tennessee, Lebanon, TN [Library symbol] [Library of
  Congress] (LCLS) .... TLebC
Cumberland College, Williamsburg, KY [Library symbol] [Library of
  Congress] (LCLS) .... KyWilC
Cumberland County Advertiser-Press, Inc., Bridgeton, NJ [Library symbol]
  [Library of Congress] (LCLS) .... NjBAP
Cumberland County Clerk, Bridgeton, NJ [Library symbol] [Library of
  Congress] (LCLS) .... NjBCoC
Cumberland County College, Vineland, NJ [Library symbol] [Library of
  Congress] (LCLS) .... NjVC
Cumberland County Historical Society and Hamilton Library Association,
  Carlisle,PA [Library symbol] [Library of Congress] (LCLS) .... PCarlH
Cumberland County Historical Society, Greenwich, NJ [Library symbol]
  [Library of Congress] (LCLS) .... NjGrHi
Cumberland County Museum, Amherst, Nova Scotia [Library symbol]
  [National Library of Canada] (NLC) .... NSCCM
Cumberland County Museum, Amherst, NS, Canada [Library symbol] [Library
  of Congress] (LCLS) .... CaNSCCM
Cumberland County Public Library, Fayetteville, NC [Library symbol] [Library
  of Congress] (LCLS) .... NcFayC
Cumberland County Public Library, North Carolina Foreign Language
  Center, Fayetteville, NC [Library symbol] [Library of Congress]
  (LCLS) .... NcFayC-F
Cumberland Gap National Historical Park [National Park Service
  designation] .... CUGA
Cumberland Holdings, Inc. [Associated Press] (SAG) .... CmbHld
Cumberland Holdings, Inc. [NASDAQ symbol] (SAG) .... CUMB
Cumberland House, SK [FM radio station call letters] (RBYB) .... CJCF
Cumberland, KY [AM radio station call letters] .... WCPM
Cumberland, KY [FM radio station call letters] .... WSEH
Cumberland Law Journal [Pennsylvania] [A publication] (DLA) .... Cumb
Cumberland Law Journal [Pennsylvania] [A publication]
  (DLA) .... Cumberland LJ (PA)
Cumberland Law Journal [Pennsylvania] [A publication] (DLA) .... Cumb Law Jrnl
Cumberland, MD [Location identifier] [FAA] (FAAL) .... RYP
Cumberland, MD [AM radio station call letters] .... WCBC
Cumberland, MD [FM radio station call letters] .... WKGO
Cumberland, MD [AM radio station call letters] .... WNTR
Cumberland, MD [FM radio station call letters] .... WROG
Cumberland, MD [AM radio station call letters] .... WTBO
Cumberland Museum, British Columbia [Library symbol] [National Library of
  Canada] (NLC) .... BCUM
Cumberland Plateau [Tennessee] [Seismograph station code, US Geological
  Survey] (SEIS) .... CPO
Cumberland Plateau Seismological Observatory .... CPSO
Cumberland Presbyterian Theological Seminary, Bethel College, McKenzie,
  TN [Library symbol] [Library of Congress] (LCLS) .... TMckB-C
Cumberland Public Library, Cumberland, WI [Library symbol] [Library of
  Congress] (LCLS) .... WCu
Cumberland Railway & Coal (MHDB) CC
Cumberland Railway & Coal Co. [AAR code] .... CDC
Cumberland Regional Library, Amherst, Nova Scotia [Library symbol]
  [National Library of Canada] (NLC) .... NSAMC
Cumberland Regional Library, Amherst, NS, Canada [Library symbol]
  [Library of Congress] (LCLS) .... CaNSAMC
Cumberland Resources Ltd. [Vancouver Stock Exchange symbol] .... CBD
Cumberland Township Library, Navan, ON, Canada [Library symbol] [Library
  of Congress] (LCLS) .... CaONCU
Cumberland Township Library, Navan, Ontario [Library symbol] [National
  Library of Canada] (BIB) .... ONCU
Cumberland Trail Library System [Library network] .... CTLS
Cumberland Trail Library System, Flora, IL [OCLC symbol] (OCLC) .... IEZ
Cumberland Trail Library System, Flora, IL [Library symbol] [Library of
  Congress] (LCLS) .... IFICL
Cumberland University (SAUO) .... CU
Cumberland University (SAUO) .... Cumb Univ
Cumberland's Law of Nature [A publication] (DLA) .... Cumb Nat

Cumberland-Samford Law Review [A publication] (DLA) .... Cumb-Sam L Rev
Cumberland-Samford Law Review [A publication] (DLA) .... Cum Sam L Rev
Cumbria [County in England] (WGA) .... CUMB
Cumbria (ADWA) .... Cumb
Cumene Hydroperoxide [Organic chemistry] .... CHP
Cumhuriyetci Turk Partisi [Republican Turkish Party] [Turkish Cyprus]
  [Political party] (PPE) .... CTP
Cumming, GA [AM radio station call letters] .... WMLB
Cumming, GA [FM radio station call letters] .... WWEV
Cummings Research Park (SAUO) .... CRP
Cummins and Dunphy's Remarkable Trials [A publication]
  (DLA) .... Cum & Dun Rem Tr
Cummins and Dunphy's Remarkable Trials [A publication] (DLA) .... Rem Tr
Cummins & Durphy, Remarkable Trials (SAUS) .... Rem Tr
Cummins Engine [NYSE symbol] (TTSB) .... CUM
Cummins Engine Co., Inc. [NYSE symbol] (SPSG) .... CUM
Cummins Engine Co., Inc. [Associated Press] (SAG) .... CumEng
Cummins' Manual of Civil Law [A publication] (DLA) .... Cum Civ L
Cummins Motor (SAUS) .... CUM
Cummins Natural Gas Engines [Cummins Engine Co., Inc.] .... CNGE
Cummins' Reports [1866-67] [Idaho] [A publication] (DLA) .... Cummins
Cummulative Abbreviated Trouble (SAUS) .... CAT
Cummulative Bulletin (SAUS) .... CB
Cummulative Elapsed Time (SAUS) .... CET
Cumulate (ABBR) .... CMULA
Cumulated (ABBR) .... CMULAD
Cumulated Index Medicus [A publication] .... CIM
Cumulated Machine-Readable Cataloging [Computer science] .... CUMARC
Cumulated Summaries .... CUMS
Cumulating (ABBR) .... CMULAG
Cumulation (ABBR) .... CMULAN
Cumulative (WGA) .... CM
Cumulative (SG) .... cm
Cumulative (ABBR) .... CMULAV
Cumulative (SAUS) .... CU
Cumulative (EBF) .... Cum
Cumulative (KSC) .... CUM
Cumulative (ADWA) .... cum
Cumulative [Banking] (TBD) .... Cuml
Cumulative Abbreviated Trouble File [Telecommunications] (TEL) .... CAT
Cumulative Amount (DNAB) .... CA
Cumulative Annual Growth Rate [Business term] .... CAGR
Cumulative Annual Regular Military Compensation (MCD) .... CARMC
Cumulative Auction-Market Preferred Stock [Investment term] .... CAMPS
Cumulative Audience [Telecommunications] .... CUME
Cumulative Average Unit Cost .... CAUC
Cumulative Bulletin [US Internal Revenue Service] [A publication] (AAGC) .... CB
Cumulative Changes (NATG) CC
Cumulative Continuation Rate (SAUS) .... CCR
Cumulative Damage Function [Nuclear energy] (NRCH) .... CDF
Cumulative Data Report (MCD) .... CDR
Cumulative Data Statistics (NASA) .... CUDS
Cumulative Density Function (SAUS) .... CDF
Cumulative Detection Probability (CAAL) .... CDP
Cumulative Discounted Cash Flow .... CDCF
Cumulative Distribution Function [Statistics] .... CDF
Cumulative Distribution of Frequency (SAUS) .... CDF
Cumulative Dividend (WDAA) .... Cum div
Cumulative Dose [Medicine] (MELL) .... CD
Cumulative Elapsed Time .... CET
Cumulative Failure Rate .... CFR
Cumulative Financial Requirements (MCD) .... CFR
Cumulative Form Inception (MCD) .... CFI
Cumulative Frequency .... CF
Cumulative Frequency Distribution (KSC) .... CFD
Cumulative Hydrologic Impact Assessment (GEOI) .... CHIA
Cumulative Index (DLA) CI
Cumulative Index to Nursing and Allied Health Literature [Database] ..... CINAHL
Cumulative List [Internal Revenue code with names of exempt organizations] CL
Cumulative List Indicator [IRS] .... CU
Cumulative Material Unaccounted For [Nuclear material] .... CUMUF
Cumulative Monthly Issue [Material] (AAG) .... CMI
Cumulative Mortality [Radiology] .... CM
Cumulative Paperback Index 1939-1959 [A publication] .... CPI
Cumulative Percentage Frequency .... CPF
Cumulative Performance Index (SAUS) .... CPI
Cumulative Pocket Parts (DLA) .... Cum PP
Cumulative Population Doubling .... CPD
Cumulative Population Doubling Level .... CPDL
Cumulative, Potency Rate (STED) .... CPR
Cumulative Preference [Commerce] (BARN) .... cum pref
Cumulative Preferred [A class of stock] [Investment term] .... CMPF
Cumulative Preferred Stock [Investment term] .... CPS
Cumulative Probability Density Function (CCCA) .... CPDF
Cumulative Probability Distribution (IEEE) .... CPD
Cumulative Probability of Success (MAE) .... CPS
Cumulative Pulmonary Toxicity Dose [Deep-sea diving] .... CPTD
Cumulative Quality Point Ratio .... CQPR
Cumulative Radiation Effect .... CRE
Cumulative Radio Audience Method (NTCM) .... CRAM
Cumulative Regulatory Effects on the Cost of Automotive Transportation
  (SAUS) .... RECAT
Cumulative Results Criterion (IEEE) .... CRC
Cumulative Sporulation [of fungal colonies] .... CSP
Cumulative Sum .... CUSUM

Cumulative Sum Control Charts [*Statistics*]	CSCC
Cumulative Sum Diagram [*Statistics*]	CSD
Cumulative Sum Techniques (MHDB)	CST
Cumulative Supplement (DLA)	Cum Supp
Cumulative Survival Rate (DB)	CSR
Cumulative Techniques and Procedures in Clinical Microbiology [*Medicine*] (DMAA)	CUMITECH
Cumulative Techniques and Procedures in Clinical Microbiology (SAUO)	CUMITECHS
Cumulative Trauma Disorder [*Medicine*]	CTD
Cumulative Urinary Excretion [*Medicine*] (STED)	CUE
Cumulative Volcano Amplitude [*Volcanology*]	CVA
Cumulative Weight Percent	CWP
Cumulative Working Level Months [*Radon exposure measure*] (ERG)	CWLM
Cumulatively (ABBR)	CMULAVY
Cumulhydroperoxyd (SAUS)	CHP
Cumuliform (SAUS)	CUF
Cumulonimbus [*Cloud*] [*Meteorology*]	CB
Cumulonimbus (ABBR)	CMULNBMS
Cumulonimbus [*Cloud*] [*Meteorology*]	CN
Cumulonimbus [*Cloud*] [*Meteorology*]	CUN
Cumulonimbus [*Cloud*] [*Meteorology*] (AIA)	Cu Nim
Cumulo-Nimbus (SAUS)	CU-NIM
Cumulonimbus Mamatus Cloud (WEAT)	CbMam
Cumulonimbus Mamma [*NWS*] (FAAC)	CBMAM
Cumulonimbus Mammatus [*Cloud*] [*Meteorology*]	CM
Cumulus [*Cloud*] [*Meteorology*]	C
Cumulus (ABBR)	CMUL
Cumulus (ABBR)	CMULS
Cumulus (ABBR)	CMULU
Cumulus [*Cloud*] [*Meteorology*]	CU
Cumulus (ADWA)	Cu
Cumulus [*Cloud*] [*Meteorology*]	K
Cumulus and Cumulonimbus [*Clouds*] [*Meteorology*]	CUCB
Cumulus Cloud (WEAT)	Cu
Cumulus Congestus Cloud (WEAT)	CuCon
Cumulus Ensemble Model (SAUS)	CEM
Cumulus Fractus [*Type of cloud*] [*Meteorology*] (DNAB)	CF
Cumulus Fractus [*NWS*] (FAAC)	CUFRA
Cumulus Humilis Cloud (WEAT)	CuHu
Cumulus Kinetic Energy (CARB)	CKE
Cumulus Media 'A' [*NASDAQ symbol*] (SG)	CMLS
Cumulus Medicoris Cloud (WEAT)	CuMed
Cumulus Technology Ltd. [*Vancouver Stock Exchange symbol*] [*Toronto Stock Exchange symbol*]	CUH
CUNA [*Credit Union National Association*] Retirement Savings Fund	CRSF
Cunagua [*Cuba*] [*ICAO location identifier*] (ICLI)	MUCC
Cunard Steamship Co. (MHDB)	CSSCO
Cunard-Eagle Airways (SAUO)	CEA
Cunard-White Star Line (SAUO)	CWRU
Cuneate Nucleus [*Neuroanatomy*]	CN
Cuneiform (VRA)	cunif
Cuneiform Inscriptions and the Old Testament (BJA)	COT
[*The*] Cuneiform Inscriptions of Western Asia [*A publication*] (BJA)	CIWA
Cuneiform Texts from Babylonian Tablets in the British Museum (BJA)	CT
Cuneiform Texts from Cappadocian Tablets in the British Museum (BJA)	CCT
Cuneo Press, Inc. (SAUO)	CUN
Cuneonavicular Joint (MELL)	CNJ
Cunnamulla [*Australia*] [*Airport symbol*] (OAG)	CMA
Cunningham & Walsh [*Advertising agency*]	C & W
Cunningham and Walsh (SAUO)	C&W
Cunningham Drug Stores, Inc. (SAUO)	CDD
Cunningham on Hindu Law [*A publication*] (DLA)	Cun Hind L
Cunningham on Simony [*A publication*] (DLA)	Cun Sim
Cunningham's Bills, Notes, and Insurances [*A publication*] (DLA)	Cun Bills
Cunningham's Dictionary [*A publication*] (DLA)	Cun Dict
Cunningham's English King's Bench Reports [*A publication*] (DLA)	Ann
Cunningham's English King's Bench Reports [*A publication*] (DLA)	Cun
Cunningham's English King's Bench Reports [*A publication*] (DLA)	Cunn
Cunningham's English King's Bench Reports [*A publication*] (DLA)	Cunningham
Cunningham's English King's Bench Reports [*A publication*] (DLA)	Cunningham (Eng)
Cunningham's Law Dictionary [*A publication*] (DLA)	Cun LD
Cunningham's Law of Notes and Bills of Exchange [*A publication*] (DLA)	Cun Bill Exch
Cunningham's Maxims and Rules of Pleading [*A publication*] (DLA)	Cun Pl
CUNY [*City University of New York*] Data Service [*Information service or system*] (IID)	CDS
Cup	C
cup to disc ratio (SAUS)	c/d
Cup to Disk [*Ratio*] [*Opthalmology*] (DAVI)	C/D
Cupboard	CPBRD
Cupboard	CPD
Cupboard	CUP
Cupboards (REAL)	cpbds
cupboards (SAUS)	cpbds
Cupertino, CA [*FM radio station call letters*]	KKUP
Cupertino National Bank [*NASDAQ symbol*] (SAG)	CUNB
Cupertino National Bank [*Associated Press*] (SAG)	CupNBk
Cupertino Natl Bancorp [*NASDAQ symbol*] (TTSB)	CUNB
Cu-Phthalocyanine (EDCT)	CPC
Cupol [*Record label*] [*Sweden*]	Cup
Cupola	CUP
Cupola (SAUS)	Cup

Cupola Trainer (SAUS)	CT
Cupola Weapon Station (SAUS)	CWS
Cupro Nickel	CN
Cuprous Oxide (SAUS)	Cuprite
Cuprum [*Copper*] [*Chemical element*]	Cu
Curacao [*Netherlands Antilles*]	CU
Curacao [*Netherlands Antilles*] [*Airport symbol*] (OAG)	CUR
Curacao [*Netherlands Antilles*] [*ICAO location identifier*] (ICLI)	TNCF
Curacao Group [*MARC geographic area code*] [*Library of Congress*] (LCCP)	nwco-
Curacao Tourist Board (EA)	CTB
Curacy [*or Curate*]	C
Curaray [*Ecuador*] [*ICAO location identifier*] (ICLI)	SECR
Curate (ROG)	CUR
Curate in Charge [*Church of England*]	CIC
Curate-in-Charge [*Church of England*]	C-in-C
Curate-in-Charge [*Church of England*] (ROG)	CUR-in-CH
Curates' Alliance [*British*]	CA
Curates' Augmentation Fund [*British*]	CAF
Curatio [*A Dressing*] [*Pharmacy*]	CURAT
Curative [*Medicine*]	CUR
Curative Dose [*Medicine*]	CD
Curative Health Services, Inc. [*NASDAQ symbol*] (SAG)	CURE
Curative Health Services, Inc. [*Associated Press*] (SAG)	CurHlth
Curative Technologies [*NASDAQ symbol*] (SPSG)	CURE
Curative Technologies, Inc. [*Associated Press*] (SAG)	CurTch
Curator	CUR
Curator (AL)	Cura
Curator Resources [*Vancouver Stock Exchange symbol*]	CUR
Curb Weight [*Automotive engineering*]	CW
Curbside (MSA)	CRBSD
Curculio [*of Plautus*] [*Classical studies*] (OCD)	Curc
Curd Firmness Tester [*For milk products*]	CFT
Curdy Dwarf Disease (SAUS)	CD Disease
Cure (DMAA)	cur
Cure AIDS [*Acquired Immune Deficiency Syndrome*] Now [*An association*] (EA)	CAN
Cure Autism Now [*An association*]	CAN
CURE [*Citizens United to Reduce Emmissions*] Formaldehyde Poisoning Association (EA)	CURE
Cure Rate Index [*Rubber technology*]	CRI
Cure to Handling	CTH
Curecanti National Recreation Area (SAUS)	CNRA
Curecanti Recreation Area [*National Park Service designation*]	CURE
Cured in Place [*Gaskets and seals*]	CIP
Cured-In- Place Pipe [*Civil Engineering*]	CIPP
Cure-In-Place Gasket	CIPG
Curettage and Desiccation [*Gynecology*] (DAVI)	C & D
Curettage and Electrodesiccation [*Fulguration*] [*Medicine*] (DAVI)	C & F
Curia [*Court*] [*Latin*] (DLA)	CUR
Curia Advisari Vult [*The Court Wishes to Consider*] [*Latin*] [*Legal term*]	CAV
Curia Advisari Vult [*The Court Wishes to Consider*] [*Latin*] [*Legal term*] (ROG)	CUR ADV VULT
Curia Phillippica [*Latin*] (DLA)	CUR PHIL
Curia Regis [*King's Court*] [*Latin*] [*Legal term*] (DLA)	CR
Curia Regis [*King's Court*] [*Latin*] [*Legal term*] (ROG)	CUR REG
Curia Regis Rolls [*British*] [*Legal term*] (DLA)	Cr R
Curia Regis Rolls [*British*]	CUR
Curia Regis Rolls [*British*] [*Legal term*] (DLA)	Cur Reg R
Curichi [*Bolivia*] [*ICAO location identifier*] (ICLI)	SLQY
Curico/General Freire [*Chile*] [*ICAO location identifier*] (ICLI)	SCIC
Curie [*Unit of radioactivity*] [*See Ci*]	C
Curie (IDOE)	c
Curie [*Unit of radioactivity*] [*Preferred unit is Bq, Becquerel*]	Ci
Curie [*Unit of radioactivity*] [*See Ci*] (AAMN)	Cu
Curie (STED)	CU
Curie (STED)	cu
Curie Hour (MAE)	Cihr
Curie Point Pyrolysis (PDAA)	CPP
Curie-Hour [*Measurement*] (DAVI)	c-hr
Curies per Liter (EEVL)	Ci/L
Curies per Year (EEVL)	Ci/yr
Curing Agent	CA
Curing, Extrusion, Plasticity, and Recovery (PDAA)	CEPAR
Curiosity (DSUE)	CURIO
Curiosity-Orientated Research (SAUS)	COR
Curious (ROG)	CUR
Curious to Know [*An inquisitive customer*] [*Merchandising slang*]	C to K
Curitiba [*Brazil*] [*Airport symbol*] (OAG)	CWB
Curitiba [*Brazil*] [*ICAO location identifier*] (ICLI)	SBCW
Curitiba/Afonso Pena [*Brazil*] [*ICAO location identifier*] (ICLI)	SBCT
Curitiba/Bacacheri [*Brazil*] [*ICAO location identifier*] (ICLI)	SBBI
Curium [*Chemical element*]	Cm
Curlew Lake [*Vancouver Stock Exchange symbol*]	CWQ
Curling Club	CC
Curling Club (SAUO)	CC
Curl's Algorithm for Logic Compression	CALC
Curly Top Virus	CTV
Curly-Coated Retriever Club of America (EA)	CCRCA
Curran Memorial Library, Port Au Port East, Newfoundland (SAUS)	NEPEC
Curran Memorial Library, Port Au Port East, Newfoundland [*Library symbol*] [*National Library of Canada*] (NLC)	NFPEC
Curran Memorial Library, Port Au Port East, NF, Canada [*Library symbol*] [*Library of Congress*] (LCLS)	CaNfPeC
Currant [*Nevada*] [*Seismograph station code, US Geological Survey*] (SEIS)	CND

Currant Yellow Dwarf (SAUS) .... CYD
Currency C
Currency .... CUR
Currency (NTIO) .... cur
Currency (ADWA) .... curr
Currency (AFM) .... CURR
Currency (EBF) .... Curr
Currency (EBF) .... Cy
Currency .... CY
Currency Adjustment and Bunkering Adjustment Factors [British] (DCTA) .... CABAF
Currency Adjustment Charge [Business term] .... CAC
Currency Adjustment Factor [Business term] .... CAF
Currency Adjustment Fee (SAUS) .... CAF
Currency Bond .... CB
Currency Clause (SAUS) CC
Currency Clearinghouse .... CCH
Currency Exchange Database [GE Information Services] [Information service or system] (CRD) .... CEDB
Currency Exploitation .... CE
Currency Forwards Contract .... CFC
Currency Market Analysis [MMS International] [Information service or system] (CRD) .... CMA
Currency Market Service [Database] [Money Market Services, Inc.] [Information service or system] (CRD) .... CMS
Currency Overprinting and Processing Equipment [Bureau of Printing and Engraving] .... COPE
Currency Regulation .... CR
Currency Sign [Telecommunications] (TEL) .... CS
Currency Transaction Report [IRS] .... CTR
Current C
Current .... CT
Current (AAG) .... CUR
Current (IDOE) .... cur
Current (EY) .... CURR
Current (EBF) .... Curr
Current (PROS) .... curr
Current (ROG) .... CURRT
Current .... CURT
Current Account [Business term] .... CA
Current Account [Business term] (IAA) .... CAC
Current Account Card (SAUS) .... CAC
Current Account Deficit [Economics] .... CAD
Current Acid Waste (ABAC) .... CAW
Current Actions Center .... CAC
Current Actions Duty Officer [Air Force] .... CADO
Current Address (DNAB) .... CA
Current Adjusting Type .... CAT
Current Advances in Plant Science [A database] [Pergamon] (NITA) .... CAPS
Current Aerospace Research Activities (KSC) .... CARA
Current Agricultural Research Information System [Food and Agriculture Organization] [United Nations] [Information service or system] (IID) .... CARIS
Current Amount (SAUS) .... CURAM
Current Amplifier (SAUS) .... CA
Current Analysis [Program] [Department of State] .... CA
Current and Account (SAUS) .... cas
Current and Past Psychopathology Scales [Psychology] .... CAPPS
Current Annotated Bibliography of Irrigation [Bet Dagan, Israel] [A publication] .... IRRICAB
Current Annual Increment (DICI) .... CAI
Current Anthropology (journ.) (SAUS) .... CAnthr
Current Anthropology. University of Chicago (journ.) (SAUS) .... UC/CA
Current Approval Plan [Army] .... CAP
Current Approved File (SAUS) .... CAF
Current ARDC [Air Research and Development Command] Technical Efforts [DoD program] .... CATE
Current Assessment Plan .... CAP
Current Asset [Business term] .... CA
Current Australian Reference Books [A publication] .... CARB
Current Awareness and Document Retrieval for Engineers (DIT) .... CADRE
Current Awareness Bibliographies [DTIC] .... CAB
Current Awareness Bulletin (SAUO) .... CA
Current Awareness Bulletin for Librarians and Information Scientists [British] [A publication] (NITA) .... CABLIS
Current Awareness in Biological Sciences [Pergamon Press] [Information service or system] (IID) .... CABS
Current Awareness Literature Service [Department of Agriculture] [Beltsville, MD] .... CALS
Current Awareness Service [Cryogenic literature bibliography] [Cryogenic Data Center] .... CAS
Current Awareness Service Individual Article Supply [Library science] (TELE) .... CAS-IAS
Current Awareness System in Coordination Chemistry .... CASCC
Current Background .... CB
Current Balance Earth Leakage (PDAA) .... CBEL
Current Balance Record [Banking] (IAA) .... CBR
Current Bibliographic Directory of the Arts and Sciences [A publication] .... CBD
Current Bibliographies in Medicine [A publication] (ADWA) .... CBM
Current Biography [A publication] .... CB
Current Biography (journ.) (SAUS) .... Cur Biog
Current Biotechnology Abstracts [Royal Society of Chemistry] [Information service or system] (IID) .... CBA
Current BIT [Binary Digit] [Computer science] (IAA) .... CB
Current Bit (SAUS) .... CB
Current BIT [Binary Digit] Monitor Unit [Computer science] .... CBMU

Current Book In Progress (SAUS) .... CBIP
Current Branch (SAUS) .... CB
Current Break-Off and Memory (OA) .... CBOM
Current Cancer Research Project Analysis Center [Database producer] .... CCRESPAC
Current Cases [1965-71] [Ghana] [A publication] (DLA) CC
Current Cash [or Cost] Equivalent (ADA) .... CCE
Current Cell Rate (VERA) .... CCR
Current Challengers CC
Current Chemical Reactions [A publication] .... CCR
Current Clinical Topics In Infectious Diseases (SAUS) .... Curr Clin Top Infect Dis
Current Clinical Trials [A publication] .... CCT
Current Comment and Legal Miscellany [A publication] (DLA) .... Cur Com
Current Comment and Legal Miscellany [A publication] (DLA) .... Current Com & Leg Mis
Current Communications (SAUS) .... CCOS
Current Complaints [Medicine] CC
Current Contact (SAUS) CC
Current Contents .... CurrCont
Current Contents Chemical Sciences (journ.) (SAUS) .... CCCS
Current Contents/Chemical Sciences [A publication] .... CC/CS
Current Contents/Clinical Practice (SAUS) .... CC/CP
Current Control Relay (DNAB) .... CCR
Current Controlled Negative Resistance [Electronics] (IAA) .... CCNR
Current Cost CC
Current Cost Accounting .... CCA
Current Cost Operating Profits [Accounting] .... CCOP
Current Data Bit (SAUS) .... CDB
Current Density .... CD
Current Density Functional Theory (SAUS) .... CDFT
Current Dental Terminology (SAUS) .... CDT
Current Depth Measurement Subsystem [National Ocean Survey] (MSC) .... CDMS
Current Design Expendable [Refers to payload type] [NASA] .... CDE
Current Design Reusable [Refers to payload type] [NASA] .... CDR
Current Device Register .... CDR
Current Dicision Ratio (SAUS) .... CDR
Current Difference Logic (DGA) .... CDI
Current Digest [A publication] .... CD
Current Directional Relay .... CDR
Current Directory Structure [Computer science] (PCM) .... CDS
Current Discharge (IAA) .... CD
Current Discharge Line (IAA) .... CDL
Current Discontinuity Device (IAA) .... CDD
Current Distribution Ratio (SAUS) .... CDR
Current Dollars (SAUO) .... CD
Current Domestic Value [of goods in the country of origin] .... CDV
Current Driver .... CD
Current Economic Reporting Program [Department of State] .... CERP
Current Efficiency [Electrochemistry] .... CE
Current Employment Statistics [Bureau of Labor Statistics] (OICC) .... CES
Current Employment Status .... CES
Current Energy Patents [A publication] .... CEP
Current Engineering and Manufacturing Services Staff [Automotive industry] .... CEMSS
Current Engineering Practice (journ.) (SAUS) .... Curr Eng Pract
Current Enlistment Date [Military] .... CED
Current Estimate (AFIT) .... CE
Current Evangelism Ministries (EA) .... CEM
Current Expendable (NASA) .... CE
Current Expenditure [Economics] C
Current Exploitation (MCD) .... CE
Current Fault File [Telecommunications] (TEL) .... CFF
Current Feedback (IAA) .... CF
Current File Disk Address (SAUS) .... CFDA
Current File User [Computer science] (OA) .... CFU
Current Files Area .... CFA
Current Fiscal Year (AFM) .... CFY
Current Flight Plan [FAA] (TAG) .... CPL
Current Flight Plan Message [Aviation code] .... CPL
Current Food Additives Legislation (SAUS) .... CFAL
Current Force (IAA) .... CF
Current Forest Conservation Action Alerts (SAUO) .... CFCAA
Current Gain .... CG
Current Gate Tube .... CGT
Current Good Manufacturing Practice [Food and Drug Administration] .... CGMP
Current History [A publication] (BRI) .... Cu H
Current History (journ.) (SAUS) .... Cur Hist
Current Hogging Integrated Logic (SAUS) .... CHIL
Current Image Diffraction (MCD) .... CID
Current Imaging Tunneling Spectroscopy .... CITS
Current Inc. Shares [NYSE symbol] (TTSB) .... CUR
Current Income Shares, Inc. [NYSE symbol] (SPSG) .... CUR
Current Income Shares, Inc. [Associated Press] (SAG) .... CurInc
Current Index to Journals in Education .... CIJE
Current Index to Legal Periodicals [University of Washington] [Information service or system] (CRD) .... CILP
Current Index to Statistics [MathSci database subfile] (IT) .... CIS
Current Indian Cases [1912-15] [A publication] (DLA) .... Cur IC
Current Indian Cases [1912-15] [A publication] (DLA) .... Cur Ind Cas
Current Indian Cases, Old Series [India] [A publication] (DLA) CIC
Current Indicator and Integrator CII
Current Industrial Reports [Census Bureau] .... CIR
Current Information Database .... CID
Current Information on Tapes for Engineers (SAUS) .... CITE
Current Information Section (ADA) .... CIS

Current Information Selection [*IBM Technical Information Retrieval Center*] [*White Plains, NY*] .... CIS
Current Information Service [*Australia*] .... CIS
Current Information Tapes for Engineering .... CITE
Current Information Tapes for Engineers (SAUS) .... CITE
Current Information Transfer in English .... CITE
Current Inhibit Logic (SAUS) CIL
Current Injection Equivalent Circuit Approach (MCD) .... CIECA
Current Injection Logic [*Computer science*] CIL
Current Injection Probe .... CIP
Current Injection Test (CCCA) .... CIT
Current Input Differential Amplifier [*Electronics*] (OA) .... CIDA
Current Instruction Address (SAUS) .... CIA
Current Instruction Register .... CIR
Current Instruction Word (SAUS) .... CIW
Current Intake Processing System (SAUS) .... CIPS
Current Intelligence Bulletin [*A publication*] .... CIB
Current Intelligence, Group (NATG) .... CIG
Current Intelligence Indication Center (CINC) CIIC
Current Intelligence Operations Center (MCD) .... CIOC
Current Intelligence Requirement List (MCD) .... CIRL
Current Intelligence Targets Groups [*Military*] .... CITG
Current Intelligence Traffic Exploitation System (PDAA) .... CITES
Current Interest Late Charge Amount (SAUS) .... CILCA
Current Interrupter [*Electronics*] (IAA) CI
Current Interruption (SAUS) CI
Current Inverting Negative Impedance Convertor (SAUS) .... CINIC
Current Laboratory Practice [*A publication*] .... CLP
Current Labour Invariance (SAUS) CLI
Current Law [*A publication*] CL
Current Law Consolidation [*England*] [*A publication*] (DLA) CLC
Current Law Index (SAUO) CLI
Current Law Monthly [*A publication*] (DLA) .... CLM
Current Law Reports [*Palestine*] [*A publication*] (DLA) .... CLR
Current Law Reports [*Ceylon*] [*A publication*] (DLA) .... Cur LR
Current Law Statutes, Annotated [*A publication*] (DLA) .... CL Stats
Current Law Year Book [*A publication*] (ILCA) .... CLY
Current Law Year Book [*A publication*] .... CLYB
Current Law Year Book [*A publication*] (DLA) .... Current LY
Current Layer (OA) CL
Current Leading Component (PDAA) CLC
Current Legal Forms with Tax Analysis [*A publication*] (DLA) .... CLF
Current Legal Information [*A publication*] CLI
Current Legal Problems [*A publication*] .... CLP
Current Legal Problems [*A publication*] (DLA) .... Curr Legal Prob
Current Liabilities [*Insurance*] CL
Current Line Pointer [*Computer science*] (IBMDP) .... CLP
Current List of Medical Literature .... CLML
Current Literature Alerting Search Service [*Biological Abstracts*] (NITA) .... CLASS
Current Literature Awareness Search Service [*BIOSIS*] [*Database*] .... CLASS
Current Literature (journ.) (SAUS) .... Cur Lit
Current Literature on Water [*Database*] [*South African Water Information Centre*] [*Information service or system*] (CRD) .... CLOW
Current Logic [*Electronics*] (IAA) CL
Current Logical Byte Address (IAA) .... CLBA
Current Loop: Interface Standard (NITA) CL
Current Market Appraisal .... CMA
Current Market Value [*Business term*] (ADA) .... CMV
Current Maximum Reimbursable Amount (ACAE) .... CMRA
Current Medical Diagnosis & Treatment (SAUO) .... CMDT
Current Medical Information and Technology (DAVI) .... CMIT
Current Medical Information and Terminology .... CMIT
Current Medical Terminology .... CMT
Current Medicine for Attorneys [*A publication*] (DLA) .... Current Med for Att'ys
Current Meter [*Marine science*] (OSRA) .... CM
Current Meter Data Base [*National Ocean Survey*] (MSC) .... CMD
Current Meter Digitizer (GEOI) .... CMD
Current Meter Intercomparison Experiment [*National Ocean Survey*] (MSC) .... CMICE
Current Meter Speed and Detection .... CUMSAD
Current Model Logic .... CML
Current Monitor [*Instrumentation*] .... CM
Current Month (SAUS) .... CM
Current Months Total Program Forecast (MCD) .... CMTPF
Current Mortality Sample [*Department of Health and Human Services*] (GFGA) .... CMS
Current Negative Immittance Converter (SAUS) .... INIC
Current New York Time (DOAD) .... CNYT
Current Notes on International Affairs [*A publication*] .... Curr No Int Aff
Current Ocean Detecting and Ranging (SAUS) .... CODAR
Current of Area (SAUS) .... CRA
Current of Record (SAUS) .... CRR
Current of Run-Unit (SAUS) .... CRU
Current Oil in Place [*Petroleum technology*] .... COIP
Current on Board (DNAB) .... COB
Current Operating Allowances .... COA
Current Operating Budget Year .... COBY
Current Operating Plan (SAUS) .... COP
Current Operating Procedure (MCD) .... COP
Current Operating Time .... COT
Current Operation Expenditure [*Business term*] .... COE
Current Operational Data System .... CODAS
Current Operational Group [*NATO*] (NATG) .... COG
Current Operations .... COPS
Current Operations Division [*Tactical Air Command*] .... COD

Current Operations Support (SAUO) .... COPS
Current Operations Value .... cov
Current Operator - Next Operator [*Computer science*] (MDG) .... CO/NO
Current Operator-Next Operator (SAUS) .... CO-NO
Current Opinion in Cardiology (SAUS) .... Curr Opin Cardiol
Current or Voltage .... CURTAGE
Current Output Station (SAUS) .... COS
Current Paper .... CP
Current Papers in Physics (journ.) (SAUS) .... CPP
Current Period .... CP
Current Perpendicular to Plane (SAUS) .... CPP
Current Perpendicular to Plane Magnetoresistance [*Physics*] .... CPP-MR
Current Physics Bibliographies [*A publication*] (MCD) .... CPB
Current Physics Information [*American Institute of Physics*] [*New York, NY*] [*Information service or system*] .... CPI
Current Physics Information (journ.) (SAUS) .... CPI
Current Physics Selected Articles [*A publication*] (MCD) .... CPSA
Current Physics Titles [*A publication*] .... CPT
Current Physis Advance Abstracts (SAUS) .... CPAA
Current Point of Purchase Survey (SAUS) .... CPPS
Current Population Survey [*Census Bureau*] .... CPS
Current Population Survey Processing Branch [*Bureau of the Census*] (GFGA) .... CPSPB
Current Practices .... CP
Current Priority Indicator .... CPI
Current Privilege Level [*Computer programs*] (BYTE) .... CPL
Current Procedural Technology [*Department of Health and Human Services*] (GFGA) .... CPT
Current Procedural Terminology [*American Medical Association*] .... CPT
Current Processor Mode .... CPM
Current Product Engineering .... CPE
Current Product Line (SAUS) .... CPL
Current Property Law [*British*] .... CPL
Current Property Law [*British*] [*A publication*] (DLA) .... Cur Prop L
Current Property Law [*British*] [*A publication*] (DLA) .... Current Prop L
Current Property Lawyer [*1852-53*] [*England*] [*A publication*] (DLA) .... CPL
Current Protocols in Immunology [*A publication*] .... CPI
Current Protocols in Molecular Biology [*A publication*] .... CPMB
Current Pulse Generator [*Electronics*] (IAA) .... CPG
Current Purchasing Power .... CPP
Current Rate [*Business term*] .... CR
Current Rate (EBF) .... C/R
Current Rate (EBF) .... cr
Current Rate for Discharge (SAUS) .... CRD
Current Ratio Forcing Element (SAUS) .... CRFE
Current Regulator Diode (SAUS) .... CRD
Current Relay (MSA) .... CR
Current Replacement Cost [*Accounting*] .... CRC
Current Requirements .... CRQ
Current Requisition File [*DoD*] .... CRF
Current Research and Development in Scientific Documentation [*A publication*] .... CRDSD
Current Research File [*NIOSH*] [*Database*] .... CRF
Current Research in Britain [*A publication*] .... CRB
Current Research Information System [*Department of Agriculture*] [*Information service or system*] .... CRIS
Current Researches in Anesthesia and Analgesia (journ.) (SAUS) .... Anesth Analg
Current Retail Trade Reports [*A publication*] .... CRTR
Current, Reverse (SAUS) .... IR
Current Routing Starting Address (SAUS) .... CRSA
Current Sector Designator (SAUS) .... CSD
Current Sensitive Relay (DNAB) .... CSR
Current Sensor Unit [*American Solenoid Co.*] [*Somerset, NJ*] .... CSU
Current Series [*Army*] .... CS
Current Ship's Maintenance Project .... CSMP
Current SIGINT [*Signal Intelligence*] Operations Center [*National Security Agency*] (MCD) .... CSOC
Current Sink Logic (IAA) .... CSL
Current Sinking Logic (SAUS) .... CSL
Current Situation Room (MCD) .... CSR
Current Sleep Walker [*Medicine*] (DMAA) .... CSW
Current Smoker (DAVI) .... CS
Current Source .... CS
Current Source (MSA) .... IGEN
Current Source Amplifier .... CSA
Current Source Inverter (SAUS) .... CSI
Current Source Logic (IAA) .... CSL
Current Sourced Schottky Logic (SAUS) .... CSyL
Current Source-Density [*Neuroelectricity*] .... CSD
Current Sourcing Logic (SAUS) .... CSL
Current State List (SAUS) .... CSL
Current Status Register (SAUS) .... CSTR
Current Steering Switch (KSC) .... CSS
Current Strength .... CS
Current Summary of Threat (MCD) .... CST
Current Switch (IAA) .... CS
Current Switch Emitter/Follower (OA) .... CSEF
Current Switch Logic (IEEE) .... CSL
Current Switching Alloy Junction Transistor Logic (SAUS) .... CSAJTL
Current Switching Diode Logic (IAA) .... CSDL
Current Switching Mode (IAA) .... CSM
Current System Description (SSD) .... CSD
Current Taper Ratio (SAUS) .... CTR
Current Tech [*Vancouver Stock Exchange symbol*] .... ONE
Current Technical Reports (SAUS) .... CTR

Current Technology [*VS, exchange symbol*] (TTSB) .... ONE
Current Technology Index [*Library science*] (TELE) .... CTI
Current, Temperature, Density .... CTD
Current, Temperature, Depth (SAUS) .... CTD
Current Therapeutic Research, Clinical and Experimental (journ.) (SAUS) .... Curr Ther Res Clin Exp
Current Time Sensing (CAAL) .... CTS
Current to Current [*Converter*] (NRCH) .... I/I
Current to Frequency Converter (SAUS) .... I/FC
Current to Pressure [*Electropneumatic*] (ACII) .... I/P
Current Topics in Microbiology and Immunology (SAUO) .... CTMI
Current Topics in Microbiology and Immunology (journ.) (SAUS) .... Curr Top Microbiol Immunol
Current Transactions (NATG) .... CT
Current Transfer Ratio [*Bell System*] .... CTR
Current Transformation Matrix (SAUS) .... CTM
Current Transformer .... CRT
Current Transformer [*Instrumentation*] .... CT
Current Transformer (SAUS) CX
Current Use Value (MHDB) .... CUV
Current Value Accounting .... CVA
Current Value/Constant Purchasing Power [*Accounting*] .... CV/CPP
Current Values Table .... CVT
Current Variable Attenuator .... CVA
Current Variable Inductor CVI
Current versus Voltage (SAUS) .... I vs V
Current Viewing Resistor .... CVR
Current Vital Signs [*Medicine*] .... CVS
Current Voltage (SAUS) IV
Current Voltage Characteristic (OA) CVC
Current Voltage Converter (IAA) CVC
Current Voltage Regulator (IAA) .... CVR
Current Wage Developments [*A publication*] .... CWD
Current Word Pointer .... CWP
Current Working Block (SAUS) .... CWB
Current Working Estimate [*Military*] .... CWE
Current Workspace Pointer [*Computer science*] (VERA) .... CWP
Current Year (DOMA) .... CY
Current Year Work Plans (SAUO) .... CYWP
Current Yield [*Banking*] .... CY
Current-Controlled Amplifier [*Electronics*] (ECII) .... CCA
Current-Controlled Current Source (SAUS) .... CCCS
Current-Controlled Current Source (SAUS) .... ICIS
Current-Controlled Inductor [*Electronics*] (IAA) CCI
Current-Controlled Negative Inductance (SAUS) .... CCNL
Current-Controlled Oscillator (IEEE) .... CCO
Current-Controlled Voltage Source (IEEE) .... CCVS
Current-Controlled Voltage Source (SAUS) .... ICVS
Current-density Voltage Temperature (SAUS) .... JVT
Current-Dependent Current Source Capacitor (SAUS) .... CDCSC
Current-Dependent Voltage Source Capacitor (SAUS) .... CDVSC
Current-Hogging Injection Logic [*Electronics*] (IEEE) .... CHIL
Current-Hogging Logic [*Electronics*] .... CHL
Currentis [*Of the Current Month or Year*] [*Latin*] C
Currentis [*Of the Current Month or Year*] [*Latin*] .... CUR
Current-Limiting Device [*Short-circuit limiter*] .... CLD
Current-Limiting Resistor (MSA) .... CLR
Current-Logic-Current-Switching [*Electronics*] .... CLCS
Current-Mode Complementary Transistor Logic [*Computer science*] (IEEE) .... CMCTL
Current-Mode Digital-to-Analog Converter [*Computer science*] .... CMDAC
Current-Mode Logic [*Computer science*] .... CML
Current-Mode Switching [*Computer science*] (MSA) .... CMS
Current-period Date (SAUS) .... CURDT
Current/Pneumatic [*Nuclear energy*] (NRCH) .... C/P
Current/Pneumatic [*Nuclear energy*] (NRCH) .... I/P
Current-Steering Logic (AAEL) .... CSL
Current-Voltage Curve (SAUS) .... I-V Curve
Current-Voltage Diagram .... CVD
Curricular-Career Information Service (SAUS) .... CCIS
Curriculum (AL) .... Cur
Curriculum .... CURR
Curriculum .... CURRIC
Curriculum (ADWA) .... curric
Curriculum, Accreditation and Registration Committee (GEOI) .... CAR
Curriculum Adaptation Network for Bilingual, Bicultural Education .... CANBBE
Curriculum Advisory Committee [*American Occupational Therapy Association*] .... CAC
Curriculum Analysis Taxonomy [*Education*] (AIE) .... CAT
Curriculum and Accreditation Secretariat [*Victoria*] [*Australia*] .... CAS
Curriculum and Education Resource Finder [*Database*] .... C.E.R.F.
Curriculum and Instruction Development [*Program*] [*National Science Foundation*] .... CID
Curriculum and Instructional Standards [*Military*] (DNAB) .... CIS
Curriculum and Research (ADA) .... C & R
Curriculum and Resource Information Service (AIE) .... CRIS
Curriculum Assessment and Teacher/Trainer Training .... CATTT
Curriculum Association (AIE) .... CA
Curriculum Commitee on Computer Education for Management (SAUS) C3EM
Curriculum Committee for Computer Education for Management (SAUO) C3EM
Curriculum Committee on Computer (SAUS) C3
Curriculum Committee on Computer Science (SAUO) C3S
Curriculum Coordinating Committees (EDAC) CCC
Curriculum Corporation [*Commercial firm*] [*Australia*] CC
Curriculum Council of Wales (WDAA) .... CCW
Curriculum Development Manager (MCD) .... CDM
Curriculum Evaluation and Management Centre [*University of Newcastle upon Tyne*] [*British*] (CB) .... CEMC
Curriculum Improvement Resulting from Creative Utilization of Instructional Two-Way Television Project [*Wisconsin*] (EDAC) .... CIRCUIT
Curriculum Led Institutional Development (AIE) .... CLID
Curriculum Materials Centre, Education Library, Memorial University, St. John's,Newfoundland [*Library symbol*] [*National Library of Canada*] (NLC) .... NFSMEC
Curriculum Perspective [*A publication*] .... Curric P
Curriculum Research and Development Group [*University of Hawaii*] [*Research center*] (RCD) .... CRDG
Curriculum Resource Materials .... CRM
Curriculum Resources Centre, Niagara South Board of Education, Allanburg, Ontario [*Library symbol*] [*National Library of Canada*] (BIB) .... OAN
Curriculum Review [*A publication*] (BRI) .... Cur R
Curriculum Review Board of the American Association of Medical Assistants (DAVI) .... CRB
Curriculum Review Integrated Product Team [*Army*] .... CRIPT
Curriculum Vitae [*Job applications*] CV
Curriculum Working Group (SAUO) .... CWG
Curriculum-Based Assessment [*Education*] .... CBA
Currie, Coopers & Lybrand Ltd., Montreal, PQ, Canada [*Library symbol*] [*Library of Congress*] (LCLS) .... CaQMCCL
Currie, Coopers & Lybrand Ltd., Montreal, Quebec [*Library symbol*] [*National Library of Canada*] (NLC) .... QMCCL
Currie, Coopers & Lybrand Ltd., Toronto, ON, Canada [*Library symbol*] [*Library of Congress*] (LCLS) .... CaOTCCL
Currie, Coopers & Lybrand Ltd., Toronto, Ontario [*Library symbol*] [*National Library of Canada*] (NLC) .... OTCCL
Currie Rose Resources, Inc. [*Vancouver Stock Exchange symbol*] .... CUI
Currituck County Public Library, Coinjock, NC [*Library symbol*] [*Library of Congress*] (LCLS) .... NcCoi
Currubin Bird Sanctuary (SAUS) .... CBS
Curry College, Milton, MA [*OCLC symbol*] (OCLC) .... CUM
Curry College, Milton, MA [*Library symbol*] [*Library of Congress*] (LCLS) .... MMiltC
Curry Public Library, Gold Beach, OR [*Library symbol*] [*Library of Congress*] (LCLS) .... OrGb
Curry's Abridgment of Blackstone [*A publication*] (DLA) .... Cur Bl
Curry's Reports [*6-19 Louisiana*] [*A publication*] (DLA) .... Curry
Curschmann-Batten-Steinert [*Syndrome*] [*Medicine*] (DB) .... CBS
Curschmann-Steinert [*Syndrome*] [*Medicine*] (DAVI) .... CS
Curse of Agade (BJA) .... CA
Cursitor Baron of the Exchequer [*British*] (ROG) .... CURS BE
Cursive (BJA) .... curs
Cursor Backward (SAUS) .... CUB
Cursor Centered [*Automotive engineering*] CC
Cursor Computer Interface Data (ACAE) .... CCID
Cursor Control [*Computer science*] (BUR) CC
Cursor Forward (SAUS) .... CUF
Cursor Home (SAUS) .... CUH
Cursor New Line (SAUS) .... CNL
Cursor Next Field (SAUS) .... CNF
Cursor On (SAUS) .... CON
Cursor Position (MCD) .... CPOS
Cursor Position (SAUS) .... CUP
Cursor Position Report (SAUS) .... CPR
Cursor Preceding Field (SAUS) .... CPF
Cursus Cancellariae [*Latin*] (DLA) .... CURS CAN
Cursus Sacrae Scripturae [*Paris*] (BJA) .... CSS
Cursus Scaccarii [*Latin*] (DLA) .... CUR SCACC
Curtain .... CRTN
Curtain (MSA) .... CURT
Curtain Sided Trailer [*Shipping*] (DCTA) .... CS
Curteis' English Ecclesiastical Reports [*A publication*] (DLA) .... Curt
Curteis' English Ecclesiastical Reports [*A publication*] (DLA) .... Curt Ecc
Curteis' English Ecclesiastical Reports [*A publication*] (DLA) .... Curt Eccl
Curteis' English Ecclesiastical Reports [*A publication*] (DLA) .... Curt Eccl (Eng)
Curtin University Environmental Studies Group [*Australia*] .... CUESG
Curtis' Admiralty Digest [*A publication*] (DLA) .... Curt Adm Dig
Curtis' American Conveyancer [*A publication*] (DLA) .... Curt Conv
Curtis Bay Railroad Co. [*AAR code*] .... CURB
Curtis' Circuit Court Reports [*United States*] [*A publication*] (DLA) .... Curt
Curtis' Circuit Court Reports [*United States*] [*A publication*] (DLA) .... Curtis
Curtis' Commentaries on the United States Courts [*A publication*] (DLA) .... Curt US Courts
Curtis Completion Form [*Psychology*] .... CCF
Curtis' Copyright [*1847*] [*A publication*] (DLA) .... Curt Cop
Curtis' Decisions of the United States Supreme Court [*A publication*] (DLA) .... Cur Dec
Curtis' Decisions of the United States Supreme Court [*A publication*] (DLA) .... Curt Cond Rep
Curtis' Decisions of the United States Supreme Court [*A publication*] (DLA) .... Curt Dec
Curtis' Decisions of the United States Supreme Court [*A publication*] (DLA) .... Curtis SC Reports
Curtis' Decisions of the United States Supreme Court [*A publication*] (DLA) .... Curtis US Sup Ct R
Curtis' Digest [*United States*] [*A publication*] (DLA) .... Curt Dig
Curtis' Edition, United States Supreme Court Reports [*A publication*] (DLA) .... Curt
Curtis' Edition, United States Supreme Court Reports [*A publication*] (DLA) .... Curt Cond

Curtis' Edition, United States Supreme Court Reports [*A publication*] (DLA) .... Curtis
Curtis' Equity Precedents [*A publication*] (DLA) .... Curt Eq Pr
Curtis High School (SAUS) .... CHS
Curtis' History of the Constitution of the United States Courts [*A publication*] (DLA) .... Curt US Const
Curtis Institute (SAUS) CI
Curtis Institute of Music [*Pennsylvania*] .... CIM
Curtis Institute of Music, Philadelphia, PA [*Library symbol*] [*Library of Congress*] (LCLS) .... PPCI
Curtis Mathes Hldg [*NASDAQ symbol*] (TTSB) .... CRTM
Curtis Mathes Holding Corp. [*Associated Press*] (SAG) .... CMathes
Curtis Mathes Holding Corp. [*NASDAQ symbol*] (SAG) .... CRTM
Curtis Memorial Public Library, Meriden, CT [*Library symbol*] [*Library of Congress*] (LCLS) .... CtMer
Curtis, Milburn & Eastern Railroad Co. [*AAR code*] .... CMER
Curtis on Patents [*A publication*] (DLA) .... Curt Pat
Curtis on the Jurisdiction of United States Courts [*A publication*] (DLA) .... Curt Jur
Curtis Publishing Co., Research Library, Philadelphia, PA [*Library symbol*] [*Library of Congress*] [*Obsolete*] (LCLS) .... PPCuP
Curtis Publishing Company (SAUO) .... CPC
Curtis' United States Circuit Court Decisions [*A publication*] (DLA) .... Curt CC
Curtis' United States Circuit Court Reports [*A publication*] (DLA) .... Cur
Curtis' United States Circuit Court Reports [*A publication*] (DLA) .... Curtis CC
Curtis-Rad (SAUS) .... C-Rad
Curtiss Aeroplane & Motor Co., Inc. (SAUO) C
Curtiss Aircraft Coporation (SAUO) .... CAC
Curtiss-Wright [*NYSE symbol*] (TTSB) .... CW
Curtiss-Wright Corp. [*Associated Press*] (SAG) .... CurtWr
Curtiss-Wright Corp. [*ICAO aircraft manufacturer identifier*] (ICAO) .... CW
Curtiss-Wright Corp. .... CWC
Curtiss-Wright Corporation (SAUO) .... CWC
Curtiss-Wright of Canada [*Toronto Stock Exchange symbol*] .... CWA
Curtiss-Wright Research Reactor .... CWRR
Curuzu Cuatia [*Argentina*] [*ICAO location identifier*] (ICLI) .... SATU
Curuzu Cuatia [*Argentina*] [*Airport symbol*] (OAG) .... UZU
Curve (SAUS) C
Curve (MSA) .... CRV
Curve .... CURV
Curve [*Commonly used*] (OPSA) .... CURVE
Curve Drawing (SAUS) .... CRV DWG
Curve Interpreter for Microprocessor (MCD) .... CIMP
Curve Lake Indian Band Library, Ontario [*Library symbol*] [*National Library of Canada*] (BIB) .... OCLI
Curve of Merit [*Electronics*] (IAA) .... COM
Curve Waring Signal (SAUS) .... CWS
Curved .... cvd
Curved Calapinto Needle [*Medicine*] (MELL) .... CCN
Curved Dash Olds Owners Club (EA) .... CDOOC
Curved End-to-End Anastomosis [*Stapler*] [*Medicine*] (DMAA) .... CEEA
Curved Motion Cutter .... CMC
Curved Orthotropic Bridge Analysis (PDAA) .... COBRA
Curvilinear Accelerator (SAUS) .... CA
Curvilinear Body [*in Batten disease*] .... CLB
Curwen's Abstract of Titles [*A publication*] (DLA) .... Cur Ab Tit
Curwen's Laws of Ohio [*1 vol.*] [*1854*] [*A publication*] (DLA) .... Curw LO
Curwen's Overruled Cases [*Ohio*] [*A publication*] (DLA) .... Cur Ov Ca
Curwen's Overruled Cases [*Ohio*] [*A publication*] (DLA) .... Curw
Curwen's Overruled Cases [*Ohio*] [*A publication*] (DLA) .... Curw Ov Cas
Curwen's Revised Statutes of Ohio [*A publication*] (DLA) .... Curw RS
Curwen's Statutes of Ohio [*A publication*] (DLA) .... Cur Stat
Curwen's Statutes of Ohio [*A publication*] (DLA) .... Curw
Curwensville, PA [*FM radio station call letters*] .... WOKW
[*The*] **Curwood Collector** [*A publication*] (EA) .... TCC
Cusac Gold Mines [*NASDAQ symbol*] (TTSB) .... CUSIF
Cusac Gold Mines Ltd. [*Associated Press*] (SAG) .... Cusac
Cusac Gold Mines Ltd. [*NASDAQ symbol*] (SAG) .... CUSI
Cusac Gold Mines Ltd. [*NASDAQ symbol*] (SAG) .... CUSW
Cusac Inds Ltd Wrrt [*NASDAQ symbol*] (TTSB) .... CUSWF
Cusac Industries Ltd. [*Toronto Stock Exchange symbol*] [*Vancouver Stock Exchange symbol*] .... CQC
Cusac Industries Ltd. [*Associated Press*] (SAG) .... Cusac
Cusco [*Peru*] [*Seismograph station code, US Geological Survey*] (SEIS) .... CUS
Cush Relief and Rehabilitation Society (SAUO) .... CRRS
Cushieri Maneuver [*Medicine*] (MELL) .... CM
Cushing, OK [*Location identifier*] [*FAA*] (FAAL) .... CUH
Cushing, OK [*AM radio station call letters*] .... KUSH
Cushing on Trustee Process [*A publication*] (DLA) .... Cush Trust Pr
Cushing, Storey, and Joselyn's Election Cases [*Massachusetts*] [*A publication*] (DLA) .... CS & J
Cushing's Election Cases in Massachusetts [*A publication*] (DLA) .... Cush Elec Cas
Cushing's Law and Practice of Legislative Assemblies [*A publication*] (DLA) .... Cush Law & Prac Leg Assem
Cushing's Law and Practice of Legislative Assemblies [*A publication*] (DLA) .... Cush Leg Ass
Cushing's Law and Practice of Legislative Assemblies [*A publication*] (DLA) .... Cush Parl Law
Cushing's Manual of Parliamentary Law [*A publication*] (DLA) .... Cush Man
Cushing's Massachusetts Supreme Judicial Court Reports [*1848-53*] [*A publication*] (DLA) .... Cush
Cushing's Reports [*1848-53*] [*A publication*] (DLA) .... Cushing
Cushing's Reports [*1848-53*] [*A publication*] (DLA) .... Cush (Mass)
Cushing's Study of the Roman Law [*A publication*] (DLA) .... Cush Rom Law
Cushing's Syndrome [*Endocrinology*] (DAVI) .... CS
Cushion .... CSHN
Cushion (MSA) .... CUSH
Cushion Aerodynamic System Parametric Assessment Research (SAUO) .... CASPAR
Cushion Air System Parametric Assessment Rig (PDAA) .... CASPAR
Cushion Air Tread Articulate [*Vehicle*] [*Army*] .... CATA
Cushion Control Point [*Navy*] (ANA) .... CCP
Cushion Craft CC
Cushion Landing Zone [*Navy*] (ANA) .... CLZ
Cushion Lift (AAG) C
Cushion-Augmentation Device (SAUS) .... CADS
Cushioning Pads .... CP
Cushitic [*MARC language code*] [*Library of Congress*] (LCCP) .... cus
Cushman Club of America (EA) .... CCA
Cushman Foundation for Foraminiferal Research (EA) .... CFFR
Cushman's Reports [*23-29 Mississippi*] [*A publication*] (DLA) .... Cush
Cushman's Reports [*23-29 Mississippi*] [*A publication*] (DLA) .... Cushm
CUSO [*Canadian University Service Overseas*], **Ottawa, Ontario** [*Library symbol*] [*National Library of Canada*] (NLC) .... OOCUS
Cusp Creek [*British Columbia*] [*Seismograph station code, US Geological Survey*] [*Closed*] (SEIS) CCC
Cusp Injection Experiment [*Nuclear energy*] [*British*] (NUCP) .... CUSIE
Cusparia [*Angustura Bark*] [*Pharmacology*] (ROG) .... CUSPAR
Cuspid (MELL) C
Cuspid [*Dentistry*] (DAVI) .... cusp
Cuspidore Hitters Association Worldwide [*Defunct*] (EA) .... CHAW
Custer Battlefield Historical and Museum Association (EA) .... CBHMA
Custer Battlefield National Monument (SAUS) .... CBNM
Custer Battlefield National Monument [*National Park Service designation*] .... CUST
Custer County Junior College [*Montana*] .... CCJC
Custer County Library, Custer, SD [*Library symbol*] [*Library of Congress*] (LCLS) .... SdCu
Custer County Public Library, Westcliffe, CO [*Library symbol*] [*Library of Congress*] (LCLS) .... CoWc
Custer, SD [*FM radio station call letters*] .... KACP
Custer, SD [*FM radio station call letters*] (RBYB) .... KAWK-FM
Custer, SD [*AM radio station call letters*] .... KFCR
Custer State Park (SAUS) .... CSP
Custer's Ecclesiastical Reports [*A publication*] (DLA) .... Cust Rep
Custodial Officer (SAUO) .... CO
Custodial Parent .... CP
Custodial, Protective, and Crafts [*US government workers*] .... CPC
Custodian [*Banking*] (AFM) .... CUST
Custodian (ADWA) .... cust
Custodian .... CUSTDN
Custodian (ADA) .... CUSTOD
Custodian (SAUS) .... Custod
Custodian Account [*Banking*] .... CA
Custodian Contractor CC
Custodian Forces, India (SAUO) .... CFI
Custodian of Allied and Enemy Property [*British*] [*World War II*] .... CAEP
Custodian of Fund .... C of F
Custodian of Postal Effects [*Military*] (AFM) .... COPE
Custodian of Records (HGAA) .... COR
Custody (AFM) .... CUST
Custody Action for Lesbian Mothers (EA) .... CALM
Custody Authorization/Custody Receipt Listing .... CA/CRL
Custody Pending Completion of Use .... CPCU
Custody Sergeant (WDAA) .... CS
Custom .... CSTM
Custom [*Automotive engineering*] .... CUST
Custom Agents Association (SAUO) .... CAA
Custom Air Transport, Inc. [*FAA designator*] (FAAC) .... CTT
Custom and Port [*International trade*] .... C/P
Custom Armoring Corp. (SAUS) .... CAC
Custom Asynchronous Receiver/Transmitter [*Automotive engineering*] .... CART
Custom Chip [*Personal computers*] CC
Custom Chrome [*NASDAQ symbol*] (TTSB) .... CSTM
Custom Chrome, Inc. [*NASDAQ symbol*] (SPSG) .... CSTM
Custom Chrome, Inc. [*Associated Press*] (SAG) .... CustCh
Custom Clothing Guild of America [*Defunct*] (EA) .... CCGA
Custom Computer System (IEEE) .... CCS
Custom Configurable Computer CCC
Custom Contract Service [*IBM Corp.*] .... CCS
Custom Control Factory [*Desaware Co.*] .... CCF
Custom Defense Package .... CDP
Custom Defined Function [*Computer science*] (PCM) .... CDF
Custom Dynamic Logic (SAUS) .... CDL
Custom Editing and Display of Reduced Information in Cartesian space (SAUS) .... CEDRIC
Custom Electronic Design Installation Association (EA) .... CEDIA
Custom Finished .... C/F
Custom House [*Business term*] .... CH
Custom House (WDAA) .... ch
Custom Input/Output Unit [*Computer science*] (IEEE) .... CIOU
Custom Install Manager (SAUS) .... CIM
Custom Integrated Circuit (PDAA) CIC
Custom Integrated System [*Computer science*] (PDAA) .... CIS
Custom Interest Profile .... CIP
Custom Large Scale Integration (ACAE) .... CLSI
Custom Local Area Signaling Services [*Telecommunications*] (ACRL) .... CLASS
Custom Logic and Array Simulation Systems for Integrated Circuits (PDAA) .... CLASSIC
Custom Logic Array [*Electronics*] (IAA) .... CLA

Custom Metallized Multigate Array [NASA] .... CMMA
Custom Microfilm Systems, Inc., Riverside, CA [Library symbol] [Library of Congress] (LCLS) .... CusM
Custom Network Broadcasting, Inc. (TSSD) .... CNB-TV
Custom of the Port [Shipping] .... COP
Custom of the Port (EBF) .... C/P
Custom of the Port (SAUS) .... CP
Custom Packages for Automation [3D Digital Design & Development Ltd.] [Software package] (NCC) .... CPFA
Custom Painted .... C/P
Custom Patrol Officer [British] .... CPO
Custom Petroleum [Vancouver Stock Exchange symbol] .... CUT
Custom Processor (SAUS) .... CP
Custom Product Operation (SAUS) .... CPO
Custom Quality Studio [Photography] .... CQS
Custom Refresh Controller .... CRC
Custom Roll Forming Institute (EA) .... CRFI
Custom Spherical Resins .... CSR
Custom Static Random Access Memory (SAUS) .... CSRAM
Custom Tailors and Designers Association of America (EA) .... CTDA
Custom, Tradition, and Usage (MCD) .... CTU
Custom Updates and Extras (SAUS) .... CUE
Custom Work Order [Telecommunications] (TEL) .... CWO
Custom Xpress Delivery .... CXD
Customary (ROG) .... CUSTMY
Customary (SAUS) .... custmy
Customary Behavior [Psychology] .... CUB
Customary, Prevailing, and Reasonable Charges [Department of Health and Human Services] (GFGA) .... CPR
Customary Quick Dispatch .... CQD
Custom-Built Installation Process Offering [Computer science] (HGAA) .... CBIPO
Customedix Corp. [AMEX symbol] (SPSG) .... CUS
Customedix Corp. [Associated Press] (SAG) .... Custmd
Customer (MSA) .... CUST
Customer (TBD) .... Cust
Customer (PROS) .... cust
Customer .... CUSTR
Customer Acceptance Readiness Review [Apollo] [NASA] .... CARR
Customer Acceptance Review Item Disposition (NASA) .... CARID
Customer Acceptance Test (SAUS) .... CAT
Customer Access Facilities [Telecommunications] .... CAF
Customer Access Line Charge [Telecommunications] .... CALC
Customer Access Network .... CAN
Customer Accommodation Plan (ACAE) .... CAP
Customer Account Library Line [Queens Borough, New York Public Library] .... CALL
Customer Account Representative (AFM) .... CAR
Customer Acquisition Unit (NASA) .... CAU
Customer Activated Terminal .... CAT
Customer Address (SAUS) .... CUSA
Customer Administration Center (SAUS) .... CAC
Customer and Product Development Office (SAUS) .... CPDO
Customer Annual Progress Summary (SAUS) .... CAPS
Customer Applicability Code (MCD) .... CAC
Customer Application Summary (IAA) .... CAS
Customer Assistance Office .... CAO
Customer Assistance Program (PCM) .... CAP
Customer Authorization for Additional Work .... CAAW
Customer Automatic Relay and Exchange (SAUS) .... Care
Customer Backorder Code (SAUS) .... CBKCD
Customer Care Consultant (ROAS) CCC
Customer Class (SAUS) .... CUSCL
Customer Code [Telecommunications] (TEL) .... CUS
Customer Communications Exchange [Bell System] CCX
Customer Control Unit (SAUS) .... CCU
Customer Controlled Reconfiguration [Telecommunications] (TSSD) .... CCR
Customer Conversion Statistics (SAUS) .... CCS
Customer Coordination Center (SSD) CCC
Customer Cost Analysis [Business term] (MHDW) .... CCA
Customer Data and Operations Language (SSD) .... CDOL
Customer Data and Operations System (SSD) .... CDOS
Customer Data Requirements List (MCD) .... CDRL
Customer Data Services Facility (SSD) .... CDSF
Customer Delivery Enterprise Model (AAEL) .... CDEM
Customer Depot Complaint System (MCD) .... CDCS
Customer Dial Pulse Receiver [Telecommunications] (TEL) .... CDPR
Customer Dialed Account Recording (SAUS) .... CDAR
Customer Digital Switching System [Telecommunications] (MHDI) .... CDSS
Customer Distributed Buglist (SAUS) .... CDB
Customer Dividend Program (SAUO) .... CDP
Customer Engineering Instruction System Diagram (SAUS) .... CEISD
Customer Engineering Letter (MCD) .... CEL
Customer Engineering Memorandum (SAUS) .... CEM
Customer Engineering Monitor [IBM Corp.] .... CEMON
Customer Engineering Product Performance Analysis (SAUS) .... CEPPA
Customer Field Service (ACAE) .... CFS
Customer File (MCD) .... CF
Customer Float Reporting Service (SAUS) .... CFRS
Customer Furnished (MCD) .... CF
Customer Furnished Equipment .... CFE
Customer Furnished Material (SAUS) .... CFM
Customer Furnished Support Equipment (ACAE) .... CFSE
Customer Gateway (SAUS) .... CGW
Customer Identification Code CIC
Customer Identifier (SAUS) .... CID

Customer Information Control System [Pronounced "kicks"] [IBM Corp.] [Computer science] .... CICS
Customer Information Control System Virtual Storage [IBM Corp.] [Computer science] .... CICS/VS
Customer Information Feed (SAUS) .... CIF
Customer Information File [Computer science] (BUR) .... CIF
Customer Information Record System (SAUS) .... CIRS
Customer Information Reference System (SAUS) .... CIRS
Customer Information Squawk Sheet .... CIS
Customer Information System [IBM Corp.] .... CIS
Customer Information Terminal (SAUS) .... CIT
Customer Initiated Entry [Banking] .... CIE
Customer Inspection Record .... CIR
Customer Integrated And/Or Reference File System (IAA) .... CIRF
Customer Integration (SSD) CI
Customer Integration Office (SSD) .... CIO
Customer Integration Panel (SSD) .... CIP
Customer Interface Control System (GFGA) .... CICS
Customer Inventory Control System (SAUS) .... CICS
Customer Item CI
Customer Item Squawks .... CIS
Customer Liaison Office (SAUS) .... CLO
Customer Local Area Signal Service (HGAA) .... CLASS
Customer Located Equipment (SAUS) .... CLE
Customer Master Card (SAUS) .... CMC
Customer Master File .... CMF
Customer Master Record (SAUS) .... CMR
Customer Material Return .... CMR
Customer Memory Update [Telecommunications] .... CMU
Customer Multiplexer (SAUS) .... CMX
Customer Must Order Direct .... CMOD
Customer Name (SAUS) .... CUSNM
Customer Name and Address (SAUS) .... CNA
Customer Name/Address (SAUS) .... CN/A
Customer Name/Address Bureau (SAUS) .... CNAB
Customer Network Access Equipment (SAUO) .... CNAE
Customer Network Control Center [Telecommunications] (TEL) .... CNCC
Customer Network Management [Telecommunications] (ACRL) .... CNM
Customer Network Management Agent [Telecommunications] (ACRL) .... CNMA
Customer Networks Control Centre [Telecommunications] .... CNCC
Customer Number (SAUS) .... CUSNR
Customer On-Line Order Processing System .... COOP
Customer Operated Automatic Checkout (SAUS) .... COACH
Customer Order Control Automated System (IAA) .... COCAS
Customer Order File (SAUS) .... COF
Customer Order Processing (BUR) .... COP
Customer Order Processing and Invoicing (SAUS) .... CPOI
Customer Order Processing System .... COPS
Customer Order Set (IAA) .... CO
Customer Oriented Manufacturing Management Systems (ACII) .... COMMS
Customer Owned and Maintained (OA) .... COAM
Customer Owned and Telephone Company Maintained [Telecommunications] (TEL) .... COTM
Customer Owned Property (SAUS) .... COP
Customer Owned Tooling (SAUS) .... COT
Customer Premise (NRCH) .... CU
Customer Premises Equipment [Telecommunications] .... CPE
Customer Premises Network [Computer science] (VERA) .... CPN
Customer Premises Node (SAUS) .... CPN
Customer Premises System [Bell System] .... CPS
Customer Programming Language (SAUS) .... CUSP
Customer Proven [GMC truck marketing] .... CP
Customer Provided Equipment [Telecommunications] .... CPE
Customer Provided Terminal [Telecommunications] (IAA) .... CPT
Customer Purchase Order (SAUS) .... CUSPO
Customer Quality Representative (SAUS) .... CQR
Customer Reaction Survey .... CRS
Customer Record Center (SAUS) .... CRC
Customer Record Information System (SAUS) .... CRIS
Customer Records and Billing [Bell System] .... CRB
Customer Relations Institute (NTPA) .... CRI
Customer Relations Manager (DCTA) .... CRM
Customer Relationship Management .... CRM
Customer Replaceable Unit (IAA) .... CRU
Customer Representative .... CR
Customer Required Date (SAUS) .... CRD
Customer Requirements Data Set (SSD) .... CRDS
Customer Requirements List (MCD) .... CRL
Customer Reservations System [Airlines] .... CRS
Customer Return For Credit (SAUS) .... CRFC
Customer Satisfaction .... CUSAT
Customer Satisfaction Index [Automotive retailing] .... CSI
Customer Satisfaction Research Institute [Lenexa, KS] [Telecommunications] (TSSD) .... CSRI
Customer Service (BUR) .... CS
Customer Service Administration Control Center (ROAS) .... CSACC
Customer Service Administration Control Center System [Telecommunications] (TEL) .... CSACCS
Customer Service Center .... CSC
Customer Service Department Procedure .... CSDP
Customer Service Division (SAUS) .... CSD
Customer Service Number (SAUO) .... CSN
Customer Service Officer .... CSO
Customer Service Representative .... CSR
Customer Service System [Computer surveillance] [British] .... CSS

Customer Service Unit (IAA) ... CSU
Customer Service Unit/Data Service Unit [*Computer science*] (ITCA) ... CSU/DSU
Customer Set-Up [*Computer science*] ... CSU
Customer Signature Required (MSA) ... CSR
Customer Software Support Facility [*IBM Corp.*] (CIST) ... CSSF
Customer Specific Dictionaries (SAUS) ... CSD
Customer Specific Integrated Circuit [*Electronics*] ... CSIC
Customer Subscriber Identification [*Telecommunications*] (PCM) ... CSID
Customer Supply Assistance [*Military*] ... CSA
Customer Supply Assistance Office [*Military*] ... CSAO
Customer Support (BUR) ... CS
Customer Support Branch (AFIT) ... CSB
Customer Support Engineer (SAUO) ... CSE
Customer Support Facility (SAUS) ... CSF
Customer Support Management System (SAUS) ... CSMS
Customer Support Operation ... CSO
Customer Support Room (SPST) ... CSR
Customer Support Team (SAUO) ... CST
Customer Support Unit (AFIT) ... CSU
Customer Switching System [*Telecommunications*] (TEL) ... CSS
Customer Technical Assistance ... CTA
Customer Telephone System (SAUS) ... CTS
Customer Test [*Army*] ... CT
Customer Trouble Report Analysis Plan [*Telecommunications*] (TEL) ... CTRAP
Customer Unit (SAUS) ... CU
Customer Use (SAUS) ... CU
Customer Utilization (SSD) ... CU
Customer Waste Solidification Facility (ABAC) ... CWSF
Customer within Country (AAGC) ... cc
Customer Work Authorization (AAG) ... CWA
Customer Work Order File (MCD) ... CWORF
Customer-Bank Communication Terminal [*Computerized banking*] ... CBCT
Customer/Campus Gateway (SAUS) ... CGW
Customer/Field Support Elements (RDA) ... C/FSE
Customer-Furnished Material (NASA) ... CFM
Customer-Initiated Call [*Marketing*] (IAA) ... CIC
Customer-Integrated Automated Procurement System (AFM) ... CIAPS
Customer-Operated Terminal [*Computer science*] ... COT
Customer-Oriented Data System (DIT) ... CODAS
Customer-Oriented Terminal [*Computer science*] ... COT
Customer-Orienting Program [*Computer science*] ... COP
Customer-Originated Change (AAG) ... COC
Customer-Owned and Maintained Equipment (SAUS) ... COAM Equip
Customer-Owned Coin-Operated Telephone (WDMC) ... COCOT
Customer-Owned Goods ... COG
Customer-Owned Tooling (AAEL) ... COT
Customer-Premises Facility (SAUS) ... CPF
Customer-Premises Facility Terminal [*Telecommunications*] (TEL) ... CPFT
Customer-Requested Earlier Due Date [*Business term*] (MHDB) ... CREDD
Customers Having Abundant Product Possibilities [*Term coined by William F. Doescher, publisher of "D & B Reports"*] [*Lifestyle classification*] ... Chapp
Customer's Other Service [*Telecommunications*] (TEL) ... COS
Customer's Own Goods (WDMC) ... COG
Customer's Own Material (WGA) ... COM
Customer's Own Merchandise (WDMC) ... COM
Customers Own Transport (DCTA) ... COT
Customer's Report [*Telecommunications*] (TEL) ... CR
Customer's Request (SAA) ... CR
Customer's Terminal Equipment [*Telecommunications*] [*British*] ... CTE
Customer-Specific IC (SAUS) ... CSIC
Customer-Vended Equipment (AAG) ... CVE
Customhouse ... Cus Ho
Customized ... CUST
Customized Assurance Plans [*Automotive engineering*] ... CAP
Customized Communications Routine (SAUS) ... CCR
Customized Health Information Project [*Computer science*] ... CHIP
Customized Intercept Service (SAUS) ... CIS
Customized Long Instruction Word (AAEL) ... CLIW
Customized Multimedia Connection ... CMC
Customized Networking Platform ... CNP
Customized Optical Reader Random Error Correction Technique (SAUS) ... CORRECT
Customized Processor [*IBM Corp.*] (IEEE) ... CP
Customized Routing Selector (SAUS) ... CRS
Customized Routing System (SAUS) ... CRS
Customized-Information-Delivery System [*Bell Communications Research Laboratory*] ... CID
Customs ... CSTMS
Customs ... CUST
Customs Accelerated Passenger Inspection System [*US Customs Service*] ... CAPIS
Customs Act [*Canada*] ... CA
Customs Acts Legislation Service [*Australia*] [*A publication*] ... CALS
Customs Additional Code (DS) ... CAC
Customs Agents' Association of Queensland [*Australia*] ... CAAQ
Customs Agents Institute of Australia (SAUO) ... CAIA
Customs and Economic Union of Central Africa ... CEUCA
Customs and Excise ... CE
Customs and Excise (SAUO) ... CE
Customs and Excise Departmental Reference and Information Computer (PDAA) ... CEDRIC
Customs and Excise Division, Department of National Revenue [*Division des Douanes et de l'Accise, Ministere du Revenu National*] **Ottawa, Ontario** [*Library symbol*] [*National Library of Canada*] (NLC) ... OONR
Customs and Excise Establishment (SAUO) ... CEE
Customs and Excise Institutions List [*Database*] (IID) ... INST
Customs and Excise Laboratory [*Canada*] ... CEL
Customs and Excise Management Act (DS) ... CEMA
Customs and Excise Preventive Staff Association (SAUO) ... CEPSA
Customs and Excise Stores Branch Association (SAUO) ... CESBA
Customs and Indirect Taxation (SAUS) ... DG XXI
Customs and International Trade Bar Association (EA) ... CITBA
Customs and Patent Appeals Reports (Customs) [*A publication*] (DLA) ... Cust & Pat App (Cust) (F)
Customs and Patent Appeals Reports (Patents) [*A publication*] (DLA) ... Cust & Pat App (Pat) (F)
Customs and Usages (DLA) ... CUS & US
Customs Annuity and Benevolent Fund (SAUO) ... CABF
Customs Appeals Decisions [*A publication*] (DLA) ... CAD
Customs Assigned Number [*Shipping*] [*British*] ... CAN
Customs Automated (or Automatic) Data Processing Intelligence Network (SAUS) ... CADPIN
Customs Automatic Data Processing Intelligence Network [*US Customs Service*] ... CADPIN
Customs Available [*Aviation*] (DA) ... CUS
Customs Border Service (SAUO) ... CBS
Customs Brokers and Forwarders Association of America (SAUO) ... CBFAA
Customs Brokers' Council of Australia ... CBCA
Customs Bulletin [*A publication*] (DLA) ... Cust Bull
Customs Bulletin and Decisions [*A publication*] (DLA) ... Cust B & Dec
Customs Bureau ... CB
Customs Clearance (DS) ... CCL
Customs Clearance Status [*British*] (DS) ... CCS
Customs Consolidation Act [*British*] ... CCA
Customs Co-Operation Council [*See also CCD*] [*Brussels, Belgium*] (EAIO) ... CCC
Customs Co-Operation Council Nomenclature [*See also BTN*] ... CCCN
Customs Court ... CUSTCT
Customs Court Decisions [*A publication*] (DLA) ... CD
Customs Court Reports [*A publication*] (DLA) ... Cu Ct
Customs Court Reports [*United States*] [*A publication*] (DLA) ... Cust Ct
Customs Court Rules [*A publication*] (DLA) ... Cust Ct R
Customs Decisions [*Department of the Treasury*] [*A publication*] (DLA) ... CD
Customs Declaration ... C/D
Customs Declaration (SAUS) ... CD
Customs Duties and Import Regulations [*A publication*] (DLA) ... Cust D
Customs Enforcement Officer [*US Customs Service*] ... CEO
Customs Entry Charge (DCTA) ... CEC
Customs Entry Processing and Cargo System (PDAA) ... CEPACS
Customs Form ... CF
Customs Handling of Import and Export Freight [*EC*] (ECED) ... CHIEF
Customs Has Been Notified [*Aviation*] (FAAC) ... CUSNO
Customs House (EBF) ... CH
Customs, Immigration, and Quarantine ... CIQ
Customs Information Exchange [*An arm of US Customs Service*] ... CIE
Customs of Port (SAUS) ... COP
Customs Officers' Association of Australia ... COAA
Customs Optical Reader Passport Systems [*A scanning device capable of reading the latest US passports*] ... CORPS
Customs Penalty Decisions [*A publication*] (DLA) ... Cust Pen Dec
Customs Port Investigator [*US Customs Service*] ... CPI
Customs Registered Number [*British*] (DS) ... CRN
Customs Regulations of the United States ... CRUS
Customs Rules Decisions [*A publication*] (DLA) ... CRD
Customs Tariff Act [*Canada*] ... CTA
Customs Transaction Code (DS) ... CTC
Customs Union [*British*] (DAS) ... CU
Customs Union (SAUO) ... CU
Customs Value per Gross Kilogram (DS) ... CVGK
Customs Value per Gross Pound (DS) ... CVGP
Customs-Assigned Number (SAUO) ... CAN
CustomTracks Corp. [*NASDAQ symbol*] (SG) ... CUST
Custos Privati Sigilli [*Keeper of the Privy Seal*] [*Latin*] ... CPS
Custos Rotulorum [*Keeper of the Rolls*] [*Latin*] ... CR
Custos Sigilli [*Keeper of the Seal*] [*Latin*] ... CS
Cut (WDAA) ... C
Cut All Round (SAUS) ... car
Cut and Paste ... C & P
Cut and Pin (SAUS) ... C&P
Cut Bank [*Montana*] [*ICAO location identifier*] (ICLI) ... KCTB
Cut Bank, MT [*Location identifier*] [*FAA*] (FAAL) ... CTB
Cut, Carat, Clarity, Color [*Factors in determining the value of a diamond*] ... 4C's
Cut, Carat, Clarity, Color [*Factors in determining the value of a diamond*] ... CCCC
Cut Down, Annoyed, Guilty, Eye-Opener [*Clinical questions asked to detect alcoholism*] ... CAGE
Cut Film [*Photography*] ... CF
Cut Holes and Sink 'Em [*Navy ammunition disposal project*] ... CHASE
Cut Image [*Computer science*] (PCM) ... CIMG
Cut In ... CI
Cut It Out (SAUS) ... CIO
Cut Length (ADA) ... CL
Cut Length (MSA) ... CLTH
Cut Off [*Military*] (AABC) ... COFF
Cut Out ... CO
Cut Out Background [*Printing*] ... COB
Cut Paraboloidal Reflector ... CPR
Cut Sizes [*Paper*] (DGA) ... CS
Cut Stone ... CUTS
Cut, Tear, and Curl [*Tea*] ... CTC
Cut to Length ... CTL

Cut to Length and Notch .... CTLN
Cutaneous Basophil Hypersensitivity [*Immunology*] .... CBH
Cutaneous Discrimination [*Psychometric test*] .... CD
Cutaneous Drug Reaction Database (SAUO) .... CDRD
Cutaneous Genuine Histiocytic Lymphoma .... CGHL
Cutaneous Germinal Center Cell-Derived Lymphomas .... CGCCL
Cutaneous Hepatic Porphyria (DB) .... CHP
Cutaneous Larva Migrans [*Medicine*] (MELL) .... CLM
Cutaneous Leukocytoclastic Vasculitis [*Medicine*] (MELL) CLV
Cutaneous Lichen Amyloidosis [*Medicine*] (MELL) .... CLA
Cutaneous Lymphocyte-Associated Antigen [*Immunology*] .... CLA
Cutaneous Lymphoid Infiltrates CLI
Cutaneous Malignant Lymphomas .... CML
Cutaneous Malignant Melanoma [*Medicine*] (MAE) .... CMM
Cutaneous Non-Epidermotropic Lymphoma (PDAA) .... CNEL
Cutaneous Occupational Infection [*Medicine*] (MELL) .... COI
Cutaneous Peripheral T-Cell-Derived Lymphomas .... CPTL
Cutaneous Squamous Cell Carcinoma [*Medicine*] (DMAA) .... CSCC
Cutaneous Stimulation [*Psychometric test*] .... CS
Cutaneous T-Cell Lymphoma [*Medicine*] .... CTCL
Cutaneous Trunci Muscle [*Anatomy*] .... CTM
Cutaneous Water Loss .... CWL
CutCo Indus [*NASDAQ symbol*] (TTSB) .... CUTC
Cutco Industries, Inc. [*NASDAQ symbol*] (NQ) .... CUTC
Cutco Industries, Inc. [*Associated Press*] (SAG) .... Cutco
Cutdown [*Cardiovascular and surgery*] (DAVI) .... CD
Cute Little Robot (SAUS) R2D2
Cute Things They Do (SAUS) .... CTTD
Cute Things They Say (SAUS) .... CTTS
Cuthbert College (ROG) .... CUTHB
Cuthbert Cudgel [*Pseudonym used by T. Houston*] CC
Cuthbert, GA [*AM radio station call letters*] .... WCUG
Cuthbert, GA [*FM radio station call letters*] (BROA) .... WMRZ-FM
Cuticle C
Cuticular Plate [*Biology*] .... CP
Cutis Laxa [*Loose skin*] (MELL) CL
Cutis Marmorata Telangiectatica Congenita [*Medicine*] (DMAA) .... CMTC
Cutis Verticis Gyrata (SAUS) .... CVG
Cutlass Bay, Cat Island [*Bahamas*] [*ICAO location identifier*] (ICLI) .... MYCX
Cutlass Industries Corp. [*Vancouver Stock Exchange symbol*] .... CUC
Cutler on Naturalization Laws [*A publication*] (DLA) .... Cut Nat
Cutler-Hammer, Inc. (SAUO) .... CEH
Cutler-Hammer, Inc. (SAUO) .... CH
Cutler's Insolvent Laws of Massachusetts [*A publication*] (DLA) .... Cut Ins L
Cutler's Legal System of the English, the Hindoos, Etc. [*A publication*] (DLA) .... Cut Leg Sys
Cutler's Trademark and Patent Cases [*A publication*] (DLA) .... Cut Pat Cas
Cutlery (MSA) .... CTLRY
Cutlery .... CUTLY
Cutlery & Allied Trades Association (WDAA) .... CATA
Cutlery and Allied Trades Research Association [*British*] (IRUK) .... CATRA
Cutlery and Silverware Association (SAUO) .... CSA
Cutlery Forgers and General Stampers Association (SAUO) .... CFGSA
Cutoff (NAKS) .... Co
Cutoff (MSA) .... CO
Cutoff [*Telecommunications*] (TEL) .... CTO
Cutoff Frequency .... COF
Cutoff Frequency (IDOE) .... f_{co}
Cutoff Frequency (SAUS) .... FCO
Cutoff Shear [*Tool*] (AAG) .... COSR
Cutoff Signal (KSC) .... COS
Cutoff Valve .... COV
Cutoff Velocity and Range .... COVER
Cut-Off Voltage (SAUS) .... COV
Cutoff Voltage (SAUS) .... E
Cut-Out (SAUS) .... CO
Cutout (SAUS) .... CO
Cut-Out Halftone [*Graphic arts*] (DGA) .... COHT
Cutout Valve .... COV
Cutral-Co [*Argentina*] [*Airport symbol*] (OAG) .... CUT
Cutral-Co [*Argentina*] [*ICAO location identifier*] (ICLI) .... SAZW
Cuts per Inch (SAUS) .... CPI
Cuttack Law Times [*India*] [*A publication*] (ILCA) .... CLT
Cuttack Law Times [*India*] [*A publication*] (DLA) .... Cut LT
Cuttack Law Times [*India*] [*A publication*] (DLA) .... Cutt LT
Cutter [*Ship*] (ROG) .... CR
Cutter (MSA) .... CTR
Cutter [*Ship*] .... CUT
Cutter (SAUS) .... Cut
Cutter & Buck [*NASDAQ symbol*] (TTSB) .... CBUK
Cutter & Buck, Inc. [*NASDAQ symbol*] (SAG) .... CBUK
Cutter & Buck, Inc. [*Associated Press*] (SAG) .... CutterB
Cutter Compensation (SAUS) .... CUTCOM
Cutter Laboratories [*Research code symbol*] CL
Cutter Laboratories, Berkeley, CA [*Library symbol*] [*Library of Congress*] (LCLS) .... CBCL
Cutter Location File CL
Cutter Location File (SAUS) .... CLFILE
Cutter Protein Hydrolysate (SAUS) .... CPH
Cutter Protein Hydrolysate Five Percent in Water [*Pharmacology*] (DAVI) .... CPH 5
Cut-Through Operate (IAA) .... CTO
Cutting (MSA) .... CTG
Cutting .... CUT
Cutting .... CUTG
Cutting and Waste (SAUS) .... C&W
Cutting and Welding Permit .... CWP
Cutting Cycle (SAUS) CC
Cutting Die Institute (EA) .... CDI
Cutting Disposal System [*Oil well drilling*] .... CDS
Cutting Edge Technologies .... CET
Cutting Fluid [*Metallurgy*] .... CF
Cutting Fluid Manufacturers Association [*Defunct*] (EA) .... CFMA
Cutting Needle Biopsy [*Medicine*] .... CNB
Cutting or Molding Machine .... CMM
Cutting Specification (AAG) .... CS
Cutting Tool Manufacturers Association [*Later, Cutting Tool Manufacturers of America*] (EA) .... CTMA
Cutting Tool Manufacturers of America (EA) .... CTMA
Cutting with Intent to Kill .... CWIK
Cutty Resources, Inc. [*Vancouver Stock Exchange symbol*] .... CUY
Cuu Long Delta Rice Research Institute (SAUO) .... CLRRI
Cuvee Extra .... CE
Cuvier Mines, Inc. [*Toronto Stock Exchange symbol*] .... CUV
Cuyahoga Community College, Cleveland, OH [*Library symbol*] [*Library of Congress*] (LCLS) .... OClCC
Cuyahoga Community College, Learning Resource Center, Cleveland, OH [*OCLC symbol*] (OCLC) .... CUL
Cuyahoga County Public Library (IID) .... CCPL
Cuyahoga County Public Library, Cleveland, OH [*OCLC symbol*] (OCLC) .... CXP
Cuyahoga County Public Library, Cleveland, OH [*Library symbol*] [*Library of Congress*] (LCLS) .... OClCo
Cuyahoga Falls, OH [*AM radio station call letters*] .... WCUE
[*The*] **Cuyahoga Valley Railway Co.** [*AAR code*] .... CUVA
Cuyahoga Valley Railway Co. (SAUO) .... CUVA
Cuyos Pies Beso [*Very Respectfully*] [*Formal correspondence*] [*Spanish*] .... CPB
Cuzco [*Peru*] [*Airport symbol*] (OAG) .... CUZ
Cuzco/Velazco Astete [*Peru*] [*ICAO location identifier*] (ICLI) .... SPZO
CV REIT, Inc. [*NYSE symbol*] (SPSG) CVI
CV REIT [*Real Estate Investment Trust*], **Inc.** [*Associated Press*] (SAG) .... CV REI
CV Sportsmark International, Inc. [*Vancouver Stock Exchange symbol*] .... SML
CV Therapeutics, Inc. [*Associated Press*] (SAG) .... CV Ther
CV Therapeutics, Inc. [*NASDAQ symbol*] (SAG) .... CVTX
CVB Financial [*AMEX symbol*] (TTSB) .... CVB
CVB Financial Corp. [*AMEX symbol*] (SPSG) .... CVB
CVB Financial Corp. [*Associated Press*] (SAG) .... CVB Fn
CVF Technologies [*AMEX symbol*] (SG) .... CNV
CVS Corp. [*NYSE symbol*] (SAG) .... CVS
CVS Corp. [*Associated Press*] (SAG) .... CVS Corp
CW Communications, Inc. [*Publisher*] .... CWCI
CW Conference Management Group [*Framingham, MA*] [*Telecommunications service*] (TSSD) .... CW/CMG
CW mixture of hydrogen cyanide and KSK (SAUS) .... AK
Cwaliton [*Qualiton*], **Swansea** [*Record label*] [*Wales*] .... Cwal
CWA/UTW Bargaining Council (EA) .... C/UBC
CWE, Inc. [*Associated Press*] (SAG) .... CWE
CWE, Inc. [*NASDAQ symbol*] (SAG) .... CWEX
CWI Multimedia Interchange Format (SAUS) .... CMIF
CWM Mortgage Hldgs [*NYSE symbol*] (TTSB) .... CWM
CWM Mortgage Holdings, Inc. [*NYSE symbol*] (SAG) .... CWM
CWM Mortgage Holdings, Inc. [*Associated Press*] (SAG) .... CWM Mt
Cwmni Cyfngedig Cyhoeddus [*Public Limited Company*] [*Welsh*] (ODBW) ccc
Cyan (WDMC) C
Cyan, Magenta, and Yellow [*Color model*] (BYTE) .... CMY
Cyan Magenta Yellow Black [*Printing*] (IGQR) .... CMYK
Cyan, Yellow, Magenta, Black [*Color model*] (PCM) .... CYMK
Cyanacetic Acid Hydrazine [*Organic chemistry*] (DAVI) .... CAH
Cyanacetic Hydrazide (SAUS) .... CAH
Cyana-Mexique (MSC) .... CYAMEX
Cyanamid (SAUS) .... Cyan
Cyanamid, Niagara Falls, ON, Canada [*Library symbol*] [*Library of Congress*] (LCLS) .... CaONfCy
Cyanamid, Niagara Falls, Ontario [*Library symbol*] [*National Library of Canada*] (NLC) .... ONFCY
Cyanic (SAUS) .... Cy
cyanic (SAUS) .... cyan
Cyanic Acid (SAUS) .... HCN
Cyanide (ABAC) .... CN
Cyanide [*Organic chemistry*] (DAVI) .... Cn
Cyanide (WDAA) .... CY
Cyanide (ADWA) .... Cy
Cyanide (KSC) .... CYN
Cyanide Amenable to Chlorination (EG) .... CNA
Cyanide Amenable to Chlorination .... CN-ATC
Cyanide Anion [*Organic chemistry*] (DAVI) .... CN
Cyanide, Chlorine and Nitrogen (SAUS) .... Cyclon Gas
Cyanide Gas (SAUS) .... CN-gas
Cyanide Total (EG) .... CNT
Cyanite (SAUS) .... cy
Cyanmethemoglobin [*Immunology*] (DAVI) .... HiCN
Cyanoacrylate Adhesive .... CA
Cyanoacrylate Adhesive .... CAA
Cyanoacrylate Tissue Adhesive [*Medicine*] .... CTA
Cyanocarbonyl m-Chlorophenylhydrazone (SAUS) .... CCP
Cyanocethydrazide [*Antihelminthic*] (ADA) .... CAH
Cyanocobalamin [*Pharmacology*] (DAVI) .... B_12
Cyanocobalamin (SAUS) .... CNB
Cyanocobalamin [*Biochemistry*] .... CNCbl
Cyano(dihydroxy)pyridine [*Biochemistry*] .... CNDP
Cyanoethyl [*Organic chemistry*] .... CE

Cyanoethyl Ethyl-M-Toluidine [*Organic chemistry*] .... CEEMT
Cyanoethyl Methylaniline [*Organic chemistry*] .... CEMA
Cyanoethylethylamine [*Organic chemistry*] .... CEEA
Cyanoethylsucrose .... CES
Cyanoethylurea [*Immunochemistry*] .... CEU
Cyanogen [*Toxic compound*] (AAMN) .... CN
Cyanogen [*Toxic compound*] .... CY
Cyanogen (SAUS) .... Cy
Cyanogen Bromide (SAUS) .... CNBr
Cyanogen Bromide (PDAA) .... CNbr
Cyanogen Chloride [*Poison gas*] [*Army symbol*] .... CK
Cyanogen Chlorite (SAUS) .... CK
Cyanogen Iodine [*Toxicity*] (LDT) .... CIN
Cyanogen Radical [*Organic chemistry*] (DAVI) .... CN
Cyanohydroxybutene [*Organic chemistry*] .... CHB
Cyanonaphthalene [*Organic chemistry*] .... CN
Cyano(nitro)quinoxalinedione [*Organic chemistry*] .... CNQX
Cyanopindolol [*Organic chemistry*] .... CYP
Cyanosis [*Medicine*] (DAVI) C
Cyanosis [*Medicine*] .... CYAN
Cyanosis, Clubbing, or Edema [*Medicine*] (MAE) .... CCE
Cyanosis Neonatorum (DB) .... CN
Cyanotech Corp. [*NASDAQ symbol*] (NQ) .... CYAN
Cyanotech Corp. [*Associated Press*] (SAG) .... Cyanotc
Cyanotic Congenital Heart Disease (DAVI) .... CCHD
Cyanotic Heart Disease [*Medicine*] (DB) .... CHD
Cyanotoluene [*Organic chemistry*] .... CNT
Cyanotrimethyl-Androsterone [*Endocrinology*] (DAVI) .... CTA
Cyano-Trimethyl-Androsterone (SAUS) .... CTA
Cyanotype (VRA) .... CTYP
Cyan-Yellow-Magenta (AEBE) .... CYM
Cyatho Theae [*In a Cup of Tea*] [*Pharmacy*] (ROG) .... CYATH THEAE
Cyathus [*Glassful*] [*Pharmacy*] .... CYATH
Cyathus Amplus [*Tumblerful*] [*Pharmacy*] .... CYATH AMP
Cyathus Vinarius [*Wineglassful*] [*Pharmacy*] (ROG) .... C VINAR
Cyathus Vinosus [*Wineglassful*] [*Pharmacy*] .... CYATH VIN
Cyathus Vinosus [*Wineglassful*] [*Pharmacy*] (ROG) .... CYATH VINOS
Cybear Group, New [*NASDAQ symbol*] .... CYBA
[*The*] **Cybele Society** (EA) .... TCS
Cybenetic Logistics (SAUS) .... Cyberlog
Cyber Optics Corp. [*Associated Press*] (SAG) .... CybrOpt
Cyber Record Manager [*Computer science*] .... CRM
CYBER Record Manager Basic Access Method [*Computer science*] (NITA) .... CRM/BAM
Cyber Sentry, Inc. [*AMEX symbol*] .... CYR
Cyber Service Unit (SAUS) .... CSU
Cyber Time Sharing System (SAUS) .... CTSS
CyberCash, Inc. [*Associated Press*] (SAG) .... CybrCsh
CyberCash, Inc. [*NASDAQ symbol*] (SAG) .... CYCH
Cyberculture (SAUS) .... Cybercult
Cybergraphics Component Manager (SAUS) .... CCM
CyberGuard Corp. [*NASDAQ symbol*] (SAG) .... CYBG
CyberGuard Corp. [*Associated Press*] (SAG) .... CybGrd
CyberMedia, Inc. [*Associated Press*] (SAG) .... CyberMd
CyberMedia, Inc. [*NASDAQ symbol*] (SAG) .... CYBR
Cybermedix, Inc. [*Toronto Stock Exchange symbol*] .... CYB
Cybernetic (ADWA) .... cyber
Cybernetic .... CYBRNTC
Cybernetic Anthropomorphous Machine [*Robot*] [*Army*] .... CAM
Cybernetic Anthropomorphous Machine System [*Robot*] [*Army*] .... CAMS
Cybernetic Data Products Corp. [*Telecommunications service*] (TSSD) .... CDP
Cybernetic Information Systems (RALS) .... CIS
Cybernetic Logistics Planning, Control, and Management Information System [*Military*] (AABC) .... CYBERLOG
Cybernetic Organism [*Concept of machine to alter man's bodily functions for space environment*] .... CYBORG
Cybernetic Organism (IGQR) .... cyborg
Cybernetica (journ.) (SAUS) .... CYBE
Cybernetics (IAA) .... CY
Cybernetics (ADA) .... CYBER
Cybernetics, Inc. (SAUO) .... CYBR
Cybernetics International (SAUO) CI
Cybernetics Products, Inc. [*NASDAQ symbol*] (NQ) .... CYBR
Cybernetics Products, Inc. [*Associated Press*] (SAG) .... Cybrnet
Cybernetics Research Consultants [*British*] (NITA) .... CRC
Cybernetics Research Consultants Information Systems (SAUS) .... CRCIS
Cybernetics Research Institute .... CRI
Cyberonics, Inc. [*Associated Press*] (SAG) .... Cyberonic
Cyberonics, Inc. [*NASDAQ symbol*] (SAG) .... CYBX
CyberOptics Corp. [*NASDAQ symbol*] (NQ) .... CYBE
Cybershop Intl. [*NASDAQ symbol*] (SG) .... CYSP
CyberSource [*Stock market symbol*] .... CYBS
Cyberspace Description Format (SAUS) .... CDF
Cyberspace Developer Kit (SAUS) .... CDK
Cyberspatial Reality Advancement Movement (SAUO) .... CRAM
Cybex Computer Products [*NASDAQ symbol*] (TTSB) .... CBXC
Cybex Corp. [*NASDAQ symbol*] (SAG) .... CBXC
Cybex Corp. [*Associated Press*] (SAG) .... Cybex
Cybex International [*AMEX symbol*] [*Formerly, Lumex, Inc.*] (SG) .... CYB
Cybex International [*Associated Press*] (SAG) .... CybexIntl
Cycad Society (EA) .... CS
CyCare Systems [*NYSE symbol*] (TTSB) .... CYS
CyCare Systems, Inc. [*Associated Press*] (SAG) .... Cycare
CyCare Systems, Inc. [*NYSE symbol*] (SPSG) .... CYS
Cychophosphamide, Hexamethylmelamine, Doxonibicin and Cisplatin (SAUS) .... CHAP
Cyclazocine [*Morphine antagonist*] .... Cyc
Cyclc3PSS Corp. [*Associated Press*] (SAG) Cyclc3pss
Cyclc3PSS Corp. [*NASDAQ symbol*] (SAG) .... OZON
Cycle [*Electricity*] C
Cycle (AAG) .... CY
Cycle (ADWA) .... cy
Cycle .... CYC
Cycle .... CYCL
Cycle .... CYL
Cycle Allocation (SAUS) .... CAL
Cycle and Motor Cycle Association (SAUO) .... CMCA
Cycle Check (SAUS) CC
Cycle Control (SAUS) .... Cy Ctl
Cycle Control Counter (SAUS) CCC
Cycle Control Unit [*IRS*] .... CCU
Cycle Count (MCD) CC
Cycle Day (ADWA) .... CD
Cycle Engineers' Institute .... CEI
Cycle Length (SAUS) CL
Cycle Line State (SAUS) .... CLS
Cycle Log Reduction [*Time required for a given amount of bacteriological kill*] .... CLR
Cycle, Major (SAUS) .... Cy Maj
Cycle, Minor (SAUS) .... Cy Mi
Cycle Model (AAEL) .... CYM
Cycle Parts and Accessories Association (EA) .... CPA
Cycle Parts and Accessories Association (EA) .... CPAA
Cycle Pressure Ratio (MCD) .... CPR
Cycle Program Control (MCD) .... CPC
Cycle Program Counter (IEEE) .... CPC
Cycle Proof Listing [*IRS*] .... CPL
Cycle Racing Club (SAUO) .... CRC
Cycle Sequence .... CS
Cycle Shift .... CS
Cycle Stealing [*Computer science*] (IAA) .... CS
Cycle Stealing Unit [*Computer science*] (IAA) .... CSU
Cycle Test Hours .... CTH
Cycle Time (NVT) .... CT
Cycle Time and Inventory Reduction (MCD) .... CIR
Cycle Time Improvement (AAEL) .... CTI
Cycle Time Management (ACAE) .... CTM
Cycle Transition Review (SAUS) .... CTR
Cycle-by-Cycle Averaging (SAUS) .... CCA
Cycles between Overhaul (MCD) .... CBO
Cycles between Scheduled Visits (MCD) .... CBSV
Cycles per Day .... CPD
Cycles per Hour .... C/H
Cycles per Instruction (SAUS) .... CPI
Cycles per Minute (ADA) .... C/M
Cycles per Minute .... C/MIN
Cycles per Minute .... CPM
Cycles Per Minute (WDMC) .... cpm
Cycles per Second [*See also HZ*] (IAA) C
Cycles per Second [*See also Hz*] .... CC/S
Cycles Per Second [*Telecommunications*] (WDMC) .... cps
Cycles per Second [*See also Hz*] .... CPS
Cycles per Second [*See also Hz*] .... C/S
Cycles Per Second (STED) .... c/s
Cycles per Second [*See also Hz*] .... CY/SEC
Cycles per Second Alternating Current (AAG) .... CPSAC
Cycle-Significant Items (MCD) .... CSI
Cycle-Speedway Council [*British*] (DBA) .... CSC
Cyclic [*Biochemistry*] c
Cyclic Acetal (SAUS) .... CA
Cyclic Address Change (SAUS) .... CAC
Cyclic Adenosine Diphosphoribose [*Biochemistry*] .... CADPR
Cyclic Adenosine Monophosphate [*Also, cAMP*] [*Biochemistry*] .... CAMP
Cyclic Adenosine Monophosphate Phosphodiesterase (PDAA) .... CAMP-PDE
Cyclic Air Sampling Monitor .... CASM
Cyclic AMP [*Adenosine Monaphorphate*] **-Dependent Protein Kinase** [*Biochemistry*] .... cAPK
Cyclic AMP [*Adenosine Monophosphate*] **Response Element Binding Proteins** [*Genetics*] (DOG) .... CREBs
Cyclic AMP [*Adenosine Monophosphate*] **Responsive Element Modulator** [*Genetics*] .... CREM
Cyclic AMP [*Adenasine Monophosphate*] **Responsive Element-Binding Protein** [*Biochemistry*] .... CREB
Cyclic Catalytic Reforming [*Chemical engineering*] (IAA) .... CCR
Cyclic Character Check (SAUS) CCC
Cyclic Check [*Computer science*] (IAA) CC
Cyclic Check BIT [*Binary Digit*] [*Computer science*] (IAA) .... CCB
Cyclic Check Character [*Computer science*] CCC
Cyclic Code (BUR) CC
Cyclic Control Time (MCD) .... CCT
Cyclic Convolution Property (SAUS) .... CCP
Cyclic Correlation (SAUS) CC
Cyclic Corrosion Test .... CCT
Cyclic Cytidine Monophosphate [*Biochemistry*] .... cCMP
Cyclic Data Management Routine [*Computer science*] .... CDMR
Cyclic Decimal Code (SAUS) .... CDC
Cyclic Error Detection Code (MCD) .... CEDC
Cyclic Fatty Acid [*Organic chemistry*] .... CFA
Cyclic Group Signal (SAUO) .... CGS

Cyclic Guanosine Monophosphate [*Biochemistry*] ... cGMP
Cyclic Instrumental Neutron Activation Analysis ... CINAA
Cyclic Lysine Anhydride [*Medicine*] (DMAA) ... CLA
Cyclic Memory (SAUS) ... CM
Cyclic Multilayered Alloy [*Electroplating technology*] ... CMA
Cyclic Neutropenia (SAUS) ... C-N
Cyclic NOR Machine (SAUS) ... CNM
Cyclic Nucleotide-Gated [*Neurobiology*] ... CNG
Cyclic Nucleotide Gated Channel (DMAA) ... CNGC
Cyclic Nucleotide Phosphohydrolase (STED) ... CNPase
Cyclic Nucleotide-Gated [*Ion channels*] [*Neurobiology*] ... CNG
Cyclic Permutated Code (SAUS) ... CP Code
Cyclic Permutation Code ... CPC
Cyclic Permuted ... CP
Cyclic Pitch Control Stick ... CPCS
Cyclic Redundancy Character (PDAA) ... CRC
Cyclic Redundancy Check [*Computer science*] ... CRC
Cyclic Redundancy Check Character [*Computer science*] (IEEE) ... CRCC
Cyclic Redundancy Check Code (SAUS) ... CRCC
Cyclic Redundancy Check Generator/Checker [*Microprocessing*] (NITA) ... CRCGR
Cyclic Redundancy Check/Longitudinal Redundancy Check (SAUS) ... CRC/LRC
Cyclic Redundancy Code (PDAA) ... CRC
Cyclic Shift Keying (SAUS) ... CCSK
Cyclic Store (SAUS) ... CS
Cyclic Strain Attenuator (NASA) ... CSA
Cyclic Time Processor (MCD) ... CTP
Cyclic Uridine 3c, 5c-Monophosphate (ADWA) ... cUMP
Cyclic Voltametric Stripping [*Electrochemistry*] ... CVS
Cyclic Voltammetry [*Analytical electrochemistry*] ... CV
Cyclic Voltammetry Stripping [*Electronics*] (AAEL) ... CVS
Cyclic Voltammogram (SAUS) ... CV
Cyclic Vomiting Syndrome Association ... CVSA
Cyclic Vomiting Syndrome Association (SAUO) ... CVSA UK
Cyclic-Adenosine Monophosphate-Responsive Element Modulator [*Genetics*] ... CREM
Cyclical Binary Code (SAUS) ... CBC
Cyclical Redundancy Character (SAUS) ... CRC
Cyclical Stress Sensitivity Limit ... CSSL
Cyclically Harvested Earth-Orbit Production System ... CHEOPS
Cyclically Magnetized (SAUS) ... CM
Cyclic-AMP [*Adenosine Monophosphate*] **Receptor Protein** [*Also, CRP*] [*Genetics*] ... CAP
Cyclic-AMP [*Adenosine Monophosphate*] **Receptor Protein** [*Also, CAP*] [*Genetics*] ... CRP
Cyclic-AMP [*Adenosine Monophosphate*] **Response Element** [*Genetics*] ... CRE
Cyclic-AMP [*Adenosine Monophosphate*]**-Responsive Transcriptional Enhancer** [*Genetics*] ... CRE
Cyclic-Nucleotide-Binding [*Neurobiology*] ... CNB
Cyclin Kinase Inhibitor [*Biochemistry*] ... CKI
Cyclin-Dependent Kinase [*An enzyme*] ... CDK
Cyclin-Dependent Kinases [*Genetics*] (DOG) ... cdks
Cycling [*Chemical engineering*] (IAA) ... CY
Cycling Air Sampling Monitor (SAUS) ... CASM
Cycling Club (SAUO) ... CC
Cycling Club ... CC
Cycling Clutch-Orifice Tube [*Automobile air-conditioning system*] ... CCOT
Cycling Council of Great Britain (SAUO) ... CCGB
Cycling Error Detection Code (SAUS) ... CEDC
Cycling Fibroblast [*Cytology*] ... CF
Cycling Oiler [*Navy*] (MCD) ... CO
Cycling Strength Test ... CST
Cyclised Rubber Master Batch (SAUS) ... CRMB
Cyclists' Rights Action Group [*Australia*] ... CRAG
Cyclists' Touring Club ... CTC
Cyclists Touring Club (SAUO) ... CTC
Cyclobutadien (SAUS) ... CBD
Cyclobutane Pyrimidine Dimer [*Organic chemistry*] ... CPD
Cyclocytidine Hydrochloric Acid [*Organic chemistry*] (DAVI) ... Cyclo C
Cyclodextrin [*Organic chemistry*] ... CD
Cyclodextrin Glucanotransferase (DMAA) ... CGT
Cyclodextrin Glycosyltransferase (DB) ... CGT
Cyclodextrin Glycosyltransferase [*An enzyme*] ... CGTase
Cyclodextrin Transglycosylase [*An enzyme*] ... CTG
Cyclodextrine Sulphate (DB) ... CDS
Cyclododecatriene [*Organic chemistry*] ... CDDT
Cyclododecatriene [*Organic chemistry*] ... CDT
Cyclogel Retinoscopy (SAUS) ... CRNS
Cyclogenesis [*NWS*] (FAAC) ... CYCLGN
Cycloheaxanediisocyanate (EDCT) ... CHDI
Cycloheptatriene [*Organic chemistry*] ... CHT
Cyclohexadiene [*Organic chemistry*] ... CHD
Cyclohexane [*Organic chemistry*] ... C
Cyclohexanedimethanol [*Organic chemistry*] ... CHDM
Cyclohexanone [*Organic chemistry*] ... CH
Cyclohexenedicarboxylic Acid [*Organic chemistry*] ... CA
Cyclohexenedicarboxylic Acid [*Organic chemistry*] ... CHDC
(Cyclohexenyl)cyclohexanone [*Organic chemistry*] ... CHCH
Cycloheximide [*Also, CHX, CXM, Cyh*] [*Fungicide*] ... CH
Cycloheximide [*Also, CH, CXM, Cyh*] [*Fungicide*] ... CHX
Cycloheximide [*Also, CH, CHX, Cyh*] [*Fungicide*] ... CXM
Cycloheximide [*Also, CH, CHX, CXM*] [*Fungicide*] ... Cyh
Cyclohexyl Isocyanate [*Organic chemistry*] ... CHI
Cyclohexyl Methacrylate [*Organic chemistry*] ... CHMA
Cyclohexyladenosine [*Biochemistry*] ... CHA
Cyclohexylamine [*Organic chemistry*] ... CHA
Cyclohexylamine Carbonate [*Corrosion prevention*] ... CHC
Cyclohexylaminoethanesulfonic Acid [*A buffer*] ... CHES
Cyclohexylaminopropanesulfonic Acid [*A buffer*] ... CAPS
Cyclohexylbenzothiazole Sulfenamide [*Organic chemistry*] ... CBS
Cyclohexylbenzothiazyl Sulphenamide (PDAA) ... CBTS
Cyclohexyldithiobenzothiazole [*Organic chemistry*] ... CDB
Cyclohexylene Diisocyanate [*Organic chemistry*] ... CHDI
(Cyclohexylenedinitrilo)tetraacetic Acid [*Organic chemistry*] ... CDTA
Cyclohexylidenecyclohexane [*Organic chemistry*] ... CCH
Cyclohexyllinoleic Acid [*Organic chemistry*] ... CHLA
Cyclohexylphenyl(piperidinylethyl)silanol [*Organic chemistry*] ... CPPS
Cyclohexylpyrrolidone [*Organic chemistry*] ... CHP
Cyclohexylthiophthalimide [*Organic chemistry*] ... CTP
Cycloidal Propeller [*on a ship*] (DS) ... CYCLD
Cyclone (EEVL) ... C
Cyclone ... CYC
Cyclone Integrated Video Interfaces Controller [*Apple*] (VERA) ... CIVIC
Cyclone Melting System [*Coal technology*] ... CMS
Cyclonene-Pyrethrene-Rodentone (EDCT) ... CPR
Cyclones (SAUS) ... Cyc
Cyclonic Extratropical Storms [*National Oceanic and Atmospheric Administration*] ... CYCLES
Cyclonic Instability of the Second Kind (SAUS) ... CISK
Cyclonite (SAUS) ... RDX
Cyclonium (MAE) ... Cy
Cyclonometer (SAUS) ... Cyclon
Cyclooctadiene [*Organic chemistry*] ... COD
Cyclooctatetraene [*or Cyclooctatetraenyl*] [*Organic chemistry*] ... COT
Cyclooctylamino-nitropyridine [*Organic chemistry*] ... COANP
Cycloolefin Copolymer ... COC
Cyclooxygenase [*An enzyme*] ... COX
Cyclooxygenase-2 ... COX-2
Cyclopaedia of Freemasonry [*A publication*] (ROG) ... C of F
Cyclopedia (ADWA) ... cyc
Cyclopedia ... CYC
Cyclopedia ... CYCL
Cyclopedia (ADWA) ... cycl
Cyclopedia ... CYCLO
Cyclopedia Law Dictionary [*A publication*] (DLA) ... Cyc Dict
Cyclopedia of Law and Procedure [*New York*] [*A publication*] (DLA) ... CYC
Cyclopedia of Law and Procedure [*A publication*] (DLA) ... Cyc Law & Proc
Cyclopedia of Law and Procedure Annotations [*A publication*] (DLA) ... Cyc Ann
Cyclopedia of Portraits ... CYP
Cyclopenta(alpha)phenanthrene [*Organic chemistry*] ... CPAP
Cyclopentadiene (EDCT) ... CP
Cyclopentadiene [*Organic chemistry*] ... CPD
Cyclopentadienyl [*Also, cp*] [*Organic radical*] ... Cp
Cyclopentane Diimide (SAUS) ... CPDI
Cyclopentanediaminetetraacetic Acid (SAUS) ... CPDTA
Cyclopentenophenanthrene [*Organic chemistry*] (AAMN) ... CPP
Cyclopentenylcytosine [*Biochemistry*] ... CPEC
Cyclopentyltheophylline [*Organic chemistry*] ... CPT
Cyclophilin [*Biochemistry*] ... CYP
Cyclophosphamid (SAUS) ... CY
Cyclophosphamide [*Cytoxan*] [*Antineoplastic drug*] ... C
Cyclophosphamide [*Cytoxan*] [*Antineoplastic drug*] ... CPA
Cyclophosphamide [*Cytoxan*] [*Antineoplastic drug*] ... CPM
Cyclophosphamide [*or Cytoxan*] [*Antineoplastic drug*] (DAVI) ... CX
Cyclophosphamide [*Cytoxan*] [*Antineoplastic drug*] ... CY
Cyclophosphamide (DB) ... Cy
Cyclophosphamide [*Cytoxan*] [*Antineoplastic drug*] ... CYC
Cyclophosphamide [*Cytoxan*] [*Antineoplastic drug*] (MAE) ... Cyclo
Cyclophosphamide [*Cytoxan*] [*Antineoplastic drug*] ... CYP
Cyclophosphamide [*Antineoplastic drug*] (DAVI) ... CYT
Cyclophosphamide, Adriamycin, Bleomycin, Oncovin [*Vincristine*], **Prednisone** [*Antineoplastic drug regimen*] ... CABOP
Cyclophosphamide, Adriamycin, Cisplatin [*Antineoplastic drug regimen*] (DAVI) ... CAP-I
Cyclophosphamide, Adriamycin, Cisplatin Hexamethylmelamire [*Antineoplastic drug regimen*] (DAVI) ... CHAD
Cyclophosphamide, Adriamycin, Dacarbazine [*Antineoplastic drug regimen*] ... CAD
Cyclophosphamide, Adriamycin, Dacarbazine [*DTIC*] [*Antineoplastic drug regimen*] (DAVI) ... CADIC
Cyclophosphamide, Adriamycin, DIC [*Dacarbazine*] [*Antineoplastic drug regimen*] ... CyADIC
Cyclophosphamide, Adriamycin, Fluorouracil [*Antineoplastic drug regimen*] ... CAF
Cyclophosphamide, Adriamycin [*Doxorubicin*], **Fluorouracil by Continuous Infusion** [*Antineoplastic drug regimen*] (DAVI) ... CAFFI
Cyclophosphamide, Adriamycin, Fluorouracil, Prednisone [*Antineoplastic drug regimen*] ... CAFP
Cyclophosphamide, Adriamycin, Fluorouracil, Vincristine, Prednisone [*Antineoplastic drug regimen*] ... CAFVP
Cyclophosphamide, Adriamycin, High-dose Cisplatin [*Antineoplastic drug regimen*] (DAVI) ... CAP-II
Cyclophosphamide, Adriamycin, High-Dose Platinol [*Cisplatin*] [*Antineoplastic drug regimen*] ... CAP-II
Cyclophosphamide, Adriamycin, Methotrexate [*Antineoplastic drug regimen*] ... CAM
Cyclophosphamide, Adriamycin, Methotrexate, Bleomycin [*Antineoplastic drug regimen*] ... CAMB
Cyclophosphamide, Adriamycin, Methotrexate, Etoposide, Oncovin [*Vincristine*] [*Antineoplastic drug regimen*] ... CAMEO

Cyclophosphamide, Adriamycin, Methotrexate, Fluorouracil [Antineoplastic drug regimen] (DAVI) .... CAMF

Cyclophosphamide, Adriamycin, Methotrexate, Folinic acid-SF [Antineoplastic drug regimen] .... CAMF

Cyclophosphamide, Adriamycin, Methotrexate, Procarbazine [Antineoplastic drug regimen] .... CAMP

Cyclophosphamide, Adriamycin, Oncovin [Vincristine] [Antineoplastic drug regimen] .... CAO

Cyclophosphamide, Adriamycin, Platinol [Cisplatin] [Antineoplastic drug regimen] .... CAP

, Cyclophosphamide, Adriamycin, Platinol [Vincristine] [Cisplatin] [Antineoplastic drug regimen] .... VOCAP

Cyclophosphamide, Adriamycin, Prednisone [Antineoplastic drug regimen] .... CAP

Cyclophosphamide, Adriamycin, Procarbazine, Bleomycin, Oncovin [Vincristine], Prednisone [Antineoplastic drug regimen] .... CAP-BOP

Cyclophosphamide, Adriamycin [Doxorubicin], Vincristine [Antineoplastic drug regimen] .... CAV

Cyclophosphamide, Adriamycin, Vincristine, Prednisone [Antineoplastic drug regimen] (DAVI) .... CAVP-I

Cyclophosphamide, Adriamycin, VM-26, Prednisone [Antineoplastic drug regimen] (DAVI) .... CAVP

Cyclophosphamide, Adriamycin, VP-16, Prednisone, Methotrexate [Antineoplastic drug regimen] (DAVI) .... CAVPM

, Cyclophosphamide, Alkeran [Lomustine] [Melphalan] [Antineoplastic drug regimen] .... MOCCA

Cyclophosphamide and VP-16 [Antineoplastic drug] (DAVI) CV

Cyclophosphamide, CCNU [Lomustine], Methotrexate [Antineoplastic drug regimen] .... CCM

Cyclophosphamide, CCNU [Lomustine] VP-16, Vincristine [Antineoplastic drug regimen] (DAVI) CCVV

Cyclophosphamide, CCNU [Lomustine], VP-16, Vincristine, Cisplatin [Antineoplastic drug regimen] (DAVI) .... CCVVP

Cyclophosphamide, Cisplatin, Fluorouracil, and Extramustine [Medicine] (DMAA) .... CCFE

Cyclophosphamide, Fluorouracil, Prednisone [Antineoplastic drug regimen] .... CFP

Cyclophosphamide, Hexamethylmelamine, Adriamycin, Cisplatin [Antineoplastic drug regimen] (DAVI) .... CHAP-S

Cyclophosphamide, Hexamethylmelamine, Adriamycin, Diamminedichloroplatinum [Cisplatin] [Antineoplastic drug regimen] .... CHAD

Cyclophosphamide, Hexamethylmelamine, Cisplatin [Antineoplastic drug regimen] (DAVI) .... CHD

Cyclophosphamide, Hexamethylmelamine, Cisplatin plus Radiotherapy [Antineoplastic drug regimen] (DAVI) .... CHD-R

Cyclophosphamide, Hexamethylmelamine, Fluorouracil [Antineoplastic drug regimen] .... CHF

Cyclophosphamide, Hexamethylmelamine, Fluorouracil, Platinol [Cisplatin] [Antineoplastic drug regimen] .... CHEX-UP

Cyclophosphamide, Hydroxydaunomycin [Adriamycin], Oncovin [Vincristine] [Antineoplastic drug regimen] .... CHO

Cyclophosphamide, Hydroxydaunomycin [Adriamycin], Oncovin , Bleomycin [Vincristine] [Antineoplastic drug regimen] .... CHOB

Cyclophosphamide, Hydroxydaunomycin [Adriamycin], Oncovin , Prednisone [Vincristine] [Antineoplastic drug regimen] .... CHOP

Cyclophosphamide, Hydroxydaunomycin [Adriamycin], Oncovin , Prednisone, Bleomycin [Vincristine] [Antineoplastic drug regimen] .... CHOP-Bleo

Cyclophosphamide, Hydroxydaunomycin [Adriamycin], Oncovin , Procarbazine, Prednisone [Vincristine] [Antineoplastic drug regimen] ..... CHOPP

Cyclophosphamide, Hydroxydaunomycin [Adriamycin], Oncovin , Radiation therapy [Vincristine] [Antineoplastic drug regimen] .... CHOR

Cyclophosphamide, Hydroxydaunomycin [Adriamycin], VM-26 , Prednisone [Teniposide] [Antineoplastic drug regimen] .... CHVP

Cyclophosphamide, Hydroxyurea, Dactinomycin Oncovin [Vincristine], Methotrexate, Adriamycin [Antineoplastic drug regimen] .... CHAMOMA

Cyclophosphamide, Mechlorethamine [Mustargen], Oncovin , Procarbazine, Prednisone [Vincristine] [Antineoplastic drug regimen] .... C-MOPP

Cyclophosphamide Methotrexate 5-Fluorouracil (SAUS) .... CMF

Cyclophosphamide [Cytoxan], Methotrexate, 5-Fluorouracil, Bleomycin [Antineoplastic drug regimen] (DAVI) .... CMF-BLEO

Cyclophosphamide [Cytoxan], Methotrexate, 5-Fluorouracil, Fluoxymesterone [Antineoplastic drug regimen] (DAVI) .... CMF-FLU

Cyclophosphamide [Cytoxan], Methotrexate, 5-Fluorouracil, Hydroxyurea [Antineoplastic drug regimen] (DAVI) .... CMFH

Cyclophosphamide, Methotrexate, 5-Fluorouracil, Prednisone, Vincristine, Adriamycin [Antineoplastic drug regimen] (DAVI) .... CMFP-VA

Cyclophosphamide [Cytoxan], Methotrexate, 5-Fluorouracil, Tamoxifen [Antineoplastic drug regimen] (DAVI) .... CMF-TAM

Cyclophosphamide [Cytoxan] Methotrexate, 5-Fluorouracil, Vincristine [Antineoplastic drug regimen] (DAVI) .... CMFV

Cyclophosphamide, Methotrexate, CCNU [Lomustine] [Antineoplastic drug regimen] .... CMC

Cyclophosphamide, Methotrexate, CCNU [Lomustine], Vincristine, Adriamycin,Procarbazine [Antineoplastic drug regimen] .... CMC-VAP

Cyclophosphamide, Methotrexate, Fluorouracil [Antineoplastic drug regimen] .... CMF

Cyclophosphamide, Methotrexate, Fluorouracil, Adriamycin, Oncovin (Vincristine) [Antineoplastic drug regimen] .... CMF/AV

Cyclophosphamide, Methotrexate, Fluorouracil, Adriamycin, Vincristine, Prednisone [Antineoplastic drug regimen] .... CMFAVP

Cyclophosphamide, Methotrexate, Fluorouracil, Prednisone [Antineoplastic drug regimen] .... CMFP

Cyclophosphamide, Methotrexate, Fluorouracil, Tamoxifen [Antineoplastic drug regimen] .... CMFT

Cyclophosphamide, Methotrexate, Fluorouracil, Vincristine, Adriamycin, Testosterone [Antineoplastic drug regimen] .... CMFVAT

Cyclophosphamide, Methotrexate, Fluorouracil, Vincristine, Prednisone [Antineoplastic drug regimen] .... CMFVP

Cyclophosphamide, Methotrexate, Prednisone, 5-Fluorouracil [Antineoplastic drug regimen] .... CMPF

Cyclophosphamide, Mitoxantrone, Fluorouracil [Antineoplastic drug regimen] (DAVI) .... CNF

Cyclophosphamide, Oncovin [Vincristine] [Antineoplastic drug regimen] .... CO

Cyclophosphamide [or Chlorambucil], Oncovin , Prednisone, Bleomycin [Vincristine] [Antineoplastic drug regimen] .... COP-BLEO

Cyclophosphamide, Oncovin [Vincristine], ara-C , Prednisone, Bleomycin [Cytarabine] [Antineoplastic drug regimen] .... COAP-BLEO

Cyclophosphamide, Oncovin [Vincristine], ara-C, Prednisone [Antineoplastic drug regimen] .... COAP

Cyclophosphamide, Oncovin [Vincristine], L-PAM , Adriamycin [Melphalan] [Antineoplastic drug regimen] .... CONPADRI

Cyclophosphamide, Oncovin [Vincristine], MeCCNU [Semustine] [Antineoplastic drug regimen] .... COM

Cyclophosphamide, Oncovin [Vincristine], MeCCNU , Bleomycin [Semustine] [Antineoplastic drug regimen] .... COMB

Cyclophosphamide, Oncovin [Vincristine], Methotrexate [Antineoplastic drug regimen] .... COM

Cyclophosphamide, Oncovin [Vincristine], Methotrexate [Antineoplastic drug regimen] .... COMe

Cyclophosphamide, Oncovin [Vincristine], Methotrexate, ara-C [Antineoplastic drug regimen] .... COMA

Cyclophosphamide, Oncovin [Vincristine], Methotrexate, Bleomycin [Antineoplastic drug regimen] .... COMB

Cyclophosphamide, Oncovin [Vincristine], Methotrexate, Fluorouracil [Antineoplastic drug regimen] .... COMF

Cyclophosphamide, Oncovin [Vincristine], Methotrexate, Prednisone [Antineoplastic drug regimen] .... COMP

Cyclophosphamide, Oncovin [Vincristine], Methotrexate with Leucovorin, araC [Antineoplastic drug regimen] .... COMLA

Cyclophosphamide, Oncovin [Vincristine], Methotrexate/citrovorum factor, Adriamycin, ara-C [Cytarabine] [Antineoplastic drug regimen] .... COMA-A

Cyclophosphamide, Oncovin [Vincristine], Prednisone [Also, CVP] [Antineoplastic drug regimen] .... COP

Cyclophosphamide, Oncovin [Vincristine], Prednisone, Adriamycin [Antineoplastic drug regimen] .... COPA

Cyclophosphamide, Oncovin [Vincristine], Prednisone, Adriamycin, Bleomycin [Antineoplastic drug regimen] .... COPA-BLEO

Cyclophosphamide, Oncovin [Vincristine], Prednisone, Bleomycin [Antineoplastic drug regimen] .... COPB

Cyclophosphamide, Oncovin [Vincristine], Prednisone, Bleomycin, Adriamycin, Matulane [Procarbazine] [Antineoplastic drug regimen] .... COP-BLAM

Cyclophosphamide, Oncovin [Vincristine], Prednisone, Doxorubicin [Adriamycin] [Antineoplastic drug regimen] .... COPAD

Cyclophosphamide, Oncovin [Vincristine], Procarbazine, Prednisone [Antineoplastic drug regimen] .... COPP

Cyclophosphamide, Platinol [Cisplatin] [Antineoplastic drug regimen] ..... CTX-PLAT

Cyclophosphamide, Prednisone [Antineoplastic drug regimen] .... CP

Cyclophosphamide, Prednisone, Oncovin [Vincristine], Bleomycin [Antineoplastic drug regimen] .... CPOB

Cyclophosphamide, Rubidazone [Zorubicin], Oncovin , Prednisone [Vincristine] [Antineoplastic drug regimen] .... CROP

Cyclophosphamide, Rubidazone, Oncovin [Vincristine], Prednisone, L-Asparaginase, Methotrexate [Antineoplastic drug regimen] (DAVI) ...... CROPAM

Cyclophosphamide, Vinblastine, Procarbazine, Prednisone [Antineoplastic drug regimen] .... CVPP

Cyclophosphamide, Vinblastine, Procarbazine, Prednisone, CCNU [Lomustine] [Antineoplastic drug regimen] .... CVPP-CCNU

Cyclophosphamide, Vincristine, Adriamycin [Antineoplastic drug regimen] ..... CVA

Cyclophosphamide, Vincristine, Adriamycin, BCNU [Carmustine], Methotrexate, Procarbazine [Antineoplastic drug regimen] .... CVA-BMP

Cyclophosphamide, Vincristine, Adriamycin, Dacarbazine [Antineoplastic drug regimen] .... CYVADIC

Cyclophosphamide, Vincristine, Adriamycin, Dactinomycin [Actinomycin D] [Antineoplastic drug regimen] .... CYVADACT

Cyclophosphamide, Vincristine, Fluorouracil, Methotrexate [Antineoplastic drug regimen] .... CVFM

Cyclophosphamide, Vincristine, Methotrexate [Antineoplastic drug regimen] .... CVM

Cyclophosphamide, Vincristine, Methotrexate, Adriamycin, Dacarbazine [Antineoplastic drug regimen] .... CYVMAD

Cyclophosphamide, Vincristine, Methotrexate, Daunomycin, and Predinisone Consolidation and Maintenance [Antineoplastic drug regimen] (DAVI) SLA-212

Cyclophosphamide [Cytoxan], Vincristine, Predinisone, Bleomycin [Antineoplastic drug regimen] (DAVI) .... CVP + Bleo

Cyclophosphamide, Vincristine, Prednisone [Also, COP] [Antineoplastic drug regimen] .... CVP

Cyclophosphamide, Vincristine, Procarbazine, and Prednisone [Medicine] .... COPP

Cyclophosphamide, Vincristine, Triflurothymidine, Papaverine [Antineoplastic drug regimen] (DAVI) N3

Cyclophosphamide, VM-26 Prednisolone [Antineoplastic drug regimen] (DAVI) .... PEP

Cyclophosphamide/Adriamycin/Bleomycin/Vincristine/Prednisone (DB) .... CABPOP

Cyclophosphamide/Etoposide/Vincristine (DB) .... CEV

Cycloporine A (SAUS) .... CSA

Cyclopropane (SAUS) .... Cyclo

Cyclopropane (Anesthetic) [Organic chemistry] ...... cyclo
Cyclopropanecarboxylic Acid [Organic chemistry] ...... CPCA
Cyclopropan-Oxygen-Nitrogen (SAUS) ...... CON
Cyclopropenoid Fatty Acid [Biochemistry] ...... CPFA
Cyclops [of Euripides] [Classical studies] (OCD) ...... Cyc
Cyclops Corp. (SAUO) ...... CYL
Cyclopss Corp. [NASDAQ symbol] (TTSB) ...... OZON
Cyclopyrophosphoglycerate [Biochemistry] ...... CPP
Cyclorama [Staging and scenery] ...... CYC
Cyclorama (SAUS) ...... Cyclo
Cycloserine [Antibacterial] (AAMN) ...... CS
Cyclosporin (STED) ...... Cys
Cyclosporin A (STED) ...... CsA
Cyclosporin A [See CYA] [An immunosuppressant drug] ...... CSA
Cyclosporin A [See CSA] [An immunosuppressant drug] ...... CYA
Cyclosporin A, Azathioprine, Prednisone [Antineoplastic drug
  regimen] ...... CSA-AZA-P
Cyclosporin C [An immunosuppressant drug] ...... CSC
Cyclosporin D [An immunosuppressant drug] ...... CSD
Cyclosporine [An immunosuppressant drug] ...... CY
Cyclostationary (SAUS) ...... CS
Cyclostomata (SAUS) ...... Cycl
Cyclotetramethylene Tetranitramine (SAUS) ...... HMX
Cyclotrimethlenetramine ...... RDX
Cyclotrimethylene Trinitramine (SAUS) ...... RDX
Cyclotron [Physics] (DAVI) ...... cyc
Cyclotron (IAA) ...... CYCLO
Cyclotron Laboratory (SAUS) CL
Cyclotron Resonance (AAEL) ...... CR
Cyclotron Unit (SAUS) ...... CU
Cyclotron Up-Scattering Process (SAUS) ...... CUSP
Cyclotron Wave Device ...... CWD
Cycocel (BARN) CCC
Cycomm International, Inc. [Associated Press] (SAG) ...... Cycom
Cycomm International, Inc. [Associated Press] (SAG) ...... Cycomm
Cycomm International, Inc. [AMEX symbol] (SPSG) ...... CYI
Cycomm Int(New) [AMEX symbol] (TTSB) ...... CYI
Cydia Pomenella Granulosis Virus ...... CpGV
Cyfeillion Cymru [Friends of Wales] [Australia] CC
Cygne Designes [NASDAQ symbol] (TTSB) ...... CYDS
Cygne Designs, Inc. [NASDAQ symbol] (SAG) ...... CYDS
Cygne Designs, Inc. [Associated Press] (SAG) ...... CygneD
Cygnus [Constellation] ...... Cyg
Cygnus [Constellation] ...... Cygn
Cygnus Therapeutic Systems [NASDAQ symbol] (SPSG) ...... CYGN
Cygnus Therapeutic Systems [Associated Press] (SAG) ...... Cygnus
Cygrus Inc. [NASDAQ symbol] (TTSB) ...... CYGN
Cylinder C
Cylinder (MCD) CL
Cylinder ...... CY
Cylinder (AAG) ...... CYL
Cylinder (STED) ...... cyl
Cylinder ...... Cyl
Cylinder Address (SAUS) ...... CA
Cylinder Address Register (SAUS) ...... CAR
Cylinder Axis [Optometry] CX
Cylinder Escape Probability (PDAA) ...... CEP
Cylinder Gas Audit ...... CGA
Cylinder, Head, and Sector [Computer science] ...... CHS
Cylinder Identification [Automotive engineering] ...... CID
Cylinder Lock ...... CYLL
Cylinder Lock (SAUS) ...... CYL L
Cylinder Manufacturers Association [Defunct] (EA) ...... CMA
Cylinder or Drum [Freight] ...... CYL DRM
Cylinder Overflow (SAUS) ...... CYFLO
Cylinder Overflow Control Record (SAUS) ...... COCR
Cylinder Rate (NVT) ...... CR
Cylinder Seek Command (SAUS) ...... CSC
Cylinder Stroke Control ...... CSC
Cylinder-Cylinder-Head-Sector [Computer science] (IBMDP) ...... CCHS
Cylinder-Head Temperature ...... CHT
Cylinder-Pressure Monitoring and Conditioning Detection System ...... CYLDET
Cylinders (RIMS) ...... Cy
Cylindric Lens (ROG) ...... CYLL
Cylindrical [Leaf characteristic] [Botany] C
Cylindrical (VRA) ...... cyl
Cylindrical (SAUS) ...... CYL
Cylindrical (ROG) ...... CYLL
Cylindrical ...... CYLNDL
Cylindrical Cartridge (SAUS) ...... CYL CART
Cylindrical Core Test Facility (SAUS) ...... CCTF
Cylindrical Electrostatic Probe [NASA] (MCD) ...... CEP
Cylindrical Electrostatic Probe Experiment [NASA] ...... CEPE
Cylindrical Film Memory (SAUS) ...... CFM
Cylindrical Fire Tube Boiler [of a ship] (DS) ...... CFTB
Cylindrical Fire Tube Boiler Survey [of a ship] (DS) ...... CFTBS
Cylindrical Horizontal Tank [Liquid gas carriers] ...... ch
Cylindrical Hydrophone Array (SAUS) ...... CHA
Cylindrical Internal Reflectance - Infrared Spectroscopy ...... CIR-IR
Cylindrical Internal Reflection [Spectroscopy] ...... CIR
Cylindrical LASER Plasma ...... CLASP
Cylindrical Laser Plasma (SAUS) ...... CLASP
Cylindrical Lens [Ophthalmology] ...... CYL
Cylindrical Lens (STED) ...... cyl
Cylindrical Magnetic Film ...... CMF

Cylindrical Mirror (SAUS) ...... CM
Cylindrical Mirror Analyser (SAUS) ...... CMA
Cylindrical Mirror Analyzer [Analytical instrumentation] ...... CMA
Cylindrical Perforated ...... CP
Cylindrical Surface (MSA) ...... CYLS
Cylindrical Tranport (SAUS) ...... CYLTRAN
Cylindrical Vertical Tank [Liquid gas carriers] cv
Cylindrical Vibration Mount ...... CVM
Cylindrical Water Tube Boiler [of a ship] (DS) ...... CWTB
Cylindrical Water Tube Boiler Survey [of a ship] (DS) ...... CWTBS
Cylindrical with Adaxial Channel [Leaf characteristics] [Botany] cc
Cylindrically Guided Wave Technique [Nuclear energy equipment] ...... CGWT
Cylindrically Symmetrical Field ...... CSF
Cylindroid (SAUS) ...... CYL
Cylink Corp. [NASDAQ symbol] (TTSB) ...... CYLK
Cylink Network Management System [Computer science] (VERA) ...... CNMS
Cymbals ...... cym
Cymbeline [Shakespearean work] ...... Cym
Cymbeline (SAUS) ...... Cymb
Cymbidium Mosaic Virus [Plant pathology] ...... CYBMV
Cymbidium Ringspot Virus [Plant pathology] ...... CYRSV
Cymbidium Society of America (EA) ...... CSA
Cymdeithas Diogelu Cymru Wledig [Council for the Protection of Rural
  Wales] (EAIO) ...... CDCW
Cymdeithas Swyddogion Addysg Bellach a Gwasanaeth Leuctid Cymru
  [Welsh Association of Further Education and Youth Service Offices] ...... CSABGC
Cymdeithas y Cymmrodorion [Honorable Society of Cymmrodorion] [British] CC
Cymdeithas yr Laith Gymraeg [Welsh Language Society] (EAIO) ...... CLG
Cymer, Inc. [NASDAQ symbol] (SG) ...... CYMI
Cymomotive Force (SAUS) ...... cmf
Cymomotive Force [Telecommunications] (TEL) ...... CMF
Cymric [Language, etc.] (ROG) ...... CYM
Cymric (ADWA) ...... Cym
Cymric Resources Ltd. [Toronto Stock Exchange symbol] ...... CYI
Cynara Virus [Plant pathology] CV
Cynarine (SAUS) ...... CYN
Cynegeticus [of Xenophon] [Classical studies] (OCD) ...... Cyn
Cynipidae [Entomology] ...... Cyn
Cynologist (SAUS) ...... Cynol
Cynology (SAUS) ...... Cynol
Cynomolgus Monkey Kidney [Medicine] ...... CMK
Cynosurus Mottle Virus [Plant pathology] ...... CYMOV
Cynthiana Argus, Cynthiana, IN [Library symbol] [Library of Congress]
  (LCLS) ...... InCyA
Cynthiana, KY [AM radio station call letters] ...... WCYN
Cynthiana, KY [FM radio station call letters] ...... WCYN-FM
Cypair Tours Ltd. [Cyprus] [ICAO designator] (FAAC) ...... CYC
Cypern (SAUO) ...... CY
Cypher Policy Board [British] [World War II] ...... CPB
Cypher Security Committee [British] [World War II] ...... CSC
Cypher Writing [Freemasonry] (ROG) ...... CW
Cyphernetics Text Processing Language [1970] [Computer science]
  (CSR) ...... CYPHERTEXT
Cypress [Botany] (ROG) ...... CYP
Cypress (VRA) ...... cyp
Cypress Airlines [Canada] [FAA designator] (FAAC) ...... CYS
Cypress Bioscience [NASDAQ symbol] (TTSB) ...... CYPB
Cypress Bioscience, Inc. [NASDAQ symbol] (SAG) ...... CYPB
Cypress Bioscience, Inc. [Associated Press] (SAG) ...... CypBio
Cypress Bioscience, Inc. [Associated Press] (SAG) ...... CyprB
Cypress Bioscience, Inc. [Associated Press] (SAG) ...... CyprBio
Cypress Bioscience Wrrt [NASDAQ symbol] (TTSB) ...... CYPBW
Cypress Gardens, FL [AM radio station call letters] ...... WHNR
Cypress Hills Provincial Park (SAUS) ...... CHPP
Cypress Hills, SK [Television station call letters] CBCP-2
Cypress Junior College, Cypress, CA [Library symbol] [Library of Congress]
  (LCLS) ...... CCyC
Cypress Semiconductor [NYSE symbol] (TTSB) ...... CY
Cypress Semiconductor [Associated Press] (SAG) ...... CypSem
Cypress Semiconductor Corp. [NYSE symbol] (SPSG) ...... CY
Cypress Semiconductor Corp. (MHDW) ...... CYPR
Cypress, TX [AM radio station call letters] ...... KYND
Cyprian (SAUS) ...... Cyp
Cyprianus Florentinus [Flourished, 12th century] [Authority cited in pre-1607
  legal work] (DSA) ...... Cy
Cyprianus Florentinus [Flourished, 12th century] [Authority cited in pre-1607
  legal work] (DSA) ...... Cyp
Cypriot Classical (BJA) CC
Cypriot Communist Party [Political party] ...... KKP
Cypriot Liberation Army ...... CLA
Cypriote (BJA) ...... Cy
Cypriote (SAUS) ...... CYP
Cypriote Archaic (BJA) ...... CA
Cypriote Geometric (BJA) ...... CG
Cyproheptadine [Antihistaminic and antipruritic] ...... CYP
Cypros Pharmaceutical [AMEX symbol] (SG) ...... CYP
Cypros Pharmaceutical [NASDAQ symbol] (TTSB) ...... CYPR
Cypros Pharmaceutical Corp. [NASDAQ symbol] (SAG) ...... CYPR
Cypros Pharmaceutical Corp. [Associated Press] (SAG) ...... Cypros
Cypros Pharmaceutical Wrrt'B' [NASDAQ symbol] (TTSB) ...... CYPRZ
Cyproterone Acetate [Endocrinology] ...... CA
Cyproterone Acetate [Endocrinology] ...... CPA
Cyproterone Acetate [Endocrinology] (MAE) ...... CTA
Cyprus [MARC geographic area code] [Library of Congress] (LCCP) ...... a-cy-
Cyprus (BARN) C

Cyprus [*IYRU nationality code*] (IYR) .... CP
Cyprus [*ANSI two-letter standard code*] (CNC) .... CY
Cyprus [*MARC country of publication code*] [*Library of Congress*] (LCCP) .... cy
Cyprus (MILB) .... Cy
Cyprus [*ANSI three-letter standard code*] (CNC) .... CYP
Cyprus (VRA) .... Cyp
Cyprus .... CYPR
Cyprus Airways (SAUO) .... CA
Cyprus Airways (SAUS) .... CAL
Cyprus Airways [*ICAO designator*] (AD) .... CY
Cyprus Airways Ltd. (IMH) .... CA
Cyprus Airways Ltd. (SAUO) .... CY
Cyprus Airways Ltd. [*ICAO designator*] (FAAC) .... CYP
Cyprus Amax Minerals [*NYSE symbol*] (SPSG) .... CYM
Cyprus Amax Minerals Co. [*Associated Press*] (SAG) .... Cyprus
Cyprus American Archaeological Research Institute [*Research center*]
    (IRC) .... CAARI
Cyprus Association (SAUO) .... CA
Cyprus Broadcasting Corp. (IMH) .... CBC
Cyprus Broadcasting Corp. .... CyBC
Cyprus Employers Consultative Organisation (SAUO) .... CECA
Cyprus Federation of America .... CFA
Cyprus International Institute of Management (ECON) .... CIIM
Cyprus Law Reports [*A publication*] (DLA) .... CLR
Cyprus Law Reports [*A publication*] (DLA) .... Cyprus LR
Cyprus Marine Environment Protection Association (SAUO) .... CYMEPA
Cyprus Minerals Co. (MHDW) .... CYPM
Cyprus Mines Corp. (SAUO) .... CYM
Cyprus National Committee of the International Association on Water
    Pollution Research and Control (EAIO) .... CNCIAWPRC
Cyprus News Agency .... CNA
Cyprus Olympic Committee (EAIO) .... COC
Cyprus Organisation for Standards and Control (SAUS) .... CYS
Cyprus Regiment (SAUO) .... CR
Cyprus Telecommunications Authority (SAUO) .... CYTA
Cyprus Tourism Organization (EA) .... CTO
Cyprus Turkish Airways [*ICAO designator*] (AD) .... YK
Cyprus Turkish Tourist Enterprises Ltd. (EY) .... CTTE
Cyrano Resources, Inc. [*Vancouver Stock Exchange symbol*] .... CYO
Cyrel Digital Imaging (SAUS) .... CDI
Cyrenaica Defence Force [*British military*] (DMA) .... CYDEF
Cyrenaican Defence Force (SAUO) .... CDF
Cyril E. King Airport [*FAA*] (TAG) .... STT
Cyril Hayes Press, Inc. [*Publisher*] .... CHP
Cyrillic Union Catalog [*Library of Congress*] .... CUC
Cyrix Corp. [*Associated Press*] (SAG) .... Cyrix Cp
Cyrix Corp. [*NASDAQ symbol*] (SAG) .... CYRX
Cyrk, Inc. [*NASDAQ symbol*] (SAG) .... CYRK
Cyropaedia [*of Xenophon*] [*Classical studies*] (OCD) .... Cyr
Cyrstallography (ADWA) .... cryst
Cyrus [*Persian emperor, d. 529BC*] (ROG) .... CYR
Cyrus Public School, Cyrus, MN [*Library symbol*] [*Library of Congress*]
    (LCLS) .... MnCyS
Cyrus Telecommunications (SAUO) .... CYRTEL
Cyrus the King [*Freemasonry*] (ROG) .... C the K
Cyst Fluid [*Biochemistry*] (DAVI) .... CYFL
Cystadenocarcinoma [*Medicine*] (MELL) .... CAC
Cystadenoma of Ovary [*Medicine*] (MELL) .... CAO
Cysteamine-S-Phosphate [*Biochemical analysis*] .... CASP
Cysteic Acid [*An amino acid*] .... Cya
Cysteine [*One-letter symbol*] [*Also, Cys, CySH*] C
Cysteine [*Also, C*] [*An amino acid*] (DOG) .... cys
Cysteine [*Also, C, CySH*] [*An amino acid*] .... Cys
Cysteine (DB) .... CYS
Cysteine [*Also, C, Cys*] [*An amino acid*] .... CySH
Cysteine Proteinase Inhibitor [*Biochemistry*] .... CPI
Cysteine Rich Neurotrophic Factor [*Neurochemistry*] .... CRNF
Cysteine String Protein [*Biochemistry*] .... CSP
Cysteine Sulfinic Acid-Decarboxylase (STED) .... CSAD
Cysteine Sulphinic Acid (PDAA) .... CSA
Cysteine-Peptone-Liver Infusion Media [*Medicine*] (MAE) .... CPLM
Cysteine-Rich Domain [*Genetics*] .... CRD
Cysteine-Rich Intestinal Protein [*Medicine*] (DMAA) .... CRIP
Cystic Adenomatoid Malformation .... CAM
Cystic Adventitial Degeneration of the Popliteal Artery [*Medicine*] .... CADPA
Cystic Disease Protein [*Biochemistry*] (DB) .... CDP
Cystic Duct [*Medicine*] .... CD
Cystic Duct Stump Syndrome [*Medicine*] (MELL) .... CDSS
Cystic Fibrosis [*Medicine*] .... CF
Cystic Fibrosis Antigen [*Medicine*] (DMAA) .... CFAG
Cystic Fibrosis Association (MELL) .... CFA
Cystic Fibrosis Chest Pain [*Medicine*] (MELL) .... CFCP
Cystic Fibrosis Factor [*Medicine*] (DB) .... CFF
Cystic Fibrosis Factor Activity [*Medicine*] (AAMN) .... CFFA
Cystic Fibrosis Foundation (SAUO) .... CF
Cystic Fibrosis Foundation (EA) .... CFF
Cystic Fibrosis of the Pancreas [*Medicine*] .... CFP
Cystic Fibrosis Pancreatic Insufficiency [*Medicine*] .... CFPI
Cystic Fibrosis Pancreatic Sufficiency [*Medicine*] .... CFPS
Cystic Fibrosis Protein [*Biochemistry*] (DAVI) .... CFP
Cystic Fibrosis Research Trust [*British*] .... CFRT
Cystic Fibrosis Society .... CFS
Cystic Fibrosis Transmembrane-Conductance Regulator [*Genetics*] .... CFTR
Cystic Medial Necrosis [*of aorta*] [*Medicine*] .... CMN
Cystic Medial Necrosis of Ascending Aorta [*Medicine*] (MAE) .... CMN-AA

Cystidine-Uridine-Guanidine [*Organic chemistry*] (DAVI) .... CUG
Cystine [*Also, CyS*] [*An amino acid*] .... Cys
Cystine [*An amino acid*] [*Also, CYS, CYSTIN*] (DAVI) .... Cys-Cys
Cystine Deficiency [*Medicine*] (MELL) .... CD
Cystine Guanine [*Medicine*] (DMAA) .... CG
Cystine Trypticase Agar [*Microbiology*] .... CTA
Cystine-Lactose-Electrolyte Deficient [*Clinical chemistry*] .... CLED
Cystine-Tellurite [*Medium*] [*Microbiology*] .... CT
Cystinosis Foundation (EA) .... CF
Cystogram [*Urology*] (DAVI) .... CYSTO
Cystoid Macular Edema [*Ophthalmology*] .... CME
Cystometrogram [*or Cystometrography*] [*Urology*] .... CMG
Cystoscope (SAUS) .... Cysto
cystoscopic exam (SAUS) .... cysto
Cystoscopic Examination (SAUS) .... Cysto
Cystoscopic Examination [*Medicine*] (MAE) .... cysto
Cystoscopy [*Medicine*] .... CYS
Cystoscopy [*Medicine*] .... Cysto
Cystoscopy + Pyelogram (SAUS) .... C + P
Cystoscopy and Dilatation [*Medicine*] .... C & D
Cystoscopy and Panendoscopy [*Medicine*] .... C & P
Cystoscopy and Pyelogram [*Medicine*] .... C & P
Cystoscopy and Voiding Urethrogram [*Radiology and urology*] (DAVI) .... CVUG
Cystourethrocele [*Medicine*] (MELL) .... CUC
Cystourethrogram [*Medicine*] .... CUG
Cystourethrography [*Medicine*] (STED) .... CUG
Cystylaminopeptidase [*An enzyme*] .... CAP
Cytarabine [*Cytosine arabinoside*] [*Also, ara-C, CAR*] [*Antineoplastic drug*] .... CA
Cytarabine [*Cytosine arabinoside*] [*Also, ara-C, CA*] [*Antineoplastic drug*] .... CAR
Cytarabine [*ara C*], Bleomycin, Oncovin , Methotrexate with Leucovorin
    [*Vincristine*] [*Antineoplastic drug regimen*] .... CytaBOM
Cytarabine, Daunorubicin [*Antineoplastic drug regimen*] .... CAD
Cytarabine, Methotrexate, Leucovorin [*Folinic acid-SF*], Oncovin [*Vincristine*]
    [*Antineoplastic drug regimen*] .... CAMELEON
Cytarabine, Thioguanine [*Antineoplastic drug*] (CDI) .... CT
Cytec Industries [*NYSE symbol*] (TTSB) .... CYT
Cytec Industries, Inc. [*NYSE symbol*] (SPSG) .... CYT
Cytec Industries, Inc. [*Associated Press*] (SAG) .... Cytec
Cytel Corp. [*Associated Press*] (SAG) .... Cytel
Cytel Corp. [*NASDAQ symbol*] (SAG) .... CYTL
Cytidine [*One-letter symbol; see Cyd*] C
Cytidine [*Also, C*] [*A nucleoside*] .... Cyd
Cytidine 5c-Triphosphate (ADWA) .... CTP
Cytidine Cyclic Phosphate [*Medicine*] (DMAA) .... CCP
Cytidine Diphosphate [*Biochemistry*] .... CDP
Cytidine Diphosphate Choline [*Biochemistry*] (MAE) .... CDPC
Cytidine Diphosphoabequose [*Biochemistry*] .... CDPAbe
Cytidine Monophosphate [*Biochemistry*] .... CMP
Cytidine Monophosphate-N-Acetylneuraminic Acid (PDAA) .... CMPNAN
Cytidine Triphosphate [*Biochemistry*] .... CTP
Cytidine Triphosphate Tritium-Labeled [*Chemistry*] (DAVI) .... CTP H
Cytidyl-Cytidyl-Adenyl (SAUS) .... CCA
Cytidyl-Cytidyl-Adenyl [*Biochemistry*] (BABM) .... C-C-A
Cytisine (SAUS) C
Cytocare, Inc. [*Associated Press*] (SAG) .... Cytocre
Cytochalasin B [*Biochemistry*] .... CB
Cytochalasin D [*Biochemistry*] .... CD
Cytochalasin D [*Biochemistry*] .... CYTD
Cytochalasin-B (SAUS) .... CB
Cytochemical Bioassay .... CBA
Cytochrome [*Biochemistry*] (MAE) C
Cytochrome [*Biochemistry*] .... Cyt
Cytochrome (DB) .... CYT
Cytochrome C Oxidase (DMAA) .... CCO
Cytochrome C Oxidase (DMAA) .... COX
Cytochrome C Reductase (DB) .... CRA
Cytochrome Oxidase [*An enzyme*] .... CO
Cytochrome Oxidase (SAUS) .... COX
Cytochrome Oxidase [*An enzyme*] .... COXI
Cytochrome Oxidase (STED) .... Cyt Ox
Cytochrome Oxidase I [*An enzyme*] .... COI
Cytochrome P450 .... CYP
Cytochrome P-450 Induction Assay (DB) .... CYPIA
Cytochrome System (SAUS) .... Cyto Syst
Cytochrome System [*Laboratory*] (DAVI) .... Cyt Sys
Cytochrome-c Peroxidase [*An enzyme*] .... CCP
Cytochromes [*Chemistry*] (MEC) .... cyt
Cytochromoxidase (SAUS) Cx
Cytoclonal Pharm Wrrt'C' [*NASDAQ symbol*] (TTSB) .... CYPHW
Cytoclonal Pharm Wrrt'D' [*NASDAQ symbol*] (TTSB) .... CYPHZ
Cytoclonal Pharmaceuticals [*NASDAQ symbol*] (TTSB) .... CYPH
Cytoclonal Pharmaceuticals, Inc. [*NASDAQ symbol*] (SAG) .... CYPH
Cytoclonal Pharmaceuticals, Inc. [*Associated Press*] (SAG) .... CytoPh
Cytocomputer Parallel Picture Processing Language (SAUS) C-3PL
cytoecologist (SAUS) .... cytoeco
cytoecology (SAUS) .... cytoeco
Cytogen Corp. [*NASDAQ symbol*] (NQ) .... CYTO
Cytogen Corp. [*Associated Press*] (SAG) .... Cytogn
Cytogen Corp. Wrrt [*NASDAQ symbol*] (TTSB) .... CYTOW
Cytogenetics .... CYTOGENET
Cytogram (STED) .... cysto
Cytokeratin [*Cytology*] .... CK
Cytokine Synthesis Inhibitory Factor [*Immunology*] .... CSIF
Cytokine-Suppressive Antiinflammatory Drug [*Biochemistry*] .... CSAID
Cytokinin [*Biochemistry*] .... CK

Cytologic Thymus-Dependent Lymphocyte [*Endocrinology*] (DAVI) ..... CTL
Cytological (ADWA) ..... cytol
cytological (SAUS) ..... cytol
Cytology ..... CYT
Cytology (STED) ..... cyt
Cytology (STED) ..... cytol
Cytology ..... CYTOL
Cytolytic Thymus (DB) ..... CT
Cytolytic Thymus-Dependent Lymphocyte [*Cell biology*] ..... CTL
Cytolytic T-Lymphocyte Line [*Cell line*] ..... CTLL
Cytolytic T-Lymphocyte Precursor [*Immunochemistry*] ..... CTLP
Cytomegalic Inclusion Bodies [*Cytology*] (DAVI) ..... CIB
Cytomegalic Inclusion Disease [*Ophthalmology*] ..... CID
Cytomegalic Inclusion Disease [*Ophthalmology*] ..... CMI
Cytomegalic Inclusion Disease [*Ophthalmology*] (MAE) ..... CMID
Cytomegalovirus [*A virus*] ..... CMV
Cytomegalovirus [*Immunology*] (DAVI) ..... CYTOMG
Cytomegalovirus Immune Globulin [*Biochemistry*] ..... CMVIG
Cytomegalovirus Immune Globulin Intravenous [*Immunology*] ..... CMV-IGIV
Cytomegalovirus Infection ..... CMV
Cytomegaloviruses (SAUS) ..... CMVs
Cytomegalovirus-Induced Thrombocytopenia and Hemolysis [*Medicine*] (MELL) ..... CITH
cytomorphologist (SAUS) ..... cytomorph
cytomorphology (SAUS) ..... cytomorph
Cytopathic Effect [*Medicine*] ..... CE
Cytopathic Human Auto Interfering Virus (SAUS) ..... CHAI-Virus
Cytopathogenic Effect (SAUS) ..... CPE
Cytopathogenic [*or Cytopathic*] **Effect** [*Microbiology*] ..... CPE
cytopathogenicity (SAUS) ..... cytopatho
cytophotometer (SAUS) ..... cytophoto
Cytophotometric Data Converter [*Instrumentation*] ..... CYDAC
cytophotometry (SAUS) ..... cytophoto
Cytoplasm (DMAA) ..... Cyt
Cytoplasm Average Optical Density [*Microscopy*] ..... CYAD
Cytoplasm Deoxyribonucleic Acid (SAUS) ..... CPDNA
Cytoplasm Sum Optical Density [*Microscopy*] ..... CYSD
Cytoplasmic (STED) ..... cyt
Cytoplasmic Androgen Binder [*Endocrinology*] ..... CAB
Cytoplasmic Hypovirulence [*Pathology*] ..... CH
Cytoplasmic Immunoglobulin [*Immunology*] ..... C-Ig
Cytoplasmic Immunoglobulin M [*Immunology*] (DAVI) ..... cIgM
Cytoplasmic Incompatibility [*Entomology*] CI
Cytoplasmic Male Sterility [*Botany*] ..... CMS
Cytoplasmic Membrane [*Botany*] ..... CM
Cytoplasmic Metabolic Factor (PDAA) ..... CMF
Cytoplasmic Microtubule Network [*Cytology*] ..... CMTN
Cytoplasmic Polyhedrosis Virus [*Medicine*] (PDAA) ..... CPV
Cytoplasmic Retinoic Acid-Binding Protein [*Biochemistry*] ..... CRABP
Cytoplasmic Shape [*Microscopy*] ..... CYSH
Cytoplasmic Size [*Microscopy*] ..... CYSZ
Cytoplasmic Tubular Aggregate (DB) ..... CTA
Cytoproct [*Protozoology*] ..... CYP
Cytosine [*Also, Cyt*] [*Biochemistry*] C
Cytosine [*Also, C*] [*Biochemistry*] ..... Cyt
Cytosine Adenine Adenine [*A triplet of bases coding for the amino acid, glutamine*] (EES) ..... CAA
Cytosine Adenine Cytosine [*A triplet of bases coding for the amino acid, histidine*] (EES) ..... CAC
Cytosine Adenine Guanine [*A triplet of bases coding for the amino acid, glutamine*] (EES) ..... CAG
Cytosine Adenine Uracil [*A triplet of bases coding for the amino acid, histidine*] (EES) ..... CAU
Cytosine Arabinoside (DB) ..... ARA-C
Cytosine Arabinoside [*Antineoplastic drug*] (MAE) ..... ara-C
Cytosine Arabinoside [*Medicine*] (DMAA) ..... CA
Cytosine Arabinoside [*ara-C*], **Adriamycin, Thioguanine** [*Antineoplastic drug regimen*] ..... CAT
Cytosine Arabinoside and Thioguanine [*Antineoplastic drug regimen*] (DAVI) ..... AT
Cytosine Arabinoside and Thioguanine [*Antineoplastic drug regimen*] (DAVI) ..... CAT
Cytosine Arabinoside, Azacytidine, Prednisone, Vincristine, Daunomycin [*Antineoplastic drug regimen*] (DAVI) ..... DZAPO
Cytosine Arabinoside Daunomycin [*Also, DA*] [*Antineoplastic drug regimen*] (DAVI) ..... AD
Cytosine Arabinoside [*ara-C*], **L-Asparaginase, Rubidomycin , Thioguanine** [*Daunorubicin*] [*Antineoplastic drug regimen*] ..... CART
Cytosine Arabinoside Monophosphate [*Biochemistry*] ..... ara-CMP
Cytosine Arabinoside Monophosphate (SAUS) ..... ara-MP
Cytosine Arabinoside Triphosphate [*Biochemistry*] ..... ara-CTP
Cytosine Arabinoside Triphosphate (SAUS) ..... ara-TP
Cytosine Arabinoside, Vincristine, L-Asparaginase, Prednisone [*Antineoplastic drug regimen*] (DAVI) ..... calasp
Cytosine Arabinoside/Daunomycin (DB) ..... CAD
Cytosine Cytosine Adenine [*A triplet of bases coding for the amino acid, proline*] (EES) ..... CCA
Cytosine Cytosine Cytosine [*A triplet of bases coding for the amino acid, proline*] (EES) CCC
Cytosine Cytosine Guanine [*A triplet of bases coding for the amino acid, proline*] (EES) ..... CCG
Cytosine Cytosine Uracil [*A triplet of bases coding for the amino acid, proline*] (EES) ..... CCU
Cytosine Diphosphate [*Biochemistry*] ..... CDP
Cytosine Guanine Adenine [*A triplet of bases coding for the amino acid, arginine*] (EES) ..... CGA
Cytosine Guanine Cytosine [*A triplet of bases coding for the amino acid, arginine*] (EES) ..... CGC
Cytosine Guanine Guanine [*A triplet of bases coding for the amino acid, arginine*] (EES) ..... CGG
Cytosine Guanine Uracil [*A triplet of bases coding for the amino acid, arginine*] (EES) ..... CGU
Cytosine Monophosphate [*Biochemistry*] ..... CMP
Cytosine Triphosphate [*Biochemistry*] ..... CTP
Cytosine Uracil Adenine [*A triplet of bases coding for the amino acid, leucine*] (EES) ..... CUA
Cytosine Uracil Cytosine [*A triplet of bases coding for the amino acid, leucine*] (EES) ..... CUC
Cytosine Uracil Guanine [*A triplet of bases coding for the amino acid, leucine*] (EES) ..... CUG
Cytoskeleton [*Cytology*] ..... CSK
Cytosolic Androgen Receptor [*Endocrinology*] ..... CAR
Cytostatic Factor [*Cytology*] ..... CSF
Cytotactin-Binding Proteoglycan ..... CTBP
cytotechnician (SAUS) ..... cyto syst
Cytotechnologist ..... CT
Cytotechnologist (HCT) ..... CYTO
cytotechnologist (SAUS) ..... cyto syst
Cytotechnologist (American Society of Clinical Pathologists) (DAVI) ..... CT(ASCP)
Cytotechnology ..... CYTECH
cytotechnology (SAUS) ..... cyto syst
Cytotechnology Programs Review Committee of the American Society of Cytology (DAVI) ..... CPRCASC
Cytotherapeutics, Inc. [*NASDAQ symbol*] (SAG) ..... CTII
Cytotherapeutics, Inc. [*Associated Press*] (SAG) ..... Cytothr
Cytotoxic Activated Macrophage [*Biochemistry*] ..... CAM
Cytotoxic Antibody (DB) ..... CA
Cytotoxic Antibody (SAUS) ..... CTA
Cytotoxic Assay (MAE) ..... CTA
Cytotoxic Dose [*Toxicology*] ..... CD
Cytotoxic Factor ..... CTF
Cytotoxic Index [*Cytochemistry*] CI
Cytotoxic Lymphocyte (DB) CL
Cytotoxic Necrotizing Factor [*Immunology*] ..... CNF
Cytotoxic T Lymphocyte [*Hematology*] ..... CTL
Cytotoxic T Lymphocyte Antigen [*Immuno chemistry*] ..... CTLA
Cytotoxic T-cell Differentiation (SAUS) ..... CTDF
Cytotoxic Thymus-Derived Lymphocyte (DB) ..... CTL
Cytotoxicity Negative - Absorption Positive [*Immunology*] ..... CYNAP
Cytotoxicity Negative Absorption Positive-Serum-Cell Reaction (SAUS) ..... CYNAP Reaction
Cytoxan [*Cyclophosphamide*] [*Also, C, CP, CPA, CPM, CY, CYC, CYP, CYT*] [*Antineoplastic drug*] ..... CTX
Cytoxan (DB) ..... CY
Cytoxan [*Cyclophosphamide*] [*Antineoplastic drug*] ..... CYT
Cytoxan, Bleomycin, Procarbazine Prednisone, Adriamycin [*Antineoplastic drug regimen*] (DAVI) ..... CBPPA
Cytoxan, Fluorouracil, Methotrexate [*Antineoplastic drug*] (CDI) ..... CFM
Cytoxan, Flurouracil, Predinose, Methotrexate [*Antineoplastic drug*] (CDI) ..... CFPT
Cytoxan, Methotrexate and 5-Fluorouracil (SAUS) ..... CMF
Cytoxan [*Cyclophosphamide*], **Oncovin , Methotrexate, Bleomycin, Adriamycin,Prednisone** [*Vincristine*] [*Antineoplastic drug regimen*] (DAVI) ..... COMBAP
Cytoxan, Oncovin, Platinol, Etoposide [*Antineoplastic drug*] (CDI) ..... COPE
Cytoxan, Vincristine, Prednisone (SAUS) ..... CVP
Cytratcyclus (SAUS) CC
Cytrax Corp. [*NASDAQ symbol*] (SAG) ..... CYTR
Cytrax Corp. [*Associated Press*] (SAG) ..... CytRx
Cytrochrom (SAUS) ..... CYT
CytRx Corp. [*NASDAQ symbol*] (TTSB) ..... CYTR
Cytyc Corp. [*NASDAQ symbol*] (TTSB) ..... CYTC
CZ [*Convergence Zone*] **Area Reduction Tactic** [*Military*] (CAAL) ..... CZARTAC
CZ [*Convergence Zone*] **Confirmation Pattern** [*Military*] (CAAL) ..... CZCP
CZ [*Convergence Zone*] **Investigation** [*Military*] (CAAL) ..... CZINVEST
CZ [*Convergence Zone*] **Investigation Pattern** [*Military*] (CAAL) ..... CZIP
CZ Scientific Instruments Ltd. (SAUO) ..... CZ
Czar Public Library, Alberta [*Library symbol*] [*National Library of Canada*] (NLC) ..... ACZ
Czar Resources Ltd. [*Toronto Stock Exchange symbol*] ..... CZR
Czech [*MARC language code*] [*Library of Congress*] (LCCP) ..... cze
Czech [*Language, etc.*] ..... CZE
Czech Accreditation Institute (SAUS) ..... CAI
Czech Air Force [*ICAO designator*] (FAAC) ..... CEF
Czech Air Handling [*Czechoslovakia*] [*ICAO designator*] (FAAC) ..... AHD
Czech Airlines JSC [*FAA designator*] (FAAC) ..... CSA
Czech American National Alliance (EA) ..... CANA
Czech and Slovak Federal Republic (RDA) ..... CSFR
Czech and Slovak Library Information Network (TELE) ..... CASLIN
Czech and Slovak Solidarity Council (EA) ..... CSSC
Czech Catholic Union (EA) ..... CCU
Czech Educational and Scientific Network (DDC) ..... CESNET
Czech Environment Management Center (SAUO) ..... CEMC
Czech Government Flying Service [*ICAO designator*] (FAAC) ..... CGF
Czech Government Flying Service [*FAA designator*] (FAAC) ..... CIE
Czech Heritage Foundation (EA) ..... CHF
Czech Inds Wrrt'A' [*NASDAQ symbol*] (TTSB) ..... CZCHW
Czech Industries [*NASDAQ symbol*] (TTSB) ..... CZCH
Czech Industries, Inc. [*NASDAQ symbol*] (SAG) ..... CZCH
Czech Industries, Inc. [*Associated Press*] (SAG) ..... Czech

Czech Ministry of Environment (SAUO) .... CME
Czech National Committee (SAUO) .... CNC
Czech Office for Standards, Metrology and Testing (SAUO) .... COSMT
Czech Republic (MILB) .... Cz
Czech Republic [*Internet country code*] .... CZ
Czech Republic Fund [*NYSE symbol*] (TTSB) .... CRF
[*The*] **Czech Republic Fund, Inc.** [*NYSE symbol*] (SAG) .... CRF
[*The*] **Czech Republic Fund, Inc.** [*Associated Press*] (SAG) .... CzechFd
Czech Society of Great Britain (SAUO) .... CSGB
Czech Telecommunications Office (SAUO) .... CTU
Czech Trade Mission (SAUO) .... CTM
Czech World Union (EA) .... CWU
Czechoslovak Academy of Sciences (GEOI) .... CSAV
Czechoslovak Airlines [*ICAO designator*] (AD) .... OK
Czechoslovak Association of Canada (EAIO) .... CAC
Czechoslovak Association of Victoria [*Australia*] .... CAV
Czechoslovak Christian Democracy (EA) .... CCD
Czechoslovak Ex-servicemen's Association [*Australia*] .... CESA
Czechoslovak Genealogical Society (EA) .... CGS
Czechoslovak Genealogical Society International (EA) .... CGSI
Czechoslovak Independent Chemical Defence Battalion (SAUS) .... CSICDB
Czechoslovak Institute (SAUO) CI
Czechoslovak Intelligence Services (SAUO) .... CIS
Czechoslovak Journal of International Law [*A publication*] (DLA) .... Czech J Int'l L
Czechoslovak Journal of Physics (journ.) (SAUS) .... Czech J Phys
**Czechoslovak National Committee of the International Association on
    Water Pollution Research and Control** (EAIO) .... CNCIAWPRC
Czechoslovak National Council (SAUO) .... CNC
Czechoslovak National Council of America (EA) .... CNCA
Czechoslovak National Group of International Association of Penal Law
    (EAIO) .... CNGIAPL
Czechoslovak Neurological Society (EAIO) .... CNS
Czechoslovak Philatelic Society [*Later, SCP*] .... CZPS
Czechoslovak Rationalist Federation of America (EA) .... CRFA

Czechoslovak Red Cross .... CRC
Czechoslovak Socialist Republic (SAUS) .... CSR
Czechoslovak Socialist Republic .... CSSR
Czechoslovak Society of America [*Later, CSA Fraternal Life*] .... CSA
Czechoslovak Society of Arts and Sciences (EA) .... CSAS
Czechoslovak Society of Arts and Sciences in America [*Later, CSAS*]
    (EA) .... CSASA
Czechoslovak Spectroscopic Society (SAUO) .... CSSS
Czechoslovak State Council (SAUO) .... CSC
Czechoslovak Yearbook of International Law [*A publication*]
    (DLA) .... Czech YB Int'l L
Czechoslovakia [*ANSI two-letter standard code*] (CNC) .... CS
Czechoslovakia [*MARC country of publication code*] [*Library of Congress*]
    (LCCP) .... cs
Czechoslovakia [*ANSI three-letter standard code*] (CNC) .... CSK
Czechoslovakia [*IYRU nationality code*] .... CZ
Czechoslovakia (SAUO) .... Cz
Czechoslovakia (SAUO) .... Czech
Czechoslovakia .... CZECH
Czechoslovakia (NTIO) .... Czech
Czechoslovakia (SAUO) .... Czia
Czechoslovakia .... CZS
Czechoslovakia (SAUO) .... Cz-SI
Czechoslovakia .... CZ-SLOV
Czechoslovakia [*MARC geographic area code*] [*Library of Congress*]
    (LCCP) .... e-cs-
Czechoslovakia [*License plate code assigned to foreign diplomats in the US*]..... PH
Czechoslovakian (SAUS) .... Czech
Czechoslovakian Air Force (SAUO) .... CSAF
Czechoslovakian Kronen [*Monetary unit*] .... CZKR
Czechoslovakian Republic (SAUS) .... CR
Czechoslovak-US Economic Council (EA) .... CUSEC
Czochralski Crystal Growth [*Crystallization process*] .... CZ
Czochralski Material (SAUS) .... CZ Material
Czochralski Process (AAEL) .... CZ